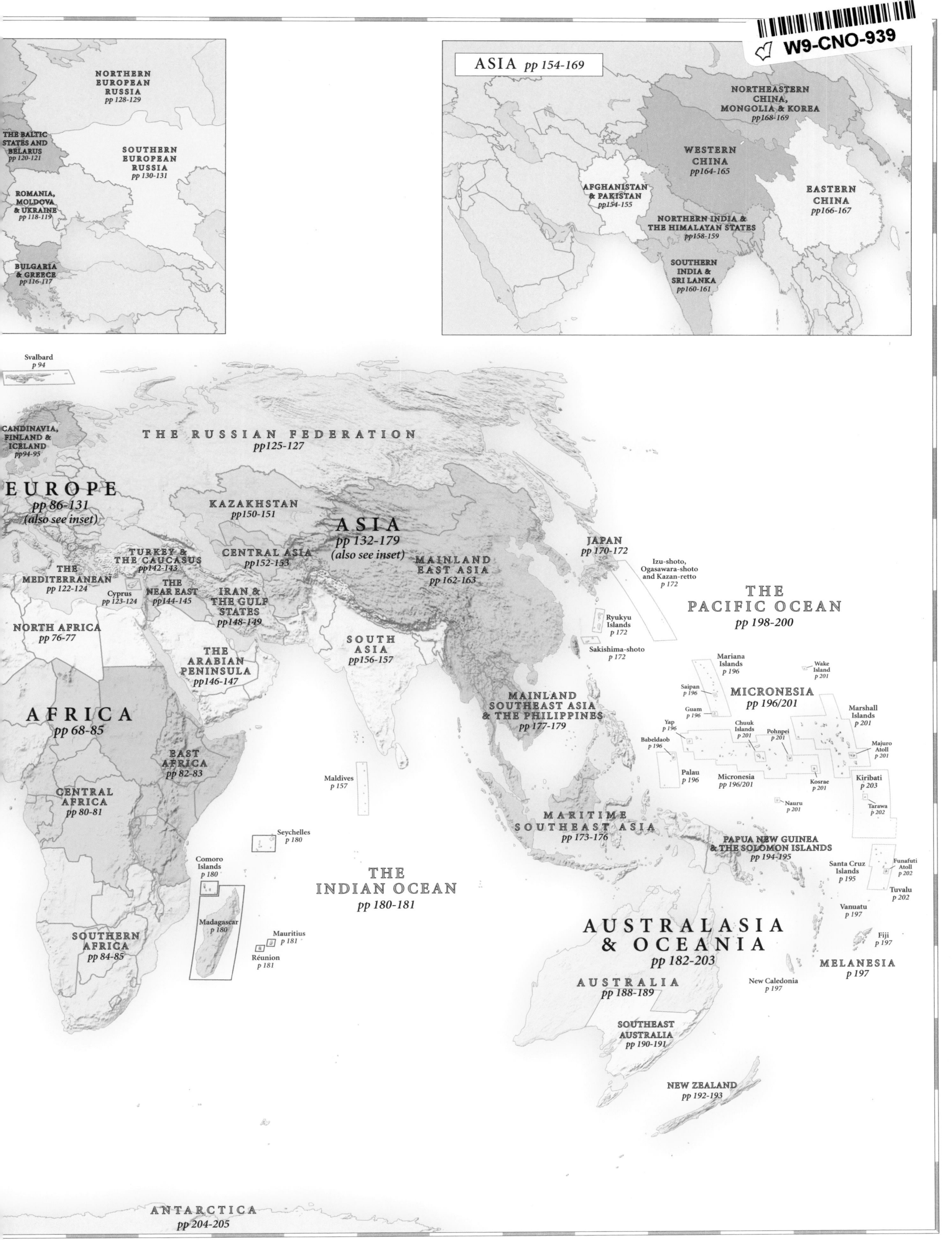

DORLING KINDERSLEY

WORLD ATLAS

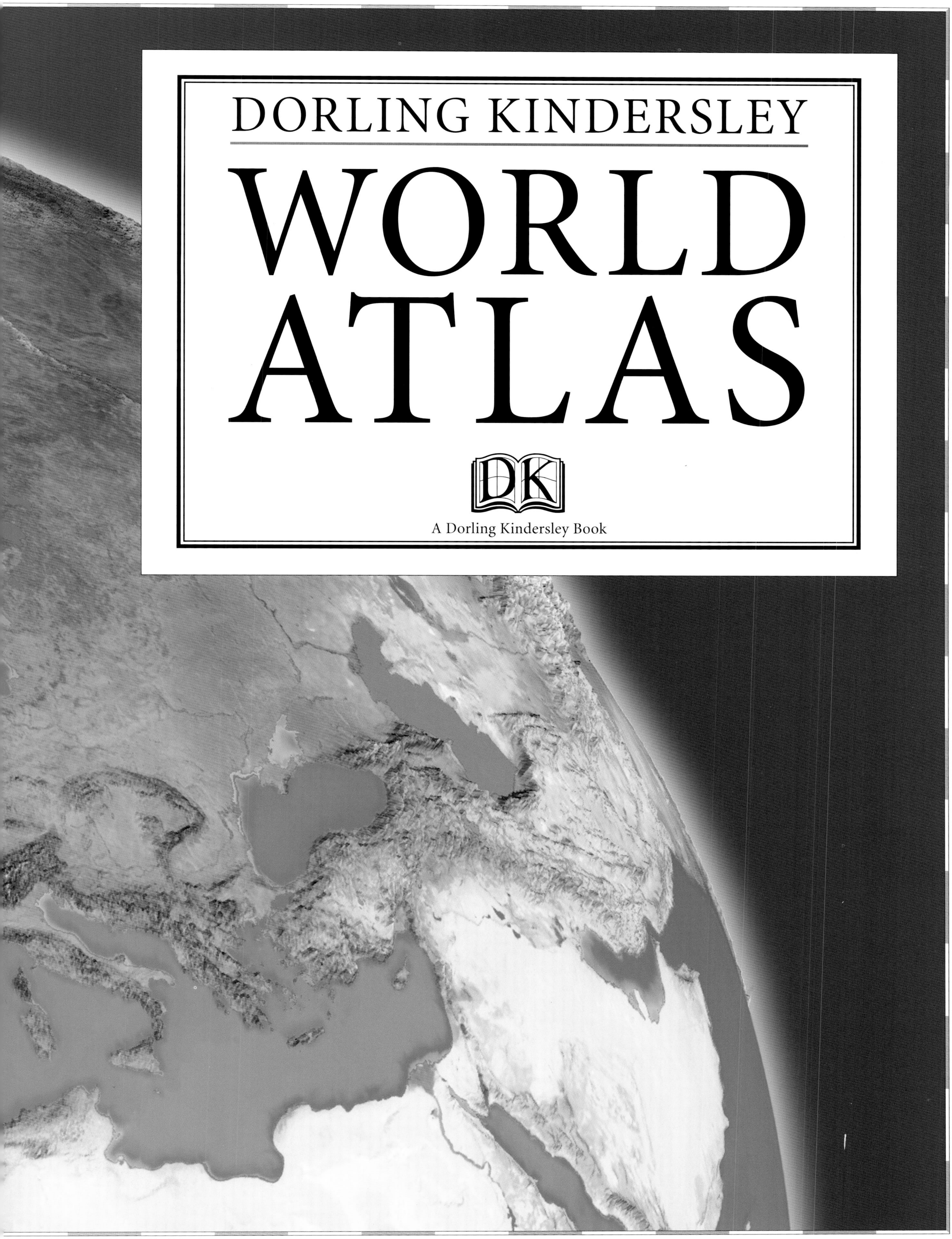

DORLING KINDERSLEY
WORLD ATLAS

A Dorling Kindersley Book

Dorling DK Kindersley

LONDON, NEW YORK, MUNICH, MELBOURNE, DELHI

GENERAL GEOGRAPHICAL CONSULTANTS

PHYSICAL GEOGRAPHY • Denys Brunsden, Emeritus Professor, Department of Geography, King's College, London

HUMAN GEOGRAPHY • Professor J Malcolm Wagstaff, Department of Geography, University of Southampton

PLACE NAMES • Caroline Burgess, Permanent Committee on Geographical Names, London

BOUNDARIES • International Boundaries Research Unit, Mountjoy Research Centre, University of Durham

DIGITAL MAPPING CONSULTANTS

DK Cartopia developed by George Galfalvi and XMap Ltd, London

Professor Jan-Peter Muller, Department of Photogrammetry and Surveying, University College, London

Cover globes, planets and information on the Solar System provided by Philip Eales and Kevin Tildsley, Planetary Visions Ltd, London

REGIONAL CONSULTANTS

NORTH AMERICA • Dr David Green, Department of Geography, King's College, London
Jim Walsh, Head of Reference, Wessell Library, Tufts University, Medford, Massachussetts

SOUTH AMERICA • Dr David Preston, School of Geography, University of Leeds

EUROPE • Dr Edward M Yates, formerly of the Department of Geography, King's College, London

AFRICA • Dr Philip Amis, Development Administration Group, University of Birmingham
Dr Ieuan Ll Griffiths, Department of Geography, University of Sussex
Dr Tony Binns, Department of Geography, University of Sussex

CENTRAL ASIA • Dr David Turnock, Department of Geography, University of Leicester

SOUTH AND EAST ASIA • Dr Jonathan Rigg, Department of Geography, University of Durham

AUSTRALASIA AND OCEANIA • Dr Robert Allison, Department of Geography, University of Durham

ACKNOWLEDGMENTS

Digital terrain data created by Eros Data Center, Sioux Falls, South Dakota, USA. Processed by GVS Images Inc, California, USA and Planetary Visions Ltd, London, UK
• Cambridge International Reference on Current Affairs (CIRCA), Cambridge, UK • Digitization by Robertson Research International, Swanley, UK • Peter Clark
British Isles maps generated from a dataset supplied by Map Marketing Ltd/European Map Graphics Ltd in combination with DK Cartopia copyright data

FOR THE FOURTH EDITION

EDITOR-IN-CHIEF
Andrew Heritage

SENIOR CARTOGRAPHIC MANAGER
David Roberts

SENIOR CARTOGRAPHIC EDITOR
Simon Mumford

DIGITAL MAPPING SUPPLIERS
Encompass Graphics

CARTOGRAPHERS
Tony Chambers • Rob Stokes • Iorwerth Watkins

SYSTEMS COORDINATOR   INDEX GAZETTEER
Phil Rowles   Roger Bullen

PRODUCTION
Elizabeth Warman

DORLING KINDERSLEY CARTOGRAPHY

EDITOR-IN-CHIEF
Andrew Heritage

MANAGING CARTOGRAPHER   SENIOR CARTOGRAPHIC EDITOR
David Roberts   Roger Bullen

CARTOGRAPHERS
Pamela Alford • James Anderson • Sarah Baker-Ede • Caroline Bowie • Dale Buckton • Tony Chambers • Jan Clark • Bob Croser • Martin Darlison • Claire Ellam
Sally Gable • Jeremy Hepworth • Geraldine Horner • Chris Jackson • Christine Johnston • Julia Lunn • Michael Martin • James Mills-Hicks • Simon Mumford • John Plumer
John Scott • Ann Stephenson • Julie Turner • Jane Voss • Scott Wallace • Iorwerth Watkins • Bryony Webb • Alan Whitaker • Peter Winfield

DIGITAL MAPS CREATED IN DK CARTOPIA BY   PLACENAMES DATABASE TEAM
Tom Coulson • Thomas Robertshaw   Natalie Clarkson • Ruth Duxbury • Caroline Falce • John Featherstone • Dan Gardiner
Philip Rowles • Rob Stokes   Ciárán Hynes • Margaret Hynes • Helen Rudkin • Margaret Stevenson • Annie Wilson

DATABASE MANAGER
Simon Lewis

MANAGING EDITOR   SENIOR MANAGING ART EDITOR
Lisa Thomas   Philip Lord

EDITORS   DESIGNERS
Thomas Heath • Wim Jenkins • Jane Oliver • Siobhán Ryan • Elizabeth Wyse   Scott David • Carol Ann Davis • David Douglas • Rhonda Fisher • Karen Gregory • Nicola Liddiard

EDITORIAL RESEARCH   ILLUSTRATIONS
Helen Dangerfield • Andrew Rebeiro-Hargrave   Ciárán Hughes • Advanced Illustration, Congleton, UK

ADDITIONAL EDITORIAL ASSISTANCE   PICTURE RESEARCH
Debra Clapson • Robert Damon • Ailsa Heritage • Constance Novis • Jayne Parsons • Chris Whitwell   Melissa Albany • James Clarke • Anna Lord • Christine Rista • Sarah Moule • Louise Thomas

EDITORIAL DIRECTION • Louise Cavanagh   ART DIRECTION • Chez Picthall

First American Edition, 1997. Reprinted with revisions 1998, 1999. Second Edition (revised) 2001. Third Edition (revised) 2003. Reprinted with revisions 2004. Fourth Edition (revised) 2005.

Published in the United States by Dorling Kindersley Publishing, Inc., 375 Hudson Street, New York, New York 10014

Copyright @ 1997, 1998, 1999, 2001, 2003, 2004, 2005 Dorling Kindersley Limited

see our complete catalogue at www.dk.com

For the very latest information, visit:
www.dk.com and click on the Maps and Atlases icon

Printed and bound by Tien Wah Press, Singapore.

DK Publishing, Inc.
DK world atlas.
p. cm.
Includes index.
ISBN 0-7566-1375-2 (alk. paper)
1. Atlases. I. Title: World atlas. II.Title
G1021 D625 2000
912--dc21

INTRODUCTION

For many, the outstanding legacy of the twentieth century was the way in which the Earth shrank. As we enter the third millennium, it is increasingly important for us to have a clear vision of the world in which we live. The human population has increased fourfold since 1900. The last scraps of *terra incognita* – the polar regions and ocean depths – have been penetrated and mapped. New regions have been colonized, and previously hostile realms claimed for habitation. The advent of aviation technology and mass tourism allows many of us to travel farther, faster, and more frequently than ever before. In doing so we are given a bird's-eye view of the Earth's surface denied to our forebears.

At the same time, the amount of information about our world has grown enormously. Telecommunications can span the greatest distances in fractions of a second: our multimedia environment hurls uninterrupted streams of data at us, on the printed page, through the airwaves, and across our television and computer screens; events from all corners of the globe reach us instantaneously, and are witnessed as they unfold. Our sense of stability and certainty has been eroded; instead, we are aware that the world is in a constant state of flux and change. Natural disasters, man-made cataclysms, and conflicts between nations remind us daily of the enormity and fragility of our domain. The events of September 11, 2001, threw into a very stark relief the levels of ignorance and inaccessibility that exist when trying to "know" or "understand" our planet and its many cultures.

The current crisis in our 'global' culture has made the need greater than ever before for everyone to possess an atlas. The *DK World Atlas* has been conceived to meet this need. At its core, like all atlases, it seeks to define where places are, to describe their main characteristics, and to locate them in relation to other places. Every attempt has been made to make the information on the maps as clear and accessible as possible. In addition, each page of the atlas provides a wealth of further information, bringing the maps to life. Using photographs, diagrams, "at-a-glance" maps, introductory texts, and captions, the atlas builds up a detailed portrait of those features – cultural, political, economic, and geomorphological – which make each region unique, and which are also the main agents of change.

This Fourth Edition of the *DK World Atlas* incorporates thousands of revisions and updates affecting every map and every page, and reflects many of the geo-political developments which continue to alter the shape of our world. Since its first publication in 1997 the *DK World Atlas* has proved extremely popular – going into 22 editions around the world –and has been translated into 13 languages, including Greek and Russian.

Andrew Heritage
Editor-in-Chief

CONTENTS

THE WORLD TODAY

ATLAS OF THE WORLD

NORTH AMERICA

SOUTH AMERICA

AFRICA

EUROPE

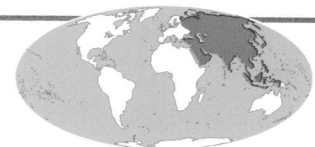

ASIA

AUSTRALASIA AND OCEANIA

INDEX–GAZETTEER

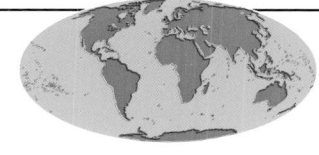

KEY TO REGIONAL MAPS

PHYSICAL FEATURES

elevation

6000m / 19,686ft
4000m / 13,124ft
3000m / 9843ft
2000m / 6562ft
1000m / 3281ft
500m / 1640ft
250m / 820ft
100m / 328ft
sea level
below sea level

▲ elevation above sea level (mountain height)
▲ volcano
✕ pass
▼ elevation below sea level (depression depth)

sand desert
lava flow
coastline
reef
atoll

sea depth

sea level
-250m / -820ft
-500m / -1640ft
-1000m / -3281ft
-2000m / -6562ft
-3000m / -9843ft

▲ seamount / guyot symbol
▼ undersea spot depth

DRAINAGE FEATURES

main river
secondary river
tertiary river
minor river
main seasonal river
secondary seasonal river
canal
waterfall
rapids
dam
perennial lake
seasonal lake
perennial salt lake
seasonal salt lake
reservoir
salt flat / salt pan
marsh / salt marsh
mangrove
wadi
∘ spring / well / waterhole / oasis

ICE FEATURES

ice cap / sheet
ice shelf
glacier / snowfield
summer pack ice limit
winter pack ice limit

COMMUNICATIONS

highway
highway (under construction)
major road
minor road
→—← tunnel (road)
main line
minor line
→—← tunnel (railroad)
✈ international airport

BORDERS

full international border
undefined international border
disputed de facto border
disputed territorial claim border
indication of country extent (Pacific only)
indication of dependent territory extent (Pacific only)
demarcation / cease-fire line
autonomous / federal region border
2nd order internal administrative border
3rd order internal administrative border

SETTLEMENTS

built-up area

settlement population symbols

◼ more than 5 million
◉ 1 million to 5 million
◎ 500,000 to 1 million
◉ 100,000 to 500,000
⊕ 50,000 to 100,000
○ 10,000 to 50,000
○ fewer than 10,000

◼●● country/dependent territory capital city
◼●● autonomous / federal region / 2nd order internal administrative center
◼●● 3rd order internal administrative center

MISCELLANEOUS FEATURES

═══ ancient wall
◇ site of interest
∘ scientific station

GRATICULE FEATURES

lines of latitude and longitude / Equator
Tropics / Polar circles
45° degrees of longitude / latitude

TYPOGRAPHIC KEY

PHYSICAL FEATURES

landscape features .. *Namib Desert*
Massif Central
ANDES

headland .... *Nordkapp*

elevation / volcano / pass .... Mount Meru 4556 m

drainage features .... *Lake Geneva*

rivers / canals spring / well / waterhole / oasis / waterfall / rapids / dam .... *Mekong*

ice features .... *Vatnajökull*

sea features........... *Golfe de Lion*
Andaman Sea
INDIAN OCEAN

undersea features ... Barracuda Fracture Zone

REGIONS

country................ **ARMENIA**

dependent territory with parent state ..... **NIUE** (to NZ)

region outside feature area.......... ANGOLA

autonomous / federal region ...... MINAS GERAIS

2nd order internal administrative region .... MINSKAYA VOBLASTS'

3rd order internal administrative region .... Vaucluse

cultural region....... New England

SETTLEMENTS

capital city............ **BEIJING**

dependent territory capital city............ FORT-DE-FRANCE

other settlements.... **Chicago**
Adana
Tizi Ozou
Yonezawa
Farnham

MISCELLANEOUS

sites of interest / miscellaneous......... Valley of the Kings

Tropics / Polar circles.......... *Antarctic Circle*

HOW TO USE THIS ATLAS

The ATLAS IS ORGANIZED BY CONTINENT, moving eastward from the International Dateline. The opening section describes the world's structure, systems, and its main features. The Atlas of the World that follows, is a continent-by-continent guide to today's world, starting with a comprehensive insight into the physical, political, and economic structure of each continent, followed by integrated mapping and descriptions of each region or country.

THE WORLD

THE INTRODUCTORY SECTION of the Atlas deals with every aspect of the planet, from physical structure to human geography, providing an overall picture of the world we live in. Complex topics such as the landscape of the Earth, climate, oceans, population, and economic patterns are clearly explained with the aid of maps and diagrams drawn from the latest information.

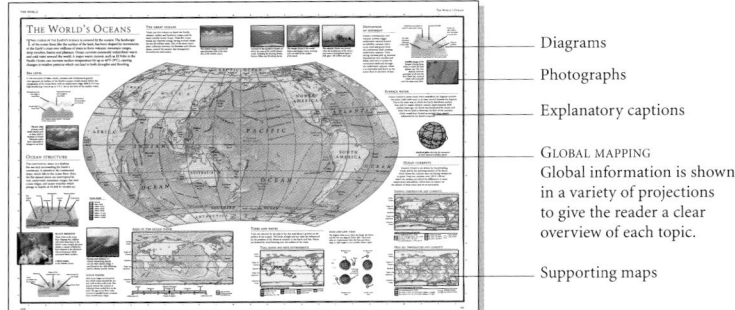

Diagrams
Photographs
Explanatory captions
GLOBAL MAPPING
Global information is shown in a variety of projections to give the reader a clear overview of each topic.
Supporting maps

THE POLITICAL CONTINENT

THE POLITICAL PORTRAIT of the continent is a vital reference point for every continental section, showing the position of countries relative to one another, and the relationship between human settlement and geographic location. The complex mosaic of languages spoken in each continent is mapped, as is the effect of communications networks on the pattern of settlement.

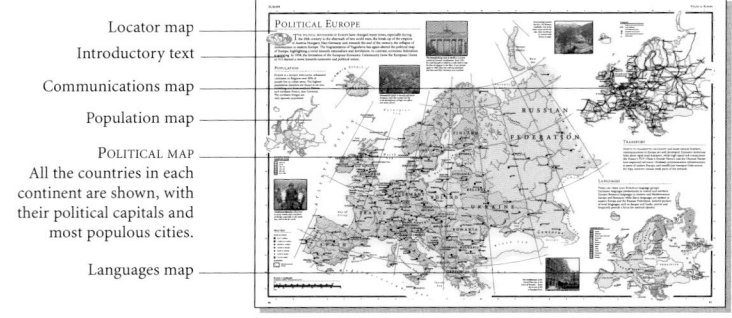

Locator map
Introductory text
Communications map
Population map
POLITICAL MAP
All the countries in each continent are shown, with their political capitals and most populous cities.
Languages map

CONTINENTAL RESOURCES

THE EARTH'S RICH NATURAL RESOURCES, including oil, gas, minerals, and fertile land, have played a key role in the development of society. These pages show the location of minerals and agricultural resources on each continent, and how they have been instrumental in dictating industrial growth and the varieties of economic activity across the continent.

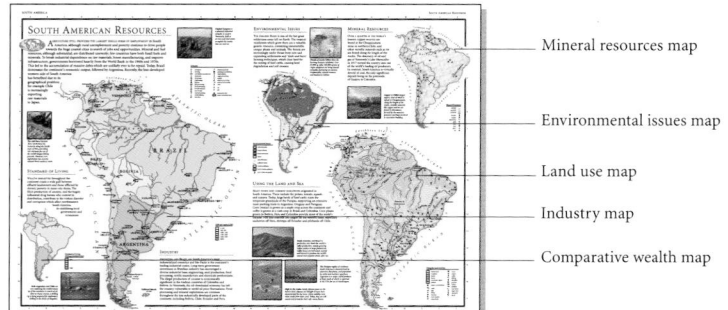

Mineral resources map
Environmental issues map
Land use map
Industry map
Comparative wealth map

THE PHYSICAL CONTINENT

THE ASTONISHING VARIETY of landforms, and the dramatic forces that created and continue to shape the landscape, are explained in the continental physical spread. Cross-sections, illustrations, and terrain maps highlight the different parts of the continent, showing how nature's forces have produced the landscapes we see today.

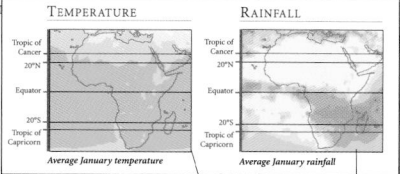

CLIMATE CHARTS
Rainfall and temperature charts clearly show the continental patterns of rainfall and temperature.

CLIMATE MAP
Climatic regions vary across each continent. The map displays the differing climatic regions, as well as daily hours of sunshine at selected weather stations.

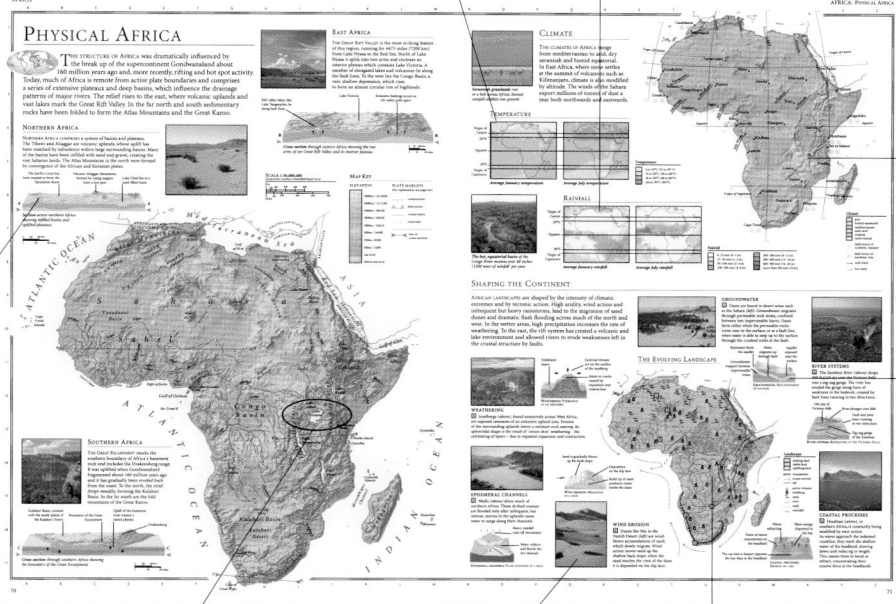

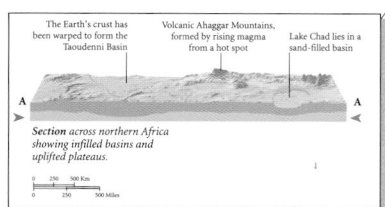

CROSS-SECTIONS
Detailed cross-sections through selected parts of the continent show the underlying geomorphic structure.

Section across northern Africa showing infilled basins and uplifted plateaus.

MAIN PHYSICAL MAP
Detailed satellite data has been used to create an accurate and visually striking picture of the surface of the continent.

PHOTOGRAPHS
A wide range of beautiful photographs bring the world's regions to life.

LANDFORM DIAGRAMS
The complex formation of many typical landforms is summarized in these easy-to-understand illustrations.

GROUNDWATER: REPLENISHMENT OF AN OASIS

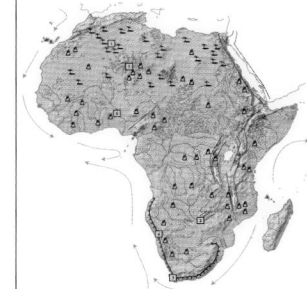

LANDSCAPE EVOLUTION MAP
The physical shape of each continent is affected by a variety of forces which continually sculpt and modify the landscape. This map shows the major processes which affect different parts of the continent.

REGIONAL MAPPING

THE MAIN BODY of the Atlas is a unique regional map set, with detailed information on the terrain, the human geography of the region and its infrastructure. Around the edge of the map, additional 'at-a-glance' maps, give an instant picture of regional industry, land use and agriculture. The detailed terrain map (shown in perspective), focuses on the main physical features of the region, and is enhanced by annotated illustrations, and photographs of the physical structure.

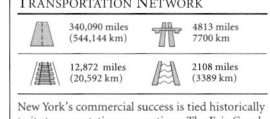

TRANSPORTATION NETWORK

340,090 miles (544,144 km)		4813 miles 7700 km	
12,872 miles (20,592 km)		2108 miles (3389 km)	

New York's commercial success is tied historically to its transportation connections. The Erie Canal, completed in 1825, opened up the Great Lakes and the interior to New York's markets and carried a stream of immigrants into the Midwest.

TRANSPORTATION NETWORK
The differing extent of the transportation network for each region is shown here, along with key facts about the transportation system.

REGIONAL LOCATOR
This small map shows the location of each country in relation to its continent.

KEY TO MAIN MAP
A key to the population symbols and land heights accompanies the main map.

WORLD LOCATOR
This locates the continent in which the region is found on a small world map.

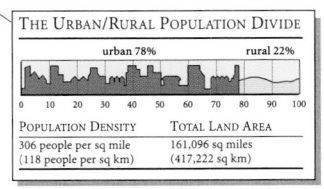

LAND USE MAP
This shows the different types of land use which characterize the region, as well as indicating the principal agricultural activities.

GRID REFERENCE
The framing grid provides a location reference for each place listed in the Index.

MAP KEYS
Each supporting map has its own key.

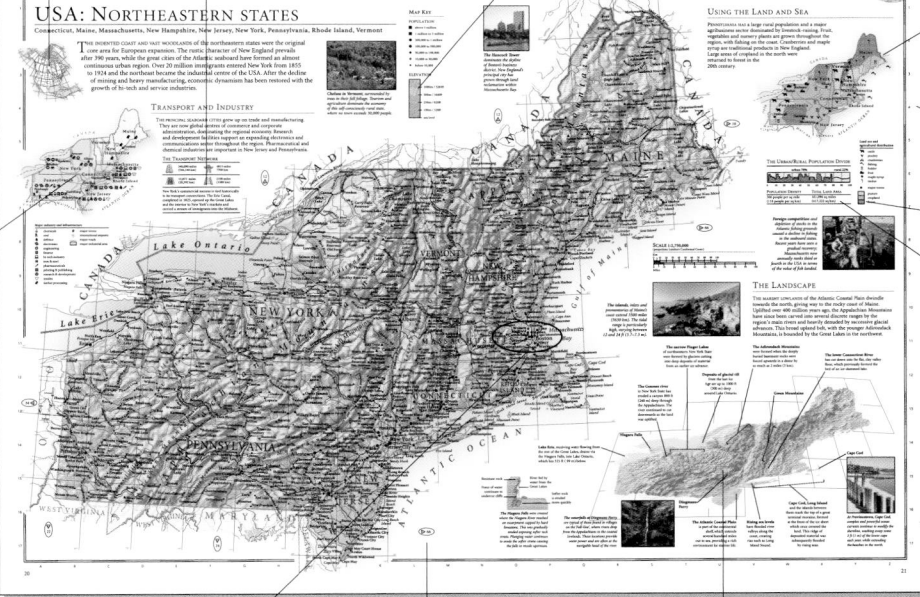

TRANSPORTATION AND INDUSTRY MAP
The main industrial areas are mapped, and the most important industrial and economic activities of the region are shown.

THE URBAN/RURAL POPULATION DIVIDE

urban 78%	rural 22%

| 0 | 10 | 20 | 30 | 40 | 50 | 60 | 70 | 80 | 90 | 100 |

POPULATION DENSITY	TOTAL LAND AREA
306 people per sq mile (118 people per sq km)	161,096 sq miles (417,222 sq km)

URBAN/RURAL POPULATION DIVIDE
The proportion of people in the region who live in urban and rural areas, as well as the overall population density and land area are clearly shown in these simple graphics.

CONTINUATION SYMBOLS
These symbols indicate where adjacent maps can be found.

LANDSCAPE MAP
The computer-generated terrain model accurately portrays an oblique view of the landscape. Annotations highlight the most important geographic features of the region.

MAIN REGIONAL MAP
A wealth of information is displayed on the main map, building up a rich portrait of the interaction between the physical landscape and the human and political geography of each region. The key to the regional maps can be found on page viii.

JUPITER

- ⊖ **Diameter:** 88,846 miles (142,984 km)
- ⊙ **Mass:** 1,900,000 million million million tons
- ○ **Temperature:** -153°C (extremes not available)
- ◑ **Distance from Sun:** 483 million miles (778 million km)
- ◐ **Length of day:** 9.84 hours
- ◑ **Length of year:** 11.86 earth years
- ○ **Surface gravity:** 1 kg = 2.53 kg

MARS

- ⊖ **Diameter:** 4,217 miles (6,786 km)
- ⊙ **Mass:** 642 million million million tons
- ○ **Temperature:** -137 to 37°C
- ◑ **Distance from Sun:** 142 million miles (228 million km)
- ◐ **Length of day:** 24.623 hours
- ◑ **Length of year:** 1.88 earth years
- ○ **Surface gravity:** 1 kg = 0.38 kg

EARTH

- ⊖ **Diameter:** 7,926 miles (12,756 km)
- ⊙ **Mass:** 5,976 million million million tons
- ○ **Temperature:** -70 to 55°C
- ◑ **Distance from Sun:** 93 million miles (150 million km)
- ◐ **Length of day:** 23.92 hours
- ◑ **Length of year:** 365.25 earth days
- ○ **Surface gravity:** 1 kg = 1 kg

VENUS

- ⊖ **Diameter:** 7,520 miles (12,102 km)
- ⊙ **Mass:** 4,870 million million million tons
- ○ **Temperature:** 457°C (extremes not available)
- ◑ **Distance from Sun:** 67 million miles (108 million km)
- ◐ **Length of day:** 243.01 earth days
- ◑ **Length of year:** 224.7 earth days
- ○ **Surface gravity:** 1 kg = 0.88 kg

MERCURY

- ⊖ **Diameter:** 3,031 miles (4,878 km)
- ⊙ **Mass:** 330 million million million tons
- ○ **Temperature:** -173 to 427°C
- ◑ **Distance from Sun:** 36 million miles (58 million km)
- ◐ **Length of day:** 58.65 earth days
- ◑ **Length of year:** 87.97 earth days
- ○ **Surface gravity:** 1 kg = 0.38 kg

THE SOLAR SYSTEM

NINE MAJOR PLANETS, their satellites, and countless minor planets (asteroids) orbit the Sun to form the Solar System. The Sun, our nearest star, creates energy from nuclear reactions deep within its interior, providing all the light and heat which make life on Earth possible. The Earth is unique in the Solar System in that it supports life: its size, gravitational pull and distance from the Sun have all created the optimum conditions for the evolution of life. The planetary images seen here are composites derived from actual spacecraft images (not shown to scale).

THE SUN

- ⊖ **Diameter:** 864,948 miles (1,392,000 km)
- ● **Mass:** 1990 million million million million tons

THE SUN was formed when a swirling cloud of dust and gas contracted, pulling matter into its center. When the temperature at the center rose to 1,000,000°C, nuclear fusion – the fusing of hydrogen into helium, creating energy – occurred, releasing a constant stream of heat and light.

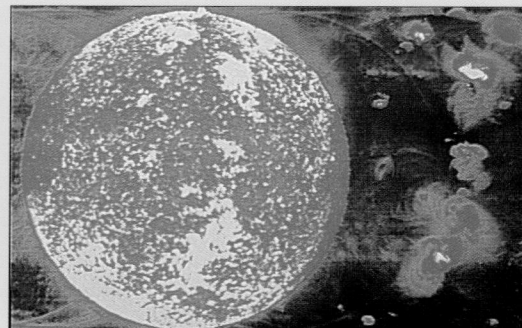

Solar flares are sudden bursts of energy from the Sun's surface. They can be 125,000 miles (200,000 km) long.

THE FORMATION OF THE SOLAR SYSTEM

The cloud of dust and gas thrown out by the Sun during its formation cooled to form the Solar System. The smaller planets nearest the Sun are formed of minerals and metals. The outer planets were formed at lower temperatures, and consist of swirling clouds of gases.

THE MILANKOVITCH CYCLE

The amount of radiation from the Sun which reaches the Earth is affected by variations in the Earth's orbit and the tilt of the Earth's axis, as well as by "wobbles" in the axis. These variations cause three separate cycles, corresponding with the durations of recent ice ages.

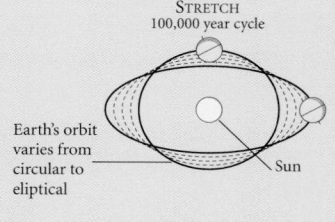

STRETCH
100,000 year cycle

Earth's orbit varies from circular to eliptical — Sun

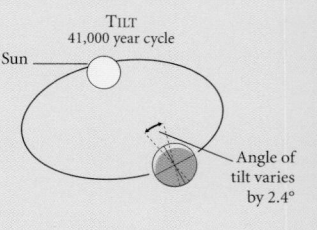

TILT
41,000 year cycle

Sun

Angle of tilt varies by 2.4°

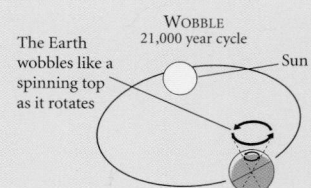

WOBBLE
21,000 year cycle

The Earth wobbles like a spinning top as it rotates — Sun

SATURN

- **Diameter:** 74,974 miles (120,660 km)
- **Mass:** 570,000 million million million tons
- **Temperature:** -185°C (extremes not available)
- **Distance from Sun:** 887 million miles (1,427 million km)
- **Length of day:** 10.23 hours
- **Length of year:** 29.46 earth years
- **Surface gravity:** 1 kg = 1.07 kg

URANUS

- **Diameter:** 31,763 miles (51,118 km)
- **Mass:** 86,800 million million million tons
- **Temperature:** -214°C (extremes not available)
- **Distance from Sun:** 1,783 million miles (2,870 million km)
- **Length of day:** 17.9 hours
- **Length of year:** 84.01 earth years
- **Surface gravity:** 1 kg = 0.92 kg

SPACE DEBRIS

MILLIONS OF OBJECTS, remnants of planetary formation, circle the Sun in a zone lying between Mars and Jupiter: the asteroid belt. Fragments of asteroids break off to form meteoroids, which can reach the Earth's surface. Comets, composed of ice and dust, originated outside our Solar System. Their elliptical orbit brings them close to the Sun and into the inner Solar System.

Meteor Crater in Arizona is 4200 ft (1300 m) wide and 660 ft (200 m) deep. It was formed over 10,000 years ago.

NEPTUNE

- **Diameter:** 30,775 miles (49,528 km)
- **Mass:** 102,000 million million million tons
- **Temperature:** -225°C (extremes not available)
- **Distance from Sun:** 2794 million miles (4497 million km)
- **Length of day:** 19.2 hours
- **Length of year:** 164.79 earth years
- **Surface gravity:** 1 kg = 1.18 kg

METEOROIDS

Meteoroids are fragments of asteroids which hurtle through space at great velocity. Although millions of meteoroids enter the Earth's atmosphere, the vast majority burn up on entry, and fall to the Earth as a meteor or shooting star. Large meteoroids traveling at speeds of 155,000 mph (250,000 kmph) can sometimes withstand the atmosphere and hit the Earth's surface with tremendous force, creating large craters on impact.

POSSIBLE AND ACTUAL METEORITE CRATERS

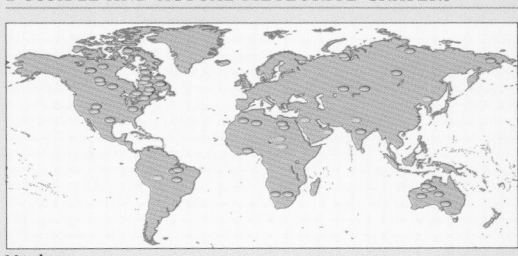

Map key

○ Possible impact craters ○ Meteorite impact craters

THE EARTH'S ATMOSPHERE

DURING THE EARLY STAGES of the Earth's formation, ash, lava, carbon dioxide, and water vapor were discharged onto the surface of the planet by constant volcanic eruptions. The water formed the oceans, while carbon dioxide entered the atmosphere or was dissolved in the oceans. Clouds, formed of water droplets, reflected some of the Sun's radiation back into space. The Earth's temperature stabilized and early life forms began to emerge, converting carbon dioxide into life-giving oxygen.

It is thought that the gases that make up the Earth's atmosphere originated deep within the interior, and were released many millions of years ago during intense volcanic actvity, similar to this eruption at Mount St. Helens.

The orbit of Halley's Comet brings it close to the Earth every 76 years. It last visited in 1986.

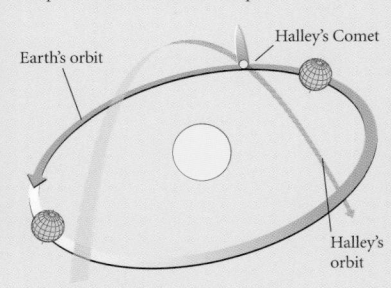

ORBIT OF HALLEY'S COMET AROUND THE SUN

PLUTO

- **Diameter:** 1,429 miles (2,300 km)
- **Mass:** 13 million million million tons
- **Temperature:** -236°C (extremes not available)
- **Distance from Sun:** 3,666 million miles (5,900 million km)
- **Length of day:** 6.39 hours
- **Length of year:** 248.54 earth years
- **Surface gravity:** 1 kg = 0.30 kg

ORDER AND RELATIVE DISTANCE FROM THE SUN OF PLANETS

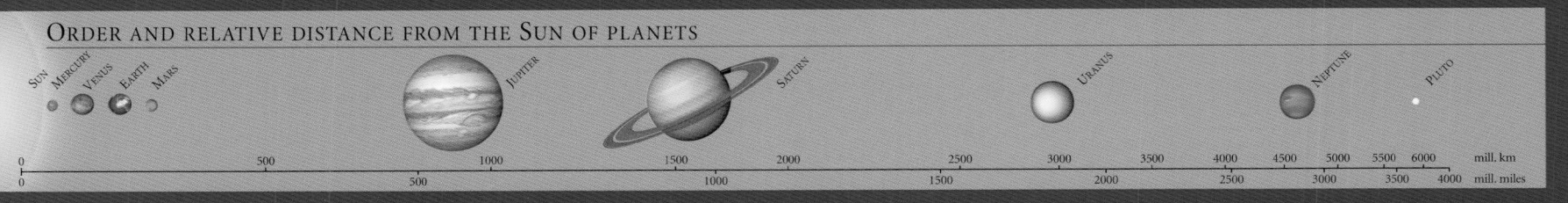

SUN MERCURY VENUS EARTH MARS JUPITER SATURN URANUS NEPTUNE PLUTO

| 0 | 500 | 1000 | 1500 | 2000 | 2500 | 3000 | 3500 | 4000 | 4500 | 5000 | 5500 | 6000 | mill. km |

| 0 | 500 | 1000 | 1500 | 2000 | 2500 | 3000 | 3500 | 4000 | mill. miles |

A B C D E F G H I J K L M

1 2 3 4 5 6 7 8 9 10 11 12 13 14 15

The Physical World

The Earth's surface is constantly being transformed: it is uplifted, folded and faulted by tectonic forces; weathered and eroded by wind, water, and ice. Sometimes change is dramatic, the spectacular results of earthquakes or floods. More often it is a slow process lasting millions of years. A physical map of the world represents a snapshot of the ever-evolving architecture of the Earth. This terrain map shows the whole surface of the Earth, both above and below the sea.

The World in Section

These cross-sections around the Earth, one in the northern hemisphere; one straddling the Equator, reveal the limited areas of land above sea level in comparison with the extent of the sea floor. The greater erosive effects of weathering by wind and water limit the upward elevation of land above sea level, while the deep oceans retain their dramatic mountain and trench profiles.

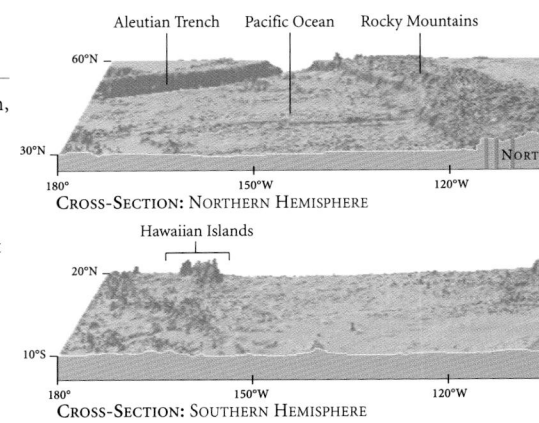

Cross-Section: Northern Hemisphere

Cross-Section: Southern Hemisphere

Map Key

Geographical regions

- ice
- tundra
- needleleaf forest
- broadleaf forest
- cultivated land
- hot desert
- cold desert
- tropical grassland
- tropical rainforest
- mountain
- submarine regions

Scale 1:60,000,000
(projection: Wagner VII)

Km 0 250 500 1,000 1,500 2,000
0 250 500 1,000 1,500 2,000 Miles

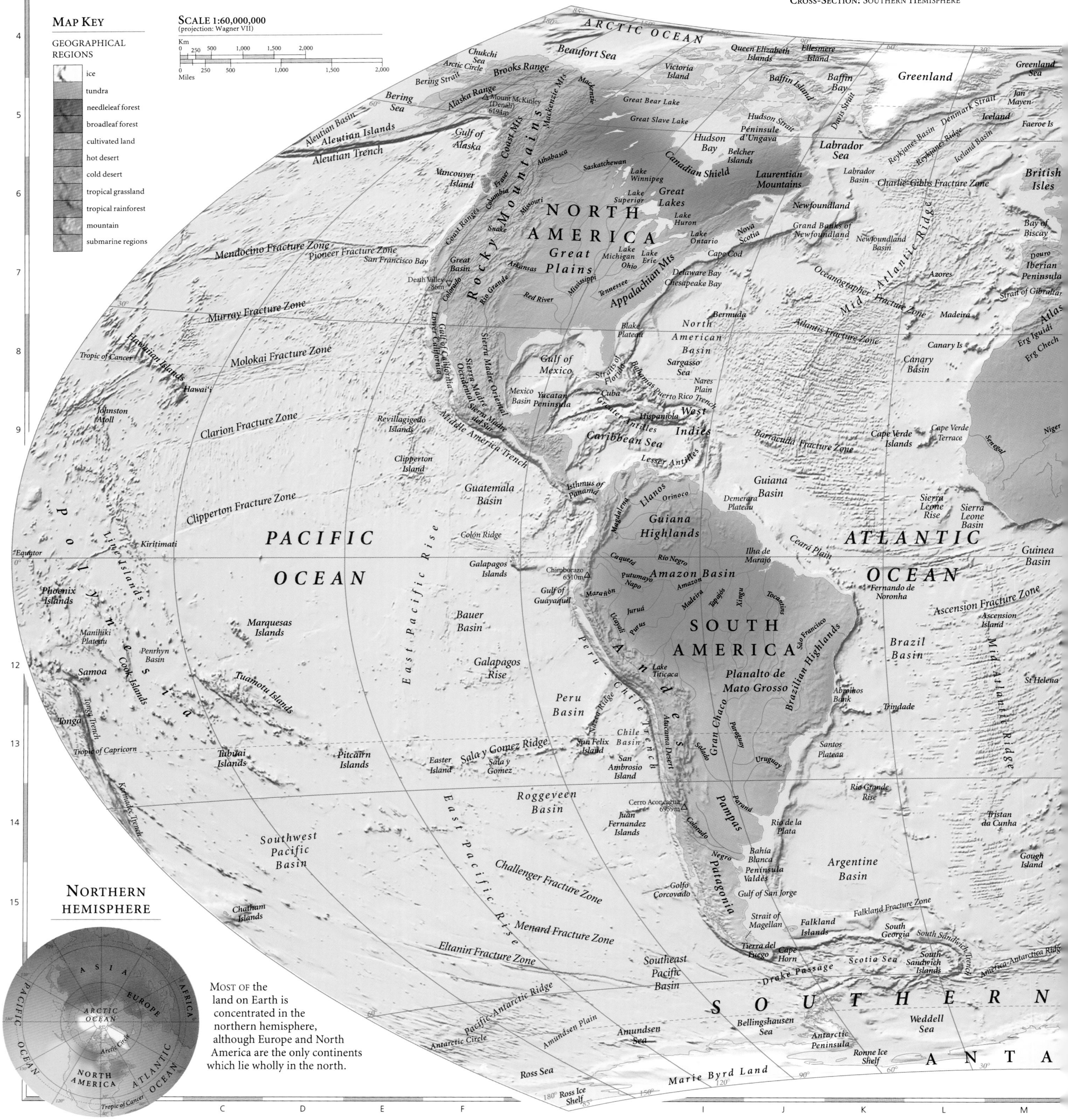

Northern Hemisphere

Most of the land on Earth is concentrated in the northern hemisphere, although Europe and North America are the only continents which lie wholly in the north.

C D E F I J K L M

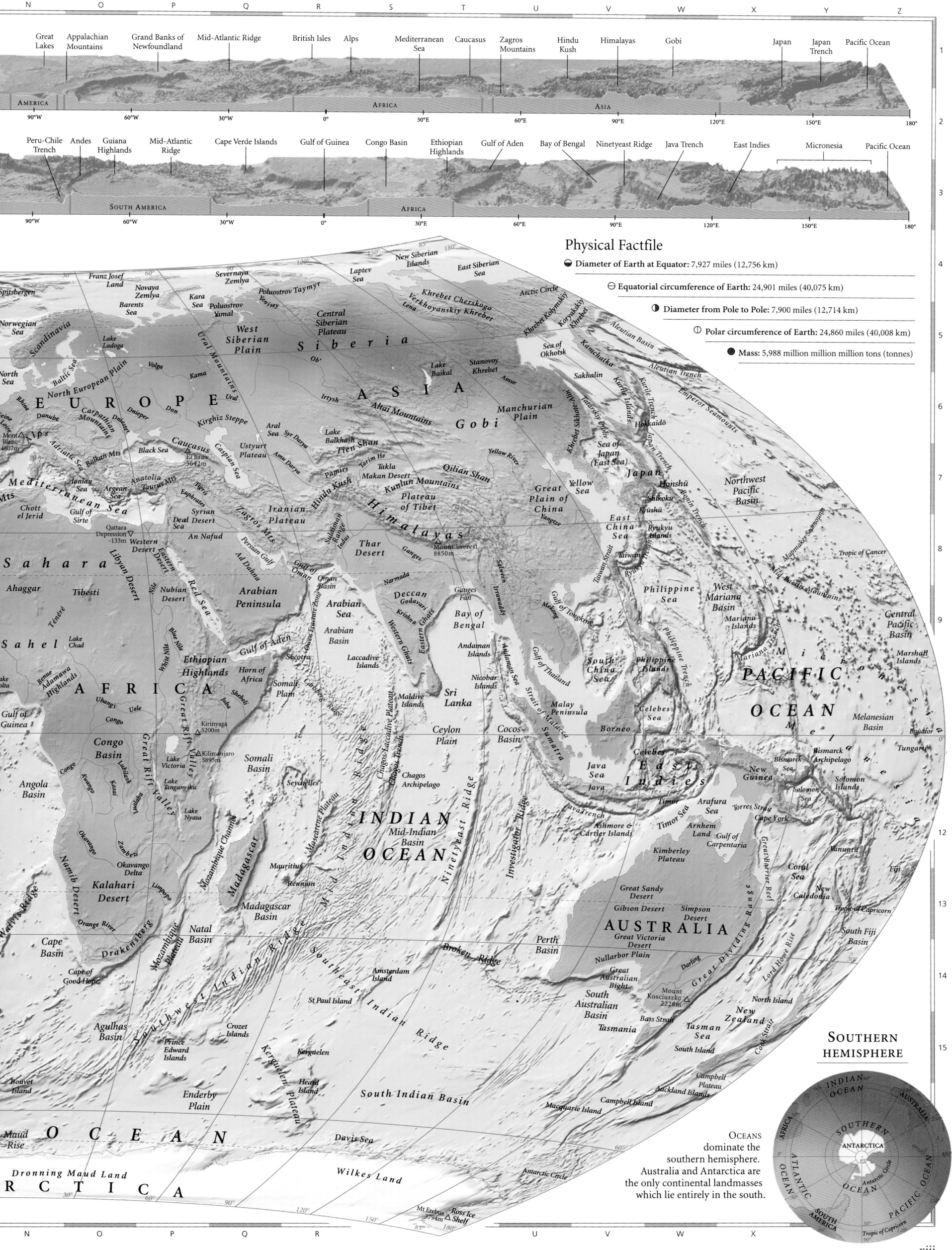

STRUCTURE OF THE EARTH

THE EARTH AS IT IS TODAY is just the latest phase in a constant process of evolution which has occurred over the past 4.5 billion years. The Earth's continents are neither fixed nor stable; over the course of the Earth's history, propelled by currents rising from the intense heat at its center, the great plates on which they lie have moved, collided, joined together, and separated. These processes continue to mold and transform the surface of the Earth, causing earthquakes and volcanic eruptions and creating oceans, mountain ranges, deep ocean trenches, and island chains.

INSIDE THE EARTH

THE EARTH'S HOT INNER CORE is made up of solid iron, while the outer core is composed of liquid iron and nickel. The mantle nearest the core is viscous, whereas the rocky upper mantle is fairly rigid. The crust is the rocky outer shell of the Earth. Together, the upper mantle and the crust form the lithosphere.

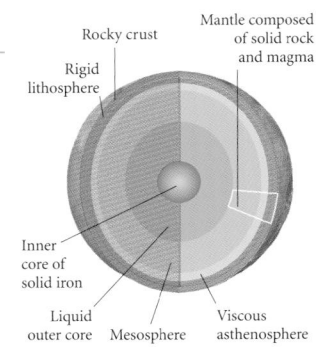

Rocky crust
Mantle composed of solid rock and magma
Rigid lithosphere
Inner core of solid iron
Liquid outer core
Mesosphere
Viscous asthenosphere

THE DYNAMIC EARTH

THE EARTH'S CRUST is made up of eight major (and several minor) rigid continental and oceanic tectonic plates, which fit closely together. The positions of the plates are not static. They are constantly moving relative to one another. The type of movement between plates affects the way in which they alter the structure of the Earth. The oldest parts of the plates, known as shields, are the most stable parts of the Earth and little tectonic activity occurs here.

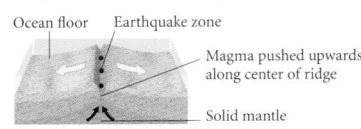

Continental plate
Oceanic plate
Plate boundary: most tectonic activity takes place here
Rigid tectonic plate
Shield area in middle of plate: little tectonic activity occurs here

CONVECTION CURRENTS

DEEP WITHIN THE EARTH, at its inner core, temperatures may exceed 8,100°F (4,500°C). This heat warms rocks in the mesosphere which rise through the partially molten mantle, displacing cooler rocks just below the solid crust, which sink, and are warmed again by the heat of the mantle. This process is continuous, creating convection currents which form the moving force beneath the Earth's crust.

Inner core
Outer core
Subduction zone
Ocean crust
Movement of plate
Mid-ocean ridge
Lithosphere
Asthenosphere
Mesosphere
Continental crust

PLATE BOUNDARIES

THE BOUNDARIES BETWEEN THE PLATES are the areas where most tectonic activity takes place. Three types of movement occur at plate boundaries: the plates can either move toward each other, move apart, or slide past each other. The effect this has on the Earth's structure depends on whether the margin is between two continental plates, two oceanic plates, or an oceanic and continental plate.

MID-OCEAN RIDGES

Mid-ocean ridges are formed when two adjacent oceanic plates pull apart, allowing magma to force its way up to the surface, which then cools to form solid rock. Vast amounts of volcanic material are discharged at these mid-ocean ridges which can reach heights of 10,000 ft (3,000 m).

The Mid-Atlantic Ridge rises above sea level in Iceland, producing geysers and volcanoes.

Ocean floor
Earthquake zone
Magma pushed upwards along center of ridge
Solid mantle

FORMATION OF A MID-OCEAN RIDGE

OCEAN PLATES MEETING

♨ ♨ Oceanic crust is denser and thinner than continental crust; on average it is 3 miles (5 km) thick, while continental crust averages 18–24 miles (30–40 km). When oceanic plates of similar density meet, the crust is contorted as one plate overrides the other, forming deep sea trenches and volcanic island arcs above sea level.

Mount Pinatubo is an active volcano, lying on the Pacific "Ring of Fire."

Overriding plate
Chain of islands
Ocean trench
Diving plate
Volcanic activity

OCEAN PLATES MEETING TO FORM AN ISLAND ARC

Tectonic Activity

- – – – – uncertain plate boundary
- ▲ volcanic zone
- ● earthquake zone
- ● hot spot
- ✕✕✕✕✕ rift valley

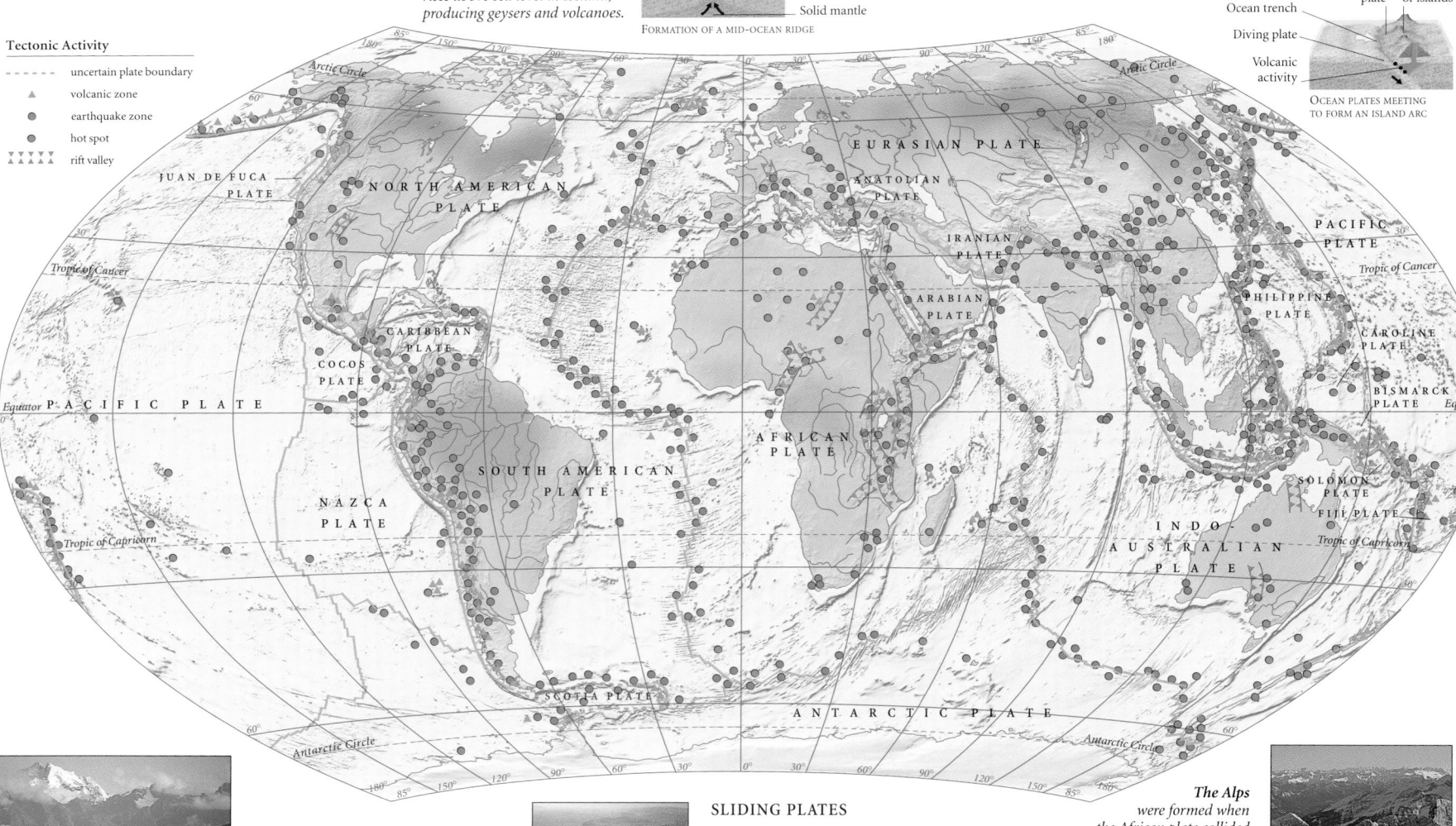

JUAN DE FUCA PLATE
NORTH AMERICAN PLATE
EURASIAN PLATE
ANATOLIAN PLATE
IRANIAN PLATE
ARABIAN PLATE
PACIFIC PLATE
PHILIPPINE PLATE
CAROLINE PLATE
CARIBBEAN PLATE
COCOS PLATE
PACIFIC PLATE
AFRICAN PLATE
BISMARCK PLATE
SOUTH AMERICAN PLATE
NAZCA PLATE
SOLOMON PLATE
FIJI PLATE
INDO-AUSTRALIAN PLATE
SCOTIA PLATE
ANTARCTIC PLATE

Arctic Circle
Tropic of Cancer
Equator
Tropic of Capricorn
Antarctic Circle

DIVING PLATES

♨ ♨ When an oceanic and a continental plate meet, the denser oceanic plate is driven underneath the continental plate, which is crumpled by the collision to form mountain ranges. As the ocean plate plunges downward, it heats up, and molten rock (magma) is forced up to the surface.

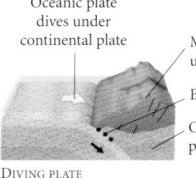

The Andean mountain chain is the typical result of the impact of a diving plate.

Oceanic plate dives under continental plate
Mountains thrust up by collision
Earthquake zone
Continental plate

DIVING PLATE

SLIDING PLATES

When two plates slide past each other, friction is caused along the fault line which divides them. The plates do not move smoothly, and the uneven movement causes earthquakes.

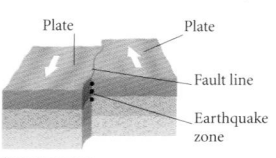

The deep fracture caused by the sliding plates of the San Andreas Fault can be clearly seen in parts of California.

Plate
Plate
Fault line
Earthquake zone

SLIDING PLATES

COLLIDING PLATES

When two continental plates collide, great mountain chains are thrust upward as the crust buckles and folds under the force of the impact.

The Alps were formed when the African plate collided with the Eurasian Plate, about 65 million years ago.

Plate buckles as it collides
Mountains thrust upwards
Earthquake zone
Crust thickens in response to the impact

CONTINENTAL PLATES COLLIDING TO FORM A MOUNTAIN RANGE

CONTINENTAL DRIFT

ALTHOUGH THE PLATES which make up the Earth's crust move only a few inches in a year, over the millions of years of the Earth's history, its continents have moved many thousands of miles, to create new continents, oceans, and mountain chains.

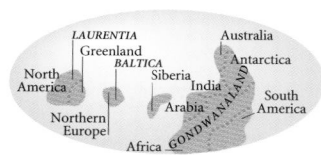

1: CAMBRIAN PERIOD

570–510 million years ago. Most continents are in tropical latitudes. The supercontinent of Gondwanaland reaches the South Pole.

2: DEVONIAN PERIOD

408–362 million years ago. The continents of Gondwanaland and Laurentia are drifting northward.

3: CARBONIFEROUS PERIOD

362–290 million years ago. The Earth is dominated by three continents; Laurentia, Angaraland, and Gondwanaland.

4: TRIASSIC PERIOD

245–208 million years ago. All three major continents have joined to form the supercontinent of Pangea.

5: JURASSIC PERIOD

208–145 million years ago. The supercontinent of Pangea begins to break up, causing an overall rise in sea levels.

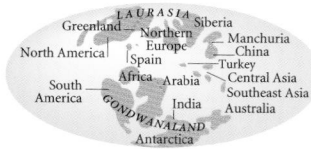

6: CRETACEOUS PERIOD

145–65 million years ago. Warm, shallow seas cover much of the land: sea levels are about 80 ft (25 m) above present levels.

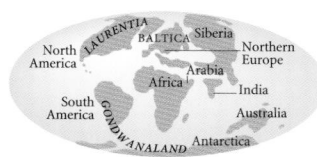

7: TERTIARY PERIOD

65–2 million years ago. Although the world's geography is becoming more recognizable, major events such as the creation of the Himalayan mountain chain, are still to occur during this period.

CONTINENTAL SHIELDS

THE CENTERS OF THE EARTH'S CONTINENTS, known as shields, were established between 2500 and 500 million years ago; some contain rocks over three billion years old. They were formed by a series of turbulent events: plate movements, earthquakes, and volcanic eruptions. Since the Pre-Cambrian period, over 570 million years ago, they have experienced little tectonic activity, and today, these flat, low-lying slabs of solidified molten rock form the stable centers of the continents. They are bounded or covered by successive belts of younger sedimentary rock.

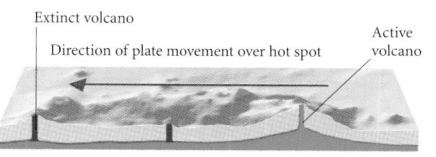

CREATION OF THE HIMALAYAS

BETWEEN 10 AND 20 MILLION YEARS AGO, the Indian subcontinent, part of the ancient continent of Gondwanaland, collided with the continent of Asia. The Indo-Australian Plate continued to move northward, displacing continental crust and uplifting the Himalayas, the world's highest mountain chain.

MOVEMENTS OF INDIA

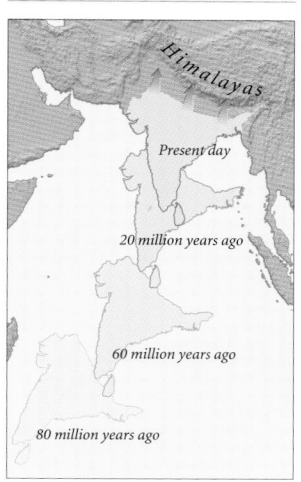

Force of collision pushes up mountains

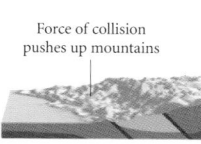

CROSS-SECTION THROUGH THE HIMALAYAS

The Himalayas were uplifted when the Indian subcontinent collided with Asia.

THE HAWAIIAN ISLAND CHAIN

A HOT SPOT lying deep beneath the Pacific Ocean pushes a plume of magma from the Earth's mantle up through the Pacific Plate to form volcanic islands. While the hot spot remains stationary, the plate on which the islands sit is moving slowly. A long chain of islands has been created as the plate passes over the hot spot.

Extinct volcano
Direction of plate movement over hot spot
Active volcano

CROSS-SECTION THROUGH THE HAWAIIAN ISLANDS

EVOLUTION OF THE HAWAIIAN ISLANDS

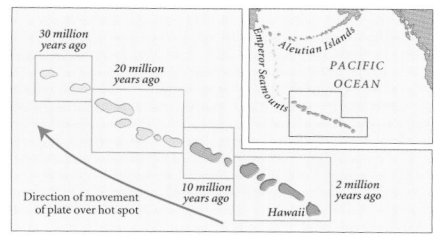

THE EARTH'S GEOLOGY

THE EARTH'S ROCKS are created in a continual cycle. Exposed rocks are weathered and eroded by wind, water and chemicals and deposited as sediments. If they pass into the Earth's crust they will be transformed by high temperatures and pressures into metamorphic rocks or they will melt and solidify as igneous rocks.

GNEISS

[1] Gneiss is a metamorphic rock made at great depth during the formation of mountain chains, when intense heat and pressure transform sedimentary or igneous rocks.

Gneiss formations in Norway's Jotunheimen Mountains.

Basalt columns at Giant's Causeway, Northern Ireland, UK.

BASALT

[2] Basalt is an igneous rock, formed when small quantities of magma lying close to the Earth's surface cool rapidly.

LIMESTONE

[3] Limestone is a sedimentary rock, which is formed mainly from the calcite skeletons of marine animals which have been compressed into rock.

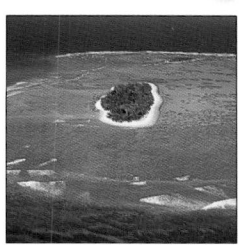

Limestone hills, Guilin, China.

CORAL

[4] Coral reefs are formed from the skeletons of millions of individual corals.

SANDSTONE

[8] Sandstones are sedimentary rocks formed mainly in deserts, beaches, and deltas. Desert sandstones are formed of grains of quartz which have been well rounded by wind erosion.

Rock stacks of desert sandstone, at Bryce Canyon National Park, Utah.

Extrusive igneous rocks are formed during volcanic eruptions, as here in Hawaii.

ANDESITE

[7] Andesite is an extrusive igneous rock formed from magma which has solidified on the Earth's crust after a volcanic eruption.

THE WORLD'S MAJOR GEOLOGICAL REGIONS

Geological Regions

- continental shield
- sedimentary cover
- coral formation
- igneous rock types

Mountain Ranges

- Alpine (new)
- Hercynian (old)
- Caledonian (ancient)

SCHIST

[6] Schist is a metamorphic rock formed during mountain building, when temperature and pressure are comparatively high. Both mudstones and shales reform into schist under these conditions.

Schist formations in the Atlas Mountains, northwestern Africa.

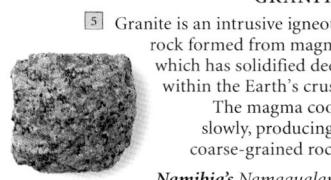

GRANITE

[5] Granite is an intrusive igneous rock formed from magma which has solidified deep within the Earth's crust. The magma cools slowly, producing a coarse-grained rock.

Namibia's Namaqualand Plateau is formed of granite.

SHAPING THE LANDSCAPE

THE BASIC MATERIAL OF THE EARTH'S SURFACE is solid rock: valleys, deserts, soil, and sand are all evidence of the powerful agents of weathering, erosion, and deposition which constantly shape and transform the Earth's landscapes. Water, either flowing continually in rivers or seas, or frozen and compacted into solid sheets of ice, has the most clearly visible impact on the Earth's surface. But wind can transport fragments of rock over huge distances and strip away protective layers of vegetation, exposing rock surfaces to the impact of extreme heat and cold.

WATER

LESS THAN 2% of the world's water is on the land, but it is the most powerful agent of landscape change. Water, as rainfall, groundwater, and rivers, can transform landscapes through both erosion and deposition. Eroded material carried by rivers forms the world's most fertile soils.

Waterfalls such as the Iguaçu Falls on the border between Argentina and southern Brazil, erode the underlying rock, causing the falls to retreat.

COASTAL WATER

THE WORLD'S COASTLINES are constantly changing; every day, tides deposit, sift and sort sand and gravel on the shoreline. Over longer periods, powerful wave action erodes cliffs and headlands and carves out bays.

A low, wide sandy beach on South Africa's Cape Peninsula is continually re-shaped by the action of the Atlantic waves.

The sheer chalk cliffs at Seven Sisters in southern England are constantly under attack from waves.

GROUNDWATER

IN REGIONS where there are porous rocks such as chalk, water is stored underground in large quantities; these reservoirs of water are known as aquifers. Rain percolates through topsoil into the underlying bedrock, creating an underground store of water. The limit of the saturated zone is called the water table.

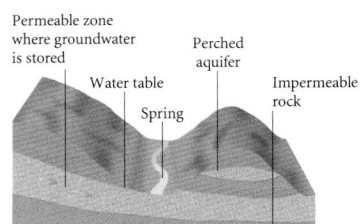

Permeable zone where groundwater is stored

Perched aquifer

Water table

Spring

Impermeable rock

STORAGE OF GROUNDWATER IN AN AQUIFER

World river systems

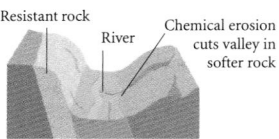

drainage basin

World river systems:
Sediment deposited annually per drainage basin

tons per sq mile per year

9120 6080 1520 760 400 200 and less 1600 2400

tonnes per sq km per year

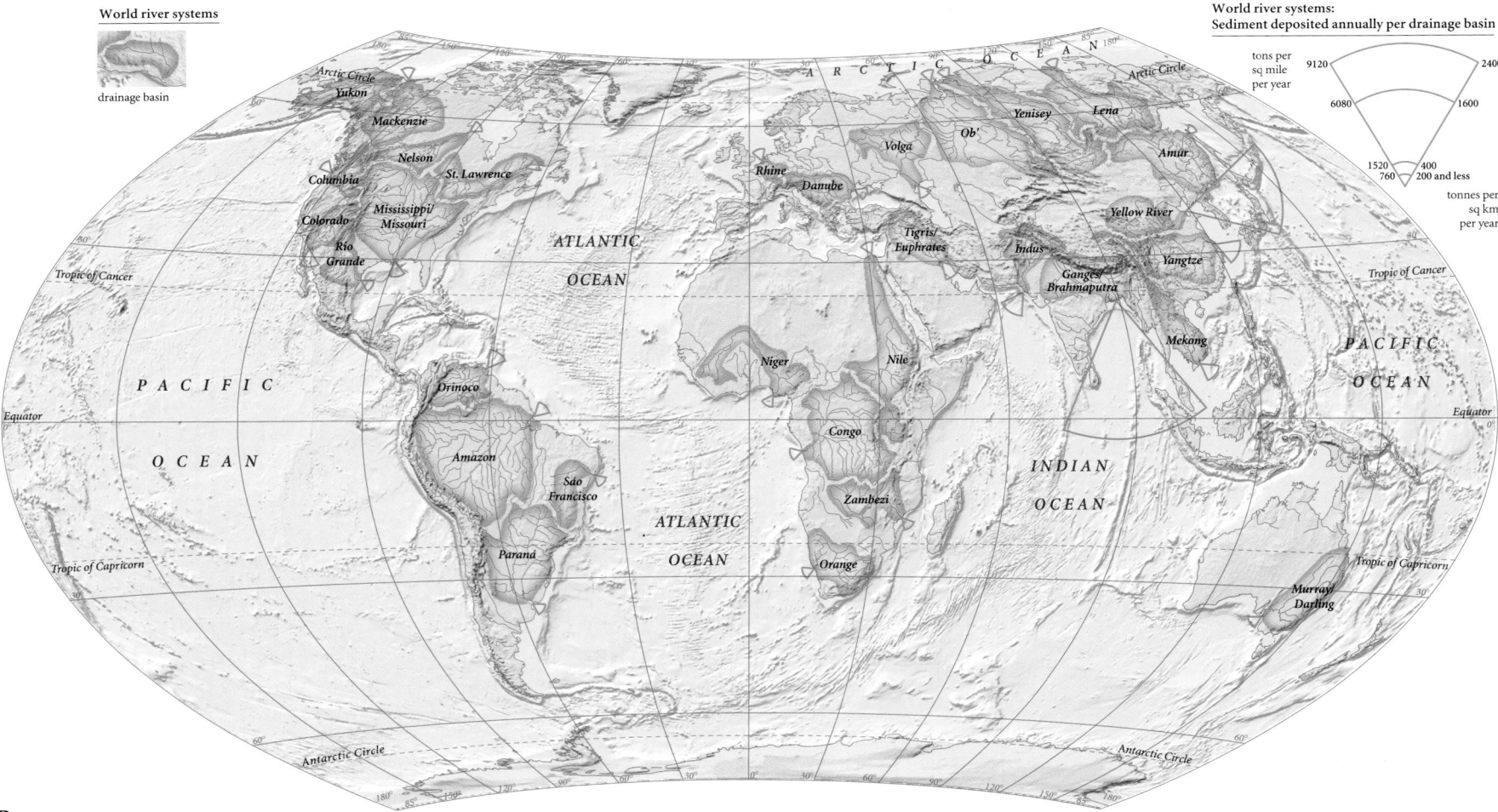

ARCTIC OCEAN

Arctic Circle

Yukon
Mackenzie
Nelson
Columbia
St. Lawrence
Mississippi/ Missouri
Colorado
Rio Grande

Rhine
Danube
Volga
Ob'
Yenisey
Lena
Amur

Tigris/ Euphrates
Indus
Yellow River
Ganges/ Brahmaputra
Yangtze
Mekong

ATLANTIC OCEAN

Tropic of Cancer

Niger
Nile
Orinoco
Amazon
São Francisco
Congo
Zambezi

PACIFIC OCEAN

Equator

Parana
Orange

ATLANTIC OCEAN

INDIAN OCEAN

PACIFIC OCEAN

Tropic of Capricorn

Murray/ Darling

Antarctic Circle

RIVERS

RIVERS ERODE THE LAND by grinding and dissolving rocks and stones. Most erosion occurs in the river's upper course as it flows through highland areas. Rock fragments are moved along the river bed by fast-flowing water and deposited in areas where the river slows down, such as flat plains, or where the river enters seas or lakes.

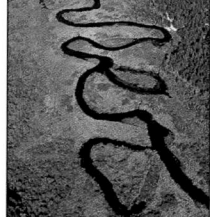

The Mississippi River forms meanders as it flows across the southern US.

MEANDERS

In their lower courses, rivers flow slowly. As they flow across the lowlands, they form looping bends called meanders.

The meanders of Utah's San Juan River have become deeply incised.

RIVER VALLEYS

Over long periods of time rivers erode uplands to form characteristic V-shaped valleys with smooth sides.

Resistant rock

River

Chemical erosion cuts valley in softer rock

RIVER VALLEY EROSION

DEPOSITION

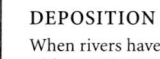

When rivers have deposited large quantities of fertile alluvium, they are forced to find new channels through the alluvium deposits, creating braided river systems.

DELTAS

When a river deposits its load of silt and sediment (alluvium) on entering the sea, it may form a delta. As this material accumulates, it chokes the mouth of the river, forcing it to create new channels to reach the sea.

The Nile forms a broad delta as it flows into the Mediterranean.

Mud is deposited by China's Yellow River in its lower course.

LANDSLIDES

Heavy rain and associated flooding on slopes can loosen underlying rocks, which crumble, causing the top layers of rock and soil to slip.

A huge landslide in the Swiss Alps has left massive piles of rocks and pebbles called scree.

DRAINAGE BASINS

The drainage basin is the area of land drained by a major trunk river and its smaller branch rivers or tributaries. Drainage basins are separated from one another by natural boundaries known as watersheds.

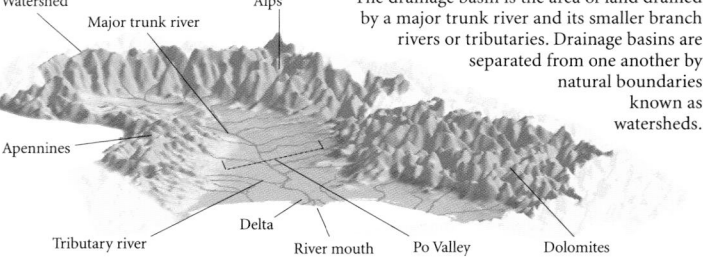

Watershed
Major trunk river
Alps
Apennines
Tributary river
Delta
River mouth
Po Valley
Dolomites

The drainage basin of the Po River, northern Italy.

GULLIES

In areas where soil is thin, rainwater is not effectively absorbed, and may flow overland. The water courses downhill in channels, or gullies, and may lead to rapid erosion of soil.

A deep gully in the French Alps caused by the scouring of upper layers of turf.

ICE

DURING ITS LONG HISTORY, the Earth has experienced a number of glacial episodes when temperatures were considerably lower than today. During the last Ice Age, 18,000 years ago, ice covered an area three times larger than it does today. Over these periods, the ice has left a remarkable legacy of transformed landscapes.

GLACIERS

GLACIERS ARE FORMED by the compaction of snow into "rivers" of ice. As they move over the landscape, glaciers pick up and carry a load of rocks and boulders which erode the landscape they pass over, and are eventually deposited at the end of the glacier.

A massive glacier advancing down a valley in southern Argentina.

POST-GLACIAL FEATURES

WHEN A GLACIAL EPISODE ENDS, the retreating ice leaves many features. These include depositional ridges called moraines, which may be eroded into low hills known as drumlins; sinuous ridges called eskers; kames, which are rounded hummocks; depressions known as kettle holes; and windblown loess deposits.

GLACIAL VALLEYS

GLACIERS CAN ERODE much more powerfully than rivers. They form steep-sided, flat-bottomed valleys with a typical U-shaped profile. Valleys created by tributary glaciers, whose floors have not been eroded to the same depth as the main glacial valley floor, are called hanging valleys.

The U-shaped profile and piles of morainic debris are characteristic of a valley once filled by a glacier.

A series of hanging valleys high up in the Chilean Andes.

The profile of the Matterhorn has been formed by three cirques lying "back-to-back."

CIRQUES

Cirques are basin-shaped hollows which mark the head of a glaciated valley. Where neighboring cirques meet, they are divided by sharp rock ridges called arêtes. It is these arêtes which give the Matterhorn its characteristic profile.

FJORDS

Fjords are ancient glacial valleys flooded by the sea following the end of a period of glaciation. Beneath the water, the valley floor can be 4,000 ft (1,300 m) deep.

A fjord fills a former glacial valley in southern New Zealand.

PAST AND PRESENT WORLD ICE-COVER AND GLACIAL FEATURES

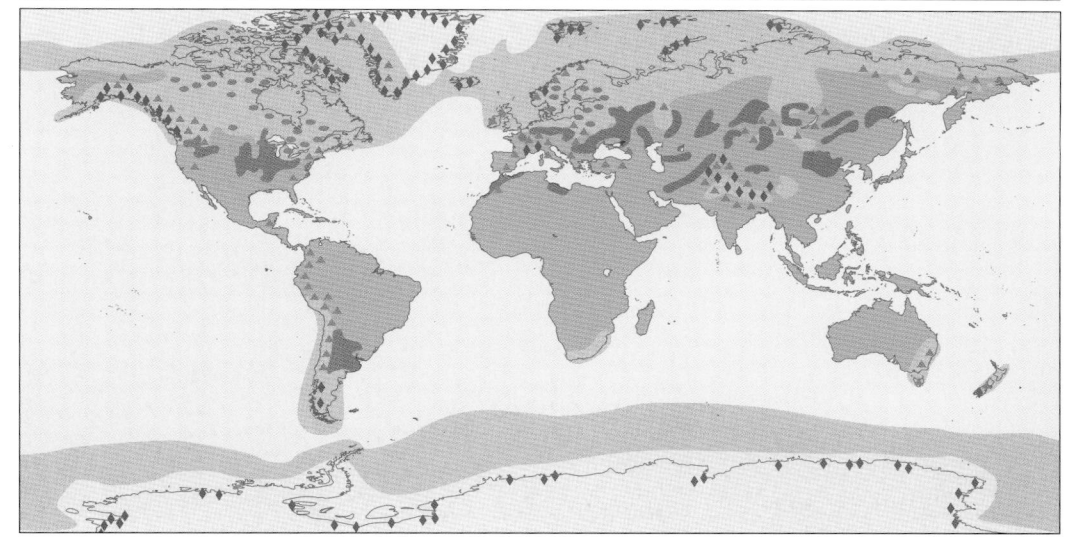

POST-GLACIAL LANDSCAPE FEATURES

Kame terrace
Kettle hole
Esker
Braided river
Windblown loess
Retreating glacier
Drumlin
Terminal moraine
Glacial till
Bedrock

Past and present world ice cover and glacial features

extent of last Ice Age
loess deposits
post-glacial feature
glacial feature
present day ice cover
glacial field

ICE SHATTERING

Water drips into fissures in rocks and freezes, expanding as it does so. The pressure weakens the rock, causing it to crack, and eventually to shatter into polygonal patterns.

Irregular polygons show through the sedge-grass tundra in the Yukon, Canada.

PERIGLACIATION

Periglacial areas occur near to the edge of ice sheets. A layer of frozen ground lying just beneath the surface of the land is known as permafrost. When the surface melts in the summer, the water is unable to drain into the frozen ground, and so "creeps" downhill, a process known as solifluction

WIND

STRONG WINDS can transport rock fragments great distances, especially where there is little vegetation to protect the rock. In desert areas, wind picks up loose, unprotected sand particles, carrying them over great distances. This powerfully abrasive debris is blasted at the surface by the wind, eroding the landscape into dramatic shapes.

PREVAILING WINDS AND DUST TRAJECTORIES

Arctic Circle
Tropic of Cancer
Equator
Tropic of Capricorn
Antarctic Circle

Prevailing winds

northeast trade
southeast trade
westerly
westerly
polar easterly
polar easterly

Dust trajectories

trajectory of aeolian dust

DEPOSITION

THE ROCKY, STONY FLOORS of the world's deserts are swept and scoured by strong winds. The smaller, finer particles of sand are shaped into surface ripples, dunes, or sand mountains, which rise to a height of 650 ft (200 m). Dunes usually form single lines, running perpendicular to the direction of the prevailing wind. These long, straight ridges can extend for over 100 miles (160 km).

Barchan dunes in the Arabian Desert.

Complex dune system in the Sahara.

DUNES

Dunes are shaped by wind direction and sand supply. Where sand supply is limited, crescent-shaped barchan dunes are formed.

TYPES OF DUNE

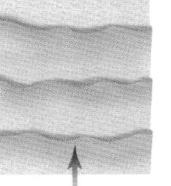
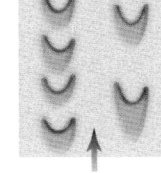
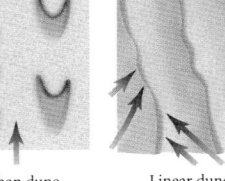

wind direction
Transverse dune
Barchan dune
Linear dune
Star dune

TEMPERATURE

HOT AND COLD DESERTS

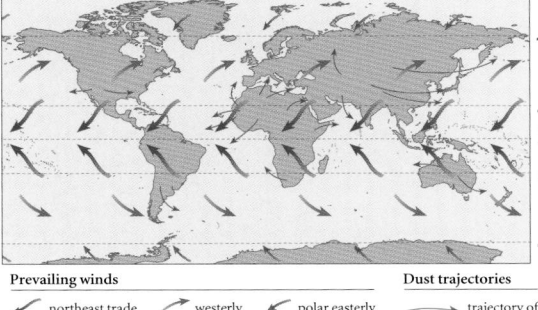

Main desert types

hot arid
semiarid
cold polar

MOST OF THE WORLD'S deserts are in the tropics. The cold deserts which occur elsewhere are arid because they are a long way from the rain-giving sea. Rock in deserts is exposed because of lack of vegetation and is susceptible to changes in temperature; extremes of heat and cold can cause both cracks and fissures to appear in the rock.

HEAT

FIERCE SUN can heat the surface of rock, causing it to expand more rapidly than the cooler, underlying layers. This creates tensions which force the rock to crack or break up. In arid regions, the evaporation of water from rock surfaces dissolves certain minerals within the water, causing salt crystals to form in small openings in the rock. The hard crystals force the openings to widen into cracks and fissures.

The cracked and parched floor of Death Valley, California. This is one of the hottest deserts on Earth.

DESERT ABRASION

Abrasion creates a wide range of desert landforms from faceted pebbles and wind ripples in the sand, to large-scale features such as yardangs (low, streamlined ridges), and scoured desert pavements.

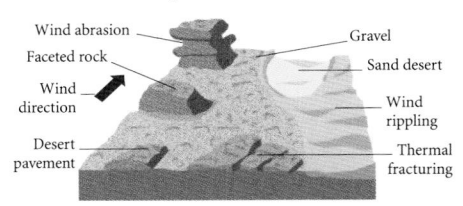

Wind abrasion
Faceted rock
Wind direction
Desert pavement
Gravel
Sand desert
Wind rippling
Thermal fracturing

FEATURES OF A DESERT SURFACE

This dry valley at Ellesmere Island in the Canadian Arctic is an example of a cold desert. The cracked floor and scoured slopes are features also found in hot deserts.

THE WORLD'S OCEANS

Two-thirds of the Earth's surface is covered by the oceans. The landscape of the ocean floor, like the surface of the land, has been shaped by movements of the Earth's crust over millions of years to form volcanic mountain ranges, deep trenches, basins, and plateaus. Ocean currents constantly redistribute warm and cold water around the world. A major warm current, such as El Niño in the Pacific Ocean, can increase surface temperature by up to 46°F (8°C), causing changes in weather patterns which can lead to both droughts and flooding.

THE GREAT OCEANS

There are five oceans on Earth: the Pacific, Atlantic, Indian, and Southern oceans, and the much smaller Arctic Ocean. These five ocean basins are relatively young, having evolved within the last 80 million years. One of the most recent plate collisions, between the Eurasian and African plates, created the present-day arrangement of continents and oceans.

The Indian Ocean accounts for approximately 20% of the total area of the world's oceans.

SEA LEVEL

If the influence of tides, winds, currents, and variations in gravity were ignored, the surface of the Earth's oceans would closely follow the topography of the ocean floor, with an underwater ridge 3,000 ft (915 m) high producing a rise of up to 3 ft (1 m) in the level of the surface water.

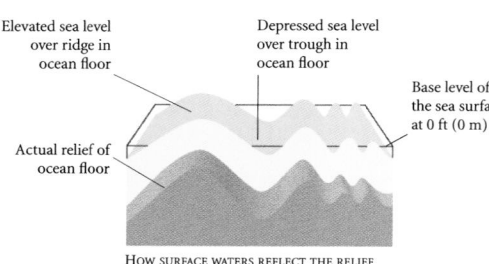

Elevated sea level over ridge in ocean floor

Depressed sea level over trough in ocean floor

Base level of the sea surface at 0 ft (0 m)

Actual relief of ocean floor

HOW SURFACE WATERS REFLECT THE RELIEF OF THE OCEAN FLOOR

The low relief of many small Pacific islands such as these atolls at Huahine in French Polynesia makes them vulnerable to changes in sea level.

OCEAN STRUCTURE

The continental shelf is a shallow, flat seabed surrounding the Earth's continents. It extends to the continental slope, which falls to the ocean floor. Here, the flat abyssal plains are interrupted by vast, underwater mountain ranges, the mid-ocean ridges, and ocean trenches which plunge to depths of 35,828 ft (10,920 m).

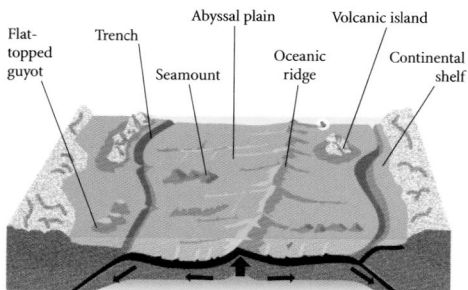

Flat-topped guyot

Trench

Abyssal plain

Seamount

Oceanic ridge

Volcanic island

Continental shelf

TYPICAL SEA-FLOOR FEATURES

Ocean depth

Sea level
200m / 656ft
1000m / 3281ft
2000m / 6562ft
3000m / 9843ft
4000m / 13,124ft
5000m / 16,400ft
6000m / 19,686ft

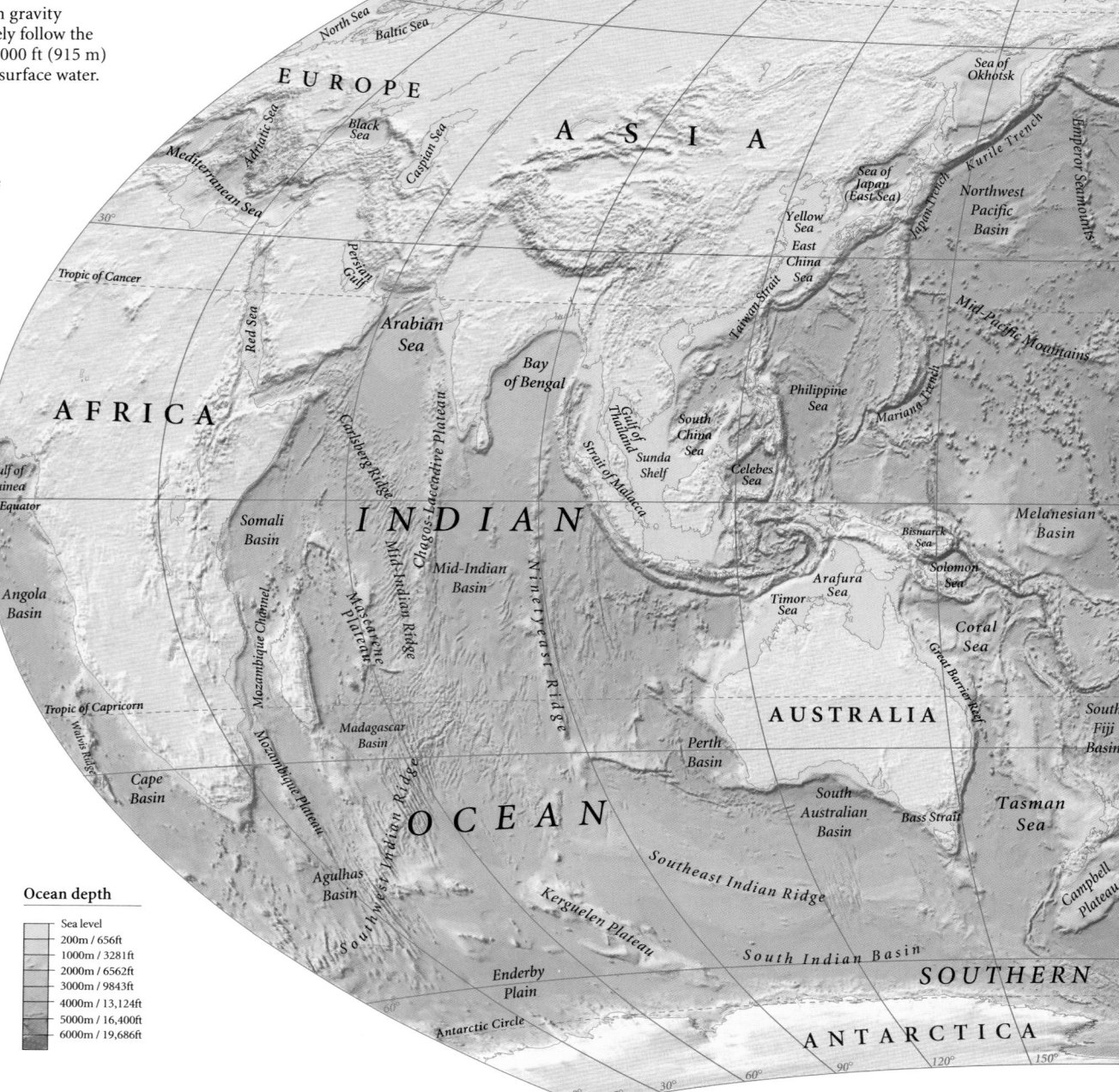

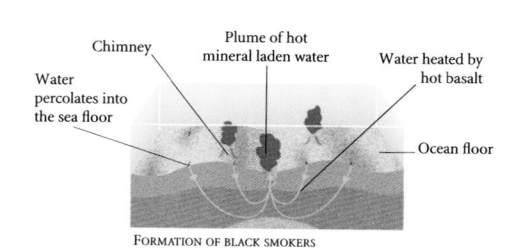

BLACK SMOKERS

These vents in the ocean floor disgorge hot, sulfur-rich water from deep in the Earth's crust. Despite the great depths, a variety of lifeforms have adapted to the chemical-rich environment which surrounds black smokers.

A black smoker in the Atlantic Ocean.

Surtsey, near Iceland, is a volcanic island lying directly over the Mid-Atlantic Ridge. It was formed in the 1960s following intense volcanic activity nearby.

OCEAN FLOORS

Mid-ocean ridges are formed by lava which erupts beneath the sea and cools to form solid rock. This process mirrors the creation of volcanoes from cooled lava on the land. The ages of sea floor rocks increase in parallel bands outward from central ocean ridges.

Chimney

Plume of hot mineral laden water

Water heated by hot basalt

Water percolates into the sea floor

Ocean floor

FORMATION OF BLACK SMOKERS

AGES OF THE OCEAN FLOOR

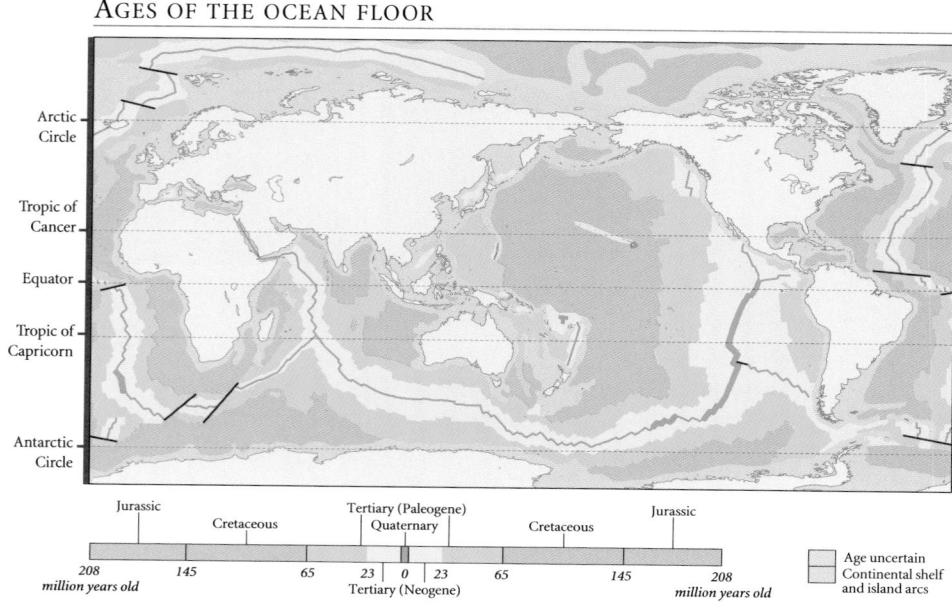

Arctic Circle

Tropic of Cancer

Equator

Tropic of Capricorn

Antarctic Circle

| Jurassic | Cretaceous | Tertiary (Paleogene) | Quaternary | Tertiary (Neogene) | Cretaceous | Jurassic |

208 million years old — 145 — 65 — 23 0 23 — 65 — 145 — 208 million years old

Age uncertain
Continental shelf and island arcs

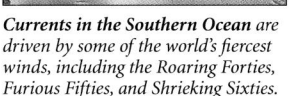

Currents in the Southern Ocean are driven by some of the world's fiercest winds, including the Roaring Forties, Furious Fifties, and Shrieking Sixties.

The Pacific Ocean is the world's largest and deepest ocean, covering over one-third of the surface of the Earth.

The Atlantic Ocean was formed when the landmasses of the eastern and western hemispheres began to drift apart 180 million years ago.

DEPOSITION OF SEDIMENT

STORMS, EARTHQUAKES, and volcanic activity trigger underwater currents known as turbidity currents which scour sand and gravel from the continental shelf, creating underwater canyons. These strong currents pick up material deposited at river mouths and deltas, and carry it across the continental shelf and through the underwater canyons, where it is eventually laid down on the ocean floor in the form of fans.

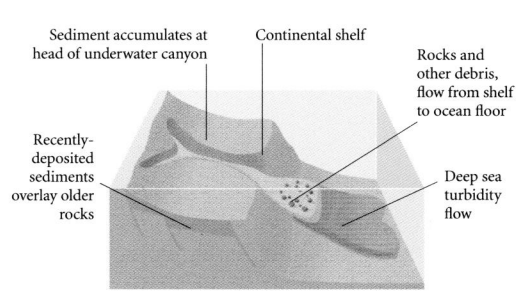

HOW SEDIMENT IS DEPOSITED ON THE OCEAN FLOOR

Sediment accumulates at head of underwater canyon
Continental shelf
Rocks and other debris, flow from shelf to ocean floor
Recently-deposited sediments overlay older rocks
Deep sea turbidity flow

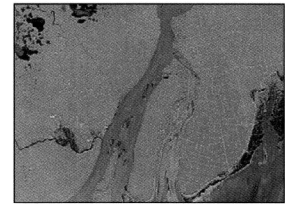

Satellite image of the Yangtze (Chang Jiang) Delta, in which the land appears red. The river deposits immense quantities of silt into the East China Sea, much of which will eventually reach the deep ocean floor.

SURFACE WATER

OCEAN CURRENTS move warm water away from the Equator toward the poles, while cold water is, in turn, moved towards the Equator. This is the main way in which the Earth distributes surface heat and is a major climatic control. Approximately 4,000 million years ago, the Earth was dominated by oceans and there was no land to interrupt the flow of the currents, which would have flowed as straight lines, simply influenced by the Earth's rotation.

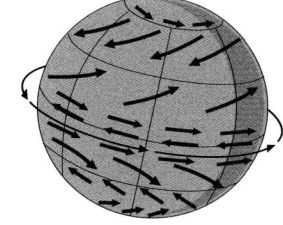

Idealized globe showing the movement of water around a landless Earth.

OCEAN CURRENTS

SURFACE CURRENTS are driven by the prevailing winds and by the spinning motion of the Earth, which drives the currents into circulating whirlpools, or gyres. Deep sea currents, over 330 ft (100 m) below the surface, are driven by differences in water temperature and salinity, which have an impact on the density of deep water and on its movement.

SURFACE TEMPERATURE AND CURRENTS

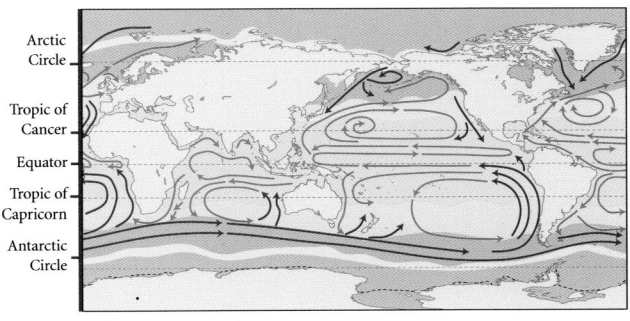

Arctic Circle
Tropic of Cancer
Equator
Tropic of Capricorn
Antarctic Circle

Surface temperature and currents

····· Ice-shelf (below 32°F / 0°C)	32–50°F / 0–10°C → warm current
Sea-ice* (average) below 28°F / -2°C	50–68°F / 10–20°C → cold current
Sea-water 28–32°F / -2–0°C	68–86°F / 20–30°C
* Sea-water freezes at 28.4°F / -1.9°C	

DEEP SEA TEMPERATURE AND CURRENTS

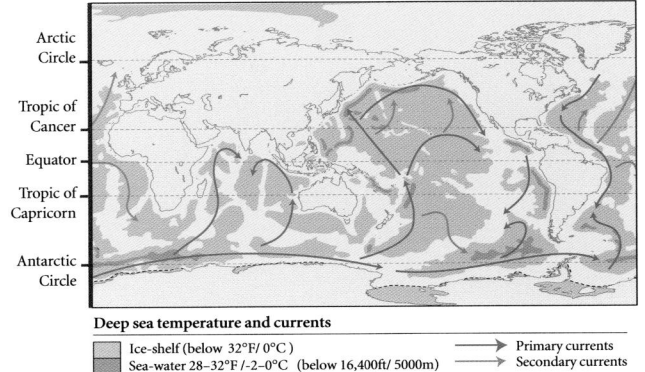

Arctic Circle
Tropic of Cancer
Equator
Tropic of Capricorn
Antarctic Circle

Deep sea temperature and currents

Ice-shelf (below 32°F / 0°C)	→ Primary currents
Sea-water 28–32°F / -2–0°C (below 16,400ft/ 5000m)	→ Secondary currents
Sea-water 32–41°F /0–5°C (below 13,120ft/4000m)	

Map labels:

OCEAN
Chukchi Sea
Beaufort Sea
Bering Sea
Gulf of Alaska
Aleutian Trench
Mendocino Fracture Zone
Murray Fracture Zone
Hawaiian Ridge
Molokai Fracture Zone
Clarion Fracture Zone
Clipperton Fracture Zone
Central Pacific Basin
PACIFIC
Tonga Trench
OCEAN
Southwest Pacific Basin
Pacific-Antarctic Ridge OCEAN
Ross Sea
Amundsen Sea
Bellingshausen Sea
Southeast Pacific Basin
East Pacific Rise

Greenland Sea
Baffin Bay
Davis Strait
Arctic Circle
Hudson Strait
Hudson Bay
Labrador Sea
NORTH AMERICA
Newfoundland Basin
Mid-Atlantic Ridge
North American Basin
Gulf of Mexico
Sargasso Sea
Yucatan Basin
Caribbean Sea
Middle America Trench
Guatemala Basin
Nazca Ridge
Peru Basin
Peru-Chile Trench
Chile Basin
Sala y Gomez Ridge
SOUTH AMERICA
ATLANTIC
Canary Basin
Tropic of Cancer
Barracuda Fracture Zone
Equator
Brazil Basin
OCEAN
Tropic of Capricorn
Rio Grande Rise
Argentine Basin
Mid-Atlantic Ridge
Scotia Sea
South Sandwich Trench
Weddell Sea
Antarctic Circle

TIDES AND WAVES

TIDES ARE CREATED by the pull of the Sun and Moon's gravity on the surface of the oceans. The levels of high and low tides are influenced by the position of the Moon in relation to the Earth and Sun. Waves are formed by wind blowing over the surface of the water.

TIDAL RANGE AND WAVE ENVIRONMENTS

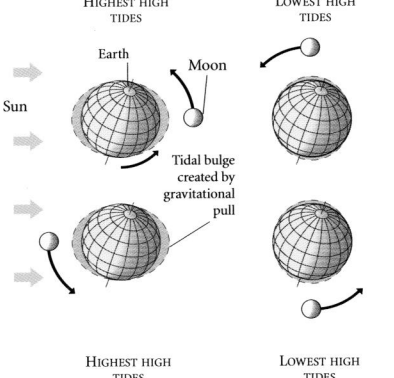

Arctic Circle
Tropic of Cancer
Equator
Tropic of Capricorn
Antarctic Circle

Tidal range and wave environments

less than 7ft / 2m	east coast swell	tropical cyclone	ice-shelf
7–13ft / 2–4m	west coast swell	storm wave	
greater than 13ft / 4m			

HIGH AND LOW TIDES

The highest tides occur when the Earth, the Moon and the Sun are aligned (*below left*). The lowest tides are experienced when the Sun and Moon align at right angles to one another (*below right*).

HIGHEST HIGH TIDES
LOWEST HIGH TIDES
Earth
Moon
Sun
Tidal bulge created by gravitational pull
HIGHEST HIGH TIDES
LOWEST HIGH TIDES

THE GLOBAL CLIMATE

THE EARTH'S CLIMATIC TYPES CONSIST of stable patterns of weather conditions averaged out over a long period of time. Different climates are categorized according to particular combinations of temperature and humidity. By contrast, weather consists of short-term fluctuations in wind, temperature, and humidity conditions. Different climates are determined by latitude, altitude, the prevailing wind, and circulation of ocean currents. Longer-term changes in climate, such as global warming or the onset of ice ages, are punctuated by shorter-term events which comprise the day-to-day weather of a region, such as frontal depressions, hurricanes, and blizzards.

THE ATMOSPHERE, WIND, AND WEATHER

THE EARTH'S ATMOSPHERE has been compared to a giant ocean of air which surrounds the planet. Its circulation patterns are similar to the currents in the oceans and are influenced by three factors; the Earth's orbit around the Sun and rotation about its axis, and variations in the amount of heat radiation received from the Sun. If both heat and moisture were not redistributed between the Equator and the poles, large areas of the Earth would be uninhabitable.

Heavy fogs, as here in southern England, form as moisture-laden air passes over cold ground.

TEMPERATURE

THE WORLD CAN BE DIVIDED into three major climatic zones, stretching like large belts across the latitudes: the tropics which are warm; the cold polar regions and the temperate zones which lie between them. Temperatures across the Earth range from above 86°F (30°C) in the deserts to as low as -70°F (-55°C) at the poles. Temperature is also controlled by altitude; because air becomes cooler and less dense the higher it gets, mountainous regions are typically colder than those areas which are at, or close to, sea level.

AVERAGE JANUARY TEMPERATURES

Arctic Circle
Tropic of Cancer
Equator
Tropic of Capricorn
Antarctic Circle

AVERAGE JULY TEMPERATURES

Arctic Circle
Tropic of Cancer
Equator
Tropic of Capricorn
Antarctic Circle

below - -22°F (30°C)
-22 to -4°F (-30 to - 20°C)
-4 to 14°F (-20 to - 10°C)
14 to 32°F (-10 to 0°C)
32 to 50°F (0 to 10°C)
50 to 68°F (10 to 20°C)
68 to 86°F (20 to 30°C)
86°F (above 30°C)

GLOBAL AIR CIRCULATION

AIR DOES NOT SIMPLY FLOW FROM THE EQUATOR TO THE POLES, it circulates in giant cells known as Hadley and Ferrel cells. As air warms it expands, becoming less dense and rising; this creates areas of low pressure. As the air rises it cools and condenses, causing heavy rainfall over the tropics and slight snowfall over the poles. This cool air then sinks, forming high pressure belts. At surface level in the tropics these sinking currents are deflected poleward as the westerlies and toward the Equator as the trade winds. At the poles they become the polar easterlies.

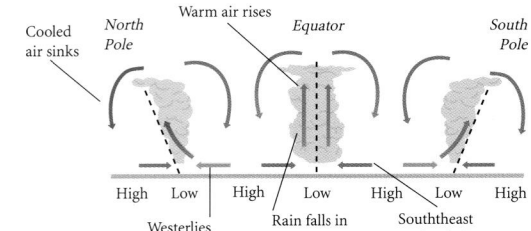

Cooled air sinks — North Pole — Warm air rises — Equator — South Pole

High — Low — High — Low — High — Low — High
Westerlies — Rain falls in the tropics — Southeast trade winds

The Antarctic pack ice expands its area by almost seven times during the winter as temperatures drop and surrounding seas freeze.

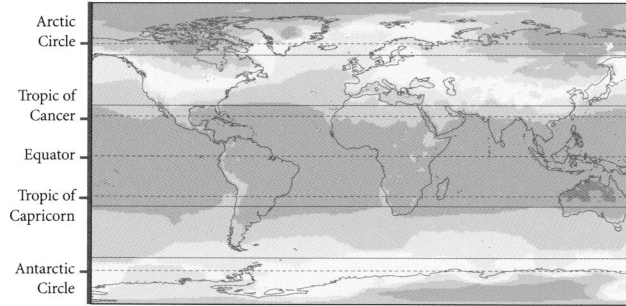

CLIMATIC CHANGE

THE EARTH IS CURRENTLY IN A WARM PHASE between ice ages. Warmer temperatures result in higher sea levels as more of the polar ice caps melt. Most of the world's population lives near coasts, so any changes which might cause sea levels to rise, could have a potentially disastrous impact.

This ice fair, painted by Pieter Brueghel the Younger in the 17th century, shows the Little Ice Age which peaked around 300 years ago.

THE GREENHOUSE EFFECT

Gases such as carbon dioxide are known as "greenhouse gases" because they allow shortwave solar radiation to enter the Earth's atmosphere, but help to stop longwave radiation from escaping. This traps heat, raising the Earth's temperature. An excess of these gases, such as that which results from the burning of fossil fuels, helps trap more heat and can lead to global warming.

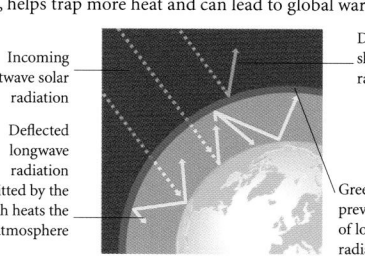

Incoming shortwave solar radiation

Deflected shortwave solar radiation

Deflected longwave radiation emitted by the Earth heats the atmosphere

Greenhouse gases prevent the escape of longwave radiation

The islands of the Caribbean, Mexico's Gulf coast and the southeastern US are often hit by hurricanes formed far out in the Atlantic.

OCEANIC WATER CIRCULATION

IN GENERAL, OCEAN CURRENTS parallel the movement of winds across the Earth's surface. Incoming solar energy is greatest at the Equator and least at the poles. So, water in the oceans heats up most at the Equator and flows poleward, cooling as it moves north or south toward the Arctic or Antarctic. The flow is eventually reversed and cold water currents move back toward the Equator. These ocean currents act as a vast system for moving heat from the Equator toward the poles and are a major influence on the distribution of the Earth's climates.

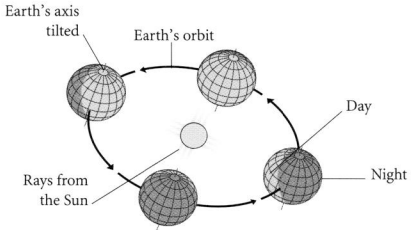

In marginal climatic zones years of drought can completely dry out the land and transform grassland to desert.

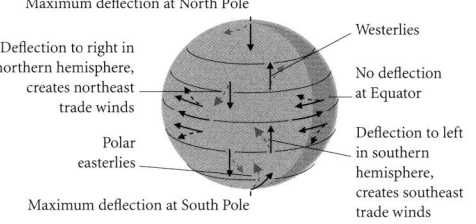

The wide range of environments found in the Andes is strongly related to their altitude, which modifies climatic influences. While the peaks are snow-capped, many protected interior valleys are semitropical.

TILT AND ROTATION

The tilt and rotation of the Earth during its annual orbit largely control the distribution of heat and moisture across its surface, which correspondingly controls its large-scale weather patterns. As the Earth annually rotates around the Sun, half its surface is receiving maximum radiation, creating summer and winter seasons. The angle of the Earth means that on average the tropics receive two and a half times as much heat from the Sun each day as the poles.

Earth's axis tilted
Earth's orbit
Day
Rays from the Sun
Night

THE CORIOLIS EFFECT

The rotation of the Earth influences atmospheric circulation by deflecting winds and ocean currents. Winds blowing in the northern hemisphere are deflected to the right and those in the southern hemisphere are deflected to the left, creating large-scale patterns of wind circulation, such as the northeast and southeast trade winds and the westerlies. This effect is greatest at the poles and least at the Equator.

Maximum deflection at North Pole
Westerlies
Deflection to right in northern hemisphere, creates northeast trade winds
No deflection at Equator
Polar easterlies
Deflection to left in southern hemisphere, creates southeast trade winds
Maximum deflection at South Pole

MAP KEY

Climate zones
- ice cap
- subarctic
- tundra
- continental
- temperate
- warm temperate
- mediterranean
- semiarid
- arid
- hot humid
- humid equatorial
- tropical

Ocean currents
- warm
- cold

Prevailing winds
- → warm
- → cold

Local winds
- → warm
- → cold
- ·ↄ·٠٠٠ → seasonal*
- * (seasonal winds which can either be warm or cold)

EASTERLIES
Buran January
January July
January
July
Mistral
Föhn
Bora
Rhine
Bora
Sirocco
Khamsin
Southwest Monsoon
April–September
Haboob
Monsoon Drift
Equatorial Counter Current
Doldrums
Northeast Monsoon October–March
South Equatorial Current
SOUTH EAST TRADES
Anguela Current
West Australian Current
WESTERLIES
Wind Drift
West Wind Drift
EASTERLIES
Antarctic Circle
Arctic Circle
January
July
KuroSiwo Current
Typhoon July–October
Tropic of Cancer
North Equatorial Current
NORTH EAST TRADES
Equatorial Counter Current
Doldrums
Equator
Southeast Monsoon October–March
South Equatorial Current
Willy Willies January
Queensland
Hurricanes January
Tropic of Capricorn

PRECIPITATION

WHEN WARM AIR EXPANDS, it rises and cools, and the water vapor it carries condenses to form clouds. Heavy, regular rainfall is characteristic of the equatorial region, while the poles are cold and receive only slight snowfall. Tropical regions have marked dry and rainy seasons, while in the temperate regions rainfall is relatively unpredictable.

Monsoon rains, which affect southern Asia from May to September, are caused by sea winds blowing across the warm land.

Heavy tropical rainstorms occur frequently in Papua New Guinea, often causing soil erosion and landslides in cultivated areas.

AVERAGE JANUARY RAINFALL

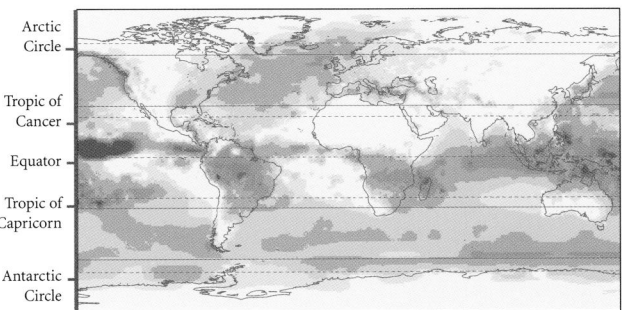

Arctic Circle
Tropic of Cancer
Equator
Tropic of Capricorn
Antarctic Circle

AVERAGE JULY RAINFALL

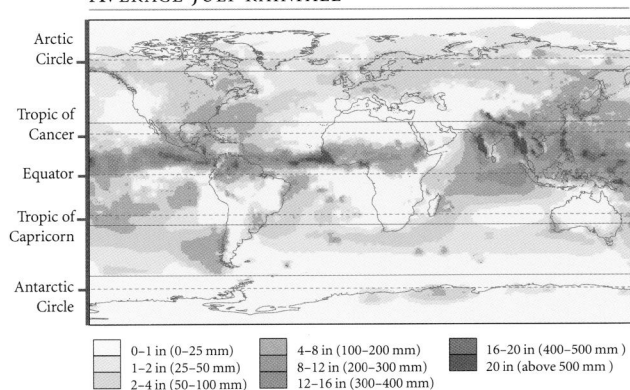

Arctic Circle
Tropic of Cancer
Equator
Tropic of Capricorn
Antarctic Circle

- 0–1 in (0–25 mm)
- 1–2 in (25–50 mm)
- 2–4 in (50–100 mm)
- 4–8 in (100–200 mm)
- 8–12 in (200–300 mm)
- 12–16 in (300–400 mm)
- 16–20 in (400–500 mm)
- 20 in (above 500 mm)

The intensity of some blizzards in Canada and the northern US can give rise to snowdrifts as high as 10 ft (3 m).

The Atacama Desert in Chile is one of the driest places on Earth, with an average rainfall of less than 2 inches (50 mm) per year.

Violent thunderstorms occur along advancing cold fronts, when cold, dry air masses meet warm, moist air, which rises rapidly, its moisture condensing into thunderclouds. Rain and hail become electrically charged, causing lightning.

THE RAINSHADOW EFFECT

When moist air is forced to rise by mountains, it cools and the water vapor falls as precipitation, either as rain or snow. Only the dry, cold air continues over the mountains, leaving inland areas with little or no rain. This is called the rainshadow effect and is one reason for the existence of the Mojave Desert in California, which lies east of the Coast Ranges.

As air rises it cools and condenses leading to cloud
Dry air in "shadow" of mountain
Moist air travels inland from the sea
THE RAINSHADOW EFFECT

LIFE ON EARTH

A UNIQUE COMBINATION of an oxygen-rich atmosphere and plentiful water is the key to life on Earth. Apart from the polar ice caps, there are few areas which have not been colonized by animals or plants over the course of the Earth's history. Plants process sunlight to provide them with their energy, and ultimately all the Earth's animals rely on plants for survival. Because of this reliance, plants are known as primary producers, and the availability of nutrients and temperature of an area is defined as its primary productivity, which affects the quantity and type of animals which are able to live there. This index is affected by climatic factors – cold and aridity restrict the quantity of life, whereas warmth and regular rainfall allow a greater diversity of species.

BIOGEOGRAPHICAL REGIONS

THE EARTH CAN BE DIVIDED into a series of biogeographical regions, or biomes, ecological communities where certain species of plant and animal coexist within particular climatic conditions. Within these broad classifications, other factors including soil richness, altitude, and human activities such as urbanization, intensive agriculture, and deforestation, affect the local distribution of living species within each biome.

POLAR REGIONS
A layer of permanent ice at the Earth's poles covers both seas and land. Very little plant and animal life can exist in these harsh regions.

TUNDRA
A desolate region, with long, dark freezing winters and short, cold summers. With virtually no soil and large areas of permanently frozen ground known as permafrost, the tundra is largely treeless, though it is briefly clothed by small flowering plants in the summer months.

NEEDLELEAF FORESTS
With milder summers than the tundra and less wind, these areas are able to support large forests of coniferous trees.

BROADLEAF FORESTS
Much of the northern hemisphere was once covered by deciduous forests, which occurred in areas with marked seasonal variations. Most deciduous forests have been cleared for human settlement.

TEMPERATE RAIN FORESTS
In warmer wetter areas, such as southern China, temperate deciduous forests are replaced by evergreen forest.

DESERTS
Deserts are areas with negligible rainfall. Most hot deserts lie within the tropics; cold deserts are dry because of their distance from the moisture-providing sea.

MEDITERRANEAN
Hot, dry summers and short winters typify these areas, which were once covered by evergreen shrubs and woodland, but have now been cleared by humans for agriculture.

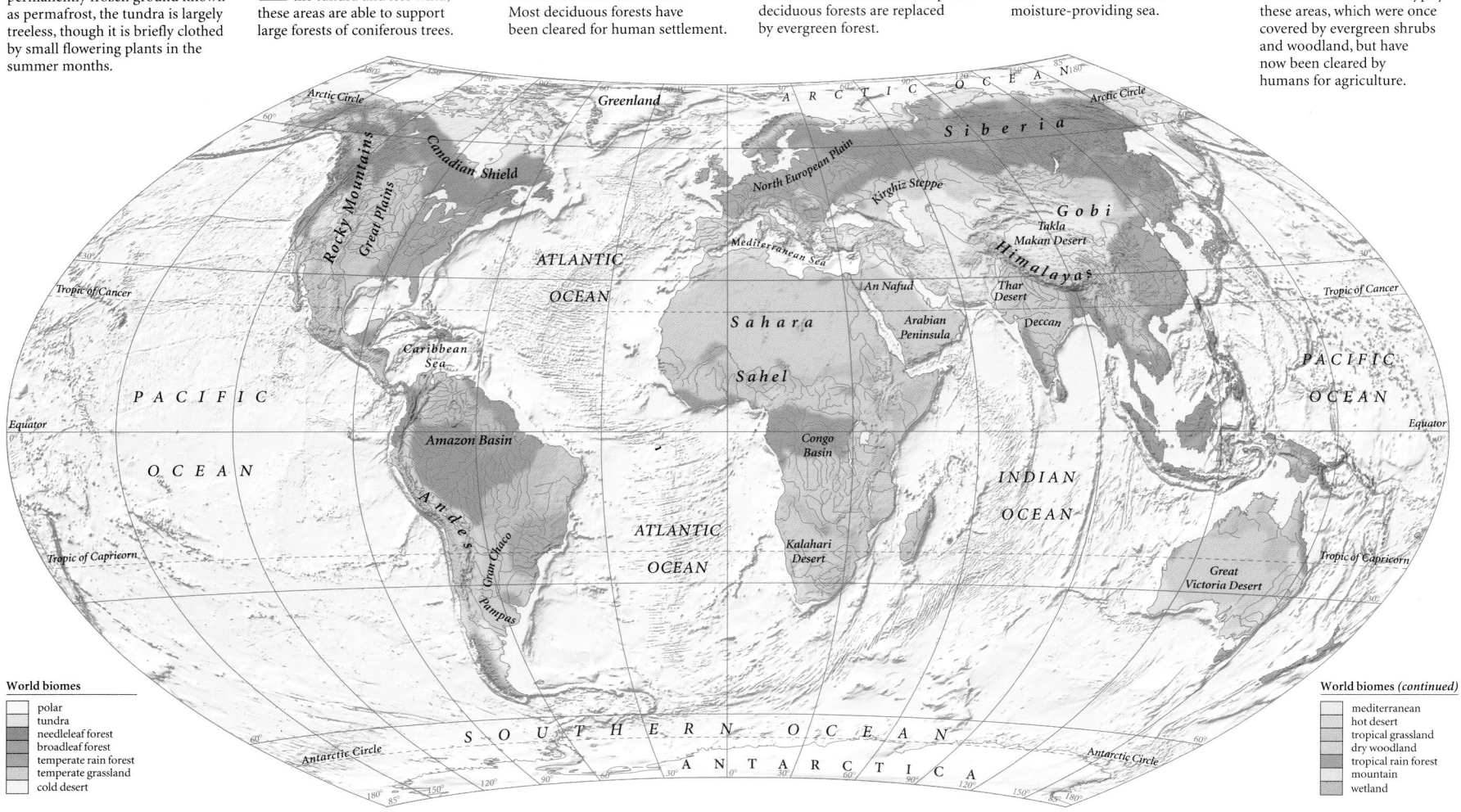

Arctic Circle · Greenland · ARCTIC OCEAN · N180° · Arctic Circle
Rocky Mountains · Canadian Shield · Siberia
Great Plains · North European Plain · Kirghiz Steppe · Gobi
Takla Makan Desert
ATLANTIC · Mediterranean Sea · Himalayas
OCEAN · An Nafud · Thar Desert
Tropic of Cancer · Sahara · Arabian Peninsula · Deccan · Tropic of Cancer
Caribbean Sea · PACIFIC · OCEAN
PACIFIC · Sahel
Equator · Congo Basin · INDIAN · Equator
OCEAN · Amazon Basin · OCEAN
Andes · Gran Chaco · ATLANTIC · Kalahari Desert
Tropic of Capricorn · OCEAN · Great Victoria Desert · Tropic of Capricorn
Pampas
Antarctic Circle · SOUTHERN OCEAN · Antarctic Circle
ANTARCTICA

World biomes
- polar
- tundra
- needleleaf forest
- broadleaf forest
- temperate rain forest
- temperate grassland
- cold desert

World biomes (continued)
- mediterranean
- hot desert
- tropical grassland
- dry woodland
- tropical rain forest
- mountain
- wetland

TROPICAL AND TEMPERATE GRASSLANDS
The major grassland areas are found in the centers of the larger continental landmasses. In Africa's tropical savannah regions, seasonal rainfall alternates with drought. Temperate grasslands, also known as steppes and prairies are found in the northern hemisphere, and in South America, where they are known as the pampas.

DRY WOODLANDS
Trees and shrubs, adapted to dry conditions, grow widely spaced from one another, interspersed by savannah grasslands.

TROPICAL RAIN FORESTS
Characterized by year-round warmth and high rainfall, tropical rain forests contain the highest diversity of plant and animal species on Earth.

MOUNTAINS
Though the lower slopes of mountains may be thickly forested, only ground-hugging shrubs and other vegetation will grow above the tree line which varies according to both altitude and latitude.

WETLANDS
Rarely lying above sea level, wetlands are marshes, swamps and tidal flats. Some, with their moist, fertile soils, are rich feeding grounds for fish and breeding grounds for birds. Others have little soil structure and are too acidic to support much plant and animal life.

BIODIVERSITY

THE NUMBER OF PLANT AND ANIMAL SPECIES, and the range of genetic diversity within the populations of each species, make up the Earth's biodiversity. The plants and animals which are endemic to a region – that is, those which are found nowhere else in the world – are also important in determining levels of biodiversity. Human settlement and intervention have encroached on many areas of the world once rich in endemic plant and animal species. Increasing international efforts are being made to monitor and conserve the biodiversity of the Earth's remaining wild places.

ANIMAL ADAPTATION

THE DEGREE OF AN ANIMAL'S ADAPTABILITY to different climates and conditions is extremely important in ensuring its success as a species. Many animals, particularly the largest mammals, are becoming restricted to ever-smaller regions as human development and modern agricultural practices reduce their natural habitats. In contrast, humans have been responsible – both deliberately and accidentally – for the spread of some of the world's most successful species. Many of these introduced species are now more numerous than the indigenous animal populations.

POLAR ANIMALS

The frozen wastes of the polar regions are able to support only a small range of species which derive their nutritional requirements from the sea. Animals such as the walrus *(left)* have developed insulating fat, stocky limbs, and double-layered coats to enable them to survive in the freezing conditions.

DIVERSITY OF ANIMAL SPECIES

DESERT ANIMALS

Many animals which live in the extreme heat and aridity of the deserts are able to survive for days and even months with very little food or water. Their bodies are adapted to lose heat quickly and to store fat and water. The Gila monster *(above)* stores fat in its tail.

AMAZON RAINFOREST

The vast Amazon Basin is home to the world's greatest variety of animal species. Animals are adapted to live at many different levels from the treetops to the tangled undergrowth which lies beneath the canopy. The sloth *(below)* hangs upside down in the branches. Its fur grows from its stomach to its back to enable water to run off quickly.

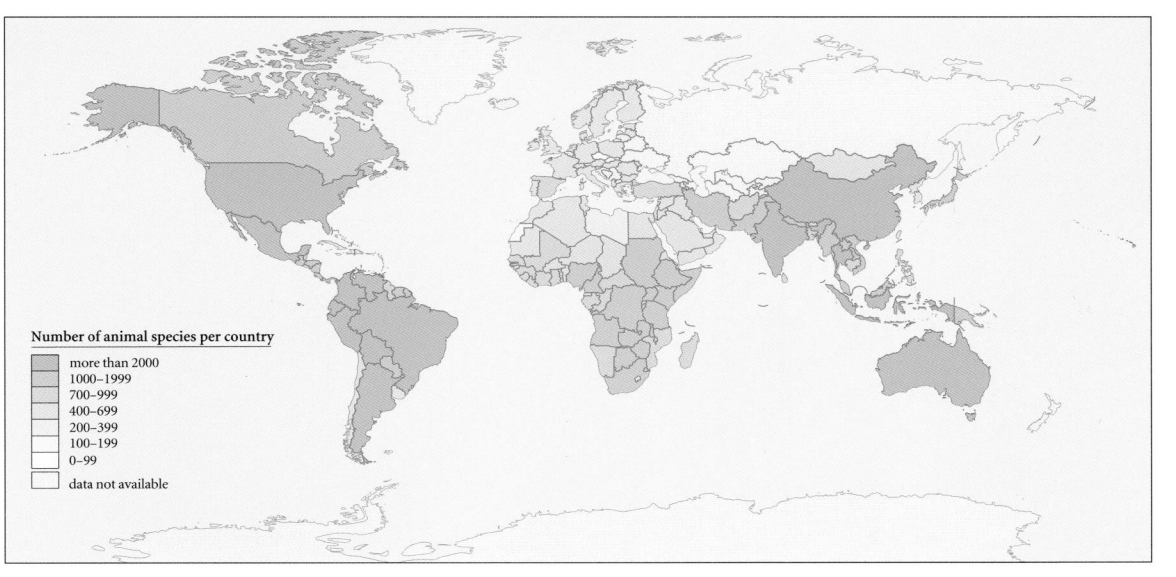

Number of animal species per country

- more than 2000
- 1000–1999
- 700–999
- 400–699
- 200–399
- 100–199
- 0–99
- data not available

MARINE BIODIVERSITY

The oceans support a huge variety of different species, from the world's largest mammals like whales and dolphins down to the tiniest plankton. The greatest diversities occur in the warmer seas of continental shelves, where plants are easily able to photosynthesize, and around coral reefs, where complex ecosystems are found. On the ocean floor, nematodes can exist at a depth of more than 10,000 ft (3,000 m) below sea level.

HIGH ALTITUDES

Few animals exist in the rarefied atmosphere of the highest mountains. However, birds of prey such as eagles and vultures *(above)*, with their superb eyesight can soar as high as 23,000 ft (7,000 m) to scan for prey below.

URBAN ANIMALS

The growth of cities has reduced the amount of habitat available to many species. A number of animals are now moving closer into urban areas to scavenge from the detritus of the modern city *(left)*. Rodents, particularly rats and mice, have existed in cities for thousands of years, and many insects, especially moths, quickly develop new coloring to provide them with camouflage.

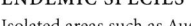

ENDEMIC SPECIES

Isolated areas such as Australia and the island of Madagascar, have the greatest range of endemic species. In Australia, these include marsupials such as the kangaroo *(below)*, which carry their young in pouches on their bodies. Destruction of habitat, pollution, hunting, and predators introduced by humans, are threatening this unique biodiversity.

PLANT ADAPTATION

ENVIRONMENTAL CONDITIONS, particularly climate, soil type, and the extent of competition with other organisms, influence the development of plants into a number of distinctive forms. Similar conditions in quite different parts of the world create similar adaptations in the plants, which may then be modified by other, local, factors specific to the region.

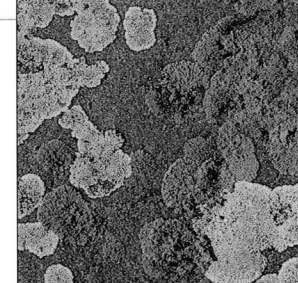

COLD CONDITIONS

In areas where temperatures rarely rise above freezing, plants such as lichens *(left)* and mosses grow densely, close to the ground.

RAIN FORESTS

Most of the world's largest and oldest plants are found in rain forests; warmth and heavy rainfall provide ideal conditions for vast plants like the world's largest flower, the rafflesia *(left)*.

HOT, DRY CONDITIONS

Arid conditions lead to the development of plants whose surface area has been reduced to a minimum to reduce water loss. In cacti *(above)*, which can survive without water for months, leaves are minimal or not present at all.

ANCIENT PLANTS

Some of the world's most primitive plants still exist today, including algae, cycads, and many ferns *(above)*, reflecting the success with which they have adapted to changing conditions.

DIVERSITY OF PLANT SPECIES

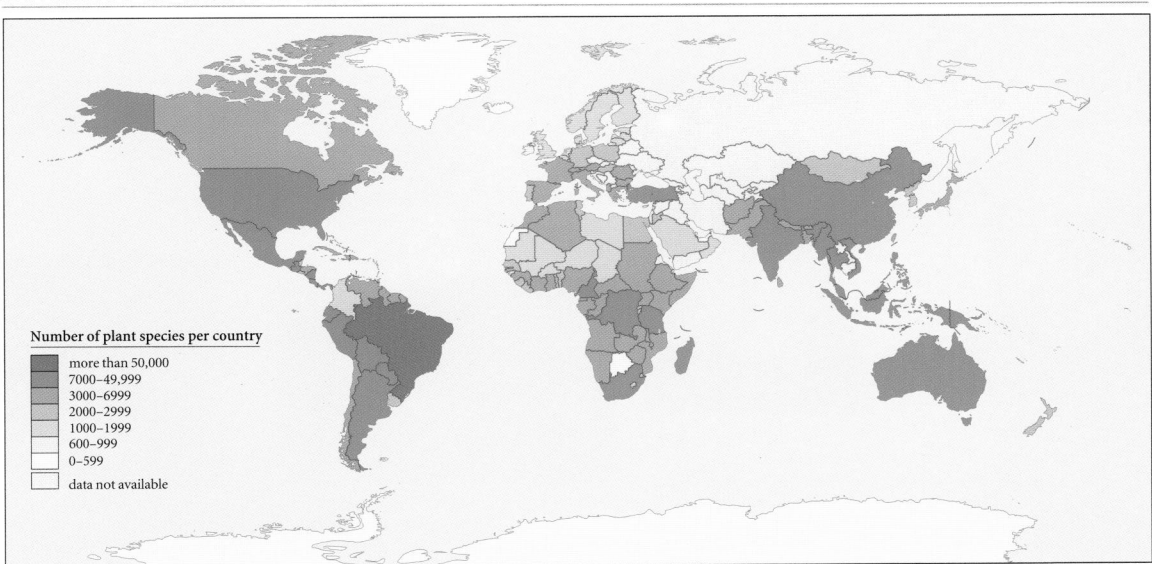

Number of plant species per country

- more than 50,000
- 7000–49,999
- 3000–6999
- 2000–2999
- 1000–1999
- 600–999
- 0–599
- data not available

RESISTING PREDATORS

A great variety of plants have developed devices including spines *(above)*, poisons, stinging hairs, and an unpleasant taste or smell to deter animal predators.

WEEDS

Weeds such as bindweed *(above)* are fast-growing, easily dispersed, and tolerant of a number of different environments, enabling them to quickly colonize suitable habitats. They are among the most adaptable of all plants.

POPULATION AND SETTLEMENT

THE EARTH'S POPULATION IS PROJECTED to rise from its current level of about 6.4 billion to reach some 10 billion by 2025. The global distribution of this rapidly growing population is very uneven, and is dictated by climate, terrain, and natural and economic resources. The great majority of the Earth's people live in coastal zones, and along river valleys. Deserts cover over 20% of the Earth's surface, but support less than 5% of the world's population. It is estimated that over half of the world's population live in cities – most of them in Asia – as a result of mass migration from rural areas in search of jobs. Many of these people live in the so-called "megacities," some with populations as great as 40 million.

PATTERNS OF SETTLEMENT

THE PAST 200 YEARS have seen the most radical shift in world population patterns in recorded history.

NOMADIC LIFE

ALL THE WORLD'S PEOPLES were hunter-gatherers 10,000 years ago. Today nomads, who live by following available food resources, account for less than 0.0001% of the world's population. They are mainly pastoral herders, moving their livestock from place to place in search of grazing land.

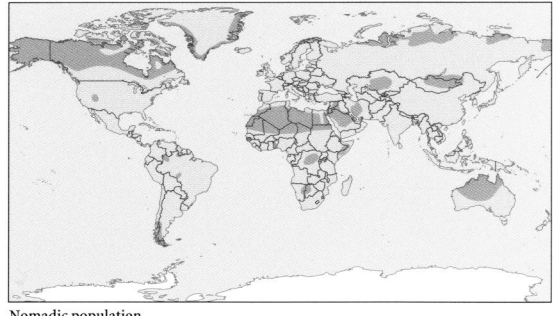

Nomadic population

▨ Nomadic population area

THE GROWTH OF CITIES

IN 1900 there were only 14 cities in the world with populations of more than a million, mostly in the northern hemisphere. Today, as more and more people in the developing world migrate to towns and cities, there are 29 cities whose population exceeds 5 million, and around 200 "million-cities."

MILLION-CITIES IN 1900

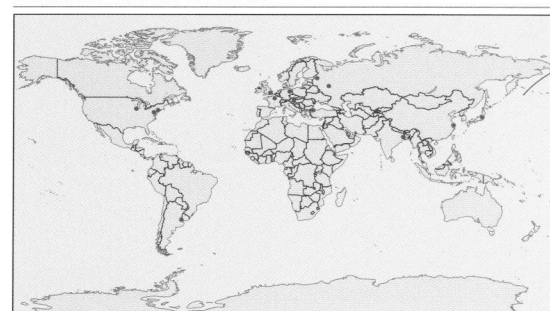

Million-cities in 1900

• Cities over 1 million population

MILLION-CITIES IN 1995

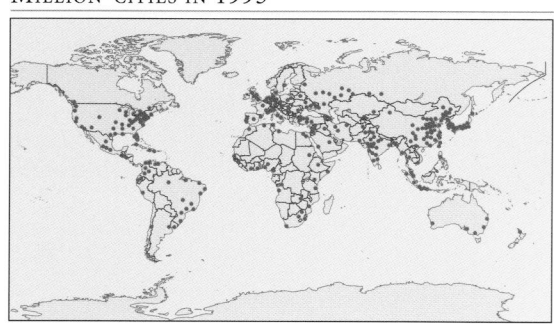

Million-cities in 1995

• Cities over 1 million population

NORTH AMERICA

THE EASTERN AND WESTERN SEABOARDS of the US, with huge expanses of interconnected cities, towns, and suburbs, are vast, densely-populated megalopolises. Central America and the Caribbean also have high population densities. Yet, away from the coasts and in the wildernesses of northern Canada the land is very sparsely settled.

Vancouver on Canada's west coast, grew up as a port city. In recent years it has attracted many Asian immigrants, particularly from the Pacific Rim.

North America's central plains, the continent's agricultural heartland, are thinly populated and highly productive.

SOUTH AMERICA

MOST SETTLEMENT IN SOUTH AMERICA is clustered in a narrow belt in coastal zones and in the northern Andes. During the 20th century, cities such as São Paulo and Buenos Aires grew enormously, acting as powerful economic magnets to the rural population. Shantytowns have grown up on the outskirts of many major cities to house these immigrants, often lacking basic amenities.

Many people in western South America live at high altitudes in the Andes, both in cities and in villages such as this one in Bolivia.

Venezuela is the most highly urbanized country in South America, with more than 90% of the population living in cities such as Caracas.

AFRICA

THE ARID CLIMATE of much of Africa means that settlement of the continent is sparse, focusing in coastal areas and fertile regions such as the Nile Valley. Africa still has a high proportion of nomadic agriculturalists, although many are now becoming settled, and the population is predominantly rural.

Cities such as Nairobi (above), Cairo and Johannesburg have grown rapidly in recent years, although only Cairo has a significant population on a global scale.

Traditional lifestyles and homes persist across much of Africa, which has a higher proportion of rural or village-based population than any other continent.

EUROPE

WITH ITS TEMPERATE CLIMATE, and rich mineral and natural resources, Europe is generally very densely settled. The continent acts as a magnet for economic migrants from the developing world, and immigration is now widely restricted. Birthrates in Europe are generally low, and in some countries, such as Germany, the populations have stabilized at zero growth, with a fast-growing elderly population.

Many European cities, like Siena, once reflected the "ideal" size for human settlements. Modern technological advances have enabled them to grow far beyond the original walls.

Within the densely-populated Netherlands the reclamation of coastal wetlands is vital to provide much-needed land for agriculture and settlement.

ASIA

MOST ASIAN SETTLEMENT originally centered around the great river valleys such as the Indus, the Ganges, and the Yangtze. Today, almost 60% of the world's population lives in Asia, many in burgeoning cities – particularly in the economically-buoyant Pacific Rim countries. Even rural population densities are high in many countries; practices such as terracing in Southeast Asia making the most of the available land.

Many of China's cities are now vast urban areas with populations of more than 5 million people.

This stilt village in Bangladesh is built to resist the regular flooding. Pressure on land, even in rural areas, forces many people to live in marginal areas.

Population density
(inhabitants per sq mile)

More than 520
260–519
130–259
55–129
28–54
15–27
1–15
Less than 1

NORTH AMERICA
Population 9%   World land area 17%

EUROPE
Population 14%   World land area 7.1%

AFRICA
Population 12%   World land area 20.2%

SOUTH AMERICA
Population 5.5%   World land area 11.8%

POPULATION STRUCTURES

POPULATION PYRAMIDS are an effective means of showing the age structures of different countries, and highlighting changing trends in population growth and decline. The typical pyramid for a country with a growing, youthful population, is broad-based *(left)*, reflecting a high birthrate and a far larger number of young rather than elderly people. In contrast, countries with populations whose numbers are stabilizing have a more balanced distribution of people in each age band, and may even have lower numbers of people in the youngest age ranges, indicating both a high life expectancy, and that the population is now barely replacing itself *(right)*. The Russian Federation *(center)* still bears the scars of World War II, reflected in the dramatically lower numbers of men than women in the 60–80+ age range.

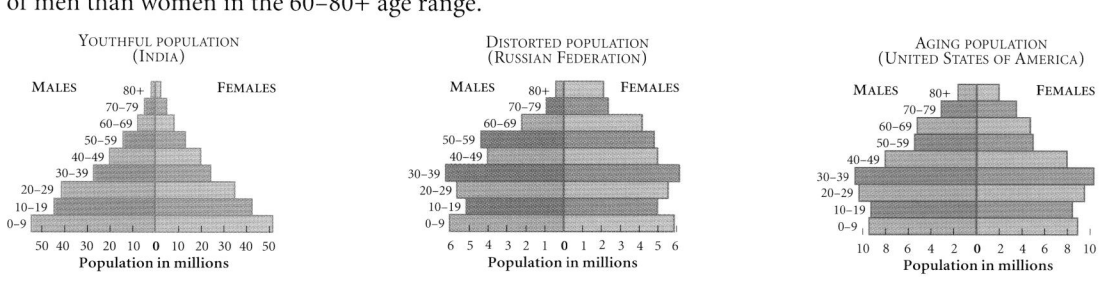

YOUTHFUL POPULATION (INDIA)

DISTORTED POPULATION (RUSSIAN FEDERATION)

AGING POPULATION (UNITED STATES OF AMERICA)

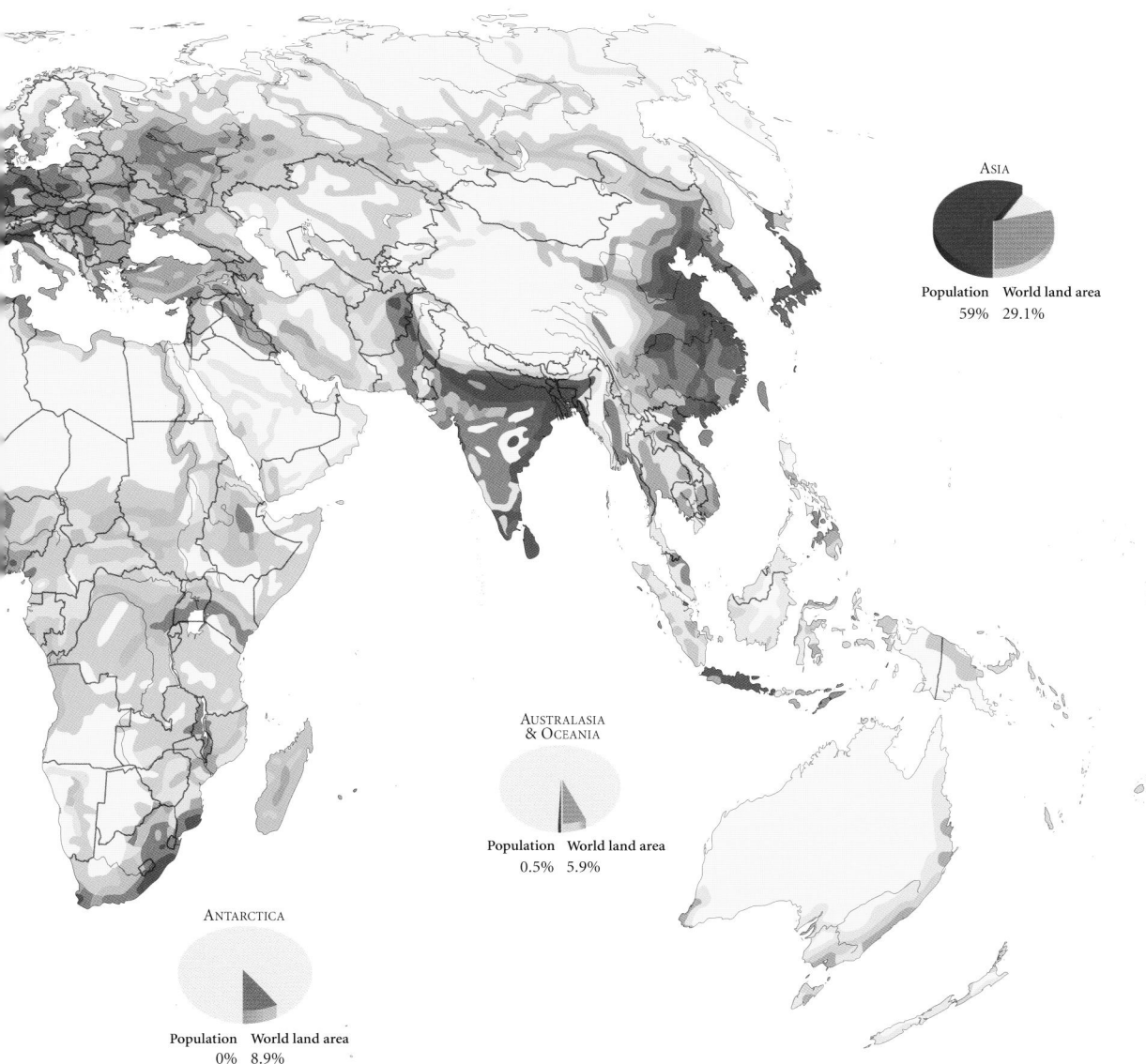

ASIA

Population 59% World land area 29.1%

AUSTRALASIA & OCEANIA

Population 0.5% World land area 5.9%

ANTARCTICA

Population 0% World land area 8.9%

AUSTRALASIA & OCEANIA

THIS IS THE WORLD'S most sparsely settled region. The peoples of Australia and New Zealand live mainly in the coastal cities, with only scattered settlements in the arid interior. The Pacific islands can only support limited populations because of their remoteness and lack of resources.

Brisbane, on Australia's Gold Coast is the most rapidly expanding city in the country. The great majority of Australia's population lives in cities near the coasts.

The remote highlands of Papua New Guinea are home to a wide variety of peoples, many of whom still subsist by traditional hunting and gathering.

AVERAGE WORLD BIRTHRATES

BIRTHRATES ARE MUCH HIGHER in Africa, Asia, and South America than in Europe and North America. Increased affluence and easy access to contraception are both factors which can lead to a significant decline in a country's birthrate.

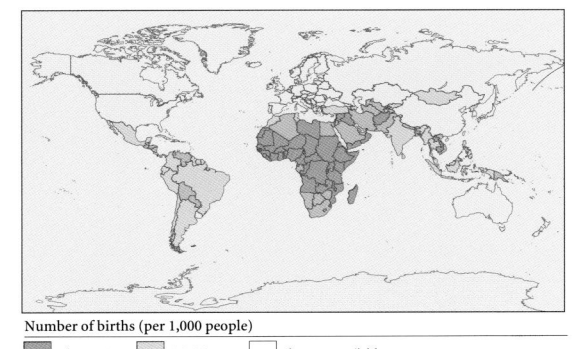

Number of births (per 1,000 people)

- above 40
- 30–39
- 20–29
- below 20
- data not available

POPULATION GROWTH

IMPROVEMENTS IN FOOD SUPPLY and advances in medicine have both played a major role in the remarkable growth in global population, which has increased five-fold over the last 150 years. Food supplies have risen with the mechanization of agriculture and improvements in crop yields. Better nutrition, together with higher standards of public health and sanitation, have led to increased longevity and higher birthrates.

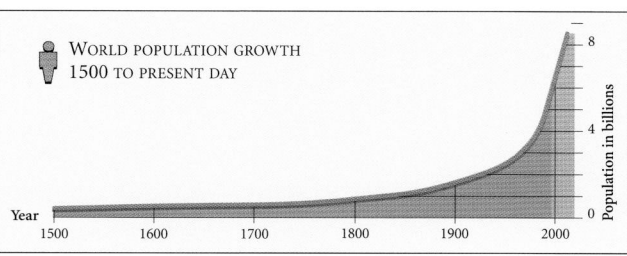

WORLD POPULATION GROWTH 1500 TO PRESENT DAY

WORLD NUTRITION

TWO-THIRDS OF THE WORLD'S food supply is consumed by the industrialized nations, many of which have a daily calorific intake far higher than is necessary for their populations to maintain a healthy body weight. In contrast, in the developing world, about 800 million people do not have enough food to meet their basic nutritional needs.

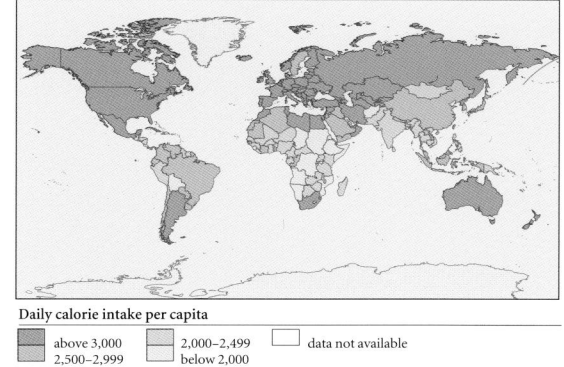

Daily calorie intake per capita

- above 3,000
- 2,500–2,999
- 2,000–2,499
- below 2,000
- data not available

WORLD LIFE EXPECTANCY

IMPROVED PUBLIC HEALTH and living standards have greatly increased life expectancy in the developed world, where people can now expect to live twice as long as they did 100 years ago. In many of the world's poorest nations, inadequate nutrition and disease, means that the average life expectancy still does not exceed 45 years.

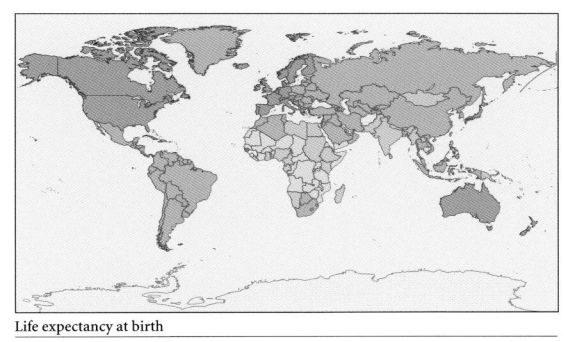

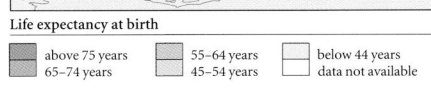

Life expectancy at birth

- above 75 years
- 65–74 years
- 55–64 years
- 45–54 years
- below 44 years
- data not available

WORLD INFANT MORTALITY

IN PARTS OF THE DEVELOPING WORLD infant mortality rates are still high; access to medical services such as immunization, adequate nutrition, and the promotion of breast-feeding have been important in combating infant mortality.

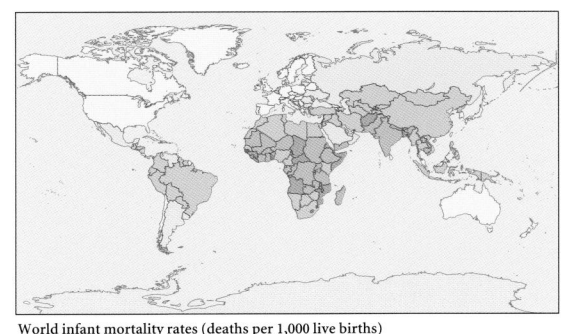

World infant mortality rates (deaths per 1,000 live births)

- above 125
- 75–124
- 35–74
- 15–43
- below 15
- data not available

THE ECONOMIC SYSTEM

The wealthy countries of the developed world, with their aggressive, market-led economies and their access to productive new technologies and international markets, dominate the world economic system. At the other extreme, many of the countries of the developing world are locked in a cycle of national debt, rising populations, and unemployment. The state-managed economies of the former communist bloc began to be dismantled during the 1990s, and China is emerging as a major economic power following decades of isolation.

Trade blocs

| EU | NAFTA | ASEAN | LAIA |
| CACM | SADC | ECOWAS | CEEAC |

TRADE BLOCS

International trade blocs are formed when groups of countries, often already enjoying close military and political ties, join together to offer mutually preferential terms of trade for both imports and exports. Increasingly, global trade is dominated by three main blocs: the EU, NAFTA, and ASEAN. They are supplanting older trade blocs such as the Commonwealth, a legacy of colonialism.

INTERNATIONAL TRADE FLOWS

World trade acts as a stimulus to national economies, encouraging growth. Over the last three decades, as heavy industries have declined, services – banking, insurance, tourism, airlines, and shipping – have taken an increasingly large share of world trade. Manufactured articles now account for nearly two-thirds of world trade; raw materials and food make up less than a quarter of the total.

SHIPPING
Ships carry 80% of international cargo, and extensive container ports, where cargo is stored, are vital links in the international transportation network.

MULTINATIONALS
Multinational companies are increasingly penetrating inaccessible markets. The reach of many American commodities is now global.

PRIMARY PRODUCTS
Many countries, particularly in the Caribbean and Africa, are still reliant on primary products such as rubber and coffee, which makes them vulnerable to fluctuating prices.

SERVICE INDUSTRIES
Service industries such as banking, tourism and insurance were the fastest-growing industrial sector in the last half of the 20th century. Lloyds of London is the center of the world insurance market.

Countries reliant on a single export
- bananas
- coffee
- oil/petroleum
- copper

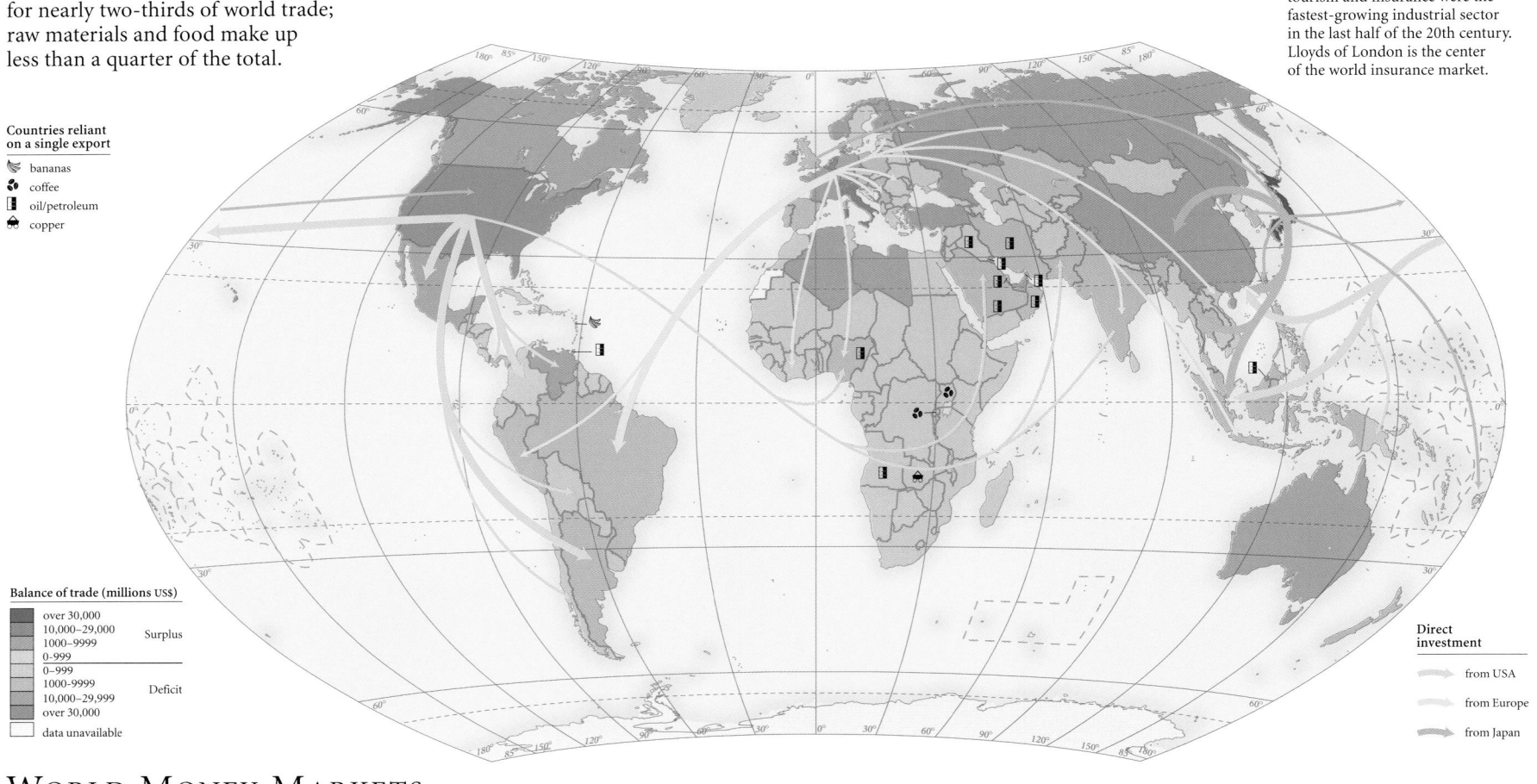

Balance of trade (millions US$)

over 30,000	
10,000–29,000	
1000–9999	Surplus
0–999	
0–999	
1000–9999	Deficit
10,000–29,999	
over 30,000	
data unavailable	

Direct investment
- from USA
- from Europe
- from Japan

WORLD MONEY MARKETS

The financial world has traditionally been dominated by three major centers – Tokyo, New York and London, which house the headquarters of stock exchanges, multinational corporations and international banks. Their geographic location means that, at any one time in a 24-hour day, one major market is open for trading in shares, currencies, and commodities. Since the late 1980s, technological advances have enabled transactions between financial centers to occur at ever-greater speed, and new markets have sprung up throughout the world.

NEW STOCK MARKETS

New stock markets are now opening in many parts of the world, where economies have recently emerged from state controls. In Moscow and Beijing, and several countries in eastern Europe, newly-opened stock exchanges reflect the transition to market-driven economies.

THE DEVELOPING WORLD

International trade in capital and currency is dominated by the rich nations of the northern hemisphere. In parts of Africa and Asia, where exports of any sort are extremely limited, home-produced commodities are simply sold in local markets.

MAJOR MONEY MARKETS

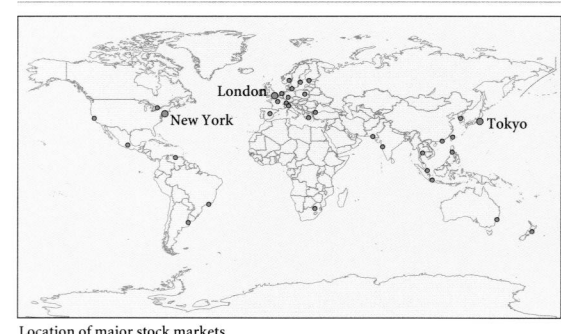

London
New York
Tokyo

Location of major stock markets
- Major stock markets

The Tokyo Stock Market *crashed in 1990, leading to a slow-down in the growth of the world's most powerful economy, and a refocusing on economic policy away from export-led growth and toward the domestic market.*

Dealers at the Kolkata Stock Market. *The Indian economy has been opened up to foreign investment and many multinationals now have bases there.*

Markets have thrived *in communist Vietnam since the introduction of a liberal economic policy.*

WORLD WEALTH DISPARITY

A GLOBAL ASSESSMENT of Gross Domestic Product (GDP) by nation reveals great disparities. The developed world, with only a quarter of the world's population, has 80% of the world's manufacturing income. Civil war, conflict, and political instability further undermine the economic self-sufficiency of many of the world's poorest nations.

Cities such as Detroit have been badly hit by the decline in heavy industry.

URBAN DECAY

ALTHOUGH THE US still dominates the global economy, it faces deficits in both the federal budget and the balance of trade. Vast discrepancies in personal wealth, high levels of unemployment, and the dismantling of welfare provisions throughout the 1980s have led to severe deprivation in several of the inner cities of North America's industrial heartland.

BOOMING CITIES

SINCE THE 1980s the Chinese government has set up special industrial zones, such as Shanghai, where foreign investment is encouraged through tax incentives. Migrants from rural China pour into these regions in search of work, creating "boomtown" economies.

Foreign investment has encouraged new infrastructure development in cities like Shanghai.

URBAN SPRAWL

CITIES ARE EXPANDING all over the developing world, attracting economic migrants in search of work and opportunities. In cities such as Rio de Janeiro, housing has not kept pace with the population explosion, and squalid shanty towns *(favelas)* rub shoulders with middle-class housing.

The favelas of Rio de Janeiro sprawl over the hills surrounding the city.

COMPARATIVE WORLD WEALTH

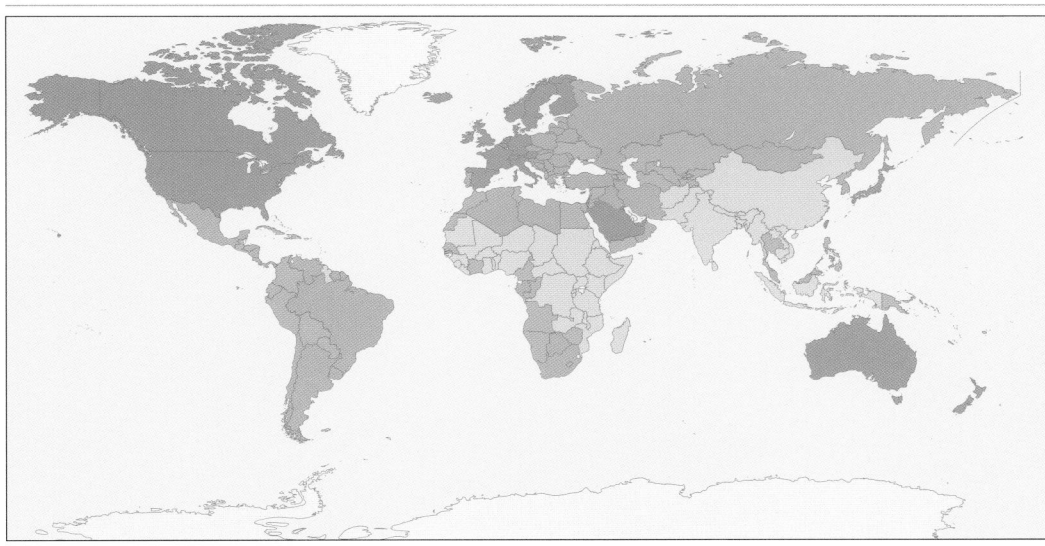

World economies
- high income
- upper-middle income
- lower-middle income
- low income
- data unavailable

ECONOMIC "TIGERS"

THE ECONOMIC "TIGERS" of the Pacific Rim – Taiwan, Singapore, and South Korea – have grown faster than Europe and the US over the last decade. Their export- and service-led economies have benefited from stable government, low labor costs, and foreign investment.

Hong Kong, with its fine natural harbor, is one of the most important ports in Asia.

AGRICULTURAL ECONOMIES

IN PARTS OF THE DEVELOPING WORLD, people survive by subsistence farming – only growing enough food for themselves and their families. With no surplus product, they are unable to exchange goods for currency, the only means of escaping the poverty trap. In other countries, farmers have been encouraged to concentrate on growing a single crop for the export market. This reliance on cash crops leaves farmers vulnerable to crop failure and to changes in the market price of the crop.

The Ugandan uplands are fertile, but poor infrastructure hampers the export of cash crops.

A shopping arcade in Paris displays a great profusion of luxury goods.

THE AFFLUENT WEST

THE CAPITAL CITIES of many countries in the developed world are showcases for consumer goods, reflecting the increasing importance of the service sector, and particularly the retail sector, in the world economy. The idea of shopping as a leisure activity is unique to the western world. Luxury goods and services attract visitors, who in turn generate tourist revenue.

TOURISM

IN 2002, THERE WERE 715 million tourists worldwide. Tourism is now the world's biggest single industry, employing over 130 million people, though frequently in low-paid unskilled jobs. While tourists are increasingly exploring inaccessible and less-developed regions of the world, the benefits of the industry are not always felt at a local level. There are also worries about the environmental impact of tourism, as the world's last wildernesses increasingly become tourist attractions.

Botswana's Okavango Delta is an area rich in wildlife. Tourists go on safaris to the region, but the impact of tourism is controlled.

MONEY FLOWS

FOREIGN INVESTMENT in the developing world during the 1970s led to a global financial crisis in the 1980s, when many countries were unable to meet their debt repayments. The International Monetary Fund (IMF) was forced to reschedule the debts and, in some cases, write them off completely. Within the developing world, austerity programs have been initiated to cope with the debt, leading in turn to high unemployment and galloping inflation. In many parts of Africa, stricken economies are now dependent on international aid.

In rural Southeast Asia, babies are given medical checks by UNICEF as part of a global aid program sponsored by the un.

TOURIST ARRIVALS

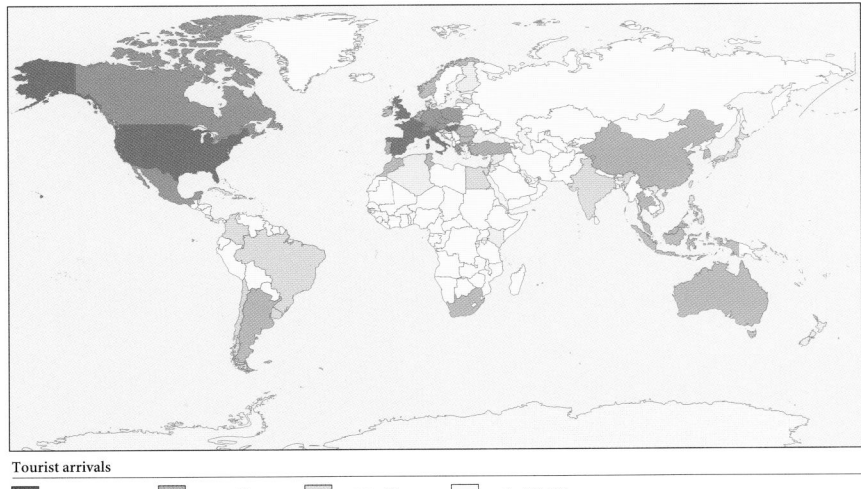

Tourist arrivals
- over 20 million
- 10–20 million
- 5–10 million
- 2.5–5 million
- 1–2.5 million
- 700,000–999,000
- under 700,000
- data unavailable

INTERNATIONAL DEBT: DONORS AND RECEIVERS

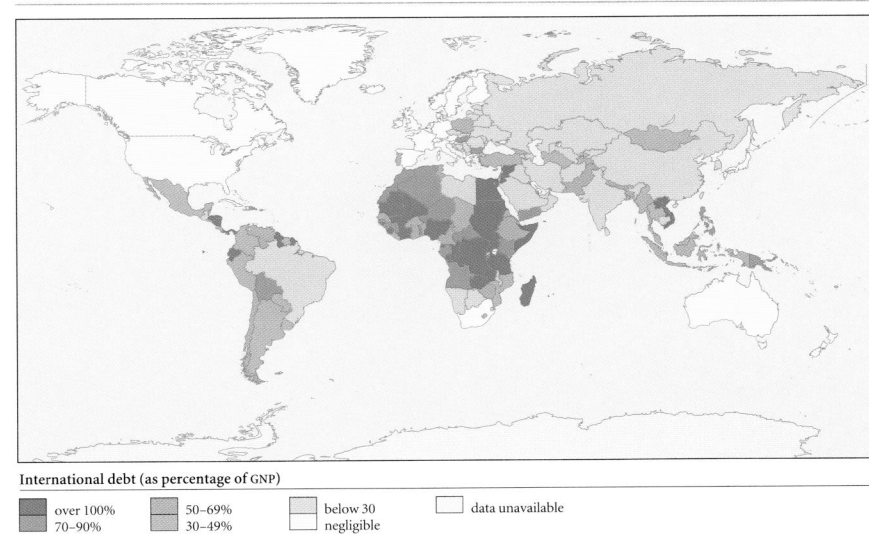

International debt (as percentage of GNP)
- over 100%
- 70–90%
- 50–69%
- 30–49%
- below 30
- negligible
- data unavailable

THE POLITICAL WORLD

There are 193 independent countries in the world today. With the exception of Antarctica, where territorial claims have been deferred by international treaty, every land area of the Earth's surface either belongs to, or is claimed by, one country or another. The largest country in the world is the Russian Federation, the smallest is Vatican City. Some 60 overseas dependent territories remain, administered variously by France, Australia, Denmark, New Zealand, Norway, Portugal, the UK, the US, and the Netherlands.

INTERNATIONAL BORDERS

The map shows three main types of boundary between states. Full borders represent internationally agreed and recognized territorial boundaries. Undefined borders exist where no fixed boundary between states has been demarcated; the boundaries indicated in this way show approximate areas of sovereignty. A disputed border is indicated where a *de facto* territorial boundary exists, which is not agreed or is subject to arbitration.

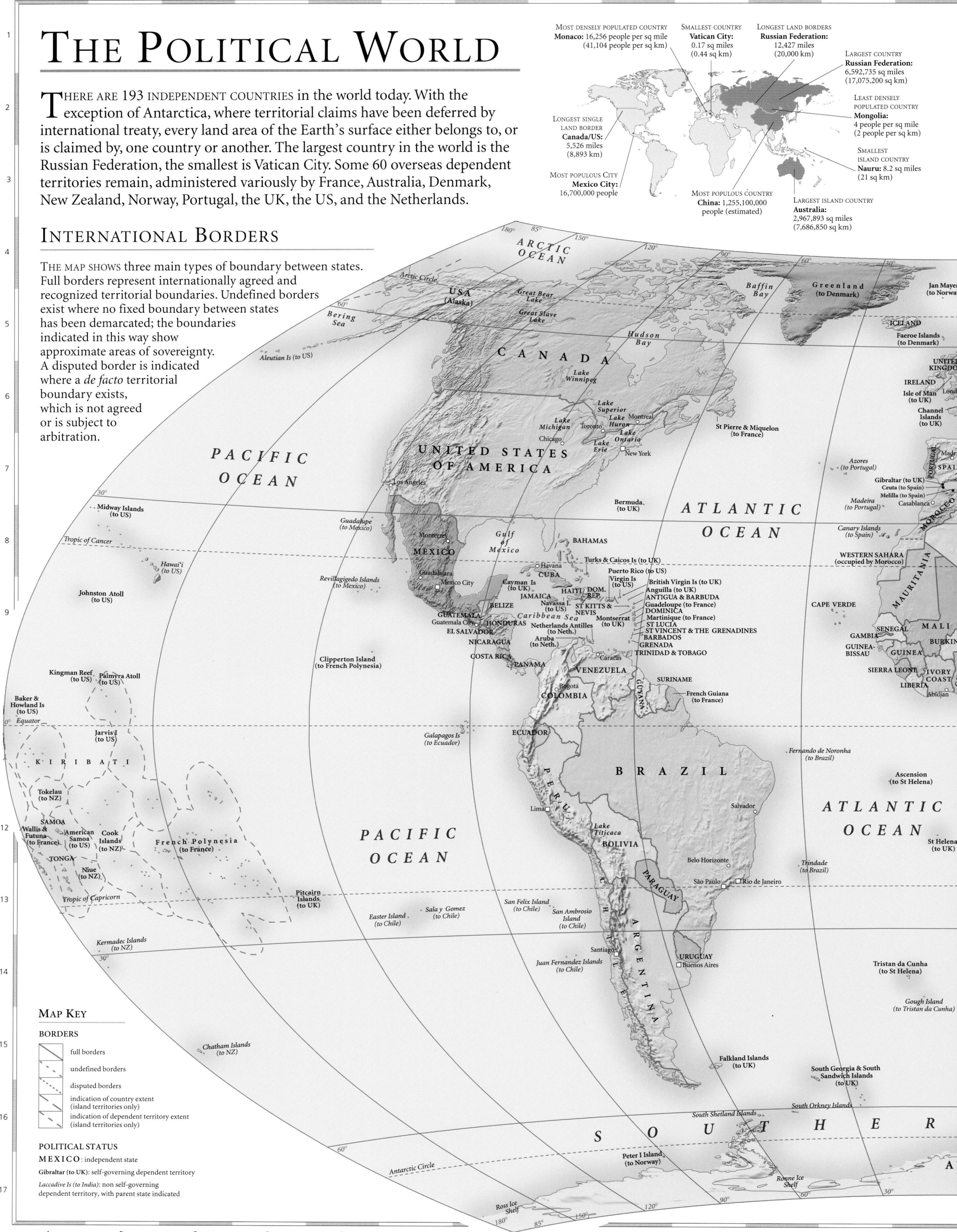

MOST DENSELY POPULATED COUNTRY
Monaco: 16,256 people per sq mile
(41,104 people per sq km)

SMALLEST COUNTRY
Vatican City:
0.17 sq miles
(0.44 sq km)

LONGEST LAND BORDERS
Russian Federation:
12,427 miles
(20,000 km)

LARGEST COUNTRY
Russian Federation:
6,592,735 sq miles
(17,075,200 sq km)

LEAST DENSELY POPULATED COUNTRY
Mongolia:
4 people per sq mile
(2 people per sq km)

SMALLEST ISLAND COUNTRY
Nauru: 8.2 sq miles
(21 sq km)

LONGEST SINGLE LAND BORDER
Canada/US:
5,526 miles
(8,893 km)

MOST POPULOUS CITY
Mexico City:
16,700,000 people

MOST POPULOUS COUNTRY
China: 1,255,100,000
people (estimated)

LARGEST ISLAND COUNTRY
Australia:
2,967,893 sq miles
(7,686,850 sq km)

MAP KEY

BORDERS

full borders

undefined borders

disputed borders

indication of country extent
(island territories only)

indication of dependent territory extent
(island territories only)

POLITICAL STATUS

MEXICO: independent state

Gibraltar (to UK): self-governing dependent territory

Laccadive Is (to India): non self-governing dependent territory, with parent state indicated

THE WORLD IN 1914

THE EARLY YEARS OF the 20th century saw the mainly European colonial empires reaching their greatest extents by 1914. Two world wars inaugurated their disintegration, but even in 1950 there were only 82 independent countries. Since then, over 100 have gained their independence, culminating in the breakup of the Soviet Union and former Yugoslavia in the early 1990s.

PERCENTAGE OF EARTH'S LAND SURFACE CONTROLLED BY COLONIAL EMPIRES IN 1914

- Independent: 29.8%
- Chinese: 6%
- Ottoman: 1.5%
- Russian: 15%
- Portuguese: 1%
- Spanish: 1%
- British: 21.5%
- French: 7.7%
- Belgian: 1.6%
- Italian: 1.8%
- German: 1.6%
- Japanese: 0.4%
- Dutch: 1.4%
- Danish: 1.5%
- United States: 7.6%

COLONIAL EMPIRES IN 1914

Colonial Empires in 1914
- Belgian
- British
- Chinese
- Danish
- Dutch
- French
- German
- Italian
- Japanese
- Ottoman
- Portuguese
- Russian
- Spanish
- United States
- Independent
- Disputed

SCALE 1:66,000,000
(projection: Wagner VII)

Km
0   250   500   1,000   1,500   2,000

Miles
0   250   500   1,000   1,500   2,000

STATES AND BOUNDARIES

THERE ARE OVER 190 SOVEREIGN STATES in the world today; in 1950 there were only 82. Over the last half-century national self-determination has been a driving force for many states with a history of colonialism and oppression. As more borders are added to the world map, the number of international border disputes increases.

In many cases, where the impetus toward independence has been religious or ethnic, disputes with minority groups have also caused violent internal conflict. While many newly-formed states have moved peacefully toward independence, successfully establishing government by multi-party democracy, dictatorship by military regime or individual despot is often the result of the internal power-struggles which characterize the early stages in the lives of new nations.

THE NATURE OF POLITICS

Democracy is a broad term: it can range from the ideal of multiparty elections and fair representation to, in countries such as Singapore and Indonesia, a thin disguise for single-party rule. In despotic regimes, on the other hand, a single, often personal authority has total power; institutions such as parliament and the military are mere instruments of the dictator.

The stars and stripes of the US flag are a potent symbol of the country's status as a federal democracy.

Types of government
- Multiparty democracy for more than 10 yrs
- Multiparty/transitional democracy within last 10 yrs
- Single-party government
- Military regime
- Theocracy
- Absolute monarchy
- ☛ Current civil unrest

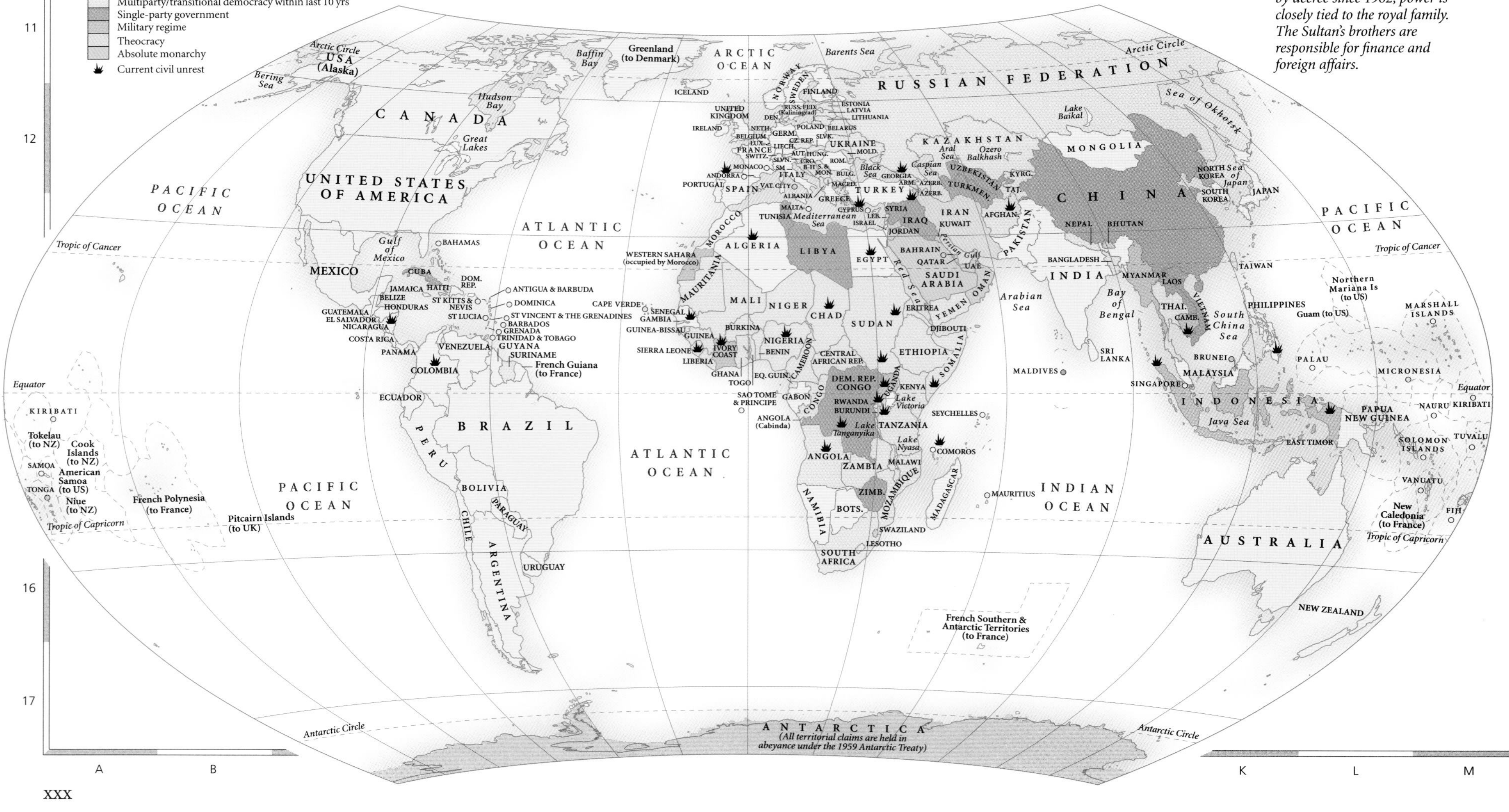

THE CHANGING WORLD MAP

DECOLONIZATION

In 1950, large areas of the world remained under the control of a handful of European countries (*page xxviii*). The process of decolonization had begun in Asia, where, following World War II, much of southern and southeastern Asia sought and achieved self-determination. In the 1960s, a host of African states achieved independence, so that by 1965, most of the larger tracts of the European overseas empires had been substantially eroded. The final major stage in decolonization came with the breakup of the Soviet Union and the Eastern bloc after 1990. The process continues today as the last toeholds of European colonialism, often tiny island nations, press increasingly for independence.

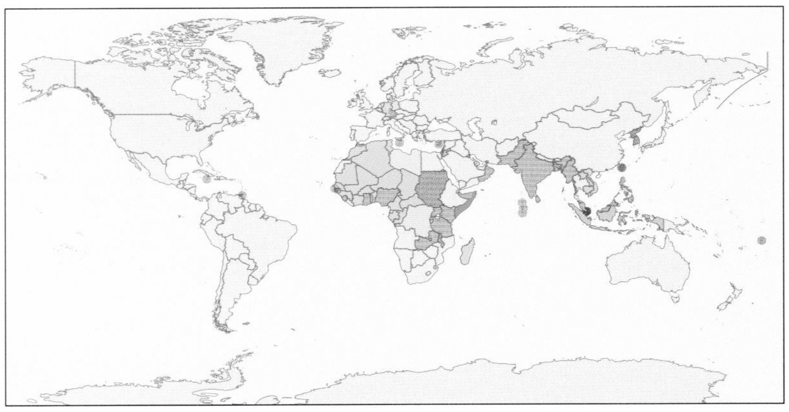

Icons of communism, including statues of former leaders such as Lenin and Stalin, were destroyed when the Soviet bloc was dismantled in 1989, creating several new nations.

Iran has been one of the modern world's few true theocracies; Islam has an impact on every aspect of political life.

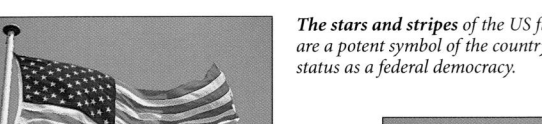
Saddam Hussein former autocratic leader of Iraq, promoted an extreme personality cult for over 20 years. He was ousted by a US-led coalition in 2003.

North Korea is an independent communist republic. Power is concentrated in the hands of Kim Jong Il.

South Africa became a democracy in 1994, when elections ended over a century of white minority rule.

NEW NATIONS 1945–1965

NEW NATIONS 1965–1996

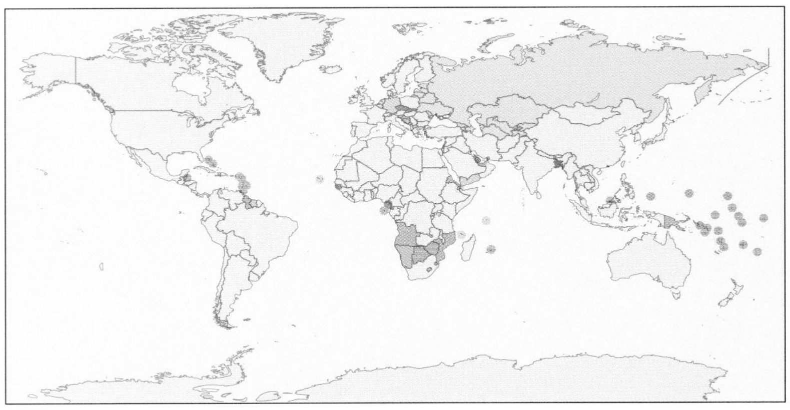

In Brunei the Sultan has ruled by decree since 1962; power is closely tied to the royal family. The Sultan's brothers are responsible for finance and foreign affairs.

Administration at the time of independence

Australia	Netherlands
Aust/NZ/UK	New Zealand
Belgium	Pakistan
China	Portugal
Czechoslovakia	South Africa
Egypt/UK	Spain
Ethiopia	UK
France	Unified country
France/UK	USA
Italy	USSR
Japan	Yugoslavia
Malaysia	

LINES ON THE MAP

THE DETERMINATION OF INTERNATIONAL BOUNDARIES can use a variety of criteria. Many of the borders between older states follow physical boundaries; some mirror religious and ethnic differences; others are the legacy of complex histories of conflict and colonialism, while others have been imposed by international agreements or arbitration.

POST-COLONIAL BORDERS

WHEN THE EUROPEAN COLONIAL EMPIRES IN AFRICA were dismantled during the second half of the 20th century, the outlines of the new African states mirrored colonial boundaries. These boundaries had been drawn up by colonial administrators, often based on inadequate geographical knowledge. Such arbitrary boundaries were imposed on people of different languages, racial groups, religions, and customs. This confused legacy often led to civil and international war.

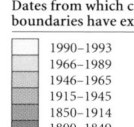

Dates from which current
boundaries have existed

1990–1993
1966–1989
1946–1965
1915–1945
1850–1914
1800–1849
Pre-1800

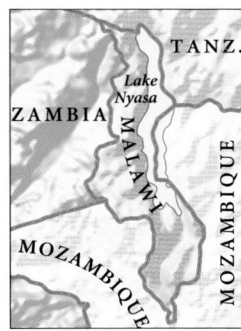

The conflict that has plagued many African countries since independence has caused millions of people to become refugees.

PHYSICAL BORDERS

MANY OF THE WORLD'S COUNTRIES are divided by physical borders: lakes, rivers, mountains. The demarcation of such boundaries can, however, lead to disputes. Control of waterways, water supplies, and fisheries are frequent causes of international friction.

ENCLAVES

THE SHIFTING POLITICAL MAP over the course of history has frequently led to anomalous situations. Parts of national territories may become isolated by territorial agreement, forming an enclave. The West German part of the city of Berlin, which until 1989 lay several hundred miles within East German territory, was a famous example.

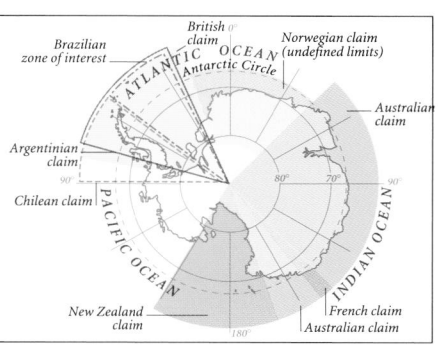

Since the independence of Lithuania and Belarus, the peoples of the Russian enclave of Kaliningrad have become physically isolated.

ANTARCTICA

WHEN ANTARCTIC EXPLORATION began a century ago, seven nations, Australia, Argentina, Britain, Chile, France, New Zealand, and Norway, laid claim to the new territory. In 1961 the Antarctic Treaty, signed by 39 nations, agreed to hold all territorial claims in abeyance.

GEOMETRIC BORDERS

STRAIGHT LINES and lines of longitude and latitude have occasionally been used to determine international boundaries; and indeed the world's longest international boundary, between Canada and the USA follows the 49th Parallel for over one-third of its course. Many Canadian, American and Australian internal administrative boundaries are similarly determined using a geometric solution.

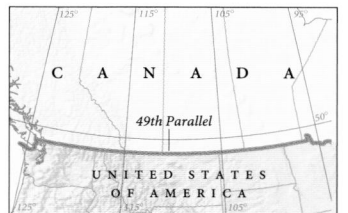

Different farming techniques in Canada and the US clearly mark the course of the international boundary in this satellite map.

WORLD BOUNDARIES

LAKE BORDERS

Countries which lie next to lakes usually fix their borders in the middle of the lake. Unusually the Lake Nyasa border between Malawi and Tanzania runs along Tanzania's shore.

Complicated agreements between colonial powers led to the awkward division of Lake Nyasa.

RIVER BORDERS

Rivers alone account for one-sixth of the world's borders. Many great rivers form boundaries between a number of countries. Changes in a river's course and interruptions of its natural flow can lead to disputes, particularly in areas where water is scarce. The center of the river's course is the nominal boundary line.

The Danube forms all or part of the border between nine European nations.

MOUNTAIN BORDERS

Mountain ranges form natural barriers and are the basis for many major borders, particularly in Europe and Asia. The watershed is the conventional boundary demarcation line, but its accurate determination is often problematic.

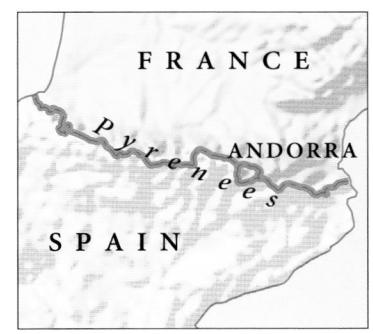

The Pyrenees form a natural mountain border between France and Spain.

SHIFTING BOUNDARIES – POLAND

BORDERS BETWEEN COUNTRIES can change dramatically over time. The nations of eastern Europe have been particularly affected by changing boundaries. Poland is an example of a country whose boundaries have changed so significantly that it has literally moved around Europe. At the start of the 16th century, Poland was the largest nation in Europe. Between 1772 and 1795, it was absorbed into Prussia, Austria, and Russia, and it effectively ceased to exist. After World War I, Poland became an independent country once more, but its borders changed again after World War II following invasions by both Soviet Russia and Nazi Germany.

In 1634, Poland was the largest nation in Europe, its eastern boundary reaching toward Moscow.

From 1772–1795, Poland was gradually partitioned between Austria, Russia, and Prussia. Its eastern boundary receded by over 100 miles (160 km).

Following World War I, Poland was reinstated as an independent state, but it was less than half the size it had been in 1634.

After World War II, the Baltic Sea border was extended westward, but much of the eastern territory was annexed by Russia.

INTERNATIONAL DISPUTES

THERE ARE MORE THAN 60 DISPUTED BORDERS or territories in the world today. Although many of these disputes can be settled by peaceful negotiation, some areas have become a focus for international conflict. Ethnic tensions have been a major source of territorial disagreement throughout history, as has the ownership of, and access to, valuable natural resources. The turmoil of the postcolonial era in many parts of Africa is partly a result of the 19th century "carve-up" of the continent, which created potential for conflict by drawing often arbitrary lines through linguistic and cultural areas.

JAMMU AND KASHMIR

DISPUTES OVER JAMMU AND KASHMIR have caused three serious wars between India and Pakistan since 1947. Pakistan wishes to annex the largely Muslim territory, while India refuses to cede any territory or to hold a referendum, and also lays claim to the entire territory. Most international maps show the "line of control" agreed in 1972 as the *de facto* border. In addition, both Pakistan and India have territorial disputes with neighboring China. The situation is further complicated by a Kashmiri independence movement, active since the late 1980s.

Indian army troops maintain their positions in the mountainous terrain of northern Kashmir.

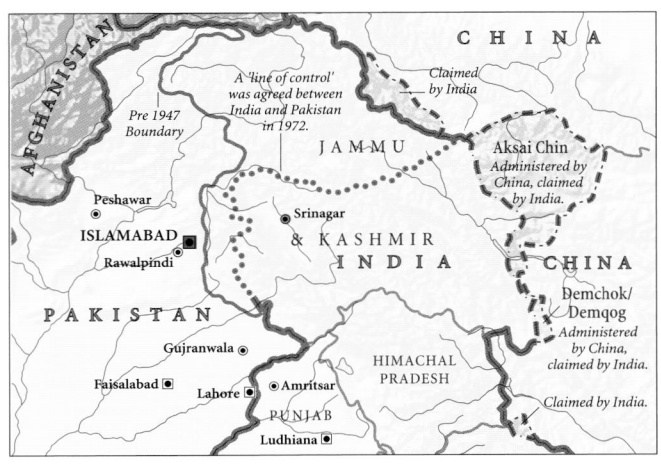

NORTH AND SOUTH KOREA

SINCE 1953, the *de facto* border between North and South Korea has been a ceasefire line which straddles the 38th Parallel and is designated as a demilitarized zone. Both countries have heavy fortifications and troop concentrations behind this zone.

Heavy fortifications on the border between North and South Korea.

CYPRUS

The so-called 'green line' divides Cyprus into Greek and Turkish sectors.

CYPRUS WAS PARTITIONED in 1974, following an invasion by Turkish troops. The south is now the Greek Cypriot Republic of Cyprus, while the self-proclaimed Turkish Republic of Northern Cyprus is recognized only by Turkey.

TURKISH REPUBLIC OF NORTHERN CYPRUS
(recognized only by Turkey)

Mediterranean Sea
Kyrenia Mountains Kyrenia
NICOSIA
CYPRUS
Troodos
UK Sovereign Base Area
Lárnaka
Mediterranean Sea
UK Sovereign Base Area
Lemesós (Limassol)

THE FALKLAND ISLANDS

THE BRITISH DEPENDENT TERRITORY of the Falkland Islands was invaded by Argentina in 1982, sparking a full-scale war with the UK. In 1995, the UK and Argentina reached an agreement on the exploitation of oil reserves around the islands.

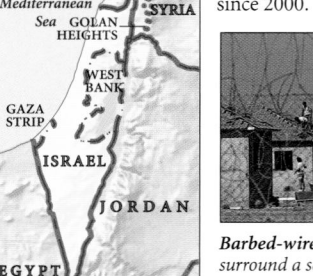

British warships in Falkland Sound during the 1982 war with Argentina.

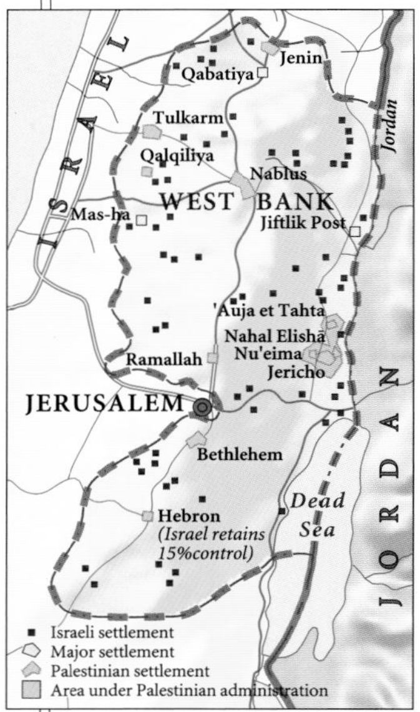

ISRAEL

ISRAEL WAS CREATED in 1948 following the 1947 UN Resolution (147) on Palestine. Until 1979 Israel had no borders, only ceasefire lines from a series of wars in 1948, 1967 and 1973. Treaties with Egypt in 1979 and Jordan in 1994 led to these borders being defined and agreed. Negotiations over Israeli settlements and Palestinian self-government have collapsed into inter-communal warfare since 2000.

Map of Israel / West Bank:
Jenin
Qabatiya
Tulkarm
Qalqiliya
Nablus
Mas-ha
WEST BANK
Jiftlik Post
'Auja et Tahta
Nahal Elisha
Nu'eima
Ramallah
Jericho
JERUSALEM
Bethlehem
Hebron (Israel retains 15% control)
Dead Sea
ISRAEL
JORDAN

- ■ Israeli settlement
- ● Major settlement
- △ Palestinian settlement
- ▦ Area under Palestinian administration

Map: LEBANON, Mediterranean Sea, GOLAN HEIGHTS, SYRIA, WEST BANK, GAZA STRIP, ISRAEL, JORDAN, EGYPT

Barbed-wire fences surround a settlement in the Golan Heights.

FORMER YUGOSLAVIA

FOLLOWING THE DISINTEGRATION in 1991 of the communist state of Yugoslavia, the breakaway states of Croatia and Bosnia-Herzegovina came into conflict with the "parent" state (consisting of Serbia and Montenegro). Warfare focused on ethnic and territorial ambitions in Bosnia. The tenuous Dayton Accord of 1995 sought to recognize the post-1990 borders, whilst providing for ethnic partition and required international peace-keeping troops to maintain the terms of the peace.

Map: CROATIA, Bihać, Banja Luka, Brčko, Sava, Bosna, Jajce, Gornji Vakuf, BOSNIA-HERZEGOVINA, Tuzla, Drina, SERB. & MON. (YUGOSLAVIA), Split, SARAJEVO, Goražde, Mostar, Adriatic Sea, Dubrovnik
- ▦ Republika Srpska
- ▦ Federacija Bosna i Hercegovina

THE SPRATLY ISLANDS

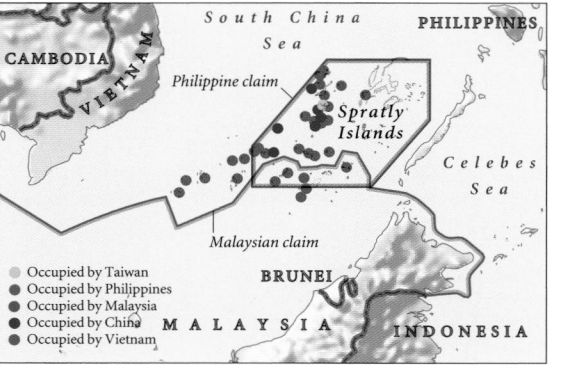

Most claimant states have small military garrisons on the Spratly Islands.

THE SITE OF POTENTIAL OIL and natural gas reserves, the Spratly Islands in the South China Sea have been claimed by China, Vietnam, Taiwan, Malaysia, and the Philippines since the Japanese gave up a wartime claim in 1951.

Map: CAMBODIA, VIETNAM, South China Sea, PHILIPPINES, Philippine claim, Spratly Islands, Celebes Sea, Malaysian claim, BRUNEI, MALAYSIA, INDONESIA
- ● Occupied by Taiwan
- ● Occupied by Philippines
- ● Occupied by Malaysia
- ● Occupied by China
- ● Occupied by Vietnam

Jammu and Kashmir map labels
AFGHANISTAN, CHINA, Claimed by India, A 'line of control' was agreed between India and Pakistan in 1972, Pre 1947 Boundary, Peshawar, JAMMU, Srinagar, & KASHMIR, Aksai Chin Administered by China, claimed by India, ISLAMABAD, Rawalpindi, INDIA, CHINA, PAKISTAN, Gujranwala, Demchok/Demqog Administered by China, claimed by India, Faisalabad, Lahore, Amritsar, HIMACHAL PRADESH, PUNJAB, Ludhiana, Claimed by India.

North/South Korea map labels
CHINA, NORTH KOREA, Sea of Japan, PYONGYANG, SEOUL, SOUTH KOREA, Yellow Sea

World map — Conflicts and international disputes legend
- (gray) Countries involved in active external conflict
- Active territorial or border disputes
- Countries involved in internal conflict
- Active territorial or border disputes and internal conflict

World map country/label list: Svalbard, ICELAND, Rockall, NORWAY, RUSSIAN FEDERATION, Northern Ireland, IRELAND, UNITED KINGDOM, UKRAINE, MOLD., Chechnya, KAZAKHSTAN, Kurile Islands, SPAIN, MACEDONIA, GEORG., ARM., UZBEKISTAN, KYRGYSTAN, Liancourt Rocks, Gibraltar, GREECE, TURKEY, AZERB., NORTH KOREA, Ceuta, Melilla, CYPRUS, SYRIA, IRAQ, IRAN, AFGHANISTAN, CHINA, SOUTH KOREA, JAPAN, MOROCCO, ISRAEL, Golan Heights, PAKISTAN, Askai Chin, Jammu and Kashmir, Senkaku Islands, UNITED STATES OF AMERICA, WESTERN SAHARA, ALGERIA, EGYPT, SAUDI ARABIA, UAE, NEPAL, BANGLADESH, Matsu, TAIWAN, Wake Island, SENEGAL, CHAD, ERITREA, Hamish Islands, INDIA, MYANMAR, LAOS, Paracel Islands, PHILIPPINES, CUBA, Guantanamo Bay, HAITI, NIGERIA, SUDAN, SRI LANKA, THAILAND, GUATEMALA, BELIZE, SIERRA LEONE, CAMEROON, LIBERIA, DEM. REP. CONGO, CONGO, UGANDA, ETHIOPIA, SOMALIA, Spratly Islands, MALAYSIA, Sipidan and Ligitan, EL SALVADOR, NICARAGUA, VENEZUELA, GUYANA, SURINAME, French Guiana, COLOMBIA, KENYA, RWANDA, BURUNDI, SINGAPORE, INDONESIA, ANGOLA, COMOROS, MADAGASCAR, ZIMBABWE, SOLOMON ISLANDS, NAMIBIA, BOTSWANA, MAURITIUS, ARGENTINA, Falkland Islands

ATLAS
OF THE
WORLD

THE MAPS IN THIS ATLAS ARE ARRANGED CONTINENT BY CONTINENT, STARTING FROM
THE INTERNATIONAL DATE LINE, AND MOVING EASTWARD. THE MAPS PROVIDE A
UNIQUE VIEW OF TODAY'S WORLD, COMBINING TRADITIONAL CARTOGRAPHIC TECHNIQUES
WITH THE LATEST REMOTE-SENSED AND DIGITAL TECHNOLOGY.

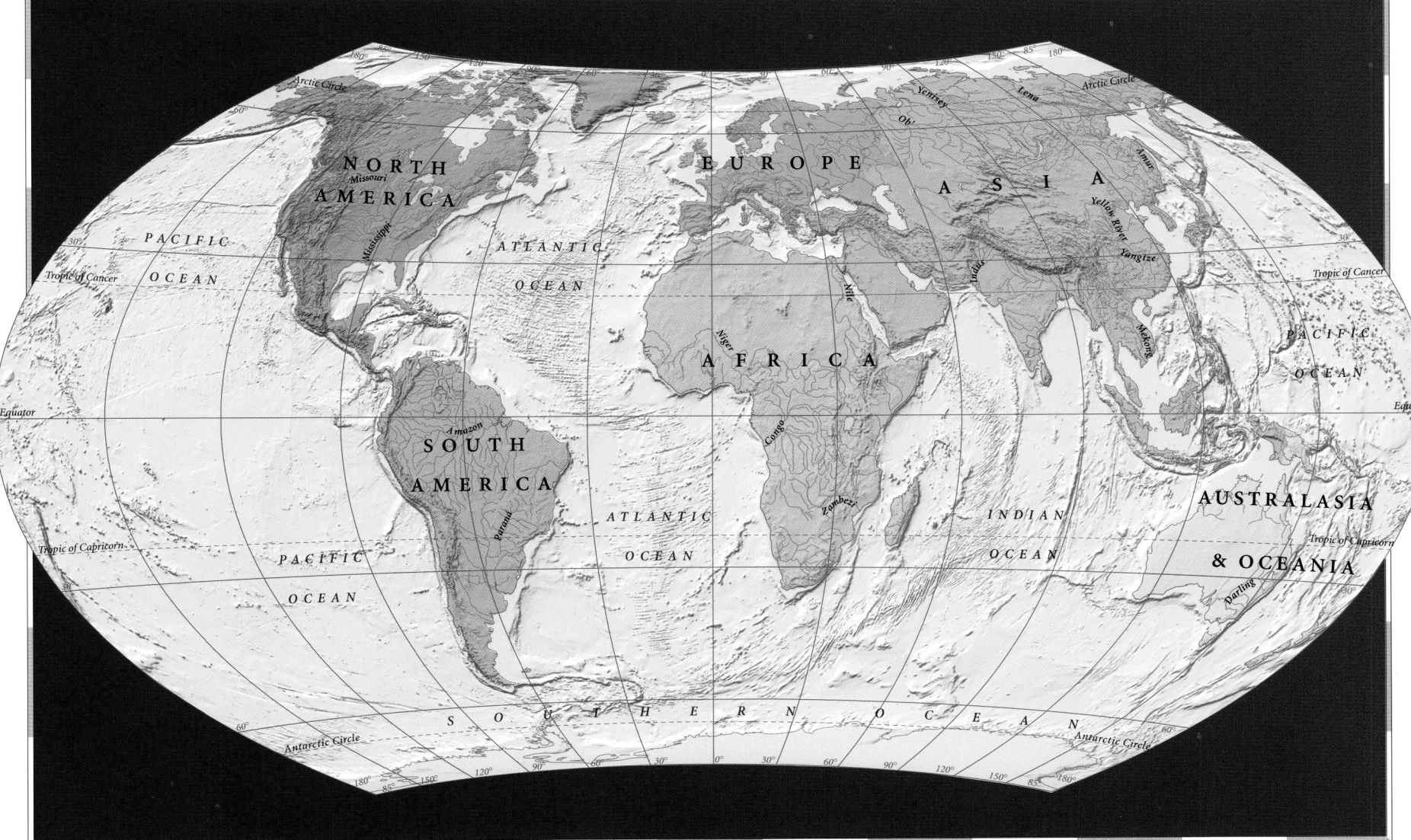

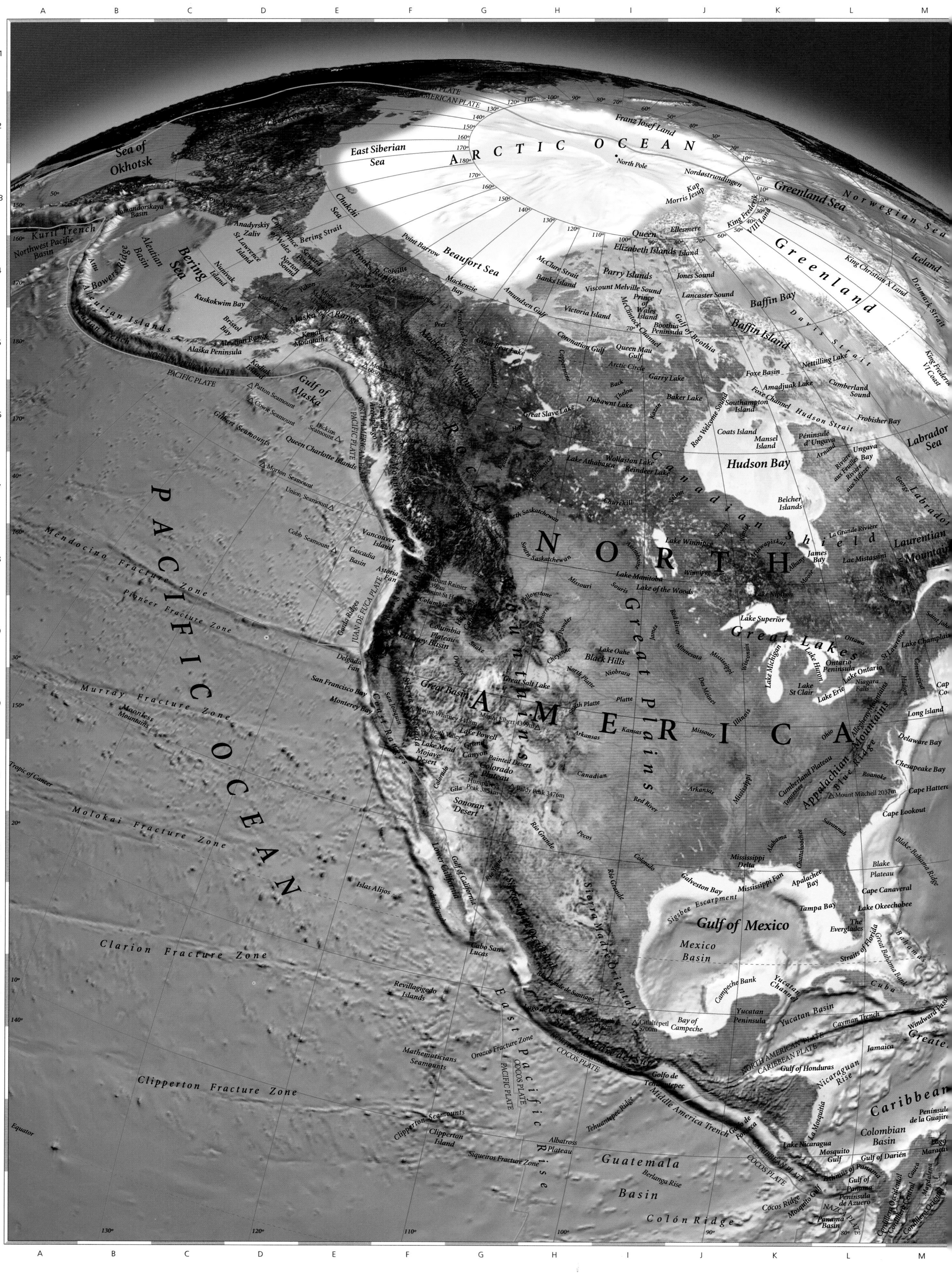

NORTH AMERICAN PLATE

ARCTIC OCEAN

Franz Josef Land

Sea of
Okhotsk

East Siberian
Sea

North Pole

Nordostrundingen

Greenland Sea

Norwegian Sea

Kap
Morris Jesup

King Frederik
VIII Land

Ellesmere
Island

Queen
Elizabeth Islands

King Christian X Land

Iceland

Kuril Trench
Northwest Pacific
Basin

Komandorskaya
Basin

Anadyrskiy
Zaliv

St Lawrence
Island

Prince of Wales

Bering Strait

Point Barrow

Beaufort Sea

McClure Strait
Banks Island

Viscount Melville Sound

Parry Islands

Jones Sound

Lancaster Sound

King Frederik
VI Coast

Denmark Strait

Aleutian
Basin

Bering
Sea

Nunivak
Island

Norton
Sound

Chukchi
Sea

Brooks Range

Colville

Mackenzie
Bay

Amundsen Gulf

Victoria Island

Prince
of
Wales
Island

McClintock
Channel

Boothia
Peninsula

Gulf of
Boothia

Baffin Bay

Greenland

Kuskokwim Bay

Yukon

Koyukuk

Peel

Arctic Red

Great Bear Lake

Coppermine

Coronation Gulf

Queen Mau
Gulf

Foxe Basin

Nettilling Lake

Baffin Island

Bowers Ridge

Aleutian Islands

Bristol
Bay

Kuskokwim

Alaska Range

Kenai
Mountains

Mackenzie Mountains

Back

Arctic Circle

Thelon

Garry Lake

Baker Lake

Foxe Channel

Amadjuak Lake

Cumberland
Sound

Frobisher Bay

Davis Strait

Alaska Peninsula

Kodiak
Island

Aleutian Range

NORTH AMERICAN PLATE

Gulf of
Alaska

Juneau

Great Slave Lake

Duhawnt Lake

Kazan

Roes Welcome Sound

Southampton
Island

Hudson Strait

Péninsule
d'Ungava

Labrador
Sea

PACIFIC PLATE

Patton Seamount

Cowie Seamount

Dickins
Seamount

Queen Charlotte Islands

PACIFIC PLATE

NORTH AMERICAN PLATE

Coats Island

Mansel
Island

Ungava
Bay

Armaud

Rivière
aux Feuilles

Rivière
aux Mélèzes

George

Gulf of Alaska

Gilbert Seamounts

Morton Seamount

Union Seamount

Cobb Seamount

Vancouver
Island

Cascadia
Basin

Astoria
Fan

Mount Rainier
4392m

Mount St Helens

Columbia

JUAN DE FUCA PLATE

Gorda Ridge

Delgada
Fan

San Francisco Bay

Monterey Bay

Astoria
Fan

Columbia
Plateau

Snake River
Plain

Yellowstone

Snake

Lake Athabasca

Wollaston Lake
Reindeer Lake

Churchill

North Saskatchewan

South Saskatchewan

Nelson

Lake Winnipeg

Belcher
Islands

La Grande Rivière

Lac Mistassini

Labrador

Laurentian
Mountains

NORTH

Canadian Shield

James
Bay

Ottawa

Missouri

Assiniboine

Lake Manitoba

Lake of the Woods

Lake Nipigon

Lake Superior

Great Lakes

Lake
Huron

Lake Ontario

St Lawrence

Lake Champlain

Connecticut

Cape
Cod

Mendocino Fracture Zone

Pioneer Fracture Zone

PACIFIC OCEAN

Murray Fracture Zone

Maarless
Mountains

Columbia
Plateau

Harney Basin

Great Basin

Mount Whitney 4418m

Death
Valley

Lake Mead

Mojave
Desert

Sierra Nevada

San Joaquin

Coast Ranges

Cheyenne

North Platte

South Platte

Humboldt

Owyhee

Green

Great Salt Lake

Colorado

Lake Powell

Grand
Canyon

Painted Desert

Colorado
Plateau

Humphreys
Peak

Baldy Peak 3476m

Gila

Wasatch Mountains

Lake Oahe

Black Hills

Niobrara

Platte

Kansas

Arkansas

Missouri

Red River

Des Moines

Minnesota

Wisconsin

Mississippi

Illinois

Lake Michigan

Lake
St Clair

Lake Erie

Niagara
Falls

Ontario

A M E R I C A

Great Plains

Sierra Madre Occidental

Ohio

Allegheny Mountains

Cumberland Plateau

Tennessee

Appalachian Mountains

Blue Ridge

Roanoke

Mount Mitchell 2037m

Delaware Bay

Chesapeake Bay

Long Island

Cape Hatteras

Cape Lookout

Molokai Fracture Zone

Tropic of Cancer

Islas Alijos

Gulf of
California

Lower California

Sonoran
Desert

Canadian

Pecos

Red River

Arkansas

Rio Grande

Colorado

Mississippi

Alabama

Chattahoochee

Savannah

Mississippi
Delta

Blake-Bahama Ridge

Clarion Fracture Zone

Cabo San
Lucas

Revillagigedo
Islands

Rio de Santiago

Sierra Madre Oriental

Galveston Bay

Mississippi Fan

Apalachee
Bay

Tampa Bay

Lake Okeechobee

The
Everglades

Blake
Plateau

Cape Canaveral

Straits of Florida

Bahamas

Sigsbee
Escarpment

Gulf of Mexico

Mexico
Basin

Campeche Bank

Yucatan
Channel

Cuba

Mathematicians
Seamounts

Orozco Fracture Zone

COCOS PLATE

PACIFIC PLATE

Citlaltépetl
5700m

Golfo de
Tehuantepec

Bay of
Campeche

Yucatan
Peninsula

Yucatan Basin

Cayman Trench

NORTH AMERICAN PLATE

CARIBBEAN PLATE

Jamaica

Greater

Clipperton Fracture Zone

Clipperton Seamounts

Clipperton
Island

Albatross
Plateau

Tehuantepec Ridge

Middle America Trench

Gulf of Honduras

Gulf of Darién

Nicaraguan
Rise

Caribbean

Peninsula
de la Guajira

Equator

East Pacific Rise

Siqueiros Fracture Zone

Berlanga Rise

**Guatemala
Basin**

Cocos Ridge

COCOS PLATE

Lake Nicaragua

Mosquito
Gulf

Isthmus of Panama

NAZCA PLATE

Colombian
Basin

Mosquito
Coast

Golfo de
Darién

Gulf of
Panama

Peninsula
de Azuero

Panama
Basin

Colón Ridge

NORTH AMERICA

North America is the world's third largest continent with a total area of 9,358,340 sq miles (24,238,000 sq km) including Greenland and the Caribbean Islands. It lies wholly within the Northern Hemisphere.

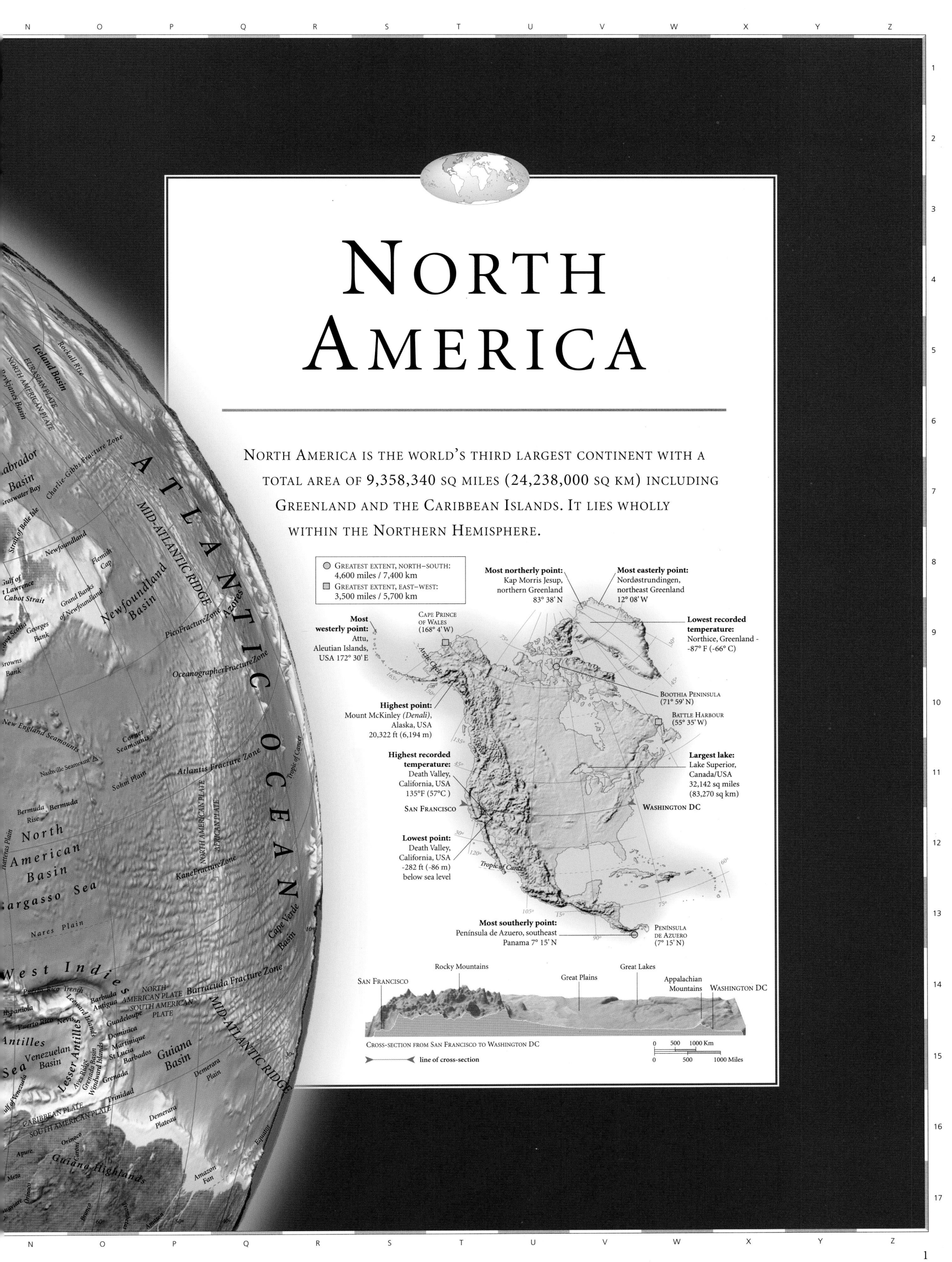

● Greatest extent, north–south: 4,600 miles / 7,400 km
□ Greatest extent, east–west: 3,500 miles / 5,700 km

Most northerly point: Kap Morris Jesup, northern Greenland 83° 38' N

Most easterly point: Nordøstrundingen, northeast Greenland 12° 08' W

Most westerly point: Attu, Aleutian Islands, USA 172° 30' E

CAPE PRINCE OF WALES (168° 4' W)

Lowest recorded temperature: Northice, Greenland - -87° F (-66° C)

Highest point: Mount McKinley (*Denali*), Alaska, USA 20,322 ft (6,194 m)

BOOTHIA PENINSULA (71° 59' N)

BATTLE HARBOUR (55° 35' W)

Highest recorded temperature: Death Valley, California, USA 135°F (57°C)

Largest lake: Lake Superior, Canada/USA 32,142 sq miles (83,270 sq km)

SAN FRANCISCO

WASHINGTON DC

Lowest point: Death Valley, California, USA -282 ft (-86 m) below sea level

Most southerly point: Península de Azuero, southeast Panama 7° 15' N

PENÍNSULA DE AZUERO (7° 15' N)

Tropic of Cancer

SAN FRANCISCO — Rocky Mountains — Great Plains — Great Lakes — Appalachian Mountains — WASHINGTON DC

CROSS-SECTION FROM SAN FRANCISCO TO WASHINGTON DC

► line of cross-section

0   500   1000 Km
0   500   1000 Miles

PHYSICAL NORTH AMERICA

THE NORTH AMERICAN CONTINENT can be divided into a number of major structural areas: the Western Cordillera, the Canadian Shield, the Great Plains, and Central Lowlands, and the Appalachians. Other smaller regions include the Gulf Atlantic Coastal Plain which borders the southern coast of North America from the southern Appalachians to the Great Plains. This area includes the expanding Mississippi Delta. A chain of volcanic islands, running in an arc around the margin of the Caribbean Plate, lie to the east of the Gulf of Mexico.

THE CANADIAN SHIELD

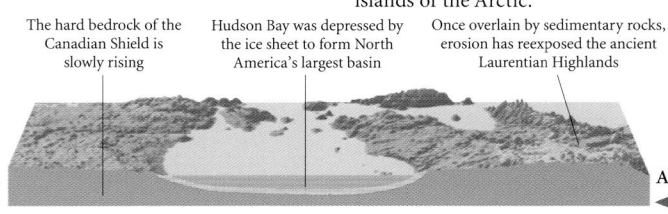

SPANNING NORTHERN CANADA and Greenland, this geologically stable plain forms the heart of the continent, containing rocks more than two billion years old. A long history of weathering and repeated glaciation has scoured the region, leaving flat plains, gentle hummocks, numerous small basins and lakes, and the bays and islands of the Arctic.

The hard bedrock of the Canadian Shield is slowly rising

Hudson Bay was depressed by the ice sheet to form North America's largest basin

Once overlain by sedimentary rocks, erosion has reexposed the ancient Laurentian Highlands

A — A

Section across the Canadian Shield showing where the ice sheet has depressed the underlying rock and formed bays and islands.

0 100 200 Km
0 100 200 Miles

THE WESTERN CORDILLERA

ABOUT 80 MILLION YEARS ago the Pacific and North American plates collided, uplifting the Western Cordillera. This consists of the Aleutian, Coast, Cascade and Sierra Nevada mountains, and the inland Rocky Mountains. These run parallel from the Arctic to Mexico.

The weight of the ice sheet, 1.8 miles (3 km) thick, has depressed the land to 0.6 miles (1 km) below sea level

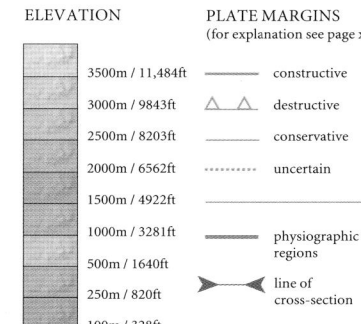

This computer-generated view shows the ice-covered island of Greenland without its ice cap.

Strata have been thrust eastward along fault lines

The Rocky Mountain Trench is the longest linear fault on the continent

B — B

Volcanic rock

Cross-section through the Western Cordillera showing direction of mountain building.

0 50 100 Km
0 50 100 Miles

MAP KEY

ELEVATION

3500m / 11,484ft
3000m / 9843ft
2500m / 8203ft
2000m / 6562ft
1500m / 4922ft
1000m / 3281ft
500m / 1640ft
250m / 820ft
100m / 328ft
sea level

PLATE MARGINS
(for explanation see page xiv)

——— constructive
△△△ destructive
——— conservative
········· uncertain

—— physiographic regions

◄—► line of cross-section

SCALE 1:38,000,000
(projection: Lambert Azimuthal Equal Area)

Km
0 100 200 400 600 800 1000
0 50 100 200 300 400 500 600 700 800 900 1000
Miles

THE APPALACHIANS

THE APPALACHIAN MOUNTAINS, uplifted about 400 million years ago, are some of the oldest in the world. They have been lowered and rounded by erosion and now slope gently toward the Atlantic across a broad coastal plain.

Horizontal strata

Sedimentary strata folded and faulted into ridges and valleys

Softer strata has been crumpled against the harder basement rock

Hard basement rock

C — C

Cross-section through the Appalachians showing the numerous folds, which have subsequently been weathered to create a rounded relief.

0 50 100 Km
0 50 100 Miles

THE GREAT PLAINS & CENTRAL LOWLANDS

DEPOSITS LEFT by retreating glaciers and rivers have made this vast flat area very fertile. In the north this is the result of glaciation, with deposits up to one mile (1.7 km) thick, covering the basement rock. To the south and west, the massive Missouri/Mississippi river system has for centuries deposited silt across the region, creating broad, flat floodplains and deltas.

Sedimentary layers overlay domed basement rock

Upland rivers drain south toward the Mississippi Basin

Confluence of the Missouri and Mississippi Rivers

D — D

Section across the Great Plains and Central Lowlands showing river systems and structure.

0 200 400 Km
0 200 400 Miles

Map labels

ATLANTIC OCEAN
Greenland
Baffin Bay
Baffin Island
Davis Strait
Labrador Sea
Labrador
Newfoundland
Nova Scotia
Cape Cod
St. Lawrence
Laurentian Mountains
Hudson Strait
Foxe Basin
Hudson Bay
CANADIAN SHIELD
Reindeer Lake
Lake Athabasca
Great Slave Lake
Lake Winnipeg
Lake Manitoba
Lake Superior
Lake Huron
Lake Michigan
Lake Ontario
Lake Erie
Great Lakes
Great Bear Lake
Beaufort Sea
Brooks Range
Mackenzie Delta
Mackenzie
Mackenzie Mountains
CENTRAL LOWLANDS
Missouri
Ohio
Arkansas
Mississippi
APPALACHIAN MOUNTAINS
APPALACHIANS
GULF ATLANTIC COASTAL PLAIN
Mississippi Delta
Gulf of Mexico
Yucatan Peninsula
WEST INDIES
Greater Antilles
Lesser Antilles
Caribbean Sea
Isthmus of Panama
SOUTH AMERICA
NORTH AMERICAN PLATE
CARIBBEAN PLATE
COCOS PLATE
SOUTH AMERICAN PLATE
Lake Nicaragua
Sierra Madre del Sur
Sierra Madre Oriental
Sierra Madre Occidental
Rio Grande
Volcán Pico de Orizaba 5700m
Lower California
Gulf of California
PACIFIC OCEAN
Sonoran Desert
Mojave Desert
Death Valley
San Joaquin Valley
San Andreas Fault
Grand Canyon
Colorado Plateau
Colorado
Great Salt Lake
Great Basin
Sierra Nevada
Cascade Range
Coast Ranges
Mount Rainier 4392m
Mount St Helens 2549m
WESTERN CORDILLERA
ROCKY MOUNTAINS
GREAT PLAINS
PACIFIC PLATE
NORTH AMERICAN PLATE
Gulf of Alaska
Coast Mountains
Aleutian Range
Alaska Range
Mount McKinley 6194m
Aleutian Islands
Bering Sea
Bering Strait
ASIA

CLIMATE

"Tornado alley" in the Mississippi Valley suffers frequent tornadoes.

NORTH AMERICA'S climate includes extremes ranging from freezing Arctic conditions in Alaska and Greenland, to desert in the southwest, and tropical conditions in southeastern Florida, the Caribbean, and Central America. Central and southern regions are prone to severe storms including tornadoes and hurricanes.

Much of the southwest is semi-desert; receiving less than 12 inches (300 mm) of rainfall a year.

Climate

- ice cap
- tundra
- subarctic
- cool continental
- warm humid
- semiarid
- arid
- humid equatorial
- tropical
- ☼ daily hours of sunshine, January
- ☼ daily hours of sunshine, July
- → direction of hurricanes
- ⊚ tornado zones

TEMPERATURE

Arctic Circle
60° N
40° N
Tropic of Cancer
20° N

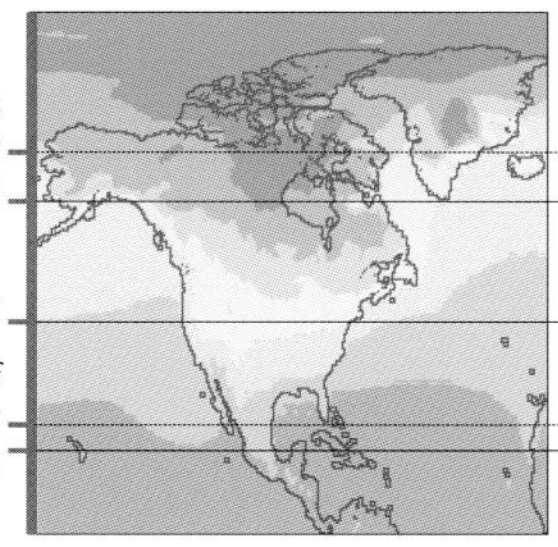

Average January temperature

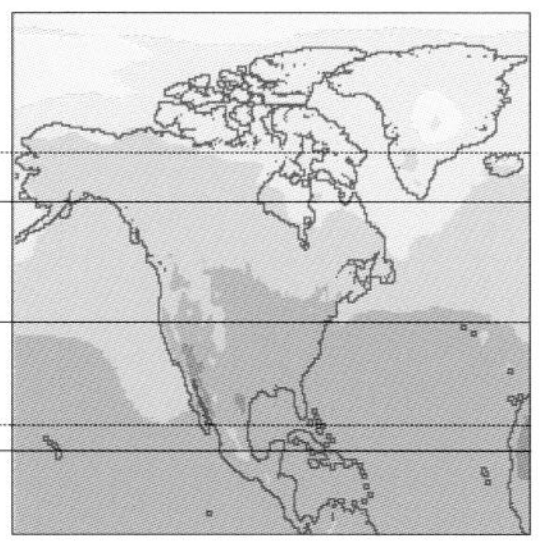

Average July temperature

Temperature

below -30°C (-22°F)	0 to 10°C (32 to 50°F)
-30 to -20°C (-22 to -4°F)	10 to 20°C (50 to 68°F)
-20 to -10°C (-4 to 14°F)	20 to 30°C (68 to 86°F)
-10 to 0°C (14 to 32°F)	above 30°C (86 °F)

RAINFALL

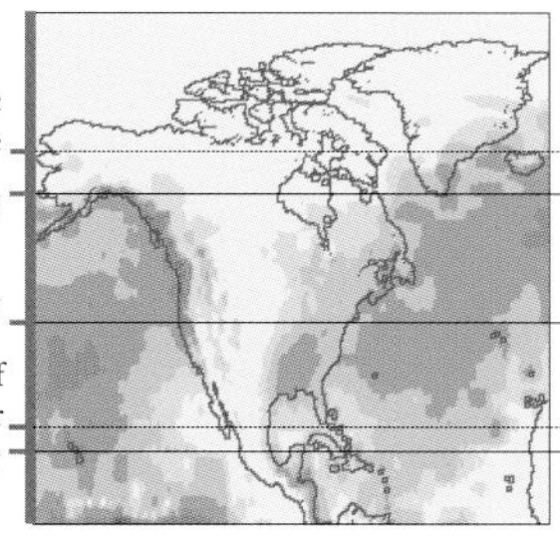

Arctic Circle
60° N
40° N
Tropic of Cancer
20° N

Average January rainfall

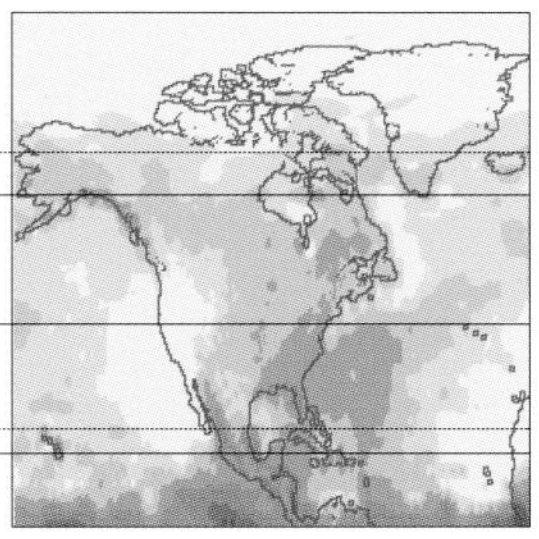

Average July rainfall

Rainfall

- 0–25 mm (0–1 in)
- 25–50 mm (1–2 in)
- 50–100 mm (2–4 in)
- 100–200 mm (4–8 in)
- 200–300 mm (8–12 in)
- 300–400 mm (12–16 in)
- 400–500 mm (16–20 in)
- more than 500 mm (20 in)

The lush, green mountains of the Lesser Antilles receive annual rainfalls of up to 360 inches (9,000 mm).

Map labels: Nome, Fairbanks, Aklavik, Kugluktuk, Resolute, Eismitte, Iqaluit, Haines Junction, Juneau, Churchill, Happy Valley - Goose Bay, Torbay, Fort Vermillon, Fort St John, Vancouver, Medicine Hat, Winnipeg, Montréal, Boise, Toronto, Sioux City, New York, Salt Lake City, Denver, San Francisco, Las Vegas, Phoenix, Atlanta, Cape Hatteras, Los Angeles, Little Rock, Guaymas, Houston, Miami, Nassau, Chihuahua, New Orleans, Santo Domingo, Fort-de-France, Mérida, Kingston, Acapulco, San Salvador, San José

SHAPING THE CONTINENT

GLACIAL PROCESSES affect much of northern Canada, Greenland and the Western Cordillera. Along the western coast of North America, Central America, and the Caribbean, underlying plates moving together lead to earthquakes and volcanic eruptions. The vast river systems, fed by mountain streams, constantly erode and deposit material along their paths.

VOLCANIC ACTIVITY

[1] Mount St. Helens volcano *(right)* in the Cascade Range erupted violently in May 1980, killing 57 people and leveling large areas of forest. The lateral blast filled a valley with debris for 15 miles (25 km).

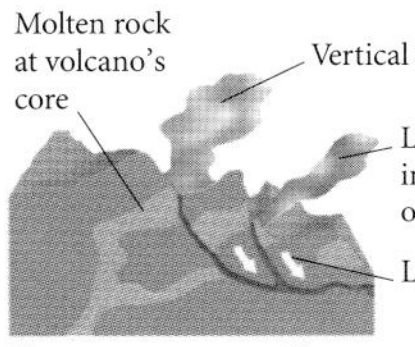

Molten rock at volcano's core
Vertical eruption
Lateral explosion increases extent of damage
Landslide fills valley

VOLCANIC ACTIVITY: ERUPTION OF MOUNT ST.. HELENS

PERIGLACIATION

[2] The ground in the far north is nearly always frozen: the surface thaws only in summer. This freeze-thaw process produces features such as pingos *(left)*, formed by the freezing of groundwater. With each successive winter ice accumulates producing a mound with a core of ice.

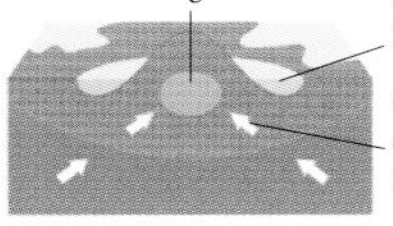

Ice core pushes up ground to form pingo
Unfrozen lake
Groundwater attracted to ice core

PERIGLACIATION: FORMATION OF A PINGO IN THE MACKENZIE DELTA

THE EVOLVING LANDSCAPE

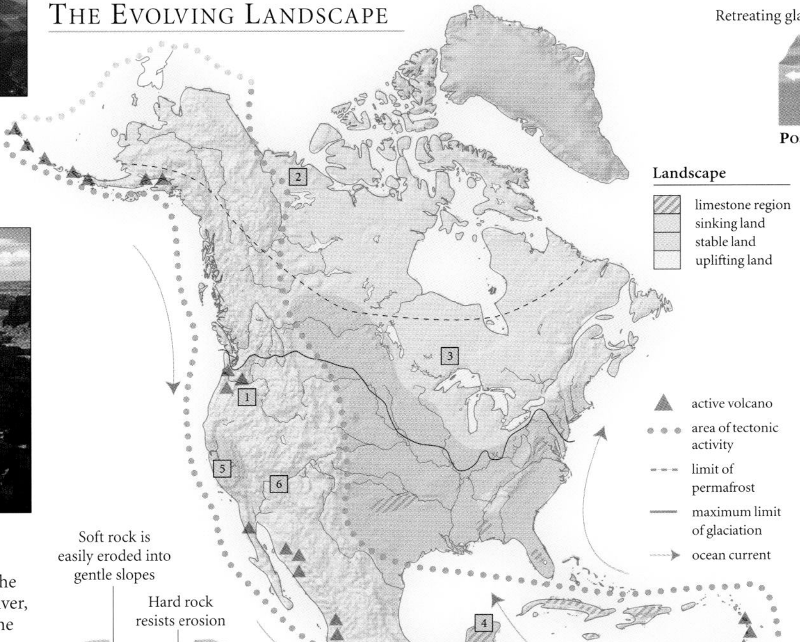

Landscape

- limestone region
- sinking land
- stable land
- uplifting land

- ▲ active volcano
- ⋯ area of tectonic activity
- --- limit of permafrost
- — maximum limit of glaciation
- → ocean current

POST-GLACIAL LAKES

[3] A chain of lakes from Great Bear Lake to the Great Lakes *(above)* was created as the ice retreated northward. Glaciers scoured hollows in the softer lowland rock. Glacial deposits at the lip of the hollows, and ridges of harder rock, trapped water to form lakes.

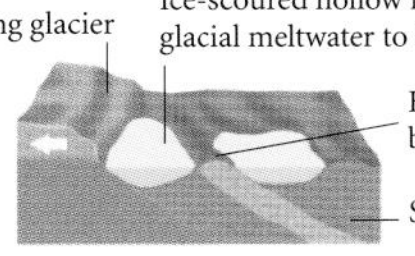

Retreating glacier
Ice-scoured hollow filled with glacial meltwater to form a lake
Harder rock creates a barrier between lakes
Softer lowland rock

POST-GLACIAL LAKES: FORMATION OF THE GREAT LAKES

WEATHERING

[4] The Yucatan Peninsula is a vast, flat limestone plateau in southern Mexico. Weathering action from both rainwater and underground streams has enlarged fractures in the rock to form caves and hollows, called sinkholes *(above)*.

Porous limestone plateau
Rainwater erodes porous rock forming sinkholes
Sea level
Underground stream further erodes rock

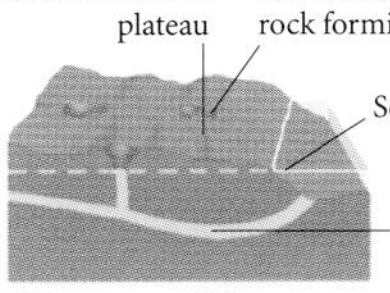

WEATHERING: WATER EROSION ON THE YUCATAN PENINSULA

SEISMIC ACTIVITY

[5] The San Andreas Fault *(above)* places much of the North America's west coast under constant threat from earthquakes. It is caused by the Pacific Plate grinding past the North American Plate at a faster rate, though in the same direction.

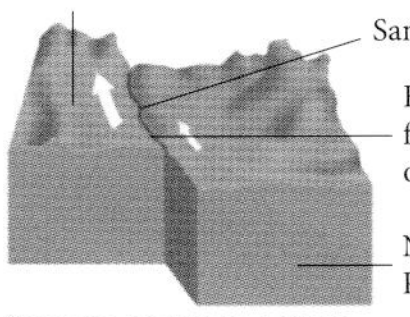

Pacific Plate
San Andreas Fault
Fault is caused by faster movement of Pacific Plate
North American Plate

SEISMIC ACTIVITY: ACTION OF THE SAN ANDREAS FAULT

RIVER EROSION

[6] The Grand Canyon *(above)* in the Colorado Plateau was created by the downward erosion of the Colorado River, combined with the gradual uplift of the plateau, over the past 30 million years. The contours of the canyon formed as the softer rock layers eroded into gentle slopes, and the hard rock layers into cliffs. The depth varies from 3,855–6,560 ft (1,175–2,000 m).

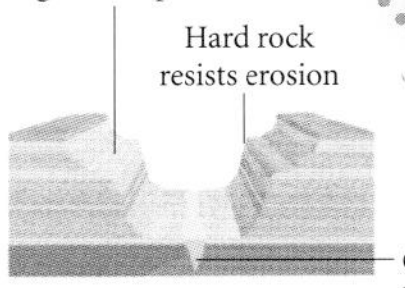

Soft rock is easily eroded into gentle slopes
Hard rock resists erosion
Colorado River cuts down through rock

RIVER EROSION: FORMATION OF THE GRAND CANYON

POLITICAL NORTH AMERICA

DEMOCRACY IS WELL ESTABLISHED in some parts of the continent but is a recent phenomenon in others. The economically dominant nations of Canada and the US have a long democratic tradition but elsewhere, notably in the countries of Central America, political turmoil has been more common. In Nicaragua and Haiti, harsh dictatorships have only recently been superseded by democratically-elected governments. North America's largest countries, Canada, Mexico, and the US have federal state systems, sharing political power between national and state governments. The US has intervened militarily on several occasions in Central America and the Caribbean to protect its strategic interests.

TRANSPORTATION

IN THE 19TH CENTURY, railroads opened up the North American continent. Air transportation is now more common for long distance passenger travel, although railroads are still extensively used for bulk freight transportation. Waterways like the Mississippi River are important for the transportation of bulk materials, and the Panama Canal is a vital link between the Pacific and Atlantic Oceans. In the 20th century, road transportation increased massively, with the introduction of cheap, mass-produced motor cars and extensive highway construction.

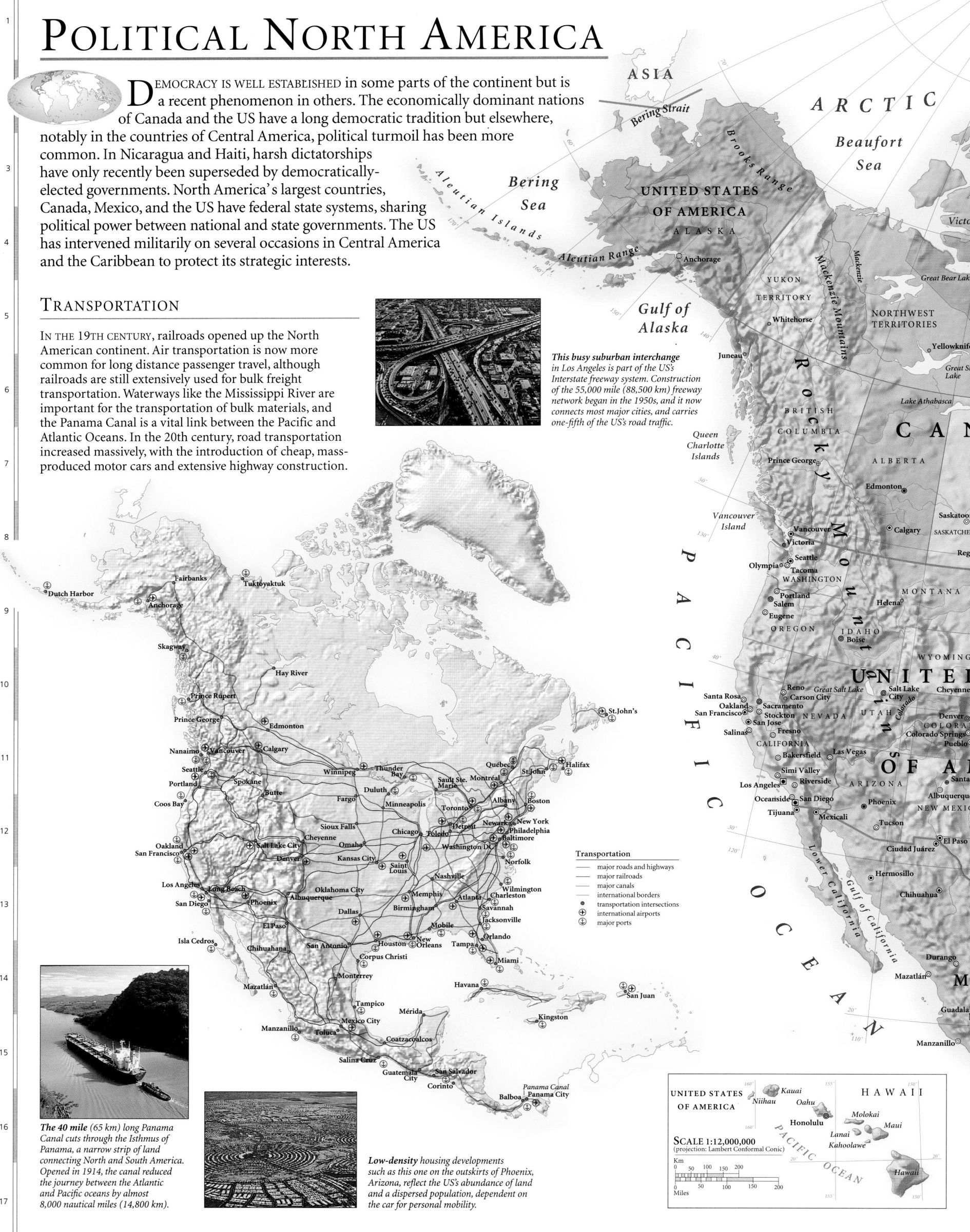

This busy suburban interchange in Los Angeles is part of the US's Interstate freeway system. Construction of the 55,000 mile (88,500 km) freeway network began in the 1950s, and it now connects most major cities, and carries one-fifth of the US's road traffic.

The 40 mile (65 km) long Panama Canal cuts through the Isthmus of Panama, a narrow strip of land connecting North and South America. Opened in 1914, the canal reduced the journey between the Atlantic and Pacific oceans by almost 8,000 nautical miles (14,800 km).

Low-density housing developments such as this one on the outskirts of Phoenix, Arizona, reflect the US's abundance of land and a dispersed population, dependent on the car for personal mobility.

Transportation

— major roads and highways
— major railroads
— major canals
— international borders
• transportation intersections
⊕ international airports
⊕ major ports

UNITED STATES OF AMERICA

SCALE 1:12,000,000
(projection: Lambert Conformal Conic)

HAWAII

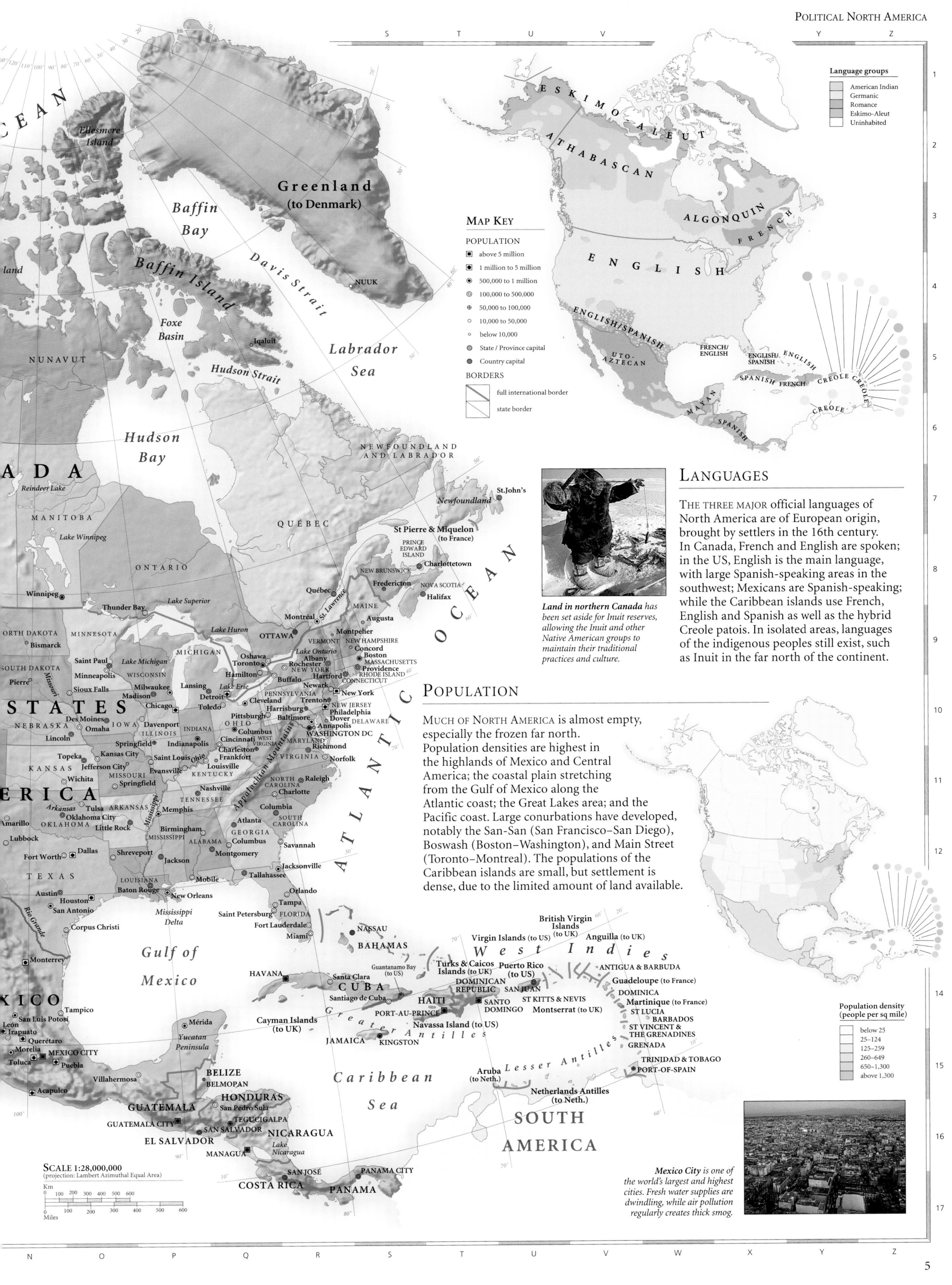

Language groups
- American Indian
- Germanic
- Romance
- Eskimo-Aleut
- Uninhabited

MAP KEY

POPULATION
- above 5 million
- 1 million to 5 million
- 500,000 to 1 million
- 100,000 to 500,000
- 50,000 to 100,000
- 10,000 to 50,000
- below 10,000
- State / Province capital
- Country capital

BORDERS
- full international border
- state border

LANGUAGES

THE THREE MAJOR official languages of North America are of European origin, brought by settlers in the 16th century. In Canada, French and English are spoken; in the US, English is the main language, with large Spanish-speaking areas in the southwest; Mexicans are Spanish-speaking; while the Caribbean islands use French, English and Spanish as well as the hybrid Creole patois. In isolated areas, languages of the indigenous peoples still exist, such as Inuit in the far north of the continent.

Land in northern Canada has been set aside for Inuit reserves, allowing the Inuit and other Native American groups to maintain their traditional practices and culture.

POPULATION

MUCH OF NORTH AMERICA is almost empty, especially the frozen far north. Population densities are highest in the highlands of Mexico and Central America; the coastal plain stretching from the Gulf of Mexico along the Atlantic coast; the Great Lakes area; and the Pacific coast. Large conurbations have developed, notably the San-San (San Francisco–San Diego), Boswash (Boston–Washington), and Main Street (Toronto–Montreal). The populations of the Caribbean islands are small, but settlement is dense, due to the limited amount of land available.

Population density (people per sq mile)
- below 25
- 25–124
- 125–259
- 260–649
- 650–1,300
- above 1,300

Mexico City is one of the world's largest and highest cities. Fresh water supplies are dwindling, while air pollution regularly creates thick smog.

SCALE 1:28,000,000
(projection: Lambert Azimuthal Equal Area)

NORTH AMERICAN RESOURCES

THE TWO NORTHERN COUNTRIES of Canada and the US are richly endowed with natural resources that have helped to fuel economic development. The US is the world's largest economy, although today it is facing stiff competition from the Far East. Mexico has relied on oil revenues but there are hopes that the North American Free Trade Agreement (NAFTA), will encourage trade growth with Canada and the US. The poorer countries of Central America and the Caribbean depend largely on cash crops and tourism.

INDUSTRY

THE MODERN, INDUSTRIALIZED economies of the US and Canada contrast sharply with those of Mexico, Central America, and the Caribbean. Manufacturing is especially important in the US; vehicle production is concentrated around the Great Lakes, while electronic and hi-tech industries are increasingly found in the western and southern states. Mexico depends on oil exports and assembly work, taking advantage of cheap labor. Many Central American and Caribbean countries rely heavily on agricultural exports.

STANDARD OF LIVING

THE US AND CANADA have one of the highest overall standards of living in the world. However, many people still live in poverty, especially in urban ghettos and some rural areas. Central America and the Caribbean are markedly poorer than their wealthier northern neighbors. Haiti is the poorest country in the western hemisphere.

After its purchase from Russia in 1867, Alaska's frozen lands were largely ignored by the US. Oil reserves similar in magnitude to those in eastern Texas were discovered in Prudhoe Bay, Alaska in 1968. Freezing temperatures and a fragile environment hamper oil extraction.

Standard of Living
(UN Human Development Index)

high

low

Fish such as cod, flounder, and plaice are caught in the Grand Banks, off the Newfoundland coast, and processed in many North Atlantic coastal settlements.

South of San Francisco, "Silicon Valley" is both a national and international center for hi-tech industries, electronic industries, and research institutions.

Multinational companies rely on cheap labor and tax benefits to assemble vehicles in Mexican factories.

The health of the Wall Street stock market in New York is the standard measure of the state of the world's economy.

Industry

✈ aerospace	📖 printing & publishing
🍺 brewing	🔬 research & development
🚗 car/vehicle manufacture	⚓ shipbuilding
⚗ chemicals	🍬 sugar processing
🛡 defense	👕 textiles
⚡ electronics	🪵 timber processing
⚙ engineering	🚬 tobacco processing
🎬 movie industry	
💲 finance	⛏ coal
🍴 food processing	♦ oil
💻 hi-tech industry	◊ gas
iron & steel	• industrial cities
💊 pharmaceuticals	▨ major industrial areas

GNP per capita (US$)

	0–1999
	2000–4999
	5000–9999
	10,000–19,999
	20,000–24,999
	25,000+

ARCTIC OCEAN

RUSS. FED.

Bering Strait

Bering Sea

Beaufort Sea

Baffin Bay

Greenland (to Denmark)

Prudhoe Bay

USA

Gulf of Alaska

Labrador Sea

Hudson Strait

Hudson Bay

PACIFIC OCEAN

CANADA

Vancouver
Calgary
Seattle
Winnipeg
Montréal
Portland

UNITED STATES OF AMERICA

Minneapolis
Milwaukee
Toronto
Buffalo
Albany
Boston
New York
Detroit
Cleveland
Chicago
Pittsburgh
Philadelphia
Baltimore
Dayton
Cincinnati
Saint Louis
Kansas City
Denver
Wichita
San Francisco
Nashville
Greensboro
Charlotte
Tulsa
Los Angeles
Phoenix
San Diego
Birmingham
Atlanta
Tijuana
Dallas
El Paso
Ciudad Juárez
Houston
Jacksonville
New Orleans
Orlando
Tampa
Miami

ATLANTIC OCEAN

Monterrey

Gulf of Mexico

MEXICO

Guadalajara

Mexico City

West Indies

BAHAMAS
Virgin Islands (to US)
Turks & Caicos Islands (to UK)
British Virgin Islands (to UK)
Anguilla (to UK)
ST KITTS & NEVIS
ANTIGUA & BARBUDA
Puerto Rico (to US)
San Juan
CUBA
HAITI
DOMINICAN REPUBLIC
Havana
Cayman Islands (to UK)
JAMAICA
Port-au-Prince
Santo Domingo
Greater Antilles
Navassa Island (to US)
Guadeloupe (to France)
Montserrat (to UK)
DOMINICA
Martinique (to France)
ST LUCIA
BARBADOS
ST VINCENT & THE GRENADINES
GRENADA
Aruba (to Neth.)
TRINIDAD & TOBAGO
Port-of-Spain
Netherlands Antilles (to Neth.)
Lesser Antilles

Caribbean Sea

BELIZE
GUATEMALA
Guatemala City
HONDURAS
Tegucigalpa
EL SALVADOR
San Salvador
NICARAGUA
Managua
San José
COSTA RICA
Panama City
PANAMA

VENEZUELA

COLOMBIA

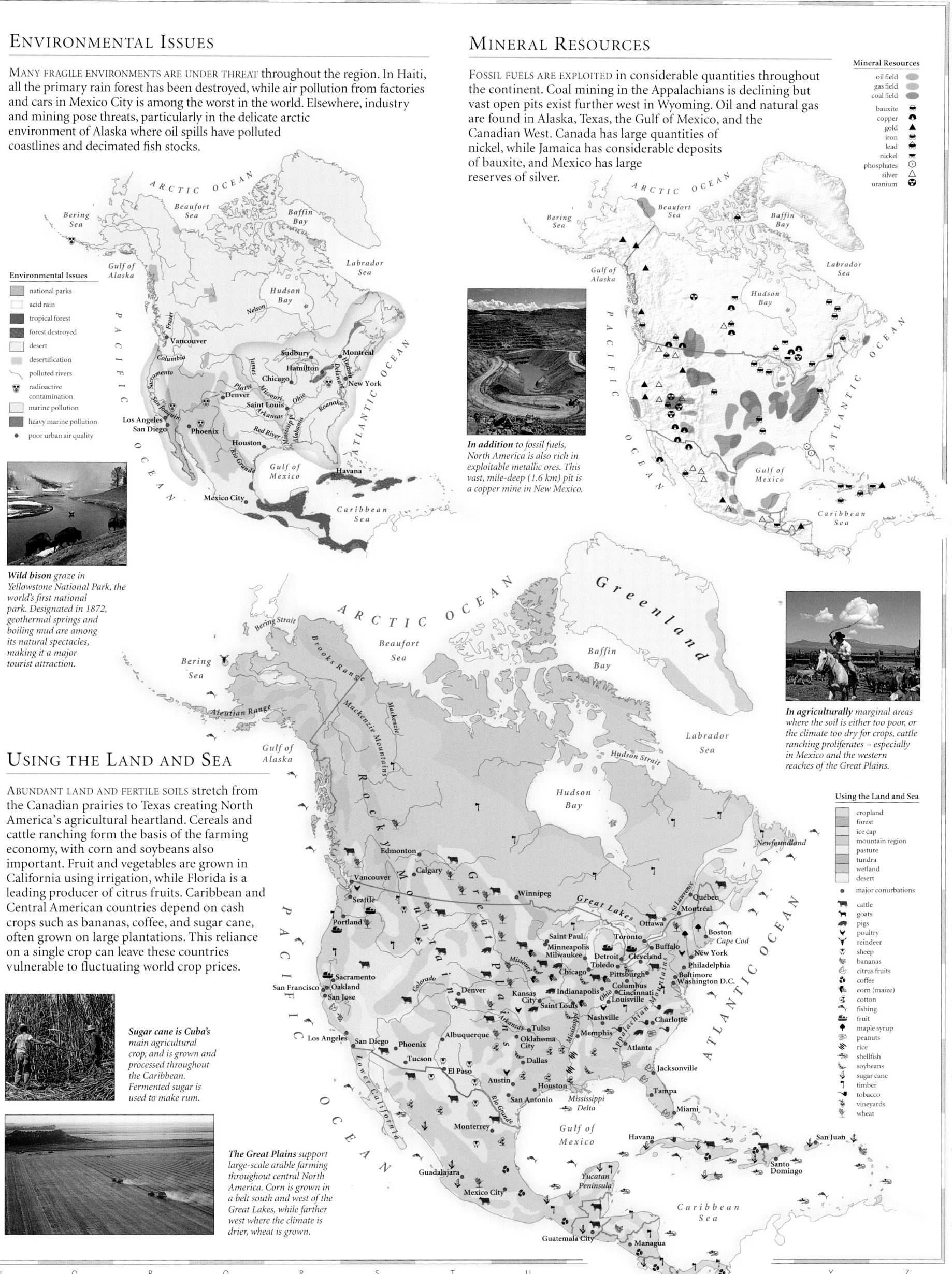

ENVIRONMENTAL ISSUES

MANY FRAGILE ENVIRONMENTS ARE UNDER THREAT throughout the region. In Haiti, all the primary rain forest has been destroyed, while air pollution from factories and cars in Mexico City is among the worst in the world. Elsewhere, industry and mining pose threats, particularly in the delicate arctic environment of Alaska where oil spills have polluted coastlines and decimated fish stocks.

Environmental Issues
- national parks
- acid rain
- tropical forest
- forest destroyed
- desert
- desertification
- polluted rivers
- radioactive contamination
- marine pollution
- heavy marine pollution
- • poor urban air quality

Wild bison graze in Yellowstone National Park, the world's first national park. Designated in 1872, geothermal springs and boiling mud are among its natural spectacles, making it a major tourist attraction.

MINERAL RESOURCES

FOSSIL FUELS ARE EXPLOITED in considerable quantities throughout the continent. Coal mining in the Appalachians is declining but vast open pits exist further west in Wyoming. Oil and natural gas are found in Alaska, Texas, the Gulf of Mexico, and the Canadian West. Canada has large quantities of nickel, while Jamaica has considerable deposits of bauxite, and Mexico has large reserves of silver.

Mineral Resources
- oil field
- gas field
- coal field
- bauxite
- copper
- gold
- iron
- lead
- nickel
- phosphates
- silver
- uranium

In addition to fossil fuels, North America is also rich in exploitable metallic ores. This vast, mile-deep (1.6 km) pit is a copper mine in New Mexico.

In agriculturally marginal areas where the soil is either too poor, or the climate too dry for crops, cattle ranching proliferates – especially in Mexico and the western reaches of the Great Plains.

USING THE LAND AND SEA

ABUNDANT LAND AND FERTILE SOILS stretch from the Canadian prairies to Texas creating North America's agricultural heartland. Cereals and cattle ranching form the basis of the farming economy, with corn and soybeans also important. Fruit and vegetables are grown in California using irrigation, while Florida is a leading producer of citrus fruits. Caribbean and Central American countries depend on cash crops such as bananas, coffee, and sugar cane, often grown on large plantations. This reliance on a single crop can leave these countries vulnerable to fluctuating world crop prices.

Sugar cane is Cuba's main agricultural crop, and is grown and processed throughout the Caribbean. Fermented sugar is used to make rum.

The Great Plains support large-scale arable farming throughout central North America. Corn is grown in a belt south and west of the Great Lakes, while farther west where the climate is drier, wheat is grown.

Using the Land and Sea
- cropland
- forest
- ice cap
- mountain region
- pasture
- tundra
- wetland
- desert
- • major conurbations
- cattle
- goats
- pigs
- poultry
- reindeer
- sheep
- bananas
- citrus fruits
- coffee
- corn (maize)
- cotton
- fishing
- fruit
- maple syrup
- peanuts
- rice
- shellfish
- soybeans
- sugar cane
- timber
- tobacco
- vineyards
- wheat

CANADA: WESTERN PROVINCES

Alberta, British Columbia, Manitoba, Saskatchewan, Yukon Territory

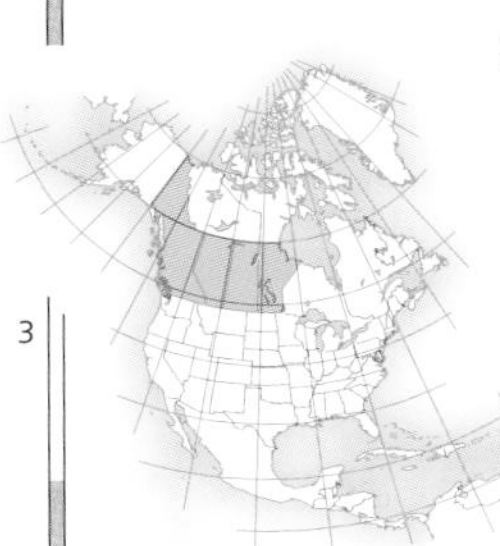

THE MOUNTAINS OF THE WEST COAST, incorporating British Columbia and the Yukon Territory, descend into the vast, flat prairies of Alberta, Saskatchewan, and Manitoba. The empty lands and fertile soils of the prairie provinces attracted migrants, and the descendants of early European immigrants still make up a large proportion of the population. The mechanization of agriculture has reduced the need for labor, and rural population densities remain low. The majority of the people live within 100 miles (160 km) of the southern Canada–US border, and in British Columbia, one of the leading Canadian provinces in terms of economic wealth. The Yukon Territory, in the far north, remains a relatively unspoiled wilderness, containing large, untapped mineral reserves. This province has a significant population of Native Americans people, many of whom maintain a traditional lifestyle.

USING THE LAND AND SEA

WHEAT FARMING IS THE ECONOMIC MAINSTAY of Alberta, Manitoba, and Saskatchewan, which contain 82% of farmland in Canada. Cattle are also raised on the prairies. Forestry and fishing are the most prominent resource-based industries in British Columbia. Despite the mountainous terrain, fruit and specialized grains can be grown in the Okanagan and Fraser valleys.

Land use and agricultural distribution

- cattle
- cereals
- fishing
- fruit
- timber
- major towns

pasture
cropland
forest
wetland
barren
tundra

THE URBAN/RURAL POPULATION DIVIDE

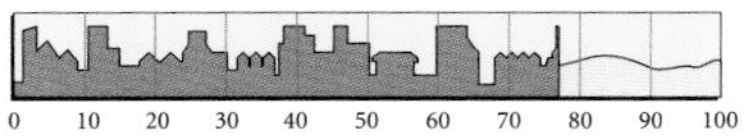

77% urban   23% rural

0 10 20 30 40 50 60 70 80 90 100

POPULATION DENSITY	TOTAL LAND AREA
7 people per sq mile	1,224,449 sq miles
(3 people per sq km)	(3,172,150 sq km)

Large, highly-mechanized and often very specialized farms, requiring huge investment but little labor, characterize modern farming in the prairies.

TRANSPORTATION & INDUSTRY

THE WESTERN PROVINCES contain a wealth of mineral resources. Alberta holds the bulk of Canada's fossil fuels; the other provinces contain reserves of metallic ores, such as zinc, lead, and silver. Isolation from markets has slowed the development of manufacturing, restricting it to the large cities like Vancouver, Winnipeg, and Calgary. Hydroelectric power is widely exploited, although there is increasing concern about potential ecological damage.

Major industry and infrastructure

- aerospace
- chemicals
- coal
- engineering
- food processing
- hydroelectric power
- mining
- oil & gas
- timber processing
- major towns
- international airports
- major roads
- major industrial areas

TRANSPORTATION NETWORK

82,438 miles (135,145 km)

6,459 miles (10,401 km)

10,811 miles (17,410 km)

None

The transportation network of the western provinces is dominated by east–west routes that weave through mountain passes and spread across the plains. Access to some northern areas is restricted to air travel.

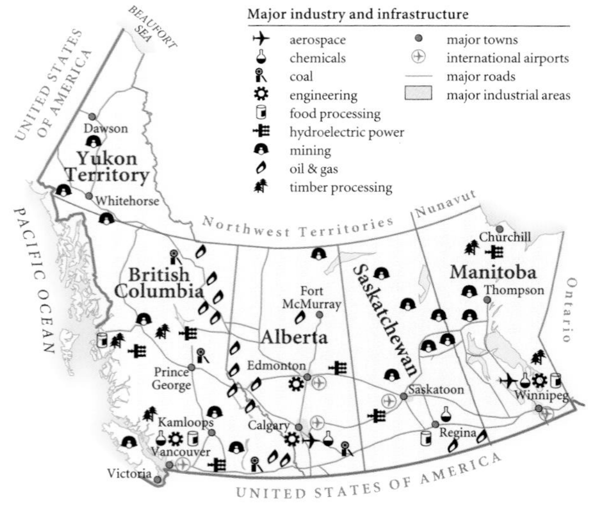

The Fraser River valley is a major area of settlement in British Columbia. Railroads cross the Rocky Mountains via this valley.

Established in 1907, Jasper National Park lies in the heart of the Rocky Mountains. It is noted for its spectacular alpine scenery and contains part of the large Columbia Icefield.

Much of the Yukon Territory is uninhabited tundra. Industry is based on the extraction of mineral resources, and to a lesser extent, on the scattered forests of the south.

THE LANDSCAPE

THE MASSIVE ROCKY MOUNTAINS form a continental divide between rivers flowing eastward and westward. The interior plains lie east of the mountains, stretching from the Arctic Circle south into the US. Covered with glacial deposits from the last Ice Age, these are interspersed with hilly regions and long, steep escarpments.

MAP KEY

POPULATION

- ◉ 500,000 to 1 million
- ◎ 100,000 to 500,000
- ⊕ 50,000 to 100,000
- ⊕ 10,000 to 50,000
- ○ below 10,000

ELEVATION

- 6000m / 19,686ft
- 4000m / 13,124ft
- 3000m / 9843ft
- 2000m / 6562ft
- 1000m / 3281ft
- 500m / 1640ft
- 250m / 820ft
- 100m / 328ft
- sea level

SCALE 1:7,500,000
(projection: Lambert Conformal Conic)

Km
0 25 50 100 150 200 250

Miles
0 25 50 100 150 200 250

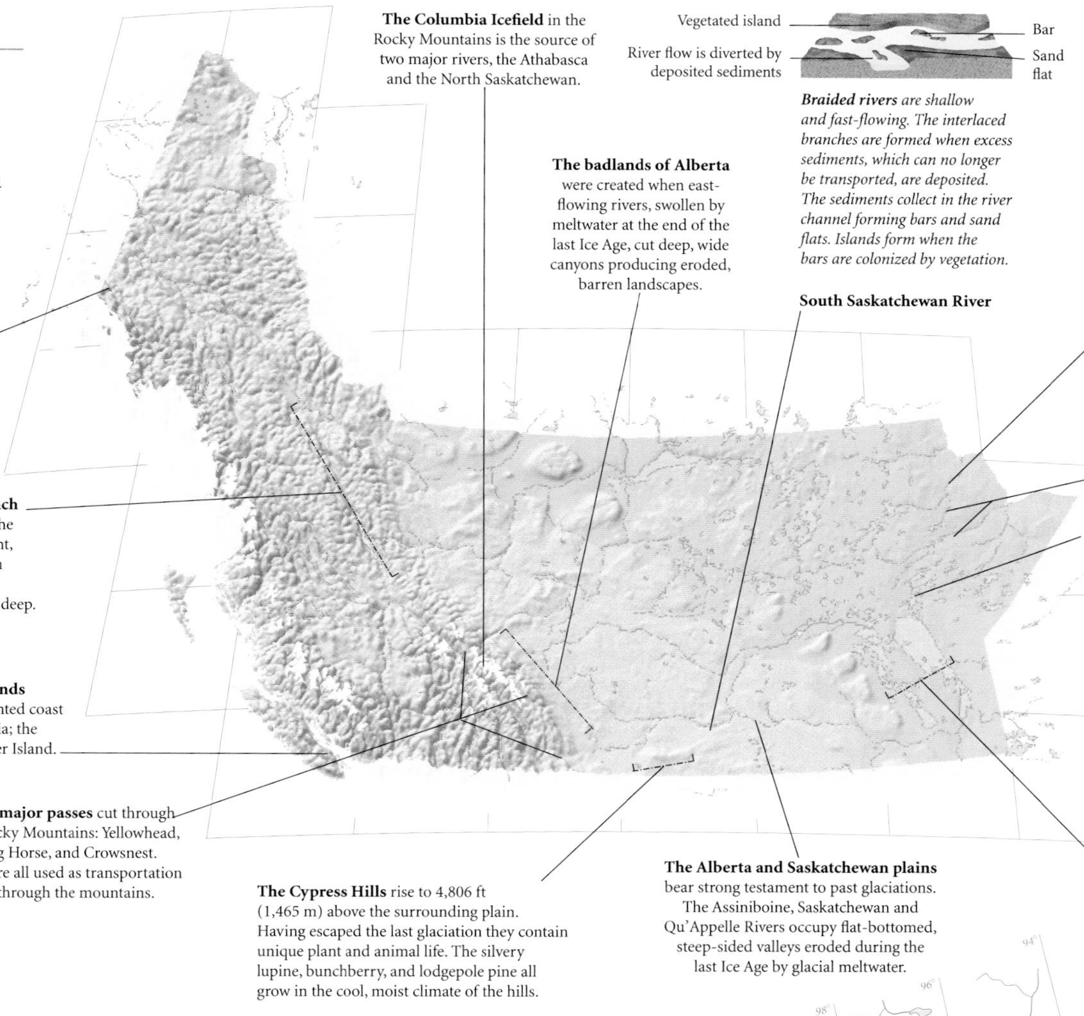

Mount Logan rises 19,551 ft (5,959 m). It is the highest peak in Canada.

The Rocky Mountain Trench is the longest linear fault in the world. It has formed a straight, flat-bottomed valley between 2–9 miles (4–15 km) wide, and up to 3,280 ft (1,000 m) deep.

Hundreds of islands dot the fjord-indented coast of British Columbia; the largest is Vancouver Island.

Three major passes cut through the Rocky Mountains: Yellowhead, Kicking Horse, and Crowsnest. They are all used as transportation routes through the mountains.

The Cypress Hills rise to 4,806 ft (1,465 m) above the surrounding plain. Having escaped the last glaciation they contain unique plant and animal life. The silvery lupine, bunchberry, and lodgepole pine all grow in the cool, moist climate of the hills.

The Columbia Icefield in the Rocky Mountains is the source of two major rivers, the Athabasca and the North Saskatchewan.

The badlands of Alberta were created when east-flowing rivers, swollen by meltwater at the end of the last Ice Age, cut deep, wide canyons producing eroded, barren landscapes.

South Saskatchewan River

Vegetated island
River flow is diverted by deposited sediments
Bar
Sand flat

Braided rivers are shallow and fast-flowing. The interlaced branches are formed when excess sediments, which can no longer be transported, are deposited. The sediments collect in the river channel forming bars and sand flats. Islands form when the bars are colonized by vegetation.

The Alberta and Saskatchewan plains bear strong testament to past glaciations. The Assiniboine, Saskatchewan and Qu'Appelle Rivers occupy flat-bottomed, steep-sided valleys eroded during the last Ice Age by glacial meltwater.

Across the tundra of northern Manitoba, widespread permafrost inhibits water from permeating the soil. This causes rivers like the Churchill to flow in many channels, which can be frozen for up to six months during the winter.

The Nelson and Churchill Rivers drain northward across the Canadian Shield to Hudson Bay. The shield covers three-fifths of Saskatchewan.

Setting Lake

Ancient granite outcrops, part of the Canadian Shield, rise above the surface of Setting Lake, which was initially formed by meltwater from the last Ice Age.

The lowlands of Manitoba are a basin that once held the vast post-glacial Lake Agassiz, remnants of which include Lake Winnipeg, Lake Winnipegosis, and Lake Manitoba.

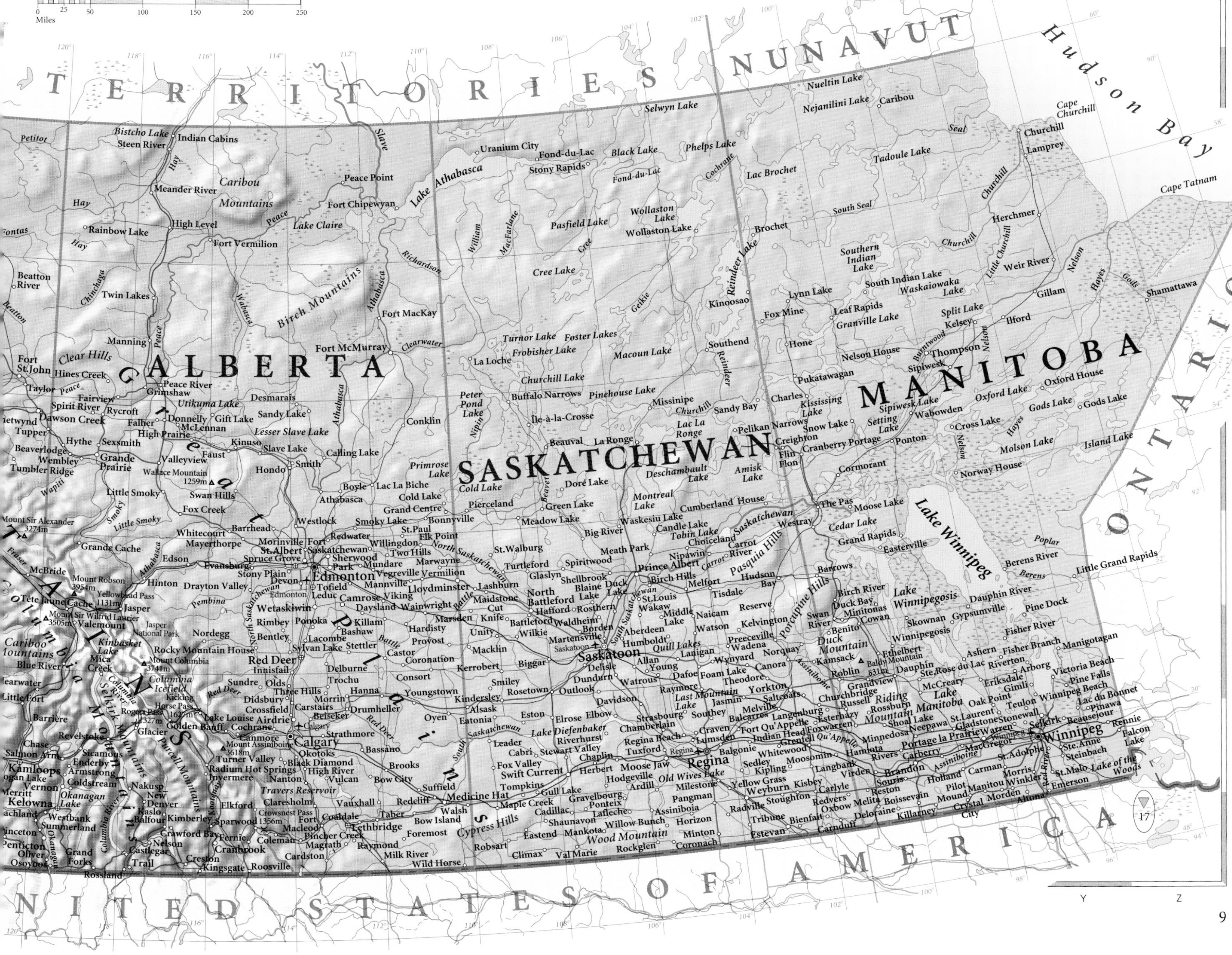

CANADA: EASTERN PROVINCES

New Brunswick, Newfoundland & Labrador, Nova Scotia, Ontario,
Prince Edward Island, Québec, *St. Pierre & Miquelon* (to France)

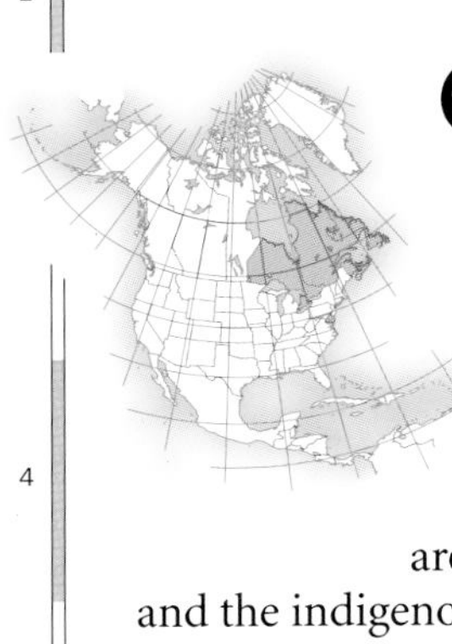

COLONIZED BY BOTH THE ENGLISH AND THE FRENCH during the 16th century, Canada's eastern provinces are still marked by their dual influences. They contain the last fragment of once-sizeable French territories, the islands of St. Pierre and Miquelon. French remains Canada's second official language and Québec's first language. The population of the eastern provinces is highly concentrated in the south, especially along the border with the US. A recent decline in fishing in the Atlantic provinces has encouraged a steady flow of westerly migration to more properous regions. The north, around Hudson Bay, remains snow-covered for most of the year and the indigenous Inuit people make up the bulk of its sparse population.

Rocher Percé, is 290 ft (88 m) high. Lying off the southeastern coast of Québec, it is a sanctuary for sea birds.

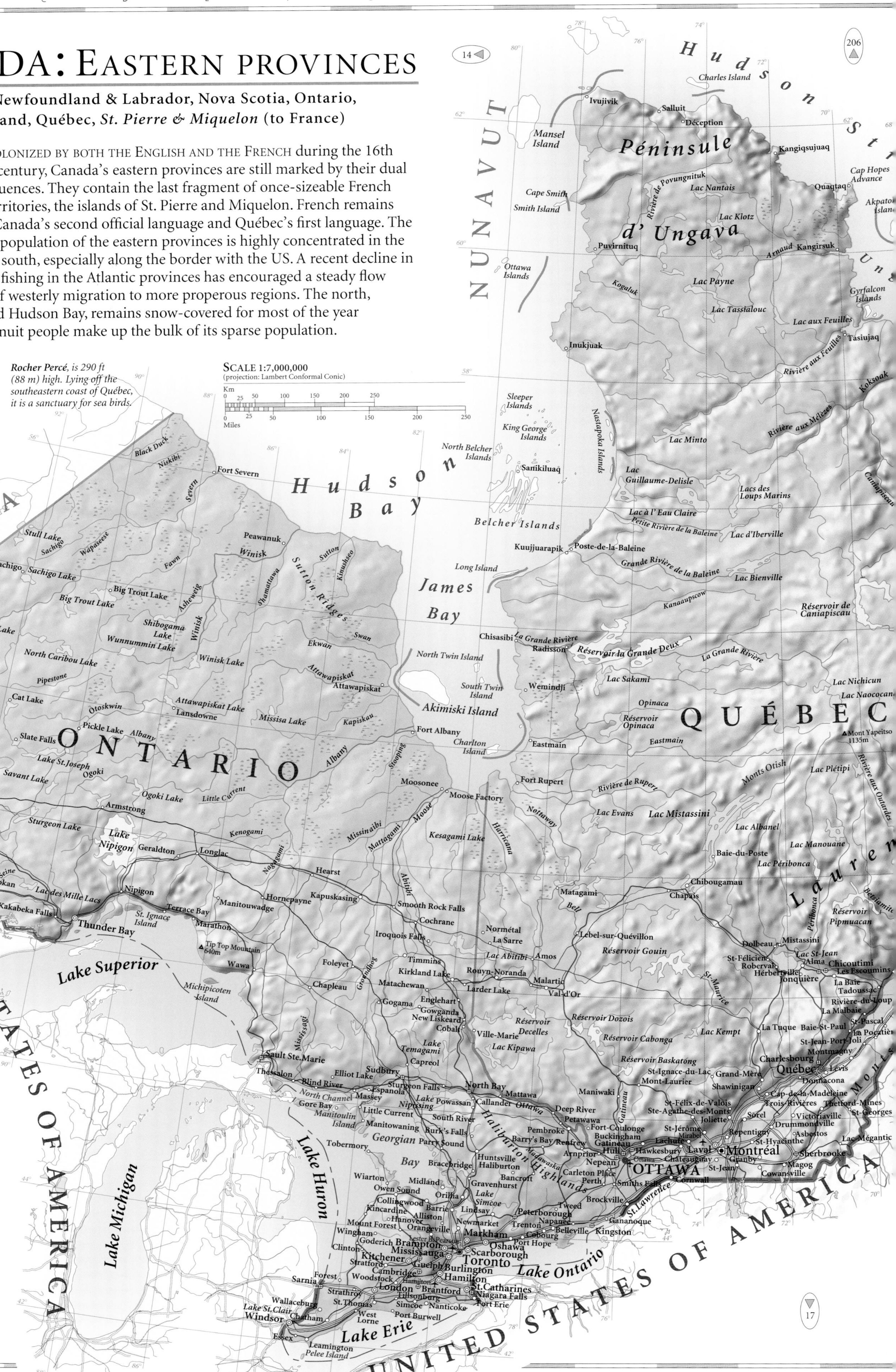

SCALE 1:7,000,000
(projection: Lambert Conformal Conic)

Km
0 25 50   100   150   200   250

Miles
0   25   50   100   150   200   250

MAP KEY

POPULATION

- ■ 1 million to 5 million
- ◉ 500,000 to 1 million
- ◉ 100,000 to 500,000
- ⊕ 50,000 to 100,000
- ○ 10,000 to 50,000
- ○ below 10,000

ELEVATION

- 500m / 1640ft
- 250m / 820ft
- 100m / 328ft
- sea level

THE LANDSCAPE

MUCH OF EASTERN CANADA is part of the Canadian Shield. Glaciers have scoured the land leaving deposits that have dammed and diverted streams, to create a rocky landscape strewn with lakes and swamps. Much of the ground is subject to permafrost, which further impedes drainage. The uplands in the far east are the most northerly extension of the Appalachian mountain chain.

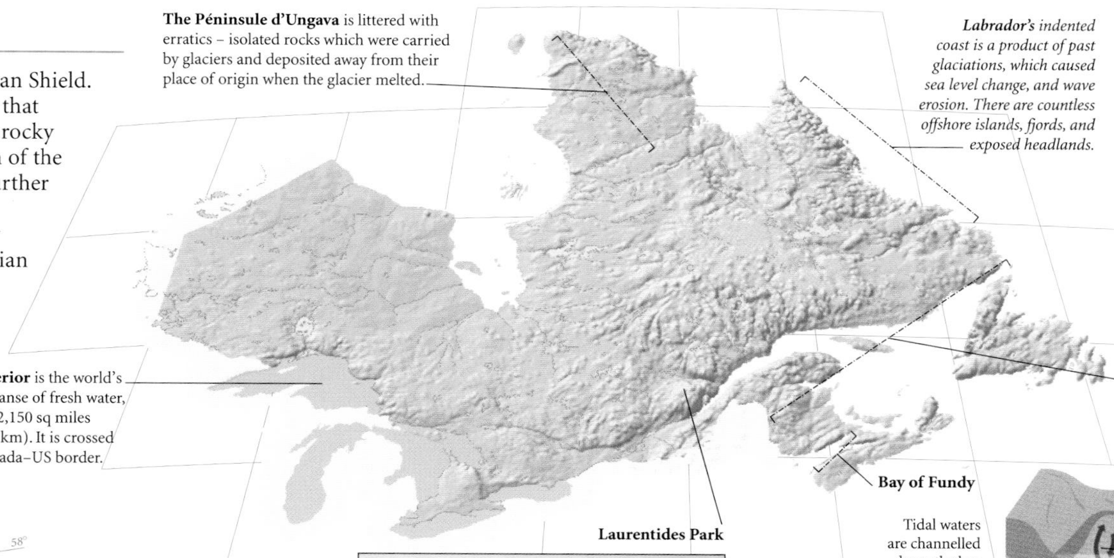

The Péninsule d'Ungava is littered with erratics – isolated rocks which were carried by glaciers and deposited away from their place of origin when the glacier melted.

Labrador's indented coast is a product of past glaciations, which caused sea level change, and wave erosion. There are countless offshore islands, fjords, and exposed headlands.

The eroded highlands of New Brunswick, Nova Scotia and Newfoundland are part of the Appalachian mountain chain, formed over 400 million years ago.

Lake Superior is the world's largest expanse of fresh water, covering 32,150 sq miles (83,270 sq km). It is crossed by the Canada–US border.

Bay of Fundy

Tidal waters are channelled down the bay

Steep cliffs bound the bay

The bay is 94 miles (151 km) long

Laurentides Park

The forested Laurentides Park incorporates part of the Laurentian Mountains. Within its boundaries are over 1,600 lakes.

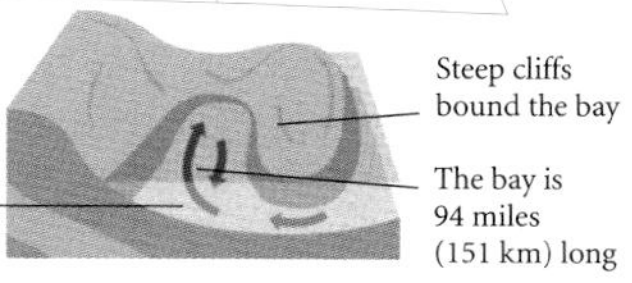

At the Bay of Fundy, incoming waves are funneled down the long, narrow, steep-sided bay. These topographical features cause fast-flowing tides which can rise 70 ft (21 m).

The tides at the Bay of Fundy are among the highest in the world. At low tide the tree-topped rocks have been likened to flowerpots.

TRANSPORTATION & INDUSTRY

BOTH QUÉBEC AND ONTARIO have a diversified manufacturing sector located in the south. Across the rest of the region, industry is largely based around local resources, which accounts for the large number of fish and timber processing plants and mines. Many of the fast-flowing rivers are also gradually being harnessed for hydroelectric power.

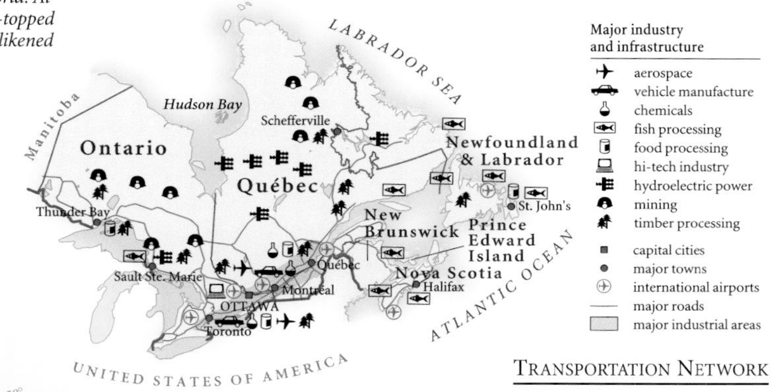

Major industry and infrastructure

- ✈ aerospace
- vehicle manufacture
- chemicals
- fish processing
- food processing
- hi-tech industry
- hydroelectric power
- mining
- timber processing
- ■ capital cities
- major towns
- ✈ international airports
- major roads
- major industrial areas

TRANSPORTATION NETWORK

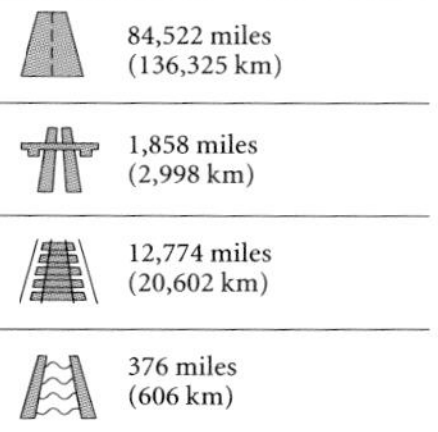

84,522 miles (136,325 km)
1,858 miles (2,998 km)
12,774 miles (20,602 km)
376 miles (606 km)

Fish processing is a major industry in the Atlantic provinces. Fogo Island, off Newfoundland, has barely a thousand inhabitants but it is able to sustain a number of cod canneries.

The majority of Canada's large ports lie in the east. Since the 1960s the region's rail network has been steadily reduced; Newfoundland recently lost its last remaining line, the Long-Cross Island line.

USING THE LAND AND SEA

WITH THIN SOILS restricting farming to the south, the forests that grow in vast unbroken tracts across eastern Canada provide an important source of revenue. Coastal communities rely heavily on the rich fishing grounds of the Atlantic Ocean, although foreign competition and overfishing have resulted in strict policies to conserve stocks.

THE URBAN/RURAL POPULATION DIVIDE

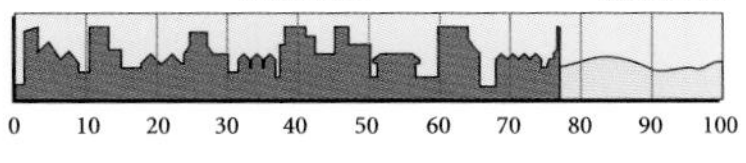

77% urban   23% rural

0 10 20 30 40 50 60 70 80 90 100

POPULATION DENSITY	TOTAL LAND AREA
17 people per sq mile (6 people per sq km)	1,061,600 sq miles (2,750,260 sq km)

Land use and agricultural distribution

- cattle
- cereals
- fishing
- fruit
- timber
- ■ capital cities
- major towns
- pasture
- cropland
- forest
- tundra

Prince Edward Island is the only Atlantic province with notable agricultural land. The island is Canada's leading producer of potatoes.

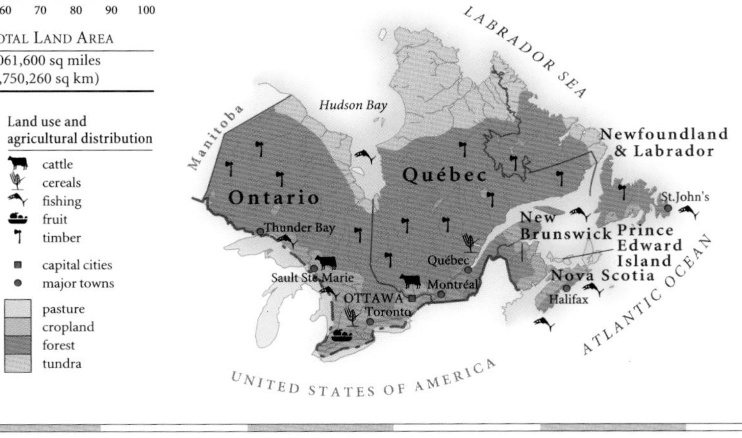

▷ 66

Map labels (main map)

Button Islands
Port Burwell
Kangiqsualujjuaq
Saglek Bay
Hebron
Cod Island
Okak Islands
South Aulatsivik Island
Nain
Tunungayualok Island
Kogaluk
Hopedale
Makkovik
Cape Harrison
Rigolet
Cartwright
Port Hope Simpson
Belle Isle
Red Bay
Cape Bauld
St.Anthony
Roddickton
Grey Islands
Forteau
Port Saunders
White Bay
Baie Verte
Fogo Island
Notre Dame Bay
Gander
Gander Bay
Bonavista Bay
Bonavista
Clarenville
Trinity Bay
Carbonear
St.John's
Placentia
Avalon Peninsula
Cape Race

Forsua Mountains
Torngat Mountains
Kangiqsualujjuaq
George
Rivière à la Baleine
Lac le Moyne
Lac Champdoré
Attikamagen Lake
Schefferville
Petitsikapau Lake
Smallwood Reservoir
Churchill Falls
Churchill
Shabogamo Lake
Lake Joseph
Atikonak Lac
Ashuanipi Lake
Labrador City
Mont Wright 899m
Lake Melville
Hamilton Inlet
North West River
Happy Valley-Goose Bay
Mealy Mountains
Eagle
Little Mecatina

LABRADOR SEA
Labrador Sea

NEWFOUNDLAND & LABRADOR

Appalachian Mountains

Réservoir Manicouagan
Monts Groulx
Petit Lac Manicouagan
Moisie
Lac-Allard
Mingan
Havre-St-Pierre
Natashquan
Romaine
Natashquan
Détroit de Jacques-Cartier
Île d'Anticosti
Honguedo Passage

Riviére-St-Paul
St-Augustin
La Tabatière
Harrington Harbour
Long Range Mountains
Sally's Cove
Gros Morne 808m
Deer Lake
Grand Lake
Buchans
Grand Falls
Red Indian Lake
Corner Brook
Stephenville
Newfoundland
Meelpaeg Lake
Table Mountain 587m
Burgeo
Harbour Breton
Marystown
Grand Bank
Placentia Bay
St-Pierre

Sept-Iles
Port-Cartier
Port-Menier
Baie-Trinité
Godbout
Baie-Comeau
Hauterive
Betsiamites
Forestville
Mont-Joli
Rimouski
Trois-Pistoles
Mont-Louis
Grande-Vallée
Cap-Chat
Ste-Anne-des-Monts
Murdochville
Gaspé
Percé
Rocher Percé
Grande-Rivière
Chandler
Îles de la Madeleine
Cabot Strait
Cape Ray
Channel-Port aux Basques

St.Lawrence
Gulf of St.Lawrence
Péninsule de Gaspé
Mont Jacques-Cartier 1268m
New-Richmond
Amqui
Campbellton
Chaleur Bay
Dalhousie
Caraquet
Shippagan
Tracadie
Neguac
Chatham
Tignish

Edmundston
St-Léonard
Grand Falls
Plaster Rock
Kedgwick
Bathurst
Newcastle
Mount Carleton 820m
Richibucto
Doaktown
Hartland
Woodstock
McAdam
NEW BRUNSWICK
Fredericton
Oromocto
Minto
Chipman
Moncton
Riverview
Northumberland Strait
PRINCE EDWARD ISLAND
Prince Edward Island
Souris
Chéticamp
Ingonish Beach
Cape Breton Island
Sydney Mines
Glace Bay
Sydney
Inverness
Kensington
Charlottetown
Summerside
Shediac
Sackville
Amherst
New Glasgow
Port Hawkesbury
Antigonish
Chedabucto Bay
Canso

St.John
Hampton
Sussex
Springhill
Truro
NOVA SCOTIA
Windsor
Minas Basin
Halifax
Dartmouth
Sheet Harbour
Grand Manan Island
St.Stephen
Saint John
Kentville
Middleton
Digby
Lake Rossignol
Bridgewater
Liverpool
Lunenburg
Sable Island
Yarmouth
Shelburne
Cape Sable
Bay of Fundy

ATLANTIC OCEAN

Cape North
Cape St.George
St.George's Bay
Trinity Bay

ST PIERRE & MIQUELON (to France)

Industry map labels

LABRADOR SEA
Hudson Bay
Manitoba
Ontario
Thunder Bay
Schefferville
Québec
Newfoundland & Labrador
St.John's
New Brunswick
Prince Edward Island
Nova Scotia
Halifax
Sault Ste.Marie
Montreal
OTTAWA
Toronto
UNITED STATES OF AMERICA
ATLANTIC OCEAN

Land use map labels

LABRADOR SEA
Hudson Bay
Manitoba
Ontario
Thunder Bay
Québec
Québec
Montréal
Sault Ste.Marie
OTTAWA
Toronto
New Brunswick
Prince Edward Island
Nova Scotia
Halifax
Newfoundland & Labrador
St.John's
UNITED STATES OF AMERICA
ATLANTIC OCEAN

SOUTHEASTERN CANADA

Southern Ontario, Southern Québec

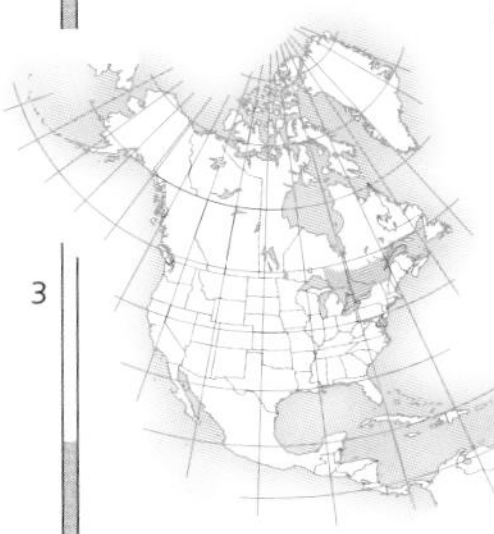

THE SOUTHERN PARTS of Québec and Ontario form the economic heart of Canada. The two provinces are divided by their language and culture; in Québec, French is the main language, whereas English is spoken in Ontario. Separatist sentiment in Québec has led to a provincial referendum on the question of a sovereignty association with Canada. The region contains Canada's capital, Ottawa and its two largest cities: Toronto, the center of commerce and Montréal, the cultural and administrative heart of French Canada.

The port at Montréal is situated on the St. Lawrence Seaway. A network of 16 locks allows sea-going vessels access to routes once plied by fur-trappers and early settlers.

Niagara Falls lies on the border between Canada and the US. It comprises a system of two falls: American Falls, in New York, is separated from Horseshoe Falls, in Ontario, by Goat Island. Horseshoe Falls, seen here, plunges 184 ft (56 m) and is 2,500 ft (762 m) wide.

TRANSPORTATION & INDUSTRY

THE CITIES OF SOUTHERN QUÉBEC AND ONTARIO, and their hinterlands, form the heart of Canadian manufacturing industry. Toronto is Canada's leading financial center, and Ontario's motor and aerospace industries have developed around the city. A major center for nickel mining lies to the north of Toronto. Most of Québec's industry is located in Montréal, the oldest port in North America. Chemicals, paper manufacture, and the construction of transportation equipment are leading industrial activities.

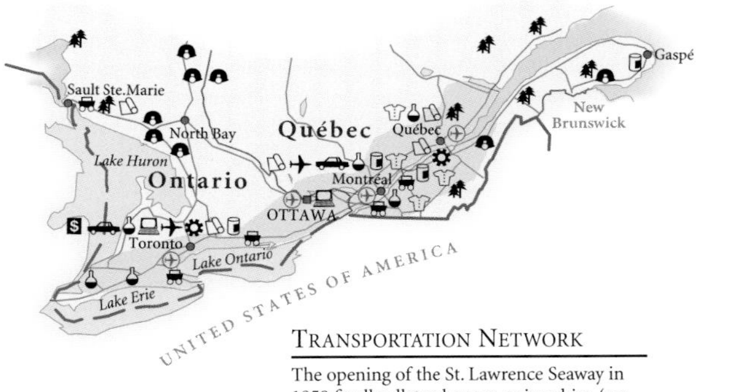

Major industry and infrastructure

- car manufacture
- chemicals
- engineering
- finance
- food processing
- hi-tech industry
- mining
- iron & steel
- textiles
- paper industry
- timber processing
- capital cities
- major towns
- international airports
- major roads
- major industrial areas

TRANSPORTATION NETWORK

The opening of the St. Lawrence Seaway in 1959 finally allowed ocean-going ships (up to 24,000 tons (tonnes)) access to the interior of Canada, creating a vital trading route.

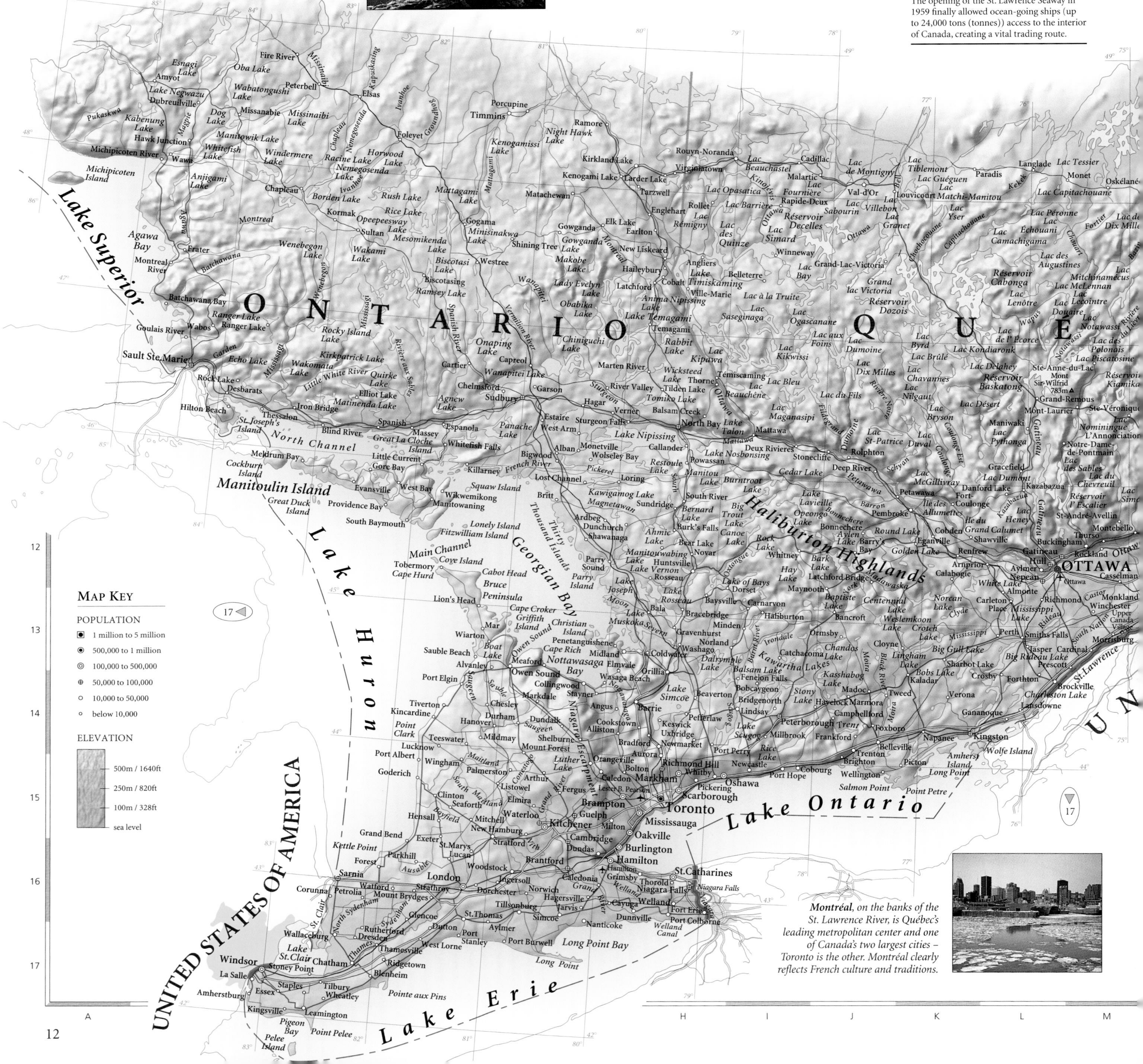

MAP KEY

POPULATION
- 1 million to 5 million
- 500,000 to 1 million
- 100,000 to 500,000
- 50,000 to 100,000
- 10,000 to 50,000
- below 10,000

ELEVATION
- 500m / 1640ft
- 250m / 820ft
- 100m / 328ft
- sea level

Montréal, on the banks of the St. Lawrence River, is Québec's leading metropolitan center and one of Canada's two largest cities – Toronto is the other. Montréal clearly reflects French culture and traditions.

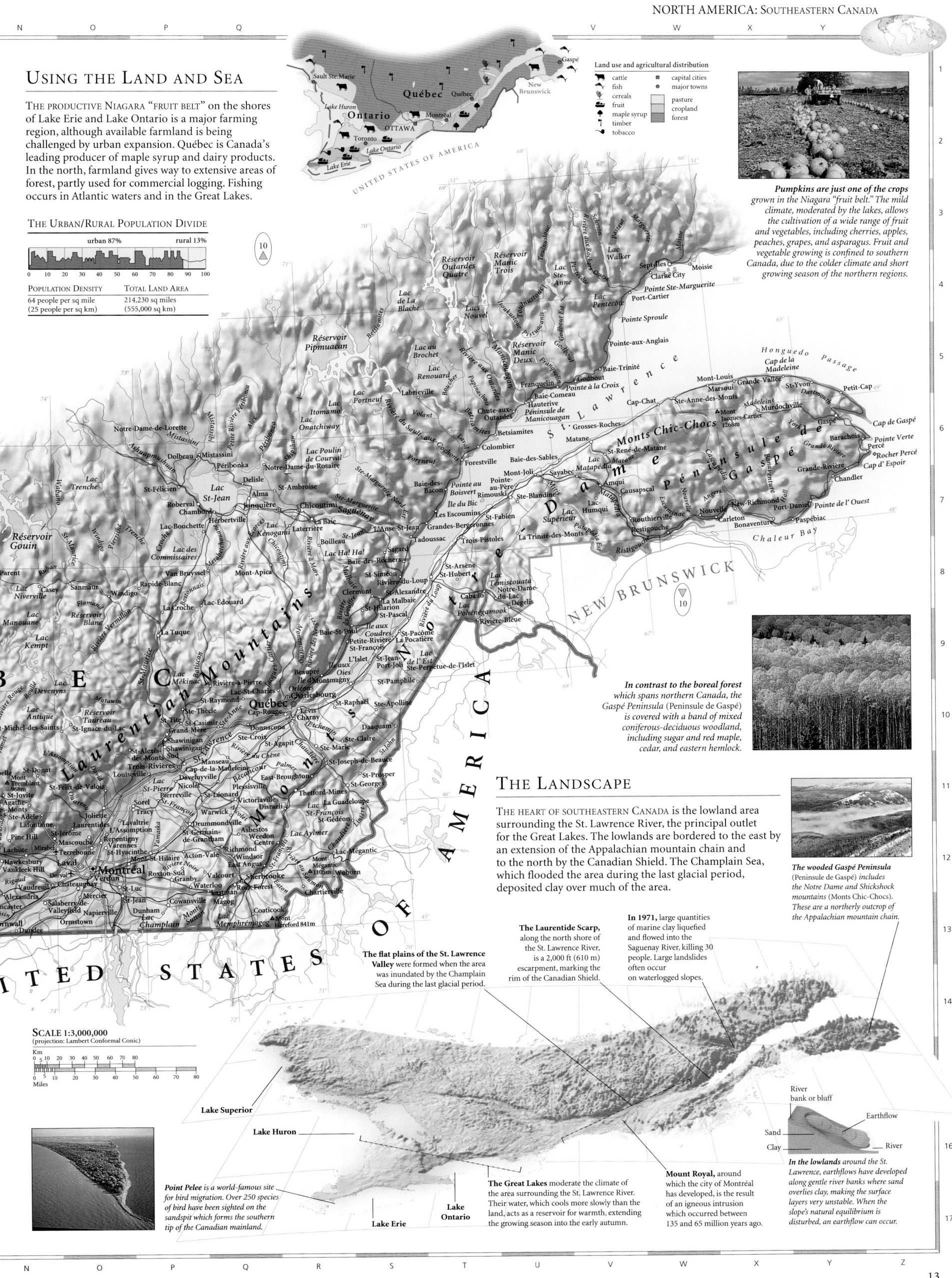

USING THE LAND AND SEA

THE PRODUCTIVE NIAGARA "FRUIT BELT" on the shores of Lake Erie and Lake Ontario is a major farming region, although available farmland is being challenged by urban expansion. Québec is Canada's leading producer of maple syrup and dairy products. In the north, farmland gives way to extensive areas of forest, partly used for commercial logging. Fishing occurs in Atlantic waters and in the Great Lakes.

THE URBAN/RURAL POPULATION DIVIDE

urban 87%   rural 13%

POPULATION DENSITY	TOTAL LAND AREA
64 people per sq mile	214,230 sq miles
(25 people per sq km)	(555,000 sq km)

Land use and agricultural distribution

cattle
fish
cereals
fruit
maple syrup
timber
tobacco

capital cities
major towns

pasture
cropland
forest

Pumpkins are just one of the crops grown in the Niagara "fruit belt." The mild climate, moderated by the lakes, allows the cultivation of a wide range of fruit and vegetables, including cherries, apples, peaches, grapes, and asparagus. Fruit and vegetable growing is confined to southern Canada, due to the colder climate and short growing season of the northern regions.

In contrast to the boreal forest which spans northern Canada, the Gaspé Peninsula (Peninsule de Gaspé) is covered with a band of mixed coniferous-deciduous woodland, including sugar and red maple, cedar, and eastern hemlock.

THE LANDSCAPE

THE HEART OF SOUTHEASTERN CANADA is the lowland area surrounding the St. Lawrence River, the principal outlet for the Great Lakes. The lowlands are bordered to the east by an extension of the Appalachian mountain chain and to the north by the Canadian Shield. The Champlain Sea, which flooded the area during the last glacial period, deposited clay over much of the area.

The wooded Gaspé Peninsula (Peninsule de Gaspé) includes the Notre Dame and Shickshock mountains (Monts Chic-Chocs). These are a northerly outcrop of the Appalachian mountain chain.

The Laurentide Scarp, along the north shore of the St. Lawrence River, is a 2,000 ft (610 m) escarpment, marking the rim of the Canadian Shield.

In 1971, large quantities of marine clay liquefied and flowed into the Saguenay River, killing 30 people. Large landslides often occur on waterlogged slopes.

The flat plains of the St. Lawrence Valley were formed when the area was inundated by the Champlain Sea during the last glacial period.

SCALE 1:3,000,000
(projection: Lambert Conformal Conic)

Km
0 5 10 20 30 40 50 60 70 80

Miles
0 10 20 30 40 50 60 70 80

Lake Superior

Lake Huron

Lake Huron

Lake Erie

Lake Ontario

River bank or bluff

Earthflow

Sand

Clay

River

In the lowlands around the St. Lawrence, earthflows have developed along gentle river banks where sand overlies clay, making the surface layers very unstable. When the slope's natural equilibrium is disturbed, an earthflow can occur.

Point Pelee is a world-famous site for bird migration. Over 250 species of bird have been sighted on the sandspit which forms the southern tip of the Canadian mainland.

The Great Lakes moderate the climate of the area surrounding the St. Lawrence River. Their water, which cools more slowly than the land, acts as a reservoir for warmth, extending the growing season into the early autumn.

Mount Royal, around which the city of Montréal has developed, is the result of an igneous intrusion which occurred between 135 and 65 million years ago.

CANADA

Canada is the second largest country in the world, and with only about one-tenth of its land area inhabited, it is one of the most sparsely populated. Canada became a confederation in 1867, though Newfoundland did not join until 1949. As a founding member of the UN and of the Commonwealth, Canada has played an important role in international affairs. A constitutional crisis, focusing on the French-speaking Québécois, and Inuit, and Native American land rights, dominated politics in the 1990s. In 1999, part of the Northwest Territories, Nunavut, became a self-governing homeland for the Inuit.

The Selwyn Mountains in northwestern Canada form part of the Rocky Mountains. The highest point, Keele Peak, rises to 9,750 ft (2,972 m).

Transportation & Industry

Abundant energy in the form of coal, oil, natural gas, and hydroelectric power underpins Canadian industry. Over 75% of manufacturing is concentrated in the Great Lakes–St. Lawrence region, including prospering aerospace, transportation, and hi-tech industries. Across Canada as a whole, manufacturing has developed around a diversified, high-quality resource base and a wide range of metallic and nonmetallic minerals.

Major industry and infrastructure

✈ aerospace		■ capital cities	
🚗 car manufacture		● major towns	
⚗ chemicals		✈ international airports	
⚙ engineering		major roads	
🍴 food processing		major industrial areas	
💻 hi-tech industry			
⌁ hydroelectric power			
◊ oil & gas			
⚒ mining			
⊤ timber processing			

Canada has one of the world's highest rates of energy consumption per person. It is endowed with vast hydroelectric potential from which more than 60% of its electricity requirements are generated.

Transportation Network

566,352 miles (912,000 km)	15,189 miles (24,459 km)
8,755 miles (14,098 km)	2,341 miles (3,769 km)

In recent years the road network has been expanded, especially links to remote areas. Meanwhile, for long-distance travel, air transportation now supersedes the declining rail network, which focuses mainly on east–west routes.

The Landscape

Glaciers on islands in the Arctic Ocean are the last remnants of the ice sheet that once covered and shaped Canada. Hudson Bay is the center of the Canadian Shield, a huge, eroded plateau marked at its southern extremity by a string of lakes running southeastward from Great Bear Lake to the Great Lakes. In contrast to the rolling relief of the Shield and the central lowland region, the Rocky Mountains rise to peaks of over 13,000 ft (4,000 m), stretching 500 miles (800 km) along the west coast.

Along the northeastern coast of Baffin Island the mountains rise to 8,000 ft (2,440 m). Glaciers move down through the valleys to the sea, eroding wide U-shaped valleys.

Top layer thaws in the summer
Permanently frozen ground

Marginal areas of permafrost thaw in summer
Unfrozen ground where temperature is more moderate

Permanently frozen ground known as permafrost is common in Canada's northern tundra. It thickens farther north, becoming hundreds of yards deep in parts of the Arctic.

The Mackenzie River, flowing north over the permafrost, forms a wide river channel with many tributaries. Together with the Peel River it has created a long, narrow delta at its mouth. The entire river freezes during the winter.

Great Bear Lake

Exposure to three phases of mountain-building and subsequent erosion over millions of years has molded the ancient Canadian Shield into a series of basins and ridges.

The Rocky Mountains were formed some 80 million years ago, when the Pacific Plate was driven southeastward under the North American Plate, forcing up the land.

Isolated pillars, known as hoodoos near Red Deer River in the badlands of Alberta are a product of wind and water erosion, especially flash floods. The badlands lie in the rain shadow of the Rocky Mountains, which creates a semiarid climate.

Fertile prairies stretch from the southern rim of the Canadian Shield, south into the US.

The Great Lakes lie on the Canada–US border. The basins they now occupy were fashioned by repeated ice advance. Once, Lakes Superior, Huron, and Michigan formed one large lake, Lake Nipissing.

The St. Lawrence River is 2,350 miles (3,782 km) long. It flows from the western shore of Lake Superior through the Great Lakes and on to the Atlantic Ocean. From December to April, the St. Lawrence Seaway freezes between Lake Ontario and Montréal.

SCALE 1:9,250,000
(projection: Lambert Azimuthal Equal Area)

Km
0 25 50   100   150   200   250   300   350

Miles
0   25 50   100   150   200   250   300   350

The Sonoran Desert in southwestern Arizona stretches into Mexico and merges to the northwest with California's Mojave Desert. Much of the southwest is very arid, especially the "rain-starved" areas between the Coast Ranges and the Rocky Mountains.

THE UNITED STATES OF AMERICA

COTERMINOUS US (FOR ALASKA AND HAWAII SEE PAGES 40-41)

THE US'S PROGRESSION FROM FRONTIER TERRITORY to economic and political superpower has taken less than 200 years. The 48 coterminous states, along with the outlying states of Alaska and Hawaii, are part of a federal union, held together by the guiding principles of the US Constitution, which embodies the ideals of democracy and liberty for all. Abundant fertile land and a rich resource-base fueled and sustained US economic development. With the spread of agriculture and the growth of trade and industry came the need for a larger workforce, which was supplied by millions of immigrants, many seeking an escape from poverty and political or religious persecution. Immigration continues today, particularly from Central America and Asia.

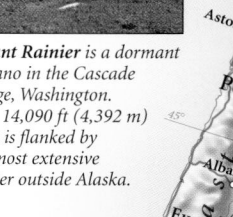

Mount Rainier is a dormant volcano in the Cascade Range, Washington. This 14,090 ft (4,392 m) peak is flanked by the most extensive glacier outside Alaska.

TRANSPORTATION & INDUSTRY

THE US HAS BEEN THE INDUSTRIAL POWERHOUSE of the world since the Second World War, pioneering mass-production and the consumer lifestyle. Initially, heavy engineering and manufacturing in the northeast led the economy. Today, heavy industry has declined and the US economy is driven by service and financial industries, with the most important being defense, hi-tech, and electronics.

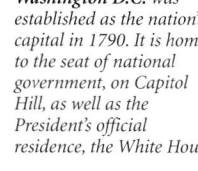

Washington D.C. was established as the nation's capital in 1790. It is home to the seat of national government, on Capitol Hill, as well as the President's official residence, the White House.

198 ◀

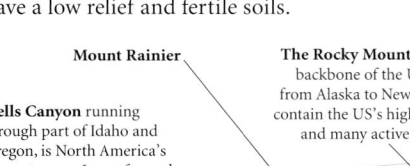

Major industry and infrastructure

- aerospace
- car manufacture
- chemicals
- coal
- electronics
- engineering
- food processing
- hi-tech industry
- oil & gas
- research & development
- textiles
- tourism
- capital cities
- major towns
- international airports
- major roads
- major industrial areas

TRANSPORTATION NETWORK

3,875,040 miles (6,240,000 km)	52,388 miles (84,361 km)
148,308 miles (235,238 km)	25,467 miles (41,009 km)

Transportation in the US is dominated by the car which, with the extensive Interstate Highway system, allows great personal mobility. Today, internal air flights between major cities provide the most rapid cross-country travel.

198 ◀

THE LANDSCAPE

THE HIGH, RUGGED MOUNTAIN RANGES of the west are about 80 million years old, geologically young compared to the old, eroded, Appalachian mountain chain, which dates from when North America and Europe were joined together as part of the supercontinent Pangaea, 400 million years ago. In contrast, the Great Plains and Mississippi Basin have a low relief and fertile soils.

Devils Tower, in Wyoming is a 1,280 ft (390 m) intrusion of basalt rock, which cooled to form octagonal pillars. In 1906 it became the first US National Monument.

Missouri River
Mississippi River
Ohio River
Mississippi Delta

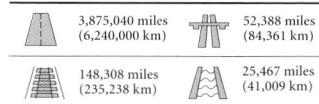

The massive drainage basin of the Mississippi covers 1,250,000 sq miles (3,200,000 sq km). It includes all areas drained by the Mississippi and its chief tributaries, the Missouri and Ohio Rivers, and drains the entire region from the Appalachians to the Rockies.

Mount Rainier

Hells Canyon running through part of Idaho and Oregon, is North America's deepest gorge. It was formed by the down-cutting of the Snake River through the thick basalt rocks of the Columbia–Snake Plateau.

The Rocky Mountains form the backbone of the US, running from Alaska to New Mexico. They contain the US's highest mountains and many active volcanoes.

The Hudson-Mohawk Gap, lying at the point where the two rivers join, allows passage from the Atlantic Ocean to the continental interior.

The Great Lakes

Death Valley, California, 282 ft (86 m) below sea level, is the lowest point in the western hemisphere, and one of the hottest places on Earth. Temperatures of 190° F (88° C) have been recorded here.

Niagara Falls

Barrier beaches, bar and spits are typica of the Atlantic coast These sand formation around Cape Hattera stretch along the coas for 200 miles (320 km)

The Great Smoky Mountains, part of the ancient Appalachian mountain chain formed a natura barrier to early settler attempting to penetrat the country's interior

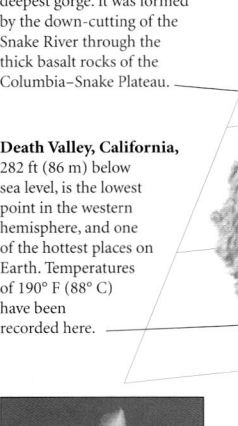

Volcanically heated water erupts every 40-80 minutes from Old Faithful geyser in Yellowstone National Park, Wyoming. The 170 ft (50 m) column of water and steam persists for 4 minutes.

Monument Valley's striking sandstone spires and pillars *(buttes)* have been formed by the action of wind, water, heat, and cold.

The deep gullies of South Dakota's badlands are created by periodic, torrential rainfall, which erodes the soft soils and rocks. Their form has been greatly affected by changes in land use.

Great Plains

Most of the US is drained by the great Mississippi River system. At its mouth, where levées are breached, floodwaters are carried to the swamps through a series of channels. This region is known as the bayou.

The US Gulf Coast is seriously affected by hurricane erosion which reshapes its beaches and sandbanks.

The Everglades are a vas area of sawgrass swamp covering 4,000 sq miles (10,300 sq km of southern Florida

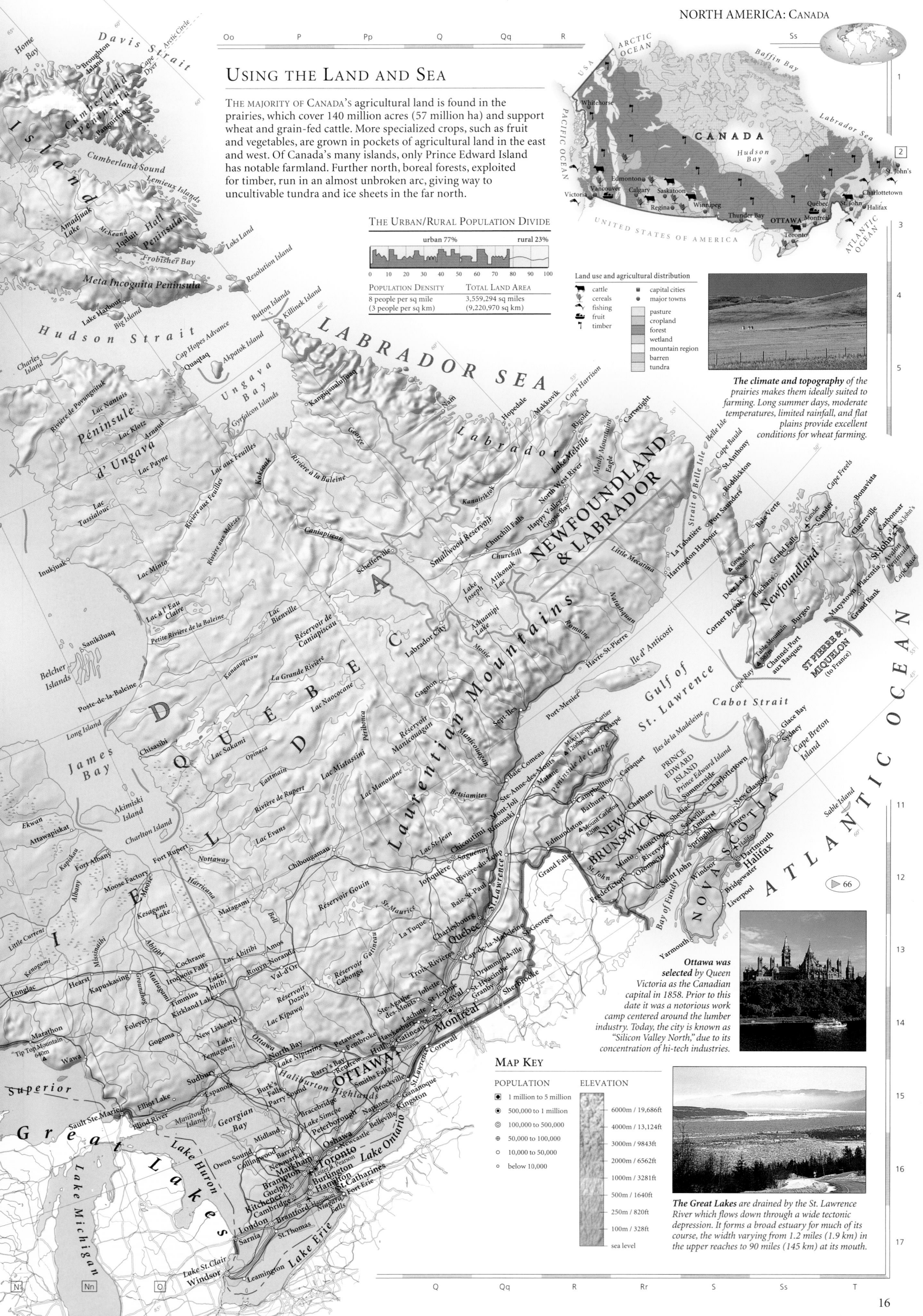

USING THE LAND AND SEA

THE MAJORITY OF CANADA's agricultural land is found in the prairies, which cover 140 million acres (57 million ha) and support wheat and grain-fed cattle. More specialized crops, such as fruit and vegetables, are grown in pockets of agricultural land in the east and west. Of Canada's many islands, only Prince Edward Island has notable farmland. Further north, boreal forests, exploited for timber, run in an almost unbroken arc, giving way to uncultivable tundra and ice sheets in the far north.

THE URBAN/RURAL POPULATION DIVIDE

urban 77%   rural 23%

0 10 20 30 40 50 60 70 80 90 100

POPULATION DENSITY	TOTAL LAND AREA
8 people per sq mile (3 people per sq km)	3,559,294 sq miles (9,220,970 sq km)

Land use and agricultural distribution

- cattle
- cereals
- fishing
- fruit
- timber
- capital cities
- major towns
- pasture
- cropland
- forest
- wetland
- mountain region
- barren
- tundra

The climate and topography of the prairies makes them ideally suited to farming. Long summer days, moderate temperatures, limited rainfall, and flat plains provide excellent conditions for wheat farming.

Ottawa was selected by Queen Victoria as the Canadian capital in 1858. Prior to this date it was a notorious work camp centered around the lumber industry. Today, the city is known as "Silicon Valley North," due to its concentration of hi-tech industries.

MAP KEY

POPULATION

- ◉ 1 million to 5 million
- ◉ 500,000 to 1 million
- ◉ 100,000 to 500,000
- ⊕ 50,000 to 100,000
- ○ 10,000 to 50,000
- ∘ below 10,000

ELEVATION

- 6000m / 19,686ft
- 4000m / 13,124ft
- 3000m / 9843ft
- 2000m / 6562ft
- 1000m / 3281ft
- 500m / 1640ft
- 250m / 820ft
- 100m / 328ft
- sea level

The Great Lakes are drained by the St. Lawrence River which flows down through a wide tectonic depression. It forms a broad estuary for much of its course, the width varying from 1.2 miles (1.9 km) in the upper reaches to 90 miles (145 km) at its mouth.

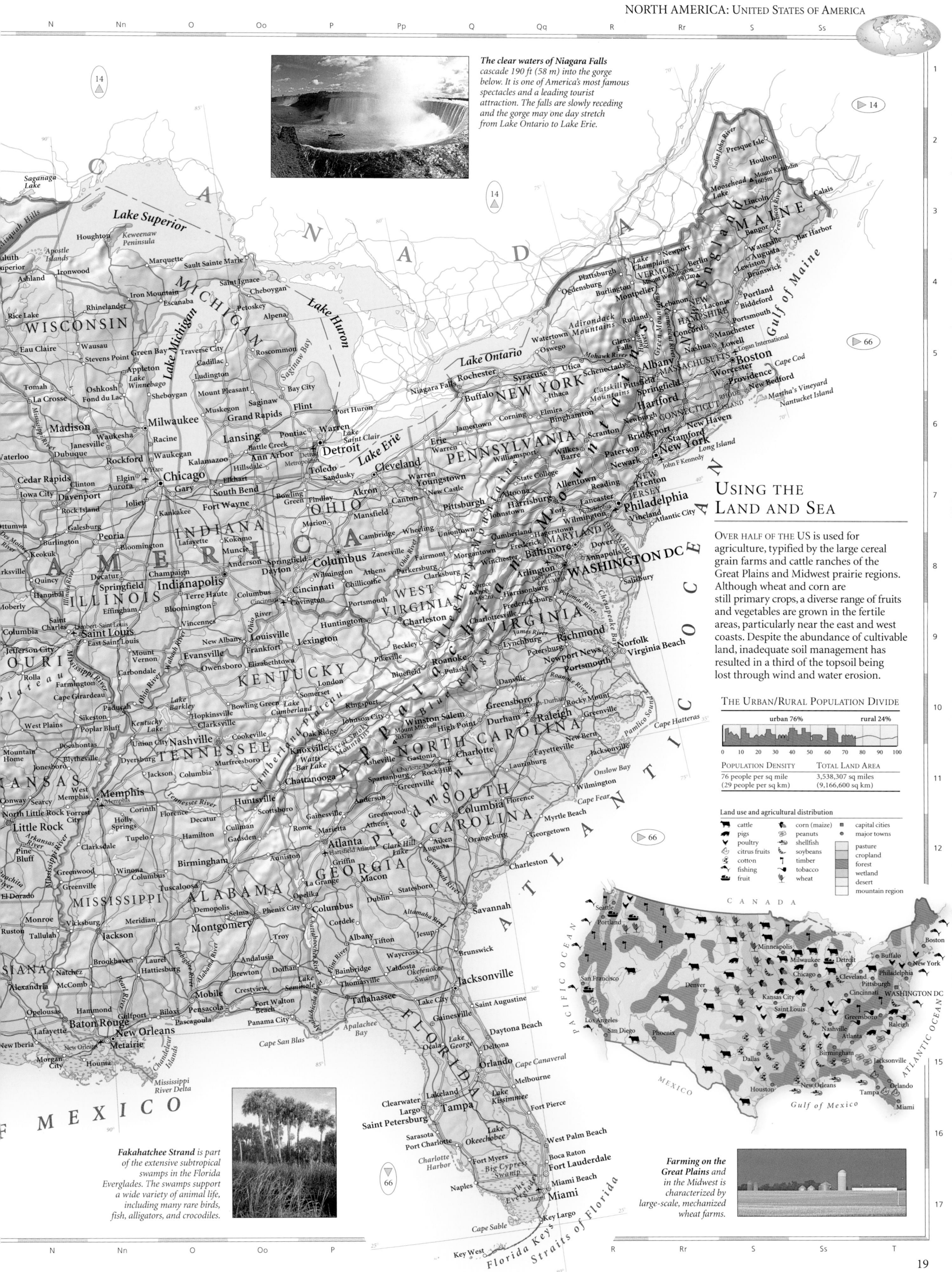

The clear waters of Niagara Falls cascade 190 ft (58 m) into the gorge below. It is one of America's most famous spectacles and a leading tourist attraction. The falls are slowly receding and the gorge may one day stretch from Lake Ontario to Lake Erie.

USING THE LAND AND SEA

OVER HALF OF THE US is used for agriculture, typified by the large cereal grain farms and cattle ranches of the Great Plains and Midwest prairie regions. Although wheat and corn are still primary crops, a diverse range of fruits and vegetables are grown in the fertile areas, particularly near the east and west coasts. Despite the abundance of cultivable land, inadequate soil management has resulted in a third of the topsoil being lost through wind and water erosion.

THE URBAN/RURAL POPULATION DIVIDE

urban 76%   rural 24%

POPULATION DENSITY
76 people per sq mile
(29 people per sq km)

TOTAL LAND AREA
3,538,307 sq miles
(9,166,600 sq km)

Land use and agricultural distribution

- cattle
- pigs
- poultry
- citrus fruits
- cotton
- fishing
- fruit
- corn (maize)
- peanuts
- shellfish
- soybeans
- timber
- tobacco
- wheat
- capital cities
- major towns
- pasture
- cropland
- forest
- wetland
- desert
- mountain region

Fakahatchee Strand is part of the extensive subtropical swamps in the Florida Everglades. The swamps support a wide variety of animal life, including many rare birds, fish, alligators, and crocodiles.

Farming on the Great Plains and in the Midwest is characterized by large-scale, mechanized wheat farms.

USA: NORTHEASTERN STATES

Connecticut, Maine, Massachusetts, New Hampshire, New Jersey, New York, Pennsylvania, Rhode Island, Vermont

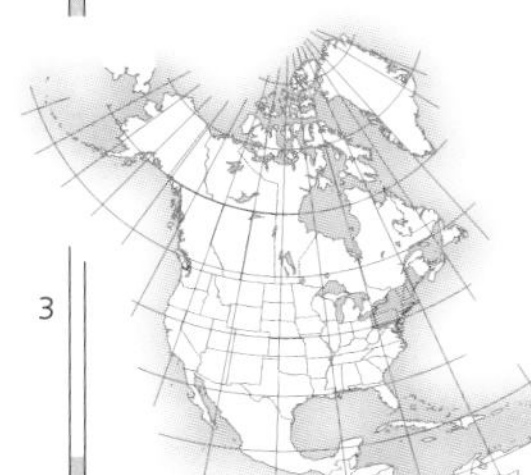

THE INDENTED COAST AND VAST WOODLANDS of the northeastern states were the original core area for European expansion. The rustic character of New England prevails after nearly four centuries, while the great cities of the Atlantic seaboard have formed an almost continuous urban region. Over 20 million immigrants entered New York from 1855 to 1924 and the northeast became the industrial center of the US. After the decline of mining and heavy manufacturing, economic dynamism has been restored with the growth of hi-tech and service industries.

Chelsea in Vermont, surrounded by trees in their fall foliage. Tourism and agriculture dominate the economy of this self-consciously rural state, where no town exceeds 30,000 people.

MAP KEY

POPULATION
- above 5 million
- 1 million to 5 million
- 500,000 to 1 million
- 100,000 to 500,000
- 50,000 to 100,000
- 10,000 to 50,000
- below 10,000

ELEVATION 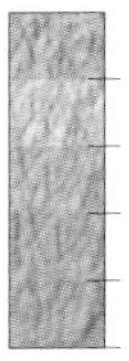
- 1000m / 3281ft
- 500m / 1640ft
- 250m / 820ft
- 100m / 328ft
- sea level

TRANSPORTATION & INDUSTRY

THE PRINCIPAL SEABOARD CITIES grew up on trade and manufacturing. They are now global centers of commerce and corporate administration, dominating the regional economy. Research and development facilities support an expanding electronics and communications sector throughout the region. Pharmaceutical and chemical industries are important in New Jersey and Pennsylvania.

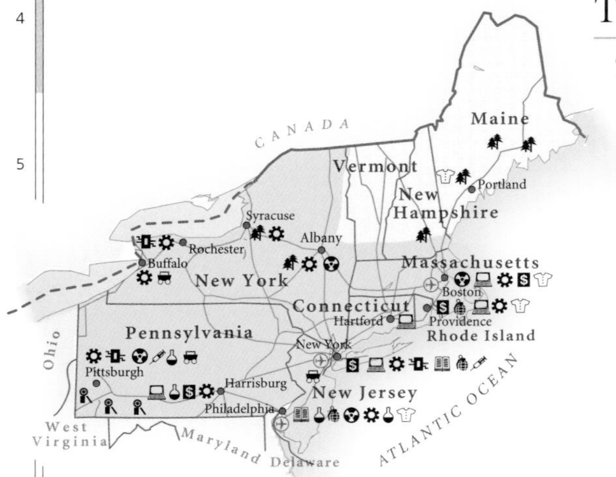

TRANSPORTATION NETWORK

340,090 miles (544,144 km)	4813 miles 7700 km
12,872 miles (20,592 km)	2108 miles (3389 km)

New York's commercial success is tied historically to its transportation connections. The Erie Canal, completed in 1825, opened up the Great Lakes and the interior to New York's markets and carried a stream of immigrants into the Midwest.

Major industry and infrastructure

- chemicals
- coal
- defense
- electronics
- engineering
- finance
- hi-tech industry
- iron & steel
- pharmaceuticals
- printing & publishing
- research & development
- textiles
- timber processing
- major towns
- international airports
- major roads
- major industrial area

(Map area with numerous place names including: Lake Ontario, Lake Erie, CANADA, NEW YORK, PENNSYLVANIA, NEW JERSEY, VERMONT, MASSACHUSETTS, CONNECTICUT, WEST VIRGINIA, MARYLAND, OHIO, Buffalo, Rochester, Syracuse, Albany, Pittsburgh, Philadelphia, Harrisburg, Scranton, New York, Newark, Trenton, Atlantic City, Cape May, and many others.)

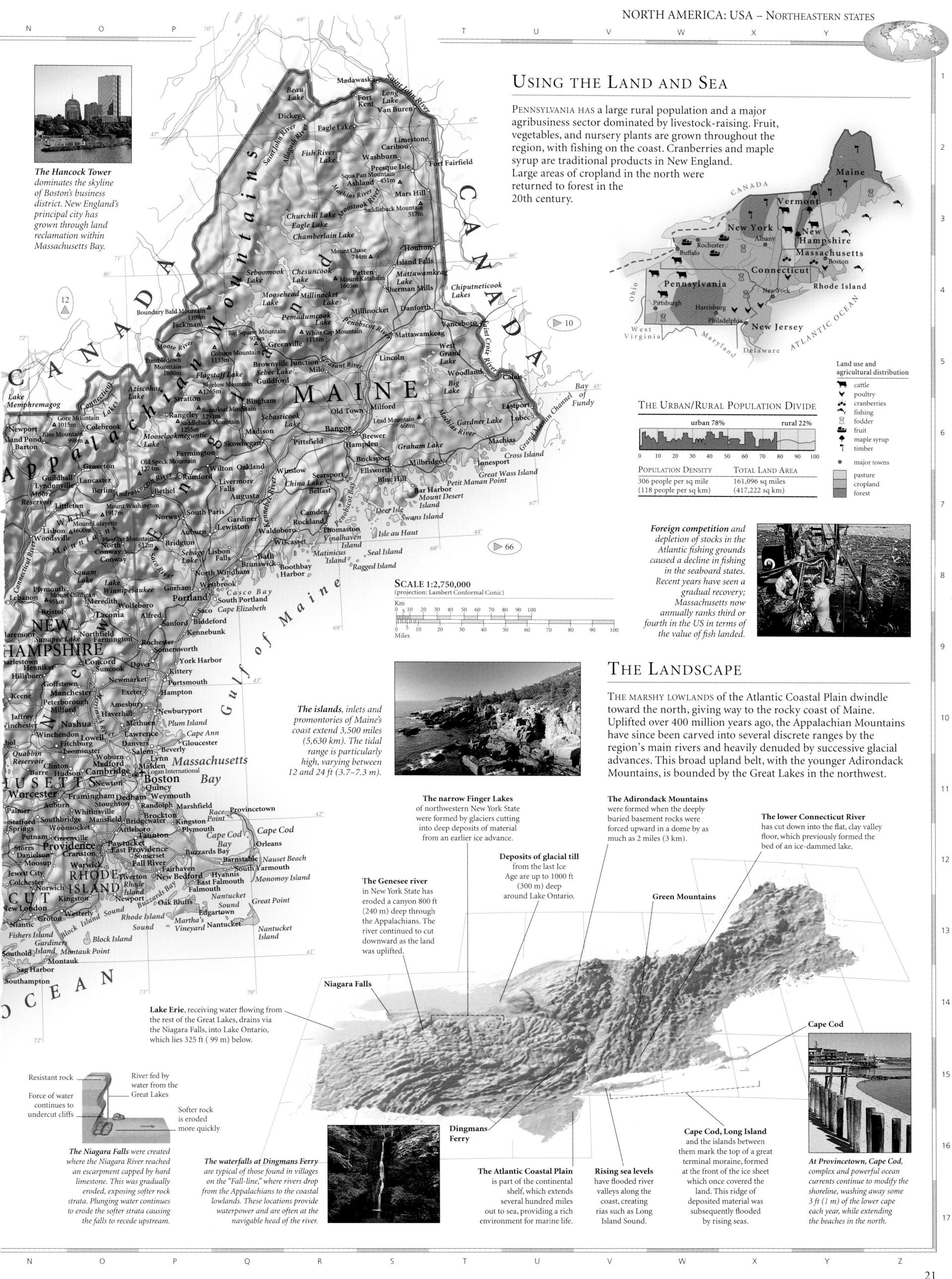

The Hancock Tower dominates the skyline of Boston's business district. New England's principal city has grown through land reclamation within Massachusetts Bay.

USING THE LAND AND SEA

PENNSYLVANIA HAS a large rural population and a major agribusiness sector dominated by livestock-raising. Fruit, vegetables, and nursery plants are grown throughout the region, with fishing on the coast. Cranberries and maple syrup are traditional products in New England. Large areas of cropland in the north were returned to forest in the 20th century.

Land use and agricultural distribution

- cattle
- poultry
- cranberries
- fishing
- fodder
- fruit
- maple syrup
- timber
- major towns

pasture
cropland
forest

THE URBAN/RURAL POPULATION DIVIDE

urban 78%   rural 22%

0 10 20 30 40 50 60 70 80 90 100

POPULATION DENSITY   TOTAL LAND AREA
306 people per sq mile   161,096 sq miles
(118 people per sq km)   (417,222 sq km)

Foreign competition and depletion of stocks in the Atlantic fishing grounds caused a decline in fishing in the seaboard states. Recent years have seen a gradual recovery; Massachusetts now annually ranks third or fourth in the US in terms of the value of fish landed.

The islands, inlets and promontories of Maine's coast extend 3,500 miles (5,630 km). The tidal range is particularly high, varying between 12 and 24 ft (3.7–7.3 m).

THE LANDSCAPE

THE MARSHY LOWLANDS of the Atlantic Coastal Plain dwindle toward the north, giving way to the rocky coast of Maine. Uplifted over 400 million years ago, the Appalachian Mountains have since been carved into several discrete ranges by the region's main rivers and heavily denuded by successive glacial advances. This broad upland belt, with the younger Adirondack Mountains, is bounded by the Great Lakes in the northwest.

The narrow Finger Lakes of northwestern New York State were formed by glaciers cutting into deep deposits of material from an earlier ice advance.

The Adirondack Mountains were formed when the deeply buried basement rocks were forced upward in a dome by as much as 2 miles (3 km).

The lower Connecticut River has cut down into the flat, clay valley floor, which previously formed the bed of an ice-dammed lake.

The Genesee river in New York State has eroded a canyon 800 ft (240 m) deep through the Appalachians. The river continued to cut downward as the land was uplifted.

Deposits of glacial till from the last Ice Age are up to 1000 ft (300 m) deep around Lake Ontario.

Green Mountains

Niagara Falls

Lake Erie, receiving water flowing from the rest of the Great Lakes, drains via the Niagara Falls, into Lake Ontario, which lies 325 ft (99 m) below.

Cape Cod

Resistant rock
River fed by water from the Great Lakes
Force of water continues to undercut cliffs
Softer rock is eroded more quickly

The Niagara Falls were created where the Niagara River reached an escarpment capped by hard limestone. This was gradually eroded, exposing softer rock strata. Plunging water continues to erode the softer strata causing the falls to recede upstream.

The waterfalls at Dingmans Ferry are typical of those found in villages on the "Fall-line," where rivers drop from the Appalachians to the coastal lowlands. These locations provide waterpower and are often at the navigable head of the river.

Dingmans Ferry

The Atlantic Coastal Plain is part of the continental shelf, which extends several hundred miles out to sea, providing a rich environment for marine life.

Rising sea levels have flooded river valleys along the coast, creating rias such as Long Island Sound.

Cape Cod, Long Island and the islands between them mark the top of a great terminal moraine, formed at the front of the ice sheet which once covered the land. This ridge of deposited material was subsequently flooded by rising seas.

At Provincetown, Cape Cod, complex and powerful ocean currents continue to modify the shoreline, washing away some 3 ft (1 m) of the lower cape each year, while extending the beaches in the north.

SCALE 1:2,750,000
(projection: Lambert Conformal Conic)

Km
0 5 10 20 30 40 50 60 70 80 90 100

Miles
0 5 10 20 30 40 50 60 70 80 90 100

USA: MID-EASTERN STATES

Delaware, District of Columbia, Kentucky, Maryland, North Carolina, South Carolina, Tennessee, Virginia, West Virginia

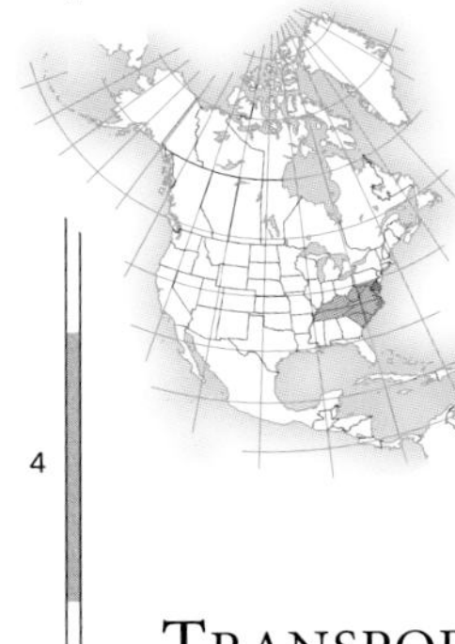

KEY EVENTS IN AMERICAN HISTORY took place in this diverse region, which became the front line between the North and the South during the Civil War of the 1860s. Strong regional contrasts exist between the fertile coastal plains, the isolated upcountry of the Appalachian Mountains, and the cotton-growing areas of the Mississippi lowlands to the west. While coal mining, a traditional industry in the Appalachians, has declined in recent years leaving much rural poverty, service industries elsewhere have increased, especially in Washington DC, the nation's capital.

MAP KEY

POPULATION
- ⊙ 500,000 to 1 million
- ◎ 100,000 to 500,000
- ⊕ 50,000 to 100,000
- ○ 10,000 to 50,000
- ○ below 10,000

ELEVATION
- 6000m / 19,686ft
- 4000m / 13,124ft
- 3000m / 9843ft
- 2000m / 6562ft
- 1000m / 3281ft
- 500m / 1640ft
- 250m / 820ft
- 100m / 328ft
- sea level

SCALE 1:3,000,000
(projection: Lambert Conformal Conic)

Km 0 5 10 20 30 40 50 60 70 80
Miles 0 5 10 20 30 40 50 60 70 80

The Bluegrass region of Kentucky centers on the town of Lexington. This exceptionally fertile rolling plain is well known for its thoroughbred horse-breeding ranches.

TRANSPORTATION & INDUSTRY

IN THE URBANIZED NORTHEAST, manufacturing remains important, alongside a burgeoning service sector. North Carolina is a major center for industrial research and development. Traditional industries include Tennessee whiskey and textiles in South Carolina. The decline of open-cast coal mining in the Appalachians has been hastened by environmental controls, although adventure-tourism is a flourishing new industry.

Major industry and infrastructure
- ⛰ adventure-tourism
- 🚗 car manufacture
- coal
- electronics
- $ finance
- food processing
- hi-tech industry
- mining
- research & development
- textiles
- ■ capital cities
- ■ major towns
- ⊕ international airports
- — major roads
- major industrial areas

TRANSPORTATION NETWORK
- 452,218 miles (723,548 km)
- 5,737 miles (8,267 km)
- 18,336 miles (29,503 km)
- 4,404 miles (7,081 km)

Tennessee's rivers are part of an important inland bulk-transportation network. Memphis connects with New Orleans in the south, and with cities as distant as Minneapolis, Sioux City, Chicago, and Pittsburgh, via the Mississippi and its tributaries.

THE LANDSCAPE

THE EASTERN TRIBUTARIES OF THE MISSISSIPPI drain the interior lowlands. The Cumberland Plateau and the parallel ranges of the Appalachians have been successively uplifted and eroded over time, with the eastern side reduced to a series of foothills known as the Piedmont. The broad coastal plain gradually falls away into salt marshes, lagoons, and offshore bars, broken by flooded estuaries along the shores of the Atlantic.

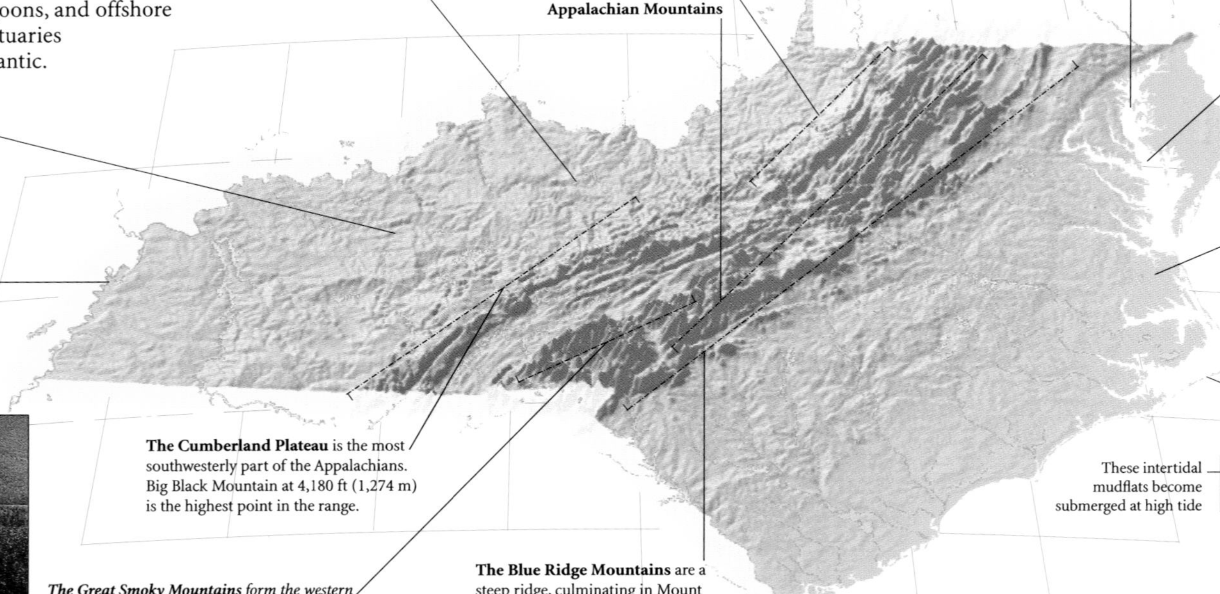

The Mammoth Cave is part of an extensive cave system in the limestone region of southwestern Kentucky. It stretches for over 300 miles (485 km) on five different levels and contains three rivers and three lakes.

The Mississippi River and its tributary the Ohio River form the western border of the region.

Natural Bridge in eastern Kentucky is an arch 78 ft (26 m) long and 65 ft (20 m) high. It has been shaped from resistant sandstone by gradual weathering processes, which removed the softer rock lying underneath.

The Allegheny Mountains form the northwestern edge of the Appalachian mountain chain. Continuous folding has formed rich seams of bituminous coal.

Appalachian Mountains

The Cumberland Plateau is the most southwesterly part of the Appalachians. Big Black Mountain at 4,180 ft (1,274 m) is the highest point in the range.

The Great Smoky Mountains form the western escarpment of the Appalachians. The region is heavily forested, with over 130 species of tree.

The Blue Ridge Mountains are a steep ridge, culminating in Mount Mitchell, the highest point in the Appalachians, at 6,684 ft (2,037 m).

Farmland on the eastern shores of Chesapeake Bay is sustained by artificial drainage. The area also provides refuge for a variety of waterfowl.

The many inlets of Chesapeake Bay are the flooded tributaries of the main river valley, which have been inundated by rising sea levels.

Salt marshes such as Great Dismal Swamp, develop where the coast is sheltered. Vast areas of such marshland have been reclaimed for farmland and settlement.

Cape Hatteras is the easternmost point of an offshore barrier island; a wave-deposited sand-bar which has become permanent, establishing its own vegetation.

Barrier islands

These intertidal mudflats become submerged at high tide
- Tidal inlet
- Barrier island

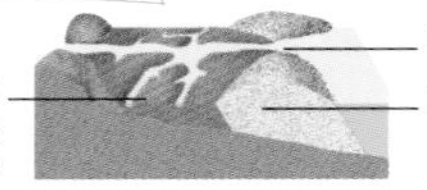

Barrier islands are common along the coasts of North and South Carolina. As sea levels rise, wave action builds up ridges of sand and pebbles parallel to the coast, separated by lagoons or intertidal mudflats, which are flooded at high tide.

Map labels (states and surrounding regions)
INDIANA, ILLINOIS, MISSOURI, ARKANSAS, MISSISSIPPI, ALABAMA, KENTUCKY, TENNESSEE

Inset regional map
Pennsylvania, Ohio, Maryland, Baltimore, WASHINGTON DC, Delaware, W. Virginia, Charleston, Virginia, Richmond, Indiana, Louisville, Illinois, Kentucky, Missouri, Nashville, Memphis, Tennessee, North Carolina, Raleigh, Arkansas, Mississippi, Alabama, Georgia, South Carolina, Columbia, ATLANTIC OCEAN

Selected place names on main map
Covington, Newport, Cincinnati, Florence, Independence, Walton, Warsaw, Carrollton, Williamstown, Owenton, Bedford, New Castle, Cynthiana, Louisville, La Grange, Eminence, Frankfort, Georgetown, Paris, Shelbyville, Valley Station, Jeffersontown, Versailles, Lexington, Brandenburg, Mount Washington, Taylorsville, Nicholasville, Irvington, Cloverport, Radcliff, Lebanon Junction, Bardstown, Harrodsburg, Richmond, Henderson, Hawesville, Whitesville, Hardinsburg, Fordsville, Elizabethtown, Springfield, Danville, Herrington Lake, Lancaster, Owensboro, Morganfield, Uniontown, Sebree, Livermore, Central City, Greenville, Morgantown, Brownsville, Munfordville, Greensburg, Horse Cave, Columbia, Russell Springs, Liberty, Mount Vernon, Sturgis, Dixon, Providence, Hartford, Smiths Grove, Cave City, Edmonton, Burkesville, Somerset, Burnside, Marion, Madisonville, Dawson Springs, Leitchfield, Rough River, Glasgow, Barren River Lake, Scottsville, Tompkinsville, Albany, Whitley City, Stearns, Paducah, Wickliffe, Crofton, Hopkinsville, Auburn, Bowling Green, Jamestown Lake, Monticello, Calvert City, Eddyville, Princeton, Cadiz, Russellville, Elkton, Franklin, Portland, Lafayette, Celina, Dale Hollow Lake, Oneida, Huntsville, Jamestown, Hickman, Fulton, South Fulton, Murray, Clarksville, Springfield, Gallatin, Hartsville, Carthage, Gainesboro, Cookeville, Algood, Sunbright, Wartburg, Oak Ridge, Union City, Martin, Dresden, Paris, Dover, Erin, Goodlettsville, Ashland, Hendersonville, Lebanon, Livingston, Monterey, Jacksboro, Tiptonville, Ridgely, Obion, Greenfield, McKenzie, Huntingdon, Camden, Waverly, Dickson, Nashville, Smyrna, Franklin, Smithville, Sparta, Crossville, Harriman, Kingston, Rockwood, Reelfoot Lake, Newbern, Dyer, Milan, Brownsville, McEwen, White Bluff, Murfreesboro, Woodbury, Spencer, McMinnville, Pikeville, Loudon, Watts Bar Lake, Lenoir City, Dyersburg, Trenton, Humboldt, Bruceton, Charlotte, Columbia, Spring Hill, Chapel Hill, Shelbyville, Manchester, Altamont, Dayton, Sweetwater, Madisonville, Halls, Alamo, Bells, Lexington, Parsons, Linden, Centerville, Decaturville, Hohenwald, Mount Pleasant, Lewisburg, Tims Ford Lake, Tullahoma, Tracy City, Soddy Daisy, Whitwell, Chickamauga Lake, Ripley, Brownsville, Jackson, Henderson, Buffalo River, Lawrenceburg, Monteagle, Winchester, Dunlap, Athens, Tellico Plains, Munford, Covington, Whiteville, Adamsville, Waynesboro, Collinwood, Lynchburg, Fayetteville, South Pittsburg, Jasper, Cleveland, Hiwassee, Millington, Bartlett, Arlington, Somerville, Bolivar, Selmer, Savannah, Pulaski, Elkton, Ardmore, Chattanooga, Ducktown, Memphis, Germantown, Moscow, Middleton, Iron City, Saint Joseph, East Ridge, Collierville, Grand Junction

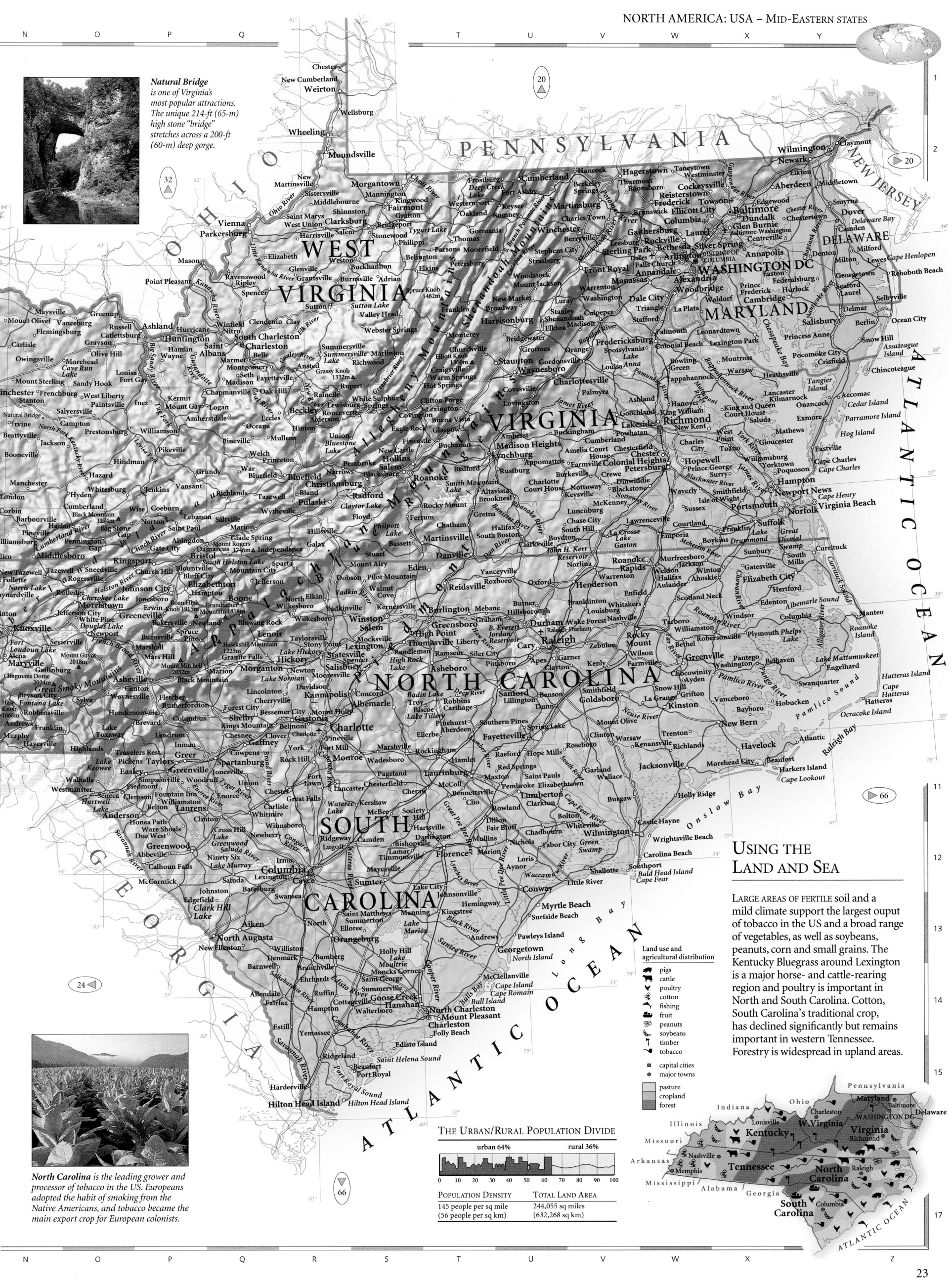

Natural Bridge
*is one of Virginia's
most popular attractions.
The unique 214-ft (65-m)
high stone "bridge"
stretches across a 200-ft
(60-m) deep gorge.*

North Carolina *is the leading grower and
processor of tobacco in the US. Europeans
adopted the habit of smoking from the
Native Americans, and tobacco became the
main export crop for European colonists.*

USING THE LAND AND SEA

LARGE AREAS OF FERTILE SOIL and a
mild climate support the largest ouput
of tobacco in the US and a broad range
of vegetables, as well as soybeans,
peanuts, corn and small grains. The
Kentucky Bluegrass around Lexington
is a major horse- and cattle-rearing
region and poultry is important in
North and South Carolina. Cotton,
South Carolina's traditional crop,
has declined significantly but remains
important in western Tennessee.
Forestry is widespread in upland areas.

**Land use and
agricultural distribution**

- pigs
- cattle
- poultry
- cotton
- fishing
- fruit
- peanuts
- soybeans
- timber
- tobacco

- ■ capital cities
- • major towns

- pasture
- cropland
- forest

THE URBAN/RURAL POPULATION DIVIDE

urban 64%	rural 36%

0 10 20 30 40 50 60 70 80 90 100

POPULATION DENSITY	TOTAL LAND AREA
145 people per sq mile (56 people per sq km)	244,055 sq miles (632,268 sq km)

23

USA: SOUTHERN STATES

Alabama, Florida, Georgia, Louisiana, Mississippi

THE SOUTH HAS MAINTAINED a separate identity and outlook throughout the history of the US. Defeat in the Civil War (1861–65) brought chronic poverty to the former confederate states, while the subsequent liberation of four million slaves began a struggle not resolved until the 1960s, when the Civil Rights movement achieved an end to legal racial segregation. Many parts of the South have experienced rapid change. Tourism and retirement communities, together with agriculture, have fueled growth in Florida, while defense-related industries have boosted the growth of cities such as Miami and Atlanta.

Many people retain a strong attachment to their history and culture, evidenced by Creole-speaking Cajuns in Louisiania and Hispanic communities in South Florida.

TRANSPORTATION & INDUSTRY

FLORIDA'S TOURIST TRADE is only part of a flourishing service sector, which has swelled the principal cities of he south. Petroleum and mineral extraction has made the Gulf Coast a major industrial region. Traditional textile production remains important in Georgia, while advanced new industries have grown from the NASA Space Program.

TRANSPORTATION NETWORK

441,625 miles (706,600 km)	
5,116 miles (8,186 km)	
16,597 miles (26,555 km)	
6,179 miles (9,942 km)	

Atlanta's Hartsfield International airport is one of the busiest in the world. A dramatic rise in the use of regional air transportation has helped to integrate the major cities of the southern states.

The French Quarter is the traditional cultural center of New Orleans, one of the historic Southern cities. The city once thrived on the cotton trade but now relies mainly on tourism and on oil from the Gulf of Mexico.

Major industry and infrastructure

- ✈ aerospace
- car manufacture
- chemicals
- coal
- defense
- electronics
- engineering
- food processing
- oil
- textiles
- tourism
- major towns
- international airports
- major roads
- major industrial areas

The cypress swamps of the Mississippi Delta form in the backswamps behind the levees of the river and in the multitude of subsiding delta basins.

THE LANDSCAPE

THE BLUE RIDGE MOUNTAINS in the north are skirted by the gentle hills of the Piedmont, whose rivers drain south on to the great flat expanse of the coastal plain. Sandy barrier beaches and islands dominate the sea shore, tracing round the swampy limestone arm of Florida. In the west, the Mississippi meanders toward its delta, crossing the thickly mantled alluvial plain of the interior lowlands.

The Yazoo River flows parallel to the Mississippi through a common floodplain. The confluence of the rivers is deferred downstream because flood deposition has built the Mississippi channel up above the level of the Yazoo.

Cathedral Caverns near Huntsville in Alabama is a system of vast limestone caves, with a main opening 1000 ft (300 m) high and 150 ft (50 m) wide.

At De Soto Falls, Alabama, the Little River descends into the deepest canyon east of the Mississippi, with sheer cliff walls up to 700 ft (230 m) high.

Brasstown Bald in the Blue Ridge mountains of Georgia is the region's highest point, at 4,784 ft (1,458 m).

The Mississippi is the world's third longest river and moves over a billion tons (tonnes) of sediment a year, creating deep alluvial plains. Flooding is a constant threat in lowland areas.

Piedmont

In Providence Canyon, Georgia, the Chattahoochee River has cut straight down through the sandy bedrock, to leave sheer rock faces and pinnacles, which have been smoothed by subsequent weathering.

Sandbars, deposited by waves breaking offshore, form barrier beaches along much of the coastline, creating sheltered lagoons and salt marshes behind them.

Mississippi Delta

Atchafalaya Bay

The delta of the Mississippi over 5,000 years ago

Present-day delta

Delta lobe

Lake Okeechobee is actually a shallow, slow-moving river, 150 miles (240 km) long and 50 miles (80 km) wide.

The Everglades lie in a limestone hollow formed over two million years ago, which has gradually become in-filled with swamp deposits.

Across Florida the coastal plain is mostly less than 75 ft (25 m) above sea level. The land is underlain by limestone, pitted with hollows which have been filled by over 10,000 lakes.

Over the last 5,000 years the lower course of the Mississippi has moved back and forth over great distances. These changes, caused by varying sediment loads and human modification, have resulted in a "bird's foot" delta with several lobes, each reflecting the river's different historic position.

Florida Keys

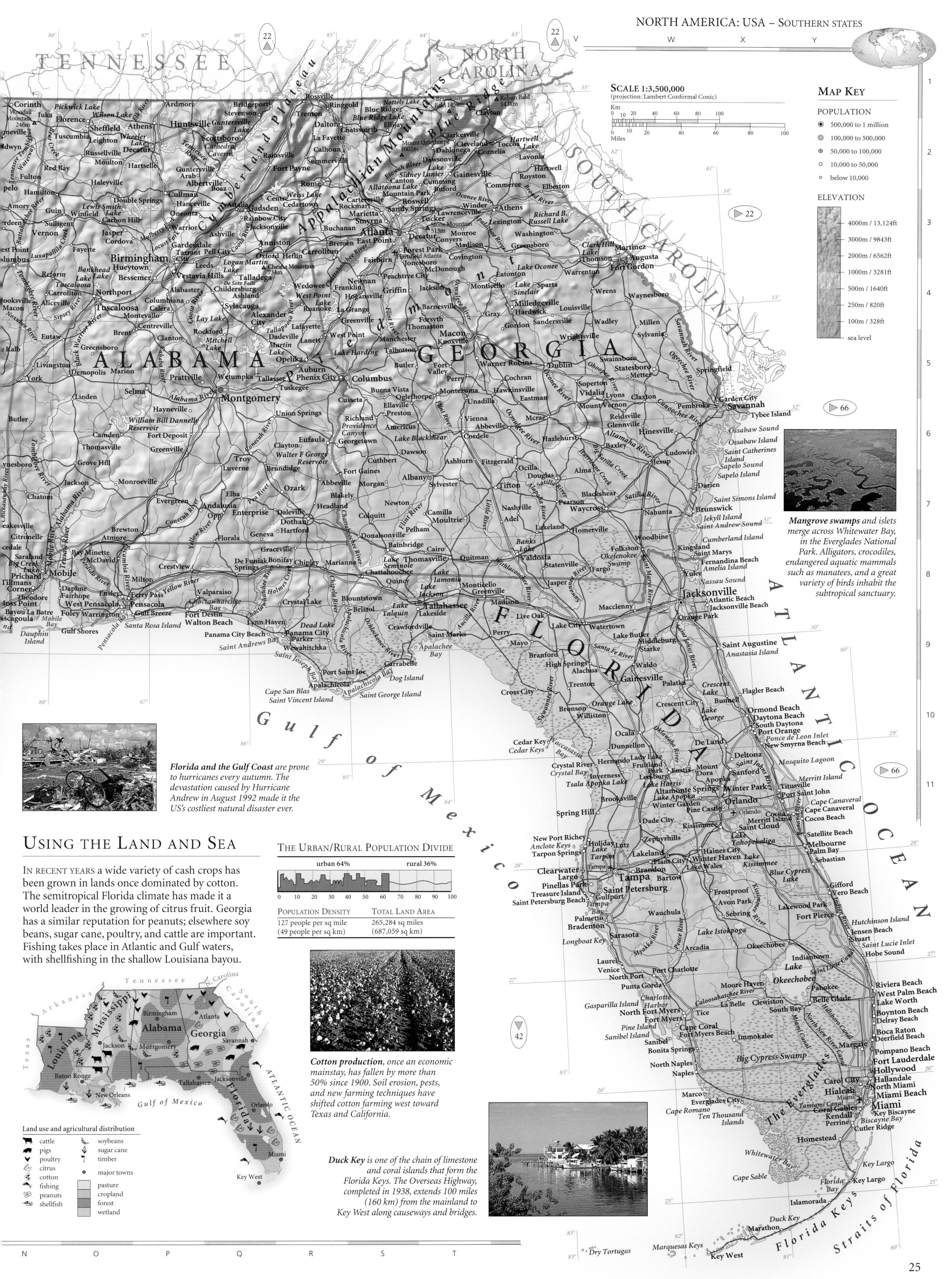

SCALE 1:3,500,000
(projection: Lambert Conformal Conic)

MAP KEY

POPULATION

- 500,000 to 1 million
- 100,000 to 500,000
- 50,000 to 100,000
- 10,000 to 50,000
- below 10,000

ELEVATION

4000m / 13,124ft
3000m / 9843ft
2000m / 6562ft
1000m / 3281ft
500m / 1640ft
250m / 820ft
100m / 328ft

sea level

Mangrove swamps and islets merge across Whitewater Bay, in the Everglades National Park. Alligators, crocodiles, endangered aquatic mammals such as manatees, and a great variety of birds inhabit the subtropical sanctuary.

Florida and the Gulf Coast are prone to hurricanes every autumn. The devastation caused by Hurricane Andrew in August 1992 made it the US's costliest natural disaster ever.

USING THE LAND AND SEA

IN RECENT YEARS a wide variety of cash crops has been grown in lands once dominated by cotton. The semitropical Florida climate has made it a world leader in the growing of citrus fruit. Georgia has a similar reputation for peanuts; elsewhere soy beans, sugar cane, poultry, and cattle are important. Fishing takes place in Atlantic and Gulf waters, with shellfishing in the shallow Louisiana bayou.

THE URBAN/RURAL POPULATION DIVIDE

urban 64%	rural 36%

0 10 20 30 40 50 60 70 80 90 100

POPULATION DENSITY	TOTAL LAND AREA
127 people per sq mile (49 people per sq km)	265,284 sq miles (687,059 sq km)

Cotton production, once an economic mainstay, has fallen by more than 50% since 1900. Soil erosion, pests, and new farming techniques have shifted cotton farming west toward Texas and California.

Duck Key is one of the chain of limestone and coral islands that form the Florida Keys. The Overseas Highway, completed in 1938, extends 100 miles (160 km) from the mainland to Key West along causeways and bridges.

Land use and agricultural distribution

- cattle
- pigs
- poultry
- citrus
- cotton
- fishing
- peanuts
- shellfish
- soybeans
- sugar cane
- timber
- major towns

pasture
cropland
forest
wetland

USA: Texas

Fᴍ First explored by Spaniards moving north from Mexico in search of gold, Texas was controlled by Spain and then by Mexico, before becoming an independent republic in 1836, and joining the Union of States in 1845. During the 19th century, many migrants who came to Texas raised cattle on the abundant land; in the 20th century, they were joined by prospectors attracted by the promise of oil riches. Today, although natural resources, especially oil, still form the basis of its wealth, the diversified Texan economy includes thriving hi-tech and financial industries. The major urban centers, home to 80% of the population, lie in the south and east, and include Houston, the "oil-city," and Dallas Fort Worth. Hispanic influences remain strong, especially in southern and western Texas.

Dallas was founded in 1841 as a prairie trading post and its development was stimulated by the arrival of railroads. Cotton and then oil funded the town's early growth. Today, the modern, high-rise skyline of Dallas reflects the city's position as a leading center of banking, insurance, and the petroleum industry in the southwest.

Using the Land

Cotton production and livestock-raising, particularly cattle, dominate farming, although crop failures and the demands of local markets have led to some diversification. Following the introduction of modern farming techniques, cotton production spread out from the east to the plains of western Texas. Cattle ranches are widespread, while sheep and goats are raised on the dry Edwards Plateau.

The huge cattle ranches of Texas developed during the 19th century when land was plentiful and could be acquired cheaply. Today, more cattle and sheep are raised in Texas than in any other state.

Land use and agricultural distribution
- cattle
- goats
- sheep
- cereals
- cotton
- • major towns

- pasture
- cropland
- forest
- barren

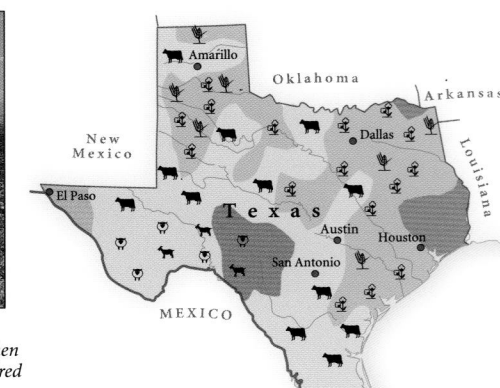

The Urban/Rural Population Divide

urban 80% rural 20%

0 10 20 30 40 50 60 70 80 90 100

POPULATION DENSITY	TOTAL LAND AREA
73 people per sq mile (28 people per sq km)	267,338 sq miles (692,402 sq km)

38 ◁

The Landscape

Texas is made up of a series of massive steps descending from the mountains and high plains of the west and northwest to the coastal lowlands in the southeast. Many of the state's borders are delineated by water. The Rio Grande flows from the Rocky Mountains to the Gulf of Mexico, marking the border with Mexico.

Cap Rock Escarpment juts out from the plains, running 200 miles (320 km) from north to south. Its height varies from 300 ft (90 m) rising to sheer cliffs up to 1,000 ft (300 m).

42 ◁

The Llano Estacado or Staked Plain in northern Texas is known for its harsh environment. In the north, freezing winds carrying ice and snow sweep down from the Rocky Mountains. To the south, sandstorms frequently blow up, scouring anything in their paths. Flash floods, in the wide, flat riverbeds that remain dry for most of the year, are another hazard.

The Guadalupe Mountains lie in the southern Rocky Mountains. They incorporate Guadalupe Peak, the highest in Texas, rising 8,749 ft (2,667 m).

The Rio Grande flows from the Rocky Mountains through semi-arid land, supporting sparse vegetation. The river actually shrinks along its course, losing more water through evaporation and seepage than it gains from its tributaries and rainfall.

Big Bend National Park

Edwards Plateau is a limestone outcrop. It is part of the Great Plains, bounded to the southeast by the Balcones Escarpment, which marks the southerly limit of the plains.

Flowing through 1,500 ft (450 m) high gorges, the shallow, muddy Rio Grande makes a 90° bend. This marks the southern border of Big Bend National Park, and gives it its name. The area is a mixture of forested mountains, deserts, and canyons.

The Red River flows for 1300 miles (2090 km), marking most of the northern border of Texas. A dam and reservoir along its course provide vital irrigation and hydro-electric power to the surrounding area.

Sabine River

Extensive forests of pine and cypress grow in the eastern corner of the coastal lowlands where the average rainfall is 45 inches (1145 mm) a year. This is higher than the rest of the state and over twice the average in the west.

In the coastal lowlands of southeastern Texas the Earth's crust is warping, causing the land to subside and allowing the sea to invade. Around Galveston, the rate of downward tilting is 6 inches (15 cm) per year. Erosion of the coast is also exacerbated by hurricanes.

Oil deposits

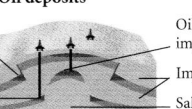

- Oil trapped by fault
- Oil deposits migrate through reservoir rocks such as shale
- Oil accumulates beneath impermeable cap rock
- Impermeable rock strata
- Salt dome

Oil deposits are found beneath much of Texas. They collect as oil migrates upward through porous layers of rock until it is trapped, either by a cap of rock above a salt dome, or by a fault line which exposes impermeable rock through which the oil cannot rise.

Laguna Madre in southern Texas has been almost completely cut off from the sea by Padre Island. This sand bank was created by wave action, carrying and depositing material along the coast. The process is known as longshore drift.

Padre Island

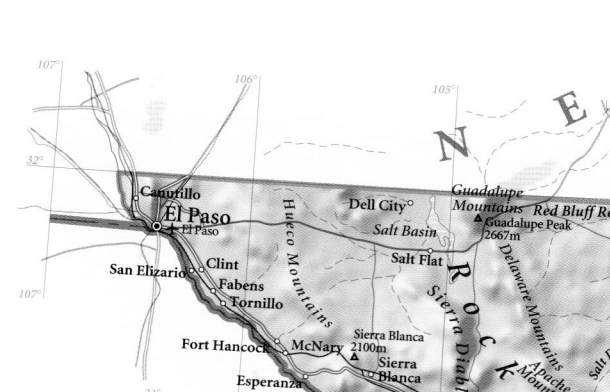

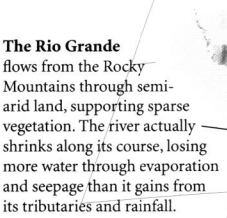

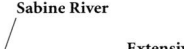

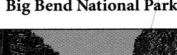

TRANSPORTATION & INDUSTRY

INDUSTRY IN THE 20TH CENTURY was largely concentrated on the processing of local raw materials, especially oil – deposits were discovered under 65% of the state's area. The technological demands of the oil industry and defense-related institutions, particularly NASA, have stimulated the development of numerous electronics and hi-tech firms which, alongside many national corporate headquarters, are based in Dallas–Fort Worth and Houston.

Major industry and infrastructure

- chemicals
- defense
- engineering
- finance
- food processing
- gas
- hi-tech industry
- mining
- oil
- textiles
- major towns
- international airports
- major roads
- major industrial areas

TRANSPORTATION NETWORK

293,509 miles (496,614 km)	3,229 miles (5,166 km)
10,681 miles (17,089 km)	845 miles (1,359 km)

The sheer size of Texas promoted the development of an extensive road and rail network. The highway system, although well-developed, is concentrated in the east.

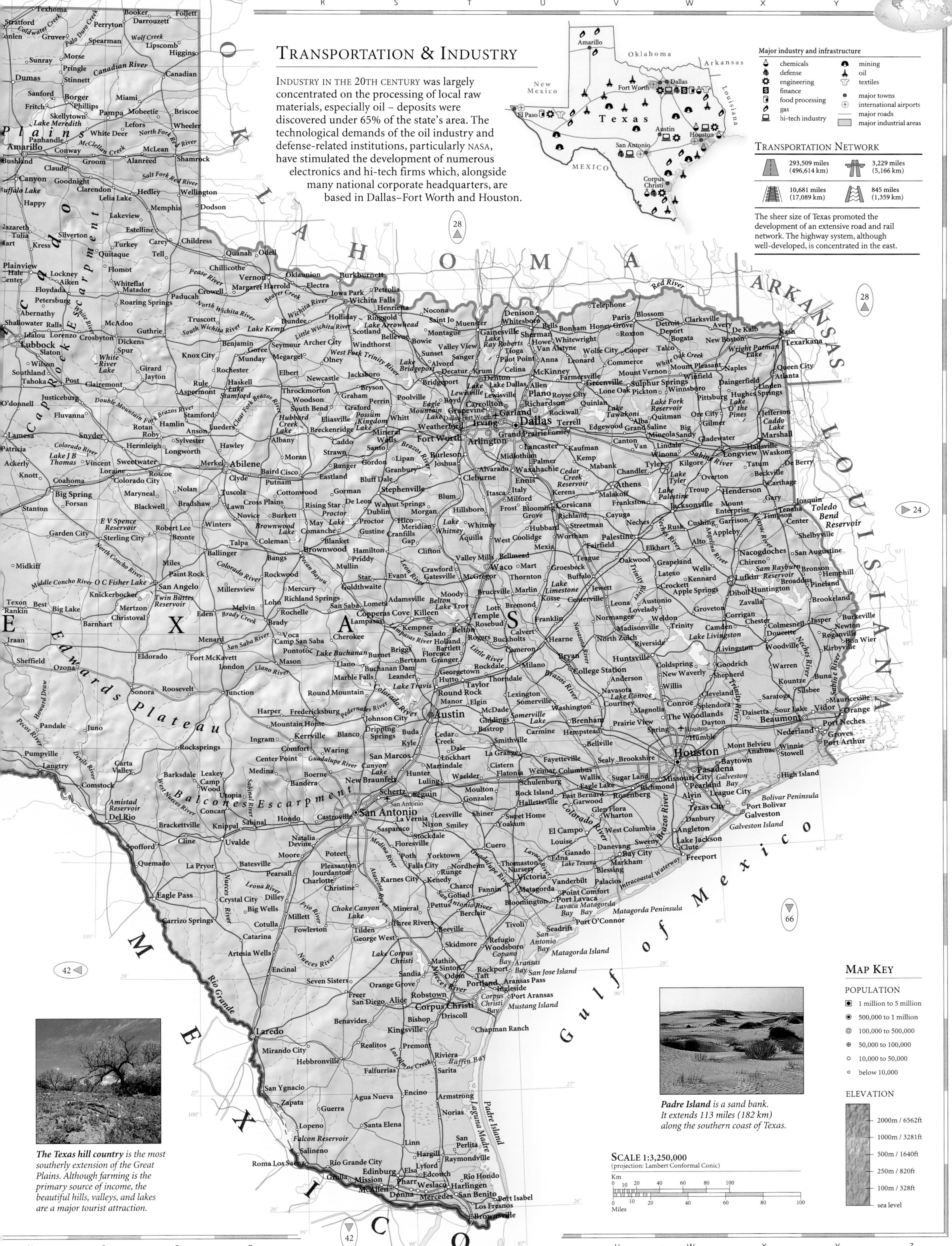

The Texas hill country is the most southerly extension of the Great Plains. Although farming is the primary source of income, the beautiful hills, valleys, and lakes are a major tourist attraction.

Padre Island is a sand bank. It extends 113 miles (182 km) along the southern coast of Texas.

MAP KEY

POPULATION
- 1 million to 5 million
- 500,000 to 1 million
- 100,000 to 500,000
- 50,000 to 100,000
- 10,000 to 50,000
- below 10,000

ELEVATION
- 2000m / 6562ft
- 1000m / 3281ft
- 500m / 1640ft
- 250m / 820ft
- 100m / 328ft
- sea level

SCALE 1:3,250,000
(projection: Lambert Conformal Conic)

Km
0 10 20 40 60 80 100
Miles
0 10 20 40 60 80 100

27

USA: South Midwestern states

Arkansas, Kansas, Missouri, Oklahoma

THE EXPANSION OF THE US focused on this region in the mid-19th century. Settlers spread from the confluence of the Missouri and Mississippi Rivers up onto the Great Plains. This treeless expanse, which early explorers had called the Great American Desert was turned into one of the world's richest agricultural regions. But periodic droughts, coupled with overintensive farming, led to the "dustbowl" soil erosion crisis of the 1930s, the abandonment of many farms, and a mass exodus to the west coast. The land has since recovered, although the mechanization of agriculture has led to a decline in the rural population. In recent years, suburban residential development has spread rapidly across the wooded Ozark Plateau in the east of the region.

TRANSPORTATION & INDUSTRY

THE PROCESSING OF AGRICULTURAL PRODUCTS, such as brewing and meatpacking, has been traditionally important in these states. In Kansas and Oklahoma, diversified manufacturing now supplements income from fossil fuels; Wichita has become a world center for aeronautical engineering, an industry which also employs many people in neighboring Missouri.

Major industry and infrastructure

- ✈ aerospace
- ✿ engineering
- Ⓢ finance
- ▣ food processing
- ◊ gas
- ◣ mining
- ⚓ oil
- 🚗 vehicle manufacture
- • major towns
- + international airports
- — major roads
- major industrial areas

Agricultural produce from the plains is moved by barges along the Mississippi. The river now carries a far greater tonnage of freight than any other waterway system in the US.

TRANSPORTATION NETWORK

380,307 miles (608,491 km)		4068 miles (6508 km)	
16,185 miles (25,896 km)		1994 miles (3208 km)	

The Arkansas River and its tributaries allow access to over half of the US's navigable inland waterways. A system of locks and dams along the river provides Tulsa, in Oklahom, with a navigable water route to the Gulf of Mexico.

MAP KEY

POPULATION

- ◎ 100,000 to 500,000
- ⊕ 50,000 to 100,000
- ⊙ 10,000 to 50,000
- ○ below 10,000

ELEVATION

- 1000m / 3281ft
- 500m / 1640ft
- 250m / 820ft
- 100m / 328ft
- sea level

THE LANDSCAPE

MOST OF THE REGION consists of high, treeless plains, which gradually descend east from the Rocky Mountains. Drainage follows this slope, with rivers flowing toward the alluvial lowlands of the Mississippi in the southeast. Between the plains and the lowlands lie various ranges of wooded hills, including the deeply incised Ozark Plateau.

The Mississippi, North America's longest river, is joined by the Missouri, its main tributary, on a flood plain which spreads south to the Gulf of Mexico.

The Ozark Plateau is a wooded, hilly region of rivers and narrow, winding lakes. The Lake of the Ozarks was created by the damming of the Osage River in 1930.

Collapsed limestone caverns led to the formation of Big Basin in Kansas; a depression 100 ft (33 m) deep and 1 mile (1.6 km) wide.

Flint Hills is the region's easternmost major escarpment. Steep, grassy uplands are interspersed with rocky, wooded ravines and outcrops of limestone and chert.

Missouri River

The Great Salt Plains of northern Oklahoma cover 45 sq miles (116 sq km). The arid, white flats were left by the gradual evaporation of an ancient salt lake.

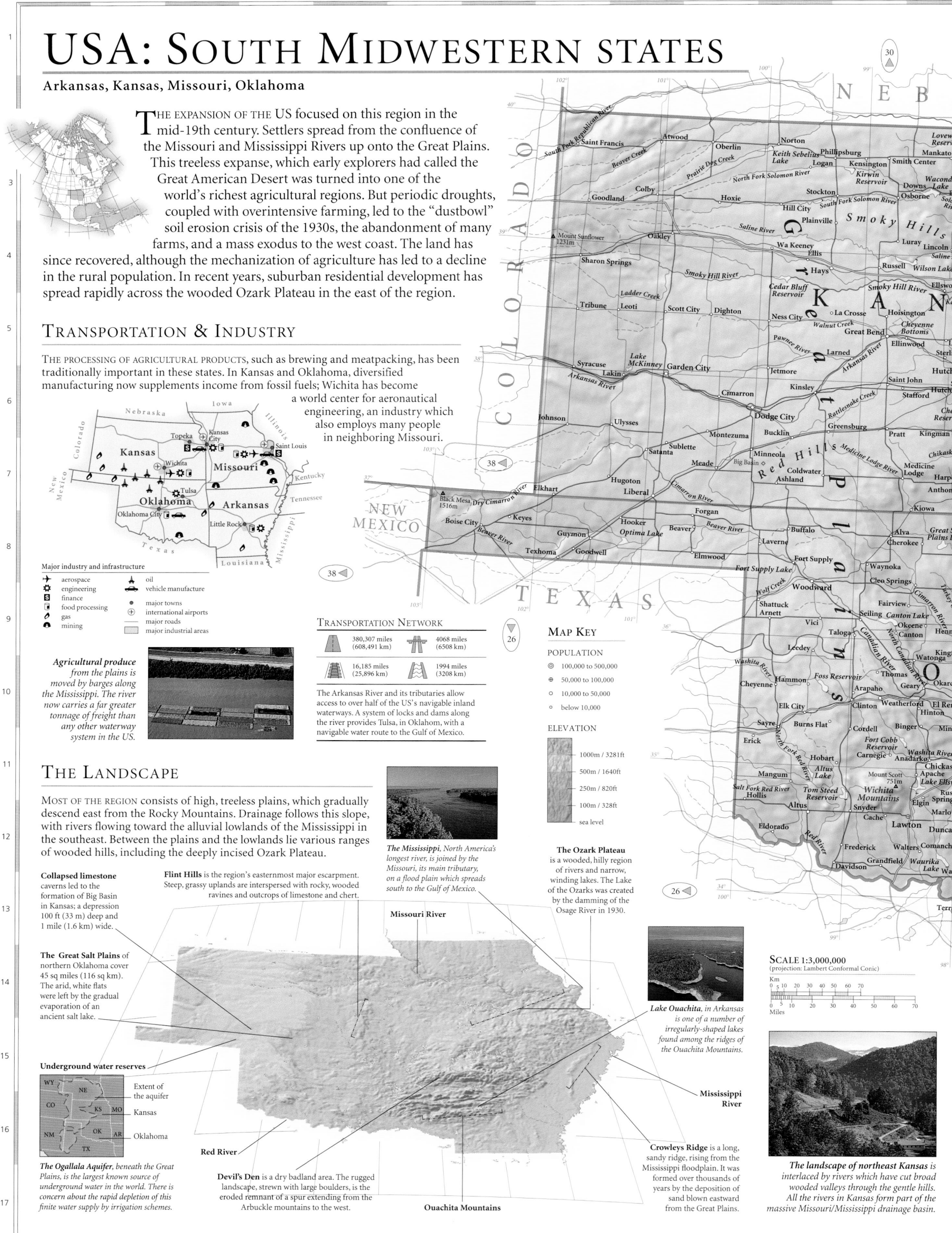

Lake Ouachita, in Arkansas is one of a number of irregularly-shaped lakes found among the ridges of the Ouachita Mountains.

Underground water reserves

- Extent of the aquifer
- Kansas
- Oklahoma

The Ogallala Aquifer, beneath the Great Plains, is the largest known source of underground water in the world. There is concern about the rapid depletion of this finite water supply by irrigation schemes.

Red River

Devil's Den is a dry badland area. The rugged landscape, strewn with large boulders, is the eroded remnant of a spur extending from the Arbuckle mountains to the west.

Ouachita Mountains

Mississippi River

Crowleys Ridge is a long, sandy ridge, rising from the Mississippi floodplain. It was formed over thousands of years by the deposition of sand blown eastward from the Great Plains.

The landscape of northeast Kansas is interlaced by rivers which have cut broad wooded valleys through the gentle hills. All the rivers in Kansas form part of the massive Missouri/Mississippi drainage basin.

SCALE 1:3,000,000
(projection: Lambert Conformal Conic)

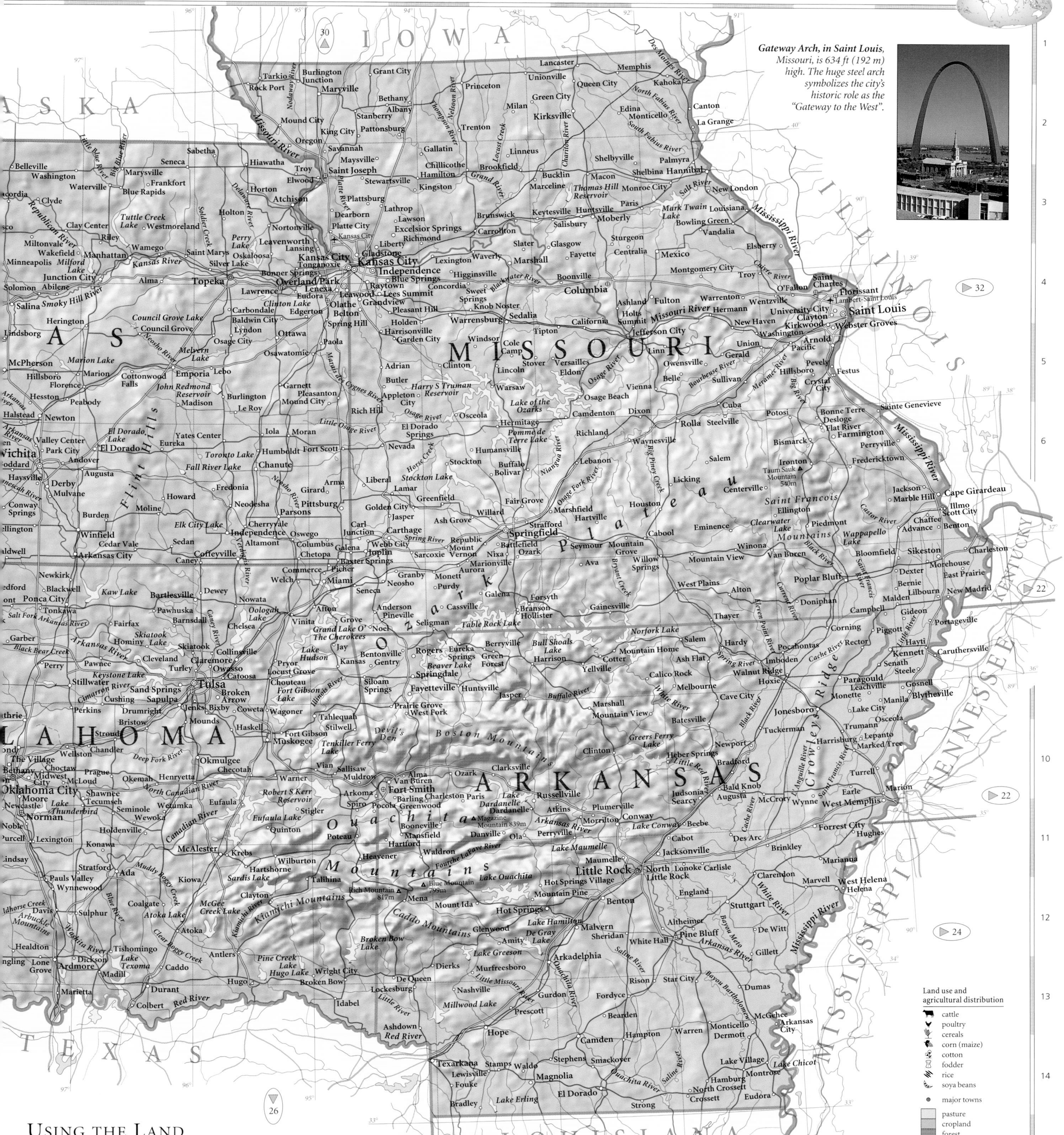

IOWA

NEBRASKA

KANSAS

MISSOURI

ILLINOIS

OKLAHOMA

ARKANSAS

TEXAS

LOUISIANA

TENNESSEE

KENTUCKY

Gateway Arch, in Saint Louis, Missouri, is 634 ft (192 m) high. The huge steel arch symbolizes the city's historic role as the "Gateway to the West".

USING THE LAND

THE PROBLEMS of a harsh continental climate, with severe winters and hot, dry summers, are partially offset by the rich soils of the plains. Kansas is a major cereal crop producer, ranking first in US production of wheat and sorghum. Rainfall increases toward the east, favoring the cultivation of soybeans, cotton, and rice, with corn concentrated in Missouri. Huge herds of cattle are raised in Oklahoma, Kansas, and Missouri.

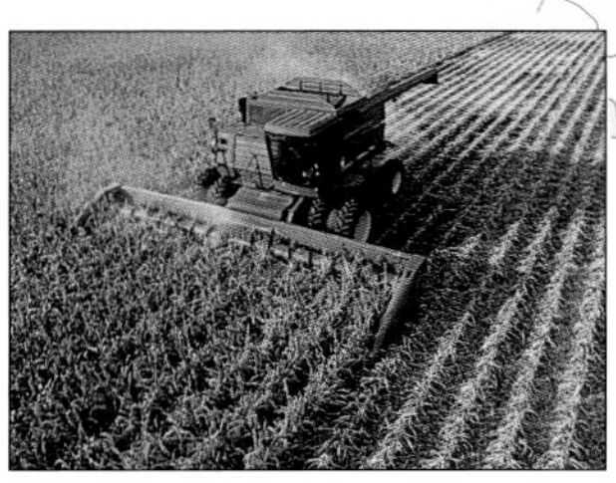

A combine harvester works the land on the great plains. A hundred years ago this region, also known as the prairies – the French word for pasture – was covered with tall, wild grasses.

THE URBAN/RURAL POPULATION DIVIDE

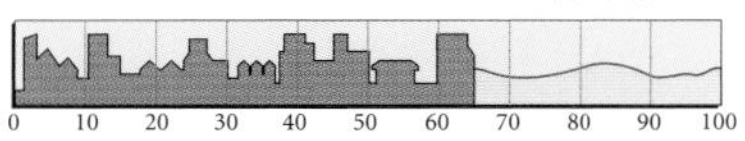

urban 65%   rural 35%

0 10 20 30 40 50 60 70 80 90 100

POPULATION DENSITY
50 people per sq mile
(19 people per sq km)

TOTAL LAND AREA
274,900 sq miles
(712,177 sq km)

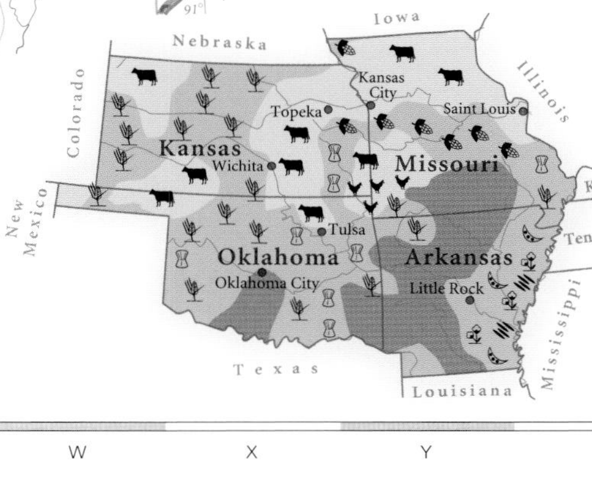

Land use and agricultural distribution
- cattle
- poultry
- cereals
- corn (maize)
- cotton
- fodder
- rice
- soya beans
- major towns

pasture
cropland
forest

Iowa
Nebraska
Colorado
Kansas
Wichita   Kansas City   Saint Louis
Topeka   Missouri
Illinois
New Mexico
Oklahoma   Tulsa   Arkansas
Oklahoma City   Little Rock
Texas   Louisiana   Mississippi   Tennessee   Kentucky

29

USA: UPPER PLAINS STATES

Iowa, Minnesota, Nebraska, North Dakota, South Dakota

LYING AT THE VERY HEART of the North American continent, much of this region was acquired from France as part of the Louisiana Purchase in 1803. The area was largely bypassed by the early waves of westward migrants. When Europeans did settle, during the 19th century, they displaced the Native Americans who lived on the plains. The settlers planted arable crops and raised cattle on the immensely fertile prairie land, founding an agrarian tradition which flourishes today. Most of this region remains rural; of the five states, only in Minnesota has there been significant diversification away from agriculture and resource-based industries into the hi-tech and service sectors.

USING THE LAND

THE POPULAR IMAGE of these states as agricultural is entirely justified; prairies stretch uninterrupted across most of the area. Croplands fall into two regions: the wheat belt of the plains, and the corn belt of the central US. Cash crops, such as soybeans, are grown to supplement incomes. Livestock, particularly pigs and cattle, are raised throughout this region.

Dark, fertile prairie soils in the southeast provide Minnesota's most productive farmland. Hot, humid summers create a long growing season for corn cultivation.

Land use and agricultural distribution
- cattle
- pigs
- corn (maize)
- soybeans
- wheat
- major towns
- pasture
- cropland
- forest
- wetland

THE URBAN/RURAL POPULATION DIVIDE

urban 64%   rural 36%

0 10 20 30 40 50 60 70 80 90 100

POPULATION DENSITY: 29 people per sq mile (11 people per sq km)

TOTAL LAND AREA: 365,287 sq miles (946,056 sq km)

TRANSPORTATION & INDUSTRY

FOOD PROCESSING and the production of farm machinery are supported by the large agricultural sector. Mineral exploitation is also an important activity: gold is mined in the ore-rich Black Hills of South Dakota, and both North Dakota and Nebraska are emerging as major petroleum producers.

Water erosion along the Little Missouri River has carried away sedimentary deposits, creating rugged landscapes known as badlands.

Major industry and infrastructure
- coal
- engineering
- electronics
- finance
- food processing
- oil & gas
- mining
- major towns
- international airports
- major roads
- major industrial areas

TRANSPORTATION NETWORK

504,522 miles (807,235 km)

3,422 miles (5,475 km)

16,940 miles (27,104 km)

683 miles (1,098 km)

Nebraska's central location has made it an important transportation artery for east–west traffic. Minnesota's road network radiates out from the hub of the twin cities, Minneapolis–Saint Paul.

THE LANDSCAPE

THESE STATES STRADDLE the Great Plains and the lowlands of the central US, with Minnesota lying in a transition zone between the eastern forests and the prairies. The region was shaped by repeated ice advances and retreats, leaving a flat relief, broken only by the numerous lakes and broad river networks that drain the prairies.

Escarpment / Ridge / In permeable strata hollows are formed by small mudslides / Water flowing into gullies erodes back the escarpment

Badlands are formed by stormwater run-off. This flows down the impermeable strata of the escarpment and saturates the permeable strata, leading to mudslides and the formation of gullies.

North Dakota Badlands

The Minnesota landscape contains many post-glacial features, including its numerous lakes, boulder-strewn hills, and mineral-rich deposits.

In the badlands of North and South Dakota, horizontal layers of sandstone have been eroded by rivers, leaving a landscape of narrow gullies, sharp crests and pinnacles.

South Dakota Badlands

Chimney Rock is a remnant of an ancient land surface, eroded by the North Platte River. The tip of its spire stands 500 ft (150 m) above the plain.

Although it escaped the last glaciation, the limestone bedrock of southeastern Minnesota has been eroded by surface and subterranean streams, leaving a network of underground caverns and steep-sided valleys.

Missouri River

Mississippi River

In northeastern Iowa, the Mississippi and its tributaries have deeply incised the underlying bedrock creating a hilly terrain, with bluffs standing 300 ft (90 m) above the valley.

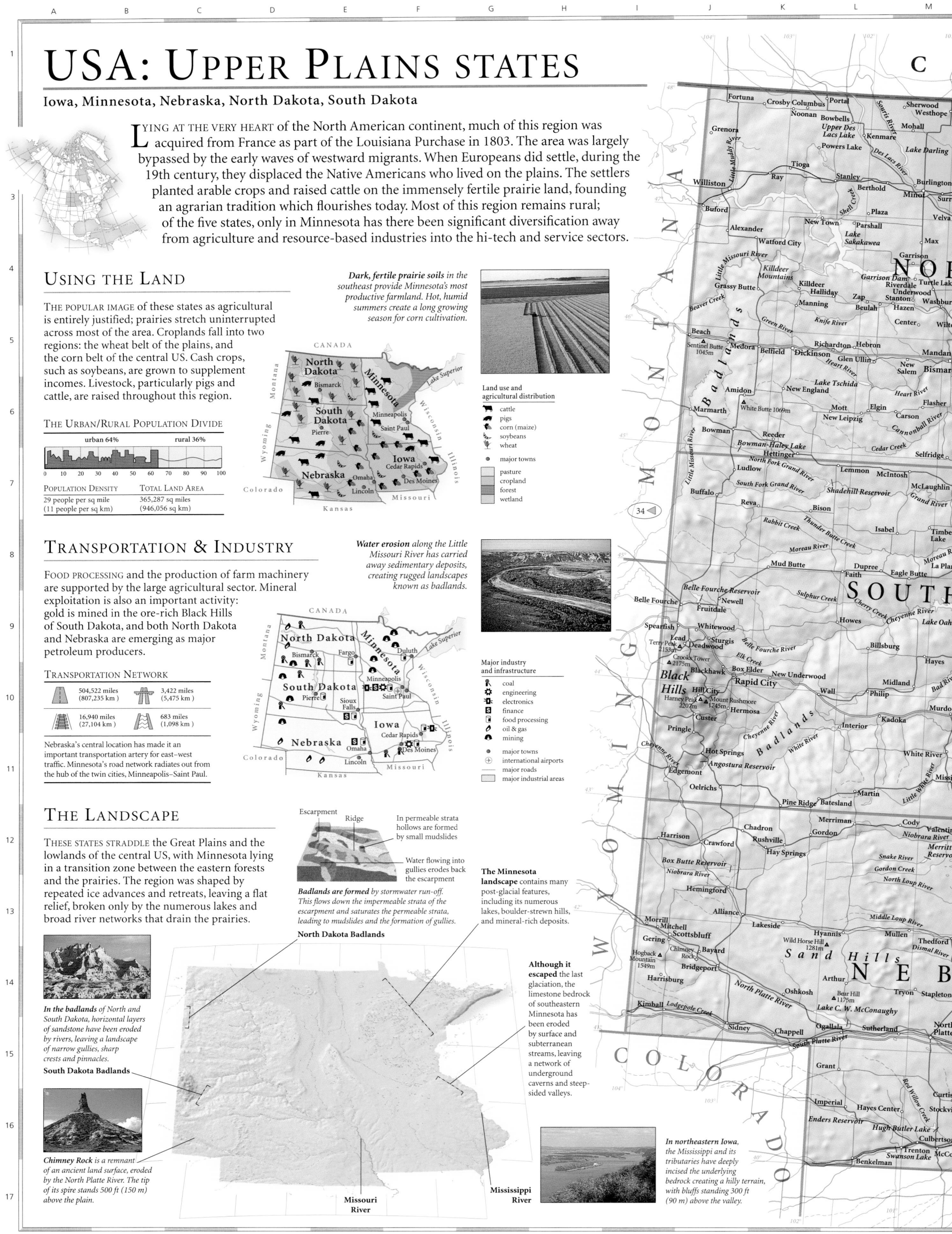

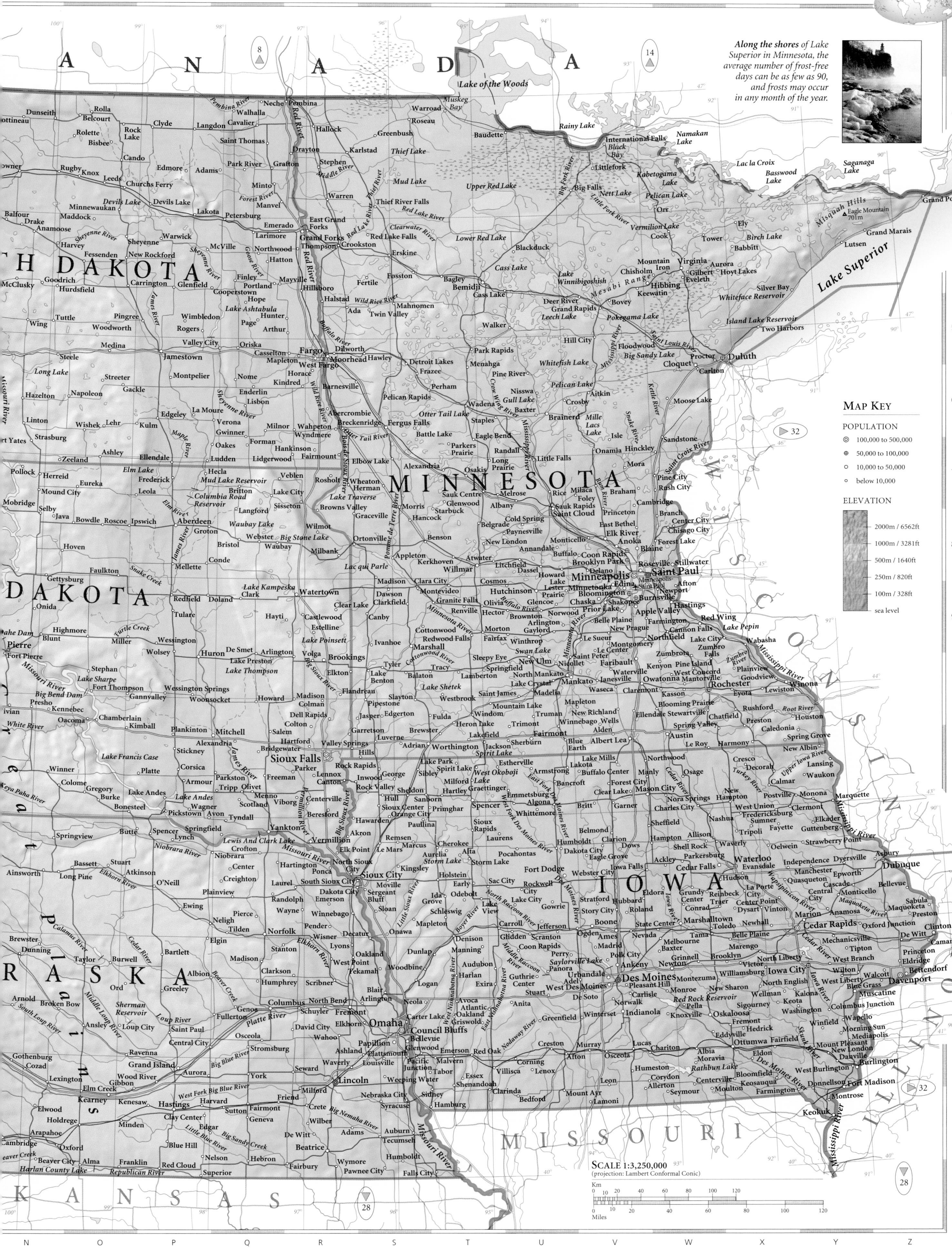

Along the shores of Lake Superior in Minnesota, the average number of frost-free days can be as few as 90, and frosts may occur in any month of the year.

CANADA

NORTH DAKOTA

SOUTH DAKOTA

MINNESOTA

WISCONSIN

NEBRASKA

IOWA

MISSOURI

KANSAS

ILLINOIS

Lake Superior

Lake of the Woods

MAP KEY

POPULATION

- ◎ 100,000 to 500,000
- ⊕ 50,000 to 100,000
- ○ 10,000 to 50,000
- ∘ below 10,000

ELEVATION

	2000m / 6562ft
	1000m / 3281ft
	500m / 1640ft
	250m / 820ft
	100m / 328ft
	sea level

SCALE 1:3,250,000
(projection: Lambert Conformal Conic)

Km
0 10 20   40   60   80   100   120

Miles
0 10 20   40   60   80   100   120

31

USA: GREAT LAKES STATES

Illinois, Indiana, Michigan, Ohio, Wisconsin

THE STATES BORDERING THE GREAT LAKES developed rapidly in the second half of the 19th century as a result of improvements in communications: railroads to the west and waterways to the south and east. Fertile land and good links with growing eastern seaboard cities encouraged the development of agriculture and food processing. Migrants from Europe and other parts of the US flooded into the region and for much of the 20th century the region's economy boomed. However, in recent years heavy industry has declined, earning the region the unwanted label the "Rustbelt."

TRANSPORTATION & INDUSTRY

THE GREAT LAKES REGION IS THE CENTER of the US car industry. Since the early part of the 20th century, its prosperity has been closely linked to the fortunes of automobile manufacturing. Iron and steel production has expanded to meet demand from this industry. In the 1970s, nationwide recession, cheaper foreign competition in the automobile sector, pollution in and around the Great Lakes, and the collapse of the meatpacking industry, centered on Chicago, forced these states to diversify their industrial base. New industries have emerged, notably electronics, service, and finance industries.

TRANSPORTATION NETWORK

540,682 miles (865,091 km)		6,550 miles (10,480 km)	
24,928 miles (39,884 km)		2,330 miles (3,748 km)	

Few areas of the US have a comparable system. Chicago is a principal transportation terminus with a dense network of roads, railroads, and Interstate freeways that radiates out from the city.

Ever since Ransom Olds and Henry Ford started mass-producing automobiles in Detroit early in the 20th century, the city's name has become synonymous with the American automotive industry.

Major industry and infrastructure

- car manufacture
- coal
- electronics
- engineering
- finance
- food processing
- iron & steel
- oil
- research & development
- textiles
- major towns
- international airports
- major roads
- major industrial areas

THE LANDSCAPE

MUCH OF THIS REGION shows the impact of glaciation which lasted until about 10,000 years ago, and extended as far south as Illinois and Ohio. Although the relief of the region slopes toward the Great Lakes, because the ice sheets blocked northerly drainage, most of the rivers today flow southward, forming part of the massive Mississippi/Missouri drainage basin.

The dunes near Sleeping Bear Point rise 400 ft (120 m) from the banks of Lake Michigan. They are constantly being resculpted by wind action.

Lake Michigan

Lake Erie is the shallowest of the five Great Lakes. Its average depth is about 62 ft (19 m). Storms sweeping across from Canada erode its shores and cause the silting of its harbors.

The many lakes and marshes of Wisconsin and Michigan are the result of glacial erosion and deposition which occurred during the last Ice Age.

Southwestern Wisconsin is known as a "driftless" area. Unlike most of the region, low hills protected it from erosion by the advancing ice sheet.

Most of the water used in northern Illinois is pumped from underground reservoirs. Due to increased demand, many areas now face a water shortage. Around Joliet, the water table was lowered by more than 700 ft (210 m) over the last century.

Illinois plains

The plains of Illinois are characteristic of drift landscapes, scoured and flattened by glacial erosion and covered with fertile glacial deposits.

Mississippi River

Relict landforms from the last glaciation, such as shallow basins and ridges, cover all but the south of this region. Ridges, known as moraines, up to 300 ft (100 m) high, lie to the south of Lake Michigan.

Ohio River

Unlike the level prairie to the north, southern Indiana is relatively rugged. Limestone in the hills has been dissolved by water, producing features such as sinkholes and underground caves.

Present-day river or stream

Channels caused by outwash from melting glacier

Glacial till

Most recent till deposits

Older till sheet

Bedrock

As a result of successive glacial depositions, the total depth of till along the former southern margin of the Laurentide ice sheet can exceed 1,300 ft (400 m).

The Appalachian plateau stretches eastward from Ohio. It is dissected by streams flowing west into the Mississippi and Ohio Rivers.

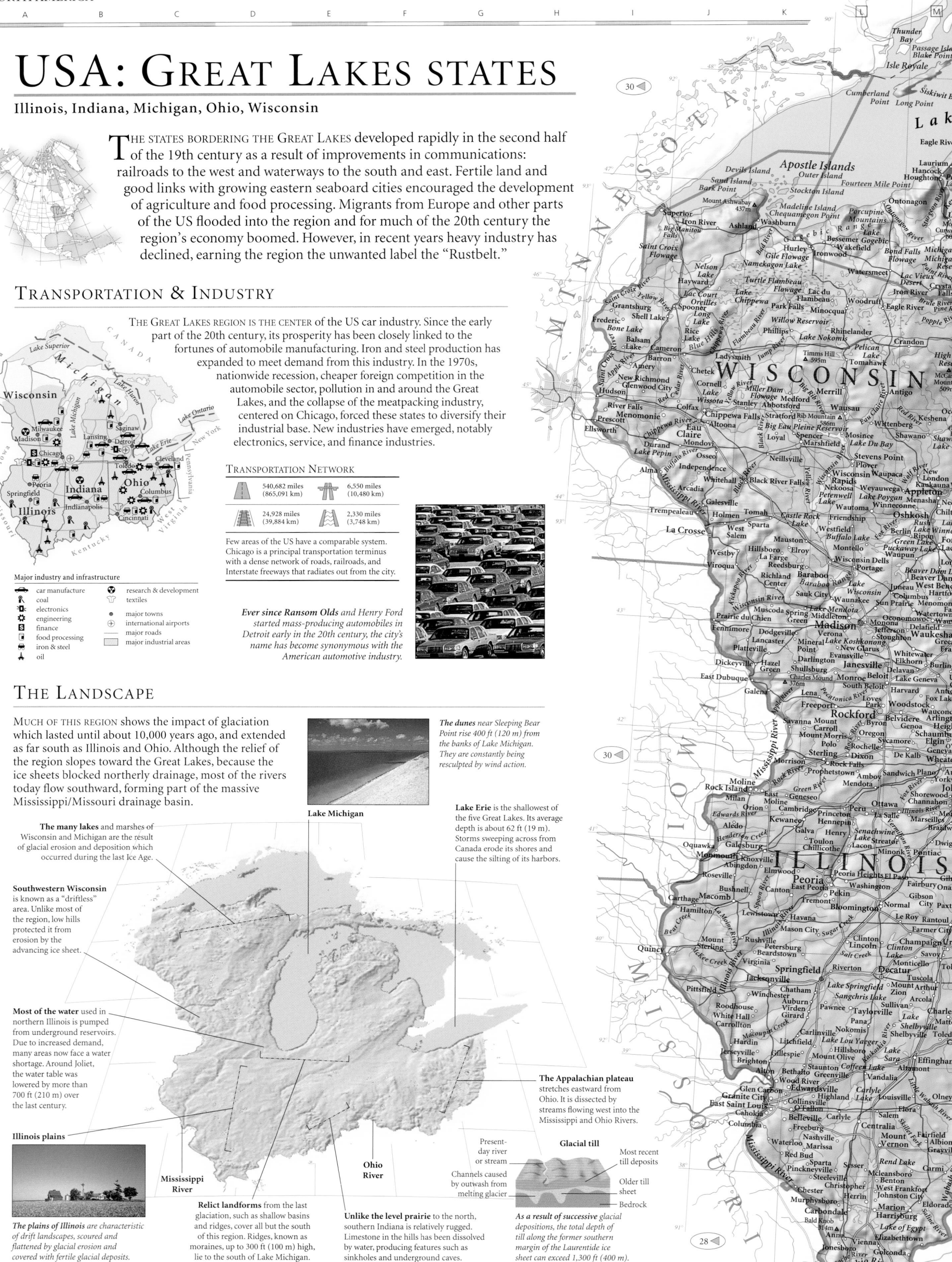

THE URBAN/RURAL POPULATION DIVIDE

urban 74%   rural 26%

POPULATION DENSITY	TOTAL LAND AREA
177 people per sq mile	248,283 sq miles
(68 people per sq km)	(643,028 sq km)

USING THE LAND

THE VARIED SOILS AND CLIMATE of this region have allowed the development of different types of agriculture. Corn and soybeans are the main crops produced, although Michigan is best known for growing fruit, particularly cherries and apples. About 80% of Wisconsin's agricultural income is derived from livestock-rearing and dairying. Pig breeding is important in both Illinois and Indiana.

Land use and agricultural distribution

cattle
pigs
poultry
corn (maize)
fruit
soybeans
timber

● major towns
pasture
cropland
forest

Farms like this one stretch across more than 80% of Illinois, covering 44,800 sq miles (116,000 sq km). The state is the leading US producer of soybeans, which are used for animal feed and oil.

Lake Superior is the largest of the Great Lakes and attracts millions of tourists each year. Valuable mineral deposits such as iron and copper are mined close to its shores.

SCALE 1:3,750,000
(projection: Lambert Conformal Conic)

Km
0 10 20 40 60 80 100

Miles
0 10 20 40 60 80 100

Although large-scale agribusiness has mostly replaced family farming in the Midwest, some communities, such as the Amish people in Ohio, retain traditional farming methods, cultivating their smallholdings using limited machinery.

MAP KEY

POPULATION

◼ 1 million to 5 million
◉ 500,000 to 1 million
◎ 100,000 to 500,000
⊕ 50,000 to 100,000
⊙ 10,000 to 50,000
○ below 10,000

ELEVATION

1000m / 3281ft
500m / 1640ft
250m / 820ft
100m / 328ft
sea level

USA: North Mountain States

Idaho, Montana, Oregon, Washington, Wyoming

The remoteness of the northwestern states, coupled with the rugged landscape, ensured that this was one of the last areas settled by Europeans in the 19th century. Fur-trappers and gold-prospectors followed the Snake River westward as it wound its way through the Rocky Mountains. The states of the northwest have pioneered many conservationist policies, with the first US National Park opened at Yellowstone in 1872. More recently, the Cascades and Rocky Mountains have become havens for adventure tourism. The mountains still serve to isolate the western seaboard from the rest of the continent. This isolation has encouraged West Coast cities to expand their trade links with countries of the Pacific Rim.

The Snake River has cut down into the basalt of the Columbia Basin to form Hells Canyon, the deepest in the US, with cliffs up to 7,900 ft (2,408 m) high.

MAP KEY

POPULATION
- ◉ 500,000 to 1 million
- ◎ 100,000 to 500,000
- ⊙ 50,000 to 100,000
- ⊡ 10,000 to 50,000
- ∘ below 10,000

ELEVATION
- 4000m / 13,124ft
- 3000m / 9843ft
- 2000m / 6562ft
- 1000m / 3281ft
- 500m / 1640ft
- 250m / 820ft
- 100m / 328ft
- sea level

Fine-textured, volcanic soils in the hilly Palouse region of eastern Washington are susceptible to erosion.

Using the Land

Wheat farming in the east gives way to cattle ranching as rainfall decreases. Irrigated farming in the Snake River valley produces large yields of potatoes and other vegetables. Dairying and fruit-growing take place in the wet western lowlands between the mountain ranges.

The Urban/Rural Population Divide

urban 70%   rural 30%

0 10 20 30 40 50 60 70 80 90 100

POPULATION DENSITY
23 people per sq mile
(9 people per sq km)

TOTAL LAND AREA
493,782 sq miles
(1,278,846 sq km)

SCALE 1:3,750,000
(projection: Lambert Conformal Conic)

Km 0 10 20 40 60 80 100
Miles 0 20 40 60 80 100

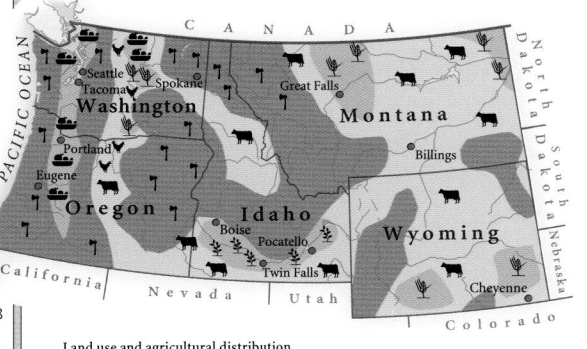

Land use and agricultural distribution
- 🐄 cattle
- 🐔 poultry
- 🌾 cereals
- 🍎 fruit
- potatoes
- 🌲 timber
- ● major towns
- pasture
- cropland
- forest

198 ◀

Transportation & Industry

Minerals and timber are extremely important in this region. Uranium, precious metals, copper, and coal are all mined, the latter in vast open-cast pits in Wyoming; oil and natural gas are extracted further north. Manufacturing, notably related to the aerospace and electronics industries, is important in western cities.

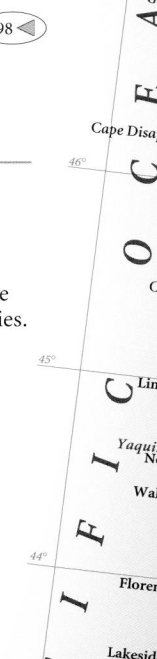

TRANSPORTATION NETWORK

- 347,857 miles (556,571 km)
- 4,200 miles (6,720 km)
- 12,354 miles (19,766 km)
- 1,108 miles (1,782 km)

Major industry and infrastructure
- ⌂ adventure tourism
- ✈ aerospace
- coal
- chemicals
- electronics
- food processing
- mining
- oil & gas
- timber processing
- ● major towns
- ✈ international airports
- major roads
- major industrial areas

The Union Pacific Railroad has been in service across Wyoming since 1867. The route through the Rocky Mountains is now shared with the Interstate 80, a major east-west highway.

Seattle lies in one of Puget Sound's many inlets. The city receives oil and other resources from Alaska, and benefits from expanding trade across the Pacific.

Crater Lake, Oregon, is 6 miles (10 km) wide and 1,800 ft (600 m) deep. It marks the site of a volcanic cone, which collapsed after an eruption within the last 7,000 years.

THE LANDSCAPE

THE ROCKY MOUNTAINS are flanked by lower parallel ranges, which spread onto the Great Plains in the east and surmount the broad lava plateau which extends westward. The Cascade Range divides the Columbia Basin from the coastlands, where the low areas around Puget Sound are broken by the steep, volcanic Olympic Mountains and the wooded hills of the Coast Ranges.

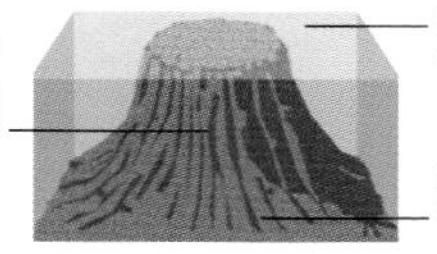

Molten rock cools, forming parallel columns

Surrounding strata eroded away

Molten rock wells up from the Earth's core

Devil's Tower in Wyoming is an igneous intrusion, formed below the Earth's surface. Molten rock intruded through cracks in the overlying strata and cooled. Over time, the softer rock layers have been eroded away, leaving only the tower standing.

Glacial valleys on the seaward side of the Olympic Mountains receive about 142 inches (3,600 mm) of rain per year, supporting the only true rain forest of the northern hemisphere.

The Cascades are glacially scoured volcanic mountains, the highest of which is Mount Rainier, a dormant volcano at 14,409 ft (4,392 m).

Coast Ranges

Mount St. Helens erupted in 1980, killing 57 people and devastating a huge area.

Puget Sound

Columbia Basin

Grand Coulee and the lesser *coulées* (ravines) were cut by cataclysmic floods, from the release of an ice-dammed lake, at the end of the last ice age.

The Continental Divide, or watershed, crosses the Lewis Range. From here, rivers flow east to Hudson Bay, south to the Gulf of Mexico and west to the Pacific Ocean.

Piney Buttes are the remnants of an older, higher land surface gradually weathered and eroded into isolated outcrops with flat tops and steep sides.

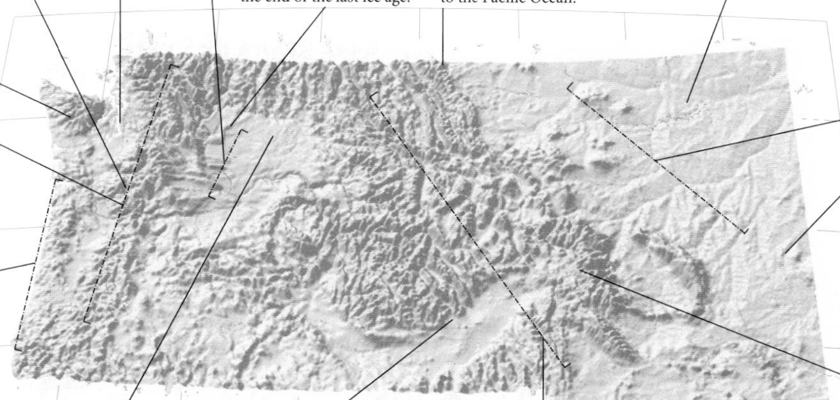

Great Plains

Devil's Tower

The plateaus of the Columbia and Snake Rivers represent one of the world's largest accumulations of lava. Over 5 million years ago, successive flows of molten basalt buried the existing land surface by up to 450 ft (150 m).

The contorted rock shapes at "Craters of the Moon" National Monument in Idaho were left 2,000 years ago by the sporadic upwelling of viscous lava from fissures in the basalt plateau.

Rocky Mountains

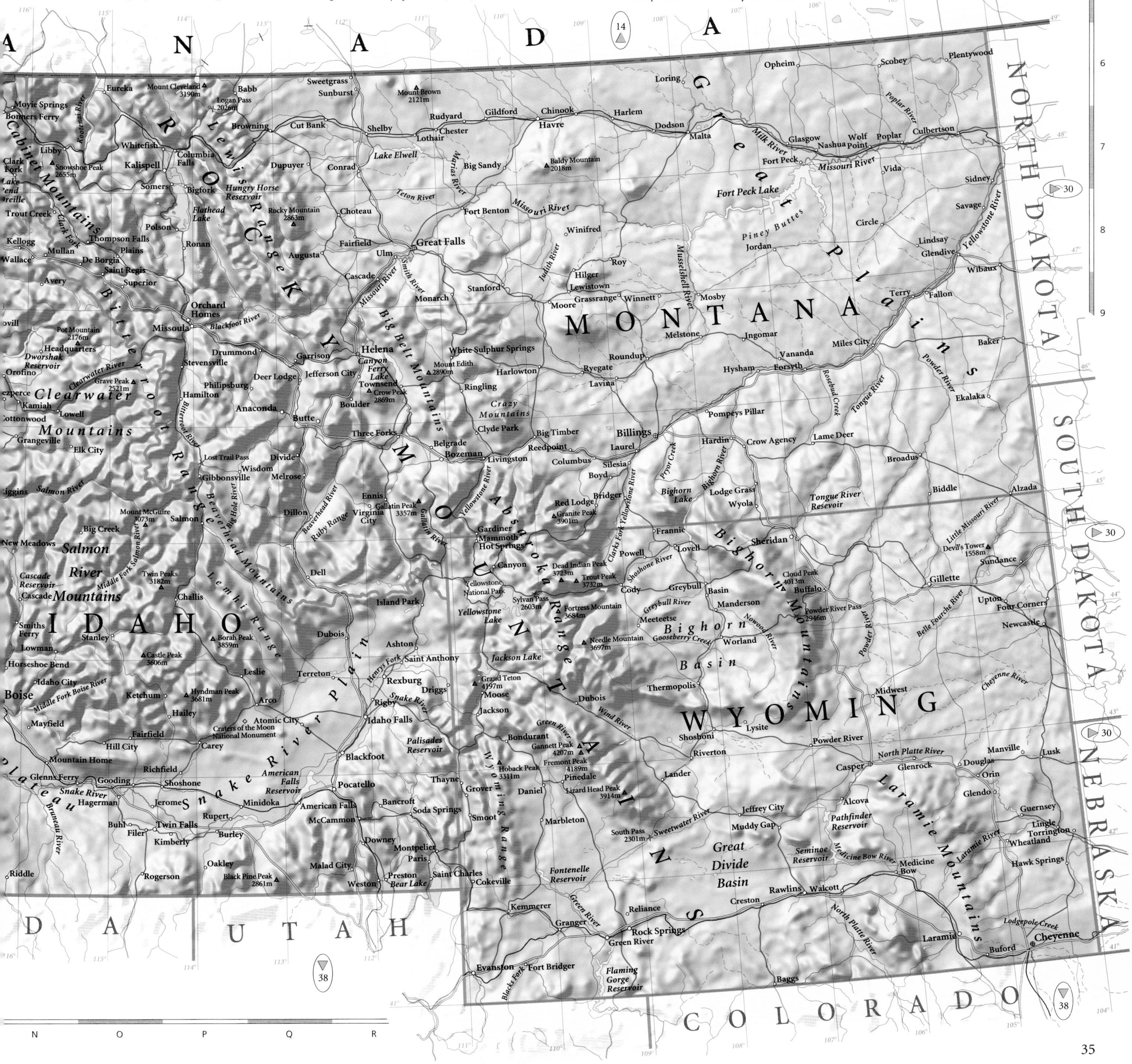

Water from the hot springs in Yellowstone National Park deposits minerals as it cools in rock pools. Long periods of deposition have created these rock terraces.

USA: California & Nevada

The Gold Rush of 1849 attracted the first major wave of European settlers to the West Coast. The pleasant climate, beautiful scenery and dynamic economy continue to attract immigrants – despite the ever-present danger of earthquakes – and California has become the US's most populous state. The overwhelmingly urban population is concentrated in the vast conurbations of Los Angeles, San Francisco, and San Diego; new immigrants include people from South Korea, the Philippines, Vietnam, and Mexico. Nevada's arid lands were initially exploited for minerals; in recent years, revenue from mining has been superseded by income from the tourist and gambling centers of Las Vegas and Reno.

Map Key

POPULATION
- ◉ 1 million to 5 million
- ◉ 500,000 to 1 million
- ◎ 100,000 to 500,000
- ⊕ 50,000 to 100,000
- ○ 10,000 to 50,000
- ○ below 10,000

ELEVATION
- 4000m / 13,124ft
- 3000m / 9843ft
- 2000m / 6562ft
- 1000m / 3281ft
- 500m / 1640ft
- 250m / 820ft
- 100m / 328ft
- sea level

SCALE 1:3,000,000
(projection: Lambert Conformal Conic)

Km 0 5 10 20 30 40 50 60 70 80
Miles 0 5 10 20 30 40 50 60 70 80

Transportation & Industry

Nevada's rich mineral reserves ushered in a period of mining wealth which has now been replaced by revenue generated from gambling. California supports a broad set of activities including defense-related industries and research and development facilities. "Silicon Valley," near San Francisco, is a world leading center for microelectronics, while tourism and the Los Angeles film industry also generate large incomes.

Gambling was legalized in Nevada in 1931. Las Vegas has since become the center of this multimillion dollar industry.

Major industry and infrastructure
- ✈ aerospace
- 🚗 car manufacture
- defense
- 🎬 movie industry
- $ finance
- food processing
- gambling
- hi-tech industry
- mining
- pharmaceuticals
- research & development
- textiles
- tourism
- major towns
- international airports
- major roads
- major industrial areas

TRANSPORTATION NETWORK
- 211,459 miles (338,334 km)
- 2,944 miles (4,710 km)
- 7,872 miles (12,595 km)
- 190 miles (306 km)

In California, the motor vehicle is a vital part of daily life, and an extensive freeway system runs throughout the state, which has a greater per capita car ownership than anywhere else in the world.

The Landscape

The broad Central Valley divides California's coastal mountains from the Sierra Nevada. The San Andreas Fault, running beneath much of the state, is the site of frequent earth tremors and sometimes more serious earthquakes. East of the Sierra Nevada, the landscape is characterized by the basin and range topography with stony deserts and many salt lakes.

Rising molten rock causes stretching of the Earth's crust

Extensive cracking (faulting) uplifted a series of ridges

As ridges are eroded they fill intervening valleys with sediments

Molten rock (magma) welling up to form a dome in the Earth's interior, causes the brittle surface rocks to stretch and crack. Some areas were uplifted to form mountains (ranges), while others sunk to form flat valleys (basins).

The General Sherman sequoia tree in Sequoia National Park is 3000 years old and at 275 ft (84 m) is one of the largest living things on earth.

Most of California's agriculture is confined to the fertile and extensively irrigated Central Valley, running between the Coast Ranges and the Sierra Nevada. It incorporates the San Joaquin and Sacramento valleys.

The dramatic granitic rock formations of Half Dome and El Capitan, and the verdant coniferous forests, attract millions of visitors annually to Yosemite National Park in the Sierra Nevada.

The Great Basin dominates most of Nevada's topography containing large open basins, punctuated by eroded features such as *buttes* and *mesas*. River flow tends to be seasonal, dependent upon spring showers and winter snow melt.

Sierra Nevada

Wheeler Peak is home to some of the world's oldest trees, bristlecone pines, which live for up to 5,000 years.

When the Hoover Dam across the Colorado River was completed in 1936, it created Lake Mead, one of the largest artificial lakes in the world, extending for 115 miles (285 km) upstream.

The San Andreas Fault is a transverse fault which extends for 650 miles (1,050 km) through California. Major earthquakes occur when the land either side of the fault moves at different rates. San Francisco was devastated by an earthquake in 1906.

Death Valley

The sparsely populated Mojave Desert receives less than 8 inches (200 mm) of rainfall a year. It is used extensively for testing weapons and other military purposes.

Amargosa Desert

Named by migrating settlers in 1849, Death Valley is the driest, hottest place in North America, as well as being the lowest point on land in the western hemisphere, at 282 ft (86 m) below sea level.

The Salton Sea was created accidentally between 1905 and 1907 when an irrigation channel from the Colorado River broke out of its banks and formed this salty 300 sq mile (777 sq km), landlocked lake.

The Sierra Nevada create a "rainshadow," preventing rain from reaching much of Nevada. Pacific air masses, passing over the mountains, are stripped of their moisture.

Using the Land

California is the leading agricultural producer in the US, although low rainfall makes irrigation essential. The long growing season and abundant sunshine allow many crops to be grown in the fertile Central Valley including grapes, citrus fruits, vegetables, and cotton. Almost 17 million acres (6.8 million hectares) of California's forests are used commercially. Nevada's arid climate and poor soil are largely unsuitable for agriculture; 85% of its land is state owned and large areas are used for underground testing of nuclear weapons.

Land use and agricultural distribution
- cattle
- citrus fruits
- fruit
- irrigation
- timber
- vineyards
- major towns
- pasture
- cropland
- forest
- desert

Without considerable irrigation, this fertile valley at Palm Springs would still be part of the Sonoran Desert. California's farmers account for about 80% of the state's total water usage.

THE URBAN/RURAL POPULATION DIVIDE

urban 92%   rural 8%

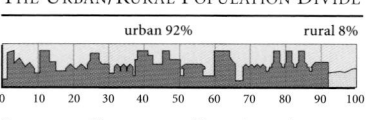

0 10 20 30 40 50 60 70 80 90 100

POPULATION DENSITY	TOTAL LAND AREA
126 people per sq mile (49 people per sq km)	269,233 sq miles (697,286 sq km)

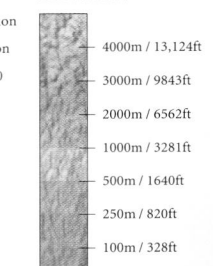

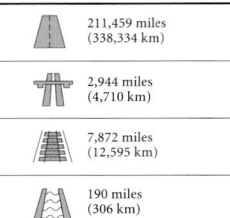

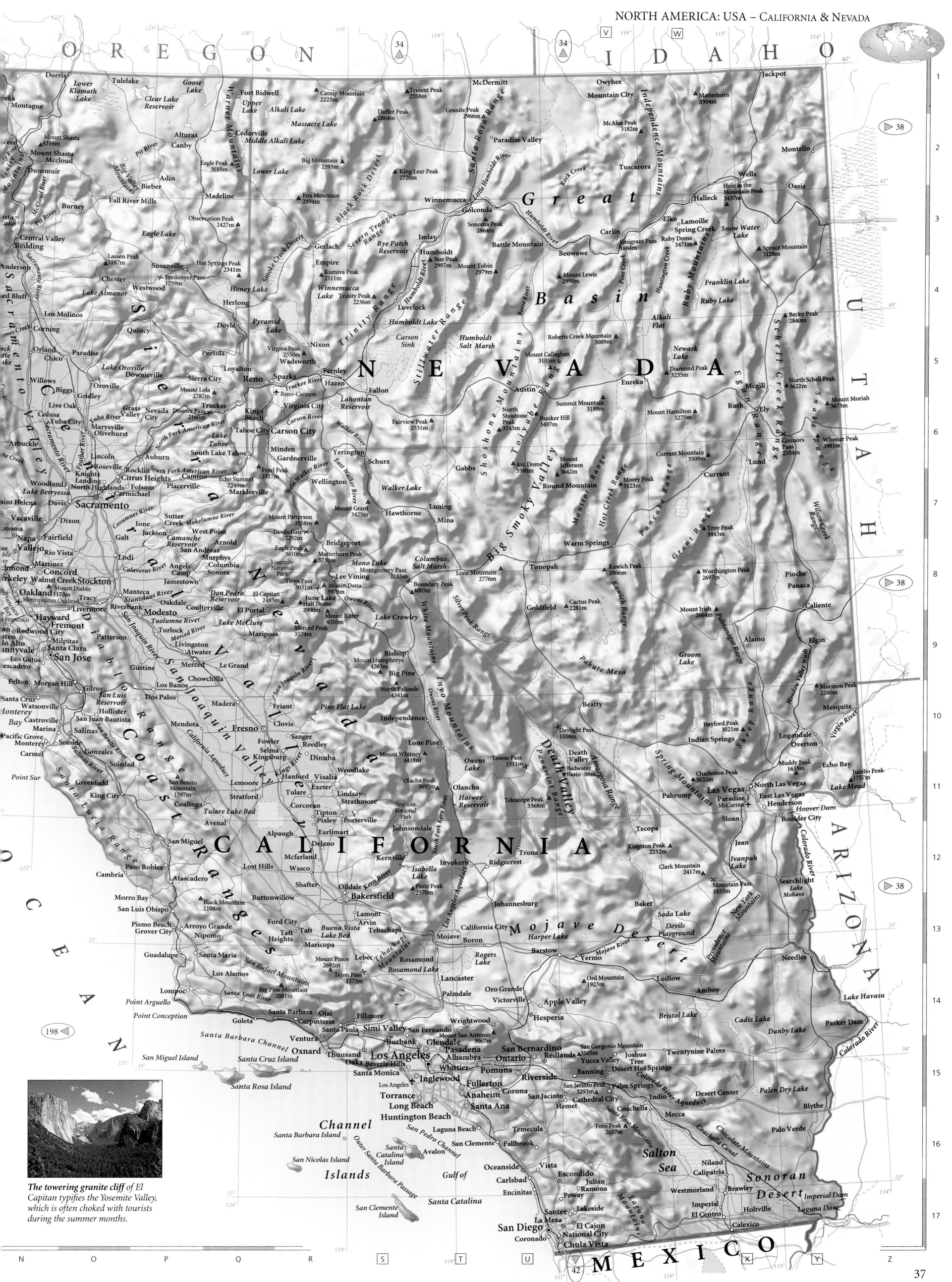

The towering granite cliff of El Capitan typifies the Yosemite Valley, which is often choked with tourists during the summer months.

USA: SOUTH MOUNTAIN STATES

Arizona, Colorado, New Mexico, Utah

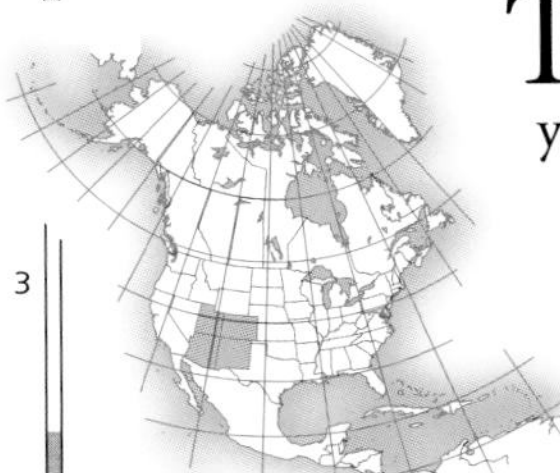

THIS ARID REGION, CHARACTERIZED BY EXPANSIVE PLATEAUS and spectacular canyons is home to several distinct peoples. The ruins of cliff dwellings built a thousand years ago by the Anasazi people still exist today, and native Americans own one-third of the land in Arizona. Spanish and Mexican conquest and settlement left a Hispanic presence which is strongest in New Mexico. The Mormons, who came to the Great Salt Lake seeking religious freedom in 1847, were among the earliest Anglo-American settlers and now make up over 70% of Utah's population. The region's mineral wealth drove rapid development in the 20th century, yet the constraints of a fragile environment, including widespread water shortages, may limit prospects for growth.

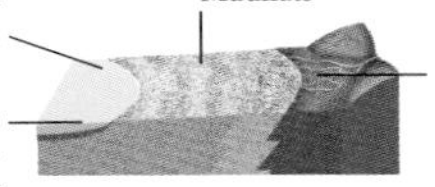

When water evaporates it leaves a salt pan

Mudflats

Lake is fed by seasonal snow melt

Water level of lake varies according to quantity of run-off received from snow melt

The Great Salt Lake is an ephemeral lake; it can remain dry for extended periods, leaving a pan of evaporated mineral salts in its center.

THE LANDSCAPE

THE ARID, ROCKY EXPANSE of the Colorado Plateau is dissected by immense canyons of the Colorado River. Desert lies to the north and south and branches of the Rocky Mountains run east and west. The Great Salt Lake and Desert lie within the Great Basin, a barren region of parallel mountain ranges that extends into Arizona.

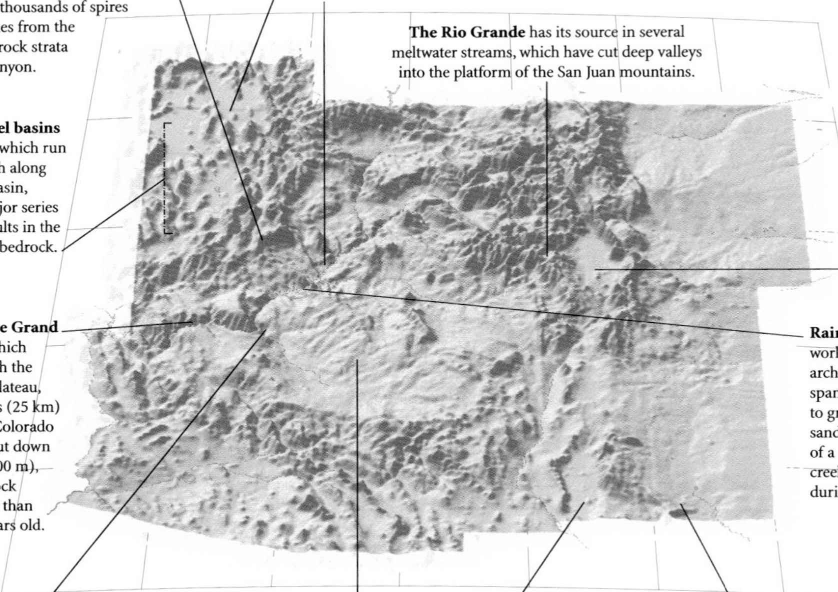

Over 13 million years of weathering has created thousands of spires and pinnacles from the alternating rock strata of Bryce Canyon.

Lake Powell

The Rio Grande has its source in several meltwater streams, which have cut deep valleys into the platform of the San Juan mountains.

The parallel basins and ridges, which run north–south along the Great Basin, reflect a major series of block-faults in the underlying bedrock.

Sand dunes, 600 ft (180 m) high, have been deposited in San Luis Valley, by winds funneled through the San Juan and Sangre de Cristo mountains in the Rockies.

Parts of the Grand Canyon, which cuts through the Colorado Plateau, are 16 miles (25 km) wide. The Colorado River has cut down 6262 ft (2000 m), exposing rock strata more than 2 billion years old.

Rainbow Bridge is the world's largest natural arch. The 309 ft (94 m) span probably began to grow when the sandstone spur of a meandering creek was breached during a flash flood.

The striking colour effects seen in the Painted Desert come from minerals such as gypsum and haematite, combined with ambient heat and dust.

Petrified Forest

Shifting gypsum sands produce a constantly changing land surface, overwhelming plants and any other obstacles in Tularosa Valley.

Carlsbad Caverns

In the arid landscape of Petrified Forest National Park, the grain of prehistoric trees has been preserved as a fossil imprint in the rocks. The bog-preserved trees were gradually turned to stone by seeping mineral-rich water.

The intricate stalactites of Carlsbad Caverns have grown with the seepage of calcium-rich water over the last 100,000 years. The huge caves are home to around 100,000 Mexican freetail bats.

TRANSPORTATION & INDUSTRY

NEW INDUSTRIES HAVE HELPED reduce the region's dependence on the extraction of minerals and fossil fuels. Precision manufacture has grown rapidly, particularly in Arizona and Colorado. Salt Lake City and Denver are well-established financial centers and New Mexico, the main US producer of uranium, is a prominent region for nuclear research. Colorado is the most important US center for winter sports.

TRANSPORTATION NETWORK

232,434 miles (373,986 km)	4,059 miles (6,515 km)
8,627 miles (13,881 km)	none

The Colorado Rockies are crossed by 32 mountain passes, some as high as 12,183 ft (3,713 m). The Eisenhower Tunnel west of Denver carries Interstate Highway 70 straight through the Continental Divide.

Major industry and infrastructure
- chemicals
- coal
- defense
- finance
- food processing
- hi-tech industry
- oil & gas
- mining
- research & development
- winter sports
- major towns
- international airports
- major roads
- major industrial areas

Glen Canyon Dam on the Colorado river was completed in 1964. it provides hydroelectric power and irrigation water as part of a long-term federal project to harness the river.

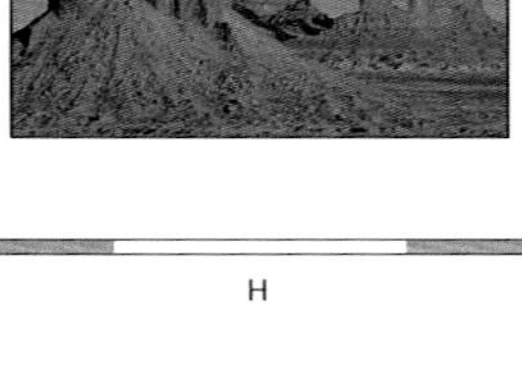

The flat tablelands (mesas), and the isolated pinnacles (buttes) which rise from the floor of Monument Valley are the resistant remnants of an earlier land surface, gradually cut back by erosion under arid conditions.

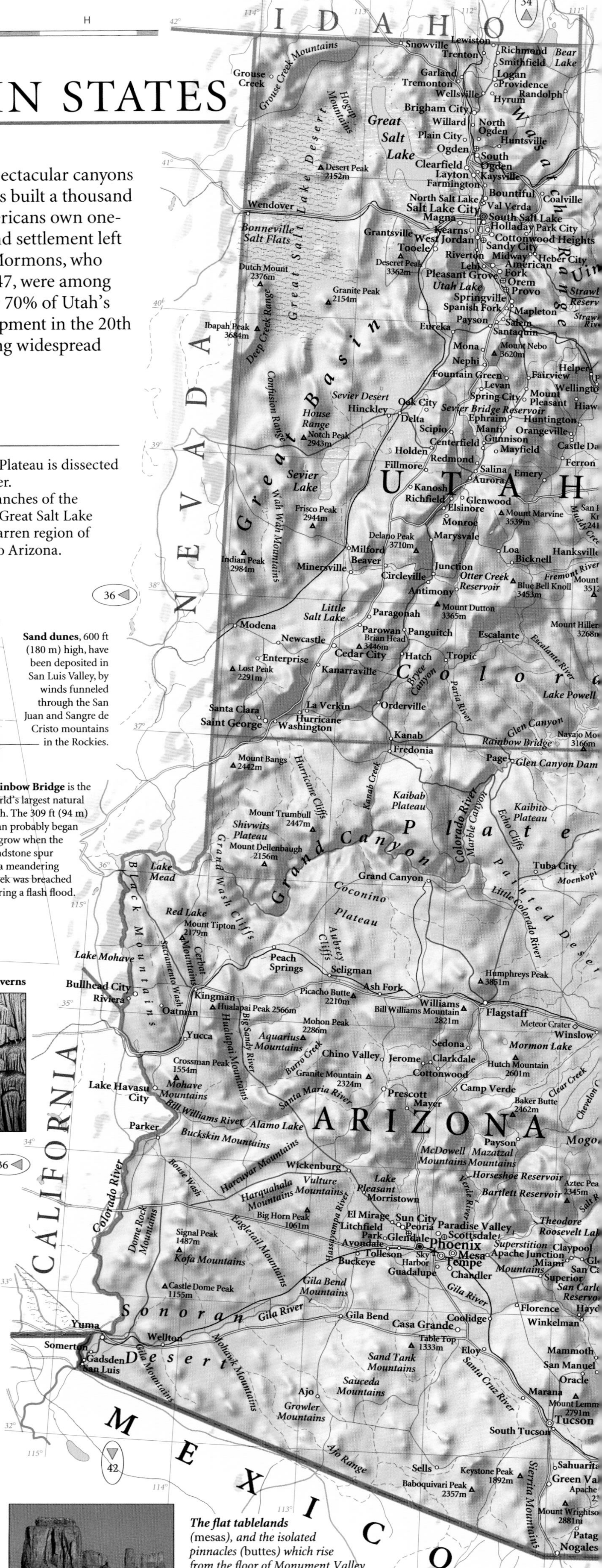

The Bonneville Salt Flats are in the Great Salt Lake. Sodium chloride (salt), magnesium, and other minerals are commercially extracted from these flats.

SCALE 1:3,500,000
(projection: Lambert Conformal Conic)

Km
Miles

MAP KEY

POPULATION

- 500,000 to 1 million
- 100,000 to 500,000
- 50,000 to 100,000
- 10,000 to 50,000
- below 10,000

ELEVATION

- 4000m / 13124ft
- 3000m / 9843ft
- 2000m / 6562ft
- 1000m / 3281ft
- 500m / 1640ft
- 250m / 820ft
- 100m / 328ft
- sea level

A glacially-eroded valley in Rocky Mountain National Park, Colorado. There are 1,500 peaks exceeding 10,000 ft (3,000 m) within the state, six times the number of major mountains found in the Swiss Alps.

USING THE LAND

LIVESTOCK, PARTICULARLY cattle-ranching, is the main source of agricultural income. The region has a long growing season and areas of rich soil, but depends heavily on water for irrigation. Crops include corn and wheat in eastern areas, and chili peppers, fruit, and cotton aided by additional irrigation.

Land use and agricultural distribution

- cattle
- cereals
- cotton
- fruit
- irrigation
- major towns
- pasture
- cropland
- forest
- desert

Cattle-ranching was introduced to New Mexico via Texas in the 19th century, and has become the principal agricultural land use across this region.

THE URBAN/RURAL POPULATION DIVIDE

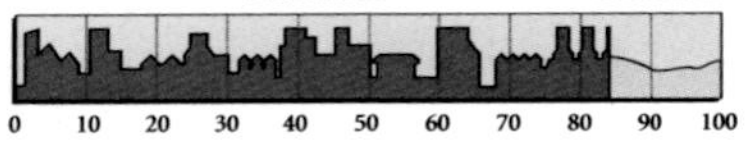

84% urban   16% rural

POPULATION DENSITY	TOTAL LAND AREA
11 people per sq mile (29 people per sq km)	424,738 sq miles (1,100,028 sq km)

WYOMING
NEBRASKA
KANSAS
COLORADO
OKLAHOMA
NEW MEXICO
TEXAS
MEXICO

USA: HAWAI'I

THE 122 ISLANDS of the Hawaiian archipelago – which are part of Polynesia – are the peaks of the world's largest volcanoes. They rise approximately 6 miles (9.7 km) from the floor of the Pacific Ocean. The largest, the island of Hawai'i, remains highly active. Hawai'i became the US's 50th state in 1959. A tradition of receiving immigrant workers is reflected in the islands' ethnic diversity, with peoples drawn from around the rim of the Pacific. Only 2% of the current population are native Polynesians.

The island of Moloka'i is formed from volcanic rock. Mature sand dunes cover the rocks in coastal areas.

TRANSPORTATION & INDUSTRY

TOURISM DOMINATES the economy, with over half of the population employed in services. The naval base at Pearl Harbor is also a major source of employment. Industry is concentrated on the island of O'ahu and relies mostly on imported materials, while agricultural produce is processed locally.

Major industry and infrastructure
- food processing
- military base
- textiles
- tourism
- major towns
- international airports
- major roads
- major industrial areas

TRANSPORTATION NETWORK

4,102 miles (6,600 km)	43 miles (69 km)
none	none

Hawai'i relies on ocean-surface transportation. Honolulu is the main focus of this network, bringing foreign trade and the markets of mainland US to Hawai'i's outer islands.

Haleakala's extinct volcanic crater is the world's largest. The giant caldera, containing many secondary cones, is 2,000 ft (600 m) deep and 20 miles (32 km) in circumference.

MAP KEY

POPULATION
- ◉ 100,000 to 500,000
- ⊕ 50,000 to 100,000
- ○ 10,000 to 50,000
- ○ below 10,000

ELEVATION
- 4000m / 13,124ft
- 3000m / 9843ft
- 2000m / 6562ft
- 1000m / 3281ft
- 500m / 1640ft
- 250m / 820ft
- 100m / 328ft
- sea level

SCALE 1:3,500,000
(projection: Lambert Conformal Conic)

USING THE LAND AND SEA

THE VOLCANIC SOILS are extremely fertile and the climate hot and humid on the lower slopes, supporting large commercial plantations growing sugar cane, bananas, pineapples, and other tropical fruit, as well as nursery plants and flowers. Some land is given to pasture, particularly for beef and dairy cattle.

Land use and agricultural distribution
- cattle
- fishing
- fruit
- sugar cane
- major towns
- pasture
- cropland
- forest
- mountain region

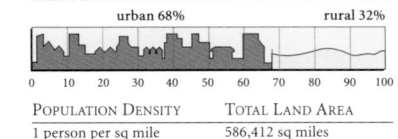
The island of Kaua'i is one of the wettest places in the world, receiving some 450 inches (11,500 mm) of rain a year.

USING THE LAND AND SEA

THE ICE-FREE COASTLINE of Alaska provides access to salmon fisheries and more than 5.5 million acres (2.2 million ha) of forest. Most of Alaska is uncultivable, and around 90% of food is imported. Barley, hay, and hothouse products are grown around Anchorage, where dairy farming is also concentrated.

THE URBAN/RURAL POPULATION DIVIDE

urban 68% rural 32%

POPULATION DENSITY	TOTAL LAND AREA
1 person per sq mile (0.4 people per sq km)	586,412 sq miles (1,518,800 sq km)

A raft of timber from the Tongass forest is hauled by a tug, bound for the pulp mills of the Alaskan coast between Juneau and Ketchikan.

THE URBAN/RURAL POPULATION DIVIDE

urban 89% rural 11%

POPULATION DENSITY	TOTAL LAND AREA
183 people per sq mile (71 people per sq km)	6,423 sq miles (16,636 sq km)

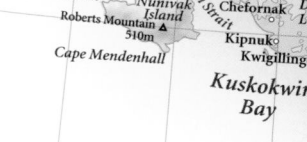

Hawaiian Islands map labels

Ni'ihau, Kaua'i, O'ahu, Honolulu, Moloka'i, Lāna'i, Kaho'olawe, Maui, Hawai'i, Hilo

PACIFIC OCEAN

Lehua Island, Kaulakahi Channel, Nohili Point, Hanalei, Kilauea, Anahola, Kekaha, Kapa'a, Kahala Point, Kii Landing, Lihu'e, Kaua'i, Ni'ihau, Waimea, 'Ele'ele, Koloa, Makahū'ena Point, Kawaihoa Point, Pu'uwai

Kaua'i Channel

Kahuku Point, Kahuku, Lā'ie, Hau'ula, Ka'a'awa, Ka'ena Point, Waimea, Waialua, Wahiawa, Pearl City, Mōkapu Point, Kāne'ohe, Makaha, Wai'anae, Waimānalo Beach, Wai'anae, Nānākuli, Honolulu, Diamond Head, Makakilo City, Ewa Beach, Pearl Harbor, O'ahu, Ilio Point

Kaiwi Channel, Kalaupapa, Kaunakakai, Cape Hālawa, Moloka'i, Kualapuu, Lā'au Point, Kalohi Channel, Nākālele Point, Pailolo Channel, Lāna'i, Lāna'i City, Wailuku, Lahaina, Pā'ia, Kailua, Kahului, Maui, Pukalani, Haleakala, Hāna, Kīhei, Haleakala (Red Hill) 3055m

Kaho'olawe, 'Alenuihāhā Channel, Cape Hanamanioa, Maui, Molokini Channel

'Upolu Point, Hāwī, Hālawa, Honoka'a, Laupāhoehoe, Waimea, Mauna Kea 4205m, Wailea, Honomū, Papa'ikou, Hilo, Keāhole Point, Kalaoa, Kailua-Kona, Hawai'i, Mountain View, Kea'au, Captain Cook, Kealakekua, Mauna Loa 4169m, Kīlauea Caldera, Cape Kumukahi, Pāhoa, Pāhala, Apua Point, Kaunā Point, Nā'ālehu, Ka Lae (South Point)

HAWAI'I

PACIFIC OCEAN

199

Bering Sea / Alaska section

CHUKCHI SEA

RUSSIAN FEDERATION

Arctic Circle

Cape Lisburne, Wevok, Point Hope, Kivalina, Shishmaref, Kotzebue Sound, Cape Espenberg, Kukpuk River, Little Diomede Island, Kougarok Mountain 875m, Cape Wales, Brooks Mountain, Brevig Mission, Cape Prince of Wales, Port Clarence, Teller, Council, Cape Douglas, Cape Rodney, Nome, Cape Nome, Solomon

BERING STRAIT

Bering Strait

Northwest Cape, Gambell, Savoonga, Saint Lawrence Island, Camp Kulowiye, Northeast Cape, Southwest Cape, Southeast Cape, Norton Sound

Pastol Bay, Kotlik, Hamilton, Emmonak, Alakanuk, Sheldons Point, Mountain Village, Scammon Bay, Hooper Bay, Chevak, Newtok, Aropuk Lake, Hazen Bay, Tununak, Toksook Bay, Nightmute, Mekoryuk, Nunivak Island, Chefornak, Roberts Mountain 510m, Kipnuk, Kwigillingok

Hall Island, Glory of Russia Cape, Saint Matthew Island, Upright Cape, Pinnacle Island, Cape Mohican, Cape Mendenhall

Kuskokwim Bay

BERING SEA

Saint Paul Island, Saint Paul, Pribilof Islands, Saint George Island, Saint George

125 ◄

199 ◄

125 ◄

Aleutian Islands section

MAP KEY

POPULATION
- ◉ 100,000 to 500,000
- ⊕ 50,000 to 100,000
- ○ 10,000 to 50,000
- ○ below 10,000

ELEVATION
- 4000m / 13,124ft
- 3000m / 9843ft
- 2000m / 6562ft
- 1000m / 3281ft
- 500m / 1640ft
- 250m / 820ft
- 100m / 328ft
- sea level

SCALE 1:8,000,000
(projection: Lambert Conformal Conic)

Cape Wrangell, Near Islands, Attu Island, Attu, Shemya Island, Agattu Strait, Agattu Island, Kruglof Point, Cape Sabak, Buldir Island, Kiska Island, Vega Point, Rat Islands, Segula Island, Little Sitkin Island, Amchitka Pass, Amchitka Island, Delarof Islands, Rat Island, Tanaga Pass, Tanaga Island, Tanaga Volcano 1806m, Cape Sasmik, Kanaga Island, Kanaga Volcano, Kagalaska Island, Adak, Andreanof Islands, Great Sitkin Island, Atka Island, Atka, Finger Pass, Amlia Island, Seguam Island, Seguam Pass, Amukta Pass, Amukta Island, Islands of Four Mountains, Herbert Island, Carlisle Island, Yunaska Island, Chuginadak Island, Nikolski, Fox Islands, Umnak Island, Makushin Volcano 2036m, Unalaska Island, Akutan, Akutan Island, Avatanak Island, Dutch Harbor, Krenitzin Islands, Sanak Island, Tigalda Island, Unimak Island, Pogromni Volcano 2002m, Shishaldin Volcano 2857m, Unimak Pass, Pauloff Harbor, False Pass, Cold Bay, Amak Island

ALEUTIAN ISLANDS

PACIFIC OCEAN

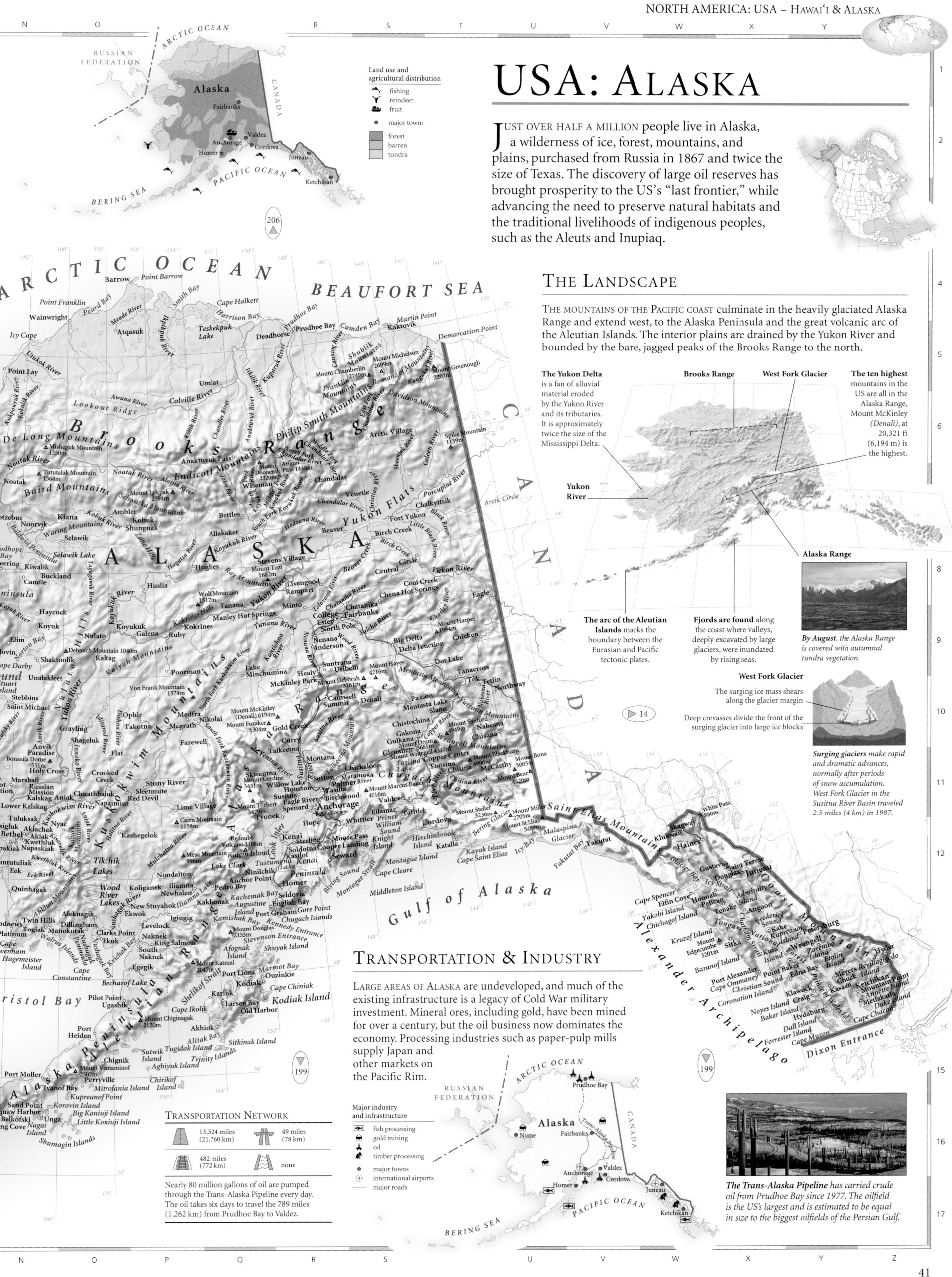

USA: ALASKA

JUST OVER HALF A MILLION people live in Alaska, a wilderness of ice, forest, mountains, and plains, purchased from Russia in 1867 and twice the size of Texas. The discovery of large oil reserves has brought prosperity to the US's "last frontier," while advancing the need to preserve natural habitats and the traditional livelihoods of indigenous peoples, such as the Aleuts and Inupiaq.

THE LANDSCAPE

THE MOUNTAINS OF THE PACIFIC COAST culminate in the heavily glaciated Alaska Range and extend west, to the Alaska Peninsula and the great volcanic arc of the Aleutian Islands. The interior plains are drained by the Yukon River and bounded by the bare, jagged peaks of the Brooks Range to the north.

The Yukon Delta is a fan of alluvial material eroded by the Yukon River and its tributaries. It is approximately twice the size of the Mississippi Delta.

Yukon River

Brooks Range

West Fork Glacier

The ten highest mountains in the US are all in the Alaska Range, Mount McKinley (Denali), at 20,321 ft (6,194 m) is the highest.

Alaska Range

The arc of the Aleutian Islands marks the boundary between the Eurasian and Pacific tectonic plates.

Fjords are found along the coast where valleys, deeply excavated by large glaciers, were inundated by rising seas.

By August, the Alaska Range is covered with autumnal tundra vegetation.

West Fork Glacier

The surging ice mass shears along the glacier margin

Deep crevasses divide the front of the surging glacier into large ice blocks

Surging glaciers make rapid and dramatic advances, normally after periods of snow accumulation. West Fork Glacier in the Susitna River Basin traveled 2.5 miles (4 km) in 1987.

TRANSPORTATION & INDUSTRY

LARGE AREAS OF ALASKA are undeveloped, and much of the existing infrastructure is a legacy of Cold War military investment. Mineral ores, including gold, have been mined for over a century, but the oil business now dominates the economy. Processing industries such as paper-pulp mills supply Japan and other markets on the Pacific Rim.

TRANSPORTATION NETWORK

13,524 miles (21,760 km)		49 miles (78 km)	
482 miles (772 km)		none	

Nearly 80 million gallons of oil are pumped through the Trans-Alaska Pipeline every day. The oil takes six days to travel the 789 miles (1,262 km) from Prudhoe Bay to Valdez.

Major industry and infrastructure
- fish processing
- gold mining
- oil
- timber processing
- major towns
- international airports
- major roads

The Trans-Alaska Pipeline has carried crude oil from Prudhoe Bay since 1977. The oilfield is the US's largest and is estimated to be equal in size to the biggest oilfields of the Persian Gulf.

Land use and agricultural distribution
- fishing
- reindeer
- fruit
- major towns
- forest
- barren
- tundra

A B C D E F G H I J K L M

SCALE 1:6,250,000
(projection: Lambert Conformal Conic)

Km
0 25 50 100 150 200
Miles
0 25 50 100 150 200

The rugged, desert landscape of the Sierra Madre del Sur is a product of complex tectonic processes, where the fold mountains in western North America, running north–south, meet the Caribbean mountain arc which runs east–west.

MEXICO

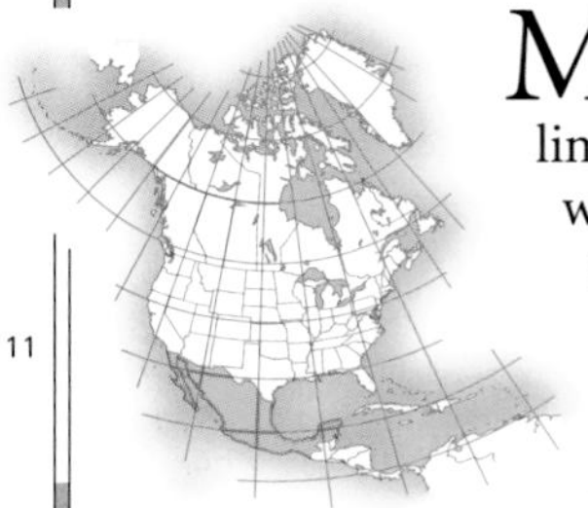

MEXICO POSSESSES rich mineral resources, limited agricultural land and the world's largest and fastest growing Spanish-speaking population. Most Mexicans are *mestizo*, although Amerindian communities still exist in the south, 400 years after Spain destroyed the Aztec empire at its height. Much of the arid north is sparsely inhabited, while Mexico City is becoming the world's most populous city. Conflict with the US has long overshadowed Mexico's development, but the North American Free Trade Agreement offers the chance for a more benign relationship, which may help to offset Mexico's problems of hyperinflation, foreign debt, unequal wealth distribution and political instability.

Wave action has cut steep cliffs into the igneous rocks of Isla Cedros, off the Pacific coast of Baja California. The island is home to sea lions, reptiles, and deer.

USING THE LAND AND SEA

CORN OCCUPIES much of the cultivated area. Commercial plantations of coffee, sugar, vanilla, and cotton are found along the Gulf coastal plain and in irrigated parts of the arid north, which is otherwise used for extensive ranching. Fishing is important, particularly shellfish for export. A soaring population has created the need for grain imports since 1980.

THE URBAN/RURAL POPULATION DIVIDE

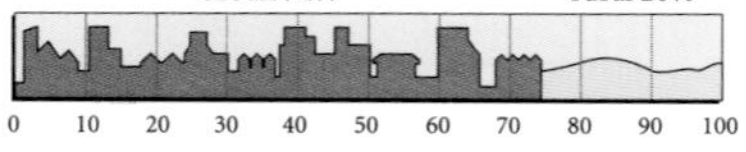

urban 74%   rural 26%

0 10 20 30 40 50 60 70 80 90 100

POPULATION DENSITY	TOTAL LAND AREA
130 people per sq mile	755,865 sq miles
(50 people per sq km)	(1,958,200 sq km)

Land use and agricultural distribution

- cattle
- coffee
- corn (maize)
- cotton
- fishing
- shellfish
- sugar cane
- timber
- vanilla

- capital cities
- major towns

- pasture
- cropland
- forest
- desert

Coffee beans spread out to dry in the sun. Coffee, grown mainly on the Gulf coastal plain, is Mexico's most valuable export crop.

MEXICO: ADMINISTRATIVE REGIONS

Ⓓ DISTRITO FEDERAL

MAP KEY

POPULATION
- ■ above 5 million
- ■ 1 million to 5 million
- ◉ 500,000 to 1 million
- ◎ 100,000 to 500,000
- ⊕ 50,000 to 100,000
- ○ 10,000 to 50,000
- ∘ below 10,000

ELEVATION
- 4000m / 13,124ft
- 3000m / 9843ft
- 2000m / 6562ft
- 1000m / 3281ft
- 500m / 1640ft
- 250m / 820ft
- 100m / 328ft
- sea level

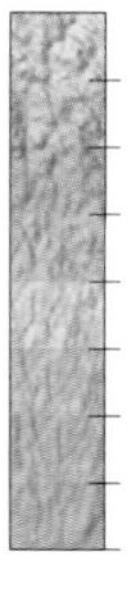

THE LANDSCAPE

THE GREAT CENTRAL PLATEAU rises gently southward from the Rio Grande, isolated from the coastal plains by the Sierra Madre Oriental and Occidental. The two ranges converge from east and west respectively, culminating in high volcanic peaks around Mexico City. Further ranges of the Sierra Madre rise to the south of the Balsas Basin, skirted by the low-lying Isthmus of Tehuantepec (*Istmo de Tehuantepec*) and Yucatan Peninsula.

The long, narrow, extremely arid peninsula of Baja (lower) California is an elongated granite block, separated from the mainland by the flooded rift valley of the Gulf of California (*Golfo de California*).

Wave action has constructed sand bars which shelter lagoons along the shore of the Gulf coastal plain.

Sierra Madre Oriental

Rio Grande

The dormant cone of Volcán Pico de Orizaba is, at 18,700 ft (5,700 m), the highest peak in Mexico. In North America, only Mount McKinley and Mount Logan are taller.

Tropical rain forest abounds in the Yucatan Peninsula, a broad, low limestone shelf. Rivers are rare due to the porous nature of limestone, so the forest is mostly fed by streams and underground water.

The heavily-forested Isthmus of Tehuantepec (*Istmo de Tehuantepec*) is a *graben;* a low-lying trough created by downward movement of the bedrock between two fault lines.

Formation of the Gulf of California

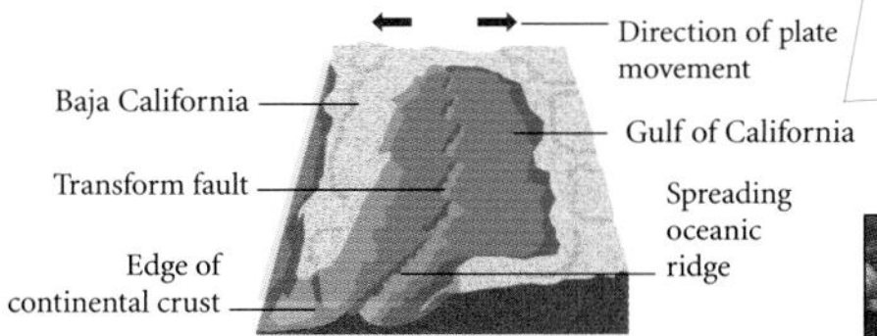

Direction of plate movement
Gulf of California
Baja California
Transform fault
Spreading oceanic ridge
Edge of continental crust

The Gulf of California (*Golfo de California*) began to open out about 4 million years ago as a result of rifting and plate displacement along transform faults.

Sierra Madre Occidental

Popocatépetl is a dormant volcano, part of the Pacific "Rim of Fire." The crater is over half a mile (1 km) wide.

Río Balsas

Popocatépetl

The unstable, earthquake-prone, upland basin around Mexico City was once a region of shallow lakes. Flood control measures and domestic consumption over the last four centuries have caused the virtual disappearance of this surface water.

The highlands of Chiapas are a series of *horsts,* blocks of land thrust upward between two fault lines. Volcanic cones have developed where lava has flowed out from the faults.

TRANSPORTATION & INDUSTRY

OIL AND GAS ON THE GULF COAST are Mexico's main sources of export income. Metal mining has declined but the country remains a leading global producer of silver. Manufacturing is heavily concentrated around the metropolitan area of Mexico City, while the duty-free movement of goods in the US border region, under the *Maquiladora* (twin plant) scheme, has created new hi-tech and service growth centers.

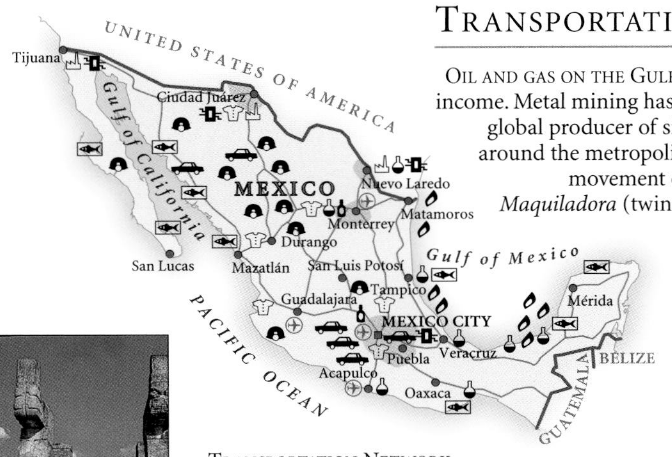

Major industry and infrastructure

- brewing
- car manufacture
- chemicals
- electronics
- fish processing
- maquiladoras
- mining
- oil & gas
- textiles
- capital cities
- major towns
- international airports
- major roads
- major industrial areas

TRANSPORTATION NETWORK

55,021 miles (88,601 km)

4,186 miles (6,740 km)

16,422 miles (26,445 km)

1,801 miles (2,900 km)

Fast, modern highways or *autopistas* now link Mexico City with Toluca, Puebla and other satellite cities, yet distant centers like Chihuahua are still served by narrow roads and an outdated railroad network.

A stone figure reclines by the Temple of Warriors, within the Mayan city of Chichén-Itzá. The Maya civilization flourished across the Yucatan Peninsula between 200 and 900 AD.

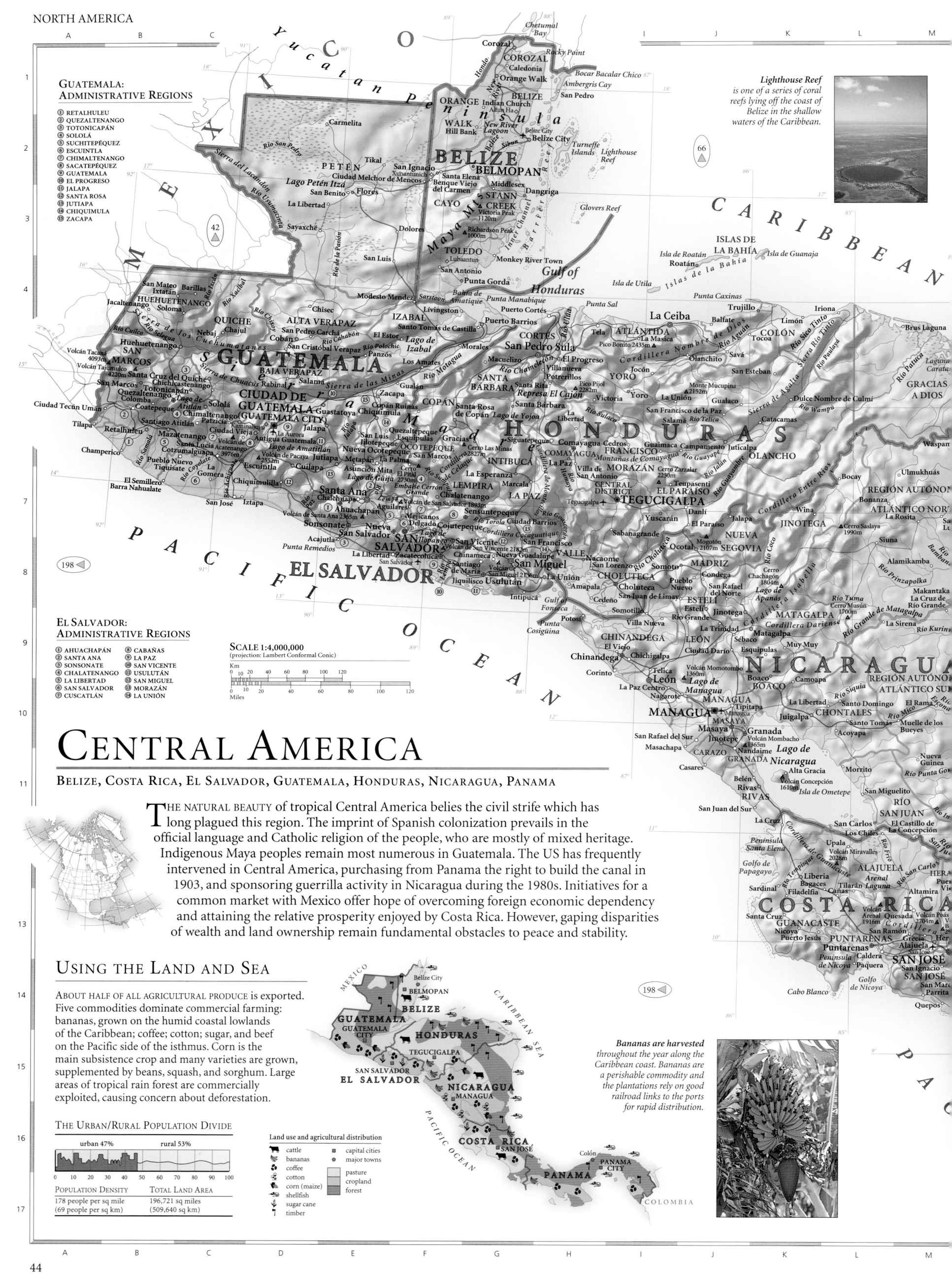

GUATEMALA: ADMINISTRATIVE REGIONS

① RETALHULEU
② QUEZALTENANGO
③ TOTONICAPÁN
④ SOLOLÁ
⑤ SUCHITEPÉQUEZ
⑥ ESCUINTLA
⑦ CHIMALTENANGO
⑧ SACATEPÉQUEZ
⑨ GUATEMALA
⑩ EL PROGRESO
⑪ JALAPA
⑫ SANTA ROSA
⑬ JUTIAPA
⑭ CHIQUIMULA
⑮ ZACAPA

Lighthouse Reef is one of a series of coral reefs lying off the coast of Belize in the shallow waters of the Caribbean.

EL SALVADOR: ADMINISTRATIVE REGIONS

① AHUACHAPÁN
② SANTA ANA
③ SONSONATE
④ CHALATENANGO
⑤ LA LIBERTAD
⑥ SAN SALVADOR
⑦ CUSCATLÁN
⑧ CABAÑAS
⑨ LA PAZ
⑩ SAN VICENTE
⑪ USULUTÁN
⑫ SAN MIGUEL
⑬ MORAZÁN
⑭ LA UNIÓN

SCALE 1:4,000,000
(projection: Lambert Conformal Conic)

Km
0 10 20   40   60   80   100   120

Miles
0 10 20   40   60   80   100   120

CENTRAL AMERICA

BELIZE, COSTA RICA, EL SALVADOR, GUATEMALA, HONDURAS, NICARAGUA, PANAMA

THE NATURAL BEAUTY of tropical Central America belies the civil strife which has long plagued this region. The imprint of Spanish colonization prevails in the official language and Catholic religion of the people, who are mostly of mixed heritage. Indigenous Maya peoples remain most numerous in Guatemala. The US has frequently intervened in Central America, purchasing from Panama the right to build the canal in 1903, and sponsoring guerrilla activity in Nicaragua during the 1980s. Initiatives for a common market with Mexico offer hope of overcoming foreign economic dependency and attaining the relative prosperity enjoyed by Costa Rica. However, gaping disparities of wealth and land ownership remain fundamental obstacles to peace and stability.

USING THE LAND AND SEA

ABOUT HALF OF ALL AGRICULTURAL PRODUCE is exported. Five commodities dominate commercial farming: bananas, grown on the humid coastal lowlands of the Caribbean; coffee; cotton; sugar; and beef on the Pacific side of the isthmus. Corn is the main subsistence crop and many varieties are grown, supplemented by beans, squash, and sorghum. Large areas of tropical rain forest are commercially exploited, causing concern about deforestation.

THE URBAN/RURAL POPULATION DIVIDE

urban 47%   rural 53%

0   10   20   30   40   50   60   70   80   90   100

POPULATION DENSITY
178 people per sq mile
(69 people per sq km)

TOTAL LAND AREA
196,721 sq miles
(509,640 sq km)

Land use and agricultural distribution

cattle
bananas
coffee
cotton
corn (maize)
shellfish
sugar cane
timber

■ capital cities
● major towns

pasture
cropland
forest

Bananas are harvested throughout the year along the Caribbean coast. Bananas are a perishable commodity and the plantations rely on good railroad links to the ports for rapid distribution.

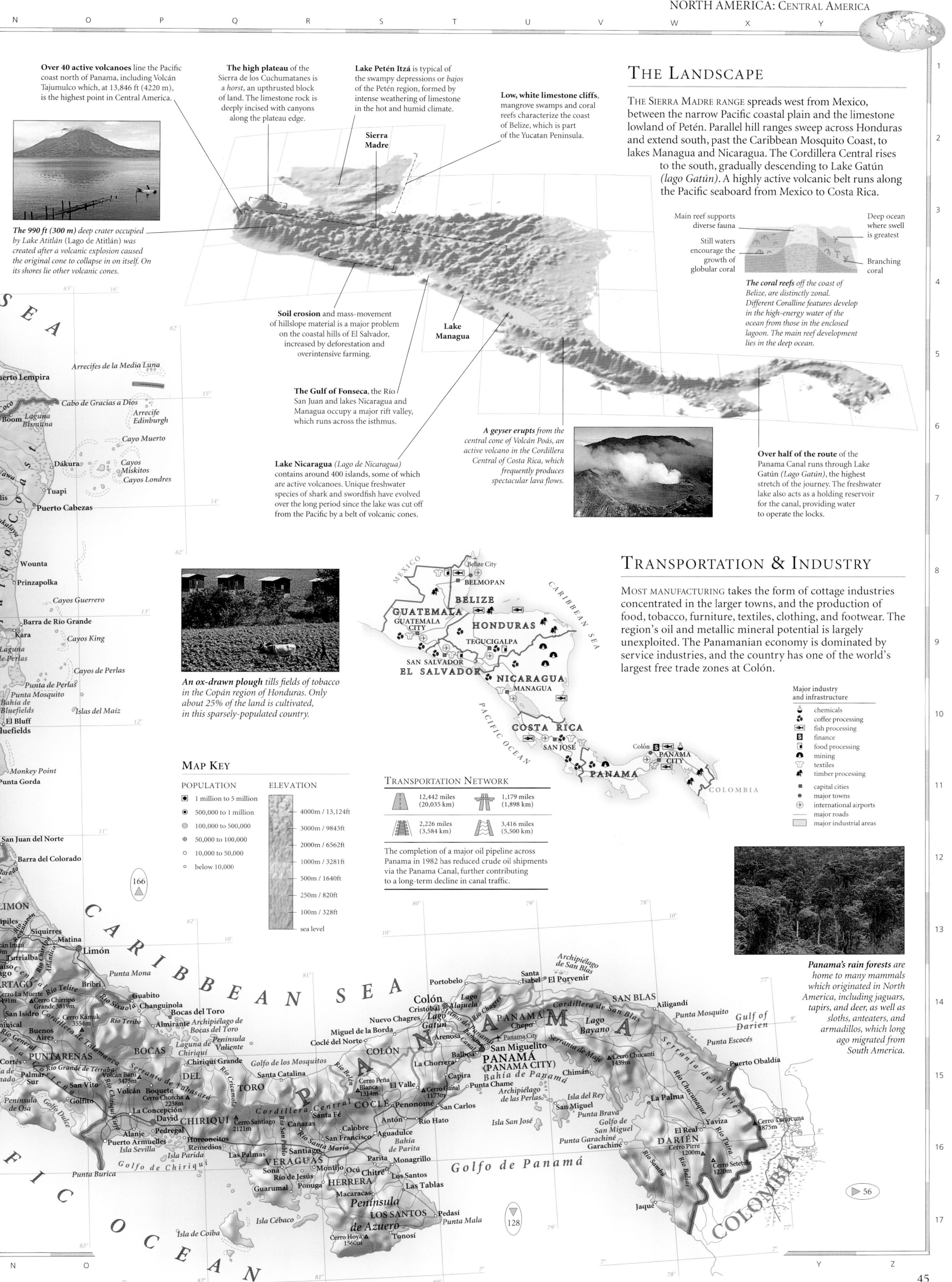

Over 40 active volcanoes line the Pacific coast north of Panama, including Volcán Tajumulco which, at 13,846 ft (4220 m), is the highest point in Central America.

The 990 ft (300 m) deep crater occupied by Lake Atitlán (Lago de Atitlán) was created after a volcanic explosion caused the original cone to collapse in on itself. On its shores lie other volcanic cones.

The high plateau of the Sierra de los Cuchumatanes is a *horst*, an upthrusted block of land. The limestone rock is deeply incised with canyons along the plateau edge.

Lake Petén Itzá is typical of the swampy depressions or *bajos* of the Petén region, formed by intense weathering of limestone in the hot and humid climate.

Low, white limestone cliffs, mangrove swamps and coral reefs characterize the coast of Belize, which is part of the Yucatan Peninsula.

Sierra Madre

Lake Managua

Soil erosion and mass-movement of hillslope material is a major problem on the coastal hills of El Salvador, increased by deforestation and overintensive farming.

The Gulf of Fonseca, the Río San Juan and lakes Nicaragua and Managua occupy a major rift valley, which runs across the isthmus.

Lake Nicaragua (Lago de Nicaragua) contains around 400 islands, some of which are active volcanoes. Unique freshwater species of shark and swordfish have evolved over the long period since the lake was cut off from the Pacific by a belt of volcanic cones.

A geyser erupts from the central cone of Volcán Poás, an active volcano in the Cordillera Central of Costa Rica, which frequently produces spectacular lava flows.

THE LANDSCAPE

THE SIERRA MADRE RANGE spreads west from Mexico, between the narrow Pacific coastal plain and the limestone lowland of Petén. Parallel hill ranges sweep across Honduras and extend south, past the Caribbean Mosquito Coast, to lakes Managua and Nicaragua. The Cordillera Central rises to the south, gradually descending to Lake Gatún (lago Gatún). A highly active volcanic belt runs along the Pacific seaboard from Mexico to Costa Rica.

Main reef supports diverse fauna

Deep ocean where swell is greatest

Still waters encourage the growth of globular coral

Branching coral

The coral reefs off the coast of Belize, are distinctly zonal. Different Coralline features develop in the high-energy water of the ocean from those in the enclosed lagoon. The main reef development lies in the deep ocean.

Over half of the route of the Panama Canal runs through Lake Gatún (Lago Gatún), the highest stretch of the journey. The freshwater lake also acts as a holding reservoir for the canal, providing water to operate the locks.

TRANSPORTATION & INDUSTRY

MOST MANUFACTURING takes the form of cottage industries concentrated in the larger towns, and the production of food, tobacco, furniture, textiles, clothing, and footwear. The region's oil and metallic mineral potential is largely unexploited. The Panamanian economy is dominated by service industries, and the country has one of the world's largest free trade zones at Colón.

An ox-drawn plough tills fields of tobacco in the Copán region of Honduras. Only about 25% of the land is cultivated, in this sparsely-populated country.

MAP KEY

POPULATION
- ▣ 1 million to 5 million
- ◉ 500,000 to 1 million
- ◎ 100,000 to 500,000
- ⊕ 50,000 to 100,000
- ○ 10,000 to 50,000
- ○ below 10,000

ELEVATION
- 4000m / 13,124ft
- 3000m / 9843ft
- 2000m / 6562ft
- 1000m / 3281ft
- 500m / 1640ft
- 250m / 820ft
- 100m / 328ft
- sea level

TRANSPORTATION NETWORK

| 12,442 miles (20,035 km) | 1,179 miles (1,898 km) |
| 2,226 miles (3,584 km) | 3,416 miles (5,500 km) |

The completion of a major oil pipeline across Panama in 1982 has reduced crude oil shipments via the Panama Canal, further contributing to a long-term decline in canal traffic.

Major industry and infrastructure
- chemicals
- coffee processing
- fish processing
- finance
- food processing
- mining
- textiles
- timber processing
- ■ capital cities
- ■ major towns
- ⊕ international airports
- — major roads
- major industrial areas

Panama's rain forests are home to many mammals which originated in North America, including jaguars, tapirs, and deer, as well as sloths, anteaters, and armadillos, which long ago migrated from South America.

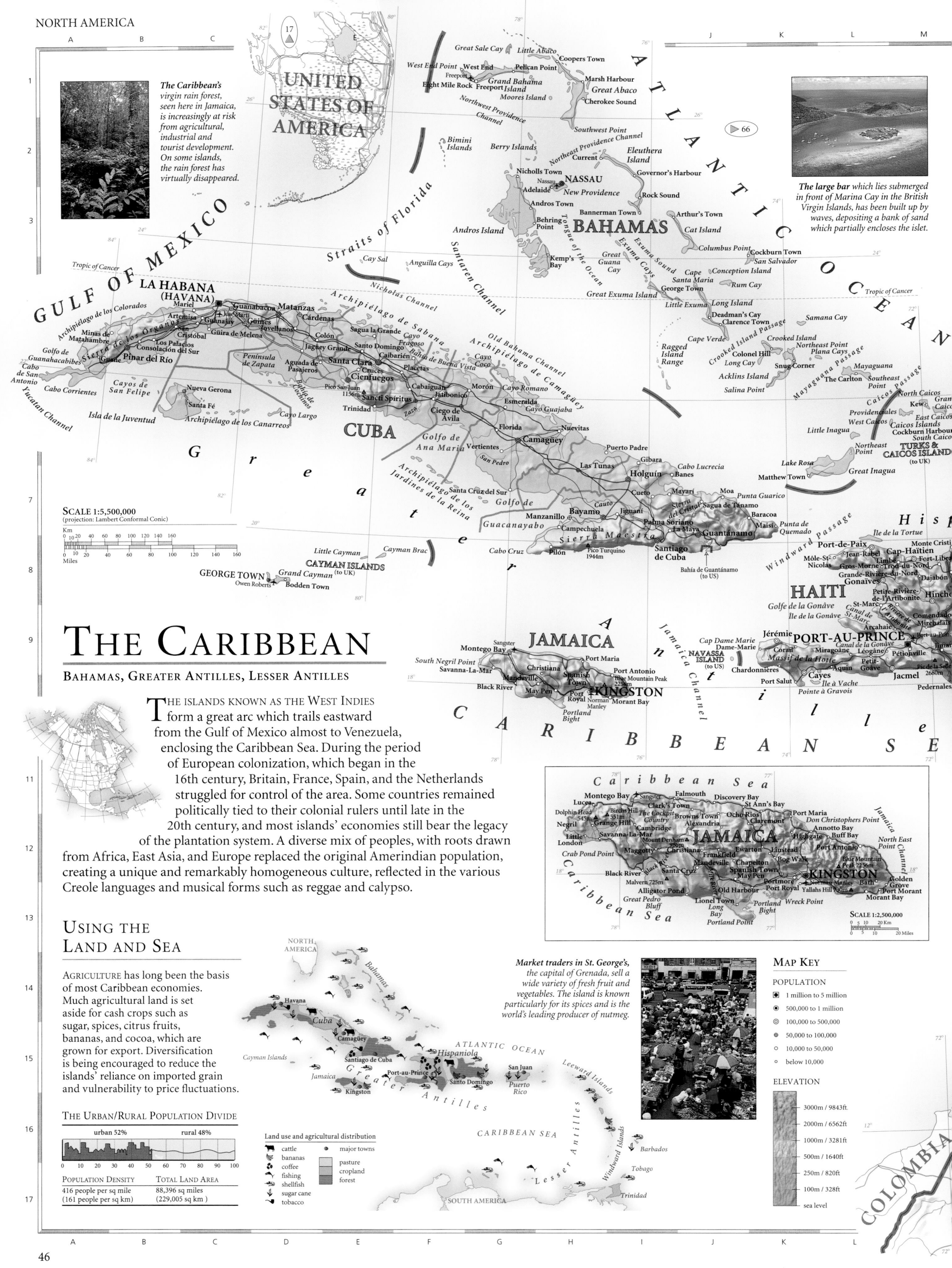

The Caribbean's virgin rain forest, seen here in Jamaica, is increasingly at risk from agricultural, industrial and tourist development. On some islands, the rain forest has virtually disappeared.

The large bar which lies submerged in front of Marina Cay in the British Virgin Islands, has been built up by waves, depositing a bank of sand which partially encloses the islet.

SCALE 1:5,500,000
(projection: Lambert Conformal Conic)

THE CARIBBEAN

BAHAMAS, GREATER ANTILLES, LESSER ANTILLES

THE ISLANDS KNOWN AS THE WEST INDIES form a great arc which trails eastward from the Gulf of Mexico almost to Venezuela, enclosing the Caribbean Sea. During the period of European colonization, which began in the 16th century, Britain, France, Spain, and the Netherlands struggled for control of the area. Some countries remained politically tied to their colonial rulers until late in the 20th century, and most islands' economies still bear the legacy of the plantation system. A diverse mix of peoples, with roots drawn from Africa, East Asia, and Europe replaced the original Amerindian population, creating a unique and remarkably homogeneous culture, reflected in the various Creole languages and musical forms such as reggae and calypso.

USING THE LAND AND SEA

AGRICULTURE has long been the basis of most Caribbean economies. Much agricultural land is set aside for cash crops such as sugar, spices, citrus fruits, bananas, and cocoa, which are grown for export. Diversification is being encouraged to reduce the islands' reliance on imported grain and vulnerability to price fluctuations.

THE URBAN/RURAL POPULATION DIVIDE

urban 52%	rural 48%

POPULATION DENSITY	TOTAL LAND AREA
416 people per sq mile (161 people per sq km)	88,396 sq miles (229,005 sq km)

Market traders in St. George's, the capital of Grenada, sell a wide variety of fresh fruit and vegetables. The island is known particularly for its spices and is the world's leading producer of nutmeg.

Land use and agricultural distribution

- cattle
- bananas
- coffee
- fishing
- shellfish
- sugar cane
- tobacco
- major towns
- pasture
- cropland
- forest

SCALE 1:2,500,000

MAP KEY

POPULATION
- 1 million to 5 million
- 500,000 to 1 million
- 100,000 to 500,000
- 50,000 to 100,000
- 10,000 to 50,000
- below 10,000

ELEVATION
- 3000m / 9843ft.
- 2000m / 6562ft.
- 1000m / 3281ft.
- 500m / 1640ft.
- 250m / 820ft.
- 100m / 328ft.
- sea level

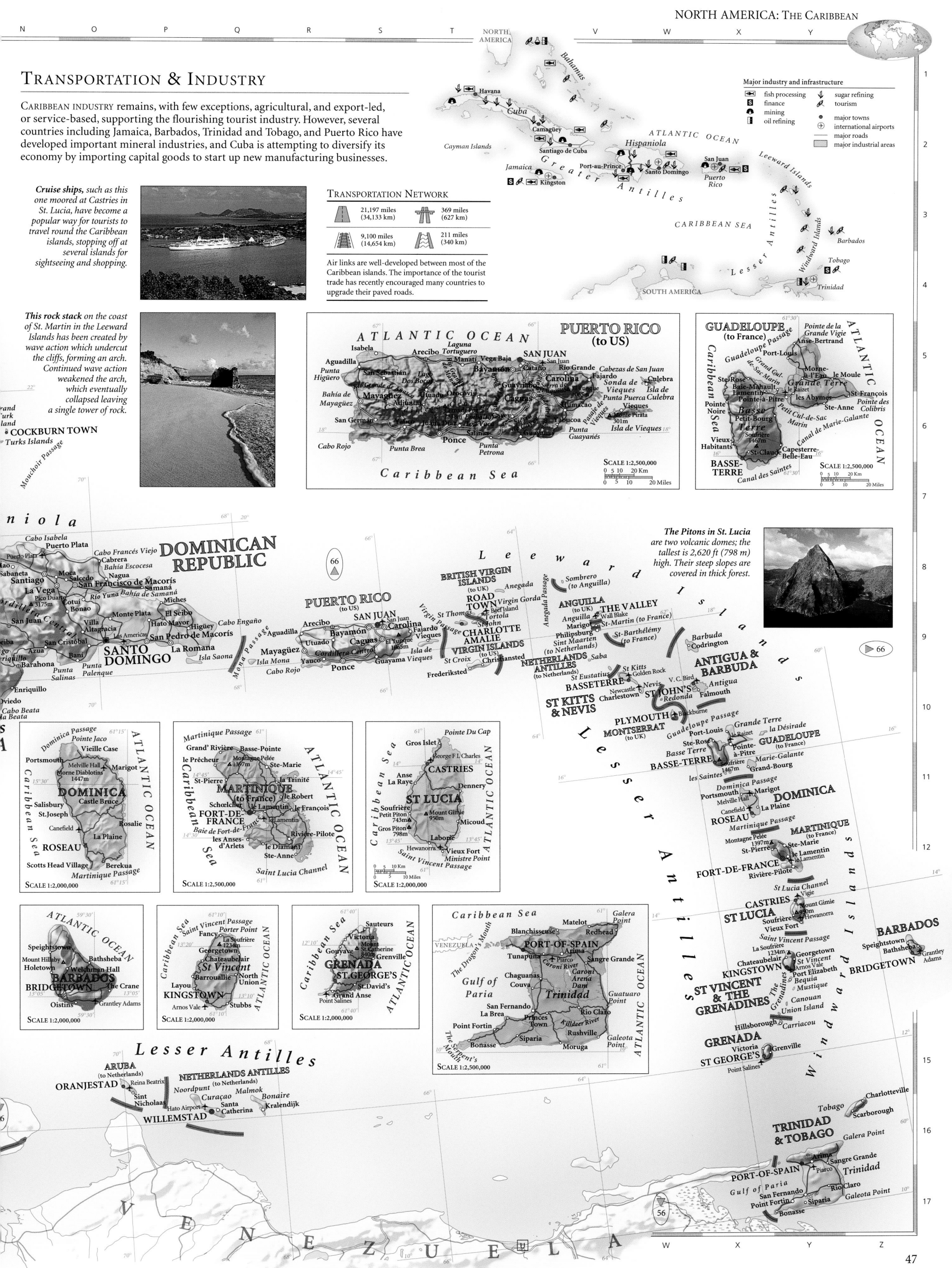

TRANSPORTATION & INDUSTRY

CARIBBEAN INDUSTRY remains, with few exceptions, agricultural, and export-led, or service-based, supporting the flourishing tourist industry. However, several countries including Jamaica, Barbados, Trinidad and Tobago, and Puerto Rico have developed important mineral industries, and Cuba is attempting to diversify its economy by importing capital goods to start up new manufacturing businesses.

Cruise ships, such as this one moored at Castries in St. Lucia, have become a popular way for tourists to travel round the Caribbean islands, stopping off at several islands for sightseeing and shopping.

This rock stack on the coast of St. Martin in the Leeward Islands has been created by wave action which undercut the cliffs, forming an arch. Continued wave action weakened the arch, which eventually collapsed leaving a single tower of rock.

Major industry and infrastructure

- fish processing
- finance
- mining
- oil refining
- sugar refining
- tourism
- major towns
- international airports
- major roads
- major industrial areas

TRANSPORTATION NETWORK

21,197 miles (34,133 km)

369 miles (627 km)

9,100 miles (14,654 km)

211 miles (340 km)

Air links are well-developed between most of the Caribbean islands. The importance of the tourist trade has recently encouraged many countries to upgrade their paved roads.

The Pitons in St. Lucia are two volcanic domes; the tallest is 2,620 ft (798 m) high. Their steep slopes are covered in thick forest.

SOUTH AMERICA

REACHING FROM THE HUMID TROPICS DOWN INTO THE COLD SOUTH ATLANTIC, SOUTH AMERICA HAS AN AREA OF 6,886,000 SQ MILES (17,835,000 SQ KM). THERE ARE 12 SEPARATE COUNTRIES, WITH THE LARGEST, BRAZIL, COVERING ALMOST HALF THE CONTINENT.

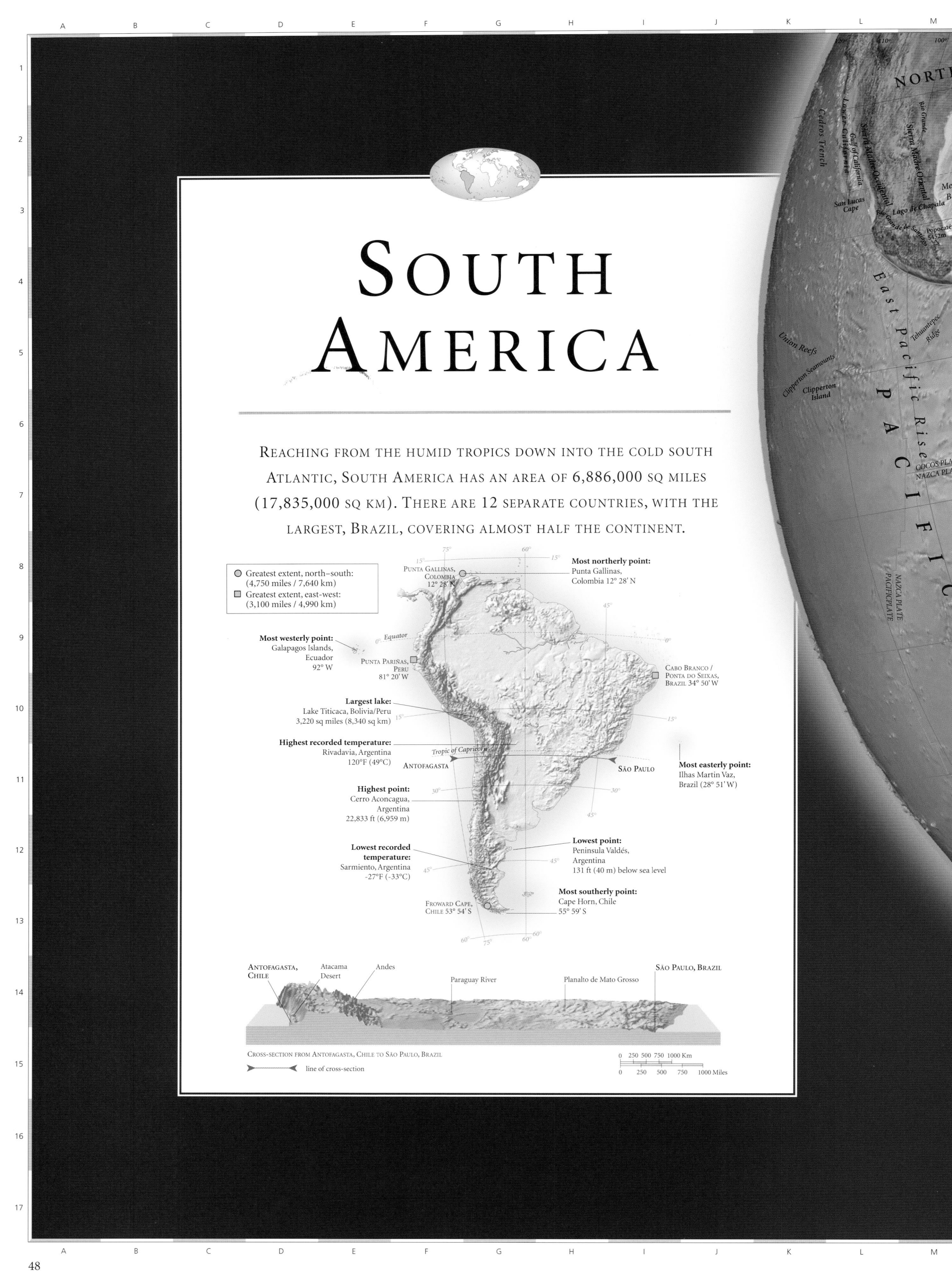

○ Greatest extent, north–south:
(4,750 miles / 7,640 km)
□ Greatest extent, east-west:
(3,100 miles / 4,990 km)

Most northerly point:
Punta Gallinas,
Colombia 12° 28' N

PUNTA GALLINAS,
COLOMBIA
12° 28' N

Most westerly point:
Galapagos Islands,
Ecuador
92° W

PUNTA PARIÑAS,
PERU
81° 20' W

CABO BRANCO /
PONTA DO SEIXAS,
BRAZIL 34° 50' W

Largest lake:
Lake Titicaca, Bolivia/Peru
3,220 sq miles (8,340 sq km)

Highest recorded temperature:
Rivadavia, Argentina
120°F (49°C)

ANTOFAGASTA

SÃO PAULO

Most easterly point:
Ilhas Martin Vaz,
Brazil (28° 51' W)

Highest point:
Cerro Aconcagua,
Argentina
22,833 ft (6,959 m)

Lowest point:
Peninsula Valdés,
Argentina
131 ft (40 m) below sea level

Lowest recorded temperature:
Sarmiento, Argentina
-27°F (-33°C)

Most southerly point:
Cape Horn, Chile
55° 59' S

FROWARD CAPE,
CHILE 53° 54' S

ANTOFAGASTA,
CHILE

Atacama
Desert

Andes

Paraguay River

Planalto de Mato Grosso

SÃO PAULO, BRAZIL

CROSS-SECTION FROM ANTOFAGASTA, CHILE TO SÃO PAULO, BRAZIL

▷──── line of cross-section

0   250 500 750 1000 Km

0   250   500   750   1000 Miles

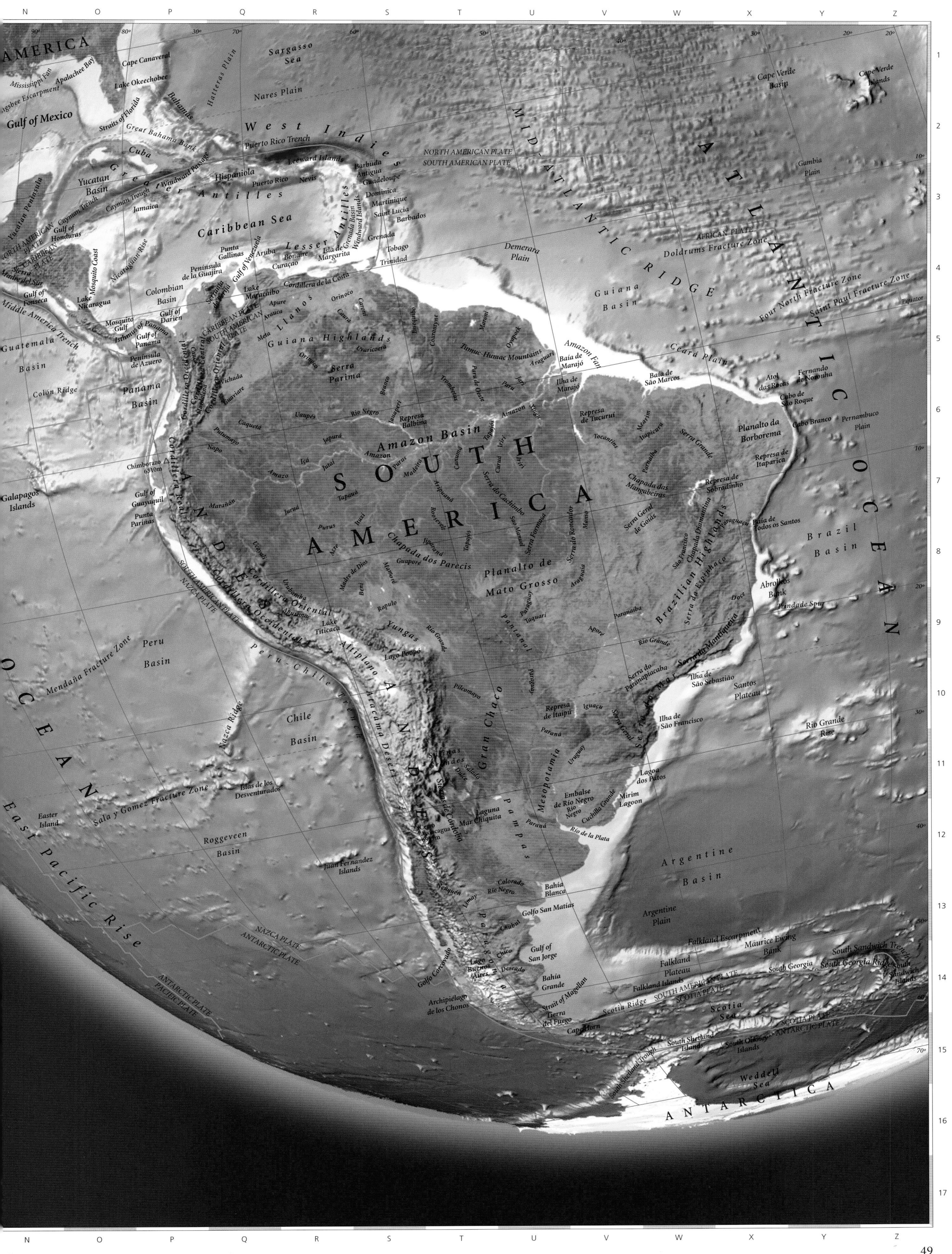

AMERICA

Cape Canaveral

Mississippi Fan

Apalachee Bay

Sigsbee Escarpment

Lake Okeechobee

Gulf of Mexico

Straits of Florida

Bahamas

Great Bahama Bank

Yucatan Peninsula

Cuba

Yucatan Basin

Cayman Trench

Gulf of Honduras

Jamaica

NORTH AMERICAN PLATE

SOUTH CARIBBEAN PLATE

Sierra Madre del Sur

Mosquito Coast

Nicaraguan Rise

Gulf of Fonseca

Lake Nicaragua

Mosquito Gulf

Gulf of Panama

Isthmus of Panama

Middle America Trench

Peninsula de Azuero

Guatemala Basin

Colón Ridge

Panama Basin

Galapagos Islands

Gulf of Guayaquil

Punta Pariñas

Chimborazo 6310m

Batteras Plain

Sargasso Sea

Nares Plain

West Indies

Puerto Rico Trench

Leeward Islands

Windward Passage

Hispaniola

Puerto Rico

Nevis

Greater Antilles

Cayman Trough

Caribbean Sea

Punta Gallinas

Peninsula de la Guajira

Bonaire

Aruba

Curaçao

Isla de Margarita

Barbuda

Antigua

Guadeloupe

Dominica

Martinique

Saint Lucia

Barbados

Lesser Antilles

Windward Islands

Grenada Basin

Grenada

Tobago

Trinidad

Gulf of Venezuela

Lake Maracaibo

Apure

Arauca

Meta

Llanos

Orinoco

Cordillera de la Costa

Caura

Cuchivero

Vichada

Guaviare

Uaupés

Putumayo

Napo

Caquetá

Rio Negro

Içá

Japurá

Jutaí

Juruá

Purus

Amazo

Tapauá

Iça

Marañón

Madre de Dios

Beni

Guaporé

Mamoré

Ucayali

Apurimac

Lago Titicaca

Altiplano

Lago Poopó

Pilcomayo

Cordillera Real

Cordillera Occidental

Cordillera Oriental

Cordillera Central

Cordillera Occidental

CARIBBEAN PLATE

SOUTH AMERICAN PLATE

SOUTH AMERICAN PLATE

NAZCA PLATE

Demerara Plain

Guiana Basin

Timuc-Humac Mountains

Amazon Fan

Baía de Marajó

Ilha de Marajó

Represa Balbina

Amazon Basin

Amazon

Represa de Tucuruí

Tocantins

Xingu

Tapajós

Trombetas

Pará de Oeste

Pará

Araguari

Araguaia

Jiparaná

Roosevelt

Chapada das Mangabeiras

Serra do Cachimbo

Serra Grande

Serra Geral de Goiás

Chapada dos Parecis

Planalto de Mato Grosso

Cuiabá

São Manuel

Serra Formosa

Serra Romador

Manso

Serra do Roncador

Paraguai

Taquari

Pantanal

Paraguay

São Francisco

Represa de Sobradinho

Represa de Itaparica

Planalto da Borborema

Chapada Diamantina

Brazilian Highlands

Serra de Espinhaço

Doce

Paranaíba

Apore

Rio Grande

Paranapanema

Serra do Paranapiacaba

Serra da Mantiqueira

Iguaçu

Paraná

Embalse de Río Negro

Río Negro

Cuchilla Grande

Lagoa dos Patos

Mirim Lagoon

Uruguay

Serra Geral

Ilha de São Sebastião

Ilha de São Francisco

Santos Plateau

Represa de Itaipú

Mesopotamia

Pampas

Río de la Plata

Mar Chiquita

Laguna Mar Chiquita

Salado

Colorado

Río Negro

Bahía Blanca

Golfo San Matías

Limay

Neuquén

Chubut

Patagonia

Gulf of San Jorge

Chico

Deseado

Desventuradas

Lago Buenos Aires

Golfo Coronado

Archipiélago de los Chonos

Strait of Magellan

Tierra del Fuego

Cape Horn

Bahía Grande

ANDES

ATLANTIC

MID-ATLANTIC RIDGE

NORTH AMERICAN PLATE

SOUTH AMERICAN PLATE

AFRICAN PLATE

Doldrums Fracture Zone

Four North Fracture Zone

Saint Paul Fracture Zone

Ceará Plain

Equator

Atol das Rocas

Fernando de Noronha

Cabo de São Roque

Cabo Branco

Pernambuco Plain

Cape Verde Basin

Cape Verde Islands

Gambia Plain

ATLANTIC OCEAN

Brazil Basin

Abrolhos Bank

Trindade Spur

Rio Grande Rise

Baía de São Marcos

Baía de Todos os Santos

Argentine Basin

Argentine Plain

Maurice Ewing Bank

Falkland Escarpment

Falkland Plateau

Falkland Islands

South Georgia

South Georgia Ridge

South Sandwich Trench

South Sandwich Islands

Scotia Ridge

SOUTH AMERICAN PLATE

SCOTIA PLATE

Scotia Sea

SCOTIA PLATE

ANTARCTIC PLATE

South Shetland Islands

South Orkney Islands

South Sandwich Trough

Weddell Sea

ANTARCTICA

SOUTH AMERICA

PERU-CHILE TRENCH

Peru Basin

Mendaña Fracture Zone

Nazca Ridge

Chile Basin

Sala y Gomez Fracture Zone

Easter Island

Roggeveen Basin

Juan Fernandez Islands

East Pacific Rise

OCEAN

NAZCA PLATE

ANTARCTIC PLATE

ANTARCTIC PLATE

PACIFIC PLATE

Atacama Desert

Yungas

Gran Chaco

Sierras Pampeanas

Sierra de Córdoba

Salado

A B C D E F G H I J K L M

PHYSICAL SOUTH AMERICA

THREE MAJOR PHYSIOGRAPHIC REGIONS characterize South America. The oldest, the ancient Brazilian Shield and the smaller Guyana and Patagonian shields, form the stable core of the continent. Stretching along the entire west coast are the younger Andean fold mountains with many summits rising to 20,000 ft (6,100 m). These two diverse regions are separated by a number of sedimentary basins carrying South America's large river systems to the sea. These include the massive Amazon Basin and the basin of the Gran Chaco.

THE AMAZON BASIN AND GUYANA SHIELD

THE RIVER AMAZON occupies a large depression in the Earth's crust, formed by the uplift of the Andes. It is covered by thick volcanic deposits and layers of alluvium – these have been laid down by the Amazon's many tributaries. To the north is the smaller Guyana Shield.

Headwaters of the Amazon rise in the Andes   Thick alluvium deposits   Mouths of the Amazon

A — — A

Section across northern South America showing Amazon Basin and its drainage pattern.

0   500   1000 Km
0   500   1000 Miles

SCALE 1:27,500,000
(projection: Lambert Azimuthal Equal Area)

Km
0 100 200   400   600   800
0 100   200   400   600   800
Miles

THE ANDEAN UPLANDS

THE ANDEAN UPLANDS run along the west coast of South America. They are being uplifted as the Nazca Plate is subducted beneath the South American Plate. They contain some of the world's largest volcanoes, such as Cotopaxi, and Lake Titicaca which occupies a dormant site. The far south has many large ice-sheets and a fragmented coastline.

Nazca Plate   South American Plate   Volcanic intrusions

B — — B

Cross-section through the Andes showing the subduction of the Nazca Plate beneath the South American Plate.

0   200   400 Km
0   200   400 Miles

MAP KEY

ELEVATION

6000m / 19,686ft
4000m / 13,124ft
3000m / 9843ft
2000m / 6562ft
1500m / 4922ft
1000m / 3281ft
500m / 1640ft
250m / 820ft
100m / 328ft
sea level

PLATE MARGINS
(for explanation see page xiv)

△▲ destructive

——— conservative

········· uncertain

——— physiographic regions

▶◀ line of cross-section

——— constructive

THE BRAZILIAN SHIELD AND GRAN CHACO

THE IMMENSE BRAZILIAN SHIELD underlies more than one-third of South America. It is pitted with numerous volcanic intrusions, and a large basaltic plateau exists between the Paraná River and the Atlantic Ocean. The flat Gran Chaco lies to the west of the shield, covered by sedimentary deposits eroded from the Andes, and transported by South America's mighty rivers.

Young, folded Andes Mountains   Volcanic intrusions   Major rivers drain to the south through the Gran Chaco   Ancient resistant shield

C — — C

Section across central South America showing the flat basin of the Gran Chaco and the ancient Brazilian Shield.

0   200   400 Km
0   200   400 Miles

CLIMATE

THE CLIMATE OF SOUTH AMERICA is influenced by three principal factors: the seasonal shift of high pressure air masses over the tropics, cold ocean currents along the western coast, affecting temperature and precipitation, and the mountain barrier produced by the Andes, which creates a rain shadow over much of the south.

Mild winters and cool summers typify the extensive Pampas grasslands of Argentina.

Chile's hyperarid Atacama Desert is renowned as one of the driest places on Earth.

Climate
- tundra
- cool continental
- warm humid
- semiarid
- arid
- humid equatorial
- tropical
- ☼ daily hours of sunshine, January
- ☼ daily hours of sunshine, July
- → cold wind

TEMPERATURE

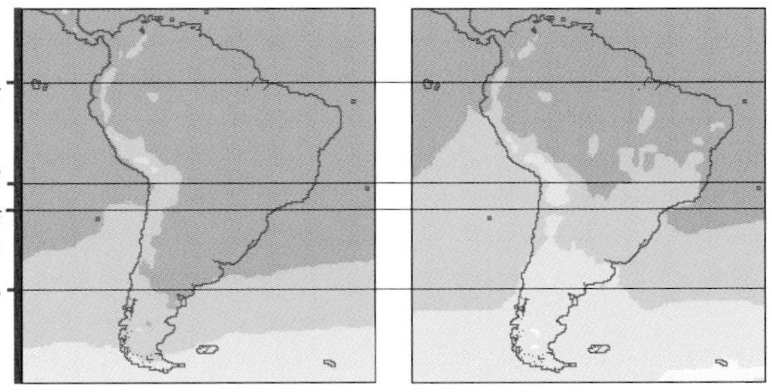

Average January temperature

Average July temperature

Temperature
- below -22°F (-30°C)
- -22 to -4°F (-30 to -20°C)
- -4 to 14°F (-20 to -10°C)
- 14 to 32°F (-10 to 0°C)
- 32 to 50°F (0 to 10°C)
- 50°F (10 to 20°C)
- 68 to 86°F (20 to 30°C)
- above 86°F (30°C)

RAINFALL

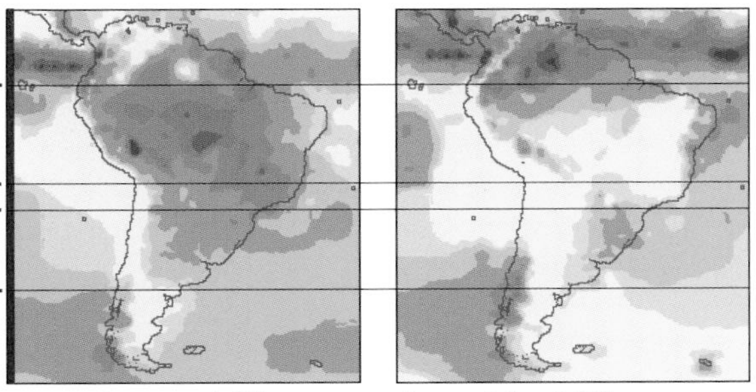

Average January rainfall

Average July rainfall

Rainfall
- 0–1 in (0–25 mm)
- 1–2 in (25–50 mm)
- 2–4 in (50–100 mm)
- 4–8 in (100–200 mm)
- 8–12 in (200–300 mm)
- 12–16 in (300–400 mm)
- 16–20 in (400–500 mm)
- more than 20 in (500 mm)

Tropical conditions are found across over half of South America. When both rainfall and temperatures are high, hot humid rain forests prevail.

SHAPING THE CONTINENT

SOUTH AMERICA'S ACTIVE TECTONIC BELT has been extensively folded over millions of years; landslides are still frequent in the mountains. The large river systems that erode the mountains flow across resistant shield areas, depositing sediment. Present-day glaciation affects the distinctive landscape of the far south.

MASS MOVEMENT

6 Debris slides are common in the highlands of South America (left). They occur where soil on a slope is saturated by rainwater and therefore less stable. The actual slides are often triggered by earthquakes.

Scarp face left after soil has moved to the base of the slope
Failure plane
Toe of debris slide

MASS MOVEMENT: A SECTION OF A DEBRIS SLIDE

CHEMICAL WEATHERING

1 Table mountains (left) are the eroded remnants of an ancient upland. As water percolates along cracks in these high, flat-topped mountains it forms intricate cave systems. Chemical weathering also isolates large blocks which then collapse, accumulating as rockfalls at the foot of scarp slopes.

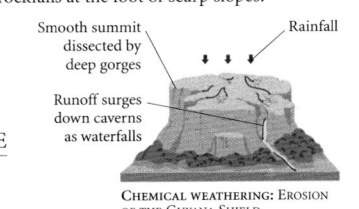

Smooth summit dissected by deep gorges
Rainfall
Runoff surges down caverns as waterfalls

CHEMICAL WEATHERING: EROSION OF THE GUYANA SHIELD

THE EVOLVING LANDSCAPE

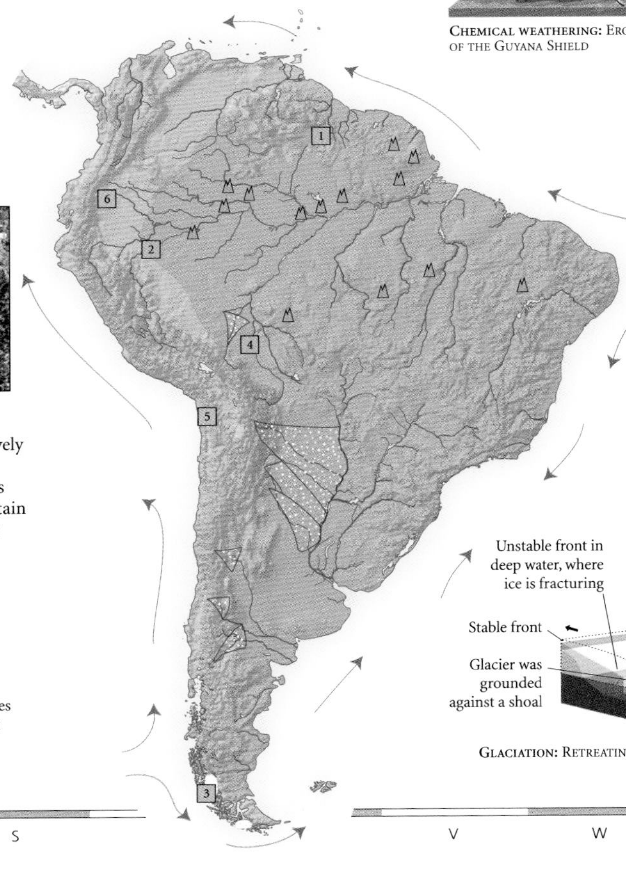

RIVER SYSTEMS

2 Along the Amazon (above) there is a great variation in rates of erosion. As the headwaters of the Amazon flow down from the Andes, they erode and transport vast quantities of sediment, and are known as whitewaters. Across the shield areas erosion rates are very low. These rivers, carrying rotting vegetation, are called blackwaters.

Whitewater river
Blackwater river
Little erosion in shield areas
Confluence of whitewater with blackwater

RIVER SYSTEMS: SUSPENDED SEDIMENTS IN THE AMAZON

Landscape
- uplifting land
- stable land
- sinking land
- glacier
- ≈ ocean current
- ◁ alluvial fan
- ⛰ inselberg
- — river

FOLDING

5 Folding occurs beneath the surface under high temperatures and pressures. Rocks become sufficiently malleable to flow and not fracture as tectonic plates collide. In the Valley of the Moon in Chile (above), anticlines (or upfolds) and synclines (or troughs) have been exploited by erosion.

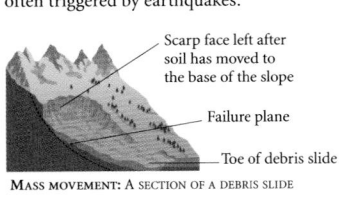

Fold axis
Anticline
Syncline
Fold axis

FOLDING: SYNCLINES AND ANTICLINES

DEPOSITION

4 Large alluvial fans are found extensively across South America (above). Confined mountain rivers, carrying large quantities of eroded material, emerge from a mountain gorge onto the plains, where they deposit their load in huge fans.

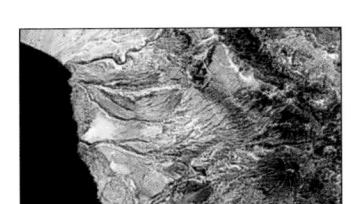

Mountain front
Subsequent fan
Confined stream in the mountains
Fan forms as stream emerges onto the plain

DEPOSITION: FORMATION OF AN ALLUVIAL FAN

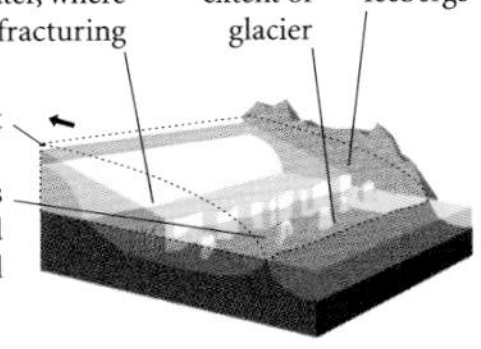

Unstable front in deep water, where ice is fracturing
Original extent of glacier
Icebergs
Stable front
Glacier was grounded against a shoal

GLACIATION: RETREATING GLACIER IN PATAGONIA

GLACIATION

3 As fjord glaciers in Patagonia (above) retreat, they become grounded on shoals. In deeper water the base of the glacier becomes unstable, and icebergs break off (calve) until the glacier snout grounds once more.

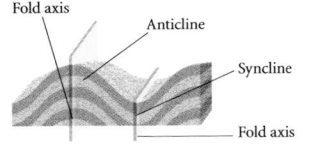
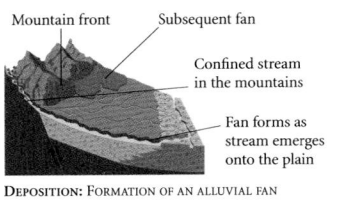
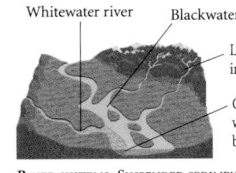

POLITICAL SOUTH AMERICA

MODERN SOUTH AMERICA'S POLITICAL BOUNDARIES have their origins in the territorial endeavors of explorers during the 16th century, who claimed almost the entire continent for Portugal and Spain. The Portuguese land in the east later evolved into the federal state of Brazil, while the Spanish vice-royalties eventually emerged as separate independent nation-states in the early 19th century. South America's growing population has become increasingly urbanized, with the growth of coastal cities into large conurbations like Rio de Janeiro and Buenos Aires. In Brazil, Argentina, Chile and Uruguay, a succession of military dictatorships has given way to fragile, but strengthening, democracies.

Europe retains a small foothold in South America. Kourou in French Guiana was the site chosen by the European Space Agency to launch the Ariane rocket. As a result of its status as a French overseas department, French Guiana is actually part of the European Union.

SCALE 1:21,500,000
(projection: Lambert Azimuthal Equal Area)

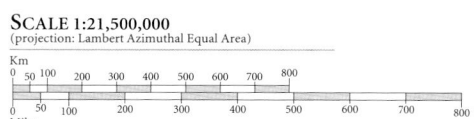

TRANSPORTATION

MOST MAJOR ROAD AND RAIL ROUTES are confined to the coastal regions by the forbidding natural barriers of the Andes Mountains and the Amazon Basin. Few major cross-continental routes exist, although Buenos Aires serves as a transportation center for the main rail links to La Paz and Valparaíso, while the construction of the Trans-Amazon and Pan-American Highways have made direct road travel possible from Recife to Lima and from Puerto Montt up the coast into central America. A new waterway project is proposed to transform the River Paraguay into a major shipping route, although it involves considerable wetland destruction.

South America's most extensive rail network is centered on the Argentinian capital, Buenos Aires. The construction of new rail lines ouward from this important port, allowed the colonization of the Pampas lands for agriculture.

LANGUAGES

PRIOR TO EUROPEAN EXPLORATION in the 16th century, a diverse range of indigenous languages were spoken across the continent. With the arrival of Iberian settlers, Spanish became the dominant language, with Portuguese spoken in Brazil, and Native American languages such as Quechua and Guaraní, becoming concentrated in the continental interior. Today this pattern persists, although successive European colonization has led to Dutch being spoken in Suriname, English in Guyana, and French in French Guiana, while in large urban areas, Japanese and Chinese are increasingly common.

Transportation

- —— major roads and highways
- —— major railroads
- —— international borders
- • transportation intersections
- ⊕ international airports
- ⊕ major ports

Language groups

- American Indian
- Germanic
- Romance

Chile's main port, Valparaíso, is a vital national shipping center, in addition to playing a key role in the growing trade with Pacific nations. The country's awkward, elongated shape means that sea transportation is frequently used for internal travel and communications in Chile.

Indigenous South American lifestyles have not been totally submerged by European cultures and languages. The continental interior, and particularly the Amazon Basin, is still home to many different ethnic peoples.

Lima's magnificent cathedral reflects South America's colonial past with its unmistakably Spanish style. In July 1821, Peru became the last Spanish colony on the mainland to declare independence.

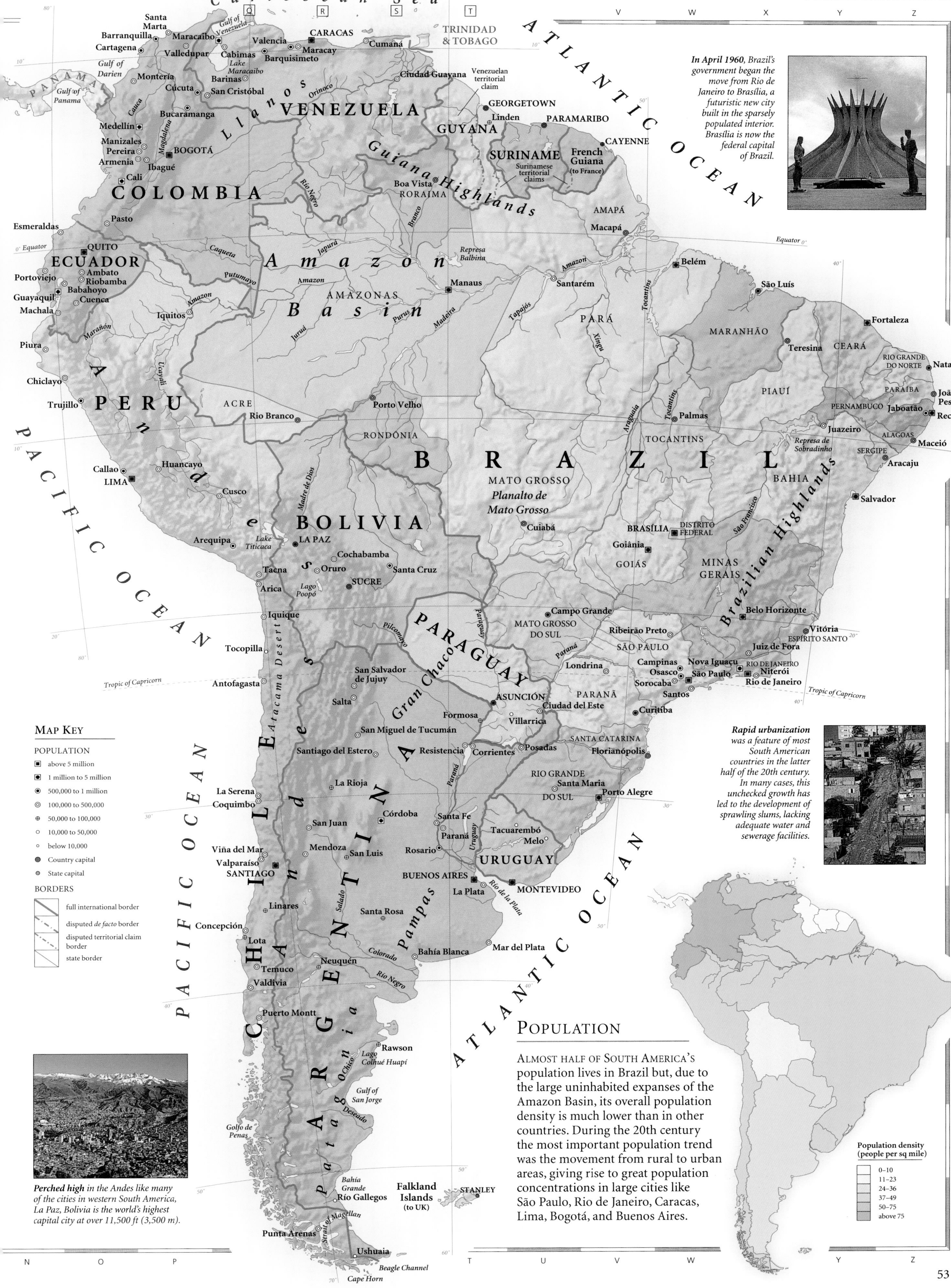

Caribbean Sea

TRINIDAD & TOBAGO

ATLANTIC OCEAN

In April 1960, Brazil's government began the move from Rio de Janeiro to Brasília, a futuristic new city built in the sparsely populated interior. Brasília is now the federal capital of Brazil.

Santa Marta
Barranquilla
Cartagena
Maracaibo
Valencia
CARACAS
Cumaná
Gulf of Venezuela
Cabimas
Maracay
Valledupar
Barquisimeto
Montería
Barinas
Ciudad Guayana
Venezuelan territorial claim
Cúcuta
San Cristóbal
GEORGETOWN
Bucaramanga
Linden
PARAMARIBO
Medellín
VENEZUELA
GUYANA
CAYENNE
Manizales
Pereira
BOGOTÁ
SURINAME
French Guiana (to France)
Armenia
Ibagué
Surinamese territorial claims
Cali
Guiana Highlands

COLOMBIA
Boa Vista
RORAIMA
AMAPÁ
Esmeraldas
Macapá
QUITO
Equator
ECUADOR
Belém
Portoviejo
Ambato
Riobamba
São Luís
Guayaquil
Babahoyo
Cuenca
AMAZONAS
Manaus
Santarém
Machala
Basin
Iquitos
PARÁ
Fortaleza
Piura
MARANHÃO
Teresina
CEARÁ
Chiclayo
RIO GRANDE DO NORTE
Natal
Trujillo
ACRE
Porto Velho
PIAUÍ
João Pessoa
PERU
Rio Branco
PARAÍBA
Jaboatão
Recife
RONDÔNIA
PERNAMBUCO
Juazeiro
Callao
LIMA
Huancayo
ALAGOAS
Maceió
Cusco
BRAZIL
SERGIPE
Aracaju
MATO GROSSO
Planalto de Mato Grosso
BAHIA
Salvador
BOLIVIA
Arequipa
Lake Titicaca
LA PAZ
Cochabamba
Cuiabá
BRASÍLIA
DISTRITO FEDERAL
Tacna
Oruro
Santa Cruz
Goiânia
MINAS GERAIS
Arica
SUCRE
GOIÁS
Lago Poopó
TOCANTINS
Palmas
Belo Horizonte
Iquique
Campo Grande
Vitória
MATO GROSSO DO SUL
ESPÍRITO SANTO
Tocopilla
Ribeirão Preto
Juiz de Fora
PARAGUAY
SÃO PAULO
Antofagasta
Londrina
Campinas
RIO DE JANEIRO
San Salvador de Jujuy
ASUNCIÓN
PARANÁ
Osasco
Niterói
Salta
Ciudad del Este
Sorocaba
São Paulo
Rio de Janeiro
Formosa
Villarrica
Santos
San Miguel de Tucumán
Curitiba
ARGENTINA
Resistencia
Corrientes
Posadas
SANTA CATARINA
Santiago del Estero
Florianópolis
La Rioja
RIO GRANDE
Santa Maria
DO SUL
Porto Alegre
San Juan
Córdoba
Santa Fe
La Serena
Coquimbo
Paraná
Tacuarembó
Melo
Viña del Mar
Mendoza
San Luis
Rosario
URUGUAY
Valparaíso
SANTIAGO
BUENOS AIRES
MONTEVIDEO
Linares
La Plata
Santa Rosa
Concepción
Lota
Neuquén
Bahía Blanca
Mar del Plata
Temuco
Valdivia
Rio Negro
Puerto Montt
Rawson
Falkland Islands (to UK)
STANLEY
Río Gallegos
Punta Arenas
Ushuaia

PACIFIC OCEAN

ATLANTIC OCEAN

Rapid urbanization was a feature of most South American countries in the latter half of the 20th century. In many cases, this unchecked growth has led to the development of sprawling slums, lacking adequate water and sewerage facilities.

MAP KEY

POPULATION
- ▪ above 5 million
- ■ 1 million to 5 million
- ◉ 500,000 to 1 million
- ◎ 100,000 to 500,000
- ⊕ 50,000 to 100,000
- ○ 10,000 to 50,000
- ○ below 10,000
- ● Country capital
- ◉ State capital

BORDERS
- full international border
- disputed de facto border
- disputed territorial claim border
- state border

Perched high in the Andes like many of the cities in western South America, La Paz, Bolivia is the world's highest capital city at over 11,500 ft (3,500 m).

POPULATION

ALMOST HALF OF SOUTH AMERICA'S population lives in Brazil but, due to the large uninhabited expanses of the Amazon Basin, its overall population density is much lower than in other countries. During the 20th century the most important population trend was the movement from rural to urban areas, giving rise to great population concentrations in large cities like São Paulo, Rio de Janeiro, Caracas, Lima, Bogotá, and Buenos Aires.

Population density (people per sq mile)
- 0–10
- 11–23
- 24–36
- 37–49
- 50–75
- above 75

SOUTH AMERICAN RESOURCES

Ciudad Guayana is a planned industrial complex in eastern Venezuela, built as an iron and steel centre to exploit the nearby iron ore reserves.

AGRICULTURE STILL PROVIDES THE LARGEST SINGLE FORM OF EMPLOYMENT in South America, although rural unemployment and poverty continue to drive people toward the huge coastal cities in search of jobs and opportunities. Mineral and fuel resources, although substantial, are distributed unevenly; few countries have both fossil fuels and minerals. To break industrial dependence on raw materials, boost manufacturing, and improve infrastructure, governments borrowed heavily from the World Bank in the 1960s and 1970s. This led to the accumulation of massive debts which are unlikely ever to be repaid. Today, Brazil dominates the continent's economic output, followed by Argentina. Recently, the less-developed western side of South America has benefited due to its geographical position; for example Chile is increasingly exporting raw materials to Japan.

Industry

✈ aerospace	pharmaceuticals
brewing	printing & publishing
car/vehicle manufacture	shipbuilding
chemicals	sugar processing
electronics	textiles
engineering	timber processing
finance	tobacco processing
fish processing	wine
food processing	oil
hi-tech industry	gas
iron & steel	industrial cities
meat processing	metal refining
metal refining	major industrial areas
narcotics	

The cold Peru Current flows north from the Antarctic along the Pacific coast of Peru, providing rich nutrients for one of the world's largest fishing grounds. Overexploitation has severely reduced Peru's anchovy catch.

STANDARD OF LIVING

WEALTH DISPARITIES throughout the continent create a wide gulf between affluent landowners and the chronically poor in inner-city slums. The illicit production of cocaine, and the hugely influential drug barons who control its distribution, contribute to the violent disorder and corruption which affect northwestern South America, de-stabilizing local governments and economies.

Standard of Living
(UN Human Development Index)

low

high

Both Argentina and Chile are now exploring the southernmost tip of the continent in search of oil. Here in Punta Arenas, a drilling rig is being prepared for exploratory drilling in the Strait of Magellen.

GNP per capita (US$)

0–499
500–999
1000–1499
1500–2999
3000–5999
6000+

INDUSTRY

ARGENTINA AND BRAZIL are South America's most industrialized countries and São Paulo is the continent's leading industrial center. Long-term government investment in Brazilian industry has encouraged a diverse industrial base; engineering, steel production, food processing, textile manufacture, and chemicals predominate. The illegal production of cocaine is economically significant in the Andean countries of Colombia and Bolivia. In Venezuela, the oil-dominated economy has left the country vulnerable to world oil price fluctuations. Food processing and mineral exploitation are common throughout the less industrially developed parts of the continent, including Bolivia, Chile, Ecuador, and Peru.

Map labels: Caribbean Sea, PANAMA, Gulf of Panama, Barranquilla, Cartagena, Maracaibo, Barquisimeto, Caracas, Valencia, VENEZUELA, Ciudad Guayana, Georgetown, Paramaribo, GUYANA, SURINAME, French Guiana (to France), Medellín, Bogotá, COLOMBIA, Cali, Quito, ECUADOR, Guayaquil, Iquitos, Amazon Basin, Manaus, Belém, Fortaleza, Natal, PERU, Chiclayo, Chimbote, Lima, Cusco, BRAZIL, Recife, Maceió, Salvador, Arequipa, La Paz, BOLIVIA, Santa Cruz, Sucre, Brasília, Arica, Iquique, Chuquicamata, Belo Horizonte, PARAGUAY, São Paulo, Rio de Janeiro, Antofagasta, Asunción, Ciudad del Este, Curitiba, San Miguel de Tucumán, Corrientes, Porto Alegre, Córdoba, Santa Fe, Rio Grande, URUGUAY, Valparaíso, Mendoza, Rosario, Buenos Aires, Montevideo, Santiago, Talca, ARGENTINA, Concepción, Valdivia, Neuquén, Bahía Blanca, INDUSTRY, Comodoro Rivadavia, Gulf of San Jorge, Falkland Islands (to UK), Bahía Grande, Punta Arenas, Strait of Magellan, Cape Horn, PACIFIC OCEAN, ATLANTIC OCEAN, CHILE

ENVIRONMENTAL ISSUES

THE AMAZON BASIN is one of the last great wilderness areas left on Earth. The tropical rain forests which grow there are a valuable genetic resource, containing innumerable unique plants and animals. The forests are increasingly under threat from new and expanding settlements and "slash and burn" farming techniques, which clear land for the raising of beef cattle, causing land degradation and soil erosion.

Clouds of smoke billow from the burning Amazon rain forest. Over 25,000 sq miles (60,000 sq km) of virgin rain forest are being cleared annually, destroying an ancient, irreplaceable, natural resource and biodiverse habitat.

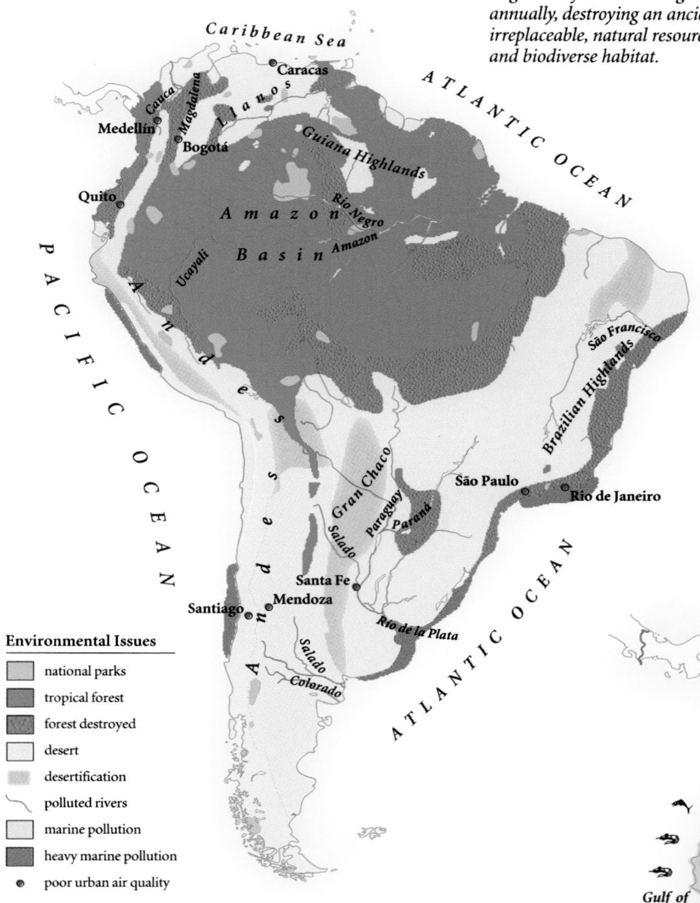

Environmental Issues
- national parks
- tropical forest
- forest destroyed
- desert
- desertification
- polluted rivers
- marine pollution
- heavy marine pollution
- poor urban air quality

MINERAL RESOURCES

OVER A QUARTER OF THE WORLD'S known copper reserves are found at the Chuquicamata mine in northern Chile, and other metallic minerals such as tin are found along the length of the Andes. The discovery of oil and gas at Venezuela's Lake Maracaibo in 1917 turned the country into one of the world's leading oil producers. In contrast, South America is virtually devoid of coal, the only significant deposit being on the peninsula of Guajira in Colombia.

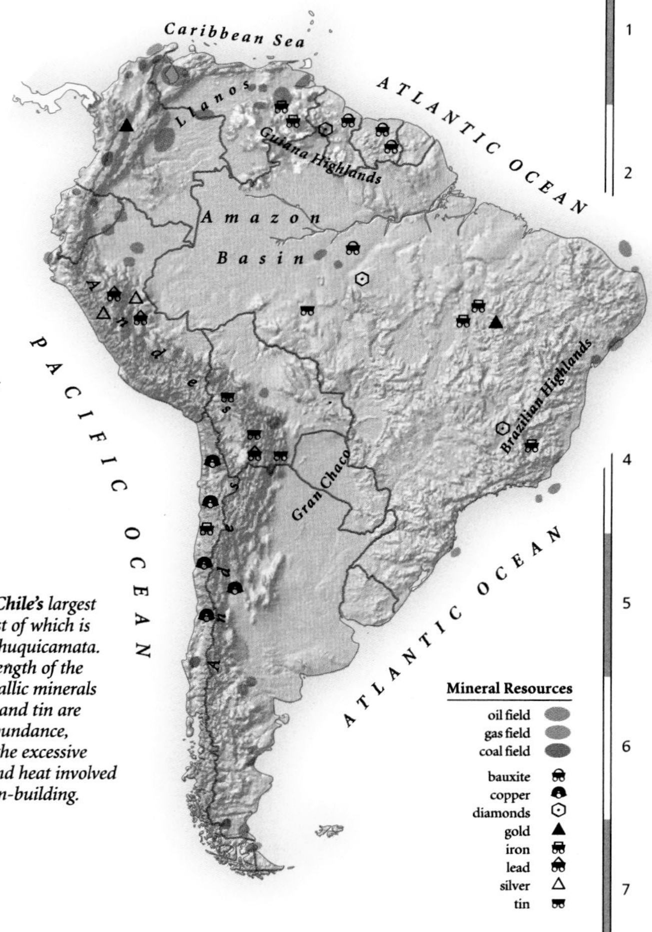

Copper is Chile's largest export, most of which is mined at Chuquicamata. Along the length of the Andes, metallic minerals like copper and tin are found in abundance, formed by the excessive pressures and heat involved in mountain-building.

Mineral Resources
- oil field
- gas field
- coal field
- bauxite
- copper
- diamonds
- gold
- iron
- lead
- silver
- tin

USING THE LAND AND SEA

MANY FOODS NOW COMMON WORLDWIDE originated in South America. These include the potato, tomato, squash, and cassava. Today, large herds of beef cattle roam the temperate grasslands of the Pampas, supporting an extensive meatpacking trade in Argentina, Uruguay and Paraguay. Corn (maize) is grown as a staple crop across the continent and coffee is grown as a cash crop in Brazil and Colombia. Coca plants grown in Bolivia, Peru, and Colombia provide most of the world's cocaine. Fish and shellfish are caught off the western coast, especially anchovies off Peru, shrimps off Ecuador and pilchards off Chile.

South America, and Brazil in particular, now leads the world in coffee production, mainly growing Coffea Arabica in large plantations. Coffee beans are harvested, roasted, and brewed to produce the world's second most popular drink, after tea.

The Pampas region of southeast South America is characterized by extensive, flat plains, and populated by cattle and ranchers (gauchos). Argentina is a major world producer of beef, much of which is exported to the US for use in hamburgers.

High in the Andes, hardy alpacas graze on the barren land. Alpacas are thought to have been domesticated by the Incas, whose nobility wore robes made from their wool. Today, they are still reared and prized for their soft, warm fleeces.

Using the Land and Sea
- barren land
- cropland
- desert
- forest
- mountain region
- pasture
- major conurbations
- cattle
- pigs
- sheep
- bananas
- corn
- citrus fruits
- cocoa
- cotton
- coffee
- fishing
- oil palms
- peanuts
- rubber
- shellfish
- soybeans
- sugar cane
- vineyards
- wheat

NORTHERN SOUTH AMERICA

COLOMBIA, GUYANA, SURINAME, VENEZUELA, *French Guiana* (to France)

FRINGED BY THE PACIFIC AND ATLANTIC OCEANS and the Caribbean Sea, South America's northern region has a rich range of natural resources, some exploited for centuries by colonial powers including the Spanish, French, Dutch, and British, others still to be fully explored.

The prospects for further economic development in Colombia, Guyana and Suriname are blighted by drug-related violence and political instability. Venezuela, despite huge incomes from its oil reserves, remains less developed in other industrial sectors.

French Guiana is an overseas *département* of France, now seeking greater autonomy. Most of the major population centers, such as Bogotá, have grown up in the temperate conditions of the high Andes or, like Caracas, at strategic points along the Caribbean coast.

Flowers grown in Colombia are exported all over the world, and include fine carnations and roses. Here, workers are cutting roses which have been grown in plastic greenhouses.

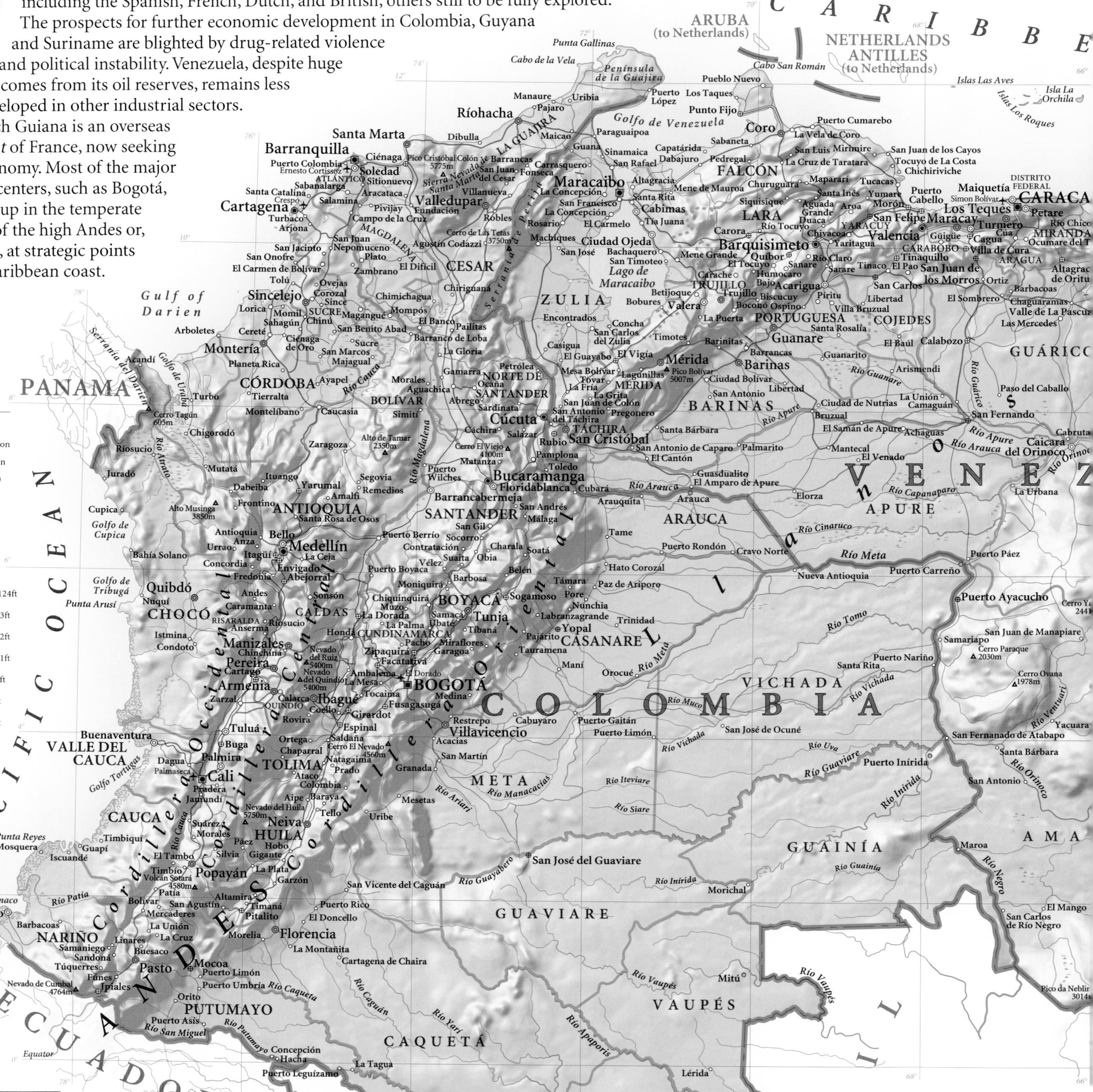

MAP KEY

POPULATION

- ▣ 1 million to 5 million
- ◉ 500,000 to 1 million
- ⊚ 100,000 to 500,000
- ⊕ 50,000 to 100,000
- ○ 10,000 to 50,000
- ○ below 10,000

ELEVATION

- 4000m / 13,124ft
- 3000m / 9843ft
- 2000m / 6562ft
- 1000m / 3281ft
- 500m / 1640ft
- 250m / 820ft
- 100m / 328ft
- sea level

44 ◁

198 ◁

58 ◁

Large open squares like the Plaza de Bolivar in Bogotá are characteristic of many cities founded by the Spanish.

Scattered farms and villages have grown up on the gentle slopes of this Colombian river valley, utilizing the fertile soils for farming.

SCALE 1:6,500,000
(projection: Lambert Azimuthal Equal Area)

Km 0 25 50 100 150 200
Miles 0 25 50 100 150 200

The River Orinoco flows from its source in the southern Guiana Highlands to form a broad delta on Venezuela's Atlantic coast. One of its distributary channels opens into a wide bay called the Serpent's Mouth.

58 ▽

60 ▽

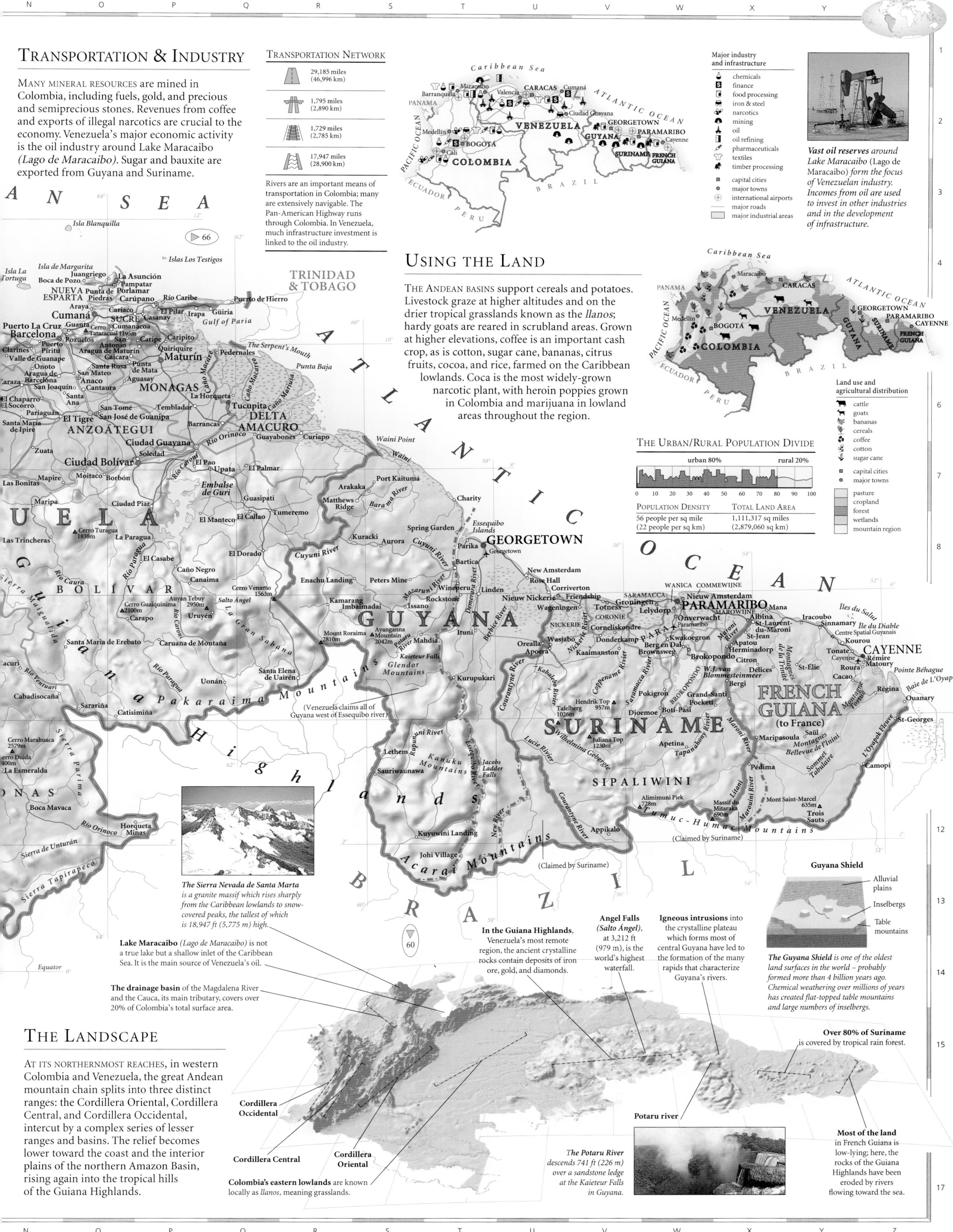

TRANSPORTATION & INDUSTRY

MANY MINERAL RESOURCES are mined in Colombia, including fuels, gold, and precious and semiprecious stones. Revenues from coffee and exports of illegal narcotics are crucial to the economy. Venezuela's major economic activity is the oil industry around Lake Maracaibo (Lago de Maracaibo). Sugar and bauxite are exported from Guyana and Suriname.

TRANSPORTATION NETWORK

29,185 miles
(46,996 km)

1,795 miles
(2,890 km)

1,729 miles
(2,785 km)

17,947 miles
(28,900 km)

Rivers are an important means of transportation in Colombia; many are extensively navigable. The Pan-American Highway runs through Colombia. In Venezuela, much infrastructure investment is linked to the oil industry.

Major industry and infrastructure

- chemicals
- finance
- food processing
- iron & steel
- narcotics
- mining
- oil
- oil refining
- pharmaceuticals
- textiles
- timber processing
- capital cities
- major towns
- international airports
- major roads
- major industrial areas

Vast oil reserves around Lake Maracaibo (Lago de Maracaibo) form the focus of Venezuelan industry. Incomes from oil are used to invest in other industries and in the development of infrastructure.

USING THE LAND

THE ANDEAN BASINS support cereals and potatoes. Livestock graze at higher altitudes and on the drier tropical grasslands known as the *llanos*; hardy goats are reared in scrubland areas. Grown at higher elevations, coffee is an important cash crop, as is cotton, sugar cane, bananas, citrus fruits, cocoa, and rice, farmed on the Caribbean lowlands. Coca is the most widely-grown narcotic plant, with heroin poppies grown in Colombia and marijuana in lowland areas throughout the region.

Land use and agricultural distribution

- cattle
- goats
- bananas
- cereals
- coffee
- cotton
- sugar cane
- capital cities
- major towns
- pasture
- cropland
- forest
- wetlands
- mountain region

THE URBAN/RURAL POPULATION DIVIDE

urban 80%   rural 20%

0 10 20 30 40 50 60 70 80 90 100

POPULATION DENSITY
56 people per sq mile
(22 people per sq km)

TOTAL LAND AREA
1,111,317 sq miles
(2,879,060 sq km)

THE LANDSCAPE

AT ITS NORTHERNMOST REACHES, in western Colombia and Venezuela, the great Andean mountain chain splits into three distinct ranges: the Cordillera Oriental, Cordillera Central, and Cordillera Occidental, intercut by a complex series of lesser ranges and basins. The relief becomes lower toward the coast and the interior plains of the northern Amazon Basin, rising again into the tropical hills of the Guiana Highlands.

The Sierra Nevada de Santa Marta is a granite massif which rises sharply from the Caribbean lowlands to snow-covered peaks, the tallest of which is 18,947 ft (5,775 m) high.

Lake Maracaibo (Lago de Maracaibo) is not a true lake but a shallow inlet of the Caribbean Sea. It is the main source of Venezuela's oil.

The drainage basin of the Magdalena River and the Cauca, its main tributary, covers over 20% of Colombia's total surface area.

(Venezuela claims all of Guyana west of Essequibo river)

Cordillera Occidental

Cordillera Central

Cordillera Oriental

Colombia's eastern lowlands are known locally as *llanos*, meaning grasslands.

The Potaru River descends 741 ft (226 m) over a sandstone ledge at the Kaieteur Falls in Guyana.

In the Guiana Highlands, Venezuela's most remote region, the ancient crystalline rocks contain deposits of iron ore, gold, and diamonds.

Angel Falls (Salto Ángel), at 3,212 ft (979 m), is the world's highest waterfall.

Igneous intrusions into the crystalline plateau which forms most of central Guyana have led to the formation of the many rapids that characterize Guyana's rivers.

(Claimed by Suriname)

(Claimed by Suriname)

Guyana Shield

- Alluvial plains
- Inselbergs
- Table mountains

The Guyana Shield is one of the oldest land surfaces in the world – probably formed more than 4 billion years ago. Chemical weathering over millions of years has created flat-topped table mountains and large numbers of inselbergs.

Potaru river

Over 80% of Suriname is covered by tropical rain forest.

Most of the land in French Guiana is low-lying; here, the rocks of the Guiana Highlands have been eroded by rivers flowing toward the sea.

WESTERN SOUTH AMERICA

BOLIVIA, ECUADOR, PERU

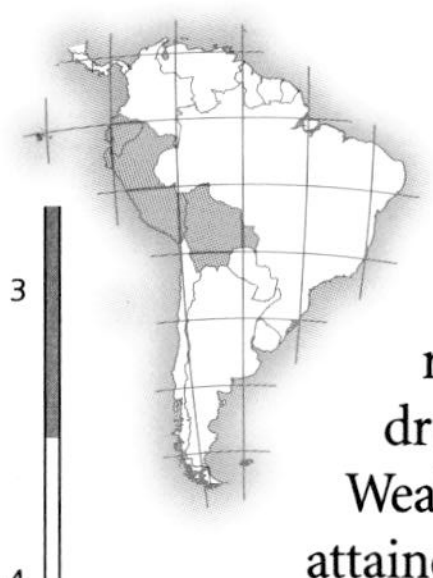

THE THREE STATES OF WESTERN SOUTH AMERICA share a similar geography and recent history. Dominated by the Inca empire until Spanish conquest in the 16th century, they achieved independence from Spain in the early 19th century. The precipitous terrain of the Andes presents severe difficulties for overland transportation and continues to be a barrier to national unity and stability. Although Ecuador is now a relatively stable democracy, the military is highly influential in Peru and Bolivia, while the drug trade and associated corruption discourages external aid and economic progress. Wealth and power are still largely concentrated in the hands of a small elite of families, who attained their position during the Spanish colonial period. Land rights and political recognition for the indigenous peoples are becoming increasingly important issues, particularly in Ecuador.

THE LANDSCAPE

BOLIVIA, PERU, AND ECUADOR each possess a high Andean mountain region and an eastern region consisting of tropical lowlands and the Andean slope leading down to them. Toward the south of the region, the mountains widen to form the high plateau of the Altiplano. Peru and Ecuador also have fertile, lowland coastal plains. A wide variety of environments include *selva* (tropical rain forest), *montaña* (mountain forest), and grassland.

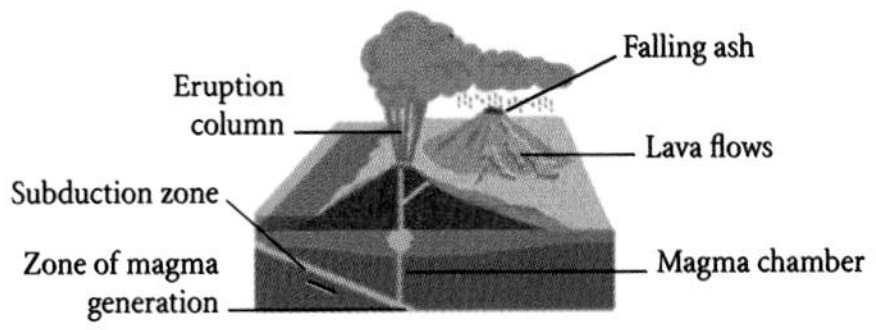

There are many large and active volcanoes in the Andes. Magma generated in the heart of the volcano erupts in a huge cloud of ash. Ash-fall deposits are common throughout the Andes and the rock produced is known as andesite. This is rapidly soaked by heavy rain, causing massive debris flows.

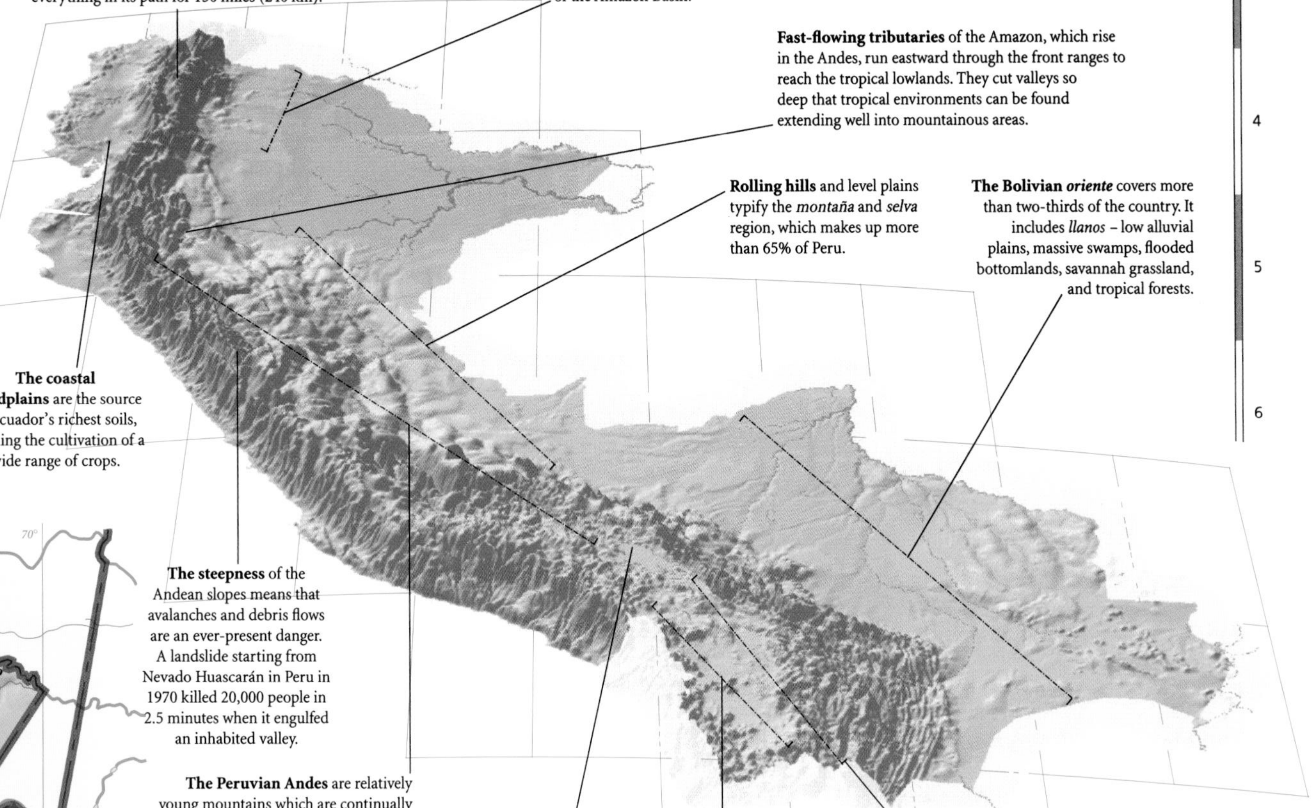

Falling ash
Lava flows
Magma chamber
Eruption column
Subduction zone
Zone of magma generation

Fast-flowing tributaries of the Amazon, which rise in the Andes, run eastward through the front ranges to reach the tropical lowlands. They cut valleys so deep that tropical environments can be found extending well into mountainous areas.

Much of eastern Ecuador is covered by the tropical rain forest of the Amazon Basin.

Cotopaxi is the world's highest active volcano, with a peak 19,347 ft (5,897 m) high. A massive eruption in 1877 caused a mudflow which destroyed everything in its path for 150 miles (240 km).

Rolling hills and level plains typify the *montaña* region, which makes up more than 65% of Peru.

The Bolivian oriente covers more than two-thirds of the country. It includes *llanos* – low alluvial plains, massive swamps, flooded bottomlands, savannah grassland, and tropical forests.

The coastal floodplains are the source of Ecuador's richest soils, enabling the cultivation of a wide range of crops.

The steepness of the Andean slopes means that avalanches and debris flows are an ever-present danger. A landslide starting from Nevado Huascarán in Peru in 1970 killed 20,000 people in 2.5 minutes when it engulfed an inhabited valley.

The Peruvian Andes are relatively young mountains which are continually being uplifted, making the area very unstable, with frequent earthquakes. The transportation difficulties that they present continue to form a barrier to national unity.

Ecuador's capital city, Quito, lies high in the Andes, nestling between snowcapped peaks. At 9,350 ft (2,850 m), Quito is the second highest capital in the world – La Paz in Bolivia is the highest.

Bolivian Andes

Nevado de Illampu and Nevado de Ancohuma, at 21,275 ft (6,485 m) and 21,490 ft (6,550 m) respectively, form Illampu, the highest mountain in the Bolivian Andes.

The Altiplano is a flat, high plateau lying between the Cordillera Oriental and the Cordillera Occidental at a height of up to 12,500 ft (3,800 m). At its margins lie many spurs and alluvial fans.

Lake Titicaca

Lake Titicaca, which forms part of the border between Peru and Bolivia, is the largest lake in South America and the highest significant body of water in the world at an altitude of 12,507 ft (3,812 m).

SCALE 1:7,750,000
(projection: Lambert Azimuthal Equal Area)

MAP KEY

POPULATION
- ■ above 5 million
- ◉ 1 million to 5 million
- ◎ 500,000 to 1 million
- ⊕ 100,000 to 500,000
- ○ 50,000 to 100,000
- ○ 10,000 to 50,000
- ○ below 10,000

ELEVATION

6000m / 19,686ft	
4000m / 13,124ft	
3000m / 9843ft	
2000m / 6562ft	
1000m / 3281ft	
500m / 1640ft	
250m / 820ft	
100m / 328ft	
sea level	

ECUADOREAN ADMINISTRATIVE REGIONS
1. CARCHI
2. TUNGURAHUA
3. BOLIVAR
4. CHIMBORAZO
5. ZAMORA CHINCHIPE

Llamas, with alpacas and vicuñas, are indigenous to South America. They thrive in Andean conditions and their wool is both exported and used in the manufacture of local textiles.

BOLIVIA'S TWO CAPITALS

LA PAZ – legislative and administrative capital
SUCRE – legal capital

THE URBAN/RURAL POPULATION DIVIDE

urban 64%   rural 36%

TOTAL LAND AREA
1,019,515 sq miles
(2,641,230 sq km)

POPULATION DENSITY
44 people per sq mile
(17 people per sq km)

Clearance of the forest in coca-growing regions is encouraged by the Bolivian government. The inaccessible terrain makes policing the growers very difficult. Coca is a popular crop because it is simple to grow and to transport, and is very profitable when illegally processed as cocaine.

USING THE LAND AND SEA

THE COASTAL REGIONS support a variety of cash crops including rice, sugar cane, bananas, coffee, and cocoa, watered by rainfall or by irrigation schemes. The grasslands of the high *sierra* are used mainly for grazing a wide range of livestock; cattle and sheep are reared, along with pigs, and the indigenous llama and alpaca. Subsistence crops, especially potatoes and cereals, are grown lower down the mountain flanks. Despite government incentives to grow alternative crops, coca, used for cocaine, is the Bolivian and Peruvian *oriente's* most profitable commercial crop.

Land use and agricultural distribution

- cattle
- sheep
- bananas
- cereals
- cocoa
- coffee
- fishing
- rubber
- sugar cane

capital cities
major towns

pasture
cropland
forest
mountain region
desert
wetlands

A colony of marine iguanas basks on the rocks of Isla Fernandina in the Galápagos Islands. Charles Darwin's theory of evolution was inspired by the differences he found between the animal species on neighboring islands in the Galápagos.

The Galápagos Islands are mainly composed of lava, with very little vegetation near to the coasts, although the wetter inland slopes are mantled with forest.

Galápagos Islands
(Archipiélago de Colón)

GALÁPAGOS
(to Ecuador)

Volcán Wolf 1646m
Volcán La Cumbre 1463m
Isla Fernandina
Volcán Darwin 1280m
Volcán Alcedo 1097m
Volcán Santo Tomás 1490m
Isla Isabela

Isla Pinta
Isla Marchena
Isla Genovesa

Isla Pinzón
Isla Santiago
Isla San Salvador
Isla Santa Cruz
Puerto Ayora
Isla Santa Fe
Isla San Cristóbal
Puerto Baquerizo Moreno
Puerto Villamil
Isla Santa María

(same scale as main map)

The ancient city of Machupicchu, in the Peruvian Andes was built prior to the Inca period. Its impressive ruins reflect a culture which had developed a high degree of sophistication.

TRANSPORTATION & INDUSTRY

THE MOUNTAIN REGIONS are rich in minerals including lead, copper, silver, gold, zinc, and tungsten, though high production and transportation costs have meant that they are expensive to extract and vulnerable to price collapses. Foreign debt remains a major burden, hampering industrial development. Manufacturing tends to be small-scale and concentrates on products for local needs, including textiles, food processing, and pharmaceuticals. Narcotics are an important, though illegal, export.

Major industry and infrastructure

- car manufacture
- chemicals
- engineering
- fish processing
- food processing
- iron & steel
- mining
- narcotics
- oil
- pharmaceuticals
- shipbuilding

capital cities
major towns
international airports
major roads
major industrial areas

At Potosí in Bolivia, silver has been mined for over 400 years.

TRANSPORTATION NETWORK

50,274 miles (80,956 km)
1,860 miles (2,995 km)

3,940 miles (6,344 km)
14,966 miles (24,100 km)

A transcontinental highway is under construction to link Ilo, on Peru's Pacific coast, to Porto Esperança in Brazil, via Puerto Suárez in Bolivia. Establishing port facilities on the Pacific coast is crucial to landlocked Bolivia's further development.

59

BRAZIL

B RAZIL IS THE LARGEST COUNTRY in South America, with a population of 179 million – greater than the combined total for the whole of the rest of the continent. The 26 states which make up the federal republic of Brazil are administered from the purpose-built capital, Brasília. Tropical rain forest, covering more than one-third of the country, contains rich natural resources, but great tracts are sacrificed to agriculture, industry and urban expansion on a daily basis. Most of Brazil's multiethnic population now live in cities, some of which are vast areas of urban sprawl; São Paulo is one of the world's biggest conurbations, with more than 17 million inhabitants. Although prosperity is a reality for some, many people still live in great poverty, and mounting foreign debts continue to damage Brazil's prospects of economic advancement.

USING THE LAND

BRAZIL HAS IMMENSE NATURAL RESOURCES, including minerals and hardwoods, many of which are found in the fragile rain forest. Brazil is the world's leading coffee grower and a major producer of livestock, sugar, and orange juice concentrate. Soybeans for animal feed, particularly for poultry feed, have become the country's most significant crop.

The fecundity of parts of Brazil's rain forest results from exceptionally high levels of rainfall and the quantities of silt deposited by the Amazon River system.

THE LANDSCAPE

THE AMAZON BASIN, containing the largest area of tropical rain forest on Earth, covers nearly half of Brazil. It is bordered by two shield areas: in the south by the Brazilian Highlands, and in the north by the Guiana Highlands. The east coast is dominated by a great escarpment which runs for 1,600 miles (2,565 km).

Brazil's highest mountain is the Pico da Neblina which was only discovered in 1962. It is 9,888 ft (3,014 m) high.

The floodplains which border the Amazon River are made up of a variety of different features including shallow lakes and swamps, mangrove forests in the tidal delta area, and fertile levels on river banks and point bars.

Pantanal swamps

The Pantanal region in the south of Brazil is an extension of the Gran Chaco plain. The swamps and marshes of this area are renowned for their beauty, and abundant and unique wildlife, including wildfowl and these caimans, a type of crocodile.

The Amazon Basin is the largest river basin in the world. The Amazon River and over a thousand tributaries drain an area of 2,375,000 sq miles (6,150,000 sq km) and carry one-fifth of the world's fresh water out to sea.

The ancient Brazilian Highlands have a varied topography. Their plateaus, hills, and deep valleys are bordered by highly-eroded mountains containing important mineral deposits. They are drained by three great river systems, the Amazon, the Paraguay–Paraná, and the São Francisco.

The São Francisco Basin has a climate unique in Brazil. Known as the "drought polygon," it has almost no rain during the dry season, leading to regular disastrous droughts.

The northeastern scrublands are known as the *caatinga*, a virtually impenetrable thorny woodland, sometimes intermixed with cacti where water is scarce.

Guiana Highlands

The famous Sugar Loaf Mountain (*Pão de Açúcar*) which overlooks Rio de Janeiro is a fine example of a volcanic plug a domed core of solidified lava left after the slopes of the original volcano have eroded away.

Deep natural harbors such as Baia de Guanabara were created where the steep slopes of the Serra da Mantiqueira plunge directly into the ocean.

Hillslope gullying

Direction of growth
Gully
Overland water flow

Rainfall

Water seeps through hillslope

Large-scale gullies are common in Brazil, particularly on hillslopes from which vegetation has been removed. Gullies grow headwards (up the slope), aided by a combination of erosion through water seepage and rainwater runoff.

The Iguaçu River surges over the spectacular Iguaçu Falls (Saltos do Iguaçu) toward the Paraná River. Falls like these are increasingly under pressure from large-scale hydroelectric projects such as that at Itaipu.

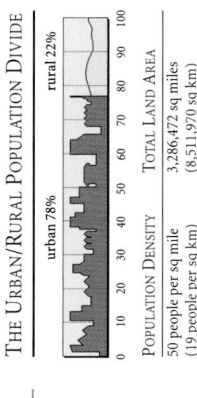

THE URBAN/RURAL POPULATION DIVIDE

urban 78%	rural 22%

POPULATION DENSITY	TOTAL LAND AREA
50 people per sq mile (19 people per sq km)	3,286,472 sq miles (8,511,970 sq km)

Land use and agricultural distribution
- cattle
- pigs
- sheep
- citrus fruits
- coffee
- cotton
- soya beans
- sugar cane
- timber
- capital cities
- major towns
- pasture
- cropland
- forest

MAP KEY

POPULATION
- ■ above 5 million
- ▣ 1 million to 5 million
- ◉ 500,000 to 1 million
- ◎ 100,000 to 500,000
- ⊕ 50,000 to 100,000
- ○ 10,000 to 50,000
- ∘ below 10,000

ELEVATION
- 3000m / 9843ft
- 2000m / 6562ft
- 1000m / 3281ft
- 500m / 1640ft
- 250m / 820ft
- 100m / 328ft
- sea level

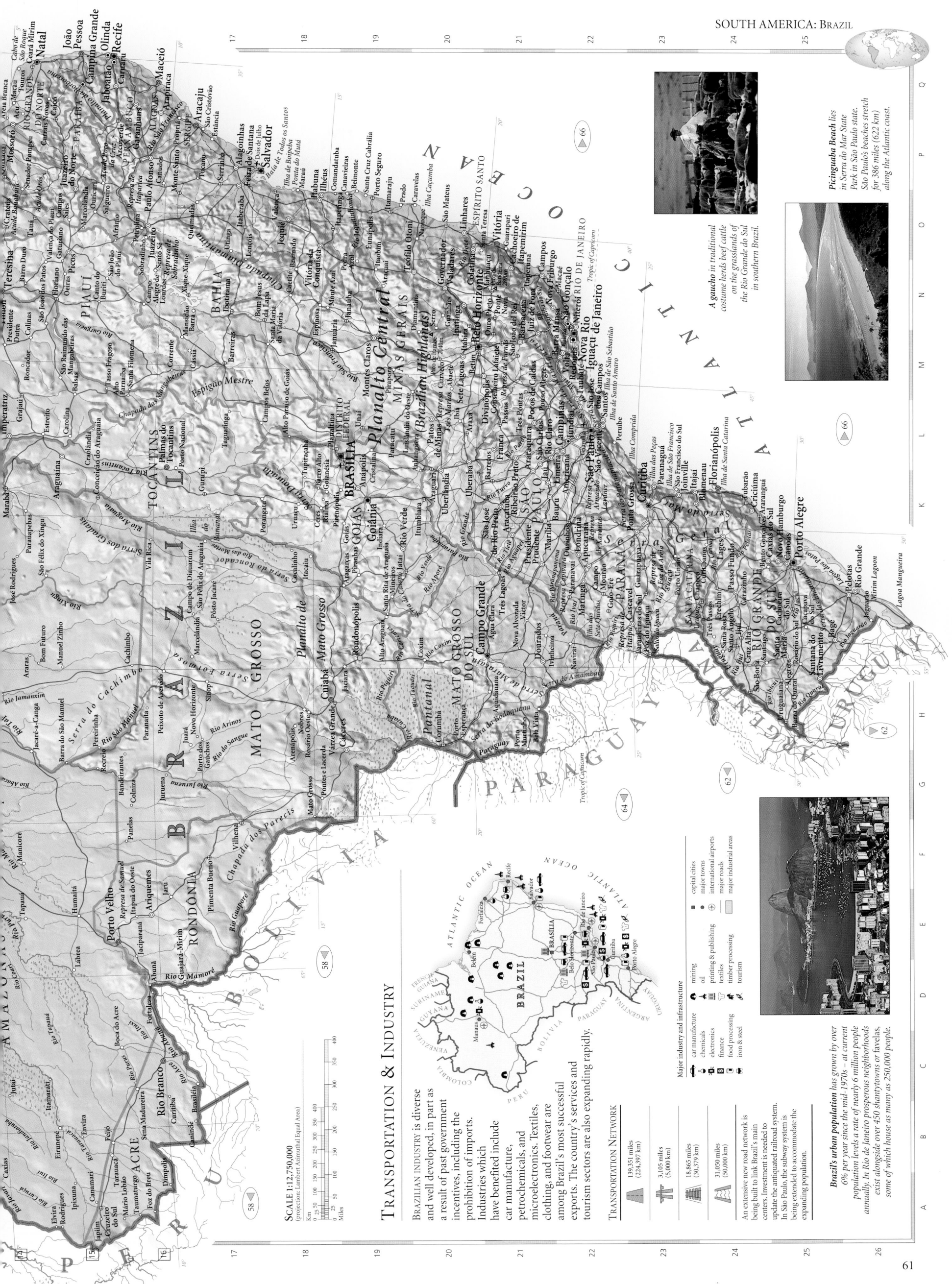

Picinguaba Beach lies in Serra do Mar State Park in São Paulo state. São Paulo's beaches stretch for 386 miles (622 km) along the Atlantic coast.

A gaucho in traditional costume herds beef cattle on the grasslands of the Rio Grande do Sul in southern Brazil.

Transportation & Industry

Brazilian industry is diverse and well developed, in part as a result of past government incentives, including the prohibition of imports. Industries which have benefited include car manufacture, petrochemicals, and microelectronics. Textiles, clothing, and footwear are among Brazil's most successful exports. The country's services and tourism sectors are also expanding rapidly.

Transportation Network

139,351 miles (224,397 km)

3,105 miles (5,000 km)

18,865 miles (30,379 km)

31,050 miles (50,000 km)

An extensive new road network is being built to link Brazil's main centers. Investment is needed to update the antiquated railroad system. In São Paulo, the subway system is being extended to accommodate the expanding population.

SCALE 1:12,750,000
(projection: Lambert Azimuthal Equal Area)

Km
0 25 50 100 150 200 250 300 350 400

Miles
0 25 50 100 150 200 250 300 350 400

Major industry and infrastructure

- car manufacture
- chemicals
- electronics
- finance
- food processing
- iron & steel
- mining
- oil
- printing & publishing
- textiles
- timber processing
- tourism

- capital cities
- major towns
- international airports
- major roads
- major industrial areas

Brazil's urban population has grown by over 6% per year since the mid-1970s – at current population levels a rate of nearly 6 million people annually. In Rio de Janeiro prosperous neighborhoods exist alongside over 450 shantytowns or favelas, some of which house as many as 250,000 people.

EASTERN SOUTH AMERICA

URUGUAY, NORTHEAST ARGENTINA, SOUTHEAST BRAZIL

THE VAST CONURBATIONS OF RIO DE JANEIRO, São Paulo, and Buenos Aires form the core of South America's highly-urbanized eastern region. São Paulo state, with almost 35 million inhabitants, is among the world's 20 most powerful economies, and São Paulo is the fastest growing city on the continent. Rio de Janeiro and Buenos Aires, transformed in the last hundred years from port cities to great metropolitan areas each with more than 10 million inhabitants, typify the unstructured growth and wealth disparities of South America's great cities.

In Uruguay, over half of the population lives in the capital, Montevideo, which faces Buenos Aires across the Plate River (*Río de la Plata*). Immigration from the countryside has created severe pressure on the urban infrastructure, particularly on available housing, leading to a profusion of crowded shanty settlements (*favelas or barrios*).

USING THE LAND

MOST OF URUGUAY and the Pampas of northern Argentina are devoted to the rearing of livestock, especially cattle and sheep, which are central to both countries' economies. Soybeans, first produced in Brazil's Rio Grande do Sul, are now more widely grown for large-scale export, as are cereals, sugar cane, and grapes. Subsistence crops, including potatoes, corn and sugar beets, are grown on the remaining arable land.

Land use and agricultural distribution

- cattle
- sheep
- cereals
- coffee
- fruit
- soybeans
- sugar cane
- capital cities
- major towns

- pasture
- cropland
- forest
- wetlands
- barren land

The rolling grasslands of Uruguay are ideally suited to the rearing of cattle, which are concentrated in great herds throughout the region.

TRANSPORTATION & INDUSTRY

SOUTHEAST BRAZIL IS HOME TO MUCH of the important motor and capital goods industry, largely based around São Paulo; iron and steel production is also concentrated in this region. Uruguay's economy continues to be based mainly on the export of livestock products including meat and leather goods. Buenos Aires is Argentina's chief port, and the region has a varied and sophisticated economic base including service-based industries such as finance and publishing, as well as primary processing.

Major industry and infrastructure

- car manufacture
- chemicals
- engineering
- finance
- food processing
- iron & steel
- meat processing
- printing & publishing
- shipbuilding
- textiles
- timber processing
- capitals/cities
- major towns
- international airports
- major industrial areas

TRANSPORTATION NETWORK

Throughout the region, road networks need to be expanded to cope with urban development. Plans are underway to build a bridge over the Plate River (*Río de la Plata*) to link Colonia and Buenos Aires.

MAP KEY

POPULATION

- ■ above 5 million
- ■ 1 million to 5 million
- ◉ 500,000 to 1 million
- ◉ 100,000 to 500,000
- ○ 50,000 to 100,000
- ○ 10,000 to 50,000
- ○ below 10,000

ELEVATION

- 2000m / 6562ft
- 1000m / 3281ft
- 500m / 1640ft
- 250m / 820ft
- 100m / 328ft
- sea level

SCALE 1: 6,250,000
(projection: Lambert Azimuthal Equal Area)

Km 0 25 50 100 150 200
Miles 0 25 50 100 150 200

Soybeans are harvested, pressed, and processed into soycake, which is used as animal feed. The cake is fed mainly to chickens on large-scale factory farms, and the growth in soy production has been an important factor in the expansion of the Brazilian poultry trade.

The Itaipú dam on the Paraná River is one of the largest hydroelectric projects in the world, jointly financed by Brazil and Paraguay.

Rio de Janeiro's annual carnival, Mardi Gras, which ushers in the start of Lent, is an extravagant five-day parade through the city, characterized by fantastically decorated floats, exuberant dancing, and samba music.

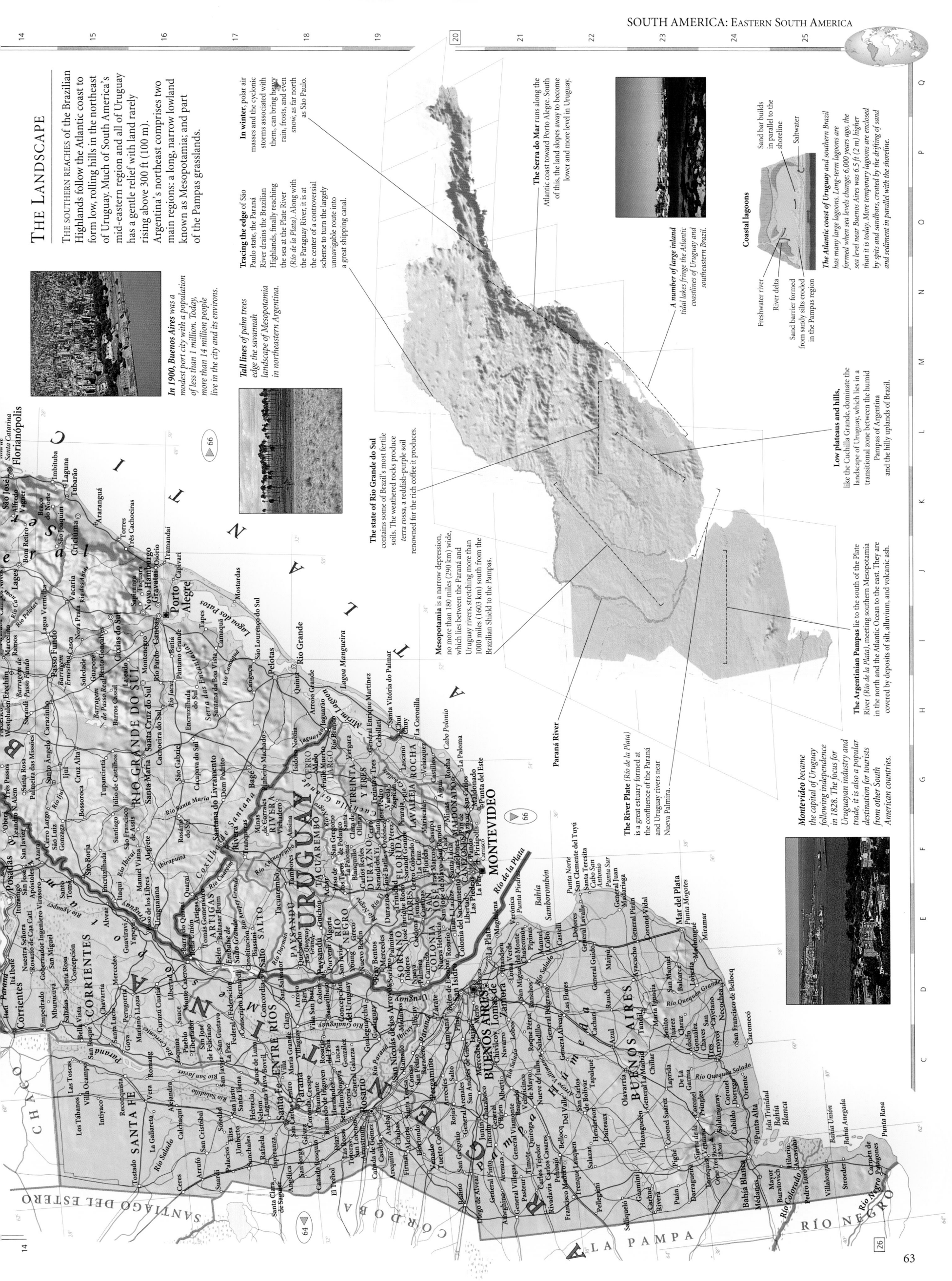

THE LANDSCAPE

THE SOUTHERN REACHES of the Brazilian Highlands follow the Atlantic coast to form low, rolling hills in the northeast of Uruguay. Much of South America's mid-eastern region and all of Uruguay has a gentle relief with land rarely rising above 300 ft (100 m). Argentina's northeast comprises two main regions: a long, narrow lowland known as Mesopotamia; and part of the Pampas grasslands.

In 1900, Buenos Aires was a modest port city with a population of less than 1 million. Today, more than 14 million people live in the city and its environs.

Tall lines of palm trees edge the savannah landscape of Mesopotamia in northeastern Argentina.

In winter, polar air masses and the cyclonic storms associated with them, can bring heavy rain, frosts, and even snow, as far north as São Paulo.

Tracing the edge of São Paulo state, the Paraná River drains the Brazilian Highlands, finally reaching the sea at the Plate River (Río de la Plata). Along with the Paraguay River, it is at the center of a controversial scheme to turn the largely unnavigable route into a great shipping canal.

The state of Rio Grande do Sul contains some of Brazil's most fertile soils. The weathered rocks produce *terra rossa*, a reddish-purple soil renowned for the rich coffee it produces.

The Serra do Mar runs along the Atlantic coast toward Porto Alegre. South of this, the land slopes away to become lower and more level in Uruguay.

A number of large inland tidal lakes fringe the Atlantic coastlines of Uruguay and southeastern Brazil.

Low plateaus and hills, like the Cuchilla Grande, dominate the landscape of Uruguay, which lies in a transitional zone between the humid Pampas of Argentina and the hilly uplands of Brazil.

Mesopotamia is a narrow depression, no more than 180 miles (290 km) wide, which lies between the Paraná and Uruguay rivers, stretching more than 1000 miles (1603 km) south from the Brazilian Shield to the Pampas.

The Argentinian Pampas lie to the south of the Plate River (Río de la Plata), meeting southern Mesopotamia in the north and the Atlantic Ocean to the east. They are covered by deposits of silt, alluvium, and volcanic ash.

Paraná River

The River Plate (Río de la Plata) is a great estuary formed at the confluence of the Paraná and Uruguay rivers near Nueva Palmira.

Montevideo became the capital of Uruguay following independence in 1828. The focus for Uruguayan industry and trade, it is also a popular destination for tourists from other South American countries.

Coastal lagoons

The Atlantic coast of Uruguay and southern Brazil has many large lagoons. Long-term lagoons are formed when sea levels change; 6,000 years ago, the sea level near Buenos Aires was 6.5 ft (2 m) higher than it is today. More temporary lagoons are enclosed by spits and sandbars, created by the drifting of sand and sediment in parallel with the shoreline.

Sand bar builds in parallel to the shoreline

Saltwater

Freshwater river

River delta

Sand barrier formed from sandy silts eroded in the Pampas region

SOUTHERN SOUTH AMERICA

ARGENTINA, CHILE, PARAGUAY

SOUTH AMERICA'S CONE-SHAPED SOUTHERN REGION is shared by Argentina and Chile, two overwhelmingly urbanized nations whose populations live mainly in or around the capital cities, Buenos Aires and Santiago. The people are largely *mestizo* or of European origin; in the early 20th century Argentina absorbed waves of new European immigrants, many from Italy and Germany. Paraguay is far less urbanized than its neighbors, with a homogeneous population of mixed Spanish and Guaraní origin, who retain their Indian roots through the Guaraní language. Though most Paraguayans live in the southeast, near Asunción, the indigenous Indians live in the sparsely populated Gran Chaco. The Gran Chaco is also home to some of Argentina's minority indigenous peoples, who otherwise live mainly in Andean regions. Chile's estimated 800,000 Mapauche Indians live almost exclusively in the south.

TRANSPORTATION & INDUSTRY

FOOD PROCESSING AND AGRICULTURAL EXPORTS remain a fundamental part of Argentina's economy. The growth of manufacturing is regularly hampered by hyperinflation and massive foreign debts. The world's most important copper-producer and one of the top ten gold producers, Chile also has a thriving wine and grape industry. Most Paraguayan exports involve primary processing, although domestic goods are produced for home markets.

Floodwaters cover the land in the Gran Chaco, partly submerging its vegetation of fan palms and hyacinths.

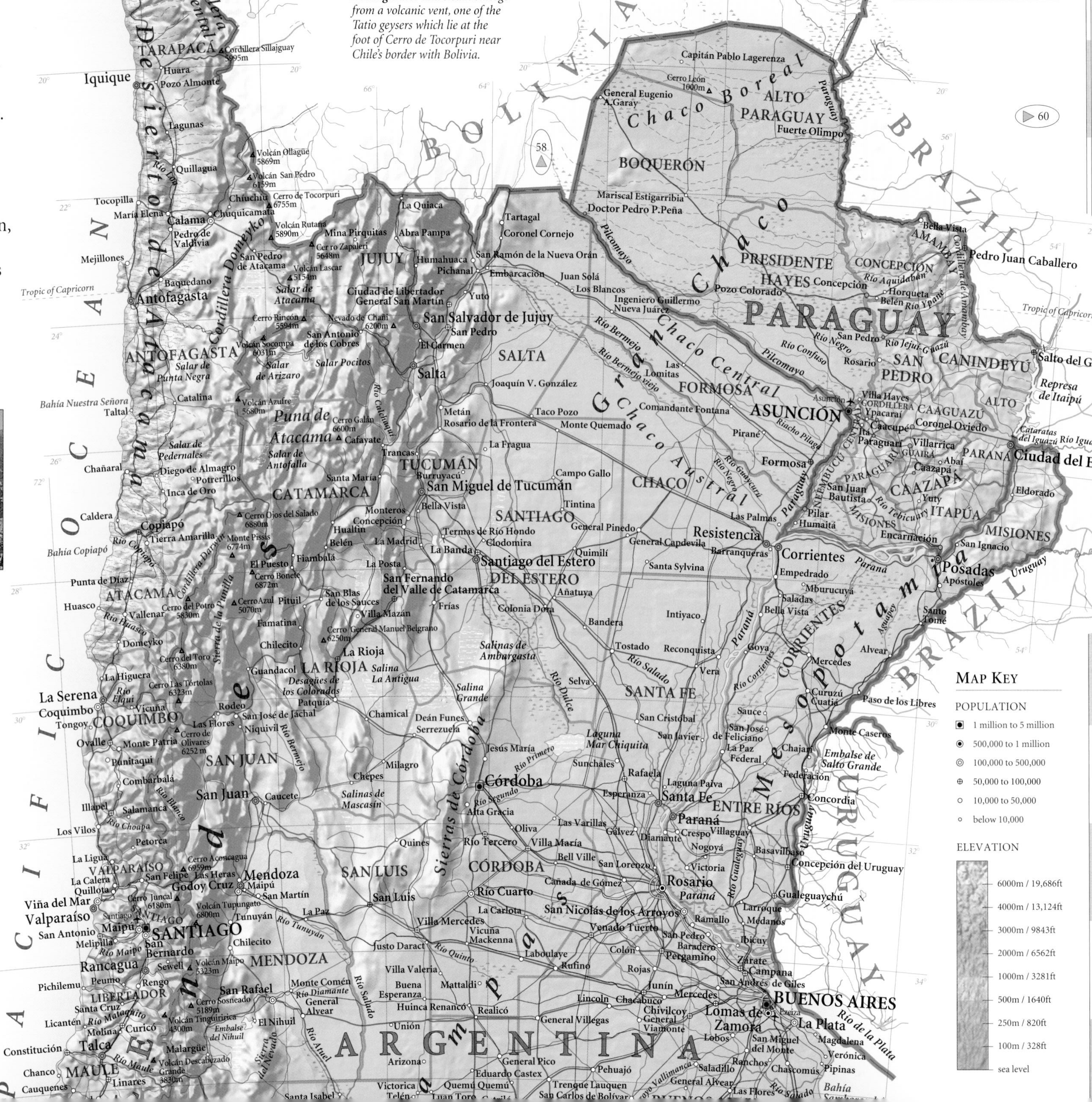

Boiling water and steam emerge from a volcanic vent, one of the Tatio geysers which lie at the foot of Cerro de Tocorpuri near Chile's border with Bolivia.

Chuquicamata copper mine, lies on a desert plateau near Calama in the Andes of northern Chile. It is the world's largest open-pit copper mine.

MAP KEY

POPULATION
- 1 million to 5 million
- 500,000 to 1 million
- 100,000 to 500,000
- 50,000 to 100,000
- 10,000 to 50,000
- below 10,000

ELEVATION
- 6000m / 19,686ft
- 4000m / 13,124ft
- 3000m / 9843ft
- 2000m / 6562ft
- 1000m / 3281ft
- 500m / 1640ft
- 250m / 820ft
- 100m / 328ft
- sea level

Major industry and infrastructure

- chemicals
- engineering
- food processing
- meat processing
- mining
- oil
- textiles
- timber processing

- capital cities
- major towns
- international airports
- major industrial areas

TRANSPORTATION NETWORK

- 89,104 miles (143,485 km)
- 2,889 miles (4,523 km)
- 23,107 miles (37,210 km)
- 9,206 miles (14,825 km)

Argentina's state transportation system is undergoing privatization, though the outmoded rail network requires updating. Paraguay requires foreign investment to upgrade its roads and railroads. Essential internal air routes, especially across the Andes, are well developed in all three countries.

Great blocks of ice break away from the jagged blue peaks of these ice mountains to form icebergs off the coast of Patagonia, Argentina's most southerly region.

Charred tree stumps surround a cattle enclosure on the island of Tierra del Fuego in southern Argentina. Forest clearance to provide grazing land for cattle is of major environmental concern.

THE LANDSCAPE

THE ANDES RUN FROM NORTH TO SOUTH, forming a precipitous natural border between Chile and Argentina. East of the Andes are the scrublands of the Gran Chaco and the plains of the Pampas, which extend northward toward Paraguay. In the far southwest, Chile's indented Pacific coastline has many features typical of areas which have been affected by glaciation.

The Atacama Desert (Desierto de Atacama) *in Chile is one of the driest places on Earth where some areas have never recorded any rain. It contains a number of salt lakes.*

Landlocked Paraguay relies on its river system for access to the sea and to produce hydroelectric power. The most important river system is the Paraguay-Paraná which provides links into neighboring countries including Brazil, Uruguay, and Argentina.

The Gran Chaco combines poor drainage, extremely hot temperatures and thorn-infested scrub to make it one of South America's most inhospitable regions.

Most of the highest mountains in Chile's northern Andes are volcanoes like Volcán Lascar and Volcán Rutana.

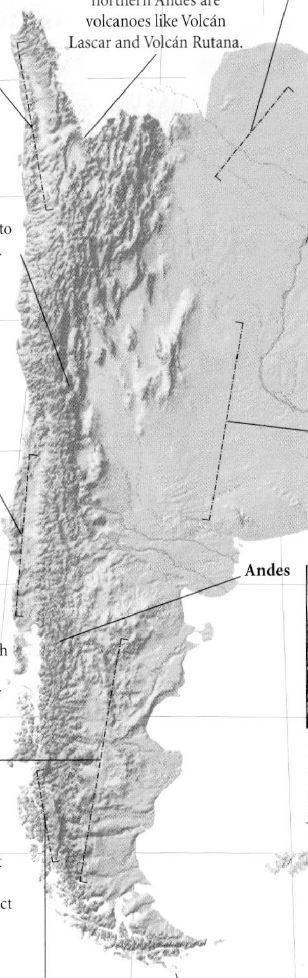

Cerro Aconcagua in the central Andes is the tallest mountain in the whole chain, rising to 22,834 ft (6,959 m).

Alluvial deposits from the many rivers in central Chile have created rich soils, ideal for a wide range of agriculture.

The Pampas derive their name from an Indian word meaning flat surface. The dry western region is largely desert, whereas the east is well-watered, supporting temperate grasses.

The Andean mountain system, which forms Argentina's western border, was created by folding and faulting, following the convergence of the Nazca and South American tectonic plates.

Cape Horn is the most southerly point of South America. The severity of the "Roaring Forties" winds makes the Horn one of the world's most treacherous shipping regions.

Patagonia divides into two zones, with the Andes in the west, and the lower main plateau, extending east toward the Atlantic. It is a desolate area with dark lava fields scattered with light bunchgrass give a "leopard skin" effect to the landscape.

The Patagonian ice sheet is the world's third largest ice field, covering 6,500 sq miles (17,000 sq km). Patagonia also contains many typical features from past glaciations. These include glacial lakes, U-shaped valleys, and deep-cut channels.

Argentinian Pampas

Ice-capped Andes is source of loess

Rainfall
Windblown particles
Thick layer of loess sediments
Jet stream

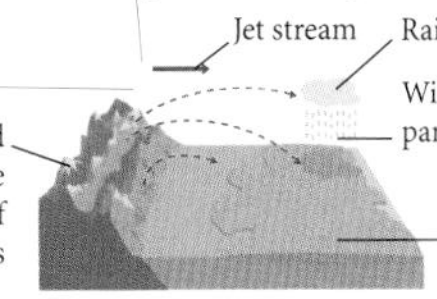

A thick, fertile layer of loess lies in the basin underlying the Argentinian Pampas. It has been laid down following successive periods of glaciation. The minute loess particles are transported as dust and deposited by a downward air motion, or following rainfall.

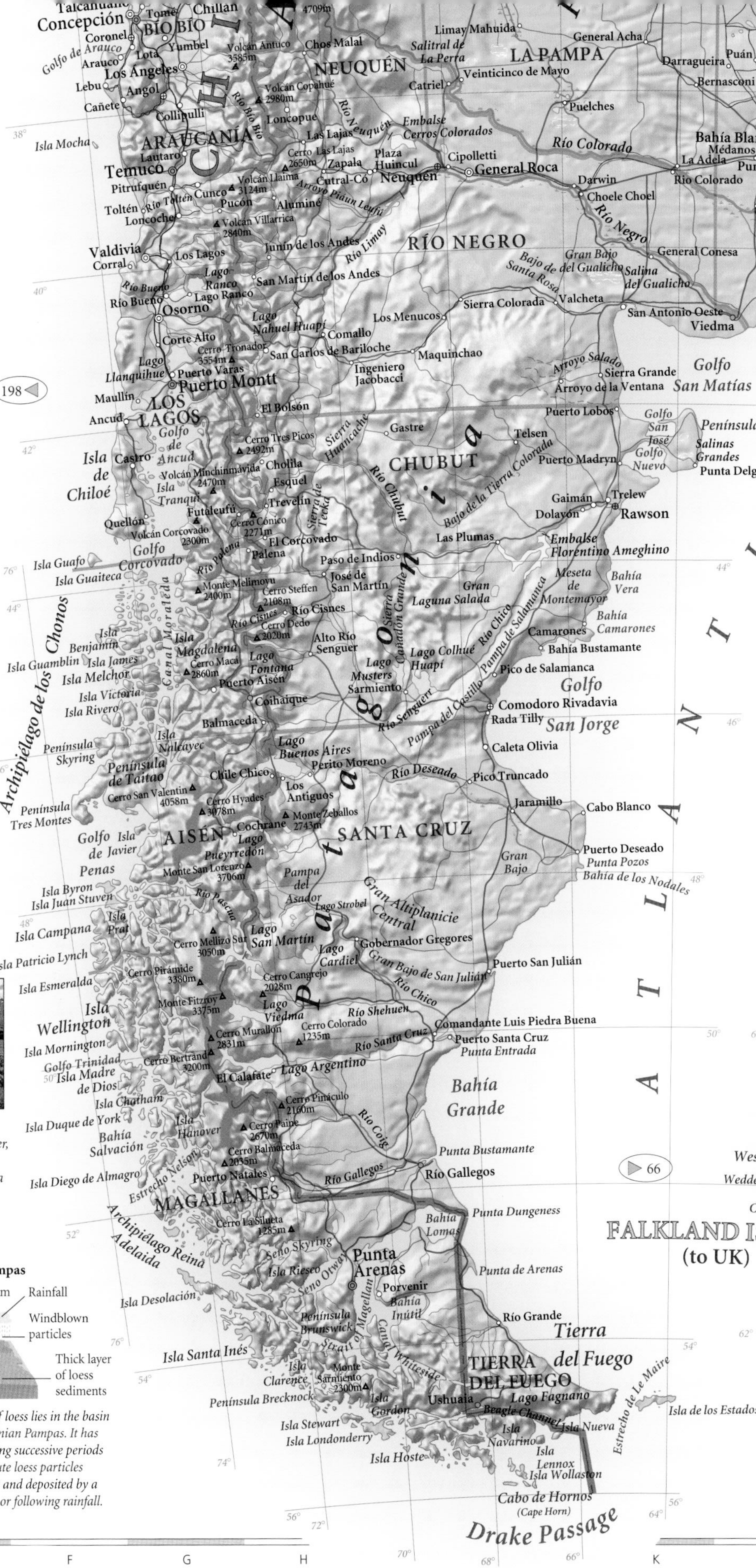

Andes

USING THE LAND AND SEA

THE RICH PLAINS OF THE PAMPAS support massive herds of cattle, producing meat, milk, and hides essential to the domestic and export markets of both Argentina and Paraguay. Wheat and fruit are Argentina's other major agricultural products. A wide range of soft fruits, citrus fruits, and more specialized crops such as walnuts, and grapes for wine and the table, are grown in Chile's fertile Central Valley, while the landscape to the south is dominated by forestry, mainly growing commercial radiata pine. Paraguay is self-sufficient in wheat and other staples. Cotton, coffee, tobacco, and oil sources such as soybeans, are the major export crops.

THE URBAN/RURAL POPULATION DIVIDE

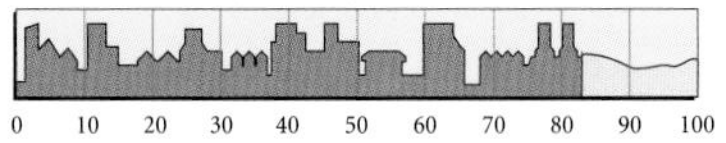

urban 84%   rural 16%

POPULATION DENSITY
37 people per sq mile
(14 people per sq km)

TOTAL LAND AREA
1,498,757 sq miles
(3,882,790 sq km)

Land use and agricultural distribution

cattle | capital cities
sheep | major towns
cereals | pasture
fruit | cropland
grapes | forest
timber | barren land
fishing | mountain region
| desert

SCALE 1:8,750,000
(projection: Lambert Azimuthal Equal Area)

FALKLAND ISLANDS
(to UK)

STANLEY

Drake Passage

THE ATLANTIC OCEAN

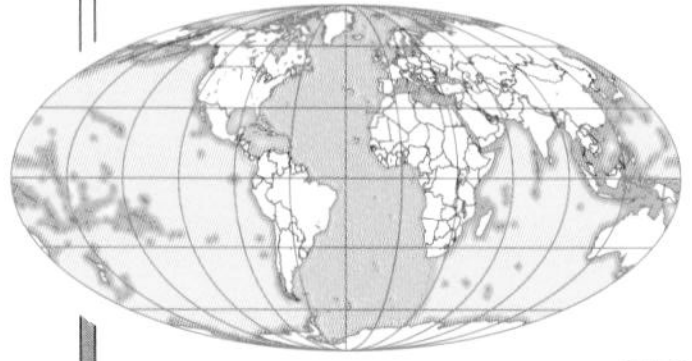

THE ATLANTIC IS THE YOUNGEST OF THE WORLD'S OCEANS, formed about 180 million years ago when the landmasses of the eastern and western hemispheres separated. Its underwater topography is dominated by the Mid-Atlantic Ridge, a huge mountain system running north to south along the center of the ocean. Although most of the ridge's peaks lie below the sea, some emerge as volcanic islands, like Iceland and the Azores. The Atlantic contains a wealth of resources, including substantial oil and gas reserves and rich fishing grounds. Until the 1950s, the north Atlantic was the world's busiest shipping route; cheaper air transportation and alternative routes have shifted patterns of world trade.

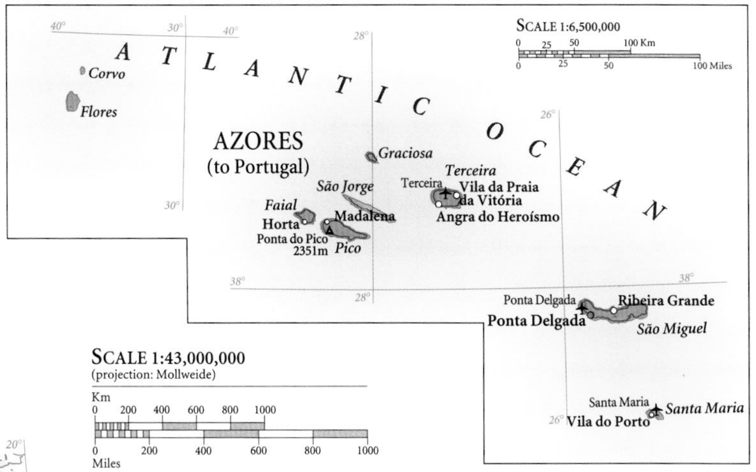

RESOURCES

DEVELOPMENT OF THE OIL AND GAS RESERVES in the Atlantic began in the 1940s around the Gulf of Mexico. Since then other areas have been exploited, including the North Sea, the west coast of Africa and the area east of Newfoundland and Nova Scotia. There is also extensive mining of sand, gravel, and shell deposits by the US and UK. For centuries, the north Atlantic's fishing grounds have been utilized more heavily than other oceans, leading to a serious decline in many fish stocks.

Resources (including wildlife)
- fish
- whales
- aggregates
- oil & gas
- major towns
- major ports

Surtsey near Iceland, lies on the Mid-Atlantic Ridge. The island was formed in 1963 following a volcanic eruption caused by sea-floor spreading.

Fishing in the seas around northwestern Europe dates back over 1,500 years. The high nutrient content of the seas makes them ideal breeding grounds for many species of fish.

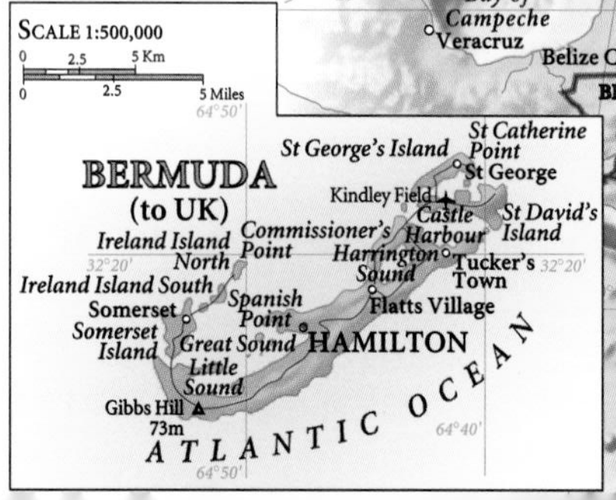

On January 5 1993, the oil tanker Braer ran aground in the Shetland Islands, spilling 83,660 tons (85,000 tonnes) of light crude oil into the ocean, devastating the local marine ecosystem.

AZORES (to Portugal)
SCALE 1:6,500,000

Corvo, Flores, Graciosa, São Jorge, Terceira, Vila da Praia, Angra do Heroísmo, Faial, Horta, Pico, 2351m Pico, Madalena, Ponta do Pico, Ribeira Grande, São Miguel, Ponta Delgada, Santa Maria, Vila do Porto

MADEIRA (to Portugal)
SCALE 1:2,500,000

Porto Santo, Camacha, Porto Santo, Ilhéu de Baixo, São Vicente, Ponta do Pargo, Porto do Moniz, 1862m, Pico Ruivo de Santana, Faial, Calheta, Machico, Ribeira Brava, Santa Cruz, Câmara de Lobos, Funchal, Ilhas Desertas, Ilheu Chão, Deserta Grande, Bugio

ISLAS CANARIAS (CANARY ISLANDS) (to Spain)
SCALE 1:6,500,000

Alegranza, Graciosa, La Oliva, Puerto del Rosario, Fuerteventura, Teguise, Arrecife, Tinajo, Lanzarote, Antigua, Tuineje, Las Palmas, Santa Cruz de Tenerife, La Palma, Santa Cruz de la Palma, Puerto de la Cruz, Orotava, Los Rodeos, Las Palmas de Gran Canaria, Gran Canaria, Los Llanos de Aridane, Villahermosa, Pico del Teide 3718m, Tenerife, Reina Sofia, Gáldar, Garajonay 1487m, Gomera, Valverde, Hierro, Santa Cruz de Tenerife

BERMUDA (to UK)
SCALE 1:500,000

St George's Island, St George, St Catherine Point, St David's, St David's Island, Town of St George, Kindley Field, Commissioner's Point, Harbour, Tucker's Town 72m, Hamilton, Ireland Island North, Spanish Point, Ireland Island South, Gibbs Hill, Somerset Island, Great Sound, Flatts Village, Somerset, Little Sound

Major features (map labels)

NORTH AMERICA, SOUTH AMERICA, EUROPE, AFRICA, ATLANTIC OCEAN, CANADA, UNITED STATES OF AMERICA, MEXICO, BELIZE, HONDURAS, GUATEMALA, NICARAGUA, COSTA RICA, PANAMA, CUBA, JAMAICA, HAITI, DOMINICAN REPUBLIC, PUERTO RICO (to USA), BAHAMAS, Turks and Caicos Islands (to UK), Leeward Islands, BARBADOS, TRINIDAD & TOBAGO, VENEZUELA, GUYANA, SURINAM, COLOMBIA

PORTUGAL, SPAIN, FRANCE, UNITED KINGDOM, IRELAND, ICELAND, Greenland (to Denmark), Faroe Islands (to Denmark), Shetland Islands, MOROCCO, Western Sahara (occupied by Morocco), ALGERIA, MAURITANIA, SENEGAL, GAMBIA, GUINEA-BISSAU, GUINEA, SIERRA LEONE, LIBERIA, IVORY COAST, GHANA, TOGO, BENIN, NIGERIA, CAMEROON, CAPE VERDE

Mid-Atlantic Ridge, Reykjanes Ridge, Denmark Strait, Baffin Bay, Baffin Basin, Labrador Sea, Labrador Basin, Davis Strait, Hudson Strait, Hudson Bay, Foxe Basin, Foxe Channel, Ungava Bay, Gulf of St Lawrence, Newfoundland Basin, Newfoundland Ridge, Grand Banks of Newfoundland, Flemish Cap, Orphan Knoll, Sohm Plain, Nares Plain, Bermuda Rise, Hatteras Plain, Sargasso Sea, Sargassos Sea, Puerto Rico Trench, Caribbean Sea, Venezuelan Basin, Colombian Basin, Demerara Plain, Demerara Plateau, Gulf of Mexico, Straits of Florida, Yucatan Channel, Campeche Bank, Bay of Campeche, Iceland Basin, Iceland-Faeroe Ridge, Faeroe-Iceland Ridge, Rockall Bank, Rockall Plateau, Rockall Trough, Porcupine Bank, Porcupine Plain, Biscay Plain, Bay of Biscay, Iberian Plain, Tagus Plain, Horseshoe Seamounts, Madeira Plain, Canary Islands (to Spain), Cape Verde Plain, Cape Verde Terrace, Sierra Leone Rise, Sierra Leone Basin, Guinea Plain, Cape Verde Basin, Azores-Biscay Rise, East Azores Fracture Zone, Oceanographer Fracture Zone, Atlantis Fracture Zone, Kane Fracture Zone, Barracuda Fracture Zone, Vema Fracture Zone, Fifteen-Twenty Fracture Zone, Doldrums Fracture Zone, Four North Fracture Zone, Charlie-Gibbs Fracture Zone, King's Trough, Great Meteor Tablemount, Cruiser Tablemount, Plato Seamounts, New England Seamounts, Nashville Seamount, Corner Seamounts, Mytilus Seamount, Milne Seamounts, Newfoundland Seamounts, Atlantic Plain, Arctic Circle, Tropic of Cancer

SCALE 1:43,000,000 (projection: Mollweide)

Reykjavik, Rotterdam, Gibraltar, Lagos, Cape Town, New York, New Orleans, Cristobal, La Guaira, Buenos Aires, Rio de Janeiro

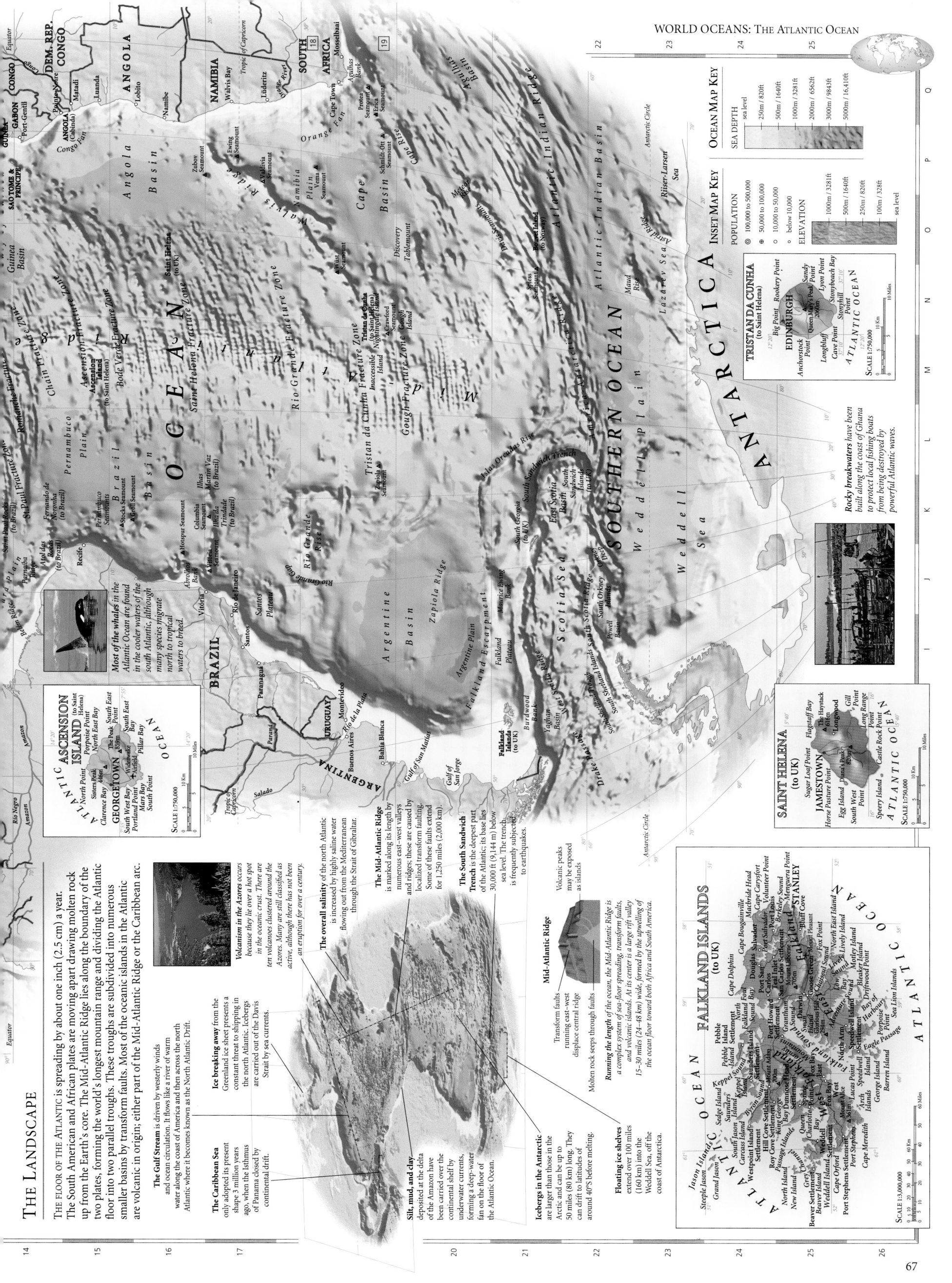

THE LANDSCAPE

THE FLOOR OF THE ATLANTIC is spreading by about one inch (2.5 cm) a year. The South American and African plates are moving apart drawing molten rock up from the Earth's core. The Mid-Atlantic Ridge lies along the boundary of the two plates, forming the world's longest mountain range and dividing the Atlantic floor into two parallel troughs. These troughs are subdivided into numerous smaller basins by transform faults. Most of the oceanic islands in the Atlantic are volcanic in origin; either part of the Mid-Atlantic Ridge or the Caribbean arc.

The Gulf Stream is driven by westerly winds and ocean circulation. It flows like a river of warm water along the coast of America and then across the north Atlantic where it becomes known as the North Atlantic Drift.

The Caribbean Sea only adopted its present shape 3 million years ago, when the Isthmus of Panama closed by continental drift.

Ice breaking away from the Greenland ice sheet presents a constant threat to shipping in the north Atlantic. Icebergs are carried out of the Davis Strait by sea currents.

Silt, mud, and clay deposited at the delta of the Amazon have been carried over the continental shelf by underwater currents, forming a deep-water fan on the floor of the Atlantic Ocean.

Icebergs in the Antarctic are larger than those in the Arctic and can be up to 50 miles (80 km) long. They can drift to latitudes of around 40°S before melting.

Floating ice shelves extend over 100 miles (160 km) into the Weddell Sea, off the coast of Antarctica.

Most of the whales in the Atlantic Ocean are found in the cooler waters of the south Atlantic, although many species migrate north to tropical waters to breed.

Volcanism in the Azores occurs because they lie over a hot spot in the oceanic crust. There are ten volcanoes clustered around the Azores. Many are still classified as active, although there has not been an eruption for over a century.

The overall salinity of the north Atlantic is increased by highly saline water flowing out from the Mediterranean through the Strait of Gibraltar.

The Mid-Atlantic Ridge is marked along its length by numerous east–west valleys and ridges; these are caused by localized transform faulting. Some of these faults extend for 1,250 miles (2,000 km).

The South Sandwich Trench is the deepest part of the Atlantic; its base lies 30,000 ft (9,144 m) below sea level. The trench is frequently subjected to earthquakes.

Volcanic peaks may be exposed as islands.

Mid-Atlantic Ridge

Transform faults running east–west displace central ridge

Molten rock seeps through faults

Running the length of the ocean, the Mid-Atlantic Ridge is a complex system of sea-floor spreading, transform faults, and volcanic islands. At its center is a large rift valley 15–30 miles (24–48 km) wide, formed by the upwelling of the ocean floor toward both Africa and South America.

Rocky breakwaters have been built along the coast of Ghana to protect local fishing boats from being destroyed by powerful Atlantic waves.

OCEAN MAP KEY

SEA DEPTH

sea level	
250m / 820ft	
500m / 1640ft	
1000m / 3281ft	
2000m / 6562ft	
3000m / 9843ft	
5000m / 16,410ft	

INSET MAP KEY

POPULATION
- ● 100,000 to 500,000
- ⊕ 50,000 to 100,000
- ○ 10,000 to 50,000
- ○ below 10,000

ELEVATION
1000m / 3281ft	
500m / 1640ft	
250m / 820ft	
100m / 328ft	
sea level	

TRISTAN DA CUNHA
(to Saint Helena)

Big Point · Rookery Point · Sandy Point
EDINBURGH · Queen Mary's Peak 2060m
Longbluff · Stonybeach Bay · Stony Point
Anchorstock Point · Lyon Point
Cave Point

ATLANTIC OCEAN

SCALE 1:750,000

SAINT HELENA
(to UK)

Sugar Loaf Point · Flagstaff Bay
Horse Pasture Point · The Haystack
JAMESTOWN · Longwood
Egg Island · Diana's Peak 820m · Long Range
South West Point · Gill Point
Speery Island · Castle Rock Point

ATLANTIC OCEAN

SCALE 1:750,000

ASCENSION ISLAND
(to Saint Helena)

North Point · The Peak 859m · South East Point
Porpoise Point · South East Bay
Sisters Peak 446m · Airfield
GEORGETOWN · Pillar Bay
South West Bay · Mars Bay
Portland Point · South Point
Clarence Bay · Widewake

ATLANTIC OCEAN

SCALE 1:750,000

FALKLAND ISLANDS
(to UK)

SCALE 1:3,000,000

SOUTHERN OCEAN

ANTARCTICA

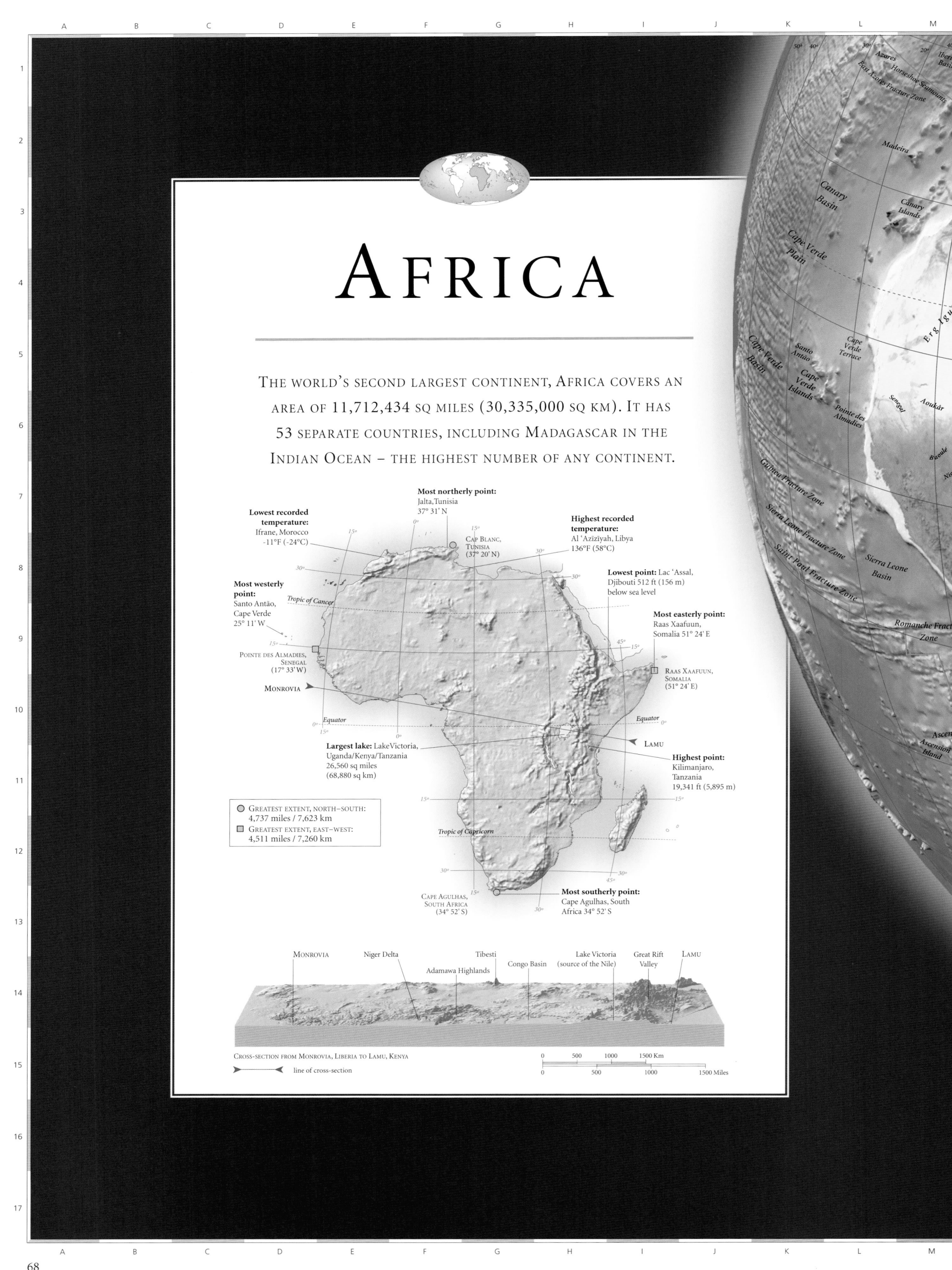

AFRICA

THE WORLD'S SECOND LARGEST CONTINENT, AFRICA COVERS AN
AREA OF 11,712,434 SQ MILES (30,335,000 SQ KM). IT HAS
53 SEPARATE COUNTRIES, INCLUDING MADAGASCAR IN THE
INDIAN OCEAN – THE HIGHEST NUMBER OF ANY CONTINENT.

Most northerly point:
Jalta, Tunisia
37° 31' N

**Lowest recorded
temperature:**
Ifrane, Morocco
-11°F (-24°C)

**Highest recorded
temperature:**
Al 'Azīzīyah, Libya
136°F (58°C)

CAP BLANC,
TUNISIA
(37° 20' N)

Lowest point: Lac 'Assal,
Djibouti 512 ft (156 m)
below sea level

**Most westerly
point:**
Santo Antão,
Cape Verde
25° 11' W

Most easterly point:
Raas Xaafuun,
Somalia 51° 24' E

Tropic of Cancer

POINTE DES ALMADIES,
SENEGAL
(17° 33' W)

RAAS XAAFUUN,
SOMALIA
(51° 24' E)

MONROVIA

Equator

Equator

LAMU

Largest lake: Lake Victoria,
Uganda/Kenya/Tanzania
26,560 sq miles
(68,880 sq km)

Highest point:
Kilimanjaro,
Tanzania
19,341 ft (5,895 m)

○ GREATEST EXTENT, NORTH–SOUTH:
4,737 miles / 7,623 km
□ GREATEST EXTENT, EAST–WEST:
4,511 miles / 7,260 km

Tropic of Capricorn

Most southerly point:
Cape Agulhas, South
Africa 34° 52' S

CAPE AGULHAS,
SOUTH AFRICA
(34° 52' S)

MONROVIA Niger Delta Tibesti Congo Basin Lake Victoria Great Rift LAMU
(source of the Nile) Valley
Adamawa Highlands

CROSS-SECTION FROM MONROVIA, LIBERIA TO LAMU, KENYA

line of cross-section

| 0 | 500 | 1000 | 1500 Km |

| 0 | 500 | 1000 | 1500 Miles |

Azores
Horseshoe Seamounts
East Azores Fracture Zone
Iberian
Basin

Madeira

Canary
Basin

Canary
Islands

Cape Verde
Plain

Cape Verde
Terrace

Cape Verde
Basin

Santo
Antão

Cape
Verde
Islands

Pointe des
Almadies

Senegal

Aoukâr

Guinea Fracture Zone

Sierra Leone Fracture Zone

Sierra Leone
Basin

Saint Paul Fracture Zone

Romanche Fracture
Zone

Ascension
Island

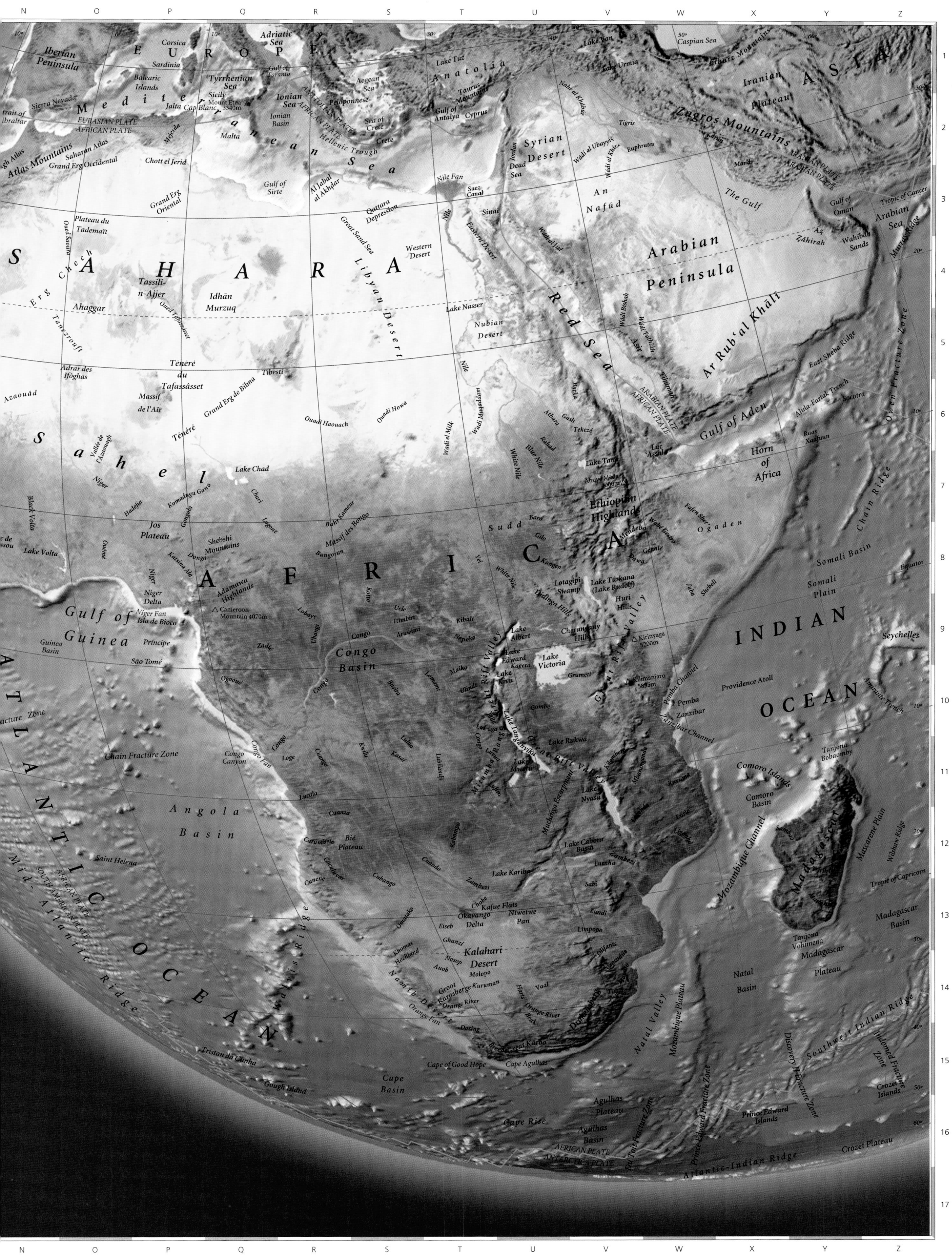

EUROPE

Iberian Peninsula
Corsica
Sardinia
Adriatic Sea
Gulf of Taranto
Caspian Sea
Lake Van
Elburz Mountains
ASIA

Sierra Nevada
Balearic Islands
Tyrrhenian Sea
Sicily
Mount Etna 3340m
Ionian Sea
Malta
Aegean Sea
Peloponnese
Ionian Basin
Lake Tuz
Anatolia
Taurus Mountains
Gulf of Antalya
Cyprus
Crete
Sea of Crete
Hellenic Trough
Nahr al Khabur
Lake Urmia
Iranian Plateau
Zagros Mountains

strait of Gibraltar
EURASIAN PLATE
AFRICAN PLATE
Mejerda
Cap Blanc
ANATOLIAN PLATE
AFRICAN PLATE
Tigris
Karun
Mand

igh Atlas
Atlas Mountains
Saharan Atlas
Grand Erg Occidental
Chott el Jerid
Gulf of Sirte
Al Jabal al Akhdar
Nile Fan
Syrian Desert
Jordan
Dead Sea
Suez Canal
Sinai
Euphrates
Wadi al Ubayyiq
Wadi al Khurr
The Gulf
Gulf of Oman
Tropic of Cancer
Arabian Sea

Plateau du Tademaït
Grand Erg Oriental
Great Sand Sea
Qattara Depression
Eastern Desert
An Nafūd
Az Zahirah
Wahibah Sands
Murray Ridge

S
Chech
A
H
A
R
A
Western Desert
Libyan Desert
Nile
Arabian
Peninsula
Wadi Bishah
Asir
Wadi Tathlith
Wadi Ad Dawasir
Hijaz
Najran

Ouad Saoura
Erg
Tassili-n-Ajjer
Idhān Murzuq
Lake Nasser
Nubian Desert
Red Sea
Ar Rub' al Khālī
East Sheba Ridge

Azaouâd
Ahaggar
Tanezrouft
Ténéré du Tafassàsset
Tibesti
Barka
Ethiopian
ARABIAN PLATE
AFRICAN PLATE
Alula-Fartak Trench
Socotra
Owen Fracture Zone

Sahel
Vallée de l'Azaouagh
Adrar des Ifôghas
Massif de l'Aïr
Grand Erg de Bilma
Ténéré
Ouadi Haouach
Ouadi Howa
Wadi el Milk
Wadi Muqaddam
Gash
Tekezé
Rahad
Lac Assal
Gulf of Aden
Horn of Africa
Raas Xaafuun

Black Volta
Niger
Hadejia
Komadugu Gana
Chari
Lake Chad
White Nile
Atbara
Lake Tana
Abay Wenz
Mendebo
Fafen Shet'
Somali Basin
Equator

de ssou
Lake Volta
Oueme
Jos Plateau
Katsina Ala
Shebshi Mountains
Donga
Legone
Bahr Kamour
Massif des Bongo
Bangoran
A
F
R
Yei
Sudd
Bard
Gilo
Kangen
I
C
Genale
Wabe Gestro
Ogaden
Somali Plain

Niger Delta
Niger Fan
Isla de Bioco
△ Cameroon Mountain 4070m
Atamawa Highlands
Lobaye
Uele
Itimbiri
Aruwimi
Kibali
Nepoko
Lotagipi Swamp
Didinga Hills
Lake Turkana (Lake Rudolf)
Huri Hills
Juba
Shabeli

Gulf of Guinea
Guinea Basin
Príncipe
São Tomé
Zadiè
Ogooué
Congo
Congo Basin
Maiko
Lomami
Ulindi
White Nile
Lake Albert
Lake Edward
Lake Kivu
Cherangany Hills
Grumeti
Kirinyaga 5200m
INDIAN
Seychelles

ATLANTIC
Fracture Zone
Congo
Congo Fan
Loge
Bomu
Kasai
Lubilandji
Lake Victoria
Kilimanjaro 5895m
Pemba Channel
Pemba
Zanzibar
Providence Atoll
Amirante Trench

Chain Fracture Zone
Congo Canyon
Lucala
Kwilu
Lake Tanganyika
Gombe
Lake Rukwa
Zanzibar Channel
OCEAN

Angola Basin
Cuanza
Kasongo
Lake Mweru
Great Rift Valley
Lake Nyasa
Tanjona Bobaomby

Saint Helena
Carumbo
Bié Plateau
Cuando
Kalahari
Muchinga Escarpment
Lake Cabora Bassa
Luangwa
Comoro Islands
Comoro Basin

Cassai
Cuanza
Lake Kariba
Zambezi
Sabi
Luni
Macarene Plain
Wilshaw Ridge

Mid-Atlantic Ridge
SOUTH AMERICAN PLATE
Walvis Ridge
Cunene
Okavango Delta
Ntwetwe Pan
Kafue Flats
Choke
Lundi
Madagascar
Tropic of Capricorn

Omaheke
Eiseb
Ghanzi
Khomas Hochland
Nosop
Kalahari Desert
Molopo
Limpopo
Mozambique Plateau
Natal Basin
Madagascar Basin

Namib Desert
Groot
Auob
Kuruman
Vaal
Dibifants
Tanjona Vohimena
Madagascar Plateau

Orange Fan
Kargsberge
Orange River
Harts
Great Karoo
Natal Valley
Southwest Indian Ridge

Tristan da Cunha
Gough Island
Cape of Good Hope
Cape Agulhas
Cape Basin
Agulhas Plateau
Prince Edward Islands
Crozet Islands

Cape Basin
Cape Rise
Agulhas Basin
AFRICAN PLATE
ANTARCTIC PLATE
Atlantic-Indian Ridge
Crozet Plateau

PHYSICAL AFRICA

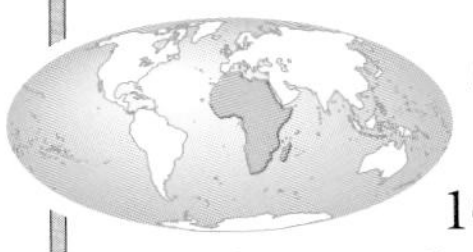

THE STRUCTURE OF AFRICA was dramatically influenced by the break up of the supercontinent Gondwanaland about 160 million years ago and, more recently, rifting and hot spot activity. Today, much of Africa is remote from active plate boundaries and comprises a series of extensive plateaus and deep basins, which influence the drainage patterns of major rivers. The relief rises to the east, where volcanic uplands and vast lakes mark the Great Rift Valley. In the far north and south sedimentary rocks have been folded to form the Atlas Mountains and the Great Karoo.

EAST AFRICA

THE GREAT RIFT VALLEY is the most striking feature of this region, running for 4,475 miles (7,200 km) from Lake Nyasa to the Red Sea. North of Lake Nyasa it splits into two arms and encloses an interior plateau which contains Lake Victoria. A number of elongated lakes and volcanoes lie along the fault lines. To the west lies the Congo Basin, a vast, shallow depression, which rises to form an almost circular rim of highlands.

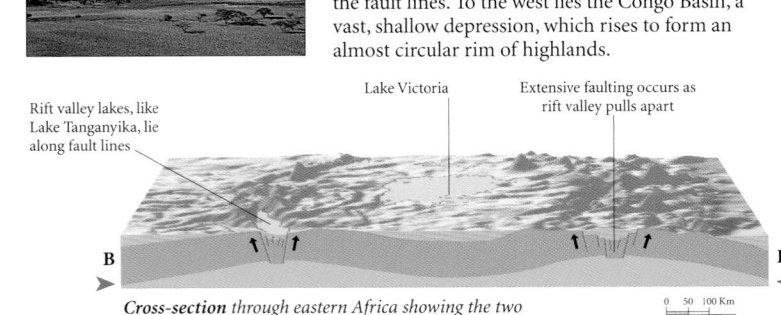

Rift valley lakes, like Lake Tanganyika, lie along fault lines

Lake Victoria

Extensive faulting occurs as rift valley pulls apart

B — B

Cross-section through eastern Africa showing the two arms of the Great Rift Valley and its interior plateau.

0   50   100 Km
0   50   100 Miles

NORTHERN AFRICA

NORTHERN AFRICA COMPRISES a system of basins and plateaus. The Tibesti and Ahaggar are volcanic uplands, whose uplift has been matched by subsidence within large surrounding basins. Many of the basins have been infilled with sand and gravel, creating the vast Saharan lands. The Atlas Mountains in the north were formed by convergence of the African and Eurasian plates.

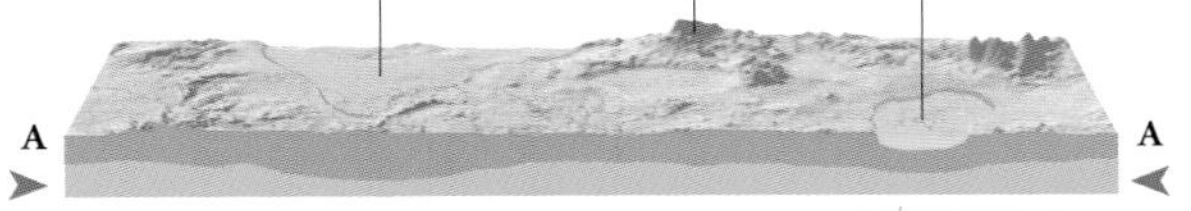

The Earth's crust has been warped to form the Taoudenni Basin

Volcanic Ahaggar Mountains, formed by rising magma from a hot spot

Lake Chad lies in a sand-filled basin

A — A

Section across northern Africa showing infilled basins and uplifted plateaus.

0   250   500 Km
0   250   500 Miles

SCALE 1:36,000,000
(projection: Lambert Azimuthal Equal Area)

Km
0 100 200   400   600   800

Miles
0   100   200   400   600   800

MAP KEY

ELEVATION

5000m / 16,405ft
4000m / 13,124ft
3000m / 9843ft
2000m / 6562ft
1000m / 3281ft
500m / 1640ft
250m / 820ft
100m / 328ft
sea level
below sea level

PLATE MARGINS
(for explanation see page xiv)

constructive
destructive
conservative
uncertain
line of cross-section

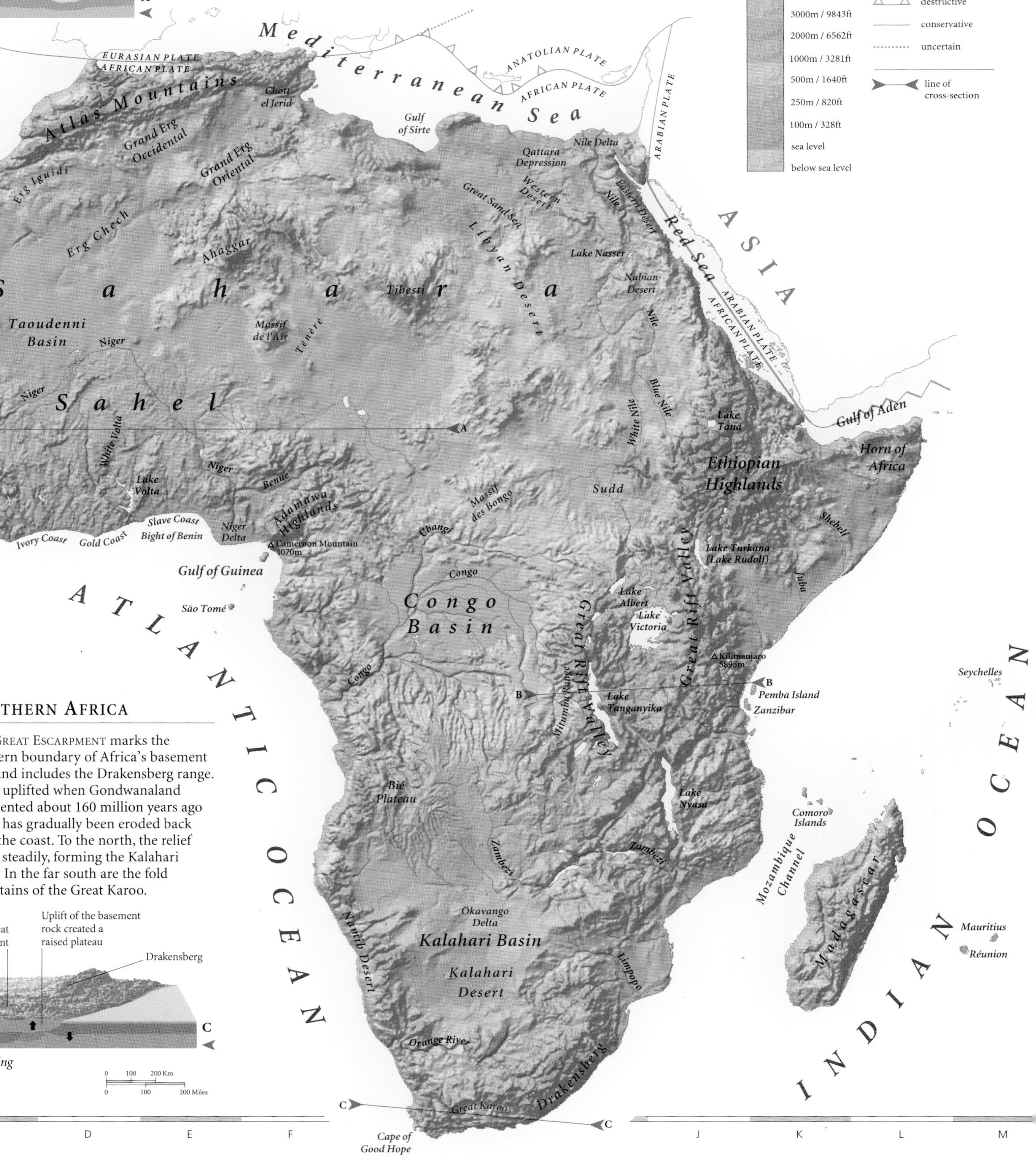

SOUTHERN AFRICA

THE GREAT ESCARPMENT marks the southern boundary of Africa's basement rock and includes the Drakensberg range. It was uplifted when Gondwanaland fragmented about 160 million years ago and it has gradually been eroded back from the coast. To the north, the relief drops steadily, forming the Kalahari Basin. In the far south are the fold mountains of the Great Karoo.

Kalahari Basin, covered with the sandy plains of the Kalahari Desert

Boundary of the Great Escarpment

Uplift of the basement rock created a raised plateau

Drakensberg

C — C

Cross-section through southern Africa showing the boundary of the Great Escarpment.

0   100   200 Km
0   100   200 Miles

Map labels

Mediterranean Sea
ATLANTIC OCEAN
EURASIAN PLATE
AFRICAN PLATE
ANATOLIAN PLATE
AFRICAN PLATE
ARABIAN PLATE
Atlas Mountains
Chott el Jerid
Gulf of Sirte
Grand Erg Occidental
Grand Erg Oriental
Erg Iguidi
Nile Delta
Qattara Depression
Western Desert
Erg Chech
Ahaggar
Libyan Desert
Great Sand Sea
Nile
Eastern Desert
Red Sea
ASIA
ARABIAN PLATE
AFRICAN PLATE
Sahara
Massif de l'Aïr
Ténéré
Tibesti
Lake Nasser
Nubian Desert
Nile
Cape Verde Islands
Senegal
Taoudenni Basin
Niger
Niger
Sahel
Blue Nile
White Nile
Lake Tana
Gulf of Aden
Horn of Africa
White Volta
Niger
Benue
Lake Volta
Sudd
Ethiopian Highlands
Grain Coast
Ivory Coast
Gold Coast
Slave Coast
Bight of Benin
Niger Delta
Adamawa Highlands
Cameroon Mountain 4070m
Massif des Bongo
Chari
Lake Turkana (Lake Rudolf)
Sheheli
Gulf of Guinea
São Tomé
Congo
Congo Basin
Congo
Lake Albert
Lake Victoria
Great Rift Valley
Juba
Kilimanjaro 5895m
B — B
Lake Tanganyika
Mitumba Range
Pemba Island
Zanzibar
Seychelles
Bié Plateau
Lake Nyasa
Comoro Islands
Madagascar
Zambezi
Zambezi
Mozambique Channel
Mauritius
Réunion
Namib Desert
Okavango Delta
Kalahari Basin
Kalahari Desert
Limpopo
INDIAN OCEAN
Orange River
Drakensberg
Great Karoo
C — C
Cape of Good Hope

CLIMATE

THE CLIMATES OF AFRICA range from mediterranean to arid, dry savannah and humid equatorial. In East Africa, where snow settles at the summit of volcanoes such as Kilimanjaro, climate is also modified by altitude. The winds of the Sahara export millions of tonnes of dust a year both northward and eastward.

Savannah grasslands run in a belt across Africa; limited rainfall inhibits tree growth.

The hot, equatorial basin of the Congo River receives over 48 inches (1,200 mm) of rainfall per year.

TEMPERATURE

Tropic of Cancer
20°N
Equator
20°S
Tropic of Capricorn

Average January temperature

Average July temperature

Temperature
- 32 to 50° F (0 to 10°C)
- 50 to 68°F (10 to 20°C)
- 68 to 86°F (20 to 30°C)
- above 86°F (30°C)

RAINFALL

Tropic of Cancer
20°N
Equator
20°S
Tropic of Capricorn

Average January rainfall

Average July rainfall

Rainfall
- 0–1 in (0–25 mm)
- 1–2 in (25–50 mm)
- 2–4 in (50–100 mm)
- 4–8 in (100–200 mm)
- 8–12 in (200–300 mm)
- 12–16 in (300–400 mm)
- 16–20 in (400–500 mm)
- more than 20 in (500 mm)

Climate
- arid
- humid equatorial
- mediterranean
- semiarid
- tropical
- warm humid
- daily hours of sunshine, January
- daily hours of sunshine, July
- cold wind
- hot wind

SHAPING THE CONTINENT

AFRICAN LANDSCAPES are shaped by the intensity of climatic extremes and by tectonic action. High aridity, wind action, and infrequent but heavy rainstorms, lead to the migration of sand dunes and dramatic flash flooding across much of the north and west. In the wetter areas, high precipitation increases the rate of weathering. To the east, the rift system has created a volcanic and lake environment and allowed rivers to erode weaknesses left in the crustal structure by faults.

GROUNDWATER

1 Oases are found in desert areas such as the Sahara (left). Groundwater migrates through permeable rock strata, confined between two impermeable layers. Oases form either when the permeable rocks come near to the surface, or at a fault line, when water is able to seep up to the surface through the crushed rocks at the fault.

Rainwater feeds the aquifer
Water migrates up through fault
Aquifer exposed near the surface
Groundwater trapped between impermeable strata

GROUNDWATER: REPLENISHMENT OF AN OASIS

THE EVOLVING LANDSCAPE

RIVER SYSTEMS

2 The Zambezi River (above) drops 360 ft (110 m) over the Victoria Falls into a zigzag gorge. The river has eroded the gorge along lines of weakness in the bedrock, created by fault lines running in two directions.

Old site of Victoria Falls
River plunges over falls
Fault and joint lines running in two directions
Zig-zag gorge of the Zambezi

RIVER SYSTEMS: RETREATING OF THE VICTORIA FALLS

WEATHERING

6 Inselbergs (above), found extensively across West Africa, are exposed remnants of an extensive upland area. Erosion of the surrounding uplands leaves a resistant rock outcrop. Its spheroidal shape is the result of "onion-skin" weathering – the exfoliating of layers – due to repeated expansion and contraction.

Exfoliated layers
External stresses act on the surface of the inselberg
Joints or cracks caused by expansion and contraction

WEATHERING: FORMATION OF AN INSELBERG

Sand is gradually blown up the back slope
Deposition on the slip face
Build up of sand produces strata inside the dune

WIND EROSION: MIGRATION OF A DUNE

Landscape
- sinking land
- stable land
- uplifting land
- escarpment
- ocean current
- rift
- active volcano
- inselberg
- oasis
- river
- wadi
- waterfall

EPHEMERAL CHANNELS

5 Wadis (above) drain much of northern Africa. These drybed courses are flooded only after infrequent, but intense, storms in the uplands cause water to surge along their channels.

Heavy rainfall runs off mountains
Water collects and floods the dry channel

EPHEMERAL CHANNELS: FLASH FLOODING OF A WADI

WIND EROSION

4 Dunes like this in the Namib Desert (left) are wind-blown accumulations of sand, which slowly migrate. Wind action moves sand up the shallow back slope; when the sand reaches the crest of the dune it is deposited on the slip face.

COASTAL PROCESSES

Waves refracting
Wave energy dispersed in the bay
Force of waves concentrates on the headland
The sea bed is deeper opposite the bay than at the headland

COASTAL PROCESSES: EROSION OF A BAY

3 Houtbaai (above), in southern Africa, is constantly being modified by wave action. As waves approach the indented coastline, they reach the shallow water of the headland, slowing down and reducing in length. This causes them to bend or refract, concentrating their erosive force at the headlands.

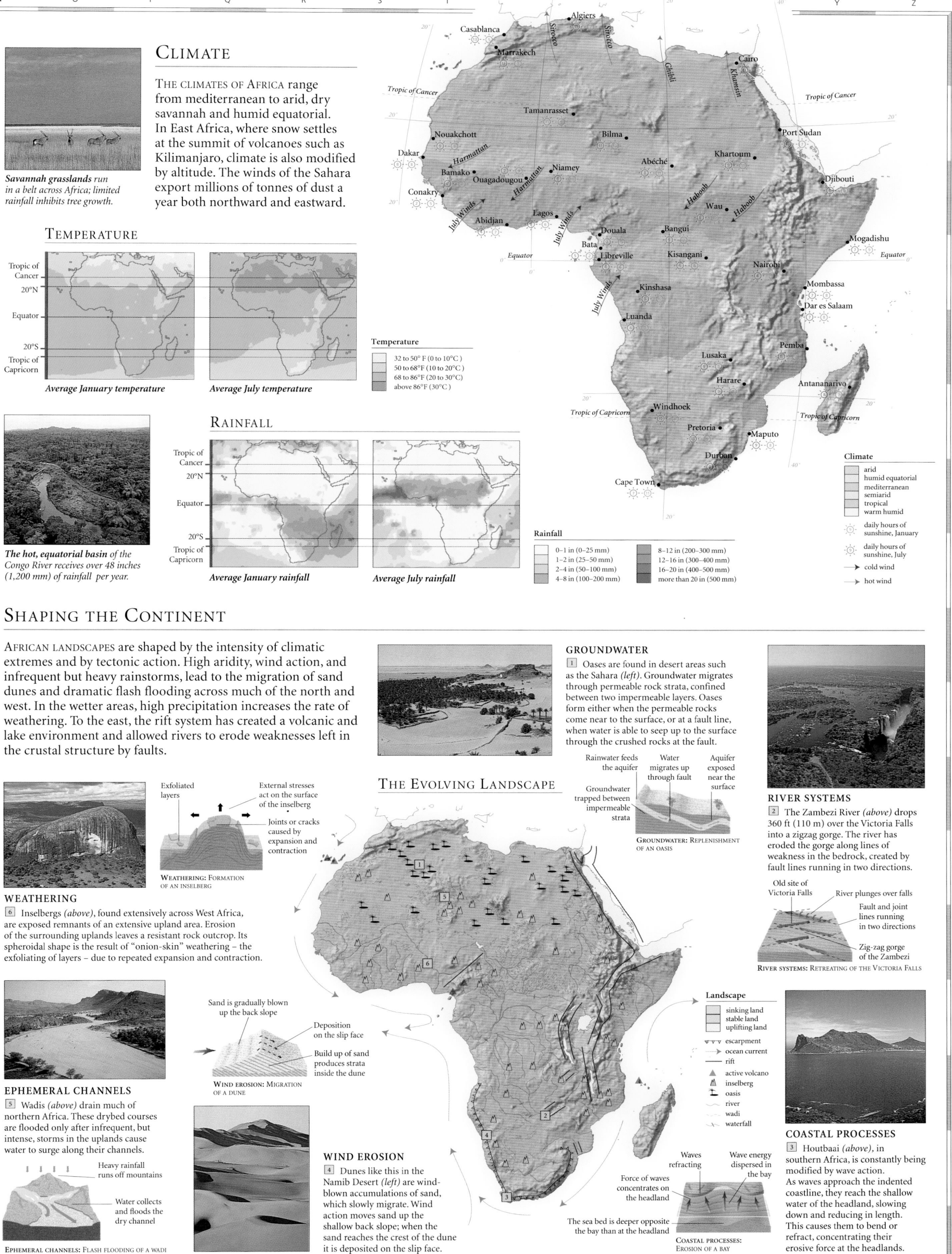

Casablanca, Algiers, Marrakech, Cairo, Tropic of Cancer, Tamanrasset, Nouakchott, Bilma, Port Sudan, Dakar, Khartoum, Djibouti, Bamako, Abéché, Ouagadougou, Niamey, Conakry, Wau, Abidjan, Lagos, Bangui, Mogadishu, Equator, Bata, Douala, Libreville, Kisangani, Nairobi, Kinshasa, Mombassa, Luanda, Dar es Salaam, Pemba, Lusaka, Harare, Antananarivo, Windhoek, Tropic of Capricorn, Pretoria, Maputo, Durban, Cape Town

Sirocco, Sirocco, Ghibli, Khamsin, Harmattan, Haboob, Haboob, July Winds, July Winds

POLITICAL AFRICA

THE POLITICAL MAP OF MODERN AFRICA only emerged following the end of the Second World War. Over the next half-century, all of the countries formerly controlled by European powers gained independence from their colonial rulers – only Liberia and Ethiopia were never colonized. The postcolonial era has not been an easy period for many countries, but there have been moves toward multiparty democracy in much of West Africa, and in Zambia, Tanzania, and Kenya. In South Africa, democratic elections replaced the internationally-condemned apartheid system only in 1994. Other countries have still to find political stability; corruption in government, and ethnic tensions are serious problems. National infrastructures, based on the colonial transportation systems built to exploit Africa's resources, are often inappropriate for independent economic development.

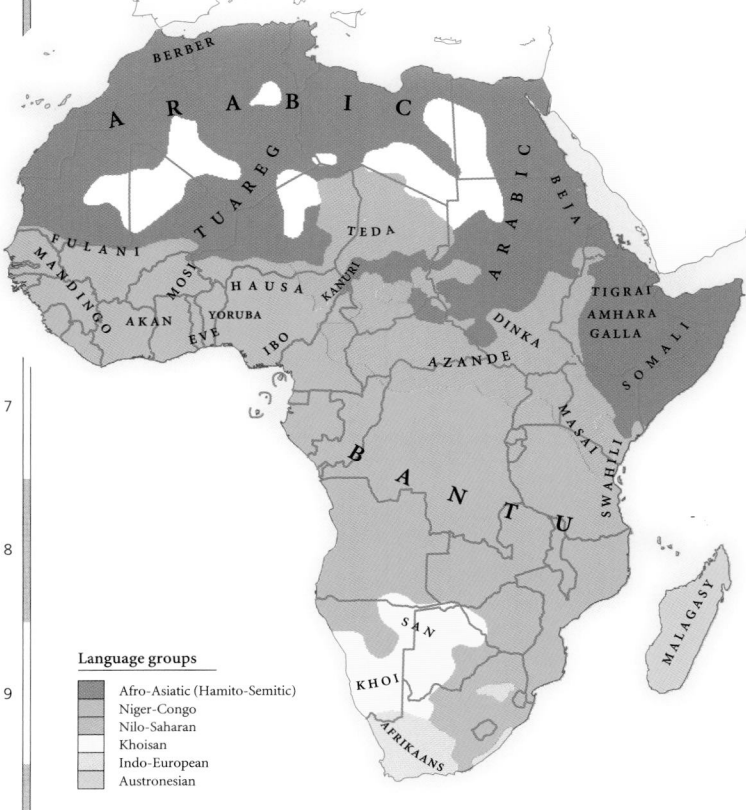

LANGUAGES

THREE MAJOR WORLD LANGUAGES act as *lingua francas* across the African continent: Arabic in North Africa; English in southern and eastern Africa and Nigeria; and French in Central and West Africa, and in Madagascar. A huge number of African languages are spoken as well – over 2,000 have been recorded, with more than 400 in Nigeria alone – reflecting the continuing importance of traditional cultures and values. In the north of the continent, the extensive use of Arabic reflects Middle Eastern influences while Bantu is widely-spoken across much of southern Africa.

Language groups
- Afro-Asiatic (Hamito-Semitic)
- Niger-Congo
- Nilo-Saharan
- Khoisan
- Indo-European
- Austronesian

OFFICIAL AFRICAN LANGUAGES

Official languages
- French
- English
- Arabic
- Portuguese
- Swahili
- Amharic
- Spanish
- French/English
- French/Arabic
- French/Malagasay
- English/Swahili
- Arabic/Somali

Islamic influences are evident throughout North Africa. The Great Mosque at Kairouan, Tunisia, is Africa's holiest Islamic place.

In northeastern Nigeria, people speak Kanuri – a dialect of the Saharan language group.

TRANSPORTATION

AFRICAN RAILROADS WERE BUILT to aid the exploitation of natural resources, and most offer passage only from the interior to the coastal cities, leaving large parts of the continent untouched – five landlocked countries have no railroads at all. The Congo, Nile, and Niger River networks offer limited access to land within the continental interior, but have a number of waterfalls and cataracts which prevent navigation from the sea. Many roads were developed in the 1960s and 1970s, but economic difficulties are making the maintenance and expansion of the networks difficult.

South Africa has the largest concentration of railroads in Africa. Over 20,000 miles (32,000 km) of routes have been built since 1870.

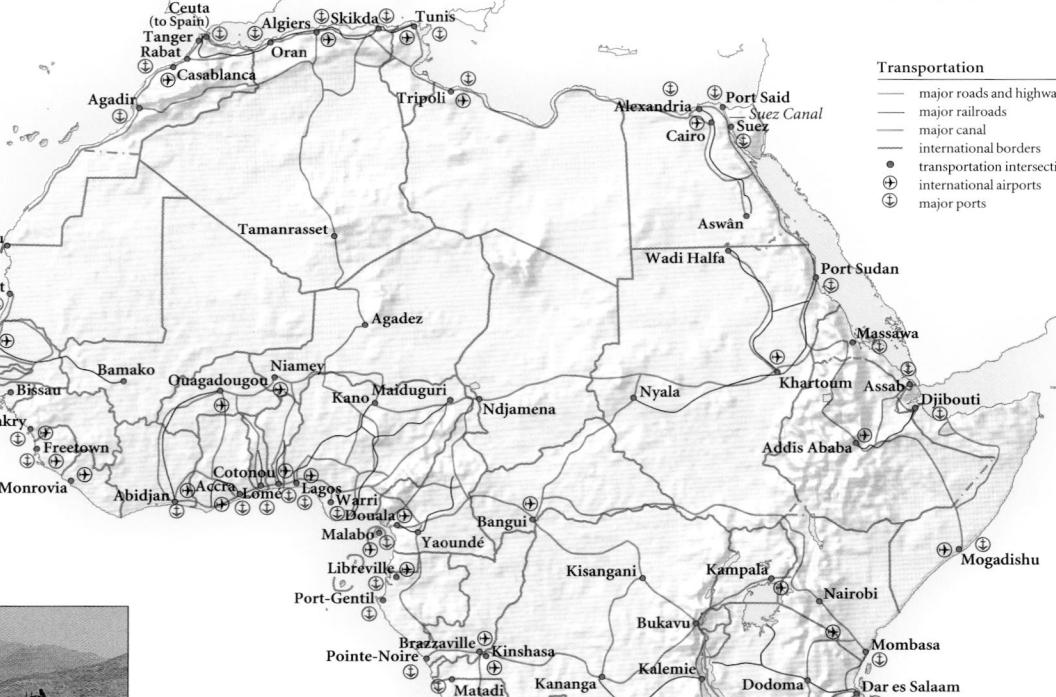

Transportation
- major roads and highways
- major railroads
- major canal
- international borders
- transportation intersections
- international airports
- major ports

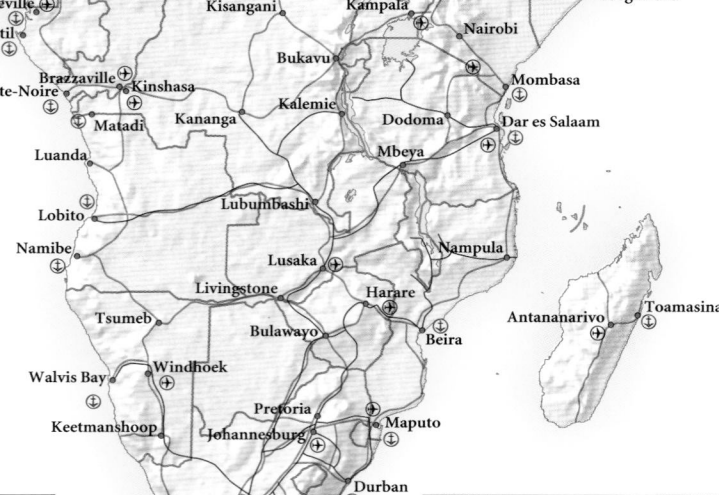

Traditional means of transportation, such as the camel, are still widely used across the less accessible parts of Africa.

The Congo River, though not suitable for river transportation along its entire length, forms a vital link for people and goods in its navigable inland reaches.

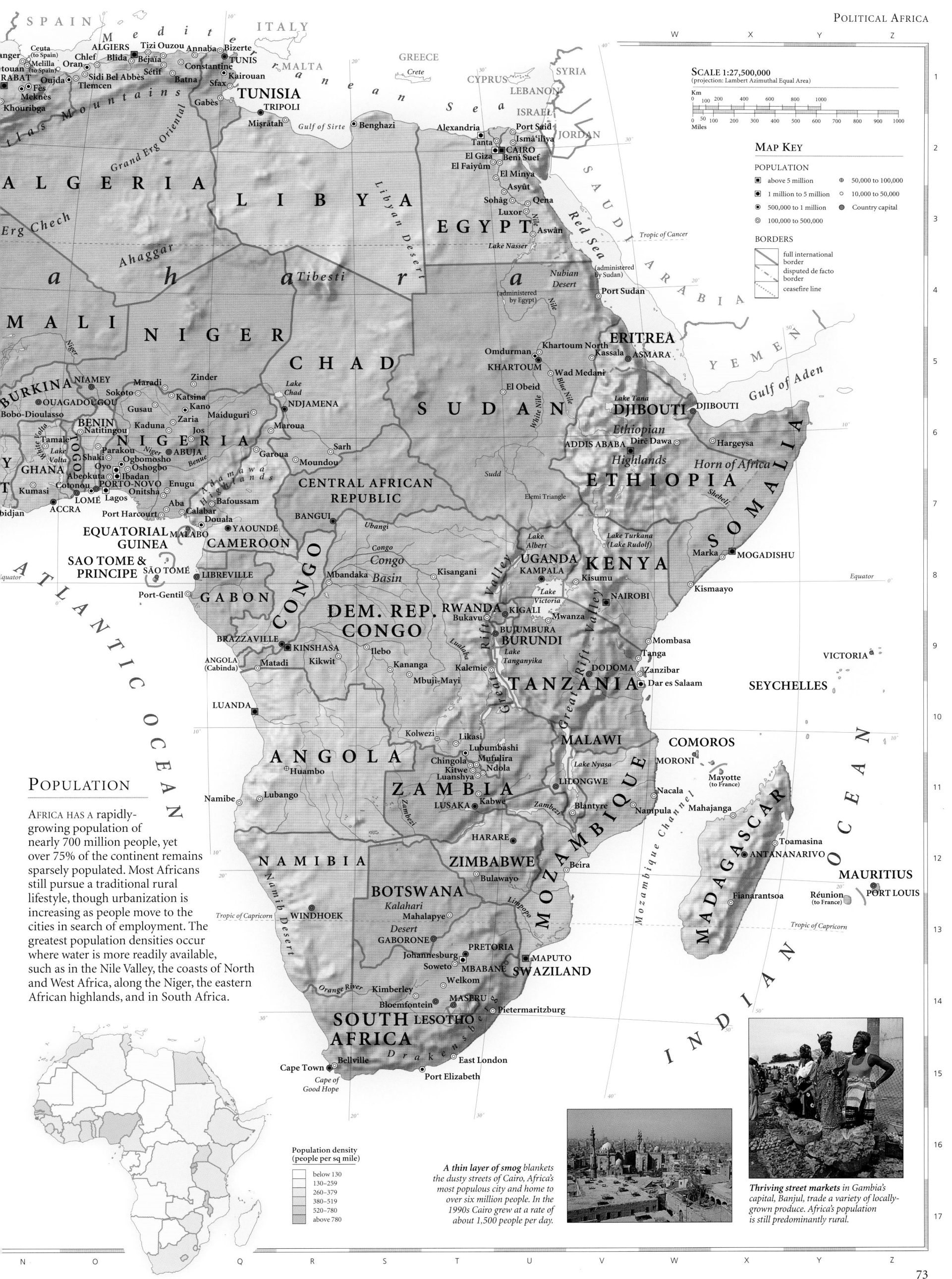

SPAIN
ITALY
GREECE
CYPRUS
SYRIA
LEBANON
ISRAEL
JORDAN

Ceuta (to Spain)
Tizi Ouzou
Annaba
Bizerte
MALTA
Tanger
Melilla (to Spain)
ALGIERS
Blida
Béjaïa
Sétif
Constantine
TUNIS
Crete
touan
RABAT
Oran
Sidi Bel Abbès
Batna
Sfax
Kairouan
Alexandria
Port Said
Ismaʻilîya
Fès
Oujda
Tlemcen
Kairouan
CAIRO
Meknès
Gabès
Tanta
El Giza
Beni Suef
Khouribga
TRIPOLI
TUNISIA
El Faiyûm
El Minya
Mişrâtah
Gulf of Sirte
Benghazi
Asyût
Sohâg
Qena
Luxor
Aswân

ALGERIA
LIBYA
EGYPT

Erg Chech
Ahaggar
Tibesti
Lake Nasser
Nubian Desert (administered by Sudan)
(administered by Egypt)
Port Sudan

MALI
NIGER
CHAD
SUDAN
ERITREA
ASMARA
DJIBOUTI
DJIBOUTI

BURKINA
NIAMEY
Maradi
Zinder
Lake Chad
NDJAMENA
Omdurman
Khartoum North
Kassala
Wad Medani
OUAGADOUGOU
Sokoto
Katsina
Kano
Zaria
Maiduguri
Maroua
KHARTOUM
El Obeid
ADDIS ABABA
Dire Dawa
Hargeysa
Bobo-Dioulasso
Gusau
Kaduna
Jos
Garoua
Sarh
Moundou
Ethiopian Highlands
Horn of Africa
BENIN
Natitingou
NIGERIA
Shaki
Oyo
Ogbomosho
ABUJA
Benue
Adamawa Highlands
CENTRAL AFRICAN REPUBLIC
Sudd
ETHIOPIA
SOMALIA
Parakou
Ibadan
Oshogbo
Enugu
GHANA
Abeokuta
PORTO-NOVO
Onitsha
Aba
Calabar
BANGUI
Ubangi
Elemi Triangle
Lake Turkana (Lake Rudolf)
Marka
MOGADISHU
Kumasi
Cotonou
LOMÉ
Lagos
Port Harcourt
Douala
YAOUNDÉ
Congo
Lake Albert
UGANDA
KENYA
ACCRA
EQUATORIAL GUINEA
MALABO
CAMEROON
Mbandaka
Congo Basin
Kisangani
KAMPALA
Kisumu
NAIROBI
SAO TOME & PRINCIPE
SÃO TOMÉ
LIBREVILLE
Lake Victoria
Port-Gentil
GABON
CONGO
DEM. REP. CONGO
RWANDA
KIGALI
Mwanza
Kismaayo
BRAZZAVILLE
KINSHASA
Ilebo
Bukavu
BUJUMBURA
BURUNDI
Mombasa
ANGOLA (Cabinda)
Matadi
Kikwit
Kananga
Kalemie
Lake Tanganyika
Tanga
VICTORIA
Mbuji-Mayi
DODOMA
Zanzibar
LUANDA
TANZANIA
Dar es Salaam
SEYCHELLES

ATLANTIC OCEAN

Equator

POPULATION

AFRICA HAS A rapidly-growing population of nearly 700 million people, yet over 75% of the continent remains sparsely populated. Most Africans still pursue a traditional rural lifestyle, though urbanization is increasing as people move to the cities in search of employment. The greatest population densities occur where water is more readily available, such as in the Nile Valley, the coasts of North and West Africa, along the Niger, the eastern African highlands, and in South Africa.

ANGOLA
Huambo
Namibe
Lubango
ZAMBIA
LUSAKA
Kolwezi
Likasi
Lubumbashi
Chingola
Mufulira
Kitwe
Ndola
Luanshya
Kabwe
MALAWI
LILONGWE
Lake Nyasa
COMOROS
MORONI
Mayotte (to France)
Nacala
Nampula
Mahajanga
NAMIBIA
ZIMBABWE
HARARE
MOZAMBIQUE
Blantyre
Namib Desert
Zambezi
Bulawayo
Beira
Toamasina
ANTANANARIVO
MADAGASCAR
MAURITIUS
BOTSWANA
Kalahari Desert
Mahalapye
WINDHOEK
GABORONE
Fianarantsoa
Réunion (to France)
PORT LOUIS
Tropic of Capricorn
PRETORIA
Johannesburg
Soweto
MBABANE
MAPUTO
SWAZILAND
Orange River
Welkom
Kimberley
MASERU
Bloemfontein
SOUTH AFRICA
LESOTHO
Pietermaritzburg
Drakensberg
Bellville
East London
Cape Town
Port Elizabeth
Cape of Good Hope

INDIAN OCEAN

Population density (people per sq mile)
- below 130
- 130–259
- 260–379
- 380–519
- 520–780
- above 780

A thin layer of smog blankets the dusty streets of Cairo, Africa's most populous city and home to over six million people. In the 1990s Cairo grew at a rate of about 1,500 people per day.

Thriving street markets *in Gambia's capital, Banjul, trade a variety of locally-grown produce. Africa's population is still predominantly rural.*

MAP KEY

POPULATION
- ■ above 5 million
- ⊕ 50,000 to 100,000
- ■ 1 million to 5 million
- ○ 10,000 to 50,000
- ⊙ 500,000 to 1 million
- ● Country capital
- ⊙ 100,000 to 500,000

BORDERS
- full international border
- disputed de facto border
- ceasefire line

AFRICAN RESOURCES

THE ECONOMIES OF MOST AFRICAN COUNTRIES are dominated by subsistence and cash crop agriculture, with limited industrialization. Manufacturing is largely confined to South Africa. Many countries depend on a single resource, such as copper or gold, or a cash crop, such as coffee, for export income, which can leave them vulnerable to fluctuations in world commodity prices. In order to diversify their economies and develop a wider industrial base, investment from overseas is being actively sought by many African governments.

INDUSTRY

MANY AFRICAN INDUSTRIES concentrate on the extraction and processing of raw materials. These include the oil industry, food processing, mining, and textile production. South Africa accounts for over half of the continent's industrial output with much of the remainder coming from the countries along the northern coast. Over 60% of Africa's workforce is employed in agriculture.

The unspoiled natural splendor *of wildlife reserves, like the Serengeti National Park in Tanzania, attract tourists to Africa from around the globe. The tourist industry in Kenya and Tanzania is particularly well developed, where it accounts for almost 10% of GNP.*

STANDARD OF LIVING

SINCE THE 1960s most countries in Africa have seen significant improvements in life expectancy, healthcare and education. However, 18 of the 20 most deprived countries in the world are African, and the continent as a whole lies well behind the rest of the world in terms of meeting many basic human needs.

Standard of Living
(UN Human Development Index)

high

low

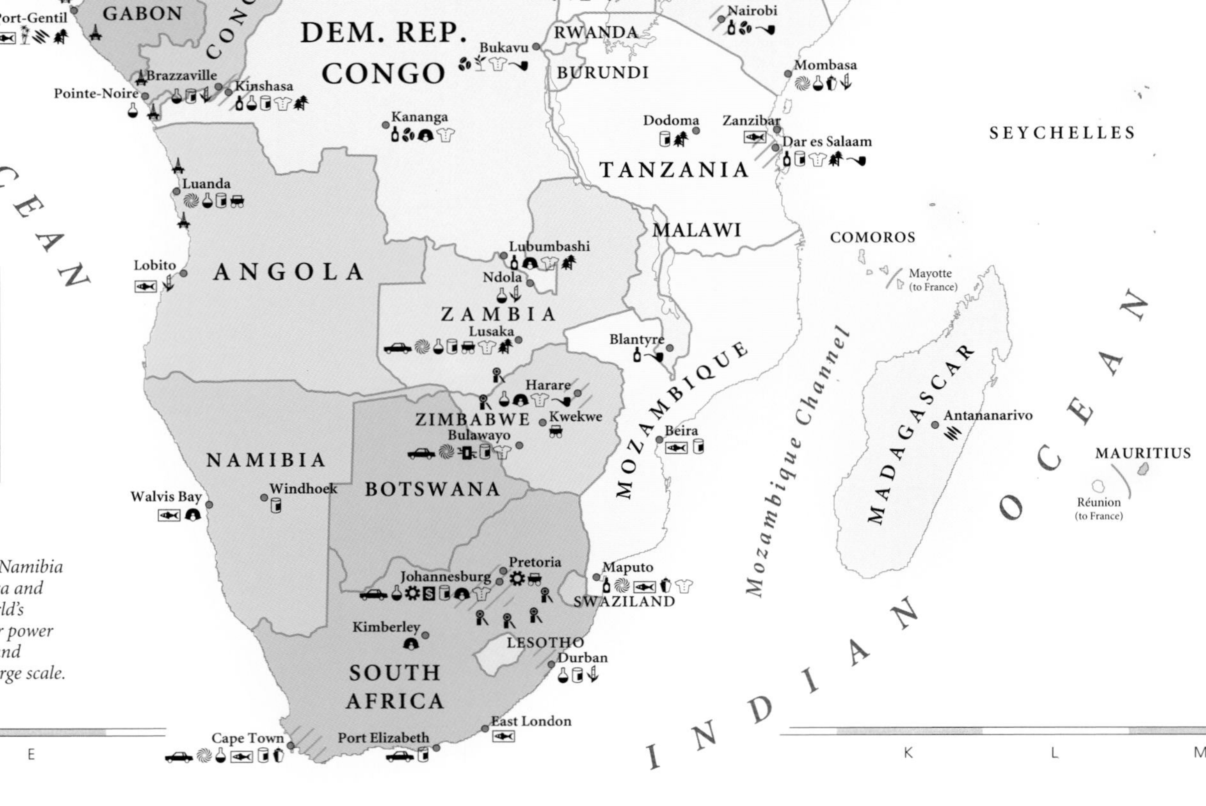

GNP per capita (US$)

0–199
200–399
400–599
600–899
900–1999
2000+

Industry

- brewing
- car/vehicle manufacture
- cement
- chemicals
- coffee processing
- electronics
- engineering
- finance
- fish processing
- food processing
- iron & steel
- mining
- palm oil processing
- peanut processing
- pharmaceuticals
- rice milling
- shipbuilding
- sugar processing
- tea processing
- textiles
- timber processing
- tobacco processing

- coal
- oil
- gas

- industrial cities
- major industrial areas

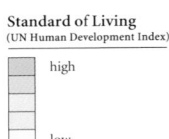

The map shows geographic place names and industry symbols across Africa, including:

PORTUGAL, SPAIN, *Mediterranean Sea*, ITALY, SYRIA, CYPRUS, LEBANON, ISRAEL

Oran, Algiers, Annaba, Tunis, Tripoli, Benghazi, Alexandria, Port Said, Cairo, Aswân

Casablanca, Rabat, Safi, MOROCCO, TUNISIA, ALGERIA, LIBYA, EGYPT

SAUDI ARABIA, *Red Sea*, YEMEN, *Gulf of Aden*

Western Sahara (occupied by Morocco)

MAURITANIA, MALI, NIGER, CHAD, SUDAN, ERITREA, Asmara, DJIBOUTI

Port Sudan, Khartoum

CAPE VERDE

Dakar, SENEGAL, Banjul, GAMBIA, GUINEA-BISSAU, Bamako, BURKINA, GUINEA, Conakry, Freetown, SIERRA LEONE, Monrovia, LIBERIA, IVORY COAST, Kumasi, GHANA, Accra, Abidjan, Sekondi-Takoradi, TOGO, BENIN, Katsina, Kano, Kaduna, NIGERIA, Ibadan, Lagos, Port Harcourt, CAMEROON, Douala

Addis Ababa, ETHIOPIA, SOMALIA, Mogadishu

CENTRAL AFRICAN REPUBLIC, Bangui

EQUATORIAL GUINEA, SAO TOME & PRINCIPE, Libreville, Port-Gentil, GABON, CONGO, DEM. REP. CONGO, Kisangani, UGANDA, Kampala, KENYA, Nairobi, Mombasa

Gulf of Guinea

ATLANTIC OCEAN

Brazzaville, Pointe-Noire, Kinshasa, Bukavu, RWANDA, BURUNDI, Kananga, Dodoma, Zanzibar, Dar es Salaam, TANZANIA, SEYCHELLES

Luanda, ANGOLA, Lobito, Lubumbashi, Ndola, ZAMBIA, Lusaka, MALAWI, Blantyre, COMOROS, Mayotte (to France)

Harare, Kwekwe, ZIMBABWE, Bulawayo, Beira, MOZAMBIQUE, *Mozambique Channel*, MADAGASCAR, Antananarivo, MAURITIUS, Réunion (to France)

NAMIBIA, Windhoek, Walvis Bay, BOTSWANA, *INDIAN OCEAN*

Johannesburg, Pretoria, Maputo, SWAZILAND, Kimberley, LESOTHO, Durban, SOUTH AFRICA, Cape Town, Port Elizabeth, East London

The discovery of oil *in the swampy Niger Delta during the 1960s made Nigeria one of Africa's richer nations. As world oil prices fell in the 1980s, the Nigerian economy faltered.*

Exotic rugs *and brightly-colored textiles are sold in a street market along the banks of the Nile River in Luxor, Egypt.*

The Rössing uranium *mines in Namibia are the largest in the world. Africa and the US produce over half the world's uranium ore, used to fuel nuclear power plants. Elsewhere, South Africa and Niger also mine uranium on a large scale.*

ENVIRONMENTAL ISSUES

ONE OF AFRICA'S most serious environmental problems occurs in marginal areas such as the Sahel where scrub and forest clearance, often for cooking fuel, combined with overgrazing, are causing desertification. Game reserves in southern and eastern Africa have helped to preserve many endangered animals, although the needs of growing populations have led to conflict over land use, and poaching is a serious problem.

Environmental Issues
- national parks
- tropical forest
- forest destroyed
- desert
- desertification
- polluted rivers
- radioactive contamination
- marine pollution
- heavy marine pollution
- poor urban air quality

The Sahel's delicate natural equilibrium is easily destroyed by the clearing of vegetation, drought, and overgrazing. This causes the Sahara to advance south, engulfing the savannah grasslands.

MINERAL RESOURCES

AFRICA'S ANCIENT PLATEAUS contain some of the world's most substantial reserves of precious stones and metals. About 30% of the world's gold is mined in South Africa; Zambia has great copper deposits; and diamonds are mined in Botswana, Dem. Rep. Congo, and South Africa. Oil has brought great economic benefits to Algeria, Libya, and Nigeria.

Mineral Resources
- oil field
- gas field
- coal field
- bauxite
- copper
- diamonds
- gold
- iron
- phosphates
- tin
- uranium

North and West Africa have large deposits of white phosphate minerals, which are used in making fertilizers. Morocco, Senegal, and Tunisia are the continent's leading producers.

Workers on a tea plantation gather one of Africa's most important cash crops, providing a valuable source of income. Coffee, rubber, bananas, cotton, and cocoa are also widely grown as cash crops.

Surrounded by desert, the fertile floodplains of the Nile Valley and Delta have been extensively irrigated, farmed, and settled since 3,000 BC.

USING THE LAND AND SEA

SOME OF AFRICA'S MOST PRODUCTIVE agricultural land is found in the eastern volcanic uplands, where fertile soils support a wide range of valuable export crops including vegetables, tea, and coffee. The most widely-grown grain is corn and peanuts are particularly important in West Africa. Without intensive irrigation, cultivation is not possible in desert regions and unreliable rainfall in other areas limits crop production. Pastoral herding is most commonly found in these marginal lands. Substantial local fishing industries are found along coasts and in vast lakes such as Lake Nyasa and Lake Victoria.

Using the Land and Sea
- cropland
- desert
- forest
- pasture
- wetland
- major conurbations
- cattle
- goats
- cereals
- sheep
- bananas
- corn (maize)
- citrus fruits
- cocoa
- cotton
- coffee
- dates
- fishing
- fruit
- oil palms
- olives
- peanuts
- rice
- rubber
- shellfish
- sugar cane
- tea
- tobacco
- vineyards
- wheat

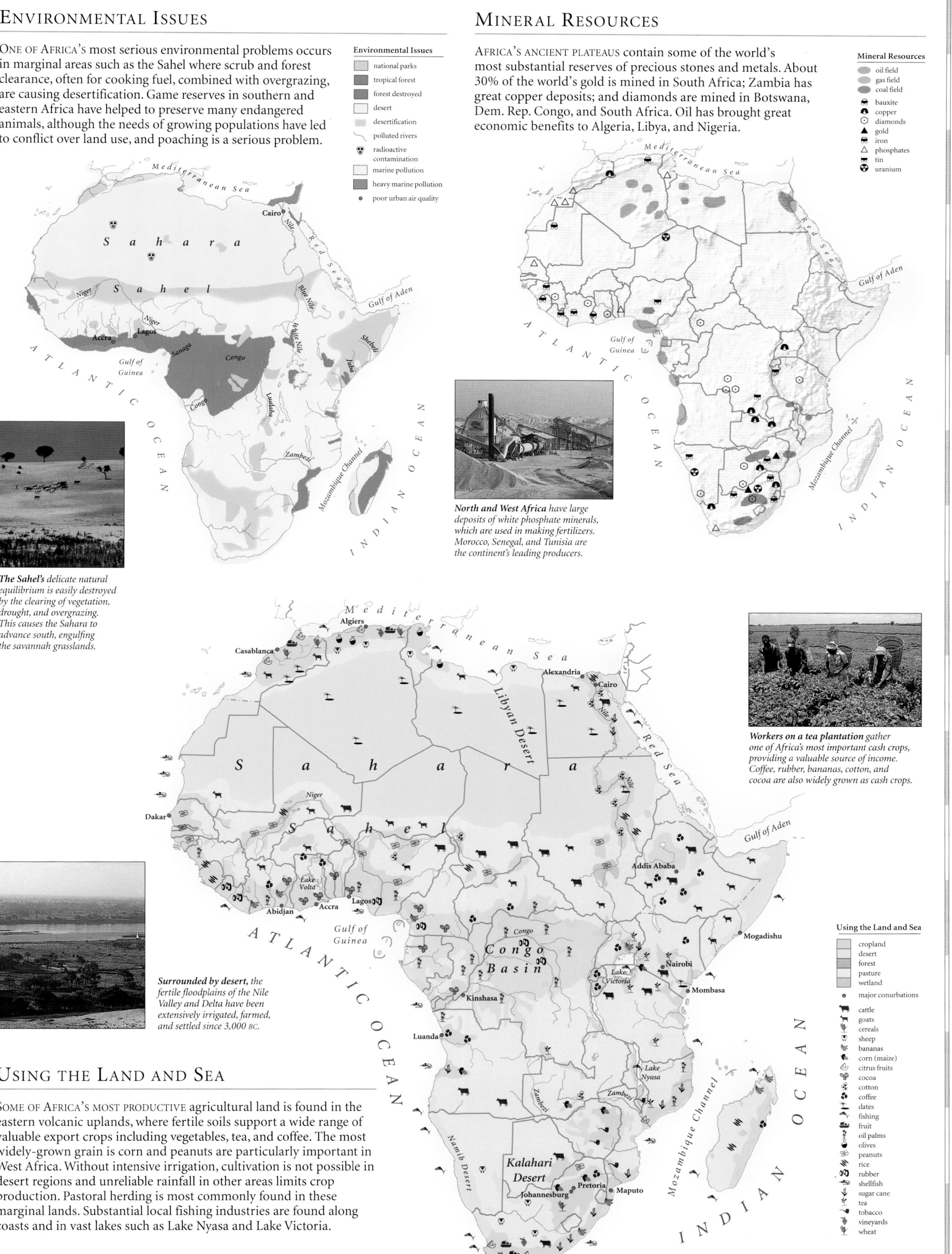

NORTH AFRICA

ALGERIA, EGYPT, LIBYA, MOROCCO, TUNISIA, WESTERN SAHARA

FRINGED BY THE MEDITERRANEAN along the northern coast and by the arid Sahara in the south, North Africa reflects the influence of many invaders, both European and, most importantly, Arab, giving the region an almost universal Islamic flavor and a common Arabic language. The countries lying to the west of Egypt are often referred to as the Maghreb, an Arabic term for "west." Today, Morocco and Tunisia exploit their culture and landscape for tourism, while rich oil and gas deposits aid development in Libya and Algeria, despite political turmoil. Egypt, with its fertile, Nile-watered agricultural land and varied industrial base, is the most populous nation.

THE LANDSCAPE

THE ATLAS MOUNTAINS, which extend across much of Morocco, northern Algeria, and Tunisia, are part of the fold mountain system which also runs through much of southern Europe. They recede to the south and east, becoming a steppe landscape before meeting the Sahara desert which covers more than 90% of the region. The sediments of the Sahara overlie an ancient plateau of crystalline rock, some of which is more than four billion years old.

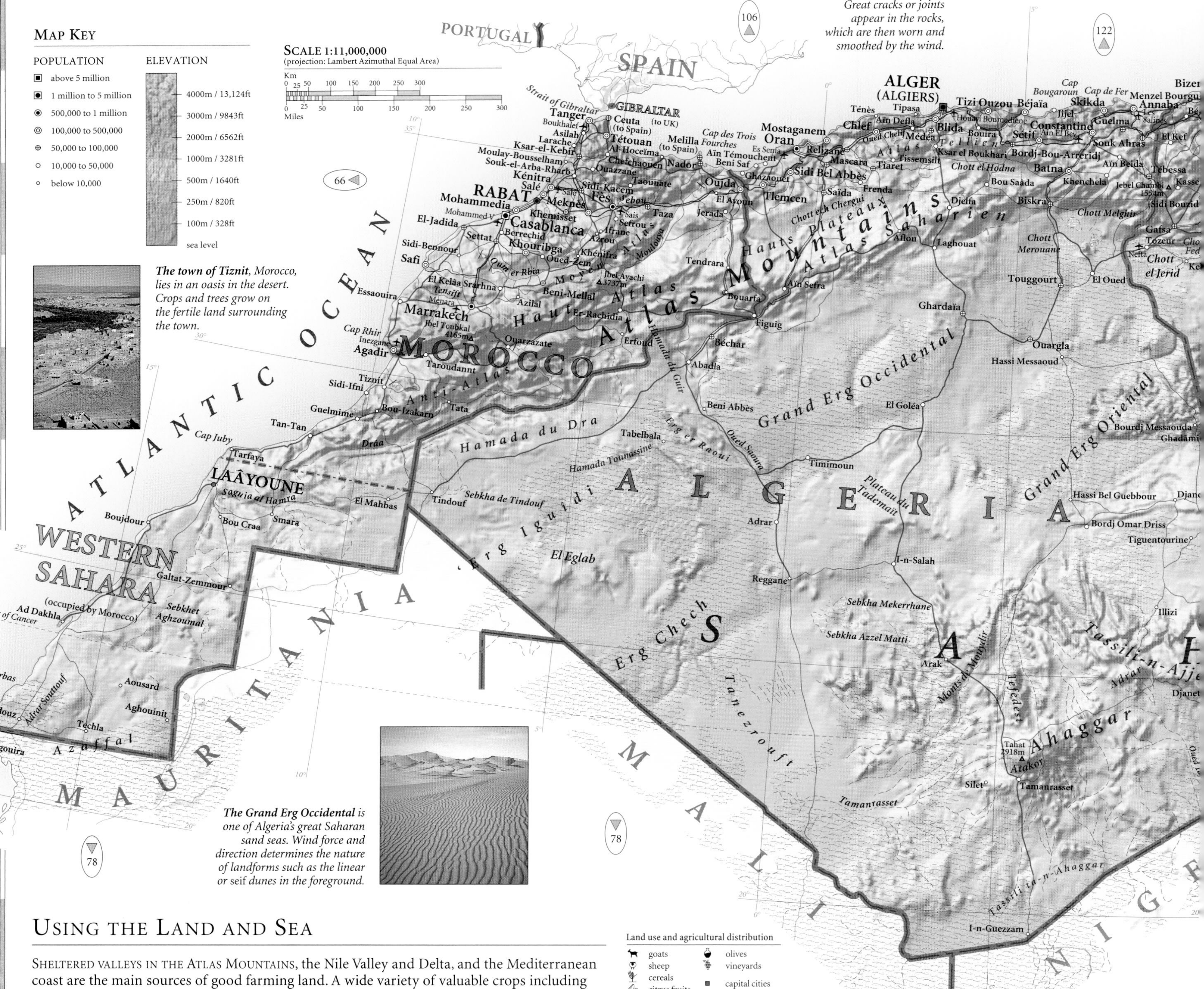

These rock piles in Algeria's Ahaggar Mountains are the result of weathering caused by extremes of temperature. Great cracks or joints appear in the rocks, which are then worn and smoothed by the wind.

MAP KEY

POPULATION

- ■ above 5 million
- ■ 1 million to 5 million
- ◙ 500,000 to 1 million
- ◉ 100,000 to 500,000
- ⊕ 50,000 to 100,000
- ○ 10,000 to 50,000
- ○ below 10,000

ELEVATION

- 4000m / 13,124ft
- 3000m / 9843ft
- 2000m / 6562ft
- 1000m / 3281ft
- 500m / 1640ft
- 250m / 820ft
- 100m / 328ft
- sea level

SCALE 1:11,000,000
(projection: Lambert Azimuthal Equal Area)

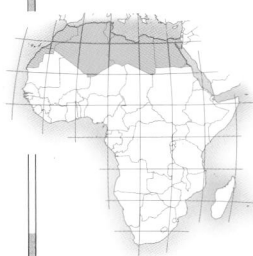

The town of Tiznit, Morocco, lies in an oasis in the desert. Crops and trees grow on the fertile land surrounding the town.

The Grand Erg Occidental is one of Algeria's great Saharan sand seas. Wind force and direction determines the nature of landforms such as the linear or seif dunes in the foreground.

USING THE LAND AND SEA

SHELTERED VALLEYS IN THE ATLAS MOUNTAINS, the Nile Valley and Delta, and the Mediterranean coast are the main sources of good farming land. A wide variety of valuable crops including cereals, rice, and cotton, and woods such as cedar and cork, are grown. Typical Mediterranean crops such as olives, figs, dates, and citrus fruits also thrive in these areas. The Nile Valley is particularly fertile, and most of Egypt's population lives close to the river. Elsewhere, irrigation is essential to improve crop yields on the desert margins.

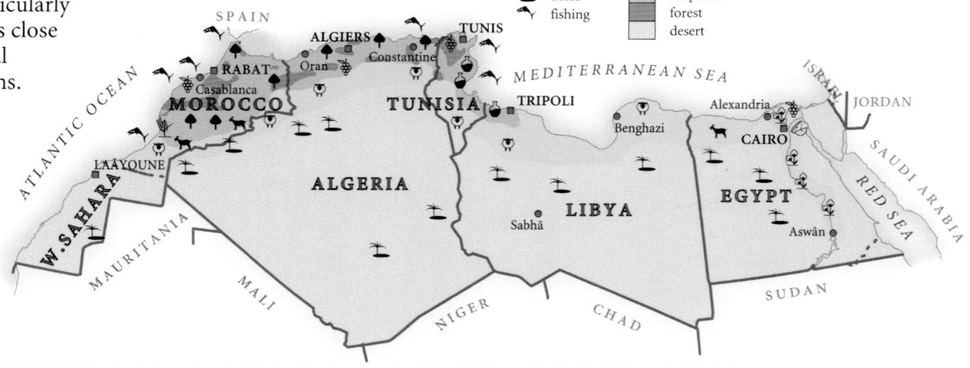

Land use and agricultural distribution

- goats
- sheep
- cereals
- citrus fruits
- cork
- cotton
- dates
- fishing
- olives
- vineyards
- ■ capital cities
- • major towns
- pasture
- cropland
- forest
- desert

THE URBAN/RURAL POPULATION DIVIDE

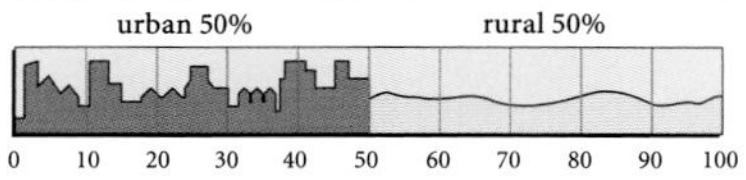

urban 50%	rural 50%

0 10 20 30 40 50 60 70 80 90 100

POPULATION DENSITY	TOTAL LAND AREA
62 people per sq mile (24 people per sq km)	2,215,020 sq miles (5,738,394 sq km)

Many North African nomads, such as the Bedouin, maintain a traditional pastoral lifestyle on the desert fringes, moving their herds of sheep, goats, and camels from place to place – crossing country borders in order to find sufficient grazing land.

The Atlas Mountains run from Morocco to Tunisia, covering more than 1,200 miles (1,931 km). The northern Tell Atlas (Atlas Tellien) are well watered, with forested slopes; the drier southern High Atlas (Haut Atlas) (left) have the highest peaks, such as Jbel Toubkal, 13,665 ft (4,165 m) high.

The spectacular sand seas of the Grand Ergs Occidental and Oriental in Algeria are only one of the varied landscapes of the Sahara. Hammadas, boulder-strewn rock plateaus, and reg, or desert pavements, plains strewn with gravel and small pebbles, are other important landforms.

Despite its outward aridity, the Sahara has several underground aquifers. Libya has built an underground pipeline, the Great Man-made River Project, to enable fuller exploitation of this valuable resource.

Split from the rest of Egypt by the Suez Canal, the Sinai Peninsula is partially dissected by countless wadis.

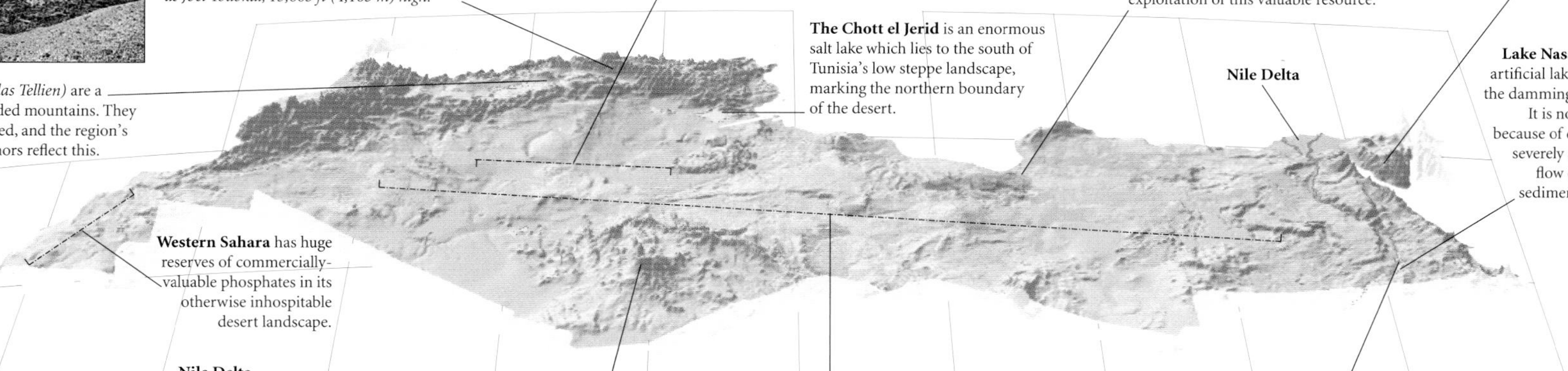

The Tell Atlas (Atlas Tellien) are a range of recent, folded mountains. They are still being formed, and the region's frequent earth tremors reflect this.

The Chott el Jerid is an enormous salt lake which lies to the south of Tunisia's low steppe landscape, marking the northern boundary of the desert.

Nile Delta

Lake Nasser is a huge artificial lake, created by the damming of the Nile. It is now silting up because of evaporation, severely affecting the flow of water and sediment to the sea.

Western Sahara has huge reserves of commercially-valuable phosphates in its otherwise inhospitable desert landscape.

Nile Delta

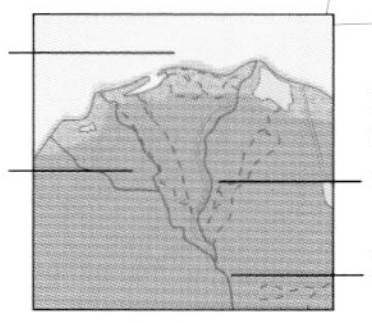

Mediterranean Sea

Fertile deposits of alluvium

Network of drainage channels

River Nile

Ahaggar

The Sahara is the largest hot desert on Earth, covering nearly a third of Africa. The sandy parts of the desert contain a wide variety of sand dunes, created by differing wind directions and strengths.

Nile Valley, Aswan

Almost all of Egypt's people – more than 99% – live close to the Nile River, or on its massive delta. The river waters the only strip of fertile land in Egypt.

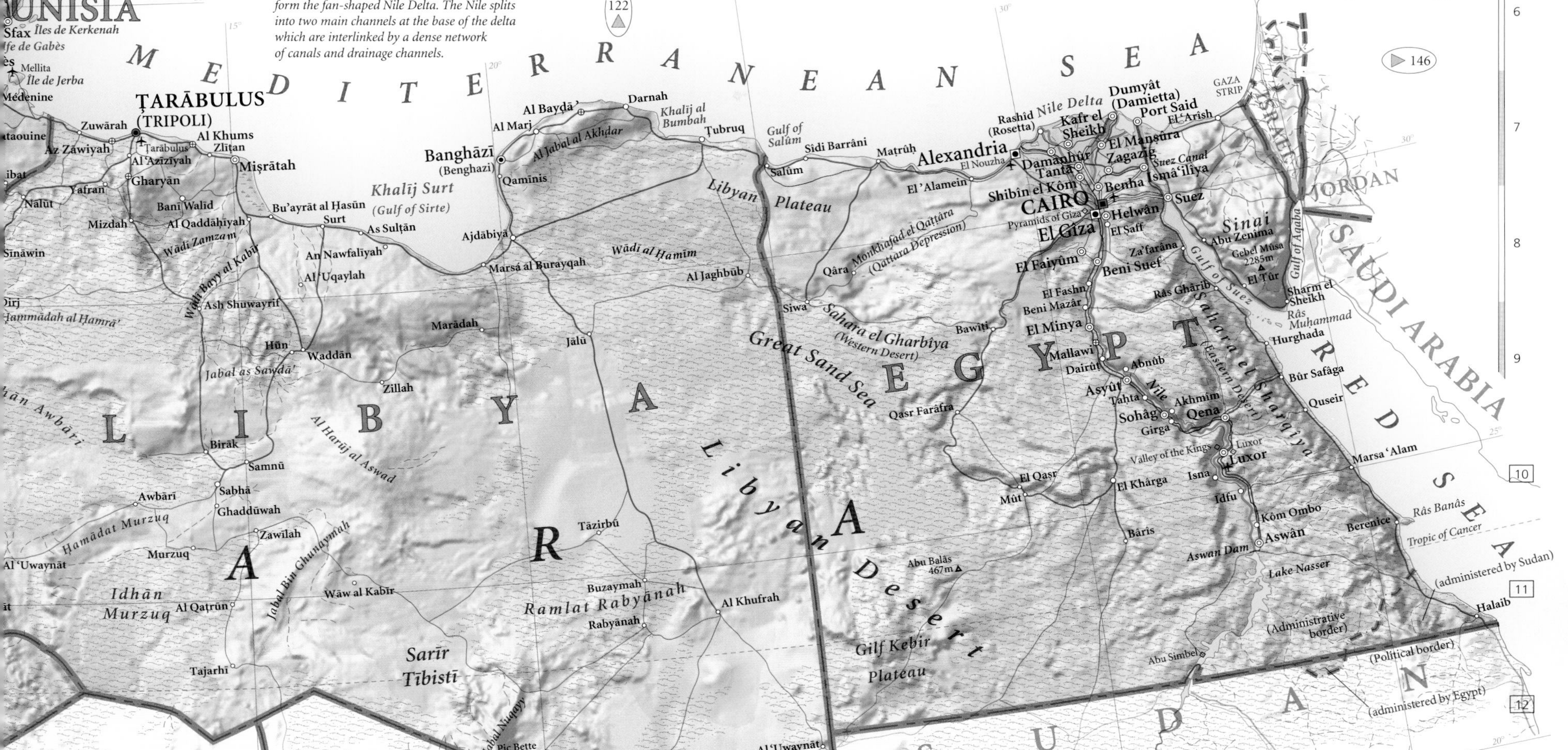

In its northernmost reaches, the Nile River has deposited huge quantities of silt and alluvium to form the fan-shaped Nile Delta. The Nile splits into two main channels at the base of the delta which are interlinked by a dense network of canals and drainage channels.

Built as great tombs for the pharaohs of ancient Egypt, the magnificent pyramids at Giza near Cairo have fascinated scholars, archaeologists, and tourists for centuries.

Oil rigs are scattered throughout the deserts of Libya and Algeria. Libyan oil is especially prized because of its low sulfur content, which means it produces much less pollution than other fuel oils.

TRANSPORTATION & INDUSTRY

THE ECONOMIES OF ALGERIA AND LIBYA were transformed by the discovery of oil and natural gas reserves in the deserts. Morocco's major exports are phosphates and agricultural produce, and as in Egypt and Tunisia, the tourist industry is essential to the economy. Egypt has the most varied industrial base, importing technology to develop electronics and engineering industries, and maintaining the reputation of its high-quality cotton textiles.

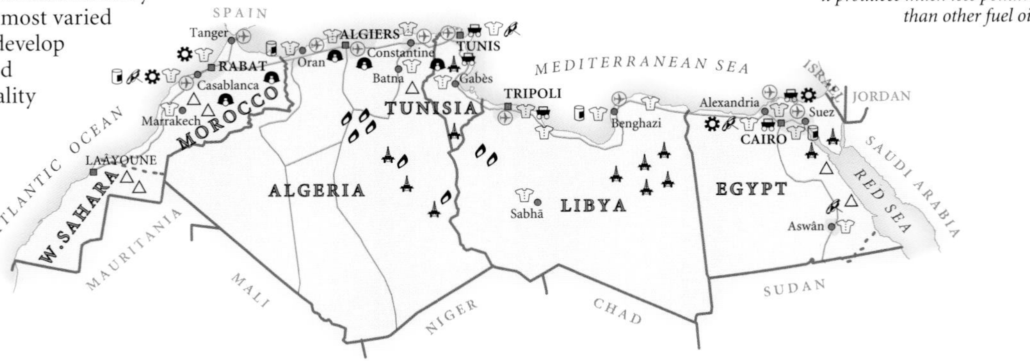

Major industry and infrastructure

- engineering
- food processing
- gas
- iron & steel
- iron ore
- oil
- phosphates
- textiles
- tourism
- capital cities
- major towns
- international airports
- major roads
- major industrial areas

TRANSPORTATION NETWORK

152,393 miles (245,400 km)		480 miles (773 km)	
8025 miles (12,922 km)		121 miles (195 km)	

Tourism and the oil industry have made improvements to the Maghreb's infrastructure – both necessary and possible. The Suez Canal is a vital artery for shipping between Europe and Asia.

WEST AFRICA

BENIN, BURKINA, CAPE VERDE, GAMBIA, GHANA, GUINEA, GUINEA-BISSAU, IVORY COAST, LIBERIA, MALI, MAURITANIA, NIGER, NIGERIA, SENEGAL, SIERRA LEONE, TOGO

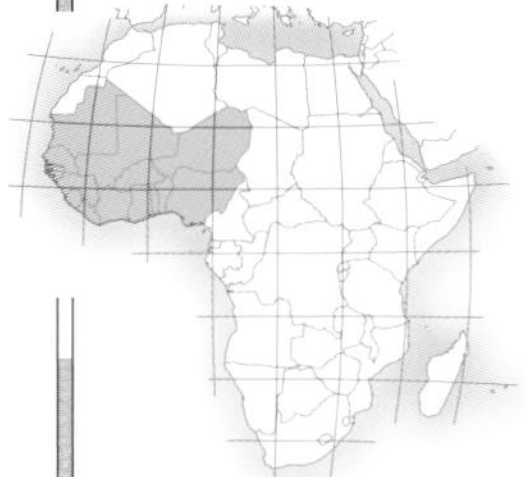

WEST AFRICA IS AN IMMENSELY DIVERSE REGION, encompassing the desert landscapes and mainly Muslim populations of the southern Saharan countries, and the tropical rain forests of the more humid south, with a great variety of local languages and cultures. The rich natural resources and accessibility of the area were quickly exploited by Europeans; most of the Africans taken by slave traders came from this region, causing serious depopulation. The very different influences of West Africa's leading colonial powers, Britain and France, remain today, reflected in the languages and institutions of the countries they once governed.

The dry scrub of the Sahel is only suitable for grazing herd animals like these cattle in Mali.

SCALE 1:9,000,000
(projection: Lambert Azimuthal Equal Area)

Km 0 25 50 100 150 200 250
Miles 0 25 50 100 150 200 250

TRANSPORTATION & INDUSTRY

ABUNDANT NATURAL RESOURCES including oil and metallic minerals are found in much of West Africa, although investment is required for their further exploitation. Nigeria experienced an oil boom during the 1970s but subsequent growth has been sporadic. Most industry in other countries has a primary basis, including mining, logging, and food processing.

TRANSPORTATION NETWORK

163,769 miles (263,719 km)	1,554 miles (2,502 km)
6,819 miles (10,980 km)	9,470 miles (15,250 km)

The road and rail systems are most developed near the coasts. Some of the landlocked countries remain disadvantaged by the difficulty of access to ports, and their poor road networks.

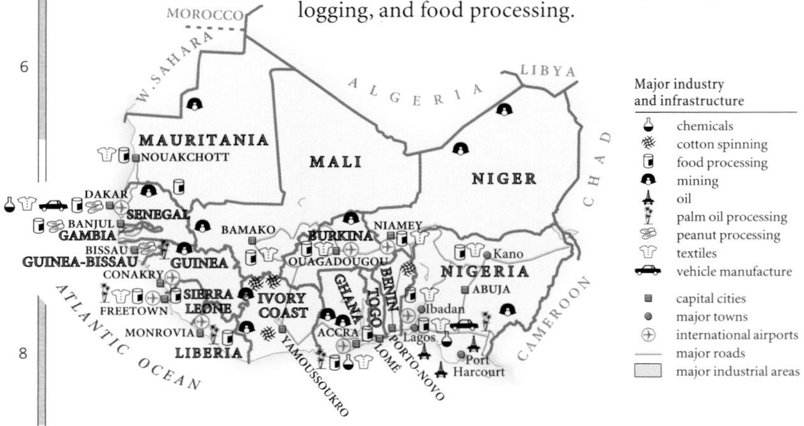

Major industry and infrastructure
- chemicals
- cotton spinning
- food processing
- mining
- oil
- palm oil processing
- peanut processing
- textiles
- vehicle manufacture

- capital cities
- major towns
- international airports
- major roads
- major industrial areas

MAP KEY

POPULATION
- 1 million to 5 million
- 500,000 to 1 million
- 100,000 to 500,000
- 50,000 to 100,000
- 10,000 to 50,000
- below 10,000

ELEVATION
- 2000m / 6562ft
- 1000m / 3281ft
- 500m / 1640ft
- 250m / 820ft
- 100m / 328ft
- sea level

CAPE VERDE

Santo Antão, Pombas, Ilhas de Barlavento, Mindelo, São Vicente, Ribeira Brava, São Nicolau, Pedra Lume, Amílcar Cabral, Sal, Boa Vista, João Barrosa

ATLANTIC OCEAN

Tarrafal, Maio, Fogo, São Filipe, Santiago, PRAIA, Maio, Ilhas de Sotavento

(same scale as main map)

The southern regions of West Africa still contain great swaths of tropical rain forest, including some of the world's most prized hardwood trees, such as mahogany and iroko.

USING THE LAND AND SEA

THE HUMID SOUTHERN REGIONS are most suitable for cultivation; in these areas, cash crops such as coffee, cotton, cocoa, and rubber are grown in large quantities. Peanuts are grown throughout West Africa. In the north, advancing desertification has made the Sahel increasingly uncultivable, and pastoral farming is more common. Great herds of sheep, cattle, and goats are grazed on the savannah grasses. Fishing is important in coastal and delta areas.

The Gambia, mainland Africa's smallest country, produces great quantities of peanuts. Winnowing is used to separate the nuts from their stalks.

Land use and agricultural distribution
- goats
- sheep
- cocoa
- coffee
- cotton
- oil palms
- peanuts
- rubber
- shellfish

- capital cities
- major towns
- pasture
- cropland
- forest
- desert

THE URBAN/RURAL POPULATION DIVIDE

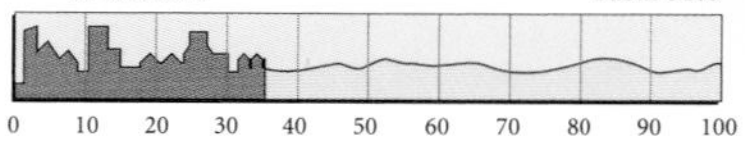

urban 36%   rural 64%

0 10 20 30 40 50 60 70 80 90 100

POPULATION DENSITY	TOTAL LAND AREA
98 people per sq mile (38 people per sq km)	2,337,137 sq miles (6,054,760 sq km)

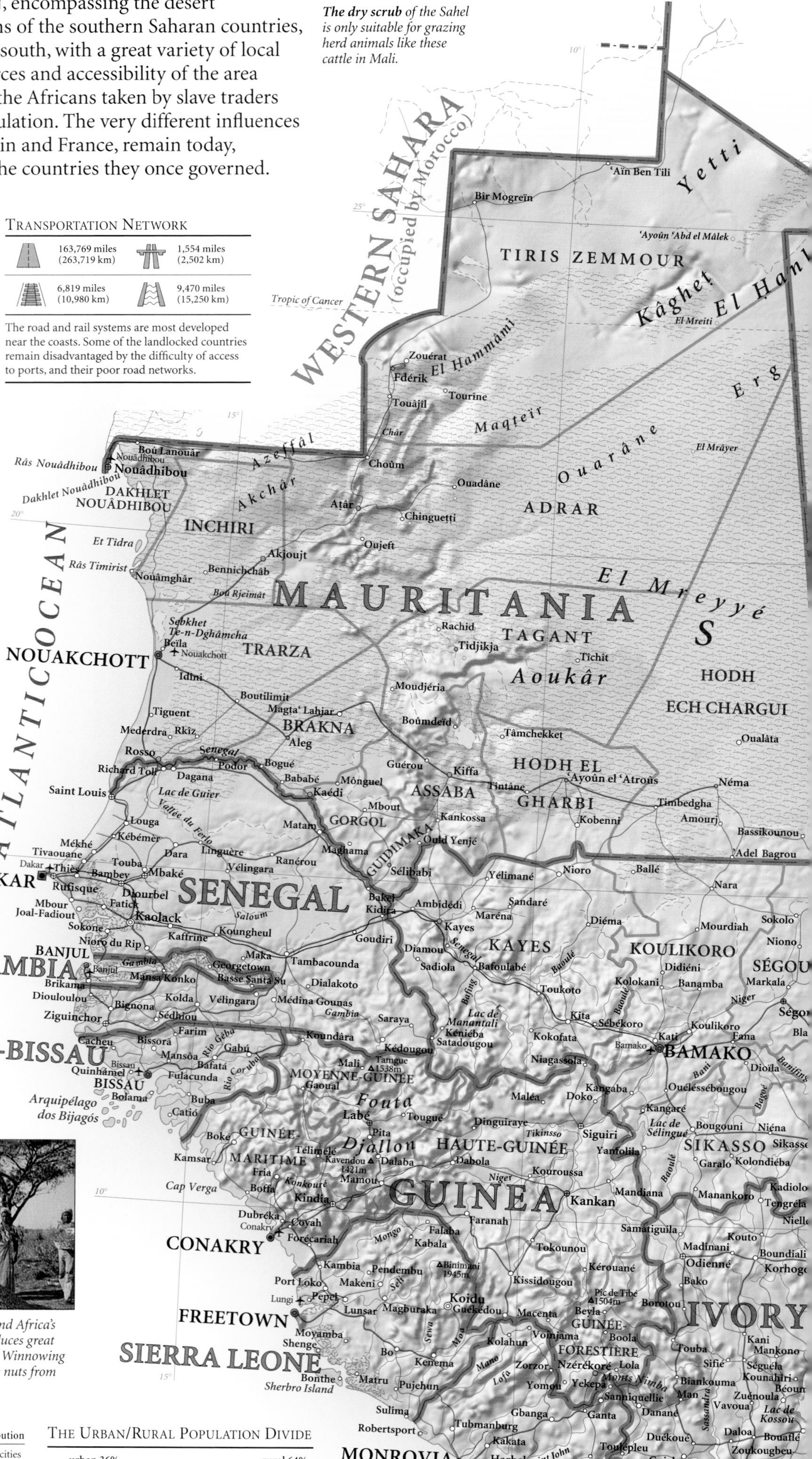

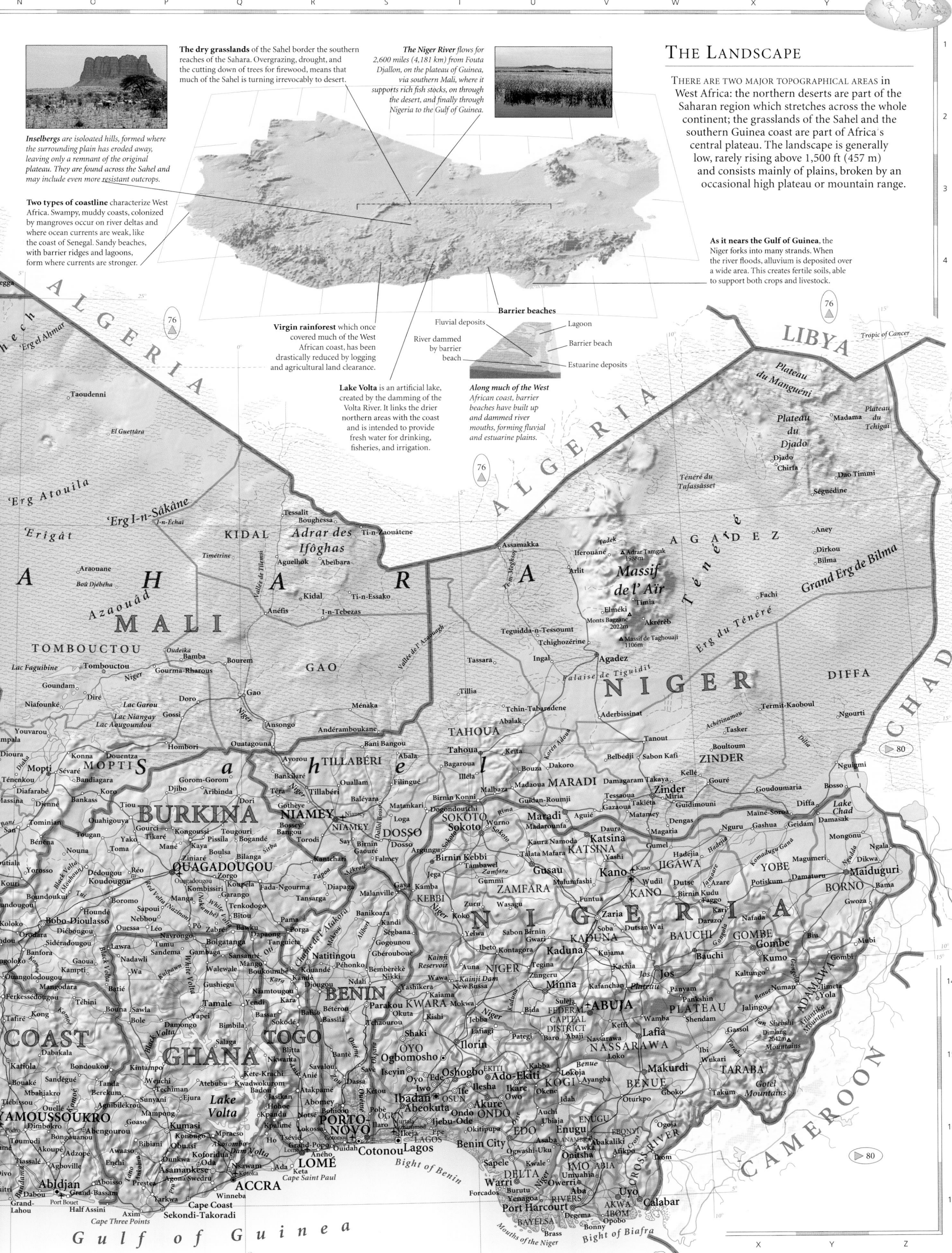

THE LANDSCAPE

THERE ARE TWO MAJOR TOPOGRAPHICAL AREAS in West Africa: the northern deserts are part of the Saharan region which stretches across the whole continent; the grasslands of the Sahel and the southern Guinea coast are part of Africa's central plateau. The landscape is generally low, rarely rising above 1,500 ft (457 m) and consists mainly of plains, broken by an occasional high plateau or mountain range.

The dry grasslands of the Sahel border the southern reaches of the Sahara. Overgrazing, drought, and the cutting down of trees for firewood, means that much of the Sahel is turning irrevocably to desert.

The Niger River flows for 2,600 miles (4,181 km) from Fouta Djallon, on the plateau of Guinea, via southern Mali, where it supports rich fish stocks, on through the desert, and finally through Nigeria to the Gulf of Guinea.

Inselbergs are isolated hills, formed where the surrounding plain has eroded away, leaving only a remnant of the original plateau. They are found across the Sahel and may include even more resistant outcrops.

Two types of coastline characterize West Africa. Swampy, muddy coasts, colonized by mangroves occur on river deltas and where ocean currents are weak, like the coast of Senegal. Sandy beaches, with barrier ridges and lagoons, form where currents are stronger.

As it nears the Gulf of Guinea, the Niger forks into many strands. When the river floods, alluvium is deposited over a wide area. This creates fertile soils, able to support both crops and livestock.

Virgin rainforest which once covered much of the West African coast, has been drastically reduced by logging and agricultural land clearance.

Barrier beaches

Fluvial deposits — Lagoon
River dammed by barrier beach — Barrier beach
— Estuarine deposits

Lake Volta is an artificial lake, created by the damming of the Volta River. It links the drier northern areas with the coast and is intended to provide fresh water for drinking, fisheries, and irrigation.

Along much of the West African coast, barrier beaches have built up and dammed river mouths, forming fluvial and estuarine plains.

CENTRAL AFRICA

CAMEROON, CENTRAL AFRICAN REPUBLIC, CHAD, CONGO, DEM. REP. CONGO, EQUATORIAL GUINEA, GABON, SAO TOME & PRINCIPE

THE GREAT RAIN FOREST BASIN of the Congo River embraces most of remote Central Africa. The interior was largely unknown to Europeans until late in the 19th century, when its tribal kingdoms were split – principally between France and Belgium – with Sao Tome and Principe the lone Portuguese territory, and Equatorial Guinea controlled by Spain. Open democracy and regional economic integration are important goals for these nations – several of which have only recently emerged from restrictive regimes – and investment is needed to improve transportation infrastructures. Many of the small, but fast-growing and increasingly urban population, speak French, the regional *lingua franca*, along with several hundred Pygmy, Bantu, and Sudanic dialects.

TRANSPORTATION & INDUSTRY

LARGE RESERVES OF VALUABLE MINERALS are found in Central Africa: copper, cobalt, zinc, and tin are mined in Dem. Rep. Congo and Cameroon; diamonds in the Central African Republic; and manganese in Gabon. Congo, Cameroon, Gabon, and Dem. Rep. Congo have oil deposits and oil has also been recently discovered in Chad. Goods such as palm oil and rubber are processed for export.

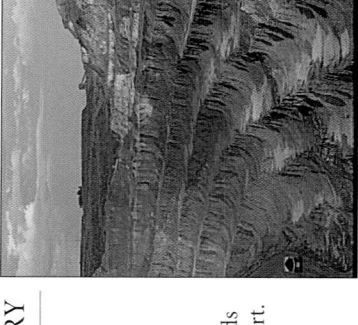

The ancient rocks of Dem. Rep. Congo hold immense and varied mineral reserves. This open pit copper mine is at Kolwezi in the far south.

Major industry and infrastructure

- brewing
- chemicals
- cobalt
- copper
- diamonds
- food processing
- manganese
- oil
- palm oil processing
- textiles
- tin
- capital cities
- major towns
- international airports
- major roads
- major industrial areas

TRANSPORTATION NETWORK

124,349 miles (200,240 km)	342 miles (550 km)
3,830 miles (6,167 km)	15,261 miles (24,575 km)

The Trans-Gabon railroad, which began operating in 1987, has opened up new sources of timber and manganese. Elsewhere, much investment is needed to update and improve road, rail, and water transportation.

THE LANDSCAPE

LAKE CHAD LIES in a desert basin bounded by the volcanic Tibesti Mountains in the north, plateaus in the east and, in the south, the broad watershed of the Congo Basin. The vast circular depression of the Congo is isolated from the coastal plain by the granite Massif du Chaillu. To the northwest, the volcanoes and fold mountains of the Cameroon Ridge (*Dorsale Camerounaise*) extend as islands into the Gulf of Guinea. The high fold mountains fringing the east of the Congo Basin fall steeply to the lakes of the Great Rift Valley.

The Tibesti Mountains are the highest in the Sahara. They were pushed up by the movement of the African Plate over a hot spot, which first formed the northern Ahaggar Mountains and is now thought to lie under the Great Rift Valley.

The Congo River is second only to the Amazon in the volume of water it carries, and in the size of its drainage basin.

Lake Tanganyika, the world's second deepest lake, is the largest of a series of linear "ribbon" lakes occupying a trench within the Great Rift Valley.

Rich mineral deposits in the "Copper Belt" of Dem. Rep. Congo were formed under intense heat and pressure when the ancient African Shield was uplifted to form the region's mountains.

Virgin tropical rain forest covers the Ruwenzori range on the borders of Dem. Rep. Congo and Uganda.

The vast sandflats surrounding Lake Chad were once covered by water. Changing climatic patterns caused the lake to shrink, and desert now covers much of its previous area.

The lake-like expansion of the Congo River at Stanley Pool is the lowest point of the interior basin, although the river still descends more than 1,000 ft (300 m) to reach the sea.

The Congo River flows sluggishly through the rain forest of the interior basin. Toward the coast, the river drops steeply in a series of waterfalls and cataracts. At this point, the erosional power of the river becomes so great that it has formed a deep submarine canyon offshore.

Broad, shallow basin

Waterfalls and cataracts

Submarine canyon

Lake Chad is the remnant of an inland sea, which once occupied much of the surrounding basin. A series of droughts since the 1970s has reduced the area of this shallow freshwater lake to about 1,000 sq miles (2,599 sq km).

*A plug of resistant lava, at the southwestern end of the Cameroon Ridge (*Dorsale Camerounaise*), is all that remains of an eroded volcano.*

The volcanic massif of Cameroon Mountain occupies an area which remains volcanically active.

Gulf of Guinea

Massif du Chaillu

MAP KEY

POPULATION

- 1 million to 5 million
- 500,000 to 1 million
- 100,000 to 500,000
- 50,000 to 100,000
- 10,000 to 50,000
- below 10,000

ELEVATION

- 4000m / 13,124ft
- 3000m / 9843ft
- 2000m / 6562ft
- 1000m / 3281ft
- 500m / 1640ft
- 250m / 820ft
- 100m / 328ft
- sea level

SCALE 1:9,500,000
(projection: Lambert Azimuthal Equal Area)

The great Congo River forms part of the border between Congo and Dem. Rep. Congo. The river is fast-flowing, and a series of falls and rapids means that it is only partly navigable.

High-quality timber is floated to Port-Gentil, Gabon, via the Ogooué River. Timber provides important export revenue for several countries, although there has been concern about the uncontrolled logging of rare tropical woods.

USING THE LAND

CASH CROPS FOR EXPORT include cocoa, coffee, and rubber. Shifting cultivation is widely practiced, and plantains are the staple food of the equatorial region, grown with yam and taro. Cassava, guinea corn (sorghum), and millet are the main subsistence crops in savannah areas. Cattle farming is limited to areas free of tsetse fly, and fish from the interior rivers are an important protein source.

THE URBAN/RURAL POPULATION DIVIDE

urban 33%   rural 67%

POPULATION DENSITY	TOTAL LAND AREA
39 people per sq mile	2,023,939 sq miles
(15 people per sq km)	(5,243,364 sq km)

Land use and agricultural distribution

cattle
cocoa
coffee
cotton
palms
peanuts
rubber
timber

capital cities
major towns

pasture
cropland
forest
desert

81

EAST AFRICA

BURUNDI, DJIBOUTI, ERITREA, ETHIOPIA, KENYA, RWANDA, SOMALIA, SUDAN, TANZANIA, UGANDA

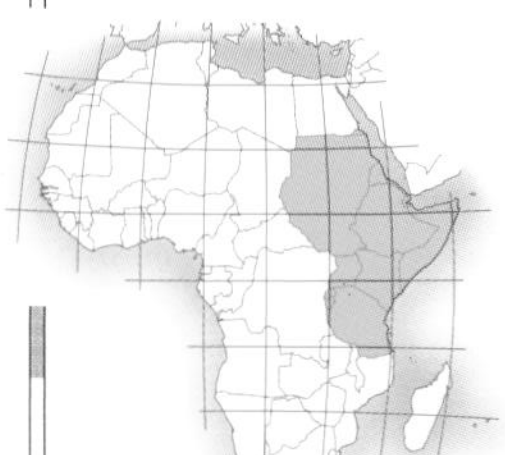

T HE COUNTRIES OF EAST AFRICA divide into two distinct cultural regions. Sudan and the "Horn" nations have been influenced by the Middle East; Ethiopia was the home of one of the earliest Christian civilizations, and Sudan reflects both Muslim and Christian influences. The southern countries share a closer cultural affinity with other sub-Saharan nations. Some of Africa's most densely populated countries lie in this region, and the needs of a growing number of people have put pressure on marginal lands and fragile environments. Although most East African economies remain strongly agricultural, Kenya has developed a varied industrial base.

THE LANDSCAPE

EAST AFRICA'S MOST SIGNIFICANT landscape feature is the Great Rift Valley, which formed during the most recent phase of continental movement when the rigid basement rocks cracked and buckled. Great blocks of land were raised and lowered, creating huge flat-bottomed valleys and steep escarpments, sometimes covered by volcanic extrusions in highland areas.

Ephemeral lake forms at far edge of slope

Boundary fault

Central block slopes towards main fault

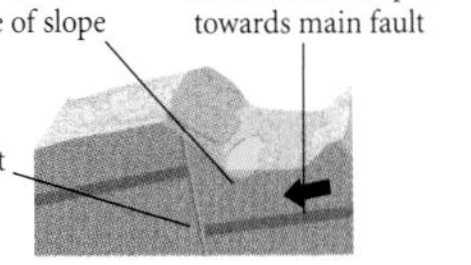

The eastern arm of the Great Rift Valley is gradually being pulled apart; however the forces on one side are greater than the other causing the land to slope. This affects regional drainage which migrates down the slope.

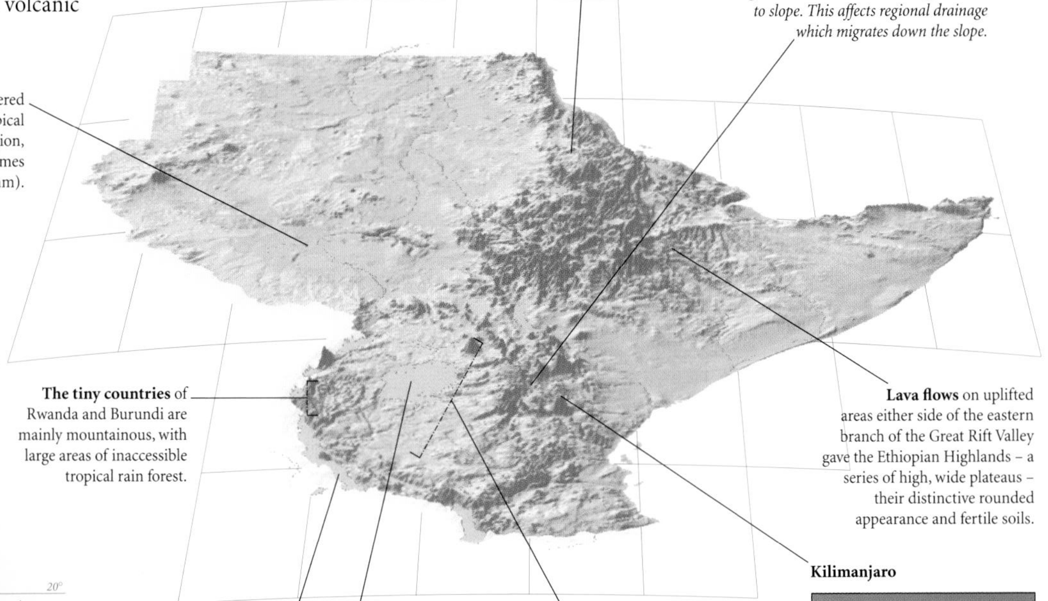

This dome at Gonder, in Ethiopia, is a volcanic intrusion, formed when molten rock pushed up the surface of the Earth and then solidified, leaving an outcrop of igneous rock.

Much of northern Sudan is covered by desert. However, in the tropical wetlands of the southern Sudd region, annual rainfall can sometimes exceed 40 inches (1,000 mm).

Lava flows on uplifted areas either side of the eastern branch of the Great Rift Valley gave the Ethiopian Highlands – a series of high, wide plateaus – their distinctive rounded appearance and fertile soils.

Kilimanjaro

An extinct volcano, Kilimanjaro is Africa's highest mountain, rising 19,340 ft (5,895 m). It is one of the few places in Africa where snow settles, allowing glacier ice to form.

A vast plateau lies between the eastern and western rift valleys in Kenya, Uganda, and western Tanzania. It has been leveled by long periods of erosion to form a peneplain, but is dotted with inselbergs – outcrops of more resistant rocks.

Lake Victoria occupies a vast basin between the two arms of the Great Rift Valley. It is the world's second largest lake in terms of surface area, extending 26,560 sq miles (68,880 sq km). The lake contains numerous islands and coral reefs.

Lake Tanganyika lies 8,202 ft (2,500 m) above sea level. It has a depth of nearly 4,700 ft (1,435 m). The lake traces the valley floor for some 400 miles (644 km) of the western arm of the Great Rift Valley.

The tiny countries of Rwanda and Burundi are mainly mountainous, with large areas of inaccessible tropical rain forest.

The Kassala region in eastern Sudan is watered by the Atbara River, an important tributary of the Nile. Most of the population is engaged in agriculture, growing cotton and cereals.

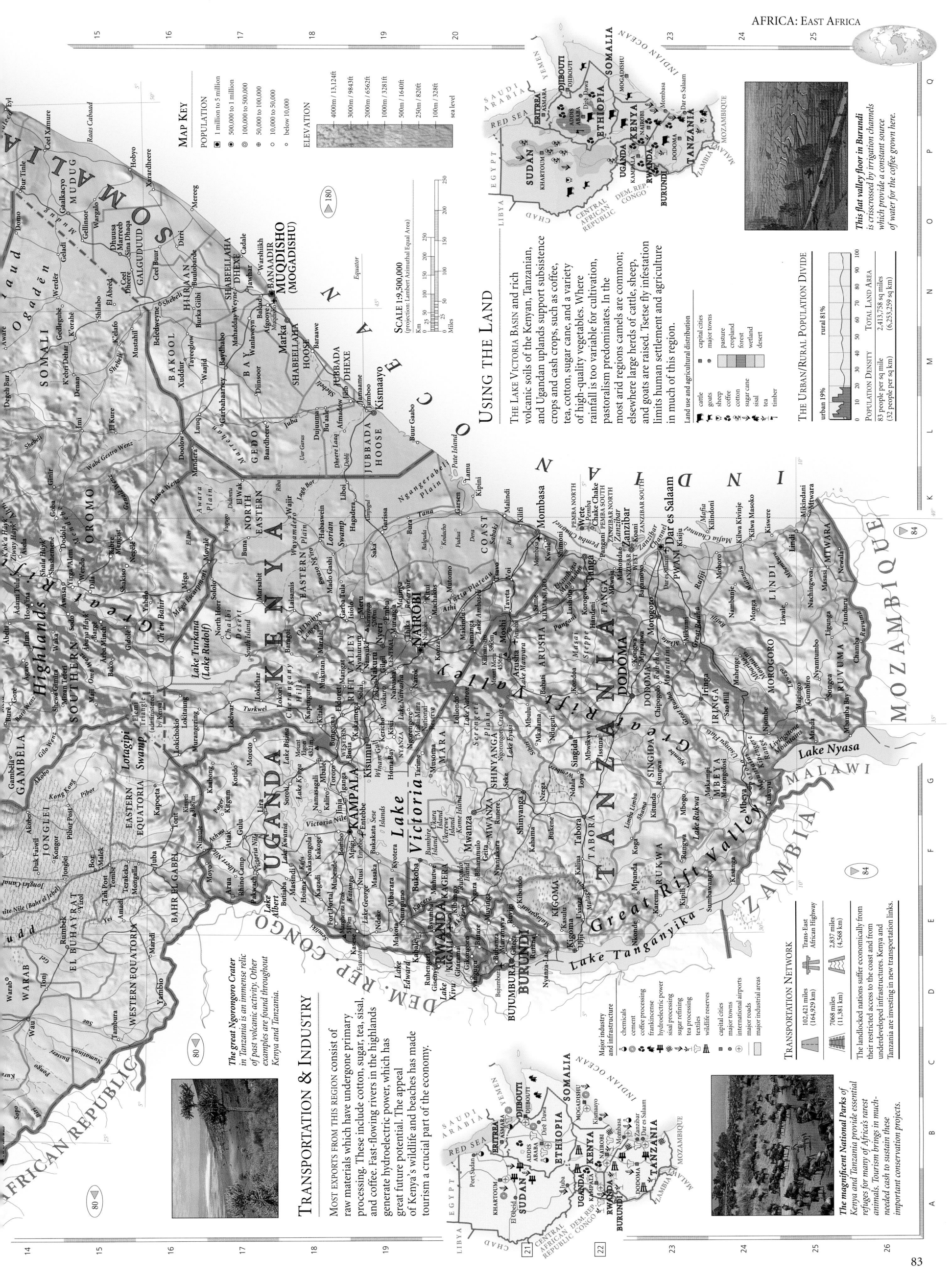

MAP KEY

POPULATION

- ◉ 1 million to 5 million
- ◎ 500,000 to 1 million
- ⊕ 100,000 to 500,000
- ⊙ 50,000 to 100,000
- ○ 10,000 to 50,000
- ∘ below 10,000

ELEVATION

- 4000m / 13,124ft
- 3000m / 9843ft
- 2000m / 6562ft
- 1000m / 3281ft
- 500m / 1640ft
- 250m / 820ft
- 100m / 328ft
- sea level

SCALE 1:9,500,000
(projection: Lambert Azimuthal Equal Area)

This flat valley floor in Burundi is crisscrossed by irrigation channels which provide a constant source of water for the coffee grown here.

USING THE LAND

THE LAKE VICTORIA BASIN and rich volcanic soils of the Kenyan, Tanzanian, and Ugandan uplands support subsistence crops and cash crops, such as coffee, tea, cotton, sugar cane, and a variety of high-quality vegetables. Where rainfall is too variable for cultivation, pastoralism predominates. In the most arid regions camels are common; elsewhere large herds of cattle, sheep, and goats are raised. Tsetse fly infestation limits human settlement and agriculture in much of this region.

Land use and agricultural distribution

- cattle
- goats
- sheep
- coffee
- cotton
- sugar cane
- sisal
- tea
- timber

- capital cities
- major towns
- pasture
- cropland
- forest
- wetland
- desert

THE URBAN/RURAL POPULATION DIVIDE

urban 19%	rural 81%	

POPULATION DENSITY	TOTAL LAND AREA
83 people per sq mile (32 people per sq km)	2,413,758 sq miles (6,253,259 sq km)

The great Ngorongoro Crater in Tanzania is an immense relic of past volcanic activity. Other examples are found throughout Kenya and Tanzania.

TRANSPORTATION & INDUSTRY

MOST EXPORTS FROM THIS REGION consist of raw materials which have undergone primary processing. These include cotton, sugar, tea, sisal, and coffee. Fast-flowing rivers in the highlands generate hydroelectric power, which has great future potential. The appeal of Kenya's wildlife and beaches has made tourism a crucial part of the economy.

Major industry and infrastructure

- chemicals
- cement
- coffee processing
- frankincense
- hydroelectric power
- sisal processing
- sugar refining
- tea processing
- textiles
- wildlife reserves
- capital cities
- major towns
- international airports
- major roads
- major industrial areas

TRANSPORTATION NETWORK

Trans-East African Highway	102,421 miles (164,929 km)
	7068 miles (11,380 km)
	2,837 miles (4,568 km)

The landlocked nations suffer economically from their restricted access to the coast and from underdeveloped infrastructures. Kenya and Tanzania are investing in new transportation links.

The magnificent National Parks of Kenya and Tanzania provide essential refuges for many of Africa's rarest animals. Tourism brings in much-needed cash to sustain these important conservation projects.

SOUTHERN AFRICA

ANGOLA, BOTSWANA, LESOTHO, MALAWI, MOZAMBIQUE, NAMIBIA,
SOUTH AFRICA, SWAZILAND, ZAMBIA, ZIMBABWE

AFRICA'S VAST SOUTHERN PLATEAU has been a contested homeland for disparate peoples for many centuries. The European incursion began with the slave trade and quickened in the 19th century, when the discovery of enormous mineral wealth secured South Africa's regional economic dominance. The struggle against white minority rule led to strife in Namibia, Zimbabwe, and the former Portuguese territories of Angola and Mozambique. South Africa's notorious apartheid laws, which denied basic human rights to more than 75% of the people, led to the state being internationally ostracized until 1994, when the first fully democratic elections inaugurated a new era of racial justice.

TRANSPORTATION & INDUSTRY

SOUTH AFRICA, the world's largest exporter of gold, has a varied economy which generates about 75% of the region's income and draws migrant labor from neighboring states. Angola exports petroleum; Botswana and Namibia rely on diamond mining; and Zambia is seeking to diversify its economy to compensate for declining copper reserves.

Almost all new mining ventures in Zimbabwe are now subject to government control. This mine at Bindura in northeastern Zimbabwe produces nickel, one of the country's top three minerals in terms of economic value.

THE LANDSCAPE

MOST OF SOUTHERN AFRICA rests on a concave plateau comprising the Kalahari basin and a mountainous fringe, skirted by a coastal plain which widens out in Mozambique. The plateau extends north, toward the Planalto de Bié in Angola, the Congo Basin and the lake-filled troughs of the Great Rift Valley. The eastern region is drained by the Zambezi and Limpopo Rivers, and the Orange is the major western river.

Thousands of years of evaporating water have produced the Etosha Pan, one of the largest salt flats in the world. Lake and river sediments in the area indicate that the region was once less arid.

Finger Rock, near Khorixas, Namibia is a remnant of a former land surface, which has been denuded by erosion over the last 5 million years. These occasional stacks of partially weathered rocks interrupt the plains of the dry southern interior.

TRANSPORTATION NETWORK

✈ 84,213 miles (135,609 km)	⬆ 746 miles (1,202 km)
🚂 23,208 miles (37,372 km)	🛣 3,815 miles (6,144 km)

Southern Africa's Cape-gauge rail network is by far the largest in the continent. About two-thirds of the 20,000 mile (32,000 km) system lies within South Africa. Lines such as the Harare–Bulawayo route have become corridors for industrial growth.

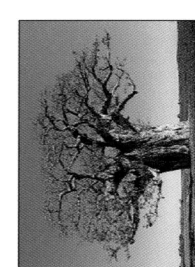

Following a series of droughts, this baobab tree in Zimbabwe now stands alone in a field once filled by sugar cane. The thick trunk and small leaves of the baobab help it to conserve water, enabling it to survive even in drought conditions.

At Victoria Falls, the Zambezi River has cut a spectacular gorge taking advantage of large joints in the basalt, which were first formed as the lava cooled and contracted.

The fast-flowing Zambezi River cuts a deep, wide channel as it flows along the Zimbabwe/Zambia border.

The Okavango/Cubango River flows from the Planalto de Bié to the swamplands of the Okavango Delta, one of the world's largest inland deltas, where it divides into countless distributary channels, feeding out into the desert.

Lake Nyasa occupies one of the deep troughs of the Great Rift Valley, where the land has been displaced downward by as much as 3,000 ft (920 m).

Great Rift Valley

Bushveld intrusion

Limpopo River

Volcanic lava, over 250 million years old, caps the peaks of the Brakensberg range, which lie on the mountainous rim of southern Africa's interior plateau.

Broad, flat-topped mountains have been cut from level rock strata under extremely arid conditions.

The mountains of the Little Karoo are composed of sedimentary rocks which have been substantially folded and faulted.

The Orange River, one of the longest in Africa, rises in Lesotho and is the only major river in the south which flows westward, rather than to the east coast.

The Kalahari Desert is the largest continuous sand surface in the world. Iron oxide gives a distinctive red color to the windblown sand, which, in eastern areas, covers the bedrock by over 200 ft (60 m).

Planalto de Bié

Namib Desert

Khorixas, Namibia

MAP KEY

POPULATION

- ◼ 1 million to 5 million
- ◉ 500,000 to 1 million
- ◎ 100,000 to 500,000
- ⊕ 50,000 to 100,000
- ⊙ 10,000 to 50,000
- ○ below 10,000

ELEVATION

	3000m / 9843ft
	2000m / 6562ft
	1000m / 3281ft
	500m / 1640ft
	250m / 820ft
	100m / 328ft
	sea level

Bushveld intrusion

Granite
Chromite
Gabbro and peridotite
Magnetite
Platinum minerals

The Bushveld intrusion lies on South Africa's high "veld" Molten magma intruded into the Earth's crust creating a saucer-shaped feature, more than 180 miles (300 km) across, containing regular layers of precious minerals, overlain by a dome of granite.

SOUTH AFRICA'S THREE CAPITALS

PRETORIA – administrative capital
CAPE TOWN – legislative capital
BLOEMFONTEIN – judicial capital

SCALE 1:9,500,000
(projection: Lambert Azimuthal Equal Area)

Major industry and infrastructure

- 🚗 car manufacture
- coal
- copper
- ⚙ diamonds
- food processing
- gold
- oil
- textiles
- uranium
- wildlife reserves

- ■ capital cities
- • major towns
- ✈ international airports
- major roads
- major industrial areas

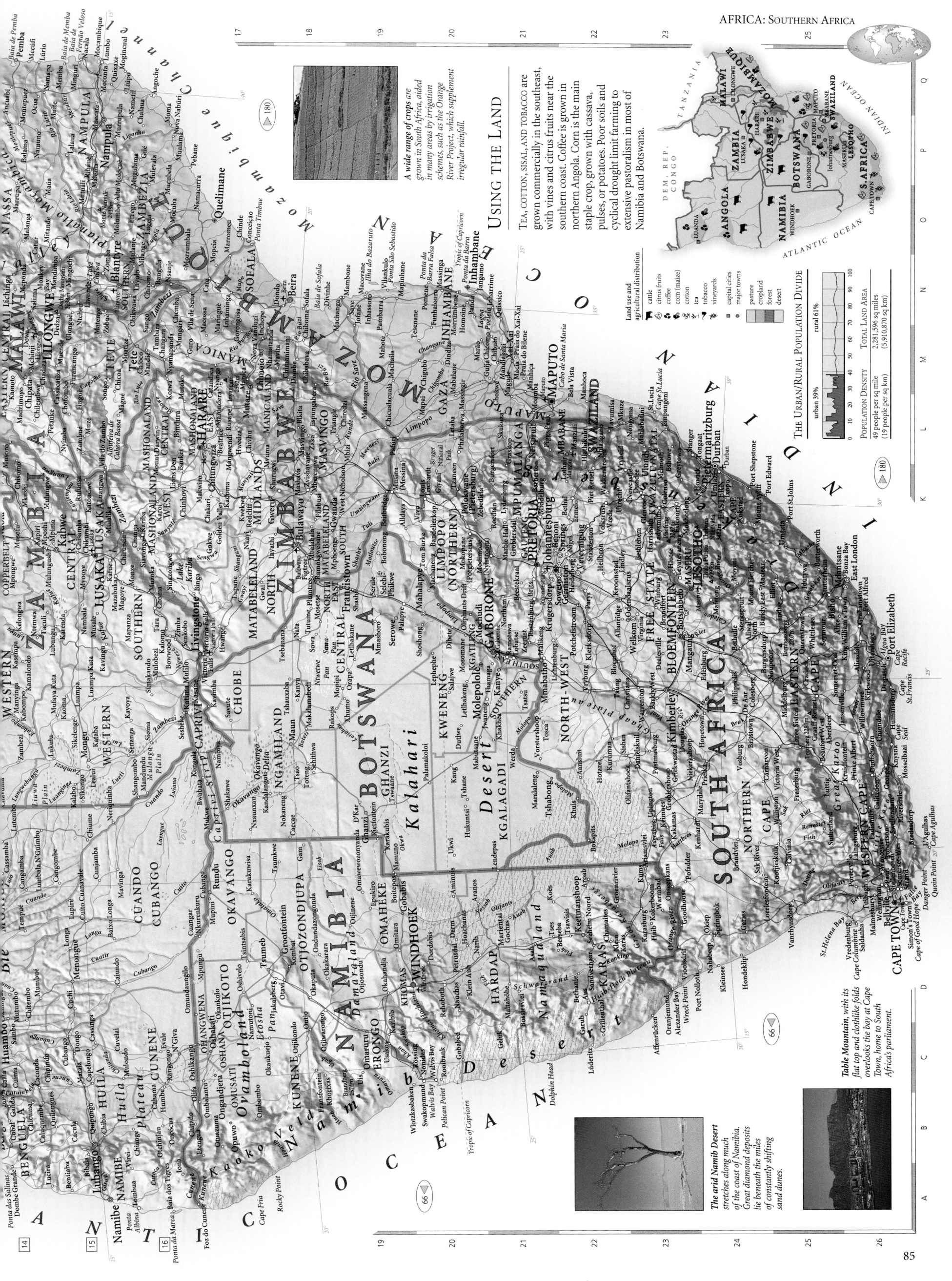

USING THE LAND

TEA, COTTON, SISAL, AND TOBACCO are grown commercially in the southeast, with vines and citrus fruits near the southern coast. Coffee is grown in northern Angola. Corn is the main staple crop, grown with cassava, pulses, or potatoes. Poor soils and cyclical drought limit farming to extensive pastoralism in most of Namibia and Botswana.

A wide range of crops are grown in South Africa, aided in many areas by irrigation schemes, such as the Orange River Project, which supplement irregular rainfall.

Land use and agricultural distribution

- cattle
- citrus fruits
- coffee
- corn (maize)
- cotton
- tea
- tobacco
- vineyards
- capital cities
- major towns

pasture
cropland
forest
desert

THE URBAN/RURAL POPULATION DIVIDE

urban 39%   rural 61%

POPULATION DENSITY	TOTAL LAND AREA
49 people per sq mile (19 people per sq km)	2,281,596 sq miles (5,910,870 sq km)

POPULATION DENSITY
0 10 20 30 40 50 60 70 80 90 100

Table Mountain, with its flat top and clothlike folds overlooks the bay at Cape Town, home to South Africa's parliament.

The arid Namib Desert stretches along much of the coast of Namibia. Great diamond deposits lie beneath the miles of constantly shifting sand dunes.

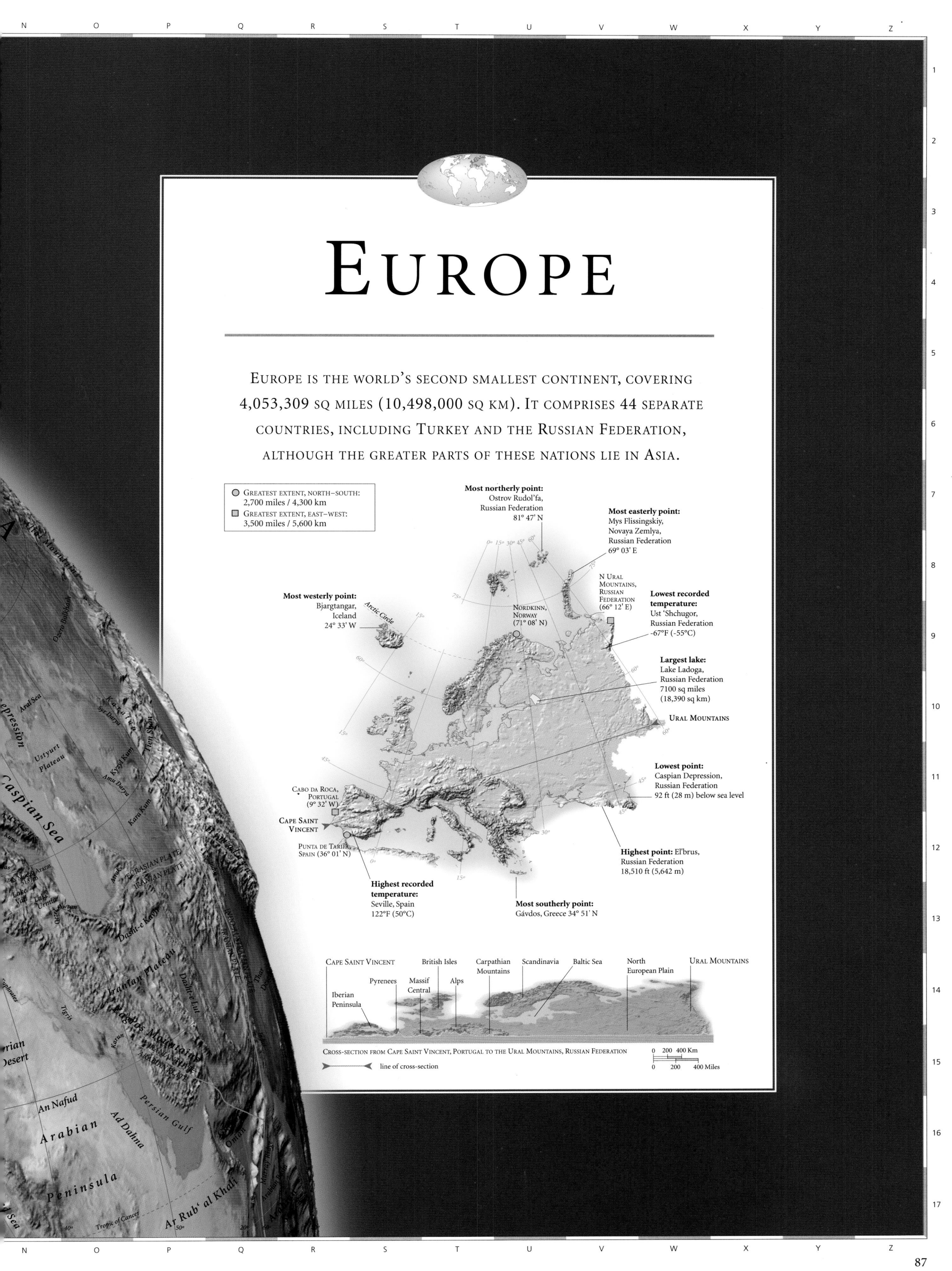

EUROPE

EUROPE IS THE WORLD'S SECOND SMALLEST CONTINENT, COVERING
4,053,309 SQ MILES (10,498,000 SQ KM). IT COMPRISES 44 SEPARATE
COUNTRIES, INCLUDING TURKEY AND THE RUSSIAN FEDERATION,
ALTHOUGH THE GREATER PARTS OF THESE NATIONS LIE IN ASIA.

○ GREATEST EXTENT, NORTH–SOUTH:
2,700 miles / 4,300 km
□ GREATEST EXTENT, EAST–WEST:
3,500 miles / 5,600 km

Most northerly point:
Ostrov Rudol'fa,
Russian Federation
81° 47' N

Most easterly point:
Mys Flissingskiy,
Novaya Zemlya,
Russian Federation
69° 03' E

N URAL
MOUNTAINS,
RUSSIAN
FEDERATION
(66° 12' E)

**Lowest recorded
temperature:**
Ust 'Shchugor,
Russian Federation
-67°F (-55°C)

Most westerly point:
Bjargtangar,
Iceland
24° 33' W

NORDKINN,
NORWAY
(71° 08' N)

Largest lake:
Lake Ladoga,
Russian Federation
7100 sq miles
(18,390 sq km)

URAL MOUNTAINS

Lowest point:
Caspian Depression,
Russian Federation
92 ft (28 m) below sea level

CABO DA ROCA,
PORTUGAL
(9° 32' W)

CAPE SAINT
VINCENT

PUNTA DE TARIFA,
SPAIN (36° 01' N)

Highest point: El'brus,
Russian Federation
18,510 ft (5,642 m)

**Highest recorded
temperature:**
Seville, Spain
122°F (50°C)

Most southerly point:
Gávdos, Greece 34° 51' N

CAPE SAINT VINCENT · British Isles · Carpathian Mountains · Scandinavia · Baltic Sea · North European Plain · URAL MOUNTAINS

Pyrenees · Massif Central · Alps

Iberian Peninsula

CROSS-SECTION FROM CAPE SAINT VINCENT, PORTUGAL TO THE URAL MOUNTAINS, RUSSIAN FEDERATION

0   200   400 Km

◄— line of cross-section

0   200   400 Miles

PHYSICAL EUROPE

THE PHYSICAL DIVERSITY of Europe belies its relatively small size. To the northwest and south it is enclosed by mountains. The older, rounded Atlantic Highlands of Scandinavia and the British Isles lie to the north and the younger, rugged peaks of the Alpine Uplands to the south. In between lies the North European Plain, stretching 2,485 miles (4,000 km) from The Fens in England to the Ural Mountains in Russia. South of the plain lies a series of gently folded sedimentary rocks separated by ancient plateaus, known as massifs.

THE NORTH EUROPEAN PLAIN

RISING LESS THAN 1,000 ft (300 m) above sea level, the North European Plain strongly reflects past glaciation. Ridges of both coarse moraine and finer, wind-blown deposits have accumulated over much of the region. The ice sheet also diverted a number of river channels from their original courses.

Glacial lakes

Rivers were diverted from their original course by the ice sheet

A layer of glacial sediments covers the North European Plain

B — B

Section across the North European Plain showing its low relief and drainage.

0 100 200 Km
0 100 200 Miles

THE ATLANTIC HIGHLANDS

THE ATLANTIC HIGHLANDS were formed by compression against the Scandinavian Shield during the Caledonian mountain-building period over 500 million years ago. The highlands were once part of a continuous mountain chain, now divided by the North Sea and a submerged rift valley.

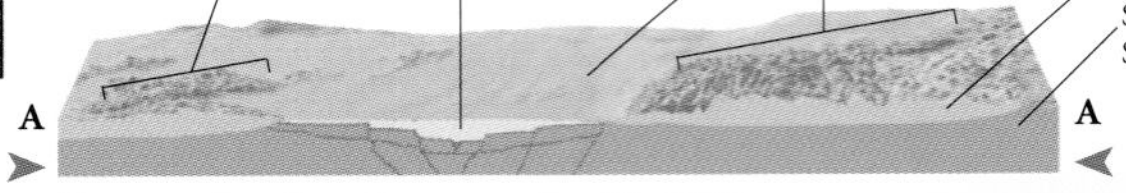

The Atlantic Highlands continue in the British Isles

Rift valley buried by sediments

North Sea

Atlantic Highlands in Norway

Rocks affected by ancient mountain-building

Scandinavian Shield

A — A

Cross-section through northeastern Europe showing the continuous mountain chain and rift valley system.

0 100 200 Km
0 100 200 Miles

SCALE 1:23,000,000
(projection: Lambert Azimuthal Equal Area)

Km
0 100 200 400 600
0 50 100 200 300 400 500 600
Miles

MAP KEY

ELEVATION

4000m / 13,124ft
3000m / 9843ft
2000m / 6562ft
1000m / 3281ft
500m / 1640ft
250m / 820ft
100m / 328ft
sea level

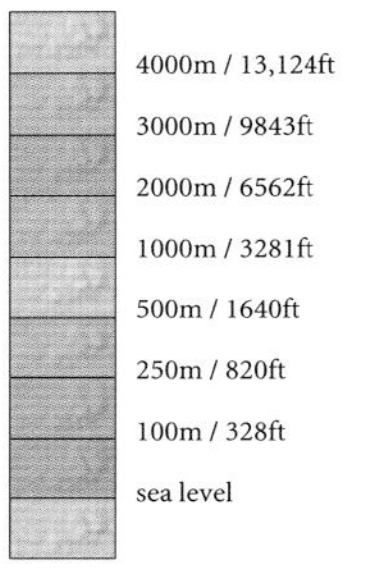

PLATE MARGINS
(for explanation see page xiv)

————— constructive
△△△ destructive
————— conservative
·········· uncertain

————— physiographic regions
▷◁ line of cross-section

THE PLATEAUS AND LOWLANDS

THE UPLIFTED PLATEAUS or massifs of southern central Europe are the result of long-term erosion, later followed by uplift. They are the source areas of many of the rivers which drain Europe's lowlands. In some of the higher reaches, fractures have enabled igneous rocks from deep in the Earth to reach the surface.

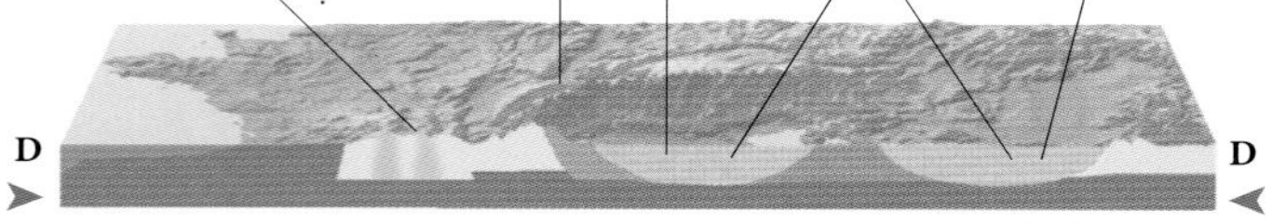

Igneous rocks have intruded into the Massif Central

Older, eroded massifs lie behind the arc of the Alps

Tectonically formed basins

Po Valley

Great Hungarian Plain

D — D

Cross-section through the plateaus and lowlands showing the lower elevation of the ancient massifs.

0 100 200 Km
0 100 200 Miles

THE ALPINE UPLANDS

THE COLLISION OF the African and European continents, which began about 65 million years ago, folded and then uplifted a series of mountain ranges running across southern Europe and into Asia. Two major lines of folding can be traced: one includes the Pyrenees, the Alps, and the Carpathian Mountains; the other incorporates the Apennines and the Dinaric Alps.

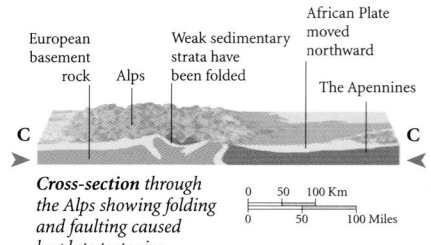

European basement rock

Alps

Weak sedimentary strata have been folded

African Plate moved northward

The Apennines

C — C

Cross-section through the Alps showing folding and faulting caused by plate tectonics.

0 50 100 Km
0 50 100 Miles

Map labels

NORTH AMERICAN PLATE
EURASIAN PLATE
Iceland
Novaya Zemlya
Kara Sea
Ostrov Kolguyev
Barents Sea
Kola Peninsula
White Sea
Scandinavian Shield
Ural Mountains
Norwegian Sea
Faeroe Islands
Shetland Islands
Outer Hebrides
British Isles
Ireland
Shannon
Britain
The Fens
The Thames
North Sea
Jylland
Vänern
Vättern
Gulf of Bothnia
Baltic Sea
Gulf of Riga
Western Dvina
Lake Onega
Lake Ladoga
Northern Dvina
Central Russian Upland
Volga Uplands
Volga
English Channel
Seine
Loire
Rhine
Ardennes
Elbe
Harz
Oder
Vistula
Dnieper
Dniester
Don
PLATEAUX AND LOWLANDS
Bay of Biscay
Massif Central
Pyrenees
Mt Blanc 4807m
Po
Garonne
Ebro
Douro
Tagus
Iberian Peninsula
Guadalquivir
Corsica
Balearic Islands
Sardinia
Tyrrhenian Sea
Apennines
Adriatic Sea
Dinaric Alps
ALPS
Great Hungarian Plain
Carpathian Mountains
Danube
Balkan Mountains
Sicily
Etna 3323m
Vesuvius 1171m
Malta
Ionian Sea
Crete
Aegean Sea
Peloponnese
EURASIAN PLATE
ANATOLIAN PLATE
AFRICAN PLATE
Mediterranean Sea
EURASIAN PLATE
AFRICAN PLATE
Black Sea
Sea of Azov
Crimea
Caucasus
Elbrus 5642m
Caspian Sea
ASIA
ATLANTIC OCEAN

CLIMATE

EUROPE EXPERIENCES few extremes in either rainfall
or temperature, with the exception of the far north
and south. Along the west coast, the warm currents
of the North Atlantic Drift moderate temperatures.
Although east–west air movement is relatively
unimpeded by relief, the Alpine Uplands halt the
progress of north–south air masses, protecting
most of the Mediterranean from cold, north winds.

*Frost grips northern and eastern
Europe during the long cold winters.
Lakes and rivers frequently freeze.*

TEMPERATURE

Arctic
Circle

60°N

40°N

Average January temperature

Average July temperature

Temperature

	below -22°F (-30°C)
	-22 to -4°F (-30 to -20°C)
	-4 to 14°F (-20 to -10°C)
	14 to 32°F (-10 to 0°C)
	32 to 50°F (0 to 10°C)
	50 to 60°F (10 to 20°C)
	68 to 86°F (20 to 30°C)
	above 86°F (30°C)

RAINFALL

Arctic
Circle

60°N

40°N

Average January rainfall

Average July rainfall

Rainfall

	0–1 in (0–25 mm)
	1–2 in (25–50 mm)
	2–4 in (50–100 mm)
	4–8 in (100–200 mm)
	8–12 in (200–300 mm)
	12–16 in (300–400 mm)
	16–20 in (400–500 mm)
	more than 20 in (500 mm)

*Mild temperatures and frequent
rainfall contribute to the fertile
farming land found over much
of northwestern Europe.*

*Dusty Sirocco winds from
Africa help create the
semiarid scrubland common
across the Mediterranean
coastlands of southern Europe.*

Reykjavík · Karasjok · Murmansk · Pechora · Bodø · Pajala · Archangel · Hoyvík · Kajaani · Kirov · Sveg · Härnösand · Ufa · Bergen · Helsinki · St Petersburg · Oslo · Stockholm · Tallinn · Moscow · Malin Head · Dundee · Vestervig · Gothenburg · Riga · Shannon · Morecambe · Malmö · Minsk · Kharkiv · Exeter · London · Hamburg · Berlin · Warsaw · Brussels · Prague · Rostov-na-Donu · Paris · Zürich · Munich · Vienna · Bratislava · Astrakhan' · A Coruña · Bordeaux · Lyon · Milan · Zagreb · Belgrade · Simferopol' · Toulouse · Monaco · Sarajevo · Bucharest · Lisbon · Madrid · Barcelona · Sofia · Constanţa · Gibraltar · Palma · Naples · Tirana · Istanbul · Cagliari · Messina · Salonica · Athens

Climate

	tundra
	subarctic
	cool continental
	warm humid
	mediterranean
	semiarid
☼	daily hours of sunshine, January
☼	daily hours of sunshine, July
→	cold wind
→	hot wind

SHAPING THE CONTINENT

SUCCESSIVE ICE AGES have left many relict landforms
across Europe. Present glaciers continue to carve peaks
and valleys in the northern Atlantic Highlands and Alpine
Uplands. Tectonic activity, both past and present, has
shaped southern Europe and Iceland. Active volcanoes
and earthquakes still occur in Italy and Greece. Europe's
extensive coastline, particularly in the northwest, is
constantly modified by wave action and fluvial deposits.

GLACIATION

1 Valley glaciers, such as this one *(left)* in
Iceland, form in hollows at the top of valleys
and flow downward, drawn by gravity. Their
growth is dynamic; new snowfall constantly
accumulates at the head of the glacier, while
the snout melts, depositing material eroded
and carried by the glacier.

Snow
accumulates at
the head of
glacier

Glacier movement
erodes valley

Glacier snout melts
depositing eroded
debris

GLACIATION: DEVELOPMENT OF A GLACIER

COASTAL PROCESSES

5 Spits are narrow bands of sand
or shingle, formed by longshore
drift; a process whereby waves carry
material along the beach. They
usually form where the coastline
changes direction, and their growth
is then halted by an opposing river
current, as at Spurn Head, in the
British Isles *(left)*. Coastal features
such as these are constantly being
created and destroyed.

Sand and
shingle spit

Original coastline

Opposing
river
current

Waves
breaking
at an angle

COASTAL PROCESSES:
FORMATION OF A SPIT

RIVER SYSTEMS

2 Rivers are continuously transporting
eroded material toward the sea.
Slow-moving, low-gradient rivers, like
this one in western Russia *(above)*, deposit
their alluvium load, infilling valleys creating
a floodplain. Subsequent climatic and
tectonic fluctuations may erode the
floodplain to form terraces.

Terrace
created by
erosion

Floodplain

Deposited
alluvium

River
channel

RIVER SYSTEMS: FORMATION OF
A FLOODPLAIN AND TERRACES

Landscape

	uplifting land
	stable land
	sinking land
	limestone region
	glacier
▲	active volcano
→	ocean current
⋯	area of tectonic activity
—	maximum limit of glaciation

THE EVOLVING LANDSCAPE

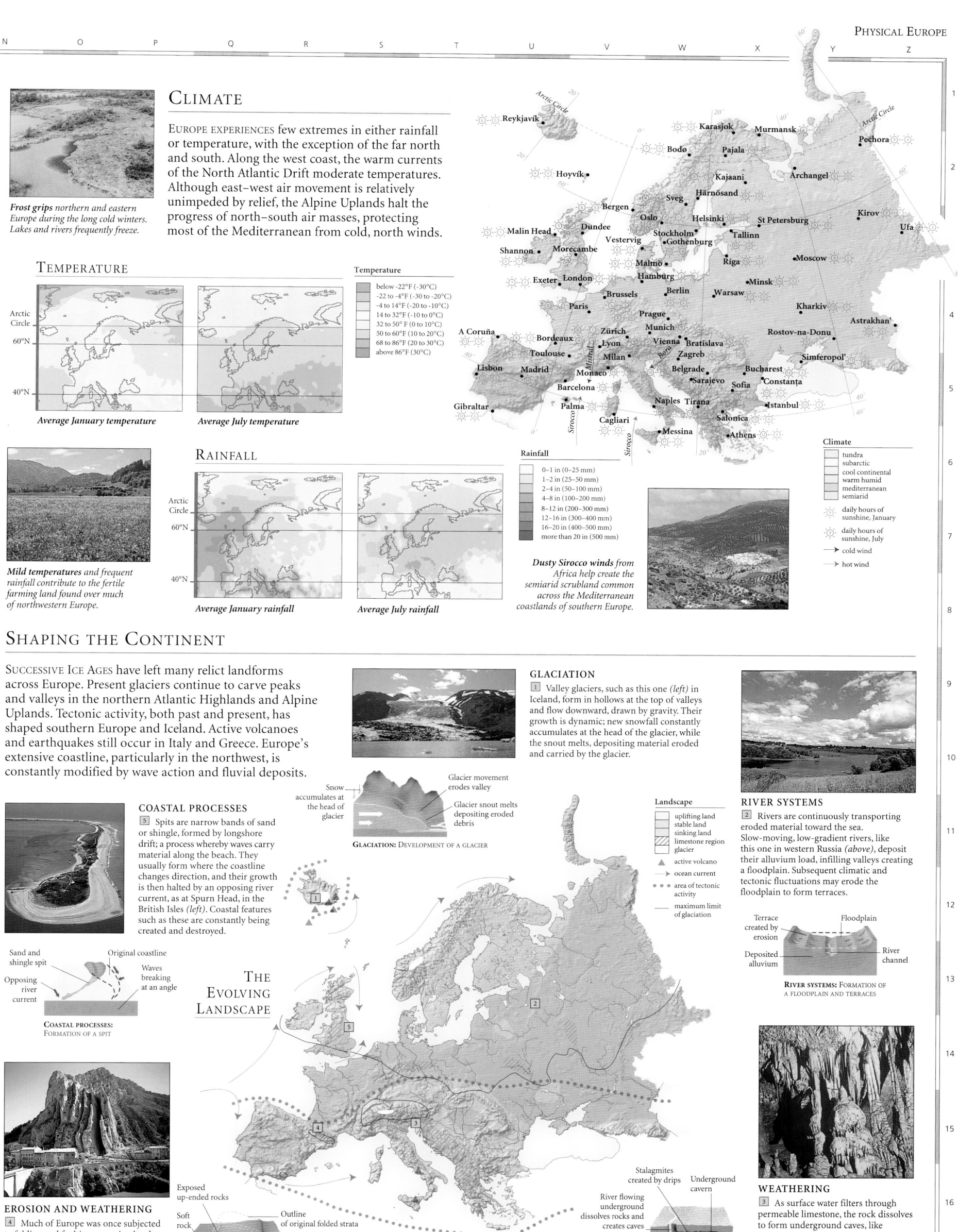

EROSION AND WEATHERING

4 Much of Europe was once subjected
to folding and faulting, exposing hard
and soft rock layers. Subsequent erosion
and weathering has worn away the softer
strata, leaving up-ended layers of hard
rock as in the French Pyrenees *(above)*.

Exposed
up-ended rocks

Soft
rock

Outline
of original folded strata

Hard rock

Fault line

Folded rock strata

EROSION AND WEATHERING: MODIFICATION OF A FOLD

WEATHERING

3 As surface water filters through
permeable limestone, the rock dissolves
to form underground caves, like
Postojna in the Karst region of Slovenia
(above). Stalactites grow downward
as lime-enriched water seeps from
roof fractures; stalagmites grow upward
where drips splash down.

Stalagmites
created by drips

Underground
cavern

River flowing
underground
dissolves rocks and
creates caves

Stalactites formed
by seeping water

WEATHERING:
FORMATION OF A CAVE

POLITICAL EUROPE

THE POLITICAL BOUNDARIES OF EUROPE have changed many times, especially during the 20th century in the aftermath of two world wars, the breakup of the empires of Austria-Hungary, Nazi Germany and, toward the end of the century, the collapse of communism in eastern Europe. The fragmentation of Yugoslavia has again altered the political map of Europe, highlighting a trend toward nationalism and devolution. In contrast, economic federalism is growing. In 1958, the formation of the European Economic Community (now the European Union or EU) started a move toward economic and political union and increasing internal migration.

The Brandenburg Gate in Berlin is a potent symbol of German reunification. From 1961, the road beneath it ended in a wall, built to stop the flow of refugees to the West. It was opened again in 1989 when the wall was destroyed and East and West Germany were reunited.

POPULATION

EUROPE IS A DENSELY POPULATED, urbanized continent; in Belgium over 90% of people live in urban areas. The highest population densities are found in an area stretching east from southern Britain and northern France, into Germany. The northern fringes are only sparsely populated.

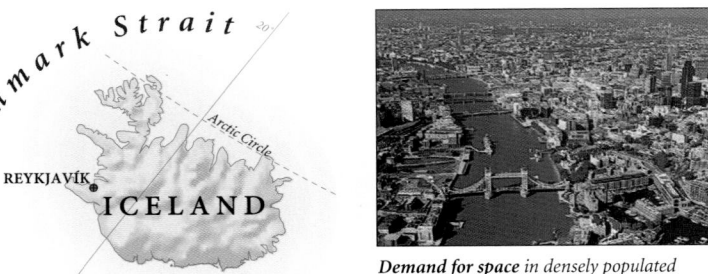

Demand for space in densely populated European cities like London has led to the development of high-rise offices and urban sprawl.

**Population density
(people per sq mile)**

- below 130
- 130–259
- 260–379
- 380–519
- 520–780
- above 780

Traditional lifestyles still persist in many remote and rural parts of Europe, especially in the south, east, and in the far north.

MAP KEY

POPULATION

- ■ above 5 million
- ◼ 1 million to 5 million
- ◉ 500,000 to 1 million
- ◎ 100,000 to 500,000
- ⊕ 50,000 to 100,000
- ○ 10,000 to 50,000
- ● Country capital

BORDERS

- full international border

SCALE 1:15,500,000
(projection: Lambert Azimuthal Equal Area)

Km
0 50 100 200 300 400 500 600 700 800 900 1000

Miles
0 50 100 200 300 400 500 600 700

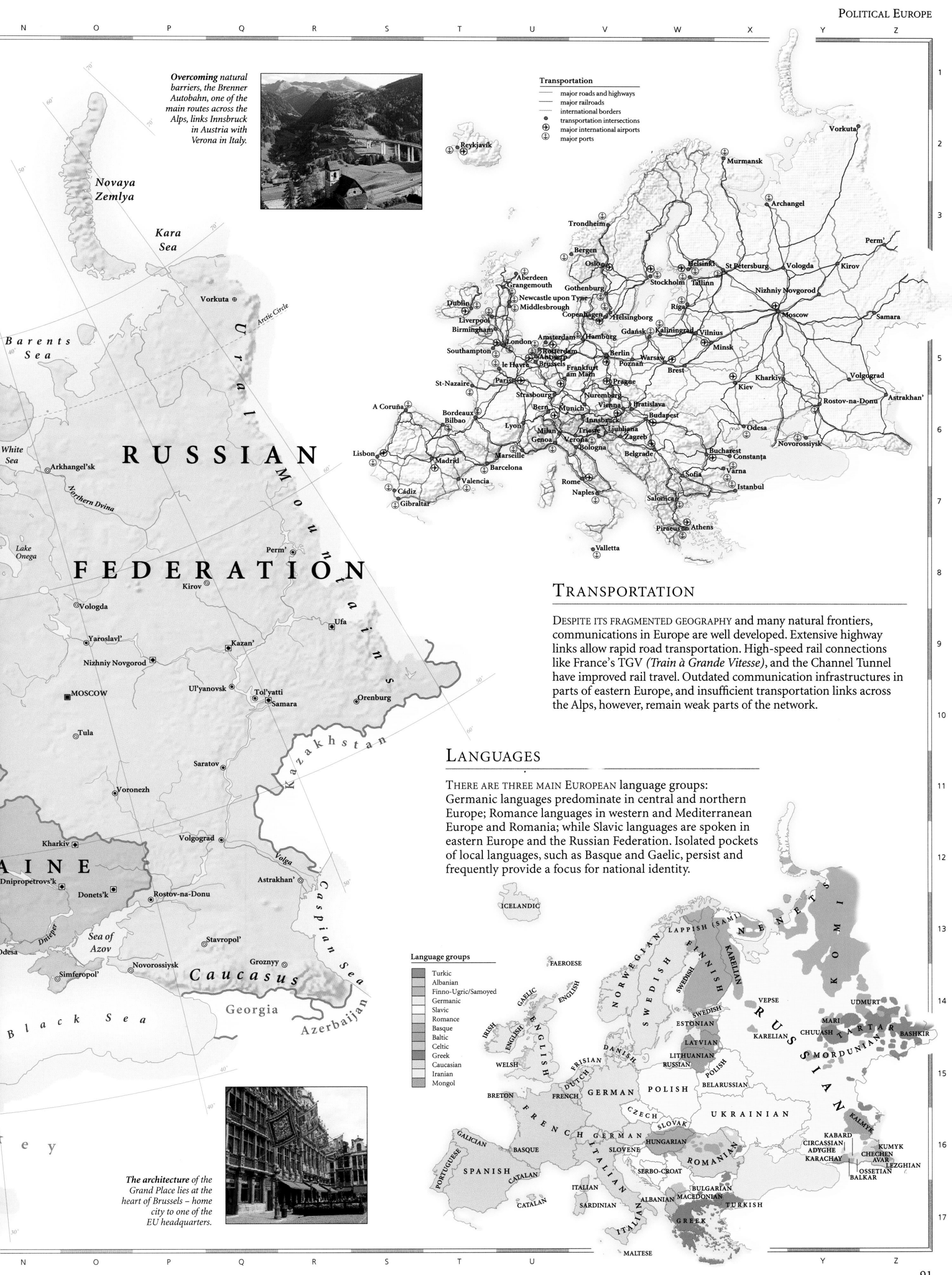

N O P Q R S T U V W X Y Z

Overcoming natural barriers, the Brenner Autobahn, one of the main routes across the Alps, links Innsbruck in Austria with Verona in Italy.

Transportation
- major roads and highways
- major railroads
- international borders
- transportation intersections
- major international airports
- major ports

Reykjavík

Novaya Zemlya

Kara Sea

Vorkuta

Murmansk

Archangel

Trondheim

Barents Sea

Bergen
Oslo
Helsinki
St Petersburg
Vologda
Perm'
Kirov

White Sea

Arkhangel'sk

Northern Dvina

Aberdeen
Grangemouth
Stockholm
Tallinn
Nizhniy Novgorod
Dublin
Newcastle upon Tyne
Gothenburg
Riga
Moscow
Samara

Liverpool
Middlesbrough
Copenhagen
Helsingborg
Gdańsk
Kaliningrad
Vilnius
Minsk
Birmingham
London
Amsterdam
Hamburg
Berlin
Warsaw
Poznań
Brest
Kiev
Kharkiv
Volgograd
Southampton
Rotterdam
Antwerp
Brussels
Frankfurt am Main
Prague
Rostov-na-Donu
Astrakhan'

le Havre
Paris
Strasbourg
Nuremberg
Bratislava
Vienna
Budapest
Odesa
St-Nazaire

A Coruña
Bordeaux
Bilbao
Bern
Munich
Innsbruck
Ljubljana
Zagreb
Bucharest
Constanța
Novorossiysk
Lyon
Milan
Genoa
Verona
Trieste
Belgrade
Varna

Lisbon
Madrid
Marseille
Bologna
Sofia
Istanbul

Barcelona
Rome
Naples
Salonica

Cádiz
Valencia

Gibraltar
Piraeus
Athens

Valletta

Russian Federation

Ural Mountains

Arctic Circle

Lake Onega
Vologda
Yaroslavl'
Kirov
Ufa

Nizhniy Novgorod
Kazan'
MOSCOW
Ul'yanovsk
Tol'yatti
Samara
Orenburg
Tula

Saratov

Voronezh

Kazakhstan

Kharkiv
Volgograd

Volga

Astrakhan'

AINE
Dnipropetrovs'k
Donets'k
Rostov-na-Donu

Dnieper
Sea of Azov
Stavropol'
Groznyy
Odesa
Simferopol'
Novorossiysk

Caucasus
Caspian Sea

Black Sea

Georgia
Azerbaijan

ey

The architecture of the Grand Place lies at the heart of Brussels – home city to one of the EU headquarters.

Transportation

DESPITE ITS FRAGMENTED GEOGRAPHY and many natural frontiers, communications in Europe are well developed. Extensive highway links allow rapid road transportation. High-speed rail connections like France's TGV *(Train à Grande Vitesse)*, and the Channel Tunnel have improved rail travel. Outdated communication infrastructures in parts of eastern Europe, and insufficient transportation links across the Alps, however, remain weak parts of the network.

Languages

THERE ARE THREE MAIN EUROPEAN language groups: Germanic languages predominate in central and northern Europe; Romance languages in western and Mediterranean Europe and Romania; while Slavic languages are spoken in eastern Europe and the Russian Federation. Isolated pockets of local languages, such as Basque and Gaelic, persist and frequently provide a focus for national identity.

ICELANDIC

FAEROESE

Language groups
- Turkic
- Albanian
- Finno-Ugric/Samoyed
- Germanic
- Slavic
- Romance
- Basque
- Baltic
- Celtic
- Greek
- Caucasian
- Iranian
- Mongol

NENETS
NORWEGIAN
LAPPISH (SAMI)
SWEDISH
FINNISH
KARELIAN
KOMI
GAELIC
ENGLISH
VEPSE
UDMURT
IRISH
ENGLISH
SWEDISH
ESTONIAN
KARELIAN
RUSSIAN
MARI
CHUUASH
TARTAR
BASHKIR
ENGLISH
WELSH
FRISIAN
DANISH
LATVIAN
LITHUANIAN
RUSSIAN
MORDUNIAN
BRETON
FRENCH
DUTCH
GERMAN
POLISH
BELARUSSIAN
GALICIAN
FRENCH
GERMAN
CZECH
SLOVAK
UKRAINIAN
KALMYK
PORTUGUESE
BASQUE
ITALIAN
SLOVENE
HUNGARIAN
ROMANIAN
KABARD
CIRCASSIAN
ADYGHE
KARACHAY
KUMYK
CHECHEN
AVAR
LEZGHIAN
SPANISH
CATALAN
SERBO-CROAT
OSSETIAN
BALKAR
CATALAN
ITALIAN
SARDINIAN
BULGARIAN
MACEDONIAN
TURKISH
ALBANIAN
GREEK
MALTESE

N O P Q R S T U

V W X Y Z

EUROPEAN RESOURCES

EUROPE'S LARGE TRACTS OF FERTILE, accessible land, combined with its generally temperate climate, have allowed a greater percentage of land to be used for agricultural purposes than in any other continent. Extensive coal and iron ore deposits were used to create steel and manufacturing industries during the 19th and 20th centuries. Today, although natural resources have been widely exploited, and heavy industry is of declining importance, the growth of hi-tech and service industries has enabled Europe to maintain its wealth.

INDUSTRY

EUROPE'S WEALTH WAS GENERATED by the rise of industry and colonial exploitation during the 19th century. The mining of abundant natural resources made Europe the industrial center of the world. Adaptation has been essential in the changing world economy, and a move to service-based industries has been widespread except in eastern Europe, where heavy industry still dominates.

Countries like Hungary are still struggling to modernize inefficient factories left over from extensive, centrally-planned industrialization during the communist era.

Other power sources are becoming more attractive as fossil fuels run out; 16% of Europe's electricity is now provided by hydroelectric power.

Frankfurt am Main is an example of a modern service-based city. The skyline is dominated by headquarters from the worlds of banking and commerce.

STANDARD OF LIVING

LIVING STANDARDS IN WESTERN EUROPE are among the highest in the world, although there is a growing sector of homeless, jobless people. Eastern Europeans have lower overall standards of living – a legacy of stagnated economies.

Standard of Living
(UN Human Development Index)
low
high

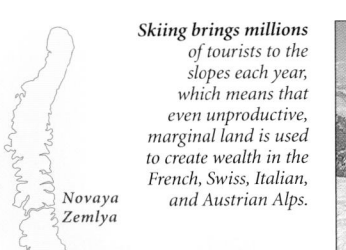
Skiing brings millions of tourists to the slopes each year, which means that even unproductive, marginal land is used to create wealth in the French, Swiss, Italian, and Austrian Alps.

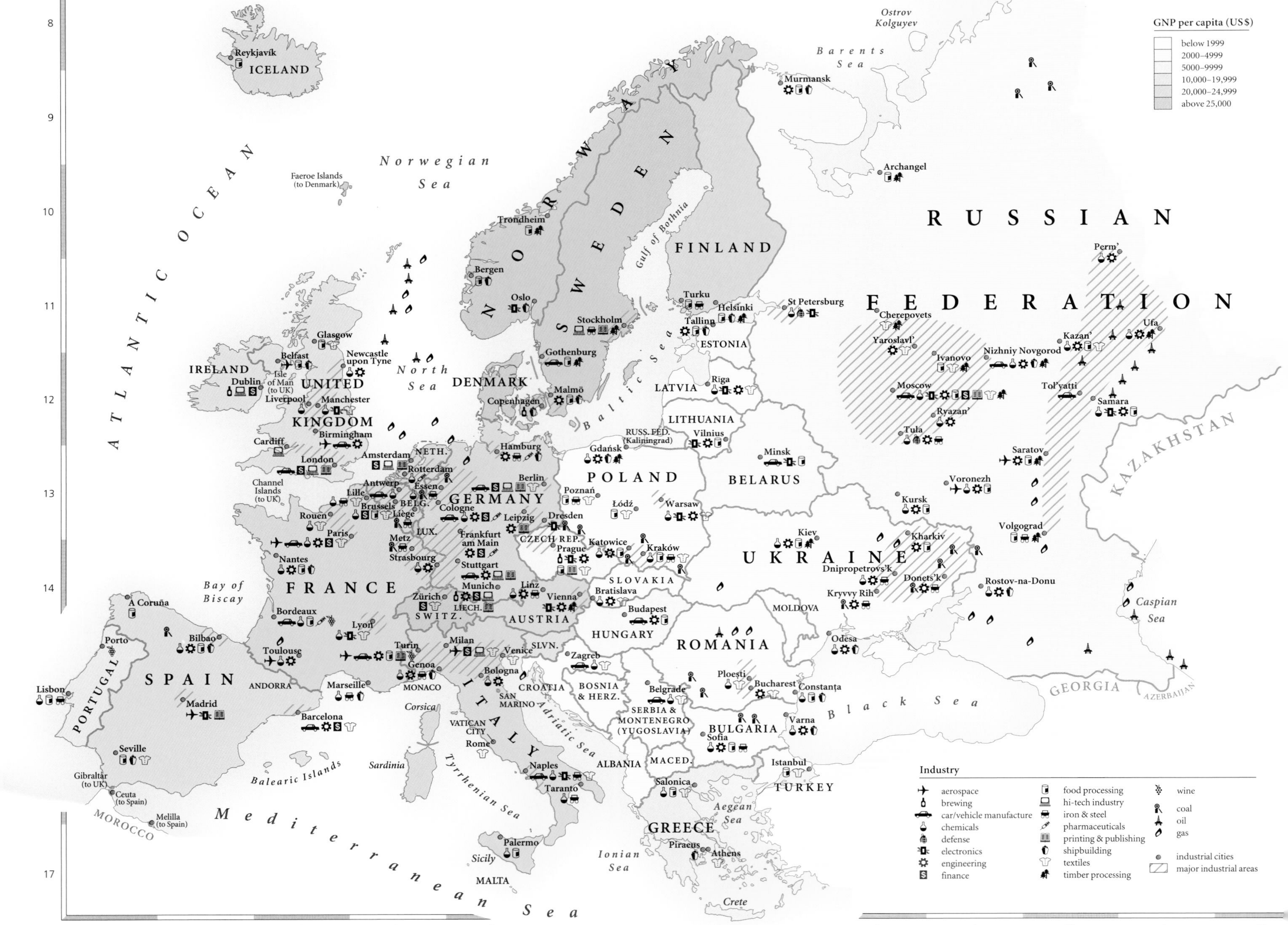

GNP per capita (US$)
below 1999
2000–4999
5000–9999
10,000–19,999
20,000–24,999
above 25,000

Industry
- aerospace
- brewing
- car/vehicle manufacture
- chemicals
- defense
- electronics
- engineering
- finance
- food processing
- hi-tech industry
- iron & steel
- pharmaceuticals
- printing & publishing
- shipbuilding
- textiles
- timber processing
- wine
- coal
- oil
- gas
- industrial cities
- major industrial areas

ATLANTIC OCEAN

ICELAND
Reykjavík

Faeroe Islands
(to Denmark)

Norwegian Sea

NORWAY
Trondheim
Bergen
Oslo

SWEDEN
Stockholm
Gothenburg

Gulf of Bothnia

FINLAND
Turku
Helsinki

Barents Sea

Ostrov Kolguyev

Novaya Zemlya

Murmansk

Archangel

RUSSIAN FEDERATION

St Petersburg
Cherepovets
Yaroslavl'
Ivanovo
Nizhniy Novgorod
Kazan'
Ufa
Perm'
Moscow
Ryazan'
Tol'yatti
Samara
Tula
Saratov
Voronezh
Volgograd
Kursk
Kharkiv
Rostov-na-Donu

IRELAND
Dublin
Liverpool

UNITED KINGDOM
Belfast
Newcastle upon Tyne
Glasgow
Isle of Man (to UK)
Manchester
Birmingham
Cardiff
London
Channel Islands (to UK)

North Sea

DENMARK
Copenhagen
Malmö

Baltic Sea

ESTONIA
Tallinn

LATVIA
Riga

LITHUANIA
Vilnius

RUSS. FED. (Kaliningrad)

POLAND
Gdańsk
Poznań
Łódź
Warsaw
Katowice
Kraków

BELARUS
Minsk

UKRAINE
Kiev
Dnipropetrovs'k
Donets'k
Kryvyy Rih

MOLDOVA
Odesa

NETH.
Amsterdam
Rotterdam

GERMANY
Hamburg
Berlin
Essen
Cologne
Leipzig
Dresden
Frankfurt am Main
Stuttgart

BELG.
Antwerp
Brussels
Liège
Lille

LUX.

CZECH REP.
Prague

SLOVAKIA
Bratislava

AUSTRIA
Vienna
Linz

SWITZ.
Zürich
Munich

LIECH.

SLVN.

HUNGARY
Budapest

FRANCE
Rouen
Paris
Metz
Strasbourg
Nantes
Bordeaux
Lyon
Toulouse
Marseille

Bay of Biscay

A Coruña
Porto
Lisbon
PORTUGAL

SPAIN
Bilbao
Madrid
Barcelona
Seville

ANDORRA

Gibraltar (to UK)
Ceuta (to Spain)
Melilla (to Spain)

MOROCCO

Balearic Islands

Corsica
Sardinia

MONACO
Turin
Milan
Genoa
Bologna
Venice
Venice
SAN MARINO
VATICAN CITY
Rome
ITALY
Naples
Taranto
Palermo
Sicily

Tyrrhenian Sea

Mediterranean Sea

CROATIA
Zagreb

BOSNIA & HERZ.

SERBIA & MONTENEGRO (YUGOSLAVIA)
Belgrade

ROMANIA
Ploesti
Bucharest
Constanța

BULGARIA
Sofia
Varna

MACED.

ALBANIA

GREECE
Salonica
Athens
Piraeus

Adriatic Sea

Ionian Sea

Aegean Sea

Crete

MALTA

Black Sea

GEORGIA

AZERBAIJAN

Caspian Sea

KAZAKHSTAN

TURKEY
Istanbul

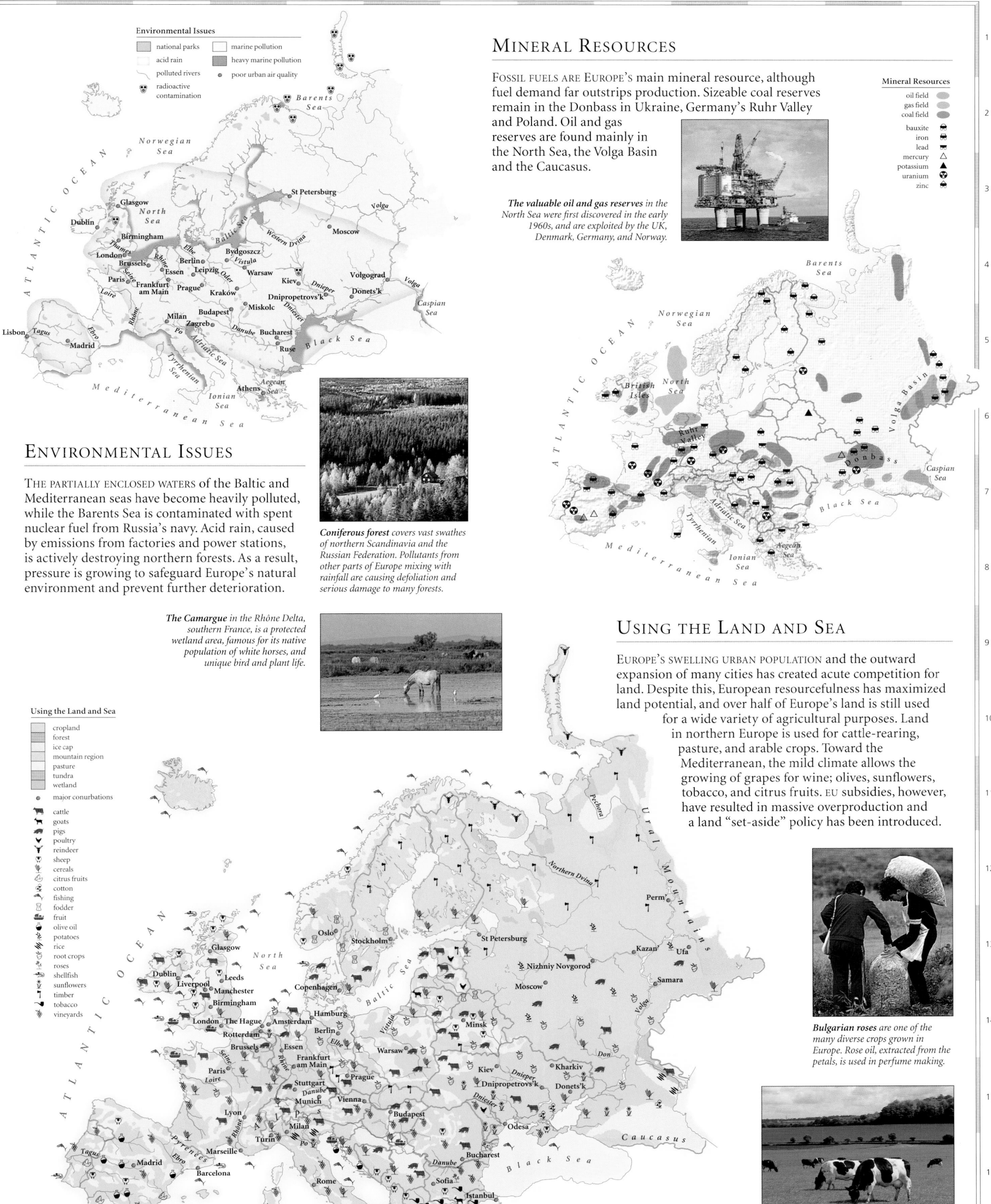

Environmental Issues

national parks	marine pollution
acid rain	heavy marine pollution
polluted rivers	poor urban air quality
radioactive contamination	

MINERAL RESOURCES

FOSSIL FUELS ARE EUROPE'S main mineral resource, although fuel demand far outstrips production. Sizeable coal reserves remain in the Donbass in Ukraine, Germany's Ruhr Valley and Poland. Oil and gas reserves are found mainly in the North Sea, the Volga Basin and the Caucasus.

Mineral Resources

- oil field
- gas field
- coal field
- bauxite
- iron
- lead
- mercury △
- potassium ▲
- uranium
- zinc

The valuable oil and gas reserves in the North Sea were first discovered in the early 1960s, and are exploited by the UK, Denmark, Germany, and Norway.

ENVIRONMENTAL ISSUES

THE PARTIALLY ENCLOSED WATERS of the Baltic and Mediterranean seas have become heavily polluted, while the Barents Sea is contaminated with spent nuclear fuel from Russia's navy. Acid rain, caused by emissions from factories and power stations, is actively destroying northern forests. As a result, pressure is growing to safeguard Europe's natural environment and prevent further deterioration.

Coniferous forest covers vast swathes of northern Scandinavia and the Russian Federation. Pollutants from other parts of Europe mixing with rainfall are causing defoliation and serious damage to many forests.

The Camargue in the Rhône Delta, southern France, is a protected wetland area, famous for its native population of white horses, and unique bird and plant life.

USING THE LAND AND SEA

EUROPE'S SWELLING URBAN POPULATION and the outward expansion of many cities has created acute competition for land. Despite this, European resourcefulness has maximized land potential, and over half of Europe's land is still used for a wide variety of agricultural purposes. Land in northern Europe is used for cattle-rearing, pasture, and arable crops. Toward the Mediterranean, the mild climate allows the growing of grapes for wine; olives, sunflowers, tobacco, and citrus fruits. EU subsidies, however, have resulted in massive overproduction and a land "set-aside" policy has been introduced.

Using the Land and Sea

- cropland
- forest
- ice cap
- mountain region
- pasture
- tundra
- wetland
- major conurbations
- cattle
- goats
- pigs
- poultry
- reindeer
- sheep
- cereals
- citrus fruits
- cotton
- fishing
- fodder
- fruit
- olive oil
- potatoes
- rice
- root crops
- roses
- shellfish
- sunflowers
- timber
- tobacco
- vineyards

Bulgarian roses are one of the many diverse crops grown in Europe. Rose oil, extracted from the petals, is used in perfume making.

Lowland pastures are used for dairy farming. Good transportation links and refrigeration allow fresh milk to be distributed throughout Europe.

SCANDINAVIA, FINLAND & ICELAND

DENMARK, NORWAY, SWEDEN, FINLAND, ICELAND

JUTTING INTO THE ARCTIC CIRCLE, this northern swath of Europe has some of the continent's harshest environments, but benefits from great reserves of oil, gas, and natural evergreen forests. While most early settlers came from the south, migrants to Finland came from the east, giving it a distinct language and culture. Since the late 19th century, the Scandinavian states have developed strong egalitarian traditions. Today, their welfare benefits systems are among the most extensive in the world, and standards of living are high. The Lapps, or Sami, maintain their traditional lifestyle in the northern regions of Norway, Sweden, and Finland.

THE LANDSCAPE

GLACIERS UP TO 10,000 ft (3,000 m) deep covered most of Scandinavia and Finland during the last Ice Age. The effects of glaciation mark the entire landscape, from the mountains to the lowlands, across the tundra landscape of Lapland, and the lake districts of Sweden and Finland.

Geysers are a by-product of Iceland's volcanic activity. Geysir, Iceland's largest spring, gives them their name.

The Lofoten Islands were one of the first areas exposed as the ice sheet melted.

Halti Mountain is Finland's highest point, at 4,356 ft (1,328 m).

Lapland, north of the Arctic Circle, is an area of undulating fells and plains known as tundra. The subsoil is permanently frozen and therefore impermeable. There are many peat bogs. Pools reappear in the summer when the surface thaws.

Finland's landscape was fashioned by ice action. Glaciers gouged out its distinctive shallow lake basins, such as Oulujärvi, and left debris called moraines in their wake.

Oulujärvi

Scandinavia is still recovering from the last Ice Age, when ice depressed the land by 2,000 ft (600 m). This gradual uplift is known as isostatic rebound.

Area of maximum yearly uplift 0.3 in/yr (9 mm/yr)

Slower rates of uplift 0.1 in/yr (3 mm/yr)

The fjords on the western coast of Norway were once gentle river valleys. Their deep floors and steep sides were carved out by glaciers during the last Ice Age, and they were later flooded by the sea.

Fjords

Sjælland coast

On the coast of Sjælland, these cliffs have been eroded by the sea, exposing layers of chalk and limestone.

USING THE LAND AND SEA

THE COLD CLIMATE, short growing season, poorly developed soil, steep slopes, and exposure to high winds across northern regions means that most agriculture is concentrated, with the population, in the south. Most of Finland and much of Norway and Sweden are covered by dense forests of pine, spruce and birch, which supply the timber industries.

Land use and agricultural distribution

capital cities
major towns

fishing
pigs
reindeer
sheep
timber

pasture
cropland
forest
tundra
mountain region

THE URBAN/RURAL POPULATION DIVIDE

urban 77%   rural 23%

POPULATION DENSITY	TOTAL LAND AREA
51 people per sq mile (20 people per sq km)	473,970 sq miles (1,227,610 sq km)

SCALE 1:8,000,000
(projection: Lambert Conformal Conic)

SCALE 1:5,000,000
(projection: Lambert Conformal Conic)

(same scale as main map)

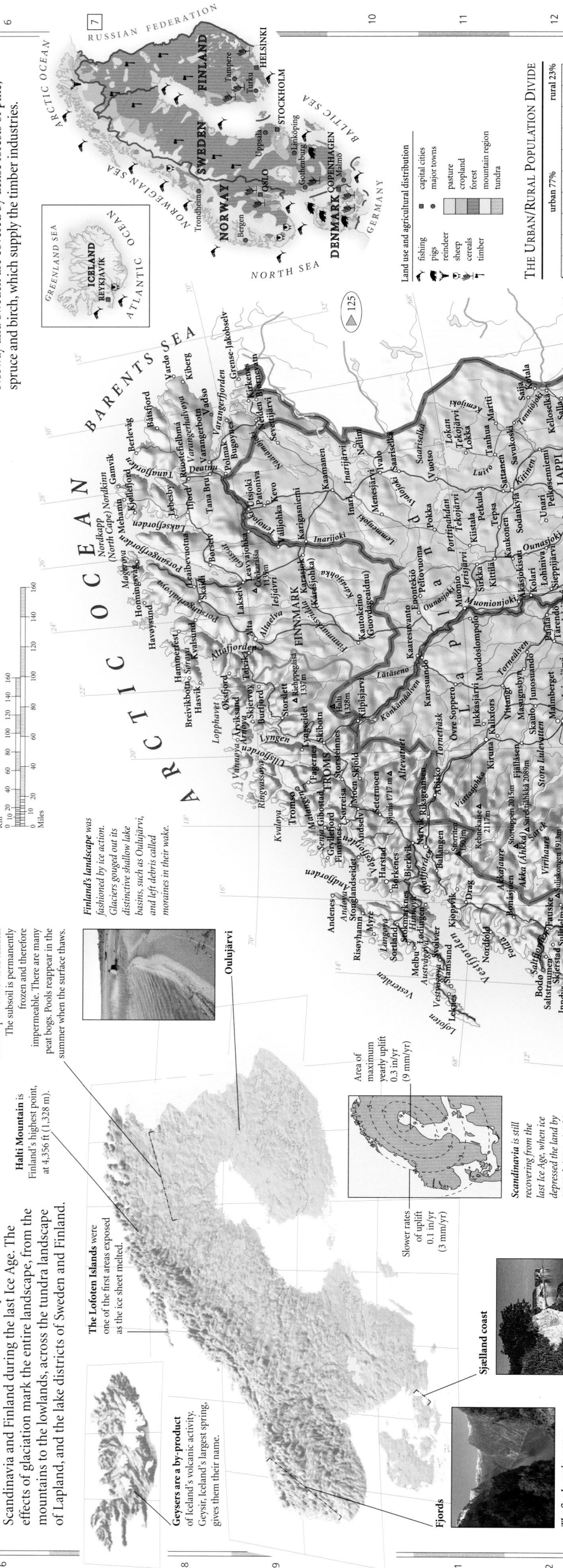

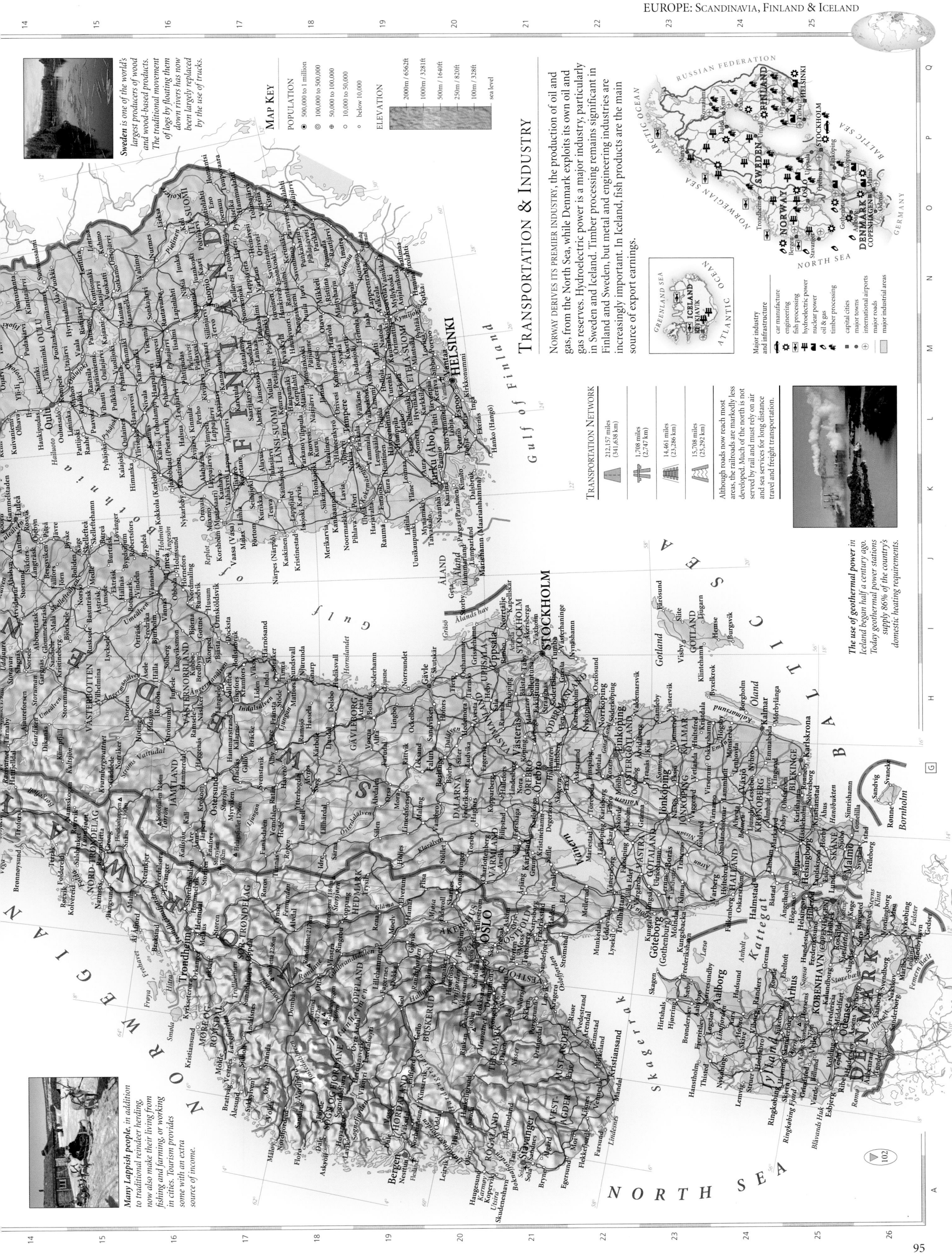

Sweden is one of the world's largest producers of wood and wood-based products. The traditional movement of logs by floating them down rivers has now been largely replaced by the use of trucks.

MAP KEY

POPULATION

- ⊙ 500,000 to 1 million
- ◎ 100,000 to 500,000
- ⊕ 50,000 to 100,000
- ○ 10,000 to 50,000
- ○ below 10,000

ELEVATION

- 2000m / 6562ft
- 1000m / 3281ft
- 500m / 1640ft
- 250m / 820ft
- 100m / 328ft
- sea level

TRANSPORTATION & INDUSTRY

NORWAY DERIVES ITS PREMIER INDUSTRY, the production of oil and gas, from the North Sea, while Denmark exploits its own oil and gas reserves. Hydroelectric power is a major industry, particularly in Sweden and Iceland. Timber processing remains significant in Finland and Sweden, but metal and engineering industries are increasingly important. In Iceland, fish products are the main source of export earnings.

Major industry and infrastructure
- car manufacture
- engineering
- fish processing
- hydroelectric power
- nuclear power
- oil & gas
- timber processing
- capital cities
- major towns
- international airports
- major roads
- major industrial areas

TRANSPORTATION NETWORK

- 212,157 miles (341,638 km)
- 1,708 miles (2,747 km)
- 14,461 miles (23,286 km)
- 15,708 miles (25,292 km)

Although roads now reach most areas, the railroads are markedly less developed. Much of the north is not served by rail and must rely on air and sea services for long distance travel and freight transportation.

The use of geothermal power in Iceland began half a century ago. Today geothermal power stations supply 86% of the country's domestic heating requirements.

Many Lappish people, in addition to traditional reindeer herding, now also make their living from fishing and farming or working in cities. Tourism provides some with an extra source of income.

95

SOUTHERN SCANDINAVIA

SOUTHERN NORWAY, SOUTHERN SWEDEN, DENMARK

S CANDINAVIA'S ECONOMIC AND POLITICAL HUB is the more habitable and
accessible southern region. Many of the area's major cities are on the
southern coasts, including Oslo and Stockholm, the capitals of Norway
and Sweden. In Denmark, most of the population and the capital,
Copenhagen, are located on its many islands. A cultural unity links the
three Scandinavian countries. Their main languages, Danish, Swedish, and
Norwegian, are mutually intelligible, and they all retain their monarchies,
although the parliaments have legislative control.

USING THE LAND

AGRICULTURE IN SOUTHERN SCANDINAVIA is highly mechanized
although farms are small. Denmark is the most intensively
farmed country and its western pastureland is used mainly
for pig farming. Cereal crops including wheat, barley, and
oats, predominate in eastern Denmark and in the far south
of Sweden. Southern Norway, and Sweden have large tracts
of forest which are exploited for logging.

THE URBAN/RURAL POPULATION DIVIDE

urban 87%   rural 13%

POPULATION DENSITY	TOTAL LAND AREA
152 people per sq mile	173,487 sq miles
(61 people per sq km)	(456,564 sq km)

Land use and agricultural distribution

- capital cities
- major towns

- pasture
- cropland
- forest
- mountain region

- cattle
- pigs
- sheep
- cereals
- fodder
- root crops
- timber

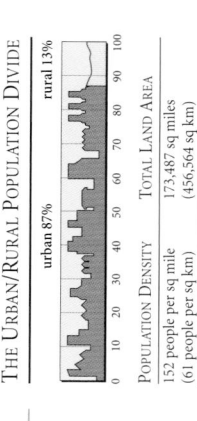

THE LANDSCAPE

SOUTHERN SCANDINAVIA, with the
exception of Norway, has a flatter
terrain than the rest of the region.
Denmark and southern Sweden are
both extensions of the North European
Plain. In this area, because of glacial
deposition rather than erosion, the
soils are deeper and more fertile.

Acid rain, caused by
industrial pollution carried
north from elsewhere in
Europe, harms plant and
animal life in Scandinavian
forests and lakes. The region's
surface rocks lack lime to
neutralize the acid, so making
the problem more serious.

*In the past, glaciers such
as this one in Olden,
Norway, were much larger.
Today, many are retreating
to yield the spectacular
glacial scenery.*

Olden

*Limestone pillars eroded by
the sea dot the coast of Gotland
and surrounding islands.*

Distinctive low ridges, called eskers,
are found across southern Sweden. They
are formed from sand and gravel
deposits left by retreating glaciers.

The peak of Glittertind
in the Jotunheimen
Mountains is 8,110 ft
(2,472 m) high.

**The lakes of southern
Sweden** remain from a
period when the land was
completely flooded.
As the ice which covered
the area melted, the land
rose, leaving lakes in
shallow, ice-scoured
depressions. Sweden
has over 90,000 lakes.

Vänern in Sweden is the largest lake
in Scandinavia. It covers an area of
2,080 sq miles (5,390 sq km).

Denmark's flat and fertile soils are
formed on glacial deposits between
100-160 ft (30-50 m) deep.

When the ice
retreated the
valley was
flooded by
the sea

Old valley floor

Erosion by glaciers
deepened existing
river valleys

Sea level

Sognefjorden

*Sognefjorden is the
deepest of Norway's
many fjords. It drops
to 4,291 ft (1,308 m)
below sea level.*

MAP KEY

POPULATION

- 500,000 to 1 million
- 100,000 to 500,000
- 50,000 to 100,000
- 10,000 to 50,000
- below 10,000

ELEVATION

- 2000m / 6562ft
- 1000m / 3281ft
- 500m / 1640ft
- 250m / 820ft
- 100m / 328ft
- sea level

SCALE 1:2,900,000 (projection: Lambert Conformal Conic)

*In Norway winters
are longer and colder
inland than in coastal
areas, where the
warm current of the
North Atlantic Drift
moderates the climate.*

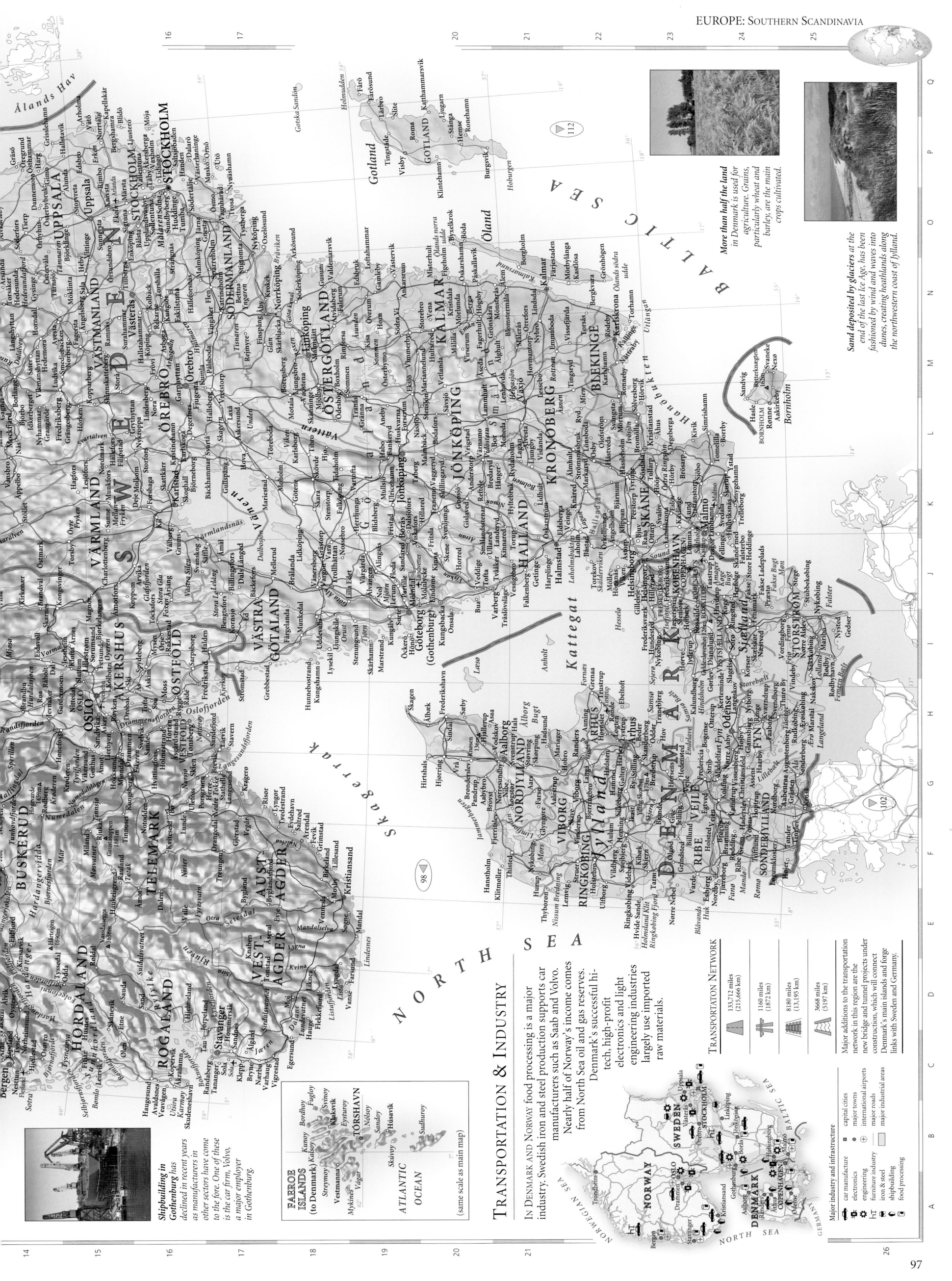

More than half the land in Denmark is used for agriculture. Grains, particularly wheat and barley, are the main crops cultivated.

Sand deposited by glaciers at the end of the last Ice Age, has been fashioned by wind and waves into dunes, creating heathlands along the northwestern coast of Jylland.

TRANSPORTATION & INDUSTRY

IN DENMARK AND NORWAY food processing is a major industry. Swedish iron and steel production supports car manufacturers such as Saab and Volvo. Nearly half of Norway's income comes from North Sea oil and gas reserves. Denmark's successful hi-tech, high-profit electronics and light engineering industries largely use imported raw materials.

Shipbuilding in Gothenburg has declined in recent years as manufacturers in other sectors have come to the fore. One of these is the car firm, Volvo, a major employer in Gothenburg.

FAEROE ISLANDS
(to Denmark)

(same scale as main map)

TRANSPORTATION NETWORK

133,712 miles (215,666 km)

1160 miles (1872 km)

8180 miles (13,195 km)

3668 miles (5197 km)

Major additions to the transportation network in this region are the new bridge and tunnel projects under construction, which will connect Denmark's main islands and forge links with Sweden and Germany.

Major industry and infrastructure

- capital cities
- major towns
- international airports
- major roads
- major industrial areas

- car manufacture
- electronics
- engineering
- furniture industry
- iron & steel
- shipbuilding
- food processing

THE BRITISH ISLES

UNITED KINGDOM, IRELAND

THE BRITISH ISLES have for centuries played a central role in European and world history. England, Wales, Scotland, and Northern Ireland together form the United Kingdom (UK), while the southern portion of Ireland is an independent country, self-governing since 1921. Although England has tended to be the politically and economically dominant partner in the UK, the Scots, Welsh and Irish maintain independent cultures, distinct national identities and languages. Southeastern England is the most densely populated part of this crowded region, with over nine million people living in and around the London area.

TRANSPORTATION AND INDUSTRY

THE BRITISH ISLES' INDUSTRIAL BASE was founded primarily on coal, iron and textiles, based largely in the north. Today, the most productive sectors include hi-tech industries clustered mainly in southeastern England, chemicals, finance and the service sector, particularly tourism.

Major industry and infrastructure

- capital cities
- major towns
- international airports
- major roads
- major industrial areas

car manufacture
chemicals
hi-tech industry
iron & steel
tourism

The UK's congested roads have become a major focus of environmental concern in recent years. No longer an island, the UK was finally linked to continental Europe by the Channel Tunnel in 1994.

TRANSPORTATION NETWORK

288,330 miles (464,300 km)	2,046 miles (3,295 km)
11,874 miles (19,121 km)	3,806 miles (6,129 km)

Clew Bay in western Ireland, is characteristic of the heavily indented west coast, where deep wide-mouthed bays separate the mountains of Mayo, Donegal, and Kerry as they thrust out into the Atlantic Ocean.

THE LANDSCAPE

RUGGED UPLANDS dominate the landscape of Scotland, Wales, and northern England. All the peaks in the British Isles over 4,000 ft (1,219 m) lie in highland Scotland. Lowland England rises into several ranges of rolling hills, including the older Mendips, and the Cotswolds and the Chilterns, which were formed at the same time as the Alps in southern Europe.

The valley of Glen Coe in the Scottish Highlands is a U-shaped valley, typical of the north and west of the British Isles, where glaciers shaped much of the landscape.

The Pennines, sometimes called "the backbone of England," are formed of limestones and grits.

Ullswater in the Lake District fills a deep valley formed by glacial erosion.

The Fens are a low-lying area reclaimed from the sea.

Chiltern Hills

The Cotswold Hills are characterized by a series of limestone ridges overlooking clay vales.

Durdle Door

Coastal erosion around the British Isles forms striking features such as this limestone arch, Durdle Door, in Dorset.

The lowlands of Scotland, drained by the Tay, Forth, and Clyde Rivers, are centred on a rift valley. The region contains valuable coal reserves.

Lake District

Mendip Hills

Ben Nevis at 4,409 ft (1,343 m) is the highest peak in the UK.

Over 600 islands, mostly uninhabited, lie west and north of the Scottish mainland.

Thousands of hexagonal basalt columns form Giant's Causeway on the north coast of Antrim. These were created by volcanic activity.

Snowdon is the highest mountain in England and Wales reaching 3,556 ft (1,085 m).

Peat bogs dot the poorly-drained Irish lowlands.

The British Isles have no large-scale river systems. The Shannon is the longest, at 230 miles (370 km).

Dartmoor, studded with tors, is an exposed part of a vast granite dome, formed when molten rock intruded into the Earth's crust.

Black Ven, Lyme Regis

Cracks
Sandstone
Clay
Limestone
Water
Mudslide
Sea

Much of the south coast is subject to landslides. Following rain, porous sandstones feed water into the underlying, less permeable clays which then crumble and slide into the sea.

MAP KEY

POPULATION
- above 5 million
- 1 million to 5 million
- 500,000 to 1 million
- 100,000 to 500,000
- 50,000 to 100,000
- 10,000 to 50,000
- below 10,000

ELEVATION
- 1000m / 3281ft
- 500m / 1640ft
- 250m / 820ft
- 100m / 328ft
- sea level

Map labels

Shetland Islands
Herma Ness, Unst, Fetlar, Out Skerries, Yell, Whalsay, Sullom Voe, Yell Sound, Hillswick, St Magnus Bay, Mainland, Papa Stour, Scalloway, West Burra, Lerwick, Bressay, Foula, Fitful Head, Sumburgh Head

Fair Isle

Orkney Islands
North Ronaldsay, Sanday, Stronsay, Westray, Papa Westray, Rousay, Eday, Shapinsay, Mainland, Kirkwall, Stromness, Hoy, Scapa Flow, Burray, St Margaret's Hope, South Ronaldsay, The North Sound, Pentland Firth, Duncansby Head, John o'Groats

North Rona
Sula Sgeir
Sule Skerry
Stack Skerry

Cape Wrath, Durness, Strathy Point, Dunnet Head, Thurso, Halladale, Tongue, Kinbrace, Helmsdale, Brora, Golspie, Dornoch, Lairg, Bonar Bridge, Tain, Tarbat Ness, Cromarty, Inverness, Nairn, Forres, Elgin, Lossiemouth, Buckie, Keith, Banff, Macduff, Turriff, Fraserburgh, Peterhead, Kinnaird Head, Buchan Ness, Aberdeen, Girdle Ness, Stonehaven, Montrose, Brechin, Forfar, Arbroath, Carnoustie, Dundee, St Andrews, Fife Ness, North Berwick

Butt of Ness, Port of Ness, Broad Bay, Carloway, Stornoway, Isle of Lewis, Loch Roag, Tarbert, Harris, North Uist, Benbecula, South Uist, Barra, Barra Head, St Kilda

Scotland, Grampian Mountains, North West Highlands, Southern Uplands

Glasgow, Edinburgh, Stirling, Perth, Oban, Fort William, Inverness, Ben Nevis

SCOTLAND

Berwick-upon-Tweed, Holy Island

ATLANTIC OCEAN

IRELAND

UNITED KINGDOM

LONDON, DUBLIN, Belfast, Cork, Glasgow, Edinburgh, Aberdeen, Dundee, Newcastle upon Tyne, Leeds, Manchester, Liverpool, Birmingham, Nottingham, Norwich, Oxford, Bristol

NORTH SEA

English Channel

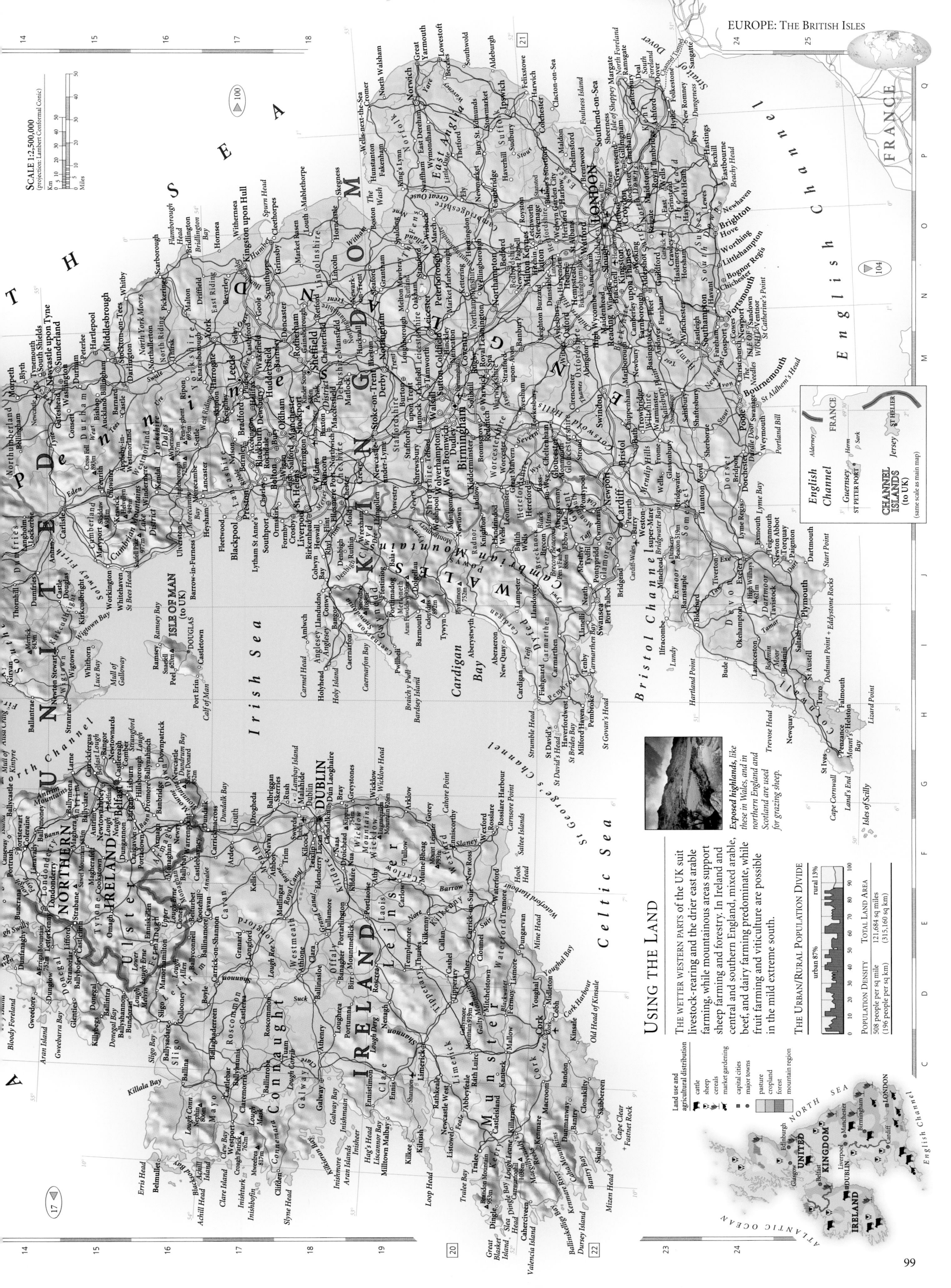

USING THE LAND

THE WETTER WESTERN PARTS of the UK suit livestock-rearing and the drier east arable farming, while mountainous areas support sheep farming and forestry. In Ireland and central and southern England, mixed arable, beef, and dairy farming predominate, while fruit farming and viticulture are possible in the mild extreme south.

Exposed highlands, like these in Wales, and in northern England and Scotland are used for grazing sheep.

THE URBAN/RURAL POPULATION DIVIDE

urban 87%   rural 13%

POPULATION DENSITY	TOTAL LAND AREA
508 people per sq mile	121,684 sq miles
(196 people per sq km)	(315,160 sq km)

Land use and agricultural distribution
- cattle
- sheep
- cereals
- market gardening
- capital cities
- major towns
- pasture
- cropland
- forest
- mountain region

SCALE 1:2,500,000
(projection: Lambert Conformal Conic)

THE LOW COUNTRIES

BELGIUM, LUXEMBOURG, NETHERLANDS

ONE OF NORTHWESTERN EUROPE's strategic crossroads, the Low Countries are united by a common history in which they have often been a battleground in European wars. For over a thousand years they were ruled by foreign powers. Even after they achieved independence, the three countries maintained close links, later forming the world's first totally free labor and goods market, the Benelux Economic Union, which became the core of the European Community (now the European Union or EU). These states have remained at the forefront of wider European cooperation; Brussels, The Hague, and Luxembourg are hosts to major institutions of the EU.

THE LANDSCAPE

THE MAIN GEOGRAPHICAL REGIONS of the Netherlands are the northern glacial heathlands, the low-lying lands of the Rhine and Maas/Meuse, the reclaimed polders, and the dune coast and islands. Belgium includes part of the Ardennes, together with the coalfields on its northern flanks, and the fertile Flanders Plain.

The loess soils of the Flanders Plain in western Belgium provide excellent conditions for arable farming.

Since the Middle Ages the people of the Netherlands have used ditches and drainage dykes to reclaim land from the sea. These reclaimed areas are known as polders.

Extensive sand dune systems along the coast have prevented flooding of the land. Behind the dunes, marshy land is drained to form polders, usable land suitable for agriculture.

Sand dunes
Polder
Drainage ditch
Dune system
Sea

Uplifted and folded 220 million years ago, the Ardennes have since been reduced to relatively level plateaus, then sharply incised by rivers such as the Maas/Meuse.

Ardennes

Hautes Fagnes is the highest part of Belgium. The bogs and streams in this upland region result from high rainfall and low temperatures.

Silts and sands eroded by the Rhine throughout its course are deposited to form a delta on the west coast of the Netherlands.

The parallel valleys of the Maas/Meuse and Rhine Rivers were created when the Rhine was deflected from its previous course by the ice sheet which formed during the last Ice Age.

One-third of the Netherlands lies below sea level and flooding is a constant threat. Barrages have been built across the mouths of many rivers to contain floodwaters.

Heathlands, like these at Schoorl, are found along the coast of the Netherlands. Much of the coast was breached by the sea in the 5th century, creating its distinctive inlets and islands.

Schoorl

TRANSPORTATION & INDUSTRY

IN THE WESTERN NETHERLANDS, a massive, sprawling industrialized zone encompasses many new hi-tech and service industries. Belgium's central region has emerged as the country's light manufacturing and services center. Luxembourg city is home to more than 160 banks and the European headquarters of many international companies.

The Low Countries hold a key position on the North Sea, containing Europe's two largest ports, Rotterdam and Antwerp, which are connected to a comprehensive system of inland waterways.

TRANSPORTATION NETWORK

	280,630 miles (451,900 km)		2,536 miles (4,083 km)
	4,037 miles (6,501 km)		4,366 miles (7,031 km)

Major industry and infrastructure:
- aerospace
- finance
- engineering
- hi-tech industry
- pharmaceuticals
- textiles
- capital cities
- major towns
- international airports
- major roads
- major industrial areas

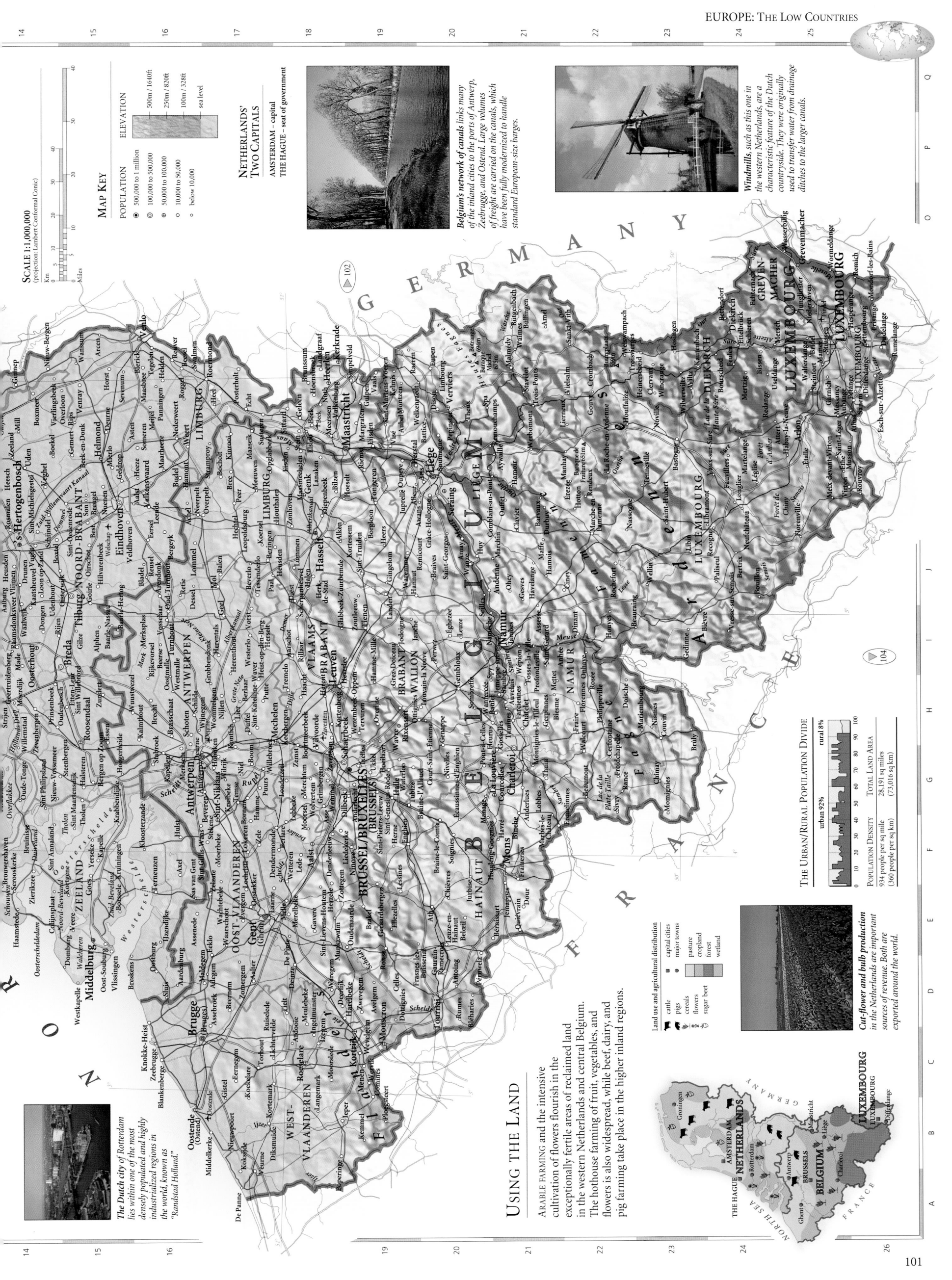

SCALE 1:1,000,000
(projection: Lambert Conformal Conic)

MAP KEY

POPULATION
- ◉ 500,000 to 1 million
- ⊙ 100,000 to 500,000
- ⊕ 50,000 to 100,000
- ○ 10,000 to 50,000
- ∘ below 10,000

ELEVATION
- 500m / 1640ft
- 250m / 820ft
- 100m / 328ft
- sea level

NETHERLANDS' TWO CAPITALS
AMSTERDAM – capital
THE HAGUE – seat of government

Belgium's network of canals links many of the inland cities to the ports of Antwerp, Zeebrugge, and Ostend. Large volumes of freight are carried on the canals, which have been fully modernized to handle standard European-size barges.

Windmills, such as this one in the western Netherlands, are a characteristic feature of the Dutch countryside. They were originally used to transfer water from drainage ditches to the larger canals.

The Dutch city of Rotterdam lies within one of the most densely populated and highly industrialized regions in the world, known as "Randstad Holland."

Cut-flower and bulb production in the Netherlands are important sources of revenue. Both are exported around the world.

USING THE LAND

ARABLE FARMING and the intensive cultivation of flowers flourish in the exceptionally fertile areas of reclaimed land in the western Netherlands and central Belgium. The hothouse farming of fruit, vegetables, and flowers is also widespread, while beef, dairy, and pig farming take place in the higher inland regions.

Land use and agricultural distribution
- cattle
- pigs
- cereals
- flowers
- sugar beet
- capital cities
- major towns
- pasture
- cropland
- forest
- wetland

THE URBAN/RURAL POPULATION DIVIDE

urban 92% / rural 8%

POPULATION DENSITY: 934 people per sq mile (360 people per sq km)
TOTAL LAND AREA: 28,191 sq miles (73,016 sq km)

101

GERMANY

DESPITE THE DEVASTATION of its industry and infrastructure during the Second World War and its separation from eastern Germany during the Cold War, West Germany made a rapid recovery in the following generation to become Europe's most formidable economic power. When the Berlin Wall was dismantled in 1989, the two halves of Germany were politically united for the first time in 40 years.

Complete social and economic unity remain a longer term goal, as East German industry and society adapt to a free market. Germany has been a key player in the creation of the European Union (EU) and in moves toward a single European currency.

USING THE LAND

GERMANY has a large, efficient agricultural sector, and produces more than three-quarters of its own food. The major crops grown are cereals and sugar beet on the more fertile soils, and root crops, rye, oats, and fodder on the poorer soils of the northern plains and central uplands. Southern Germany is also a principal producer of high quality wines. Vineyards cover the slopes surrounding the Rhine and its tributaries.

Land use and agricultural distribution

- cattle
- pigs
- cereals
- sugar beet
- vineyards
- capital cities
- major towns
- pasture
- cropland
- forest

THE URBAN/RURAL POPULATION DIVIDE

urban 87%   rural 13%

POPULATION DENSITY
598 people per sq mile
(231 people per sq km)

TOTAL LAND AREA
13,804 sq miles
(356,910 sq km)

The Moselle River flows through the Rhine State Uplands (Rheinisches Schiefergebirge). During a period of uplift, preexisting river meanders were deeply incised, to form its present dramatic contours.

THE LANDSCAPE

THE PLAINS OF NORTHERN GERMANY, the volcanic plateaus and mountains of the central uplands, and the Bavarian Alps are the three principal geographic regions in Germany. North to south the land rises steadily from barely 300 ft (90 m) in the plains to 6,500 ft (2,000 m) in the Bavarian Alps, which are a small but distinct region in the far south.

Lüneburg Heath
(*Lüneburger Heide*)

The heathlands of northern Germany are covered by glacial deposits of sandy outwash soil which makes them largely infertile. They support only sheep and solitary trees.

Much of the landscape of northern Germany has been shaped by glaciation. During the last Ice Age, the ice sheet advanced as far the northern slopes of the central uplands.

Rhine Rift Valley

Part of the floor of the Rhine Rift Valley was let down between two parallel faults in the Earth's crust.

Fault lines
Rhine
Downfaulted block

Müritz lake covers 45 sq miles (117 sq km), but is only 1.08 ft (33 m) deep. It lies in a shallow valley formed by meltwater flowing out from a retreating ice sheet. These valleys are known as *Urstromtäler*.

The Harz Mountains were formed 300 million years ago. They are block-faulted mountains, formed when a section of the Earth's crust was thrust up between two faults.

Elbe River

The Elbe flows in wide meanders across the north German plain to the North Sea. At its mouth it is 10 miles (16 km) wide.

The Rhine is Germany's principal waterway and one of Europe's longest rivers, flowing 820 miles (1,320 km).

The Danube rises in the Black Forest (*Schwarzwald*) and flows east, across a wide valley, on its course to the Black Sea.

Zugspitze, the highest peak in Germany at 9,719 ft (2,962 m), was formed during the Alpine mountain-building period, 30 million years ago.

SCALE 1:2,250,000
(projection: Lambert Conformal Conic)

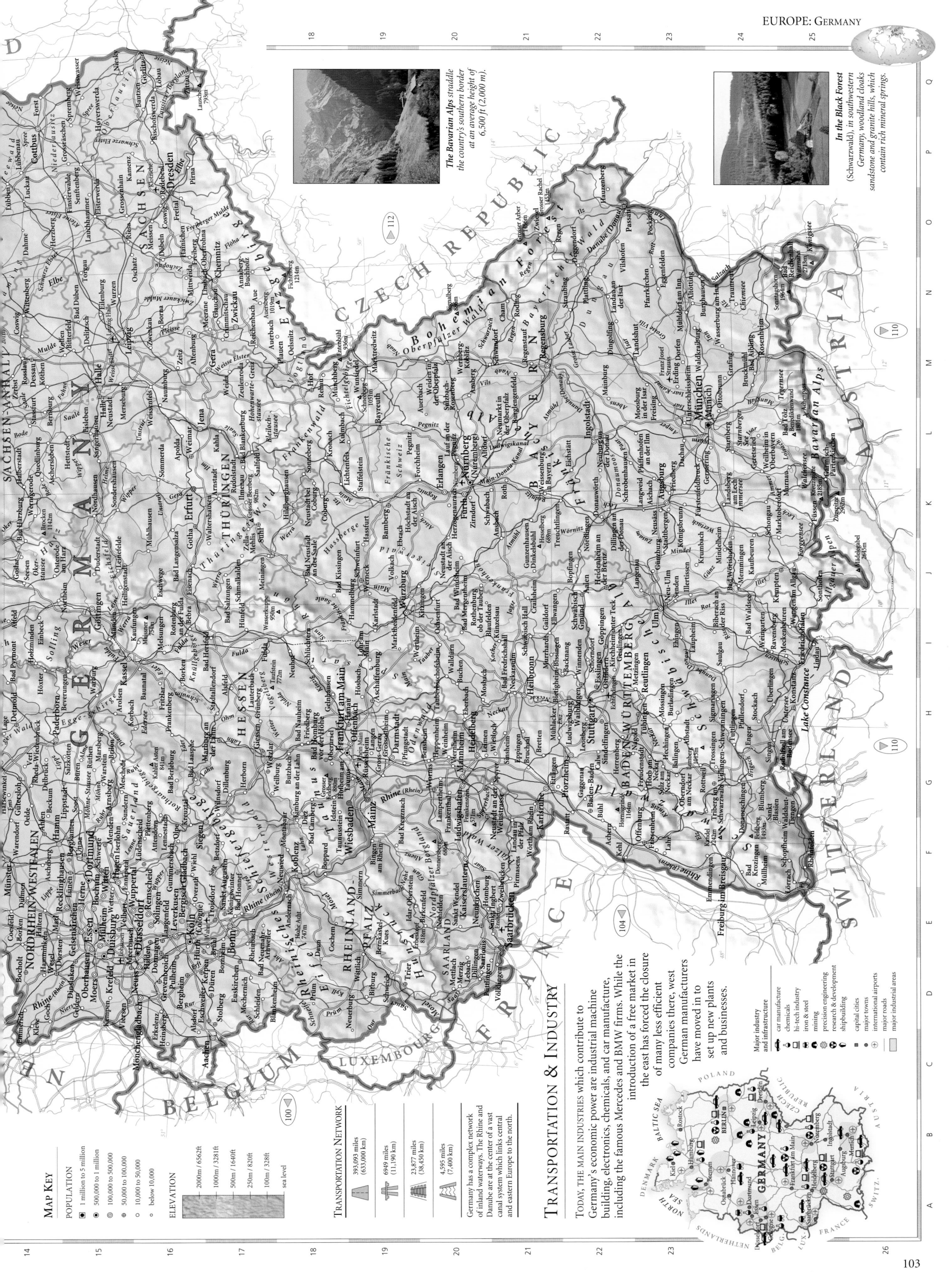

The Bavarian Alps straddle the country's southern border at an average height of 6,500 ft (2,000 m).

In the Black Forest (Schwarzwald), in southwestern Germany, woodland cloaks sandstone and granite hills, which contain rich mineral springs.

TRANSPORTATION & INDUSTRY

TODAY, THE MAIN INDUSTRIES which contribute to Germany's economic power are industrial machine building, electronics, chemicals, and car manufacture, including the famous Mercedes and BMW firms. While the introduction of a free market in the east has forced the closure of many less efficient companies there, west German manufacturers have moved in to set up new plants and businesses.

TRANSPORTATION NETWORK

393,093 miles (633,000 km)

6949 miles (11,190 km)

23,877 miles (38,450 km)

4,595 miles (7,400 km)

Germany has a complex network of inland waterways. The Rhine and Danube are at the center of a vast canal system which links central and eastern Europe to the north.

MAP KEY

POPULATION

- 1 million to 5 million
- 500,000 to 1 million
- 100,000 to 500,000
- 50,000 to 100,000
- 10,000 to 50,000
- below 10,000

ELEVATION

- 2000m/6562ft
- 1000m/3281ft
- 500m/1640ft
- 250m/820ft
- 100m/328ft
- sea level

Major industry and infrastructure

- car manufacture
- chemicals
- hi-tech industry
- iron & steel
- mining
- precision engineering
- research & development
- shipbuilding
- capital cities
- major towns
- international airports
- major roads
- major industrial areas

FRANCE

FRANCE, MONACO

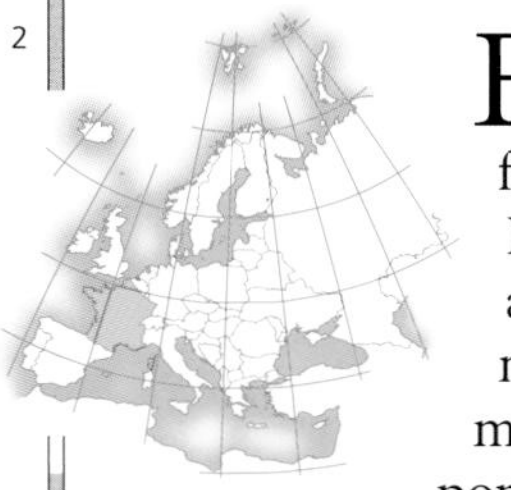

Europe's second largest nation and the founder of modern Republican government, France is a major center of culture and fashion, and a leading producer of both agricultural and industrial goods. It has played a leading role in European events for centuries, and remains a key player in the push toward European unity. The Paris Basin is the most highly populated area; Île de France is home to over nine million people. Large parts of France remain thinly populated, particularly the mountainous Massif Central, Pyrenees, and southern Alps.

THE LANDSCAPE

FRANCE'S LANDSCAPE was fashioned by two phases of mountain-building. The northwestern peninsula, the Massif Central, and the Vosges date from 220 million years ago. The complex folds of the Alps and Pyrenees, the gently-folded Jura, and the low-lying sedimentary areas of the Paris, Garonne, and Rhône basins started to form 65 million years ago.

The chalk cliffs of Normandy (Normandie) and southeastern England form part of a single geological region, now divided in two by the English Channel.

The coast of Brittany (Bretagne) is highly indented where deep valleys in the northwestern peninsula were drowned by the sea.

The Normandy (Normandie) coastline is characterized by high chalk cliffs.

The coastline of France is 2,141 miles (3,427 km) long.

The Paris Basin consists of a layered sequence of sedimentary rocks. Fertile soils over much of the area make good agricultural land.

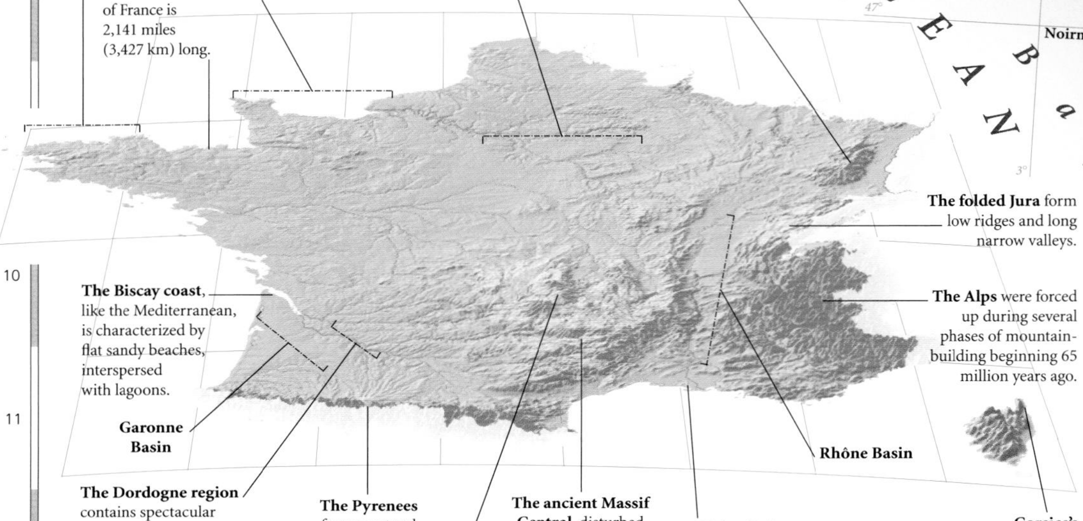

The gently rounded summits of the Vosges are over 200 million years old.

The folded Jura form low ridges and long narrow valleys.

The Alps were forced up during several phases of mountain-building beginning 65 million years ago.

The Biscay coast, like the Mediterranean, is characterized by flat sandy beaches, interspersed with lagoons.

Garonne Basin

The Dordogne region contains spectacular examples of limestone scenery including caves and gorges.

The Pyrenees form a natural border between France and Spain.

The ancient Massif Central, disturbed by the formation of the Alps, was subject to volcanism that only ceased during the last 10,000 years.

Rhône Basin

Rhône Delta

Rhône

Delta plain

The marshes of the Camargue

Deposition in the Rhône Delta is wave-dominated. Sea currents carry river sediments extending the delta plain westwards.

Corsica's northeastern peninsula has dramatic cliffs of folded limestone.

The volcanic landscape of the Auvergne where the cones of its extinct volcanoes have worn away to leave "plugs" of lava.

TRANSPORTATION & INDUSTRY

TODAY THE MAIN FRENCH GROWTH INDUSTRIES are hi-tech, including microelectronics, telecommunications, and aerospace. Other important sectors are the nuclear industry, only rivalled in scale by that of the USA, car manufacture, dominated by the giants Renault and Peugeot and a highly diversified tourist industry.

Major industry and infrastructure

- aerospace industry
- car manufacture
- chemicals
- engineering
- hi-tech industry
- nuclear power
- tourism

- capital cities
- major towns
- international airports
- major roads
- major industrial areas

TRANSPORTATION NETWORK

599,017 miles (964,600 km)	5,900 miles (9,500 km)
19,761 miles (31,821 km)	5,279 miles (8,500 km)

The French TGV (Train à Grande Vitesse) leads the world in high-speed train technology, and provides a service which is faster, door-to-door, than air travel.

SCALE 1:2,750,000
(projection: Lambert Conformal Conic)

Km
0 10 20 30 40 50 60 70 80

Miles
0 5 10 20 30 40 50 60 70 80

MAP KEY

POPULATION

- ■ above 5 million
- ◉ 1 million to 5 million
- ◉ 500,000 to 1 million
- ◉ 100,000 to 500,000
- ⊕ 50,000 to 100,000
- ○ 10,000 to 50,000
- ○ below 10,000

ELEVATION

4000m / 13,124ft
3000m / 9843ft
2000m / 6562ft
1000m / 3281ft
500m / 1640ft
250m / 820ft
100m / 328ft
sea level

USING THE LAND

FRANCE IS WESTERN EUROPE's leading agricultural producer, and benefits from high levels of EU subsidy. The variation in climate and soils across the country provides great potential for agriculture and forestry, reflected in the range of products cultivated, including cereals, olives, herbs, and grapes for its famous wines.

Land use and agricultural distribution

- cattle
- cereals
- market gardening
- sugar beet
- vineyards
- ■ capital cities
- ● major towns

pasture
cropland
forest
mountain region

The Romans first introduced winemaking to France when they occupied the region. Traditional vineyards can be found all over France, producing many of the world's classic wines.

THE URBAN/RURAL POPULATION DIVIDE

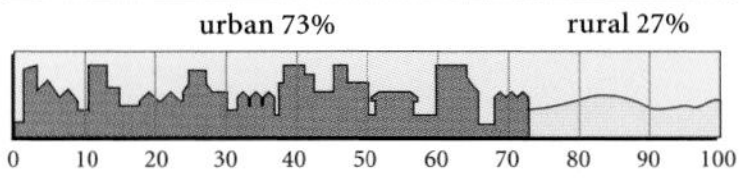

urban 73%   rural 27%

0 10 20 30 40 50 60 70 80 90 100

POPULATION DENSITY
276 people per sq mile
(106 people per sq km)

TOTAL LAND AREA
212,930 sq mile
(551,500 sq km)

The rugged hills and cliffs of Corsica were uplifted when the African and Eurasian plates collided. Frost action during the Ice Age created their present form.

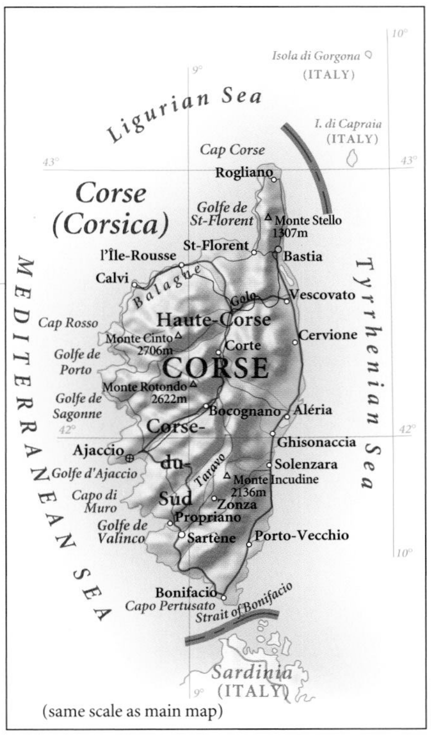

Corse (Corsica)

(same scale as main map)

In the sunny climate of southern France olives, vines, peppers, garlic, and lavender now grow in place of the forests that once covered much of the area.

THE IBERIAN PENINSULA

ANDORRA, GIBRALTAR, PORTUGAL, SPAIN *(Azores, Canary Islands, Madeira on p.66)*

THE IBERIAN PENINSULA is separated from the rest of Europe by the Pyrenees, and at its most southerly point is only 5 miles (8 km) from North Africa. The location of Iberia has been central to its diverse history. The Greeks, Carthaginians, Romans, Visigoths, and most recently the Moors, invaded Iberia at various times. For much of the 20th century, both Spain and Portugal were governed by right-wing dictators. Since the establishment of democratic governments in the mid-1970s, modernization has been rapid and both countries are now among the most popular of European holiday destinations.

USING THE LAND

THE PRINCIPAL CROPS grown in Iberia are cereals, especially wheat and barley. Both countries are major wine producers, most notably of Rioja, sherry, and port. Sheep are kept throughout the region, and citrus fruits thrive on the Mediterranean coast. The successful forest industry in Iberia produces two-thirds of the world's cork.

The steep, terraced slopes of the Douro Valley in northern Portugal, are used to cultivate vines. The grapes harvested produce Portugal's famous port wine.

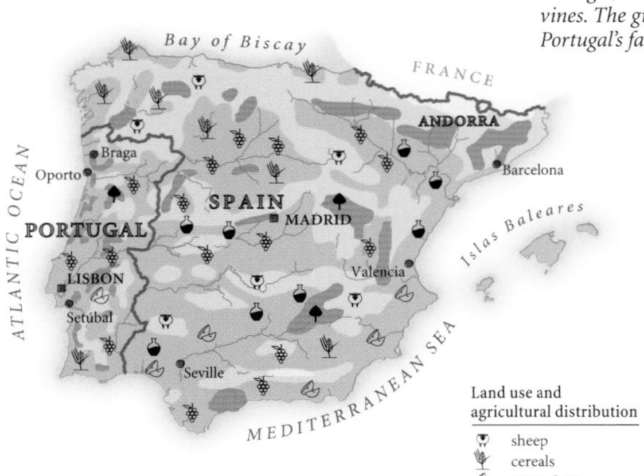

Land use and agricultural distribution

- sheep
- cereals
- citrus fruit
- olives
- vineyards
- cork

- capital cities
- major towns

- pasture
- cropland
- forest
- mountain region

THE URBAN/RURAL POPULATION DIVIDE

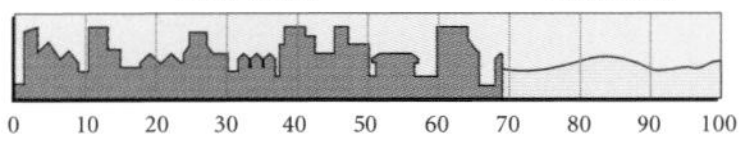

urban 68%   rural 32%

0 10 20 30 40 50 60 70 80 90 100

POPULATION DENSITY	TOTAL LAND AREA
215 people per sq mile (83 people per sq km)	230,569 sq miles (597,170 sq km)

TRANSPORTATION & INDUSTRY

SINCE THE 1970s, the economies of Spain and Portugal have expanded and diversified. In both countries, tourism has outstripped agriculture in economic importance. Spain's resource base is varied, including coal, iron, and the world's largest reserves of mercury. Portugal is a leading producer of tungsten ore.

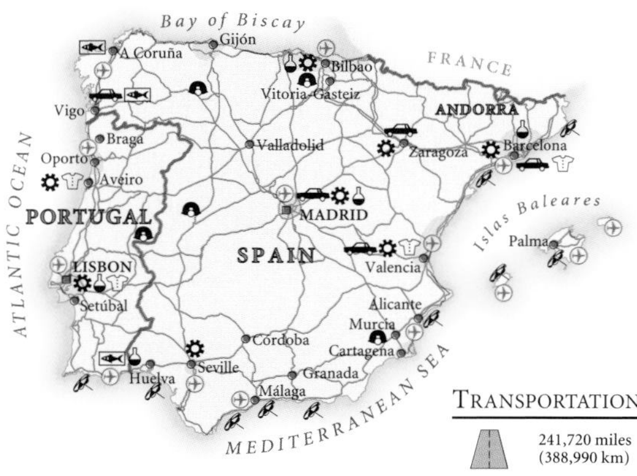

Major industry and infrastructure

- car manufacture
- chemicals
- engineering
- fish processing
- mining
- textiles
- tourism

- capital cities
- major towns
- international airports
- major roads
- major industrial areas

TRANSPORTATION NETWORK

241,720 miles (388,990 km)	1,552 miles (2,529 km)
11,793 miles (18,979 km)	1,159 miles (1,865 km)

Radiating from Madrid, the road network in Spain dates from the 18th century, but now includes many highways. Portugal's road system has been completely modernized in recent years.

The eroded cliffs of the Algarve in southern Portugal were carved by Atlantic waves. The numerous rocky bays and beaches, and the region's pleasant climate, have made it a popular tourist destination.

66 ◀

76

THE ITALIAN PENINSULA

ITALY, SAN MARINO, VATICAN CITY

THE ITALIAN PENINSULA is a land of great contrasts. Until unification in 1861, Italy was a collection of independent states, whose competitiveness during the Renaissance resulted in the architectural and artistic magnificence of cities such as Rome, Florence, and Venice. The majority of Italy's population and economic activity is concentrated in the north, centered on the sophisticated industrial city of Milan. Southern Italy, the *Mezzogiorno*, has a harsh terrain, and remains far less developed than the north. Attempts to attract industry and investment in the south are frequently deterred by the entrenched network of organized crime and corruption.

Costa Smeralda

THE LANDSCAPE

THE MAINLY MOUNTAINOUS and hilly Italian peninsula took its present form following a collision between the African and Eurasian tectonic plates. The Alps in the northwest rise to a high point of 15,772 ft (4,807 m) at Mont Blanc (*Monte Bianco*) on the French border, while the Apennines (*Appennino*) form a rugged backbone, running along the entire length of the country.

The island of Sardinia is an ancient land mass, an uplifted section of very old igneous rocks. Its rugged mountainous regions provide pasture for sheep and goats, while its valleys support some agriculture.

Mont Blanc (*Monte Bianco*)

The Dolomites (*Alpi Dolomitiche*) *are formed of thick limestones, overlying weaker marine strata. They have distinctive serrated peaks and many massive landslides occur.*

The distinctive square shape of the Gulf of Taranto (*Golfo di Taranto*) was defined by numerous block faults. Earthquakes are common in this region.

Vesuvius (*Vesuvio*)

The Apennines (*Appennino*) are the source of most of Italy's rivers. They run 823 miles (1324 km) down the length of the peninsula.

The Pontine Marshes (*Agro Pontino*) are bounded by low sand hills which prevent natural drainage.

The Po Valley once formed part of the Adriatic Sea. Sediments of gravel, sand, and clay washed down from the Alps gradually filling the bay and forming a broad, cultivable plain.

The Strait of Messina (*Stretto di Messina*) is between 2 and 12 miles (3–19 km) wide, and is a rich fishing ground.

Sardinia is the second largest island in the Mediterranean Sea. The highest point is Punta La Marmora at 6,017 ft (1,834 m).

Sicily is the largest island in the Mediterranean at 9,926 sq miles (25,708 sq km).

The southwestern tip of Sicily lies 95 miles (152 km) from the north African mainland and is part of the same geological region.

Present-day crater has developed within the old crater of Monte Somma

Old crater

Vesuvius (*Vesuvio*)

Monte Somma

Old crater

There have been four volcanoes on the site of Vesuvius since volcanic activity began here more than 10,000 years ago.

USING THE LAND

ITALY PRODUCES 95% of its own food. The best farming land is in the Po Valley in northern Italy, where soft wheat and rice are grown. Irrigation is essential to agriculture in much of the south. Italy is a major producer and exporter of citrus fruits, olives, tomatoes, and wine.

THE URBAN/RURAL POPULATION DIVIDE

urban 67%

rural 33%

POPULATION DENSITY	TOTAL LAND AREA
492 people per sq mile	116,320 sq miles
(190 people per sq km)	(301,270 sq km)

Land use and agricultural distribution

- capital cities
- major towns
- cattle
- cereals
- citrus fruits
- olive oil
- rice
- vineyards
- pasture
- cropland
- forest
- mountain region

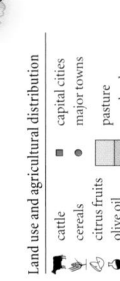

ITALY

ROME

SAN MARINO

AUSTRIA

SLOVENIA

CROATIA

SWITZERLAND

FRANCE

Milan

Turin

Genoa

Bologna

Florence

Naples

Bari

Palermo

Sicily

Catania

Sardinia

Cagliari

Sassari

Adriatic Sea

Tyrrhenian Sea

Ionian Sea

MEDITERRANEAN SEA

SCALE 1:2,500,000
(projection: Lambert Conformal Conic)

Km

Miles

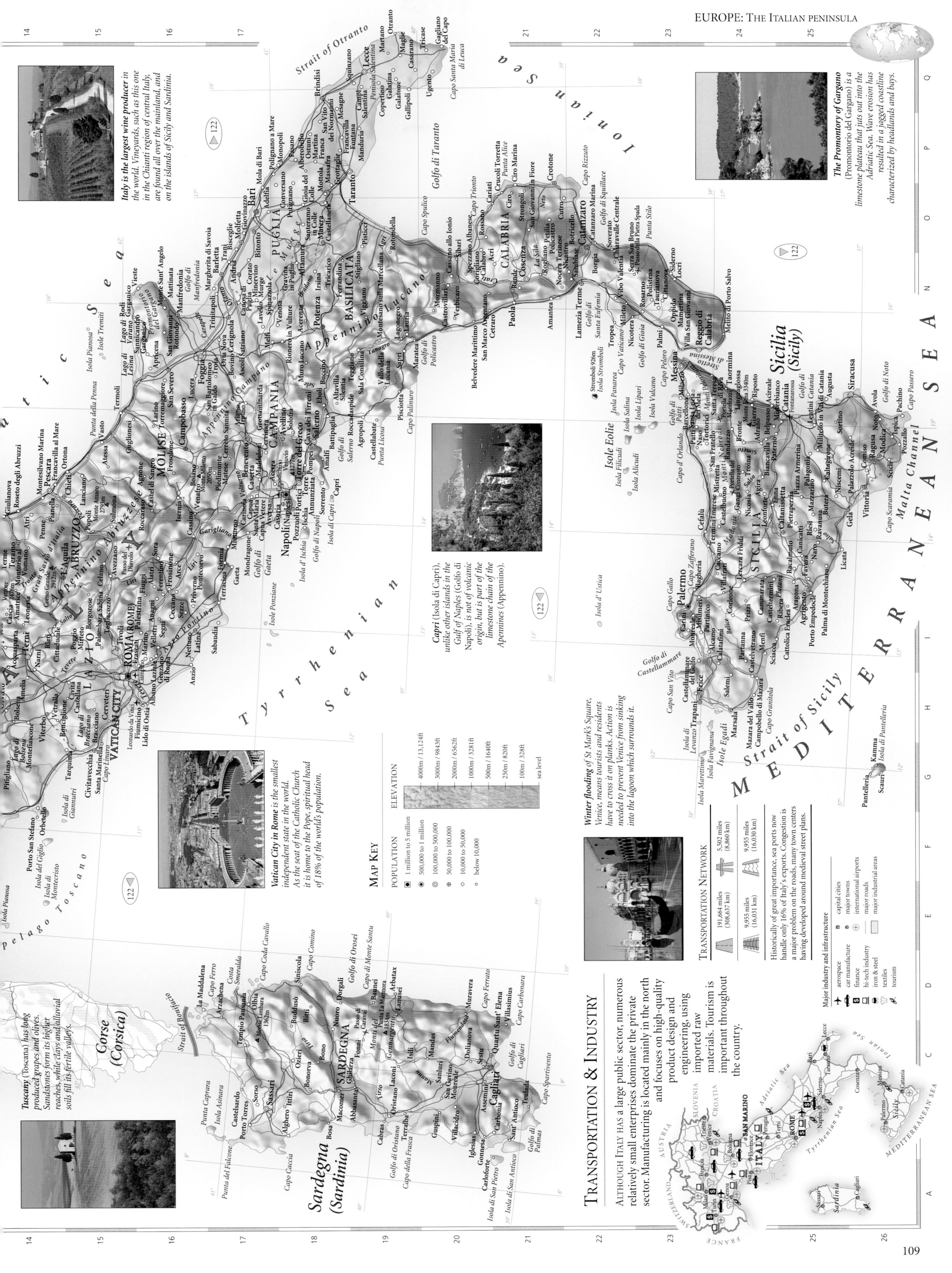

Italy is the largest wine producer in the world. Vineyards, such as this one, are found all over the mainland, and on the islands of Sicily and Sardinia. The Chianti region of central Italy,

The Promontory of Gargano (Promontorio del Gargano) is a limestone plateau that juts out into the Adriatic Sea. Wave erosion has resulted in a jagged coastline characterized by headlands and bays.

Capri (Isola di Capri), unlike other islands in the Gulf of Naples (Golfo di Napoli), is not of volcanic origin, but is part of the limestone chain of the Apennines (Appennino).

Winter flooding of St Mark's Square, Venice, means tourists and residents have to cross it on planks. Action is needed to prevent Venice from sinking into the lagoon which surrounds it.

Vatican City in Rome is the smallest independent state in the world. As the seat of the Catholic Church it is home to the Pope, spiritual head of 18% of the world's population.

Tuscany (Toscana) has long produced grapes and olives. Sandstones form its higher reaches, while clays and alluvial soils fill its fertile valleys.

MAP KEY

POPULATION

- 1 million to 5 million
- 500,000 to 1 million
- 100,000 to 500,000
- 50,000 to 100,000
- 10,000 to 50,000
- below 10,000

ELEVATION

4000m / 13,124ft	
3000m / 9843ft	
2000m / 6562ft	
1000m / 3281ft	
500m / 1640ft	
250m / 820ft	
100m / 328ft	
sea level	

TRANSPORTATION & INDUSTRY

ALTHOUGH ITALY HAS a large public sector, numerous relatively small enterprises dominate the private sector. Manufacturing is located mainly in the north and focuses on high-quality product design and engineering, using imported raw materials. Tourism is important throughout the country.

TRANSPORTATION NETWORK

191,664 miles (308,637 km)	capital cities	5,502 miles (8,860 km)	international airports
9,955 miles (16,031 km)	major roads	9,955 miles (16,030 km)	major industrial areas

Historically of great importance, sea ports now handle only 16% of Italy's exports. Congestion is a major problem on the roads; many town centers having developed around medieval street plans.

Major industry and infrastructure

- aerospace
- car manufacture
- finance
- hi-tech industry
- iron & steel
- textiles
- tourism
- capital cities
- major towns
- international airports
- major roads
- major industrial areas

THE ALPINE STATES

AUSTRIA, LIECHTENSTEIN, SLOVENIA, SWITZERLAND

THE ALPINE COUNTRIES of Austria, Switzerland, Liechtenstein, and Slovenia form a narrow strip across western Europe's geographical core, lying on the main north–south trading routes across the Alps. Switzerland, politically neutral since 1815, is an important international meeting place and houses one of the headquarters of the United Nations, although not itself a member. Austria, once at the heart of the great Habsburg Empire has been a fully independent nation since 1955, and maintains a deserved reputation as an international center of culture. Slovenia declared independence from the former Yugoslavia in 1991 and despite initial economic hardship, is now starting to achieve the prosperity enjoyed by its Alpine neighbors.

USING THE LAND

THE ALPINE REGION's mountainous terrain discourages cultivation over much of the land area. The primary agricultural activity is the raising of dairy and beef cattle on the pasture land of the lower mountain slopes. Austria is self-supporting in grains, and crops such as wheat, barley, and grapes are grown on the east Austrian lowlands. Woodlands are more prevalent in the eastern Alps; both Austria and Slovenia have large tracts of forest.

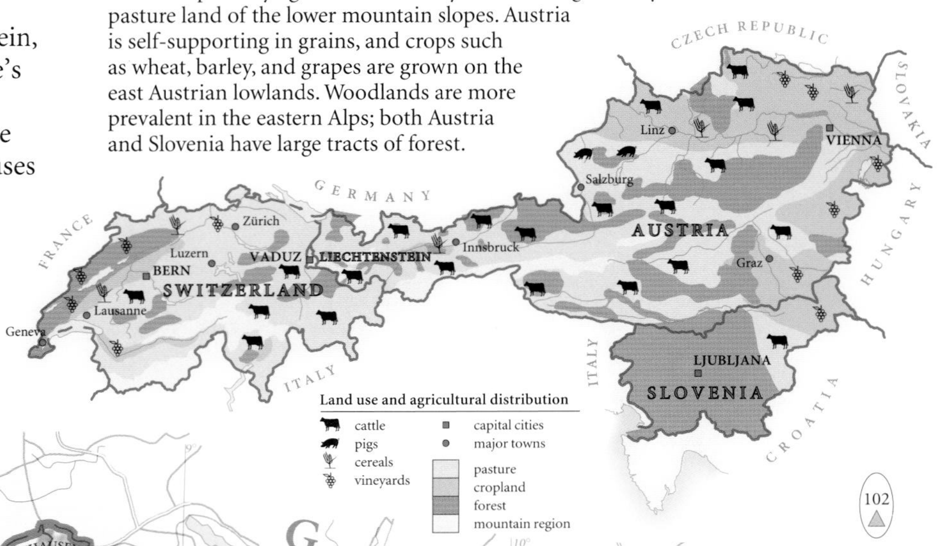

Land use and agricultural distribution

- cattle
- pigs
- cereals
- vineyards
- capital cities
- major towns
- pasture
- cropland
- forest
- mountain region

The Matterhorn, on the Swiss-Italian border, is one of the highest mountains in the Alps, at 14,692 ft (4,478 m). The term "horn" refers to its distinctive peak, formed by three glaciers eroding hollows, known as cirques, in each of its sides.

THE LANDSCAPE

THE ALPS OCCUPY THREE-FIFTHS OF SWITZERLAND, most of southern Austria and the northwest of Slovenia. They were formed by the collision of the African and Eurasian tectonic plates, which began 65 million years ago. Their complex geology is reflected in the differing heights and rock types of the various ranges. The Rhine flows along Liechtenstein's border with Switzerland, creating a broad floodplain in the north and west of Liechtenstein. In the far northeast and east are a number of lowland regions, including the Vienna Basin, Burgenland, and the plain of the Danube. Slovenia's major rivers flow across the lower eastern regions; in the west, the rivers flow underground through the limestone Karst region.

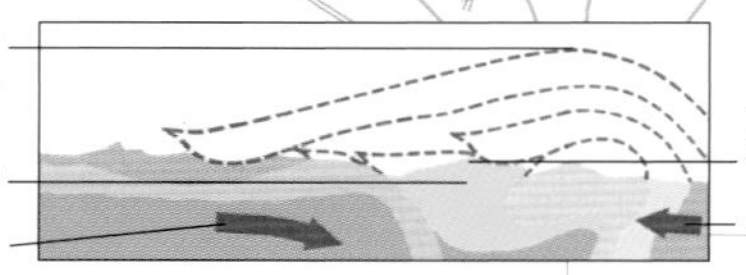

Original height after uplift and folding

Folded strata are overturned creating a *nappe*

Eurasian Plate

Present-day height of Alps

African Plate

The convergence of the African and Eurasian plates compressed and folded huge masses of rock strata. As the plates continued to move together, the folded strata were overturned, creating complex nappes. Much of the rock strata has since been eroded, resulting in the current topography of the Alps.

Constricted as it cuts through ridges in the Alps, the Danube meanders across the lowlands, where uplift combined with river erosion has deepened meanders.

The Vienna Basin lies mainly below 390 ft (120 m). It gradually subsided and filled with sediment as the Alps were uplifted.

Neusiedler See straddles the border of Austria and Hungary; the area around it provides some of the best wine-growing land in Austria.

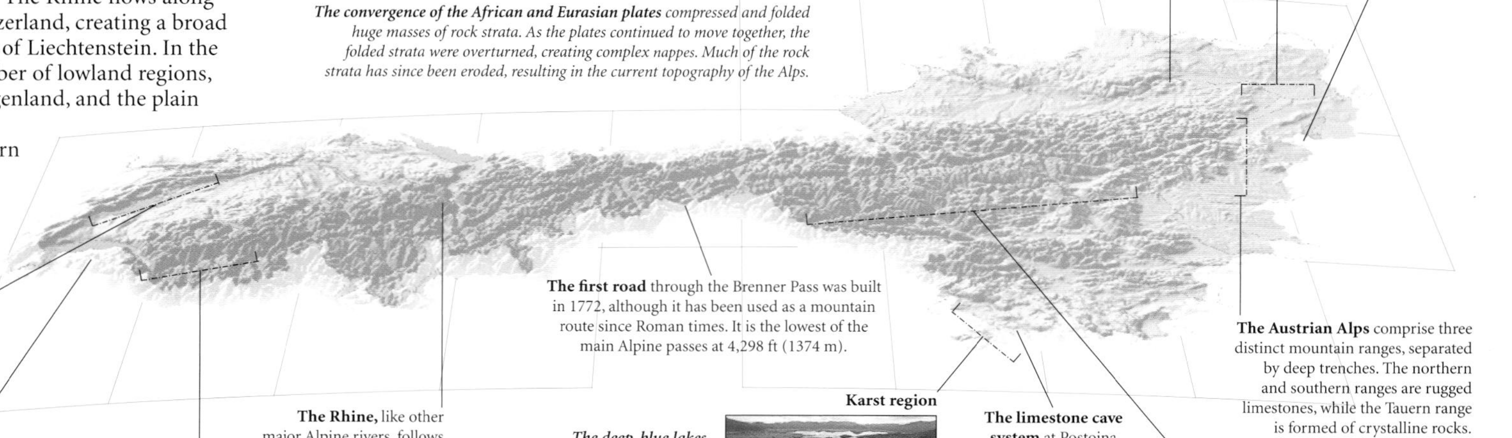

The mountains of the Jura form a natural border between Switzerland and France. Their marine limestones date from over 200 million years ago. When the Alps were formed the Jura were folded into a series of parallel ridges and troughs.

Tectonic activity has resulted in dramatic changes in land height over very short distances. Lake Geneva, lying at 1,221 ft (372 m) is only 43 miles (70 km) away from the 15,772 ft (4,807 m) peak of Mont Blanc, on the France–Italy border.

The Bernese Alps (*Berner Alpen*) contain the Aletsch, which at 15 miles (24 km) is the longest Alpine glacier.

The Rhine, like other major Alpine rivers, follows a broad, flat trough between the mountains. Along part of its course, the Rhine forms the boundary between Switzerland and Liechtenstein.

The deep, blue lakes of the Karst region are part of a drainage network which runs largely underground through this limestone area.

Karst region

The first road through the Brenner Pass was built in 1772, although it has been used as a mountain route since Roman times. It is the lowest of the main Alpine passes at 4,298 ft (1374 m).

The limestone cave system at Postojna extends for more than 10 miles (16 km) and includes caverns reaching 125 ft (40 m) in height and width.

The Austrian Alps comprise three distinct mountain ranges, separated by deep trenches. The northern and southern ranges are rugged limestones, while the Tauern range is formed of crystalline rocks.

The Tauern range in the central Austrian Alps contains the highest mountain in Austria, the towering Grossglockner, rising 12,461 ft (3,798 m).

THE URBAN/RURAL POPULATION DIVIDE

58% urban   42% rural

POPULATION DENSITY   TOTAL LAND AREA

310 people per sq mile   56,135 sq miles
(120 people per sq km)   (145,390 sq km)

In this mountainous region, the flatter, more accessible areas are often used for both cattle grazing and recreation.

These converging glaciers are marked by dark lines of moraine. This eroded material is carried by glaciers, and deposited as the ice melts.

SCALE 1:1,750,000
(projection: Lambert Conformal Conic)

MAP KEY

POPULATION

- ◉ 1 million to 5 million
- ◎ 500,000 to 1 million
- ⊚ 100,000 to 500,000
- ⊕ 50,000 to 100,000
- ○ 10,000 to 50,000
- ∘ below 10,000

ELEVATION

- 4000m / 13,124ft
- 3000m / 9843ft
- 2000m / 6562ft
- 1000m / 3281ft
- 500m / 1640ft
- 250m / 820ft
- 100m / 328ft
- sea level

The Austrian Tirol contains some of the most spectacular Alpine scenery. Snow cover is a permanent feature in the highest reaches.

TRANSPORTATION & INDUSTRY

ALL FOUR NATIONS concentrate on high-quality manufacturing and services. Austrian iron and steel production is complemented by construction industries; and Slovenia, traditionally the industrial powerhouse of the western Balkans has increasingly diversified industries. Liechtenstein and Switzerland, lacking raw materials, produce pharmaceuticals and precision instruments, such as watches, and act as international banking centers. The spectacular scenery of the region encourages tourism all year round.

TRANSPORTATION NETWORK

- 119,805 miles (192,923 km)
- 2044 miles (3292 km)
- 6227 miles (10,028 km)
- 984 miles (1584 km)

Tunnels and passes through the Alps are an important feature of this region. The NEAT project, providing two new high-speed rail links between Basel and Milan, was given approval in 1992.

Major industry and infrastructure

- car manufacture
- chemicals
- engineering
- finance
- food processing
- iron & steel
- pharmaceuticals
- textiles
- tourism
- watch making
- winter sports
- ■ capital cities
- • major towns
- ✈ international airports
- major roads
- major industrial areas

The Schönbrunn Palace in Vienna was the summer residence of the Habsburg monarchy. Today, it is a major tourist attraction.

CENTRAL EUROPE

CZECH REPUBLIC, HUNGARY, POLAND, SLOVAKIA

WHEN SLOVAKIA AND THE CZECH REPUBLIC became separate countries in 1993, they joined Hungary and Poland in a new role as independent nation states, following centuries of shifting boundaries and imperial strife. This turbulent history bequeathed the region a rich cultural heritage, shared through the works of its many great writers and composers, and celebrated in the vibrant historic capitals of Prague, Budapest, and Warsaw. Having shaken off years of Soviet domination in 1989, these states are confronting the challenge of winning commercial investment to modernize outmoded industries as they integrate their economies with those of the European Union.

TRANSPORTATION & INDUSTRY

HEAVY INDUSTRY HAS DOMINATED POSTWAR LIFE in Central Europe. Poland has large coal reserves, having inherited the Silesian coalfield from Germany after the Second World War, allowing the export of large quantities of coal, along with other minerals. Hungary specializes in consumer goods and services, while Slovakia's industrial base is still relatively small. The Czech Republic's traditional glassworks and breweries bring some stability to its precarious Soviet-built manufacturing sector.

Major industry and infrastructure

- car manufacture
- chemicals
- engineering
- food processing
- mining
- shipbuilding
- tourism

- capital cities
- major towns
- ⊕ international airports
- major roads
- major industrial areas

TRANSPORTATION NETWORK

213,997 miles (344,600 km)	817 miles (1,315 km)
27,479 miles (44,249 km)	3,784 miles (6,094 km)

The huge growth of tourism and business has prompted major investment in the transportation infrastructure, with new roadbuilding schemes within and between the main cities of the region.

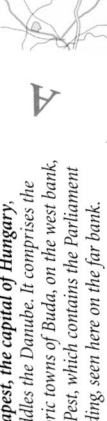

Budapest, the capital of Hungary, straddles the Danube. It comprises the historic towns of Buda, on the west bank, and Pest, which contains the Parliament Building, seen here on the far bank.

THE LANDSCAPE

THE FORESTED Carpathian Mountains, uplifted with the Alps, lie southeast of the older Bohemian massif, which contains the Sudeten and Krušné Hory (*Erzgebirge*) ranges. They divide the fertile plains of the Danube to the south and the Vistula (*Wisła*), which flows north across vast expanses of glacial deposits into the Baltic Sea.

The Biebrza River has left meanders and oxbow lakes as it flows across low-lying ground.

Gerlachovský štít, in the Tatra Mountains, is Slovakia's highest mountain, at 8,711ft (2,655 m).

Carpathian Mountains

Danube River

Slip-off slope

Meanders form as rivers flow across plains at a low gradient. A steep cliff or bluff, forms on the outside curve, and a gentler slip-off slope on the inside bend.

Bluff

Direction of flow

▲ 120

Longshore currents moving east along the Baltic coast have built a 40 mile (65 km) spit composed of material from the Vistula (*Wisła*) River.

Pomerania is a sandy coastal region of glacially-formed lakes stretching west from the Vistula (*Wisła*).

Hot mineral springs occur where geothermally heated water wells up through faults and fractures in the rocks of the Sudeten Mountains.

The Great Hungarian Plain formed by the floodplain of the Danube is a mixture of steppe and cultivated land, covering nearly half of Hungary's total area.

The Slovak Ore Mountains (*Slovenské Rudohorie*) are noted for their mineral resources, including high-grade iron ore.

Bohemian Massif

Krušné Hory (Erzgebirge)

The Berounka River cuts through the precipitous wooded landscape of the Bohemian massif, banked by a broad floodplain.

MAP KEY

POPULATION
- 1 million to 5 million
- 500,000 to 1 million
- 100,000 to 500,000
- 50,000 to 100,000
- 10,000 to 50,000
- below 10,000

ELEVATION
- 2000m / 6562ft
- 1000m / 3281ft
- 500m / 1640ft
- 250m / 820ft
- 100m / 328ft
- sea level

SCALE 1:2,500,000
(projection: Lambert Conformal Conic)

The upper Dunajec River of Poland and eastern Slovakia forms a gorge through the Pieniny range of the Carpathian Mountains.

USING THE LAND

Cereals, sugar beet, and potatoes are Central Europe's main crops, along with hops for the Czech breweries, sweet peppers for paprika, sunflowers and vines in milder areas. The plains of Poland and Hungary are well-suited to livestock-rearing, while forestry is important in the mountains of Slovakia.

Land use and agricultural distribution
- cattle
- pigs
- cereals
- potatoes
- root crops
- timber
- vineyards

- capital cities
- major towns
- pasture
- cropland
- forest

Hay, used to feed livestock, is one of the major crops grown on the fertile foothills of Slovakia's Tatra Mountains.

THE URBAN/RURAL POPULATION DIVIDE

urban 65%   rural 35%

POPULATION DENSITY
312 people per sq mile
(120 people per sq km)

TOTAL LAND AREA
201,561 sq miles
(522,180 sq km)

113

SOUTHEAST EUROPE

ALBANIA, BOSNIA & HERZEGOVINA, CROATIA, MACEDONIA, SERBIA & MONTENEGRO (YUGOSLAVIA)

FOR 46 YEARS THE FEDERATION of Yugoslavia held together the most diverse ethnic region in Europe, along the picturesque mountain hinterland of the Dalmatian coast. Economic collapse resulted in internal tensions. In the early 1990s, civil war broke out in both Croatia and Bosnia as the ethnic populations struggled to establish their own exclusive territories. Peace was only restored by the UN after NATO launched air strikes in 1995. In the province of Kosovo, attempts to gain autonomy from Yugoslavia in 1998 were crushed by the Serbian government. The slaughter of ethnic Albanians in Kosovo provoked the West to launch NATO air strikes yet again in the region, and Yugoslav forces withdrew. The flood of refugees from Kosovo has severely strained Albania.

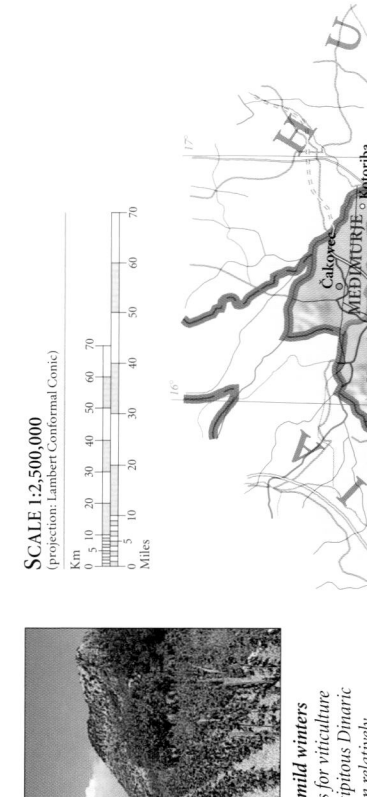

Hot, dry summers and mild winters offer excellent conditions for viticulture in Montenegro. The precipitous Dinaric Alps have kept this region relatively isolated for centuries.

THE LANDSCAPE

THE TISZA, SAVA, AND DRAVA RIVERS drain the broad northern lowland, meeting the Danube after it crosses the Hungarian border. In the west, the Dinaric Alps divide the Adriatic Sea from the interior. Mainland valleys and elongated islands run parallel to the steep Dalmatian (*Dalmacija*) coastline, following alternating bands of resistant limestone.

Pol-jes in the Kosovo region

Sheer limestone walls enclose all sides

Flat polje floor

Rain and underground water dissolve limestone along massive vertical joints (cracks). This creates pol-jes: depressions several miles across with steep walls and broad, flat floors.

Underground drainage along joints in the rock

Spring at foot of cliff

At Iron Gate (*Ðerdap*), on the border with Romania, the Danube narrows and cuts through foothills of the Balkan and Carpathian mountains, forming the deepest gorge in Europe.

The river floodplains of the Pannonian Basin are flanked by terraces of gravel and wind-blown glacial deposits known as loess.

Tisza River

A major earthquake at Skopje, Macedonia, in 1963 killed 1,000 people. The whole region lies on an active crustal plate margin.

Lake Ohrid

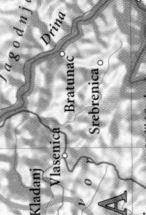
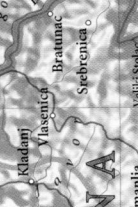
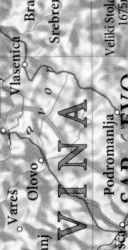

Lake Ohrid borders Albania and Macedonia. Ohrid is the deepest lake in the Western Balkans, reaching depths of 938 ft (286 m).

At least 70% of the fresh water in the Western Balkans drains eastward into the Black Sea, mostly via the Danube (*Dunav*).

Drava River

A series of river valleys breaking through the Dinaric Alps from the lowlands of western Albania, give access to the interior.

Dalmatian (*Dalmacija*) coast

The elongated islands, promontories and straits of the Dalmatian (*Dalmacija*) coast were formed as the Adriatic Sea rose to flood valleys running parallel to the shore.

Limestone cliffs along the Dalmatian (Dalmacija) shoreline are heavily eroded, as salt water dissolves the rock along existing horizontal cracks, or joints. This tends to form a platform of rock at the foot of the cliff.

Sava River

SCALE 1:2,500,000
(projection: Lambert Conformal Conic)

Km
0 5 10 20 30 40 50 60 70

Miles
0 10 20 30 40 50

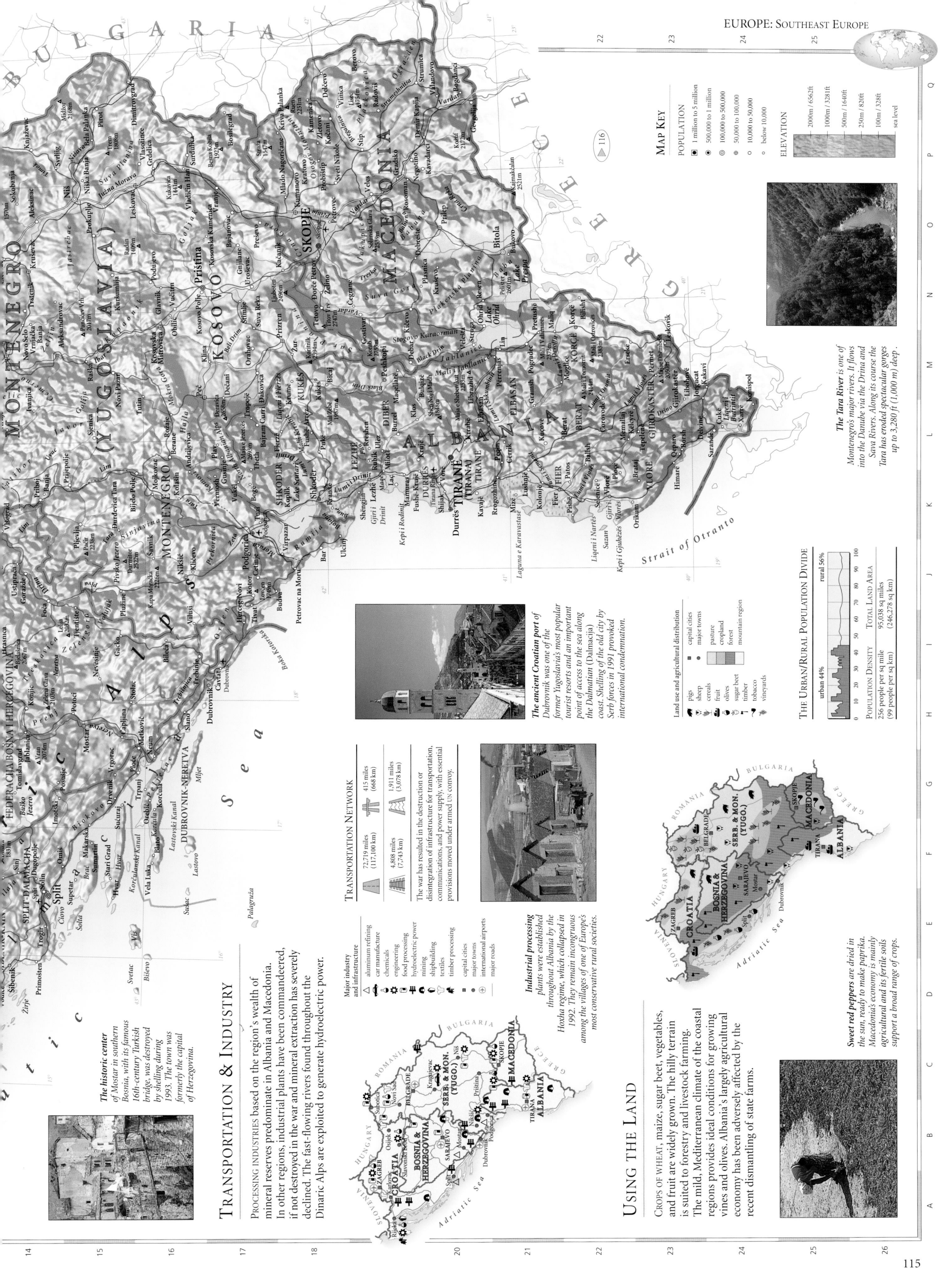

MAP KEY

POPULATION

- ■ 1 million to 5 million
- ◉ 500,000 to 1 million
- ◎ 100,000 to 500,000
- ⊕ 50,000 to 100,000
- ○ 10,000 to 50,000
- ○ below 10,000

ELEVATION

	2000m / 6562ft
	1000m / 3281ft
	500m / 1640ft
	250m / 820ft
	100m / 328ft
	sea level

The Tara River is one of Montenegro's major rivers. It flows into the Danube via the Drina and Sava Rivers. Along its course the Tara has eroded spectacular gorges up to 3,280 ft (1,000 m) deep.

The ancient Croatian port of Dubrovnik was one of the former Yugoslavia's most popular tourist resorts and an important point of access to the sea along the Dalmatian (Dalmacija) coast. Shelling of the old city by Serb forces in 1991 provoked international condemnation.

Land use and agricultural distribution

- pigs
- sheep
- cereals
- fruit
- olives
- sugar beet
- timber
- tobacco
- vineyards

- ● capital cities
- major towns
- pasture
- cropland
- forest
- mountain region

THE URBAN/RURAL POPULATION DIVIDE

urban 44%	rural 56%

POPULATION DENSITY	TOTAL LAND AREA
256 people per sq mile	95,038 sq miles
(99 people per sq km)	(246,278 sq km)

TRANSPORTATION NETWORK

⚞	72,219 miles (117,100 km)	415 miles (668 km)
⚟	4,808 miles (7,743 km)	1,911 miles (3,078 km)

The war has resulted in the destruction or disintegration of infrastructure for transportation, communications, and power supply, with essential provisions moved under armed UN convoy.

Industrial processing plants were established throughout Albania by the Hoxha regime, which collapsed in 1992. They remain incongruous among the villages of one of Europe's most conservative rural societies.

TRANSPORTATION & INDUSTRY

PROCESSING INDUSTRIES based on the region's wealth of mineral reserves predominate in Albania and Macedonia. In other regions, industrial plants have been commandeered, if not destroyed in the war and mineral extraction has severely declined. The fast-flowing rivers found throughout the Dinaric Alps are exploited to generate hydroelectric power.

Major industry and infrastructure

- aluminum refining
- car manufacture
- chemicals
- engineering
- food processing
- hydroelectric power
- mining
- shipbuilding
- textiles
- timber processing
- ■ capital cities
- ● major towns
- ⊕ international airports
- major roads

The historic center of Mostar in southern Bosnia, with its famous 16th-century Turkish bridge, was destroyed by shelling during 1993. The town was formerly the capital of Herzegovina.

USING THE LAND

CROPS OF WHEAT, maize, sugar beet, vegetables, and fruit are widely grown. The hilly terrain is suited to forestry and livestock farming. The mild, Mediterranean climate of the coastal regions provides ideal conditions for growing vines and olives. Albania's largely agricultural economy has been adversely affected by the recent dismantling of state farms.

Sweet red peppers are dried in the sun, ready to make paprika. Macedonia's economy is mainly agricultural and its fertile soils support a broad range of crops.

115

BULGARIA & GREECE

Including EUROPEAN TURKEY

G REECE IS RENOWNED as the original hearth of Western civilization. The rugged terrain and numerous islands have profoundly affected its development, creating a strong agricultural and maritime tradition. In the past 50 years, this formerly rural society has rapidly urbanized, with more than half the population now living in the capital, Athens, and in the northern city of Salonica. Bulgaria, dominated for centuries by the Ottoman Turks, became part of the eastern bloc after the Second World War, only slowly emerging from Soviet influence in 1989. Moves toward democracy led to some instability in Bulgaria and Greece, now outweighed by the challenge of integration with the European Union.

TRANSPORTATION & INDUSTRY

SOVIET INVESTMENT introduced heavy industry into Bulgaria, and the processing of agricultural produce, such as tobacco, is important throughout the country. Both countries have substantial shipyards and Greece has one of the world's largest merchant fleets. Many small craft workshops, producing textiles and processed foods, are clustered around Greek cities. The service and construction sectors have profited from the successful tourist industry.

Major industry and infrastructure

- chemicals
- engineering
- food processing
- shipbuilding
- textiles
- tourism
- capital cities
- major towns
- international airports
- major roads
- major industrial areas

TRANSPORTATION NETWORK

103,930 miles (167,630 km)

345 miles (557 km)

4,346 miles (6,995 km)

294 miles (474 km)

Bulgaria's railroads require investment to revive an outdated infrastructure. In Greece, despite a developing road network, ferry-boats remain the most effective form of transportation in many areas.

THE LANDSCAPE

BULGARIA'S BALKAN MOUNTAINS divide the Danubian Plain (*Dunavska Ravnina*) and Maritsa Basin, meeting the Black Sea in the east along sandy beaches. The steep Rhodope Mountains form a natural barrier with Greece, while the younger Pindus form a rugged central spine which descends into the Aegean Sea to give a vast archipelago of over 2000 islands, the largest of which is Crete.

Mount Olympus is the mythical home of the Greek Gods and, at 9,570 ft (2,917 m), is the highest mountain in Greece.

Mount Olympus is a composite of rocks formed by two major tectonic events. First the older metamorphic rocks were thrust over the limestones, then two million years ago regional warping and subsequent erosion, reexposed the limestone.

Mount Olympus

Younger limestones created in shallow seas

Limestone rocks exposed by erosion of metamorphic rocks

Ancient metamorphic rock, formed miles below the surface

The Peloponnese consist of several mountainous peninsulas, linked to the mainland by the Isthmus of Corinth. The Corinth Canal (*Dioryga Korinthou*), built in 1893, cuts through the isthmus, linking the Aegean and Ionian Seas.

The Arda river cuts through the Rhodope mountains in rugged, rocky gorges.

The Danube, Europe's second longest river, forms most of Bulgaria's northern border. The Danubian Plain (*Dunavska Ravnina*), extending from the southern bank, is extremely fertile.

The islands of Crete, Kythira, Karpathos, and Rhodes are part of an arc which bends southeastward from the Peloponnese, forming the southern boundary of the Aegean.

Layers of black volcanic ash still cover the island of Thira. This volcano last erupted 3,500 years ago, but still shows signs of volcanic activity.

Balkan Mountains

Maritsa Basin

Rhodope Mountains

Pindus Mountains

Corinth Canal (*Dioryga Korinthou*)

Kythira

Crete

Karpathos

Rhodes

SCALE 1:2,500,000 (projection: Lambert Conformal Conic)

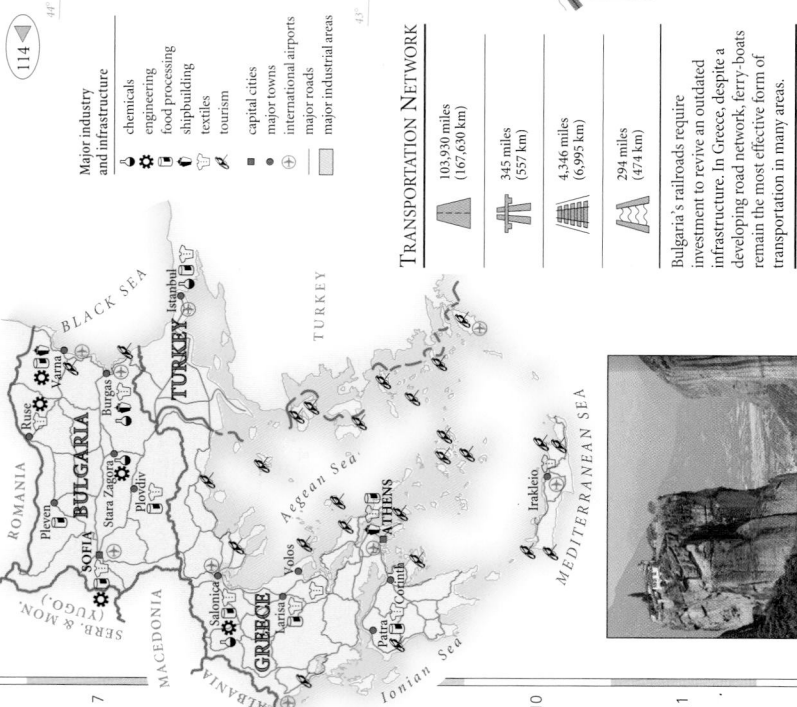

A towering pinnacle at Metéora in central Greece is home to the monastery of Roussanou. The 24 rock towers which dominate the plain of Thessaliá (Thessalia) are remnants of an old plateau. Long-term weathering along fissures in the rock has worn away the rest of the plateau.

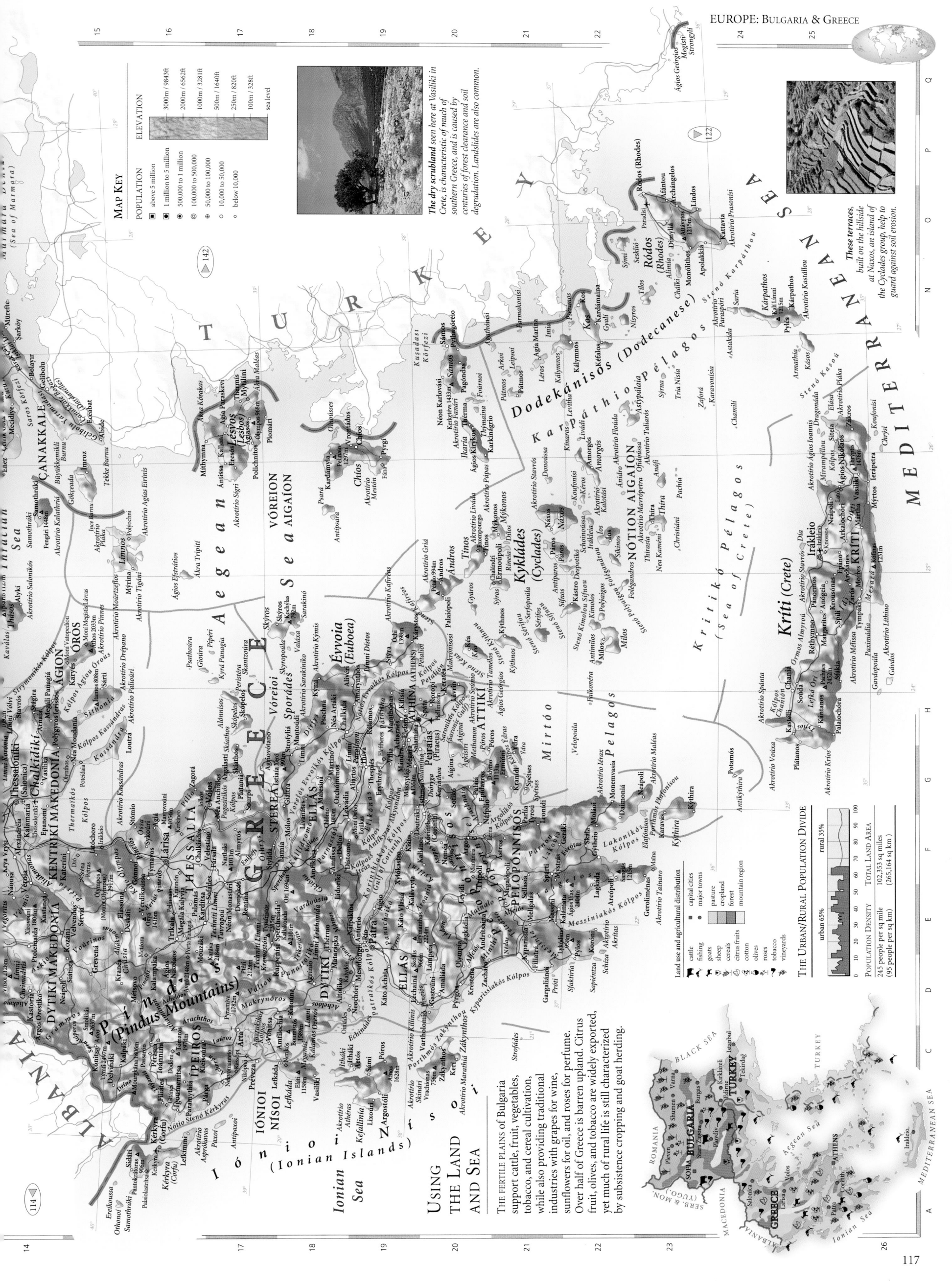

MAP KEY

POPULATION

- ■ above 5 million
- ▣ 1 million to 5 million
- ◉ 500,000 to 1 million
- ◎ 100,000 to 500,000
- ⊕ 50,000 to 100,000
- ○ 10,000 to 50,000
- ° below 10,000

ELEVATION

	3000m / 9843ft
	2000m / 6562ft
	1000m / 3281ft
	500m / 1640ft
	250m / 820ft
	100m / 328ft
	sea level

The dry scrubland seen here at Vasiliki in Crete, is characteristic of much of southern Greece, and is caused by centuries of forest clearance and soil degradation. Landslides are also common.

These terraces, built on the hillside at Naxos, an island of the Cyclades group, help to guard against soil erosion.

Using The Land and Sea

THE FERTILE PLAINS of Bulgaria support cattle, fruit, vegetables, tobacco, and cereal cultivation, while also providing traditional industries with grapes for wine, and sunflowers for oil, and roses for perfume. Citrus fruit, olives, and tobacco are widely exported, yet much of rural life is still characterized by subsistence cropping and goat herding.

THE URBAN/RURAL POPULATION DIVIDE

urban 65% rural 35%

0	10	20	30	40	50	60	70	80	90	100

POPULATION DENSITY	TOTAL LAND AREA
245 people per sq mile	102,353 sq miles
(95 people per sq km)	(265,164 sq km)

Land use and agricultural distribution

- cattle
- fishing
- goats
- sheep
- cereals
- cotton
- citrus fruits
- olives
- roses
- tobacco
- vineyards

- capital cities
- major towns
- pasture
- cropland
- forest
- mountain region

ROMANIA, MOLDOVA & UKRAINE

THE INDUSTRIAL, SOCIAL, AND CULTURAL make-up of Romania and the former Soviet states of Moldova and Ukraine still bear the imprint of their communist past. As part of the USSR, Ukraine was a leading agricultural, industrial, and energy producer. These industries, like those in Moldova and Romania, are now being reoriented more firmly toward Western markets. As a result of shifting borders, and Soviet policy actively encouraging Russian immigration into other Soviet states like Ukraine and Moldova, all three countries now contain large numbers of foreign nationals. Moldovans and Romanians are still close in terms of language and culture, although Moldova is striving to remain an independent nation.

USING THE LAND

THE FERTILE BLACK SOILS of Ukraine, often called "the breadbasket of Europe," have enabled the cultivation of a variety of cereals and vegetables, which are widely exported. Romania and Moldova also grow cereals, sunflowers, and vegetables, and are noted for the quality of their wines.

The fertile lands and tolerant climate of Moldova are ideally suited to growing grapes for wine.

Land use and agricultural distribution
- cattle
- pigs
- poultry
- sheep
- cereals
- cotton
- sugar beet
- sunflowers
- vineyards
- capital cities
- major towns

- pasture
- cropland
- forest
- wetland

THE URBAN/RURAL POPULATION DIVIDE

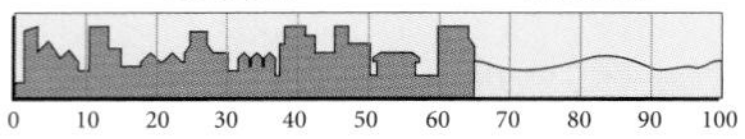

urban 65%   rural 35%

0 10 20 30 40 50 60 70 80 90 100

POPULATION DENSITY
232 people per sq mile
(89 people per sq km)

TOTAL LAND AREA
334,947 sq miles
(867,740 sq km)

Glacial lakes are found throughout the Transylvanian Alps (Carpaţii Meridionali), although the mountains no longer have any permanent snow cover.

TRANSPORTATION & INDUSTRY

HEAVY INDUSTRY using local raw materials characterizes much of this region. The industrial heartland of Ukraine, specializing in metal and machine-building industries, is based around its vast mineral reserves in the Donbass region. In Moldova, food processing draws on produce from its agricultural sector. Romanian industry relies both on local raw materials and imported iron, steel, and oil.

Major industry and infrastructure
- car manufacture
- chemicals
- coal
- engineering
- food processing
- mining
- oil & gas
- textiles
- tourism
- capital cities
- major towns
- international airports
- major roads
- major industrial areas

TRANSPORTATION NETWORK

151,089 miles (243,300 km)		70 miles (113 km)	
21,889 miles (35,248 km)		3803 miles (6124 km)	

Increased industrialization has necessitated the upgrading of road and rail networks in all three countries. Modernization has tended to focus only on major cities and industrial areas.

During the 1960s and 1970s, many industries, like this carbon factory, developed using the mineral resources on the flanks of the Transylvanian Alps (Carpaţii Meridionali).

SCALE 1:3,250,000
(projection: Lambert Conformal Conic)

MAP KEY

POPULATION
- 1 million to 5 million
- 500,000 to 1 million
- 100,000 to 500,000
- 50,000 to 100,000
- 10,000 to 50,000
- below 10,000

ELEVATION
- 2000m / 6562ft
- 1000m / 3281ft
- 500m / 1640ft
- 250m / 820ft
- 100m / 328ft
- sea level

The Swallow's Nest castle at Yalta is one of many tourist resorts on the Crimean (Krym) coast, dubbed the "Russian Riviera."

THE LANDSCAPE

VAST FLAT LOWLANDS and gently rolling hills cover most of southeastern Europe. In the southwest, the Carpathian Mountains form a gentle arc. To the south of the Carpathian Mountains lies the Danube Plain, across which the Danube River flows to the Black Sea. To the north and east, the hills of Moldova level out into low plains, running east to the steppes of Ukraine.

Divided into crystalline massifs, the southern arm of the Carpathian Mountains, the Transylvanian Alps (Carpații Meridionali), extend 170 miles (274 km) across southwestern Romania.

The Codrii Hills dominate the landscape of central Moldova; they are intersected by deep, flat valleys and ravines.

Steppe landscape covers two-thirds of Ukraine. These flat, treeless grasslands extend from central Europe to central Asia.

Most of the major rivers in southeastern Europe, like the Danube, the Dniester and Dnieper flow south and east to the Black Sea.

Uplifted and folded at the same time as the Alps, some 250 miles (400 km) of the eastern Carpathian Mountains contain ancient volcanic cones and craters.

The Apuseni Mountains (Munții Apuseni) are rich in mineral deposits, including gold and iron ore.

Transylvanian Alps (Carpații Meridionali)

The Danube forms a natural border between Romania and Bulgaria.

The three branches of the Danube Delta (Delta Dunării) form a triangle of wetlands covering some 1,950 sq miles (5,050 sq km).

At Kryms'ki Hory, three flat-topped, parallel limestone ridges run 80 miles (128 km) along the southern coast of the Crimean (Krym) Peninsula.

Water has eroded a new post-glacial valley

Old glaciated valley

Balkas are common throughout Ukraine. They are large U-shaped valleys, formed during the last Ice Age, which contain narrower, deep valleys. These were incised by a sudden flow of water, following an ice melt.

Counterclockwise currents have created the sandspits which fringe the Sea of Azov.

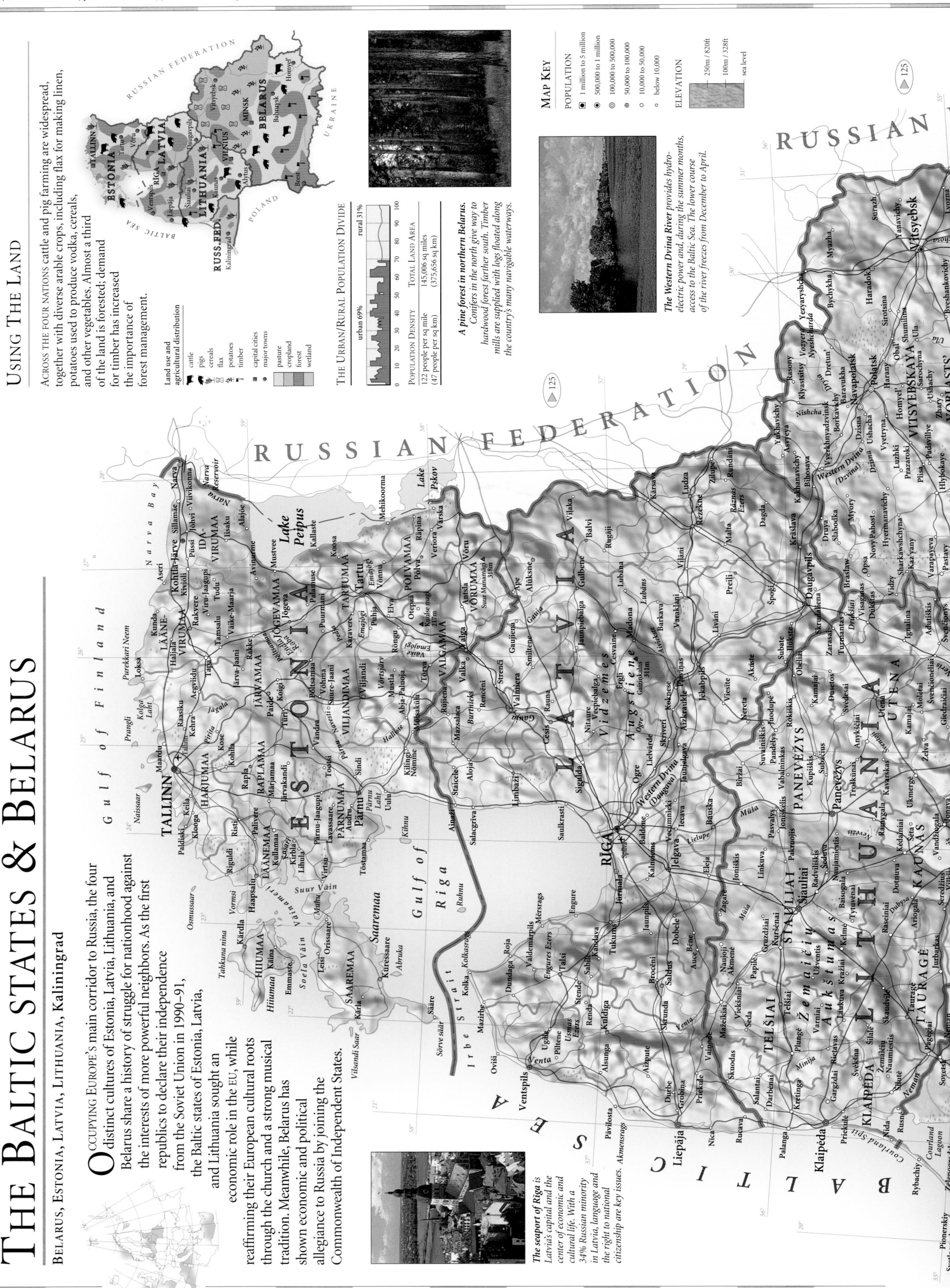

The Baltic States & Belarus

BELARUS, ESTONIA, LATVIA, LITHUANIA, Kaliningrad

Occupying Europe's main corridor to Russia, the four distinct cultures of Estonia, Latvia, Lithuania, and Belarus share a history of struggle for nationhood against the interests of more powerful neighbors. As the first republics to declare their independence from the Soviet Union in 1990–91, the Baltic states of Estonia, Latvia, and Lithuania sought an economic role in the EU, while reaffirming their European cultural roots through the church and a strong musical tradition. Meanwhile, Belarus has shown economic and political allegiance to Russia by joining the Commonwealth of Independent States.

The seaport of Riga is Latvia's capital and the center of economic and cultural life. With a 34% Russian minority in Latvia, language and the right to national citizenship are key issues.

USING THE LAND

ACROSS THE FOUR NATIONS cattle and pig farming are widespread, together with diverse arable crops, including flax for making linen, potatoes used to produce vodka, cereals, and other vegetables. Almost a third of the land is forested; demand for timber has increased the importance of forest management.

Land use and agricultural distribution

- cattle
- pigs
- cereals
- flax
- potatoes
- timber
- capital cities
- major towns

- pasture
- cropland
- forest
- wetland

A pine forest in northern Belarus. Conifers in the north give way to hardwood forest farther south. Timber mills are supplied with logs floated along the country's many navigable waterways.

The Western Dvina River provides hydro-electric power and, during the summer months, access to the Baltic Sea. The lower course of the river freezes from December to April.

THE URBAN/RURAL POPULATION DIVIDE

urban 69%   rural 31%

POPULATION DENSITY	TOTAL LAND AREA
122 people per sq mile (47 people per sq km)	145,006 sq miles (375,656 sq km)

MAP KEY

POPULATION
- 1 million to 5 million
- 500,000 to 1 million
- 100,000 to 500,000
- 50,000 to 100,000
- 10,000 to 50,000
- below 10,000

ELEVATION
- 250m / 820ft
- 100m / 328ft
- sea level

Rich oil shale deposits in northern Estonia are quarried, crushed, and heated to produce almost 32,000 barrels of oil a day.

Major industry and infrastructure

- capital cities
- major towns
- ⊕ international airports
- major roads
- major industrial areas

amber mining
car manufacture
chemicals
electrical goods
oil shale
food processing
light engineering
paper industry

RUSSIAN FEDERATION

ESTONIA
TALLINN
Tartu
Võru

LATVIA
RIGA
Daugavpils
Ventspils
Liepāja

LITHUANIA
VILNIUS
Šiauliai
Kaunas

BELARUS
MINSK
Vitsyebsk
Babruysk
Homyel'
Brest

RUSS.FED.
Kaliningrad

POLAND

UKRAINE

BALTIC SEA

TRANSPORTATION & INDUSTRY

RECENT ECONOMIC RESTRUCTURING has meant modernizing old Soviet industries such as vehicle production and the paper industry, and expanding the light engineering and electronics sectors. There has also been a revival of traditional crafts like carpentry and amber work. Although Estonia has oil shale reserves, the Baltic economies still rely heavily on Russian raw materials and energy.

TRANSPORTATION NETWORK

242,810 miles (391,630 km)	40 miles (64 km)
6830 miles (11,016 km)	376 miles (606 km)

Railroads are being superseded by roads linking the ports with eastern Europe and Russia. A highway connecting the three Baltic capitals with Warsaw has been proposed.

Nuclear fallout from the 1986 Chernobyl (*Chornobyl'*) disaster in Ukraine has contaminated large areas of agricultural land in Belarus.

The Dnieper River is the third longest in Europe and forms the heart of Belarus's drainage system.

Pripet Marshes

A network of streams and creeks drains across the marshes

Peat deposits

Glacial deposits

Broad tectonic basin

This large area of marshland lies in a broad tectonic depression, mantled by glacial deposits. Peat deposits have developed below the marshes, which are prone to spring flooding.

The Pripet Marshes form the largest area of "unreclaimed" marshland in Europe. They also provide a network of navigable waterways across southern Belarus.

Byelavyezhskaya Pushcha

Courland Spit

Courland Spit is one of the largest of its kind on the Baltic coast, created by longshore currents moving eastward.

THE LANDSCAPE

ROCK-STREWN GLACIAL PLAINS meet the Baltic Sea along a coast of cliffs and sandy beaches. Hundreds of islands ranging from tiny, rocky outcrops to the large island of Saaremaa, lie scattered off the Estonian mainland, creating an archipelago. Lakes and marshes in low-lying areas give way to mixed woodland on fertile, undulating ground, with remnants of the primeval forest which once covered most of Europe preserved at Byelavyezhskaya Pushcha in western Belarus.

SCALE 1:2,500,000
(projection: Lambert Conformal Conic)

Saaremaa is the largest island in the Estonian archipelago. The southeastern parts are flat and fertile, giving way to numerous low hills and ridges toward the northwest.

Saaremaa Island

There are many shallow depressions across Estonia. These formed as the ice sheet retreated and water from the melting ice was concentrated into lake basins, which eventually found outlets in the Baltic Sea.

A small delta has formed where the Neman River flows into the protected waters of Courland Lagoon, behind Courland Spit.

Suur Munamägi in southern Estonia is, at 1,088 ft (318 m), the highest point in the low-lying Baltic states.

The Vidzeme Uplands (*Vidzemes Augstiene*) is a region of mixed forest and pasture.

121

THE MEDITERRANEAN

THE MEDITERRANEAN SEA stretches over 2,500 miles (4,000 km) east to west, separating Europe from Africa. At its westernmost point it is connected to the Atlantic Ocean through the Strait of Gibraltar. In the east, the Suez Canal, opened in 1869, gives passage to the Indian Ocean. In the northeast, linked by the Sea of Marmara, lies the Black Sea. The Mediterranean is bordered by 28 states and territories, and more than 100 million people live on its shores and islands. Throughout history, the Mediterranean has been a focal area for many great empires and civilizations, reflected in the variety of cultures found on its shores. Since the 1960s, development along the southern coast of Europe has expanded rapidly to accommodate increasing numbers of tourists and to enable the exploitation of oil and gas reserves. This has resulted in rising levels of pollution, threatening the future of the sea.

USING THE LAND AND SEA

A QUARTER OF THE FISH SPECIES found in the Mediterranean are economically important. Sardines are the main catch in northern and western regions and aquaculture, including oyster farming, is becoming increasingly important in the eastern Mediterranean. Olives, citrus fruit, cork trees, and vines thrive in the Mediterranean climate, enjoying hot, dry summers and mild, wet winters. Italy and Spain are world leaders in commercial olive production.

The growing of citrus fruit such as lemons, limes, oranges, and grapefruit is common along the coasts surrounding the Mediterranean.

Land use and agricultural distribution

- goats
- sheep
- cereals
- citrus fruits
- cork
- fishing
- olives
- sunflowers
- tobacco
- vineyards
- major towns
- pasture
- cropland
- forest
- mountain region
- wetland
- desert

THE LANDSCAPE

THE MEDITERRANEAN SEA IS ALMOST TOTALLY LANDLOCKED, joined to the Atlantic Ocean through the Strait of Gibraltar, which is only 8 miles (13 km) wide. Lying on an active plate margin, sea floor movements have formed a variety of basins, troughs, and ridges. A submarine ridge running from Tunisia to the island of Sicily divides the Mediterranean into two distinct basins. The western basin is characterized by broad, smooth abyssal (or ocean) plains. In contrast, the eastern basin is dominated by a large ridge system, running east to west.

The narrow Strait of Gibraltar inhibits water exchange between the Mediterranean Sea and the Atlantic Ocean, producing a high degree of salinity and a low tidal range within the Mediterranean. The lack of tides has encouraged the build-up of pollutants in many semienclosed bays.

Main surface current
Denser, more saline currents flow back to Atlantic
Dense currents sink below surface

Because the Mediterranean is almost enclosed by land, its circulation is quite different to the oceans. There is one major current which flows in from the Atlantic and moves east. Currents flowing back to the Atlantic are denser and flow below the main current.

The Dalmatian (Dalmacija) coast has many long, elongated islands running parallel to the mainland. These resulted when rising sea levels drowned valleys running parallel with the coast.

TRANSPORTATION & INDUSTRY

THE OPENING OF THE SUEZ CANAL in 1869 made the Mediterranean a key shipping route to Asia. Oil and gas reserves, although comparatively small on a world scale, are being explored and exploited off the coasts of Libya, Greece, Italy, Spain, and Tunisia. The Mediterranean's greatest natural resources are its miles of beaches and warm sea. Over half the world's income from tourism is generated in the Mediterranean.

Benidorm is one of the most popular resorts on Spain's Costa Blanca. Many of the Mediterranean's coastal resorts have grown up since the 1950s, expanding from small fishing villages to large resorts catering almost exclusively for tourists.

The Ionian Basin is the deepest in the Mediterranean, reaching depths of 16,800 ft (5,121 m).

Industrial pollution flowing from the Dnieper and Danube Rivers has destroyed a large proportion of the fish population that used to inhabit the upper layers of the Black Sea.

The eastern basin of the Mediterranean contains many features which indicate the force of a colliding plate margin, including volcanoes, earthquake zones, ridges, and seamounts.

The Atlas Mountains are a range of fold mountains that lie in Morocco and Algeria. They run parallel to the Mediterranean, forming a topographical and climatic divide between the Mediterranean coast and the western Sahara.

The edge of the Eurasian Plate is edged by a continental shelf. In the Mediterranean Sea this is widest at the Ebro Fan where it extends 60 miles (96 km).

Beneath the Strait of Sicily lies a submarine ridge which rises to 1,200 ft (360 m) below sea level. It divides the eastern and western basins of the Mediterranean.

An arc of active submarine, island and mainland volcanoes, including Etna and Vesuvius, lie in and around southern Italy. The area is also susceptible to earthquakes and landslides.

The shallow basin of the Aegean contains numerous small islands, many of volcanic origin.

Nutrient flows into the eastern Mediterranean, and sediment flows to the Nile Delta have been severely lowered by the building of the Aswan Dam across the Nile in Egypt. This is causing the delta to shrink.

A **fishing trawler** lies at anchor in the icy waters of Karaginskiy Zaliv, at the northern end of the Kamchatka Peninsula (Poluostrov Kamchatka) in eastern Siberia. The Russian Federation's fishing fleet is the largest in the world and operates worldwide.

The **shores of Lake Baikal** (Ozero Baykal) are a mixture of forest and the grassy steppe seen here. The lake freezes to a depth of 33 ft (10 m) in winter.

SCALE 1:13,800,000
(projection: Lambert Conformal Conic)

Monte Carlo is just one of the luxurious resorts scattered along the Riviera, which stretches along the coast from Cannes in France to La Spezia in Italy. The region's mild winters and hot summers have attracted wealthy tourists since the early 19th century.

Major industry and infrastructure

- fishing port
- oil & gas
- tourism
- major towns
- international airports
- major roads
- major industrial areas

Oxygen in the Black Sea is dissolved only in its upper layers; at depths below 230–300 ft (70–100 m) the sea is "dead" and can support no lifeforms other than specially-adapted bacteria.

The city of Venice is built on an archipelago of islands and mud-flats in the middle of a lagoon at the head of the Adriatic Sea. The city's numerous canals follow water routes between the original 118 islands.

Cyprus is the third largest Mediterranean island after Sardinia and Sicily. The island is mountainous; containing two main ranges, the Troodos and the Kyrenia mountains.

Both the Dead Sea in Jordan and the Gulf of Aqaba are extensions of the Great Rift Valley which runs through eastern Africa.

The Suez Canal, opened in 1869, extends 100 miles (160 km) from Port Said to the Gulf of Suez.

Commercial fisheries are found throughout the Mediterranean. Operations have traditionally been small-scale. As elsewhere, high demand has caused a decline in fish stocks.

MALTA

SCALE 1:900,000
(projection: Lambert Conformal Conic)

CYPRUS

IN 1974 TU... Cyprus wh... of the south... and a UN b... areas. In 19... itself the T... It was only...

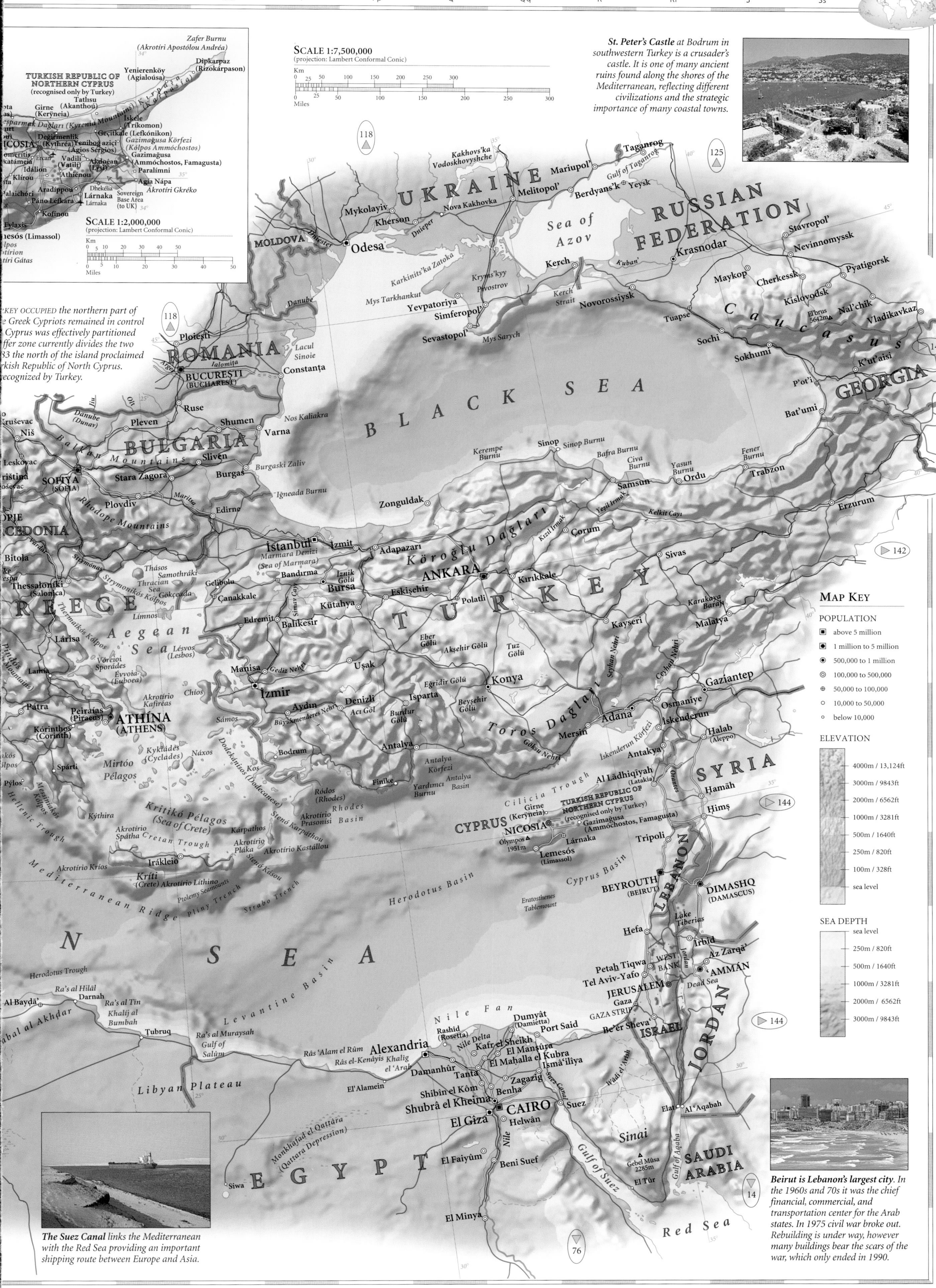

St. Peter's Castle at Bodrum in southwestern Turkey is a crusader's castle. It is one of many ancient ruins found along the shores of the Mediterranean, reflecting different civilizations and the strategic importance of many coastal towns.

SCALE 1:7,500,000
(projection: Lambert Conformal Conic)

TURKISH REPUBLIC OF NORTHERN CYPRUS
(recognised only by Turkey)

Zafer Burnu
(Akrotíri Apostólou Andréa)
Dípkarpaz
(Rizokárpason)
Yenierenköy
(Agialoúsa)
Tathsu
Girne (Akanthoú)
(Kerýnia)
İskele
(Tríkomon)
Geçitkale (Lefkónikon)
Gazimağusa Körfezi
(Kólpos Ammóchostos)
Gazimağusa
(Ammóchostos, Famagusta)
Paralímni
Agía Nápa
Akrotíri Gkréko
Dhekélia
Lárnaka
Sovereign Base Area (to UK)

SCALE 1:2,000,000
(projection: Lambert Conformal Conic)

TURKEY OCCUPIED the northern part of the Greek Cypriots remained in control. Cyprus was effectively partitioned. A buffer zone currently divides the two. In 1983 the north of the island proclaimed the Turkish Republic of North Cyprus. Recognized by Turkey.

MAP KEY

POPULATION
- above 5 million
- 1 million to 5 million
- 500,000 to 1 million
- 100,000 to 500,000
- 50,000 to 100,000
- 10,000 to 50,000
- below 10,000

ELEVATION
4000m / 13,124ft
3000m / 9843ft
2000m / 6562ft
1000m / 3281ft
500m / 1640ft
250m / 820ft
100m / 328ft
sea level

SEA DEPTH
sea level
250m / 820ft
500m / 1640ft
1000m / 3281ft
2000m / 6562ft
3000m / 9843ft

The Suez Canal links the Mediterranean with the Red Sea providing an important shipping route between Europe and Asia.

Beirut is Lebanon's largest city. In the 1960s and 70s it was the chief financial, commercial, and transportation center for the Arab states. In 1975 civil war broke out. Rebuilding is under way, however many buildings bear the scars of the war, which only ended in 1990.

124

THE RUSSIAN FEDERATION

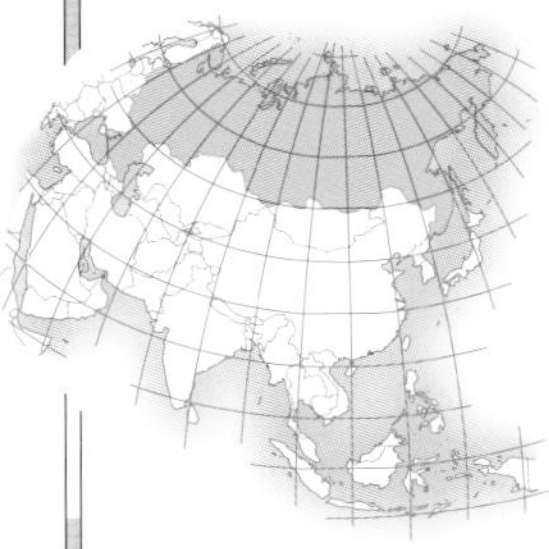

THE COLD WAR ERA OF GLOBAL RELATIONS was concluded in 1991 with the formal dissolution of the Soviet Union. The Russian Federation declared its separate sovereignty from the foundering communist empire following independence declarations from a number of former Soviet republics. As the leading member of the Commonwealth of Independent States, the Russian Federation has a central role in the development of post-Soviet Eurasia. Crossing 11 time zones, the Russian Federation is almost twice the size of the US, and with more than 150 ethnic minorities and 21 autonomous republics, regionalist dissent within its own territory remains a danger.

Summer beds of moss and lichen scatter a 90% surface cover of ice across the islands of Franz Josef Land (Zemlya Frantsa-Iosifa), the northernmost land in the eastern hemisphere.

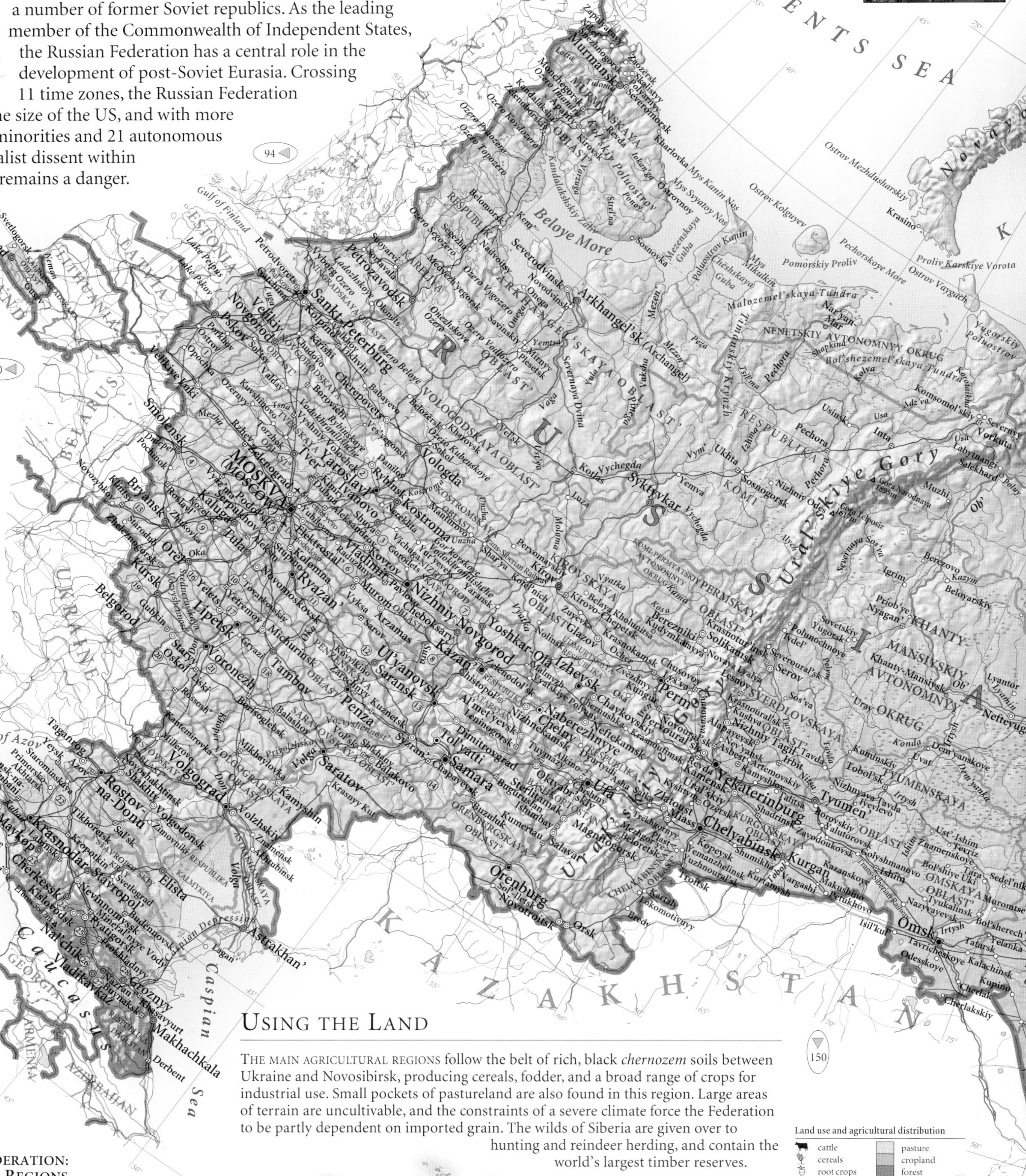

MAP KEY

POPULATION

- ■ above 5 million
- ■ 1 million to 5 million
- ◉ 500,000 to 1 million
- ◎ 100,000 to 500,000
- ⊕ 50,000 to 100,000
- ○ 10,000 to 50,000
- ○ below 10,000

ELEVATION

- 4000m / 13,124ft
- 3000m / 9843ft
- 2000m / 6562ft
- 1000m / 3281ft
- 500m / 1640ft
- 250m / 820ft
- 100m / 328ft
- sea level

USING THE LAND

THE MAIN AGRICULTURAL REGIONS follow the belt of rich, black *chernozem* soils between Ukraine and Novosibirsk, producing cereals, fodder, and a broad range of crops for industrial use. Small pockets of pastureland are also found in this region. Large areas of terrain are uncultivable, and the constraints of a severe climate force the Federation to be partly dependent on imported grain. The wilds of Siberia are given over to hunting and reindeer herding, and contain the world's largest timber reserves.

Land use and agricultural distribution

- cattle
- cereals
- root crops
- timber
- capital cities
- major towns
- pasture
- cropland
- forest
- desert
- mountain region
- barren

THE RUSSIAN FEDERATION: ADMINISTRATIVE REGIONS

① PSKOVSKAYA OBLAST'
② YAROSLAVSKAYA OBLAST'
③ IVANOVSKAYA OBLAST'
④ SMOLENSKAYA OBLAST'
⑤ MOSKOVSKAYA OBLAST
⑥ VLADIMIRSKAYA OBLAST'
⑦ RESPUBLIKA MARIY EL
⑧ CHAVASH RESPUBLIKI
⑨ KALUZHSKAYA OBLAST'
⑩ TUL'SKAYA OBLAST'
⑪ RYAZANSKAYA OBLAST'
⑫ RESPUBLIKA MORDOVIYA
⑬ UL'YANOVSKAYA OBLAST'
⑭ SAMARSKAYA OBLAST'
⑮ BRYANSKAYA OBLAST'
⑯ ORLOVSKAYA OBLAST'
⑰ LIPETSKAYA OBLAST'
⑱ TAMBOVSKAYA OBLAST'
⑲ KURSKAYA OBLAST'
⑳ BELGORODSKAYA OBLAST'
㉑ VORONEZHSKAYA OBLAST'
㉒ KRASNODARSKIY KRAY
㉓ RESPUBLIKA ADYGEYA
㉔ KARACHAYEVO-CHERKESSKAYA RESPUBLIKA
㉕ KABARDINO-BALKARSKAYA RESPUBLIKA
㉖ RESPUBLIKA SEVERNAYA OSETIYA - ALANIYA
㉗ INGUSHSKAYA RESPUBLIKA
㉘ CHECHENSKAYA RESPUBLIKA
㉙ YEVREYSKAYA AVTONOMNAYA OBLAST'

THE URBAN/RURAL POPULATION DIVIDE

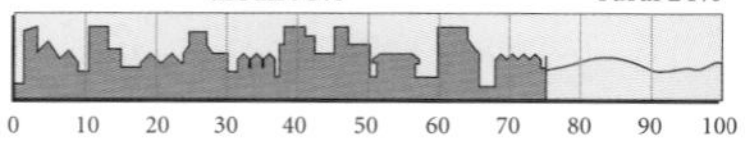

urban 76%   rural 24%

POPULATION DENSITY	TOTAL LAND AREA
22 people per sq mile (9 people per sq km)	65,592,800 sq miles (17,075,400 sq km)

The Kamchatka Peninsula
(Poluostrov Kamchatka) *is a volcanic area on the margins of the Eurasian Plate, forming part of the Pacific "Ring of Fire." The volcano Vulkan Klyuchevskaya Sopka, at 15,585 ft (4,750 m), is the highest mountain in Siberia.*

TRANSPORTATION & INDUSTRY

RAW MATERIALS, particularly fossil fuels, ores, and precious metals are abundant, yet often found at sites far from habitation. This inherent "friction of distance" problem was met starting in the 1930s by Soviet commitment to heavy industry and the strategic location of plants east of the Urals. It has left a pattern of isolated and often vast industrial complexes, in remote areas from Vladivostok to Murmansk, in the far north and across European Russia, with lighter manufacturing concentrated in urban areas.

Major industry and infrastructure

- ✈ aerospace
- 🚗 car manufacture
- ⚗ chemicals
- ⚙ engineering
- gas
- iron & steel
- mining
- oil
- textiles
- timber processing
- ■ capital cities
- • major towns
- ⊕ international airports
- major roads
- major industrial areas

TRANSPORTATION NETWORK

🛣	598,023 miles (963,000 km)
🛣	None
🚆	53,816 miles (86,660 km)
🚆	62,721 miles (101,000 km)

The recent growth of trade with China and East Asia has put pressure on Siberia's inadequate road and rail network, prompting increased use of the Amur River for freight transportation.

Novosibirsk was established at the point where the Trans–Siberian railroad crosses the Ob' River. It grew as an industrial center under the Soviet Union and is now Siberia's largest city.

THE LANDSCAPE

THE URAL MOUNTAINS (*Ural'skiye Gory*) divide the fertile North European Plain from the West Siberian Plain (*Zapadno-Sibirskaya Ravnina*), the world's largest area of flat ground, crossed by giant rivers flowing north to the Kara Sea (*Karskoye More*). The land rises to the Central Siberian Plateau (*Srednesibirskoye Ploskogor'ye*) and becomes more mountainous to the southeast. These immense topographic regions intersect with latitudinal vegetation bands. The tundra of the extreme north gives way to a vast area of coniferous woodland, which is known as *taiga*, larger than the Amazon rain forest. This belt turns to mixed forest and then steppe grasslands toward the south.

Polygon shapes create patterned ground

Permafrost

Permanent ice wedges up to 16 ft (5 m) deep

Patterned ground is a permafrost feature found extensively across northern Russia. Seasonal contraction of the permafrost creates polygonal cracks, which are filled by ice wedges.

The Khatanga River meanders slowly across the Poluostrov Taymyr, a low-lying tundra landscape which floods in the spring thaw, until the water can escape to the sea.

Poluostrov Taymyr

The mountains of Verkhoyanskiy Khrebet were formed by movement between the Eurasian and North American plates, during the same period of folding that created the Urals.

Kara Sea (Karskoye More)

Central Siberian Plateau (Srednesibirskoye Ploskogor'ye)

West Siberian Plain (Zapadno-Sibirskaya Ravnina)

The North European Plain is marked by huge moraine ridges left by the Scandinavian Ice Sheet and by long intermoraine drainage channels, known as *Urstromtäler*.

The Ural Mountains (*Ural'skiye Gory*) extend 1,550 miles (2,500 km). They were formed over 280 million years ago, folded as the East European and Siberian plates moved closer together.

The Yenisey is one of the world's longest rivers, and also among the most languid, dropping only 500 ft (152 m) over 1,200 miles (2,000 km).

Lake Baikal (*Ozero Baykal*), occupies a rift valley and is the world's deepest lake, over 1 mile (1.6 km) in depth. It is fed by over 300 rivers and drained by just one, the Angara.

Yukagirskoye Ploskogor'ye is a rolling plain with isolated drumlins, domelike features resulting from glacial deposition.

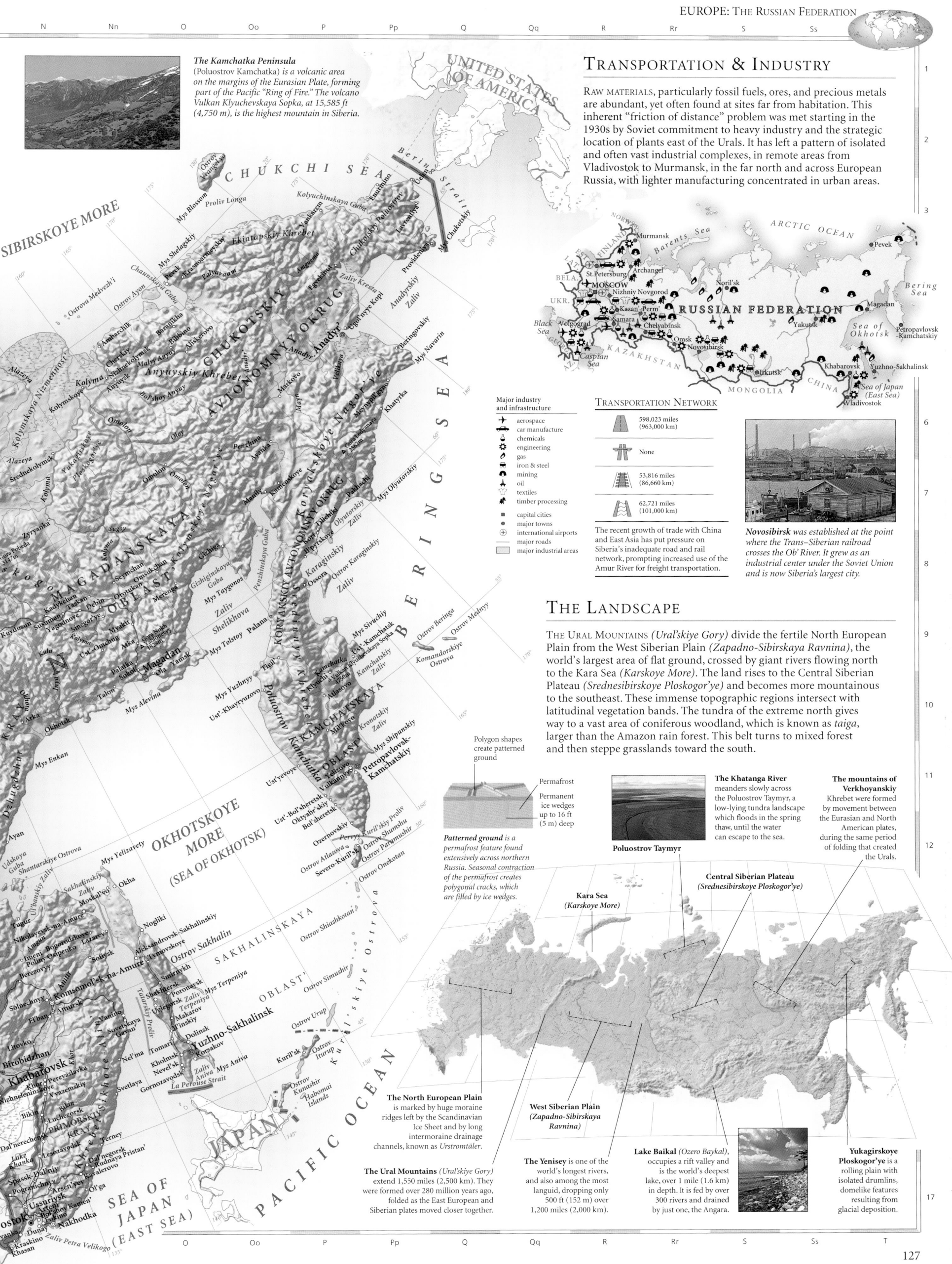

NORTHERN EUROPEAN RUSSIA

REACHING INTO THE ARCTIC CIRCLE, this region of lakeland, forest, and tundra is historically bound to Europe by St. Petersburg, the old imperial capital of Tsarist Russia and home to a third of the region's population. Communist rule from Moscow left the north politically marginalized, contributing to the present problems of outmoded industry, poor infrastructure, and serious environmental neglect. However, with borders embracing Finland, Norway, the Baltic, and the northern sea route to the Atlantic, the region's success in foreign trade is now of prime importance to the Russian economy.

St. Peter and Paul Fortress is the oldest building in St. Petersburg, founded by Peter the Great in 1703 as a modern, European capital for Russia.

THE LANDSCAPE

THE ANCIENT BEDROCK of the Scandinavian Shield lies exposed across the glacially scoured Khibiny Mountains of the Kola Peninsula *(Kol'skiy Poluostrov)*, becoming mantled with till toward the North European Plain. The Valdai Hills *(Valdayskaya Vozvyshennost')* form an important watershed for the plain's rivers, while thick forest veils a complicated topography of moraines, lakes, and ground disturbed by frost action. The Ural Mountains *(Ural'skiye Gory)* form a border with Asia in the east.

The Khibiny Mountains were formed by volcanic intrusions into the Scandinavian Shield, over 570 million years ago.

Kola Peninsula *(Kol'skiy Poluostrov)*

The Kola Peninsula (Kol'skiy Poluostrov) *is part of the Scandinavian Shield, an area of ancient bedrock underlying Scandinavia. Rocks in excess of 2,500 million years old are exposed across the peninsula.*

Karst features, including sinkholes, lakes, and caverns, are found in limestone outcrops across the plain of the Severnaya Dvina and Mezen' Rivers.

The low-lying plains of the Pechora, Mezen', and Severnaya Dvina Rivers were flooded by the sea while the land was still isostatically depressed following the last Ice Age, a process which has hidden the landforms created by glacial deposition.

Retreating glacier

Meltwater channels

Terminal moraine

Terminal moraines are crescent-shaped ridges of glacial deposits, widely found in central Russia. Detritus is carried by the glacier and deposited at its terminus (snout) as it melts, marking the limit of the ice advance.

Lake Onega (Onezhskoye Ozero) *is the remnant of a body of water which, 12,000 years ago, connected the White Sea (Beloye More) with the Gulf of Finland and the Baltic Sea.*

Ural Mountains *(Ural'skiye Gory)*

Two of Europe's biggest rivers, the Volga and Western Dvina, rise in the swampy uplands of the Valdai Hills *(Valdayskaya Vozvyshennost')*.

USING THE LAND AND SEA

THE COLD CLIMATE confines agriculture mainly to southern and western provinces, where dairy farming predominates and arable land is given over to fodder crops as well as flax, potatoes, oats, and rye. Areas beyond the northern margins of cultivation are used for forestry, hunting, herding, and fishing, with some vegetables grown in hothouses around urban areas.

Land use and agricultural distribution

- cattle
- fishing
- reindeer
- timber
- fodder
- major towns

pasture
cropland
forest
mountain region
wetland
tundra
barren
ice

THE URBAN/RURAL POPULATION DIVIDE

urban 74% rural 26%

0 10 20 30 40 50 60 70 80 90 100

POPULATION DENSITY	TOTAL LAND AREA
26 people per sq mile	829,398 sq miles
10 people per sq km	(2,148,700 sq km)

Many rapids are found along the 175 mile (280 km) course of the Suna River.

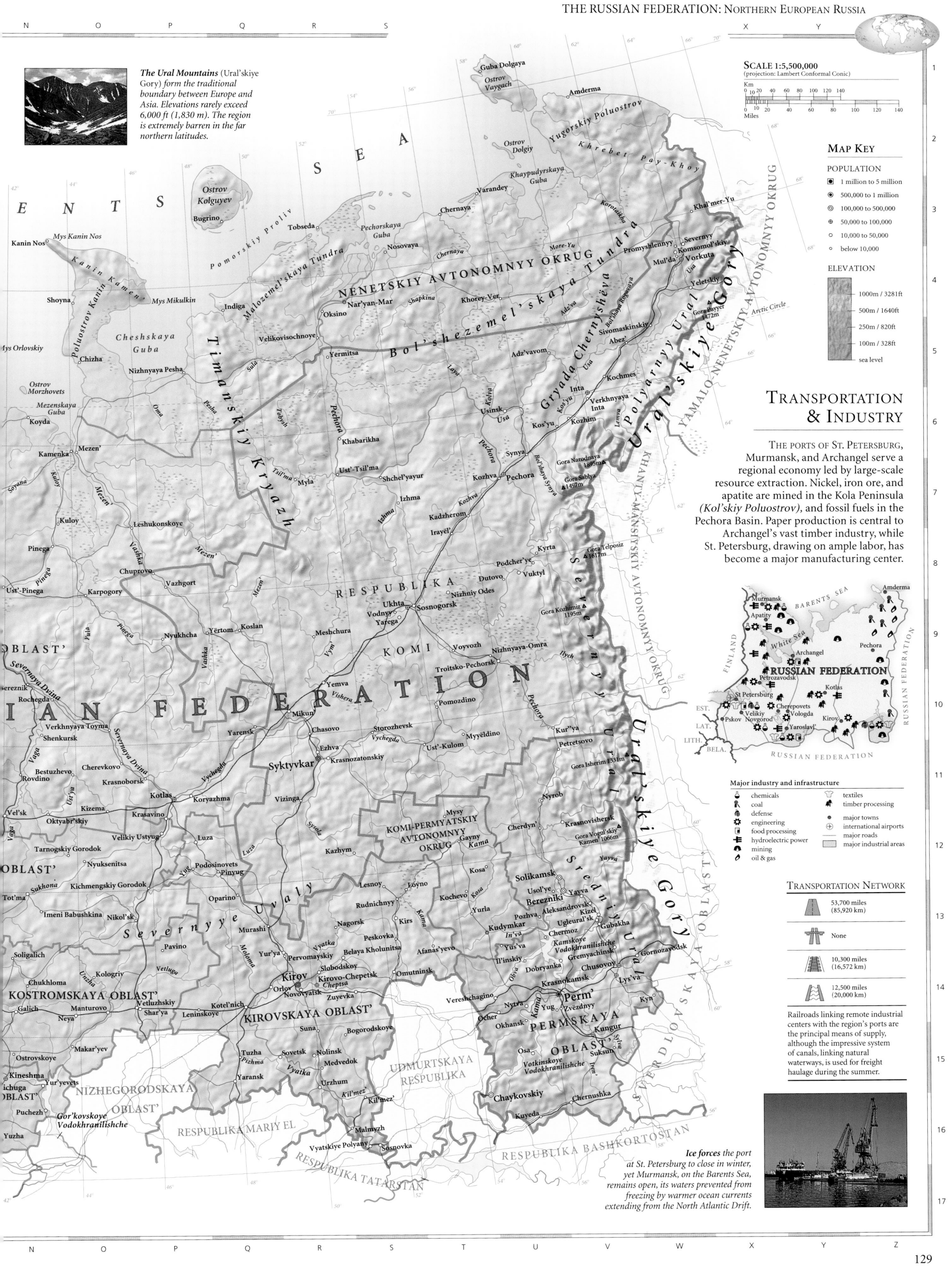

The Ural Mountains (Ural'skiye Gory) form the traditional boundary between Europe and Asia. Elevations rarely exceed 6,000 ft (1,830 m). The region is extremely barren in the far northern latitudes.

SCALE 1:5,500,000
(projection: Lambert Conformal Conic)

MAP KEY

POPULATION

- 1 million to 5 million
- 500,000 to 1 million
- 100,000 to 500,000
- 50,000 to 100,000
- 10,000 to 50,000
- below 10,000

ELEVATION

- 1000m / 3281ft
- 500m / 1640ft
- 250m / 820ft
- 100m / 328ft
- sea level

TRANSPORTATION & INDUSTRY

THE PORTS OF ST. PETERSBURG, Murmansk, and Archangel serve a regional economy led by large-scale resource extraction. Nickel, iron ore, and apatite are mined in the Kola Peninsula (*Kol'skiy Poluostrov*), and fossil fuels in the Pechora Basin. Paper production is central to Archangel's vast timber industry, while St. Petersburg, drawing on ample labor, has become a major manufacturing center.

Major industry and infrastructure

- chemicals
- coal
- defense
- engineering
- food processing
- hydroelectric power
- mining
- oil & gas
- textiles
- timber processing
- major towns
- international airports
- major roads
- major industrial areas

TRANSPORTATION NETWORK

roads	53,700 miles (85,920 km)
highways	None
	10,300 miles (16,572 km)
railroads	12,500 miles (20,000 km)

Railroads linking remote industrial centers with the region's ports are the principal means of supply, although the impressive system of canals, linking natural waterways, is used for freight haulage during the summer.

Ice forces the port at St. Petersburg to close in winter, yet Murmansk, on the Barents Sea, remains open, its waters prevented from freezing by warmer ocean currents extending from the North Atlantic Drift.

Kaliningrad has been a Russian enclave since 1945. The port is an important center for the Russian Federation's Baltic fishing fleet.

St Basil's Cathedral, completed in 1561, stands in Moscow's Red Square next to the Kremlin; the original fortified stronghold of the city.

SOUTHERN EUROPEAN RUSSIA

THIS REGION, DIVIDED FROM ASIA by desert, seas, and mountains, has exerted a powerful influence both east and west since the 13th century. Over 70 years of Communist rule produced a highly urbanized, industrial society dominated by Moscow, which was the capital of the Soviet Union until 1991. Almost two-thirds of the Russian Federation's population live in this core area, with a relatively high *per capita* share of its wealth. However, the rapid growth of a market economy has caused great social upheaval, with rising crime and political instability.

THE LANDSCAPE

ANCIENT FOLDS in the deep sedimentary strata of the North European Plain have created a sequence of high and low regions. The Central Russian Upland (*Srednerusskaya Vozvyshennost'*) in the west is deeply incised by rivers draining into the lowland of the Oka and Don Rivers. In the east the Volga, Europe's longest river flows south to the Caspian Sea, dividing the Volga Uplands (*Privolzhskaya Vozvyshennost'*) from the foothills of the Ural Mountains (*Ural'skiye Gory*). The Caucasus Mountains and the Black Sea form a natural border to the southwest.

A plantation of Scots pine helps consolidate the loose sandy soils of the Meshchera Lowland (Meshcherskaya Nizina), which lies on the bed of an old glacial lake.

The Smolensk-Moscow Upland (*Smolensko-Moskovskaya Vozvyshennost'*) is a series of terminal moraine ridges marking the southern extent of the last glaciation.

Glacial till covers the bedrock to the north of the North European Plain, giving a gentle surface relief.

The lowland of the Oka and Don Rivers lies over a broad trough, between the upfolds of the Volga Uplands (*Privolzhskaya Vozvyshennost'*) to the east, and the Central Russian Upland (*Srednerusskaya Vozvyshennost'*) to the west.

The southern Ural Mountains (*Ural'skiye Gory*) consist of several parallel ranges of ancient fold mountains running from north to south.

Central Russian Upland (*Srednerusskaya Vozvyshennost'*).

The floodplain of the Volga forms a long oasis of verdant vegetation, contrasting with the aridity of the surrounding Caspian hinterland.

The marshlands of the Volga Delta are visited by over 260 species of bird each year, migrating between South Africa and Arctic Siberia.

The Caspian Depression is a large downfold (or syncline) which became flooded, forming the Caspian Sea. The shoreline is 98 ft (30 m) below sea level.

The Caucasus Mountains run from the Black Sea to the Caspian Sea. They include El'brus which, at 18,511 ft (5,642 m), is the highest point in Europe. It is still uplifting at a rate of 0.4 inches (10 mm/yr).

Drifting sand occupies large areas of the south, forming dunes up to 50 ft (15 m) high.

Salt dome

Salt dome is forced up and through the rock strata

Sedimentary strata

Salts are forced upwards by denser overlying strata

Salt domes, rounded hills up to 500 ft (150 m) high, are produced as less dense rock salts are displaced under the extreme pressure of denser, overlying strata and forced up toward the surface creating domes. They are widespread in the Caspian Depression.

SCALE 1:5,500,000
(projection: Lambert Conformal Conic)

MAP KEY

POPULATION

- ■ above 5 million
- ▣ 1 million to 5 million
- ◉ 500,000 to 1 million
- ◎ 100,000 to 500,000
- ⊕ 50,000 to 100,000
- ○ 10,000 to 50,000
- ○ below 10,000

ELEVATION

- 4000m / 13,124ft
- 3000m / 9843ft
- 2000m / 6562ft
- 1000m / 3281ft
- 500m / 1640ft
- 250m / 820ft
- 100m / 328ft
- sea level

USING THE LAND

IN THE COLD, HUMID NORTH and in the southern Urals *(Ural'skiye Gory)*, small grains, potatoes and flax are commonly rotated with legumes which support livestock farming. The rich chernozem (or black earth) areas support diverse crops such as sugar beet, hemp, sunflowers, millet and vegetables. Further south, aridity restricts husbandry to extensive grazing, with intensive fruit and rice cultivation along the oasis of the Volga.

THE URBAN/RURAL POPULATION DIVIDE

urban 65% rural 35%

0 10 20 30 40 50 60 70 80 90 100

POPULATION DENSITY TOTAL LAND AREA
119 people per sq mile 705,916 sq miles
(46 people per sq km) (1,828,800 sq km)

Land use and agricultural distribution

- sheep
- flax
- potatoes
- rice
- sunflowers
- sugar beet
- timber
- ■ capital cities
- • major towns
- pasture
- cropland
- forest
- wetland
- mountain region
- tundra

TRANSPORTATION & INDUSTRY

MANUFACTURING is largely based around Moscow and the Volga region, which became a major industrial area during the Second World War. Both Moscow and Nizhniy Novgorod are centers of skilled labor for light manufacturing and engineering. Most of Russia's main chemical plants are located along the Volga, and one of the world's largest car factories was recently opened in Tol'yatti. Processing and machine construction plants use oil, gas, and hydroelectric power from the Volga Basin and metallic minerals from the Urals *(Ural'skiye Gory)* and Kursk.

Industrial plants are massed along the Volga. Environmental stress from decades of unbridled industrial development has prompted widespread concern about pollution levels.

TRANSPORTATION NETWORK

| 250,000 miles (402,000 km) | None |
| 28,000 miles (44,800 km) | 16,300 miles (26,080 km) |

Seventy private and national flag airlines have been created from the reorganization of the state airline Aeroflot, which maintained the world's largest fleet of aircraft during the Soviet era.

Major industry and infrastructure

- ✈ aerospace
- 🚗 car manufacture
- chemicals
- defense
- electronics
- engineering
- gas
- mining
- oil
- textiles
- ■ capital cities
- • major towns
- ⊕ international airports
- major roads
- major industrial areas

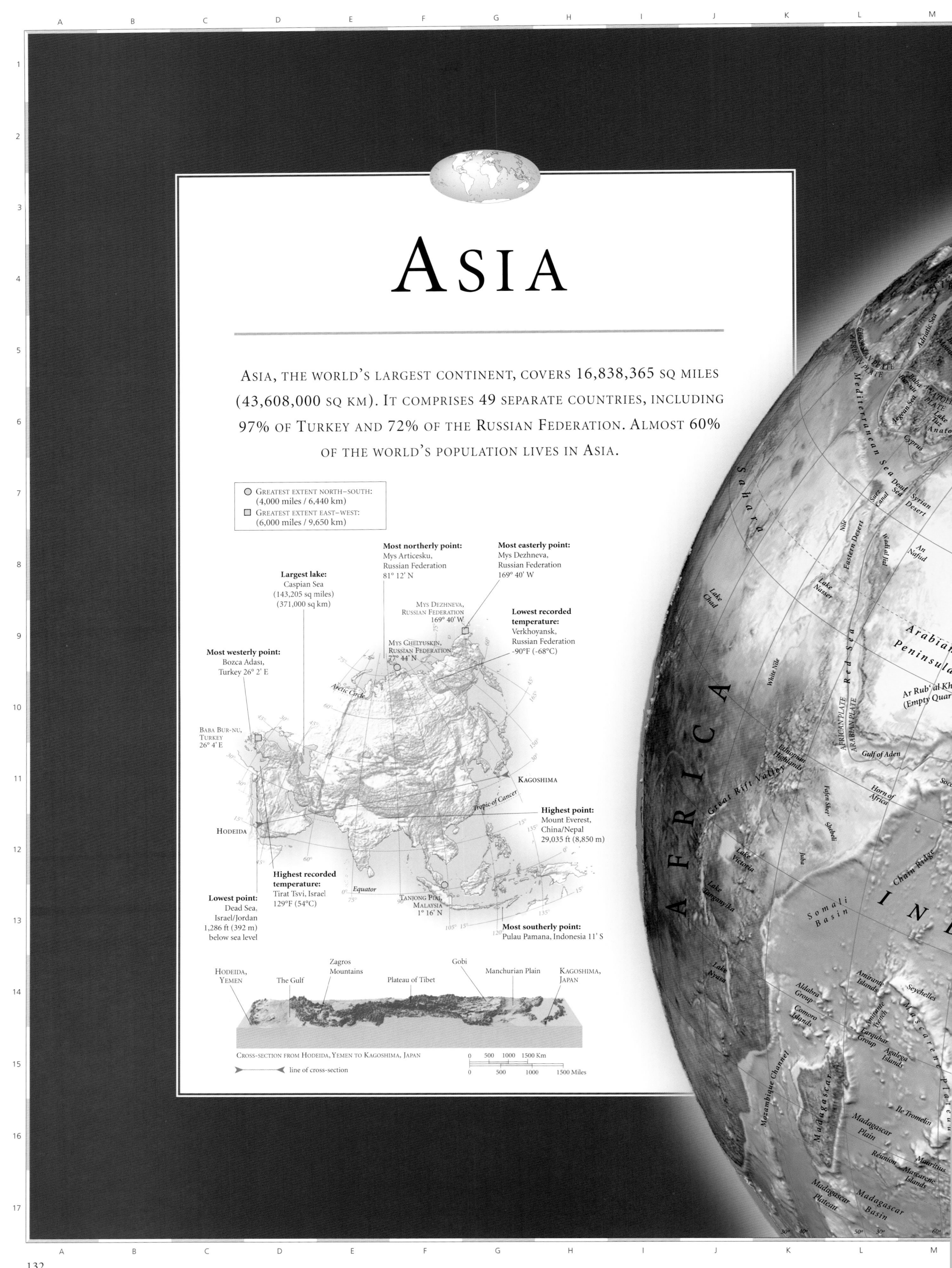

ASIA

ASIA, THE WORLD'S LARGEST CONTINENT, COVERS 16,838,365 SQ MILES (43,608,000 SQ KM). IT COMPRISES 49 SEPARATE COUNTRIES, INCLUDING 97% OF TURKEY AND 72% OF THE RUSSIAN FEDERATION. ALMOST 60% OF THE WORLD'S POPULATION LIVES IN ASIA.

○ GREATEST EXTENT NORTH–SOUTH:
(4,000 miles / 6,440 km)
□ GREATEST EXTENT EAST–WEST:
(6,000 miles / 9,650 km)

Most northerly point:
Mys Articesku,
Russian Federation
81° 12' N

Most easterly point:
Mys Dezhneva,
Russian Federation
169° 40' W

Largest lake:
Caspian Sea
(143,205 sq miles)
(371,000 sq km)

MYS DEZHNEVA,
RUSSIAN FEDERATION
169° 40' W

**Lowest recorded
temperature:**
Verkhoyansk,
Russian Federation
-90°F (-68°C)

Most westerly point:
Bozca Adasi,
Turkey 26° 2' E

MYS CHELYUSKIN,
RUSSIAN FEDERATION
77° 44' N

BABA BUR-NU,
TURKEY
26° 4' E

Arctic Circle

KAGOSHIMA

HODEIDA

Tropic of Cancer

Highest point:
Mount Everest,
China/Nepal
29,035 ft (8,850 m)

**Highest recorded
temperature:**
Tirat Tsvi, Israel
129°F (54°C)

Equator

TANJONG PIAI,
MALAYSIA
1° 16' N

Lowest point:
Dead Sea,
Israel/Jordan
1,286 ft (392 m)
below sea level

Most southerly point:
Pulau Pamana, Indonesia 11' S

HODEIDA,
YEMEN

Zagros
Mountains

Gobi

The Gulf

Plateau of Tibet

Manchurian Plain

KAGOSHIMA,
JAPAN

CROSS-SECTION FROM HODEIDA, YEMEN TO KAGOSHIMA, JAPAN

◄ line of cross-section

| 0 | 500 | 1000 | 1500 Km |
| 0 | 500 | 1000 | 1500 Miles |

ARCTIC OCEAN
North Pole
NORTH AMERICAN PLATE
EURASIAN PLATE

Norwegian Sea
Scandinavia
North Sea
Gulf of Bothnia
Baltic Sea
Gulf of Finland
Lake Ladoga
Lake Onega
White Sea
Kola Peninsula
North Cape
Barents Sea
Novaya Zemlya
Kara Sea
Severnaya Zemlya
Franz Josef Land
Mys Chelyuskin
Laptev Sea
New Siberian Islands
East Siberian Sea
Long Strait
Chukot Range
Bering Strait
Bering Sea
Aleutian Basin

EUROPE
North European Plain
Central Russian Upland
Ural Mountains
West Siberian Plain
North Siberian Lowland
Putorana Mountains
Central Siberian Plateau
Verkhoyanskiy Khrebet
Khrebet Cherskogo
Kolyma
Koryak Range
Kamchatka

Rhine
Vistula
Dnieper
Dniester
Don
Sea of Azov
Black Sea
Caspian Sea
Caspian Depression
Caucasus
Lake Van
Lake Urmia
Elburz Mountains
Zagros Mountains
Great Salt Desert
Iranian Plateau
Persian Gulf
Strait of Hormuz
Gulf of Oman
Central Makran Range
Hamun
Jaz Murian
Oman Basin

Khalij Masirah
ARABIAN PLATE
INDIAN PLATE
INDO-AUSTRALIAN PLATE

Arabian Sea
Arabian Basin
Laccadive Islands
Malabar Coast
Cape Comorin
Gulf of Mannar
Maldives
Sri Lanka
Ceylon Plain
Chagos-Laccadive Plateau
Chagos Bank
Chagos Trench
Mid-Indian Basin
Mid-Indian Ridge

INDIAN OCEAN

Kirghiz Steppe
Turan Lowland
Aral Sea
Syr Darya
Amu Darya
Kara Kum
Kyzyl Kum
Lake Balkhash
Lake Zaysan
Ozero Alakol
Ozero Issyk-Kul
Tien Shan
Pamirs
Hindu Kush
Karakoram Range
Sulaiman Range
Rigestan
Kuh-e-Baba
5143m
Takla Makan Desert
Tarim Basin
Tarim He
Kongi He
Qarqan He
Lop Nur
Shule He
Nan Shan
Altun Shan
Qilian Shan
Kunlun Mountains
Plateau of Tibet
Himalayas
Mount Everest 8850m
Annapurna 8091m
K2 8611m

ASIA
Altai Mountains
Dzungaria
Plateau of Mongolia
Gobi
Ordos Desert
Qinghai Hu
Bayan Har Shan
Xiqing Shan
Yellow River
Han Shui
Wutai Shan
Great Plain of China
Yangtze
Yellow Sea
Bo Hai
Korea Bay
Korea Strait
Cheju-do

Siberia
Lake Baikal
Stanovoy Khrebet
Zeya Reservoir
Amur
Sea of Okhotsk
Manchurian Plain
Hulun Nur
Kerulen
Great Khingan Range
Lake Khanka
Hokkaido
Sea of Japan (East Sea)
Honshu
Shikoku
Kyushu
Japan
Japan Trench
Kurile Islands
Kurile Trench
PACIFIC OCEAN

Thar Desert
Punjab Plains
Indus
Sutlej
Ganges
Yamuna
Brahmaputra
Siling Co
Tangra Yumco
Nam Co
Dogai Coring

Gulf of Kachchh
Gulf of Khambhat
Sabarmati
Mahi
Banas
Chambal
Narmada
Vindhya Range
Satpura Range
Ajanta Range
Godavari
Deccan
Western Ghats
Eastern Ghats
Krishna
Kaveri
Coromandel Coast
Bay of Bengal
Mouths of the Ganges
Arakan Yoma
Irrawaddy
Chindwin
Salween
Gulf of Martaban
Andaman Islands
Andaman Sea
Nicobar Islands
Mouths of the Mekong

Xi Jiang
Dongting Hu
Wuyi Shan
Hainan Strait
Hainan
Gulf of Tongking
Red River
Black River
Mekong
Chao Phraya
Gulf of Thailand
Isthmus of Kra
Tônlé Sap
Malay Peninsula
Strait of Malacca
Sumatra
Danau Toba
Gunung Kerinci 3800m
Anambas Islands
Natuna Islands
Sunda Shelf
Greater Sunda Islands
Borneo
Gunung Kinabalu 4101m
Kapuas Sungai
Java Sea
Java
Bali
Lesser Sunda Islands
Sumba Islands
Java Trough
Sunda Trough
Timor Trough
Christmas Island
Cocos Islands

Taiwan
Taiwan Strait
East China Sea
Ryukyu Islands
Luzon Strait
Luzon
Philippine Sea
Mindoro
Philippine Basin
Panay
Negros
Palawan
Sulu Sea
Mindanao
Celebes Sea
Celebes
Halmahera
Molucca Sea
Buru
Seram
Banda Sea
Flores Sea
Flores
Timor
Arafura Sea
Torres Strait

PHILIPPINE PLATE
Philippine Trench
Kyushu-Palau Ridge
Euripik Rise
CAROLINE PLATE
New Guinea Trench
BISMARCK PLATE

SOUTH CHINA SEA
South China Basin
East Indies

AUSTRALIA

ASIAN RESOURCES

ALTHOUGH AGRICULTURE REMAINS THE ECONOMIC MAINSTAY of most Asian countries, the number of people employed in agriculture has steadily declined, as new industries have been developed during the past 30 years. China, Indonesia, Malaysia, Thailand, and Turkey have all experienced far-reaching structural change in their economies, while the breakup of the Soviet Union has created a new economic challenge in the Central Asian republics. The countries of the Persian Gulf illustrate the rapid transformation from rural nomadism to modern, urban society which oil wealth has brought to parts of the continent. Asia's most economically dynamic countries, Japan, Singapore, South Korea, and Taiwan, fringe the Pacific Ocean and are known as the Pacific Rim. In contrast, other Southeast Asian countries like Laos and Cambodia remain both economically and industrially underdeveloped.

INDUSTRY

JAPANESE INDUSTRY LEADS THE CONTINENT in both productivity and efficiency; electronics, hi-tech industries, car manufacture and shipbuilding are important. In recent years, the so-called economic "tigers" of the Pacific Rim such as Taiwan and South Korea are now challenging Japan's economic dominance. Heavy industries such as engineering, chemicals, and steel typify the industrial complexes along the corridor created by the Trans-Siberian Railway, the Fergana Valley in Central Asia, and also much of the huge industrial plain of east China. The discovery of oil in the Persian Gulf brought immense wealth and international pressure to countries that previously relied on subsistence agriculture.

STANDARD OF LIVING

DESPITE JAPAN'S HIGH STANDARDS OF LIVING, and Southwest Asia's oil-derived wealth, immense disparities exist across the continent. Afghanistan remains one of the world's most underdeveloped nations, as do the mountain states of Nepal and Bhutan. Further rapid population growth is exacerbating poverty and overcrowding in many parts of India and Bangladesh.

Standard of Living
(UN Human Development Index)

low

high

On a small island at the southern tip of the Malay Peninsula lies Singapore, one of the Pacific Rim's most vibrant economic centers. Multinational banking and finance form the core of the city's wealth.

GNP per capita (US$)

0–499
500–999
1000–4999
5000–9999
10000–19999
20000+

Industry

aerospace	printing & publishing
brewing	shipbuilding
car/vehicle manufacture	sugar processing
cement	tea processing
chemicals	textiles
electronics	timber processing
engineering	tobacco processing
finance	coal
fish processing	oil
food processing	gas
hi-tech industry	industrial cities
iron & steel	major industrial areas
pharmaceuticals	

Iron and steel, engineering, and shipbuilding typify the heavy industry found in eastern China's industrial cities, especially the nation's leading manufacturing center, Shanghai.

Traditional industries are still crucial to many rural economies across Asia. Here, on the Vietnamese coast, salt has been extracted from seawater by evaporation and is being loaded into a van to take to market.

ARCTIC OCEAN

PACIFIC OCEAN

RUSSIAN FEDERATION

Yakutsk

Sea of Okhotsk

Trans-Siberian Railway

Khabarovsk

Yekaterinburg

Chelyabinsk Trans-Siberian Railway

Magnitogorsk

Omsk Novosibirsk

Krasnoyarsk

Bratsk

Kemerovo

Novokuznetsk

Irkutsk

Vladivostok

Harbin

JAPAN

Istanbul

Izmir

Ankara

TURKEY

GEORGIA Tbilisi

ARMENIA Yerevan AZERB.

Baku

CYPRUS

LEBANON Beirut

SYRIA Damascus

Tel Aviv-Yafo

ISRAEL Amman

JORDAN

Kirkuk

Baghdad

IRAQ Basra

SAUDI ARABIA

Kuwait KUWAIT

Ad Damman BAHRAIN

Jedda

Riyadh

QATAR Persian Gulf

Abu Dhabi Dubai

UAE

YEMEN

OMAN

Red Sea

Gulf of Aden

Caspian Sea

Aral Sea

KAZAKHSTAN

Karaganda

UZBEKISTAN

Tashkent

TURKMENISTAN

Asgabat

Ashgabat

Dushanbe

TAJIKISTAN

Almaty

KYRGYZSTAN

Fergana

Urumqi

MONGOLIA

Ulan Bator

Shenyang

NORTH KOREA

Pyongyang

Beijing

Tianjin

Dalian

Seoul

SOUTH KOREA

Pusan

Tokyo

Nagoya

Kobe

Jinan

Qingdao

Taiyuan

Zhengzhou

Nanjing

Shanghai

CHINA

Lanzhou

Xi'an

Wuhan

Chengdu

Chongqing

Taipei

TAIWAN

Tehran

Isfahan

IRAN

Rawalpindi

Lahore

AFGHANISTAN

PAKISTAN

Delhi

Karachi

Ahmadabad

Indore

Jamshedpur

Nagpur

Mumbai (Bombay)

INDIA

NEPAL

Kanpur

BHUTAN

BANGLADESH

Dhaka

Kolkata (Calcutta)

Chittagong

Kunming

Guangzhou

Hong Kong

MYANMAR

Mandalay

Hanoi

LAOS

VIETNAM

Da Nang

South China Sea

Manila

PHILIPPINES

Rangoon

THAILAND

Bangkok

CAMBODIA

Ho Chi Minh City

Chennai (Madras)

Bangalore

SRI LANKA

Arabian Sea

INDIAN OCEAN

Gulf of Oman

Kuala Lumpur

MALAYSIA

BRUNEI

Singapore

SINGAPORE

INDONESIA

Jakarta

Surabaya

EAST TIMOR

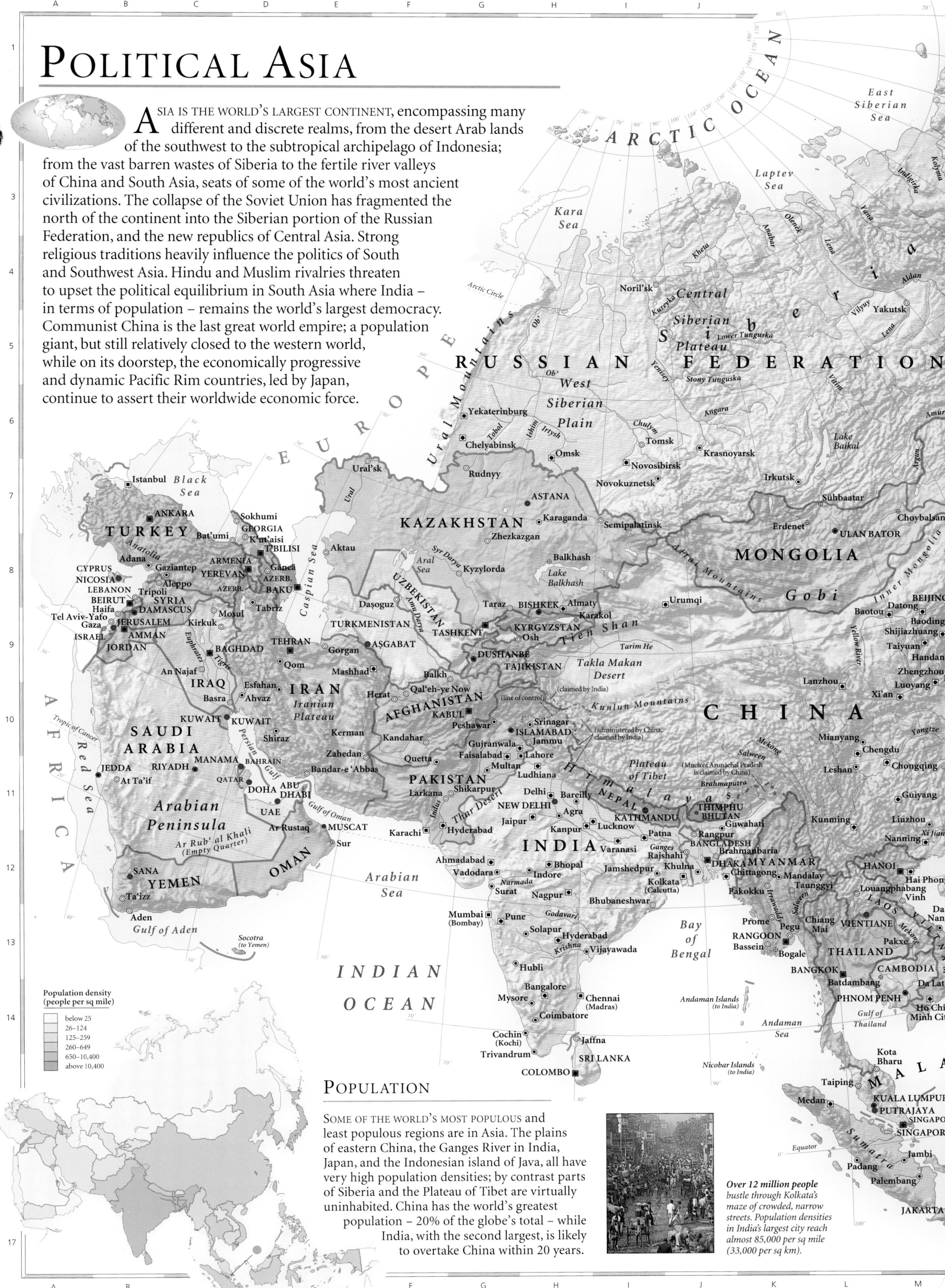

POLITICAL ASIA

ASIA IS THE WORLD'S LARGEST CONTINENT, encompassing many different and discrete realms, from the desert Arab lands of the southwest to the subtropical archipelago of Indonesia; from the vast barren wastes of Siberia to the fertile river valleys of China and South Asia, seats of some of the world's most ancient civilizations. The collapse of the Soviet Union has fragmented the north of the continent into the Siberian portion of the Russian Federation, and the new republics of Central Asia. Strong religious traditions heavily influence the politics of South and Southwest Asia. Hindu and Muslim rivalries threaten to upset the political equilibrium in South Asia where India – in terms of population – remains the world's largest democracy. Communist China is the last great world empire; a population giant, but still relatively closed to the western world, while on its doorstep, the economically progressive and dynamic Pacific Rim countries, led by Japan, continue to assert their worldwide economic force.

POPULATION

SOME OF THE WORLD'S MOST POPULOUS and least populous regions are in Asia. The plains of eastern China, the Ganges River in India, Japan, and the Indonesian island of Java, all have very high population densities; by contrast parts of Siberia and the Plateau of Tibet are virtually uninhabited. China has the world's greatest population – 20% of the globe's total – while India, with the second largest, is likely to overtake China within 20 years.

Over 12 million people bustle through Kolkata's maze of crowded, narrow streets. Population densities in India's largest city reach almost 85,000 per sq mile (33,000 per sq km).

Population density (people per sq mile)
- below 25
- 26–124
- 125–259
- 260–649
- 650–10,400
- above 10,400

PHYSICAL ASIA

T HE STRUCTURE OF ASIA can be divided into two distinct regions. The landscape of northern Asia consists of old mountain chains, shields, plateaus, and basins, like the Ural Mountains in the west and the Central Siberian Plateau to the east. To the south of this region, are a series of plateaux and basins, including the vast Plateau of Tibet and the Tarim Basin. In contrast, the landscapes of southern Asia are much younger, formed by tectonic activity beginning about 65 million years ago, leading to an almost continuous mountain chain running from Europe, across much of Asia, and culminating in the mighty Himalayan mountain belt, formed when the Indo-Australian Plate collided with the Eurasian Plate. They are still being uplifted today. North of the mountains lies a belt of deserts, including the Gobi and the Takla Makan. In the far south, tectonic activity has formed narrow island arcs, extending over 4,000 miles (7,000 km). To the west lies the Arabian Shield, once part of the African Plate. As it was rifted apart from Africa, the Arabian Plate collided with the Eurasian Plate, uplifting the Zagros Mountains.

SHAPING THE LANDSCAPE

IN THE NORTH, melting of extensive permafrost leads to typical periglacial features such as thermokarst. In the arid areas wind action transports sand creating extensive dune systems. An active tectonic margin in the south causes continued uplift, and volcanic and seismic activity, but also high rates of weathering and erosion. Across the continent, huge rivers erode and transport vast quantities of sediment depositing it on the plains or forming large deltas.

PERIGLACIATION

1 Permafrost is widespread across northern Siberia. When ground ice, which makes up a large proportion of the soil layer, melts, it contracts and extensive ground subsidence occurs. Over time this process leads to depressions in the landscape and the gradual movement of soil down slopes. Eventually the accumulation of water in the depressions leads to thermokarstic lakes (left).

PERIGLACIATION: FORMATION OF THERMOKARST

THE EVOLVING LANDSCAPE

Landscape
- limestone region
- sinking land
- stable land
- uplifting land
- ▲ active volcano
- • • • area of tectonic activity
- – – limit of permafrost
- → ocean current

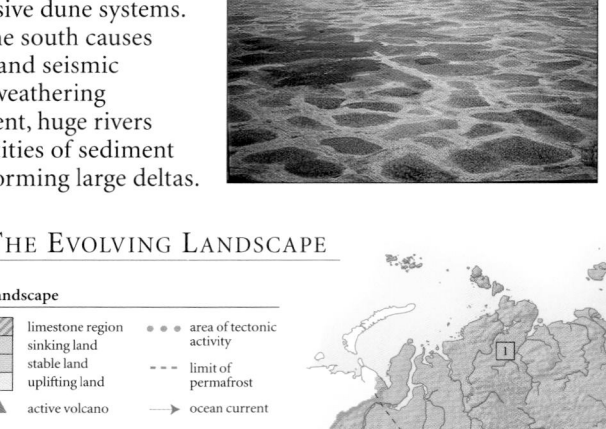

RIVER SYSTEMS

2 Vast river systems flow across Asia, many originating in the Himalayas and the Plateau of Tibet. Seasonal melting of snow and monsoon rains swell the river flow leading to flooding and erosion. The Yellow River (above) gets its color from the high level of eroded material from the loess plateau.

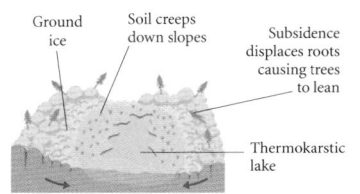

RIVER SYSTEMS: EROSION OF THE LOESS PLATEAU BY THE YELLOW RIVER

TECTONIC ACTIVITY

7 The Dead Sea (above) lies in a pull-apart basin. The sliding of the African Plate against the Arabian Plate, at unequal rates, led to the sinking of blocks of crust. This depression has been filled by the waters of the Dead Sea and Lake Tiberias (Sea of Galilee). The plates continue to move causing intermittent earthquakes.

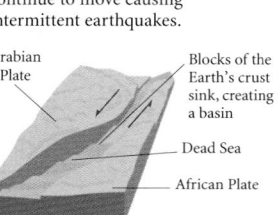

TECTONIC ACTIVITY: THE FORMATION OF A PULL-APART BASIN

CHEMICAL WEATHERING

3 Tower karsts are widespread across south China (above) and Vietnam. It is thought the karstic towers were formed under a soil cover, where small depressions in the limestone bedrock began to be weathered by soil water acids, eventually creating larger hollows. This process continued over millions of years, deepening the hollows and leaving steep-sided limestone hills.

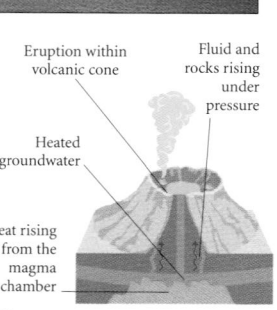

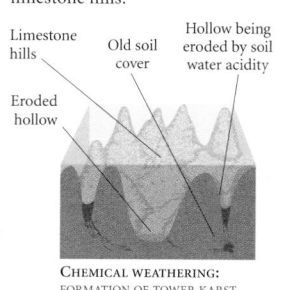

SEDIMENTATION

6 The Ganges/Brahmaputra is a tide-dominated delta (above). The two rivers transport huge quantities of mountain sediment, which is deposited on the delta plain. This debris is then redistributed by tidal currents, to form extensions to the bars, beach ridges, and deltaic deposits.

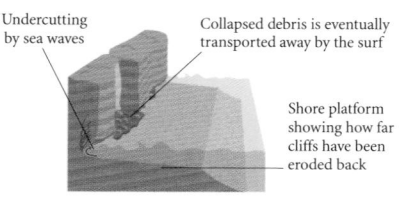

SEDIMENTATION: THE DESTRUCTION OF A DELTA

COASTAL EROSION

5 The erosion of cliffs along the coast of Indonesia (above) and Thailand occurs when waves and currents undermine the base leading to collapse of material. The surf then gradually erodes this material away, exposing the cliff to further undercutting. This process eventually creates shore platforms.

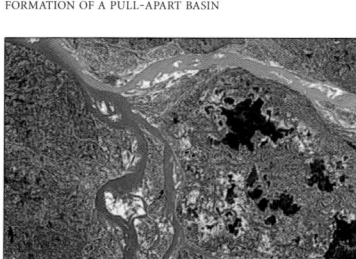
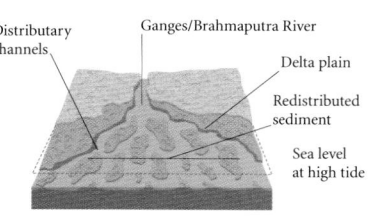

COASTAL EROSION: THE UNDERCUTTING OF A CLIFF

VOLCANIC ACTIVITY

4 Volcanic eruptions occur frequently across Southeast Asia's island arcs (above). Low-level eruptions occur when groundwater, superheated by underlying magma, becomes pressurized, forcing hot fluid and rocks up through cracks in the volcanic cone. This is known as a phreatic eruption.

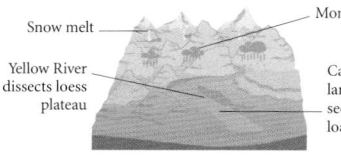
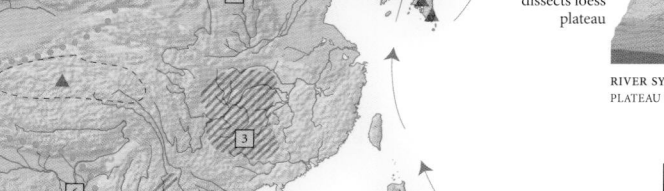

VOLCANIC ACTIVITY: A PHREATIC ERUPTION

CHEMICAL WEATHERING: FORMATION OF TOWER KARST

SIBERIAN PLATEAU AND PLAIN

THE WEST SIBERIAN PLAIN is one of the largest in the world, and contains a vast system of marshes. The whole area is covered by glacial deposits, underlain by the Angara Shield, a remnant of the ancient continent of Laurasia. The flat relief of the region and thick surface deposits result in poor drainage; this, combined with the freezing and thawing of the extensive permafrost layer leads to the formation of the vast swamps which cover the area. Many of the north-flowing rivers are also frozen for up to half the year.

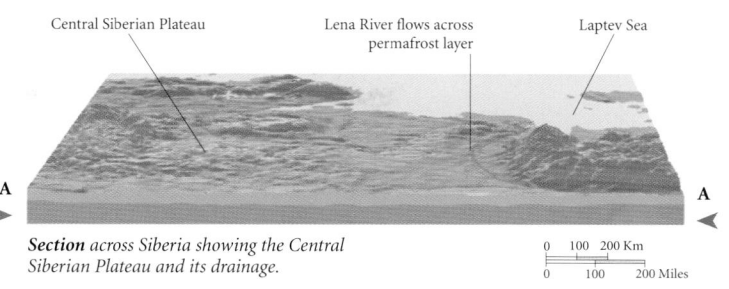

Section across Siberia showing the Central Siberian Plateau and its drainage.

THE ARABIAN SHIELD AND IRANIAN PLATEAU

APPROXIMATELY FIVE MILLION YEARS AGO, rifting of the continental crust split the Arabian Plate from the African Plate and flooded the Red Sea. As this rift spread, the Arabian Plate collided with the Eurasian Plate, transforming part of the Tethys seabed into the Zagros Mountains which run northwest-southeast across western Iran.

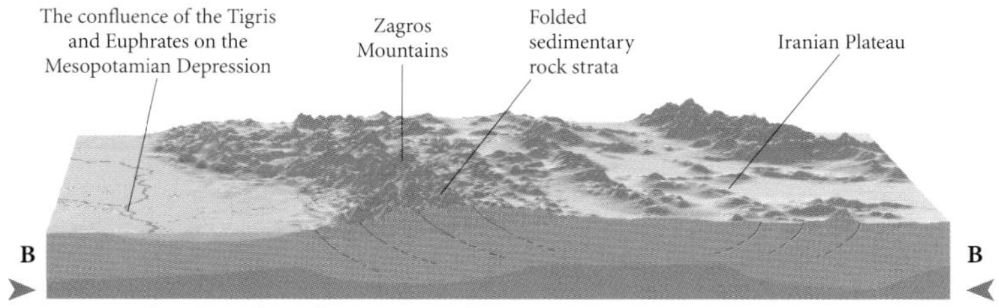

Cross-section through southwestern Asia, showing the Mesopotamian Depression, the folded Zagros Mountains, and the Iranian Plateau.

THE TURAN BASIN AND KAZAKH UPLANDS

THE TURAN BASIN AND KAZAKH UPLANDS are a complex mixture of mountain foothills, an arid limestone plateau, and deserts including the Kyzl Kum and Kara Kum. In the center of the Turan Lowland – an area of inland drainage – is the desiccated Aral Sea, reduced to a fraction of its former size because of the diversion of its flow into irrigation channels. The only rivers with sufficient water to cross this arid region are the Syr Dayra and Amu Dayra.

THE INDIAN SHIELD AND HIMALAYAN SYSTEM

THE LARGE SHIELD AREA beneath the Indian subcontinent is between 2.5 and 3.5 billion years old. As the floor of the southern Indian Ocean spread, it pushed the Indian Shield north. This was eventually driven beneath the Plateau of Tibet. This process closed up the ancient Tethys Sea and uplifted the world's highest mountain chain, the Himalayas. Much of the uplifted rock strata was from the seabed of the Tethys Sea, partly accounting for the weakness of the rocks and the high levels of erosion found in the Himalayas.

Cross-section through the Himalayas showing thrust faulting of the rock strata.

CENTRAL ASIAN PLATEAUS AND BASINS

THE PLATEAU OF TIBET lies north of the Himalayas and covers 965,250 sq miles (2,500,000 sq km); its average elevation is 16,500 ft (5,000 m). The region is noted for its extreme aridity. In the south, the Himalayan mountain belt blocks moisture-bearing winds. The pressure from the Indo-Australian Plate against the plateau is causing both uplift and, when combined with the downward force caused by weight of the plateau, extension east and west of the of the more malleable underlying crust. The brittle upper rock layers are extensively faulted.

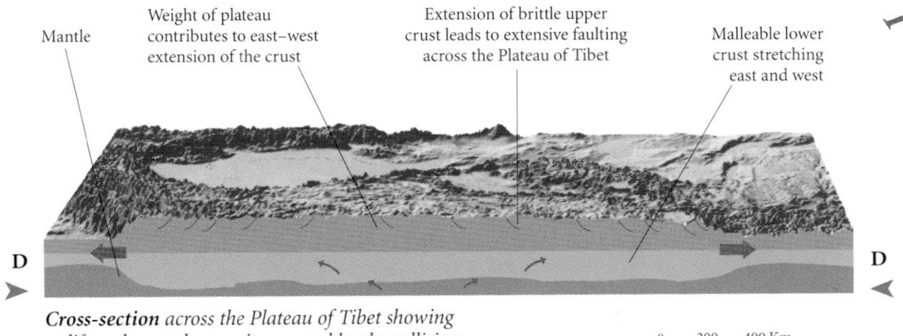

Cross-section across the Plateau of Tibet showing uplift and crustal extension caused by the collision of the Indo-Australian and Eurasian plates.

ENVIRONMENTAL ISSUES

THE TRANSFORMATION OF UZBEKISTAN by the former Soviet Union into the world's second largest producer of cotton led to the diversion of several major rivers for irrigation. Starved of this water, the Aral Sea diminished in volume by over 50% in 30 years, irreversibly altering the ecology of the area. Heavy industries in eastern China have polluted coastal waters, rivers, and urban air, while in Myanmar, Malaysia, and Indonesia, ancient hardwood rain forests are felled faster than they can regenerate.

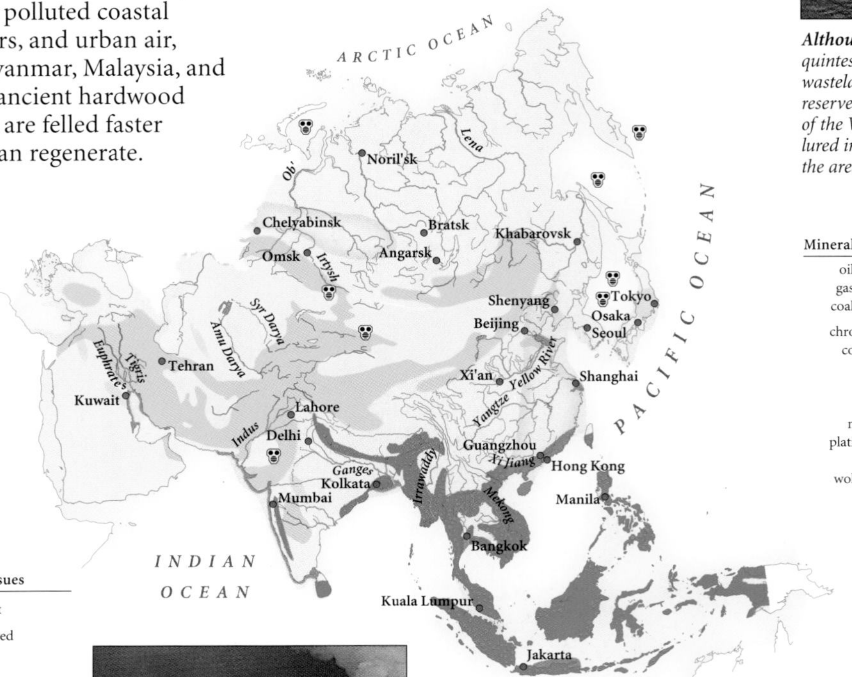

Although Siberia remains a quintessentially frozen, inhospitable wasteland, vast untapped mineral reserves – especially the oil and gas of the West Siberian Plain – have lured industrial development to the area since the 1950s and 1960s.

MINERAL RESOURCES

AT LEAST 60% OF THE WORLD'S known oil and gas deposits are found in Asia; notably the vast oil fields of the Persian Gulf, and the less-exploited oil and gas fields of the Ob' Basin in west Siberia. Immense coal reserves in Siberia and China have been utilized to support large steel industries. Southeast Asia has some of the world's largest deposits of tin, found in a belt running down the Malay Peninsula to Indonesia.

Environmental Issues

- tropical forest
- forest destroyed
- desert
- desertification
- acid rain
- polluted rivers
- marine pollution
- heavy marine pollution
- radioactive contamination
- poor urban air quality

Mineral Resources

- oil field
- gas field
- coal field
- chromite
- copper
- gold
- iron
- lead
- nickel
- platinum
- tin
- wolfram

The long-term environmental impact of the Gulf War (1991) is still uncertain. As Iraqi troops left Kuwait, equipment was abandoned to rust and thousands of oil wells were set alight, pouring crude oil into the Persian Gulf.

USING THE LAND AND SEA

VAST AREAS OF ASIA REMAIN UNCULTIVATED as a result of unsuitable climatic and soil conditions. In favorable areas such as river deltas, farming is intensive. Rice is the staple crop of most Asian countries, grown in paddy fields on waterlogged alluvial plains and terraced hillsides, and often irrigated for higher yields. Across the black earth region of the Eurasian steppe in southern Siberia and Kazakhstan, wheat farming is the dominant activity. Cash crops, like tea in Sri Lanka and dates in the Arabian Peninsula, are grown for export, and provide valuable income. The sovereignty of the rich fishing grounds in the South China Sea is disputed by China, Malaysia, Taiwan, the Philippines, and Vietnam, because of potential oil reserves.

Using the Land and Sea

- cropland
- desert
- forest
- mountain region
- pasture
- tundra
- wetland
- major conurbations

- cattle
- pigs
- goats
- sheep
- coconuts
- corn
- cotton
- dates
- fishing
- fruit
- jute
- peanuts
- rice
- rubber
- shellfish
- soybeans
- sugar beet
- sugar cane
- tea
- timber
- wheat

Date palms have been cultivated in oases throughout the Arabian Peninsula since antiquity. In addition to the fruit, palms are used for timber, fuel, rope, and for making vinegar, syrup, and a liquor known as arrack.

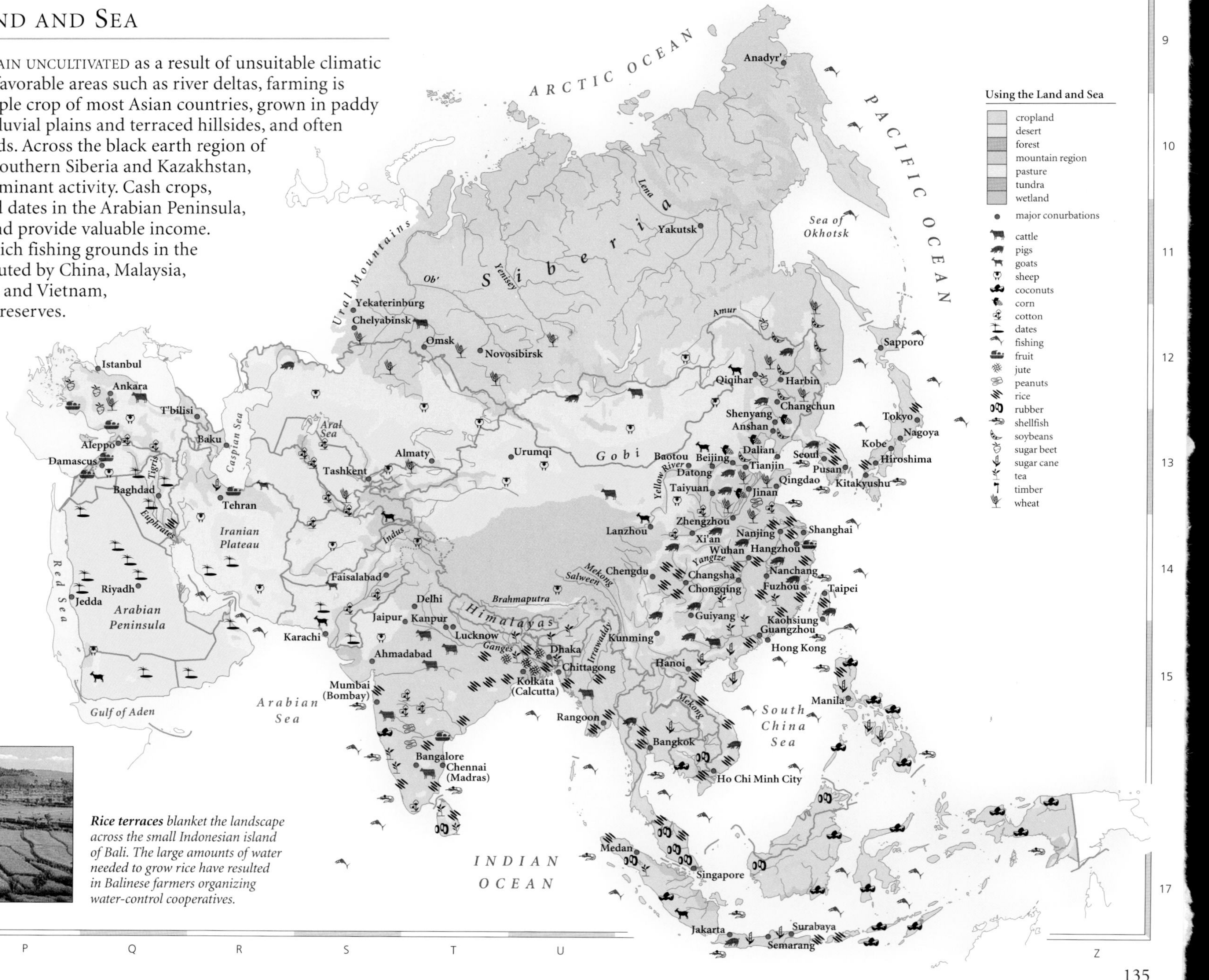

Rice terraces blanket the landscape across the small Indonesian island of Bali. The large amounts of water needed to grow rice have resulted in Balinese farmers organizing water-control cooperatives.

The Near East

Iraq, Israel, Jordan, Lebanon, Syria

Some of the world's oldest civilizations developed in this region – the Fertile Crescent – which is venerated by Jews, Muslims, and Christians, but torn by competing religious, ethnic, and national claims to the land. Turkish Ottoman rule ended with World War I and the region was divided into areas administered by Britain and France. The UN endorsed calls for a Jewish homeland in what was then Palestine and in 1948 the state of Israel was declared. Hostility toward the Jewish state led to a series of wars with its Arab neighbors. After 2000, attempts to broker peaceful resolutions with both the Palestinian population and with adjacent Arab states were hampered by a revival of Islamic militarism and conflicting international interests in the oil-rich region. This led to an Israeli retrenchment and culminated in a US-led invasion of Iraq in 2003, which toppled the Ba'athist regime of Saddam Hussein in the name of a "war on terror."

Using the Land and Sea

Water scarcity limits cropland to the north and to areas watered principally by the Tigris, Euphrates, and Jordan Rivers. In Israel, new irrigation techniques are allowing cultivation in the arid Negev. Wheat is the chief grain and large areas of scrub support livestock herding. Commercial produce includes dates, tobacco, citrus fruits, olives, grapes, and cotton, which is Syria's main export crop. Fishing is still important in the Mediterranean.

The Urban/Rural Population Divide

urban 70%   rural 30%

0 10 20 30 40 50 60 70 80 90 100

POPULATION DENSITY	TOTAL LAND AREA
163 people per sq mile	325,460 sq miles
(63 people per sq km)	(843,160 sq km)

Land use and agricultural distribution

- sheep
- cereals
- citrus fruits
- cotton
- dates
- fishing
- rice
- tobacco
- capital cities
- major towns
- pasture
- cropland
- wetland
- desert

Transportation & Industry

The petrochemical industry is well established, and central to the economies of Syria and Iraq, which was the world's second largest oil exporter before the war with Iran which began in 1980. Lebanon has traditionally been a center for commerce, while Israel has a well-diversified economy with an expanding tourist industry, despite few natural resources.

Transportation Network

	75,427 miles (121,461 km)	
	1,468 miles (2,364 km)	
	3,271 miles (5,267 km)	
	498 miles (802 km)	

Jordan's seaport of Al 'Aqabah is connected to Damascus in Syria by road and rail. This route to the Red Sea provides for large exports of phosphate and trade with states in The Persian Gulf.

Major industry and infrastructure

- car manufacture
- cement
- chemicals
- electronics
- finance
- food processing
- iron & steel
- oil
- oil refining
- textiles
- capital cities
- major towns
- international airports
- major roads
- major industrial areas

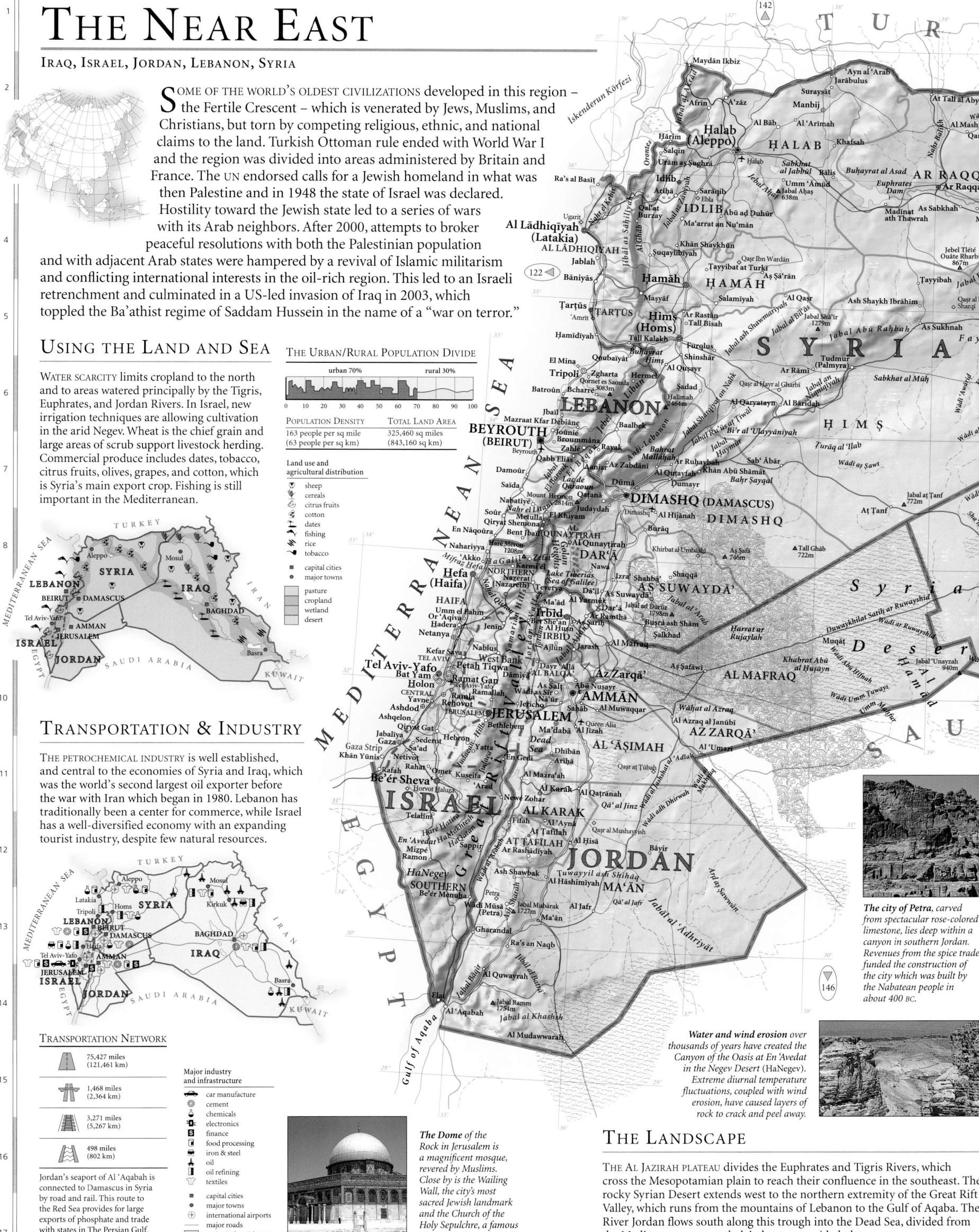

The Dome of the Rock in Jerusalem is a magnificent mosque, revered by Muslims. Close by is the Wailing Wall, the city's most sacred Jewish landmark and the Church of the Holy Sepulchre, a famous Christian place of worship.

The city of Petra, carved from spectacular rose-colored limestone, lies deep within a canyon in southern Jordan. Revenues from the spice trade funded the construction of the city which was built by the Nabatean people in about 400 BC.

Water and wind erosion over thousands of years have created the Canyon of the Oasis at En 'Avedat in the Negev Desert (HaNegev). Extreme diurnal temperature fluctuations, coupled with wind erosion, have caused layers of rock to crack and peel away.

The Landscape

The Al Jazirah plateau divides the Euphrates and Tigris Rivers, which cross the Mesopotamian plain to reach their confluence in the southeast. The rocky Syrian Desert extends west to the northern extremity of the Great Rift Valley, which runs from the mountains of Lebanon to the Gulf of Aqaba. The River Jordan flows south along this trough into the Dead Sea, divided from the Mediterranean coastal plain by a steep-sided plateau.

THE LANDSCAPE

THE DEEPLY ERODED HILLS and salty basins of the Anatolian Plateau are bordered by several mountain ranges along the Black Sea coast, and the limestone Taurus Mountains (*Toros Dağlari*) in the south. A lowland trough divides the Caucasus and the Lesser Caucasus, which form a formidable barrier of peaks in the north.

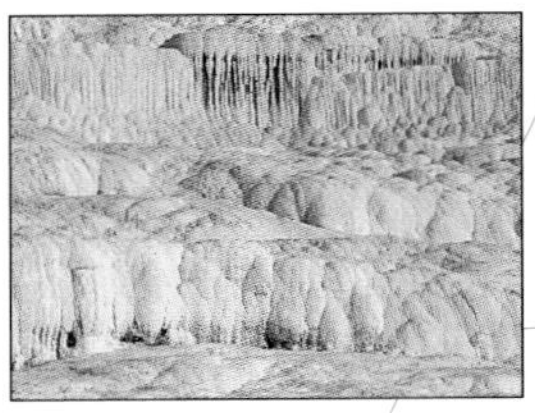

Limestone weathering in the Anatolian Plateau

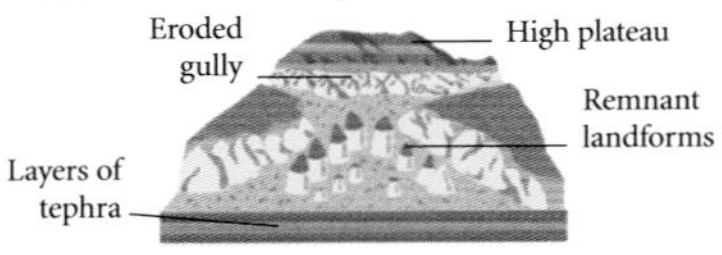

Eroded gully
High plateau
Remnant landforms
Layers of tephra

In central Turkey, rainwater has chemically weathered away numerous layers of limestone, leaving isolated outcrops and pinnacles and deep eroded gullies.

The Caucasus are fold mountains, which formed around the same time as the Taurus Mountains (*Toros Dağlari*) around 65 million years ago and have since been modified by volcanic erruptions.

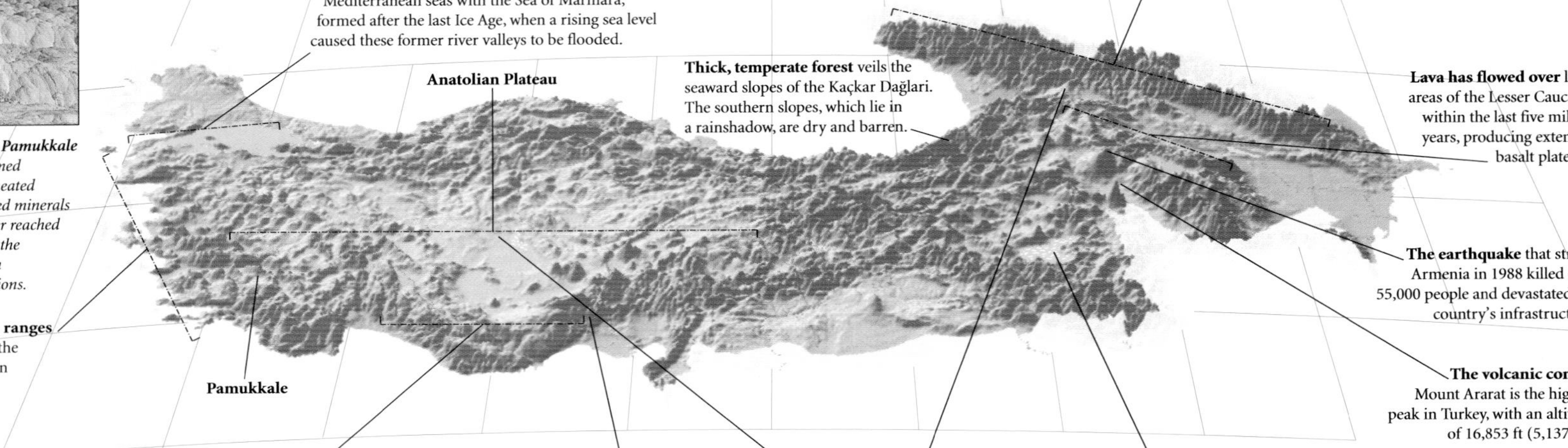

The white rock terraces at Pamukkale in western Turkey were formed when underground water, heated by volcanic activity, dissolved minerals in the rocks. When the water reached the surface and evaporated, the minerals were left behind in these extraordinary formations.

The straits of the Bosporus and the Dardanelles, respectively linking the Black and Mediterranean seas with the Sea of Marmara, formed after the last Ice Age, when a rising sea level caused these former river valleys to be flooded.

Anatolian Plateau

Thick, temperate forest veils the seaward slopes of the Kaçkar Dağlari. The southern slopes, which lie in a rainshadow, are dry and barren.

Lava has flowed over large areas of the Lesser Caucasus within the last five million years, producing extensive basalt plateaus.

Long, parallel mountain ranges run from east to west into the Aegean Sea, which has risen since the last Ice Age to form a drowned coastline of numerous islands and extended inlets.

Pamukkale

The earthquake that struck Armenia in 1988 killed over 55,000 people and devastated the country's infrastructure.

The volcanic cone of Mount Ararat is the highest peak in Turkey, with an altitude of 16,853 ft (5,137 m).

The folded peaks of the Taurus Mountains (*Toros Dağlari*) were formed 60–65 million years ago, at the same time as the Alps. The rock is mainly limestone, with deep caves, gorges, and underground rivers.

The Cilician Gates (*Gŕlek Boğazi*), a major pass through the Taurus Mountains (*Toros Dağlari*), is the point where streams flow from the interior plateau onto the lowland of Adana.

Many of the rivers crossing the Anatolian Plateau never reach the sea, but drain into salt marshes and shallow salt lakes such as Lake Tuz (*Tuz Gölü*), where much of the water is lost to evaporation.

The granite massif near Suram divides the lowlands of Georgia from the oil-rich basin of Azerbaijan's Kura River, which has built a large delta into the Caspian Sea.

The shallow, saline Lake Van (*Van Gölü*) is the largest lake in Turkey. Dry terraces mark a previous shoreline 181 ft (55 m) above the present water level.

Since the 6th century BC, the pinnacles and caves of east-central Anatolia have been utilized as dwellings. Many are still inhabited today.

MAP KEY

POPULATION

- ▪ above 5 million
- ◼ 1 million to 5 million
- ◉ 500,000 to 1 million
- ◎ 100,000 to 500,000
- ⊕ 50,000 to 100,000
- ⊙ 10,000 to 50,000
- ○ below 10,000

ELEVATION

- 4000m / 13,124ft
- 3000m / 9843ft
- 2000m / 6562ft
- 1000m / 3281ft
- 500m / 1640ft
- 250m / 820ft
- 100m / 328ft
- sea level

SCALE 1:4,000,000
(projection: Lambert Conformal Conic)

Km
0 10 20   40   60   80   100   120
Miles
0   10   20   40   60   80   100   120

The fisheries of Azerbaijan are noted for their hauls of sturgeon, and the Caspian Sea accounts for 80% of the world's total catch. Sturgeon roe is used to make internationally-famed caviar.

Traditional steam baths are found throughout the region, and are used for socializing as well as for bathing.

TURKEY & THE CAUCASUS

ARMENIA, AZERBAIJAN, GEORGIA, TURKEY

THIS REGION OCCUPIES THE FRAGMENTED JUNCTION between Europe, Asia, and the Russian Federation. Sunni Islam provides a common identity for the secular state of Turkey, which the revered leader Kemal Atatürk established from the remnants of the Ottoman Empire after the First World War. Turkey has a broad resource base and expanding trade links with Europe, but the east is relatively undeveloped and strife between the state and a large Kurdish minority has yet to be resolved. Georgia is similarly challenged by ethnic separatism, while the Christian state of Armenia and the mainly Muslim and oil-rich Azerbaijan are locked in conflict over the territory of Nagornyy Karabakh.

TRANSPORTATION & INDUSTRY

TURKEY LEADS THE REGION'S well-diversified economy. Petrochemicals, textiles, engineering, and food processing are the main industries. Azerbaijan is able to export oil, while the other states rely heavily on hydro-electric power and imported fuel. Georgia produces precision machinery. War and earthquake damage have devastated Armenia's infrastructure.

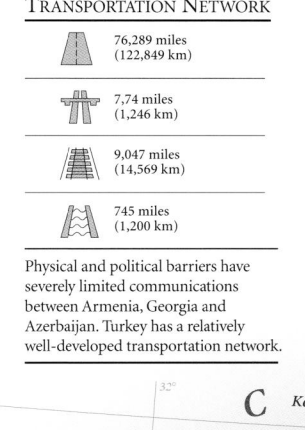

Azerbaijan has substantial oil reserves, located in and around the Caspian Sea. They were some of the earliest oilfields in the world to be exploited.

Major industry and infrastructure

- 🧵 carpet weaving
- ⚗ cement
- 🧪 chemicals
- coal
- ⚙ engineering
- food processing
- oil
- textiles
- tourism
- vehicle manufacture
- ■ capital cities
- ● major towns
- ⊕ international airports
- major roads
- major industrial areas

TRANSPORTATION NETWORK

76,289 miles (122,849 km)	
7,74 miles (1,246 km)	
9,047 miles (14,569 km)	
745 miles (1,200 km)	

Physical and political barriers have severely limited communications between Armenia, Georgia and Azerbaijan. Turkey has a relatively well-developed transportation network.

USING THE LAND AND SEA

TURKEY IS LARGELY SELF-SUFFICIENT in food. The irrigated Black Sea coastlands have the world's highest yields of hazelnuts. Tobacco, cotton, sultanas, tea, and figs are the region's main cash crops and a great range of fruit and vegetables are grown. Wine grapes are among the labor-intensive crops which allow full use of limited agricultural land in the Caucasus. Sturgeon fishing is particularly important in Azerbaijan.

Land use and agricultural distribution

- cattle
- goats
- cotton
- fishing
- fruit
- hazelnuts
- olives
- sugar beet
- tobacco
- vineyards
- ■ capital cities
- ● major towns
- pasture
- cropland
- forest

THE URBAN/RURAL POPULATION DIVIDE

urban 67%   rural 23%

0 10 20 30 40 50 60 70 80 90 100

POPULATION DENSITY	TOTAL LAND AREA
218 people per sq mile (84 people per sq km)	368,912 sq miles (955,730 sq km)

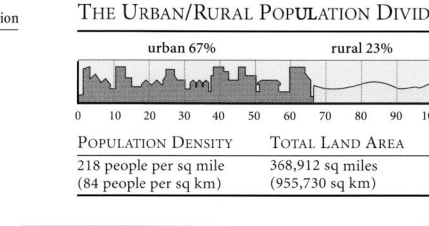

For many centuries, Istanbul has held tremendous strategic importance as a crucial gateway between Europe and Asia. Founded by the Greeks as Byzantium, the city became the center of the East Roman Empire and was known as Constantinople to the Romans. From the 15th century onward the city became the center of the great Ottoman Empire.

116 ▲

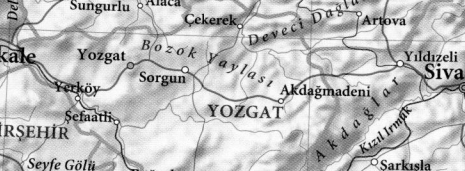

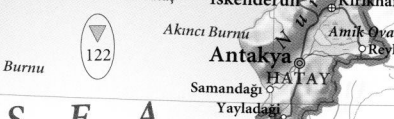

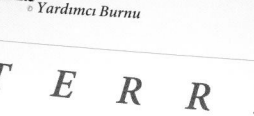

116 ◀

122 ▽

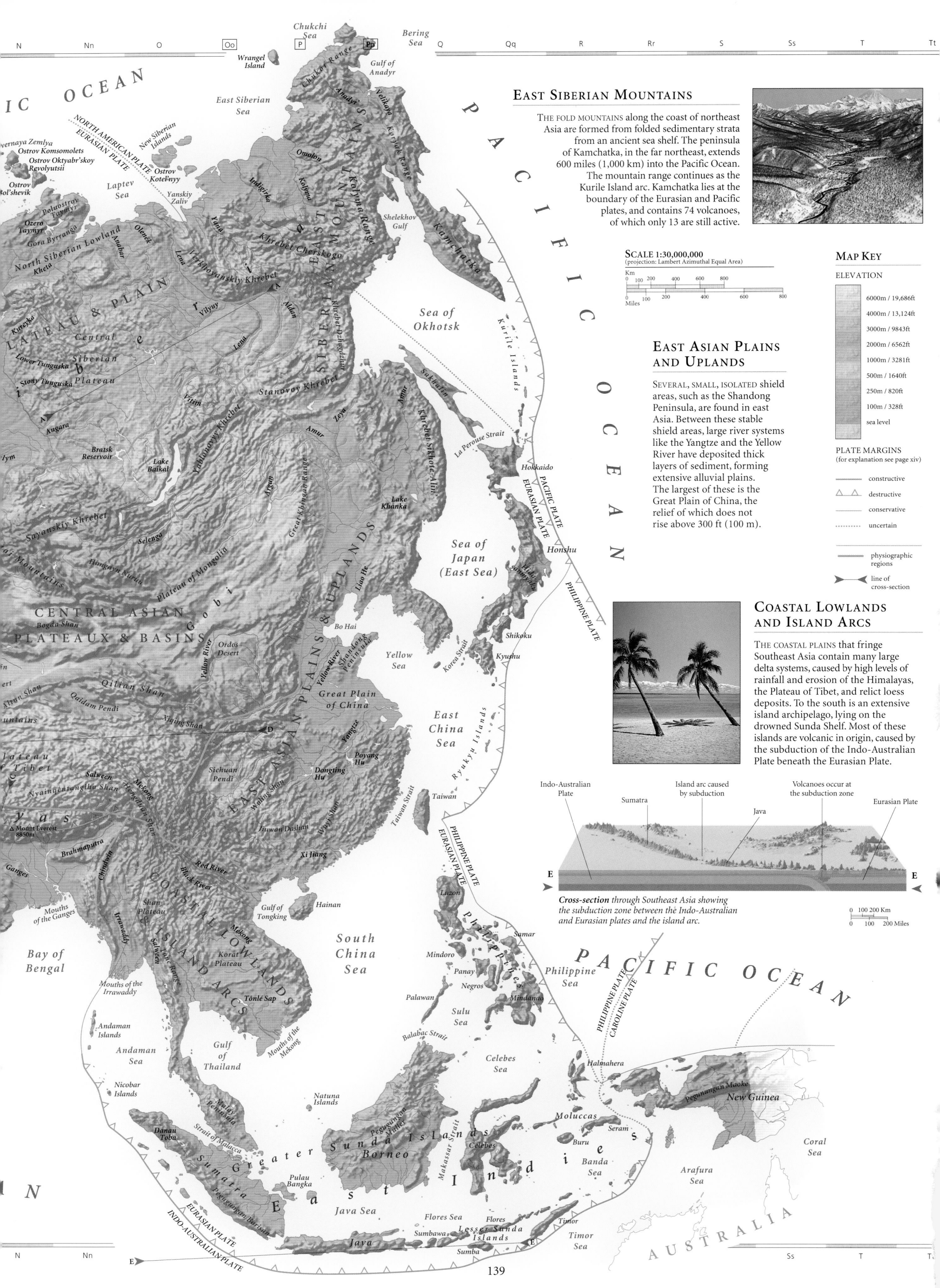

EAST SIBERIAN MOUNTAINS

THE FOLD MOUNTAINS along the coast of northeast Asia are formed from folded sedimentary strata from an ancient sea shelf. The peninsula of Kamchatka, in the far northeast, extends 600 miles (1,000 km) into the Pacific Ocean. The mountain range continues as the Kurile Island arc. Kamchatka lies at the boundary of the Eurasian and Pacific plates, and contains 74 volcanoes, of which only 13 are still active.

SCALE 1:30,000,000
(projection: Lambert Azimuthal Equal Area)

Km
0 100 200   400   600   800

Miles
0 100   200   400   600   800

MAP KEY

ELEVATION

6000m / 19,686ft
4000m / 13,124ft
3000m / 9843ft
2000m / 6562ft
1000m / 3281ft
500m / 1640ft
250m / 820ft
100m / 328ft
sea level

PLATE MARGINS
(for explanation see page xiv)

constructive
destructive
conservative
uncertain

physiographic regions
line of cross-section

EAST ASIAN PLAINS AND UPLANDS

SEVERAL, SMALL, ISOLATED shield areas, such as the Shandong Peninsula, are found in east Asia. Between these stable shield areas, large river systems like the Yangtze and the Yellow River have deposited thick layers of sediment, forming extensive alluvial plains. The largest of these is the Great Plain of China, the relief of which does not rise above 300 ft (100 m).

COASTAL LOWLANDS AND ISLAND ARCS

THE COASTAL PLAINS that fringe Southeast Asia contain many large delta systems, caused by high levels of rainfall and erosion of the Himalayas, the Plateau of Tibet, and relict loess deposits. To the south is an extensive island archipelago, lying on the drowned Sunda Shelf. Most of these islands are volcanic in origin, caused by the subduction of the Indo-Australian Plate beneath the Eurasian Plate.

Indo-Australian Plate   Island arc caused by subduction   Volcanoes occur at the subduction zone

Sumatra   Java   Eurasian Plate

E   E

Cross-section through Southeast Asia showing the subduction zone between the Indo-Australian and Eurasian plates and the island arc.

0 100 200 Km
0 100   200 Miles

CLIMATE

THE CLIMATE OF ASIA exhibits marked differences from region to region, with freezing polar conditions in the north, hot and cold deserts in central regions and subtropical conditions throughout the south. Much of this variation can be attributed to enormous mountain barriers and internal depressions found across the continent. Monsoon winds, which reverse semiannually, cause alternate wet and dry seasons across southern Asia. These air masses moving north from the ocean are stripped of their moisture over the Himalayas causing arid conditions across the Plateau of Tibet. Both the south and east are susceptible to tropical cyclones or typhoons.

Treeless, frozen plains, with permanently frozen soil layers characterize much of Siberia. Even during the summer only the top 2–3 ft (1 m) of soil thaws.

Tundra-like marshes are found alongside vast sand dunes in the Takla Makan Desert in China. In the spring, windstorms of hurricane-force can send dust as high as 13,000 ft (4,000 m) in the air.

The Gobi Desert experiences major extremes in climate, with winter temperatures sometimes falling below -40°C (-40°F) and summer temperatures exceeding 45°C (113°F).

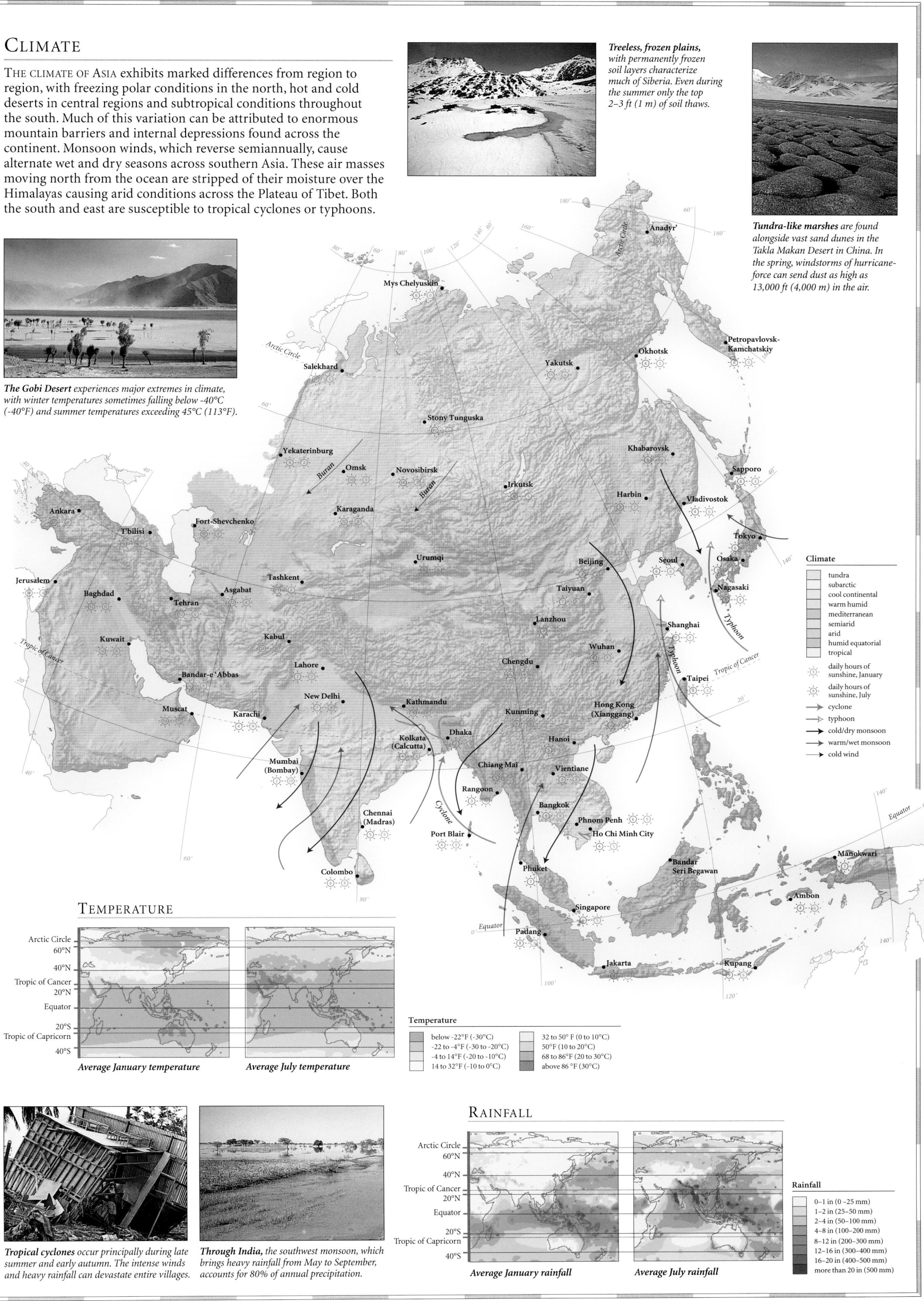

Climate

	tundra
	subarctic
	cool continental
	warm humid
	mediterranean
	semiarid
	arid
	humid equatorial
	tropical

☀ daily hours of sunshine, January
☀ daily hours of sunshine, July
→ cyclone
→ typhoon
→ cold/dry monsoon
→ warm/wet monsoon
→ cold wind

TEMPERATURE

Average January temperature

Average July temperature

Temperature

below -22°F (-30°C)	32 to 50° F (0 to 10°C)
-22 to -4°F (-30 to -20°C)	50°F (10 to 20°C)
-4 to 14°F (-20 to -10°C)	68 to 86°F (20 to 30°C)
14 to 32°F (-10 to 0°C)	above 86 °F (30°C)

RAINFALL

Average January rainfall

Average July rainfall

Rainfall

	0–1 in (0 –25 mm)
	1–2 in (25–50 mm)
	2–4 in (50–100 mm)
	4–8 in (100–200 mm)
	8–12 in (200–300 mm)
	12–16 in (300–400 mm)
	16–20 in (400–500 mm)
	more than 20 in (500 mm)

Tropical cyclones occur principally during late summer and early autumn. The intense winds and heavy rainfall can devastate entire villages.

Through India, the southwest monsoon, which brings heavy rainfall from May to September, accounts for 80% of annual precipitation.

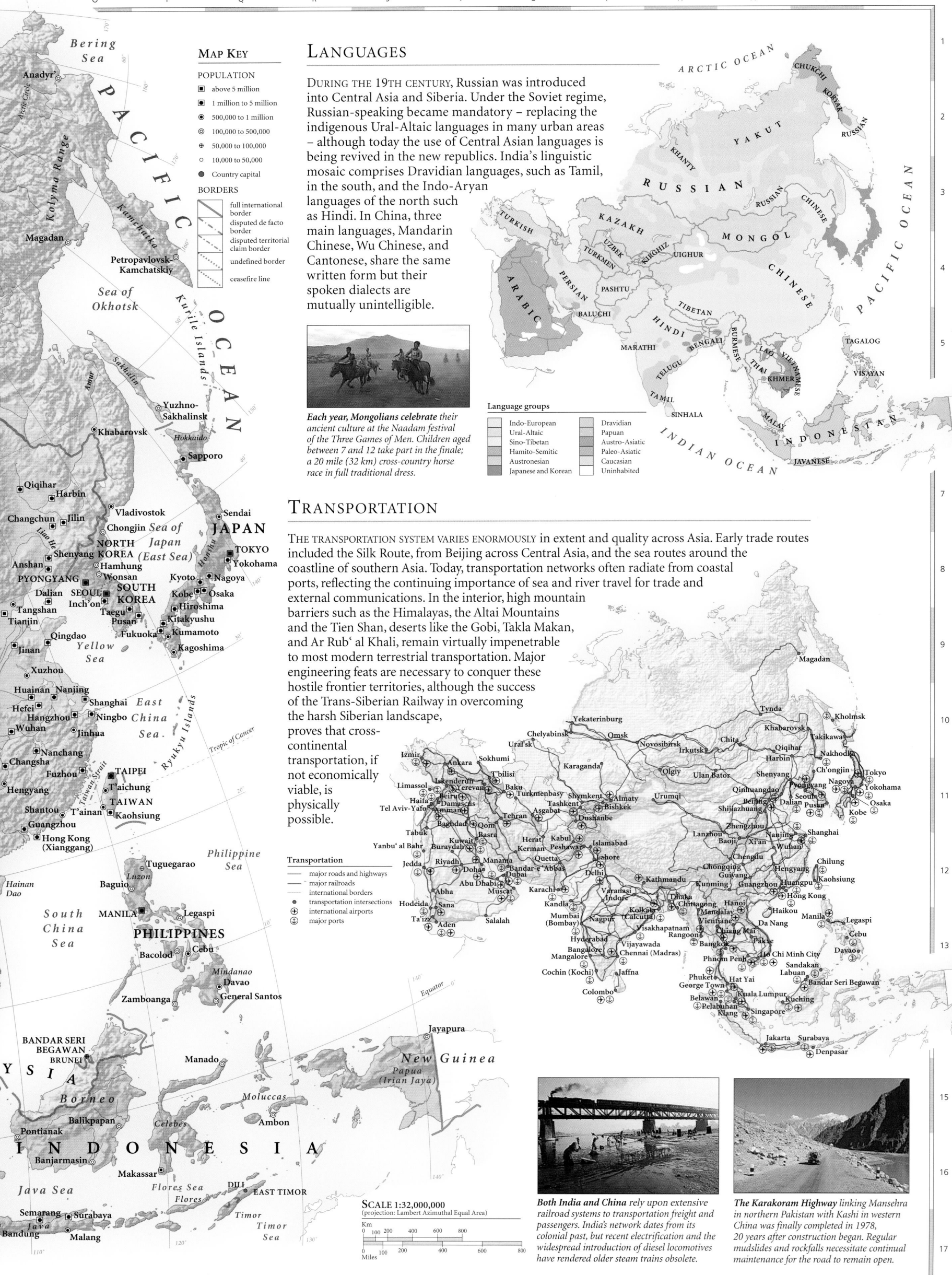

MAP KEY

POPULATION
- ◼ above 5 million
- ◼ 1 million to 5 million
- ◉ 500,000 to 1 million
- ◎ 100,000 to 500,000
- ⊕ 50,000 to 100,000
- ○ 10,000 to 50,000
- ● Country capital

BORDERS
- full international border
- disputed de facto border
- disputed territorial claim border
- undefined border
- ceasefire line

LANGUAGES

DURING THE 19TH CENTURY, Russian was introduced into Central Asia and Siberia. Under the Soviet regime, Russian-speaking became mandatory – replacing the indigenous Ural-Altaic languages in many urban areas – although today the use of Central Asian languages is being revived in the new republics. India's linguistic mosaic comprises Dravidian languages, such as Tamil, in the south, and the Indo-Aryan languages of the north such as Hindi. In China, three main languages, Mandarin Chinese, Wu Chinese, and Cantonese, share the same written form but their spoken dialects are mutually unintelligible.

Each year, Mongolians celebrate their ancient culture at the Naadam festival of the Three Games of Men. Children aged between 7 and 12 take part in the finale; a 20 mile (32 km) cross-country horse race in full traditional dress.

Language groups
- Indo-European
- Ural-Altaic
- Sino-Tibetan
- Hamito-Semitic
- Austronesian
- Japanese and Korean
- Dravidian
- Papuan
- Austro-Asiatic
- Paleo-Asiatic
- Caucasian
- Uninhabited

TRANSPORTATION

THE TRANSPORTATION SYSTEM VARIES ENORMOUSLY in extent and quality across Asia. Early trade routes included the Silk Route, from Beijing across Central Asia, and the sea routes around the coastline of southern Asia. Today, transportation networks often radiate from coastal ports, reflecting the continuing importance of sea and river travel for trade and external communications. In the interior, high mountain barriers such as the Himalayas, the Altai Mountains and the Tien Shan, deserts like the Gobi, Takla Makan, and Ar Rub' al Khali, remain virtually impenetrable to most modern terrestrial transportation. Major engineering feats are necessary to conquer these hostile frontier territories, although the success of the Trans-Siberian Railway in overcoming the harsh Siberian landscape, proves that cross-continental transportation, if not economically viable, is physically possible.

Transportation
- major roads and highways
- major railroads
- international borders
- ● transportation intersections
- ⊕ international airports
- ⊕ major ports

Both India and China rely upon extensive railroad systems to transportation freight and passengers. India's network dates from its colonial past, but recent electrification and the widespread introduction of diesel locomotives have rendered older steam trains obsolete.

The Karakoram Highway linking Mansehra in northern Pakistan with Kashi in western China was finally completed in 1978, 20 years after construction began. Regular mudslides and rockfalls necessitate continual maintenance of the road to remain open.

SCALE 1:32,000,000
(projection: Lambert Azimuthal Equal Area)

Km
0 100 200 400 600 800

Miles
0 100 200 400 600 800

141

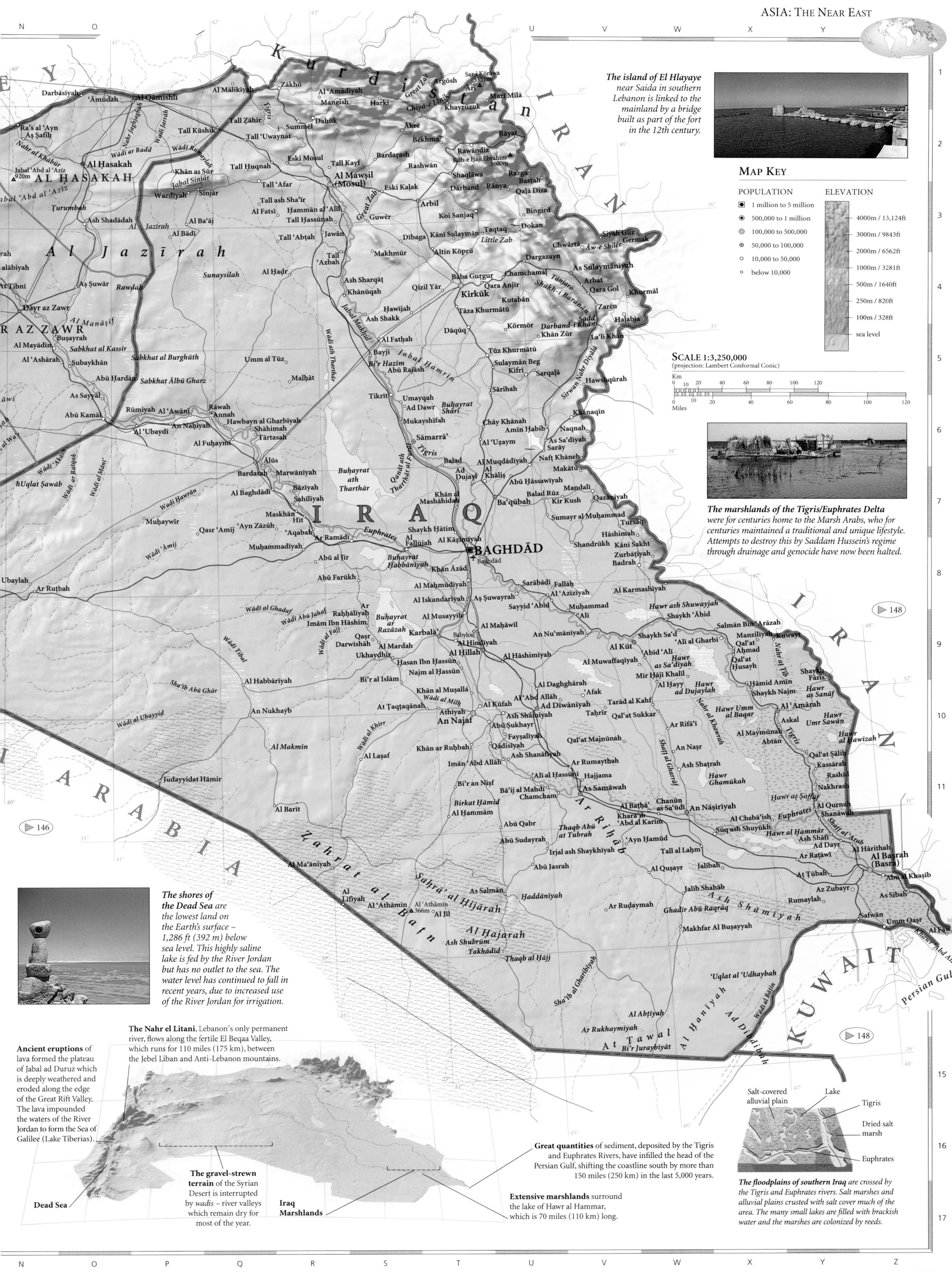

The island of El Hlayaye near Saida in southern Lebanon is linked to the mainland by a bridge built as part of the fort in the 12th century.

MAP KEY

POPULATION

⬛	1 million to 5 million
◉	500,000 to 1 million
◉	100,000 to 500,000
⊕	50,000 to 100,000
○	10,000 to 50,000
○	below 10,000

ELEVATION

	4000m / 13,124ft
	3000m / 9843ft
	2000m / 6562ft
	1000m / 3281ft
	500m / 1640ft
	250m / 820ft
	100m / 328ft
	sea level

SCALE 1:3,250,000
(projection: Lambert Conformal Conic)

Km 0 10 20 40 60 80 100 120

Miles 0 10 20 40 60 80 100 120

The marshlands of the Tigris/Euphrates Delta were for centuries home to the Marsh Arabs, who for centuries maintained a traditional and unique lifestyle. Attempts to destroy this by Saddam Hussein's regime through drainage and genocide have now been halted.

▶ 148

▶ 146

▶ 148

The shores of the Dead Sea are the lowest land on the Earth's surface – 1,286 ft (392 m) below sea level. This highly saline lake is fed by the River Jordan but has no outlet to the sea. The water level has continued to fall in recent years, due to increased use of the River Jordan for irrigation.

Ancient eruptions of lava formed the plateau of Jabal ad Duruz which is deeply weathered and eroded along the edge of the Great Rift Valley. The lava impounded the waters of the River Jordan to form the Sea of Galilee (Lake Tiberias).

The Nahr el Litani, Lebanon's only permanent river, flows along the fertile El Beqaa Valley, which runs for 110 miles (175 km), between the Jebel Liban and Anti-Lebanon mountains.

Dead Sea

The gravel-strewn terrain of the Syrian Desert is interrupted by wadis – river valleys which remain dry for most of the year.

Iraq Marshlands

Great quantities of sediment, deposited by the Tigris and Euphrates Rivers, have infilled the head of the Persian Gulf, shifting the coastline south by more than 150 miles (250 km) in the last 5,000 years.

Extensive marshlands surround the lake of Hawr al Hammar, which is 70 miles (110 km) long.

Salt-covered alluvial plain — Lake — Tigris — Dried salt marsh — Euphrates

The floodplains of southern Iraq are crossed by the Tigris and Euphrates rivers. Salt marshes and alluvial plains crusted with salt cover much of the area. The many small lakes are filled with brackish water and the marshes are colonized by reeds.

THE ARABIAN PENINSULA

BAHRAIN, KUWAIT, OMAN, QATAR, SAUDI ARABIA, UNITED ARAB EMIRATES (UAE), YEMEN

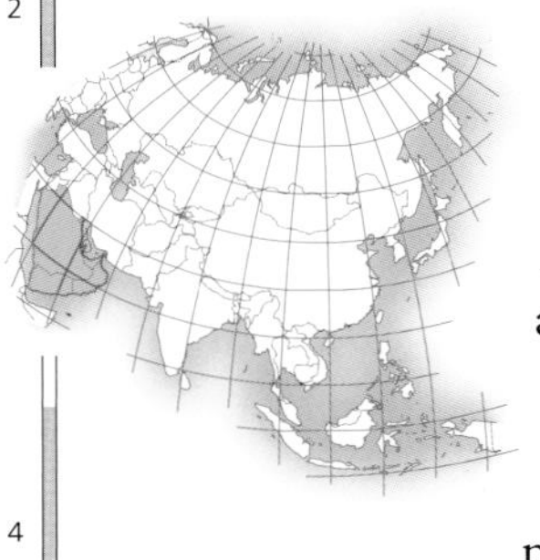

HUGE EXPANSES OF DESERT cover much of the Arabian Peninsula, limiting settlement to oases, the mountains along the Red Sea and coastal belts. The most populous area is the fertile highlands of Yemen. The Islamic faith and Arabic language give the region a cultural and religious unity, and the Saudi city of Mecca (Makkah) is Islam's most holy place, visited by over two million pilgrims each year. More than half the world's oil reserves are contained in this region, and the exploitation of oil and gas has brought great wealth, particularly to Saudi Arabia. Yemen and Oman are the least developed of the Arabian states, with large rural populations. Within Saudi Arabia over two-thirds of the people live in urban areas.

USING THE LAND

MOST OF THE ARABIAN PENINSULA is unsuited to settled agriculture, making irrigation and land reclamation projects essential. The narrow coastal plain and isolated oases, commonly amounting to less than 1% of the land area, are used to cultivate grains, coffee, and exotic fruits. Goats, sheep, and camels are widespread throughout the region.

THE URBAN/RURAL POPULATION DIVIDE

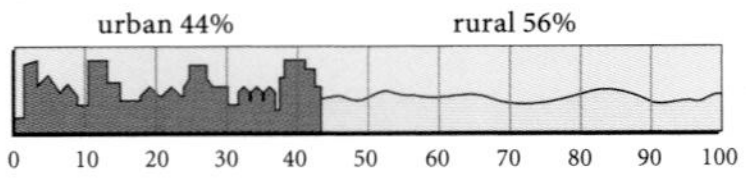

urban 44%   rural 56%

0 10 20 30 40 50 60 70 80 90 100

POPULATION DENSITY	TOTAL LAND AREA
37 people per sq mile (14 people per sq km)	1,147,856 sq miles (2,973,720 sq km)

Land use and agricultural distribution

- goats
- sheep
- cereals
- coffee
- dates
- fruit
- capital cities
- major towns
- pasture
- cropland
- desert

The fertile soils of Yemen have encouraged settlement of almost all of the land from sea level up to the mountains at 10,000 ft (3,050 m). In the higher reaches elaborate terraces have been constructed to facilitate crop cultivation.

THE LANDSCAPE

A PLATEAU MORE THAN 2,500 ft (760 m) high extends across much of the Arabian Peninsula. The plateau slopes eastward from the massive, rifted escarpment along the coast of the Red Sea, to the shallow waters of the Persian Gulf. The interior is characterized by *cuestas* and valleys, drained by a system of *wadis*. A crescent of sand and gravel deserts lies to the east.

The An Nafud Desert is covered with *barchan* dunes varying between 30–100 ft (10–30 m) high. The "horns" of the crescent-shaped dunes reflect the direction in which they are being moved by the wind.

Inselbergs are dotted over a wide area of the Najd Plateau. These resistant remnants of the ancient basement rock are left standing when the softer weathered rock has been worn away.

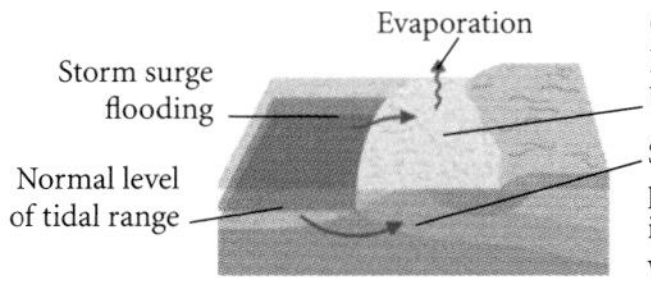

Evaporation
Storm surge flooding
Normal level of tidal range
Crusted layer left behind
Salt wedge penetrates inland water

A sabkha is a flat, salt-encrusted plain which occurs near the coast just above the high water mark. Flooding by sea water leads to saturation of the land with saline-rich groundwater. As this evaporates, a cracked layer of sand, cemented together with salt, gypsum, and calcium carbonate is left behind.

Few areas in the Arabian Peninsula have rivers flowing through them. Most are drained by ephemeral watercourses called *wadis*.

The Hejaz (Al Ḥijāz) and Asir Mountains form part of the same geological region as the highlands of Sudan and Eritrea, to which they were once joined. They were separated when faulting opened the Red Sea, over 50 million years ago.

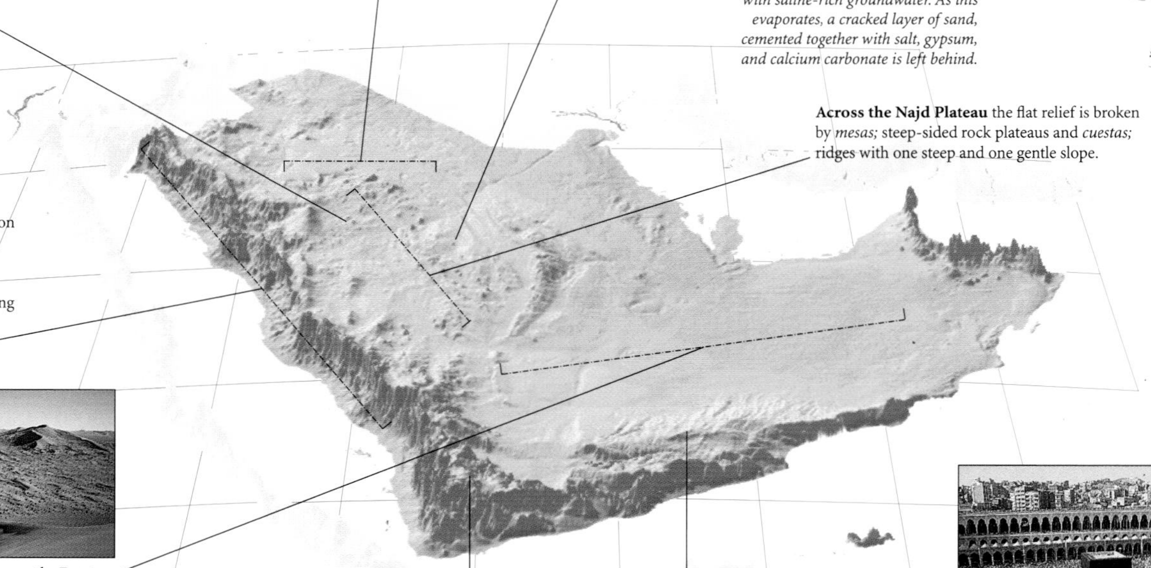

Across the Najd Plateau the flat relief is broken by *mesas*; steep-sided rock plateaus and *cuestas*; ridges with one steep and one gentle slope.

Ar Rub' al Khali, also known as the Empty Quarter, is the most arid part of the Arabian Peninsula. It is the largest uninterrupted sand desert in the world. Ridges of sand up to 25 miles (40 km) long, run northeast–southwest, giving characteristic linear dunes.

The Jabal an Nabi Shu'ayb in Yemen is the highest point on the peninsula, rising to 12,336 ft (3,760 m).

The Arabian Shield underpins the west of the peninsula. It is a fragment of the ancient continent, Gondwanaland, which was separated by rifting millions of years ago.

Every Muslim must make at least one pilgrimage or hajj to Mecca (Makkah), in Saudi Arabia, during their lifetime. The cloth-covered shrine is called the Ka'bah, and is regarded by Muslims as the most sacred place on Earth.

TRANSPORTATION & INDUSTRY

THE EXTRACTION AND REFINING OF OIL AND GAS are the major industrial activities in the Arabian Peninsula. The region also has an active construction sector, with many Arab cities reflecting the wealth generated by the oil industry. The service sector is dominated by financial and technical institutions, which, like the construction sector, mainly serve the oil industry. Traditional handicrafts such as carpet-weaving are found in rural areas.

Saudi Arabia contains the world's largest oil reserves, lying mainly along the Persian Gulf coast. Each day the region produces 8.3 million barrels of oil. Here, in the desert, excess oil is being burnt off.

TRANSPORTATION NETWORK

🛣	65,239 miles (105,054 km)	🛤	2,071 miles (3,333 km)
🚂	864 miles (1,392 km)		none

Internal surface transportation is poorly developed across the peninsula. Along the coast, commercial routes have developed, but connections between bordering states rely on major airports.

Major industry and infrastructure

- ⚙ cement
- 🧪 chemicals
- ⚒ iron & steel
- ⛽ oil
- 🏭 oil refining
- 🍴 food processing
- ■ capital cities
- ● major towns
- ✈ international airports
- — major roads
- ▨ major industrial areas

MAP KEY

POPULATION

- ■ 1 million to 5 million
- ◉ 500,000 to 1 million
- ◎ 100,000 to 500,000
- ⊕ 50,000 to 100,000
- ○ 10,000 to 50,000
- ∘ below 10,000

ELEVATION

- 3000m / 9843ft
- 2000m / 6562ft
- 1000m / 3281ft
- 500m / 1640ft
- 250m / 820ft
- 100m / 328ft
- sea level

Seasonal watercourses or wadis drain much of the interior of the Arabian Peninsula. Although they remain dry for much of the year, they are prone to flash floods after heavy rains.

SCALE 1:7,500,000
(projection: Lambert Conformal Conic)

A B C D E F G H M

IRAN & THE GULF STATES

BAHRAIN, IRAN, KUWAIT, QATAR, UNITED ARAB EMIRATES (UAE)

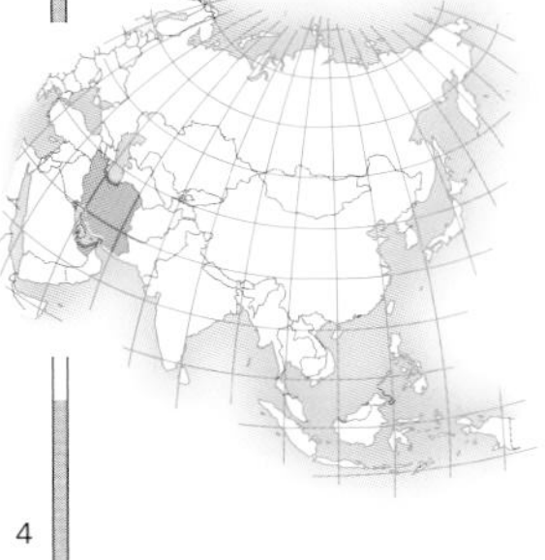

THE DISCOVERY OF OIL in the Persian Gulf in the 1930s brought great wealth to the surrounding states. The revenue was largely used to modernize industry and infrastructure, initiating great social change in these formerly agrarian countries. Today, over 80% of the people in the Gulf states live in urban areas, and foreign nationals make up a sizeable proportion of the population in Kuwait, Qatar, and the United Arab Emirates. The importance of control of the oil reserves has led to a number of territorial disputes, including most recently the Iran–Iraq War (1980-88) and the First Gulf War (1991). Islam is practiced almost exclusively throughout the region and two distinct strands are found; Sunni Muslims in Qatar, Kuwait, and UAE, and Shi'a Muslims in Iran and Bahrain. In 1979 Iran became the world's largest theocracy.

THE LANDSCAPE

THE LAND RISES STEEPLY from the fragmented coastal lowlands bordering the Persian Gulf, to reach Iran's interior plateau, bounded by heavily-eroded mountain chains. An unstable plate boundary runs northwest to southeast across Iran causing frequent earthquakes. On the sandy west coast of the Persian Gulf, the relief is generally flat, with patches of salt marsh. Bahrain consists of two groups of islands, which are mostly small and rocky.

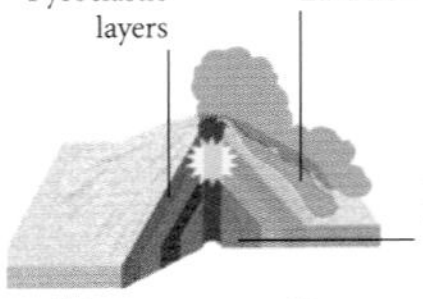

Pyroclastic layers
Lava flow
Lava flow layers

Qolleh-ye Damavand in the Elburz Mountains is a composite volcano. It comprises layers of lava and pyroclasts fragmentary rocks which accumulate on the slopes of the volcano after being ejected into the air.

Marine sediments from deep beneath the ancient Tethys Sea have been uplifted to form the Elburz Mountains, which stretch along the shores of the Caspian Sea, northern Iran.

Lava and ash from previous volcanic activity covers a 200-mile (320-km) stretch from the border with Azerbaijan to the Caspian Sea.

Iran's two mountain chains, the Zagros and Elburz, were uplifted at the same time as the Alps in Europe, when the African Plate collided with the Eurasian Plate.

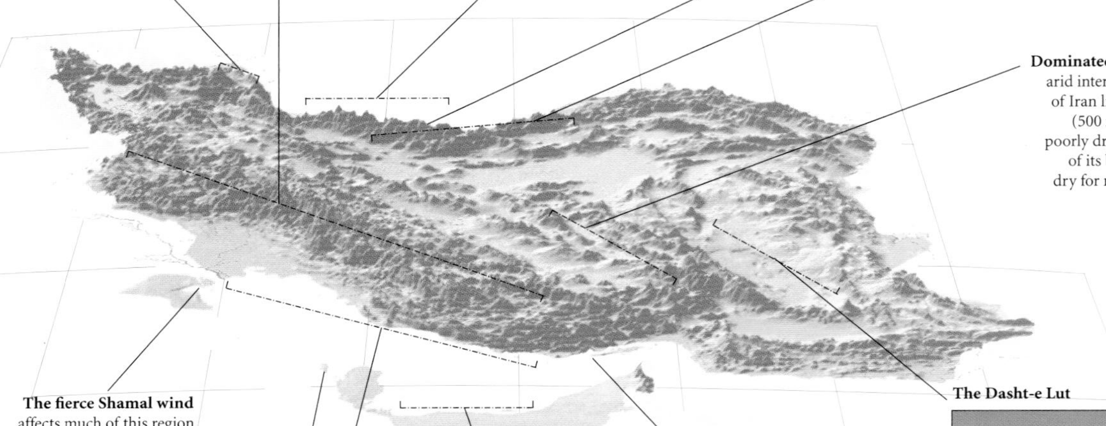

Caspian Sea

Qolleh-ye Damavand

Dominated by a vast, semi-arid interior plateau, most of Iran lies above 1,640 ft (500 m). The region is poorly drained with many of its basins remaining dry for months at a time.

The fierce Shamal wind affects much of this region. Every summer it blows dust south from the flood plains of the Tigris and Euphrates, reducing visibility to such an extent that Kuwait International Airport is frequently forced to close.

The oilfields of The Gulf are formed from marine shale deposits lying in sedimentary basins at the margins of the Zagros Mountains.

Autumn winds blowing across The Gulf can reach speeds of up to 95 mph (150 kmph) causing severe storms, squalls, and waterspouts.

The Dasht-e Lut

Prolific springs tapping artesian water make cultivation possible across the north of Bahrain's main island. This provides a sharp contrast to the sandy plains in the south and west.

Numerous islands lie along the southern coast of the Persian Gulf. Some of these are salt domes, created when less dense salts were displaced and forced up to the surface by denser, overlying strata.

The Dasht-e Lut covers a large portion of eastern Iran with its dry, wind-eroded plain of scattered sandstone pillars and salty depressions. During the summer, temperatures soar, making it one of the world's hottest, driest places.

USING THE LAND AND SEA

ALONG THE COAST of the Caspian Sea, desalinated water allows fruits and vegetables to be produced, although water shortages and desert soils still limit farming. Sheep are the most important livestock raised in Iran and commercial forests cover the northwest of the country. Shrimp stocks were decimated by pollution during the Gulf War, but fishing remains important for domestic and export markets.

All of the Gulf states have commercial fishing fleets. Before the discovery of oil, fishing was the region's leading industry.

The Kuwait Towers in the centre of Kuwait are symbols of the vast wealth oil has brought to the country. Before 1960, the city had only one main street and was surrounded by a mud wall.

Land use and agricultural distribution

- goats
- sheep
- cereals
- citrus fruits
- cotton
- dates
- fishing
- timber

- capital cities
- major towns

pasture
cropland
forest
desert
wetland

THE URBAN/RURAL POPULATION DIVIDE

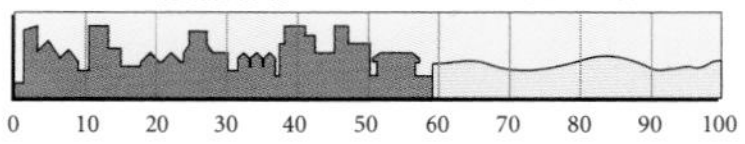

urban 59%   rural 41%

0 10 20 30 40 50 60 70 80 90 100

POPULATION DENSITY
118 people per sq mile
(46 people per sq km)

TOTAL LAND AREA
642,883 sq miles
(1,665,500 sq km)

Many volcanoes lie in Iran's 1,200 mile (1930 km) volcanic belt, including the country's highest peak, the now-extinct Qolleh-ye Damavand at 18,600 ft (5,671 m).

Extensive oil and gas exploitation in the Gulf region has allowed the economic transformation of the Gulf states. Kuwait and the United Arab Emirates today have the highest per capita incomes in the world.

TRANSPORTATION & INDUSTRY

BOTH ONSHORE AND OFFSHORE oil reserves are exploited throughout the region. Kuwait not only extracts but also refines 80% of its oil. Bahrain has diversified its economy to become the main commercial and financial center in the Persian Gulf. Iran produces a wide range of products: textile mills are widespread and carpet weaving is an important export industry.

Major industry and infrastructure

carpet manufacture	capital city
chemicals	major towns
finance	international airports
food processing	major roads
oil	major industrial areas
oil refining	
textiles	

TRANSPORTATION NETWORK

50,340 miles (81,063 km)		466 miles (750 km)	
3723 miles (5995 km)		81 miles (130 km)	

Major towns and neighboring countries are linked by adequate road networks, although rural areas are less well served. Bahrain is linked to the mainland by a 15 mile (25 km) long causeway.

MAP KEY

POPULATION	ELEVATION
above 5 million	4000m / 13,124ft
1 million to 5 million	3000m / 9843ft
500,000 to 1 million	2000m / 6562ft
100,000 to 500,000	1000m / 3281ft
50,000 to 100,000	500m / 1640ft
10,000 to 50,000	250m / 820ft
below 10,000	100m / 328ft
	sea level

SCALE 1:5,500,000
(projection: Lambert Conformal Conic)

Km
0 10 20 40 60 80 100 120 140 160 180 200
Miles
0 10 20 40 60 80 100 120 140 160 180 200

Tropic of Cancer

KAZAKHSTAN

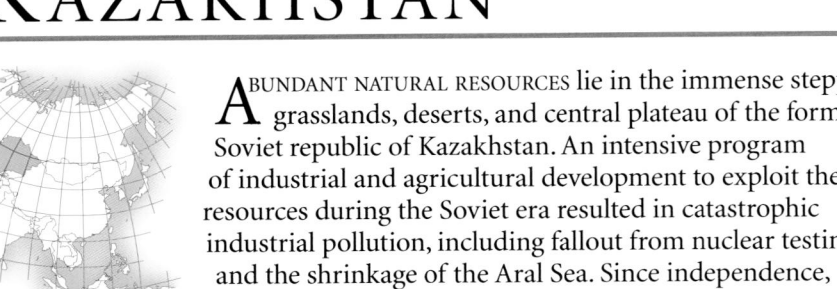

ABUNDANT NATURAL RESOURCES lie in the immense steppe grasslands, deserts, and central plateau of the former Soviet republic of Kazakhstan. An intensive program of industrial and agricultural development to exploit these resources during the Soviet era resulted in catastrophic industrial pollution, including fallout from nuclear testing and the shrinkage of the Aral Sea. Since independence, the government has encouraged foreign investment and liberalized the economy to promote growth. The adoption of Kazakh as the national language is intended to encourage a new sense of national identity in a state where living conditions for the majority remain harsh, both in cramped urban centers and impoverished rural areas.

TRANSPORTATION & INDUSTRY

THE SINGLE MOST IMPORTANT INDUSTRY in Kazakhstan is mining, based around extensive oil deposits near the Caspian Sea, the world's largest chromium mine, and vast reserves of iron ore. Recent foreign investment has helped to develop industries including food processing and steel manufacture, and to expand the exploitation of mineral resources. The Russian space program is still based at Baykonur, near Zhezkazgan in central Kazakhstan.

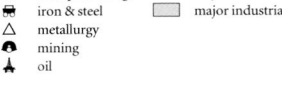

Major industry and infrastructure

- chemicals
- engineering
- fish processing
- food processing
- iron & steel
- metallurgy
- mining
- oil
- capital cities
- major towns
- international airports
- major roads
- major industrial areas

TRANSPORTATION NETWORK

87,561 miles (141,000 km)	
none	
8,483 miles (13,660 km)	
none	

Industrial areas in the north and east are well-connected to Russia. Air and rail links with Germany and China have been established through foreign investment. Better access to Baltic ports is being sought.

An open-cast coal mine in Kazakhstan. Foreign investment is being actively sought by the Kazakh government in order to fully exploit the potential of the country's rich mineral reserves.

MAP KEY

POPULATION
- 1 million to 5 million
- 500,000 to 1 million
- 100,000 to 500,000
- 50,000 to 100,000
- 10,000 to 50,000
- below 10,000

ELEVATION
- 4000m / 13,124ft
- 3000m / 9843ft
- 2000m / 6562ft
- 1000m / 3281ft
- 500m / 1640ft
- 250m / 820ft
- 100m / 328ft
- sea level

USING THE LAND AND SEA

THE REARING OF LARGE HERDS of sheep and goats on the steppe grasslands forms the core of Kazakh agriculture. Arable cultivation and cotton-growing in pasture and desert areas was encouraged during the Soviet era, but relative yields are low. The heavy use of fertilizers and the diversion of natural water sources for irrigation has degraded much of the land.

THE URBAN/RURAL POPULATION DIVIDE

urban 60%   rural 40%

POPULATION DENSITY	TOTAL LAND AREA
16 people per sq mile (6 people per sq km)	1,048,878 sq miles (2,717,300 sq km)

Land use and agricultural distribution
- cattle
- goats
- sheep
- cotton
- fishing
- wheat
- capital cities
- major towns
- pasture
- cropland
- forest
- mountain region
- desert

The nomadic peoples who moved their herds around the steppe grasslands are now largely settled, although echoes of their traditional lifestyle, in particular their superb riding skills, remain.

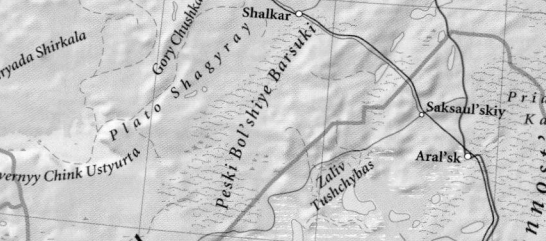

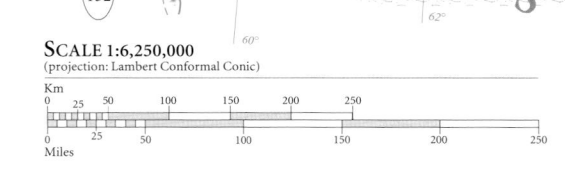

SCALE 1:6,250,000
(projection: Lambert Conformal Conic)

THE LANDSCAPE

STRETCHING MORE THAN 1,250 MILES (2,000 km) from the Caspian Sea in the west to China in the east, more than 40% of Kazakhstan is covered by steppe grasslands which give way to barren desert in the south. The land rises eastward towards the mineral-rich central plateau, to form the Altai Mountains.

1960	1996	2010

Since 1960, the Aral Sea has shrunk by 40%, become extremely saline, and lost all but five of its once-abundant fish species. Factors in this ecological disaster include the excessive use of fertilizers, defoliants and the diversion of its main source rivers for the irrigation of desert lands.

The Caspian Sea is the largest body of inland water in the world.

The desert of Peski Bol'shiye Barsuki is mainly sandy, displaying a number of classic dune formations. Groundwater supports a small amount of vegetation.

A large number of salt lakes fill depressions in the rolling uplands of central Kazakhstan.

The Altai Mountains lie on Kazakhstan's eastern borders with China and the Russian Federation. Cold and largely barren, they are the source of many of the rivers which flow across the steppe.

Altai Mountains

Tien Shan

Aral Sea

Khrebet Kanchingiz

Its waters taken for industry and irrigation, the Syr Darya, one of Kazakhstan's major rivers, now barely reaches the Aral Sea which it used to fill. Like many Kazakh rivers it has been heavily polluted with chemicals and its flow has been restricted by up to 60%.

The waters of Lake Balkhash (*Ozero Balkhash*), unlike those of the Aral Sea, are still able to support a fishing industry.

The central Kazakh Uplands (*Kazakhskiy Melkosopochnik*) contain much of the country's mineral riches. The landscape is largely flat with occasional rocky outcrops and hillocks.

Immense stretches of steppe grasslands characterize much of the Kazak landscape. These lowland areas have been used for arable cultivation in recent years, although problems with irrigation have meant that much of the land is being allowed to revert to its natural vegetation and pastoral usage.

Rows of pine trees edge this valley near Almaty. The snow-covered slopes in the background are used for skiing.

CENTRAL ASIA

KYRGYZSTAN, TAJIKISTAN, TURKMENISTAN, UZBEKISTAN

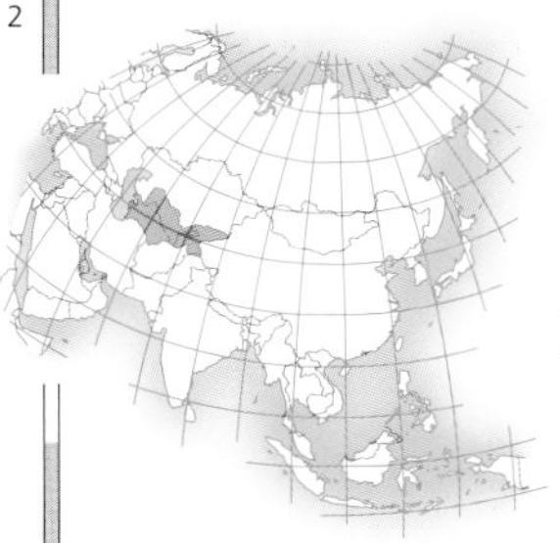

THE FOUR REPUBLICS that declared independence in 1991 were created in the early years of the Soviet Union, promoting ethnic divisions in a region whose common focus, since the 8th century, has been Islam. Traditional rural, nomadic ways of life have survived the Soviet era, while the benefits of modern industry and grand irrigation schemes have resulted in severe pollution in the delicate, arid environment of the steppe, particularly in Uzbekistan. Many ethnic minority groups are scattered among the four republics, with isolated communities in the mountains of Kyrgyzstan. The current Islamic revival has brought hope of greater regional unity, in spite of religious factionalism which, in 1992, plunged Tajikistan into civil war.

The southern shoreline of the Aral Sea has retreated over 30 miles (48 km) since 1960. A major cause is the diversion of water from the Amu Darya River for irrigation via the Kara Kum Canal (Garagum Kanaly).

The desert of the Kara Kum (Garagum) occupies over 70% of Turkmenistan; its wind-scoured surface of dune ridges and depressions severely limits human settlement.

MAP KEY

POPULATION

- ◉ 1 million to 5 million
- ◎ 500,000 to 1 million
- ⊚ 100,000 to 500,000
- ⊕ 50,000 to 100,000
- ○ 10,000 to 50,000
- ○ below 10,000

ELEVATION

6000m / 19,686ft
4000m / 13,124ft
3000m / 9843ft
2000m / 6562ft
1000m / 3281ft
500m / 1640ft
250m / 820ft
100m / 328ft
sea level

TRANSPORTATION & INDUSTRY

FOSSIL FUELS ARE extracted and processed in all four states, with scope for further exploitation. Agriculture provides raw materials for many industries, including food and textiles processing, and the manufacture of leather goods, clothing, and carpets. Farm machinery is also produced.

TRANSPORTATION NETWORK

🛣	85,574 miles (137,800 km)	🛤	None
🚂	4,184 miles (6,738 km)	⚓	1,180 miles (1,900 km)

The Kara Kum Canal (Garagum Kanaly) runs for 870 miles (1,400 km) from the Amu Darya River to the Caspian Sea. The canal is principally used for irrigation but is navigable for 280 miles (450 km).

Major industry and infrastructure

- ⌇ carpet weaving
- ⚗ chemicals
- ⚙ engineering
- 🗇 food processing
- ⬦ oil & gas
- ⊤ textiles
- ■ capital cities
- ● major towns
- ⊕ international airports
- ▬ major roads
- ▨ major industrial areas

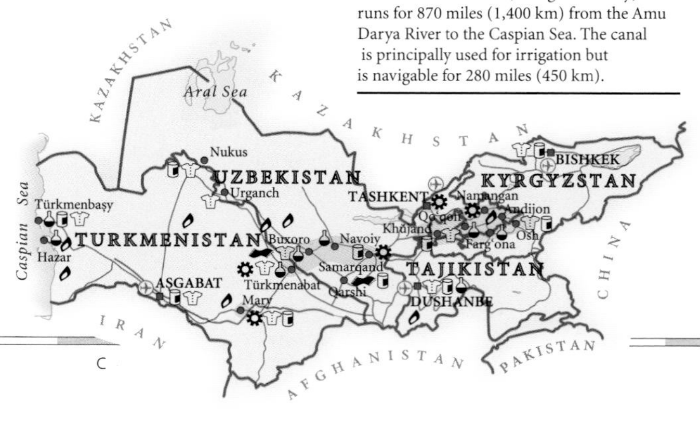

152

THE LANDSCAPE

THE GREAT TIEN SHAN and Pamir Ranges meet in a succession of high mountain chains. These mountains encircle the fertile Fergana Valley and reach west into the desert of the Kyzyl Kum, dividing the Syr Darya and Amu Darya Rivers. Sandy steppeland extends to the shores of the Caspian Sea, with the desert of the Kara Kum (Garagum) in the south. The Amu Darya drains into the Aral Sea in the north.

Salt marshes fill many of the depressions in the Ustyurt Plateau, a barren, rocky tableland about 650 ft (200 m) above sea level.

Some of the world's largest deposits of marine salts are found in Garabogaz Aylagy. This shallow, saline gulf has an average depth of only 33 ft (10 m), and a very high evaporation rate, producing the salty deposits.

The Kara Kum (Garagum) is one of the world's largest expanses of sand. Wind action has created a terrain of shifting, crescent-shaped sand dunes known as barchans.

The Amu Darya is the only river in Central Asia with a sufficient volume of water to cross the desert of the Kara Kum (Garagum) from the Pamirs to the Aral Sea, where it forms a delta largely vegetated by scrub grasses.

A series of major rock faults has created the Fergana Valley, a deep depression surrounded by high mountains. Water from the Syr Darya River and from underground sources supports intensive agriculture, despite minimal rainfall.

In the heavily-fractured and faulted mountain region, earthquakes are common, caused by the sudden release of tension along active fault lines.

Mount Communism (Qullai Kommunizm), in the northern Pamirs, was so named for being the highest point in the former Soviet Union, rising to 24,590 ft (7,495 m).

Shock waves travel through ground — Epicentre — Fault

Kyzyl Kum

Earthquake zone

Syr Darya

Naryn River

Qarokŭl

Bare mountains provide a stark background to the croplands along the Naryn River in Kyrgyzstan. Irrigation is essential for cultivation in this dry region.

Ozero Issyk-Kul' lies at an altitude of 5,193 ft (1,584 m). The lake remains ice-free throughout the year, due to the slight salinity of the water.

Tien Shan

The Tien Shan extend from China in the east, reaching heights over 24,400 ft (7,439 m) and branching into many parallel ranges in the west.

Nestling high in the Pamir range, and fed by glacial meltwater, Qarokŭl is the largest of the lakes in this region.

SCALE 1:4,250,000
(projection: Lambert Conformal Conic)

USING THE LAND

CROPLAND OUTSIDE Kyrgyzstan is restricted to irrigated areas such as the Fergana Valley. Central Asia is a leading global producer of cotton, and traditional silk-farming remains widespread. A wide range of fruits, vegetables, and grains are grown and livestock raised includes horses, goats, and karakul sheep.

Land use and agricultural distribution
- cattle
- goats
- sheep
- cereals
- cotton
- fruit
- capital cities
- major towns
- pasture
- cropland
- mountain region
- desert
- wetland

Plentiful sunshine, rich soils and massive irrigation schemes have made Uzbekistan the world's third largest cotton producer, although water shortages now prevent any further expansion of irrigated land.

THE URBAN/RURAL POPULATION DIVIDE

urban 40% | rural 60%

0 10 20 30 40 50 60 70 80 90 100

POPULATION DENSITY
79 people per sq mile
(31 people per sq km)

TOTAL LAND AREA
492,961 sq miles
(1,277,100 sq km)

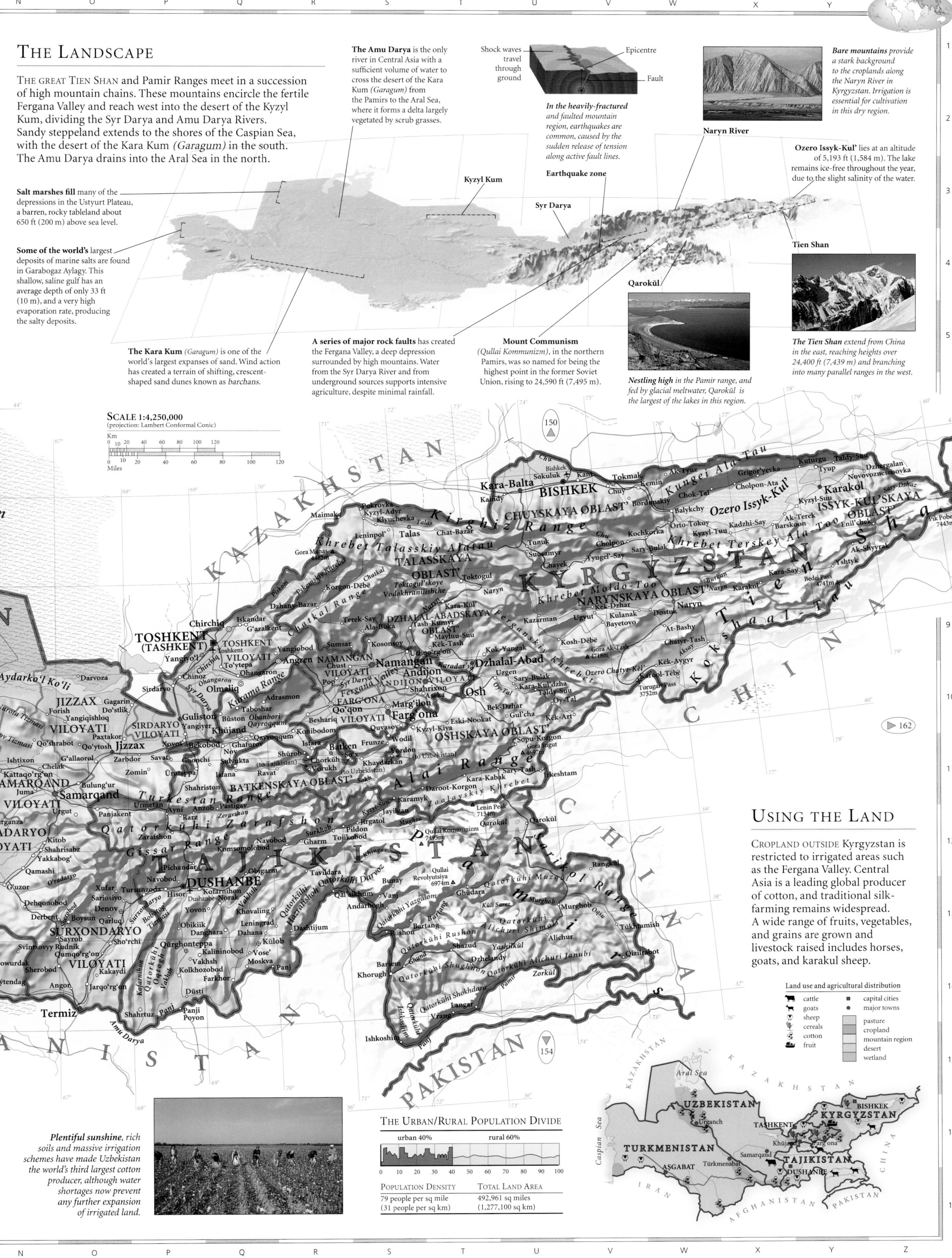

AFGHANISTAN & PAKISTAN

PAKISTAN WAS CREATED by the partition of British India in 1947, becoming the western arm of a new Islamic state for Indian Muslims; the eastern sector, in Bengal, seceded to become the separate country of Bangladesh in 1971. Over half of Pakistan's 154 million people live in the Punjab, at the fertile head of the great Indus Basin. The river sustains a national economy based on irrigated agriculture, including cotton for the vital textiles industry. Afghanistan, a mountainous, landlocked country, with an ancient and independent culture, has been wracked by war since 1979. Factional strife escalated into an international conflict in late 2001, as US-led troops ousted the miltant and fundamentally Islamist *taliban* regime as part of their "war on terror."

The town of Bamian lies high in the Hindu Kush west of Kabul. Between the 2nd and 5th centuries two huge statues of Buddha were carved into the nearby rock, the largest of which stood 125ft (38m) high. The statues were destroyed by the taliban regime in March 2001.

TRANSPORTATION & INDUSTRY

PAKISTAN IS HIGHLY dependent on the cotton textiles industry, although diversified manufacture is expanding around cities such as Karachi and Lahore. Afghanistan's limited industry is based mainly on the processing of agricultural raw materials and includes traditional crafts such as carpet weaving.

Major industry and infrastructure

	carpet weaving	■	capital cities
	chemicals	■	major towns
	engineering	⊕	international airports
	finance		major roads
	food processing		major industrial areas
	iron & steel		
	oil & gas		
	textiles		

TRANSPORTATION NETWORK

141,340 miles (227,600 km)	
211 miles (340 km)	
4,852 miles (7,814 km)	
745 miles (1,200 km)	

The Karakoram Highway was completed after 20 years of construction in 1978. It breaches the Himalayan mountain barrier providing a commercial motor route linking lowland Pakistan and China.

The Karakoram Highway is one of the highest major roads in the world. It took over 24,000 workers almost 20 years to complete.

THE LANDSCAPE

AFGHANISTAN'S TOPOGRAPHY is dominated by the mountains of the Hindu Kush, which spread south and west into numerous mountain spurs. The dry plateau of southwestern Afghanistan extends into Pakistan and the hills which overlook the great Indus Basin. In northern Pakistan the Hindu Kush, Himalayan and Karakoram ranges meet to form one of the world's highest mountain regions.

The arid Hindu Kush makes much of Afghanistan uninhabitable, with over 50% of the land lying above 6,500 ft (2,000 m).

Frequent earthquakes mean that mountain-building processes are continuing in this region, as the Indo-Australian Plate drifts northward, colliding with the Eurasian Plate.

Mountain chains running southwest from the Hindu Kush into Pakistan form a barrier to the humid winds which blow from the Indian Ocean, creating arid conditions across southern Afghanistan.

The plains and foothills which extend from the northern slopes of the Hindu Kush are part of the great grassy steppe lands of Central Asia.

The Hunza River rises in the northern Karakoram Range, running for 120 miles (193 km) before joining the Gilgit River.

Hunza River

K2 (Mount Godwin Austen), in the Karakoram Range, is the second highest mountain in the world, at an altitude of 28,251 ft (8,611 m).

Some of the largest glaciers outside the polar regions are found in the Karakoram Range, including Siachen Glacier (*Siachen Muztagh*), which is 40 miles (72 km) long.

Hindu Kush

Himalayas

The soils of the Punjab Plain are nourished by enormous quantities of sediment, carried from the Himalayas by the five tributaries of the Indus River.

The Indus Basin is part of the Indus-Ganges lowland, a vast depression which has been filled with layers of sediment over the last 50 million years. These deposits are estimated to be over 16,400 ft (5,000 m) deep.

The Indus Delta is prone to heavy flooding and high levels of salinity. It remains a largely uncultivated wilderness area.

Glacis covered by coarse-grained sediment

Sediments washed down from mountains accumulate on glacis slopes

Bedrock

Fine sediments deposited on salt flats are removed by wind erosion

Glacis are gentle, debris-covered slopes which lead into saltflats or deserts. They typically occur at the base of mountains in arid regions such as Afghanistan.

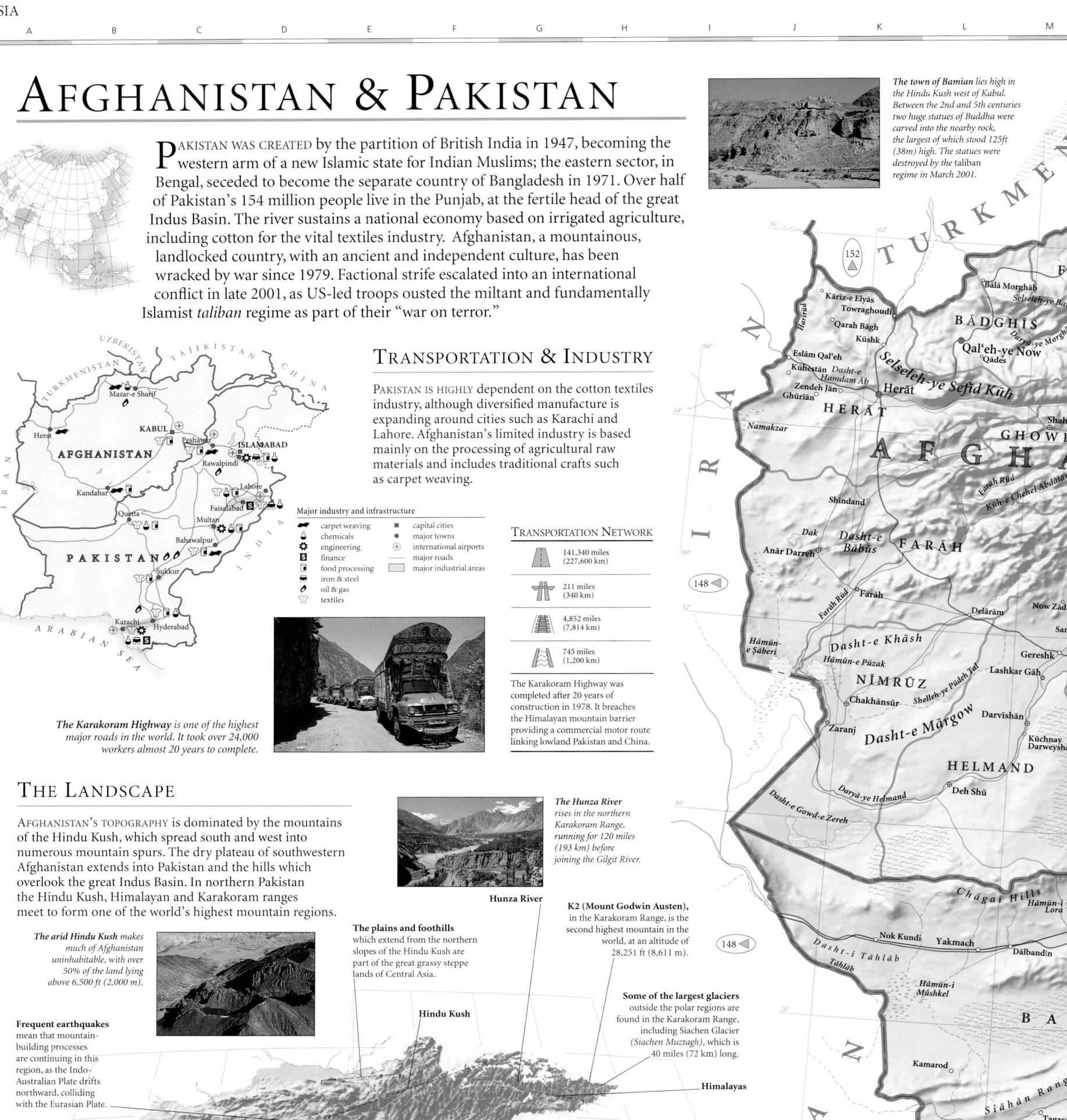

SCALE 1:4,500,000
(projection: Lambert Conformal Conic)

Km
0 10 20 40 60 80 100 120 140 160 180 200

0 10 20 40 60 80 100 120 140 160 180 200
Miles

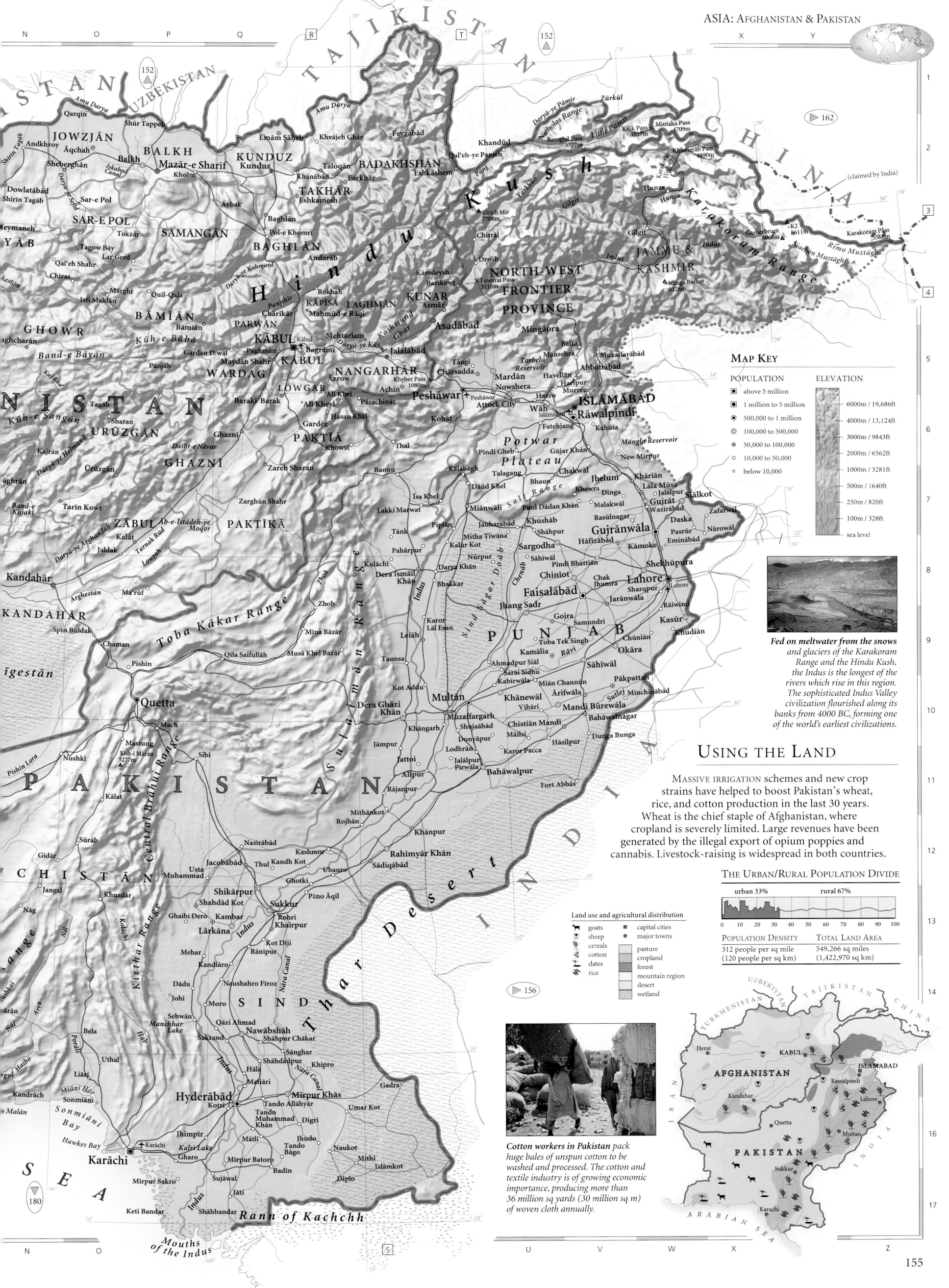

MAP KEY

POPULATION
- above 5 million
- 1 million to 5 million
- 500,000 to 1 million
- 100,000 to 500,000
- 50,000 to 100,000
- 10,000 to 50,000
- below 10,000

ELEVATION
- 6000m / 19,686ft
- 4000m / 13,124ft
- 3000m / 9843ft
- 2000m / 6562ft
- 1000m / 3281ft
- 500m / 1640ft
- 250m / 820ft
- 100m / 328ft
- sea level

Fed on meltwater from the snows and glaciers of the Karakoram Range and the Hindu Kush, the Indus is the longest of the rivers which rise in this region. The sophisticated Indus Valley civilization flourished along its banks from 4000 BC, forming one of the world's earliest civilizations.

USING THE LAND

MASSIVE IRRIGATION schemes and new crop strains have helped to boost Pakistan's wheat, rice, and cotton production in the last 30 years. Wheat is the chief staple of Afghanistan, where cropland is severely limited. Large revenues have been generated by the illegal export of opium poppies and cannabis. Livestock-raising is widespread in both countries.

THE URBAN/RURAL POPULATION DIVIDE

urban 33%   rural 67%

POPULATION DENSITY
312 people per sq mile
(120 people per sq km)

TOTAL LAND AREA
549,266 sq miles
(1,422,970 sq km)

Land use and agricultural distribution
- goats
- sheep
- cereals
- cotton
- dates
- rice
- capital cities
- major towns
- pasture
- cropland
- forest
- mountain region
- desert
- wetland

Cotton workers in Pakistan pack huge bales of unspun cotton to be washed and processed. The cotton and textile industry is of growing economic importance, producing more than 36 million sq yards (30 million sq m) of woven cloth annually.

SOUTH ASIA

BANGLADESH, BHUTAN, INDIA, MALDIVES, NEPAL, PAKISTAN, SRI LANKA

MORE THAN ONE-FIFTH of the world's population lives in the south Asian subcontinent. Great cultural diversity has come from a long succession of foreign invaders, including Hindu Aryans, Islamic Moguls, and the British, whose empire incorporated the princely states of the Maharajas and extended to the borders of Nepal and Bhutan in the Himalayas. Half a century after independence, India is the world's largest democracy, and at the current rate of growth, may overtake China as the world's most populous country within the next century. There are points of tension in the region over claims for independence by the Sikhs in the Indian Punjab and the Tamil separatists in Sri Lanka, and the long-standing dispute with Pakistan over Jammu and Kashmir in the north.

THE LANDSCAPE

SOUTH ASIA is effectively isolated from the rest of Asia by desert along the western flank of Pakistan, and a continuous wall of mountains, dominated by the Himalayas, to the north and east. The great basins of the Indus and Ganges separate this mountain fringe from the rolling plateau of the Indian peninsula, which is bordered by a line of coastal hills, the Eastern and Western Ghats.

The towering Karakoram and Hindu Kush ranges, formed at the same time as the Himalayas, dominate Pakistan's northern borders. K2 on the border of northern Pakistan is the second highest mountain on Earth, at 28,251 ft (8,611 m).

The Himalayas are the highest and most extensive mountain system in the world. They were formed when the Indo-Australian Plate collided with the Eurasian Plate about 40 million years ago, thrusting up huge masses of land and creating a "ripple" effect, which formed lesser mountain ranges in Tibet and Southeast Asia. Mount Everest at 29,035 ft (8,850 m).

Almost all of Bangladesh lies in the immense delta formed by the Ganges and the Brahmaputra which merge and flow out into the Bay of Bengal.

Ganges Delta

Deccan Plateau

The Deccan Plateau covers an area of more than 123,553 sq miles (320,000 sq km). It is formed of deep layers of volcanic basalt, reaching thicknesses of more than 9,880 ft (3,000 m) toward the coast. Distinctive stepped valleys cut in the basalt plateau by rivers are known as "traps."

Layers of volcanic basalt

Stepped valleys or 'traps'

Eastern Ghats

Coastal deposition has formed many typical features along the western coast of Sri Lanka. These include spits and bars, sometimes enclosing lagoons.

Trivandrum in southern India normally receives the first of the monsoon rains, which are essential to south Asian agriculture and moderate the extreme summer heat. The monsoon then moves northward over a period of about two months.

The Indus Valley near Skardu in northern Pakistan has been partially infilled by great quantities of eroded sediment. Most of this is carried from the region's bare slopes by swollen rivers during the spring thaw and mass movement activity.

The Western Ghats are formed by a fault scarp which runs unbroken for more than 930 miles (1,500 km). They reach their highest point at the southern Cardamon Hills.

The Indus River flows more than 1,970 miles (3,180 km) from southwestern Tibet to its mouth on the Arabian Sea. It has an estimated catchment area of 450,000 sq miles (1,165,500 sq km).

The coast of western Pakistan is a staircase of folded rock strata caused by successive periods of rapid uplift.

Bharatpur

Rivers flowing from the Himalayas into a broad depression in northern India have formed marshes around Bharatpur. They are now a sanctuary for numerous bird species.

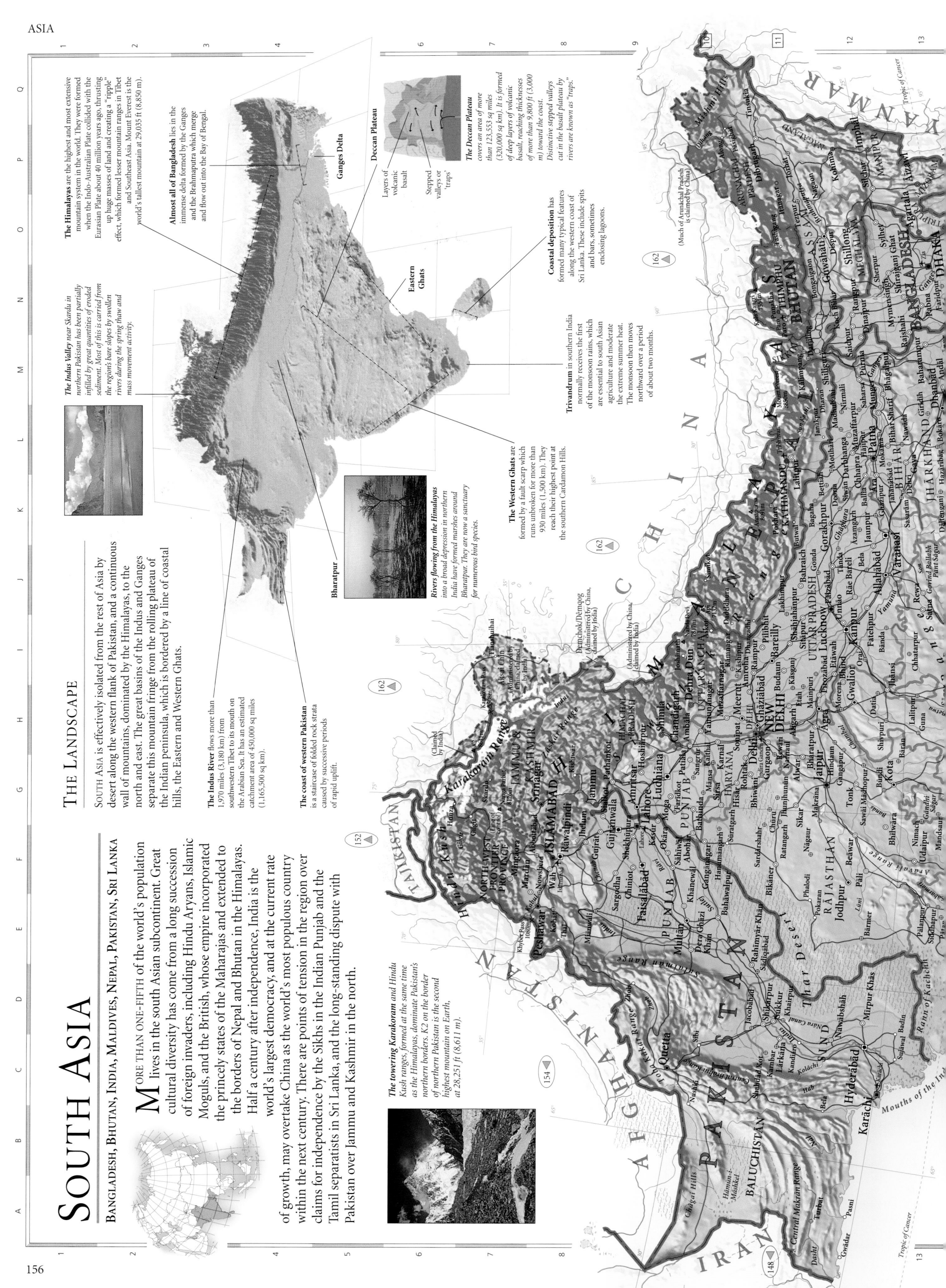

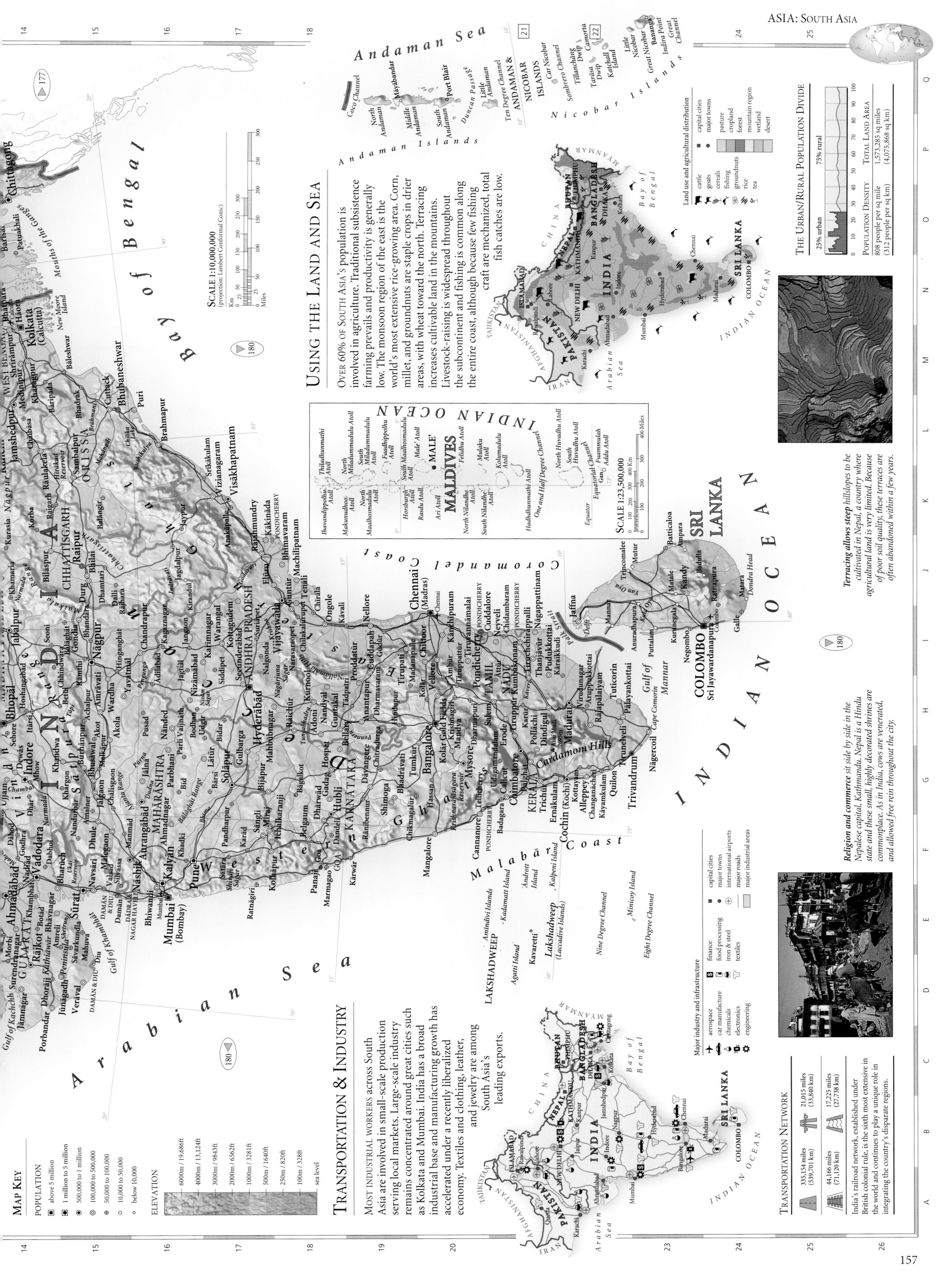

USING THE LAND AND SEA

OVER 60% OF SOUTH ASIA's population is involved in agriculture. Traditional subsistence farming prevails and productivity is generally low. The monsoon region of the east is the world's most extensive rice-growing area. Corn, millet, and groundnuts are staple crops in drier areas, with wheat toward the north. Terracing increases cultivable land in the mountains. Livestock-raising is widespread throughout the subcontinent and fishing is common along the entire coast, although few fishing craft are mechanized, total fish catches are low.

Land use and agricultural distribution

- cattle
- goats
- cereals
- fishing
- groundnuts
- rice
- tea
- capital cities
- major towns
- pasture
- cropland
- forest
- mountain region
- wetland
- desert

THE URBAN/RURAL POPULATION DIVIDE

25% urban   75% rural

POPULATION DENSITY
808 people per sq mile
(312 people per sq km)

TOTAL LAND AREA
1,573,285 sq miles
(4,075,868 sq km)

0 10 20 30 40 50 60 70 80 90 100

Terracing allows steep hillslopes to be cultivated in Nepal, a country where agricultural land is very limited. Because of poor soil quality, these terraces are often abandoned within a few years.

Religion and commerce sit side by side in the Nepalese capital, Kathmandu. Nepal is a Hindu state and these small, highly decorated shrines are commonplace. As in India, cows are venerated, and allowed free rein throughout the city.

TRANSPORTATION & INDUSTRY

MOST INDUSTRIAL WORKERS across South Asia are involved in small-scale production serving local markets. Large-scale industry remains concentrated around great cities such as Kolkata and Mumbai. India has a broad industrial base and manufacturing growth has accelerated under a recently liberalized economy. Textiles and clothing, leather, and jewelry are among South Asia's leading exports.

Major industry and infrastructure
- aerospace
- car manufacture
- chemicals
- electronics
- engineering
- finance
- food processing
- iron & steel
- textiles
- capital cities
- major towns
- international airports
- major roads
- major industrial areas

TRANSPORTATION NETWORK

335,154 miles (539,701 km)   21,015 miles (33,840 km)
17,225 miles (27,738 km)   44,166 miles (71,120 km)

India's railroad network, established under British colonial rule, is the sixth most extensive in the world and continues to play a unique role in integrating the country's disparate regions.

MAP KEY

POPULATION
- ■ above 5 million
- ■ 1 million to 5 million
- ◉ 500,000 to 1 million
- ◉ 100,000 to 500,000
- ⊕ 50,000 to 100,000
- ○ 10,000 to 50,000
- ○ below 10,000

ELEVATION
- 6000m / 19,686ft
- 4000m / 13,124ft
- 3000m / 9843ft
- 2000m / 6562ft
- 1000m / 3281ft
- 500m / 1640ft
- 250m / 820ft
- 100m / 328ft
- sea level

SCALE 1:10,000,000
(projection: Lambert Conformal Conic)

SCALE 1:23,500,000

SCALE 1:23,500,000

NORTHERN INDIA & THE HIMALAYAN STATES

BANGLADESH, BHUTAN, NEPAL, Arunachal Pradesh, Assam, Bihar, Chandigarh, Delhi, Haryana, Himachal Pradesh, Jammu & Kashmir, Jharkhand, Manipur, Meghalaya, Mizoram, Nagaland, Punjab, Rajasthan, Sikkim, Tripura, Uttaranchal, Uttar Pradesh, West Bengal

THE GANGES AND BRAHMAPUTRA river basins and the massive mountain barrier of the Himalayas define this region's landscape and have served to reinforce potent cultural and religious differences among its people. Hinduism pervades most aspects of national life and is a growing political force within India, a secular country which also encompasses the center of Sikhism at Amritsar and the world's largest Muslim minority. Nepal is a crowded mountain state, which faces severe ecological problems from deforestation, while the tiny Himalayan Buddhist kingdom of Bhutan is emerging from long-term isolation, to welcome selected visitors. The Muslim state of Bangladesh, formerly East Pakistan, is one of the world's most densely populated countries and one of the poorest, with more than 120 million people living largely on the massive Ganges/Brahmaputra Delta. Many Bangladeshis live under threat of repeated, catastrophic floods.

The Golden Temple in Amritsar, the most sacred shrine of the Sikh religion, was the scene of violent clashes between Sikh separatists and government forces in 1984.

MAP KEY

POPULATION
- 1 million to 5 million
- 500,000 to 1 million
- 100,000 to 500,000
- 50,000 to 100,000
- 10,000 to 50,000
- below 10,000

ELEVATION
- 6000m / 19,686ft
- 4000m / 13,124ft
- 3000m / 9843ft
- 2000m / 6562ft
- 1000m / 3281ft
- 500m / 1640ft
- 250m / 820ft
- 100m / 328ft
- sea level

TRANSPORTATION & INDUSTRY

TEXTILES, ENGINEERING, chemicals, and electronics are leading industries in north India. The plateau of Chota Nagpur provides ore for iron and steel production in the major industrial region northeast of Kolkata. Bangladesh processes jute and Nepal has a small manufacturing sector based on agricultural produce, while Bhutan's limited industry is concentrated in the southern lowland area.

SCALE 1:5,750,000
(projection: Lambert Conformal Conic)

Major industry and infrastructure
- adventure tourism
- car manufacture
- chemicals
- coal
- electronics
- engineering
- finance
- food processing
- iron & steel
- jute processing
- oil
- tea processing
- textiles
- capital cities
- major towns
- international airports
- major roads
- major industrial areas

TRANSPORTATION NETWORK

Over 60% of Bangladesh's internal trade is carried by boat. The country has a very disjointed land transportation network, with no bridges over the Brahmaputra and few road crossings on the Ganges River.

THE LANDSCAPE

MOST OF THE REGION is drained by the Ganges River, which meets the Brahmaputra in Bangladesh to form an immense delta before flowing into the Bay of Bengal. The Himalayas extend eastward over 1,500 miles (2,400 km), from the parallel ranges running through Jammu and Kashmir. The Thar Desert occupies the southwest.

The Indian Punjab lies mainly to the west of the Ganges watershed and its rivers flow into the Indus. Control of this water resource has been a source of great friction with neighboring Pakistan.

The border between India and Pakistan runs through the Thar Desert, an area of sandy *seif* dunes 50–100 ft (15–30 m) in height. Fossils found in the desert indicate that the dunes, stabilized by vegetation, have been in their current position for about 3,000 years.

Sambhar Salt Lake in Rajasthan is India's largest lake. Unlike most of the Himalayan lakes which are glacial in origin – formed in ice-scoured basins or as the result of depositional damming – it is an ephemeral salt lake filled periodically by flash flooding.

The Pir Panjal Range in southwestern Kashmir rises to elevations of 12,500 ft (3,810 m). Despite the freezing conditions, settlements and extensive pastures are found above the tree line.

The Ganges River, sacred to the Hindu people, drains a vast lowland area at the base of the Himalayas. The northern plains are covered by sandy deposits, broken by mud-banks formed when the river floods.

The rapid deforestation of Himalayan valleys has led to acute soil erosion and increased rates of rainwater runoff, both cited as possible causes of the worsening floods downstream in the Ganges/Brahmaputra Delta, although natural rates are high and may be the real cause.

The northern ranges of the Himalayas contain the highest mountains in the world, with average heights of more than 23,000 ft (7,000 m) and many peaks higher than 26,000 ft (8,000 m).

In the last 40 million years, the course of the Brahmaputra has been diverted hundreds of miles to the east by the rising landmass of the Himalayas.

Over half of the great Ganges/Brahmaputra Delta floods each year during the monsoon as rivers, swollen by meltwater from the Himalayas and by excess rainwater, break their banks and fertilize the land with nutrient-rich sediment.

The Khasi Hills are an example of a *horst*, a fractured block of bedrock which has been thrust upward.

The summit of Machhapuchhre rises to 22,942 ft (6,993 m). It is also known as the "Fish's Tail" because of its distinctive peak.

Debris slides in the middle Himalayas

Soil blocks
Debris fans at base of slope
Slide plain

Soil loss in the middle Himalayas has largely been attributed to debris slides, where large blocks of soil are mobilized by saturation along a slide plane. Once mobile, the soil slides down the slope, gaining speed and thinning to form a fan at the base of the slope.

USING THE LAND

GRAIN PRODUCTION dominates land use. Rice is most widely grown in the east. Irrigation and new crop strains have dramatically increased yields in the Punjab, a major wheat-producing area. River floodplains are intensively farmed and livestock-herding is widespread, particularly in Bhutan. Regional crops include jute in Bangladesh, tea in Assam, cardamom in Sikkim, and saffron in Kashmir.

THE URBAN/RURAL POPULATION DIVIDE

urban 23% rural 77%

POPULATION DENSITY	TOTAL LAND AREA
782 people per sq mile (302 people per sq km)	665,104 sq miles (1,723,068 sq km)

Land use and agricultural distribution

cattle
goats
sheep
cereals
jute
rice
tea

capital cities
major towns

pasture
cropland
forest
mountain region
wetland
desert

An adverse climate, steep slopes, and poor soils limit crop cultivation in Bhutan, which is a largely agrarian economy. Rice, corn, and wheat are the main staples, although orchards are being established as the soil and climate suit this type of farming.

Flooded streets in Dhaka, Bangladesh are a testament to the region's vulnerability to flooding. In 1988 alone, 75% of the country was flooded, leaving thousands of people dead and over 25 million homeless.

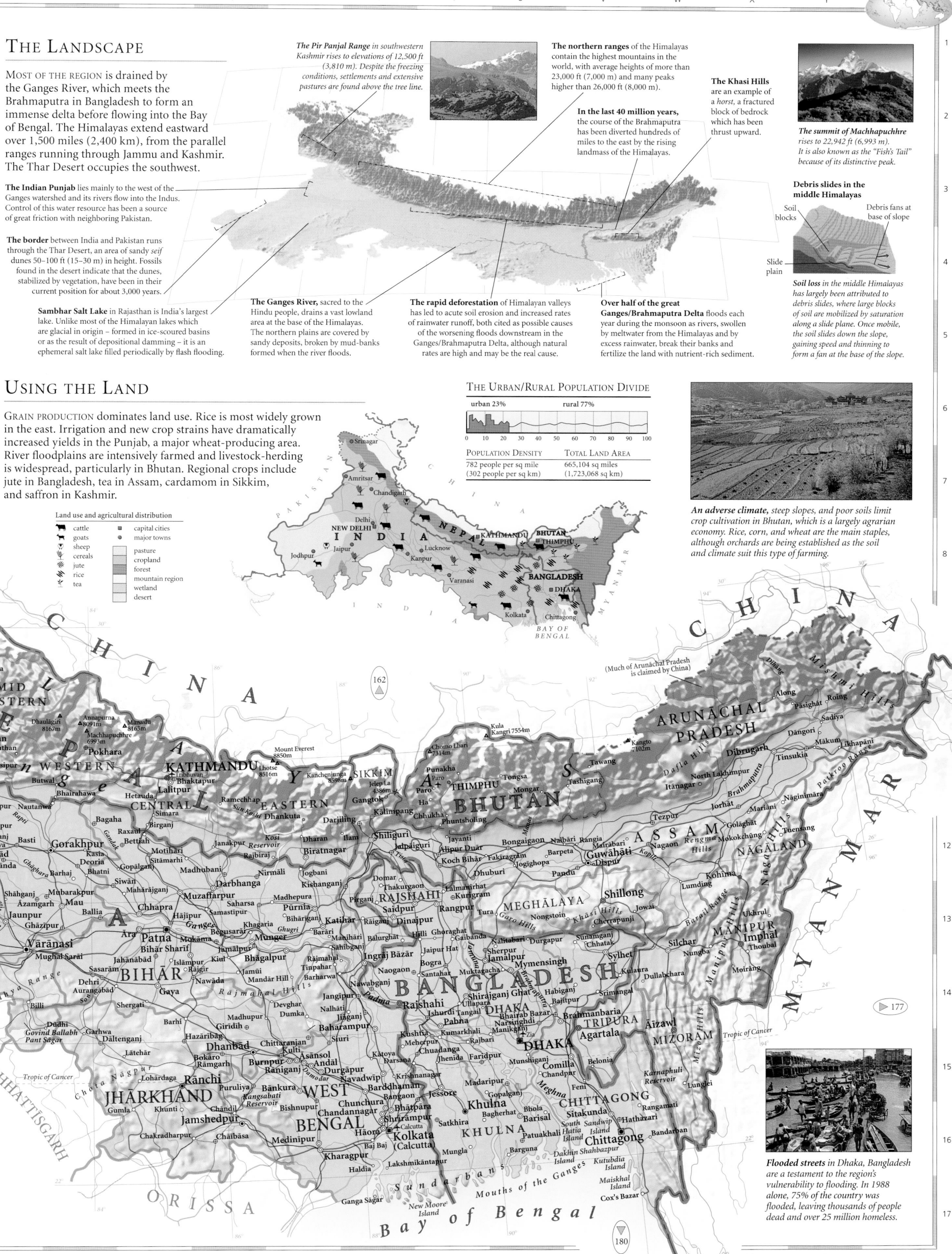

Southern India & Sri Lanka

Sri Lanka, Andhra Pradesh, Chhattisgarh, Dadra & Nagar Haveli, Daman & Diu, Goa, Gujarat, Karnataka, Kerala, Lakshadweep, Madhya Pradesh, Maharashtra, Orissa, Pondicherry, Tamil Nadu

The unique and highly independent southern states reflect the diverse and decentralized nature of India, which has fourteen official languages. The southern half of the peninsula lay beyond the reach of early invaders from the north and retained the distinct and ancient culture of Dravidian peoples such as the Tamils, whose language is spoken in preference to Hindi throughout southern India. The interior plateau of southern India is less densely populated than the coastal lowlands, where the European colonial imprint is strongest. Urban and industrial growth is accelerating, but southern India's vast population remains predominantly rural. The island of Sri Lanka has two distinct cultural groups; the mainly Buddhist Sinhalese majority, and the Tamil minority whose struggle for a homeland in the northeast has led to prolonged civil war.

The Landscape

The undulating Deccan Plateau underlies most of southern India; it slopes gently down toward the east and is largely enclosed by the Ghats coastal hill ranges. The Western Ghats run continuously along the Arabian Sea coast, while the Eastern Ghats are interrupted by rivers which follow the slope of the plateau and flow across broad lowlands into the Bay of Bengal. The plateaus and basins of Sri Lanka's central highlands are surrounded by a broad plain.

Along the northern boundary of the Deccan Plateau, old basement rocks are interspersed with younger sedimentary strata. This creates spectacular scarplands, cut by numerous waterfalls along the softer sedimentary strata.

The interior uplands of southern India are broadly known as the Deccan Plateau. River erosion of the plateau's volcanic rock has created distinctive stepped valleys called *traps*.

Deep layers of river sediment have created a broad lowland plain along the eastern coast, with rivers such as the Krishna forming extensive deltas.

The island of Sri Lanka is essentially an extension of the Deccan Plateau. It lies on the Indian continental shelf and is composed of the same hard, crystalline rocks.

The Rann of Kachchh tidal marshes encircle the low-lying Kachchh Peninsula. For several months during the rainy season the water level of the marshes rises and Kachchh becomes an island.

The Konkan coast, which runs between Daman and Goa, is characterized by rocky headlands, and bays with crescent-shaped beaches. Flooded river valleys known as *rias* extend inland.

The Western Ghats run north–south marking the western boundary of the Deccan Plateau. Their height rises to the south where their summits reach altitudes of 8,000 ft (2,500 m).

Adam's Bridge

Ocean currents cause sediment build up

Sri Lanka

Relict of ancient tombolo

Adam's Bridge

Adam's Bridge (Rama's Bridge) is a chain of sandy shoals lying about 4 ft (1.2 m) under the sea between India and Sri Lanka. They once formed the world's longest tombolo, or land bridge, before the sea level began to rise several thousand years ago.

Using the Land and Sea

Rice is the main staple in the east, in Sri Lanka and along the humid Malabar Coast. Peanuts are grown on the Deccan Plateau, with wheat, corn, and chickpeas, toward the north. Sri Lanka is a leading exporter of tea, coconuts and rubber. Cotton plantations supply local mills around Nagpur and Mumbai (Bombay). Fishing supports many communities in Kerala and the Laccadive Islands.

Commercial plantations, growing tea, (seen here), cardamom, coffee, coconuts, and rubber, occupy about half the agricultural land in Kerala, necessitating food imports for local consumption.

Land use and agricultural distribution

- ◼ capital cities
- ● major towns

- pasture
- cropland
- forest
- wetland

- cattle
- goats
- cereals
- cotton
- fishing
- groundnuts
- rice
- rubber
- tea

The Urban/Rural Population Divide

urban 29%	rural 71%

Population Density	Total Land Area
715 people per sq mile (276 people per sq km)	698,295 sq miles (1,809,054 sq km)

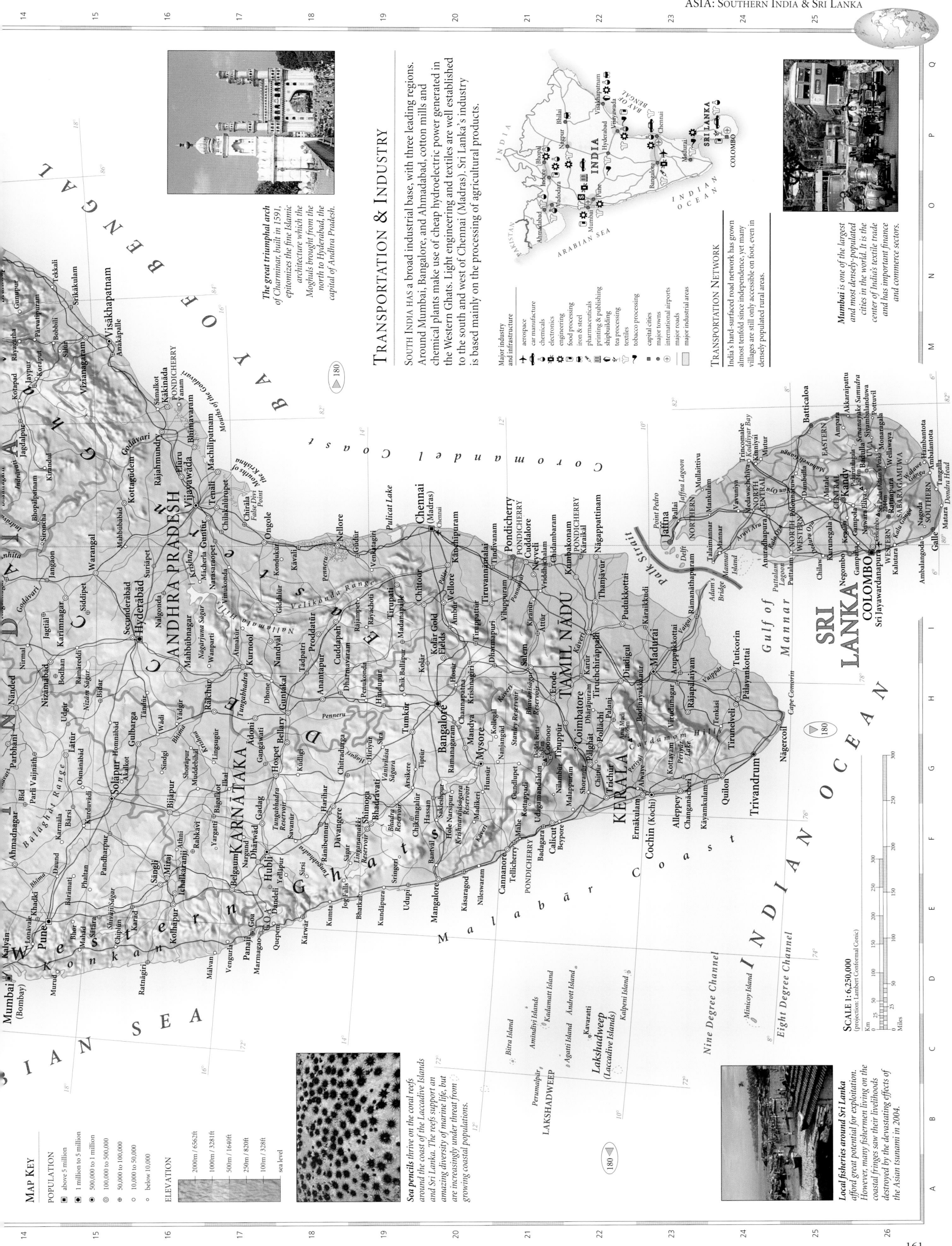

The great triumphal arch of Charminar, built in 1591, epitomizes the fine Islamic architecture which the Moghuls brought from the north to Hyderabad, the capital of Andhra Pradesh.

TRANSPORTATION & INDUSTRY

SOUTH INDIA HAS a broad industrial base, with three leading regions. Around Mumbai, Bangalore, and Ahmadabad, cotton mills and chemical plants make use of cheap hydroelectric power generated in the Western Ghats. Light engineering and textiles are well established to the south and west of Chennai (Madras). Sri Lanka's industry is based mainly on the processing of agricultural products.

Major industry and infrastructure

aerospace
car manufacture
chemicals
electronics
engineering
food processing
iron & steel
pharmaceuticals
printing & publishing
shipbuilding
textiles
tobacco processing
capital cities
major towns
international airports
major roads
major industrial areas

TRANSPORTATION NETWORK

India's hard-surfaced road network has grown almost tenfold since independence, yet many villages are still only accessible on foot, even in densely populated rural areas.

Mumbai is one of the largest and most densely-populated cities in the world. It is the center of India's textile trade and has important finance and commerce sectors.

Sea pencils thrive on the coral reefs around the coast of the Laccadive Islands and Sri Lanka. The reefs support an amazing diversity of marine life, but are increasingly under threat from growing coastal populations.

Local fisheries around Sri Lanka afford great potential for exploitation. However, many fishermen living on the coastal fringes saw their livelihoods destroyed by the devastating effects of the Asian tsunami in 2004.

MAP KEY

POPULATION
■ above 5 million
◉ 1 million to 5 million
◎ 500,000 to 1 million
⊚ 100,000 to 500,000
⊕ 50,000 to 100,000
○ 10,000 to 50,000
∘ below 10,000

ELEVATION
2000m / 6562ft
1000m / 3281ft
500m / 1640ft
250m / 820ft
100m / 328ft
sea level

SCALE 1:6,250,000
(projection: Lambert Conformal Conic)

Mainland East Asia

China, Mongolia, North Korea, South Korea, Taiwan

CHINA, THE WORLD'S MOST POPULOUS NATION, has an unbroken cultural history, longer than that of any other country, and is rapidly emerging as a leading world power. When Mao Zedong established Communist rule in 1949, China had become a backward feudal empire, stricken by civil war and over a century of European and Japanese incursions. The closed regime withstood the traumas of rapid industrialization, communal farming, and the brutal purges of the Cultural Revolution. Since the 1980s has introduced economic reforms, led by expanded foreign trade. China's population is heavily concentrated in the east and, despite accelerating urban growth, remains predominantly rural. One cultural group, the Han, make up over 90% of the people, while five "Autonomous Regions" have been established in the south and west for the main ethnic minorities.

Transportation & Industry

LARGE-SCALE INDUSTRIAL growth has always been a priority of the Communist government. Metals and machine production, chemicals, and engineering are among the leading industries, concentrated in the major cities of the east coast. Textiles and clothing manufacture, the main consumer goods sector, is relatively well dispersed, with a few significant centers such as Shanghai, Beijing, and Hong Kong.

Major industry and infrastructure

- car manufacture
- chemicals
- electronics
- engineering
- finance
- food processing
- iron & steel
- shipbuilding
- textiles
- capital cities
- major towns
- international airports
- major roads
- major industrial areas

Transportation Network

734,473 miles (1,182,727 km)	1,182 miles (1,904 km)
41,798 miles (67,308 km)	70,495 miles (113,519 km)

Steam trains use China's abundant coal and are still the main form of passenger and goods transportation. The railroad network is now struggling to meet an ever-growing demand.

Coal is China's most abundant mineral resource. This mine at Fuxin in Liaoning province is used to provide coal for a nearby power station.

The Landscape

THE EAST ASIAN LANDMASS is arranged in three distinct levels, the highest of which is the Plateau of Tibet in the southwest. The arid uplands of northwestern China form a barren middle step. The main rivers flow eastward from these two platforms to the East China and South China sea coasts, across a broad region of alluvial lowlands and low hills.

Gansu province, through which the ancient Silk Route passes on its way to the west, is characterized by extensive loess deposits which are terraced and used for crop cultivation.

Paektu-san, at 9,023 ft (2,750 m), is North Korea's highest peak; an extinct volcanic cone now filled by a crater lake.

The loess plateau of northern China is the world's greatest expanse of loess, a loose soil made up of wind-blown material. The plateau has been heavily eroded by tributaries of the Yellow River.

Shifting sand dunes are found in the arid west of the northeast China Plain, while the eastern part of this great expanse is wet and swampy.

Because of its very small grain-size, loess has been easily transported and deposited by winds which scour the plains, and in northern China, deposits of loess can be up to 3,000 ft (1,000 m) thick. Loess-based soils are very fertile, but clearing land for agriculture quickly destabilizes the soil and allows it to be eroded.

River-eroded fine soils

Thick blanket of loess

The Gobi Desert extends across the Nei Mongol Gaoyuan; a vast saucer-shaped upland surrounded by a rim of higher mountains.

Tarim Basin (Tarim Pendi)

Plateau of Tibet

Paektu-san

North China Plain

The Yangtze is China's longest river and the principal navigable waterway.

The Plateau of Tibet occupies about a quarter of China's total area. The Yangtze, Mekong, Indus, and Brahmaputra Rivers all originate in the south and east of the plateau.

The Himalayas extend along the southwestern edge of the Plateau of Tibet, forming a continuous mountain barrier over 1,500 miles (2,500 km) long.

Warm, humid conditions have caused intensive erosion of south China's karst areas, producing spectacular jagged peaks and vast caves in the limestone.

Sichuan Pendi

Although it is over 20 years since his death, the legacy of Chairman Mao Zedong, architect of the Great Proletariat Cultural Revolution, is still very much in evidence across China's landscape. In 1959 Mao launched a 20-year period of industrialization and socioeconomic realignment, rejecting western ideals and social codes.

The Great Wall of China remains one of the world's largest-ever construction projects, and is so vast that it is visible from space. Finally completed in AD 214, it runs for over 4,000 miles (6,400 km) from the Yellow Sea, stretching into Central Asia.

SCALE 1:12,500,000
(projection: Lambert Conformal Conic)

MAP KEY

POPULATION

- ■ above 5 million
- ■ 1 million to 5 million
- ◉ 500,000 to 1 million
- ◎ 100,000 to 500,000
- ⊙ 50,000 to 100,000
- ○ 10,000 to 50,000
- · below 10,000

ELEVATION

- 6000m / 19,686ft
- 4000m / 13,124ft
- 3000m / 9843ft
- 2000m / 6562ft
- 1000m / 3281ft
- 500m / 1640ft
- 250m / 820ft
- 100m / 328ft
- sea level

USING THE LAND AND SEA

AROUND 90% OF China is unsuitable for cultivation, being either climatically or topographically adverse, or lacking sufficiently fertile soils. Most of the west is used for nomadic herding, while farmland is concentrated in the eastern monsoon region, with rice grown in the tropical and subtropical south. Cereals and soybeans predominate as rainfall and temperatures decline further north.

Land use and agricultural distribution

- ᛗ pigs
- ᛙ sheep
- ᛘ corn
- ᛚ cotton
- ᛛ fishing
- ᛜ fruit
- ᛝ rice
- ᛞ sugar cane
- ᛟ soybeans
- ● capital cities
- ◦ major towns
- pasture
- cropland
- forest
- mountain region

Beijing (formerly Peking), is China's capital city and, with Shanghai, one of its leading industrial and cultural centers. The morning and evening rush-hours are dominated by bicycles, which constitute the bulk of traffic.

THE URBAN/RURAL POPULATION DIVIDE

urban 32%   rural 68%

0 10 20 30 40 50 60 70 80 90 100

POPULATION DENSITY
297 people per sq mile
(115 people per sq km)

TOTAL LAND AREA
4,288,672 sq miles
(11,110,550 sq km)

RUSSIAN FEDERATION

WESTERN CHINA

Gansu, Ningxia, Qinghai, Tibet, Xinjiang

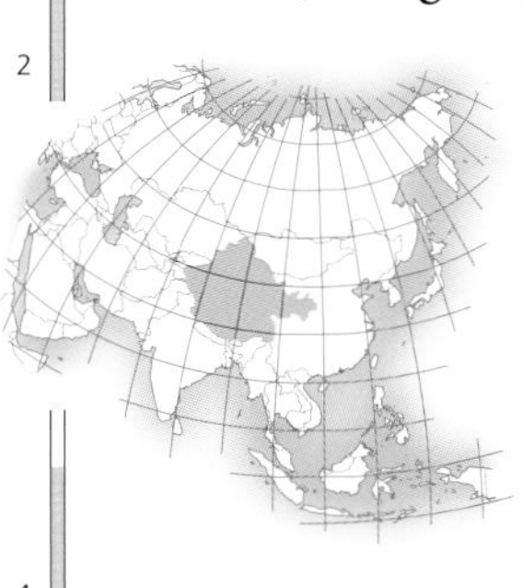

THE PLATEAUS AND BASINS of China's dry, desolate western domain are sparsely populated and largely undeveloped, although they have rich mineral reserves; they also form a critical buffer zone for China, in a geographically important and culturally sensitive part of the Asian continent. Across most of the west, the Han Chinese are outnumbered by a range of cultural groups, including the Uygur, the largest group of the various seminomadic Muslim peoples from Central Asia. The remote, inhospitable Plateau of Tibet is the world's coldest and highest plateau. It has been occupied by the Chinese since 1950. Tibet is one of western China's five "Autonomous Regions," but its reclusive Buddhist culture has been systematically undermined by the Chinese government.

MAP KEY

POPULATION

- ⬛ 1 million to 5 million
- ◉ 500,000 to 1 million
- ◎ 100,000 to 500,000
- ⊕ 50,000 to 100,000
- ○ 10,000 to 50,000
- ○ below 10,000

ELEVATION

- 6000m / 19,686ft
- 4000m / 13,124ft
- 3000m / 9843ft
- 2000m / 6562ft
- 1000m / 3281ft
- 500m / 1640ft
- 250m / 820ft
- 100m / 328ft
- sea level

SCALE 1:7,000,000
(projection: Lambert Conformal Conic)

Km 0 25 50 100 150 200 250 300
Miles 0 25 50 100 150 200 250 300

The Lhasa He is one of the many rivers that drain the vast Plateau of Tibet. From its source in the Nyainqêntanglha Shan range and fed by the spring meltwater, it eventually joins the upper Brahmaputra 40 miles (65 km) southwest of Lhasa.

USING THE LAND

AGRICULTURE IS CONSTRAINED by the cold, dry climate and lack of fertile soils in the region, although irrigation and glasshouse farming are increasing agricultural potential. Large quantities of fruit, like melons and grapes, are grown at the oases of Hami and Turpan in Xinjiang, and new irrigation schemes have greatly increased cotton and wheat production in the Tarim Basin (Tarim Pendi). Most of the great area of Tibet and Qinghai is devoted to pastoralism. Sheep are the principal livestock.

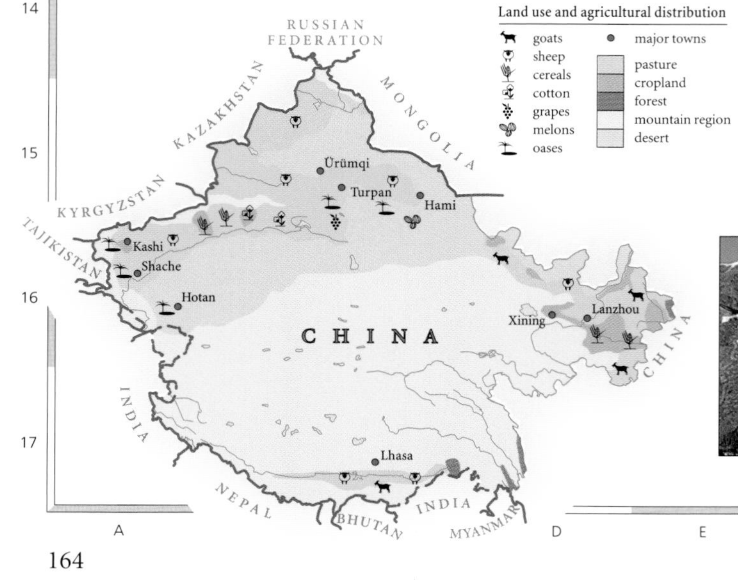

Land use and agricultural distribution

- goats
- sheep
- cereals
- cotton
- grapes
- melons
- oases
- major towns
- pasture
- cropland
- forest
- mountain region
- desert

The Potala Palace, in Tibet's capital, Lhasa, was the former residence of the Dalai Lama, Tibetan Buddhism's spiritual leader. Tibet remains only sparsely populated; forming over 20% of China's landmass, it supports fewer than 1% of its population.

KAZAKHSTAN
KYRGYZSTAN
TAJIKISTAN
AFGHANISTAN
RUSSIAN FEDERATION

Altai Mountain
Habahe
Jeminay · Burqin
Ertix He · Altay
Ulungur Hu · Fuhai
Tacheng · Hoboksar · Utubulak
Emin · Emin He
Yumin · Düre · Ulungur He
Toli · Urho · Kok Kuduk
Manas Hu · Shaqiuhe
Wenquan · Bole · Ebinur Hu · Karamay · Junggar Pendi
Sayram Hu · Gurbantünggüt Shamo
Huocheng · Jinghe · Usu · Kuytun · Shihezi · Hutubi · Fukang
Yining · Nilka · Shawan · Manas · Changji · Miquan · Jimsar
Qapqal · Ili He · Kax He · Bayanbulak · Ürümqi · Bogda Feng 5445m
Tekes · Zhaosu · Gongliu · Xinyuan · Künes He · Narat · Xiaocaohu · Yongfengqu
Tekes He · Balguntay · Ewirgol · Turpan Zhan · Turpan
Tömür Feng 7443m · Kaidu He · Hejing · Toksun · Aydingkol Hu · Turpan Pendi -154m
Hantengri Feng 6995m · Baicheng · Muzat He · Yanqi · Hoxud · Kümüx
Wensu · Aksu · Xinhe · Kuqa · Luntai · Korla · Bosten Hu
Akqi · Aksu He · Aral · Yuli · Konqi He · Kuruktag · Biratar
Kalpin · Awat · Tarim He · Tikanlik · Lop
Turugart Shankou 3752m · Sugun · Sanchakou · XINJIANG UYGUR ZIZHIQU
Ulugqat · Baykurt · Artux · Jiashi · Bachu · Tarim Pendi · Argan
Kashi · Kaxgar He · Shufu · Shule · Yopurga · Yarkant He · Qarqan He
Akto · Yengisar · Markit · Taklimakan Shamo · Miran · Baxkorg
Kongur Shan 7649m · Shache · Ruoqiang
Muztagata 7509m · Zepu · Yecheng · Waxxari
Taxkorgan · Yarkant He · Pishan · Hotan · Qiemo · Altun Shan
Kunjirap Daban 4890m · Akmeqit · Kokyar · Lop · Andirlangar
Mazar · Karakax He · Qira · Yutian · Minfeng · Bostan · Karamiran He · Aqqikkol Hu
Xaidulla (Claimed by India) · Moyu · Qira · Muztag 7282m · Muz Tag 6973m
Karakoram Range · Dahongliutan · Keriya He · Yeyik · Hoh Xil She
Karakoram Pass 5575m · Quanshuigou · Pulu · Kunlun Shan
Aksai Chin (Administered by China, claimed by India) · Tielongtan · Gozha Co · Bairab Co · Rola Co
Aksayqin Hu · Tumajiangdong Co · Orba Co · Dogai Coring
Bangong Co · Qingzang Gaoyuan (Plat
Rutog · Lungdo · Gomo
Zapug · Lugu
Denchok/Dêmqog (Administered by China, claimed by India) · Nganglong Kangri 6596m · XIZANG ZIZHIQU (TIBET)
Dêmqog · Qagcaka · Ge'gyai · Yibug Caka
Gar · Sênggê Zangbo · Oma · Gêrzê · Zhari Namco · Lhazhong · Nyima · Siling Co
Zanda · Gangdisê Shan · Coqên · Bogcang Zangbo · Tangra Yumco · Gyaring Co
Langqên Zangbo · Ngangla Ringco · Xainza
La'nga Co · Barga · Zhari Namco · Ngangzê Co
Mapam Yumco · Lunggar · Kangmar
Paryang · Zhongba · Saga · Dogxung Zangbo · Namling · Lungsang
Gangdisê Shan · Zhabdün · Xaitongmoin · Ngamring · Xigazê · Rinb
Cho Oyu 8201m · Lhaze · Bainang · Gyangzê
Xixabangma Feng 8027m · Tingri · Dinggyê · Gamba
Mount Everest 8850m · Lhotse 8516m · Makalu 8463m · Kula Ka
NEPAL · BHUTAN · INDIA · MYANMAR

RUSSIAN FEDERATION
MONGOLIA
KAZAKHSTAN
KYRGYZSTAN
TAJIKISTAN
Ürümqi · Turpan · Hami
Kashi · Shache
Hotan · Xining · Lanzhou
CHINA
Lhasa
NEPAL · BHUTAN · INDIA · MYANMAR

THE LANDSCAPE

THE HIMALAYAS MARK the southwestern edge of the Plateau of Tibet, an extreme mountain wilderness which occupies nearly a quarter of China's total area. A large structural depression, the Qaidam Pendi, lies at its northeastern edge. The Kunlun mountain chain isolates the plateau from the desert to the north, where the Tien Shan range forms a spur between the Tarim Basin (*Tarim Pendi*) and Dzungarian Basin (*Junggar Pendi*).

The Tien Shan reach elevations of over 24,419 ft (7443 m) and have permanent ice fields, from which large glaciers extend.

Dzungarian Basin (*Junggar Pendi*)

The Bogda Shan, an eastward arm of the Tien Shan range, rise high above the Turpan Depression (Turpan Pendi).

The Turpan Depression (*Turpan Pendi*) is the lowest and hottest place in China. Temperatures can exceed 117°F (47°C) around the lake of Aydingkol Hu, which lies 505 ft (154 m) below sea level.

Northwestern China is largely a region of internal drainage. The Tarim He flows only as far as Lop Nur, where its water is lost by evapotranspiration from the lake and land surface.

A vast glacial lake filled much of the Tarim Basin (*Tarim Pendi*) during the last Ice Age. This area is now occupied by the Takla Makan Desert (*Taklimakan Shamo*). A remnant of the lake, Lop Nur, forms the eastern margin, where it is fed by the Tarim He.

The terrain of the Plateau of Tibet consists of mountain peaks and open plateaus, dotted with brackish lakes. These are probably remnants of the Tethys Sea, which covered the area before it was uplifted following the collision of the Indo-Australian and Eurasian plates.

Mount Everest is the world's highest peak, at 29,035 ft (8,850 m). The summit marks the border between China and Nepal.

Sand dunes cover western parts of the the basin of Qaidam Pendi. Strong winds frequently carry the sands east, threatening the agricultural areas around the lake of Qinghai Hu.

Tarim Basin (*Tarim Pendi*)

Barchan sand dunes in Takla Makan Desert (*Taklimakan Shamo*)

Oases at edge of basin

Lop Nur

The Tarim Basin (Tarim Pendi) *has no permanent rivers. Rainfall from the surrounding Plateau of Tibet and Tien Shan ranges drains into the basin's sand and gravel floor.*

From its source, high in eastern Qinghai, the Yellow River starts on a 3,395 mile (5,464 km) journey to the Yellow Sea.

TRANSPORTATION & INDUSTRY

OIL EXTRACTION AT Yumen and in the Dzungarian and Qaidam basins has led to the growth of the petrochemical industry and a range of heavy manufacturing plants in the cities of Lanzhou and Urumqi. Tibet, and most of Xinjiang, have little industry beyond traditional handicrafts, especially textiles at Hotan and Kashi, located along the ancient Silk Route. Nuclear and space-research testing are carried out at Lop Nur in Xinjiang.

Major industry and infrastructure

- agribusiness
- chemicals
- coal
- engineering
- food processing
- iron & steel
- nuclear testing
- oil
- textiles
- major towns
- major roads
- major industrial areas

TRANSPORTATION NETWORK

The construction of roads connecting Lhasa in Tibet with Sichuan, Qinghai, and Xinjiang was achieved in the 1950s, in spite of the extreme physical conditions of the Plateau of Tibet.

EASTERN CHINA

Taiwan, Anhui, Beijing, Chongqing, Fujian, Guangdong, Guangxi, Guizhou, Hainan, Hebei, Henan, Hubei, Hunan, Jiangsu, Jiangxi, Shaanxi, Shandong, Shanghai, Shanxi, Sichuan, Tianjin, Yunnan, Zhejiang

THE EAST IS CHINA'S HEARTLAND. Massive industrial development since 1949 has transformed much of the densely populated rural landscape, in a region still prone to flooding and drought. Over 20 cities have populations of over a million, including the giant metropolis of Shanghai and the capital Beijing, which has been China's cultural and political center since the 13th century. The ethnically diverse southwest and the oil-rich interior provinces of Sichuan and Shaanxi have largely missed out on the remarkable economic growth occurring in designated free-trade areas along the coasts of the South and East China seas. The republic of Taiwan was established in 1949 by Chinese nationalists ousted from the mainland by the victorious Communist forces. Taiwan now has one of the strongest economies in the world but its sovereignty is not recognized by China. Hong Kong provides a major international trade link for China; a 99-year "lease" period of British control was concluded in 1997.

North of the Qin Ling range in Shaanxi province, is an agriculturally fertile region covered with fine, wind-blown deposits and known as the loess plateau. The loose sediments are vulnerable to water erosion.

USING THE LAND AND SEA

THIS IS A REGION of intensive cultivation. Wheat, millet, sorghum, and cotton are the main crops of the Yellow River basin. South from Sichuan, rice becomes the principal crop, grown with wheat, corn, and cotton along the Yangtze River. Tea is produced in the hills and sugar cane along the coast of the southeast, where flat land is limited. Pigs and poultry are raised in great numbers.

On the hills above the North China Plain, slopes are terraced to utilize the rich loess soils of the Taihang Shan range.

MAP KEY

POPULATION

- ■ above 5 million
- ■ 1 million to 5 million
- ◉ 500,000 to 1 million
- ◎ 100,000 to 500,000
- ⊕ 50,000 to 100,000
- ○ 10,000 to 50,000
- ○ below 10,000

ELEVATION

- 6000m / 19,686ft
- 4000m / 13,124ft
- 3000m / 9843ft
- 2000m / 6562ft
- 1000m / 3281ft
- 500m / 1640ft
- 250m / 820ft
- 100m / 328ft
- sea level

Land use and agricultural distribution

- cattle
- pigs
- cereals
- corn (maize)
- cotton
- fishing
- peanuts
- rice
- sugar cane
- tea
- ■ capital cities
- ● major towns
- pasture
- cropland
- forest
- mountain region

SCALE 1:7,750,000
(projection: Lambert Conformal Conic)

Km
0 25 50 100 150 200 250 300
Miles
0 25 50 100 150 200 250 300

The former Portuguese territory of Macao, with its colonial architecture, bars and casinos, reverted to Chinese rule in 1999.

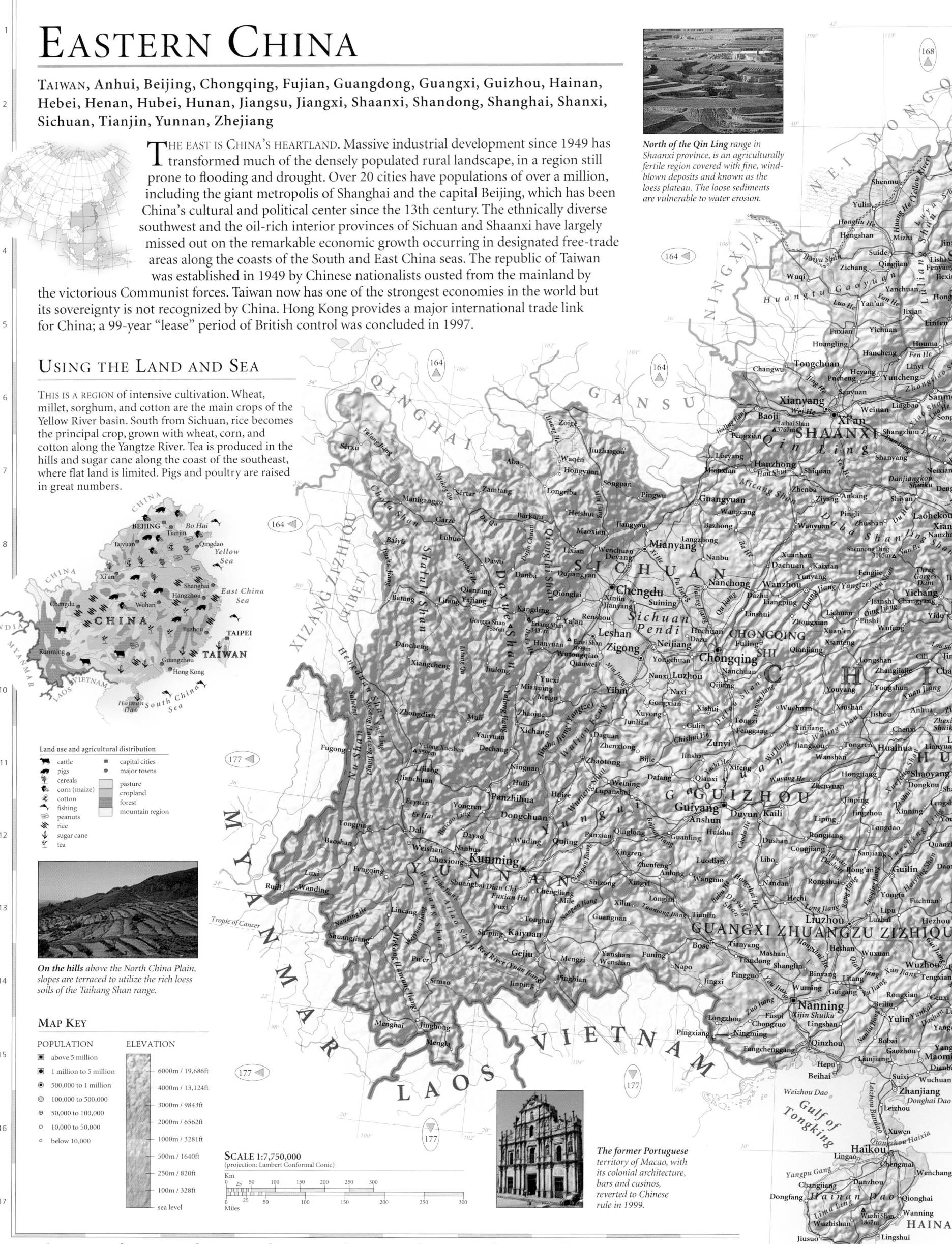

R S T U V W X Y

THE LANDSCAPE

THE SICHUAN PENDI (Red Basin), lies at the foot of the Plateau of Tibet between the Qin Ling range in the north and the limestone uplands of Yunnan and Guizhou to the south. Hills extend from Yunnan to the rocky southeast coast, dividing the Yangtze and Xi Jiang basins. The North China Plain is composed of sediment carried by the Yellow River from the loess plateau in the northwest.

The Yellow River carries more sediment than any other river on Earth – approximately 1,600 million tons (tonnes) per year. Floods caused by the breaching of the river's high banks have claimed many millions of human lives through history.

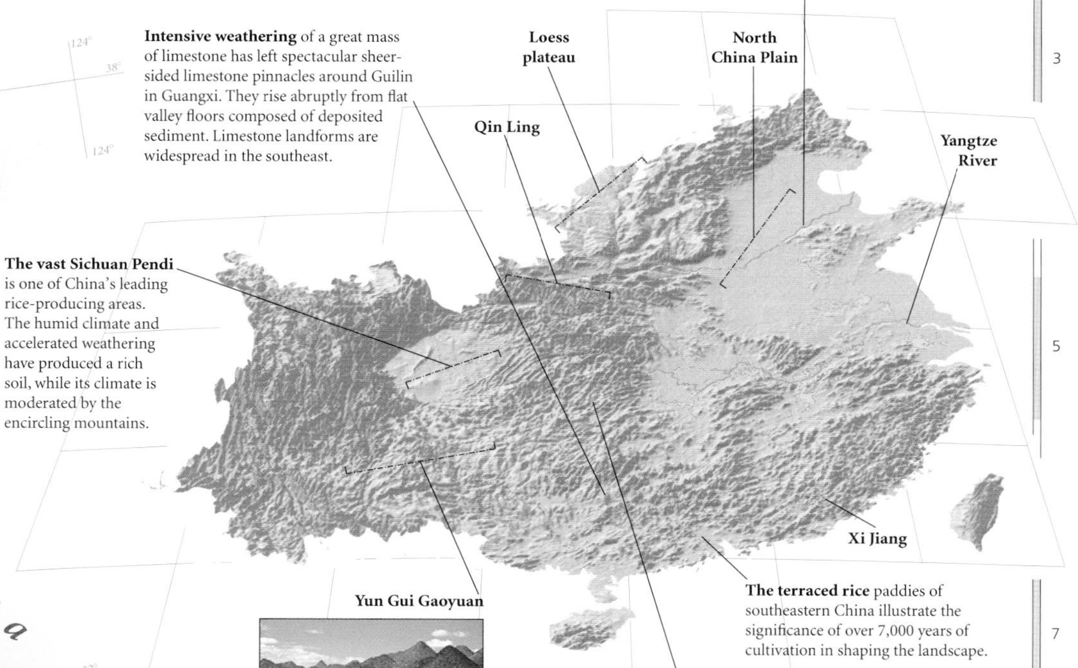

Intensive weathering of a great mass of limestone has left spectacular sheer-sided limestone pinnacles around Guilin in Guangxi. They rise abruptly from flat valley floors composed of deposited sediment. Limestone landforms are widespread in the southeast.

Loess plateau

North China Plain

Qin Ling

Yangtze River

The vast Sichuan Pendi is one of China's leading rice-producing areas. The humid climate and accelerated weathering have produced a rich soil, while its climate is moderated by the encircling mountains.

Xi Jiang

The terraced rice paddies of southeastern China illustrate the significance of over 7,000 years of cultivation in shaping the landscape.

Yun Gui Gaoyuan

Wu Jiang Gorge

The eroded rocky features of the Yungui Gaoyuan are testament to the Earth's forces which have folded and eroded this limestone region to produce dramatic, incised river valleys, gorges, and karst features.

The Wu Jiang Gorge is the result of tectonic uplift on the Yungui Gaoyuan Plateau which has caused the rapid downcutting of rivers across the region, creating deep, steep-sided valleys.

Course of the Yellow River

Pre 4BC

4BC–AD1

1234–1891

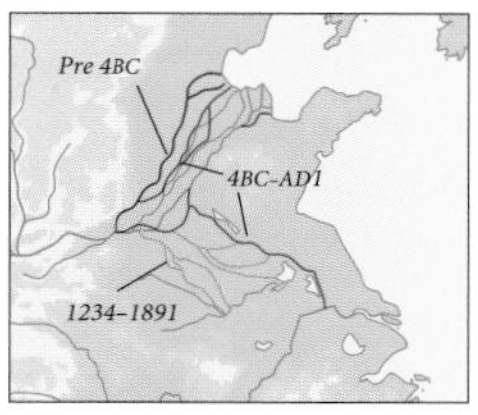

Over the past 2,000 years, the downstream course of the Yellow River has altered dramatically, veering unpredictably to the north and south across the North China Plain, and flooding vast expanses of land.

TRANSPORTATION & INDUSTRY

MODERN INDUSTRY IS CONCENTRATED in the coastal provinces, with dramatic new growth in Guangdong, based on foreign investment. Chemicals, iron and steel, engineering, and textiles are leading activities around Beijing and Shanghai, the two largest industrial centers. In the interior provinces, large fossil fuel reserves support heavy industry around major cities such as Wuhan and Chengdu. Taiwan's broad-based manufacturing economy specializes in hi-tech goods. Hong Kong is a major financial center and international entrepôt.

Major industry and infrastructure

- car manufacture
- chemicals
- electronics
- engineering
- finance
- food processing
- iron & steel
- pharmaceuticals
- shipbuilding
- textiles
- capital cities
- major towns
- international airports
- major roads
- major industrial areas

The former British colony of Hong Kong was ceded to China in 1997, marking the beginning of a new chapter in the history of this small territory. A vibrant mixture of eastern and western cultures, the booming textile industry, and subsequent electronics and financial industries, have driven immense growth and brought economic prosperity since the 1950s.

Taiwan is one of the Pacific Rim's economic "tigers," specializing in hi-tech and electronics industries.

THE TRANSPORTATION NETWORK

China's Grand Canal (Da Yunhe), built in the 13th century, is the world's longest artificial waterway, running 1,100 miles (1,770 km) from Beijing to Hangzhou. Despite restoration work, not all of the canal is currently navigable.

NORTHEASTERN CHINA, MONGOLIA & KOREA

MONGOLIA, NORTH KOREA, SOUTH KOREA, Heilongjiang, Inner Mongolia, Jilin, Liaoning

THIS NORTHERLY REGION has been a domain of shifting borders and competing colonial powers for centuries. Mongolia was the heartland of Chinghiz Khan's vast Mongol empire in the 13th century, while northeastern China was home to the Manchus, China's last ruling dynasty (1644–1911). The mineral and forest wealth of the northeast helped make this China's principal region of heavy industry, although the outdated state factories now face decline. South Korea's state-led market economy has grown dramatically and Seoul is now one of the world's largest cities. The austere communist regime of North Korea has isolated itself from the expanding markets of the Pacific Rim and faces continuing economic stagnation.

The Eurasian steppe stretches from the mouth of the Danube in Europe, to Mongolia. In Mongolia, nomadic people have lived in felt huts called yurts or gers, for thousands of years.

MAP KEY

POPULATION

- ▪ above 5 million
- ◼ 1 million to 5 million
- ◉ 500,000 to 1 million
- ◎ 100,000 to 500,000
- ⊕ 50,000 to 100,000
- ⊕ 10,000 to 50,000
- ○ below 10,000

ELEVATION

- 4000m / 13,124ft
- 3000m / 9843ft
- 2000m / 6562ft
- 1000m / 3281ft
- 500m / 1640ft
- 250m / 820ft
- 100m / 328ft
- sea level

SCALE 1:7,000,000
(projection: Lambert Conformal Conic)

THE LANDSCAPE

THE GREAT NORTH CHINA PLAIN is largely enclosed by mountain ranges including the Great and Lesser Khingan Ranges (*Da Hinggan Ling* and *Xiao Hinggan Ling*) in the north, and the Changbai Shan, which extend south into the rugged peninsula of Korea. The broad steppeland plateau of Nei Mongol Gaoyuan borders the southeastern edge of the great cold desert of the Gobi which extends west across the southern reaches of Mongolia. In northwest Mongolia the Altai Mountains and various lesser ranges are interspersed with lakeland basins.

Much of Mongolia and Inner Mongolia is a vast desert area. To the south and east, a semiarid region extends into China proper.

The Gobi Desert stretches from Central Asia, through Mongolia and into China. Bare rock surfaces, rather than sand dunes, typify the cold desert landscape of the Gobi.

Tributaries of the Amur River follow U-shaped valleys through the Great Khingan Range (*Da Hinggan Ling*). These were cut by ice-age glaciers between 3 and 10 million years ago.

Lesser Khingan Range (*Xiao Hinggan Ling*)

Changbai Shan

T'aebaek-sanmaek

The Altai Mountains are the highest and longest of the mountain ranges that extend into Mongolia from the northwest. These mountains provide one of the last refuges for the endangered snow leopard.

The Yellow River sweeps north around the Ordos Desert (*Mu Us Shadi*), bringing water to an otherwise barren region.

Columns of basalt rock protrude in occasional clusters from the flat surface of the eastern Gobi. Their regular, six-sided form was produced when the rock cooled and contracted from its molten state.

Great Khingan Range (*Da Hinggan Ling*)

A crater lake occupies the 9,023 ft (2,750 m) snowy summit of the extinct volcano Paektu-san, the highest peak in the mountains of the Changbai Shan.

The wooded mountain range of T'aebaek-sanmaek forms the backbone of the Korean peninsula, running north–south along the eastern coastline.

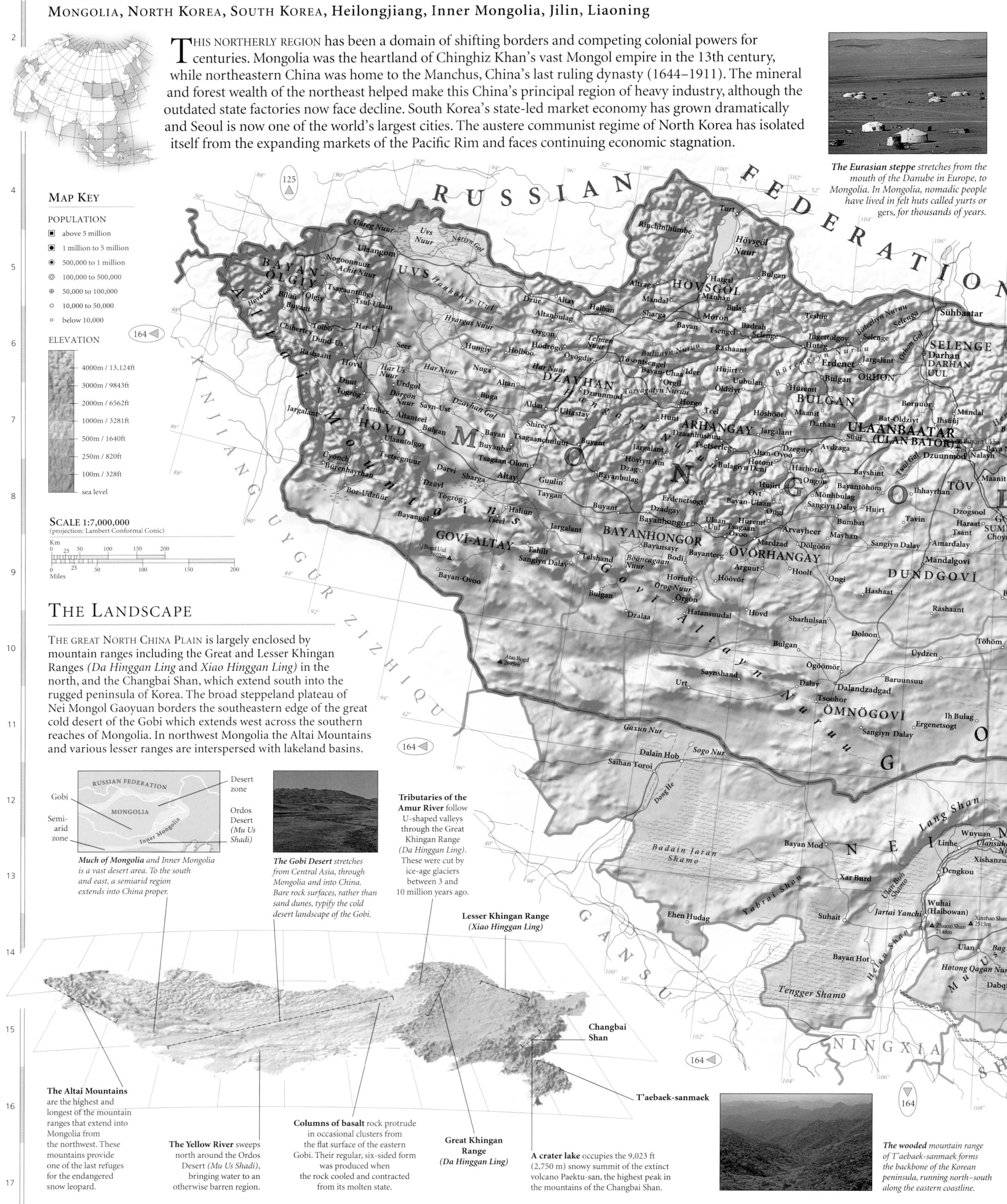

TRANSPORTATION & INDUSTRY

NORTH KOREA'S CENTRALLY-PLANNED ECONOMY is strongly oriented toward heavy industry, while South Korea has a broad manufacturing base which includes textiles, steel, electronics, and one of the world's largest shipbuilding industries. Mongolia and Inner Mongolia's great mineral resource potential is largely undeveloped. The heavy industrial region around Shenyang produces iron, steel, chemicals, and cement on a massive scale.

Major industry and infrastructure

- car manufacture
- chemicals
- coal
- electronics
- engineering
- finance
- food processing
- iron & steel
- pharmaceuticals
- shipbuilding
- textiles
- Rice
- capital cities
- major towns
- international airports
- major roads
- major industrial areas

TRANSPORTATION NETWORK

Liaoning has China's most comprehensive railroad network, the legacy of the Japanese occupation of Manchuria in the 20th century. The railroads are used primarily for freight transportation.

Ulan Bator, the Mongolian capital bears many of the hallmarks of Soviet-style central planning, the result of economic and industrial assistance from the Soviet Union following Mongolian independence in 1921.

While North Korea has remained politically and economically isolated from the rest of the world, South Korea has enjoyed immense economic growth. It has benefited considerably from US economic aid in the aftermath of the Korean war of 1950–1953.

USING THE LAND AND SEA

MONGOLIA AND INNER MONGOLIA rely heavily on livestock farming, with only about 1% of the land area cultivated. Northeastern China produces wheat, corn, soybeans, and sugar beet. The cool climate limits the range of crops and large upland areas of the northeast remain forested. Rice is the staple food of North and South Korea. The latter has become a leading ocean-fishing nation.

Land use and agricultural distribution

- goats
- pigs
- sheep
- corn
- fishing
- rice
- soybeans
- sugar beet
- wheat
- capital cities
- major towns
- pasture
- cropland
- forest
- mountain region
- desert

JAPAN

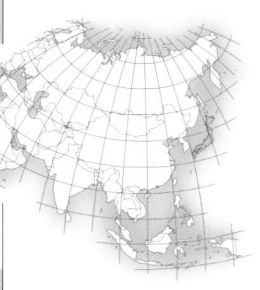

IN THE YEARS SINCE THE END of the Second World War, Japan has become the world's most dynamic industrial nation. The country comprises a string of over 4,000 islands which lie in a great northeast to southwest arc in the northwest Pacific. Four major islands: Hokkaido, Honshu, Shikoku, and Kyushu are home to the great majority of Japan's population of 128 million people, although the mountainous terrain of the central region means that most cities are situated on the coast. A densely populated industrial belt stretches along much of Honshu's southern coast, including Japan's crowded capital, Tokyo. Alongside its spectacular economic growth and the increasing westernization of its cities, Japan still maintains a highly individual culture, reflected in its traditional food, formal behavioral codes, unique Shinto religion, and a deep reverence for the emperor.

TRANSPORTATION & INDUSTRY

JAPAN IS THE WORLD'S second largest market economy, outranked only by the US. Technological development, particularly of computers, electronic goods, cars, and motorcycles is second to none. Japanese industry invests in its workforce and in long-term research and development to maintain the high standard of its products and a reputation for innovation. Japanese businesses are now global both in their manufacturing bases and in the distribution of goods.

TRANSPORTATION NETWORK

720,360 miles (1,160,000 km)	6,070 miles (12,529 km)
12,529 miles (20,175 km)	1,099 miles (1,770 km)

Japanese road construction traditionally lagged behind that of its extensive and technologically advanced railroad network. The road network's relative lack of development has led to severe urban congestion, although expressways have now been built in some cities.

USING THE LAND AND SEA

ALTHOUGH ONLY ABOUT 11% OF JAPAN is suitable for cultivation, substantial government support, a favorable climate and intensive farming methods enable the country to be virtually self-sufficient in rice production. Northern Hokkaido, the largest and most productive farming region, has an open terrain and climate similar to that of the American Midwest, and produces over half of Japan's cereal requirements. Farmers are being encouraged to diversify by growing fruit, vegetables, and wheat, as well as raising livestock.

Land use and agricultural distribution

- cattle
- pigs
- fishing
- cereals
- citrus fruits
- fruit
- herbs
- rice
- root crops
- tobacco
- capital cities
- major towns
- pasture
- cropland
- forest

THE URBAN/RURAL POPULATION DIVIDE

urban 78% rural 22%

0 10 20 30 40 50 60 70 80 90 100

POPULATION DENSITY	TOTAL LAND AREA
863 people per sq mile (333 people per sq km)	145,869 sq miles (377,800 sq km)

Cutting terraces maximizes the limited agricultural land, enabling Japan to produce large quantities of rice.

The Kobe earthquake in January 1995 highlighted Japan's vulnerability to earthquakes, despite technological advances. It shattered much of the infrastructure of this important port. More than 5,000 people died as buildings and overhead highways collapsed and fires broke out.

Major industry and infrastructure

- brewing
- car manufacture
- chemicals
- hi-tech industry
- engineering
- finance
- iron & steel
- research & development
- shipbuilding
- textiles
- winter sports
- capital cities
- major towns
- international airports
- major roads
- major industrial areas

Known in the west as the "bullet train," the Shinkansen is the second-fastest train in the world. It speeds past the snowcapped peak of Mount Fuji between the cities of Tokyo and Osaka.

A number of new volcanoes emerged in Japan during the 20th century. They exist alongside older cones like this one in Aso-Kuju National Park on Kyushu, now dormant and grass-covered.

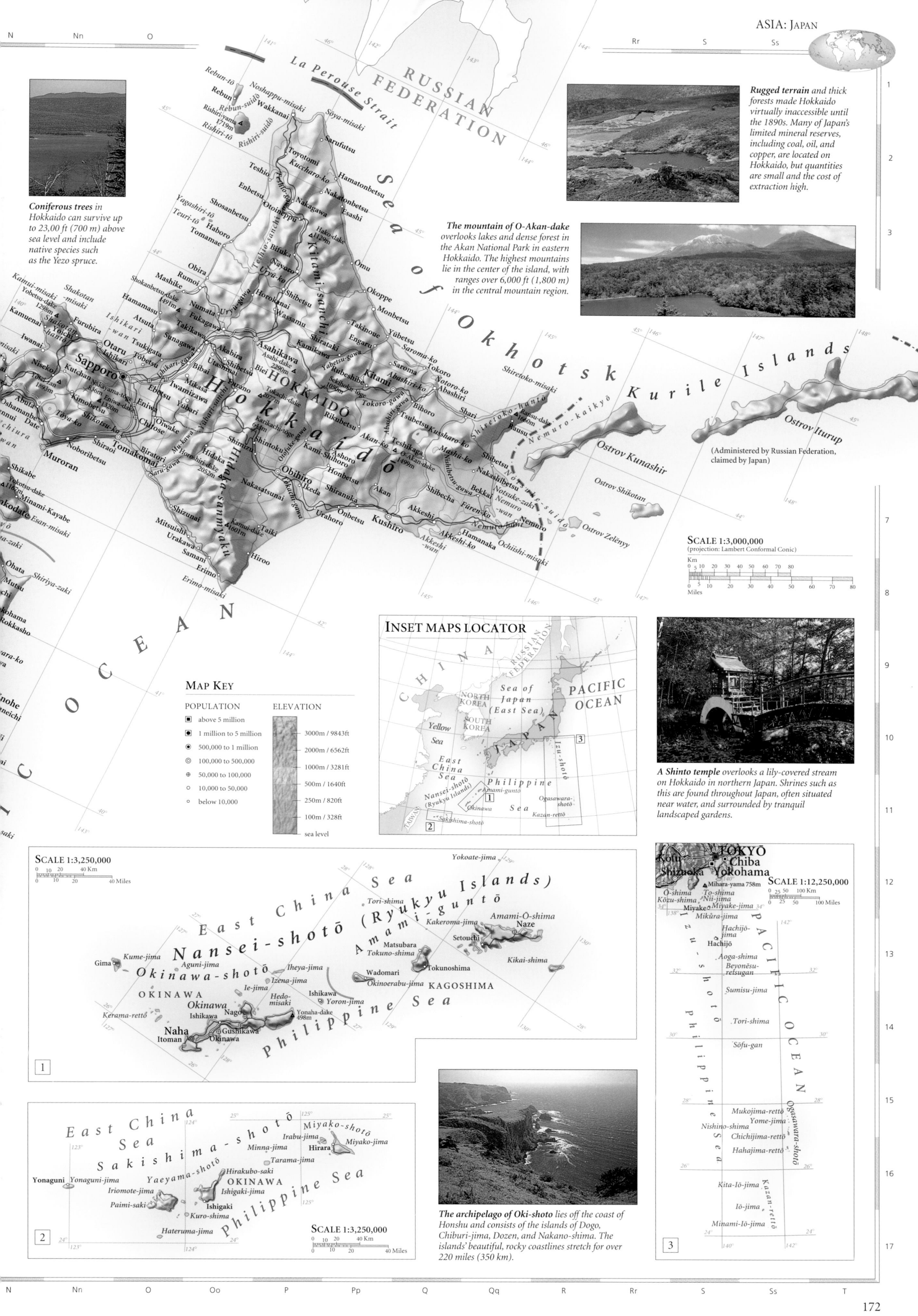

Coniferous trees in Hokkaido can survive up to 23,00 ft (700 m) above sea level and include native species such as the Yezo spruce.

Rugged terrain and thick forests made Hokkaido virtually inaccessible until the 1890s. Many of Japan's limited mineral reserves, including coal, oil, and copper, are located on Hokkaido, but quantities are small and the cost of extraction high.

The mountain of O-Akan-dake overlooks lakes and dense forest in the Akan National Park in eastern Hokkaido. The highest mountains lie in the center of the island, with ranges over 6,000 ft (1,800 m) in the central mountain region.

A Shinto temple overlooks a lily-covered stream on Hokkaido in northern Japan. Shrines such as this are found throughout Japan, often situated near water, and surrounded by tranquil landscaped gardens.

The archipelago of Oki-shoto lies off the coast of Honshu and consists of the islands of Dogo, Chiburi-jima, Dozen, and Nakano-shima. The islands' beautiful, rocky coastlines stretch for over 220 miles (350 km).

MAP KEY

POPULATION
- above 5 million
- 1 million to 5 million
- 500,000 to 1 million
- 100,000 to 500,000
- 50,000 to 100,000
- 10,000 to 50,000
- below 10,000

ELEVATION
- 3000m / 9843ft
- 2000m / 6562ft
- 1000m / 3281ft
- 500m / 1640ft
- 250m / 820ft
- 100m / 328ft
- sea level

INSET MAPS LOCATOR

SCALE 1:3,000,000
(projection: Lambert Conformal Conic)

SCALE 1:3,250,000

SCALE 1:3,250,000

SCALE 1:12,250,000

MARITIME SOUTHEAST ASIA

BRUNEI, EAST TIMOR, INDONESIA, MALAYSIA, SINGAPORE

THE INTRICATE ARC OF ISLANDS which runs from peninsular Malaysia east to Irian Jaya in western New Guinea sustains a huge variety of peoples, languages, and cultures. Indonesia is by far the largest country in the region, and 87% of its huge, predominantly Muslim, population is crowded onto Java, the most habitable of Indonesia's 13,677 islands. Malaysia, split between the mainland and the east Malaysian states of Sabah and Sarawak on Borneo, has a diverse population, as well as a fast-growing economy, although the pace of its development is still far outstripped by that of Singapore. This small island nation is the financial and commercial capital of Southeast Asia, and an Asian "tiger" economy. The Sultanate of Brunei in northern Borneo, one of the world's last princely states, also has an extremely high standard of living, based on its oil revenues.

USING THE LAND AND SEA

RICE IS THE MOST IMPORTANT ARABLE CROP in Indonesia and Malaysia, and both countries manage to meet almost all of their domestic demand. Malaysian rubber accounts for 25% of world production and is the main cash crop, grown on plantations and small farms, along with oil palms and copra. Timber is exported from both Malaysia and Indonesia. Modern agricultural techniques enable Singapore to produce fruit and vegetables despite a shortage of suitable land.

Spiral cuts in the bark of this rubber palm show where it has been tapped. Sophisticated "cloning" techniques mean that trees which produce consistently high quantities of rubber can be easily reproduced.

THE URBAN/RURAL POPULATION DIVIDE

urban 38%   rural 62%

0 10 20 30 40 50 60 70 80 90 100

POPULATION DENSITY
262 people per sq mile
(101 people per sq km)

TOTAL LAND AREA
828,356 sq miles
(2,146,000 sq km)

Land use and agricultural distribution

- coconuts
- fishing
- oil palms
- rice
- rubber
- shellfish
- sugar cane
- timber
- capital cities
- major towns
- pasture
- cropland
- forest
- wetland

MALAYSIA'S TWO CAPITALS

KUALA LUMPUR – capital
PUTRAJAYA – administrative capital

THE LANDSCAPE

FROM SUMATRA IN THE WEST, the volcanic islands of Indonesia run for nearly 3,100 miles (5,000 km). The Sunda Shelf, an extension of the Eurasian Plate, lies between Java, Bali, Sumatra, Lombok, and Borneo. Their volcanic mountains rise from a base below the sea and they were once joined together by dry land, which has since been submerged by rising sea levels.

Malay Peninsula has a rugged east coast, but the west coast, fronting the Strait of Malacca, has many sheltered beaches and bays. The two coasts are divided by the Banjaran Titiwangsa, which run the length of the peninsula.

The river of Sungai Mahakam cuts through the central highlands of Borneo, the third largest island in the world, with a total area of 290,000 sq miles (757,050 sq km). Although mountainous, Borneo is one of the most stable of the Indonesian islands, with little volcanic activity.

Borneo
Malay Peninsula
Sumatra
Drowned rivers
Broad, shallow valleys on sea floor
Present sea level
Quaternary sea level, 460 ft (140 m) below present sea level

The Sunda Shelf underlies this whole region. It is one of the largest submarine shelves in the world, covering an area of 714,285 sq miles (1,850,000 sq km). During the early Quaternary period, when sea levels were lower, the shelf was exposed.

Gunung Kinabalu is the highest peak in Malaysia, rising 13,455 ft (4,101 m).

The four-pronged island of Celebes is the product of complex tectonic activity which ruptured and then reattached small fragments of the Earth's crust to form the island's many peninsulas.

Papua (Irian Jaya) contains some of the most dense and least explored tropical rain forests in the world, inhabited by many rare species of plants and animals.

The island of Krakatau (Pulau Rakata), lying between Sumatra and Java, was all but destroyed in 1883, when the volcano erupted. The release of gas and dust into the atmosphere disrupted cloud cover and global weather patterns for several years.

Gunung Semeru

The volcano of Gunung Semeru in eastern Java lies on the Pacific "Rim of Fire." It is part of the ancient Tennegger volcano and remains highly active.

Indonesia has more than 220 volcanoes, most of which are still active. They are strung out along the island arc from Sumatra through the Lesser Sunda Islands, into the Moluccas and Celebes.

Coral islands such as Timor in eastern Indonesia show evidence of very recent and dramatic movements of the Earth's plates. Reefs in Timor have risen by as much as 4,000 ft (1,300 m) in the last million years.

The Pegunungan Jayawijaya range in central papua (Irian Jaya) contains the world's highest range of limestone mountains, some with peaks more than 16,400 ft (5,000 m) high. Heavy rainfall and high temperatures, which promote rapid weathering, have led to the creation of large underground caves and river systems such as the river of Sungai Baliem.

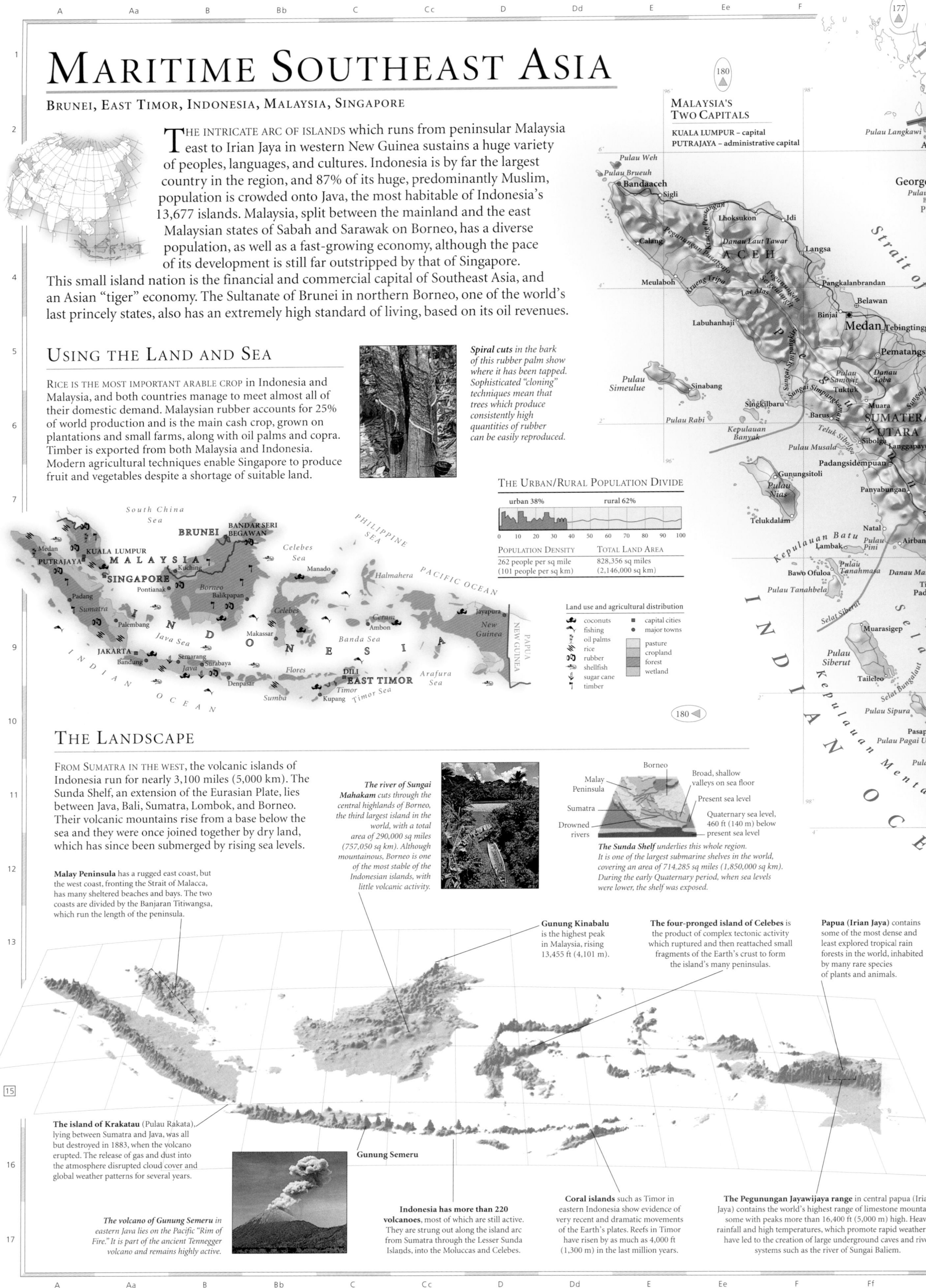

Malaysia exports a greater tonnage of tropical timber than anywhere else in the world. Much of it comes from Sarawak in Borneo. Although in principle logging is only allowed on a sustainable basis, environmentalists fear that the rainforest in Sarawak will have disappeared by the early 21st century.

This tiny island near Kota Kinabalu, in Sabah, eastern Malaysia, is a part of a designated national park. Thickly forested, it is surrounded by broad, sandy beaches and shallow inland seas.

Throughout Southeast Asia, where agricultural land is at a premium, terraces are cut into the slopes to maximize the area available for cultivation. These terraces on the Indonesian island of Bali are used to support rice paddies.

MAP KEY

POPULATION
- above 5 million
- 1 million to 5 million
- 500,000 to 1 million
- 100,000 to 500,000
- 50,000 to 100,000
- 10,000 to 50,000
- below 10,000

ELEVATION
- 4000m / 13,124ft
- 3000m / 9843ft
- 2000m / 6562ft
- 1000m / 3281ft
- 500m / 1640ft
- 250m / 820ft
- 100m / 328ft
- sea level

SCALE 1:6,250,000
(projection: Mercator)

Km
0 25 50 100 150
Miles
0 25 50 100 150

THE LANDSCAPE

THE ISLANDS OF JAPAN LIE on the Pacific "Ring of Fire," and form a series of clearly defined arcs. The largely mountainous landscape was formed very recently in geological terms. Volcanic eruptions and earthquakes continue to reshape the terrain and shake the country's complex infrastructure. There is no single continuous mountain range; the mountains divide into many small land blocks separated by lowlands and dissected by numerous river valleys.

Japan is part of an arc of volcanic islands, formed by the Pacific Plate diving under the Eurasian Plate. This process generates intense stress which is periodically released as earthquakes.

Sea of Japan (East Sea)
Active volcanic island
Japan Trench (subduction zone)

A number of rivers which emerge from the volcanic parts of northeastern Honshu are so highly acidic that their water is unsuitable for irrigation and consumption.

Calderas are the wide, flat-bottomed craters of volcanoes. Many Japanese calderas are filled by lakes such as Towada-ko in northern Honshu.

Trees cling to the sheer slopes of the waterfalls on the northern island of Hokkaido. The island's climate is similar to that in northern Europe, with long, cold winters and short, warm summers.

The long, narrow, steep-sided islands which make up Japan give rise to numerous short, fast-flowing rivers. The river of Shinano-gawa is the longest, at 228 miles (367 km).

The Inland Sea *(Seto-naikai)* has resulted from the depression of faulted blocks which has allowed sea water to invade the region between northern Shikoku and western Honshu.

There are over 60 active volcanoes – like Asahi-dake, Hokkaido's highest peak – throughout Japan. This accounts for more than 10% of the world's total.

Rising land on the Pacific coast of Honshu leads to typical features such as raised beaches, some lying over 1,000 ft (300 m) above sea level.

In much of Kyushu the coast is subsiding, giving a highly indented coastline. In some places, former hilltops are barely visible above the current sea level.

Strong northwesterly winds blowing onshore during the winter create sand dunes which extend for miles along the western coasts.

Biwa-ko is the largest lake in Japan, covering 260 sq miles (673 sq km) in central Honshu. The depression in which it lies was created by recent faulting of the underlying rocks.

Mount Fuji

Japan experiences earthquakes on an almost daily basis. They can cause fast-moving landslides and immense sea waves called *tsunami*. One that hit Sagami-nada in 1923, reached heights of 40 ft (12 m).

Mount Fuji is Japan's highest mountain, rising 12,388 ft (3,776 m) above the Kanto Plain in the central region of Honshu. The flat land below is suitable for growing crops such as tea. Like many Japanese mountains, it is revered as a sacred site.

Autumnal trees near Gifu, on central Honshu, create a spectacular display. Native trees on this island include camphor, pasania, Japanese evergreen oak, camellia and holly.

Modern tower blocks overlook the docks in Tokyo, Japan's teeming capital. Over 8 million people live in the city, straining the infrastructure to its limits.

USING THE LAND AND SEA

THE FERTILE FLOODPLAINS of rivers such as the Mekong and Salween, and the humid climate, enable the production of rice throughout the region. Cambodia, Myanmar and Laos still have substantial forests, producing hardwoods such as teak and rosewood. Cash crops include tropical fruits such as coconuts, bananas, and pineapples, rubber, oil palm, sugar cane, and the jute substitute, kenaf. Pigs and cattle are the main livestock raised. Large quantities of marine and freshwater fish are caught throughout the region.

Land use and agricultural distribution

- cattle
- pigs
- bananas
- coconuts
- fishing
- oil palms
- rice
- rubber
- sugar cane
- timber

- ■ capital cities
- • major towns

pasture
cropland
forest
wetland

THE URBAN/RURAL POPULATION DIVIDE

urban 30%   rural 70%

POPULATION DENSITY	TOTAL LAND AREA
322 people per sq mile (124 people per sq km)	733,828 sq miles (1,901,110 sq km)

The Paracel Islands and the Spratly Islands are two strategically sensitive island groups, disputed by several surrounding countries. The Paracels are claimed by China, Taiwan and Vietnam, though only China has actually occupied them. The Spratlys are claimed by China, Taiwan, Vietnam, Malaysia and the Philippines and are particularly important as they lie on oil and gas deposits.

The city of Hue in central Vietnam was the country's capital under the 13 emperors of the Nguyen dynasty from 1802 to 1945. It is the site of a number of religious monuments, including the Thien-Mu Pagoda.

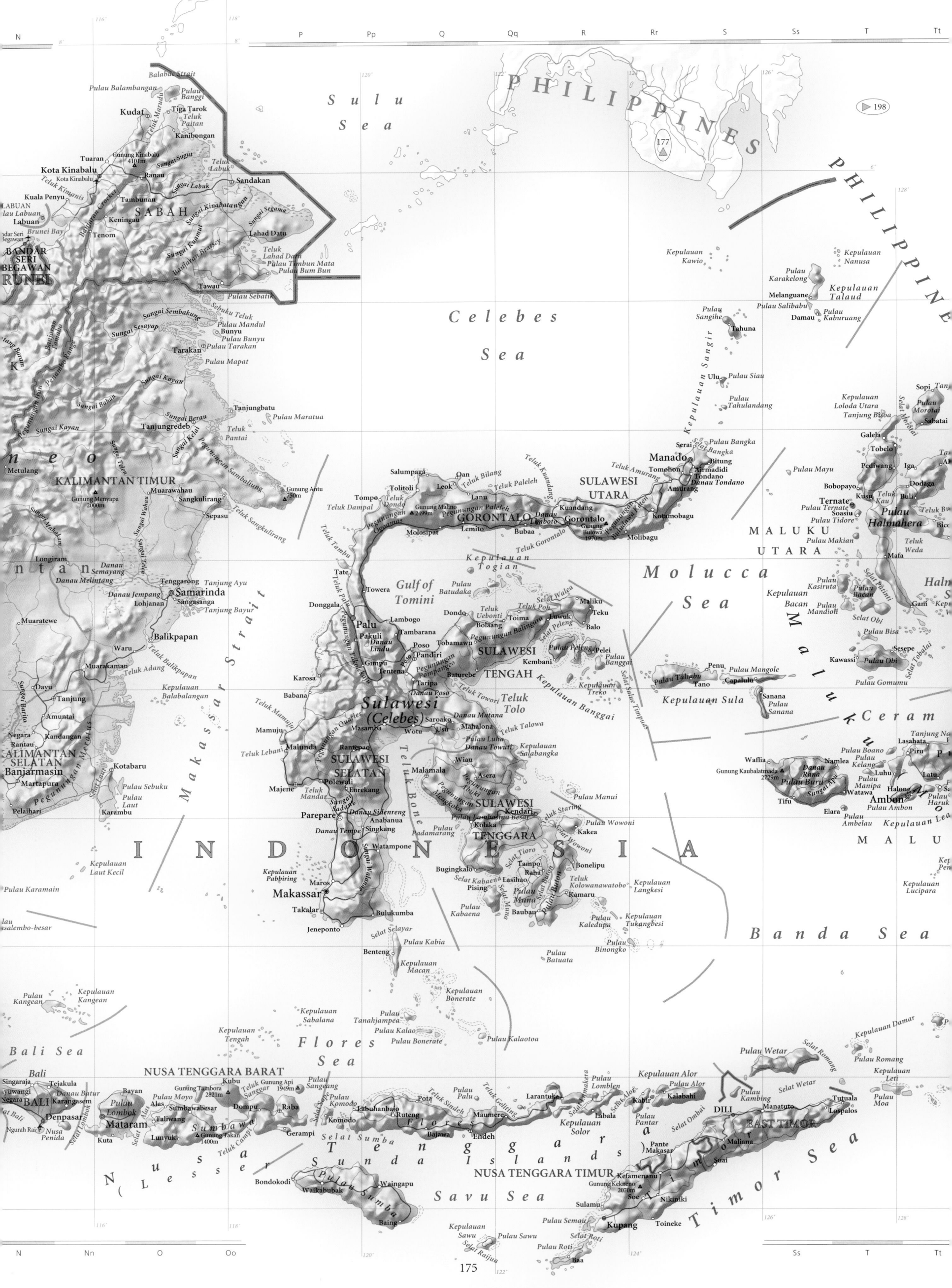

▷ 198

S u l u
S e a

PHILIPPINES

PHILIPPINE

PHILIPPINES

Pulau Balambangan

Pulau
Banggi

Kudat
Tiga Tarok
Teluk
Paitan
Kanibongan

Kepulauan
Kawio

Kepulauan
Nanusa

Tuaran
Gunung Kinabalu
4101m
Ranau
Sandakan

Pulau
Karakelong

Kota Kinabalu
Kota Kinabalu

Kuala Penyu
Tambunan
SABAH
Sungai Labuk
Teluk
Labuk

Melanguane
Kepulauan Talaud
Pulau Salibabu
Pulau
Kaburuang

LABUAN
Keningau
Sungai Kinabatangan

Labuan
Sungai Segama

Bandar Seri
Begawan
Tenom
Lahad Datu

BRUNEI
Brunei Bay

C e l e b e s

S e a

Damau

Pulau Sangihe
Tahuna

Batiatan Brassey
Teluk
Lahad Datu
Pulau Timbun Mata
Pulau Bum Bun

Tawau

Pulau Sebatik

Sebuku Teluk

Pulau Siau

Sungai Sembakung
Pulau Mandul
Bunyu
Pulau Bunyu

Sopi
Tan

Sungai Sesayap
Tarakan
Pulau Tarakan

Pulau
Tahulandang

Kepulauan
Loloda Utara
Tanjung Bisoa
Sabatai

Pulau Mapat

Galela

Sungai Kayan

Serai
Pulau Bangka
Tobelo
Iga

Tanjungbatu

Manado
Bitung
Pediwang
Dodaga

Sungai Berau
Tanjungredeb

Teluk
Pantai
Pulau Maratua

Teluk Amurang
Tomohon
Ahmaddadi
Tondano
Danau Tondano

Pulau Mayu
Bobopayo

neo

SULAWESI
UTARA
Amurang
Kotamobagu

Ternate
Pulau Ternate
Soasiu
Pulau Tidore

Kusu
Teluk
Kau

Pulau
Halmahera

KALIMANTAN TIMUR

Salumpaga
Oan

Teluk Bilang

MALUKU

Muarawahau
Sangkulirang

Gunung Antu
750m
Tompo
Tolitoli
Leok
Teluk Paleleh
Kuandang

UTARA
Pulau Makian

Gunung Menyapa
2000m
Sepasu
Teluk Dampal
Teluk
Dondo
Gunung Malino
2499m
Pegunungan Paleleh
Danau
Limboto
Gunung
Bulowa
1970m

Mafa

Molosipat
GORONTALO
Gorontalo

Teluk Weda

Longiram
Danau
Semayang
Tenggarong
Tanjung Ayu
Lemito
Bubaa
Molibagu

Halm
S

Danau Jempang
Lohjanan
Sangasanga
Tanjung Bayur

Kepulauan
Togian

M o l u c c a

Muaratewe
Samarinda

Tate
Towera
Pulau
Batudaka

Kepulauan
Kasiruta

Gulf of
Tomini

Teluk Walea

Pulau
Bacan
Pulau
Mandioli

Maluku

Waru
Teluk Balikpapan

Donggala
Lambogo
Dondo
Teluk
Uebonti
Toima
Maliku
Teku

Muarakaman
Balikpapan

Palu
Pakuli
Tambarana
Bolaang
Luwuk
Balo

Pulau Bisa

ntan

Dayu
Teluk Adang

Danau
Lindu
Poso
Tobamawu
Pegunungan Balingara

SULAWESI

Sesepe
Pulau Obi

Kepulauan
Balabalangan

Gimpu
Pandiri
Pulau Peleng
Pelei

Selat Obi

Tanjung
Amuntai

Karosa
Tentena
Taripa

TENGAH
Kembani

Penu
Pulau Mangole

Kawassi
Pulau Gomumu

Negara
Rantau
Kandangan

Babana
Baturebe

Pulau Taliabu
Tano
Capalulu

C e r a m

KALIMANTAN
SELATAN
Banjarmasin
Martapura

Teluk Poso
Danau Poso

Teluk Tolo
Kepulauan Banggai

Kepulauan
Treko

Selat Salue Timpaus

Kepulauan Sula

Tanjung Na
Lasahata

Pegunungan Meratus

Mamuju
Masamba
Saroako
Danau Matana

Sanana
Pulau Sanana

Maluku

Pulau Boano
Piru

Wotu
Usu
Teluk Talowa

Pulau Sebuku

Sulawesi
(Celebes)

Pulau Luha
Danau Towuti
Mahalona

Pulau Manipa
Kelang

Kotabaru

Malunda
Rantepang

Wiau
Kepulauan
Salabangka

Waflia
Pulau
Manipa

Pulau Laut
Karambu

Pulau
Buru

Pelaihari

Majene

SULAWESI
SELATAN
Polewali

Asera
Pegunungan
Abuki

Gunung Kaubalatmada
2729m

Namlea
Luhu
Latu

Danau
Rana

Tifu
Watawa

Halong
Pulau Haruk

I   N   D   O   N   E   S   I   A

Parepare
Enrekang

SULAWESI
Kendari
Kolaka

Elara

Tifu
Pulau Ambon

Ambon

Anabanua
Danau Sidenreng
Singkang

TENGGARA

Ambelau

Pulau
Padamarang

Teluk Staring
Kakea

Kepulauan Lea

MALU

Kepulauan
Pabbiring

Watampone
Pulau
Wowoni

Maros
Kepulauan
Laut Kecil

Bugingkalo
Raha
Tampo
Bonelipu

Kepulauan
Langkesi

Pulau Karamain

Makassar

Selat Tioro
Pising
Lasihao
Pulau
Muna
Kamaru

Kepulauan
Lucipara

lau
salembo-besar

Takalar

Bukumba

Pulau
Kabaena
Bauban

Teluk
Kolonawanatobo

Jeneponto

Selat Selayar

Pulau Kabia

Pulau
Binongko

B a n d a   S e a

Benteng

Kepulauan
Macan

Pulau
Batuata

F l o r e s

Kepulauan
Sabalana
Pulau Kalao

Kepulauan
Bonerate

Pulau
Kangean

Kepulauan
Kangean

Kepulauan
Tengah
Tanahjampea
Pulau Kalaotoa

S e a

Pulau Bonerate

B a l i   S e a

Pulau Wetar

Kepulauan Damar

Selat Romang
Pulau Romang

Bali
Singaraja
Tejakula

NUSA TENGGARA BARAT

Kubu
Teluk
Gunung Api
1949m

Pulau
Sangeang

Pulau
Lomblen
Kepulauan Alor
Pulau Alor

Kalabahi

Pulau
Kambing
Selat Wetar
Manatuto

Kepulauan
Leti
Pulau
Moa

yuwangi
Negara

Bayan
Gunung Tambora
2821m
Dompu
Pota

Larantuka
Labala

DILI

Denpasar
BALI
Karangasem

Pulau Lombok
Alas
Sumbawabesar
Raba

Teluk
Komodo
Ruteng
Maumere

Kabir
Pante
Makasar

EAST TIMOR
Tutuala
Lospalos

Nusa
Penida
Mataram
Lunyuk
Gunung Tukan
1400m

Labuhanbajo
Bajawa
Endeh

Kefamenanu
Maliana
Suai

Kuta
Taliwang

Komodo
Gerampi

Flores

NUSA TENGGARA TIMUR

Soe
Nikiniki

Bondokodi
Waikabubak
Selat Sumba

Waingapu

Gunung Kekneno
2070m

Baing

S a v u   S e a

Sulamu

Pulau Semau
Kupang
Toineke

Kepulauan
Sawu
Pulau Sawu
Selat Roti

T i m o r   S e a

Iba
Pulau Roti

U Uu V Vv W Ww X Xx Y Yy Z

TRANSPORTATION & INDUSTRY

SINGAPORE HAS A THRIVING ECONOMY based on international trade and finance. Annual trade through the port is among the highest of any port in the world. Indonesia still depends on natural resources, particularly wood, petroleum, and gas, although the economy is rapidly diversifying, with manufactured exports including garments, consumer electronics, and footwear; a high-profile aircraft industry has developed at Bandung. In Malaysia, although oil, gas, and timber remain important resource-based industries, it has a fast-growing and varied manufacturing sector.

Major industry and infrastructure

- aerospace
- copra processing
- chemicals
- electronics
- engineering
- finance
- food processing
- iron & steel
- oil
- ship building
- timber processing
- textiles
- capital cities
- major towns
- international airports
- major roads
- major industrial areas

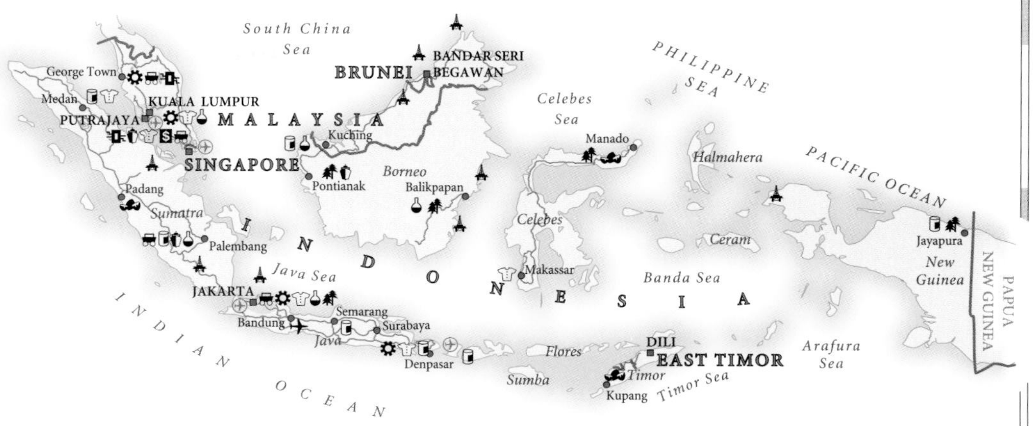

South China Sea

George Town
Medan
KUALA LUMPUR
PUTRAJAYA
MALAYSIA
Kuching
SINGAPORE
Padang
Sumatra
Pontianak
Balikpapan
Borneo
Palembang
Java Sea
JAKARTA
Bandung
Java
Semarang
Surabaya
Denpasar
Sumba
Kupang
Timor
DILI
EAST TIMOR
Timor Sea

BRUNEI
BANDAR SERI BEGAWAN
Manado
Celebes Sea
Halmahera
Celebes
Makassar
Banda Sea
Flores

PHILIPPINE SEA
PACIFIC OCEAN

Ceram
Jayapura
PAPUA NEW GUINEA
New Guinea

Arafura Sea

INDIAN OCEAN

INDONESIA

Ranks of gleaming skyscrapers, new highways and infrastructure construction reflect the investment which is pouring into Southeast Asian cities like the Malaysian capital, Kuala Lumpur. Traditional housing and markets still exist amidst the new developments. Many of the city's inhabitants subsist at a level far removed from the prosperity implied by its outward modernity.

TRANSPORTATION NETWORK

160,350 miles (258,213 km)

188 miles (302 km)

5,482 miles (8,828 km)

15,523 miles (32,903km)

Singapore's subway system is among the most efficient in the world. Malaysia has several fast, modern highways and most roads are paved. Indonesia's many islands make improvement of the shipping infrastructure a priority.

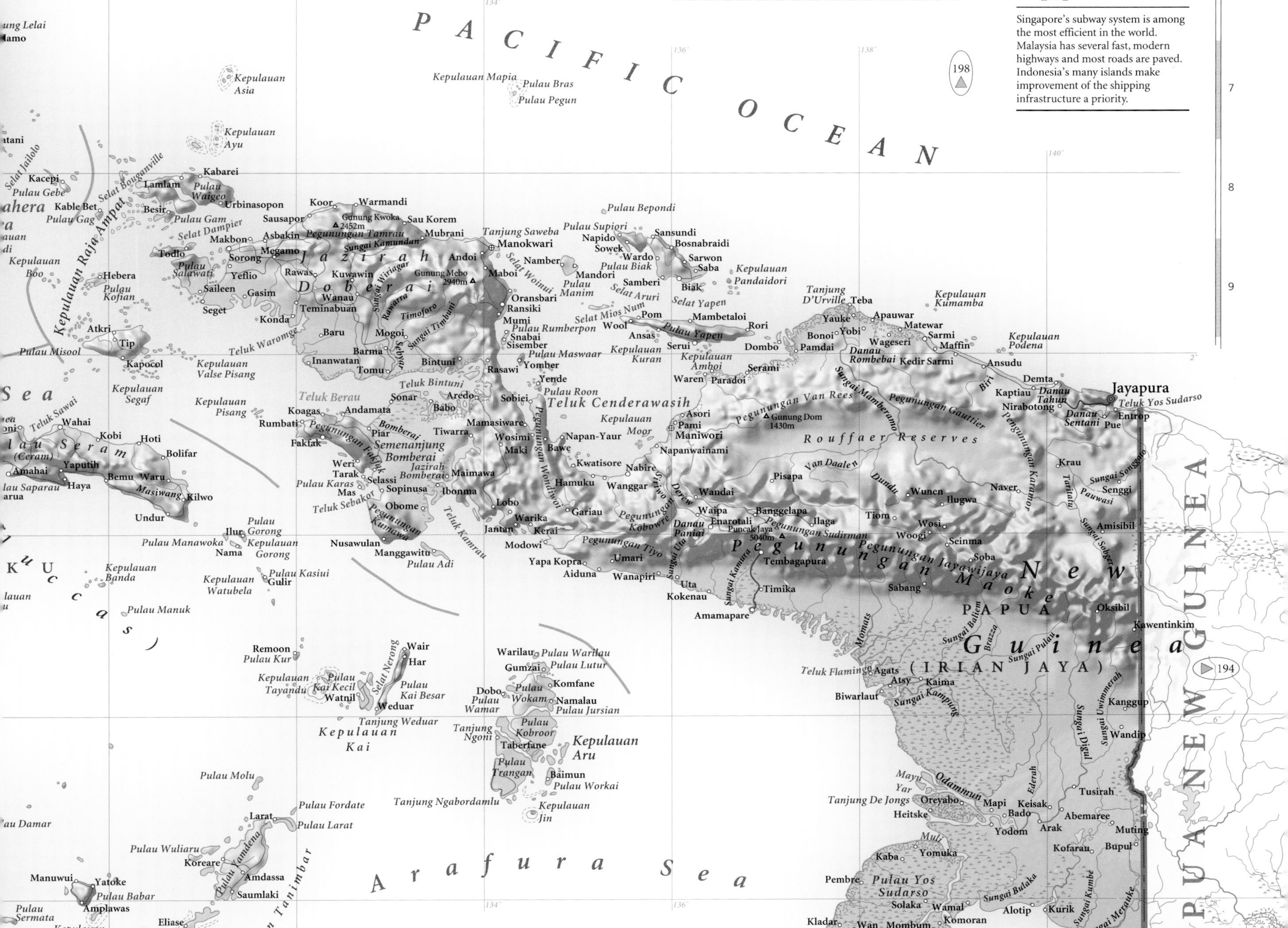

PACIFIC OCEAN

SEA
ng Sopi
Pulau Gebe
Kacepi
Pulau Gebe
Kable Bet.
Pulau Gag
Kepulauan Boo
Hebera
Pulau Kofiau
Atkri
Pulau Misool
Kapocol
Pulau Seram
Wahai
(Ceram)
Kobi
Hoti
Yaputih
Amahai
Bolifar
Bemu
Waru
Masiwang
Kilwo
Haya
Undur
Pulau Manawoka
Nama
Ilur
Kepulauan Gorong
Pulau Gorong
Kepulauan Banda
Kepulauan Watubela
Pulau Kasiui
Gulir
Pulau Manuk

Kepulauan Asia
Kepulauan Ayu
Kepulauan Mapia
Pulau Bras
Pulau Pegun

Kabarei
Lamlam
Pulau Waigeo
Urbinasopon
Warmandi
Besir
Pulau Gam
Koor
Gunung Kwoka 2452m
Sau Korem
Sausapor
Asbakin
Megamo
Mubrani
Makbon
Sorong
Manokwari
Todlo
Pulau Salawati
Saileen
Gasim
Maboi
Gunung Mebo 2940m
Andoi
Yeflio
Teminabuan
Segat
Konda
Baru
Mogoi
Inanwatan
Barma
Tomu
Rasawi
Sorong
Ransiki
Mumi
Wool
Seget
Kapocol
Tip
Kepulauan Valse Pisang
Kepulauan Segaf
Kepulauan Pisang
Teluk Waronge
Teluk Berau
Sonar
Koagas
Andamata
Rumbati
Pegunungan Fakfak
Piar
Faktak
Weri
Tarak
Selassi
Pulau Karas
Mas
Sopinusa
Obome
Pulau Gorong
Kepulauan Kumawa
Lobo
Warika
Jantan
Kerai
Modowi
Nusawulan
Manggawitu
Pulau Adi
Yapa Kopra
Aiduna
Umari
Wanapiri
Uta
Kokenau
Amamapare

Jazirah Doberai
Pegunungan Tamrau
Mubrani
Napido
Sowek
Sansundi
Bosnabraidi
Sarwon
Saba
Kepulauan Pandaidori
Pulau Biak
Namber
Yauke
Wardo
Mandori
Samberi
Biak
Rori
Manim
Ransiki
Pulau Rumberpon
Snabai
Sisember
Pulau Maswaar
Pulau Roon
Kepulauan Kuran
Serui
Kepulauan Ambpi
Serami
Waren
Paradoi
Pulau Yapen
Selat Mios Num
Pom
Ansas
Selat Aruri
Selat Yapen
Mambetaloi
Teba
Apauwer
Matewer
Sarmi
Maffin
Kepulauan Kumamba
Kepulauan Podena
Ansudu
Demta
Kaptiau
Nirabotong
Danau Tahun
Jayapura
Teluk Yos Sudarso
Entrop
Pue
Krau
Danau Sentani
Tanjung D'Urville
Bonoi
Yobi
Dombo
Pamdai
Wageseri
Danau Rombebai
Kedir
Sarmi

Teluk Cenderawasih
Kepulauan Mapia
Kepulauan Yamdena

Rouffaer Reserves
Pegunungan Van Rees
Pegunungan Gautier
Pegunungan Karanrang
Sungai Mamberamo
Sungai Idenburg
Gunung Dom 1430m
Asori
Pami
Maniwori
Napanwainami
Wosimi
Napan-Yaur
Maki
Bawe
Kwatisore
Hamuku
Wanggar
Gariau
Pegunungan Weyland
Pegunungan Kobowre
Waipa
Enarotali
Banggelapa
Ilaga
Puncak Jaya 5040m
Tiom
Wosi
Woogi
Tembagapura
Sabang
Timika
Pegunungan Tiyo
Pegunungan Sudirman
Pegunungan Jayawijaya
Pegunungan Maoke
Seinma
Soba
Oksibil
Kawentinkim

PAPUA (IRIAN JAYA)
New Guinea

Remoon
Pulau Kur
Kepulauan Tayandu
Kai Kecil
Watnil
Wair
Har
Pulau Nerong
Selat Nerong
Pulau Kai Besar
Weduar
Weduar
Tanjung Weduar
Kepulauan Kai
Pulau Molu
Pulau Fordate
Larat
Pulau Larat
Pulau Wuliaru
Koreare
Amdassa
Saumlaki
Selat Yamdena
Pulau Selaru
Tanjung Aro Usu
Eliase

Warilau
Gumzai
Dobo
Pulau Wokam
Namalau
Pulau Wamar
Pulau Kobroor
Taberfane
Pulau Trangan
Baimun
Tanjung Ngabordamlu
Pulau Warilau
Pulau Lutur
Komfane
Pulau Jursian
Pulau Ngoni
Kepulauan Aru
Pulau Workai
Kepulauan Jin

Teluk Flamingo
Agats
Atsy
Biwarlaut
Sungai Kampong
Sungai Pulau
Sungai Digul
Kaima
Mayn
Yar
Tanjung De Jongs
Heitske
Muli
Kaba
Yomuka
Pembre
Pulau Yos Sudarso
Solaka
Kladar
Wan
Mombum
Pulau Komoran
Tanjung Vals
Komoran
Wamal
Kurik
Alotip
Kondomirat
Sakiramke
Merauke
Sungai Merauke
Sungai Kumbi
Bupul
Muting
Kofarau
Arak
Yodom
Bado
Keisak
Abemaree
Tusirah
Wandip
Kanggup
Oreyabo
Mapi
Eldrah
Odammun

Pulau Damar
Manuwui
Yatoke
Pulau Babar
Amplawas
Pulau Sermata
Kepulauan Babar

Arafura Sea

Torres Strait

Although Indonesia is now a mainly Muslim country, relics of other civilizations are found throughout its many islands. These scattered columns are the ruins of a Hindu settlement which flourished on Java more than a thousand years ago.

PAPUA NEW GUINEA

MAINLAND SOUTHEAST ASIA & THE PHILIPPINES

CAMBODIA, LAOS, MYANMAR, PHILIPPINES, THAILAND, VIETNAM

THICKLY FORESTED MOUNTAINS, intercut by the broad valleys of five great rivers characterize the landscape of Southeast Asia's mainland countries. Agriculture remains the main activity for much of the population, which is concentrated in the river floodplains and deltas. Linked ethnic and cultural roots give the region a distinct identity. Most people on the mainland are Theravada Buddhists, and the Philippines is the only predominantly Christian country in Southeast Asia. Foreign intervention began in the 16th century with the opening of the spice trade; Cambodia, Laos, and Vietnam were French colonies until the end of the Second World War, Myanmar was under British control; and the Philippines was controlled by Spain and the US in the 20th century. Only Thailand was never colonized. Today, Thailand and the Philippines are poised to play a leading role in the economic development of the Pacific Rim, and Laos and Vietnam have begun to mend the devastation of the Vietnam War, and to develop their economies. With continuing political instability and a shattered infrastructure, Cambodia faces an uncertain future, while Myanmar is seeking investment and the ending of its 42-year isolation from the world community.

The Irrawaddy River is Myanmar's vital central artery, watering the rice paddies and providing a rich source of fish, as well as an important transportation link, particularly for local traffic.

Commercial logging – still widespread in Myanmar – has now been stopped in Thailand because of overexploitation of the tropical rain forest.

THE LANDSCAPE

A SERIES OF MOUNTAIN RANGES runs north–south through the mainland, formed as the result of the collision between the Eurasian Plate and the Indian subcontinent, which created the Himalayas. They are interspersed by the valleys of a number of great rivers. On their passage to the sea these rivers have deposited sediment, forming huge, fertile floodplains and deltas. The Philippines' 7,000 islands are mountainous and volcanic, with narrow coastal plains.

Lake Taal on the Philippine island of Luzon lies within the crater of an immense volcano which erupted twice in the 20th century, first in 1911 and again in 1965, causing the deaths of more than 3,200 people.

The Irrawaddy River runs virtually north–south, draining the plains of northern Myanmar. The Irrawaddy Delta is the country's main rice-growing area.

Hkakabo Razi is the highest point in mainland Southeast Asia. It rises 19,300 ft (5,885 m) at the border between China and Myanmar.

Mountains dominate the Laotian landscape with more than 90% of the land lying more than 600 ft (180 m) above sea level. The mountains of the Chaîne Annamitique form the country's eastern border.

The Red River Delta in northern Vietnam is fringed to the north by steep-sided, round-topped limestone hills, typical of karst scenery.

Mindanao has five mountain ranges, many of which have large numbers of active volcanoes. Lying just west of the Philippine Trench, which forms the boundary between the colliding Philippine and Eurasian plates, the entire island chain is subject to earthquakes and volcanic activity.

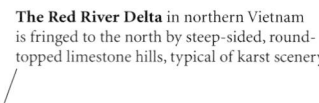

The fast-flowing waters of the Mekong River cascade over this waterfall in Champasak province in Laos. The force of the water erodes rocks at the base of the fall.

Salween River

Malay Peninsula

The Mekong River flows through southern China and Myanmar, then for much of its length forms the border between Laos and Thailand, flowing through Cambodia before terminating in a vast delta on the southern Vietnamese coast.

Tonle Sap, a freshwater lake, drains into the Mekong Delta via the Mekong River. It is the largest lake in Southeast Asia.

Thailand

The coastline of the Isthmus of Kra

Longshore drift

Spit

Eroded coastline

Lagoon

Wave attack

The east and west coasts of the Isthmus of Kra differ greatly. The tectonically uplifting west coast is exposed to the harsh south-westerly monsoon and is heavily eroded. On the east coast, longshore currents produce depositional features such as spits and lagoons.

Bohol

Bohol in the southern Philippines is famous for its so-called "chocolate hills". There are more than 1,000 of these regular mounds on the island. The hills are limestone in origin, the smoothed remains of an earlier cycle of erosion. Their brown appearance in the dry season gives the hills their name.

The coast of the Isthmus of Kra, in southeast Thailand has many small, precipitous islands like these, formed by chemical erosion on limestone, which is weathered along vertical cracks. The humidity of the climate in Southeast Asia increases the rate of weathering.

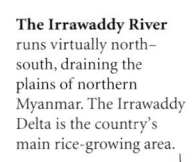

TRANSPORTATION & INDUSTRY

INDUSTRIAL MANUFACTURING has become increasingly important in Thailand, Vietnam, and the Philippines in recent years. The assembling of component-based electrical and electronic goods is becoming more common throughout this region, with foreign companies benefiting from low labor costs and the upgrading of technology. The economies of Myanmar and Cambodia are still based on agricultural produce and the processing of raw materials. Tin is the region's most important metal, and nickel, copper, and chromite are also mined, although the quantities produced are not significant on a global scale. Thailand's successful tourist industry is the country's highest earner of foreign exchange.

TRANSPORTATION NETWORK

131,566 miles (211,845 km)	267 miles (430 km)
7,785 miles (12,536 km)	28,393 miles (45,722 km)

Transportation development has concentrated on the building of road networks. Water and sea transportation remain important, although air links have improved, particularly in Thailand and the Philippines.

Major industry and infrastructure

- chemicals
- electronics
- engineering
- finance
- food processing
- iron & steel
- oil & gas
- mining
- shipbuilding
- textiles
- timber processing
- capital cities
- major towns
- international airports
- major roads
- major industrial areas

BANGLADESH
INDIA
CHINA
Mandalay
MYANMAR
Chiang Mai
HANOI
Hai Phong
Gulf of Tongking
VIENTIANE
LAOS
Bay of Bengal
RANGOON
Moulmein
THAILAND
Hue
Da Nang
Andaman Sea
BANGKOK
CAMBODIA
VIETNAM
PHNOM PENH
Gulf of Thailand
Ho Chi Minh City
South China Sea
Hat Yai
MALAYSIA
BRUNEI
Luzon Strait
Luzon
Philippine Sea
MANILA
PHILIPPINES
Cebu
Sulu Sea
Mindanao
Davao
Zamboanga
Celebes Sea

***Opium poppies** are destroyed under army supervision in Thailand. This action is part of a government-sponsored initiative to reduce the trade in drugs such as heroin, which is derived from these plants. Drug trafficking is a major problem throughout the region; the area is known as the "Golden Triangle," and Laos is the third-largest producer of opium poppies in the world.*

***The terracing of land** to restrict soil erosion and create flat surfaces for agriculture is a common practice throughout Southeast Asia, particularly where land is scarce. These terraces are on Luzon in the Philippines.*

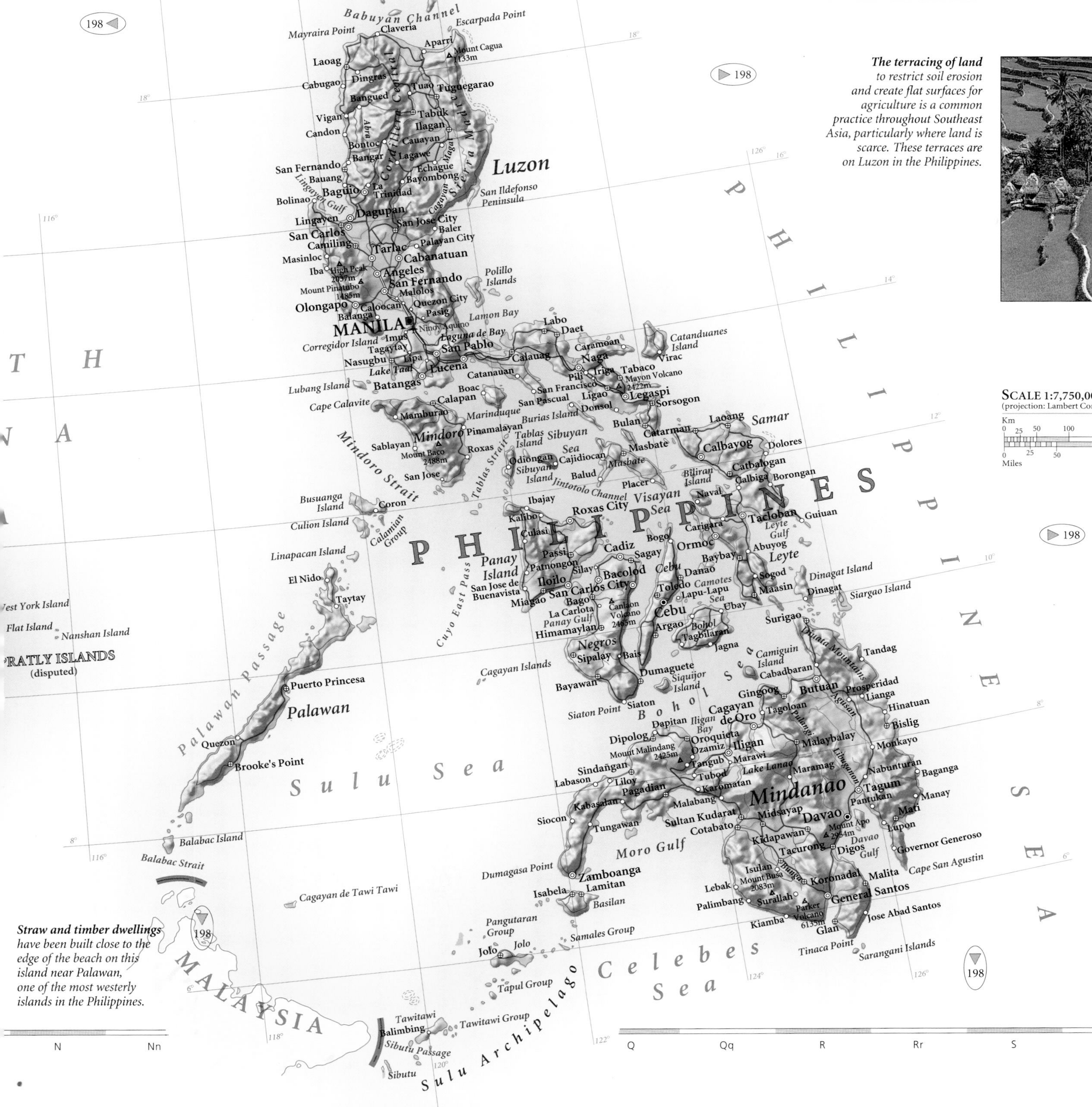
Bashi Channel
Batan Islands
Luzon Strait
Balintang Channel
Babuyan Island
Babuyan Channel
Escarpada Point
Mayraira Point
Claveria
Aparri
Laoag
Cabugao
Tuguegarao
Vigan
Candon
Luzon
San Fernando
Baguio
Dagupan
Lingayen
San Carlos
Cabanatuan
Angeles
Olongapo
Quezon City
MANILA
Batangas
Lucena
Naga
Legaspi
Sorsogon
Calapan
Mindoro
Masbate
Samar
Calbayog
Catbalogan
Tacloban
Leyte
Roxas City
Iloilo
Bacolod
Cebu
Negros
Dumaguete
Bohol
Surigao
Butuan
Cagayan de Oro
Iligan
Mindanao
Davao
Cotabato
General Santos
Zamboanga
Puerto Princesa
Palawan
Sulu Sea
Celebes Sea
PHILIPPINES
PHILIPPINE SEA
SOUTH CHINA SEA
SPRATLY ISLANDS (disputed)
MALAYSIA
Sulu Archipelago
Tawitawi
Jolo
198

***Straw and timber dwellings** have been built close to the edge of the beach on this island near Palawan, one of the most westerly islands in the Philippines.*

SCALE 1:7,750,000
(projection: Lambert Conformal Conic)

Km 0 25 50 100 150 200
Miles 0 25 50 100 150 200

MAP KEY

POPULATION

- above 5 million
- 1 million to 5 million
- 500,000 to 1 million
- 100,000 to 500,000
- 50,000 to 100,000
- 10,000 to 50,000
- below 10,000

ELEVATION

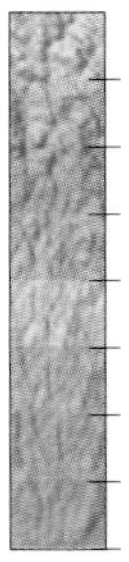

- 4000m / 13,124ft
- 3000m / 9843ft
- 2000m / 6562ft
- 1000m / 3281ft
- 500m / 1640ft
- 250m / 820ft
- 100m / 328ft
- sea level

THE INDIAN OCEAN

DESPITE BEING THE SMALLEST of the three major oceans, the evolution of the Indian Ocean was the most complex. The ocean basin was formed during the breakup of the supercontinent Gondwanaland, when the Indian subcontinent moved northeast, Africa moved west and Australia separated from Antarctica. Like the Pacific Ocean, the warm waters of the Indian Ocean are punctuated by coral atolls and islands. About one-fifth of the world's population – over a billion people – live on its shores. In 2004, over 290,000 died and millions more were left homeless after a tsunami devastated large stretches of the ocean's coastline.

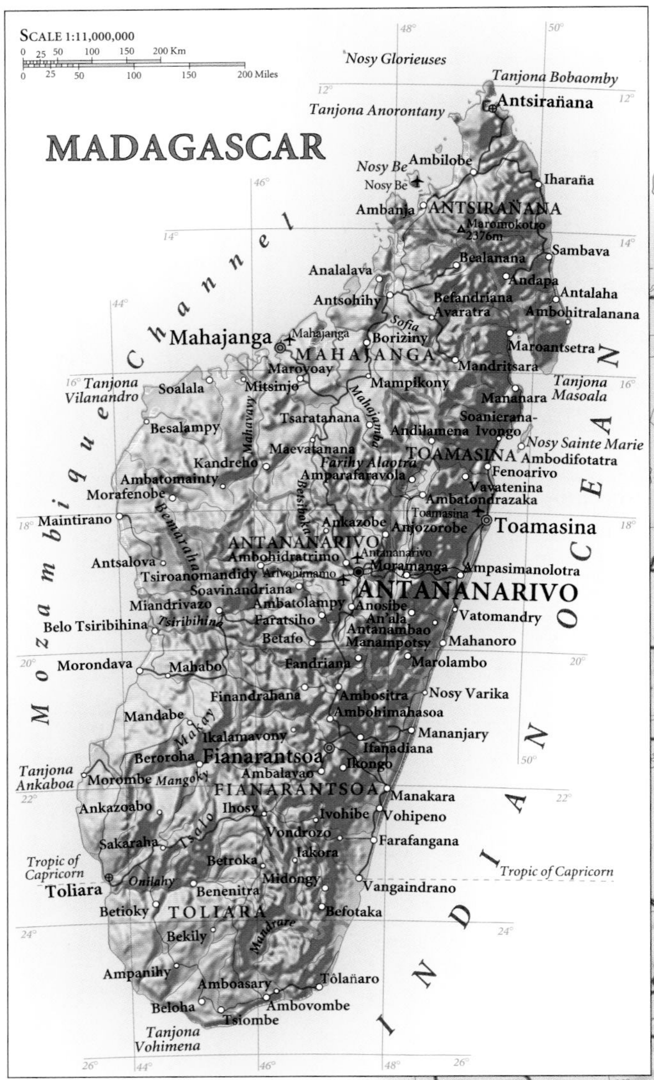

THE LANDSCAPE

THE INDIAN OCEAN BEGAN FORMING about 150 million years ago, but in its present form it is relatively young, only about 36 million years old. Along the three subterranean mountain chains of its mid-ocean ridge the seafloor is still spreading. The Indian Ocean has fewer trenches than other oceans and only a narrow continental shelf around most of its surrounding land.

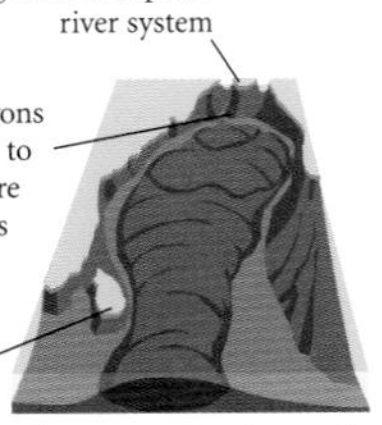

Sediments come from Ganges/Brahmaputra river system

Submarine canyons transport sediment to fan – some of these are more than 1,500 miles (2,500 km) long

Sri Lanka

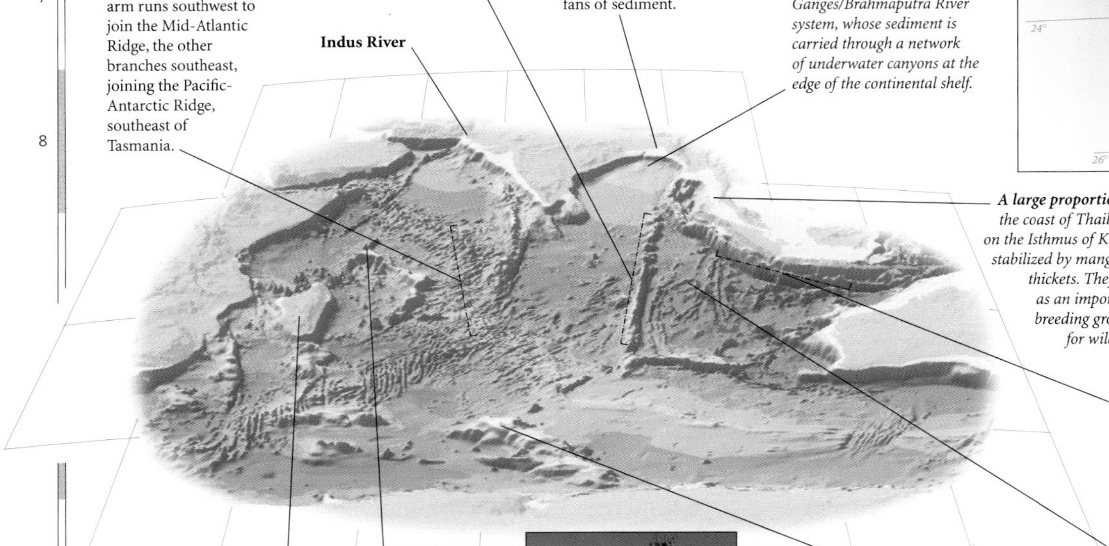

The mid-oceanic ridge runs from the Arabian Sea. It diverges east of Madagascar. One arm runs southwest to join the Mid-Atlantic Ridge, the other branches southeast, joining the Pacific-Antarctic Ridge, southeast of Tasmania.

The Ninetyeast Ridge takes its name from the line of longitude it follows. It is the world's longest and straightest under-sea ridge.

Two of the world's largest rivers flow into the Indian Ocean; the Indus and the Ganges/Brahmaputra. Both have deposited enormous fans of sediment.

The Ganges Fan is one of the world's largest submarine accumulations of sediment, extending far beyond Sri Lanka. It is fed by the Ganges/Brahmaputra River system, whose sediment is carried through a network of underwater canyons at the edge of the continental shelf.

Indus River

A large proportion of the coast of Thailand, on the Isthmus of Kra, is stabilized by mangrove thickets. They act as an important breeding ground for wildlife.

The Java Trench is the world's longest, it runs 1,600 miles (2,570 km) from the southwest of Java, but is only 50 miles (80 km) wide.

The relief of Madagascar rises from a low-lying coastal strip in the east, to the central plateau. The plateau is also a major watershed separating Madagascar's three main river basins.

The central group of the Seychelles are mountainous, granite islands. They have a narrow coastal belt and lush, tropical vegetation cloaks the highlands.

The Kerguelen Islands in the Southern Ocean were created by a hot spot in the Earth's crust. The islands were formed in succession as the Antarctic Plate moved slowly over the hot spot.

The circulation in the northern Indian Ocean is controlled by the monsoon winds. Biannually these winds reverse their pattern, causing a reversal in the surface currents and alternative high and low pressure conditions over Asia and Australia.

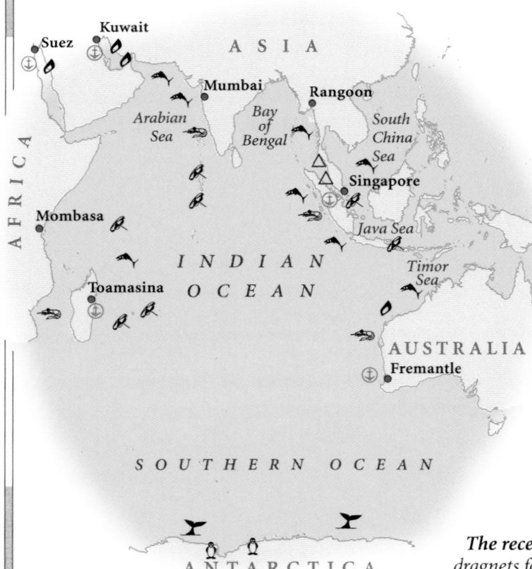

RESOURCES

MANY OF THE SMALL ISLANDS in the Indian Ocean rely exclusively on tuna-fishing and tourism to maintain their economies. Most fisheries are artisanal, although large-scale tuna-fishing does take place in the Seychelles, Mauritius and the western Indian Ocean. Nonliving resources include oil in the Persian Gulf, pearls in the Red Sea, and tin from deposits off the shores of Myanmar, Thailand, and Indonesia.

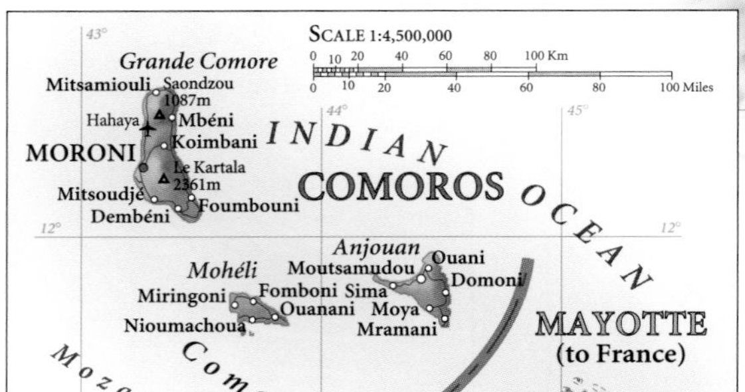

The recent use of large dragnets for tuna-fishing has not only threatened the livelihoods of many small-scale fisheries, but also caused widespread environmental concern about the potential impact on other marine species.

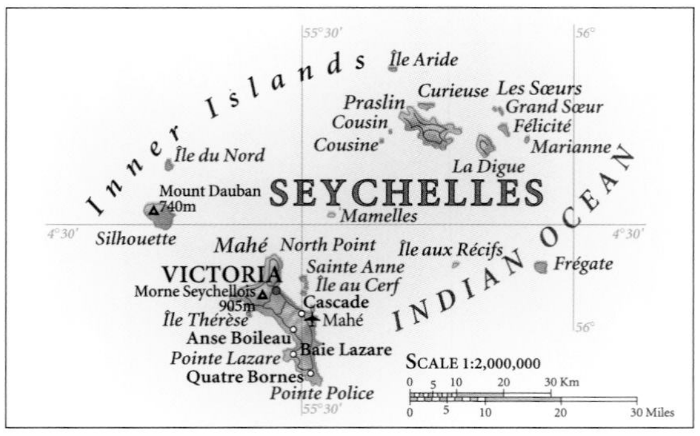

Resources (including wildlife)
- fish
- penguins
- shellfish
- whales
- oil & gas
- tin deposits
- tourism
- major towns
- major ports

Coral reefs support an enormous diversity of animal and plant life. Many species of tiny tropical fish, like these squirrel fish, live and feed around the profusion of reefs and atolls in the Indian Ocean.

SCALE 1:11,000,000

MADAGASCAR

SCALE 1:4,500,000

MORONI
COMOROS
MAYOTTE (to France)
MAMOUDZOU

Inner Islands
SEYCHELLES
VICTORIA

SCALE 1:2,000,000

The steeper eastern side of Madagascar is drained by numerous short, fast-flowing rivers. In contrast, larger, more languid rivers flow across the west. Both erode huge quantities of Madagascar's reddish soil.

There are over 1,300 small coral islands in the Maldives, but only about 200 are inhabited. They are based around an ancient submerged volcanic mountain range and all the islands are low-lying, none rising more than 6 ft (1.8 m) above sea level.

SCALE 1:42,000,000
(projection: Mollweide)

Km
Miles

Labels on main map

KUWAIT
IRAN
Ad Dammam
AHRAIN
Doha
QATAR
Abu Dhabi
UAE
Dubai
OMAN
Bandar-e 'Abbās
Gulf of Oman
OMAN
Muscat
Minā' Qābūs
PAKISTAN
Karachi
Gwadar
Persian Gulf
ARABIA
YEMEN
Salalah
Socotra
(to Yemen)
Error
Tablemount
Andrew
Tablemount

ASIA
Indus
Bhavnagar
Narmada
Mumbai (Bombay)
INDIA
Ganges
Godavari
Krishna
BANGLADESH
Dhaka
Kolkata (Calcutta)
Chittagong
Brahmaputra
Ganges Fan
Visākhapatnam
Bay of Bengal
MYANMAR
Rangoon
Salween
Irrawaddy
LAOS
THAILAND
CAMBODIA
VIETNAM
CHINA
Mekong
Gulf of Tongking
TAIWAN
East China Sea
Ryukyu Islands
Tropic of Cancer
Philippine Sea

Arabian Basin
Arabian Sea
Indus Fan
Owen Fracture Zone
Carlsberg Ridge
Chain Ridge
Mid-Indian Ridge
Laccadive Islands (to India)
Mangalore
Chennai (Madras)
Cochin
Tuticorin
Trincomalee
Sri Lanka
SRI LANKA
Colombo
MALDIVES
Laccadive Plateau
Ceylon Plain
Andaman Islands (to India)
Andaman Basin
Andaman Sea
Nicobar Islands (to India)
Bedawan
Strait of Malacca
Sumatra
Klang
Singapore
MALAYSIA
Borneo
South China Sea
PHILIPPINES
Sulu Sea
Celebes Sea
INDONESIA
Celebes
Molucca Sea
Ceram Sea
New Guinea

Somali Basin
Cosmoledo Seamounts
Mahé
Madingley Rise
SEYCHELLES
Amirante Islands
Mascarene Plateau
Saya de Malha Bank
Cocos-Keeling
Chagos-Laccadive Plateau
Chagos Archipelago
Diego Garcia
British Indian Ocean Territory (to UK)
Chagos Trench
Mid-Indian Basin
Cocos Basin
Investigator Ridge
Java Trench
Java Ridge
Java
Bali
Sumbawa
Lombok Basin
Pulau Sumba
Timor
EAST TIMOR
Timor Sea
Banda Sea
Arafura Sea
Darwin
Gulf of Carpentaria

INDIAN OCEAN
West Indian Ridge
Madagascar Basin
MAURITIUS
Rodrigues (to Mauritius)
Mascarene Islands
Réunion (to France)
Mascarene Basin
Nazareth Bank
Cargados Carajos Bank
Agalega Islands (to Mauritius)
Farquhar Group
Mascarene Plain
Mauritius Trench
Egeria Fracture Zone
Central Indian Ridge
Ninetyeast Ridge
Osborn Plateau
East Indian Ridge
Batavia Seamount
Gulden Draak Seamount
Wharton Basin
Wallaby Plateau
Broken Ridge
Ob' Trench
Naturaliste Plateau
Diamantina Fracture Zone
Perth Basin
Geraldton
Fremantle
Bunbury
Albany
Great Australian Bight
AUSTRALIA
North Australian Basin
Gascoyne Plain
Exmouth Plateau
Cuvier Basin
Cuvier Plateau
Shark Bay
Rowley Shoals
Sahul Shelf
King Sound
Ahmore & Cartier Islands (to Australia)
Joseph Bonaparte Gulf
Wyndham
Broome
Port Hedland
Tropic of Capricorn
Christmas Island (to Australia)
Cocos Islands (to Australia)
Roo Rise

Crozet Basin
Crozet Plateau
Crozet Islands
Amsterdam Fracture Zone
Amsterdam Island
St. Paul Island
French Southern & Antarctic Territories (to France)
Kerguelen Plateau
Kerguelen
Heard & McDonald Islands (to Australia)
Ob' Tablemount
Lena Tablemount
Southeast Indian Ridge
South Australian Basin
South Australian Plain
Spencer Gulf
Port Augusta
Kangaroo Island
Adelaide
Melbourne
King Island
Bass Strait
Tasmania
Tasman Plateau
Murray
Darling

SOUTHERN OCEAN
Derby Plain
Banzare Seamounts
South Indian Basin

ANTARCTICA
Prydz Bay
Antarctic Circle

Inset: RÉUNION (to France)

RÉUNION (to France)
SCALE 1:2,000,000
0 5 10 20 30 Km
0 10 20 30 Miles

ST-DENIS
Le Port
Ste-Marie
Gillot
St-Paul
Ste-Suzanne
St-André
Salazie
St-Benoît
Pointe des Aigrettes
St-Gilles-les-Bains
Piton des Neiges 3070m
Trois-Bassins
St-Leu
Cilaos
La Plaine-des-Palmistes
Ste-Rose
Pointe au Sel
Le Tampon
Piton de la Fournaise 2632m
St-Louis
St-Pierre
Pointe de la Table
Point de la Rivière St-Étienne
St-Joseph
St-Philippe
INDIAN OCEAN

INSET MAP KEY

POPULATION
- ◉ 500,000 to 1 million
- ◎ 100,000 to 500,000
- ⊕ 50,000 to 100,000
- ⊙ 10,000 to 50,000
- ○ below 10,000

ELEVATION
- 3000m / 9843ft
- 2000m / 6562ft
- 1000m / 3281ft
- 500m / 1640ft
- 250m / 820ft
- 100m / 328ft
- sea level

OCEAN MAP KEY

SEA DEPTH
- sea level
- 250m / 820ft
- 500m / 1640ft
- 1000m / 3281ft
- 2000m / 6562ft
- 3000m / 9843ft

Inset: MAURITIUS

MAURITIUS

Round Island
Flat Island
Gunner's Quoin
Canonniers Point
Ile D'Ambre
Goodlands
Triolet
Pamplemousses
Rivière du Rempart
PORT LOUIS
Beau Bassin
Quatre Bornes
Centre de Flacq
Rose Hill
Bel Air
Mont du Rempart 545m
Vacoas
Tamarin
Curepipe
Piton de la Petite
Rivière Noire 828m
Rose Belle
Mahebourg
Pointe Sud Ouest
Chemin Grenier
Seewoosagur Ramgoolam
Souillac
INDIAN OCEAN
SCALE 1:2,000,000
0 5 10 20 30 Km
0 5 10 20 30 Miles

*The island of **Mauritius** is volcanic in origin. Its central plateau is bounded by mountains which may once have formed the rim of a volcanic crater.*

181

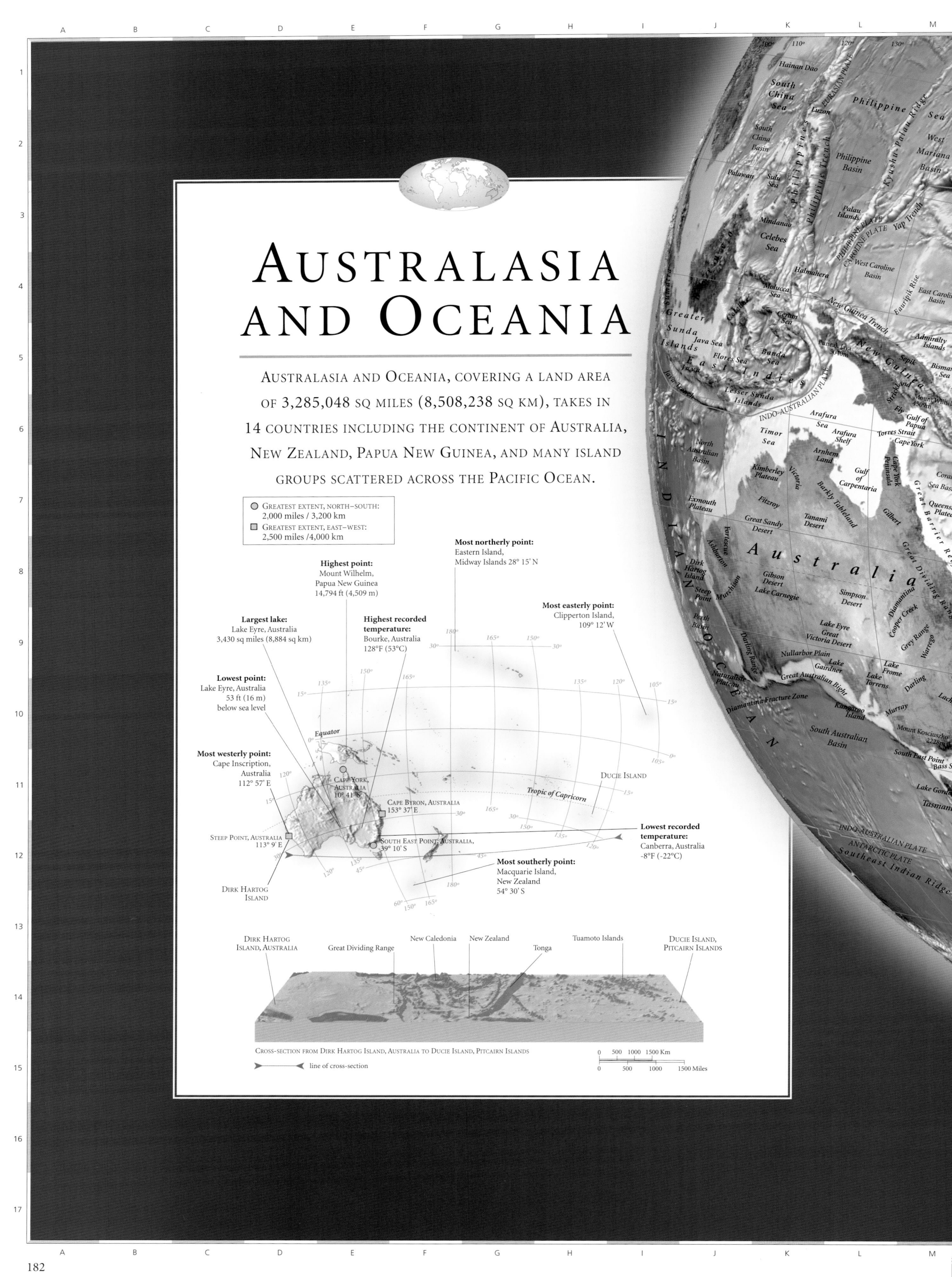

AUSTRALASIA AND OCEANIA

AUSTRALASIA AND OCEANIA, COVERING A LAND AREA OF 3,285,048 SQ MILES (8,508,238 SQ KM), TAKES IN 14 COUNTRIES INCLUDING THE CONTINENT OF AUSTRALIA, NEW ZEALAND, PAPUA NEW GUINEA, AND MANY ISLAND GROUPS SCATTERED ACROSS THE PACIFIC OCEAN.

⊙ GREATEST EXTENT, NORTH–SOUTH:
2,000 miles / 3,200 km

▢ GREATEST EXTENT, EAST–WEST:
2,500 miles /4,000 km

Most northerly point:
Eastern Island,
Midway Islands 28° 15' N

Highest point:
Mount Wilhelm,
Papua New Guinea
14,794 ft (4,509 m)

Most easterly point:
Clipperton Island,
109° 12' W

Largest lake:
Lake Eyre, Australia
3,430 sq miles (8,884 sq km)

Highest recorded temperature:
Bourke, Australia
128°F (53°C)

Lowest point:
Lake Eyre, Australia
53 ft (16 m)
below sea level

Most westerly point:
Cape Inscription,
Australia
112° 57' E

CAPE YORK,
AUSTRALIA
10° 41' S

CAPE BYRON, AUSTRALIA
153° 37' E

DUCIE ISLAND

Tropic of Capricorn

STEEP POINT, AUSTRALIA
113° 9' E

SOUTH EAST POINT, AUSTRALIA,
39° 10' S

Lowest recorded temperature:
Canberra, Australia
-8°F (-22°C)

DIRK HARTOG
ISLAND

Most southerly point:
Macquarie Island,
New Zealand
54° 30' S

DIRK HARTOG
ISLAND, AUSTRALIA

Great Dividing Range

New Caledonia

New Zealand

Tonga

Tuamoto Islands

DUCIE ISLAND,
PITCAIRN ISLANDS

CROSS-SECTION FROM DIRK HARTOG ISLAND, AUSTRALIA TO DUCIE ISLAND, PITCAIRN ISLANDS

0   500   1000 1500 Km

0   500   1000   1500 Miles

→ ← line of cross-section

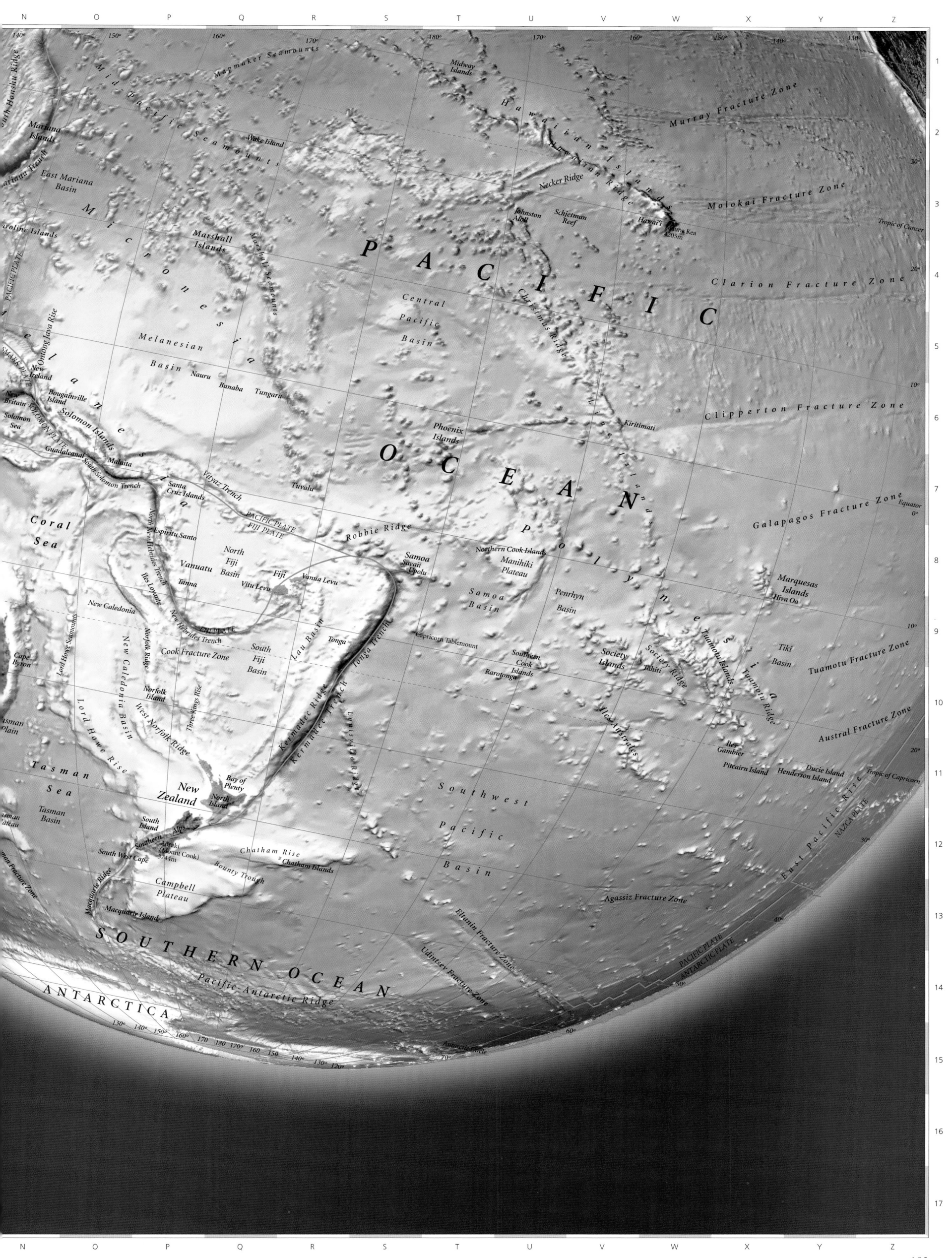

PACIFIC

OCEAN

N O P Q R S T U V W X Y Z

North Honshu Ridge
Mapmaker Seamounts
Midway Islands
Hawaiian Islands
Murray Fracture Zone

Mariana Islands
Wake Island
Necker Ridge
Molokai Fracture Zone

Marianna Trench
East Mariana Basin
Johnston Atoll
Schjetman Reef
Hawai'i Mauna Kea 4205m
Tropic of Cancer

Caroline Islands
Marshall Islands
Christmas Ridge
Clarion Fracture Zone

Micronesia
Central Pacific Basin

Melanesian Basin
Nauru Banaba Tungaru
Clipperton Fracture Zone

New Ireland
Bougainville Island
Solomon Islands
Phoenix Islands
Kiritimati

New Britain
Solomon Sea
Guadalcanal
Malaita
South Solomon Trench
Santa Cruz Islands
Vityaz Trench
Tuvalu
Galapagos Fracture Zone
Equator

Coral Sea
Espiritu Santo
PACIFIC PLATE
FIJI PLATE
Robbie Ridge
Northern Cook Islands
Manihiki Plateau
Marquesas Islands
Hiva Oa

Vanuatu
North Fiji Basin
Fiji
Vanua Levu
Samoa Savai'i Upolu
Samoa Basin
Penrhyn Basin

Tanna
Vitu Levu
Iles Loyaute
New Caledonia
New Hebrides Trench
South Fiji Basin
Tonga
Capricorn Tablemount
Southern Cook Islands
Rarotonga
Society Islands
Tahiti
Tiki Basin
Tuamotu Fracture Zone

Cape Byron
Lord Howe Seamounts
New Caledonia
Norfolk Ridge
Cook Fracture Zone
Lau Basin
Kermadec Ridge
Iles Australes
Iles Gambier
Pitcairn Island
Austral Fracture Zone

Tasman Plain
Lord Howe Rise
Norfolk Island
West Norfolk Ridge
Three Kings Rise
Kermadec Trench
Louisville Ridge
Southwest
Ducie Island
Henderson Island
Tropic of Capricorn

Tasman Sea
New Caledonia Basin
New Zealand
Southern Alps
Bay of Plenty
North Island
Pacific

Tasman Basin
South Island
Aoraki (Mount Cook) 3744m
Chatham Rise
Chatham Islands
Basin
NAZCA PLATE

Tasman Plateau
South West Cape
Campbell Plateau
Bounty Trough
Agassiz Fracture Zone
East Pacific Rise

Macquarie Ridge
Macquarie Island
Eltanin Fracture Zone
PACIFIC PLATE
ANTARCTIC PLATE

SOUTHERN OCEAN
Udintsev Fracture Zone

ANTARCTICA
Pacific-Antarctic Ridge
Antarctic Circle

POLITICAL AUSTRALASIA AND OCEANIA

V AST EXPANSES OF OCEAN separate this geographically fragmented realm, characterized more by each country's isolation than by any political unity. Australia's and New Zealand's traditional ties with the United Kingdom, as members of the Commonwealth, are now being called into question as Australasian and Oceanian nations are increasingly looking to forge new relationships with neighboring Asian countries like Japan. External influences have featured strongly in the politics of the Pacific Islands; the various territories of Micronesia were largely under US control until the late 1980s, and France, New Zealand, the US, and the UK still have territories under colonial rule in Polynesia. Nuclear weapons-testing by Western superpowers was widespread during the Cold War period, but has now been discontinued.

POPULATION

DENSITY OF SETTLEMENT in the region is generally low. Australia is one of the least densely populated countries on Earth with over 80% of its population living within 25 miles (40 km) of the coast – mostly in the southeast of the country. New Zealand, and the island groups of Melanesia, Micronesia, and Polynesia, are much more densely populated, although many of the smaller islands remain uninhabited.

Western Australia's mineral wealth has transformed its state capital, Perth, into one of Australia's major cities. Perth is one of the world's most isolated cities – over 2,500 miles (4,000 km) from the population centers of the eastern seaboard.

Population density
(people per sq mile)

- below 10
- 10-62
- 63-130
- 131-259
- 260-519
- 520-780
- above 780

The myriad of small coral islands that are scattered across the Pacific Ocean are often uninhabited, as they offer little shelter from the weather, often no fresh water, and only limited food supplies.

The planes of the Australian Royal Flying Doctor Service are able to cover large expanses of barren land quickly, bringing medical treatment to the most inaccessible and far-flung places.

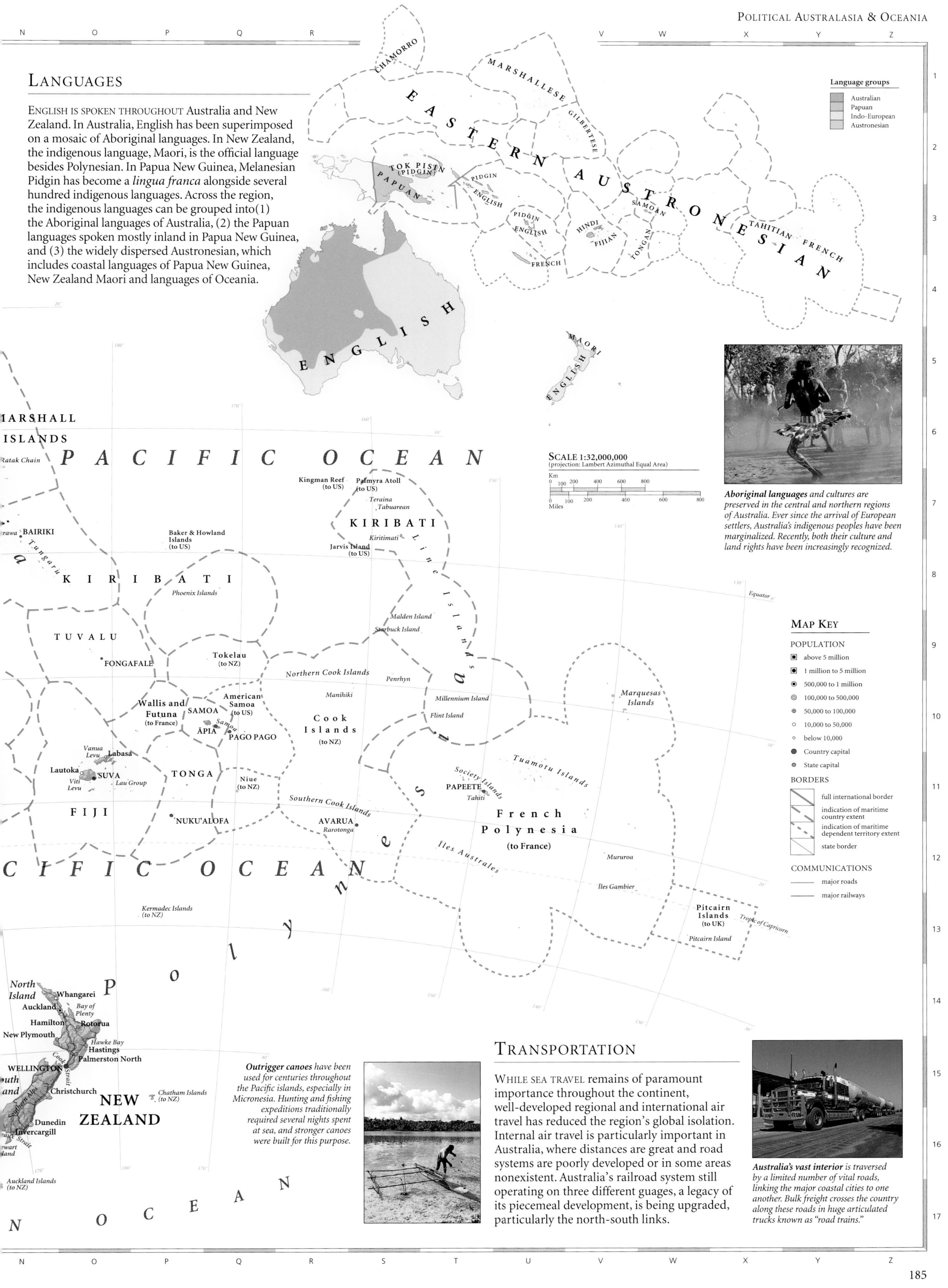

LANGUAGES

ENGLISH IS SPOKEN THROUGHOUT Australia and New Zealand. In Australia, English has been superimposed on a mosaic of Aboriginal languages. In New Zealand, the indigenous language, Maori, is the official language besides Polynesian. In Papua New Guinea, Melanesian Pidgin has become a *lingua franca* alongside several hundred indigenous languages. Across the region, the indigenous languages can be grouped into (1) the Aboriginal languages of Australia, (2) the Papuan languages spoken mostly inland in Papua New Guinea, and (3) the widely dispersed Austronesian, which includes coastal languages of Papua New Guinea, New Zealand Maori and languages of Oceania.

Language groups
- Australian
- Papuan
- Indo-European
- Austronesian

SCALE 1:32,000,000
(projection: Lambert Azimuthal Equal Area)

Km
0 100 200   400   600   800

Miles
0 100 200   400   600   800

Aboriginal languages and cultures are preserved in the central and northern regions of Australia. Ever since the arrival of European settlers, Australia's indigenous peoples have been marginalized. Recently, both their culture and land rights have been increasingly recognized.

MAP KEY

POPULATION
- ▣ above 5 million
- ◨ 1 million to 5 million
- ◉ 500,000 to 1 million
- ◎ 100,000 to 500,000
- ⊕ 50,000 to 100,000
- ○ 10,000 to 50,000
- ∘ below 10,000
- ● Country capital
- ◉ State capital

BORDERS
- full international border
- indication of maritime country extent
- indication of maritime dependent territory extent
- state border

COMMUNICATIONS
- major roads
- major railways

Outrigger canoes have been used for centuries throughout the Pacific islands, especially in Micronesia. Hunting and fishing expeditions traditionally required several nights spent at sea, and stronger canoes were built for this purpose.

TRANSPORTATION

WHILE SEA TRAVEL remains of paramount importance throughout the continent, well-developed regional and international air travel has reduced the region's global isolation. Internal air travel is particularly important in Australia, where distances are great and road systems are poorly developed or in some areas nonexistent. Australia's railroad system still operating on three different guages, a legacy of its piecemeal development, is being upgraded, particularly the north-south links.

Australia's vast interior is traversed by a limited number of vital roads, linking the major coastal cities to one another. Bulk freight crosses the country along these roads in huge articulated trucks known as "road trains."

AUSTRALASIAN AND OCEANIAN RESOURCES

NATURAL RESOURCES ARE OF MAJOR ECONOMIC IMPORTANCE throughout Australasia and Oceania. Australia in particular is a major world exporter of raw materials such as coal, iron ore, and bauxite, while New Zealand's agricultural economy is dominated by sheep-raising. Trade with western Europe has declined significantly in the last 20 years, and the Pacific Rim countries of Southeast Asia are now the main trading partners, as well as a source of new settlers to the region. Australasia and Oceania's greatest resources are its climate and environment; tourism increasingly provides a vital source of income for the whole continent.

The largely unpolluted waters of the Pacific Ocean support rich and varied marine life, much of which is farmed commercially. Here, oysters are gathered for market off the coast of New Zealand's South Island.

Huge flocks of sheep are a common sight in New Zealand, where they outnumber people by 20 to 1. New Zealand is one of the world's largest exporters of wool and frozen lamb.

STANDARD OF LIVING

IN MARKED CONTRAST TO ITS NEIGHBOR, Australia, with one of the world's highest life expectancies and standards of living, Papua New Guinea is one of the world's least developed countries. In addition, high population growth and urbanization rates throughout the Pacific islands contribute to overcrowding. In Australia and New Zealand, the Aboriginal and Maori people have been isolated, although recently their traditional land ownership rights have begun to be legally recognized in an effort to ease their social and economic isolation, and to improve living standards.

Standard of Living
(UN Human Development Index)

low

high

figures unavailable

ENVIRONMENTAL ISSUES

THE PROSPECT OF RISING SEA LEVELS poses a threat to many low-lying islands in the Pacific. The testing of nuclear weapons, once common throughout the region, was finally discontinued in 1996. Australia's ecological balance has been irreversibly altered by the introduction of alien species. Although it has the world's largest underground water reserve, the Great Artesian Basin, the availability of fresh water in Australia remains critical. Periodic droughts combined with overgrazing lead to desertification and increase the risk of devastating bush fires, and occasional flash floods.

Environmental Issues

national parks
tropical forest
forest destroyed
desert
desertification
polluted rivers
radioactive contamination
marine pollution
heavy marine pollution
poor urban air quality

In 1946 Bikini Atoll, in the Marshall Islands, was chosen as the site for Operation Crossroads – investigating the effects of atomic bombs upon naval vessels. Further nuclear tests continued until the early 1990s. The long-term environmental effects are unknown.

Northern Mariana Islands (to US)

Saipan

Guam (to US)

MICRO

PALAU

Me

PAPUA NEW GUINEA

New Guinea

Port More

Arafura Sea

Torres Strait

Timor Sea

Darwin

Gulf of Carpentaria

Great Barrier R

Townsville

AUSTRALIA

INDIAN OCEAN

Adelaide

Geele

Perth

Bikini Atoll

Eniwetak Atoll

Malden Island

SOUTHERN

Fangataufa

INDIAN OCEAN

Coral Sea

PACIFIC OCEAN

Murchison

Darling

Murray

Mackenzie

Sydney

Tasman Sea

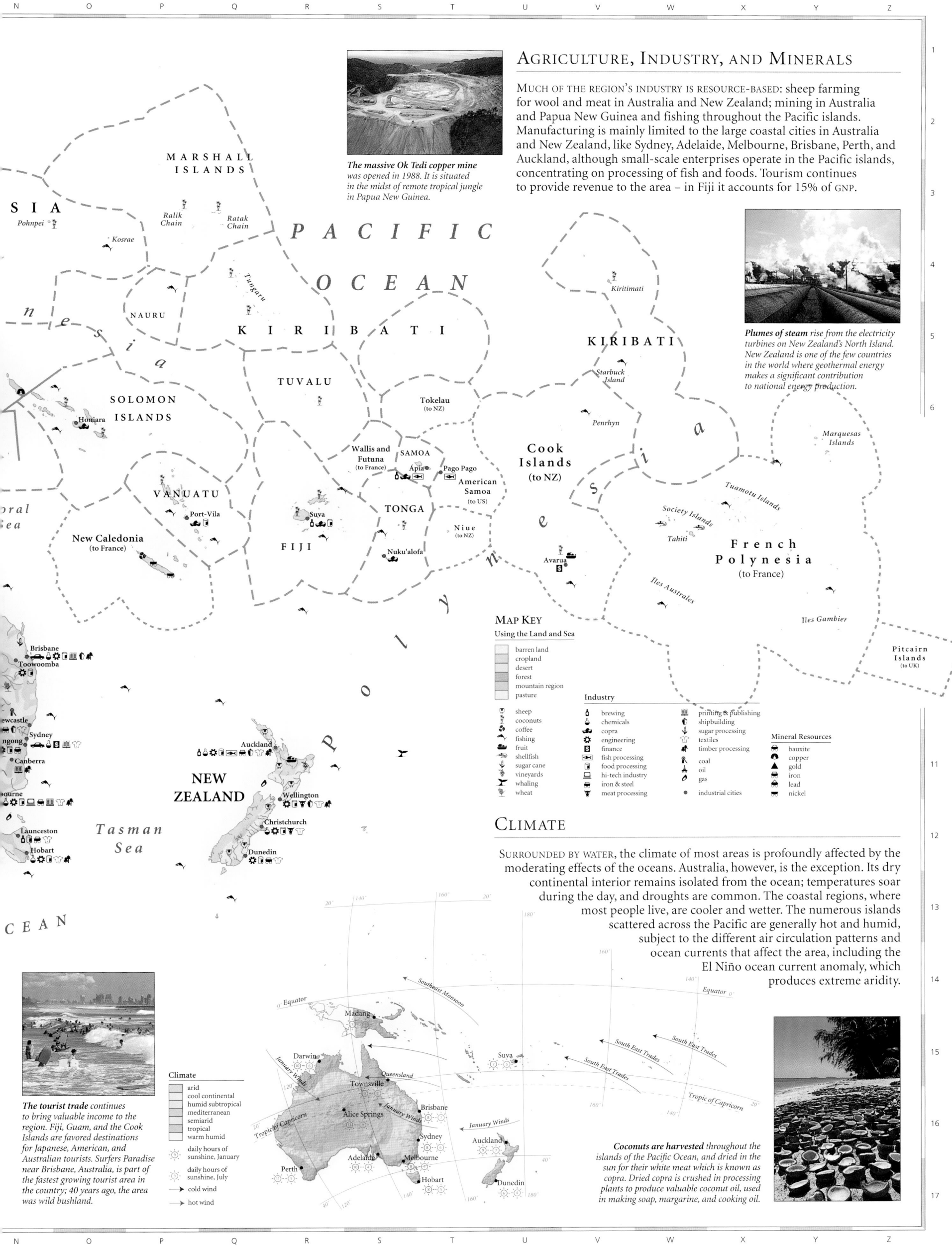

AGRICULTURE, INDUSTRY, AND MINERALS

MUCH OF THE REGION'S INDUSTRY IS RESOURCE-BASED: sheep farming for wool and meat in Australia and New Zealand; mining in Australia and Papua New Guinea and fishing throughout the Pacific islands. Manufacturing is mainly limited to the large coastal cities in Australia and New Zealand, like Sydney, Adelaide, Melbourne, Brisbane, Perth, and Auckland, although small-scale enterprises operate in the Pacific islands, concentrating on processing of fish and foods. Tourism continues to provide revenue to the area – in Fiji it accounts for 15% of GNP.

The massive Ok Tedi copper mine was opened in 1988. It is situated in the midst of remote tropical jungle in Papua New Guinea.

Plumes of steam rise from the electricity turbines on New Zealand's North Island. New Zealand is one of the few countries in the world where geothermal energy makes a significant contribution to national energy production.

MAP KEY

Using the Land and Sea

- barren land
- cropland
- desert
- forest
- mountain region
- pasture

Industry

- sheep
- coconuts
- coffee
- fishing
- fruit
- shellfish
- sugar cane
- vineyards
- whaling
- wheat

- brewing
- chemicals
- copra
- engineering
- finance
- fish processing
- food processing
- hi-tech industry
- iron & steel
- meat processing

- printing & publishing
- shipbuilding
- sugar processing
- textiles
- timber processing
- coal
- oil
- gas
- industrial cities

Mineral Resources

- bauxite
- copper
- gold
- iron
- lead
- nickel

CLIMATE

SURROUNDED BY WATER, the climate of most areas is profoundly affected by the moderating effects of the oceans. Australia, however, is the exception. Its dry continental interior remains isolated from the ocean; temperatures soar during the day, and droughts are common. The coastal regions, where most people live, are cooler and wetter. The numerous islands scattered across the Pacific are generally hot and humid, subject to the different air circulation patterns and ocean currents that affect the area, including the El Niño ocean current anomaly, which produces extreme aridity.

Climate

- arid
- cool continental
- humid subtropical
- mediterranean
- semiarid
- tropical
- warm humid

- daily hours of sunshine, January
- daily hours of sunshine, July
- cold wind
- hot wind

The tourist trade continues to bring valuable income to the region. Fiji, Guam, and the Cook Islands are favored destinations for Japanese, American, and Australian tourists. Surfers Paradise near Brisbane, Australia, is part of the fastest growing tourist area in the country; 40 years ago, the area was wild bushland.

Coconuts are harvested throughout the islands of the Pacific Ocean, and dried in the sun for their white meat which is known as copra. Dried copra is crushed in processing plants to produce valuable coconut oil, used in making soap, margarine, and cooking oil.

AUSTRALIA

AUSTRALIA IS THE WORLD'S smallest continent, a stable landmass lying between the Indian and Pacific oceans. Previously home to its aboriginal peoples only, since the end of the 18th century immigration has transformed the face of the country. Initially settlers came mainly from western Europe, particularly the UK, and for years Australia remained wedded to its British colonial past. More recent immigrants have come from eastern Europe, and from Asian countries such as Japan, South Korea, and Indonesia. Australia is now forging strong trading links with these "Pacific Rim" countries and its economic future seems to lie with Asia and the Americas, rather than Europe, its traditional partner.

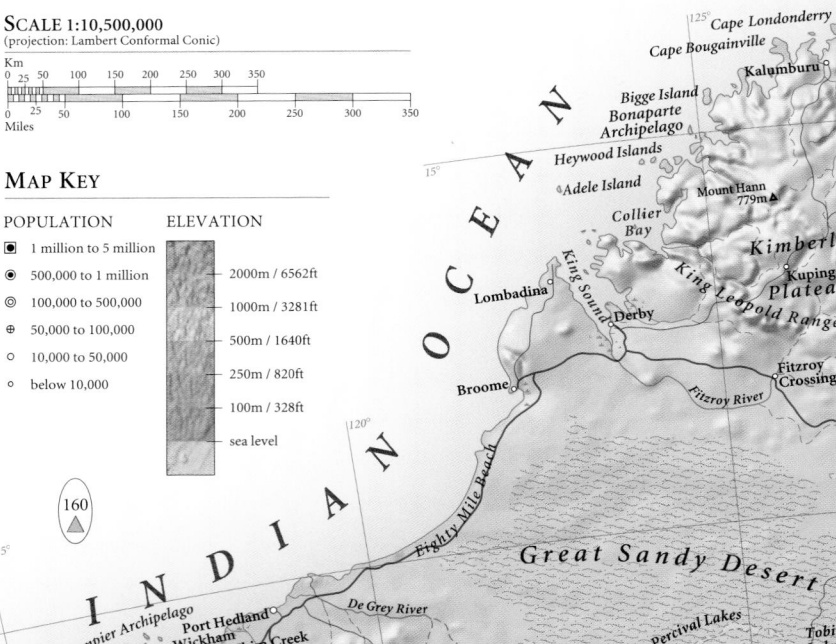

Uluru (Ayers Rock), the world's largest free-standing rock, is a massive outcrop of red sandstone in Australia's desert center. Wind and sandstorms have ground the rock into the smooth curves seen here. Uluru is revered as a sacred site by many aboriginal peoples.

SCALE 1:10,500,000
(projection: Lambert Conformal Conic)

Km 0 25 50 100 150 200 250 300 350
Miles 0 25 50 100 150 200 250 300 350

MAP KEY

POPULATION
- ▣ 1 million to 5 million
- ◉ 500,000 to 1 million
- ◎ 100,000 to 500,000
- ⊕ 50,000 to 100,000
- ○ 10,000 to 50,000
- · below 10,000

ELEVATION
- 2000m / 6562ft
- 1000m / 3281ft
- 500m / 1640ft
- 250m / 820ft
- 100m / 328ft
- sea level

USING THE LAND

OVER 165 MILLION SHEEP are dispersed in vast herds around the country, contributing to a major export industry. Cattle-ranching is important, particularly in the west. Wheat, and grapes for Australia's wine industry, are grown mainly in the south. Much of the country is desert, unsuitable for agriculture unless irrigation is used.

THE URBAN/RURAL POPULATION DIVIDE

urban 85%   rural 15%

0 10 20 30 40 50 60 70 80 90 100

POPULATION DENSITY	TOTAL LAND AREA
6 people per sq mile	2,967,893 sq miles
(2 people per sq km)	(7,686,850 sq km)

Land use and agricultural distribution
- cattle
- sheep
- cereals
- sugar cane
- timber
- vineyards
- capital cities
- major towns
- pasture
- cropland
- forest
- desert
- mountain region

Lines of ripening vines stretch for miles in Barossa Valley, a major wine-growing region near Adelaide.

THE LANDSCAPE

AUSTRALIA CONSISTS OF MANY ERODED PLATEAUS, lying firmly in the middle of the Indo-Australian Plate. It is the world's flattest continent, and the driest, after Antarctica. The coasts tend to be more hilly and fertile, especially in the east. The mountains of the Great Dividing Range form a natural barrier between the eastern coastal areas and the flat, dry plains and desert regions of the Australian "outback."

The Great Barrier Reef is the world's largest area of coral islands and reefs. It runs for about 1,240 miles (2,000 km) along the Queensland coast.

The Pinnacles are a series of rugged sandstone pillars. Their strange shapes have been formed by water and wind erosion.

The ancient Kimberley Plateau is the source of some of Australia's richest mineral deposits, including diamonds.

Arnhem Land

Uluru (Ayers Rock)

The tropical rainforest of the Cape York Peninsula contains more than 600 different varieties of tree.

Great Artesian Basin

More than half of Australia rests on a uniform shield over 600 million years old. It is one of the Earth's original geological plates.

The Simpson Desert has a number of large salt pans, created by the evaporation of past rivers and now sourced by seasonal rains. Some are crusted with gypsum, but most are covered by common salt crystals.

The Nullarbor Plain is a low-lying limestone plateau which is so flat that the Trans-Australian Railway runs through it in a straight line for more than 300 miles (483 km).

The Lake Eyre basin, lying 51 ft (16 m) below sea level, is one of the largest inland drainage systems in the world, covering an area of more than 500,000 sq miles (1,300,000 sq km).

Australian Alps

Tasmania has the same geological structure as the Australian Alps. During the last period of glaciation, 18,000 years ago, sea levels were some 300 ft (100 m) lower and it was joined to the mainland.

The Great Dividing Range forms a watershed between east- and west-flowing rivers. Erosion has created deep valleys, gorges, and waterfalls where rivers tumble over escarpments on their way to the sea.

Great Artesian Basin

Rainwater replenishes aquifer

Lake Eyre

Aquifers from which artesian water is obtained

Underground water movements

The Great Artesian Basin underlies nearly 20% of the total area of Australia, providing a valuable store of underground water, essential to Australian agriculture. The ephemeral rivers which drain the northern part of the basin have highly braided courses and, in consequence, the area is known as "channel country."

Map labels

Cape Londonderry, Cape Bougainville, Kalumburu, Bigge Island, Bonaparte Archipelago, Heywood Islands, Adele Island, Mount Hann 779m, Kimberley, Collier Bay, King Leopold Ranges, Kupingarri, Lombadina, Derby, Plateau, Fitzroy Crossing, Broome, Fitzroy River, INDIAN OCEAN, Eighty Mile Beach, Great Sandy Desert, De Grey River, Port Hedland, Wickham, Whim Creek, Percival Lakes, Tobin Lake, Dampier Archipelago, Dampier, Karratha, Roebourne, Marble Bar, Lake Dora, Lake Auld, Barrow Island, Fortescue River, Wittenoom, Lake Disappointment, Hamersley Range, Little Sandy Desert, Gibson Desert, North West Cape, Exmouth, Onslow, Tom Price, Mount Bruce, Mehania 1251m, Newman, WESTERN, Learmonth, Paraburdoo, Kumarina Roadhouse, Coral Bay, Kenneth Range, Mount Augustus 1105m, Carnarvon Range, Lake Gregory, Lake Carnegie, Minilya, Barlee Range, Waldburg Range, Tropic of Capricorn, Lake Macleod, Gascoyne River, Robinson Range, Lake Wells, Bernier Island, Carnarvon, Gascoyne Junction, Wiluna, Lake Throssell, Dorre Island, Shark Bay, Meekatharra, Lake Way, Lake Yeo, Denham, Murchison River, Lake Annean, Lake Austin, AUSTRALIA, Dirk Hartog Island, Kalbarri, Lake Magnet, Leonora, Lake Carey, Yalgoo, Lake Ballard, Menzies, Lake Rebecca, Geraldton, Mongers Lake, Lake Moore, Kalgoorlie, Coolgardie, Kitchener, Wubin, Pithara, Kambalda, Lake Lefroy, Moora, Southern Cross, Merredin, Lake Cowan, The Pinnacles, Gingin, Northam, Lake Johnston, Norseman, Lake Dundas, Balladonia, Wanneroo, Brookton, Kondinin, Lake Hope, Tower Peak 594m, Perth, Fremantle, York, Rockingham, Narrogin, Lake King, Ravensthorpe, Esperance, Mandurah, Wagin, Bunbury, Katanning, Busselton, Bridgetown, Manjimup, Mount Barker, Margaret River, Augusta, Pemberton, Albany, Cape Leeuwin

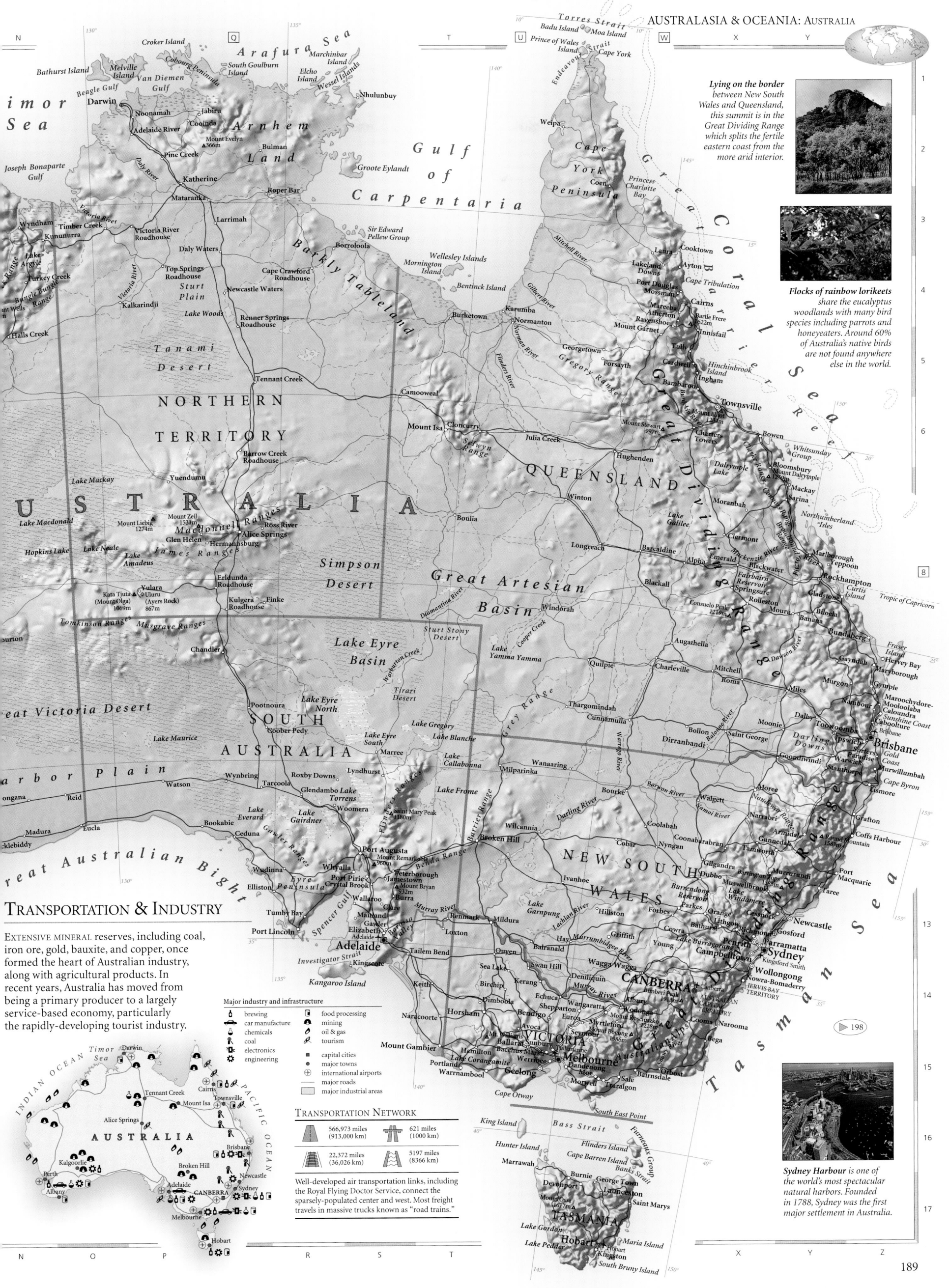

Lying on the border between New South Wales and Queensland, this summit is in the Great Dividing Range which splits the fertile eastern coast from the more arid interior.

Flocks of rainbow lorikeets share the eucalyptus woodlands with many bird species including parrots and honeyeaters. Around 60% of Australia's native birds are not found anywhere else in the world.

TRANSPORTATION & INDUSTRY

EXTENSIVE MINERAL reserves, including coal, iron ore, gold, bauxite, and copper, once formed the heart of Australian industry, along with agricultural products. In recent years, Australia has moved from being a primary producer to a largely service-based economy, particularly the rapidly-developing tourist industry.

Major industry and infrastructure

brewing	food processing
car manufacture	mining
chemicals	oil & gas
coal	tourism
electronics	capital cities
engineering	major towns
	international airports
	major roads
	major industrial areas

TRANSPORTATION NETWORK

566,973 miles (913,000 km)	621 miles (1000 km)
22,372 miles (36,026 km)	5197 miles (8366 km)

Well-developed air transportation links, including the Royal Flying Doctor Service, connect the sparsely-populated center and west. Most freight travels in massive trucks known as "road trains."

Sydney Harbour is one of the world's most spectacular natural harbors. Founded in 1788, Sydney was the first major settlement in Australia.

▶ 198

189

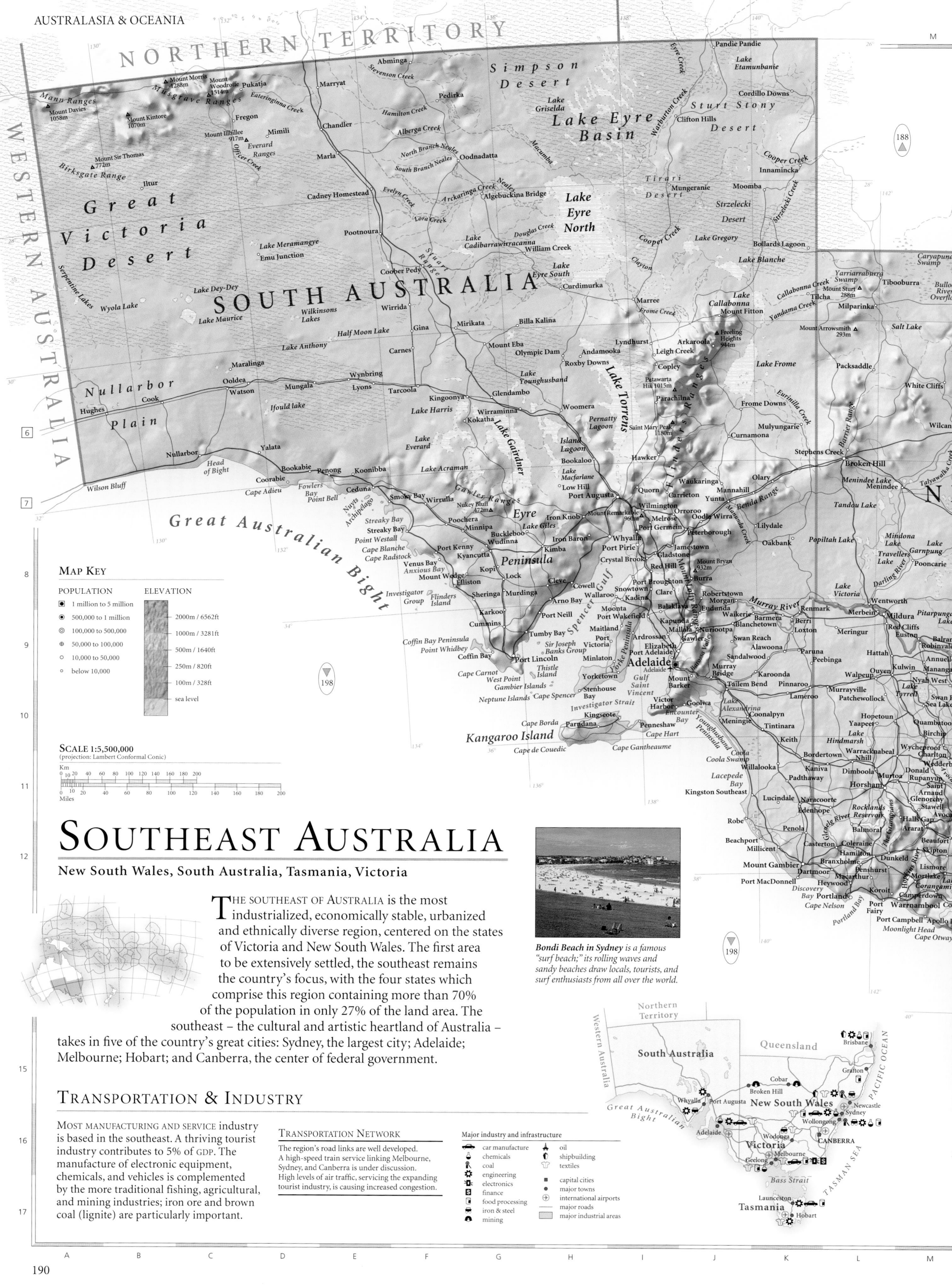

SOUTHEAST AUSTRALIA

New South Wales, South Australia, Tasmania, Victoria

THE SOUTHEAST OF AUSTRALIA is the most industrialized, economically stable, urbanized and ethnically diverse region, centered on the states of Victoria and New South Wales. The first area to be extensively settled, the southeast remains the country's focus, with the four states which comprise this region containing more than 70% of the population in only 27% of the land area. The southeast – the cultural and artistic heartland of Australia – takes in five of the country's great cities: Sydney, the largest city; Adelaide; Melbourne; Hobart; and Canberra, the center of federal government.

Bondi Beach in Sydney is a famous "surf beach;" its rolling waves and sandy beaches draw locals, tourists, and surf enthusiasts from all over the world.

TRANSPORTATION & INDUSTRY

MOST MANUFACTURING AND SERVICE industry is based in the southeast. A thriving tourist industry contributes to 5% of GDP. The manufacture of electronic equipment, chemicals, and vehicles is complemented by the more traditional fishing, agricultural, and mining industries; iron ore and brown coal (lignite) are particularly important.

TRANSPORTATION NETWORK

The region's road links are well developed.
A high-speed train service linking Melbourne, Sydney, and Canberra is under discussion.
High levels of air traffic, servicing the expanding tourist industry, is causing increased congestion.

Major industry and infrastructure

- car manufacture
- chemicals
- coal
- engineering
- electronics
- finance
- food processing
- iron & steel
- mining
- oil
- shipbuilding
- textiles
- capital cities
- major towns
- international airports
- major roads
- major industrial areas

MAP KEY

POPULATION

- 1 million to 5 million
- 500,000 to 1 million
- 100,000 to 500,000
- 50,000 to 100,000
- 10,000 to 50,000
- below 10,000

ELEVATION

- 2000m / 6562ft
- 1000m / 3281ft
- 500m / 1640ft
- 250m / 820ft
- 100m / 328ft
- sea level

SCALE 1:5,500,000
(projection: Lambert Conformal Conic)

USING THE LAND AND SEA

THE WESTERN FLANKS of the Great Dividing Range and the northern deserts of South Australia support massive herds of sheep and cattle, while more intensive stockrearing occurs near the cities. Sugar cane is the most important industrial crop, and cereal grains including wheat, corn, barley, and sorghum are also grown. Grapes, citrus, and orchard fruits are among the wide range of fruit and vegetables cultivated in this region. Tasmania's forestry and fishing contributes to over one-third of the state's exports.

The fertile Darling Downs, known as the "breadbasket of Australia," support a wide range of crops including cereals, sugar cane, and fruit.

The Murray River has its source in the eastern uplands of the Great Dividing Range. Fed by melting snow, it runs for 1,609 miles (2,589 km), and has sufficient volume to reach the ocean southeast of Adelaide despite a minimal gradient for most of its lower reaches.

THE URBAN/RURAL POPULATION DIVIDE

89% urban 11% rural

0 10 20 30 40 50 60 70 80 90 100

POPULATION DENSITY	TOTAL LAND AREA
16 people per sq mile (6 people per sq km)	778,022 sq miles (2,015,600 sq km)

Land use and agricultural distribution
- cattle
- sheep
- bananas
- fishing
- fruit
- vineyards
- wheat
- capital cities
- major towns
- pasture
- cropland
- forest
- desert
- mountain region

THE LANDSCAPE

THE SOUTHERN HALF of the Great Dividing Range runs parallel to the eastern coast of Victoria and New South Wales as far as Tasmania, which, though divided from the mainland is part of the same mountain chain. South Australia comprises the Australian Shield and half of the dry, flat Nullarbor Plain. The Murray/Darling River Basin is the only major river system.

The heavily folded Flinders Range is part of an arc of sedimentary rocks reaching northward from Kangaroo Island.

Lake Eyre is the largest of southern Australia's dry lakes. Lying -51 ft (-16 m) below sea level, it has flooded only three times in the last century.

The Musgrave and Everard ranges form bare, rounded hills made up of ancient granite and gneiss.

The Murray/Darling is Australia's longest river at 1,703 miles (2,739 km).

Shallow continental shelf
Past land link
Bass Strait
Tasmania

Tasmania is part of Australia's eastern highlands, separated from the mainland by 155 miles (250 km) of the Bass Strait. In the recent geological past, dry land links between Tasmania and Victoria would have been possible during periods of world-wide glaciation, when the sea level was more than 1,80 ft (55 m) below that of present sea levels.

Great Dividing Range

The eastern part of the Nullarbor Plain has many sinkholes, eroded by rainwater, which run underground to form a system of long caves in the limestone rocks.

The world's largest deposit of brown coal (lignite) is sited beneath Victoria's La Trobe Valley.

Though temperate rain forest grows in the wettest parts of Tasmania, extreme variations in the levels of rainfall over the island mean that some drier areas may experience forest fires.

The glaciated central plateau of Tasmania has many lakes, including Lake St. Clair, a piedmont lake more than 700 ft (200 m) deep.

The eastern coastal plains of New South Wales rise into a series of plateaus known as the tableland.

Mount Kosciuszko, the highest point in the Snowy Mountains, is the tallest mountain in Australia at 7,316 ft (2,228 m).

▶ 198

NEW ZEALAND

L YING 1,500 MILES EAST-SOUTHEAST OF AUSTRALIA, New Zealand was originally settled by the Maori people of Polynesia. It was visited by Europeans for the first time only as recently as the 1770s. The islands' rugged topography means that most settlement has concentrated in coastal areas. People of European origin make up more than 85% of the population of 3.9 million, following immigration which began in the 1920s. Many recent settlers have come from Asia, including India and China, and a number of the Pacific islands. The Maori now make up a minority of less than half a million. Their ancient claims to at least half of national territory, however, are gaining increasing legal credence.

THE LANDSCAPE

NEW ZEALAND comprises two large islands and many scattered smaller islands. On South Island the Alpine Fault marks the boundary between the Pacific and Indo-Australian plates. Tectonic activity has strongly influenced the formation of the Southern Alps, snowcapped mountains with several peaks over 9,800 ft (3,000 m). North Island has a lower and less extensive mountain region, containing forested hills, a central volcanic plateau, and downlands.

Mountain-building in the Southern Alps

North Island

Alpine Fault

Pacific Plate

Southern Alps

Indo-Australian Plate

The Southern Alps have been formed by 'slip' faulting. The Indo-Australian and Pacific plates run in opposite directions along the Alpine Fault. Although they slide past each other, they are also being thrust over one another, causing the continental crust of the Pacific Plate to be uplifted to form the Alps.

The Southern Alps run for more than 300 miles (483 km) forming the backbone of South Island. They were uplifted following the collision of the Pacific and Indo-Australian plates.

Probable location of Alpine Fault

Fiordland, in the far south west, contains a large number of flooded glacial valleys.

Sutherland Falls

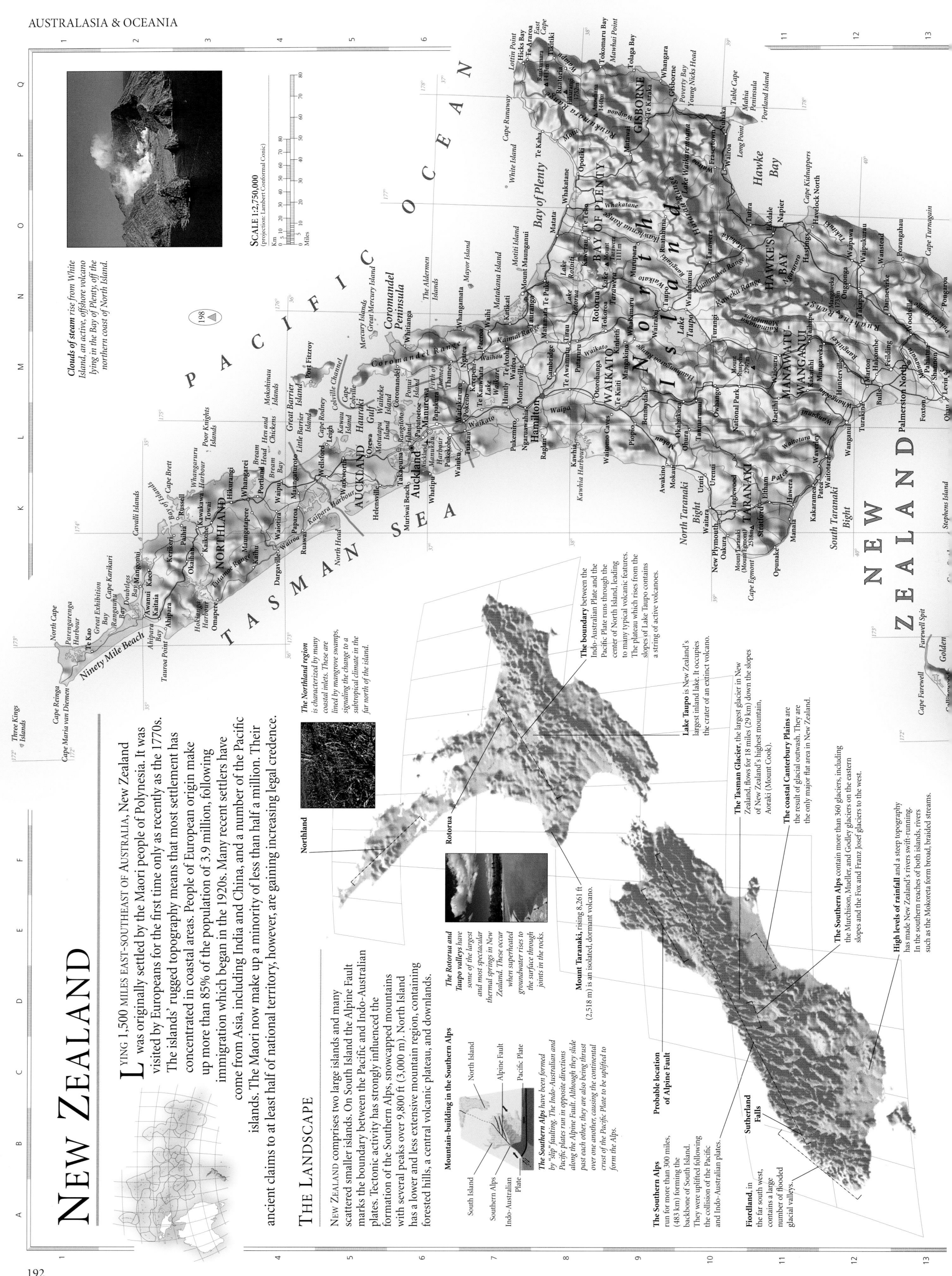

Clouds of steam rise from White Island, an active, offshore volcano lying in the Bay of Plenty, off the northern coast of North Island.

SCALE 1:2,750,000
(projection: Lambert Conformal Conic)

The Northland region is characterized by many coastal inlets. These are lined by mangrove swamps, signaling the change to a subtropical climate in the far north of the island.

Northland

Rotorua

The Rotorua and Taupo valleys have some of the largest and most spectacular thermal springs in New Zealand. These occur when superheated groundwater rises to the surface through joints in the rocks.

Mount Taranaki, rising 8,261 ft (2,518 m) is an isolated, dormant volcano.

The boundary between the Indo-Australian Plate and the Pacific Plate runs through the center of North Island, leading to many typical volcanic features. The plateau which rises from the slopes of Lake Taupo contains a string of active volcanoes.

Lake Taupo is New Zealand's largest inland lake. It occupies the crater of an extinct volcano.

The Tasman Glacier, the largest glacier in New Zealand, flows for 18 miles (29 km) down the slopes of New Zealand's highest mountain, Aoraki (Mount Cook).

The coastal Canterbury Plains are the result of glacial outwash. They are the only major flat area in New Zealand.

The Southern Alps contain more than 360 glaciers, including the Murchison, Mueller, and Godley glaciers on the eastern slopes and the Fox and Franz Josef glaciers to the west.

High levels of rainfall and a steep topography has made New Zealand's rivers swift-running. In the southern reaches of both islands, rivers such as the Mokoreta form broad, braided streams.

PACIFIC OCEAN

TASMAN SEA

NORTH ISLAND

NEW ZEALAND

SOUTH ISLAND

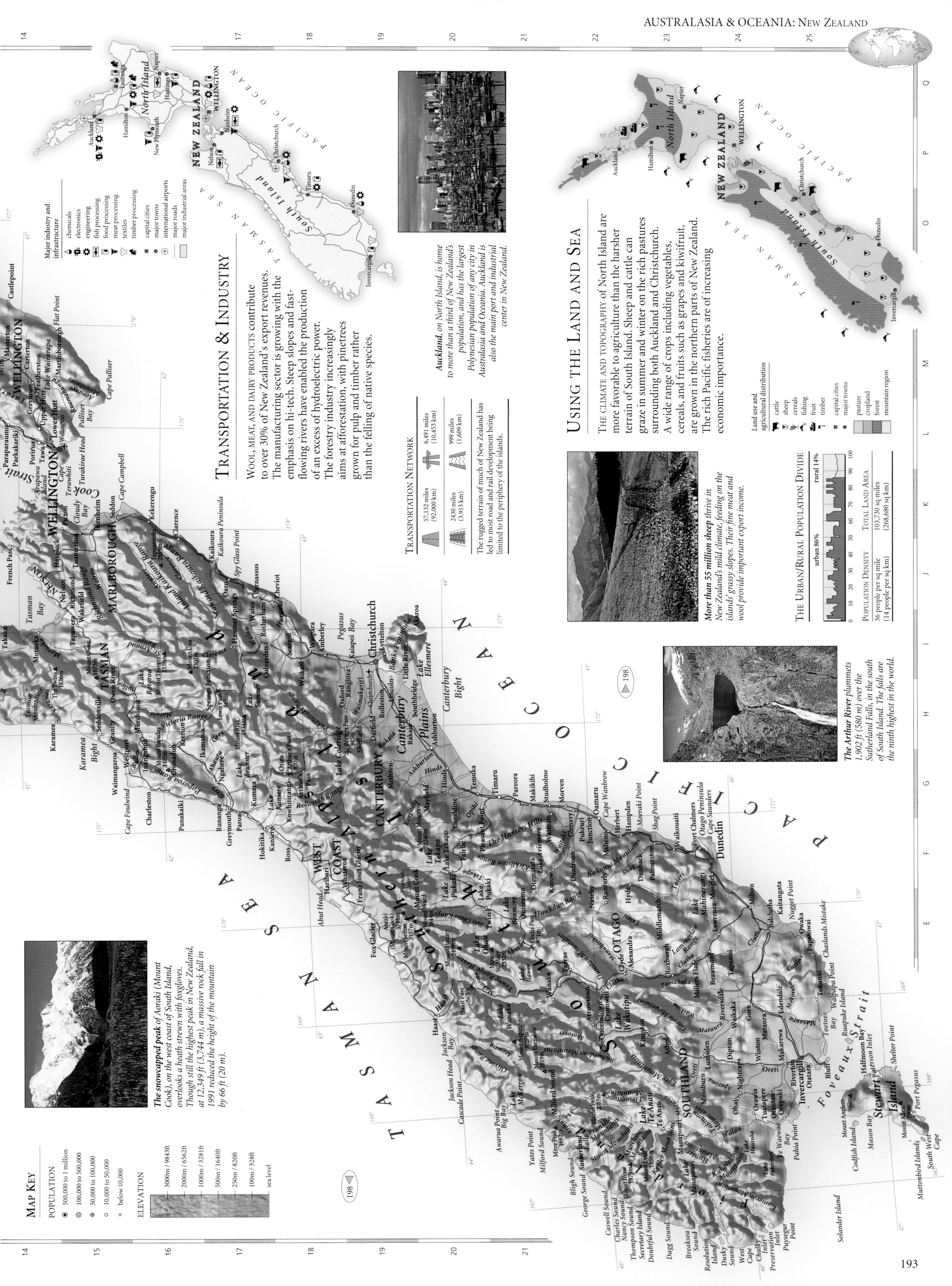

Map Key

POPULATION

- ● 500,000 to 1 million
- ◎ 100,000 to 500,000
- ⊕ 50,000 to 100,000
- ○ 10,000 to 50,000
- ○ below 10,000

ELEVATION

- 3000m / 9843ft
- 2000m / 6562ft
- 1000m / 3281ft
- 500m / 1640ft
- 250m / 820ft
- 100m / 328ft
- sea level

The snowcapped peak of Aoraki (Mount Cook), on the west coast of South Island, overlooks a heath strewn with foxgloves. Though still the highest peak in New Zealand, at 12,349 ft (3,744 m), a massive rock fall in 1991 reduced the height of the mountain by 66 ft (20 m).

Transportation & Industry

WOOL, MEAT, AND DAIRY PRODUCTS contribute to over 30% of New Zealand's export revenues. The manufacturing sector is growing with the emphasis on hi-tech. Steep slopes and fast-flowing rivers have enabled the production of an excess of hydroelectric power. The forestry industry increasingly aims at afforestation, with pinetrees grown for pulp and timber rather than the felling of native species.

Major industry and infrastructure

- chemicals
- electronics
- engineering
- fish processing
- food processing
- meat processing
- textiles
- timber processing
- capital cities
- major towns
- international airports
- major industrial areas

Auckland, on North Island, is home to more than a third of New Zealand's population, and has the largest Polynesian population of any city in Australasia and Oceania. Auckland is also the main port and industrial center in New Zealand.

Transportation Network

57,132 miles (92,000 km)		6,491 miles (10,453 km)
2430 miles (3,913 km)		999 miles (1,609 km)

The rugged terrain of much of New Zealand has led to most road and rail development being limited to the periphery of the islands.

Using the Land and Sea

THE CLIMATE AND TOPOGRAPHY of North Island are more favorable to agriculture than the harsher terrain of South Island. Sheep and cattle can graze in summer and winter on the rich pastures surrounding both Auckland and Christchurch. A wide range of crops including vegetables, cereals, and fruits such as grapes and kiwifruit, are grown in the northern parts of New Zealand. The rich Pacific fisheries are of increasing economic importance.

Land use and agricultural distribution

- cattle
- sheep
- cereals
- fishing
- fruit
- timber
- capital cities
- major towns

Land use
- pasture
- cropland
- forest
- mountain region

More than 55 million sheep thrive in New Zealand's mild climate, feeding on the islands' grassy slopes. Their fine meat and wool provide important export income.

The Arthur River plummets 1,902 ft (580 m) over the Sutherland Falls, in the south of South Island. The falls are the ninth highest in the world.

The Urban/Rural Population Divide

	urban 86%	rural 14%

POPULATION DENSITY	TOTAL LAND AREA
36 people per sq mile (14 people per sq km)	103,730 sq miles (268,680 sq km)

193

PAPUA NEW GUINEA & THE SOLOMON ISLANDS

CUT OFF BY INACCESSIBLE, largely mountainous terrain, the peoples of Papua New Guinea have maintained a remarkable diversity of language and culture. There are over 750 separate languages, and yet more distinct tribes. Much of the country remains isolated, with many of the indigenous inhabitants of the interior living as hunter-gatherers. To the east of Papua New Guinea, the Solomons form an archipelago of several hundred islands, scattered over an area of 252,897 sq miles (655,000 sq km). The Solomon Islanders, a mainly Melanesian people, live on the six largest islands.

TRANSPORTATION & INDUSTRY

PAPUA NEW GUINEA has substantial mineral resources including the world's largest copper reserves at Panguna on Bougainville Island; gold, and potential oil and natural gas. Political instability on Bougainville and an undeveloped infrastructure deters the investment necessary for exploition of these reserves. The Solomon Islanders rely mainly on copra and timber with some production of palm oil and cocoa. Traditional crafts are made for the tourist market and for export.

TRANSPORTATION NETWORK

	460 miles (740 km)
	None
	None
	6,794 miles (10,940 km)

Much of Papua New Guinea and the Solomons is inaccessible by road. A network of airstrips serves even remote villages on the islands. The Solomons' airport has been extended to take jumbo jets to improve connections for tourism.

USING THE LAND AND SEA

MOST AGRICULTURE IN Papua New Guinea is at a subsistence level, with more than two-thirds of the land used for rough grazing, particularly for pigs. The tropical rain forest is a rich timber resource. The Solomon Islanders rely heavily on coconuts for export revenue and fishing, mainly for tuna, is a staple industry.

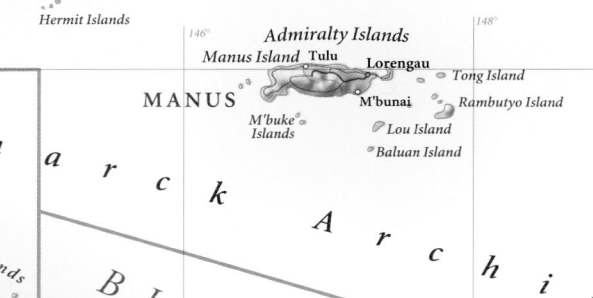

The slopes of this extinct volcano near Talasea on the island of New Britain have been almost entirely colonized by rain forest vegetation.

Major industry and infrastructure

- beverages
- coffee processing
- copra processing
- food processing
- mining
- textiles
- timber processing
- capital cities
- major towns
- international airports
- major roads

Land use and agricultural distribution

- bananas
- cocoa
- coconuts
- fishing
- oil palms
- rubber
- timber
- capital cities
- major towns
- cropland
- forest
- wetland

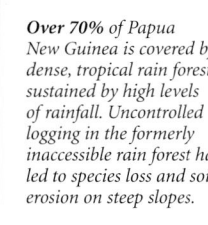

Over 70% of Papua New Guinea is covered by dense, tropical rain forest, sustained by high levels of rainfall. Uncontrolled logging in the formerly inaccessible rain forest has led to species loss and soil erosion on steep slopes.

THE URBAN/RURAL POPULATION DIVIDE

urban 16%	rural 84%

0 10 20 30 40 50 60 70 80 90 100

POPULATION DENSITY	TOTAL LAND AREA
17 people per sq mile (7 people per sq km)	290,210 sq miles (751,840 sq km)

MAP KEY

POPULATION

- ◎ 100,000 to 500,000
- ⊕ 50,000 to 100,000
- ○ 10,000 to 50,000
- ○ below 10,000

ELEVATION

- 4000m / 13,124ft
- 3000m / 9843ft
- 2000m / 6562ft
- 1000m / 3281ft
- 500m / 1640ft
- 250m / 820ft
- 100m / 328ft
- sea level

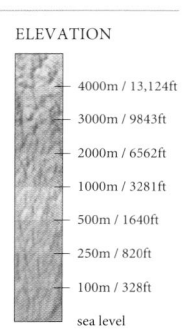

Huli tribesmen from Southern Highlands Province in Papua New Guinea parade in ceremonial dress, their powdered wigs decorated with exotic plumage and their faces and bodies painted with colored pigments.

SCALE 1:5,500,000
(projection: Mercator)

Km
0 10 20 40 60 80 100 120 140 160 180 200

0 10 20 40 60 80 100 120 140 160 180 200
Miles

MICRONESIA

MARSHALL ISLANDS, MICRONESIA, NAURU, PALAU, *Guam, Northern Mariana Islands, Wake Island*

THE MICRONESIAN ISLANDS lie in the western reaches of the Pacific Ocean and are all part of the same volcanic zone. The Federated States of Micronesia is the largest group, with more than 600 atolls and forested volcanic islands in an area of more than 1,120 sq miles (2,900 sq km). Micronesia is a mixture of former colonies, overseas territories, and dependencies. Most of the region still relies on aid and subsidies to sustain economies limited by resources, isolation, and an emigrating population, drawn to New Zealand and Australia by the attractions of a western lifestyle.

PALAU

PALAU IS AN ARCHIPELAGO OF OVER 200 ISLANDS, only eight of which are inhabited. It was the last remaining UN trust territory in the Pacific, controlled by the US until 1994, when it became independent. The economy operates on a subsistence level, with coconuts and cassava the principal crops. Fishing licenses and tourism provide foreign currency.

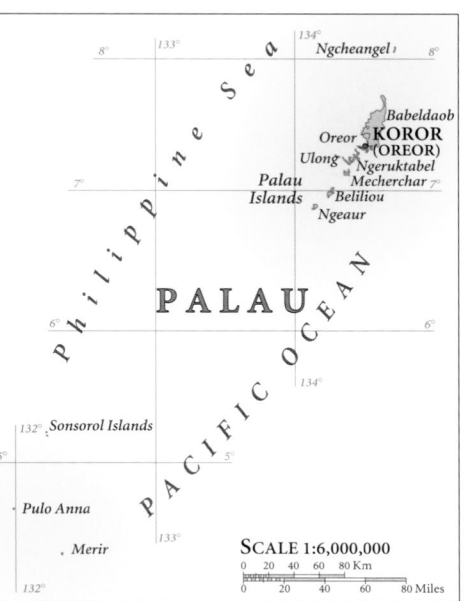

SCALE 1:6,000,000

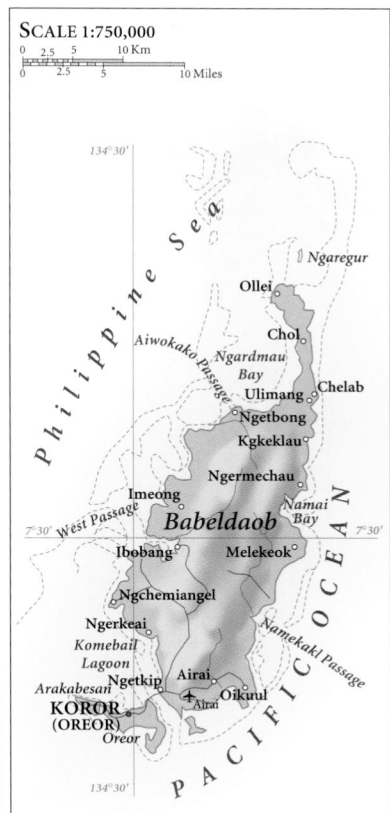

SCALE 1:750,000

The Palau Islands have numerous hidden lakes and lagoons. These sustain their own ecosystems which have developed in isolation. This has produced adaptations in the animals and plants that are often unique to each lake.

GUAM (to US)

LYING AT THE SOUTHERN END of the Mariana Islands, Guam is an important US military base and tourist destination. Social and political life is dominated by the indigenous Chamorro, who make up just under half the population, although the increasing prevalence of western culture threatens Guam's traditional social stability.

The tranquillity of these coastal lagoons, at Inarajan in southern Guam, belies the fact that the island lies in a region where typhoons are common.

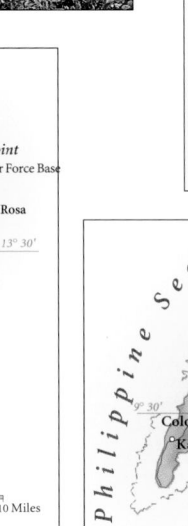

SCALE 1:825,000

NORTHERN MARIANA ISLANDS (to US)

A US COMMONWEALTH TERRITORY, the Northern Marianas comprise the whole of the Mariana archipelago except for Guam. The islands retain their close links with the US and continue to receive American aid. Tourism, though bringing in much-needed revenue, has speeded the decline of the traditional subsistence economy. Most of the population lives on Saipan.

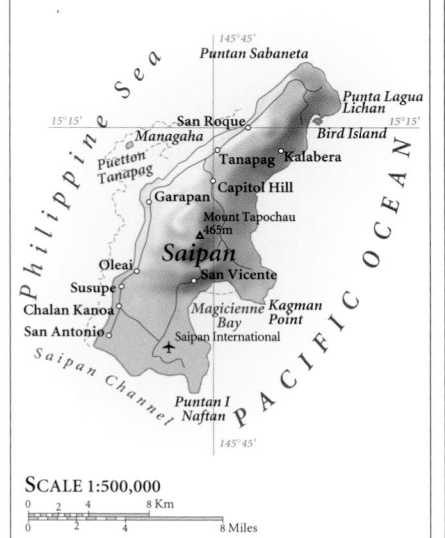

SCALE 1:500,000

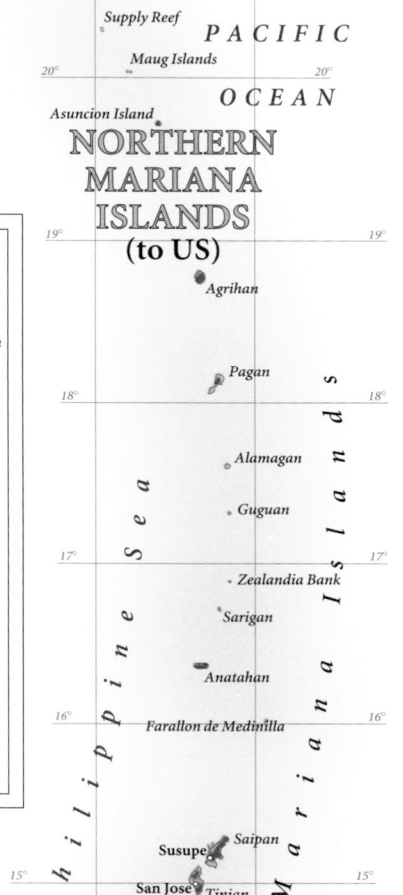

SCALE 1:5,000,000

MICRONESIA

A MIXTURE OF HIGH VOLCANIC ISLANDS and low-lying coral atolls, the Federated States of Micronesia include all the Caroline Islands except Palau. Pohnpei, Kosrae, Chuuk, and Yap are the four main island cluster states, each of which has its own language, with English remaining the official language. Nearly half the population is concentrated on Pohnpei, the largest island. Independent since 1986, the islands continue to receive considerable aid from the US which supplements an economy based primarily on fishing and copra processing.

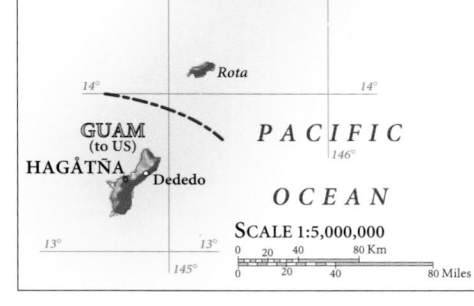

SCALE 1:825,000

Ulithi Atoll, lying in the state of Yap, the most westerly part of Micronesia, is a typical coral island, with a series of reefs enclosing a large lagoon.

Melanesia

Fiji, Vanuatu, *New Caledonia* (to France)

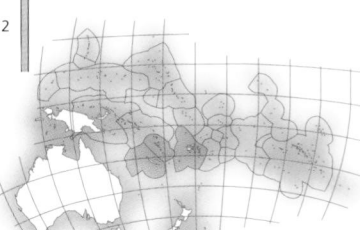

Three Main Island groups make up the area of southern Melanesia in the southwestern Pacific: the independent countries of Fiji and Vanuatu and the French overseas territory of New Caledonia. The major Melanesian island group, the Solomon Islands, lies to the east of Papua New Guinea (pages 194–95). Most of the larger islands are volcanic in origin; the smaller ones are mainly coral atolls and are largely uninhabited. The economy in all three island groups is increasingly driven by tourism, not necessarily to the benefit of other economic activities.

Vanuatu

A string of mountainous volcanic islands covering more than 4,706 sq miles (12,190 sq km) of the south Pacific, Vanuatu achieved independence from France and the UK in 1980. The majority of the population relies on subsistence fishing and agriculture. Once-important copra and cocoa exports are declining as a result of cost-effective substitutes from elsewhere, and alternatives are being explored. There is further resource potential in the forests and fishing grounds, and beef and arable farming are of growing importance. Tourism, accounting for 40% of GDP, is the fastest-growing sector of the economy, and further expansion is planned.

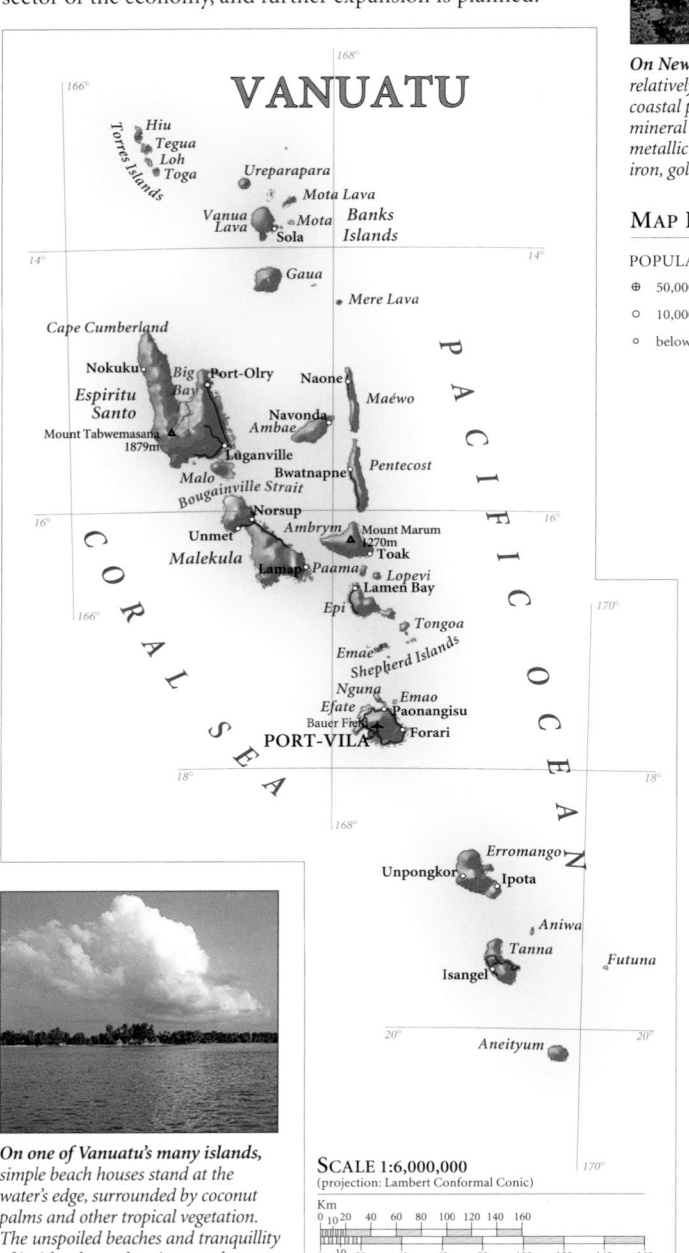

New Caledonia (to France)

New Caledonia, a French overseas territory known as Kanaky by its indigenous peoples, comprises a large main island, 260 miles (418 km) long, and many smaller islands and atolls. Socioeconomic inequality, unemployment, and the issue of independence have caused tension between the Kanaks and the French-speaking expatriate population. This resulted in a long history of political violence, although the Nouméa accord, signed in 1998, allowed for greater autonomy. New Caledonia produces 25% of the world's nickel, and improved incomes from tourism and agriculture have benefited the economy.

On New Caledonia's main island, relatively high interior plateaus descend to coastal plains. Nickel is the most important mineral resource, but the hills also harbor metallic deposits including chrome, cobalt, iron, gold, silver, and copper.

Map Key

POPULATION
- ⊕ 50,000 to 100,000
- ○ 10,000 to 50,000
- ○ below 10,000

ELEVATION
- 1000m / 3281ft
- 500m / 1640ft
- 250m / 820ft
- 100m / 328ft
- sea level

Fiji

Fiji is a volcanic archipelago in the southwestern Pacific consisting of two large islands and 880 smaller islets, and covering a total area of 7,054 sq miles (18,270 sq km). The majority of the population lives on the two largest islands. The people are split fairly evenly between Indo-Fijians, who arrived when Fiji was still a British colony, and the indigenous Fijians who have, since 1987, controlled the government. Sugar and copra are the most important crops in a diversified agricultural base and forestry is becoming increasingly important. A relatively varied economy has potential for mineral and hydroelectric exploitation, while Fiji's climate and location on the main Pacific air routes are an impetus to tourism.

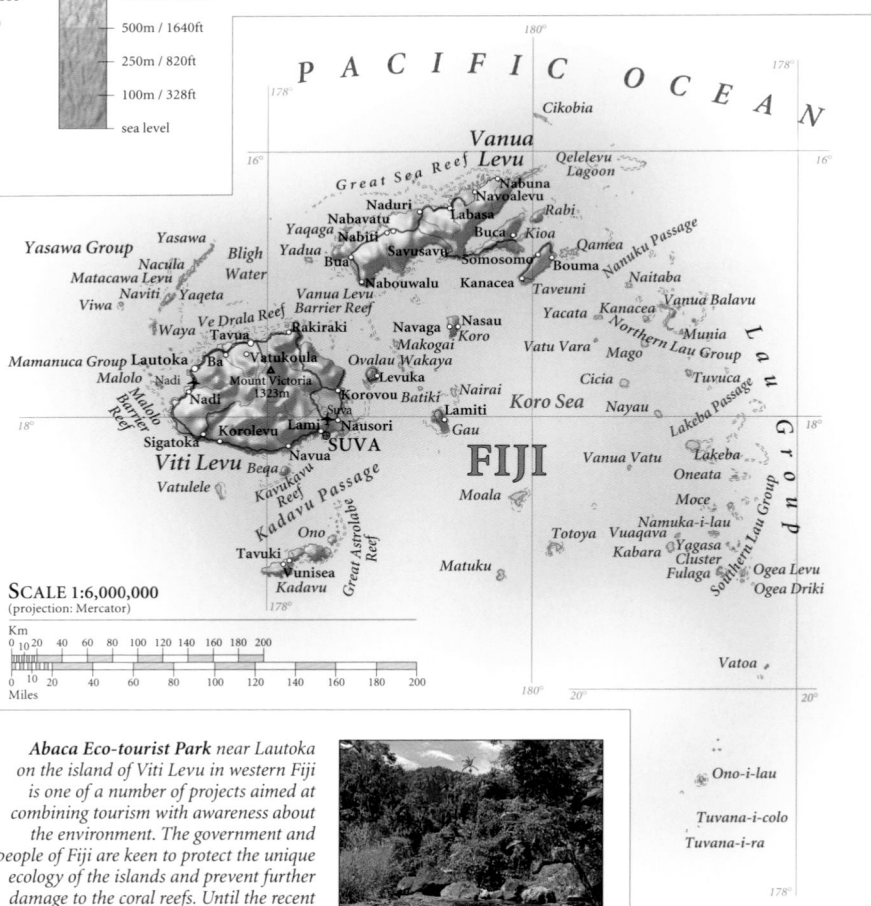

Abaca Eco-tourist Park near Lautoka on the island of Viti Levu in western Fiji is one of a number of projects aimed at combining tourism with awareness about the environment. The government and people of Fiji are keen to protect the unique ecology of the islands and prevent further damage to the coral reefs. Until the recent ending of nuclear testing in the Pacific by Western nations, Fiji lay downwind of some of the main testing sites.

On one of Vanuatu's many islands, simple beach houses stand at the water's edge, surrounded by coconut palms and other tropical vegetation. The unspoiled beaches and tranquillity of its islands are drawing ever-larger numbers of tourists to Vanuatu.

PACIFIC OCEAN

THE PACIFIC IS THE WORLD'S LARGEST AND DEEPEST OCEAN. It is nearly twice the area of the Atlantic and contains almost three times as much water. The ocean is dotted with islands and surrounded by some of the world's most populous states; over half the world's population lives on its shores. The Pacific is bordered by active plate margins known as the "Ring of Fire," causing earthquakes and tsunamis, and creating volcanic islands and subterranean mountain chains. The largest underwater mountains break the surface as island arcs. The fisheries of the Pacific are some of the most productive in the world and provide a vital resource for many of the Pacific islands. Since the Second World War there has been a shift in trading patterns, with a considerable growth in trade between the US and the countries of the Pacific Rim.

INSET MAP KEY

POPULATION
○ below 10,000

ELEVATION

1000m / 3281ft
500m / 1640ft
250m / 820ft
100m / 328ft
sea level

OCEAN MAP KEY

SEA DEPTH

sea level
250m / 820ft
500m / 1640ft
1000m / 3281ft
2000m / 6562ft
3000m / 9843ft
5000m / 16410ft

SCALE 1:50,000,000
(projection: Mollweide)

Km   0 200 400 600 800 1000
Miles 0   200   400   600 800 100

AMERICAN SAMOA AND SAMOA

AMERICAN SAMOA AND SAMOA are part of the island archipelago of Polynesia. The two most populous islands are Tutuila in American Samoa and Upolu in Samoa. Although the economies of both these states remain predominantly resource-based, both are expanding their light manufacturing sectors, and the US administration is the primary employer in American Samoa. Tuna fishing is particularly important: 25% of all tuna consumed in the US is processed and canned in Pago Pago.

Japan is one of the major trading nations within the Pacific, importing iron and steel from Australia, and grain from the US. The major exports from the 'Pacific Rim' are electronics, precision equipment, and motor cars.

SCALE 1:3,000,000

0 10 20 40 Km
0   10   20 40 Miles

SAMOA — Sàmoa — AMERICAN SAMOA (to US)

Savai'i, Fagamálo, Faleálupo, Sátaua, Cape Puava, Silisili 1858m, Tuasivi, Pu'apu'a, Fálelima, Sala'ilua, Salelologa, Cape Ásuisui, Taga, Satupaiteau, ÁPIA Upolu, Feleolo, Fito 1113m, Matautu, Poutasi, Lotofaga, Salani, Safata Bay, Palauli Bay, Apolima Strait, Fagaloa Bay, Ti'avea, PAGO PAGO, Cape Matátula, Cape Taputapu, Steps Point, Tutuila, Aunu'u Island, Manua Islands, Olosega, Ofu, Luma, Ta'ū

PACIFIC OCEAN

Many of the buildings in Samoa reflect the country's colonial past. Once a colony of New Zealand, Samoa is now an independent state; American Samoa remains an unincorporated territory of the United States.

RESOURCES

MANY OF THE SMALL ISLANDS in the Pacific rely heavily on marine resources to provide valuable export incomes. These fisheries tend to be small-scale and are forced to compete with the large commerical fleets from Japan and the Russian Federation. Although many metallic mineral deposits have been discovered in the Pacific, few are exploited. The major areas of oil and gas extraction are off the coast of Vietnam, along the Kamchatka Peninsula and off the coast of Alaska. The numerous reefs which fringe the islands of the Pacific are harvested for corals.

Farms such as this black pearl oyster farm in Tahiti are widespread throughout the Pacific. The culturing or farming of marine organisms, such as mollusks and crustaceans, has been practiced for hundreds of years.

ASIA, Vancouver, Seattle, NORTH AMERICA, Shanghai, Ōsaka, Tokyo, San Francisco, Long Beach, Hong Kong, Honolulu, Manila, PACIFIC OCEAN, Panama City, Guayaquil, SOUTH AMERICA, Callao, AUSTRALIA, Brisbane, Sydney, Wellington, OCEAN, Valparaiso, ANTARCTICA

Resources
⌐ fish
⚓ shellfish
⌐ whales
◊ oil & gas
● major towns
⚓ major ports

THE RING OF FIRE

THE ACTIVE PLATE MARGINS surrounding the Pacific have created numerous land and island volcanoes along its border. The actual basin of the Pacific is made up of a number of separate tectonic plates which move away from each other, colliding with other plates. When they collide, the oceanic plates, being thinner, are forced beneath the thicker continental plates, forming deep ocean trenches and high ridges. These collision zones are known as subduction zones and are characterized by intense seismic and volcanic activity.

Vulkan Klyuchevskaya Sopka, Mount Katmai, Mount Rainier, Mount Saint Helens, Mount Fuji, Popocatépetl, Mount Pinatubo, Mauna Loa, Pagan, Volcán El Chichonal, Mayon Volcano, Nevado del Ruiz, Mount Sinewit, Cotopaxi, Volcán Antofalla, Tupungato, Mount Tarawera, Mount Erebus

Ring of Fire
— plate boundaries
● major volcanoes

Mayon Volcano in the Philippines is one of many active volcanoes on the Pacific "Ring of Fire." It is noted for its perfect conical shape; the base of the cone is 80 miles (130 km) in circumference.

The Hawaiian volcanoes lie in the center of a plate, not on a plate margin, and are known as intraplate volcanoes. They are associated with hot spots, whereby a plume of hot molten rock rises to the surface as the plate moves over it.

ASIA, CHINA, Yellow River, Qingdao, Lianyungang, Yangtze, Shanghai, Fuzhou, LAOS, THAILAND, Bangkok, Hai Phong, Gulf of Tongking, Hainan Dao, Da Nang, CAMBODIA, VIETNAM, Kâmpóng Saôm, Hồ Chí Minh, Guangzhou, Hong Kong, Kaohsiung, TAIWAN, Luzon Strait, Luzon, Manila, PHILIPPINES, Paracel Islands (disputed), South China Sea, Spratly Islands (disputed), Palawan, Andaman Sea, Gulf of Thailand, Kuantan, Klang, Kepulauan Natuna (to Indonesia), BRUNEI, Bintulu, Kuching, Kota Kinabalu, Sulu Sea, Celebes Sea, Celebes Basin, MALAYSIA, SINGAPORE, Straits of Malacca, Borneo, INDONESIA, Java Sea, Jakarta, Java, Makassar, Makassar Strait, Surabaya, Bali, Flores Sea, Sumbawa, Flores, EAST TIMOR, Sumatra, INDIAN OCEAN

N O P Q R S T U V W X Y

The Sepik River drains the lowlands north of the Central Range, flowing eastward into the Bismarck Sea.

The Bismarck Range is precipitous, rugged and covered in dense vegetation, rising to 14,793 ft (4,509 m) at Mount Wilhelm in central Papua New Guinea.

Most of Papua New Guinea's outlying islands, including New Britain, Bougainville Island, and New Ireland, are precipitous and of volcanic origin.

THE LANDSCAPE

THE PLATE MARGIN between the Pacific and Indo-Australian plates runs through the mainland of Papua New Guinea, which is dominated by steep and forested mountain ranges. The 600 or so outer islands are mainly high, volcanic islands, fringed by coral reefs. The Solomons comprise six large volcanic islands which form two parallel chains, and several hundred small islands and atolls.

The Star Mountains include some of the most remote terrain on Earth. The area is rich in gold and copper.

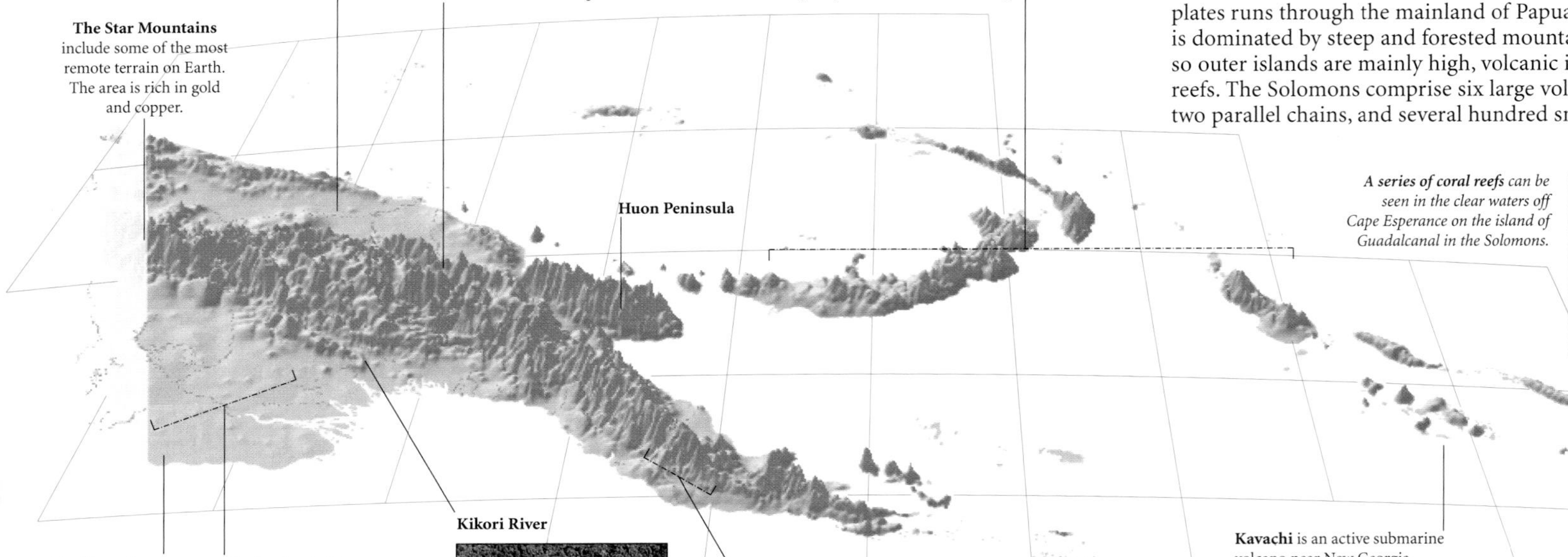

Huon Peninsula

A series of coral reefs can be seen in the clear waters off Cape Esperance on the island of Guadalcanal in the Solomons.

Cape Esperance

Kikori River

Southern Papua New Guinea is part of the Indo-Australian Plate. New Guinea only became separated physically from Australia about 8,000 years ago following the flooding of the Torres Strait.

The lowland plains in the south and north of the main island are swampy, and contain some fertile alluvial soils. This contrasts with the mountainous islands in the rest of Papua New Guinea where soils are generally thin and nutrients are retained in the existing vegetation.

Papua New Guinea's rivers, though fairly short, carry extremely high sediment loads, largely due to soil erosion. This is caused by a combination of very steep slopes and heavy rainfall, and is made worse by forest clearance, particularly "slash and burn" techniques and road or mine operations.

The Owen Stanley Range contains several of Papua New Guinea's highest peaks, the greatest of which is Mount Victoria at 13,200 ft (4,035 m).

Kavachi is an active submarine volcano near New Georgia, which erupts every few years.

The Louisiade Archipelago contains 10 volcanic islands and numerous coral islets. Tagula Island is the largest of the islands, containing the archipelago's highest peak at 2,645 ft (806 m).

Huon Peninsula

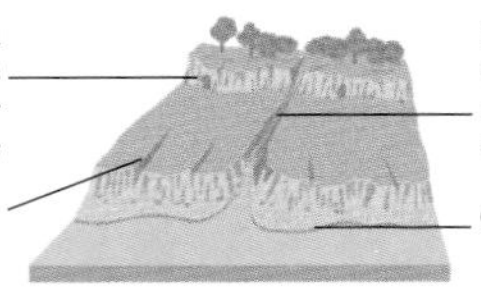

Caves and undercut cliffs mark former shoreline

Stream cuts down through recently exposed land

Former level of beach

Current beach

Uplift of the land in tectonically active regions can lead to former coastlines being lifted beyond the reach of the sea. New cliffs and caves are formed at a lower level, and rivers cut down through the lower land to reach sea level once more.

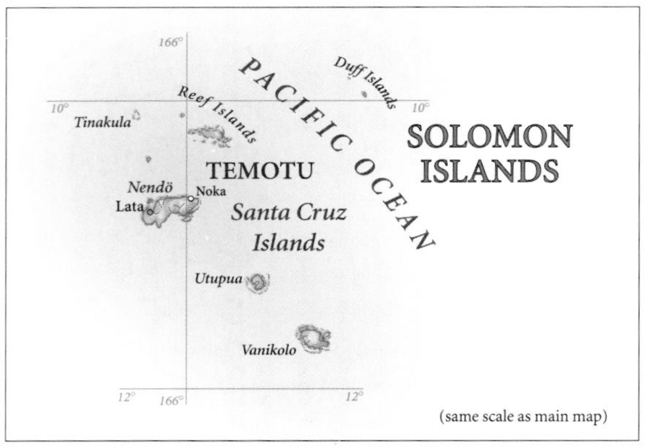

SOLOMON ISLANDS

PACIFIC OCEAN

Duff Islands
Reef Islands
Tinakula
TEMOTU
Nendö Noka
Lata
Santa Cruz Islands
Utupua
Vanikolo

(same scale as main map)

St. Matthias Group
Emirau Island

Isabel Channel

PACIFIC OCEAN

New Hanover
Taskul
North Cape
Kavieng
Tatau Island
Tabar Island
Simberi Island
Tabar Islands
Meteran
Konos
Lihir Group
Lihir Island
Nuguria Islands
Dyaul Island
Tanga Islands
Boang Island
Malendok Island
NEW IRELAND
Konogogo
Namatanai
New Ireland
Feni Islands
Mount Konogaiang 1860m
Ambitle Island
Babase Island
Green Islands
Pinipel Island
Nissan Island

Cape Lambert
Rabaul
Kokopo
Gazelle Peninsula
Taron
Toriu
Cape St.George
Open Bay
Lolobau Island
Willaumez Peninsula
Wide Bay
Mount Sinewit 1360m
Sampun
Lemankoa
Buka Island
Hutjena
NORTH SOLOMONS
Tulun Islands
Takuu Islands
Ontong Java Atoll
Nukumanu Islands

Talasea
Kimbe Bay
Hoskins
Nakanai Mountains
Wakunai
Mount Balbi 2685m
Kimbe
Ubai
EAST NEW BRITAIN
Torokina
Arawa
Kieta
Empress Augusta Bay
Panguna
Roncador Reef
Gasmata
New Britain
Bougainville Island
Buin
Nukiki
Fauro
Panggoe
Choiseul
Luti
Rob Roy
GUINEA
SOLOMON SEA
Shortland Island
Shortland Islands Strait
Treasury Islands
WESTERN
Vaghena
Kia
Baolo
ISABEL
Santa Isabel
Dai Island
MALAITA
Lusancay Islands and Reefs
Kiriwina Island
Vella Lavella
Mongga
Kolombangara
New Georgia Sound
Buala
Mount Sasari 1219m
Maluu
Kwailibesi
Losuia
Kitava Island
Gizo
Ringgi
New Georgia
Kaolo
San Jorge
Auki
Olomburi
Sikaiana
D'Entrecasteaux Islands
Vakuta Island
Gawa Island
Madau Island
Woodlark Island
Ranongga
Gizo
Munda
Rendova
Vangunu
Nggatokae
Russell Islands
CENTRAL
Florida Islands
Tulaghi
Malaita
Bannoni
Goodenough Island
Bolubolu
Fergusson Island
Yanaba Island
Guasopa
New Georgia Islands
Tetepare
Blanche Channel
Cape Esperance
Savo
Iron Bottom Sound
Tarapaina
Maramasike
Cape Vogel
Esa'ala
Normanby Island
HONIARA
Tangarare
Yandina
Tambea
Ulawa Island
Alotau
Ahioma
Sehulea
SOLOMON ISLANDS
Guadalcanal
Nduindui
Aola
Mount Popomanaseu 2330m
Avuavu
Heuru
Three Sisters Islands
Samarai
Sideia Island
Misima Island
MILNE BAY
Louisiade Archipelago
Pocklington Reef
GUADALCANAL
Kirakira
San Cristobal
Suau
Basilaki Island
Conflict Group
Bwagaoia
CENTRAL
Star Harbour
The Calvados Chain
Tagula
Rossel Island
Bellona
Haurahas
MAKIRA
SEA
Tagula Island
Lavanggu
Rennell

198

Lying close to the banks of the Sepik River in northern Papua New Guinea, this building is known as the Spirit House. It is constructed from leaves and twigs, ornately woven and trimmed into geometric patterns. The house is decorated with a mask and topped by a carved statue.

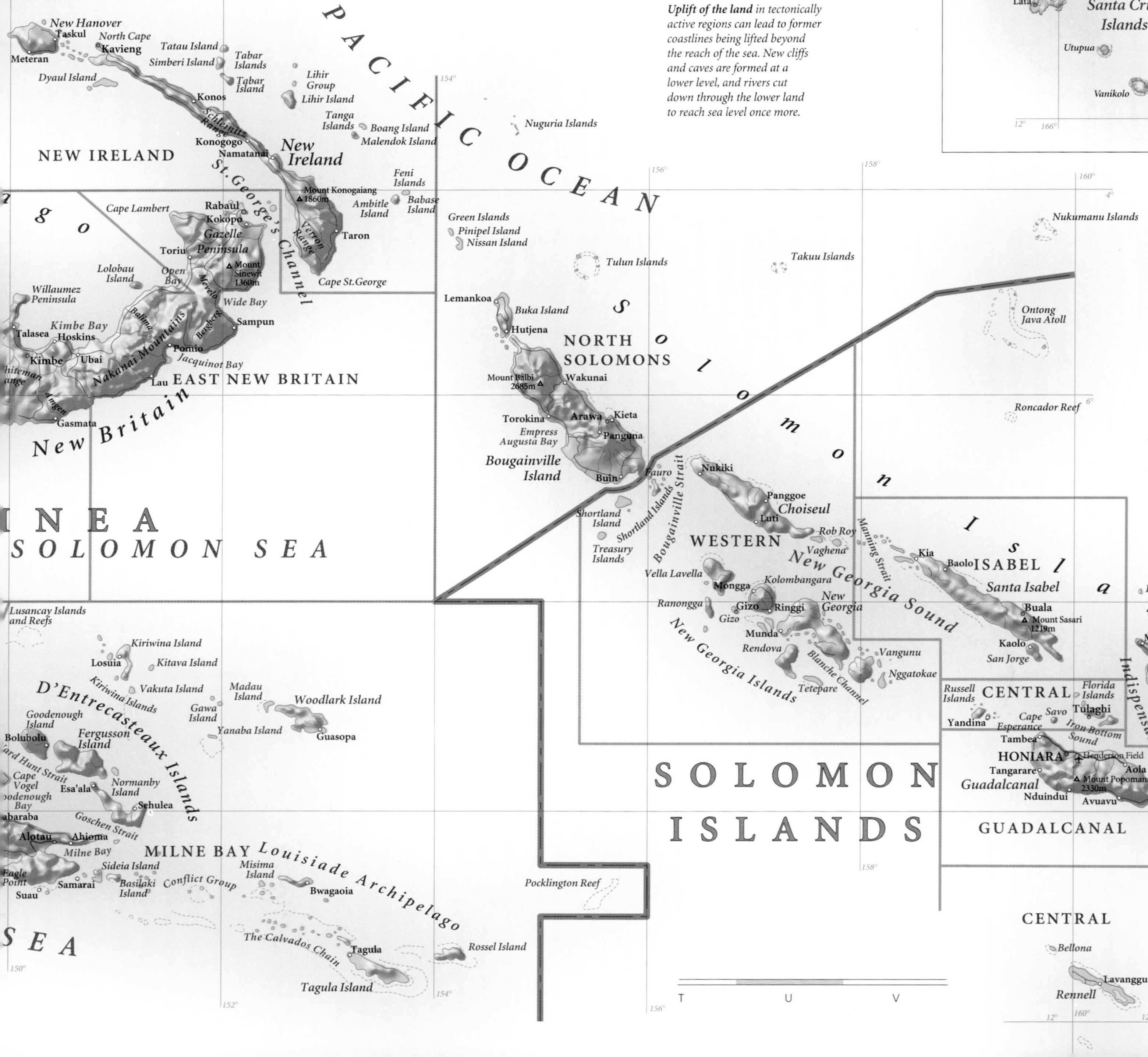

POLYNESIA

Kiribati, Tuvalu, *Cook Islands, Easter Island, French Polynesia, Niue,
Pitcairn Islands, Tokelau, Wallis & Futuna*

THE NUMEROUS ISLAND GROUPS OF POLYNESIA lie to the east of Australia, scattered over a vast area in the south Pacific. The islands are a mixture of low-lying coral atolls, some of which enclose lagoons, and the tips of great underwater volcanoes. The populations on the islands are small, and most people are of Polynesian origin, as are the Maori of New Zealand. Local economies remain simple, relying mainly on subsistence crops, mineral deposits, many now exhausted, fishing, and tourism.

KIRIBATI

A FORMER BRITISH COLONY, Kiribati became independent in 1979. Banaba's phosphate deposits ran out in 1980, following decades of exploitation by the British. Economic development remains slow and most agriculture is at a subsistence level, though coconuts provide export income, and underwater agriculture is being developed.

SCALE 1:1,000,000

With the exception of Banaba all the islands in Kiribati's three groups are low-lying, coral atolls. This aerial view shows the sparsely vegetated islands, intercut by many small lagoons.

TUVALU

A CHAIN of nine coral atolls, 360 miles (579 km) long with a land area of just over 9 sq miles (23 sq km), Tuvalu is one of the world's smallest and most isolated states. As the Ellice Islands, Tuvalu was linked to the Gilbert Islands (now part of Kiribati) as a British colony until independence in 1978. Politically and socially conservative, Tuvaluans live by fishing and subsistence farming.

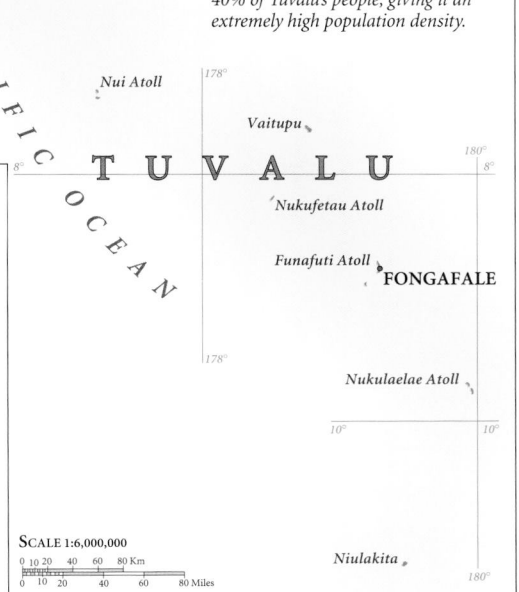

Funafuti Atoll contains more than 40% of Tuvalu's people, giving it an extremely high population density.

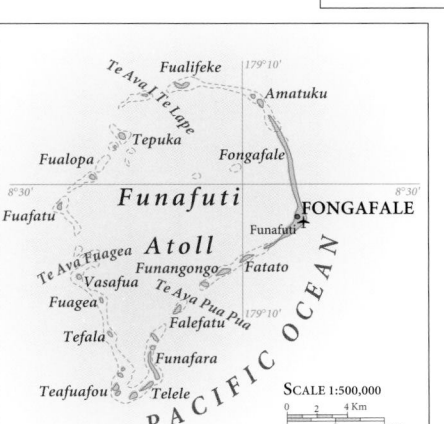
SCALE 1:500,000

SCALE 1:6,000,000

TOKELAU (to New Zealand)

A LOW-LYING CORAL ATOLL, Tokelau is a dependent territory of New Zealand with few natural resources. Although a 1990 cyclone destroyed crops and infrastructure, a tuna cannery and the sale of fishing licenses have raised revenue and a catamaran link between the islands has increased their tourism potential. Tokelau's small size and economic weakness makes independence from New Zealand unlikely.

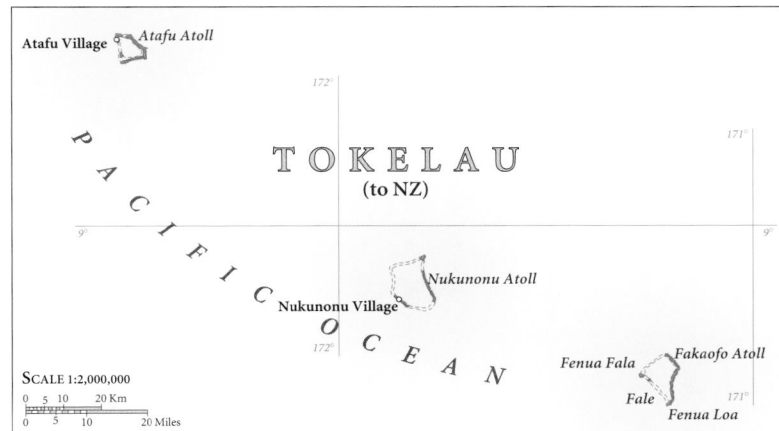

Fishermen cast their nets to catch small fish in the shallow waters off Atafu Atoll, the most westerly island in Tokelau.

SCALE 1:2,000,000

WALLIS & FUTUNA (to France)

IN CONTRAST TO OTHER FRENCH overseas territories in the south Pacific, the inhabitants of Wallis and Futuna have shown little desire for greater autonomy. A subsistence economy produces a variety of tropical crops, while foreign currency remittances come from expatriates and from the sale of licenses to Japanese and Korean fishing fleets.

SCALE 1:1,000,000

SCALE 1:1,000,000

COOK ISLANDS (to New Zealand)

A MIXTURE OF CORAL ATOLLS and volcanic peaks, the Cook Islands achieved self-government in 1965 but exist in free association with New Zealand. A diverse economy includes pearl and giant clam farming, and an ostrich farm, plus tourism and banking. A 1991 friendship treaty with France provides for French surveillance of territorial waters.

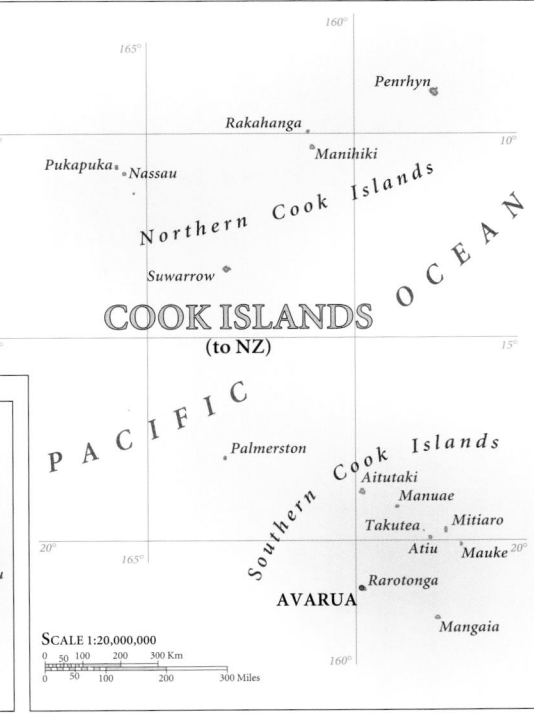
COOK ISLANDS (to NZ)

NIUE (to New Zealand)

NIUE, the world's largest coral island, is self-governing but exists in free association with New Zealand. Tropical fruits are grown for local consumption; tourism and the sale of postage stamps provide foreign currency. The lack of local job prospects has led more than 10,000 Niueans to emigrate to New Zealand, which has now invested heavily in Niue's economy in the hope of reversing this trend.

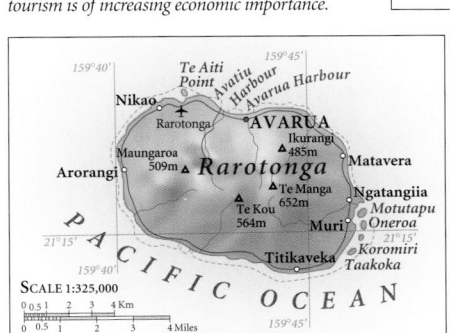

Palm trees fringe the white sands of a beach on Aitutaki in the Southern Cook Islands, where tourism is of increasing economic importance.

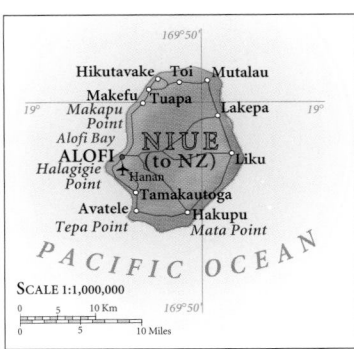
NIUE (to NZ)
SCALE 1:1,000,000

Waves have cut back the original coastline, exposing a sandy beach, near Mutalau in the northeast corner of Niue.

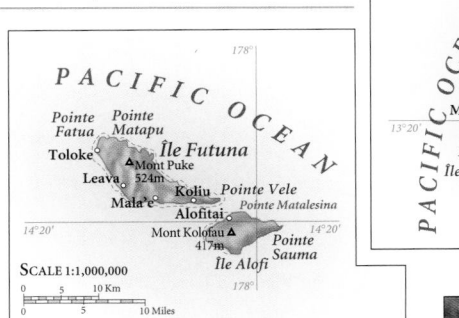

SCALE 1:325,000

SCALE 1:20,000,000

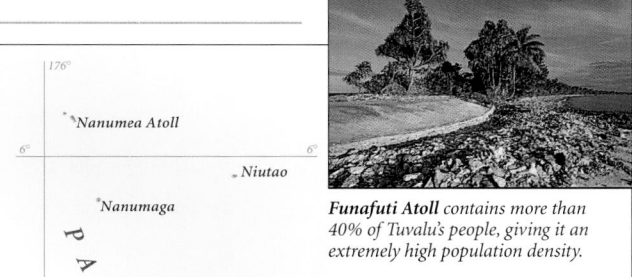

Wave action has eroded this shoreline near Port Campbell in southeastern Australia leaving isolated pinnacles of rock cut off from the main coastline. They are known as the "Twelve Apostles."

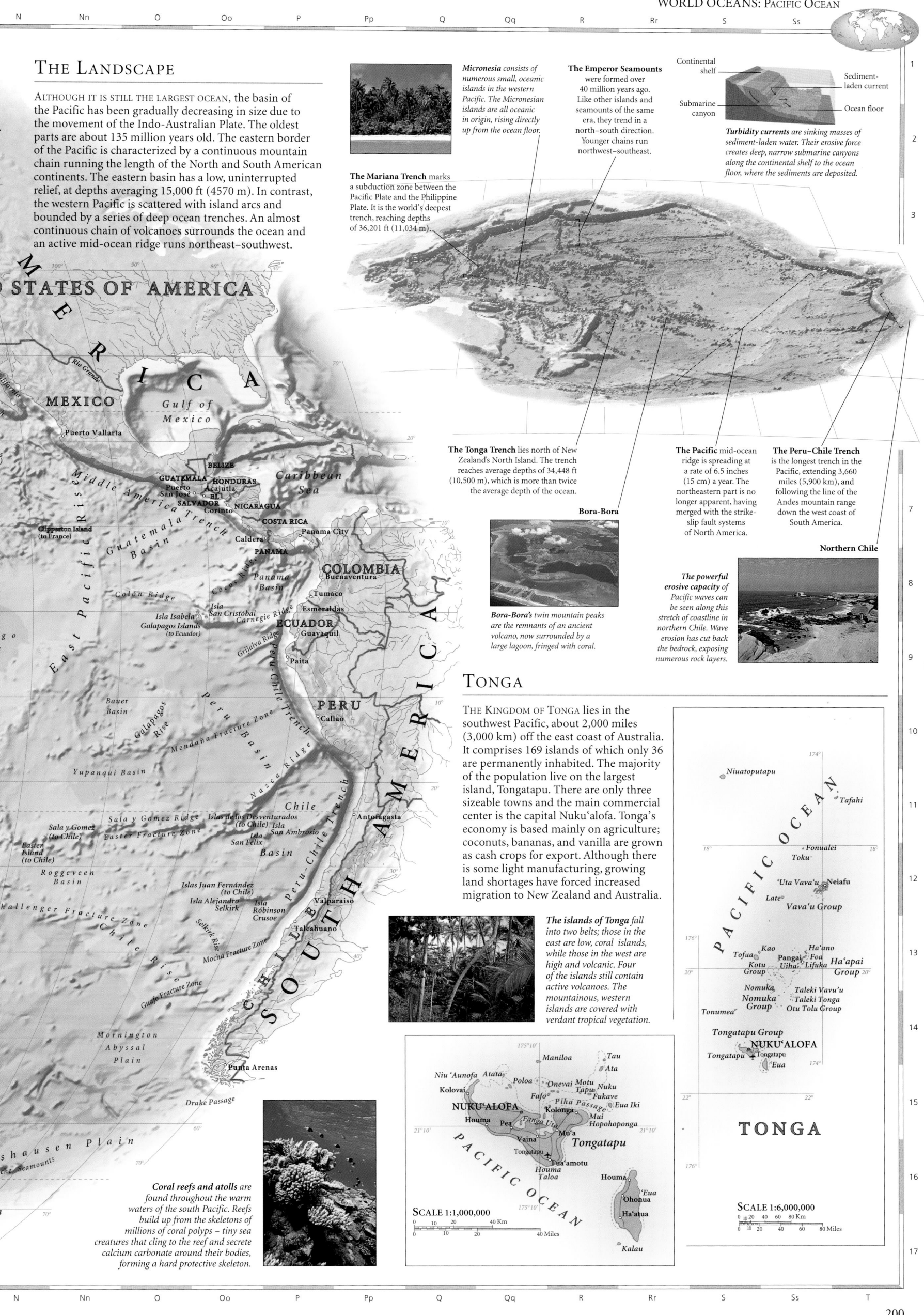

THE LANDSCAPE

ALTHOUGH IT IS STILL THE LARGEST OCEAN, the basin of the Pacific has been gradually decreasing in size due to the movement of the Indo-Australian Plate. The oldest parts are about 135 million years old. The eastern border of the Pacific is characterized by a continuous mountain chain running the length of the North and South American continents. The eastern basin has a low, uninterrupted relief, at depths averaging 15,000 ft (4570 m). In contrast, the western Pacific is scattered with island arcs and bounded by a series of deep ocean trenches. An almost continuous chain of volcanoes surrounds the ocean and an active mid-ocean ridge runs northeast–southwest.

Micronesia consists of numerous small, oceanic islands in the western Pacific. The Micronesian islands are all oceanic in origin, rising directly up from the ocean floor.

The Emperor Seamounts were formed over 40 million years ago. Like other islands and seamounts of the same era, they trend in a north–south direction. Younger chains run northwest–southeast.

Turbidity currents are sinking masses of sediment-laden water. Their erosive force creates deep, narrow submarine canyons along the continental shelf to the ocean floor, where the sediments are deposited.

The Mariana Trench marks a subduction zone between the Pacific Plate and the Philippine Plate. It is the world's deepest trench, reaching depths of 36,201 ft (11,034 m).

The Tonga Trench lies north of New Zealand's North Island. The trench reaches average depths of 34,448 ft (10,500 m), which is more than twice the average depth of the ocean.

The Pacific mid-ocean ridge is spreading at a rate of 6.5 inches (15 cm) a year. The northeastern part is no longer apparent, having merged with the strike-slip fault systems of North America.

The Peru–Chile Trench is the longest trench in the Pacific, extending 3,660 miles (5,900 km), and following the line of the Andes mountain range down the west coast of South America.

Bora-Bora

Bora-Bora's twin mountain peaks are the remnants of an ancient volcano, now surrounded by a large lagoon, fringed with coral.

Northern Chile

The powerful erosive capacity of Pacific waves can be seen along this stretch of coastline in northern Chile. Wave erosion has cut back the bedrock, exposing numerous rock layers.

TONGA

THE KINGDOM OF TONGA lies in the southwest Pacific, about 2,000 miles (3,000 km) off the east coast of Australia. It comprises 169 islands of which only 36 are permanently inhabited. The majority of the population live on the largest island, Tongatapu. There are only three sizeable towns and the main commercial center is the capital Nuku'alofa. Tonga's economy is based mainly on agriculture; coconuts, bananas, and vanilla are grown as cash crops for export. Although there is some light manufacturing, growing land shortages have forced increased migration to New Zealand and Australia.

The islands of Tonga fall into two belts; those in the east are low, coral islands, while those in the west are high and volcanic. Four of the islands still contain active volcanoes. The mountainous, western islands are covered with verdant tropical vegetation.

Coral reefs and atolls are found throughout the warm waters of the south Pacific. Reefs build up from the skeletons of millions of coral polyps – tiny sea creatures that cling to the reef and secrete calcium carbonate around their bodies, forming a hard protective skeleton.

SCALE 1:1,000,000

SCALE 1:6,000,000

TONGA

N O P Q R S T W X Y

MARSHALL ISLANDS

A GROUP OF 34 WIDELY-SCATTERED ATOLLS in the central Pacific Ocean, the Marshall Islands include some of the largest atolls in the world, formed from low coral islands with sandy beaches and enclosing vast lagoons. Formerly under US protection as part of the UN Trust Territory of the Pacific Islands, and including the former US nuclear testing sites of Bikini Atoll and Enewetak Atoll, the Marshall Islands became self-governing in 1979. The economy is reliant on US aid and on the rent paid by the US for its missile base on Kwajalein Atoll.

SCALE 1:1,000,000

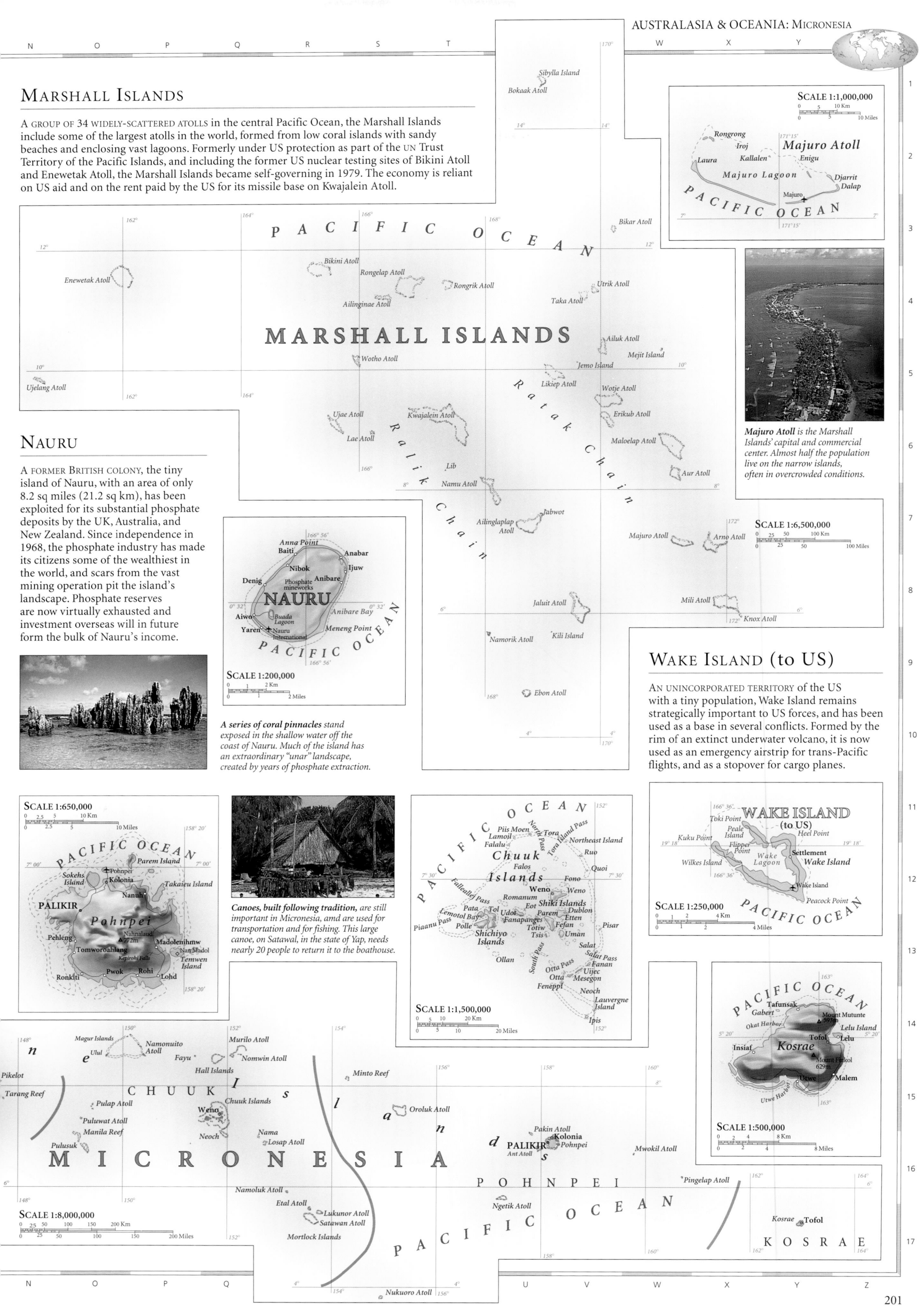

Majuro Atoll is the Marshall Islands' capital and commercial center. Almost half the population live on the narrow islands, often in overcrowded conditions.

NAURU

A FORMER BRITISH COLONY, the tiny island of Nauru, with an area of only 8.2 sq miles (21.2 sq km), has been exploited for its substantial phosphate deposits by the UK, Australia, and New Zealand. Since independence in 1968, the phosphate industry has made its citizens some of the wealthiest in the world, and scars from the vast mining operation pit the island's landscape. Phosphate reserves are now virtually exhausted and investment overseas will in future form the bulk of Nauru's income.

SCALE 1:200,000

A series of coral pinnacles stand exposed in the shallow water off the coast of Nauru. Much of the island has an extraordinary "unar" landscape, created by years of phosphate extraction.

SCALE 1:6,500,000

SCALE 1:650,000

Canoes, built following tradition, are still important in Micronesia, amd are used for transportation and for fishing. This large canoe, on Satawal, in the state of Yap, needs nearly 20 people to return it to the boathouse.

WAKE ISLAND (to US)

AN UNINCORPORATED TERRITORY of the US with a tiny population, Wake Island remains strategically important to US forces, and has been used as a base in several conflicts. Formed by the rim of an extinct underwater volcano, it is now used as an emergency airstrip for trans-Pacific flights, and as a stopover for cargo planes.

WAKE ISLAND (to US)

SCALE 1:250,000

SCALE 1:1,500,000

SCALE 1:500,000

SCALE 1:8,000,000

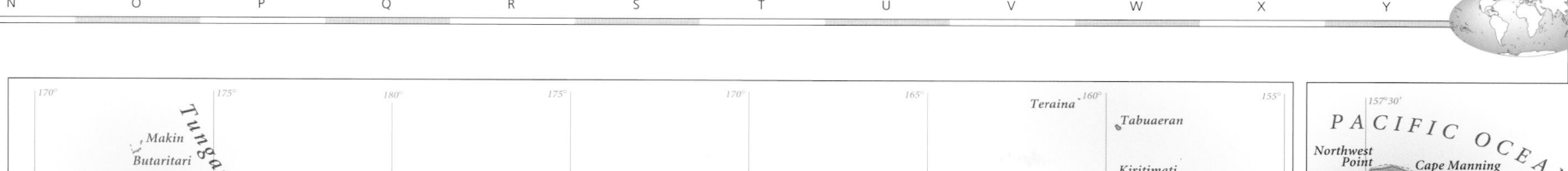

FRENCH POLYNESIA (to France)

THE 130 ISLANDS OF FRENCH POLYNESIA cover 4 million sq miles (10.5 million sq km). Nearly 75% of the people live on Tahiti. The use of Mururoa as a nuclear testing site by the French military transformed the economy, creating many jobs. The end of testing led to calls from the Polynesian majority for greater autonomy from France, the rebuilding of indigenous trade, and a reduction in tourism to stop the erosion of the islands' traditional culture.

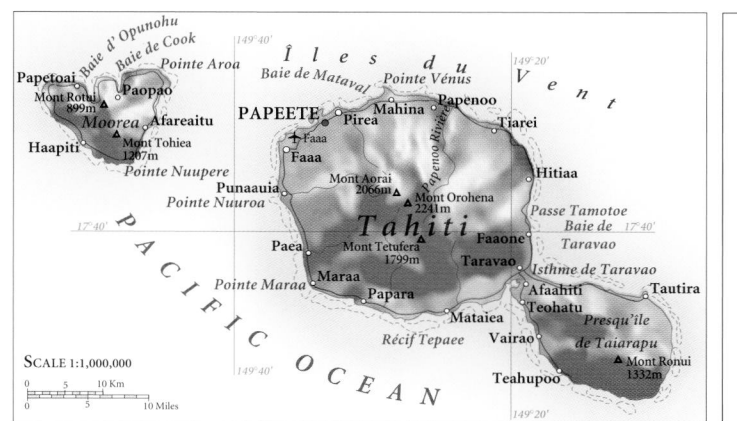

The traditional Tahitian welcome for visitors, who are greeted by parties of canoes, has become a major tourist attraction.

PITCAIRN ISLANDS (to UK)

BRITAIN'S MOST ISOLATED DEPENDENCY, Pitcairn Island was first populated by mutineers from the HMS *Bounty* in 1790. Emigration is further depleting the already limited gene pool of the island's inhabitants, with associated social and health problems. Barter, fishing, and subsistence farming form the basis of the economy although postage stamp sales provide foreign currency earnings, and offshore mineral exploitation may boost the economy in future.

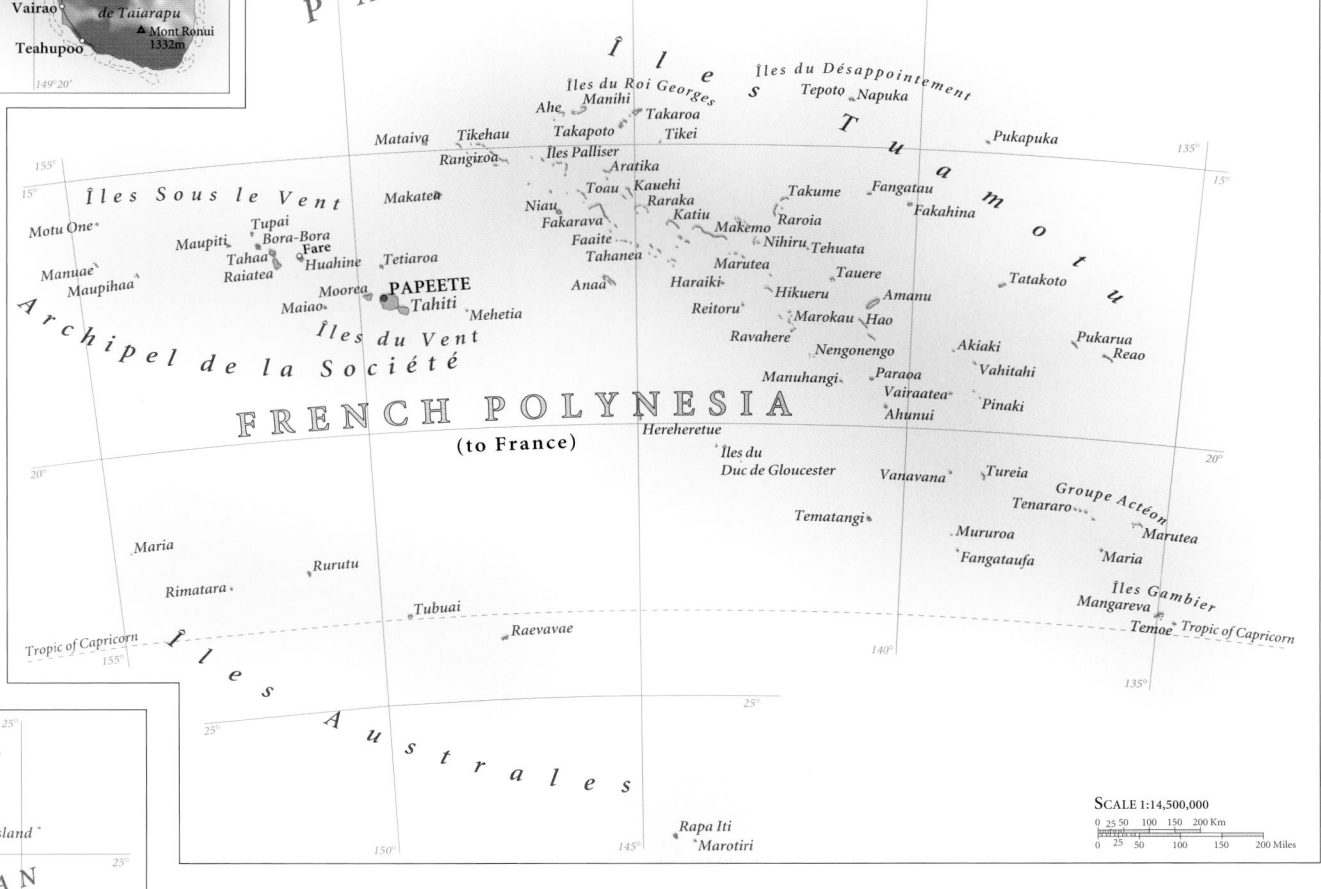

The Pitcairn Islanders rely on regular airdrops from New Zealand and periodic visits by supply vessels to provide them with basic commodities.

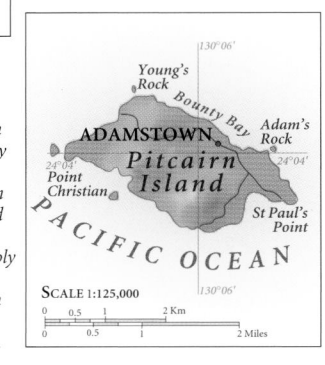

EASTER ISLAND (to Chile)

ONE OF THE MOST EASTERLY ISLANDS in Polynesia, Easter Island *(Isla de Pascua)* – also known as Rapa Nui, is part of Chile. The mainly Polynesian inhabitants support themselves by farming, which is mainly of a subsistence nature, and includes cattle rearing and crops such as sugar cane, bananas, corn, gourds, and potatoes. In recent years, tourism has become the most important source of income and the island sustains a small commercial airport.

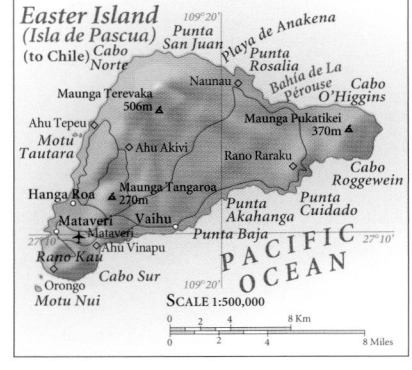

The Naunau, a series of huge stone statues overlook Playa de Anakena, on Easter Island. Carved from a soft volcanic rock, they were erected between 400 and 900 years ago.

A B C D E F G

ANTARCTICA

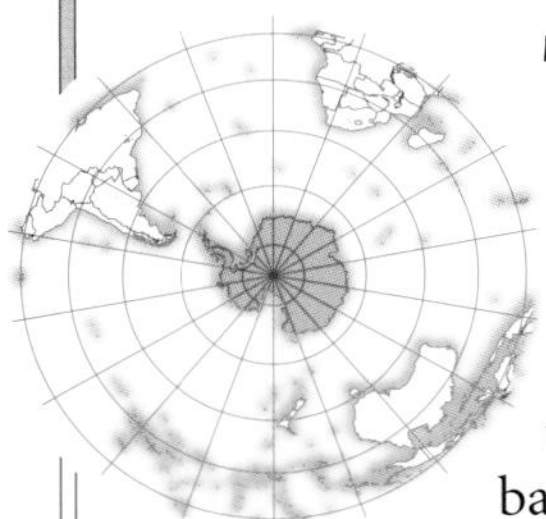

THE ICE-COVERED CONTINENT of Antarctica, which is the Earth's most southerly region, has drawn explorers and entrepreneurs seeking challenge and riches in its wintry lands for over 200 years. The extreme climate has deterred any large-scale settlement of the continent, and though commercial hunters built outposts in the past, habitation is now limited to scientific bases. The Antarctic Treaty, which came into force in 1961, provides for international governance and scientific cooperation in place of potential territorial conflict.

RESOURCES

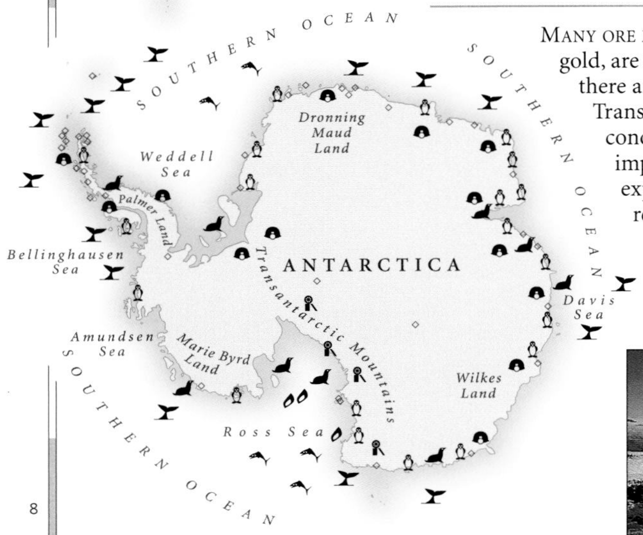

MANY ORE MINERALS, including iron and gold, are found in the Antarctic, and there are also coal reserves in the Transantarctic Mountains. The severe conditions and environmental importance of the region mean that exploitation of potential mineral resources is both uneconomic and undesirable. The unique wildlife and landscape draw a small number of tourists annually.

Most settlements in Antarctica are research bases such as this one at Rothera on Adelaide Island, although there is a small Chilean settlement on King George Island.

Resources (including wildlife)
- coal
- fish
- minerals
- oil & gas
- penguins
- seals
- whales
- ◇ polar research base

THE LANDSCAPE

THERE ARE TWO DISTINCT PARTS to Antarctica: Lesser Antarctica, a series of ice-covered, mountainous islands, joined together by the ice; and the high plateau of Greater Antarctica. The Ross Sea and the Weddell Sea are outliers of the Southern Ocean – deep bays partially covered by thick ice shelves.

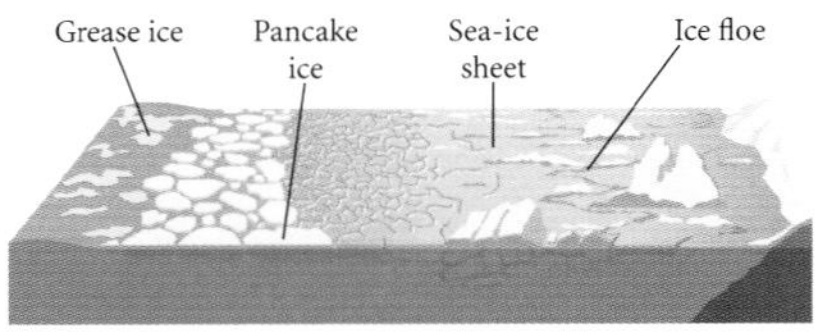

On Elephant Island, the coast is edged by glaciers, although the land is not permanently covered by ice.

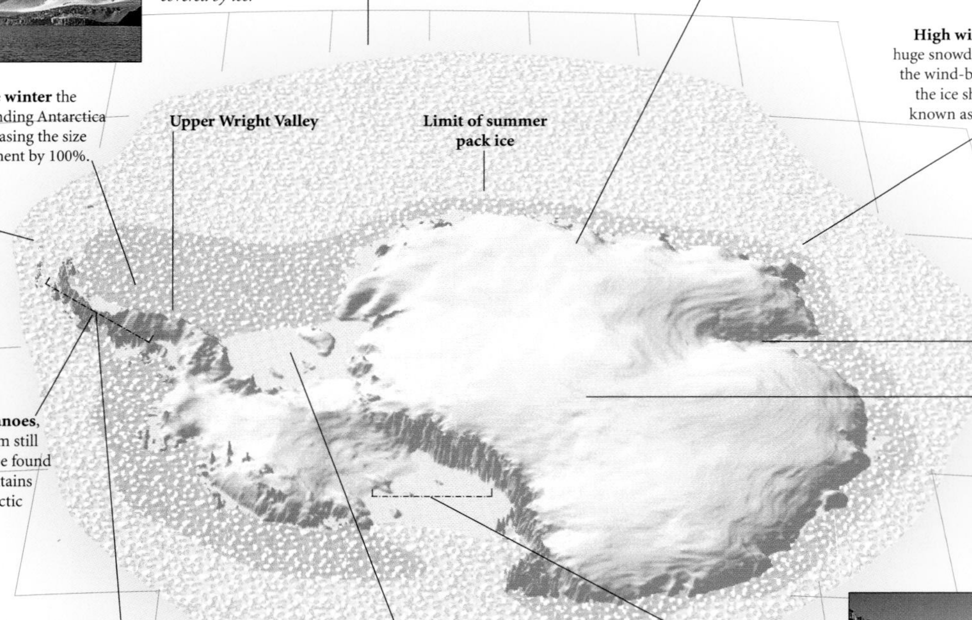

Grease ice | Pancake ice | Sea-ice sheet | Ice floe

Pack ice forms out at sea in freezing temperatures. At the outer limits, grease ice congeals on the surface of the ocean. This is then spun around by wind and waves into irregular "pancakes," freezing and breaking up several times before bonding together again to form sea-ice sheets, which finally cement into enormous ice floes.

During the winter the seas surrounding Antarctica freeze, increasing the size of the continent by 100%.

Elephant Island

Upper Wright Valley

Limit of winter pack ice

Limit of summer pack ice

High winds carrying snow form huge snowdrifts. The erosive power of the wind-borne snow can also sculpt the ice sheet to produce landforms known as sastrugi which align with the direction of the wind.

Many volcanoes, some of them still active, can be found in the mountains of the Antarctic Peninsula.

The Lambert Glacier is the largest glacier system in the world, up to 50 miles (80 km) wide at its seaward limit, and reaching 180 miles (300 km) into the interior by way of the Prince Charles Mountains.

Antarctica is the highest continent on Earth, because of the great thickness of ice which overlays the land. In places the ice alone can reach up to 15,700 ft (4,800 m) thick. Much of the basement rock of west Antarctica lies below sea level, pushed down by the weight of the ice.

The mountainous Antarctic Peninsula is formed of rocks 65–225 million years old, overlain by more recent rocks and glacial deposits. It is connected to the Andes in South America by a submarine ridge.

Nearly half – 44% – of the Antarctic coastline is bounded by ice shelves, like the Ronne Ice Shelf, which float on the Ocean. These are joined to the inland ice sheet by dome-shaped ice "rises."

More than 30% of Antarctic ice is contained in the Ross Ice Shelf.

The barren, flat-bottomed Upper Wright Valley was once filled by a glacier, but is now dry, strewn with boulders and pebbles. In some dry valleys, there has been no rain for over 2 million years.

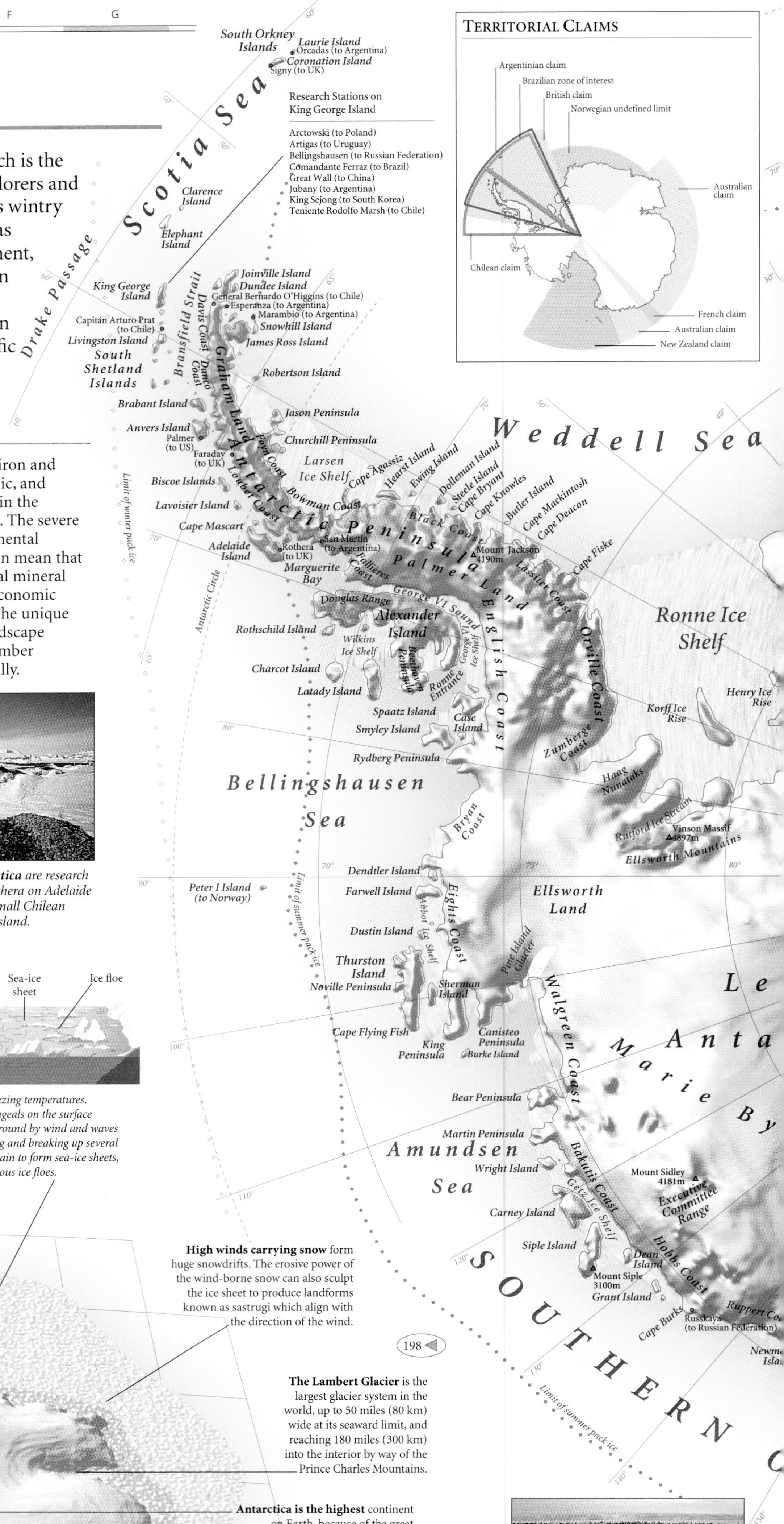

Large colonies of seabirds live in the extremely harsh Antarctic climate. The Emperor penguins seen here, the smaller Adélie penguin, the Antarctic petrel and the South Polar skua are the only birds that breed exclusively on the continent.

TERRITORIAL CLAIMS

Argentinian claim
Brazilian zone of interest
British claim
Norwegian undefined limit
Australian claim
Chilean claim
French claim
Australian claim
New Zealand claim

Map labels

South Orkney Islands
Laurie Island
Orcadas (to Argentina)
Coronation Island
Signy (to UK)
Scotia Sea

Research Stations on King George Island
Arctowski (to Poland)
Artigas (to Uruguay)
Bellingshausen (to Russian Federation)
Comandante Ferraz (to Brazil)
Great Wall (to China)
Jubany (to Argentina)
King Sejong (to South Korea)
Teniente Rodolfo Marsh (to Chile)

Clarence Island
Elephant Island
Joinville Island
Dundee Island
General Bernardo O'Higgins (to Chile)
Esperanza (to Argentina)
Marambio (to Argentina)
Snowhill Island
James Ross Island
Robertson Island

Drake Passage

King George Island
Capitán Arturo Prat (to Chile)
Livingston Island
South Shetland Islands

Bransfield Strait
Davis Coast
Danco Coast
Graham Land

Brabant Island
Anvers Island
Palmer (to US)
Faraday (to UK)
Biscoe Islands
Lavoisier Island
Cape Mascart
Adelaide Island
Rothera (to UK)
San Martín (to Argentina)
Marguerite Bay
Rothschild Island
Charcot Island
Latady Island

Churchill Peninsula
Larsen Ice Shelf
Cape Agassiz
Hearst Island
Jason Peninsula
Bowman Coast
Foyn Coast
Wilkins Coast
Black Coast
Fallieres Coast

Weddell Sea

Ewing Island
Dolleman Island
Steele Island
Cape Bryant
Cape Knowles
Cape Mackintosh
Butler Island
Cape Fiske
Cape Deacon

Antarctic Peninsula
Palmer Land
English Coast
George VI Sound
Alexander Island
Douglas Range
Wilkins Ice Shelf
Orville Coast

Ronne Ice Shelf

Spaatz Island
Smyley Island
Case Island
Rydberg Peninsula
Zumberge Coast
Haag Nunataks
Korff Ice Rise
Henry Ice Rise

Antarctic Circle

Bellingshausen Sea

Dendtler Island
Farwell Island
Peter I Island (to Norway)
Dustin Island
Thurston Island
Noville Peninsula
Bryan Coast
Rutford Ice Stream
Vinson Massif 4892m
Ellsworth Mountains
Ellsworth Land

Cape Flying Fish
King Peninsula
Canisteo Peninsula
Burke Island
Eights Coast
Abbot Ice Shelf
Pine Island Glacier

Bear Peninsula
Walgreen Coast

Martin Peninsula
Amundsen Sea
Wright Island
Carney Island

Mount Sidley 4181m
Executive Committee Range
Marie Byrd Land

Getz Ice Shelf
Bakutis Coast
Siple Island

Mount Siple 3100m
Grant Island
Dean Island
Hobbs Coast
Cape Burks
Russkaya (to Russian Federation)
Ruppert Coast
Newman Island

Southern Ocean

(map inset, small)
Dronning Maud Land
Weddell Land
Palmer Land
Bellingshausen Sea
Amundsen Sea
Marie Byrd Land
Ross Sea
ANTARCTICA
Transantarctic Mountains
Wilkes Land
Davis Sea
SOUTHERN OCEAN

198 ◄

A B C D E F G H I J K L M

The sun sets over the Antarctic Peninsula for more than six months during the winter. However, there are more hours of sunshine during the brief Antarctic summer than most equatorial countries experience in a whole year.

Immense, flat-topped icebergs are formed when blocks of ice break away from the main ice sheet. Though the exposed area is enormous, the volume of ice concealed beneath the water may be many times greater.

MAP KEY

ELEVATION

ice cap
ice shelf
exposed land

SCALE 1:14,750,000
(projection: Lambert Azimuthal Equal Area)

205

THE ARCTIC

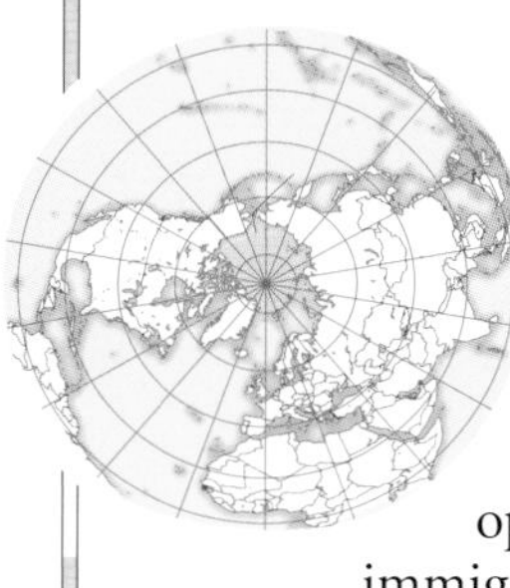

THREE CONTINENTS, ASIA, NORTH AMERICA, AND EUROPE, reach into the Arctic Circle at their northernmost limits, almost entirely encircling the Arctic Ocean. Despite the region's extraordinarily harsh climate, it has been inhabited for thousands of years by peoples such as the European Lapps, the Russian Nenet, and the North American Inuit, who draw a living from fishing, herding, and hunting. More recently, particularly in the Russian Arctic, opportunities to exploit oil and other mineral reserves have encouraged immigration. Pollution of the Arctic's unique ecology and damage to the traditional lifestyles of many native peoples have been the unfortunate results of this activity, and international cooperation is needed to safeguard the future of the region.

MAP KEY

POPULATION
- ■ above 5 million
- ◉ 1 million to 5 million
- ◍ 500,000 to 1 million
- ◎ 100,000 to 500,000
- ⊕ 50,000 to 100,000
- ○ 10,000 to 50,000
- ○ below 10,000

SEA DEPTH
sea level
- 250m / 820ft
- 500m / 1640ft
- 1000m / 3281ft
- 2000m / 6562ft
- 3000m / 9843ft

SCALE 1:21,000,000
(projection: Lambert Azimuthal Equal Area)

Windblown snow etches deep patterns in the ice sheet known as sastrugi. They align with the direction of the wind

RESOURCES

LARGE QUANTITIES of coal, oil, and natural gas are to be found in the basins of the Arctic Ocean, and in northern Canada, Alaska and the Russian Federation. The cost and difficulty of extraction and, more recently, awareness of damage to the environment, have limited exploitation to coastal regions. The unfrozen waters have stocks of fish including cod, flounder, and haddock. Quotas have now been put in place to restrict the number of fish caught annually. Reindeer are herded in large numbers by many of the native Arctic peoples. Most grain and vegetables are imported from elsewhere.

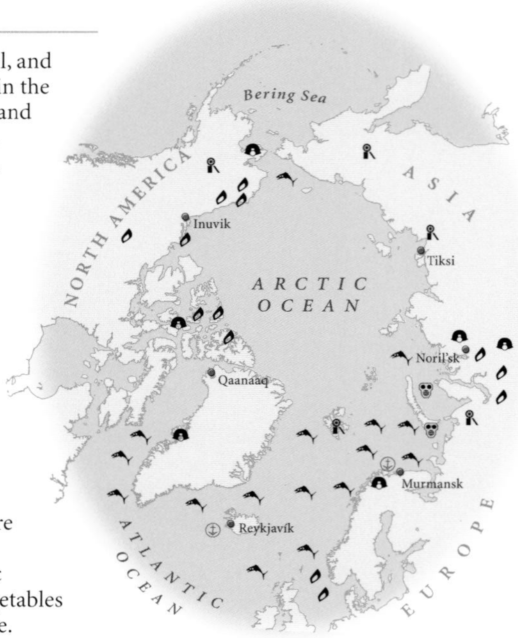

Icebreakers are ships with specially strengthened hulls, designed to break a path through the ice. They are used to keep important routes open during the winter, when falling temperatures cause much of the Arctic Ocean to freeze over.

Resources
- ⚒ coal
- ⚓ fish
- ◣ mining
- ◔ oil & gas
- ☢ radioactive contamination
- ⊕ major towns
- ⊕ major ports

THE LANDSCAPE

THE ARCTIC OCEAN comprises two large ocean basins divided by three submarine ridges, the greatest of which, the Lomonosov Ridge, is a huge underwater mountain range which has an average height of more than 10,000 ft (3,000 m). The lands which encircle the Arctic Ocean are underlain by great shield areas of ancient rocks, which were heavily glaciated during the last Ice Age.

Icebergs are constantly broken up and reshaped by wind and the oceans. This flat-topped iceberg has been undercut, leaving a craggy ice cliff.

A complex and ancient mountain system, extending from the Queen Elizabeth Islands to eastern Greenland was formed more than 245 million years ago.

The Canadian Shield underlies almost all of the Canadian Arctic. It is a very stable plateau of ancient rock, now covered by glacial lakes and sediment, which supports tundra vegetation.

The Arctic Ocean is the world's smallest ocean with a total area of 5,440,000 sq miles (15,100,000 sq km).

At a latitude of more than 75° N, the Arctic Ocean is almost permanently covered by pack-ice, though high winds and the movement of the seas may cause the ice to crack and break up.

In the more southerly reaches of the Arctic, like Siberia, much of the land is covered by permafrost. In the summer, higher temperatures warm the frozen ground, causing a number of typical phenomena. These include solifluction, the fast downhill movement of top soil layers; freeze/thaw activity, which patterns the ground into regular polygonal shapes, and the formation of large domes with a frozen ice core, known as pingos.

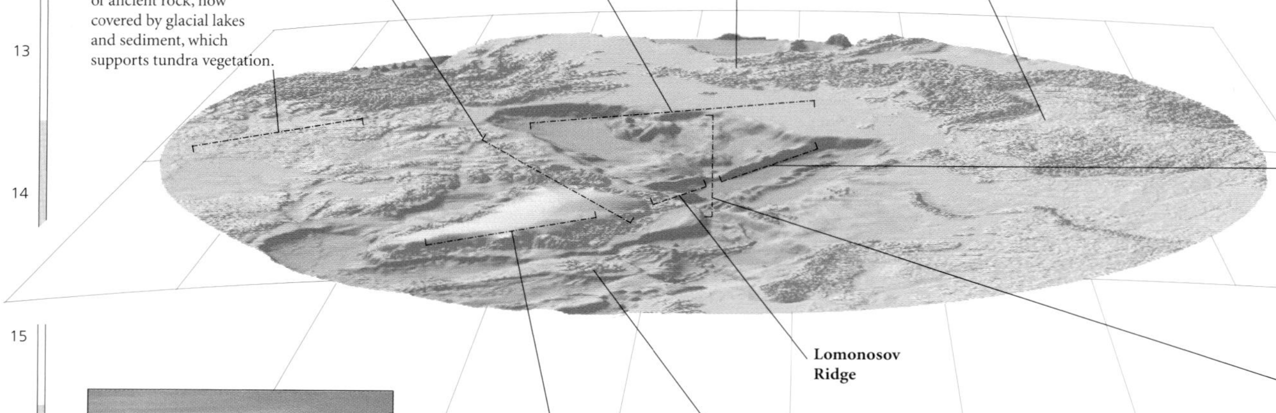

Lomonosov Ridge

Lomonosov Ridge

Arctic ice shelf

Ice sheet

Iceberg

Crevasses occur at the edge of the ice sheet

Sea water melts the edge of the ice sheet

Much of Greenland is covered by a massive ice sheet more than 650,000 sq miles (1,683,400 sq km) in extent. The weight of the ice has depressed the central land area to form a basin lying more than 1,000 ft (300 m) below sea level. Only at the edges of the island is bare rock visible.

Iceland has five major glaciers, sustained by heavy snowfall. Parts of the ice cap cover active volcanoes, such as Bárdharbunga, which periodically erupt causing the melted ice to form a great lake at the glacier margins.

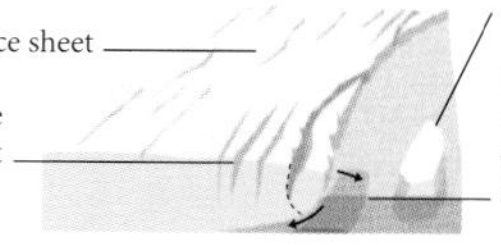

At the boundary of the Arctic ice shelves, sea water flows under the ice causing melting and forming crevasses on the surface. This eventually weakens blocks of ice which break away as icebergs. This process is known as calving.

Map labels
Bering Sea · NORTH AMERICA · ASIA · ARCTIC OCEAN · Inuvik · Tiksi · Noril'sk · Qaanaaq · Murmansk · Reykjavík · ATLANTIC OCEAN · EUROPE

Great Bear Lake · Great Slave Lake · Kugluktuk · Bathurst Inlet · Cambridge Bay · King William Island · Boothia Peninsula · Churchill · Nelson · Southampton Island · Coats Island · Repulse Bay · Melville Peninsula · Hudson Bay · Mansel Island · Foxe Basin · Prince Charles Island · Ivujivik · Inukjuak · Baffin Island · Lake Harbour · Ungava Bay · Cape Chidley · Davis Strait · Nain · Labrador Sea · Maniitsoq · NUUK · Paamiut · Labrador Basin · Ivittuut · Qaqortoq · Nanortalik · Nunap Isua (Kap Farvel) · Eirik Ridge · ATLANTIC · NORTH AMERICA · CANADA

198

14

14

66

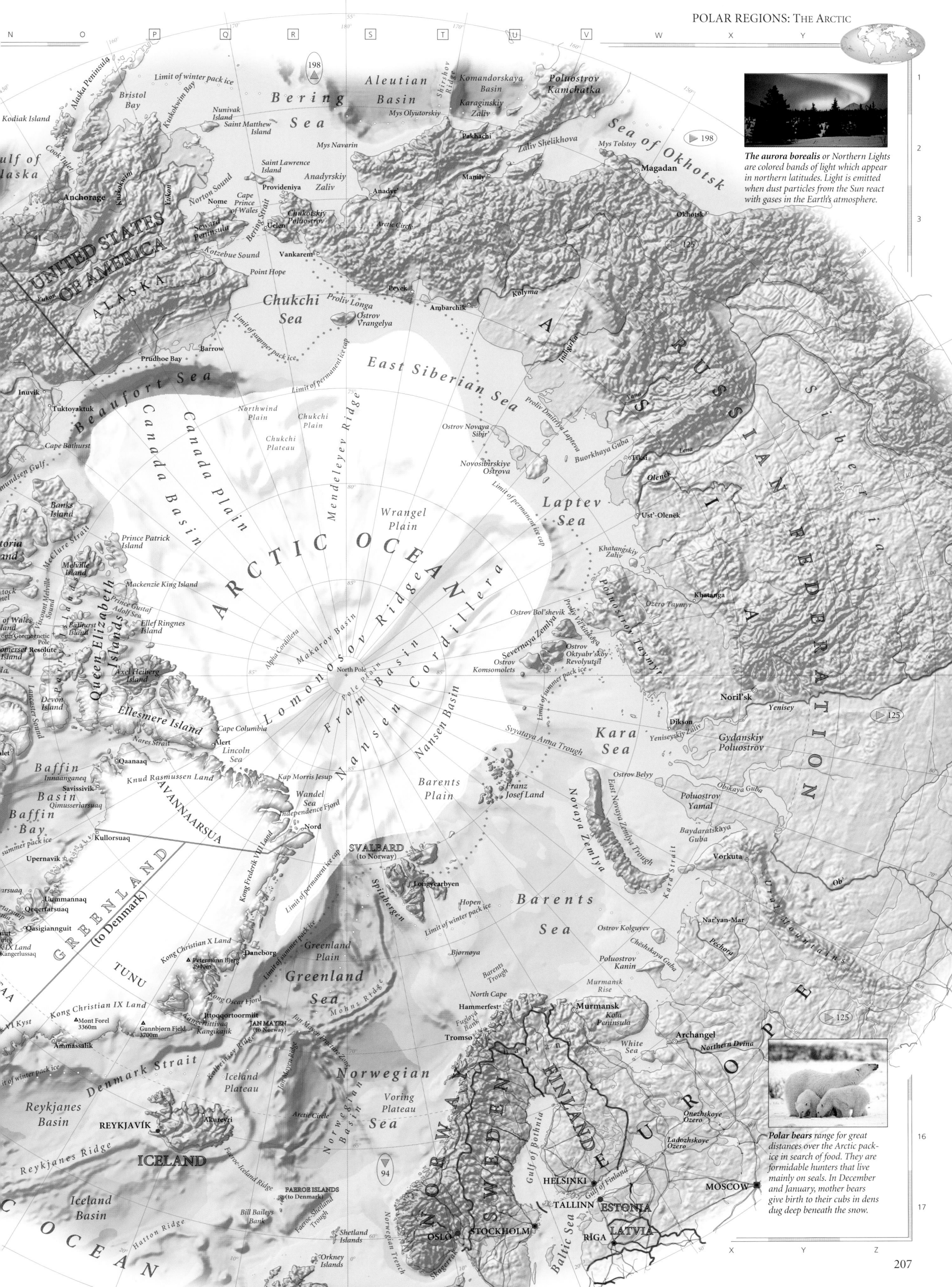

The aurora borealis or Northern Lights are colored bands of light which appear in northern latitudes. Light is emitted when dust particles from the Sun react with gases in the Earth's atmosphere.

Polar bears range for great distances over the Arctic pack-ice in search of food. They are formidable hunters that live mainly on seals. In December and January, mother bears give birth to their cubs in dens dug deep beneath the snow.

GEOGRAPHICAL COMPARISONS

LARGEST COUNTRIES

Russian Federation	6,592,735 sq miles	(17,075,200 sq km)
Canada	3,855,171 sq miles	(9,984,670 sq km)
USA	3,717,792 sq miles	(9,629,091 sq km)
China	3,705,386 sq miles	(9,596,960 sq km)
Brazil	3,286,470 sq miles	(8,511,965 sq km)
Australia	2,967,893 sq miles	(7,686,850 sq km)
India	1,269,339 sq miles	(3,287,590 sq km)
Argentina	1,068,296 sq miles	(2,766,890 sq km)
Kazakhstan	1,049,150 sq miles	(2,717,300 sq km)
Sudan	967,493 sq miles	(2,505,810 sq km)

SMALLEST COUNTRIES

Vatican City	0.17 sq miles	(0.44 sq km)
Monaco	0.75 sq miles	(1.95 sq km)
Nauru	8 sq miles	(21 sq km)
Tuvalu	10 sq miles	(26 sq km)
San Marino	24 sq miles	(61 sq km)
Liechtenstein	62 sq miles	(160 sq km)
Marshall Islands	70 sq miles	(181 sq km)
St. Kitts & Nevis	101 sq miles	(261 sq km)
Maldives	116 sq miles	(300 sq km)
Malta	122 sq miles	(316 sq km)

LARGEST ISLANDS

(TO THE NEAREST 1000 - OR 100,000 FOR THE LARGEST)

Greenland	849,400 sq miles	(2,200,000 sq km)
New Guinea	312,000 sq miles	(808,000 sq km)
Borneo	292,222 sq miles	(757,050 sq km)
Madagascar	229,300 sq miles	(594,000 sq km)
Sumatra	202,300 sq miles	(524,000 sq km)
Baffin Island	183,800 sq miles	(476,000 sq km)
Honshu	88,800 sq miles	(230,000 sq km)
Britain	88,700 sq miles	(229,800 sq km)
Victoria Island	81,900 sq miles	(212,000 sq km)
Ellesmere Island	75,700 sq miles	(196,000 sq km)

RICHEST COUNTRIES

(GNP PER CAPITA, IN US$)

Liechtenstein	50,000
Luxembourg	39,470
Norway	38,730
Switzerland	36,170
USA	35,400
Japan	34,010
Denmark	30,260
Iceland	27,960
Monaco	27,500
Sweden	25,970

POOREST COUNTRIES

(GNP PER CAPITA, IN US$)

Burundi	100
Congo, Dem. Rep.	100
Ethiopia	100
Somalia	120
Guinea-Bissau	130
Liberia	140
Sierra Leone	140
Malawi	160
Tajikistan	180
Niger	180
Eritrea	190
Mozambique	200

MOST POPULOUS COUNTRIES

China	1,304,200,000
India	1,065,500,000
USA	294,000,000
Indonesia	219,900,000
Brazil	178,500,000
Pakistan	153,600,000
Bangladesh	146,700,000
Russian Federation	143,200,000
Japan	127,700,000
Nigeria	124,000,000

LEAST POPULOUS COUNTRIES

Vatican City	921
Tuvalu	11,305
Nauru	12,570
Palau	19,717
San Marino	28,119
Monaco	32,130
Liechtenstein	33,145
St Kitts & Nevis	38,763
Marshall Islands	56,429
Antigua & Barbuda	67,897
Andorra	69,150
Dominica	69,655

MOST DENSELY POPULATED COUNTRIES

Monaco	42,840 people per sq mile	(16,477 per sq km)
Singapore	18,220 people per sq mile	(7,049 per sq km)
Vatican City	5,359 people per sq mile	(2,070 per sq km)
Malta	3,177 people per sq mile	(1,231 per sq km)
Bangladesh	2,837 people per sq mile	(1,096 per sq km)
Maldives	2,741 people per sq mile	(1,060 per sq km)
Bahrain	2,652 people per sq mile	(1,025 per sq km)
Taiwan	1,815 people per sq mile	(701 per sq km)
Mauritius	1,671 people per sq mile	(645 per sq km)
Barbados	1,627 people per sq mile	(628 per sq km)

MOST SPARSELY POPULATED COUNTRIES

Mongolia	4 people per sq mile	(2 per sq km)
Namibia	6 people per sq mile	(2 per sq km)
Australia	7 people per sq mile	(3 per sq km)
Iceland	7 people per sq mile	(3 per sq km)
Mauritania	7 people per sq mile	(3 per sq km)
Suriname	7 people per sq mile	(3 per sq km)
Botswana	8 people per sq mile	(3 per sq km)
Libya	8 people per sq mile	(3 per sq km)
Canada	9 people per sq mile	(3 per sq km)
Guyana	10 people per sq mile	(4 per sq km)

MOST WIDELY SPOKEN LANGUAGES

1. Chinese (Mandarin)	6. Arabic
2. English	7. Bengali
3. Hindi	8. Portuguese
4. Spanish	9. Malay-Indonesian
5. Russian	10. French

COUNTRIES WITH THE MOST LAND BORDERS

14: China (Afghanistan, Bhutan, India, Kazakhstan, Kyrgyzstan, Laos, Mongolia, Myanmar, Nepal, North Korea, Pakistan, Russian Federation, Tajikistan, Vietnam)

14: Russian Federation (Azerbaijan, Belarus, China, Estonia, Finland, Georgia, Kazakhstan, Latvia, Lithuania, Mongolia, North Korea, Norway, Poland, Ukraine)

10: Brazil (Argentina, Bolivia, Colombia, French Guiana, Guyana, Paraguay, Peru, Suriname, Uruguay, Venezuela)

9: Congo, Dem. Rep. (Angola, Burundi, Central African Republic, Congo, Rwanda, Sudan, Tanzania, Uganda, Zambia)

9: Germany (Austria, Belgium, Czech Republic, Denmark, France, Luxembourg, Netherlands, Poland, Switzerland)

9: Sudan (Central African Republic, Chad, Congo, Dem. Rep., Egypt, Eritrea, Ethiopia, Kenya, Libya, Uganda)

8: Austria (*Czech Republic, Germany, Hungary, Italy, Liechtenstein, Slovakia, Slovenia, Switzerland*)

8: France (*Andorra, Belgium, Germany, Italy, Luxembourg, Monaco, Spain, Switzerland*)

8: Tanzania (*Burundi, Congo, Dem. Rep., Kenya, Malawi, Mozambique, Rwanda, Uganda, Zambia*)

8: Turkey (*Armenia, Azerbaijan, Bulgaria, Georgia, Greece, Iran, Iraq, Syria*)

8: Zambia (*Angola, Botswana, Congo, Dem. Rep., Malawi, Mozambique, Namibia, Tanzania, Zimbabwe*)

LONGEST RIVERS

Nile (NE Africa)	4,160 miles	(6,695 km)
Amazon (South America)	4,049 miles	(6,516 km)
Yangtze (China)	3,915 miles	(6,299 km)
Mississippi/Missouri (USA)	3,710 miles	(5,969 km)
Ob'-Irtysh (Russian Federation)	3,461 miles	(5,570 km)
Yellow River (China)	3,395 miles	(5,464 km)
Congo (Central Africa)	2,900 miles	(4,667 km)
Mekong (Southeast Asia)	2,749 miles	(4,425 km)
Lena (Russian Federation)	2,734 miles	(4,400 km)
Mackenzie (Canada)	2,640 miles	(4,250 km)
Yenisey (Russian Federation)	2,541 miles	(4,090 km)

HIGHEST MOUNTAINS
(HEIGHT ABOVE SEA LEVEL)

Everest	29,035 ft	(8,850 m)
K2	28,253 ft	(8,611 m)
Kanchenjunga I	28,210 ft	(8,598 m)
Makalu I	27,767 ft	(8,463 m)
Cho Oyu	26,907 ft	(8,201 m)
Dhaulagiri I	26,796 ft	(8,167 m)
Manaslu I	26,783 ft	(8,163 m)
Nanga Parbat I	26,661 ft	(8,126 m)
Annapurna I	26,547 ft	(8,091 m)
Gasherbrum I	26,471 ft	(8,068 m)

LARGEST BODIES OF INLAND WATER
(WITH AREA AND DEPTH)

Caspian Sea	143,243 sq miles (371,000 sq km)	3,215 ft (980 m)
Lake Superior	31,151 sq miles (83,270 sq km)	1,289 ft (393 m)
Lake Victoria	26,560 sq miles (68,880 sq km)	328 ft (100 m)
Lake Huron	23,436 sq miles (60,700 sq km)	751 ft (229 m)
Lake Michigan	22,402 sq miles (58,020 sq km)	922 ft (281 m)
Lake Tanganyika	12,703 sq miles (32,900 sq km)	4,700 ft (1,435 m)
Great Bear Lake	12,274 sq miles (31,790 sq km)	1,047 ft (319 m)
Lake Baikal	11,776 sq miles (30,500 sq km)	5,712 ft (1,741 m)
Great Slave Lake	10,981 sq miles (28,440 sq km)	459 ft (140 m)
Lake Erie	9,915 sq miles (25,680 sq km)	197 ft (60 m)

DEEPEST OCEAN FEATURES

Challenger Deep, Marianas Trench (Pacific)	36,201 ft	(11,034 m)
Vityaz III Depth, Tonga Trench (Pacific)	35,704 ft	(10,882 m)
Vityaz Depth, Kurile-Kamchatka Trench (Pacific)	34,588 ft	(10,542 m)
Cape Johnson Deep, Philippine Trench (Pacific)	34,441 ft	(10,497 m)
Kermadec Trench (Pacific)	32,964 ft	(10,047 m)
Ramapo Deep, Japan Trench (Pacific)	32,758 ft	(9,984 m)
Milwaukee Deep, Puerto Rico Trench (Atlantic)	30,185 ft	(9,200 m)
Argo Deep, Torres Trench (Pacific)	30,070 ft	(9,165 m)
Meteor Depth, South Sandwich Trench (Atlantic)	30,000 ft	(9,144 m)
Planet Deep, New Britain Trench (Pacific)	29,988 ft	(9,140 m)

GREATEST WATERFALLS
(MEAN FLOW OF WATER)

Boyoma (Congo, Dem. Rep.)	600,400 cu. ft/sec	(17,000 cu.m/sec)
Khône (Laos/Cambodia)	410,000 cu. ft/sec	(11,600 cu.m/sec)
Niagara (USA/Canada)	195,000 cu. ft/sec	(5,500 cu.m/sec)
Grande (Uruguay)	160,000 cu. ft/sec	(4,500 cu.m/sec)
Paulo Afonso (Brazil)	100,000 cu. ft/sec	(2,800 cu.m/sec)
Urubupunga (Brazil)	97,000 cu. ft/sec	(2,750 cu.m/sec)
Iguaçu (Argentina/Brazil)	62,000 cu. ft/sec	(1,700 cu.m/sec)
Maribondo (Brazil)	53,000 cu. ft/sec	(1,500 cu.m/sec)
Kabalega (Uganda)	42,000 cu. ft/sec	(1,200 cu.m/sec)
Victoria (Zimbabwe)	39,000 cu. ft/sec	(1,100 cu.m/sec)
Churchill (Canada)	35,000 cu. ft/sec	(1,000 cu.m/sec)
Cauvery (India)	33,000 cu. ft/sec	(900 cu.m/sec)

HIGHEST WATERFALLS

Angel (Venezuela)	3,212 ft	(979 m)
Tugela (South Africa)	3,110 ft	(948 m)
Utigard (Norway)	2,625 ft	(800 m)
Mongefossen (Norway)	2,539 ft	(774 m)
Mtarazi (Zimbabwe)	2,500 ft	(762 m)
Yosemite (USA)	2,425 ft	(739 m)
Ostre Mardola Foss (Norway)	2,156 ft	(657 m)
Tyssestrengane (Norway)	2,119 ft	(646 m)
*Cuquenan (Venezuela)	2,001 ft	(610 m)
Sutherland (New Zealand)	1,903 ft	(580 m)
*Kjellfossen (Norway)	1,841 ft	(561 m)

* indicates that the total height is a single leap

LARGEST DESERTS

Sahara	3,450,000 sq miles	(9,065,000 sq km)
Gobi	500,000 sq miles	(1,295,000 sq km)
Ar Rub al Khali	289,600 sq miles	(750,000 sq km)
Great Victorian	249,800 sq miles	(647,000 sq km)
Sonoran	120,000 sq miles	(311,000 sq km)
Kalahari	120,000 sq miles	(310,800 sq km)
Kara Kum	115,800 sq miles	(300,000 sq km)
Takla Makan	100,400 sq miles	(260,000 sq km)
Namib	52,100 sq miles	(135,000 sq km)
Thar	33,670 sq miles	(130,000 sq km)

NB – Most of Antarctica is a polar desert, with only 50 mm of precipitation annually

HOTTEST INHABITED PLACES

Djibouti (Djibouti)	86° F	(30 °C)
Timbouctou (Mali)	84.7° F	(29.3 °C)
Tirunelveli (India)		
Tuticorin (India)		
Nellore (India)	84.5° F	(29.2 °C)
Santa Marta (Colombia)		
Aden (Yemen)	84° F	(28.9 °C)
Madurai (India)		
Niamey (Niger)		
Hodeida (Yemen)	83.8° F	(28.8 °C)
Ouagadougou (Burkina)		
Thanjavur (India)		
Tiruchchirappalli (India)		

DRIEST INHABITED PLACES

Aswân (Egypt)	0.02 in	(0.5 mm)
Luxor (Egypt)	0.03 in	(0.7 mm)
Arica (Chile)	0.04 in	(1.1 mm)
Ica (Peru)	0.1 in	(2.3 mm)
Antofagasta (Chile)	0.2 in	(4.9 mm)
El Minya (Egypt)	0.2 in	(5.1 mm)
Asyût (Egypt)	0.2 in	(5.2 mm)
Callao (Peru)	0.5 in	(12.0 mm)
Trujillo (Peru)	0.55 in	(14.0 mm)
El Faiyûm (Egypt)	0.8 in	(19.0 mm)

WETTEST INHABITED PLACES

Buenaventura (Colombia)	265 in	(6,743 mm)
Monrovia (Liberia)	202 in	(5,131 mm)
Pago Pago (American Samoa)	196 in	(4,990 mm)
Moulmein (Myanmar)	191 in	(4,852 mm)
Lae (Papua New Guinea)	183 in	(4,645 mm)
Baguio (Luzon Island, Philippines)	180 in	(4,573 mm)
Sylhet (Bangladesh)	176 in	(4,457 mm)
Bogor (Java, Indonesia)	166 in	(4,225 mm)
Padang (Sumatra, Indonesia)	166 in	(4,225 mm)
Conakry (Guinea)	171 in	(4,341 mm)

THE TIME ZONES

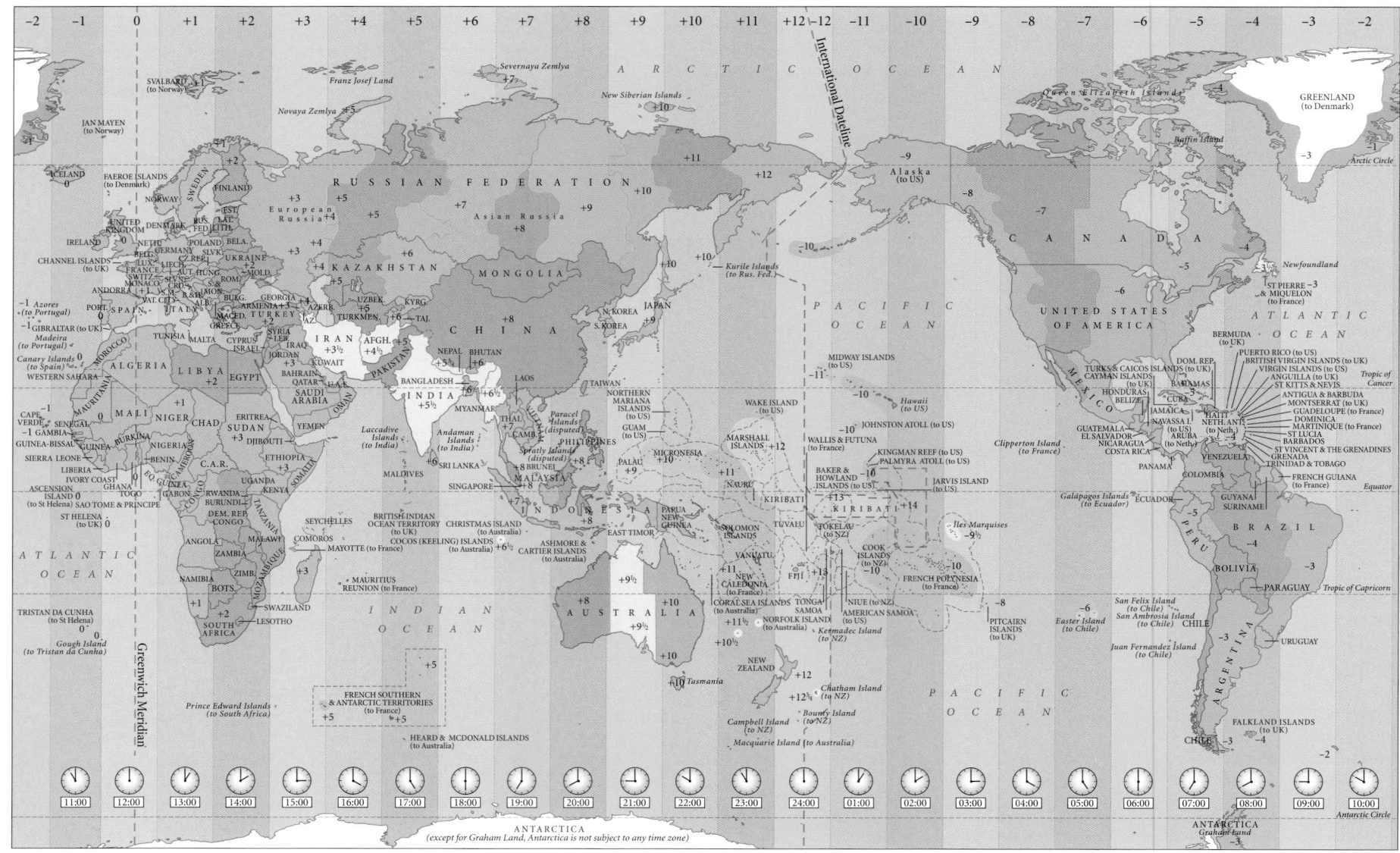

The numbers at the top of the map indicate the number of hours each time zone is ahead or behind Greenwich Mean Time (GMT). The clocks and 24-hour times given at the bottom of the map show the time in each time zone when it is 12:00 hours noon GMT.

TIME ZONES

The present system of international timekeeping divides the world into 24 time zones by means of 24 standard meridians of longitude, each 15° apart. Time is measured in each zone as so many hours ahead or behind the time at the Greenwich Meridian (GMT). Countries, or parts of countries, falling in the vicinity of each zone, adopt its time as shown on the map above. Therefore, using the map, when it is 12:00 noon GMT, it will be 2:00 pm in Zambia; similarly, when it is 4:30 pm. GMT, it will be 11:30 am in Peru.

GREENWICH MEAN TIME (GMT)

Greenwich Mean Time (or Universal Time, as it is more correctly called) has been the internationally accepted basis for calculating solar time – measured in relation to the Earth's rotation around the Sun – since 1884. Greenwich Mean Time is specifically the solar time at the site of the former Royal Observatory in the London Borough of Greenwich, United Kingdom. The Greenwich Meridian is an imaginary line around the world that runs through the North and South poles. It corresponds to 0° of longitude, which lies on this site at Greenwich. Time is measured around the world in relation to the official time along the Meridian.

STANDARD TIME

Standard time is the official time, designated by law, in any specific country or region. Standard time was initiated in 1884, after it became apparent that the practice of keeping various systems of local time was causing confusion – particularly in the USA and Canada, where several railroad routes passed through scores of areas which calculated local time by different rules. The standard time of a particular region is calculated in reference to the longitudinal time zone in which it falls. In practice, these zones do not always match their longitudinal position; in some places the area of the zone has been altered in shape for the convenience of inhabitants, as can be seen in the map. For example, while Greenland occupies three time zones, the majority of the territory uses a standard time of -3 hours GMT. Similarly China, which spans five time zones, is standardized at +8 hours GMT.

THE INTERNATIONAL DATELINE

The International Dateline is an imaginary line that extends from pole to pole, and roughly corresponds to a line of 180° longitude for much of its length. This line is the arbitrary marker between calendar days. By moving from east to west across the line, a traveller will need to set their calendar back one day, while those travelling in the opposite direction will need to add a day. This is to compensate for the use of standard time around the world, which is based on the time at noon along the Greenwich Meridian, approximately halfway around the world. Wide deviations from 180° longitude occur through the Bering Strait – to avoid dividing Siberia into two separate calendar days – and in the Pacific Ocean – to allow certain Pacific islands the same calendar day as New Zealand. Changes were made to the International Dateline in 1995 that made Millennium Island (formerly Caroline Island) in Kiribati the first land area to witness the beginning of the year 2000.

DAYLIGHT SAVING TIME

Also known as summer time, daylight saving is a system of advancing clocks in order to extend the waking day during periods of later daylight hours. This normally means advancing clocks by one hour in early spring, and reverting back to standard time in early autumn. The system of daylight saving is used throughout much of Europe, the USA, Australia, and many other countries worldwide, although there are no standardized dates for the changeover to summer time due to the differences in hours of daylight at different latitudes. Daylight saving was first introduced in certain countries during the First World War, to decrease the need for artificial light and heat – the system stayed in place after the war, as it proved practical. During the Second World War, some countries went so far as to keep their clocks an hour ahead of standard time continuously, and the UK temporarily introduced 'double summer time', which advanced clocks two hours ahead of standard time during the summer months.

COUNTRIES OF THE WORLD

THERE ARE CURRENTLY 193 independent countries in the world – more than at any previous time – and 59 dependencies. Antarctica is the only land area on Earth that is not officially part of, and does not belong to, any single country.

In 1950, the world comprised 82 countries. In the decades following, many more states came into being as they achieved independence from their former colonial rulers. Most recent additions were caused by the breakup of the former Soviet Union in 1991, and the former Yugoslavia in 1992, which swelled the ranks of independent states. In 2002 East Timor became the latest country to gain independence.

COUNTRY FACTFILE KEY

Formation Date of independence / date current borders were established
Population Total population / population density – based on total *land* area / percentage of urban-based population
Languages An asterisk (*) denotes the official language(s)
Calorie consumption Average number of calories consumed daily per person

AFGHANISTAN
Central Asia

Official name Islamic State of Afghanistan
Formation 1919 / 1919
Capital Kabul
Population 23.9 million / 95 people per sq mile (37 people per sq km) / 22%
Total area 250,000 sq miles (647,500 sq km)
Languages Pashtu*, Dari, Farsi, Tajik, Turkmen, Uzbek,
Religions Sunni Muslim 84%, Shi'a Muslim 15%, other 1%
Ethnic mix Pashtun 38%, Tajik 25%, Hazara 19%, Uzbek and Turkmen 15%, other 3%
Government Transitional regime
Currency New afghani = 100 puls
Literacy rate 36%
Calorie consumption 1,539 calories

ALBANIA
Southeast Europe

Official name Republic of Albania
Formation 1912 / 1921
Capital Tirana
Population 3.2 million / 302 people per sq mile (117 people per sq km) / 42%
Total area 11,100 sq miles (28,748 sq km)
Languages Albanian*, Greek
Religions Sunni Muslim 70%, Orthodox Christian 20%, Roman Catholic 10%
Ethnic mix Albanian 86%, Greek 12%, other 2%
Government Parliamentary system
Currency Lek = 100 qindarka (qintars)
Literacy rate 99%
Calorie consumption 2,900 calories

ALGERIA
North Africa

Official name People's Democratic Republic of Algeria
Formation 1962 / 1962
Capital Algiers
Population 31.8 million / 35 people per sq mile (13 people per sq km) / 60%
Total area 919,590 sq miles (2,381,740 sq km)
Languages Arabic*, French, Tamazight
Religions Sunni Muslim 99%, Christian and Jewish 1%
Ethnic mix Arab 75%, Berber 24%, other 1%
Government Presidential system
Currency Algerian dinar = 100 centimes
Literacy rate 69%
Calorie consumption 2,987 calories

ANDORRA
Southwest Europe

Official name Principality of Andorra
Formation 1278 / 1278
Capital Andorra la Vella
Population 69,150 / 384 people per sq mile (149 people per sq km) / 63%
Total area 181 sq miles (468 sq km)
Languages Catalan*, French, Portuguese, Spanish
Religions Roman Catholic 94%, other 6%
Ethnic mix Spanish 46%, Andorran 28%, French 8%, other 18%
Government Parliamentary system
Currency Euro = 100 cents
Literacy rate 99%
Calorie consumption Not available

ANGOLA
Southern Africa

Official name Republic of Angola
Formation 1975 / 1975
Capital Luanda
Population 13.6 million / 28 people per sq mile (11 people per sq km) / 34%
Total area 481,351 sq miles (1,246,700 sq km)
Languages Portuguese*, Kikongo, Kimbundu, Umbundu
Religions Roman Catholic 50%, Protestant 20%, other 30%
Ethnic mix Ovimbundu 37%, Kimbundu 25%, Bakongo 13%, other 25%
Government Presidential system
Currency Readjusted kwanza = 100 lwei
Literacy rate 40%
Calorie consumption 1,953 calories

ANTIGUA & BARBUDA
West Indies

Official name Antigua and Barbuda
Formation 1981 / 1981
Capital St. John's
Population 67,897 / 399 people per sq mile (154 people per sq km) / 37%
Total area 170 sq miles (442 sq km)
Languages English*, English patois
Religions Anglican 45%, other Protestant 42%, Roman Catholic 10%, Rastafarian 1%, other 2%
Ethnic mix Black African 95%, other 5%
Government Parliamentary system
Currency Eastern Caribbean dollar = 100 cents
Literacy rate 87%
Calorie consumption 2,381 calories

ARGENTINA
South America

Official name Republic of Argentina
Formation 1816 / 1816
Capital Buenos Aires
Population 38.4 million / 36 people per sq mile (14 people per sq km) / 90%
Total area 1,068,296 sq miles (2,766,890 sq km)
Languages Spanish*, Amerindian languages, Italian
Religions Roman Catholic 90%, Protestant 2%, Jewish 2%, other 6%
Ethnic mix Indo-European 83%, Mestizo 14%, Jewish 2%, Amerindian 1%
Government Presidential system
Currency Argentine peso = 100 centavos
Literacy rate 97%
Calorie consumption 3,171 calories

ARMENIA
Southwest Asia

Official name Republic of Armenia
Formation 1991 / 1991
Capital Yerevan
Population 3.1 million / 269 people per sq mile (104 people per sq km) / 70%
Total area 11,506 sq miles (29,800 sq km)
Languages Armenian*, Azeri, Russian
Religions Armenian Apostolic Church 94%, other Christian and Muslim 6%
Ethnic mix Armenian 93%, Azeri 3%, Russian 2%, other 2%
Government Presidential system
Currency Dram = 100 luma
Literacy rate 99%
Calorie consumption 1991 calories

AUSTRALIA
Australasia & Oceania

Official name Commonwealth of Australia
Formation 1901 / 1901
Capital Canberra
Population 19.7 million / 7 people per sq mile (3 people per sq km) / 85%
Total area 2,967,893 sq miles (7,686,850 sq km)
Languages English*, Aboriginal languages, Arabic, Cantonese, Greek, Italian, Vietnamese,
Religions Christian 64%, other 36%
Ethnic mix European 92%, Asian 5%, Aboriginal and other 3%
Government Parliamentary system
Currency Australian dollar = 100 cents
Literacy rate 99%
Calorie consumption 3,126 calories

AUSTRIA
Central Europe

Official name Republic of Austria
Formation 1918 / 1919
Capital Vienna
Population 8.1 million / 254 people per sq mile (98 people per sq km) / 65%
Total area 32,378 sq miles (83,858 sq km)
Languages German*, Croatian, Hungarian (Magyar), Slovenian
Religions Roman Catholic 78%, non-religious 9%, Protestant 5%, other 8%
Ethnic mix Austrian 93%, Croat, Slovene, and Hungarian 6%, other 1%
Government Parliamentary system
Currency Euro = 100 cents
Literacy rate 99%
Calorie consumption 3,799 calories

AZERBAIJAN
Southwest Asia

Official name Republic of Azerbaijan
Formation 1991 / 1991
Capital Baku
Population 8.4 million / 251 people per sq mile (97 people per sq km) / 57%
Total area 33,436 sq miles (86,600 sq km)
Languages Azeri, Russian
Religions Shi'a Muslim 68%, Sunni Muslim 26%, Russian Orthodox 3%, Armenian Apostolic Church (Orthodox) 2%, other 1%
Ethnic mix Azeri 90%, Dagestani 3%, Russian 3%, Armenian 2%, other 2%,
Government Presidential system
Currency Manat = 100 gopik
Literacy rate 97%
Calorie consumption 2,474 calories

BAHAMAS
West Indies

Official name Commonwealth of the Bahamas
Formation 1973 / 1973
Capital Nassau
Population 314,000 / 81 people per sq mile (31 people per sq km) / 89%
Total area 5,382 sq miles (13,940 sq km)
Languages English*, English Creole, French Creole
Religions Baptist 32%, Anglican 20%, Roman Catholic 19%, Methodist 6%, Church of God 6%, other 17%
Ethnic mix Black African 85%, other 15%
Government Parliamentary system
Currency Bahamian dollar = 100 cents
Literacy rate 96%
Calorie consumption 2,777 calorie

BAHRAIN
Southwest Asia

Official name Kingdom of Bahrain
Formation 1971 / 1971
Capital Manama
Population 724,000 / 2,652 people per sq mile (1025 people per sq km) / 97%
Total area 239 sq miles (620 sq km)
Languages Arabic*
Religions Muslim (mainly Shi'a) 99%, other 1%
Ethnic mix Bahraini 70%, Iranian, Indian, and Pakistani 24%, other Arab 4%, European 2%
Government Monarchy
Currency Bahraini dinar = 1,000 fils
Literacy rate 89%
Calorie consumption Not available

BANGLADESH
South Asia

Official name People's Republic of Bangladesh
Formation 1971 / 1971
Capital Dhaka
Population 147 million / 2,837 people per sq mile (1,096 people per sq km) / 25%
Total area 55,598 sq miles (144,000 sq km)
Languages Bengali*, Chakma, Garo, Khasi, Marma (Magh), Mro, Santhali, Tripuri, Urdu
Religions Muslim (mainly Sunni) 87%, Hindu 12%, other 1%
Ethnic mix Bengali 98%, other 2%
Government Parliamentary system
Currency Taka = 100 poisha
Literacy rate 41%
Calorie consumption 2,187 calories

BARBADOS
West Indies

Official name Barbados
Formation 1966 / 1966
Capital Bridgetown
Population 270,000 / 1,627 people per sq mile (628 people per sq km) / 50%
Total area 166 sq miles (430 sq km)
Languages English*, Bajan (Barbadian English)
Religions Anglican 40%, non-religious 17%, Pentecostal 8%, Methodist 7%, Roman Catholic 4%, other 24%
Ethnic mix Black African 90%, other 10%
Government Parliamentary system
Currency Barbados dollar = 100 cents
Literacy rate 99%
Calorie consumption 2,992 calories

BELARUS
Eastern Europe

Official name Republic of Belarus
Formation 1991 / 1991
Capital Minsk
Population 9.9 million / 124 people per sq mile (48 people per sq km) / 71%
Total area 80,154 sq miles (207,600 sq km)
Languages Belarussian*, Russian
Religions Orthodox Christian 60%, other (including Muslim, Jews and Protestant) 32%, Roman Catholic 8%
Ethnic mix Belarussian 78%, Russian 13%, Polish 4%, Ukrainian 3%, other 2%
Government Presidential system
Currency Belarussian rouble = 100 kopeks
Literacy rate 99%
Calorie consumption 2,925 calories

BELGIUM
Northwest Europe

Official name Kingdom of Belgium
Formation 1830 / 1919
Capital Brussels
Population 10.3 million / 813 people per sq mile (314 people per sq km) / 97%
Total area 11,780 sq miles (30,510 sq km)
Languages Dutch (Flemish)*, French*, German
Religions Roman Catholic 88%, Muslim 2%, other 10%
Ethnic mix Fleming 58%, Walloon 33%, Italian 2%, Moroccan 1%, other 6%
Government Parliamentary system
Currency Euro = 100 cents
Literacy rate 99%
Calorie consumption 3,682 calories

BELIZE
Central America

Official name Belize
Formation 1981 / 1981
Capital Belmopan
Population 256,000 / 29 people per sq mile (11 people per sq km) / 54%
Total area 8,867 sq miles (22,966 sq km)
Languages English*, English Creole, Garifuna (Carib), Mayan, Spanish
Religions Roman Catholic 62%, Anglican 12%, Methodist 6%, Mennonite 4%, other 16%
Ethnic mix Mestizo 44%, Creole 30%, Maya 11%, Garifuna 7%, Asian Indian 4%, other 4%
Government Parliamentary system
Currency Belizean dollar = 100 cents
Literacy rate 77%
Calorie consumption 2,886 calories

BENIN
West Africa

Official name Republic of Benin
Formation 1960 / 1960
Capital Porto-Novo
Population 6.7 million / 157 people per sq mile (61 people per sq km) / 42%
Total area 43,483 sq miles (112,620 sq km)
Languages French*, Adja, Bariba, Fon, Houeda, Somba, Yoruba
Religions Voodoo 50%, Muslim 30%, Christian 20%
Ethnic mix Fon 47%, Adja 12%, Bariba 10%, other 31%
Government Presidential system
Currency CFA franc = 100 centimes
Literacy rate 40%
Calorie consumption 2,455 calories

BHUTAN
South Asia

Official name Kingdom of Bhutan
Formation 1656 / 1865
Capital Thimphu
Population 2.3 million / 127 people per sq mile (49 people per sq km) / 7%
Total area 18,147 sq miles (47,000 sq km)
Languages Dzongkha*, Nepali, Assamese
Religions Mahayana Buddhist 70%, Hindu 24%, other 6%
Ethnic mix Bhute 50%, Nepalese 25%, other 25%
Government Monarchy
Currency Ngultrum = 100 chetrum
Literacy rate 47%
Calorie consumption Not available

BOLIVIA
South America

Official name Republic of Bolivia
Formation 1825 / 1938
Capital La Paz (administrative) / Sucre (judicial)
Population 8.8 million / 21 people per sq mile (8 people per sq km) / 63%
Total area 424,162 sq miles (1,098,580 sq km)
Languages Aymara*, Quechua*, Spanish*
Religions Roman Catholic 93%, other 7%
Ethnic mix Quechua 37%, Aymara 32%, mixed race 13%, European 10%, other 8%
Government Presidential system
Currency Boliviano = 100 centavos
Literacy rate 87%
Calorie consumption 2,267 calories

BOSNIA & HERZEGOVINA
Southeast Europe

Official name Bosnia and Herzegovina
Formation 1992 / 1992
Capital Sarajevo
Population 4.2 million / 213 people per sq mile (82 people per sq km) / 43%
Total area 19,741 sq miles (51,129 sq km)
Languages Serbo-Croat*
Religions Muslim (mainly Sunni) 40%, Orthodox Christian 31%, Roman Catholic 15%, Protestant 4%, other 10%
Ethnic mix Bosniak 48%, Serb 38%, Croat 14%
Government Parliamentary system
Currency Marka = 100 pfeninga
Literacy rate 95%
Calorie consumption 2,845 calories

BOTSWANA
Southern Africa

Official name Republic of Botswana
Formation 1966 / 1966
Capital Gaborone
Population 1.8 million / 8 people per sq mile (3 people per sq km) / 50%
Total area 231,803 sq miles (600,370 sq km)
Languages English*, isiNdebele, Khoikhoi, San, Setswana, Shona
Religions Traditional beliefs 50%, Christian (mainly Protestant) 30%, other (including Muslim) 20%
Ethnic mix Tswana 98%, other 2%
Government Presidential system
Currency Pula = 100 thebe
Literacy rate 79%
Calorie consumption 2,292 calories

BRAZIL
South America

Official name Federative Republic of Brazil
Formation 1822 / 1828
Capital Brasília
Population 179 million / 55 people per sq mile (21 people per sq km) / 81%
Total area 3,286,470 sq miles (8,511,965 sq km)
Languages Portuguese*, Amerindian languages, German, Italian, Japanese, Polish, Spanish
Religions Roman Catholic 74%, Protestant 15%, Atheist 7%, other 4%
Ethnic mix Black 53%, mixed race 40%, White 6%, other 1%
Government Presidential system
Currency Real = 100 centavos
Literacy rate 86%
Calorie consumption 3,002 calories

BRUNEI
Southeast Asia

Official name Sultanate of Brunei
Formation 1984 / 1984
Capital Bandar Seri Begawan
Population 358,000 / 176 people per sq mile (68 people per sq km) / 72%
Total area 2,228 sq miles (5,770 sq km)
Languages Malay*, Chinese, English
Religions Muslim (mainly Sunni) 66%, Buddhist 14%, Christian 10%, other 10%
Ethnic mix Malay 67%, Chinese 16%, Indigenous 6%, other 11%
Government Monarchy
Currency Brunei dollar = 100 cents
Literacy rate 94%
Calorie consumption 2,814 calories

BULGARIA
Southeast Europe

Official name Republic of Bulgaria
Formation 1908 / 1947
Capital Sofia
Population 7.9 million / 185 people per sq mile (71 people per sq km) / 70%
Total area 42,822 sq miles (110,910 sq km)
Languages Bulgarian*, Romani, Turkish
Religions Orthodox Christian 83%, Muslim 12%, Roman Catholic 1%, other 4%
Ethnic mix Bulgarian 84%, Turkish 9%, Roma 5%, other 2%
Government Parliamentary system
Currency Lev = 100 stotinki
Literacy rate 99%
Calorie consumption 2,626 calories

BURKINA
West Africa

Official name Burkina Faso
Formation 1960 / 1960
Capital Ouagadougou
Population 13 million / 123 people per sq mile (47 people per sq km) / 19%
Total area 105,869 sq miles (274,200 sq km)
Languages French*, Dyula, Fulani, Mossi, Songhai, Tuareg
Religions Muslim 55%, Traditional beliefs 35%, Roman Catholic 9%, other Christian 1%
Ethnic mix Mossi 50%, other 50%
Government Presidential system
Currency CFA franc = 100 centimes
Literacy rate 25%
Calorie consumption 2,485 calories

BURUNDI
Central Africa

Official name Republic of Burundi
Formation 1962 / 1962
Capital Bujumbura
Population 6.8 million / 687 people per sq mile (265 people per sq km) / 9%
Total area 10,745 sq miles (27,830 sq km)
Languages French*, Kirundi*, Kiswahili
Religions Christian (mainly Roman Catholic) 60%, Traditional beliefs 39%, Muslim 1%
Ethnic mix Hutu 85%, Tutsi 14%, Twa 1%
Government Transitional regime
Currency Burundi franc = 100 centimes
Literacy rate 50%
Calorie consumption 1,612 calories

CAMBODIA
Southeast Asia

Official name Kingdom of Cambodia
Formation 1953 / 1953
Capital Phnom Penh
Population 14.1 million / 207 people per sq mile (80 people per sq km) / 16%
Total area 69,900 sq miles (181,040 sq km)
Languages Khmer*, Cham, Chinese, French, Vietnamese
Religions Buddhist 93%, Muslim 6%, Christian 1%
Ethnic mix Khmer 90%, Vietnamese 4%, Chinese 1%, other 5%
Government Parliamentary system
Currency Riel = 100 sen
Literacy rate 69%
Calorie consumption 1,967 calories

CAMEROON
Central Africa

Official name Republic of Cameroon
Formation 1960 / 1961
Capital Yaoundé
Population 16 million / 89 people per sq mile (34 people per sq km) / 49%
Total area 183,567 sq miles (475,400 sq km)
Languages English*, French*, Bamileke, Fang, Fulani
Religions Roman Catholic 35%, Traditional beliefs 25%, Muslim 22%, Protestant 18%
Ethnic mix Cameroon highlanders 31%, Equatorial Bantu 19%, Kirdi 11%, other 39%
Government Presidential system
Currency CFA franc = 100 centimes
Literacy rate 68%
Calorie consumption 2,242 calories

CANADA
North America

Official name Canada
Formation 1867 / 1949
Capital Ottawa
Population 31.5 million / 9 people per sq mile (3 people per sq km) / 77%
Total area 3,717,792 sq miles (9,984,670 sq km)
Languages English*, French*, Chinese, Cree, German, Inuktitut, Italian, Portuguese, Ukrainian
Religions Roman Catholic 44%, Protestant 29%, other and non-religious 27%
Ethnic mix British origin 44%, French origin 25%, other European 20%, other 11%
Government Parliamentary system
Currency Canadian dollar = 100 cents
Literacy rate 99%
Calorie consumption 3,176 calories

CAPE VERDE
Atlantic Ocean

Official name Republic of Cape Verde
Formation 1975 / 1975
Capital Praia
Population 463,000 / 298 people per sq mile (115 people per sq km) / 62%
Total area 1,557 sq miles (4,033 sq km)
Languages Portuguese*, Portuguese Creole
Religions Roman Catholic 97%, Protestant (Church of the Nazarene) 1%, other 2%
Ethnic mix Mestiço 60%, African 30%, other 10%
Government Mixed presidential–parliamentary system
Currency Cape Verde escudo = 100 centavos
Literacy rate 76%
Calorie consumption 3,308 calories

CENTRAL AFRICAN REPUBLIC
Central Africa

Official name Central African Republic
Formation 1960 / 1960
Capital Bangui
Population 3.9 million / 16 people per sq mile (6 people per sq km) / 41%
Total area 240,534 sq miles (622,984 sq km)
Languages French*, Banda, Gbaya, Sango
Religions Traditional beliefs 60%, Christian (mainly Roman Catholic) 35%, Muslim 5%
Ethnic mix Baya 34%, Banda 27%, Mandjia 21%, Sara 10%, other 8%
Government Transitional regime
Currency CFA franc = 100 centimes
Literacy rate 49%
Calorie consumption 1,949 calories

CHAD
Central Africa

Official name Republic of Chad
Formation 1960 / 1960
Capital N'Djamena
Population 8.6 million / 18 people per sq mile (7 people per sq km) / 24%
Total area 495,752 sq miles (1,284,000 sq km)
Languages Arabic*, French*, Maba, Sara
Religions Muslim 55%, Traditional beliefs 35%, Christian 10%
Ethnic mix Nomads (Tuareg and Toubou) 38%, Sara 30%, Arab 15%, other 17%
Government Presidential system
Currency CFA franc = 100 centimes
Literacy rate 46%
Calorie consumption 2,245 calories

CHILE
South America

Official name Republic of Chile
Formation 1818 / 1883
Capital Santiago
Population 15.8 million / 55 people per sq mile (21 people per sq km) / 86%
Total area 292,258 sq miles (756,950 sq km)
Languages Spanish*, Amerindian languages
Religions Roman Catholic 80%, other and non-religious 20%
Ethnic mix Mixed race and European 90%, Amerindian 10%
Government Presidential system
Currency Chilean peso = 100 centavos
Literacy rate 96%
Calorie consumption 2,868 calories

CHINA
East Asia

Official name People's Republic of China
Formation 960 / 1999
Capital Beijing
Population 1.3 billion / 362 people per sq mile (140 people per sq km) / 32%
Total area 3,705,386 sq miles (9,596,960 sq km)
Languages Mandarin*, Cantonese, Hakka, Hsiang, Kan, Min, Wu
Religions Non-religious 59%, Traditional beliefs 20%, Buddhist 6%, Muslim 2%, other 13%
Ethnic mix Han 92%, Zhuang 1%, Hui 1%, other 6%
Government One-party state
Currency Renminbi (Yuan) = 10 jiao
Literacy rate 91%
Calorie consumption 2,963 calories

COLOMBIA
South America

Official name Republic of Colombia
Formation 1819 / 1903
Capital Bogotá
Population 44.2 million / 110 people per sq mile (43 people per sq km) / 74%
Total area 439,733 sq miles (1,138,910 sq km)
Languages Spanish*, Wayuu, Páez, and other Amerindian languages
Religions Roman Catholic 95%, other 5%
Ethnic mix Mestizo 58%, White 20%, European–African 14%, African 4%, African–Amerindian 3%, Amerindian 1%
Government Presidential system
Currency Colombian peso = 100 centavos
Literacy rate 92%
Calorie consumption 2,580 calories

COMOROS
Indian Ocean

Official name Union of the Comoros
Formation 1975 / 1975
Capital Moroni
Population 768,000 / 892 people per sq mile (344 people per sq km) / 33%
Total area 838 sq miles (2,170 sq km)
Languages Arabic*, French*, Comoran
Religions Muslim (mainly Sunni) 98%, Roman Catholic 1%, other 1%
Ethnic mix Comoran 97%, other 3%
Government Presidential system
Currency Comoros franc = 100 centimes
Literacy rate 56%
Calorie consumption 1,735 calories

CONGO
Central Africa

Official name Republic of the Congo
Formation 1960 / 1960
Capital Brazzaville
Population 3.7 million / 28 people per sq mile (11 people per sq km) / 63%
Total area 132,046 sq miles (342,000 sq km)
Languages French*, Kongo, Lingala, Teke
Religions Traditional beliefs 50%, Roman Catholic 25%, Protestant 23%, Muslim 2%
Ethnic mix Bakongo 48%, Sangha 20%, Teke 17%, Mbochi 12%, other 3%
Government Presidential system
Currency CFA franc = 100 centimes
Literacy rate 83%
Calorie consumption 2,221 calories

CONGO, DEM. REP.
Central Africa

Official name Democratic Republic of the Congo
Formation 1960/ 1960
Capital Kinshasa
Population 52.8 million / 60 people per sq mile (23 people per sq km) / 30%
Total area 905,563 sq miles (2,345,410 sq km)
Languages French*, Kiswahili, Tshiluba, Kikongo, Lingala
Religions Roman Catholic 50%, Protestant 20%, Traditional beliefs and other 10%, Muslim 10%, Kimbanguist 10%
Ethnic mix Bantu and Hamitic 45%, other 55%
Government Transitional regime
Currency Congolese franc = 100 centimes
Literacy rate 63%
Calorie consumption 1,535 calories

COSTA RICA
Central America

Official name Republic of Costa Rica
Formation 1838 / 1838
Capital San José
Population 4.2 million / 213 people per sq mile (82 people per sq km) / 52%
Total area 19,730 sq miles (51,100 sq km)
Languages Spanish*, Bribri, Cabecar, English Creole
Religions Roman Catholic 76%, other (including Protestant) 24%
Ethnic mix Mestizo and European 96%, Black 2%, Chinese 1%, Amerindian 1%
Government Presidential system
Currency Costa Rican colón = 100 centimos
Literacy rate 96%
Calorie consumption 2,761 calories

CROATIA
Southeast Europe

Official name Republic of Croatia
Formation 1991 / 1991
Capital Zagreb
Population 4.4 million / 202 people per sq mile (78 people per sq km) / 58%
Total area 21,831 sq miles (56,542 sq km)
Languages Croatian*
Religions Roman Catholic 88%, Orthodox Christian 4%, Muslim 1%, other 7%
Ethnic mix Croat 90%, Serb 4%, Bosniak 1%, other 5%
Government Parliamentary system
Currency Kuna = 100 lipas
Literacy rate 98%
Calorie consumption 2,678 calories

CUBA
West Indies

Official name Republic of Cuba
Formation 1902 / 1902
Capital Havana
Population 11.3 million / 264 people per sq mile (102 people per sq km) / 75%
Total area 42,803 sq miles (110,860 sq km)
Languages Spanish*
Religions non-religious 49%, Roman Catholic 40%, Atheist 6%, Protestant 1%, other 4%
Ethnic mix White 66%, European–African 22%, Black 12%
Government One-party state
Currency Cuban peso = 100 centavos
Literacy rate 97%
Calorie consumption 2,643 calories

CYPRUS
Southeast Europe

Official name Republic of Cyprus
Formation 1960 / 1960
Capital Nicosia
Population 802,000 / 225 people per sq mile (87 people per sq km) / 57%
Total area 3,571 sq miles (9,250 sq km)
Languages Greek, Turkish
Religions Orthodox Christian 78%, Muslim 18%, other 4%
Ethnic mix Greek 85%, Turkish 12%, other 3%
Government Presidential system
Currency Cyprus pound (Turkish lira in TRNC) = 100 cents (Cyprus pound); 100 kurus (Turkish lira)
Literacy rate 97%
Calorie consumption 3,302 calories

CZECH REPUBLIC
Central Europe

Official name Czech Republic
Formation 1993 / 1993
Capital Prague
Population 10.2 million / 335 people per sq mile (129 people per sq km) / 75%
Total area 30,450 sq miles (78,866 sq km)
Languages Czech*, Hungarian (Magyar), Slovak,
Religions Roman Catholic 39%, Atheist 38%, Protestant 3%, Hussite 2%, other 18%
Ethnic mix Czech 81%, Moravian 13%, Slovak 6%
Government Parliamentary system
Currency Czech koruna = 100 haleru
Literacy rate 99%
Calorie consumption 3,097 calories

DENMARK
Northern Europe

Official name Kingdom of Denmark
Formation 950 / 1944
Capital Copenhagen
Population 5.4 million / 330 people per sq mile (127 people per sq km) / 85%
Total area 16,639 sq miles (43,094 sq km)
Languages Danish*
Religions Evangelical Lutheran 89%, Roman Catholic 1%, other 10%
Ethnic mix Danish 96%, Faeroese and Inuit 1%, other (including Scandinavian and Turkish) 3%
Government Parliamentary system
Currency Danish krone = 100 øre
Literacy rate 99%
Calorie consumption 3,454 calories

DJIBOUTI
East Africa

Official name Republic of Djibouti
Formation 1977 / 1977
Capital Djibouti
Population 703,000 / 79 people per sq mile (30 people per sq km) / 83%
Total area 8,494 sq miles (22,000 sq km)
Languages Arabic*, French*, Afar, Somali
Religions Muslim (mainly Sunni) 94%, Christian 6%
Ethnic mix Issa 60%, Afar 35%, other 5%
Government Presidential system
Currency Djibouti franc = 100 centimes
Literacy rate 66%
Calorie consumption 2,218 calories

DOMINICA
West Indies

Official name Commonwealth of Dominica
Formation 1978 / 1978
Capital Roseau
Population 69,655 / 240 people per sq mile (93 people per sq km) / 71%
Total area 291 sq miles (754 sq km)
Languages English*, French Creole
Religions Roman Catholic 77%, Protestant 15%, other 8%
Ethnic mix Black 91%, mixed race 6%, Carib 2%, other 1%
Government Parliamentary system
Currency Eastern Caribbean dollar = 100 cents
Literacy rate 76%
Calorie consumption 2,995 calories

DOMINICAN REPUBLIC
West Indies

Official name Dominican Republic
Formation 1865 / 1865
Capital Santo Domingo
Population 8.7 million / 466 people per sq mile (180 people per sq km) / 65%
Total area 18,679 sq miles (48,380 sq km)
Languages Spanish*, French Creole
Religions Roman Catholic 92%, other and non-religious 8%
Ethnic mix Mixed race 75%, White 15%, Black 10%
Government Presidential system
Currency Dominican Republic peso = 100 centavos
Literacy rate 84%
Calorie consumption 2,333 calories

EAST TIMOR
Southeast Asia

Official name Democratic Republic of Timor-Leste
Formation 2002 / 2002
Capital Dili
Population 778,000 / 138 people per sq mile (53 people per sq km) / 8%
Total area 5,756 sq miles (14,874 sq km)
Languages Portuguese*, Tetum (Portuguese/Austronesian)*, Bahasa Indonesia
Religions Roman Catholic 95%, other 5%
Ethnic mix Papuan groups 85%, Indonesian 13%, Chinese 2%
Government Parliamentary system
Currency US dollar = 100 cents
Literacy rate 59%
Calorie consumption Not available

ECUADOR
South America

Official name Republic of Ecuador
Formation 1830 / 1941
Capital Quito
Population 13 million / 122 people per sq mile (47 people per sq km) / 45%
Total area 109,483 sq miles (283,560 sq km)
Languages Quechua*, Spanish*, other Amerindian languages
Religions Roman Catholic 93%, Protestant, Jewish, and other 7%
Ethnic mix Mestizo 55%, Amerindian 25%, Black 10%, White 10%
Government Presidential system
Currency US dollar = 100 cents
Literacy rate 91%
Calorie consumption 2,792 calories

EGYPT
North Africa

Official name Arab Republic of Egypt
Formation 1936 / 1982
Capital Cairo
Population 71.9 million / 187 people per sq mile (72 people per sq km) / 45%
Total area 386,660 sq miles (1,001,450 sq km)
Languages Arabic*, Berber, English, French
Religions Muslim (mainly Sunni) 94%, Coptic Christian and other 6%
Ethnic mix Eastern Hamitic 90%, Nubian, Armenian, and Greek 10%
Government Presidential system
Currency Egyptian pound = 100 piastres
Literacy rate 56%
Calorie consumption 3,385 calories

EL SALVADOR
Central America

Official name Republic of El Salvador
Formation 1841 / 1841
Capital San Salvador
Population 6.5 million / 812 people per sq mile (314 people per sq km) / 47%
Total area 8,124 sq miles (21,040 sq km)
Languages Spanish*
Religions Roman Catholic 80%, Evangelical 18%, other 2%
Ethnic mix Mestizo 94%, Amerindian 5%, White 1%
Government Presidential system
Currency Salvadorean colón & US dollar = 100 centavos (colón); 100 cents (US dollar)
Literacy rate 80%
Calorie consumption 2,512 calories

EQUATORIAL GUINEA
Central Africa

Official name Republic of Equatorial Guinea
Formation 1968 / 1968
Capital Malabo
Population 494,000 / 46 people per sq mile (18 people per sq km) / 48%
Total area 10,830 sq miles (28,051 sq km)
Languages Spanish*, Bubi, Fang
Religions Roman Catholic 90%, other 10%
Ethnic mix Fang 85%, Bubi 4%, other 11%
Government Presidential system
Currency CFA franc = 100 centimes
Literacy rate 84%
Calorie consumption Not available

ERITREA
East Africa

Official name State of Eritrea
Formation 1993 / 2002
Capital Asmara
Population 4.1 million / 90 people per sq mile (35 people per sq km) / 19%
Total area 46,842 sq miles (121,320 sq km)
Languages Arabic*, Tigrinya*, Afar, Bilen,English, Hadareb, Kunama, Nara, Saho, Tigre
Religions Christian 45%, Muslim 45%, other 10%
Ethnic mix Tigray 50%, Tigray and Kunama 40%, Afar 4%, Saho 3%, other 3%
Government Transitional regime
Currency Nakfa = 100 cents
Literacy rate 57%
Calorie consumption 1,690 calories

ESTONIA

Northeast Europe

Official name Republic of Estonia
Formation 1991 / 1991
Capital Tallinn
Population 1.3 million / 75 people per sq mile (29 people per sq km) / 69%
Total area 17,462 sq miles (45,226 sq km)
Languages Estonian*, Russian
Religions Evangelical Lutheran 56%, Orthodox Christian 25%, other 19%
Ethnic mix Estonian 62%, Russian 30%, other 8%
Government Parliamentary system
Currency Kroon = 100 senti
Literacy rate 99%
Calorie consumption 3,048 calories

ETHIOPIA

East Africa

Official name Federal Democratic Republic of Ethiopia
Formation 1896 / 2002
Capital Addis Ababa
Population 70.7 million / 165 people per sq mile (64 people per sq km) / 18%
Total area 435,184 sq miles (1,127,127 sq km)
Languages Amharic*, Tigrinya, Galla
Religions Muslim 40%, Orthodox Christian 40%, Traditional beliefs 15%, other 5%
Ethnic mix Oromo 40%, Amhara 25%, Sidamo 9%, Berta 6%, Somali 6%, other 14%
Government Parliamentary system
Currency Ethiopian birr = 100 cents
Literacy rate 42%
Calorie consumption 2,037 calories

FIJI

Australasia & Oceania

Official name Republic of the Fiji Islands
Formation 1970 / 1970
Capital Suva
Population 839,000 / 119 people per sq mile (46 people per sq km) / 49%
Total area 7,054 sq miles (18,270 sq km)
Languages English*, Fijian*, Hindi, Tamil, Telugu, Urdu
Religions Hindu 38%, Methodist 37%, Roman Catholic 9%, Muslim 8%, other 8%
Ethnic mix Melanesian 48%, Indian 46%, other 6%
Government Parliamentary system
Currency Fiji dollar = 100 cents
Literacy rate 93%
Calorie consumption 2,789 calories

FINLAND

Northern Europe

Official name Republic of Finland
Formation 1917 / 1947
Capital Helsinki
Population 5.2 million / 44 people per sq mile (17 people per sq km) / 67%
Total area 130,127 sq miles (337,030 sq km)
Languages Finnish*, Swedish*, Sámi
Religions Evangelical Lutheran 89%, Orthodox Christian 1%, Roman Catholic 1%, other 9%
Ethnic mix Finnish 93%, other (including Sámi) 7%
Government Parliamentary system
Currency Euro = 100 cents
Literacy rate 99%
Calorie consumption 3,202 calories

FRANCE

Western Europe

Official name French Republic
Formation 987 / 1919
Capital Paris
Population 60.1 million / 283 people per sq mile (109 people per sq km) / 76%
Total area 211,208 sq miles (547,030 sq km)
Languages French*, Basque, Breton, Catalan, German, Provençal
Religions Roman Catholic 88%, Muslim 8%, Protestant 2%, Jewish 1%, Buddhist 1%
Ethnic mix French 90%, North African 6%, German 2%, other 2%
Government Presidential–parliamentary system
Currency Euro = 100 cents
Literacy rate 99%
Calorie consumption 3,629 calories

GABON

Central Africa

Official name Gabonese Republic
Formation 1960 / 1960
Capital Libreville
Population 1.3 million / 13 people per sq mile (5 people per sq km) / 81%
Total area 103,346 sq miles (267,667 sq km)
Languages French*, Fang, Mpongwe, Nzebi, Punu, Sira,
Religions Christian 55%, Traditional beliefs 40%, Muslim 1%, other 4%
Ethnic mix Fang 35%, other Bantu 29%, Eshira 25%, European and other African 9%, French 2%
Government Presidential system
Currency CFA franc = 100 centimes
Literacy rate 71%
Calorie consumption 2,602 calories

GAMBIA

West Africa

Official name Republic of the Gambia
Formation 1965 / 1965
Capital Banjul
Population 1.4 million / 363 people per sq mile (140 people per sq km) / 33%
Total area 4,363 sq, miles (11,300 sq km)
Languages English*, Fulani, Jola, Mandinka, Soninke, Wolof
Religions Sunni Muslim 90%, Christian 9%, Traditional beliefs 1%
Ethnic mix Mandinka 42%, Fulani 18%, Wolof 16%, Jola 10%, Serahuli 9%, other 5%
Government Presidential system
Currency Dalasi = 100 butut
Literacy rate 38%
Calorie consumption 2,300 calories

GEORGIA

Southwest Asia

Official name Georgia
Formation 1991 / 1991
Capital Tbilisi
Population 5.1 million / 190 people per sq mile (73 people per sq km) / 61%
Total area 26,911 sq miles (69,700 sq km)
Languages Georgian*, Russian
Religions Georgian Orthodox 65%, Muslim 11%, Russian Orthodox 10%, Armenian Orthodox 8%, other 6%
Ethnic mix Georgian 70%, Armenian 8%, Russian 6%, Azeri 6%, Ossetian 3%, other 7%
Government Presidential system
Currency Lari = 100 tetri
Literacy rate 99%
Calorie consumption 2,247 calories

GERMANY

Northern Europe

Official name Federal Republic of Germany
Formation 1871 / 1990
Capital Berlin
Population 82.5 million / 611 people per sq mile (236 people per sq km) /88%
Total area 137,846 sq miles (357,021 sq km)
Languages German*, Turkish
Religions Protestant 34%, Roman Catholic 33%, Muslim 3%, other 30%
Ethnic mix German 92%, other European 3%, Turkish 2%, other 3%
Government Parliamentary system
Currency Euro = 100 cents
Literacy rate 99%
Calorie consumption 3,567 calories

GHANA

West Africa

Official name Republic of Ghana
Formation 1957 / 1957
Capital Accra
Population 20.9 million / 235 people per sq mile (91 people per sq km) / 38%
Total area 92,100 sq miles (238,540 sq km)
Languages English*, Adangbe, Dagomba (Dagbani), Ewe, Fanti, Ga, Gurma, Twi
Religions Christian 69%, Muslim 16%, Traditional beliefs 9%, other 6%
Ethnic mix Ashanti and Fanti 52%, Moshi-Dagomba 16%, Ewe 12%, Ga 8%, other 12%
Government Presidential system
Currency Cedi = 100 psewas
Literacy rate 74%
Calorie consumption 2,670 calories

GREECE

Southeast Europe

Official name Hellenic Republic
Formation 1829 / 1947
Capital Athens
Population 11 million / 218 people per sq mile (84 people per sq km) / 60%
Total area 50,942 sq miles (131,940 sq km)
Languages Greek*, Albanian, Macedonian, Turkish
Religions Orthodox Christian 98%, Muslim 1%, other 1%
Ethnic mix Greek 98%, other 2%
Government Parliamentary system
Currency Euro = 100 cents
Literacy rate 97%
Calorie consumption 3,754 calories

GRENADA

West Indies

Official name Grenada
Formation 1974 / 1974
Capital St. George's
Population 89,258 / 681 people per sq mile (263 people per sq km) / 38%
Total area 131 sq miles (340 sq km)
Languages English*, English Creole
Religions Roman Catholic 68%, Anglican 17%, other 15%
Ethnic mix Black African 82%, Mulatto (mixed race) 13%, East Indian 3%, other 2%
Government Parliamentary system
Currency Eastern Caribbean dollar = 100 cents
Literacy rate 94%
Calorie consumption 2,749 calories

GUATEMALA

Central America

Official name Republic of Guatemala
Formation 1838 / 1838
Capital Guatemala City
Population 12.3 million / 294 people per sq mile (113 people per sq km) / 40%
Total area 42,042 sq miles (108,890 sq km)
Languages Spanish*, Cakchiquel, Kekchí, Mam, Quiché,
Religions Roman Catholic 65%, Protestant 33%, other and non-religious 2%
Ethnic mix Amerindian 60%, Mestizo 30%, other 10%
Government Presidential system
Currency Quetzal = 100 centavos
Literacy rate 70%
Calorie consumption 2,203 calories

GUINEA

West Africa

Official name Republic of Guinea
Formation 1958 / 1958
Capital Conakry
Population 8.5 million / 90 people per sq mile (35 people per sq km) / 33%
Total area 94,925 sq miles (245,857 sq km)
Languages French*, Fulani, Malinke, Soussou
Religions Muslim 65%, Traditional beliefs 33%, Christian 2%
Ethnic mix Fulani 30%, Malinke 30%, Soussou 15%, Kissi 10%, other tribes 10%, other 5%
Government Presidential system
Currency Guinea franc = 100 centimes
Literacy rate 41%
Calorie consumption 2,362 calories

GUINEA-BISSAU

West Africa

Official name Republic of Guinea-Bissau
Formation 1974 / 1974
Capital Bissau
Population 1.5 million / 138 people per sq mile (53 people per sq km) / 24%
Total area 13,946 sq miles (36,120 sq km)
Languages Portuguese*, Balante, Fulani, Malinke, Portuguese Creole,
Religions Traditional beliefs 52%, Muslim 40%, Christian 8%
Ethnic mix Other tribes 31%, Balante 25%, Fula 20%, Mandinka 12%, Mandyako 11%, other 1%
Government Transitional regime
Currency CFA franc = 100 centimes
Literacy rate 40%
Calorie consumption 2,481 calories

GUYANA

South America

Official name Cooperative Republic of Guyana
Formation 1966 / 1966
Capital Georgetown
Population 765,000 / 10 people per sq mile (4 people per sq km) / 38%
Total area 83,000 sq miles (214,970 sq km)
Languages English*, Amerindian languages, English Creole, Hindi, Tamil
Religions Christian 57%, Hindu 33%, Muslim 9%, other 1%
Ethnic mix East Indian 52%, Black African 38%, other 10%
Government Presidential system
Currency Guyana dollar = 100 cents
Literacy rate 97%
Calorie consumption 2,515 calories

HAITI

West Indies

Official name Republic of Haiti
Formation 1804 / 1844
Capital Port-au-Prince
Population 8.3 million / 780 people per sq mile (301 people per sq km) / 36%
Total area 10,714 sq miles (27,750 sq km)
Languages French*, French Creole*
Religions Roman Catholic 80%, Protestant 16%, non-religious 1%, other (including Voodoo) 3%
Ethnic mix Black African 95%, Mulatto (mixed race) and European 5%
Government Transitional regime
Currency Gourde = 100 centimes
Literacy rate 52%
Calorie consumption 2,045 calories

HONDURAS

Central America

Official name Republic of Honduras
Formation 1838 / 1838
Capital Tegucigalpa
Population 6.9 million / 160 people per sq mile (62 people per sq km) / 53%
Total area 43,278 sq miles (112,090 sq km)
Languages Spanish*, English Creole, Garífuna (Carib)
Religions Roman Catholic 97%, Protestant 3%
Ethnic mix Mestizo 90%, Black African 5%, Amerindian 4%, White 1%
Government Presidential system
Currency Lempira = 100 centavos
Literacy rate 80%
Calorie consumption 2,406 calories

HUNGARY

Central Europe

Official name Republic of Hungary
Formation 1918 / 1947
Capital Budapest
Population 9.9 million / 278 people per sq mile (107 people per sq km) / 64%
Total area 35,919 sq miles (93,030 sq km)
Languages Hungarian (Magyar)*
Religions Roman Catholic 52%, Calvinist 16%, non-religious 14%, Lutheran 3%, other 15%
Ethnic mix Magyar 90%, Roma 2%, German 1%, other 7%
Government Parliamentary system
Currency Forint = 100 fillér
Literacy rate 99%
Calorie consumption 3,520 calories

ICELAND

Northwest Europe

Official name Republic of Iceland
Formation 1944 / 1944
Capital Reykjavík
Population 290,000 / 7 people per sq mile (3 people per sq km) / 93%
Total area 39,768 sq miles (103,000 sq km)
Languages Icelandic*
Religions Evangelical Lutheran 93%, non-religious 6%, other (mostly Christian) 1%
Ethnic mix Icelandic 94%, Danish 1%, other 5%
Government Parliamentary system
Currency Icelandic króna = 100 aurar
Literacy rate 99%
Calorie consumption 3,231 calories

INDIA

South Asia

Official name Republic of India
Formation 1947 / 1947
Capital New Delhi
Population 1.07 billion / 928 people per sq mile (358 people per sq km) / 28%
Total area 1,269,338 sq miles (3,287,590 sq km)
Languages English*, Hindi*, Bengali, Bihari, Gujarati, Kanarese, Marathi, Tamil, Telugu, Urdu,
Religions Hindu 83%, Muslim 11%, Christian 2%, Sikh 2%, Buddhist 1%, other 1%
Ethnic mix Indo-Aryan 72%, Dravidian 25%, Mongoloid and other 3%
Government Parliamentary system
Currency Indian rupee = 100 paise
Literacy rate 61%
Calorie consumption 2,487 calories

INDONESIA

Southeast Asia

Official name Republic of Indonesia
Formation 1949 / 1999
Capital Jakarta
Population 220 million / 317 people per sq mile (122 people per sq km) / 41%
Total area 741,096 sq miles (1,919,440 sq km)
Languages Bahasa Indonesia*, Dutch, Javanese, Madurese, Sundanese
Religions Sunni Muslim 87%, Protestant 6%, Roman Catholic 3%, Hindu 2%, Buddhist 1%, other 1%
Ethnic mix Javanese 45%, Sundanese 14%, Coastal Malays 8%, Madurese 8%, other 25%
Government Presidential system
Currency Rupiah = 100 sen
Literacy rate 88%
Calorie consumption 2,904 calories

IRAN

Southwest Asia

Official name Islamic Republic of Iran
Formation 1502 / 1990
Capital Tehran
Population 68.9 million / 109 people per sq mile (42 people per sq km) / 62%
Total area 636,293 sq miles (1,648,000 sq km)
Languages Farsi*, Arabic, Azeri, Baluchi, Gilaki, Kurdish, Luri, Mazanderani, Turkmen
Religions Shi'a Muslim 93%, Sunni Muslim 6%, other 1%
Ethnic mix Persian 50%, Azari 24%, Kurdish 8%, Lur and Bakhtiari 8%, other 10%
Government Islamic theocracy
Currency Iranian rial = 100 dinars
Literacy rate 77%
Calorie consumption 2,931 calories

IRAQ

Southwest Asia

Official name Republic of Iraq
Formation 1932 / 1990
Capital Baghdad
Population 25.2 million / 149 people per sq mile (58 people per sq km) / 77%
Total area 168,753 sq miles (437,072 sq km)
Languages Arabic*, Armenian, Assyrian, Kurdish, Turkic languages
Religions Shi'a Muslim 62%, Sunni Muslim 33%, other (including Christian) 5%
Ethnic mix Arab 79%, Kurdish 16%, Persian 3%, Turkmen 2%
Government Transitional regime
Currency New Iraqi dinar = 1,000 fils
Literacy rate 40%
Calorie consumption 2,197 calories

IRELAND

Northwest Europe

Official name Ireland
Formation 1922 / 1922
Capital Dublin
Population 4 million / 150 people per sq mile (58 people per sq km) / 59%
Total area 27,135 sq miles (70,280 sq km)
Languages English*, Irish Gaelic*
Religions Roman Catholic 88%, Anglican 3%, other and non-religious 9%
Ethnic mix Irish 93%, British 3%, other 4%
Government Parliamentary system
Currency Euro = 100 cents
Literacy rate 99%
Calorie consumption 3,666 calories

ISRAEL

Southwest Asia

Official name State of Israel
Formation 1948 / 1994
Capital Jerusalem
Population 6.4 million / 815 people per sq mile (315 people per sq km) / 91%
Total area 8,019 sq miles (20,770 sq km)
Languages Hebrew*, Arabic, German, Persian, Polish, Romanian, Russian, Yiddish
Religions Jewish 80%, Muslim (mainly Sunni) 16%, Druze and other 2%, Christian 2%
Ethnic mix Jewish 80%, other (mostly Arab) 20%
Government Parliamentary system
Currency Shekel = 100 agorat
Literacy rate 95%
Calorie consumption 3,512 calories

ITALY

Southern Europe

Official name Italian Republic
Formation 1861 / 1947
Capital Rome
Population 57.4 million / 506 people per sq mile (195 people per sq km) / 67%
Total area 116,305 sq miles (301,230 sq km)
Languages Italian*, French, German, Rhaeto-Romanic, Sardinian
Religions Roman Catholic 85%, Muslim 2%, other and non-religious 13%
Ethnic mix Italian 94%, Sardinian 2%, other 4%
Government Parliamentary system
Currency Euro = 100 cents
Literacy rate 99%
Calorie consumption 3,680 calories

IVORY COAST

West Africa

Official name Republic of Côte d'Ivoire
Formation 1960 / 1960
Capital Yamoussoukro
Population 16.6 million / 135 people per sq mile (52 people per sq km) / 46%
Total area 124,502 sq miles (322,460 sq km)
Languages French*, Akan, Kru, Voltaic
Religions Muslim 38%, Roman Catholic 25%, Traditional beliefs 25%, Protestant 6%, other 6%
Ethnic mix Baoulé 23%, Bété 18%, Senufo 15%, Agni-Ashanti 14%, Mandinka 11%, other 19%
Government Presidential system
Currency CFA franc = 100 centimes
Literacy rate 50%
Calorie consumption 2,594 calories

JAMAICA

West Indies

Official name Jamaica
Formation 1962 /1962
Capital Kingston
Population 2.7 million / 646 people per sq mile (249 people per sq km) / 56%
Total area 4,243 sq miles (10,990 sq km)
Languages English*, English Creole
Religions Christian 55%, other and non-religious 45%
Ethnic mix Black African 75%, Mulatto (mixed race) 13%, European and Chinese 11%, East Indian 1%
Government Parliamentary system
Currency Jamaican dollar = 100 cents
Literacy rate 88%
Calorie consumption 2,705 calories

JAPAN

East Asia

Official name Japan
Formation 1590 / 1972
Capital Tokyo
Population 128 million / 878 people per sq mile (339 people per sq km) / 79%
Total area 145,882 sq miles (377,835 sq km)
Languages Japanese, Korean, Chinese
Religions Shinto and Buddhist 76%, Buddhist 16%, other (including Christian) 8%
Ethnic mix Japanese 99%, other (mainly Korean) 1%
Government Parliamentary system
Currency Yen = 100 sen
Literacy rate 99%
Calorie consumption 2,746 calories

JORDAN
Southwest Asia

Official name Hashemite Kingdom of Jordan
Formation 1946 / 1967
Capital Amman
Population 5.5 million / 160 people per sq mile (62 people per sq km) / 74%
Total area 35,637 sq miles (92,300 sq km)
Languages Arabic*
Religions Muslim (mainly Sunni) 92%, other (mostly Christian) 8%
Ethnic mix Arab 98%, Circassian 1%, Armenian 1%
Government Monarchy
Currency Jordanian dinar = 1,000 fils
Literacy rate 91%
Calorie consumption 2,769 calories

KAZAKHSTAN
Central Asia

Official name Republic of Kazakhstan
Formation 1991 / 1991
Capital Astana
Population 15.4 million / 15 people per sq mile (6 people per sq km) / 56%
Total area 1,049,150 sq miles (2,717,300 sq km)
Languages Kazakh*, Russian*, German, Tatar, Uighur, Ukrainian, Uzbek
Religions Muslim (mainly Sunni) 47%, Orthodox Christian 44%, other 9%
Ethnic mix Kazakh 53%, Russian 30%, Ukrainian 4%, German 2%, Tatar 2%, other 9%
Government Presidential system
Currency Tenge = 100 tiyn
Literacy rate 99%
Calorie consumption 2,477 calories

KENYA
East Africa

Official name Republic of Kenya
Formation 1963 / 1963
Capital Nairobi
Population 32 million / 146 people per sq mile (56 people per sq km) / 33%
Total area 224,961 sq miles (582,650 sq km)
Languages Kiswahili*, English*, Kalenjin, Kamba, Kikuyu, Luo
Religions Christian 60%, Traditional beliefs 25%, Muslim 6%, other 9%
Ethnic mix Kikuyu 21%, Luhya 14%, Luo 13%, Kalenjin 11%, Kamba 11%, other 30%
Government Presidential system
Currency Kenya shilling = 100 cents
Literacy rate 84%
Calorie consumption 2058 calories

KIRIBATI
Australasia & Oceania

Official name Republic of Kiribati
Formation 1979 / 1979
Capital Bairiki (Tarawa Atoll)
Population 98,549 / 360 people per sq mile (139 people per sq km) / 36%
Total area 277 sq miles (717 sq km)
Languages English*, Kiribati
Religions Roman Catholic 53%, Kiribati Protestant Church 39%, other 8%
Ethnic mix Micronesian 96%, other 4%
Government Non-party system
Currency Australian dollar = 100 cents
Literacy rate 99%
Calorie consumption 2,922 calories

KUWAIT
Southwest Asia

Official name State of Kuwait
Formation 1961 / 1961
Capital Kuwait City
Population 2.5 million / 363 people per sq mile (140 people per sq km) / 98%
Total area 6,880 sq miles (17,820 sq km)
Languages Arabic*, English
Religions Sunni Muslim 45%, Shi'a Muslim 40%, Christian, Hindu, and other 15%
Ethnic mix Kuwaiti 45%, other Arab 35%, South Asian 9%, Iranian 4%, other 7%
Government Monarchy
Currency Kuwaiti dinar = 1,000 fils
Literacy rate 83%
Calorie consumption 3,170 calories

KYRGYZSTAN
Central Asia

Official name Kyrgyz Republic
Formation 1991 / 1991
Capital Bishkek
Population 5.1 million / 67 people per sq mile (26 people per sq km) / 33%
Total area 76,641 sq miles (198,500 sq km)
Languages Kyrgyz*, Russian*, Tatar, Ukrainian, Uzbek
Religions Muslim (mainly Sunni) 70%, Orthodox Christian 30%
Ethnic mix Kyrgyz 57%, Russian 19%, Uzbek 13%, Tatar 2%, Ukrainian 2%, other 7%
Government Presidential system
Currency Som = 100 tyyn
Literacy rate 97%
Calorie consumption 2,882 calories

LAOS
Southeast Asia

Official name Lao People's Democratic Republic
Formation 1953 / 1953
Capital Vientiane
Population 5.7 million / 64 people per sq mile (25 people per sq km) / 24%
Total area 91,428 sq miles (236,800 sq km)
Languages Lao*, Chinese, French, Mon-Khmer, Vietnamese, Yao
Religions Buddhist 85%, other (including Animist) 15%
Ethnic mix Lao Loum 66%, Lao Theung 30%, Lao Soung 2%, other 2%
Government One-party state
Currency New kip = 100 at
Literacy rate 66%
Calorie consumption 2309 calories

LATVIA
Northeast Europe

Official name Republic of Latvia
Formation 1991 / 1991
Capital Riga
Population 2.3 million / 92 people per sq mile (36 people per sq km) / 69%
Total area 24,938 sq miles (64,589 sq km)
Languages Latvian*, Russian
Religions Lutheran 55%, Roman Catholic 24%, Orthodox Christian 9%, other 12%
Ethnic mix Latvian 57%, Russian 32%, Belarussian 4%, Ukrainian 3%, other 4%
Government Parliamentary system
Currency Lats = 100 santims
Literacy rate 99%
Calorie consumption 2,809 calories

LEBANON
Southwest Asia

Official name Republic of Lebanon
Formation 1941 / 1941
Capital Beirut
Population 3.7 million / 937 people per sq mile (362 people per sq km) / 90%
Total area 4,015 sq miles (10,400 sq km)
Languages Arabic*, Armenian, Assyrian, French
Religions Muslim 70%, Christian 30%
Ethnic mix Arab 94%, Armenian 4%, other 2%
Government Parliamentary system
Currency Lebanese pound = 100 piastres
Literacy rate 87%
Calorie consumption 3,184 calories

LESOTHO
Southern Africa

Official name Kingdom of Lesotho
Formation 1966 / 1966
Capital Maseru
Population 1.8 million / 154 people per sq mile (59 people per sq km) / 28%
Total area 11,720 sq miles (30,355 sq km)
Languages English*, Sesotho*, isiZulu
Religions Christian 90%, Traditional beliefs 10%
Ethnic mix Sotho 97%, European and Asian 3%
Government Parliamentary system
Currency Loti = 100 lisente
Literacy rate 81%
Calorie consumption 2,320 calories

LIBERIA
West Africa

Official name Republic of Liberia
Formation 1847 / 1847
Capital Monrovia
Population 3.4 million / 91 people per sq mile (35 people per sq km) / 45%
Total area 43,000 sq miles (111,370 sq km)
Languages English*, Bassa, Gola, Grebo, Kissi, Kpelle, Kru, Loma, Vai
Religions Christian 68%, Traditional beliefs 18%, Muslim 14%
Ethnic mix Indigenous tribes (16 main groups) 95%, Americo-Liberians 5%
Government Transitional regime
Currency Liberian dollar = 100 cents
Literacy rate 56%
Calorie consumption 1,946 calories

LIBYA
North Africa

Official name Great Socialist People's Libyan Arab Jamahariyah
Formation 1951 / 1951
Capital Tripoli
Population 5.6 million / 8 people per sq mile (3 people per sq km) / 88%
Total area 679,358 sq miles (1,759,540 sq km)
Languages Arabic*, Tuareg
Religions Muslim (mainly Sunni) 97%, other 3%
Ethnic mix Arab and Berber 95%, other 5%
Government One-party state
Currency Libyan dinar = 1,000 dirhams
Literacy rate 82%
Calorie consumption 3,333 calories

LIECHTENSTEIN
Central Europe

Official name Principality of Liechtenstein
Formation 1719 / 1719
Capital Vaduz
Population 33,145 / 535 people per sq mile (207 people per sq km) / 21%
Total area 62 sq miles (160 sq. km)
Languages German*, Alemannish dialect, Italian
Religions Roman Catholic 81%, Protestant 7%, other 12%
Ethnic mix Liechtensteiner 62%, Foreign residents 38%
Government Parliamentary system
Currency Swiss franc = 100 rappen/centimes
Literacy rate 99%
Calorie consumption Not available

LITHUANIA
Northeast Europe

Official name Republic of Lithuania
Formation 1991 / 1991
Capital Vilnius
Population 3.4 million / 135 people per sq mile (52 people per sq km) / 68%
Total area 25,174 sq miles (65,200 sq km)
Languages Lithuanian*, Russian
Religions Roman Catholic 83%, Protestant 5%, other 12%
Ethnic mix Lithuanian 80%, Russian 9%, Polish 7%, Belarussian 2%, other 2%
Government Parliamentary system
Currency Litas = 100 centu (euro is also legal tender)
Literacy rate 99%
Calorie consumption 3,384 calories

LUXEMBOURG
Northwest Europe

Official name Grand Duchy of Luxembourg
Formation 1867 / 1867
Capital Luxembourg
Population 453,000 / 454 people per sq mile (175 people per sq km) / 92%
Total area 998 sq miles (2,586 sq km)
Languages French*, German*, Luxembourgish*
Religions Roman Catholic 97%, Protestant, Orthodox Christian, and Jewish 3%
Ethnic mix Luxembourger 73%, Foreign residents 27%
Government Parliamentary system
Currency Euro = 100 cents
Literacy rate 99%
Calorie consumption 3,701 calories

MACEDONIA
Southeast Europe

Official name Republic of Macedonia
Formation 1991 / 1991
Capital Skopje
Population 2.02 million / 204 people per sq mile (79 people per sq km) / 62%
Total area 9,781 sq miles (25,333 sq km)
Languages Macedonian, Albanian, Serbo-Croat
Religions Orthodox Christian 59%, Muslim 26%, Roman Catholic 4%, Protestant 1%, other 10%
Ethnic mix Macedonian 64%, Albanian 25%, Turkish 4%, Roma 3%, Serb 2%, other 2%
Government Mixed presidential–parliamentary system
Currency Macedonian denar = 100 deni
Literacy rate 94%
Calorie consumption 2,552 calories

MADAGASCAR
Indian Ocean

Official name Republic of Madagascar
Formation 1960 / 1960
Capital Antananarivo
Population 17.4 million / 77 people per sq mile (30 people per sq km) / 30%
Total area 226,656 sq miles (587,040 sq km)
Languages Malagasy*, French*
Religions Traditional beliefs 52%, Christian (mainly Roman Catholic) 41%, Muslim 7%
Ethnic mix Other Malay 46%, Merina 26%, Betsimisaraka 15%, Betsileo 12%, other 1%
Government Presidential system
Currency Ariary = 5 iraimbilanja
Literacy rate 67%
Calorie consumption 2,072 calories

MALAWI
Southern Africa

Official name Republic of Malawi
Formation 1964 / 1964
Capital Lilongwe
Population 12.1 million / 333 people per sq mile (129 people per sq km) / 25%
Total area 45,745 sq miles (118,480 sq km)
Languages English*, Chewa*, Lomwe, Ngoni, Yao
Religions Protestant 55%, Roman Catholic 20%, Muslim 20%, Traditional beliefs 5%
Ethnic mix Bantu 99%, other 1%
Government Presidential system
Currency Malawi kwacha = 100 tambala
Literacy rate 62%
Calorie consumption 2,168 calories

MALAYSIA
Southeast Asia

Official name Federation of Malaysia
Formation 1963 / 1965
Capital Kuala Lumpur; Putrajaya (administrative)
Population 24.4 million / 192 people per sq mile (74 people per sq km) / 57%
Total area 127,316 sq. miles (329,750 sq. km)
Languages Malay*, Chinese*, Bahasa Malaysia, Tamil, English
Religions Muslim 53%, Buddhist 19%, Chinese faiths 12%, Christian 7%, other 9%
Ethnic mix Malay 48%, Chinese 29%, Indigenous tribes 12%, Indian 6%, other 5%
Government Parliamentary system
Currency Ringgit = 100 sen
Literacy rate 89%
Calorie consumption 2,927 calories

MALDIVES
Indian Ocean

Official name Republic of Maldives
Formation 1965 / 1965
Capital Male'
Population 318,000 / 2,741 people per sq mile (1,060 people per sq km) / 30%
Total area 116 sq miles (300 sq km)
Languages Dhivehi (Maldivian)*, Arabic, Sinhala, Tamil
Religions Sunni Muslim 100%
Ethnic mix Arab–Sinhalese–Malay 100%
Government Non-party system
Currency Rufiyaa = 100 lari
Literacy rate 97%
Calorie consumption 2,587 calories

MALI
West Africa

Official name Republic of Mali
Formation 1960 / 1960
Capital Bamako
Population 13 million / 28 people per sq mile (11 people per sq km) / 30%
Total area 478,764 sq miles (1,240,000 sq km)
Languages French*, Bambara, Fulani, Senufo, Soninke
Religions Muslim (mainly Sunni) 80%, Traditional beliefs 18%, Christian 1%, other 1%
Ethnic mix Bambara 32%, Fulani 14%, Senufu 12%, Soninka 9%, Tuareg 7%, other 26%
Government Presidential system
Currency CFA franc = 100 centimes
Literacy rate 26%
Calorie consumption 2,376 calories

MALTA
Southern Europe

Official name Republic of Malta
Formation 1964 / 1964
Capital Valletta
Population 394,000 / 3,177 people per sq mile (1,231 people per sq km) / 91%
Total area 122 sq miles (316 sq km)
Languages Maltese*, English
Religions Roman Catholic 98%, other and non-religious 2%
Ethnic mix Maltese 96%, other 4%
Government Parliamentary system
Currency Maltese lira = 100 cents
Literacy rate 93%
Calorie consumption 3,496 calories

MARSHALL ISLANDS
Australasia & Oceania

Official name Republic of the Marshall Islands
Formation 1986 / 1986
Capital Majuro
Population 56,429 / 806 people per sq mile (312 people per sq km) / 69%
Total area 70 sq miles (181 sq km)
Languages Marshallese*, English*, German, Japanese
Religions Protestant 90%, Roman Catholic 8%, other 2%
Ethnic mix Micronesian 97%, other 3%
Government Presidential system
Currency US dollar = 100 cents
Literacy rate 91%
Calorie consumption Not available

MAURITANIA
West Africa

Official name Islamic Republic of Mauritania
Formation 1960 / 1960
Capital Nouakchott
Population 2.9 million / 7 people per sq mile (3 people per sq km) / 58%
Total area 397,953 sq miles (1,030,700 sq km)
Languages French*, Hassaniyah Arabic, Wolof
Religions Sunni Muslim 100%
Ethnic mix Maure 81%, Wolof 7%, Tukolor 5%, Soninka 3%, other 4%
Government Presidential system
Currency Ouguiya = 5 khoums
Literacy rate 41%
Calorie consumption 2,764 calories

MAURITIUS
Indian Ocean

Official name Republic of Mauritius
Formation 1968 / 1968
Capital Port Louis
Population 1.2 million / 1,671 people per sq mile (645 people per sq km) / 41%
Total area 718 sq miles (1,860 sq km)
Languages English*, Chinese, French, French Creole, Hindi, Tamil, Urdu
Religions Hindu 52%, Roman Catholic 26%, Muslim 17%, Protestant 2%, other 3%
Ethnic mix Indo-Mauritian 68%, Creole 27%, Sino-Mauritian 3%, Franco-Mauritian 2%
Government Parliamentary system
Currency Mauritian rupee = 100 cents
Literacy rate 84%
Calorie consumption 2,995 calories

MEXICO
North America

Official name United Mexican States
Formation 1836 / 1848
Capital Mexico City
Population 104 million / 140 people per sq mile (54 people per sq km) / 74%
Total area 761,602 sq miles (1,972,550 sq km)
Languages Spanish*, Mayan, Mixtec, Nahuatl, Otomi, Totonac, Tzeltal, Tzotzil, Zapotec
Religions Roman Catholic 88%, Protestant 5%, other 7%
Ethnic mix Mestizo 60%, Amerindian 30%, European 9%, other 1%
Government Presidential system
Currency Mexican peso = 100 centavos
Literacy rate 91%
Calorie consumption 3,160 calories

MICRONESIA
Australasia & Oceania

Official name Federated States of Micronesia
Formation 1986 / 1986
Capital Palikir (Pohnpei Island)
Population 108,143 / 399 people per sq mile (154 people per sq km) / 28%
Total area 271 sq miles (702 sq km)
Languages English, Kosraean, Mortlockese, Pohnpeian, Trukese
Religions Roman Catholic 50%, Protestant 48%, other 2%
Ethnic mix Micronesian 100%
Government Non-party system
Currency US dollar = 100 cents
Literacy rate 81%
Calorie consumption Not available

MOLDOVA
Southeast Europe

Official name Republic of Moldova
Formation 1991 / 1991
Capital Chisinau
Population 4.3 million / 330 people per sq mile (128 people per sq km) / 46%
Total area 13,067 sq miles (33,843 sq km)
Languages Moldovan*, Russian, Ukrainian
Religions Orthodox Christian 98%, Jewish 2%
Ethnic mix Moldovan 65%, Ukrainian 14%, Russian 13%, Gagauz 4%, other 4%
Government Parliamentary system
Currency Moldovan leu = 100 bani
Literacy rate 99%
Calorie consumption 2,712 calories

MONACO
Southern Europe

Official name Principality of Monaco
Formation 1861 / 1861
Capital Monaco-Ville
Population 32,130 / 42,840 people per sq mile (16,477 people per sq km) / 100%
Total area 0.75 sq miles (1.95 sq km)
Languages French*, Italian, Monégasque, English
Religions Roman Catholic 89%, Protestant 6%, other 5%
Ethnic mix French 47%, Monégasque 17%, Italian 16%, other 20%
Government Monarchy
Currency Euro = 100 cents
Literacy rate 99%
Calorie consumption Not available

MONGOLIA
East Asia

Official name Mongolia
Formation 1924 / 1924
Capital Ulan Bator
Population 2.6 million / 4 people per sq mile (2 people per sq km) / 64%
Total area 604,247 sq miles (1,565,000 sq km)
Languages Khalkha Mongolian*, Kazakh, Chinese, Russian
Religions Tibetan Buddhist 96%, Muslim 4%
Ethnic mix Mongol 90%, Kazakh 4%, Chinese 2%, Russian 2%, other 2%
Government Mixed presidential–parliamentary system
Currency Tugrik (tögrög) = 100 möngö
Literacy rate 98%
Calorie consumption 1,974 calories

MOROCCO
North Africa

Official name Kingdom of Morocco
Formation 1956 / 1956
Capital Rabat
Population 30.6 million / 178 people per sq mile (69 people per sq km) / 56%
Total area 172,316 sq. miles (446,300 sq. km)
Languages Arabic*, French, Spanish, Tamazight (Berber)
Religions Muslim (mainly Sunni) 99%, other (mostly Christian) 1%
Ethnic mix Arab 70%, Berber 29%, European 1%
Government Monarchy
Currency Moroccan dirham = 100 centimes
Literacy rate 51%
Calorie consumption 3,046 calories

MOZAMBIQUE
Southern Africa

Official name Republic of Mozambique
Formation 1975 / 1975
Capital Maputo
Population 18.9 million / 62 people per sq mile (24 people per sq km) / 40%
Total area 309,494 sq miles (801,590 sq km)
Languages Portuguese*, Lomwe, Makua, Sena, Xitsonga
Religions Traditional beliefs 56%, Christian 30%, Muslim 14%
Ethnic mix Makua Lomwe 47%, Tsonga 23%, Malawi 12%, Shona 11%, Yao 4%, other 3%
Government Presidential system
Currency Metical = 100 centavos
Literacy rate 47%
Calorie consumption 1,980 calories

MYANMAR
Southeast Asia

Official name Union of Myanmar
Formation 1948 /1948
Capital Rangoon (Yangon)
Population 49.5 million / 195 people per sq mile (75 people per sq km) / 28%
Total area 261,969 sq miles (678,500 sq km)
Languages Burmese*, Chin, Kachin, Karen, Mon, Rakhine, Shan, Yangbye
Religions Buddhist 87%, Christian 6%, Muslim 4%, Hindu 1%, other 2%
Ethnic mix Burman (Bamah) 68%, Shan 9%, Karen 6%, Rakhine 4%, other 13%
Government Military-based regime
Currency Kyat = 100 pyas
Literacy rate 85%
Calorie consumption 2,822 calories

NAMIBIA
Southern Africa

Official name Republic of Namibia
Formation 1990 / 1994
Capital Windhoek
Population 2 million / 6 people per sq mile (2 people per sq km) / 31%
Total area 318,694 sq miles (825,418 sq km)
Languages English*, Afrikaans, Bergdama, German, Kavango, Ovambo
Religions Christian 90%, Traditional beliefs 10%
Ethnic mix Ovambo 50%, other tribes 16%, Kavango 9%, Damara 8%, Herero 8%, other 9%
Government Presidential system
Currency Namibian dollar = 100 cents
Literacy rate 83%
Calorie consumption 2,745 calories

NAURU
Australasia & Oceania

Official name Republic of Nauru
Formation 1968 / 1968
Capital None
Population 12,570 / 1,552 people per sq mile (599 people per sq km) / 100%
Total area 8.1 sq miles (21 sq km)
Languages Nauruan*, Chinese, English, Kiribati, Tuvaluan
Religions Nauruan Congregational Church 60%, Roman Catholic 35%, other 5%
Ethnic mix Nauruan 62%, other Pacific islanders 25%, Chinese and Vietnamese 8%, European 5%
Government Parliamentary system
Currency Australian dollar = 100 cents
Literacy rate 95%
Calorie consumption Not available

NEPAL
South Asia

Official name Kingdom of Nepal
Formation 1769 / 1769
Capital Kathmandu
Population 25.2 million / 477 people per sq mile (184 people per sq km) / 12%
Total area 54,363 sq miles (140,800 sq km)
Languages Nepali*, Bhojpuri, Maithili
Religions Hindu 90%, Buddhist 5%, Muslim 3%, other (including Christian) 2%
Ethnic mix Nepalese 52%, Maithili 11%, Tibeto-Burmese 10%, Bhojpuri 8%, other 19%
Government Monarchy
Currency Nepalese rupee = 100 paise
Literacy rate 44%
Calorie consumption 2,459 calories

NETHERLANDS
Northwest Europe

Official name Kingdom of the Netherlands
Formation 1648 / 1839
Capital Amsterdam; The Hague (administrative)
Population 16.1 million / 1,229 people per sq mile (475 people per sq km) / 89%
Total area 16,033 sq miles (41,526 sq km)
Languages Dutch*, Frisian
Religions Roman Catholic 36%, Protestant 27%, Muslim 3%, other 34%
Ethnic mix Dutch 82%, Moroccan 2%, Surinamese 2%, Turkish 2%, other 12%
Government Parliamentary system
Currency Euro = 100 cents
Literacy rate 97%
Calorie consumption 3,282 calories

NEW ZEALAND
Australasia & Oceania

Official name New Zealand
Formation 1947 / 1947
Capital Wellington
Population 3.9 million / 38 people per sq mile (15 people per sq km) / 86%
Total area 103,737 sq miles (268,680 sq km)
Languages English*, Maori
Religions Anglican 24%, Presbyterian 18%, non-religious 16%, Roman Catholic 15%, Methodist 5%, other 22%
Ethnic mix European 77%, Maori 12%, other immigrant 6%, Pacific islanders 5%
Government Parliamentary system
Currency New Zealand dollar = 100 cents
Literacy rate 99%
Calorie consumption 3,235 calories

NICARAGUA
Central America

Official name Republic of Nicaragua
Formation 1838 / 1838
Capital Managua
Population 5.5 million / 120 people per sq mile (46 people per sq km) / 65%
Total area 49,998 sq miles (129,494 sq km)
Languages Spanish*, English Creole, Miskito
Religions Roman Catholic 80%, Protestant Evangelical 17%, other 3%
Ethnic mix Mestizo 69%, White 14%, Black 8%, Amerindian 5%, Zambo 4%
Government Presidential system
Currency Córdoba oro = 100 centavos
Literacy rate 77%
Calorie consumption 2,256 calories

NIGER
West Africa

Official name Republic of Niger
Formation 1960 / 1960
Capital Niamey
Population 12 million / 25 people per sq mile (9 people per sq km) / 21%
Total area 489,188 sq miles (1,267,000 sq km)
Languages French*, Djerma, Fulani, Hausa, Teda, Tuareg
Religions Muslim 85%, Traditional beliefs 14%, other (including Christian) 1%
Ethnic mix Hausa 54%, Djerma and Songhai 21%, Fulani 10%, Tuareg 9%, other 6%
Government Presidential system
Currency CFA franc = 100 centimes
Literacy rate 17%
Calorie consumption 2,118 calories

NIGERIA
West Africa

Official name Federal Republic of Nigeria
Formation 1960 / 1961
Capital Abuja
Population 124 million / 353 people per sq mile (136 people per sq km) / 44%
Total area 356,667 sq miles (923,768 sq km)
Languages English*, Hausa, Ibo, Yoruba
Religions Muslim 50%, Christian 40%, Traditional beliefs 10%
Ethnic mix Hausa 21%, Yoruba 21%, Ibo 18%, Fulani 11%, other 29%
Government Presidential system
Currency Naira = 100 kobo
Literacy rate 67%
Calorie consumption 2,747 calories

NORTH KOREA
East Asia

Official name Democratic People's Republic of Korea
Formation 1948 / 1953
Capital Pyongyang
Population 22.7 million / 488 people per sq mile (189 people per sq km) / 60%
Total area 46,540 sq miles (120,540 sq km)
Languages Korean*, Chinese
Religions Atheist 100%
Ethnic mix Korean 100%
Government One-party state
Currency North Korean won = 100 chon
Literacy rate 99%
Calorie consumption 2,201 calories

NORWAY
Northern Europe

Official name Kingdom of Norway
Formation 1905 / 1905
Capital Oslo
Population 4.5 million / 38 people per sq mile (15 people per sq km) / 76%
Total area 125,181 sq miles (324,220 sq km)
Languages Norwegian* (Bokmål and Nynorsk), Sámi
Religions Evangelical Lutheran 89%, Roman Catholic 1%, other and non-religious 10%
Ethnic mix Norwegian 93%, Sámi 1%, other 6%
Government Parliamentary system
Currency Norwegian krone = 100 øre
Literacy rate 99%
Calorie consumption 3,382 calories

OMAN
Southwest Asia

Official name Sultanate of Oman
Formation 1951 / 1951
Capital Muscat
Population 2.9 million / 35 people per sq mile (14 people per sq km) / 84%
Total area 82,031 sq miles (212,460 sq km)
Languages Arabic*, Baluchi, Farsi, Hindi, Punjabi
Religions Ibadi Muslim 75%, other Muslim and Hindu 25%
Ethnic mix Arab 88%, Baluchi 4%, Persian 3%, Indian and Pakistani 3%, African 2%
Government Monarchy
Currency Omani rial = 1,000 baizas
Literacy rate 74%
Calorie consumption Not available

PAKISTAN
South Asia

Official name Islamic Republic of Pakistan
Formation 1947 / 1971
Capital Islamabad
Population 154 million / 516 people per sq mile (199 people per sq km) / 37%
Total area 310,401 sq miles (803,940 sq km)
Languages Urdu*, Baluchi, Brahui, Pashtu, Punjabi, Sindhi
Religions Sunni Muslim 77%, Shi'a Muslim 20%, Hindu 2%, Christian 1%
Ethnic mix Punjabi 56%, Pathan (Pashtun) 15%, Sindhi 14%, Mohajir 7%, Baluchi 4%, other 4%
Government Presidential system
Currency Pakistani rupee = 100 paisa
Literacy rate 44%
Calorie consumption 2,457 calories

PALAU
Australasia & Oceania

Official name Republic of Palau
Formation 1994 / 1994
Capital Koror (Oreor)
Population 19,717 / 101 people per sq mile (39 people per sq km) / 70%
Total area 177 sq miles (458 sq km)
Languages Angaur, English, Japanese, Palauan, Sonsorolese, Tobi
Religions Christian 66%, Modekngei 34%
Ethnic mix Micronesian 87%, Filipino 8%, Chinese and other Asian 5%
Government Non-party system
Currency US dollar = 100 cents
Literacy rate 98%
Calorie consumption Not available

PANAMA
Central America

Official name Republic of Panama
Formation 1903 / 1903
Capital Panama City
Population 3.1 million / 106 people per sq mile (41 people per sq km) / 56%
Total area 30,193 sq miles (78,200 sq km)
Languages Spanish*, Amerindian languages, Chibchan languages, English Creole
Religions Roman Catholic 86%, Protestant 6%, other 8%
Ethnic mix Mestizo 60%, White 14%, Black 12%, Amerindian 8%, Asian 4%, other 2%
Government Presidential system
Currency Balboa = 100 centesimos
Literacy rate 92%
Calorie consumption 2,386 calories

PAPUA NEW GUINEA
Australasia & Oceania

Official name Independent State of Papua New Guinea
Formation 1975 / 1975
Capital Port Moresby
Population 5.7 million / 33 people per sq mile (13 people per sq km) / 17%
Total area 178,703 sq miles (462,840 sq km)
Languages Papuan*, Pidgin English*, English, Motu, 750 (est.) native languages
Religions Protestant 60%, Roman Catholic 37%, other 3%
Ethnic mix Melanesian and mixed race 100%
Government Parliamentary system
Currency Kina = 100 toeas
Literacy rate 65%
Calorie consumption 2,193 calories

PARAGUAY
South America

Official name Republic of Paraguay
Formation 1811 / 1938
Capital Asunción
Population 5.9 million / 38 people per sq mile (15 people per sq km) / 56%
Total area 157,046 sq miles (406,750 sq km)
Languages Guaraní*, Spanish*, German
Religions Roman Catholic 96%, Protestant (including Mennonite) 4%
Ethnic mix Mestizo 90%, Amerindian 2%, other 8%
Government Presidential system
Currency Guaraní = 100 centimos
Literacy rate 92%
Calorie consumption 2,576 calories

PERU
South America

Official name Republic of Peru
Formation 1824 / 1941
Capital Lima
Population 27.2 million / 55 people per sq mile (21 people per sq km) / 73%
Total area 496,223 sq miles (1,285,200 sq km)
Languages Spanish*, Quechua*, Aymara*
Religions Roman Catholic 95%, other 5%
Ethnic mix Amerindian 50%, Mestizo 40%, White 7%, other 3%
Government Presidential system
Currency New sol = 100 centimos
Literacy rate 85%
Calorie consumption 2,610 calories

PHILIPPINES
Southeast Asia

Official name Republic of the Philippines
Formation 1946 / 1946
Capital Manila
Population 80 million / 695 people per sq mile (268 people per sq km) / 59%
Total area 115,830 sq miles (300,000 sq km)
Languages Filipino*, English*, Bicolano, Cebuano, Hiligaynon, Ilocano, Samaran, Tagalog
Religions Roman Catholic 83%, Protestant 9%, Muslim 5%, other (including Buddhist) 3%
Ethnic mix Malay 95%, Chinese 2%, other 3%
Government Presidential system
Currency Philippine peso = 100 centavos
Literacy rate 93%
Calorie consumption 2,372 calories

POLAND
Northern Europe

Official name Republic of Poland
Formation 1918 / 1945
Capital Warsaw
Population 38.6 million / 328 people per sq mile (127 people per sq km) / 66%
Total area 120,728 sq miles (312,685 sq km)
Languages Polish*
Religions Roman Catholic 93%, Orthodox Christian 2%, other and non-religious 5%
Ethnic mix Polish 97%, Silesian 1%, other 2%
Government Parliamentary system
Currency Zloty = 100 groszy
Literacy rate 99%
Calorie consumption 3,397 calories

PORTUGAL
Southwest Europe

Official name Republic of Portugal
Formation 1139 / 1640
Capital Lisbon
Population 10.1 million / 284 people per sq mile (110 people per sq km) / 38%
Total area 35,672 sq miles (92,391 sq km)
Languages Portuguese*
Religions Roman Catholic 97%, Protestant 1%, other 2%
Ethnic mix Portuguese 98%, African and other 2%
Government Parliamentary system
Currency Euro = 100 cents
Literacy rate 93%
Calorie consumption 3,751 calories

QATAR
Southwest Asia

Official name State of Qatar
Formation 1971 / 1971
Capital Doha
Population 610,000 / 144 people per sq mile (55 people per sq km) / 93%
Total area 4,416 sq miles (11,437 sq km)
Languages Arabic*
Religions Muslim (mainly Sunni) 95%, other 5%
Ethnic mix Arab 40%, Indian 18%, Pakistani 18%, Iranian 10%, other 14%
Government Monarchy
Currency Qatar riyal = 100 dirhams
Literacy rate 82%
Calorie consumption Not available

ROMANIA
Southeast Europe

Official name Romania
Formation 1878 / 1947
Capital Bucharest
Population 22.3 million / 251 people per sq mile (97 people per sq km) / 56%
Total area 91,699 sq miles (237,500 sq km)
Languages Romanian*, Hungarian (Magyar), Romani, German
Religions Romanian Orthodox 87%, Roman Catholic 5%, other 8%
Ethnic mix Romanian 89%, Magyar 7%, Roma 3%, other 1%
Government Presidential system
Currency Romanian leu = 100 bani
Literacy rate 97%
Calorie consumption 3,407 calories

RUSSIAN FEDERATION
Europe / Asia

Official name Russian Federation
Formation 1480 / 1991
Capital Moscow
Population 143 million / 22 people per sq mile (8 people per sq km) / 78%
Total area 6,592,735 sq miles (17,075,200 sq km)
Languages Russian*, Chavash, Tatar, Ukrainian, various other national languages
Religions Orthodox Christian 75%, Muslim 10%, other 15%
Ethnic mix Russian 82%, Tatar 4%, Ukrainian 3%, Chavash 1%, other 10%
Government Presidential system
Currency Russian rouble = 100 kopeks
Literacy rate 99%
Calorie consumption 3,014 calories

RWANDA
Central Africa

Official name Republic of Rwanda
Formation 1962 / 1962
Capital Kigali
Population 8.4 million / 872 people per sq mile (337 people per sq km) / 6%
Total area 10,169 sq miles (26,338 sq km)
Languages French*, Kinyarwanda*, Kiswahili, English
Religions Roman Catholic 56%, Traditional beliefs 25%, Muslim 10%, Protestant 9%
Ethnic mix Hutu 90%, Tutsi 9%, other (including Twa) 1%
Government Presidential system
Currency Rwanda franc = 100 centimes
Literacy rate 69%
Calorie consumption 2,086 calories

SAINT KITTS & NEVIS
West Indies

Official name Federation of Saint Christopher and Nevis
Formation 1983 / 1983
Capital Basseterre
Population 38,763 / 279 people per sq mile (108 people per sq km) / 34%
Total area 101 sq miles (261 sq km)
Languages English*, English Creole
Religions Anglican 33%, Methodist 29%, other 22%, Moravian 9%, Roman Catholic 7%
Ethnic mix Black 94%, Mixed race 3%, White 1%, other and Amerindian 2%
Government Parliamentary system
Currency Eastern Caribbean dollar = 100 cents
Literacy rate 98%
Calorie consumption 2,997 calories

SAINT LUCIA
West Indies

Official name Saint Lucia
Formation 1979 / 1979
Capital Castries
Population 162,157 / 687 people per sq mile (266 people per sq km) / 38%
Total area 239 sq miles (620 sq km)
Languages English*, French Creole
Religions Roman Catholic 90%, other 10%
Ethnic mix Black 90%, Mulatto (mixed race) 6%, Asian 3%, White 1%
Government Parliamentary system
Currency Eastern Caribbean dollar = 100 cents
Literacy rate 95%
Calorie consumption 2,849 calories

SAINT VINCENT & THE GRENADINES *West Indies*

Official name Saint Vincent and the Grenadines
Formation 1979 / 1979
Capital Kingstown
Population 116,812 / 892 people per sq mile (344 people per sq km) / 55%
Total area 150 sq miles (389 sq km)
Languages English*, English Creole
Religions Anglican 47%, Methodist 28%, Roman Catholic 13%, other 12%
Ethnic mix Black 66%, Mulatto (mixed race) 19%, Asian 6%, White 4%, other 5%
Government Parliamentary system
Currency Eastern Caribbean dollar = 100 cents
Literacy rate 83%
Calorie consumption 2,609 calories

Samoa
Australasia & Oceania

Official name Independent State of Samoa
Formation 1962 / 1962
Capital Apia
Population 178,000 / 163 people per sq mile (63 people per sq km) / 22%
Total area 1,104 sq miles (2,860 sq km)
Languages Samoan*, English*
Religions Christian 99%, other 1%
Ethnic mix Polynesian 90%, Euronesian 9%, other 1%
Government Parliamentary system
Currency Tala = 100 sene
Literacy rate 99%
Calorie consumption Not available

San Marino
Southern Europe

Official name Republic of San Marino
Formation 1631 / 1631
Capital San Marino
Population 28,119 / 1,172 people per sq mile (461 people per sq km) / 94%
Total area 23.6 sq miles (61 sq km)
Languages Italian*
Religions Roman Catholic 93%, other and non-religious 7%
Ethnic mix Sammarinese 80%, Italian 19%, other 1%
Government Parliamentary system
Currency Euro = 100 cents
Literacy rate 99%
Calorie consumption Not available

Sao Tome & Principe
West Africa

Official name Democratic Republic of São Tomé and Príncipe
Formation 1975 / 1975
Capital São Tomé
Population 175,883 / 474 people per sq mile (183 people per sq km) / 47%
Total area 386 sq. miles (1,001 sq. km)
Languages Portuguese*, Portuguese Creole
Religions Roman Catholic 84%, other 16%
Ethnic mix Black 90%, Portuguese and Creole 10%
Government Presidential system
Currency Dobra = 100 centimos
Literacy rate 83%
Calorie consumption 2,567 calories

Saudi Arabia
Southwest Asia

Official name Kingdom of Saudi Arabia
Formation 1932 / 1932
Capital Riyadh; Jedda (administrative)
Population 24.2 million / 30 people per sq mile (11 people per sq km) / 86%
Total area 756,981 sq miles (1,960,582 sq km)
Languages Arabic*
Religions Sunni Muslim 85%, Shi'a Muslim 15%
Ethnic mix Arab 90%, Afro-Asian 10%
Government Monarchy
Currency Saudi riyal = 100 halalat
Literacy rate 78%
Calorie consumption 2,841 calories

Senegal
West Africa

Official name Republic of Senegal
Formation 1960 / 1960
Capital Dakar
Population 10.1 million / 136 people per sq mile (52 people per sq km) / 47%
Total area 75,749 sq miles (196,190 sq km)
Languages French*, Diola, Malinke, Mandinka, Pulaar, Serer, Soninke, Wolof
Religions Sunni Muslim 90%, Christian (mainly Roman Catholic) 5%, Traditional beliefs 5%
Ethnic mix Wolof 43%, Toucouleur 24%, Serer 15%, Diola 4%, Malinke 3%, other 11%
Government Presidential system
Currency CFA franc = 100 centimes
Literacy rate 39%
Calorie consumption 2,277 calories

Serbia & Montenegro (Yugoslavia) *SE Europe*

Official name Serbia and Montenegro
Formation 1992 / 1992
Capital Belgrade
Population 10.5 million / 266 people per sq mile (103 people per sq km) / 52%
Total area 39,517 sq miles (102,350 sq km)
Languages Serbo-Croat*, Albanian, Hungarian
Religions Orthodox Christian 65%, Muslim 19%, Roman Catholic 4%, Protestant 1%, other 11%
Ethnic mix Serb 62%, Albanian 17%, Montenegrin 5%, Magyar 3%, Bosniak 3%, other 10%
Government Parliamentary system
Currency Dinar (Serbia); euro (Montenegro) = 100 para (dinar); 100 cents (euro)
Literacy rate 98%
Calorie consumption 2,778 calories

Seychelles
Indian Ocean

Official name Republic of Seychelles
Formation 1976 / 1976
Capital Victoria
Population 80,469 / 774 people per sq mile (298 people per sq km) / 64%
Total area 176 sq miles (455 sq km)
Languages French Creole*, English, French
Religions Roman Catholic 90%, Anglican 8%, other (including Muslim) 2%
Ethnic mix Creole 89%, Indian 5%, Chinese 2%, other 4%
Government Presidential system
Currency Seychelles rupee = 100 cents
Literacy rate 92%
Calorie consumption 2,461 calories

Sierra Leone
West Africa

Official name Republic of Sierra Leone
Formation 1961 / 1961
Capital Freetown
Population 5 million / 181 people per sq mile (70 people per sq km) / 37%
Total area 27,698 sq miles (71,740 sq km)
Languages English*, Mende, Temne, Krio
Religions Muslim 30%, Traditional beliefs 30%, Christian 10%, other 30%
Ethnic mix Mende 35%, Temne 32%, Limba 8%, Kuranko 4%, other 21%
Government Presidential system
Currency Leone = 100 cents
Literacy rate 36%
Calorie consumption 1,913 calories

Singapore
Southeast Asia

Official name Republic of Singapore
Formation 1965 / 1965
Capital Singapore
Population 4.3 million / 18,220 people per sq mile (7,049 people per sq km) / 100%
Total area 250 sq miles (648 sq km)
Languages English*, Malay*, Mandarin*, Tamil*
Religions Buddhist 55%, Taoist 22%, Muslim 16%, Hindu, Christian, and Sikh 7%
Ethnic mix Chinese 77%, Malay 14%, Indian 8%, other 1%
Government Parliamentary system
Currency Singapore dollar = 100 cents
Literacy rate 93%
Calorie consumption Not available

Slovakia
Central Europe

Official name Slovak Republic
Formation 1993 / 1993
Capital Bratislava
Population 5.4 million / 285 people per sq mile (110 people per sq km) / 57%
Total area 18,859 sq miles (48,845 sq km)
Languages Slovak*, Hungarian (Magyar), Czech
Religions Roman Catholic 60%, Atheist 10%, Protestant 8%, Orthodox Christian 4%, other 18%
Ethnic mix Slovak 85%, Magyar 11%, Czech 1%, Roma 1%, other 2%
Government Parliamentary system
Currency Slovak koruna = 100 halierov
Literacy rate 99%
Calorie consumption 2,894 calories

Slovenia
Central Europe

Official name Republic of Slovenia
Formation 1991 / 1991
Capital Ljubljana
Population 2 million / 256 people per sq mile (99 people per sq km) / 50%
Total area 7,820 sq miles (20,253 sq km)
Languages Slovene*, Serbo-Croat
Religions Roman Catholic 96%, Muslim 1%, other 3%
Ethnic mix Slovene 83%, Serb 2%, Croat 2%, Bosniak 1%, other 12%
Government Parliamentary system
Currency Tolar = 100 stotinov
Literacy rate 99%
Calorie consumption 2,935 calories

Solomon Islands
Australasia & Oceania

Official name Solomon Islands
Formation 1978 / 1978
Capital Honiara
Population 477,000 / 44 people per sq mile (17 people per sq km) / 20%
Total area 10,985 sq miles (28,450 sq km)
Languages English*, Melanesian Pidgin, Pidgin English
Religions Anglican 34%, Roman Catholic 19%, South Seas Evangelical Church 17%, Methodist 11%, Seventh-day Adventist 10%, other 9%
Ethnic mix Melanesian 94%, other 6%
Government Parliamentary system
Currency Solomon Islands dollar = 100 cents
Literacy rate 77%
Calorie consumption 2,272 calories

Somalia
East Africa

Official name Somalia
Formation 1960 / 1960
Capital Mogadishu
Population 9.9 million / 41 people per sq mile (16 people per sq km) / 28%
Total area 246,199 sq miles (637,657 sq km)
Languages Somali*, Arabic*, English, Italian
Religions Sunni Muslim 98%, Christian 2%
Ethnic mix Somali 85%, other 15%
Government Transitional regime
Currency Somali shilling = 100 centesimi
Literacy rate 24%
Calorie consumption 1,628 calories

South Africa
Southern Africa

Official name Republic of South Africa
Formation 1934 / 1994
Capital Pretoria; Cape Town; Bloemfontein
Population 45 million / 95 people per sq mile (37 people per sq km) / 55%
Total area 471,008 sq miles (1,219,912 sq km)
Languages Afrikaans, English, 9 other African languages
Religions Christian 68%, Traditional beliefs and animist 29%, Muslim 2%, Hindu 1%
Ethnic mix Black 79%, White 10%, Coloured 9%, Asian 2%
Government Presidential system
Currency Rand = 100 cents
Literacy rate 86%
Calorie consumption 2,921 calories

South Korea
East Asia

Official name Republic of Korea
Formation 1948 / 1953
Capital Seoul
Population 47.7 million / 1,251 people per sq mile (483 people per sq km) / 82%
Total area 38,023 sq miles (98,480 sq km)
Languages Korean*, Chinese
Religions Mahayana Buddhist 47%, Protestant 38%, Roman Catholic 11%, Confucianist 3%, other 1%
Ethnic mix Korean 100%
Government Presidential system
Currency South Korean won = 100 chon
Literacy rate 98%
Calorie consumption 3,055 calories

Spain
Southwest Europe

Official name Kingdom of Spain
Formation 1492 / 1713
Capital Madrid
Population 41.1 million / 213 people per sq mile (82 people per sq km) / 78%
Total area 194,896 sq miles (504,782 sq km)
Languages Spanish*, Catalan*, Galician*, Basque*
Religions Roman Catholic 96%, other 4%
Ethnic mix Castilian Spanish 72%, Catalan 17%, Galician 6%, Basque 2%, Roma 1%, other 2%
Government Parliamentary system
Currency Euro = 100 cents
Literacy rate 98%
Calorie consumption 3,422 calories

Sri Lanka
South Asia

Official name Democratic Socialist Republic of Sri Lanka
Formation 1948 / 1948
Capital Colombo
Population 19.1 million / 764 people per sq mile (295 people per sq km) / 24%
Total area 25,332 sq miles (65,610 sq km)
Languages Sinhala, Tamil, Sinhala-Tamil, English
Religions Buddhist 69%, Hindu 15%, Muslim 8%, Christian 8%
Ethnic mix Sinhalese 74%, Tamil 18%, Moor 7%, Burgher, Malay, and Veddha 1%
Government Mixed presidential–parliamentary system
Currency Sri Lanka rupee = 100 cents
Literacy rate 92%
Calorie consumption 2,274 calories

Sudan
East Africa

Official name Republic of the Sudan
Formation 1956 / 1956
Capital Khartoum
Population 33.6 million / 35 people per sq mile (13 people per sq km) / 36%
Total area 967,493 sq miles (2,505,810 sq km)
Languages Arabic*, Bari, Beja, Dinka, Fur, Lotuko, Nubian, Nuer, Shilluk, Zande
Religions Muslim (mainly Sunni) 70%, Traditional beliefs 20%, Christian 9%, other 1%
Ethnic mix Other Black 52%, Arab 40%, Dinka and Beja 7%, other 1%
Government Presidential system
Currency Sudanese pound or dinar = 100 piastres
Literacy rate 60%
Calorie consumption 2,288 calories

Suriname
South America

Official name Republic of Suriname
Formation 1975 / 1975
Capital Paramaribo
Population 436,000 / 7 people per sq mile (3 people per sq km) / 74%
Total area 63,039 sq miles (163,270 sq km)
Languages Dutch*, Chinese, Carib, Javanese, Saramaccan, Sarnami Hindi, Sranan (Creole)
Religions Hindu 27%, Protestant 25%, Roman Catholic 23%, Muslim 20%, Traditional beliefs 5%
Ethnic mix Creole 34%, South Asian 34%, Javanese 18%, Black 9%, other 5%
Government Parliamentary system
Currency Surinam dollar (guilder until 2004) = 100 cents
Literacy rate 94%
Calorie consumption 2,643 calories

Swaziland
Southern Africa

Official name Kingdom of Swaziland
Formation 1968 / 1968
Capital Mbabane
Population 1.1 million / 166 people per sq mile (64 people per sq km) / 26%
Total area 6,704 sq miles (17,363 sq km)
Languages English*, siSwati*, isiZulu, Xitsonga
Religions Christian 60%, Traditional beliefs 40%
Ethnic mix Swazi 97%, other 3%
Government Monarchy
Currency Lilangeni = 100 cents
Literacy rate 81%
Calorie consumption 2,593 calories

Sweden
Northern Europe

Official name Kingdom of Sweden
Formation 1523 / 1905
Capital Stockholm
Population 8.9 million / 56 people per sq mile (22 people per sq km) / 83%
Total area 173,731 sq miles (449,964 sq km)
Languages Swedish*, Finnish, Sámi
Religions Evangelical Lutheran 82%, Roman Catholic 2%, Muslim 2%, Orthodox Christian 1%, other 13%
Ethnic mix Swedish 88%, Foreign-born or first-generation immigrant 10%, Finnish and Sámi 2%
Government Parliamentary system
Currency Swedish krona = 100 öre
Literacy rate 99%
Calorie consumption 3,164 calories

Switzerland
Central Europe

Official name Swiss Confederation
Formation 1291 / 1857
Capital Bern
Population 7.2 million / 469 people per sq mile (181 people per sq km) / 68%
Total area 15,942 sq miles (41,290 sq km)
Languages French*, German*, Italian*, Romansch*, Swiss-German
Religions Roman Catholic 46%, Protestant 40%, Muslim 2%, other and non-religious 12%
Ethnic mix German 65%, French 18%, Italian 10%, Romansch 1%, other 6%
Government Parliamentary system
Currency Swiss franc = 100 rappen/centimes
Literacy rate 99%
Calorie consumption 3,440 calories

Syria
Southwest Asia

Official name Syrian Arab Republic
Formation 1941 / 1967
Capital Damascus
Population 17.8 million / 250 people per sq mile (97 people per sq km) / 55%
Total area 71,498 sq miles (184,180 sq km)
Languages Arabic*, Armenian, Circassian, French, Kurdish, Turkic languages, Assyrian, Aramaic
Religions Sunni Muslim 74%, Other Muslim 16%, Christian 10%
Ethnic mix Arab 89%, Kurdish 6%, Armenian, Turkmen, and Circassian 2%, other 3%
Government One-party state
Currency Syrian pound = 100 piasters
Literacy rate 83%
Calorie consumption 3,038 calories

Taiwan
East Asia

Official name Republic of China (ROC)
Formation 1949 / 1949
Capital Taipei
Population 22.6 million / 1,815 people per sq mile (701 people per sq km) / 69%
Total area 13,892 sq miles (35,980 sq km)
Languages Mandarin*, Amoy, Hakka
Religions Buddhist, Confucianist, and Taoist 93%, Christian 5%, other 2%
Ethnic mix Indigenous Chinese 84%, Mainland Chinese 14%, Aboriginal 2%
Government Presidential system
Currency Taiwan dollar = 100 cents
Literacy rate 96%
Calorie consumption Not available

Tajikistan
Central Asia

Official name Republic of Tajikistan
Formation 1991 / 1991
Capital Dushanbe
Population 6.2 million / 112 people per sq mile (43 people per sq km) / 28%
Total area 55,251 sq miles (143,100 sq km)
Languages Tajik*, Russian, Uzbek
Religions Sunni Muslim 80%, Shi'a Muslim 5%, other 15%
Ethnic mix Tajik 62%, Uzbek 24%, Russian 8%, Tatar 1%, Kyrgyz 1%, other 4%
Government Presidential system
Currency Somoni = 100 diram
Literacy rate 99%
Calorie consumption 1,662 calories

Tanzania
East Africa

Official name United Republic of Tanzania
Formation 1964 / 1964
Capital Dodoma
Population 37 million / 108 people per sq mile (42 people per sq km) / 33%
Total area 364,898 sq miles (945,087 sq km)
Languages English*, Kiswahili*, Chagga, Hehe, Makonde, Nyamwezi, Sandawe, Sukuma, Yao
Religions Muslim 33%, Christian 33%, Traditional beliefs 30%, other 4%
Ethnic mix Native African (over 120 tribes) 99%, European and Asian 1%
Government Presidential system
Currency Tanzanian shilling = 100 cents
Literacy rate 77%
Calorie consumption 1,997 calories

Thailand
Southeast Asia

Official name Kingdom of Thailand
Formation 1238 / 1907
Capital Bangkok
Population 62.8 million / 318 people per sq mile (123 people per sq km) / 22%
Total area 198,455 sq miles (514,000 sq km)
Languages Thai*, Chinese, Karen, Khmer, Malay, Miao, Mon
Religions Buddhist 95%, Muslim 4%, other (including Christian) 1%
Ethnic mix Thai 83%, Chinese 12%, Malay 3%, Khmer and other 2%
Government Parliamentary system
Currency Baht = 100 stang
Literacy rate 93%
Calorie consumption 2,486 calories

Togo
West Africa

Official name Republic of Togo
Formation 1960 / 1960
Capital Lomé
Population 4.9 million / 233 people per sq mile (90 people per sq km) / 33%
Total area 21,924 sq miles (56,785 sq km)
Languages French*, Ewe, Gurma, Kabye
Religions Traditional beliefs 50%, Christian 35%, Muslim 15%
Ethnic mix Ewe 46%, Kabye 27%, other African 26%, European 1%
Government Presidential system
Currency CFA franc = 100 centimes
Literacy rate 60%
Calorie consumption 2,287 calories

Tonga
Australasia & Oceania

Official name Kingdom of Tonga
Formation 1970 / 1970
Capital Nuku'alofa
Population 108,141 / 389 people per sq mile (150 people per sq km) / 43%
Total area 289 sq miles (748 sq km)
Languages Tongan*, English
Religions Free Wesleyan 41%, Roman Catholic 16%, Church of Jesus Christ of Latter-day Saints 14%, Free Church of Tonga 12%, other 17%
Ethnic mix Polynesian 99%, other 1%
Government Monarchy
Currency Pa'anga (Tongan dollar) = 100 seniti
Literacy rate 99%
Calorie consumption Not available

Trinidad & Tobago
West Indies

Official name Republic of Trinidad and Tobago
Formation 1962 / 1962
Capital Port-of-Spain
Population 1.3 million / 656 people per sq mile (253 people per sq km) / 74%
Total area 1,980 sq miles (5,128 sq km)
Languages English*, English Creole, French, Hindi, Spanish
Religions Christian 60%, Hindu 24%, Muslim 7%, other and non-religious 9%
Ethnic mix East Indian 41%, Black 40%, mixed race 19%, White and Chinese 1%
Government Parliamentary system
Currency Trinidad and Tobago dollar = 100 cents
Literacy rate 99%
Calorie consumption 2,756 calories

TUNISIA
North Africa

Official name Republic of Tunisia
Formation 1956 / 1956
Capital Tunis
Population 9.8 million / 163 people per sq mile
  (63 people per sq km) / 68%
Total area 63,169 sq miles (163,610 sq km)
Languages Arabic*, French
Religions Muslim (mainly Sunni) 98%,
  Christian 1%, Jewish 1%
Ethnic mix Arab and Berber 98%, Jewish 1%,
  European 1%
Government Presidential system
Currency Tunisian dinar = 1,000 millimes
Literacy rate 73%
Calorie consumption 3,293 calories

TURKEY
Asia / Europe

Official name Republic of Turkey
Formation 1923 / 1939
Capital Ankara
Population 71.3 million / 240 people per sq mile
  (93 people per sq km) / 75%
Total area 301,382 sq miles (780,580 sq km)
Languages Turkish*, Arabic, Armenian, Circassian,
  Georgian, Greek, Kurdish, Ladino
Religions Muslim (mainly Sunni) 99%, other 1%
Ethnic mix Turkish 70%, Kurdish 20%, Arab 2%,
  other 8%
Government Parliamentary system
Currency Turkish lira = 100 kurus
Literacy rate 87%
Calorie consumption 3,343 calories

TURKMENISTAN
Central Asia

Official name Turkmenistan
Formation 1991 / 1991
Capital Asgabat
Population 4.9 million / 26 people per sq mile
  (10 people per sq km) / 45%
Total area 188,455 sq miles (488,100 sq km)
Languages Turkmen*, Kazakh, Russian, Tatar,
  Uzbek
Religions Sunni Muslim 87%,
  Orthodox Christian 11%, other 2%
Ethnic mix Turkmen 77%, Uzbek 9%, Russian 7%,
  Kazakh 2%, Tatar 1%, other 4%
Government One-party state
Currency Manat = 100 tenga
Literacy rate 98%
Calorie consumption 2,738 calories

TUVALU
Australasia & Oceania

Official name Tuvalu
Formation 1978 / 1978
Capital Fongafale
Population 11,305 / 1,130 people per sq mile
  (435 people per sq km) / 45%
Total area 10 sq miles (26 sq km)
Languages English, Kiribati, Tuvaluan
Religions Church of Tuvalu 97%, Baha'i 1%,
  Seventh-day Adventist 1%, other 1%
Ethnic mix Polynesian 96%, other 4%
Government Non-party system
Currency Australian dollar and Tuvaluan dollar =
  100 cents
Literacy rate 98%
Calorie consumption Not available

UGANDA
East Africa

Official name Republic of Uganda
Formation 1962 / 1962
Capital Kampala
Population 25.8 million / 335 people per sq mile
  (129 people per sq km) / 14%
Total area 91,135 sq miles (236,040 sq km)
Languages English*, Acholi, Chiga, Lango,
  Luganda, Lugbara, Nkole, Teso
Religions Roman Catholic 38%, Protestant 33%,
  Traditional beliefs 13%, Muslim (mainly Sunni)
  8%, other 8%
Ethnic mix Bantu tribes 50%, other 50%
Government Non-party system
Currency New Uganda shilling = 100 cents
Literacy rate 69%
Calorie consumption 2,398 calories

UKRAINE
Eastern Europe

Official name Ukraine
Formation 1991 / 1991
Capital Kiev
Population 47.7 million / 205 people per sq mile
  (79 people per sq km) / 68%
Total area 223,089 sq miles (603,700 sq km)
Languages Ukrainian*, Russian, Tatar
Religions Christian (mainly Orthodox) 95%,
  Jewish 1%, other 4%
Ethnic mix Ukrainian 73%, Russian 22%,
  Jewish 1%, other 4%
Government Presidential system
Currency Hryvna = 100 kopiykas
Literacy rate 99%
Calorie consumption 3,008 calories

UNITED ARAB EMIRATES
Southwest Asia

Official name United Arab Emirates
Formation 1971 / 1972
Capital Abu Dhabi
Population 3 million / 93 people per sq mile
  (36 people per sq km) / 86%
Total area 32,000 sq miles (82,880 sq km)
Languages Arabic*, English, Farsi, Indian and
  Pakistani languages
Religions Muslim (mainly Sunni) 96%,
  Christian, Hindu, and other 4%
Ethnic mix Asian 60%, Emirian 25%,
  other Arab 12%, European 3%
Government Monarchy
Currency UAE dirham = 100 fils
Literacy rate 77%
Calorie consumption 3,340 calories

UNITED KINGDOM
Northwest Europe

Official name United Kingdom of Great Britain
  and Northern Ireland
Formation 1707 / 1922
Capital London
Population 59.3 million / 636 people per sq mile
  (245 people per sq km) / 90%
Total area 94,525 sq miles (244,820 sq km)
Languages English*, Gaelic, Scottish, Welsh
Religions Anglican 45%, Roman Catholic 9%,
  Presbyterian 4%, other and non-religious 42%
Ethnic mix English 80%, Scottish 9%, West Indian,
  Asian, and other 5%, Northern Irish 3%, Welsh 3%
Government Parliamentary system
Currency Pound sterling = 100 pence
Literacy rate 99%
Calorie consumption 3,368 calories

UNITED STATES
North America

Official name United States of America
Formation 1776 / 1959
Capital Washington DC
Population 294 million / 83 people per sq mile
  (32 people per sq km) / 77%
Total area 3,717,792 sq miles (9,626,091 sq km)
Languages English*, Spanish, Chinese, French,
  German, Italian, Polish
Religions Protestant 52%, Roman Catholic 25%,
  Jewish 2%, other and non-religious 21%
Ethnic mix White 69%, Hispanic 13%,
  Black American/African 13%, Asian 4%,
  Native American 1%
Government Presidential system
Currency US dollar = 100 cents
Literacy rate 99%
Calorie consumption 3,766 calories

URUGUAY
South America

Official name Eastern Republic of Uruguay
Formation 1828 / 1828
Capital Montevideo
Population 3.4 million / 50 people per sq mile
  (19 people per sq km) / 91%
Total area 68,039 sq miles (176,220 sq km)
Languages Spanish*
Religions Roman Catholic 66%, Jewish 2%,
  Protestant 2%, other and non-religious 30%
Ethnic mix White 90%, Mestizo 6%, Black 4%
Government Presidential system
Currency Uruguayan peso = 100 centésimos
Literacy rate 98%
Calorie consumption 2,848 calories

UZBEKISTAN
Central Asia

Official name Republic of Uzbekistan
Formation 1991 / 1991
Capital Tashkent
Population 26.1 million / 151 people per sq mile
  (58 people per sq km) / 37%
Total area 172,741 sq miles (447,400 sq km)
Languages Uzbek*, Kazakh, Russian, Tajik
Religions Sunni Muslim 88%, Orthodox Christian
  9%, other 3%
Ethnic mix Uzbek 71%, Russian 8%, Tajik 5%,
  Kazakh 4%, other 12%
Government Presidential system
Currency Som = 100 tiyin
Literacy rate 99%
Calorie consumption 2,197 calories

VANUATU
Australasia & Oceania

Official name Republic of Vanuatu
Formation 1980 / 1980
Capital Port Vila
Population 212,000 / 45 people per sq mile
  (17 people per sq km) / 20%
Total area 4,710 sq miles (12,200 sq km)
Languages Bislama*, English*, French*,
  other indigenous languages
Religions Presbyterian 37%, Anglican 15%,
  Roman Catholic 15%, Traditional beliefs 8%,
  Seventh-day Adventist 6%, other 19%
Ethnic mix Melanesian 94%, Polynesian 3%,
  other 3%
Government Parliamentary system
Currency Vatu = 100 centimes
Literacy rate 34%
Calorie consumption 2,565 calories

VATICAN CITY
Southern Europe

Official name State of the Vatican City
Formation 1929 / 1929
Capital Vatican City
Population 911 / 5,359 people per sq mile
  (2,070 people per sq km) / 100%
Total area 0.17 sq miles (0.44 sq km)
Languages Italian*, Latin*
Religions Roman Catholic 100%
Ethnic mix The current pope is Polish, Cardinals
  are from many nationalities, most of the resident
  lay persons are Italian.
Government Papal state
Currency Euro = 100 cents
Literacy rate 99%
Calorie consumption Not available

VENEZUELA
South America

Official name Bolivarian Republic of Venezuela
Formation 1830 / 1830
Capital Caracas
Population 25.7 million / 75 people per sq mile
  (29 people per sq km) / 87%
Total area 352,143 sq miles (912,050 sq km)
Languages Spanish*, Amerindian languages
Religions Roman Catholic 89%,
  Protestant and other 11%
Ethnic mix Mestizo 69%, White 20%, Black 9%,
  Amerindian 2%
Government Presidential system
Currency Bolívar = 100 centimos
Literacy rate 93%
Calorie consumption 2,376 calories

VIETNAM
Southeast Asia

Official name Socialist Republic of Vietnam
Formation 1976 / 1976
Capital Hanoi
Population 81.4 million / 648 people per sq mile
  (250 people per sq km) / 20%
Total area 127,243 sq miles (329,560 sq km)
Languages Vietnamese*, Chinese, Jarai, Khmer,
  Miao, Muong, Nung, Thai, Yao
Religions Buddhist 55%, Christian 7%,
  other and non-religious 38%
Ethnic mix Vietnamese 88%, Chinese 4%,
  Thai 2%, other 6%
Government One-party state
Currency Dông = 10 hao = 100 xu
Literacy rate 93%
Calorie consumption 2,533 calories

YEMEN
Southwest Asia

Official name Republic of Yemen
Formation 1990 / 1990
Capital Sana
Population 20 million / 92 people per sq mile
  (36 people per sq km) / 25%
Total area 203,849 sq miles (527,970 sq km)
Languages Arabic*
Religions Sunni Muslim 55%, Shi'a Muslim 42%,
  Christian, Hindu, and Jewish 3%
Ethnic mix Arab 95%, Afro-Arab 3%, Indian,
  Somali, and European 2%
Government Presidential system
Currency Yemeni rial = 100 sene
Literacy rate 49%
Calorie consumption 2,050 calories

ZAMBIA
Southern Africa

Official name Republic of Zambia
Formation 1964 / 1964
Capital Lusaka
Population 10.8 million / 38 people per sq mile
  (15 people per sq km) / 45%
Total area 290,584 sq miles (752,614 sq km)
Languages English*, Bemba, Lala-Bisa, Lozi,
  Nsenga, Nyanja, Tonga
Religions Christian 63%, Traditional beliefs 36%,
  Muslim and Hindu 1%
Ethnic mix Bemba 34%, other African 26%,
  Tonga 16%, Nyanja 14%, Lozi 9%, European 1%
Government Presidential system
Currency Zambian kwacha = 100 ngwee
Literacy rate 80%
Calorie consumption 1,885 calories

ZIMBABWE
Southern Africa

Official name Republic of Zimbabwe
Formation 1980 / 1980
Capital Harare
Population 12.9 million / 86 people per sq mile
  (33 people per sq km) / 35%
Total area 150,803 sq miles (390,580 sq km)
Languages English*, isiNdebele, Shona
Religions Syncretic (Christian/traditional beliefs)
  50%, Christian 25%, Traditional beliefs 24%,
  other (including Muslim) 1%
Ethnic mix Shona 71%, Ndebele 16%,
  other African 11%, White 1%, Asian 1%
Government Presidential system
Currency Zimbabwe dollar = 100 cents
Literacy rate 90%
Calorie consumption 2,133 calories

Geographical Names

The following glossary lists all geographical terms occurring on the maps and in main-entry names in the Index-Gazetteer. These terms may precede, follow or be run together with the proper element of the name; where they precede it the term is reversed for indexing purposes – thus Poluostrov Yamal is indexed as Yamal, Poluostrov.

Key
Geographical term *Language,* Term

A

Å *Danish, Norwegian,* River
Āb *Persian,* River
Adrar *Berber,* Mountains
Agía, Ágios *Greek,* Saint
Air *Indonesian,* River
Ákra *Greek,* Cape, point
Alpen *German,* Alps
Alt- *German,* Old
Altiplanicie *Spanish,* Plateau
Älve(en) *Swedish,* River
-ån *Swedish,* River
Anse *French,* Bay
'Aqabat *Arabic,* Pass
Archipiélago *Spanish,* Archipelago
Arcipelago *Italian,* Archipelago
Arquipélago *Portuguese,* Archipelago
Arrecife(s) *Spanish,* Reef(s)
Aru *Tamil,* River
Augstiene *Latvian,* Upland
Aukštuma *Lithuanian,* Upland
Aust- *Norwegian,* Eastern
Avtonomnyy Okrug *Russian,* Autonomous district
Āw *Kurdish,* River
'Ayn *Arabic,* Spring, well
'Ayoûn *Arabic,* Wells

B

Baelt *Danish,* Strait
Bahía *Spanish,* Bay
Baḥr *Arabic,* River
Baía *Portuguese,* Bay
Baie *French,* Bay
Bañado *Spanish,* Marshy land
Bandao *Chinese,* Peninsula
Banjaran *Malay,* Mountain range
Barajı *Turkish,* Dam
Barragem *Portuguese,* Reservoir
Bassin *French,* Basin
Batang *Malay,* Stream
Beinn, Ben *Gaelic,* Mountain
-berg *Afrikaans, Norwegian,* Mountain
Besar *Indonesian, Malay,* Big
Birkat, Birket *Arabic,* Lake, well
Blato *Croatian,* Muddy lake
Boğazi *Turkish,* Lake
Boka *Serbo-Croatian,* Bay
Bol'sh-aya, -iye, -oy, -oye *Russian,* Big
Botigh(i) *Uzbek,* Depression basin
-bre(en) *Norwegian,* Glacier
Bredning *Danish,* Bay
Bucht *German,* Bay
Bugt(en) *Danish,* Bay
Buḥayrat *Arabic,* Lake, reservoir
Buḥeiret *Arabic,* Lake
Bukit *Malay,* Mountain
-bukta *Norwegian,* Bay
bukten *Swedish,* Bay
Bulag *Mongolian,* Spring
Bulak *Uighur,* Spring
Burnu *Turkish,* Cape, point
Buuraha *Somali,* Mountains

C

Cabo *Portuguese,* Cape
Caka *Tibetan,* Salt lake
Canal *Spanish,* Channel
Cap *French,* Cape
Capo *Italian,* Cape, headland
Cascada *Portuguese,* Waterfall
Cayo(s) *Spanish,* Islet(s), rock(s)
Cerro *Spanish,* Mountain
Chaîne *French,* Mountain range
Chapada *Portuguese,* Hills, upland
Chau *Cantonese,* Island
Chāy *Turkish,* River
Chhâk *Cambodian,* Bay
Chhu *Tibetan,* River
-chŏsuji *Korean,* Reservoir
Chott *Arabic,* Depression, salt lake
Chŭli *Uzbek,* Grassland, steppe
Ch'ün-tao *Chinese,* Island group
Chuŏr Phnum *Cambodian,* Mountains
Ciudad *Spanish,* City, town
Co *Tibetan,* Lake
Colline(s) *French,* Hill(s)
Cordillera *Spanish,* Mountain range
Costa *Spanish,* Coast
Côte *French,* Coast
Coxilha *Portuguese,* Mountains
Cuchilla *Spanish,* Mountains

D

Daban *Mongolian, Uighur,* Pass
Daği *Azerbaijani, Turkish,* Mountain
Dağlari *Azerbaijani, Turkish,* Mountains
-dake *Japanese,* Peak
-dal(en) *Norwegian,* Valley
Danau *Indonesian,* Lake
Dao *Chinese,* Island
Đao *Vietnamese,* Island
Daryā *Persian,* River
Daryācheh *Persian,* Lake
Dasht *Persian,* Desert, plain
Dawḥat *Arabic,* Bay
Denizi *Turkish,* Sea
Dere *Turkish,* Stream
Desierto *Spanish,* Desert
Dili *Azerbaijani,* Spit
Ding *Chinese,* Peak
-do *Korean,* Island
Donj-a, -i *Croatian,* Lower
Dooxo *Somali,* Valley
Düzü *Azerbaijani,* Steppe
-dwīp *Bengali,* Island

E

-eilanden *Dutch,* Islands
Embalse *Spanish,* Reservoir
Encoro *Galician,* Reservoir
Ensenada *Spanish,* Bay
Erg *Arabic,* Dunes
Estany *Catalan,* Lake
Estero *Spanish,* Inlet
Estrecho *Spanish,* Strait
Étang *French,* Lagoon, lake
-ey *Icelandic,* Island
Ezero *Bulgarian, Macedonian,* Lake
Ezers *Latvian,* Lake

F

Feng *Chinese,* Peak
Fjord *Danish,* Fjord
-fjord(en) *Danish, Norwegian, Swedish,* fjord
-fjørdhur *Faeroese,* Fjord
Fleuve *French,* River
Fliegu *Maltese,* Channel
-fljór *Icelandic,* River
-flói *Icelandic,* Bay
Forêt *French,* Forest

G

-gan *Japanese,* Rock
-gang *Korean,* River
Ganga *Hindi, Nepali, Sinhala,* River
Gaoyuan *Chinese,* Plateau
Garagumy *Turkmen,* Sands
-gawa *Japanese,* River
Gebel *Arabic,* Mountain
-gebirge *German,* Mountain range
Ghadīr *Arabic,* Well
Ghubbat *Arabic,* Bay
Gjiri *Albanian,* Bay
Gol *Mongolian,* River
Golfe *French,* Gulf
Golfo *Italian, Spanish,* Gulf
Göl(ü) *Turkish,* Lake
Golyam, -a *Bulgarian,* Big
Gora *Russian, Serbo-Croatian,* Mountain
Góra *Polish,* Mountain
Gorica *Croatian,* Mountains
Gorje *Croatian,* Mountains
Gornj-a, -e, -i *Croatian,* Upper
Gory *Russian,* Mountain
Grad *Croatian,* Town, city
Griā *Croatian,* Rock
Gryada *Russian,* Ridge
Guba *Russian,* Bay
-gundo *Korean,* Island group
Gunung *Malay,* Mountain

H

Ḥadd *Arabic,* Spit
-haehyŏp *Korean,* Strait
Haff *German,* Lagoon
Hai *Chinese,* Bay, lake, sea
Haixia *Chinese,* Strait
Hamada *Arabic,* Plateau
Ḥammādat *Arabic,* Plateau
Hāmūn *Persian,* Lake
-hantō *Japanese,* Peninsula
Har, Haré *Hebrew,* Mountain
Ḥarrat *Arabic,* Lava-field
Hav(et) *Danish, Swedish,* Sea
Hawr *Arabic,* Lake
Hāyk' *Amharic,* Lake
He *Chinese,* River
-hegység *Hungarian,* Mountain range
Heide *German,* Heath, moorland
Helodrano *Malagasy,* Bay
Higashi- *Japanese,* East(ern)
Ḥiṣā' *Arabic,* Well
Hka *Burmese,* River
-ho *Korean,* Lake
Hô *Korean,* Reservoir
Ḥolot *Hebrew,* Dunes
Hora *Belorussian, Czech,* Mountain
Hrada *Belorussian,* Mountain, ridge
Hrvatsk-a, -i, -o *Croatian,* Croatian
Hsi *Chinese,* River
Hu *Chinese,* Lake
Huk *Danish,* Point

I

Île(s) *French,* Island(s)
Ilha(s) *Portuguese,* Island(s)
Ilhéu(s) *Portuguese,* Islet(s)
Imeni *Russian,* In the name of
Inish- *Gaelic,* Island
Insel(n) *German,* Island(s)
Irmağı, Irmak *Turkish,* River
Isla(s) *Spanish,* Island(s)
Isola (Isole) *Italian,* Island(s)

J

Jabal *Arabic,* Mountain
Jāl *Arabic,* Ridge
-järv *Estonian,* Lake
-järvi *Finnish,* Lake
Jazā'ir *Arabic,* Islands
Jazīrat *Arabic,* Island
Jazīreh *Persian,* Island
Jebel *Arabic,* Mountain
Jezero *Serbo-Croatian,* Lake
Jezioro *Polish,* Lake
Jiang *Chinese,* River
-jima *Japanese,* Island
Jižní *Czech,* Southern
-jõgi *Estonian,* River
-joki *Finnish,* River
-jökull *Icelandic,* Glacier
Jūn *Arabic,* Bay
Juzur *Arabic,* Islands

K

Kaikyō *Japanese,* Strait
-kaise *Lappish,* Mountain
Kali *Nepali,* River
Kalnas *Lithuanian,* Mountain
Kalns *Latvian,* Mountain
Kanal *Croatian,* Strait, inlet
Kang *Chinese,* Harbor
Kangri *Tibetan,* Mountain(s)
Kaôh *Cambodian,* Island
Kapp *Norwegian,* Cape
Káto *Greek,* Lower
Kavīr *Persian,* Desert
K'edi *Georgian,* Mountain range
Kediet *Arabic,* Mountain
Kepi *Albanian,* Cape, point
Kepulauan *Indonesian, Malay,* Island group
Khalīg, Khalīj *Arabic,* Gulf
Khawr *Arabic,* Inlet
Khola *Nepali,* River
Khrebet *Russian,* Mountain range
Ko *Thai,* Island
-ko *Japanese,* Inlet, lake
Kólpos *Greek,* Bay
-kopf *German,* Peak
Körfäzi *Azerbaijani,* Bay
Körfezi *Turkish,* Bay
Kõrgustik *Estonian,* Upland
Kosa *Russian, Ukrainian,* Spit
Koshi *Nepali,* River
Kotlina *Croatian,* Valley
Kou *Chinese,* River-mouth
Kowtal *Persian,* Pass
Kray *Russian,* Region, territory
Kryazh *Russian,* Ridge
Kuduk *Uighur,* Well
Kūh(hā) *Persian,* Mountain(s)
-kul' *Russian,* Lake
Kŭl(i) *Tajik, Uzbek,* Lake
-kundo *Korean,* Island group
-kysten *Norwegian,* Coast
Kyun *Burmese,* Island

L

Laaq *Somali,* Watercourse
Lac *French,* Lake
Lacul *Romanian,* Lake
Lagh *Somali,* Stream
Lago *Italian, Portuguese, Spanish,* Lake
Lagoa *Portuguese,* Lagoon
Laguna *Italian, Spanish,* Lagoon, lake
Laht *Estonian,* Bay
Laut *Indonesian,* Bay
Lembalemba *Malagasy,* Plateau
Lerr *Armenian,* Mountain
Lerrnashghht'a *Armenian,* Mountain range
Les *Czech,* Forest
Lich *Armenian,* Lake
Liehtao *Chinese,* Island group
Liqeni *Albanian,* Lake
Límni *Greek,* Lake
Ling *Chinese,* Mountain range
Llano *Spanish,* Plain, prairie
Lumi *Albanian,* River
Lyman *Ukrainian,* Estuary

M

Madīnat *Arabic,* City, town
Mae Nam *Thai,* River
-mägi *Estonian,* Hill
Maja *Albanian,* Mountain
Mal *Albanian,* Mountains
Mal-aya, -oye, -yy, *Russian,* Small
-man *Korean,* Bay
Mar *Spanish,* Lake
Marios *Lithuanian,* Lake
Massif *French,* Mountains
Meer *German,* Lake
-meer *Dutch,* Lake
Melkosopochnik *Russian,* Plain
-meri *Estonian,* Sea
Mifraẓ *Hebrew,* Bay
Minami- *Japanese,* South(ern)
-misaki *Japanese,* Cape, point
Monkhafad *Arabic,* Depression
Montagne(s) *French,* Mountain(s)
Montañas *Spanish,* Mountains
Mont(s) *French,* Mountain(s)
Monte *Italian, Portuguese,* Mountain
More *Croatian,* Russian, Sea, lagoon
Mörön *Mongolian,* River
Mys *Russian,* Cape, point

N

Nacionalni Park *Croatian,* National park
-nada *Japanese,* Open stretch of water
Nagor'ye *Russian,* Upland
Naḥal *Hebrew,* River
Nahr *Arabic,* River
Nam *Laotian,* River
Namakzār *Persian,* Salt desert
Né-a, -on, -os *Greek,* New
Nedre- *Norwegian,* Lower
-neem *Estonian,* Cape, point
Nehri *Turkish,* River
-nes *Norwegian,* Cape, point
Nevado *Spanish,* Mountain (snow-capped)
Nieder- *German,* Lower
Nishi- *Japanese,* West(ern)
-nísi *Greek,* Island
Nisoi *Greek,* Islands
Nizhn-eye, -iy, -iye, -yaya *Russian,* Lower
Nizmennost' *Russian,* Lowland, plain
Nord *Danish, French, German,* North
Norte *Portuguese, Spanish,* North
Nos *Bulgarian,* Point, spit
Nosy *Malagasy,* Island
Nov-a, -i, *Bulgarian, Serbo-Croatian,* New
Nov-aya, -o, -oye, -yy, -yye *Russian,* New
Now-a, -e, -y *Polish,* New
Nur *Mongolian,* Lake
Nuruu *Mongolian,* Mountains
Nuur *Mongolian,* Lake
Nyzovyna *Ukrainian,* Lowland, plain

O

-ø *Danish,* Island
Ober- *German,* Upper
Oblast' *Russian,* Province
Órmos *Greek,* Bay
Orol(i) *Uzbek,* Island
Øster- *Norwegian,* Eastern
Ostrov(a) *Russian,* Island(s)
Otok *Serbo-Croatian,* Island
Oued *Arabic,* Watercourse
-oy *Faeroese,* Island
-øy(a) *Norwegian,* Island
Oya *Sinhala,* River
Ozero *Russian, Ukrainian,* Lake

P

Passo *Italian,* Pass
Pegunungan *Indonesian, Malay,* Mountain range
Pélagos *Greek,* Sea
Pendi *Chinese,* Basin
Penisola *Italian,* Peninsula
Pertuis *French,* Strait
Peski *Russian,* Sands
Phanom *Thai,* Mountain
Phou *Laotian,* Mountain
Pi *Chinese,* Point
Pic *Catalan, French,* Peak
Pico *Portuguese, Spanish,* Peak
-piggen *Danish,* Peak
Pik *Russian,* Peak
Pivostriv *Ukrainian,* Peninsula
Planalto *Portuguese,* Plateau
Planina, Planini *Bulgarian, Macedonian, Serbo-Croatian,* Mountain range
Plato *Russian,* Plateau
Ploskogor'ye *Russian,* Upland
Polje *Croatian,* Plain, lowlands
Poluostrov *Russian,* Peninsula
Ponta *Portuguese,* Point
Porthmós *Greek,* Strait
Pótamos *Greek,* River
Presa *Spanish,* Dam
Prokhod *Bulgarian,* Pass
Prolaz *Croatian,* Passage
Proliv *Russian,* Strait
Pulau *Indonesian, Malay,* Island
Pulu *Malay,* Island
Punta *Croatian,* Spanish, Point
Pushcha *Belarussian,* Forest
Puszcza *Polish,* Forest

Q

Qā' *Arabic,* Depression
Qalamat *Arabic,* Well
Qatorkŭh(i) *Tajik,* Mountain
Qiuling *Chinese,* Hills
Qolleh *Persian,* Mountain
Qu *Tibetan,* Stream
Quan *Chinese,* Well
Qulla(i) *Tajik,* Peak
Qundao *Chinese,* Island group

R

Raas *Somali,* Cape
-rags *Latvian,* Cape
Ramlat *Arabic,* Sands
Ra's *Arabic,* Cape, headland, point
Ravnina *Bulgarian, Russian,* Plain
Récif *French,* Reef
Recife *Portuguese,* Reef
Reka *Bulgarian,* River
Represa (Rep.) *Portuguese, Spanish,* Reservoir
Reshteh *Persian,* Mountain range
Respublika *Russian,* Republic, first-order administrative division
Respublika(si) *Uzbek,* Republic, first-order administrative division
-retsugan *Japanese,* Chain of rocks
-rettō *Japanese,* Island chain
Riacho *Spanish,* Stream
Riban' *Malagasy,* Mountains
Rio *Portuguese,* River
Río *Spanish,* River
Riu *Catalan,* River
Rivier *Dutch,* River
Rivière *French,* River
Rowd *Pashtu,* River
Rt *Serbo-Croatian,* Point
Rūd *Persian,* River
Rūdkhāneh *Persian,* River
Rudohorie *Slovak,* Mountains
Ruisseau *French,* Stream

S

-saar *Estonian,* Island
-saari *Finnish,* Island
Sabkhat *Arabic,* Salt marsh
Sāgar(a) *Hindi,* Lake, reservoir
Ṣaḥrā' *Arabic,* Desert
Saint, Sainte *French,* Saint
Salar *Spanish,* Salt-pan
Salto *Portuguese, Spanish,* Waterfall
Samudra *Sinhala,* Reservoir
-san *Japanese, Korean,* Mountain
-sanchi *Japanese,* Mountains
-sandur *Icelandic,* Beach
Sankt *German, Swedish,* Saint
-sanmaek *Korean,* Mountain range
-sanmyaku *Japanese,* Mountain range
San, Santa, Santo *Italian, Portuguese, Spanish,* Saint
São *Portuguese,* Saint
Sarīr *Arabic,* Desert
Sebkha, Sebkhet *Arabic,* Depression, salt marsh
Sedlo *Czech,* Pass
See *German,* Lake
Selat *Indonesian,* Strait
Selatan *Indonesian,* Southern
-selkä *Finnish,* Lake, ridge
Selo *Croatian,* Village
Selseleh *Persian,* Mountain range
Serra *Portuguese,* Mountain
Serranía *Spanish,* Mountain
-seto *Japanese,* Channel, strait
Sever-naya, -noye, -nyy, -o *Russian,* Northern
Sha'īb *Arabic,* Watercourse
Shākh *Kurdish,* Mountain
Shamo *Chinese,* Desert
Shan *Chinese,* Mountain(s)
Shankou *Chinese,* Pass
Shanmo *Chinese,* Mountain range
Shaṭṭ *Arabic,* Distributary
Shet' *Amharic,* River
Shi *Chinese,* Municipality
-shima *Japanese,* Island
Shiqqat *Arabic,* Depression
-shotō *Japanese,* Group of islands
Shuiku *Chinese,* Reservoir
Shūrkhog(i) *Uzbek,* Salt marsh
Sierra *Spanish,* Mountains
Sint *Dutch,* Saint
-sjø(en) *Norwegian,* Lake
-sjön *Swedish,* Lake
Solonchak *Russian,* Salt lake
Solonchakovyye Vpadiny *Russian,* Salt basin, wetlands
Sơn *Vietnamese,* Mountain
Sông *Vietnamese,* River
Sør- *Norwegian,* Southern
-spitze *German,* Peak
Star-á, -é *Czech,* Old
Star-a, -i, -o *Croatian,* Old
Star-aya, -oye, -yy, -yye *Russian,* Old
Stenó *Greek,* Strait
Step' *Russian,* Steppe
Štít *Slovak,* Peak
Stœng *Cambodian,* River
Stolovaya Strana *Russian,* Plateau
Stredné *Slovak,* Middle
Střední *Czech,* Middle
Stretto *Italian,* Strait
Su Anbari *Azerbaijani,* Reservoir
-suidō *Japanese,* Channel, strait
Sund *Swedish,* Sound, strait
Sungai *Indonesian, Malay,* River
Suu *Turkish,* River
Sveti *Croatian,* Saint

T

Tag *Turkic,* Peak
Tal *Mongolian,* Plain
Tandavan' *Malagasy,* Mountain range
Tangorombohitr' *Malagasy,* Mountain massif
Tanjung *Indonesian, Malay,* Cape, point
Tao *Chinese,* Island
Ṭaraq *Arabic,* Hills
Tassili *Berber,* Mountain, plateau
Tau *Russian,* Mountain(s)
Taungdan *Burmese,* Mountain range
Techníti Límni *Greek,* Reservoir
Tekojärvi *Finnish,* Reservoir
Teluk *Indonesian, Malay,* Bay
Tengah *Indonesian,* Middle
Terara *Amharic,* Mountain
Timur *Indonesian,* Eastern
-tind(an) *Norwegian,* Peak
Tizma(si) *Uzbek,* Mountain range, ridge
-tō *Japanese,* Island
Tog *Somali,* Valley
-tōge *Japanese,* Pass
Togh(i) *Uzbek,* Mountain
Tônlé *Cambodian,* Lake
Top *Dutch,* Peak
-tunturi *Finnish,* Mountain
Ṭurāq *Arabic,* Hills
Tur'at *Arabic,* Channel

U

Udde(n) *Swedish,* Cape, point
'Uqlat *Arabic,* Well
Utara *Indonesian,* Northern
Uul *Mongolian,* Mountains

V

Väin *Estonian,* Strait
Vallée *French,* Valley
-vatn *Icelandic,* Lake
-vatnet *Norwegian,* Lake
Velayat *Turkmen,* Province
Velik-a, -e, -i, -o *Croatian,* Big
-vesi *Finnish,* Lake
Vestre- *Norwegian,* Western
-vidda *Norwegian,* Plateau
-vík *Icelandic,* Bay
-viken *Swedish,* Bay, inlet
Vinh *Vietnamese,* Bay
Víztárloló *Hungarian,* Reservoir
Vodaskhovishcha *Belarussian,* Reservoir
Vodokhranilishche (Vdkhr.) *Russian,* Reservoir
Vodoskhovyshche (Vdskh.) *Ukrainian,* Reservoir
Volcán *Spanish,* Volcano
Vostochn-o, yy *Russian,* Eastern
Vozvyshennost' *Russian,* Upland, plateau
Vozyera *Belarussian,* Lake
Vpadina *Russian,* Depression
Vrata *Croatian,* Pass, marine passage
Vrchovina *Czech,* Mountains
Vrh *Croatian,* Peak
Vrha *Macedonian,* Peak
Vychodné *Slovak,* Eastern
Vysochyna *Ukrainian,* Upland
Vysočina *Czech,* Upland

W

Waadi *Somali,* Watercourse
Wādī *Arabic* Watercourse
Wāḥat, Wâhat *Arabic,* Oasis
Wald *German,* Forest
Wan *Chinese,* Bay
Way *Indonesian,* River
Webi *Somali,* River
Wenz *Amharic,* River
Wiloyat(i) *Uzbek,* Province
Wyżyna *Polish,* Upland
Wzgórza *Polish,* Upland
Wzvyshsha *Belarussian,* Upland

X

Xé *Laotian,* River
Xi *Chinese,* Stream
Xueshan *Chinese,* Snow-peak

Y

-yama *Japanese,* Mountain
Yanchi *Chinese,* Salt lake
Yang *Chinese,* Bay
Yanhu *Chinese,* Salt lake
Yarımadası *Azerbaijani, Turkish,* Peninsula
Yaylası *Turkish,* Plateau
Yazovir *Bulgarian,* Reservoir
Yoma *Burmese,* Mountains
Ytre- *Norwegian,* Outer
Yü *Chinese,* Island
Yunhe *Chinese,* Canal
Yuzhn-o, -yy *Russian,* Southern

Z

Zagorje *Croatian,* Uplands
-zaki *Japanese,* Cape, point
Zaliv *Bulgarian, Russian,* Bay
Zaljev *Croatian,* Bay
-zan *Japanese,* Mountain
Zangbo *Tibetan,* River
Zapadn-aya, -o, -yy *Russian,* Western
Západné *Slovak,* Western
Západní *Czech,* Western
Zatoka *Polish, Ukrainian,* Bay
-zee *Dutch,* Sea
Zemlya *Russian,* Earth, land
Zizhiqu *Chinese,* Autonomous region

25 de Mayo – Abū Şukhayr

Index

Glossary of Abbreviations

This glossary provides a comprehensive guide to the abbreviations used in this Atlas, and in the Index.

A
abbrev. abbreviated
AD Anno Domini
Afr. Afrikaans
Alb. Albanian
Amh. Amharic
anc. ancient
approx. approximately
Ar. Arabic
Arm. Armenian
ASEAN Association of South East Asian Nations
ASSR Autonomous Soviet Socialist Republic
Aust. Australian
Az. Azerbaijani
Azerb. Azerbaijan

B
Basq. Basque
BC before Christ
Bel. Belorussian
Ben. Bengali
Ber. Berber
B-H Bosnia-Herzegovina
bn billion (one thousand million)
BP British Petroleum
Bret. Breton
Brit. British
Bul. Bulgarian
Bur. Burmese

C
C central
C. Cape
°C degrees Centigrade
CACM Central America Common Market
Cam. Cambodian
Cant. Cantonese
CAR Central African Republic
Cast. Castilian
Cat. Catalan
CEEAC Central America Common Market
Chin. Chinese
CIS Commonwealth of Independent States
cm centimetre(s)
Cro. Croat
Cz. Czech
Czech Rep. Czech Republic

D
Dan. Danish
Div. Divehi
Dom. Rep. Dominican Republic
Dut. Dutch

E
E east
EC *see* EU
EEC *see* EU
ECOWAS Economic Community of West African States
ECU European Currency Unit
EMS European Monetary System
Eng. English
est estimated
Est. Estonian
EU European Union (previously European Community [EC], European Economic Community [EEC])

F
°F degrees Fahrenheit
Faer. Faeroese
Fij. Fijian
Fin. Finnish
Fr. French
Fris. Frisian
ft foot/feet
FYROM Former Yugoslav Republic of Macedonia

G
g gram(s)
Gael. Gaelic
Gal. Galician
GDP Gross Domestic Product (the total value of goods and services produced by a country excluding income from foreign countries)
Geor. Georgian
Ger. German
Gk Greek
GNP Gross National Product (the total value of goods and services produced by a country)

H
Heb. Hebrew
HEP hydro-electric power
Hind. Hindi
hist. historical
Hung. Hungarian

I
I. Island
Icel. Icelandic
in inch(es)
In. Inuit (Eskimo)
Ind. Indonesian
Intl International
Ir. Irish
Is Islands
It. Italian

J
Jap. Japanese

K
Kaz. Kazakh
kg kilogram(s)
Kir. Kirghiz
km kilometre(s)
km² square kilometre (singular)
Kor. Korean
Kurd. Kurdish

L
L. Lake
LAIA Latin American Integration Association
Lao. Laotian
Lapp. Lappish
Lat. Latin
Latv. Latvian
Liech. Liechtenstein
Lith. Lithuanian
Lus. Lusatian
Lux. Luxembourg

M
m million/metre(s)
Mac. Macedonian
Maced. Macedonia
Mal. Malay
Malg. Malagasy
Malt. Maltese
mi. mile(s)
Mong. Mongolian
Mt. Mountain
Mts Mountains

N
N north
NAFTA North American Free Trade Agreement
Nep. Nepali
Neth. Netherlands
Nic. Nicaraguan
Nor. Norwegian
NZ New Zealand

P
Pash. Pashtu
PNG Papua New Guinea
Pol. Polish
Poly. Polynesian
Port. Portuguese
prev. previously

R
Rep. Republic
Res. Reservoir
Rmsch Romansch
Rom. Romanian
Rus. Russian
Russ. Fed. Russian Federation

S
S south
SADC Southern Africa Development Community
SCr. Serbian, Croatian
Sinh. Sinhala
Slvk Slovak
Slvn. Slovene
Som. Somali
Sp. Spanish
St., St Saint
Strs Straits
Swa. Swahili
Swe. Swedish
Switz. Switzerland

T
Taj. Tajik
Th. Thai
Thai. Thailand
Tib. Tibetan
Turk. Turkish
Turkm. Turkmenistan

U
UAE United Arab Emirates
Uigh. Uighur
UK United Kingdom
Ukr. Ukrainian
UN United Nations
Urd. Urdu
US/USA United States of America
USSR Union of Soviet Socialist Republics
Uzb. Uzbek

V
var. variant
Vdkhr. Vodokhranilishche (Russian for reservoir)
Vdskh. Vodoskhovyshche (Ukrainian for reservoir)
Vtn. Vietnamese

W
W west
Wel. Welsh

Y
Yugo. Yugoslavia

This index lists all the placenames and features shown on the regional and continental maps in this Atlas. Placenames are referenced to the largest scale map on which they appear. The policy followed throughout the Atlas is to use the local spelling or local name at regional level; commonly-used English language names may occasionally be added (in parentheses) where this is an aid to identification e.g. Firenze (Florence). English names, where they exist, have been used for all international features e.g. oceans and country names; they are also used on the continental maps and in the introductory World Today section; these are then fully cross-referenced to the local names found on the regional maps. The index also contains commonly-found alternative names and variant spellings, which are also fully cross-referenced.

All main entry names are those of settlements unless otherwise indicated by the use of italicized definitions or representative symbols, which are keyed at the foot of each page.

1

25 de Mayo *see* Veinticinco de Mayo
143 *Y13* **26 Bakı Komissarı** *Rus.* Imeni 26 Bakinskikh Komissarov. SE Azerbaijan *39.18N 49.13E*
26 Baku Komissarlary Adyndaky *see* Uzboý
8 *M16* **100 Mile House** *var.* Hundred Mile House. British Columbia, SW Canada *51.39N 121.19W*

A

Aa *see* Gauja
97 *G24* **Aabenraa** *var.* Åbenrå, *Ger.* Apenrade. Sønderjylland, SW Denmark *55.03N 9.25E*
97 *G20* **Aabybro** *var.* Åbybro. Nordjylland, N Denmark *57.09N 9.45E*
103 *C16* **Aachen** *Dut.* Aken, *Fr.* Aix-la-Chapelle; *anc.* Aquae Grani, Aquisgranum. Nordrhein-Westfalen, W Germany *50.47N 6.06E*
Aaiún *see* Laâyoune
97 *M24* **Aakirkeby** *var.* Åkirkeby. Bornholm, E Denmark *55.04N 14.55E*
Ãak Nông *see* Gia Nghia
97 *G20* **Aalborg** *var.* Ålborg, Ålborg-Nørresundby; *anc.* Alburgum. Nordjylland, N Denmark *57.03N 9.55E*
Aalborg Bugt *see* Ålborg Bugt
103 *J21* **Aalen** Baden-Württemberg, S Germany *48.49N 10.06E*
97 *G21* **Aalestrup** *var.* Ålestrup. Viborg, NW Denmark *56.42N 9.31E*
100 *I11* **Aalsmeer** Noord-Holland, C Netherlands *52.16N 4.43E*
101 *F18* **Aalst** *Fr.* Alost. Oost-Vlaanderen, C Belgium *50.57N 4.03E*
101 *K18* **Aalst** Noord-Brabant, S Netherlands *51.46N 5.07E*
100 *O12* **Aalten** Gelderland, E Netherlands *51.55N 6.34E*
101 *D17* **Aalter** Oost-Vlaanderen, NW Belgium *51.04N 3.28E*
Aanaar *see* Inari
Aanaarjävri *see* Inarijärvi
95 *M17* **Äänekoski** Länsi-Suomi, W Finland *62.33N 25.44E*
144 *H7* **Aanjar** *var.* 'Anjar. C Lebanon *33.45N 35.56E*
85 *G21* **Aansluit** Northern Cape, N South Africa *26.41S 22.24E*
Aar *see* Aare
110 *F7* **Aarau** Aargau, N Switzerland *47.22N 8.00E*
110 *D8* **Aarberg** Bern, W Switzerland *47.02N 7.15E*
101 *D16* **Aardenburg** Zeeland, SW Netherlands *51.16N 3.27E*
110 *D8* **Aare** *var.* Aar. ≈ W Switzerland
110 *F7* **Aargau** *Fr.* Argovie. ◐ *canton* N Switzerland
Aarhus *see* Århus
Aarlen *see* Arlon
97 *G21* **Aars** *var.* Års. Nordjylland, N Denmark *56.49N 9.31E*
101 *I17* **Aarschot** Vlaams Brabant, C Belgium *50.58N 4.49E*
Aassi, Nahr el *see* Orontes
Aat *see* Ath
166 *G7* **Aba** *prev.* Ngawa. Sichuan, C China *32.51N 101.46E*
79 *V17* **Aba** Abia, S Nigeria *5.06N 7.22E*
81 *P16* **Aba** Orientale, NE Dem. Rep. Congo *3.52N 30.13E*
146 *J6* **Abā al Qazāz, Bi'r** *well* NW Saudi Arabia *26.37N 36.50E*
Abā as Su'ūd *see* Najrān
61 *G14* **Abacaxis, Rio** ≈ NW Brazil
Abaco Island *see* Great Abaco/Little Abaco
Abaco Island *see* Great Abaco, N Bahamas
148 *K10* **Ābādān** Khūzestān, SW Iran *30.24N 48.18E*
149 *O10* **Ābādeh** Fārs, C Iran *31.10N 52.39E*
76 *H8* **Abadla** W Algeria *31.04N 2.39W*
61 *M20* **Abaeté** Minas Gerais, SE Brazil *19.10S 45.24W*
Abag Qi *see* Xin Hot
64 *P7* **Abaí** Caazapá, S Paraguay *25.58S 55.54W*
203 *O2* **Abaiang** *var.* Apia; *prev.* Charlotte Island. *atoll* Tungaru, W Kiribati
Abaj *see* Abay
79 *U15* **Abaji** Federal Capital District, C Nigeria *8.35N 6.54E*
39 *O7* **Abajo Peak** ▲ Utah, W USA *37.51N 109.28W*
79 *V16* **Abakaliki** Ebonyi, SE Nigeria *6.18N 8.07E*
126 *Hh15* **Abakan** Respublika Khakasiya, S Russian Federation *53.43N 91.25E*
126 *Hh15* **Abakan** ≈ S Russian Federation
79 *S11* **Abala** Tillabéri, SW Niger *14.55N 3.27E*
79 *U* **Abalak** Tahoua, C Niger *15.28N 6.18E*
121 *N14* **Abalyanka** *Rus.* Obolyanka. ≈ N Belarus
126 *Ii14* **Aban** Krasnoyarskiy Kray, S Russian Federation *56.41N 96.04E*
149 *P9* **Āb Anbār-e Kān Sorkh** Yazd, C Iran *31.22N 53.37E*
59 *G16* **Abancay** Apurímac, SE Peru *13.37S 72.52W*
202 *H2* **Abaokoro** *atoll* Tungaru, W Kiribati
Abariringa *see* Kanton
149 *P10* **Abarkū** Yazd, C Iran
172 *Qq5* **Abashiri** *var.* Abasiri. Hokkaidō, NE Japan *44.00N 144.15E*
172 *Q6* **Abashiri-gawa** ≈ Hokkaidō, NE Japan
172 *Q5* **Abashiri-ko** ◎ Hokkaidō, NE Japan
Abasiri *see* Abashiri
43 *P10* **Abasolo** Tamaulipas, C Mexico *24.02N 98.18W*
194 *L16* **Abau** Central, S PNG *10.09S 148.40E*
151 *R10* **Abay** *var.* Abaj. Karaganda, C Kazakhstan *49.34N 72.54E*
83 *I15* **Ābaya Hāyk'** *Eng.* Lake Margherita, *It.* Abbaia. ◎ SW Ethiopia
Ābay Wenz *see* Blue Nile
126 *Hh15* **Abaza** Respublika Khakasiya, S Russian Federation *52.40N 89.58E*
Abbaia *see* Ābaya Hāyk'
149 *Q13* **Āb Bārīk** Fārs, S Iran
109 *C18* **Abbasanta** Sardegna, Italy, C Mediterranean Sea *40.08N 8.49E*
Abbatis Villa *see* Abbeville
32 *M3* **Abbaye, Point** *headland* Michigan, N USA *46.58N 88.08W*
Abbazia *see* Opatija
Abbé, Lake *see* Abhe, Lake
105 *N2* **Abbeville** *anc.* Abbatis Villa. Somme, N France *50.06N 1.50E*
25 *R7* **Abbeville** Alabama, S USA *31.34N 85.16W*
25 *U6* **Abbeville** Georgia, SE USA *31.58N 83.18W*
24 *I9* **Abbeville** Louisiana, S USA *29.58N 92.08W*
23 *P12* **Abbeville** South Carolina, SE USA *34.10N 82.22W*
99 *B20* **Abbeyfeale** *Ir.* Mainistir na Féile. SW Ireland *52.24N 9.21W*
108 *D8* **Abbiategrasso** Lombardia, NW Italy *45.24N 9.04E*
95 *I14* **Abborrträsk** Norrbotten, N Sweden *65.24N 19.33E*
204 *J9* **Abbot Ice Shelf** *ice shelf* Antarctica
8 *M17* **Abbotsford** British Columbia, SW Canada *49.01N 122.18W*
32 *K6* **Abbotsford** Wisconsin, N USA *44.57N 90.19W*
155 *U5* **Abbottābād** North-West Frontier Province, NW Pakistan *34.08N 73.10E*
121 *M14* **Abchuha** *Rus.* Obchuga. Minskaya Voblasts', NW Belarus *54.30N 29.23E*
100 *I10* **Abcoude** Utrecht, C Netherlands *52.16N 4.58E*
145 *N2* **'Abd al 'Azīz, Jabal** ▲▲ NE Syria
147 *U17* **'Abd al Kūrī** *island* SE Yemen
145 *Z13* **'Abd Allāh, Khawr** *bay* Iraq/Kuwait
131 *U6* **Abdulino** Orenburgskaya Oblast', W Russian Federation *53.37N 53.39E*
80 *J10* **Abéché** *var.* Abécher, Abeshr. Ouaddaï, SE Chad *13.49N 20.49E*
Abécher *see* Abéché
149 *S8* **Āb-e Garm va Sard** Yazd, E Iran
79 *R8* **Abeïbara** Kidal, NE Mali *19.07N 1.52E*
107 *P5* **Abejar** Castilla-León, N Spain *41.48N 2.46W*
56 *E9* **Abejorral** Antioquia, W Colombia *5.52N 75.34W*
Abela *see* Ávila
Abellinum *see* Avellino
94 *Q2* **Abeløya** *island* Kong Karls Land, E Svalbard
82 *I13* **Ābeltī** Oromo, C Ethiopia *8.09N 37.31E*
203 *O2* **Abemama** *var.* Apamama; *prev.* Roger Simpson Island. *atoll* Tungaru, W Kiribati
176 *Yy14* **Abemaree** *var.* Abemarre. Papua, E Indonesia *7.03S 140.10E*
79 *O16* **Abengourou** E Ivory Coast *6.42N 3.27W*
Åbenrå *see* Aabenraa
103 *L22* **Abens** ≈ SE Germany
79 *S16* **Abeokuta** Ogun, SW Nigeria *7.07N 3.21E*
99 *I20* **Aberaeron** SW Wales, UK *52.15N 4.15W*
Aberbrothock *see* Arbroath
Abercorn *see* Mbala
31 *R6* **Abercrombie** North Dakota, N USA *46.25N 96.42W*
191 *T7* **Aberdeen** New South Wales, SE Australia *32.09S 150.55E*
9 *T15* **Aberdeen** Saskatchewan, S Canada *52.15N 106.19W*
85 *H25* **Aberdeen** Eastern Cape, S South Africa *32.30S 24.00E*
98 *L9* **Aberdeen** *anc.* Devana. NE Scotland, UK *57.10N 2.04W*
23 *X2* **Aberdeen** Maryland, NE USA *39.28N 76.09W*
25 *N3* **Aberdeen** Mississippi, S USA *33.49N 88.32W*
23 *T10* **Aberdeen** North Carolina, SE USA *35.07N 79.25W*
31 *P8* **Aberdeen** South Dakota, N USA *45.27N 98.29W*
34 *F8* **Aberdeen** Washington, NW USA *46.57N 123.48W*
98 *K9* **Aberdeen** *cultural region* NE Scotland, UK
15 *K6* **Aberdeen Lake** ◎ Nunavut, NE Canada
98 *J10* **Aberfeldy** C Scotland, UK *56.38N 3.48W*
99 *K21* **Abergavenny** *anc.* Gobannium. SE Wales, UK *51.50N 3.00W*
Abergwaun *see* Fishguard
Abermarre *see* Abemaree
27 *N5* **Abernathy** Texas, SW USA *33.49N 101.50W*
Abersee *see* Wolfgangsee
Abertawe *see* Swansea
Aberteifi *see* Cardigan
34 *I15* **Abert, Lake** ◎ Oregon, NW USA
99 *I20* **Aberystwyth** W Wales, UK *52.25N 4.04W*
Abeshr *see* Abéché
Ábeskovvu *see* Abisko
108 *F10* **Abetone** Toscana, C Italy *44.09N 10.42E*
129 *V5* **Abez'** Respublika Komi, NW Russian Federation *66.32N 61.41E*
148 *M5* **Āb Garm** Qazvin, N Iran
147 *N12* **Abhā** 'Asīr, SW Saudi Arabia *18.16N 42.31E*
148 *M5* **Abhar** Zanjān, NW Iran *36.07N 49.19E*
Abhé Bad/Ābhē Bid Hāyk' *see* Abhe, Lake
82 *K12* **Abhe, Lake** *var.* Lake Abbé, *Amh.* Ābhē Bid Hāyk', *Som.* Abhé Bad. ◎ Djibouti/Ethiopia
79 *V17* **Abia** ◐ *state* SE Nigeria
145 *V9* **'Abīd 'Alī** E Iraq *32.20N 45.58E*
121 *O17* **Abidavichy** *Rus.* Obidovichi. Mahilyowskaya Voblasts', E Belarus *53.21N 30.24E*
117 *L15* **Abide** Çanakkale, NW Turkey *40.04N 26.13E*
79 *N17* **Abidjan** S Ivory Coast *5.19N 4.01W*
Āb-i-Istāda *see* Īstādeh-ye Moqor, Āb-e-
29 *N4* **Abilene** Kansas, C USA *38.55N 97.12W*
27 *Q7* **Abilene** Texas, SW USA *32.27N 99.43W*
Abindonia *see* Abingdon
99 *M21* **Abingdon** *anc.* Abindonia. S England, UK *51.40N 1.16W*
32 *K12* **Abingdon** Illinois, N USA *40.48N 90.24W*
23 *P8* **Abingdon** Virginia, NE USA *36.42N 81.58W*
Abingdon *see* Pinta, Isla
20 *J15* **Abington** Pennsylvania, NE USA *40.06N 75.05W*
130 *K14* **Abinsk** Krasnodarskiy Kray, SW Russian Federation *44.51N 38.12E*
39 *R9* **Abiquiu Reservoir** ⊠ New Mexico, SW USA
94 *I10* **Abisko** *Lapp.* Ábeskovvu. Norrbotten, N Sweden *68.21N 18.49E*
10 *G12* **Abitibi** ≈ Ontario, S Canada
10 *H12* **Abitibi, Lac** ◎ Ontario/Québec, S Canada
82 *J10* **Ābīy Ādī** Tigray, N Ethiopia *13.40N 38.57E*
120 *H6* **Abja-Paluoja** Viljandimaa, S Estonia *58.07N 25.19E*
143 *Q8* **Abkhazia** ◐ *autonomous republic* NW Georgia
190 *F1* **Abminga** South Australia *26.07S 134.49E*
77 *W9* **Abnûb** C Egypt *27.18N 31.09E*
Åbo *see* Turku
158 *G9* **Abohar** Punjab, N India *30.10N 74.12E*
79 *O17* **Aboisso** SE Ivory Coast *5.27N 3.06W*
80 *H5* **Abo, Massif d'** ▲▲ NW Chad
79 *R16* **Abomey** S Benin *7.14N 2.00E*
81 *F16* **Abong Mbang** Est, SE Cameroon *3.58N 13.10E*
113 *L23* **Abony** Pest, C Hungary *47.10N 20.00E*
80 *J11* **Abou-Déïa** Salamat, SE Chad *11.30N 19.18E*
Aboudouhour *see* Abū aḍ Ḍuhūr
Abou Kémal *see* Abū Kamāl
Abou Simbel *see* Abu Simbel
143 *T12* **Abovyan** C Armenia *40.16N 44.33E*
179 *P8* **Abra** ≈ Luzon, N Philippines
147 *P15* **Abrād, Wādī** *seasonal river* W Yemen
Abraham Bay *see* The Carlton
106 *G10* **Abrantes** *var.* Abrántes. Santarém, C Portugal *39.28N 8.12W*
64 *J4* **Abra Pampa** Jujuy, N Argentina *22.46S 65.40W*
Abrashlare *see* Brezovo
56 *G7* **Abrego** Norte de Santander, N Colombia *8.07N 73.15W*
Abrene *see* Pytalovo
42 *C7* **Abreojos, Punta** *headland* W Mexico *26.43N 113.36W*
67 *J16* **Abrolhos Bank** *undersea feature* W Atlantic Ocean
121 *H19* **Abrova** *Rus.* Obrovo. Brestskaya Voblasts', SW Belarus *52.30N 25.31E*
118 *G11* **Abrud** *Ger.* Gross-Schlatten, *Hung.* Abrudbánya. Alba, SW Romania *46.15N 23.07E*
Abrudbánya *see* Abrud
120 *E6* **Abruka** *island* SW Estonia
109 *J15* **Abruzzese, Appennino** ▲▲ C Italy
109 *J14* **Abruzzo** ◐ *region* C Italy
147 *N14* **'Abs** *var.* Sūq 'Abs. W Yemen *16.42N 42.55E*
35 *T12* **Absaroka Range** ▲▲ Montana/Wyoming, NW USA
143 *Z11* **Abşeron Yarımadası** *Rus.* Apsheronskiy Poluostrov. *peninsula* E Azerbaijan
149 *N6* **Āb Shīrīn** Eşfahān, C Iran
145 *X10* **Abtān** SE Iraq *31.37N 47.06E*
111 *R6* **Abtenau** Salzburg, NW Austria *47.33N 13.21E*
170 *Dd12* **Abu** Yamaguchi, Honshū, SW Japan *34.30N 131.26E*
158 *E14* **Ābu** Rājasthān, N India *24.40N 72.49E*
144 *I4* **Abū aḍ Ḍuhūr** *Fr.* Aboudouhour. Idlib, NW Syria *35.30N 37.00E*
149 *P17* **Abū al Abyaḍ** *island* C UAE
144 *K10* **Abū al Ḩuşayn, Khabrat** ◎ N Jordan
145 *R8* **Abū al Jīr** C Iraq *33.16N 42.55E*
145 *Y12* **Abū al Khaşīb** *var.* Abul Khasib. SE Iraq *30.26N 48.00E*
145 *U12* **Abū at Tubrah, Thaqb** *well* S Iraq *30.54N 45.02E*
77 *V11* **Abu Balâs** ▲ SW Egypt *24.28N 27.36E*
Abu Dhabi *see* Abū Z̧aby
145 *R8* **Abū Farūkh** C Iraq *33.06N 43.18E*
82 *C12* **Abu Gabra** Southern Darfur, W Sudan *11.01N 26.49E*
145 *P10* **Abū Ghār, Sha'īb** *dry watercourse* S Iraq
82 *G7* **Abu Hamed** River Nile, N Sudan *19.31N 33.19E*
145 *O5* **Abū Ḩardān** *var.* Hajîne. Dayr az Zawr, E Syria *34.45N 40.49E*
145 *T7* **Abū Ḩāssawīyah** E Iraq *33.52N 44.47E*
144 *K10* **Abū Ḩifnah, Wādī** *dry watercourse* N Jordan
79 *V15* **Abuja** ● (Nigeria) Federal Capital District, C Nigeria *9.04N 7.28E*
145 *R9* **Abū Jahaf, Wādī** *dry watercourse* C Iraq
58 *F12* **Abujao, Río** ≈ E Peru
145 *U12* **Abū Jasrah** S Iraq *30.43N 44.50E*
145 *O6* **Abū Kamāl** *Fr.* Abou Kémal. Dayr az Zawr, E Syria *34.28N 40.55E*
175 *Q11* **Abuki, Pegunungan** ▲▲ Sulawesi, C Indonesia
171 *Ll14* **Abukuma-gawa** ≈ Honshū, C Japan
171 *Ll15* **Abukuma-sanchi** ▲▲ Honshū, C Japan
Abula *see* Ávila
Abul Khasib *see* Abū al Khaşīb
81 *K16* **Abumombazi** *var.* Abumonbazi. Equateur, N Dem. Rep. Congo *3.43N 22.06E*
Abumonbazi *see* Abumombazi
61 *D15* **Abunã** Rondônia, W Brazil *9.40S 65.19W*
58 *K13* **Abunã, Rio** *var.* Río Abuná. ≈ Bolivia/Brazil
144 *G10* **Abū Nuşayr** *var.* Abu Nuseir. Al 'Āşimah, W Jordan *32.03N 35.58E*
Abu Nuseir *see* Abū Nuşayr
145 *T12* **Abū Qabr** S Iraq *31.03N 44.34E*
144 *K5* **Abū Raḩbah, Jabal** ▲▲ C Syria
145 *S5* **Abū Rajāsh** N Iraq *34.47N 43.36E*
145 *W13* **Abū Raqrāq, Ghadīr** *well* S Iraq *30.15N 45.57E*
158 *E14* **Ābu Road** Rājasthān, N India *24.28N 72.46E*
82 *I6* **Abu Shagara, Ras** *headland* NE Sudan *18.04N 38.31E*
77 *W12* **Abu Simbel** *var.* Abou Simbel, Abū Sunbul. *ancient monument* S Egypt *22.25N 31.37E*
145 *U12* **Abū Sudayrah** S Iraq *30.55N 44.58E*
145 *T10* **Abū Şukhayr** S Iraq *31.54N 44.27E*

◆ COUNTRY   ◇ DEPENDENT TERRITORY   ◈ ADMINISTRATIVE REGION   ▲ MOUNTAIN   ▲ VOLCANO   ◎ LAKE
● COUNTRY CAPITAL   ○ DEPENDENT TERRITORY CAPITAL   ● ADMINISTRATIVE REGION CAPITAL   ▲ MOUNTAIN RANGE   ★ INTERNATIONAL AIRPORT   ↗ RIVER   ▨ RESERVOIR

AÏN TÉMOUCHENT – ALCOUTIM

76 H5 **Aïn Témouchent** N Algeria 35.18N 1.09W
194 H11 **Aiome** Madang, N PNG 5.04S 144.43E
Aïoun el Atrous/Aïoun el Atroûss see 'Ayoûn el 'Atroûs
56 E11 **Aipe** Huila, C Colombia 3.15N 75.16W
58 D9 **Aipena, Río** ~ N Peru
59 L19 **Aiquile** Cochabamba, C Bolivia 18.10S 65.10W
Aïr see Aïr, Massif de l'
196 E10 **Airai** Babeldaob, C Palau
196 E10 **Airai** ✈ (Oreor) Babeldaob, N Palau 7.22N 134.34E
173 Ff8 **Airbangis** Sumatera, NW Indonesia 0.12N 99.22E
9 Q16 **Airdrie** Alberta, SW Canada 51.20N 114.00W
98 I12 **Airdrie** S Scotland, UK 55.52N 3.58W
Air du Azbine see Aïr, Massif de l'
99 M17 **Aire** ~ N England, UK
104 K15 **Aire-sur-l'Adour** Landes, SW France 43.43N 0.16W
105 O1 **Aire-sur-la-Lys** Pas-de-Calais, N France 50.39N 2.24E
16 N2 **Air Force Island** island Baffin Island, Nunavut, NE Canada
174 L11 **Airhitam, Teluk** bay Borneo, C Indonesia
175 Rr7 **Airmadidi** Sulawesi, N Indonesia 1.25N 124.58E
79 V8 **Aïr, Massif de l'** var. Aïr, Air du Azbine, Asben. ▲ NC Niger
110 G10 **Airolo** Ticino, S Switzerland 46.32N 8.38E
104 K9 **Airvault** Deux-Sèvres, W France 46.51N 0.07W
103 K19 **Aisch** ~ S Germany
65 G20 **Aisén** off. Región Aisén del General Carlos Ibañez del Campo, var. Aysen. ◆ region S Chile
8 H7 **Aishihik Lake** ◎ Yukon Territory, W Canada
105 P3 **Aisne** ◆ department N France
105 R4 **Aisne** ~ NE France
111 T4 **Aist** ~ N Austria
116 K13 **Aisými** Anatolikí Makedonía kai Thráki, NE Greece 41.00N 25.55E
107 S11 **Aitana** ▲ E Spain 38.39N 0.15W
194 F9 **Aitape** var. Eitape. Sandaun, NW PNG 3.07S 142.22E
Aiti see Aichi
31 V6 **Aitkin** Minnesota, N USA 46.31N 93.42W
117 D18 **Aitolikó** var. Etoliko; prev. Aitolikón. Dytikí Ellás, C Greece 38.25N 21.21E
Aitolikón see Aitolikó
202 L15 **Aitutaki** island S Cook Islands
118 H11 **Aiud** Ger. Strassburg, Hung. Nagyenyed; prev. Engeten. Alba, SW Romania 46.16N 23.42E
120 I9 **Aiviekste** ~ C Latvia
201 Q8 **Aiwo** SW Nauru 0.32S 166.54E
196 E8 **Aiwokako Passage** passage Babeldaob, N Palau
Aix see Aix-en-Provence
105 S15 **Aix-en-Provence** var. Aix; anc. Aquae Sextiae. Bouches-du-Rhône, SE France 43.31N 5.27E
Aix-la-Chapelle see Aachen
105 T11 **Aix-les-Bains** Savoie, E France 45.40N 5.55E
194 E11 **Aiyang, Mount** ▲ NW PNG 5.03S 141.15E
Aiyina see Aígina
Aiyion see Aígio
159 W15 **Āīzawl** Mizoram, NE India 23.40N 92.45E
120 H9 **Aizkraukle** Aizkraukle, S Latvia 56.36N 25.06E
120 C9 **Aizpute** Liepāja, W Latvia 56.43N 21.32E
171 L14 **Aizu-Wakamatsu** var. Aizuwakamatu. Fukushima, Honshū, C Japan 37.27N 139.55E
Aizuwakamatu see Aizu-Wakamatsu
105 X15 **Ajaccio** Corse, France, C Mediterranean Sea 41.54N 8.43E
105 X15 **Ajaccio, Golfe d'** gulf Corse, France, C Mediterranean Sea
43 Q15 **Ajalpán** Puebla, S Mexico 18.25N 97.19W
160 F13 **Ajanta Range** ▲▲ C India
143 R10 **Ajaria** ◆ autonomous republic SW Georgia
Ajastan see Armenia
95 G14 **Ajaureforsen** Västerbotten, N Sweden 65.31N 15.43E
193 H17 **Ajax, Mount** ▲ South Island, NZ 42.34S 172.06E
168 F9 **Aj Bogd Uul** ▲ SW Mongolia 44.49N 95.01E
77 R8 **Ajdābiyā** var. Agedabia, Ajdābiyah. NE Libya 30.46N 20.13E
Ajdābiyah see Ajdābiyā
111 S12 **Ajdovščina** Ger. Haidenschaft, It. Aidussina. W Slovenia 45.52N 13.55E
171 Mm8 **Ajigasawa** Aomori, Honshū, C Japan 40.45N 140.11E
Ajjinena see El Geneina
113 H23 **Ajka** Veszprém, W Hungary 47.07N 17.31E
144 G9 **'Ajlūn** Irbid, N Jordan 32.19N 35.45E
144 H9 **'Ajlūn, Jabal** ▲▲ W Jordan
Ajluokta see Drag
149 R15 **'Ajmān** var. Ajman, 'Ujmān. 'Ajmān, NE UAE 25.36N 55.42E
158 G12 **Ajmer** var. Ajmere. Rājasthān, N India 26.28N 74.40E
38 J15 **Ajo** Arizona, SW USA 32.22N 112.51W
107 N2 **Ajo, Cabo de** headland N Spain 43.31N 3.36W
38 J16 **Ajo Range** ▲▲ Arizona, SW USA
152 C14 **Ajyguýy** Rus. Adzhikui. Balkan Welaýaty, W Turkmenistan 39.46N 53.57E
Akaba see Al 'Aqabah
172 P5 **Akabira** Hokkaidō, NE Japan 43.31N 142.03E
171 K12 **Akadomari** Niigata, Sado, C Japan 37.54N 138.24E
83 E20 **Akagera** var. Kagera. ~ Rwanda/Tanzania see also Kagera
203 W16 **Akahanga, Punta** headland Easter Island, Chile, E Pacific Ocean
171 Ii16 **Akaishi-dake** ▲ Honshū, S Japan 35.26N 138.09E
171 J16 **Akaishi-sanmyaku** ▲▲ Honshū, S Japan
82 J13 **Āk'ak'i** Oromo, C Ethiopia 8.50N 38.51E
161 G15 **Akalkot** Mahārāshtra, W India 17.36N 76.10E
Akamagaseki see Shimonoseki
172 Q7 **Akan** Hokkaidō, NE Japan 43.09N 144.08E
172 Q6 **Akan-ko** ◎ Hokkaidō, NE Japan
Akanthoú see Tatlısu
193 I19 **Akaroa** Canterbury, South Island, NZ 43.48S 172.58E
82 E6 **Akasha** Northern, N Sudan 21.03N 30.45E
170 G14 **Akashi** var. Akasi. Hyōgo, Honshū, SW Japan 34.37N 134.59E
145 N7 **'Akāsh, Wādī** var. Wādī 'Ukash. dry watercourse W Iraq
Akasi see Akashi
94 K11 **Äkäsjokisuu** Lappi, N Finland 67.28N 23.44E
143 S11 **Akbaba Dağı** ▲ Armenia/Turkey 41.04N 43.28E
Akbük Limanı see Güllük Körfezi
131 V8 **Akbulak** Orenburgskaya Oblast', W Russian Federation 51.01N 55.35E
143 O11 **Akçaabat** Trabzon, NE Turkey 41.00N 39.36E
143 N15 **Akçadağ** Malatya, C Turkey 38.21N 37.58E
142 G11 **Akçakoca** Bolu, NW Turkey 41.04N 31.07E
Akchakaya, Vpadina see Akdzhakaya, Vpadina
78 H7 **Akchâr** desert W Mauritania
151 S12 **Akchatau** Kaz. Aqshataū. Karaganda, C Kazakhstan 47.58N 74.01E
142 L13 **Akdağlar** ▲▲ C Turkey
142 E17 **Ak Dağları** ▲▲ SW Turkey
142 K13 **Akdağmadeni** Yozgat, C Turkey 39.39N 35.48E
152 G8 **Akdepe** prev. Ak-Tepe, Leninsk, Turkm. Lenin. Daşoguz Welaýaty, N Turkmenistan 42.10N 59.17E
Ak-Dere see Byala
124 O3 **Akdoğan** Gk. Lýsi. C Cyprus 35.06N 33.42E
126 Hh16 **Ak-Dovurak** Respublika Tyva, S Russian Federation 51.09N 90.36E
152 F9 **Akdzhakaya, Vpadina** var. Vpadina Akchakaya. depression N Turkmenistan
175 Tt7 **Akelamo** Pulau Halmahera, E Indonesia 1.27N 128.39E
Aken see Aachen
Akermanceaster see Bath
97 P15 **Åkersberga** Stockholm, C Sweden 59.28N 18.19E
97 H15 **Akershus** ◆ county S Norway
81 L16 **Aketi** Orientale, N Dem. Rep. Congo 2.46N 23.42E
152 C10 **Akgyr Erezi** Rus. Gryada Akkyr. hill range NW Turkmenistan
Akhalskiy Velayat see Ahal Welaýaty
143 S10 **Akhalts'ikhe** SW Georgia 41.38N 43.03E
Akhangaran see Ohangaron
Akharnaí see Acharnés
77 R7 **Akhḑar, Al Jabal al** hill range NE Libya
Akhelóös see Achelóos
41 Q15 **Akhiok** Kodiak Island, Alaska, USA 56.57N 154.12W
142 C13 **Akhisar** Manisa, W Turkey 38.54N 27.49E
77 X10 **Akhmīm** anc. Panopolis. C Egypt 26.43N 31.50E
158 H6 **Akhnūr** Jammu and Kashmir, NW India 32.57N 74.43E
Akhsu see Ağsu
131 P11 **Akhtuba** ~ SW Russian Federation
131 P11 **Akhtubinsk** Astrakhanskaya Oblast', SW Russian Federation 48.16N 46.13E
Akhtyrka see Okhtyrka
170 F15 **Aki** Kōchi, Shikoku, SW Japan 33.30N 133.54E
41 N12 **Akiachak** Alaska, USA 60.54N 161.25W
41 N12 **Akiak** Alaska, USA 60.54N 161.12W
203 X11 **Akiaki** atoll Îles Tuamotu, E French Polynesia
10 H9 **Akimiski Island** island Nunavut, C Canada
142 K17 **Akıncı Burnu** headland S Turkey 36.21N 35.47E
Akıncılar see Selçuk
119 U10 **Akinovka** Zaporiz'ka Oblast', S Ukraine
Akirkeby see Aakirkeby
171 M10 **Akita** Akita, Honshū, C Japan 39.44N 140.06E
171 M10 **Akita** off. Akita-ken. ◆ prefecture Honshū, C Japan
78 H8 **Akjoujt** prev. Fort-Repoux. Inchiri, W Mauritania 19.42N 14.28W
94 H11 **Akka** Lapp. Áhkká. ▲ N Sweden
94 H11 **Akkajaure** ◎ N Sweden
Akkala see Oqqal'a
161 L25 **Akkaraipattu** Eastern Province, E Sri Lanka 7.13N 81.51E
151 P13 **Akkense** Karaganda, C Kazakhstan 46.39N 68.06E
Akkerman see Bilhorod-Dnistrovs'kyy
131 W8 **Akkermanovka** Orenburgskaya Oblast', W Russian Federation 51.11N 58.03E
172 Qq7 **Akkeshi** Hokkaidō, NE Japan 43.03N 144.48E
172 Qq7 **Akkeshi-ko** ◎ Hokkaidō, NE Japan
172 Qq8 **Akkeshi-wan** bay NW Pacific Ocean
144 F8 **'Akko** Eng. Acre, Fr. Saint-Jean-d'Acre; Bibl. Accho, Ptolemaïs. Northern, N Israel 32.55N 35.04E
151 Q8 **Akkol'** Kaz. Aqköl; prev. Alekseyevka, Kaz. Alekseevka. Akmola, C Kazakhstan 51.58N 70.58E
151 T14 **Akkol'** Kaz. Aqköl. Almaty, SE Kazakhstan 45.01N 75.38E
151 Q16 **Akkol'** Kaz. Aqköl. Zhambyl, S Kazakhstan 43.25N 70.46E
150 M11 **Akkol', Ozero** prev. Ozero Zhaman-Akkol'. ◎ C Kazakhstan
100 L6 **Akkrum** Friesland, N Netherlands 53.01N 5.52E
151 U8 **Akku** prev. Lebyazh'ye. Pavlodar, NE Kazakhstan 51.29N 77.48E
150 F12 **Akkystau** Kaz. Aqqystaū. Atyrau, SW Kazakhstan 47.13N 51.01E
14 Ff3 **Aklavik** Northwest Territories, NW Canada 68.15N 135.01W
Akmenrags see Akmensrags
120 B9 **Akmensrags** prev. Akmenrags. headland W Latvia 56.49N 21.03E
164 E9 **Akmeqit** Xinjiang Uygur Zizhiqu, NW China 37.10N 76.59E
152 J14 **Akmeydan** Mary Welaýaty, C Turkmenistan 37.50N 62.08E
Akmola see Astana
151 P9 **Akmola** off. Akmolinskaya Oblast', Kaz. Aqmola Oblysy; prev. Tselinogradskaya Oblast. ◆ province C Kazakhstan
Akmolinsk see Astana
Akmolinskaya Oblast' see Akmola
Aknavásár see Târgu Ocna
120 I11 **Aknīste** Jēkabpils, S Latvia 56.09N 25.43E
170 G14 **Akō** Hyōgo, Honshū, SW Japan 34.44N 134.22E
83 G14 **Akobo** Jonglei, SE Sudan 7.49N 33.04E
83 G14 **Akobo** var. Åkobowenz. ~ Ethiopia/Sudan
Åkobowenz see Akobo
160 H12 **Akola** Mahārāshtra, C India 20.44N 77.00E
Akordat see Akurdet
79 Q16 **Akosombo Dam** dam SE Ghana 6.23N 0.06E
160 H12 **Akot** Mahārāshtra, C India 20.45N 77.00E
79 N16 **Akoupé** SE Ivory Coast 6.19N 3.54W
10 M3 **Akpatok Island** island Nunavut, E Canada
164 G7 **Akqi** Xinjiang Uygur Zizhiqu, NW China 40.51N 78.20E
144 I2 **Akrād, Jabal al** ▲ N Syria
Akragas see Agrigento
94 H3 **Akranes** Vesturland, W Iceland 64.19N 22.01W
145 S2 **Ākrē** Ar. 'Aqrah. N Iraq 36.46N 43.52E
97 C16 **Åkrehamn** Rogaland, S Norway 59.15N 5.12E
79 V9 **Akréréb** Agadez, C Niger 17.45N 9.01E
117 D22 **Akrítas, Akrotírio** headland S Greece 36.43N 21.52E
39 V3 **Akron** Colorado, C USA 40.09N 103.12W
31 R12 **Akron** Iowa, C USA 42.49N 96.33W
33 U12 **Akron** Ohio, N USA 41.04N 81.31W
Akrotiri see Akrotírion
Akrotiri Bay see Akrotírion, Kólpos
124 N4 **Akrotírion** var. Akrotiri. UK air base S Cyprus 34.36N 32.57E
124 Nn4 **Akrotírion, Kólpos** var. Akrotiri Bay. bay S Cyprus
123 Mm4 **Akrotiri Sovereign Base Area** UK military installation S Cyprus 34.34N 32.58E
164 F11 **Aksai Chin** Chin. Aksayqin. disputed region China/India
Aksaj see Aksay
142 I15 **Aksaray** Aksaray, C Turkey 38.23N 33.50E
142 I15 **Aksaray** ◆ province C Turkey
150 G8 **Aksay** var. Aksaj, Kaz. Aqsay. Zapadnyy Kazakhstan, NW Kazakhstan 51.10N 53.03E
131 O11 **Aksay** Volgogradskaya Oblast', SW Russian Federation 47.59N 43.54E
153 W10 **Aksay** var. Toxkan He. ~ China/Kyrgyzstan
Aksay/Aksay Kazakskiy Zizhixian see Boluozhuanjing/Hongliuwan
Aksayqin see Aksai Chin
164 G11 **Aksayqin Hu** ◎ NW China
142 G14 **Akşehir** Konya, W Turkey 38.22N 31.24E
142 G14 **Akşehir Gölü** ◎ C Turkey
142 G16 **Akseki** Antalya, SW Turkey 37.03N 31.46E
126 L15 **Aksenovo-Zilovskoye** Chitinskaya Oblast', S Russian Federation 53.01N 117.26E
126 Kk16 **Aksha** Chitinskaya Oblast', S Russian Federation 50.16N 113.22E
151 V11 **Akshatau, Khrebet** ▲▲ E Kazakhstan
153 Y8 **Ak-Shyyrak** Issyk-Kul'skaya Oblast', E Kyrgyzstan 41.46N 78.34E
Akstafa see Ağstafa
164 H7 **Aksu** Xinjiang Uygur Zizhiqu, NW China 41.16N 80.15E
151 R8 **Aksu** Kaz. Aqsū. Akmola, N Kazakhstan 52.31N 72.00E
151 T8 **Aksu** var. Jermak, Kaz. Ermak; prev. Yermak. Pavlodar, NE Kazakhstan 52.03N 76.55E
151 W13 **Aksu** Kaz. Aqsū. Almaty, SE Kazakhstan 45.31N 79.28E
151 V13 **Aksu** Kaz. Aqsū. ~ SE Kazakhstan
151 X11 **Aksuat** Kaz. Aqsūat. Vostochnyy Kazakhstan, E Kazakhstan 47.46N 82.49E
151 Y11 **Aksuat** Kaz. Aqsūat. Vostochnyy Kazakhstan, SE Kazakhstan 48.16N 83.39E
131 S4 **Aksubayevo** Respublika Tatarstan, W Russian Federation 54.52N 50.50E
164 H7 **Aksu He** Rus. Sary-Dzhaz. ~ China/Kyrgyzstan see also Sary-Dzhaz
82 J10 **Āksum** Tigray, N Ethiopia 14.06N 38.42E
151 O12 **Aktas** Kaz. Aqtas. Karaganda, C Kazakhstan 48.03N 66.21E
Aktash see Oqtosh
153 V9 **Ak-Tash, Gora** ▲ C Kyrgyzstan 40.53N 74.39E
151 R10 **Aktau** Kaz. Aqtaū. Karaganda, C Kazakhstan 50.13N 73.06E
150 E11 **Aktau** Kaz. Aqtaū; prev. Shevchenko. Mangistau, W Kazakhstan 43.37N 51.13E
Aktau, Khrebet see Oqtogh, SW Tajikistan
Aktau, Khrebet see Oqtov Tizmasi, C Uzbekistan
Akte see Ágion Óros
Ak-Tepe see Akdepe
153 X7 **Ak-Terek** Issyk-Kul'skaya Oblast', E Kyrgyzstan 42.14N 77.46E
Aktí see Ágion Óros
164 E8 **Akto** Xinjiang Uygur Zizhiqu, NW China 39.07N 75.43E
150 I10 **Aktobe** Kaz. Aqtöbe, prev. Aktyubinsk. Aktyubinsk, NW Kazakhstan 50.18N 57.09E
151 V12 **Aktogay** Kaz. Aqtoghay. Vostochnyy Kazakhstan, E Kazakhstan 46.56N 79.40E
121 M18 **Aktsyabrski** Rus. Oktyabr'skiy; prev. Karpilovka. Homyel'skaya Voblasts', SE Belarus 52.37N 28.52E
Aktyubinsk see Aktobe
150 H11 **Aktyubinsk** off. Aktyubinskaya Oblast', Kaz. Aqtöbe Oblysy. ◆ province W Kazakhstan
Aktyubinsk see Aktobe
153 W7 **Ak-Tyuz** var. Aktyuz. Chuyskaya Oblast', N Kyrgyzstan 42.50N 76.05E
81 J17 **Akula** Equateur, NW Dem. Rep. Congo 2.21N 20.13E
170 Bb15 **Akune** Kagoshima, Kyūshū, SW Japan 31.59N 130.11E
40 L16 **Akun Island** island Aleutian Islands, Alaska, USA
82 J9 **Akurdet** var. Agordat, Akordat. C Eritrea 15.33N 38.01E
79 T16 **Akure** Ondo, SW Nigeria 7.18N 5.12E
94 J2 **Akureyri** Nordhurland Eystra, N Iceland 65.40N 18.06W
40 L17 **Akutan** Akutan Island, Alaska, USA 54.08N 165.47W
40 K17 **Akutan Island** island Aleutian Islands, Alaska, USA
79 V17 **Akwa Ibom** ◆ state SE Nigeria
Akyab see Sittwe
131 W7 **Ak"yar** Respublika Bashkortostan, W Russian Federation 51.51N 58.13E
150 J10 **Akzhar** prev. Novorossiyskiy, Novorossiyskoye. Aktyubinsk, NW Kazakhstan 50.13N 57.57E
151 Y11 **Akzhar** Kaz. Aqzhar. Vostochnyy Kazakhstan, E Kazakhstan 47.36N 83.37E
96 F13 **Ål** Buskerud, S Norway 60.37N 8.34E
121 N18 **Ala** Rus. Ola. ~ SE Belarus
22 H11 **Alabama** off. State of Alabama; also known as Camellia State, Heart of Dixie, The Cotton State, Yellowhammer State. ◆ state S USA
25 P6 **Alabama River** ~ Alabama, S USA
25 P4 **Alabaster** Alabama, S USA 33.14N 86.49W
145 U10 **Al 'Abd Allāh** var. Al Abdullah. S Iraq 32.06N 45.08E
Al Abdullah see Al 'Abd Allāh
145 W14 **Al Abṭīyah** well S Iraq 29.27N 45.56E
153 S9 **Ala-Buka** Dzhalal-Abadskaya Oblast', W Kyrgyzstan 41.22N 71.27E
194 K15 **Alabule** ~ C PNG
142 J12 **Alaca** Çorum, N Turkey 40.10N 34.52E
142 K10 **Alaçam** Samsun, N Turkey 41.35N 35.37E
Alacant see Alicante
25 V10 **Alachua** Florida, SE USA 29.48N 82.29W
143 S13 **Aladağlar** ▲▲ W Turkey
142 K15 **Ala Dağları** ▲▲ C Turkey
131 O16 **Alagir** Respublika Severnaya Osetiya, SW Russian Federation 43.02N 44.10E
108 B6 **Alagna Valsesia** Valle d'Aosta, NW Italy 45.51N 7.50E
105 P12 **Alagnon** ~ C France
61 P16 **Alagoas** off. Estado de Alagoas. ◆ state E Brazil
61 P17 **Alagoinhas** Bahia, E Brazil 12.09S 38.21W
107 R5 **Alagón** Aragón, NE Spain 41.46N 1.07W
106 J9 **Alagón** ~ W Spain
95 K16 **Alahärmä** Länsi-Suomi, W Finland 63.15N 22.49E
al Ahdar see Al Akhḑar
Álahеaieatnu see Altaelva
148 K12 **Al Aḥmadī** var. Ahmadi. E Kuwait 29.02N 48.01E
Al Ain see Al 'Ayn
107 Z8 **Alaior** prev. Alayor. Menorca, Spain, W Mediterranean Sea 39.55N 4.07E
153 T11 **Alai Range** Rus. Alayskiy Khrebet. ▲▲ Kyrgyzstan/Tajikistan
Alais see Alès
147 X11 **Al 'Ajā'iz** E Oman 19.33N 57.12E
147 X11 **Al 'Ajā'iz** oasis SE Oman 19.40N 57.13E
95 L16 **Alajärvi** Länsi-Suomi, W Finland 63.00N 23.50E
120 K4 **Alajõe** Ida-Virumaa, NE Estonia 59.00N 27.26E
44 M13 **Alajuela** Alajuela, C Costa Rica 10.00N 84.12W
44 L12 **Alajuela** off. Provincia de Alajuela. ◆ province N Costa Rica
45 T14 **Alajuela, Lago** ◎ C Panama
40 M11 **Alakanuk** Alaska, USA 62.41N 164.37W
146 K5 **Al Akhḑar** var. al Ahdar. Tabūk, NW Saudi Arabia 28.04N 37.13E
Alaköl see Alakol', Ozero
151 X13 **Alakol', Ozero** Kaz. Alaköl. ◎ SE Kazakhstan
128 I5 **Alakurtti** Murmanskaya Oblast', NW Russian Federation 66.57N 30.27E
40 F10 **'Alalākeiki Channel** var. Alalakeiki Channel. channel Hawai'i, USA, C Pacific Ocean
Al 'Alamayn see El 'Alamein
145 R1 **Al 'Amādīyah** N Iraq 37.09N 43.27E
196 K5 **Alamagan** island C Northern Mariana Islands
145 X10 **Al 'Amārah** var. Amara. E Iraq 31.51N 47.10E
82 J11 **Ālamat'ā** Tigray, N Ethiopia 12.22N 39.32E
39 R11 **Alameda** New Mexico, SW USA 35.09N 106.37W
124 Pp15 **'Alam el Rûm, Râs** headland N Egypt 31.21N 27.23E
Alamícamba see Alamikamba
44 M8 **Alamikamba** var. Alamícamba. Región Autónoma Atlántico Norte, NE Nicaragua 13.29N 84.17W
26 K11 **Alamito Creek** ~ Texas, SW USA
42 M8 **Alamitos, Sierra de los** ▲ NE Mexico 26.15N 102.14W
37 X9 **Alamo** Nevada, W USA 37.21N 115.07W
22 F9 **Alamo** Tennessee, S USA 35.46N 89.07W
43 Q12 **Álamo** Veracruz-Llave, C Mexico 20.55N 97.40W
39 S14 **Alamogordo** New Mexico, SW USA 32.52N 105.57W
38 J12 **Alamo Lake** ⊠ Arizona, SW USA
42 H7 **Alamos** Sonora, NW Mexico 26.59N 108.53W
39 S7 **Alamosa** Colorado, C USA 37.25N 105.51W
95 J20 **Åland** var. Aland Islands, Fin. Ahvenanmaa. ◆ province SW Finland
95 J19 **Åland** Fin. Ahvenanmaa. island SW Finland
90 K9 **Åland** var. Aland Islands, Fin. Ahvenanmaa. island group SW Finland
Aland Islands see Åland
Aland Sea see Ålands Hav
97 Q14 **Ålands Hav** var. Aland Sea. strait Baltic Sea/Gulf of Bothnia
45 P16 **Alanje** Chiriquí, SW Panama 8.22N 82.36W
27 O2 **Alanreed** Texas, SW USA 35.12N 100.45W
142 G17 **Alanya** Antalya, S Turkey 36.31N 32.01E
25 U7 **Alapaha River** ~ Florida/Georgia, SE USA
125 Ee11 **Alapayevsk** Sverdlovskaya Oblast', C Russian Federation 57.48N 61.50E
Alappuzha see Alleppey
144 F14 **Al 'Aqabah** var. Akaba, Aqaba, 'Aqaba; anc. Aelana, Elath. Ma'ān, SW Jordan 29.32N 35.00E
Al 'Arabīyah as Su'ūdīyah see Saudi Arabia
al Araïch see Larache
107 Q10 **Alarcón** Castilla-La Mancha, C Spain 39.33N 2.04W
107 Q9 **Alarcón, Embalse de** ⊠ C Spain
144 J2 **Al 'Arīmah** Fr. Arime. Ḥalab, N Syria 36.27N 37.41E
Al 'Arīsh see El 'Arîsh
147 P6 **Al Arṭāwīyah** Ar Riyāḑ, N Saudi Arabia 26.33N 45.19E
175 O16 **Alas** Sumbawa, S Indonesia 8.27S 117.04E
Alasca, Golfo de see Alaska, Gulf of
142 D14 **Alaşehir** Manisa, W Turkey 38.19N 28.30E
145 N5 **Al 'Ashārah** var. Ashara. Dayr az Zawr, E Syria 34.51N 40.36E
144 H10 **Al 'Āṣimah** prev. Muḥāfaẓat 'Ammān. ◆ governorate NW Jordan
Al Ashkhara see Al Ashkharah
147 Z9 **Al Ashkharah** var. Al Ashkhara. NE Oman 21.46N 59.30E
41 P8 **Alaska** off. State of Alaska; also known as Land of the Midnight Sun, The Last Frontier, Seward's Folly; prev. Russian America. ◆ state NW USA
41 T13 **Alaska, Gulf of** var. Golfo de Alasca. gulf Canada/USA
41 O15 **Alaska Peninsula** peninsula Alaska, USA
41 Q11 **Alaska Range** ▲▲ Alaska, USA
173 Ee4 **Alas, Lae** ~ Sumatera, NW Indonesia
Al-Asnam see Chlef
175 O16 **Alas, Selat** strait Nusa Tenggara, C Indonesia
108 B10 **Alassio** Liguria, NW Italy 44.01N 8.12E
Alat see Olot
143 Y12 **Ālāt** Rus. Alyat; prev. Alyaty-Pristan'. SE Azerbaijan 39.57N 49.24E
145 T13 **Al 'Athāmīn** S Iraq 30.27N 43.40E
41 P7 **Alatna River** ~ Alaska, USA
109 J15 **Alatri** Lazio, C Italy 41.43N 13.21E
Alattio see Alta
131 P5 **Alatyr'** Chavash Respubliki, W Russian Federation 54.50N 46.28E
58 C7 **Alausí** Chimborazo, C Ecuador 2.07S 78.44W
107 O3 **Álava** Basq. Araba. ◆ province País Vasco, N Spain
143 T11 **Alaverdi** N Armenia 41.06N 44.37E
Alavo see Alavus
95 N14 **Ala-Vuokki** Oulu, E Finland 64.46N 29.29E
95 K17 **Alavus** Swe. Alavo. Länsi-Suomi, W Finland 62.33N 23.38E
Al 'Awābī see Awābī
145 P6 **Al 'Awānī** W Iraq 34.28N 41.43E
Al Awaynāt see Al 'Uwaynāt
190 K9 **Alawoona** South Australia 34.45S 140.28E
Alaykel'/Alay-Kuu see Këk-Art
149 R17 **Al 'Ayn** var. Al Ain. Abū Ẓaby, E UAE 24.13N 55.44E
149 R17 **Al 'Ayn** var. Al Ain. ✈ Abū Ẓaby, E UAE 24.16N 55.31E
144 G12 **Al 'Aynā** Al Karak, W Jordan 30.59N 35.43E
Alayor see Alaior
Alayskiy Khrebet see Alai Range
127 N7 **Alazeya** ~ NE Russian Federation
145 U8 **Al 'Azīzīyah** var. Aziziya. E Iraq 32.54N 45.05E
123 L14 **Al 'Azīzīyah** NW Libya 32.31N 13.01E
144 I10 **Al Azraq al Janūbī** Az Zarqā', N Jordan 31.49N 36.48E
108 B9 **Alba** anc. Alba Pompeia. Piemonte, NW Italy 44.40N 8.01E
27 V6 **Alba** Texas, SW USA 32.47N 95.37W
118 G11 **Alba** ◆ county W Romania
145 P3 **Al Ba'āj** N Iraq 36.02N 41.43E
144 J2 **Al Bāb** Ḥalab, N Syria 36.24N 37.31E
118 G10 **Albac** Hung. Fehérvölgy; prev. Álbák. Alba, SW Romania 46.25N 22.58E
107 Q11 **Albacete** Castilla-La Mancha, C Spain 39.00N 1.52W
107 P11 **Albacete** ◆ province Castilla-La Mancha, C Spain
146 I4 **Al Bad'** Tabūk, NW Saudi Arabia 28.28N 35.00E
106 L7 **Alba de Tormes** Castilla-León, N Spain 40.49N 5.30W
145 P3 **Al Bādī** N Iraq 35.57N 41.37E
147 V8 **Al Badī'ah** ✈ (Abū Ẓaby) Abū Ẓaby, C UAE 24.27N 54.39E
149 P17 **Al Badī'ah** var. Al Bedei'ah. spring/well C UAE 23.44N 53.50E
145 Q7 **Al Baghdādī** var. Khān al Baghdādī. SW Iraq 33.19N 44.22E
Al Bāha see Al Bāḩah
146 M11 **Al Bāḩah** var. Al Bāha. Al Bāḩah, SW Saudi Arabia 20.00N 41.29E
146 M11 **Al Bāḩah** off. Minṭaqat al Bāḩah. ◆ province W Saudi Arabia
Al Baḩrayn see Bahrain
107 S11 **Albaida** País Valenciano, E Spain 38.51N 0.31W
118 H11 **Alba Iulia** Ger. Weissenburg, Hung. Gyulafehérvár; prev. Bălgrad, Karlsburg, Károly-Fehérvár. Alba, W Romania 46.06N 23.33E
Álbák see Albac
144 G10 **Al Balqā'** off. Muḥāfaẓat al Balqā', var. Balqā'. ◆ governorate NW Jordan
12 F11 **Alban** Ontario, S Canada 46.07N 80.37W
105 O15 **Alban** Tarn, S France 43.52N 2.30E
10 K11 **Albanel, Lac** ◎ Québec, SE Canada
115 L20 **Albania** off. Republic of Albania, Alb. Republika e Shqipërisë, Shqipëria; prev. People's Socialist Republic of Albania. ◆ republic SE Europe
Albania see Aubagne
109 H15 **Albano Laziale** Lazio, C Italy 41.43N 12.40E
188 J14 **Albany** Western Australia 35.03S 117.54E
25 S7 **Albany** Georgia, SE USA 31.34N 84.09W
33 P13 **Albany** Indiana, N USA 40.18N 85.14W
22 L8 **Albany** Kentucky, S USA 36.41N 85.07W
31 U7 **Albany** Minnesota, N USA 45.39N 94.33W
29 R2 **Albany** Missouri, C USA 40.15N 94.15W
20 L10 **Albany** state capital New York, NE USA 42.39N 73.45W
34 G12 **Albany** Oregon, NW USA 44.38N 123.06W
27 Q6 **Albany** Texas, SW USA 32.43N 99.18W
10 F10 **Albany** ~ Ontario, S Canada
Alba Pompeia see Alba
Alba Regia see Székesfehérvár
144 J6 **Al Bāridah** var. Bāridah. Ḥimṣ, C Syria 34.15N 37.39E
145 Q11 **Al Barīt** S Iraq 31.16N 42.28E
107 R8 **Albarracín** Aragón, NE Spain 40.24N 1.25W
145 Y12 **Al Başrah** Eng. Basra; hist. Busra, Bussora. SE Iraq 30.30N 47.49E
145 V11 **Al Baṭḩā'** SE Iraq 31.06N 45.49E
147 X8 **Al Bāṭinah** var. Batinah. coastal region N Oman
(0) H16 **Albatross Plateau** undersea feature E Pacific Ocean
Al Batrūn see Batroûn
124 Nn14 **Al Bayḑā'** var. Beida. NE Libya 32.46N 21.43E
147 P16 **Al Bayḑā'** var. Al Beida. SW Yemen 13.58N 45.38E
Al Bedei'ah see Al Badī'ah
Al Beida see Al Bayḑā'
23 S10 **Albemarle** var. Albermarle. North Carolina, SE USA 35.21N 80.12W
Albemarle Island see Isabela, Isla
23 N8 **Albemarle Sound** inlet W Atlantic Ocean
108 B10 **Albenga** Liguria, NW Italy 44.04N 8.13E
106 L8 **Alberche** ~ C Spain
105 O17 **Albères, Chaîne des** var. les Albères, Montes Albères. ▲▲ France/Spain
Albères, Montes see Albères, Chaîne des
190 F2 **Alberga Creek** seasonal river South Australia
106 G7 **Albergaria-a-Velha** Aveiro, N Portugal 40.42N 8.28W
107 S10 **Alberic** País Valenciano, E Spain 39.07N 0.31W
Albermarle see Albemarle
109 P18 **Alberobello** Puglia, SE Italy 40.47N 17.14E
110 J7 **Alberschwende** Vorarlberg, W Austria 47.28N 9.49E
105 O3 **Albert** Somme, N France 50.00N 2.37E
9 O12 **Alberta** ◆ province SW Canada
194 K14 **Albert Edward, Mount** ▲ S PNG 8.23S 147.23E
Albert Edward Nyanza see Edward, Lake
63 C20 **Alberti** Buenos Aires, E Argentina 35.03S 60.15W
113 K23 **Albertirsa** Pest, C Hungary 47.15N 19.36E
101 I16 **Albertkanaal** canal N Belgium
81 P17 **Albert, Lake** var. Albert Nyanza, Lac Mobutu Sese Seko. ◎ Uganda/Dem. Rep. Congo
31 V11 **Albert Lea** Minnesota, N USA 43.39N 93.22W
83 F16 **Albert Nile** ~ NW Uganda
Albert Nyanza see Albert, Lake
105 T11 **Albertville** Savoie, E France 45.41N 6.24E
25 Q2 **Albertville** Alabama, S USA 34.16N 86.12W
Albertville see Kalemie
105 N15 **Albi** anc. Albiga. Tarn, S France 43.55N 2.09E
31 W15 **Albia** Iowa, C USA 41.01N 92.48W
Albiga see Albi
57 X9 **Albina** Marowijne, NE Suriname 5.31N 54.04W
85 A15 **Albina, Ponta** headland SW Angola 15.52S 11.45E
32 M16 **Albion** Illinois, N USA 38.22N 88.03W
33 P11 **Albion** Indiana, N USA 41.22N 85.23W
31 P14 **Albion** Nebraska, C USA 41.41N 98.00W
20 E9 **Albion** New York, NE USA 43.13N 78.09W
20 B12 **Albion** Pennsylvania, NE USA 41.52N 80.18W
Al Biqā' see El Beqaa
146 J4 **Al Bi'r** var. Bi'r Ibn Hirmās. Tabūk, NW Saudi Arabia 28.52N 36.16E
146 M12 **Al Birk** Makkah, SW Saudi Arabia 18.12N 41.36E
147 Q9 **Al Biyāḑ** desert C Saudi Arabia
100 H13 **Alblasserdam** Zuid-Holland, SW Netherlands 51.52N 4.40E
107 T8 **Albocácer** var. Albocasser. País Valenciano, E Spain 40.21N 0.01E
Albocasser see Albocácer
97 H19 **Ålbæk** Nordjylland, N Denmark 57.33N 10.24E
Albona see Labin
107 O17 **Alborán, Isla de** island S Spain
Alborán, Mar de see Alboran Sea
107 N17 **Alboran Sea** Sp. Mar de Alborán. sea SW Mediterranean Sea
Ålborg see Aalborg
97 H21 **Ålborg Bugt** var. Aalborg Bugt. bay N Denmark
Ålborg-Nørresundby see Aalborg
149 O5 **Alborz, Reshteh-ye Kūhhā-ye** Eng. Elburz Mountains. ▲▲ N Iran
107 Q14 **Albox** Andalucía, S Spain 37.22N 2.08W
103 H23 **Albstadt** Baden-Württemberg, SW Germany 48.13N 9.01E
106 G14 **Albufeira** Beja, S Portugal 37.04N 8.15W
145 P5 **Ālbū Gharz, Sabkhat** ◎ W Iraq
107 O15 **Albuñol** Andalucía, S Spain 36.48N 3.10W
39 Q11 **Albuquerque** New Mexico, SW USA 35.04N 106.37W
147 W8 **Al Buraymī** var. Buraimi. N Oman 24.16N 55.48E
149 R17 **Al Buraymī** var. Buraimi. spring/well Oman/UAE 24.27N 55.33E
Al Burayqah see Marsá al Burayqah
Alburgum see Aalborg
106 I10 **Alburquerque** Extremadura, W Spain 39.12N 7.00W
189 V14 **Albury** New South Wales, SE Australia 36.03S 146.52E
147 T14 **Al Buzūn** SE Yemen 15.40N 50.53E
95 G17 **Alby** Västernorrland, C Sweden 62.30N 15.25E
Albyn, Glen see Mor, Glen
106 G12 **Alcácer do Sal** Setúbal, W Portugal 38.21N 8.29W
Alcalá de Chisvert see Alcalà de Xivert
107 T8 **Alcalà de Xivert** var. Alcalá de Chisvert. País Valenciano, E Spain 40.19N 0.13E
106 K14 **Alcalá de Guadaira** Andalucía, S Spain 37.19N 5.49W
107 O8 **Alcalá de Henares** Ar. Alkal'a; anc. Complutum. Madrid, C Spain 40.28N 3.22W
106 K16 **Alcalá de los Gazules** Andalucía, S Spain 36.28N 5.43W
107 N14 **Alcalá La Real** Andalucía, S Spain 37.28N 3.55W
109 I23 **Alcamo** Sicilia, Italy, C Mediterranean Sea 37.58N 12.58E
107 T4 **Alcanadre** ~ NE Spain
107 T8 **Alcanar** Cataluña, NE Spain 40.33N 0.28E
106 J5 **Alcañices** Castilla-León, N Spain 41.40N 6.21W
107 T7 **Alcañiz** Aragón, NE Spain 41.03N 0.09W
106 I9 **Alcántara** Extremadura, W Spain 39.42N 6.54W
106 J9 **Alcántara, Embalse de** ⊠ W Spain
107 R13 **Alcantarilla** Murcia, SE Spain 37.58N 1.12W
107 P11 **Alcaraz** Castilla-La Mancha, C Spain 38.40N 2.28W
107 P12 **Alcaraz, Sierra de** ▲▲ C Spain
106 I12 **Alcarrache** ~ SW Spain
107 T6 **Alcarràs** Cataluña, NE Spain 41.34N 0.31E
107 N14 **Alcaudete** Andalucía, S Spain 37.34N 4.04W
Alcázar see Ksar-el-Kebir
107 O10 **Alcázar de San Juan** anc. Alce. Castilla-La Mancha, C Spain 39.24N 3.12W
Alcazarquivir see Ksar-el-Kebir
Alce see Alcázar de San Juan
59 B17 **Alcebo, Volcán** ▲ Galapagos Islands, Ecuador, E Pacific Ocean 0.25S 91.06W
145 X12 **Al Chabā'ish** var. Al Kaba'ish. SE Iraq 30.58N 47.01E
119 Y7 **Alchevs'k** prev. Kommunarsk, Voroshilovsk. Luhans'ka Oblast', E Ukraine 48.29N 38.52E
Alcira see Alzira
23 N9 **Alcoa** Tennessee, S USA 35.47N 83.58W
106 F9 **Alcobaça** Leiria, C Portugal 39.31N 8.58W
107 N8 **Alcobendas** Madrid, C Spain 40.31N 3.37W
Alcoi see Alcoy
107 P7 **Alcolea del Pinar** Castilla-La Mancha, C Spain 41.01N 2.28W
106 I11 **Alconchel** Extremadura, W Spain 38.31N 7.04W
107 S9 **Alcora** País Valenciano, E Spain 40.04N 0.13W
107 N8 **Alcorcón** Madrid, C Spain 40.20N 3.52W
107 S7 **Alcorisa** Aragón, NE Spain 40.52N 0.22W
63 B19 **Alcorta** Santa Fe, C Argentina 33.31S 61.07W
106 H14 **Alcoutim** Faro, S Portugal 37.28N 7.28W

◆ Country ● Country Capital ◇ Dependent Territory ○ Dependent Territory Capital ◆ Administrative Region ✈ International Airport ▲ Mountain ▲▲ Mountain Range ▲ Volcano ~ River ◎ Lake ⊠ Reservoir

◆ COUNTRY ◇ DEPENDENT TERRITORY ◆ ADMINISTRATIVE REGION ▲ MOUNTAIN ▲ VOLCANO ⊗ LAKE
● COUNTRY CAPITAL ○ DEPENDENT TERRITORY CAPITAL ✈ INTERNATIONAL AIRPORT ▲ MOUNTAIN RANGE ↗ RIVER ⊠ RESERVOIR

◆ COUNTRY   ◇ DEPENDENT TERRITORY   ◆ ADMINISTRATIVE REGION   ▲ MOUNTAIN   ⋌ VOLCANO   ⊠ LAKE
◆ COUNTRY CAPITAL   ○ DEPENDENT TERRITORY CAPITAL   ✕ INTERNATIONAL AIRPORT   ▲ MOUNTAIN RANGE   ⊷ RIVER   ⊠ RESERVOIR

37 T15 **Anaheim** California, W USA 33.50N 117.54W
8 L15 **Anahim Lake** British Columbia, SW Canada 52.26N 125.13W
40 B8 **Anahola** Kaua'i, Hawai'i, USA, C Pacific Ocean 22.09N 159.19W
27 X11 **Anahuac** Texas, SW USA 29.46N 94.40W
43 O7 **Anáhuac** Nuevo León, NE Mexico 27.13N 100.09W
161 G22 **Anai Mudi** ▲ S India 10.16N 77.08E
Anaiza *see* 'Unayzah
161 M15 **Anakāpalle** Andhra Pradesh, E India 17.42N 83.06E
203 W15 **Anakena, Playa de** *beach* Easter Island, Chile, E Pacific Ocean
41 Q7 **Anaktuvuk Pass** Alaska, USA 68.08N 151.44W
41 Q6 **Anaktuvuk River** ≈ Alaska, USA
180 J3 **Analalava** Mahajanga, NW Madagascar 14.37S 47.46E
46 F6 **Ana Maria, Golfo de** *gulf* C Cuba
Anambas Islands *see* Anambas, Kepulauan
174 Ii5 **Anambas, Kepulauan** *var.* Anambas Islands *island group* W Indonesia
79 U17 **Anambra** ◆ *state* SE Nigeria
31 N4 **Anamoose** North Dakota, N USA 47.50N 100.14W
31 Y13 **Anamosa** Iowa, C USA 42.06N 91.17W
142 H17 **Anamur** İçel, S Turkey 36.06N 32.49E
142 H17 **Anamur Burnu** *headland* S Turkey 36.03N 32.49E
170 Ff16 **Anan** Tokushima, Shikoku, SW Japan 33.54N 134.40E
160 O12 **Ānandadur** Orissa, E India 21.13N 86.08E
161 H18 **Anantapur** Andhra Pradesh, S India 14.40N 77.36E
158 H5 **Anantnāg** *var.* Islamabad. Jammu and Kashmir, NW India 33.43N 75.10E
Ananyev *see* Anan'yiv
119 O9 **Anan'yiv** *Rus.* Ananyev. Odes'ka Oblast', SW Ukraine 47.43N 29.51E
130 J14 **Anapa** Krasnodarskiy Kray, SW Russian Federation 44.55N 37.20E
Anaphe *see* Anáfi
61 K18 **Anápolis** Goiás, C Brazil 16.19S 48.58W
149 R10 **Anār** Kermān, C Iran 30.48N 55.17E
Anár *see* Inari
149 P7 **Anārak** Eşfahān, C Iran 33.21N 53.43E
Anar Dara *see* Anār Darreh
154 J7 **Anār Darreh** *var.* Anar Dara. Farāh, W Afghanistan 32.45N 61.37E
Anárjohka *see* Inarijoki
25 X9 **Anastasia Island** *island* Florida, SE USA
196 K7 **Anatahan** *island* C Northern Mariana Islands
132 M6 **Anatolia** *plateau* C Turkey
88 F14 **Anatolian Plate** *tectonic feature* Asia/Europe
116 H13 **Anatolikí Makedonía kai Thráki** *Eng.* Macedonia East and Thrace. ◆ *region* NE Greece
Anatom *see* Aneityum
64 L8 **Añatuya** Santiago del Estero, N Argentina 28.27S 62.52W
An Baile Meánach *see* Ballymena
An Bhearú *see* Barrow
An Bhóinn *see* Boyne
An Blascaod Mór *see* Great Blasket Island
An Cabhán *see* Cavan
An Caisleán Nua *see* Newcastle
An Caisleán Riabhach *see* Castlereagh, Northern Ireland, UK
An Caisleán Riabhach *see* Castlerea, Ireland
58 C13 **Ancash** *off.* Departamento de Ancash. ◆ *department* W Peru
An Cathair *see* Caher
104 J8 **Ancenis** Loire-Atlantique, NW France 47.22N 1.10W
An Chanáil Ríoga *see* Royal Canal
An Cheacha *see* Caha Mountains
41 R11 **Anchorage** Alaska, USA 61.12N 149.52W
41 R12 **Anchorage** ✈ Alaska, USA 61.08N 150.00W
41 Q13 **Anchor Point** Alaska, USA 59.46N 151.49W
An Chorr Chríochach *see* Cookstown
67 M24 **Anchorstack Point** *headland* W Tristan da Cunha 37.07S 12.21W
An Clár *see* Clare
An Clochán *see* Clifden
An Clochán Liath *see* Dunglow
25 U12 **Anclote Keys** *island group* Florida, SE USA
An Cóbh *see* Cobh
59 J17 **Ancohuma, Nevado de** ▲ W Bolivia 15.51S 68.33W
An Comar *see* Comber
59 D14 **Ancón** Lima, W Peru 11.47S 77.09W
108 J12 **Ancona** Marche, C Italy 43.37N 13.30E
Ancuabe *see* Ancuabi
84 Q13 **Ancuabi** *var.* Ancuabe. Cabo Delgado, NE Mozambique 12.57S 39.54E
65 F17 **Ancud** *prev.* San Carlos de Ancud. Los Lagos, S Chile 41.52S 73.49W
65 G17 **Ancud, Golfo de** *gulf* S Chile
Ancyra *see* Ankara
169 V8 **Anda** Heilongjiang, NE China 46.22N 125.15E
59 G16 **Andahuaylas** Apurímac, S Peru 13.38S 73.20W
An Daingean *see* Dingle
159 R15 **Andāl** West Bengal, NE India 23.34N 87.13E
96 E9 **Åndalsnes** Møre og Romsdal, S Norway 62.33N 7.42E
106 K13 **Andalucía** *Eng.* Andalusia. ◆ *autonomous community* S Spain
25 P7 **Andalusia** Alabama, S USA 31.18N 86.29W
Andalusia *see* Andalucía
157 Q21 **Andaman and Nicobar Islands** *var.* Andamans and Nicobars. ◇ *union territory* India, NE Indian Ocean
181 T4 **Andaman Basin** *undersea feature* NE Indian Ocean
157 P19 **Andaman Islands** *island group* India, NE Indian Ocean
181 T4 **Andaman Sea** *sea* NE Indian Ocean
59 K19 **Andamarca** Oruro, C Bolivia 18.50S 67.24W
176 V10 **Andamata** Papua, E Indonesia 2.40S 132.30E
190 H5 **Andamooka** South Australia 30.26S 137.12E
147 Y9 **'Andām, Wādī** *seasonal river* NE Oman
180 J3 **Andapa** Antsirañana, NE Madagascar 14.39S 49.40E
155 R4 **Andarāb** *var.* Banow. Baghlān, NE Afghanistan 35.36N 69.18E
Andarbag *see* Andarbogh
153 S13 **Andarbogh** *Rus.* Andarbag, Anderbak. S Tajikistan 37.51N 71.45E
111 Z5 **Andau** Burgenland, E Austria 47.46N 17.03E
110 I10 **Andeer** Graubünden, S Switzerland 46.36N 9.24E
94 H9 **Andenes** Nordland, C Norway 69.18N 16.06E
101 J20 **Andenne** Namur, SE Belgium 50.28N 5.06E
79 S11 **Andéramboukane** Gao, E Mali 15.24N 3.03E
Anderbak *see* Andarbogh
101 G18 **Anderlecht** Brussels, C Belgium 50.50N 4.18E
101 G21 **Anderlues** Hainaut, S Belgium 50.24N 4.16E
110 G9 **Andermatt** Uri, C Switzerland 46.39N 8.36E
103 E17 **Andernach** *anc.* Antunnacum. Rheinland-Pfalz, SW Germany 50.25N 7.25E
196 D15 **Andersen Air Force Base** *air base* NE Guam 13.34N 144.55E
41 R9 **Anderson** Alaska, USA 64.20N 149.11W
37 N4 **Anderson** California, W USA 40.26N 122.21W
33 P13 **Anderson** Indiana, N USA 40.06N 85.40W
29 R8 **Anderson** Missouri, C USA 36.39N 94.26W
23 P11 **Anderson** South Carolina, SE USA 34.30N 82.39W
27 V10 **Anderson** Texas, SW USA 30.29N 96.00W
15 Gg3 **Anderson** ≈ Northwest Territories, NW Canada
97 K20 **Anderstorp** Jönköping, S Sweden 57.16N 13.46E
56 D9 **Andes** Antioquia, W Colombia 5.40N 75.55W
49 P7 **Andes** ▲▲ W South America
31 P12 **Andes, Lake** ◎ South Dakota, N USA
94 H9 **Andfjorden** *fjord* E Norwegian Sea
161 H16 **Andhra Pradesh** ◆ *state* E India
100 J8 **Andijk** Noord-Holland, NW Netherlands 52.38N 5.00E
153 S10 **Andijon** *Rus.* Andizhan. Andijon Viloyati, E Uzbekistan 40.46N 72.19E
153 S10 **Andijon Viloyati** *Rus.* Andizhanskaya Oblast'. ◆ *province* E Uzbekistan
Andikíthira *see* Antikýthira
180 J4 **Andilamena** Toamasina, C Madagascar 17.00S 48.35E
148 L8 **Andīmeshk** *var.* Andimishk; *prev.* Salehābād. Khūzestān, SW Iran 32.28N 48.21E
Andimishk *see* Andīmeshk
Andipáros *see* Antíparos
Andipaxi *see* Antípaxoi
Andípsara *see* Antípsara
142 L16 **Andırın** Kahramanmaraş, S Turkey 37.33N 36.18E
164 J8 **Andirlangar** Xinjiang Uygur Zizhiqu, NW China 37.38N 83.40E
Andírrion *see* Antírrio
Andissa *see* Ántissa
Andizhan *see* Andijon
Andizhanskaya Oblast' *see* Andijon Viloyati
155 N2 **Andkhvoy** Fāryāb, N Afghanistan 36.55N 65.07E
107 Q2 **Andoain** País Vasco, N Spain 43.13N 2.01W
176 W9 **Andoi** Papua, E Indonesia 0.53S 133.59E
169 Y15 **Andong** *Jap.* Antō. E South Korea 36.34N 128.43E
111 R4 **Andorf** Oberösterreich, N Austria 48.22N 13.33E
107 S7 **Andorra** Aragón, NE Spain 40.58N 0.27W
107 V4 **Andorra** *off.* Principality of Andorra, *Cat.* Valls d'Andorra, *Fr.* Vallée d'Andorre. ◆ *monarchy* SW Europe
Andorra *see* Andorra la Vella
107 V4 **Andorra la Vella** *var.* Andorra, *Fr.* Andorre la Vielle, *Sp.* Andorra la Vieja. ● (Andorra) C Andorra 42.30N 1.30E
Andorra la Vieja *see* Andorra la Vella
Andorra, Valls d'/Andorre, Vallée d' *see* Andorra
Andorre la Vielle *see* Andorra la Vella
99 M22 **Andover** S England, UK 51.13N 1.28W
29 N6 **Andover** Kansas, C USA 37.42N 97.08W
94 G10 **Andøya** *island* C Norway
62 I8 **Andradina** São Paulo, S Brazil 20.54S 51.25W
41 N10 **Andreafsky River** ≈ Alaska, USA
40 H17 **Andreanof Islands** *island group* Aleutian Islands, Alaska, USA
128 H16 **Andreapol'** Tverskaya Oblast', W Russian Federation 56.38N 32.17E
Andreas, Cape *see* Zafer Burnu
Andreevka *see* Kabanbay
23 N10 **Andrews** North Carolina, SE USA 35.19N 84.01W
23 T13 **Andrews** South Carolina, SE USA 33.27N 79.33W
26 M7 **Andrews** Texas, SW USA 32.19N 102.33W
181 N5 **Andrew Tablemount** *var.* Gora Andryu. *undersea feature* W Indian Ocean 6.45N 50.30E
Andreyevka *see* Kabanbay
109 N17 **Andria** Puglia, SE Italy 41.13N 16.16E
115 K16 **Andrijevica** Montenegro, SW Serbia and Montenegro (Yugoslavia) 42.45N 19.45E
117 E20 **Andrítsaina** Pelopónnisos, S Greece 37.29N 21.52E
An Droichead Nua *see* Newbridge
Andropov *see* Rybinsk
117 J19 **Ándros** Ándros, Kykládes, Greece, Aegean Sea 37.49N 24.55E
117 J20 **Ándros** *island* Kykládes, Greece, Aegean Sea
21 O7 **Androscoggin River** ≈ Maine/New Hampshire, NE USA
46 F3 **Andros Island** *island* NW Bahamas
131 R7 **Androsovka** Samarskaya Oblast', W Russian Federation 52.41N 49.34E
46 G3 **Andros Town** Andros Island, NW Bahamas 24.40N 77.47W
161 D21 **Āndrott Island** *island* Lakshadweep, India, N Indian Ocean
119 N5 **Andrushivka** Zhytomyrs'ka Oblast', N Ukraine 50.01N 29.02E
113 K17 **Andrychów** Małopolskie, S Poland 49.51N 19.23E
Andryu, Gora *see* Andrew Tablemount
94 I10 **Andselv** Troms, N Norway 69.05N 18.30E
81 O17 **Andudu** Orientale, NE Dem. Rep. Congo 2.25N 28.39E
107 N13 **Andújar** *anc.* Illiturgis. Andalucía, SW Spain 38.01N 4.03W
84 C12 **Andulo** Bié, W Angola 11.28S 16.43E
105 Q14 **Anduze** Gard, S France 44.03N 3.59E
An Earagail *see* Errigal Mountain
97 L19 **Aneby** Jönköping, S Sweden 57.49N 14.45E
Anécho *see* Aného
79 Q9 **Anéfis** Kidal, NE Mali 18.05N 0.38E
47 U8 **Anegada** *island* NE British Virgin Islands
63 B25 **Anegada, Bahía** *bay* E Argentina
47 U9 **Anegada Passage** *passage* Anguilla/British Virgin Islands
79 R17 **Aného** *var.* Anécho; *prev.* Petit-Popo. S Togo 6.13N 1.36E
197 D17 **Aneityum** *var.* Anatom; *prev.* Kéamu. *island* S Vanuatu
119 N10 **Anenii Noi** *Rus.* Novyye Aneny. C Moldova 46.52N 29.10E
194 L12 **Anepmete** New Britain, E PNG 5.47S 148.37E
107 U4 **Aneto** ▲ NE Spain 42.36N 0.37E
152 F13 **Änew** *Rus.* Annau. Ahal Welaýaty, C Turkmenistan 37.51N 58.22E
Änewetak *see* Enewetak Atoll
79 Y8 **Aney** Agadez, NE Niger 19.22N 13.00E
An Fheoir *see* Nore
126 Ii13 **Angara** ≈ C Russian Federation
126 J15 **Angarsk** Irkutskaya Oblast', S Russian Federation 52.31N 103.55E
95 G17 **Ånge** Västernorrland, C Sweden 62.31N 15.40E
Angel *see* Úhlava
42 D4 **Ángel de la Guarda, Isla** *island* NW Mexico
179 P10 **Angeles** *off.* Angeles City. Luzon, N Philippines 15.16N 120.37E
Angeles City *see* Angeles
Angel Falls *see* Ángel, Salto
97 J22 **Ängelholm** Skåne, S Sweden 56.14N 12.52E
63 A17 **Angélica** Santa Fe, C Argentina 31.33S 61.33W
27 W8 **Angelina River** ≈ Texas, SW USA
57 Q9 **Ángel, Salto** *Eng.* Angel Falls. *waterfall* E Venezuela 5.52N 62.19W
97 M15 **Ängelsberg** Västmanland, C Sweden 59.57N 16.01E
37 P8 **Angels Camp** California, W USA 38.03N 120.31W
111 W7 **Anger** Steiermark, SE Austria 47.16N 15.41E
Angerapp *see* Ozersk
Angerburg *see* Węgorzewo
95 H15 **Ångermanälven** ≈ N Sweden
102 P11 **Angermünde** Brandenburg, NE Germany 53.01N 13.59E
104 K7 **Angers** *anc.* Juliomagus. Maine-et-Loire, NW France 47.30N 0.33W
13 W7 **Angers** ≈ Québec, SE Canada
95 J16 **Ångesön** *island* N Sweden
Angistro *see* Ágkistro
116 H13 **Angítis** ≈ NE Greece
178 J14 **Ângk Tasaôm** *prev.* Angtassom. Takêv, S Cambodia 10.59N 104.39E
193 C25 **Anglem, Mount** ▲ Stewart Island, Southland, SW NZ 46.44S 167.56E
99 I18 **Anglesey** *cultural region* NW Wales, UK
99 I18 **Anglesey** *island* NW Wales, UK
104 I15 **Anglet** Pyrénées-Atlantiques, SW France 43.28N 1.30W
27 W12 **Angleton** Texas, SW USA 29.10N 95.25W
Anglia *see* England
12 H9 **Angliers** Québec, SE Canada 47.33N 79.17W
Anglo-Egyptian Sudan *see* Sudan
Angmagssalik *see* Ammassalik
178 Ii8 **Ang Nam Ngum** ◎ C Laos
81 N16 **Ango** Orientale, N Dem. Rep. Congo 4.02N 25.49E
85 Q15 **Angoche** Nampula, E Mozambique 16.12S 39.55E
65 G14 **Angol** Araucanía, C Chile 37.48S 72.40W
33 Q11 **Angola** Indiana, N USA 41.37N 85.00W
84 A9 **Angola** *off.* Republic of Angola; *prev.* People's Republic of Angola, Portuguese West Africa. ◆ *republic* SW Africa
67 P15 **Angola Basin** *undersea feature* E Atlantic Ocean
41 X13 **Angoon** Admiralty Island, Alaska, USA 57.33N 134.30W
153 O14 **Angor** Surkhondaryo Viloyati, S Uzbekistan 37.30N 67.06E
Angora *see* Ankara
194 H10 **Angoram** East Sepik, NW PNG 4.01S 144.03E
42 H8 **Angostura** Sinaloa, C Mexico 25.18N 108.10W
Angostura *see* Ciudad Bolívar
43 U17 **Angostura, Presa de la** ⊠ SE Mexico
30 J11 **Angostura Reservoir** ⊠ South Dakota, N USA
104 L11 **Angoulême** *anc.* Iculisma. Charente, W France 45.39N 0.10E
104 K11 **Angoumois** *cultural region* W France
66 O2 **Angra do Heroísmo** Terceira, Azores, Portugal, NE Atlantic Ocean 38.40N 27.13W
62 O10 **Angra dos Reis** Rio de Janeiro, SE Brazil 22.58S 44.16W
Angra Pequena *see* Lüderitz
153 Q10 **Angren** Toshkent Viloyati, E Uzbekistan 41.04N 70.17E
Angtassom *see* Ângk Tasaôm
178 Hh11 **Ang Thong** *var.* Angthong. Ang Thong, C Thailand 14.34N 100.25E
81 M16 **Angu** Orientale, N Dem. Rep. Congo 3.38N 24.14E
107 S5 **Angües** Aragón, NE Spain 42.07N 0.10W
47 U9 **Anguilla** ◇ *UK dependent territory* E West Indies
47 V9 **Anguilla** *island* E West Indies
46 F4 **Anguilla Cays** *islets* SW Bahamas
Angul *see* Anugul
167 N1 **Anguli Nur** ◎ E China
81 O18 **Angumu** Orientale, E Dem. Rep. Congo 0.10S 27.42E
12 G14 **Angus** Ontario, S Canada 44.19N 79.52W
98 J10 **Angus** *cultural region* E Scotland, UK
61 K19 **Anhangüera** Goiás, S Brazil 18.12S 48.19W
101 I21 **Anhée** Namur, S Belgium 50.18N 4.52E
97 I21 **Anholt** *island* C Denmark
166 M11 **Anhua** *var.* Dongping. Hunan, S China 28.25N 111.10E
167 P8 **Anhui** *var.* Anhui Sheng, Anhwei, Wan. ◆ *province* E China
Anhui Sheng/Anhwei *see* Anhui
41 O11 **Aniak** Alaska, USA 61.34N 159.31W
41 O12 **Aniak River** ≈ Alaska, USA
An Iarmhí *see* Westmeath
201 R8 **Anibare** E Nauru 0.31S 166.56E
201 R8 **Anibare Bay** *bay* E Nauru, W Pacific Ocean
Anicium *see* le Puy
117 K22 **Ánidro** *island* Kykládes, Greece, Aegean Sea
79 R15 **Anié** C Togo 7.48N 1.12E
79 Q15 **Anié** ≈ C Togo
104 J16 **Anie, Pic d'** ▲ SW France 42.56N 0.44W
131 Y7 **Anikhovka** Orenburgskaya Oblast', W Russian Federation 51.27N 60.17E
12 G9 **Anima Nipissing Lake** ◎ Ontario, S Canada
39 O16 **Animas** New Mexico, SW USA 31.55N 108.49W
39 P16 **Animas Peak** ▲ New Mexico, SW USA 31.34N 108.46W
39 P16 **Animas Valley** *valley* New Mexico, SW USA
118 F13 **Anina** *Ger.* Steierdorf, *Hung.* Stájerlakanina; *prev.* Ştaierdorf-Anina, Steierdorf-Anina, Steyerlak-Anina. Caraş-Severin, SW Romania 45.04N 21.51E
31 U14 **Anita** Iowa, C USA 41.27N 94.45W
127 Oo16 **Aniva, Mys** *headland* Ostrov Sakhalin, SE Russian Federation 46.02N 143.25E
127 Oo16 **Aniva, Zaliv** *bay* SE Russian Federation
197 E16 **Aniwa** *island* S Vanuatu
95 M19 **Anjalankoski** Etelä-Suomi, S Finland 60.39N 26.54E
'Anjar *see* Aanjar
Anjiangying *see* Luanping
12 B8 **Anjigami Lake** ◎ Ontario, S Canada
171 Hh16 **Anjō** *var.* Anzyō. Aichi, Honshū, SW Japan 34.58N 137.07E
104 J8 **Anjou** *cultural region* NW France
180 I13 **Anjouan** *var.* Nzwani, Johanna Island. *island* SE Comoros
180 J4 **Anjozorobe** Antananarivo, C Madagascar 18.22S 47.52E
169 W13 **Anju** W North Korea 39.36N 125.44E
100 M5 **Anjum** *Fris.* Eanjum. Friesland, N Netherlands 53.22N 6.09E
180 G6 **Ankaboa, Tanjona** *headland* W Madagascar 21.57S 43.16E
166 L7 **Ankang** *prev.* Xing'an. Shaanxi, C China 32.45N 109.00E
142 I12 **Ankara** *prev.* Angora, *anc.* Ancyra. ● (Turkey) Ankara, C Turkey 39.55N 32.49E
142 H12 **Ankara** ◆ *province* C Turkey
97 N19 **Ankarsrum** Kalmar, S Sweden 57.40N 16.19E
180 H6 **Ankazoabo** Toliara, SW Madagascar 22.18S 44.30E
180 J4 **Ankazobe** Antananarivo, C Madagascar 18.19S 47.07E
31 V14 **Ankeny** Iowa, C USA 41.43N 93.37W
178 Kk11 **An Khê** Gia Lai, C Vietnam 13.57N 108.39E
102 O9 **Anklam** Mecklenburg-Vorpommern, NE Germany 53.51N 13.42E
82 K13 **Ānkober** Amhara, N Ethiopia 9.36N 39.44E
79 O17 **Ankobra** ≈ S Ghana
81 N22 **Ankoro** Katanga, SE Dem. Rep. Congo 6.45S 26.58E
101 L24 **Anlier, Forêt d'** *forest* SE Belgium
166 I13 **Anlong** Guizhou, S China 25.05N 105.29E
An Longfort *see* Longford
178 Ii11 **Ânlong Vêng** Siĕmréab, NW Cambodia 14.16N 104.07E
An Lorgain *see* Lurgan
167 N8 **Anlu** Hubei, C China 31.15N 113.41E
An Mhí *see* Meath
An Mhuir Cheilteach *see* Celtic Sea
An Muileann gCearr *see* Mullingar
95 F16 **Ånn** Jämtland, C Sweden 63.19N 12.34E
130 M8 **Anna** Voronezhskaya Oblast', W Russian Federation 51.31N 40.23E
32 L17 **Anna** Illinois, N USA 37.27N 89.15W
27 U5 **Anna** Texas, SW USA 33.21N 96.33W
76 L5 **Annaba** *prev.* Bône. NE Algeria 36.55N 7.46E
An Nabatīyah at Taḥtā *see* Nabatîyé
103 N17 **Annaberg-Buchholz** Sachsen, E Germany 50.34N 13.01E
111 T9 **Annabichl** ✈ (Klagenfurt) Kärnten, S Austria 46.39N 14.21E
146 M5 **An Nafūd** *desert* NW Saudi Arabia
145 P6 **'Annah** *var.* 'Ānah. NW Iraq 33.27N 43.19E
145 P6 **An Nāḩiyah** W Iraq 34.24N 41.33E
145 T10 **An Najaf** *var.* Najaf. S Iraq 31.58N 44.19E
23 V5 **Anna, Lake** ⊠ Virginia, NE USA
99 E16 **Annalee** ≈ N Ireland
178 Jj9 **Annamitique, Chaîne** ▲▲ C Laos
99 J14 **Annan** S Scotland, UK 55.00N 3.19W
31 U8 **Annandale** Minnesota, N USA 45.15N 94.07W
23 W4 **Annandale** Virginia, NE USA 38.48N 77.10W
201 Q7 **Anna Point** *headland* N Nauru 0.30S 166.56E
23 X3 **Annapolis** *state capital* Maryland, NE USA 38.58N 76.29W
196 A10 **Anna, Pulo** *island* S Palau
159 O10 **Annapurna** ▲ C Nepal 28.30N 83.49E
An Nāqūrah *see* En Nâqoûra
33 R10 **Ann Arbor** Michigan, N USA 42.16N 83.45W
An Nās *see* Naas
145 W12 **An Nāşirīyah** *var.* Nasiriya. SE Iraq 31.04N 46.16E
145 W11 **An Naşr** E Iraq 31.34N 46.08E
Annau *see* Änew
123 Mm16 **An Nawfalīyah** *var.* Al Nūwfalīyah. N Libya 30.46N 17.48E
21 P10 **Ann, Cape** *headland* Massachusetts, NE USA 42.39N 70.35W
188 I10 **Annean, Lake** ◎ Western Australia
Anneciacum *see* Annecy
105 T11 **Annecy** *anc.* Anneciacum. Haute-Savoie, E France 45.53N 6.09E
105 T11 **Annecy, Lac d'** ◎ E France
105 T10 **Annemasse** Haute-Savoie, E France 46.10N 6.13E
41 Z14 **Annette Island** *island* Alexander Archipelago, Alaska, USA
An Nhon *see* Binh Đinh
An Nīl al Abyaḍ *see* White Nile
An Nīl al Azraq *see* Blue Nile
25 Q3 **Anniston** Alabama, S USA 33.39N 85.49W
81 A19 **Annobón** *island* W Equatorial Guinea
105 R12 **Annonay** Ardèche, E France 45.15N 4.40E
46 K12 **Annotto Bay** C Jamaica 18.16N 76.45W
147 R5 **An Nu'ayrīyah** *var.* Narıya. Ash Sharqīyah, NE Saudi Arabia 27.30N 48.30E
190 M9 **Annuello** Victoria, SE Australia 34.54S 142.50E
145 Q10 **An Nukhayb** S Iraq 32.01N 42.15E
145 U9 **An Nu'mānīyah** E Iraq 32.34N 45.22E
Áno Arkhánai *see* Epáno Archánes
117 J25 **Anógeia** *var.* Anogia, Anóyia. Kríti, Greece, E Mediterranean Sea 35.17N 24.55E
Anogia *see* Anógeia
31 V8 **Anoka** Minnesota, N USA 45.15N 93.26W
An Ómaigh *see* Omagh
180 I1 **Anorontany, Tanjona** *headland* N Madagascar
180 J5 **Anosibe An'Ala** Toamasina, E Madagascar 19.24S 48.10E
Anóyia *see* Anógeia
An Pointe *see* Warrenpoint
167 P9 **Anqing** Anhui, E China 30.31N 116.58E
167 Q5 **Anqiu** Shandong, E China 36.25N 119.10E
An Ráth *see* Ráth Luirc
An Ribhéar *see* Kenmare River
An Ros *see* Rush
101 K19 **Ans** Liège, E Belgium 50.39N 5.31E
Ansāb *see* Nişāb
176 Ww10 **Ansas** Papua, E Indonesia 1.44S 135.52E
103 J20 **Ansbach** Bayern, SE Germany 49.15N 10.34E
An Sciobairín *see* Skibbereen
An Scoil *see* Skull
An Seancheann *see* Old Head of Kinsale
47 Y5 **Anse-Bertrand** Grande Terre, N Guadeloupe 16.28N 61.30W
180 H17 **Anse Boileau** Mahé, NE Seychelles 4.43S 55.28E
47 S11 **Anse La Raye** NW Saint Lucia 13.57N 61.01W
56 D9 **Anserma** Caldas, W Colombia 5.15N 75.46W
111 T4 **Ansfelden** Oberösterreich, N Austria 48.12N 14.17E
169 U12 **Anshan** Liaoning, NE China 41.06N 122.55E
166 J12 **Anshun** Guizhou, S China 26.15N 105.58E
63 F17 **Ansina** Tacuarembó, C Uruguay 31.58S 55.28W
31 O15 **Ansley** Nebraska, C USA 41.16N 99.22W
27 P6 **Anson** Texas, SW USA 32.45N 99.54W
79 Q10 **Ansongo** Gao, E Mali 15.39N 0.33E
An Srath Bán *see* Strabane
23 R5 **Ansted** West Virginia, NE USA 38.08N 81.06W
176 Yy10 **Ansudu** Papua, E Indonesia 2.09S 139.19E
59 G15 **Anta** Cusco, S Peru 13.31S 72.12W
59 G16 **Antabamba** Apurímac, C Peru 14.26S 72.51W
Antafalva *see* Kovačica
142 L17 **Antakya** *anc.* Antioch, Antiochia. Hatay, S Turkey 36.12N 36.10E
180 K3 **Antalaha** Antsirañana, NE Madagascar 14.52S 50.16E
142 F17 **Antalya** *prev.* Adalia, *anc.* Attaleia, *Bibl.* Attalia. Antalya, SW Turkey 36.52N 30.42E
142 F17 **Antalya** ◆ *province* SW Turkey
142 F16 **Antalya** ✈ Antalya, SW Turkey 36.53N 30.45E
124 Qq11 **Antalya Basin** *undersea feature* E Mediterranean Sea
Antalya, Gulf of *see* Antalya Körfezi
142 F16 **Antalya Körfezi** *var.* Gulf of Adalia, *Eng.* Gulf of Antalya. *gulf* SW Turkey
180 J5 **Antanambao Manampotsy** Toamasina, E Madagascar 19.30S 48.36E
180 I5 **Antananarivo** *prev.* Tananarive. ● (Madagascar) Antananarivo, C Madagascar 18.52S 47.30E
180 I4 **Antananarivo** ◆ *province* C Madagascar
180 J5 **Antananarivo** ✈ Antananarivo, C Madagascar 18.52S 47.30E
An tAonach *see* Nenagh
204-205 **Antarctica** *continent*
204 I5 **Antarctic Peninsula** *peninsula* Antarctica
63 J15 **Antas, Rio das** ≈ S Brazil
201 U16 **Ant Atoll** *atoll* Caroline Islands, E Micronesia
An Teampall Mór *see* Templemore
Antep *see* Gaziantep
106 M15 **Antequera** *anc.* Anticaria, Antiquaria. Andalucía, S Spain 37.01N 4.34W
Antequera *see* Oaxaca
39 S5 **Antero Reservoir** ⊠ Colorado, C USA
28 M7 **Anthony** Kansas, C USA 37.09N 98.01W
39 R16 **Anthony** New Mexico, SW USA 32.00N 106.36W
190 D5 **Anthony, Lake** *salt lake* South Australia
76 E8 **Anti-Atlas** ▲▲ SW Morocco
105 U15 **Antibes** *anc.* Antipolis. Alpes-Maritimes, SE France 43.34N 7.07E
105 U15 **Antibes, Cap d'** *headland* SE France 43.33N 7.08E
Anticaria *see* Antequera
11 Q11 **Anticosti, Île d'** *Eng.* Anticosti Island. *island* Québec, E Canada
Anticosti Island *see* Anticosti, Île d'
104 K3 **Antifer, Cap d'** *headland* N France 49.43N 0.10E
32 L6 **Antigo** Wisconsin, N USA 45.10N 89.10W
11 Q15 **Antigonish** Nova Scotia, SE Canada 45.39N 62.00W
66 P11 **Antigua** Fuerteventura, Islas Canarias, NE Atlantic Ocean
47 X10 **Antigua** *island* S Antigua and Barbuda, Leeward Islands
Antigua *see* Antigua Guatemala
47 W9 **Antigua and Barbuda** ◆ *commonwealth republic* E West Indies
44 C6 **Antigua Guatemala** *var.* Antigua. Sacatepéquez, SW Guatemala 14.33N 90.39W
43 P11 **Antiguo Morelos** *var.* Antiguo-Morelos. Tamaulipas, C Mexico 22.34N 99.06W
117 F19 **Antíkyras, Kólpos** *gulf* C Greece
117 G24 **Antikýthira** *var.* Andikíthira. *island* S Greece
144 I7 **Anti-Lebanon** *var.* Jebel esh Sharqi, *Ar.* Al Jabal ash Sharqī, *Fr.* Anti-Liban. ▲▲ Lebanon/Syria
Anti-Liban *see* Anti-Lebanon
117 I22 **Antímilos** *island* Kykládes, Greece, Aegean Sea
38 L6 **Antimony** Utah, W USA 38.07N 112.00W
An tInbhear Mór *see* Arklow
32 M10 **Antioch** Illinois, N USA 42.28N 88.06W
Antioch *see* Antakya
104 I10 **Antioche, Pertuis d'** *inlet* W France
Antiochia *see* Antakya
56 D8 **Antioquia** Antioquia, C Colombia 6.24N 75.54W
56 E8 **Antioquia** *off.* Departamento de Antioquia. ◆ *province* C Colombia
117 J21 **Antíparos** *var.* Andipáros. *island* Kykládes, Greece, Aegean Sea
117 B17 **Antípaxoi** *var.* Andipaxi. *island* Iónioi Nísoi, Greece, C Mediterranean Sea
126 H7 **Antipayuta** Yamalo-Nenetskiy Avtonomnyy Okrug, N Russian Federation 69.08N 76.43E
199 J14 **Antipodes Islands** *island group* S NZ
Antipolis *see* Antibes
117 J18 **Antípsara** *var.* Andípsara. *island* E Greece
Antiquaria *see* Antequera
13 N10 **Antique, Lac** ◎ Québec, SE Canada
117 E18 **Antírrio** *var.* Andírrion. Dytikí Elláda, C Greece 38.20N 21.46E
117 K16 **Ántissa** *var.* Ándissa. Lésvos, E Greece 39.15N 25.59E
An tIúr *see* Newry
Antivari *see* Bar
58 C6 **Antizana** ▲ N Ecuador 0.29S 78.08W
29 Q13 **Antlers** Oklahoma, C USA 34.13N 95.37W
95 J14 **Antnäs** Norrbotten, N Sweden 65.32N 21.53E
Antō *see* Andong
64 G5 **Antofagasta** Antofagasta, N Chile 23.40S 70.22W
64 G6 **Antofagasta** *off.* Región de Antofagasta. ◆ *region* N Chile
64 I7 **Antofalla, Salar de** *salt lake* NW Argentina
101 D20 **Antoing** Hainaut, SW Belgium 50.34N 3.26E
26 M5 **Anton** Texas, SW USA 33.48N 102.09W
45 S16 **Antón** Coclé, C Panama 8.23N 80.15W
39 T11 **Anton Chico** New Mexico, SW USA 35.12N 105.09W
62 K12 **Antonina** Paraná, S Brazil 25.28S 48.43W
105 O5 **Antony** Hauts-de-Seine, N France 48.45N 2.16E
Antratsit *see* Antratsyt
119 Y8 **Antratsyt** *Rus.* Antratsit. Luhans'ka Oblast', E Ukraine 48.07N 39.04E
99 G15 **Antrim** *Ir.* Aontroim. NE Northern Ireland, UK 54.43N 6.13W
99 G14 **Antrim** *Ir.* Aontroim. *cultural region* NE Northern Ireland, UK
99 G14 **Antrim Mountains** ▲▲ NE Northern Ireland, UK
180 H5 **Antsalova** Mahajanga, W Madagascar 18.40S 44.37E
Antserana *see* Antsirañana
An tSionainn *see* Shannon
180 J2 **Antsirañana** *var.* Antserana; *prev.* Antsirane, Diégo-Suarez. Antsirañana, N Madagascar 12.19S 49.16E
180 J2 **Antsirañana** ◆ *province* N Madagascar
Antsirane *see* Antsirañana
An tSiúir *see* Suir
120 I7 **Antsla** *Ger.* Anzen. Võrumaa, SE Estonia 57.49N 26.34E
An tSláine *see* Slaney
180 J3 **Antsohihy** Mahajanga, NW Madagascar 14.49S 47.58E
65 G14 **Antuco, Volcán** ▲ C Chile 37.29S 71.25W
175 P7 **Antu, Gunung** ▲ Borneo, N Indonesia 0.57N 118.51E
An Tullach *see* Tullow
An-tung *see* Dandong
Antunnacum *see* Andernach
Antwerp *see* Antwerpen
101 G16 **Antwerpen** *Eng.* Antwerp, *Fr.* Anvers. Antwerpen, N Belgium 51.13N 4.25E
101 H16 **Antwerpen** *Eng.* Antwerp. ◆ *province* N Belgium
An Uaimh *see* Navan
160 N12 **Anugul** *var.* Angul. Orissa, E India 20.51N 84.59E
158 F9 **Anūpgarh** Rājasthān, NW India 29.10N 73.13E
160 K10 **Anūppur** Madhya Pradesh, C India 23.06N 81.45E
161 K24 **Anuradhapura** North Central Province, C Sri Lanka 8.19N 80.25E
Anvers *see* Antwerpen
204 G4 **Anvers Island** *island* Antarctica
41 N11 **Anvik** Alaska, USA 62.39N 160.12W
41 N10 **Anvik River** ≈ Alaska, USA
40 F17 **Anvil Peak** ▲ Semisopochnoi Island, Alaska, USA 51.59N 179.36E
165 P7 **Anxi** *var.* Yuanquan. Gansu, N China 40.31N 95.45E
190 F8 **Anxious Bay** *bay* South Australia
167 O5 **Anyang** Henan, C China 36.10N 114.18E
165 S11 **A'nyêmaqên Shan** ▲▲ C China
120 H12 **Anykščiai** Utena, E Lithuania 55.30N 25.34E
167 P13 **Anyuan** *var.* Xinshan. Jiangxi, S China 25.10N 115.25E
127 O6 **Anyuysk** Chukotskiy Avtonomnyy Okrug, NE Russian Federation 68.22N 161.33E
127 Oo5 **Anyuyskiy Khrebet** ▲▲ NE Russian Federation
56 D8 **Anza** Antioquia, C Colombia 6.18N 75.54W
Anzen *see* Antsla
126 H13 **Anzhero-Sudzhensk** Kemerovskaya Oblast', S Russian Federation 56.00N 85.42E
109 I16 **Anzio** Lazio, C Italy 41.27N 12.37E
57 O6 **Anzoátegui** *off.* Estado Anzoátegui. ◆ *state* NE Venezuela
153 P12 **Anzob** W Tajikistan 39.24N 68.55E
Anzyō *see* Anjō
Aoba *see* Ambae
172 Ss13 **Aoga-shima** *island* Izu-shotō, SE Japan
Aohan Qi *see* Xinhui
Aoiz *see* Agoiz
195 X16 **Aola** *var.* Tenaghau. Guadalcanal, C Solomon Islands 9.32S 160.28E
178 Gg15 **Ao Luk Nua** Krabi, SW Thailand 8.21N 98.43E
Aomen *see* Macao
172 N8 **Aomori** Aomori, Honshū, C Japan 40.49N 140.43E
171 Mm9 **Aomori** *off.* Aomori-ken. ◆ *prefecture* Honshū, C Japan
Aontroim *see* Antrim
117 C15 **Aóos** *var.* Vijosa, Vijosë, *Alb.* Lumi i Vjosës. ≈ Albania/Greece *see also* Vjosës, Lumi i
203 Q7 **Aorai, Mont** ▲ Tahiti, W French Polynesia 17.36S 149.28W
193 E19 **Aoraki** *prev.* Aorangi, Mount Cook. ▲ South Island, NZ 43.38S 170.05E
178 Ii13 **Aôral, Phnum** *prev.* Phnom Aural. ▲ W Cambodia 12.01N 104.10E
Aorangi *see* Aoraki
193 L15 **Aorangi Mountains** ▲▲ North Island, NZ
192 H13 **Aorere** ≈ South Island, NZ
108 A7 **Aosta** *anc.* Augusta Praetoria. Valle d'Aosta, NW Italy 45.43N 7.19E
79 O11 **Aougoundou, Lac** ◎ S Mali
78 K9 **Aoukâr** *var.* Aouker. *plateau* C Mauritania
80 J13 **Aouk, Bahr** ≈ Central African Republic/Chad
Aouker *see* Aoukâr
76 B11 **Aousard** SE Western Sahara 22.42N 14.22W
170 G12 **Aoya** Tottori, Honshū, SW Japan 35.31N 134.01E
Aoyang *see* Shanggao
80 H5 **Aozou** Borkou-Ennedi-Tibesti, N Chad 22.00N 17.11E
28 M11 **Apache** Oklahoma, C USA 34.57N 98.21W
38 L14 **Apache Junction** Arizona, SW USA 33.25N 111.33W
26 J9 **Apache Mountains** ▲▲ Texas, SW USA
38 M16 **Apache Peak** ▲ Arizona, SW USA 31.50N 110.25W

◆ Country ● Country Capital ◇ Dependent Territory ○ Dependent Territory Capital ◆ Administrative Region ✈ International Airport ▲ Mountain ▲▲ Mountain Range Volcano ≈ River ◎ Lake ⊠ Reservoir

APAHIDA – ARMSTRONG

118 *H10* **Apahida** Cluj, NW Romania *46.49N 23.45E*
25 *T9* **Apalachee Bay** *bay* Florida, SE USA
25 *T3* **Apalachee River** ≈ Georgia, SE USA
25 *S10* **Apalachicola** Florida, SE USA *29.43N 84.58W*
25 *S10* **Apalachicola Bay** *bay* Florida, SE USA
25 *R9* **Apalachicola River** ≈ Florida, SE USA
Apam *see* Apan
Apamama *see* Abemama
43 *P14* **Apan** *var.* Apam. Hidalgo, C Mexico *19.41N 98.24W*
44 *J8* **Apanás, Lago de** ◎ NW Nicaragua
56 *H14* **Apaporis, Río** ≈ Brazil/Colombia
193 *C23* **Aparima** ≈ South Island, NZ
179 *P7* **Aparri** Luzon, N Philippines *18.16N 121.42E*
114 *J9* **Apatin** Serbia, NW Serbia and Montenegro (Yugoslavia) *45.40N 19.01E*
128 *J4* **Apatity** Murmanskaya Oblast', NW Russian Federation *67.33N 33.26E*
57 *X9* **Apatou** NW French Guiana *5.07N 54.20W*
42 *M14* **Apatzingán** *var.* Apatzingán de la Constitución. Michoacán de Ocampo, SW Mexico *19.04N 102.19W*
176 *Y9* **Apauwar** Papua, E Indonesia *1.36S 138.10E*
Apaxtla *see* Apaxtla de Castrejón
43 *O15* **Apaxtla de Castrejón** *var.* Apaxtla. Guerrero, S Mexico *18.06N 99.55W*
120 *J7* **Ape** Alūksne, NE Latvia *57.32N 26.42E*
100 *L11* **Apeldoorn** Gelderland, E Netherlands *52.13N 5.57E*
Apennines *see* Appennino
Apenrade *see* Aabenraa
59 *L17* **Apere, Río** ≈ C Bolivia
57 *W11* **Apetina** Sipaliwini, SE Suriname *3.30N 55.03W*
23 *U9* **Apex** North Carolina, SE USA *35.43N 78.51W*
81 *M16* **Api Orientale,** N Dem. Rep. Congo *3.42N 25.22E*
158 *M9* **Api** ▲ NW Nepal *30.07N 80.57E*
Apia *see* Abaiang
198 *Bb8* **Āpia** ● (Samoa) Upolu, SE Samoa *13.49S 171.46W*
62 *K11* **Apiaí** São Paulo, S Brazil *24.28S 48.51W*
175 *P16* **Api, Gunung** ▲ Pulau Sangeang, S Indonesia *8.09S 119.03E*
195 *Y16* **Apio** Maramasike Island, N Solomon Islands *9.36S 161.25E*
43 *O15* **Apipilulco** Guerrero, S Mexico *18.10N 99.40W*
43 *P14* **Apizaco** Tlaxcala, S Mexico *19.24N 98.10W*
106 *I4* **A Pobla de Trives** *Cast.* Puebla de Trives. Galicia, NW Spain *42.21N 7.16W*
57 *U9* **Apoera** Sipaliwini, NW Suriname *5.10N 57.08W*
117 *O23* **Apolakkiá** Ródos, Dodekánisos, Greece, Aegean Sea *36.02N 27.48E*
103 *L16* **Apolda** Thüringen, C Germany *51.01N 11.31E*
198 *B8* **Apolima Strait** *strait* C Pacific Ocean
190 *M13* **Apollo Bay** Victoria, SE Australia *38.40S 143.44E*
Apollonia *see* Sozopol
59 *J16* **Apolo** La Paz, W Bolivia *14.40S 68.33W*
59 *J16* **Apolobamba, Cordillera** ▲▲ Bolivia/Peru
179 *Rr16* **Apo, Mount** ⛰ Mindanao, S Philippines *6.54N 125.16E*
25 *W11* **Apopka** Florida, SE USA *28.40N 81.30W*
25 *W11* **Apopka, Lake** ◎ Florida, SE USA
61 *J19* **Aporé, Rio** ≈ SW Brazil
32 *K2* **Apostle Islands** *island group* Wisconsin, N USA
Apostolas Andreas, Cape *see* Zafer Burnu
63 *F14* **Apóstoles** Misiones, NE Argentina *27.54S 55.45W*
Apostólou Andréa, Akrotíri *see* Zafer Burnu
119 *S9* **Apostolove** *Rus.* Apostolovo. Dnipropetrovs'ka Oblast', E Ukraine *47.40N 33.45E*
Apostolovo *see* Apostolove
19 *Qq9* **Appalachian Mountains** ▲▲ E USA
97 *K14* **Äppelbo** Dalarna, C Sweden *60.30N 14.00E*
100 *N7* **Appelscha** *Fris.* Appelskea. Friesland, N Netherlands *52.57N 6.19E*
Appelskea *see* Appelscha
108 *G11* **Appennino** *Eng.* Apennines. ▲▲ Italy/San Marino
109 *L17* **Appennino Campano** ▲▲ C Italy
110 *I7* **Appenzell** Appenzell, NW Switzerland *47.19N 9.25E*
110 *H7* **Appenzell** ◈ *canton* NE Switzerland
57 *V12* **Appikalo** Sipaliwini, S Suriname *2.07N 56.16W*
100 *O5* **Appingedam** Groningen, NE Netherlands *53.18N 6.52E*
27 *X8* **Appleby** Texas, SW USA *31.43N 94.36W*
99 *L15* **Appleby-in-Westmorland** NW England, UK *54.34N 2.26W*
32 *K10* **Apple River** ≈ Illinois, N USA
32 *I5* **Apple River** ≈ Wisconsin, N USA
27 *W9* **Apple Springs** Texas, SW USA *31.13N 94.57W*
31 *S8* **Appleton** Minnesota, N USA *45.12N 96.01W*
32 *M7* **Appleton** Wisconsin, N USA *44.16N 88.24W*
29 *S5* **Appleton City** Missouri, C USA *38.11N 94.01W*
37 *U14* **Apple Valley** California, W USA *34.30N 117.11W*
31 *V9* **Apple Valley** Minnesota, N USA *44.43N 93.13W*
23 *U6* **Appomattox** Virginia, NE USA *37.21N 78.49W*
196 *B16* **Apra Harbour** *harbor* W Guam
196 *B16* **Apra Heights** W Guam
108 *F6* **Aprica, Passo dell'** *pass* N Italy *46.10N 10.08E*
109 *M15* **Apricena** *anc.* Hadria Picena. Puglia, SE Italy *41.46N 15.27E*
130 *L14* **Apsheronsk** Krasnodarskiy Kray, SW Russian Federation *44.27N 39.45E*
Apsheronskiy Poluostrov *see* Abşeron Yarımadası
105 *S15* **Apt** *anc.* Apta Julia. Vaucluse, SE France *43.54N 5.24E*
Apta Julia *see* Apt
40 *H12* **'Āpua Point** *var.* Apua Point *headland* Hawai'i, USA, C Pacific Ocean *19.15N 155.13W*
62 *I10* **Apucarana** Paraná, S Brazil *23.34S 51.28W*
Apulia *see* Puglia
56 *K8* **Apure** *off.* Estado Apure. ◈ *state* C Venezuela
56 *J7* **Apure, Río** ≈ W Venezuela
59 *F16* **Apurímac** *off.* Departamento de Apurímac. ◈ *department* C Peru
59 *F15* **Apurímac, Río** ≈ S Peru
118 *G10* **Apuseni, Munții** ▲▲ W Romania
Aqaba/'Aqaba *see* Al 'Aqabah
144 *F15* **Aqaba, Gulf of** *var.* Gulf of Elat, *Ar.* Khalīj al 'Aqabah; *anc.* Sinus Aelaniticus. *gulf* NE Red Sea
145 *R7* **'Aqabah** C Iraq *33.33N 42.55E*
'Aqabah, Khalīj al *see* Aqaba, Gulf of
155 *O2* **Āqchah** *var.* Āqcheh. Jowzjān, N Afghanistan *36.59N 66.07E*
Āqcheh *see* Āqchah
Aqköl *see* Akkol'
Aqmola *see* Astana
Aqmola Oblysy *see* Akmola
164 *L10* **Aqqikkol Hu** ◎ NW China
Aqqystaū *see* Akkystau
'Aqrah *see* Ākrē
Aqsay *see* Aksay
Aqshataū *see* Akchatau
Aqsū *see* Aksu
Aqsūat *see* Aksuat
Aqtas *see* Aktas
Aqtaū *see* Aktau
Aqtöbe/Aqtöbe Oblysy *see* Aktobe
Aqtoghay *see* Aktogay
Aquae Augustae *see* Dax
Aquae Calidae *see* Bath
Aquae Flaviae *see* Chaves
Aquae Grani *see* Aachen
Aquae Panoniae *see* Baden
Aquae Sextiae *see* Aix-en-Provence
Aquae Solis *see* Bath
Aquae Tarbelicae *see* Dax
38 *J11* **Aquarius Mountains** ▲▲ Arizona, SW USA
64 *O5* **Aquidabán, Río** ≈ E Paraguay
61 *H20* **Aquidauana** Mato Grosso do Sul, S Brazil *20.27S 55.45W*
42 *L15* **Aquila** Michoacán de Ocampo, S Mexico *18.36N 103.32W*
Aquila/Aquila degli Abruzzi *see* L'Aquila
27 *T8* **Aquilla** Texas, SW USA *31.51N 97.13W*
46 *L9* **Aquin** S Haiti *18.16N 73.24W*
Aquisgranum *see* Aachen
104 *J13* **Aquitaine** ◈ *region* SW France
Aqzhar *see* Akzhar
159 *P13* **Āra** *prev.* Arrah. Bihār, N India *25.34N 84.40E*
107 *S4* **Ara** ≈ NE Spain
25 *P2* **Arab** Alabama, S USA *34.19N 86.30W*
Araba *see* Álava
144 *G12* **'Arabah, Wādī al** *Heb.* Ha'Arava. *dry watercourse* Israel/Jordan
119 *U12* **Arabats'ka Strilka, Kosa** *spit* S Ukraine
119 *U12* **Arabats'ka Zatoka** *gulf* S Ukraine
'Arab, Baḩr al *see* Arab, Bahr el
82 *C12* **Arab, Bahr el** *var.* Baḩr al 'Arab. ≈ S Sudan
58 *E7* **Arabela, Río** ≈ N Peru
181 *O4* **Arabian Basin** *undersea feature* N Arabian Sea
Arabian Desert *see* Sahara el Sharqîya
147 *N9* **Arabian Peninsula** *peninsula* SW Asia
87 *P15* **Arabian Plate** *tectonic feature* Africa/Asia/Europe
147 *W14* **Arabian Sea** *sea* NW Indian Ocean
Arabicus, Sinus *see* Red Sea
'Arabī, Khalīj al *see* Persian Gulf
Arabistan *see* Khūzestān
'Arabīyah as Su'ūdīyah, Al Mamlakah al *see* Saudi Arabia
'Arabīyah Jumhūrīyah, Mişr al *see* Egypt
144 *I9* **'Arab, Jabal al** ▲▲ S Syria
124 *Pp14* **'Arab, Khalîg el** *Eng.* Arabs Gulf. *gulf* N Egypt
Arab Republic of Egypt *see* Egypt
Arabs Gulf *see* 'Arab, Khalîg el
145 *Y12* **'Arab, Shaţţ al** *Eng.* Shatt al Arab, *Per.* Arvand Rūd. ≈ Iran/Iraq
142 *I11* **Araç** Kastamonu, N Turkey *41.13N 33.19E*
61 *P16* **Aracaju** *state capital* Sergipe, E Brazil *10.45S 37.07W*
56 *F5* **Aracataca** Magdalena, N Colombia *10.36N 74.13W*
60 *P13* **Aracati** Ceará, E Brazil *4.31S 37.45W*
62 *J8* **Araçatuba** São Paulo, S Brazil *21.12S 50.24W*
106 *J13* **Aracena** Andalucía, S Spain *37.54N 6.33W*
117 *F20* **Arachnaío** ▲▲ S Greece
117 *D16* **Árachthos** *var.* Arta; *prev.* Árakhthos, *anc.* Arachthus. ≈ W Greece
Arachthus *see* Árachthos
61 *N19* **Araçuai** Minas Gerais, SE Brazil *16.52S 42.03W*
142 *I11* **Araç Çayı** ≈ N Turkey
144 *F11* **'Arad** Southern, S Israel *31.16N 35.09E*
118 *F11* **Arad** Arad, W Romania *46.12N 21.20E*
118 *F11* **Arad** ◈ *county* W Romania
80 *J9* **Arada** Biltine, NE Chad *15.00N 20.38E*
149 *P18* **'Arādah** Abū Z̧aby, S UAE *22.57N 53.24E*
Aradhippou *see* Aradíppou
124 *O3* **Aradíppou** *var.* Aradhippou. SE Cyprus *34.57N 33.37E*
182 *K6* **Arafura Sea** *Ind.* Laut Arafuru. *sea* W Pacific Ocean
182 *L6* **Arafura Shelf** *undersea feature* C Arafura Sea
Arafuru, Laut *see* Arafura Sea
61 *J18* **Aragarças** Goiás, C Brazil *15.55S 52.12W*
Aragats, Gora *see* Aragats Lerr
143 *T12* **Aragats Lerr** *Rus.* Gora Aragats. ▲ W Armenia *40.31N 44.06E*
34 *E14* **Arago, Cape** *headland* Oregon, NW USA *43.17N 124.25W*
107 *R6* **Aragón** ◈ *autonomous community* E Spain
107 *Q4* **Aragón** ≈ NE Spain
109 *I24* **Aragona** Sicilia, Italy, C Mediterranean Sea *37.25N 13.37E*
107 *Q7* **Aragoncillo** ▲ C Spain *40.59N 2.01W*
56 *L5* **Aragua** *off.* Estado Aragua. ◈ *state* N Venezuela
57 *N6* **Aragua de Barcelona** Anzoátegui, NE Venezuela *9.30N 64.45W*
57 *O5* **Aragua de Maturín** Monagas, NE Venezuela *9.58N 63.30W*
61 *K15* **Araguaia, Río** *var.* Araguaya. ≈ C Brazil
61 *K19* **Araguari** Minas Gerais, SE Brazil *18.37S 48.13W*
60 *J11* **Araguari, Rio** ≈ SW Brazil
Araguaya *see* Araguaia, Río
106 *K14* **Arahal** Andalucía, S Spain *37.15N 5.33W*
171 *Jj13* **Arai** Niigata, Honshū, C Japan *36.58N 138.14E*
Árainn *see* Inishmore
Árainn Mhór *see* Aran Island
Ara Jovis *see* Aranjuez
76 *J11* **Arak** C Algeria *25.17N 3.45E*
176 *Yy15* **Arak** Papua, E Indonesia *7.14S 139.40E*
148 *M7* **Arāk** *prev.* Sultānābād. Markazī, W Iran *34.07N 49.39E*
196 *D10* **Arakabesan** *island* Palau Islands, N Palau
57 *S7* **Arakaka** NW Guyana *7.37N 59.58W*
177 *Ff6* **Arakan State** *var.* Rakhine State. ◈ *state* W Myanmar
177 *Ff5* **Arakan Yoma** ▲▲ W Myanmar
171 *Kk12* **Arakawa** Niigata, Honshū, C Japan *38.06N 139.25E*
Árakhthos *see* Árachthos
Araks/Arak's *see* Aras
164 *H7* **Aral** Xinjiang Uygur Zizhiqu, NW China *40.40N 81.19E*
Aral *see* Aral'sk, Kazakhstan
Aral *see* Vose', Tajikistan
Aral-Bukhorskiy Kanal *see* Amu-Buxoro Kanali
143 *T12* **Aralik** Iğdır, E Turkey *39.54N 44.28E*
152 *H5* **Aral Sea** *Kaz.* Aral Tengizi, *Rus.* Aral'skoye More, *Uzb.* Orol Dengizi. *inland sea* Kazakhstan/Uzbekistan
150 *L13* **Aral'sk** *Kaz.* Aral. Kzylorda, SW Kazakhstan *46.48N 61.40E*
Aral'skoye More/Aral Tengizi *see* Aral Sea
43 *O10* **Aramberri** Nuevo León, NE Mexico *24.05N 99.52W*
194 *F14* **Aramia** ≈ SW PNG
149 *N6* **Ārān** *var.* Golārā. Eşfahān, C Iran *34.03N 51.30E*
107 *N5* **Aranda de Duero** Castilla-León, N Spain *41.40N 3.40W*
114 *M12* **Aranđelovac** *prev.* Arandjelovac. Serbia, C Serbia and Montenegro (Yugoslavia) *44.18N 20.32E*
Arandjelovac *see* Aranđelovac
99 *J19* **Aran Fawddwy** ▲ NW Wales, UK *52.48N 3.42W*
99 *C14* **Aran Island** *Ir.* Árainn Mhór. *island* NW Ireland
99 *A18* **Aran Islands** *island group* W Ireland
107 *N9* **Aranjuez** *anc.* Ara Jovis. Madrid, C Spain *40.01N 3.37W*
85 *E20* **Aranos** Hardap, SE Namibia *24.11S 19.07E*
27 *U14* **Aransas Bay** *inlet* Texas, SW USA
27 *T14* **Aransas Pass** Texas, SW USA *27.54N 97.09W*
203 *O3* **Aranuka** *prev.* Nanouki. *atoll* Tungaru, W Kiribati
178 *I11* **Aranyaprathet** Prachin Buri, S Thailand *13.42N 102.32E*
Aranyosasztal *see* Zlatý Stôl
Aranyosgyéres *see* Câmpia Turzii
Aranyosmarót *see* Zlaté Moravce
170 *Cc14* **Arao** Kumamoto, Kyūshū, SW Japan *33.16N 130.25E*
79 *O8* **Araouane** Tombouctou, N Mali *18.58N 3.39W*
28 *L10* **Arapaho** Oklahoma, C USA *35.34N 98.57W*
31 *N16* **Arapahoe** Nebraska, C USA *40.18N 99.54W*
59 *I16* **Arapa, Laguna** ◎ SE Peru
193 *K14* **Arapawa Island** *island* C NZ
63 *E17* **Arapey Grande, Río** ≈ N Uruguay
61 *P16* **Arapiraca** Alagoas, E Brazil *9.45S 36.40W*
146 *M3* **'Ar'ar** Al Ḩudūd ash Shamālīyah, NW Saudi Arabia *31.00N 41.00E*
56 *G15* **Araracuara** Caquetá, S Colombia *0.36S 72.24W*
63 *K15* **Araranguá** Santa Catarina, S Brazil *28.55S 49.30W*
62 *L8* **Araraquara** São Paulo, S Brazil *21.46S 48.07W*
61 *O13* **Araras** Ceará, E Brazil *4.08S 40.30W*
60 *I14* **Araras** Pará, N Brazil *6.03S 54.34W*
62 *L9* **Araras** São Paulo, S Brazil *22.21S 47.21W*
62 *H11* **Araras, Serra das** ▲▲ S Brazil
143 *U12* **Ararat** S Armenia *39.49N 44.45E*
190 *M12* **Ararat** Victoria, SE Australia *37.18S 142.57E*
Ararat, Mount *see* Büyükağrı Dağı
146 *M3* **'Ar'ar, Wādī** *dry watercourse* Iraq/Saudi Arabia
133 *N7* **Aras** *Arm.* Arak's, *Az.* Araz Nehri, *Per.* Rūd-e Aras, *Rus.* Araks; *prev.* Araxes. ≈ SW Asia
107 *R9* **Aras de Alpuente** País Valenciano, E Spain *39.55N 1.09W*
143 *S13* **Aras Güneyi Dağları** ▲▲ NE Turkey
Aras, Rūd-e *see* Aras
203 *U9* **Aratika** *atoll* Îles Tuamotu, C French Polynesia
Aratürük *see* Yiwu
56 *I8* **Arauca** Arauca, NE Colombia *7.03N 70.46W*
56 *I8* **Arauca** *off.* Intendencia de Arauca. ◈ *province* NE Colombia
65 *G15* **Araucanía** *off.* Región de la Araucanía. ◈ *region* C Chile
56 *L7* **Arauca, Río** ≈ Colombia/Venezuela
65 *F14* **Arauco** Bío Bío, C Chile *37.16S 73.15W*
65 *F14* **Arauco, Golfo de** *gulf* S Chile
56 *H8* **Arauquita** Arauca, C Colombia *7.01N 71.20W*
Arausio *see* Orange
158 *F13* **Arāvali Range** ▲▲ N India
195 *S12* **Arawa** Bougainville Island, NE PNG *6.13S 155.37E*
193 *C20* **Arawata** ≈ South Island, NZ
194 *L12* **Arawe Islands** *island group* E PNG
61 *L20* **Araxá** Minas Gerais, SE Brazil *19.37S 46.49W*
Araxes *see* Aras
57 *O5* **Araya** Sucre, N Venezuela *10.34N 64.15W*
107 *R4* **Arba** ≈ N Spain
83 *I15* **Ārba Minch'** Southern, S Ethiopia *6.02N 37.34E*
145 *U4* **Arbat** NE Iraq *35.26N 45.34E*
109 *D19* **Arbatax** Sardegna, Italy, C Mediterranean Sea *39.57N 9.42E*
Arbe *see* Rab
Arbela *see* Arbīl
145 *S3* **Arbīl** *var.* Erbil, Irbīl, *Kurd.* Hawlēr; *anc.* Arbela. N Iraq *36.12N 44.01E*
97 *M16* **Arboga** Västmanland, C Sweden *59.24N 15.49E*
97 *M16* **Arbogaån** ≈ C Sweden
105 *S9* **Arbois** Jura, E France *46.54N 5.45E*
56 *D6* **Arboletes** Antioquia, NW Colombia *8.52N 76.25W*
9 *X15* **Arborg** Manitoba, S Canada *50.52N 97.20W*
96 *N12* **Arbrå** Gävleborg, C Sweden *61.27N 16.21E*
98 *K10* **Arbroath** *anc.* Aberbrothock. E Scotland, UK *56.34N 2.34W*
37 *N6* **Arbuckle** California, W USA *39.00N 122.05W*
29 *N12* **Arbuckle Mountains** ▲▲ Oklahoma, C USA
Arbuzinka *see* Arbyzynka
119 *Q8* **Arbyzynka** *Rus.* Arbuzinka. Mykolayivs'ka Oblast', S Ukraine *47.54N 31.19E*
105 *U12* **Arc** ≈ E France
104 *J13* **Arcachon** Gironde, SW France *44.40N 1.10W*
104 *J13* **Arcachon, Bassin d'** *inlet* SW France
20 *E10* **Arcade** New York, NE USA *42.32N 78.19W*
25 *W14* **Arcadia** Florida, SE USA *27.13N 81.51W*
24 *H5* **Arcadia** Louisiana, S USA *32.33N 92.55W*
32 *J7* **Arcadia** Wisconsin, N USA *44.15N 91.30W*
Arcae Remorum *see* Châlons-en-Champagne
46 *L9* **Arcahaie** C Haiti *18.46N 72.32W*
36 *K3* **Arcata** California, W USA *40.51N 124.06W*
37 *U6* **Arc Dome** ▲ Nevada, W USA *38.52N 117.20W*
109 *J16* **Arce** Lazio, C Italy *41.35N 13.34E*
43 *O15* **Arcelia** Guerrero, S Mexico *18.19N 100.16W*
101 *M15* **Arcen** Limburg, SE Netherlands *51.28N 6.10E*
Archangel *see* Arkhangel'sk
Archangel Bay *see* Chëshskaya Guba
117 *O23* **Archángelos** *var.* Arhangelos, Arkhángelos. Ródos, Dodekánisos, Greece, Aegean Sea *36.13N 28.07E*
116 *F7* **Archar** ≈ NW Bulgaria
33 *R11* **Archbold** Ohio, N USA *41.31N 84.18W*
107 *R12* **Archena** Murcia, SE Spain *38.07N 1.16W*
27 *R5* **Archer City** Texas, SW USA *33.36N 98.37W*
106 *M14* **Archidona** Andalucía, S Spain *37.06N 4.22W*
67 *B25* **Arch Islands** *island group* SW Falkland Islands
108 *G13* **Arcidosso** Toscana, C Italy *42.52N 11.30E*
105 *Q5* **Arcis-sur-Aube** Aube, N France *48.32N 4.09E*
190 *F3* **Arckaringa Creek** *seasonal river* South Australia
108 *G7* **Arco** Trentino-Alto Adige, N Italy *45.53N 10.51E*
35 *Q14* **Arco** Idaho, NW USA *43.38N 113.18W*
32 *M14* **Arcola** Illinois, N USA *39.39N 88.19W*
107 *P6* **Arcos de Jalón** Castilla-León, N Spain *41.12N 2.13W*
106 *K15* **Arcos de la Frontera** Andalucía, S Spain *36.45N 5.49W*
106 *G5* **Arcos de Valdevez** Viana do Castelo, N Portugal *41.51N 8.25W*
61 *P15* **Arcoverde** Pernambuco, E Brazil *08.23S 37.00W*
104 *H5* **Arcovest, Pointe de l'** *headland* NW France *48.49N 2.58W*
Arctic-Mid Oceanic Ridge *see* Nansen Cordillera
207 *R8* **Arctic Ocean** *ocean*
14 *G4* **Arctic Red River** ≈ Northwest Territories/Yukon Territory, NW Canada
Arctic Red River *see* Tsiigehtchic
41 *S6* **Arctic Village** Alaska, USA *68.07N 145.32W*
204 *H1* **Arctowski** *Polish research station* South Shetland Islands, Antarctica *61.57S 58.23W*
116 *I12* **Arda** *var.* Ardhas, *Gk.* Ardas. ≈ Bulgaria/Greece *see also* Ardas
148 *L2* **Ardabīl** *var.* Ardebil. Ardabīl, NW Iran *38.15N 48.18E*
148 *L2* **Ardabīl** *off.* Ostān-e Ardabīl. ◈ *province* NW Iran
143 *R11* **Ardahan** Ardahan, NE Turkey *41.07N 42.40E*
143 *S11* **Ardahan** ◈ *province* NE Turkey
149 *P8* **Ardakān** Yazd, C Iran *32.20N 54.02E*
96 *E12* **Årdalstangen** Sogn og Fjordane, S Norway *61.13N 7.43E*
143 *R11* **Ardanuç** Artvin, NE Turkey *41.07N 42.04E*
116 *L12* **Ardas** *var.* Ardhas, *Bul.* Arda. ≈ Bulgaria/Greece *see also* Arda
144 *I13* **Arḑ aş Şawwān** *var.* Ardh es Suwwān. *plain* S Jordan
131 *P5* **Ardatov** Respublika Mordoviya, W Russian Federation *54.49N 46.13E*
12 *G12* **Ardbeg** Ontario, S Canada *45.38N 80.05W*
Ardeal *see* Transylvania
Ardebil *see* Ardabīl
105 *Q13* **Ardèche** ≈ C France
105 *Q13* **Ardèche** ◈ *department* E France
99 *F17* **Ardee** *Ir.* Baile Átha Fhirdhia. NE Ireland *53.52N 6.33W*
105 *Q3* **Ardennes** ◈ *department* NE France
101 *J23* **Ardennes** *physical region* Belgium/France
143 *Q11* **Ardeşen** Rize, NE Turkey *41.12N 41.02E*
149 *O7* **Ardestān** *var.* Ardistan. Eşfahān, C Iran *33.29N 52.16E*
110 *J9* **Ardez** Graubünden, SE Switzerland *46.47N 10.09E*
Ardhas *see* Arda/Ardas
Ardh es Suwwān *see* Arḑ aş Şawwān
106 *I12* **Ardila, Ribeira de** *Sp.* Ardilla. ≈ Portugal/Spain *see also* Ardilla
9 *T17* **Ardill** Saskatchewan, S Canada *49.56N 105.49W*
106 *I12* **Ardilla** *Port.* Ribeira de Ardila. ≈ Portugal/Spain *see also* Ardila, Ribeira de
42 *M11* **Ardilla, Cerro la** ▲ C Mexico *22.15N 102.33W*
116 *J12* **Ardino** Kŭrdzhali, S Bulgaria *41.38N 25.22E*
Ardistan *see* Ardestān
191 *P9* **Ardlethan** New South Wales, SE Australia *34.24S 146.52E*
Ard Mhacha *see* Armagh
25 *P1* **Ardmore** Alabama, S USA *34.59N 86.51W*
29 *N13* **Ardmore** Oklahoma, C USA *34.10N 97.08W*
22 *J10* **Ardmore** Tennessee, S USA *35.00N 86.48W*
98 *G10* **Ardnamurchan, Point of** *headland* N Scotland, UK *56.42N 6.15W*
Árdni *see* Arnøya
101 *C17* **Ardooie** West-Vlaanderen, W Belgium *50.59N 3.10E*
190 *I9* **Ardrossan** South Australia *34.27S 137.54E*
118 *H9* **Ardusat** *Hung.* Erdőszáda. Maramureş, N Romania *47.36N 23.25E*
95 *F16* **Åre** Jämtland, C Sweden *63.25N 13.04E*
81 *P16* **Arebi** Orientale, NE Dem. Rep. Congo *2.46N 29.34E*
47 *T5* **Arecibo** C Puerto Rico *18.28N 66.43W*
176 *W10* **Aredo** Papua, E Indonesia *2.27S 133.59E*
61 *P14* **Areia Branca** Rio Grande do Norte, E Brazil *4.53S 37.03W*
121 *O14* **Arekhawsk** *Rus.* Orekhovsk. Vitsyebskaya Voblasts', N Belarus *54.42N 30.30E*
Arel *see* Arlon
Arelas/Arelate *see* Arles
Arenal, Embalse de *see* Arenal Laguna
44 *L12* **Arenal Laguna** *var.* Embalse de Arenal. ◎ NW Costa Rica
44 *L13* **Arenal, Volcán** ⛰ NW Costa Rica *10.21N 84.42W*
36 *K6* **Arena, Point** *headland* California, W USA *38.57N 123.44W*
61 *H17* **Arenápolis** Mato Grosso, W Brazil *14.25S 56.52W*
42 *G10* **Arena, Punta** *headland* W Mexico *23.28N 109.24W*
106 *L8* **Arenas de San Pedro** Castilla-León, N Spain *40.12N 5.04W*
65 *I24* **Arenas, Punta de** *headland* S Argentina *53.10S 68.15W*
63 *B20* **Arenaza** Buenos Aires, E Argentina *34.55S 61.45W*
97 *F17* **Arendal** Aust-Agder, S Norway *58.27N 8.45E*
101 *J16* **Arendonk** Antwerpen, N Belgium *51.18N 5.06E*
45 *T15* **Arenosa** Panamá, N Panama *9.02N 79.57W*
Arensburg *see* Kuressaare
107 *W5* **Arenys de Mar** Cataluña, NE Spain *41.34N 2.33E*
108 *C9* **Arenzano** Liguria, NW Italy *44.25N 8.43E*
117 *F22* **Areópoli** *prev.* Areópolis. Pelopónnisos, S Greece *36.39N 22.24E*
Areópolis *see* Areópoli
59 *H18* **Arequipa** Arequipa, SE Peru *16.24S 71.33W*
59 *G17* **Arequipa** *off.* Departamento de Arequipa. ◈ *department* SW Peru
63 *B19* **Arequito** Santa Fe, C Argentina *33.09S 61.28W*
106 *M7* **Arévalo** Castilla-León, N Spain *41.04N 4.43W*
108 *H12* **Arezzo** *anc.* Arretium. Toscana, C Italy *43.28N 11.49E*
107 *Q4* **Arga** ≈ N Spain
Argaeus *see* Erciyes Dağı
117 *G17* **Argalastí** Thessalía, C Greece *39.13N 23.14E*
107 *O10* **Argamasilla de Alba** Castilla-La Mancha, C Spain *39.07N 3.04W*
164 *L8* **Argan** Xinjiang Uygur Zizhiqu, NW China *40.09N 88.16E*
107 *O8* **Arganda** Madrid, C Spain *40.19N 3.25W*
106 *H8* **Arganil** Coimbra, N Portugal *40.13N 8.03W*
179 *Qq14* **Argao** Cebu, C Philippines *9.52N 123.33E*
159 *V15* **Argartala** Tripura, NE India
126 *K9* **Arga-Sala** ≈ NE Russian Federation
105 *P17* **Argelès-sur-Mer** Pyrénées-Orientales, S France *42.33N 3.01E*
105 *T15* **Argens** ≈ SE France
108 *H9* **Argenta** Emilia-Romagna, N Italy *44.37N 11.49E*
104 *K5* **Argentan** Orne, N France *48.45N 0.01W*
105 *N12* **Argentat** Corrèze, C France *45.06N 1.57E*
108 *A9* **Argentera** Piemonte, NE Italy *44.25N 6.57E*
105 *N5* **Argenteuil** Val-d'Oise, N France *48.57N 2.13E*
64 *K13* **Argentina** *off.* Republic of Argentina. ◆ *republic* S South America
Argentina Basin *see* Argentine Basin
Argentine Abyssal Plain *see* Argentine Plain
67 *I19* **Argentine Basin** *var.* Argentina Basin. *undersea feature* SW Atlantic Ocean
67 *I20* **Argentine Plain** *var.* Argentine Abyssal Plain. *undersea feature* SW Atlantic Ocean
Argentine Rise *see* Falkland Plateau
65 *H22* **Argentino, Lago** ◎ S Argentina
104 *K8* **Argenton-Château** Deux-Sèvres, W France *46.59N 0.22W*
104 *M9* **Argenton-sur-Creuse** Indre, C France *46.34N 1.32E*
Argentoratum *see* Strasbourg
118 *I12* **Argeş** ◈ *county* S Romania
118 *K14* **Argeş** ≈ S Romania
155 *O8* **Arghandāb, Daryā-ye** ≈ SE Afghanistan
Arghastān *see* Arghestān
155 *O8* **Arghestān** *Pash.* Arghastān. ≈ SE Afghanistan
Argirocastro *see* Gjirokastër
82 *E7* **Argo** Northern, N Sudan *19.31N 30.25E*
181 *P7* **Argo Fracture Zone** *tectonic feature* C Indian Ocean
117 *F20* **Argolikós Kólpos** *gulf* S Greece
105 *R4* **Argonne** *physical region* NE France
174 *Mm15* **Argopuro, Gunung** ▲ Jawa, S Indonesia *7.57S 113.32E*
117 *F20* **Árgos** Pelopónnisos, S Greece *37.38N 22.42E*
145 *S1* **Argōsh** N Iraq *37.07N 44.13E*
117 *D14* **Árgos Orestikó** Dytikí Makedonía, N Greece *40.27N 21.15E*
117 *B19* **Argostóli** *var.* Argostólion. Kefallinía, Iónioi Nísoi, Greece, C Mediterranean Sea *38.10N 20.29E*
Argostólion *see* Argostóli
Argovie *see* Aargau
37 *O14* **Arguello, Point** *headland* California, W USA *34.34N 120.39W*
131 *P16* **Argun** Chechenskaya Respublika, SW Russian Federation *43.16N 45.53E*
163 *T2* **Argun** *Chin.* Ergun He, *Rus.* Argun'. ≈ China/Russian Federation
79 *T12* **Argungu** Kebbi, NW Nigeria *12.45N 4.24E*
168 *J9* **Arguut** Övörhangay, C Mongolia *45.27N 102.25E*
189 *N3* **Argyle, Lake** *salt lake* Western Australia
98 *G12* **Argyll** *cultural region* W Scotland, UK
Argyrokastron *see* Gjirokastër
168 *I7* **Arhangay** ◈ *province* C Mongolia
Arhangelos *see* Archángelos
97 *P14* **Arholma** Stockholm, C Sweden *59.51N 19.01E*
97 *G22* **Århus** *var.* Aarhus. Århus, C Denmark *56.09N 10.10E*
97 *G22* **Århus** ◈ *county* C Denmark
145 *T1* **Ārī** E Iraq *37.07N 44.34E*
194 *M12* **Aria** ≈ New Britain, E PNG
Aria *see* Herāt
170 *C13* **Ariake-kai** *bay* NE East China Sea
85 *F22* **Ariamsvlei** Karas, SE Namibia *28.07S 19.49E*
109 *L17* **Ariano Irpino** Campania, S Italy *41.08N 15.00E*
56 *F11* **Ariari, Río** ≈ C Colombia
157 *K19* **Ari Atoll** *atoll* C Maldives
79 *P11* **Aribinda** N Burkina *14.12N 0.50W*
64 *G2* **Arica** *hist.* San Marcos de Arica. Tarapacá, N Chile *18.30S 70.18W*
56 *H16* **Arica** Amazonas, S Colombia *2.09S 71.48W*
64 *G2* **Arica** ✈ Tarapacá, N Chile *18.30S 70.19W*
170 *G16* **Arida** Wakayama, Honshū, SW Japan *34.05N 135.07E*
116 *E13* **Aridaía** *var.* Aridea, Aridhaía. Dytikí Makedonía, N Greece *40.58N 22.04E*
Aridea *see* Aridaía
180 *I15* **Aride, Île** *island* Inner Islands, NE Seychelles
Aridhaía *see* Aridaía
105 *N17* **Ariège** ◈ *department* S France
104 *M16* **Ariège** *var.* la Riege. ≈ Andorra/France
118 *H11* **Arieş** ≈ W Romania
155 *U10* **Ārifwāla** Punjab, E Pakistan *30.14N 73.04E*
Ariguaní *see* El Difícil
144 *G11* **Arīhā** Al Karak, W Jordan *31.25N 35.46E*
144 *I3* **Arīḩā** *var.* Arīhā. Idlib, W Syria *35.49N 36.36E*
Arīḩā *see* Jericho
39 *W4* **Arikaree River** ≈ Colorado/Nebraska, C USA
170 *Bb12* **Arikawa** Nagasaki, Nakadōri-jima, SW Japan *32.58N 129.06E*
114 *L13* **Arilje** Serbia, W Serbia and Montenegro (Yugoslavia) *43.45N 20.06E*
47 *U14* **Arima** Trinidad, Trinidad and Tobago *10.38N 61.16W*
Arime *see* Al 'Arīmah
Ariminum *see* Rimini
61 *H16* **Arinos, Rio** ≈ W Brazil
42 *M14* **Ario de Rosales** *var.* Ario de Rosáles. Michoacán de Ocampo, SW Mexico *19.12N 101.43W*
120 *F12* **Ariogala** Kaunas, C Lithuania *55.16N 23.30E*
49 *T7* **Aripuanã** ≈ W Brazil
61 *E15* **Ariquemes** Rondônia, W Brazil *9.55S 63.06W*
124 *Rr15* **'Arîsh, Wâdi el** ≈ NE Egypt
56 *K6* **Arismendi** Barinas, C Venezuela *8.28N 68.22W*
8 *J14* **Aristazabal Island** *island* SW Canada
62 *F13* **Aristóbulo del Valle** Misiones, NE Argentina *27.09S 54.54W*
180 *I5* **Arivonimamo** ✈ (Antananarivo) Antananarivo, C Madagascar *19.00S 47.11E*
Arixang *see* Wenquan
107 *Q6* **Ariza** Aragón, NE Spain *41.19N 2.03W*
64 *I6* **Arizaro, Salar de** *salt lake* NW Argentina
64 *K13* **Arizona** San Luis, C Argentina *35.43S 65.16W*
38 *J12* **Arizona** *off.* State of Arizona; also known as Copper State, Grand Canyon State. ◈ *state* SW USA
42 *G4* **Arizpe** Sonora, NW Mexico *30.19N 110.11W*
97 *J16* **Årjäng** Värmland, C Sweden *59.24N 12.09E*
149 *P8* **Arjenān** Yazd, C Iran *32.19N 53.48E*
94 *I13* **Arjeplog** Norrbotten, N Sweden *66.04N 18.00E*
56 *E5* **Arjona** Bolívar, N Colombia *10.13N 75.22W*
107 *N13* **Arjona** Andalucía, S Spain *37.55N 4.04W*
127 *N11* **Arka** Khabarovskiy Kray, E Russian Federation *60.04N 142.17E*
24 *L2* **Arkabutla Lake** ⊞ Mississippi, S USA
131 *O7* **Arkadak** Saratovskaya Oblast', W Russian Federation *51.55N 43.29E*
29 *T13* **Arkadelphia** Arkansas, C USA *34.07N 93.03W*
117 *J25* **Arkalochóri** *prev.* Arkalohori, Arkalokhórion. Kríti, Greece, E Mediterranean Sea *35.09N 25.15E*
Arkalohori/Arkalokhórion *see* Arkalochóri
151 *O10* **Arkalyk** *Kaz.* Arqalyq. Kostanay, N Kazakhstan *50.15N 66.52E*
29 *U10* **Arkansas** *off.* State of Arkansas; also known as The Land of Opportunity. ◈ *state* S USA
29 *W14* **Arkansas City** Arkansas, C USA *33.36N 91.12W*
29 *O7* **Arkansas City** Kansas, C USA *37.03N 97.02W*
18 *Kk10* **Arkansas River** ≈ C USA
190 *J5* **Arkaroola** South Australia *30.21S 139.20E*
Arkhángelos *see* Archángelos
128 *L8* **Arkhangel'sk** *Eng.* Archangel. Arkhangel'skaya Oblast', NW Russian Federation *64.31N 40.40E*
128 *L9* **Arkhangel'skaya Oblast'** ◈ *province* NW Russian Federation
131 *O14* **Arkhangel'skoye** Stavropol'skiy Kray, SW Russian Federation *44.37N 44.03E*
127 *N16* **Arkhara** Amurskaya Oblast', S Russian Federation *49.20N 130.04E*
99 *G19* **Arklow** *Ir.* An tInbhear Mór. SE Ireland *52.48N 6.09W*
117 *M20* **Arkoí** *island* Dodekánisos, Greece, Aegean Sea
29 *R11* **Arkoma** Oklahoma, C USA *35.19N 94.27W*
102 *O7* **Arkona, Kap** *headland* NE Germany *54.40N 13.24E*
97 *N17* **Arkösund** Östergötland, S Sweden *58.28N 16.55E*
126 *H4* **Arkticheskogo Instituta, Ostrova** *island* N Russian Federation
97 *O15* **Arlanda** ✈ (Stockholm) Stockholm, C Sweden *59.40N 17.58E*
152 *C11* **Arlandag** *Rus.* Gora Arlan. ▲ W Turkmenistan *39.39N 54.28E*
Arlan, Gora *see* Arlandag
107 *O5* **Arlanza** ≈ N Spain
107 *N5* **Arlanzón** ≈ N Spain
105 *R15* **Arles** *var.* Arles-sur-Rhône; *anc.* Arelas, Arelate. Bouches-du-Rhône, SE France *43.40N 4.37E*
Arles-sur-Rhône *see* Arles
105 *O17* **Arles-sur-Tech** Pyrénées-Orientales, S France *42.27N 2.37E*
31 *U9* **Arlington** Minnesota, N USA *44.36N 94.04W*
31 *R15* **Arlington** Nebraska, C USA *41.27N 96.21W*
34 *J11* **Arlington** Oregon, NW USA *45.43N 120.10W*
31 *R10* **Arlington** South Dakota, N USA *44.21N 97.07W*
22 *E10* **Arlington** Tennessee, S USA *35.17N 89.40W*
27 *T6* **Arlington** Texas, SW USA *32.43N 97.04W*
23 *W4* **Arlington** Virginia, NE USA *38.54N 77.09W*
34 *H7* **Arlington** Washington, NW USA *48.12N 122.07W*
32 *M10* **Arlington Heights** Illinois, N USA *42.08N 88.03W*
79 *U8* **Arlit** Agadez, C Niger *18.54N 7.25E*
101 *L24* **Arlon** *Dut.* Aarlen, *Ger.* Arel; *Lat.* Orolaunum. Luxembourg, SE Belgium *49.40N 5.49E*
29 *R7* **Arma** Kansas, C USA *37.32N 94.42W*
99 *F16* **Armagh** *Ir.* Ard Mhacha. S Northern Ireland, UK *54.15N 6.33W*
99 *F16* **Armagh** *cultural region* S Northern Ireland, UK
104 *K15* **Armagnac** *cultural region* S France
105 *Q7* **Armançon** ≈ C France
62 *K10* **Armando Laydner, Represa** ⊞ S Brazil
117 *M24* **Armathía** *island* SE Greece
130 *M14* **Armavir** Krasnodarskiy Kray, SW Russian Federation *44.59N 41.07E*
143 *T12* **Armavir** *prev.* Hoktemberyan, *Rus.* Oktemberyan. SW Armenia *40.09N 43.58E*
56 *E10* **Armenia** Quindío, W Colombia *4.31N 75.40W*
143 *T12* **Armenia** *off.* Republic of Armenia, *var.* Ajastan, *Arm.* Hayastani Hanrapetut'yun; *prev.* Armenian Soviet Socialist Republic. ◆ *republic* SW Asia
Armenierstadt *see* Gherla
105 *O1* **Armentières** Nord, N France *50.40N 2.52E*
42 *K14* **Armería** Colima, SW Mexico *18.55N 103.55W*
191 *T5* **Armidale** New South Wales, SE Australia *30.31S 151.40E*
31 *P11* **Armour** South Dakota, N USA *43.19N 98.21W*
63 *B18* **Armstrong** Santa Fe, C Argentina *32.46S 61.39W*

◆ Country
● Country Capital
◇ Dependent Territory
○ Dependent Territory Capital
◈ Administrative Region
✈ International Airport
▲ Mountain
▲▲ Mountain Range
⛰ Volcano
≈ River
◎ Lake
⊞ Reservoir

ARMSTRONG – ATHABASCA

9 N16 **Armstrong** British Columbia, SW Canada *50.27N 119.13W*
10 D11 **Armstrong** Ontario, S Canada *50.19N 89.01W*
31 U11 **Armstrong** Iowa, C USA *43.24N 94.28W*
27 S16 **Armstrong** Texas, SW USA *26.55N 97.47W*
119 S11 **Armyans'k** *Rus.* Armyansk. Respublika Krym, S Ukraine *46.05N 33.43E*
117 H14 **Arnaía** *var.* Arnea. Kentrikí Makedonía, N Greece *40.30N 23.36E*
123 Mm3 **Arnaoúti, Akrotíri** *var.* Arnaoutis, Cape Arnaouti. *headland* W Cyprus *35.06N 32.16E*
Arnaouti, Cape/Arnaoútis *see* Arnaoúti, Akrotíri
10 L4 **Arnaud** ≈ Québec, E Canada
105 Q8 **Arnay-le-Duc** Côte d'Or, C France *47.08N 4.27E*
Arnea *see* Arnaía
107 Q4 **Arnedo** La Rioja, N Spain *42.13N 2.04W*
97 I14 **Årnes** Akershus, S Norway *60.07N 11.28E*
Årnes *see* Åi Åfjord
28 K9 **Arnett** Oklahoma, C USA *36.07N 99.46W*
100 L12 **Arnhem** Gelderland, SE Netherlands *51.58N 5.54E*
189 Q2 **Arnhem Land** *physical region* Northern Territory, N Australia
108 F11 **Arno** ≈ C Italy
Arno *see* Arno Atoll
201 W7 **Arno Atoll** *var.* Arno. *atoll* Ratak Chain, NE Marshall Islands
190 H8 **Arno Bay** South Australia *33.55S 136.31E*
37 Q8 **Arnold** California, W USA *38.15N 120.19W*
29 X5 **Arnold** Missouri, C USA *38.25N 90.22W*
31 N15 **Arnold** Nebraska, C USA *41.25N 100.11W*
111 R10 **Arnoldstein** *Slvn.* Pod Klošter. Kärnten, S Austria *46.34N 13.43E*
105 N9 **Arnon** ≈ C France
47 P14 **Arnos Vale** ✕ (Kingstown) Saint Vincent, SE Saint Vincent and the Grenadines *13.08N 61.13W*
94 I8 **Arnøya** *Lapp.* Árdni. *island* N Norway
12 L12 **Arnprior** Ontario, SE Canada *45.31N 76.11W*
103 G15 **Arnsberg** Nordrhein-Westfalen, W Germany *51.24N 8.04E*
103 K16 **Arnstadt** Thüringen, C Germany *50.49N 10.57E*
Arnswalde *see* Choszczno
56 K5 **Aroa** Yaracuy, N Venezuela *10.25N 68.54W*
85 E21 **Aroab** Karas, SE Namibia *26.47S 19.37E*
117 E19 **Aroánia** ▲ S Greece
203 O6 **Aroa, Pointe** *headland* Moorea, W French Polynesia *17.27S 149.45W*
Aroe Islands *see* Aru, Kepulauan
103 H15 **Arolsen** Niedersachsen, C Germany *51.23N 9.00E*
108 C7 **Arona** Piemonte, NE Italy *45.45N 8.33E*
21 R3 **Aroostook River** ≈ Canada/USA
Arop Island *see* Long Island
40 M12 **Aropuk Lake** ⊚ Alaska, USA
203 P4 **Arorae** *atoll* Tungaru, W Kiribati
202 G16 **Arorangi** Rarotonga, S Cook Islands *21.13S 159.49W*
110 I9 **Arosa** Graubünden, S Switzerland *46.48N 9.42E*
106 F4 **Arousa, Ría de** *estuary* E Atlantic Ocean
176 Uu16 **Aro Usu, Tanjung** *headland* Pulau Selaru, SE Indonesia *8.19S 130.45E*
192 P8 **Arowhana** ▲ North Island, NZ *38.07S 177.52E*
143 V12 **Arp'a** *Az.* Arpaçay. ≈ Armenia/Azerbaijan
143 S11 **Arpaçay** Kars, NE Turkey *40.51N 43.19E*
Arpaçay *see* Arp'a
Arqalyq *see* Arkalyk
155 N14 **Arra** ≈ SW Pakistan
Arrabona *see* Győr
Arrah *see* Āra
Ar Rahad *see* Er Rahad
145 R9 **Ar Raḩḩālīyah** C Iraq *32.53N 43.21E*
62 Q10 **Arraial do Cabo** Rio de Janeiro, SE Brazil *22.57S 42.00W*
106 H11 **Arraiolos** Évora, S Portugal *38.43N 7.58W*
145 R8 **Ar Ramādī** *var.* Ramadi, Rumadiya. SW Iraq *33.27N 43.19E*
144 J6 **Ar Rāmī** Ḩimş, C Syria *34.32N 37.54E*
Ar Rams *see* Rams
144 H9 **Ar Ramthā** *var.* Ramtha. Irbid, N Jordan *32.34N 36.00E*
98 H13 **Arran, Isle of** *island* SW Scotland, UK
144 L3 **Ar Raqqah** *var.* Rakka; *anc.* Nicephorium. Ar Raqqah, N Syria *35.57N 39.03E*
144 L3 **Ar Raqqah** *off.* Muḩāfaẓat al Raqqah, *var.* Raqqah, *Fr.* Rakka. ◐ *governorate* N Syria
105 O2 **Arras** *anc.* Nemetocenna. Pas-de-Calais, N France *50.16N 2.46E*
Arrasate *see* Mondragón
144 G12 **Ar Rashādīyah** Aţ Ţafīlah, W Jordan *30.42N 35.37E*
144 I5 **Ar Rastān** *var.* Rastâne. Ḩimş, W Syria *34.57N 36.43E*
145 X12 **Ar Raţāwī** E Iraq *30.37N 47.12E*
104 L15 **Arrats** ≈ S France
147 N10 **Ar Rawḑah** Makkah, S Saudi Arabia *21.19N 42.48E*
147 Q15 **Ar Rawḑah** S Yemen *14.26N 47.13E*
148 K11 **Ar Rawḑatayn** *var.* Raudhatain. N Kuwait *29.52N 47.42E*
149 N16 **Ar Rayyān** *var.* Al Rayyan. C Qatar *25.18N 51.29E*
104 L17 **Arreau** Hautes-Pyrénées, S France *42.55N 0.21E*
66 Q11 **Arrecife** *var.* Arrecife de Lanzarote, Puerto Arrecife. Lanzarote, Islas Canarias, NE Atlantic Ocean *28.57N 13.33W*
Arrecife de Lanzarote *see* Arrecife
45 P6 **Arrecife Edinburgh** *reef* NE Nicaragua
63 C19 **Arrecifes** Buenos Aires, E Argentina *34.06S 60.09W*
104 F6 **Arrée, Monts d'** ▲▲ NW France
Ar Refā'ī *see* Ar Rifā'ī
Arretium *see* Arezzo
Arriaca *see* Guadalajara
111 S9 **Arriach** Kärnten, S Austria *46.43N 13.52E*
43 T16 **Arriaga** Chiapas, SE Mexico *16.13N 93.54W*
43 N12 **Arriaga** San Luis Potosí, C Mexico *21.55N 101.22W*
145 W10 **Ar Rifā'ī** *var.* Ar Refā'ī. SE Iraq *31.46N 46.07E*
145 V12 **Ar Riḩāb** *salt flat* S Iraq
106 L2 **Arriondas** Asturias, N Spain *43.22N 5.10W*
147 Q7 **Ar Riyāḑ** *Eng.* Riyadh. ● (Saudi Arabia) Ar Riyāḑ, C Saudi Arabia *24.49N 46.49E*
147 O8 **Ar Riyāḑ** *off.* Minţaqat ar Riyāḑ. ◐ *province* C Saudi Arabia
147 S15 **Ar Riyān** S Yemen *14.43N 49.18E*
Arrö *see* Ærø
63 H18 **Arroio Grande** Rio Grande do Sul, S Brazil *32.15S 53.02W*
104 K15 **Arros** ≈ S France
105 Q9 **Arroux** ≈ C France
27 R5 **Arrowhead, Lake** ⊟ Texas, SW USA
190 L5 **Arrowsmith, Mount** *hill* New South Wales, SE Australia *30.07S 141.37E*
193 D21 **Arrowtown** Otago, South Island, NZ *44.57S 168.51E*
63 D17 **Arroyo Barú** Entre Ríos, E Argentina *31.52S 58.25W*
106 J10 **Arroyo de la Luz** Extremadura, W Spain *39.28N 6.36W*
65 J16 **Arroyo de la Ventana** Río Negro, SE Argentina *41.41S 66.03W*
37 P13 **Arroyo Grande** California, W USA *35.07N 120.35W*
Ar Ru'ays *see* Ar Ruways
147 R11 **Ar Rub' al Khālī** *Eng.* Empty Quarter, Great Sandy Desert. *desert* SW Asia
145 V13 **Ar Ruḑaymah** S Iraq *30.19N 45.25E*
63 A16 **Arrufó** Santa Fe, C Argentina *30.15S 61.45W*
144 I7 **Ar Ruḩaybah** *var.* Ruhaybeh, *Fr.* Rouhaïbé. Dimashq, W Syria *33.45N 36.40E*
145 V15 **Ar Rukhaymīyah** *well* S Iraq *29.22N 45.43E*
145 U11 **Ar Rumaythah** *var.* Rumaitha. S Iraq *31.31N 45.15E*
147 X8 **Ar Rustāq** *var.* Rostak, Rustaq. N Oman *23.34N 57.25E*
145 N8 **Ar Ruţbah** *var.* Rutba. SW Iraq *33.03N 40.16E*
146 M3 **Ar Rūthīyah** *spring/well* NW Saudi Arabia *31.18N 41.23E*
ar-Ruwaida *see* Ar Ruwaydah
147 O8 **Ar Ruwaydah** *var.* ar-Ruwaida. Jīzān, C Saudi Arabia *23.48N 44.44E*
149 N15 **Ar Ruways** *var.* Al Ruweis, Ar Ru'ays, Ruwais. N Qatar *26.07N 51.13E*
149 O17 **Ar Ruways** *var.* Ar Ru'ays, Ruwaisv. Abū Ẓaby, W UAE *24.09N 52.57E*
Ārs *see* Aars
Arsanias *see* Murat Nehri
127 Nn18 **Arsen'yev** Primorskiy Kray, SE Russian Federation *44.09N 133.28E*
161 G19 **Arsikere** Karnātaka, W India *13.18N 76.15E*
131 R3 **Arsk** Respublika Tatarstan, W Russian Federation *56.07N 49.54E*
96 N10 **Årskogen** Gävleborg, C Sweden *62.07N 17.19E*
124 N3 **Ársos** C Cyprus *34.51N 32.46E*
96 N13 **Ärsunda** Gävleborg, C Sweden *60.31N 16.45E*
Árta *see* Árachthos
117 C17 **Árta** *anc.* Ambracia. Ípeiros, W Greece *39.07N 20.59E*
143 T12 **Artashat** S Armenia *39.57N 44.34E*
42 M15 **Arteaga** Michoacán de Ocampo, SW Mexico *18.20N 102.18W*
127 Nn18 **Artem** Primorskiy Kray, SE Russian Federation *43.24N 132.20E*
46 C4 **Artemisa** La Habana, W Cuba *22.49N 82.46W*
119 W7 **Artemivs'k** Donets'ka Oblast', E Ukraine *48.35N 37.58E*
126 I14 **Artemovsk** Krasnoyarskiy Kray, S Russian Federation *54.22N 93.24E*
126 Kk13 **Artemovskiy** Irkutskaya Oblast', C Russian Federation *58.15N 114.51E*
125 Ee13 **Artemovskiy** Sverdlovskaya Oblast', C Russian Federation *57.22N 61.55E*
107 U5 **Artesa de Segre** Cataluña, NE Spain *41.54N 1.03E*
39 U14 **Artesia** New Mexico, SW USA *32.50N 104.24W*
27 Q14 **Artesia Wells** Texas, SW USA *28.13N 99.18W*
110 G8 **Arth** Schwyz, C Switzerland *47.05N 8.39E*
12 F15 **Arthur** Ontario, S Canada *43.49N 80.31W*
32 M14 **Arthur** Illinois, N USA *39.42N 88.28W*
30 L14 **Arthur** Nebraska, C USA *41.32N 101.42W*
31 Q5 **Arthur** North Dakota, N USA *47.03N 97.12W*
193 B21 **Arthur** ≈ South Island, NZ
20 B13 **Arthur, Lake** ⊟ Pennsylvania, NE USA
191 N15 **Arthur River** ≈ Tasmania, SE Australia
193 G18 **Arthur's Pass** Canterbury, South Island, NZ *42.59S 171.33E*
193 G17 **Arthur's Pass** *pass* South Island, NZ *42.57S 171.33E*
46 I3 **Arthur's Town** Cat Island, C Bahamas *24.34N 75.39W*
46 M9 **Artibonite, Rivière de l'** ≈ C Haiti
63 E16 **Artigas** *prev.* San Eugenio, San Eugenio del Cuareim. Artigas, N Uruguay *30.25S 56.28W*
63 E16 **Artigas** ◐ *department* N Uruguay
204 H1 **Artigas** *Uruguayan research station* Antarctica *61.57S 58.23W*
143 T11 **Art'ik** W Armenia *40.38N 43.57E*
197 G4 **Art, Île** *island* Îles Belep, W New Caledonia
105 O2 **Artois** *cultural region* N France
142 L12 **Artova** Tokat, N Turkey *40.06N 36.18E*
107 Y9 **Artrutx, Cap d'** *var.* Cabo Dartuch. *headland* Menorca, Spain, W Mediterranean Sea *39.55N 3.49E*
Artsiz *see* Artsyz
119 N11 **Artsyz** *Rus.* Artsiz. Odes'ka Oblast', SW Ukraine *45.58N 29.25E*
164 E7 **Artux** Xinjiang Uygur Zizhiqu, NW China *39.45N 76.09E*
143 R11 **Artvin** Artvin, NE Turkey *41.12N 41.48E*
143 R11 **Artvin** ◐ *province* NE Turkey
152 G14 **Artyk** Ahal Welaýaty, C Turkmenistan *37.32N 59.16E*
81 Q16 **Aru** Orientale, NE Dem. Rep. Congo *2.52N 30.49E*
83 E17 **Arua** NW Uganda *3.01N 30.55E*
106 I4 **A Rúa de Valdeorras** *var.* La Rúa. Galicia, NW Spain *42.22N 7.12W*
Aruângua *see* Luangwa
47 O15 **Aruba** *var.* Oruba. ◇ *Dutch autonomous region* S West Indies
49 Q4 **Aruba** *island* Aruba, Lesser Antilles
Aru Islands *see* Aru, Kepulauan
176 Ww14 **Aru, Kepulauan** *Eng.* Aru Islands; *prev.* Aroe Islands. *island group* E Indonesia
159 W10 **Arunāchal Pradesh** *prev.* North East Frontier Agency, North East Frontier Agency of Assam. ◐ *state* NE India
Arun Qi *see* Naji
161 H23 **Aruppukkottai** Tamil Nādu, SE India *9.31N 78.03E*
176 Ww9 **Aruri, Selat** *strait* Papua, E Indonesia
83 I20 **Arusha** Arusha, N Tanzania *3.22S 36.40E*
83 I21 **Arusha** ◐ *region* E Tanzania
83 I20 **Arusha** ✕ Arusha, N Tanzania *3.26S 37.07E*
56 C9 **Arusí, Punta** *headland* NW Colombia *5.36N 77.30W*
174 Ll10 **Arut, Sungai** ≈ Borneo, C Indonesia
162 J23 **Aruvi Aru** ≈ NW Sri Lanka
81 M17 **Aruwimi** *var.* Ituri (upper course). ≈ NE Dem. Rep. Congo
Árva *see* Orava
39 T4 **Arvada** Colorado, C USA *39.48N 105.06W*
Arvand Rūd *see* 'Arab, Shaţţ al
168 J8 **Arvayheer** Övörhangay, C Mongolia *46.13N 102.47E*
15 L8 **Arviat** *prev.* Eskimo Point. Nunavut, C Canada *61.10N 94.15W*
95 I14 **Arvidsjaur** Norrbotten, N Sweden *65.34N 19.12E*
97 J15 **Arvika** Värmland, C Sweden *59.40N 12.37E*
94 J8 **Årviksand** Troms, N Norway *70.10N 20.30E*
37 S13 **Arvin** California, W USA *35.12N 118.52W*
169 S8 **Arxan** Nei Mongol Zizhiqu, N China *47.11N 119.58E*
151 P7 **Arykbalyk** *Kaz.* Aryqbalyq. Severnyy Kazakhstan, N Kazakhstan *53.00N 68.11E*
Aryqbalyq *see* Arykbalyk
151 P17 **Arys'** *Kaz.* Arys. Yuzhnyy Kazakhstan, S Kazakhstan *42.25N 68.49E*
Arys *see* Orzysz
Arys Köli *see* Arys, Ozero
151 O14 **Arys, Ozero** *Kaz.* Arys Köli. ⊚ C Kazakhstan
109 D16 **Arzachena** Sardegna, Italy, C Mediterranean Sea *41.05N 9.21E*
131 O4 **Arzamas** Nizhegorodskaya Oblast', W Russian Federation *55.25N 43.51E*
147 V13 **Arzāt** S Oman *17.03N 54.19E*
106 H3 **Arzúa** Galicia, NW Spain *42.55N 8.10W*
113 A16 **Aš** *Ger.* Asch. Karlovarský Kraj, W Czech Republic *50.12N 12.12E*
97 H15 **Ås** Akershus, S Norway *59.39N 10.48E*
Aså *see* Asaa
97 H20 **Asaa** *var.* Aså. Nordjylland, N Denmark *57.07N 10.24E*
85 E21 **Asab** Karas, S Namibia *25.28S 17.58E*
79 U16 **Asaba** Delta, S Nigeria *6.10N 6.44E*
155 S4 **Asadābād** *var.* Asadābād; *prev.* Chaghasarāy. Kunar, E Afghanistan *34.52N 71.09E*
144 K3 **Asad, Buḩayrat al** ⊚ N Syria
65 H20 **Asador, Pampa del** *plain* S Argentina
171 Kk17 **Asahi** Chiba, Honshū, S Japan *36.08N 140.37E*
171 J13 **Asahi** Toyama, Honshū, SW Japan *36.56N 137.34E*
172 Pp5 **Asahi-dake** ▲ Hokkaidō, N Japan *43.42N 142.50E*
170 Ff13 **Asahi-gawa** ≈ Honshū, SW Japan
172 P5 **Asahikawa** Hokkaidō, N Japan *43.46N 142.22E*
153 S10 **Asaka** *Rus.* Assake; *prev.* Leninsk. Andijon Viloyati, E Uzbekistan *40.39N 72.16E*
79 P17 **Asamankese** SE Ghana *5.46N 0.41W*
171 Jj15 **Asama-yama** ▲ Honshū, S Japan *36.25N 138.34E*
196 B15 **Asan** W Guam *13.28N 144.43E*
196 B15 **Asan Point** *headland* W Guam
159 R15 **Āsansol** West Bengal, NE India *23.40N 86.58E*
82 K12 **Āsayita** Afar, NE Ethiopia *11.35N 41.23E*
176 V9 **Asbakin** Papua, E Indonesia *0.45S 131.40E*
Asben *see* Aïr, Massif de l'
125 Ee11 **Asbest** Sverdlovskaya Oblast', C Russian Federation *57.12N 61.18E*
13 Q12 **Asbestos** Québec, SE Canada *45.46N 71.55W*
31 Y13 **Asbury** Iowa, C USA *42.30N 90.45W*
20 K15 **Asbury Park** New Jersey, NE USA *40.13N 74.00W*
43 Z12 **Ascención, Bahía de la** *bay* NW Caribbean Sea
42 I3 **Ascensión** Chihuahua, N Mexico *31.07N 107.58W*
67 M14 **Ascension Fracture Zone** *tectonic feature* C Atlantic Ocean
67 G14 **Ascension Island** ◇ *dependency of St. Helena* C Atlantic Ocean
67 N16 **Ascension Island** *island* C Atlantic Ocean
Asch *see* Aš
111 S3 **Aschach an der Donau** Oberösterreich, N Austria *48.22N 14.00E*
103 H18 **Aschaffenburg** Bayern, SW Germany *49.58N 9.09E*
103 F14 **Ascheberg** Nordrhein-Westfalen, W Germany *51.46N 7.36E*
103 L14 **Aschersleben** Sachsen-Anhalt, C Germany *51.46N 11.28E*
108 G12 **Asciano** Toscana, C Italy *43.15N 11.32E*
108 J13 **Ascoli Piceno** *anc.* Asculum Picenum. Marche, C Italy *42.51N 13.34E*
109 M17 **Ascoli Satriano** *anc.* Asculub, Ausculum Apulum. Puglia, SE Italy *41.13N 15.31E*
110 G11 **Ascona** Ticino, S Switzerland *46.10N 8.45E*
Asculub *see* Ascoli Satriano
Asculum Picenum *see* Ascoli Piceno
82 L11 **Aseb** *var.* Assab, *Amh.* Āseb. SE Eritrea *13.03N 42.36E*
97 M20 **Åseda** Kronoberg, S Sweden *57.10N 15.19E*
131 T6 **Asekeyevo** Orenburgskaya Oblast', W Russian Federation *53.36N 52.53E*
194 J13 **Aseki** Morobe, C PNG *7.18S 156.16E*
83 J14 **Āsela** *var.* Asella, Aselle, Asselle. Oromo, C Ethiopia *7.55N 39.08E*
95 H15 **Åsele** Västerbotten, N Sweden *64.10N 17.19E*
Asella/Aselle *see* Āsela
96 K12 **Åsen** Dalarna, C Sweden *61.18N 13.49E*
116 J11 **Asenovgrad** *prev.* Stanimaka. Plovdiv, C Bulgaria *42.01N 24.54E*
175 Q11 **Asera** Sulawesi, C Indonesia *3.24S 121.42E*
97 E17 **Åseral** Vest-Agder, S Norway *58.37N 7.27E*
120 J3 **Aseri** *var.* Asserien, *Ger.* Asserin. Ida-Virumaa, NE Estonia *59.28N 26.50E*
42 J10 **Aserradero** Durango, W Mexico
152 F13 **Aşgabat** *prev.* Ashgabat, Ashkhabad, Poltoratsk. ● (Turkmenistan) Ahal Welaýaty, C Turkmenistan *37.58N 58.22E*
152 F13 **Aşgabat** ✕ Ahal Welaýaty, C Turkmenistan *38.06N 58.10E*
97 H16 **Åsgårdstrand** Vestfold, S Norway *59.19N 10.28E*
125 E11 **Asha** Chelyabinskaya Oblast', C Russian Federation *55.01N 57.11E*
Ashara *see* Al 'Ashārah
25 T6 **Ashburn** Georgia, SE USA *31.42N 83.39W*
193 G19 **Ashburton** Canterbury, South Island, NZ *43.55S 171.46E*
193 G19 **Ashburton** ≈ South Island, NZ
188 H8 **Ashburton River** ≈ Western Australia
151 V10 **Ashchysu** ≈ E Kazakhstan
8 M16 **Ashcroft** British Columbia, SW Canada *50.40N 121.16W*
144 E10 **Ashdod** *anc.* Azotos, *Lat.* Azotus. Central, W Israel *31.48N 34.37E*
29 S14 **Ashdown** Arkansas, C USA *33.40N 94.07W*
23 T9 **Asheboro** North Carolina, SE USA *35.42N 79.48W*
9 X15 **Ashern** Manitoba, S Canada *51.10N 98.22W*
23 P10 **Asheville** North Carolina, SE USA *35.36N 82.33W*
10 E8 **Asheweig** ≈ Ontario, C Canada
29 V9 **Ash Flat** Arkansas, C USA *36.13N 91.36W*
191 T4 **Ashford** New South Wales, SE Australia *29.18S 151.09E*
99 P22 **Ashford** SE England, UK *51.09N 0.52E*
38 K11 **Ash Fork** Arizona, SW USA *35.12N 112.31W*
Ashgabat *see* Aşgabat
29 T7 **Ash Grove** Missouri, C USA *37.19N 93.35W*
171 K15 **Ashikaga** *var.* Asikaga. Tochigi, Honshū, S Japan *36.19N 139.26E*
171 Mm10 **Ashiro** Iwate, Honshū, C Japan *40.04N 141.00E*
170 E16 **Ashizuri-misaki** *headland* Shikoku, SW Japan *32.43N 132.59E*
Ashkelon *see* Ashqelon
Ashkhabad *see* Aşgabat
25 Q4 **Ashland** Alabama, S USA *33.16N 85.50W*
28 K7 **Ashland** Kansas, C USA *37.11N 99.46W*
23 P5 **Ashland** Kentucky, S USA *38.28N 82.39W*
21 S2 **Ashland** Maine, NE USA *46.36N 68.24W*
24 M1 **Ashland** Mississippi, S USA *34.51N 89.10W*
29 U4 **Ashland** Missouri, C USA *38.46N 92.15W*
31 S15 **Ashland** Nebraska, C USA *41.01N 96.21W*
33 T12 **Ashland** Ohio, N USA *40.52N 82.19W*
34 G15 **Ashland** Oregon, NW USA *42.11N 122.42W*
23 W6 **Ashland** Virginia, NE USA *37.45N 77.28W*
32 K3 **Ashland** Wisconsin, N USA *46.34N 90.54W*
22 I8 **Ashland City** Tennessee, S USA *36.16N 87.03W*
191 S4 **Ashley** New South Wales, SE Australia *29.21S 149.49E*
31 O7 **Ashley** North Dakota, N USA *46.00N 99.22W*
181 W7 **Ashmore and Cartier Islands** ◇ *Australian external territory* E Indian Ocean
121 I14 **Ashmyany** *Rus.* Oshmyany. Hrodzyenskaya Voblasts', W Belarus *54.24N 25.57E*
20 K12 **Ashokan Reservoir** ⊟ New York, NE USA
172 Pp6 **Ashoro** Hokkaidō, NE Japan *43.16N 143.33E*
144 E10 **Ashqelon** *var.* Ashkelon. Southern, C Israel *31.40N 34.34E*
Ashraf *see* Behshahr
145 O3 **Ash Shadādah** *var.* Ash Shaddādah, Jisr ash Shadadi, Shaddādī, Shedadi, Tell Shedadi. Al Ḩasakah, NE Syria *36.00N 40.42E*
Ash Shaddādah *see* Ash Shadādah
145 Y12 **Ash Shāfī** E Iraq *30.49N 47.30E*
145 R4 **Ash Shakk** *var.* Shaykh. C Iraq *35.15N 43.27E*
Ash Sham/Ash Shām *see* Dimashq
145 T10 **Ash Shāmīyah** *var.* Shamiya. C Iraq *31.55N 44.37E*
145 Y13 **Ash Shāmīyah** *var.* Al Bādiyah al Janūbīyah. *desert* S Iraq
145 T11 **Ash Shanāfīyah** *var.* Ash Shināfīyah. S Iraq *31.34N 44.38E*
144 G13 **Ash Sharāh** *var.* Esh Sharā. ▲▲ W Jordan
149 R16 **Ash Shāriqah** *Eng.* Sharjah. Ash Shāriqah, NE UAE *25.22N 55.28E*
149 R16 **Ash Shāriqah** *var.* Sharjah. ✕ Ash Shāriqah, NE UAE *25.19N 55.37E*
146 I4 **Ash Sharmah** *var.* Šarma. Tabūk, NW Saudi Arabia *28.01N 35.16E*
145 R4 **Ash Sharqāţ** NW Iraq *35.30N 43.15E*
147 S10 **Ash Sharqīyah** *off.* Al Minţaqah ash Sharqīyah, *Eng.* Eastern Region. ◐ *province* E Saudi Arabia
145 W11 **Ash Shaţrah** *var.* Shatra. SE Iraq *31.25N 46.10E*
144 G13 **Ash Shawbak** Ma'ān, W Jordan *30.31N 35.34E*
144 L5 **Ash Shaykh Ibrāhīm** Ḩimş, C Syria *35.03N 38.50E*
147 O17 **Ash Shaykh 'Uthmān** SW Yemen *12.53N 45.00E*
147 S15 **Ash Shiḩr** SE Yemen *14.45N 49.24E*
Ash Shināfīyah *see* Ash Shanāfīyah
147 V12 **Ash Shişar** *var.* Shisur. SW Oman *18.13N 53.34E*
145 S13 **Ash Shubrūm** *well* S Iraq *30.09N 43.59E*
147 R10 **Ash Shuqqān** *desert* E Saudi Arabia
77 O9 **Ash Shuwayrif** *var.* Ash Shwayrif. N Libya *29.54N 14.16E*
Ash Shwayrif *see* Ash Shuwayrif
33 U10 **Ashtabula** Ohio, N USA *41.54N 80.46W*
31 Q5 **Ashtabula, Lake** ⊟ North Dakota, N USA
143 T12 **Ashtarak** W Armenia *40.18N 44.22E*
148 M6 **Āshtiān** *var.* Āshtiyān. Markazī, W Iran *34.24N 49.55E*
Āshtiyān *see* Āshtiān
35 R13 **Ashton** Idaho, NW USA *44.04N 111.27W*
11 O10 **Ashuanipi Lake** ⊚ Newfoundland and Labrador, E Canada
13 P6 **Ashuapmushuan** ≈ Québec, SE Canada
25 Q3 **Ashville** Alabama, S USA *33.50N 86.15W*
33 S14 **Ashville** Ohio, N USA *39.43N 82.57W*
32 K3 **Ashwabay, Mount** *hill* Wisconsin, N USA *46.49N 90.57W*
176 Uu7 **Asia, Kepulauan** *island group* E Indonesia
160 N13 **Āsika** Orissa, E India *19.37N 84.40E*
Asikaga *see* Ashikaga
95 M18 **Asikkala** *var.* Vääksy. Etelä-Suomi, S Finland *61.09N 25.36E*
76 G5 **Asilah** N Morocco *35.18N 6.04W*
'Aşī, Nahr al *see* Orontes
109 B16 **Asinara, Isola** *island* W Italy
126 H13 **Asino** Tomskaya Oblast', C Russian Federation *56.56N 86.02E*
121 O14 **Asintorf** *Rus.* Osintorf. Vitsyebskaya Voblasts', N Belarus *54.43N 30.35E*
121 L17 **Asipovichy** *Rus.* Osipovichi. Mahilyowskaya Voblasts', C Belarus *53.18N 28.40E*
147 N12 **'Asīr** *off.* Minţaqat 'Asīr. ◐ *province* SW Saudi Arabia
146 M11 **'Asīr** *Eng.* Asir. ▲▲ SW Saudi Arabia
145 X10 **Askal** E Iraq *31.45N 47.07E*
143 P13 **Aşkale** Erzurum, NE Turkey *39.56N 40.39E*
119 T11 **Askaniya-Nova** Khersons'ka Oblast', S Ukraine *46.27N 33.54E*
97 H15 **Asker** Akershus, S Norway *59.49N 10.29E*
97 L17 **Askersund** Örebro, C Sweden *58.55N 14.55E*
Askī Kalak *see* Eski Kaļak
97 I15 **Askim** Østfold, S Norway *59.34N 11.10E*
131 V3 **Askino** Respublika Bashkortostan, W Russian Federation *56.07N 56.39E*
117 D14 **Áskio** ▲ N Greece
158 L9 **Askot** Uttaranchal, N India *29.43N 80.19E*
96 C12 **Askvoll** Sogn og Fjordane, S Norway *61.21N 5.04E*
142 A13 **Aslan Burnu** *headland* W Turkey *38.44N 26.43E*
142 L16 **Aslantaş Barajı** ⊟ S Turkey
155 S4 **Asmār** *var.* Bar Kunar. Kunar, E Afghanistan *34.58N 71.28E*
82 I9 **Asmara** *Amh.* Āsmera. ● (Eritrea) C Eritrea *15.15N 38.57E*
Āsmera *see* Asmara
97 L21 **Åsnen** ⊚ S Sweden
117 F19 **Asopós** ≈ S Greece
176 X10 **Asori** Papua, E Indonesia *2.37S 136.06E*
82 G12 **Āsosa** Benishangul, W Ethiopia *10.06N 34.27E*
34 M10 **Asotin** Washington, NW USA *46.18N 117.03W*
Aspadana *see* Eşfahān
Aspang *see* Aspang Markt
111 X6 **Aspang Markt** *var.* Aspang. Niederösterreich, E Austria *47.34N 16.06E*
107 S12 **Aspe** País Valenciano, E Spain *38.21N 0.43W*
39 R5 **Aspen** Colorado, C USA *39.12N 106.49W*
27 P6 **Aspermont** Texas, SW USA *33.07N 100.13W*
Asphaltites, Lacus *see* Dead Sea
Aspinwall *see* Colón
193 C20 **Aspiring, Mount** ▲ South Island, NZ *44.21S 168.47E*
117 B16 **Asprókavos, Akrotírio** *headland* Kérkyra, Iónioi Nísoi, Greece, C Mediterranean Sea *39.22N 20.07E*
Aspropótamos *see* Achelóos
Assab *see* Aseb
78 J10 **Assaba** *var.* Açâba. ◐ *region* S Mauritania
144 L4 **As Sabkhah** *var.* Sabkha. Ar Raqqah, NE Syria *35.30N 35.54E*
145 U6 **As Sa'dīyah** E Iraq *34.11N 45.09E*
Assad, Lake *see* Asad, Buḩayrat al
144 I8 **Aş Şafā** ▲ S Syria *33.03N 37.07E*
144 I10 **Aş Şafāwī** Al Mafraq, N Jordan *37.12N 32.30E*
Aş Şaff *see* El Şaff
145 N2 **Aş Şafiḩ** Al Ḩasakah, N Syria *36.42N 40.12E*
Aş Şaḩrā' al Gharbīyah *see* Sahara el Gharbîya
Aş Şaḩrā' ash Sharqīyah *see* Sahara el Sharqîya
Assake *see* Asaka
As Salamīyah *see* Salamīyah
147 Q4 **As Sālimī** *var.* Salemy. SW Kuwait *29.07N 46.41E*
69 W7 **'Assal, Lac** ⊚ C Djibouti
As Sallūm *see* Salûm
145 T13 **As Salmān** S Iraq *30.28N 44.34E*
144 G10 **As Salţ** *var.* Salt. Al Balqā', NW Jordan *32.03N 35.43E*
148 M16 **As Salwā** *var.* Salwa, Salwah. S Qatar *24.43N 50.52E*
159 V12 **Assam** ◐ *state* NE India
Assamaka *see* Assamakka
79 T8 **Assamakka** *var.* Assamaka. Agadez, NW Niger *19.24N 5.52E*
145 U11 **As Samāwah** *var.* Samawa. S Iraq *31.17N 45.05E*
As Saqia al Hamra *see* Saguia al Hamra
144 J4 **Aş Şā'rān** Ḩamāh, C Syria *35.15N 37.28E*
144 G9 **Aş Şarīḩ** Irbid, N Jordan *32.31N 35.54E*
23 Z5 **Assateague Island** *island* Maryland, NE USA
145 O6 **As Sayyāl** *var.* Sayyāl. Dayr az Zawr, E Syria *34.37N 40.52E*
101 G18 **Asse** Vlaams Brabant, C Belgium *50.55N 4.12E*
101 D16 **Assebroek** West-Vlaanderen, NW Belgium *51.12N 3.16E*
Asselle *see* Āsela
109 C20 **Assemini** Sardegna, Italy, C Mediterranean Sea *39.16N 8.58E*
100 N7 **Assen** Drenthe, NE Netherlands *53.00N 6.34E*
101 E16 **Assenede** Oost-Vlaanderen, NW Belgium *51.15N 3.43E*
97 G24 **Assens** Fyn, C Denmark *55.16N 9.54E*
Asserien/Asserin *see* Aseri
101 I21 **Assesse** Namur, SE Belgium *50.22N 5.01E*
147 Y8 **As Sīb** *var.* Seeb. NE Oman *23.40N 58.03E*
145 Z13 **As Sībah** *var.* Sibah. SE Iraq *30.13N 47.24E*
9 T17 **Assiniboia** Saskatchewan, S Canada *49.39N 105.58W*
9 V15 **Assiniboine** ≈ Manitoba, S Canada
9 P16 **Assiniboine, Mount** ▲ Alberta/British Columbia, SW Canada *50.54N 115.43W*
Assiout *see* Asyût
62 J9 **Assis** São Paulo, S Brazil *22.37S 50.25W*
108 I13 **Assisi** Umbria, C Italy *43.04N 12.36E*
Assiut *see* Asyût
Assling *see* Jesenice
Assouan *see* Aswân
Assu *see* Açu
Assuan *see* Aswân
148 K12 **Aş Şubayḩīyah** *var.* Subiyah. S Kuwait *28.55N 47.57E*
147 R16 **As Sufāl** S Yemen *14.06N 48.42E*
144 L5 **As Sukhnah** *var.* Sukhne, *Fr.* Soukhné. Ḩimş, C Syria *34.55N 38.52E*
145 U4 **As Sulaymānīyah** *var.* Sulaimaniya, *Kurd.* Slēmānī. NE Iraq *35.31N 45.27E*
147 P11 **As Sulayyil** Ar Riyāḑ, S Saudi Arabia *20.28N 45.33E*
123 M16 **As Sulţān** N Libya *31.01N 17.21E*
147 Q5 **Aş Şummān** *desert* N Saudi Arabia
147 Q16 **Aş Şurrah** SW Yemen *13.56N 46.23E*
145 N4 **Aş Şuwār** *var.* Şuwār. Dayr az Zawr, E Syria *35.31N 40.37E*
144 H9 **As Suwaydā'** *var.* El Suweida, Es Suweida, Suweida, *Fr.* Soueida. As Suwaydā', SW Syria *32.43N 36.33E*
144 H9 **As Suwaydā'** *off.* Muḩāfaẓat as Suwaydā', *var.* As Suwaydā, Suwaydā, Suweida, *Fr.* Soueida. ◐ *governorate* S Syria
147 Z9 **As Suwayḩ** NE Oman *22.07N 59.42E*
147 X8 **As Suwayq** *var.* Suwaik. N Oman *23.51N 57.20E*
145 T8 **Aş Şuwayrah** *var.* Suwaira. E Iraq *32.57N 44.46E*
As Suways *see* Suez
Asta Colonia *see* Asti
Astacus *see* İzmit
117 M23 **Astakída** *island* SE Greece
151 Q9 **Astana** *prev.* Akmola, Akmolinsk, Tselinograd, Aqmola. ● (Kazakhstan) Akmola, N Kazakhstan *51.12N 71.25E*
148 M3 **Āstāneh** Gīlān, NW Iran *37.16N 49.58E*
Asta Pompeia *see* Asti
143 Y14 **Astara** S Azerbaijan *38.28N 48.51E*
Astarabad *see* Gorgān
101 L15 **Asten** Noord-Brabant, SE Netherlands *51.24N 5.45E*
Asterābād *see* Gorgān
108 C8 **Asti** *anc.* Asta Colonia, Asta Pompeia, Hasta Colonia, Hasta Pompeia. Piemonte, NW Italy *44.54N 8.10E*
Astigi *see* Ecija
Astipálaia *see* Astypálaia
154 L16 **Astola Island** *island* SW Pakistan
158 H4 **Astor** Jammu and Kashmir, NW India *35.21N 74.52E*
106 K4 **Astorga** *anc.* Asturica Augusta. Castilla-León, N Spain *42.27N 6.04W*
34 F10 **Astoria** Oregon, NW USA *46.12N 123.49W*
(0) F8 **Astoria Fan** *undersea feature* E Pacific Ocean
97 J22 **Åstorp** Skåne, S Sweden *56.09N 12.57E*
Astrabad *see* Gorgān
131 Q13 **Astrakhan'** Astrakhanskaya Oblast', SW Russian Federation *46.20N 48.00E*
Astrakhan-Bazar *see* Cälilabad
131 Q11 **Astrakhanskaya Oblast'** ◐ *province* SW Russian Federation
95 J15 **Åsträsk** Västerbotten, N Sweden *64.38N 20.00E*
Astrida *see* Butare
67 O22 **Astrid Ridge** *undersea feature* S Atlantic Ocean
194 J11 **Astrolabe Bay** *inlet* N PNG
197 I4 **Astrolabe, Récifs de l'** *reef* C New Caledonia
124 Nn3 **Astromerítis** N Cyprus *35.09N 33.02E*
117 F20 **Ástros** Pelopónnisos, S Greece *37.24N 22.43E*
121 G16 **Astryna** *Rus.* Ostryna. Hrodzyenskaya Voblasts', W Belarus *53.44N 24.33E*
106 J2 **Asturias** ◐ *autonomous community* NW Spain
Asturias *see* Oviedo
Asturica Augusta *see* Astorga
117 L22 **Astypálaia** *var.* Astipálaia, *It.* Stampalia. *island* Kykládes, Greece, Aegean Sea
198 Aa8 **Āsuisui, Cape** *headland* Savai'i, W Samoa *13.43S 172.28W*
205 S2 **Asuka** *Japanese research station* Antarctica *71.49S 23.52E*
64 O6 **Asunción** ● (Paraguay) Central, S Paraguay *25.16S 57.36W*
64 O6 **Asunción** ✕ Central, S Paraguay *25.15S 57.40W*
196 K3 **Asuncion Island** *island* N Northern Mariana Islands
44 E6 **Asunción Mita** Jutiapa, SE Guatemala *14.19N 89.42W*
Asunción Nochixtlán *see* Nochixtlán
42 E3 **Asunción, Río** ≈ NW Mexico
97 M18 **Åsunden** ⊚ S Sweden
120 K11 **Asveyeya** *Rus.* Osveya. Vitsyebskaya Voblasts', N Belarus *56.00N 28.05E*
Aswa *see* Achwa
77 X11 **Aswân** *var.* Assouan, Assuan; *anc.* Syene. SE Egypt *24.03N 32.58E*
77 X11 **Aswân High Dam** *dam* SE Egypt *23.54N 32.51E*
77 W9 **Asyût** *var.* Assiout, Assiut, Siut; *anc.* Lycopolis. C Egypt *27.06N 31.10E*
200 R15 **Ata** *island* Tongatapu Group, SW Tonga
64 G8 **Atacama** *off.* Región de Atacama. ◐ *region* C Chile
Atacama Desert *see* Atacama, Desierto de
64 H4 **Atacama, Desierto de** *Eng.* Atacama Desert. *desert* N Chile
64 I6 **Atacama, Puna de** ▲▲ NW Argentina
64 I5 **Atacama, Salar de** *salt lake* N Chile
56 E11 **Ataco** Tolima, C Colombia *3.33N 75.25W*
202 H8 **Atafu Atoll** *island* NW Tokelau
202 H8 **Atafu Village** Atafu Atoll, NW Tokelau *8.40S 172.40W*
76 K12 **Atakor** ▲ SE Algeria
79 R14 **Atakora, Chaîne de l'** *var.* Atakora Mountains. ▲▲ N Benin
Atakora Mountains *see* Atakora, Chaîne de l'
79 R16 **Atakpamé** C Togo *7.31N 1.07E*
152 F11 **Atakui** Ahal Welaýaty, C Turkmenistan *40.04N 58.03E*
60 B13 **Atalaia do Norte** Amazonas, N Brazil *4.22S 70.10W*
171 J17 **Atami** Shizuoka, Honshū, S Japan *35.04N 139.03E*
152 M14 **Atamyrat** *prev.* Kerki. Lebap Welaýaty, E Turkmenistan *37.51N 65.06E*
78 I7 **Aţâr** Adrar, W Mauritania *20.30N 13.03W*
168 G10 **Atas Bogd** ▲ SW Mongolia *43.17N 96.47E*
37 P12 **Atascadero** California, W USA *35.28N 120.40W*
27 S13 **Atascosa River** ≈ Texas, SW USA
151 R11 **Atasu** Karaganda, C Kazakhstan *48.42N 71.27E*
151 R12 **Atasu** ≈ C Kazakhstan
200 Qq15 **Atata** *island* Tongatapu Group, S Tonga
142 H10 **Atatürk** ✕ (İstanbul) İstanbul, NW Turkey *40.58N 28.50E*
143 N16 **Atatürk Barajı** ⊟ S Turkey
Atax *see* Aude
82 G8 **Atbara** *var.* 'Aţbārah. River Nile, NE Sudan *17.42N 34.00E*
82 H8 **Atbara** *var.* Nahr 'Aţbarah. ≈ Eritrea/Sudan
'Aţbārah/'Aţbarah, Nahr *see* Atbara
151 P9 **Atbasar** Akmola, N Kazakhstan *51.49N 68.18E*
At-Bashi *see* At-Bashy
153 W9 **At-Bashy** *var.* At-Bashi. Narynskaya Oblast', C Kyrgyzstan *41.07N 75.48E*
24 I10 **Atchafalaya Bay** *bay* Louisiana, S USA
24 I8 **Atchafalaya River** ≈ Louisiana, S USA
Atchin *see* Aceh
29 Q3 **Atchison** Kansas, C USA *39.31N 95.07W*
79 P16 **Atebubu** C Ghana *7.47N 1.00W*
107 Q6 **Ateca** Aragón, N Spain *41.19N 1.49W*
42 K11 **Atengo, Río** ≈ C Mexico
Aternum *see* Pescara
109 K15 **Atessa** Abruzzo, C Italy *42.03N 14.25E*
Ateste *see* Este
101 E19 **Ath** *var.* Aat. Hainaut, SW Belgium *50.37N 3.46E*
9 Q13 **Athabasca** Alberta, SW Canada *54.43N 113.15W*

◆ Country ● Country Capital ◇ Dependent Territory ○ Dependent Territory Capital ◐ Administrative Region ✕ International Airport ▲ Mountain ▲▲ Mountain Range ⊼ Volcano ≈ River ⊚ Lake ⊟ Reservoir

ATHABASCA – ĀZROW

9 Q12 **Athabasca** *var.* Athabaska. ≈ Alberta, SW Canada
9 R10 **Athabasca, Lake** ◎ Alberta/Saskatchewan, SW Canada
Athabaska *see* Athabasca
117 C16 **Athamánon** ▲▲ C Greece
99 F17 **Athboy** *Ir.* Baile Átha Buí. E Ireland *53.37N 6.54W*
Athenae *see* Athína
99 C18 **Athenry** *Ir.* Baile Átha an Rí. W Ireland *53.19N 8.49W*
25 P2 **Athens** Alabama, S USA *34.48N 86.58W*
25 T3 **Athens** Georgia, SE USA *33.57N 83.24W*
33 T14 **Athens** Ohio, N USA *39.19N 82.06W*
22 M10 **Athens** Tennessee, S USA *35.26N 84.35W*
27 V7 **Athens** Texas, SW USA *32.12N 95.51W*
Athens *see* Athína
117 B18 **Athéras, Akrotírio** *headland* Kefallinía, Iónioi Nísoi, Greece, C Mediterranean Sea *38.20N 20.24E*
189 W4 **Atherton** Queensland, NE Australia *17.18S 145.29E*
83 I19 **Athi** ≈ S Kenya
124 O3 **Athiénou** SE Cyprus *35.01N 33.31E*
117 H19 **Athína** *Eng.* Athens; ***prev.*** Athínai, ***anc.*** Athenae. ● (Greece) Attikí, C Greece *37.58N 23.44E*
Athínai *see* Athína
145 S10 **Athīyah** C Iraq *32.01N 44.04E*
99 D18 **Athlone** *Ir.* Baile Átha Luain. C Ireland *53.25N 7.55W*
161 F16 **Athni** Karnātaka, W India *16.43N 75.04E*
193 C23 **Athol** Southland, South Island, NZ *45.30S 168.35E*
21 N11 **Athol** Massachusetts, NE USA *42.35N 72.11W*
117 I15 **Áthos** ▲ NE Greece *40.10N 24.21E*
Athos, Mount *see* Ágion Óros
Ath Thawrah *see* Madīnat ath Thawrah
147 P5 **Ath Thumāmī** *spring/well* N Saudi Arabia *27.56N 45.06E*
101 L25 **Athus** Luxembourg, SE Belgium *49.34N 5.49E*
99 E19 **Athy** *Ir.* Baile Átha Í. C Ireland *52.58N 6.58W*
80 I10 **Ati** Batha, C Chad *13.10N 18.19E*
83 F16 **Atiak** NW Uganda *3.13N 32.04E*
59 G17 **Atico** Arequipa, SW Peru *16.13S 73.13W*
107 O6 **Atienza** Castilla-La Mancha, C Spain *41.12N 2.52W*
41 Q6 **Atigun Pass** *pass* Alaska, USA *68.01N 149.36W*
10 B12 **Atikokan** Ontario, S Canada *48.45N 91.37W*
11 O9 **Atikonak Lac** ◎ Newfoundland and Labrador, E Canada
44 C6 **Atitlán, Lago de** ◎ W Guatemala
202 L16 **Atiu** *island* S Cook Islands
Atjeh *see* Aceh
127 O9 **Atka** Magadanskaya Oblast', E Russian Federation *60.45N 151.34E*
40 H17 **Atka** Atka Island, Alaska, USA *52.12N 174.13W*
40 H17 **Atka Island** *island* Aleutian Islands, Alaska, USA
131 O7 **Atkarsk** Saratovskaya Oblast', W Russian Federation *52.15N 43.48E*
29 U11 **Atkins** Arkansas, C USA *35.15N 92.56W*
31 O13 **Atkinson** Nebraska, C USA *42.31N 98.57W*
176 U10 **Atkri** Papua, E Indonesia *1.45S 130.04E*
43 O13 **Atlacomulco** *var.* Atlacomulco de Fabela. México, C Mexico *19.48N 99.52W*
Atlacomulco de Fabela *see* Atlacomulco
25 S3 **Atlanta** *state capital* Georgia, SE USA *33.45N 84.22W*
33 R6 **Atlanta** Michigan, N USA *45.01N 84.07W*
27 X6 **Atlanta** Texas, SW USA *33.06N 94.09W*
31 T15 **Atlantic** Iowa, C USA *41.24N 95.00W*
23 Y10 **Atlantic** North Carolina, SE USA *34.52N 76.20W*
25 W8 **Atlantic Beach** Florida, SE USA *30.19N 81.24W*
20 J17 **Atlantic City** New Jersey, NE USA *39.22N 74.27W*
180 L14 **Atlantic-Indian Basin** *undersea feature* SW Indian Ocean
180 K13 **Atlantic-Indian Ridge** *undersea feature* SW Indian Ocean
56 E4 **Atlántico** ***off.*** Departamento del Atlántico. ◈ *province* NW Colombia
66-67 **Atlantic Ocean** *ocean*
44 K7 **Atlántico Norte, Región Autónoma** ***prev.*** Zelaya Norte. ◈ *autonomous region* NE Nicaragua
44 L10 **Atlántico Sur, Región Autónoma** ***prev.*** Zelaya *Sur.* ◈ *autonomous region* SE Nicaragua
44 I5 **Atlántida** ◈ *department* N Honduras
79 Y15 **Atlantika Mountains** ▲▲ E Nigeria
66 J10 **Atlantis Fracture Zone** *tectonic feature* NW Atlantic Ocean
76 H7 **Atlas Mountains** ▲▲ NW Africa
127 Pp13 **Atlasova, Ostrov** *island* SE Russian Federation
127 Pp10 **Atlasovo** Kamchatskaya Oblast', E Russian Federation *55.42N 159.34E*
123 H13 **Atlas Saharien** *var.* Saharan Atlas. ▲▲ Algeria/Morocco
Atlas, Tell *see* Atlas Tellien
123 Gg10 **Atlas Tellien** *Eng.* Tell Atlas. ▲▲ N Algeria
8 I9 **Atlin** British Columbia, W Canada *59.31N 133.40W*
8 I9 **Atlin Lake** ◎ British Columbia, W Canada
43 P14 **Atlixco** Puebla, S Mexico *18.55N 98.25W*
96 B11 **Atløyna** *island* S Norway
161 I17 **Ātmakūr** Andhra Pradesh, C India *15.52N 78.42E*
25 O8 **Atmore** Alabama, S USA *31.01N 87.29W*
103 J20 **Atmühl** ≈ S Germany
96 H11 **Atna** ≈ S Norway
170 E12 **Atō** Yamaguchi, Honshū, SW Japan *34.24N 131.42E*
59 L21 **Atocha** Potosí, S Bolivia *20.55S 66.13W*
29 P12 **Atoka** Oklahoma, C USA *34.23N 96.07W*
29 O12 **Atoka Lake** *var.* Atoka Reservoir. ⊠ Oklahoma, C USA
Atoka Reservoir *see* Atoka Lake
35 Q14 **Atomic City** Idaho, NW USA *43.26N 112.48W*
42 L10 **Atotonilco** Zacatecas, C Mexico *24.12N 102.46W*
42 M13 **Atotonilco el Alto** *var.* Atotonilco. Jalisco, SW Mexico *20.32N 102.27W*
79 N7 **Atouila, 'Erg** *desert* N Mali
43 N16 **Atoyac** *var.* Atoyac de Alvarez. Guerrero, S Mexico *17.10N 100.27W*
Atoyac de Alvarez *see* Atoyac
43 P15 **Atoyac, Río** ≈ S Mexico
41 O5 **Atqasuk** Alaska, USA *70.28N 157.24W*
Atrak/Atrak, Rūd-e *see* Etrek
97 J20 **Ätran** ≈ S Sweden
56 C7 **Atrato, Río** ≈ NW Colombia
Atrek *see* Etrek
109 K14 **Atri** Abruzzo, C Italy *42.34N 13.58E*
Atria *see* Adria
171 Jj16 **Atsugi** *var.* Atugi. Kanagawa, Honshū, S Japan *35.27N 139.21E*
171 L12 **Atsumi** Yamagata, Honshū, C Japan *38.38N 139.36E*
172 Oo4 **Atsuta** Hokkaidō, NE Japan *43.28N 141.24E*
176 Y13 **Atsy** Papua, E Indonesia *5.40S 138.19E*
149 Q17 **Aṭ Ṭaff** *desert* C UAE
144 G12 **Aṭ Ṭafīlah** *var.* Et Tafila, Tafila. Aṭ Ṭafīlah, W Jordan *30.52N 35.36E*
144 G12 **Aṭ Ṭafīlah** ***off.*** Muḩāfaẓat aṭ Ṭafīlah. ◈ *governorate* W Jordan
146 L10 **Aṭ Ṭā'if** Makkah, W Saudi Arabia *21.49N 40.49E*
Attaleia/Attalia *see* Antalya
25 Q3 **Attalla** Alabama, S USA *34.01N 86.05W*
144 L2 **At Tall al Abyaḍ** *var.* Tall al Abyaḍ, Tell Abyad, ***Fr.*** Tell Abiad. Ar Raqqah, N Syria *36.36N 34.00E*
144 L7 **Aṭ Ṭanf** Ḩimş, S Syria *33.29N 38.39E*
Attapu *see* Samakhixai
145 S10 **At Taqtaqānah** C Iraq *32.03N 43.54E*
117 O23 **Attávytos** ▲ Ródos, Dodekánisos, Greece, Aegean Sea *36.10N 27.50E*
145 V15 **At Tawal** *desert* Iraq/Saudi Arabia
10 G9 **Attawapiskat** Ontario, C Canada *52.55N 82.25W*
10 F9 **Attawapiskat** ≈ Ontario, S Canada
10 D9 **Attawapiskat Lake** ◎ Ontario, C Canada
At Taybé *see* Ţayyibah
103 F16 **Attendorn** Nordrhein-Westfalen, W Germany *51.07N 7.54E*
111 R5 **Attersee** Salzburg, NW Austria *47.55N 13.31E*
111 R5 **Attersee** ◎ N Austria
101 L24 **Attert** Luxembourg, SE Belgium *49.45N 5.47E*
144 M4 **At Tibnī** *var.* Tibnī. Dayr az Zawr, NE Syria *35.30N 39.48E*
33 N13 **Attica** Indiana, N USA *40.17N 87.15W*
20 E10 **Attica** New York, NE USA *42.51N 78.13W*
Attica *see* Attikí
11 N7 **Attikamagen Lake** ◎ Newfoundland and Labrador, E Canada
117 H20 **Attikí** *Eng.* Attica. ◈ *region* C Greece
21 O12 **Attleboro** Massachusetts, NE USA *41.55N 71.15W*
111 R5 **Attnang** Oberösterreich, N Austria *48.01N 13.43E*
155 U6 **Attock City** Punjab, E Pakistan *33.52N 72.19E*
Attopeu *see* Samakhixai
27 X8 **Attoyac River** ≈ Texas, SW USA
40 D16 **Attu** Attu Island, Alaska, USA *52.53N 173.18E*
145 Y12 **Aṭ Ṭūbah** E Iraq *30.29N 47.28E*
146 K4 **Aṭ Ṭubayq** *plain* Jordan/Saudi Arabia
40 C16 **Attu Island** *island* Aleutian Islands, Alaska, USA
Aṭ Ṭūr *see* El Ţûr
161 I21 **Āttūr** Tamil Nādu, SE India *11.34N 78.39E*
147 N17 **At Turbah** SW Yemen *12.42N 43.31E*
64 I12 **Atuel, Río** ≈ C Argentina
Atugi *see* Atsugi
203 X7 **Atuona** Hiva Oa, NE French Polynesia *9.46S 139.03W*
Aturus *see* Adour
97 M18 **Åtvidaberg** Östergötland, S Sweden *58.12N 16.00E*
37 P9 **Atwater** California, W USA *37.19N 120.33W*
31 T8 **Atwater** Minnesota, N USA *45.08N 94.48W*
28 I2 **Atwood** Kansas, C USA *39.48N 101.02W*
33 U12 **Atwood Lake** ⊠ Ohio, N USA
131 P5 **Atyashevo** Respublika Mordoviya, W Russian Federation *54.36N 46.04E*
150 F12 **Atyrau** ***prev.*** Gur'yev. Atyrau, W Kazakhstan *47.07N 51.55E*
150 E11 **Atyrau** ***off.*** Atyrauskaya Oblast', ***var. Kaz.*** Atyraū Oblysy; ***prev.*** Gur'yevskaya Oblast'. ◈ *province* W Kazakhstan
Atyraū Oblysy/Atyrauskaya Oblast' *see* Atyrau
110 J7 **Au** Vorarlberg, NW Austria *47.19N 10.01E*
194 G8 **Aua Island** *island* NW PNG
105 S16 **Aubagne** ***anc.*** Albania. Bouches-du-Rhône, SE France *43.16N 5.34E*
101 L25 **Aubange** Luxembourg, SE Belgium *49.34N 5.48E*
105 Q6 **Aube** ◈ *department* N France
105 R6 **Aube** ≈ N France
101 L19 **Aubel** Liège, E Belgium *50.45N 5.49E*
105 Q13 **Aubenas** Ardèche, E France *44.37N 4.24E*
105 O8 **Aubigny-sur-Nère** Cher, C France *47.30N 2.27E*
105 O13 **Aubin** Aveyron, S France *44.30N 2.18E*
105 O13 **Aubrac, Monts d'** ▲▲ S France
38 J10 **Aubrey Cliffs** *cliff* Arizona, SW USA
25 R5 **Auburn** Alabama, S USA *32.37N 85.30W*
37 P6 **Auburn** California, W USA *38.53N 121.03W*
32 K14 **Auburn** Illinois, N USA *39.35N 89.45W*
33 Q11 **Auburn** Indiana, N USA *41.22N 85.03W*
22 J7 **Auburn** Kentucky, S USA *36.52N 86.42W*
21 P8 **Auburn** Maine, NE USA *44.05N 70.15W*
21 N11 **Auburn** Massachusetts, NE USA *42.11N 71.47W*
31 S16 **Auburn** Nebraska, C USA *40.23N 95.50W*
20 H10 **Auburn** New York, NE USA *42.55N 76.31W*
34 H8 **Auburn** Washington, NW USA *47.18N 122.13W*
105 N11 **Aubusson** Creuse, C France *45.58N 2.10E*
120 E10 **Auce** *Ger.* Autz. Dobele, SW Latvia *56.28N 22.54E*
104 L15 **Auch** *Lat.* Augusta Auscorum, Elimberrum. Gers, S France *43.39N 0.37E*
79 U16 **Auchi** Edo, S Nigeria *7.01N 6.17E*
25 T9 **Aucilla River** ≈ Florida/Georgia, SE USA
192 L6 **Auckland** Auckland, North Island, NZ *36.53S 174.46E*
192 K5 **Auckland** ***off.*** Auckland Region. ◈ *region* North Island, NZ
192 L6 **Auckland** ✕ Auckland, North Island, NZ *37.01S 174.49E*
199 Ii15 **Auckland Islands** *island group* S NZ
105 O16 **Aude** ◈ *department* S France
105 N16 **Aude** ***anc.*** Atax. ≈ S France
Audenarde *see* Oudenaarde
Audern *see* Audru
104 E6 **Audierne** Finistère, NW France *48.01N 4.30W*
104 E6 **Audierne, Baie d'** *bay* NW France
105 U7 **Audincourt** Doubs, E France *47.28N 6.49E*
120 G5 **Audru** *Ger.* Audern. Pärnumaa, SW Estonia *58.25N 24.21E*
31 T14 **Audubon** Iowa, C USA *41.44N 94.56W*
103 N17 **Aue** Sachsen, E Germany *50.34N 12.42E*
102 H12 **Aue** ≈ NW Germany
102 L9 **Auerbach** Bayern, SE Germany *49.41N 11.41E*
103 M17 **Auerbach** Sachsen, E Germany *50.30N 12.24E*
110 I10 **Auererrhein** ≈ SW Switzerland
103 N17 **Auersberg** ▲ E Germany *50.30N 12.42E*
189 W9 **Augathella** Queensland, E Australia *25.54S 146.38E*
33 Q12 **Auglaize River** ≈ Ohio, N USA
85 F22 **Augrabies Falls** *waterfall* W South Africa *28.37S 20.24E*
33 R7 **Au Gres River** ≈ Michigan, N USA
Augsbourg *see* Augsburg
103 K22 **Augsburg** *Fr.* Augsbourg; ***anc.*** Augusta Vindelicorum. Bayern, S Germany *48.22N 10.54E*
188 I14 **Augusta** Western Australia *34.18S 115.10E*
109 L25 **Augusta** *It.* Agosta. Sicilia, Italy, C Mediterranean Sea *37.19N 15.13E*
29 W11 **Augusta** Arkansas, C USA *35.16N 91.22W*
25 V3 **Augusta** Georgia, SE USA *33.29N 81.58W*
29 O6 **Augusta** Kansas, C USA *37.40N 96.59W*
21 Q7 **Augusta** *state capital* Maine, NE USA *44.19N 69.44W*
35 Q8 **Augusta** Montana, NW USA *47.28N 112.23W*
Augusta *see* London
Augusta Auscorum *see* Auch
Augusta Emerita *see* Mérida
Augusta Praetoria *see* Aosta
Augusta Suessionum *see* Soissons
Augusta Trajana *see* Stara Zagora
Augusta Treverorum *see* Trier
Augusta Vangionum *see* Worms
Augusta Vindelicorum *see* Augsburg
97 G24 **Augustenborg** *Ger.* Augustenburg. Sønderjylland, SW Denmark *54.57N 9.52E*
Augustenburg *see* Augustenborg
41 Q13 **Augustine Island** *island* Alaska, USA
12 L9 **Augustines, Lac des** ◎ Québec, SE Canada
Augustobona Tricassium *see* Troyes
Augustodunum *see* Autun
Augustodurum *see* Bayeux
Augustoritum Lemovicensium *see* Limoges
112 O8 **Augustów** *Rus.* Avgustov. Podlaskie, NE Poland *53.51N 22.58E*
Augustow Canal *see* Augustowski, Kanał
112 O8 **Augustowski, Kanał** *Eng.* Augustow Canal, ***Rus.*** Avgustovskiy Kanal. *canal* NE Poland
188 I9 **Augustus, Mount** ▲ Western Australia *24.42S 117.42E*
195 X15 **Auki** Malaita, N Solomon Islands *8.48S 160.45E*
23 W8 **Aulander** North Carolina, SE USA *36.15N 77.16W*
188 L7 **Auld, Lake** *salt lake* Western Australia
Aulie Ata/Auliye-Ata *see* Taraz
150 M8 **Auliyekol'** ***prev.*** Semiozernoye. Kostanay, N Kazakhstan *52.22N 64.06E*
108 E10 **Aulla** Toscana, C Italy *44.15N 10.00E*
104 F6 **Aulne** ≈ NW France
Aulong *see* Ulong
39 T3 **Ault** Colorado, C USA *40.34N 104.43W*
97 F22 **Aulum** *var.* Avlum. Ringkøbing, C Denmark *56.16N 8.48E*
105 N3 **Aumale** Seine-Maritime, N France *49.45N 1.43E*
Auminzatau, Gory *see* Ovminzatovo Tog'lari
79 T14 **Auna** Niger, W Nigeria *10.13N 4.43E*
97 H21 **Auning** Århus, C Denmark *56.25N 10.22E*
198 Cc9 **Aunu'u Island** *island* W American Samoa
85 E20 **Auob** *var.* Oup. ≈ Namibia/South Africa
95 K19 **Aura** Länsi-Suomi, W Finland *60.37N 22.34E*
111 R5 **Aurach** ≈ N Austria
Aural, Phnom *see* Aôral, Phnum
159 O14 **Aurangābād** Bihār, N India *24.48N 84.22E*
160 F13 **Aurangābād** Mahārāshtra, C India *19.52N 75.22E*
201 V7 **Aur Atoll** *atoll* E Marshall Islands
104 G7 **Auray** Morbihan, NW France *47.40N 2.58W*
96 G13 **Aurdal** Oppland, S Norway *60.51N 9.25E*
96 F8 **Aure** Møre og Romsdal, S Norway *63.16N 8.31E*
31 T12 **Aurelia** Iowa, C USA *42.42N 95.26W*
Aurelia Aquensis *see* Baden-Baden
Aurelianum *see* Orléans
123 J12 **Aurès, Massif de l'** ▲▲ NE Algeria
102 F10 **Aurich** Niedersachsen, NW Germany *53.28N 7.28E*
105 O13 **Aurillac** Cantal, C France *44.55N 2.25E*
Aurine, Alpi *see* Zillertaler Alpen
Aurium *see* Ourense
12 H15 **Aurora** Ontario, S Canada *44.00N 79.26W*
57 S8 **Aurora** NW Guyana *6.46N 59.45W*
39 T4 **Aurora** Colorado, C USA *39.42N 104.51W*
32 M11 **Aurora** Illinois, N USA *41.45N 88.19W*
33 Q15 **Aurora** Indiana, N USA *39.01N 84.55W*
31 W4 **Aurora** Minnesota, N USA *47.31N 92.14W*
29 S8 **Aurora** Missouri, C USA *36.58N 93.43W*
31 P16 **Aurora** Nebraska, C USA *40.52N 98.00W*
38 J5 **Aurora** Utah, W USA *38.55N 111.55W*
Aurora *see* Maéwo, Vanuatu
Aurora *see* San Francisco, Philippines
96 F10 **Aursjøen** ◎ S Norway
96 I9 **Aursunden** ◎ S Norway
85 D21 **Aus** Karas, SW Namibia *26.37S 16.18E*
Ausa *see* Vic
12 E16 **Ausable** ≈ Ontario, S Canada
33 O3 **Au Sable Point** *headland* Michigan, N USA *46.40N 86.08W*
33 S7 **Au Sable Point** *headland* Michigan, N USA *44.19N 83.20W*
33 R6 **Au Sable River** ≈ Michigan, N USA
59 H16 **Ausangate, Nevado** ▲ C Peru *13.46S 71.13W*
Auschwitz *see* Oświęcim
Ausculum Apulum *see* Ascoli Satriano
107 Q4 **Ausejo** La Rioja, N Spain *42.21N 2.10W*
Aussig *see* Ústí nad Labem
97 F17 **Aust-Agder** ◈ *county* S Norway
94 P2 **Austfonna** *glacier* NE Svalbard
33 P15 **Austin** Indiana, N USA *38.45N 85.48W*
31 W11 **Austin** Minnesota, N USA *43.40N 92.58W*
37 U5 **Austin** Nevada, W USA *39.28N 117.04W*
27 S10 **Austin** *state capital* Texas, S USA *30.16N 97.44W*
188 J10 **Austin, Lake** *salt lake* Western Australia
33 V11 **Austintown** Ohio, N USA *41.06N 80.45W*
27 V9 **Austonio** Texas, SW USA *31.09N 95.39W*
Australes, Archipel des *see* Australes, Îles
Australes et Antarctiques Françaises, Terres *see* French Southern and Antarctic Territories
203 T14 **Australes, Îles** *var.* Archipel des Australes, Îles Tubuai, Tubuai Islands, ***Eng.*** Austral Islands. *island group* SW French Polynesia
183 Y11 **Austral Fracture Zone** *tectonic feature* S Pacific Ocean
189 O7 **Australia** ***off.*** Commonwealth of Australia. ◆ *commonwealth republic*
182 M8 **Australia** *continent*
191 Q12 **Australian Alps** ▲▲ SE Australia
191 R11 **Australian Capital Territory** ***prev.*** Federal Capital Territory. ◈ *territory* SE Australia
Australie, Bassin Nord de l' *see* North Australian Basin
Austral Islands *see* Australes, Îles
Austrava *see* Ostrov
111 T6 **Austria** ***off.*** Republic of Austria, ***Ger.*** Österreich. ◆ *republic* C Europe
94 K3 **Austurland** ◈ *region* SE Iceland
94 G10 **Austvågøya** *island* C Norway
60 G13 **Autazes** Amazonas, N Brazil *3.37S 59.07W*
104 M16 **Auterive** Haute-Garonne, S France *43.22N 1.28E*
Autesiodorum *see* Auxerre
105 N2 **Authie** ≈ N France
Autissiodorum *see* Auxerre
42 K14 **Autlán** *var.* Autlán de Navarro. Jalisco, SW Mexico *19.46N 104.22W*
Autlán de Navarro *see* Autlán
Autricum *see* Chartres
105 Q9 **Autun** ***anc.*** Ædua, Augustodunum. Saône-et-Loire, C France *46.57N 4.18E*
Autz *see* Auce
101 H20 **Auvelais** Namur, S Belgium *50.27N 4.37E*
105 P11 **Auvergne** ◈ *region* C France
104 M12 **Auvézère** ≈ W France
105 P7 **Auxerre** ***anc.*** Autesiodorum, Autissiodorum. Yonne, C France *47.48N 3.34E*
105 N2 **Auxi-le-Château** Pas-de-Calais, N France *50.14N 2.06E*
105 S8 **Auxonne** Côte d'Or, C France *47.12N 5.22E*
57 P9 **Auyan Tebuy** ▲ SE Venezuela *5.48N 62.27W*
105 O10 **Auzances** Creuse, C France *46.01N 2.29E*
29 U8 **Ava** Missouri, C USA *36.57N 92.39W*
148 M5 **Āvaj** Qazvin, N Iran
97 C15 **Avaldsnes** Rogaland, S Norway *59.21N 5.16E*
105 Q8 **Avallon** Yonne, C France *47.30N 3.54E*
104 K6 **Avaloirs, Mont des** ▲ NW France *48.27N 0.11W*
37 S16 **Avalon** Santa Catalina Island, California, W USA *33.20N 118.19W*
20 J17 **Avalon** New Jersey, NE USA *39.04N 74.42W*
11 V13 **Avalon Peninsula** *peninsula* Newfoundland and Labrador, E Canada
207 Q11 **Avannaarsua** ◈ *province* N Greenland
62 K10 **Avaré** São Paulo, S Brazil *23.06S 48.57W*
Avaricum *see* Bourges
202 H16 **Avarua** ○ (Cook Islands) Rarotonga, S Cook Islands *21.12S 159.46E*
202 H16 **Avarua Harbour** *harbor* Rarotonga, S Cook Islands
Avasfelsőfalu *see* Negrești-Oaș
40 L17 **Avatanak Island** *island* Aleutian Islands, Alaska, USA
202 B16 **Avatele** S Niue *19.06S 169.55E*
202 H16 **Avatiu** Rarotonga, S Cook Islands *21.12S 159.46W*
202 H15 **Avatiu Harbour** *harbor* Rarotonga, S Cook Islands
Avdeyevka *see* Avdiyivka
116 J13 **Ávdira** Anatolikí Makedonía kai Thráki, NE Greece *40.58N 24.58E*
119 X8 **Avdiyivka** *Rus.* Avdeyevka. Donets'ka Oblast', SE Ukraine *48.05N 37.45E*
168 K7 **Avdzaga** C Mongolia *47.43N 103.30E*
106 G6 **Ave** ≈ N Portugal
106 G7 **Aveiro** ***anc.*** Talabriga. Aveiro, W Portugal *40.37N 8.40W*
106 G7 **Aveiro** ◈ *district* N Portugal
Avela *see* Ávila
101 D18 **Avelgem** West-Vlaanderen, W Belgium *50.46N 3.25E*
63 D20 **Avellaneda** Buenos Aires, E Argentina *34.43S 58.23W*
109 L17 **Avellino** ***anc.*** Abellinum. Campania, S Italy *40.54N 14.46E*
37 Q12 **Avenal** California, W USA *36.00N 120.07W*
Avenio *see* Avignon
96 E8 **Averoya** *island* S Norway
109 K17 **Aversa** Campania, S Italy *40.58N 14.10E*
35 N9 **Avery** Idaho, NW USA *47.14N 115.48W*
27 W5 **Avery** Texas, SW USA *33.33N 94.46W*
Aves, Islas de *see* Las Aves, Islas
Avesnes *see* Avesnes-sur-Helpe
105 Q2 **Avesnes-sur-Helpe** *var.* Avesnes. Nord, N France *50.07N 3.57E*
66 G12 **Aves Ridge** *undersea feature* SE Caribbean Sea
97 M14 **Avesta** Dalarna, C Sweden *60.09N 16.10E*
105 O14 **Aveyron** ◈ *department* S France
105 N14 **Aveyron** ≈ S France
109 J15 **Avezzano** Abruzzo, C Italy *42.01N 13.25E*
117 D16 **Avgó** ▲ C Greece *39.31N 21.24E*
Avgustov *see* Augustów
Avgustovskiy Kanal *see* Augustowski, Kanał
98 J9 **Aviemore** N Scotland, UK *57.06N 4.01W*
193 F21 **Aviemore, Lake** ◎ South Island, NZ
105 R15 **Avignon** ***anc.*** Avenio. Vaucluse, SE France *43.57N 4.49E*
106 M7 **Ávila** *var.* Avila; ***anc.*** Abela, Abula, Abyla, Avela. Castilla-León, C Spain *40.39N 4.42W*
106 L8 **Ávila** ◈ *province* Castilla-León, C Spain
106 K2 **Avilés** Asturias, NW Spain *43.33N 5.55W*
120 J4 **Avinurme** *Ger.* Awwinorm. Ida-Virumaa, NE Estonia *58.58N 26.52E*
106 H10 **Avis** Portalegre, C Portugal *39.03N 7.52W*
Avlum *see* Aulum
190 M11 **Avoca** Victoria, SE Australia *37.09S 143.34E*
31 T14 **Avoca** Iowa, C USA *41.27N 95.20W*
190 M11 **Avoca River** ≈ Victoria, SE Australia
109 L25 **Avola** Sicilia, Italy, C Mediterranean Sea *36.54N 15.07E*
20 F10 **Avon** New York, NE USA *42.53N 77.41W*
31 P12 **Avon** South Dakota, N USA *43.00N 98.03W*
99 M23 **Avon** ≈ S England, UK
99 L20 **Avon** ≈ C England, UK
38 K13 **Avondale** Arizona, SW USA *33.25N 112.20W*
25 X13 **Avon Park** Florida, SE USA *27.36N 81.30W*
104 J5 **Avranches** Manche, N France *48.42N 1.21W*
105 O3 **Avre** ≈ N France
195 X16 **Avuavu** *var.* Kolotambu. Guadalcanal, C Solomon Islands *9.52S 160.25E*
Avveel *see* Ivalo, Finland
Avveel *see* Ivalojoki, Finland
Avvil *see* Ivalo
79 O17 **Awaaso** *var.* Awaso. SW Ghana *6.10N 2.18W*
147 X8 **Awābī** *var.* Al 'Awābī. NE Oman *23.19N 57.34E*
170 G15 **Awaji-shima** *island* SW Japan
192 L9 **Awakino** Waikato, North Island, NZ *38.40S 174.37E*
148 M15 **'Awālī** C Bahrain *26.06N 50.33E*
101 K19 **Awans** Liège, E Belgium *50.39N 5.30E*
192 I2 **Awanui** Northland, North Island, NZ *35.01S 173.16E*
154 M14 **Awārān** Baluchistān, SW Pakistan *26.31N 65.10E*
83 K16 **Awara Plain** *plain* NE Kenya
82 M13 **Āwarē** Somali, E Ethiopia *8.12N 44.09E*
144 M6 **'Awāriḍ, Wādī** *dry watercourse* E Syria
193 B20 **Awarua Point** *headland* South Island, NZ *44.15S 168.03E*
83 J14 **Āwasa** Southern, S Ethiopia *6.54N 38.26E*
82 K13 **Āwash** Afar, NE Ethiopia *8.59N 40.15E*
82 K12 **Āwash** *var.* Hawash. ≈ C Ethiopia
171 Kk11 **Awa-shima** *island* C Japan
Awaso *see* Awaaso
164 H7 **Awat** Xinjiang Uygur Zizhiqu, NW China *40.36N 80.22E*
193 J15 **Awatere** ≈ South Island, NZ
77 O10 **Awbārī** SW Libya *26.34N 12.46E*
77 N9 **Awbāri, Idhān** *var.* Edeyen d'Oubari. *desert* Algeria/Libya
82 C13 **Aweil** Northern Bahr el Ghazal, SW Sudan *8.44N 27.25E*
98 H11 **Awe, Loch** ◎ W Scotland, UK
79 U16 **Awka** Anambra, SW Nigeria *6.12N 7.04E*
41 O6 **Awuna River** ≈ Alaska, USA
Awwinorm *see* Avinurme
Ax *see* Dax
Axarfjördhur *see* Öxarfjördhur
105 N17 **Axat** Aude, S France *42.46N 2.13E*
101 F16 **Axel** Zeeland, SW Netherlands *51.16N 3.55E*
207 P9 **Axel Heiberg Island** *var.* Axel Heiburg. *island* Nunavut, N Canada
Axel Heiburg *see* Axel Heiberg Island
79 O17 **Axim** S Ghana *4.52N 2.13W*
116 F13 **Axiós** *var.* Vardar. ≈ Greece/FYR Macedonia **see also** Vardar
105 N17 **Ax-les-Thermes** Ariège, S France *42.43N 1.49E*
171 Gg14 **Ayabe** Kyōto, Honshū, SW Japan *35.16N 135.15E*
122 F13 **Ayachi, Jbel** ▲ C Morocco *32.30N 5.00W*
63 D22 **Ayacucho** Buenos Aires, E Argentina *37.09S 58.30W*
59 F15 **Ayacucho** Ayacucho, S Peru *13.10S 74.15W*
59 E16 **Ayacucho** ***off.*** Departamento de Ayacucho. ◈ *department* SW Peru
151 W11 **Ayagoz** *var.* Ayaguz, ***Kaz.*** Ayaköz; ***prev.*** Sergiopol. Vostochnyy Kazakhstan, E Kazakhstan *47.54N 80.25E*
151 V12 **Ayagoz** *var.* Ayaguz, ***Kaz.*** Ayaköz. ≈ E Kazakhstan
Ayaguz *see* Ayagoz
Ayakagytma *see* Oyoqog'itma
Ayakkuduk *see* Oyoqquduq
164 L10 **Ayakkum Hu** ◎ NW China
Ayaköz *see* Ayagoz
106 H14 **Ayamonte** Andalucía, S Spain *37.13N 7.24W*
127 N12 **Ayan** Khabarovskiy Kray, E Russian Federation *56.27N 138.09E*
142 J10 **Ayancık** Sinop, N Turkey *41.55N 34.34E*
57 S9 **Ayanganna Mountain** ▲ C Guyana *5.21N 59.54W*
79 U16 **Ayangba** Kogi, C Nigeria *7.36N 7.10E*
127 P6 **Ayanka** Koryakskiy Avtonomnyy Okrug, E Russian Federation *63.42N 167.31E*
56 E7 **Ayapel** Córdoba, NW Colombia *8.17N 75.13W*
142 H12 **Ayaş** Ankara, N Turkey *40.01N 32.21E*
59 I16 **Ayaviri** Puno, S Peru *14.52S 70.34W*
155 P3 **Āybak** *var.* Aibak, Haibak; ***prev.*** Samangān. Samangān, NE Afghanistan *36.16N 68.04E*
153 N10 **Aydarko'l Ko'li** ***Rus.*** Ozero Aydarkul'. ◎ C Uzbekistan
Aydarkul', Ozero *see* Aydarko'l Ko'li
23 W10 **Ayden** North Carolina, SE USA *35.28N 77.25W*
142 C15 **Aydın** *var.* Aïdin; ***anc.*** Tralles. Aydın, SW Turkey *37.51N 27.51E*
142 C15 **Aydın** *var.* Aïdin. ◈ *province* SW Turkey
142 I17 **Aydıncık** İçel, S Turkey *36.10N 33.16E*
142 C15 **Aydın Dağları** ▲▲ W Turkey
164 L6 **Aydingkol Hu** ◎ NW China
131 X7 **Aydyrlinskiy** Orenburgskaya Oblast', W Russian Federation *52.03N 59.54E*
107 S4 **Ayerbe** Aragón, NE Spain *42.16N 0.40W*
Ayers Rock *see* Uluru
Ayeyarwady *see* Irrawaddy
Ayia Napa *see* Agía Nápa
Ayia Phyla *see* Agía Fýlaxis
Ayiásos/Ayiássos *see* Agiasós
Áyios Evstrátios *see* Ágios Efstrátios
Áyios Kírikos *see* Ágios Kírykos
Áyios Nikólaos *see* Ágios Nikólaos
Ayios Seryios *see* Yeniboğaziçi
82 I11 **Āykel** Amhara, N Ethiopia *12.33N 37.01E*
126 K10 **Aykhal** Respublika Sakha (Yakutiya), NE Russian Federation *66.07N 110.25E*
12 J12 **Aylen Lake** ◎ Ontario, SE Canada
99 N21 **Aylesbury** SE England, UK *51.49N 0.49W*
107 O6 **Ayllón** Castilla-León, N Spain *41.25N 3.22W*
12 F17 **Aylmer** Ontario, S Canada *42.46N 80.57W*
12 L12 **Aylmer** Québec, SE Canada *45.22N 75.51W*
13 R12 **Aylmer, Lac** ◎ Québec, SE Canada
15 J6 **Aylmer Lake** ◎ Northwest Territories, NW Canada
151 V14 **Aynabulak** Almaty, SE Kazakhstan *44.37N 77.58E*
144 K2 **'Ayn al 'Arab** Ḩalab, N Syria *36.55N 38.21E*
Aynayn *see* 'Aynīn
145 V12 **'Ayn Ḩamūd** S Iraq *30.51N 45.37E*
153 P12 **Ayní** ***prev. Rus.*** Varzimanor Ayni. W Tajikistan *39.24N 68.30E*
146 M10 **'Aynīn** *var.* Aynayn. *spring/well* SW Saudi Arabia *20.52N 41.41E*
23 U12 **Aynor** South Carolina, SE USA *33.59N 79.11W*
145 Q7 **'Ayn Zāzūh** C Iraq *33.29N 42.34E*
159 N12 **Ayodhya** Uttar Pradesh, N India *26.46N 82.12E*
127 O5 **Ayon, Ostrov** *island* NE Russian Federation
107 R11 **Ayora** País Valenciano, E Spain *39.04N 1.04W*
79 Q11 **Ayorou** Tillabéri, W Niger *14.44N 0.54E*
81 E16 **Ayos** Centre, S Cameroon *3.52N 12.31E*
78 L5 **'Ayoûn 'Abd el Mâlek** *well* N Mauritania *24.51N 7.38W*
78 K10 **'Ayoûn el 'Atroûs** *var.* Aïoun el Atrous, Aïoun el Atroûss. Hodh el Gharbi, SE Mauritania *16.37N 9.36W*
98 I13 **Ayr** W Scotland, UK *55.28N 4.37W*
98 I13 **Ayr** ≈ W Scotland, UK
98 I13 **Ayrshire** *cultural region* SW Scotland, UK
Aysen *see* Aisén
82 L12 **Āysha** Somali, E Ethiopia *10.36N 42.31E*
150 L14 **Ayteke Bi** *Kaz.* Zhangaqazaly ***prev.*** Novokazalinsk. Kyzylorda, SW Kazakhstan *45.52N 62.09E*
152 K8 **Aytim** Navoiy Viloyati, N Uzbekistan *42.15N 63.25E*
189 W4 **Ayton** Queensland, NE Australia *15.54S 145.19E*
116 M9 **Aytos** Burgas, E Bulgaria *42.43N 27.13E*
176 Uu7 **Ayu, Kepulauan** *island group* E Indonesia
A Yun Pa *see* Cheo Reo
175 O8 **Ayu, Tanjung** *headland* Borneo, N Indonesia *0.25N 117.34E*
42 K13 **Ayutla** Jalisco, C Mexico *20.07N 104.18W*
43 P16 **Ayutlá** *var.* Ayutla de los Libres. Guerrero, S Mexico *16.56N 99.22W*
Ayutla de los Libres *see* Ayutlá
178 H11 **Ayutthaya** *var.* Phra Nakhon Si Ayutthaya. Phra Nakhon Si Ayutthaya, C Thailand *14.19N 100.34E*
142 B13 **Ayvalık** Balıkesir, W Turkey *39.18N 26.42E*
101 L20 **Aywaille** Liège, E Belgium *50.28N 5.40E*
147 R13 **'Aywat aş Şay'ar, Wādī** *seasonal river* N Yemen
Azaffal *see* Azeffâl
107 T9 **Azahar, Costa del** *coastal region* E Spain
107 S6 **Azaila** Aragón, NE Spain *41.16N 0.30W*
106 F10 **Azambuja** Lisboa, C Portugal *39.04N 8.52W*
159 N13 **Āzamgarh** Uttar Pradesh, N India *26.03N 83.10E*
79 O9 **Azaouâd** *desert* C Mali
79 S10 **Azaouagh, Vallée de l'** *var.* Azaouak. ≈ W Niger
Azaouak *see* Azaouagh, Vallée de l'
63 F14 **Azara** Misiones, NE Argentina *28.03S 55.42W*
148 K3 **Āzarān** Āẕarbāyjān-e Khāvarī, N Iran *37.34N 47.10E*
Azärbaycan/Azärbaycan Respublikası *see* Azerbaijan
Āẕarbāyjān-e Bākhtarī *see* Āẕarbāyjān-e Gharbī
148 I4 **Āẕarbāyjān-e Gharbī** ***off.*** Ostān-e Āẕarbāyjān-e Gharbī ***Eng.*** West Azerbaijan ***prev.*** Āẕarbāyjān-e Bākhtarī . ◈ *province* NW Iran
Āẕarbāyjān-e Khāvarī *see* Āẕarbāyjān-e Sharqī
148 J3 **Āẕarbāyjān-e Sharqī** ***off.*** Ostān-e Āẕarbāyjān-e Sharqī, ***Eng.*** East Azerbaijan; ***prev.*** Āẕarbāyjān-e Sharqī. ◈ *province* NW Iran
79 W13 **Azare** Bauchi, N Nigeria *11.41N 10.09E*
121 M19 **Azarychy** *Rus.* Ozarichi. Homyel'skaya Voblasts', SE Belarus *52.31N 29.19E*
104 L8 **Azay-le-Rideau** Indre-et-Loire, C France *47.16N 0.25E*
144 I2 **A'zāz** Ḩalab, NW Syria *36.34N 37.03E*
78 H7 **Azeffâl** *var.* Azaffal. *desert* Mauritania/Western Sahara
143 V12 **Azerbaijan** ***off.*** Azerbaijani Republic, ***Az.*** Azärbaycan, Azärbaycan Respublikası; ***prev.*** Azerbaijan SSR. ◆ *republic* SW Asia
151 T7 **Azhbulat, Ozero** ◎ NE Kazakhstan
76 F7 **Azilal** C Morocco *31.58N 6.53W*
Azimabad *see* Patna
21 O6 **Aziscohos Lake** ⊠ Maine, NE USA
Azizbekov *see* Vayk'
Azizie *see* Telish
Aziziya *see* Al 'Azīzīyah
131 T4 **Aznakayevo** Respublika Tatarstan, W Russian Federation *54.55N 53.15E*
58 C8 **Azogues** Cañar, S Ecuador *2.41S 78.54W*
66 N2 **Azores** *var.* Açores, Ilhas dos Açores, ***Port.*** Arquipélago dos Açores. *island group* Portugal, NE Atlantic Ocean
66 L8 **Azores-Biscay Rise** *undersea feature* E Atlantic Ocean
Azotos/Azotus *see* Ashdod
80 K11 **Azoum, Bahr** *seasonal river* SE Chad
130 L12 **Azov** Rostovskaya Oblast', SW Russian Federation *47.06N 39.26E*
130 J13 **Azov, Sea of** *Rus.* Azovskoye More, ***Ukr.*** Azovs'ke More. *sea* NE Black Sea
Azovs'ke More/Azovskoye More *see* Azov, Sea of
144 I10 **Azraq, Wāḩat al** *oasis* N Jordan *31.51N 36.51E*
Āzro *see* Āzrow
76 G6 **Azrou** C Morocco *33.30N 5.12W*
155 R5 **Āzrow** *var.* Āzro. Lowgar, E Afghanistan *34.10N 69.39E*

◆ Country
● Country Capital
◇ Dependent Territory
○ Dependent Territory Capital
◈ Administrative Region
✕ International Airport
▲ Mountain
▲▲ Mountain Range
Volcano
≈ River
◎ Lake
⊠ Reservoir

BĀLĀ MORGHĀB – BARAMA RIVER

154 *L3* **Bālā Morghāb** Laghmān, NW Afghanistan *35.37N 63.21E*
158 *E11* **Bālān** *prev.* Bāhla. Rājasthān, NW India *27.45N 71.31E*
118 *J10* **Bălan** *Hung.* Balánbánya. Harghita, C Romania *46.39N 25.45E*
Balánbánya *see* Bălan
179 *P10* **Balanga** Luzon, N Philippines *14.40N 120.32E*
160 *M12* **Balāngīr** *prev.* Bolangir. Orissa, E India *20.46N 83.31E*
131 *N8* **Balashov** Saratovskaya Oblast', W Russian Federation *51.31N 43.14E*
Balasore *see* Bāleshwar
113 *K21* **Balassagyarmat** Nógrád, N Hungary *48.04N 19.16E*
31 *S10* **Balaton** Minnesota, N USA *44.13N 95.52W*
113 *H24* **Balaton** *var.* Lake Balaton, *Ger.* Plattensee. ◎ W Hungary
113 *I23* **Balatonfüred** *var.* Füred. Veszprém, W Hungary *46.56N 17.51E*
Balaton, Lake *see* Balaton
118 *I11* **Bălăuşeri** *Ger.* Bladenmarkt, *Hung.* Balavásár. Mureş, C Romania *46.24N 24.41E*
Balavásár *see* Bălăuşeri
107 *Q11* **Balazote** Castilla-La Mancha, C Spain *38.54N 2.09W*
Balázsfalva *see* Blaj
121 *F14* **Balbieriškis** Kaunas, S Lithuania *54.29N 23.52E*
195 *S12* **Balbi, Mount** ▲ Bougainville Island, NE PNG *5.51S 154.58E*
60 *F11* **Balbina, Represa** ▣ NW Brazil
45 *T15* **Balboa** Panamá, C Panama *8.55N 79.36W*
99 *G17* **Balbriggan** *Ir.* Baile Brigín. E Ireland *53.37N 6.10W*
Balbunar *see* Kubrat
83 *N17* **Balcad** Shabeellaha Dhexe, C Somalia *2.19N 45.19E*
63 *D23* **Balcarce** Buenos Aires, E Argentina *37.51S 58.16W*
9 *U16* **Balcarres** Saskatchewan, S Canada *50.49N 103.31W*
116 *O8* **Balchik** Dobrich, NE Bulgaria *43.25N 28.11E*
193 *E24* **Balclutha** Otago, South Island, NZ *46.15S 169.44E*
27 *Q12* **Balcones Escarpment** *escarpment* Texas, SW USA
20 *F14* **Bald Eagle Creek** ≈ Pennsylvania, NE USA
Baldenburg *see* Biały Bór
23 *V12* **Bald Head Island** *island* North Carolina, SE USA
29 *W10* **Bald Knob** Arkansas, C USA *35.18N 91.34W*
32 *K17* **Bald Knob** *hill* Illinois, N USA *37.33N 89.21W*
Baldohn *see* Baldone
120 *G9* **Baldone** *Ger.* Baldohn. Rīga, W Latvia *56.46N 24.18E*
24 *I9* **Baldwin** Louisiana, S USA *29.50N 91.32W*
33 *P7* **Baldwin** Michigan, N USA *43.54N 85.49W*
29 *Q4* **Baldwin City** Kansas, C USA *38.43N 95.12W*
41 *N8* **Baldwin Peninsula** *headland* Alaska, USA *66.45N 162.19W*
20 *H9* **Baldwinsville** New York, NE USA *43.09N 76.19W*
25 *N2* **Baldwyn** Mississippi, S USA *34.30N 88.38W*
9 *W15* **Baldy Mountain** ▲ Manitoba, S Canada *51.29N 100.46W*
35 *T7* **Baldy Mountain** ▲ Montana, NW USA *48.09N 109.39W*
39 *O13* **Baldy Peak** ▲ Arizona, SW USA *33.56N 109.37W*
Bâle *see* Basel
107 *X9* **Baleares** ◈ *autonomous community* E Spain
107 *X11* **Baleares, Islas** *Eng.* Balearic Islands. *island group* Spain, W Mediterranean Sea
Baleares Major *see* Mallorca
Balearic Islands *see* Baleares, Islas
Balearic Plain *see* Algerian Basin
Balearis Minor *see* Menorca
174 *M6* **Baleh, Batang** ≈ East Malaysia
10 *J8* **Baleine, Grande Rivière de la** ≈ Québec, E Canada
10 *K7* **Baleine, Petite Rivière de la** ≈ Québec, SE Canada
11 *N6* **Baleine, Rivière à la** ≈ Québec, E Canada
101 *J16* **Balen** Antwerpen, N Belgium *51.11N 5.12E*
179 *P9* **Baler** Luzon, N Philippines *15.47N 121.30E*
160 *P11* **Bāleshwar** *prev.* Balasore. Orissa, E India *21.31N 86.58E*
126 *L16* **Baley** Chitinskaya Oblast', S Russian Federation *51.30N 116.16E*
79 *S12* **Baléyara** Tillabéri, W Niger *13.48N 2.57E*
131 *T1* **Balezino** Udmurtskaya Respublika, NW Russian Federation *57.57N 53.03E*
44 *J4* **Balfate** Colón, N Honduras *15.47N 86.24W*
9 *O17* **Balfour** British Columbia, SW Canada *49.39N 116.57W*
31 *N3* **Balfour** North Dakota, N USA *47.55N 100.34W*
Balfrush *see* Bābol
126 *I16* **Balgazyn** Respublika Tyva, S Russian Federation *50.53N 95.12E*
9 *U16* **Balgonie** Saskatchewan, S Canada *50.30N 104.12W*
Bălgrad *see* Alba Iulia
83 *J19* **Balguda** *spring/well* S Kenya *1.28S 39.50E*
164 *K6* **Balguntay** Xinjiang Uygur Zizhiqu, NW China *42.51N 86.19E*
147 *R16* **Balḩāf** S Yemen *14.02N 48.15E*
158 *F13* **Bāli** Rājasthān, N India *25.17N 73.16E*
175 *N15* **Bali** ◈ *province* S Indonesia
175 *N16* **Bali** *island* C Indonesia
113 *K16* **Balice** ✈ (Kraków) Małopolskie, S Poland *49.57N 19.49E*
176 *Yy13* **Baliem, Sungai** ≈ Papua, E Indonesia
142 *C12* **Balıkesir** Balıkesir, W Turkey *39.38N 27.52E*
142 *C12* **Balıkesir** ◈ *province* NW Turkey
144 *L3* **Balīkh, Nahr** ≈ N Syria
175 *O9* **Balikpapan** Borneo, C Indonesia *1.15S 116.49E*
175 *O9* **Balikpapan, Teluk** *bay* Borneo, C Indonesia
Bali, Laut *see* Bali Sea
195 *O11* **Balima** ≈ New Britain, C PNG
179 *P17* **Balimbing** Tawitawi, SW Philippines *5.10N 120.00E*
194 *G14* **Balimo** Western, SW PNG *8.01S 142.52E*
Bálinc *see* Balinţ
175 *Qq9* **Balingara, Pegunungan** ⛰ Sulawesi, N Indonesia
103 *H23* **Balingen** Baden-Württemberg, SW Germany *48.16N 8.51E*
118 *F11* **Balinţ** *Hung.* Bálinc. Timiş, W Romania *45.52N 21.54E*
179 *Pp6* **Balintang Channel** *channel* N Philippines
144 *K3* **Bālis** Ḩalab, N Syria *36.01N 38.03E*
175 *N15* **Bali Sea** *Ind.* Laut Bali. *sea* C Indonesia
175 *N16* **Bali, Selat** *strait* C Indonesia
100 *K7* **Balk** Friesland, N Netherlands *52.54N 5.34E*
152 *B11* **Balkanabat** *Rus.* Nebitdag. Balkan Welaýaty, W Turkmenistan *39.33N 54.19E*
124 *O7* **Balkan Mountains** *Bul./SCr.* Stara Planina. ⛰ Bulgaria/Serbia and Montenegro (Yugoslavia)
Balkanskiy Velayat *see* Balkan Welaýaty
152 *B9* **Balkan Welaýaty** *Rus.* Balkanskiy Velayat. ◈ *province* W Turkmenistan
151 *P8* **Balkashino** Akmola, N Kazakhstan *52.32N 68.43E*
155 *O2* **Balkh** *anc.* Bactra. Balkh, N Afghanistan *36.46N 66.54E*
155 *P2* **Balkh** ◈ *province* N Afghanistan
151 *T13* **Balkhash** *Kaz.* Balqash. Karaganda, SE Kazakhstan *46.52N 74.54E*
Balkhash, Lake *see* Balkhash, Ozero
151 *T13* **Balkhash, Ozero** *Eng.* Lake Balkhash, *Kaz.* Balqash. ◎ SE Kazakhstan
Balla Balla *see* Mbalabala
98 *H10* **Ballachulish** N Scotland, UK *56.40N 5.10W*
188 *M12* **Balladonia** Western Australia *32.21S 123.31E*
99 *C16* **Ballaghaderreen** *Ir.* Bealach an Doirín. C Ireland *53.51N 8.29W*
94 *H10* **Ballangen** *Lapp.* Bálák. Nordland, NW Norway *68.18N 16.48E*
99 *H14* **Ballantrae** W Scotland, UK *55.04N 5.00W*
191 *N12* **Ballarat** Victoria, SE Australia *37.36S 143.51E*
188 *K11* **Ballard, Lake** *salt lake* Western Australia
Ballari *see* Bellary
78 *L11* **Ballé** Koulikoro, W Mali *15.18N 8.31W*
42 *D7* **Ballenas, Bahía de** *bay* W Mexico
42 *D5* **Ballenas, Canal de** *channel* NW Mexico
205 *R17* **Balleny Islands** *island group* Antarctica
42 *J7* **Balleza** *var.* San Pablo Balleza. Chihuahua, N Mexico *26.55N 106.21W*
116 *M13* **Ballı** Tekirdağ, NW Turkey *40.48N 27.03E*
159 *O13* **Ballia** Uttar Pradesh, N India *25.45N 84.09E*
191 *V4* **Ballina** New South Wales, SE Australia *28.49S 153.33E*
99 *C16* **Ballina** *Ir.* Béal an Átha. W Ireland *54.07N 9.09W*
99 *D16* **Ballinamore** *Ir.* Béal an Átha Móir. NW Ireland *54.03N 7.46W*
99 *D18* **Ballinasloe** *Ir.* Béal Átha na Sluaighe. W Ireland *53.19N 8.13W*
27 *P8* **Ballinger** Texas, SW USA *31.44N 99.57W*
99 *C17* **Ballinrobe** *Ir.* Baile an Róba. W Ireland *53.37N 9.14W*
99 *A21* **Ballinskelligs Bay** *Ir.* Bá na Scealg. *inlet* SW Ireland
99 *D15* **Ballintra** *Ir.* Baile an tSratha. NW Ireland *54.34N 8.07W*
105 *T7* **Ballon d'Alsace** ▲ NE France *47.50N 6.54E*
Ballon de Guebwiller *see* Grand Ballon
115 *K21* **Ballsh** *var.* Ballshi. Fier, SW Albania *40.35N 19.45E*
Ballshi *see* Ballsh
100 *K4* **Ballum** Friesland, N Netherlands *53.27N 5.40E*
99 *F16* **Ballybay** *Ir.* Béal Átha Beithe. N Ireland *54.07N 6.54W*
99 *E14* **Ballybofey** *Ir.* Bealach Féich. NW Ireland *54.48N 7.46W*
99 *G14* **Ballycastle** *Ir.* Baile an Chaistil. N Northern Ireland, UK *55.12N 6.13W*
99 *G15* **Ballyclare** *Ir.* Bealach Cláir. E Northern Ireland, UK *54.45N 6.00W*
99 *E16* **Ballyconnell** *Ir.* Béal Átha Conaill. N Ireland *54.07N 7.34W*
99 *C17* **Ballyhaunis** *Ir.* Beál Átha hAmhnais. W Ireland *53.45N 8.45W*
99 *G14* **Ballymena** *Ir.* An Baile Meánach. NE Northern Ireland, UK *54.52N 6.16W*
99 *F14* **Ballymoney** *Ir.* Baile Monaidh. NE Northern Ireland, UK *55.10N 6.30W*
99 *G15* **Ballynahinch** *Ir.* Baile na hInse. SE Northern Ireland, UK *54.24N 5.54W*
99 *D16* **Ballysadare** *Ir.* Baile Easa Dara. NW Ireland *54.13N 8.30W*
99 *D15* **Ballyshannon** *Ir.* Béal Átha Seanaidh. NW Ireland *54.30N 8.10W*
65 *H19* **Balmaceda** Aisén, S Chile *45.54S 71.47W*
65 *G23* **Balmaceda, Cerro** ▲ S Chile *51.27S 73.26W*
113 *N22* **Balmazújváros** Hajdú-Bihar, E Hungary *47.36N 21.18E*
110 *E10* **Balmhorn** ▲ SW Switzerland *46.27N 7.41E*
190 *L12* **Balmoral** Victoria, SE Australia *37.16S 141.38E*
26 *K9* **Balmorhea** Texas, SW USA *30.58N 103.44W*
Balneario Claromecó *see* Claromecó
175 *R9* **Balo** Sulawesi, N Indonesia *0.58S 123.19E*
Balochistān *see* Baluchistān
84 *B13* **Balombo** *Port.* Norton de Matos, Vila Norton de Matos. Benguela, W Angola *12.21S 14.46E*
84 *B13* **Balombo** ≈ W Angola
189 *X10* **Balonne River** ≈ Queensland, E Australia
158 *E13* **Bālotra** Rājasthān, N India *25.51N 72.18E*
151 *V14* **Balpyk Bi** *prev.* Kirovskiy *Kaz.* Kīrov. Almaty, SE Kazakhstan *44.52N 78.10E*
Balqā'/Balqā', Muḩāfaẓat al *see* Al Balqā'
Balqash *see* Balkhash/Balkhash, Ozero
158 *M12* **Balrāmpur** Uttar Pradesh, N India *27.25N 82.10E*
190 *M9* **Balranald** New South Wales, SE Australia *34.39S 143.33E*
118 *H14* **Balş** Olt, S Romania *44.19N 24.06E*
12 *H11* **Balsam Creek** Ontario, S Canada *46.26N 79.10W*
32 *I5* **Balsam Lake** Wisconsin, N USA *45.27N 92.28W*
12 *I14* **Balsam Lake** ◎ Ontario, SE Canada
61 *M14* **Balsas** Maranhão, E Brazil *07.30S 46.00W*
42 *M15* **Balsas, Río** *var.* Río Mexcala. ≈ S Mexico
45 *W16* **Balsas, Río** ≈ SE Panama
121 *O18* **Bal'shavik** *Rus.* Bol'shevik. Homyel'skaya Voblasts', SE Belarus *52.34N 30.49E*
97 *O15* **Bålsta** Uppsala, C Sweden *59.33N 17.35E*
110 *E7* **Balsthal** Solothurn, NW Switzerland *47.20N 7.50E*
119 *O8* **Balta** Odes'ka Oblast', SW Ukraine *47.58N 29.39E*
107 *N5* **Baltanás** Castilla-León, N Spain *41.56N 4.12W*
63 *E16* **Baltasar Brum** Artigas, N Uruguay *30.43S 57.19W*
118 *M9* **Bălţi** *Rus.* Bel'tsy. N Moldova *47.45N 27.57E*
Baltic Port *see* Paldiski
120 *B10* **Baltic Sea** *Ger.* Ostee, *Rus.* Baltiskoye More. *sea* N Europe
23 *X3* **Baltimore** Maryland, NE USA *39.17N 76.36W*
33 *T13* **Baltimore** Ohio, N USA *39.48N 82.33W*
23 *X3* **Baltimore-Washington** ✈ Maryland, E USA *39.10N 76.40W*
Baltischport/Baltiski *see* Paldiski
Baltiskoye More *see* Baltic Sea
121 *A14* **Baltiysk** *Ger.* Pillau. Kaliningradskaya Oblast', W Russian Federation *54.39N 19.54E*
Baltkrievija *see* Belarus
121 *H14* **Baltoji Vokė** Vilnius, SE Lithuania *54.35N 25.13E*
194 *K9* **Baluan Island** *island* N PNG
Balūchestān va Sīstān *see* Sīstān va Balūchestān
154 *M12* **Baluchistān** *var.* Balochistān, Beluchistan. ◈ *province* SW Pakistan
179 *Q12* **Balud** Masbate, N Philippines *12.03N 123.12E*
174 *Mm6* **Balui, Batang** ≈ East Malaysia
159 *S13* **Bālurghat** West Bengal, NE India *25.14N 88.43E*
120 *J8* **Balvi** Balvi, NE Latvia *57.07N 27.14E*
194 *H12* **Balyer River** Western Highlands, C PNG
153 *W7* **Balykchy** *Kir.* Ysyk-Köl; *prev.* Issyk-Kul', Rybach'ye. Issyk-Kul'skaya Oblast', NE Kyrgyzstan *42.28N 76.08E*
58 *B7* **Balzar** Guayas, W Ecuador *1.25S 79.54W*
110 *I8* **Balzers** S Liechtenstein *47.04N 9.31E*
149 *T12* **Bam** Kermān, SE Iran *29.08N 58.27E*
79 *Y13* **Bama** Borno, NE Nigeria *11.28N 13.46E*
78 *L12* **Bamako** ● (Mali) Capital District, SW Mali *12.39N 8.01W*
79 *P10* **Bamba** Gao, C Mali *17.03N 1.19W*
44 *M8* **Bambana, Río** ≈ NE Nicaragua
81 *J15* **Bambari** Ouaka, C Central African Republic *5.45N 20.37E*
189 *W5* **Bambaroo** Queensland, NE Australia *19.00S 146.16E*
103 *K19* **Bamberg** Bayern, SE Germany *49.54N 10.52E*
23 *R14* **Bamberg** South Carolina, SE USA *33.18N 81.02W*
81 *M16* **Bambesa** Orientale, N Dem. Rep. Congo *3.25N 25.43E*
78 *G11* **Bambey** W Senegal *14.43N 16.26W*
81 *H16* **Bambio** Sangha-Mbaéré, SW Central African Republic *3.57N 16.54E*
85 *I24* **Bamboesberge** ▲ S South Africa *31.24S 26.10E*
81 *D14* **Bamenda** Nord-Ouest, W Cameroon *5.55N 10.09E*
8 *K17* **Bamfield** Vancouver Island, British Columbia, SW Canada *48.48N 125.05W*
Bami *see* Bamy
155 *P4* **Bāmīān** *var.* Bāmiān. Bāmīān, NE Afghanistan *34.50N 67.51E*
155 *O4* **Bāmīān** ◈ *province* C Afghanistan
81 *J14* **Bamingui** Bamingui-Bangoran, C Central African Republic *7.38N 20.06E*
80 *J13* **Bamingui** ≈ N Central African Republic
80 *J13* **Bamingui-Bangoran** ◈ *prefecture* N Central African Republic
149 *V13* **Bampūr** Sīstān va Balūchestān, SE Iran *27.13N 60.28E*
194 *G14* **Bamu** ≈ SW PNG
152 *E12* **Bamy** *Rus.* Bami. Ahal Welaýaty, C Turkmenistan *38.42N 56.47E*
Bán *see* Bánovce nad Bebravou
83 *N17* **Banaadir** *off.* Gobolka Banaadir. ◈ *region* S Somalia
203 *N3* **Banaba** *var.* Ocean Island. *island* Tungaru, W Kiribati
61 *O14* **Banabuiú, Açude** ▣ NE Brazil
59 *O19* **Bañados del Izozog** *salt lake* SE Bolivia
99 *D18* **Banagher** *Ir.* Beannchar. C Ireland *53.12N 7.56W*
81 *M17* **Banalia** Orientale, N Dem. Rep. Congo *1.39N 25.19E*
78 *L12* **Banamba** Koulikoro, W Mali *13.33N 7.25W*
42 *G4* **Banámichi** Sonora, NW Mexico *30.01N 110.13W*
189 *Y9* **Banana** Queensland, E Australia *24.33S 150.07E*
203 *Z2* **Banana** *prev.* Main Camp. Kiritimati, E Kiribati *02.00N 157.25W*
61 *K16* **Bananal, Ilha do** *island* C Brazil
25 *Y12* **Banana River** *lagoon* Florida, SE USA
157 *Q22* **Bananga** Andaman and Nicobar Islands, India, NE Indian Ocean *6.57N 93.54E*
Banaras *see* Vārānasi
116 *N13* **Banarlı** Tekirdağ, NW Turkey *41.04N 27.21E*
158 *H12* **Banās** ≈ N India
77 *Z11* **Banâs, Râs** *headland* E Egypt *23.55N 35.47E*
114 *N10* **Banatski Karlovac** Serbia, NE Serbia and Montenegro (Yugoslavia) *45.03N 21.02E*
147 *P16* **Banā, Wādī** *dry watercourse* SW Yemen
142 *E14* **Banaz** Uşak, W Turkey *38.46N 29.46E*
142 *E14* **Banaz Çayı** ≈ W Turkey
165 *P14* **Banbar** *var.* Coka. Xizang Zizhiqu, W China *31.01N 94.43E*
99 *G15* **Banbridge** *Ir.* Droichead na Banna. SE Northern Ireland, UK *54.21N 6.16W*
Ban Bua Yai *see* Bua Yai
99 *M21* **Banbury** S England, UK *52.04N 1.19W*
178 *H7* **Ban Chiang Dao** Chiang Mai, NW Thailand *19.22N 98.59E*
98 *K9* **Banchory** NE Scotland, UK *58.04N 0.35W*
12 *J13* **Bancroft** Ontario, SE Canada *45.04N 77.49W*
35 *R15* **Bancroft** Idaho, NW USA *42.43N 111.54W*
31 *U11* **Bancroft** Iowa, C USA *43.17N 94.13W*
160 *I9* **Banda** Madhya Pradesh, C India *24.04N 78.57E*
158 *L13* **Bānda** Uttar Pradesh, N India *25.28N 80.19E*
173 *E3* **Bandaaceh** *var.* Banda Atjeh; *prev.* Koetaradja, Kutaradja, Kutaraja. Sumatera, W Indonesia *5.30N 95.19E*
Banda Atjeh *see* Bandaaceh
176 *U12* **Banda, Kepulauan** *island group* E Indonesia
Banda, Laut *see* Banda Sea
79 *N17* **Bandama** *var.* Bandama Fleuve. ≈ S Ivory Coast
79 *N15* **Bandama Blanc** ≈ C Ivory Coast
Bandama Fleuve *see* Bandama
Bandar 'Abbās *see* Bandar-e 'Abbās
159 *W16* **Bandarban** Chittagong, SE Bangladesh *22.13N 92.13E*
82 *Q13* **Bandarbeyla** *var.* Bender Beila, Bender Beyla. Bari, NE Somalia *9.28N 50.48E*
149 *R14* **Bandar-e 'Abbās** *var.* Bandar 'Abbās; *prev.* Gombroon. Hormozgān, S Iran *27.10N 56.10E*
148 *M3* **Bandar-e Anzalī** Gīlān, NW Iran *37.25N 49.28E*
149 *N12* **Bandar-e Būshehr** *var.* Būshehr, *Eng.* Bushire. Būshehr, S Iran *28.58N 50.49E*
148 *M11* **Bandar-e Gonāveh** *var.* Ganāveh; *prev.* Gonāveh. Būshehr, SW Iran *29.33N 50.39E*
149 *R14* **Bandar-e Khamīr** Hormozgān, S Iran *26.59N 55.30E*
149 *Q14* **Bandar-e Langeh** *var.* Bandar-e Lengeh, Lingeh. Hormozgān, S Iran *26.34N 54.52E*
Bandar-e Lengeh *see* Bandar-e Langeh
148 *L10* **Bandar-e Māhshahr** *var.* Māh-Shahr; *prev.* Bandar-e Ma'shūr. Khūzestān, SW Iran *30.33N 49.10E*
Bandar-e Ma'shūr *see* Bandar-e Māhshahr
149 *O14* **Bandar-e Nakhīlū** Hormozgān, S Iran
Bandar-e Shāh *see* Bandar-e Torkaman
149 *P4* **Bandar-e Torkaman** *var.* Bandar-e Torkeman, Bandar-e Torkman; *prev.* Bandar-e Shāh. Golestān, N Iran *36.55N 54.04E*
Bandar-e Torkeman/Bandar-e Torkman *see* Bandar-e Torkaman
Bandar Kassim *see* Boosaaso
174 *Ii13* **Bandarlampung** *prev.* Tanjungkarang, Teloekbetoeng, Telukbetung. Sumatera, W Indonesia *5.28N 105.16E*
Bandar Maharani *see* Muar
Bandar Masulipatnam *see* Machilīpatnam
Bandar Penggaram *see* Batu Pahat
175 *N3* **Bandar Seri Begawan** *prev.* Brunei Town. ● (Brunei) N Brunei *4.55N 114.58E*
174 *Mm3* **Bandar Seri Begawan** ✈ N Brunei *4.55N 114.58E*
175 *Ss13* **Banda Sea** *var.* Laut Banda. *sea* E Indonesia
106 *H5* **Bande** Galicia, NW Spain *42.01N 7.58W*
61 *G15* **Bandeirantes** Mato Grosso, W Brazil *9.04S 57.53W*
61 *N20* **Bandeira, Pico da** ▲ SE Brazil *20.25S 41.45W*
85 *K19* **Bandelierkop** Limpopo, NE South Africa *23.21S 29.46E*
64 *L8* **Bandera** Santiago del Estero, N Argentina *28.52S 62.15W*
27 *Q11* **Bandera** Texas, SW USA *29.43N 99.07W*
42 *J13* **Banderas, Bahía de** *bay* W Mexico
79 *O11* **Bandiagara** Mopti, C Mali *14.22N 3.42W*
158 *I12* **Bāndīkūi** Rājasthān, N India *27.07N 76.34E*
142 *C11* **Bandırma** *var.* Penderma. Balıkesir, NW Turkey *40.21N 27.58E*
Bandjarmasin *see* Banjarmasin
Bandoeng *see* Bandung
99 *C21* **Bandon** *Ir.* Droicheadna Bandan. SW Ireland *51.43N 8.43W*
34 *E14* **Bandon** Oregon, NW USA *43.07N 124.24W*
178 *J8* **Ban Dong Bang** Nong Khai, E Thailand *18.00N 104.08E*
178 *I6* **Ban Donkon** Oudômxai, N Laos *20.20N 101.37E*
180 *J14* **Bandrélé** SE Mayotte
81 *H20* **Bandundu** *prev.* Banningville. Bandundu, W Dem. Rep. Congo *3.18S 17.24E*
81 *I21* **Bandundu** *off.* Région de Bandundu. ◈ *region* W Dem. Rep. Congo
174 *Jj14* **Bandung** *prev.* Bandoeng. Jawa, C Indonesia *6.47S 107.28E*
118 *L15* **Băneasa** Constanţa, SW Romania *44.03N 27.42E*
148 *J4* **Bāneh** Kordestān, N Iran *35.58N 45.54E*
46 *I7* **Banes** Holguín, E Cuba *20.58N 75.43W*
9 *P16* **Banff** Alberta, SW Canada *51.10N 115.34W*
98 *K8* **Banff** NE Scotland, UK *57.39N 2.33W*
98 *K8* **Banff** *cultural region* NE Scotland, UK
Bánffyhunyad *see* Huedin
79 *N14* **Banfora** SW Burkina *10.36N 4.45W*
161 *H19* **Bangalore** Karnātaka, S India *12.58N 77.34E*
159 *S16* **Bangaon** West Bengal, NE India *23.01N 88.49E*
179 *P9* **Bangar** Luzon, N Philippines *16.51N 120.25E*
81 *L15* **Bangassou** Mbomou, SE Central African Republic *4.51N 22.55E*
194 *K12* **Bangeta, Mount** ▲ C PNG *6.11S 147.02E*
175 *Qq10* **Banggai, Kepulauan** *island group* C Indonesia
175 *R9* **Banggai, Pulau** *island* Kepulauan Banggai, N Indonesia
176 *X11* **Banggelapa** Papua, E Indonesia *3.47S 136.53E*
Banggi *see* Banggi, Pulau
175 *O1* **Banggi, Pulau** *var.* Banggi. *island* East Malaysia
124 *N15* **Banghāzī** *Eng.* Bengazi, Benghazi, *It.* Bengasi. NE Libya *32.07N 20.04E*
Bang Hieng *see* Xé Banghiang
174 *J10* **Bangka-Belitung** *off.* Propinsi Bangka-Belitung. ◈ *province* W Indonesia
174 *K8* **Bangkai, Tanjung** *var.* Bankai. *headland* Borneo, N Indonesia *0.21N 108.53E*
174 *M14* **Bangkalan** Pulau Madura, C Indonesia *7.04S 112.43E*
175 *S6* **Bangka, Pulau** *island* N Indonesia
174 *J10* **Bangka, Pulau** *island* W Indonesia
174 *Ii10* **Bangka, Selat** *strait* Sumatera, W Indonesia
175 *Rr6* **Bangka, Selat** *var.* Selat Likupang. *strait* Sulawesi, N Indonesia
174 *Gg8* **Bangkinang** Sumatera, W Indonesia *0.21N 100.56E*
174 *H10* **Bangko** Sumatera, W Indonesia *2.03S 102.15E*
Bangkok *see* Krung Thep
Bangkok, Bight of *see* Krung Thep, Ao
159 *T14* **Bangladesh** *off.* People's Republic of Bangladesh; *prev.* East Pakistan. ◆ *republic* S Asia
178 *Kk13* **Ba Ngoi** Khanh Hoa, S Vietnam *11.55N 109.07E*
158 *K5* **Bangong Co** *var.* Pangong Tso. ◎ China/India
see also Pangong Tso
99 *G15* **Bangor** *Ir.* Beannchar. E Northern Ireland, UK *54.40N 5.40W*
99 *I18* **Bangor** NW Wales, UK *53.13N 4.07W*
21 *R6* **Bangor** Maine, NE USA *44.48N 68.46W*
20 *I14* **Bangor** Pennsylvania, NE USA *40.52N 75.12W*
69 *R8* **Bangoran** ≈ S Central African Republic
Bang Phra *see* Trat
Bang Pla Soi *see* Chon Buri
27 *Q8* **Bangs** Texas, SW USA *31.43N 99.07W*
178 *H13* **Bang Saphan** *var.* Bang Saphan Yai. Prachuap Khiri Khan, SW Thailand *11.10N 99.27E*
Bang Saphan Yai *see* Bang Saphan
38 *I8* **Bangs, Mount** ▲ Arizona, SW USA *36.47N 113.51W*
95 *E15* **Bangsund** Nord-Trøndelag, C Norway *64.22N 11.22E*
179 *P8* **Bangued** Luzon, N Philippines *17.36N 120.40E*
81 *I15* **Bangui** ● (Central African Republic) Ombella-Mpoko, SW Central African Republic *4.21N 18.31E*
81 *I15* **Bangui** ✈ Ombella-Mpoko, SW Central African Republic *4.19N 18.34E*
85 *N16* **Bangula** Southern, S Malawi *16.38S 35.04E*
Bangwaketse *see* Southern
84 *K12* **Bangweulu, Lake** *var.* Lake Bengweulu. ◎ N Zambia
Banhā *see* Benha
Ban Hat Yai *see* Hat Yai
178 *I8* **Ban Hin Heup** Viangchan, C Laos *18.37N 102.19E*
Ban Houayxay/Ban Houei Sai *see* Houayxay
178 *H12* **Ban Hua Hin** *var.* Hua Hin. Prachuap Khiri Khan, SW Thailand *12.29N 99.55E*
81 *L14* **Bani** Haute-Kotto, E Central African Republic *7.06N 22.51E*
79 *N12* **Bani** ≈ S Mali
47 *O9* **Baní** S Dominican Republic *18.14N 70.18W*
Banias *see* Bāniyās
79 *S11* **Bani Bangou** Tillabéri, SW Niger *15.04N 2.40E*
78 *M12* **Banifing** *var.* Ngorolaka. ≈ Burkina/Mali
79 *R13* **Banikoara** N Benin *11.18N 2.25E*
Banī Mazār *see* Beni Mazâr
116 *K8* **Baniski Lom** ≈ N Bulgaria
23 *U7* **Banister River** ≈ Virginia, NE USA
Banī Suwayf *see* Beni Suef
77 *O8* **Banī Walīd** NW Libya *31.46N 13.58E*
144 *H5* **Bāniyās** *var.* Banias, Baniyas, Paneas. Ţarţūs, W Syria *35.12N 35.57E*
115 *K14* **Banja** Serbia, W Serbia and Montenegro (Yugoslavia) *43.33N 19.35E*
Banjak, Kepulauan *see* Banyak, Kepulauan
114 *J12* **Banja Koviljača** Serbia, W Serbia and Montenegro (Yugoslavia) *44.31N 19.11E*
114 *G11* **Banja Luka** Republika Srpska, NW Bosnia and Herzegovina *44.46N 17.10E*
175 *N11* **Banjarmasin** *prev.* Bandjarmasin. Borneo, C Indonesia *3.22S 114.33E*
Banjoewangi *see* Banyuwangi
78 *F11* **Banjul** *prev.* Bathurst. ● (Gambia) W Gambia *13.25N 16.43W*
78 *F11* **Banjul** ✈ W Gambia *13.18N 16.39W*
Banjuwangi *see* Banyuwangi
Bank *see* Bankä
143 *Y13* **Bankä** *Rus.* Bank. SE Azerbaijan *39.25N 49.13E*
178 *Jj11* **Ban Kadian** *var.* Ban Kadiene. Champasak, S Laos *14.25N 105.42E*
Ban Kadiene *see* Ban Kadian
Bankai *see* Bangkai, Tanjung
178 *Gg15* **Ban Kam Phuam** Phangnga, SW Thailand *9.16N 98.24E*
Ban Kantang *see* Kantang
79 *O11* **Bankass** Mopti, S Mali *14.05N 3.30W*
97 *L19* **Bankeryd** Jönköping, S Sweden *57.51N 14.07E*
85 *K16* **Banket** Mashonaland West, N Zimbabwe *17.25S 30.25E*
178 *Jj11* **Ban Khamphô** Attapu, S Laos *14.35N 106.18E*
25 *O4* **Bankhead Lake** ▣ Alabama, S USA
79 *Q11* **Bankilaré** Tillabéri, SW Niger *14.34N 0.41E*
Banks, Îles *see* Banks Islands
8 *I14* **Banks Island** *island* British Columbia, SW Canada
15 *Hh1* **Banks Island** *island* Banks Island, Northwest Territories, NW Canada
197 *C10* **Banks Islands** *Fr.* Îles Banks. *island group* N Vanuatu
25 *U8* **Banks Lake** ◎ Georgia, SE USA
34 *K8* **Banks Lake** ▣ Washington, NW USA
193 *I19* **Banks Peninsula** *peninsula* South Island, NZ
191 *Q15* **Banks Strait** *strait* SW Tasman Sea
Ban Kui Nua *see* Kui Buri
159 *R16* **Bānkura** West Bengal, NE India *23.13N 87.04E*
178 *J8* **Ban Lakxao** *var.* Lak Sao. Bolikhamxai, C Laos *18.10N 104.58E*
178 *H17* **Ban Lam Phai** Songkhla, SW Thailand *6.43N 100.57E*
Ban Mae Sot *see* Mae Sot
Ban Mae Suai *see* Mae Suai
Ban Mak Khaeng *see* Udon Thani
177 *G3* **Banmauk** Sagaing, N Myanmar *24.25N 95.54E*
Banmo *see* Bhamo
178 *Jj10* **Ban Mun-Houamuang** S Laos *15.11N 106.44E*
99 *F14* **Bann** *var.* Lower Bann, Upper Bann. ≈ N Northern Ireland, UK
178 *Jj10* **Ban Nadou** Salavan, S Laos *15.51N 105.37E*
178 *J10* **Ban Nakala** Savannakhét, S Laos *16.14N 105.09E*
178 *I8* **Ban Nakha** Viangchan, C Laos *18.13N 102.29E*
178 *Jj9* **Ban Nakham** Khammouan, S Laos *17.10N 105.25E*
178 *I8* **Ban Namoun** Xaignabouli, N Laos *18.40N 101.34E*
178 *Hh17* **Ban Nang Sata** Yala, SW Thailand *6.15N 101.13E*
178 *Gg15* **Ban Na San** Surat Thani, SW Thailand *8.52N 99.21E*
178 *Ii7* **Ban Nasi** Xiangkhoang, N Laos *19.37N 103.33E*
46 *I3* **Bannerman Town** Eleuthera Island, C Bahamas *24.38N 76.09W*
37 *V15* **Banning** California, W USA *33.55N 116.52W*
Banningville *see* Bandundu
178 *Jj11* **Ban Nongsim** Champasak, S Laos *14.45N 106.00E*
155 *S7* **Bannu** *prev.* Edwardesabad. North-West Frontier Province, NW Pakistan *32.00N 70.36E*
Bañolas *see* Banyoles
58 *C7* **Baños** Tungurahua, C Ecuador *1.20S 78.24W*
Bánovce *see* Bánovce nad Bebravou
113 *I19* **Bánovce nad Bebravou** *var.* Bánovce, *Hung.* Bán. Trenčiansky Kraj, W Slovakia *48.43N 18.15E*
114 *I12* **Banovići** Federacija Bosna I Hercegovina, E Bosnia and Herzegovina *44.25N 18.31E*
Banow *see* Andarāb
Ban Pak Phanang *see* Pak Phanang
178 *Hh7* **Ban Pan Nua** Lampang, NW Thailand *18.51N 99.57E*
178 *I10* **Ban Phai** Khon Kaen, E Thailand *16.00N 102.42E*
178 *Jj9* **Ban Phou A Douk** Khammouan, C Laos *17.12N 106.07E*
178 *I8* **Ban Phu** Uthai Thani, W Thailand
178 *H11* **Ban Pong** Ratchaburi, W Thailand *13.49N 99.52E*
202 *I3* **Banraeaba** Tarawa, W Kiribati *1.19N 173.01E*
178 *Gg11* **Ban Sai Yok** Kanchanaburi, W Thailand *14.24N 98.54E*
Ban Sattahip/Ban Sattahipp *see* Sattahip
Ban Sichon *see* Sichon
Ban Si Racha *see* Siracha
113 *J19* **Banská Bystrica** *Ger.* Neusohl, *Hung.* Besztercebánya. Banskobystrický Kraj, C Slovakia *48.45N 19.08E*
113 *K20* **Banskobystrický Kraj** ◈ *region* C Slovakia
178 *J8* **Ban Sôppheung** Bolikhamxai, C Laos *18.33N 104.18E*
Ban Sop Prap *see* Sop Prap
158 *G15* **Bānswāra** Rājasthān, N India *23.31N 74.28E*
178 *Gg15* **Ban Ta Khun** Surat Thani, SW Thailand *8.53N 98.52E*
Ban Takua Pa *see* Takua Pa
178 *Jj9* **Ban Talak** Khammouan, C Laos *17.33N 105.40E*
79 *R15* **Bantè** W Benin *8.21N 1.55E*
174 *Ii14* **Banten** *off.* Propinsi Banten. ◈ *province* W Indonesia
178 *Ii8* **Ban Thabôk** Bolikhamxai, C Laos *18.21N 103.12E*
178 *Jj10* **Ban Tôp** Savannakhét, S Laos *16.07N 106.07E*
99 *B21* **Bantry** *Ir.* Beanntraí. SW Ireland *51.40N 9.27W*
99 *A21* **Bantry Bay** *Ir.* Bá Bheanntraí. *bay* SW Ireland
174 *L15* **Bantul** *prev.* Bantoel. Jawa, C Indonesia *7.55S 110.21E*
161 *F19* **Bantvāl** *var.* Bantwāl. Karnātaka, E India *12.57N 75.04E*
Bantwāl *see* Bantvāl
116 *N9* **Banya** Burgas, E Bulgaria *42.46N 27.49E*
173 *Ee6* **Banyak, Kepulauan** *prev.* Kepulauan Banjak. *island group* NW Indonesia
107 *U8* **Banya, La** *headland* E Spain *40.34N 0.37E*
81 *E14* **Banyo** Adamaoua, NW Cameroon *6.46N 11.49E*
107 *X4* **Banyoles** *var.* Bañolas. Cataluña, NE Spain *42.07N 2.46E*
178 *H16* **Ban Yong Sata** Trang, SW Thailand *7.09N 99.42E*
174 *Mm16* **Banyuwangi** *var.* Banjuwangi; *prev.* Banjoewangi. Jawa, S Indonesia *8.12S 114.22E*
205 *X14* **Banzare Coast** *physical region* Antarctica
181 *Q14* **Banzare Seamounts** *undersea feature* S Indian Ocean
Banzart *see* Bizerte
169 *Q12* **Baochang** *var.* Taibus Qi. Nei Mongol Zizhiqu, N China *41.55N 115.22E*
167 *O3* **Baoding** *var.* Pao-ting; *prev.* Tsingyuan. Hebei, E China *38.52N 115.28E*
Baoebaoe *see* Baubau
Baoi, Oileán *see* Dursey Island
166 *J6* **Baoji** *var.* Pao-chi, Paoki. Shaanxi, C China *34.22N 107.16E*
169 *U9* **Baokang** *var.* Hoqin Zuoyi Zhongji. Nei Mongol Zizhiqu, N China *44.08N 123.18E*
195 *V14* **Baolo** Santa Isabel, N Solomon Islands *7.41S 158.47E*
178 *K13* **Bao Lôc** Lâm Đông, S Vietnam *11.33N 107.48E*
169 *Z7* **Baoqing** Heilongjiang, NE China *46.15N 132.12E*
Baoqing *see* Shaoyang
81 *H15* **Baoro** Nana-Mambéré, W Central African Republic *5.40N 16.00E*
166 *E12* **Baoshan** *var.* Pao-shan. Yunnan, SW China *25.04N 99.07E*
169 *N13* **Baotou** *var.* Pao-t'ou, Paotow. Nei Mongol Zizhiqu, N China *40.37N 109.58E*
78 *L14* **Baoulé** ≈ S Mali
78 *K12* **Baoulé** ≈ W Mali
105 *O2* **Bapaume** Pas-de-Calais, N France *50.06N 2.50E*
12 *J13* **Baptiste Lake** ◎ Ontario, SE Canada
Bapu *see* Meigu
Baqanas *see* Bakanas
Baqbaqty *see* Bakbakty
165 *P14* **Baqên** *var.* Dartang. Xizang Zizhiqu, W China *31.50N 94.08E*
144 *F14* **Bāqir, Jabal** ⛰ S Jordan
145 *T7* **Ba'qūbah** *var.* Qubba. C Iraq *33.45N 44.40E*
64 *H5* **Baquedano** Antofagasta, N Chile *23.19S 69.49W*
118 *M6* **Bar** Vinnyts'ka Oblast', C Ukraine *49.04N 27.39E*
115 *J18* **Bar** *It.* Antivari. Montenegro, SW Serbia and Montenegro (Yugoslavia) *42.02N 19.09E*
82 *E10* **Bara** Northern Kordofan, C Sudan *13.42N 30.21E*
83 *M18* **Baraawe** *It.* Brava. Shabeellaha Hoose, S Somalia *1.09N 43.59E*
158 *M12* **Bāra Banki** Uttar Pradesh, N India *26.55N 81.10E*
125 *G13* **Barabinsk** Novosibirskaya Oblast', C Russian Federation *55.19N 78.01E*
32 *L8* **Baraboo** Wisconsin, N USA *43.27N 89.45W*
32 *K8* **Baraboo Range** *hill range* Wisconsin, N USA
Baracaldo *see* San Vicente de Barakaldo
13 *Y6* **Barachois** Québec, SE Canada *48.37N 64.14W*
46 *J7* **Baracoa** Guantánamo, E Cuba *20.19N 74.31W*
63 *C19* **Baradero** Buenos Aires, E Argentina *33.47S 59.29W*
191 *R6* **Baradine** New South Wales, SE Australia *30.55S 149.03E*
Baraf Daja Islands *see* Damar, Kepulauan
160 *M12* **Baragarh** Orissa, E India *21.20N 83.36E*
83 *I17* **Baragoi** Rift Valley, W Kenya *1.39N 36.46E*
47 *N9* **Barahona** SW Dominican Republic *18.13N 71.07W*
159 *W13* **Barail Range** ⛰ NE India
82 *I9* **Baraka** *var.* Barka, *Ar.* Khawr Barakah. *seasonal river* Eritrea/Sudan
82 *G10* **Barakat** Gezira, C Sudan *14.18N 33.31E*
Barakī *see* Barakī Barak
155 *Q6* **Barakī Barak** *var.* Barakī, Baraki Rajan. Lowgar, E Afghanistan *33.58N 68.58E*
Baraki Rajan *see* Barakī Barak
160 *N11* **Bārākot** Orissa, E India *21.35N 85.00E*
Baram *see* Baram, Batang
57 *S7* **Barama River** ≈ N Guyana

◆ Country
● Country Capital
◇ Dependent Territory
○ Dependent Territory Capital
◈ Administrative Region
✈ International Airport
▲ Mountain
⛰ Mountain Range
Volcano
≈ River
◎ Lake
▣ Reservoir

BĀRĀMATI – BAYAN HOT

161 E14 **Bārāmati** Mahārāshtra, W India 18.12N 74.39E
174 Mm4 **Baram, Batang** *var.* Baram, Barram. ≈ East Malaysia
158 H5 **Bārāmūla** Jammu and Kashmir, NW India 34.15N 74.24E
121 N14 **Baran'** Vitsyebskaya Voblasts', NE Belarus 54.28N 30.18E
158 I14 **Bārān** Rājasthān, N India 25.07N 76.31E
145 U4 **Barānān, Shākh-i** ▲ E Iraq
121 I17 **Baranavichy** *Pol.* Baranowicze, *Rus.* Baranovichi. Brestskaya Voblasts', SW Belarus 53.07N 26.01E
127 Oo5 **Baranikha** Chukotskiy Avtonomnyy Okrug, NE Russian Federation 68.29N 168.13E
118 M4 **Baranivka** Zhytomyrs'ka Oblast', N Ukraine 50.16N 27.40E
41 W14 **Baranof Island** *island* Alexander Archipelago, Alaska, USA
Baranovichi/Baranowicze *see* Baranavichy
113 N15 **Baranów Sandomierski** Podkarpackie, SE Poland 50.28N 21.31E
113 I26 **Baranya** *off.* Baranya Megye. ◈ *county* S Hungary
159 R13 **Barāri** Bihār, NE India 25.31N 87.22E
24 L10 **Barataria Bay** *bay* Louisiana, S USA
Barat Daya, Kepulauan *see* Damar, Kepulauan
120 L12 **Baravukha** *Rus.* Borovukha. Vitsyebskaya Voblasts', N Belarus 55.36N 28.33E
56 E11 **Baraya** Huila, C Colombia 3.10N 75.04W
61 M21 **Barbacena** Minas Gerais, SE Brazil 21.13S 43.46W
56 B13 **Barbacoas** Nariño, SW Colombia 1.37N 78.07W
56 L6 **Barbacoas** Aragua, N Venezuela 9.28N 66.58W
47 Z13 **Barbados** ◆ *commonwealth republic* SE West Indies
49 S3 **Barbados** *island* Barbados
107 U11 **Barbaria, Cap de** *var.* Cabo de Berberia. *headland* Formentera, E Spain 38.39N 1.24E
116 N13 **Barbaros** Tekirdağ, NW Turkey 40.55N 27.28E
76 A11 **Barbas, Cap** *headland* S Western Sahara 22.14N 16.45W
107 T5 **Barbastro** Aragón, NE Spain 42.01N 0.07E
106 K16 **Barbate** ≈ SW Spain
106 K16 **Barbate de Franco** Andalucía, S Spain 36.11N 5.55W
85 K21 **Barberton** Mpumalanga, NE South Africa 25.45S 31.01E
33 U12 **Barberton** Ohio, N USA 41.02N 81.37W
104 K12 **Barbezieux-St-Hilaire** Charente, W France 45.28N 0.09W
56 G9 **Barbosa** Boyaca, C Colombia 5.57N 73.37W
23 N7 **Barbourville** Kentucky, S USA 36.52N 83.53W
47 W9 **Barbuda** *island* N Antigua and Barbuda
189 W8 **Barcaldine** Queensland, E Australia 23.33S 145.20E
Barcarozsnyó *see* Râşnov
106 I11 **Barcarrota** Extremadura, W Spain 38.31N 6.51W
Barcău *see* Berettyó
Barce *see* Al Marj
109 L23 **Barcellona** *var.* Barcellona Pozzo di Gotto. Sicilia, Italy, C Mediterranean Sea 38.09N 15.15E
Barcellona Pozzo di Gotto *see* Barcellona
107 W6 **Barcelona** *anc.* Barcino, Barcinona. Cataluña, E Spain 41.25N 2.10E
57 N5 **Barcelona** Anzoátegui, NE Venezuela 10.07N 64.43W
107 S5 **Barcelona** ◈ *province* Cataluña, NE Spain
107 W6 **Barcelona** ✕ Cataluña, E Spain 41.25N 2.10E
105 U14 **Barcelonnette** Alpes-de-Haute-Provence, SE France 44.24N 6.37E
60 E12 **Barcelos** Amazonas, N Brazil 0.58S 62.58W
106 G5 **Barcelos** Braga, N Portugal 41.31N 8.37W
112 I10 **Barcin** *Ger.* Bartschin. Kujawski-pomorskie, C Poland 52.51N 17.55E
Barcino/Barcinona *see* Barcelona
Barcoo *see* Cooper Creek
113 H26 **Barcs** Somogy, SW Hungary 45.57N 17.26E
143 W11 **Bärdä** *Rus.* Barda. C Azerbaijan 40.25N 47.07E
80 H5 **Bardaï** Borkou-Ennedi-Tibesti, N Chad 21.21N 16.55E
145 R2 **Bardaraşh** N Iraq 36.32N 43.36E
145 Q7 **Bardasah** SW Iraq 34.02N 42.28E
159 S16 **Barddhamān** West Bengal, NE India 23.10N 88.03E
113 N18 **Bardejov** *Ger.* Bartfeld, *Hung.* Bártfa. Prešovský Kraj, E Slovakia 49.17N 21.18E
107 R4 **Bárdenas Reales** *physical region* N Spain
Bardera/Bardere *see* Baardheere
Bardesīr *see* Bardsīr
94 K3 **Bárdharbunga** ▲ C Iceland 64.39N 17.30W
Bardhë, Drini i *see* Beli Drim
108 E9 **Bardi** Emilia-Romagna, C Italy 44.39N 9.44E
108 A8 **Bardonecchia** Piemonte, W Italy 45.04N 6.40E
99 H19 **Bardsey Island** *island* NW Wales, UK
149 S11 **Bardsīr** *var.* Bardesīr, Mashīz. Kermān, C Iran 29.58N 56.29E
22 L6 **Bardstown** Kentucky, S USA 37.48N 85.28W
Barduli *see* Barletta
22 G7 **Bardwell** Kentucky, S USA 36.52N 89.01W
158 K11 **Bareilly** *var.* Bareli. Uttar Pradesh, N India 28.19N 79.24E
Bareli *see* Bareilly
100 H13 **Barendrecht** Zuid-Holland, SW Netherlands 51.52N 4.31E
104 M3 **Barentin** Seine-Maritime, N France 49.33N 0.57E
94 N3 **Barentsburg** Spitsbergen, W Svalbard 78.01N 14.19E
Barentsevo More/Barents Havet *see* Barents Sea
94 O3 **Barentsøya** *island* E Svalbard
207 T11 **Barents Plain** *undersea feature* N Barents Sea
129 P3 **Barents Sea** *Nor.* Barents Havet, *Rus.* Barentsevo More. *sea* Arctic Ocean
207 U14 **Barents Trough** *undersea feature* SW Barents Sea
82 I9 **Barentu** W Eritrea 15.08N 37.35E
104 J3 **Barfleur** Manche, N France 49.41N 1.18W
104 J3 **Barfleur, Pointe de** *headland* N France 49.46N 1.09W
Barfrush/Barfurush *see* Bābol
164 H14 **Barga** Xizang Zizhiqu, W China 30.51N 81.19E
107 N9 **Bargas** Castilla-La Mancha, C Spain 39.56N 4.00W
83 I15 **Bargē** Southern, S Ethiopia 6.11N 37.04E
108 A9 **Barge** Piemonte, NE Italy 44.49N 7.21E
159 U16 **Barguna** Khulna, S Bangladesh 22.09N 90.07E
Bärgușad *see* Vorotan
126 K15 **Barguzin** Respublika Buryatiya, S Russian Federation 53.37N 109.47E
159 O13 **Barhaj** Uttar Pradesh, N India 26.16N 83.43E
191 N10 **Barham** New South Wales, SE Australia 35.39S 144.09E
158 J12 **Barhan** Uttar Pradesh, N India 27.21N 78.10E
21 S7 **Bar Harbor** Mount Desert Island, Maine, NE USA 44.23N 68.14W
159 R14 **Barharwa** Jhārkhand, NE India 24.52N 87.46E
159 P15 **Barhi** Jhārkhand, N India 24.19N 85.25E
109 O17 **Bari** *var.* Bari delle Puglie; *anc.* Barium. Puglia, SE Italy 41.06N 16.52E
82 P12 **Bari** *off.* Gobolka Bari. ◈ *region* NE Somalia
178 K14 **Ba Ria** Ba Ria-Vung Tau, S Vietnam 10.30N 107.10E
Bāridah *see* Al Bāridah
Bari delle Puglie *see* Bari
Barikot *see* Barīkowţ
155 T4 **Barīkowţ** *var.* Barikot. Kunar, NE Afghanistan 35.18N 71.36E
44 C4 **Barillas** *var.* Santa Cruz Barillas. Huehuetenango, NW Guatemala 15.49N 91.19W
56 J6 **Barinas** Barinas, W Venezuela 8.36N 70.15W
56 I7 **Barinas** *off.* Estado Barinas; *prev.* Zamora. ◈ *state* C Venezuela
56 I6 **Barinitas** Barinas, NW Venezuela 8.47N 70.26W
160 P11 **Bāripada** Orissa, E India 21.58N 86.45E
62 K9 **Bariri** São Paulo, S Brazil 22.04S 48.46W
77 W11 **Bârîs** S Egypt 24.28N 30.39E
158 G14 **Bari Sādri** Rājasthān, N India 24.25N 74.28E
159 U16 **Barisal** Khulna, S Bangladesh 22.40N 90.19E
173 G7 **Barisan, Pegunungan** ▲▲ Sumatera, W Indonesia
175 N10 **Barito, Sungai** ≈ Borneo, C Indonesia
Barium *see* Bari
Bårjås *see* Porjus
Barka *see* Baraka
Barka *see* Al Marj
166 H8 **Barkam** Sichuan, C China 31.56N 102.22E
120 J9 **Barkava** Madona, C Latvia 56.43N 26.34E
8 M15 **Barkerville** British Columbia, SW Canada 53.06N 121.34W
12 J12 **Bark Lake** ◎ Ontario, SE Canada
22 H7 **Barkley, Lake** ▣ Kentucky/Tennessee, S USA
8 K17 **Barkley Sound** *inlet* British Columbia, W Canada
85 J24 **Barkly East** *Afr.* Barkly-Oos. Eastern Cape, SE South Africa 30.58S 27.34E
Barkly-Oos *see* Barkly East
189 S4 **Barkly Tableland** *plateau* Northern Territory/Queensland, N Australia
Barkly-Wes *see* Barkly West
85 H22 **Barkly West** *Afr.* Barkly-Wes. Northern Cape, N South Africa 28.31S 24.31E
165 O5 **Barkol** *var.* Barkol Kazak Zizhixian. Xinjiang Uygur Zizhiqu, NW China 43.37N 93.01E
165 O5 **Barkol Hu** ◎ NW China
Barkol Kazak Zizhixian *see* Barkol
32 J3 **Bark Point** *headland* Wisconsin, N USA 46.53N 91.11W
27 P11 **Barksdale** Texas, SW USA 29.43N 100.03W
Bar Kunar *see* Asmār
118 L11 **Bârlad** *prev.* Bîrlad. Vaslui, E Romania 46.12N 27.39E
118 M11 **Bârlad** *prev.* Bîrlad. ≈ E Romania
78 D9 **Barlavento, Ilhas de** *var.* Windward Islands. *island group* N Cape Verde
105 R5 **Bar-le-Duc** *var.* Bar-sur-Ornain. Meuse, NE France 48.46N 5.10E
188 K11 **Barlee, Lake** ◎ Western Australia
188 H8 **Barlee Range** ▲▲ Western Australia
109 N16 **Barletta** *anc.* Barduli. Puglia, SE Italy 41.19N 16.16E
112 E10 **Barlinek** *Ger.* Berlinchen. Zachodnio-pomorskie, NW Poland 53.00N 15.11E
29 S11 **Barling** Arkansas, C USA 35.19N 94.18W
176 Vv10 **Barma** Papua, E Indonesia 1.55S 132.57E
191 Q9 **Barmedman** New South Wales, SE Australia 34.09S 147.21E
Barmen-Elberfeld *see* Wuppertal
158 D12 **Bārmer** Rājasthān, NW India 25.46N 71.24E
190 K9 **Barmera** South Australia 34.15S 140.26E
99 I19 **Barmouth** NW Wales, UK 52.44N 4.03W
160 F10 **Barnagar** Madhya Pradesh, C India 23.01N 75.28E
158 H9 **Barnāla** Punjab, NW India 30.19N 75.33E
99 L15 **Barnard Castle** N England, UK 54.34N 1.55W
191 O6 **Barnato** New South Wales, SE Australia 31.39S 145.01E
126 H14 **Barnaul** Altayskiy Kray, C Russian Federation 53.21N 83.45E
111 V8 **Bärnbach** Steiermark, SE Austria 47.05N 15.07E
20 K16 **Barnegat** New Jersey, NE USA 39.43N 74.12W
25 S4 **Barnesville** Georgia, SE USA 33.03N 84.09W
31 R6 **Barnesville** Minnesota, N USA 46.39N 96.25W
33 U13 **Barnesville** Ohio, N USA 39.59N 81.10W
100 K11 **Barneveld** *var.* Barnveld. Gelderland, C Netherlands 52.10N 5.34E
27 O9 **Barnhart** Texas, SW USA 31.07N 101.09W
29 P8 **Barnsdall** Oklahoma, C USA 36.33N 96.09W
99 M17 **Barnsley** N England, UK 53.34N 1.28W
21 Q12 **Barnstable** Massachusetts, NE USA 41.42N 70.16W
99 I23 **Barnstaple** SW England, UK 51.04N 4.04W
Barnveld *see* Barneveld
23 Q14 **Barnwell** South Carolina, SE USA 33.14N 81.21W
69 U8 **Baro** *var.* Baro Wenz. ≈ Ethiopia/Sudan
79 U15 **Baro** Niger, C Nigeria 8.35N 6.28E
Baro *see* Baro Wenz
Baroda *see* Vadodara
155 U2 **Baroghil Pass** *var.* Kowtal-e Barowghīl. *pass* Afghanistan/Pakistan 36.54N 73.22E
121 Q17 **Baron'ki** *Rus.* Boron'ki. Mahilyowskaya Voblasts', E Belarus 53.07N 32.09E
190 J9 **Barossa Valley** *valley* South Australia
Barouì *see* Salisbury
83 H14 **Baro Wenz** *var.* Baro, Nahr Barū. ≈ Ethiopia/Sudan
159 U12 **Barpeta** Assam, NE India 26.19N 91.05E
33 S7 **Barques, Pointe Aux** *headland* Michigan, N USA 44.04N 82.57W
56 I5 **Barquisimeto** Lara, NW Venezuela 10.03N 69.18W
61 N16 **Barra** Bahia, E Brazil 11.06S 43.15W
98 E9 **Barra** *island* NW Scotland, UK
191 T5 **Barraba** New South Wales, SE Australia 30.24S 150.37E
62 L9 **Barra Bonita** São Paulo, S Brazil 22.30S 48.34W
66 J12 **Barracuda Fracture Zone** *var.* Fifteen Twenty Fracture Zone. *tectonic feature* SW Atlantic Ocean
66 G11 **Barracuda Ridge** *undersea feature* N Atlantic Ocean
45 N12 **Barra del Colorado** Limón, NE Costa Rica 10.44N 83.35W
45 N9 **Barra de Río Grande** Región Autónoma Atlántico Sur, E Nicaragua 12.56N 83.30W
84 A11 **Barra do Cuanza** Luanda, NW Angola 9.12S 13.08E
62 O9 **Barra do Piraí** Rio de Janeiro, SE Brazil 22.30S 43.47W
63 D16 **Barra do Quaraí** Rio Grande do Sul, SE Brazil 31.03S 58.10W
61 G14 **Barra do São Manuel** Pará, N Brazil 7.12S 58.03W
85 N19 **Barra Falsa, Ponta da** *headland* S Mozambique 22.57S 35.36E
98 E10 **Barra Head** *headland* NW Scotland, UK 56.46N 7.37W
62 O9 **Barra Mansa** Rio de Janeiro, SE Brazil 22.25S 44.03W
59 D14 **Barranca** Lima, W Peru 10.46S 77.46W
56 F8 **Barrancabermeja** Santander, N Colombia 7.00N 73.51W
56 H4 **Barrancas** La Guajira, N Colombia 10.58N 72.46W
56 J6 **Barrancas** Barinas, NW Venezuela 8.46N 70.07W
57 Q6 **Barrancas** Monagas, NE Venezuela 8.45N 62.12W
56 F6 **Barranco de Loba** Bolívar, N Colombia 8.55N 74.07W
106 I12 **Barrancos** Beja, S Portugal 38.07N 6.58W
64 N7 **Barranqueras** Chaco, N Argentina 27.31S 58.53W
56 E4 **Barranquilla** Atlántico, N Colombia 10.58N 74.48W
85 N20 **Barra, Ponta da** *headland* S Mozambique 23.46S 35.33E
107 P11 **Barrax** Castilla-La Mancha, C Spain 39.04N 2.12W
21 N11 **Barre** Massachusetts, NE USA 42.24N 72.06W
20 M7 **Barre** Vermont, NE USA 44.09N 72.25W
61 M17 **Barreiras** Bahia, E Brazil 12.09S 44.58W
106 F11 **Barreiro** Setúbal, W Portugal 38.40N 9.04W
67 C26 **Barren Island** *island* S Falkland Islands
22 K7 **Barren River Lake** ▣ Kentucky, S USA
62 L7 **Barretos** São Paulo, S Brazil 20.33S 48.33W
9 P14 **Barrhead** Alberta, SW Canada 54.10N 114.28W
12 G14 **Barrie** Ontario, S Canada 44.24N 79.39W
9 N16 **Barrière** British Columbia, SW Canada 51.10N 120.06W
12 H8 **Barrière, Lac** ◎ Québec, SE Canada
190 L6 **Barrier Range** *hill range* New South Wales, SE Australia
44 G3 **Barrier Reef** *reef* E Belize
196 C16 **Barrigada** C Guam 13.27N 144.48E
Barrington Island *see* Santa Fe, Isla
191 T7 **Barrington Tops** ▲ New South Wales, SE Australia 32.06S 151.18E
191 O4 **Barringun** New South Wales, SE Australia 29.02S 145.45E
61 K18 **Barro Alto** Goiás, S Brazil 15.07S 48.56W
61 N14 **Barro Duro** Piauí, NE Brazil 5.49S 42.30W
32 I5 **Barron** Wisconsin, N USA 45.24N 91.49W
12 J12 **Barron** ≈ Ontario, SE Canada
63 H15 **Barros Cassal** Rio Grande do Sul, S Brazil 29.12S 52.33W
47 P14 **Barrouallie** Saint Vincent, W Saint Vincent and the Grenadines 13.13N 61.16W
41 O4 **Barrow** Alaska, USA 71.17N 156.47W
99 E20 **Barrow** *Ir.* An Bhearú. ≈ SE Ireland
189 Q6 **Barrow Creek Roadhouse** Northern Territory, N Australia 21.30S 133.52E
99 J16 **Barrow-in-Furness** NW England, UK 54.07N 3.13W
188 G7 **Barrow Island** *island* Western Australia
41 O4 **Barrow, Point** *headland* Alaska, USA 71.23N 156.28W
9 V14 **Barrows** Manitoba, S Canada 52.49N 101.36W
99 J22 **Barry** S Wales, UK 51.24N 3.18W
12 J12 **Barry's Bay** Ontario, SE Canada 45.28N 77.40W
150 K14 **Barsakel'mes, Ostrov** *island* SW Kazakhstan
Barsč Łužyca *see* Forst
153 S14 **Barsem** S Tajikistan 37.36N 71.43E
151 V11 **Barshatas** Vostochnyy Kazakhstan, E Kazakhstan 48.04N 78.38E
161 F14 **Bārsi** Mahārāshtra, W India 18.13N 75.42E
102 I13 **Barsinghausen** Niedersachsen, C Germany 53.19N 9.30E
153 X8 **Barskoon** Issyk-Kul'skaya Oblast', E Kyrgyzstan 42.07N 77.34E
102 F10 **Barssel** Niedersachsen, NW Germany 53.10N 7.46E
37 U14 **Barstow** California, W USA 34.52N 117.00W
26 L8 **Barstow** Texas, SW USA 31.27N 103.23W
105 R6 **Bar-sur-Aube** Aube, NE France 48.13N 4.43E
Bar-sur-Ornain *see* Bar-le-Duc
105 Q6 **Bar-sur-Seine** Aube, N France 48.06N 4.22E
153 S13 **Bartang** S Tajikistan 38.06N 71.48E
153 T13 **Bartang** ≈ SE Tajikistan
Bartenstein *see* Bartoszyce
Bártfa/Bartfeld *see* Bardejov
102 N7 **Barth** Mecklenburg-Vorpommern, NE Germany 54.21N 12.43E
29 W13 **Bartholomew, Bayou** ≈ Arkansas/Louisiana, S USA
57 T8 **Bartica** N Guyana 6.24N 58.36W
142 H10 **Bartın** Bartin, NW Turkey 41.37N 32.19E
142 H10 **Bartın** ◈ *province* NW Turkey
189 W4 **Bartle Frere** ▲ Queensland, E Australia 17.15S 145.43E
29 P8 **Bartlesville** Oklahoma, C USA 36.45N 95.58W
31 P14 **Bartlett** Nebraska, C USA 41.51N 98.32W
22 E10 **Bartlett** Tennessee, S USA 35.12N 89.52W
27 T9 **Bartlett** Texas, SW USA 30.47N 97.25W
38 L13 **Bartlett Reservoir** ▣ Arizona, SW USA
21 N6 **Barton** Vermont, NE USA 44.44N 72.09W
112 L7 **Bartoszyce** *Ger.* Bartenstein. Warmińsko-Mazurskie, NE Poland, 54.16N 20.49E
25 W12 **Bartow** Florida, SE USA 27.54N 81.50W
Bartschin *see* Barcin
176 V10 **Baru** Papua, E Indonesia 1.44S 132.16E
173 G6 **Barumun, Sungai** ≈ Sumatera, W Indonesia
Barū, Nahr *see* Baro Wenz
174 M16 **Barung, Nusa** *island* S Indonesia
173 Ff6 **Barus** Sumatera, NW Indonesia 2.08N 98.15E
168 L10 **Baruunsuu** Ömnögovĭ, S Mongolia 43.46N 105.28E
169 P8 **Baruun-Urt** Sühbaatar, E Mongolia 46.39N 113.17E
45 P15 **Barú, Volcán** *var.* Volcán de Chiriquí. ⊛ W Panama 8.49N 82.32W
101 K21 **Barvaux** Luxembourg, SE Belgium 50.21N 5.30E
44 M13 **Barva, Volcán** ⊛ NW Costa Rica 10.07N 84.08W
119 W6 **Barvinkove** Kharkivs'ka Oblast', E Ukraine 48.54N 37.03E
160 G11 **Barwāh** Madhya Pradesh, C India 22.17N 76.01E
Bärwalde Neumark *see* Mieszkowice
160 F11 **Barwāni** Madhya Pradesh, C India 22.01N 74.55E
191 P5 **Barwon River** ≈ New South Wales, SE Australia
121 L15 **Barysaw** *Rus.* Borisov. Minskaya Voblasts', NE Belarus 54.14N 28.30E
131 Q6 **Barysh** Ul'yanovskaya Oblast', W Russian Federation 53.32N 47.06E
119 Q4 **Baryshivka** Kyyivs'ka Oblast', N Ukraine 50.21N 31.21E
81 J17 **Basankusu** Equateur, NW Dem. Rep. Congo 1.12N 19.49E
119 N11 **Basarabeasca** *Rus.* Bessarabka. SE Moldova 46.22N 28.56E
118 M14 **Basarabi** Constanţa, SW Romania 44.07N 28.27E
42 H6 **Basaseachic** Chihuahua, NW Mexico 28.18N 108.13W
107 O2 **Basauri** País Vasco, N Spain 43.13N 2.54W
63 D18 **Basavilbaso** Entre Ríos, E Argentina 32.23S 58.48W
81 F21 **Bas-Congo** *off.* Région du Bas-Congo; *prev.* Bas-Zaïre. ◈ *region* SW Dem. Rep. Congo
110 E6 **Basel** *Eng.* Basle, *Fr.* Bâle. Basel-Stadt, NW Switzerland 47.33N 7.36E
110 E7 **Basel** *Eng.* Basle, *Fr.* Bâle. ◈ *canton* NW Switzerland
149 T14 **Bashākerd, Kūhhā-ye** ▲▲ SE Iran
9 Q15 **Bashaw** Alberta, SW Canada 52.40N 112.53W
152 K16 **Bashbedeng** Mary Welaýaty, S Turkmenistan 35.44N 63.07E
167 T15 **Bashi Channel** *Chin.* Pa-shih Hai-hsia. *channel* Philippines/Taiwan
Bashkiria *see* Bashkortostan, Respublika
125 Dd12 **Bashkortostan, Respublika** *prev.* Bashkiria. ◈ *autonomous republic* W Russian Federation
131 N6 **Bashmakovo** Penzenskaya Oblast', W Russian Federation 53.13N 43.00E
152 J10 **Bashsakarba** Lebap Welaýaty, NE Turkmenistan 40.25N 62.16E
119 R9 **Bashtanka** Mykolayivs'ka Oblast', S Ukraine 47.24N 32.27E
195 O17 **Basilaki Island** *island* SE PNG
24 H8 **Basile** Louisiana, S USA 30.29N 92.36W
109 M18 **Basilicata** ◈ *region* S Italy
35 V13 **Basin** Wyoming, C USA 44.22N 108.02W
99 N22 **Basingstoke** S England, UK 51.16N 1.08W
149 U8 **Başīrān** Khorāsān, E Iran 31.57N 59.10E
114 B10 **Baška** *It.* Bescanuova. Primorje-Gorski Kotar, NW Croatia 44.58N 14.46E
143 T15 **Başkale** Van, SE Turkey 38.03N 44.01E
12 L10 **Baskatong, Réservoir** ▣ Québec, SE Canada
143 O14 **Baskil** Elazığ, E Turkey 38.35N 38.52E
Basle *see* Basel
160 H9 **Bāsoda** Madhya Pradesh, C India 23.54N 77.58E
81 L17 **Basoko** Orientale, N Dem. Rep. Congo 1.13N 23.25E
Basque Country, The *see* País Vasco
Basra *see* Al Başrah
105 U5 **Bas-Rhin** ◈ *department* NE France
Bassam *see* Grand-Bassam
9 Q16 **Bassano** Alberta, SW Canada 50.48N 112.28W
108 H7 **Bassano del Grappa** Veneto, NE Italy 45.45N 11.45E
79 Q15 **Bassar** *var.* Bassari. NW Togo 9.15N 0.46E
Bassari *see* Bassar
180 L9 **Bassas da India** *island group* W Madagascar
110 D7 **Bassecourt** Jura, W Switzerland 47.20N 7.16E
177 Ff8 **Bassein** *var.* Pathein. Irrawaddy, SW Myanmar 16.46N 94.45E
81 J15 **Basse-Kotto** ◈ *prefecture* S Central African Republic
107 V5 **Bassella** Cataluña, NE Spain 42.01N 1.16E
104 J5 **Basse-Normandie** *Eng.* Lower Normandy. ◈ *region* N France
47 Q11 **Basse-Pointe** N Martinique 14.52N 61.07W
78 H12 **Basse Santa Su** E Gambia 13.18N 14.10W
Basse-Saxe *see* Niedersachsen
47 X6 **Basse-Terre** ○ (Guadeloupe) Basse Terre, SW Guadeloupe 16.07N 61.40W
47 X6 **Basse Terre** *island* W Guadeloupe
47 V10 **Basseterre** ● (Saint Kitts and Nevis) Saint Kitts, Saint Kitts and Nevis 17.15N 62.45W
31 O13 **Bassett** Nebraska, C USA 42.34N 99.32W
23 S7 **Bassett** Virginia, NE USA 36.45N 79.59W
39 N15 **Bassett Peak** ▲ Arizona, SW USA 32.30N 110.16W
78 M10 **Bassikounou** Hodh ech Chargui, SE Mauritania 15.55N 5.58W
79 R15 **Bassila** W Benin 9.01N 1.46E
Bass, Îlots de *see* Marotiri
33 O11 **Bass Lake** Indiana, N USA 41.12N 86.35W
191 O14 **Bass Strait** *strait* SE Australia
102 H12 **Bassum** Niedersachsen, NW Germany 52.51N 8.43E
31 X3 **Basswood Lake** ◎ Canada/USA
97 J21 **Båstad** Skåne, S Sweden 56.25N 12.49E
145 U2 **Basţah** E Iraq 36.20N 45.14E
159 N12 **Basti** Uttar Pradesh, N India 26.48N 82.43E
105 X14 **Bastia** Corse, France, C Mediterranean Sea 42.42N 9.27E
101 L23 **Bastogne** Luxembourg, SE Belgium 50.00N 5.43E
24 I5 **Bastrop** Louisiana, S USA 32.46N 91.54W
27 T11 **Bastrop** Texas, SW USA 30.06N 97.19W
95 J15 **Bastuträsk** Västerbotten, N Sweden 64.46N 20.05E
121 J19 **Bastyn'** *Rus.* Bostyn'. Brestskaya Voblasts', SW Belarus 52.23N 26.46E
Basuo *see* Dongfang
Basutoland *see* Lesotho
121 O15 **Basya** ≈ E Belarus
119 V8 **Basyl'kivka** Dnipropetrovs'ka Oblast', E Ukraine 48.12N 36.00E
81 D17 **Bata** NW Equatorial Guinea 1.50N 9.47E
81 D17 **Bata** ✕ S Equatorial Guinea 1.55N 9.48E
Batae Coritanorum *see* Leicester
126 M8 **Batagay** Respublika Sakha (Yakutiya), NE Russian Federation 67.36N 134.44E
126 Ll8 **Batagay-Alyta** Respublika Sakha (Yakutiya), NE Russian Federation 67.48N 130.15E
114 L10 **Batajnica** Serbia, N Serbia and Montenegro (Yugoslavia) 44.55N 20.17E
142 H15 **Bataklık Gölü** ◎ S Turkey
116 H11 **Batak, Yazovir** ▣ SW Bulgaria
158 H7 **Batāla** Punjab, N India 31.50N 75.10E
106 F9 **Batalha** Leiria, C Portugal 39.40N 8.49W
81 N17 **Batama** Orientale, NE Dem. Rep. Congo 0.54N 26.25E
126 Ll10 **Batamay** Respublika Sakha (Yakutiya), NE Russian Federation 63.28N 129.33E
174 I7 **Batam, Pulau** *island* Kepulauan Riau, W Indonesia
166 F9 **Batang** *var.* Bazhong. Sichuan, C China 30.04N 99.10E
174 Kk14 **Batang** Jawa, C Indonesia 6.55S 109.42E
81 I14 **Batangafo** Ouham, NW Central African Republic 7.19N 18.22E
179 P11 **Batangas** *off.* Batangas City. Luzon, N Philippines 13.47N 121.02E
Bătania *see* Battonya
179 Pp6 **Batan Islands** *island group* N Philippines
62 L8 **Batatais** São Paulo, S Brazil 20.54S 47.37W
20 E10 **Batavia** New York, NE USA 43.00N 78.11W
Batavia *see* Jakarta
181 T9 **Batavia Seamount** *undersea feature* E Indian Ocean 27.42S 100.36E
130 L12 **Bataysk** Rostovskaya Oblast', SW Russian Federation 47.10N 39.46E
12 B9 **Batchawana** ≈ Ontario, S Canada
12 B9 **Batchawana Bay** Ontario, S Canada 46.55N 84.36W
178 Ii12 **Bătdâmbâng** *prev.* Battambang. Bătdâmbâng, NW Cambodia 13.06N 103.13E
81 G20 **Batéké, Plateaux** *plateau* S Congo
191 S11 **Batemans Bay** New South Wales, SE Australia 35.45S 150.09E
23 Q13 **Batesburg** South Carolina, SE USA 33.54N 81.33W
30 K12 **Batesland** South Dakota, N USA 43.05N 102.07W
29 V10 **Batesville** Arkansas, C USA 35.47N 91.37W
33 Q14 **Batesville** Indiana, N USA 39.18N 85.13W
24 L2 **Batesville** Mississippi, S USA 34.18N 89.56W
27 Q13 **Batesville** Texas, SW USA 28.56N 99.38W
46 L13 **Bath** E Jamaica 17.56N 76.20W
99 L22 **Bath** *hist.* Akermanceaster, *anc.* Aquae Calidae, Aquae Solis. SW England, UK 51.22N 2.22W
21 Q8 **Bath** Maine, NE USA 43.54N 69.49W
20 F11 **Bath** New York, NE USA 42.20N 77.16W
Bath *see* Berkeley Springs
80 I10 **Batha** *off.* Préfecture du Batha. ◈ *prefecture* C Chad
80 I10 **Batha** *seasonal river* C Chad
147 Y8 **Baţhā', Wādī al** *dry watercourse* NE Oman
158 H9 **Bathinda** Punjab, NW India 30.13N 74.54E
100 M11 **Bathmen** Overijssel, E Netherlands 52.15N 6.16E
47 Z14 **Bathsheba** E Barbados 13.12N 59.31W
191 R8 **Bathurst** New South Wales, SE Australia 33.32S 149.34E
11 O13 **Bathurst** New Brunswick, SE Canada 47.37N 65.40W
Bathurst *see* Banjul
15 Gg2 **Bathurst, Cape** *headland* Northwest Territories, NW Canada 70.33N 128.00W
206 L8 **Bathurst Inlet** Nunavut, N Canada 66.23N 107.00W
15 J4 **Bathurst Inlet** *inlet* Nunavut, N Canada
189 N1 **Bathurst Island** *island* Northern Territory, N Australia
207 O9 **Bathurst Island** *island* Parry Islands, Nunavut, N Canada
79 O14 **Batié** SW Burkina 9.53N 2.57W
197 J14 **Batiki** *prev.* Mbatiki. *island* C Fiji
Batinah *see* Al Bāţinah
147 Y9 **Bāţin, Wādī al** *dry watercourse* SW Asia
13 P9 **Batiscan** ≈ Québec, SE Canada
142 F16 **Batı Toroslar** ▲▲ SW Turkey
Batjan *see* Bacan, Pulau
153 R11 **Batken** Batkenskaya Oblast', SW Kyrgyzstan 40.03N 70.50E
Batken Oblasty *see* Batkenskaya Oblast'
153 Q11 **Batkenskaya Oblast'** *Kir.* Batken Oblasty. ◈ *province* SW Kyrgyzstan
Batlle y Ordóñez *see* José Batlle y Ordóñez
191 Q10 **Batlow** New South Wales, SE Australia 35.32S 148.09E
143 Q15 **Batman** *var.* Iluh. Batman, SE Turkey 37.52N 41.06E
143 Q15 **Batman** ◈ *province* SE Turkey
76 L6 **Batna** NE Algeria 35.34N 6.10E
Batoe *see* Batu, Kepulauan
168 K7 **Bat-Öldziyt** Töv, C Mongolia 48.10N 104.49E
24 J8 **Baton Rouge** *state capital* Louisiana, S USA 30.28N 91.09W
81 G15 **Batouri** Est, E Cameroon 4.26N 14.24E
144 G14 **Batrā', Jibāl al** ▲ S Jordan
144 G6 **Batroûn** *var.* Al Batrūn. N Lebanon 34.15N 35.42E
Batsch *see* Bač
Batsevichi *see* Batsevichy
121 M17 **Batsevichy** *Rus.* Batsevichi. Mahilyowskaya Voblasts', E Belarus 53.24N 29.13E
94 M7 **Båtsfjord** Finnmark, N Norway 70.37N 29.42E
Battambang *see* Bătdâmbâng
205 X3 **Batterbee, Cape** *headland* Antarctica
161 L24 **Batticaloa** Eastern Province, E Sri Lanka 7.43N 81.43E
101 L19 **Battice** Liège, E Belgium 50.39N 5.50E
109 L18 **Battipaglia** Campania, S Italy 40.36N 14.58E
9 R15 **Battle** ≈ Alberta/Saskatchewan, SW Canada
Battle Born State *see* Nevada
33 Q10 **Battle Creek** Michigan, N USA 42.19N 85.10W
29 T7 **Battlefield** Missouri, C USA 37.07N 93.22W
9 S15 **Battleford** Saskatchewan, S Canada 52.45N 108.19W
31 S6 **Battle Lake** Minnesota, N USA 46.16N 95.42W
37 U3 **Battle Mountain** Nevada, W USA 40.37N 116.55W
113 M25 **Battonya** *Rom.* Bătania. Békés, SE Hungary 46.16N 21.00E
175 Qq14 **Batuata, Pulau** *island* C Indonesia
175 Q8 **Batudaka, Pulau** *island* N Indonesia
173 F8 **Batu, Kepulauan** *prev.* Batoe. *island group* W Indonesia
143 Q10 **Bat'umi** W Georgia 41.39N 41.37E
174 H6 **Batu Pahat** *prev.* Bandar Penggaram. Johor, Peninsular Malaysia 1.51N 102.55E
175 Q10 **Baturebe** Sulawesi, N Indonesia 1.43S 121.43E
126 H13 **Baturino** Tomskaya Oblast', C Russian Federation 57.46N 85.08E
119 R3 **Baturyn** Chernihivs'ka Oblast', N Ukraine 51.20N 32.54E
144 F10 **Bat Yam** Tel Aviv, C Israel 32.01N 34.45E
131 Q4 **Batyrevo** Chuvashskaya Respublika, W Russian Federation 55.04N 47.34E
Batys Qazaqstan Oblysy *see* Zapadnyy Kazakhstan
104 F5 **Batz, Île de** *island* NW France
174 L7 **Bau** Sarawak, East Malaysia 1.25N 110.10E
179 P9 **Bauang** Luzon, N Philippines 16.33N 120.19E
175 Qq13 **Baubau** *var.* Baoebaoe. Pulau Buton, C Indonesia 5.30S 122.37E
79 W14 **Bauchi** Bauchi, NE Nigeria 10.18N 9.46E
79 W14 **Bauchi** ◈ *state* C Nigeria
104 H7 **Baud** Morbihan, NW France 47.52N 2.59W
31 T2 **Baudette** Minnesota, N USA 48.42N 94.36W
200 Nn10 **Bauer Basin** *undersea feature* E Pacific Ocean
197 C14 **Bauer Field** *var.* Port Vila. ✕ (Port-Vila) Éfaté, C Vanuatu 17.42S 168.21E
11 T9 **Bauld, Cape** *headland* Newfoundland and Labrador, E Canada 51.35N 55.22W
105 T8 **Baume-les-Dames** Doubs, E France 47.22N 6.20E
195 X15 **Baunani** Malaita, N Solomon Islands 9.06S 160.52E
103 I15 **Baunatal** Hessen, C Germany 51.15N 9.25E
109 D18 **Baunei** Sardegna, Italy, C Mediterranean Sea 40.04N 9.36E
59 M15 **Baures, Río** ≈ N Bolivia
62 K9 **Bauru** São Paulo, S Brazil 22.19S 49.07W
Baushar *see* Bawshar
120 G10 **Bauska** *Ger.* Bauske. Bauska, S Latvia 56.24N 24.11E
Bauske *see* Bauska
103 Q15 **Bautzen** *Lus.* Budyšin. Sachsen, E Germany 51.10N 14.28E
151 Q16 **Bauyrzhan Momyshuly** *Kaz.* Baūyrzhan Momyshuly; *prev.* Burnoye. Zhambyl, S Kazakhstan 42.36N 70.46E
Bauzanum *see* Bolzano
Bavaria *see* Bayern
111 N7 **Bavarian Alps** *Ger.* Bayrische Alpen. ▲▲ Austria/Germany
Bavière *see* Bayern
42 H4 **Bavispe, Río** ≈ NW Mexico
131 T5 **Bavly** Respublika Tatarstan, W Russian Federation 54.20N 53.21E
174 Kk10 **Bawal, Pulau** *island* N Indonesia
174 Mm10 **Bawan** Borneo, C Indonesia 1.36S 113.55E
191 O12 **Baw Baw, Mount** ▲ Victoria, SE Australia 37.49S 146.16E
176 W11 **Bawe** Papua, E Indonesia 2.56S 134.39E
174 M13 **Bawean, Pulau** *island* S Indonesia
174 L15 **Bawen** Jawa, S Indonesia 7.13S 110.25E
77 V9 **Bawīţī** N Egypt 28.18N 28.52E
79 Q13 **Bawku** N Ghana 11.00N 0.12W
178 Gg7 **Bawlakè** Kayah State, C Myanmar 19.10N 97.19E
173 Ff8 **Bawo Ofuloa** Pulau Tanahmasa, W Indonesia 0.10S 98.24E
147 Y8 **Bawshar** *var.* Baushar. NE Oman 23.26N 58.19E
Ba Xian *see* Bazhou
164 M8 **Baxkorgan** Xinjiang Uygur Zizhiqu, W China 39.05N 90.00E
25 V6 **Baxley** Georgia, SE USA 31.46N 82.21W
165 R15 **Baxoi** *var.* Baima. Xizang Zizhiqu, W China 30.01N 96.53E
31 W14 **Baxter** Iowa, C USA 41.49N 93.09W
31 U6 **Baxter** Minnesota, N USA 46.21N 94.18W
29 R8 **Baxter Springs** Kansas, C USA 37.01N 94.45W
83 M17 **Bay** *off.* Gobolka Bay. ◈ *region* SW Somalia
Bay *see* Baicheng
46 H7 **Bayamo** Granma, E Cuba 20.21N 76.38W
47 U5 **Bayamón** E Puerto Rico 18.24N 66.09W
169 W8 **Bayan** Heilongjiang, NE China 46.04N 127.24E
175 Nn16 **Bayan** *prev.* Bajan. Pulau Lombok, C Indonesia 8.16S 116.28E
168 I6 **Bayan** Arhangay, C Mongolia 49.36N 99.36E
169 P7 **Bayan** Dornod, E Mongolia 47.56N 112.58E
169 N9 **Bayan** Dornogovĭ, SE Mongolia 46.15N 110.16E
168 F7 **Bayan** Govĭ-Altay, W Mongolia 47.05N 95.13E
169 O8 **Bayan** Hentiy, C Mongolia 47.13N 110.57E
158 I12 **Bayāna** Rājasthān, N India 26.55N 77.18E
155 N5 **Bāyan, Band-e** ▲▲ C Afghanistan
168 H8 **Bayanbulag** Bayanhongor, C Mongolia 46.46N 98.07E
169 N7 **Bayanbulag** Hentiy, C Mongolia 47.54N 109.51E
164 J5 **Bayanbulak** Xinjiang Uygur Zizhiqu, W China 43.04N 84.04E
126 Jj15 **Bayanday** Ust'-Ordynskiy Buryatskiy Avtonomnyy Okrug, S Russian Federation 53.01N 105.24E
Bayan Gol *see* Dengkou
168 F8 **Bayangol** Govĭ-Altay, SW Mongolia 45.33N 94.22E
165 R12 **Bayan Har Shan** *var.* Bayan Khar. ▲▲ C China
168 I8 **Bayanhongor** Bayanhongor, C Mongolia 46.07N 100.42E
168 H9 **Bayanhongor** ◈ *province* C Mongolia
166 K14 **Bayan Hot** *var.* Alxa Zuoqi. Nei Mongol Zizhiqu, N China 38.49N 105.40E

◆ Country ● Country Capital ◇ Dependent Territory ○ Dependent Territory Capital ◈ Administrative Region ✕ International Airport ▲ Mountain ▲▲ Mountain Range ⊛ Volcano ≈ River ◎ Lake ▣ Reservoir

Bayan Huxu – Belostok

169 T9 Bayan Huxu var. Horqin Zuoyi Zhongji. Nei Mongol Zizhiqu, N China 45.02N 121.33E
Bayan Khar see Bayan Har Shan
173 G3 Bayan Lepas ✈ (George Town) Pinang, Peninsular Malaysia 5.18N 100.15E
168 K13 Bayan Mod Nei Mongol Zizhiqu, N China 40.45N 104.29E
Bayan Nuru see Xar Burd
169 N12 Bayan Obo Nei Mongol Zizhiqu, N China 41.45N 109.58E
45 V15 Bayano, Lago ⊚ E Panama
168 C5 Bayan-Ölgiy ◐ province NW Mongolia
168 F9 Bayan-Ovoo Govĭ-Altay, SW Mongolia 44.39N 94.45E
168 H9 Bayansayr Bayanhongor, C Mongolia 45.36N 99.27E
165 Q9 Bayan Shan ▲ C China 37.36N 96.23E
168 J9 Bayanteeg Övörhangay, C Mongolia 45.39N 101.30E
168 L8 Bayantöhöm Töv, C Mongolia 46.57N 105.09E
Bayan Tumen see Choybalsan
168 H6 Bayan-Uhaa Dzavhan, C Mongolia 48.41N 98.46E
168 J8 Bayan-Ulaan Övörhangay, C Mongolia 46.38N 102.30E
169 R10 Bayan Ul var. Xi Ujimqin Qi. Nei Mongol Zizhiqu, N China 44.31N 117.36E
30 J14 Bayard Nebraska, C USA 41.45N 103.19W
39 P15 Bayard New Mexico, SW USA 32.45N 108.07W
105 T13 Bayard, Col pass SE France 44.37N 6.04E
169 O8 Bayasgalant Sühbaatar, E Mongolia 46.55N 112.11E
142 J12 Bayat Çorum, N Turkey 40.34N 34.07E
179 Q14 Bayawan Negros, C Philippines 9.22N 122.50E
149 R10 Bayāẕ Kermān, C Iran 30.40N 55.28E
179 R13 Baybay Leyte, C Philippines 10.41N 124.49E
23 X10 Bayboro North Carolina, SE USA 35.06N 76.46W
143 P12 Bayburt Bayburt, NE Turkey 40.15N 40.16E
143 P12 Bayburt ◐ province NE Turkey
33 R8 Bay City Michigan, N USA 43.34N 83.52W
27 V12 Bay City Texas, SW USA 28.59N 96.00W
125 G7 Baydaratskaya Guba var. Baydarata Bay. bay N Russian Federation
83 M16 Baydhabo var. Baydhowa, Isha Baydhabo, It. Baidoa. Bay, SW Somalia 3.07N 43.39E
Baydhowa see Baydhabo
103 N21 Bayerischer Wald ▲ SE Germany
103 K21 Bayern Eng. Bavaria, Fr. Bavière. ◐ state SE Germany
153 V9 Bayetovo Narynskaya Oblast', C Kyrgyzstan 41.14N 74.55E
104 K4 Bayeux anc. Augustodurum. Calvados, N France 49.16N 0.42W
12 E15 Bayfield ≈ Ontario, S Canada
151 O15 Baygekum Kaz. Bäygequm. Kzylorda, S Kazakhstan 44.15N 66.34E
Bäygequm see Baygekum
142 C14 Bayındır İzmir, SW Turkey 38.14N 27.37E
144 H12 Bāyir var. Bā'ir. Ma'ān, S Jordan 30.46N 36.40E
Bay Islands see Bahía, Islas de la
145 R5 Bayjī var. Baiji. N Iraq 34.55N 43.28E
Baykadam see Saudakent
126 K15 Baykal, Ozero Eng. Lake Baikal. ⊚ S Russian Federation
126 J16 Baykal'sk Irkutskaya Oblast', S Russian Federation 51.30N 104.03E
143 R15 Baykan Siirt, SE Turkey 38.07N 41.43E
126 Ii12 Baykit Evenkiyskiy Avtonomnyy Okrug, C Russian Federation 61.37N 96.23E
151 N12 Baykonur var. Baykonyr. Karaganda, C Kazakhstan 47.50N 75.33E
150 M14 Baykonyr var. Baykonur Kaz. Bayqongyr; prev. Leninsk. Kyzylorda, S Kazakhstan 45.38N 63.20E
Baykonyr see Baykonur
164 E7 Baykurt Xinjiang Uygur Zizhiqu, W China 39.55N 75.33E
12 I9 Bay, Lac ⊚ Québec, SE Canada
179 Pp11 Bay, Laguna de ⊚ Luzon, N Philippines
131 W6 Baymak Respublika Bashkortostan, W Russian Federation 52.34N 58.20E
25 O8 Bay Minette Alabama, S USA 30.52N 87.46W
149 O17 Baynūnah desert W UAE
192 O8 Bay of Plenty off. Bay of Plenty Region. ◐ region North Island, NZ
203 Z3 Bay of Wrecks bay Kiritimati, E Kiribati
179 P9 Bayombong Luzon, N Philippines 16.29N 121.08E
104 I15 Bayonne anc. Lapurdum. Pyrénées-Atlantiques, SW France 43.30N 1.28W
24 H4 Bayou D'Arbonne Lake ⊠ Louisiana, S USA
25 N9 Bayou La Batre Alabama, S USA 30.24N 88.15W
Bayou State see Mississippi
Bayqadam see Saudakent
Bayqongyr see Baykonyr
Bayram-Ali see Baýramaly
152 J14 Baýramaly var. Bayramaly; prev. Bayram-Ali. Mary Welaýaty, S Turkmenistan 37.33N 62.08E
103 L19 Bayreuth var. Baireuth. Bayern, SE Germany 49.57N 11.34E
Bayrische Alpen see Bavarian Alps
Bayrūt see Beyrouth
24 L9 Bay Saint Louis Mississippi, S USA 30.18N 89.19W
Baysān see Bet She'an
168 L8 Bayshint Töv, C Mongolia 47.22N 105.04E
12 H13 Bays, Lake of ⊚ Ontario, S Canada
24 M6 Bay Springs Mississippi, S USA 31.58N 89.17W
Bay State see Massachusetts
Baysun see Boysun
12 H13 Baysville Ontario, S Canada 45.10N 79.03W
147 N15 Bayt al Faqīh W Yemen 14.30N 43.20E
164 M4 Baytik Shan ▲▲ China/Mongolia
Bayt Laḥm see Bethlehem
27 W11 Baytown Texas, SW USA 29.44N 94.58W
175 O9 Bayur, Tanjung headland Borneo, N Indonesia 0.43S 117.32E
123 Ll16 Bayy al Kabīr, Wādī dry watercourse NW Libya
Bayyrqum see Bairkum
107 P14 Baza Andalucía, S Spain 37.30N 2.45W
143 X10 Bazardüzü Dağı Rus. Gora Bazardyuzyu. ▲ N Azerbaijan 41.13N 47.50E
Bazardyuzyu, Gora see Bazardüzü Dağı
Bazargic see Dobrich
85 N18 Bazaruto, Ilha do island SE Mozambique
104 K14 Bazas Gironde, SW France 44.27N 0.11W
107 O14 Baza, Sierra de ▲▲ S Spain
166 J8 Bazhong Sichuan, C China 31.55N 106.44E
Bazhong see Batang
167 P3 Bazhou prev. Baxian, Ba Xian. Hebei, E China 39.04N 116.24E
12 M9 Bazin ≈ Québec, SE Canada
Bazin see Pezinok
145 Q7 Bāzīyah C Iraq 33.49N 42.41E
144 H6 Bcharré var. Bcharreh, Bsharrī, Bsherri. NE Lebanon 34.16N 36.01E
Bcharreh see Bcharré
30 J5 Beach North Dakota, N USA 46.55N 104.00W
190 K12 Beachport South Australia 37.29S 140.03E
99 O23 Beachy Head headland SE England, UK 50.44N 0.16E
20 K13 Beacon New York, NE USA 41.30N 73.54W
65 J25 Beagle Channel channel Argentina/Chile
189 O1 Beagle Gulf gulf Northern Territory, N Australia
Bealach an Doirín see Ballaghaderreen
Bealach Cláir see Ballyclare
Bealach Féich see Ballybofey
180 J3 Bealanana Mahajanga, NE Madagascar 14.33S 48.43E
Béal an Átha see Ballina
Béal an Átha Móir see Ballinamore
Béal an Mhuirhead see Belmullet
Béal Átha Beithe see Ballybay
Béal Átha Conaill see Ballyconnell
Beál Átha hAmhnais see Ballyhaunis
Béal Átha na Sluaighe see Ballinasloe
Béal Átha Seanaidh see Ballyshannon
Bealdovuopmi see Peltovuoma
Béal Feirste see Belfast
Béal Tairbirt see Belturbet
Beanna Boirche see Mourne Mountains
Beannchar see Banagher, Ireland
Beannchar see Bangor, Northern Ireland, UK
Beanntraí see Bantry
Bearalváhki see Berlevåg
25 N2 Bear Creek ≈ Alabama/Mississippi, S USA
32 J13 Bear Creek ≈ Illinois, N USA
29 U13 Bearden Arkansas, C USA 33.43N 92.37W
205 Q10 Beardmore Glacier glacier Antarctica
32 K13 Beardstown Illinois, N USA 40.01N 90.25W
30 L14 Bear Hill ▲ Nebraska, C USA 41.24N 101.49W
Bear Island see Bjørnøya
12 H12 Bear Lake Ontario, S Canada 45.28N 79.31W
38 M1 Bear Lake ⊚ Idaho/Utah, NW USA
41 U11 Bear, Mount ▲ Alaska, USA 61.16N 141.09W
104 J16 Béarn cultural region SW France
204 J11 Bear Peninsula peninsula Antarctica
158 I7 Beās ≈ India/Pakistan
107 P3 Beasain País Vasco, N Spain 43.03N 2.10W
107 O12 Beas de Segura Andalucía, S Spain 38.16N 2.53W
47 N10 Beata, Cabo headland SW Dominican Republic 17.34N 71.25W
47 N10 Beata, Isla island SW Dominican Republic
66 F11 Beata Ridge undersea feature N Caribbean Sea
31 R17 Beatrice Nebraska, C USA 40.14N 96.43W
85 L16 Beatrice Mashonaland East, NE Zimbabwe 18.13S 30.52E
9 N11 Beatton ≈ British Columbia, W Canada
9 N11 Beatton River British Columbia, W Canada 57.35N 121.10W
37 V10 Beatty Nevada, W USA 36.53N 116.44W
23 N6 Beattyville Kentucky, S USA 37.34N 83.39W
181 X16 Beau Bassin W Mauritius 20.13S 57.27E
105 R15 Beaucaire Gard, S France 43.49N 4.37E
12 I8 Beauchastel, Lac ⊚ Québec, SE Canada
12 I10 Beauchêne, Lac ⊚ Québec, SE Canada
191 V3 Beaudesert Queensland, E Australia 28.00S 152.27E
190 M12 Beaufort Victoria, SE Australia 37.27S 143.24E
23 X11 Beaufort North Carolina, SE USA 34.45N 76.50W
23 R15 Beaufort South Carolina, SE USA 32.25N 80.40W
40 M11 Beaufort Sea sea Arctic Ocean
Beaufort-Wes see Beaufort West
85 G25 Beaufort West Afr. Beaufort-Wes. Western Cape, SW South Africa 32.21S 22.34E
105 N7 Beaugency Loiret, C France 47.46N 1.38E
21 R1 Beau Lake ⊠ Maine, NE USA
98 I8 Beauly N Scotland, UK 57.28N 4.28W
101 G21 Beaumont Hainaut, S Belgium 50.12N 4.13E
193 E23 Beaumont Otago, South Island, NZ 45.48S 169.32E
24 M7 Beaumont Mississippi, S USA 31.10N 88.55W
27 X10 Beaumont Texas, SW USA 30.05N 94.06W
104 M15 Beaumont-de-Lomagne Tarn-et-Garonne, S France 43.54N 1.00E
104 L6 Beaumont-sur-Sarthe Sarthe, NW France 48.15N 0.07E
105 R8 Beaune Côte d'Or, C France 47.01N 4.49E
13 R9 Beaupré Québec, SE Canada 47.03N 70.52W
104 J8 Beaupréau Maine-et-Loire, NW France 47.13N 0.57W
101 I22 Beauraing Namur, SE Belgium 50.07N 4.57E
105 R12 Beaurepaire Isère, E France 45.20N 5.03E
9 Y16 Beausejour Manitoba, S Canada 50.04N 96.30W
105 N4 Beauvais anc. Bellovacum, Caesaromagus. Oise, N France 49.27N 2.04E
9 S13 Beauval Saskatchewan, C Canada 55.10N 107.37W
104 I9 Beauvoir-sur-Mer Vendée, NW France 46.54N 2.03W
41 R8 Beaver Alaska, USA 66.22N 147.31W
28 J8 Beaver Oklahoma, C USA 36.49N 100.31W
20 B14 Beaver Pennsylvania, NE USA 40.39N 80.19W
38 K6 Beaver Utah, W USA 38.16N 112.38W
8 L9 Beaver ≈ British Columbia/Yukon Territory, W Canada
9 S13 Beaver ≈ Saskatchewan, C Canada
31 N17 Beaver City Nebraska, C USA 40.08N 99.49W
8 G6 Beaver Creek Yukon Territory, W Canada 62.19N 140.45W
33 R14 Beavercreek Ohio, N USA 39.42N 83.58W
41 S8 Beaver Creek ≈ Alaska, USA
28 H3 Beaver Creek ≈ Kansas/Nebraska, C USA
30 J5 Beaver Creek ≈ Montana/North Dakota, N USA
31 Q14 Beaver Creek ≈ Nebraska, C USA
27 Q4 Beaver Creek ≈ Texas, SW USA
32 M8 Beaver Dam Wisconsin, N USA 43.28N 88.49W
32 M8 Beaver Dam Lake ⊚ Wisconsin, N USA
20 B14 Beaver Falls Pennsylvania, NE USA 40.45N 80.20W
35 P12 Beaverhead Mountains ▲▲ Idaho/Montana, NW USA
35 Q12 Beaverhead River ≈ Montana, NW USA
67 A25 Beaver Island island W Falkland Islands
33 P5 Beaver Island island Michigan, N USA
29 S9 Beaver Lake ⊠ Arkansas, C USA
9 N13 Beaverlodge Alberta, W Canada 55.10N 119.28W
20 I8 Beaver River ≈ New York, NE USA
28 J8 Beaver River ≈ Oklahoma, C USA
20 B13 Beaver River ≈ Pennsylvania, NE USA
67 A25 Beaver Settlement Beaver Island, W Falkland Islands 51.30S 61.15W
Beaver State see Oregon
12 H14 Beaverton Ontario, S Canada 44.24N 79.07W
34 G11 Beaverton Oregon, NW USA 45.29N 122.48W
158 G12 Beāwar Rājasthān, N India 26.07N 74.21E
Bebas, Dasht-i see Bābūs, Dasht-e
62 L8 Bebedouro São Paulo, S Brazil 20.58S 48.28W
103 I16 Bebra Hessen, C Germany 50.59N 9.46E
43 W12 Becal Campeche, SE Mexico 19.49N 90.28W
13 Q11 Bécancour ≈ Québec, SE Canada
99 Q19 Beccles E England, UK 52.27N 1.32E
114 L9 Bečej Ger. Altbetsche, Hung. Óbecse, Rácz-Becse; prev. Magyar-Becse, Stari Bečej. Serbia, N Serbia and Montenegro (Yugoslavia) 45.36N 20.02E
106 I3 Becerreá Galicia, NW Spain 42.51N 7.10W
76 H7 Béchar prev. Colomb-Béchar. W Algeria 31.38N 2.10W
41 O14 Becharof Lake ⊚ Alaska, USA
118 H15 Bechet var. Bechetu. Dolj, SW Romania 43.45N 23.57E
Bechetu see Bechet
23 R6 Beckley West Virginia, NE USA 37.46N 81.11W
103 G14 Beckum Nordrhein-Westfalen, W Germany 51.45N 8.03E
27 X7 Beckville Texas, SW USA 32.14N 94.27W
37 X4 Becky Peak ▲ Nevada, W USA 39.59N 114.33W
118 I9 Beclean Hung. Bethlen; prev. Betlen. Bistriţa-Năsăud, N Romania 47.10N 24.10E
Bécs see Wien
113 H18 Bečva Ger. Betschau, Pol. Beczwa. ≈ E Czech Republic
Beczwa see Bečva
105 P15 Bédarieux Hérault, S France 43.37N 3.10E
122 Dd12 Beddouza, Cap headland W Morocco 32.35N 9.16W
82 I13 Bedelē Oromo, C Ethiopia 8.25N 36.21E
153 Y8 Bedel Pass Rus. Pereval Bedel. pass China/Kyrgyzstan 41.22N 78.19E
Bedel, Pereval see Bedel Pass
97 H22 Beder Århus, C Denmark 56.03N 10.13E
99 N20 Bedford E England, UK 52.07N 0.28W
33 O15 Bedford Indiana, N USA 38.51N 86.29W
31 U16 Bedford Iowa, C USA 40.40N 94.43W
22 L4 Bedford Kentucky, S USA 38.34N 85.18W
20 D15 Bedford Pennsylvania, NE USA 40.00N 78.29W
23 T6 Bedford Virginia, NE USA 37.19N 79.31W
99 N20 Bedfordshire cultural region E England, UK
131 N5 Bednodem'yanovsk Penzenskaya Oblast', W Russian Federation 53.55N 43.14E
100 N5 Bedum Groningen, NE Netherlands 53.18N 6.36E
29 V11 Beebe Arkansas, C USA 35.04N 91.52W
47 T9 Beef Island ✈ (Road Town) Tortola, E British Virgin Islands 18.25N 64.31W
Beehive State see Utah
101 L18 Beek Limburg, SE Netherlands 50.55N 5.46E
101 L18 Beek ✈ (Maastricht) Limburg, SE Netherlands 50.55N 5.47E
101 K14 Beek-en-Donk Noord-Brabant, S Netherlands 51.31N 5.37E
144 F13 Be'ér Menuḥa var. Be'er Menukha. Southern, S Israel 30.21N 35.09E
Be'er Menukha see Be'ér Menuḥa
101 D16 Beernem West-Vlaanderen, NW Belgium 51.09N 3.18E
101 I16 Beerse Antwerpen, N Belgium 51.20N 4.52E
Beersheba see Be'ér Sheva'
144 E11 Be'ér Sheva' var. Beersheba, Ar. Bir es Saba. Southern, S Israel 31.15N 34.46E
100 J13 Beesd Gelderland, C Netherlands 51.52N 5.12E
101 M16 Beesel Limburg, SE Netherlands 51.16N 6.01E
85 J21 Beestekraal North-West, N South Africa 25.21S 27.40E
204 J7 Beethoven Peninsula peninsula Alexander Island, Antarctica
Beetstersweach see Beetsterzwaag
100 M6 Beetsterzwaag Fris. Beetstersweach. Friesland, N Netherlands 53.03N 6.04E
27 S13 Beeville Texas, SW USA 28.25N 97.46W
81 J18 Befale Equateur, NW Dem. Rep. Congo 0.25N 20.48E
Befandriana see Befandriana Avaratra
180 J3 Befandriana Avaratra var. Befandriana, Befandriana Nord. Mahajanga, NW Madagascar 15.13S 48.33E
Befandriana Nord see Befandriana Avaratra
81 K18 Befori Equateur, N Dem. Rep. Congo 0.09N 22.18E
180 I7 Befotaka Fianarantsoa, S Madagascar 23.49S 47.00E
191 R11 Bega New South Wales, SE Australia 36.43S 149.49E
104 G5 Bégard Côtes d'Armor, NW France 48.37N 3.18W
114 M9 Begejski Kanal canal NE Serbia and Montenegro (Yugoslavia)
96 G13 Begna ≈ S Norway
Begoml' see Byahoml'
Begovat see Bekobod
159 Q13 Begusarai Bihār, NE India 25.25N 86.07E
149 R9 Behābād Yazd, C Iran 32.22N 59.49E
Behagle see Laï
57 Z10 Béhague, Pointe headland E French Guiana 4.37N 51.52W
Behar see Bihār
148 M10 Behbahān var. Behbehān. Khūzestān, SW Iran 30.37N 50.07E
Behbehān see Behbahān
46 G3 Behring Point Andros Island, W Bahamas 24.28N 77.44W
149 P4 Behshahr prev. Ashraf. Māzandarān, N Iran 36.42N 53.36E
169 V6 Bei'an Heilongjiang, NE China 48.16N 126.28E
Beibunar see Sredishte
Beibu Wan see Tongking, Gulf of
Beida see Al Bayḍā'
82 H13 Beigi Oromo, C Ethiopia 9.13N 34.48E
166 L16 Beihai Guangxi Zhuangzu Zizhiqu, S China 21.28N 109.10E
165 Q10 Bei Hulsan Hu ⊚ C China
167 N13 Bei Jiang ≈ S China
167 O2 Beijing var. Pei-ching, Eng. Peking; prev. Pei-p'ing. country/municipality capital (China) Beijing Shi, E China 39.58N 116.22E
167 P2 Beijing ✈ Beijing Shi, E China 39.54N 116.22E
Beijing see Beijing Shi
167 O2 Beijing Shi var. Beijing, Jing, Pei-ching, Eng. Peking; prev. Pei-p'ing. ◐ municipality E China
78 G8 Beïla Trarza, W Mauritania 18.07N 15.55W
100 N7 Beilen Drenthe, NE Netherlands 52.52N 6.27E
166 L15 Beiliu Guangxi Zhuangzu Zizhiqu, S China 22.43N 110.21E
165 O12 Beilu He ≈ W China
Beilul see Beylul
169 U12 Beining prev. Beizhen. Liaoning, NE China 41.34N 121.51E
98 H8 Beinn Dearg ▲ N Scotland, UK 57.47N 4.52W
Beinn MacDuibh see Ben Macdui
166 I12 Beipan Jiang ≈ S China
169 T12 Beipiao Liaoning, NE China 41.46N 120.51E
85 N17 Beira Sofala, C Mozambique 19.45S 34.55E
85 N17 Beira ✈ Sofala, C Mozambique 19.39S 35.05E
106 I7 Beira Alta former province N Portugal
106 H9 Beira Baixa former province C Portugal
106 G8 Beira Litoral former province N Portugal
Beirut see Beyrouth
Beisān see Bet She'an
9 Q16 Beiseker Alberta, SW Canada 51.20N 113.34W
Beitai Ding see Wutai Shan
85 K19 Beitbridge Matabeleland South, S Zimbabwe 22.10S 30.02E
118 G10 Beiuş Hung. Belényes. Bihor, NW Romania 46.40N 22.18E
Beizhen see Beining
106 H12 Beja anc. Pax Julia. Beja, SE Portugal 38.01N 7.52W
106 G13 Beja ◐ district S Portugal
76 M5 Béja var. Bājah. N Tunisia 36.45N 9.04E
123 Ii11 Béjaïa var. Bejaïa, Fr. Bougie; anc. Saldae. NE Algeria 36.45N 5.02E
106 K8 Béjar Castilla-León, N Spain 40.24N 5.45W
Bejraburi see Phetchaburi
Bekaa Valley see El Beqaa
Bekabad see Bekobod
Békás see Bicaz
174 J14 Bekasi Jawa, C Indonesia 6.13S 106.59E
Bek-Budi see Qarshi
152 A8 Bekdaş Rus. Bekdash. Balkan Welaýaty, NW Turkmenistan 41.33N 52.33E
Bekdash see Bekdaş
153 T10 Bek-Dzhar Oshskaya Oblast', SW Kyrgyzstan 40.22N 73.08E
113 N24 Békés Rom. Bichiş. Békés, SE Hungary 46.47N 21.07E
113 M24 Békés off. Békés Megye. ◐ county SE Hungary
113 M24 Békéscsaba Rom. Bichiş-Ciaba. Békés, SE Hungary 46.40N 21.04E
145 S2 Bēkhma E Iraq 36.40N 44.15E
180 H7 Bekily Toliara, S Madagascar 24.12S 45.19E
172 Qq7 Bekkai Hokkaidō, NE Japan 43.23N 145.07E
153 Q11 Bekobod Rus. Bekabad; prev. Begovat. Toshkent Viloyati, E Uzbekistan 40.17N 69.10E
131 O7 Bekovo Penzenskaya Oblast', W Russian Federation 52.27N 43.41E
Bél see Beliu
158 M13 Bela Uttar Pradesh, N India 25.55N 82.00E
155 N15 Bela Baluchistān, SW Pakistan 26.12N 66.22E
81 F15 Bélabo Est, C Cameroon 4.54N 13.10E
114 N10 Bela Crkva Ger. Weisskirchen, Hung. Fehértemplom. Serbia, W Serbia and Montenegro (Yugoslavia) 44.55N 21.28E
181 Y16 Bel Air var. Rivière Sèche. E Mauritius
106 L12 Belalcázar Andalucía, S Spain 38.33N 5.07W
115 P15 Bela Palanka Serbia, SE Serbia and Montenegro (Yugoslavia) 43.13N 22.19E
121 H16 Belarus off. Republic of Belarus, var. Belorussia, Latv. Baltkrievija; prev. Belorussian SSR, Rus. Belorusskaya SSR. ◆ republic E Europe
Belau see Palau
61 H21 Bela Vista Mato Grosso do Sul, SW Brazil 22.04S 56.25W
85 L21 Bela Vista Maputo, S Mozambique 26.19S 32.40E
173 Ff4 Belawan Sumatera, W Indonesia 3.44N 98.39E
Běla Woda see Weisswasser
131 U4 Belaya ≈ W Russian Federation
127 N7 Belaya Gora Respublika Sakha (Yakutiya), NE Russian Federation 68.25N 146.12E
130 M11 Belaya Kalitva Rostovskaya Oblast', SW Russian Federation 48.09N 40.43E
129 R14 Belaya Kholunitsa Kirovskaya Oblast', NW Russian Federation 58.54N 50.52E
Belaya Tserkov' see Bila Tserkva
79 V11 Belbédji Zinder, S Niger 14.35N 8.00E
112 K13 Belchatów var. Belchatow. Łodzkie, C Poland 51.22N 19.19E
Belcher, Îles see Belcher Islands
10 H7 Belcher Islands Fr. Îles Belcher. island group Nunavut, SE Canada
107 S6 Belchite Aragón, NE Spain 41.18N 0.45W
31 O2 Belcourt North Dakota, N USA 48.50N 99.44W
33 P9 Belding Michigan, N USA 43.06N 85.13W
131 U5 Belebey Respublika Bashkortostan, W Russian Federation 54.04N 54.13E
83 N16 Beledweyne var. Belet Huen, It. Belet Uen. Hiiraan, C Somalia 4.39N 45.12E
152 B10 Belek Balkan Welaýaty, W Turkmenistan 39.57N 53.51E
60 L12 Belém var. Pará. state capital Pará, N Brazil 1.27S 48.28W
67 I14 Belém Ridge undersea feature C Atlantic Ocean
39 R12 Belen New Mexico, SW USA 34.37N 106.46W
64 I7 Belén Catamarca, NW Argentina 27.40S 67.01W
56 G9 Belén Boyacá, C Colombia 5.59N 72.55W
44 J11 Belén Rivas, SW Nicaragua 11.30N 85.55W
64 O5 Belén Concepción, C Paraguay 23.25S 57.13W
63 D16 Belén Salto, N Uruguay 30.46S 57.46W
63 D20 Belén de Escobar Buenos Aires, E Argentina 34.21S 58.46W
116 J7 Belene Pleven, N Bulgaria 43.39N 25.09E
116 J7 Belene, Ostrov island N Bulgaria
45 R15 Belén, Río ≈ C Panama
Belényes see Beiuş
197 G4 Belep, Îles island group W New Caledonia
Belesar, Embalse de see Belesar, Encoro de
106 H3 Belesar, Encoro de Sp. Embalse de Belesar. ⊠ NW Spain
Belet Huen/Belet Uen see Beledweyne
130 J5 Belëv Tul'skaya Oblast', W Russian Federation 53.48N 36.07E
99 G15 Belfast Ir. Béal Feirste. ● E Northern Ireland, UK 54.34N 5.55W
21 R7 Belfast Maine, NE USA 44.25N 69.02W
99 G15 Belfast ✈ E Northern Ireland, UK 54.37N 6.11W
99 G15 Belfast Lough Ir. Loch Lao inlet E Northern Ireland, UK
30 K5 Belfield North Dakota, N USA 46.53N 103.12W
105 U7 Belfort Territoire-de-Belfort, E France 47.37N 6.52E
Belgard see Białogard
161 E17 Belgaum Karnātaka, W India 15.52N 74.30E
Belgian Congo see Congo (Democratic Republic of)
205 T3 Belgica Mountains ▲ Antarctica
België/Belgique see Belgium
101 F20 Belgium off. Kingdom of Belgium, Dut. België, Fr. Belgique. ◆ monarchy NW Europe
130 J8 Belgorod Belgorodskaya Oblast', W Russian Federation 50.37N 36.37E
Belgorod-Dnestrovskiy see Bilhorod-Dnistrovs'kyy
130 J8 Belgorodskaya Oblast' ◐ province W Russian Federation
Belgrad see Beograd
31 T8 Belgrade Minnesota, N USA 45.27N 94.59W
35 S11 Belgrade Montana, NW USA 45.46N 111.10W
Belgrade see Beograd
205 N5 Belgrano II Argentinian research station Antarctica 77.50S 35.25W
Belgrano, Cabo see Meredith, Cape
23 X9 Belhaven North Carolina, SE USA 35.36N 76.50W
109 I23 Belice anc. Hypsas. ≈ Sicilia, Italy, C Mediterranean Sea
Belice see Belize/Belize City
115 M16 Beli Drim Alb. Drini i Bardhë. ≈ Albania/Serbia and Montenegro (Yugoslavia)
Beligrad see Berat
196 C8 Beliliou prev. Peleliu. island S Palau
116 L8 Beli Lom, Yazovir ⊠ NE Bulgaria
114 I8 Beli Manastir Hung. Pélmonostor; prev. Monostor. Osijek-Baranja, NE Croatia 45.46N 16.38E
104 J13 Bélin-Béliet Gironde, SW France 44.30N 0.48W
81 F17 Bélinga Ogooué-Ivindo, NE Gabon 1.05N 13.12E
23 S4 Belington West Virginia, NE USA 39.01N 79.57W
131 O6 Belinskiy Penzenskaya Oblast', W Russian Federation 52.58N 43.25E
174 Ii9 Belinyu Pulau Bangka, W Indonesia 1.34S 105.45E
174 Jj11 Belitung, Pulau island W Indonesia
118 F10 Beliu Hung. Bél. Arad, W Romania 46.31N 21.57E
116 I9 Beli Vit ≈ NW Bulgaria
44 G2 Belize Sp. Belice; prev. British Honduras, Colony of Belize. ◆ commonwealth republic Central America
44 F2 Belize Sp. Belice. ◐ district NE Belize
44 G2 Belize ≈ Belize/Guatemala
Belize see Belize City
44 G2 Belize City var. Belize, Sp. Belice. Belize, NE Belize 17.28N 88.10W
44 G2 Belize City ✈ Belize, NE Belize 17.31N 88.15W
Beljak see Villach
41 N16 Belkofski Alaska, USA 55.06N 162.03W
126 L4 Bel'kovskiy, Ostrov island Novosibirskiye Ostrova, NE Russian Federation
12 J8 Bell ≈ Québec, SE Canada
8 J15 Bella Bella British Columbia, SW Canada 52.04N 128.07W
104 M10 Bellac Haute-Vienne, C France 46.07N 1.04E
8 K15 Bella Coola British Columbia, SW Canada 52.22N 126.46W
108 D6 Bellagio Lombardia, N Italy 45.58N 9.15E
33 P6 Bellaire Michigan, N USA 44.58N 85.12W
108 D6 Bellano Lombardia, N Italy 46.06N 9.21E
161 G17 Bellary var. Ballari. Karnātaka, S India 15.10N 76.54E
191 S5 Bellata New South Wales, SE Australia 29.58S 149.49E
63 D16 Bella Unión Artigas, N Uruguay 30.18S 57.34W
63 C14 Bella Vista Corrientes, NE Argentina 28.34S 58.58W
64 J7 Bella Vista Tucumán, N Argentina 27.04S 65.19W
64 P4 Bella Vista Amambay, C Paraguay 22.12S 56.30W
58 B10 Bellavista Cajamarca, N Peru 5.43S 78.46W
58 D11 Bellavista San Martín, N Peru 7.02S 76.36W
191 U6 Bellbrook New South Wales, SE Australia 30.48S 152.32E
29 V5 Belle Missouri, C USA 38.17N 91.43W
23 Q5 Belle West Virginia, NE USA 38.13N 81.32W
33 R13 Bellefontaine Ohio, N USA 40.21N 83.45W
20 F14 Bellefonte Pennsylvania, NE USA 40.54N 77.43W
30 J9 Belle Fourche South Dakota, N USA 44.40N 103.49W
30 J9 Belle Fourche Reservoir ⊠ South Dakota, N USA
30 K9 Belle Fourche River ≈ South Dakota/Wyoming, N USA
105 S10 Bellegarde-sur-Valserine Ain, E France 46.06N 5.49E
25 Y14 Belle Glade Florida, SE USA 26.40N 80.40W
104 G8 Belle Île island NW France
11 T9 Belle Isle island Belle Isle, Newfoundland and Labrador, E Canada
11 S10 Belle Isle, Strait of strait Newfoundland and Labrador, E Canada
Bellenz see Bellinzona
31 W14 Belle Plaine Iowa, C USA 41.54N 92.16W
31 V9 Belle Plaine Minnesota, N USA 44.39N 93.47W
12 I9 Belleterre Québec, SE Canada 47.24N 78.40W
12 J15 Belleville Ontario, SE Canada 44.10N 77.22W
105 R10 Belleville Rhône, E France 46.09N 4.42E
32 K15 Belleville Illinois, N USA 38.31N 89.58W
29 N3 Belleville Kansas, C USA 39.46N 97.37W
31 Z13 Bellevue Iowa, C USA 42.15N 90.25W
31 S15 Bellevue Nebraska, C USA 41.08N 95.53W
33 S11 Bellevue Ohio, N USA 41.16N 82.50W
27 S5 Bellevue Texas, SW USA 33.38N 98.00W
34 H8 Bellevue Washington, NW USA 47.36N 122.12W
57 Y11 Bellevue de l'Inini, Montagnes ▲ S French Guiana
105 S11 Belley Ain, E France 45.46N 5.40E
Bellin see Kangirsuk
191 V6 Bellingen New South Wales, SE Australia 30.27S 152.53E
99 L14 Bellingham N England, UK 55.09N 2.16W
34 H6 Bellingham Washington, NW USA 48.45N 122.29W
Belling Hausen Mulde see Southeast Pacific Basin
204 H2 Bellingshausen Russian research station South Shetland Islands, Antarctica 61.57S 58.23W
Bellingshausen see Motu One
Bellingshausen Abyssal Plain see Bellingshausen Plain
200 N16 Bellingshausen Plain var. Bellingshausen Abyssal Plain. undersea feature SE Pacific Ocean
204 I8 Bellingshausen Sea sea Antarctica
100 P6 Bellingwolde Groningen, NE Netherlands 53.07N 7.10E
110 H11 Bellinzona Ger. Bellenz. Ticino, S Switzerland 46.12N 9.01E
27 T8 Bellmead Texas, SW USA 31.36N 97.02W
56 E8 Bello Antioquia, W Colombia 6.19N 75.34W
63 B21 Bellocq Buenos Aires, E Argentina 35.55S 61.31W
Bello Horizonte see Belo Horizonte
195 W17 Bellona var. Mungiki. island S Solomon Islands
Bellovacum see Beauvais
190 D7 Bell, Point headland South Australia 32.13S 133.08E
22 F9 Bells Tennessee, S USA 35.42N 89.05W
27 U5 Bells Texas, SW USA 33.36N 96.24W
94 N3 Bellsund inlet SW Svalbard
108 H6 Belluno Veneto, NE Italy 46.07N 12.06E
64 L11 Bell Ville Córdoba, C Argentina 32.42S 62.42W
85 E26 Bellville Western Cape, SW South Africa 33.49S 18.43E
27 U11 Bellville Texas, SW USA 29.57N 96.15W
106 L12 Belmez Andalucía, S Spain 38.16N 5.12W
31 V12 Belmond Iowa, C USA 42.51N 93.36W
20 E11 Belmont New York, NE USA 42.13N 78.01W
23 R10 Belmont North Carolina, SE USA 35.13N 81.01W
61 O18 Belmonte Bahia, E Brazil 15.52S 38.54W
106 I8 Belmonte Castelo Branco, C Portugal 40.21N 7.19W
107 P10 Belmonte Castilla-La Mancha, C Spain 39.34N 2.43W
44 G2 Belmopan ● (Belize) Cayo, C Belize 17.13N 88.48W
99 B16 Belmullet Ir. Béal an Mhuirhead. W Ireland 54.13N 9.58W
126 Mm15 Belogorsk Amurskaya Oblast', SE Russian Federation 50.53N 128.24E
Belogorsk see Bilohirs'k
116 F7 Belogradchik Vidin, NW Bulgaria 43.37N 22.42E
180 H8 Beloha Toliara, S Madagascar 25.09S 45.04E
61 M20 Belo Horizonte prev. Bello Horizonte. state capital Minas Gerais, SE Brazil 19.54S 43.54W
28 M3 Beloit Kansas, C USA 39.27N 98.06W
32 L9 Beloit Wisconsin, N USA 42.31N 89.01W
Belokorovichi see Bilokorovychi
126 H15 Belokurikha Altayskiy Kray, S Russian Federation 51.57N 84.56E
128 J8 Belomorsk Respublika Kareliya, NW Russian Federation 64.30N 34.43E
128 J8 Belomorsko-Baltiyskiy Kanal Eng. White Sea-Baltic Canal, White Sea Canal. canal NW Russian Federation
159 V15 Belonia Tripura, NE India 23.15N 91.25E
Belopol'ye see Bilopillya
107 O4 Belorado Castilla-León, N Spain 42.25N 3.10W
130 L14 Belorechensk Krasnodarskiy Kray, SW Russian Federation 44.46N 39.53E
131 W5 Beloretsk Respublika Bashkortostan, W Russian Federation
Belorussia/Belorussian SSR see Belarus
Belorusskaya Gryada see Byelaruskaya Hrada
Belorusskaya SSR see Belarus
Beloshchel'ye see Nar'yan-Mar
116 N8 Beloslav Varna, E Bulgaria 43.13N 27.42E
Belostok see Białystok

◆ Country ● Country Capital ◇ Dependent Territory ○ Dependent Territory Capital ◐ Administrative Region ✈ International Airport ▲ Mountain ▲▲ Mountain Range Volcano ≈ River ⊚ Lake ⊠ Reservoir
231

BELO TSIRIBIHINA – BHATKAL

180 *H5* **Belo Tsiribihina** *var.* Belo-sur-Tsiribihina. Toliara, W Madagascar *19.40S 44.30E*
Belovár *see* Bjelovar
Belovezhskaya Pushcha *see* Białowieska, Puszcza/Byelavyezhskaya Pushcha
116 *H10* **Belovo** Pazardzhik, C Bulgaria *42.12N 24.02E*
126 *H14* **Belovo** Kemerovskaya Oblast', S Russian Federation *54.25N 86.13E*
Belovodsk *see* Bilovods'k
125 *Ff9* **Beloyarskiy** Khanty-Mansiyskiy Avtonomnyy Okrug, N Russian Federation *63.40N 66.31E*
128 *K7* **Beloye More** *Eng.* White Sea. *sea* NW Russian Federation
128 *K13* **Beloye, Ozero** ◎ NW Russian Federation
116 *J10* **Belozem** Plovdiv, C Bulgaria *42.11N 25.00E*
128 *K13* **Belozërsk** Vologodskaya Oblast', NW Russian Federation *59.58N 37.49E*
101 *E20* **Belœil** Hainaut, SW Belgium *50.33N 3.45E*
110 *D8* **Belp** Bern, W Switzerland *46.54N 7.31E*
110 *D8* **Belp** ✈ (Bern) Bern, C Switzerland *46.55N 7.29E*
109 *L24* **Belpasso** Sicilia, Italy, C Mediterranean Sea *37.34N 14.58E*
33 *U14* **Belpre** Ohio, N USA *39.14N 81.34W*
100 *M8* **Belterwijde** ◎ N Netherlands
29 *R4* **Belton** Missouri, C USA *38.48N 94.31W*
23 *P11* **Belton** South Carolina, SE USA *34.31N 82.29W*
27 *T9* **Belton** Texas, SW USA *31.03N 97.27W*
27 *S9* **Belton Lake** ▣ Texas, SW USA
Bel'tsy *see* Bălți
99 *E16* **Belturbet** *Ir.* Béal Tairbirt. N Ireland *54.06N 7.25W*
Beluchistan *see* Baluchistān
151 *Z9* **Belukha, Gora** ▲ Kazakhstan/Russian Federation *49.42N 86.33E*
109 *M20* **Belvedere Marittimo** Calabria, SW Italy *39.37N 15.52E*
32 *L10* **Belvidere** Illinois, N USA *42.15N 88.50W*
20 *J14* **Belvidere** New Jersey, NE USA *40.49N 75.03W*
Bely *see* Belyy
131 *V8* **Belyayevka** Orenburgskaya Oblast', W Russian Federation *51.25N 56.26E*
Belynichi *see* Byalynichy
128 *H17* **Belyy** *var.* Bely, Beyj. Tverskaya Oblast', W Russian Federation *55.51N 32.57E*
130 *I6* **Belyye Berega** Bryanskaya Oblast', W Russian Federation *53.11N 34.42E*
126 *H5* **Belyy, Ostrov** *island* N Russian Federation
126 *H12* **Belyy Yar** Tomskaya Oblast', C Russian Federation *58.26N 84.57E*
102 *N13* **Belzig** Brandenburg, NE Germany *52.09N 12.37E*
24 *K4* **Belzoni** Mississippi, S USA *33.10N 90.29W*
180 *H4* **Bemaraha** *var.* Plateau du Bemaraha. ▲▲ W Madagascar
84 *B10* **Bembe** Uíge, NW Angola *7.01S 14.18E*
79 *S14* **Bembèrèkè** *var.* Bimbéréké. N Benin *10.10N 2.40E*
106 *K12* **Bembézar** ~ SW Spain
106 *J3* **Bembibre** Castilla-León, N Spain *42.37N 6.25W*
31 *T4* **Bemidji** Minnesota, N USA *47.27N 94.53W*
100 *L12* **Bemmel** Gelderland, SE Netherlands *51.52N 5.54E*
176 *U11* **Bemu** Pulau Seram, E Indonesia *3.21S 129.58E*
Benāb *see* Bonāb
107 *T5* **Benabarre** *var.* Benavarn. Aragón, NE Spain *42.06N 0.28E*
Benaco *see* Garda, Lago di
81 *L20* **Bena-Dibele** Kasai Oriental, C Dem. Rep. Congo *4.01S 22.50E*
107 *R9* **Benageber, Embalse de** ▣ E Spain
191 *O11* **Benalla** Victoria, SE Australia *36.33S 146.00E*
106 *M14* **Benamejí** Andalucía, S Spain *37.16N 4.33W*
Benares *see* Vārānasi
Benavarn *see* Benabarre
106 *F10* **Benavente** Santarém, C Portugal *38.58N 8.49W*
106 *K5* **Benavente** Castilla-León, N Spain *42.00N 5.40W*
27 *S15* **Benavides** Texas, SW USA *27.36N 98.24W*
98 *F8* **Benbecula** *island* NW Scotland, UK
Bencovazzo *see* Benkovac
34 *H13* **Bend** Oregon, NW USA *44.03N 121.18W*
190 *K7* **Benda Range** ▲▲ South Australia
191 *T6* **Bendemeer** New South Wales, SE Australia *30.54S 151.12E*
Bender *see* Tighina
Bender Beila/Bender Beyla *see* Bandarbeyla
Bender Cassim/Bender Qaasim *see* Boosaaso
Bendery *see* Tighina
191 *N11* **Bendigo** Victoria, SE Australia *36.46S 144.18E*
120 *E10* **Bēne** Dobele, SW Latvia *56.30N 23.04E*
100 *K13* **Beneden-Leeuwen** Gelderland, C Netherlands *51.52N 5.32E*
103 *L24* **Benediktenwand** ▲ S Germany *47.39N 11.28E*
Benemérita de San Cristóbal *see* San Cristóbal
79 *N12* **Bénéna** Ségou, S Mali *13.04N 4.20W*
180 *I7* **Benenitra** Toliara, S Madagascar *23.25S 45.06E*
Beneschau *see* Benešov
Beneški Zaliv *see* Venice, Gulf of
113 *D17* **Benešov** *Ger.* Beneschau. Středočeský Kraj, W Czech Republic *49.48N 14.40E*
126 *Ll3* **Benetta, Ostrov** *island* Novosibirskiye Ostrova, NE Russian Federation
109 *L17* **Benevento** *anc.* Beneventum, Malventum. Campania, S Italy *41.07N 14.45E*
Beneventum *see* Benevento
181 *S3* **Bengal, Bay of** *bay* N Indian Ocean
81 *M17* **Bengamisa** Orientale, N Dem. Rep. Congo *0.58N 25.10E*
Bengasi *see* Banghāzī
174 *Ll15* **Bengawan, Sungai** ~ Jawa, S Indonesia
Bengazi *see* Banghāzī
167 *P7* **Bengbu** *var.* Peng-pu. Anhui, E China *32.57N 117.17E*
34 *L9* **Benge** Washington, NW USA *46.55N 118.01W*
Benghazi *see* Banghāzī
174 *H7* **Bengkalis** Pulau Bengkalis, W Indonesia *1.29N 102.07E*
174 *H6* **Bengkalis, Pulau** *island* W Indonesia
174 *Kk7* **Bengkayang** Borneo, C Indonesia *0.45N 109.28E*
Bengkoelen/Bengkoeloe *see* Bengkulu
174 *H12* **Bengkulu** *prev.* Bengkoeloe, Benkoelen, Benkulen. Sumatera, W Indonesia *3.46S 102.16E*
174 *H11* **Bengkulu** *off.* Propinsi Bengkulu; *prev.* Bengkoelen, Benkoelen, Benkulen. ◈ *province* W Indonesia
84 *A11* **Bengo** ◈ *province* W Angola
97 *J16* **Bengtsfors** Västra Götaland, S Sweden *59.03N 12.13E*
84 *B13* **Benguela** *var.* Benguella. Benguela, W Angola *12.34S 13.30E*
85 *A14* **Benguela** ◈ *province* W Angola
Benguella *see* Benguela
Bengweulu, Lake *see* Bangweulu, Lake
124 *Qq15* **Benha** *var.* Banhā. N Egypt *30.22N 31.16E*
198 *G6* **Benham Seamount** *undersea feature* W Philippine Sea *15.48N 124.15E*
98 *H6* **Ben Hope** ▲ N Scotland, UK *58.25N 4.36W*
81 *P18* **Beni** Nord Kivu, NE Dem. Rep. Congo *0.31N 29.29E*
59 *L15* **Beni** *var.* El Beni. ◈ *department* N Bolivia
76 *H8* **Beni Abbès** W Algeria *30.07N 2.09W*
107 *T8* **Benicarló** País Valenciano, E Spain *40.25N 0.25E*
107 *T9* **Benicasim** País Valenciano, E Spain *40.03N 0.03E*
107 *T12* **Benidorm** País Valenciano, SE Spain *38.33N 0.09W*
77 *W9* **Beni Mazâr** *var.* Banī Mazār. C Egypt *28.24N 30.38E*
122 *F12* **Beni-Mellal** C Morocco *32.20N 6.21W*
79 *R14* **Benin** *off.* Republic of Benin; *prev.* Dahomey. ◆ *republic* W Africa
79 *S17* **Benin, Bight of** *gulf* W Africa
79 *U16* **Benin City** Edo, SW Nigeria *6.22N 5.39E*
59 *K16* **Beni, Río** ~ N Bolivia
123 *Gg11* **Beni Saf** *var.* Beni-Saf. NW Algeria *35.16N 1.33W*
82 *H12* **Benishangul** ◈ *region* W Ethiopia
107 *T11* **Benissa** País Valenciano, E Spain *38.43N 0.03E*
124 *Qq17* **Beni Suef** *var.* Banī Suwayf. N Egypt *29.09N 31.03E*
9 *V15* **Benito** Manitoba, S Canada *51.57N 101.24W*
Benito *see* Uolo, Río
63 *C23* **Benito Juárez** Buenos Aires, E Argentina *37.43S 59.48W*
43 *P14* **Benito Juaréz Internacional** ✈ (México) México, S Mexico *19.24N 99.02W*
27 *P5* **Benjamin** Texas, SW USA *33.34N 99.47W*
60 *B13* **Benjamin Constant** Amazonas, N Brazil *4.22S 70.01W*
42 *F4* **Benjamín Hill** Sonora, NW Mexico *30.13N 111.07W*
65 *F19* **Benjamín, Isla** *island* Archipiélago de los Chonos, S Chile
172 *N5* **Benkei-misaki** *headland* Hokkaidō, NE Japan *42.49N 140.10E*
30 *L17* **Benkelman** Nebraska, C USA *40.04N 101.30W*
98 *I7* **Ben Klibreck** ▲ N Scotland, UK *58.15N 4.23W*
Benkoelen *see* Bengkulu
114 *D13* **Benkovac** *It.* Bencovazzo. Zadar, SW Croatia *44.02N 15.36E*
Benkulen *see* Bengkulu
98 *I11* **Ben Lawers** ▲ C Scotland, UK *56.33N 4.13W*
98 *J9* **Ben Macdui** *var.* Beinn MacDuibh. ▲ C Scotland, UK *57.02N 3.42W*
98 *G11* **Ben More** ▲ W Scotland, UK *56.26N 6.00W*
98 *I11* **Ben More** ▲ C Scotland, UK *56.22N 4.31W*
98 *H7* **Ben More Assynt** ▲ N Scotland, UK *58.09N 4.51W*
193 *E20* **Benmore, Lake** ◎ South Island, NZ
100 *L12* **Bennekom** Gelderland, SE Netherlands *52.00N 5.40E*
23 *T11* **Bennettsville** South Carolina, SE USA *34.37N 79.41W*
98 *H10* **Ben Nevis** ▲ N Scotland, UK *56.46N 5.01W*
192 *M9* **Benneydale** Waikato, North Island, NZ *38.31S 175.22E*
Bennichab *see* Bennichchâb
78 *H8* **Bennichchâb** *var.* Bennichab. Inchiri, W Mauritania *19.25N 15.21W*
20 *L10* **Bennington** Vermont, NE USA *42.51N 73.09W*
193 *E20* **Ben Ohau Range** ▲▲ South Island, NZ
85 *J21* **Benoni** Gauteng, NE South Africa *26.04S 28.18E*
180 *J2* **Be, Nosy** *var.* Nossi-Bé. *island* NW Madagascar
Bénoué *see* Benue
44 *F2* **Benque Viejo del Carmen** Cayo, W Belize *17.04N 89.08W*
103 *G19* **Bensheim** Hessen, W Germany *49.40N 8.37E*
39 *N16* **Benson** Arizona, SW USA *31.55N 110.16W*
31 *S8* **Benson** Minnesota, N USA *45.19N 95.36W*
23 *U10* **Benson** North Carolina, SE USA *35.22N 78.33W*
175 *Pp14* **Benteng** Pulau Selayar, C Indonesia *6.07S 120.28E*
85 *A14* **Bentiaba** Namibe, SW Angola *14.18S 12.27E*
189 *T4* **Bentinck Island** *island* Wellesley Islands, Queensland, N Australia
82 *E13* **Bentiu** Wahda, S Sudan *9.13N 29.49E*
144 *G8* **Bent Jbaïl** *var.* Bint Jubayl. S Lebanon *33.07N 35.25E*
9 *Q15* **Bentley** Alberta, SW Canada *52.27N 114.02W*
63 *I15* **Bento Gonçalves** Rio Grande do Sul, S Brazil *29.06S 51.29W*
29 *U12* **Benton** Arkansas, C USA *34.33N 92.35W*
32 *L16* **Benton** Illinois, N USA *38.00N 88.55W*
22 *H7* **Benton** Kentucky, S USA *36.51N 88.21W*
24 *G5* **Benton** Louisiana, S USA *32.41N 93.44W*
29 *Y7* **Benton** Missouri, C USA *37.05N 89.34W*
22 *M10* **Benton** Tennessee, S USA *35.10N 84.39W*
33 *O10* **Benton Harbor** Michigan, N USA *42.07N 86.27W*
29 *S9* **Bentonville** Arkansas, C USA *36.22N 94.12W*
79 *V16* **Benue** ◈ *state* SE Nigeria
80 *F13* **Benue** *Fr.* Bénoué. ~ Cameroon/Nigeria
174 *Hh6* **Benut** Johor, Peninsular Malaysia *1.37N 103.15E*
169 *V12* **Benxi** *prev.* Pen-ch'i, Penhsihu, Penki. Liaoning, NE China *41.11N 123.46E*
Benyakoni *see* Byenyakoni
114 *K10* **Beočin** Serbia, N Serbia and Montenegro (Yugoslavia) *45.13N 19.43E*
Beodericsworth *see* Bury St Edmunds
114 *M11* **Beograd** *Eng.* Belgrade, *Ger.* Belgrad; *anc.* Singidunum. ● (Serbia and Montenegro (Yugoslavia)) Serbia, N Serbia and Montenegro (Yugoslavia) *44.48N 20.27E*
114 *L11* **Beograd** *Eng.* Belgrade. ✈ Serbia, N Serbia and Montenegro (Yugoslavia) *44.45N 20.21E*
78 *M16* **Béoumi** C Ivory Coast *7.40N 5.34W*
37 *V3* **Beowawe** Nevada, W USA *40.33N 116.31W*
176 *Ww8* **Bepondi, Pulau** *see* Bepondi, Pulau
170 *D13* **Beppu** Ōita, Kyūshū, SW Japan *33.16N 131.28E*
170 *Dd14* **Beppu-wan** *bay* SW Japan
197 *H15* **Beqa** *prev.* Mbengga. *island* W Fiji
Beqa Barrier Reef *see* Kavukavu Reef
47 *Y14* **Bequia** *island* C Saint Vincent and the Grenadines
115 *L16* **Berane** *prev.* Ivangrad. Montenegro, SW Serbia and Montenegro (Yugoslavia) *42.51N 19.51E*
115 *L21* **Berat** *var.* Berati, *SCr.* Beligrad. Berat, C Albania *40.42N 19.57E*
115 *L21* **Berat** ◈ *district* C Albania
Berătău *see* Berettyó
Berati *see* Berat
Beraun *see* Berounka, Czech Republic
Beraun *see* Beroun, Czech Republic
175 *O6* **Berau, Sungai** ~ Borneo, N Indonesia
176 *V10* **Berau, Teluk** *var.* MacCluer Gulf. *bay* Papua, E Indonesia
82 *G8* **Berber** River Nile, NE Sudan *18.01N 34.00E*
82 *N12* **Berbera** Woqooyi Galbeed, NW Somalia *10.24N 45.01E*
81 *H16* **Berbérati** Mambéré-Kadéï, SW Central African Republic *4.13N 15.49E*
Berberia, Cabo de *see* Barbaria, Cap de
57 *T9* **Berbice River** ~ NE Guyana
Berchid *see* Berrechid
105 *N2* **Berck-Plage** Pas-de-Calais, N France *50.24N 1.34E*
27 *T13* **Berclair** Texas, SW USA *28.33N 97.32W*
119 *W10* **Berda** ~ SE Ukraine
Berdichev *see* Berdychiv
126 *Ll11* **Berdigestyakh** Respublika Sakha (Yakutiya), NE Russian Federation *62.02N 127.03E*
126 *H14* **Berdsk** Novosibirskaya Oblast', C Russian Federation *54.42N 82.56E*
119 *W10* **Berdyans'k** *Rus.* Berdyansk; *prev.* Osipenko. Zaporiz'ka Oblast', SE Ukraine *46.46N 36.48E*
119 *W10* **Berdyans'ka Kosa** *spit* SE Ukraine
119 *V10* **Berdyans'ka Zatoka** *gulf* S Ukraine
119 *N5* **Berdychiv** *Rus.* Berdichev. Zhytomyrs'ka Oblast', N Ukraine *49.52N 28.39E*
22 *M6* **Berea** Kentucky, S USA *37.34N 84.18W*
Beregovo/Beregszász *see* Berehove
118 *G8* **Berehove** *Cz.* Berehovo, *Hung.* Beregszász, *Rus.* Beregovo. Zakarpats'ka Oblast', W Ukraine *48.13N 22.39E*
Berehovo *see* Berehove
194 *J15* **Bereina** Central, S PNG *8.33S 146.25E*
152 *C11* **Bereket** *prev. Rus.* Gazandzhyk, Kazandzhik, *Turkm.* Gazanjyk. Balkan Welaýaty, W Turkmenistan *39.16N 55.27E*
47 *O12* **Berekua** S Dominica *15.14N 61.19W*
79 *O16* **Berekum** W Ghana *7.27N 2.34W*
77 *Y11* **Berenice** *var.* Mînâ Baranîs. SE Egypt *23.58N 35.29E*
15 *L14* **Berens** ~ Manitoba/Ontario, C Canada
9 *X14* **Berens River** Manitoba, C Canada *52.22N 97.00W*
31 *R12* **Beresford** South Dakota, N USA *43.02N 96.45W*
118 *J4* **Berestechko** Volyns'ka Oblast', NW Ukraine *50.21N 25.06E*
118 *M11* **Bereşti** Galaţi, E Romania *46.04N 27.54E*
119 *U6* **Berestova** ~ E Ukraine
Beretău *see* Berettyó
113 *N23* **Berettyó** *Rom.* Barcău; *prev.* Berătău, Beretău. ~ Hungary/Romania
113 *N23* **Berettyóújfalu** Hajdú-Bihar, E Hungary *47.15N 21.33E*
Berëza/Bereza Kartuska *see* Byaroza
119 *Q4* **Berezan'** Kyyivs'ka Oblast', N Ukraine *50.18N 31.30E*
119 *Q10* **Berezanka** Mykolayivs'ka Oblast', S Ukraine *46.51N 31.24E*
118 *J6* **Berezhany** *Pol.* Brzeżany. Ternopil's'ka Oblast', W Ukraine *49.29N 25.00E*
Berezina *see* Byerezino
Berezino *see* Byerazino
119 *P10* **Berezivka** *Rus.* Berezovka. Odes'ka Oblast', SW Ukraine *47.12N 30.55E*
119 *Q2* **Berezna** Chernihivs'ka Oblast', NE Ukraine *51.35N 31.50E*
118 *L3* **Berezne** Rivnens'ka Oblast', NW Ukraine *51.00N 26.46E*
119 *R9* **Bereznehuvate** Mykolayivs'ka Oblast', S Ukraine *47.18N 32.52E*
129 *N10* **Bereznik** Arkhangel'skaya Oblast', NW Russian Federation *62.50N 42.40E*
129 *U13* **Berezniki** Permskaya Oblast', NW Russian Federation *59.25N 56.49E*
Berezovka *see* Berezivka
125 *Ff9* **Berezovo** Khanty-Mansiyskiy Avtonomnyy Okrug, N Russian Federation *63.48N 64.38E*
131 *O9* **Berezovskaya** Volgogradskaya Oblast', SW Russian Federation *50.17N 43.58E*
126 *H14* **Berezovskiy** Kemerovskaya Oblast', S Russian Federation *55.40N 86.06E*
127 *N14* **Berezovyy** Khabarovskiy Kray, E Russian Federation *51.42N 135.39E*
85 *E25* **Berg** ~ W South Africa
Berg *see* Berg bei Rohrbach
107 *V4* **Berga** Cataluña, NE Spain *42.06N 1.40E*
97 *N20* **Berga** Kalmar, S Sweden *57.13N 16.03E*
142 *B13* **Bergama** İzmir, W Turkey *39.07N 27.10E*
108 *E7* **Bergamo** *anc.* Bergomum. Lombardia, N Italy *45.42N 9.40E*
107 *P3* **Bergara** País Vasco, N Spain *43.05N 2.25W*
111 *S3* **Berg bei Rohrbach** *var.* Berg. Oberösterreich, N Austria *48.34N 14.02E*
195 *O11* **Bergberg** ~ New Britain, C Papau New Guinea
102 *O6* **Bergen** Mecklenburg-Vorpommern, NE Germany *54.25N 13.24E*
103 *I11* **Bergen** Niedersachsen, NW Germany *52.49N 9.57E*
100 *H8* **Bergen** Noord-Holland, NW Netherlands *52.40N 4.42E*
96 *C13* **Bergen** Hordaland, S Norway *60.24N 5.19E*
Bergen *see* Mons
57 *W9* **Berg en Dal** Brokopondo, C Suriname *5.15N 55.20W*
101 *G15* **Bergen op Zoom** Noord-Brabant, S Netherlands *51.30N 4.18E*
104 *L13* **Bergerac** Dordogne, SW France *44.51N 0.30E*
101 *J16* **Bergeyk** Noord-Brabant, S Netherlands *51.19N 5.21E*
103 *D16* **Bergheim** Nordrhein-Westfalen, W Germany *50.57N 6.39E*
57 *X10* **Bergi** Sipaliwini, E Suriname *4.36N 54.24W*
103 *E16* **Bergisch Gladbach** Nordrhein-Westfalen, W Germany *50.59N 7.07E*
103 *F14* **Bergkamen** Nordrhein-Westfalen, W Germany *51.36N 7.39E*
97 *N21* **Bergkvara** Kalmar, S Sweden *56.22N 16.04E*
Bergomum *see* Bergamo
100 *K13* **Bergse Maas** ~ S Netherlands
97 *P15* **Bergshamra** Stockholm, C Sweden *59.37N 18.40E*
96 *N10* **Bergsjö** Gävleborg, C Sweden *62.00N 17.10E*
95 *J14* **Bergsviken** Norrbotten, N Sweden *65.16N 21.24E*
100 *L6* **Bergum** *Fris.* Burgum. Friesland, N Netherlands *53.12N 5.58E*
100 *M6* **Bergumer Meer** ◎ N Netherlands
96 *N12* **Bergviken** ◎ C Sweden
174 *I9* **Berhala, Selat** *strait* Sumatera, W Indonesia
Berhampore *see* Baharampur
127 *Q9* **Beringa, Ostrov** *island* E Russian Federation
101 *J17* **Beringen** Limburg, NE Belgium *51.04N 5.13E*
41 *T12* **Bering Glacier** *glacier* Alaska, USA
Beringov Proliv *see* Bering Strait
127 *Q5* **Beringovskiy** Chukotskiy Avtonomnyy Okrug, NE Russian Federation *63.04N 179.09E*
199 *K2* **Bering Sea** *sea* N Pacific Ocean
40 *L9* **Bering Strait** *Rus.* Beringov Proliv. *strait* Bering Sea/Chukchi Sea
Berislav *see* Beryslav
107 *O15* **Berja** Andalucía, S Spain *36.51N 2.55W*
96 *H9* **Berkåk** Sør-Trøndelag, S Norway *62.50N 10.01E*
100 *N11* **Berkel** ~ Germany/Netherlands
37 *N8* **Berkeley** California, W USA *37.52N 122.16W*
67 *E24* **Berkeley Sound** *sound* NE Falkland Islands
23 *V2* **Berkeley Springs** *var.* Bath. West Virginia, NE USA *39.36N 78.12W*
205 *N6* **Berkner Island** *island* Antarctica
116 *G8* **Berkovitsa** Montana, NW Bulgaria *43.16N 23.07E*
99 *M22* **Berkshire** *cultural region* S England, UK
101 *H17* **Berlaar** Antwerpen, N Belgium *51.08N 4.39E*
Berlanga *see* Berlanga de Duero
107 *P6* **Berlanga de Duero** *var.* Berlanga. Castilla-León, N Spain *41.28N 2.51W*
(0) *I16* **Berlanga Rise** *undersea feature* E Pacific Ocean
101 *F17* **Berlare** Oost-Vlaanderen, NW Belgium *51.01N 4.01E*
106 *E9* **Berlenga, Ilha da** *island* C Portugal
94 *M7* **Berlevåg** *Lapp.* Bearalváhki. Finnmark, N Norway *70.51N 29.04E*
102 *O12* **Berlin** ● (Germany) Berlin, NE Germany *52.31N 13.26E*
23 *Z4* **Berlin** Maryland, NE USA *38.19N 75.13W*
21 *O7* **Berlin** New Hampshire, NE USA *44.27N 71.13W*
20 *D16* **Berlin** Pennsylvania, NE USA *39.54N 78.57W*
32 *L7* **Berlin** Wisconsin, N USA *43.57N 88.59W*
102 *O12* **Berlin** ◈ *state* NE Germany
Berlinchen *see* Barlinek
33 *U12* **Berlin Lake** ▣ Ohio, N USA
191 *R11* **Bermagui** New South Wales, SE Australia *36.26S 150.01E*
42 *L8* **Bermejillo** Durango, C Mexico *25.55N 103.39W*
64 *M6* **Bermejo (viejo), Río** ~ N Argentina
64 *L5* **Bermejo, Río** ~ N Argentina
64 *I10* **Bermejo, Río** ~ W Argentina
107 *P2* **Bermeo** País Vasco, N Spain *43.25N 2.43W*
106 *K6* **Bermillo de Sayago** Castilla-León, N Spain *41.22N 6.07W*
108 *E6* **Bermina, Pizzo** *Rmsch.* Piz Bernina. ▲ Italy/Switzerland **see also** Bernina, Piz *46.22N 9.52E*
66 *A12* **Bermuda** *var.* Bermuda Islands, Bermudas; *prev.* Somers Islands. ◇ *UK crown colony* NW Atlantic Ocean
1 *N11* **Bermuda** *var.* Great Bermuda, Long Island, Main Island. *island* Bermuda
Bermuda Islands *see* Bermuda
Bermuda-New England Seamount Arc *see* New England Seamounts
1 *N11* **Bermuda Rise** *undersea feature* C Sargasso Sea
Bermudas *see* Bermuda
110 *D8* **Bern** *Fr.* Berne. ● (Switzerland) Bern, W Switzerland *46.57N 7.25E*
110 *D9* **Bern** *Fr.* Berne. ◈ *canton* W Switzerland
39 *R11* **Bernalillo** New Mexico, SW USA *35.18N 106.33W*
12 *H12* **Bernard Lake** ◎ Ontario, S Canada
63 *B18* **Bernardo de Irigoyen** Santa Fe, NE Argentina *32.09S 61.06W*
20 *J14* **Bernardsville** New Jersey, NE USA *40.43N 74.34W*
65 *K14* **Bernasconi** La Pampa, C Argentina *37.55S 63.43W*
102 *O12* **Bernau** Brandenburg, NE Germany *52.40N 13.36E*
104 *L4* **Bernay** Eure, N France *49.04N 0.36E*
103 *L14* **Bernburg** Sachsen-Anhalt, C Germany *51.46N 11.45E*
111 *X5* **Berndorf** Niederösterreich, NE Austria *47.55N 16.10E*
33 *Q12* **Berne** Indiana, N USA *40.39N 84.57W*
Berne *see* Bern
110 *D10* **Berner Alpen** *var.* Berner Oberland, *Eng.* Bernese Oberland. ▲▲ SW Switzerland
Berner Oberland/Bernese Oberland *see* Berner Alpen
111 *Y2* **Bernhardsthal** Niederösterreich, N Austria *48.40N 16.51E*
24 *H4* **Bernice** Louisiana, S USA *32.49N 92.39W*
29 *Y8* **Bernie** Missouri, C USA *36.40N 89.58W*
188 *G9* **Bernier Island** *island* Western Australia
Bernina Pass *see* Bernina, Passo del
110 *J10* **Bernina, Passo del** *Eng.* Bernina Pass. *pass* SE Switzerland *46.23N 10.00E*
110 *J10* **Bernina, Piz** *It.* Pizzo Bermina. ▲ Italy/Switzerland **see also** Bermina, Pizzo *46.22N 9.55E*
101 *E20* **Bérnissart** Hainaut, SW Belgium *50.29N 3.37E*
103 *E18* **Bernkastel-Kues** Rheinland-Pfalz, W Germany *49.55N 7.04E*
Beroea *see* Ḥalab
180 *H6* **Beroroha** Toliara, SW Madagascar *21.40S 45.10E*
Béroubouay *see* Gbéroubouè
113 *C17* **Beroun** *Ger.* Beraun. Středočeský Kraj, W Czech Republic *49.58N 14.04E*
113 *C16* **Berounka** *Ger.* Beraun. ~ W Czech Republic
115 *Q18* **Berovo** E FYR Macedonia *41.45N 22.50E*
76 *F6* **Berrechid** *var.* Berchid. W Morocco *33.16N 7.32W*
105 *R15* **Berre, Étang de** ◎ SE France
105 *S15* **Berre-l'Étang** Bouches-du-Rhône, SE France *43.28N 5.10E*
190 *K9* **Berri** South Australia *34.16S 140.35E*
33 *O10* **Berrien Springs** Michigan, N USA *41.57N 86.20W*
191 *O10* **Berrigan** New South Wales, SE Australia *35.41S 145.50E*
105 *N9* **Berry** *cultural region* C France
37 *N7* **Berryessa, Lake** ◎ California, W USA
46 *G2* **Berry Islands** *island group* N Bahamas
29 *T9* **Berryville** Arkansas, C USA *36.21N 93.30W*
23 *V3* **Berryville** Virginia, NE USA *39.09N 77.58W*
85 *D21* **Berseba** Karas, S Namibia *26.00S 17.46E*
119 *O8* **Bershad'** Vinnyts'ka Oblast', C Ukraine *48.19N 29.28E*
30 *L3* **Berthold** North Dakota, N USA *48.16N 101.48W*
39 *T3* **Berthoud** Colorado, C USA *40.18N 105.04W*
39 *S4* **Berthoud Pass** *pass* Colorado, C USA *39.48N 105.46W*
81 *F15* **Bertoua** Est, E Cameroon *4.34N 13.42E*
27 *S10* **Bertram** Texas, SW USA *30.44N 98.03W*
65 *G22* **Bertrand, Cerro** ▲ S Argentina *50.00S 73.27W*
101 *J23* **Bertrix** Luxembourg, SE Belgium *49.52N 5.15E*
203 *P3* **Beru** *var.* Peru. *atoll* Tungaru, W Kiribati
Beruni *see* Beruniy
152 *I9* **Beruniy** *var.* Biruni, *Rus.* Beruni. Qoraqalpog'iston Respublikasi, W Uzbekistan *41.48N 60.39E*
60 *F13* **Beruri** Amazonas, NW Brazil *3.44S 61.13W*
20 *H14* **Berwick** Pennsylvania, NE USA *41.03N 76.13W*
98 *K12* **Berwick** *cultural region* SE Scotland, UK
98 *L12* **Berwick-upon-Tweed** N England, UK *55.46N 2.00W*
119 *S10* **Beryslav** *Rus.* Berislav. Khersons'ka Oblast', S Ukraine *46.51N 33.27E*
Berytus *see* Beyrouth
180 *H4* **Besalampy** Mahajanga, W Madagascar *16.43S 44.28E*
105 *T8* **Besançon** *anc.* Besontium, Vesontio. Doubs, E France *47.13N 6.01E*
105 *P10* **Besbre** ~ C France
Bescanuova *see* Baška
Besdan *see* Bezdan
Besed' *see* Byesyedz'
153 *R10* **Beshariq** *Rus.* Besharyk; *prev.* Kirovo. Farg'ona Viloyati, E Uzbekistan *40.26N 70.33E*
Besharyk *see* Beshariq
152 *L9* **Beshbuloq** *Rus.* Beshulak. Navoiy Viloyati, N Uzbekistan *41.55N 64.13E*
Beshenkovichi *see* Byeshankovichy
152 *M13* **Beshkent** Qashqadaryo Viloyati, S Uzbekistan *38.47N 65.42E*
Beshulak *see* Beshbuloq
176 *Uu8* **Besir** Papua, E Indonesia *0.25S 130.38E*
114 *L10* **Beška** Serbia, N Serbia and Montenegro (Yugoslavia) *45.09N 20.04E*
Beskra *see* Biskra
131 *O16* **Beslan** Respublika Severnaya Osetiya, SW Russian Federation *43.12N 44.33E*
115 *P16* **Besna Kobila** ▲ SE Serbia and Montenegro (Yugoslavia) *42.30N 22.16E*
143 *N16* **Besni** Adıyaman, S Turkey *37.42N 37.52E*
Besontium *see* Besançon
124 *Nn2* **Beşparmak Dağları** *Eng.* Kyrenia Mountains. ▲▲ N Cyprus
Bessarabka *see* Basarabeasca
94 *O2* **Bessels, Kapp** *headland* C Svalbard *78.36N 21.43E*
25 *P4* **Bessemer** Alabama, S USA *33.24N 86.57W*
32 *K3* **Bessemer** Michigan, N USA *46.28N 90.03W*
23 *Q10* **Bessemer City** North Carolina, SE USA *35.16N 81.16W*
104 *M10* **Bessines-sur-Gartempe** Haute-Vienne, C France *46.06N 1.22E*
101 *K15* **Best** Noord-Brabant, S Netherlands *51.31N 5.24E*
27 *N9* **Best** Texas, SW USA *31.13N 101.34W*
129 *O11* **Bestuzhevo** Arkhangel'skaya Oblast', NW Russian Federation *61.36N 43.54E*
126 *M11* **Bestyakh** Respublika Sakha (Yakutiya), NE Russian Federation *61.25N 129.05E*
Beszterce *see* Bistriţa
Besztercebánya *see* Banská Bystrica
180 *I5* **Betafo** Antananarivo, C Madagascar *19.49S 46.49E*
106 *H2* **Betanzos** Galicia, NW Spain *43.16N 8.16W*
106 *G2* **Betanzos, Ría de** *estuary* NW Spain
81 *G15* **Bétaré Oya** Est, E Cameroon *5.34N 14.09E*
107 *S9* **Bétera** País Valenciano, E Spain *39.34N 0.28W*
79 *R15* **Bétérou** C Benin *9.13N 2.18E*
85 *K21* **Bethal** Mpumalanga, NE South Africa *26.27S 29.28E*
32 *K15* **Bethalto** Illinois, N USA *38.54N 90.02W*
85 *D21* **Bethanie** *var.* Bethanien, Bethany. Karas, S Namibia *26.26S 17.06E*
Bethanien *see* Bethanie
29 *S2* **Bethany** Missouri, C USA *40.15N 94.03W*
29 *N10* **Bethany** Oklahoma, C USA *35.31N 97.37W*
Bethany *see* Bethanie
41 *N12* **Bethel** Alaska, USA *60.47N 161.45W*
21 *P7* **Bethel** Maine, NE USA *44.24N 70.47W*
23 *W9* **Bethel** North Carolina, SE USA *35.46N 77.21W*
20 *B15* **Bethel Park** Pennsylvania, NE USA *40.21N 80.03W*
23 *W3* **Bethesda** Maryland, NE USA *38.58N 77.06W*
85 *J22* **Bethlehem** Free State, C South Africa *28.11S 28.16E*
20 *I14* **Bethlehem** Pennsylvania, NE USA *40.36N 75.22W*
144 *F10* **Bethlehem** *Ar.* Bayt Laḥm, *Heb.* Bet Leḥem. C West Bank *31.43N 35.12E*
Bethlen *see* Beclean
85 *I24* **Bethulie** Free State, C South Africa *30.29S 25.54E*
105 *O1* **Béthune** Pas-de-Calais, N France *50.31N 2.37E*
104 *M3* **Béthune** ~ N France
106 *M14* **Béticos, Sistemas** *var.* Sistema Penibético, *Eng.* Baetic Cordillera, Baetic Mountains. ▲▲ S Spain
56 *I6* **Betijoque** Trujillo, NW Venezuela *9.27N 70.47W*
61 *M20* **Betim** Minas Gerais, SE Brazil *19.55S 44.10W*
202 *H3* **Betio** Tarawa, W Kiribati *1.21N 172.55E*
180 *H7* **Betioky** Toliara, S Madagascar *23.42S 44.22E*
Bet Leḥem *see* Bethlehem
Betlen *see* Beclean
178 *H17* **Betong** Yala, SW Thailand *5.47N 101.04E*
81 *I16* **Bétou** La Likouala, N Congo *3.07N 18.30E*
151 *P14* **Betpak-Dala** *Kaz.* Betpaqdala. *plateau* S Kazakhstan
Betpaqdala *see* Betpak-Dala
180 *H7* **Betroka** Toliara, S Madagascar *23.15S 46.07E*
Betschau *see* Bečva
144 *G9* **Bet She'an** *Ar.* Baysān, Beisān; *anc.* Scythopolis. Northern, N Israel *32.29N 35.25E*
13 *T6* **Betsiamites** Québec, SE Canada *48.55N 68.40W*
13 *T6* **Betsiamites** ~ Québec, SE Canada
180 *I4* **Betsiboka** ~ N Madagascar
101 *M25* **Bettembourg** Luxembourg, S Luxembourg *49.31N 6.06E*
101 *M23* **Bettendorf** Diekirch, NE Luxembourg *49.52N 6.13E*
31 *Z14* **Bettendorf** Iowa, C USA *41.31N 90.31W*
77 *R13* **Bette, Pic** *var.* Bīkkū Bīttī, *It.* Picco Bette. ▲ S Libya *22.02N 19.07E*
Bette, Picco *see* Bette, Pic
159 *P12* **Bettiah** Bihār, N India *26.49N 84.30E*
41 *Q7* **Bettles** Alaska, USA *66.54N 151.40W*
97 *N17* **Bettna** Södermanland, C Sweden *58.52N 16.40E*
160 *H11* **Betūl** *prev.* Badnur. Madhya Pradesh, C India *21.55N 77.54E*
160 *H9* **Betwa** ~ C India
103 *F16* **Betzdorf** Rheinland-Pfalz, W Germany *50.47N 7.50E*
84 *C9* **Béu** Uíge, NW Angola *6.16S 15.28E*
33 *P6* **Beulah** Michigan, N USA *44.37N 86.04W*
30 *L5* **Beulah** North Dakota, N USA *47.16N 101.48W*
100 *M8* **Beulakerwijde** ◎ N Netherlands
100 *L13* **Beuningen** Gelderland, SE Netherlands *51.52N 5.47E*
Beuthen *see* Bytom
105 *N7* **Beuvron** ~ C France
101 *F16* **Beveren** Oost-Vlaanderen, N Belgium *51.13N 4.15E*
23 *T9* **B.Everett Jordan Reservoir** *var.* Jordan Lake. ▣ North Carolina, SE USA
99 *N17* **Beverley** E England, UK *53.51N 0.25W*
Beverley *see* Beverly
101 *J17* **Beverlo** Limburg, NE Belgium *51.06N 5.14E*
21 *P11* **Beverly** Massachusetts, NE USA *42.33N 70.49W*
34 *J9* **Beverly** *var.* Beverley. Washington, NW USA *46.50N 119.57W*
37 *S15* **Beverly Hills** California, W USA *34.02N 118.25W*
103 *I14* **Beverungen** Nordrhein-Westfalen, C Germany *51.39N 9.22E*
100 *H9* **Beverwijk** Noord-Holland, W Netherlands *52.28N 4.37E*
110 *C10* **Bex** Vaud, W Switzerland *46.15N 7.00E*
99 *P23* **Bexhill** *var.* Bexhill-on-Sea. SE England, UK *50.49N 0.28E*
Bexhill-on-Sea *see* Bexhill
142 *E17* **Bey Dağları** ▲▲ SW Turkey
Beyj *see* Belyy
142 *E10* **Beykoz** İstanbul, NW Turkey *41.09N 29.06E*
78 *K15* **Beyla** Guinée-Forestière, SE Guinea *8.43N 8.41W*
143 *X12* **Beyläqan** *prev.* Zhdanov. SW Azerbaijan *39.43N 47.38E*
82 *L10* **Beylul** *var.* Beilul. SE Eritrea *13.10N 42.27E*
150 *H14* **Beyneu** *Kaz.* Beyneū. Mangistau, SW Kazakhstan *45.19N 55.11E*
Beyneū *see* Beyneu
172 *Ss14* **Beyonēsu-retsugan** *Eng.* Bayonnaise Rocks. *island group* SE Japan
142 *G12* **Beypazarı** Ankara, NW Turkey *40.10N 31.55E*
161 *F21* **Beypore** Kerala, SW India *11.10N 75.49E*
144 *G7* **Beyrouth** *var.* Bayrūt, *Eng.* Beirut; *anc.* Berytus. ● (Lebanon) W Lebanon *33.54N 35.31E*
144 *G7* **Beyrouth** ✈ W Lebanon *33.52N 35.30E*
142 *G15* **Beyşehir** Konya, SW Turkey *37.39N 31.42E*
142 *G15* **Beyşehir Gölü** ◎ C Turkey
110 *J7* **Bezau** Vorarlberg, NW Austria *47.24N 9.55E*
114 *J8* **Bezdan** *Ger.* Besdan, *Hung.* Bezdán. Serbia, NW Serbia and Montenegro (Yugoslavia) *45.51N 19.00E*
Bezdezh *see* Byezdzyezh
128 *G15* **Bezhanitsy** Pskovskaya Oblast', W Russian Federation *56.57N 29.53E*
128 *K15* **Bezhetsk** Tverskaya Oblast', W Russian Federation *57.47N 36.42E*
105 *P16* **Béziers** *anc.* Baeterrae, Baeterrae Septimanorum, Julia Beterrae. Hérault, S France *43.21N 3.13E*
Bezmein *see* Büzmeýin
Bezwada *see* Vijayawāda
160 *P12* **Bhadrak** *var.* Bhadrakh. Orissa, E India *21.06N 86.31E*
Bhadrakh *see* Bhadrak
161 *F19* **Bhadra Reservoir** ▣ SW India
161 *F18* **Bhadrāvati** Karnātaka, SW India *13.52N 75.43E*
159 *R14* **Bhāgalpur** Bihār, NE India *25.13N 86.58E*
Bhairab *see* Bhairab Bazar
159 *U14* **Bhairab Bazar** *var.* Bhairab. Dhaka, C Bangladesh *24.04N 91.00E*
159 *O11* **Bhairahawa** Western, S Nepal *27.31N 83.27E*
155 *S8* **Bhakkar** Punjab, E Pakistan *31.41N 71.04E*
159 *P11* **Bhaktapur** Central, C Nepal *27.47N 85.21E*
178 *Gg3* **Bhamo** *var.* Banmo. Kachin State, N Myanmar *24.15N 97.15E*
Bhāmragad *see* Bhāmragarh
160 *K13* **Bhāmragarh** *var.* Bhāmragad. Mahārāshtra, C India *19.28N 80.39E*
160 *J12* **Bhandāra** Mahārāshtra, C India *21.10N 79.40E*
Bhārat *see* India
158 *J12* **Bharatpur** *prev.* Bhurtpore. Rājasthān, N India *27.13N 77.28E*
160 *D11* **Bharūch** Gujarāt, W India *21.48N 72.54E*
161 *E18* **Bhatkal** Karnātaka, W India *13.59N 74.34E*

◆ COUNTRY
● COUNTRY CAPITAL
◇ DEPENDENT TERRITORY
○ DEPENDENT TERRITORY CAPITAL
◈ ADMINISTRATIVE REGION
✈ INTERNATIONAL AIRPORT
▲ MOUNTAIN
▲▲ MOUNTAIN RANGE
VOLCANO
~ RIVER
◎ LAKE
▣ RESERVOIR

Bhatni – Blackpool

159 O13 **Bhatni** *var.* Bhatni Junction. Uttar Pradesh, N India *26.22N 83.55E*
Bhatni Junction *see* Bhatni
159 S16 **Bhātpāra** West Bengal, NE India *22.55N 88.30E*
155 U7 **Bhaun** Punjab, E Pakistan *32.53N 72.45E*
Bhaunagar *see* Bhāvnagar
160 M13 **Bhavānīpātna** Orissa, E India *19.56N 83.09E*
161 H21 **Bhavānīsāgar Reservoir** ⊠ S India
160 D11 **Bhāvnagar** *prev.* Bhaunagar. Gujarāt, W India *21.46N 72.13E*
Bheanntraí, Bá *see* Bantry Bay
Bheara, Béal an *see* Gweebarra Bay
160 K12 **Bhilai** Chhattīsgarh, C India *21.13N 81.26E*
158 G13 **Bhīlwāra** Rājasthān, N India *25.22N 74.39E*
161 E14 **Bhīma** ⁓ S India
161 K16 **Bhīmavaram** Andhra Pradesh, E India *16.34N 81.34E*
160 I7 **Bhind** Madhya Pradesh, C India *26.33N 78.46E*
158 E13 **Bhīnmāl** Rājasthān, N India *25.01N 72.22E*
Bhir *see* Bīd
160 D13 **Bhiwandi** Mahārāshtra, W India *19.21N 73.07E*
158 H10 **Bhiwāni** Haryāna, N India *28.49N 76.07E*
158 L13 **Bhognipur** Uttar Pradesh, N India *26.12N 79.48E*
159 U16 **Bhola** Khulna, S Bangladesh *22.42N 90.43E*
160 H10 **Bhopāl** Madhya Pradesh, C India *23.16N 77.24E*
161 J14 **Bhopālpatnam** Chhattīsgarh, C India *18.51N 80.22E*
161 E14 **Bhor** Mahārāshtra, W India *18.10N 73.55E*
160 O12 **Bhubaneshwar** *prev.* Bhubaneswar, Bhuvaneshwar. Orissa, E India *20.16N 85.51E*
Bhubaneswar *see* Bhubaneshwar
160 B9 **Bhuj** Gujarāt, W India *23.16N 69.40E*
Bhuket *see* Phuket
Bhurtpore *see* Bharatpur
Bhusawal *see* Bhusāwal
160 G12 **Bhusāwal** *prev.* Bhusawal. Mahārāshtra, C India *21.01N 75.49E*
159 T12 **Bhutan** *off.* Kingdom of Bhutan, *var.* Druk-yul. ◆ *monarchy* S Asia
Bhuvaneshwar *see* Bhubaneshwar
149 T15 **Biābān, Kūh-e** ▲ S Iran
79 V18 **Biafra, Bight of** *var.* Bight of Bonny. *bay* W Africa
176 X9 **Biak** Papua, E Indonesia *1.10S 136.04E*
176 Ww9 **Biak, Pulau** *island* E Indonesia
112 P12 **Biała Podlaska** Lubelskie, E Poland *52.03N 23.08E*
112 F7 **Białogard** *Ger.* Belgard. Zachodnio-pomorskie, NW Poland *54.00N 15.58E*
112 P10 **Białowieska, Puszcza** *Bel.* Byelavyezhskaya Pushcha, *Rus.* Belovezhskaya Pushcha. *physical region* Belarus/Poland *see also* Byelavyezhskaya Pushcha
112 G8 **Biały Bór** *Ger.* Baldenburg. Zachodnio-pomorskie, NW Poland *53.53N 16.49E*
112 P9 **Białystok** *Rus.* Belostok, Bielostok. Podlaskie, NE Poland *53.08N 23.09E*
109 L24 **Biancavilla** *prev.* Inessa. Sicilia, Italy, C Mediterranean Sea *37.37N 14.52E*
Bianco, Monte *see* Blanc, Mont
78 L15 **Biankouma** W Ivory Coast *7.43N 7.37W*
178 Ii7 **Bia, Phou** *var.* Pou Bia. ▲ C Laos *18.59N 103.09E*
Bia, Pou *see* Bia, Phou
149 R5 **Biārjmand** Semnān, N Iran *36.04N 55.49E*
107 P4 **Biarra** ⁓ NE Spain
104 I15 **Biarritz** Pyrénées-Atlantiques, SW France *43.24N 1.39W*
110 H10 **Biasca** Ticino, S Switzerland *46.22N 8.59E*
63 E17 **Biassini** Salto, N Uruguay *31.18S 57.05W*
172 Oo5 **Bibai** Hokkaidō, NE Japan *43.22N 141.52E*
85 B15 **Bibala** *Port.* Vila Arriaga. Namibe, SW Angola *14.45S 13.18E*
106 I4 **Bibéi** ⁓ NW Spain
Biberach *see* Biberach an der Riss
103 I23 **Biberach an der Riss** *var.* Biberach, *Ger.* Biberach an der Riß. Baden-Württemberg, S Germany *48.06N 9.46E*
110 E7 **Biberist** Solothurn, NW Switzerland *47.10N 7.34E*
79 O16 **Bibiani** SW Ghana *6.28N 2.19W*
114 C13 **Bibinje** Zadar, SW Croatia *44.04N 15.17E*
Biblical Gebal *see* Jbail
118 I5 **Bibrka** *Pol.* Bóbrka, *Rus.* Bobrka. L'vivs'ka Oblast', NW Ukraine *49.39N 24.16E*
119 N10 **Bic** ⁓ S Moldova
115 M18 **Bicaj** Kukës, NE Albania *42.00N 20.24E*
118 K10 **Bicaz** *Hung.* Békás. Neamţ, NE Romania *46.53N 26.04E*
191 Q16 **Bicheno** Tasmania, SE Australia *41.56S 148.15E*
Bichiş *see* Békés
Bichiş-Ciaba *see* Békéscsaba
Bichitra *see* Phichit
143 P8 **Bichvint'a** *Rus.* Pitsunda. NW Georgia *43.12N 40.21E*
13 T7 **Bic, Île du** *island* Québec, SE Canada
34 J10 **Bickleton** Washington, NW USA *46.00N 120.16W*
38 L6 **Bicknell** Utah, W USA *38.20N 111.32W*
175 Tt7 **Bicoli** Pulau Halmahera, E Indonesia *0.34N 128.33E*
113 J22 **Bicske** Fejér, C Hungary *47.28N 18.38E*
161 F14 **Bīd** *prev.* Bhir. Mahārāshtra, W India *19.17N 75.22E*
79 U15 **Bida** Niger, C Nigeria *9.06N 6.02E*
161 H15 **Bīdar** Karnātaka, C India *17.55N 77.34E*
147 Y8 **Bidbid** NE Oman *23.25N 58.07E*
21 P9 **Biddeford** Maine, NE USA *43.28N 70.27W*
100 L9 **Biddinghuizen** Flevoland, C Netherlands *52.28N 5.41E*
35 X11 **Biddle** Montana, NW USA *45.04N 105.21W*
99 J23 **Bideford** SW England, UK *51.01N 4.12W*
84 D13 **Bié** ◆ *province* C Angola
37 Q2 **Bieber** California, W USA *41.07N 121.09W*
112 O9 **Biebrza** ⁓ NE Poland
172 P5 **Biei** Hokkaidō, NE Japan *43.33N 142.28E*
110 D8 **Biel** *Fr.* Bienne. Bern, W Switzerland *47.09N 7.16E*
102 G13 **Bielefeld** Nordrhein-Westfalen, NW Germany *52.01N 8.31E*
110 D8 **Bieler See** *Fr.* Lac de Bienne. ⊚ W Switzerland
Bielitz/Bielitz-Biala *see* Bielsko-Biała
108 C7 **Biella** Piemonte, N Italy *45.33N 8.03E*
Bielostok *see* Białystok
113 J17 **Bielsko-Biała** *Ger.* Bielitz, Bielitz-Biala. Śląskie, S Poland *49.48N 19.01E*
112 P10 **Bielsk Podlaski** Białystok, E Poland *52.45N 23.11E*
Bien Bien *see* Điện Biên
Biên Đông *see* South China Sea
9 V17 **Bienfait** Saskatchewan, S Canada *49.06N 102.47W*
178 Jj14 **Biên Hoa** Đông Nai, S Vietnam *10.58N 106.49E*
Bienne *see* Biel
Bienne, Lac de *see* Bieler See
10 K8 **Bienville, Lac** ⊚ Québec, C Canada
84 D13 **Bié, Planalto do** *var.* Bié Plateau. *plateau* C Angola
Bié Plateau *see* Bié, Planalto do
110 B9 **Bière** Vaud, W Switzerland *46.32N 6.19E*
100 O4 **Bierum** Groningen, NE Netherlands *53.25N 6.51E*
100 I13 **Biesbos** *var.* Biesbosch. *wetland* S Netherlands
Biesbosch *see* Biesbos
101 H21 **Biesme** Namur, S Belgium *50.19N 4.43E*
103 H21 **Bietigheim-Bissingen** Baden-Württemberg, SW Germany *48.57N 9.07E*
101 I23 **Bièvre** Namur, SE Belgium *49.56N 5.01E*
81 D18 **Bifoun** Moyen-Ogooué, NW Gabon *0.15S 10.24E*
172 Pp3 **Bifuka** Hokkaidō, NE Japan *44.28N 142.20E*
142 C11 **Biga** Çanakkale, NW Turkey *40.13N 27.13E*
142 C13 **Bigadiç** Balıkesir, W Turkey *39.24N 28.07E*
28 J7 **Big Basin** *basin* Kansas, C USA
193 B20 **Big Bay** *bay* South Island, NZ
197 B12 **Big Bay** *bay* C Vanuatu
33 O5 **Big Bay de Noc** ⊚ Michigan, N USA
33 N3 **Big Bay Point** *headland* Michigan, N USA *46.51N 87.40W*
35 R10 **Big Belt Mountains** ▲ Montana, NW USA
31 N10 **Big Bend Dam** *dam* South Dakota, N USA *44.03N 99.27W*
26 K12 **Big Bend National Park** *national park* Texas, S USA
24 K5 **Big Black River** ⁓ Mississippi, S USA
29 O3 **Big Blue River** ⁓ Kansas/Nebraska, C USA
26 M10 **Big Canyon** ⁓ Texas, SW USA
35 N12 **Big Creek** Idaho, NW USA *45.05N 115.20W*
25 N8 **Big Creek Lake** ⊠ Alabama, S USA
25 X15 **Big Cypress Swamp** *wetland* Florida, SE USA
41 S9 **Big Delta** Alaska, USA *64.09N 145.50W*
32 K6 **Big Eau Pleine Reservoir** ⊠ Wisconsin, N USA
21 P5 **Bigelow Mountain** ▲ Maine, NE USA *45.09N 70.17W*
31 U3 **Big Falls** Minnesota, N USA *48.13N 93.48W*
35 P8 **Bigfork** Montana, NW USA *48.03N 114.04W*
31 U3 **Big Fork River** ⁓ Minnesota, N USA
9 S15 **Biggar** Saskatchewan, S Canada *52.03N 107.58W*
188 L3 **Bigge Island** *island* Western Australia
37 O5 **Biggs** California, W USA *39.24N 121.44W*
34 I11 **Biggs** Oregon, NW USA *45.39N 120.49W*
12 K13 **Big Gull Lake** ⊚ Ontario, SE Canada
39 P16 **Big Hachet Peak** ▲ New Mexico, SW USA *31.38N 108.24W*
35 P11 **Big Hole River** ⁓ Montana, NW USA
35 V13 **Bighorn Basin** *basin* Wyoming, C USA
35 U11 **Bighorn Lake** ⊚ Montana/Wyoming, N USA
35 W13 **Bighorn Mountains** ▲ Wyoming, C USA
38 J13 **Big Horn Peak** ▲ Arizona, SW USA *33.40N 113.01W*
35 V11 **Bighorn River** ⁓ Montana/Wyoming, NW USA
15 L5 **Big Island** *island* Nunavut, NE Canada
41 O16 **Big Koniuji Island** *island* Shumagin Islands, Alaska, USA
27 N9 **Big Lake** Texas, SW USA *31.11N 101.27W*
21 T5 **Big Lake** ⊚ Maine, NE USA
32 I3 **Big Manitou Falls** *waterfall* Wisconsin, N USA *46.32N 92.07W*
37 R2 **Big Mountain** ▲ Nevada, W USA *41.18N 119.03W*
110 G10 **Bignasco** Ticino, S Switzerland *46.21N 8.37E*
31 R16 **Big Nemaha River** ⁓ Nebraska, C USA
78 G12 **Bignona** SW Senegal *12.49N 16.16W*
Bigorra *see* Tarbes
Bigosovo *see* Bihosava
37 S10 **Big Pine** California, W USA *37.09N 118.18W*
37 Q14 **Big Pine Mountain** ▲ California, W USA *34.41N 119.37W*
29 V6 **Big Piney Creek** ⁓ Missouri, C USA
67 M24 **Big Point** *headland* N Tristan da Cunha
33 P8 **Big Rapids** Michigan, N USA *43.42N 85.28W*
32 K6 **Big Rib River** ⁓ Wisconsin, N USA
12 L14 **Big Rideau Lake** ⊚ Ontario, SE Canada
9 T14 **Big River** Saskatchewan, C Canada *53.48N 106.55W*
29 X5 **Big River** ⁓ Missouri, C USA
33 N7 **Big Sable Point** *headland* Michigan, N USA *44.03N 86.30W*
35 S7 **Big Sandy** Montana, NW USA *48.08N 110.09W*
27 W6 **Big Sandy** Texas, SW USA *32.34N 95.06W*
39 V5 **Big Sandy Creek** ⁓ Colorado, C USA
31 Q16 **Big Sandy Creek** ⁓ Nebraska, C USA
31 V5 **Big Sandy Lake** ⊚ Minnesota, N USA
38 J11 **Big Sandy River** ⁓ Arizona, SW USA
23 P5 **Big Sandy River** ⁓ S USA
25 V6 **Big Satilla Creek** ⁓ Georgia, SE USA
31 R12 **Big Sioux River** ⁓ Iowa/South Dakota, N USA
37 U7 **Big Smoky Valley** *valley* Nevada, W USA
27 N7 **Big Spring** Texas, SW USA *32.15N 101.30W*
21 Q5 **Big Squaw Mountain** ▲ Maine, NE USA *45.28N 69.42W*
23 O7 **Big Stone Gap** Virginia, NE USA *36.52N 82.45W*
31 Q8 **Big Stone Lake** ⊚ Minnesota/South Dakota, N USA
24 K4 **Big Sunflower River** ⁓ Mississippi, S USA
35 T11 **Big Timber** Montana, NW USA *45.50N 109.57W*
10 D8 **Big Trout Lake** Ontario, C Canada *53.40N 90.00W*
12 I12 **Big Trout Lake** ⊚ Ontario, SE Canada
37 O2 **Big Valley Mountains** ▲ California, W USA
27 Q13 **Big Wells** Texas, SW USA *28.34N 99.34W*
12 F11 **Bigwood** Ontario, S Canada *46.03N 80.37W*
114 D11 **Bihać** Federacija Bosna I Hercegovina, NW Bosnia and Herzegovina *44.49N 15.53E*
159 P13 **Bihār** *prev.* Behar. ◆ *state* N India
Bihār *see* Bihār Sharīf
83 F20 **Biharamulo** Kagera, NW Tanzania *2.37S 31.19E*
159 R13 **Bihārīganj** Bihār, NE India *25.43N 86.58E*
159 P14 **Bihār Sharīf** *var.* Bihār. Bihār, N India *25.13N 85.31E*
118 F10 **Bihor** ◆ *county* NW Romania
172 Q6 **Bihoro** Hokkaidō, NE Japan *43.50N 144.05E*
120 K11 **Bihosava** *Rus.* Bigosovo. Vitsyebskaya Voblasts', NW Belarus *55.50N 27.45E*
Bijagos Archipelago *see* Bijagós, Arquipélago dos
78 G13 **Bijagós, Arquipélago dos** *var.* Bijagos Archipelago. *island group* W Guinea-Bissau
161 F16 **Bījāpur** Karnātaka, C India *16.49N 75.42E*
148 K5 **Bījār** Kordestān, W Iran *35.54N 47.36E*
114 J11 **Bijeljina** Republika Srpska, NE Bosnia and Herzegovina *44.46N 19.13E*
115 K15 **Bijelo Polje** Montenegro, SW Serbia and Montenegro (Yugoslavia) *43.03N 19.44E*
166 I11 **Bijie** Guizhou, S China *27.18N 105.15E*
158 J10 **Bijnor** Uttar Pradesh, N India *29.22N 78.09E*
158 F11 **Bīkaner** Rājasthān, NW India *28.01N 73.22E*
201 V3 **Bikar Atoll** *var.* Pikaar. *atoll* Ratak Chain, N Marshall Islands
202 H3 **Bikeman** *atoll* Tungaru, W Kiribati
202 I3 **Bikenebu** Tarawa, W Kiribati
127 Nn16 **Bikin** Khabarovskiy Kray, SE Russian Federation *46.45N 134.06E*
127 Nn16 **Bikin** ⁓ SE Russian Federation
201 R3 **Bikini Atoll** *var.* Pikinni. *atoll* Ralik Chain, NW Marshall Islands
85 L17 **Bikita** Masvingo, E Zimbabwe *20.04S 31.38E*
Bīkkū Bīttī *see* Bette, Pic
81 I19 **Bikoro** Equateur, W Dem. Rep. Congo *0.45S 18.09E*
147 Z9 **Bilād Banī Bū 'Alī** NE Oman *22.01N 59.18E*
147 Z9 **Bilād Banī Bū Ḩasan** NE Oman *22.09N 59.13E*
147 X9 **Bilād Manaḩ** *var.* Manaḩ. NE Oman *22.37N 57.27E*
79 Q12 **Bilanga** C Burkina *12.35N 0.08W*
175 Q7 **Bilang, Teluk** *bay* Sulawesi, N Indonesia
158 F12 **Bilāra** Rājasthān, N India *26.14N 73.48E*
158 K10 **Bilāri** Uttar Pradesh, N India *28.37N 78.48E*
144 J5 **Bil'ās, Jabal al** ▲ C Syria
160 L11 **Bilāspur** Chhattīsgarh, C India *22.06N 82.08E*
158 I8 **Bilāspur** Himāchal Pradesh, N India *31.19N 76.46E*
173 G6 **Bila, Sungai** ⁓ Sumatera, W Indonesia
143 Y13 **Biläsuvar** *Rus.* Bilyasuvar; *prev.* Pushkino. SE Azerbaijan *39.26N 48.33E*
119 O5 **Bila Tserkva** *Rus.* Belaya Tserkov'. Kyyivs'ka Oblast', N Ukraine *49.48N 30.07E*
178 H11 **Bilauktaung Range** *var.* Thanintari Taungdan. ▲ Myanmar/Thailand
107 O2 **Bilbao** *Basq.* Bilbo. País Vasco, N Spain *43.15N 2.55W*
Bilbo *see* Bilbao
94 H2 **Bíldudalur** Vestfirdhir, NW Iceland *65.40N 23.35W*
115 I16 **Bileća** Republika Srpska, S Bosnia and Herzegovina *42.53N 18.27E*
142 E12 **Bilecik** Bilecik, NW Turkey *39.59N 29.54E*
142 F12 **Bilecik** ◆ *province* NW Turkey
118 E11 **Biled** *Ger.* Billed, *Hung.* Billéd. Timiş, W Romania *45.55N 20.55E*
113 O15 **Biłgoraj** Lubelskie, E Poland *50.32N 22.42E*
119 P11 **Bilhorod-Dnistrovs'kyy** *Rus.* Belgorod-Dnestrovskiy, *Rom.* Cetatea Albă; *prev.* Akkerman, *anc.* Tyras. Odes'ka Oblast', SW Ukraine *46.10N 30.18E*
81 M16 **Bili** Orientale, N Dem. Rep. Congo *4.07N 25.09E*
127 Oo5 **Bilibino** Chukotskiy Avtonomnyy Okrug, NE Russian Federation *67.56N 166.45E*
178 Gg8 **Bilin** Mon State, S Myanmar *17.13N 97.12E*
179 Qq12 **Biliran Island** *island* C Philippines
115 N21 **Bilisht** *var.* Bilishti. Korçë, SE Albania *40.36N 21.00E*
Bilishti *see* Bilisht
191 N10 **Billabong Creek** *var.* Moulamein Creek. *seasonal river* New South Wales, SE Australia
190 G4 **Billa Kalina** South Australia *29.57S 136.13E*
207 Q17 **Bill Baileys Bank** *undersea feature* N Atlantic Ocean *60.34N 10.15W*
Billed/Billéd *see* Biled
159 N14 **Billi** Uttar Pradesh, N India *24.30N 82.58E*
99 M15 **Billingham** N England, UK *54.36N 1.16W*
35 U11 **Billings** Montana, NW USA *45.47N 108.32W*
97 J16 **Billingsfors** Västra Götaland, S Sweden *58.57N 12.14E*
Bill of Cape Clear, The *see* Clear, Cape
30 L9 **Billsburg** South Dakota, N USA *44.22N 101.40W*
97 F23 **Billund** Ribe, W Denmark *55.43N 9.07E*
38 L11 **Bill Williams Mountain** ▲ Arizona, SW USA *35.12N 112.12W*
38 I12 **Bill Williams River** ⁓ Arizona, SW USA
79 Y8 **Bilma** Agadez, NE Niger *18.22N 13.01E*
79 Y8 **Bilma, Grand Erg de** *desert* NE Niger
189 Y9 **Biloela** Queensland, E Australia *24.27S 150.31E*
114 G8 **Bilo Gora** ▲ N Croatia
119 U13 **Bilohirs'k** *Rus.* Belogorsk; *prev.* Karasubazar. Respublika Krym, S Ukraine *45.01N 34.45E*
118 M3 **Bilokorovychi** *Rus.* Belokorovichi. Zhytomyrs'ka Oblast', N Ukraine *51.07N 28.02E*
119 X5 **Bilokurakine** Luhans'ka Oblast', E Ukraine *49.32N 38.44E*
119 T3 **Bilopillya** *Rus.* Belopol'ye. Sums'ka Oblast', NE Ukraine *51.09N 34.16E*
119 Y6 **Bilovods'k** *Rus.* Belovodsk. Luhans'ka Oblast', E Ukraine *49.10N 39.34E*
24 M9 **Biloxi** Mississippi, S USA *30.24N 88.53W*
119 R10 **Bilozerka** Khersons'ka Oblast', S Ukraine *46.36N 32.23E*
119 W7 **Bilozers'ke** Donets'ka Oblast', E Ukraine *48.29N 37.03E*
100 J11 **Bilthoven** Utrecht, C Netherlands *52.07N 5.12E*
80 K9 **Biltine** Biltine, E Chad *14.30N 20.52E*
80 J9 **Biltine** *off.* Préfecture de Biltine. ◆ *prefecture* E Chad
168 D5 **Biluu** Bayan-Ölgiy, W Mongolia *48.54N 89.40E*
Bilwi *see* Puerto Cabezas
Bilyasuvar *see* Biläsuvar
119 O11 **Bilyayivka** Odes'ka Oblast', SW Ukraine *46.28N 30.11E*
101 K18 **Bilzen** Limburg, NE Belgium *50.52N 5.31E*
Bimbéréké *see* Bembèrèkè
191 R10 **Bimberi Peak** ▲ New South Wales, SE Australia *35.42S 148.46E*
79 Q15 **Bimbila** E Ghana *8.54N 0.04E*
81 I15 **Bimbo** Ombella-Mpoko, SW Central African Republic *4.19N 18.27E*
46 F2 **Bimini Islands** *island group* W Bahamas
160 I9 **Bīna** Madhya Pradesh, C India *24.09N 78.10E*
149 T4 **Bīnālūd, Kūh-e** ▲ NE Iran
101 F20 **Binche** Hainaut, S Belgium *50.25N 4.10E*
Bindloe Island *see* Marchena, Isla
85 L16 **Bindura** Mashonaland Central, NE Zimbabwe *17.18S 31.13E*
107 T5 **Binefar** Aragón, NE Spain *41.51N 0.16E*
85 J16 **Binga** Matabeleland North, W Zimbabwe *17.42S 27.21E*
191 T5 **Bingara** New South Wales, SE Australia *29.54S 150.36E*
103 F18 **Bingen am Rhein** Rheinland-Pfalz, SW Germany *49.58N 7.54E*
28 M11 **Binger** Oklahoma, C USA *35.19N 98.19W*
Bingerau *see* Węgrów
Bin Ghalfān, Jazā'ir *see* Ḩalāniyāt, Juzur al
21 Q6 **Bingham** Maine, NE USA *45.01N 69.51W*
20 H11 **Binghamton** New York, NE USA *42.06N 75.55W*
Bin Ghanīmah, Jabal *see* Bin Ghunaymah, Jabal
77 P11 **Bin Ghunaymah, Jabal** *var.* Jabal Bin Ghanīmah. ▲ C Libya
145 U3 **Bingird** NE Iraq *36.03N 45.03E*
Bingmei *see* Congjiang
143 P14 **Bingöl** Bingöl, E Turkey *38.54N 40.28E*
143 P14 **Bingöl** ◆ *province* E Turkey
167 R6 **Binhai** *var.* Binhai Xian. Dongkan. Jiangsu, E China *34.03N 119.46E*
Binhai Xian *see* Binhai
178 Kk12 **Binh Đinh** *var.* An Nhon. Binh Đinh, C Vietnam *13.52N 109.07E*
178 Kk10 **Binh Sơn** *var.* Châu Ô. Quang Ngai, C Vietnam *15.18N 108.45E*
Binimani *see* Bintimani
173 Ff5 **Binjai** Sumatera, W Indonesia *3.37N 98.30E*
191 R6 **Binnaway** New South Wales, SE Australia *31.34S 149.24E*
110 E6 **Binningen** Basel-Land, NW Switzerland *47.31N 7.34E*
175 R13 **Binongko, Pulau** *island* Kepulauan Tukangbesi, C Indonesia
174 Gg3 **Bintang, Banjaran** ▲ Peninsular Malaysia
174 I7 **Bintan, Pulau** *island* Kepulauan Riau, W Indonesia
78 J14 **Bintimani** *var.* Binimani. ▲ NE Sierra Leone *9.21N 11.09W*
Bint Jubayl *see* Bent Jbaïl
174 M5 **Bintulu** Sarawak, East Malaysia *3.12N 113.01E*
176 Vv10 **Bintuni** *prev.* Steenkool. Papua, E Indonesia *2.03S 133.45E*
176 Vv10 **Bintuni, Teluk** *bay* Papua, E Indonesia
169 W8 **Binxian** Heilongjiang, NE China *45.43N 127.24E*
166 K14 **Binyang** *var.* Binzhou. Guangxi Zhuangzu Zizhiqu, S China *23.15N 108.47E*
167 Q4 **Binzhou** Shandong, E China *37.22N 118.03E*
Binzhou *see* Binyang
65 G14 **Bío Bío** *off.* Región del Bío Bío. ◆ *region* C Chile
65 G14 **Bío Bío, Río** ⁓ C Chile
81 C16 **Bioco, Isla de** *var.* Bioko, *Eng.* Fernando Po, *Sp.* Fernando Póo; *prev.* Macías Nguema Biyogo. *island* NW Equatorial Guinea
114 D13 **Biograd na Moru** *It.* Zaravecchia. Zadar, SW Croatia *43.57N 15.27E*
Bioko *see* Bioco, Isla de
115 F14 **Biokovo** ▲ S Croatia
Biorra *see* Birr
Bipontium *see* Zweibrücken
149 W13 **Birag, Kūh-e** ▲ SE Iran
77 O10 **Birāk** *var.* Brak. C Libya *27.31N 14.16E*
145 S10 **Bi'r al Islām** C Iraq *32.15N 43.40E*
160 N11 **Biramitrapur** Orissa, E India *22.24N 84.42E*
145 T11 **Bi'r an Nişf** S Iraq *31.22N 44.07E*
80 L12 **Birao** Vakaga, NE Central African Republic *10.14N 22.49E*
152 J10 **Birata** *Rus.* Darganata, Dargan-Ata. Lebap Welaýaty, NE Turkmenistan *40.30N 62.09E*
164 M6 **Biratar Bulak** *well* NW China *42.00N 90.26E*
159 R12 **Birātnagar** Eastern, SE Nepal *26.28N 87.16E*
172 Oo6 **Biratori** Hokkaidō, NE Japan *42.35N 142.07E*
41 S8 **Birch Creek** Alaska, USA *66.17N 145.54W*
40 M11 **Birch Creek** ⁓ Alaska, USA
9 T14 **Birch Hills** Saskatchewan, S Canada *52.58N 105.22W*
190 M10 **Birchip** Victoria, SE Australia *36.01S 142.55E*
31 X4 **Birch Lake** ⊚ Minnesota, N USA
9 Q11 **Birch Mountains** ▲ Alberta, W Canada
9 V15 **Birch River** Manitoba, S Canada *52.22N 101.03W*
46 H12 **Birchs Hill** *hill* W Jamaica *18.27N 78.05W*
41 R11 **Birchwood** Alaska, USA *61.24N 149.28W*
196 I5 **Bird Island** *island* S Northern Mariana Islands
143 N16 **Birecik** Şanlıurfa, S Turkey *37.02N 38.01E*
158 M10 **Birendranagar** *var.* Surkhet. Mid Western, W Nepal *28.35N 81.36E*
Bir es Saba *see* Be'ér Sheva'
76 A12 **Bir-Gandouz** SW Western Sahara *21.35N 16.27W*
159 P12 **Birganj** Central, C Nepal *27.03N 84.53E*
83 B14 **Biri** ⁓ W Sudan
Bi'r Ibn Hirmās *see* Al Bi'r
176 Yy10 **Biri, Sungai** ⁓ Papua, E Indonesia
149 U8 **Birjand** Khorāsān, E Iran *32.54N 59.13E*
145 T11 **Birkat Ḩāmid** *well* S Iraq *31.16N 44.04E*
97 F18 **Birkeland** Aust-Agder, S Norway *58.18N 8.13E*
103 E19 **Birkenfeld** Rheinland-Pfalz, SW Germany *49.39N 7.09E*
99 K18 **Birkenhead** NW England, UK *53.24N 3.01W*
111 W7 **Birkfeld** Steiermark, SE Austria *47.21N 15.40E*
190 A2 **Birksgate Range** ▲ South Australia
Bîrlad *see* Bârlad
99 K20 **Birmingham** C England, UK *52.30N 1.49W*
25 P4 **Birmingham** Alabama, S USA *33.30N 86.47W*
99 M20 **Birmingham** ✕ C England, UK *52.27N 1.46W*
Bir Moghreïn *see* Bîr Mogreïn
78 J4 **Bîr Mogreïn** *var.* Bir Moghreïn; *prev.* Fort-Trinquet. Tiris Zemmour, N Mauritania *25.10N 11.34W*
203 S4 **Birnie Island** *atoll* Phoenix Islands, C Kiribati
Birni-Ngaouré *see* Birnin Gaouré
79 S12 **Birnin Gaouré** *var.* Birni-Ngaouré. Dosso, SW Niger *12.59N 3.02E*
79 S12 **Birnin Kebbi** Kebbi, NW Nigeria *12.28N 4.08E*
Birni-Nkonni *see* Birnin Konni
79 T12 **Birnin Konni** *var.* Birni-Nkonni. Tahoua, SW Niger *13.50N 5.14E*
79 W13 **Birnin Kudu** Jigawa, N Nigeria *11.28N 9.29E*
127 N16 **Birobidzhan** Yevreyskaya Avtonomnaya Oblast', SE Russian Federation *48.41N 132.55E*
99 D18 **Birr** *var.* Parsonstown, *Ir.* Biorra. C Ireland *53.06N 7.54W*
191 P4 **Birrie River** ⁓ New South Wales/Queensland, SE Australia
110 D7 **Birse** ⁓ NW Switzerland
Birsen *see* Biržai
110 E6 **Birsfelden** Basel-Land, NW Switzerland *47.33N 7.37E*
131 U4 **Birsk** Respublika Bashkortostan, W Russian Federation *55.24N 55.33E*
121 F14 **Birštonas** Kaunas, C Lithuania *54.37N 24.00E*
165 P14 **Biru** Xinjiang Uygur Zizhiqu, W China *31.30N 93.55E*
Biruni *see* Beruniy
126 Ii14 **Biryusa** ⁓ C Russian Federation
126 Ii14 **Biryusinsk** Irkutskaya Oblast', C Russian Federation *55.52N 97.48E*
120 G10 **Biržai** *Ger.* Birsen. Panevėžys, NE Lithuania *56.12N 24.47E*
123 Jj17 **Birżebbuġa** SE Malta *35.50N 14.32E*
Bisanthe *see* Tekirdağ
175 T9 **Bisa, Pulau** *island* Maluku, E Indonesia
39 N17 **Bisbee** Arizona, SW USA *31.27N 109.55W*
31 O2 **Bisbee** North Dakota, N USA *48.36N 99.21W*
Biscaia, Baía de *see* Biscay, Bay of
104 I13 **Biscarrosse et de Parentis, Étang de** ⊚ SW France
106 M1 **Biscay, Bay of** *Sp.* Golfo de Vizcaya, *Port.* Baía de Biscaia. *bay* France/Spain
25 Z16 **Biscayne Bay** *bay* Florida, SE USA
66 M7 **Biscay Plain** *undersea feature* SE Bay of Biscay
109 N17 **Bisceglie** Puglia, SE Italy *41.13N 16.31E*
Bischofflack *see* Škofja Loka
Bischofsburg *see* Biskupiec
111 Q7 **Bischofshofen** Salzburg, NW Austria *47.25N 13.13E*
103 P15 **Bischofswerda** Sachsen, E Germany *51.07N 14.13E*
105 V5 **Bischwiller** Bas-Rhin, NE France *48.46N 7.52E*
23 T10 **Biscoe** North Carolina, SE USA *35.20N 79.46W*
204 G5 **Biscoe Islands** *island group* Antarctica
12 E9 **Biscotasi Lake** ⊚ Ontario, S Canada
12 E9 **Biscotasing** Ontario, S Canada *47.16N 82.04W*
56 J6 **Biscucuy** Portuguesa, NW Venezuela *9.22N 69.58W*
116 K11 **Biser** Khaskovo, S Bulgaria *41.52N 25.58E*
115 D15 **Biševo** *It.* Busi. *island* SW Croatia
147 N12 **Bīshah, Wādī** *dry watercourse* C Saudi Arabia
153 U7 **Bishkek** *var.* Pishpek; *prev.* Frunze. ● (Kyrgyzstan) Chuyskaya Oblast', N Kyrgyzstan *42.53N 74.26E*
153 U7 **Bishkek** ✕ Chuyskaya Oblast', N Kyrgyzstan *42.55N 74.37E*
159 R16 **Bishnupur** West Bengal, NE India *23.04N 87.19E*
85 J25 **Bisho** Eastern Cape, S South Africa *32.46S 27.21E*
37 S9 **Bishop** California, W USA *37.22N 118.24W*
27 S15 **Bishop** Texas, SW USA *27.36N 97.49W*
99 L15 **Bishop Auckland** N England, UK *54.40N 1.40W*
Bishop's Lynn *see* King's Lynn
99 O21 **Bishop's Stortford** E England, UK *51.45N 0.12E*
23 S12 **Bishopville** South Carolina, SE USA *34.13N 80.15W*
144 M5 **Bishrī, Jabal** ▲ E Syria
169 U4 **Bishui** Heilongjiang, NE China *52.06N 123.42E*
83 G17 **Bisina, Lake** *prev.* Lake Salisbury. ⊚ E Uganda
Biskara *see* Biskra
76 L6 **Biskra** *var.* Beskra, Biskara. NE Algeria *34.51N 5.44E*
112 M8 **Biskupiec** *Ger.* Bischofsburg. Warmińsko-Mazurskie, NE Poland *53.51N 20.56E*
179 Rr15 **Bislig** Mindanao, S Philippines *8.10N 126.18E*
29 X6 **Bismarck** Missouri, C USA *37.46N 90.37W*
30 M5 **Bismarck** *state capital* North Dakota, N USA *46.48N 100.46W*
194 K9 **Bismarck Archipelago** *island group* NE PNG
133 Z16 **Bismarck Plate** *tectonic feature* W Pacific Ocean
194 I12 **Bismarck Range** ▲ N PNG
194 J10 **Bismarck Sea** *sea* W Pacific Ocean
143 P15 **Bismil** Dıyarbakır, SE Turkey *37.52N 40.37E*
45 N6 **Bismuna, Laguna** *lagoon* NE Nicaragua
Bisnulok *see* Phitsanulok
175 T6 **Bisoa, Tanjung** *headland* Pulau Halmahera, N Indonesia *2.15N 127.57E*
30 K7 **Bison** South Dakota, N USA *45.30N 102.25W*
95 H17 **Bispfors** Jämtland, C Sweden *63.00N 16.40E*
78 G13 **Bissau** ● (Guinea-Bissau) W Guinea-Bissau *11.52N 15.39W*
78 G13 **Bissau** ✕ W Guinea-Bissau *11.53N 15.41W*
101 M24 **Bissen** Luxembourg, C Luxembourg *49.46N 6.04E*
Bissojohka *see* Børselv
78 G12 **Bissorã** W Guinea-Bissau *12.16N 15.34W*
9 O10 **Bistcho Lake** ⊚ Alberta, W Canada
24 G5 **Bistineau, Lake** ⊠ Louisiana, S USA
Bistrica *see* Ilirska Bistrica
118 I9 **Bistriţa** *Ger.* Bistritz, *Hung.* Beszterce; *prev.* Nösen. Bistriţa-Năsăud, N Romania *47.10N 24.30E*
118 K10 **Bistriţa** *Ger.* Bistritz. ⁓ NE Romania
118 I9 **Bistriţa-Năsăud** ◆ *county* N Romania
Bistritz *see* Bistriţa
Bistritz ober Pernstein *see* Bystřice nad Pernštejnem
158 L11 **Biswān** Uttar Pradesh, N India *27.30N 81.00E*
112 M7 **Bisztynek** Warmińsko-Mazurskie, NE Poland *54.05N 20.53E*
81 E17 **Bitam** Woleu-Ntem, N Gabon *2.04N 11.30E*
103 D18 **Bitburg** Rheinland-Pfalz, SW Germany *49.57N 6.31E*
105 U4 **Bitche** Moselle, NE France *49.01N 7.27E*
80 I11 **Bitkine** Guéra, C Chad *11.58N 18.13E*
143 R15 **Bitlis** Bitlis, SE Turkey *38.22N 42.04E*
143 R14 **Bitlis** ◆ *province* E Turkey
Bitoeng *see* Bitung
115 N20 **Bitola** *Turk.* Monastir; *prev.* Bitolj. S FYR Macedonia *41.01N 21.21E*
Bitolj *see* Bitola
109 O17 **Bitonto** *anc.* Butuntum. Puglia, SE Italy *41.07N 16.40E*
79 Q13 **Bitou** *var.* Bittou. SE Burkina *11.19N 0.16W*
161 C20 **Bitra Island** *island* Lakshadweep, India, N Indian Ocean
103 M14 **Bitterfeld** Sachsen-Anhalt, E Germany *51.36N 12.18E*
34 O9 **Bitterroot Range** ▲ Idaho/Montana, NW USA
35 P10 **Bitterroot River** ⁓ Montana, NW USA
109 D18 **Bitti** Sardegna, Italy, C Mediterranean Sea *40.30N 9.31E*
Bittou *see* Bitou
175 S7 **Bitung** *prev.* Bitoeng. Sulawesi, C Indonesia *1.28N 125.13E*
62 I12 **Bituruna** Paraná, S Brazil *26.11S 51.34W*
79 Y13 **Biu** Borno, E Nigeria *10.35N 12.13E*
Biumba *see* Byumba
171 H14 **Biwa-ko** ⊚ Honshū, SW Japan
176 Y13 **Biwarlaut** Papua, E Indonesia *5.44S 138.14E*
29 P10 **Bixby** Oklahoma, C USA *35.56N 95.52W*
126 H15 **Biya** ⁓ S Russian Federation
Biy-Khem *see* Bol'shoy Yenisey
126 H15 **Biysk** Altayskiy Kray, S Russian Federation *52.34N 85.09E*
170 Ff14 **Bizen** Okayama, Honshū, SW Japan *34.43N 134.10E*
Bizerta *see* Bizerte
123 K11 **Bizerte** *Ar.* Banzart, *Eng.* Bizerta. N Tunisia *37.18N 9.48E*
Bizkaia *see* Vizcaya
94 G2 **Bjargtangar** *headland* W Iceland *63.30N 24.28W*
Bjärnå *see* Perniö
97 K22 **Bjärnum** Skåne, S Sweden *56.15N 13.45E*
95 I16 **Bjästa** Västernorrland, C Sweden *63.12N 18.30E*
115 I14 **Bjelašnica** ▲ SE Bosnia and Herzegovina *43.13N 18.18E*
114 C10 **Bjelolasica** ▲ NW Croatia *45.13N 14.56E*
114 F8 **Bjelovar** *Hung.* Belovár. Bjelovar-Bilogora, N Croatia *45.54N 16.49E*
114 F8 **Bjelovar-Bilogora** *off.* Bjelovarsko-Bilogorska Županija. ◆ *province* NE Croatia
Bjelovarsko-Bilogorska Županija *see* Bjelovar-Bilogora
94 H10 **Bjerkvik** Nordland, C Norway *68.31N 16.08E*
97 G21 **Bjerringbro** Viborg, NW Denmark *56.22N 9.40E*
Bjeshkët e Namuna *see* North Albanian Alps
97 L14 **Björbo** Dalarna, C Sweden *60.28N 14.44E*
97 I15 **Bjørkelangen** Akershus, S Norway *59.52N 11.34E*
97 O14 **Björklinge** Uppsala, C Sweden *60.03N 17.33E*
95 I14 **Björkselse** Västerbotten, N Sweden *64.58N 18.30E*
95 I16 **Björna** Västernorrland, C Sweden *63.34N 18.38E*
97 C14 **Bjørnafjorden** *fjord* S Norway
97 L16 **Björneborg** Värmland, C Sweden *59.13N 14.15E*
Björneborg *see* Pori
97 E14 **Bjornesfjorden** ⊚ S Norway
94 M9 **Bjørnevatn** Finnmark, N Norway *69.40N 29.57E*
207 T13 **Bjørnøya** *Eng.* Bear Island. *island* N Norway
95 I15 **Bjurholm** Västerbotten, N Sweden *63.57N 19.16E*
97 J22 **Bjuv** Skåne, S Sweden *56.04N 12.57E*
78 M12 **Bla** Ségou, W Mali *12.58N 5.45W*
189 W8 **Blackall** Queensland, E Australia *24.25S 145.31E*
31 V2 **Black Bay** *lake bay* Minnesota, N USA
29 N9 **Black Bear Creek** ⁓ Oklahoma, C USA
99 K17 **Blackburn** NW England, UK *53.45N 2.28W*
47 W10 **Blackburne** ✕ (Plymouth) E Montserrat *16.45N 62.09W*
41 T11 **Blackburn, Mount** ▲ Alaska, USA *61.43N 143.25W*
37 N5 **Black Butte Lake** ⊠ California, W USA
204 J5 **Black Coast** *physical region* Antarctica
9 Q16 **Black Diamond** Alberta, SW Canada *50.42N 114.09W*
20 K11 **Black Dome** ▲ New York, NE USA *42.16N 74.07W*
115 L18 **Black Drin** *Alb.* Lumi i Drinit të Zi, *SCr.* Crni Drim. ⁓ Albania/FYR Macedonia
10 D6 **Black Duck** ⁓ Ontario, C Canada
31 U4 **Blackduck** Minnesota, N USA *47.45N 94.33W*
35 R14 **Blackfoot** Idaho, NW USA *43.11N 112.20W*
35 P9 **Blackfoot River** ⁓ Montana, NW USA
Black Forest *see* Schwarzwald
30 J10 **Blackhawk** South Dakota, N USA *44.09N 103.18W*
30 I10 **Black Hills** ▲ South Dakota/Wyoming, N USA
9 T10 **Black Lake** ⊚ Saskatchewan, C Canada
33 Q5 **Black Lake** ⊚ Michigan, N USA
20 I7 **Black Lake** ⊚ New York, NE USA
24 G6 **Black Lake** ⊠ Louisiana, S USA
28 F7 **Black Mesa** ▲ Oklahoma, C USA *37.00N 103.07W*
23 P10 **Black Mountain** North Carolina, SE USA *35.37N 82.19W*
37 P13 **Black Mountain** ▲ California, W USA *35.22N 120.21W*
39 Q2 **Black Mountain** ▲ Colorado, C USA *40.47N 107.23W*
23 O7 **Black Mountain** ▲ Kentucky, E USA *36.54N 82.53W*
98 K1 **Black Mountains** ▲ SE Wales, UK
38 H10 **Black Mountains** ▲ Arizona, SW USA
35 Q16 **Black Pine Peak** ▲ Idaho, NW USA *42.07N 113.07W*
99 K17 **Blackpool** NW England, UK *53.49N 3.03W*

◆ Country ● Country Capital ◇ Dependent Territory ○ Dependent Territory Capital ◆ Administrative Region ✕ International Airport ▲ Mountain ▲ Mountain Range ⛰ Volcano ⁓ River ⊚ Lake ⊠ Reservoir

233

Black Range – Bombarral

39 Q14 **Black Range** ▲ New Mexico, SW USA
46 I12 **Black River** W Jamaica *18.01N 77.52W*
12 J14 **Black River** ≈ Ontario, SE Canada
133 U12 **Black River** *Chin.* Babian Jiang, Lixian Jiang, *Fr.* Rivière Noire, *Vtn.* Sông Đa. ≈ China/Vietnam
46 I12 **Black River** ≈ W Jamaica
41 T7 **Black River** ≈ Alaska, USA
39 N13 **Black River** ≈ Arizona, SW USA
29 X7 **Black River** ≈ Arkansas/Missouri, C USA
24 I7 **Black River** ≈ Louisiana, S USA
33 S8 **Black River** ≈ Michigan, N USA
33 Q5 **Black River** ≈ Michigan, N USA
20 I8 **Black River** ≈ New York, NE USA
23 T13 **Black River** ≈ South Carolina, SE USA
32 J7 **Black River** ≈ Wisconsin, N USA
32 J7 **Black River Falls** Wisconsin, N USA *44.18N 90.51W*
37 R3 **Black Rock Desert** *desert* Nevada, W USA
Black Sand Desert *see* Garagum
23 S7 **Blacksburg** Virginia, NE USA *37.16N 80.24W*
142 H10 **Black Sea** *var.* Euxine Sea, *Bul.* Cherno More, *Rom.* Marea Neagră, *Rus.* Chernoye More, *Turk.* Karadeniz, *Ukr.* Chorne More. *sea* Asia/Europe
119 Q10 **Black Sea Lowland** *Ukr.* Prychornomors'ka Nyzovyna. *depression* SE Europe
35 S17 **Blacks Fork** ≈ Wyoming, C USA
25 V7 **Blackshear** Georgia, SE USA *31.18N 82.14W*
25 S6 **Blackshear, Lake** ⊠ Georgia, SE USA
99 A16 **Blacksod Bay** *Ir.* Cuan an Fhóid Duibh. *inlet* W Ireland
23 V7 **Blackstone** Virginia, NE USA *37.04N 78.00W*
79 O14 **Black Volta** *var.* Borongo, Mouhoun, Moun Hou, *Fr.* Volta Noire. ≈ W Africa
25 O5 **Black Warrior River** ≈ Alabama, S USA
189 X8 **Blackwater** Queensland, E Australia *23.34S 148.51E*
99 D20 **Blackwater** *Ir.* An Abhainn Mhór. ≈ S Ireland
29 T4 **Blackwater River** ≈ Missouri, C USA
23 W7 **Blackwater River** ≈ Virginia, NE USA
Blackwater State *see* Nebraska
24 N8 **Blackwell** Oklahoma, C USA *36.48N 97.16W*
27 P7 **Blackwell** Texas, SW USA *32.05N 100.19W*
101 J15 **Bladel** Noord-Brabant, S Netherlands *51.22N 5.13E*
Bladenmarkt *see* Bălăuşeri
116 G11 **Blagoevgrad** *prev.* Gorna Dzhumaya. Blagoevgrad, SW Bulgaria *42.01N 23.04E*
116 G11 **Blagoevgrad** ◈ *province* SW Bulgaria
126 Gg14 **Blagoveshchenka** Altayskiy Kray, S Russian Federation *52.49N 79.54E*
126 M16 **Blagoveshchensk** Amurskaya Oblast', SE Russian Federation *50.19N 127.30E*
131 V4 **Blagoveshchensk** Respublika Bashkortostan, W Russian Federation *55.03N 56.01E*
104 I7 **Blain** Loire-Atlantique, NW France *47.26N 1.47W*
31 V8 **Blaine** Minnesota, N USA *45.09N 93.13W*
34 H6 **Blaine** Washington, NW USA *48.59N 122.45W*
9 T15 **Blaine Lake** Saskatchewan, S Canada *52.49N 106.48W*
31 S14 **Blair** Nebraska, C USA *41.32N 96.07W*
98 J10 **Blairgowrie** C Scotland, UK *56.18N 3.24W*
20 C15 **Blairsville** Pennsylvania, NE USA *40.25N 79.12W*
118 H11 **Blaj** *Ger.* Blasendorf, *Hung.* Balázsfalva. Alba, SW Romania *46.10N 23.56E*
66 F9 **Blake-Bahama Ridge** *undersea feature* W Atlantic Ocean
25 S7 **Blakely** Georgia, SE USA *31.22N 84.55W*
66 E10 **Blake Plateau** *var.* Blake Terrace. *undersea feature* W Atlantic Ocean
32 M1 **Blake Point** *headland* Michigan, N USA *48.11N 88.25W*
Blake Terrace *see* Blake Plateau
63 B24 **Blanca, Bahía** *bay* E Argentina
58 C12 **Blanca, Cordillera** ▲▲ W Peru
107 T12 **Blanca, Costa** *physical region* SE Spain
39 S7 **Blanca Peak** ▲ Colorado, C USA *37.34N 105.29W*
26 I9 **Blanca, Sierra** ▲ Texas, SW USA *31.15N 105.26W*
123 K11 **Blanc, Cap** *headland* N Tunisia *37.20N 9.41E*
Blanc, Cap *see* Nouâdhibou, Râs
33 R12 **Blanchard River** ≈ Ohio, N USA
190 E8 **Blanche, Cape** *headland* South Australia *33.03S 134.10E*
195 U15 **Blanche Channel** *channel* NW Solomon Islands
190 J4 **Blanche, Lake** ◎ South Australia
33 R14 **Blanchester** Ohio, N USA *39.17N 83.59W*
190 J9 **Blanchetown** South Australia *34.21S 139.36E*
47 U13 **Blanchisseuse** Trinidad, Trinidad and Tobago *10.47N 61.18W*
105 T11 **Blanc, Mont** *It.* Monte Bianco. ▲ France/Italy *45.45N 6.51E*
27 R11 **Blanco** Texas, SW USA *30.06N 98.25W*
44 K14 **Blanco, Cabo** *headland* NW Costa Rica *9.34N 85.06W*
34 D14 **Blanco, Cape** *headland* Oregon, NW USA *42.49N 124.33W*
64 H10 **Blanco, Río** ≈ W Argentina
58 F10 **Blanco, Río** ≈ NE Peru
13 O9 **Blanc, Réservoir** ⊠ Québec, SE Canada
23 R7 **Bland** Virginia, NE USA *37.06N 81.07W*
94 I2 **Blanda** ≈ N Iceland
39 O7 **Blanding** Utah, W USA *37.37N 109.28W*
107 X5 **Blanes** Cataluña, NE Spain *41.40N 2.48E*
105 N3 **Blangy-sur-Bresle** Seine-Maritime, N France *49.55N 1.37E*
113 C18 **Blanice** *Ger.* Blanitz. ≈ SE Czech Republic
Blanitz *see* Blanice
101 C16 **Blankenberge** West-Vlaanderen, NW Belgium *51.19N 3.07E*
103 D17 **Blankenheim** Nordrhein-Westfalen, W Germany *50.25N 6.41E*
27 R8 **Blanket** Texas, SW USA *31.49N 98.47W*
57 O3 **Blanquilla, Isla** *var.* La Blanquilla. *island* N Venezuela
Blanquilla, La *see* Blanquilla, Isla
63 F18 **Blanquillo** Durazno, C Uruguay *32.52S 55.37W*
113 G18 **Blansko** *Ger.* Blanz. Jihomoravský Kraj, SE Czech Republic *49.22N 16.39E*
85 N15 **Blantyre** *var.* Blantyre-Limbe. Southern, S Malawi *15.45S 35.03E*
85 N15 **Blantyre** ✈ Southern, S Malawi *15.34S 35.03E*
Blantyre-Limbe *see* Blantyre
Blanz *see* Blansko
100 J10 **Blaricum** Noord-Holland, C Netherlands *52.16N 5.15E*
Blasendorf *see* Blaj
Blatnitsa *see* Durankulak
115 F15 **Blato** *It.* Blatta. Dubrovnik-Neretva, S Croatia *42.57N 16.47E*
Blatta *see* Blato
110 E10 **Blatten** Valais, SW Switzerland *46.22N 8.00E*
103 J20 **Blaufelden** Baden-Württemberg, SW Germany *49.21N 10.01E*
97 E23 **Blåvands Huk** *headland* W Denmark *55.33N 8.04E*
104 G6 **Blavet** ≈ NW France
104 J12 **Blaye** Gironde, SW France *45.07N 0.36W*
191 R8 **Blayney** New South Wales, SE Australia *33.33S 149.13E*
67 D25 **Bleaker Island** *island* SE Falkland Islands
111 T10 **Bled** *Ger.* Veldes. NW Slovenia *46.23N 14.06E*
101 D20 **Bléharies** Hainaut, SW Belgium *50.31N 3.25E*
111 U9 **Bleiburg** *Slvn.* Pliberk. Kärnten, S Austria *46.36N 14.49E*
103 L17 **Bleiloch-Stausee** ⊠ C Germany
100 H12 **Bleiswijk** Zuid-Holland, W Netherlands *52.01N 4.31E*
97 L22 **Blekinge** ◈ *county* S Sweden
12 D17 **Blenheim** Ontario, S Canada *42.19N 81.58W*
193 K15 **Blenheim** Marlborough, South Island, NZ *41.31S 174.00E*
101 M15 **Blerick** Limburg, SE Netherlands *51.22N 6.10E*
Blesae *see* Blois
27 V13 **Blessing** Texas, SW USA *28.52N 96.12W*
12 I10 **Bleu, Lac** ◎ Québec, SE Canada
Blibba *see* Blitta
123 I11 **Blida** *var.* El Boulaida, El Boulaïda. N Algeria *36.32N 2.49E*
97 P15 **Blidö** Stockholm, C Sweden *59.37N 18.55E*
97 K18 **Blidsberg** Västra Götaland, S Sweden *57.55N 13.30E*
193 A21 **Bligh Sound** *sound* South Island, NZ
197 H13 **Bligh Water** *strait* NW Fiji
12 D11 **Blind River** Ontario, S Canada *46.11N 82.55W*
33 R11 **Blissfield** Michigan, N USA *41.49N 83.51W*
174 Ll16 **Blitar** Jawa, C Indonesia *8.06S 112.12E*
79 R15 **Blitta** *prev.* Blibba. C Togo *8.19N 0.58E*
21 O13 **Block Island** *island* Rhode Island, NE USA
21 O13 **Block Island Sound** *sound* Rhode Island, NE USA
100 H10 **Bloemendaal** Noord-Holland, W Netherlands *52.23N 4.39E*
85 H23 **Bloemfontein** *var.* Mangaung. ● (South Africa-judicial capital) Free State, C South Africa *29.07S 26.13E*
85 I22 **Bloemhof** North-West, NW South Africa *27.38S 25.33E*
104 M7 **Blois** *anc.* Blesae. Loir-et-Cher, C France *47.36N 1.19E*
100 L8 **Blokzijl** Overijssel, N Netherlands *52.46N 5.58E*
97 N20 **Blomstermåla** Kalmar, S Sweden *56.58N 16.19E*
94 I2 **Blönduós** Nordhurland Vestra, N Iceland *65.39N 20.15W*
112 L11 **Błonie** Mazowieckie, C Poland *52.13N 20.36E*
99 C14 **Bloody Foreland** *Ir.* Cnoc Fola. *headland* NW Ireland *55.09N 8.18W*
33 N15 **Bloomfield** Indiana, N USA *39.01N 86.58W*
31 X16 **Bloomfield** Iowa, C USA *40.45N 92.24W*
29 Y8 **Bloomfield** Missouri, C USA *36.53N 89.55W*
39 P9 **Bloomfield** New Mexico, SW USA *36.42N 108.00W*
27 U7 **Blooming Grove** Texas, SW USA *32.05N 96.43W*
31 W10 **Blooming Prairie** Minnesota, N USA *43.52N 93.03W*
32 L13 **Bloomington** Illinois, N USA *40.28N 88.59W*
33 O15 **Bloomington** Indiana, N USA *39.10N 86.31W*
31 V9 **Bloomington** Minnesota, N USA *44.50N 93.18W*
27 U13 **Bloomington** Texas, SW USA *28.39N 96.53W*
20 H14 **Bloomsburg** Pennsylvania, NE USA *40.58N 76.27W*
189 X7 **Bloomsbury** Queensland, NE Australia *20.46S 148.34E*
174 Ll14 **Blora** Jawa, C Indonesia *6.55S 111.28E*
20 G12 **Blossburg** Pennsylvania, NE USA *41.38N 77.00W*
27 V5 **Blossom** Texas, SW USA *33.39N 95.23W*
127 Oo3 **Blossom, Mys** *headland* Ostrov Vrangelya, NE Russian Federation *70.49N 178.49E*
25 R8 **Blountstown** Florida, SE USA *30.26N 85.03W*
23 P8 **Blountville** Tennessee, S USA *36.31N 82.19W*
23 Q9 **Blowing Rock** North Carolina, SE USA *36.15N 81.53W*
110 J8 **Bludenz** Vorarlberg, W Austria *47.10N 9.49E*
38 L6 **Blue Bell Knoll** ▲ Utah, W USA *38.11N 111.31W*
25 Y12 **Blue Cypress Lake** ◎ Florida, SE USA
31 U11 **Blue Earth** Minnesota, N USA *43.38N 94.06W*
23 Q7 **Bluefield** Virginia, NE USA *37.15N 81.16W*
23 R7 **Bluefield** West Virginia, NE USA *37.16N 81.13W*
45 N10 **Bluefields** Región Autónoma Atlántico Sur, SE Nicaragua *12.01N 83.47W*
45 N10 **Bluefields, Bahía de** *bay* W Caribbean Sea
31 Z14 **Blue Grass** Iowa, C USA *41.30N 90.46W*
Bluegrass State *see* Kentucky
Blue Hen State *see* Delaware
21 S7 **Blue Hill** Maine, NE USA *44.25N 68.36W*
31 P16 **Blue Hill** Nebraska, C USA *40.19N 98.27W*
32 J5 **Blue Hills** *hill range* Wisconsin, N USA
36 L3 **Blue Lake** California, W USA *40.52N 124.00W*
Blue Law State *see* Connecticut
39 Q6 **Blue Mesa Reservoir** ⊠ Colorado, C USA
29 S12 **Blue Mountain** ▲ Arkansas, C USA *34.42N 94.04W*
21 O6 **Blue Mountain** ▲ New Hampshire, NE USA *44.48N 71.26W*
20 K8 **Blue Mountain** ▲ New York, NE USA *43.52N 74.24W*
20 H15 **Blue Mountain** *ridge* Pennsylvania, NE USA
46 H10 **Blue Mountain Peak** ▲ E Jamaica *18.02N 76.34W*
191 S8 **Blue Mountains** ▲ New South Wales, SE Australia
34 L11 **Blue Mountains** ▲▲ Oregon/Washington, NW USA
82 G12 **Blue Nile** ◈ *state* E Sudan
82 H12 **Blue Nile** *var.* Abai, Bahr el Azraq, *Amh.* Ābay Wenz, *Ar.* An Nīl al Azraq. ≈ Ethiopia/Sudan
15 Hh4 **Bluenose Lake** ◎ Nunavut, NW Canada
29 O3 **Blue Rapids** Kansas, C USA *39.39N 96.38W*
25 S1 **Blue Ridge** Georgia, SE USA *34.51N 84.19W*
19 Q10 **Blue Ridge** *var.* Blue Ridge Mountains. ▲▲ North Carolina/Virginia, E USA
25 S1 **Blue Ridge Lake** ⊠ Georgia, SE USA
Blue Ridge Mountains *see* Blue Ridge
9 N15 **Blue River** British Columbia, SW Canada *52.03N 119.21W*
29 O12 **Blue River** ≈ Oklahoma, C USA
29 R4 **Blue Springs** Missouri, C USA *39.01N 94.16W*
23 R6 **Bluestone Lake** ⊠ West Virginia, NE USA
193 C25 **Bluff** Southland, South Island, NZ *46.36S 168.22E*
39 O8 **Bluff** Utah, W USA *37.15N 109.36W*
23 P8 **Bluff City** Tennessee, S USA *36.28N 82.15W*
67 E24 **Bluff Cove** East Falkland, Falkland Islands *51.45S 58.10W*
27 S7 **Bluff Dale** Texas, SW USA *32.18N 98.01W*
191 N15 **Bluff Hill Point** *headland* Tasmania, SE Australia *41.03S 144.35E*
33 Q12 **Bluffton** Indiana, N USA *40.44N 85.10W*
33 R12 **Bluffton** Ohio, N USA *40.54N 83.53W*
27 T7 **Blum** Texas, SW USA *32.08N 97.24W*
103 G24 **Blumberg** Baden-Württemberg, SW Germany *47.48N 8.31E*
62 K13 **Blumenau** Santa Catarina, S Brazil *26.55S 49.07W*
31 N9 **Blunt** South Dakota, N USA *44.30N 99.58E*
34 H15 **Bly** Oregon, NW USA *42.22N 121.04W*
41 R13 **Blying Sound** *sound* Alaska, USA
99 M14 **Blyth** N England, UK *55.07N 1.30W*
37 Y16 **Blythe** California, W USA *33.35N 114.36W*
29 Y9 **Blytheville** Arkansas, C USA *35.55N 89.55W*
119 V7 **Blyznyuky** Kharkivs'ka Oblast', E Ukraine *48.51N 36.32E*
78 I15 **Bo** S Sierra Leone *7.58N 11.45W*
97 G16 **Bø** Telemark, S Norway *59.24N 9.04E*
179 Pp11 **Boac** Marinduque, N Philippines *13.26N 121.50E*
44 K10 **Boaco** Boaco, S Nicaragua *12.27N 85.45W*
44 J10 **Boaco** ◈ *department* C Nicaragua
79 I15 **Boali** Ombella-Mpoko, SW Central African Republic *4.52N 18.00E*
Boalsert *see* Bolsward
194 K13 **Boana** Morobe, C PNG *6.30S 146.54E*
195 Q10 **Boang Island** *island* Tanga Islands, NE PNG
33 V12 **Boardman** Ohio, N USA *41.01N 80.39W*
34 J11 **Boardman** Oregon, NW USA *45.50N 119.42W*
12 F13 **Boat Lake** ◎ Ontario, S Canada
60 F10 **Boa Vista** *state capital* Roraima, NW Brazil *2.51N 60.43W*
78 D9 **Boa Vista** *island* Ilhas de Barlavento, E Cape Verde
25 Q2 **Boaz** Alabama, S USA *34.12N 86.10W*
166 L15 **Bobai** Guangxi Zhuangzu Zizhiqu, S China *22.09N 109.57E*
180 J1 **Bobaomby, Tanjona** *Fr.* Cap d'Ambre. *headland* N Madagascar *11.58S 49.13E*
161 M14 **Bobbili** Andhra Pradesh, E India *18.31N 83.28E*
108 D9 **Bobbio** Emilia-Romagna, C Italy *44.48N 9.27E*
12 I14 **Bobcaygeon** Ontario, SE Canada *44.31N 78.33W*
Bober *see* Bóbr
105 O5 **Bobigny** Seine-St-Denis, N France *48.55N 2.27E*
79 N13 **Bobo-Dioulasso** SW Burkina *11.12N 4.21W*
112 G8 **Bobolice** *Ger.* Bublitz. Zachodnio-pomorskie, NW Poland *53.56N 16.37E*
85 J19 **Bobonong** Central, E Botswana *21.56S 28.24E*
175 T7 **Bobopayo** Pulau Halmahera, E Indonesia *1.07N 127.26E*
116 G10 **Bobovdol** Kyustendil, W Bulgaria *42.21N 22.58E*
121 M15 **Bobr** Minskaya Voblasts', NW Belarus *54.20N 29.18E*
121 M15 **Bobr** ≈ C Belarus
113 E14 **Bóbr** *Eng.* Bobrawa, *Ger.* Bober. ≈ SW Poland
Bobrawa *see* Bóbr
Bobrik *see* Bobryk
Bobrinets *see* Bobrynets'
Bobrka/Bóbrka *see* Bibrka
130 L8 **Bobrov** Voronezhskaya Oblast', W Russian Federation *51.10N 40.03E*
119 Q4 **Bobrovytsya** Chernihivs'ka Oblast', N Ukraine *50.43N 31.24E*
Bobruysk *see* Babruysk
121 J19 **Bobryk** *Rus.* Bobrik. ≈ SW Belarus
119 Q8 **Bobrynets'** *Rus.* Bobrinets. Kirovohrads'ka Oblast', C Ukraine *48.01N 32.09E*
12 K14 **Bobs Lake** ◎ Ontario, SE Canada
56 I6 **Bobures** Zulia, NW Venezuela *9.15N 71.10W*
44 H1 **Boca Bacalar Chico** *headland* N Belize *15.05N 82.12W*
114 G11 **Bočac** Republika Srpska, NW Bosnia and Herzegovina *44.32N 17.09E*
43 R14 **Boca del Río** Veracruz-Llave, S Mexico *19.07N 96.07W*
57 O4 **Boca de Pozo** Nueva Esparta, NE Venezuela *11.01N 64.21W*
61 C15 **Boca do Acre** Amazonas, N Brazil *8.45S 67.22W*
57 N12 **Boca Mavaca** Amazonas, S Venezuela *2.30N 65.10W*
81 G14 **Bocaranga** Ouham-Pendé, W Central African Republic *7.07N 15.40E*
25 Z15 **Boca Raton** Florida, SE USA *26.22N 80.04W*
45 P14 **Bocas del Toro** Bocas del Toro, NW Panama *9.21N 82.14W*
45 P15 **Bocas del Toro** *off.* Provincia de Bocas del Toro. ◈ *province* NW Panama
45 P15 **Bocas del Toro, Archipiélago de** *island group* NW Panama
44 L7 **Bocay** Jinotega, N Nicaragua *14.19N 85.07W*
107 N6 **Boceguillas** Castilla-León, N Spain *41.23N 3.37W*
Bocheykovo *see* Bacheykava
113 L17 **Bochnia** Małopolskie, SE Poland *49.58N 20.27E*
101 K16 **Bocholt** Limburg, NE Belgium *51.10N 5.37E*
103 D14 **Bocholt** Nordrhein-Westfalen, W Germany *51.49N 6.37E*
103 E15 **Bochum** Nordrhein-Westfalen, W Germany *51.28N 7.13E*
105 Y15 **Bocognano** Corse, France, C Mediterranean Sea *42.04N 9.03E*
56 I6 **Boconó** Trujillo, NW Venezuela *9.12N 70.16W*
118 F12 **Bocşa** *Ger.* Bokschen, *Hung.* Boksánbánya. Caraş-Severin, SW Romania *45.24N 21.46E*
81 H15 **Boda** Lobaye, SW Central African Republic *4.17N 17.25E*
96 L12 **Boda** Dalarna, C Sweden *61.00N 15.15E*
97 O20 **Böda** Kalmar, S Sweden *57.16N 17.04E*
97 L19 **Bodafors** Jönköping, S Sweden *57.30N 14.40E*
126 Kk13 **Bodaybo** Irkutskaya Oblast', E Russian Federation *57.52N 114.04E*
24 G5 **Bodcau, Bayou** *var.* Bodcau Creek. ≈ Louisiana, S USA
Bodcau Creek *see* Bodcau, Bayou
46 D8 **Bodden Town** *var.* Boddentown. Grand Cayman, SW Cayman Islands *19.17N 81.10W*
103 K14 **Bode** ≈ C Germany
36 L7 **Bodega Head** *headland* California, W USA *38.16N 123.04W*
Bodegas *see* Babahoyo
100 H11 **Bodegraven** Zuid-Holland, C Netherlands *52.04N 4.45E*
80 H8 **Bodélé** *depression* W Chad
94 J13 **Boden** Norrbotten, N Sweden *65.49N 21.43E*
Bodensee *see* Constance, Lake, C Europe
67 M15 **Bode Verde Fracture Zone** *tectonic feature* E Atlantic Ocean
161 H14 **Bodhan** Andhra Pradesh, C India *18.40N 77.51E*
168 I9 **Bodĭ** Bayanhongor, C Mongolia *45.25N 100.33E*
161 H22 **Bodināyakkanūr** Tamil Nādu, SE India *10.01N 77.18E*
110 H10 **Bodio** Ticino, S Switzerland *46.23N 8.55E*
99 I24 **Bodmin** SW England, UK *50.28N 4.43W*
99 I24 **Bodmin Moor** *moorland* SW England, UK
94 G12 **Bodø** Nordland, C Norway *67.16N 14.22E*
61 H20 **Bodoquena, Serra da** ▲▲ SW Brazil
142 B16 **Bodrum** Muğla, SW Turkey *37.03N 27.28E*
Bodzafordulő *see* Întorsura Buzăului
101 L14 **Boekel** Noord-Brabant, SE Netherlands *51.35N 5.42E*
Boeloekoemba *see* Bulukumba
105 Q11 **Boën** Loire, E France *45.45N 4.01E*
81 K18 **Boende** Equateur, C Dem. Rep. Congo *0.12S 20.54E*
27 R11 **Boerne** Texas, SW USA *29.47N 98.43W*
Boeroe *see* Buru, Pulau
Boetoeng *see* Buton, Pulau
24 I5 **Boeuf River** ≈ Arkansas/Louisiana, S USA
78 H14 **Boffa** Guinée-Maritime, W Guinea *10.12N 14.01W*
Bó Finne, Inis *see* Inishbofin
Boga *see* Bogë
177 Ff9 **Bogale** Irrawaddy, SW Myanmar *16.16N 95.21E*
24 L8 **Bogalusa** Louisiana, S USA *30.47N 89.51W*
79 Q12 **Bogandé** C Burkina *13.01N 0.07W*
81 I15 **Bogangolo** Ombella-Mpoko, C Central African Republic *5.36N 18.17E*
191 Q7 **Bogan River** ≈ New South Wales, SE Australia
27 W5 **Bogata** Texas, SW USA *33.28N 95.12W*
113 D14 **Bogatynia** *Ger.* Reichenau. Dolnośląskie, SW Poland *50.52N 14.54E*
142 K13 **Boğazlıyan** Yozgat, C Turkey *39.13N 35.16E*
81 J17 **Bogbonga** Equateur, NW Dem. Rep. Congo *1.36N 19.24E*
164 J14 **Bogcang Zangbo** ≈ W China
164 L5 **Bogda Feng** ▲ NW China *43.51N 88.14E*
116 I9 **Bogdan** ▲ C Bulgaria *42.37N 24.28E*
115 Q20 **Bogdanci** SE FYR Macedonia *41.12N 22.34E*
164 M5 **Bogda Shan** *var.* Po-ko-to Shan. ▲▲ NW China
115 K17 **Bogë** *var.* Boga. Shkodër, N Albania *42.25N 19.38E*
Bogendorf *see* Łuków
97 G23 **Bogense** Fyn, C Denmark *55.34N 10.06E*
191 T3 **Boggabilla** New South Wales, SE Australia *28.37S 150.21E*
191 S6 **Boggabri** New South Wales, SE Australia *30.44S 150.00E*
194 I10 **Bogia** Madang, N PNG *4.12S 144.55E*
99 N23 **Bognor Regis** SE England, UK *50.46N 0.40W*
179 Qq13 **Bogo** Cebu, C Philippines *11.04N 123.59E*
Bogodukhov *see* Bohodukhiv
189 V15 **Bogong, Mount** ▲ Victoria, SE Australia *36.43S 147.19E*
174 J14 **Bogor** *Dut.* Buitenzorg. Jawa, C Indonesia *6.34S 106.45E*
130 L5 **Bogoroditsk** Tul'skaya Oblast', W Russian Federation *53.46N 38.09E*
131 O3 **Bogorodsk** Nizhegorodskaya Oblast', W Russian Federation *56.06N 43.29E*
Bogorodskoje *see* Bogorodskoye
127 Nn14 **Bogorodskoye** Khabarovskiy Kray, SE Russian Federation *52.22N 140.33E*
129 R15 **Bogorodskoye** *var.* Bogorodskoje. Kirovskaya Oblast', NW Russian Federation *57.50N 50.41E*
56 F10 **Bogotá** *prev.* Santa Fe, Santa Fe de Bogotá. ● (Colombia) Cundinamarca, C Colombia *4.37N 74.04W*
159 T14 **Bogra** Rajshahi, N Bangladesh *24.52N 89.28E*
Boguschan *see* Boldu
126 Ii13 **Boguchany** Krasnoyarskiy Kray, C Russian Federation *58.20N 97.20E*
130 M9 **Boguchar** Voronezhskaya Oblast', W Russian Federation *49.57N 40.34E*
78 H10 **Bogué** Brakna, SW Mauritania *16.36N 14.15W*
24 K8 **Bogue Chitto** ≈ Louisiana/Mississippi, S USA
Bogushëvsk *see* Bahushewsk
Boguslav *see* Bohuslav
46 K12 **Bog Walk** C Jamaica *18.06N 77.01W*
167 Q3 **Bo Hai** *var.* Gulf of Chihli. *gulf* NE China
167 R3 **Bohai Haixia** *strait* NE China
167 Q3 **Bohai Wan** *bay* NE China
113 C17 **Bohemia** *Cz.* Čechy, *Ger.* Böhmen. *cultural and historical region* W Czech Republic
113 B18 **Bohemian Forest** *Cz.* Český Les, Šumava, *Ger.* Böhmerwald. ▲▲ C Europe
Bohemian-Moravian Highlands *see* Českomoravská Vrchovina
79 R16 **Bohicon** S Benin *7.08N 2.07E*
111 S11 **Bohinjska Bistrica** *Ger.* Wocheiner Feistritz. NW Slovenia *46.16N 13.55E*
Bohkká *see* Pokka
Böhmen *see* Bohemia
Böhmerwald *see* Bohemian Forest
Böhmisch-Krumau *see* Český Krumlov
Böhmisch-Leipa *see* Česká Lípa
Böhmisch-Mährische Höhe *see* Českomoravská Vrchovina
Böhmisch-Trübau *see* Česká Třebová
119 U5 **Bohodukhiv** *Rus.* Bogodukhov. Kharkivs'ka Oblast', E Ukraine *50.09N 35.31E*
179 Qq14 **Bohol** *island* C Philippines
179 Qq15 **Bohol Sea** *var.* Mindanao Sea. *sea* S Philippines
118 I7 **Bohorodchany** Ivano-Frankivs'ka Oblast', W Ukraine *48.46N 24.31E*
168 M9 **Böhöt** Dundgovĭ, C Mongolia *45.13N 108.12E*
164 K6 **Bohu** *var.* Bagrax. Xinjiang Uygur Zizhiqu, NW China *42.00N 86.28E*
113 I17 **Bohumín** *Ger.* Oderberg; *prev.* Neuoderberg, Nový Bohumín. Moravskoslezský Kraj, E Czech Republic *49.55N 18.19E*
119 P6 **Bohuslav** *Rus.* Boguslav. Kyyivs'ka Oblast', N Ukraine *49.33N 30.53E*
60 F11 **Boiaçu** Roraima, N Brazil *0.27S 61.46W*
109 K16 **Boiano** Molise, C Italy *41.28N 14.28E*
13 R8 **Boilleau** Québec, SE Canada *48.06N 70.49W*
61 O17 **Boipeba, Ilha de** *island* SE Brazil
106 G3 **Boiro** Galicia, NW Spain *42.39N 8.53W*
33 Q5 **Bois Blanc Island** *island* Michigan, N USA
31 R7 **Bois de Sioux River** ≈ Minnesota, N USA
35 N14 **Boise** *var.* Boise City. *state capital* Idaho, NW USA *43.38N 116.14W*
28 G8 **Boise City** Oklahoma, C USA *36.43N 102.30W*
35 N14 **Boise River, Middle Fork** ≈ Idaho, NW USA
Bois, Lac des *see* Woods, Lake of the
Bois-le-Duc *see* 's-Hertogenbosch
9 W17 **Boissevain** Manitoba, S Canada *49.13N 100.01W*
13 T7 **Boisvert, Pointe au** *headland* Québec, SE Canada *48.34N 69.07W*
102 K10 **Boizenburg** Mecklenburg-Vorpommern, N Germany *53.23N 10.43E*
Bojador *see* Boujdour
115 K18 **Bojana** *Alb.* Bunë. ≈ Albania/Serbia and Montenegro (Yugoslavia) *see also* Bunë
149 S3 **Bojnūrd** *var.* Bujnurd. Khorāsān, N Iran *37.30N 57.24E*
174 Ll15 **Bojonegoro** *prev.* Bodjonegoro. Jawa, C Indonesia *7.06S 111.49E*
201 T1 **Bokaak Atoll** *var.* Bokak, Taongi. *atoll* Ratak Chain, NE Marshall Islands
Bokak *see* Bokaak Atoll
152 K8 **Bo'kantov Tog'lari** *Rus.* Gory Bukantau. ▲ N Uzbekistan
159 Q15 **Bokāro** Jhārkhand, N India *23.46N 85.55E*
81 I18 **Bokatola** Equateur, NW Dem. Rep. Congo *0.37S 18.45E*
78 H13 **Boké** Guinée-Maritime, W Guinea *10.55N 14.18W*
Bokhara *see* Buxoro
191 Q4 **Bokharra River** ≈ New South Wales/Queensland, SE Australia
97 C16 **Boknafjorden** *fjord* S Norway
80 H11 **Bokoro** Chari-Baguirmi, W Chad *12.22N 17.03E*
81 K19 **Bokota** Equateur, NW Dem. Rep. Congo *0.56S 22.20E*
178 Gg13 **Bokpyin** Tenasserim, S Myanmar *11.16N 98.47E*
Boksánbánya/Bokschen *see* Bocşa
85 F21 **Bokspits** Kgalagadi, SW Botswana *26.50S 20.41E*
81 K18 **Bokungu** Equateur, C Dem. Rep. Congo *0.41S 22.19E*
152 F12 **Bokurdak** *Rus.* Bakhardok. Ahal Welaýaty, C Turkmenistan *38.51N 58.34E*
80 G10 **Bol** Lac, W Chad *13.27N 14.40E*
175 Qq9 **Bolaang** Sulawesi, N Indonesia *0.58S 122.10E*
78 G13 **Bolama** SW Guinea-Bissau *11.34N 15.32W*
Bolangir *see* Balāngīr
Bolanos *see* Bolanos, Mount, Guam
Bolaños *see* Bolaños de Calatrava, Spain
107 N11 **Bolaños de Calatrava** *var.* Bolaños. Castilla-La Mancha, C Spain *38.55N 3.39W*
196 B17 **Bolanos, Mount** *var.* Bolaños. ▲ S Guam *13.18N 144.41E*
42 L12 **Bolaños, Río** ≈ C Mexico
117 M14 **Bolayır** Çanakkale, NW Turkey *40.31N 26.46E*
104 L3 **Bolbec** Seine-Maritime, N France *49.34N 0.31E*
118 L13 **Boldu** *var.* Bogschan. Buzău, SE Romania *45.18N 27.15E*
152 H8 **Boldumsaz** *prev.* Kalinin, Kalininsk, Porsy. Daşoguz Welaýaty, N Turkmenistan *42.12N 59.33E*
164 I4 **Bole** *var.* Bortala. Xinjiang Uygur Zizhiqu, NW China *44.52N 82.06E*
79 O15 **Bole** NW Ghana *9.01N 2.28W*
81 J19 **Boleko** Equateur, W Dem. Rep. Congo *1.27S 19.52E*
113 E14 **Bolesławiec** *Ger.* Bunzlau. Dolnośląskie, SW Poland *51.16N 15.34E*
131 R4 **Bolgar** *prev.* Kuybyshev. Respublika Tatarstan, W Russian Federation *54.58N 49.03E*
79 P14 **Bolgatanga** N Ghana *10.45N 0.52W*
Bolgrad *see* Bolhrad
119 N12 **Bolhrad** *Rus.* Bolgrad. Odes'ka Oblast', SW Ukraine *45.42N 28.34E*
169 Y8 **Boli** Heilongjiang, NE China *45.45N 130.32E*
81 I19 **Bolia** Bandundu, W Dem. Rep. Congo *1.34S 18.24E*
95 J14 **Boliden** Västerbotten, N Sweden *64.52N 20.19E*
176 Uu11 **Bolifar** Pulau Seram, E Indonesia *3.08S 130.34E*
179 Oo9 **Bolinao** Luzon, N Philippines *16.22N 119.52E*
29 T6 **Bolivar** Missouri, C USA *37.36N 93.24W*
22 F10 **Bolivar** Tennessee, S USA *35.15N 88.59W*
56 C12 **Bolívar** Cauca, SW Colombia *1.49N 76.58W*
56 F7 **Bolívar** *off.* Departmento de Bolívar. ◈ *province* N Colombia
58 A13 **Bolívar** ◈ *province* C Ecuador
57 N9 **Bolívar** *off.* Estado Bolívar. ◈ *state* SE Venezuela
27 X12 **Bolivar Peninsula** *headland* Texas, SW USA *29.26N 94.41W*
56 I6 **Bolívar, Pico** ▲ W Venezuela *8.33N 71.05W*
59 K17 **Bolivia** *off.* Republic of Bolivia. ◆ *republic* W South America
114 O13 **Boljevac** Serbia, E Serbia and Montenegro (Yugoslavia) *43.50N 21.57E*
Bolkenhain *see* Bolków
130 J5 **Bolkhov** Orlovskaya Oblast', W Russian Federation *53.28N 36.00E*
113 F14 **Bolków** *Ger.* Bolkenhain. Dolnośląskie, SW Poland *50.55N 15.49E*
190 K3 **Bollards Lagoon** South Australia *28.58S 140.52E*
105 R14 **Bollène** Vaucluse, SE France *44.16N 4.45E*
96 N12 **Bollnäs** Gävleborg, C Sweden *61.18N 16.27E*
189 W10 **Bollon** Queensland, C Australia *28.07S 147.28E*
199 Jj14 **Bollons Tablemount** *undersea feature* S Pacific Ocean *49.40S 176.10W*
95 H17 **Bollstabruk** Västernorrland, C Sweden *63.00N 17.41E*
Bolluilos de Par del Condado *see* Bollullos Par del Condado
106 J14 **Bollullos Par del Condado** *var.* Bolluilos de Par del Condado. Andalucía, S Spain *37.19N 6.31W*
97 K21 **Bolmen** ◎ S Sweden
143 T10 **Bolnisi** S Georgia *41.28N 44.34E*
81 H19 **Bolobo** Bandundu, W Dem. Rep. Congo *2.10S 16.16E*
108 G10 **Bologna** Emilia-Romagna, N Italy *44.30N 11.19E*
128 I15 **Bologoye** Tverskaya Oblast', W Russian Federation *57.54N 34.04E*
81 J18 **Bolomba** Equateur, NW Dem. Rep. Congo *0.24N 19.10E*
43 X13 **Bolonchén de Rejón** *var.* Bolonchén de Rejón. Campeche, SE Mexico *20.00N 89.34W*
126 H14 **Bolotnoye** Novosibirskaya Oblast', C Russian Federation *55.39N 84.19E*
116 J13 **Boloústra, Akrotírio** *headland* NE Greece *40.56N 24.58E*
178 Jj10 **Bolovens, Plateau des** *plateau* S Laos
108 H13 **Bolsena** Lazio, C Italy *42.39N 11.59E*
109 G14 **Bolsena, Lago di** ◎ C Italy
130 B3 **Bol'shakovo** *Ger.* Kreuzingen; *prev.* Gross-Skaisgirren. Kaliningradskaya Oblast', W Russian Federation *54.53N 21.38E*
126 J6 **Bol'shaya Balakhnya** ≈ N Russian Federation
Bol'shaya Berëstovitsa *see* Vyalikaya Byerastavitsa
131 S7 **Bol'shaya Chernigovka** Samarskaya Oblast', W Russian Federation *52.07N 50.49E*
131 S7 **Bol'shaya Glushitsa** Samarskaya Oblast', W Russian Federation *52.22N 50.29E*
150 H9 **Bol'shaya Khobda** *Kaz.* Ülkenqobda. ≈ Kazakhstan/Russian Federation
126 Jj8 **Bol'shaya Kuonamka** ≈ NE Russian Federation
130 M12 **Bol'shaya Martynovka** Rostovskaya Oblast', SW Russian Federation *47.19N 41.40E*
126 I13 **Bol'shaya Murta** Krasnoyarskiy Kray, C Russian Federation *56.51N 93.10E*
129 V4 **Bol'shaya Rogovaya** ≈ NW Russian Federation
129 U7 **Bol'shaya Synya** ≈ NW Russian Federation
151 V9 **Bol'shaya Vladimirovka** Vostochnyy Kazakhstan, E Kazakhstan *50.52N 79.28E*
125 G13 **Bol'sherech'ye** Omskaya Oblast', C Russian Federation *56.03N 74.37E*
127 Pp12 **Bol'sheretsk** Kamchatskaya Oblast', E Russian Federation *52.20N 156.24E*
131 W3 **Bol'sheust'ikinskoye** Respublika Bashkortostan, W Russian Federation *56.00N 58.13E*
Bol'shevik *see* Bal'shavik
126 I13 **Bol'shevik, Ostrov** *island* Severnaya Zemlya, N Russian Federation
129 U4 **Bol'shezemel'skaya Tundra** *physical region* NW Russian Federation
150 J13 **Bol'shiye Barsuki, Peski** *desert* SW Kazakhstan
125 Ff12 **Bol'shiye Uki** Omskaya Oblast', C Russian Federation *56.57N 72.26E*
127 O6 **Bol'shoy Anyuy** ≈ NE Russian Federation
126 K6 **Bol'shoy Begichev, Ostrov** *island* NE Russian Federation
127 N17 **Bol'shoy Kamen'** Primorskiy Kray, SE Russian Federation *43.06N 132.21E*
131 O4 **Bol'shoye Murashkino** Nizhegorodskaya Oblast', W Russian Federation *55.46N 44.48E*
131 W4 **Bol'shoy Iremel'** ▲ W Russian Federation *54.31N 58.47E*
131 R7 **Bol'shoy Irgiz** ≈ W Russian Federation
126 M5 **Bol'shoy Lyakhovskiy, Ostrov** *island* NE Russian Federation
126 Ll13 **Bol'shoy Nimnyr** Respublika Sakha (Yakutiya), NE Russian Federation *57.55N 125.34E*
Bol'shoy Rozhan *see* Vyaliki Rozhan
150 E10 **Bol'shoy Uzen'** *Kaz.* Ülkenözen. ≈ Kazakhstan/Russian Federation
126 Ii15 **Bol'shoy Yenisey** *var.* Biy-Khem. ≈ S Russian Federation
42 K6 **Bolson de Mapimi** ▲▲ NW Mexico
100 K6 **Bolsward** *Fris.* Boalsert. Friesland, N Netherlands *53.04N 5.31E*
107 T4 **Boltaña** Aragón, NE Spain *42.28N 0.02E*
12 G15 **Bolton** Ontario, S Canada *43.52N 79.45W*
99 K17 **Bolton** *prev.* Bolton-le-Moors. NW England, UK *53.34N 2.25W*
23 V12 **Bolton** North Carolina, SE USA *34.22N 78.26W*
Bolton-le-Moors *see* Bolton
142 G11 **Bolu** Bolu, NW Turkey *40.45N 31.37E*
142 G11 **Bolu** ◈ *province* NW Turkey
195 N15 **Bolubolu** Goodenough Island, S PNG *9.22S 150.22E*
94 H1 **Bolungarvík** Vestfirdhir, NW Iceland *66.09N 23.16W*
165 O10 **Boluntay** Qinghai, W China *36.30N 92.10E*
165 P8 **Boluozhuanjing** *var.* Aksay, Aksay Kazakzu Zizhixian. Gansu, N China *39.25N 94.09E*
142 F14 **Bolvadin** Afyon, W Turkey *38.43N 31.01E*
116 M10 **Bolyarovo** *prev.* Pashkeni. Yambol, E Bulgaria *42.09N 26.49E*
108 G6 **Bolzano** *Ger.* Bozen; *anc.* Bauzanum. Trentino-Alto Adige, N Italy *46.30N 11.22E*
81 F22 **Boma** Bas-Congo, W Dem. Rep. Congo *5.42S 13.05E*
191 R12 **Bombala** New South Wales, SE Australia *36.54S 149.15E*
106 F10 **Bombarral** Leiria, C Portugal *39.15N 9.09W*

◆ Country ● Country Capital ◇ Dependent Territory ○ Dependent Territory Capital ◈ Administrative Region ✈ International Airport ▲ Mountain ▲▲ Mountain Range Volcano ≈ River ◎ Lake ⊠ Reservoir

Bombay – Bracciano

Bombay *see* Mumbai
176 *Vv11* **Bomberai** ≈ Papua, E Indonesia
176 *Vv11* **Bomberai, Jazirah** *peninsula* Papua, E Indonesia
176 *Vv11* **Bomberai, Semenanjung** *headland* Papua, E Indonesia *3.01S 133.25E*
83 *F18* **Bombo** S Uganda *0.38N 32.31E*
81 *I17* **Bomboma** Equateur, NW Dem. Rep. Congo *2.22N 19.03E*
61 *I14* **Bom Futuro** Pará, N Brazil *6.27S 54.44W*
165 *Q15* **Bomi** *var.* Bowo, Zhamo. Xizang Zizhiqu, W China *29.43N 96.12E*
81 *N17* **Bomili** Orientale, NE Dem. Rep. Congo *1.45N 27.01E*
61 *N17* **Bom Jesus da Lapa** Bahia, E Brazil *13.16S 43.22W*
62 *Q8* **Bom Jesus do Itabapoana** Rio de Janeiro, SE Brazil *21.07S 41.43W*
97 *C15* **Bømlafjorden** *fjord* S Norway
97 *B15* **Bømlo** *island* S Norway
126 *M14* **Bomnak** Amurskaya Oblast', SE Russian Federation *54.43N 128.50E*
81 *I17* **Bomongo** Equateur, NW Dem. Rep. Congo *1.22N 18.21E*
63 *K14* **Bom Retiro** Santa Catarina, S Brazil *27.52S 49.33W*
81 *L15* **Bomu** *var.* Mbomou, Mbomu, M'Bomu. ≈ Central African Republic/Dem. Rep. Congo
148 *J3* **Bonāb** *var.* Benāb, Bunab. Āzarbāyjān-e Khāvarī, N Iran *37.24N 45.59E*
47 *Q16* **Bonaire** *island* E Netherlands Antilles
41 *U11* **Bona, Mount** ▲ Alaska, USA *61.22N 141.45W*
194 *M16* **Bonando** ≈ SE Papau New Guinea
191 *Q12* **Bonang** Victoria, SE Australia *37.13S 148.43E*
44 *L7* **Bonanza** Región Autónoma Atlántico Norte, NE Nicaragua *13.58N 84.37W*
39 *O4* **Bonanza** Utah, W USA *40.01N 109.12W*
47 *O9* **Bonao** C Dominican Republic *18.55N 70.25W*
188 *L3* **Bonaparte Archipelago** *island group* Western Australia
34 *K6* **Bonaparte, Mount** ▲ Washington, NW USA *48.47N 119.07W*
41 *N11* **Bonasila Dome** ▲ Alaska, USA *62.24N 160.28W*
94 *H11* **Bonåsjøen** Nordland, C Norway *67.35N 15.39E*
47 *T15* **Bonasse** Trinidad, Trinidad and Tobago *10.02N 61.48W*
13 *X7* **Bonaventure** Québec, SE Canada *48.03N 65.30W*
13 *X7* **Bonaventure** ≈ Québec, SE Canada
11 *V11* **Bonavista** Newfoundland and Labrador, SE Canada *48.36N 53.07W*
11 *U11* **Bonavista Bay** *inlet* NW Atlantic Ocean
123 *Kk11* **Bon, Cap** *headland* N Tunisia *37.05N 11.04E*
81 *E19* **Bonda** Ogooué-Lolo, C Gabon *0.50S 12.28E*
131 *N6* **Bondari** Tambovskaya Oblast', W Russian Federation *52.58N 42.02E*
108 *G9* **Bondeno** Emilia-Romagna, C Italy *44.53N 11.24E*
32 *L4* **Bond Falls Flowage** ◎ Michigan, N USA
81 *L16* **Bondo** Orientale, N Dem. Rep. Congo *3.51N 23.41E*
175 *P17* **Bondokodi** Pulau Sumba, S Indonesia *9.36S 119.01E*
79 *O15* **Bondoukou** E Ivory Coast *8.03N 2.45W*
Bondoukui/Bondoukuy *see* Boundoukui
174 *Mm15* **Bondowoso** Jawa, C Indonesia *7.54S 113.49E*
35 *S14* **Bondurant** Wyoming, C USA *43.14N 110.26W*
Bone *see* Watampone, Indonesia
Bône *see* Annaba, Algeria
32 *I5* **Bone Lake** ◎ Wisconsin, N USA
175 *R12* **Bonelipu** Pulau Buton, C Indonesia *4.42S 123.09E*
175 *Q14* **Bonerate, Kepulauan** *var.* Macan. *island group* C Indonesia
175 *Pp15* **Bonerate, Pulau** *island* Kepulauan Bonerate, C Indonesia
31 *O12* **Bonesteel** South Dakota, N USA *43.01N 98.55W*
64 *I8* **Bonete, Cerro** ▲ N Argentina *27.58S 68.22W*
175 *Pp11* **Bone, Teluk** *bay* Sulawesi, C Indonesia
110 *D6* **Bonfol** Jura, NW Switzerland *47.28N 7.08E*
159 *U12* **Bongaigaon** Assam, NE India *26.30N 90.30E*
81 *K17* **Bongandanga** Equateur, NW Dem. Rep. Congo *1.30N 21.03E*
80 *L13* **Bongo, Massif des** *var.* Chaîne des Mongos. ▲▲ NE Central African Republic
80 *G12* **Bongor** Mayo-Kébbi, SW Chad *10.18N 15.19E*
79 *N16* **Bongouanou** E Ivory Coast *6.39N 4.12W*
178 *Kk11* **Bông Sơn** *var.* Hoai Nhơn. Binh Đinh, C Vietnam *14.28N 109.00E*
27 *U5* **Bonham** Texas, SW USA *33.34N 96.10W*
Bonhard *see* Bonyhád
105 *U6* **Bonhomme, Col du** *pass* NE France *48.10N 7.07E*
105 *Y16* **Bonifacio** Corse, France, C Mediterranean Sea *41.23N 9.09E*
Bonifacio, Bocche de/Bonifacio, Bouches de *see* Bonifacio, Strait of
105 *Y16* **Bonifacio, Strait of** *Fr.* Bouches de Bonifacio, *It.* Bocche de Bonifacio. *strait* C Mediterranean Sea
25 *Q8* **Bonifay** Florida, SE USA *30.49N 85.42W*
Bonin Islands *see* Ogasawara-shotō
199 *H6* **Bonin Trench** *undersea feature* NW Pacific Ocean
25 *W15* **Bonita Springs** Florida, SE USA *26.19N 81.48W*
44 *I5* **Bonito, Pico** ▲ N Honduras *15.33N 86.55W*
103 *E17* **Bonn** Nordrhein-Westfalen, W Germany *50.43N 7.06E*
12 *J12* **Bonnechere** Ontario, SE Canada *45.39N 77.36W*
12 *J12* **Bonnechere** ≈ Ontario, SE Canada
35 *N7* **Bonners Ferry** Idaho, NW USA *48.41N 116.19W*
29 *R4* **Bonner Springs** Kansas, C USA *39.03N 94.52W*
104 *L6* **Bonnétable** Sarthe, NW France *48.09N 0.24E*
29 *X6* **Bonne Terre** Missouri, C USA *37.55N 90.33W*
8 *J5* **Bonnet Plume** ≈ Yukon Territory, NW Canada
104 *M6* **Bonneval** Eure-et-Loir, C France *48.12N 1.23E*
105 *T10* **Bonneville** Haute-Savoie, E France *46.04N 6.25E*
38 *J3* **Bonneville Salt Flats** *salt flat* Utah, W USA
79 *U18* **Bonny** Rivers, S Nigeria *4.25N 7.13E*
Bonny, Bight of *see* Biafra, Bight of
39 *W4* **Bonny Reservoir** ▣ Colorado, C USA
9 *R14* **Bonnyville** Alberta, SW Canada *54.16N 110.46W*
109 *C18* **Bono** Sardegna, Italy, C Mediterranean Sea *40.24N 9.01E*
176 *Xx10* **Bonoi** Papua, E Indonesia *1.46S 137.45E*
Bononia *see* Vidin, Bulgaria
Bononia *see* Boulogne-sur-Mer, France
109 *B18* **Bonorva** Sardegna, Italy, C Mediterranean Sea *40.27N 8.46E*
32 *M15* **Bonpas Creek** ≈ Illinois, N USA
202 *I3* **Bonriki** Tarawa, W Kiribati *1.22N 173.09E*
191 *T4* **Bonshaw** New South Wales, SE Australia *29.06S 151.15E*
78 *I16* **Bonthe** SW Sierra Leone *7.26N 12.32W*
179 *P8* **Bontoc** Luzon, N Philippines *17.04N 120.58E*
194 *M16* **Bonua** ≈ S PNG
27 *Y9* **Bon Wier** Texas, SW USA *30.43N 93.40W*
113 *J25* **Bonyhád** *Ger.* Bonhard. Tolna, S Hungary *46.17N 18.31E*
Bonzabaai *see* Bonza Bay
85 *J25* **Bonza Bay** *Afr.* Bonzabaai. Eastern Cape, S South Africa *32.58S 27.58E*
190 *D7* **Bookabie** South Australia *31.49S 132.41E*
190 *H6* **Bookaloo** South Australia *31.56S 137.21E*
39 *P5* **Book Cliffs** *cliff* Colorado/Utah, W USA
175 *Tt9* **Boo, Kepulauan** *island group* E Indonesia
27 *P1* **Booker** Texas, SW USA *36.27N 100.32W*
78 *K15* **Boola** Guinée-Forestière, SE Guinea *8.22N 8.40W*
191 *O8* **Booligal** New South Wales, SE Australia *33.56S 144.54E*
101 *G17* **Boom** Antwerpen, N Belgium *51.05N 4.24E*
45 *N6* **Boom** *var.* Boon. Región Autónoma Atlántico Norte, NE Nicaragua *14.52N 83.36W*
191 *S3* **Boomi** New South Wales, SE Australia *28.43S 149.35E*
Boon *see* Boom
31 *V13* **Boone** Iowa, C USA *42.04N 93.52W*
23 *Q8* **Boone** North Carolina, SE USA *36.13N 81.40W*
29 *S11* **Booneville** Arkansas, C USA *35.08N 93.55W*
23 *N6* **Booneville** Kentucky, S USA *37.27N 83.41W*
25 *N2* **Booneville** Mississippi, S USA *34.39N 88.34W*
23 *V3* **Boonsboro** Maryland, NE USA *39.30N 77.39W*
168 *H9* **Böön Tsagaan Nuur** ◎ S Mongolia
36 *L6* **Boonville** California, W USA *38.58N 123.21W*
33 *N16* **Boonville** Indiana, N USA *38.03N 87.16W*
29 *U4* **Boonville** Missouri, C USA *38.58N 92.44W*
20 *I9* **Boonville** New York, NE USA *43.28N 75.17W*
82 *M12* **Boorama** Woqooyi Galbeed, NW Somalia *9.58N 43.15E*
191 *O6* **Booroondarra, Mount** *hill* New South Wales, SE Australia *31.07S 145.20E*
191 *N9* **Booroorban** New South Wales, SE Australia *34.55S 144.45E*
191 *R9* **Boorowa** New South Wales, SE Australia *34.26S 148.42E*
101 *H17* **Boortmeerbeek** Vlaams Brabant, C Belgium *50.58N 4.27E*
82 *P11* **Boosaaso** *var.* Bandar Kassim, Bender Qaasim, Bosaso, *It.* Bender Cassim. Bari, N Somalia *11.26N 49.37E*
21 *Q8* **Boothbay Harbor** Maine, NE USA *43.52N 69.35W*
Boothia Felix *see* Boothia Peninsula
15 *Kk2* **Boothia, Gulf of** *gulf* Nunavut, NE Canada
15 *K2* **Boothia Peninsula** *prev.* Boothia Felix. *peninsula* Nunavut, NE Canada
81 *E18* **Booué** Ogooué-Ivindo, NE Gabon *0.03S 11.58E*
103 *J21* **Bopfingen** Baden-Württemberg, S Germany *48.51N 10.21E*
103 *F18* **Boppard** Rheinland-Pfalz, W Germany *50.13N 7.35E*
64 *M4* **Boquerón** *off.* Departamento de Boquerón. ◈ *department* W Paraguay
45 *P15* **Boquete** *var.* Bajo Boquete. Chiriquí, W Panama *8.45N 82.26W*
42 *J6* **Boquilla, Presa de la** ▣ N Mexico
42 *L5* **Boquillas** *var.* Boquillas del Carmen. Coahuila de Zaragoza, NE Mexico *29.10N 102.55W*
Boquillas del Carmen *see* Boquillas
126 *I11* **Bor** Krasnoyarskiy Kray, C Russian Federation *61.28N 90.09E*
83 *F15* **Bor** Jonglei, S Sudan *6.12N 31.33E*
97 *L20* **Bor** Jönköping, S Sweden *57.04N 14.10E*
142 *J15* **Bor** Niğde, S Turkey *37.48N 34.30E*
114 *P12* **Bor** Serbia, E Serbia and Montenegro (Yugoslavia) *44.05N 22.06E*
203 *S10* **Bora-Bora** *island* Îles Sous le Vent, W French Polynesia
178 *Ii10* **Borabu** Maha Sarakham, E Thailand *16.01N 103.06E*
35 *P13* **Borah Peak** ▲ Idaho, NW USA *44.21N 113.53W*
151 *U16* **Boralday** *prev.* Burunday. Almaty, SE Kazakhstan *43.21N 76.48E*
150 *G13* **Borankul** *prev.* Opornyy. Mangistau, SW Kazakhstan *46.09N 54.32E*
97 *J19* **Borås** Västra Götaland, S Sweden *57.43N 12.55E*
149 *N11* **Borāzjān** *var.* Borazjān. Būshehr, S Iran *29.19N 51.12E*
Borazjān *see* Borāzjān
60 *G13* **Borba** Amazonas, N Brazil *4.39S 59.34W*
106 *H11* **Borba** Évora, S Portugal *38.48N 7.28W*
Borbetomagus *see* Worms
57 *O7* **Borbón** Bolívar, E Venezuela *7.55N 64.03W*
61 *Q15* **Borborema, Planalto da** *plateau* NE Brazil
118 *M14* **Borcea, Braţul** ≈ S Romania
Borchalo *see* Marneuli
205 *R15* **Borchgrevink Coast** *physical region* Antarctica
143 *Q11* **Borçka** Artvin, NE Turkey *41.24N 41.37E*
100 *N11* **Borculo** Gelderland, E Netherlands *52.07N 6.31E*
190 *G10* **Borda, Cape** *headland* South Australia *35.45S 136.34E*
104 *K13* **Bordeaux** *anc.* Burdigala. Gironde, SW France *44.49N 0.33W*
9 *T15* **Borden** Saskatchewan, S Canada *52.23N 107.10W*
12 *D8* **Borden Lake** ◎ Ontario, S Canada
15 *L1* **Borden Peninsula** *peninsula* Baffin Island, Nunavut, NE Canada
190 *K11* **Bordertown** South Australia *36.21S 140.48E*
94 *H2* **Bordheyri** Vestfirdhir, NW Iceland *65.12N 21.09W*
97 *B18* **Bordhoy** *Dan.* Bordø *Island* Faeroe Islands *62.17N 6.30W*
108 *B11* **Bordighera** Liguria, NW Italy *43.48N 7.40E*
76 *K5* **Bordj-Bou-Arreridj** *var.* Bordj Bou Arreridj, Bordj Bou Arréridj. N Algeria *36.04N 4.45E*
123 *I10* **Bordj El Bahri, Cap de** *headland* N Algeria *36.52N 3.13E*
76 *L10* **Bordj Omar Driss** E Algeria *28.09N 6.52E*
149 *N13* **Bord Khūn** Hormozgān, S Iran
153 *V7* **Bordunskiy** Chuyskaya Oblast', N Kyrgyzstan *42.37N 75.31E*
97 *M17* **Borensberg** Östergötland, S Sweden *58.33N 15.15E*
Borgå *see* Porvoo
94 *L2* **Borgarfjördhur** Austurland, NE Iceland *65.32N 13.46W*
94 *H3* **Borgarnes** Vesturland, W Iceland *64.33N 21.54W*
95 *G14* **Børgefjell** ▲▲ C Norway
100 *O7* **Borger** Drenthe, NE Netherlands *52.54N 6.48E*
27 *N2* **Borger** Texas, SW USA *35.40N 101.24W*
97 *N20* **Borgholm** Kalmar, S Sweden *56.50N 16.40E*
109 *N22* **Borgia** Calabria, SW Italy *38.48N 16.28E*
101 *J18* **Borgloon** Limburg, NE Belgium *50.48N 5.21E*
205 *P2* **Borg Massif** ▲▲ Antarctica
24 *L9* **Borgne, Lake** ◎ Louisiana, S USA
108 *C7* **Borgomanero** Piemonte, NE Italy *45.42N 8.33E*
108 *G10* **Borgo Panigale** ✕ (Bologna) Emilia-Romagna, N Italy *44.33N 11.16E*
109 *J15* **Borgorose** Lazio, C Italy *42.10N 13.15E*
108 *A9* **Borgo San Dalmazzo** Piemonte, N Italy *44.19N 7.28E*
108 *G11* **Borgo San Lorenzo** Toscana, C Italy *43.58N 11.22E*
108 *C7* **Borgosesia** Piemonte, NE Italy *45.41N 8.21E*
108 *E9* **Borgo Val di Taro** Emilia-Romagna, C Italy *44.29N 9.48E*
108 *G6* **Borgo Valsugana** Trentino-Alto Adige, N Italy *46.04N 11.31E*
169 *O11* **Borhoyn Tal** Dornogovĭ, SE Mongolia *43.43N 111.53E*
178 *Ii8* **Borikhan** *var.* Borikhane. Bolikhamxai, C Laos *18.36N 103.43E*
Borikhane *see* Borikhan
Borislav *see* Boryslav
131 *N8* **Borisoglebsk** Voronezhskaya Oblast', W Russian Federation *51.23N 42.00E*
Borisov *see* Barysaw
Borisovgrad *see* Pŭrvomay
Borispol' *see* Boryspil'
180 *I3* **Boriziny** Mahajanga, NW Madagascar *15.31S 47.40E*
107 *Q5* **Borja** Aragón, NE Spain *41.49N 1.31W*
Borjas Blancas *see* Les Borges Blanques
143 *S10* **Borjomi** *Rus.* Borzhomi. C Georgia *41.50N 43.24E*
120 *L12* **Borkavichy** *Rus.* Borkovichi. Vitsyebskaya Voblasts', N Belarus *55.40N 28.18E*
103 *H16* **Borken** Hessen, C Germany *51.01N 9.16E*
103 *E14* **Borken** Nordrhein-Westfalen, W Germany *51.51N 6.51E*
94 *H10* **Borkenes** Troms, N Norway *68.46N 16.10E*
80 *H7* **Borkou-Ennedi-Tibesti** *off.* Préfecture du Borkou-Ennedi-Tibesti. ◈ *prefecture* N Chad
Borkovichi *see* Borkavichy
102 *E9* **Borkum** *island* NW Germany
83 *K17* **Bor, Lagh** *var.* Lak Bor. *dry watercourse* NE Kenya
Bor, Lak *see* Bor, Lagh
97 *M14* **Borlänge** Dalarna, C Sweden *60.28N 15.25E*
108 *C9* **Bormida** ≈ NW Italy
108 *F6* **Bormio** Lombardia, N Italy *46.27N 10.24E*
103 *M16* **Borna** Sachsen, E Germany *51.07N 12.30E*
100 *O10* **Borne** Overijssel, E Netherlands *52.18N 6.45E*
101 *F17* **Bornem** Antwerpen, N Belgium *51.06N 4.13E*
174 *M6* **Borneo** *island* Brunei/Indonesia/Malaysia
103 *E16* **Bornheim** Nordrhein-Westfalen, W Germany *50.46N 6.58E*
97 *L24* **Bornholm** ◈ *county* E Denmark
97 *L24* **Bornholm** *island* E Denmark
79 *Y13* **Borno** ◈ *state* NE Nigeria
106 *K15* **Bornos** Andalucía, S Spain *36.49N 5.42W*
168 *L7* **Bornuur** Töv, C Mongolia *48.28N 106.15E*
119 *O4* **Borodyanka** Kyyivs'ka Oblast', N Ukraine *50.40N 29.54E*
126 *M10* **Borogontsy** Respublika Sakha (Yakutiya), NE Russian Federation *62.42N 131.01E*
164 *I5* **Borohoro Shan** ▲▲ NW China
79 *O13* **Boromo** SW Burkina *11.46N 2.54W*
37 *T13* **Boron** California, W USA *35.00N 117.42W*
179 *R12* **Borongan** Samar, C Philippines *11.26N 125.30E*
Borongo *see* Black Volta
Boron'ki *see* Baron'ki
Borosjenő *see* Ineu
Borossebes *see* Sebiş
78 *L15* **Borotou** NW Ivory Coast *8.46N 7.30W*
119 *W6* **Borova** Kharkivs'ka Oblast', E Ukraine *49.22N 37.39E*
116 *H8* **Borovan** Vratsa, NW Bulgaria *43.25N 23.45E*
128 *I14* **Borovichi** Novgorodskaya Oblast', W Russian Federation *58.23N 33.56E*
Borovlje *see* Ferlach
114 *J9* **Borovo** Vukovar-Srijem, NE Croatia *45.22N 18.57E*
151 *Q7* **Borovoye** *Kaz.* Būrabay. Akmola, N Kazakhstan *53.07N 70.19E*
130 *K4* **Borovsk** Kaluzhskaya Oblast', W Russian Federation *55.12N 36.22E*
125 *F12* **Borovskiy** Tyumenskaya Oblast', C Russian Federation *57.04N 65.37E*
151 *N7* **Borovskoy** Kostanay, N Kazakhstan *53.49N 64.12E*
Borovukha *see* Baravukha
97 *L23* **Borrby** Skåne, S Sweden *55.27N 14.10E*
189 *R3* **Borroloola** Northern Territory, N Australia *16.09S 136.18E*
118 *F9* **Borş** Bihor, NW Romania *47.06N 21.47E*
118 *I9* **Borşa** *Hung.* Borsa. Maramureş, N Romania *47.40N 24.37E*
118 *J10* **Borsec** *Ger.* Bad Borseck, *Hung.* Borszék. Harghita, C Romania *46.57N 25.32E*
94 *K8* **Børselv** *Lapp.* Bissojohka. Finnmark, N Norway *70.18N 25.35E*
115 *L23* **Borsh** *var.* Borshi. Vlorë, S Albania *40.04N 19.51E*
Borshchev *see* Borshchiv
118 *K7* **Borshchiv** *Pol.* Borszczów, *Rus.* Borshchev. Ternopil's'ka Oblast', W Ukraine *48.48N 26.00E*
Borshi *see* Borsh
113 *L20* **Borsod-Abaúj-Zemplén** *off.* Borsod-Abaúj-Zemplén Megye. ◈ *county* NE Hungary
101 *E15* **Borssele** Zeeland, SW Netherlands *51.26N 3.45E*
Borszczów *see* Borshchiv
Borszék *see* Borsec
Bortala *see* Bole
105 *O12* **Bort-les-Orgues** Corrèze, C France *45.28N 2.31E*
Bor u České Lípy *see* Nový Bor
168 *E8* **Bor-Udzüür** Hovd, W Mongolia *45.46N 92.13E*
149 *N9* **Borūjen** Chahār Maḩall va Bakhtīārī, C Iran *32.00N 51.08E*
148 *L7* **Borūjerd** *var.* Burujird. Lorestān, W Iran *33.55N 48.45E*
118 *H6* **Boryslav** *Pol.* Borysław, *Rus.* Borislav. L'vivs'ka Oblast', NW Ukraine *49.18N 23.28E*
Borysław *see* Boryslav
119 *P4* **Boryspil'** *Rus.* Borispol'. Kyyivs'ka Oblast', N Ukraine *50.20N 30.58E*
119 *P4* **Boryspil'** *Rus.* Borispol'. ✕ (Kyyiv) Kyyivs'ka Oblast', N Ukraine *50.21N 30.46E*
Borzhomi *see* Borjomi
119 *R3* **Borzna** Chernihivs'ka Oblast', NE Ukraine *51.15N 32.25E*
126 *L16* **Borzya** Chitinskaya Oblast', S Russian Federation *50.18N 116.24E*
109 *B18* **Bosa** Sardegna, Italy, C Mediterranean Sea *40.18N 8.28E*
114 *F10* **Bosanska Dubica** *var.* Kozarska Dubica. Republika Srpska, NW Bosnia and Herzegovina *45.09N 16.47E*
114 *G10* **Bosanska Gradiška** *var.* Gradiška. Republika Srpska, N Bosnia and Herzegovina *45.09N 17.14E*
114 *F10* **Bosanska Kostajnica** *var.* Srpska Kostajnica. Republika Srpska, NW Bosnia and Herzegovina *45.12N 16.33E*
114 *E11* **Bosanska Krupa** *var.* Krupa, Krupa na Uni. Federacija Bosna I Hercegovina, NW Bosnia and Herzegovina *44.52N 16.09E*
114 *H10* **Bosanski Brod** *var.* Srpski Brod. Republika Srpska, N Bosnia and Herzegovina *45.07N 17.59E*
114 *E10* **Bosanski Novi** *var.* Novi Grad. Republika Srpska, NW Bosnia and Herzegovina *45.03N 16.22E*
114 *E11* **Bosanski Petrovac** *var.* Petrovac. Federacija Bosna I Hercegovina, NW Bosnia and Herzegovina *44.34N 16.21E*
114 *N12* **Bosanski Petrovac** Serbia, E Serbia and Montenegro (Yugoslavia) *44.22N 21.25E*
114 *I10* **Bosanski Šamac** *var.* Šamac. Republika Srpska, N Bosnia and Herzegovina *45.03N 18.27E*
114 *E12* **Bosansko Grahovo** *var.* Grahovo, Hrvatsko Grahovo. Federacija Bosna I Hercegovina, W Bosnia and Herzegovina *44.10N 16.22E*
Bosaso *see* Boosaaso
194 *G13* **Bosavi, Mount** ◬ W PNG *6.33S 142.50E*
166 *J14* **Bose** Guangxi Zhuangzu Zizhiqu, S China *23.55N 106.31E*
167 *Q5* **Boshan** Shandong, E China *36.31N 117.46E*
115 *P16* **Bosilegrad** *prev.* Bosiljgrad. Serbia, SE Serbia and Montenegro (Yugoslavia) *42.30N 22.30E*
Bosiljgrad *see* Bosilegrad
Bösing *see* Pezinok
100 *H12* **Boskoop** Zuid-Holland, C Netherlands *52.04N 4.40E*
113 *G18* **Boskovice** *Ger.* Boskowitz. Jihomoravský Kraj, SE Czech Republic *49.30N 16.39E*
Boskowitz *see* Boskovice
114 *I10* **Bosna** ≈ N Bosnia and Herzegovina
176 *X9* **Bosnabraidi** Papua, E Indonesia *0.49S 136.00E*
115 *G14* **Bosna I Hercegovina, Federacija** ◈ *republic* Bosnia and Herzegovina
114 *H12* **Bosnia and Herzegovina** *off.* Republic of Bosnia and Herzegovina. ◆ *republic* SE Europe
81 *J16* **Bosobolo** Equateur, NW Dem. Rep. Congo *4.10N 19.55E*
171 *K17* **Bōsō-hantō** *peninsula* Honshū, S Japan
Bosora *see* Buşrá ash Shām
Bosphorus/Bosporus *see* İstanbul Boğazı
Bosporus Cimmerius *see* Kerch Strait
Bosporus Thracius *see* İstanbul Boğazı
Bosra *see* Buşrá ash Shām
81 *H14* **Bossangoa** Ouham, C Central African Republic *6.31N 17.24E*
Bossé Bangou *see* Bossey Bangou
81 *I15* **Bossembélé** Ombella-Mpoko, C Central African Republic *5.13N 17.39E*
81 *H15* **Bossentélé** Ouham-Pendé, W Central African Republic *5.36N 16.37E*
79 *R12* **Bossey Bangou** *var.* Bossé Bangou. Tillabéri, SW Niger *13.22N 1.18E*
24 *G5* **Bossier City** Louisiana, S USA *32.31N 93.43W*
85 *D20* **Bossiesvlei** Hardap, S Namibia *25.01S 16.45E*
79 *Y11* **Bosso** Diffa, SE Niger *13.42N 13.18E*
63 *F15* **Bossoroca** Rio Grande do Sul, S Brazil *28.45S 54.54W*
164 *J10* **Bostan** Xinjiang Uygur Zizhiqu, W China *41.19N 83.15E*
148 *K3* **Bostānābād** Āzarbāyjān-e Khāvarī, N Iran *37.52N 46.51E*
164 *K6* **Bosten Hu** *var.* Bagrax Hu. ◎ NW China
99 *O18* **Boston** *prev.* St.Botolph's Town. E England, UK *52.58N 0.01W*
21 *O11* **Boston** *state capital* Massachusetts, NE USA *42.21N 71.03W*
152 *I9* **Bo'ston** *Rus.* Bustan. Qoraqalpog'iston Respublikasi, W Uzbekistan *41.49N 60.51E*
8 *M17* **Boston Bar** British Columbia, SW Canada *49.54N 121.22W*
29 *T10* **Boston Mountains** ▲▲ Arkansas, C USA
13 *P8* **Bostonnais** ≈ Québec, SE Canada
Bostyn' *see* Bastyn'
114 *J10* **Bosut** ≈ E Croatia
160 *C11* **Botād** Gujarāt, W India *22.12N 71.43E*
191 *T9* **Botany Bay** *inlet* New South Wales, SE Australia
85 *G18* **Boteti** *var.* Botletle. ≈ N Botswana
116 *J9* **Botev** ▲ C Bulgaria *42.45N 24.57E*
116 *H9* **Botevgrad** *prev.* Orkhaniye. Sofiya, W Bulgaria *42.55N 23.46E*
95 *J16* **Bothnia, Gulf of** *Fin.* Pohjanlahti, *Swe.* Bottniska Viken. *gulf* N Baltic Sea
191 *P17* **Bothwell** Tasmania, SE Australia *42.24S 147.01E*
106 *H5* **Boticas** Vila Real, N Portugal *41.40N 7.40W*
57 *W10* **Boti-Pasi** Sipaliwini, C Suriname *4.08N 55.27W*
Botletle *see* Boteti
131 *P16* **Botlikh** Chechenskaya Respublika, SW Russian Federation *42.39N 46.12E*
119 *N10* **Botna** ≈ E Moldova
153 *P13* **Botogot', Tizmasi** *Rus.* Khrebet Babatag. ▲▲ Tajikistan/Uzbekistan
118 *I9* **Botoşani** *Hung.* Botosány. Botoşani, NE Romania *47.43N 26.40E*
118 *K8* **Botoşani** ◈ *county* NE Romania
Botosány *see* Botoşani
167 *P4* **Botou** *prev.* Bozhen. Hebei, E China *38.09N 116.37E*
101 *M20* **Botrange** ▲ E Belgium *50.30N 6.03E*
109 *O21* **Botricello** Calabria, SW Italy *38.56N 16.51E*
85 *I23* **Botshabelo** Free State, C South Africa *29.15S 26.51E*
95 *J15* **Botsmark** Västerbotten, N Sweden *64.15N 20.15E*
85 *G19* **Botswana** *off.* Republic of Botswana. ◆ *republic* S Africa
31 *N2* **Bottineau** North Dakota, N USA *48.49N 100.28W*
Bottniska Viken *see* Bothnia, Gulf of
62 *L9* **Botucatu** São Paulo, S Brazil *22.52S 48.30W*
78 *M16* **Bouaflé** C Ivory Coast *6.58N 5.45W*
79 *N16* **Bouaké** *var.* Bwake. C Ivory Coast *7.39N 5.01W*
81 *G14* **Bouar** Nana-Mambéré, W Central African Republic *5.58N 15.38E*
76 *H7* **Bouarfa** NE Morocco *32.33N 1.54W*
113 *B19* **Boubín** ▲ SW Czech Republic *49.00N 13.51E*
81 *I14* **Bouca** Ouham, W Central African Republic *6.57N 18.18E*
13 *T5* **Boucher** ≈ Québec, SE Canada
105 *R15* **Bouches-du-Rhône** ◈ *department* SE France
76 *C9* **Bou Craa** *var.* Bu Craa. NW Western Sahara *26.31N 12.52W*
79 *O9* **Boû Djébéha** *oasis* C Mali *18.39N 3.45W*
110 *C8* **Boudry** Neuchâtel, W Switzerland *46.57N 6.46E*
188 *L2* **Bougainville, Cape** *headland* Western Australia *13.53S 126.01E*
67 *E24* **Bougainville, Cape** *headland* East Falkland, Falkland Islands *51.18S 58.28W*
Bougainville, Détroit de *see* Bougainville Strait, Vanuatu
195 *S13* **Bougainville Island** *island* NE PNG
195 *T13* **Bougainville Strait** *strait* N Solomon Islands
197 *B12* **Bougainville Strait** *Fr.* Détroit de Bougainville. *strait* C Vanuatu
176 *U8* **Bouganville, Selat** *strait* Papua, E Indonesia
123 *J11* **Bougaroun, Cap** *headland* NE Algeria *37.07N 6.18E*
79 *R8* **Boughessa** Kidal, NE Mali *20.05N 2.13E*
Bougie *see* Béjaïa
78 *L13* **Bougouni** Sikasso, SW Mali *11.22N 7.24W*
101 *J24* **Bouillon** Luxembourg, SE Belgium *49.46N 5.04E*
76 *K5* **Bouira** *var.* Bouïra. N Algeria *36.22N 3.55E*
76 *D8* **Bou-Izakarn** SW Morocco *29.12N 9.43W*
76 *B9* **Boujdour** *var.* Bojador. W Western Sahara *26.06N 14.28W*
76 *G5* **Boukhalef** ✕ (Tanger) N Morocco *35.45N 5.53W*
Boukombé *see* Boukoumbé
79 *R14* **Boukoumbé** *var.* Boukombé. C Benin *10.13N 1.09E*
78 *G6* **Boû Lanouâr** Dakhlet Nouâdhibou, W Mauritania *21.16N 16.28W*
39 *T4* **Boulder** Colorado, C USA *40.01N 105.18W*
35 *R10* **Boulder** Montana, NW USA *46.14N 112.07W*
37 *X12* **Boulder City** Nevada, W USA *35.58N 114.49W*
189 *T7* **Boulia** Queensland, C Australia *23.02S 139.58E*
13 *N10* **Boullé** ≈ Québec, SE Canada
104 *J9* **Boulogne** ≈ NW France
Boulogne *see* Boulogne-sur-Mer
104 *L16* **Boulogne-sur-Gesse** Haute-Garonne, S France *43.18N 0.39E*
105 *N1* **Boulogne-sur-Mer** *var.* Boulogne; *anc.* Bononia, Gesoriacum, Gessoriacum. Pas-de-Calais, N France *50.43N 1.36E*
197 *I7* **Bouloupari** Province Sud, S New Caledonia *21.54S 166.04E*
79 *Q12* **Boulsa** C Burkina *12.40N 0.28W*
79 *W11* **Boultoum** Zinder, C Niger *14.43N 10.22E*
197 *K13* **Bouma** Taveuni, N Fiji *16.49S 179.50W*
81 *G16* **Boumba** ≈ SE Cameroon
78 *J9* **Boûmdeïd** *var.* Boumdeït. Assaba, S Mauritania *17.25N 11.21W*
Boumdeït *see* Boûmdeïd
117 *C17* **Boumistós** ▲ W Greece *38.48N 20.59E*
79 *O15* **Bouna** NE Ivory Coast *9.16N 3.00W*
21 *P4* **Boundary Bald Mountain** ▲ Maine, NE USA *45.45N 70.10W*
37 *S8* **Boundary Peak** ▲ Nevada, W USA *37.50N 118.21W*
78 *M14* **Boundiali** N Ivory Coast *9.31N 6.28W*
81 *G19* **Boundji** Cuvette, C Congo *1.04S 15.18E*
79 *O13* **Boundoukui** *var.* Bondoukui, Bondoukuy. W Burkina *11.51N 3.47W*
38 *L2* **Bountiful** Utah, W USA *40.53N 111.52W*
Bounty Basin *see* Bounty Trough
203 *Q16* **Bounty Bay** *bay* Pitcairn Island, C Pacific Ocean
199 *Jj14* **Bounty Islands** *island group* S NZ
183 *Q13* **Bounty Trough** *var.* Bounty Basin. *undersea feature* S Pacific Ocean
197 *I6* **Bourail** Province Sud, C New Caledonia *21.35S 165.29E*
29 *V5* **Bourbeuse River** ≈ Missouri, C USA
105 *Q9* **Bourbon-Lancy** Saône-et-Loire, C France *46.39N 3.48E*
33 *N11* **Bourbonnais** Illinois, N USA *41.08N 87.52W*
105 *O10* **Bourbonnais** *cultural region* C France
105 *S7* **Bourbonne-les-Bains** Haute-Marne, N France *48.00N 5.43E*
Bourbon Vendée *see* la Roche-sur-Yon
76 *M8* **Bourdj Messaouda** E Algeria *30.18N 9.19E*
79 *Q10* **Bourem** Gao, C Mali *16.56N 0.21W*
Bourg *see* Bourg-en-Bresse
105 *N11* **Bourganeuf** Creuse, C France *45.57N 1.47E*
Bourgas *see* Burgas
Bourge-en-Bresse *see* Bourg-en-Bresse
105 *S10* **Bourg-en-Bresse** *var.* Bourg, Bourge-en-Bresse. Ain, E France *46.12N 5.13E*
105 *O8* **Bourges** *anc.* Avaricum. Cher, C France *47.06N 2.24E*
105 *T11* **Bourget, Lac du** ◎ E France
105 *P8* **Bourgogne** *Eng.* Burgundy. ◈ *region* E France
105 *S11* **Bourgoin-Jallieu** Isère, E France *45.34N 5.16E*
105 *R14* **Bourg-St-Andéol** Ardèche, E France *44.24N 4.36E*
105 *U11* **Bourg-St-Maurice** Savoie, E France *45.37N 6.49E*
110 *C11* **Bourg St.Pierre** Valais, SW Switzerland *45.54N 7.10E*
78 *H8* **Boû Rjeimât** *well* W Mauritania *19.06N 15.16W*
191 *P5* **Bourke** New South Wales, SE Australia *30.07S 145.57E*
99 *M24* **Bournemouth** S England, UK *50.43N 1.54W*
101 *M23* **Bourscheid** Diekirch, NE Luxembourg *49.55N 6.04E*
76 *K6* **Bou Saâda** *var.* Bou Saada. N Algeria *35.13N 4.09E*
38 *I13* **Bouse Wash** ≈ Arizona, SW USA
105 *N10* **Boussac** Creuse, C France *46.20N 2.12E*
104 *M16* **Boussens** Haute-Garonne, S France *43.10N 0.58E*
80 *H12* **Bousso** *prev.* Fort-Bretonnet. Chari-Baguirmi, S Chad *10.31N 16.45E*
78 *H9* **Boutilimit** Trarza, SW Mauritania *17.33N 14.42W*
67 *D21* **Bouvet Island** ◇ *Norwegian dependency* S Atlantic Ocean
79 *U11* **Bouza** Tahoua, SW Niger *14.25N 6.09E*
111 *R10* **Bovec** *Ger.* Flitsch, *It.* Plezzo. NW Slovenia *46.21N 13.33E*
100 *J8* **Bovenkarspel** Noord-Holland, NW Netherlands *52.33N 5.03E*
31 *V5* **Bovey** Minnesota, N USA *47.18N 93.25W*
34 *M9* **Bovill** Idaho, NW USA *46.50N 116.24W*
26 *L4* **Bovina** Texas, SW USA *34.30N 102.52W*
109 *M17* **Bovino** Puglia, SE Italy *41.14N 15.19E*
63 *C17* **Bovril** Entre Ríos, E Argentina *31.24S 59.25W*
30 *L2* **Bowbells** North Dakota, N USA *48.48N 102.15W*
9 *Q16* **Bow City** Alberta, SW Canada *50.27N 112.16W*
31 *O8* **Bowdle** South Dakota, N USA *45.27N 99.39W*
189 *X6* **Bowen** Queensland, NE Australia *20.00S 148.10E*
198 *B4* **Bowers Ridge** *undersea feature* S Bering Sea
15 *Jj4* **Bowes Point** *headland* Nunavut, N Canada *67.46N 101.51W*
27 *S5* **Bowie** Texas, SW USA *33.33N 97.51W*
9 *R17* **Bow Island** Alberta, SW Canada *49.52N 111.24W*
Bowkān *see* Būkān
22 *J7* **Bowling Green** Kentucky, S USA *36.59N 86.26W*
29 *V3* **Bowling Green** Missouri, C USA *39.20N 91.12W*
33 *R11* **Bowling Green** Ohio, N USA *41.22N 83.40W*
23 *W5* **Bowling Green** Virginia, NE USA *38.01N 77.20W*
30 *J6* **Bowman** North Dakota, N USA *46.10N 103.25W*
16 *N3* **Bowman Bay** *bay* NW Atlantic Ocean
204 *I5* **Bowman Coast** *physical region* Antarctica
30 *J7* **Bowman-Haley Lake** ▣ North Dakota, N USA
205 *Z11* **Bowman Island** *island* Antarctica
Bowo *see* Bomi
191 *S9* **Bowral** New South Wales, SE Australia *34.29S 150.28E*
194 *K14* **Bowutu Mountains** ▲▲ C PNG
85 *I16* **Bowwood** Southern, S Zambia *17.09S 26.16E*
30 *I12* **Box Butte Reservoir** ▣ Nebraska, C USA
30 *J10* **Box Elder** South Dakota, N USA *44.06N 103.04W*
97 *M18* **Boxholm** Östergötland, S Sweden *58.12N 15.04E*
Bo Xian/Boxian *see* Bozhou
167 *Q4* **Boxing** Shandong, E China *37.06N 118.05E*
101 *L14* **Boxmeer** Noord-Brabant, SE Netherlands *51.39N 5.57E*
101 *J14* **Boxtel** Noord-Brabant, S Netherlands *51.36N 5.19E*
142 *J10* **Boyabat** Sinop, N Turkey *41.27N 34.45E*
56 *F9* **Boyacá** *off.* Departamento de Boyacá. ◈ *province* C Colombia
119 *O4* **Boyarka** Kyyivs'ka Oblast', N Ukraine *50.19N 30.19E*
24 *H7* **Boyce** Louisiana, S USA *31.23N 92.40W*
35 *U11* **Boyd** Montana, NW USA *45.27N 109.03W*
27 *S6* **Boyd** Texas, SW USA *33.01N 97.33W*
23 *V8* **Boydton** Virginia, NE USA *36.40N 78.24W*
Boyer Ahmadī va Kohkīlūyeh *see* Kohgīlūyeh va Būyer Aḩmad
31 *T13* **Boyer River** ≈ Iowa, C USA
23 *W8* **Boykins** Virginia, NE USA *36.35N 77.11W*
9 *Q13* **Boyle** Alberta, SW Canada *54.38N 112.45W*
99 *D16* **Boyle** *Ir.* Mainistirna Búille. C Ireland *53.58N 8.18W*
99 *F17* **Boyne** *Ir.* An Bhóinn. ≈ E Ireland
33 *Q5* **Boyne City** Michigan, N USA *45.13N 85.00W*
25 *Z14* **Boynton Beach** Florida, SE USA *26.31N 80.04W*
153 *O13* **Boysun** *Rus.* Baysun. Surkhondaryo Viloyati, S Uzbekistan *38.13N 67.07E*
Bozau *see* Întorsura Buzăului
142 *B12* **Bozcaada** *island* Çanakkale, NW Turkey
142 *C14* **Boz Dağları** ▲▲ W Turkey
35 *S11* **Bozeman** Montana, NW USA *45.40N 111.02W*
Bozen *see* Bolzano
81 *J16* **Bozene** Equateur, NW Dem. Rep. Congo *2.55N 19.15E*
167 *P7* **Bozhou** *var.* Boxian, Bo Xian. Anhui, E China *33.49N 115.49E*
142 *H16* **Bozkır** Konya, S Turkey *37.10N 32.15E*
142 *K13* **Bozok Yaylası** *plateau* C Turkey
81 *H14* **Bozoum** Ouham-Pendé, W Central African Republic *6.17N 16.26E*
143 *N16* **Bozova** Sanlıurfa, S Turkey *37.22N 38.33E*
Bozrah *see* Buşrá ash Shām
142 *E12* **Bozüyük** Bilecik, NW Turkey *39.55N 30.01E*
108 *B9* **Bra** Piemonte, NW Italy *44.42N 7.51E*
204 *G4* **Brabant Island** *island* Antarctica
101 *I20* **Brabant Wallon** ◈ *province* C Belgium
115 *F15* **Brač** *var.* Brach, *It.* Brazza; *anc.* Brattia. *island* S Croatia
Bracara Augusta *see* Braga
109 *H15* **Bracciano** Lazio, C Italy *42.04N 12.12E*

◆ Country
● Country Capital
◇ Dependent Territory
○ Dependent Territory Capital
◈ Administrative Region
✕ International Airport
▲ Mountain
▲▲ Mountain Range
◬ Volcano
≈ River
◎ Lake
▣ Reservoir

BRACCIANO, LAGO DI – BRYUKHOVETSKAYA

109 H14 Bracciano, Lago di ◎ C Italy
12 H13 Bracebridge Ontario, S Canada 45.01N 79.19W
Brach see Brač
95 G17 Bräcke Jämtland, C Sweden 62.42N 15.30E
27 P12 Brackettville Texas, SW USA 29.18N 100.25W
99 N22 Bracknell S England, UK 51.25N 0.46W
63 K14 Braço do Norte Santa Catarina, S Brazil 28.16S 49.11W
118 G11 Brad Hung. Brád. Hunedoara, SW Romania 45.52N 23.00E
109 N18 Bradano ≈ S Italy
25 V13 Bradenton Florida, SE USA 27.30N 82.34W
12 H14 Bradford Ontario, S Canada 44.09N 79.34W
99 L17 Bradford N England, UK 53.48N 1.45W
29 W10 Bradford Arkansas, C USA 35.25N 91.27W
20 D12 Bradford Pennsylvania, NE USA 41.57N 78.38W
29 T15 Bradley Arkansas, C USA 33.06N 93.39W
27 P7 Bradshaw Texas, SW USA 32.06N 99.52W
27 Q9 Brady Texas, SW USA 31.07N 99.22W
27 Q9 Brady Creek ≈ Texas, SW USA
98 J10 Braemar NE Scotland, UK 57.12N 2.52W
118 K8 Brăeşti Botoşani, NW Romania 47.50N 26.26E
106 G5 Braga anc. Bracara Augusta. Braga, NW Portugal 41.31N 8.25W
106 G5 Braga ◐ district N Portugal
118 J15 Bragadiru Teleorman, S Romania 43.43N 25.32E
63 C20 Bragado Buenos Aires, E Argentina 35.10S 60.28W
106 J5 Bragança Eng. Braganza; anc. Julio Briga. Bragança, NE Portugal 41.46N 6.46W
106 I5 Bragança ◐ district N Portugal
62 N9 Bragança Paulista São Paulo, S Brazil 22.55S 46.30W
Braganza see Bragança
Bragin see Brahin
31 V7 Braham Minnesota, N USA 45.43N 93.10W
Brahe see Brda
Brahestad see Raahe
121 O20 Brahin Rus. Bragin. Homyel'skaya Voblasts', SE Belarus 51.46N 30.16E
159 U15 Brahmanbaria Chittagong, E Bangladesh 23.58N 91.04E
160 O12 Brāhmani ≈ E India
160 N13 Brahmapur Orissa, E India 19.21N 84.51E
133 S10 Brahmaputra var. Padma, Tsangpo, Ben. Jamuna, Chin. Yarlung Zangbo Jiang, Ind. Bramaputra, Dihang, Siang. ≈ S Asia
99 H19 Braich y Pwll headland NW Wales, UK 52.47N 4.46W
191 R10 Braidwood New South Wales, SE Australia 35.26S 149.48E
32 M11 Braidwood Illinois, N USA 41.16N 88.12W
118 M13 Brăila Brăila, E Romania 45.17N 27.57E
118 L13 Brăila ◐ county SE Romania
101 G19 Braine-l'Alleud Brabant Wallon, C Belgium 50.40N 4.22E
101 F19 Braine-le-Comte Hainaut, SW Belgium 50.37N 4.07E
31 U6 Brainerd Minnesota, N USA 46.22N 94.10W
101 J19 Braives Liège, E Belgium 50.37N 5.09E
85 H23 Brak ≈ C South Africa
Brak see Birāk
101 E18 Brakel Oost-Vlaanderen, SW Belgium 50.50N 3.48E
100 J13 Brakel Gelderland, C Netherlands 51.49N 5.05E
78 H9 Brakna ◐ region S Mauritania
97 J17 Brålanda Västra Götaland, S Sweden 58.32N 12.18E
Bramaputra see Brahmaputra
97 F23 Bramming Ribe, W Denmark 55.28N 8.42E
12 G15 Brampton Ontario, S Canada 43.42N 79.46W
102 F12 Bramsche Niedersachsen, NW Germany 52.25N 7.58E
118 J12 Bran Ger. Törzburg, Hung. Törcsvár. Braşov, S Romania 45.31N 25.23E
31 W8 Branch Minnesota, N USA 45.29N 92.57W
23 R14 Branchville South Carolina, SE USA 33.15N 80.49W
49 Y6 Branco, Cabo headland E Brazil 7.07S 34.45W
60 F11 Branco, Rio ≈ N Brazil
110 J8 Brand Vorarlberg, W Austria 47.07N 9.45E
85 B18 Brandberg ▲ NW Namibia 21.20S 14.22E
97 H14 Brandbu Oppland, S Norway 60.24N 10.30E
97 F22 Brande Ringkøbing, W Denmark 55.57N 9.07E
Brandebourg see Brandenburg
102 M12 Brandenburg var. Brandenburg an der Havel. Brandenburg, NE Germany 52.25N 12.34E
22 K5 Brandenburg Kentucky, S USA 37.58N 86.11W
102 N12 Brandenburg off. Freie und Hansestadt Hamburg, Fr. Brandebourg. ◐ state NE Germany
Brandenburg an der Havel see Brandenburg
85 I23 Brandfort Free State, C South Africa 28.42S 26.28E
9 W16 Brandon Manitoba, S Canada 49.49N 99.57W
25 V12 Brandon Florida, SE USA 27.56N 82.17W
24 L6 Brandon Mississippi, S USA 32.16N 90.01W
99 A20 Brandon Mountain Ir. Cnoc Bréanainn. ▲ SW Ireland 52.13N 10.16W
Brandsen see Coronel Brandsen
97 I14 Brandval Hedmark, S Norway 60.18N 12.01E
85 F24 Brandvlei Northern Cape, W South Africa 30.19S 20.31E
25 U9 Branford Florida, SE USA 29.57N 82.54W
112 K7 Braniewo Ger. Braunsberg. Warmińsko-Mazurskie, NE Poland 54.24N 19.49E
204 H3 Bransfield Strait strait Antarctica
39 U8 Branson Colorado, C USA 37.01N 103.52W
29 T8 Branson Missouri, C USA 36.38N 93.13W
12 G16 Brantford Ontario, S Canada 43.04N 80.21W
104 L12 Brantôme Dordogne, SW France 45.21N 0.37E
190 L12 Branxholme Victoria, SE Australia 37.51S 141.48E
Brasil see Brazil
61 C16 Brasiléia Acre, W Brazil 10.58S 48.45W
61 K18 Brasília ● (Brazil) Distrito Federal, C Brazil 15.45S 47.57W
Braslav see Braslaw
120 J12 Braslaw Pol. Brasław, Rus. Braslav. Vitsyebskaya Voblasts', N Belarus 55.37N 27.01E
118 J12 Braşov Ger. Kronstadt, Hung. Brassó; prev. Oraşul Stalin. Braşov, C Romania 45.40N 25.34E
118 I12 Braşov ◐ county C Romania
176 W7 Bras, Pulau island Kepulauan Mapia, E Indonesia
79 U18 Brass Bayelsa, S Nigeria 4.19N 6.21E
101 H16 Brasschaat var. Brasschaet. Antwerpen, N Belgium 51.16N 4.30E
Brasschaet see Brasschaat
175 O4 Brassey, Banjaran var. Brassey Range. ▲▲ East Malaysia
Brassey Range see Brassey, Banjaran
Brassó see Braşov
25 T1 Brasstown Bald ▲ Georgia, SE USA 34.52N 83.48W
115 K22 Brataj Vlorë, SW Albania 40.18N 19.37E
116 J10 Bratan var. Morozov. ▲ C Bulgaria 42.31N 25.08E
113 F21 Bratislava Ger. Pressburg, Hung. Pozsony. ● (Slovakia) Bratislavský Kraj, W Slovakia 48.10N 17.10E
113 H21 Bratislavský Kraj ◐ region W Slovakia
116 H10 Bratiya ▲ C Bulgaria 42.36N 24.08E
126 J14 Bratsk Irkutskaya Oblast', C Russian Federation 56.19N 101.49E
119 Q8 Brats'ke Mykolayivs'ka Oblast', S Ukraine 47.52N 31.34E
126 J14 Bratskoye Vodokhranilishche Eng. Bratsk Reservoir. ▣ S Russian Federation
Bratsk Reservoir see Bratskoye Vodokhranilishche
Brattia see Brač
96 D9 Brattvåg Møre og Romsdal, S Norway 62.36N 6.21E
114 K12 Bratunac Republika Srpska, E Bosnia and Herzegovina 44.10N 19.21E
116 J10 Bratya Daskalovi prev. Grozdovo. Stara Zagora, C Bulgaria 42.13N 25.21E
111 U2 Braunau ≈ N Austria
Braunau see Braunau am Inn
111 Q4 Braunau am Inn var. Braunau. Oberösterreich, N Austria 48.16N 13.03E
Braunsberg see Braniewo
102 J13 Braunschweig Eng./Fr. Brunswick. Niedersachsen, N Germany 52.16N 10.31E
Brava see Baraawe
107 Y6 Brava, Costa coastal region NE Spain
45 V16 Brava, Punta headland E Panama 8.21N 78.22W
97 N17 Bråviken inlet S Sweden
58 B10 Bravo, Cerro ▲ N Peru 5.33S 79.10W
Bravo del Norte, Río/Bravo, Río see Grande, Rio
37 X17 Brawley California, W USA 32.58N 115.31W
99 G18 Bray Ir. Bré. E Ireland 53.12N 6.06W
61 G16 Brazil off. Federative Republic of Brazil, Port. República Federativa do Brasil, Sp. Brasil; prev. United States of Brazil. ◆ federal republic South America
67 K15 Brazil Basin var. Brazilian Basin, Brazil'skaya Kotlovina. undersea feature W Atlantic Ocean
Brazilian Basin see Brazil Basin
Brazilian Highlands see Central, Planalto
Brazil'skaya Kotlovina see Brazil Basin
27 U10 Brazos River ≈ Texas, SW USA
176 Yy13 Brazza ≈ Papua, E Indonesia
Brazza see Brač
81 G21 Brazzaville ● (Congo) Capital District, S Congo 4.13S 15.13E
81 G21 Brazzaville ✕ Le Pool, S Congo 4.15S 15.15E
114 J11 Brčko Republika Srpska, NE Bosnia and Herzegovina 44.52N 18.49E
112 H8 Brda Ger. Brahe. ≈ N Poland
Bré see Bray
193 A23 Breaksea Sound sound South Island, NZ
192 L4 Bream Bay bay North Island, NZ
192 L4 Bream Head headland North Island, NZ 35.51S 174.35E
Bréanainn, Cnoc see Brandon Mountain
47 S6 Brea, Punta headland W Puerto Rico 17.56N 66.55W
24 I9 Breaux Bridge Louisiana, S USA 30.16N 91.54W
118 J13 Breaza Prahova, SE Romania 45.06N 25.44E
174 K14 Brebes Jawa, C Indonesia 6.54S 109.00E
98 K10 Brechin E Scotland, UK 56.44N 2.38W
101 H15 Brecht Antwerpen, N Belgium 51.21N 4.32E
39 S4 Breckenridge Colorado, C USA 39.28N 106.02W
31 R6 Breckenridge Minnesota, N USA 46.15N 96.35W
27 R6 Breckenridge Texas, SW USA 32.45N 98.54W
99 J21 Brecknock cultural region SE Wales, UK
65 G25 Brecknock, Península headland S Chile 54.39S 71.48W
113 G19 Břeclav Ger. Lundenburg. Jihomoravský Kraj, SE Czech Republic 49.04N 16.51E
99 J21 Brecon E Wales, UK 51.57N 3.26W
99 J21 Brecon Beacons ▲▲ S Wales, UK
101 I14 Breda Noord-Brabant, S Netherlands 51.34N 4.46E
97 K20 Bredaryd Jönköping, S Sweden 57.10N 13.45E
85 F26 Bredasdorp Western Cape, SW South Africa 34.28S 20.03E
95 H16 Bredbyn Västernorrland, N Sweden 63.28N 18.04E
125 E13 Bredy Chelyabinskaya Oblast', C Russian Federation 52.23N 60.24E
101 K17 Bree Limburg, NE Belgium 51.07N 5.36E
69 T15 Breede ≈ S South Africa
100 I7 Breezand Noord-Holland, NW Netherlands 52.52N 4.47E
115 P18 Bregalnica ≈ E FYR Macedonia
110 I6 Bregenz anc. Brigantium. Vorarlberg, W Austria 47.31N 9.44E
110 J7 Bregenzer Wald ▲▲ W Austria
116 F6 Bregovo Vidin, NW Bulgaria 44.07N 22.40E
104 H5 Bréhat, Île de island NW France
94 H2 Breidhafjördhur bay W Iceland
94 L3 Breidhdalsvík Austurland, E Iceland 64.48N 14.02W
110 H9 Breil Ger. Brigels. Graubünden, S Switzerland 46.46N 9.04E
94 J8 Breivikbotn Finnmark, N Norway 70.36N 22.19E
96 I9 Brekken Sør-Trøndelag, S Norway 62.39N 11.49E
96 G7 Brekstad Sør-Trøndelag, S Norway 63.42N 9.40E
96 B10 Bremangerlandet island S Norway
Brême see Bremen
102 H11 Bremen Fr. Brême. Bremen, NW Germany 53.05N 8.48E
25 R3 Bremen Georgia, SE USA 33.43N 85.09W
33 O11 Bremen Indiana, N USA 41.24N 86.07W
102 H10 Bremen off. Freie Hansestadt Bremen, Fr. Brême. ◐ state N Germany
102 G9 Bremerhaven Bremen, NW Germany 53.33N 8.34E
Bremersdorp see Manzini
34 G8 Bremerton Washington, NW USA 47.34N 122.37W
102 H10 Bremervörde Niedersachsen, NW Germany 53.29N 9.06E
27 U9 Bremond Texas, SW USA 31.10N 96.40W
27 U10 Brenham Texas, SW USA 30.10N 96.24W
110 M8 Brenner Tirol, W Austria 47.10N 11.51E
Brenner, Col du/Brennero, Passo del see Brenner Pass
110 M8 Brenner Pass var. Brenner Sattel, Fr. Col du Brenner, Ger. Brennerpass, It. Passo del Brennero. pass Austria/Italy 47.00N 11.29E
Brenner Sattel see Brenner Pass
110 G10 Brenno ≈ SW Switzerland
108 F7 Breno Lombardia, N Italy 45.58N 10.18E
25 O5 Brent Alabama, S USA 32.54N 87.10W
108 H7 Brenta ≈ NE Italy
99 P21 Brentwood E England, UK 51.38N 0.21E
20 L14 Brentwood Long Island, New York, NE USA 40.46N 73.12W
108 F7 Brescia anc. Brixia. Lombardia, N Italy 45.33N 10.13E
101 D15 Breskens Zeeland, SW Netherlands 51.24N 3.33E
Breslau see Dolnośląskie
108 H5 Bressanone Ger. Brixen. Trentino-Alto Adige, N Italy 46.43N 11.41E
98 M2 Bressay island NE Scotland, UK
104 K9 Bressuire Deux-Sèvres, W France 46.50N 0.29W
121 F20 Brest Pol. Brześć nad Bugiem, Rus. Brest-Litovsk; prev. Brześć Litewski. Brestskaya Voblasts', SW Belarus 52.06N 23.42E
104 F5 Brest Finistère, NW France 48.24N 4.30W
Brest-Litovsk see Brest
114 A10 Brestova Istra, NW Croatia 45.09N 14.13E
Brestskaya Oblast' see Brestskaya Voblasts'
121 G19 Brestskaya Voblasts' prev. Rus. Brestskaya Oblast'. ◐ province SW Belarus
104 G6 Bretagne Eng. Brittany; Lat. Britannia Minor. ◐ region NW France
118 G12 Bretea-Română Hung. Oláhbrettye; prev. Bretea-Romînă. Hunedoara, W Romania 45.39N 23.00E
Bretea-Romînă see Bretea-Română
105 O3 Breteuil Oise, N France 49.37N 2.18E
104 I10 Breton, Pertuis inlet W France
24 L10 Breton Sound sound Louisiana, S USA
192 K2 Brett, Cape headland North Island, NZ 35.11S 174.21E
103 G21 Bretten Baden-Württemberg, SW Germany 49.01N 8.42E
101 K15 Breugel Noord-Brabant, S Netherlands 51.30N 5.30E
108 B6 Breuil-Cervinia It. Cervinia. Valle d'Aosta, NW Italy 45.57N 7.37E
100 I11 Breukelen Utrecht, C Netherlands 52.11N 5.01E
23 P10 Brevard North Carolina, SE USA 35.13N 82.43W
40 L9 Brevig Mission Alaska, USA 65.19N 166.29W
97 G16 Brevik Telemark, S Norway 59.03N 9.40E
191 P5 Brewarrina New South Wales, SE Australia 30.01S 146.50E
21 R6 Brewer Maine, NE USA 44.46N 68.44W
31 T11 Brewster Minnesota, N USA 43.43N 95.28W
31 N14 Brewster Nebraska, C USA 41.54N 99.52W
33 U12 Brewster Ohio, N USA 40.42N 81.36W
191 O8 Brewster, Lake ◎ New South Wales, SE Australia
25 P7 Brewton Alabama, S USA 31.06N 87.04W
Brezhnev see Naberezhnyye Chelny
111 W12 Brežice Ger. Rann. E Slovenia 45.54N 15.35E
116 G9 Breznik Pernik, W Bulgaria 42.45N 22.54E
113 K19 Brezno Ger. Bries, Briesen, Hung. Breznóbánya; prev. Brezno nad Hronom. Banskobystrický Kraj, C Slovakia 48.49N 19.40E
Breznóbánya/Brezno nad Hronom see Brezno
118 I12 Brezoi Vâlcea, SW Romania 45.18N 24.15E
116 J10 Brezovo prev. Abrashlare. Plovdiv, C Bulgaria 42.19N 25.05E
81 K14 Bria Haute-Kotto, C Central African Republic 6.30N 22.00E
105 U13 Briançon anc. Brigantio. Hautes-Alpes, SE France 44.55N 6.37E
38 K7 Brian Head ▲ Utah, W USA 37.40N 112.49W
105 O7 Briare Loiret, C France 47.35N 2.46E
191 V2 Bribie Island island Queensland, E Australia
45 O14 Bribrí Limón, E Costa Rica 9.37N 82.51W
118 L8 Briceni var. Brinceni, Rus. Brichany. N Moldova 48.21N 27.02E
Bricgstow see Bristol
Brichany see Briceni
101 M24 Bridel Luxembourg, C Luxembourg 49.40N 6.03E
99 J22 Bridgend S Wales, UK 51.30N 3.37W
12 I14 Bridgenorth Ontario, SE Canada 44.21N 78.22W
25 Q1 Bridgeport Alabama, S USA 34.57N 85.42W
37 R8 Bridgeport California, W USA 38.14N 119.13W
20 L13 Bridgeport Connecticut, NE USA 41.10N 73.12W
33 N15 Bridgeport Illinois, N USA 38.42N 87.45W
30 J14 Bridgeport Nebraska, C USA 41.37N 103.07W
27 S6 Bridgeport Texas, SW USA 33.12N 97.45W
23 S3 Bridgeport West Virginia, NE USA 39.17N 80.15W
27 S5 Bridgeport, Lake ◎ Texas, SW USA
35 U11 Bridger Montana, NW USA 45.16N 108.55W
20 I17 Bridgeton New Jersey, NE USA 39.24N 75.10W
188 J14 Bridgetown Western Australia 34.01S 116.07E
47 Y14 Bridgetown ● (Barbados) SW Barbados 13.05N 59.36W
191 P17 Bridgewater Tasmania, SE Australia 42.47S 147.15E
11 P16 Bridgewater Nova Scotia, SE Canada 44.19N 64.30W
21 P12 Bridgewater Massachusetts, NE USA 41.59N 70.58W
31 Q11 Bridgewater South Dakota, N USA 43.33N 97.30W
23 U5 Bridgewater Virginia, NE USA 38.22N 78.58W
21 P8 Bridgton Maine, NE USA 44.04N 70.43W
99 K23 Bridgwater SW England, UK 51.08N 3.00W
99 K22 Bridgwater Bay bay SW England, UK
99 O16 Bridlington E England, UK 54.04N 0.12W
99 O16 Bridlington Bay bay E England, UK
191 P15 Bridport Tasmania, SE Australia 41.03S 147.26E
99 K24 Bridport S England, UK 50.43N 2.43W
105 O5 Brie cultural region N France
Brieg see Brzeg
Briel see Brielle
100 G12 Brielle var. Briel, Bril, Eng. The Brill. Zuid-Holland, SW Netherlands 51.54N 4.10E
110 E9 Brienz Bern, C Switzerland 46.45N 8.00E
110 E9 Brienzer See ◎ SW Switzerland
Bries/Briesen see Brezno
Brietzig see Brzesko
105 S4 Briey Meurthe-et-Moselle, NE France 49.15N 5.57E
110 E10 Brig Fr. Brigue, It. Briga. Valais, SW Switzerland 46.19N 8.00E
Briga see Brig
103 G24 Brigach ≈ S Germany
20 K17 Brigantine New Jersey, NE USA 39.23N 74.21W
Brigantio see Briançon
Brigantium see Bregenz
Brigels see Breil
27 S9 Briggs Texas, SW USA 30.52N 97.55W
38 L1 Brigham City Utah, W USA 41.30N 112.00W
12 J15 Brighton Ontario, SE Canada 44.01N 77.44W
99 O23 Brighton SE England, UK 50.49N 0.10W
39 T4 Brighton Colorado, C USA 39.58N 104.46W
32 K15 Brighton Illinois, N USA 39.01N 90.09W
105 T16 Brignoles Var, W France 43.25N 6.03E
Brigue see Brig
107 O7 Brihuega Castilla-La Mancha, C Spain 40.45N 2.52W
114 A10 Brijuni It. Brioni. island group NW Croatia
78 G12 Brikama W Gambia 13.13N 16.37W
Bril see Brielle
Brill, The see Brielle
103 G15 Brilon Nordrhein-Westfalen, W Germany 51.24N 8.34E
Brinceni see Briceni
109 Q18 Brindisi anc. Brundisium, Brundusium. Puglia, SE Italy 40.39N 17.55E
29 W11 Brinkley Arkansas, C USA 34.53N 91.11W
Brioni see Brijuni
105 P12 Brioude anc. Brivas. Haute-Loire, C France 45.18N 3.22E
Briovera see St-Lô
191 U2 Brisbane state capital Queensland, E Australia 27.30S 153.00E
191 V2 Brisbane ✕ Queensland, E Australia 27.30S 153.00E
27 P2 Briscoe Texas, SW USA 35.34N 100.17W
108 H10 Brisighella Emilia-Romagna, C Italy 44.12N 11.45E
110 G11 Brissago Ticino, S Switzerland 46.07N 8.40E
99 K22 Bristol anc. Bricgstow. SW England, UK 51.27N 2.34W
20 M12 Bristol Connecticut, NE USA 41.40N 72.56W
25 R9 Bristol Florida, SE USA 30.25N 84.58W
21 N9 Bristol New Hampshire, NE USA 43.34N 71.42W
31 Q8 Bristol South Dakota, N USA 45.18N 97.45W
23 P8 Bristol Tennessee, S USA 36.36N 82.11W
20 M8 Bristol Vermont, NE USA 44.07N 73.00W
41 N14 Bristol Bay bay Alaska, USA
99 I22 Bristol Channel inlet England/Wales, UK
37 W14 Bristol Lake ◎ California, W USA
29 P10 Bristow Oklahoma, C USA 35.49N 96.23W
88 C10 Britain var. Great Britain. island UK
Britannia Minor see Bretagne
8 L12 British Columbia Fr. Colombie-Britannique. ◐ province SW Canada
British Guiana see Guyana
British Honduras see Belize
181 Q7 British Indian Ocean Territory ◇ UK dependent territory C Indian Ocean
88 B9 British Isles island group NW Europe
8 I1 British Mountains ▲▲ Yukon Territory, NW Canada
British North Borneo see Sabah
British Solomon Islands Protectorate see Solomon Islands
47 S8 British Virgin Islands var. Virgin Islands. ◇ UK dependent territory E West Indies
85 J21 Brits North-West, N South Africa 25.39S 27.46E
85 H24 Britstown Northern Cape, W South Africa 30.36S 23.30E
12 F12 Britt Ontario, S Canada 45.46N 80.34W
31 V12 Britt Iowa, C USA 43.06N 93.48W
Brittany see Bretagne
31 Q7 Britton South Dakota, N USA 45.47N 97.45W
Briva Curretia see Brive-la-Gaillarde
Briva Isarae see Pontoise
Brivas see Brioude
Brive see Brive-la-Gaillarde
104 M12 Brive-la-Gaillarde prev. Brive, anc. Briva Curretia. Corrèze, C France 45.09N 1.31E
107 O4 Briviesca Castilla-León, N Spain 42.33N 3.19W
Brixen see Bressanone
Brixia see Brescia
151 S15 Brlik prev. Novotroickoje, Novotroitskoye. Zhambyl, SE Kazakhstan 43.39N 73.45E
Brněnský Kraj see Jihomoravský Kraj
113 G18 Brno Ger. Brünn. Jihomoravský Kraj, SE Czech Republic 49.10N 16.35E
98 G7 Broad Bay bay NW Scotland, UK
27 X8 Broaddus Texas, SW USA 31.18N 94.16W
191 O12 Broadford Victoria, SE Australia 37.07S 145.04E
98 G9 Broadford N Scotland, UK 57.14N 5.54W
98 J13 Broad Law ▲ S Scotland, UK 55.30N 3.22W
25 U3 Broad River ≈ Georgia, SE USA
23 N8 Broad River ≈ North Carolina/South Carolina, SE USA
189 Y8 Broadsound Range ▲▲ Queensland, E Australia
35 X11 Broadus Montana, NW USA 45.28N 105.22W
23 U4 Broadway Virginia, NE USA 38.36N 78.48W
120 E9 Broceni Saldus, SW Latvia 56.41N 22.31E
9 U11 Brochet Manitoba, C Canada 57.55N 101.40W
9 U10 Brochet, Lac ◎ Manitoba, C Canada
13 S5 Brochet, Lac au ◎ Québec, SE Canada
103 K14 Brocken ▲ C Germany 51.48N 10.38E
21 O12 Brockton Massachusetts, NE USA 42.04N 71.01W
12 L14 Brockville Ontario, SE Canada 44.36N 75.42W
20 D13 Brockway Pennsylvania, NE USA 41.14N 78.45W
Brod/Bród see Slavonski Brod
15 Kk1 Brodeur Peninsula peninsula Baffin Island, Nunavut, NE Canada
98 H13 Brodick W Scotland, UK 55.34N 5.09W
Brod na Savi see Slavonski Brod
112 K9 Brodnica Ger. Buddenbrock. Kujawski-pomorskie, C Poland 53.15N 19.22E
114 G10 Brod-Posavina off. Brodsko-Posavska Županija. ◐ province NE Croatia
118 J5 Brody L'vivs'ka Oblast', NW Ukraine 50.04N 25.07E
97 G22 Brædstrup Vejle, C Denmark 55.58N 9.37E
100 I10 Broek-in-Waterland Noord-Holland, C Netherlands 52.27N 4.58E
34 L13 Brogan Oregon, NW USA 44.15N 117.34W
112 N10 Brok Mazowieckie, C Poland 52.42N 21.53E
29 P9 Broken Arrow Oklahoma, C USA 36.03N 95.47W
191 T9 Broken Bay bay New South Wales, SE Australia
31 N15 Broken Bow Nebraska, C USA 41.24N 99.38W
29 R13 Broken Bow Oklahoma, C USA 34.01N 94.44W
29 R12 Broken Bow Lake ▣ Oklahoma, C USA
190 L6 Broken Hill New South Wales, SE Australia 31.58S 141.27E
181 S10 Broken Ridge undersea feature S Indian Ocean
194 H10 Broken Water Bay bay W Bismarck Sea
57 W10 Brokopondo Brokopondo, NE Suriname 05.04N 55.00W
57 W10 Brokopondo ◐ district C Suriname
Bromberg see Bydgoszcz
97 L22 Bromölla Skåne, S Sweden 56.04N 14.28E
99 L20 Bromsgrove W England, UK 52.19N 2.03W
97 G20 Brønderslev Nordjylland, N Denmark 57.16N 9.58E
108 D8 Broni Lombardia, N Italy 45.04N 9.18E
8 K11 Bronlund Peak ▲ British Columbia, W Canada 57.27N 126.43W
95 F14 Brønnøysund Nordland, C Norway 65.28N 12.13E
25 V10 Bronson Florida, SE USA 29.25N 82.38W
33 Q11 Bronson Michigan, N USA 41.52N 85.11W
27 X8 Bronson Texas, SW USA 31.20N 94.00W
109 L24 Bronte Sicilia, Italy, C Mediterranean Sea 37.46N 14.49E
27 P8 Bronte Texas, SW USA 31.53N 100.17W
27 Y9 Brookeland Texas, SW USA 31.05N 93.57W
179 O15 Brooke's Point Palawan, W Philippines 8.54N 117.54E
29 T3 Brookfield Missouri, C USA 39.46N 93.04W
24 K7 Brookhaven Mississippi, S USA 31.34N 90.26W
34 E16 Brookings Oregon, NW USA 42.03N 124.16W
31 R10 Brookings South Dakota, N USA 44.15N 96.46W
31 W14 Brooklyn Iowa, C USA 41.43N 92.27W
31 U8 Brooklyn Park Minnesota, N USA 45.06N 93.18W
23 U7 Brookneal Virginia, NE USA 37.03N 78.56W
9 R16 Brooks Alberta, SW Canada 50.34N 111.54W
27 V11 Brookshire Texas, SW USA 29.47N 95.57W
40 L8 Brooks Mountain ▲ Alaska, USA 65.31N 167.24W
40 M11 Brooks Range ▲▲ Alaska, USA
33 O12 Brookston Indiana, N USA 40.34N 86.53W
25 V11 Brooksville Florida, SE USA 28.33N 82.23W
25 N4 Brooksville Mississippi, S USA 33.13N 88.34W
188 J13 Brookton Western Australia 32.24S 117.04E
33 Q14 Brookville Indiana, N USA 39.25N 85.00W
20 D13 Brookville Pennsylvania, NE USA 41.07N 79.05W
33 Q14 Brookville Lake ▣ Indiana, N USA
188 K5 Broome Western Australia 17.58S 122.15E
39 S4 Broomfield Colorado, C USA 39.55N 105.05W
Broos see Orăştie
98 J7 Brora N Scotland, UK 57.58N 4.00W
98 I7 Brora ≈ N Scotland, UK
97 F23 Brørup Ribe, W Denmark 55.28N 9.01E
97 L23 Brösarp Skåne, S Sweden 55.43N 14.10E
118 J9 Broşteni Suceava, NE Romania 47.13N 25.43E
104 M6 Brou Eure-et-Loir, C France 48.12N 1.10E
Broucsella see Brussel/Bruxelles
Broughton Bay see Tongjosŏn-man
16 O1 Broughton Island Nunavut, NE Canada 67.34N 63.55W
144 G7 Broummâna C Lebanon 33.53N 35.39E
24 I9 Broussard Louisiana, S USA 30.09N 91.57W
100 E13 Brouwersdam dam SW Netherlands 51.46N 3.51E
100 E13 Brouwershaven Zeeland, SW Netherlands 51.44N 3.50E
119 P4 Brovary Kyyivs'ka Oblast', N Ukraine 50.30N 30.43E
97 G20 Brovst Nordjylland, N Denmark 57.06N 9.31E
33 S8 Brown City Michigan, N USA 43.12N 82.50W
26 M6 Brownfield Texas, SW USA 33.10N 102.16W
35 Q7 Browning Montana, NW USA 48.33N 113.00W
35 R6 Brown, Mount ▲ Montana, NW USA 48.52N 111.08W
194 K15 Brown River ≈ S PNG
(0) M9 Browns Bank undersea feature NW Atlantic Ocean
33 O14 Brownsburg Indiana, N USA 39.50N 86.24W
20 J16 Browns Mills New Jersey, NE USA 39.58N 74.33W
46 J12 Browns Town C Jamaica 18.28N 77.22W
33 P15 Brownstown Indiana, N USA 38.52N 86.02W
31 R8 Browns Valley Minnesota, N USA 45.36N 96.49W
22 K7 Brownsville Kentucky, S USA 37.09N 86.13W
22 F9 Brownsville Tennessee, S USA 35.34N 89.15W
27 T17 Brownsville Texas, SW USA 25.55N 97.28W
57 W10 Brownsweg Brokopondo, C Suriname
31 U9 Brownton Minnesota, N USA 44.43N 94.21W
21 R5 Brownville Junction Maine, NE USA 45.20N 69.04W
27 R8 Brownwood Texas, SW USA 31.41N 98.59W
27 R8 Brownwood Lake ▣ Texas, SW USA
106 I9 Brozas Extremadura, W Spain 39.37N 6.48W
121 M18 Brozha Mahilyowskaya Voblasts', E Belarus 52.57N 29.07E
105 O2 Bruay-en-Artois Pas-de-Calais, N France 50.31N 2.30E
105 P2 Bruay-sur-l'Escaut Nord, N France 50.24N 3.33E
12 F13 Bruce Peninsula peninsula Ontario, S Canada
22 H9 Bruceton Tennessee, S USA 36.02N 88.14W
27 T9 Bruceville Texas, SW USA 31.17N 97.15W
103 G21 Bruchsal Baden-Württemberg, SW Germany 49.07N 8.34E
111 Q7 Bruck Salzburg, NW Austria 47.18N 12.51E
Bruck see Bruck an der Mur
111 Y4 Bruck an der Leitha Niederösterreich, NE Austria 48.02N 16.47E
111 V7 Bruck an der Mur var. Bruck. Steiermark, C Austria 47.26N 15.13E
103 M24 Bruckmühl Bayern, SE Germany 47.52N 11.54E
173 Dd3 Brueuh, Pulau island NW Indonesia
Bruges see Brugge
110 F6 Brugg Aargau, NW Switzerland 47.28N 8.13E
101 C16 Brugge Fr. Bruges. West-Vlaanderen, NW Belgium 51.13N 3.13E
111 R9 Bruggen Kärnten, S Austria 46.46N 13.13E
103 E16 Brühl Nordrhein-Westfalen, W Germany 50.49N 6.54E
101 F14 Bruinisse Zeeland, SW Netherlands 51.40N 4.04E
174 L5 Bruit, Pulau island East Malaysia
12 K10 Brûlé, Lac ◎ Québec, SE Canada
32 M4 Brule River ≈ Michigan/Wisconsin, N USA
101 H23 Brûly Namur, S Belgium 49.55N 4.31E
61 N17 Brumado Bahia, E Brazil 14.13S 41.37W
100 M11 Brummen Gelderland, E Netherlands 52.04N 6.10E
96 H13 Brumunddal Hedmark, S Norway 60.52N 10.55E
25 Q6 Brundidge Alabama, S USA 31.43N 85.49W
Brundisium/Brundusium see Brindisi
35 N15 Bruneau River ≈ Idaho, NW USA
Bruneck see Brunico
174 Mm4 Brunei off. Sultanate of Brunei, Mal. Negara Brunei Darussalam. ◆ monarchy SE Asia
175 N3 Brunei Bay var. Teluk Brunei. bay N Brunei
Brunei, Teluk see Brunei Bay
Brunei Town see Bandar Seri Begawan
108 H5 Brunico Ger. Bruneck. Trentino-Alto Adige, N Italy 46.49N 11.57E
Brünn see Brno
193 G17 Brunner, Lake ◎ South Island, NZ
101 M18 Brunssum Limburg, SE Netherlands 50.57N 5.58E
25 W7 Brunswick Georgia, SE USA 31.09N 81.30W
21 Q8 Brunswick Maine, NE USA 43.54N 69.58W
23 V3 Brunswick Maryland, NE USA 39.18N 77.37W
29 T3 Brunswick Missouri, C USA 39.25N 93.07W
33 T11 Brunswick Ohio, N USA 41.14N 81.50W
Brunswick see Braunschweig
65 H24 Brunswick, Península headland S Chile 53.30S 71.27W
113 H17 Bruntál Ger. Freudenthal. Moravskoslezský Kraj, E Czech Republic 50.00N 17.27E
205 N3 Brunt Ice Shelf ice shelf Antarctica
Brusa see Bursa
39 U3 Brush Colorado, C USA 40.15N 103.37W
44 M5 Brus Laguna Gracias a Dios, E Honduras 15.46N 84.31W
62 K13 Brusque Santa Catarina, S Brazil 27.07S 48.54W
Brussa see Bursa
101 E18 Brussel var. Brussels, Fr. Bruxelles, Ger. Brüssel; anc. Broucsella. ● (Belgium) Brussels, C Belgium see also Bruxelles 50.52N 4.21E
Brüssel/Brussels see Brussel/Bruxelles
119 O5 Brusyliv Zhytomyrs'ka Oblast', N Ukraine 50.16N 29.31E
191 Q12 Bruthen Victoria, SE Australia 37.43S 147.49E
Bruttium see Calabria
Brüx see Most
101 E18 Bruxelles var. Brussels, Dut. Brussel, Ger. Brüssel; anc. Broucsella. ● (Belgium) Brussels, C Belgium see also Brussel 50.52N 4.21E
56 J7 Bruzual Apure, W Venezuela 7.59N 69.18W
33 Q11 Bryan Ohio, N USA 41.28N 84.33W
27 U10 Bryan Texas, SW USA 30.40N 96.22W
204 J4 Bryan Coast physical region Antarctica
126 I13 Bryanka Krasnoyarskiy Kray, C Russian Federation 59.01N 93.13E
119 Y7 Bryanka Luhans'ka Oblast', E Ukraine 48.30N 38.45E
190 J8 Bryan, Mount ▲ South Australia 33.25S 138.59E
130 I6 Bryansk Bryanskaya Oblast', W Russian Federation 53.15N 34.06E
130 H6 Bryanskaya Oblast' ◐ province W Russian Federation
204 J5 Bryant, Cape headland Antarctica
29 U8 Bryant Creek ≈ Missouri, C USA
38 K8 Bryce Canyon canyon Utah, W USA
121 O15 Bryli Rus. Bryli. Mahilyowskaya Voblasts', E Belarus 53.55N 30.31E
97 C17 Bryne Rogaland, S Norway 58.43N 5.37E
27 R6 Bryson Texas, SW USA 33.09N 98.23W
23 N10 Bryson City North Carolina, SE USA 35.25N 83.27W
12 K11 Bryson, Lac ◎ Québec, SE Canada
130 K13 Bryukhovetskaya Krasnodarskiy Kray, SW Russian Federation 45.49N 38.01E

◆ Country ● Country Capital ◇ Dependent Territory ○ Dependent Territory Capital ◐ Administrative Region ✕ International Airport ▲ Mountain ▲▲ Mountain Range ⩚ Volcano ≈ River ◎ Lake ▣ Reservoir

Brzeg – Buyant

113 H15 **Brzeg** Ger. Brieg; anc. Civitas Altae Ripae. Opolskie, S Poland 50.52N 17.27E
113 G14 **Brzeg Dolny** Ger. Dyhernfurth. Dolnośląskie, SW Poland 51.15N 16.42E
Brześć Litewski/Brzešć nad Bugiem see Brest
113 L17 **Brzesko** Ger. Brietzig. Małopolskie, S Poland 49.57N 20.35E
Brzeżany see Berezhany
112 K12 **Brzeziny** Łódzkie, C Poland 51.48N 19.42E
Brzostowica Wielka see Vyalikaya Byerastavitsa
113 O17 **Brzozów** Podkarpackie, SE Poland 49.38N 22.00E
Bsharrī/Bsherri see Bcharré
197 I13 **Bua** Vanua Levu, N Fiji 16.48S 178.36E
97 J20 **Bua** Halland, S Sweden 57.13N 12.07E
84 M13 **Bua** ~ C Malawi
Bua see Čiovo
83 L18 **Bu'aale** It. Buale. Jubbada Dhexe, SW Somalia 0.52N 42.37E
201 Q8 **Buada Lagoon** lagoon Nauru, C Pacific Ocean
195 W14 **Buala** Santa Isabel, E Solomon Islands 8.06S 159.31E
Buale see Bu'aale
202 H1 **Buariki** atoll Tungaru, W Kiribati
178 I10 **Bua Yai** var. Ban Bua Yai. Nakhon Ratchasima, E Thailand 15.34N 102.25E
77 P8 **Bu'ayrāt al Ḩasūn** var. Buwayrāt al Hasūn. C Libya 31.22N 15.41E
78 H13 **Buba** S Guinea-Bissau 11.36N 14.55W
175 Qq7 **Bubaa** Sulawesi, N Indonesia 0.32N 122.27E
83 D20 **Bubanza** NW Burundi 3.04S 29.22E
85 K18 **Bubi** prev. Bubye. ~ S Zimbabwe
148 L11 **Būbīyan, Jazīrat** island E Kuwait
Bublitz see Bobolice
Bubye see Bubi
197 J13 **Buca** prev. Mbutha. Vanua Levu, N Fiji 16.39S 179.51E
142 F16 **Bucak** Burdur, SW Turkey 37.26N 30.32E
56 G8 **Bucaramanga** Santander, N Colombia 7.07N 73.10W
109 M18 **Buccino** Campania, S Italy 40.37N 15.25E
118 K9 **Bucecea** Botoşani, NE Romania 47.43N 26.24E
118 J6 **Buchach** Pol. Buczacz. Ternopil's'ka Oblast', W Ukraine 49.04N 25.22E
191 Q12 **Buchan** Victoria, SE Australia 37.26S 148.11E
78 J17 **Buchanan** prev. Grand Bassa. SW Liberia 5.52N 10.03W
25 R3 **Buchanan** Georgia, SE USA 33.48N 85.11W
33 O11 **Buchanan** Michigan, N USA 41.49N 86.21W
23 T6 **Buchanan** Virginia, NE USA 37.31N 79.40W
27 R10 **Buchanan Dam** Texas, SW USA 30.42N 98.24W
27 R10 **Buchanan, Lake** ⊡ Texas, SW USA
98 L8 **Buchan Ness** headland NE Scotland, UK 57.28N 1.46W
11 T12 **Buchans** Newfoundland and Labrador, SE Canada 48.49N 56.44W
Bucharest see București
103 H20 **Buchen** Baden-Württemberg, SW Germany 49.31N 9.18E
102 I10 **Buchholz in der Nordheide** Niedersachsen, NW Germany 53.19N 9.52E
110 F7 **Buchs** Aargau, N Switzerland 47.24N 8.03E
110 I8 **Buchs** Sankt Gallen, NE Switzerland 47.10N 9.26E
102 H13 **Bückeburg** Niedersachsen, NW Germany 52.16N 9.03E
38 K14 **Buckeye** Arizona, SW USA 33.22N 112.34W
Buckeye State see Ohio
23 S4 **Buckhannon** West Virginia, NE USA 38.59N 80.13W
27 T9 **Buckholts** Texas, SW USA 30.52N 97.07W
98 K8 **Buckie** NE Scotland, UK 57.39N 2.55W
12 M12 **Buckingham** Québec, SE Canada 45.34N 75.25W
23 U6 **Buckingham** Virginia, NE USA 37.33N 78.33W
99 N21 **Buckinghamshire** cultural region SE England, UK
41 N8 **Buckland** Alaska, USA 65.58N 161.07W
190 G7 **Buckleboo** South Australia 32.55S 136.11E
28 K7 **Bucklin** Kansas, C USA 37.33N 99.37W
29 T3 **Bucklin** Missouri, C USA 39.46N 92.53W
38 I12 **Buckskin Mountains** ▲ Arizona, SW USA
21 R7 **Bucksport** Maine, NE USA 44.34N 68.46W
84 A9 **Buco Zau** Cabinda, NW Angola 4.47S 12.32E
Bu Craa see Bou Craa
118 K14 **București** Eng. Bucharest, Ger. Bukarest; prev. Altenburg, anc. Cetatea Damboviței. ● (Romania) București, S Romania 44.27N 26.06E
33 S12 **Bucyrus** Ohio, N USA 40.48N 82.58W
Buczacz see Buchach
96 E9 **Bud** Møre og Romsdal, S Norway 62.55N 6.55E
27 S11 **Buda** Texas, SW USA 30.05N 97.50W
121 O18 **Buda-Kashalyova** Rus. Buda-Koshelëvo. Homyel'skaya Voblasts', SE Belarus 52.43N 30.34E
Buda-Koshelëvo see Buda-Kashalyova
177 G4 **Budalin** Sagaing, C Myanmar 22.24N 95.07E
113 J22 **Budapest** off. Budapest Főváros, SCr. Budimpešta. ● (Hungary) Pest, N Hungary 47.30N 19.03E
158 K11 **Budaun** Uttar Pradesh, N India 28.01N 79.07E
147 O9 **Budayyi'ah** oasis C Saudi Arabia 23.04N 43.29E
205 Y12 **Budd Coast** physical region Antarctica
Buddenbrock see Brodnica
109 C17 **Budduso** Sardegna, Italy, C Mediterranean Sea 40.37N 9.19E
99 I23 **Bude** SW England, UK 50.49N 4.33W
24 J7 **Bude** Mississippi, S USA 31.27N 90.51W
Budějovický Kraj see Jihočeský Kraj
101 K16 **Budel** Noord-Brabant, SE Netherlands 51.16N 5.34E
102 I8 **Büdelsdorf** Schleswig-Holstein, N Germany 54.20N 9.40E
131 O14 **Budënnovsk** Stavropol'skiy Kray, SW Russian Federation 44.46N 44.07E
118 K14 **Budeşti** Călăraşi, SE Romania 44.13N 26.31E
Budgewoi see Budgewoi Lake
191 T8 **Budgewoi Lake** var. Budgewoi. New South Wales, SE Australia 33.13S 151.34E
94 I2 **Búdhardalur** Vesturland, W Iceland 65.07N 21.45W
Budimpešta see Budapest
81 J16 **Budjala** Equateur, NW Dem. Rep. Congo 2.39N 19.42E
108 G10 **Budrio** Emilia-Romagna, C Italy 44.33N 11.34E
Budslav see Budslaw
121 K14 **Budslaw** Rus. Budslav. Minskaya Voblasts', N Belarus 54.46N 27.26E
Budua see Budva
174 Ll5 **Budu, Tanjung** headland East Malaysia 2.51N 111.42E
115 J17 **Budva** It. Budua. Montenegro, SW Serbia and Montenegro (Yugoslavia) 42.17N 18.49E
Budweis see České Budějovice
Budyšin see Bautzen
81 D16 **Buea** Sud-Ouest, SW Cameroon 4.09N 9.13E
105 S13 **Buëch** ~ SE France
20 J17 **Buena** New Jersey, NE USA 39.30N 74.55W
64 K12 **Buena Esperanza** San Luis, C Argentina 34.45S 65.15W
56 C11 **Buenaventura** Valle del Cauca, W Colombia 3.54N 77.01W
42 I4 **Buenaventura** Chihuahua, N Mexico 29.52N 107.25W
59 M18 **Buena Vista** Santa Cruz, C Bolivia 17.27S 63.40W
42 G10 **Buenavista** Baja California Sur, W Mexico 23.39N 109.40W
39 S5 **Buena Vista** Colorado, C USA 38.50N 106.07W
25 S5 **Buena Vista** Georgia, SE USA 32.19N 84.31W
23 T6 **Buena Vista** Virginia, NE USA 37.43N 79.21W
46 F5 **Buena Vista, Bahia de** bay N Cuba
37 R13 **Buena Vista Lake Bed** ◎ California, W USA
107 P8 **Buendía, Embalse de** ⊡ C Spain
65 F16 **Bueno, Río** ~ S Chile
64 N12 **Buenos Aires** hist. Santa Maria del Buen Aire. ● (Argentina) Buenos Aires, E Argentina 34.40S 58.30W
45 O15 **Buenos Aires** Puntarenas, SE Costa Rica 9.09N 83.15W
63 C20 **Buenos Aires** off. Provincia de Buenos Aires. ◆ province E Argentina
65 H19 **Buenos Aires, Lago** var. Lago General Carrera. ◎ Argentina/Chile
56 C13 **Buesaco** Nariño, SW Colombia 1.22N 77.07W
31 U8 **Buffalo** Minnesota, N USA 45.10N 93.49W
28 T6 **Buffalo** Missouri, C USA 37.38N 93.05W
20 D10 **Buffalo** New York, NE USA 42.53N 78.52W
29 K8 **Buffalo** Oklahoma, C USA 36.50N 99.37W
30 J7 **Buffalo** South Dakota, N USA 45.35N 103.32W
27 V8 **Buffalo** Texas, SW USA 31.25N 96.04W
35 W12 **Buffalo** Wyoming, C USA 44.21N 106.40W
31 U11 **Buffalo Center** Iowa, C USA 43.23N 93.57W
26 M3 **Buffalo Lake** ⊡ Texas, SW USA
32 K7 **Buffalo Lake** ⊡ Wisconsin, N USA
9 S12 **Buffalo Narrows** Saskatchewan, C Canada 55.52N 108.28W
29 U9 **Buffalo River** ~ Arkansas, C USA
31 R5 **Buffalo River** ~ Minnesota, N USA
22 I10 **Buffalo River** ~ Tennessee, S USA
32 J6 **Buffalo River** ~ Wisconsin, N USA
46 L12 **Buff Bay** E Jamaica 18.18N 76.40W
25 T3 **Buford** Georgia, SE USA 34.07N 84.00W
30 J3 **Buford** North Dakota, N USA 48.00N 103.58W
35 Y17 **Buford** Wyoming, C USA 41.05N 105.17W
118 J14 **Buftea** București, S Romania 44.34N 25.57E
86 I9 **Bug** Bel. Zakhodni Buh, Eng. Western Bug, Rus. Zapadnyy Bug, Ukr. Zakhidnyy Buh. ~ E Europe
56 D11 **Buga** Valle del Cauca, W Colombia 3.52N 76.16W
168 F7 **Buga** Dzavhan, W Mongolia 47.42N 94.53E
105 O17 **Bugarach, Pic du** ▲ S France 42.52N 2.23E
152 B12 **Bugdaýly** Rus. Bugdayly. Balkan Welaýaty, W Turkmenistan 38.42N 54.14E
Buggs Island Lake see John H.Kerr Reservoir
Bughotu see Santa Isabel
175 Q12 **Bugingkalo** Sulawesi, C Indonesia 4.49S 121.42E
66 P6 **Bugio** island Madeira, Portugal, NE Atlantic Ocean
94 M8 **Bugøynes** Finnmark, N Norway 69.57N 29.34E
129 Q3 **Bugrino** Nenetskiy Avtonomnyy Okrug, NW Russian Federation 68.48N 49.12E
131 T5 **Bugul'ma** Respublika Tatarstan, W Russian Federation 54.31N 52.45E
Bügür see Luntai
131 T6 **Buguruslan** Orenburgskaya Oblast', W Russian Federation 53.37N 52.30E
165 R9 **Buh He** ~ C China
35 O15 **Buhl** Idaho, NW USA 42.36N 114.45W
103 F22 **Bühl** Baden-Württemberg, SW Germany 48.42N 8.07E
118 K10 **Buhuşi** Bacău, E Romania 46.34N 26.55E
Buie d'Istria see Buje
99 J20 **Builth Wells** E Wales, UK 52.07N 3.27W
195 S13 **Buin** Bougainville Island, NE PNG 6.50S 155.42E
110 J9 **Buin, Piz** ▲ Austria/Switzerland 46.51N 10.07E
131 Q4 **Buinsk** Chuvashskaya Respublika, W Russian Federation 55.09N 47.00E
131 Q4 **Buinsk** Respublika Tatarstan, W Russian Federation 54.58N 48.16E
169 R8 **Buir Nur** Mong. Buyr Nuur. ◎ China/Mongolia see also Buyr Nuur
100 M5 **Buitenpost** Fris. Bûtenpost. Friesland, N Netherlands 53.15N 6.09E
Buitenzorg see Bogor
85 F19 **Buitepos** Omaheke, E Namibia 22.17S 19.59E
107 N7 **Buitrago del Lozoya** Madrid, C Spain 41.00N 3.38W
Buj see Buy
106 M13 **Bujalance** Andalucía, S Spain 37.54N 4.22W
115 O17 **Bujanovac** Serbia, SE Serbia and Montenegro (Yugoslavia) 42.29N 21.43E
107 S6 **Bujaraloz** Aragón, NE Spain 41.29N 0.10W
114 A9 **Buje** It. Buie d'Istria. Istra, NW Croatia 45.23N 13.40E
Bujnurd see Bojnūrd
83 D21 **Bujumbura** prev. Usumbura. ● (Burundi) W Burundi 3.25S 29.23E
83 D20 **Bujumbura** ✕ W Burundi 3.21S 29.19E
126 L15 **Bukachacha** Chitinskaya Oblast', S Russian Federation 52.49N 116.39E
165 N11 **Buka Daban** var. Bukadaban Feng. ▲ C China 36.09N 90.52E
Bukadaban Feng see Buka Daban
195 R11 **Buka Island** island NE PNG
83 F18 **Bukakata** S Uganda 0.18S 31.57E
81 N24 **Bukama** Katanga, SE Dem. Rep. Congo 9.13S 25.52E
148 J4 **Būkān** var. Bowkān. Āžarbāyjān-e Bākhtarī, NW Iran 36.31N 46.14E
Bukantau, Gory see Bo'kantov Tog'lari
Bukarest see București
81 O19 **Bukavu** prev. Costermansville. Sud Kivu, E Dem. Rep. Congo 2.18S 28.49E
83 F21 **Bukene** Tabora, NW Tanzania 4.15S 32.51E
147 W8 **Bū Khābī** var. Bakhābī. NW Oman 23.28N 56.06E
Bukhara see Buxoro
Bukharskaya Oblast' see Buxoro Viloyati
174 I12 **Bukitkemuning** Sumatera, W Indonesia 4.43S 104.27E
173 G8 **Bukittinggi** prev. Fort de Kock. Sumatera, W Indonesia 0.18S 100.19E
113 L21 **Bükk** ▲ NE Hungary
83 F19 **Bukoba** Kagera, NW Tanzania 1.19S 31.49E
115 N20 **Bukovo** S FYR Macedonia 40.59N 21.20E
110 G6 **Bülach** Zürich, NW Switzerland 47.31N 8.30E
Bŭlaevo see Bulayevo
168 I6 **Bulag** Hövsgöl, N Mongolia 49.51N 100.41E
168 M7 **Bulag** Töv, C Mongolia 48.09N 108.33E
168 I8 **Bulagiyn Denj** Arhangay, C Mongolia 47.14N 100.56E
191 U7 **Bulahdelah** New South Wales, SE Australia 32.24S 152.13E
176 Yy15 **Bulaka, Sungai** ~ Papua, E Indonesia
179 Qq12 **Bulan** Luzon, N Philippines 12.40N 123.55E
143 N11 **Bulancak** Giresun, N Turkey 40.57N 38.13E
158 J10 **Bulandshahr** Uttar Pradesh, N India 28.30N 77.49E
143 R14 **Bulanık** Muş, E Turkey 39.04N 42.16E
131 V7 **Bulanovo** Orenburgskaya Oblast', W Russian Federation 52.27N 55.08E
85 J17 **Bulawayo** var. Buluwayo. Matabeleland North, SW Zimbabwe 20.08S 28.36E
85 J17 **Bulawayo** ✕ Matabeleland North, SW Zimbabwe 20.00S 28.36E
151 Q6 **Bulayevo** Kaz. Bŭlaevo. Severnyy Kazakhstan, N Kazakhstan 54.55N 70.28E
142 D15 **Buldan** Denizli, SW Turkey 38.03N 28.49E
160 G12 **Buldāna** Mahārāshtra, C India 20.31N 76.18E
40 E16 **Buldir Island** island Aleutian Islands, Alaska, USA
Buldur see Burdur
168 H9 **Bulgan** Bayanhongor, C Mongolia 44.48N 98.39E
168 K6 **Bulgan** Bulgan, N Mongolia 50.31N 101.30E
168 F7 **Bulgan** Hovd, W Mongolia 46.57N 93.40E
168 J5 **Bulgan** Hövsgöl, N Mongolia 50.30N 101.28E
168 J10 **Bulgan** Ömnögovĭ, S Mongolia 44.07N 103.28E
168 J7 **Bulgan** ◆ province N Mongolia
116 H10 **Bulgaria** off. Republic of Bulgaria, Bul. Bŭlgariya; prev. People's Republic of Bulgaria. ◆ republic SE Europe
Bŭlgariya see Bulgaria
116 L9 **Bŭlgarka** ▲ E Bulgaria 42.43N 26.19E
175 T7 **Buli** Pulau Halmahera, E Indonesia 0.56N 128.17E
175 Tt7 **Buli, Teluk** bay Pulau Halmahera, E Indonesia
166 J13 **Buliu He** ~ S China
Bullange see Büllingen
Bulla, Ostrov see Xärä Zirä Adası
106 M11 **Bullaque** ~ C Spain
107 Q13 **Bullas** Murcia, SE Spain 38.01N 1.40W
82 M12 **Bullaxaar** Woqooyi Galbeed, NW Somalia 10.28N 44.15E
110 C9 **Bulle** Fribourg, SW Switzerland 46.37N 7.04E
193 G15 **Buller** ~ South Island, NZ
191 P12 **Buller, Mount** ▲ Victoria, SE Australia 37.10S 146.31E
38 H11 **Bullhead City** Arizona, SW USA 35.07N 114.32W
101 N21 **Büllingen** Fr. Bullange. Liège, E Belgium 50.23N 6.15E
Bullion State see Missouri
23 T14 **Bull Island** island South Carolina, SE USA
190 M4 **Bulloo River Overflow** wetland New South Wales, SE Australia
192 M12 **Bulls** Manawatu-Wanganui, North Island, NZ 40.10S 175.22E
23 T14 **Bulls Bay** bay South Carolina, SE USA
29 U9 **Bull Shoals Lake** ⊡ Arkansas/Missouri, C USA
189 Q2 **Bulman** Northern Territory, N Australia 13.39S 134.21E
168 I6 **Bulnayn Nuruu** ▲ N Mongolia
194 I13 **Bulolo** Morobe, C PNG 7.11S 146.34E
175 Qq7 **Bulowa, Gunung** ▲ Sulawesi, N Indonesia 0.33N 123.39E
Bulqiza see Bulqizë
115 L19 **Bulqizë** var. Bulqiza. Dibër, C Albania 41.30N 20.16E
Bulsar see Valsād
175 R7 **Buludawa Keten, Pegunungan** ▲ Sulawesi, N Indonesia
175 Pp13 **Bulukumba** prev. Boeloekoemba. Sulawesi, C Indonesia 5.34S 120.13E
153 O11 **Bulung'ur** Rus. Bulungur; prev. Krasnogvardeysk. Samarqand Viloyati, C Uzbekistan 39.46N 67.18E
81 I21 **Bulungu** Bandundu, SW Dem. Rep. Congo 4.34S 18.34E
Bulungur see Bulung'ur
Buluwayo see Bulawayo
81 K17 **Bumba** Equateur, N Dem. Rep. Congo 2.14N 22.25E
124 O15 **Bumbah, Khalīj al** gulf N Libya
168 K8 **Bumbat** Övörhangay, C Mongolia 46.30N 104.08E
83 F19 **Bumbire Island** island N Tanzania
175 Oo4 **Bum Bun, Pulau** island East Malaysia
83 J17 **Buna** North Eastern, NE Kenya 2.40N 39.34E
27 Y10 **Buna** Texas, SW USA 30.25N 94.00W
Bunab see Bonāb
Bunai see M'bunai
153 S13 **Bunay** S Tajikistan 38.29N 71.41E
188 I13 **Bunbury** Western Australia 33.24S 115.43E
99 E14 **Buncrana** Ir. Bun Cranncha. NW Ireland 55.07N 7.27W
Bun Cranncha see Buncrana
189 Z9 **Bundaberg** Queensland, E Australia 24.49S 152.16E
191 T5 **Bundarra** New South Wales, SE Australia 30.12S 151.06E
102 G13 **Bünde** Nordrhein-Westfalen, NW Germany 52.12N 8.34E
158 H13 **Būndi** Rājasthān, N India 25.28N 75.42E
194 I12 **Bundi** Madang, N PNG 5.40S 145.10E
Bun Dobhráin see Bundoran
99 D15 **Bundoran** Ir. Bun Dobhráin. NW Ireland 54.28N 8.16W
115 K18 **Bunë** SCr. Bojana. ~ Albania/Serbia and Montenegro (Yugoslavia) see also Bojana
179 R16 **Bunga** ~ Mindanao, S Philippines
173 Ff10 **Bungalaut, Selat** strait W Indonesia
178 Ii8 **Bung Kan** Nong Khai, E Thailand 18.19N 103.39E
189 N4 **Bungle Bungle Range** ▲ Western Australia
84 C10 **Bungo** Uíge, NW Angola 7.30S 15.24E
83 G18 **Bungoma** Western, W Kenya 0.34N 34.34E
170 Dd15 **Bungo-suidō** strait SW Japan
170 Dd13 **Bungo-Takada** Ōita, Kyūshū, SW Japan 33.36N 131.28E
102 K8 **Bungsberg** hill N Germany 54.12N 10.45E
Bungur see Bunyu
81 P17 **Bunia** Orientale, NE Dem. Rep. Congo 1.33N 30.16E
37 U6 **Bunker Hill** ▲ Nevada, W USA 39.16N 117.06W
24 I7 **Bunkie** Louisiana, S USA 30.58N 92.12W
25 X10 **Bunnell** Florida, SE USA 29.28N 81.15W
107 S10 **Buñol** País Valenciano, E Spain 39.25N 0.46W
100 K11 **Bunschoten** Utrecht, C Netherlands 52.15N 5.22E
142 K14 **Bünyan** Kayseri, C Turkey 38.51N 35.49E
175 Oo5 **Bunyu** var. Bungur. Borneo, N Indonesia 3.33N 117.50E
175 Oo5 **Bunyu, Pulau** island N Indonesia
Bunzlau see Bolesławiec
Buoddobohki see Patoniva
126 Ll6 **Buorkhaya Guba** bay N Russian Federation
176 Z15 **Bupul** Papua, E Indonesia 7.24S 140.57E
83 K19 **Bura** Coast, SE Kenya 1.06S 40.01E
82 P12 **Buraan** Sanaag, N Somalia 10.03N 49.08E
Būrabay see Borovoye
Buraida see Buraydah
Buraimi see Al Buraymī
151 Y11 **Buran** Vostochnyy Kazakhstan, E Kazakhstan 48.00N 85.09E
164 G15 **Burang** Xizang Zizhiqu, W China 30.28N 81.13E
Burao see Burco
144 H8 **Burāq** Dar'ā, S Syria 33.10N 36.28E
147 O6 **Buraydah** var. Buraida. Al Qaşim, N Saudi Arabia 26.50N 44.00E
37 S15 **Burbank** California, W USA 34.10N 118.19W
33 N11 **Burbank** Illinois, N USA 41.45N 87.48W
191 Q8 **Burcher** New South Wales, SE Australia 33.29S 147.16E
82 N13 **Burco** var. Burao, Bur'o. Togdheer, NW Somalia 9.29N 45.30E
152 L13 **Burdalyk** Lebap Welaýaty, E Turkmenistan 38.31N 64.21E
189 W6 **Burdekin River** ~ Queensland, NE Australia
29 O7 **Burden** Kansas, C USA 37.18N 96.45W
Burdigala see Bordeaux
142 E15 **Burdur** var. Buldur. Burdur, SW Turkey 37.43N 30.16E
142 E15 **Burdur** var. Buldur. ◆ province SW Turkey
142 E15 **Burdur Gölü** salt lake SW Turkey
67 H21 **Burdwood Bank** undersea feature SW Atlantic Ocean
82 I12 **Burē** Amhara, N Ethiopia 10.43N 37.09E
82 H13 **Burē** Oromo, C Ethiopia 8.13N 35.09E
95 J15 **Bureå** Västerbotten, N Sweden 64.36N 21.15E
103 G14 **Büren** Nordrhein-Westfalen, W Germany 51.34N 8.34E
168 K6 **Bürengiyn Nuruu** ▲ N Mongolia
168 E8 **Bürenhayrhan** Hovd, W Mongolia 46.04N 91.34E
Bürewāla see Mandi Bürewāla
127 N17 **Bureya** ~ SE Russian Federation
94 J9 **Burfjord** Troms, N Norway 69.55N 21.54E
102 L13 **Burg** var. Burg an der Ihle, Burg bei Magdeburg. Sachsen-Anhalt, C Germany 52.16N 11.51E
Burg an der Ihle see Burg
116 N10 **Burgas** var. Bourgas. Burgas, E Bulgaria 42.31N 27.30E
116 N9 **Burgas** ✕ Burgas, E Bulgaria 42.35N 27.33E
116 M10 **Burgas** ◆ province E Bulgaria
116 N10 **Burgaski Zaliv** gulf E Bulgaria
116 M10 **Burgasko Ezero** lagoon E Bulgaria
23 V11 **Burgaw** North Carolina, SE USA 34.33N 77.54W
Burg bei Magdeburg see Burg
110 E8 **Burgdorf** Bern, NW Switzerland 47.03N 7.37E
111 Y7 **Burgenland** off. Land Burgenland. ◆ state SE Austria
11 S13 **Burgeo** Newfoundland and Labrador, SE Canada 47.42N 57.29W
85 I24 **Burgersdorp** Eastern Cape, SE South Africa 31.00S 26.20E
85 K20 **Burgersfort** Mpumalanga, NE South Africa 24.39S 30.18E
103 N23 **Burghausen** Bayern, SE Germany 48.10N 12.48E
145 O5 **Burghūth, Sabkhat al** ◎ E Syria
103 M20 **Burglengenfeld** Bayern, SE Germany 49.11N 12.01E
43 P9 **Burgos** Tamaulipas, C Mexico 24.55N 98.46W
107 N4 **Burgos** Castilla-León, N Spain 42.21N 3.40W
107 N4 **Burgos** ◆ province Castilla-León, N Spain
Burgstadlberg see Hradiště
97 P20 **Burgsvik** Gotland, SE Sweden 57.01N 18.18E
Burgum see Bergum
Burgundy see Bourgogne
165 Q11 **Burhan Budai Shan** ▲ C China
142 B12 **Burhaniye** Balıkesir, W Turkey 39.28N 26.58E
160 G12 **Burhānpur** Madhya Pradesh, C India 21.18N 76.13E
179 Q11 **Burias Island** island C Philippines
131 W7 **Buribay** Respublika Bashkortostan, W Russian Federation 51.57N 58.11E
45 O17 **Burica, Punta** headland Costa Rica/Panama 8.02N 82.53W
178 Ii10 **Buriram** var. Buri Ram, Puriramya. Buri Ram, E Thailand 15.01N 103.06E
107 S10 **Burjassot** País Valenciano, E Spain 39.33N 0.25W
83 N16 **Burka Giibi** Hiiraan, C Somalia 3.52N 45.07E
153 X8 **Burkan** ~ E Kyrgyzstan
27 R4 **Burkburnett** Texas, SW USA 34.06N 98.34W
31 O12 **Burke** South Dakota, N USA 43.09N 99.18W
8 K15 **Burke Channel** channel British Columbia, W Canada
204 J10 **Burke Island** island Antarctica
22 L7 **Burkesville** Kentucky, S USA 36.47N 85.22W
189 T4 **Burketown** Queensland, NE Australia 17.48S 139.28E
27 Q8 **Burkett** Texas, SW USA 32.01N 99.17W
27 Y9 **Burkeville** Texas, SW USA 30.58N 93.41W
23 V7 **Burkeville** Virginia, NE USA 37.11N 78.12W
79 O12 **Burkina** off. Burkina Faso; prev. Upper Volta. ◆ republic W Africa
Burkina Faso see Burkina
204 L13 **Burks, Cape** headland Antarctica
12 H12 **Burk's Falls** Ontario, S Canada 45.38N 79.25W
103 H23 **Burladingen** Baden-Württemberg, S Germany 48.18N 9.05E
27 T7 **Burleson** Texas, SW USA 32.32N 97.19W
35 P15 **Burley** Idaho, NW USA 42.32N 113.47W
150 G8 **Burlin** Zapadnyy Kazakhstan, NW Kazakhstan 51.25N 52.42E
12 G16 **Burlington** Ontario, S Canada 43.21N 79.45W
39 W4 **Burlington** Colorado, C USA 39.16N 102.16W
31 Y15 **Burlington** Iowa, C USA 40.48N 91.05W
29 P5 **Burlington** Kansas, C USA 38.11N 95.44W
23 T9 **Burlington** North Carolina, SE USA 36.06N 79.26W
30 M3 **Burlington** North Dakota, N USA 48.16N 101.25W
20 L7 **Burlington** Vermont, NE USA 44.28N 73.13W
32 M9 **Burlington** Wisconsin, N USA 42.38N 88.12W
29 Q1 **Burlington Junction** Missouri, C USA 40.27N 95.04W
Burma see Myanmar
8 L17 **Burnaby** British Columbia, SW Canada 49.16N 122.58W
119 O12 **Burnas, Ozero** ◎ SW Ukraine
27 S10 **Burnet** Texas, SW USA 30.45N 98.13W
37 O3 **Burney** California, W USA 40.52N 121.42W
191 O16 **Burnie** Tasmania, SE Australia 41.06S 145.52E
99 L17 **Burnley** NW England, UK 53.48N 2.13W
Burnoye see Bauyrzhan Momyshuly
159 R15 **Burnpur** West Bengal, NE India 23.39N 86.55E
34 K14 **Burns** Oregon, NW USA 43.35N 119.03W
28 K11 **Burns Flat** Oklahoma, C USA 35.21N 99.10W
22 M7 **Burnside** Kentucky, S USA 36.55N 84.34W
15 I5 **Burnside** ~ Nunavut, NW Canada
34 L15 **Burns Junction** Oregon, NW USA 42.46N 117.51W
8 L13 **Burns Lake** British Columbia, SW Canada 54.13N 125.45W
31 V9 **Burnsville** Minnesota, N USA 44.49N 93.14W
23 P9 **Burnsville** North Carolina, SE USA 35.55N 82.18W
23 R4 **Burnsville** West Virginia, NE USA 38.50N 80.39W
12 I13 **Burnt River** ~ Ontario, SE Canada
12 I11 **Burntroot Lake** ◎ Ontario, SE Canada
9 W12 **Burntwood** ~ Manitoba, C Canada
Bur'o see Burco
164 L2 **Burqin** Xinjiang Uygur Zizhiqu, NW China 47.42N 86.49E
190 J8 **Burra** South Australia 33.41S 138.54E
191 S9 **Burragorang, Lake** ⊡ New South Wales, SE Australia
98 K5 **Burray** island NE Scotland, UK
115 L19 **Burrel** var. Burreli. Dibër, C Albania 41.36N 20.00E
Burreli see Burrel
191 R8 **Burrendong Reservoir** ⊡ New South Wales, SE Australia
191 R5 **Burren Junction** New South Wales, SE Australia 30.06S 149.01E
107 T9 **Burriana** País Valenciano, E Spain 39.54N 0.04W
191 R10 **Burrinjuck Reservoir** ⊡ New South Wales, SE Australia
38 J12 **Burro Creek** ~ Arizona, SW USA
42 M5 **Burro, Serranías del** ▲ NW Mexico
64 K7 **Burruyacú** Tucumán, N Argentina 26.28S 64.30W
142 E12 **Bursa** var. Brussa; prev. Brusa, anc. Prusa. Bursa, NW Turkey 40.12N 29.04E
142 D12 **Bursa** var. Brusa, Brussa. ◆ province NW Turkey
77 Y9 **Būr Safāga** var. Būr Safājah. E Egypt 26.41N 33.58E
Būr Safājah see Būr Safāga
Būr Sa'īd see Port Said
83 O14 **Bur Tinle** Mudug, C Somalia 7.50N 48.01E
33 Q5 **Burt Lake** ◎ Michigan, N USA
120 H7 **Burtnieks** var. Burtnieks Ezers. ◎ N Latvia
Burtnieks Ezers see Burtnieks
33 Q9 **Burton** Michigan, N USA 43.00N 84.16W
Burton on Trent see Burton upon Trent
99 M19 **Burton upon Trent** var. Burton on Trent, Burton-upon-Trent. C England, UK 52.48N 1.36W
95 J15 **Burträsk** Västerbotten, N Sweden 64.31N 20.40E
151 S14 **Burubaytal** prev. Burylbaytal. Zhambyl, SE Kazakhstan 45.01N 73.58E
Burujird see Borūjerd
Burultokay see Fuhai
147 R15 **Burūm** SE Yemen 14.22N 48.53E
Burunday see Boralday
83 D21 **Burundi** off. Republic of Burundi; prev. Kingdom of Burundi, Urundi. ◆ republic C Africa
175 S11 **Buru, Pulau** prev. Boeroe. island E Indonesia
79 T17 **Burutu** Delta, S Nigeria 5.18N 5.32E
8 G7 **Burwash Landing** Yukon Territory, W Canada 61.26N 139.12W
31 O14 **Burwell** Nebraska, C USA 41.46N 99.04W
99 L17 **Bury** NW England, UK 53.36N 2.16W
126 K15 **Buryatiya, Respublika** prev. Buryatskaya ASSR. ◆ autonomous republic S Russian Federation
Buryatskaya ASSR see Buryatiya, Respublika
Burylbaytal see Burubaytal
119 S3 **Buryn'** Sums'ka Oblast', NE Ukraine 51.12N 33.49E
99 P20 **Bury St Edmunds** hist. Beodericsworth. E England, UK 52.15N 0.43E
116 G8 **Būrziya** ~ NW Bulgaria
108 D9 **Busalla** Liguria, NW Italy 44.35N 8.55E
179 R17 **Busa, Mount** ▲ Mindanao, S Philippines 6.19N 124.29E
Busan see Pusan
145 N5 **Buşayrah** Dayr az Zawr, E Syria 35.03N 40.28E
Busen see Baba
149 N12 **Būshehr** off. Ostān-e Būshehr. ◆ province SW Iran
Būshehr/Bushire see Bandar-e Būshehr
27 N2 **Bushland** Texas, SW USA 35.11N 102.04W
32 J12 **Bushnell** Illinois, N USA 40.33N 90.30W
Busi see Biševo
83 G18 **Busia** SE Uganda 1.20N 34.48E
Busiasch see Buziaş
81 K16 **Businga** Equateur, NW Dem. Rep. Congo 3.19N 20.52E
81 J18 **Busira** ~ NW Dem. Rep. Congo
118 I5 **Bus'k** Rus. Busk. L'vivs'ka Oblast', W Ukraine 49.59N 24.34E
97 E14 **Buskerud** ◆ county S Norway
115 F14 **Buško Jezero** ⊡ SW Bosnia and Herzegovina
113 M15 **Busko-Zdrój** Świętokrzyskie, C Poland 50.28N 20.43E
Busra see Al Başrah, Iraq
Buşrá see Buşrá ash Shām, Syria
144 H9 **Buşrá ash Shām** var. Bosora, Bosra, Bozrah, Buşrá. Dar'ā, S Syria 32.31N 36.31E
188 I13 **Busselton** Western Australia 33.43S 115.15E
83 C14 **Busseri** ~ W Sudan
108 E9 **Busseto** Emilia-Romagna, C Italy 45.00N 10.06E
108 A8 **Bussoleno** Piemonte, NE Italy 45.11N 7.07E
Bussora see Al Başrah
100 J10 **Bussum** Noord-Holland, C Netherlands 52.16N 5.10E
43 N7 **Bustamante** Nuevo León, NE Mexico 26.29N 100.30W
65 I23 **Bustamante, Punta** headland S Argentina 51.34S 68.58W
Bustan see Bo'ston
118 J12 **Buşteni** Prahova, SE Romania 45.23N 25.31E
108 D7 **Busto Arsizio** Lombardia, N Italy 45.37N 8.49E
153 Q10 **Būston** Rus. Buston. NW Tajikistan 40.31N 69.21E
179 P12 **Busuanga Island** island Calamian Group, W Philippines
102 H8 **Büsum** Schleswig-Holstein, N Germany 54.08N 8.52E
81 M16 **Buta** Orientale, N Dem. Rep. Congo 2.50N 24.41E
83 E20 **Butare** prev. Astrida. S Rwanda 2.39S 29.44E
203 O2 **Butaritari** atoll Tungaru, W Kiribati
Butawal see Butwal
98 H13 **Bute** cultural region SW Scotland, UK
168 K6 **Büteeliyn Nuruu** ▲ N Mongolia
8 L16 **Bute Inlet** fjord British Columbia, W Canada
98 H12 **Bute, Island of** island SW Scotland, UK
81 P18 **Butembo** Nord Kivu, NE Dem. Rep. Congo 0.09N 29.16E
Bûtenpost see Buitenpost
109 K25 **Butera** Sicilia, Italy, C Mediterranean Sea 37.12N 14.12E
101 M20 **Bütgenbach** Liège, E Belgium 50.25N 6.12E
Butha Qi see Zalantun
177 F5 **Buthidaung** Arakan State, W Myanmar 20.52N 92.32E
63 I16 **Butiá** Rio Grande do Sul, S Brazil 30.09S 51.55W
83 F17 **Butiaba** NW Uganda 1.48N 31.21E
25 N6 **Butler** Alabama, S USA 32.05N 88.13W
25 S5 **Butler** Georgia, SE USA 32.33N 84.14W
33 Q11 **Butler** Indiana, N USA 41.25N 84.52W
29 R5 **Butler** Missouri, C USA 38.15N 94.19W
20 B14 **Butler** Pennsylvania, NE USA 40.51N 79.52W
204 K5 **Butler Island** island Antarctica
23 U8 **Butner** North Carolina, SE USA 36.07N 78.45W
175 Qq13 **Buton, Pulau** var. Pulau Butung; prev. Boetoeng. island C Indonesia
175 Qq13 **Buton, Selat** strait C Indonesia
Bütow see Bytów
115 L23 **Butrintit, Liqeni i** ◎ S Albania
25 N3 **Buttahatchee River** ~ Alabama/Mississippi, S USA
35 Q10 **Butte** Montana, NW USA 46.01N 112.33W
31 O12 **Butte** Nebraska, C USA 42.54N 98.51W
173 G3 **Butterworth** Pinang, Peninsular Malaysia 5.24N 100.22E
85 J25 **Butterworth** var. Gcuwa. Eastern Cape, SE South Africa 32.19S 28.09E
11 O3 **Button Islands** island group Nunavut, NE Canada
37 R13 **Buttonwillow** California, W USA 35.24N 119.26W
179 R14 **Butuan** off. Butuan City. Mindanao, S Philippines 8.56N 125.32E
Butung, Pulau see Buton, Pulau
Butuntum see Bitonto
130 M8 **Buturlinovka** Voronezhskaya Oblast', W Russian Federation 50.48N 40.33E
159 O11 **Butwal** var. Butawal. Western, C Nepal 27.41N 83.28E
103 G17 **Butzbach** Hessen, W Germany 50.26N 8.40E
102 L9 **Bützow** Mecklenburg-Vorpommern, N Germany 53.49N 11.58E
82 N13 **Buuhoodle** Togdheer, N Somalia 8.18N 46.15E
83 N16 **Buulobarde** var. Buulo Berde. Hiiraan, C Somalia Africa 3.52N 45.36E
Buulo Berde see Buulobarde
82 P12 **Buuraha Cal Miskaat** ▲ NE Somalia
83 L19 **Buur Gaabo** Jubbada Hoose, S Somalia 1.14S 41.48E
101 M22 **Buurgplaatz** ▲ N Luxembourg 50.09N 6.02E
Buwayrāt al Hasūn see Bu'ayrāt al Ḩasūn
152 L11 **Buxoro** var. Bokhara, Rus. Bukhara. Buxoro Viloyati, C Uzbekistan 39.50N 64.22E
152 J11 **Buxoro Viloyati** Rus. Bukharskaya Oblast'. ◆ province C Uzbekistan
102 I10 **Buxtehude** Niedersachsen, NW Germany 53.28N 9.42E
99 L18 **Buxton** C England, UK 53.18N 1.52W
128 M14 **Buy** var. Buj. Kostromskaya Oblast', NW Russian Federation 58.27N 41.31E
168 G7 **Buyanbat** Govĭ-Altay, W Mongolia 47.00N 95.57E
168 H8 **Buyant** Bayanhongor, C Mongolia 46.07N 98.45E
168 D6 **Buyant** Bayan-Ölgiy, W Mongolia 48.31N 89.36E

◆ Country ● Country Capital ◇ Dependent Territory ○ Dependent Territory Capital ◆ Administrative Region ✕ International Airport ▲ Mountain ▲ Mountain Range Volcano ~ River ◎ Lake ⊡ Reservoir

BUYANT – CAMOAPA

168 *H7* **Buyant** Dzavhan, C Mongolia *47.14N 97.14E*
169 *N9* **Buyant** Hentiy, C Mongolia *46.15N 110.50E*
169 *N10* **Buyant-Uhaa** Dornogovĭ, SE Mongolia *44.52N 110.12E*
168 *M7* **Buyant Ukha** ✕ (Ulaanbaatar) Töv, N Mongolia
131 *Q16* **Buynaksk** Respublika Dagestan, SW Russian Federation *42.52N 47.03E*
121 *L20* **Buynavichy** ***Rus.*** Buynovichi. Homyel'skaya Voblasts', SE Belarus *51.53N 28.31E*
Buynovichi *see* Buynavichy
78 *L16* **Buyo** SW Ivory Coast *6.23N 7.04W*
78 *L16* **Buyo, Lac de** ⊠ W Ivory Coast
169 *R7* **Buyr Nuur** ***var.*** Buir Nur. ◎ China /Mongolia ***see also*** Buir Nur
143 *T13* **Büyükağrı Dağı** ***var.*** Aghri Dagh, Agri Dagi, Koh I Noh, Masis, ***Eng.*** Great Ararat, Mount Ararat. ▲ E Turkey *39.43N 44.19E*
143 *R15* **Büyük Çayı** ≈ NE Turkey
116 *O13* **Büyük Çekmece** İstanbul, NW Turkey *41.02N 28.36E*
116 *N12* **Büyükkarıştıran** Kırklareli, NW Turkey *41.17N 27.33E*
117 *L14* **Büyükkemikli Burnu** *headland* NW Turkey *40.19N 26.14E*
142 *E15* **Büyükmenderes Nehri** ≈ SW Turkey
Büyükzap Suyu *see* Great Zab
104 *M9* **Buzançais** Indre, C France *46.53N 1.25E*
118 *K13* **Buzău** Buzău, SE Romania *45.08N 26.51E*
118 *K13* **Buzău** ◈ *county* SE Romania
118 *L12* **Buzău** ≈ E Romania
77 *S11* **Buzaymah** ***var.*** Bzīmah. SE Libya *24.53N 22.01E*
170 *D13* **Buzen** Fukuoka, Kyūshū, SW Japan *33.30N 131.26E*
118 *F12* **Buziaş** ***Ger.*** Busiasch, ***Hung.*** Buziásfürdő; ***prev.*** Buziás. Timiş, W Romania *45.38N 21.37E*
Buziásfürdő *see* Buziaş
85 *M18* **Búzi, Rio** ≈ C Mozambique
119 *Q10* **Buz'kyy Lyman** *bay* S Ukraine
152 *F13* **Büzmeýin** ***Rus.*** Byuzmeyin; ***prev.*** Bezmein. Ahal Welaýaty, C Turkmenistan *38.07N 57.52E*
151 *O8* **Buzuluk** Akmola, C Kazakhstan *51.52N 66.09E*
131 *T6* **Buzuluk** Orenburgskaya Oblast', W Russian Federation *52.47N 52.15E*
131 *N8* **Buzuluk** ≈ SW Russian Federation
21 *P12* **Buzzards Bay** Massachusetts, NE USA *41.45N 70.37W*
21 *P13* **Buzzards Bay** *bay* Massachusetts, NE USA
85 *G16* **Bwabata** Caprivi, NE Namibia *17.52S 22.39E*
195 *P17* **Bwagaoia** Misima Island, SE PNG *10.39S 152.48E*
Bwake *see* Bouaké
197 *C12* **Bwatnapne** Pentecost, C Vanuatu *15.42S 168.07E*
121 *K14* **Byahoml'** ***Rus.*** Begoml'. Vitsyebskaya Voblasts', N Belarus *54.44N 28.03E*
116 *J8* **Byala** Ruse, N Bulgaria *43.32N 27.51E*
116 *N9* **Byala** ***prev.*** Ak-Dere. Varna, E Bulgaria *42.52N 27.53E*
Byala Reka *see* Erydropótamos
116 *H8* **Byala Slatina** Vratsa, NW Bulgaria *43.28N 23.57E*
121 *N15* **Byalynichy** ***Rus.*** Belynichi. Mahilyowskaya Voblasts', E Belarus *53.58N 29.44E*
121 *G19* **Byaroza** ***Pol.*** Bereza Kartuska, ***Rus.*** Berëza. Brestskaya Voblasts', SW Belarus *52.33N 24.58E*
Bybles *see* Jbaïl
113 *O14* **Bychawa** Lubelskie, SE Poland *51.06N 22.34E*
Bychikha *see* Bychykha
120 *N11* **Bychykha** ***Rus.*** Bychikha. Vitsyebskaya Voblasts', NE Belarus *55.40N 29.58E*
113 *I14* **Byczyna** ***Ger.*** Pitschen. Opolskie, S Poland *51.06N 18.13E*
112 *I10* **Bydgoszcz** ***Ger.*** Bromberg. Kujawski-pomorskie, C Poland *53.16N 18.00E*
121 *I17* **Byelaruskaya Hrada** ***Rus.*** Belorusskaya Gryada. *ridge* N Belarus
121 *G18* **Byelavyezhskaya Pushcha** ***Pol.*** Puszcza Białowieska, ***Rus.*** Belovezhskaya Pushcha. *forest* Belarus/Poland ***see also*** Białowieska, Puszcza
121 *H15* **Byenyakoni** ***Rus.*** Benyakoni. Hrodzyenskaya Voblasts', W Belarus *54.15N 25.22E*
121 *M16* **Byerazino** ***Rus.*** Berezino. Minskaya Voblasts', C Belarus *53.49N 28.58E*
120 *L13* **Byerazino** ***Rus.*** Berezino. Vitsyebskaya Voblasts', N Belarus *54.54N 28.12E*
121 *L14* **Byerezino** ***Rus.*** Berezina. ≈ C Belarus
120 *M13* **Byeshankovichy** ***Rus.*** Beshenkovichi. Vitsyebskaya Voblasts', N Belarus *55.03N 29.28E*
33 *U13* **Byesville** Ohio, N USA *39.58N 81.32W*
121 *P18* **Byesyedz'** ***Rus.*** Besed'. ≈ SE Belarus
121 *H19* **Byezdzyezh** ***Rus.*** Bezdezh. Brestskaya Voblasts', SW Belarus *52.18N 25.16E*
95 *J15* **Bygdeå** Västerbotten, N Sweden *64.03N 20.49E*
96 *F12* **Bygdin** ◎ S Norway
95 *J15* **Bygdsiljum** Västerbotten, N Sweden *64.20N 20.31E*
97 *E17* **Bygland** Aust-Agder, S Norway *58.46N 7.50E*
97 *E17* **Byglandsfjord** Aust-Agder, S Norway *58.42N 7.51E*
121 *N16* **Bykhaw** ***Rus.*** Bykhov. Mahilyowskaya Voblasts', E Belarus *53.31N 30.15E*
Bykhov *see* Bykhaw
131 *P9* **Bykovo** Volgogradskaya Oblast', SW Russian Federation *49.52N 45.24E*
126 *L6* **Bykovskiy** Respublika Sakha (Yakutiya), NE Russian Federation *71.57N 129.07E*
205 *R12* **Byrd Glacier** *glacier* Antarctica
12 *K10* **Byrd, Lac** ◎ Québec, SE Canada
191 *P5* **Byrock** New South Wales, SE Australia *30.40S 146.24E*
32 *L10* **Byron** Illinois, N USA *42.06N 89.15W*
191 *V4* **Byron Bay** New South Wales, SE Australia *28.39S 153.34E*
191 *V4* **Byron, Cape** *headland* New South Wales, E Australia *28.37S 153.40E*
65 *F21* **Byron, Isla** *island* S Chile
Byron Island *see* Nikunau
67 *B24* **Byron Sound** *sound* NW Falkland Islands
126 *J5* **Byrranga, Gora** ▲▲ N Russian Federation
95 *J14* **Byske** Västerbotten, N Sweden *64.58N 21.10E*
113 *K18* **Bystrá** ▲ N Slovakia *49.10N 19.49E*
113 *F18* **Bystřice nad Pernštejnem** ***Ger.*** Bistritz ober Pernstein. Vysočina, C Czech Republic *49.30N 16.16E*
Bystrovka *see* Kemin
113 *G16* **Bystrzyca Kłodzka** ***Ger.*** Habelschwerdt. Wałbrzych, SW Poland *50.19N 16.39E*
113 *I18* **Bytča** Žilinský Kraj, N Slovakia *49.15N 18.31E*
121 *L15* **Bytcha** ***Rus.*** Bytcha. Minskaya Voblasts', NE Belarus *54.19N 28.24E*
Byteń/Byten' *see* Bytsyen'
113 *J16* **Bytom** ***Ger.*** Beuthen. Śląskie, S Poland *50.21N 18.51E*
112 *H7* **Bytów** ***Ger.*** Bütow. Pomorskie, N Poland *54.09N 17.30E*
121 *H18* **Bytsyen'** ***Pol.*** Byteń, ***Rus.*** Byten'. Brestskaya Voblasts', SW Belarus *52.53N 25.32E*
83 *E19* **Byumba** ***var.*** Biumba. N Rwanda *1.37S 30.05E*
Byuzmeyin *see* Büzmeýin
121 *O20* **Byval'ki** Homyel'skaya Voblasts', SE Belarus *51.51N 30.37E*
97 *O20* **Byxelkrok** Kalmar, S Sweden *57.18N 17.01E*
Byzantium *see* İstanbul
Bzīmah *see* Buzaymah

C

64 *O6* **Caacupé** Cordillera, S Paraguay *25.22S 57.04W*
64 *P6* **Caaguazú** ***off.*** Departamento de Caaguazú. ◈ *department* C Paraguay
84 *C13* **Caála** ***var.*** Kaala, Robert Williams, ***Port.*** Vila Robert Williams. Huambo, C Angola *12.51S 15.33E*
64 *P7* **Caazapá** Caazapá, S Paraguay *26.09S 56.21W*
64 *P7* **Caazapá** ***off.*** Departamento de Caazapá. ◈ *department* SE Paraguay
83 *P15* **Cabaad, Raas** *headland* C Somalia *6.13N 49.01E*
179 *R14* **Cabadbaran** Mindanao, S Philippines *9.07N 125.34E*
57 *N10* **Cabadisocaña** Amazonas, S Venezuela *4.28N 64.45W*
46 *F5* **Cabaiguán** Sancti Spíritus, C Cuba *22.04N 79.31W*
Caballeria, Cabo *see* Cavalleria, Cap de
39 *Q14* **Caballo Reservoir** ⊠ New Mexico, SW USA
42 *L6* **Caballos Mesteños, Llano de los** *plain* N Mexico
106 *L2* **Cabañaquinta** Asturias, N Spain *43.10N 5.37W*
44 *B9* **Cabañas** ◈ *department* E El Salvador
179 *P10* **Cabanatuan** ***off.*** Cabanatuan City. Luzon, N Philippines *15.27N 120.57E*
13 *T8* **Cabano** Québec, SE Canada *47.40N 68.55W*
106 *L11* **Cabeza del Buey** Extremadura, W Spain *38.43N 5.13W*
47 *V5* **Cabezas de San Juan** *headland* E Puerto Rico *18.23N 65.37W*
107 *N2* **Cabezón de la Sal** Cantabria, N Spain *43.19N 4.13W*
Cabhán *see* Cavan
63 *B23* **Cabildo** Buenos Aires, E Argentina *38.28S 61.49W*
Cabillonum *see* Chalon-sur-Saône
56 *H5* **Cabimas** Zulia, NW Venezuela *10.25N 71.27W*
84 *A9* **Cabinda** ***var.*** Kabinda. Cabinda, NW Angola *5.34S 12.12E*
84 *A9* **Cabinda** ***var.*** Kabinda. ◈ *province* NW Angola
35 *N7* **Cabinet Mountains** ▲▲ Idaho/Montana, NW USA
84 *B11* **Cabiri** Bengo, NW Angola *8.50S 13.42E*
65 *J20* **Cabo Blanco** Santa Cruz, SE Argentina *47.13S 65.43W*
84 *P13* **Cabo Delgado** ***off.*** Província de Capo Delgado. ◈ *province* NE Mozambique
12 *L9* **Cabonga, Réservoir** ⊠ Québec, SE Canada
29 *V7* **Cabool** Missouri, C USA *37.07N 92.06W*
191 *V2* **Caboolture** Queensland, E Australia *27.05S 152.56E*
Cabora Bassa, Lake *see* Cahora Bassa, Albufeira de
42 *F3* **Caborca** Sonora, NW Mexico *30.44N 112.06W*
Cabo San Lucas *see* San Lucas
29 *V11* **Cabot** Arkansas, C USA *34.58N 92.01W*
12 *F12* **Cabot Head** *headland* Ontario, S Canada *45.13N 81.17W*
16 *Ss10* **Cabot Strait** *strait* E Canada
Cabo Verde, Ilhas do *see* Cape Verde
106 *M14* **Cabra** Andalucía, S Spain *37.28N 4.28W*
109 *B19* **Cabras** Sardegna, Italy, C Mediterranean Sea *39.55N 8.30E*
196 *A15* **Cabras Island** *island* W Guam
47 *O8* **Cabrera** N Dominican Republic *19.34N 69.55W*
107 *X10* **Cabrera** ***anc.*** Capraria. *island* Islas Baleares, Spain, W Mediterranean Sea
106 *J4* **Cabrera** ≈ NW Spain
107 *Q15* **Cabrera, Sierra** ▲▲ S Spain
9 *S16* **Cabri** Saskatchewan, S Canada *50.37N 108.28W*
107 *R10* **Cabriel** ≈ E Spain
56 *M7* **Cabruta** Guárico, C Venezuela *7.39N 66.19W*
179 *Oo8* **Cabugao** Luzon, N Philippines *17.55N 120.29E*
56 *G10* **Cabuyaro** Meta, C Colombia *4.16N 72.47W*
62 *I13* **Caçador** Santa Catarina, S Brazil *26.47S 51.00W*
44 *G8* **Cacaguatique, Cordillera** ***var.*** Cordillera. ▲▲ NE El Salvador
114 *L13* **Čačak** Serbia, C Serbia and Montenegro (Yugoslavia) *43.52N 20.23E*
57 *Y10* **Cacao** NE French Guiana *4.37N 52.28W*
63 *H16* **Caçapava do Sul** Rio Grande do Sul, S Brazil *30.28S 53.28W*
23 *U3* **Cacapon River** ≈ West Virginia, NE USA
109 *J23* **Caccamo** Sicilia, Italy, C Mediterranean Sea *37.55N 13.40E*
109 *A17* **Caccia, Capo** *headland* Sardegna, Italy, C Mediterranean Sea *40.34N 8.09E*
152 *H15* **Çäçe** ***var.*** Chäche, ***Rus.*** Chaacha. Ahal Welaýaty, S Turkmenistan *36.49N 60.33E*
61 *G18* **Cáceres** Mato Grosso, W Brazil *16.04S 57.40W*
106 *J10* **Cáceres** ***Ar.*** Qazris. Extremadura, W Spain *39.28N 6.22W*
106 *J9* **Cáceres** ◈ *province* Extremadura, W Spain
Cachacrou *see* Scotts Head Village
63 *C21* **Cacharí** Buenos Aires, E Argentina *36.24S 59.31W*
28 *L12* **Cache** Oklahoma, C USA *34.37N 98.37W*
8 *M16* **Cache Creek** British Columbia, SW Canada *50.49N 121.19W*
37 *N6* **Cache Creek** ≈ California, W USA
39 *S3* **Cache La Poudre River** ≈ Colorado, C USA
Cacheo *see* Cacheu
29 *W11* **Cache River** ≈ Arkansas, C USA
32 *L17* **Cache River** ≈ Illinois, N USA
78 *G12* **Cacheu** ***var.*** Cacheo. W Guinea-Bissau *12.12N 16.10W*
61 *I15* **Cachimbo** Pará, NE Brazil *9.21S 54.58W*
61 *H15* **Cachimbo, Serra do** ▲▲ C Brazil
84 *D13* **Cachingues** Bié, C Angola *13.05S 16.48E*
56 *G7* **Cáchira** Norte de Santander, N Colombia *7.46N 73.03W*
63 *H16* **Cachoeira do Sul** Rio Grande do Sul, S Brazil *29.58S 52.54W*
61 *O20* **Cachoeiro de Itapemirim** Espírito Santo, SE Brazil *20.51S 41.07W*
84 *E12* **Cacolo** Lunda Sul, NE Angola *10.09S 19.17E*
85 *C14* **Caconda** Huíla, C Angola *13.43S 15.03E*
84 *A9* **Cacongo** Cabinda, NW Angola *5.16S 12.10E*
37 *U9* **Cactus Peak** ▲ Nevada, W USA *37.42N 116.51W*
84 *A11* **Cacuaco** Luanda, NW Angola *8.49S 13.24E*
85 *B14* **Cacula** Huíla, SW Angola *14.31S 14.07E*
69 *R12* **Caculuvar** ≈ SW Angola
61 *O19* **Caçumba, Ilha** *island* SE Brazil
57 *N10* **Cacuri** Amazonas, S Venezuela
83 *N17* **Cadale** Shabeellaha Dhexe, E Somalia *2.48N 46.19E*
107 *X4* **Cadaqués** Cataluña, NE Spain *42.16N 3.16E*
113 *J18* **Čadca** ***Hung.*** Csaca. Žilinský Kraj, N Slovakia *49.27N 18.46E*
29 *P13* **Caddo** Oklahoma, C USA *34.07N 96.15W*
27 *R6* **Caddo** Texas, SW USA *32.42N 98.40W*
27 *X6* **Caddo Lake** ⊠ Louisiana/Texas, SW USA
29 *S12* **Caddo Mountains** ▲▲ Arkansas, C USA
43 *O8* **Cadereyta** Nuevo León, NE Mexico *25.35N 99.54W*
99 *J19* **Cader Idris** ▲ NW Wales, United Kingdom *52.43N 3.57W*
190 *F3* **Cadibarrawirracanna, Lake** *salt lake* South Australia
12 *I7* **Cadillac** Québec, SE Canada *48.12N 78.23W*
9 *T17* **Cadillac** Saskatchewan, S Canada *49.43N 107.41W*
104 *K13* **Cadillac** Gironde, SW France *44.37N 0.16W*
33 *P7* **Cadillac** Michigan, N USA *44.16N 85.22W*
107 *V4* **Cadí, Torre de** ▲ NE Spain *42.16N 1.38E*
179 *Q13* **Cadiz** ***off.*** Cadiz City. Negros, C Philippines *10.58N 123.18E*
22 *H7* **Cadiz** Kentucky, S USA *36.53N 87.49W*
33 *U13* **Cadiz** Ohio, N USA *40.16N 81.00W*
106 *J15* **Cádiz** ***anc.*** Gades, Gadier, Gadir, Gadire. Andalucía, SW Spain *36.31N 6.18W*
106 *K15* **Cádiz** ◈ *province* Andalucía, SW Spain
106 *I15* **Cadiz, Bahía de** *bay* SW Spain
Cadiz City *see* Cadiz
106 *H15* **Cádiz, Golfo de** ***Eng.*** Gulf of Cadiz. *gulf* Portugal/Spain
Cadiz, Gulf of *see* Cádiz, Golfo de
37 *X14* **Cadiz Lake** ◎ California, W USA
190 *E2* **Cadney Homestead** South Australia *27.52S 134.03E*
Cadurcum *see* Cahors
85 *F17* **Caecae** Ngamiland, NW Botswana *19.52S 21.04E*
104 *K4* **Caen** Calvados, N France *49.10N 0.19W*
Caene/Caenepolis *see* Qena
Caerdydd *see* Cardiff
Caer Glou *see* Gloucester
Caer Gybi *see* Holyhead
Caerleon *see* Chester
Caer Luel *see* Carlisle
99 *I18* **Caernarfon** ***var.*** Caernarvon, Carnarvon. NW Wales, UK *53.07N 4.16W*
99 *H18* **Caernarfon Bay** *bay* NW Wales, UK
99 *I19* **Caernarvon** *cultural region* NW Wales, UK
Caernarvon *see* Caernarfon
Caesaraugusta *see* Zaragoza
Caesarea Mazaca *see* Kayseri
Caesarobriga *see* Talavera de la Reina
Caesarodunum *see* Tours
Caesaromagus *see* Beauvais
Caesena *see* Cesena
61 *N17* **Caetité** Bahia, E Brazil *14.04S 42.28W*
64 *J6* **Cafayate** Salta, N Argentina *26.02S 66.00W*
179 *Pp9* **Cagayan** ≈ Luzon, N Philippines
179 *R15* **Cagayan de Oro** ***off.*** Cagayan de Oro City. Mindanao, S Philippines *8.28N 124.38E*
179 *Oo17* **Cagayan de Tawi Tawi** *island* S Philippines
179 *Pp14* **Cagayan Islands** *island group* C Philippines
33 *O14* **Cagles Mill Lake** ⊠ Indiana, N USA
108 *I12* **Cagli** Marche, C Italy *43.33N 12.39E*
109 *C20* **Cagliari** ***anc.*** Caralis. Sardegna, Italy, C Mediterranean Sea *39.15N 9.06E*
109 *C20* **Cagliari, Golfo di** *gulf* Sardegna, Italy, C Mediterranean Sea
105 *U15* **Cagnes-sur-Mer** Alpes-Maritimes, SE France *43.40N 7.09E*
56 *L5* **Cagua** Aragua, N Venezuela *10.09N 67.27W*
179 *Pp8* **Cagua, Mount** ▲ Luzon, N Philippines *18.10N 122.03E*
56 *F13* **Caguán, Río** ≈ SW Colombia
47 *U6* **Caguas** E Puerto Rico *18.13N 66.02W*
152 *C9* **Çagyl** ***Rus.*** Chagyl. Balkan Welaýaty, NW Turkmenistan *40.48N 55.21E*
25 *P5* **Cahaba River** ≈ Alabama, S USA
44 *E5* **Cahabón, Río** ≈ C Guatemala
85 *B15* **Cahama** Cunene, SW Angola *16.16S 14.19E*
99 *B21* **Caha Mountains** ***Ir.*** An Cheacha. ▲▲ SW Ireland
99 *D20* **Caher** ***Ir.*** An Cathair. S Ireland *52.21N 7.58W*
99 *A21* **Cahersiveen** ***Ir.*** Cathair Saidhbhín. SW Ireland *51.56N 10.12W*
32 *K15* **Cahokia** Illinois, N USA *38.34N 90.11W*
85 *L15* **Cahora Bassa, Albufeira de** ***var.*** Lake Cabora Bassa. ⊠ NW Mozambique
99 *G20* **Cahore Point** ***Ir.*** Rinn Chathóir. *headland* SE Ireland *52.33N 6.11W*
104 *M14* **Cahors** ***anc.*** Cadurcum. Lot, S France *44.26N 1.27E*
58 *D9* **Cahuapanas, Río** ≈ N Peru
118 *M12* **Cahul** ***Rus.*** Kagul. S Moldova *45.52N 28.13E*
Cahul, Lacul *see* Kahul, Ozero
85 *N16* **Caia** Sofala, C Mozambique *17.51S 35.22E*
61 *J19* **Caiapó, Serra do** ▲▲ C Brazil
46 *F5* **Caibarién** Villa Clara, C Cuba *22.31N 79.28W*
57 *O5* **Caicara** Monagas, NE Venezuela *9.49N 63.37W*
56 *L5* **Caicara del Orinoco** Bolívar, C Venezuela *7.38N 66.10W*
61 *P14* **Caicó** Rio Grande do Norte, E Brazil *6.25S 37.04W*
46 *M6* **Caicos Islands** *island group* W Turks and Caicos Islands
46 *L5* **Caicos Passage** *strait* Bahamas/Turks and Caicos Islands
167 *O9* **Caidian** ***prev.*** Hanyang. Hubei, C China *30.33N 114.03E*
Caiffa *see* Hefa
188 *M12* **Caiguna** Western Australia *32.14S 125.33E*
Caillí, Ceann *see* Hag's Head
42 *J11* **Caimanero, Laguna del** ***var.*** Laguna del Camaronero. *lagoon* E Pacific Ocean
119 *N10* **Căinari** ***Rus.*** Kaynary. C Moldova *46.43N 29.00E*
59 *L19* **Caine, Río** ≈ C Bolivia
Caiphas *see* Hefa
205 *N4* **Caird Coast** *physical region* Antarctica
98 *J9* **Cairn Gorm** ▲ C Scotland, UK *57.07N 3.38W*
98 *J9* **Cairngorm Mountains** ▲▲ C Scotland, UK
41 *P12* **Cairn Mountain** ▲ Alaska, USA *61.07N 155.23W*
189 *W4* **Cairns** Queensland, NE Australia *16.51S 145.43E*
124 *Qq16* **Cairo** ***Ar.*** Al Qāhirah, ***var.*** El Qâhira. ● (Egypt) N Egypt *30.01N 31.18E*
25 *T8* **Cairo** Georgia, SE USA *30.52N 84.12W*
32 *L17* **Cairo** Illinois, N USA *37.00N 89.10W*
77 *V8* **Cairo** ✕ C Egypt *30.06N 31.36E*
Caiseal *see* Cashel
Caisleán an Bharraigh *see* Castlebar
Caisleán na Finne *see* Castlefinn
98 *J6* **Caithness** *cultural region* N Scotland, UK
85 *D15* **Caiundo** Cuando Cubango, S Angola *15.41S 17.28E*
58 *C11* **Cajamarca** ***prev.*** Caxamarca. Cajamarca, NW Peru *7.09S 78.31W*
58 *B11* **Cajamarca** ***off.*** Departamento de Cajamarca. ◈ *department* N Peru
105 *N14* **Cajarc** Lot, S France *44.28N 1.51E*
179 *Q12* **Cajidiocan** Sibuyan Island, C Philippines *12.20N 122.39E*
44 *G6* **Cajón, Represa El** ⊠ NW Honduras
60 *N12* **Caju, Ilha do** *island* NE Brazil
Cakaubalavu Reef *see* Kavukavu Reef
165 *R10* **Caka Yanhu** ◎ C China
114 *E7* **Čakovec** ***Ger.*** Csakathurn, ***Hung.*** Csáktornya; ***prev. Ger.*** Tschakathurn. Međimurje, N Croatia *46.24N 16.29E*
79 *V17* **Calabar** Cross River, S Nigeria *4.55N 8.25E*
12 *K13* **Calabogie** Ontario, SE Canada *45.18N 76.43W*
56 *L6* **Calabozo** Guárico, C Venezuela *8.53N 67.28W*
109 *N20* **Calabria** ***anc.*** Bruttium. ◈ *region* SW Italy
106 *M16* **Calaburra, Punta de** *headland* S Spain *36.30N 4.38W*
118 *G14* **Calafat** Dolj, SW Romania *43.55N 23.01E*
Calafate *see* El Calafate
107 *Q4* **Calahorra** La Rioja, N Spain *42.19N 1.58W*
105 *N1* **Calais** Pas-de-Calais, N France *51.00N 1.53E*
21 *T5* **Calais** Maine, NE USA *45.09N 67.15W*
Calais, Pas de *see* Dover, Strait of
Calalen *see* Kallalen
64 *H4* **Calama** Antofagasta, N Chile *22.25S 68.54W*
Calamianes *see* Calamian Group
179 *P13* **Calamian Group** ***var.*** Calamianes. *island group* W Philippines
107 *R7* **Calamocha** Aragón, NE Spain *40.54N 1.18W*
31 *N14* **Calamus River** ≈ Nebraska, C USA
118 *G12* **Călan** ***Ger.*** Kalan, ***Hung.*** Pusztakalán. Hunedoara, SW Romania *45.45N 22.59E*
107 *S7* **Calanda** Aragón, NE Spain *40.55N 0.15W*
173 *E4* **Calang** Sumatera, W Indonesia *4.37N 95.37E*
179 *P11* **Calapan** Mindoro, N Philippines *13.23N 121.08E*
Călăras *see* Călăraşi
118 *M9* **Călăraşi** ***var.*** Călăras, ***Rus.*** Kalarash. C Moldova *47.19N 28.13E*
118 *L14* **Călăraşi** Călăraşi, SE Romania *44.18N 26.52E*
118 *K14* **Călăraşi** ◈ *county* SE Romania
56 *E10* **Calarca** Quindío, W Colombia *4.31N 75.37W*
107 *Q12* **Calasparra** Murcia, SE Spain *38.13N 1.40W*
109 *I23* **Calatafimi** Sicilia, Italy, C Mediterranean Sea *37.54N 12.52E*
107 *Q6* **Calatayud** Aragón, NE Spain *41.21N 1.39W*
179 *Pp11* **Calauag** Luzon, N Philippines *13.57N 122.18E*
37 *P8* **Calaveras River** ≈ California, W USA
179 *Oo11* **Calavite, Cape** *headland* Mindoro, N Philippines *13.25N 120.16E*
179 *Qq12* **Calbayog** ***off.*** Calbayog City. Samar, C Philippines *12.07N 124.35E*
179 *R12* **Calbiga** Samar, C Philippines *11.37N 125.00E*
24 *G9* **Calcasieu Lake** ◎ Louisiana, S USA
24 *H8* **Calcasieu River** ≈ Louisiana, S USA
58 *B6* **Calceta** Manabí, W Ecuador *0.51S 80.09W*
63 *B16* **Calchaquí** Santa Fe, C Argentina *29.55S 60.13W*
64 *J6* **Calchaquí, Río** ≈ NW Argentina
60 *J10* **Calçoene** Amapá, NE Brazil *2.29N 51.01W*
159 *S16* **Calcutta** ✕ West Bengal, N India *22.30N 88.19E*
Calcutta *see* Kolkata
56 *E9* **Caldas** ***off.*** Departamento de Caldas. ◈ *province* W Colombia
106 *F10* **Caldas da Rainha** Leiria, W Portugal *39.24N 9.07W*
106 *G3* **Caldas de Reis** ***var.*** Caldas de Reyes. Galicia, NW Spain *42.36N 8.39W*
Caldas de Reyes *see* Caldas de Reis
60 *F13* **Caldeirão** Amazonas, NW Brazil *3.18S 60.22W*
64 *G7* **Caldera** Atacama, N Chile *27.04S 70.48W*
44 *L14* **Caldera** Puntarenas, W Costa Rica *9.55N 84.42W*
107 *N10* **Calderina** ▲ C Spain *39.18N 3.49W*
143 *T13* **Çaldıran** Van, E Turkey *39.10N 43.52E*
34 *M14* **Caldwell** Idaho, NW USA *43.39N 116.41W*
29 *N8* **Caldwell** Kansas, C USA *37.01N 97.36W*
12 *G15* **Caledon** Ontario, S Canada *43.51N 79.58W*
85 *I23* **Caledon** ***var.*** Mohokare. ≈ Lesotho/South Africa
44 *G1* **Caledonia** Corozal, N Belize *18.13N 88.27W*
12 *G16* **Caledonia** Ontario, S Canada *43.04N 79.57W*
31 *X11* **Caledonia** Minnesota, N USA *43.37N 91.30W*
107 *X5* **Calella** ***var.*** Calella de la Costa. Cataluña, NE Spain *41.37N 2.40E*
Calella de la Costa *see* Calella
25 *P4* **Calera** Alabama, S USA *33.06N 86.45W*
65 *I19* **Caleta Olivia** Santa Cruz, SE Argentina *46.21S 67.37W*
37 *X17* **Calexico** California, W USA *32.39N 115.28W*
99 *H16* **Calf of Man** *island* SW Isle of Man
9 *Q16* **Calgary** Alberta, SW Canada *51.04N 114.04W*
9 *Q16* **Calgary** ✕ Alberta, SW Canada *51.15N 114.03W*
39 *U5* **Calhan** Colorado, C USA *39.00N 104.18W*
66 *O5* **Calheta** Madeira, Portugal, NE Atlantic Ocean *32.42N 17.12W*
25 *R2* **Calhoun** Georgia, SE USA *34.30N 84.57W*
22 *I6* **Calhoun** Kentucky, S USA *37.32N 87.10W*
24 *M3* **Calhoun City** Mississippi, S USA *33.51N 89.18W*
23 *P12* **Calhoun Falls** South Carolina, SE USA *34.05N 82.36W*
56 *D11* **Cali** Valle del Cauca, W Colombia *3.24N 76.30W*
29 *V9* **Calico Rock** Arkansas, C USA *36.07N 92.08W*
161 *F21* **Calicut** ***var.*** Kozhikode. Kerala, SW India *11.17N 75.49E*
37 *Y9* **Caliente** Nevada, W USA *37.37N 114.30W*
29 *U5* **California** Missouri, C USA *38.38N 92.33W*
20 *B15* **California** Pennsylvania, NE USA *40.02N 79.52W*
37 *Q12* **California** ***off.*** State of California; also known as El Dorado, The Golden State. ◈ *state* W USA
37 *P11* **California Aqueduct** *aqueduct* California, W USA
37 *T13* **California City** California, W USA *35.06N 117.55W*
42 *F6* **California, Golfo de** ***Eng.*** Gulf of California; ***prev.*** Sea of Cortez. *gulf* W Mexico
California, Gulf of *see* California, Golfo de
143 *Y13* **Cälilabad** ***Rus.*** Dzhalilabad; ***prev.*** Astrakhan-Bazar. S Azerbaijan *39.15N 48.30E*
118 *I12* **Călimăneşti** Vâlcea, SW Romania *45.13N 24.19E*
118 *J9* **Călimani, Munţii** ▲▲ N Romania
Calinisc *see* Cupcina
37 *X17* **Calipatria** California, W USA *33.07N 115.30W*
Calisia *see* Kalisz
36 *M7* **Calistoga** California, W USA *38.34N 122.37W*
85 *G25* **Calitzdorp** Western Cape, SW South Africa *33.31S 21.40E*
43 *W12* **Calkiní** Campeche, E Mexico *20.21N 90.03W*
190 *K4* **Callabonna Creek** ***var.*** Tilcha Creek. *seasonal river* New South Wales/South Australia
190 *J4* **Callabonna, Lake** ◎ South Australia
104 *G5* **Callac** Côtes d'Armor, NW France *48.28N 3.22W*
37 *U5* **Callaghan, Mount** ▲ Nevada, W USA *39.38N 116.57W*
Callain *see* Callan
99 *E19* **Callan** ***Ir.*** Callain. S Ireland *52.33N 7.22W*
12 *H11* **Callander** Ontario, S Canada *46.12N 79.20W*
98 *I11* **Callander** C Scotland, UK *56.14N 4.16W*
100 *H7* **Callantsoog** Noord-Holland, NW Netherlands *52.51N 4.41E*
59 *D14* **Callao** Callao, W Peru *12.03S 77.09W*
59 *D15* **Callao** ***off.*** Departamento del Callao. ◈ *constitutional province* W Peru
58 *F11* **Callaria, Río** ≈ E Peru
Callatis *see* Mangalia
9 *Q13* **Calling Lake** Alberta, W Canada *55.12N 113.07W*
Callosa de Ensarriá *see* Callosa d'En Sarrià
107 *T11* **Callosa d'En Sarrià** ***var.*** Callosa de Ensarriá. País Valenciano, E Spain *38.40N 0.07W*
107 *S12* **Callosa de Segura** País Valenciano, E Spain *38.07N 0.52W*
31 *X11* **Calmar** Iowa, C USA *43.10N 91.51W*
Calmar *see* Kalmar
45 *R16* **Calobre** Veraguas, C Panama *8.18N 80.49W*
179 *P10* **Caloocan** *municipality* Luzon, N Philippines *14.37N 120.58E*
25 *X14* **Caloosahatchee River** ≈ Florida, SE USA
191 *V2* **Caloundra** Queensland, E Australia *26.48S 153.07E*
Calp *see* Calpe
107 *T11* **Calpe** ***Cat.*** Calp. País Valenciano, E Spain *38.39N 0.03E*
43 *P14* **Calpulalpan** Tlaxcala, S Mexico *19.36N 98.30W*
109 *K25* **Caltagirone** Sicilia, Italy, C Mediterranean Sea *37.13N 14.31E*
109 *J24* **Caltanissetta** Sicilia, Italy, C Mediterranean Sea *37.30N 14.00E*
84 *E11* **Caluango** Lunda Norte, NE Angola *8.16S 19.36E*
84 *C12* **Calucinga** Bié, W Angola *11.18S 16.10E*
84 *B12* **Calulo** Cuanza Sul, NW Angola *9.58S 14.56E*
85 *B14* **Caluquembe** Huíla, W Angola *13.46S 14.40E*
82 *Q11* **Caluula** Bari, NE Somalia *11.55N 50.51E*
104 *K4* **Calvados** ◈ *department* N France
195 *P17* **Calvados Chain, The** *island group* SE PNG
27 *U9* **Calvert** Texas, SW USA *30.58N 96.40W*
22 *H7* **Calvert City** Kentucky, S USA *37.01N 88.21W*
105 *X14* **Calvi** Corse, France, C Mediterranean Sea *42.34N 8.44E*
42 *L12* **Calvillo** Aguascalientes, C Mexico *21.51N 102.42W*
85 *F24* **Calvinia** Northern Cape, W South Africa *31.26S 19.45E*
106 *K8* **Calvitero** ▲ W Spain *40.16N 5.48W*
103 *G22* **Calw** Baden-Württemberg, SW Germany *48.43N 8.43E*
Calydon *see* Kalydón
107 *N11* **Calzada de Calatrava** Castilla-La Mancha, C Spain *38.42N 3.46W*
Cama *see* Kama
84 *C11* **Camabatela** Cuanza Norte, NW Angola *8.13S 15.22E*
66 *Q5* **Camacha** Porto Santo, Madeira, Portugal, NE Atlantic Ocean *32.40N 16.52W*
12 *L8* **Camachigama, Lac** ◎ Québec, SE Canada
42 *M9* **Camacho** Zacatecas, C Mexico *24.23N 102.20W*
84 *D13* **Camacupa** ***var.*** General Machado, ***Port.*** Vila General Machado. Bié, C Angola *11.59S 17.30E*
56 *L7* **Camaguán** Guárico, C Venezuela *8.05N 67.34W*
46 *G6* **Camagüey** ***prev.*** Puerto Príncipe. Camagüey, C Cuba *21.24N 77.54W*
46 *G5* **Camagüey, Archipiélago de** *island group* C Cuba
42 *D5* **Camalli, Sierra de** ▲ NW Mexico *28.21N 113.26W*
59 *G18* **Camana** ***var.*** Camaná. Arequipa, SW Peru *16.37S 72.42W*
31 *Z14* **Camanche** Iowa, C USA *41.47N 90.15W*
37 *P8* **Camanche Reservoir** ⊠ California, W USA
63 *I16* **Camaquã** Rio Grande do Sul, S Brazil *30.49S 51.46W*
63 *H16* **Camaquã, Rio** ≈ S Brazil
66 *P6* **Câmara de Lobos** Madeira, Portugal, NE Atlantic Ocean *32.37N 16.58W*
105 *U16* **Camarat, Cap** *headland* SE France *43.12N 6.42E*
43 *O8* **Camargo** Tamaulipas, C Mexico *26.16N 98.49W*
105 *R15* **Camargue** *physical region* SE France
106 *F2* **Camariñas** Galicia, NW Spain *43.07N 9.10W*
Camaronero, Laguna del *see* Caimanero, Laguna del
65 *J18* **Camarones** Chaco, S Argentina *44.48S 65.42W*
65 *J18* **Camarones, Bahía** *bay* S Argentina
106 *J14* **Camas** Andalucía, S Spain *37.24N 6.01W*
178 *J15* **Ca Mau** ***prev.*** Quan Long. Minh Hai, S Vietnam *9.11N 105.09E*
84 *E11* **Camaxilo** Lunda Norte, NE Angola *8.19S 18.52E*
106 *G3* **Cambados** Galicia, NW Spain *42.31N 8.49W*
Cambay, Gulf of *see* Khambhāt, Gulf of
Camberia *see* Chambéry
99 *N22* **Camberley** SE England, UK *51.21N 0.45W*
178 *Ii12* **Cambodia** ***off.*** Kingdom of Cambodia, ***var.*** Democratic Kampuchea, Roat Kampuchea, ***Cam.*** Kampuchea; ***prev.*** People's Democratic Republic of Kampuchea. ◆ *republic* SE Asia
104 *I16* **Cambo-les-Bains** Pyrénées-Atlantiques, SW France *43.22N 1.24W*
105 *P2* **Cambrai** ***Flem.*** Kambryk; ***prev.*** Cambray, ***anc.*** Cameracum. Nord, N France *50.10N 3.13E*
Cambray *see* Cambrai
106 *H2* **Cambre** Galicia, NW Spain *43.18N 8.21W*
37 *O12* **Cambria** California, W USA *35.33N 121.04W*
99 *J20* **Cambrian Mountains** ▲▲ C Wales, UK
12 *G16* **Cambridge** Ontario, S Canada *43.22N 80.16W*
46 *I12* **Cambridge** W Jamaica *18.19N 77.54W*
192 *M8* **Cambridge** Waikato, North Island, NZ *37.53S 175.28E*
99 *O20* **Cambridge** ***Lat.*** Cantabrigia. E England, UK *52.12N 0.07E*
34 *M12* **Cambridge** Idaho, NW USA *44.34N 116.42W*
32 *K11* **Cambridge** Illinois, N USA *41.18N 90.11W*
23 *Y4* **Cambridge** Maryland, NE USA *38.33N 76.04W*
21 *O11* **Cambridge** Massachusetts, NE USA *42.21N 71.05W*
31 *V7* **Cambridge** Minnesota, N USA *45.34N 93.13W*
31 *N16* **Cambridge** Nebraska, C USA *40.18N 100.10W*
33 *U13* **Cambridge** Ohio, NE USA *40.00N 81.34W*
15 *J3* **Cambridge Bay** Victoria Island, Nunavut, NW Canada *68.55N 105.08W*
99 *O20* **Cambridgeshire** *cultural region* E England, UK
107 *U6* **Cambrils de Mar** Cataluña, NE Spain *41.06N 1.02E*
Cambundi-Catembo *see* Nova Gaia
143 *N11* **Çam Burnu** *headland* N Turkey *41.07N 37.48E*
191 *S9* **Camden** New South Wales, SE Australia *34.04S 150.40E*
25 *O6* **Camden** Alabama, S USA *31.59N 87.17W*
29 *U14* **Camden** Arkansas, C USA *33.34N 92.49W*
23 *Y3* **Camden** Delaware, NE USA *39.06N 75.30W*
21 *R7* **Camden** Maine, NE USA *44.12N 69.04W*
20 *I16* **Camden** New Jersey, NE USA *39.55N 75.07W*
20 *I9* **Camden** New York, NE USA *43.21N 75.45W*
23 *R12* **Camden** South Carolina, SE USA *34.15N 80.36W*
22 *H8* **Camden** Tennessee, S USA *36.03N 88.06W*
27 *X9* **Camden** Texas, SW USA *30.55N 94.43W*
41 *S5* **Camden Bay** *bay* S Beaufort Sea
29 *U6* **Camdenton** Missouri, C USA *38.01N 92.44W*
Camellia State *see* Alabama
20 *M7* **Camels Hump** ▲ Vermont, NE USA *44.18N 72.50W*
119 *N8* **Camenca** ***Rus.*** Kamenka. N Moldova *48.01N 28.43E*
Cameracum *see* Cambrai
24 *G9* **Cameron** Louisiana, S USA *29.48N 93.19W*
27 *T9* **Cameron** Texas, SW USA *30.51N 96.58W*
32 *J5* **Cameron** Wisconsin, N USA *45.25N 91.42W*
8 *M12* **Cameron** ≈ British Columbia, W Canada
193 *A24* **Cameron Mountains** ▲▲ South Island, NZ
81 *D15* **Cameroon** ***off.*** Republic of Cameroon, ***Fr.*** Cameroun. ◆ *republic* W Africa
81 *D15* **Cameroon Mountain** ▲ SW Cameroon *4.12N 9.00E*
Cameroon Ridge *see* Camerounaise, Dorsale
Cameroun *see* Cameroon
81 *E14* **Camerounaise, Dorsale** ***Eng.*** Cameroon Ridge. *ridge* NW Cameroon
179 *R14* **Camiguin Island** *island* S Philippines
179 *P10* **Camiling** Luzon, N Philippines *15.41N 120.22E*
25 *T7* **Camilla** Georgia, SE USA *31.13N 84.12W*
106 *G5* **Caminha** Viana do Castelo, N Portugal *41.52N 8.49W*
37 *P7* **Camino** California, W USA *38.43N 120.39W*
142 *B15* **Çamiçi Gölü** ◎ SW Turkey
109 *J24* **Cammarata** Sicilia, Italy, C Mediterranean Sea *37.36N 13.39E*
44 *K10* **Camoapa** Boaco, S Nicaragua *12.24N 85.32W*

238

◆ Country ● Country Capital ◇ Dependent Territory ○ Dependent Territory Capital ◈ Administrative Region ✕ International Airport ▲ Mountain ▲▲ Mountain Range Volcano ≈ River ◎ Lake ⊠ Reservoir

Camocim – Carol City

60 O13 **Camocim** Ceará, E Brazil 2.55S 40.49W
108 D10 **Camogli** Liguria, NW Italy 44.21N 9.10E
189 S5 **Camooweal** Queensland, C Australia 19.57S 138.14E
57 Y11 **Camopi** E French Guiana 3.12N 52.19W
157 Q22 **Camorta** *island* Nicobar Islands, India, NE Indian Ocean
179 R13 **Camotes Sea** *sea* C Philippines
44 I6 **Campamento** Olancho, C Honduras 14.33N 86.37W
63 D19 **Campana** Buenos Aires, E Argentina 34.06S 59.04W
65 F21 **Campana, Isla** *island* S Chile
106 K11 **Campanario** Extremadura, W Spain 38.52N 5.36W
109 L17 **Campania** *Eng.* Champagne. ◈ *region* S Italy
29 Y8 **Campbell** Missouri, C USA 36.29N 90.04W
193 K15 **Campbell, Cape** *headland* South Island, NZ 41.44S 174.16E
12 J14 **Campbellford** Ontario, SE Canada 44.18N 77.48W
33 R13 **Campbell Hill** *hill* Ohio, N USA 40.22N 83.43W
199 J14 **Campbell Island** *island* S NZ
183 P13 **Campbell Plateau** *undersea feature* SW Pacific Ocean
8 K17 **Campbell River** Vancouver Island, British Columbia, SW Canada 49.58N 125.18W
22 L6 **Campbellsville** Kentucky, S USA 37.20N 85.20W
11 O13 **Campbellton** New Brunswick, SE Canada 48.00N 66.41W
191 P16 **Campbell Town** Tasmania, SE Australia 41.57S 147.30E
191 S9 **Campbelltown** New South Wales, SE Australia 34.04S 150.46E
98 G13 **Campbeltown** W Scotland, UK 55.25N 5.37W
43 W13 **Campeche** Campeche, SE Mexico 19.46N 90.28W
43 W14 **Campeche** ◈ *state* SE Mexico
43 T14 **Campeche, Bahía de** *Eng.* Bay of Campeche. *bay* E Mexico
Campeche, Banco de *see* Campeche Bank
66 C11 **Campeche Bank** *Sp.* Banco de Campeche, Sonda de Campeche. *undersea feature* S Gulf of Mexico
Campeche, Bay of *see* Campeche, Bahía de
Campeche, Sonda de *see* Campeche Bank
46 H7 **Campechuela** Granma, E Cuba 20.11N 77.14W
190 M13 **Camperdown** Victoria, SE Australia 38.16S 143.10E
178 K6 **Cẩm Pha** Quang Ninh, N Vietnam 21.04N 107.20E
118 H10 **Câmpia Turzii** *Ger.* Jerischmarkt, *Hung.* Aranyosgyéres; *prev.* Cîmpia Turzii, Ghiriş, Gyéres. Cluj, NW Romania 46.33N 23.53E
106 K12 **Campillo de Llerena** Extremadura, W Spain 38.30N 5.48W
106 L15 **Campillos** Andalucía, S Spain 37.04N 4.51W
118 J13 **Câmpina** *prev.* Cîmpina. Prahova, SE Romania 45.08N 25.44E
61 Q15 **Campina Grande** Paraíba, E Brazil 7.15S 35.49W
62 L9 **Campinas** São Paulo, S Brazil 22.54S 47.06W
40 L10 **Camp Kulowiye** Saint Lawrence Island, Alaska, USA 63.15N 168.45W
81 D17 **Campo** *var.* Kampo. Sud, SW Cameroon 2.22N 9.49E
Campo *see* Ntem
61 N15 **Campo Alegre de Lourdes** Bahia, E Brazil 9.28S 43.01W
109 L16 **Campobasso** Molise, C Italy 41.34N 14.40E
109 H24 **Campobello di Mazara** Sicilia, Italy, C Mediterranean Sea 37.37N 12.45E
Campo Criptana *see* Campo de Criptana
107 O10 **Campo de Criptana** *var.* Campo Criptana. Castilla-La Mancha, C Spain 39.25N 3.07W
61 I16 **Campo de Diauarum** *var.* Pôsto Diuarum. Mato Grosso, W Brazil 11.08S 53.16W
56 E5 **Campo de la Cruz** Atlántico, N Colombia 10.22N 74.52W
107 P11 **Campo de Montiel** *physical region* C Spain
Campo dos Goitacazes *see* Campos
62 H12 **Campo Erê** Santa Catarina, S Brazil 26.24S 53.04W
64 L7 **Campo Gallo** Santiago del Estero, N Argentina 26.36S 62.50W
61 I20 **Campo Grande** *state capital* Mato Grosso do Sul, SW Brazil 20.24S 54.34W
62 K12 **Campo Largo** Paraná, S Brazil 25.27S 49.29W
60 N13 **Campo Maior** Piauí, E Brazil 4.49S 42.12W
106 I10 **Campo Maior** Portalegre, C Portugal 39.01N 7.04W
62 H10 **Campo Mourão** Paraná, S Brazil 24.01S 52.24W
62 Q9 **Campos** *var.* Campo dos Goitacazes. Rio de Janeiro, SE Brazil 21.46S 41.21W
61 L17 **Campos Belos** Goiás, S Brazil 13.11S 46.46W
62 N9 **Campos do Jordão** São Paulo, S Brazil 22.45S 45.36W
62 I13 **Campos Novos** Santa Catarina, S Brazil 27.22S 51.11W
61 O14 **Campos Sales** Ceará, E Brazil 7.01S 40.21W
27 Q9 **Camp San Saba** Texas, SW USA 30.57N 99.16W
23 N6 **Campton** Kentucky, S USA 37.43N 83.28W
118 I13 **Câmpulung** *prev.* Câmpulung-Muşcel, Cîmpulung. Argeş, S Romania 45.16N 25.03E
118 J9 **Câmpulung Moldovenesc** *var.* Cîmpulung Moldovenesc, *Ger.* Kimpolung, *Hung.* Hosszúmezjő. Suceava, NE Romania 47.31N 25.34E
Câmpulung-Muşcel *see* Câmpulung
Campus Stellae *see* Santiago
38 L12 **Camp Verde** Arizona, SW USA 34.33N 111.52W
27 P11 **Camp Wood** Texas, SW USA 29.40N 100.00W
178 Kk13 **Cam Ranh** Khanh Hoa, S Vietnam 11.54N 109.13E
9 Q15 **Camrose** Alberta, SW Canada 53.01N 112.48W
Camulodunum *see* Colchester
142 B12 **Çan** Çanakkale, NW Turkey 40.01N 26.59E
20 L12 **Canaan** Connecticut, NE USA 42.00N 73.17W
15 Kk13 **Canada** ◆ *commonwealth republic* N North America
207 P6 **Canada Basin** *undersea feature* Arctic Ocean
63 B18 **Cañada de Gómez** Santa Fe, C Argentina 32.49S 61.22W
207 P6 **Canada Plain** *undersea feature* Arctic Ocean
63 A18 **Cañada Rosquín** Santa Fe, C Argentina 32.04S 61.35W
27 P1 **Canadian** Texas, SW USA 35.54N 100.22W
18 Kk11 **Canadian River** ~ SW USA
15 K12 **Canadian Shield** *physical region* Canada
65 I18 **Cañadón Grande, Sierra** ▲▲ S Argentina
57 P9 **Canaima** Bolívar, SE Venezuela 9.40N 72.33W
142 B11 **Çanakkale** *var.* Dardanelli; *prev.* Chanak, Kale Sultanie. Çanakkale, W Turkey 40.09N 26.25E
142 B12 **Çanakkale** ◈ *province* NW Turkey
142 B11 **Çanakkale Boğazı** *Eng.* Dardanelles. *strait* NW Turkey
197 I6 **Canala** Province Nord, C New Caledonia 21.31S 165.57E
61 A15 **Canamari** Amazonas, W Brazil 7.37S 72.33W
20 G10 **Canandaigua** New York, NE USA 42.52N 77.14W
20 F10 **Canandaigua Lake** ◎ New York, NE USA
42 G3 **Cananea** Sonora, NW Mexico 30.58N 110.19W
58 B8 **Cañar** ◈ *province* C Ecuador
66 N10 **Canarias, Islas** *Eng.* Canary Islands. ◈ *autonomous community* Spain, NE Atlantic Ocean
Canaries Basin *see* Canary Basin
46 C6 **Canarreos, Archipiélago de los** *island group* W Cuba
68 K3 **Canary Basin** *var.* Canaries Basin, Monaco Basin. *undersea feature* E Atlantic Ocean
Canary Islands *see* Canarias, Islas
44 L13 **Cañas** Guanacaste, NW Costa Rica 10.25N 85.07W
20 I10 **Canastota** New York, NE USA 43.04N 75.45W
42 K9 **Canatlán** Durango, C Mexico 24.33N 104.45W
106 J9 **Cañaveral** Extremadura, W Spain 39.46N 6.24W
25 Y11 **Canaveral, Cape** *headland* Florida, SE USA 28.27N 80.31W
61 O18 **Canavieiras** Bahia, E Brazil 15.43S 38.58W
45 R16 **Cañazas** Veraguas, W Panama 8.19N 81.09W
108 H6 **Canazei** Trentino-Alto Adige, N Italy 46.29N 11.50E
191 P6 **Canbelego** New South Wales, SE Australia 31.36S 146.20E
191 R10 **Canberra** ● (Australia) Australian Capital Territory, SE Australia 35.21S 149.08E
191 R10 **Canberra** ✕ Australian Capital Territory, SE Australia 35.19S 149.12E
37 P2 **Canby** California, W USA 41.27N 120.51W
31 S9 **Canby** Minnesota, N USA 44.42N 96.17W
105 N2 **Canche** ~ N France
104 L13 **Cancon** Lot-et-Garonne, SW France 44.33N 0.37E
43 Z11 **Cancún** Quintana Roo, SE Mexico 21.05N 86.48W
106 K2 **Candás** Asturias, N Spain 43.35N 5.45W
104 J7 **Cande** Maine-et-Loire, NW France 47.33N 1.03W
43 W14 **Candelaria** Campeche, SE Mexico 18.10N 91.00W
26 J11 **Candelaria** Texas, SW USA 30.05N 104.40W
43 W15 **Candelaria, Río** ~ Guatemala/Mexico
106 L8 **Candeleda** Castilla-León, N Spain 40.10N 5.13W
Candia *see* Irákleio
43 P8 **Cándido Aguilar** Tamaulipas, C Mexico 25.30N 97.57W
41 N8 **Candle** Alaska, USA 65.54N 161.55W
9 T14 **Candle Lake** Saskatchewan, C Canada 53.43N 105.09W
20 L13 **Candlewood, Lake** ▣ Connecticut, NE USA
31 O3 **Cando** North Dakota, N USA 48.29N 99.12W
179 P8 **Candon** Luzon, N Philippines 17.15N 120.25E
Canea *see* Chaniá
47 O12 **Canefield** ✕ (Roseau) SW Dominica 15.20N 61.24W
63 F20 **Canelones** *prev.* Guadalupe. Canelones, S Uruguay 34.31S 56.16W
63 E20 **Canelones** ◈ *department* S Uruguay
Canendiyú *see* Canindeyú
65 F14 **Cañete** Bío Bío, C Chile 37.48S 73.21W
107 Q9 **Cañete** Castilla-La Mancha, C Spain 40.03N 1.39W
Cañete *see* San Vicente de Cañete
29 P8 **Caney** Kansas, C USA 37.00N 95.56W
29 P8 **Caney River** ~ Kansas/Oklahoma, C USA
107 S3 **Canfranc-Estación** Aragón, NE Spain 42.42N 0.31W
85 E14 **Cangamba** *Port.* Vila de Aljustrel. Moxico, E Angola 13.39S 19.57E
84 C12 **Cangandala** Malanje, NW Angola 9.46S 16.27E
106 G4 **Cangas** Galicia, NW Spain 42.16N 8.46W
106 J2 **Cangas del Narcea** Asturias, N Spain 43.10N 6.31W
106 L2 **Cangas de Onís** Asturias, N Spain 43.21N 5.07W
167 S11 **Cangnan** *var.* Lingxi. Zhejiang, SE China 27.29N 120.23E
84 C10 **Cangola** Uíge, NW Angola 7.54S 15.57E
85 E14 **Cangombe** Moxico, E Angola 14.27S 20.05E
65 H21 **Cangrejo, Cerro** ▲ S Argentina 49.19S 72.18W
63 H17 **Canguçu** Rio Grande do Sul, S Brazil 31.25S 52.37W
167 P3 **Cangzhou** Hebei, E China 38.19N 116.54E
10 M7 **Caniapiscau** ~ Québec, E Canada
10 M8 **Caniapiscau, Réservoir de** ▣ Québec, C Canada
109 J24 **Canicattì** Sicilia, Italy, C Mediterranean Sea 37.22N 13.51E
142 L11 **Canik Dağları** ▲▲ N Turkey
107 P14 **Caniles** Andalucía, S Spain 37.24N 2.41W
61 B16 **Canindé** Acre, W Brazil 10.55S 69.45W
64 P6 **Canindeyú** *var.* Canendiyú, Canindiyú. ◈ *department* E Paraguay
Canindiyú *see* Canindeyú
204 J10 **Canisteo Peninsula** *peninsula* Antarctica
20 F11 **Canisteo River** ~ New York, NE USA
42 M10 **Cañitas** *var.* Cañitas de Felipe Pescador. Zacatecas, C Mexico 23.35N 102.39W
Cañitas de Felipe Pescador *see* Cañitas
107 P15 **Canjáyar** Andalucía, S Spain 37.00N 2.45W
142 I12 **Çankırı** *var.* Chankiri; *anc.* Gangra, Germanicopolis. Çankın, N Turkey 40.36N 33.35E
142 I11 **Çankırı** *var.* Chankiri. ◈ *province* N Turkey
179 Qq13 **Canlaon Volcano** ✶ Negros, C Philippines 10.24N 123.05E
9 P16 **Canmore** Alberta, SW Canada 51.07N 115.18W
98 F9 **Canna** *island* NW Scotland, UK
161 F20 **Cannanore** *var.* Kananur, Kannur. Kerala, SW India 11.52N 75.22E
33 O17 **Cannelton** Indiana, N USA 37.54N 86.44W
105 U15 **Cannes** Alpes-Maritimes, SE France 43.33N 6.58E
41 R5 **Canning River** ~ Alaska, USA
108 C6 **Cannobio** Piemonte, NE Italy 46.04N 8.39E
99 L19 **Cannock** C England, UK 52.40N 2.03W
30 M6 **Cannonball River** ~ North Dakota, N USA
31 W9 **Cannon Falls** Minnesota, N USA 44.30N 92.54W
20 I11 **Cannonsville Reservoir** ▣ New York, NE USA
191 R12 **Cann River** Victoria, SE Australia 37.34S 149.11E
63 I16 **Canoas** Rio Grande do Sul, S Brazil 29.42S 51.07W
63 I14 **Canoas, Rio** ~ S Brazil
12 I12 **Canoe Lake** ◎ Ontario, SE Canada
62 J12 **Canoinhas** Santa Catarina, S Brazil 26.12S 50.24W
39 T6 **Canon City** Colorado, C USA 38.25N 105.14W
57 P8 **Caño Negro** Bolívar, SE Venezuela
181 X15 **Canonniers Point** *headland* N Mauritius
25 W6 **Canoochee River** ~ Georgia, SE USA
9 V15 **Canora** Saskatchewan, S Canada 51.37N 102.28W
47 Y14 **Canouan** *island* S Saint Vincent and the Grenadines
11 R15 **Canso** Nova Scotia, SE Canada 45.20N 61.00W
106 M3 **Cantabria** ◈ *autonomous community* N Spain
106 K3 **Cantábrica, Cordillera** ▲▲ N Spain
Cantabrigia *see* Cambridge
105 O12 **Cantal** ◈ *department* C France
107 N6 **Cantalejo** Castilla-León, N Spain 41.15N 3.57W
105 O12 **Cantal, Monts du** ▲▲ C France
106 G8 **Cantanhede** Coimbra, C Portugal 40.21N 8.37W
Cantaño *see* Cataño
57 O6 **Cantaura** Anzoátegui, NE Venezuela 9.18N 64.21W
118 M11 **Cantemir** *Rus.* Kantemir. S Moldova 46.17N 28.12E
99 Q22 **Canterbury** *hist.* Cantwaraburh, *anc.* Durovernum, *Lat.* Cantuaria. SE England, UK 51.16N 1.04E
193 F19 **Canterbury** *off.* Canterbury Region. ◈ *region* South Island, NZ
193 H20 **Canterbury Bight** *bight* South Island, NZ
193 H19 **Canterbury Plains** *plain* South Island, NZ
178 Jj15 **Cần Thơ** Cần Thơ, S Vietnam 10.03N 105.46E
106 K13 **Cantillana** Andalucía, S Spain 37.34N 5.48W
61 N15 **Canto do Buriti** Piauí, NE Brazil 8.07S 43.00W
25 S2 **Canton** Georgia, SE USA 34.14N 84.29W
32 K12 **Canton** Illinois, N USA 40.33N 90.02W
24 L5 **Canton** Mississippi, S USA 32.36N 90.02W
29 V2 **Canton** Missouri, C USA 40.07N 91.31W
20 J7 **Canton** New York, NE USA 44.36N 75.10W
23 O10 **Canton** North Carolina, SE USA 35.31N 82.50W
33 U12 **Canton** Ohio, N USA 40.48N 81.22W
28 L9 **Canton** Oklahoma, C USA 36.03N 98.35W
20 G12 **Canton** Pennsylvania, NE USA 41.38N 76.49W
31 R11 **Canton** South Dakota, N USA 43.19N 96.33W
27 V7 **Canton** Texas, SW USA 32.34N 95.50W
Canton *see* Guangzhou
Canton Island *see* Kanton
28 L9 **Canton Lake** ▣ Oklahoma, C USA
108 D7 **Cantù** Lombardia, N Italy 45.43N 9.07E
Cantuaria/Cantwaraburh *see* Canterbury
41 R10 **Cantwell** Alaska, USA 63.23N 148.57W
61 O16 **Canudos** Bahia, E Brazil 9.51S 39.07W
49 T7 **Canumã, Rio** ~ N Brazil
Canusium *see* Puglia, Canosa di
26 G7 **Canutillo** Texas, SW USA 31.53N 106.34W
27 N3 **Canyon** Texas, SW USA 34.58N 101.55W
35 S12 **Canyon** Wyoming, C USA 44.44N 110.30W
34 K13 **Canyon City** Oregon, NW USA 44.22N 118.58W
35 R10 **Canyon Ferry Lake** ▣ Montana, NW USA
27 S11 **Canyon Lake** ▣ Texas, SW USA
178 Jj5 **Cao Bằng** *var.* Caobang. Cao Bằng, N Vietnam 22.40N 106.16E
166 J12 **Caodu He** ~ S China
178 J14 **Cao Lanh** Đồng Tháp, S Vietnam 10.35N 105.25E
84 C11 **Caombo** Malanje, NW Angola 8.42S 16.33E
Caorach, Cuan na g *see* Sheep Haven
Caozhou *see* Heze
175 S10 **Capalulu** Pulau Mangole, E Indonesia 1.51S 125.53E
56 K8 **Capanaparo, Río** ~ Colombia/Venezuela
60 L12 **Capanema** Pará, NE Brazil 1.07S 47.07W
62 L10 **Capão Bonito** São Paulo, S Brazil 24.01S 48.22W
62 I13 **Capão Doce, Morro do** ▲ S Brazil 26.37S 51.28W
56 I4 **Capatárida** Falcón, N Venezuela 11.10N 70.38W
104 I15 **Capbreton** Landes, SW France 43.40N 1.25W
Cap-Breton, Île du *see* Cape Breton Island
13 W6 **Cap-Chat** Québec, SE Canada 49.04N 66.43W
13 P11 **Cap-de-la-Madeleine** Québec, SE Canada 46.22N 72.31W
105 N13 **Capdenac** Aveyron, S France 44.35N 2.06E
191 Q15 **Cape Barren Island** *island* Furneaux Group, Tasmania, SE Australia
67 O18 **Cape Basin** *undersea feature* S Atlantic Ocean
11 R14 **Cape Breton Island** *Fr.* Île du Cap-Breton. *island* Nova Scotia, SE Canada
25 Y11 **Cape Canaveral** Florida, SE USA 28.24N 80.36W
23 Y6 **Cape Charles** Virginia, NE USA 37.16N 76.01W
79 P17 **Cape Coast** *prev.* Cape Coast Castle. S Ghana 5.10N 1.13W
Cape Coast Castle *see* Cape Coast
21 Q12 **Cape Cod Bay** *bay* Massachusetts, NE USA
25 W15 **Cape Coral** Florida, SE USA 26.33N 81.57W
189 R4 **Cape Crawford Roadhouse** Northern Territory, N Australia 16.39S 135.44E
16 N4 **Cape Dorset** Baffin Island, Nunavut, NE Canada 64.12N 76.31W
23 N8 **Cape Fear River** ~ North Carolina, SE USA
29 Y7 **Cape Girardeau** Missouri, C USA 37.17N 89.31W
23 T14 **Cape Island** *island* South Carolina, SE USA
194 E11 **Capella** ▲ NW PNG 5.00S 141.09E
100 H12 **Capelle aan den IJssel** Zuid-Holland, SW Netherlands 51.55N 4.36E
85 C15 **Capelongo** Huíla, C Angola 14.45S 15.02E
20 J17 **Cape May** New Jersey, NE USA 38.54N 74.54W
20 J17 **Cape May Court House** New Jersey, NE USA 39.03N 74.46W
Cape Palmas *see* Harper
15 H2 **Cape Parry** Northwest Territories, N Canada 70.10N 124.33W
67 P19 **Cape Rise** *undersea feature* SW Indian Ocean
Cape Saint Jacques *see* Vung Tau
Capesterre *see* Capesterre-Belle-Eau
47 Y6 **Capesterre-Belle-Eau** *var.* Capesterre. Basse Terre, S Guadeloupe 16.03N 61.33W
85 D26 **Cape Town** *var.* Ekapa, *Afr.* Kaapstad, Kapstad. ● (South Africa-legislative capital) Western Cape, SW South Africa 33.55S 18.28E
85 E26 **Cape Town** ✕ Western Cape, SW South Africa 31.51S 21.06E
78 D9 **Cape Verde** *off.* Republic of Cape Verde, *Port.* Cabo Verde, Ilhas do Cabo Verde. ◆ *republic* E Atlantic Ocean
66 L11 **Cape Verde Basin** *undersea feature* E Atlantic Ocean
68 K5 **Cape Verde Islands** *island group* E Atlantic Ocean
66 L10 **Cape Verde Plain** *undersea feature* E Atlantic Ocean
Cape Verde Plateau/Cape Verde Rise *see* Cape Verde Terrace
66 L11 **Cape Verde Terrace** *var.* Cape Verde Plateau, Cape Verde Rise. *undersea feature* E Atlantic Ocean
189 V2 **Cape York Peninsula** *peninsula* Queensland, N Australia
46 M8 **Cap-Haïtien** *var.* Le Cap. N Haiti 19.43N 72.12W
45 T15 **Capira** Panamá, C Panama 8.45N 79.52W
12 K8 **Capitachouane** ~ Québec, SE Canada
12 L8 **Capitachouane, Lac** ◎ Québec, SE Canada
39 T13 **Capitan** New Mexico, SW USA 33.33N 105.34W
204 G3 **Capitán Arturo Prat** *Chilean research station* South Shetland Islands, Antarctica 62.24S 59.42W
39 S13 **Capitan Mountains** ▲▲ New Mexico, SW USA
64 M3 **Capitán Pablo Lagerenza** *var.* Mayor Pablo Lagerenza. Chaco, N Paraguay 19.55S 60.46W
39 T13 **Capitan Peak** ▲ New Mexico, SW USA 33.35N 105.15W
196 H5 **Capitol Hill** Saipan, S Northern Mariana Islands
62 I9 **Capivara, Represa** ▣ S Brazil
63 J16 **Capivari** Rio Grande do Sul, S Brazil 30.08S 50.32W
115 H15 **Čapljina** Federacija Bosna I Hercegovina, S Bosnia and Herzegovina 43.07N 17.42E
85 M15 **Capoche** *var.* Kapoche. ~ Mozambique/Zambia
Capo Delgado, Província de *see* Cabo Delgado
109 K17 **Capodichino** ✕ (Napoli) Campania, S Italy 40.53N 14.15E
Capodistria *see* Koper
108 E12 **Capraia, Isola** *island* Archipelago Toscano, C Italy
109 B16 **Caprara, Punta** *var.* Punta dello Scorno. *headland* Isola Asinara, W Italy 41.07N 8.19E
Capraria, Isola di to Capraia, Isola *see* Cabrera
12 F10 **Capreol** Ontario, S Canada 46.43N 80.55W
109 K18 **Capri** Campania, S Italy 40.33N 14.14E
183 S9 **Capricorn Tablemount** *undersea feature* W Pacific Ocean 18.34S 172.12W
109 J18 **Capri, Isola di** *island* S Italy
85 G16 **Caprivi** ◈ *district* NE Namibia
Caprivi Concession *see* Caprivi Strip
85 F16 **Caprivi Strip** *Ger.* Caprivizipfel; *prev.* Caprivi Concession. *cultural region* NE Namibia
Caprivizipfel *see* Caprivi Strip
27 O5 **Cap Rock Escarpment** *cliffs* Texas, SW USA
13 R10 **Cap-Rouge** Québec, SE Canada 46.45N 71.18W
Cap Saint-Jacques *see* Vung Tau
40 F12 **Captain Cook** Hawai'i, USA, C Pacific Ocean 19.30N 155.55W
191 R10 **Captains Flat** New South Wales, SE Australia 35.37S 149.28E
104 K14 **Captieux** Gironde, SW France 44.16N 0.15W
109 K17 **Capua** Campania, S Italy 41.06N 14.13E
56 F14 **Caquetá** *off.* Departamento del Caquetá. ◈ *province* S Colombia
56 E13 **Caquetá, Río** *var.* Rio Japurá, Yapurá. ~ Brazil/Colombia *see also* Japurá, Rio
CAR *see* Central African Republic
Cara *see* Kara
59 I16 **Carabaya, Cordillera** ▲▲ E Peru
56 K5 **Carabobo** *off.* Estado Carabobo. ◈ *state* N Venezuela
118 I14 **Caracal** Olt, S Romania 44.07N 24.18E
60 F10 **Caracaraí** Rondônia, W Brazil 1.46N 61.10W
56 L5 **Caracas** ● (Venezuela) Distrito Federal, N Venezuela 10.28N 66.53W
56 I5 **Carache** Trujillo, N Venezuela 9.40N 70.15W
62 N10 **Caraguatatuba** São Paulo, S Brazil 23.37S 45.24W
50 I7 **Carajás, Serra dos** ▲▲ N Brazil
Caralis *see* Cagliari
56 E9 **Caramanta** Antioquia, W Colombia 5.36N 75.37W
179 Q11 **Caramoan** Catanduanes Island, N Philippines 13.47N 123.49E
Caramurat *see* Mihail Kogălniceanu
118 F12 **Caransebeş** *Ger.* Karansebesch, *Hung.* Karánsebes. Caraş-Severin, SW Romania 45.23N 22.13E
Carapella *see* Carapelle
109 M16 **Carapelle** *var.* Carapella. ~ SE Italy
57 O9 **Carapo** Bolívar, SE Venezuela
11 P13 **Caraquet** New Brunswick, SE Canada 47.48N 64.58W
Caras *see* Caraz
118 F12 **Caraşova** *Hung.* Krassóvár. Caraş-Severin, SW Romania 45.10N 21.51E
118 F12 **Caraş-Severin** ◈ *county* SW Romania
44 M5 **Caratasca, Laguna de** *lagoon* NE Honduras
60 C13 **Carauari** Amazonas, NW Brazil 4.55S 66.57W
Caravaca *see* Caravaca de la Cruz
107 Q12 **Caravaca de la Cruz** *var.* Caravaca. Murcia, SE Spain 38.06N 1.51W
108 E7 **Caravaggio** Lombardia, N Italy 45.31N 9.39E
109 C18 **Caravai, Passo di** *pass* Sardegna, Italy, C Mediterranean Sea 40.10N 9.16E
61 O19 **Caravelas** Bahia, E Brazil 17.45S 39.15W
58 C12 **Caraz** *var.* Caras. Ancash, W Peru 9.01S 77.48W
63 H14 **Carazinho** Rio Grande do Sul, S Brazil 28.16S 52.46W
44 J11 **Carazo** ◈ *department* SW Nicaragua
Carballiño *see* O Carballiño
106 G2 **Carballo** Galicia, NW Spain 43.13N 8.42W
9 W16 **Carberry** Manitoba, S Canada 49.52N 99.19W
42 F4 **Carbó** Sonora, NW Mexico 29.40N 110.54W
109 C20 **Carbonara, Capo** *headland* Sardegna, Italy, C Mediterranean Sea 39.06N 9.31E
39 Q5 **Carbondale** Colorado, C USA 39.24N 107.12W
32 L17 **Carbondale** Illinois, N USA 37.43N 89.13W
29 Q4 **Carbondale** Kansas, C USA 38.49N 95.41W
20 I13 **Carbondale** Pennsylvania, NE USA 41.34N 75.30W
11 V12 **Carbonear** Newfoundland and Labrador, SE Canada 47.45N 53.16W
107 Q9 **Carboneras de Guadazaón** *var.* Carboneras de Guadazón. Castilla-La Mancha, C Spain 39.54N 1.49W
Carboneras de Guadazón *see* Carboneras de Guadazaón
25 O3 **Carbon Hill** Alabama, S USA 33.53N 87.31W
109 B20 **Carbonia** *var.* Carbonia Centro. Sardegna, Italy, C Mediterranean Sea 39.10N 8.31E
Carbonia Centro *see* Carbonia
107 S10 **Carcaixent** País Valenciano, E Spain 39.07N 0.28W
Carcaso *see* Carcassonne
67 B24 **Carcass Island** *island* NW Falkland Islands
105 O16 **Carcassonne** *anc.* Carcaso. Aude, S France 43.13N 2.21E
107 R12 **Carche** ▲ S Spain 38.24N 1.11W
58 A13 **Carchi** ◈ *province* N Ecuador
8 I8 **Carcross** Yukon Territory, W Canada 60.10N 134.40W
Cardamomes, Chaîne des *see* Krâvanh, Chuŏr Phnum
161 G22 **Cardamom Hills** ▲▲ SW India
Cardamom Mountains *see* Krâvanh, Chuŏr Phnum
106 M12 **Cardeña** Andalucía, S Spain 38.16N 4.19W
46 D4 **Cárdenas** Matanzas, W Cuba 23.01N 81.12W
43 O11 **Cárdenas** San Luis Potosí, C Mexico 22.03N 99.30W
43 U15 **Cárdenas** Tabasco, SE Mexico 18.00N 93.21W
65 H21 **Cardiel, Lago** ◎ S Argentina
99 K22 **Cardiff** *Wel.* Caerdydd. ◈ S Wales, UK 51.30N 3.13W
99 J22 **Cardiff-Wales** ✕ S Wales, UK 51.24N 3.22W
99 I21 **Cardigan** *Wel.* Aberteifi. SW Wales, UK 52.06N 4.40W
99 I20 **Cardigan** *cultural region* W Wales, UK
99 I20 **Cardigan Bay** *bay* W Wales, UK
21 N8 **Cardigan, Mount** ▲ New Hampshire, NE USA 43.39N 71.52W
12 M13 **Cardinal** Ontario, SE Canada 44.48N 75.22W
107 V5 **Cardona** Cataluña, NE Spain 41.55N 1.40E
63 E19 **Cardona** Soriano, SW Uruguay 33.52S 57.18W
107 V4 **Cardoner** ~ NE Spain
9 Q17 **Cardston** Alberta, SW Canada 49.13N 113.19W
189 W5 **Cardwell** Queensland, NE Australia 18.24S 146.06E
118 G8 **Carei** *Ger.* Gross-Karol, Karol, *Hung.* Nagykároly; *prev.* Careii-Mari. Satu Mare, NW Romania 47.40N 22.27E
Careii-Mari *see* Carei
60 F13 **Careiro** Amazonas, NW Brazil 3.39S 60.22W
104 J4 **Carentan** Manche, N France 49.18N 1.15W
106 M2 **Cares** ~ N Spain
35 P14 **Carey** Idaho, NW USA 43.17N 113.58W
33 S12 **Carey** Ohio, N USA 40.57N 83.22W
27 P4 **Carey** Texas, SW USA 34.28N 100.18W
188 L11 **Carey, Lake** ◎ Western Australia
181 O8 **Cargados Carajos Bank** *undersea feature* C Indian Ocean
104 G6 **Carhaix-Plouguer** Finistère, NW France 48.16N 3.34W
63 A22 **Carhué** Buenos Aires, E Argentina 37.10S 62.45W
57 O5 **Cariaco** Sucre, NE Venezuela 10.28N 63.33W
109 O20 **Cariati** Calabria, SW Italy 39.30N 16.57E
2 H17 **Caribbean Plate** *tectonic feature*
46 I11 **Caribbean Sea** *sea* W Atlantic Ocean
9 N15 **Cariboo Mountains** ▲▲ British Columbia, SW Canada
9 W9 **Caribou** Manitoba, C Canada 59.27N 97.43W
21 S2 **Caribou** Maine, NE USA 46.51N 68.00W
9 P10 **Caribou Mountains** ▲▲ Alberta, SW Canada
Caribrod *see* Dimitrovgrad
42 I6 **Carichic** Chihuahua, N Mexico 27.57N 107.01W
179 Qq13 **Carigara** Leyte, C Philippines 11.15N 124.43E
105 R3 **Carignan** Ardennes, N France 49.38N 5.08E
191 Q5 **Carinda** New South Wales, SE Australia 30.26S 147.45E
107 R6 **Cariñena** Aragón, NE Spain 41.19N 1.13W
109 I23 **Carini** Sicilia, Italy, C Mediterranean Sea 38.06N 13.09E
109 K17 **Carinola** Campania, S Italy 41.14N 14.03E
Carinthi *see* Kärnten
57 O5 **Caripe** Monagas, NE Venezuela 10.06N 63.30W
57 P5 **Caripito** Monagas, NE Venezuela 10.03N 63.05W
13 W7 **Carleton** Québec, SE Canada 48.07N 66.07W
33 S10 **Carleton** Michigan, N USA 42.03N 83.23W
11 O14 **Carleton, Mount** ▲ New Brunswick, SE Canada 47.10N 66.54W
12 L13 **Carleton Place** Ontario, SE Canada 45.09N 76.07W
37 V3 **Carlin** Nevada, W USA 40.40N 116.09W
32 K14 **Carlinville** Illinois, N USA 39.16N 89.52W
99 K14 **Carlisle** *anc.* Caer Luel, Luguvallium, Luguvallum. NW England, UK 54.54N 2.55W
29 V11 **Carlisle** Arkansas, C USA 34.46N 91.45W
33 N15 **Carlisle** Indiana, N USA 38.57N 87.23W
31 V14 **Carlisle** Iowa, C USA 41.30N 93.29W
23 N5 **Carlisle** Kentucky, S USA 38.19N 83.59W
20 F15 **Carlisle** Pennsylvania, NE USA 40.10N 77.10W
23 Q11 **Carlisle** South Carolina, SE USA 34.35N 81.27W
40 J17 **Carlisle Island** *island* Aleutian Islands, Alaska, USA
29 R7 **Carl Junction** Missouri, C USA 37.10N 94.34W
109 A20 **Carloforte** Sardegna, Italy, C Mediterranean Sea 39.10N 8.17E
Carlopago *see* Karlobag
63 B21 **Carlos Casares** Buenos Aires, E Argentina 35.39S 61.28W
63 E18 **Carlos Reyles** Durazno, C Uruguay 33.04S 56.28W
63 A21 **Carlos Tejedor** Buenos Aires, E Argentina 35.23S 62.31W
99 F19 **Carlow** *Ir.* Ceatharlach. SE Ireland 52.49N 6.55W
99 F19 **Carlow** *Ir.* Cheatharlach. *cultural region* SE Ireland
98 F7 **Carloway** NW Scotland, UK 58.16N 6.48W
Carlsbad *see* Karlovy Vary
37 U17 **Carlsbad** California, W USA 33.09N 117.21W
39 U15 **Carlsbad** New Mexico, SW USA 32.24N 104.14W
133 N13 **Carlsberg Ridge** *undersea feature* S Arabian Sea
Carlsruhe *see* Karlsruhe
31 W6 **Carlton** Minnesota, N USA 46.39N 92.25W
9 V17 **Carlyle** Saskatchewan, S Canada 49.39N 102.18W
32 L15 **Carlyle** Illinois, N USA 38.36N 89.22W
32 L15 **Carlyle Lake** ▣ Illinois, N USA
8 H7 **Carmacks** Yukon Territory, W Canada 62.04N 136.21W
108 B9 **Carmagnola** Piemonte, NW Italy 44.50N 7.43E
9 X16 **Carman** Manitoba, S Canada 49.31N 97.58W
Carmana/Carmania *see* Kermān
99 I21 **Carmarthen** SW Wales, UK 51.52N 4.19W
99 I21 **Carmarthen** *cultural region* SW Wales, UK
99 I22 **Carmarthen Bay** *inlet* SW Wales, UK
105 N14 **Carmaux** Tarn, S France 44.03N 2.09E
37 N11 **Carmel** California, W USA 36.32N 121.54W
33 O13 **Carmel** Indiana, N USA 39.58N 86.07W
20 L13 **Carmel** New York, NE USA 41.25N 73.40W
99 H18 **Carmel Head** *headland* NW Wales, UK 53.24N 4.35W
44 E2 **Carmelita** Petén, N Guatemala 17.33N 90.10W
63 D19 **Carmelo** Colonia, SW Uruguay 34.00S 58.20W
43 V14 **Carmen** *var.* Ciudad del Carmen. Campeche, SE Mexico 18.37N 91.49W
63 A25 **Carmen de Patagones** Buenos Aires, E Argentina 40.45S 63.00W
42 F8 **Carmen, Isla** *island* W Mexico
42 M5 **Carmen, Sierra del** ▲▲ NW Mexico
32 M16 **Carmi** Illinois, N USA 38.05N 88.09W
37 O7 **Carmichael** California, W USA 38.36N 121.21W
Carmiel *see* Karmi'ēl
27 U11 **Carmine** Texas, SW USA 30.07N 96.40W
106 K14 **Carmona** Andalucía, S Spain 37.28N 5.37W
Carmona *see* Uíge
Carnaro *see* Kvarner
12 I13 **Carnarvon** Ontario, SE Canada 45.03N 78.41W
85 G24 **Carnarvon** Northern Cape, W South Africa 30.58S 22.07E
Carnarvon *see* Caernarfon
188 K9 **Carnarvon Range** ▲▲ Western Australia
188 G9 **Carnarvon** Western Australia 24.57S 113.37E
Carn Domhnach *see* Carndonagh
98 E13 **Carndonagh** *Ir.* Carn Domhnach. NW Ireland 55.15N 7.15W
9 V17 **Carnduff** Saskatchewan, S Canada 49.10N 101.49W
28 L11 **Carnegie** Oklahoma, C USA 35.06N 98.36W
188 L9 **Carnegie, Lake** *salt lake* Western Australia
200 Oo8 **Carnegie Ridge** *undersea feature* E Pacific Ocean
98 H9 **Carn Eige** ▲ N Scotland, UK 57.18N 5.04W
190 F5 **Carnes** South Australia 30.12S 134.31E
204 J12 **Carney Island** *island* Antarctica
20 H16 **Carneys Point** New Jersey, NE USA 39.38N 75.29W
Carniche, Alpi *see* Karnische Alpen
157 Q21 **Car Nicobar** *island* Nicobar Islands, India, NE Indian Ocean
81 H15 **Carnot** Mambéré-Kadéï, W Central African Republic 4.58N 15.55E
190 F10 **Carnot, Cape** *headland* South Australia 34.57S 135.39E
98 K11 **Carnoustie** E Scotland, UK 56.29N 2.42W
99 F20 **Carnsore Point** *Ir.* Ceann an Chairn. *headland* SE Ireland 52.10N 6.22W
15 Gg4 **Carnwath** ~ Northwest Territories, NW Canada
33 R8 **Caro** Michigan, N USA 43.29N 83.24W
25 Z15 **Carol City** Florida, SE USA 25.56N 80.15W

◆ Country ● Country Capital ◇ Dependent Territory ○ Dependent Territory Capital ◈ Administrative Region ✕ International Airport ▲ Mountain ▲▲ Mountain Range ✶ Volcano ~ River ◎ Lake ▣ Reservoir
239

CAROLINA – CENTERFIELD

61 L14 **Carolina** Maranhão, E Brazil 7.19S 47.25W
47 U5 **Carolina** E Puerto Rico 18.22N 65.57W
23 V12 **Carolina Beach** North Carolina, SE USA 34.02N 77.53W
Caroline Island see Millennium Island
201 N15 **Caroline Islands** island group C Micronesia
133 Z14 **Caroline Plate** tectonic feature
199 H7 **Caroline Ridge** undersea feature E Philippine Sea
Carolopois see Châlons-en-Champagne
47 V14 **Caroni Arena Dam** ⊠ Trinidad, Trinidad and Tobago
Caronie, Monti see Nebrodi, Monti
57 P7 **Caroní, Río** ⇝ E Venezuela
47 U14 **Caroni River** ⇝ Trinidad, Trinidad and Tobago
Caronium see A Coruña
56 J5 **Carora** Lara, N Venezuela 10.09N 70.06W
88 F12 **Carpathian Mountains** var. Carpathians, Cz./Pol. Karpaty, Ger. Karpaten. ▲ E Europe
Carpathians see Carpathian Mountains
Carpathos/Carpathus see Kárpathos
118 H12 **Carpaţii Meridionali** var. Alpi Transilvaniei, Carpaţii Sudici, Eng. South Carpathians, Transylvanian Alps, Ger. Südkarpaten, Transsylvanische Alpen, Hung. Déli-Kárpátok, Erdélyi-Havasok. ▲ C Romania
Carpaţii Sudici see Carpaţii Meridionali
182 L7 **Carpentaria, Gulf of** gulf N Australia
Carpentoracte see Carpentras
105 R14 **Carpentras** anc. Carpentoracte. Vaucluse, SE France 44.03N 5.03E
108 F9 **Carpi** Emilia-Romagna, N Italy 44.46N 10.52E
118 E11 **Cărpiniş** Hung. Gyertyámos. Timiş, W Romania 45.46N 20.51E
37 R14 **Carpinteria** California, W USA 34.24N 119.30W
25 S9 **Carrabelle** Florida, SE USA 29.51N 84.39W
Carraig Aonair see Fastnet Rock
Carraig Fhearghais see Carrickfergus
Carraig Mhachaire Rois see Carrickmacross
Carraig na Siúire see Carrick-on-Suir
Carrantual see Carrauntoohil
108 E10 **Carrara** Toscana, C Italy 44.04N 10.07E
63 F20 **Carrasco** ✕ (Montevideo) Canelones, S Uruguay 34.51S 56.00W
107 P9 **Carrascosa del Campo** Castilla-La Mancha, C Spain 40.01N 2.34W
56 H4 **Carrasquero** Zulia, NW Venezuela 11.00N 72.01W
191 O9 **Carrathool** New South Wales, SE Australia 34.25S 145.30E
Carrauntohil see Carrauntoohil
99 B21 **Carrauntoohil** Ir. Carrantual, Carrauntohil, Corrán Tuathail. ▲ SW Ireland 51.59N 9.45W
47 Y15 **Carriacou** island N Grenada
99 G15 **Carrickfergus** Ir. Carraig Fhearghais. NE Northern Ireland, UK 54.43N 5.49W
99 F16 **Carrickmacross** Ir. Carraig Mhachaire Rois. N Ireland 53.58N 6.43W
99 D16 **Carrick-on-Shannon** Ir. Cora Droma Rúisc. NW Ireland 53.37N 8.04W
99 E20 **Carrick-on-Suir** Ir. Carraig na Siúire. S Ireland 52.21N 7.25W
190 I7 **Carrieton** South Australia 32.27S 138.33E
42 L7 **Carrillo** Chihuahua, N Mexico 25.53N 103.54W
31 O4 **Carrington** North Dakota, N USA 47.27N 99.07W
106 M4 **Carrión** ⇝ N Spain
106 M4 **Carrión de los Condes** Castilla-León, N Spain 42.19N 4.37W
27 P13 **Carrizo Springs** Texas, SW USA 28.31N 99.51W
39 S13 **Carrizozo** New Mexico, SW USA 33.38N 105.52W
31 T13 **Carroll** Iowa, C USA 42.04N 94.52W
25 N4 **Carrollton** Alabama, S USA 33.13N 88.05W
25 R3 **Carrollton** Georgia, SE USA 33.33N 85.04W
32 K14 **Carrollton** Illinois, N USA 39.18N 90.24W
22 L4 **Carrollton** Kentucky, S USA 38.40N 85.10W
33 R8 **Carrollton** Michigan, N USA 43.27N 83.55W
29 T3 **Carrollton** Missouri, C USA 39.21N 93.30W
33 U12 **Carrollton** Ohio, N USA 40.34N 81.05W
27 T6 **Carrollton** Texas, SW USA 32.57N 96.53W
9 U14 **Carrot** ⇝ Saskatchewan, S Canada
9 U14 **Carrot River** Saskatchewan, C Canada 53.18N 103.31W
20 J7 **Carry Falls Reservoir** ⊠ New York, NE USA
142 L11 **Çarşamba** Samsun, N Turkey 41.13N 36.43E
30 L6 **Carson** North Dakota, N USA 46.21N 101.33W
37 Q6 **Carson City** state capital Nevada, W USA 39.10N 119.46W
37 R6 **Carson River** ⇝ Nevada, W USA
37 S5 **Carson Sink** salt flat Nevada, W USA
9 Q16 **Carstairs** Alberta, SW Canada 51.34N 114.01W
Carstensz, Puntjak see Jaya, Puncak
56 E5 **Cartagena** var. Cartagena de los Indes. Bolívar, NW Colombia 10.24N 75.33W
107 R13 **Cartagena** anc. Carthago Nova. Murcia, SE Spain 37.36N 0.58W
Cartagena de los Indes see Cartagena
56 D10 **Cartago** Valle del Cauca, W Colombia 4.45N 75.55W
45 N14 **Cartago** Cartago, C Costa Rica 9.49N 83.53W
44 M14 **Cartago** off. Provincia de Cartago. ◆ province C Costa Rica
27 O11 **Carta Valley** Texas, SW USA 29.46N 100.37W
106 F10 **Cartaxo** Santarém, C Portugal 39.10N 8.46W
106 I14 **Cartaya** Andalucía, S Spain 37.16N 7.09W
Carteret Islands see Tulun Islands
31 S15 **Carter Lake** Iowa, C USA 41.17N 95.55W
25 S3 **Cartersville** Georgia, SE USA 34.10N 84.48W
193 M14 **Carterton** Wellington, North Island, NZ 41.01S 175.32E
32 J13 **Carthage** Illinois, N USA 40.25N 91.09W
24 L5 **Carthage** Mississippi, S USA 32.43N 89.31W
29 R7 **Carthage** Missouri, C USA 37.10N 94.18W
20 I8 **Carthage** New York, NE USA 43.58N 75.36W
23 T10 **Carthage** North Carolina, SE USA 35.19N 79.24W
22 K8 **Carthage** Tennessee, S USA 36.16N 85.57W
27 X7 **Carthage** Texas, SW USA 32.09N 94.20W
76 M5 **Carthage** ✕ (Tunis) N Tunisia 36.51N 10.12E
Carthago Nova see Cartagena
12 E10 **Cartier** Ontario, S Canada 46.40N 81.31W
56 E13 **Cartagena de Chaira** Caquetá, S Colombia 1.19N 74.52W
11 S8 **Cartwright** Newfoundland and Labrador, E Canada 53.40N 57.00W
57 P9 **Caruana de Montaña** Bolívar, SE Venezuela 5.16N 63.12W
61 Q15 **Caruaru** Pernambuco, E Brazil 8.15S 35.55W
57 P5 **Carúpano** Sucre, NE Venezuela 10.39N 63.13W
Carusbur see Cherbourg
60 M12 **Carutapera** Maranhão, E Brazil 1.12S 45.57W
29 Y9 **Caruthersville** Missouri, C USA 36.07N 89.38W
105 O1 **Carvin** Pas-de-Calais, N France 50.31N 3.00E
60 E12 **Carvoeiro** Amazonas, NW Brazil 1.24S 61.59W
106 E10 **Carvoeiro, Cabo** headland C Portugal 39.19N 9.27W
23 U9 **Cary** North Carolina, SE USA 35.47N 78.46W
190 M3 **Caryapundy Swamp** wetland New South Wales/Queensland, SE Australia
67 E24 **Carysfort, Cape** headland East Falkland, Falkland Islands 51.25S 57.49W
76 F6 **Casablanca** Ar. Dar-el-Beida. NW Morocco 33.39N 7.30W
62 M8 **Casa Branca** São Paulo, S Brazil 21.47S 47.05W
38 L14 **Casa Grande** Arizona, SW USA 32.52N 111.45W
108 C8 **Casale Monferrato** Piemonte, NW Italy 45.07N 8.28E
108 E8 **Casalpusterlengo** Lombardia, N Italy 45.10N 9.37E
56 H10 **Casanare** off. Intendencia de Casanare. ◆ province C Colombia
57 P5 **Casanay** Sucre, NE Venezuela 10.30N 63.25W
26 K11 **Casa Piedra** Texas, SW USA 29.43N 104.03W
109 Q19 **Casarano** Puglia, SE Italy 40.01N 18.10E
44 J11 **Casares** Carazo, W Nicaragua 11.37N 86.19W
107 R10 **Casas Ibáñez** Castilla-La Mancha, C Spain 39.16N 1.28W
63 I14 **Casca** Rio Grande do Sul, S Brazil 28.39S 51.55W
180 I17 **Cascade** Mahé, NE Seychelles 4.39S 55.28E
35 N13 **Cascade** Idaho, NW USA 44.31N 116.02W
31 Y13 **Cascade** Iowa, C USA 42.18N 91.00W
35 R9 **Cascade** Montana, NW USA 47.15N 111.46W
193 B20 **Cascade Point** headland South Island, NZ 44.00S 168.23E
34 G13 **Cascade Range** ▲ Oregon/Washington, NW USA
35 N12 **Cascade Reservoir** ⊠ Idaho, NW USA
(0) E8 **Cascadia Basin** undersea feature NE Pacific Ocean
106 E11 **Cascais** Lisboa, C Portugal 38.41N 9.25W
13 W7 **Cascapédia** ⇝ Québec, SE Canada
61 I22 **Cascavel** Ceará, E Brazil 4.10S 38.15W
62 G11 **Cascavel** Paraná, S Brazil 24.55S 53.28W
108 I13 **Cascia** Umbria, C Italy 42.45N 13.01E
108 F11 **Cascina** Toscana, C Italy 43.40N 10.33E
21 Q8 **Casco Bay** bay Maine, NE USA
204 J7 **Case Island** island Antarctica
108 B8 **Caselle** ✕ (Torino) Piemonte, NW Italy 45.06N 7.41E
109 K17 **Caserta** Campania, S Italy 41.04N 14.19E
13 N8 **Casey** Québec, SE Canada 47.50N 74.09W
32 M14 **Casey** Illinois, N USA 39.18N 87.59W
205 Y12 **Casey** Australian research station Antarctica 65.58S 111.04E
205 W3 **Casey Bay** bay Antarctica
82 Q11 **Caseyr, Raas** headland NE Somalia 11.51N 51.16E
99 D20 **Cashel** Ir. Caiseal. S Ireland 52.31N 7.52W
56 G6 **Casigua** Zulia, W Venezuela 8.46N 72.30W
63 B19 **Casilda** Santa Fe, C Argentina 33.04S 61.10W
Casim see General Toshevo
191 V4 **Casino** New South Wales, SE Australia 28.49S 153.01E
Casinum see Cassino
113 E17 **Čáslav** Ger. Tschaslau. Střední Čechy, C Czech Republic 49.54N 15.22E
58 C13 **Casma** Ancash, C Peru 9.27S 78.21W
178 J7 **Ca, Sông** ⇝ N Vietnam
109 K17 **Casoria** Campania, S Italy 40.54N 14.28E
107 T6 **Caspe** Aragón, NE Spain 41.13N 0.03W
35 X15 **Casper** Wyoming, C USA 42.48N 106.22W
86 M10 **Caspian Depression** Kaz. Kaspiy Mangy Oypaty, Rus. Prikaspiyskaya Nizmennost'. depression Kazakhstan/Russian Federation
138 Kk9 **Caspian Sea** Az. Xäzär Dänizi, Kaz. Kaspiy Tengizi, Per. Baḩr-e Khazar, Daryā-ye Khazar, Rus. Kaspiyskoye More. inland sea Asia/Europe
85 L14 **Cassacatiza** Tete, NW Mozambique 14.20S 32.24E
Cassai see Kasai
84 F13 **Cassamba** Moxico, E Angola 13.07S 20.22E
109 N20 **Cassano allo Ionio** Calabria, SE Italy 39.46N 16.16E
33 S8 **Cass City** Michigan, N USA 43.36N 83.10W
Cassel see Kassel
12 M13 **Casselman** Ontario, SE Canada 45.19N 75.04W
31 R5 **Casselton** North Dakota, N USA 46.53N 97.10W
61 M16 **Cássia** var. Santa Rita de Cassia. Bahia, E Brazil 11.03S 44.16W
8 J9 **Cassiar** British Columbia, W Canada 59.16N 129.45W
8 K10 **Cassiar Mountains** ▲ British Columbia, W Canada
85 C15 **Cassinga** Huíla, SW Angola 15.06S 16.05E
109 J16 **Cassino** prev. San Germano; anc. Casinum. Lazio, C Italy 41.28N 13.49E
31 T4 **Cass Lake** Minnesota, N USA 47.22N 94.36W
31 T4 **Cass Lake** ◎ Minnesota, N USA
33 P10 **Cassopolis** Michigan, N USA 41.56N 86.00W
33 S8 **Cass River** ⇝ Michigan, N USA
29 S8 **Cassville** Missouri, C USA 36.40N 93.52W
Castamoni see Kastamonu
60 L12 **Castanhal** Pará, NE Brazil 1.16S 47.55W
106 G8 **Castanheira de Pêra** Leiria, C Portugal 40.01N 8.12W
43 N7 **Castaños** Coahuila de Zaragoza, NE Mexico 26.48N 101.25W
110 I10 **Castasegna** Graubünden, SE Switzerland 46.21N 9.30E
108 D8 **Casteggio** Lombardia, N Italy 45.01N 9.10E
109 K23 **Castelbuono** Sicilia, Italy, C Mediterranean Sea 37.55N 14.04E
109 K15 **Castel di Sangro** Abruzzo, C Italy 41.46N 14.03E
108 H7 **Castelfranco Veneto** Veneto, NE Italy 45.40N 11.55E
104 K14 **Casteljaloux** Lot-et-Garonne, SW France 44.19N 0.03E
109 L18 **Castellabate** var. Santa Maria di Castellabate. Campania, S Italy 40.16N 14.57E
109 I23 **Castellammare del Golfo** Sicilia, Italy, C Mediterranean Sea 38.01N 12.52E
109 H22 **Castellammare, Golfo di** gulf Sicilia, Italy, C Mediterranean Sea
105 U15 **Castellane** Alpes-de-Haute-Provence, SE France 43.49N 6.34E
109 O18 **Castellaneta** Puglia, SE Italy 40.37N 16.57E
108 E9 **Castel l'Arquato** Emilia-Romagna, C Italy 44.52N 9.51E
63 E21 **Castelli** Buenos Aires, E Argentina 36.07S 57.46W
107 T9 **Castelló de la Plana** var. Castellón. País Valenciano, E Spain 39.58N 0.03W
107 S8 **Castellón** ◆ province País Valenciano, E Spain
Castellón see Castelló de la Plana
107 S7 **Castellote** Aragón, NE Spain 40.46N 0.18W
105 N16 **Castelnaudary** Aude, S France 43.18N 1.57E
104 L16 **Castelnau-Magnoac** Hautes-Pyrénées, S France 43.18N 0.30E
108 F10 **Castelnovo ne' Monti** Emilia-Romagna, C Italy 44.26N 10.24E
Castelnuovo see Herceg-Novi
106 H9 **Castelo Branco** Castelo Branco, C Portugal 39.49N 7.30W
106 H8 **Castelo Branco** ◆ district C Portugal
106 I10 **Castelo de Vide** Portalegre, C Portugal 39.25N 7.27W
106 G9 **Castelo do Bode, Barragem do** ⊠ C Portugal
108 G10 **Castel San Pietro Terme** Emilia-Romagna, C Italy 44.22N 11.34E
109 B17 **Castelsardo** Sardegna, Italy, C Mediterranean Sea 40.54N 8.42E
104 M14 **Castelsarrasin** Tarn-et-Garonne, S France 44.01N 1.06E
109 I24 **Casteltermini** Sicilia, Italy, C Mediterranean Sea 37.33N 13.37E
109 H24 **Castelvetrano** Sicilia, Italy, C Mediterranean Sea 37.40N 12.46E
190 L12 **Casterton** Victoria, SE Australia 37.37S 141.22E
104 J15 **Castets** Landes, SW France 43.55N 1.08W
108 H12 **Castiglione del Lago** Umbria, C Italy 43.07N 12.02E
108 F13 **Castiglione della Pescaia** Toscana, C Italy 42.46N 10.53E
108 F8 **Castiglione delle Stiviere** Lombardia, N Italy 45.24N 10.31E
106 M9 **Castilla-La Mancha** ◆ autonomous community NE Spain
106 L5 **Castilla-León** var. Castillia y Leon. ◆ autonomous community NW Spain
107 N10 **Castilla Nueva** cultural region C Spain
107 N6 **Castilla Vieja** cultural region N Spain
Castillia y Leon see Castilla-León
Castillo de Locubim see Castillo de Locubín
107 N14 **Castillo de Locubín** var. Castillo de Locubim. Andalucía, S Spain 37.31N 3.55W
104 K13 **Castillon-la-Bataille** Gironde, SW France 44.51N 0.01W
65 I19 **Castillo, Pampa del** plain S Argentina
63 G19 **Castillos** Rocha, SE Uruguay 34.12S 53.52W
99 B16 **Castlebar** Ir. Caisleán an Bharraigh. W Ireland 53.52N 9.16W
99 F16 **Castleblayney** Ir. Baile na Lorgan. N Ireland 54.07N 6.43W
47 O11 **Castle Bruce** E Dominica 15.25N 61.15W
38 M5 **Castle Dale** Utah, W USA 39.10N 111.02W
38 I14 **Castle Dome Peak** ▲ Arizona, SW USA 33.04N 114.08W
99 J14 **Castle Douglas** S Scotland, UK 54.56N 3.55W
99 E14 **Castlefinn** Ir. Caisleán na Finne. NW Ireland 54.48N 7.36W
99 M17 **Castleford** N England, UK 53.43N 1.21W
9 O17 **Castlegar** British Columbia, SW Canada 49.18N 117.48W
66 B12 **Castle Harbour** inlet Bermuda, NW Atlantic Ocean
23 V12 **Castle Hayne** North Carolina, SE USA 34.23N 78.07W
99 B20 **Castleisland** Ir. Oileán Ciarraí. SW Ireland 52.12N 9.30W
191 N12 **Castlemaine** Victoria, SE Australia 37.06S 144.13E
39 R5 **Castle Peak** ▲ Colorado, C USA 39.00N 106.51W
35 O13 **Castle Peak** ▲ Idaho, NW USA 44.02N 114.42W
192 N13 **Castlepoint** Wellington, North Island, NZ 40.54S 176.13E
99 D17 **Castlerea** Ir. An Caisleán Riabhach. W Ireland 53.45N 8.31W
99 G15 **Castlereagh** Ir. An Caisleán Riabhach. N Northern Ireland, UK 54.33N 5.53W
191 R6 **Castlereagh River** ⇝ New South Wales, SE Australia
39 T5 **Castle Rock** Colorado, C USA 39.22N 104.51W
32 K7 **Castle Rock Lake** ⊠ Wisconsin, N USA
67 G25 **Castle Rock Point** headland S Saint Helena 16.01S 5.45W
99 I16 **Castletown** SE Isle of Man 54.04N 4.39W
31 R9 **Castlewood** South Dakota, N USA 44.43N 97.01W
9 R15 **Castor** Alberta, SW Canada 52.13N 111.54W
12 M13 **Castor** ⇝ Ontario, SE Canada
29 X7 **Castor River** ⇝ Missouri, C USA
Castra Albiensium see Castres
Castra Regina see Regensburg
105 N15 **Castres** anc. Castra Albiensium. Tarn, S France 43.36N 2.15E
100 H9 **Castricum** Noord-Holland, W Netherlands 52.33N 4.40E
47 S11 **Castries** ● (Saint Lucia) N Saint Lucia 14.01N 60.59W
62 J11 **Castro** Paraná, S Brazil 24.45S 50.58W
65 F17 **Castro** Los Lagos, W Chile 42.27S 73.48W
106 H7 **Castro Daire** Viseu, N Portugal 40.54N 7.55W
106 M13 **Castro del Río** Andalucía, S Spain 37.40N 4.28W
Castrogiovanni see Enna
106 H14 **Castro Marim** Faro, S Portugal 37.13N 7.25W
106 J2 **Castropol** Asturias, N Spain 43.30N 7.01W
107 O2 **Castro-Urdiales** var. Castro Urdiales. Cantabria, N Spain 43.22N 3.10W
106 G13 **Castro Verde** Beja, S Portugal 37.42N 8.04W
109 N19 **Castrovillari** Calabria, SW Italy 39.48N 16.12E
37 N10 **Castroville** California, W USA 36.46N 121.46W
27 R12 **Castroville** Texas, SW USA 29.21N 98.52W
106 K11 **Castuera** Extremadura, W Spain 38.43N 5.33W
63 F19 **Casupá** Florida, S Uruguay 34.04S 55.39W
193 A22 **Caswell Sound** sound South Island, NZ
143 Q13 **Çat** Erzurum, NE Turkey 39.40N 41.03E
44 K6 **Catacamas** Olancho, C Honduras 14.50N 85.54W
58 A10 **Catacaos** Piura, NW Peru 5.22S 80.40W
24 I7 **Catahoula Lake** ◎ Louisiana, S USA
143 S15 **Çatak** Van, SE Turkey 38.01N 43.04E
143 S15 **Çatak Çayi** ⇝ SE Turkey
116 O12 **Çatalca** İstanbul, NW Turkey 41.09N 28.28E
116 O12 **Çatalca Yarımadası** physical region NW Turkey
64 H6 **Catalina** Antofagasta, N Chile 25.19S 69.37W
Catalonia see Cataluña
107 U5 **Cataluña** Cat. Catalunya; Eng. Catalonia. ◆ autonomous community N Spain
Catalunya see Cataluña
64 J7 **Catamarca** off. Provincia de Catamarca. ◆ province NW Argentina
Catamarca see San Fernando del Valle de Catamarca
179 Pp11 **Catanauan** Luzon, N Philippines 13.36N 122.19E
85 M16 **Catandica** Manica, C Mozambique 18.04S 33.10E
179 Qq11 **Catanduanes Island** island N Philippines
62 K8 **Catanduva** São Paulo, S Brazil 21.06S 48.57W
109 L24 **Catania** Sicilia, Italy, C Mediterranean Sea 37.31N 15.04E
109 M24 **Catania, Golfo di** gulf Sicilia, Italy, C Mediterranean Sea
47 U5 **Cataño** var. Cantaño. E Puerto Rico 18.26N 66.06W
109 O21 **Catanzaro** Calabria, SW Italy 38.53N 16.36E
109 O22 **Catanzaro Marina** var. Marina di Catanzaro. Calabria, S Italy 38.48N 16.33E
27 Q14 **Catarina** Texas, SW USA 28.19N 99.36W
179 Qq12 **Catarman** Samar, C Philippines 12.29N 124.34E
107 S10 **Catarroja** País Valenciano, E Spain 39.24N 0.24W
23 R11 **Catawba River** ⇝ North Carolina/South Carolina, SE USA
179 R12 **Catbalogan** Samar, C Philippines 11.49N 124.55E
12 I14 **Catchacoma** Ontario, SE Canada 44.43N 78.19W
43 S15 **Catemaco** Veracruz-Llave, SE Mexico 18.28N 95.10W
Cathair na Mart see Westport
Cathair Saidhbhín see Cahersiveen
33 P5 **Cat Head Point** headland Michigan, N USA 45.11N 85.37W
25 Q2 **Cathedral Caverns** cave Alabama, S USA 34.36N 86.11W
37 V16 **Cathedral City** California, W USA 33.45N 116.27W
26 K10 **Cathedral Mountain** ▲ Texas, SW USA 30.10N 103.39W
34 G10 **Cathlamet** Washington, NW USA 46.12N 123.24W
78 G13 **Catió** S Guinea-Bissau 11.17N 15.16W
57 O10 **Catisimiña** Bolívar, SE Venezuela 4.07N 63.40W
46 J3 **Cat Island** island C Bahamas
10 B9 **Cat Lake** Ontario, S Canada 51.47N 91.52W
23 P5 **Catlettsburg** Kentucky, S USA 38.24N 82.37W
193 D24 **Catlins** ⇝ South Island, NZ
37 R1 **Catnip Mountain** ▲ Nevada, W USA 41.53N 119.19W
43 Z11 **Catoche, Cabo** headland SE Mexico 21.36N 87.04W
29 P9 **Catoosa** Oklahoma, C USA 36.11N 95.45W
43 N10 **Catorce** San Luis Potosí, C Mexico 23.42N 100.49W
65 I14 **Catriel** Río Negro, C Argentina 37.54S 67.52W
64 K13 **Catriló** La Pampa, C Argentina 36.24S 63.25W
60 F11 **Catrimani** Roraima, N Brazil 0.24N 61.30W
60 E10 **Catrimani, Rio** ⇝ N Brazil
20 K11 **Catskill** New York, NE USA 42.13N 73.52W
20 K11 **Catskill Creek** ⇝ New York, NE USA
20 J11 **Catskill Mountains** ▲ New York, NE USA
20 D11 **Cattaraugus Creek** ⇝ New York, NE USA
Cattaro see Kotor
Cattaro, Bocche di see Kotorska, Boka
109 I24 **Cattolica Eraclea** Sicilia, Italy, C Mediterranean Sea 37.27N 13.24E
85 B14 **Catumbela** ⇝ W Angola
85 N14 **Catur** Niassa, N Mozambique 13.50S 35.43E
84 C10 **Cauale** ⇝ NE Angola
179 Pp9 **Cauayan** Luzon, N Philippines 16.55N 121.46E
56 C12 **Cauca** off. Departamento del Cauca. ◆ province SW Colombia
49 P5 **Cauca** ⇝ SE Venezuela
60 P13 **Caucaia** Ceará, E Brazil 3.43S 38.45W
56 E7 **Cauca, Río** ⇝ N Colombia
56 E7 **Caucasia** Antioquia, NW Colombia 7.58N 75.13W
143 Q8 **Caucasus** Rus. Kavkaz. ▲ Georgia/Russian Federation
64 I10 **Caucete** San Juan, W Argentina 31.37S 68.16W
107 R11 **Caudete** Castilla-La Mancha, C Spain 38.42N 1.00W
105 P2 **Caudry** Nord, N France 50.07N 3.24E
84 D11 **Caungula** Lunda Norte, NE Angola 8.22S 18.37E
64 G13 **Cauquenes** Maule, C Chile 35.58S 72.22W
57 N8 **Caura, Río** ⇝ C Venezuela
13 V7 **Causapscal** Québec, SE Canada 48.22N 67.13W
119 N10 **Căuşeni** Rus. Kaushany. E Moldova 46.37N 29.21E
104 M14 **Caussade** Tarn-et-Garonne, S France 44.10N 1.31E
104 K17 **Cauterets** Hautes-Pyrénées, S France 42.53N 0.08W
8 J15 **Caution, Cape** headland British Columbia, SW Canada 51.10N 127.43W
46 H7 **Cauto** ⇝ E Cuba
Cauvery see Kāveri
104 L3 **Caux, Pays de** physical region N France
109 L18 **Cava dei Tirreni** Campania, S Italy 40.42N 14.42E
106 G6 **Cávado** ⇝ N Portugal
Cavaia see Kavajë
105 R15 **Cavaillon** Vaucluse, SE France 43.51N 5.01E
105 U16 **Cavalaire-sur-Mer** Var, SE France 43.10N 6.31E
108 G6 **Cavalese** Ger. Gablös. Trentino-Alto Adige, N Italy 46.18N 11.29E
31 Q2 **Cavalier** North Dakota, N USA 48.47N 97.37W
78 L17 **Cavalla** var. Cavally, Cavally Fleuve. ⇝ Ivory Coast/Liberia
107 Y8 **Cavalleria, Cap de** var. Cabo Caballeria. headland Menorca, Spain, W Mediterranean Sea 40.04N 4.06E
192 K2 **Cavalli Islands** island group N NZ
Cavally/Cavally Fleuve see Cavalla
99 E16 **Cavan** Ir. Cabhán. N Ireland 54.00N 7.21W
99 E16 **Cavan** Ir. An Cabhán. cultural region N Ireland
108 H8 **Cavarzere** Veneto, NE Italy 45.07N 12.04E
29 W9 **Cave City** Arkansas, C USA 35.56N 91.33W
22 K7 **Cave City** Kentucky, S USA 37.08N 85.57W
67 M25 **Cave Point** headland S Tristan da Cunha
23 N5 **Cave Run Lake** ⊠ Kentucky, S USA
60 K11 **Caviana de Fora, Ilha** var. Ilha Caviana. island N Brazil
Caviana, Ilha see Caviana de Fora, Ilha
115 I16 **Cavtat** It. Ragusavecchia. Dubrovnik-Neretva, SE Croatia 42.36N 18.13E
Cawnpore see Kānpur
Caxamarca see Cajamarca
60 A13 **Caxias** Amazonas, W Brazil 4.27S 71.27W
60 N13 **Caxias** Maranhão, E Brazil 4.52S 43.19W
63 I15 **Caxias do Sul** Rio Grande do Sul, S Brazil 29.13S 51.10W
44 J4 **Caxinas, Punta** headland N Honduras 16.01N 86.02W
84 B11 **Caxito** Bengo, NW Angola 8.34S 13.37E
142 F14 **Çay** Afyon, W Turkey 38.34N 31.01E
42 L15 **Cayacal, Punta** var. Punta Mongrove. headland S Mexico 17.55N 102.09W
58 C6 **Cayambe** Pichincha, N Ecuador 0.01N 78.10W
58 C6 **Cayambe** ▲ N Ecuador 0.00N 77.58W
23 R12 **Cayce** South Carolina, SE USA 33.58N 81.04W
57 Y10 **Cayenne** ○ (French Guiana) NE French Guiana 4.55N 52.18W
57 Y10 **Cayenne** ✕ NE French Guiana 4.55N 52.18W
46 K10 **Cayes** var. Les Cayes. SW Haiti 18.10N 73.48W
47 U6 **Cayey** C Puerto Rico 18.06N 66.09W
47 U6 **Cayey, Sierra de** ▲ E Puerto Rico
105 N14 **Caylus** Tarn-et-Garonne, S France 44.13N 1.42E
46 E8 **Cayman Brac** island E Cayman Islands
46 D8 **Cayman Islands** ◇ UK dependent territory W West Indies
66 D11 **Cayman Trench** undersea feature NW Caribbean Sea
49 O3 **Cayman Trough** undersea feature NW Caribbean Sea
82 O13 **Caynabo** Togdheer, N Somalia 8.55N 46.28E
44 F3 **Cayo** ◆ district SW Belize
Cayo see San Ignacio
45 N9 **Cayos Guerrero** reef E Nicaragua
45 O9 **Cayos King** reef E Nicaragua
46 E4 **Cay Sal** islet SW Bahamas
12 G16 **Cayuga** Ontario, S Canada 42.57N 79.49W
27 V8 **Cayuga** Texas, SW USA 31.55N 95.57W
20 G10 **Cayuga Lake** ◎ New York, NE USA
106 K13 **Cazalla de la Sierra** Andalucía, S Spain 37.56N 5.46W
118 L14 **Căzăneşti** Ialomiţa, SE Romania 44.36N 27.02E
104 M16 **Cazères** Haute-Garonne, S France 43.15N 1.11E
114 E10 **Cazin** Federacija Bosna I Hercegovina, NW Bosnia and Herzegovina 44.58N 15.58E
84 G13 **Cazombo** Moxico, E Angola 11.53S 22.52E
107 O13 **Cazorla** Andalucía, S Spain 37.55N 3.00W
Cazza see Sušac
106 L4 **Cea** ⇝ NW Spain
Ceadâr-Lunga see Ciadîr-Lunga
Ceanannas see Kells
Ceann Toirc see Kanturk
60 O13 **Ceará** off. Estado do Ceará. ◆ state C Brazil
Ceará see Fortaleza
Ceara Abyssal Plain see Ceará Plain
61 Q14 **Ceará Mirim** Rio Grande do Norte, E Brazil 5.30S 35.50W
66 J13 **Ceará Plain** var. Ceara Abyssal Plain. undersea feature W Atlantic Ocean
66 I13 **Ceará Ridge** undersea feature C Atlantic Ocean
Ceatharlach see Carlow
45 Q17 **Cébaco, Isla** island SW Panama
42 K7 **Ceballos** Durango, C Mexico 26.33N 104.07W
63 G19 **Cebollatí** Rocha, E Uruguay 33.15S 53.49W
63 G19 **Cebollatí, Río** ⇝ E Uruguay
107 P5 **Cebollera** ▲ N Spain 42.01N 2.40W
106 M8 **Cebreros** Castilla-León, N Spain 40.27N 4.28W
179 Qq14 **Cebu** off. Cebu City. Cebu, C Philippines 10.16N 123.45E
179 Qq13 **Cebu** island C Philippines
109 J16 **Ceccano** Lazio, C Italy 41.34N 13.19E
Čechy see Bohemia
108 F12 **Cecina** Toscana, C Italy 43.19N 10.31E
28 K4 **Cedar Bluff Reservoir** ⊠ Kansas, C USA
32 M8 **Cedarburg** Wisconsin, N USA 43.18N 87.58W
38 J7 **Cedar City** Utah, W USA 37.40N 113.03W
27 T11 **Cedar Creek** Texas, SW USA 30.04N 97.30W
30 L7 **Cedar Creek** ⇝ North Dakota, N USA
27 U7 **Cedar Creek Reservoir** ⊠ Texas, SW USA
31 W13 **Cedar Falls** Iowa, C USA 42.31N 92.27W
33 N8 **Cedar Grove** Wisconsin, N USA 43.31N 87.48W
23 Y6 **Cedar Island** island Virginia, NE USA
25 U11 **Cedar Key** Cedar Keys, Florida, SE USA 29.08N 83.03W
25 U11 **Cedar Keys** island group Florida, SE USA
9 V14 **Cedar Lake** ◎ Manitoba, C Canada
12 I11 **Cedar Lake** ◎ Ontario, SE Canada
26 M6 **Cedar Lake** ◎ Texas, SW USA
31 X13 **Cedar Rapids** Iowa, C USA 41.58N 91.39W
31 X14 **Cedar River** ⇝ Iowa/Minnesota, C USA
31 O14 **Cedar River** ⇝ Nebraska, C USA
33 P8 **Cedar Springs** Michigan, N USA 43.13N 85.33W
25 R3 **Cedartown** Georgia, SE USA 34.00N 85.16W
29 O7 **Cedar Vale** Kansas, C USA 37.06N 96.30W
37 Q2 **Cedarville** California, W USA 41.30N 120.10W
106 H1 **Cedeira** Galicia, NW Spain 43.40N 8.03W
44 H8 **Cedeño** Choluteca, S Honduras 13.10N 87.25W
43 N10 **Cedral** San Luis Potosí, C Mexico 23.47N 100.40W
44 I6 **Cedros** Francisco Morazán, C Honduras 14.38N 87.09W
42 M9 **Cedros** Zacatecas, C Mexico 24.39N 101.47W
42 B5 **Cedros, Isla** island W Mexico
199 Mm6 **Cedros Trench** undersea feature E Pacific Ocean
190 E7 **Ceduna** South Australia 32.09S 133.43E
112 D10 **Cedynia** Ger. Zehden. Zachodnio-pomorskie, W Poland 52.54N 14.15E
82 P12 **Ceelaayo** Sanaag, N Somalia 11.18N 49.20E
83 O16 **Ceel Buur** It. El Bur; Galguduud, C Somalia 4.36N 46.33E
83 N15 **Ceel Dheere** var. Ceel Dher, It. El Dere. Galguduud, C Somalia 5.18N 46.07E
Ceel Dher see Ceel Dheere
83 P14 **Ceel Xamure** Mudug, E Somalia 7.15N 48.55E
82 O12 **Ceerigaabo** var. Erigabo, Erigavo. Sanaag, N Somalia 10.34N 47.22E
109 J23 **Cefalù** anc. Cephaloedium. Sicilia, Italy, C Mediterranean Sea 38.01N 14.01E
107 N6 **Cega** ⇝ N Spain
113 K23 **Cegléd** prev. Czegléd. Pest, C Hungary 47.10N 19.45E
115 N18 **Čegrane** W FYR Macedonia 41.50N 20.59E
107 Q13 **Cehegín** Murcia, SE Spain 38.06N 1.48W
142 K12 **Çekerek** Yozgat, N Turkey 40.04N 35.30E
152 B13 **Çekiçler** Rus. Chekishlyar, Turkm. Chekichler. Balkan Welaýaty, W Turkmenistan 37.35N 53.52E
109 J15 **Celano** Abruzzo, C Italy 42.06N 13.33E
106 H4 **Celanova** Galicia, NW Spain 42.09N 7.58W
44 F6 **Celaque, Cordillera de** ▲ W Honduras
43 N13 **Celaya** Guanajuato, C Mexico 20.31N 100.48W
Celebes see Sulawesi
198 Ff8 **Celebes Basin** undersea feature SE South China Sea
175 Qq4 **Celebes Sea** Ind. Laut Sulawesi. sea Indonesia/Philippines
43 W12 **Celestún** Yucatán, E Mexico 20.49N 90.22W
33 Q12 **Celina** Ohio, N USA 40.33N 84.34W
22 L8 **Celina** Tennessee, S USA 36.30N 85.30W
27 U5 **Celina** Texas, SW USA 33.19N 96.46W
114 G11 **Čelinac Donji** Republika Srpska, N Bosnia and Herzegovina 44.43N 17.19E
111 V10 **Celje** Ger. Cilli. C Slovenia 46.16N 15.14E
113 G23 **Celldömölk** Vas, W Hungary 47.16N 17.10E
102 J12 **Celle** var. Zelle. Niedersachsen, N Germany 52.37N 10.04E
101 D19 **Celles** Hainaut, SW Belgium 50.42N 3.25E
106 I7 **Celorico da Beira** Guarda, N Portugal 40.37N 7.24W
Celovec see Klagenfurt
66 M7 **Celtic Sea** Ir. An Mhuir Cheilteach. sea SW British Isles
66 N7 **Celtic Shelf** undersea feature E Atlantic Ocean
116 L13 **Çeltik Gölu** ◎ NW Turkey
152 J17 **Çemenibit** prev. Rus. Chemenibit. Mary Welaýaty, S Turkmenistan 35.27N 62.19E
115 M14 **Čemerno** ▲ C Serbia and Montenegro (Yugoslavia)
175 Oo16 **Cempi, Teluk** bay Nusa Tenggara, S Indonesia
107 Q12 **Cenajo, Embalse del** ⊠ S Spain
176 Ww10 **Cenderawasih, Teluk** var. Teluk Irian, Teluk Sarera. bay W Pacific Ocean
107 P4 **Cenicero** La Rioja, N Spain 42.28N 2.37W
108 E9 **Ceno** ⇝ NW Italy
104 K13 **Cenon** Gironde, SW France 44.51N 0.33W
12 K13 **Centennial Lake** ◎ Ontario, SE Canada
Centennial State see Colorado
39 S7 **Center** Colorado, C USA 37.45N 106.06W
31 Q13 **Center** Nebraska, C USA 42.33N 97.51W
30 M5 **Center** North Dakota, N USA 47.07N 101.18W
27 X8 **Center** Texas, SW USA 31.46N 94.10W
31 W8 **Center City** Minnesota, N USA 45.22N 92.46W
38 L5 **Centerfield** Utah, W USA 39.07N 111.49W

◆ Country ● Country Capital ◇ Dependent Territory ○ Dependent Territory Capital ◆ Administrative Region ✕ International Airport ▲ Mountain ▲ Mountain Range Volcano ⇝ River ◎ Lake ⊠ Reservoir

CENTER HILL LAKE – CHARLOTTE TOWN

22 K9 **Center Hill Lake** ⊡ Tennessee, S USA
31 X13 **Center Point** Iowa, C USA 42.11N 91.47W
27 R11 **Center Point** Texas, SW USA 29.56N 99.01W
31 W16 **Centerville** Iowa, C USA 40.42N 92.49W
29 W7 **Centerville** Missouri, C USA 37.27N 91.01W
31 R12 **Centerville** South Dakota, N USA 43.07N 96.57W
22 I9 **Centerville** Tennessee, S USA 35.43N 87.27W
27 V9 **Centerville** Texas, SW USA 31.15N 95.58W
42 M5 **Centinela, Picacho del** ▲ NE Mexico 29.07N 102.40W
108 G9 **Cento** Emilia-Romagna, N Italy 44.43N 11.16E
Centrafricaine, République see Central African Republic
41 S8 **Central** Alaska, USA 65.34N 144.48W
39 P15 **Central** New Mexico, SW USA 32.46N 108.09W
85 H18 **Central** ◆ district E Botswana
144 E10 **Central** ◆ district C Israel
83 I19 **Central** ◆ province C Kenya
84 M13 **Central** ◆ region C Malawi
159 P12 **Central** ◆ zone C Nepal
194 J15 **Central** ◆ province S PNG
65 I21 **Central** ◆ department C Paraguay
195 W15 **Central** off. Central Province. ◆ province S Solomon Islands
85 J14 **Central** ◆ province C Zambia
119 P11 **Central** ✕ (Odesa) Odes'ka Oblast', SW Ukraine 46.26N 30.41E
Central see Centre
81 H14 **Central African Republic** var. République Centrafricaine, abbrev. CAR; prev. Ubangi-Shari, Oubangui-Chari, Territoire de l'Oubangui-Chari. ◆ republic C Africa
198 G6 **Central Basin Trough** undersea feature W Pacific Ocean
Central Borneo see Kalimantan Tengah
155 P12 **Central Brāhui Range** ▲▲ W Pakistan
Central Celebes see Sulawesi Tengah
31 Y13 **Central City** Iowa, C USA 42.12N 91.31W
22 I6 **Central City** Kentucky, S USA 37.17N 87.07W
31 P15 **Central City** Nebraska, C USA 41.04N 97.59W
50 D6 **Central, Cordillera** ▲▲ W Bolivia
56 D11 **Central, Cordillera** ▲▲ W Colombia
44 M13 **Central, Cordillera** ▲▲ C Costa Rica
47 N9 **Central, Cordillera** ▲▲ C Dominican Republic
45 R16 **Central, Cordillera** ▲▲ C Panama
179 P8 **Central, Cordillera** ▲▲ Luzon, N Philippines
47 S6 **Central, Cordillera** ▲▲ Puerto Rico
44 H7 **Central District** var. Tegucigalpa. ◆ district C Honduras
32 L15 **Centralia** Illinois, N USA 38.31N 89.07W
29 U4 **Centralia** Missouri, C USA 39.12N 92.08W
34 G9 **Centralia** Washington, NW USA 46.43N 122.57W
Central Indian Ridge see Mid-Indian Ridge
Central Java see Jawa Tengah
Central Kalimantan see Kalimantan Tengah
154 L14 **Central Makrān Range** ▲▲ W Pakistan
199 J8 **Central Pacific Basin** undersea feature C Pacific Ocean
61 M19 **Central, Planalto** var. Brazilian Highlands. ▲▲ E Brazil
34 F15 **Central Point** Oregon, NW USA 42.22N 122.55W
161 K25 **Central Province** ◆ province C Sri Lanka
Central Provinces and Berar see Madhya Pradesh
194 G11 **Central Range** ▲▲ NW PNG
Central Russian Upland see Srednerusskaya Vozvyshennost'
Central Siberian Plateau/Central Siberian Uplands see Srednesibirskoye Ploskogor'ye
106 K8 **Central, Sistema** ▲▲ C Spain
Central Sulawesi see Sulawesi Tengah
37 N3 **Central Valley** California, W USA 40.39N 122.21W
37 P8 **Central Valley** valley California, W USA
25 Q3 **Centre** Alabama, S USA 34.09N 85.40W
81 E15 **Centre** Eng. Central. ◆ province C Cameroon
104 M8 **Centre** ◆ region N France
181 Y16 **Centre de Flacq** E Mauritius 20.12S 57.43E
57 Y9 **Centre Spatial Guyanais** space station N French Guiana 5.11N 52.42W
25 O5 **Centreville** Alabama, S USA 32.58N 87.08W
23 X3 **Centreville** Maryland, NE USA 39.02N 76.04W
24 J7 **Centreville** Mississippi, S USA 31.05N 91.04W
Centum Cellae see Civitavecchia
166 M14 **Cenxi** Guangxi Zhuangzu Zizhiqu, S China 22.58N 111.00E
Ceos see Kéa
Cephaloedium see Cefalu
114 I9 **Čepin** Hung. Csepén. Osijek-Baranja, E Croatia 45.32N 18.33E
174 Ll15 **Cepu** prev. Tjepoe, Tjepu. Jawa, C Indonesia 7.07S 111.34E
Ceram see Seram, Pulau
175 T10 **Ceram Sea** Ind. Laut Seram. sea E Indonesia
198 G9 **Ceram Trough** undersea feature W Pacific Ocean
Cerasus see Giresun
38 I10 **Cerbat Mountains** ▲▲ Arizona, SW USA
105 P17 **Cerbère, Cap** headland S France 42.28N 3.15E
106 F13 **Cercal do Alentejo** Setúbal, S Portugal 37.48N 8.40W
113 A18 **Čerchov** Ger. Czerkow. ▲ W Czech Republic 49.24N 12.47E
105 O13 **Cère** ≈ C France
63 A16 **Ceres** Santa Fe, C Argentina 29.55S 61.55W
61 K18 **Ceres** Goiás, C Brazil 15.21S 49.34W
Ceresio see Lugano, Lago di
105 O17 **Céret** Pyrénées-Orientales, S France 42.30N 2.43E
56 E6 **Cereté** Córdoba, NW Colombia 8.51N 75.48W
180 I17 **Cerf, Île au** island Inner Islands, NE Seychelles
101 G22 **Cerfontaine** Namur, S Belgium 50.08N 4.25E
Cergy-Pontoise see Pontoise
109 N16 **Cerignola** Puglia, SE Italy 41.16N 15.52E
Cerigo see Kýthira
105 O9 **Cérilly** Allier, C France 46.38N 2.51E
142 I11 **Çerkeş** Çankırı, N Turkey 40.51N 32.52E
142 D10 **Çerkezköy** Tekirdağ, NW Turkey 41.18N 27.58E
111 T12 **Cerknica** Ger. Zirknitz. SW Slovenia 45.48N 14.21E
111 S11 **Cerkno** W Slovenia 46.07N 13.58E
118 F10 **Cermei** Hung. Csermő. Arad, W Romania 46.33N 21.50E
143 O15 **Çermik** Diyarbakır, SE Turkey 38.09N 39.27E
114 I10 **Cerna** Vukovar-Srijem, E Croatia 45.10N 18.36E
Cernăuţi see Chernivtsi
118 M14 **Cernavodă** Constanţa, SW Romania 44.19N 28.01E
105 U7 **Cernay** Haut-Rhin, NE France 47.49N 7.10E
Černice see Schwarzach
43 O8 **Cerralvo** Nuevo León, NE Mexico 26.01N 99.37W
42 G9 **Cerralvo, Isla** island W Mexico
109 L16 **Cerreto Sannita** Campania, S Italy 41.17N 14.39E
115 L20 **Cërrik** var. Cerriku. Elbasan, C Albania 41.01N 19.55E
Cerriku see Cërrik
43 O11 **Cerritos** San Luis Potosí, C Mexico 22.25N 100.16W
62 K11 **Cerro Azul** Paraná, S Brazil 24.48S 49.13W
63 F18 **Cerro Chato** Treinta y Tres, E Uruguay 33.08S 55.07W
63 F19 **Cerro Colorado** Florida, S Uruguay 33.52S 55.33W
58 E13 **Cerro de Pasco** Pasco, C Peru 10.43S 76.15W
63 G18 **Cerro Largo** ◆ department NE Uruguay
63 G14 **Cêrro Largo** Rio Grande do Sul, S Brazil 28.10S 54.43W
44 E7 **Cerrón Grande, Embalse** ⊡ N El Salvador
65 I14 **Cerros Colorados, Embalse** ⊡ W Argentina
107 V5 **Cervera** Cataluña, NE Spain 41.40N 1.16E
106 M3 **Cervera del Pisuerga** Castilla-León, N Spain 42.51N 4.30W
107 Q5 **Cervera del Río Alhama** La Rioja, N Spain 42.01N 1.58W
109 H15 **Cerveteri** Lazio, C Italy 42.00N 12.06E
108 H10 **Cervia** Emilia-Romagna, N Italy 44.15N 12.22E
108 J7 **Cervignano del Friuli** Friuli-Venezia Giulia, NE Italy 45.49N 13.18E
109 L17 **Cervinara** Campania, S Italy 41.01N 14.36E
Cervinia see Breuil-Cervinia
108 B6 **Cervino, Monte** var. Matterhorn. ▲ Italy/Switzerland see also Matterhorn 46.00N 7.39E
105 Y14 **Cervione** Corse, France, C Mediterranean Sea 42.22N 9.28E
106 I1 **Cervo** Galicia, NW Spain 43.39N 7.25W
56 F5 **Cesar** off. Departamento del Cesar. ◆ province N Colombia
108 H10 **Cesena** anc. Caesena. Emilia-Romagna, N Italy 44.09N 12.13E
108 I10 **Cesenatico** Emilia-Romagna, N Italy 44.12N 12.24E
120 H8 **Cēsis** Ger. Wenden. Cēsis, C Latvia 57.19N 25.17E
113 D15 **Česká Lípa** Ger. Böhmisch-Leipa. Liberecký Kraj, N Czech Republic 50.40N 14.32E
Česká Republika see Czech Republic
113 F17 **Česká Třebová** Ger. Böhmisch-Trübau. Pardubický Kraj, C Czech Republic 49.54N 16.27E
113 D19 **České Budějovice** Ger. Budweis. Jihočeský Kraj, S Czech Republic 48.58N 14.28E
113 D19 **České Velenice** Jihočeský Kraj, S Czech Republic 48.49N 14.57E
113 E18 **Českomoravská Vrchovina** var. Českomoravská Vysočina, Eng. Bohemian-Moravian Highlands, Ger. Böhmisch-Mährische Höhe. ▲▲ S Czech Republic
Českomoravská Vysočina see Českomoravská Vrchovina
113 C19 **Český Krumlov** var. Böhmisch-Krumau, Ger. Krummau. Jihočeský Kraj, S Czech Republic 48.48N 14.18E
Český Les see Bohemian Forest
114 F8 **Česma** ≈ N Croatia
142 A14 **Çeşme** İzmir, W Turkey 38.19N 26.19E
Cess see Cestos
191 T8 **Cessnock** New South Wales, SE Australia 32.51S 151.21E
78 K17 **Cestos** var. Cess. ≈ S Liberia
120 I9 **Cesvaine** Madona, E Latvia 56.58N 26.15E
118 G14 **Cetate** Dolj, SW Romania 44.06N 23.03E
Cetatea Albă see Bilhorod-Dnistrovs'kyy
115 J17 **Cetinje** It. Cettigne. Montenegro, SW Serbia and Montenegro (Yugoslavia) 42.23N 18.55E
109 N20 **Cetraro** Calabria, S Italy 39.30N 15.59E
Cette see Sète
196 A17 **Cetti Bay** bay SW Guam
Cettigne see Cetinje
106 L17 **Ceuta** var. Sebta. Ceuta, Spain, N Africa 35.52N 5.19W
90 C15 **Ceuta** enclave Spain, N Africa
108 B9 **Ceva** Piemonte, NE Italy 44.24N 8.01E
105 P14 **Cévennes** ▲▲ S France
110 G10 **Cevio** Ticino, S Switzerland 46.18N 8.36E
142 K16 **Ceyhan** Adana, S Turkey 37.01N 35.48E
142 K17 **Ceyhan Nehri** ≈ S Turkey
143 P17 **Ceylanpınar** Şanlıurfa, SE Turkey 36.53N 40.01E
Ceylon see Sri Lanka
181 R6 **Ceylon Plain** undersea feature N Indian Ocean
Ceyre to the Caribs see Marie-Galante
105 Q14 **Cèze** ≈ S France
Chaacha see Çäçe
131 P6 **Chaadayevka** Penzenskaya Oblast', W Russian Federation 53.07N 45.55E
178 H12 **Cha-Am** Phetchaburi, SW Thailand 12.48N 99.58E
149 W15 **Chābahār** var. Chāh Bahār, Chahbar. Sīstān va Balūchestān, SE Iran 25.21N 60.38E
63 B19 **Chabas** Santa Fe, C Argentina 33.16S 61.22W
105 T10 **Chablais** physical region E France
63 B20 **Chacabuco** Buenos Aires, E Argentina 34.38S 60.31W
44 K8 **Chachagón, Cerro** ▲ N Nicaragua 13.18N 85.39W
58 C10 **Chachapoyas** Amazonas, NW Peru 6.13S 77.54W
Chăche see Çäçe
121 O18 **Chachersk** Rus. Chechersk. Homyel'skaya Voblasts', SE Belarus 52.54N 30.54E
121 N16 **Chachevichy** Rus. Chechevichi. Mahilyowskaya Voblasts', E Belarus 53.31N 29.49E
63 B14 **Chaco** off. Provincia de Chaco. ◆ province NE Argentina
Chaco see Gran Chaco
64 M6 **Chaco Austral** physical region N Argentina
64 M3 **Chaco Boreal** physical region N Paraguay
64 M6 **Chaco Central** physical region N Argentina
41 Y15 **Chacon, Cape** headland Prince of Wales Island, Alaska, USA 54.41N 132.00W
80 H9 **Chad** off. Republic of Chad, Fr. Tchad. ◆ republic C Africa
126 Hh16 **Chadan** Respublika Tyva, S Russian Federation 51.16N 91.25E
23 U12 **Chadbourn** North Carolina, SE USA 34.19N 78.49W
85 L14 **Chadiza** Eastern, E Zambia 14.04S 32.27E
69 Q7 **Chad, Lake** Fr. Lac Tchad. ◎ C Africa
126 J13 **Chadobets** ≈ C Russian Federation
30 J12 **Chadron** Nebraska, C USA 42.48N 102.57W
Chadyr-Lunga see Ciadîr-Lunga
169 W14 **Chaeryŏng** SW North Korea 38.22N 125.35E
107 P17 **Chafarinas, Islas** island group S Spain
29 Y7 **Chaffee** Missouri, C USA 37.10N 89.39W
154 L12 **Chāgai Hills** var. Chāh Gay. ▲▲ Afghanistan/Pakistan
126 M12 **Chagda** Respublika Sakha (Yakutiya), NE Russian Federation 58.43N 130.38E
Chaghasarāy see Asadābād
155 N5 **Chaghcharān** var. Chakhcharan, Cheghcheran, Qala Āhangarān. Ghowr, C Afghanistan 34.28N 65.18E
105 R9 **Chagny** Saône-et-Loire, C France 46.54N 4.45E
181 Q7 **Chagos Archipelago** var. Oil Islands. island group British Indian Ocean Territory
133 O15 **Chagos Bank** undersea feature C Indian Ocean
133 O14 **Chagos-Laccadive Plateau** undersea feature N Indian Ocean
181 Q7 **Chagos Trench** undersea feature N Indian Ocean
45 T14 **Chagres, Río** ≈ C Panama
47 U14 **Chaguanas** Trinidad, Trinidad and Tobago 10.29N 61.24W
56 M6 **Chaguaramas** Guárico, N Venezuela 9.21N 66.15W
Chagyl see Çagyl
Chahārmahāl and Bakhtiyāri see Chahār Maḩall va Bakhtīārī
148 M9 **Chahār Maḩall va Bakhtīārī** off. Ostān-e Chahār Maḩall va Bakhtīārī, var. Chahārmahāl and Bakhtiyāri. ◆ province SW Iran
Chāh Bahār/Chahbar see Chābahār
149 V13 **Chāh Derāz** Sīstān va Balūchestān, SE Iran 27.07N 60.01E
Chāh Gay see Chāgai Hills
178 Hh10 **Chai Badan** Lop Buri, C Thailand 15.07N 101.03E
159 Q16 **Chāībāsa** Jhārkhand, N India 22.34N 85.48E
81 E19 **Chaillu, Massif du** ▲▲ C Gabon
178 Hh10 **Chai Nat** var. Chainat, Jainat, Jayanath. Chai Nat, C Thailand 15.12N 100.12E
67 M14 **Chain Fracture Zone** tectonic feature E Atlantic Ocean
181 N5 **Chain Ridge** undersea feature W Indian Ocean
Chairn, Ceann an see Carnsore Point
164 L5 **Chaiwopu** Xinjiang Uygur Zizhiqu, W China 43.31N 87.55E
178 I10 **Chaiyaphum** var. Jayabum. Chaiyaphum, C Thailand 15.49N 102.03E
64 N10 **Chajarí** Entre Ríos, E Argentina 30.45S 57.57W
44 C5 **Chajul** Quiché, W Guatemala 15.28N 91.02W
85 K16 **Chakari** Mashonaland West, N Zimbabwe 18.04S 29.49E
154 J9 **Chakhānsūr** Nīmrūz, SW Afghanistan 31.11N 62.06E
Chakhānsūr see Nīmrūz
Chakhcharan see Chaghcharān
155 V8 **Chak Jhumra** var. Jhumra. Punjab, E Pakistan 31.33N 73.13E
152 I16 **Chaknakdysonga** Ahal Welaýaty, S Turkmenistan 35.39N 61.24E
159 P16 **Chakradharpur** Jhārkhand, N India 22.37N 85.28E
158 J8 **Chakrāta** Uttaranchal, N India 30.42N 77.52E
155 U7 **Chakwāl** Punjab, NE Pakistan 32.56N 72.49E
59 F17 **Chala** Arequipa, SW Peru 15.52S 74.13W
104 K12 **Chalais** Charente, W France 45.16N 0.02E
110 D10 **Chalais** Valais, SW Switzerland 46.18N 7.37E
117 J20 **Chalándri** var. Halandri; prev. Khalándrion. prehistoric site Sýros, Kykládes, Greece, Aegean Sea 37.28N 24.56E
196 H6 **Chalan Kanoa** Saipan, S Northern Mariana Islands 15.07S 145.43E
196 C16 **Chalan Pago** C Guam
Chalap Dalam/Chalap Dalan see Chehel Abdālān, Kūh-e
44 F7 **Chalatenango** Chalatenango, N El Salvador 14.03N 88.54W
44 A9 **Chalatenango** ◆ department NW El Salvador
85 P15 **Chalaua** Nampula, NE Mozambique 16.04S 39.08E
83 I16 **Chalbi Desert** desert N Kenya
44 D7 **Chalchuapa** Santa Ana, W El Salvador 13.58N 89.39W
Chalcidice see Chalkidikí
Chalcis see Chalkída
105 N6 **Châlette-sur-Loing** Loiret, C France 48.01N 2.45E
13 X8 **Chaleur Bay** Fr. Baie des Chaleurs. bay New Brunswick/Québec, E Canada
Chaleurs, Baie des see Chaleur Bay
59 G16 **Chalhuanca** Apurímac, S Peru 14.21S 73.16W
160 F12 **Chālisgaon** Mahārāshtra, C India 20.28N 75.10E
117 N23 **Chálki** island Dodekánisos, Greece, Aegean Sea
117 F16 **Chalkiádes** Thessalía, C Greece 39.24N 22.25E
117 H18 **Chalkída** var. Halkida; prev. Khalkís, anc. Chalcis. Evvoia, E Greece 38.27N 23.37E
117 G14 **Chalkidikí** var. Khalkidhikí; anc. Chalcidice. peninsula NE Greece
193 A24 **Chalky Inlet** inlet South Island, NZ
41 S7 **Chalkyitsik** Alaska, USA 66.39N 143.43W
104 I9 **Challans** Vendée, NW France 46.51N 1.52W
59 K19 **Challapata** Oruro, SW Bolivia 19.02S 66.46W
199 H7 **Challenger Deep** undersea feature W Pacific Ocean
200 Nn12 **Challenger Fracture Zone** tectonic feature SE Pacific Ocean
199 Ii13 **Challenger Plateau** undersea feature E Tasman Sea
35 P13 **Challis** Idaho, NW USA 44.31N 114.14W
24 L9 **Chalmette** Louisiana, S USA 29.56N 89.57W
128 J11 **Chalna** Respublika Kareliya, NW Russian Federation 61.53N 33.59E
105 Q5 **Châlons-en-Champagne** prev. Châlons-sur-Marne, hist. Arcae Remorum, anc. Carolopois. Marne, NE France 48.58N 4.22E
Châlons-sur-Marne see Châlons-en-Champagne
105 R9 **Chalon-sur-Saône** anc. Cabillonum. Saône-et-Loire, C France 46.46N 4.51E
Chaltel, Cerro see Fitzroy, Monte
149 N4 **Chālūs** Māzandarān, N Iran 36.40N 51.25E
104 M11 **Châlus** Haute-Vienne, C France 45.38N 1.00E
103 N20 **Cham** Bayern, SE Germany 49.13N 12.40E
110 F7 **Cham** Zug, N Switzerland 47.10N 8.28E
39 R8 **Chama** New Mexico, SW USA 36.54N 106.34W
Cha Mai see Thung Song
85 E22 **Chamaites** Karas, S Namibia 27.13S 17.55E
155 O9 **Chaman** Baluchistān, SW Pakistan 30.55N 66.27E
39 R9 **Chama, Rio** ≈ New Mexico, SW USA
158 I6 **Chamba** Himāchal Pradesh, N India 32.33N 76.10E
85 I25 **Chamba** Ruvuma, S Tanzania 11.33S 37.01E
156 H12 **Chambal** ≈ C India
9 U16 **Chamberlain** Saskatchewan, S Canada 50.49N 105.29W
31 O11 **Chamberlain** South Dakota, N USA 43.48N 99.19W
21 R3 **Chamberlain Lake** ◎ Maine, NE USA
41 S5 **Chamberlin, Mount** ▲ Alaska, USA 69.16N 144.54W
39 O11 **Chambers** Arizona, SW USA 35.11N 109.25W
20 F16 **Chambersburg** Pennsylvania, NE USA 39.54N 77.39W
33 N5 **Chambers Island** island Wisconsin, N USA
105 T11 **Chambéry** anc. Camberia. Savoie, E France 45.34N 5.55E
84 L12 **Chambeshi** Northern, NE Zambia 10.55S 31.07E
84 L12 **Chambeshi** ≈ NE Zambia
76 M6 **Chambi, Jebel** var. Jabal ash Sha'nabī. ▲ W Tunisia 35.16N 8.39E
13 Q7 **Chambord** Québec, SE Canada 48.25N 72.02W
194 G10 **Chambri Lake** ◎ W PNG
145 U11 **Chamcham** S Iraq 31.17N 45.05E
145 T4 **Chamchamāl** N Iraq 35.31N 44.49E
42 J14 **Chamela** Jalisco, SW Mexico 19.33N 105.04W
44 G5 **Chamelecón, Río** ≈ NW Honduras
64 J9 **Chamical** La Rioja, C Argentina 30.21S 66.19W
117 L23 **Chamilí** island Kykládes, Greece, Aegean Sea
178 Ii13 **Châmnar** Kaôh Kông, SW Cambodia 11.45N 103.32E
158 K9 **Chamoli** Uttaranchal, N India 30.22N 79.19E
105 U11 **Chamonix-Mont-Blanc** Haute-Savoie, E France 45.55N 6.52E
160 L11 **Chāmpa** Chhattisgarh, C India 22.01N 82.42E
8 H8 **Champagne** Yukon Territory, W Canada 60.48N 136.22W
105 Q5 **Champagne** cultural region N France
Champagne see Campania
105 Q5 **Champagne-Ardenne** ◆ region N France
105 S9 **Champagnole** Jura, E France 46.43N 5.55E
32 M13 **Champaign** Illinois, N USA 40.07N 88.14W
178 Jj11 **Champasak** Champasak, S Laos 14.50N 105.51E
105 U6 **Champ de Feu** ▲ NE France 48.24N 7.15E
11 O7 **Champdoré, Lac** ◎ Québec, NE Canada
44 B6 **Champerico** Retalhuleu, SW Guatemala 14.18N 91.54W
110 C11 **Champéry** Valais, SW Switzerland 46.12N 6.52E
20 L6 **Champlain** New York, NE USA 44.58N 73.25W
20 L9 **Champlain Canal** canal New York, NE USA
13 P13 **Champlain, Lac** ◎ Quebec, Canada/USA see also Champlain, Lake
20 L7 **Champlain, Lake** ◎ Canada/USA see also Champlain, Lac
105 S7 **Champlitte** Haute-Saône, E France 47.36N 5.31E
43 W13 **Champotón** Campeche, SE Mexico 19.18N 90.43W
106 G10 **Chamusca** Santarém, C Portugal 39.21N 8.29W
121 O20 **Chamyarysy** Rus. Chemerisy. Homyel'skaya Voblasts', SE Belarus 51.42N 30.26E
131 P5 **Chamzinka** Respublika Mordoviya, W Russian Federation 54.22N 45.22E
Chanáil Mhór, An see Grand Canal
Chanak see Çanakkale
64 G7 **Chañaral** Atacama, N Chile 26.19S 70.34W
106 H13 **Chança, Rio** var. Chanza. ≈ Portugal/Spain
59 D14 **Chancay** Lima, W Peru 11.33S 77.16W
Chan-chiang/Chanchiang see Zhanjiang
64 G13 **Chanco** Maule, Chile 35.43S 72.35W
41 R7 **Chandalar** Alaska, USA 67.30N 148.29W
41 R6 **Chandalar River** ≈ Alaska, USA
158 L10 **Chandan Chauki** Uttar Pradesh, N India 28.31N 80.43E
159 S16 **Chandannagar** prev. Chandernagore. West Bengal, E India 22.52N 88.21E
158 K10 **Chandausi** Uttar Pradesh, N India 28.27N 78.43E
24 M10 **Chandeleur Islands** island group Louisiana, S USA
24 M9 **Chandeleur Sound** sound N Gulf of Mexico
158 I8 **Chandigarh** Punjab, N India 30.41N 76.51E
159 Q16 **Chāndil** Jhārkhand, NE India 22.58N 86.04E
190 D2 **Chandler** South Australia 26.59S 133.22E
13 Y7 **Chandler** Québec, SE Canada 48.21N 64.40W
38 L14 **Chandler** Arizona, SW USA 33.18N 111.50W
29 O10 **Chandler** Oklahoma, C USA 35.42N 96.52W
27 V7 **Chandler** Texas, SW USA 32.18N 95.28W
41 Q6 **Chandler River** ≈ Alaska, USA
58 H13 **Chandles, Río** ≈ E Peru
169 N9 **Chandmanĭ** Dornogovĭ, SE Mongolia 45.36N 110.30E
12 J13 **Chandos Lake** ◎ Ontario, SE Canada
159 U15 **Chandpur** Chittagong, C Bangladesh 23.13N 90.43E
160 I13 **Chandrapur** Mahārāshtra, C India 19.58N 79.21E
85 J15 **Changa** Southern, S Zambia 16.24S 28.27E
Changan see Xi'an, Shaanxi, China
Chang'an see Rong'an, Guangxi Zhuangzu Zizhiqu, China
161 G23 **Changanācheri** Kerala, SW India 9.27N 76.34E
85 M19 **Changane** ≈ S Mozambique
85 M16 **Changara** Tete, NW Mozambique 16.54S 33.15E
169 X11 **Changbai** var. Changbai Chosenzu Zizhixian. Jilin, NE China 41.25N 128.08E
Changbai Chosenzu Zizhixian see Changbai
169 X11 **Changbai Shan** ▲▲ NE China
169 V10 **Changchun** var. Ch'angch'un, Ch'ang-ch'un; prev. Hsinking. Jilin, NE China 43.52N 125.18E
166 M10 **Changde** Hunan, S China 29.04N 111.42E
167 S13 **Changhua** Jap. Shōka. C Taiwan 24.06N 120.31E
174 I7 **Changi** ✕ (Singapore) E Singapore 1.22N 103.58E
164 L5 **Changji** Xinjiang Uygur Zizhiqu, NW China 44.02N 87.12E
166 L17 **Changjiang** var. Changjiang Lizu Zizhixian, Shiliu. Hainan, S China 19.16N 109.09E
163 O13 **Chang Jiang** var. Yangtze Kiang, Eng. Yangtze. ≈ C China
167 S8 **Changjiang Kou** delta E China
Changjiang Lizu Zizhixian see Changjiang
178 I13 **Chang, Ko** island S Thailand
167 Q2 **Changli** Hebei, E China 39.43N 119.13E
169 V10 **Changling** Jilin, NE China 44.15N 124.03E
Changning see Xunwu
167 N11 **Changsha** var. Ch'angsha, Ch'ang-sha. Hunan, S China 28.10N 113.00E
167 Q10 **Changshan** Zhejiang, SE China 28.54N 118.26E
169 V14 **Changshan Qundao** island group NE China
167 S8 **Changshu** var. Ch'ang-shu. Jiangsu, E China 31.36N 120.42E
169 V11 **Changtu** Liaoning, NE China 42.49N 123.58E
45 P14 **Changuinola** Bocas del Toro, NW Panama 9.25N 82.31W
165 N9 **Changweiliang** Qinghai, W China 38.24N 92.07E
166 K6 **Changwu** var. Zhaoren. Shaanxi, C China 35.12N 107.45E
169 U13 **Changxing Dao** island N China
166 M9 **Changyang** var. Longzhouping. Hubei, C China 30.45N 111.13E
169 W14 **Changyŏn** SW North Korea 38.19N 125.14E
167 N5 **Changzhi** Shanxi, C China 36.09N 113.01E
167 R8 **Changzhou** Jiangsu, E China 31.53N 119.50E
117 H24 **Chaniá** var. Hania, Khaniá, Eng. Canea; anc. Cydonia. Kríti, Greece, E Mediterranean Sea 35.31N 24.01E
64 J5 **Chañi, Nevado de** ▲ NW Argentina 24.09S 65.44W
117 H24 **Chanión, Kólpos** gulf Kríti, Greece, E Mediterranean Sea
Chankiri see Çankırı
32 M11 **Channahon** Illinois, N USA 41.25N 88.13W
161 H20 **Channapatna** Karnātaka, E India 12.43N 77.13E
99 K26 **Channel Islands** Fr. Îles Normandes. island group S English Channel
37 R16 **Channel Islands** island group California, W USA
11 S13 **Channel-Port aux Basques** Newfoundland and Labrador, SE Canada 47.35N 59.02W
Channel, The see English Channel
99 Q23 **Channel Tunnel** tunnel France/UK
26 M2 **Channing** Texas, SW USA 35.40N 102.19W
Chantabun/Chantaburi see Chanthaburi
106 H3 **Chantada** Galicia, NW Spain 42.36N 7.46W
178 I12 **Chanthaburi** var. Chantabun, Chantaburi. Chantaburi, S Thailand 12.34N 102.07E
105 O4 **Chantilly** Oise, N France 49.12N 2.28E
15 Kk4 **Chantrey Inlet** inlet Nunavut, N Canada
145 V12 **Chanūn as Sa'ūdī** S Iraq 31.04N 46.00E
29 Q6 **Chanute** Kansas, C USA 37.40N 95.27W
125 G13 **Chany, Ozero** ◎ C Russian Federation
Chanza see Chança, Rio
Ch'ao-an/Chaochow see Chaozhou
167 P8 **Chao Hu** ◎ E China
178 Hh11 **Chao Phraya, Mae Nam** ≈ C Thailand
Chaor He see Qulin Gol
Chaouèn see Chefchaouen
167 P14 **Chaoyang** Guangdong, S China 23.17N 116.30E
169 T12 **Chaoyang** Liaoning, NE China 41.33N 120.28E
Chaoyang see Huinan, Jilin, China
Chaoyang see Jiayin, Heilongjiang, China
167 Q14 **Chaozhou** var. Chaoan, Chao'an, Ch'ao-an; prev. Chaochow. Guangdong, SE China 23.39N 116.34E
60 N13 **Chapadinha** Maranhão, E Brazil 3.45S 43.22W
10 K12 **Chapais** Québec, SE Canada 49.46N 74.54W
42 L13 **Chapala** Jalisco, SW Mexico 20.17N 103.13W
42 L13 **Chapala, Lago de** ◎ C Mexico
152 F13 **Chapan, Gora** ▲ C Turkmenistan 37.48N 58.03E
59 M18 **Chapare, Río** ≈ C Bolivia
56 E11 **Chaparral** Tolima, C Colombia 3.44N 75.33W
126 Kk12 **Chapayevo** Respublika Sakha (Yakutiya), NE Russian Federation 60.03N 117.19E
150 F9 **Chapayev** Zapadnyy Kazakhstan, NW Kazakhstan 50.13N 51.05E
131 R6 **Chapayevsk** Samarskaya Oblast', W Russian Federation 52.57N 49.41E
62 H13 **Chapecó** Santa Catarina, S Brazil 27.06S 52.39W
62 I13 **Chapecó, Rio** ≈ S Brazil
22 J9 **Chapel Hill** Tennessee, S USA 35.38N 86.40W
46 J12 **Chapelton** C Jamaica 18.04N 77.16W
12 C8 **Chapleau** Ontario, SE Canada 47.49N 83.24W
12 D7 **Chapleau** ≈ Ontario, S Canada
9 T16 **Chaplin** Saskatchewan, S Canada 50.27N 106.37W
130 M6 **Chaplygin** Lipetskaya Oblast', W Russian Federation 53.13N 39.58E
119 S11 **Chaplynka** Khersons'ka Oblast', S Ukraine 46.20N 33.34E
15 L3 **Chapman, Cape** headland Nunavut, NE Canada 69.15N 89.09W
27 T15 **Chapman Ranch** Texas, SW USA 27.32N 97.25W
Chapman's see Okwa
23 P5 **Chapmanville** West Virginia, NE USA 37.58N 82.01W
30 K15 **Chappell** Nebraska, C USA 41.05N 102.28W
Chapra see Chhapra
58 D9 **Chapuli, Río** ≈ N Peru
78 I6 **Châr** well N Mauritania 21.31N 12.55W
126 Kk13 **Chara** Chitinskaya Oblast', S Russian Federation 56.57N 118.05E
126 Kk13 **Chara** ≈ C Russian Federation
56 G8 **Charala** Santander, C Colombia 6.16N 73.09W
43 N10 **Charcas** San Luis Potosí, C Mexico 23.09N 101.04W
27 T13 **Charco** Texas, SW USA 28.42N 97.35E
204 H7 **Charcot Island** island Antarctica
66 M8 **Charcot Seamounts** undersea feature E Atlantic Ocean
Chardara see Shardara
151 P17 **Chardarinskoye Vodokhranilishche** ⊡ S Kazakhstan
33 U11 **Chardon** Ohio, N USA 41.33N 81.10W
46 K9 **Chardonnières** SW Haiti 18.17N 74.09W
Chardzhev see Türkmenabat
Chardzhevskaya Oblast' see Lebap Welaýaty
Chardzhou/Chardzhui see Türkmenabat
104 L11 **Charente** ◆ department W France
104 J11 **Charente** ≈ W France
104 J10 **Charente-Maritime** ◆ department W France
143 U12 **Ch'arents'avan** C Armenia 40.23N 44.41E
80 I12 **Chari** var. Shari. ≈ Central African Republic/Chad
80 G11 **Chari-Baguirmi** off. Préfecture du Chari-Baguirmi. ◆ prefecture SW Chad
155 Q4 **Chārīkār** Parwān, NE Afghanistan 35.01N 69.10E
31 V15 **Chariton** Iowa, C USA 41.00N 93.18W
29 U3 **Chariton River** ≈ Missouri, C USA
57 T7 **Charity** NW Guyana 7.22N 58.34W
33 R7 **Charity Island** island Michigan, N USA
Chärjew see Türkmenabat
Chärjew Oblasty see Lebap Welaýaty
Charkhlik/Charkhliq see Ruoqiang
101 G20 **Charleroi** Hainaut, S Belgium 50.25N 4.27E
9 V12 **Charles** Manitoba, C Canada 55.27N 100.58W
13 R10 **Charlesbourg** Québec, SE Canada 46.49N 71.14W
23 Y7 **Charles, Cape** headland Virginia, NE USA 37.09N 75.57W
31 W12 **Charles City** Iowa, C USA 43.04N 92.40W
23 W6 **Charles City** Virginia, NE USA 37.19N 77.01W
105 O5 **Charles de Gaulle** ✕ (Paris) Seine-et-Marne, N France 49.04N 2.36E
10 K1 **Charles Island** island Nunavut, NE Canada
Charles Island see Santa María, Isla
18 Mm5 **Charles-Lindbergh** ✕ (Minneapolis/Saint Paul) Minnesota, N USA 44.47N 93.12W
32 K9 **Charles Mound** hill Illinois, N USA 42.30N 90.14W
193 A22 **Charles Sound** sound South Island, NZ
193 G15 **Charleston** West Coast, South Island, NZ 41.54S 171.25E
29 S11 **Charleston** Arkansas, C USA 35.18N 94.02W
32 M14 **Charleston** Illinois, N USA 39.30N 88.10W
24 L3 **Charleston** Mississippi, S USA 34.00N 90.03W
29 Z7 **Charleston** Missouri, C USA 36.55N 89.21W
23 T15 **Charleston** South Carolina, SE USA 32.48N 79.57W
23 Q5 **Charleston** state capital West Virginia, NE USA 38.21N 81.37W
12 L14 **Charleston Lake** ◎ Ontario, SE Canada
37 W11 **Charleston Peak** ▲ Nevada, W USA 36.16N 115.40W
47 W10 **Charlestown** Nevis, Saint Kitts and Nevis 17.05N 62.35W
33 P16 **Charlestown** Indiana, N USA 38.27N 85.40W
20 M9 **Charlestown** New Hampshire, NE USA 43.14N 72.23W
23 V3 **Charles Town** West Virginia, NE USA 39.17N 77.51W
189 W9 **Charleville** Queensland, E Australia 26.24S 146.18E
105 R3 **Charleville-Mézières** Ardennes, N France 49.45N 4.43E
33 P5 **Charlevoix** Michigan, N USA 45.19N 85.15W
33 Q6 **Charlevoix, Lake** ◎ Michigan, N USA
41 T9 **Charley River** ≈ Alaska, USA
66 J6 **Charlie-Gibbs Fracture Zone** tectonic feature N Atlantic Ocean
105 Q10 **Charlieu** Loire, E France 46.11N 4.10E
33 Q9 **Charlotte** Michigan, N USA 42.33N 84.50W
23 R10 **Charlotte** North Carolina, SE USA 35.13N 80.50W
22 I8 **Charlotte** Tennessee, S USA 36.11N 87.18W
27 R13 **Charlotte** Texas, SW USA 28.51N 98.42W
23 R10 **Charlotte** ✕ North Carolina, SE USA 35.12N 80.54W
47 T9 **Charlotte Amalie** prev. Saint Thomas. ○ (Virgin Islands (US)) Saint Thomas, N Virgin Islands (US) 18.22N 64.55W
23 U7 **Charlotte Court House** Virginia, NE USA 37.04N 78.37W
25 W14 **Charlotte Harbor** inlet Florida, SE USA
Charlotte Island see Abaiang
97 J15 **Charlottenberg** Värmland, C Sweden 59.52N 12.16E
Charlottenhof see Aegviidu
23 U5 **Charlottesville** Virginia, NE USA 38.01N 78.28W
Charlotte Town see Roseau, Dominica

◆ Country ● Country Capital ◇ Dependent Territory ○ Dependent Territory Capital ◆ Administrative Region ✕ International Airport ▲ Mountain ▲▲ Mountain Range Volcano ≈ River ◎ Lake ⊡ Reservoir

Charlotte Town – Chiloquin

Charlotte Town see Gouyave, Grenada
11 Q14 Charlottetown Prince Edward Island, Prince Edward Island, SE Canada 46.13N 63.09W
47 Z16 Charlotteville Tobago, Trinidad and Tobago 11.16N 60.33W
190 M11 Charlton Victoria, SE Australia 36.18S 143.19E
10 H10 Charlton Island island Nunavut, C Canada
105 T6 Charmes Vosges, NE France 48.19N 6.19E
121 F19 Charnawchytsy Rus. Chernavchitsy. Brestskaya Voblasts', SW Belarus 52.13N 23.43E
13 R10 Charny Québec, SE Canada 46.43N 71.14W
155 T5 Chārsadda North-West Frontier Province, NW Pakistan 34.12N 71.46E
Charshanga/Charshangngy/Charshangy see Köýtendag
Charsk see Shar
189 W6 Charters Towers Queensland, NE Australia 20.01S 146.19E
13 R12 Chartierville Québec, SE Canada 45.19N 71.13W
104 M6 Chartres anc. Autricum, Civitas Carnutum. Eure-et-Loir, C France 48.27N 1.27E
151 W15 Charyn Kaz. Sharyn. Almaty, SE Kazakhstan 43.48N 79.22E
63 D21 Chascomús Buenos Aires, E Argentina 35.34S 58.01W
9 N16 Chase British Columbia, SW Canada 50.49N 119.40W
23 U7 Chase City Virginia, NE USA 36.48N 78.27W
21 S4 Chase, Mount ▲ Maine, NE USA 46.06N 68.30W
120 M13 Chashniki Rus. Chashniki. Vitsyebskaya Voblasts', N Belarus 54.51N 29.09E
117 D15 Chásia ▲ C Greece
31 V9 Chaska Minnesota, N USA 44.47N 93.36W
193 D25 Chaslands Mistake headland South Island, NZ 46.37S 169.21E
129 R11 Chasovo Respublika Komi, NW Russian Federation 61.58N 50.34E
Chasovo see Vazhgort
128 H14 Chastova Novgorodskaya Oblast', NW Russian Federation 58.37N 32.04E
149 R3 Chāt Golestān, N Iran 37.52N 55.27E
Chatak see Chhatak
Chatang see Zhanang
41 R9 Chatanika Alaska, USA 65.06N 147.28W
41 R9 Chatanika River ≈ Alaska, USA
153 T8 Chat-Bazar Talasskaya Oblast', NW Kyrgyzstan 42.29N 72.37E
47 Y14 Chateaubelair Saint Vincent, W Saint Vincent and the Grenadines 13.16N 61.14W
104 J7 Châteaubriant Loire-Atlantique, NW France 47.43N 1.22W
105 Q8 Château-Chinon Nièvre, C France 47.04N 3.50E
110 C10 Château d'Oex Vaud, W Switzerland 46.28N 7.09E
104 L7 Château-du-Loir Sarthe, NW France 47.40N 0.25E
104 M6 Châteaudun Eure-et-Loir, C France 48.04N 1.19E
104 K7 Château-Gontier Mayenne, NW France 47.49N 0.42W
13 O13 Châteauguay Québec, SE Canada 45.21N 73.46W
104 F6 Châteaulin Finistère, NW France 48.12N 4.07W
105 N9 Châteaumeillant Cher, C France 46.33N 2.10E
104 K11 Châteauneuf-sur-Charente Charente, W France 45.34N 0.33W
104 M7 Château-Renault Indre-et-Loire, C France 47.34N 0.52E
105 N9 Châteauroux prev. Indreville. Indre, C France 46.50N 1.42E
105 T5 Château-Salins Moselle, NE France 48.50N 6.29E
105 P4 Château-Thierry Aisne, N France 49.03N 3.24E
101 H21 Châtelet Hainaut, S Belgium 50.24N 4.31E
Châtelherault see Châtellerault
104 L9 Châtellerault var. Châtelherault. Vienne, W France 46.49N 0.33E
31 X10 Chatfield Minnesota, N USA 43.51N 92.11W
11 O14 Chatham New Brunswick, SE Canada 47.01N 65.30W
12 D17 Chatham Ontario, S Canada 42.24N 82.10W
99 P22 Chatham SE England, UK 51.22N 0.31E
32 K14 Chatham Illinois, N USA 39.40N 89.42W
23 T7 Chatham Virginia, NE USA 36.49N 79.24W
65 F22 Chatham, Isla island S Chile
183 R12 Chatham Island island Chatham Islands, NZ
Chatham Island see San Cristóbal, Isla
Chatham Island Rise see Chatham Rise
199 Jj14 Chatham Islands island group NZ, SW Pacific Ocean
183 Q12 Chatham Rise var. Chatham Island Rise. undersea feature S Pacific Ocean
41 X13 Chatham Strait strait Alaska, USA
Chathóir, Rinn see Cahore Point
104 M9 Châtillon-sur-Indre Indre, C France 46.58N 1.10E
105 Q7 Châtillon-sur-Seine Côte d'Or, C France 47.51N 4.30E
153 S8 Chatkal Uzb. Chotqol. ≈ Kyrgyzstan/Uzbekistan
153 R9 Chatkal Range Rus. Chatkal'skiy Khrebet. ▲ Kyrgyzstan/Uzbekistan
Chatkal'skiy Khrebet see Chatkal Range
25 N7 Chatom Alabama, S USA 31.28N 88.15W
Chatrapur see Chhatrapur
149 S10 Chatrūd Kermān, C Iran 30.39N 56.57E
25 S2 Chatsworth Georgia, SE USA 34.46N 84.46W
Chāttagām see Chittagong
25 S8 Chattahoochee Florida, SE USA 30.40N 84.51W
25 R8 Chattahoochee River ≈ SE USA
22 L10 Chattanooga Tennessee, S USA 35.05N 85.16W
153 V10 Chatyr-Kël', Ozero ◎ C Kyrgyzstan
153 W9 Chatyr-Tash Narynskaya Oblast', C Kyrgyzstan 40.54N 76.22E
13 R12 Chaudière ≈ Québec, SE Canada
178 J14 Châu Đốc var. Chauphu, Chau Phu. An Giang, S Vietnam 10.52N 105.07E
158 D13 Chauhtan prev. Chohtan. Rājasthān, NW India 25.27N 71.07E
117 Ff5 Chauk Magwe, W Myanmar 20.52N 94.49E
105 R6 Chaumont prev. Chaumont-en-Bassigny. Haute-Marne, N France 48.07N 5.07E
Chaumont-en-Bassigny see Chaumont
127 O4 Chaunskaya Guba bay NE Russian Federation
105 P3 Chauny Aisne, N France 49.37N 3.13E
Châu Ô see Binh Sơn
Chau Phu see Châu Đốc
104 I5 Chausey, Îles island group N France
Chausy see Chavusy
20 C11 Chautauqua Lake ◎ New York, NE USA
104 L9 Chauvigny Vienne, W France 46.35N 0.37E
128 L6 Chavan'ga Murmanskaya Oblast', NW Russian Federation 66.07N 37.44E
12 K10 Chavannes, Lac ◎ Québec, SE Canada
Chavantes, Represa de see Xavantes, Represa de
63 D15 Chavarría Corrientes, NE Argentina 28.57S 58.34W
131 P4 Chavash Respubliki var. Chuvashskaya Respublika, Eng. Chuvashia. ◈ autonomous republic W Russian Federation
106 I5 Chaves anc. Aquae Flaviae. Vila Real, N Portugal 41.43N 7.28W
Chávez, Isla see Santa Cruz, Isla
84 G13 Chavuma North Western, NW Zambia 13.04S 22.43E
121 O16 Chavusy Rus. Chausy. Mahilyowskaya Voblasts', E Belarus 53.49N 30.59E
Chayan see Shayan
153 U8 Chayek Narynskaya Oblast', C Kyrgyzstan 41.54N 74.28E
145 T6 Chāy Khānah E Iraq 34.19N 44.33E
129 T16 Chaykovskiy Permskaya Oblast', NW Russian Federation 56.45N 54.09E
178 K12 Chbar Môndól Kiri, E Cambodia 12.46N 107.10E
25 Q4 Cheaha Mountain ▲ Alabama, S USA 33.29N 85.48W
Cheatharlach see Carlow
23 S2 Cheat River ≈ NE USA
113 A16 Cheb Ger. Eger. Karlovarský Kraj, W Czech Republic 50.04N 12.23E
131 Q3 Cheboksary Chavash Respubliki, W Russian Federation 56.06N 47.14E
33 Q5 Cheboygan Michigan, N USA 45.40N 84.28W
Chechaouèn see Chefchaouen
Chechenia see Chechenskaya Respublika
131 O15 Chechenskaya Respublika Eng. Chechenia, Chechnia, Rus. Chechnya. ◈ autonomous republic SW Russian Federation
69 N4 Chech, Erg desert Algeria/Mali
Chechersk see Chachersk
Chechevichi see Chachevichy
Che-chiang see Zhejiang
Chechnia/Chechnya see Chechenskaya Respublika
169 Y15 Chech'ŏn Jap. Teisen. N South Korea 37.06N 128.15E
113 L15 Chęciny Świętokrzyskie, S Poland 50.51N 20.31E
29 Q10 Checotah Oklahoma, C USA 35.28N 95.31W
11 R15 Chedabucto Bay inlet Nova Scotia, E Canada
177 F7 Cheduba Island island W Myanmar
39 T5 Cheesman Lake ⊠ Colorado, C USA
205 S16 Cheetham, Cape headland Antarctica 70.25S 162.40E
76 G5 Chefchaouen var. Chaouèn, Chechaouèn, Sp. Xauen. N Morocco 35.09N 5.16W
Chefoo see Yantai
40 M12 Chefornak Alaska, USA 60.09N 164.09W
126 Mm15 Chegdomyn Khabarovskiy Kray, SE Russian Federation 51.09N 132.58E
78 M4 Chegga Tiris Zemmour, NE Mauritania 25.27N 5.49W
Cheghcheran see Chaghcharān
34 G9 Chehalis Washington, NW USA 46.39N 122.57W
34 G9 Chehalis River ≈ Washington, NW USA
154 M6 Chehel Abdālān, Kūh-e var. Chalap Dalam, Pash. Chalap Dalan. ▲ C Afghanistan
117 D14 Cheimadítis, Límni ◎ N Greece
105 U15 Cheiron, Mont ▲ SE France 43.49N 7.00E
169 X17 Cheju Jap. Saishū. S South Korea 33.31N 126.34E
169 Y17 Cheju ✕ S South Korea 33.31N 126.28E
169 Y17 Cheju-do Jap. Saishū; prev. Quelpart. island S South Korea
169 X17 Cheju-haehyŏp strait S South Korea
Chekiang see Zhejiang
Chekichler/Chekishlyar see Çekiçler
196 F8 Chelab Babeldaob, N Palau
153 N11 Chelak Rus. Chelek. Samarqand Viloyati, C Uzbekistan 39.55N 66.45E
34 J7 Chelan, Lake ⊠ Washington, NW USA
Chelek see Chelak
Cheleken see Hazar
Chélif/Chéliff see Chelif, Oued
76 J5 Chelif, Oued var. Chélif, Chéliff, Chellif, Shellif. ≈ N Algeria
Chelkar see Shalkar
Chelkar, Ozero see Shalkar, Ozero
Chellif see Chelif, Oued
113 P14 Chełm Rus. Kholm. Lubelskie, SE Poland 51.07N 23.28E
112 I9 Chełmno Ger. Culm, Kulm. Kujawski-pomorskie, C Poland 53.21N 18.27E
12 F10 Chelmsford Ontario, S Canada 46.33N 81.16W
99 P21 Chelmsford E England, UK 51.43N 0.28E
112 J9 Chełmża Ger. Culmsee, Kulmsee. Kujawski-pomorskie, C Poland 53.12N 18.36E
29 Q8 Chelsea Oklahoma, C USA 36.32N 95.25W
20 M8 Chelsea Vermont, NE USA 43.57N 72.24W
99 L21 Cheltenham C England, UK 51.54N 2.04W
107 R9 Chelva País Valenciano, E Spain 39.45N 1.00W
125 Ee12 Chelyabinsk Chelyabinskaya Oblast', C Russian Federation 55.12N 61.25E
125 E12 Chelyabinskaya Oblast' ◈ province C Russian Federation
126 Jj4 Chelyuskin, Mys headland N Russian Federation 77.42N 104.13E
126 H15 Chemal Altayskiy Kray, S Russian Federation 51.22N 85.08E
43 Y12 Chemax Yucatán, SE Mexico 20.41N 87.54W
85 N16 Chemba Sofala, C Mozambique 17.10S 34.52E
84 J13 Chembe Luapula, NE Zambia 11.58S 28.45E
Chemenibit see Çemenibit
Chemerisy see Chamyarysy
118 K7 Chemerivtsi Khmel'nyts'ka Oblast', W Ukraine 49.00N 26.21E
104 J8 Chemillé Maine-et-Loire, NW France 47.15N 0.42W
181 X17 Chemin Grenier S Mauritius 20.28S 57.28E
103 N16 Chemnitz prev. Karl-Marx-Stadt. Sachsen, E Germany 50.49N 12.55E
Chemulpo see Inch'ŏn
34 H14 Chemult Oregon, NW USA 43.14N 121.48W
20 G12 Chemung River ≈ New York/Pennsylvania, NE USA
155 U8 Chenāb ≈ India/Pakistan
41 S9 Chena Hot Springs Alaska, USA 65.06N 146.02W
20 I11 Chenango River ≈ New York, NE USA
174 Gg3 Chenderoh, Tasik ◎ Peninsular Malaysia
13 Q11 Chêne, Rivière du ≈ Québec, SE Canada
34 L8 Cheney Washington, NW USA 47.29N 117.34W
28 M6 Cheney Reservoir ⊠ Kansas, C USA
Chengchiatun see Liaoyuan
Ch'eng-chou/Chengchow see Zhengzhou
167 P1 Chengde var. Jehol. Hebei, E China 41.00N 117.57E
166 I9 Chengdu var. Chengtu, Ch'eng-tu. Sichuan, C China 30.40N 104.03E
167 Q14 Chenghai Guangdong, S China 23.33N 116.42E
Chenghsien see Zhengzhou
166 H13 Chengjiang Yunnan, SW China 24.40N 102.55E
Chengjiang see Taihe
166 L17 Chengmai var. Jinjiang. Hainan, S China 19.45N 109.56E
Chengtu/Ch'eng-tu see Chengdu
165 W12 Chengxian var. Cheng Xian. Gansu, C China 33.42N 105.45E
Chengyang see Juxian
Chengzhong see Ningming
Chenkiang see Zhenjiang
161 J19 Chennai prev. Madras. Tamil Nādu, S India 13.04N 80.18E
161 J19 Chennai ✕ Tamil Nādu, S India 13.07N 80.13E
105 R8 Chenôve Côte d'Or, C France 47.16N 5.00E
Chenstokhov see Częstochowa
166 L11 Chenxi var. Chenyang. Hunan, S China 28.01N 110.15E
Chen Xian/Chenxian/Chen Xiang see Chenzhou
Chenyang see Chenxi
167 N12 Chenzhou var. Chenxian, Chen Xian, Chen Xiang. Hunan, S China 25.51N 113.01E
178 Kk12 Cheo Reo var. A Yun Pa. Gia Lai, S Vietnam 13.19N 108.27E
116 I11 Chepelare Smolyan, S Bulgaria 41.43N 24.40E
116 J11 Chepelarska Reka ≈ S Bulgaria
58 B11 Chepén La Libertad, C Peru 7.12S 79.24W
64 J10 Chepes La Rioja, C Argentina 31.23S 66.34W
167 O15 Chep Lap Kok ✕ (Hong Kong) S China 22.23N 114.11E
45 U14 Chepo Panamá, C Panama 9.10N 79.05W
Chepping Wycombe see High Wycombe
129 R14 Cheptsa ≈ NW Russian Federation
32 K3 Chequamegon Point headland Wisconsin, N USA 46.42N 90.45W
105 O8 Cher ◈ department C France
104 M8 Cher ≈ C France
Cherangani Hills see Cherangany Hills
83 H17 Cherangany Hills var. Cherangani Hills. ▲ W Kenya
23 S11 Cheraw South Carolina, SE USA 34.42N 79.52W
104 I3 Cherbourg anc. Carusbur. Manche, N France 49.39N 1.36W
131 R5 Cherdakly Ul'yanovskaya Oblast', W Russian Federation 54.21N 48.54E
129 U12 Cherdyn' Permskaya Oblast', NW Russian Federation 60.21N 56.39E
128 J14 Cherekha ≈ W Russian Federation
126 J15 Cheremkhovo Irkutskaya Oblast', S Russian Federation 53.16N 102.44E
126 Hh15 Cheremushki Respublika Khakasiya, S Russian Federation 52.48N 91.20E
Cheren see Keren
128 K14 Cherepovets Vologodskaya Oblast', NW Russian Federation 59.09N 37.49E
129 O11 Cherevkovo Arkhangel'skaya Oblast', NW Russian Federation 61.45N 45.16E
76 I6 Chergui, Chott ech salt lake NW Algeria
Cherikov see Cherykaw
119 P6 Cherkas'ka Oblast' var. Cherkasy, Rus. Cherkasskaya Oblast'. ◈ province C Ukraine
Cherkasskaya Oblast' see Cherkas'ka Oblast'
Cherkassy see Cherkasy
119 Q6 Cherkasy Rus. Cherkassy. Cherkas'ka Oblast', C Ukraine 49.25N 32.04E
Cherkasy see Cherkas'ka Oblast'
130 M15 Cherkessk Karachayevo-Cherkesskaya Respublika, SW Russian Federation 44.12N 42.06E
125 G13 Cherlak Omskaya Oblast', C Russian Federation 54.06N 74.59E
125 Ff14 Cherlakskiy Omskaya Oblast', C Russian Federation 53.42N 74.23E
129 U13 Chermoz Permskaya Oblast', NW Russian Federation 58.49N 56.07E
Chernavchitsy see Charnawchytsy
129 T3 Chernaya Nenetskiy Avtonomnyy Okrug, NW Russian Federation 68.36N 56.34E
129 T4 Chernaya ≈ NW Russian Federation
Chernigov see Chernihiv
Chernigovskaya Oblast' see Chernihivs'ka Oblast'
119 Q2 Chernihiv Rus. Chernigov. Chernihivs'ka Oblast', NE Ukraine 51.28N 31.19E
Chernihiv see Chernihivs'ka Oblast'
119 V9 Chernihivka Zaporiz'ka Oblast', SE Ukraine 47.11N 36.10E
119 P2 Chernihivs'ka Oblast' var. Chernihiv, Rus. Chernigovskaya Oblast'. ◈ province NE Ukraine
116 I9 Cherni Osŭm ≈ N Bulgaria
118 J8 Chernivets'ka Oblast' var. Chernivtsi, Rus. Chernovitskaya Oblast'. ◈ province W Ukraine
116 I9 Cherni Vit ≈ NW Bulgaria
116 G10 Cherni Vrŭkh ▲ W Bulgaria 42.33N 23.18E
118 K8 Chernivtsi Ger. Czernowitz, Rom. Cernăuţi, Rus. Chernovtsy. Chernivets'ka Oblast', W Ukraine 48.18N 25.55E
118 M7 Chernivtsi Vinnyts'ka Oblast', C Ukraine 48.33N 28.06E
Chernivtsi see Chernivets'ka Oblast'
Chernobyl' see Chornobyl'
126 Hh15 Chernogorsk Respublika Khakasiya, S Russian Federation 53.48N 91.03E
Cherno More see Black Sea
Chernomorskoye see Chornomors'ke
151 T7 Chernoretskoye Pavlodar, NE Kazakhstan 52.51N 76.37E
Chernovitskaya Oblast' see Chernivets'ka Oblast'
Chernovtsy see Chernivtsi
151 U8 Chernoye Pavlodar, NE Kazakhstan 51.40N 77.33E
Chernoye More see Black Sea
129 U16 Chernushka Permskaya Oblast', NW Russian Federation 56.30N 56.07E
119 N4 Chernyakhiv Rus. Chernyakhov. Zhytomyrs'ka Oblast', N Ukraine 50.31N 28.38E
Chernyakhov see Chernyakhiv
121 C14 Chernyakhovsk Ger. Insterburg. Kaliningradskaya Oblast', W Russian Federation 54.36N 21.49E
130 K8 Chernyanka Belgorodskaya Oblast', W Russian Federation 50.59N 37.54E
129 V5 Chernyshëva, Gryada ▲ NW Russian Federation
150 J14 Chernyshëva, Zaliv gulf SW Kazakhstan
126 L15 Chernyshevsk Chitinskaya Oblast', S Russian Federation 52.28N 116.52E
126 K11 Chernyshevskiy Respublika Sakha (Yakutiya), NE Russian Federation 62.57N 112.29E
131 P13 Chërnyye Zemli plain SW Russian Federation
Chërnyy Irtysh see Ertix He
131 V7 Chernyy Otrog Orenburgskaya Oblast', W Russian Federation 52.03N 56.09E
31 T12 Cherokee Iowa, C USA 42.45N 95.33W
28 M8 Cherokee Oklahoma, C USA 36.45N 98.22W
27 R9 Cherokee Texas, SW USA 30.56N 98.42W
23 O8 Cherokee Lake ⊠ Tennessee, S USA
Cherokees, Lake O' The see Grand Lake O' The Cherokees
46 H1 Cherokee Sound Great Abaco, N Bahamas 26.16N 77.03W
159 V13 Cherrapunji Meghālaya, NE India 25.16N 91.42E
30 L9 Cherry Creek ≈ South Dakota, N USA
20 J16 Cherry Hill New Jersey, NE USA 39.55N 75.01W
29 Q7 Cherryvale Kansas, C USA 37.16N 95.33W
23 Q10 Cherryville North Carolina, SE USA 35.22N 81.22W
Cherski Range see Cherskogo, Khrebet
127 O5 Cherskiy Respublika Sakha (Yakutiya), NE Russian Federation 68.45N 161.15E
126 Mm8 Cherskogo, Khrebet var. Cherski Range. ▲ NE Russian Federation
Cherso see Cres
130 L10 Chertkovo Rostovskaya Oblast', SW Russian Federation 49.22N 40.10E
Cherven' see Chervyen'
116 H8 Cherven Bryag Pleven, N Bulgaria 43.17N 24.06E
118 M4 Chervonoarmiys'k Zhytomyrs'ka Oblast', N Ukraine 50.27N 28.15E
Chervonograd see Chervonohrad
118 I4 Chervonohrad Rus. Chervonograd. L'vivs'ka Oblast', NW Ukraine 50.27N 24.11E
119 W6 Chervonooskil's'ke Vodoskhovyshche Rus. Krasnooskol'skoye Vodokhranilishche. ⊠ NE Ukraine
Chervonoye, Ozero see Chyrvonaye, Vozyera
119 S4 Chervonozavods'ke Poltavs'ka Oblast', C Ukraine 50.24N 33.22E
121 L16 Chervyen' Rus. Cherven'. Minskaya Voblasts', C Belarus 53.42N 28.23E
121 P16 Cherykaw Rus. Cherikov. Mahilyowskaya Voblasts', E Belarus 53.34N 31.19E
33 R9 Chesaning Michigan, N USA 43.10N 84.07W
23 X5 Chesapeake Bay inlet NE USA
Cheshevlya see Tsyeshawlya
99 K18 Cheshire cultural region C England, UK
129 P5 Chëshskaya Guba var. Archangel Bay, Chesha Bay, Dvina Bay. bay NW Russian Federation
12 F14 Chesley Ontario, S Canada 44.17N 81.06W
23 Q10 Chesnee South Carolina, SE USA 35.09N 81.51W
99 K18 Chester Wel. Caerleon; hist. Legaceaster, Lat. Deva, Devana Castra. C England, UK 53.12N 2.54W
37 O4 Chester California, W USA 40.18N 121.14W
32 K16 Chester Illinois, N USA 37.54N 89.49W
35 S7 Chester Montana, NW USA 48.30N 110.59W
20 I16 Chester Pennsylvania, NE USA 39.51N 75.21W
23 R1 Chester South Carolina, SE USA 34.42N 81.12W
27 X9 Chester Texas, SW USA 30.55N 94.36W
23 W6 Chester Virginia, NE USA 37.22N 77.27W
23 R11 Chester West Virginia, NE USA 40.34N 80.33W
99 M18 Chesterfield C England, UK 53.15N 1.25W
23 S11 Chesterfield South Carolina, SE USA 34.44N 80.05W
23 W6 Chesterfield Virginia, NE USA 37.22N 77.31W
199 I10 Chesterfield, Îles island group NW New Caledonia
15 Ll6 Chesterfield Inlet Nunavut, NW Canada 63.19N 90.57W
15 L6 Chesterfield Inlet inlet Nunavut, N Canada
23 Y3 Chester River ≈ Delaware/Maryland, NE USA
23 X3 Chestertown Maryland, NE USA 39.12N 76.04W
21 R4 Chesuncook Lake ◎ Maine, NE USA
32 J5 Chetek Wisconsin, N USA 45.19N 91.37W
11 R14 Chéticamp Nova Scotia, SE Canada 46.13N 61.19W
29 Q8 Chetopa Kansas, C USA 37.02N 95.05W
43 Y14 Chetumal var. Payo Obispo. Quintana Roo, SE Mexico 18.32N 88.15W
Chetumal, Bahia/Chetumal, Bahía de see Chetumal Bay
44 G1 Chetumal Bay Sp. Bahia Chetumal, Bahía de Chetumal. bay Belize/Mexico
8 M13 Chetwynd British Columbia, W Canada 55.42N 121.36W
40 M11 Chevak Alaska, USA 61.31N 165.35W
38 M12 Chevelon Creek ≈ Arizona, SW USA
193 J17 Cheviot Canterbury, South Island, NZ 42.48S 173.17E
98 L13 Cheviot Hills hill range England/Scotland, UK
98 L13 Cheviot, The ▲ NE England, UK 55.28N 2.10W
12 M11 Chevreuil, Lac du ◎ Québec, SE Canada
83 I16 Ch'ew Bahir var. Lake Stefanie. ◎ Ethiopia/Kenya
34 L7 Chewelah Washington, NW USA 48.16N 117.42W
28 K10 Cheyenne Oklahoma, C USA 35.38N 99.40W
35 Z17 Cheyenne state capital Wyoming, C USA 41.08N 104.45W
28 L5 Cheyenne Bottoms ◎ Kansas, C USA
18 Kk6 Cheyenne River ≈ South Dakota/Wyoming, N USA
39 W5 Cheyenne Wells Colorado, C USA 38.49N 102.21W
110 C9 Cheyres Vaud, W Switzerland 46.48N 6.48E
Chezdi-Oşorheiu see Târgu Secuiesc
159 P13 Chhapra prev. Chapra. Bihār, N India 25.49N 84.42E
159 V13 Chhatak var. Chatak. Chittagong, NE Bangladesh 25.02N 91.33E
160 J9 Chhatarpur Madhya Pradesh, C India 24.54N 79.34E
160 N13 Chhatrapur prev. Chatrapur; Orissa, E India 19.25N 85.01E
160 L12 Chhattīsgarh plain C India
160 K12 Chhattīsgarh ◈ state E India
160 I11 Chhindwāra Madhya Pradesh, C India 22.04N 78.58E
159 T12 Chhukha SW Bhutan 27.01N 89.36E
167 S14 Chiai var. Chia-i, Chiayi, Kiayi, Jiayi, Jap. Kagi. C Taiwan 23.28N 120.27E
Chia-mu-ssu see Jiamusi
85 B15 Chiange Port. Vila de Almoster. Huíla, SW Angola 15.49S 13.52E
Chiang-hsi see Jiangxi
167 S12 Chiang Kai-shek ✕ (T'aipei) N Taiwan 25.09N 121.20E
178 I8 Chiang Khan Loei, E Thailand 17.51N 101.43E
178 H7 Chiang Mai var. Chiangmai, Chiengmai, Kiangmai. Chiang Mai, NW Thailand 18.48N 98.58E
178 H7 Chiang Mai ✕ Chiang Mai, NW Thailand 18.44N 98.53E
178 Hh6 Chiang Rai var. Chianpai, Chienrai, Muang Chiang Rai. Chiang Rai, NW Thailand 19.55N 99.51E
Chiang-su see Jiangsu
Chianning/Chian-ning see Nanjing
Chianpai see Chiang Rai
108 G12 Chianti cultural region C Italy
Chiapa see Chiapa de Corzo
43 U16 Chiapa de Corzo var. Chiapa. Chiapas, SE Mexico 16.42N 92.58W
43 V16 Chiapas ◈ state SE Mexico
108 J12 Chiaravalle Marche, C Italy 43.36N 13.19E
109 N22 Chiaravalle Centrale Calabria, SW Italy 38.40N 16.25E
108 E7 Chiari Lombardia, N Italy 45.33N 10.00E
110 H12 Chiasso Ticino, S Switzerland 45.51N 9.01E
143 S9 Chiat'ura C Georgia 42.13N 43.11E
43 P15 Chiautla var. Chiautla de Tapia. Puebla, S Mexico 18.16N 98.31W
Chiautla de Tapia see Chiautla
108 D10 Chiavari Liguria, NW Italy 44.19N 9.19E
108 E6 Chiavenna Lombardia, N Italy 46.19N 9.22E
Chiayi see Chiai
Chiazza see Piazza Armerina
172 Ss12 Chiba var. Tiba. Chiba, Honshū, S Japan 35.37N 140.05E
171 K17 Chiba off. Chiba-ken, var. Tiba. ◈ prefecture Honshū, S Japan
85 M18 Chibabava Sofala, C Mozambique 20.16S 33.39E
167 O10 Chibi prev. Puqi. Hubei, C China 29.45N 114.02E
85 B15 Chibia Port. João de Almeida, Vila João de Almeida. Huíla, SW Angola 15.09S 13.45E
85 M18 Chiboma Sofala, C Mozambique 20.06S 33.54E
84 J12 Chibondo Luapula, N Zambia 10.42S 28.42E
84 K11 Chibote Luapula, NE Zambia 9.52S 29.33E
10 K12 Chibougamau Québec, SE Canada 49.55N 74.24W
170 Ff11 Chiburi-jima island Oki-shotō, SW Japan
85 M20 Chibuto Gaza, S Mozambique 24.40S 33.33E
33 N11 Chicago Illinois, N USA 41.51N 87.39W
33 N11 Chicago Heights Illinois, N USA 41.30N 87.38W
13 W6 Chic-Chocs, Monts Eng. Shickshock Mountains. ▲ Québec, SE Canada
41 W13 Chichagof Island island Alexander Archipelago, Alaska, USA
59 K20 Chichas, Cordillera de ▲ SW Bolivia
43 X12 Chichén-Itzá, Ruinas ruins Yucatán, SE Mexico 20.35N 88.34W
99 N23 Chichester SE England, UK 50.49N 0.48W
171 Jj16 Chichibu var. Titibu. Saitama, Honshū, S Japan 35.58N 139.06E
44 C5 Chichicastenango Quiché, W Guatemala 14.55N 91.06W
44 I9 Chichigalpa Chinandega, NW Nicaragua 12.34N 87.04W
Ch'i-ch'i-ha-erh see Qiqihar
172 T16 Chichijima-rettō Eng. Beechy Group. island group SE Japan
56 K4 Chichiriviche Falcón, N Venezuela 10.58N 68.16W
41 R11 Chickaloon Alaska, USA 61.48N 148.27W
22 L10 Chickamauga Lake ⊠ Tennessee, S USA
25 N7 Chickasawhay River ≈ Mississippi, S USA
28 M11 Chickasha Oklahoma, C USA 35.03N 97.56W
41 T9 Chicken Alaska, USA 64.04N 141.56W
106 J16 Chiclana de la Frontera Andalucía, S Spain 36.25N 6.09W
58 B11 Chiclayo Lambayeque, NW Peru 6.46S 79.46W
37 N5 Chico California, W USA 39.42N 121.51W
85 L15 Chicoa Tete, NW Mozambique 15.45S 32.25E
85 M20 Chicomo Gaza, S Mozambique 24.29S 34.15E
20 M11 Chicopee Massachusetts, NE USA 42.08N 72.34W
65 I19 Chico, Río ≈ SE Argentina
65 I21 Chico, Río ≈ S Argentina
29 W14 Chicot, Lake ◎ Arkansas, C USA
13 R7 Chicoutimi Québec, SE Canada 48.24N 71.04W
13 Q8 Chicoutimi ≈ Québec, SE Canada
85 L19 Chicualacuala Gaza, SW Mozambique 22.06S 31.42E
85 B14 Chicuma Benguela, C Angola 13.33S 14.41E
161 J21 Chidambaram Tamil Nādu, SE India 11.25N 79.42E
206 K13 Chidley, Cape headland Newfoundland and Labrador, E Canada 60.25N 64.39W
103 N24 Chiemsee ◎ SE Germany
Chiengmai see Chiang Mai
Chienrai see Chiang Rai
108 B8 Chieri Piemonte, NW Italy 45.01N 7.49E
108 F8 Chiese ≈ N Italy
109 K14 Chieti var. Teate. Abruzzo, C Italy 42.22N 14.10E
101 E19 Chièvres Hainaut, SW Belgium 50.34N 3.49E
169 S12 Chifeng var. Ulanhad. Nei Mongol Zizhiqu, N China 42.16N 118.55E
84 F13 Chifumage ≈ E Angola
84 M13 Chifunda Eastern, NE Zambia 11.57S 32.36E
151 S14 Chiganak var. Ĉiganak. Zhambyl, SE Kazakhstan 45.10N 73.55E
41 P15 Chiginagak, Mount ▲ Alaska, USA 57.10N 157.00W
Chigirin see Chyhyryn
43 P13 Chignahuapan Puebla, S Mexico 19.52N 98.03W
41 O15 Chignik Alaska, USA 56.18N 158.24W
85 M19 Chigombe ≈ S Mozambique
56 D7 Chigorodó Antioquia, NW Colombia 7.42N 76.45W
85 M19 Chigubo Gaza, S Mozambique 22.50S 33.30E
168 D6 Chihertey Bayan-Ölgiy, W Mongolia 48.10N 89.35E
Chih-fu see Yantai
Chihli see Hebei
Chihli, Gulf of see Bo Hai
42 J6 Chihuahua Chihuahua, NW Mexico 28.40N 106.06W
42 I6 Chihuahua ◈ state N Mexico
151 O15 Chiili Kzylorda, S Kazakhstan 44.09N 66.44E
28 M7 Chikaskia River ≈ Kansas/Oklahoma, C USA
161 H19 Chik Ballāpur Karnātaka, W India 13.28N 77.42E
128 G15 Chikhachevo Pskovskaya Oblast', W Russian Federation 57.17N 29.51E
161 F19 Chikmagalūr Karnātaka, W India 13.19N 75.46E
133 V7 Chikoy ≈ C Russian Federation
85 J15 Chikumbi Lusaka, C Zambia 15.16S 28.18E
84 M13 Chikwa Eastern, NE Zambia 11.39S 32.45E
Chikwana see Chikwawa
85 N15 Chikwawa var. Chikwana. Southern, S Malawi 16.01S 34.51E
161 J16 Chilakalūrupet Andhra Pradesh, E India 16.09N 80.13E
152 L14 Chilan Lebap Welaýaty, E Turkmenistan 37.57N 64.58E
Chilapa see Chilapa de Alvarez
43 P16 Chilapa de Alvarez var. Chilapa. Guerrero, S Mexico 17.36N 99.09W
161 J25 Chilaw North Western Province, W Sri Lanka 7.34N 79.49E
59 D15 Chilca Lima, W Peru 12.33S 76.44W
25 Q4 Childersburg Alabama, S USA 33.16N 86.21W
27 P4 Childress Texas, SW USA 34.25N 100.13W
65 G14 Chile off. Republic of Chile. ◆ republic SW South America
49 R10 Chile Basin undersea feature E Pacific Ocean
65 H20 Chile Chico Aisén, W Chile 46.34S 71.43W
64 I9 Chilecito La Rioja, NW Argentina 29.10S 67.30W
64 H12 Chilecito Mendoza, W Argentina 33.52S 69.03W
85 L14 Chilembwe Eastern, E Zambia 13.54S 31.38E
200 O13 Chile Rise undersea feature SE Pacific Ocean
119 N13 Chilia Braţul ≈ SE Romania
Chilia-Nouă see Kiliya
151 V15 Chilik Almaty, SE Kazakhstan 43.35N 78.17E
151 V15 Chilik ≈ SE Kazakhstan
160 O13 Chilika Lake var. Chilka Lake. ◎ E India
84 J13 Chililabombwe Copperbelt, C Zambia 12.19S 27.52E
Chi-lin see Jilin
Chilka Lake see Chilika Lake
8 H9 Chilkoot Pass pass British Columbia, W Canada 59.41N 135.14W
Chill Ala, Cuan see Killala Bay
64 G13 Chillán Bío Bío, C Chile 36.37S 72.10W
63 C22 Chillar Buenos Aires, E Argentina 37.16S 59.58W
Chill Chiaráin, Cuan see Kilkieran Bay
32 K12 Chillicothe Illinois, N USA 40.55N 89.29W
29 S3 Chillicothe Missouri, C USA 39.48N 93.33W
33 S14 Chillicothe Ohio, N USA 39.19N 82.58W
27 Q4 Chillicothe Texas, SW USA 34.15N 99.31W
8 M17 Chilliwack British Columbia, SW Canada 49.09N 121.54W
Chill Mhantáin, Ceann see Wicklow Head
Chill Mhantáin, Sléibhte see Wicklow Mountains
110 C10 Chillon Vaud, W Switzerland 46.24N 6.56E
Chil'mamedkum, Peski/Chilmämetgum see Çilmämetgum
65 F17 Chiloé, Isla de var. Isla Grande de Chiloé. island W Chile
34 H15 Chiloquin Oregon, NW USA 42.33N 121.33W

◆ Country ● Country Capital ◇ Dependent Territory ○ Dependent Territory Capital ◈ Administrative Region ✕ International Airport ▲ Mountain ▲ Mountain Range ☒ Volcano ≈ River ◎ Lake ⊠ Reservoir

Chilpancingo – Cill Rois

43 O16 **Chilpancingo** *var.* Chilpancingo de los Bravos. Guerrero, S Mexico 17.33N 99.30W
Chilpancingo de los Bravos *see* Chilpancingo
99 N21 **Chiltern Hills** *hill range* S England, UK
32 M7 **Chilton** Wisconsin, N USA 44.04N 88.10W
84 F11 **Chiluage** Lunda Sul, NE Angola 9.32S 21.48E
84 N12 **Chilumba** *prev.* Deep Bay. Northern, N Malawi 10.27S 34.12E
167 T12 **Chilung** *var.* Keelung, *Jap.* Kirun, Kirun'; *prev. Sp.* Santissima Trinidad. N Taiwan 25.10N 121.43E
85 N15 **Chilwa, Lake** *var.* Lago Chirua, Lake Shirwa. ◎ SE Malawi
178 J10 **Chi, Mae Nam** ≈ E Thailand
44 C6 **Chimaltenango** Chimaltenango, C Guatemala 14.37N 90.48W
44 A2 **Chimaltenango** *off.* Departamento de Chimaltenango. ◆ *department* S Guatemala
45 V15 **Chimán** Panamá, E Panama 8.41N 78.37W
85 M17 **Chimanimani** *prev.* Mandidzudzure, Melsetter. Manicaland, E Zimbabwe 19.48S 32.52E
101 G22 **Chimay** Hainaut, S Belgium 50.03N 4.19E
39 S10 **Chimayo** New Mexico, SW USA 36.00N 105.55W
Chimbay *see* Chimboy
58 A13 **Chimborazo** ◆ *province* C Ecuador
58 C7 **Chimborazo** ※ C Ecuador 1.29S 78.50W
58 C12 **Chimbote** Ancash, W Peru 9.04S 78.34W
152 H7 **Chimboy** *Rus.* Chimbay. Qoraqalpog'iston Respublikasi, NW Uzbekistan 43.03N 59.52E
194 H12 **Chimbu** ◆ *province* C PNG
56 F6 **Chimichagua** Cesar, N Colombia 9.19N 73.51W
Chimishliya *see* Cimişlia
Chimkent *see* Shymkent
Chimkentskaya Oblast' *see* Yuzhnyy Kazakhstan
30 I14 **Chimney Rock** *rock* Nebraska, C USA 41.40N 103.21W
85 M17 **Chimoio** Manica, C Mozambique 19.07S 33.28E
84 K11 **Chimpembe** Northern, NE Zambia 9.33S 29.30E
43 O8 **China** Nuevo León, NE Mexico 25.44N 99.09W
162 M9 **China** *off.* People's Republic of China, *Chin.* Chung-hua Jen-min Kung-ho-kuo, Zhonghua Renmin Gongheguo; *prev.* Chinese Empire. ◆ *republic* E Asia
21 Q7 **China Lake** ◎ Maine, NE USA
44 F8 **Chinameca** San Miguel, E El Salvador 13.28N 88.21W
Chi-nan/Chinan *see* Jinan
44 H9 **Chinandega** Chinandega, NW Nicaragua 12.37N 87.07W
44 H9 **Chinandega** ◆ *department* NW Nicaragua
China, People's Republic of *see* China
China, Republic of *see* Taiwan
26 J11 **Chinati Mountains** ▲▲ Texas, SW USA
Chinaz *see* Chinoz
59 E15 **Chincha Alta** Ica, SW Peru 13.25S 76.08W
9 N11 **Chinchaga** ≈ Alberta, SW Canada
Chin-chiang *see* Quanzhou
Chinchilla *see* Chinchilla de Monte Aragón
107 Q11 **Chinchilla de Monte Aragón** *var.* Chinchilla. Castilla-La Mancha, C Spain 38.55N 1.43W
56 D10 **Chinchiná** Caldas, W Colombia 4.58N 75.37W
107 O8 **Chinchón** Madrid, C Spain 40.07N 3.25W
43 Z14 **Chinchorro, Banco** *island* SE Mexico
Chin-chou/Chinchow *see* Jinzhou
23 Z5 **Chincoteague** Assateague Island, Virginia, NE USA 37.55N 75.22W
85 O17 **Chinde** Zambézia, NE Mozambique 18.34S 36.25E
169 X17 **Chin-do** *Jap.* Chin-tō. *island* SW South Korea
165 R13 **Chindu** *var.* Chuqung. Qinghai, C China 33.19N 97.08E
177 G2 **Chindwin** ≈ N Myanmar
Chinese Empire *see* China
Ch'ing Hai *see* Qinghai Hu
Chinghai *see* Qinghai
Chingildi *see* Shengeldi
150 H9 **Chingirlau** *Kaz.* Shyngghyrlaū. Zapadnyy Kazakhstan, W Kazakhstan 51.10N 53.44E
84 J13 **Chingola** Copperbelt, C Zambia 12.31S 27.52E
Ching-Tao/Ch'ing-tao *see* Qingdao
84 C13 **Chinguar** Huambo, C Angola 12.33S 16.22E
78 I7 **Chinguețți** *var.* Chinguetti. Adrar, C Mauritania 20.25N 12.24W
169 Z16 **Chinhae** *Jap.* Chinkai. S South Korea 35.06N 128.48E
177 Ff4 **Chin Hills** ▲▲ W Myanmar
85 K16 **Chinhoyi** *prev.* Sinoia. Mashonaland West, N Zimbabwe 17.19S 30.06E
Chinhsien *see* Jinzhou
41 Q14 **Chiniak, Cape** *headland* Kodiak Island, Alaska, USA 57.37N 152.10W
12 G10 **Chiniguchi Lake** ◎ Ontario, S Canada
155 U8 **Chiniot** Punjab, NE Pakistan 31.40N 73.00E
169 Y16 **Chinju** *Jap.* Shinshū. S South Korea 35.11N 128.06E
Chinkai *see* Chinhae
80 M13 **Chinko** ≈ E Central African Republic
39 O9 **Chinle** Arizona, SW USA 36.09N 109.33W
167 R13 **Chinmen Tao** *var.* Jinmen Dao, Quemoy. *island* W Taiwan
Chinnchâr *see* Shinshār
Chinnereth *see* Tiberias, Lake
171 J15 **Chino** *var.* Tino. Nagano, Honshū, S Japan 36.00N 138.10E
104 L8 **Chinon** Indre-et-Loire, C France 47.10N 0.15E
35 T7 **Chinook** Montana, NW USA 48.35N 109.13W
Chinook State *see* Washington
199 Jj3 **Chinook Trough** *undersea feature* N Pacific Ocean
38 K11 **Chino Valley** Arizona, SW USA 34.45N 112.27W
153 P10 **Chinoz** *Rus.* Chinaz. Toshkent Viloyati, E Uzbekistan 40.58N 68.46E
84 L12 **Chinsali** Northern, NE Zambia 10.33S 32.04E
177 F4 **Chin State** ◆ *state* W Myanmar
Chinsura *see* Chunchura
Chin-tō *see* Chin-do
56 E6 **Chinú** Córdoba, NW Colombia 9.07N 75.25W
101 K24 **Chiny, Forêt de** *forest* SE Belgium
85 M15 **Chioco** Tete, NW Mozambique 16.22S 32.50E
108 H8 **Chioggia** *anc.* Fossa Claudia. Veneto, NE Italy 45.13N 12.16E
116 H12 **Chionótrypa** ▲ NE Greece 41.16N 24.06E
117 L18 **Chíos** *var.* Hios, Khíos, *It.* Scio, *Turk.* Sakiz-Adasi. Chíos, E Greece 38.22N 26.07E
117 K18 **Chíos** *var.* Khíos. *island* E Greece
85 M14 **Chipata** *prev.* Fort Jameson. Eastern, E Zambia 13.40S 32.42E
85 C14 **Chipindo** Huíla, C Angola 13.53S 15.47E
25 R8 **Chipley** Florida, SE USA 30.46N 85.32W
161 D15 **Chiplūn** Mahārāshtra, W India 17.31N 73.31E
83 H22 **Chipogolo** Dodoma, C Tanzania 6.52S 36.03E
25 R8 **Chipola River** ≈ Florida, SE USA
99 L22 **Chippenham** S England, UK 51.28N 2.07W
32 J6 **Chippewa Falls** Wisconsin, N USA 44.55N 91.25W
32 J4 **Chippewa, Lake** ▣ Wisconsin, N USA
33 Q8 **Chippewa River** ≈ Michigan, N USA
32 I6 **Chippewa River** ≈ Wisconsin, N USA
Chipping Wycombe *see* High Wycombe
116 G8 **Chiprovtsi** Montana, NW Bulgaria 43.23N 22.53E
21 T4 **Chiputneticook Lakes** *lakes* Canada/USA
58 D13 **Chiquián** Ancash, W Peru 10.03S 77.11W
43 Y11 **Chiquilá** Quintana Roo, SE Mexico 21.25N 87.20W
44 E6 **Chiquimula** Chiquimula, SE Guatemala 14.45N 89.31W
44 A3 **Chiquimula** *off.* Departamento de Chiquimula. ◆ *department* SE Guatemala
44 D7 **Chiquimulilla** Santa Rosa, S Guatemala 14.06N 90.22W
56 F9 **Chiquinquirá** Boyacá, C Colombia 5.37N 73.51W
161 J17 **Chīrāla** Andhra Pradesh, E India 15.49N 80.21E
155 N4 **Chīras** Ghowr, N Afghanistan 35.15N 65.39E
158 H11 **Chirāwa** Rājasthān, N India 28.15N 75.42E
Chirchik *see* Chirchiq
153 Q9 **Chirchiq** *Rus.* Chirchik. Toshkent Viloyati, E Uzbekistan 41.30N 69.31E
153 P10 **Chirchiq** ≈ E Uzbekistan
Chire *see* Shire
85 L18 **Chiredzi** Masvingo, SE Zimbabwe 21.03S 31.40E
27 X8 **Chireno** Texas, SW USA 31.30N 94.21W
79 X7 **Chirfa** Agadez, NE Niger 21.01N 12.41E
39 O16 **Chiricahua Mountains** ▲▲ Arizona, SW USA
39 O16 **Chiricahua Peak** ▲ Arizona, SW USA 31.51N 109.17W
56 F6 **Chiriguaná** Cesar, N Colombia 9.24N 73.37W
41 P15 **Chirikof Island** *island* Alaska, USA
45 P16 **Chiriquí** *off.* Provincia de Chiriquí. ◆ *province* SW Panama
45 P17 **Chiriquí, Golfo de** *Eng.* Chiriqui Gulf. *gulf* SW Panama
45 P15 **Chiriquí Grande** Bocas del Toro, W Panama 8.55N 82.08W
Chiriqui Gulf *see* Chiriquí, Golfo de
45 P15 **Chiriquí, Laguna de** *lagoon* NW Panama
45 O16 **Chiriquí Viejo, Río** ≈ W Panama
Chiriquí, Volcán de *see* Barú, Volcán
85 N15 **Chiromo** Southern, S Malawi 16.32S 35.07E
116 J10 **Chirpan** Stara Zagora, C Bulgaria 42.13N 25.22E
45 N14 **Chirripó Atlántico, Río** ≈ E Costa Rica
Chirripó, Cerro *see* Chirripó Grande, Cerro
45 N14 **Chirripó Grande, Cerro** *var.* Cerro Chirripó. ▲ SE Costa Rica 9.31N 83.28W
45 N13 **Chirripó, Río** *var.* Río Chirripó del Pacífico. ≈ NE Costa Rica
Chirua, Lago *see* Chilwa, Lake
85 J15 **Chirundu** Southern, S Zambia 16.01S 28.52E
31 W8 **Chisago City** Minnesota, N USA 45.22N 92.53W
85 J14 **Chisamba** Central, C Zambia 14.58S 28.21E
41 T10 **Chisana** Alaska, USA 62.09N 142.07W
84 I13 **Chisasa** North Western, NW Zambia 12.09S 25.30E
10 I9 **Chisasibi** Québec, C Canada 53.45N 79.01W
44 D4 **Chisec** Alta Verapaz, C Guatemala 15.47N 90.13W
131 U5 **Chishmy** Respublika Bashkortostan, W Russian Federation 54.33N 55.21E
31 V4 **Chisholm** Minnesota, N USA 47.29N 92.52W
166 I11 **Chishui He** ≈ C China
Chisimaio/Chisimayu *see* Kismaayo
119 N10 **Chişinău** *Rus.* Kishinev. ● (Moldova) C Moldova 47.00N 28.50E
119 N10 **Chişinău** ✈ S Moldova 46.54N 28.56E
Chişinău-Criş *see* Chişineu-Criş
118 F10 **Chişineu-Criş** *Hung.* Kisjenő; *prev.* Chişinău-Criş. Arad, W Romania 46.33N 21.29E
85 K14 **Chisomo** Central, C Zambia 13.30S 30.37E
108 A8 **Chisone** ≈ NW Italy
26 K12 **Chisos Mountains** ▲▲ Texas, SW USA
155 U10 **Chistian Mandi** Punjab, E Pakistan 29.52N 72.46E
41 T10 **Chistochina** Alaska, USA 62.34N 144.39W
131 R4 **Chistopol'** Respublika Tatarstan, W Russian Federation 55.20N 50.39E
151 O8 **Chistopol'ye** Severnyy Kazakhstan, N Kazakhstan 52.37N 67.13E
126 Kk16 **Chita** Chitinskaya Oblast', S Russian Federation 52.03N 113.34E
85 B16 **Chitado** Cunene, SW Angola 17.16S 13.54E
Chitaldroog/Chitaldrug *see* Chitradurga
85 C15 **Chitanda** ≈ S Angola
Chitangwiza *see* Chitungwiza
84 F10 **Chitato** Lunda Norte, NE Angola 7.23S 20.45E
85 C14 **Chitembo** Bié, C Angola 13.33S 16.44E
41 T11 **Chitina** Alaska, USA 61.31N 144.26W
41 T11 **Chitina River** ≈ Alaska, USA
126 Kk14 **Chitinskaya Oblast'** ◆ *province* S Russian Federation
84 M11 **Chitipa** Northern, NW Malawi 9.40S 33.19E
172 Oo6 **Chitose** *var.* Titose. Hokkaidō, NE Japan 42.50N 141.39E
161 G18 **Chitradurga** *prev.* Chitaldroog, Chitaldrug. Karnātaka, W India 14.15N 76.24E
155 T3 **Chitrāl** North-West Frontier Province, NW Pakistan 35.51N 71.46E
45 S16 **Chitré** Herrera, S Panama 7.57N 80.25W
159 V16 **Chittagong** *Ben.* Châttagām. Chittagong, SE Bangladesh 22.19N 91.48E
159 U16 **Chittagong** ◆ *division* E Bangladesh
159 Q15 **Chittaranjan** West Bengal, NE India 23.52N 86.40E
158 G14 **Chittaurgarh** Rājasthān, N India 24.54N 74.42E
161 I19 **Chittoor** Andhra Pradesh, E India 13.13N 79.06E
161 G21 **Chittūr** Kerala, SW India 10.42N 76.46E
85 K16 **Chitungwiza** *prev.* Chitangwiza. Mashonaland East, NE Zimbabwe 18.00S 31.06E
64 H4 **Chíuchíu** Antofagasta, N Chile 22.13S 68.34W
84 F12 **Chiumbe** *var.* Tshiumbe. ≈ Angola/Dem. Rep. Congo
85 F15 **Chiume** Moxico, E Angola 15.08S 21.09E
84 K13 **Chiundaponde** Northern, NE Zambia 12.14S 30.40E
108 H13 **Chiusi** Toscana, C Italy 43.00N 11.56E
56 J5 **Chivacoa** Yaracuy, N Venezuela 10.10N 68.54W
108 B8 **Chivasso** Piemonte, NW Italy 45.13N 7.54E
85 L17 **Chivhu** *prev.* Enkeldoorn. Midlands, C Zimbabwe 19.01S 30.54E
63 C20 **Chivilcoy** Buenos Aires, E Argentina 34.55S 60.00W
84 N12 **Chiweta** Northern, N Malawi 10.36S 34.09E
44 D4 **Chixoy, Río** *var.* Río Negro, Río Salinas. ≈ Guatemala/Mexico
84 H13 **Chizela** North Western, NW Zambia 13.11S 24.59E
129 O5 **Chizha** Nenetskiy Avtonomnyy Okrug, NW Russian Federation 67.04N 44.19E
167 Q9 **Chizhou** *var.* Guichi. Anhui, E China 30.39N 117.29E
170 G13 **Chizu** Tottori, Honshū, SW Japan 35.15N 134.14E
Chkalov *see* Orenburg
76 J5 **Chlef** *var.* Ech Cheliff, Ech Chleff; *prev.* Al-Asnam, El Asnam, Orléansville. NW Algeria 36.10N 1.21E
117 G18 **Chlómo** ▲ C Greece 38.36N 22.57E
113 M15 **Chmielnik** Świętokrzyskie, C Poland 50.37N 20.43E
178 J11 **Chŏâm Khsant** Preăh Vihéar, N Cambodia 14.13N 104.55E
64 G10 **Choapa, Río** *var.* Choapo. ≈ C Chile
Choapas *see* Las Choapas
Choarta *see* Chwārtā
85 H17 **Chobe** ◆ *district* NE Botswana
69 T13 **Chobe** ≈ N Botswana
12 K8 **Chochocouane** ≈ Québec, SE Canada
112 E13 **Chocianów** *Ger.* Kotzenan. Dolnośląskie, SW Poland 51.23N 15.55E
56 C9 **Chocó** *off.* Departamento del Chocó. ◆ *province* W Colombia
37 X16 **Chocolate Mountains** ▲▲ California, W USA
23 W9 **Chocowinity** North Carolina, SE USA 35.33N 77.03W
29 N10 **Choctaw** Oklahoma, C USA 35.30N 97.16W
25 Q8 **Choctawhatchee Bay** *bay* Florida, SE USA
25 Q8 **Choctawhatchee River** ≈ Florida, SE USA
Chodau *see* Chodov
169 V14 **Chŏ-do** *island* SW North Korea
Chodorów *see* Khodoriv
113 A16 **Chodov** *Ger.* Chodau. Karlovarský Kraj, W Czech Republic 50.15N 12.45E
112 G10 **Chodzież** Wielkopolskie, C Poland 53.00N 16.55E
65 J15 **Choele Choel** Río Negro, C Argentina 39.18S 65.42W
85 L14 **Chofombo** Tete, NW Mozambique 14.43S 31.48E
Chohtan *see* Chauhtan
9 U14 **Choiceland** Saskatchewan, C Canada 53.28N 104.26W
195 U13 **Choiseul** *var.* Lauru. *island* NW Solomon Islands
65 M23 **Choiseul Sound** *sound* East Falkland, Falkland Islands
42 H7 **Choix** Sinaloa, C Mexico 26.43N 108.20W
112 D10 **Chojna** Zachodnio-pomorskie, W Poland 52.56N 14.25E
112 H8 **Chojnice** *Ger.* Konitz. Pomorskie, N Poland 53.41N 17.34E
113 F14 **Chojnów** *Ger.* Hainau, Haynau. Dolnośląskie, SW Poland 51.16N 15.55E
171 Ll11 **Chōkai-san** ▲ Honshū, C Japan 39.06N 140.02E
178 I11 **Chok Chai** Nakhon Ratchasima, C Thailand 14.45N 102.10E
82 I12 **Ch'ok'ē** *var.* Choke Mountains. ▲▲ NW Ethiopia
27 R13 **Choke Canyon Lake** ▣ Texas, SW USA
Choke Mountains *see* Ch'ok'ē
151 T15 **Chokpar** *Kaz.* Shoqpar. Zhambyl, S Kazakhstan 43.49N 74.25E
153 W7 **Chok-Tal** *var.* Choktal. Issyk-Kul'skaya Oblast', E Kyrgyzstan 42.37N 76.45E
Chókué *see* Chokwé
126 Mm6 **Chokurdakh** Respublika Sakha (Yakutiya), NE Russian Federation 70.38N 148.18E
85 L20 **Chokwé** *var.* Chókué. Gaza, S Mozambique 24.36S 33.06E
196 F8 **Chol** Babeldaob, N Palau
166 E8 **Chola Shan** ▲▲ C China
104 J8 **Cholet** Maine-et-Loire, NW France 47.03N 0.52W
65 H17 **Cholila** Chubut, W Argentina 42.33S 71.28W
Cholo *see* Thyolo
153 V8 **Cholpon** Narynskaya Oblast', C Kyrgyzstan 42.07N 75.25E
153 X7 **Cholpon-Ata** Issyk-Kul'skaya Oblast', E Kyrgyzstan 42.39N 77.05E
43 P14 **Cholula** Puebla, S Mexico 19.03N 98.19W
44 I8 **Choluteca** Choluteca, S Honduras 13.16N 87.11W
44 H8 **Choluteca** ◆ *department* S Honduras
44 G6 **Choluteca, Río** ≈ SW Honduras
85 I15 **Choma** Southern, S Zambia 16.47S 26.58E
159 T11 **Chomo Lhari** ▲ NW Bhutan 27.59N 89.24E
178 H7 **Chom Thong** Chiang Mai, NW Thailand 18.28N 98.41E
113 B15 **Chomutov** *Ger.* Komotau. Ústecký Kraj, NW Czech Republic 50.28N 13.24E
126 K12 **Chona** ≈ C Russian Federation
169 X15 **Ch'ŏnan** *Jap.* Tenan. W South Korea 36.51N 127.10E
178 Hh12 **Chon Buri** *prev.* Bang Pla Soi. Chon Buri, S Thailand 13.17N 100.58E
58 B6 **Chone** Manabí, W Ecuador 0.41S 80.06W
169 W13 **Ch'ŏngch'ŏn-gang** ≈ W North Korea
169 Y11 **Ch'ŏngjin** NE North Korea 41.48N 129.43E
169 W13 **Chŏngju** W North Korea 39.43N 125.13E
167 S8 **Chongming Dao** *island* E China
166 J10 **Chongqing** *var.* Ch'ung-ching, Ch'ung-ch'ing, Chungking, Pahsien, Tchongking, Yuzhou. Chongqing Shi, C China 29.34N 106.27E
Chŏngup *see* Chŏnju
167 O10 **Chongyang** *var.* Tiancheng. Hubei, C China 29.34N 114.03E
166 J15 **Chongzuo** Guangxi Zhuangzu Zizhiqu, S China 22.18N 107.23E
169 Y16 **Chŏnju** *prev.* Chŏngup, *Jap.* Seiyu. SW South Korea 35.51N 127.08E
169 Y15 **Chŏnju** *Jap.* Zenshū. SW South Korea 35.51N 127.08E
Chonnacht *see* Connaught
169 Q9 **Chonogol** Sühbaatar, E Mongolia 45.55N 115.19E
65 F19 **Chonos, Archipiélago de los** *island group* S Chile
44 K10 **Chontales** ◆ *department* S Nicaragua
178 Jj14 **Chơn Thanh** Sông Be, S Vietnam 11.25N 106.37E
164 K17 **Cho Oyu** *var.* Qowowuyag. ▲ China/Nepal 28.07N 86.37E
118 G7 **Chop** *Cz.* Čop, *Hung.* Csap. Zakarpats'ka Oblast', W Ukraine 48.25N 22.13E
23 Y3 **Choptank River** ≈ Maryland, NE USA
Chorcaí, Cuan *see* Cork Harbour
45 P15 **Chorcha, Cerro** ▲ W Panama 8.39N 82.07W
Chorku *see* Chorkŭh
153 R11 **Chorkŭh** *Rus.* Chorku. N Tajikistan 40.04N 70.30E
99 K17 **Chorley** NW England, UK 53.40N 2.37W
Chorne More *see* Black Sea
119 R5 **Chornobay** Cherkas'ka Oblast', C Ukraine 49.40N 32.20E
119 O3 **Chornobyl'** *Rus.* Chernobyl'. Kyyivs'ka Oblast', N Ukraine 51.16N 30.15E
119 R12 **Chornomors'ke** *Rus.* Chernomorskoye. Respublika Krym, S Ukraine 45.29N 32.45E
119 R4 **Chornukhy** Poltavs'ka Oblast', C Ukraine 50.15N 32.57E
Chorokh/Chorokhi *see* Çoruh Nehri
112 O9 **Choroszcz** Podlaskie, NE Poland 53.09N 22.59E
118 K6 **Chortkiv** *Rus.* Chortkov. Ternopil's'ka Oblast', W Ukraine 49.01N 25.45E
Chortkov *see* Chortkiv
Chorum *see* Çorum
112 M9 **Chorzele** Mazowieckie, C Poland 53.16N 20.53E
113 J16 **Chorzów** *Ger.* Königshütte; *prev.* Królewska Huta. Śląskie, S Poland 50.17N 18.57E
169 W12 **Ch'osan** N North Korea 40.45N 125.52E
Chośebuz *see* Cottbus
Chōsen-kaikyō *see* Korea Strait
171 Kk17 **Chōshi** *var.* Tyôsi. Chiba, Honshū, S Japan 35.43N 140.48E
65 H14 **Chos Malal** Neuquén, W Argentina 37.22S 70.16W
Chosŏn-minjujuŭi-inmin-kanghwaguk *see* North Korea
112 E9 **Choszczno** *Ger.* Arnswalde. Zachodnio-pomorskie, NW Poland 53.10N 15.24E
159 O15 **Chota Nāgpur** *plateau* N India
35 R8 **Choteau** Montana, NW USA 47.48N 112.40W
Chotqol *see* Chatkal
12 M8 **Chouart** ≈ Québec, SE Canada
78 I7 **Choûm** Adrar, C Mauritania 21.18N 12.58W
29 Q9 **Chouteau** Oklahoma, C USA 36.11N 95.20W
23 X8 **Chowan River** ≈ North Carolina, SE USA
37 Q10 **Chowchilla** California, W USA 37.06N 120.15W
169 P7 **Choybalsan** *prev.* Bayan Tumen. Dornod, E Mongolia 48.02N 114.31E
168 M9 **Choyr** Govĭ Sumber, C Mongolia 46.20N 108.21E
193 I19 **Christchurch** Canterbury, South Island, NZ 43.31S 172.39E
99 M24 **Christchurch** S England, UK 50.43N 1.45W
193 I18 **Christchurch** ✈ Canterbury, South Island, NZ 43.28S 172.33E
46 J12 **Christiana** C Jamaica 18.13N 77.28W
85 H22 **Christiana** Free State, C South Africa 27.55S 25.10E
117 J23 **Christiáni** *island* Kykládes, Greece, Aegean Sea
Christiania *see* Oslo
12 G13 **Christian Island** *island* Ontario, S Canada
203 P16 **Christian, Point** *headland* Pitcairn Island, Pitcairn Islands 25.04S 130.07E
40 M11 **Christian River** ≈ Alaska, USA
Christiansand *see* Kristiansand
23 S7 **Christiansburg** Virginia, NE USA 37.07N 80.24W
97 G23 **Christiansfeld** Sønderjylland, SW Denmark 55.21N 9.30E
Christianshåb *see* Qasigiannguit
41 X14 **Christian Sound** *inlet* Alaska, USA
47 T9 **Christiansted** Saint Croix, S Virgin Islands (US) 17.43N 64.42W
Christiansund *see* Kristiansund
27 R13 **Christine** Texas, SW USA 28.47N 98.30W
181 U7 **Christmas Island** ◇ *Australian external territory* E Indian Ocean
133 T17 **Christmas Island** *island* E Indian Ocean
Christmas Island *see* Kiritimati
199 K8 **Christmas Ridge** *undersea feature* C Pacific Ocean
32 L16 **Christopher** Illinois, N USA 37.58N 89.03W
27 P9 **Christoval** Texas, SW USA 31.09N 100.30W
113 F17 **Chrudim** Pardubický Kraj, C Czech Republic 49.58N 15.49E
117 K25 **Chrýsi** *island* SE Greece
123 Mm3 **Chrysochoú, Kólpos** *var.* Khrysokhou Bay. *bay* E Mediterranean Sea
116 I13 **Chrysoúpoli** *var.* Hrisoupoli; *prev.* Khrisoúpolis. Anatolikí Makedonía kai Thráki, NE Greece 40.58N 24.42E
113 K16 **Chrzanów** *var.* Chrzanow, *Ger.* Zaumgarten. Śląskie, S Poland 50.09N 19.18E
133 Q7 **Chu** *Kaz.* Shū. ≈ Kazakhstan/Kyrgyzstan
44 C5 **Chuacús, Sierra de** ▲▲ W Guatemala
159 S15 **Chuadanga** Khulna, W Bangladesh 23.37N 88.52E
Chuan *see* Sichuan
Ch'uan-chou *see* Quanzhou
41 O11 **Chuathbaluk** Alaska, USA 61.36N 159.14W
194 I12 **Chuave** Chimbu, W PNG 6.06S 145.06E
Chubek *see* Moskva
65 I17 **Chubut** *off.* Provincia de Chubut. ◆ *province* S Argentina
65 I17 **Chubut, Río** ≈ SE Argentina
45 V15 **Chucanti, Cerro** ▲ E Panama 8.48N 78.27W
Ch'u-chiang *see* Shaoguan
45 W15 **Chucunaque, Río** ≈ E Panama
Chudin *see* Chudzin
118 M5 **Chudniv** Zhytomyrs'ka Oblast', N Ukraine 50.02N 28.06E
128 H13 **Chudovo** Novgorodskaya Oblast', W Russian Federation 59.07N 31.42E
Chudskoye Ozero *see* Peipus, Lake
121 J18 **Chudzin** *Rus.* Chudin. Brestskaya Voblasts', SW Belarus 52.43N 26.56E
41 Q13 **Chugach Islands** *island group* Alaska, USA
41 S11 **Chugach Mountains** ▲▲ Alaska, USA
170 Ee12 **Chūgoku-sanchi** ▲▲ Honshū, SW Japan
Chugqênsumdo *see* Jigzhi
Chuguyev *see* Chuhuyiv
119 V5 **Chuhuyiv** *var.* Chuguyev. Kharkivs'ka Oblast', E Ukraine 49.51N 36.44E
63 H19 **Chuí** Rio Grande do Sul, S Brazil 33.40S 53.24W
Chuí *see* Chuy
151 S15 **Chu-Iliyskiye Gory** *Kaz.* Shū-Ile Taūlary. ▲▲ S Kazakhstan
Chukai *see* Cukai
Chukchi Avtonomnyy Okrug *see* Chukotskiy Avtonomnyy Okrug
Chukchi Peninsula *see* Chukotskiy Poluostrov
207 R6 **Chukchi Plain** *undersea feature* Arctic Ocean
207 R6 **Chukchi Plateau** *undersea feature* Arctic Ocean
207 R4 **Chukchi Sea** *Rus.* Chukotskoye More. *sea* Arctic Ocean
129 N14 **Chukhloma** Kostromskaya Oblast', NW Russian Federation 58.42N 42.39E
Chukotka *see* Chukotskiy Avtonomnyy Okrug
Chukot Range *see* Anadyrskiy Khrebet
127 Oo5 **Chukotskiy Avtonomnyy Okrug** *var.* Chukchi Avtonomnyy Okrug, Chukotka. ◆ *autonomous district* NE Russian Federation
127 Q4 **Chukotskiy, Mys** *headland* NE Russian Federation 64.15N 173.03W
127 Pp4 **Chukotskiy Poluostrov** *Eng.* Chukchi Peninsula. *peninsula* NE Russian Federation
Chukotskoye More *see* Chukchi Sea
Chukurkak *see* Chuqurqoq
Chulakkurgan *see* Sholakkorgan
37 U17 **Chula Vista** California, W USA 32.38N 117.04W
126 Ll13 **Chul'man** Respublika Sakha (Yakutiya), NE Russian Federation 56.50N 124.47E
58 B9 **Chulucanas** Piura, NW Peru 5.07S 80.10W
126 Gg14 **Chulym** Novosibirskaya Oblast', C Russian Federation 55.03N 80.53E
126 H13 **Chulym** ≈ C Russian Federation
158 K6 **Chumar** Jammu and Kashmir, N India 32.37N 78.36E
116 K9 **Chumerna** ▲ C Bulgaria 42.45N 25.58E
127 N13 **Chumikan** Khabarovskiy Kray, E Russian Federation 54.41N 135.12E
178 I9 **Chum Phae** Khon Kaen, C Thailand 16.31N 102.09E
178 Gg14 **Chumphon** *var.* Jumporn. Chumphon, SW Thailand 10.30N 99.10E
178 Hh10 **Chumsaeng** *var.* Chum Saeng. Nakhon Sawan, C Thailand 15.52N 100.20E
126 H14 **Chumysh** ≈ S Russian Federation
126 I13 **Chuna** ≈ C Russian Federation
167 R9 **Chun'an** *var.* Pailing. Zhejiang, SE China 29.37N 118.59E
167 S13 **Chunan** N Taiwan 24.44N 120.51E
169 Y14 **Ch'unch'ŏn** *Jap.* Shunsen. N South Korea 37.52N 127.48E
159 S16 **Chunchura** *prev.* Chinsura. West Bengal, NE India 22.54N 88.19E
151 W15 **Chundzha** Almaty, SE Kazakhstan 43.31N 79.28E
Ch'ung-ch'ing/Ch'ung-ching *see* Chongqing
Chung-hua Jen-min Kung-ho-kuo *see* China
169 Y15 **Ch'ungju** *Jap.* Chūshū. C South Korea 36.57N 127.49E
Chungking *see* Chongqing
167 T14 **Chungyang Shanmo** *Chin.* Taiwan Shan. ▲▲ C Taiwan
155 V9 **Chūniān** Punjab, E Pakistan 30.57N 74.01E
126 Ii14 **Chunskiy** Irkutskaya Oblast', S Russian Federation 56.10N 99.15E
126 J11 **Chunya** ≈ C Russian Federation
128 J6 **Chupa** Respublika Kareliya, NW Russian Federation 66.15N 33.02E
129 P8 **Chuprovo** Respublika Komi, NW Russian Federation 64.16N 46.27E
59 G17 **Chuquibamba** Arequipa, SW Peru 15.54S 72.37W
64 H4 **Chuquicamata** Antofagasta, N Chile 22.19S 68.55W
59 L21 **Chuquisaca** ◆ *department* S Bolivia
Chuquisaca *see* Sucre
Chuqung *see* Chindu
152 I8 **Chuqurqoq** *Rus.* Chukurkak. Qoraqalpog'iston Respublikasi, NW Uzbekistan 42.44N 61.33E
131 T2 **Chur** Udmurtskaya Respublika, NW Russian Federation 57.06N 52.57E
110 I9 **Chur** *Fr.* Coire, *It.* Coira, *Rmsch.* Cuera, Quera; *anc.* Curia Rhaetorum. Graubünden, E Switzerland 46.52N 9.31E
126 M11 **Churapcha** Respublika Sakha (Yakutiya), NE Russian Federation 61.59N 132.06E
9 V16 **Churchbridge** Saskatchewan, S Canada 50.55N 101.53W
23 O8 **Church Hill** Tennessee, S USA 36.31N 82.42W
9 X9 **Churchill** Manitoba, C Canada 58.46N 94.10W
9 X10 **Churchill** ≈ Manitoba/Saskatchewan, C Canada
11 P9 **Churchill** ≈ Newfoundland and Labrador, E Canada
9 Y9 **Churchill, Cape** *headland* Manitoba, C Canada 58.42N 93.12W
11 P9 **Churchill Falls** Newfoundland and Labrador, E Canada 53.38N 64.00W
9 S12 **Churchill Lake** ◎ Saskatchewan, C Canada
21 Q3 **Churchill Lake** ▣ Maine, NE USA
204 I5 **Churchill Peninsula** *peninsula* Antarctica
24 H8 **Church Point** Louisiana, S USA 30.24N 92.13W
31 O3 **Churchs Ferry** North Dakota, N USA 48.15N 99.12W
152 G12 **Churchuri** Ahal Welaýaty, C Turkmenistan 38.55N 59.13E
23 T5 **Churchville** Virginia, NE USA 38.13N 79.10W
158 G10 **Chūru** Rājasthān, NW India 28.18N 75.00E
56 J4 **Churuguara** Falcón, N Venezuela 10.48N 69.30W
150 J12 **Chushkakul, Gory** ▲▲ SW Kazakhstan
178 K12 **Chư Sê** Gia Lai, C Vietnam 13.38N 108.06E
Chūshū *see* Ch'ungju
39 O9 **Chuska Mountains** ▲▲ Arizona/New Mexico, SW USA
Chu, Sông *see* Sam, Nam
125 Ee11 **Chusovaya** ≈ W Russian Federation
129 V14 **Chusovoy** Permskaya Oblast', NW Russian Federation 58.17N 57.54E
153 R10 **Chust** Namangan Viloyati, E Uzbekistan 40.58N 71.12E
Chust *see* Khust
13 U6 **Chute-aux-Outardes** Québec, SE Canada 49.07N 68.25W
119 U5 **Chutove** Poltavs'ka Oblast', C Ukraine 49.45N 35.11E
201 O15 **Chuuk** *var.* Truk. ◆ *state* C Micronesia
201 P15 **Chuuk Islands** *var.* Hogoley Islands; *prev.* Truk Islands. *island group* Caroline Islands, C Micronesia
Chuvashia *see* Chavash Respubliki
Chuvashskaya Respublika *see* Chavash Respubliki
Chuwārtah *see* Chwārtā
Chu Xian/Chuxian *see* Chuzhou
166 G13 **Chuxiong** Yunnan, SW China 25.01N 101.31E
153 V7 **Chuy** Chuyskaya Oblast', N Kyrgyzstan 42.45N 75.11E
63 H19 **Chuy** *var.* Chuí. Rocha, E Uruguay 33.42S 53.27W
126 K12 **Chuya** Respublika Sakha (Yakutiya), NE Russian Federation 59.30N 112.26E
Chüy Oblasty *see* Chuyskaya Oblast'
153 U8 **Chuyskaya Oblast'** *Kir.* Chüy Oblasty. ◆ *province* N Kyrgyzstan
167 Q7 **Chuzhou** *var.* Chuxian, Chu Xian. Anhui, E China 32.21N 118.15E
145 U3 **Chwārtā** *var.* Choarta, Chuwārtah. NE Iraq 35.10N 45.58E
121 N16 **Chyhirynskaye Vodaskhovishcha** ▣ E Belarus
119 R6 **Chyhyryn** *Rus.* Chigirin. Cherkas'ka Oblast', N Ukraine 49.03N 32.40E
Chyrvonaya Slabada *see* Krasnaya Slabada
121 L19 **Chyrvonaye, Vozyera** *Rus.* Ozero Chervonoye. ◎ SE Belarus
119 N11 **Ciadîr-Lunga** *var.* Ceadâr-Lunga, *Rus.* Chadyr-Lunga. S Moldova 46.03N 28.50E
174 K15 **Ciamis** *prev.* Tjiamis. Jawa, C Indonesia 7.19S 108.21E
109 I16 **Ciampino** ✈ Lazio, C Italy 41.48N 12.36W
174 J14 **Cianjur** *prev.* Tjiandjoer. Jawa, C Indonesia 6.49S 107.09E
62 H10 **Cianorte** Paraná, S Brazil 23.37S 52.38W
Ciarraí *see* Kerry
114 N13 **Ćićevac** Serbia, E Serbia and Montenegro (Yugoslavia) 43.44N 21.25E
197 K14 **Cicia** *prev.* Thithia. *island* Lau Group, E Fiji
107 P4 **Cidacos** ≈ N Spain
142 I10 **Cide** Kastamonu, N Turkey 41.52N 33.01E
112 L10 **Ciechanów** *prev.* Zichenau. Mazowieckie, C Poland 52.53N 20.36E
112 O10 **Ciechanowiec** *Ger.* Rudelstadt. Podlaskie, E Poland 52.43N 22.30E
112 J10 **Ciechocinek** Kujawskio-pomorskie, C Poland 52.53N 18.48E
46 F6 **Ciego de Ávila** Ciego de Ávila, C Cuba 21.50N 78.44W
56 F4 **Ciénaga** Magdalena, N Colombia 10.58N 74.15W
56 E6 **Ciénaga de Oro** Córdoba, NW Colombia 8.52N 75.37W
46 E5 **Cienfuegos** Cienfuegos, C Cuba 22.10N 80.27W
106 F4 **Cíes, Illas** *island group* NW Spain
113 P16 **Cieszanów** Podkarpackie, SE Poland 50.15N 23.09E
113 J17 **Cieszyn** *Cz.* Těšín, *Ger.* Teschen. Śląskie, S Poland 49.45N 18.37E
107 R12 **Cieza** Murcia, SE Spain 38.13N 1.25W
142 F13 **Çifteler** Eskişehir, W Turkey 39.25N 31.00E
107 P7 **Cifuentes** Castilla-La Mancha, C Spain 40.46N 2.37W
Çiganak *see* Chiganak
107 P9 **Cigüela** ≈ C Spain
142 H14 **Cihanbeyli** Konya, C Turkey 38.40N 32.55E
142 H14 **Cihanbeyli Yaylası** *plateau* C Turkey
106 L10 **Cíjara, Embalse de** ▣ C Spain
174 K15 **Cikalong** Jawa, S Indonesia 7.46S 108.13E
174 Ii14 **Cikawung** Jawa, S Indonesia 6.49S 105.29E
197 K12 **Cikobia** *prev.* Thikombia. *island* N Fiji
174 K15 **Cilacap** *prev.* Tjilatjap. Jawa, C Indonesia 7.44S 109.00E
181 O16 **Cilaos** C Réunion 21.07S 55.28E
143 S11 **Çıldır** Ardahan, NE Turkey 41.07N 43.07E
143 S11 **Çıldır Gölü** ◎ NE Turkey
174 K14 **Ciledug** *prev.* Tjiledoeg. Jawa, SW Indonesia 6.55S 108.43E
166 M10 **Cili** Hunan, S China 29.27N 111.03E
124 R12 **Cilicia Trough** *undersea feature* E Mediterranean Sea
Cill Airne *see* Killarney
Cill Chainnigh *see* Kilkenny
Cill Chaoi *see* Kilkee
Cill Choca *see* Kilcock
Cill Dara *see* Kildare
107 N3 **Cilleruelo de Bezana** Castilla-León, N Spain 42.58N 3.50W
Cilli *see* Celje
Cill Mhantáin *see* Wicklow
Cill Rois *see* Kilrush

◆ Country ● Country Capital ◇ Dependent Territory ○ Dependent Territory Capital ◆ Administrative Region ✈ International Airport ▲ Mountain ▲▲ Mountain Range ※ Volcano ≈ River ◎ Lake ▣ Reservoir

Çilmämmetgum – Coleambally

152 C11 Çilmämmetgum Rus. Peski Chil'mamedkum, Turkm. Chilmämmetgum. desert W Turkmenistan
143 Z11 Çiloy Adası Rus. Ostrov Zhiloy. island E Azerbaijan
28 J6 Cimarron Kansas, C USA 37.49N 100.20W
39 T9 Cimarron New Mexico, SW USA 36.30N 104.55W
28 M9 Cimarron River Kansas/Oklahoma, C USA
119 N11 Cimişlia Rus. Chimishliya. S Moldova 46.31N 28.45E
Cîmpia Turzii see Câmpia Turzii
Cîmpina see Câmpina
Cîmpulung see Câmpulung
Cîmpulung Moldovenesc see Câmpulung Moldovenesc
143 P15 Çınar Diyarbakır, SE Turkey 37.45N 40.22E
56 J8 Cinaruco, Río Colombia/Venezuela
Cina Selatan, Laut see South China Sea
107 T5 Cinca NE Spain
114 G13 Cincar ▲ SW Bosnia and Herzegovina 43.55N 17.05E
33 Q15 Cincinnati Ohio, N USA 39.04N 84.33W
23 M4 Cincinnati ✕ Kentucky, S USA 39.03N 84.39W
Cinco de Outubro see Xá-Muteba
142 C15 Çine Aydın, SW Turkey 37.37N 28.03E
101 J21 Ciney Namur, SE Belgium 50.16N 5.06E
106 H6 Cinfães Viseu, N Portugal 41.04N 8.06W
108 J12 Cingoli Marche, C Italy 43.25N 13.09E
43 U16 Cintalapa var. Cintalapa de Figueroa. Chiapas, SE Mexico 16.42N 93.40W
Cintalapa de Figueroa see Cintalapa
105 X14 Cinto, Monte ▲ Corse, France, C Mediterranean Sea 42.22N 8.57E
Cintra see Sintra
107 Q5 Cintruénigo Navarra, N Spain 42.04N 1.49W
Cionn tSáile see Kinsale
118 K13 Ciorani Prahova, SE Romania 44.48N 26.25E
115 E14 Čiovo It. Bua. island S Croatia
174 J14 Cipanas Jawa, S Indonesia
Cipiúr see Kippure
65 I15 Cipolletti Río Negro, C Argentina 38.55S 68.00W
123 L8 Circeo, Capo headland C Italy 41.15N 13.03E
41 S8 Circle var. Circle City. Alaska, USA 65.51N 144.04W
35 X8 Circle Montana, NW USA 47.25N 105.32W
Circle City see Circle
33 S14 Circleville Ohio, N USA 39.36N 82.57W
38 K6 Circleville Utah, W USA 38.10N 112.16W
174 K14 Cirebon prev. Tjirebon. Jawa, S Indonesia 6.46S 108.33E
99 L21 Cirencester anc. Corinium, Corinium Dobunorum. C England, UK 51.43N 1.58W
Cirkvenica see Crikvenica
109 O20 Ciro Calabria, SW Italy 39.22N 17.02E
109 O20 Ciro Marina Calabria, S Italy 39.21N 17.07E
104 K14 Ciron SW France
Cirquenizza see Crikvenica
27 R7 Cisco Texas, SW USA 32.23N 98.58W
118 I12 Cisnădie Ger. Heltau, Hung. Nagydisznód. Sibiu, SW Romania 45.42N 24.08E
65 G18 Cisnes, Río S Chile
27 T11 Cistern Texas, SW USA 29.46N 97.12W
106 L3 Cistierna Castilla-León, N Spain 42.46N 5.07W
174 Ii14 Citeureup Jawa, S Indonesia 6.34S 105.41E
Citharista see la Ciotat
Citlaltépetl see Orizaba, Volcán Pico de
57 X10 Citron NW French Guiana 4.49N 53.56W
25 N7 Citronelle Alabama, S USA 31.05N 88.13W
37 O7 Citrus Heights California, W USA 38.42N 121.18W
108 H7 Cittadella Veneto, NE Italy 45.37N 11.46E
108 H13 Città della Pieve Umbria, C Italy 42.57N 12.01E
108 H12 Città di Castello Umbria, C Italy 43.27N 12.13E
109 I14 Cittaducale Lazio, C Italy 42.24N 12.55E
109 N22 Cittanova Calabria, SW Italy 38.21N 16.04E
Cittavecchia see Starigrad
118 G10 Ciucea Hung. Csucsa. Cluj, NW Romania 46.57N 22.51E
118 M13 Ciucurova Tulcea, SE Romania 44.57N 28.24E
Ciudad Acuña see Villa Acuña
43 N15 Ciudad Altamirano Guerrero, S Mexico 18.22N 100.39W
44 G7 Ciudad Barrios San Miguel, NE El Salvador 13.46N 88.13W
56 I7 Ciudad Bolívar Barinas, NW Venezuela 8.23N 70.34W
57 N7 Ciudad Bolívar prev. Angostura. Bolívar, E Venezuela 8.07N 63.31W
42 K6 Ciudad Camargo Chihuahua, N Mexico 27.42N 105.10W
42 E8 Ciudad Constitución Baja California Sur, W Mexico 25.06N 111.42W
Ciudad Cortés see Cortés
43 V17 Ciudad Cuauhtémoc Chiapas, SE Mexico 15.23N 91.11W
44 J9 Ciudad Darío var. Dario. Matagalpa, W Nicaragua 12.42N 86.06W
Ciudad de Dolores Hidalgo see Dolores Hidalgo
44 C6 Ciudad de Guatemala Eng. Guatemala City; prev. Santiago de los Caballeros. ● (Guatemala) Guatemala, C Guatemala 14.37N 90.29W
Ciudad del Carmen see Carmen
64 Q6 Ciudad del Este prev. Cuidad Presidente Stroessner, Presidente Stroessner, Puerto Presidente Stroessner. Alto Paraná, SE Paraguay 25.34S 54.40W
64 K5 Ciudad de Libertador General San Martín var. Libertador General San Martín. Jujuy, C Argentina 23.49S 64.45W
Ciudad Delicias see Delicias
43 O11 Ciudad del Maíz San Luis Potosí, C Mexico 22.25N 99.36W
Ciudad de México see México
56 J7 Ciudad de Nutrias Barinas, NW Venezuela 8.03N 69.17W
Ciudad de Panamá see Panamá
57 P7 Ciudad Guayana prev. San Tomé de Guayana, Santo Tomé de Guayana. Bolívar, NE Venezuela 8.22N 62.37W
42 K14 Ciudad Guzmán Jalisco, SW Mexico 19.40N 103.30W
43 V17 Ciudad Hidalgo Chiapas, SE Mexico 14.45N 92.13W
43 N14 Ciudad Hidalgo Michoacán de Ocampo, SW Mexico 19.40N 100.34W
42 J3 Ciudad Juárez Chihuahua, N Mexico 31.39N 106.25W
42 L8 Ciudad Lerdo Durango, C Mexico 25.34N 103.30W
43 Q11 Ciudad Madero var. Villa Cecilia. Tamaulipas, C Mexico 22.18N 97.55W
43 P11 Ciudad Mante Tamaulipas, C Mexico 22.43N 99.01W
44 F2 Ciudad Melchor de Mencos var. Melchor de Mencos. Petén, NE Guatemala 17.03N 89.12W
43 P8 Ciudad Miguel Alemán Tamaulipas, C Mexico 26.19N 98.55W
Ciudad Mutis see Bahía Solano
42 G6 Ciudad Obregón Sonora, NW Mexico 27.32N 109.52W
56 I5 Ciudad Ojeda Zulia, NW Venezuela 10.09N 71.15W
57 P7 Ciudad Piar Bolívar, E Venezuela 7.25N 63.19W
Ciudad Porfirio Díaz see Piedras Negras
Ciudad Quesada see Quesada
107 N11 Ciudad Real Castilla-La Mancha, C Spain 38.58N 3.55W
107 N11 Ciudad Real ◆ province Castilla-La Mancha, C Spain
106 J7 Ciudad-Rodrigo Castilla-León, N Spain 40.36N 6.33W
44 A6 Ciudad Tecún Umán San Marcos, SW Guatemala 14.40N 92.06W
Ciudad Trujillo see Santo Domingo
43 P12 Ciudad Valles San Luis Potosí, C Mexico 21.58N 99.00W
43 O10 Ciudad Victoria Tamaulipas, C Mexico 23.43N 99.07W
44 C6 Ciudad Vieja Suchitepéquez, S Guatemala 14.30N 90.46W
118 L8 Ciuhuru var. Reuţel. N Moldova
Ciutadella see Ciutadella de Menorca
107 Z8 Ciutadella de Menorca var. Ciutadella. Menorca, Spain, W Mediterranean Sea 40.00N 3.50E
142 L11 Civa Burnu headland N Turkey 41.22N 36.39E
108 J7 Cividale del Friuli Friuli-Venezia Giulia, NE Italy 46.06N 13.25E
109 H14 Civita Castellana Lazio, C Italy 42.16N 12.24E
108 J12 Civitanova Marche Marche, C Italy 43.18N 13.40E
Civitas Altae Ripae see Brzeg
Civitas Carnutum see Chartres
Civitas Eburovicum see Évreux
Civitas Nemetum see Speyer
109 G15 Civitavecchia anc. Centum Cellae, Trajani Portus. Lazio, C Italy 42.04N 11.46E
104 L10 Civray Vienne, W France 46.10N 0.18E
142 E14 Çivril Denizli, W Turkey 38.18N 29.43E
167 O5 Cixian Hebei, E China 36.19N 114.22E
143 R16 Cizre Şırnak, SE Turkey 37.21N 42.10E
Clacton see Clacton-on-Sea
99 Q21 Clacton-on-Sea var. Clacton. E England, UK 51.48N 1.09E
24 H5 Claiborne, Lake ⊠ Louisiana, S USA
104 L10 Clain W France
9 Q11 Claire, Lake ◎ Alberta, C Canada
27 O6 Clairemont Texas, SW USA 33.09N 100.45W
36 M3 Clair Engle Lake ⊠ California, W USA
20 B15 Clairton Pennsylvania, NE USA 40.17N 79.52W
34 F7 Clallam Bay Washington, NW USA 48.13N 124.16W
105 P8 Clamecy Nièvre, C France 47.28N 3.30E
25 P5 Clanton Alabama, S USA 32.50N 86.37W
63 D17 Clara Entre Ríos, E Argentina 31.49S 58.48W
99 E18 Clara Ir. Clóirtheach. C Ireland 53.19N 7.36W
31 T9 Clara City Minnesota, N USA 44.57N 95.22W
63 D23 Claraz Buenos Aires, E Argentina 37.55S 59.18W
Clár Chlainne Mhuiris see Claremorris
190 I8 Clare South Australia 33.49S 138.35E
99 C19 Clare Ir. An Clár. cultural region W Ireland
99 C18 Clare W Ireland
99 A16 Clare Island Ir. Cliara. island W Ireland
46 J12 Claremont C Jamaica 18.22N 77.10W
31 W10 Claremont Minnesota, N USA 44.01N 93.00W
21 N9 Claremont New Hampshire, NE USA 43.21N 72.18W
29 Q9 Claremore Oklahoma, C USA 36.18N 95.37W
99 C17 Claremorris Ir. Clár Chlainne Mhuiris. W Ireland 53.47N 9.00W
193 J16 Clarence Canterbury, South Island, NZ 42.07S 173.54E
193 J16 Clarence South Island, NZ
67 F15 Clarence Bay bay Ascension Island, C Atlantic Ocean
65 H25 Clarence, Isla island S Chile
204 H2 Clarence Island island South Shetland Islands, Antarctica
191 V5 Clarence River New South Wales, SE Australia
46 J5 Clarence Town Long Island, C Bahamas 23.03N 74.57W
29 W12 Clarendon Arkansas, C USA 34.41N 91.18W
27 O3 Clarendon Texas, SW USA 34.56N 100.53W
11 U12 Clarenville Newfoundland and Labrador, SE Canada 48.12N 54.01W
9 Q17 Claresholm Alberta, SW Canada 50.01N 113.33W
31 T16 Clarinda Iowa, C USA 40.44N 95.02W
57 N5 Clarines Anzoátegui, NE Venezuela 9.55N 65.10W
31 V12 Clarion Iowa, C USA 42.43N 93.43W
20 C13 Clarion Pennsylvania, NE USA 41.11N 79.21W
199 L7 Clarion Fracture Zone tectonic feature NE Pacific Ocean
20 D13 Clarion River Pennsylvania, NE USA
31 Q9 Clark South Dakota, N USA 44.50N 97.44W
38 K11 Clarkdale Arizona, SW USA 34.46N 112.03W
13 W4 Clarke City Québec, SE Canada 50.09N 66.36W
191 Q15 Clarke Island island Furneaux Group, Tasmania, SE Australia
189 X6 Clarke Range ▲ Queensland, E Australia
25 T2 Clarkesville Georgia, SE USA 34.36N 83.31W
31 S9 Clarkfield Minnesota, N USA 44.48N 95.49W
35 N7 Clark Fork Idaho, NW USA 48.06N 116.10W
35 N8 Clark Fork Idaho/Montana, NW USA
41 Q12 Clark, Lake ◎ Alaska, USA
37 W12 Clark Mountain ▲ California, W USA 35.30N 115.34W
39 S3 Clark Peak ▲ Colorado, C USA 40.36N 105.57W
12 D14 Clark, Point headland Ontario, S Canada 44.04N 81.45W
23 S3 Clarksburg West Virginia, NE USA 39.16N 80.19W
24 K2 Clarksdale Mississippi, S USA 34.12N 90.34W
35 U12 Clarks Fork Yellowstone River Montana/Wyoming, NW USA
23 P13 Clark Hill Lake var. J.Storm Thurmond Reservoir. ⊠ Georgia/South Carolina, SE USA
31 R14 Clarkson Nebraska, C USA 41.42N 97.07W
41 O13 Clarks Point Alaska, USA 58.50N 158.33W
20 I13 Clarks Summit Pennsylvania, NE USA 41.29N 75.42W
34 M10 Clarkston Washington, NW USA 46.25N 117.02W
46 J12 Clark's Town C Jamaica 18.25N 77.32W
29 T10 Clarksville Arkansas, C USA 35.28N 93.28W
33 P13 Clarksville Indiana, N USA 40.01N 85.54W
22 I8 Clarksville Tennessee, S USA 36.31N 87.21W
27 W5 Clarksville Texas, SW USA 33.36N 95.03W
23 U8 Clarksville Virginia, NE USA 36.36N 78.36W
23 U11 Clarkton North Carolina, SE USA 34.28N 78.39W
63 C24 Claromecó var. Balneario Claromecó. Buenos Aires, E Argentina 38.51S 60.01W
27 N3 Claude Texas, SW USA 35.06N 101.21W
Clausentum see Southampton
179 P7 Claveria Luzon, N Philippines 18.36N 121.04E
101 J20 Clavier Liège, E Belgium 50.27N 5.21E
25 W6 Claxton Georgia, SE USA 32.09N 81.54W
23 R4 Clay West Virginia, NE USA 38.28N 81.04W
29 N3 Clay Center Kansas, C USA 39.22N 97.08W
31 P16 Clay Center Nebraska, C USA 40.31N 98.03W
23 Y2 Claymont Delaware, NE USA 39.48N 75.27W
38 M14 Claypool Arizona, SW USA 33.24N 110.50W
25 R6 Clayton Alabama, S USA 31.52N 85.27W
25 T1 Clayton Georgia, SE USA 34.52N 83.24W
24 J5 Clayton Louisiana, S USA 31.43N 91.32W
29 X5 Clayton Missouri, C USA 38.39N 90.21W
39 V9 Clayton New Mexico, SW USA 36.27N 103.12W
23 V9 Clayton North Carolina, SE USA 35.39N 78.27W
29 Q12 Clayton Oklahoma, C USA 34.35N 95.21W
190 I4 Clayton River seasonal river South Australia
23 R7 Claytor Lake ⊠ Virginia, NE USA
29 P13 Clear Boggy Creek Oklahoma, C USA
99 B22 Clear, Cape var. The Bill of Cape Clear, Ir. Ceann Cléire. headland SW Ireland 51.25N 9.31W
38 M12 Clear Creek Arizona, SW USA
41 S12 Cleare, Cape headland Montague Island, Alaska, USA 59.46N 147.54W
20 E13 Clearfield Pennsylvania, NE USA 41.01N 78.27W
38 L2 Clearfield Utah, W USA 41.06N 112.03W
27 Q6 Clear Fork Brazos River Texas, SW USA
33 T12 Clear Fork Reservoir ⊠ Ohio, N USA
9 N12 Clear Hills ▲ Alberta, SW Canada
31 V12 Clear Lake Iowa, C USA 43.07N 93.27W
31 R9 Clear Lake South Dakota, N USA 44.45N 96.40W
36 M6 Clear Lake ◎ California, W USA
24 G6 Clear Lake ⊠ Louisiana, S USA
36 M6 Clearlake California, W USA 38.57N 122.38W
37 P1 Clear Lake Reservoir ⊠ California, W USA
9 N16 Clearwater British Columbia, SW Canada 51.37N 120.01W
25 U12 Clearwater Florida, SE USA 27.58N 82.46W
9 R12 Clearwater Alberta/Saskatchewan, C Canada
29 W7 Clearwater Lake ⊠ Missouri, C USA
35 N10 Clearwater Mountains ▲ Idaho, NW USA
35 N10 Clearwater River Idaho, NW USA
31 S4 Clearwater River Minnesota, N USA
27 T7 Cleburne Texas, SW USA 32.21N 97.23W
34 I9 Cle Elum Washington, NW USA 47.12N 120.56W
99 O17 Cleethorpes E England, UK 53.34N 0.01W
Cléire, Ceann see Clear, Cape
23 O11 Clemson South Carolina, SE USA 34.40N 82.50W
23 Q4 Clendenin West Virginia, NE USA 38.29N 81.21W
28 M9 Cleo Springs Oklahoma, C USA 36.25N 98.25W
Clerk Island see Onotoa
189 X8 Clermont Queensland, E Australia 22.46S 147.40E
13 S8 Clermont Québec, SE Canada 47.41N 70.15W
105 O4 Clermont Oise, N France 49.22N 2.25E
31 X12 Clermont Iowa, C USA 43.00N 91.39W
105 P11 Clermont-Ferrand Puy-de-Dôme, C France 45.46N 3.04E
105 Q15 Clermont-l'Hérault Hérault, S France 43.37N 3.25E
101 M22 Clervaux Diekirch, N Luxembourg 50.03N 6.01E
108 G6 Cles Trentino-Alto Adige, N Italy 46.22N 11.04E
190 H8 Cleve South Australia 33.43S 136.30E
Cleve see Kleve
25 T2 Cleveland Georgia, SE USA 34.36N 83.45W
24 K3 Cleveland Mississippi, S USA 33.45N 90.43W
33 T11 Cleveland Ohio, N USA 41.30N 81.42W
29 O9 Cleveland Oklahoma, C USA 36.18N 96.27W
22 L10 Cleveland Tennessee, S USA 35.09N 84.52W
27 W10 Cleveland Texas, SW USA 30.19N 95.06W
33 N7 Cleveland Wisconsin, N USA 43.58N 87.45W
33 O4 Cleveland Cliffs Basin ◎ Michigan, N USA
33 U11 Cleveland Heights Ohio, N USA 41.31N 81.33W
35 P6 Cleveland, Mount ▲ Montana, NW USA 48.55N 113.51W
Cleves see Kleve
99 B16 Clew Bay Ir. Cuan Mó. inlet W Ireland
25 Y14 Clewiston Florida, SE USA 26.45N 80.55W
Cliara see Clare Island
99 A17 Clifden Ir. An Clochán. W Ireland 53.28N 10.13W
39 O14 Clifton Arizona, SW USA 33.03N 109.18W
20 K14 Clifton New Jersey, NE USA 40.50N 74.28W
27 S8 Clifton Texas, SW USA 31.43N 97.36W
23 S6 Clifton Forge Virginia, NE USA 37.49N 79.49W
190 I1 Clifton Hills South Australia 27.03S 138.49E
9 S17 Climax Saskatchewan, S Canada 49.12N 108.22W
23 O8 Clinch River Tennessee/Virginia, S USA
27 P12 Cline Texas, SW USA 29.14N 100.07W
23 N10 Clingmans Dome ▲ North Carolina/Tennessee, SE USA 35.33N 83.30W
26 H8 Clint Texas, SW USA 31.35N 106.13W
8 M16 Clinton British Columbia, SW Canada 51.06N 121.31W
12 E15 Clinton Ontario, S Canada 43.37N 81.31W
29 U10 Clinton Arkansas, C USA 35.36N 92.26W
32 L10 Clinton Illinois, N USA 40.09N 88.57W
31 Z14 Clinton Iowa, C USA 41.50N 90.11W
22 G7 Clinton Kentucky, S USA 36.39N 89.00W
24 J8 Clinton Louisiana, S USA 30.52N 91.01W
21 N11 Clinton Massachusetts, NE USA 42.25N 71.40W
33 R10 Clinton Michigan, N USA 42.04N 83.58W
24 K5 Clinton Mississippi, S USA 32.22N 90.22W
29 S5 Clinton Missouri, C USA 38.22N 93.51W
23 V10 Clinton North Carolina, SE USA 35.00N 78.19W
28 L10 Clinton Oklahoma, C USA 35.31N 98.58W
23 Q12 Clinton South Carolina, SE USA 34.28N 81.52W
23 M9 Clinton Tennessee, S USA 36.06N 84.07W
15 J7 Clinton-Colden Lake ◎ Northwest Territories, NW Canada
8 H5 Clinton Creek Yukon Territory, NW Canada 64.24N 140.35W
32 L13 Clinton Lake ⊠ Illinois, N USA
29 Q4 Clinton Lake ⊠ Kansas, N USA
23 T11 Clio South Carolina, SE USA 34.34N 79.33W
199 Ll7 Clipperton Fracture Zone tectonic feature E Pacific Ocean
200 N7 Clipperton Island ◇ French dependency of French Polynesia E Pacific Ocean
48 K6 Clipperton Island island E Pacific Ocean
(0) F16 Clipperton Seamounts undersea feature E Pacific Ocean
104 J8 Clisson Loire-Atlantique, NW France 47.06N 1.19W
64 K7 Clodomira Santiago del Estero, N Argentina 27.33S 64.07W
Cloich na Coillte see Clonakilty
Clóirtheach see Clara
99 C21 Clonakilty Ir. Cloich na Coillte. SW Ireland 51.37N 8.54W
189 T6 Cloncurry Queensland, C Australia 20.44S 140.30E
99 F18 Clondalkin Ir. Cluain Dolcáin. E Ireland 53.19N 6.24W
99 E16 Clones Ir. Cluain Eois. N Ireland 54.10N 7.13W
99 D20 Clonmel Ir. Cluain Meala. S Ireland 52.21N 7.42W
102 G11 Cloppenburg Niedersachsen, NW Germany 52.51N 8.03E
31 W6 Cloquet Minnesota, N USA 46.43N 92.27W
39 S14 Cloudcroft New Mexico, SW USA 32.57N 105.44W
35 W12 Cloud Peak ▲ Wyoming, C USA 44.22N 107.10W
193 K14 Cloudy Bay inlet South Island, NZ
23 R10 Clover South Carolina, SE USA 35.06N 81.13W
36 M6 Cloverdale California, W USA 38.49N 123.03W
22 J5 Cloverport Kentucky, S USA 37.50N 86.37W
37 Q10 Clovis California, W USA 36.48N 119.43W
39 W12 Clovis New Mexico, SW USA 34.22N 103.12W
12 K13 Cloyne Ontario, SE Canada 44.48N 77.09W
Cluain Dolcáin see Clondalkin
Cluain Eois see Clones
Cluainín see Manorhamilton
Cluain Meala see Clonmel
118 H10 Cluj ◆ county NW Romania
Cluj see Cluj-Napoca
118 H10 Cluj-Napoca Ger. Klausenburg, Hung. Kolozsvár; prev. Cluj. Cluj, NW Romania 46.47N 23.36E
Clunia see Feldkirch
105 R10 Cluny Saône-et-Loire, C France 46.25N 4.38E
105 T10 Cluses Haute-Savoie, E France 46.04N 6.34E
108 E7 Clusone Lombardia, N Italy 45.56N 10.00E
27 W12 Clute Texas, SW USA 29.01N 95.24W
193 D23 Clutha South Island, NZ
99 J18 Clwyd cultural region NE Wales, UK
193 D22 Clyde Otago, South Island, NZ 45.12S 169.21E
29 N3 Clyde Kansas, C USA 39.35N 97.24W
31 P2 Clyde North Dakota, N USA 48.44N 98.51W
33 S11 Clyde Ohio, N USA 41.18N 82.58W
27 Q7 Clyde Texas, SW USA 32.24N 99.29W
12 K13 Clyde Ontario, SE Canada
98 J13 Clyde W Scotland, UK
98 H12 Clydebank S Scotland, UK 55.54N 4.24W
98 H13 Clyde, Firth of inlet S Scotland, UK
35 S11 Clyde Park Montana, NW USA 45.56N 110.39W
106 I7 Côa, Rio N Portugal
37 W16 Coachella California, W USA 33.38N 116.10W
37 W16 Coachella Canal canal California, W USA
42 I9 Coacoyole Durango, C Mexico 24.30N 106.33W
27 N7 Coahoma Texas, SW USA 32.18N 101.18W
8 K8 Coal Yukon Territory, NW Canada
42 L14 Coalcomán var. Coalcomán de Matamoros. Michoacán de Ocampo, S Mexico 18.49N 103.13W
Coalcomán de Matamoros see Coalcomán
41 T8 Coal Creek Alaska, USA 65.21N 143.08W
9 Q17 Coaldale Alberta, SW Canada 49.42N 112.36W
29 P12 Coalgate Oklahoma, C USA 34.33N 96.14W
37 P11 Coalinga California, W USA 36.08N 120.21W
8 L9 Coal River British Columbia, W Canada 59.38N 126.45W
23 Q6 Coal River West Virginia, NE USA
38 M2 Coalville Utah, W USA 40.56N 111.22W
60 E13 Coari Amazonas, N Brazil 4.07S 63.07W
61 D14 Coari, Rio NW Brazil
83 J20 Coast ◆ province SE Kenya
Coast see Pwani
14 F11 Coast Mountains Fr. Chaîne Côtière. ▲ Canada/USA
17 Ff3 Coast Ranges ▲ W USA
98 I12 Coatbridge S Scotland, UK 55.52N 4.01W
44 B6 Coatepeque Quezaltenango, SW Guatemala 14.42N 91.49W
20 H16 Coatesville Pennsylvania, NE USA 39.58N 75.47W
13 Q13 Coaticook Québec, SE Canada 45.07N 71.46W
15 Mm6 Coats Island island Nunavut, NE Canada
205 O4 Coats Land physical region Antarctica
43 T14 Coatzacoalcos var. Quetzalcoalco; prev. Puerto México. Veracruz-Llave, E Mexico 18.06N 94.25W
43 S14 Coatzacoalcos, Río SE Mexico
118 M15 Cobadin Constanța, SW Romania 44.02N 28.29E
12 H9 Cobalt Ontario, S Canada 47.23N 79.40W
44 D5 Cobán Alta Verapaz, C Guatemala 15.28N 90.19W
191 O6 Cobar New South Wales, SE Australia 31.31S 145.50E
20 F12 Cobb Hill ▲ Pennsylvania, NE USA 41.52N 77.52W
(0) D8 Cobb Seamount undersea feature E Pacific Ocean 47.00N 131.00W
12 K12 Cobden Ontario, SE Canada 45.36N 76.54W
99 D21 Cobh Ir. An Cóbh; prev. Cove of Cork, Queenstown. SW Ireland 51.51N 8.16W
59 J14 Cobija Pando, NW Bolivia 11.04S 68.49W
Coblence/Coblenz see Koblenz
20 J10 Cobleskill New York, NE USA 42.40N 74.29W
12 I15 Cobourg Ontario, SE Canada 43.57N 78.06W
189 P1 Cobourg Peninsula headland Northern Territory, N Australia 11.27S 132.33E
191 O10 Cobram Victoria, SE Australia 35.56S 145.36E
84 N13 Cóbuè Niassa, N Mozambique 12.08S 34.46E
103 K18 Coburg Bayern, SE Germany 50.16N 10.58E
21 Q5 Coburn Mountain ▲ Maine, NE USA 45.28N 70.07W
Coca see Puerto Francisco de Orellana
59 H18 Cocachacra Arequipa, SW Peru 17.09S 71.46W
61 J17 Cocalinho Mato Grosso, W Brazil 14.22S 51.00W
Cocanada see Kākināda
107 S11 Cocentaina País Valenciano, E Spain 38.44N 0.27W
59 L18 Cochabamba hist. Oropeza. Cochabamba, C Bolivia 17.23S 66.10W
59 K18 Cochabamba ◆ department C Bolivia
59 L18 Cochabamba, Cordillera de ▲ C Bolivia
103 E18 Cochem Rheinland-Pfalz, W Germany 50.09N 7.09E
39 R6 Cochetopa Hills ▲ Colorado, C USA
161 G22 Cochin var. Kochi. Kerala, SW India 9.55N 76.15E
46 D5 Cochinos, Bahía de Eng. Bay of Pigs. bay SE Cuba
39 O16 Cochise Head ▲ Arizona, SW USA 32.03N 109.19W
25 U5 Cochran Georgia, SE USA 32.23N 83.21W
9 P16 Cochrane Alberta, SW Canada 51.15N 114.25W
10 G12 Cochrane Ontario, S Canada 49.04N 81.01W
65 G20 Cochrane Aisén, S Chile 47.16S 72.33W
9 U10 Cochrane Manitoba/Saskatchewan, C Canada
Cochrane, Lago see Pueyrredón, Lago
Cocibolca see Nicaragua, Lago de
Cockade State see Maryland
46 M6 Cockburn Harbour South Caicos, S Turks and Caicos Islands 21.28N 71.30W
12 C11 Cockburn Island island Ontario, S Canada
46 J3 Cockburn Town San Salvador, E Bahamas 24.01N 74.30W
23 X2 Cockeysville Maryland, NE USA 39.29N 76.34W
189 N12 Cocklebiddy Western Australia 32.02S 125.54E
46 I12 Cockpit Country, The physical region W Jamaica
45 S16 Coclé off. Provincia de Coclé. ◆ province C Panama
45 S15 Coclé del Norte Colón, C Panama 9.04N 80.32W
25 Y12 Cocoa Florida, SE USA 28.23N 80.44W
25 Y12 Cocoa Beach Florida, SE USA 28.19N 80.36W
81 D17 Cocobeach Estuaire, NW Gabon 0.58N 9.34E
46 G5 Coco, Cayo island C Cuba
157 Q19 Coco Channel strait Andaman Sea/Bay of Bengal
181 N6 Coco-de-Mer Seamounts undersea feature W Indian Ocean
38 K10 Coconino Plateau plain Arizona, SW USA
45 N6 Coco, Río var. Río Wanki, Segoviao Wangkí. Honduras/Nicaragua
181 T8 Cocos (Keeling) Islands ◇ Australian external territory E Indian Ocean
181 T7 Cocos Basin undersea feature E Indian Ocean
196 B17 Cocos Island island S Guam
Cocos Island Ridge see Cocos Ridge
133 S17 Cocos Islands island group E Indian Ocean
(0) G15 Cocos Plate tectonic feature
200 Oo8 Cocos Ridge var. Cocos Island Ridge. undersea feature E Pacific Ocean
42 K13 Cocula Jalisco, SW Mexico 20.25N 103.52W
109 D17 Coda Cavallo, Capo headland Sardegna, Italy, C Mediterranean Sea 40.49N 9.43E
60 E13 Codajás Amazonas, N Brazil 3.49S 62.12W
Codazzi see Agustín Codazzi
21 Q12 Cod, Cape headland Massachusetts, NE USA 41.50N 69.56W
193 B25 Codfish Island island SW NZ
108 H9 Codigoro Emilia-Romagna, N Italy 44.49N 12.07E
11 P5 Cod Island island Newfoundland and Labrador, E Canada
118 J12 Codlea Ger. Zeiden, Hung. Feketehalom. Braşov, C Romania 45.42N 25.27E
60 M13 Codó Maranhão, E Brazil 4.28S 43.51W
108 E8 Codogno Lombardia, N Italy 45.10N 9.42E
118 M10 Codrii hill range C Moldova
47 W9 Codrington Barbuda, Antigua and Barbuda 17.37N 61.49W
108 J7 Codroipo Friuli-Venezia Giulia, NE Italy 45.58N 13.00E
30 M12 Cody Nebraska, C USA 42.54N 101.13W
35 U12 Cody Wyoming, C USA 43.31N 109.04W
23 P7 Coeburn Virginia, NE USA 36.56N 82.27W
56 E10 Coello Tolima, W Colombia 4.16N 74.54W
Coemba see Cuemba
189 V2 Coen Queensland, NE Australia 14.03S 143.16E
103 E14 Coesfeld Nordrhein-Westfalen, W Germany 51.55N 7.10E
34 M8 Coeur d'Alene Idaho, NW USA 47.40N 116.46W
34 M8 Coeur d'Alene Lake ⊠ Idaho, NW USA
100 O8 Coevorden Drenthe, NE Netherlands 52.39N 6.45E
8 H6 Coffee Creek Yukon Territory, W Canada 62.52N 139.05W
32 L15 Coffeen Lake ⊠ Illinois, N USA
24 L3 Coffeeville Mississippi, S USA 33.58N 89.40W
29 Q8 Coffeyville Kansas, C USA 37.02N 95.37W
190 G9 Coffin Bay South Australia 34.39S 135.30E
190 F9 Coffin Bay Peninsula peninsula South Australia
191 V5 Coffs Harbour New South Wales, SE Australia 30.18S 153.07E
107 R10 Cofrentes País Valenciano, E Spain 39.13N 1.04W
Cogilnic see Kohyl'nyk
104 K11 Cognac anc. Compniacum. Charente, W France 45.42N 0.19W
108 B7 Cogne Valle d'Aosta, NW Italy 45.37N 7.27E
105 U16 Cogolin Var, SE France 43.15N 6.30E
107 O7 Cogolludo Castilla-La Mancha, C Spain 40.58N 3.05W
Cohalm see Rupea
94 L8 Čohkarášša var. Cuokkaraša. ▲ N Norway 69.57N 24.38E
Čohkkiras see Jukkasjärvi
F11 Cohocton River New York, NE USA
20 L10 Cohoes New York, NE USA 42.46N 73.42W
191 N10 Cohuna Victoria, SE Australia 35.51S 144.15E
45 P17 Coiba, Isla de island SW Panama
65 H23 Coig, Río S Argentina
65 G19 Coihaique var. Coyhaique. Aisén, S Chile 45.31S 72.00W
161 G21 Coimbatore Tamil Nādu, S India 11.00N 76.57E
106 G8 Coimbra anc. Conimbria, Conimbriga. Coimbra, W Portugal 40.12N 8.25W
106 G8 Coimbra ◆ district N Portugal
106 L15 Coín Andalucía, S Spain 36.40N 4.45W
59 J20 Coipasa, Laguna ◎ W Bolivia
59 J20 Coipasa, Salar de salt lake W Bolivia
Coira/Coire see Chur
Coirib, Loch see Corrib, Lough
56 K6 Cojedes off. Estado Cojedes. ◆ state N Venezuela
44 F7 Cojutepeque Cuscatlán, C El Salvador 13.44N 88.55W
Coka see Banbar
35 S16 Cokeville Wyoming, C USA 42.03N 110.55W
190 M13 Colac Victoria, SE Australia 38.22S 143.37E
61 O20 Colatina Espírito Santo, SE Brazil 19.34S 40.37W
29 O13 Colbert Oklahoma, C USA 33.51N 96.30W
102 L12 Colbitz-Letzinger Heide heathland N Germany
28 I3 Colby Kansas, C USA 39.24N 101.03W
59 H17 Colca, Río SW Peru
99 P21 Colchester hist. Colneceaste, anc. Camulodunum. E England, UK 51.54N 0.54E
21 N13 Colchester Connecticut, NE USA 41.34N 72.17W
40 M16 Cold Bay Alaska, USA 55.11N 162.43W
9 R14 Cold Lake Alberta, SW Canada 54.25N 110.16W
9 R13 Cold Lake ◎ Alberta/Saskatchewan, S Canada
31 U8 Cold Spring Minnesota, N USA 45.27N 94.25W
27 W10 Coldspring Texas, SW USA 30.35N 95.07W
9 N17 Coldstream British Columbia, SW Canada 50.13N 119.09W
98 L13 Coldstream SE Scotland, UK 55.39N 2.19W
12 H13 Coldwater Ontario, S Canada 44.43N 79.36W
28 K7 Coldwater Kansas, C USA 37.15N 99.21W
33 Q10 Coldwater Michigan, N USA 41.56N 85.00W
27 N1 Coldwater Creek Oklahoma/Texas, SW USA
24 K2 Coldwater River Mississippi, S USA
191 O9 Coleambally New South Wales, SE Australia 34.48S 145.54E

◆ Country ● Country Capital ◇ Dependent Territory ○ Dependent Territory Capital ◆ Administrative Region ✕ International Airport ▲ Mountain ▲ Mountain Range Volcano River ◎ Lake ⊠ Reservoir

Colebrook – Corneliskondre

21 O6 **Colebrook** New Hampshire, NE USA 44.52N 71.27W
29 T5 **Cole Camp** Missouri, C USA 38.27N 93.12W
41 T6 **Coleen River** ≈ Alaska, USA
9 P17 **Coleman** Alberta, SW Canada 49.36N 114.26W
27 Q8 **Coleman** Texas, SW USA 31.49N 99.25W
Çölemerik see Hakkâri
85 K22 **Colenso** KwaZulu/Natal, E South Africa 28.39S 29.49E
190 L12 **Coleraine** Victoria, SE Australia 37.39S 141.42E
99 F14 **Coleraine** *Ir.* Cúil Raithin. N Northern Ireland, UK 55.07N 6.40W
193 G18 **Coleridge, Lake** ◎ South Island, NZ
85 H24 **Colesberg** Northern Cape, C South Africa 30.41S 25.08E
24 H7 **Colfax** Louisiana, S USA 31.31N 92.42W
34 L9 **Colfax** Washington, NW USA 46.52N 117.21W
32 J6 **Colfax** Wisconsin, N USA 45.00N 91.44W
65 I19 **Colhué Huapí, Lago** ◎ S Argentina
47 Z6 **Colibris, Pointe des** *headland* Grande Terre, E Guadeloupe 16.15N 61.10W
108 D6 **Colico** Lombardia, N Italy 46.08N 9.24E
101 E14 **Colijnsplaat** Zeeland, SW Netherlands 51.36N 3.47E
42 L14 **Colima** Colima, S Mexico 19.12N 103.45W
42 K14 **Colima** ◐ *state* SW Mexico
42 L14 **Colima, Nevado de** ⋀ C Mexico 19.36N 103.36W
61 M14 **Colinas** Maranhão, E Brazil 6.01S 44.15W
98 F10 **Coll** *island* W Scotland, UK
107 N7 **Collado Villalba** *var.* Villalba. Madrid, C Spain 40.37N 3.58W
191 R4 **Collarenebri** New South Wales, SE Australia 29.31S 148.33E
39 P5 **Collbran** Colorado, C USA 39.14N 107.57W
108 G12 **Colle di Val d'Elsa** Toscana, C Italy 43.26N 11.06E
41 R9 **College** Alaska, USA 64.49N 148.06W
34 K10 **College Place** Washington, NW USA 46.03N 118.23W
27 U10 **College Station** Texas, SW USA 30.36N 96.21W
191 P4 **Collerina** New South Wales, SE Australia 29.41S 146.36E
188 I13 **Collie** Western Australia 33.19S 116.06E
188 L4 **Collier Bay** *bay* Western Australia
23 F10 **Collierville** Tennessee, S USA 35.02N 89.39W
108 F11 **Collina, Passo della** *pass* C Italy 44.02N 10.55E
12 G14 **Collingwood** Ontario, S Canada 44.28N 80.12W
192 I13 **Collingwood** Tasman, South Island, NZ 40.40S 172.40E
194 M15 **Collingwood Bay** *bay* SE PNG
24 L7 **Collins** Mississippi, S USA 31.39N 89.33W
32 K15 **Collinsville** Illinois, N USA 38.40N 89.58W
29 P9 **Collinsville** Oklahoma, C USA 36.21N 95.50W
22 H10 **Collinwood** Tennessee, S USA 35.10N 87.44W
Collipo see Leiria
65 G14 **Collipulli** Araucanía, C Chile 37.55S 72.30W
99 D16 **Collooney** *Ir.* Cúil Mhuine. NW Ireland 54.10N 8.28W
31 R10 **Colman** South Dakota, N USA 43.58N 96.48W
105 U6 **Colmar** *Ger.* Kolmar. Haut-Rhin, NE France 48.04N 7.21E
106 M15 **Colmenar** Andalucía, S Spain 36.54N 4.19W
Colmenar see Colmenar de Oreja
107 O9 **Colmenar de Oreja** *var.* Colmenar. Madrid, C Spain 40.06N 3.25W
107 N7 **Colmenar Viejo** Madrid, C Spain 40.39N 3.46W
27 X9 **Colmesneil** Texas, SW USA 30.54N 94.25W
Cöln see Köln
Colneceaste see Colchester
42 C3 **Colnet** Baja California, NW Mexico
61 G15 **Colniza** Mato Grosso, W Brazil 9.16S 59.25W
Cologne see Köln
44 B6 **Colomba** Quezaltenango, SW Guatemala 14.45N 91.39W
Colomb-Béchar see Béchar
56 E11 **Colombia** Huila, C Colombia 3.24N 74.49W
56 G10 **Colombia** *off.* Republic of Colombia. ◆ *republic* N South America
66 E12 **Colombian Basin** *undersea feature* SW Caribbean Sea
Colombie-Britannique see British Columbia
13 T6 **Colombier** Québec, SE Canada 48.51N 68.52W
161 J25 **Colombo** ● (Sri Lanka) Western Province, W Sri Lanka 6.55N 79.52E
161 J25 **Colombo** ✖ Western Province, SW Sri Lanka 6.50N 79.59E
31 N11 **Colome** South Dakota, N USA 43.13N 99.42W
63 D18 **Colon** Entre Ríos, E Argentina 32.13S 58.15W
63 B19 **Colón** Buenos Aires, E Argentina 33.53S 61.06W
46 D5 **Colón** Matanzas, C Cuba 22.42N 80.54W
45 T14 **Colón** *prev.* Aspinwall. Colón, C Panama 9.04N 80.32W
44 K5 **Colón** ◐ *department* NE Honduras
45 S15 **Colón** *off.* Provincia de Colón. ◐ *province* N Panama
59 A16 **Colón, Archipiélago de** *var.* Islas de los Galápagos, *Eng.* Galapagos Islands, Tortoise Islands. *island group* Ecuador, E Pacific Ocean
46 K5 **Colonel Hill** Crooked Island, SE Bahamas 22.43N 74.12W
42 B3 **Colonet, Cabo** *headland* NW Mexico 30.57N 116.19W
196 G14 **Colonia** Yap, W Micronesia 9.29N 138.06E
63 D19 **Colonia** ◐ *department* SW Uruguay
Colonia see Kolonia, Micronesia
Colonia see Colonia del Sacramento, Uruguay
Colonia Agrippina see Köln
63 D20 **Colonia del Sacramento** *var.* Colonia. Colonia, SW Uruguay 34.28S 57.48W
64 L8 **Colonia Dora** Santiago del Estero, N Argentina 28.34S 62.58W
Colonia Julia Fanestris see Fano
23 W5 **Colonial Beach** Virginia, NE USA 38.15N 76.57W
23 V6 **Colonial Heights** Virginia, NE USA 37.15N 77.24W
200 Oo8 **Colón Ridge** *undersea feature* E Pacific Ocean
98 F12 **Colonsay** *island* W Scotland, UK
59 K22 **Colorada, Laguna** ◎ SW Bolivia
39 R6 **Colorado** *off.* State of Colorado; also known as Centennial State, Silver State. ◐ *state* C USA
65 H22 **Colorado, Cerro** ▲ S Argentina 49.58S 71.38W
27 O7 **Colorado City** Texas, SW USA 32.23N 100.51W
38 M7 **Colorado Plateau** *plateau* W USA
63 A24 **Colorado, Río** ≈ E Argentina
45 N12 **Colorado, Río** ≈ NE Costa Rica
Colorado, Río see Colorado River
18 Hh10 **Colorado River** *var.* Río Colorado. ≈ Mexico/USA
18 Ll15 **Colorado River** ≈ Texas, SW USA
37 W15 **Colorado River Aqueduct** *aqueduct* California, W USA
46 A4 **Colorados, Archipiélago de los** *island group* NW Cuba
64 J9 **Colorados, Desagües de los** ◎ W Argentina
39 T5 **Colorado Springs** Colorado, C USA 38.49N 104.46W
42 L11 **Colotlán** Jalisco, SW Mexico 22.07N 103.15W
59 L19 **Colquechaca** Potosí, C Bolivia 18.39S 66.12W
25 S7 **Colquitt** Georgia, SE USA 31.10N 84.43W
31 R11 **Colton** South Dakota, N USA 43.47N 96.55W
34 M10 **Colton** Washington, NW USA 46.34N 117.10W
37 P8 **Columbia** California, W USA 38.01N 120.22W
32 K16 **Columbia** Illinois, N USA 38.26N 90.12W
22 L7 **Columbia** Kentucky, S USA 37.06N 85.18W
24 I6 **Columbia** Louisiana, S USA 32.05N 92.03W
23 W3 **Columbia** Maryland, NE USA 39.11N 76.52W
24 L7 **Columbia** Mississippi, S USA 31.15N 89.50W
29 U4 **Columbia** Missouri, C USA 38.55N 92.19W
23 Y9 **Columbia** North Carolina, SE USA 35.53N 76.16W
20 G16 **Columbia** Pennsylvania, NE USA 40.01N 76.30W
23 Q12 **Columbia** *state capital* South Carolina, SE USA 34.00N 81.00W
22 I9 **Columbia** Tennessee, S USA 35.37N 87.02W
(0) F9 **Columbia** ≈ Canada/USA
34 K9 **Columbia Basin** *basin* Washington, NW USA
207 Q10 **Columbia, Cape** *headland* Ellesmere Island, Nunavut, NE Canada
33 Q12 **Columbia City** Indiana, N USA 41.09N 85.29W
23 W3 **Columbia, District of** ◐ *federal district* NE USA
35 P7 **Columbia Falls** Montana, NW USA 48.22N 114.10W
9 O15 **Columbia Icefield** *icefield* Alberta/British Columbia, S Canada
9 O15 **Columbia, Mount** ▲ Alberta/British Columbia, SW Canada 52.07N 117.30W
9 N15 **Columbia Mountains** ▲▲ British Columbia, SW Canada
25 P4 **Columbiana** Alabama, S USA 33.10N 86.36W
33 V12 **Columbiana** Ohio, N USA 40.53N 80.41W
34 M14 **Columbia Plateau** *plateau* Idaho/Oregon, NW USA
31 P7 **Columbia Road Reservoir** ⊠ South Dakota, N USA
67 K16 **Columbia Seamount** *undersea feature* C Atlantic Ocean 20.30S 32.00W
85 D25 **Columbine, Cape** *headland* SW South Africa 32.50S 17.39E
107 U9 **Columbretes, Islas** *island group* E Spain
25 R5 **Columbus** Georgia, SE USA 32.28N 84.58W
33 P14 **Columbus** Indiana, N USA 39.12N 85.55W
29 R7 **Columbus** Kansas, C USA 37.10N 94.50W
25 N4 **Columbus** Mississippi, S USA 33.30N 88.25W
35 U11 **Columbus** Montana, NW USA 45.38N 109.15W
31 Q15 **Columbus** Nebraska, C USA 41.25N 97.22W
39 Q16 **Columbus** New Mexico, SW USA 31.49N 107.38W
23 P10 **Columbus** North Carolina, SE USA 35.15N 82.09W
30 K2 **Columbus** North Dakota, N USA 48.52N 102.47W
33 S13 **Columbus** *state capital* Ohio, N USA 39.57N 83.00W
27 U11 **Columbus** Texas, SW USA 29.42N 96.32W
32 L8 **Columbus** Wisconsin, N USA 43.21N 89.00W
33 R12 **Columbus Grove** Ohio, N USA 40.55N 84.03W
31 Y15 **Columbus Junction** Iowa, C USA 41.16N 91.21W
46 J3 **Columbus Point** *headland* Cat Island, C Bahamas 24.07N 75.19W
37 T8 **Columbus Salt Marsh** *salt marsh* Nevada, W USA
37 N6 **Colusa** California, W USA 39.10N 122.03W
34 L7 **Colville** Washington, NW USA 48.33N 117.54W
192 M5 **Colville, Cape** *headland* North Island, NZ 36.28S 175.20E
192 M5 **Colville Channel** *channel* North Island, NZ
41 P6 **Colville River** ≈ Alaska, USA
99 J18 **Colwyn Bay** N Wales, UK 53.18N 3.43W
108 H9 **Comacchio** *var.* Commachio; *anc.* Comactium. Emilia-Romagna, N Italy 44.40N 12.10E
108 H9 **Comacchio, Valli di** *lagoon* Adriatic Sea, N Mediterranean Sea
Comactium see Comacchio
43 V17 **Comalapa** Chiapas, SE Mexico 15.42N 92.06W
43 U15 **Comalcalco** Tabasco, SE Mexico 18.16N 93.05W
65 H16 **Comallo** Río Negro, SW Argentina 40.58S 70.13W
28 M12 **Comanche** Oklahoma, C USA 34.22N 97.57W
27 R8 **Comanche** Texas, SW USA 31.54N 98.36W
204 H2 **Comandante Ferraz** *Brazilian research station* Antarctica 61.57S 58.23W
64 N6 **Comandante Fontana** Formosa, N Argentina 25.19S 59.42W
65 I22 **Comandante Luis Peidra Buena** Santa Cruz, S Argentina 50.04S 68.55W
61 O18 **Comandatuba** Bahia, SE Brazil 15.13S 39.00W
118 K11 **Comănești** *Hung.* Kománfalva. Bacău, SW Romania 46.24N 26.27E
59 M19 **Comarapa** Santa Cruz, C Bolivia 17.52S 64.34W
118 J13 **Comarnic** Prahova, SE Romania 45.13N 25.36E
44 H6 **Comayagua** Comayagua, W Honduras 14.33N 87.37W
44 H6 **Comayagua** ◐ *department* W Honduras
44 I6 **Comayagua, Montañas de** ▲▲ C Honduras
23 R15 **Combahee River** ≈ South Carolina, SE USA
64 G10 **Combarbalá** Coquimbo, C Chile 31.15S 71.03W
105 S7 **Combeaufontaine** Haute-Saône, E France 47.43N 5.52E
99 G15 **Comber** *Ir.* An Comar. E Northern Ireland, UK 54.33N 5.45W
101 K20 **Comblain-au-Pont** Liège, E Belgium 50.29N 5.36E
104 I6 **Combourg** Ille-et-Vilaine, NW France 48.21N 1.44W
46 M9 **Comendador** *prev.* Elías Piña. W Dominican Republic 18.51N 71.40W
Comer See see Como, Lago di
27 R11 **Comfort** Texas, SW USA 29.58N 98.54W
159 V15 **Comilla** *Ben.* Kumillā. Chittagong, E Bangladesh 23.28N 91.10E
101 B18 **Comines** Hainaut, W Belgium 50.46N 2.58E
123 J16 **Comino** *Malt.* Kemmuna. *island* C Malta
109 D18 **Comino, Capo** *headland* Sardegna, Italy, C Mediterranean Sea 40.32N 9.49E
109 K25 **Comiso** Sicilia, Italy, C Mediterranean Sea 36.57N 14.37E
43 V16 **Comitán** *var.* Comitán de Domínguez. Chiapas, SE Mexico 16.14N 92.06W
Comitán de Domínguez see Comitán
Commachio see Comacchio
Commander Islands see Komandorskiye Ostrova
105 O10 **Commentry** Allier, C France 46.18N 2.46E
25 T2 **Commerce** Georgia, SE USA 34.12N 83.27W
29 R8 **Commerce** Oklahoma, C USA 36.55N 94.52W
27 V5 **Commerce** Texas, SW USA 33.16N 95.52W
39 T4 **Commerce City** Colorado, C USA 39.45N 104.54W
105 S5 **Commercy** Meuse, NE France 48.46N 5.36E
57 W9 **Commewijne** *var.* Commewyne. ◐ *district* NE Suriname
Commewyne see Commewijne
13 P8 **Commissaires, Lac des** ◎ Québec, SE Canada
66 A12 **Commissioner's Point** *headland* W Bermuda
15 Ll3 **Committee Bay** *bay* Nunavut, N Canada
108 D7 **Como** *anc.* Comum. Lombardia, N Italy 45.48N 9.04E
65 J19 **Comodoro Rivadavia** Chubut, SE Argentina 45.49S 67.30W
108 D6 **Como, Lago di** *var.* Lario, *Eng.* Lake Como, *Ger.* Comer See. ◎ N Italy
Como, Lake see Como, Lago di
42 E7 **Comondú** Baja California Sur, W Mexico 26.01N 111.50W
118 F12 **Comorâște** *Hung.* Komornok. Caraș-Severin, SW Romania 45.13N 21.34E
Comores, République Fédérale Islamique des see Comoros
161 G24 **Comorin, Cape** *headland* SE India 8.00N 77.10E
180 M8 **Comoro Basin** *undersea feature* SW Indian Ocean
180 K14 **Comoro Islands** *island group* W Indian Ocean
180 H13 **Comoros** *off.* Federal Islamic Republic of the Comoros, *Fr.* République Fédérale Islamique des Comores. ◆ *republic* W Indian Ocean
8 L17 **Comox** Vancouver Island, British Columbia, SW Canada 49.40N 124.55W
105 O4 **Compiègne** Oise, N France 49.25N 2.49E
Complutum see Alcalá de Henares
Compniacum see Cognac
42 K12 **Compostela** Nayarit, C Mexico 21.14N 104.52W
Compostella see Santiago
62 L11 **Comprida, Ilha** *island* S Brazil
119 N11 **Comrat** *Rus.* Komrat. S Moldova 46.18N 28.40E
27 O11 **Comstock** Texas, SW USA 29.39N 101.10W
33 P9 **Comstock Park** Michigan, N USA 43.00N 85.40W
199 Kk3 **Comstock Seamount** *undersea feature* N Pacific Ocean 48.15N 156.55W
Comum see Como
165 N17 **Cona** Xizang Zizhiqu, W China 27.58N 91.54E
78 H14 **Conakry** ● (Guinea) Conakry, SW Guinea 9.31N 13.43W
78 H14 **Conakry** ✖ Conakry, SW Guinea 9.37N 13.32W
Conamara see Connemara
Conca see Cuenca
27 Q12 **Concan** Texas, SW USA 29.27N 99.43W
104 F6 **Concarneau** Finistère, NW France 47.52N 3.55W
85 O17 **Conceição** Sofala, C Mozambique 18.47S 36.18E
61 K15 **Conceição do Araguaia** Pará, NE Brazil 8.15S 49.15W
60 F10 **Conceição do Maú** Roraima, W Brazil 3.34N 59.52W
63 D14 **Concepción** *var.* Concepcion. Corrientes, NE Argentina 28.25S 57.54W
64 J8 **Concepción** Tucumán, N Argentina 27.19S 65.34W
59 O17 **Concepción** Santa Cruz, E Bolivia 16.15S 62.07W
64 G13 **Concepción** Bío Bío, C Chile 36.47S 73.01W
56 E14 **Concepción** Putumayo, S Colombia 0.03N 75.39W
64 O5 **Concepción** *var.* Villa Concepción. Concepción, C Paraguay 23.26S 57.23W
64 O5 **Concepción** *off.* Departamento de Concepción. ◐ *department* E Paraguay
Concepción see La Concepción
Concepción de la Vega see La Vega
43 N9 **Concepción del Oro** Zacatecas, C Mexico 24.37N 101.25W
63 D18 **Concepción del Uruguay** Entre Ríos, E Argentina 32.30S 58.15W
44 K11 **Concepción, Volcán** ⋀ SW Nicaragua 11.31N 85.37W
46 J4 **Conception Island** *island* C Bahamas
37 P14 **Conception, Point** *headland* California, W USA 34.27N 120.28W
56 H6 **Concha** Zulia, W Venezuela 9.01N 71.45W
62 L9 **Conchas** São Paulo, S Brazil 23.00S 47.58W
39 U11 **Conchas Dam** New Mexico, SW USA 35.21N 104.11W
39 U10 **Conchas Lake** ⊠ New Mexico, SW USA
104 M5 **Conches-en-Ouche** Eure, N France 49.00N 1.00E
39 N12 **Concho** Arizona, SW USA 34.28N 109.33W
42 J5 **Conchos, Río** ≈ NW Mexico
43 O8 **Conchos, Río** ≈ C Mexico
110 C8 **Concise** Vaud, W Switzerland 46.52N 6.40E
37 N8 **Concord** California, W USA 37.58N 122.01W
21 O9 **Concord** *state capital* New Hampshire, NE USA 43.10N 71.31W
23 R10 **Concord** North Carolina, SE USA 35.30N 80.34W
63 D17 **Concordia** Entre Ríos, E Argentina 31.25S 58.00W
56 D9 **Concordia** Antioquia, W Colombia 6.03N 75.57W
42 J10 **Concordia** Sinaloa, C Mexico 23.18N 106.03W
59 I19 **Concordia** Tacna, SW Peru 18.12S 70.19W
29 N3 **Concordia** Kansas, C USA 39.34N 97.39W
29 S4 **Concordia** Missouri, C USA 38.58N 93.34W
62 I13 **Concórdia** Santa Catarina, S Brazil 27.13S 52.01W
178 J7 **Con Cuông** Nghê An, N Vietnam 19.02N 104.54E
178 Jj16 **Côn Đao** *var.* Con Son. *island* S Vietnam
Condate see St-Claude, Jura, France
Condate see Rennes, Ille-et-Vilaine, France
Condate see Montereau-Faut-Yonne, Seine-St-Denis, France
31 P8 **Conde** South Dakota, N USA 45.08N 98.07W
44 J8 **Condega** Estelí, NW Nicaragua 13.21N 86.23W
105 P2 **Condé-sur-l'Escaut** Nord, N France 50.27N 3.36E
104 K5 **Condé-sur-Noireau** Calvados, N France 48.52N 0.31W
Condivincum see Nantes
191 P8 **Condobolin** New South Wales, SE Australia 33.04S 147.08E
104 L15 **Condom** Gers, S France 43.58N 0.23E
34 J11 **Condon** Oregon, NW USA 45.13N 120.11W
56 D9 **Condoto** Chocó, W Colombia 5.06N 76.37W
25 P7 **Conecuh River** ≈ Alabama/Florida, SE USA
108 H7 **Conegliano** Veneto, NE Italy 45.52N 12.18E
63 C19 **Conesa** Buenos Aires, E Argentina 33.36S 60.21W
12 F15 **Conestogo** ≈ Ontario, S Canada
195 O17 **Conflict Group** *island group* SE PNG
Confluentes see Koblenz
104 L10 **Confolens** Charente, W France 46.00N 0.40E
38 J4 **Confusion Range** ▲▲ Utah, W USA
64 N6 **Confuso, Río** ≈ C Paraguay
23 R12 **Congaree River** ≈ South Carolina, SE USA
Công Hoa Xa Hôi Chu Nghia Viêt Nam see Vietnam
166 K12 **Congjiang** *var.* Bingmei. Guizhou, S China 25.48N 108.55E
81 K19 **Congo** *off.* Democratic Republic of Congo; *prev.* Zaire, Belgian Congo, Congo (Kinshasa). ◆ *republic* C Africa
81 G18 **Congo** *off.* Republic of the Congo, *Fr.* Moyen-Congo; *prev.* Middle Congo. ◆ *republic* C Africa
69 T11 **Congo** *var.* Kongo, *Fr.* Zaire. ≈ C Africa
Congo see Zaire (province, Angola)
Congo/Congo (Kinshasa) see Congo (Democratic Republic of)
70 G12 **Congo Basin** *drainage basin* W Dem. Rep. Congo
69 Q11 **Congo Canyon** *var.* Congo Seavalley, Congo Submarine Canyon. *undersea feature* E Atlantic Ocean
Congo Cone see Congo Fan
67 P15 **Congo Fan** *var.* Congo Cone. *undersea feature* E Atlantic Ocean
Coni see Cuneo
65 H18 **Cónico, Cerro** ▲ SW Argentina 43.12S 71.42W
Conimbria/Conimbriga see Coimbra
Conjeeveram see Kānchipuram
9 R13 **Conklin** Alberta, C Canada 55.36N 111.06W
26 M1 **Conlen** Texas, SW USA 36.16N 102.10W
Con, Loch see Conn, Lough
Connacht see Connaught
99 B17 **Connaught** *var.* Connacht, *Ir.* Chonnacht, Cúige. *cultural region* W Ireland
33 V10 **Conneaut** Ohio, N USA 41.56N 80.32W
20 L13 **Connecticut** *off.* State of Connecticut; also known as Blue Law State, Constitution State, Land of Steady Habits, Nutmeg State. ◐ *state* NE USA
21 N8 **Connecticut** ≈ Canada/USA
21 O6 **Connecticut Lakes** *lakes* New Hampshire, NE USA
34 K9 **Connell** Washington, NW USA 46.39N 118.51W
99 B17 **Connemara** *Ir.* Conamara. *region* W Ireland
33 Q14 **Connersville** Indiana, N USA 39.38N 85.15W
99 B16 **Conn, Lough** *Ir.* Loch Con. ◎ W Ireland
37 X6 **Connors Pass** *pass* Nevada, W USA 39.01N 114.37W
189 X7 **Connors Range** ▲▲ Queensland, E Australia
58 E7 **Cononaco, Río** ≈ E Ecuador
31 W13 **Conrad** Iowa, C USA 42.13N 92.52W
35 R7 **Conrad** Montana, NW USA 48.10N 111.58W
27 W10 **Conroe** Texas, SW USA 30.18N 95.27W
27 V10 **Conroe, Lake** ⊠ Texas, SW USA
63 C17 **Conscripto Bernardi** Entre Ríos, E Argentina 31.03S 59.04W
61 M20 **Conselheiro Lafaiete** Minas Gerais, SE Brazil 20.40S 43.48W
Consentia see Cosenza
99 L14 **Consett** N England, UK 54.49N 1.52W
46 B5 **Consolación del Sur** Pinar del Río, W Cuba 22.29N 83.31W
Con Son see Côn Đao
9 R15 **Consort** Alberta, SW Canada 51.58N 110.44W
Constance see Konstanz
110 I6 **Constance, Lake** *Ger.* Bodensee. ◎ C Europe
106 G9 **Constância** Santarém, C Portugal 39.28N 8.22W
119 N14 **Constanța** *var.* Küstendje, *Eng.* Constanza, *Ger.* Konstanza, *Turk.* Küstence. Constanța, SE Romania 44.09N 28.36E
118 L14 **Constanța** ◐ *county* SE Romania
Constantia see Coutances, France
Constantia see Konstanz, Germany
106 K13 **Constantina** Andalucía, S Spain 37.54N 5.36W
76 L5 **Constantine** *var.* Qacentina, *Ar.* Qoussantina. NE Algeria 36.22N 6.43E
41 O14 **Constantine, Cape** *headland* Alaska, USA 58.23N 158.53W
Constantinople see İstanbul
Constantiola see Oltenișa
Constanz see Konstanz
Constanza see Constanța
64 G13 **Constitución** Maule, C Chile 35.25S 72.19W
63 D17 **Constitución** Salto, N Uruguay 31.04S 57.51W
Constitution State see Connecticut
107 N10 **Consuegra** Castilla-La Mancha, C Spain 39.28N 3.36W
189 X9 **Consuelo Peak** ▲ Queensland, E Australia 24.45S 148.01E
58 E11 **Contamana** Loreto, N Peru 7.19S 75.04W
Contrasto, Colle del see Contrasto, Portella del
109 K23 **Contrasto, Portella del** *var.* Colle del Contrasto. *pass* Sicilia, Italy, C Mediterranean Sea 37.51N 14.22E
56 G8 **Contratación** Santander, C Colombia 6.18N 73.27W
104 M8 **Contres** Loir-et-Cher, C France 47.24N 1.30E
109 O17 **Conversano** Puglia, SE Italy 40.58N 17.07E
29 U11 **Conway** Arkansas, C USA 35.05N 92.26W
21 O8 **Conway** New Hampshire, NE USA 43.58N 71.05W
23 U13 **Conway** South Carolina, SE USA 33.50N 79.03W
27 N2 **Conway** Texas, SW USA 35.10N 101.23W
29 U11 **Conway, Lake** ⊠ Arkansas, C USA
29 N7 **Conway Springs** Kansas, C USA 37.23N 97.38W
99 J18 **Conwy** N Wales, UK 53.16N 3.51W
25 T3 **Conyers** Georgia, SE USA 33.40N 84.01W
Coo see Kos
190 F4 **Coober Pedy** South Australia 29.01S 134.46E
189 P2 **Cooinda** Northern Territory, N Australia 12.54S 132.31E
190 B6 **Cook** South Australia 30.37S 130.26E
31 W4 **Cook** Minnesota, N USA 47.51N 92.41W
203 N6 **Cook, Baie de** *bay* Moorea, W French Polynesia
8 J16 **Cook, Cape** *headland* Vancouver Island, British Columbia, SW Canada 50.04N 127.52W
39 Q15 **Cookes Peak** ▲ New Mexico, SW USA 32.32N 107.43W
22 L8 **Cookeville** Tennessee, S USA 36.09N 85.30W
183 P9 **Cook Fracture Zone** *tectonic feature* S Pacific Ocean
Cook, Grand Récif de see Cook, Récif de
41 Q12 **Cook Inlet** *inlet* Alaska, USA
203 X2 **Cook Island** *island* Line Islands, E Kiribati
202 J14 **Cook Islands** ◇ *territory in free association with NZ* S Pacific Ocean
Cook, Mount see Aoraki
197 G4 **Cook, Récif de** *var.* Grand Récif de Cook. *reef* S New Caledonia
12 G14 **Cookstown** Ontario, S Canada 44.12N 79.39W
99 F15 **Cookstown** *Ir.* An Chorr Chríochach. C Northern Ireland, UK 54.39N 6.45W
193 K14 **Cook Strait** *var.* Raukawa. *strait* NZ
189 W3 **Cooktown** Queensland, NE Australia 15.28S 145.15E
191 P6 **Coolabah** New South Wales, SE Australia 31.03S 146.42E
190 J11 **Coola Coola Swamp** *wetland* South Australia
191 S7 **Coolah** New South Wales, SE Australia 31.49S 149.43E
191 P9 **Coolamon** New South Wales, SE Australia 34.49S 147.13E
191 T4 **Coolatai** New South Wales, SE Australia 29.16S 150.45E
188 K12 **Coolgardie** Western Australia 31.00S 121.12E
38 L14 **Coolidge** Arizona, SW USA 32.58N 111.29W
27 U8 **Coolidge** Texas, SW USA 31.45N 96.39W
191 Q11 **Cooma** New South Wales, SE Australia 36.16S 149.09E
Coomassie see Kumasi
191 R6 **Coonabarabran** New South Wales, SE Australia 31.19S 149.18E
190 J10 **Coonalpyn** South Australia 35.43S 139.50E
191 R6 **Coonamble** New South Wales, SE Australia 30.56S 148.22E
Coondapoor see Kundāpura
161 G21 **Coonoor** Tamil Nādu, SE India 11.21N 76.46E
31 U14 **Coon Rapids** Iowa, C USA 41.52N 94.40W
31 V8 **Coon Rapids** Minnesota, N USA 45.12N 93.18W
27 V5 **Cooper** Texas, SW USA 33.22N 95.41W
189 U9 **Cooper Creek** *var.* Barcoo, Cooper's Creek. *seasonal river* Queensland/South Australia
41 R12 **Cooper Landing** Alaska, USA 60.27N 149.59W
23 T14 **Cooper River** ≈ South Carolina, SE USA
Cooper's Creek see Cooper Creek
46 H1 **Coopers Town** Great Abaco, N Bahamas 26.46N 77.27W
20 J10 **Cooperstown** New York, NE USA 42.43N 74.55W
31 P4 **Cooperstown** North Dakota, N USA 47.26N 98.07W
33 P9 **Coopersville** Michigan, N USA 43.03N 85.55W
190 D7 **Coorabie** South Australia 31.57S 132.18E
25 Q3 **Coosa River** ≈ Alabama/Georgia, S USA
34 E14 **Coos Bay** Oregon, NW USA 43.22N 124.13W
191 Q9 **Cootamundra** New South Wales, SE Australia 34.40S 148.03E
99 E16 **Cootehill** *Ir.* Muinchille. N Ireland 54.04N 7.04W
Čop see Chop
59 J17 **Copacabana** La Paz, W Bolivia 16.11S 69.02W
65 H14 **Copahué, Volcán** ⋀ C Chile 37.56S 71.04W
43 U16 **Copainalá** Chiapas, SE Mexico 17.04N 93.13W
34 F8 **Copalis Beach** Washington, NW USA 47.05N 124.11W
44 F6 **Copán** ◐ *department* W Honduras
Copán see Copán Ruinas
27 T14 **Copano Bay** *bay* NW Gulf of Mexico
44 F6 **Copán Ruinas** *var.* Copán. Copán, W Honduras 14.51N 89.07W
Copenhagen see København
109 Q19 **Copertino** Puglia, SE Italy 40.16N 18.03E
64 H7 **Copiapó** Atacama, N Chile 27.17S 70.25W
64 G8 **Copiapó, Bahía** *bay* N Chile
64 G7 **Copiapó, Río** ≈ N Chile
116 M12 **Çöpköy** Edirne, NW Turkey 41.14N 26.51E
190 I5 **Copley** South Australia 30.36S 138.26E
108 H9 **Copparo** Emilia-Romagna, C Italy 44.53N 11.53E
57 V10 **Coppename Rivier** *var.* Koppename. ≈ C Suriname
27 S9 **Copperas Cove** Texas, SW USA 31.07N 97.54W
84 J13 **Copperbelt** ◐ *province* C Zambia
41 S11 **Copper Center** Alaska, USA 61.57N 145.21W
Coppermine see Kugluktuk
15 I5 **Coppermine** ≈ Northwest Territories/Nunavut, N Canada
41 T11 **Copper River** ≈ Alaska, USA
Copper State see Arizona
118 I11 **Copșa Mică** *Ger.* Kleinkopisch, *Hung.* Kiskapus. Sibiu, C Romania 45.48N 24.08E
164 J14 **Coqên** Xizang Zizhiqu, W China 31.13N 85.12E
Coquilhatville see Mbandaka
34 E14 **Coquille** Oregon, NW USA 43.10N 124.11W
64 G9 **Coquimbo** Coquimbo, N Chile 29.59S 71.18W
64 G9 **Coquimbo** *off.* Región de Coquimbo. ◐ *region* C Chile
118 I15 **Corabia** Olt, S Romania 43.46N 24.31E
59 F17 **Coracora** Ayacucho, SW Peru 15.07S 73.45W
Cora Droma Rúisc see Carrick-on-Shannon
46 K9 **Corail** SW Haiti 18.32N 73.54W
191 V4 **Coraki** New South Wales, SE Australia 29.01S 153.15E
188 G8 **Coral Bay** Western Australia 23.02S 113.51E
25 Y16 **Coral Gables** Florida, SE USA 25.43N 80.16W
15 M5 **Coral Harbour** Southampton Island, Northwest Territories, NE Canada 64.10N 83.15W
199 I10 **Coral Sea** *sea* SW Pacific Ocean
182 M7 **Coral Sea Basin** *undersea feature* N Coral Sea
199 Hh10 **Coral Sea Islands** ◇ *Australian external territory* SW Pacific Ocean
190 M12 **Corangamite, Lake** ◎ Victoria, SE Australia
Corantijn Rivier see Courantyne River
20 B14 **Coraopolis** Pennsylvania, NE USA 40.28N 80.08W
109 N17 **Corato** Puglia, SE Italy 41.09N 16.25E
105 O17 **Corbières** ▲▲ S France
105 P8 **Corbigny** Nièvre, C France 47.15N 3.42E
23 N7 **Corbin** Kentucky, S USA 36.57N 84.06W
106 L14 **Corbones** ≈ SW Spain
Corcaigh see Cork
37 R11 **Corcoran** California, W USA 36.06N 119.33W
49 T14 **Corcovado, Golfo** *gulf* S Chile
65 G18 **Corcovado, Volcán** ▲ S Chile 43.13S 72.45W
106 F3 **Corcubión** Galicia, NW Spain 42.55N 9.12W
Corcyra Nigra see Korčula
62 Q9 **Cordeiro** Rio de Janeiro, SE Brazil 22.01S 42.20W
25 T6 **Cordele** Georgia, SE USA 31.58N 83.49W
28 L11 **Cordell** Oklahoma, C USA 35.18N 98.58W
105 N14 **Cordes** Tarn, S France 44.03N 1.57E
64 O6 **Cordillera** *off.* Departamento de la Cordillera. ◐ *department* C Paraguay
190 K1 **Cordillo Downs** South Australia 26.44S 140.37E
64 K10 **Córdoba** Córdoba, C Argentina 31.25S 64.10W
43 R14 **Córdoba** Veracruz-Llave, E Mexico 18.52N 96.48W
106 M13 **Córdoba** *var.* Cordoba, *Eng.* Cordova; *anc.* Corduba. Andalucía, SW Spain 37.52N 4.46W
64 K11 **Córdoba** *off.* Provincia de Córdoba. ◐ *province* C Argentina
56 D7 **Córdoba** *off.* Departamento de Córdoba. ◐ *province* NW Colombia
106 L13 **Córdoba** ◐ *province* Andalucía, S Spain
64 K10 **Córdoba, Sierras de** ▲▲ C Argentina
25 O3 **Cordova** Alabama, S USA 33.45N 87.10W
41 S12 **Cordova** Alaska, USA 60.32N 145.45W
Cordova/Corduba see Córdoba
Corentyne River see Courantyne River
Corfu see Kérkyra
106 J9 **Coria** Extremadura, W Spain 39.58N 6.31W
106 J14 **Coria del Río** Andalucía, S Spain 37.18N 6.04W
191 S8 **Coricudgy, Mount** ▲ New South Wales, SE Australia 32.49S 150.28E
109 N20 **Corigliano Calabro** Calabria, SW Italy 39.35N 16.30E
Corinium/Corinium Dobunorum see Cirencester
25 N1 **Corinth** Mississippi, S USA 34.56N 88.29W
Corinth see Kórinthos
Corinth Canal see Dióryga Korinthou
Corinth, Gulf of/Corinthiacus Sinus see Korinthiakós Kólpos
Corinthus see Kórinthos
44 I9 **Corinto** Chinandega, NW Nicaragua 12.28N 87.12W
99 C21 **Cork** *Ir.* Corcaigh. S Ireland 51.54N 7.06W
99 C21 **Cork** *Ir.* Corcaigh. *cultural region* SW Ireland
99 C21 **Cork** ✖ SW Ireland 51.52N 8.25W
99 D21 **Cork Harbour** *Ir.* Cuan Chorcaí. *inlet* SW Ireland
109 I23 **Corleone** Sicilia, Italy, C Mediterranean Sea 37.49N 13.18E
116 N13 **Çorlu** Tekirdağ, NW Turkey 41.10N 27.48E
116 N12 **Çorlu Çayı** ≈ NW Turkey
Cormaiore see Courmayeur
9 V13 **Cormorant** Manitoba, C Canada 54.12N 100.33W
25 T2 **Cornelia** Georgia, SE USA 34.30N 83.31W
62 J10 **Cornélio Procópio** Paraná, S Brazil 23.07S 50.40W
57 V9 **Corneliskondre** Sipaliwini, N Suriname 5.21N 56.10W

◆ Country ● Country Capital ◇ Dependent Territory ○ Dependent Territory Capital ◐ Administrative Region ✖ International Airport ▲ Mountain ▲▲ Mountain Range ⋀ Volcano ≈ River ◎ Lake ⊠ Reservoir

CORNELL – CUENCA

32 *J5* **Cornell** Wisconsin, N USA *45.09N 91.10W*
11 *S12* **Corner Brook** Newfoundland and Labrador, E Canada *48.58N 57.58W*
Corner Rise Seamounts *see* Corner Seamounts
66 *I9* **Corner Seamounts** ***var.*** Corner Rise Seamounts. *undersea feature* NW Atlantic Ocean
118 *M9* **Cornești** ***Rus.*** Korneshty. C Moldova *47.23N 28.00E*
Corneto *see* Tarquinia
Cornhusker State *see* Nebraska
29 *X8* **Corning** Arkansas, C USA *36.25N 90.35W*
37 *N5* **Corning** California, W USA *39.54N 122.12W*
31 *U15* **Corning** Iowa, C USA *40.58N 94.46W*
20 *G11* **Corning** New York, NE USA *42.08N 77.03W*
Corn Islands *see* Maíz, Islas del
109 *J14* **Corno Grande** ▲ C Italy *42.26N 13.29E*
13 *N13* **Cornwall** Ontario, SE Canada *45.01N 74.45W*
99 *H25* **Cornwall** *cultural region* SW England, UK
99 *G25* **Cornwall, Cape** *headland* SW England, UK *50.11N 5.39W*
56 *J4* **Coro** ***prev.*** Santa Ana de Coro. Falcón, NW Venezuela *11.27N 69.40W*
59 *J18* **Corocoro** La Paz, W Bolivia *17.10S 68.28W*
59 *K17* **Coroico** La Paz, W Bolivia *16.09S 67.41W*
192 *M5* **Coromandel** Waikato, North Island, NZ *36.47S 175.30E*
161 *K20* **Coromandel Coast** *coast* E India
192 *M5* **Coromandel Peninsula** *peninsula* North Island, NZ
192 *M6* **Coromandel Range** ⛰ North Island, NZ
179 *P12* **Coron** Busuanga Island, W Philippines *12.02N 120.10E*
37 *T15* **Corona** California, W USA *33.52N 117.34W*
39 *T12* **Corona** New Mexico, SW USA *34.15N 105.36W*
9 *U17* **Coronach** Saskatchewan, S Canada *49.07N 105.33W*
37 *U17* **Coronado** California, W USA *32.41N 117.10W*
45 *N15* **Coronado, Bahía de** *bay* S Costa Rica
9 *R15* **Coronation** Alberta, SW Canada *52.06N 111.25W*
15 *Ii4* **Coronation Gulf** *gulf* Nunavut, N Canada
204 *I1* **Coronation Island** *island* Antarctica
41 *X14* **Coronation Island** *island* Alexander Archipelago, Alaska, USA
63 *B18* **Coronda** Santa Fe, C Argentina *31.58S 60.55W*
65 *F14* **Coronel** Bío Bío, C Chile *37.01S 73.07W*
63 *D20* **Coronel Brandsen** ***var.*** Brandsen. Buenos Aires, E Argentina *35.07S 58.15W*
64 *K4* **Coronel Cornejo** Salta, N Argentina *22.46S 63.49W*
63 *B24* **Coronel Dorrego** Buenos Aires, E Argentina *38.38S 61.15W*
64 *P6* **Coronel Oviedo** Caaguazú, SE Paraguay *25.30S 56.27W*
63 *B23* **Coronel Pringles** Buenos Aires, E Argentina *37.58S 61.26W*
63 *B23* **Coronel Suárez** Buenos Aires, E Argentina *37.27S 61.57W*
63 *E22* **Coronel Vidal** Buenos Aires, E Argentina *37.28S 57.45W*
57 *V9* **Coronie** ◈ *district* NW Suriname
59 *G17* **Coropuna, Nevado** ▲ S Peru *15.31S 72.31W*
Çorovoda *see* Çorovodë
115 *L22* **Çorovodë** ***var.*** Çorovoda. Berat, S Albania *40.29N 20.15E*
191 *P11* **Corowa** New South Wales, SE Australia *36.01S 146.22E*
44 *G1* **Corozal** Corozal, N Belize *18.22N 88.22W*
56 *E6* **Corozal** Sucre, NW Colombia *9.18N 75.19W*
44 *G1* **Corozal** ◈ *district* N Belize
27 *T14* **Corpus Christi** Texas, SW USA *27.48N 97.24W*
27 *T14* **Corpus Christi Bay** *inlet* Texas, SW USA
27 *R14* **Corpus Christi, Lake** ▣ Texas, SW USA
65 *F16* **Corral** Los Lagos, C Chile *39.55S 73.30W*
107 *O9* **Corral de Almaguer** Castilla-La Mancha, C Spain *39.45N 3.10W*
106 *K6* **Corrales** Castilla-León, N Spain *41.22N 5.43W*
39 *R11* **Corrales** New Mexico, SW USA *35.11N 106.37W*
Corrán Tuathail *see* Carrauntoohil
108 *F9* **Correggio** Emilia-Romagna, C Italy *44.47N 10.46E*
179 *P11* **Corregidor Island** *island* NW Philippines
61 *M16* **Corrente** Piauí, E Brazil *10.28S 45.10W*
61 *I19* **Correntes, Rio** ∿ SW Brazil
105 *N12* **Corrèze** ◈ *department* C France
99 *C17* **Corrib, Lough** ***Ir.*** Loch Coirib. ◎ W Ireland
63 *C14* **Corrientes** Corrientes, NE Argentina *27.28S 58.42W*
63 *D15* **Corrientes** ***off.*** Provincia de Corrientes. ◈ *province* NE Argentina
46 *A5* **Corrientes, Cabo** *headland* W Cuba *21.48N 84.30W*
42 *I13* **Corrientes, Cabo** *headland* SW Mexico *20.25N 105.42W*
Corrientes, Provincia de *see* Corrientes
63 *C16* **Corrientes, Río** ∿ NE Argentina
58 *E8* **Corrientes, Río** ∿ Ecuador/Peru
27 *W9* **Corrigan** Texas, SW USA *31.00N 94.49W*
57 *U9* **Corriverton** E Guyana *5.55N 57.09W*
Corriza *see* Korçë
191 *Q11* **Corryong** Victoria, SE Australia *36.14S 147.54E*
105 *Y12* **Corse** ***Eng.*** Corsica. ◈ *region* France, C Mediterranean Sea
105 *X13* **Corse** ***Eng.*** Corsica. *island* France, C Mediterranean Sea
105 *Y13* **Corse, Cap** *headland* Corse, France, C Mediterranean Sea *43.01N 9.25E*
105 *X15* **Corse-du-Sud** ◈ *department* Corse, France, C Mediterranean Sea
31 *P11* **Corsica** South Dakota, N USA *43.25N 98.24W*
Corsica *see* Corse
27 *U7* **Corsicana** Texas, SW USA *32.04N 96.27W*
105 *Y15* **Corte** Corse, France, C Mediterranean Sea *42.19N 9.09E*
65 *G16* **Corte Alto** Los Lagos, S Chile *40.58S 73.04W*
106 *I13* **Cortegana** Andalucía, S Spain *37.55N 6.49W*
45 *N15* **Cortés** ***var.*** Ciudad Cortés. Puntarenas, SE Costa Rica *8.59N 83.32W*
44 *G5* **Cortés** ◈ *department* NW Honduras
39 *P8* **Cortez** Colorado, C USA *37.22N 108.36W*
Cortez, Sea of *see* California, Golfo de
108 *H6* **Cortina d'Ampezzo** Veneto, NE Italy *46.33N 12.09E*
20 *H11* **Cortland** New York, NE USA *42.34N 76.09W*
33 *V11* **Cortland** Ohio, N USA *41.19N 80.43W*
108 *H12* **Cortona** Toscana, C Italy *43.15N 12.01E*
78 *H13* **Corubal, Rio** ∿ E Guinea-Bissau
106 *G10* **Coruche** Santarém, C Portugal *38.58N 8.31W*
Çoruh *see* Rize
143 *R11* **Çoruh Nehri** ***Geor.*** Chorokhi, ***Rus.*** Chorokh. ∿ Georgia/Turkey
142 *K12* **Çorum** ***var.*** Chorum. Çorum, N Turkey *40.31N 34.57E*
142 *J12* **Çorum** ***var.*** Chorum. ◈ *province* N Turkey
61 *H19* **Corumbá** Mato Grosso do Sul, S Brazil *19.00S 57.35W*
12 *D16* **Corunna** Ontario, S Canada *42.49N 82.25W*
Corunna *see* A Coruña
34 *F12* **Corvallis** Oregon, NW USA *44.34N 122.36W*
66 *M1* **Corvo** ***var.*** Ilha do Corvo. *island* Azores, Portugal, NE Atlantic Ocean
Corvo, Ilha do *see* Corvo
33 *O16* **Corydon** Indiana, N USA *38.12N 86.07W*
31 *V16* **Corydon** Iowa, C USA *40.45N 93.19W*
Cos *see* Kos
42 *I9* **Cosalá** Sinaloa, C Mexico *24.25N 106.39W*
43 *R15* **Cosamaloapan** ***var.*** Cosamaloapan de Carpio. Veracruz-Llave, E Mexico *18.21N 95.50W*
Cosamaloapan de Carpio *see* Cosamaloapan
109 *N21* **Cosenza** ***anc.*** Consentia. Calabria, SW Italy *39.16N 16.15E*
33 *T13* **Coshocton** Ohio, N USA *40.16N 81.51W*
44 *H9* **Cosigüina, Punta** *headland* NW Nicaragua *12.53N 87.42W*
31 *T9* **Cosmos** Minnesota, N USA *44.56N 94.42W*
105 *O8* **Cosne-sur-Loire** Nièvre, C France *47.25N 2.56E*
110 *B9* **Cossonay** Vaud, W Switzerland *46.37N 6.28E*
Cossyra *see* Pantelleria
49 *R4* **Costa, Cordillera de la** ***var.*** Cordillera de Venezuela. ⛰ N Venezuela
44 *K13* **Costa Rica** ***off.*** Republic of Costa Rica. ◆ *republic* Central America
45 *N15* **Costeña, Fila** ⛰ S Costa Rica
Costermansville *see* Bukavu
118 *I14* **Costești** Argeș, SW Romania *44.38N 24.52E*
39 *S8* **Costilla** New Mexico, SW USA *36.58N 105.31W*
37 *O7* **Cosumnes River** ∿ California, W USA
103 *O16* **Coswig** Sachsen, E Germany *51.07N 13.36E*
103 *M14* **Coswig** Sachsen-Anhalt, E Germany *51.53N 12.26E*
Cosyra *see* Pantelleria
179 *R16* **Cotabato** Mindanao, S Philippines *7.13N 124.12E*
58 *C5* **Cotacachi** ▲ N Ecuador *0.29N 78.17W*
59 *L21* **Cotagaita** Potosí, S Bolivia *20.46S 65.40W*
105 *V15* **Côte d'Azur** ***prev.*** Nice. ✕ (Nice) Alpes-Maritimes, SE France *43.40N 7.12E*
Côte d'Ivoire *see* Ivory Coast
105 *R8* **Côte d'Or** *cultural region* C France
105 *R7* **Côte d'Or** ◈ *department* E France
Côte Française des Somalis *see* Djibouti
104 *J4* **Cotentin** *peninsula* N France
104 *G6* **Côtes d'Armor** ***prev.*** Côtes-du-Nord. ◈ *department* NW France
Côtes-du Nord *see* Côtes d'Armor
Cöthen *see* Köthen
Côtière, Chaîne *see* Coast Mountains
42 *M13* **Cotija** ***var.*** Cotija de la Paz. Michoacán de Ocampo, SW Mexico *19.49N 102.39W*
Cotija de la Paz *see* Cotija
79 *R16* **Cotonou** ***var.*** Kotonu. S Benin *6.24N 2.25E*
79 *R16* **Cotonou** ✕ S Benin *6.31N 2.18E*
58 *B6* **Cotopaxi** ***prev.*** León. ◈ *province* C Ecuador
58 *C6* **Cotopaxi** ⊼ N Ecuador *0.42S 78.24W*
Cotrone *see* Crotone
99 *L21* **Cotswold Hills** ***var.*** Cotswolds. *hill range* S England, UK
Cotswolds *see* Cotswold Hills
34 *F13* **Cottage Grove** Oregon, NW USA *43.48N 123.03W*
23 *S14* **Cottageville** South Carolina, SE USA *32.55N 80.28W*
103 *P14* **Cottbus** ***Lus.*** Chośebuz; ***prev.*** Kottbus. Brandenburg, E Germany *51.42N 14.22E*
29 *U9* **Cotter** Arkansas, C USA *36.16N 92.30W*
108 *A9* **Cottian Alps** ***Fr.*** Alpes Cottiennes, ***It.*** Alpi Cozie. ⛰ France/Italy
Cottiennes, Alpes *see* Cottian Alps
Cotton State, The *see* Alabama
24 *G4* **Cotton Valley** Louisiana, S USA *32.49N 93.25W*
38 *L12* **Cottonwood** Arizona, SW USA *34.43N 112.00W*
34 *M10* **Cottonwood** Idaho, NW USA *46.01N 116.20W*
31 *S9* **Cottonwood** Minnesota, N USA *44.37N 95.41W*
27 *Q7* **Cottonwood** Texas, SW USA *32.12N 99.14W*
29 *O5* **Cottonwood Falls** Kansas, C USA *38.22N 96.32W*
38 *L3* **Cottonwood Heights** Utah, W USA *40.37N 111.48W*
31 *S10* **Cottonwood River** ∿ Minnesota, N USA
47 *O9* **Cotuí** C Dominican Republic *19.04N 70.10W*
27 *Q13* **Cotulla** Texas, SW USA *28.26N 99.13W*
Cotyora *see* Ordu
104 *I11* **Coubre, Pointe de la** *headland* W France *45.39N 1.23W*
20 *E12* **Coudersport** Pennsylvania, NE USA *41.45N 78.00W*
13 *S9* **Coudres, Île aux** *island* Québec, SE Canada
190 *G11* **Couedic, Cape de** *headland* South Australia *36.04S 136.43E*
Couentrey *see* Coventry
104 *I6* **Couesnon** ∿ NW France
34 *H10* **Cougar** Washington, NW USA *46.03N 122.18W*
104 *L10* **Couhé** Vienne, W France *46.18N 0.10E*
34 *K8* **Coulee City** Washington, NW USA *47.36N 119.18W*
205 *Q15* **Coulman Island** *island* Antarctica
105 *P5* **Coulommiers** Seine-et-Marne, N France *48.49N 3.04E*
12 *K11* **Coulonge** ∿ Québec, SE Canada
12 *K11* **Coulonge Est** ∿ Québec, SE Canada
37 *Q9* **Coulterville** California, W USA *37.41N 120.10W*
40 *M9* **Council** Alaska, USA *64.54N 163.40W*
34 *M12* **Council** Idaho, NW USA *44.45N 116.26W*
31 *S15* **Council Bluffs** Iowa, C USA *41.15N 95.51W*
29 *O5* **Council Grove** Kansas, C USA *38.37N 96.27W*
29 *O5* **Council Grove Lake** ▣ Kansas, C USA
34 *G7* **Coupeville** Washington, NW USA *48.13N 122.41W*
57 *U12* **Courantyne River** ***var.*** Corantijn Rivier, Corentyne River. ∿ Guyana/Suriname
101 *G21* **Courcelles** Hainaut, S Belgium *50.28N 4.22E*
110 *C7* **Courgenay** Jura, NW Switzerland *47.24N 7.09E*
130 *B2* **Courland Lagoon** ***Ger.*** Kurisches Haff, ***Rus.*** Kurskiy Zaliv. *lagoon* Lithuania/Russian Federation
120 *B12* **Courland Spit** ***Lith.*** Kuršių Nerija, ***Rus.*** Kurshskaya Kosa. *spit* Lithuania/Russian Federation
108 *A6* **Courmayeur** ***prev.*** Cormaiore. Valle d'Aosta, NW Italy *45.48N 7.00E*
110 *D7* **Courroux** Jura, NW Switzerland *47.22N 7.22E*
8 *K17* **Courtenay** Vancouver Island, British Columbia, SW Canada *49.40N 124.58W*
23 *W7* **Courtland** Virginia, NE USA *36.41N 77.01W*
27 *V10* **Courtney** Texas, SW USA *30.16N 96.04W*
32 *J4* **Court Oreilles, Lac** ◎ Wisconsin, N USA
Courtrai *see* Kortrijk
101 *H19* **Court-Saint-Étienne** Wallon Brabant, C Belgium *50.38N 4.34E*
24 *G6* **Coushatta** Louisiana, S USA *32.00N 93.20W*
180 *I16* **Cousin** *island* Inner Islands, NE Seychelles
180 *I16* **Cousine** *island* Inner Islands, NE Seychelles
104 *J4* **Coutances** ***anc.*** Constantia. Manche, N France *49.04N 1.27W*
104 *K12* **Coutras** Gironde, SW France *45.01N 0.07W*
47 *U14* **Couva** Trinidad, Trinidad and Tobago *10.25N 61.27W*
110 *B8* **Couvet** Neuchâtel, W Switzerland *46.57N 6.41E*
101 *H22* **Couvin** Namur, S Belgium *50.03N 4.30E*
118 *K12* **Covasna** ***Ger.*** Kowasna, ***Hung.*** Kovászna. Covasna, E Romania *45.51N 26.09E*
118 *J11* **Covasna** ◈ *county* E Romania
12 *E12* **Cove Island** *island* Ontario, S Canada
36 *M5* **Covelo** California, W USA *39.46N 123.16W*
99 *M20* **Coventry** ***anc.*** Couentrey. C England, UK *52.25N 1.30W*
Cove of Cork *see* Cobh
23 *U5* **Covesville** Virginia, NE USA *37.52N 78.41W*
106 *I8* **Covilhã** Castelo Branco, E Portugal *40.16N 7.30W*
25 *T3* **Covington** Georgia, SE USA *33.34N 83.52W*
33 *N13* **Covington** Indiana, N USA *40.08N 87.23W*
22 *M3* **Covington** Kentucky, S USA *39.04N 84.30W*
24 *K8* **Covington** Louisiana, S USA *30.28N 90.06W*
33 *Q13* **Covington** Ohio, N USA *40.07N 84.21W*
22 *F9* **Covington** Tennessee, S USA *35.33N 89.39W*
23 *S6* **Covington** Virginia, NE USA *37.47N 79.59W*
191 *Q8* **Cowal, Lake** *seasonal lake* New South Wales, SE Australia
9 *W15* **Cowan** Manitoba, S Canada *51.59N 100.36W*
20 *F12* **Cowanesque River** ∿ New York/Pennsylvania, NE USA
188 *L12* **Cowan, Lake** ◎ Western Australia
13 *P13* **Cowansville** Québec, SE Canada *45.13N 72.43W*
190 *H8* **Cowell** South Australia *33.43S 136.53E*
99 *M23* **Cowes** S England, UK *50.45N 1.19W*
29 *Q10* **Coweta** Oklahoma, C USA *35.57N 95.39W*
(0) *D6* **Cowie Seamount** *undersea feature* NE Pacific Ocean *54.15N 149.30W*
34 *G10* **Cowlitz River** ∿ Washington, NW USA
23 *Q11* **Cowpens** South Carolina, SE USA *35.01N 81.48W*
191 *R8* **Cowra** New South Wales, SE Australia *33.52S 148.36E*
Coxen Hole *see* Roatán
61 *I19* **Coxim** Mato Grosso do Sul, S Brazil *18.28S 54.45W*
61 *I19* **Coxim, Rio** ∿ SW Brazil
Coxin Hole *see* Roatán
159 *V17* **Cox's Bazar** Chittagong, S Bangladesh *21.25N 92.01E*
78 *H14* **Coyah** Conakry, W Guinea *9.45N 13.25W*
42 *K5* **Coyame** Chihuahua, N Mexico *29.28N 105.01W*
26 *L9* **Coyanosa Draw** ∿ Texas, SW USA
Coyhaique *see* Coihaique
44 *C7* **Coyolate, Río** ∿ S Guatemala
Coyote State *see* South Dakota
42 *I10* **Coyotitán** Sinaloa, C Mexico *23.44N 106.34W*
43 *N15* **Coyuca** ***var.*** Coyuca de Catalán. Guerrero, S Mexico *18.21N 100.39W*
43 *O16* **Coyuca** ***var.*** Coyuca de Benítez. Guerrero, S Mexico *16.57N 100.01W*
Coyuca de Benítez/Coyuca de Catalán *see* Coyuca
31 *N15* **Cozad** Nebraska, C USA *40.52N 99.58W*
Cozie, Alpi *see* Cottian Alps
Cozmeni *see* Kitsman'
42 *E3* **Cozón, Cerro** ▲ NW Mexico *31.16N 112.29W*
43 *Z12* **Cozumel** Quintana Roo, E Mexico *20.28N 86.54W*
43 *Z12* **Cozumel, Isla** *island* SE Mexico
34 *K8* **Crab Creek** ∿ Washington, NW USA
46 *H12* **Crab Pond Point** *headland* W Jamaica *18.07N 78.01W*
Cracovia/Cracow *see* Małopolskie
85 *I25* **Cradock** Eastern Cape, S South Africa *32.06S 25.37E*
41 *Y14* **Craig** Prince of Wales Island, Alaska, USA *55.29N 133.04W*
39 *Q3* **Craig** Colorado, C USA *40.31N 107.33W*
99 *F15* **Craigavon** C Northern Ireland, UK *54.28N 6.25W*
23 *T5* **Craigsville** Virginia, NE USA *38.07N 79.21W*
103 *J21* **Crailsheim** Baden-Württemberg, S Germany *49.07N 10.04E*
118 *H14* **Craiova** Dolj, SW Romania *44.19N 23.49E*
8 *K12* **Cranberry Junction** British Columbia, SW Canada *55.35N 128.21W*
20 *J8* **Cranberry Lake** ◎ New York, NE USA
9 *V13* **Cranberry Portage** Manitoba, C Canada *54.34N 101.22W*
9 *P17* **Cranbrook** British Columbia, SW Canada *49.28N 115.48W*
32 *M5* **Crandon** Wisconsin, N USA *45.34N 88.54W*
34 *K14* **Crane** Oregon, NW USA *43.24N 118.35W*
26 *M9* **Crane** Texas, SW USA *31.24N 102.21W*
Crane *see* The Crane
27 *S8* **Cranfills Gap** Texas, SW USA *31.46N 97.49W*
21 *O12* **Cranston** Rhode Island, NE USA *41.46N 71.26W*
Cranz *see* Zelenogradsk
61 *L15* **Craolândia** Tocantins, E Brazil *7.17S 47.23W*
104 *J7* **Craon** Mayenne, NW France *47.52N 0.57W*
205 *V16* **Crary, Cape** *headland* Antarctica
Crasna *see* Kraszna
34 *G14* **Crater Lake** ◎ Oregon, NW USA
194 *I13* **Crater Mount** ▲ C PNG *6.23S 145.18E*
35 *P14* **Craters of the Moon National Monument** *national park* Idaho, NW USA
61 *O14* **Crateús** Ceará, E Brazil *5.10S 40.39W*
Crathis *see* Crati
109 *N20* **Crati** ***anc.*** Crathis. ∿ S Italy
9 *U16* **Craven** Saskatchewan, S Canada *50.43N 104.49W*
56 *I8* **Cravo Norte** Arauca, E Colombia *6.17N 70.15W*
30 *J12* **Crawford** Nebraska, C USA *42.40N 103.24W*
27 *T8* **Crawford** Texas, SW USA *31.31N 97.26W*
9 *O17* **Crawford Bay** British Columbia, SW Canada *49.39N 116.44W*
67 *M19* **Crawford Seamount** *undersea feature* S Atlantic Ocean *40.30S 10.00W*
33 *O13* **Crawfordsville** Indiana, N USA *40.02N 86.52W*
25 *S9* **Crawfordville** Florida, SE USA *30.10N 84.22W*
99 *O23* **Crawley** SE England, UK *51.07N 0.12W*
35 *S10* **Crazy Mountains** ⛰ Montana, NW USA
9 *T11* **Cree** ∿ Saskatchewan, C Canada
39 *R7* **Creede** Colorado, C USA *37.51N 106.55W*
42 *I6* **Creel** Chihuahua, N Mexico *27.45N 107.36W*
9 *S11* **Cree Lake** ◎ Saskatchewan, C Canada
9 *V13* **Creighton** Saskatchewan, C Canada *54.46N 101.54W*
31 *Q13* **Creighton** Nebraska, C USA *42.28N 97.54W*
105 *O4* **Creil** Oise, N France *49.16N 2.28E*
108 *E8* **Crema** Lombardia, N Italy *45.22N 9.40E*
108 *E8* **Cremona** Lombardia, N Italy *45.07N 10.01E*
Creole State *see* Louisiana
114 *M10* **Crepaja** ***Hung.*** Cserépalja. Serbia, N Serbia and Montenegro (Yugoslavia) *45.02N 20.36E*
105 *O4* **Crépy-en-Valois** Oise, N France *49.13N 2.54E*
114 *B10* **Cres** ***It.*** Cherso. Primorje-Gorski Kotar, NW Croatia *44.57N 14.24E*
114 *A11* **Cres** ***It.*** Cherso; ***anc.*** Crexa. *island* W Croatia
34 *H14* **Crescent** Oregon, NW USA *43.27N 121.40W*
36 *K1* **Crescent City** California, W USA *41.45N 124.13W*
25 *W10* **Crescent City** Florida, SE USA *29.25N 81.30W*
178 *M10* **Crescent Group** *island group* C Paracel Islands
25 *W10* **Crescent Lake** ◎ Florida, SE USA
31 *X11* **Cresco** Iowa, C USA *43.22N 92.06W*
63 *B18* **Crespo** Entre Ríos, E Argentina *32.02S 60.22W*
56 *E5* **Crespo** ✕ (Cartagena) Bolívar, NW Colombia *10.27N 75.31W*
105 *R13* **Crest** Drôme, E France *44.45N 5.00E*
39 *R5* **Crested Butte** Colorado, C USA *38.52N 106.59W*
33 *S12* **Crestline** Ohio, N USA *40.47N 82.44W*
9 *O17* **Creston** British Columbia, SW Canada *49.04N 116.31W*
31 *U15* **Creston** Iowa, C USA *41.03N 94.21W*
35 *V16* **Creston** Wyoming, C USA *41.40N 107.43W*
39 *S7* **Crestone Peak** ▲ Colorado, C USA *37.58N 105.34W*
25 *P8* **Crestview** Florida, SE USA *30.43N 86.34W*
123 *Gg10* **Cretan Trough** *undersea feature* Aegean Sea, C Mediterranean Sea
31 *R16* **Crete** Nebraska, C USA *40.36N 96.58W*
Crete *see* Kríti
105 *O5* **Créteil** Val-de-Marne, N France *48.46N 2.28E*
Crete, Sea of/Creticum, Mare *see* Kritikó Pélagos
107 *X4* **Creus, Cap de** *headland* NE Spain *42.18N 3.18E*
105 *N10* **Creuse** ◈ *department* C France
104 *L9* **Creuse** ∿ C France
105 *T4* **Creutzwald** Moselle, NE France *49.13N 6.41E*
107 *S12* **Crevillente** País Valenciano, E Spain *38.12N 0.47W*
99 *L18* **Crewe** C England, UK *53.04N 2.27W*
23 *V7* **Crewe** Virginia, NE USA *37.10N 78.07W*
Crexa *see* Cres
45 *Q15* **Cricamola, Río** ∿ NW Panama
63 *K14* **Criciúma** Santa Catarina, S Brazil *28.39S 49.22W*
98 *J11* **Crieff** C Scotland, UK *56.22N 3.49W*
114 *B10* **Crikvenica** ***It.*** Cirquenizza; ***prev.*** Cirkvenica, Crjkvenica. Primorje-Gorski Kotar, NW Croatia *45.12N 14.40E*
Crimea/Crimean Oblast *see* Krym, Respublika
103 *M16* **Crimmitschau** ***var.*** Krimmitschau. Sachsen, E Germany *50.48N 12.22E*
118 *G11* **Crișcior** ***Hung.*** Kristyor. Hunedoara, W Romania *46.09N 22.54E*
23 *Y5* **Crisfield** Maryland, NE USA *37.58N 75.51W*
33 *P3* **Crisp Point** *headland* Michigan, N USA *46.45N 85.15W*
61 *L19* **Cristalina** Goiás, C Brazil *16.43S 47.37W*
46 *J7* **Cristal, Sierra del** ⛰ E Cuba
45 *T14* **Cristóbal** Colón, C Panama *9.18N 79.52W*
56 *F4* **Cristóbal Colón, Pico** ▲ N Colombia *10.52N 73.46W*
Cristur/Cristuru Săcuiesc *see* Cristuru Secuiesc
118 *I11* **Cristuru Secuiesc** ***prev.*** Cristur, Cristuru Săcuiesc, Sitaș Cristuru, ***Ger.*** Kreutz, ***Hung.*** Székelykeresztúr, Szitás-Keresztúr. Harghita, C Romania *46.16N 25.01E*
118 *F10* **Crișul Alb** ***var.*** Weisse Kreisch, ***Ger.*** Weisse Körös, ***Hung.*** Fehér-Körös. ∿ Hungary/Romania
118 *F10* **Crișul Negru** ***Ger.*** Schwarze Körös, ***Hung.*** Fekete-Körös. ∿ Hungary/Romania
118 *G10* **Crișul Repede** ***var.*** Schnelle Kreisch, ***Ger.*** Schnelle Körös, ***Hung.*** Sebes-Körös. ∿ Hungary/Romania
119 *N10* **Criuleni** ***Rus.*** Kriulyany. C Moldova *47.12N 29.09E*
Crivadia Vulcanului *see* Vulcan
Crjkvenica *see* Crikvenica
115 *O17* **Crna Gora** ⛰ FYR Macedonia/Serbia and Montenegro (Yugoslavia)
Crna Gora *see* Montenegro
115 *O20* **Crna Reka** ∿ S FYR Macedonia
Crni Drim *see* Black Drin
111 *V10* **Črni vrh** ▲ NE Slovenia *46.28N 15.14E*
111 *V13* **Črnomelj** ***Ger.*** Tschernembl. SE Slovenia *45.32N 15.12E*
99 *A17* **Croagh Patrick** ***Ir.*** Cruach Phádraig. ▲ W Ireland *53.45N 9.39W*
114 *D9* **Croatia** ***off.*** Republic of Croatia, ***Ger.*** Kroatien, ***SCr.*** Hrvatska. ◆ *republic* SE Europe
Croce, Picco di *see* Wilde Kreuzspitze
13 *P8* **Croche** ∿ Québec, SE Canada
175 *Nn3* **Crocker, Banjaran** ***var.*** Crocker Range. ⛰ East Malaysia
Crocker Range *see* Crocker, Banjaran
27 *V9* **Crockett** Texas, SW USA *31.19N 95.27W*
69 *V14* **Crocodile** ***var.*** Krokodil. ∿ N South Africa
Crocodile *see* Limpopo
22 *I7* **Crofton** Kentucky, S USA *37.01N 87.25W*
31 *Q12* **Crofton** Nebraska, C USA *42.43N 97.30W*
Croia *see* Krujë
105 *R16* **Croisette, Cap** *headland* SE France *43.12N 5.21E*
104 *G8* **Croisic, Pointe du** *headland* NW France *47.16N 2.42W*
105 *S13* **Croix Haute, Col de la** *pass* E France *44.43N 5.39E*
13 *U5* **Croix, Pointe à la** *headland* Québec, SE Canada *49.16N 67.46W*
12 *F13* **Croker, Cape** *headland* Ontario, S Canada *44.56N 80.57W*
189 *P1* **Croker Island** *island* Northern Territory, N Australia
98 *I8* **Cromarty** N Scotland, UK *57.40N 4.01W*
101 *M21* **Crombach** Liège, E Belgium *50.14N 6.07E*
99 *Q18* **Cromer** E England, UK *52.55N 1.06E*
193 *D22* **Cromwell** Otago, South Island, NZ *45.03S 169.13E*
193 *H16* **Cronadun** West Coast, South Island, NZ *42.03S 171.52E*
41 *O11* **Crooked Creek** Alaska, USA *61.52N 158.06W*
46 *K5* **Crooked Island** *island* SE Bahamas
46 *J5* **Crooked Island Passage** *channel* SE Bahamas
34 *I13* **Crooked River** ∿ Oregon, NW USA
31 *R4* **Crookston** Minnesota, N USA *47.46N 96.36W*
30 *I10* **Crooks Tower** ▲ South Dakota, N USA *44.09N 103.55W*
33 *T14* **Crooksville** Ohio, N USA *39.46N 82.05W*
191 *R9* **Crookwell** New South Wales, SE Australia *34.28S 149.27E*
12 *L14* **Crosby** Ontario, SE Canada *44.39N 76.13W*
99 *K17* **Crosby** ***var.*** Great Crosby. NW England, UK *53.30N 3.01W*
31 *U6* **Crosby** Minnesota, N USA *46.30N 93.58W*
30 *K2* **Crosby** North Dakota, N USA *48.54N 103.17W*
27 *O5* **Crosbyton** Texas, SW USA *33.39N 101.14W*
79 *V16* **Cross** ∿ Cameroon/Nigeria
25 *U10* **Cross City** Florida, SE USA *29.37N 83.08W*
Crossen *see* Krosno Odrzańskie
29 *V14* **Crossett** Arkansas, C USA *33.08N 91.58W*
99 *K15* **Cross Fell** ▲ N England, UK *54.42N 2.30W*
9 *P16* **Crossfield** Alberta, SW Canada *51.24N 114.03W*
23 *Q12* **Cross Hill** South Carolina, SE USA *34.18N 81.58W*
21 *U6* **Cross Island** *island* Maine, NE USA
9 *X13* **Cross Lake** Manitoba, C Canada *54.37N 97.34W*
24 *F5* **Cross Lake** ▣ Louisiana, S USA
38 *I12* **Crossman Peak** ▲ Arizona, SW USA *34.33N 114.09W*
27 *Q7* **Cross Plains** Texas, SW USA *32.07N 99.10W*
79 *V17* **Cross River** ◈ *state* SE Nigeria
22 *L9* **Crossville** Tennessee, S USA *35.57N 85.01W*
33 *S8* **Croswell** Michigan, N USA *43.16N 82.37W*
12 *K13* **Crotch Lake** ◎ Ontario, SE Canada
Croton/Crotona *see* Crotone
109 *O21* **Crotone** ***var.*** Cotrone; ***anc.*** Croton, Crotona. Calabria, SW Italy *39.04N 17.07E*
35 *V11* **Crow Agency** Montana, NW USA *45.35N 107.28W*
191 *U7* **Crowdy Head** *headland* New South Wales, SE Australia *31.52S 152.45E*
27 *Q4* **Crowell** Texas, SW USA *33.58N 99.43W*
191 *O6* **Crowl Creek** *seasonal river* New South Wales, SE Australia
24 *H9* **Crowley** Louisiana, S USA *30.11N 92.21W*
37 *S9* **Crowley, Lake** ▣ California, W USA
29 *X10* **Crowleys Ridge** *hill range* Arkansas, C USA
194 *J11* **Crown Island** *island* N Papau New Guinea
33 *N11* **Crown Point** Indiana, N USA *41.25N 87.22W*
39 *P10* **Crownpoint** New Mexico, SW USA *35.40N 108.09W*
35 *R10* **Crow Peak** ▲ Montana, NW USA *46.17N 111.54W*
9 *P17* **Crowsnest Pass** *pass* Alberta/British Columbia, SW Canada *49.38N 114.43W*
31 *T6* **Crow Wing River** ∿ Minnesota, N USA
99 *O22* **Croydon** SE England, UK *51.21N 0.06W*
181 *P11* **Crozet Basin** *undersea feature* S Indian Ocean
181 *O12* **Crozet Islands** *island group* French Southern and Antarctic Territories
181 *N12* **Crozet Plateau** ***var.*** Crozet Plateaus. *undersea feature* SW Indian Ocean
Crozet Plateaus *see* Crozet Plateau
104 *E6* **Crozon** Finistère, NW France *48.14N 4.31W*
Cruacha Dubha, Na *see* Macgillycuddy's Reeks
Cruach Phádraig *see* Croagh Patrick
118 *M14* **Crucea** Constanța, SE Romania *44.30N 28.18E*
46 *E5* **Cruces** Cienfuegos, C Cuba *22.18N 80.18W*
109 *O20* **Crucoli Torretta** Calabria, SW Italy *39.26N 17.03E*
43 *P9* **Cruillas** Tamaulipas, C Mexico *24.43N 98.26W*
66 *K9* **Cruiser Tablemount** *undersea feature* E Atlantic Ocean *32.00N 28.00W*
63 *G14* **Cruz Alta** Rio Grande do Sul, S Brazil *28.37S 53.37W*
46 *G8* **Cruz, Cabo** *headland* S Cuba *19.50N 77.43W*
62 *N9* **Cruzeiro** São Paulo, S Brazil *22.33S 44.55W*
62 *H10* **Cruzeiro do Oeste** Paraná, S Brazil *23.45S 53.03W*
61 *A15* **Cruzeiro do Sul** Acre, W Brazil *7.40S 72.39W*
25 *U11* **Crystal Bay** *bay* Florida, SE USA
190 *I8* **Crystal Brook** South Australia *33.24S 138.10E*
9 *X17* **Crystal City** Manitoba, S Canada *49.07N 98.54W*
29 *X5* **Crystal City** Missouri, C USA *38.13N 90.22W*
27 *P13* **Crystal City** Texas, SW USA *28.40N 99.49W*
32 *M4* **Crystal Falls** Michigan, N USA *46.06N 88.19W*
25 *Q8* **Crystal Lake** Florida, SE USA *30.26N 85.41W*
33 *O6* **Crystal Lake** ◎ Michigan, N USA
25 *V11* **Crystal River** Florida, SE USA *28.54N 82.35W*
39 *Q5* **Crystal River** ∿ Colorado, C USA
24 *K6* **Crystal Springs** Mississippi, S USA *31.59N 90.21W*
Csaca *see* Čadca
Csakathurn/Csáktornya *see* Čakovec
Csap *see* Chop
Csepén *see* Čepin
Cserépalja *see* Crepaja
Csermő *see* Cermei
Csíkszereda *see* Miercurea-Ciuc
113 *L24* **Csongrád** Csongrád, SE Hungary *46.42N 20.05E*
113 *L24* **Csongrád** ***off.*** Csongrád Megye. ◈ *county* SE Hungary
113 *H22* **Csorna** Győr-Moson-Sopron, NW Hungary *47.37N 17.13E*
Csucsa *see* Ciucea
113 *G25* **Csurgó** Somogy, SW Hungary *46.16N 17.09E*
Csurog *see* Čurug
56 *L5* **Cúa** Miranda, N Venezuela *10.07N 66.53W*
84 *C11* **Cuale** Malanje, NW Angola *8.13S 16.11E*
69 *T12* **Cuando** ***var.*** Kwando. ∿ S Africa
85 *E15* **Cuando Cubango** ***var.*** Kuando-Kubango. ◈ *province* SE Angola
85 *E16* **Cuangar** Cuando Cubango, S Angola *17.34S 18.39E*
84 *D11* **Cuango** Lunda Norte, NE Angola *9.09S 18.01E*
84 *C10* **Cuango** Uíge, NW Angola *6.17S 16.41E*
84 *C10* **Cuango** ***var.*** Kwango. ∿ Angola/Dem. Rep. Congo ***see also*** Kwango
Cuan, Loch *see* Strangford Lough
84 *C12* **Cuanza** ***var.*** Kwanza. ∿ C Angola
84 *B11* **Cuanza Norte** ***var.*** Kuanza Norte. ◈ *province* NE Angola
84 *B12* **Cuanza Sul** ***var.*** Kuanza Sul. ◈ *province* NE Angola
63 *E16* **Cuareim, Río** ***var.*** Rio Quaraí. ∿ Brazil/Uruguay ***see also*** Quaraí, Rio
85 *D15* **Cuatir** ∿ S Angola
42 *M7* **Cuatro Ciénegas** ***var.*** Cuatro Ciénegas de Carranza. Coahuila de Zaragoza, NE Mexico *26.59N 102.04W*
Cuatro Ciénegas de Carranza *see* Cuatro Ciénegas
42 *I6* **Cuauhtémoc** Chihuahua, N Mexico *28.22N 106.51W*
43 *P14* **Cuautla** Morelos, S Mexico *18.47N 98.56W*
106 *H12* **Cuba** Beja, S Portugal *38.10N 7.54W*
29 *W6* **Cuba** Missouri, C USA *38.03N 91.24W*
39 *R10* **Cuba** New Mexico, SW USA *36.01N 106.57W*
46 *E6* **Cuba** ***off.*** Republic of Cuba. ◆ *republic* W West Indies
49 *O2* **Cuba** *island* W West Indies
84 *B13* **Cubal** Benguela, W Angola *12.58S 14.16E*
85 *C15* **Cubango** ***var.*** Kuvango, ***Port.*** Vila Artur de Paiva, Vila da Ponte. Huíla, SW Angola *14.27S 16.17E*
85 *D16* **Cubango** ***var.*** Kavango, Kavengo, Kubango, Okavango, Okavanggo. ∿ S Africa ***see also*** Okavango
56 *H8* **Cubará** Boyacá, N Colombia *7.01N 72.07W*
142 *I12* **Çubuk** Ankara, N Turkey *40.13N 33.01E*
85 *D14* **Cuchi** Cuando Cubango, C Angola *14.40S 16.58E*
44 *C5* **Cuchumatanes, Sierra de los** ⛰ W Guatemala
Cuculaya, Rio *see* Kukalaya, Rio
84 *E12* **Cucumbi** ***prev.*** Trás-os-Montes. Lunda Sul, NE Angola *10.13S 19.04E*
56 *G7* **Cúcuta** ***var.*** San José de Cúcuta. Norte de Santander, N Colombia *7.55N 72.31W*
33 *N9* **Cudahy** Wisconsin, N USA *42.54N 87.51W*
161 *J21* **Cuddalore** Tamil Nādu, SE India *11.43N 79.46E*
161 *I18* **Cuddapah** Andhra Pradesh, S India *14.30N 78.49E*
106 *M6* **Cuéllar** Castilla-León, N Spain *41.24N 4.19W*
84 *D13* **Cuemba** ***var.*** Coemba. Bié, C Angola *12.09S 18.07E*
58 *B8* **Cuenca** Azuay, S Ecuador *02.54S 79.00W*
107 *Q9* **Cuenca** ***anc.*** Conca. Castilla-La Mancha, C Spain *40.04N 2.07W*
107 *P9* **Cuenca** ◈ *province* Castilla-La Mancha, C Spain

◆ COUNTRY
● COUNTRY CAPITAL
◇ DEPENDENT TERRITORY
○ DEPENDENT TERRITORY CAPITAL
◈ ADMINISTRATIVE REGION
✕ INTERNATIONAL AIRPORT
▲ MOUNTAIN
⛰ MOUNTAIN RANGE
⊼ VOLCANO
∿ RIVER
◎ LAKE
▣ RESERVOIR

CUENCAMÉ – DANVILLE

42 L9 **Cuencamé** *var.* Cuencamé de Ceniceros. Durango, C Mexico *24.51N 103.42W*
Cuencamé de Ceniceros *see* Cuencamé
107 Q8 **Cuenca, Serranía de** ▲▲ C Spain
Cuera *see* Chur
107 P5 **Cuerda del Pozo, Embalse de la** ⊠ N Spain
43 O14 **Cuernavaca** Morelos, S Mexico *18.57N 99.15W*
27 T12 **Cuero** Texas, SW USA *29.04N 97.16W*
46 I7 **Cueto** Holguín, E Cuba *20.39N 75.55W*
43 Q13 **Cuetzalán** *var.* Cuetzalán del Progreso. Puebla, S Mexico *20.00N 97.27W*
Cuetzalán del Progreso *see* Cuetzalán
107 Q14 **Cuevas de Almanzora** Andalucía, S Spain *37.19N 1.52W*
107 T8 **Cuevas de Vinromá** País Valenciano, E Spain *40.18N 0.07E*
118 H12 **Cugir** *Hung.* Kudzsir. Alba, SW Romania *45.48N 23.24E*
61 H18 **Cuiabá** *prev.* Cuyabá. *state capital* Mato Grosso, SW Brazil *15.31S 56.04W*
61 H19 **Cuiabá, Rio** ~ SW Brazil
43 R15 **Cuicatlán** *var.* San Juan Bautista Cuicatlán. Oaxaca, SE Mexico *17.48N 96.57W*
203 W16 **Cuidado, Punta** *headland* Easter Island, Chile, E Pacific Ocean *27.07S 109.18W*
Cuidad Presidente Stroessner *see* Ciudad del Este
Cúige *see* Connaught
Cúige Laighean *see* Leinster
Cúige Mumhan *see* Munster
Cuihua *see* Daguan
100 L13 **Cuijck** Noord-Brabant, SE Netherlands *51.40N 5.55E*
Cúil an tSúdaire *see* Portarlington
44 D7 **Cuilapa** Santa Rosa, S Guatemala *14.15N 90.17W*
44 B5 **Cuilco, Río** ~ W Guatemala
Cúil Mhuine *see* Collooney
Cúil Raithin *see* Coleraine
85 C14 **Cuima** Huambo, C Angola *13.16S 15.39E*
85 E16 **Cuito** *var.* Kwito. ~ SE Angola
85 E15 **Cuito Cuanavale** Cuando Cubango, E Angola *15.01S 19.07E*
41 N14 **Cuitzeo, Lago de** ◎ C Mexico
29 W4 **Cuivre River** ~ Missouri, C USA
Čuka *see* Çukë
174 Hh4 **Cukai** *var.* Chukai, Kemaman. Terengganu, Peninsular Malaysia *4.15N 103.25E*
115 L23 **Çukë** *var.* Çuka. Vlorë, S Albania *39.50N 20.01E*
Cularo *see* Grenoble
179 Pp13 **Culasi** Panay Island, C Philippines *11.21N 122.05E*
35 Y7 **Culbertson** Montana, NW USA *48.09N 104.30W*
30 M16 **Culbertson** Nebraska, C USA *40.13N 100.50W*
191 P10 **Culcairn** New South Wales, SE Australia *35.41S 147.01E*
47 W5 **Culebra** *var.* Dewey. E Puerto Rico *18.19N 65.17W*
47 W6 **Culebra, Isla de** *island* E Puerto Rico
39 T8 **Culebra Peak** ▲ Colorado, C USA *37.07N 105.11W*
106 J5 **Culebra, Sierra de la** ▲▲ NW Spain
100 J12 **Culemborg** Gelderland, C Netherlands *51.57N 5.17E*
143 V14 **Culfa** *Rus.* Dzhul'fa. SW Azerbaijan *38.58N 45.37E*
191 P4 **Culgoa River** ~ New South Wales/Queensland, SE Australia
42 I9 **Culiacán** *var.* Culiacán Rosales, Culiacán-Rosales. Sinaloa, C Mexico *24.48N 107.25W*
Culiacán-Rosales/Culiacán Rosales *see* Culiacán
179 P13 **Culion Island** *island* Calamian Group, W Philippines
107 P14 **Cúllar-Baza** Andalucía, S Spain *37.34N 2.34W*
107 S10 **Cullera** País Valenciano, E Spain *39.10N 0.15W*
25 P3 **Cullman** Alabama, S USA *34.10N 86.50W*
110 B10 **Cully** Vaud, W Switzerland *46.58N 6.46E*
Culm *see* Chełmno
Culmsee *see* Chełmża
23 V4 **Culpeper** Virginia, NE USA *38.28N 78.00W*
193 I17 **Culverden** Canterbury, South Island, NZ *42.46S 172.51E*
57 N5 **Cumaná** Sucre, NE Venezuela *10.28N 64.12W*
57 O5 **Cumanacoa** Sucre, NE Venezuela *10.16N 63.58W*
56 C13 **Cumbal, Nevado de** *elevation* S Colombia *0.51N 77.58W*
23 O7 **Cumberland** Kentucky, S USA *36.55N 83.00W*
23 U2 **Cumberland** Maryland, NE USA *39.39N 78.45W*
23 V6 **Cumberland** Virginia, NE USA *37.30N 78.13W*
197 A11 **Cumberland, Cape** *var.* Cape Nahoi. *headland* Espiritu Santo, N Vanuatu *14.39S 166.35E*
9 V14 **Cumberland House** Saskatchewan, C Canada *53.57N 102.21W*
25 W8 **Cumberland Island** *island* Georgia, SE USA
22 L7 **Cumberland, Lake** ⊠ Kentucky, S USA
16 O1 **Cumberland Peninsula** *peninsula* Baffin Island, Nunavut, NE Canada
2 N9 **Cumberland Plateau** *plateau* E USA
32 L1 **Cumberland Point** *headland* Michigan, N USA *47.51N 89.14W*
23 O7 **Cumberland River** ~ Kentucky/Tennessee, S USA
16 O2 **Cumberland Sound** *inlet* Baffin Island, Nunavut, NE Canada
98 I12 **Cumbernauld** S Scotland, UK *55.57N 4.00W*
99 K15 **Cumbria** *cultural region* NW England, UK
99 K15 **Cumbrian Mountains** ▲▲ NW England, UK
25 S2 **Cumming** Georgia, SE USA *34.12N 84.08W*
Cummin in Pommern *see* Kamień Pomorski
190 G9 **Cummins** South Australia *34.17S 135.43E*
98 I13 **Cumnock** W Scotland, UK *55.31N 4.28W*
42 G4 **Cumpas** Sonora, NW Mexico *30.00N 109.48W*
142 H16 **Çumra** Konya, C Turkey *37.32N 32.52E*
65 G15 **Cunco** Araucanía, C Chile *38.57S 72.13W*
56 E9 **Cundinamarca** *off.* Departamento de Cundinamarca. ◆ *province* C Colombia
43 U15 **Cunduacán** Tabasco, SE Mexico *18.00N 93.07W*
85 C16 **Cunene** ◆ *province* S Angola
85 A16 **Cunene** *var.* Kunene. ~ Angola/Namibia *see also* Kunene
108 A9 **Cuneo** *Fr.* Coni. Piemonte, NW Italy *44.22N 7.31E*
85 E15 **Cunjamba** Cuando Cubango, E Angola *15.22S 20.07E*
189 V10 **Cunnamulla** Queensland, E Australia *28.09S 145.43E*
Čunusavvon *see* Junosuando
Cuokkarašša *see* Čohkarášša
108 B7 **Cuorgne** Piemonte, NE Italy *45.23N 7.34E*
98 K11 **Cupar** E Scotland, UK *56.19N 3.01W*
118 L8 **Cupcina** *Rus.* Kupchino; *prev.* Calinisc, Kalinisk. N Moldova *48.07N 27.22E*
56 C8 **Cupica** Chocó, W Colombia *6.43N 77.31W*
56 C8 **Cupica, Golfo de** *gulf* W Colombia
114 N13 **Ćuprija** Serbia, E Serbia and Montenegro (Yugoslavia) *43.57N 21.21E*
Cura *see* Villa de Cura
47 P16 **Curaçao** *island* Netherlands Antilles
58 H13 **Curanja, Río** ~ E Peru
58 F7 **Curaray, Río** ~ Ecuador/Peru
118 K14 **Curcani** Călărași, SE Romania *44.04N 26.39E*
190 H4 **Curdimurka** South Australia *29.27S 136.56E*
105 P7 **Cure** ~ C France
181 Y16 **Curepipe** C Mauritius *20.19S 57.31E*
57 R6 **Curiapo** Delta Amacuro, NE Venezuela *10.03N 63.05W*
Curia Rhaetorum *see* Chur
64 G12 **Curicó** Maule, C Chile *35.00S 71.15W*
Curieta *see* Krk
180 I15 **Curieuse** *island* Inner Islands, NE Seychelles
61 C16 **Curitiba** Acre, W Brazil *10.08S 69.00W*
62 K12 **Curitiba** *prev.* Curytiba. *state capital* Paraná, S Brazil *25.25S 49.25W*
62 J13 **Curitibanos** Santa Catarina, S Brazil *27.18S 50.34W*
191 S6 **Curlewis** New South Wales, SE Australia *31.09S 150.18E*
190 J6 **Curnamona** South Australia *31.39S 139.35E*
85 A15 **Curoca** ~ SW Angola
191 T6 **Currabubula** New South Wales, SE Australia *31.17S 150.43E*
61 Q14 **Currais Novos** Rio Grande do Norte, E Brazil *6.12S 36.30W*
37 W7 **Currant** Nevada, W USA *38.43N 115.27W*
37 W6 **Currant Mountain** ▲ Nevada, W USA *38.56N 115.19W*
46 H2 **Current** Eleuthera Island, C Bahamas *25.24N 76.44W*
29 W8 **Current River** ~ Arkansas/Missouri, C USA
190 M14 **Currie** Tasmania, SE Australia *39.59S 143.51E*
23 Y8 **Currituck** North Carolina, SE USA *36.27N 76.02W*
23 Y8 **Currituck Sound** *sound* North Carolina, SE USA
41 R11 **Curry** Alaska, USA *62.36N 150.00W*
Curtbunar *see* Tervel
118 I13 **Curtea de Argeș** *var.* Curtea-de-Arges. Argeș, S Romania *45.06N 24.40E*
118 E10 **Curtici** *Ger.* Kurtitsch, *Hung.* Kürtös. Arad, W Romania *46.21N 21.17E*
30 M16 **Curtis** Nebraska, C USA *40.36N 100.27W*
106 H2 **Curtis-Estación** Galicia, NW Spain *43.09N 8.10W*
191 O14 **Curtis Group** *island group* Tasmania, SE Australia
189 Y8 **Curtis Island** *island* Queensland, SE Australia
60 K11 **Curuá, Ilha do** *island* NE Brazil
49 U7 **Curuá, Rio** ~ N Brazil
61 A14 **Curuçá, Rio** ~ NW Brazil
114 L9 **Čurug** *Hung.* Csurog. Serbia, N Serbia and Montenegro (Yugoslavia) *45.30N 20.02E*
63 D16 **Curuzú Cuatiá** Corrientes, NE Argentina *29.45S 58.01W*
61 M19 **Curvelo** Minas Gerais, SE Brazil *18.45S 44.27W*
20 E14 **Curwensville** Pennsylvania, NE USA *40.57N 78.29W*
32 M3 **Curwood, Mount** ▲ Michigan, N USA *46.42N 88.14W*
Curytiba *see* Curitiba
Curzola *see* Korčula
44 A10 **Cuscatlán** ◆ *department* C El Salvador
59 H15 **Cusco** *var.* Cuzco. Cusco, C Peru *13.34S 72.01W*
59 H15 **Cusco** *off.* Departamento de Cusco; *var.* Cuzco. ◆ *department* C Peru
29 O9 **Cushing** Oklahoma, C USA *36.01N 96.46W*
27 W8 **Cushing** Texas, SW USA *31.48N 94.50W*
42 I6 **Cusihuiriachic** Chihuahua, N Mexico *28.16N 106.46W*
105 P10 **Cusset** Allier, C France *46.07N 3.27E*
25 S6 **Cusseta** Georgia, SE USA *32.18N 84.46W*
30 J10 **Custer** South Dakota, N USA *43.46N 103.36W*
Cüstrin *see* Kostrzyn
35 Q7 **Cut Bank** Montana, NW USA *48.37N 112.19W*
Cutch, Gulf of *see* Kachchh, Gulf of
25 S6 **Cuthbert** Georgia, SE USA *31.46N 84.47W*
9 S15 **Cut Knife** Saskatchewan, S Canada *52.40N 108.54W*
25 Y16 **Cutler Ridge** Florida, SE USA *25.34N 80.21W*
24 K10 **Cut Off** Louisiana, S USA *29.32N 90.20W*
65 I15 **Cutral-Có** Neuquén, C Argentina *38.55S 69.13W*
109 O21 **Cutro** Calabria, SW Italy *39.01N 16.59E*
191 O4 **Cuttaburra Channels** *seasonal river* New South Wales, SE Australia
160 O12 **Cuttack** Orissa, E India *20.28N 85.52E*
85 C15 **Cuvelai** Cunene, SW Angola *15.40S 15.48E*
81 G18 **Cuvette** *var.* Région de la Cuvette. ◆ *province* C Congo
181 V9 **Cuvier Basin** *undersea feature* E Indian Ocean
181 U9 **Cuvier Plateau** *undersea feature* E Indian Ocean
84 B12 **Cuvo** ~ W Angola
102 H9 **Cuxhaven** Niedersachsen, NW Germany *53.51N 8.42E*
Cuyabá *see* Cuiabá
179 Pp13 **Cuyo East Pass** *passage* C Philippines
179 P13 **Cuyo West Pass** *passage* C Philippines
Cuyuni, Río *see* Cuyuni River
57 S8 **Cuyuni River** *var.* Río Cuyuni. ~ Guyana/Venezuela
Cuzco *see* Cusco
99 K22 **Cwmbran** *Wel.* Cwmbrân. SW Wales, UK *51.39N 3.00W*
30 K15 **C.W.McConaughy, Lake** ⊠ Nebraska, C USA
83 D20 **Cyangugu** SW Rwanda *2.27S 29.00E*
112 D11 **Cybinka** *Ger.* Ziebingen. Lubuskie, W Poland *52.11N 14.46E*
Cyclades *see* Kykládes
Cydonia *see* Chaniá
Cymru *see* Wales
22 M5 **Cynthiana** Kentucky, S USA *38.23N 84.17W*
9 S17 **Cypress Hills** ▲▲ Alberta/Saskatchewan, SW Canada
Cypro-Syrian Basin *see* Cyprus Basin
123 Mm1 **Cyprus** *off.* Republic of Cyprus, *Gk.* Kypros, *Turk.* Kıbrıs, Kıbrıs Cumhuriyeti. ◆ *republic* E Mediterranean Sea
86 L14 **Cyprus** *Gk.* Kypros, *Turk.* Kıbrıs. *island* E Mediterranean Sea
123 Gg10 **Cyprus Basin** *var.* Cypro-Syrian Basin. *undersea feature* E Mediterranean Sea
Cythera *see* Kýthira
Cythnos *see* Kýthnos
112 F9 **Czaplinek** *Ger.* Tempelburg. Zachodnio-pomorskie, NW Poland *53.33N 16.14E*
Czarna Woda *see* Wda
112 G8 **Czarne** Pomorskie, N Poland *53.40N 17.00E*
112 G10 **Czarnków** Wielkopolskie, C Poland *52.52N 16.31E*
113 E17 **Czech Republic** *Cz.* Česká Republika. ◆ *republic* C Europe
Czegléd *see* Cegléd
112 G12 **Czempiń** Wielkopolskie, C Poland *52.10N 16.46E*
Czenstochau *see* Częstochowa
Czerkow *see* Čerchov
Czernowitz *see* Chernivtsi
112 I8 **Czersk** Pomorskie, N Poland *53.48N 17.58E*
113 J15 **Częstochowa** *Ger.* Czenstochau, Tschenstochau, *Rus.* Chenstokhov. Śląskie, S Poland *50.51N 19.09E*
112 F10 **Człopa** *Ger.* Schloppe. Zachodnio-pomorskie, NW Poland *53.04N 16.04E*
112 H8 **Człuchów** *Ger.* Schlochau. Pomorskie, NW Poland *53.40N 17.19E*

D

169 V9 **Da'an** *var.* Dalai. Jilin, NE China *45.28N 124.18E*
13 S10 **Daaquam** Québec, SE Canada *46.36N 70.03W*
Daawo, Webi *see* Dawa Wenz
56 I4 **Dabajuro** Falcón, NW Venezuela *11.00N 70.41W*
79 N15 **Dabakala** NE Ivory Coast *8.19N 4.24W*
169 S11 **Daban** *var.* Bairin Youqi. Nei Mongol Zizhiqu, N China *43.33N 118.40E*
113 K23 **Dabas** Pest, C Hungary *47.13N 19.18E*
166 L8 **Daba Shan** ▲▲ C China
Dabba *see* Daocheng
146 J5 **Dabbāgh, Jabal** ▲ NW Saudi Arabia *27.52N 35.48E*
56 D8 **Dabeiba** Antioquia, NW Colombia *6.57N 76.13W*
160 E11 **Dabhoi** Gujarāt, W India *22.07N 73.28E*
167 P8 **Dabie Shan** ▲▲ C China
78 J13 **Dabola** Haute-Guinée, C Guinea *10.48N 11.01W*
79 N17 **Dabou** S Ivory Coast *5.19N 4.22W*
168 M15 **Dabqig** *var.* Uxin Qi. Nei Mongol Zizhiqu, N China *38.29N 108.48E*
112 P8 **Dąbrowa Białostocka** Podlaskie, NE Poland *53.38N 23.18E*
113 M16 **Dąbrowa Tarnowska** Małopolskie, S Poland *50.10N 21.00E*
121 M20 **Dabryn'** *Rus.* Dobryn'. Homyel'skaya Voblasts', SE Belarus *51.46N 29.12E*
165 P10 **Dabsan Hu** ◎ C China
167 Q13 **Dabu** *var.* Huliao. Guangdong, S China *24.19N 116.07E*
118 H15 **Dăbuleni** Dolj, SW Romania *43.47N 24.05E*
Dacca *see* Dhaka
103 L23 **Dachau** Bayern, SE Germany *48.16N 11.25E*
166 K8 **Dachuan** *prev.* Daxian, Da Xian. Sichuan, C China *31.16N 107.31E*
Dacia Bank *see* Dacia Seamount
66 M10 **Dacia Seamount** *var.* Dacia Bank. *undersea feature* E Atlantic Ocean *31.10N 13.42W*
39 T3 **Dacono** Colorado, C USA *40.04N 104.56W*
Đắc Tô *see* Đak Tô
Dacura *see* Dákura
25 W12 **Dade City** Florida, SE USA *28.21N 82.12W*
158 L10 **Dadeldhura** *var.* Dandeldhura. Far Western, W Nepal *29.12N 80.31E*
25 Q5 **Dadeville** Alabama, S USA *32.49N 85.45W*
Dadong *see* Donggang
105 N15 **Dadou** ~ S France
160 D12 **Dādra and Nagar Haveli** ◆ *union territory* W India
155 P14 **Dādu** Sind, SE Pakistan *26.42N 67.48E*
178 K11 **Da Du Boloc** Kon Tum, C Vietnam *14.06N 107.40E*
166 G9 **Dadu He** ~ C China
Daegu *see* Taegu
Daerah Istimewa Aceh *see* Aceh
179 Q11 **Daet** Luzon, N Philippines *14.06N 122.57E*
166 I11 **Dafang** Guizhou, S China *27.07N 105.40E*
Dafeng *see* Shanglin
159 W11 **Dafla Hills** ▲▲ NE India
9 U15 **Dafoe** Saskatchewan, S Canada *51.46N 104.11W*
78 G10 **Dagana** N Senegal *16.28N 15.35W*
Dagana *see* Dahana, Tajikistan
Dagana *see* Massakory, Chad
Dagcagoin *see* Zoigê
120 K11 **Dagda** Krāslava, SE Latvia *56.06N 27.36E*
Dagden *see* Hiiumaa
Dagden-Sund *see* Soela Väin
131 P16 **Dagestan, Respublika** *prev.* Dagestanskaya ASSR, *Eng.* Daghestan. ◆ *autonomous republic* SW Russian Federation
Dagestanskaya ASSR *see* Dagestan, Respublika
131 R17 **Dagestanskiye Ogni** Respublika Dagestan, SW Russian Federation *42.09N 48.08E*
193 A23 **Dagg Sound** *sound* South Island, NZ
Daghestan *see* Dagestan, Respublika
147 Y8 **Daghmar** NE Oman *23.09N 59.01E*
Dağliq Qarabağ *see* Nagorno-Karabakh
Dagö *see* Hiiumaa
56 D11 **Dagua** Valle del Cauca, W Colombia *3.37N 76.42W*
166 H11 **Daguan** *var.* Cuihua. Yunnan, SW China *27.42N 103.51E*
179 P9 **Dagupan** *off.* Dagupan City. Luzon, N Philippines *16.04N 120.21E*
165 N16 **Dagzê** *var.* Dêqên. Xizang Zizhiqu, W China *29.38N 91.15E*
153 Q13 **Dahana** *Rus.* Dagana, Dakhana. SW Tajikistan *38.03N 69.51E*
169 V10 **Dahei Shan** ▲▲ N China
169 T7 **Da Hinggan Ling** *Eng.* Great Khingan Range. ▲▲ NE China
Dahlac Archipelago *see* Dahlak Archipelago
82 K9 **Dahlak Archipelago** *var.* Dahlac Archipelago. *island group* E Eritrea
25 T2 **Dahlonega** Georgia, SE USA *34.31N 83.59W*
103 O14 **Dahme** Brandenburg, E Germany *51.52N 13.47E*
102 O13 **Dahme** ~ E Germany
147 O14 **Dahm, Ramlat** *desert* NW Yemen
160 E10 **Dāhod** *prev.* Dohad. Gujarāt, W India *22.48N 74.18E*
Dahomey *see* Benin
164 G10 **Dahongliutan** Xinjiang Uygur Zizhiqu, NW China *35.59N 79.12E*
Dahra *see* Dara
145 R2 **Dahūk** *var.* Dohuk, *Kurd.* Dihōk. N Iraq *36.52N 43.01E*
118 J15 **Daia** Giurgiu, S Romania *44.00N 25.59E*
171 L15 **Daigo** Ibaraki, Honshū, S Japan *36.43N 140.22E*
169 O13 **Dai Hai** ◎ N China
Daihoku *see* T'aipei
195 X14 **Dai Island** *island* N Solomon Islands
177 G8 **Daik-u** Pegu, SW Myanmar *17.46N 96.40E*
144 H9 **Dā'īl** Dar'ā, S Syria *32.45N 36.07E*
178 Kk12 **Dai Lanh** Khanh Hoa, S Vietnam *12.49N 109.20E*
167 Q13 **Daimao Shan** ▲▲ SE China
107 N11 **Daimiel** Castilla-La Mancha, C Spain *39.04N 3.37W*
117 F22 **Daimoniá** Pelopónnisos, S Greece *36.38N 22.54E*
Dainan *see* T'ainan
27 W6 **Daingerfield** Texas, SW USA *33.01N 94.43W*
Daingin, Bá an *see* Dingle Bay
165 R13 **Dainkognubma** Xizang Zizhiqu, W China *32.25N 97.58E*
171 Hh17 **Daiō-zaki** *headland* Honshū, SW Japan *34.15N 136.50E*
Dairbhre *see* Valencia Island
63 B22 **Daireaux** Buenos Aires, E Argentina *36.36S 61.42W*
Dairen *see* Dalian
77 W9 **Dairūṭ** *var.* Dayrūṭ. C Egypt *27.34N 30.48E*
170 Ff12 **Dai-sen** ▲ Kyūshū, SW Japan *35.22N 133.32E*
27 X10 **Daisetta** Texas, SW USA *30.06N 94.38W*
199 Gg5 **Daitō-jima** *island group* SW Japan
199 Gg5 **Daitō Ridge** *undersea feature* N Philippine Sea
167 N3 **Daixian** *var.* Dai Xian. Shanxi, C China *39.07N 112.54E*
Daiyue *see* Shanyin
167 Q12 **Daiyun Shan** ▲▲ SE China
46 M8 **Dajabón** NW Dominican Republic *19.29N 71.40W*
166 G8 **Dajin Chuan** ~ C China
154 J6 **Dak** ◎ W Afghanistan
78 F11 **Dakar** ● (Senegal) W Senegal *14.43N 17.27W*
78 F11 **Dakar** ✕ W Senegal *14.42N 17.27W*
178 K11 **Đak Glây** Kon Tum, C Vietnam *15.05N 107.42E*
Dakhana *see* Dahana
159 U16 **Dakhin Shahbazpur Island** *island* S Bangladesh
Dakhla *see* Ad Dakhla
78 F7 **Dakhlet Nouâdhibou** ◆ *region* NW Mauritania
Đak Lap *see* Kiên Đuc
178 K13 **Đak Nông** Đăc Lăc, S Vietnam *11.58N 107.42E*
79 U11 **Dakoro** Maradi, S Niger *14.28N 6.45E*
31 U12 **Dakota City** Iowa, C USA *42.42N 94.13W*
31 R13 **Dakota City** Nebraska, C USA *42.25N 96.25W*
115 M17 **Đakovica** *var.* Djakovica, *Alb.* Gjakovë. Serbia, S Serbia and Montenegro (Yugoslavia) *42.22N 20.30E*
114 I10 **Đakovo** *var.* Djakovo, *Hung.* Diakovár. Osijek-Baranja, E Croatia *45.18N 18.24E*
Dakshin *see* Deccan
178 K11 **Đak Tô** *var.* Đắc Tô. Kon Tum, C Vietnam *14.35N 107.55E*
45 N7 **Dákura** *var.* Dacura. Región Autónoma Atlántico Norte, NE Nicaragua *14.22N 83.13W*
97 I14 **Dal** Akershus, S Norway *60.19N 11.16E*
84 E12 **Dala** Lunda Sul, E Angola *11.03S 20.12E*
110 I8 **Dalaas** Vorarlberg, W Austria *47.08N 10.03E*
78 I13 **Dalaba** Moyenne-Guinée, W Guinea *10.46N 12.12W*
Dalai *see* Da'an
168 I12 **Dalain Hob** *var.* Ejin Qi. Nei Mongol Zizhiqu, N China *41.59N 101.04E*
Dalai Nor *see* Hulun Nur
169 Q11 **Dalai Nur** *salt lake* N China
Dala-Jarna *see* Järna
97 M14 **Dalälven** ~ C Sweden
142 C16 **Dalaman** Muğla, SW Turkey *36.46N 28.46E*
142 C16 **Dalaman** ✕ Muğla, SW Turkey *36.37N 28.51E*
142 D16 **Dalaman Çayı** ~ SW Turkey
168 K11 **Dalandzadgad** Ömnögovĭ, S Mongolia *43.35N 104.23E*
97 D17 **Dalane** *physical region* S Norway
201 Z2 **Dalap-Uliga-Djarrit** *var.* Delap-Uliga-Darrit, D-U-D. *island group* Ratak Chain, SE Marshall Islands
96 J12 **Dalarna** *prev.* Kopparberg ◆ *county* C Sweden
96 L13 **Dalarna** *prev. Eng.* Dalecarlia. *cultural region* C Sweden
97 P16 **Dalarö** Stockholm, C Sweden *59.07N 18.25E*
178 Kk13 **Đa Lat** Lâm Đông, S Vietnam *11.55N 108.25E*
168 J11 **Dalay** Ömnögovĭ, S Mongolia *43.27N 103.30E*
154 L12 **Dālbandīn** *var.* Dāl Bandin. Baluchistān, SW Pakistan *28.48N 64.08E*
97 J17 **Dalbosjön** *lake bay* S Sweden
189 Y10 **Dalby** Queensland, E Australia *27.14S 151.16E*
96 D13 **Dale** Hordaland, S Norway *60.34N 5.48E*
96 C12 **Dale** Sogn og Fjordane, S Norway *61.22N 5.24E*
34 K12 **Dale** Oregon, NW USA *44.58N 118.56W*
27 T11 **Dale** Texas, SW USA *29.56N 97.34W*
Dalecarlia *see* Dalarna
23 W4 **Dale City** Virginia, NE USA *38.38N 77.18W*
22 L8 **Dale Hollow Lake** ⊠ Kentucky/Tennessee, S USA
100 O8 **Dalen** Drenthe, NE Netherlands *52.42N 6.45E*
97 E15 **Dalen** Telemark, S Norway *59.25N 7.58E*
177 F4 **Daletme** Chin State, W Myanmar *21.44N 92.48E*
25 Q7 **Daleville** Alabama, S USA *31.18N 85.42W*
100 M9 **Dalfsen** Overijssel, E Netherlands *52.31N 6.16E*
26 M1 **Dalhart** Texas, SW USA *36.04N 102.31W*
11 O13 **Dalhousie** New Brunswick, SE Canada *48.03N 66.22W*
158 I6 **Dalhousie** Himāchal Pradesh, N India *32.31N 76.01E*
166 F12 **Dali** *var.* Xiaguan. Yunnan, SW China *25.33N 100.10E*
Dali *see* Idálion
169 U14 **Dalian** *var.* Dairen, Dalien, Lüda, Ta-lien, *Rus.* Dalny. Liaoning, NE China *38.53N 121.36E*
107 O15 **Dalías** Andalucía, S Spain *36.49N 2.50W*
Dalien *see* Dalian
Dalijan *see* Delījān
114 J9 **Dalj** *Hung.* Dalja. Osijek-Baranja, E Croatia *45.29N 19.00E*
Dalja *see* Dalj
34 F12 **Dallas** Oregon, NW USA *44.55N 123.19W*
27 U6 **Dallas** Texas, SW USA *32.46N 96.48W*
27 T7 **Dallas-Fort Worth** ✕ Texas, SW USA *32.37N 97.16W*
160 K12 **Dalli Rājhara** Chhattīsgarh, C India *20.33N 81.06E*
41 X15 **Dall Island** *island* Alexander Archipelago, Alaska, USA
40 M12 **Dall Lake** ◎ Alaska, USA
Dállogilli *see* Korpilombolo
79 S12 **Dallol Bosso** *seasonal river* W Niger
147 U7 **Dalmā** *island* W UAE
115 E14 **Dalmacija** *Eng.* Dalmatia, *Ger.* Dalmatien, *It.* Dalmazia. *cultural region* S Croatia
Dalmatia/Dalmatien/Dalmazia *see* Dalmacija
127 Nn17 **Dal'negorsk** Primorskiy Kray, SE Russian Federation *44.27N 135.30E*
127 Nn17 **Dal'nerechensk** Primorskiy Kray, SE Russian Federation *45.57N 133.42E*
Dalny *see* Dalian
78 M16 **Daloa** C Ivory Coast *6.52N 6.28W*
166 J11 **Dalou Shan** ▲▲ S China
189 X7 **Dalrymple Lake** ◎ Queensland, E Australia
12 H14 **Dalrymple Lake** ◎ Ontario, S Canada
189 X7 **Dalrymple, Mount** ▲ Queensland, E Australia *21.01S 148.34E*
95 K20 **Dalsbruk** *Fin.* Taalintehdas. Länsi-Suomi, W Finland *60.01N 22.33E*
97 K19 **Dalsjöfors** Västra Götaland, S Sweden *57.43N 13.04E*
97 J17 **Dals Långed** *var.* Långed. Västra Götaland, S Sweden *58.54N 12.20E*
159 O15 **Dāltenganj** *prev.* Daltonganj. Jhārkhand, N India *23.59N 84.07E*
25 R2 **Dalton** Georgia, SE USA *34.46N 84.58W*
Daltonganj *see* Dāltenganj
205 X14 **Dalton Iceberg Tongue** *ice feature* Antarctica
Dálvvadis *see* Jokkmokk
94 J1 **Dalvík** Nordhurland Eystra, N Iceland *65.58N 18.31W*
37 N8 **Daly City** California, W USA *37.44N 122.27W*
189 P2 **Daly River** ~ Northern Territory, N Australia
189 Q3 **Daly Waters** Northern Territory, N Australia *16.21S 133.21E*
121 F20 **Damachava** *var.* Damachova, *Pol.* Domaczewo, *Rus.* Domachëvo. Brestskaya Voblasts', SW Belarus *51.45N 23.36E*
Damachova *see* Damachava
79 W11 **Damagaram Takaya** Zinder, S Niger *14.02N 9.28E*
160 D12 **Damān** Damān and Diu, W India *20.25N 72.58E*
160 B12 **Damān and Diu** ◆ *union territory* W India
77 V7 **Damanhûr** *anc.* Hermopolis Parva. N Egypt *31.02N 30.34E*
Damão *see* Damān
167 O1 **Damaqun Shan** ▲▲ E China
81 I15 **Damara** Ombella-Mpoko, S Central African Republic *5.00N 18.45E*
85 D18 **Damaraland** *physical region* C Namibia
175 T15 **Damar, Kepulauan** *var.* Baraf Daja Islands, Kepulauan Barat Daya. *island group* C Indonesia
174 Gg4 **Damar Laut** Perak, Peninsular Malaysia *4.13N 100.36E*
175 Tt15 **Damar, Pulau** *island* Maluku, E Indonesia
Damas *see* Dimashq
79 Y12 **Damasak** Borno, NE Nigeria *13.10N 12.40E*
Damasco *see* Dimashq
23 Q8 **Damascus** Virginia, NE USA *36.37N 81.46W*
Damascus *see* Dimashq
79 X13 **Damaturu** Yobe, NE Nigeria *11.44N 11.58E*
175 Ss4 **Damau** Pulau Kaburuang, N Indonesia *3.46N 126.49E*
149 O5 **Damāvand, Qolleh-ye** ▲ N Iran *35.59N 52.06E*
84 B10 **Damba** Uíge, NW Angola *6.42S 15.07E*
116 M12 **Dambaslar** Tekirdağ, NW Turkey *41.13N 27.13E*
118 J13 **Dâmbovița** *prev.* Dîmbovița. ◆ *county* SE Romania
118 J13 **Dâmbovița** *prev.* Dîmbovița. ~ S Romania
181 Y15 **D'Ambre, Île** *island* NE Mauritius
161 K24 **Dambulla** Central Province, C Sri Lanka *7.51N 80.40E*
46 K9 **Dame-Marie** SW Haiti *18.31N 74.24W*
46 J9 **Dame Marie, Cap** *headland* SW Haiti *18.37N 74.24W*
149 Q4 **Dāmghān** Semnān, N Iran *36.13N 54.22E*
Damietta *see* Dumyāt
144 G10 **Dāmiyā** Al Balqā', NW Jordan *32.07N 35.33E*
152 G11 **Damla** Daşoguz Welaýaty, N Turkmenistan *40.05N 59.15E*
Dammām *see* Ad Dammān
102 G12 **Damme** Niedersachsen, NW Germany *52.31N 8.12E*
159 R15 **Dāmodar** ~ NE India
160 J9 **Damoh** Madhya Pradesh, C India *23.50N 79.24E*
79 P15 **Damongo** NW Ghana *9.06N 1.46W*
144 G7 **Damoûr** *var.* Ad Dāmūr. W Lebanon *33.36N 35.30E*
175 Pp7 **Dampal, Teluk** *bay* Sulawesi, C Indonesia
188 H7 **Dampier** Western Australia *20.40S 116.40E*
188 H6 **Dampier Archipelago** *island group* Western Australia
176 Uu9 **Dampier, Selat** *strait* Papua, E Indonesia
194 L12 **Dampier Strait** *strait* NE PNG
147 U14 **Damqawt** *var.* Damqut. E Yemen *16.35N 52.39E*
165 O13 **Dam Qu** ~ C China
Damqut *see* Damqawt
178 I13 **Dâmrei, Chuŏr Phmun** *Fr.* Chaîne de l'Éléphant. ▲▲ SW Cambodia
110 C7 **Damvant** Jura, NW Switzerland *47.22N 6.55E*
Damwâld *see* Damwoude
100 L5 **Damwoude** *Fris.* Damwâld. Friesland, N Netherlands *53.18N 5.59E*
165 N15 **Damxung** *var.* Gongtang. Xizang Zizhiqu, W China *30.28N 91.01E*
82 K11 **Danakil Desert** *var.* Afar Depression, Danakil Plain. *desert* E Africa
Danakil Plain *see* Danakil Desert
37 R8 **Dana, Mount** ▲ California, W USA *37.54N 119.13W*
78 L16 **Danané** W Ivory Coast *7.16N 8.09W*
178 Kk10 **Đa Nẵng** *prev.* Tourane. Quang Nam-Đa Nẵng, C Vietnam *16.04N 108.13E*
179 Qq13 **Danao** *var.* Danao City. Cebu, C Philippines *10.34N 124.00E*
166 G9 **Danba** *var.* Zhanggu, *Tib.* Rongzhag. Sichuan, C China *30.54N 101.49E*
Danborg *see* Daneborg
20 L13 **Danbury** Connecticut, NE USA *41.21N 73.27W*
27 W12 **Danbury** Texas, SW USA *29.13N 95.20W*
37 X15 **Danby Lake** ◎ California, W USA
204 H4 **Danco Coast** *physical region* Antarctica
84 B11 **Dande** ~ NW Angola
Dandeldhura *see* Dadeldhura
161 E17 **Dandeli** Karnātaka, W India *15.18N 74.42E*
191 O12 **Dandenong** Victoria, SE Australia *38.01S 145.13E*
169 V13 **Dandong** *var.* Tan-tung; *prev.* An-tung. Liaoning, NE China *40.09N 124.23E*
207 Q14 **Daneborg** *var.* Danborg. Tunu, N Greenland *74.34N 19.51W*
118 I14 **Draganesti-Olt** Olt, S Romania *44.06N 25.00E*
27 V12 **Danevang** Texas, SW USA *29.03N 96.11W*
Dänew *see* Galkynyş
Danfeng *see* Shizong
12 L12 **Danford Lake** Québec, SE Canada *45.55N 76.12W*
21 T4 **Danforth** Maine, NE USA *45.39N 67.54W*
39 P3 **Danforth Hills** ▲▲ Colorado, C USA
Dangara *see* Danghara
165 V12 **Dangchang** Gansu, C China *34.01N 104.19E*
165 P8 **Dangchengwan** *var.* Subei, Subei Mongolzu Zizhixian. Gansu, N China *39.33N 94.50E*
84 B10 **Dange** Uíge, NW Angola *7.55S 15.01E*
Dangerous Archipelago *see* Tuamotu, Îles
85 E26 **Danger Point** *headland* SW South Africa *34.37S 19.20E*
153 Q13 **Danghara** *Rus.* Dangara. SW Tajikistan *38.04N 69.14E*
165 P8 **Danghe Nanshan** ▲▲ W China
82 I12 **Dangila** *var.* Dānglā. Amhara, NW Ethiopia *11.08N 36.51E*
165 P8 **Dangjin Shankou** *pass* N China *39.22N 94.19E*
Dangla *see* Tanggula Shan, China
Dang La *see* Tanggula Shankou, China
Dānglā *see* Dangila, Ethiopia
Dangme Chu *see* Manās
159 Y11 **Dāngori** Assam, NE India *27.40N 95.34E*
Dang Raek, Phanom/Dangrek, Chaîne des *see* Dângrêk, Chuŏr Phnum
178 Ii11 **Dângrêk, Chuŏr Phnum** *var.* Phanom Dang Raek, Phanom Dong Rak, *Fr.* Chaîne des Dangrek. ▲▲ Cambodia/Thailand
44 G3 **Dangriga** *prev.* Stann Creek. Stann Creek, E Belize *16.58N 88.13W*
167 P6 **Dangshan** Anhui, E China *34.28N 116.24E*
35 T15 **Daniel** Wyoming, C USA *42.49N 110.04W*
85 H22 **Daniëlskuil** Northern Cape, N South Africa *28.07S 23.35E*
21 N12 **Danielson** Connecticut, NE USA *41.48N 71.53W*
128 M15 **Danilov** Yaroslavskaya Oblast', W Russian Federation *58.11N 40.11E*
131 O9 **Danilovka** Volgogradskaya Oblast', SW Russian Federation *50.21N 44.03E*
Danish West Indies *see* Virgin Islands (US)
166 L7 **Dan Jiang** ~ C China
166 M7 **Danjiangkou Shuiku** ⊠ C China
147 W8 **Ḍank** *var.* Dhank. NW Oman *23.34N 56.16E*
158 J7 **Dankhar** Himāchal Pradesh, N India *32.07N 78.12E*
130 L6 **Dankov** Lipetskaya Oblast', W Russian Federation *53.17N 39.07E*
44 J7 **Danlí** El Paraíso, S Honduras *14.02N 86.34W*
Danmark *see* Denmark
Danmarksstraedet *see* Denmark Strait
97 O14 **Dannemora** Uppsala, C Sweden *60.13N 17.49E*
20 L6 **Dannemora** New York, NE USA *44.42N 73.42W*
102 K11 **Dannenberg** Niedersachsen, N Germany *53.05N 11.06E*
192 N12 **Dannevirke** Manawatu-Wanganui, North Island, NZ *40.13S 176.04E*
23 U8 **Dan River** ~ Virginia, NE USA
178 Hh9 **Dan Sai** Loei, C Thailand *17.15N 101.04E*
20 F10 **Dansville** New York, NE USA *42.34N 77.40W*
Dantzig *see* Gdańsk
88 E12 **Danube** *Bul.* Dunav, *Cz.* Dunaj, *Ger.* Donau, *Hung.* Duna, *Rom.* Dunărea. ~ C Europe
Danubian Plain *see* Dunavska Ravnina
177 Ff8 **Danubyu** Irrawaddy, SW Myanmar *17.15N 95.34E*
Danum *see* Doncaster
21 P11 **Danvers** Massachusetts, NE USA *42.34N 70.54W*
29 T11 **Danville** Arkansas, C USA *35.03N 93.22W*
33 N13 **Danville** Illinois, N USA *40.10N 87.37W*
33 O14 **Danville** Indiana, N USA *39.45N 86.31W*

◆ Country ● Country Capital ◇ Dependent Territory ○ Dependent Territory Capital ◆ Administrative Region ✕ International Airport ▲ Mountain ▲▲ Mountain Range Volcano ~ River ◎ Lake ⊠ Reservoir

DANVILLE – DEMOTTE

31 Y15 **Danville** Iowa, C USA *40.52N 91.18W*
22 M6 **Danville** Kentucky, S USA *37.39N 84.46W*
20 G14 **Danville** Pennsylvania, NE USA *40.57N 76.36W*
23 T6 **Danville** Virginia, NE USA *36.35N 79.24W*
Danxian/Dan Xian *see* Danzhou
166 L17 **Danzhou** ***prev.*** Danxian, Dan Xian, Nada. Hainan, S China *19.31N 109.31E*
Danzig *see* Gdańsk
Danziger Bucht *see* Danzig, Gulf of
112 J6 **Danzig, Gulf of** ***var.*** Gulf of Gdańsk, ***Ger.*** Danziger Bucht, ***Pol.*** Zakota Gdańska, ***Rus.*** Gdan'skaya Bukhta. *gulf* N Poland
166 F10 **Daocheng** ***var.*** Jinzhu, ***Tib.*** Dabba. Sichuan, C China *29.05N 100.14E*
Daojiang *see* Daoxian
Daokou *see* Huaxian
106 H7 **Dão, Rio** ≈ N Portugal
Daosa *see* Dausa
79 Y7 **Dao Timmi** Agadez, NE Niger *20.31N 13.34E*
166 M13 **Daoxian** ***var.*** Daojiang, Dao Xian. Hunan, S China *25.30N 111.37E*
79 Q14 **Dapaong** N Togo *10.52N 0.12E*
25 N8 **Daphne** Alabama, S USA *30.36N 87.54W*
179 Qq15 **Dapitan** Mindanao, S Philippines *8.39N 123.25E*
165 P9 **Da Qaidam** Qinghai, C China *37.49N 95.18E*
169 V8 **Daqing** ***var.*** Sartu. Heilongjiang, NE China *46.29N 125.07E*
169 O13 **Daqing Shan** ▲▲ N China
169 T11 **Daqin Tal** ***var.*** Naiman Qi. Nei Mongol Zizhiqu, N China *42.51N 120.41E*
Daqm *see* Duqm
166 G8 **Da Qu** ***var.*** Do Qu. ≈ C China
145 T5 **Dāqūq** ***var.*** Tāwūq. N Iraq *35.07N 44.27E*
78 G10 **Dara** ***var.*** Dahra. NW Senegal *15.20N 15.28W*
144 H9 **Dar'ā** ***var.*** Der'a, ***Fr.*** Déraa. Dar'ā, SW Syria *32.37N 36.06E*
144 H8 **Dar'ā** ***off.*** Muḩāfaẓat Dar'ā, ***var.*** Dará, Derá, Derrá. ⬖ *governorate* S Syria
149 Q12 **Dārāb** Fārs, S Iran *28.52N 54.25E*
118 K8 **Darabani** Botoşani, NW Romania *48.10N 26.40E*
Daraj *see* Dirj
148 M8 **Dārān** Eşfahān, W Iran *33.02N 50.27E*
178 Kk12 **Đa Răng, Sông** ***var.*** Ba. ≈ S Vietnam
126 Kk16 **Darasun** Chitinskaya Oblast', S Russian Federation *51.36N 113.58E*
Daraut-Kurgan *see* Daroot-Korgon
79 W13 **Darazo** Bauchi, E Nigeria *11.01N 10.27E*
145 S3 **Darband** N Iraq *36.15N 44.17E*
145 V4 **Darband-i Khān, Sadd** *dam* NE Iraq *35.07N 45.42E*
145 N1 **Darbāsīyah** ***var.*** Derbisīye. Al Ḩasakah, N Syria *37.06N 40.42E*
120 C11 **Darbėnai** Klaipėda, NW Lithuania *56.02N 21.16E*
159 Q13 **Darbhanga** Bihār, N India *26.10N 85.54E*
40 M9 **Darby, Cape** *headland* Alaska, USA *64.19N 162.46W*
114 I9 **Darda** ***Hung.*** Dárda. Osijek-Baranja, E Croatia *45.37N 18.41E*
29 T11 **Dardanelle** Arkansas, C USA *35.13N 93.09W*
29 S11 **Dardanelle, Lake** ▣ Arkansas, C USA
Dardanelles *see* Çanakkale Boğazı
Dardanelli *see* Çanakkale
Dardo *see* Kangding
Dar-el-Beida *see* Casablanca
142 M14 **Darende** Malatya, C Turkey *38.33N 37.31E*
83 J22 **Dar es Salaam** Dar es Salaam, E Tanzania *6.51S 39.18E*
83 J22 **Dar es Salaam** ✕ Pwani, E Tanzania *6.57S 39.17E*
193 H18 **Darfield** Canterbury, South Island, NZ *43.28S 172.07E*
108 F7 **Darfo** Lombardia, N Italy *45.54N 10.12E*
82 B10 **Darfur** ***var.*** Darfur Massif. *cultural region* W Sudan
Darfur Massif *see* Darfur
Darganata/Dargan-Ata *see* Birata
149 T3 **Dargaz** ***var.*** Darreh Gaz; ***prev.*** Moḩammadābād. Khorāsān, NE Iran *37.28N 59.08E*
145 U4 **Dargazayn** NE Iraq *35.39N 45.00E*
191 P12 **Dargo** Victoria, SE Australia *37.29S 147.15E*
168 K7 **Darhan** Bulgan, C Mongolia *48.07N 103.54E*
168 L6 **Darhan** Darhan Uul, N Mongolia *49.24N 105.57E*
169 N8 **Darhan** Hentiy, C Mongolia *46.38N 109.25E*
Darhan Muminggan Lianheqi *see* Bailingmiao
168 L6 **Darhan Uul** ⬖ *province* N Mongolia
25 W7 **Darien** Georgia, SE USA *31.22N 81.25W*
45 W16 **Darién** ***off.*** Provincia del Darién. ⬖ *province* SE Panama
Darién, Golfo del *see* Darien, Gulf of
45 X14 **Darien, Gulf of** ***Sp.*** Golfo del Darién. *gulf* S Caribbean Sea
Darien, Isthmus of *see* Panamá, Istmo de
44 K9 **Dariense, Cordillera** ▲▲ C Nicaragua
45 W15 **Darién, Serranía del** ▲▲ Colombia/Panama
Dario *see* Ciudad Darío
Dariorigum *see* Vannes
Dariv *see* Darvi
Darj *see* Dirj
Darjeeling *see* Darjiling
159 S12 **Darjiling** ***prev.*** Darjeeling. West Bengal, NE India *27.00N 88.13E*
Darkehnen *see* Ozersk
165 S12 **Darlag** ***var.*** Gümai. Qinghai, C China *33.43N 99.42E*
191 T3 **Darling Downs** *hill range* Queensland, E Australia
30 M2 **Darling, Lake** ▣ North Dakota, N USA
188 I12 **Darling Range** ▲▲ Western Australia
190 L8 **Darling River** ≈ New South Wales, SE Australia
99 M15 **Darlington** N England, UK *54.31N 1.34W*
23 T12 **Darlington** South Carolina, SE USA *34.18N 79.52W*
32 K9 **Darlington** Wisconsin, N USA *42.40N 90.07W*
112 G7 **Darłowo** Zachodnio-pomorskie, NW Poland *54.24N 16.21E*
103 G19 **Darmstadt** Hessen, SW Germany *49.52N 8.39E*
77 S7 **Darnah** ***var.*** Dérna. NE Libya *32.46N 22.39E*
105 S6 **Darney** Vosges, NE France *48.06N 5.58E*
190 M7 **Darnick** New South Wales, SE Australia *32.52S 143.38E*
205 Y6 **Darnley, Cape** *headland* Antarctica *67.36S 70.04E*
107 R7 **Daroca** Aragón, NE Spain *41.07N 1.25W*
153 S11 **Daroot-Korgon** ***var.*** Daraut-Kurgan. Oshskaya Oblast', SW Kyrgyzstan *39.34N 72.13E*
63 A23 **Darragueira** ***var.*** Darregueira. Buenos Aires, E Argentina *37.40S 63.12W*
Darregueira *see* Darragueira
Darreh Gaz *see* Dargaz
148 K7 **Darreh Shahr** ***var.*** Darreh-ye Shahr. Īlām, W Iran *33.10N 47.18E*
Darreh-ye Shahr *see* Darreh Shahr
34 I7 **Darrington** Washington, NW USA *48.15N 121.36W*
27 P1 **Darrouzett** Texas, SW USA *36.27N 100.19W*
159 S15 **Darsana** ***var.*** Darshana. Khulna, N Bangladesh *23.31N 88.49E*
Darshana *see* Darsana
102 M7 **Darss** *peninsula* NE Germany
102 M7 **Darsser Ort** *headland* NE Germany *54.28N 12.31E*
99 J24 **Dart** ≈ SW England, UK
Dartang *see* Baqên
99 P22 **Dartford** SE England, UK *51.27N 0.13E*
190 L12 **Dartmoor** Victoria, SE Australia *37.56S 141.18E*
99 I24 **Dartmoor** *moorland* SW England, UK
11 Q15 **Dartmouth** Nova Scotia, SE Canada *44.40N 63.34W*
99 J24 **Dartmouth** SW England, UK *50.20N 3.34W*
13 Y6 **Dartmouth** ≈ Québec, SE Canada
191 Q11 **Dartmouth Reservoir** ◎ Victoria, SE Australia
Dartuch, Cabo *see* Artrutx, Cap d'
194 G15 **Daru** Western, SW PNG *9.04S 143.12E*
114 G9 **Daruvar** ***Hung.*** Daruvár. Bjelovar-Bilogora, NE Croatia *45.34N 17.12E*
Darvaza *see* Darvoza, Uzbekistan
Darvaza *see* Derweze, Turkmenistan
Darvazskiy Khrebet *see* Darvoz, Qatorkŭhi
168 F8 **Darvi** ***var.*** Dariv. Govĭ-Altay, W Mongolia *46.20N 94.11E*
154 L9 **Darvīshān** ***var.*** Darweshan, Garmser. Helmand, S Afghanistan *31.01N 64.12E*
153 R13 **Darvoz, Qatorkŭhi** ***Rus.*** Darvazskiy Khrebet. ▲▲ C Tajikistan
153 O10 **Darvoza** ***Rus.*** Darvaza. Jizzax Viloyati, C Uzbekistan *40.59N 67.19E*
Darweshan *see* Darvīshān
65 J15 **Darwin** Río Negro, S Argentina *39.13S 65.41W*
189 O1 **Darwin** ***prev.*** Palmerston, Port Darwin. *territory capital* Northern Territory, N Australia *12.27S 130.52E*
67 D24 **Darwin** ***var.*** Darwin Settlement. East Falkland, Falkland Islands *51.51S 58.55W*
64 H8 **Darwin, Cordillera** ▲▲ N Chile
59 B17 **Darwin, Volcán** Ѫ Galapagos Islands, Ecuador, E Pacific Ocean *0.12S 91.17W*
155 S8 **Darya Khān** Punjab, E Pakistan *31.48N 71.05E*
151 O15 **Dar'yalyktakyr, Ravnina** *plain* S Kazakhstan
149 T11 **Dārzīn** Kermān, S Iran *29.10N 58.09E*
Dashennongjia *see* Shennong Ding
Dashhowuz *see* Daşoguz
Dashhowuz Welayaty *see* Daşoguz Welaýaty
121 O16 **Dashkawka** ***Rus.*** Dashkovka. Mahilyowskaya Voblasts', E Belarus *53.42N 30.17E*
Dashkhovuz *see* Daşoguz/Daşoguz Welaýaty
Dashkhovuzskiy Velayat *see* Daşoguz Welaýaty
Dashköpri *see* Daşköpri
Dashkovka *see* Dashkawka
154 J15 **Dasht** ≈ SW Pakistan
Dashtidzhum *see* Dashtijum
153 R13 **Dashtijum** ***Rus.*** Dashtidzhum. SW Tajikistan *38.06N 70.11E*
155 W7 **Daska** Punjab, NE Pakistan *32.21N 74.20E*
152 J16 **Daşköpri** ***var.*** Dashköpri, ***Rus.*** Tashkepri. Mary Welaýaty, S Turkmenistan *36.15N 62.37E*
152 H8 **Daşoguz** ***Rus.*** Dashkhovuz, ***Turkm.*** Dashhowuz; ***prev.*** Tashauz. Daşoguz Welaýaty, N Turkmenistan *41.51N 59.52E*
152 E9 **Daşoguz Welaýaty** ***var.*** Dashhowuz Welayaty, ***Rus.*** Dashkhovuz, Dashkhovuzskiy Velayat. ⬖ *province* N Turkmenistan
Đa,Sông *see* Black River
79 R15 **Dassa** ***var.*** Dassa-Zoumé. S Benin *7.46N 2.15E*
Dassa-Zoumé *see* Dassa
31 U8 **Dassel** Minnesota, N USA *45.06N 94.18W*
158 H3 **Dastegil Sar** ***var.*** Disteghil Sār. ▲ N India
142 C16 **Datça** Muğla, SW Turkey *36.46N 27.40E*
172 Nn6 **Date** Hokkaidō, NE Japan *42.28N 140.51E*
160 I8 **Datia** ***prev.*** Duttia. Madhya Pradesh, C India *25.40N 78.28E*
Dåtnejaevrie *see* Tunnsjøen
165 T10 **Datong** ***var.*** Qiaotou. Qinghai, C China *37.01N 101.33E*
167 N2 **Datong** ***var.*** Tatung, Ta-t'ung. Shanxi, C China *40.09N 113.16E*
Datong *see* Tong'an
165 S9 **Datong He** ≈ C China
165 S9 **Datong Shan** ▲▲ C China
174 Kk6 **Datu, Tanjung** *headland* Indonesia/Malaysia *2.01N 109.37E*
Daua *see* Dawa Wenz
180 H16 **Dauban, Mount** ▲ Silhouette, NE Seychelles
155 T7 **Dāūd Khel** Punjab, E Pakistan *32.52N 71.34E*
121 G15 **Daugai** Alytus, S Lithuania *54.22N 24.20E*
Daugava *see* Western Dvina
120 J11 **Daugavpils** ***Ger.*** Dünaburg; ***prev. Rus.*** Dvinsk. *municipality* Daugvapils, SE Latvia *55.53N 26.33E*
Dauka *see* Dawkah
Daulatabad *see* Malāyer
103 D18 **Daun** Rheinland-Pfalz, W Germany *50.13N 6.50E*
161 E14 **Daund** ***prev.*** Dhond. Mahārāshtra, W India *18.28N 74.37E*
178 Gg12 **Daung Kyun** *island* S Myanmar
9 W15 **Dauphin** Manitoba, S Canada *51.09N 100.04W*
105 S13 **Dauphiné** *cultural region* E France
25 N9 **Dauphin Island** *island* Alabama, S USA
9 X15 **Dauphin River** Manitoba, S Canada *51.55N 98.03W*
79 V12 **Daura** Katsina, N Nigeria *13.03N 8.18E*
158 H12 **Dausa** ***prev.*** Daosa. Rājasthān, N India *26.54N 76.18E*
Dauwa *see* Dawwah
143 Y10 **Däväçi** ***Rus.*** Divichi. NE Azerbaijan *41.15N 48.58E*
161 F18 **Dāvangere** Karnātaka, W India *14.30N 75.52E*
179 Rr16 **Davao** ***off.*** Davao City. Mindanao, S Philippines *7.06N 125.35E*
179 Rr16 **Davao Gulf** *gulf* Mindanao, S Philippines
13 Q11 **Daveluyville** Québec, SE Canada *46.12N 72.07W*
31 Z14 **Davenport** Iowa, C USA *41.31N 90.34W*
34 L8 **Davenport** Washington, NW USA *47.39N 118.09W*
45 P16 **David** Chiriquí, W Panama *8.25N 82.25W*
13 O11 **David** ≈ Québec, SE Canada
31 R15 **David City** Nebraska, C USA *41.15N 97.07W*
David-Gorodok *see* Davyd-Haradok
9 T16 **Davidson** Saskatchewan, S Canada *51.15N 105.58W*
23 R10 **Davidson** North Carolina, SE USA *35.29N 80.49W*
28 K12 **Davidson** Oklahoma, C USA *34.15N 99.06W*
41 S6 **Davidson Mountains** ▲▲ Alaska, USA
180 M8 **Davie Ridge** *undersea feature* W Indian Ocean
190 A1 **Davies, Mount** ▲ South Australia *26.14S 129.14E*
37 O7 **Davis** California, W USA *38.31N 121.46W*
29 N12 **Davis** Oklahoma, C USA *34.30N 97.07W*
205 Y7 **Davis** *Australian research station* Antarctica *68.30S 78.15E*
204 H3 **Davis Coast** *physical region* Antarctica
20 C16 **Davis, Mount** ▲ Pennsylvania, NE USA *39.47N 79.10W*
26 K9 **Davis Mountains** ▲▲ Texas, SW USA
205 Z9 **Davis Sea** *sea* Antarctica
67 O20 **Davis Seamounts** *undersea feature* S Atlantic Ocean
206 M13 **Davis Strait** *strait* Baffin Bay/Labrador Sea
131 U5 **Davlekanovo** Respublika Bashkortostan, W Russian Federation *54.13N 55.06E*
110 J9 **Davos** ***Rmsch.*** Tavau. Graubünden, E Switzerland *46.48N 9.50E*
121 J20 **Davyd-Haradok** ***Pol.*** Dawidgródek, ***Rus.*** David-Gorodok. Brestskaya Voblasts', SW Belarus *52.03N 27.13E*
169 U12 **Dawa** Liaoning, NE China *40.55N 122.02E*
147 O11 **Dawāsir, Wādī ad** *dry watercourse* S Saudi Arabia
83 K15 **Dawa Wenz** ***var.*** Daua, Webi Daawo. ≈ E Africa
Dawaymah, Birkat ad *see* Umm al Baqar, Hawr
Dawei *see* Tavoy
121 K14 **Dawhinava** ***Rus.*** Dolginovo. Minskaya Voblasts', N Belarus *54.39N 27.28E*
Dawidgródek *see* Davyd-Haradok
147 V12 **Dawkah** ***var.*** Dauka. SW Oman *18.32N 54.03E*
Dawlat Qaṭar *see* Qatar
26 M3 **Dawn** Texas, SW USA *34.54N 102.10W*
Dawo *see* Maqên
146 M11 **Daws** Al Bāḩah, SW Saudi Arabia *20.19N 41.12E*
8 H5 **Dawson** ***var.*** Dawson City. Yukon Territory, NW Canada *64.04N 139.24W*
25 S6 **Dawson** Georgia, SE USA *31.46N 84.27W*
31 S9 **Dawson** Minnesota, N USA *44.55N 96.03W*
Dawson City *see* Dawson
9 N13 **Dawson Creek** British Columbia, W Canada *55.48N 120.18W*
8 H7 **Dawson Range** ▲▲ Yukon Territory, W Canada
189 Y9 **Dawson River** ≈ Queensland, E Australia
8 J15 **Dawsons Landing** British Columbia, SW Canada *51.33N 127.38W*
22 I7 **Dawson Springs** Kentucky, S USA *37.10N 87.41W*
25 S2 **Dawsonville** Georgia, SE USA *34.28N 84.07W*
166 G8 **Dawu** ***var.*** Xianshui. Sichuan, C China *30.55N 101.08E*
Dawu *see* Maqên
Dawukou *see* Shizuishan
147 Y10 **Dawwah** ***var.*** Dauwa. W Oman *20.36N 58.52E*
104 J15 **Dax** ***var.*** Ax; ***anc.*** Aquae Augustae, Aquae Tarbelicae. Landes, SW France *43.43N 1.03W*
Da Xian/Daxian *see* Dachuan
Daxue *see* Wencheng
166 G9 **Daxue Shan** ▲▲ C China
Dayan *see* Lijiang
166 G12 **Dayao** ***var.*** Jinbi. Yunnan, SW China *25.41N 101.23E*
Dayishan *see* Gaoyou
191 N12 **Daylesford** Victoria, SE Australia *37.24S 144.07E*
37 U10 **Daylight Pass** *pass* California, W USA *36.44N 116.55W*
63 D17 **Daymán, Río** ≈ N Uruguay
Dayr *see* Ad Dayr
144 G10 **Dayr 'Allā** ***var.*** Deir 'Alla. Al Balqā', N Jordan *32.39N 36.06E*
145 N4 **Dayr az Zawr** ***var.*** Deir ez Zor. Dayr az Zawr, E Syria *35.12N 40.12E*
144 M5 **Dayr az Zawr** ***off.*** Muḩāfaẓat Dayr az Zawr, ***var.*** Dayr Az-Zor. ⬖ *governorate* E Syria
Dayr Az-Zor *see* Dayr az Zawr
Dayrūṭ *see* Dairûṭ
9 Q15 **Daysland** Alberta, SW Canada *52.53N 112.19W*
33 R14 **Dayton** Ohio, N USA *39.45N 84.11W*
22 L10 **Dayton** Tennessee, S USA *35.30N 85.01W*
27 W11 **Dayton** Texas, SW USA *30.03N 94.53W*
34 L10 **Dayton** Washington, NW USA *46.19N 117.58W*
25 X10 **Daytona Beach** Florida, SE USA *29.12N 81.03W*
175 N10 **Dayu** Borneo, C Indonesia *1.58S 115.04E*
167 O13 **Dayu Ling** ▲▲ S China
167 R7 **Da Yunhe** ***Eng.*** Grand Canal. *canal* E China
167 S11 **Dayu Shan** *island* SE China
166 J9 **Dazhu** ***var.*** Zhuyang. Sichuan, C China *30.45N 107.10E*
166 J9 **Dazu** ***var.*** Longgang. Chongqing Shi, C China *29.48N 105.46E*
85 H24 **De Aar** Northern Cape, C South Africa *30.40S 24.01E*
204 K5 **Deacon, Cape** *headland* Antarctica
41 R5 **Deadhorse** Alaska, USA *70.15N 148.28W*
35 T12 **Dead Indian Peak** ▲ Wyoming, C USA *44.36N 109.45W*
25 R9 **Dead Lake** ◎ Florida, SE USA
46 J4 **Deadman's Cay** Long Island, C Bahamas *23.09N 75.06W*
144 G11 **Dead Sea** ***var.*** Bahret Lut, Lacus Asphaltites, ***Ar.*** Al Baḩr al Mayyit, Baḩrat Lūt, ***Heb.*** Yam HaMelaḥ. *salt lake* Israel/Jordan
30 J9 **Deadwood** South Dakota, N USA *44.22N 103.43W*
99 Q22 **Deal** SE England, UK *51.14N 1.22E*
85 I22 **Dealesville** Free State, C South Africa *28.40S 25.46E*
167 P10 **De'an** ***var.*** Puting. Jiangxi, S China *29.24N 115.46E*
64 K9 **Deán Funes** Córdoba, C Argentina *30.25S 64.22W*
204 L12 **Dean Island** *island* Antarctica
Deanuvuotna *see* Tanafjorden
33 S10 **Dearborn** Michigan, N USA *42.16N 83.13W*
29 R3 **Dearborn** Missouri, C USA *39.31N 94.46W*
Deargget *see* Tärendö
34 K9 **Deary** Idaho, NW USA *46.46N 118.33W*
34 M9 **Deary** Washington, NW USA *46.42N 116.36W*
8 J10 **Dease** ≈ British Columbia, W Canada
8 J10 **Dease Lake** British Columbia, W Canada *58.28N 130.04W*
37 U11 **Death Valley** California, W USA *36.25N 116.50W*
37 U11 **Death Valley** *valley* California, W USA
94 M8 **Deatnu** ***Fin.*** Tenojoki, ***Nor.*** Tana. ≈ Finland/Norway ***see also*** Tenojoki
104 L4 **Deauville** Calvados, N France *49.21N 0.06E*
119 X7 **Debal'tseve** ***Rus.*** Debal'tsevo. Donets'ka Oblast', SE Ukraine *48.21N 38.25E*
Debal'tsevo *see* Debal'tseve
115 M19 **Debar** ***Ger.*** Dibra, ***Turk.*** Debre. W FYR Macedonia *41.32N 20.33E*
41 O9 **Debauch Mountain** ▲ Alaska, USA *64.31N 159.52W*
De Behagle *see* Laï
27 X7 **De Berry** Texas, SW USA *32.18N 94.09W*
131 T2 **Debessy** Udmurtskaya Respublika, NW Russian Federation *57.41N 53.56E*
113 N16 **Dębica** Podkarpackie, SE Poland *50.03N 21.24E*
De Bildt *see* De Bilt
100 J11 **De Bilt** ***var.*** De Bildt. Utrecht, C Netherlands *52.06N 5.10E*
127 O9 **Debin** Magadanskaya Oblast', E Russian Federation *62.18N 150.42E*
112 N13 **Dęblin** ***Rus.*** Ivangorod. Lubelskie, E Poland *51.34N 21.49E*
112 D10 **Dębno** Zachodnio-pomorskie, NW Poland *52.44N 14.42E*
41 S10 **Deborah, Mount** ▲ Alaska, USA *63.38N 147.13W*
35 N8 **De Borgia** Montana, NW USA *47.23N 115.24W*
Debra Birhan *see* Debre Birhan
Debra Marcos *see* Debre Mark'os
Debra Tabor *see* Debre Tabor
Debre *see* Debar
82 J13 **Debre Birhan** ***var.*** Debra Birhan. Amhara, N Ethiopia *9.45N 39.40E*
113 N22 **Debrecen** ***Ger.*** Debreczin, ***Rom.*** Debreţin; ***prev.*** Debreczen. Hajdú-Bihar, E Hungary *47.31N 21.37E*
Debreczen/Debreczin *see* Debrecen
82 I12 **Debre Mark'os** ***var.*** Debra Marcos. Amhara, N Ethiopia *10.18N 37.48E*
115 N19 **Debrešte** SW FYR Macedonia *41.29N 21.20E*
82 J11 **Debre Tabor** ***var.*** Debra Tabor. Amhara, N Ethiopia *11.46N 38.06E*
Debreţin *see* Debrecen
82 J13 **Debre Zeyt** Oromo, C Ethiopia *8.41N 39.00E*
115 L16 **Dečani** Serbia, S Serbia and Montenegro (Yugoslavia) *42.33N 20.18E*
25 P2 **Decatur** Alabama, S USA *34.36N 86.58W*
25 S3 **Decatur** Georgia, SE USA *33.46N 84.18W*
32 L13 **Decatur** Illinois, N USA *39.50N 88.57W*
33 Q12 **Decatur** Indiana, N USA *40.48N 84.55W*
24 M5 **Decatur** Mississippi, S USA *32.26N 89.06W*
31 S14 **Decatur** Nebraska, C USA *42.00N 96.19W*
27 S6 **Decatur** Texas, SW USA *33.14N 97.32W*
22 H9 **Decaturville** Tennessee, S USA *35.34N 88.07W*
105 O13 **Decazeville** Aveyron, S France *44.34N 2.18E*
161 H17 **Deccan** ***Hind.*** Dakshin. *plateau* C India
12 J8 **Decelles, Réservoir** ▣ Québec, SE Canada
10 K2 **Déception** Québec, NE Canada *62.06N 74.36W*
166 G11 **Dechang** ***var.*** Dezhou. Sichuan, C China *27.24N 102.09E*
113 C15 **Děčín** ***Ger.*** Tetschen. Ústecký Kraj, NW Czech Republic *50.48N 14.15E*
105 P9 **Decize** Nièvre, C France *46.51N 3.25E*
100 I6 **De Cocksdorp** Noord-Holland, NW Netherlands *53.09N 4.52E*
31 X11 **Decorah** Iowa, C USA *43.18N 91.47W*
Dedeagaç/Dedeagach *see* Alexandroúpoli
196 C15 **Dededo** N Guam *13.30N 144.51E*
100 N9 **Dedemsvaart** Overijssel, E Netherlands *52.36N 6.28E*
21 O11 **Dedham** Massachusetts, NE USA *42.14N 71.10W*
65 H19 **Dedo, Cerro** ▲ SW Argentina *44.46S 71.48W*
79 O13 **Dédougou** W Burkina *12.25N 3.27W*
128 G15 **Dedovichi** Pskovskaya Oblast', W Russian Federation *57.31N 29.53E*
Dedu *see* Wudalianchi
161 J24 **Deduru Oya** ≈ W Sri Lanka
85 N14 **Dedza** Central, S Malawi *14.24S 34.15E*
85 N14 **Dedza Mountain** ▲ C Malawi *14.22S 34.16E*
99 J19 **Dee** ***Wel.*** Afon Dyfrdwy. ≈ England/Wales, UK
98 K9 **Dee** ≈ NE Scotland, UK
Deep Bay *see* Chilumba
23 T3 **Deep Creek Lake** ▣ Maryland, NE USA
38 J4 **Deep Creek Range** ▲▲ Utah, W USA
29 P10 **Deep Fork** ≈ Oklahoma, C USA
12 J11 **Deep River** Ontario, SE Canada *46.05N 77.28W*
23 T10 **Deep River** ≈ North Carolina, SE USA
191 U4 **Deepwater** New South Wales, SE Australia *29.27S 151.52E*
33 S14 **Deer Creek Lake** ◎ Ohio, N USA
25 Z15 **Deerfield Beach** Florida, SE USA *26.19N 80.06W*
41 N8 **Deering** Alaska, USA *66.04N 162.43W*
40 M16 **Deer Island** *island* Alaska, USA
21 S7 **Deer Isle** *island* Maine, NE USA
11 S11 **Deer Lake** Newfoundland and Labrador, SE Canada *49.10N 57.18W*
101 D18 **Deerlijk** West-Vlaanderen, W Belgium *50.52N 3.21E*
35 Q10 **Deer Lodge** Montana, NW USA *46.24N 112.43W*
34 L8 **Deer Park** Washington, NW USA *47.55N 117.28W*
31 U5 **Deer River** Minnesota, N USA *47.19N 93.47W*
Deés *see* Dej
Defeng *see* Liping
33 R11 **Defiance** Ohio, N USA *41.16N 84.21W*
25 Q8 **De Funiak Springs** Florida, SE USA *30.43N 86.07W*
97 L23 **Degeberga** Skåne, S Sweden *55.48N 14.06E*
106 H12 **Degebe, Ribeira** ≈ S Portugal
82 M13 **Degeh Bur** Somali, E Ethiopia *8.08N 43.35E*
13 U9 **Dégelis** Québec, SE Canada *47.30N 68.38W*
79 U17 **Degema** Rivers, S Nigeria *4.46N 6.47E*
97 L16 **Degerfors** Örebro, C Sweden *59.13N 14.25E*
200 N16 **De Gerlache Seamounts** *undersea feature* SE Pacific Ocean
103 N21 **Deggendorf** Bayern, SE Germany *48.49N 12.58E*
124 Nn2 **Değirmenlik** ***Gk.*** Kythréa. N Cyprus *35.14N 33.28E*
82 I11 **Degoma** Amhara, N Ethiopia *12.22N 37.36E*
De Gordyk *see* Gorredijk
29 T12 **De Gray Lake** ▣ Arkansas, C USA
188 J6 **De Grey River** ≈ Western Australia
130 M10 **Degtevo** Rostovskaya Oblast', SW Russian Federation *49.12N 40.39E*
149 X13 **Dehak** Sīstān va Balūchestān, SE Iran *27.10N 62.34E*
149 R9 **Deh 'Alī** Kermān, C Iran *31.40N 56.10E*
149 S13 **Dehbārez** ***var.*** Rūdān. Hormozgān, S Iran *27.30N 57.10E*
149 P10 **Deh Bīd** Fārs, C Iran *30.37N 53.11E*
148 M10 **Deh Dasht** Kohgīlūyeh va Būyer Aḩmad, SW Iran *30.49N 50.36E*
77 N8 **Dehibat** SE Tunisia *31.58N 10.43E*
Dehli *see* Delhi
148 K8 **Dehlorān** Īlām, W Iran *32.40N 47.18E*
153 N13 **Dehqonobod** ***Rus.*** Dekhkanabad. Qashqadaryo Viloyati, S Uzbekistan *38.24N 66.31E*
158 J9 **Dehra Dūn** Uttaranchal, N India *30.18N 78.03E*
159 O14 **Dehri** Bihār, N India *24.55N 84.10E*
154 K10 **Deh Shū** ***var.*** Deshu. Helmand, S Afghanistan *30.28N 63.21E*
101 D17 **Deinze** Oost-Vlaanderen, NW Belgium *50.58N 3.31E*
Deir 'Alla *see* Dayr 'Allā
Deir ez Zor *see* Dayr az Zawr
Deirgeirt, Loch *see* Derg, Lough
118 H9 **Dej** ***Hung.*** Dés; ***prev.*** Deés. Cluj, NW Romania *47.08N 23.55E*
97 K15 **Deje** Värmland, C Sweden *59.34N 13.28E*
176 Y14 **De Jongs, Tanjung** *headland* Papua, SE Indonesia *6.55S 138.31E*
De Jouwer *see* Joure
32 M10 **De Kalb** Illinois, N USA *41.55N 88.45W*
24 M5 **De Kalb** Mississippi, S USA *32.46N 88.39W*
27 W5 **De Kalb** Texas, SW USA *33.30N 94.34W*
Dekéleia *see* Dhekélia
81 K20 **Dekese** Kasai Occidental, C Dem. Rep. Congo *3.28S 21.24E*
Dekhkanabad *see* Dehqonobod
81 I14 **Dékoa** Kémo, C Central African Republic *6.17N 19.07E*
100 H6 **De Koog** Noord-Holland, NW Netherlands *53.06N 4.43E*
32 M9 **Delafield** Wisconsin, N USA *43.03N 88.22W*
63 C23 **De La Garma** Buenos Aires, E Argentina *37.58S 60.25W*
12 K10 **Delahey, Lac** ◎ Québec, SE Canada
82 E11 **Delami** Southern Kordofan, C Sudan *11.51N 30.30E*
25 X11 **De Land** Florida, SE USA *29.01N 81.18W*
37 R12 **Delano** California, W USA *35.46N 119.15W*
31 V8 **Delano** Minnesota, N USA *45.03N 93.46W*
38 K6 **Delano Peak** ▲ Utah, W USA *38.22N 112.21W*
Delap-Uliga-Darrit *see* Dalap-Uliga-Djarrit
154 L7 **Delārām** Farāh, SW Afghanistan *32.10N 63.27E*
40 F17 **Delarof Islands** *island group* Aleutian Islands, Alaska, USA
32 M9 **Delavan** Wisconsin, N USA *42.37N 88.37W*
33 S13 **Delaware** Ohio, N USA *40.18N 83.04W*
20 I17 **Delaware** ***off.*** State of Delaware; also known as Blue Hen State, Diamond State, First State. ⬖ *state* NE USA
20 I17 **Delaware Bay** *bay* NE USA
26 J8 **Delaware Mountains** ▲▲ Texas, SW USA
20 I12 **Delaware River** ≈ NE USA
29 Q3 **Delaware River** ≈ Kansas, C USA
20 J14 **Delaware Water Gap** *valley* New Jersey/Pennsylvania, NE USA
103 G14 **Delbrück** Nordrhein-Westfalen, W Germany *51.46N 8.34E*
9 Q15 **Delburne** Alberta, SW Canada *52.09N 113.11W*
180 M12 **Del Cano Rise** *undersea feature* SW Indian Ocean
115 Q18 **Delčevo** NE FYR Macedonia *41.57N 22.45E*
Delcommune, Lac *see* Nzilo, Lac
100 O10 **Delden** Overijssel, E Netherlands *52.16N 6.40E*
191 R12 **Delegate** New South Wales, SE Australia *37.04S 148.57E*
De Lemmer *see* Lemmer
110 D7 **Delémont** ***Ger.*** Delsberg. Jura, NW Switzerland *47.22N 7.21E*
27 R7 **De Leon** Texas, SW USA *32.06N 98.33W*
117 F18 **Delfoí** Stereá Ellás, C Greece *38.28N 22.31E*
100 G12 **Delft** Zuid-Holland, W Netherlands *52.01N 4.22E*
161 J23 **Delft** *island* NW Sri Lanka
100 O5 **Delfzijl** Groningen, NE Netherlands *53.19N 6.55E*
(0) E9 **Delgada Fan** *undersea feature* NE Pacific Ocean
44 F7 **Delgado** San Salvador, SW El Salvador *13.44N 89.07W*
84 Q12 **Delgado, Cabo** *headland* N Mozambique *10.41S 40.40E*
82 E6 **Delgo** Northern, N Sudan *20.07N 30.34E*
165 R10 **Delhi** ***var.*** Delingha. Qinghai, C China *37.19N 97.22E*
158 I10 **Delhi** ***var.*** Dehli, ***Hind.*** Dilli; ***hist.*** Shahjahanabad. Delhi, N India *28.40N 77.11E*
24 J5 **Delhi** Louisiana, S USA *32.28N 91.29W*
20 J11 **Delhi** New York, NE USA *42.16N 74.55W*
158 I10 **Delhi** ⬖ *union territory* NW India
142 J17 **Deli Burnu** *headland* S Turkey *36.43N 34.55E*
57 X10 **Délices** C French Guiana *4.46N 53.42W*
142 J12 **Delice Çayı** ≈ C Turkey
42 J6 **Delicias** ***var.*** Ciudad Delicias. Chihuahua, N Mexico *28.08N 105.22W*
149 N7 **Delījān** ***var.*** Dalijan, Dilijan. Markazī, W Iran *34.01N 50.39E*
114 P12 **Deli Jovan** ▲▲ E Serbia and Montenegro (Yugoslavia)
Déli-Kárpátok *see* Carpaţii Meridionali
15 H6 **Délįne** ***prev.*** Fort Franklin. Northwest Territories, NW Canada *65.10N 123.30W*
Delingha *see* Delhi
13 Q7 **Delisle** Québec, SE Canada *48.39N 71.42W*
9 T15 **Delisle** Saskatchewan, S Canada *51.54N 107.01W*
103 M15 **Delitzsch** Sachsen, E Germany *51.31N 12.19E*
35 Q12 **Dell** Montana, NW USA *44.41N 112.42W*
26 I7 **Dell City** Texas, SW USA *31.56N 105.12W*
105 U7 **Delle** Territoire-de-Belfort, E France *47.30N 7.00E*
38 J9 **Dellenbaugh, Mount** ▲ Arizona, SW USA *36.06N 113.32W*
31 R11 **Dell Rapids** South Dakota, N USA *43.50N 96.42W*
23 Y4 **Delmar** Maryland, NE USA *38.26N 75.32W*
20 K11 **Delmar** New York, NE USA *42.37N 73.49W*
102 G11 **Delmenhorst** Niedersachsen, NW Germany *53.03N 8.37E*
114 C9 **Delnice** Primorje-Gorski Kotar, NW Croatia *45.24N 14.49E*
39 R7 **Del Norte** Colorado, C USA *37.40N 106.21W*
41 N6 **De Long Mountains** ▲▲ Alaska, USA
191 P16 **Deloraine** Tasmania, SE Australia *41.34S 146.43E*
9 W17 **Deloraine** Manitoba, S Canada *49.12N 100.28W*
33 O12 **Delphi** Indiana, N USA *40.35N 86.40W*
33 Q12 **Delphos** Ohio, N USA *40.49N 84.20W*
25 Z15 **Delray Beach** Florida, SE USA *26.27N 80.04W*
27 O12 **Del Rio** Texas, SW USA *29.22N 100.55W*
Delsberg *see* Delémont
96 N11 **Delsbo** Gävleborg, C Sweden *61.49N 16.34E*
39 P6 **Delta** Colorado, C USA *38.44N 108.04W*
38 K5 **Delta** Utah, W USA *39.21N 112.34W*
79 T17 **Delta** ⬖ *state* S Nigeria
57 Q6 **Delta Amacuro** ***off.*** Territorio Delta Amacuro. ⬖ *federal district* NE Venezuela
41 S9 **Delta Junction** Alaska, USA *64.02N 145.43W*
25 X11 **Deltona** Florida, SE USA *28.54N 81.15W*
191 T5 **Delungra** New South Wales, SE Australia *29.40S 150.49E*
160 C12 **Delvāda** Gujarāt, W India *20.46N 71.01E*
63 B21 **Del Valle** Buenos Aires, E Argentina *35.55S 60.42W*
Delvina *see* Delvinë
117 C15 **Delvináki** ***var.*** Dhelvinákion; ***prev.*** Pogónion. Ípeiros, W Greece *39.56N 20.27E*
115 L23 **Delvinë** ***var.*** Delvina, ***It.*** Delvino. Vlorë, S Albania *39.56N 20.07E*
Delvino *see* Delvinë
118 I7 **Delyatyn** Ivano-Frankivs'ka Oblast', W Ukraine *48.32N 24.38E*
131 U5 **Dëma** ≈ W Russian Federation
107 O5 **Demanda, Sierra de la** ▲▲ W Spain
41 T5 **Demarcation Point** *headland* Alaska, USA *69.40N 141.19W*
81 K21 **Demba** Kasai Occidental, C Dem. Rep. Congo *5.24S 22.16E*
180 H13 **Dembéni** Grande Comore, NW Comoros *11.49S 43.25E*
81 M15 **Dembia** Mbomou, SE Central African Republic *5.08N 24.25E*
Dembidollo *see* Dembī Dolo
82 H13 **Dembī Dolo** ***var.*** Dembidollo. Oromo, C Ethiopia *8.33N 34.49E*
158 K6 **Demchok** ***var.*** Dêmqog. China/India ***see also*** Dêmqog *32.30N 79.42E*
158 L6 **Demchok** ***var.*** Dêmqog. *disputed region* China/India ***see also*** Dêmqog
100 I12 **De Meern** Utrecht, C Netherlands *52.06N 5.00E*
101 I17 **Demer** ≈ C Belgium
66 H12 **Demerara Plain** *undersea feature* W Atlantic Ocean
66 H12 **Demerara Plateau** *undersea feature* W Atlantic Ocean
57 T9 **Demerara River** ≈ NE Guyana
130 H3 **Demidov** Smolenskaya Oblast', W Russian Federation *55.15N 31.30E*
39 Q15 **Deming** New Mexico, SW USA *32.13N 107.46W*
34 H6 **Deming** Washington, NW USA *48.49N 122.13W*
60 E10 **Demini, Rio** ≈ NW Brazil
142 D13 **Demirci** Manisa, W Turkey *39.03N 28.40E*
115 P19 **Demir Kapija** ***prev.*** Železna Vrata. SE FYR Macedonia *41.25N 22.15E*
116 N11 **Demirköy** Kırklareli, NW Turkey *41.49N 27.47E*
102 N9 **Demmin** Mecklenburg-Vorpommern, NE Germany *53.53N 13.03E*
25 O5 **Demopolis** Alabama, S USA *32.31N 87.50W*
33 N11 **Demotte** Indiana, N USA *41.13N 87.07W*

◆ Country
● Country Capital
◇ Dependent Territory
○ Dependent Territory Capital
⬖ Administrative Region
✕ International Airport
▲ Mountain
▲▲ Mountain Range
Ѫ Volcano
≈ River
◎ Lake
▣ Reservoir

DÊMQOG – DISCOVERY SEAMOUNT/DISCOVERY SEAMOUNTS

164 F13 **Dêmqog** *var.* Demchok. China/India 32.36N 79.28E *see also* Demchok
158 L6 **Dêmqog** *var.* Demchok. *disputed region* China/India *see also* Demchok
176 Yy10 **Demta** Papua, E Indonesia 2.19S 140.06E
125 G11 **Dem'yanka** ≈ C Russian Federation
128 H15 **Demyansk** Novgorodskaya Oblast', W Russian Federation 57.39N 32.31E
125 Ff11 **Dem'yanskoye** Tyumenskaya Oblast', C Russian Federation 59.39N 69.15E
105 P2 **Denain** Nord, N France 50.19N 3.24E
41 S10 **Denali** Alaska, USA 63.08N 147.33W
Denali *see* McKinley, Mount
83 M14 **Denan** Somali, E Ethiopia 6.40N 43.31E
Denau *see* Denov
99 J18 **Denbigh** *Wel.* Dinbych. NE Wales, UK 53.10N 3.25W
99 J18 **Denbigh** *cultural region* N Wales, UK
100 I6 **Den Burg** Noord-Holland, NW Netherlands 53.03N 4.46E
101 F18 **Dender** *Fr.* Dendre. ≈ W Belgium
101 F18 **Denderleeuw** Oost-Vlaanderen, NW Belgium 50.52N 4.04E
101 F17 **Dendermonde** *Fr.* Termonde. Oost-Vlaanderen, NW Belgium 51.01N 4.07E
Dendre *see* Dender
204 I9 **Dendtler Island** *island* Antarctica
100 P10 **Denekamp** Overijssel, E Netherlands 52.23N 7.00E
79 W12 **Dengas** Zinder, S Niger 13.15N 9.43E
Dêngkagoin *see* Têwo
168 L13 **Dengkou** *var.* Bayan Gol. Nei Mongol Zizhiqu, N China 40.15N 106.58E
165 Q14 **Dêngqên** *var.* Gyamotang. Xizang Zizhiqu, W China 31.28N 95.28E
Deng Xian *see* Dengzhou
166 M7 **Dengzhou** *prev.* Deng Xian. Henan, C China 32.43N 112.02E
Dengzhou *see* Penglai
Den Haag *see* 's-Gravenhage
100 N9 **Den Ham** Overijssel, E Netherlands 52.30N 6.30E
188 H10 **Denham** Western Australia 25.56S 113.35E
46 J12 **Denham, Mount** ▲ C Jamaica 18.13N 77.33W
24 J8 **Denham Springs** Louisiana, S USA 30.29N 90.57W
100 I7 **Den Helder** Noord-Holland, NW Netherlands 52.54N 4.45E
107 T11 **Dénia** País Valenciano, E Spain 38.51N 0.07E
201 Q8 **Denig** W Nauru
191 N10 **Deniliquin** New South Wales, SE Australia 35.33S 144.58E
31 T14 **Denison** Iowa, C USA 42.00N 95.22W
27 U5 **Denison** Texas, SW USA 33.45N 96.32W
150 L8 **Denisovka** *prev.* Ordzhonikidze. Kostanay, N Kazakhstan 52.24N 61.40E
142 D15 **Denizli** Denizli, SW Turkey 37.46N 29.04E
142 D15 **Denizli** ◈ *province* SW Turkey
Denjong *see* Sikkim
191 S7 **Denman** New South Wales, SE Australia 32.24S 150.43E
205 Y10 **Denman Glacier** *glacier* Antarctica
23 R14 **Denmark** South Carolina, SE USA 33.19N 81.08W
97 G23 **Denmark** *off.* Kingdom of Denmark, *Dan.* Danmark; *anc.* Hafnia. ◆ *monarchy* N Europe
94 H1 **Denmark Strait** *var.* Danmarksstraedet. *strait* Greenland/Iceland
47 T11 **Dennery** E Saint Lucia 13.55N 60.53W
100 I7 **Den Oever** Noord-Holland, NW Netherlands 52.56N 5.01E
153 O13 **Denov** *Rus.* Denau. Surkhondaryo Viloyati, S Uzbekistan 38.19N 67.48E
175 N16 **Denpasar** *prev.* Paloe. Bali, C Indonesia 8.40S 115.13E
118 E12 **Denta** Timiş, W Romania 45.18N 21.14E
23 Y3 **Denton** Maryland, NE USA 38.52N 75.49W
27 T6 **Denton** Texas, SW USA 33.10N 97.08W
195 O15 **D'Entrecasteaux Islands** *island group* SE PNG
39 T4 **Denver** *state capital* Colorado, C USA 39.44N 105.00W
18 K8 **Denver** × Colorado, C USA 39.57N 104.38W
26 L6 **Denver City** Texas, SW USA 32.57N 102.49W
158 J9 **Deoband** Uttar Pradesh, N India 29.40N 77.40E
Deoghar *see* Devghar
160 E13 **Deolāli** Mahārāshtra, W India 19.55N 73.49E
160 I10 **Deori** Madhya Pradesh, C India 23.09N 78.39E
159 O12 **Deoria** Uttar Pradesh, N India 26.31N 83.48E
101 A17 **De Panne** West-Vlaanderen, W Belgium 51.06N 2.34E
56 M5 **Dependencia Federal** *off.* Territorio Dependencia Federal. ◈ *federal dependency* N Venezuela
Dependencia Federal, Territorio *see* Dependencia Federal
32 M7 **De Pere** Wisconsin, N USA 44.26N 88.03W
20 D10 **Depew** New York, NE USA 42.54N 78.41W
101 E17 **De Pinte** Oost-Vlaanderen, NW Belgium 51.00N 3.37E
27 V5 **Deport** Texas, SW USA 33.31N 95.19W
126 M7 **Deputatskiy** Respublika Sakha (Yakutiya), NE Russian Federation 69.18N 139.48E
Dêqên *see* Dagzê
29 S13 **De Queen** Arkansas, C USA 34.02N 94.20W
24 G8 **De Quincy** Louisiana, S USA 30.27N 93.25W
83 J20 **Dera** *spring/well* S Kenya 2.39S 39.52E
Der'a/Derá/Déraa *see* Dar'ā
155 S10 **Dera Ghāzi Khān** *var.* Dera Ghāzikhān. Punjab, C Pakistan 30.01N 70.37E
155 S8 **Dera Ismāīl Khān** North-West Frontier Province, C Pakistan 31.51N 70.55E
115 L16 **Đeravica** ▲ S Serbia and Montenegro (Yugoslavia) 42.33N 20.08E
118 L6 **Derazhnya** Khmel'nyts'ka Oblast', W Ukraine 49.16N 27.24E
131 R17 **Derbent** Respublika Dagestan, SW Russian Federation 42.01N 48.16E
153 N13 **Derbent** Surkhondaryo Viloyati, S Uzbekistan 38.15N 66.59E
Derbisîye *see* Darbāsīyah
81 M15 **Derbissaka** Mbomou, SE Central African Republic 5.43N 24.48E
188 L4 **Derby** Western Australia 17.18S 123.36E
99 M19 **Derby** C England, UK 52.55N 1.30W
29 N7 **Derby** Kansas, C USA 37.33N 97.16W
99 L18 **Derbyshire** *cultural region* C England, UK
114 O11 **Đerdap** *physical region* E Serbia and Montenegro (Yugoslavia)
Dereli *see* Gónnoi
176 X11 **Derew** ≈ Papua, E Indonesia
131 R8 **Dergachi** Saratovskaya Oblast', W Russian Federation 51.15N 48.58E
Dergachi *see* Derhachi
99 C19 **Derg, Lough** *Ir.* Loch Deirgeirt. ◎ W Ireland
119 V5 **Derhachi** *Rus.* Dergachi. Kharkivs'ka Oblast', E Ukraine 50.08N 36.10E
24 G8 **De Ridder** Louisiana, S USA 30.51N 93.18W
143 P16 **Derik** Mardin, SE Turkey 37.22N 40.16E
85 E20 **Derm** Hardap, C Namibia 23.38S 18.12E
150 M14 **Dermentobe** *prev.* Dyurmen'tyube. Kzylorda, S Kazakhstan 45.46N 63.42E
29 W14 **Dermott** Arkansas, C USA 33.31N 91.26W
Dérna *see* Darnah
Dernberg, Cape *see* Dolphin Head
24 J11 **Dernieres, Isles** *island group* Louisiana, S USA
Dernis *see* Drniš
104 I4 **Déroute, Passage de la** *strait* Channel Islands/France
Derrá *see* Dar'ā
Derry *see* Londonderry
Dertona *see* Tortona
Dertosa *see* Tortosa
82 H8 **Derudeb** Red Sea, NE Sudan 17.28N 36.04E
114 H10 **Derventa** Republika Srpska, N Bosnia and Herzegovina 44.57N 17.55E
191 O16 **Derwent Bridge** Tasmania, SE Australia 42.10S 146.13E
191 O17 **Derwent, River** ≈ Tasmania, SE Australia
152 F10 **Derweze** *Rus.* Darvaza. Ahal Welaýaty, C Turkmenistan 40.10N 58.27E
Deržavinsk *see* Derzhavinsk
151 O9 **Derzhavinsk** *var.* Deržavinsk. Akmola, C Kazakhstan 51.04N 66.19E
Dés *see* Dej
59 J18 **Desaguadero** Puno, S Peru 16.31S 69.01W
59 J18 **Desaguadero, Río** ≈ Bolivia/Peru
203 W9 **Désappointement, Îles du** *island group* Îles Tuamotu, C French Polynesia
29 W11 **Des Arc** Arkansas, C USA 34.58N 91.30W
12 C10 **Desbarats** Ontario, S Canada 46.20N 83.52W
64 H13 **Descabezado Grande, Volcán** ☒ C Chile 35.34S 70.40W
42 B2 **Descanso** Baja California, NW Mexico 32.08N 116.51W
104 L9 **Descartes** Indre-et-Loire, C France 46.58N 0.40E
9 T13 **Deschambault Lake** ◎ Saskatchewan, C Canada
Deschnaer Koppe *see* Velká Deštná
34 I11 **Deschutes River** ≈ Oregon, NW USA
82 J12 **Desē** *var.* Desse, *It.* Dessie. Amhara, N Ethiopia 11.01N 39.39E
65 I20 **Deseado, Río** ≈ S Argentina
108 F8 **Desenzano del Garda** Lombardia, N Italy 45.28N 10.31E
38 K3 **Deseret Peak** ▲ Utah, W USA 40.27N 112.37W
66 P6 **Deserta Grande** *island* Madeira, Portugal, NE Atlantic Ocean
66 P6 **Desertas, Ilhas** *island group* Madeira, Portugal, NE Atlantic Ocean
37 X16 **Desert Center** California, W USA 33.42N 115.22W
37 V15 **Desert Hot Springs** California, W USA 33.57N 116.33W
12 K10 **Désert, Lac** ◎ Québec, SE Canada
38 J2 **Desert Peak** ▲ Utah, W USA 41.03N 113.22W
33 R11 **Deshler** Ohio, N USA 41.12N 83.55W
Deshu *see* Deh Shū
Desiderii Fanum *see* St-Dizier
108 D7 **Desio** Lombardia, N Italy 45.37N 9.12E
117 E15 **Deskáti** *var.* Dheskáti. Dytikí Makedonía, N Greece 39.55N 21.49E
30 L2 **Des Lacs River** ≈ North Dakota, N USA
29 X6 **Desloge** Missouri, C USA 37.52N 90.31W
9 Q12 **Desmarais** Alberta, W Canada 55.58N 113.55W
31 Q10 **De Smet** South Dakota, N USA 44.23N 97.33W
31 V14 **Des Moines** *state capital* Iowa, C USA 41.36N 93.36W
19 N8 **Des Moines River** ≈ C USA
119 P4 **Desna** ≈ Russian Federation/Ukraine
118 G14 **Desnăţui** ≈ S Romania
65 F24 **Desolación, Isla** *island* S Chile
31 V14 **De Soto** Iowa, C USA 41.31N 94.00W
25 Q4 **De Soto Falls** *waterfall* Alabama, S USA 33.22N 86.12W
85 I25 **Despatch** Eastern Cape, S South Africa 33.48S 25.28E
107 N12 **Despeñaperros, Desfiladero de** *pass* S Spain 38.25N 3.26W
33 N10 **Des Plaines** Illinois, N USA 42.01N 87.52W
117 J21 **Despotikó** *island* Kykládes, Greece, Aegean Sea
114 N12 **Despotovac** Serbia, E Serbia and Montenegro (Yugoslavia) 44.06N 21.25E
103 M14 **Dessau** Sachsen-Anhalt, E Germany 51.51N 12.15E
Desse *see* Desē
101 J16 **Dessel** Antwerpen, N Belgium 51.15N 5.07E
Dessie *see* Desē
Destêrro *see* Florianópolis
25 P9 **Destin** Florida, SE USA 30.23N 86.30W
Deštná *see* Velká Deštná
200 Oo11 **Desventurados, Islas de los** *island group* W Chile
105 N1 **Desvres** Pas-de-Calais, N France 50.41N 1.48E
118 E12 **Deta** *Ger.* Detta. Timiş, W Romania 45.22N 21.13E
103 H14 **Detmold** Nordrhein-Westfalen, W Germany 51.55N 8.52E
33 S10 **Detroit** Michigan, N USA 42.19N 83.03W
27 W5 **Detroit** Texas, SW USA 33.39N 95.16W
33 S10 **Detroit** ≈ Canada/USA
31 S6 **Detroit Lakes** Minnesota, N USA 46.49N 95.49W
33 S10 **Detroit Metropolitan** × Michigan, N USA 42.12N 83.16W
Detta *see* Deta
178 J11 **Det Udom** Ubon Ratchathani, E Thailand 14.54N 105.03E
113 K20 **Detva** *Hung.* Gyeva. Banskobystrický Kraj, C Slovakia 48.34N 19.25E
160 G13 **Deūlgaon Rāja** Mahārāshtra, C India 20.04N 76.08E
101 L15 **Deurne** Noord-Brabant, SE Netherlands 51.28N 5.46E
101 H16 **Deurne** × (Antwerpen) Antwerpen, N Belgium 51.10N 4.28E
Deutsch-Brod *see* Havlíčkův Brod
Deutschendorf *see* Poprad
Deutsch-Eylau *see* Iława
111 Y6 **Deutschkreutz** Burgenland, E Austria 47.36N 16.38E
Deutsch Krone *see* Wałcz
Deutschland/Deutschland, Bundesrepublik *see* Germany
111 V9 **Deutschlandsberg** Steiermark, SE Austria 46.52N 15.13E
Deutsch-Südwestafrika *see* Namibia
111 Y3 **Deutsch-Wagram** Niederösterreich, E Austria 48.19N 16.33E
Deux-Ponts *see* Zweibrücken
12 I11 **Deux Rivieres** Ontario, SE Canada 46.13N 78.16W
104 K9 **Deux-Sèvres** ◈ *department* W France
118 G11 **Deva** *Ger.* Diemrich, *Hung.* Déva. Hunedoara, W Romania 45.55N 22.54E
Deva *see* Chester
Devana *see* Aberdeen
Devana Castra *see* Chester
Đevđelija *see* Gevgelija
142 L12 **Deveci Dağları** ▲▲ N Turkey
143 P15 **Devegeçidi Barajı** ⊠ SE Turkey
142 K15 **Develi** Kayseri, C Turkey 38.22N 35.28E
100 M11 **Deventer** Overijssel, E Netherlands 52.15N 6.10E
13 O10 **Devenyns, Lac** ◎ Québec, SE Canada
98 K8 **Deveron** ≈ NE Scotland, UK
159 R14 **Devghar** *prev.* Deoghar. Jhārkhand, NE India
29 R10 **Devil's Den** *plateau* Arkansas, C USA
37 R7 **Devils Gate** *pass* California, W USA 38.20N 119.23W
32 J2 **Devils Island** *island* Apostle Islands, Wisconsin, N USA
Devil's Island *see* Diable, Île du
31 P3 **Devils Lake** North Dakota, N USA 48.07N 98.49W
33 R10 **Devils Lake** ◎ Michigan, N USA
31 O3 **Devils Lake** ◎ North Dakota, N USA
37 W13 **Devils Playground** *desert* California, W USA
27 O11 **Devils River** ≈ Texas, SW USA
35 Y12 **Devils Tower** ▲ Wyoming, C USA 44.33N 104.45W
116 I11 **Devin** *prev.* Dovlen. Smolyan, SW Bulgaria 41.45N 24.24E
27 R12 **Devine** Texas, SW USA 29.08N 98.54W
158 H13 **Devli** Rājasthān, N India 25.46N 75.22E
Devne *see* Devnya
116 N8 **Devnya** *prev.* Devne. Varna, E Bulgaria 43.13N 27.36E
33 U14 **Devola** Ohio, N USA 39.28N 81.28W
Devoll *see* Devollit, Lumi i
115 M21 **Devollit, Lumi i** *var.* Devoll. ≈ SE Albania
9 Q14 **Devon** Alberta, SW Canada 53.21N 113.47W
99 I23 **Devon** *cultural region* SW England, UK
207 N10 **Devon Island** *prev.* North Devon Island. *island* Parry Islands, Nunavut, NE Canada
191 O16 **Devonport** Tasmania, SE Australia 41.14S 146.20E
142 H11 **Devrek** Zonguldak, N Turkey 41.13N 31.57E
160 G10 **Dewās** Madhya Pradesh, C India 22.58N 76.03E
De Westerein *see* Zwaagwesteinde
29 P8 **Dewey** Oklahoma, C USA 36.48N 95.56W
Dewey *see* Culebra
100 M8 **De Wijk** Drenthe, NE Netherlands 52.41N 6.13E
29 W12 **De Witt** Arkansas, C USA 34.17N 91.20W
31 Z14 **De Witt** Iowa, C USA 41.49N 90.32W
31 R16 **De Witt** Nebraska, C USA 40.23N 96.55W
99 M17 **Dewsbury** N England, UK 53.42N 1.37W
167 Q10 **Dexing** Jiangxi, S China 28.49N 117.37E
29 Y8 **Dexter** Missouri, C USA 36.48N 89.57W
39 U14 **Dexter** New Mexico, SW USA 33.12N 104.25W
166 I8 **Deyang** Sichuan, C China 31.07N 104.24E
190 C4 **Dey-Dey, Lake** *salt lake* South Australia
149 S7 **Deyhūk** Yazd, E Iran 33.18N 57.30E
Deynau *see* Galkynyş
148 L8 **Dezfūl** *var.* Dizful. Khūzestān, SW Iran 32.22N 48.28E
133 X4 **Dezhneva, Mys** *headland* NE Russian Federation 66.07N 169.40W
167 P4 **Dezhou** Shandong, E China 37.28N 116.18E
Dezhou *see* Dechang
Dezh Shāhpūr *see* Marīvān
Dhahran *see* Az Zahrān
Dhahran Al Khobar *see* Az Zahrān al Khubar
159 U14 **Dhaka** *prev.* Dacca. ● (Bangladesh) Dhaka, C Bangladesh 23.42N 90.22E
159 T15 **Dhaka** ◈ *division* C Bangladesh
Dhali *see* Idálion
147 O15 **Dhamār** W Yemen 14.31N 44.25E
Dhambul *see* Taraz
160 K12 **Dhamtari** Chhattīsgarh, C India 20.43N 81.36E
159 Q15 **Dhanbād** Jhārkhand, NE India 23.48N 86.27E
158 L10 **Dhangadhi** *var.* Dhangarhi. Far Western, W Nepal 28.45N 80.38E
Dhangarhi *see* Dhangadhi
Dhank *see* Dank
159 R12 **Dhankuta** Eastern, E Nepal 27.06N 87.21E
158 I6 **Dhaola Dhār** ▲▲ NE India
160 F10 **Dhār** Madhya Pradesh, C India 22.36N 75.23E
159 R12 **Dharan** *var.* Dharan Bazar. Eastern, E Nepal 26.51N 87.18E
161 H21 **Dhārāpuram** Tamil Nādu, SE India 10.45N 77.33E
161 H20 **Dharmapuri** Tamil Nādu, SE India 12.10N 78.07E
161 H18 **Dharmavaram** Andhra Pradesh, E India 14.27N 77.43E
160 M11 **Dharmjaygarh** Chhattīsgarh, C India 22.27N 83.16E
Dharmsāla *see* Dharmshāla
158 I7 **Dharmshāla** *prev.* Dharmsāla. Himāchal Pradesh, N India 32.13N 76.24E
161 F17 **Dhārwād** *prev.* Dharwar. Karnātaka, SW India 15.30N 75.04E
Dharwar *see* Dhārwād
159 O10 **Dhaulāgiri** ▲ C Nepal 28.45N 83.27E
83 L18 **Dheere Laaq** *var.* Lak Dera, *It.* Lach Dera. *seasonal river* Kenya/Somalia
124 O3 **Dhekéleia Sovereign Base Area** *UK military installation* E Cyprus 34.59N 33.45E
124 O3 **Dhekélia** *Eng.* Dhekelia, *Gk.* Dekéleia. *UK air base* SE Cyprus 35.00N 33.45E
Dhelvinákion *see* Delvináki
115 M22 **Dhëmbelit, Majae** ▲ S Albania 40.10N 20.22E
160 O12 **Dhenkānāl** Orissa, E India 20.40N 85.36E
Dheskáti *see* Deskáti
144 G11 **Dhībān** Al 'Āşimah, NW Jordan 31.30N 35.46E
Dhidhimótikhon *see* Didymóteicho
Dhíkti Ori *see* Díkti
144 I12 **Dhirwah, Wādī adh** *dry watercourse* C Jordan
Dhístomon *see* Dístomo
Dhodhekánisos *see* Dodekánisos
Dhodhóni *see* Dodóni
Dhofar *see* Zufār
Dhomokós *see* Domokós
Dhond *see* Daund
161 H17 **Dhone** Andhra Pradesh, C India 15.25N 77.52E
160 B11 **Dhorāji** Gujarāt, W India 21.43N 70.27E
Dhráma *see* Dráma
160 C10 **Dhrāngadhra** Gujarāt, W India 22.58N 71.31E
Dhrepanon, Akrotírio *see* Drépano, Akrotírio
159 T13 **Dhuburi** Assam, NE India 26.06N 89.55E
160 F12 **Dhule** *prev.* Dhulia. Mahārāshtra, C India 20.54N 74.46E
Dhulia *see* Dhule
Dhún Dealgan, Cuan *see* Dundalk Bay
Dhún Droma, Cuan *see* Dundrum Bay
Dhún na nGall, Bá *see* Donegal Bay
Dhū Shaykh *see* Qazānīyah
82 Q13 **Dhuudo** Bari, NE Somalia 9.21N 50.19E
83 N15 **Dhuusa Marreeb** *var.* Dusa Marreb, *It.* Dusa Mareb. Galguduud, C Somalia 5.33N 46.24E
117 J24 **Día** *island* SE Greece
57 Y9 **Diable, Île du** *var.* Devil's Island. *island* N French Guiana
13 N12 **Diable, Rivière du** ≈ Québec, SE Canada
37 N8 **Diablo, Mount** ▲ California, W USA 37.52N 121.57W
37 O9 **Diablo Range** ▲▲ California, W USA
26 I8 **Diablo, Sierra** ▲▲ Texas, SW USA
47 O11 **Diablotins, Morne** ▲ N Dominica 15.30N 61.23W
79 N11 **Diafarabé** Mopti, C Mali 14.12N 5.01W
79 N11 **Diaka** ≈ SW Mali
Diakovár *see* Đakovo
78 I12 **Dialakoto** S Senegal 13.21N 13.19W
63 B18 **Diamante** Entre Ríos, E Argentina 32.04S 60.40W
64 I12 **Diamante, Río** ≈ C Argentina
61 M19 **Diamantina** Minas Gerais, SE Brazil 18.16S 43.37W
61 N17 **Diamantina, Chapada** ▲▲ E Brazil
181 U11 **Diamantina Fracture Zone** *tectonic feature* E Indian Ocean
189 T8 **Diamantina River** ≈ Queensland/South Australia
40 D9 **Diamond Head** *headland* O'ahu, Hawai'i, USA, C Pacific Ocean 21.15N 157.48W
39 P2 **Diamond Peak** ▲ Colorado, C USA 40.56N 108.56W
37 W5 **Diamond Peak** ▲ Nevada, W USA 39.34N 115.46W
Diamond State *see* Delaware
78 J11 **Diamou** Kayes, SW Mali 14.04N 11.16W
97 I23 **Dianalund** Vestsjælland, C Denmark 55.31N 11.30E
67 G25 **Diana's Peak** ▲ C Saint Helena
166 M16 **Dianbai** *var.* Shuidong. Guangdong, S China 21.33N 110.58E
166 G13 **Dian Chi** ⊠ SW China
108 B10 **Diano Marina** Liguria, NW Italy 43.55N 8.06E
169 V11 **Diaobingshan** *var.* Tiefa. Liaoning, NE China 42.25N 123.39E
79 R13 **Diapaga** E Burkina 12.04N 1.47E
Diarbekr *see* Diyarbakır
109 J15 **Diavolo, Passo del** *pass* C Italy 41.55N 13.42E
63 B18 **Díaz** Santa Fe, C Argentina 32.22S 61.04W
147 W6 **Dibā al Ḩişn** *var.* Dibāh, Dibba. Ash Shāriqah, NE UAE 25.34N 56.16E
145 S3 **Dībaga** N Iraq 35.51N 43.49E
Dibāh *see* Dibā al Ḩişn
81 L22 **Dibaya** Kasai Occidental, S Dem. Rep. Congo 6.31S 22.57E
Dibba *see* Dibā al Ḩişn
205 W15 **Dibble Iceberg Tongue** *ice feature* Antarctica
115 L19 **Dibër** ◈ *district* E Albania
85 I20 **Dibete** Central, SE Botswana 23.45S 26.29E
27 W9 **Diboll** Texas, SW USA 31.11N 94.46W
Dibra *see* Debar
159 X11 **Dibrugarh** Assam, NE India 27.29N 94.49E
56 G4 **Dibulla** La Guajira, N Colombia 11.14N 73.22W
27 O5 **Dickens** Texas, SW USA 33.37N 100.50W
21 R2 **Dickey** Maine, NE USA 47.04N 69.05W
32 K9 **Dickeyville** Wisconsin, N USA 42.37N 90.36W
30 K5 **Dickinson** North Dakota, N USA 46.54N 102.48W
(0) E6 **Dickins Seamount** *undersea feature* NE Pacific Ocean
29 O13 **Dickson** Oklahoma, C USA 34.11N 96.58W
22 I9 **Dickson** Tennessee, S USA 36.04N 87.23W
Dicle *see* Tigris
Dicsőszentmárton *see* Târnăveni
100 M12 **Didam** Gelderland, E Netherlands 51.55N 6.07E
169 Y8 **Didao** Heilongjiang, NE China 45.20N 130.54E
78 L12 **Didiéni** Koulikoro, W Mali 13.48N 8.01W
Didimo *see* Dídymo
Didimotiho *see* Didymóteicho
83 K17 **Didimtu** *spring/well* NE Kenya 2.58N 40.07E
69 U9 **Didinga Hills** ▲ S Sudan
9 Q16 **Didsbury** Alberta, SW Canada 51.39N 114.09W
158 G11 **Dīdwāna** Rājasthān, N India 27.22N 74.36E
117 G20 **Dídymo** *var.* Didimo. ▲ S Greece 37.28N 23.12E
116 L12 **Didymóteicho** *var.* Dhidhimótikhon, Didimotiho. Anatolikí Makedonía kai Thráki, NE Greece 41.22N 26.28E
105 S13 **Die** Drôme, E France 44.46N 5.21E
79 O13 **Diébougou** SW Burkina 11.00N 3.12W
Diedenhofen *see* Thionville
9 S16 **Diefenbaker, Lake** ⊠ Saskatchewan, S Canada
64 H7 **Diego de Almagro** Atacama, N Chile 26.24S 70.10W
65 F23 **Diego de Almagro, Isla** *island* S Chile
63 A20 **Diego de Alvear** Santa Fe, C Argentina 34.24S 62.04W
181 Q7 **Diego Garcia** *island* S British Indian Ocean Territory
Diégo-Suarez *see* Antsirañana
101 M23 **Diekirch** Diekirch, C Luxembourg 49.52N 6.10E
101 L23 **Diekirch** ◈ *district* N Luxembourg
78 K11 **Diéma** Kayes, W Mali 14.28N 9.10W
103 H15 **Diemel** ≈ W Germany
100 I10 **Diemen** Noord-Holland, C Netherlands 52.21N 4.58E
Diemrich *see* Deva
178 Ii6 **Điện Biên** *var.* Bien Bien, Dien Bien Phu. Lai Châu, N Vietnam 21.22N 103.01E
Dien Bien Phu *see* Điện Biên
178 Jj8 **Diễn Châu** Nghê An, N Vietnam 18.54N 105.35E
101 K18 **Diepenbeek** Limburg, NE Belgium 50.54N 5.25E
100 N11 **Diepenheim** Overijssel, E Netherlands 52.10N 6.37E
100 M10 **Diepenveen** Overijssel, E Netherlands 52.18N 6.09E
102 G12 **Diepholz** Niedersachsen, NW Germany 52.36N 8.22E
104 M3 **Dieppe** Seine-Maritime, N France 49.55N 1.04E
100 M12 **Dieren** Gelderland, E Netherlands 52.03N 6.06E
29 S13 **Dierks** Arkansas, C USA 34.07N 94.01W
101 J17 **Diest** Vlaams Brabant, C Belgium 50.58N 5.03E
110 F7 **Dietikon** Zürich, NW Switzerland 47.24N 8.25E
105 R13 **Dieulefit** Drôme, E France 44.30N 5.01E
105 T5 **Dieuze** Moselle, NE France 48.49N 6.41E
121 H15 **Dievenišķes** Vilnius, SE Lithuania 54.12N 25.38E
100 N7 **Diever** Drenthe, NE Netherlands 52.49N 6.19E
103 F17 **Diez** Rheinland-Pfalz, W Germany 50.22N 8.01E
79 Y12 **Diffa** Diffa, SE Niger 13.20N 12.39E
79 Y10 **Diffa** ◈ *department* SE Niger
101 L25 **Differdange** Luxembourg, SW Luxembourg 49.31N 5.52E
11 O16 **Digby** Nova Scotia, SE Canada 44.37N 65.46W
28 J5 **Dighton** Kansas, C USA 38.28N 100.28W
Dignano d'Istria *see* Vodnjan
105 T14 **Digne** *var.* Digne-les-Bains. Alpes-de-Haute-Provence, SE France 44.04N 6.13E
Digne-les-Bains *see* Digne
Digoel *see* Digul, Sungai
105 Q10 **Digoin** Saône-et-Loire, C France 46.30N 3.59E
179 Rr16 **Digos** Mindanao, S Philippines 6.46N 125.21E
155 Q16 **Digri** Sind, SE Pakistan 25.10N 69.10E
176 Z13 **Digul Barat, Sungai** ≈ Papua, E Indonesia
176 Z14 **Digul, Sungai** *prev.* Digoel. ≈ Papua, E Indonesia
176 Z13 **Digul Timur, Sungai** ≈ Papua, E Indonesia
Dihang *see* Brahmaputra
159 X10 **Dihāng** ≈ NE India
Dihōk *see* Dahūk
83 L17 **Diinsoor** Bay, S Somalia 2.28N 43.00E
Dijlah *see* Tigris
101 H17 **Dijle** ≈ C Belgium
105 R8 **Dijon** *anc.* Dibio. Côte d'Or, C France 47.21N 5.03E
95 H14 **Dikanäs** Västerbotten, N Sweden 65.15N 16.00E
82 L12 **Dikhil** SW Djibouti 11.07N 42.18E
142 B13 **Dikili** İzmir, W Turkey 39.04N 26.52E
101 B17 **Diksmuide** *var.* Dixmuide, *Fr.* Dixmude. West-Vlaanderen, W Belgium 51.01N 2.52E
126 Hh6 **Dikson** Taymyrskiy (Dolgano-Nenetskiy) Avtonomnyy Okrug, N Russian Federation 73.30N 80.35E
117 K25 **Díkti** *var.* Dhíkti Ori. ▲▲ Kríti, Greece, E Mediterranean Sea
79 Z13 **Dikwa** Borno, NE Nigeria 12.00N 13.57E
83 J15 **Dīla** Southern, S Ethiopia 6.19N 38.16E
101 G18 **Dilbeek** Vlaams Brabant, C Belgium 50.51N 4.16E
175 S16 **Dili** *var.* Dilli, Dilly. ● (East Timor) N East Timor 8.33S 125.34E
79 Y11 **Dilia** *var.* Dillia. ≈ SE Niger
Dilijan *see* Dilijan
178 K13 **Di Linh** Lâm Đông, S Vietnam 11.34N 108.04E
103 G16 **Dillenburg** Hessen, W Germany 50.45N 8.16E
27 Q13 **Dilley** Texas, SW USA 28.40N 99.10W
Dilli *see* Delhi, India
Dilli *see* Dili, East Timor
Dillia *see* Dilia
82 E11 **Dilling** *var.* Ad Dalanj. Southern Kordofan, C Sudan 12.01N 29.40E
103 D20 **Dillingen** Saarland, SW Germany 49.20N 6.43E
Dillingen *see* Dillingen an der Donau
103 J22 **Dillingen an der Donau** *var.* Dillingen. Bayern, S Germany 48.34N 10.29E
41 O13 **Dillingham** Alaska, USA 59.03N 158.30W
35 Q12 **Dillon** Montana, NW USA 45.13N 112.37W
23 T12 **Dillon** South Carolina, SE USA 34.25N 79.22W
33 T13 **Dillon Lake** ⊠ Ohio, N USA
Dilly *see* Dili
Dilman *see* Salmās
81 K24 **Dilolo** Katanga, S Dem. Rep. Congo 10.42S 22.21E
117 J20 **Dílos** *island* Kykládes, Greece, Aegean Sea
147 Y11 **Ḑil', Ra's aḑ** *headland* E Oman 19.12N 57.53E
31 R5 **Dilworth** Minnesota, N USA 46.53N 96.38W
144 H7 **Dimashq** *var.* Ash Shām, Esh Sham, *Eng.* Damascus, *Fr.* Damas, *It.* Damasco. ● (Syria) Dimashq, SW Syria 33.30N 36.19E
144 I8 **Dimashq** *off.* Muḩāfaẓat Dimashq, *var.* Damascus, *Ar.* Ash Sham, Ash Shām, Damasco, Esh Sham, *Fr.* Damas. ◈ *governorate* S Syria
144 I7 **Dimashq** × Dimashq, S Syria 33.30N 36.19E
81 L21 **Dimbelenge** Kasai Occidental, C Dem. Rep. Congo 5.36S 23.04E
79 N16 **Dimbokro** E Ivory Coast 6.39N 4.43W
190 L11 **Dimboola** Victoria, SE Australia 36.29S 142.03E
Dîmboviţa *see* Dâmboviţa
Dimitrov *see* Dymytrov
116 K11 **Dimitrovgrad** Khaskovo, S Bulgaria 42.03N 25.36E
131 R5 **Dimitrovgrad** Ul'yanovskaya Oblast', W Russian Federation 54.14N 49.37E
115 Q15 **Dimitrovgrad** *prev.* Caribrod. Serbia, SE Serbia and Montenegro (Yugoslavia) 43.01N 22.46E
Dimitrovo *see* Pernik
Dimlang *see* Vogel Peak
26 M3 **Dimmitt** Texas, SW USA 34.33N 102.18W
116 F7 **Dimovo** Vidin, NW Bulgaria 43.46N 22.46E
61 A16 **Dimpolis** Acre, W Brazil 9.52S 71.51W
117 O23 **Dimyliá** Ródos, Dodekánisos, Greece, Aegean Sea 36.17N 27.59E
179 R13 **Dinagat** Dinagat Island, S Philippines 10.00N 125.36E
179 Rr13 **Dinagat Island** *island* S Philippines
159 S13 **Dinajpur** Rajshahi, NW Bangladesh 25.37N 88.39E
104 I6 **Dinan** Côtes d'Armor, NW France 48.27N 2.01W
101 I21 **Dinant** Namur, S Belgium 50.16N 4.55E
142 E15 **Dinar** Afyon, SW Turkey 38.04N 30.09E
114 F13 **Dinara** ▲ W Croatia 43.49N 16.42E
Dinara *see* Dinaric Alps
104 I5 **Dinard** Ille-et-Vilaine, NW France 48.38N 2.04W
114 F13 **Dinaric Alps** *var.* Dinara. ▲▲ Bosnia and Herzegovina/Croatia
149 N10 **Dīnār, Kūh-e** ▲ C Iran 30.51N 51.36E
Dinbych *see* Denbigh
161 H22 **Dindigul** Tamil Nādu, SE India 10.23N 78.00E
85 M19 **Dindiza** Gaza, S Mozambique 23.22S 33.28E
155 V7 **Dinga** Punjab, E Pakistan 32.37N 73.45E
81 H21 **Dinga** Bandundu, SW Dem. Rep. Congo 5.00S 16.29E
164 L16 **Dinggyê** *var.* Gyangkar. Xizang Zizhiqu, W China 28.18N 88.06E
99 A20 **Dingle** *Ir.* An Daingean. SW Ireland 52.08N 10.16W
99 A20 **Dingle Bay** *Ir.* Bá an Daingin. *bay* SW Ireland
20 I13 **Dingmans Ferry** Pennsylvania, NE USA 41.12N 74.51W
103 N22 **Dingolfing** Bayern, SE Germany 48.37N 12.28E
179 P8 **Dingras** Luzon, N Philippines 18.06N 120.43E
78 J13 **Dinguiraye** Haute-Guinée, N Guinea 11.19N 10.49W
98 I8 **Dingwall** N Scotland, UK 57.36N 4.25W
165 V10 **Dingxi** Gansu, C China 35.36N 104.33E
167 Q7 **Dingyuan** Anhui, E China 32.30N 117.40E
167 O3 **Dingzhou** *prev.* Ding Xian. Hebei, E China 38.31N 114.52E
178 K6 **Đinh Lập** Lang Sơn, N Vietnam 21.33N 107.03E
178 K14 **Đinh Quan** Đồng Nai, S Vietnam 11.11N 107.20E
102 E13 **Dinkel** ≈ Germany/Netherlands
103 J21 **Dinkelsbühl** Bayern, S Germany 49.06N 10.18E
103 D14 **Dinslaken** Nordrhein-Westfalen, W Germany 51.34N 6.43E
37 R11 **Dinuba** California, W USA 36.32N 119.23W
23 W7 **Dinwiddie** Virginia, NE USA 37.04N 77.34W
100 N13 **Dinxperlo** Gelderland, E Netherlands 51.51N 6.30E
117 F14 **Dió** *anc.* Dium. *site of ancient city* Kentrikí Makedonía, N Greece 40.13N 22.30E
Diófás *see* Nucet
78 M12 **Dioïla** Koulikoro, W Mali 12.28N 6.43W
117 G19 **Dióryga Korinthou** *Eng.* Corinth Canal. *canal* S Greece
78 G12 **Diouloulou** SW Senegal 13.00N 16.34W
79 N11 **Dioura** Mopti, W Mali 14.48N 5.20W
78 G11 **Diourbel** W Senegal 14.38N 16.12W
158 L10 **Dipayal** Far Western, W Nepal 29.09N 80.46E
124 Oo2 **Dipkarpaz** *Gk.* Rizokarpaso, Rizokárpason. NE Cyprus 35.36N 34.23E
155 R17 **Diplo** Sind, SE Pakistan 24.29N 69.36E
179 Qq15 **Dipolog** *var.* Dipolog City. Mindanao, S Philippines 8.31N 123.20E
193 C23 **Dipton** Southland, South Island, NZ 45.55S 168.21E
79 O10 **Diré** Tombouctou, C Mali 16.12N 3.31W
82 L13 **Dirē Dawa** Dirē Dawa, E Ethiopia 9.34N 41.53E
Dirfis *see* Dírfys
117 H18 **Dírfys** *var.* Dirfis. ▲▲ Évvoia, C Greece
77 N9 **Dirj** *var.* Daraj, Darj. W Libya 30.09N 10.25E
188 G10 **Dirk Hartog Island** *island* Western Australia
79 Y8 **Dirkou** Agadez, NE Niger 18.45N 13.00E
189 X11 **Dirranbandi** Queensland, E Australia 28.37S 148.13E
83 O16 **Dirri** Galguduud, C Somalia 4.15N 46.31E
Dirschau *see* Tczew
39 N6 **Dirty Devil River** ≈ Utah, W USA
34 E10 **Disappointment, Cape** *headland* Washington, NW USA 46.16N 124.06W
188 L8 **Disappointment, Lake** *salt lake* Western Australia
191 R12 **Disaster Bay** *bay* New South Wales, SE Australia
46 J11 **Discovery Bay** C Jamaica 18.27N 77.23W
190 K13 **Discovery Bay** *inlet* SE Australia
69 Y15 **Discovery II Fracture Zone** *tectonic feature* SW Indian Ocean
Discovery Seamount/ Discovery Seamounts *see* Discovery Tablemount

◆ Country ● Country Capital ◇ Dependent Territory ○ Dependent Territory Capital ◈ Administrative Region × International Airport ▲ Mountain ▲▲ Mountain Range ☒ Volcano ≈ River ◎ Lake ⊠ Reservoir

DISCOVERY TABLEMOUNT – DOWNPATRICK

67 O19 **Discovery Tablemount** var. Discovery Seamount, Discovery Seamounts. undersea feature SW Indian Ocean 42.00S 0.10E
110 G9 **Disentis** Rmsch. Mustér. Graubünden, S Switzerland 46.43N 8.52E
41 O10 **Dishna River** ≈ Alaska, USA
205 X4 **Dismal Mountains** ▲ Antarctica
30 M14 **Dismal River** ≈ Nebraska, C USA
Disna see Dzisna
101 L19 **Dison** Liège, E Belgium 50.37N 5.52E
159 V12 **Dispur** Assam, NE India 26.03N 91.52E
13 R11 **Disraeli** Québec, SE Canada 45.58N 71.21W
117 F18 **Dístomo** prev. Dhístomon. Stereá Ellás, C Greece 38.25N 22.40E
117 H18 **Dístos, Límni** ◎ Évvoia, C Greece
61 L18 **Distrito Federal** Eng. Federal District. ◆ federal district C Brazil
43 P14 **Distrito Federal** ◆ federal district S Mexico
56 L4 **Distrito Federal** off. Territorio Distrito Federal. ◆ federal district N Venezuela
Distrito Federal, Territorio see Distrito Federal
118 J10 **Ditrău** Hung. Ditró. Harghita, C Romania 46.47N 25.30E
Ditró see Ditrău
160 B12 **Diu** Damān and Diu, W India 20.42N 70.58E
179 Rr14 **Diuata Mountains** ▲ Mindanao, S Philippines
Dium see Dió
111 S13 **Divača** SW Slovenia 45.40N 13.58E
104 K5 **Dives** ≈ N France
Divichi see Däväçi
35 Q11 **Divide** Montana, NW USA 45.44N 112.47W
Divin see Dzivin
85 N18 **Divinhe** Sofala, E Mozambique 20.41S 34.46E
61 L20 **Divinópolis** Minas Gerais, SE Brazil 20.07S 44.55W
131 N13 **Divnoye** Stavropol'skiy Kray, SW Russian Federation 45.54N 43.18E
78 M17 **Divo** S Ivory Coast 5.49N 5.22W
Divodurum Mediomatricum see Metz
143 N13 **Divriği** Sivas, C Turkey 39.22N 38.06E
Diwaniyah see Ad Dīwānīyah
12 J10 **Dix Milles, Lac** ◎ Québec, SE Canada
12 M8 **Dix Milles, Lac des** ◎ Québec, SE Canada
Dixmude/Dixmuide see Diksmuide
37 N7 **Dixon** California, W USA 38.19N 121.49W
32 L10 **Dixon** Illinois, N USA 41.51N 89.26W
22 I6 **Dixon** Kentucky, S USA 37.30N 87.39W
29 V6 **Dixon** Missouri, C USA 37.59N 92.05W
39 S9 **Dixon** New Mexico, SW USA 36.10N 105.49W
41 Y15 **Dixon Entrance** strait Canada/USA
20 D14 **Dixonville** Pennsylvania, NE USA 40.43N 79.01W
143 T13 **Diyadin** Ağrı, E Turkey 39.33N 43.40E
145 V5 **Diyālá, Nahr** var. Rudkhaneh-ye Sīrvān, Sīrwan. ≈ Iran/Iraq see also Sīrvān, Rudkhaneh-ye
143 P15 **Diyarbakır** var. Diarbekr; anc. Amida. Diyarbakır, SE Turkey 37.55N 40.13E
143 P15 **Diyarbakır** var. Diarbekr. ◆ province SE Turkey
Dizful see Dezfūl
81 F16 **Dja** ≈ SE Cameroon
Djadié see Zadié
79 X7 **Djado** Agadez, NE Niger 21.00N 12.11E
79 X6 **Djado, Plateau du** ▲ NE Niger
Djailolo see Halmahera, Pulau
Djajapura see Jayapura
Djakarta see Jakarta
Djakovica see Đakovica
Djakovo see Đakovo
81 G20 **Djambala** Plateaux, C Congo 2.31S 14.43E
Djambi see Jambi
Djambi see Hari, Batang, Sumatera, W Indonesia
76 M9 **Djanet** E Algeria 28.43N 8.57E
76 M11 **Djanet** prev. Fort Charlet. SE Algeria 24.34N 9.33E
Djatiwangi see Jatiwangi
Djaul see Dyaul Island
Djawa see Jawa
Djéblé see Jablah
80 I10 **Djédaa** Batha, C Chad 13.31N 18.34E
76 J6 **Djelfa** var. El Djelfa. N Algeria 34.42N 3.16E
81 M14 **Djéma** Haut-Mbomou, E Central African Republic 6.03N 25.19E
Djeneponto see Jeneponto
79 N12 **Djenné** var. Jenné. Mopti, C Mali 13.55N 4.34W
Djérablous see Jarābulus
Djerba see Jerba, Île de
81 F15 **Djérem** ≈ C Cameroon
Djevdjelija see Gevgelija
79 P11 **Djibo** N Burkina 14.09N 1.37W
82 L12 **Djibouti** var. Jibuti. ● (Djibouti) E Djibouti 11.32N 42.55E
82 L12 **Djibouti** off. Republic of Djibouti, var. Jibuti; prev. French Somaliland, French Territory of the Afars and Issas, Fr. Côte Française des Somalis, Territoire Français des Afars et des Issas. ◆ republic E Africa
82 L12 **Djibouti** ✕ C Djibouti 11.29N 42.54E
Djidjel/Djidjelli see Jijel
57 W10 **Djoemoe** Sipaliwini, C Suriname 4.00N 55.27W
Djokjakarta see Yogyakarta
81 K21 **Djoku-Punda** Kasai Occidental, S Dem. Rep. Congo 5.27S 20.58E
81 K18 **Djolu** Equateur, N Dem. Rep. Congo 0.42N 22.23E
Djorče Petrov see Đorče Petrov
81 F17 **Djoua** ≈ Congo/Gabon
79 R14 **Djougou** W Benin 9.42N 1.38E
81 F16 **Djoum** Sud, S Cameroon 2.38N 12.51E
80 I8 **Djourab, Erg du** dunes N Chad
81 P17 **Djugu** Orientale, NE Dem. Rep. Congo 1.55N 30.31E
Djumbir see Ďumbier
94 L3 **Djúpivogur** Austurland, SE Iceland 64.39N 14.18W
96 L13 **Djura** Dalarna, C Sweden 60.37N 15.00E
Djurdjevac see Đurđevac
85 G18 **D'Kar** Ghanzi, NW Botswana 21.31S 21.55E
207 U6 **Dmitriya Lapteva, Proliv** strait N Russian Federation
130 J7 **Dmitriyev-L'govskiy** Kurskaya Oblast', W Russian Federation 52.08N 35.09E
Dmitriyevsk see Makiyivka
130 K3 **Dmitrov** Moskovskaya Oblast', W Russian Federation 56.23N 37.30E
Dmitrovichi see Dzmitravichy
130 J6 **Dmitrovsk-Orlovskiy** Orlovskaya Oblast', W Russian Federation 52.28N 35.01E
119 R3 **Dmytrivka** Chernihivs'ka Oblast', N Ukraine 50.56N 32.57E
Dnepr see Dnieper
Dneprodzerzhinsk see Dniprodzerzhyns'k
Dneprodzerzhinskoye Vodokhranilishche see Dniprodzerzhyns'ke Vodoskhovyshche
Dnepropetrovsk see Dnipropetrovs'k
Dnepropetrovskaya Oblast' see Dnipropetrovs'ka Oblast'
Dneprorudnoye see Dniprorudne
Dneprovskiy Liman see Dniprovs'kyy Lyman
Dneprovsko-Bugskiy Kanal see Dnyaprowska-Buhski, Kanal
Dnestr see Dniester
Dnestrovskiy Liman see Dnistrovs'kyy Lyman
88 H11 **Dnieper** Bel. Dnyapro, Rus. Dnepr, Ukr. Dnipro. ≈ E Europe
119 P3 **Dnieper Lowland** Bel. Prydnyaprowskaya Nizina, Ukr. Prydniprovs'ka Nyzovyna. lowlands Belarus/Ukraine
118 M8 **Dniester** Rom. Nistru, Rus. Dnestr, Ukr. Dnister; anc. Tyras. ≈ Moldova/Ukraine
Dnipro see Dnieper
119 T7 **Dniprodzerzhyns'k** Rus. Dneprodzerzhinsk; prev. Kamenskoye. Dnipropetrovs'ka Oblast', E Ukraine 48.30N 34.35E
119 T7 **Dniprodzerzhyns'ke Vodoskhovyshche** Rus. Dneprodzerzhinskoye Vodokhranilishche. ⊠ C Ukraine
119 U7 **Dnipropetrovs'k** Rus. Dnepropetrovsk; prev. Yekaterinoslav. Dnipropetrovs'ka Oblast', E Ukraine 48.28N 34.59E
119 U8 **Dnipropetrovs'k** ✕ Dnipropetrovs'ka Oblast', S Ukraine 48.20N 35.04E
Dnipropetrovs'k see Dnipropetrovs'ka Oblast'
119 T7 **Dnipropetrovs'ka Oblast'** var. Dnipropetrovs'k, Rus. Dnepropetrovskaya Oblast'. ◆ province E Ukraine
119 U9 **Dniprorudne** Rus. Dneprorudnoye. Zaporiz'ka Oblast', SE Ukraine 47.21N 35.00E
119 Q11 **Dniprovs'kyy Lyman** Rus. Dneprovskiy Liman. bay S Ukraine
Dnister see Dniester
119 O11 **Dnistrovs'kyy Lyman** Rus. Dnestrovskiy Liman. inlet S Ukraine
128 G14 **Dno** Pskovskaya Oblast', W Russian Federation 57.48N 29.58E
Dnyapro see Dnieper
121 H20 **Dnyaprowska-Buhski, Kanal** Rus. Dneprovsko-Bugskiy Kanal. canal SW Belarus
11 O14 **Doaktown** New Brunswick, SE Canada 46.34N 66.06W
80 H13 **Doba** Logone-Oriental, S Chad 8.40N 16.49E
120 E9 **Dobele** Ger. Doblen. Dobele, W Latvia 56.36N 23.14E
103 N16 **Döbeln** Sachsen, E Germany 51.07N 13.07E
176 Vv9 **Doberai, Jazirah** Dut. Vogelkop. peninsula Papua, E Indonesia
112 F10 **Dobiegniew** Ger. Lubuskie, W Poland 52.58N 15.43E
Doblen see Dobele
83 K18 **Dobli** spring/well SW Somalia 0.24N 41.18E
176 W13 **Dobo** Pulau Wamar, E Indonesia 5.45S 134.12E
114 H11 **Doboj** Republika Srpska, N Bosnia and Herzegovina 44.45N 18.03E
112 L8 **Dobre Miasto** Ger. Guttstadt. Warmińsko-Mazurskie, NE Poland 53.59N 20.25E
116 N7 **Dobrich** Rom. Bazargic; prev. Tolbukhin. Dobrich, NE Bulgaria 43.34N 27.49E
116 N7 **Dobrich** ◆ province NE Bulgaria
130 M8 **Dobrinka** Lipetskaya Oblast', W Russian Federation 52.10N 40.30E
130 M7 **Dobrinka** Volgogradskaya Oblast', SW Russian Federation 50.52N 41.48E
Dobrla Vas see Eberndorf
113 I15 **Dobrodzień** Ger. Guttentag. Opolskie, S Poland 50.43N 18.24E
Dobrogea see Dobruja
119 W7 **Dobropillya** Rus. Dobropol'ye. Donets'ka Oblast', SE Ukraine 48.29N 37.06E
Dobropol'ye see Dobropillya
119 P8 **Dobrovelychkivka** Kirovohrads'ka Oblast', C Ukraine 48.22N 31.12E
Dobrudja/Dobrudzha see Dobruja
116 O7 **Dobruja** var. Dobrudja, Bul. Dobrudzha, Rom. Dobrogea. physical region Bulgaria/Romania
121 P19 **Dobrush** Homyel'skaya Voblasts', SE Belarus 52.25N 31.21E
129 U14 **Dobryanka** Permskaya Oblast', NW Russian Federation 58.28N 56.27E
119 P2 **Dobryanka** Chernihivs'ka Oblast', N Ukraine 52.03N 31.09E
Dobryn' see Dabryn'
23 R8 **Dobson** North Carolina, SE USA 36.23N 80.54W
61 N20 **Doce, Rio** ≈ SE Brazil
95 I16 **Docksta** Västernorrland, C Sweden 63.06N 18.22E
43 N10 **Doctor Arroyo** Nuevo León, NE Mexico 23.40N 100.09W
64 L4 **Doctor Pedro P. Peña** Boquerón, W Paraguay 22.22S 62.22W
175 T7 **Dodaga** Pulau Halmahera, E Indonesia 1.06N 128.10E
161 G21 **Dodda Betta** ▲ S India 11.28N 76.44E
Dodecanese see Dodekánisos
117 M22 **Dodekánisos** var. Nóties Sporádes, Eng. Dodecanese; prev. Dhodhekánisos. island group SE Greece
28 J6 **Dodge City** Kansas, C USA 37.45N 100.01W
32 K9 **Dodgeville** Wisconsin, N USA 42.57N 90.07W
99 H25 **Dodman Point** headland SW England, UK 50.13N 4.47W
83 J14 **Dodola** Oromo, C Ethiopia 7.00N 39.15E
83 H22 **Dodoma** ● (Tanzania) Dodoma, C Tanzania 6.10S 35.45E
83 H22 **Dodoma** ◆ region C Tanzania
117 C16 **Dodóni** var. Dhodhóni. site of ancient city Ípeiros, W Greece 39.33N 20.47E
35 U7 **Dodson** Montana, NW USA 48.25N 108.18W
27 P3 **Dodson** Texas, SW USA 34.46N 100.01W
100 M12 **Doesburg** Gelderland, E Netherlands 52.01N 6.07E
100 N12 **Doetinchem** Gelderland, E Netherlands 51.58N 6.16E
164 L12 **Dogai Coring** var. Lake Montcalm. ◎ W China
143 N15 **Doğanşehir** Malatya, C Turkey 38.06N 37.52E
86 E9 **Dogger Bank** undersea feature C North Sea
25 S10 **Dog Island** island Florida, SE USA
12 C7 **Dog Lake** ◎ Ontario, S Canada
108 B9 **Dogliani** Piemonte, NE Italy 44.33N 7.55E
170 G11 **Dōgo** island Oki-shotō, SW Japan
Do Gonbadān see Dow Gonbadān
79 S12 **Dogondoutchi** Dosso, SW Niger 13.37N 4.03E
Dōgo-san see Dōgo-yama
170 F13 **Dōgo-yama** var. Dōgo-san. ▲ Kyūshū, SW Japan 35.03N 133.12E
Dogrular see Pravda
143 T13 **Doğubayazıt** Ağrı, E Turkey 39.33N 44.07E
143 P12 **Doğu Karadeniz Dağları** var. Anadolu Dağları. ▲ NE Turkey
164 K16 **Dogxung Zangbo** ≈ W China
Doha see Ad Dawḩah
Dohad see Dāhod
Dohuk see Dahūk
165 N16 **Doilungdêqên** var. Namka. Xizang Zizhiqu, W China 29.41N 90.58E
116 F12 **Doïranis, Límnis** Bul. Ezero Doyransko. ◎ N Greece
Doire see Londonderry
101 H22 **Doische** Namur, S Belgium 50.09N 4.43E
61 P17 **Dois de Julho** ✕ (Salvador) Bahia, NE Brazil 12.04S 38.58W
62 H12 **Dois Vizinhos** Paraná, S Brazil 25.47S 53.03W
82 H10 **Doka** Gedaref, E Sudan 13.30N 35.46E
Doka see Kéita, Bahr
145 T3 **Dokan** var. Dūkān. E Iraq 35.55N 44.58E
96 H13 **Dokka** Oppland, S Norway 60.49N 10.04E
100 L5 **Dokkum** Friesland, N Netherlands 53.20N 6.00E
100 L5 **Dokkumer Ee** ≈ N Netherlands
78 K13 **Doko** Haute-Guinée, NE Guinea 11.46N 8.58W
Dokshitsy see Dokshytsy
120 K13 **Dokshytsy** Rus. Dokshitsy. Vitsyebskaya Voblasts', N Belarus 54.54N 27.46E
119 X8 **Dokuchayevs'k** var. Dokuchayevsk. Donets'ka Oblast', SE Ukraine 47.43N 37.40E
Dolak, Pulau see Yos Sudarso, Pulau
31 P9 **Doland** South Dakota, N USA 44.51N 98.06W
65 J18 **Dolavón** Chaco, S Argentina 43.20S 65.42W
13 P6 **Dolbeau** Québec, SE Canada 48.52N 72.15W
104 I5 **Dol-de-Bretagne** Ille-et-Vilaine, NW France 48.33N 1.45W
66 J13 **Doldrums Fracture Zone** tectonic feature W Atlantic Ocean
105 S8 **Dôle** Jura, E France 47.04N 5.30E
99 J19 **Dolgellau** NW Wales, UK 52.44N 3.54W
Dolginovo see Dawhinava
Dolgi, Ostrov see Dolgiy, Ostrov
129 U2 **Dolgiy, Ostrov** var. Ostrov Dolgi. island NW Russian Federation
168 J9 **Dölgöön** Övörhangay, C Mongolia 45.57N 103.14E
109 C20 **Dolianova** Sardegna, Italy, C Mediterranean Sea 39.23N 9.08E
Dolina see Dolyna
127 Oo15 **Dolinsk** Ostrov Sakhalin, Sakhalinskaya Oblast', SE Russian Federation 47.20N 142.52E
Dolinskaya see Dolyns'ka
81 F21 **Dolisie** prev. Loubomo. Le Niari, S Congo 4.12S 12.40E
118 G14 **Dolj** ◆ county SW Romania
100 P5 **Dollard** bay NW Germany
204 J5 **Dolleman Island** island Antarctica
116 I8 **Dolni Dŭbnik** Pleven, N Bulgaria 43.24N 24.25E
116 F8 **Dolni Lom** Vidin, NW Bulgaria 43.31N 22.46E
Dolnja Lendava see Lendava
116 K9 **Dolno Panicherevo** var. Panicherevo. Sliven, C Bulgaria 42.36N 25.51E
113 F14 **Dolnośląskie** ◆ province SW Poland
113 K18 **Dolný Kubín** Hung. Alsókubin. Žilinský Kraj, N Slovakia 49.13N 19.16E
108 H8 **Dolo** Veneto, NE Italy 45.25N 12.06E
Dolomites/Dolomiti see Dolomitiche, Alpi
108 H6 **Dolomitiche, Alpi** var. Dolomiti, Eng. Dolomites. ▲ NE Italy
Dolonnur see Duolun
168 K10 **Doloon** Ömnögovĭ, S Mongolia 44.28N 105.22E
63 E21 **Dolores** Buenos Aires, E Argentina 36.21S 57.39W
44 E3 **Dolores** Petén, N Guatemala 16.33N 89.25W
179 R12 **Dolores** Samar, C Philippines 12.01N 125.27E
107 S12 **Dolores** País Valenciano, E Spain 38.09N 0.45W
63 D19 **Dolores** Soriano, SW Uruguay 33.34S 58.15W
43 N12 **Dolores Hidalgo** var. Ciudad de Dolores Hidalgo. Guanajuato, C Mexico 21.10N 100.55W
15 Hh3 **Dolphin and Union Strait** strait Northwest Territories/Nunavut, N Canada
67 D23 **Dolphin, Cape** headland East Falkland, Falkland Islands 51.15S 58.57W
46 H12 **Dolphin Head** hill W Jamaica 18.21N 78.08W
85 B21 **Dolphin Head** var. Cape Dernberg. headland SW Namibia 25.33S 14.36E
112 G12 **Dolsk** Ger. Dolzig. Wielkolpolskie, C Poland 51.59N 17.03E
178 J8 **Đô Lương** Nghê An, N Vietnam 18.51N 105.19E
118 I6 **Dolyna** Rus. Dolina. Ivano-Frankivs'ka Oblast', W Ukraine 48.58N 24.01E
119 R8 **Dolyns'ka** Rus. Dolinskaya. Kirovohrads'ka Oblast', S Ukraine 48.06N 32.46E
Dolzig see Dolsk
Domachëvo/Domaczewo see Damachava
119 P9 **Domanivka** Mykolayivs'ka Oblast', S Ukraine 47.40N 30.56E
159 S13 **Domar** Rajshahi, N Bangladesh 26.09N 88.49E
110 I9 **Domat/Ems** Graubünden, SE Switzerland 46.49N 9.28E
113 A18 **Domažlice** Ger. Taus. Plzeňský Kraj, W Czech Republic 49.25N 12.55E
131 X8 **Dombarovskiy** Orenburgskaya Oblast', W Russian Federation 50.53N 59.18E
96 G10 **Dombås** Oppland, S Norway 62.04N 9.07E
85 M17 **Dombe** Manica, C Mozambique 19.59S 33.24E
84 A13 **Dombe Grande** Benguela, C Angola 12.57S 13.07E
105 R10 **Dombes** physical region E France
176 Xx10 **Dombo** Papua, E Indonesia 1.52S 137.09E
113 I25 **Dombóvár** Tolna, S Hungary 46.24N 18.09E
101 D14 **Domburg** Zeeland, SW Netherlands 51.34N 3.30E
60 L13 **Dom Eliseu** Pará, NE Brazil 4.02S 47.31W
Domel Island see Letsôk-aw Kyun
105 O11 **Dôme, Puy de** ▲ C France 45.46N 3.00E
38 H13 **Dome Rock Mountains** ▲ Arizona, SW USA
Domesnes, Cape see Kolkasrags
64 G8 **Domeyko** Atacama, N Chile 28.57S 70.54W
64 H5 **Domeyko, Cordillera** ▲ N Chile
104 K5 **Domfront** Orne, N France 48.35N 0.39W
176 Xx10 **Dom, Gunung** ▲ Papua, E Indonesia 2.41S 137.00E
47 X11 **Dominica** off. Commonwealth of Dominica. ◆ republic E West Indies
49 S3 **Dominica** island Dominica
Dominica Channel see Martinique Passage
45 N15 **Dominical** Puntarenas, SE Costa Rica 9.16N 83.52W
47 Q8 **Dominican Republic** ◆ republic C West Indies
47 X11 **Dominica Passage** passage E Caribbean Sea
101 K14 **Dommel** ≈ S Netherlands
83 O14 **Domo** Somali, E Ethiopia 7.53N 46.55E
130 L4 **Domodedovo** ✕ (Moskva) Moskovskaya Oblast', W Russian Federation 55.19N 37.55E
108 C6 **Domodossola** Piemonte, NE Italy 46.07N 8.20E
117 F17 **Domokós** var. Dhomokós. Stereá Ellás, C Greece 39.07N 22.18E
180 I14 **Domoni** Anjouan, SE Comoros 12.15S 44.39E
63 G16 **Dom Pedrito** Rio Grande do Sul, S Brazil 30.55S 54.39W
Dompoe see Dompu
175 Oo16 **Dompu** prev. Dompoe. Sumbawa, C Indonesia 8.30S 118.28E
Domschale see Domžale
64 H13 **Domuyo, Volcán** ▲ W Argentina 36.36S 70.22W
111 U11 **Domžale** Ger. Domschale. C Slovenia 46.09N 14.33E
131 O10 **Don** var. Duna, Tanais. ≈ SW Russian Federation
98 K9 **Don** ≈ NE Scotland, UK
190 M11 **Donald** Victoria, SE Australia 36.27S 143.03E
24 J9 **Donaldsonville** Louisiana, S USA 30.06N 90.59W
25 S8 **Donalsonville** Georgia, SE USA 31.02N 84.52W
Donau see Danube
103 G23 **Donaueschingen** Baden-Württemberg, SW Germany 47.57N 8.30E
103 K22 **Donaumoos** wetland S Germany
103 K22 **Donauwörth** Bayern, S Germany 48.43N 10.46E
111 U7 **Donawitz** Steiermark, SE Austria 47.23N 15.00E
119 X7 **Donbass** industrial region Russian Federation/Ukraine
106 K11 **Don Benito** Extremadura, W Spain 38.57N 5.52W
99 M17 **Doncaster** anc. Danum. N England, UK 53.31N 1.07W
46 K12 **Don Christophers Point** headland C Jamaica 18.19N 76.48W
57 V9 **Donderkamp** Sipaliwini, NW Suriname 5.18N 56.22W
84 B12 **Dondo** Cuanza Norte, NW Angola 9.40S 14.24E
175 Q9 **Dondo** Sulawesi, N Indonesia 0.54S 121.33E
85 N17 **Dondo** Sofala, C Mozambique 19.36S 34.46E
175 Pp7 **Dondo, Teluk** bay Sulawesi, N Indonesia
161 K26 **Dondra Head** headland S Sri Lanka 5.57N 80.33E
Donduşani see Donduşeni
118 M8 **Donduşeni** var. Donduşani, Rus. Dondyushany. N Moldova 48.13N 27.38E
Dondyushany see Donduşeni
99 D15 **Donegal** Ir. Dún na nGall. NW Ireland 54.39N 8.06W
99 D14 **Donegal** Ir. Dún na nGall. cultural region NW Ireland
99 C15 **Donegal Bay** Ir. Bá Dhún na nGall. bay NW Ireland
86 K10 **Donets** ≈ Russian Federation/Ukraine
119 X8 **Donets'k** Rus. Donetsk; prev. Stalino. Donets'ka Oblast', E Ukraine 47.58N 37.49E
119 W8 **Donets'k** ✕ Donets'ka Oblast', E Ukraine 48.03N 37.44E
Donets'k see Donets'ka Oblast'
119 W8 **Donets'ka Oblast'** var. Donets'k, Rus. Donetskaya Oblast'; prev. Rus. Stalinskaya Oblast'. ◆ province SE Ukraine
Donetskaya Oblast' see Donets'ka Oblast'
69 P8 **Donga** ≈ Cameroon/Nigeria
163 O13 **Dongchuan** Yunnan, SW China 26.09N 103.10E
101 I14 **Dongen** Noord-Brabant, S Netherlands 51.37N 4.55E
166 K17 **Dongfang** var. Basuo. Hainan, S China 19.05N 108.40E
169 Z7 **Dongfanghong** Heilongjiang, NE China 46.13N 133.13E
169 W11 **Dongfeng** Jilin, NE China 42.39N 125.33E
175 P9 **Donggala** Sulawesi, C Indonesia 0.40S 119.43E
169 V13 **Donggang** var. Dadong, prev. Donggou. Liaoning, NE China 39.52N 124.07E
Donggou see Donggang
167 O14 **Dongguan** Guangdong, S China 23.03N 113.43E
178 K9 **Đông Hà** Quang Tri, C Vietnam 16.45N 107.10E
Dong Hai see East China Sea
166 M16 **Donghai Dao** island S China
168 I12 **Dong He** Mong. Narin Gol. ≈ N China
178 Jj9 **Đông Hơi** Quang Binh, C Vietnam 17.30N 106.34E
110 H10 **Dongio** Ticino, S Switzerland 46.27N 8.58E
Dongkan see Binhai
166 L11 **Dongkou** Hunan, S China 27.06N 110.34E
Dongliao see Liaoyuan
Dong-nai see Đồng Nai, Sông
178 K13 **Đồng Nai, Sông** var. Dong-nai, Dong Noi, Donnai. ≈ S Vietnam
167 N14 **Dongnan Qiuling** plateau SE China
169 Y9 **Dongning** Heilongjiang, NE China 44.01N 131.03E
Dong Noi see Đồng Nai, Sông
85 C14 **Dongo** Huíla, C Angola 14.35S 15.51E
82 E7 **Dongola** var. Dongola, Dunqulah. Northern, N Sudan 19.10N 30.27E
81 I17 **Dongou** La Likouala, NE Congo 2.04N 18.00E
Đông Phu see Đông Xoai
Dongping see Anhua
Dong Rak, Phanom see Dângrêk, Chuŏr Phnum
167 Q14 **Dongshan Dao** island SE China
Dongsheng see Ordos
167 R7 **Dongtai** Jiangsu, E China 32.52N 120.13E
167 N10 **Dongting Hu** var. Tung-t'ing Hu. ◎ S China
167 P10 **Dongxiang** var. Xiaogang. Jiangxi, S China 28.17N 116.36E
178 Jj13 **Đông Xoai** var. Đông Phu. Sông Be, S Vietnam 11.31N 106.55E
167 Q4 **Dongying** Shandong, E China 37.27N 118.01E
29 X8 **Doniphan** Missouri, C USA 36.37N 90.49W
Donja Łużyca see Niederlausitz
8 G7 **Donjek** ≈ Yukon Territory, W Canada
114 E11 **Donji Lapac** Lika-Senj, W Croatia 44.33N 15.58E
114 H8 **Donji Miholjac** Osijek-Baranja, NE Croatia 45.45N 18.10E
114 P12 **Donji Milanovac** Serbia, E Serbia and Montenegro (Yugoslavia) 44.27N 22.06E
114 G12 **Donji Vakuf** var. Srbobran. Federacija Bosna I Hercegovina, C Bosnia & Herzegovina 44.08N 17.23E
100 M6 **Donkerbroek** Friesland, N Netherlands 52.58N 5.15E
178 Hh11 **Don Muang** ✕ (Krung Thep) Nonthaburi, C Thailand 13.51N 100.40E
27 S17 **Donna** Texas, SW USA 26.10N 98.03W
13 Q10 **Donnacona** Québec, SE Canada 46.41N 71.46W
Donnai see Đồng Nai, Sông
31 Y16 **Donnellson** Iowa, C USA 40.38N 91.33W
9 O13 **Donnelly** Alberta, W Canada 55.42N 117.06W
37 P6 **Donner Pass** pass California, W USA 39.19N 120.19W
103 F19 **Donnersberg** ▲ W Germany 49.37N 7.54E
Donoso see Miguel de la Borda
107 P2 **Donostia-San Sebastián** País Vasco, N Spain 43.19N 1.58W
117 K21 **Donoússa** island Kykládes, Greece, Aegean Sea
37 P8 **Don Pedro Reservoir** ⊠ California, W USA
Donqola see Dongola
130 L5 **Donskoy** Tul'skaya Oblast', W Russian Federation 54.02N 38.27E
179 Q11 **Donsol** Luzon, N Philippines 12.56N 123.34E
83 L16 **Doolow** Somali, E Ethiopia 4.10N 42.04E
41 Q7 **Doonerak, Mount** ▲ Alaska, USA 67.54N 150.33W
100 J12 **Doorn** Utrecht, C Netherlands 52.01N 5.21E
Doornik see Tournai
33 N6 **Door Peninsula** peninsula Wisconsin, N USA
82 P13 **Dooxo Nugaaleed** var. Nogal Valley. valley E Somalia
Do Qu see Da Qu
108 B7 **Dora Baltea** anc. Duria Major. ≈ NW Italy
188 K7 **Dora, Lake** salt lake Western Australia
108 A8 **Dora Riparia** anc. Duria Minor. ≈ NW Italy
Dorbiljin see Emin
Dorbod/Dorbod Mongolzu Zizhixian see Taikang
115 N18 **Đorče Petrov** var. Djorče Petrov, Gorče Petrov. N FYR Macedonia 42.01N 21.21E
12 F16 **Dorchester** Ontario, S Canada 43.00N 81.04W
99 L24 **Dorchester** anc. Durnovaria. S England, UK 50.43N 2.25W
15 Mm4 **Dorchester, Cape** headland Baffin Island, Nunavut, NE Canada 65.25N 77.25W
85 D19 **Dordabis** Khomas, C Namibia 22.57S 17.39E
104 L12 **Dordogne** ◆ department SW France
105 N12 **Dordogne** ≈ W France
100 H13 **Dordrecht** var. Dordt, Dort. Zuid-Holland, SW Netherlands 51.48N 4.40E
Dordt see Dordrecht
105 P11 **Dore** ≈ C France
9 S13 **Doré Lake** Saskatchewan, C Canada 54.37N 107.36W
105 O12 **Dore, Monts** ▲ C France
103 M23 **Dorfen** Bayern, SE Germany 48.16N 12.06E
109 D18 **Dorgali** Sardegna, Italy, C Mediterranean Sea 40.18N 9.34E
165 N11 **Dorgê Co** var. Elsen Nur. ◎ C China
168 F7 **Dörgön Nuur** ◎ NW Mongolia
79 Q12 **Dori** N Burkina 14.03N 0.01W
85 E24 **Doring** ≈ S South Africa
103 E16 **Dormagen** Nordrhein-Westfalen, W Germany 51.06N 6.49E
105 P4 **Dormans** Marne, N France 49.03N 3.44E
110 E6 **Dornach** Solothurn, NW Switzerland 47.28N 7.37E
Dorna Watra see Vatra Dornei
110 J7 **Dornbirn** Vorarlberg, W Austria 47.25N 9.46E
98 I7 **Dornoch** N Scotland, UK 57.52N 4.00W
98 J7 **Dornoch Firth** inlet N Scotland, UK
169 P7 **Dornod** ◆ province E Mongolia
169 N10 **Dornogovĭ** ◆ province SE Mongolia
79 P10 **Doro** Tombouctou, S Mali 16.07N 0.57W
118 L14 **Dorobanţu** Călăraşi, S Romania 44.15N 26.55E
113 J22 **Dorog** Komárom-Esztergom, N Hungary 47.42N 18.44E
130 I4 **Dorogobuzh** Smolenskaya Oblast', W Russian Federation 54.56N 33.16E
118 K8 **Dorohoi** Botoşani, NE Romania 47.57N 26.24E
95 H15 **Dorotea** Västerbotten, N Sweden 64.16N 16.30E
Dorpat see Tartu
188 G10 **Dorre Island** island Western Australia
191 U5 **Dorrigo** New South Wales, SE Australia 30.22S 152.43E
37 N1 **Dorris** California, W USA 41.58N 121.54W
12 H13 **Dorset** Ontario, SE Canada 45.12N 78.52W
99 K23 **Dorset** cultural region S England, UK
103 E14 **Dorsten** Nordrhein-Westfalen, W Germany 51.40N 6.58E
Dort see Dordrecht
103 F15 **Dortmund** Nordrhein-Westfalen, W Germany 51.31N 7.28E
102 F12 **Dortmund-Ems-Kanal** canal W Germany
142 L17 **Dörtyol** Hatay, S Turkey 36.51N 36.10E
148 L7 **Do Rūd** var. Dow Rūd, Durud. Lorestān, W Iran 33.31N 49.03E
81 O15 **Doruma** Orientale, N Dem. Rep. Congo 4.35N 27.43E
13 O12 **Dorval** ✕ (Montréal) Québec, SE Canada 45.27N 73.46W
47 T5 **Dos Bocas, Lago** ◎ C Puerto Rico
106 K14 **Dos Hermanas** Andalucía, S Spain 37.16N 5.55W
Dospad Dagh see Rhodope Mountains
37 P10 **Dos Palos** California, W USA 37.00N 120.39W
116 I11 **Dospat** Smolyan, S Bulgaria 41.39N 24.10E
116 H11 **Dospat, Yazovir** ⊠ SW Bulgaria
102 M11 **Dosse** ≈ NE Germany
79 S12 **Dosso** Dosso, SW Niger 13.03N 3.13E
79 S12 **Dosso** ◆ department SW Niger
150 G12 **Dossor** Atyrau, SW Kazakhstan 47.32N 52.58E
153 O10 **Do'stlik** Jizzax Viloyati, C Uzbekistan 40.37N 67.59E
153 V9 **Dostuk** Narynskaya Oblast', C Kyrgyzstan 41.19N 75.40E
151 X13 **Dostyk** prev. Druzhba. Almaty, SE Kazakhstan 45.15N 82.28E
25 R7 **Dothan** Alabama, S USA 31.13N 85.23W
41 T9 **Dot Lake** Alaska, USA 63.39N 144.10W
120 F12 **Dotnuva** Kaunas, C Lithuania 55.22N 23.52E
101 D19 **Dottignies** Hainaut, W Belgium 50.43N 3.16E
105 P2 **Douai** prev. Douay, anc. Duacum. Nord, N France 50.22N 3.04E
12 L9 **Douaire, Lac** ◎ Québec, SE Canada
81 D16 **Douala** var. Duala. Littoral, W Cameroon 4.04N 9.43E
81 D16 **Douala** ✕ Littoral, W Cameroon 3.57N 9.48E
104 F6 **Douarnenez** Finistère, NW France 48.04N 4.19W
104 E6 **Douarnenez, Baie de** bay NW France
Douay see Douai
27 O6 **Double Mountain Fork Brazos River** ≈ Texas, SW USA
25 O3 **Double Springs** Alabama, S USA 34.09N 87.24W
105 T8 **Doubs** ◆ department E France
110 C8 **Doubs** ≈ France/Switzerland
193 A22 **Doubtful Sound** sound South Island, NZ
192 J2 **Doubtless Bay** bay North Island, NZ
27 X9 **Doucette** Texas, SW USA 30.48N 94.25W
104 K8 **Doué-la-Fontaine** Maine-et-Loire, NW France 47.12N 0.16W
79 O11 **Douentza** Mopti, S Mali 14.59N 2.57W
40 L9 **Douglas** East Falkland, Falkland Islands
99 I16 **Douglas** ○ (Isle of Man) E Isle of Man 54.09N 4.28W
85 H23 **Douglas** Northern Cape, C South Africa 29.03S 23.46E
41 X13 **Douglas** Alexander Archipelago, Alaska, USA 58.12N 134.18W
39 O17 **Douglas** Arizona, SW USA 31.20N 109.32W
25 U7 **Douglas** Georgia, SE USA 31.30N 82.51W
35 Y15 **Douglas** Wyoming, C USA 42.48N 105.22W
23 O7 **Douglas, Cape** headland Alaska USA 64.59N 166.41W
8 J14 **Douglas Channel** channel British Columbia, W Canada
190 G3 **Douglas Creek** seasonal river South Australia
33 P5 **Douglas Lake** ◎ Michigan, N USA
23 O9 **Douglas Lake** ⊠ Tennessee, S USA
41 Q13 **Douglas, Mount** ▲ Alaska, USA 58.51N 153.31W
204 I6 **Douglas Range** ▲ Alexander Island, Antarctica
124 N10 **Doukáto, Akrotírio** headland Lefkáda, W Greece 38.35N 20.33E
105 O2 **Doullens** Somme, N France 50.09N 2.21E
Douma see Dūmā
81 F15 **Doumé** Est, E Cameroon 4.13N 13.27E
101 E21 **Dour** Hainaut, S Belgium 50.24N 3.46E
61 K18 **Dourada, Serra** ▲ S Brazil
61 I21 **Dourados** Mato Grosso do Sul, S Brazil 22.09S 54.52W
105 N5 **Dourdan** Essonne, N France 48.33N 1.58E
106 I6 **Douro** Sp. Duero. ≈ Portugal/Spain see also Duero
106 G6 **Douro Litoral** former province N Portugal
Douvres see Dover
104 K15 **Douze** ≈ SW France
191 P17 **Dover** Tasmania, SE Australia 43.19S 147.01E
99 Q22 **Dover** Fr. Douvres; Lat. Dubris Portus. SE England, UK 51.08N 1.19E
19 Rr8 **Dover** state capital Delaware, NE USA 39.09N 75.31W
21 P9 **Dover** New Hampshire, NE USA 43.10N 70.50W
20 J14 **Dover** New Jersey, NE USA 40.51N 74.33W
33 U12 **Dover** Ohio, N USA 40.31N 81.28W
22 H8 **Dover** Tennessee, S USA 36.29N 87.50W
99 Q23 **Dover, Strait of** var. Straits of Dover, Fr. Pas de Calais. strait England, UK/France
Dover, Straits of see Dover, Strait of
Dovlen see Devin
96 G11 **Dovre** Oppland, S Norway 61.59N 9.16E
96 G10 **Dovrefjell** plateau S Norway
Dovsk see Dowsk
85 M14 **Dowa** Central, C Malawi 13.42S 33.55E
33 O10 **Dowagiac** Michigan, N USA 41.58N 86.06W
149 N10 **Dow Gonbadān** var. Do Gonbadān, Gonbadān. Kohgīlūyeh va Būyer Aḩmad, SW Iran 30.24N 50.45E
154 M2 **Dowlatābād** Fāryāb, N Afghanistan 36.30N 64.51E
99 G16 **Down** cultural region SE Northern Ireland, UK
35 R16 **Downey** Idaho, NW USA 42.25N 112.06W
37 P5 **Downieville** California, W USA 39.33N 120.49W
99 G16 **Downpatrick** Ir. Dún Pádraig. SE Northern Ireland, UK 54.19N 5.43W

◆ Country ● Country Capital ◇ Dependent Territory ○ Dependent Territory Capital ◆ Administrative Region ✕ International Airport ▲ Mountain ▲ Mountain Range ▲ Volcano ≈ River ◎ Lake ⊠ Reservoir

DOWNS – DYATLOVO

28 *M3* **Downs** Kansas, C USA *39.50N 98.33W*
20 *J12* **Downsville** New York, NE USA *42.03N 74.59W*
Dow Rūd *see* Do Rūd
31 *V12* **Dows** Iowa, C USA *42.39N 93.30W*
121 *O17* **Dowsk** *Rus.* Dovsk. Homyel'skaya Voblasts', SE Belarus *53.09N 30.27E*
37 *Q4* **Doyle** California, W USA *40.00N 120.06W*
20 *I15* **Doylestown** Pennsylvania, NE USA *40.18N 75.07W*
Doyransko, Ezero *see* Doïranis, Límnis
116 *I8* **Doyrentsi** Lovech, N Bulgaria *43.13N 24.46E*
170 *Ff11* **Dōzen** *island* Oki-shotō, SW Japan
12 *K9* **Dozois, Réservoir** ⊠ Québec, SE Canada
76 *D9* **Drâa** *seasonal river* S Morocco
Drâa, Hammada du *see* Dra, Hamada du
Drabble *see* José Enrique Rodó
119 *Q5* **Drabiv** Cherkas'ka Oblast', C Ukraine *49.57N 32.10E*
Drable *see* José Enrique Rodó
105 *S13* **Drac** ↝ E France
Drač/Draç *see* Durrës
62 *I8* **Dracena** São Paulo, S Brazil *21.27S 51.30W*
100 *M6* **Drachten** Friesland, N Netherlands *53.07N 6.06E*
94 *H11* **Drag** *Lapp.* Ájluokta. Nordland, C Norway *68.02N 16.00E*
118 *L14* **Dragalina** Călărași, SE Romania *44.25N 27.17E*
118 *J14* **Drăgănești-Vlașca** Teleorman, S Romania *44.05N 25.39E*
118 *I13* **Drăgășani** Vâlcea, SW Romania *44.40N 24.16E*
116 *G9* **Dragoman** Sofiya, W Bulgaria *42.57N 22.53E*
117 *L25* **Dragonáda** *island* SE Greece
Dragonera, Isla *see* Sa Dragonera
47 *T14* **Dragon's Mouths, The** *strait* Trinidad and Tobago/Venezuela
97 *J23* **Dragør** København, E Denmark *55.36N 12.42E*
116 *F10* **Dragovishtitsa** Kyustendil, W Bulgaria *42.22N 22.39E*
105 *U15* **Draguignan** Var, SE France *43.31N 6.31E*
76 *E9* **Dra, Hamada du** *var.* Hammada du Drâa, Haut Plateau du Dra. *plateau* W Algeria
Dra, Haut Plateau du *see* Dra, Hamada du
121 *H19* **Drahichyn** *Pol.* Drohiczyn Poleski, *Rus.* Drogichin. Brestskaya Voblasts', SW Belarus *52.10N 25.10E*
31 *N4* **Drake** North Dakota, N USA *47.54N 100.23W*
85 *K23* **Drakensberg** ▲▲ Lesotho/South Africa
204 *F3* **Drake Passage** *passage* Atlantic Ocean/Pacific Ocean
116 *L8* **Dralfa** Tŭrgovishte, N Bulgaria *43.17N 26.25E*
116 *I12* **Dráma** *var.* Dhráma. Anatolikí Makedonía kai Thráki, NE Greece *41.09N 24.10E*
Dramburg *see* Drawsko Pomorskie
97 *H15* **Drammen** Buskerud, S Norway *59.43N 10.12E*
97 *H15* **Drammensfjorden** *fjord* S Norway
94 *H1* **Drangajökull** ▲ NW Iceland *66.13N 22.18W*
97 *F16* **Drangedal** Telemark, S Norway *59.04N 9.01E*
94 *I2* **Drangsnes** Vestfirdhir, NW Iceland *65.42N 21.27W*
Drann *see* Dravinja
111 *T10* **Drau** *var.* Drava, *Eng.* Drave, *Hung.* Dráva. ↝ C Europe *see also* Drava
86 *I11* **Drava** *var.* Drau, *Eng.* Drave, *Hung.* Dráva. ↝ C Europe *see also* Drau
Dráva/Drave *see* Drau/Drava
111 *W10* **Dravinja** *Ger.* Drann. ↝ NE Slovenia
111 *V9* **Dravograd** *Ger.* Unterdrauburg; *prev.* Spodnji Dravograd. N Slovenia *46.36N 15.00E*
112 *F10* **Drawa** ↝ NW Poland
112 *F9* **Drawno** Zachodnio-pomorskie, NW Poland *53.12N 15.44E*
112 *F9* **Drawsko Pomorskie** *Ger.* Dramburg. Zachodnio-pomorskie, NW Poland *53.31N 15.48E*
31 *R3* **Drayton** North Dakota, N USA *48.34N 97.10W*
9 *P14* **Drayton Valley** Alberta, SW Canada *53.15N 115.00W*
194 *F10* **Dreikikir** East Sepik, NW PNG *3.34S 142.44E*
Dreikirchen *see* Teiuș
100 *N7* **Drenthe** ◈ *province* NE Netherlands
117 *H15* **Drépano, Akrotírio** *var.* Akra Dhrepanon. *headland* N Greece *39.56N 23.57E*
Drepanum *see* Trapani
12 *D17* **Dresden** Ontario, S Canada *42.34N 82.09W*
103 *O16* **Dresden** Sachsen, E Germany *51.02N 13.43E*
22 *G8* **Dresden** Tennessee, S USA *36.17N 88.42W*
120 *M11* **Dretun'** *Rus.* Dretun'. Vitsyebskaya Voblasts', N Belarus *55.42N 29.12E*
104 *M5* **Dreux** *anc.* Drocae, Durocasses. Eure-et-Loir, C France *48.43N 1.22E*
96 *I11* **Drevsjø** Hedmark, S Norway *61.52N 12.01E*
24 *K3* **Drew** Mississippi, S USA *33.48N 90.31W*
112 *F10* **Drezdenko** *Ger.* Driesen. Lubuskie, W Poland *52.51N 15.49E*
100 *J12* **Driebergen** *var.* Driebergen-Rijsenburg. Utrecht, C Netherlands *52.03N 5.16E*
Driebergen-Rijsenburg *see* Driebergen
Driesen *see* Drezdenko
99 *N16* **Driffield** E England, UK *54.00N 0.28W*
67 *D25* **Driftwood Point** *headland* East Falkland, Falkland Islands *52.15S 59.00W*
35 *S14* **Driggs** Idaho, NW USA *43.44N 111.06W*
Drin *see* Drinit, Lumi i
114 *K12* **Drina** ↝ Bosnia and Herzegovina/Serbia and Montenegro (Yugoslavia)
Drin, Gulf of *see* Drinit, Gjiri i
115 *K18* **Drinit, Gjiri i** *var.* Pellg i Drinit, *Eng.* Gulf of Drin. *gulf* NW Albania
115 *L17* **Drinit, Lumi i** *var.* Drin. ↝ NW Albania
Drinit, Pellg i *see* Drinit, Gjiri i
Drinit të Zi, Lumi i *see* Black Drin
115 *L22* **Drino** *var.* Drino, Drínos Pótamos, *Alb.* Lumi i Drinos. ↝ Albania/Greece
Drinos, Lumi i/Drínos Pótamos *see* Drino
27 *S11* **Dripping Springs** Texas, SW USA *30.11N 98.04W*
27 *S15* **Driscoll** Texas, SW USA *27.40N 97.45W*
24 *H5* **Driskill Mountain** ▲ Louisiana, S USA *32.25N 92.54W*
Drissa *see* Drysa
96 *G10* **Driva** ↝ S Norway
114 *E13* **Drniš** *It.* Šibenik-Knin, S Croatia *43.51N 16.10E*
97 *H15* **Drøbak** Akershus, S Norway *59.40N 10.37E*
118 *G13* **Drobeta-Turnu Severin** *prev.* Turnu Severin. Mehedinți, SW Romania *44.39N 22.39E*
Drocae *see* Dreux
118 *M8* **Drochia** *Rus.* Drokiya. N Moldova *48.02N 27.46E*
99 *F17* **Drogheda** *Ir.* Droichead Átha. NE Ireland *53.43N 6.21W*
Drogichin *see* Drahichyn
Drogobych *see* Drohobych
Drohiczyn Poleski *see* Drahichyn
118 *H6* **Drohobych** *Pol.* Drohobycz, *Rus.* Drogobych. L'vivs'ka Oblast', NW Ukraine *49.22N 23.34E*
Drohobycz *see* Drohobych
Droichead Átha *see* Drogheda
Droicheadna Bandan *see* Bandon
Droichead na Banna *see* Banbridge
Droim Mór *see* Dromore
Drokiya *see* Drochia
105 *R13* **Drôme** ◈ *department* E France
105 *S13* **Drôme** ↝ E France
99 *G15* **Dromore** *Ir.* Droim Mór. SE Northern Ireland, UK *54.25N 6.09W*
108 *A9* **Dronero** Piemonte, NE Italy *44.28N 7.25E*
104 *L12* **Dronne** ↝ SW France
205 *Q3* **Dronning Maud Land** *physical region* Antarctica
100 *K6* **Dronrijp** *Fris.* Dronryp. Friesland, N Netherlands *53.12N 5.37E*
Dronryp *see* Dronrijp
100 *L9* **Dronten** Flevoland, C Netherlands *52.31N 5.40E*
Drontheim *see* Trondheim
104 *L13* **Dropt** ↝ SW France
155 *T4* **Drosh** North-West Frontier Province, NW Pakistan *35.33N 71.48E*
Drossen *see* Ośno Lubuskie
Drug *see* Durg
Drujba *see* Pitnak
120 *I12* **Drūkšiai** ◎ NE Lithuania
Druk-yul *see* Bhutan
9 *Q16* **Drumheller** Alberta, SW Canada *51.28N 112.42W*
35 *Q10* **Drummond** Montana, NW USA *46.39N 113.12W*
33 *R4* **Drummond Island** *island* Michigan, N USA
Drummond Island *see* Tabiteuea
23 *X7* **Drummond, Lake** ◎ Virginia, NE USA
13 *P12* **Drummondville** Québec, SE Canada *45.52N 72.28W*
41 *T11* **Drum, Mount** ▲ Alaska, USA *62.11N 144.37W*
29 *O9* **Drumright** Oklahoma, C USA *35.59N 96.36W*
101 *J14* **Drunen** Noord-Brabant, S Netherlands *51.40N 5.07E*
Druskienniki *see* Druskininkai
121 *F15* **Druskininkai** *Pol.* Druskienniki. Alytus, S Lithuania *54.00N 24.00E*
100 *K13* **Druten** Gelderland, SE Netherlands *51.52N 5.37E*
120 *K11* **Druya** Vitsyebskaya Voblasts', NW Belarus *55.48N 27.27E*
119 *S2* **Druzhba** Sums'ka Oblast', NE Ukraine *52.01N 33.56E*
Druzhba *see* Dostyk, Kazakhstan
Druzhba *see* Pitnak, Uzbekistan
126 *Mm7* **Druzhina** Respublika Sakha (Yakutiya), NE Russian Federation *68.01N 144.58E*
119 *X7* **Druzhkivka** Donets'ka Oblast', E Ukraine *48.38N 37.31E*
114 *E12* **Drvar** Federacija Bosna I Hercegovina, Bosnia and Herzegovina *44.21N 16.24E*
115 *G15* **Drvenik** Split-Dalmacija, SE Croatia *43.10N 17.13E*
116 *K9* **Dryanovo** Gabrovo, N Bulgaria *42.58N 25.28E*
28 *G7* **Dry Cimarron River** ↝ Kansas/Oklahoma, C USA
10 *B11* **Dryden** Ontario, C Canada *49.48N 92.48W*
26 *M11* **Dryden** Texas, SW USA *30.01N 102.06W*
205 *Q14* **Drygalski Ice Tongue** *ice feature* Antarctica
120 *L11* **Drysa** *Rus.* Drissa. ↝ N Belarus
25 *V17* **Dry Tortugas** *island* Florida, SE USA
81 *D15* **Dschang** Ouest, W Cameroon *5.28N 10.01E*
56 *J5* **Duaca** Lara, N Venezuela *10.16N 69.12W*
Duacum *see* Douai
Duala *see* Douala
47 *N9* **Duarte, Pico** ▲ C Dominican Republic *19.02N 70.57W*
146 *J5* **Ḑubā** Tabūk, NW Saudi Arabia *27.25N 35.42E*
Dubai *see* Dubayy
119 *N9* **Dubăsari** *Rus.* Dubossary. NE Moldova *47.16N 29.07E*
119 *N9* **Dubăsari Reservoir** ⊠ NE Moldova
15 *Jj8* **Dubawnt** ↝ Nunavut, NW Canada
15 *K7* **Dubawnt Lake** ◎ Northwest Territories/Nunavut, N Canada
32 *L6* **Du Bay, Lake** ⊠ Wisconsin, N USA
147 *U7* **Dubayy** *Eng.* Dubai. Dubayy, NE UAE *25.10N 55.18E*
147 *W7* **Dubayy** *Eng.* Dubai. ✕ Dubayy, NE UAE *25.15N 55.22E*
191 *R7* **Dubbo** New South Wales, SE Australia *32.16S 148.40E*
110 *G7* **Dübendorf** Zürich, NW Switzerland *47.24N 8.36E*
99 *F18* **Dublin** *Ir.* Baile Átha Cliath; *anc.* Eblana. ● (Ireland), E Ireland *53.19N 6.15W*
25 *U5* **Dublin** Georgia, SE USA *32.32N 82.54W*
27 *R7* **Dublin** Texas, SW USA *32.05N 98.20W*
99 *G18* **Dublin** *Ir.* Baile Átha Cliath; *anc.* Eblana. *cultural region* E Ireland
99 *G18* **Dublin Airport** ✕ E Ireland *53.25N 6.18W*
201 *V12* **Dublon** *var.* Tonoas. *island* Chuuk Islands, C Micronesia
130 *K2* **Dubna** Moskovskaya Oblast', W Russian Federation *56.45N 37.09E*
113 *G19* **Dubňany** *Ger.* Dubnian. Jihomoravský Kraj, SE Czech Republic *48.54N 17.00E*
Dubnian *see* Dubňany
113 *I19* **Dubnica nad Váhom** *Hung.* Máriatölgyes; *prev.* Dubnicz. Trenčiansky Kraj, W Slovakia *48.58N 18.10E*
Dubnicz *see* Dubnica nad Váhom
118 *K4* **Dubno** Rivnens'ka Oblast', NW Ukraine *50.27N 25.39E*
20 *D13* **Du Bois** Pennsylvania, NE USA *41.07N 78.45W*
35 *R13* **Dubois** Idaho, NW USA *44.10N 112.13W*
35 *T14* **Dubois** Wyoming, C USA *43.31N 109.37W*
Dubossary *see* Dubăsari
131 *O10* **Dubovka** Volgogradskaya Oblast', SW Russian Federation *49.10N 48.49E*
78 *H14* **Dubréka** Guinée-Maritime, SW Guinea *9.48N 13.31W*
12 *B7* **Dubreuilville** Ontario, S Canada *48.21N 84.31W*
Dubris Portus *see* Dover
121 *L20* **Dubrova** *Rus.* Dubrova. Homyel'skaya Voblasts', SE Belarus *51.46N 28.13E*
130 *I5* **Dubrovka** Bryanskaya Oblast', W Russian Federation *53.44N 33.27E*
115 *H16* **Dubrovnik** *It.* Ragusa. Dubrovnik-Neretva, SE Croatia *42.39N 18.06E*
115 *I16* **Dubrovnik** ✕ Dubrovnik-Neretva, SE Croatia *42.34N 18.17E*
115 *F16* **Dubrovnik-Neretva** *off.* Dubrovačko-Neretvanska Županija. ◈ *province* SE Croatia
Dubrovno *see* Dubrowna
118 *L2* **Dubrovytsya** Rivnens'ka Oblast', NW Ukraine *51.34N 26.37E*
121 *O14* **Dubrowna** *Rus.* Dubrovno. Vitsyebskaya Voblasts', N Belarus *54.34N 30.40E*
31 *Z13* **Dubuque** Iowa, C USA *42.30N 90.39W*
120 *E12* **Dubysa** ↝ C Lithuania
178 *K12* **Đức Cơ** Gia Lai, C Vietnam *13.48N 107.41E*
203 *V12* **Duc de Gloucester, Îles du** *Eng.* Duke of Gloucester Islands. *island group* C French Polynesia
113 *C15* **Duchcov** *Ger.* Dux. Ústecký Kraj, NW Czech Republic *50.37N 13.40E*
39 *N3* **Duchesne** Utah, W USA *40.09N 110.24W*
203 *P17* **Ducie Island** *atoll* E Pitcairn Islands
9 *W15* **Duck Bay** Manitoba, S Canada *52.11N 100.08W*
25 *X17* **Duck Key** *island* Florida Keys, Florida, SE USA
9 *T14* **Duck Lake** Saskatchewan, S Canada *52.52N 106.12W*
9 *V15* **Duck Mountain** ▲▲ Manitoba, S Canada
22 *I9* **Duck River** ↝ Tennessee, S USA
22 *M10* **Ducktown** Tennessee, S USA *35.01N 84.24W*
178 *Kk11* **Đức Phổ** Quang Ngai, C Vietnam *14.55N 108.55E*
Đức Tho *see* Lin Camh
178 *Kk13* **Đức Trong** *var.* Liên Nghia. Lâm Đồng, S Vietnam *11.45N 108.24E*
D-U-D *see* Dalap-Uliga-Djarrit
101 *M25* **Dudelange** *var.* Forge du Sud, *Ger.* Dudelingen. Luxembourg, S Luxembourg *49.28N 6.04E*
Dudelingen *see* Dudelange
103 *J15* **Duderstadt** Niedersachsen, C Germany *51.31N 10.16E*
159 *N15* **Dūdhi** Uttar Pradesh, N India *24.13N 83.18E*
126 *I8* **Dudinka** Taymyrskiy (Dolgano-Nenetskiy) Avtonomnyy Okrug, N Russian Federation *69.27N 86.13E*
99 *L20* **Dudley** C England, UK *52.30N 2.04W*
160 *G13* **Dudna** ↝ C India
78 *L16* **Duékoué** W Ivory Coast *6.45N 7.21W*
106 *M5* **Dueñas** Castilla-León, N Spain *41.52N 4.33W*
106 *K4* **Duerna** ↝ NW Spain
107 *O6* **Duero** *Port.* Douro. ↝ Portugal/Spain *see also* Douro
Duesseldorf *see* Düsseldorf
23 *P12* **Due West** South Carolina, SE USA *34.19N 82.23W*
205 *P11* **Dufek Coast** *physical region* Antarctica
101 *H17* **Duffel** Antwerpen, C Belgium *51.06N 4.30E*
37 *S2* **Duffer Peak** ▲ Nevada, W USA *41.40N 118.45W*
195 *X7* **Duff Islands** *island group* E Solomon Islands
Dufour, Pizzo/Dufour, Punta *see* Dufour Spitze
110 *E12* **Dufour Spitze** *It.* Pizzo Dufour, Punta Dufour. ▲ Italy/Switzerland *45.54N 7.50E*
114 *D9* **Duga Resa** Karlovac, C Croatia *45.25N 15.30E*
24 *H5* **Dugdemona River** ↝ Louisiana, S USA
160 *J12* **Duggīpar** Mahārāshtra, C India *21.06N 80.10E*
114 *B13* **Dugi Otok** *var.* Isola Grossa, *It.* Isola Lunga. *island* W Croatia
115 *F14* **Dugopolje** Split-Dalmacija, S Croatia *43.35N 16.35E*
166 *L8* **Du He** ↝ C China
56 *M11* **Duida, Cerro** ▲ S Venezuela *3.21N 65.45W*
Duinekerke *see* Dunkerque
103 *E15* **Duisburg** *prev.* Duisburg-Hamborn. Nordrhein-Westfalen, W Germany *51.24N 6.47E*
Duisburg-Hamborn *see* Duisburg
101 *F14* **Duiveland** *island* SW Netherlands
100 *M12* **Duiven** Gelderland, E Netherlands *51.57N 6.02E*
145 *W10* **Dujaylah, Hawr ad** ◎ S Iraq
166 *H9* **Dujiangyan** *var.* Guanxian, Guan Xian. Sichuan, C China *31.01N 103.40E*
83 *L18* **Dujuuma** Shabeellaha Hoose, S Somalia *1.04N 42.37E*
Dūkān *see* Dokan
41 *Z14* **Duke Island** *island* Alexander Archipelago, Alaska, USA
Dukelský Priesmy/Dukelský Průsmyk *see* Dukla Pass
Duke of Gloucester Islands *see* Duc de Gloucester, Îles du
83 *F14* **Duk Faiwil** Jonglei, SE Sudan *7.30N 31.27E*
147 *T7* **Dukhān** C Qatar *25.29N 50.48E*
Dukhan Heights *see* Dukhān, Jabal
149 *N16* **Dukhān, Jabal** *var.* Dukhan Heights. *hill range* S Qatar
131 *Q7* **Dukhovnitskoye** Saratovskaya Oblast', W Russian Federation *52.31N 48.32E*
130 *H4* **Dukhovshchina** Smolenskaya Oblast', W Russian Federation *55.15N 32.22E*
Dukielska, Przełęcz *see* Dukla Pass
113 *N17* **Dukla** Podkarpackie, SE Poland *49.33N 21.40E*
Duklai Hág *see* Dukla Pass
113 *N18* **Dukla Pass** *Cz.* Dukelský Průsmyk, *Ger.* Dukla-Pass, *Hung.* Duklai Hág, *Pol.* Przełęcz Dukielska, *Slvk.* Dukelský Priesmy. *pass* Poland/Slovakia *49.25N 21.42E*
Dukou *see* Panzhihua
120 *I12* **Dūkštas** Utena, E Lithuania *55.32N 26.21E*
168 *M8* **Dulaan** Hentiy, C Mongolia *47.09N 108.48E*
165 *R10* **Dulan** *var.* Qagan Us. Qinghai, C China *36.11N 97.51E*
39 *R8* **Dulce** New Mexico, SW USA *36.55N 107.00W*
45 *N16* **Dulce, Golfo** *gulf* S Costa Rica
Dulce, Golfo *see* Izabal, Lago de
44 *K6* **Dulce Nombre de Culmí** Olancho, C Honduras *15.04N 85.35W*
64 *L9* **Dulce, Río** ↝ C Argentina
126 *M9* **Dulgalakh** ↝ NE Russian Federation
116 *M8* **Dŭlgopol** Varna, E Bulgaria *43.05N 27.24E*
159 *V14* **Dullabchara** Assam, NE India *24.25N 92.22E*
22 *D3* **Dulles** ✕ (Washington DC) Virginia, NE USA *39.00N 77.27W*
103 *E14* **Dülmen** Nordrhein-Westfalen, W Germany *51.51N 7.17E*
116 *M7* **Dulovo** Silistra, NE Bulgaria *43.50N 27.10E*
31 *W5* **Duluth** Minnesota, N USA *46.46N 92.06W*
144 *H7* **Dūmā** *Fr.* Douma. Dimashq, SW Syria *33.33N 36.24E*
179 *Pp16* **Dumagasa Point** *headland* Mindanao, S Philippines *7.01N 121.54E*
179 *Qq14* **Dumaguete** *var.* Dumaguete City. Negros, C Philippines *9.16N 123.17E*
174 *Gg6* **Dumai** Sumatera, W Indonesia *1.40N 101.27E*
191 *T4* **Dumaresq River** ↝ New South Wales/Queensland, SE Australia
29 *W13* **Dumas** Arkansas, C USA *33.53N 91.29W*
27 *N1* **Dumas** Texas, SW USA *35.51N 101.57W*
144 *I7* **Ḑumayr** Dimashq, W Syria *33.36N 36.28E*
98 *I12* **Dumbarton** W Scotland, UK *55.57N 4.34W*
98 *I12* **Dumbarton** *cultural region* C Scotland, UK
197 *J7* **Dumbéa** Province Sud, S New Caledonia *22.11S 166.27E*
113 *K19* **Ďumbier** *Ger.* Djumbir, *Hung.* Gyömbér. ▲ C Slovakia *48.54N 19.36E*
118 *I11* **Dumbrăveni** *Ger.* Elisabethstedt, *Hung.* Erzsébetváros; *prev.* Ebesfalva, Eppeschdorf, Ibașfalău. Sibiu, C Romania *46.14N 24.34E*
118 *L12* **Dumbrăveni** Vrancea, E Romania *45.30N 27.08E*
99 *J14* **Dumfries** S Scotland, UK *55.04N 3.37W*
99 *J14* **Dumfries** *cultural region* SW Scotland, UK
159 *R15* **Dumka** Jhārkhand, NE India *24.16N 87.15E*
Dümmer *see* Dümmersee
102 *G12* **Dümmersee** *var.* Dümmer. ◎ NW Germany
12 *J11* **Dumoine** ↝ Québec, SE Canada
12 *J10* **Dumoine, Lac** ◎ Québec, SE Canada
205 *V16* **Dumont d'Urville** *French research station* Antarctica *66.24S 139.38E*
205 *W15* **Dumont d'Urville Sea** S Pacific Ocean
12 *K11* **Dumont, Lac** ◎ Québec, SE Canada
77 *W7* **Dumyât** *Eng.* Damietta. N Egypt *31.25N 31.48E*
Duna *see* Don, Russian Federation
Duna *see* Danube, C Europe
Düna *see* Western Dvina
Dünaburg *see* Daugavpils
113 *J24* **Dunaföldvár** Tolna, C Hungary *46.16N 18.54E*
Dunaj *see* Wien, Austria
Dunaj *see* Danube, C Europe
113 *L18* **Dunajec** ↝ S Poland
113 *H21* **Dunajská Streda** *Hung.* Dunaszerdahely. Trnavský Kraj, W Slovakia *48.00N 17.28E*
Dunapentele *see* Dunaújváros
Dunărea *see* Danube
118 *M13* **Dunărea Veche, Brațul** ↝ SE Romania
119 *N13* **Dunării, Delta** *delta* SE Romania
Dunaszerdahely *see* Dunajská Streda
113 *J23* **Dunaújváros** *prev.* Dunapentele, Sztálinváros. Fejér, C Hungary *47.00N 18.55E*
Dunav *see* Danube
116 *J8* **Dunavska Ravnina** *Eng.* Danubian Plain. *plain* N Bulgaria
116 *G7* **Dunavtsi** Vidin, NW Bulgaria *43.56N 22.49E*
127 *N17* **Dunay** Primorskiy Kray, SE Russian Federation *42.53N 132.20E*
Dunayevtsy *see* Dunayivtsi
118 *L7* **Dunayivtsi** *Rus.* Dunayevtsy. Khmel'nyts'ka Oblast', NW Ukraine *48.54N 26.51E*
193 *F22* **Dunback** Otago, South Island, NZ *45.22S 170.37E*
8 *L17* **Duncan** Vancouver Island, British Columbia, SW Canada *48.46N 123.10W*
39 *O15* **Duncan** Arizona, SW USA *32.43N 109.06W*
28 *M12* **Duncan** Oklahoma, C USA *34.30N 97.57W*
Duncan Island *see* Pinzón, Isla
157 *Q20* **Duncan Passage** *strait* Andaman Sea/Bay of Bengal
98 *K6* **Duncansby Head** *headland* N Scotland, UK *58.37N 3.01W*
12 *G12* **Dunchurch** Ontario, S Canada *45.36N 79.54W*
120 *D7* **Dundaga** Talsi, NW Latvia *57.29N 22.19E*
12 *G14* **Dundalk** Ontario, S Canada *44.11N 80.22W*
99 *F16* **Dundalk** *Ir.* Dún Dealgan. NE Ireland *54.01N 6.25W*
23 *X3* **Dundalk** Maryland, NE USA *39.15N 76.31W*
99 *F16* **Dundalk Bay** *Ir.* Cuan Dhún Dealgan. *bay* NE Ireland
12 *G16* **Dundas** Ontario, S Canada *43.16N 79.55W*
188 *L12* **Dundas, Lake** *salt lake* Western Australia
169 *O7* **Dundbürd** Hentiy, E Mongolia *47.55N 111.37E*
Dún Dealgan *see* Dundalk
13 *N13* **Dundee** Québec, SE Canada *45.01N 74.27W*
85 *K22* **Dundee** KwaZulu/Natal, E South Africa *28.08S 30.12E*
98 *K11* **Dundee** E Scotland, UK *56.28N 3.00W*
33 *R10* **Dundee** Michigan, N USA *41.57N 83.39W*
27 *R5* **Dundee** Texas, SW USA *33.43N 98.52W*
204 *H3* **Dundee Island** *island* Antarctica
168 *L9* **Dundgovĭ** ◈ *province* C Mongolia
99 *G16* **Dundrum Bay** *Ir.* Cuan Dhún Droma. *inlet* NW Irish Sea
176 *Y11* **Dundu** ↝ Papua, E Indonesia
9 *T15* **Dundurn** Saskatchewan, S Canada *51.43N 106.27W*
168 *E6* **Dund-Us** Hovd, W Mongolia *48.06N 91.22E*
193 *F23* **Dunedin** Otago, South Island, NZ *45.51S 170.31E*
191 *R7* **Dunedoo** New South Wales, SE Australia *32.04S 149.23E*
99 *D14* **Dunfanaghy** *Ir.* Dún Fionnachaidh. NW Ireland *55.10N 7.58W*
98 *J12* **Dunfermline** C Scotland, UK *56.04N 3.28W*
Dún Fionnachaidh *see* Dunfanaghy
155 *V10* **Dunga Bunga** Punjab, E Pakistan *29.51N 73.19E*
99 *F15* **Dungannon** *Ir.* Dún Geanainn. C Northern Ireland, UK *54.31N 6.46W*
Dun Garbháin *see* Dungarvan
158 *F15* **Dūngarpur** Rājasthān, N India *23.53N 73.39E*
99 *E21* **Dungarvan** *Ir.* Dun Garbháin. S Ireland *52.04N 7.37W*
103 *N21* **Dungau** *cultural region* SE Germany
Dún Geanainn *see* Dungannon
99 *P23* **Dungeness** *headland* SE England, UK *50.55N 0.58E*
65 *I23* **Dungeness, Punta** *headland* S Argentina *52.25S 68.25W*
Dungloe *see* Dunglow
99 *D14* **Dunglow** *var.* Dungloe, *Ir.* An Clochán Liath. NW Ireland *54.57N 8.22W*
191 *T7* **Dungog** New South Wales, SE Australia *32.24S 151.45E*
81 *O16* **Dungu** Orientale, NE Dem. Rep. Congo *3.40N 28.31E*
174 *Hh3* **Dungun** *var.* Kuala Dungun. Terengganu, Peninsular Malaysia *4.46N 103.25E*
82 *I6* **Dungûnab** Red Sea, NE Sudan *21.06N 37.06E*
13 *P13* **Dunham** Québec, SE Canada *45.08N 72.48W*
Dunheved *see* Launceston
Dunholme *see* Durham
169 *X10* **Dunhua** Jilin, NE China *43.22N 128.12E*
165 *P8* **Dunhuang** Gansu, N China *40.10N 94.43E*
190 *L12* **Dunkeld** Victoria, SE Australia *37.41S 142.19E*
105 *O1* **Dunkerque** *Eng.* Dunkirk, *Flem.* Duinekerke; *prev.* Dunquerque. Nord, N France *51.06N 2.34E*
99 *K23* **Dunkery Beacon** ▲ SW England, UK *51.10N 3.36W*
20 *C11* **Dunkirk** New York, NE USA *42.28N 79.19W*
Dunkirk *see* Dunkerque
79 *P17* **Dunkwa** SW Ghana *5.58N 1.45W*
99 *G18* **Dún Laoghaire** *Eng.* Dunleary; *prev.* Kingstown. E Ireland *53.16N 6.07W*
31 *S14* **Dunlap** Iowa, C USA *41.51N 95.36W*
22 *L10* **Dunlap** Tennessee, S USA *35.22N 85.23W*
Dunleary *see* Dún Laoghaire
Dún Mánmhaí *see* Dunmanway
99 *B21* **Dunmanway** *Ir.* Dún Mánmhaí. SW Ireland *51.43N 9.07W*
20 *I13* **Dunmore** Pennsylvania, NE USA *41.25N 75.37W*
23 *U10* **Dunn** North Carolina, SE USA *35.18N 78.36W*
Dún na nGall *see* Donegal
25 *V11* **Dunnellon** Florida, SE USA *29.03N 82.27W*
98 *J6* **Dunnet Head** *headland* N Scotland, UK *58.40N 3.27W*
31 *N14* **Dunning** Nebraska, C USA *41.49N 100.04W*
67 *B24* **Dunnose Head Settlement** West Falkland, Falkland Islands *51.24S 60.28W*
12 *G17* **Dunnville** Ontario, S Canada *42.54N 79.36W*
Dún Pádraig *see* Downpatrick
Dunquerque *see* Dunkerque
Dunqulah *see* Dongola
98 *L12* **Duns** SE Scotland, UK *55.46N 2.13W*
31 *N2* **Dunseith** North Dakota, N USA *48.48N 100.03W*
37 *N2* **Dunsmuir** California, W USA *41.12N 122.19W*
99 *N21* **Dunstable** *Lat.* Durocobrivae. E England, UK *51.52N 0.31W*
193 *D21* **Dunstan Mountains** ▲▲ South Island, NZ
105 *O9* **Dun-sur-Auron** Cher, C France *46.52N 2.40E*
193 *F21* **Duntroon** Canterbury, South Island, NZ *44.52S 170.40E*
155 *T10* **Dunyāpur** Punjab, E Pakistan *29.48N 71.48E*
169 *U5* **Duobukur He** ↝ NE China
169 *R12* **Duolun** *var.* Dolonnur. Nei Mongol Zizhiqu, N China *42.11N 116.30E*
178 *Ii14* **Dương Đông** Kiên Giang, S Vietnam *10.15N 103.58E*
116 *G10* **Dupnitsa** *prev.* Marek, Stanke Dimitrov. Kyustendil, W Bulgaria *42.15N 23.09E*
30 *L8* **Dupree** South Dakota, N USA *45.03N 101.36W*
35 *Q7* **Dupuyer** Montana, NW USA *48.13N 112.34W*
147 *Y11* **Duqm** *var.* Daqm. E Oman *19.42N 57.39E*
65 *F23* **Duque de York, Isla** *island* S Chile
189 *N4* **Durack Range** ▲▲ Western Australia
142 *K10* **Durağan** Sinop, N Turkey *41.25N 35.03E*
105 *S15* **Durance** ↝ SE France
33 *R9* **Durand** Michigan, N USA *42.54N 83.58W*
32 *I6* **Durand** Wisconsin, N USA *44.37N 91.55W*
197 *L7* **Durand, Récif** *reef* SE New Caledonia
42 *K10* **Durango** *var.* Victoria de Durango. Durango, W Mexico *24.03N 104.37W*
107 *P3* **Durango** País Vasco, N Spain *43.10N 2.37W*
39 *Q8* **Durango** Colorado, C USA *37.13N 107.51W*
42 *J9* **Durango** ◈ *state* C Mexico
116 *O7* **Durankulak** *Rom.* Răcari; *prev.* Blatnitsa, Duranulac. Dobrich, NE Bulgaria *43.41N 28.31E*
24 *L4* **Durant** Mississippi, S USA *33.04N 89.51W*
29 *P13* **Durant** Oklahoma, C USA *33.59N 96.22W*
Duranulac *see* Durankulak
107 *N6* **Duratón** ↝ N Spain
63 *E19* **Durazno** *var.* San Pedro de Durazno. Durazno, C Uruguay *33.24S 56.28W*
63 *E19* **Durazno** ◈ *department* C Uruguay
Durazzo *see* Durrës
85 *K23* **Durban** *var.* Port Natal. KwaZulu/Natal, E South Africa *29.51S 31.00E*
85 *K23* **Durban** ✕ KwaZulu/Natal, E South Africa *29.55S 31.01E*
120 *C9* **Durbe** *Ger.* Durben. Liepāja, W Latvia *56.34N 21.22E*
Durben *see* Durbe
101 *K21* **Durbuy** Luxembourg, SE Belgium *50.21N 5.27E*
107 *N15* **Dúrcal** Andalucía, S Spain *37.00N 3.24W*
114 *F8* **Đurđevac** *Ger.* Sankt Georgen, *Hung.* Szentgyörgy; *prev.* Djurdjevac, Gjurgjevac. Koprivnica-Križevci, N Croatia *46.02N 17.03E*
115 *K15* **Đurđevica Tara** Montenegro, SW Serbia and Montenegro (Yugoslavia) *43.09N 19.18E*
99 *L24* **Durdle Door** *natural arch* S England, UK
164 *L3* **Dure** Xinjiang Uygur Zizhiqu, W China *46.30N 88.25E*
103 *D16* **Düren** *anc.* Marcodurum. Nordrhein-Westfalen, W Germany *50.48N 6.28E*
160 *K12* **Durg** *prev.* Drug. Chhattīsgarh, C India *21.12N 81.19E*
159 *U13* **Durgapur** Dhaka, N Bangladesh *25.10N 90.41E*
159 *R15* **Durgāpur** West Bengal, NE India *23.30N 87.19E*
12 *F14* **Durham** Ontario, S Canada *44.10N 80.48W*
99 *M14* **Durham** *hist.* Dunholme. N England, UK *54.46N 1.34W*
23 *U9* **Durham** North Carolina, SE USA *35.59N 78.54W*
99 *L15* **Durham** *cultural region* N England, UK
174 *Gg7* **Duri** Sumatera, W Indonesia *1.13N 101.13E*
Duria Major *see* Dora Baltea
Duria Minor *see* Dora Riparia
Durlas *see* Thurles
147 *P8* **Ḑurmā** Ar Riyāḑ, C Saudi Arabia *24.37N 46.06E*
115 *J15* **Durmitor** ▲ N Serbia and Montenegro (Yugoslavia) *43.06N 19.00E*
98 *H6* **Durness** N Scotland, UK *58.34N 4.45W*
111 *Y3* **Dürnkrut** Niederösterreich, E Austria *48.28N 16.50E*
Durnovaria *see* Dorchester
Durobrivae *see* Rochester
Durocasses *see* Dreux
Durocobrivae *see* Dunstable
Durocortorum *see* Reims
Durostorum *see* Silistra
Durovernum *see* Canterbury
115 *K20* **Durrës** *var.* Durrësi, Dursi, *It.* Durazzo, *SCr.* Drač, *Turk.* Draç. Durrës, W Albania *41.19N 19.25E*
115 *K19* **Durrës** ◈ *district* W Albania
Durrësi *see* Durrës
99 *A21* **Dursey Island** *Ir.* Oileán Baoi. *island* SW Ireland
Dursi *see* Durrës
Duru *see* Wuchuan
Durud *see* Do Rūd
116 *P12* **Durusu** İstanbul, NW Turkey *41.18N 28.41E*
116 *O12* **Durusu Gölü** ◎ NW Turkey
144 *I9* **Durūz, Jabal ad** ▲ SW Syria *37.00N 32.30E*
192 *K13* **D'Urville Island** *island* C NZ
176 *Xx9* **D'Urville, Tanjung** *headland* Papua, E Indonesia *1.26S 137.52E*
152 *H14* **Duşak** *Rus.* Dushak. Ahal Welaýaty, S Turkmenistan *37.15N 59.57E*
Dusa Mareb/Dusa Marreb *see* Dhuusa Marreeb
120 *I11* **Dusetos** Utena, NE Lithuania *55.44N 25.49E*
Dushak *see* Duşak
166 *K12* **Dushan** Guizhou, S China *25.45N 107.33E*
153 *P13* **Dushanbe** *var.* Dyushambe; *prev.* Stalinabad, *Taj.* Stalinobod. ● (Tajikistan) W Tajikistan *38.35N 68.43E*
153 *P13* **Dushanbe** ✕ W Tajikistan *38.31N 68.49E*
143 *T9* **Dushet'i** E Georgia *42.07N 44.44E*
20 *H13* **Dushore** Pennsylvania, NE USA *41.30N 76.23W*
193 *A23* **Dusky Sound** *sound* South Island, NZ
103 *E15* **Düsseldorf** *var.* Duesseldorf. Nordrhein-Westfalen, W Germany *51.13N 6.49E*
153 *P14* **Dŭsti** *Rus.* Dusti. SW Tajikistan *37.22N 68.41E*
204 *I9* **Dustin Island** *island* Antarctica
Dutch East Indies *see* Indonesia
Dutch Guiana *see* Suriname
40 *L17* **Dutch Harbor** Unalaska Island, Alaska, USA *53.50N 166.33W*
38 *J3* **Dutch Mount** ▲ Utah, W USA *40.16N 113.56W*
Dutch New Guinea *see* Papua
Dutch West Indies *see* Netherlands Antilles
85 *H20* **Dutlwe** Kweneng, S Botswana *23.56S 23.53E*
69 *V16* **Du Toit Fracture Zone** *tectonic feature* SW Indian Ocean
129 *U8* **Dutovo** Respublika Komi, NW Russian Federation *63.45N 56.38E*
79 *V13* **Dutsan Wai** *var.* Dutsen Wai. Kaduna, C Nigeria *10.49N 8.15E*
79 *W13* **Dutse** Jigawa, N Nigeria *11.43N 9.25E*
Dutsen Wai *see* Dutsan Wai
Duttia *see* Datia
12 *E17* **Dutton** Ontario, S Canada *42.40N 81.28W*
38 *L7* **Dutton, Mount** ▲ Utah, W USA *38.00N 112.10W*
168 *E7* **Duut** Hovd, W Mongolia *47.28N 91.52E*
12 *K11* **Duval, Lac** ◎ Québec, SE Canada
131 *W3* **Duvan** Respublika Bashkortostan, W Russian Federation *55.42N 57.56E*
144 *L9* **Duwaykhilat Satīḩ ar Ruwayshid** *seasonal river* SE Jordan
Dux *see* Duchcov
166 *J13* **Duyang Shan** ▲▲ S China
178 *Jj15* **Duyên Hai** Tra Vinh, S Vietnam *9.39N 106.28E*
166 *K12* **Duyun** Guizhou, S China *26.16N 107.28E*
142 *G11* **Düzce** Bolu, NW Turkey *40.51N 31.09E*
Duzdab *see* Zāhedān
Duzenkyr, Khrebet *see* Duzkyr, Khrebet
152 *I16* **Duzkyr, Khrebet** *prev.* Khrebet Duzenkyr. ▲▲ S Turkmenistan
Dvina Bay *see* Chëshskaya Guba
Dvinsk *see* Daugavpils
128 *L7* **Dvinskaya Guba** *bay* NW Russian Federation
114 *E10* **Dvor** Sisak-Moslavina, C Croatia *45.05N 16.22E*
119 *W5* **Dvorichna** Kharkivs'ka Oblast', E Ukraine *49.52N 37.43E*
113 *F16* **Dvůr Králové nad Labem** *Ger.* Königinhof an der Elbe. Královéhradecký Kraj, NE Czech Republic *50.25N 15.48E*
160 *A10* **Dwārka** Gujarāt, W India *22.13N 68.58E*
32 *M12* **Dwight** Illinois, N USA *41.05N 88.25W*
100 *N8* **Dwingeloo** Drenthe, NE Netherlands *52.49N 6.20E*
35 *N10* **Dworshak Reservoir** ⊠ Idaho, NW USA
Dyal *see* Dyaul Island
Dyanev *see* Galkynyş
Dyatlovo *see* Dzyatlava

◆ Country ● Country Capital ◇ Dependent Territory ○ Dependent Territory Capital ◈ Administrative Region ✕ International Airport ▲ Mountain ▲▲ Mountain Range Volcano ↝ River ◎ Lake ⊠ Reservoir

251

DYAUL ISLAND – EIVISSA

195 N9 Dyaul Island var. Djaul, Dyal. island NE PNG
22 G8 Dyer Tennessee, S USA 36.04N 88.59W
16 O1 Dyer, Cape headland Baffin Island, Nunavut, NE Canada 66.37N 61.13W
22 F8 Dyersburg Tennessee, S USA 36.01N 89.23W
31 Y13 Dyersville Iowa, C USA 42.29N 91.07W
99 I21 Dyfed cultural region SW Wales, UK
Dyfrdwy, Afon see Dee
Dyhernfurth see Brzeg Dolny
113 E19 Dyje var. Thaya. ≈ Austria/Czech Republic see also Thaya
119 T5 Dykanska Poltavs'ka Oblast', C Ukraine 49.48N 34.33E
194 L15 Dyke Ackland Bay inlet E PNG
131 N16 Dykhtau ▲ SW Russian Federation 43.01N 42.56E
113 A16 Dyleń Ger. Tillenberg. ▲ NW Czech Republic 49.58N 12.31E
112 K9 Dylewska Góra ▲ N Poland 53.33N 19.57E
119 O4 Dymer Kyyivs'ka Oblast', N Ukraine 50.50N 30.21E
119 W7 Dymytrov Rus. Dimitrov. Donets'ka Oblast', SE Ukraine 48.18N 37.19E
113 O17 Dynów Podkarpackie, SE Poland 49.49N 22.14E
31 X13 Dysart Iowa, C USA 42.10N 92.18W
Dysna see Dzisna
117 D18 Dytikí Ellás Eng. Greece West. ◆ region C Greece
117 C14 Dytikí Makedonía Eng. Macedonia West. ◆ region N Greece
Dyurmen'tyube see Dermentobe
131 U4 Dyurtyuli Respublika Bashkortostan, W Russian Federation 55.31N 54.49E
Dyushambe see Dushanbe
168 I7 Dzaanhushuu Arhangay, C Mongolia 47.36N 101.06E
Dza Chu see Mekong
168 I8 Dzadgay Bayanhongor, C Mongolia 46.12N 99.29E
168 H8 Dzag Bayanhongor, C Mongolia 46.54N 99.11E
168 H10 Dzalaa Bayanhongor, C Mongolia 44.29N 99.19E
180 J14 Dzaoudzi E Mayotte 12.48S 45.18E
Dzaudzhikau see Vladikavkaz
168 G7 Dzavhan ◆ province NW Mongolia
168 G7 Dzavhan Gol ≈ NW Mongolia
168 J7 Dzegstey Arhangay, C Mongolia 47.38N 102.31E
131 O3 Dzerzhinsk Nizhegorodskaya Oblast', W Russian Federation 56.20N 43.22E
Dzerzhinsk see Dzyarzhynsk, Belarus
Dzerzhinsk see Dzerzhyns'k, Ukraine
Dzerzhinskiy see Nar'yan-Mar
Dzerzhinskoye see Tokzhaylau
119 X7 Dzerzhyns'k Rus. Dzerzhinsk. Donets'ka Oblast', SE Ukraine 48.21N 37.50E
118 M5 Dzerzhyns'k Zhytomyrs'ka Oblast', N Ukraine 50.07N 27.56E
Dzhailgan see Jayilgan
151 N14 Dzhalagash Kaz. Zhalashash. Kzylorda, S Kazakhstan 45.06N 64.40E
153 T10 Dzhalal-Abad Kir. Jalal-Abad. Dzhalal-Abadskaya Oblast', W Kyrgyzstan 40.55N 73.00E
153 S9 Dzhalal-Abadskaya Oblast' Kir. Jalal-Abad Oblasty. ◆ province W Kyrgyzstan
Dzhalilabad see Cälilabad
126 Ll15 Dzhalinda Amurskaya Oblast', SE Russian Federation 53.29N 123.53E
Dzhambeyty see Zhympity
Dzhambulskaya Oblast' see Zhambyl
150 D9 Dzhanibek var. Dzhanybek, Kaz. Zhanibek, Zhänibek. Zapadnyy Kazakhstan, W Kazakhstan 49.27N 46.51E
Dzhankel'dy see Jongeldi
119 T12 Dzhankoy Respublika Krym, S Ukraine 45.42N 34.24E
151 V14 Dzhansugurov Kaz. Zhansügirov. Almaty, SE Kazakhstan 45.25N 79.23E
153 R9 Dzhany-Bazar var. Yangibazar. Dzhalal-Abadskaya Oblast', W Kyrgyzstan 41.40N 70.49E
Dzhanybek see Dzhanibek
126 L8 Dzhardzhan Respublika Sakha (Yakutiya), NE Russian Federation 68.47N 123.51E
Dzharkurgan see Jarqo'rg'on
119 S11 Dzharylhats'ka Zatoka gulf S Ukraine
Dzhayilgan see Jayilgan
Dzhebel see Jebel
153 T14 Dzhelandy SE Tajikistan 37.34N 72.34E
153 Y7 Dzhergalan Kir. Jyrgalan. Issyk-Kul'skaya Oblast', NE Kyrgyzstan 42.37N 78.55E
Dzherzinskoye see Tokzhaylau
Dzhetygara see Zhitikara
Dzhetysay see Zhetysay.
Dzhezkazgan see Zhezkazgan
Dzhigirbent see Jigerbent
Dzhirgatal' see Jirgatol
Dzhizak see Jizzax
Dzhizakskaya Oblast' see Jizzax Viloyati
127 N12 Dzhugdzhur, Khrebet ▲ E Russian Federation
Dzhul'fa see Culfa
Dzhuma see Juma
151 W14 Dzhungarskiy Alatau ▲ China/Kazakhstan
150 M14 Dzhusaly Kaz. Zholsaly. Kzylorda, SW Kazakhstan 45.28N 64.04E
152 J12 Dzhynlykum, Peski desert E Turkmenistan
112 L9 Działdowo Warmińsko-Mazurskie, C Poland 53.13N 20.11E
113 L16 Działoszyce Swiętokrzyskie, C Poland 50.21N 20.19E
43 X11 Dzidzantún Yucatán, E Mexico 21.18N 89.00W
113 G15 Dzierżoniów Ger. Reichenbach. Dolnośląskie, SW Poland 50.43N 16.40E
43 X11 Dzilam de Bravo Yucatán, E Mexico 21.24N 88.52W
120 L12 Dzisna Rus. Disna. Vitsyebskaya Voblasts', N Belarus 55.33N 28.13E
120 K12 Dzisna Lith. Dysna, Rus. Disna. ≈ Belarus/Lithuania
121 G20 Dzivin Rus. Divin. Brestskaya Voblasts', SW Belarus 51.58N 24.33E
121 M15 Dzmitravichy Rus. Dmitrovichi. Minskaya Voblasts', C Belarus 53.58N 29.14E
168 M8 Dzogsool Töv, C Mongolia 46.46N 107.18E
133 S8 Dzungaria var. Sungaria, Zungaria. physical region W China
Dzungarian Basin see Junggar Pendi
168 G5 Dzür Dzavhan, W Mongolia 49.36N 95.46E
169 Q8 Dzüünbulag Dornod, E Mongolia 46.48N 115.21E
169 O8 Dzüünbulag Sühbaatar, E Mongolia 46.30N 112.22E
168 H7 Dzuunmod Dzavhan, C Mongolia 48.09N 97.22E
168 L8 Dzuunmod Töv, C Mongolia 47.45N 107.00E
Dzüün Soyoni Nuruu see Eastern Sayans
168 F8 Dzüyl Govĭ-Altay, SW Mongolia 46.09N 93.55E
Dzvina see Western Dvina
121 J16 Dzyarzhynsk Rus. Dzerzhinsk; prev. Kaydanovo. Minskaya Voblasts', C Belarus 53.41N 27.09E
121 H17 Dzyatlava Pol. Zdzięcioł, Rus. Dyatlovo. Hrodzyenskaya Voblasts', W Belarus 53.27N 25.23E

E

E see Hubei
Éadan Doire see Edenderry
39 W6 Eads Colorado, C USA 38.28N 102.46W
39 O13 Eagar Arizona, SW USA 34.05N 109.17W
41 T8 Eagle Alaska, USA 64.47N 141.12W
11 S8 Eagle ≈ Newfoundland and Labrador, E Canada
8 I3 Eagle ≈ Yukon Territory, NW Canada
31 T7 Eagle Bend Minnesota, N USA 46.10N 95.02W
30 M8 Eagle Butte South Dakota, N USA 44.58N 101.13W
31 V12 Eagle Grove Iowa, C USA 42.39N 93.54W
21 R2 Eagle Lake Maine, NE USA 47.01N 68.35W
27 U11 Eagle Lake Texas, SW USA 29.35N 96.19W
10 A11 Eagle Lake ◎ Ontario, S Canada
37 P3 Eagle Lake ◎ California, W USA
21 R3 Eagle Lake ◎ Maine, NE USA
31 Y3 Eagle Mountain ▲ Minnesota, N USA 47.54N 90.33W
27 T6 Eagle Mountain Lake ⊡ Texas, SW USA
39 S9 Eagle Nest Lake ⊡ New Mexico, SW USA
27 P13 Eagle Pass Texas, SW USA 28.43N 100.31W
67 C25 Eagle Passage passage SW Atlantic Ocean
37 R8 Eagle Peak ▲ California, W USA 38.11N 119.22W
37 Q2 Eagle Peak ▲ California, W USA 41.16N 120.12W
39 P13 Eagle Peak ▲ New Mexico, SW USA 33.39N 109.36W
8 I4 Eagle Plain Yukon Territory, NW Canada 66.23N 136.42W
34 G15 Eagle Point Oregon, NW USA 42.28N 122.48W
195 N17 Eagle Point headland SE PNG 10.31S 149.53E
41 R11 Eagle River Alaska, USA 61.18N 149.38W
32 M2 Eagle River Michigan, N USA 47.24N 88.18W
32 L4 Eagle River Wisconsin, N USA 45.55N 89.15W
23 S6 Eagle Rock Virginia, NE USA 37.40N 79.46W
38 J13 Eagletail Mountains ▲ Arizona, SW USA
178 Kk12 Ea Hleo Đăc Lăc, S Vietnam 13.09N 108.14E
178 Kk12 Ea Kar Đăc Lăc, S Vietnam 12.47N 108.26E
Eanjum see Anjum
Eanodat see Enontekiö
10 B10 Ear Falls Ontario, C Canada 50.37N 93.13W
29 X10 Earle Arkansas, C USA 35.16N 90.28W
37 R12 Earlimart California, W USA 35.52N 119.17W
22 I6 Earlington Kentucky, S USA 37.16N 87.30W
12 H8 Earlton Ontario, S Canada 47.41N 79.46W
31 T13 Early Iowa, C USA 42.27N 95.09W
98 J11 Earn ≈ N Scotland, UK
193 C21 Earnslaw, Mount ▲ South Island, NZ 44.34S 168.26E
26 M4 Earth Texas, SW USA 34.13N 102.24W
23 P11 Easley South Carolina, SE USA 34.49N 82.36W
East see Est
East Açores Fracture Zone see East Azores Fracture Zone
99 P19 East Anglia physical region E England, UK
13 Q12 East Angus Québec, SE Canada 45.29N 71.39W
East Antarctica see Greater Antarctica
20 E10 East Aurora New York, NE USA 42.44N 78.36W
East Australian Basin see Tasman Basin
East Azerbaijan see Āzarbāyjān-e Sharqī
66 L9 East Azores Fracture Zone var. East Açores Fracture Zone. tectonic feature E Atlantic Ocean
24 M11 East Bay bay Louisiana, S USA
27 V11 East Bernard Texas, SW USA 29.31N 96.04W
31 V8 East Bethel Minnesota, N USA 45.24N 93.14W
East Borneo see Kalimantan Timur
99 P23 Eastbourne SE England, UK 50.46N 0.16E
13 R11 East-Broughton Québec, SE Canada 46.13N 71.03W
46 M6 East Caicos island E Turks and Caicos Islands
192 R7 East Cape headland North Island, NZ 37.40S 178.31E
182 M4 East Caroline Basin undersea feature SW Pacific Ocean
198 G5 East China Sea Chin. Dong Hai. sea W Pacific Ocean
99 P19 East Dereham E England, UK 52.40N 0.55E
32 J9 East Dubuque Illinois, N USA 42.29N 90.38W
9 S17 Eastend Saskatchewan, S Canada 49.29N 108.48W
200 Nn11 Easter Fracture Zone tectonic feature E Pacific Ocean
Easter Island see Pascua, Isla de
83 J18 Eastern ◆ province Kenya
159 Q12 Eastern ◆ zone E Nepal
84 L13 Eastern ◆ province E Zambia
85 H24 Eastern Cape off. Eastern Cape Province, Afr. Oos-Kaap. ◆ province SE South Africa
Eastern Desert see Sahara el Sharqîya
83 F15 Eastern Equatoria ◆ state SE Sudan
Eastern Euphrates see Murat Nehri
161 J17 Eastern Ghats ▲ SE India
194 I13 Eastern Highlands ◆ province C PNG
161 K25 Eastern Province ◆ province E Sri Lanka
Eastern Region see Ash Sharqiyah
126 I15 Eastern Sayans Mong. Dzüün Soyoni Nuruu, Rus. Vostochnyy Sayan. ▲ Mongolia/Russian Federation
Eastern Scheldt see Oosterschelde
Eastern Sierra Madre see Madre Oriental, Sierra
Eastern Transvaal see Mpumalanga
9 W14 Easterville Manitoba, C Canada 53.06N 99.52W
Easterwâlde see Oosterwolde
65 M23 East Falkland var. Isla Soledad. island E Falkland Islands
21 P12 East Falmouth Massachusetts, NE USA 41.34N 70.31W
East Fayu see Fayu
East Flanders see Oost Vlaanderen
41 S6 East Fork Chandalar River ≈ Alaska, USA
31 U12 East Fork Des Moines River ≈ Iowa/Minnesota, C USA
East Frisian Islands see Ostfriesische Inseln
20 K10 East Glenville New York, NE USA 42.53N 73.55W
31 R4 East Grand Forks Minnesota, N USA 47.54N 97.59W
99 O23 East Grinstead SE England, UK 51.07N 0.00W
20 M12 East Hartford Connecticut, NE USA 41.45N 72.36W
20 M13 East Haven Connecticut, NE USA 41.16N 72.52W
181 T9 East Indiaman Ridge undersea feature E Indian Ocean
133 V16 East Indies island group SE Asia
East Java see Jawa Timur
33 Q6 East Jordan Michigan, N USA 45.09N 85.07W
East Kalimantan see Kalimantan Timur
East Kazakhstan see Vostochnyy Kazakhstan
98 I12 East Kilbride S Scotland, UK 55.46N 4.10W
27 R7 Eastland Texas, SW USA 32.24N 98.49W
33 Q9 East Lansing Michigan, N USA 42.44N 84.28W
37 X11 East Las Vegas Nevada, W USA 36.05N 115.02W
99 M23 Eastleigh S England, UK 50.58N 1.22W
33 V12 East Liverpool Ohio, N USA 40.37N 80.34W
85 J25 East London Afr. Oos-Londen; prev. Emonti, Port Rex. Eastern Cape, S South Africa 33.00S 27.54E
98 K12 East Lothian cultural region SE Scotland, UK
10 I10 Eastmain Québec, E Canada 52.11N 78.27W
10 J10 Eastmain ≈ Québec, C Canada
13 P13 Eastman Québec, SE Canada 45.19N 72.18W
25 U6 Eastman Georgia, SE USA 32.12N 83.10W
183 O3 East Mariana Basin undersea feature W Pacific Ocean
32 K11 East Moline Illinois, N USA 41.30N 90.26W
195 O12 East New Britain ◆ province E PNG
31 T15 East Nishnabotna River ≈ Iowa, C USA
207 V12 East Novaya Zemlya Trough var. Novaya Zemlya Trough. undersea feature W Kara Sea
East Nusa Tenggara see Nusa Tenggara Timur
23 X4 Easton Maryland, NE USA 38.46N 76.04W
20 I14 Easton Pennsylvania, NE USA 40.40N 75.13W
200 N8 East Pacific Rise undersea feature E Pacific Ocean
East Pakistan see Bangladesh
33 V12 East Palestine Ohio, N USA 40.49N 80.32W
32 L12 East Peoria Illinois, N USA 40.40N 89.34W
25 S3 East Point Georgia, SE USA 33.40N 84.26W
21 U6 Eastport Maine, NE USA 44.54N 66.59W
29 Z8 East Prairie Missouri, C USA 36.46N 89.23W
21 O12 East Providence Rhode Island, NE USA 41.48N 71.20W
22 L11 East Ridge Tennessee, S USA 35.00N 85.15W
99 N16 East Riding cultural region N England, UK
20 F9 East Rochester New York, NE USA 43.06N 77.29W
32 K15 East Saint Louis Illinois, N USA 38.35N 90.07W
67 K21 East Scotia Basin undersea feature SE Scotia Sea
133 Y8 East Sea var. Sea of Japan, Rus. Yapanskoye More. sea NW Pacific Ocean see also Japan, Sea of
194 F11 East Sepik ◆ province NW PNG
181 N4 East Sheba Ridge undersea feature W Arabian Sea
East Siberian Sea see Vostochno-Sibirskoye More
20 I14 East Stroudsburg Pennsylvania, NE USA 41.00N 75.10W
East Tasmanian Rise/East Tasmania Plateau/East Tasmania Rise see East Tasman Plateau
199 Hh13 East Tasman Plateau var. East Tasmanian Rise, East Tasmania Plateau, East Tasmania Rise. undersea feature SW Tasman Sea
66 L7 East Thulean Rise undersea feature N Atlantic Ocean
175 S16 East Timor var Loro Sae prev. Portuguese Timor, Timor Timur ◆ country SE Asia
23 Y6 Eastville Virginia, NE USA 37.18N 75.57W
37 R7 East Walker River ≈ California/Nevada, W USA
190 D1 Eateringinna Creek ≈ South Australia
39 T3 Eaton Colorado, C USA 40.31N 104.42W
13 Q12 Eaton ≈ Québec, SE Canada
9 S16 Eatonia Saskatchewan, S Canada 51.13N 109.22W
33 Q10 Eaton Rapids Michigan, N USA 42.30N 84.39W
25 U4 Eatonton Georgia, SE USA 33.19N 83.23W
34 H9 Eatonville Washington, NW USA 46.51N 122.19W
32 J6 Eau Claire Wisconsin, N USA 44.49N 91.30W
Eau Claire, Lac à L' see St.Clair, Lake
10 J7 Eau Claire, Lac à l' ◎ Québec, SE Canada
32 L6 Eau Claire River ≈ Wisconsin, N USA
196 J16 Eauripik Atoll atoll Caroline Islands, C Micronesia
199 H8 Eauripik Rise undersea feature W Pacific Ocean
104 K15 Eauze Gers, S France 43.52N 0.06E
43 P11 Ébano San Luis Potosí, C Mexico 22.13N 98.22W
99 K21 Ebbw Vale SE Wales, UK 51.48N 3.13W
81 E17 Ebebiyin NE Equatorial Guinea 2.08N 11.15E
97 H22 Ebeltoft Århus, C Denmark 56.10N 10.42E
111 X5 Ebenfurth Niederösterreich, E Austria 47.51N 16.21E
20 D14 Ebensburg Pennsylvania, NE USA 40.28N 78.42W
111 S5 Ebensee Oberösterreich, N Austria 47.48N 13.45E
103 H20 Eberbach Baden-Württemberg, SW Germany 49.28N 8.58E
124 Q9 Eber Gölü salt lake C Turkey
111 U9 Eberndorf Slvn. Dobrla Vas. Kärnten, S Austria 46.33N 14.35E
111 R4 Eberschwang Oberösterreich, N Austria 48.09N 13.37E
102 O11 Eberswalde-Finow Brandenburg, E Germany 52.49N 13.48E
Ebesfalva see Dumbrăveni
172 Oo5 Ebetsu var. Ebetu. Hokkaidō, NE Japan 43.08N 141.37E
Ebetu see Ebetsu
Ebinayon see Evinayong
164 I4 Ebinur Hu ◎ NW China
144 I3 Ebla Ar. Tell Mardikh. site of ancient city Idlib, NW Syria
Eblana see Dublin
110 H7 Ebnat Sankt Gallen, NE Switzerland 47.16N 9.07E
109 L18 Eboli Campania, S Italy 40.39N 15.01E
81 E16 Ebolowa Sud, S Cameroon 2.55N 11.10E
81 N21 Ebombo Kasai Oriental, C Dem. Rep. Congo 5.42S 26.07E
201 T9 Ebon Atoll var. Epoon. atoll Ralik Chain, S Marshall Islands
Ebora see Évora
Eboracum see York
Eborodunum see Yverdon
103 J19 Ebrach Bayern, C Germany 49.49N 10.30E
111 X5 Ebreichsdorf Niederösterreich, E Austria 47.58N 16.24E
107 S6 Ebro ≈ NE Spain
107 N3 Ebro, Embalse del ⊡ N Spain
123 Hh8 Ebro Fan undersea feature W Mediterranean Sea
Eburacum see York
Ebusus see Eivissa
101 F20 Écaussinnes-d'Enghien Hainaut, SW Belgium 50.34N 4.10E
Ecbatana see Hamadān
23 Q6 Eccles West Virginia, NE USA 37.46N 81.16W
117 L14 Eceabat Çanakkale, NW Turkey 40.12N 26.22E
179 P9 Echague Luzon, N Philippines 16.42N 121.37E
Ech Cheliff/Ech Chleff see Chlef
Echeng see Ezhou
171 Kk13 Echigo-sanmyaku ▲ Honshū, C Japan
117 C18 Echinádes island group W Greece
116 J12 Echínos var. Ehinos, Ekhínos. Anatolikí Makedonía kai Thráki, NE Greece 41.16N 25.00E
171 H13 Echizen-misaki headland Honshū, SW Japan 35.59N 135.57E
Echmiadzin see Ejmiatsin
15 Hh5 Echo Bay Northwest Territories, NW Canada 66.04N 118.00W
37 Y11 Echo Bay Nevada, W USA 36.19N 114.27W
38 L9 Echo Cliffs cliff Arizona, SW USA
12 C10 Echo Lake ◎ Ontario, S Canada
37 Q7 Echo Summit ▲ California, W USA 38.47N 120.06W
12 L8 Échouani, Lac ◎ Québec, SE Canada
101 L17 Echt Limburg, SE Netherlands 51.07N 5.52E
103 H22 Echterdingen ✕ (Stuttgart) Baden-Württemberg, SW Germany 48.40N 9.13E
101 N24 Echternach Grevenmacher, E Luxembourg 49.49N 6.25E
191 N11 Echuca Victoria, SE Australia 36.10S 144.46E
106 L14 Ecija anc. Astigi. Andalucía, SW Spain 37.33N 5.04W
Eckengraf see Viesīte
102 I7 Eckernförde Schleswig-Holstein, N Germany 54.28N 9.49E
102 J7 Eckernförder Bucht inlet N Germany
104 L7 Écommoy Sarthe, NW France 47.51N 0.15E
12 L10 Écorce, Lac de l' ◎ Québec, SE Canada
13 Q8 Écorces, Rivière aux ≈ Québec, SE Canada
58 C7 Ecuador off. Republic of Ecuador. ◆ republic NW South America
82 L10 Ed var. Edd. SE Eritrea 13.54N 41.39E
97 I17 Ed Västra Götaland, S Sweden 58.55N 11.55E
100 I9 Edam Noord-Holland, C Netherlands 52.31N 5.03E
98 K4 Eday island NE Scotland, UK
27 S17 Edcouch Texas, SW USA 26.17N 97.57W
Edd see Ed
82 C11 Ed Da'ein Southern Darfur, W Sudan 11.25N 26.07E
82 G11 Ed Damazin var. Ad Damazīn. Blue Nile, E Sudan 11.45N 34.20E
82 G8 Ed Damer var. Ad Damar, Ad Dāmir. River Nile, NE Sudan 17.37N 33.58E
82 E8 Ed Debba Northern, N Sudan 18.01N 30.55E
82 F10 Ed Dueim var. Ad Duwaym, Ad Duwēm. White Nile, C Sudan 13.38N 32.36E
191 Q16 Eddystone Point headland Tasmania, SE Australia 41.01S 148.18E
99 I25 Eddystone Rocks rocks SW England, UK
31 W15 Eddyville Iowa, C USA 41.09N 92.37W
22 H7 Eddyville Kentucky, S USA 37.05N 88.04W
100 L12 Ede Gelderland, C Netherlands 52.03N 5.40E
79 T16 Ede Osun, SW Nigeria 7.40N 4.21E
81 D16 Edéa Littoral, SW Cameroon 3.46N 10.07E
113 M20 Edelény Borsod-Abaúj-Zemplén, NE Hungary 48.19N 20.44E
191 R12 Eden New South Wales, SE Australia 37.04S 149.51E
23 T8 Eden North Carolina, SE USA 36.29N 79.46W
27 P9 Eden Texas, SW USA 31.13N 99.51W
99 K14 Eden ≈ NW England, UK
85 I23 Edenburg Free State, C South Africa 29.43S 25.54E
193 D24 Edendale Southland, South Island, NZ 46.18S 168.48E
99 E18 Edenderry Ir. Éadan Doire. C Ireland 53.21N 7.03W
190 L11 Edenhope Victoria, SE Australia 37.04S 141.15E
23 X8 Edenton North Carolina, SE USA 36.06N 76.46W
103 G16 Eder ≈ NW Germany
176 Yy14 Ederah ≈ Papua, E Indonesia
103 H15 Edersee ⊡ W Germany
Edessa see Şanlıurfa
116 E13 Édessa var. Édhessa. Kentrikí Makedonía, N Greece 40.48N 22.03E
Edfu see Idfu
31 P16 Edgar Nebraska, C USA 40.22N 97.58W
21 P13 Edgartown Martha's Vineyard, Massachusetts, NE USA 41.22N 70.30W
41 X13 Edgecumbe, Mount ▲ Baranof Island, Alaska, USA 57.03N 135.45W
23 Q13 Edgefield South Carolina, SE USA 33.47N 81.55W
31 P6 Edgeley North Dakota, N USA 46.19N 98.42W
30 I11 Edgemont South Dakota, N USA 43.18N 103.49W
94 O3 Edgeøya island S Svalbard
29 Q4 Edgerton Kansas, C USA 38.45N 95.00W
31 S10 Edgerton Minnesota, N USA 43.52N 96.07W
23 X3 Edgewood Maryland, NE USA 39.20N 76.21W
27 V6 Edgewood Texas, SW USA 32.42N 95.53W
Édhessa see Édessa
31 V9 Edina Minnesota, N USA 44.53N 93.21W
29 U2 Edina Missouri, C USA 40.10N 92.10W
27 S17 Edinburg Texas, SW USA 26.18N 98.09W
67 M24 Edinburgh var. Settlement of Edinburgh. O (Tristan da Cunha) NW Tristan da Cunha 37.03S 12.18W
98 J12 Edinburgh ● S Scotland, UK 55.57N 3.13W
33 P14 Edinburgh Indiana, N USA 39.19N 86.00W
98 J12 Edinburgh ✕ S Scotland, UK 55.57N 3.22W
118 L8 Edineţ var. Edineţi, Rus. Yedintsy. NW Moldova 48.10N 27.18E
Edineţi see Edineţ
Edingen see Enghien
142 B9 Edirne Eng. Adrianople; anc. Adrianopolis, Hadrianopolis. Edirne, NW Turkey 41.40N 26.34E
142 B11 Edirne ◆ province NW Turkey
20 K15 Edison New Jersey, NE USA 40.31N 74.24W
23 S15 Edisto Island South Carolina, SE USA 32.34N 80.17W
23 R14 Edisto River ≈ South Carolina, SE USA
35 S10 Edith, Mount ▲ Montana, NW USA 46.25N 111.10W
29 N10 Edmond Oklahoma, C USA 35.40N 97.27W
34 H8 Edmonds Washington, NW USA 47.48N 122.22W
9 Q14 Edmonton Alberta, SW Canada 53.34N 113.25W
22 K7 Edmonton Kentucky, S USA 36.57N 85.37W
9 Q14 Edmonton ✕ Alberta, SW Canada 53.22N 113.43W
31 P3 Edmore North Dakota, N USA 48.22N 98.26W
11 N13 Edmundston New Brunswick, SE Canada 47.22N 68.19W
27 U12 Edna Texas, SW USA 28.58N 96.39W
41 X14 Edna Bay Kosciusko Island, Alaska, USA 55.54N 133.40W
79 U16 Edo ◆ state S Nigeria
108 F6 Edolo Lombardia, N Italy 46.12N 10.19E
66 L6 Edoras Bank undersea feature C Atlantic Ocean
98 G7 Edrachillis Bay bay NW Scotland, UK
142 B12 Edremit Balıkesir, NW Turkey 39.34N 27.01E
142 B12 Edremit Körfezi gulf NW Turkey
97 P14 Edsbro Stockholm, C Sweden 59.54N 18.30E
97 N18 Edsbruk Kalmar, S Sweden 58.01N 16.30E
96 M12 Edsbyn Gävleborg, C Sweden 61.22N 15.45E
9 O14 Edson Alberta, SW Canada 53.36N 116.28W
64 K13 Eduardo Castex La Pampa, C Argentina 35.52S 64.15W
60 F12 Eduardo Gomes ✕ (Manaus) Amazonas, NW Brazil 5.55S 35.15W
Edwardesabad see Bannu
69 U9 Edward, Lake var. Albert Edward Nyanza, Edward Nyanza, Lac Idi Amin, Lake Rutanzige. ◎ Uganda/Dem. Rep. Congo
Edward Nyanza see Edward, Lake
24 K5 Edwards Mississippi, S USA 32.19N 90.36W
27 O10 Edwards Plateau plain Texas, SW USA
32 J11 Edwards River ≈ Illinois, N USA
32 K15 Edwardsville Illinois, N USA 38.48N 89.57W
205 O13 Edward VII Peninsula peninsula Antarctica
205 X4 Edward VIII Gulf bay Antarctica
8 J11 Edziza, Mount ▲ British Columbia, W Canada 57.43N 130.39W
25 H16 Edzo prev. Rae-Edzo. Northwest Territories, NW Canada 62.43N 115.55W
41 N12 Eek Alaska, USA 60.13N 162.01W
101 D16 Eeklo var. Eekloo. Oost-Vlaanderen, NW Belgium 51.10N 3.34E
Eekloo see Eeklo
41 N12 Eek River ≈ Alaska, USA
100 N6 Eelde Drenthe, NE Netherlands 53.07N 6.30E
36 L5 Eel River ≈ California, W USA
33 P12 Eel River ≈ Indiana, N USA
Eems see Ems
100 O4 Eemshaven Groningen, NE Netherlands 53.27N 6.50E
100 O5 Eems Kanaal canal NE Netherlands
100 M11 Eerbeek Gelderland, E Netherlands 52.07N 6.04E
101 C17 Eernegem West-Vlaanderen, W Belgium 51.08N 3.03E
101 J15 Eersel Noord-Brabant, S Netherlands 51.22N 5.19E
Eesti Vabariik see Estonia
197 C14 Efate var. Éfaté, Fr. Vaté prev. Sandwich Island. island C Vanuatu
111 S4 Eferding Oberösterreich, N Austria 48.18N 14.00E
32 M15 Effingham Illinois, N USA 39.07N 88.32W
119 N15 Eforie-Nord Constanța, SE Romania 44.04N 28.37E
119 N15 Eforie Sud Constanța, E Romania 44.00N 28.38E
Efyrnwy, Afon see Vyrnwy
169 N7 Eg Hentiy, N Mongolia 48.42N 110.07E
109 G23 Egadi, Isole island group S Italy
37 X6 Egan Range ▲ Nevada, W USA
12 K12 Eganville Ontario, SE Canada 45.33N 77.03W
Ege Denizi see Aegean Sea
41 O14 Egegik Alaska, USA 58.13N 157.22W
113 L21 Eger Ger. Erlau. Heves, NE Hungary 47.54N 20.21E
Eger see Cheb, Czech Republic
Eger see Ohre, Czech Republic/Germany
181 P8 Egeria Fracture Zone tectonic feature W Indian Ocean
97 C17 Egersund Rogaland, S Norway 58.27N 6.01E
110 J7 Egg Vorarlberg, NW Austria 47.27N 9.55E
103 H14 Egge-gebirge ▲ C Germany
111 Q4 Eggelsberg Oberösterreich, N Austria 48.04N 13.00E
111 W2 Eggenburg Niederösterreich, NE Austria 48.36N 15.49E
103 N22 Eggenfelden Bayern, SE Germany 48.24N 12.45E
20 J17 Egg Harbor City New Jersey, NE USA 39.31N 74.39W
67 G25 Egg Island island W Saint Helena
191 N14 Egg Lagoon Tasmania, SE Australia 39.42S 143.57E
101 I20 Éghezèe Namur, C Belgium 50.36N 4.55E
94 L2 Egilsstadhir Austurland, E Iceland 65.14N 14.21W
Egina see Aígina
Egindibulaq see Yegindybulak
Egio see Aígio
105 N12 Égletons Corrèze, C France 45.24N 2.01E
100 H9 Egmond aan Zee Noord-Holland, NW Netherlands 52.37N 4.37E
Egmont see Taranaki, Mount
192 J10 Egmont, Cape headland North Island, NZ 39.18S 173.44E
Egoli see Johannesburg
Eğri Palanka see Kriva Palanka
97 G23 Egtved Vejle, C Denmark 55.34N 9.18E
127 Pp4 Egvekinot Chukotskiy Avtonomnyy Okrug, NE Russian Federation 66.13N 178.55W
77 V9 Egypt off. Arab Republic of Egypt, Ar. Jumhūrīyah Mişr al 'Arabīyah; prev. United Arab Republic, anc. Aegyptus. ◆ republic NE Africa
32 L17 Egypt, Lake Of ◎ Illinois, N USA
168 I14 Ehen Hudag var. Alx Youqi. Nei Mongol Zizhiqu, N China 39.12N 101.40E
170 E15 Ehime off. Ehime-ken. ◆ prefecture Shikoku, SW Japan
103 I23 Ehingen Baden-Württemberg, S Germany 48.16N 9.43E
Ehinos see Echínos
23 R14 Ehrhardt South Carolina, SE USA 33.06N 81.00W
110 L7 Ehrwald Tirol, W Austria 47.24N 10.52E
203 W6 Eiao island Îles Marquises, NE French Polynesia
107 P2 Eibar País Vasco, N Spain 43.10N 2.28W
100 O11 Eibergen Gelderland, E Netherlands 52.06N 6.39E
111 V9 Eibiswald Steiermark, SE Austria 46.40N 15.15E
111 P8 Eichham ▲ SW Austria 47.04N 12.24E
103 J15 Eichsfeld hill range C Germany
103 K21 Eichstätt Bayern, SE Germany 48.53N 11.11E
102 H8 Eider ≈ N Germany
96 E13 Eidfjord Hordaland, S Norway 60.26N 7.05E
96 D13 Eidfjorden fjord S Norway
96 F9 Eidsvåg Møre og Romsdal, S Norway 62.46N 8.00E
97 I14 Eidsvoll Akershus, S Norway 60.19N 11.16E
94 N2 Eidsvollfjellet ▲ NW Svalbard 79.13N 13.23E
Eier-Berg see Suur Munamägi
103 D18 Eifel plateau W Germany
110 E9 Eiger ▲ C Switzerland 46.33N 8.02E
98 G10 Eigg island W Scotland, UK
161 D24 Eight Degree Channel channel India/Maldives
46 G1 Eight Mile Rock Grand Bahama Island, N Bahamas 26.28N 78.43W
204 J9 Eights Coast physical region Antarctica
188 K6 Eighty Mile Beach beach Western Australia
101 L18 Eijsden Limburg, SE Netherlands 50.47N 5.43E
97 G15 Eikeren ◎ S Norway
Eil see Eyl
Eilat see Elat
191 O12 Eildon Victoria, SE Australia 37.17S 145.57E
191 O12 Eildon, Lake ◎ Victoria, SE Australia
82 E8 Eilei Northern Kordofan, C Sudan 16.33N 30.54E
103 N15 Eilenburg Sachsen, E Germany 51.28N 12.37E
96 H13 Eina Oppland, S Norway 60.37N 10.37E
Ein 'Avedat see En 'Avedat
103 I14 Einbeck Niedersachsen, C Germany 51.49N 9.52E
101 K15 Eindhoven Noord-Brabant, S Netherlands 51.25N 5.30E
110 G8 Einsiedeln Schwyz, NE Switzerland 47.06N 8.44E
Eipel see Ipel'
Éire see Ireland, Republic of
Éireann, Muir see Irish Sea
Eirik Outer Ridge see Eirik Ridge
66 I6 Eirik Ridge var. Eirik Outer Ridge. undersea feature E Labrador Sea
94 I3 Eiríksjökull ▲ C Iceland 64.47N 20.23W
61 B14 Eirunepé Amazonas, N Brazil 6.37S 69.52W
101 L17 Eisden Limburg, NE Belgium 51.05N 5.42E
85 F18 Eiseb ≈ Botswana/Namibia
Eisen see Yŏngch'ŏn
103 J16 Eisenach Thüringen, C Germany 50.58N 10.19E
Eisenburg see Vasvár
111 U6 Eisenerz Steiermark, SE Austria 47.33N 14.52E
102 Q13 Eisenhüttenstadt Brandenburg, E Germany 52.09N 14.36E
111 U10 Eisenkappel Slvn. Železna Kapela. Kärnten, S Austria 46.27N 14.33E
Eisenmarkt see Hunedoara
111 Y5 Eisenstadt Burgenland, E Austria 47.49N 16.31E
Eishū see Yŏngju
121 H15 Eišiškės Vilnius, SE Lithuania 54.10N 24.59E
103 L15 Eisleben Sachsen-Anhalt, C Germany 51.31N 11.33E
202 I3 Eita Tarawa, W Kiribati 1.21N 173.04E
Eitape see Aitape
107 V11 Eivissa var. Iviza, Cast. Ibiza; anc. Ebusus. Eivissa, Spain, W Mediterranean Sea 38.54N 1.25E

252
◆ Country ● Country Capital ◇ Dependent Territory O Dependent Territory Capital ◆ Administrative Region ✕ International Airport ▲ Mountain ▲ Mountain Range Volcano ≈ River ◎ Lake ⊡ Reservoir

Eivissa – Emonti

107 V10 **Eivissa** *var.* Iviza, *Cast.* Ibiza; *anc.* Ebusus. *island* Islas Baleares, Spain, W Mediterranean Sea
107 R4 **Ejea de los Caballeros** Aragón, NE Spain 42.07N 1.09W
42 E8 **Ejido Insurgentes** Baja California Sur, W Mexico 25.14N 111.45W
Ejin Qi *see* Dalain Hob
Ejmiadzın *see* Ejmiatsin
143 T12 **Ejmiatsin** *var.* Ejmiadzın, Etchmiadzin, *Rus.* Echmiadzin. W Armenia 40.10N 44.17E
79 P16 **Ejura** C Ghana 7.22N 1.22W
43 R16 **Ejutla** *var.* Ejutla de Crespo. Oaxaca, SE Mexico 16.30N 96.40W
Ejutla de Crespo *see* Ejutla
35 Y10 **Ekalaka** Montana, NW USA 45.52N 104.32W
Ekapa *see* Cape Town
130 **Ekaterinodar** *see* Krasnodar
95 L20 **Ekenäs** *Fin.* Tammisaari. Etelä-Suomi, SW Finland 60.00N 23.30E
152 B13 **Ekerem** *Rus.* Okarem. Balkan Welaýaty, W Turkmenistan 38.06N 53.52E
192 M13 **Eketahuna** Manawatu-Wanganui, North Island, NZ 40.41S 175.40E
Ekhínos *see* Echínos
127 P3 **Ekiatapskiy Khrebet** ▲▲ NE Russian Federation
151 T8 **Ekibastuz** Pavlodar, NE Kazakhstan 51.45N 75.22E
127 N14 **Ekimchan** Amurskaya Oblast', SE Russian Federation 53.04N 132.56E
97 O15 **Ekoln** ◎ C Sweden
82 I7 **Ekowit** Red Sea, NE Sudan 18.46N 37.07E
97 L19 **Eksjö** Jönköping, S Sweden 57.40N 15.00E
95 I15 **Ekträsk** Västerbotten, N Sweden 64.28N 19.49E
41 O13 **Ekuk** Alaska, USA 58.48N 158.25W
10 F9 **Ekwan** ≈ Ontario, C Canada
41 O13 **Ekwok** Alaska, USA 59.21N 157.28W
177 G6 **Ela** Mandalay, C Myanmar 19.37N 96.15E
El Aaiun *see* El Ayoun
83 N15 **Ēl Ābrēd** Somali, E Ethiopia 5.33N 45.12E
117 F22 **Elafónisos** *island* S Greece
117 F22 **Elafonísou, Porthmós** *strait* S Greece
El-Aïoun *see* El Ayoun
77 U8 **El 'Alamein** *var.* Al 'Alamayn. N Egypt 30.46N 28.58E
43 Q12 **El Alazán** Veracruz-Llave, C Mexico 21.06N 97.43W
59 J18 **El Alto** *var.* La Paz. ✕ (La Paz) La Paz, W Bolivia 16.31S 68.07W
Elam *see* Īlām
El Amparo *see* El Amparo de Apure
56 I8 **El Amparo de Apure** *var.* El Amparo. Apure, C Venezuela 7.03N 70.46W
175 Ss12 **Elara** Pulau Ambelau, E Indonesia 3.49S 127.10E
El Araïch/El Araïche *see* Larache
42 D6 **El Arco** Baja California, NW Mexico 28.03N 113.25W
77 X7 **El 'Arîsh** *var.* Al 'Arīsh. NE Egypt 33.00N 31.00E
117 L25 **Elása** *island* SE Greece
El Asnam *see* Chlef
Elassón *see* Elassóna
117 E15 **Elassóna** *prev.* Elassón. Thessalía, C Greece 39.54N 22.11E
107 N2 **El Astillero** Cantabria, N Spain 43.23N 3.45W
144 F14 **Elat** *var.* Eilat, Elath. Southern, S Israel 29.33N 34.57E
Elat, Gulf of *see* Aqaba, Gulf of
Elath *see* Elat, Israel
Elath *see* Al 'Aqabah, Jordan
117 C17 **Eláti** ▲ Lefkáda, Iónioi Nísoi, Greece, C Mediterranean Sea 38.43N 20.38E
196 L16 **Elato Atoll** *atoll* Caroline Islands, C Micronesia
82 C7 **El'Atrun** Northern Darfur, NW Sudan 18.10N 26.40E
76 H6 **El Ayoun** *var.* El Aaiun, El-Aïoun, La Youne. NE Morocco 34.38N 2.28W
143 N14 **Elazığ** *var.* Elâzığ, Elâziz. Elazig, E Turkey 38.40N 39.13E
143 O14 **Elazığ** *var.* Elâzığ, Elâziz. ◈ *province* C Turkey
Elâziz *see* Elazığ
Azraq, Bahr el *see* Blue Nile
25 Q7 **Elba** Alabama, S USA 31.24N 86.04W
108 E13 **Elba, Isola d'** *island* Archipelago Toscano, C Italy
127 Nn15 **El'ban** Khabarovskiy Kray, E Russian Federation 50.03N 136.34E
56 F6 **El Banco** Magdalena, N Colombia 9.00N 74.01W
El Barco *see* O Barco
106 L8 **El Barco de Ávila** Castilla-León, N Spain 40.21N 5.31W
El Barco de Valdeorras *see* O Barco
144 H7 **El Barouk, Jabal** ▲▲ C Lebanon
115 L20 **Elbasan** *var.* Elbasani. Elbasan, C Albania 41.07N 20.04E
115 L20 **Elbasan** ◈ *district* C Albania
Elbasani *see* Elbasan
56 K6 **El Baúl** Cojedes, C Venezuela 8.55N 68.17W
88 D11 **Elbe** *Cz.* Labe. ≈ Czech Republic/Germany
102 L13 **Elbe-Havel-Kanal** *canal* E Germany
102 K9 **Elbe-Lübeck-Kanal** *canal* N Germany
El Beni *see* Beni
144 H7 **El Beqaa** *var.* Al Biqā', Bekaa Valley. *valley* E Lebanon
27 R6 **Elbert** Texas, SW USA 33.15N 98.58W
39 R5 **Elbert, Mount** ▲ Colorado, C USA 39.07N 106.26W
25 U3 **Elberton** Georgia, SE USA 34.06N 82.52W
102 K11 **Elbe-Seiten-Kanal** *canal* N Germany
104 M4 **Elbeuf** Seine-Maritime, N France 49.16N 1.01E
Elbing *see* Elbląg
142 M15 **Elbistan** Kahramanmaraş, S Turkey 38.13N 37.10E
112 K7 **Elbląg** *var.* Elblag, *Ger.* Elbing. Warmińsko-Mazurskie, NE Poland 54.10N 19.25E
45 N10 **El Bluff** Región Autónoma Atlántico Sur, SE Nicaragua 12.01N 83.41W
65 H17 **El Bolsón** Río Negro, W Argentina 41.57S 71.33W
107 P11 **El Bonillo** Castilla-La Mancha, C Spain 38.57N 2.31W
El Bordo *see* Patía
El Boulaida/El Boulaïda *see* Blida
9 T16 **Elbow** Saskatchewan, S Canada 51.07N 106.30W
31 S7 **Elbow Lake** Minnesota, N USA 45.59N 95.58W
131 N16 **El'brus** *var.* Gora El'brus. ▲ SW Russian Federation 43.18N 42.21E
El'brus, Gora *see* El'brus
130 M15 **El'brusskiy** Karachayevo-Cherkesskaya Respublika, SW Russian Federation 43.36N 42.06E
83 D14 **El Buhayrat** *var.* Lakes State. ◈ *state* S Sudan
El Bur *see* Ceel Buur
100 L10 **Elburg** Gelderland, E Netherlands 52.27N 5.46E
107 O6 **El Burgo de Osma** Castilla-León, C Spain 41.36N 3.04W
Elburz Mountains *see* Alborz, Reshteh-ye Kūhhā-ye
37 V17 **El Cajon** California, W USA 32.46N 116.52W
65 H22 **El Calafate** *var.* Calafate. Santa Cruz, S Argentina 50.19S 72.12W
57 Q8 **El Callao** Bolívar, E Venezuela 7.18N 61.48W
27 U12 **El Campo** Texas, SW USA 29.12N 96.16W
56 I7 **El Cantón** Barinas, W Venezuela 7.25N 71.16W
37 Q8 **El Capitan** ▲ California, W USA 37.46N 119.39W
56 H5 **El Carmelo** Zulia, NW Venezuela 10.21N 71.46W
64 J5 **El Carmen** Jujuy, NW Argentina 24.24S 65.16W
56 E5 **El Carmen de Bolívar** Bolívar, NW Colombia 9.45N 75.11W
57 O8 **El Casabe** Bolívar, SE Venezuela 6.25N 63.34W
44 M12 **El Castillo de La Concepción** Río San Juan, SE Nicaragua 10.58N 84.24W
El Cayo *see* San Ignacio
37 X17 **El Centro** California, W USA 32.47N 115.33W
57 N6 **El Chaparro** Anzoátegui, NE Venezuela 9.08N 65.01W
107 S12 **Elche** *Cat.* Elx; *anc.* Ilici, *Lat.* Illicis. País Valenciano, E Spain 38.16N 0.40W
107 Q12 **Elche de la Sierra** Castilla-La Mancha, C Spain 38.27N 2.03W
43 U15 **El Chichonal, Volcán** ⛰ SE Mexico 17.20N 93.12W
42 C2 **El Chinero** Baja California, NW Mexico
189 R1 **Elcho Island** *island* Wessel Islands, Northern Territory, N Australia
65 H18 **El Corcovado** Chubut, SW Argentina 43.31S 71.30W
107 R12 **Elda** País Valenciano, E Spain 38.28N 0.46W
102 M10 **Elde** ≈ NE Germany
100 L12 **Elden** Gelderland, E Netherlands 51.57N 5.53E
83 J16 **El Der** *spring/well* S Ethiopia 3.55N 39.48E
El Dere *see* Ceel Dheere
42 E3 **El Desemboque** Sonora, NW Mexico 30.33N 112.59W
56 F5 **El Difícil** *var.* Ariguaní. Magdalena, N Colombia 9.49N 74.16W
126 Mm11 **El'dikan** Respublika Sakha (Yakutiya), NE Russian Federation 60.46N 135.04E
El Djazaïr *see* Alger
El Djelfa *see* Djelfa
31 X15 **Eldon** Iowa, C USA 40.55N 92.13W
29 U5 **Eldon** Missouri, C USA 38.21N 92.34W
56 E13 **El Doncello** Caquetá, S Colombia 1.43N 75.16W
31 W13 **Eldora** Iowa, C USA 42.21N 93.06W
62 G12 **Eldorado** Misiones, NE Argentina 26.22S 54.33W
42 I9 **El Dorado** Sinaloa, C Mexico 24.19N 107.22W
29 U14 **El Dorado** Arkansas, C USA 33.12N 92.40W
32 M17 **Eldorado** Illinois, N USA 37.48N 88.26W
29 O6 **El Dorado** Kansas, C USA 37.49N 96.51W
28 K12 **Eldorado** Oklahoma, C USA 34.28N 99.39W
27 O9 **Eldorado** Texas, SW USA 30.51N 100.36W
57 Q8 **El Dorado** Bolívar, E Venezuela 6.45N 61.37W
56 F10 **El Dorado** ✕ (Bogotá) Cundinamarca, C Colombia 1.15N 71.52W
El Dorado *see* California
29 O6 **El Dorado Lake** ▣ Kansas, C USA
29 S6 **El Dorado Springs** Missouri, C USA 37.53N 94.01W
83 H18 **Eldoret** Rift Valley, W Kenya 0.31N 35.16E
31 Z14 **Eldridge** Iowa, C USA 41.39N 90.34W
97 J21 **Eldsberga** Halland, S Sweden 56.36N 13.00E
27 R4 **Electra** Texas, SW USA 34.01N 98.55W
39 Q7 **Electra Lake** ▣ Colorado, C USA
40 B8 **'Ele'ele** *var.* Eleele. Kaua'i, Hawai'i, USA, C Pacific Ocean 21.54N 159.35W
Elefantes *see* Olifants
117 H19 **Elefsína** *prev.* Elevsís. Attikí, C Greece 38.02N 23.33E
117 G19 **Eléftheres** *anc.* Eleutherae. *site of ancient city* Attikí/Stereá Ellás, C Greece 38.12N 23.24E
116 I13 **Eleftheroúpoli** *prev.* Elevtheroúpolis. Anatolikí Makedonía kai Thráki, NE Greece 40.56N 24.16E
76 F10 **El Eglab** ▲▲ SW Algeria
120 F10 **Eleja** Jelgava, C Latvia 56.24N 23.41E
Elek *see* Ilek
121 G14 **Elektrėnai** Vilnius, SE Lithuania 54.47N 24.35E
130 L3 **Elektrostal'** Moskovskaya Oblast', W Russian Federation 55.46N 38.23E
83 H15 **Elemi Triangle** *disputed region* Kenya/Sudan
56 G16 **El Encanto** Amazonas, S Colombia 1.45S 73.12W
39 R14 **Elephant Butte Reservoir** ▣ New Mexico, SW USA
Éléphant, Chaîne de l' *see* Dâmrei, Chuŏr Phmun
204 G2 **Elephant Island** *island* South Shetland Islands, Antarctica
Elephant River *see* Olifants
El Escorial *see* San Lorenzo de El Escorial
Élesd *see* Aleşd
116 F11 **Eleshnitsa** ≈ W Bulgaria
143 S13 **Eleşkirt** Ağrı, E Turkey 39.22N 42.48E
44 F5 **El Estor** Izabal, E Guatemala 15.31N 89.19W
Eleutherae *see* Eléftheres
46 I2 **Eleuthera Island** *island* N Bahamas
39 S5 **Elevenmile Canyon Reservoir** ▣ Colorado, C USA
29 W8 **Eleven Point River** ≈ Arkansas/Missouri, C USA
Elevsís *see* Elefsína
Elevtheroúpolis *see* Eleftheroúpoli
77 W8 **El Faiyûm** *var.* Al Fayyūm. N Egypt 29.24N 30.52E
82 B10 **El Fasher** *var.* Al Fāshir. Northern Darfur, W Sudan 13.37N 25.22E
77 W8 **El Fashn** *var.* Al Fashn. C Egypt 28.49N 30.54E
El Ferrol/El Ferrol del Caudillo *see* Ferrol
41 W13 **Elfin Cove** Chichagof Island, Alaska, USA 58.09N 136.16W
107 W4 **El Fluvià** ≈ NE Spain
42 H7 **El Fuerte** Sinaloa, W Mexico 26.28N 108.34W
82 D11 **El Fula** Western Kordofan, C Sudan 11.43N 28.19E
El Gedaref *see* Gedaref
82 A10 **El Geneina** *var.* Ajjinena, Al-Genain, Al Junaynah. Western Darfur, W Sudan 13.27N 22.30E
98 J8 **Elgin** NE Scotland, UK 57.39N 3.19W
32 M10 **Elgin** Illinois, N USA 42.02N 88.16W
31 P14 **Elgin** Nebraska, C USA 41.58N 98.04W
37 Y9 **Elgin** Nevada, W USA 37.19N 114.30W
30 L6 **Elgin** North Dakota, N USA 46.24N 101.51W
28 M12 **Elgin** Oklahoma, C USA 34.46N 98.17W
27 T10 **Elgin** Texas, SW USA 30.21N 97.22W
127 N9 **El'ginskiy** Respublika Sakha (Yakutiya), NE Russian Federation 64.27N 141.57E
77 W8 **El Gîza** *var.* Al Jīzah, Gîza, Gizeh. N Egypt 30.01N 31.13E
76 J8 **El Goléa** *var.* Al Golea. C Algeria 30.35N 2.58E
42 D2 **El Golfo de Santa Clara** Sonora, NW Mexico 31.44N 114.34W
83 G18 **Elgon, Mount** ▲ E Uganda 1.07N 34.29E
107 T4 **El Grado** Aragón, NE Spain 42.09N 0.13E
96 I10 **Elgspiggen** ▲ S Norway 62.13N 11.18E
42 L6 **El Guaje, Laguna** ▣ NE Mexico
56 H6 **El Guayabo** Zulia, W Venezuela 8.37N 72.19W
79 O6 **El Gueṭṭâra** *oasis* N Mali 22.01N 3.00W
78 J6 **El Ḥammâmi** *desert* N Mauritania
78 M5 **El Ḥank** *cliff* N Mauritania
El Haseke *see* Al Ḩasakah
82 H10 **El Hawata** Gedaref, E Sudan 13.25N 34.42E
El Higo *see* Higos
176 Uu16 **Eliase** Pulau Selaru, E Indonesia 8.16S 130.49E
Elías Piña *see* Comendador
27 R6 **Eliasville** Texas, SW USA 32.55N 98.46W
Elichpur *see* Achalpur
39 V13 **Elida** New Mexico, SW USA 33.57N 103.39W
117 F18 **Elikónas** ▲▲ C Greece
69 T10 **Elila** ≈ W Dem. Rep. Congo
41 N9 **Elim** Alaska, USA 64.37N 162.15W
Elimberrum *see* Auch
Eliocroca *see* Lorca
63 B16 **Elisa** Santa Fe, C Argentina 30.42S 61.04W
Elisabethstedt *see* Dumbrăveni
Élisabethville *see* Lubumbashi
131 O13 **Elista** Respublika Kalmykiya, SW Russian Federation 46.17N 44.09E
190 I9 **Elizabeth** South Australia 34.44S 138.39E
23 Q3 **Elizabeth** West Virginia, NE USA 39.03N 81.22W
21 Q9 **Elizabeth, Cape** *headland* Maine, NE USA 43.34N 70.12W
23 Y8 **Elizabeth City** North Carolina, SE USA 36.18N 76.13W
23 P8 **Elizabethton** Tennessee, S USA 36.21N 82.12W
32 M17 **Elizabethtown** Illinois, N USA 37.24N 88.21W
22 K6 **Elizabethtown** Kentucky, S USA 37.41N 85.51W
20 L7 **Elizabethtown** New York, NE USA 44.13N 73.37W
23 U11 **Elizabethtown** North Carolina, SE USA 34.37N 78.36W
20 G15 **Elizabethtown** Pennsylvania, NE USA 40.08N 76.36W
76 E6 **El-Jadida** *prev.* Mazagan. W Morocco 33.15N 8.27W
El Jafr *see* Jafr, Qā' al
82 F11 **El Jebelein** White Nile, E Sudan 12.37N 32.51E
112 N8 **Ełk** *Ger.* Lyck. Warmińsko-Mazurskie, NE Poland 53.51N 22.19E
112 O8 **Ełk** ≈ NE Poland
31 Y12 **Elkader** Iowa, C USA 42.51N 91.24W
82 G9 **El Kamlin** Gezira, C Sudan 15.01N 33.02E
35 N11 **Elk City** Idaho, NW USA 45.50N 115.28W
28 K10 **Elk City** Oklahoma, C USA 35.24N 99.24W
29 P7 **Elk City Lake** ▣ Kansas, C USA
36 M5 **Elk Creek** California, W USA 39.34N 122.34W
30 J10 **Elk Creek** ≈ South Dakota, N USA
76 M5 **El Kef** *var.* Al Kāf, Le Kef. NW Tunisia 36.13N 8.44E
76 F7 **El Kelâa Srarhna** *var.* Kal al Sraghna. C Morocco 32.05N 7.20W
El Kerak *see* Al Karak
9 P17 **Elkford** British Columbia, SW Canada 49.58N 114.57W
El Khalil *see* Hebron
82 E7 **El Khandaq** Northern, N Sudan 18.34N 30.34E
77 W10 **El Khârga** *var.* Al Khārijah. C Egypt 25.31N 30.36E
33 P11 **Elkhart** Indiana, N USA 41.40N 85.58W
28 H7 **Elkhart** Kansas, C USA 37.00N 101.51W
27 V8 **Elkhart** Texas, SW USA 31.37N 95.34W
32 M7 **Elkhart Lake** ◎ Wisconsin, N USA
El Khartûm *see* Khartoum
39 Q3 **Elkhead Mountains** ▲▲ Colorado, C USA
20 I12 **Elk Hill** ▲ Pennsylvania, NE USA 41.42N 75.33W
144 G8 **El Khiyam** *var.* Al Khiyām, Khiam. S Lebanon 33.12N 35.42E
31 S15 **Elkhorn** Nebraska, C USA 41.17N 96.13W
32 M9 **Elkhorn** Wisconsin, N USA 42.40N 88.34W
31 R14 **Elkhorn River** ≈ Nebraska, C USA
131 O16 **El'khotovo** Respublika Severnaya Osetiya, SW Russian Federation 43.18N 44.17E
116 L10 **Elkhovo** *prev.* Kizilagach. Yambol, E Bulgaria 42.12N 26.36E
23 R8 **Elkin** North Carolina, SE USA 36.14N 80.51W
23 S4 **Elkins** West Virginia, NE USA 38.55N 79.51W
205 X3 **Elkins, Mount** ▲ Antarctica 66.25S 53.54E
12 G8 **Elk Lake** Ontario, S Canada 47.44N 80.19W
33 P6 **Elk Lake** ◎ Michigan, N USA
20 F12 **Elkland** Pennsylvania, NE USA 41.59N 77.16W
37 W3 **Elko** Nevada, W USA 40.48N 115.46W
9 R14 **Elk Point** Alberta, SW Canada 53.52N 110.49W
31 R12 **Elk Point** South Dakota, N USA 42.42N 96.37W
31 V8 **Elk River** Minnesota, N USA 45.18N 93.34W
22 J10 **Elk River** ≈ Alabama/Tennessee, S USA
23 R4 **Elk River** ≈ West Virginia, NE USA
22 I7 **Elkton** Kentucky, S USA 36.48N 87.07W
23 Y2 **Elkton** Maryland, NE USA 39.36N 75.49W
31 R10 **Elkton** South Dakota, N USA 44.14N 96.28W
22 I10 **Elkton** Tennessee, S USA 35.01N 86.51W
23 U5 **Elkton** Virginia, NE USA 38.22N 78.35W
El Kuneitra *see* Al Qunayṭirah
83 L15 **El Kure** Somali, E Ethiopia 5.37N 42.05E
82 D12 **El Lagowa** Western Kordofan, C Sudan 11.22N 29.10E
41 S12 **Ellamar** Alaska, USA 60.54N 146.37W
Ellás *see* Greece
25 S6 **Ellaville** Georgia, SE USA 32.14N 84.18W
207 P9 **Ellef Ringnes Island** *island* Nunavut, N Canada
31 V10 **Ellendale** Minnesota, N USA 43.53N 93.19W
31 P7 **Ellendale** North Dakota, N USA 45.57N 98.33W
38 M6 **Ellen, Mount** ▲ Utah, W USA 38.06N 110.48W
34 I9 **Ellensburg** Washington, NW USA 47.00N 124.34W
20 K12 **Ellenville** New York, NE USA 41.43N 74.24W
Ellep *see* Lib
23 T10 **Ellerbe** North Carolina, SE USA 35.04N 79.45W
207 P10 **Ellesmere Island** *island* Queen Elizabeth Islands, Nunavut, N Canada
193 H19 **Ellesmere, Lake** ◎ South Island, NZ
99 K18 **Ellesmere Port** C England, UK 53.16N 2.54W
33 O14 **Ellettsville** Indiana, N USA 39.13N 86.37W
101 E19 **Ellezelles** Hainaut, SW Belgium 50.44N 3.40E
15 Jj4 **Ellice** ≈ Nunavut, NE Canada
Ellice Islands *see* Tuvalu
Ellichpur *see* Achalpur
23 W3 **Ellicott City** Maryland, NE USA 39.16N 76.48W
25 S2 **Ellijay** Georgia, SE USA 34.42N 84.28W
29 W7 **Ellington** Missouri, C USA 37.14N 90.58W
28 L5 **Ellinwood** Kansas, C USA 38.21N 98.34W
85 J24 **Elliot** Eastern Cape, SE South Africa 31.19S 27.51E
12 D10 **Elliot Lake** Ontario, S Canada 46.24N 82.37W
189 X6 **Elliot, Mount** ▲ Queensland, E Australia 19.36S 147.02E
23 T5 **Elliott Knob** ▲ Virginia, NE USA 38.10N 79.18W
28 K4 **Ellis** Kansas, C USA 38.56N 99.33W
190 F8 **Elliston** South Australia 33.39S 134.56E
24 M7 **Ellisville** Mississippi, S USA 31.36N 89.12W
107 V5 **El Llobregat** ≈ NE Spain
98 L9 **Ellon** NE Scotland, UK 57.22N 2.06W
Ellore *see* Elūru
23 S13 **Elloree** South Carolina, SE USA 33.34N 80.37W
28 M4 **Ellsworth** Kansas, C USA 38.43N 98.13W
21 S7 **Ellsworth** Maine, NE USA 44.32N 68.25W
32 I6 **Ellsworth** Wisconsin, N USA 44.43N 92.28W
28 M11 **Ellsworth, Lake** ▣ Oklahoma, C USA
204 K9 **Ellsworth Land** *physical region* Antarctica
204 L9 **Ellsworth Mountains** ▲▲ Antarctica
103 J21 **Ellwangen** Baden-Württemberg, S Germany 48.58N 10.07E
20 B14 **Ellwood City** Pennsylvania, NE USA 40.49N 80.15W
110 H8 **Elm** Glarus, NE Switzerland 46.55N 9.09E
34 G9 **Elma** Washington, NW USA 47.00N 123.24W
124 Qq15 **El Maḥalla el Kubra** *var.* Al Maḥallah al Kubrá, Mahalla el Kubra. N Egypt 30.58N 31.10E
76 E9 **El Mahbas** *var.* Mahbés. SW Western Sahara 27.25N 9.09W
65 H17 **El Maitén** Chubut, W Argentina 42.03S 71.10W
142 E16 **Elmalı** Antalya, SW Turkey 36.40N 29.54E
82 G10 **El Manaqil** Gezira, C Sudan 14.12N 33.01E
56 M12 **El Mango** Amazonas, S Venezuela 1.55N 66.34W
77 W7 **El Manṣûra** *var.* Al Manṣūrah, Manṣûra. N Egypt 31.02N 31.30E
57 P8 **El Manteco** Bolívar, E Venezuela 7.17N 62.31W
31 O16 **Elm Creek** Nebraska, C USA 40.43N 99.22W
El Mediyya *see* Médéa
79 V9 **Elméki** Agadez, C Niger 17.52N 8.07E
110 K7 **Elmen** Tirol, W Austria 47.22N 10.34E
20 I16 **Elmer** New Jersey, NE USA 39.34N 75.09W
144 G6 **El Mina** *var.* Al Mīnā'. N Lebanon 34.28N 35.49E
77 W9 **El Minya** *var.* Al Minyā, Minya. C Egypt 28.06N 30.40E
12 F15 **Elmira** Ontario, S Canada 43.35N 80.34W
20 G11 **Elmira** New York, NE USA 42.06N 76.49W
38 K13 **El Mirage** Arizona, SW USA 33.36N 112.19W
31 O7 **Elm Lake** ▣ South Dakota, N USA
El Moján *see* San Rafael
107 N7 **El Molar** Madrid, C Spain 40.43N 3.34W
78 L7 **El Mrâyer** *well* C Mauritania 21.40N 7.50W
78 L5 **El Mreiti** *well* N Mauritania 23.40N 7.23W
78 L8 **El Mreyyé** *desert* E Mauritania
31 P8 **Elm River** ≈ North Dakota/South Dakota, N USA
102 I9 **Elmshorn** Schleswig-Holstein, N Germany 53.45N 9.39E
82 D12 **El Muglad** Western Kordofan, C Sudan 11.01N 27.43E
El Muwaqqar *see* Al Muwaqqar
12 G14 **Elmvale** Ontario, S Canada 44.34N 79.53W
32 K12 **Elmwood** Illinois, N USA 40.46N 89.58W
28 J8 **Elmwood** Oklahoma, C USA 36.37N 100.31W
105 P17 **Elne** *anc.* Illiberis. Pyrénées-Orientales, S France 42.36N 2.58E
56 F11 **El Nevado, Cerro** *elevation* C Colombia 3.56N 74.20W
179 Oo13 **El Nido** Palawan, W Philippines 11.10N 119.25E
64 I12 **El Nihuil** Mendoza, W Argentina 35.07S 68.38W
77 W7 **El Nouzha** ✕ (Alexandria) N Egypt 31.06N 29.58E
82 E10 **El Obeid** *var.* Al Obayyid, Al Ubayyiḍ. Northern Kordofan, C Sudan 13.10N 30.10E
43 O13 **El Oro** México, S Mexico 19.51N 100.07W
58 B8 **El Oro** ◈ *province* SW Ecuador
63 B19 **Elortondo** Santa Fe, C Argentina 33.42S 61.37W
56 J8 **Elorza** Apure, C Venezuela 7.01N 69.30W
El Ouâdi *see* El Oued
76 L7 **El Oued** *var.* Al Oued, El Ouâdi, El Wad. NE Algeria 33.19N 6.52E
38 L15 **Eloy** Arizona, SW USA 32.47N 111.33W
57 Q7 **El Palmar** Bolívar, E Venezuela 8.03N 61.51W
42 K8 **El Palmito** Durango, W Mexico 25.40N 104.58W
57 P7 **El Pao** Bolívar, E Venezuela 8.02N 62.38W
56 K5 **El Pao** Cojedes, N Venezuela 9.42N 68.12W
44 J7 **El Paraíso** El Paraíso, S Honduras 13.52N 86.32W
44 I7 **El Paraíso** ◈ *department* SE Honduras
32 L12 **El Paso** Illinois, N USA 40.44N 89.01W
26 G8 **El Paso** Texas, SW USA 31.45N 106.30W
26 G8 **El Paso** ✕ Texas, SW USA 31.48N 106.24W
107 U7 **El Perello** Cataluña, NE Spain 40.52N 0.43E
57 P5 **El Pilar** Sucre, NE Venezuela 10.33N 63.13W
44 F7 **El Pital, Cerro** ▲ El Salvador/Honduras 14.19N 89.06W
37 Q9 **El Portal** California, W USA 37.40N 119.46W
42 J3 **El Porvenir** Chihuahua, N Mexico 31.13N 105.51W
45 U14 **El Porvenir** San Blas, N Panama 9.33N 78.55W
107 W6 **El Prat de Llobregat** Cataluña, NE Spain 41.19N 2.04E
44 H5 **El Progreso** Yoro, NW Honduras 15.25N 87.49W
44 A2 **El Progreso** *off.* Departamento de El Progreso. ◈ *department* C Guatemala
El Progreso *see* Guastatoya
106 L9 **El Puente del Arzobispo** Castilla-La Mancha, C Spain 39.48N 5.10W
106 J15 **El Puerto de Santa María** Andalucía, S Spain 36.36N 6.13W
64 I8 **El Puesto** Catamarca, NW Argentina 27.57S 67.37W
El Qâhira *see* Cairo
77 V10 **El Qaṣr** *var.* Al Qaṣr. C Egypt 25.39N 28.54E
El Qatrani *see* Al Qaṭrānah
42 I10 **El Quelite** Sinaloa, C Mexico 23.37N 106.26W
64 G9 **Elqui, Río** ≈ N Chile
El Quneitra *see* Al Qunayṭirah
El Quseir *see* Al Quṣayr
El Quweira *see* Al Quwayrah
147 O15 **El-Rahaba** ✕ (Ṣan'ā') W Yemen 15.28N 44.12E
44 M10 **El Rama** Región Autónoma Atlántico Sur, SE Nicaragua 12.12N 84.13W
45 W16 **El Real** *var.* El Real de Santa María. Darién, SE Panama 8.07N 77.42W
El Real de Santa María *see* El Real
28 M10 **El Reno** Oklahoma, C USA 35.31N 97.57W
42 K9 **El Rodeo** Durango, C Mexico 25.08N 104.34W
106 J13 **El Ronquillo** Andalucía, S Spain 37.43N 6.09W
9 S16 **Elrose** Saskatchewan, S Canada 51.07N 107.59W
32 K8 **Elroy** Wisconsin, N USA 43.43N 90.16W
27 S17 **Elsa** Texas, SW USA 26.17N 97.59W
77 W8 **El Ṣaff** *var.* Aş Şaff. N Egypt 29.26N 31.19E
42 J10 **El Salto** Durango, C Mexico 23.46N 105.22W
44 D8 **El Salvador** *off.* Republica de El Salvador. ◆ *republic* Central America
56 K7 **El Samán de Apure** Apure, C Venezuela 7.51N 68.47W
12 D7 **Elsas** Ontario, S Canada 48.31N 82.53W
42 F3 **El Sásabe** *var.* Aduana del Sásabe. Sonora, NW Mexico 31.27N 111.31W
Elsass *see* Alsace
42 J5 **El Sáuz** Chihuahua, N Mexico 29.03N 106.15W
29 W4 **Elsberry** Missouri, C USA 39.10N 90.46W
47 P9 **El Seibo** *var.* Santa Cruz de El Seibo, Santa Cruz del Seibo. E Dominican Republic 18.45N 69.04W
44 B7 **El Semillero Barra Nahualate** Escuintla, SW Guatemala 14.01N 91.28W
Elsene *see* Ixelles
Elsen Nur *see* Dorgê Co
38 L6 **Elsinore** Utah, W USA 38.40N 112.09W
Elsinore *see* Helsingør
101 L18 **Elsloo** Limburg, SE Netherlands 50.57N 5.46E
62 G13 **El Soberbio** Misiones, NE Argentina 27.15S 54.04W
57 N6 **El Socorro** Guárico, C Venezuela 9.00N 65.42W
56 L6 **El Sombrero** Guárico, N Venezuela 9.25N 67.06W
100 L10 **Elspeet** Gelderland, E Netherlands 52.19N 5.47E
100 L12 **Elst** Gelderland, E Netherlands 51.55N 5.51E
103 O15 **Elsterwerda** Brandenburg, E Germany 51.27N 13.32E
42 J4 **El Sueco** Chihuahua, N Mexico 29.52N 106.23W
El Suweida *see* As Suwaydā'
El Suweis *see* Suez
56 D12 **El Tambo** Cauca, SW Colombia 2.25N 76.49W
183 T13 **Eltanin Fracture Zone** *tectonic feature* SE Pacific Ocean
107 X5 **El Ter** ≈ NE Spain
192 K11 **Eltham** Taranaki, North Island, NZ 39.25S 174.17E
57 O6 **El Tigre** Anzoátegui, NE Venezuela 8.55N 64.15W
El Tigrito *see* San José de Guanipa
56 J5 **El Tocuyo** Lara, N Venezuela 9.47N 69.48W
131 Q10 **El'ton** Volgogradskaya Oblast', SW Russian Federation 49.07N 46.50E
34 K10 **Eltopia** Washington, NW USA 46.33N 118.59W
107 Z8 **El Toro** *var.* Mare de Déu del Toro. ▲ Menorca, Spain, W Mediterranean Sea 39.59N 4.06E
63 A18 **El Trébol** Santa Fe, C Argentina 32.12S 61.40W
42 J13 **El Tuito** Jalisco, SW Mexico 20.20N 105.19W
77 X8 **El Ṭûr** *var.* Aṭ Ṭūr. NE Egypt 28.18N 33.37E
161 K16 **Elūru** *prev.* Ellore. Andhra Pradesh, E India 16.45N 81.10E
120 H13 **Elva** *Ger.* Elwa. Tartumaa, SE Estonia 58.13N 26.27E
39 R9 **El Vado Reservoir** ▣ New Mexico, SW USA
45 S15 **El Valle** Coclé, C Panama 8.39N 80.07W
106 I11 **Elvas** Portalegre, C Portugal 38.52N 7.10W
56 K7 **El Venado** Apure, C Venezuela 7.25N 68.46W
107 V6 **El Vendrell** Cataluña, NE Spain 41.13N 1.31E
96 I13 **Elverum** Hedmark, S Norway 60.52N 11.34E
44 I9 **El Viejo** Chinandega, NW Nicaragua 12.37N 87.09W
56 G7 **El Viejo, Cerro** ▲ C Colombia 7.31N 72.56W
56 H6 **El Vigía** Mérida, NW Venezuela 8.37N 71.39W
107 Q4 **El Villar de Arnedo** La Rioja, N Spain 42.19N 2.05W
61 A14 **Elvira** Amazonas, W Brazil 7.12S 69.56W
Elwa *see* Elva
El Wad *see* El Oued
83 K17 **El Wak** North Eastern, NE Kenya 2.46N 40.57E
35 R7 **Elwell, Lake** ▣ Montana, NW USA
33 P13 **Elwood** Indiana, N USA 40.16N 85.50W
29 R3 **Elwood** Kansas, C USA 39.43N 94.52W
31 N16 **Elwood** Nebraska, C USA 40.35N 99.51W
Elx *see* Elche
99 O20 **Ely** E England, UK 52.23N 0.15E
31 X4 **Ely** Minnesota, N USA 47.54N 91.52W
37 X6 **Ely** Nevada, W USA 39.15N 114.53W
El Yopal *see* Yopal
33 T11 **Elyria** Ohio, N USA 41.22N 82.06W
47 S9 **El Yunque** ▲ E Puerto Rico 18.15N 65.46W
103 F23 **Elz** ≈ SW Germany
197 C14 **Emae** *island* Shepherd Islands, C Vanuatu
120 I5 **Emajõgi** *Ger.* Embach. ≈ SE Estonia
Emāmrūd *see* Shāhrūd
155 Q2 **Emām Şāḩeb** *var.* Emam Saheb, Hazarat Imam. Kunduz, NE Afghanistan 37.10N 68.55E
Emāmshahr *see* Shāhrūd
97 M20 **Emån** ≈ S Sweden
197 D14 **Emao** *island* C Vanuatu
150 J11 **Emba** *Kaz.* Embi. Aktyubinsk, W Kazakhstan 48.49N 58.10E
150 H12 **Emba** *Kaz.* Zhem. ≈ W Kazakhstan
Embach *see* Emajõgi
64 K5 **Embarcación** Salta, N Argentina 23.15S 64.04W
32 M15 **Embarras River** ≈ Illinois, N USA
Embi *see* Emba
83 I19 **Embu** Eastern, C Kenya 0.30N 37.30E
102 E10 **Emden** Niedersachsen, NW Germany 53.22N 7.12E
166 H9 **Emei Shan** ▲ Sichuan, C China 29.32N 103.21E
31 Q4 **Emerado** North Dakota, N USA 47.55N 97.21W
189 X8 **Emerald** Queensland, E Australia 23.33S 148.10E
Emerald Isle *see* Montserrat
59 J15 **Emero, Río** ≈ W Bolivia
9 Y17 **Emerson** Manitoba, S Canada 49.01N 97.07W
31 T15 **Emerson** Iowa, C USA 41.00N 95.22W
31 R13 **Emerson** Nebraska, C USA 42.16N 96.43W
38 M5 **Emery** Utah, W USA 38.54N 111.16W
Emesa *see* Ḩimş
142 E13 **Emet** Kütahya, W Turkey 39.21N 29.15E
194 G14 **Emeti** Western, SW PNG 7.51S 143.14E
37 V3 **Emigrant Pass** *pass* Nevada, W USA 40.39N 116.15W
80 I6 **Emi Koussi** ▲ N Chad 19.52N 18.34E
Emilia *see* Emilia-Romagna
43 V15 **Emiliano Zapata** Chiapas, SE Mexico 17.45N 91.45W
108 E9 **Emilia-Romagna** *prev.* Emilia, *anc.* Æmilia. ◈ *region* N Italy
164 J3 **Emin** *var.* Dorbiljin. Xinjiang Uygur Zizhiqu, NW China 46.31N 83.35E
155 W8 **Eminābād** Punjab, E Pakistan 32.01N 73.51E
23 L5 **Eminence** Kentucky, S USA 38.22N 85.10W
29 W7 **Eminence** Missouri, C USA 37.09N 91.21W
116 N9 **Emine, Nos** *headland* E Bulgaria 42.43N 27.53E
164 I3 **Emin He** ≈ NW China
195 N8 **Emirau Island** *island* N PNG
142 F13 **Emirdağ** Afyon, W Turkey 39.01N 31.09E
97 M21 **Emmaboda** Kalmar, S Sweden 56.36N 15.30E
120 E5 **Emmaste** Hiiumaa, W Estonia 58.43N 22.36E
20 I15 **Emmaus** Pennsylvania, NE USA 40.32N 75.28W
191 U4 **Emmaville** New South Wales, SE Australia 29.26S 151.38E
110 E9 **Emme** ≈ W Switzerland
100 L8 **Emmeloord** Flevoland, N Netherlands 52.43N 5.46E
100 O8 **Emmen** Drenthe, NE Netherlands 52.48N 6.57E
110 F8 **Emmen** Luzern, C Switzerland 47.03N 8.14E
103 F23 **Emmendingen** Baden-Württemberg, SW Germany 48.07N 7.51E
100 P8 **Emmer-Compascuum** Drenthe, NE Netherlands 52.47N 7.03E
103 D14 **Emmerich** Nordrhein-Westfalen, W Germany 51.49N 6.16E
31 U12 **Emmetsburg** Iowa, C USA 43.06N 94.40W
34 M14 **Emmett** Idaho, NW USA 43.52N 116.30W
40 M10 **Emmonak** Alaska, USA 62.46N 164.31W
Emona *see* Ljubljana
Emonti *see* East London

◆ Country
● Country Capital
◇ Dependent Territory
○ Dependent Territory Capital
◈ Administrative Region
✕ International Airport
▲ Mountain
▲▲ Mountain Range
⛰ Volcano
≈ River
◎ Lake
▣ Reservoir

EMORY PEAK – ETHIOPIAN PLATEAU

26 L12 **Emory Peak** ▲ Texas, SW USA 29.15N 103.18W
42 F6 **Empalme** Sonora, NW Mexico 27.57N 110.49W
85 L23 **Empangeni** KwaZulu/Natal, E South Africa 28.40S 31.57E
63 C14 **Empedrado** Corrientes, NE Argentina 27.57S 58.46W
199 I13 **Emperor Seamounts** undersea feature NW Pacific Ocean
199 J3 **Emperor Trough** undersea feature N Pacific Ocean
37 R4 **Empire** Nevada, W USA 40.26N 119.21W
Empire State of the South see Georgia
Emplawas see Amplawas
108 F11 **Empoli** Toscana, C Italy 43.43N 10.57E
29 P5 **Emporia** Kansas, C USA 38.24N 96.10W
23 W7 **Emporia** Virginia, NE USA 36.41N 77.32W
20 E13 **Emporium** Pennsylvania, NE USA 41.31N 78.13W
195 S12 **Empress Augusta Bay** inlet Bougainville Island, PNG
Empty Quarter see Ar Rub' al Khālī
102 E10 **Ems** Dut. Eems. ~ NW Germany
102 F13 **Emsdetten** Nordrhein-Westfalen, NW Germany 52.10N 7.31E
Ems-Hunte Canal see Küstenkanal
102 F10 **Ems-Jade-Kanal** canal NW Germany
102 F11 **Emsland** cultural region NW Germany
190 D3 **Emu Junction** South Australia 28.39S 132.13E
169 T3 **Emur He** ~ NE China
57 R8 **Enachu Landing** NW Guyana 6.09N 60.01W
95 F16 **Enafors** Jämtland, C Sweden 63.16N 12.24E
96 N11 **Enånger** Gävleborg, C Sweden 61.30N 17.10E
98 G7 **Enard Bay** bay NW Scotland, UK
Enareträsk see Inarijärvi
176 X12 **Enarotali** Papua, E Indonesia 3.55S 136.21E
171 I15 **Ena-san** ▲ Honshū, S Japan 35.27N 137.36E
144 E12 **En 'Avedat** var. Ein 'Avedat, well S Israel
172 P2 **Enbetsu** Hokkaidō, NE Japan 44.44N 141.47E
63 H16 **Encantadas, Serra das** ▲▲ S Brazil
42 E7 **Encantado, Cerro** ▲ NW Mexico 26.46N 112.33W
64 P7 **Encarnación** Itapúa, S Paraguay 27.19S 55.49W
42 M12 **Encarnación de Díaz** Jalisco, SW Mexico 21.33N 102.13W
79 O17 **Enchi** SW Ghana 5.52N 2.48W
27 Q14 **Encinal** Texas, SW USA 28.02N 99.21W
37 U17 **Encinitas** California, W USA 33.02N 117.17W
27 S16 **Encino** Texas, SW USA 26.58N 98.06W
56 H6 **Encontrados** Zulia, NW Venezuela 9.01N 72.16W
190 I10 **Encounter Bay** inlet South Australia
63 F15 **Encruzilhada** Rio Grande do Sul, S Brazil 28.58S 55.31W
63 H16 **Encruzilhada do Sul** Rio Grande do Sul, S Brazil 30.30S 52.31W
113 M20 **Encs** Borsod-Abaúj-Zemplén, NE Hungary 48.21N 21.09E
199 M3 **Endeavour Seamount** undersea feature N Pacific Ocean 48.15N 129.04W
189 V1 **Endeavour Strait** strait Queensland, NE Australia
175 Q16 **Endeh** Flores, S Indonesia 8.48S 121.37E
97 G23 **Endelave** island C Denmark
203 T4 **Enderbury Island** atoll Phoenix Islands, C Kiribati
9 N16 **Enderby** British Columbia, SW Canada 50.34N 119.09W
205 W4 **Enderby Land** physical region Antarctica
181 N14 **Enderby Plain** undersea feature S Indian Ocean
31 Q6 **Enderlin** North Dakota, N USA 46.37N 97.36W
Endersdorf see Jędrzejów
30 K16 **Enders Reservoir** ⊠ Nebraska, C USA
20 H11 **Endicott** New York, NE USA 42.06N 76.03W
41 P7 **Endicott Mountains** ▲▲ Alaska, USA
120 I5 **Endla Raba** wetland C Estonia
119 T9 **Enerhodar** Zaporiz'ka Oblast', SE Ukraine 47.30N 34.40E
57 F14 **Ene, Río** ~ C Peru
201 N4 **Enewetak Atoll** var. Ānewetak, Eniwetok. atoll Ralik Chain, W Marshall Islands
116 L13 **Enez** Edirne, NW Turkey 40.43N 26.04E
23 W8 **Enfield** North Carolina, SE USA 36.10N 77.40W
194 G12 **Enga** ◐ province W PNG
47 Q9 **Engaño, Cabo** headland E Dominican Republic 18.36N 68.19W
172 Q5 **Engaru** Hokkaidō, NE Japan 44.06N 143.30E
144 F11 **'En Gedi** Southern, E Israel 31.23N 35.21E
110 F9 **Engelberg** Unterwalden, C Switzerland 46.51N 8.25E
23 Y9 **Engelhard** North Carolina, SE USA 35.30N 76.00W
131 P8 **Engel's** Saratovskaya Oblast', W Russian Federation 51.27N 46.09E
103 G24 **Engen** Baden-Württemberg, SW Germany 47.52N 8.46E
Engeten see Aiud
174 H13 **Enggano, Pulau** island W Indonesia
82 J8 **Enghershatu** ▲ N Eritrea 16.41N 38.21E
101 F19 **Enghien** Dut. Edingen. Hainaut, SW Belgium 50.42N 4.03E
29 V12 **England** Arkansas, C USA 34.32N 91.58W
99 M20 **England** Lat. Anglia. national region UK
15 L2 **Englefield, Cape** headland Nunavut, NE Canada 69.51N 85.31W
12 H8 **Englehart** Ontario, S Canada 47.49N 79.52W
39 T4 **Englewood** Colorado, C USA 39.39N 104.59W
33 O16 **English** Indiana, N USA 38.19N 86.28W
41 Q13 **English Bay** Alaska, USA 59.21N 151.55W
English Bazar see Ingrāj Bāzār
99 N25 **English Channel** var. The Channel, Fr. la Manche. channel NW Europe
204 J7 **English Coast** physical region Antarctica
107 S11 **Enguera** País Valenciano, E Spain 38.58N 0.42W
120 E8 **Engure** Tukums, W Latvia 57.09N 23.13E
120 E8 **Engures Ezers** ◎ NW Latvia
143 R9 **Enguri** Rus. Inguri. ~ NW Georgia
Engyum see Gangi
28 M9 **Enid** Oklahoma, C USA 36.24N 97.52W
24 L3 **Enid Lake** ⊠ Mississippi, S USA
201 Y2 **Enigu** island Ratak Chain, SE Marshall Islands
Enikale Strait see Kerch Strait
153 Z8 **Enil'chek** Issyk-Kul'skaya Oblast', E Kyrgyzstan 42.04N 79.01E
117 F17 **Enipéfs** ~ C Greece
172 O6 **Eniwa** Hokkaidō, NE Japan 42.54N 141.33E
172 O6 **Eniwa-dake** ✶ Hokkaidō, NE Japan 42.48N 141.15E
Eniwetok see Enewetak Atoll
Enjiang see Yongfeng
127 Nn11 **Enkan, Mys** headland NE Russian Federation 58.29N 141.27E
Enkeldoorn see Chivhu
100 J8 **Enkhuizen** Noord-Holland, NW Netherlands 52.34N 5.03E
111 Q4 **Enknach** ~ N Austria
97 N15 **Enköping** Uppsala, C Sweden 59.39N 17.07E
109 K24 **Enna** var. Castrogiovanni, Henna. Sicilia, Italy, C Mediterranean Sea 37.34N 14.18E
82 D11 **En Nahud** Western Kordofan, C Sudan 12.40N 28.28E
144 F8 **En Nâqoûra** var. An Nāqūrah. SW Lebanon 33.06N 33.30E
En Nazira see Nagerat
80 K8 **Ennedi** plateau E Chad
103 E15 **Ennepetal** Nordrhein-Westfalen, W Germany 51.18N 7.22E
191 P4 **Enngonia** New South Wales, SE Australia 29.19S 145.52E
99 C19 **Ennis** Ir. Inis. W Ireland 52.49N 8.58W
35 R11 **Ennis** Montana, NW USA 45.21N 111.45W
27 U7 **Ennis** Texas, SW USA 32.19N 96.37W
99 F20 **Enniscorthy** Ir. Inis Córthaidh. SE Ireland 52.30N 6.34W
99 E15 **Enniskillen** var. Inniskilling, Ir. Inis Ceithleann. SW Northern Ireland, UK 54.21N 7.37W
99 B19 **Ennistimon** Ir. Inis Díomáin. W Ireland 52.56N 9.17W
111 T4 **Enns** Oberösterreich, N Austria 48.12N 14.29E
111 T4 **Enns** ~ C Austria
95 O16 **Eno** Itä-Suomi, E Finland 62.45N 30.15E
26 M5 **Enochs** Texas, SW USA 33.51N 102.46W
95 N17 **Enonkoski** Isä-Suomi, E Finland 62.04N 28.53E
94 K10 **Enontekiö** Lapp. Eanodat. Lappi, N Finland 68.25N 23.40E
23 Q11 **Enoree** South Carolina, SE USA 34.39N 81.58W
23 P11 **Enoree River** ~ South Carolina, SE USA
20 M6 **Enosburg Falls** Vermont, NE USA 44.54N 72.50W
175 P11 **Enrekang** Sulawesi, C Indonesia 3.33S 119.46E
47 N10 **Enriquillo** SW Dominican Republic 17.53N 71.13W
47 N9 **Enriquillo, Lago** ◎ SW Dominican Republic
100 L9 **Ens** Flevoland, N Netherlands 52.39N 5.49E
100 P11 **Enschede** Overijssel, E Netherlands 52.13N 6.55E
42 B2 **Ensenada** Baja California, NW Mexico 31.52N 116.31W
103 E20 **Ensheim** ✕ (Saarbrücken) Saarland, W Germany 49.13N 7.09E
166 L9 **Enshi** Hubei, C China 30.16N 109.25E
171 Hh17 **Enshū-nada** gulf SW Japan
25 O8 **Ensley** Florida, SE USA 30.31N 87.16W
Enso see Svetogorsk
83 F18 **Entebbe** S Uganda 0.07N 32.29E
83 F18 **Entebbe** ✕ C Uganda 0.04N 32.29E
103 M18 **Entenbühl** ▲ Czech Republic/Germany 50.09N 12.10E
100 N10 **Enter** Overijssel, E Netherlands 52.19N 6.34E
25 Q7 **Enterprise** Alabama, S USA 31.19N 85.50W
34 L11 **Enterprise** Oregon, NW USA 45.25N 117.16W
38 J7 **Enterprise** Utah, W USA 37.33N 113.42W
34 J8 **Entiat** Washington, NW USA 47.39N 120.15W
107 P15 **Entinas, Punta de las** headland S Spain 36.40N 2.44W
110 F8 **Entlebuch** Luzern, W Switzerland 47.02N 8.04E
110 F8 **Entlebuch** valley C Switzerland
65 I22 **Entrada, Punta** headland S Argentina
105 O13 **Entraygues-sur-Truyère** Aveyron, S France 44.39N 2.36E
197 G3 **Entrecasteaux, Récifs d'** reef N New Caledonia
63 C17 **Entre Ríos** off. Provincia de Entre Ríos. ◐ province NE Argentina
44 K7 **Entre Ríos, Cordillera** ▲▲ Honduras/Nicaragua
106 G9 **Entroncamento** Santarém, C Portugal 39.28N 8.28W
176 Z10 **Entrop** Papua, E Indonesia 2.37S 140.43E
79 V16 **Enugu** Enugu, S Nigeria 6.24N 7.24E
79 U16 **Enugu** ◐ state SE Nigeria
127 Pp3 **Enurmino** Chukotskiy Avtonomnyy Okrug, NE Russian Federation 66.46N 171.40W
56 E9 **Envigado** Antioquia, W Colombia 6.09N 75.37W
61 B15 **Envira** Amazonas, W Brazil 7.12S 69.58W
Enyélé see Enyellé
81 I16 **Enyellé** var. Enyélé. La Likouala, NE Congo 2.48N 18.01E
103 H21 **Enz** ~ SW Germany
171 J16 **Enzan** Yamanashi, Honshū, S Japan 35.42N 138.43E
106 I2 **Eo** ~ NW Spain
Eochaill see Youghal
Eochaille, Cuan see Youghal Bay
109 K22 **Eolie, Isole** var. Isole Lipari, Eng. Aeolian Islands, Lipari Islands. island group S Italy
201 U12 **Eot** island Chuuk, C Micronesia
117 J25 **Epáno Archánes** var. Áno Arkhánai; prev. Epáno Arkhánai. Kríti, Greece, E Mediterranean Sea 35.12N 25.10E
Epáno Arkhánai see Epáno Archánes
117 G14 **Epanomí** Kentrikí Makedonía, N Greece 40.25N 22.55E
100 M10 **Epe** Gelderland, E Netherlands 52.21N 5.58E
79 S16 **Epe** Lagos, S Nigeria 6.37N 4.01E
81 I17 **Epéna** La Likouala, NE Congo 1.27N 17.28E
Eperies/Eperjes see Prešov
105 Q4 **Épernay** anc. Sparnacum. Marne, N France 49.01N 3.58E
38 L5 **Ephraim** Utah, W USA 39.21N 111.35W
20 H15 **Ephrata** Pennsylvania, NE USA 40.09N 76.08W
34 J8 **Ephrata** Washington, NW USA 47.19N 119.33W
197 C13 **Epi** var. Épi. island C Vanuatu
107 R6 **Épila** Aragón, NE Spain 41.34N 1.19W
105 T6 **Épinal** Vosges, NE France 48.10N 6.28E
Epiphania see Ḩamāh
Epirus see Ípeiros
124 N4 **Episkopí** SW Cyprus 34.37N 32.53E
Episkopi Bay see Episkopí, Kólpos
124 N4 **Episkopí, Kólpos** var. Episkopi Bay. bay SE Cyprus
Epitoli see Pretoria
Epoon see Ebon Atoll
Eporedia see Ivrea
Eppeschdorf see Dumbrăveni
103 H21 **Eppingen** Baden-Württemberg, SW Germany 49.09N 8.54E
85 E18 **Epukiro** Omaheke, E Namibia 21.40S 19.09E
31 Y13 **Epworth** Iowa, C USA 42.27N 90.55W
149 O10 **Eqlīd** var. Iqlid. Fārs, C Iran 30.54N 52.43E
Equality State see Wyoming
81 J18 **Equateur** off. Région de l' Equateur. ◐ region N Dem. Rep. Congo
157 K22 **Equatorial Channel** channel S Maldives
81 B17 **Equatorial Guinea** off. Republic of Equatorial Guinea. ◆ republic C Africa
194 H14 **Era** ~ S PNG
124 R13 **Eratosthenes Tablemount** undersea feature E Mediterranean Sea 33.48N 32.53E
Erautini see Johannesburg
194 H13 **Erave** Southern Highlands, W PNG 6.36S 143.55E
142 L12 **Erbaa** Tokat, N Turkey 40.39N 36.37E
103 E19 **Erbeskopf** ▲ W Germany 49.43N 7.04E
Erbil see Arbīl
124 Nn3 **Ercan** ✕ (Nicosia) N Cyprus 35.07N 33.30E
Ercegnovi see Herceg-Novi
143 T14 **Erçek Gölü** ◎ E Turkey
143 S14 **Erciş** Van, E Turkey 39.02N 43.21E
142 K14 **Erciyes Dağı** anc. Argaeus. ▲ C Turkey 38.35N 35.27E
113 J22 **Érd** Ger. Hanselbeck. Pest, C Hungary 47.22N 18.55E
Erdaobaihe see Baihe
165 O12 **Erdaogou** Qinghai, W China 34.30N 92.49E
169 X11 **Erdao Jiang** ~ NE China
Erdăt-Sângeorz see Sângeorgiu de Pădure
142 C11 **Erdek** Balıkesir, NW Turkey 40.25N 27.49E
Erdély see Transylvania
Erdélyi-Havasok see Carpații Meridionali
142 J17 **Erdemli** İçel, S Turkey 36.39N 34.18E
168 K6 **Erdenet** Orhon, N Mongolia 49.01N 104.06E
168 I8 **Erdenetsogt** Bayanhongor, C Mongolia 46.27N 100.53E
80 K7 **Erdi** plateau NE Chad
80 L7 **Erdi Ma** desert NE Chad
103 M23 **Erding** Bayern, SE Germany 48.18N 11.54E
Erdőszáda see Ardusat
Erdőszentgyörgy see Sângeorgiu de Pădure
104 I7 **Erdre** ~ NW France
205 R13 **Erebus, Mount** ▲ Ross Island, Antarctica 78.11S 165.09E
63 H14 **Erechim** Rio Grande do Sul, S Brazil 27.34S 52.15W
169 O7 **Ereen Davaanī Nuruu** ▲▲ NE Mongolia
169 Q6 **Ereentsav** Dornod, NE Mongolia 49.51N 115.41E
142 I16 **Ereğli** Konya, S Turkey 37.30N 34.01E
142 I15 **Ereğli Gölü** ◎ W Turkey
117 A15 **Ereíkoussa** island Iónioi Nísoi, Greece, C Mediterranean Sea
169 O11 **Erenhot** var. Erlian. Nei Mongol Zizhiqu, NE China 43.35N 112.00E
106 M6 **Eresma** ~ N Spain
117 K17 **Eresós** var. Eressós. Lésvos, E Greece 39.10N 25.57E
Eressós see Eresós
Erevan see Yerevan
Ereymentaū see Yereymentau
101 K21 **Érezée** Luxembourg, SE Belgium 50.16N 5.34E
76 G7 **Erfoud** SE Morocco 31.29N 4.18W
103 D16 **Erft** ~ W Germany
103 K16 **Erfurt** Thüringen, C Germany 50.59N 11.02E
143 P15 **Ergani** Dıyarbakır, SE Turkey 38.16N 39.43E
169 N11 **Ergel** Dornogovĭ, SE Mongolia 43.10N 109.13E
Ergene Irmağı see Ergene Çayı
168 L11 **Ergenetsogt** Ömnögovĭ, S Mongolia 42.54N 106.16E
142 C10 **Ergene Çayı** var. Ergene Irmağı. ~ NW Turkey
120 I9 **Ērgli** Madona, C Latvia 56.54N 25.37E
80 H11 **Erguig, Bahr** ~ SW Chad
169 S5 **Ergun** var. Labudalin, prev. Ergun Youqi. Nei Mongol Zizhiqu, N China 50.13N 120.09E
Ergun He see Argun
Ergun Youqi see Ergun
Erguo Zuoqi see Genhe
166 F12 **Er Hai** ◎ SW China
104 G4 **Er, Îles d'** island group NW France
106 K4 **Ería** ~ NW Spain
82 H8 **Eriba** Kassala, NE Sudan 16.37N 36.04E
98 I6 **Eriboll, Loch** inlet NW Scotland, UK
67 Q18 **Erica Seamount** undersea feature SW Indian Ocean 38.15S 14.30E
109 H23 **Erice** Sicilia, Italy, C Mediterranean Sea 38.02N 12.35E
106 E10 **Ericeira** Lisboa, C Portugal 38.58N 9.25W
98 H10 **Ericht, Loch** ◎ C Scotland, UK
28 J11 **Erick** Oklahoma, C USA 35.13N 99.52W
20 B11 **Erie** Pennsylvania, NE USA 42.06N 80.03W
20 E9 **Erie Canal** canal New York, NE USA
Érié, Lac see Erie, Lake
33 T10 **Erie, Lake** Fr. Lac Érié. ◎ Canada/USA
Erigabo see Ceerigaabo
79 N8 **'Erîgât** desert N Mali
Erigavo see Ceerigaabo
94 P2 **Erik Eriksenstretet** strait E Svalbard
9 X15 **Eriksdale** Manitoba, S Canada 50.52N 98.07W
201 V6 **Erikub Atoll** var. Ādkup. atoll Ratak Chain, C Marshall Islands
Erimanthos see Erýmanthos
172 P8 **Erimo** Hokkaidō, NE Japan 42.01N 143.07E
172 Oo8 **Erimo-misaki** headland Hokkaidō, NE Japan 41.57N 143.12E
22 H8 **Erin** Tennessee, S USA 36.19N 87.41W
98 E9 **Eriskay** island NW Scotland, UK
Erithraí see Erythrés
82 I9 **Eritrea** off. State of Eritrea, Tig. Ērtra. ◆ transitional government E Africa
Erivan see Yerevan
103 D16 **Erkelenz** Nordrhein-Westfalen, W Germany 51.04N 6.19E
97 P15 **Erken** ◎ C Sweden
103 K19 **Erlangen** Bayern, S Germany 49.35N 11.00E
166 G9 **Erlang Shan** ▲ C China 29.56N 102.24E
Erlau see Eger
111 V5 **Erlauf** ~ NE Austria
189 Q8 **Erldunda Roadhouse** Northern Territory, N Australia 25.13S 133.13E
Erlian see Erenhot
29 T15 **Erling, Lake** ⊠ Arkansas, USA
111 O8 **Erlsbach** Tirol, W Austria 46.54N 12.15E
Ermak see Aksu
100 K10 **Ermelo** Gelderland, C Netherlands 52.18N 5.37E
85 K21 **Ermelo** Mpumalanga, NE South Africa 26.31S 29.58E
142 H17 **Ermenek** Karaman, S Turkey 36.37N 32.55E
Érmihályfalva see Valea lui Mihai
117 G20 **Ermióni** Pelopónnisos, S Greece 37.24N 23.15E
117 J20 **Ermoúpoli** var. Hermoupolis; prev. Ermoúpolis. Sýros, Kykládes, Greece, Aegean Sea 37.26N 24.55E
Ermoúpolis see Ermoúpoli
Ernabella see Pukatja
161 G22 **Ernākulam** Kerala, SW India 10.04N 76.18E
104 J6 **Ernée** Mayenne, NW France 48.18N 0.54W
63 H14 **Ernestina, Barragem** ⊠ S Brazil
56 E4 **Ernesto Cortissoz** ✕ (Barranquilla) Atlántico, N Colombia
161 H21 **Erode** Tamil Nādu, SE India 11.21N 77.43E
Eroj see Iroj
85 C19 **Erongo** ◐ district W Namibia
101 F21 **Erquelinnes** Hainaut, S Belgium 50.18N 4.07E
76 G7 **Er-Rachidia** var. Ksar al Soule. E Morocco 31.58N 4.22W
82 E11 **Er Rahad** var. Ar Rahad. Northern Kordofan, C Sudan 12.42N 30.33E
Er Ramle see Ramla
85 O15 **Errego** Zambézia, NE Mozambique 16.02S 37.12E
Errenteria see Rentería
Er Rif/Er Riff see Rif
99 D14 **Errigal Mountain** Ir. An Earagail. ▲ N Ireland 55.03N 8.09W
99 A15 **Erris Head** Ir. Ceann Iorrais. headland W Ireland 54.18N 10.01W
197 D15 **Erromango** island S Vanuatu
Error Guyot see Error Tablemount
181 O4 **Error Tablemount** var. Error Guyot. undersea feature W Indian Ocean 10.19N 56.04E
82 G11 **Er Roseires** Blue Nile, E Sudan 11.52N 34.22E
Erseka see Ersekë
115 M22 **Ersekë** var. Erseka, Kolonjë. Korçë, SE Albania 40.19N 20.39E
Érsekújvár see Nové Zámky
31 S4 **Erskine** Minnesota, N USA 47.42N 96.00W
105 V6 **Erstein** Bas-Rhin, NE France 48.24N 7.39E
110 G9 **Erstfeld** Uri, C Switzerland 46.49N 8.41E
164 M3 **Ertai** Xinjiang Uygur Zizhiqu, NW China 46.04N 90.06E
130 M7 **Ertil'** Voronezhskaya Oblast', W Russian Federation 51.51N 40.46E
Ertis see Irtysh, C Asia
Ertis see Irtyshsk, Kazakhstan
164 K2 **Ertix He** Rus. Chërnyy Irtysh. ~ China/Kazakhstan
Ērtra see Eritrea
23 P9 **Erwin** North Carolina, SE USA 35.19N 78.40W
116 L12 **Erydropótamos** Bul. Byala Reka. ~ Bulgaria/Greece
117 E19 **Erýmanthos** var. Erimanthos. ▲ S Greece 37.57N 21.51E
117 G19 **Erythrés** prev. Erithraí. Stereá Ellás, C Greece 38.19N 23.20E
166 F12 **Eryuan** var. Yuhu. Yunnan, SW China 26.09N 100.01E
111 U6 **Erzbach** ~ W Austria
Erzerum see Erzurum
103 N17 **Erzgebirge** Cz. Krušné Hory, Eng. Ore Mountains. ▲▲ Czech Republic/Germany see also Krušné Hory
126 I16 **Erzin** Respublika Tyva, S Russian Federation 50.17N 95.03E
143 O13 **Erzincan** var. Erzinjan. Erzincan, E Turkey 39.43N 39.30E
143 N13 **Erzincan** var. Erzinjan. ◐ province NE Turkey
Erzinjan see Erzincan
Erzsébetváros see Dumbrăveni
143 Q13 **Erzurum** prev. Erzerum. Erzurum, NE Turkey 39.57N 41.16E
143 Q12 **Erzurum** prev. Erzerum. ◐ province NE Turkey
195 N16 **Esa'ala** Normanby Island, SE PNG 9.45S 150.47E
172 Nn7 **Esan-misaki** headland Hokkaidō, N Japan 41.49N 141.12E
172 Pp3 **Esashi** Hokkaidō, NE Japan 44.57N 142.32E
171 M11 **Esashi** var. Esasi. Iwate, Honshū, C Japan 39.13N 141.08E
171 Mm6 **Esasho** Hokkaidō, N Japan
Esasi see Esashi
97 F23 **Esbjerg** Ribe, W Denmark 55.28N 8.28E
Esbo see Espoo
38 L7 **Escalante** Utah, W USA 37.46N 111.36W
38 M7 **Escalante River** ~ Utah, W USA
12 L12 **Escalier, Réservoir l'** ⊠ Québec, SE Canada
42 K7 **Escalón** Chihuahua, N Mexico 26.43N 104.20W
106 M8 **Escalona** Castilla-La Mancha, C Spain 40.10N 4.24W
25 O8 **Escambia River** ~ Florida, SE USA
33 N5 **Escanaba** Michigan, N USA 45.45N 87.03W
33 N4 **Escanaba River** ~ Michigan, N USA
107 R8 **Escandón, Puerto de** pass E Spain 40.17N 0.57W
43 W14 **Escárcega** Campeche, SE Mexico 18.33N 90.41W
179 Pp7 **Escarpada Point** headland Luzon, N Philippines 18.28N 122.10E
25 N8 **Escatawpa River** ~ Alabama/Mississippi, S USA
105 P2 **Escaut** ~ N France
Escaut see Scheldt
101 M25 **Esch-sur-Alzette** Luxembourg, S Luxembourg 49.30N 5.58E
103 J15 **Eschwege** Hessen, C Germany 51.10N 10.03E
103 D16 **Eschweiler** Nordrhein-Westfalen, W Germany 50.48N 6.15E
Esclaves, Grand Lac des see Great Slave Lake
47 O8 **Escocesa, Bahía** bay N Dominican Republic
45 W15 **Escocés, Punta** headland NE Panama 8.50N 77.37W
37 U17 **Escondido** California, W USA 33.07N 117.05W
44 M10 **Escondido, Río** ~ SE Nicaragua
13 S7 **Escoumins, Rivière des** ~ Québec, SE Canada
39 O13 **Escudilla Mountain** ▲ Arizona, SW USA 33.57N 109.07W
42 J11 **Escuinapa** var. Escuinapa de Hidalgo. Sinaloa, C Mexico 22.49N 105.46W
Escuinapa de Hidalgo see Escuinapa
44 C6 **Escuintla** Escuintla, S Guatemala 14.16N 90.46W
43 V17 **Escuintla** Chiapas, SE Mexico 15.15N 92.39W
44 A2 **Escuintla** off. Departamento de Escuintla. ◐ department S Guatemala
13 W7 **Escuminac** ~ Québec, SE Canada
81 D16 **Eséka** Centre, SW Cameroon 3.40N 10.48E
142 I12 **Esenboğa** ✕ (Ankara) Ankara, C Turkey 40.05N 33.01E
152 B13 **Esenguly** Rus. Gasan-Kuli. Balkan Welaýaty, W Turkmenistan 37.29N 53.56E
142 D17 **Eşen Çayı** ~ SW Turkey
107 T4 **Ésera** ~ NE Spain
149 N8 **Eşfahān** Eng. Isfahan; anc. Aspadana. Eşfahān, C Iran 32.40N 51.40E
149 O7 **Eşfahān** off. Ostān-e Eşfahān. ◐ province C Iran
107 N5 **Esgueva** ~ N Spain
155 Q3 **Eshkamesh** Takhār, NE Afghanistan 36.25N 69.10E
155 T2 **Eshkāshem** Badakhshān, NE Afghanistan 36.43N 71.34E
85 L23 **Eshowe** KwaZulu/Natal, E South Africa 28.49S 31.29E
149 T5 **'Eshqābād** Khorāsān, NE Iran 36.00N 59.01E
Esh Sham see Dimashq
Esh Sharā see Ash Sharāh
Esik see Yesik
Esil see Ishim, Kazakhstan/Russian Federation
Esil see Yesil', Kazakhstan
191 V2 **Esk** Queensland, E Australia 27.15S 152.22E
192 O11 **Eskdale** Hawke's Bay, North Island, NZ 39.24S 176.51E
Eski Dzhumaya see Türgovishte
94 L2 **Eskifjördhur** Austurland, E Iceland 65.04N 14.01W
145 S3 **Eski Kalak** var. Askī Kalak, Kalak. N Iraq 36.16N 43.40E
97 N16 **Eskilstuna** Södermanland, C Sweden 59.22N 16.31E
14 G2 **Eskimo Lakes** lakes Northwest Territories, NW Canada
15 L8 **Eskimo Point** headland Nunavut, E Canada 61.19N 93.49W
Eskimo Point see Arviat
145 Q2 **Eski Mosul** N Iraq 36.31N 42.45E
153 T10 **Eski-Nookat** var. Iski-Nauket. Oshskaya Oblast', SW Kyrgyzstan 40.18N 72.29E
142 F12 **Eskişehir** var. Eskishehr. Eskişehir, W Turkey 39.46N 30.30E
142 F13 **Eskişehir** var. Eski shehr. ◐ province NW Turkey
Eskishehr see Eskişehir
106 K5 **Esla** ~ NW Spain
148 J6 **Eslāmābād** var. Eslāmābād-e Gharb; prev. Harunabad, Shāhābād. Kermānshāhān, W Iran 34.07N 46.34E
Eslāmābād-e Gharb see Eslāmābād
154 J4 **Eslām Qal'eh** Pash. Islam Qala. Herāt, W Afghanistan 34.41N 61.03E
97 K23 **Eslöv** Skåne, S Sweden 55.49N 13.19E
149 S12 **Esmā'īlābād** Kermān, S Iran 28.48N 56.39E
149 U8 **Esmā'īlābād** Khorāsān, E Iran 35.19N 60.30E
142 D14 **Eşme** Uşak, W Turkey 38.25N 28.58E
46 G6 **Esmeralda** Camagüey, E Cuba 21.51N 78.10W
65 F21 **Esmeralda, Isla** island S Chile
58 B5 **Esmeraldas** Esmeraldas, N Ecuador 0.55N 79.40W
58 B5 **Esmeraldas** ◐ province NW Ecuador
Esna see Isna
12 B6 **Esnagi Lake** ◎ Ontario, S Canada
149 V14 **Espakeh** Sīstān va Balūchestān, SE Iran 26.54N 60.09E
105 O13 **Espalion** Aveyron, S France 44.31N 2.45E
España see Spain
12 E11 **Espanola** Ontario, S Canada 46.15N 81.46W
39 S10 **Espanola** New Mexico, SW USA 35.59N 106.04W
59 C18 **Española, Isla** var. Hood Island. island Galapagos Islands, Ecuador, E Pacific Ocean
106 M13 **Espejo** Andalucía, S Spain 37.40N 4.34W
96 C13 **Espeland** Hordaland, S Norway 60.22N 5.27E
102 G12 **Espelkamp** Nordrhein-Westfalen, NW Germany 52.22N 8.37E
40 M8 **Espenberg, Cape** headland Alaska, USA 66.33N 163.36W
188 L13 **Esperance** Western Australia 33.49S 121.52E
195 W15 **Esperance, Cape** headland Guadacanal, C Solomon Islands 9.09S 159.38E
59 P18 **Esperancita** Santa Cruz, E Bolivia
63 B17 **Esperanza** Santa Fe, C Argentina 31.25S 60.59W
42 G6 **Esperanza** Sonora, NW Mexico 27.37N 109.51W
26 H9 **Esperanza** Texas, SW USA 31.09N 105.40W
204 H3 **Esperanza** Argentinian research station Antarctica 63.29S 56.53W
106 E12 **Espichel, Cabo** headland S Portugal 38.25N 9.15W
56 E10 **Espinal** Tolima, C Colombia 4.09N 74.54W
50 K10 **Espinhaço, Serra do** ▲▲ SE Brazil
106 G6 **Espinho** Aveiro, N Portugal 41.01N 8.37W
61 N18 **Espinosa** Minas Gerais, SE Brazil 14.58S 42.49W
105 O15 **Espinouse** ▲ S France
62 Q8 **Espírito Santo** off. Estado do Espírito Santo. ◐ state E Brazil
197 B12 **Espiritu Santo** var. Santo. island W Vanuatu
43 Z13 **Espíritu Santo, Bahía del** bay SE Mexico
42 F9 **Espíritu Santo, Isla del** island W Mexico
43 Y12 **Espita** Yucatán, SE Mexico 21.00N 88.17W
13 Y7 **Espoir, Cap d'** headland Québec, SE Canada 48.24N 64.21W
Esponsede/Esponsende see Esposende
95 L20 **Espoo** Swe. Esbo. Etelä-Suomi, S Finland 60.10N 24.42E
106 G5 **Esposende** var. Esponsede, Esponsende. Braga, N Portugal 41.30N 8.46W
85 M18 **Espungabera** Manica, SW Mozambique 20.27S 32.48E
65 H17 **Esquel** Chubut, SW Argentina 42.55S 71.19W
8 L17 **Esquimalt** Vancouver Island, British Columbia, SW Canada 48.25N 123.27W
63 C16 **Esquina** Corrientes, NE Argentina 30.00S 59.30W
44 E6 **Esquipulas** Chiquimula, SE Guatemala 14.34N 89.20W
44 K9 **Esquipulas** Matagalpa, C Nicaragua 12.39N 85.48W
96 I8 **Essandjøen** ◎ S Norway
76 E7 **Essaouira** prev. Mogador. W Morocco 31.33N 9.40W
Esseg see Osijek
Es Semara see Smara
101 G15 **Essen** Antwerpen, N Belgium 51.28N 4.28E
103 E15 **Essen** var. Essen an der Ruhr. Nordrhein-Westfalen, W Germany 51.28N 7.01E
Essen an der Ruhr see Essen
76 I5 **Es Senia** ✕ (Oran) NW Algeria 35.34N 0.42W
57 T8 **Essequibo Islands** island group N Guyana
57 T11 **Essequibo River** ~ C Guyana
12 C18 **Essex** Ontario, S Canada 42.06N 82.52W
31 T16 **Essex** Iowa, C USA 40.49N 95.18W
99 P21 **Essex** cultural region E England, UK
33 R8 **Essexville** Michigan, N USA 43.37N 83.50W
103 H22 **Esslingen** var. Esslingen am Neckar. Baden-Württemberg, SW Germany 48.45N 9.18E
Esslingen am Neckar see Esslingen
105 N6 **Essonne** ◐ department N France
Es Suweida see As Suwaydā'
81 F16 **Est** Eng. East. ◐ province SE Cameroon
106 I1 **Estaca de Bares, Punta da** point NW Spain 43.46N 7.40W
26 M5 **Estacado, Llano** plain New Mexico/Texas, SW USA
65 K25 **Estados, Isla de los** prev. Eng. Staten Island. island S Argentina
149 P12 **Eşţahbān** Fārs, S Iran
12 F11 **Estaire** Ontario, S Canada 46.19N 80.47W
39 S12 **Estancia** New Mexico, SW USA 34.45N 106.03W
61 P16 **Estância** Sergipe, E Brazil 11.15S 37.28W
106 G7 **Estarreja** Aveiro, N Portugal 40.45N 8.34W
104 M17 **Estats, Pic d'** Sp. Pico d'Estats. ▲ France/Spain 42.39N 1.24E
Estats, Pico d' see Estats, Pic d'
85 K23 **Estcourt** KwaZulu/Natal, E South Africa 28.58S 29.54E
108 H8 **Este** anc. Ateste. Veneto, NE Italy 45.14N 11.40E
44 J9 **Estelí** Estelí, NW Nicaragua 13.04N 86.21W
44 J9 **Estelí** ◐ department NW Nicaragua
107 Q4 **Estella** Bas. Lizarra. Navarra, N Spain 42.40N 2.01W
31 R9 **Estelline** South Dakota, N USA 44.34N 96.54W
27 P4 **Estelline** Texas, SW USA 34.33N 100.26W
106 L14 **Estepa** Andalucía, S Spain 37.16N 4.52W
106 L16 **Estepona** Andalucía, S Spain 36.25N 5.09W
41 R9 **Ester** Alaska, USA 64.49N 148.03W
9 V16 **Esterhazy** Saskatchewan, S Canada 50.40N 102.01W
39 S3 **Estes Park** Colorado, C USA 40.22N 105.31W
9 V17 **Estevan** Saskatchewan, S Canada 49.07N 103.04W
31 T11 **Estherville** Iowa, C USA 43.24N 94.49W
23 R15 **Estill** South Carolina, SE USA 32.45N 81.14W
105 Q6 **Estissac** Aube, N France 48.17N 3.51E
13 T9 **Est, Lac de l'** ◎ Québec, SE Canada
Estland see Estonia
9 S16 **Eston** Saskatchewan, S Canada 51.09N 108.41W
120 G5 **Estonia** off. Republic of Estonia, Est. Eesti Vabariik, Ger. Estland, Latv. Igaunija; prev. Estonian SSR, Rus. Estonskaya SSR. ◆ republic NE Europe
Estonskaya SSR see Estonia
106 E11 **Estoril** Lisboa, W Portugal 38.42N 9.22W
61 L14 **Estreito** Maranhão, E Brazil 6.34S 47.22W
106 I8 **Estrela, Serra da** ▲▲ C Portugal
42 D3 **Estrela, Punta** headland NW Mexico 30.53N 114.45W
Estremadura see Extremadura
106 F10 **Estremadura** cultural and historical region W Portugal
106 H11 **Estremoz** Évora, S Portugal 38.49N 7.34W
81 D18 **Estuaire** off. Province de l'Estuaire, var. L'Estuaire. ◐ province NW Gabon
Eszék see Osijek
113 I22 **Esztergom** Ger. Gran; anc. Strigonium. Komárom-Esztergom, N Hungary 47.46N 18.44E
158 K11 **Etah** Uttar Pradesh, N India 27.33N 78.39E
201 R17 **Etal Atoll** atoll Mortlock Islands, C Micronesia
101 K24 **Étalle** Luxembourg, SE Belgium 49.40N 5.36E
105 N6 **Étampes** Essonne, N France 48.25N 2.10E
190 J1 **Etamunbanie, Lake** salt lake South Australia
105 N1 **Étaples** Pas-de-Calais, N France 50.31N 1.37E
158 K12 **Etāwah** Uttar Pradesh, N India 26.46N 79.01E
13 R10 **Etchemin** ~ Québec, SE Canada
Etchmiadzin see Ejmiatsin
42 G7 **Etchojoa** Sonora, NW Mexico 26.54N 109.37W
95 L19 **Etelä-Suomi** ◐ province S Finland
85 B16 **Etengua** Kunene, NW Namibia 17.24S 13.05E
101 K25 **Éthe** Luxembourg, SE Belgium 49.34N 5.32E
9 W15 **Ethelbert** Manitoba, S Canada 51.30N 100.22W
82 H12 **Ethiopia** off. Federal Democratic Republic of Ethiopia; prev. Abyssinia, People's Democratic Republic of Ethiopia. ◆ republic E Africa
82 I13 **Ethiopian Highlands** var. Ethiopian Plateau. plateau N Ethiopia
Ethiopian Plateau see Ethiopian Highlands

◆ Country
◆ Country Capital
◇ Dependent Territory
○ Dependent Territory Capital
◐ Administrative Region
✕ International Airport
▲ Mountain
▲▲ Mountain Range
✶ Volcano
~ River
◎ Lake
⊠ Reservoir

ETNA – FEALE

36 M2 **Etna** California, W USA 41.25N 122.53W
20 B14 **Etna** Pennsylvania, NE USA 40.29N 79.55W
96 G12 **Etna** ≈ S Norway
109 L24 **Etna, Monte** *Eng.* Mount Etna. ☒ Sicilia, Italy, C Mediterranean Sea 37.46N 15.00E
Etna, Mount *see* Etna, Monte
97 C15 **Etne** Hordaland, S Norway 59.40N 5.55E
Etoliko *see* Aitolikó
41 Y14 **Etolin Island** *island* Alexander Archipelago, Alaska, USA
40 L12 **Etolin Strait** *strait* Alaska, USA
85 C17 **Etosha Pan** *salt lake* N Namibia
81 G18 **Etoumbi** Cuvette, NW Congo 0.01N 14.57E
22 M10 **Etowah** Tennessee, S USA 35.19N 84.31W
25 S2 **Etowah River** ≈ Georgia, SE USA
152 B13 **Etrek** *var.* Gyzyletrek, *Rus.* Kizyl-Atrek. Balkan Welaýaty, W Turkmenistan 37.40N 54.44E
152 C13 **Etrek** *Per.* Rūd-e Atrak, *Rus.* Atrak, Atrek. ≈ Iran/Turkmenistan
104 L3 **Étretat** Seine-Maritime, N France 49.46N 0.23E
116 H9 **Etropole** Sofiya, W Bulgaria 42.50N 24.00E
Etsch *see* Adige
Et Tafila *see* Aţ Ţafilah
101 M23 **Ettelbrück** Diekirch, C Luxembourg 49.51N 6.06E
201 V12 **Etten** *atoll* Chuuk Islands, C Micronesia
101 H14 **Etten-Leur** Noord-Brabant, S Netherlands 51.34N 4.37E
78 G7 **Et Tidra** *var.* Île Tidra. *island* Dakhlet Nouâdhibou, NW Mauritania
103 G21 **Ettlingen** Baden-Württemberg, SW Germany 48.57N 8.25E
104 M2 **Eu** Seine-Maritime, N France 50.01N 1.24E
200 Rr16 **'Eua** *prev.* Middleburg Island. *island* Tongatapu Group, SE Tonga
200 R15 **Eua Iki** *island* Tongatapu Group, S Tonga
Euboea *see* Évvoia
189 O12 **Eucla** Western Australia 31.40S 128.50E
33 U11 **Euclid** Ohio, N USA 41.35N 81.31W
29 W14 **Eudora** Arkansas, C USA 33.06N 91.15W
29 Q4 **Eudora** Kansas, C USA 38.56N 95.06W
190 J9 **Eudunda** South Australia 34.11S 139.03E
25 R6 **Eufaula** Alabama, S USA 31.53N 85.09W
29 Q11 **Eufaula** Oklahoma, C USA 35.17N 95.34W
29 Q11 **Eufaula Lake** *var.* Eufaula Reservoir. ▣ Oklahoma, C USA
Eufaula Reservoir *see* Eufaula Lake
34 F13 **Eugene** Oregon, NW USA 44.03N 123.05W
42 B6 **Eugenia, Punta** *headland* W Mexico 27.48N 115.03W
191 Q8 **Eugowra** New South Wales, SE Australia 33.28S 148.21E
106 I2 **Eume** ≈ NW Spain
106 H2 **Eume, Embalse do** ▣ NW Spain
Eumolpias *see* Plovdiv
61 O18 **Eunápolis** Bahia, SE Brazil 16.19S 39.36W
24 H8 **Eunice** Louisiana, S USA 30.29N 92.25W
39 W15 **Eunice** New Mexico, SW USA 32.26N 103.09W
101 M19 **Eupen** Liège, E Belgium 50.37N 6.01E
138 Jj9 **Euphrates** *Ar.* Al Furāt, *Turk.* Firat Nehri. ≈ SW Asia
144 L3 **Euphrates Dam** *dam* N Syria 35.52N 38.34E
24 M4 **Eupora** Mississippi, S USA 33.32N 89.16W
95 K19 **Eura** Länsi-Suomi, W Finland 61.06N 22.12E
95 K19 **Eurajoki** Länsi-Suomi, W Finland 61.13N 21.44E
0-1 **Eurasian Plate** *tectonic feature*
104 L4 **Eure** ◈ *department* N France
104 M4 **Eure** ≈ N France
104 M6 **Eure-et-Loir** ◈ *department* C France
36 K3 **Eureka** California, W USA 40.47N 124.12W
29 P6 **Eureka** Kansas, C USA 37.47N 96.15W
35 O6 **Eureka** Montana, NW USA 48.52N 115.03W
37 V5 **Eureka** Nevada, W USA 39.30N 115.58W
31 O7 **Eureka** South Dakota, N USA 45.46N 99.37W
38 L4 **Eureka** Utah, W USA 39.57N 112.07W
34 K10 **Eureka** Washington, NW USA 46.21N 118.41W
29 S9 **Eureka Springs** Arkansas, C USA 36.25N 93.43W
190 K6 **Eurinilla Creek** *seasonal river* South Australia
191 O11 **Euroa** Victoria, SE Australia 36.46S 145.35E
180 M9 **Europa** *island* W Madagascar
106 L3 **Europa, Picos de** ▲▲ N Spain
106 L16 **Europa Point** *headland* S Gibraltar 36.07N 5.20W
86-87 **Europe** *continent*
100 F12 **Europoort** Zuid-Holland, W Netherlands 51.59N 4.08E
Euskadi *see* País Vasco
103 D17 **Euskirchen** Nordrhein-Westfalen, W Germany 50.40N 6.47E
25 W11 **Eustis** Florida, SE USA 28.51N 81.41W
190 M9 **Euston** New South Wales, SE Australia 34.34S 142.45E
25 N5 **Eutaw** Alabama, S USA 32.50N 87.53W
102 K8 **Eutin** Schleswig-Holstein, N Germany 54.07N 10.37E
8 K14 **Eutsuk Lake** ◎ British Columbia, SW Canada
Euxine Sea *see* Black Sea
85 C16 **Evale** Cunene, SW Angola 16.36S 15.46E
39 T3 **Evans** Colorado, C USA 40.22N 104.41W
9 P14 **Evansburg** Alberta, SW Canada 53.34N 114.57W
31 X13 **Evansdale** Iowa, C USA 42.28N 92.16W
191 V4 **Evans Head** New South Wales, SE Australia 29.07S 153.27E
10 J11 **Evans, Lac** ◎ Québec, SE Canada
39 S5 **Evans, Mount** ▲ Colorado, C USA 39.15N 106.10W
15 Mm6 **Evans Strait** *strait* Nunavut, N Canada
33 N10 **Evanston** Illinois, N USA 42.02N 87.41W
35 S17 **Evanston** Wyoming, C USA 41.16N 110.57W
12 D11 **Evansville** Manitoulin Island, Ontario, S Canada 45.48N 82.34W
33 N16 **Evansville** Indiana, N USA 37.58N 87.33W
32 L9 **Evansville** Wisconsin, N USA 42.46N 89.16W
27 S8 **Evant** Texas, SW USA 31.28N 98.09W
149 P13 **Evaz** Fārs, S Iran 27.48N 53.58E
31 W4 **Eveleth** Minnesota, N USA 47.27N 92.32W
190 E3 **Evelyn Creek** *seasonal river* South Australia
189 Q2 **Evelyn, Mount** ▲ Northern Territory, N Australia 13.28S 132.50E
126 I11 **Evenkiyskiy Avtonomnyy Okrug** ◈ *autonomous district* N Russian Federation
191 R13 **Everard, Cape** *headland* Victoria, SE Australia 37.48S 149.21E
190 F6 **Everard, Lake** *salt lake* South Australia
190 C2 **Everard Ranges** ▲▲ South Australia
159 R11 **Everest, Mount** *Chin.* Qomolangma Feng, *Nep.* Sagarmatha. ▲ China/Nepal 27.58N 86.57E
20 E15 **Everett** Pennsylvania, NE USA 40.00N 78.22W
34 H7 **Everett** Washington, NW USA 47.58N 122.12W
101 E17 **Evergem** Oost-Vlaanderen, NW Belgium 51.07N 3.43E
25 X16 **Everglades City** Florida, SE USA 25.51N 81.22W
25 Y16 **Everglades, The** *wetland* Florida, SE USA
25 P7 **Evergreen** Alabama, S USA 31.25N 86.55W
39 T4 **Evergreen** Colorado, C USA 39.37N 105.19W
Evergreen State *see* Washington
99 L21 **Evesham** C England, UK 52.06N 1.57W
105 T10 **Évian-les-Bains** Haute-Savoie, E France 46.22N 6.34E
95 K16 **Evijärvi** Länsi-Suomi, W Finland 63.22N 23.30E
81 D17 **Evinayong** *var.* Ebinayon, Evinayoung. C Equatorial Guinea 1.28N 10.17E
Evinayoung *see* Evinayong
117 E18 **Évinos** ≈ C Greece
97 E17 **Evje** Aust-Agder, S Norway 58.34N 7.49E
Evmolpia *see* Plovdiv
106 H11 **Évora** *anc.* Ebora, *Lat.* Liberalitas Julia. Évora, C Portugal 38.34N 7.54W
106 G11 **Évora** ◈ *district* S Portugal
104 M4 **Évreux** *anc.* Civitas Eburovicum. Eure, N France 49.01N 1.09E
104 K6 **Évron** Mayenne, NW France 48.10N 0.24W
116 L13 **Évros** *Bul.* Maritsa, *Turk.* Meriç; *anc.* Hebrus. ≈ SE Europe *see also* Maritsa/Meriç
117 F21 **Evrótas** ≈ S Greece
105 O5 **Évry** Essonne, N France 48.38N 2.27E
27 O8 **E.V.Spence Reservoir** ▣ Texas, SW USA
117 I18 **Évvoia** *Lat.* Euboea. *island* C Greece
40 D9 **'Ewa Beach** *var.* Ewa Beach. O'ahu, Hawai'i, USA, C Pacific Ocean 21.19N 158.00W
34 L9 **Ewan** Washington, NW USA 47.06N 117.46W
46 K12 **Ewarton** C Jamaica 18.10N 77.04W
83 J18 **Ewaso Ng'iro** *var.* Nyiro. ≈ C Kenya
194 E13 **Ewe** ≈ W PNG
31 P13 **Ewing** Nebraska, C USA 42.13N 98.20W
204 J5 **Ewing Island** *island* Antarctica
67 P17 **Ewing Seamount** *undersea feature* E Atlantic Ocean 23.19S 8.45E
164 L6 **Ewirgol** Xinjiang Uygur Zizhiqu, W China 42.55N 87.39E
81 G19 **Ewo** Cuvette, W Congo 0.55S 14.49E
29 S3 **Excelsior Springs** Missouri, C USA 39.20N 94.13W
99 J23 **Exe** ≈ SW England, UK
204 L12 **Executive Committee Range** ▲▲ Antarctica
12 E16 **Exeter** Ontario, S Canada 43.19N 81.26W
99 J24 **Exeter** *anc.* Isca Damnoniorum. SW England, UK 50.43N 3.31W
37 R11 **Exeter** California, W USA 36.17N 119.08W
21 P10 **Exeter** New Hampshire, NE USA 42.57N 70.55W
Exin *see* Kcynia
31 T14 **Exira** Iowa, C USA 41.36N 94.55W
99 J23 **Exmoor** *moorland* SW England, UK
23 Y6 **Exmore** Virginia, NE USA 37.31N 75.48W
188 G8 **Exmouth** Western Australia 22.00S 114.06E
99 J24 **Exmouth** SW England, UK 50.36N 3.24W
188 G8 **Exmouth Gulf** *gulf* Western Australia
181 V8 **Exmouth Plateau** *undersea feature* E Indian Ocean
117 J20 **Exompourgo** *ancient monument* Tínos, Kykládes, Greece, Aegean Sea 37.34N 25.12E
106 I10 **Extremadura** *var.* Estremadura. ◈ *autonomous community* W Spain
80 F12 **Extrême-Nord** *Eng.* Extreme North. ◈ *province* N Cameroon
Extreme North *see* Extrême-Nord
46 I3 **Exuma Cays** *islets* C Bahamas
46 I3 **Exuma Sound** *sound* C Bahamas
83 H20 **Eyasi, Lake** ◎ N Tanzania
97 F17 **Eydehavn** Aust-Agder, S Norway 58.31N 8.52E
98 L12 **Eyemouth** SE Scotland, UK 55.51N 2.06W
98 G7 **Eye Peninsula** *peninsula* NW Scotland, UK
82 Q13 **Eyl** *It.* Eil. Nugaal, E Somalia 8.03N 49.49E
105 N11 **Eymoutiers** Haute-Vienne, C France 45.45N 1.43E
Eyo (lower course) *see* Uolo, Río
31 X10 **Eyota** Minnesota, N USA 44.00N 92.13W
190 H2 **Eyre Basin, Lake** *salt lake* South Australia
190 I1 **Eyre Creek** *seasonal river* Northern Territory/South Australia
182 L9 **Eyre, Lake** *salt lake* South Australia
193 C22 **Eyre Mountains** ▲▲ South Island, NZ
190 H3 **Eyre North, Lake** *salt lake* South Australia
190 G7 **Eyre Peninsula** *peninsula* South Australia
190 H4 **Eyre South, Lake** *salt lake* South Australia
97 B18 **Eysturoy** *Dan.* Østerø *Island* Faeroe Islands 62.15N 6.55W
63 D20 **Ezeiza** ✕ (Buenos Aires) Buenos Aires, E Argentina 34.49S 58.30W
Ezeres *see* Ezeriş
118 F12 **Ezeriş** *Hung.* Ezeres. Caraş-Severin, W Romania 45.21N 21.55E
167 O9 **Ezhou** *prev.* Echeng. Hubei, C China 30.22N 114.52E
129 R11 **Ezhva** Respublika Komi, NW Russian Federation 61.45N 50.43E
142 B12 **Ezine** Çanakkale, NW Turkey 39.46N 26.19E
Ezo *see* Hokkaidō
Ezra/Ezraa *see* Izra'

F

203 P7 **Faaa** Tahiti, W French Polynesia 17.31S 149.36W
203 P7 **Faaa** ✕ (Papeete) Tahiti, W French Polynesia 17.31S 149.36W
97 H24 **Faaborg** *var.* Fåborg. Fyn, C Denmark 55.06N 10.15E
157 K19 **Faadhippolhu Atoll** *var.* Fadiffolu, Lhaviyani Atoll. *atoll* N Maldives
203 U10 **Faaite** *atoll* Îles Tuamotu, C French Polynesia
203 Q8 **Faaone** Tahiti, W French Polynesia 17.39S 149.18W
26 H8 **Fabens** Texas, SW USA 31.30N 106.09W
96 H12 **Fåberg** Oppland, S Norway 61.15N 10.21E
Fåborg *see* Faaborg
108 I12 **Fabriano** Marche, C Italy 43.19N 15.52E
151 U16 **Fabrichnyy** Almaty, SE Kazakhstan 43.12N 76.19E
56 F10 **Facatativá** Cundinamarca, C Colombia 4.52N 74.27W
79 X9 **Fachi** Agadez, C Niger 18.01N 11.36E
196 B16 **Facpi Point** *headland* W Guam
20 I13 **Factoryville** Pennsylvania, NE USA 41.34N 75.45W
80 K8 **Fada** Borkou-Ennedi-Tibesti, E Chad 17.13N 21.31E
79 Q13 **Fada-Ngourma** E Burkina 12.07N 0.20E
126 Jj4 **Faddeya, Zaliv** *bay* N Russian Federation
126 M4 **Faddeyevskiy, Ostrov** *island* Novosibirskiye Ostrova, NE Russian Federation
147 W12 **Fadhī** S Oman 17.54N 55.30E
108 H10 **Faenza** *anc.* Faventia. Emilia-Romagna, N Italy 44.16N 11.52E
66 M5 **Faeroe-Iceland Ridge** *undersea feature* NW Norwegian Sea
66 M5 **Faeroe Islands** *Dan.* Færøerne, *Faer.* Føroyar. ◇ *Danish external territory* N Atlantic Ocean
88 C8 **Faeroe Islands** *island group* N Atlantic Ocean
Færøerne *see* Faeroe Islands
66 N6 **Faeroe-Shetland Trough** *undersea feature* NE Atlantic Ocean
106 H6 **Fafe** Braga, N Portugal 41.27N 8.10W
82 K13 **Fafen Shet'** ≈ E Ethiopia
200 Qq15 **Fafo** *island* Tongatapu Group, S Tonga
198 Bb8 **Fagaloa Bay** *bay* Upolu, E Samoa
198 B7 **Fagamālo** Savai'i, N Samoa 13.27S 172.22W
118 I12 **Făgăraş** *Ger.* Fogarasch, *Hung.* Fogaras. Braşov, C Romania 45.49N 24.58E
97 M20 **Fagerhult** Kalmar, S Sweden 57.07N 15.40E
96 G13 **Fagernes** Oppland, S Norway 60.58N 9.13E
94 I9 **Fagernes** Troms, N Norway 69.31N 19.16E
97 M14 **Fagersta** Västmanland, C Sweden 59.58N 15.49E
79 W13 **Faggo** *var.* Foggo. Bauchi, N Nigeria 11.22N 9.55E
Faghman *see* Fughmah
Fagibina, Lake *see* Faguibine, Lac
65 J25 **Fagnano, Lago** ◎ S Argentina
101 G22 **Fagne** *hill range* S Belgium
79 N10 **Faguibine, Lac** *var.* Lake Fagibina. ◎ NW Mali
Fahaheel *see* Al Fuḩayḩīl
Fahlun *see* Falun
149 U12 **Fahraj** Kermān, SE Iran 29.03N 58.54E
66 P5 **Faial** Madeira, Portugal, NE Atlantic Ocean 32.46N 16.52W
66 N2 **Faial** *var.* Ilha do Faial. *island* Azores, Portugal, NE Atlantic Ocean
Faial, Ilha do *see* Faial
110 G10 **Faido** Ticino, S Switzerland 46.30N 8.48E
Faifo *see* Hôi An
Failaka Island *see* Faylakah
202 G12 **Faioa, Île** *island* N Wallis and Futuna
189 W8 **Fairbairn Reservoir** ▣ Queensland, E Australia
41 R9 **Fairbanks** Alaska, USA 64.48N 147.47W
23 U12 **Fair Bluff** North Carolina, SE USA 34.18N 79.02W
33 R14 **Fairborn** Ohio, N USA 39.49N 84.01W
25 S3 **Fairburn** Georgia, SE USA 33.34N 84.34W
32 M12 **Fairbury** Illinois, N USA 40.45N 88.30W
31 Q17 **Fairbury** Nebraska, C USA 40.08N 97.10W
31 T9 **Fairfax** Minnesota, N USA 44.31N 94.43W
29 O8 **Fairfax** Oklahoma, C USA 36.34N 96.42W
23 R14 **Fairfax** South Carolina, SE USA 32.57N 81.14W
37 N8 **Fairfield** California, W USA 38.14N 122.03W
35 O14 **Fairfield** Idaho, NW USA 43.20N 114.45W
32 M16 **Fairfield** Illinois, N USA 38.22N 88.22W
31 X15 **Fairfield** Iowa, C USA 41.00N 91.57W
35 R8 **Fairfield** Montana, NW USA 47.36N 111.59W
33 Q14 **Fairfield** Ohio, N USA 39.21N 84.33W
27 U8 **Fairfield** Texas, SW USA 31.43N 96.10W
29 T7 **Fair Grove** Missouri, C USA 37.22N 93.09W
21 P12 **Fairhaven** Massachusetts, NE USA 41.38N 70.51W
25 N8 **Fairhope** Alabama, S USA 30.31N 87.54W
98 L4 **Fair Isle** *island* NE Scotland, UK
193 F20 **Fairlie** Canterbury, South Island, NZ 44.05S 170.50E
31 U11 **Fairmont** Minnesota, N USA 43.40N 94.27W
31 Q16 **Fairmont** Nebraska, C USA 40.37N 97.36W
23 S3 **Fairmont** West Virginia, NE USA 39.29N 80.08W
33 P13 **Fairmount** Indiana, N USA 40.25N 85.39W
20 H10 **Fairmount** New York, NE USA 43.03N 76.14W
31 R7 **Fairmount** North Dakota, N USA 46.02N 96.36W
39 S5 **Fairplay** Colorado, C USA 39.13N 106.00W
20 F9 **Fairport** New York, NE USA 43.06N 77.26W
9 O12 **Fairview** Alberta, W Canada 56.03N 118.28W
28 L9 **Fairview** Oklahoma, C USA 36.16N 98.28W
38 L4 **Fairview** Utah, W USA 39.37N 111.26W
37 T6 **Fairview Peak** ▲ Nevada, W USA 39.13N 118.09W
196 H14 **Fais** *atoll* Caroline Islands, W Micronesia
155 U8 **Faisalābād** *prev.* Lyallpur. Punjab, NE Pakistan 31.25N 73.06E
Faisaliya *see* Fayşalīyah
30 L8 **Faith** South Dakota, N USA 45.01N 102.02W
159 N12 **Faizābād** Uttar Pradesh, N India 26.46N 82.07E
Faizabad/Faizābād *see* Feyzābād
47 S9 **Fajardo** E Puerto Rico 18.20N 65.39W
145 R9 **Fajj, Wādī al** *dry watercourse* S Iraq
146 K4 **Fajr, Bi'r** *well* NW Saudi Arabia 28.46N 37.51E
203 W10 **Fakahina** *atoll* Îles Tuamotu, C French Polynesia
202 L10 **Fakaofo Atoll** *island* SE Tokelau
203 U10 **Fakarava** *atoll* Îles Tuamotu, C French Polynesia
131 T2 **Fakel** Udmurtskaya Respublika, NW Russian Federation 57.35N 53.00E
99 P19 **Fakenham** E England, UK 52.50N 0.51E
176 V11 **Fakfak** Papua, E Indonesia 2.55S 132.16E
176 V11 **Fakfak, Pegunungan** ▲▲ Papua, E Indonesia
159 T12 **Fakīragrām** Assam, NE India 26.22N 90.15E
116 M10 **Fakiyska Reka** ≈ SE Bulgaria
97 J24 **Fakse** Storstrøm, SE Denmark 55.16N 12.07E
97 J24 **Fakse Bugt** *bay* SE Denmark
97 J24 **Fakse Ladeplads** Storstrøm, SE Denmark 55.13N 12.10E
169 V11 **Faku** Liaoning, NE China 42.30N 123.27E
78 J14 **Falaba** N Sierra Leone 9.54N 11.22W
104 K5 **Falaise** Calvados, N France 48.52N 0.12W
116 H12 **Falakró** ▲ NE Greece
201 T12 **Falalu** *island* Chuuk, C Micronesia
177 Ff4 **Falam** Chin State, W Myanmar 22.58N 93.45E
149 N8 **Falāvarjān** Eşfahān, C Iran 32.33N 51.28E
118 M11 **Fălciu** Vaslui, E Romania 46.19N 28.10E
56 I4 **Falcón** *off.* Estado Falcón. ◈ *state* NW Venezuela
108 J12 **Falconara Marittima** Marche, C Italy 43.37N 13.22E
Falcone, Capo del *see* Falcone, Punta del
109 A16 **Falcone, Punta del** *var.* Capo del Falcone. *headland* Sardegna, Italy, C Mediterranean Sea 40.57N 8.12E
9 Y16 **Falcon Lake** Manitoba, S Canada 49.43N 95.18W
Falcon Lake *see* Falcón, Presa/Falcon Reservoir
43 O7 **Falcón, Presa** *var.* Falcon Lake, Falcon Reservoir. ▣ Mexico/USA *see also* Falcon Reservoir
27 Q16 **Falcon Reservoir** *var.* Falcon Lake, Presa Falcón. ▣ Mexico/USA *see also* Falcón, Presa
202 L10 **Fale** *island* Fakaofo Atoll, SE Tokelau
198 Aa7 **Faleālupo** Savai'i, NW Samoa 13.30S 172.46W
202 B10 **Falefatu** *island* Funafuti Atoll, C Tuvalu
198 Aa7 **Fālelima** Savai'i, NW Samoa 13.30S 172.40W
97 N18 **Falerum** Östergötland, S Sweden 58.07N 16.15E
Faleshty *see* Făleşti
118 M9 **Făleşti** *Rus.* Faleshty. NW Moldova 47.33N 27.43E
27 S15 **Falfurrias** Texas, SW USA 27.13N 98.08W
9 O13 **Falher** Alberta, W Canada 55.45N 117.18W
Falkenau an der Eger *see* Sokolov
97 J21 **Falkenberg** Halland, S Sweden 56.55N 12.30E
Falkenberg *see* Niemodlin
Falkenburg in Pommern *see* Złocieniec
102 N12 **Falkensee** Brandenburg, NE Germany 52.34N 13.04E
98 J12 **Falkirk** C Scotland, UK 56.00N 3.48W
67 I20 **Falkland Escarpment** *undersea feature* SW Atlantic Ocean
65 K24 **Falkland Islands** *var.* Falklands, Islas Malvinas. ◇ *UK dependent territory* SW Atlantic Ocean
49 W14 **Falkland Islands** *island group* SW Atlantic Ocean
67 I20 **Falkland Plateau** *var.* Argentine Rise. *undersea feature* SW Atlantic Ocean
Falklands *see* Falkland Islands
65 M23 **Falkland Sound** *var.* Estrecho de San Carlos. *strait* C Falkland Islands
Falknov nad Ohří *see* Sokolov
117 H21 **Falkonéra** *island* S Greece
97 K18 **Falköping** Västra Götaland, S Sweden 58.10N 13.31E
145 U8 **Fallāḩ** E Iraq 32.58N 45.09E
37 U16 **Fallbrook** California, W USA 33.22N 117.15W
201 U12 **Falleallej Pass** *passage* Chuuk Islands, C Micronesia
95 J14 **Fällfors** Västerbotten, N Sweden 65.07N 20.46E
204 I6 **Fallières Coast** *physical region* Antarctica
102 I11 **Fallingbostel** Niedersachsen, NW Germany 52.52N 9.42E
35 X9 **Fallon** Montana, NW USA 46.49N 105.07W
37 S5 **Fallon** Nevada, W USA 39.28N 118.46W
21 O12 **Fall River** Massachusetts, NE USA 41.42N 71.09W
29 P6 **Fall River Lake** ▣ Kansas, C USA
37 O3 **Fall River Mills** California, W USA 41.00N 121.28W
23 W4 **Falls Church** Virginia, NE USA 38.53N 77.11W
31 S17 **Falls City** Nebraska, C USA 40.03N 95.36W
27 S12 **Falls City** Texas, SW USA 28.58N 98.01W
Falluja *see* Al Fallūjah
79 S12 **Falmey** Dosso, SW Niger 12.29N 2.58E
47 W10 **Falmouth** Antigua, Antigua and Barbuda 16.59N 61.48W
46 J11 **Falmouth** W Jamaica 18.28N 77.39W
99 H25 **Falmouth** SW England, UK 50.07N 5.04W
22 M4 **Falmouth** Kentucky, S USA 38.40N 84.19W
21 P13 **Falmouth** Massachusetts, NE USA 41.31N 70.36W
23 W5 **Falmouth** Virginia, NE USA 38.19N 77.28W
201 U12 **Falos** *island* Chuuk, C Micronesia
85 E26 **False Bay** *Afr.* Valsbaai. *bay* SW South Africa
161 K17 **False Divi Point** *headland* E India 15.46N 80.43E
40 M16 **False Pass** Unimak Island, Alaska, USA 54.52N 163.15W
160 P12 **False Point** *headland* E India 20.23N 86.52E
107 U6 **Falset** Cataluña, NE Spain 41.07N 0.49E
97 I25 **Falster** *island* SE Denmark
118 K9 **Fălticeni** *Hung.* Faltiscsén. Suceava, NE Romania 47.27N 26.18E
Falticsén *see* Fălticeni
96 M13 **Falun** *var.* Fahlun. Dalarna, C Sweden 60.36N 15.36E
Famagusta *see* Gazimağusa
Famagusta Bay *see* Gazimağusa Körfezi
64 I8 **Famatina** La Rioja, NW Argentina 28.53S 67.31W
101 J21 **Famenne** *physical region* SE Belgium
115 D22 **Fan** *var.* Fani. ≈ N Albania
79 X15 **Fan** ≈ E Nigeria
78 M12 **Fana** Koulikoro, SW Mali 12.45N 6.55W
117 K19 **Fána** *ancient harbor* Chíos, SE Greece 38.11N 25.35E
201 V13 **Fanan** *island* Chuuk, C Micronesia
201 U12 **Fanapanges** *island* Chuuk, C Micronesia
117 L20 **Fanári, Akrotírio** *headland* Ikaría, Dodekánisos, Greece, Aegean Sea 37.40N 26.21E
47 Q13 **Fancy** Saint Vincent, Saint Vincent and the Grenadines 13.22N 61.10W
180 I5 **Fandriana** Fianarantsoa, SE Madagascar 20.13S 47.21E
178 H6 **Fang** Chiang Mai, NW Thailand 19.55N 99.13E
82 E13 **Fangak** Jonglei, SE Sudan 9.04N 30.52E
203 W10 **Fangatau** *atoll* Îles Tuamotu, C French Polynesia
203 X12 **Fangataufa** *island* Îles Tuamotu, SE French Polynesia
200 Qq15 **Fanga Uta** *bay* S Tonga
167 N7 **Fangcheng** Henan, C China 33.18N 113.03E
166 K15 **Fangchenggang** *var.* Fangcheng Gezu Zizhixian; *prev.* Fangcheng. Guangxi Zhuangzu Zizhiqu, S China 21.49N 108.21E
167 S15 **Fangshan** S Taiwan 22.19N 120.41E
169 X8 **Fangzheng** Heilongjiang, NE China 45.49N 128.49E
Fani *see* Fan
121 K16 **Fanipal'** *Rus.* Fanipol'. Minskaya Voblasts', C Belarus 53.43N 27.17E
Fanipol' *see* Fanipal'
27 T13 **Fannin** Texas, SW USA 28.41N 97.13W
Fanning Island *see* Tabuaeran
96 G8 **Fannrem** Sør-Trøndelag, S Norway 63.16N 9.48E
108 I11 **Fano** *anc.* Colonia Julia Fanestris, Fanum Fortunae. Marche, C Italy 43.51N 13.01E
97 E23 **Fanø** *island* W Denmark
178 Ii5 **Fan Si Pan** ▲ N Vietnam 22.18N 103.36E
Fanum Fortunae *see* Fano
Fao *see* Al Fāw
147 W7 **Faq'** *var.* Al Faqa. Dubayy, E UAE 24.42N 55.37E
Farab *see* Farap
204 H5 **Faraday** *UK research station* Antarctica 65.35S 64.09W
193 G16 **Faraday, Mount** ▲ South Island, NZ 42.01S 171.37E
81 P16 **Faradje** Orientale, NE Dem. Rep. Congo 3.45N 29.43E
Faradofay *see* Tôlañaro
180 I7 **Farafangana** Fianarantsoa, SE Madagascar 22.49S 47.49E
154 J7 **Farāh** *var.* Farah, Fararud. Farāh, W Afghanistan 32.22N 62.07E
154 K7 **Farāh** ◈ *province* W Afghanistan
154 J7 **Farāh Rūd** ≈ W Afghanistan
196 K7 **Farallon de Medinilla** *island* C Northern Mariana Islands
196 J2 **Farallon de Pajaros** *var.* Uracas. *island* N Northern Mariana Islands
78 J14 **Faranah** Haute-Guinée, S Guinea 10.01N 10.43W
152 K12 **Farap** *Rus.* Farab. Lebap Welaýaty, NE Turkmenistan 39.15N 63.32E
Fararud *see* Farāh
146 M13 **Farasān, Jazā'ir** *island group* SW Saudi Arabia
180 I5 **Faratsiho** Antananarivo, C Madagascar 19.24S 46.57E
196 K15 **Faraulep Atoll** *atoll* Caroline Islands, C Micronesia
101 H20 **Farciennes** Hainaut, S Belgium 50.25N 4.33E
107 O14 **Fardes** ≈ S Spain
203 S10 **Fare** Huahine, W French Polynesia 16.42S 151.01W
99 M23 **Fareham** S England, UK 50.51N 1.10W
41 P11 **Farewell** Alaska, USA 62.35N 153.59W
192 H13 **Farewell, Cape** *headland* South Island, NZ 40.30S 172.39E
Farewell, Cape *see* Nunap Isua
192 I13 **Farewell Spit** *spit* South Island, NZ
97 J17 **Färgelanda** Västra Götaland, S Sweden 58.34N 11.58E
Farghona Valley *see* Fergana Valley
Farghona, Wodii/Farghona Wodiysi *see* Fergana Valley
25 V8 **Fargo** Georgia, SE USA 30.42N 82.33W
31 R5 **Fargo** North Dakota, N USA 46.52N 96.47W
153 S10 **Farg'ona** *Rus.* Fergana; *prev.* Novyy Margilan. Farg'ona Viloyati, E Uzbekistan 40.27N 71.43E
153 R10 **Farg'ona Viloyati** *Rus.* Ferganskaya Oblast'. ◈ *province* E Uzbekistan
31 V10 **Faribault** Minnesota, N USA 44.18N 93.16W
158 J11 **Farīdābād** Haryāna, N India 28.26N 77.18E
158 H8 **Farīdkot** Punjab, NW India 30.42N 74.46E
159 T15 **Faridpur** Dhaka, C Bangladesh 23.28N 89.49E
124 N16 **Fārigh, Wādī al** ≈ N Libya
180 I4 **Farihy Alaotra** ◎ C Madagascar
96 M11 **Färila** Gävleborg, C Sweden 61.48N 15.55E
106 E9 **Farilhões** *island* C Portugal
78 G12 **Farim** NW Guinea-Bissau 12.29N 15.14W
Farish *see* Forish
147 T11 **Fāris, Qalamat** *well* SE Saudi Arabia 19.59N 50.57E
97 N21 **Färjestaden** Kalmar, S Sweden 56.37N 16.30E
155 R2 **Farkhār** Takhār, NE Afghanistan 36.39N 69.43E
153 Q14 **Farkhor** *Rus.* Parkhar. SW Tajikistan 37.31N 69.21E
118 F12 **Fârliug** *prev.* Fîrliug, *Hung.* Furluk. Caraş-Severin, SW Romania 45.21N 21.55E
117 M21 **Farmakonísi** *island* Dodekánisos, Greece, Aegean Sea
32 M13 **Farmer City** Illinois, N USA 40.14N 88.38W
33 N14 **Farmersburg** Indiana, N USA 39.14N 87.21W
27 U6 **Farmersville** Texas, SW USA 33.09N 96.21W
24 H5 **Farmerville** Louisiana, S USA 32.46N 92.24W
31 X16 **Farmington** Iowa, C USA 40.37N 91.43W
21 Q6 **Farmington** Maine, NE USA 44.40N 70.09W
31 V9 **Farmington** Minnesota, N USA 44.39N 93.09W
29 X6 **Farmington** Missouri, C USA 37.46N 90.25W
21 O9 **Farmington** New Hampshire, NE USA 43.23N 71.04W
39 P9 **Farmington** New Mexico, SW USA 36.43N 108.13W
38 L2 **Farmington** Utah, W USA 40.58N 111.53W
23 W9 **Farmville** North Carolina, SE USA 35.37N 77.36W
23 U6 **Farmville** Virginia, NE USA 37.18N 78.23W
99 N22 **Farnborough** S England, UK 51.16N 0.46W
99 N22 **Farnham** S England, UK 51.13N 0.49W
8 J7 **Faro** Yukon Territory, W Canada 62.15N 133.30W
106 G14 **Faro** Faro, S Portugal 37.01N 7.55W
106 G14 **Faro** ◈ *district* S Portugal
106 G14 **Faro** ✕ Faro, S Portugal 37.02N 8.01W
80 F13 **Faro** ≈ Cameroon/Nigeria
97 Q18 **Fårö** Gotland, SE Sweden 57.55N 19.10E
Faro, Punta del *see* Peloro, Capo
97 Q18 **Fårösund** Gotland, SE Sweden 57.51N 19.02E
181 N7 **Farquhar Group** *island group* S Seychelles
20 B13 **Farrell** Pennsylvania, NE USA 41.12N 80.28W
158 K11 **Farrukhābād** Uttar Pradesh, N India 27.24N 79.34E
149 P11 **Fārs** *off.* Ostān-e Fārs; *anc.* Persis. ◈ *province* S Iran
117 F16 **Fársala** Thessalía, C Greece 39.18N 22.22E
149 R4 **Fārsīān** Golestān, N Iran
Fars, Khalīj-e *see* Persian Gulf
97 G21 **Farsø** Nordjylland, N Denmark 56.46N 9.21E
97 D18 **Farsund** Vest-Agder, S Norway 58.04N 6.48E
147 U14 **Fartak, Ra's** *headland* E Yemen 15.34N 52.19E
62 H13 **Fartura, Serra da** ▲▲ S Brazil
Farvel, Kap *see* Nunap Isua
26 L4 **Farwell** Texas, SW USA 34.22N 103.02W
204 I9 **Farwell Island** *island* Antarctica
158 L9 **Far Western** ◈ *zone* W Nepal
154 M3 **Fāryāb** ◈ *province* N Afghanistan
149 P12 **Fasā** Fārs, S Iran 28.55N 53.39E
147 U12 **Fasad, Ramlat** *desert* SW Oman
109 P17 **Fasano** Puglia, SE Italy 40.49N 17.21E
94 L3 **Fáskrúðsfjörður** Austurland, E Iceland 64.55N 14.01W
119 O5 **Fastiv** *Rus.* Fastov. Kyyivs'ka Oblast', NW Ukraine 50.08N 29.59E
99 B22 **Fastnet Rock** *Ir.* Carraig Aonair. *island* SW Ireland
Fastov *see* Fastiv
202 C9 **Fatato** *island* Funafuti Atoll, C Tuvalu
158 K12 **Fatehgarh** Uttar Pradesh, N India 27.22N 79.37E
155 U6 **Fatehjang** Punjab, E Pakistan 33.33N 72.39E
158 G11 **Fatehpur** Rājasthān, N India 27.58N 74.58E
158 L13 **Fatehpur** Uttar Pradesh, N India 25.55N 80.55E
130 J7 **Fatezh** Kurskaya Oblast', W Russian Federation 52.01N 35.51E
78 G11 **Fatick** W Senegal 14.20N 16.29W
106 G9 **Fátima** Santarém, W Portugal 39.37N 8.39W
142 M11 **Fatsa** Ordu, N Turkey 41.01N 37.31E
Fatshan *see* Foshan
202 D12 **Fatua, Pointe** *var.* Pointe Nord. *headland* Île Futuna, S Wallis and Futuna
203 X7 **Fatu Hiva** *island* Îles Marquises, NE French Polynesia
Fatunda *see* Fatundu
81 H21 **Fatundu** *var.* Fatunda. Bandundu, W Dem. Rep. Congo 4.07S 17.13E
31 O8 **Faulkton** South Dakota, N USA 45.02N 99.07W
118 L13 **Făurei** *prev.* Filimon Sîrbu. Brăila, SE Romania 45.04N 27.15E
195 T13 **Fauro** *island* Shortland Islands, NW Solomon Islands
94 G12 **Fauske** Nordland, C Norway 67.15N 15.27E
9 P13 **Faust** Alberta, W Canada 55.19N 115.33W
101 L23 **Fauvillers** Luxembourg, SE Belgium 49.52N 5.40E
109 J24 **Favara** Sicilia, Italy, C Mediterranean Sea 37.19N 13.39E
Faventia *see* Faenza
109 G23 **Favignana, Isola** *island* Isole Egadi, S Italy
10 D8 **Fawn** ≈ Ontario, SE Canada
Faxa Bay *see* Faxaflói
94 H3 **Faxaflói** *Eng.* Faxa Bay. *bay* W Iceland
80 I7 **Faya** *prev.* Faya-Largeau, Largeau. Borkou-Ennedi-Tibesti, N Chad 17.58N 19.06E
Faya-Largeau *see* Faya
197 J5 **Fayaoué** Province des Îles Loyauté, C New Caledonia 20.41S 166.31E
144 M5 **Fayḍāt** *hill range* E Syria
25 O3 **Fayette** Alabama, S USA 33.40N 87.49W
31 X12 **Fayette** Iowa, C USA 42.50N 91.48W
24 J6 **Fayette** Mississippi, S USA 31.42N 91.03W
29 U4 **Fayette** Missouri, C USA 39.09N 92.40W
29 S9 **Fayetteville** Arkansas, C USA 36.03N 94.09W
23 U10 **Fayetteville** North Carolina, SE USA 35.03N 78.52W
22 J10 **Fayetteville** Tennessee, S USA 35.09N 86.34W
27 U11 **Fayetteville** Texas, SW USA 29.52N 96.40W
23 R5 **Fayetteville** West Virginia, NE USA 38.03N 81.06W
147 R4 **Faylakah** *var.* Failaka Island. *island* E Kuwait
145 T10 **Fayşalīyah** *var.* Faisaliya. S Iraq 31.48N 44.36E
201 P15 **Fayu** *var.* East Fayu. *island* Hall Islands, C Micronesia
158 G8 **Fāzilka** Punjab, NW India 30.25N 74.04E
Fdérick *see* Fdérik
78 I6 **Fdérik** *var.* Fdérick, *Fr.* Fort Gouraud. Tiris Zemmour, NW Mauritania 22.40N 12.40W
Feabhail, Loch *see* Foyle, Lough
99 B20 **Feale** ≈ SW Ireland

◆ Country ● Country Capital ◇ Dependent Territory ○ Dependent Territory Capital ◈ Administrative Region ✕ International Airport ▲ Mountain ▲▲ Mountain Range ☒ Volcano ≈ River ◎ Lake ▣ Reservoir

FEAR, CAPE – FOREL, MONT

23 V12 **Fear, Cape** headland Bald Head Island, North Carolina, SE USA 33.50N 77.57W
37 O6 **Feather River** ≈ California, W USA
193 M14 **Featherston** Wellington, North Island, NZ 41.07S 175.19E
104 L3 **Fécamp** Seine-Maritime, N France 49.45N 0.22E
Fédala see Mohammedia
63 D17 **Federación** Entre Ríos, E Argentina 30.57S 58.04W
63 D17 **Federal** Entre Ríos, E Argentina 30.53S 58.45W
79 T15 **Federal Capital District** ◈ capital territory C Nigeria
Federal Capital Territory see Australian Capital Territory
Federal District see Distrito Federal
23 Y4 **Federalsburg** Maryland, NE USA 38.41N 75.46W
76 M6 **Fedjaj, Chott el** var. Chott el Fejaj, Shaṭṭ al Fijāj. salt lake C Tunisia
96 B13 **Fedje** island S Norway
150 M7 **Fedorovka** Kostanay, N Kazakhstan 51.12N 52.00E
131 U6 **Fedorovka** Respublika Bashkortostan, W Russian Federation 53.09N 55.07E
Fëdory see Fyadory
119 U11 **Fedotova Kosa** spit SE Ukraine
201 V13 **Fefan** atoll Chuuk Islands, C Micronesia
113 O21 **Fehérgyarmat** Szabolcs-Szatmár-Bereg, E Hungary 47.58N 22.28E
Fehér-Körös see Crişul Alb
Fehértemplom see Bela Crkva
Fehérvölgy see Albac
102 L7 **Fehmarn** island N Germany
97 H25 **Fehmarn Belt** Dan. Femern Bælt, Ger. Fehmarnbelt. strait Denmark/Germany see also Femern Bælt
Fehmarnbelt see Fehmarn Belt/Femern Bælt
111 X8 **Fehring** Steiermark, SE Austria 46.56N 16.00E
61 B15 **Feijó** Acre, W Brazil 8.07S 70.27W
192 M12 **Feilding** Manawatu-Wanganui, North Island, NZ 40.14S 175.34E
Feira see Feira de Santana
61 O17 **Feira de Santana** var. Feira. Bahia, E Brazil 12.16S 38.52W
111 X7 **Feistritz** ≈ SE Austria
Feistritz see Ilirska Bistrica
167 P8 **Feixi** var. Shangpai. Anhui, E China 31.40N 117.08E
Fejaj, Chott el see Fedjaj, Chott el
113 I23 **Fejér** off. Fejér Megye. ◈ county W Hungary
97 I24 **Fejø** island SE Denmark
142 K15 **Feke** Adana, S Turkey 37.49N 35.55E
Feketehalom see Codlea
Fekete-Körös see Crişul Negru
111 T3 **Feldaist** ≈ N Austria
111 W8 **Feldbach** Steiermark, SE Austria 46.57N 15.52E
103 F24 **Feldberg** ▲ SW Germany 47.52N 8.01E
118 J12 **Feldioara** Ger. Marienburg, Hung. Földvár. Braşov, C Romania 45.48N 25.37E
110 I7 **Feldkirch** anc. Clunia. Vorarlberg, W Austria 47.15N 9.37E
111 S9 **Feldkirchen in Kärnten** Slvn. Trg. Kärnten, S Austria 46.42N 14.01E
Félegyháza see Kiskunfélegyháza
198 B8 **Feleolo** ✈ (Āpia) Upolu, C Samoa 13.49S 171.59W
106 H6 **Felgueiras** Porto, N Portugal 41.22N 8.12W
Felicitas Julia see Lisboa
180 J16 **Félicité** island Inner Islands, NE Seychelles
157 K20 **Felidhu Atoll** atoll C Maldives
43 Y13 **Felipe Carrillo Puerto** Quintana Roo, SE Mexico 19.33N 88.01W
99 Q21 **Felixstowe** E England, UK 51.58N 1.19E
105 N11 **Felletin** Creuse, C France 45.53N 2.12E
Fellin see Viljandi
Felsőbánya see Baia Sprie
Felsőmuzslya see Mužlja
Felsővisó see Vişeu de Sus
37 N10 **Felton** California, W USA 37.03N 122.04W
108 H7 **Feltre** Veneto, NE Italy 46.01N 11.55E
97 H25 **Femern Bælt** Ger. Fehmarnbelt. Fehmarn Belt. strait Denmark/Germany see also Fehmarn Belt
97 I24 **Femø** island SE Denmark
96 I10 **Femunden** ◎ S Norway
106 H2 **Fene** Galicia, NW Spain 43.28N 8.10W
12 I14 **Fenelon Falls** Ontario, SE Canada 44.34N 78.43W
201 U13 **Feneppi** atoll Chuuk Islands, C Micronesia
143 O11 **Fener Burnu** headland N Turkey 41.07N 39.26E
117 J14 **Fengári** ▲ Samothráki, E Greece 40.27N 25.37E
169 V13 **Fengcheng** var. Feng-cheng, Fenghwangcheng. Liaoning, NE China 40.28N 124.01E
166 K11 **Fenggang** var. Longquan. Guizhou, S China 27.57N 107.42E
167 S9 **Fenghua** Zhejiang, SE China 29.38N 121.23E
Fenghwangcheng see Fengcheng
Fengjiaba see Wangcang
166 L9 **Fengjie** var. Yong'an. Chongqing Shi, C China 31.03N 109.29E
166 M14 **Fengkai** var. Jiangkou. Guangdong, S China 23.26N 111.28E
167 T13 **Fenglin** Jap. Hōrin. C Taiwan 23.52N 121.30E
167 P1 **Fengning** prev. Dagezhen. Hebei, E China 41.12N 116.37E
166 E13 **Fengqing** var. Fengshan. Yunnan, SW China 24.38N 99.54E
167 O6 **Fengqiu** Henan, C China 35.01N 114.24E
167 Q2 **Fengrun** Hebei, E China 39.49N 118.10E
Fengshan see Fengqing, Yunnan, China
Fengshan see Luoyuan, Fujian, China
169 T4 **Fengshui Shan** ▲ NE China 52.20N 123.22E
167 P14 **Fengshun** Guangdong, S China 23.51N 116.11E
Fengtien see Liaoning, China
Fengtien see Shenyang, China
166 J7 **Fengxian** var. Feng Xian; prev. Shuangshipu. Shaanxi, C China 33.50N 106.33E
Fengxiang see Luobei
169 P13 **Fengzhen** Nei Mongol Zizhiqu, N China 40.25N 113.09E
166 M6 **Fen He** ≈ C China
159 V15 **Feni** Chittagong, E Bangladesh 23.00N 91.24E
195 Q10 **Feni Islands** island group NE PNG
40 H17 **Fenimore Pass** strait Aleutian Islands, Alaska, USA
86 B9 **Feni Ridge** undersea feature N Atlantic Ocean
Fennern see Vändra
32 J9 **Fennimore** Wisconsin, N USA 42.58N 90.39W
180 J4 **Fenoarivo** Toamasina, E Madagascar 20.52S 46.52E
97 I24 **Fensmark** Storstrøm, SE Denmark 55.16N 11.48E
99 O19 **Fens, The** wetland E England, UK
33 R9 **Fenton** Michigan, N USA 42.48N 83.42W
202 K10 **Fenua Fala** island SE Tokelau
202 F12 **Fenuafo'ou, Île** island E Wallis and Futuna
202 L10 **Fenua Loa** island Fakaofo Atoll, E Tokelau
166 M4 **Fenyang** Shanxi, C China 37.14N 111.40E
119 U13 **Feodosiya** var. Kefe, It. Kaffa; anc. Theodosia. Respublika Krym, S Ukraine 45.03N 35.23E
96 I10 **Feragen** ◎ S Norway
76 L5 **Fer, Cap de** headland NE Algeria 37.05N 7.10E
33 O16 **Ferdinand** Indiana, N USA 38.13N 86.51W
Ferdinand see Montana, Bulgaria
Ferdinand see Mihail Kogălniceanu, Romania
Ferdinandsberg see Oţelu Roşu
149 T7 **Ferdows** var. Firdaus; prev. Tūn. Khorāsān, E Iran 34.00N 58.09E
105 Q5 **Fère-Champenoise** Marne, N France 48.45N 3.59E
Ferencz-Jósef Csúcs see Gerlachovský štít
109 J16 **Ferentino** Lazio, C Italy 41.40N 13.16E
116 L13 **Féres** Anatolikí Makedonía kai Thráki, NE Greece 40.54N 26.12E
Fergana see Farg'ona
153 S10 **Fergana Valley** var. Farghona Valley, Rus. Ferganskaya Dolina, Taj. Wodii Farghona, Uzb. Farghona Wodiysi. basin Tajikistan/Uzbekistan
Ferganskaya Dolina see Fergana Valley
Ferganskaya Oblast' see Farg'ona Viloyati
153 U9 **Ferganskiy Khrebet** ▲▲ C Kyrgyzstan
12 F15 **Fergus** Ontario, S Canada 43.42N 80.22W
31 S6 **Fergus Falls** Minnesota, N USA 46.15N 96.02W
195 N15 **Fergusson Island** var. Kaluwawa. island SE PNG
113 K22 **Ferihegy** ✈ (Budapest) Budapest, C Hungary 47.25N 19.13E
Ferizaj see Uroševac
79 N14 **Ferkessédougou** N Ivory Coast 9.36N 5.12W
111 T10 **Ferlach** Slvn. Borovlje. Kärnten, S Austria 46.31N 14.18E
99 E16 **Fermanagh** cultural region SW Northern Ireland, UK
108 J13 **Fermo** anc. Firmum Picenum. Marche, C Italy 43.09N 13.43E
106 J6 **Fermoselle** Castilla-León, N Spain 41.19N 6.24W
99 D20 **Fermoy** Ir. Mainistir Fhear Maí. SW Ireland 52.07N 8.16W
25 W8 **Fernandina Beach** Amelia Island, Florida, SE USA 30.40N 81.27W
59 A17 **Fernandina, Isla** var. Narborough Island. island Galapagos Islands, Ecuador, E Pacific Ocean
49 Y5 **Fernando de Noronha** island E Brazil
Fernando Po/Fernando Póo see Bioco, Isla de
62 J7 **Fernandópolis** São Paulo, S Brazil 20.12S 50.14W
106 M13 **Fernán Núñez** Andalucía, S Spain 37.40N 4.43W
85 Q14 **Fernão Veloso, Baia de** bay NE Mozambique
36 K3 **Ferndale** California, W USA 40.34N 124.16W
34 H6 **Ferndale** Washington, NW USA 48.51N 122.35W
9 P17 **Fernie** British Columbia, SW Canada 49.30N 115.00W
37 R5 **Fernley** Nevada, W USA 39.35N 119.15W
Ferozepore see Firozpur
109 N18 **Ferrandina** Basilicata, S Italy 40.30N 16.25E
108 G9 **Ferrara** anc. Forum Alieni. Emilia-Romagna, N Italy 44.49N 11.36E
123 H11 **Ferrat, Cap** headland NW Algeria 35.52N 0.24W
109 D20 **Ferrato, Capo** headland Sardegna, Italy, C Mediterranean Sea 39.18N 9.37E
106 G12 **Ferreira do Alentejo** Beja, S Portugal 38.04N 8.06W
58 B11 **Ferreñafe** Lambayeque, W Peru 6.37S 79.45W
110 C12 **Ferret** Valais, SW Switzerland 45.57N 7.04E
104 I13 **Ferret, Cap** headland W France 44.37N 1.15W
24 I6 **Ferriday** Louisiana, S USA 31.37N 91.33W
Ferro see Hierro
109 D16 **Ferro, Capo** headland Sardegna, Italy, C Mediterranean Sea 41.09N 9.31E
106 H2 **Ferrol** var. El Ferrol; prev. El Ferrol del Caudillo. Galicia, NW Spain 43.28N 8.13W
58 B12 **Ferrol, Península de** peninsula W Peru
38 M5 **Ferron** Utah, W USA 39.05N 111.07W
23 S7 **Ferrum** Virginia, NE USA 36.54N 80.01W
25 O8 **Ferry Pass** Florida, SE USA 30.30N 87.12W
Ferryville see Menzel Bourguiba
31 S4 **Fertile** Minnesota, N USA 47.32N 96.16W
Fertő see Neusiedler See
100 L5 **Ferwerd** Fris. Ferwert. Friesland, N Netherlands 53.21N 5.46E
Ferwert see Ferwerd
76 G6 **Fès** Eng. Fez. N Morocco 34.06N 4.57W
81 I22 **Feshi** Bandundu, SW Dem. Rep. Congo 6.07S 18.12E
31 O4 **Fessenden** North Dakota, N USA 47.36N 99.37W
Festenberg see Twardogóra
29 X5 **Festus** Missouri, C USA 38.13N 90.24W
118 M14 **Feteşti** Ialomiţa, SE Romania 44.22N 27.51E
142 D17 **Fethiye** Muğla, SW Turkey 36.37N 29.07E
98 M1 **Fetlar** island NE Scotland, UK
97 I15 **Fetsund** Akershus, S Norway 59.55N 11.03E
10 L5 **Feuilles, Lac aux** ◎ Québec, E Canada
10 L5 **Feuilles, Rivière aux** ≈ Québec, E Canada
101 M23 **Feulen** Diekirch, C Luxembourg 49.52N 6.03E
105 Q11 **Feurs** Loire, E France 45.44N 4.14E
97 F18 **Fevik** Aust-Agder, S Norway 58.22N 8.40E
126 Mm14 **Fevral'sk** Amurskaya Oblast', SE Russian Federation 52.25N 131.06E
155 S2 **Feyzābād** var. Faizabad, Faizābād, Feyzābād, Fyzabad. Badakhshān, NE Afghanistan 37.06N 70.34E
Fez see Fès
99 J19 **Ffestiniog** NW Wales, UK 52.55N 3.54W
Fhóid Duibh, Cuan an see Blacksod Bay
64 I8 **Fiambalá** Catamarca, NW Argentina 27.45S 67.37W
180 I6 **Fianarantsoa** Fianarantsoa, C Madagascar 21.27S 47.04E
180 H6 **Fianarantsoa** ◈ province SE Madagascar
80 G12 **Fianga** Mayo-Kébbi, SW Chad 9.57N 15.09E
Ficce see Fichē
82 J12 **Fichē** It. Ficce. Oromo, C Ethiopia 9.48N 38.43E
103 N17 **Fichtelberg** ▲ Czech Republic/Germany 50.26N 12.57E
103 M18 **Fichtelgebirge** ▲▲ SE Germany
103 M19 **Fichtelnaab** ≈ SE Germany
108 E9 **Fidenza** Emilia-Romagna, N Italy 44.52N 10.04E
115 K21 **Fier** var. Fieri. Fier, SW Albania 40.44N 19.34E
115 K21 **Fier** ◈ district W Albania
Fieri see Fier
Fierza see Fierzë
115 L17 **Fierzë** var. Fierza. Shkodër, N Albania 42.15N 20.02E
115 L17 **Fierzës, Liqeni i** ◎ N Albania
110 F10 **Fiesch** Valais, SW Switzerland 46.25N 8.09E
108 G11 **Fiesole** Toscana, C Italy 43.50N 11.18E
144 G12 **Fifah** Aṭ Ṭafilah, W Jordan 30.55N 35.25E
98 K11 **Fife** var. Kingdom of Fife. cultural region E Scotland, UK
98 K11 **Fife Ness** headland E Scotland, UK 56.16N 2.35W
Fifteen Twenty Fracture Zone see Barracuda Fracture Zone
105 N13 **Figeac** Lot, S France 44.37N 2.01E
97 N19 **Figeholm** Kalmar, SE Sweden 57.12N 16.34E
Figig see Figuig
85 J18 **Figtree** Matabeleland South, SW Zimbabwe 20.20S 28.20E
106 F8 **Figueira da Foz** Coimbra, W Portugal 40.09N 8.51W
107 X4 **Figueres** Cataluña, E Spain 42.16N 2.57E
76 H7 **Figuig** var. Figig. E Morocco 32.09N 1.13W
Fijāj, Shaṭṭ al see Fedjaj, Chott el
197 J14 **Fiji** off. Sovereign Democratic Republic of Fiji, Fij. Viti. ◆ republic SW Pacific Ocean
197 J13 **Fiji** island group SW Pacific Ocean
183 Q8 **Fiji Plate** tectonic feature
107 P14 **Filabres, Sierra de los** ▲▲ SE Spain
85 K18 **Filabusi** Matabeleland South, S Zimbabwe 20.31S 29.16E
44 K13 **Filadelfia** Guanacaste, W Costa Rica 10.24N 85.33W
113 K20 **Fil'akovo** Hung. Fülek. Banskobystrický Kraj, C Slovakia 48.15N 19.53E
205 N5 **Filchner Ice Shelf** ice shelf Antarctica
12 J11 **Fildegrand** ≈ Québec, SE Canada
96 E12 **Filefjell** ▲▲ S Norway
35 O15 **Filer** Idaho, NW USA 42.34N 114.36W
Filevo see Vŭrbitsa
118 H14 **Filiaşi** Dolj, SW Romania 44.32N 23.30E
117 B16 **Filiátes** Ípeiros, W Greece 39.36N 20.19E
117 D21 **Filiatrá** Pelopónnisos, S Greece 37.10N 21.35E
109 K22 **Filicudi, Isola** island Isole Eolie, S Italy
147 Y10 **Filim** E Oman 20.37N 58.11E
Filimon Sîrbu see Făurei
79 S11 **Filingué** Tillabéri, W Niger 14.12N 3.16E
116 K13 **Filiouri** ≈ NE Greece
116 I13 **Fílippoi** anc. Philippi. site of ancient city Anatolikí Makedonía kai Thráki, NE Greece 41.01N 24.16E
97 L15 **Filipstad** Värmland, C Sweden 59.43N 14.10E
110 I9 **Filisur** Graubünden, S Switzerland 46.40N 9.43E
37 R14 **Fillmore** California, W USA 34.23N 118.56W
38 K5 **Fillmore** Utah, W USA 38.57N 112.19W
12 J10 **Fils, Lac du** ◎ Québec, SE Canada
142 H11 **Filyos Çayı** ≈ N Turkey
205 Q2 **Fimbulheimen** physical region Antarctica
205 Q1 **Fimbul Ice Shelf** ice shelf Antarctica
108 G9 **Finale Emilia** Emilia-Romagna, C Italy 44.50N 11.17E
108 C10 **Finale Ligure** Liguria, NW Italy 44.11N 8.21E
107 P14 **Fiñana** Andalucía, S Spain 37.09N 2.47W
180 I6 **Finandrahana** Fianarantsoa, SE Madagascar
23 S6 **Fincastle** Virginia, NE USA 37.29N 79.51W
101 M25 **Findel** ✈ (Luxembourg) Luxembourg, C Luxembourg 49.39N 6.16E
98 J9 **Findhorn** ≈ N Scotland, UK
33 R12 **Findlay** Ohio, N USA 41.02N 83.39W
20 G11 **Finger Lakes** lakes New York, NE USA
85 L14 **Fingoè** Tete, NW Mozambique 15.01S 31.52E
142 E17 **Finike** Antalya, SW Turkey 36.18N 30.07E
104 F6 **Finistère** ◈ department NW France
194 J12 **Finisterre, Mount** ▲ C PNG 5.58S 146.30E
194 J12 **Finisterre Range** ▲▲ N PNG
189 Q8 **Finke** Northern Territory, N Australia 25.37S 134.35E
111 S10 **Finkenstein** Kärnten, S Austria 46.34N 13.53E
201 Y15 **Finkol, Mount** var. Mount Crozer. ▲ Kosrae, E Micronesia 5.18N 163.00E
95 L17 **Finland** off. Republic of Finland, Fin. Suomen Tasavalta, Suomi. ◆ republic N Europe
128 F12 **Finland, Gulf of** Est. Soome Laht, Fin. Suomenlahti, Ger. Finnischer Meerbusen, Rus. Finskiy Zaliv, Swe. Finska Viken. gulf E Baltic Sea
8 L11 **Finlay** ≈ British Columbia, W Canada
191 O10 **Finley** New South Wales, SE Australia 35.41S 145.33E
31 Q4 **Finley** North Dakota, N USA 47.30N 97.50W
Finnischer Meerbusen see Finland, Gulf of
94 K9 **Finnmark** ◈ county N Norway
94 K9 **Finnmarksvidda** physical region N Norway
94 I9 **Finnsnes** Troms, N Norway 69.13N 17.58E
194 K13 **Finschhafen** Morobe, C PNG 6.38S 147.49E
96 E13 **Finse** Hordaland, S Norway 60.35N 7.33E
Finska Viken/Finskiy Zaliv see Finland, Gulf of
97 M17 **Finspång** Östergötland, S Sweden 58.42N 15.45E
110 F10 **Finsteraarhorn** ▲ Switzerland 46.33N 8.07E
103 O14 **Finsterwalde** Brandenburg, E Germany 51.37N 13.43E
193 A23 **Fiordland** physical region South Island, NZ
108 E9 **Fiorenzuola d'Arda** Emilia-Romagna, C Italy 44.57N 9.53E
Firat Nehri see Euphrates
Firdaus see Ferdows
20 M14 **Fire Island** island New York, NE USA
108 G11 **Firenze** Eng. Florence; anc. Florentia. Toscana, C Italy 43.46N 11.15E
108 G10 **Firenzuola** Toscana, C Italy 44.07N 11.22E
12 C6 **Fire River** Ontario, S Canada 48.46N 83.34W
Firling see Fârliug
63 B19 **Firmat** Santa Fe, C Argentina 33.28S 61.28W
105 Q12 **Firminy** Loire, E France 45.22N 4.18E
Firmum Picenum see Fermo
158 J12 **Firozābād** Uttar Pradesh, N India 27.09N 78.24E
158 G8 **Firozpur** var. Ferozepore. Punjab, NW India 30.55N 74.37E
First State see Delaware
149 O12 **Fīrūzābād** Fārs, S Iran 28.51N 52.36E
Fischamend see Fischamend Markt
111 Y4 **Fischamend Markt** var. Fischamend. Niederösterreich, NE Austria 48.06N 16.37E
111 W6 **Fischbacher Alpen** ▲▲ E Austria
Fischhausen see Primorsk
85 D21 **Fish** var. Vis. ≈ S Namibia
85 F24 **Fish** Afr. Vis. ≈ SW South Africa
9 X15 **Fisher Branch** Manitoba, S Canada 51.09N 97.34W
9 X15 **Fisher River** Manitoba, S Canada 51.25N 97.23W
21 N13 **Fishers Island** island New York, NE USA
39 U8 **Fishers Peak** ▲ Colorado, C USA 37.06N 104.27W
15 M6 **Fisher Strait** strait Nunavut, N Canada
99 H21 **Fishguard** Wel. Abergwaun. SW Wales, UK 51.58N 4.49W
21 R2 **Fish River Lake** ◎ Maine, NE USA
204 K6 **Fiske, Cape** headland Antarctica 74.27S 60.28W
105 P4 **Fismes** Marne, N France 49.19N 3.41E
106 F3 **Fisterra, Cabo** headland NW Spain 42.53N 9.16W
21 N11 **Fitchburg** Massachusetts, NE USA 42.34N 71.48W
98 L3 **Fitful Head** headland NE Scotland, UK 59.57N 1.24W
97 C14 **Fitjar** Hordaland, S Norway 59.55N 5.19E
198 Bb8 **Fito** ▲ Upolu, C Samoa 13.57S 171.42W
25 U6 **Fitzgerald** Georgia, SE USA 31.42N 83.15W
188 M5 **Fitzroy Crossing** Western Australia 18.10S 125.40E
65 G21 **Fitzroy, Monte** var. Cerro Chaltel. ▲ S Argentina 49.18S 73.06W
189 Y8 **Fitzroy River** ≈ Queensland, E Australia
188 L5 **Fitzroy River** ≈ Western Australia
12 E12 **Fitzwilliam Island** island Ontario, S Canada
109 J15 **Fiuggi** Lazio, C Italy 41.47N 13.16E
Fiume see Rijeka
109 H15 **Fiumicino** Lazio, C Italy 41.46N 12.13E
Fiumicino see Leonardo da Vinci
108 E10 **Fivizzano** Toscana, C Italy 44.13N 10.06E
81 O21 **Fizi** Sud Kivu, E Dem. Rep. Congo 4.15S 28.57E
Fizuli see Füzuli
94 I11 **Fjällåsen** Norrbotten, N Sweden 67.31N 20.08E
97 G20 **Fjerritslev** Nordjylland, N Denmark 57.06N 9.16E
F.J.S. see Franz Josef Strauss
97 L16 **Fjugesta** Örebro, C Sweden 59.10N 14.50E
Fladstrand see Frederikshavn
39 V5 **Flagler** Colorado, C USA 39.17N 103.04W
25 X10 **Flagler Beach** Florida, SE USA 29.28N 81.07W
38 L11 **Flagstaff** Arizona, SW USA 35.12N 111.39W
67 H24 **Flagstaff Bay** bay Saint Helena, C Atlantic Ocean
21 P5 **Flagstaff Lake** ◎ Maine, NE USA
96 E13 **Flåm** Sogn og Fjordane, S Norway 60.51N 7.06E
13 O8 **Flamand** ≈ Québec, SE Canada
32 J5 **Flambeau River** ≈ Wisconsin, N USA
99 O16 **Flamborough Head** headland E England, UK 54.06N 0.03W
102 N13 **Fläming** hill range NE Germany
18 I17 **Flaming Gorge Reservoir** ⊡ Utah/Wyoming, NW USA
176 Xx13 **Flamingo, Teluk** bay N Arafura Sea
101 B18 **Flanders** Dut. Vlaanderen, Fr. Flandre. cultural region Belgium/France
Flandre see Flanders
31 R10 **Flandreau** South Dakota, N USA 44.03N 96.36W
98 D6 **Flannan Isles** island group NW Scotland, UK
30 M6 **Flasher** North Dakota, N USA 46.25N 101.12W
95 G15 **Flåsjön** ◎ N Sweden
41 O11 **Flat** Alaska, USA 62.27N 158.00W
14 G7 **Flat** ≈ Northwest Territories, NW Canada
94 H1 **Flateyri** Vestfirdhir, NW Iceland 66.03N 23.28W
35 P8 **Flathead Lake** ◎ Montana, NW USA
181 Y15 **Flat Island** Fr. Île Plate. island N Mauritius
179 N14 **Flat Island** island NE Spratly Islands
27 T11 **Flatonia** Texas, SW USA 29.41N 97.06W
193 M14 **Flat Point** headland North Island, NZ 41.12S 176.03E
29 X6 **Flat River** Missouri, C USA 37.51N 90.31W
33 P8 **Flat River** ≈ Michigan, N USA
33 P14 **Flatrock River** ≈ Indiana, N USA
34 E6 **Flattery, Cape** headland Washington, NW USA 48.22N 124.43W
66 B12 **Flatts Village** var. The Flatts Village. C Bermuda 32.19N 64.43W
110 H7 **Flawil** Sankt Gallen, NE Switzerland 47.25N 9.12E
99 N22 **Fleet** S England, UK 51.16N 0.49W
99 K16 **Fleetwood** NW England, UK 53.55N 3.01W
20 H15 **Fleetwood** Pennsylvania, NE USA 40.27N 75.49W
97 D18 **Flekkefjord** Vest-Agder, S Norway 58.16N 6.40E
23 N5 **Flemingsburg** Kentucky, S USA 38.25N 83.43W
20 J15 **Flemington** New Jersey, NE USA 40.30N 74.51W
66 I7 **Flemish Cap** undersea feature NW Atlantic Ocean
97 N16 **Flen** Södermanland, C Sweden 59.03N 16.37E
102 I6 **Flensburg** Schleswig-Holstein, N Germany 54.46N 9.25E
102 J6 **Flensburger Förde** inlet Denmark/Germany
104 K5 **Flers** Orne, N France 48.45N 0.34W
97 C14 **Flesland** ✈ (Bergen) Hordaland, S Norway 60.18N 5.15E
Flessingue see Vlissingen
23 P10 **Fletcher** North Carolina, SE USA 35.24N 82.29W
33 R6 **Fletcher Pond** ◎ Michigan, N USA
104 L15 **Fleurance** Gers, S France 43.50N 0.39E
110 B8 **Fleurier** Neuchâtel, W Switzerland 46.55N 6.37E
101 H20 **Fleurus** Hainaut, S Belgium 50.28N 4.33E
105 N7 **Fleury-les-Aubrais** Loiret, C France 47.55N 1.55E
100 K10 **Flevoland** ◈ province C Netherlands
Flickertail State see North Dakota
110 H9 **Flims** Glarus, NE Switzerland 46.50N 9.16E
190 F8 **Flinders Island** island Investigator Group, South Australia
191 P14 **Flinders Island** island Furneaux Group, Tasmania, SE Australia
190 I6 **Flinders Ranges** ▲▲ South Australia
189 U5 **Flinders River** ≈ Queensland, NE Australia
9 V13 **Flin Flon** Manitoba, C Canada 54.46N 101.51W
99 K18 **Flint** NE Wales, UK 53.15N 3.09W
33 R9 **Flint** Michigan, N USA 43.00N 83.41W
99 J18 **Flint** cultural region NE Wales, UK
29 O7 **Flint Hills** hill range Kansas, C USA
203 Y6 **Flint Island** island Line Islands, E Kiribati
25 S4 **Flint River** ≈ Georgia, SE USA
33 R9 **Flint River** ≈ Michigan, N USA
201 X12 **Flipper Point** headland C Wake Island 19.18N 166.37E
96 I13 **Flisa** Hedmark, S Norway 60.36N 12.01E
96 J13 **Flisa** ≈ S Norway
126 Hh4 **Flissingskiy, Mys** headland Novaya Zemlya, NW Russian Federation 76.43N 69.01E
Flitsch see Bovec
107 U6 **Flix** Cataluña, NE Spain 41.13N 0.32E
97 J19 **Floda** Västra Götaland, S Sweden 57.46N 12.19E
103 O16 **Flöha** ≈ E Germany
27 O4 **Flomot** Texas, SW USA 34.13N 100.58W
31 V5 **Floodwood** Minnesota, N USA 46.55N 92.55W
32 M15 **Flora** Illinois, N USA 38.40N 88.29W
105 P14 **Florac** Lozère, S France 44.18N 3.35E
25 Q8 **Florala** Alabama, S USA 31.00N 86.19W
105 S4 **Florange** Moselle, NE France 49.21N 6.06E
Floreana, Isla see Santa María, Isla
25 O2 **Florence** Alabama, S USA 34.48N 87.40W
38 L14 **Florence** Arizona, SW USA 33.01N 111.23W
39 T6 **Florence** Colorado, C USA 38.20N 105.06W
29 O5 **Florence** Kansas, C USA 38.13N 96.56W
22 M4 **Florence** Kentucky, S USA 39.00N 84.37W
34 E13 **Florence** Oregon, NW USA 43.58N 124.06W
23 T12 **Florence** South Carolina, SE USA 34.12N 79.45W
27 S9 **Florence** Texas, SW USA 30.50N 97.47W
Florence see Firenze
56 E13 **Florencia** Caquetá, S Colombia 1.37N 75.37W
101 H21 **Florennes** Namur, S Belgium 50.15N 4.36E
Florentia see Firenze
65 J18 **Florentino Ameghino, Embalse** ⊡ S Argentina
101 J24 **Florenville** Luxembourg, SE Belgium 49.42N 5.19E
44 E3 **Flores** Petén, N Guatemala 16.54N 89.55W
63 E19 **Flores** ◈ department S Uruguay
175 Pp16 **Flores** island Nusa Tenggara, C Indonesia
66 M1 **Flores** island Azores, Portugal, NE Atlantic Ocean
Floreshty see Floreşti
Flores, Lago de see Petén Itzá, Lago
Flores, Laut see Flores Sea
175 P15 **Flores Sea** Ind. Laut Flores. sea C Indonesia
118 M8 **Floreşti** Rus. Floreshty. N Moldova 47.52N 28.19E
27 S12 **Floresville** Texas, SW USA 29.07N 98.09W
61 N14 **Floriano** Piauí, E Brazil 6.45S 43.00W
63 K14 **Florianópolis** prev. Destêrro. state capital Santa Catarina, S Brazil 27.34S 48.31W
46 G6 **Florida** Camagüey, C Cuba 21.31N 78.13W
63 F19 **Florida** Florida, S Uruguay 34.04S 56.13W
63 F19 **Florida** ◈ department S Uruguay
25 U9 **Florida** off. State of Florida; also known as Peninsular State, Sunshine State. ◈ state SE USA
25 Y17 **Florida Bay** bay Florida, SE USA
56 G8 **Floridablanca** Santander, N Colombia 7.04N 73.06W
195 X15 **Florida Islands** island group C Solomon Islands
25 Y17 **Florida Keys** island group Florida, SE USA
39 Q16 **Florida Mountains** ▲▲ New Mexico, SW USA
66 D10 **Florida, Straits of** strait Atlantic Ocean/Gulf of Mexico
116 D13 **Flórina** var. Phlórina. Dytikí Makedonía, N Greece 40.48N 21.25E
29 X4 **Florissant** Missouri, C USA 38.47N 90.19W
96 C11 **Florø** Sogn og Fjordane, S Norway 61.34N 5.01E
117 L22 **Floúda, Akrotírio** headland Astypálaia, Kykládes, Greece, Aegean Sea 36.38N 26.23E
23 S7 **Floyd** Virginia, NE USA 36.53N 80.21W
27 N4 **Floydada** Texas, SW USA 33.58N 101.20W
Flüela Wisshorn see Weisshorn
100 K7 **Fluessen** ◎ N Netherlands
107 S5 **Flumen** ≈ NE Spain
109 C20 **Flumendosa** ≈ Sardegna, Italy, C Mediterranean Sea
33 R9 **Flushing** Michigan, N USA 43.03N 83.51W
Flushing see Vlissingen
27 O6 **Fluvanna** Texas, SW USA 32.54N 101.06W
194 F14 **Fly** ≈ Indonesia/PNG
204 I10 **Flying Fish, Cape** headland Thurston Island, Antarctica 72.00S 102.25W
Flylân see Vlieland
200 Ss13 **Foa** island Ha'apai Group, C Tonga
9 U15 **Foam Lake** Saskatchewan, S Canada 51.37N 103.31W
115 J14 **Foča** var Srbinje, Republika Srpska, Bosnia and Herzegovina 43.32N 18.45E
118 L12 **Focşani** Vrancea, E Romania 45.45N 27.13E
Fogaras/Fogarasch see Făgăraş
109 M16 **Foggia** Puglia, SE Italy 41.28N 15.31E
Foggo see Faggo
78 D10 **Fogo** island Ilhas de Sotavento, SW Cape Verde
11 U11 **Fogo Island** island Newfoundland and Labrador, E Canada
111 U7 **Fohnsdorf** Steiermark, SE Austria 47.13N 14.40E
102 G7 **Föhr** island NW Germany
106 F14 **Fóia** ▲ S Portugal 37.19N 8.39W
12 I10 **Foins, Lac aux** ◎ Québec, SE Canada
105 N17 **Foix** Ariège, S France 42.58N 1.39E
130 I5 **Fokino** Bryanskaya Oblast', W Russian Federation 53.22N 34.22E
127 N17 **Fokino** Primorskiy Kray, SE Russian Federation 42.58N 132.25E
Fola, Cnoc see Bloody Foreland
96 E13 **Folarskardnuten** ▲ S Norway 60.34N 7.18E
94 G11 **Folda** fjord C Norway
95 E14 **Folda** fjord C Norway
Földvár see Feldioara
95 F14 **Foldereid** Nord-Trøndelag, C Norway 64.58N 12.09E
117 J22 **Folégandros** island Kykládes, Greece, Aegean Sea
25 O9 **Foley** Alabama, S USA 30.24N 87.40W
31 U7 **Foley** Minnesota, N USA 45.39N 93.54W
12 E7 **Foleyet** Ontario, S Canada 48.15N 82.25W
97 D14 **Folgefonni** glacier S Norway
108 I13 **Foligno** Umbria, C Italy 42.58N 12.40E
99 Q23 **Folkestone** SE England, UK 51.04N 1.10E
25 W8 **Folkston** Georgia, SE USA 30.49N 82.00W
96 H10 **Folldal** Hedmark, S Norway 62.08N 10.00E
27 P1 **Follett** Texas, SW USA 36.25N 100.08W
108 F13 **Follonica** Toscana, C Italy 42.55N 10.45E
23 T15 **Folly Beach** South Carolina, SE USA 32.39N 79.56W
37 O7 **Folsom** California, W USA 38.40N 121.11W
118 M12 **Folteşti** Galaţi, E Romania 45.45N 28.00E
180 H14 **Fomboni** Mohéli, S Comoros 12.18S 43.46E
20 K10 **Fonda** New York, NE USA 42.57N 74.24W
9 S10 **Fond-du-Lac** Saskatchewan, C Canada 59.19N 107.09W
32 M8 **Fond du Lac** Wisconsin, N USA 43.48N 88.27W
9 T10 **Fond-du-Lac** ≈ Saskatchewan, C Canada
202 C9 **Fongafale** var. Funafuti. ● (Tuvalu) Funafuti Atoll, SE Tuvalu 8.31N 179.11E
202 G8 **Fongafale** atoll C Tuvalu
109 C18 **Fonni** Sardegna, Italy, C Mediterranean Sea 40.07N 9.17E
201 V12 **Fono** island Chuuk, C Micronesia
56 G4 **Fonseca** La Guajira, N Colombia 10.54N 72.54W
Fonseca, Golfo de see Fonseca, Gulf of
44 H8 **Fonseca, Gulf of** Sp. Golfo de Fonseca. gulf Central America
105 O6 **Fontainebleau** Seine-et-Marne, N France 48.24N 2.42E
65 G19 **Fontana, Lago** ◎ W Argentina
23 N10 **Fontana Lake** ⊡ North Carolina, SE USA
109 L24 **Fontanarossa** ✈ (Catania) Sicilia, Italy, C Mediterranean Sea 37.28N 15.04E
9 N11 **Fontas** ≈ British Columbia, W Canada
60 D12 **Fonte Boa** Amazonas, N Brazil 2.31S 66.01W
104 J10 **Fontenay-le-Comte** Vendée, NW France 46.28N 0.48W
35 T16 **Fontenelle Reservoir** ⊡ Wyoming, C USA
200 Ss12 **Fonualei** island Vava'u Group, N Tonga
113 H24 **Fonyód** Somogy, W Hungary 46.43N 17.31E
Foochow see Fuzhou
41 Q10 **Foraker, Mount** ▲ Alaska, USA 62.57N 151.24W
197 D14 **Forari** Éfaté, C Vanuatu 17.42S 168.33E
105 U4 **Forbach** Moselle, NE France 49.10N 6.54E
191 Q8 **Forbes** New South Wales, SE Australia 33.24S 148.00E
79 T17 **Forcados** Delta, S Nigeria 5.16N 5.25E
105 S14 **Forcalquier** Alpes-de-Haute-Provence, SE France 43.57N 5.46E
103 K19 **Forchheim** Bayern, SE Germany 49.43N 11.07E
176 V14 **Fordate, Pulau** island Kepulauan Tanimbar, E Indonesia
37 R13 **Ford City** California, W USA 35.09N 119.27W
96 D11 **Førde** Sogn og Fjordane, S Norway 61.27N 5.49E
33 N4 **Ford River** ≈ Michigan, N USA
191 O4 **Fords Bridge** New South Wales, SE Australia 29.44S 145.25E
22 J6 **Fordsville** Kentucky, S USA 37.36N 86.39W
29 U13 **Fordyce** Arkansas, C USA 33.49N 92.24W
78 I14 **Forécariah** Guinée-Maritime, SW Guinea 9.28N 13.06W
207 O14 **Forel, Mont** ▲ SE Greenland 66.55N 36.45W

◆ Country ● Country Capital ◇ Dependent Territory ○ Dependent Territory Capital ◈ Administrative Region ✈ International Airport ▲ Mountain ▲▲ Mountain Range Volcano ≈ River ◎ Lake ⊡ Reservoir

9 R17 **Foremost** Alberta, SW Canada *49.30N 111.34W*

12 D16 **Forest** Ontario, S Canada *43.05N 82.00W*

24 L5 **Forest** Mississippi, S USA *32.22N 89.30W*

33 S12 **Forest** Ohio, N USA *40.47N 83.26W*

31 V11 **Forest City** Iowa, C USA *43.15N 93.38W*

23 Q10 **Forest City** North Carolina, SE USA *35.19N 81.52W*

34 G11 **Forest Grove** Oregon, NW USA *45.31N 123.06W*

191 P17 **Forestier Peninsula** *peninsula* Tasmania, SE Australia

31 V8 **Forest Lake** Minnesota, N USA *45.16N 92.59W*

25 S3 **Forest Park** Georgia, SE USA *33.37N 84.22W*

31 Q3 **Forest River** ⇝ North Dakota, N USA

13 T6 **Forestville** Québec, SE Canada *48.45N 69.04W*

105 Q11 **Forez, Monts du** ▲▲ C France

98 K10 **Forfar** E Scotland, UK *56.37N 2.54W*

28 J8 **Forgan** Oklahoma, C USA *36.54N 100.32W*

Forge du Sud *see* Dudelange

103 J24 **Forggensee** ◎ S Germany

153 N10 **Forish** ***Rus.*** Farish. Jizzax Viloyati, C Uzbekistan *40.33N 66.52E*

22 F9 **Forked Deer River** ⇝ Tennessee, S USA

34 F7 **Forks** Washington, NW USA *47.57N 124.22W*

94 N2 **Forlandsundet** *sound* W Svalbard

108 H10 **Forlì** ***anc.*** Forum Livii. Emilia-Romagna, N Italy *44.13N 12.01E*

31 Q7 **Forman** North Dakota, N USA *46.07N 97.39W*

99 K17 **Formby** NW England, UK *53.34N 3.04W*

107 V11 **Formentera** ***anc.*** Ophiusa, ***Lat.*** Frumentum. *island* Islas Baleares, Spain, W Mediterranean Sea

Formentor, Cabo de *see* Formentor, Cap de

107 Y9 **Formentor, Cap de** ***var.*** Cabo de Formentor, Cape Formentor. *headland* Mallorca, Spain, W Mediterranean Sea *39.57N 3.12E*

Formentor, Cape *see* Formentor, Cap de

109 J16 **Formia** Lazio, C Italy *41.16N 13.37E*

64 O7 **Formosa** Formosa, NE Argentina *26.07S 58.13W*

64 M6 **Formosa** ***off.*** Provincia de Formosa. ◐ *province* NE Argentina

Formosa/Formo'sa *see* Taiwan

61 I17 **Formosa, Serra** ▲▲ C Brazil

Formosa Strait *see* Taiwan Strait

97 H15 **Fornebu** ✕ (Oslo) Akershus, S Norway *59.54N 10.37E*

27 U6 **Forney** Texas, SW USA *32.45N 96.28W*

97 H21 **Fornæs** *headland* C Denmark *56.26N 10.57E*

108 E9 **Fornovo di Taro** Emilia-Romagna, C Italy *44.42N 10.07E*

119 T14 **Foros** Respublika Krym, S Ukraine *44.24N 33.47E*

Føroyar *see* Faeroe Islands

98 J8 **Forres** NE Scotland, UK *57.32N 3.37W*

29 X11 **Forrest City** Arkansas, C USA *35.01N 90.48W*

41 Y15 **Forrester Island** *island* Alexander Archipelago, Alaska, USA

27 N7 **Forsan** Texas, SW USA *32.06N 101.22W*

189 V5 **Forsayth** Queensland, NE Australia *18.31S 143.37E*

97 L19 **Forserum** Jönköping, S Sweden *57.42N 14.28E*

97 K15 **Forshaga** Värmland, C Sweden *59.33N 13.28E*

95 L19 **Forssa** Etelä-Suomi, S Finland *60.49N 23.40E*

103 Q14 **Forst** ***Lus.*** Baršć Łužyca. Brandenburg, E Germany *51.43N 14.38E*

191 U7 **Forster-Tuncurry** New South Wales, SE Australia *32.13S 152.31E*

25 T4 **Forsyth** Georgia, SE USA *33.00N 83.57W*

29 T8 **Forsyth** Missouri, C USA *36.41N 93.07W*

35 W10 **Forsyth** Montana, NW USA *46.16N 106.40W*

155 U11 **Fort Abbās** Punjab, E Pakistan *29.11N 72.54E*

10 G10 **Fort Albany** Ontario, C Canada *52.15N 81.34W*

58 L13 **Fortaleza** Pando, N Bolivia *9.48S 65.28W*

60 P13 **Fortaleza** ***prev.*** Ceará. *state capital* Ceará, NE Brazil *3.45S 38.34W*

61 D16 **Fortaleza** Rondônia, W Brazil *8.45S 64.06W*

58 C13 **Fortaleza, Río** ⇝ W Peru

Fort-Archambault *see* Sarh

23 U3 **Fort Ashby** West Virginia, NE USA *39.30N 78.46W*

98 I9 **Fort Augustus** N Scotland, UK *57.13N 4.37W*

Fort-Bayard *see* Zhanjiang

35 S8 **Fort Benton** Montana, NW USA *47.49N 110.40W*

37 Q1 **Fort Bidwell** California, W USA *41.50N 120.07W*

36 L5 **Fort Bragg** California, W USA *39.25N 123.48W*

33 N16 **Fort Branch** Indiana, N USA *38.15N 87.34W*

Fort-Bretonnet *see* Bousso

35 T17 **Fort Bridger** Wyoming, C USA *41.18N 110.19W*

Fort-Cappolani *see* Tidjikja

Fort Charlet *see* Djanet

Fort-Chimo *see* Kuujjuaq

9 R10 **Fort Chipewyan** Alberta, C Canada *58.42N 111.07W*

Fort Cobb Lake *see* Fort Cobb Reservoir

28 L11 **Fort Cobb Reservoir** ***var.*** Fort Cobb Lake. ⊠ Oklahoma, C USA

39 T3 **Fort Collins** Colorado, C USA *40.35N 105.04W*

12 K12 **Fort-Coulonge** Québec, SE Canada *45.51N 76.43W*

Fort-Crampel *see* Kaga Bandoro

Fort-Dauphin *see* Tôlañaro

26 K10 **Fort Davis** Texas, SW USA *30.34N 103.55W*

39 O10 **Fort Defiance** Arizona, SW USA *35.44N 109.04W*

47 Q12 **Fort-de-France** ***prev.*** Fort-Royal. ○ (Martinique) W Martinique *14.36N 61.04W*

47 P12 **Fort-de-France, Baie de** *bay* W Martinique

Fort de Kock *see* Bukittinggi

25 P6 **Fort Deposit** Alabama, S USA *31.58N 86.34W*

31 U13 **Fort Dodge** Iowa, C USA *42.30N 94.10W*

11 S10 **Forteau** Quebec, E Canada *51.30N 56.55W*

108 E11 **Forte dei Marmi** Toscana, C Italy *43.59N 10.10E*

12 H17 **Fort Erie** Ontario, S Canada *42.55N 78.55W*

188 H7 **Fortescue River** ⇝ Western Australia

21 S2 **Fort Fairfield** Maine, NE USA *46.45N 67.51W*

Fort-Foureau *see* Kousséri

10 A11 **Fort Frances** Ontario, S Canada *48.37N 93.22W*

Fort Franklin *see* Délįne

25 R7 **Fort Gaines** Georgia, SE USA *31.36N 85.03W*

39 T8 **Fort Garland** Colorado, C USA *37.22N 105.24W*

23 P5 **Fort Gay** West Virginia, NE USA *38.06N 82.35W*

Fort George *see* La Grande Rivière

29 Q10 **Fort Gibson** Oklahoma, C USA *35.48N 95.15W*

29 Q9 **Fort Gibson Lake** ⊠ Oklahoma, C USA

15 Gg5 **Fort Good Hope** ***var.*** Good Hope. Northwest Territories, NW Canada *66.16N 128.37W*

25 V4 **Fort Gordon** Georgia, SE USA *33.25N 82.09W*

Fort Gouraud *see* Fdérik

98 I11 **Forth** ⇝ C Scotland, UK

Fort Hall *see* Murang'a

26 H8 **Fort Hancock** Texas, SW USA *31.18N 105.49W*

Fort Hertz *see* Putao

98 K12 **Forth, Firth of** *estuary* E Scotland, UK

12 L14 **Forthton** Ontario, SE Canada *44.43N 75.31W*

12 M8 **Fortier** ⇝ Québec, SE Canada

Fortín General Eugenio Garay *see* General Eugenio A. Garay

Fort Jameson *see* Chipata

Fort Johnston *see* Mangochi

21 R1 **Fort Kent** Maine, NE USA *47.15N 68.33W*

Fort-Lamy *see* Ndjamena

25 Z15 **Fort Lauderdale** Florida, SE USA *26.07N 80.08W*

23 R11 **Fort Lawn** South Carolina, SE USA *34.43N 80.46W*

15 Gg9 **Fort Liard** ***var.*** Liard. Northwest Territories, W Canada *60.13N 123.28W*

46 M8 **Fort-Liberté** NE Haiti *19.37N 71.51W*

23 N9 **Fort Loudoun Lake** ⊠ Tennessee, S USA

39 T3 **Fort Lupton** Colorado, C USA *40.04N 104.48W*

9 R12 **Fort MacKay** Alberta, C Canada *57.12N 111.40W*

9 Q17 **Fort Macleod** ***var.*** MacLeod. Alberta, SW Canada *49.43N 113.24W*

31 Y16 **Fort Madison** Iowa, C USA *40.37N 91.15W*

Fort Manning *see* Mchinji

27 P9 **Fort McKavett** Texas, SW USA *30.50N 100.07W*

9 R12 **Fort McMurray** Alberta, C Canada *56.43N 111.22W*

14 Ff3 **Fort McPherson** ***var.*** McPherson. Northwest Territories, NW Canada *67.28N 134.49W*

23 R11 **Fort Mill** South Carolina, SE USA *35.00N 80.57W*

Fort-Millot *see* Ngouri

39 U3 **Fort Morgan** Colorado, C USA *40.13N 103.48W*

25 W14 **Fort Myers** Florida, SE USA *26.39N 81.52W*

25 W15 **Fort Myers Beach** Florida, SE USA *26.27N 81.57W*

8 M10 **Fort Nelson** British Columbia, W Canada *58.48N 122.43W*

8 M10 **Fort Nelson** ⇝ British Columbia, W Canada

Fort Norman *see* Tulita.

25 Q2 **Fort Payne** Alabama, S USA *34.23N 85.43W*

35 W7 **Fort Peck** Montana, NW USA *48.00N 106.28W*

35 V8 **Fort Peck Lake** ⊠ Montana, NW USA

25 Y13 **Fort Pierce** Florida, SE USA *27.28N 80.19W*

31 N10 **Fort Pierre** South Dakota, N USA *44.21N 100.22W*

83 E18 **Fort Portal** SW Uganda *0.39N 30.16E*

15 Hh8 **Fort Providence** ***var.*** Providence. Northwest Territories, W Canada *61.21N 117.39W*

9 U16 **Fort Qu'Appelle** Saskatchewan, S Canada *50.49N 103.52W*

Fort-Repoux *see* Akjoujt

15 I8 **Fort Resolution** ***var.*** Resolution. Northwest Territories, W Canada *61.10N 113.39W*

35 T13 **Fortress Mountain** ▲ Wyoming, C USA *44.20N 109.51W*

Fort Rosebery *see* Mansa

Fort-Rousset *see* Owando

Fort-Royal *see* Fort-de-France

10 I10 **Fort Rupert** ***prev.*** Rupert House. Québec, SE Canada *51.30N 79.45W*

14 G12 **Fort St.James** British Columbia, SW Canada *54.25N 124.15W*

9 N12 **Fort St.John** British Columbia, W Canada *56.16N 120.51W*

Fort Sandeman *see* Zhob

9 Q14 **Fort Saskatchewan** Alberta, SW Canada *53.42N 113.12W*

29 R6 **Fort Scott** Kansas, C USA *37.49N 94.42W*

10 E6 **Fort Severn** Ontario, C Canada *56.00N 87.40W*

33 R12 **Fort Shawnee** Ohio, N USA *40.41N 84.08W*

150 E14 **Fort-Shevchenko** Mangistau, W Kazakhstan *44.28N 50.16E*

Fort-Sibut *see* Sibut

15 H8 **Fort Simpson** ***var.*** Simpson. Northwest Territories, W Canada *61.52N 121.22W*

15 Ii9 **Fort Smith** *district capital* Northwest Territories, W Canada *60.01N 111.55W*

29 R10 **Fort Smith** Arkansas, C USA *35.23N 94.24W*

39 T13 **Fort Stanton** New Mexico, SW USA *33.28N 105.31W*

26 L9 **Fort Stockton** Texas, SW USA *30.54N 102.54W*

39 U12 **Fort Sumner** New Mexico, SW USA *34.28N 104.15W*

28 K8 **Fort Supply** Oklahoma, C USA *36.34N 99.34W*

28 K8 **Fort Supply Lake** ⊠ Oklahoma, C USA

31 O10 **Fort Thompson** South Dakota, N USA *44.01N 99.22W*

Fort-Trinquet *see* Bîr Mogreïn

107 R12 **Fortuna** Murcia, SE Spain *38.10N 1.07W*

36 K3 **Fortuna** California, W USA *40.35N 124.07W*

30 J2 **Fortuna** North Dakota, N USA *48.53N 103.46W*

25 T5 **Fort Valley** Georgia, SE USA *32.33N 83.53W*

9 P11 **Fort Vermilion** Alberta, W Canada *58.22N 115.58W*

Fort Victoria *see* Masvingo

33 P13 **Fortville** Indiana, N USA *39.55N 85.51W*

25 P9 **Fort Walton Beach** Florida, SE USA *30.24N 86.37W*

33 P12 **Fort Wayne** Indiana, N USA *41.07N 85.07W*

98 H10 **Fort William** N Scotland, UK *56.49N 5.07W*

27 T6 **Fort Worth** Texas, SW USA *32.43N 97.19W*

30 M7 **Fort Yates** North Dakota, N USA *46.05N 100.37W*

41 S7 **Fort Yukon** Alaska, USA *66.35N 145.05W*

Forum Alieni *see* Ferrara

Forum Julii *see* Fréjus

Forum Livii *see* Forlì

149 Q15 **Forūr, Jazīreh-ye** *island* S Iran

96 H7 **Fosen** *physical region* S Norway

167 N14 **Foshan** ***var.*** Fatshan, Fo-shan, Namhoi. Guangdong, S China *23.03N 113.05E*

Fossa Claudia *see* Chioggia

108 B9 **Fossano** Piemonte, NW Italy *44.33N 7.43E*

101 H21 **Fosses-la-Ville** Namur, S Belgium *50.24N 4.42E*

34 J12 **Fossil** Oregon, NW USA *44.58N 120.15W*

Foss Lake *see* Foss Reservoir

108 I11 **Fossombrone** Marche, C Italy *43.42N 12.48E*

28 K10 **Foss Reservoir** ***var.*** Foss Lake. ⊠ Oklahoma, C USA

31 S4 **Fosston** Minnesota, N USA *47.34N 95.45W*

191 O13 **Foster** Victoria, SE Australia *38.40S 146.15E*

9 T12 **Foster Lakes** ◎ Saskatchewan, C Canada

33 S12 **Fostoria** Ohio, N USA *41.09N 83.25W*

81 D19 **Fougamou** Ngounié, C Gabon *1.15S 10.37E*

104 J6 **Fougères** Ille-et-Vilaine, NW France *48.21N 1.12W*

Fou-hsin *see* Fuxin

29 S14 **Fouke** Arkansas, C USA *33.15N 93.53W*

98 K2 **Foula** *island* NE Scotland, UK

67 D24 **Foul Bay** *bay* East Falkland, Falkland Islands

99 P21 **Foulness Island** *island* SE England, UK

193 F15 **Foulwind, Cape** *headland* South Island, NZ *41.45S 171.28E*

81 E15 **Foumban** Ouest, NW Cameroon *5.43N 10.49E*

180 H13 **Foumbouni** Grande Comore, NW Comoros *11.49S 43.30E*

205 N8 **Foundation Ice Stream** *glacier* Antarctica

39 T6 **Fountain** Colorado, C USA *38.40N 104.42W*

38 L4 **Fountain Green** Utah, W USA *39.37N 111.37W*

23 P11 **Fountain Inn** South Carolina, SE USA *34.41N 82.12W*

29 S11 **Fourche LaFave River** ⇝ Arkansas, C USA

35 Z13 **Four Corners** Wyoming, C USA *44.04N 104.08W*

105 Q2 **Fourmies** Nord, N France *50.01N 4.03E*

40 J17 **Four Mountains, Islands of** *island group* Aleutian Islands, Alaska, USA

181 P17 **Fournaise, Piton de la** ▲ SE Réunion *21.13S 55.43E*

12 J8 **Fournière, Lac** ◎ Québec, SE Canada

117 L20 **Foúrnoi** *island* Dodekánisos, Greece, Aegean Sea

66 K13 **Four North Fracture Zone** *tectonic feature* W Atlantic Ocean

Fouron-Saint-Martin *see* Sint-Martens-Voeren

32 L3 **Fourteen Mile Point** *headland* Michigan, N USA *46.59N 89.07W*

78 I13 **Fouta Djallon** ***var.*** Futa Jallon. ▲▲ W Guinea

193 C25 **Foveaux Strait** *strait* S NZ

37 Q11 **Fowler** California, W USA *36.35N 119.40W*

39 U6 **Fowler** Colorado, C USA *38.07N 104.01W*

33 N12 **Fowler** Indiana, N USA *40.36N 87.20W*

190 D7 **Fowlers Bay** *bay* South Australia

27 R13 **Fowlerton** Texas, SW USA *28.27N 98.48W*

148 M3 **Fowman** ***var.*** Fuman, Fumen. Gīlān, NW Iran *37.15N 49.19E*

67 C25 **Fox Bay East** West Falkland, Falkland Islands

67 C25 **Fox Bay West** West Falkland, Falkland Islands

12 J14 **Foxboro** Ontario, SE Canada *44.16N 77.23W*

9 O14 **Fox Creek** Alberta, W Canada *54.25N 116.57W*

66 G5 **Foxe Basin** *sea* Nunavut, N Canada

66 G5 **Foxe Channel** *channel* Nunavut, N Canada

97 I16 **Foxen** ◎ C Sweden

16 N4 **Foxe Peninsula** *peninsula* Baffin Island, Nunavut, NE Canada

193 E19 **Fox Glacier** West Coast, South Island, NZ *43.28S 170.00E*

40 L17 **Fox Islands** *island* Aleutian Islands, Alaska, USA

32 M10 **Fox Lake** Illinois, N USA *42.24N 88.10W*

9 V12 **Fox Mine** Manitoba, C Canada *56.36N 101.48W*

37 R3 **Fox Mountain** ▲ Nevada, W USA *41.01N 119.30W*

67 E25 **Fox Point** *headland* East Falkland, Falkland Islands *51.55S 58.24W*

32 M11 **Fox River** ⇝ Illinois/Wisconsin, N USA

32 L7 **Fox River** ⇝ Wisconsin, N USA

192 L13 **Foxton** Manawatu-Wanganui, North Island, NZ *40.30S 175.17E*

9 S16 **Fox Valley** Saskatchewan, S Canada *50.28N 109.28W*

9 W16 **Foxwarren** Manitoba, S Canada *50.30N 101.09W*

99 E14 **Foyle, Lough** ***Ir.*** Loch Feabhail. *inlet* N Ireland

204 H5 **Foyn Coast** *physical region* Antarctica

106 I2 **Foz** Galicia, NW Spain *43.33N 7.16W*

62 I12 **Foz do Areia, Represa de** ⊠ S Brazil

61 A16 **Foz do Breu** Acre, W Brazil *9.21S 72.40W*

85 A16 **Foz do Cunene** Namibe, SW Angola *17.11S 11.52E*

62 G12 **Foz do Iguaçu** Paraná, S Brazil *25.33S 54.31W*

60 C12 **Foz do Mamoriá** Amazonas, NW Brazil *2.28S 66.06W*

107 T6 **Fraga** Aragón, NE Spain *41.31N 0.21E*

46 F5 **Fragoso, Cayo** *island* C Cuba

63 G18 **Fraile Muerto** Cerro Largo, NE Uruguay *32.30S 54.30W*

101 H21 **Fraire** Namur, S Belgium *50.16N 4.30E*

101 L21 **Fraiture, Baraque de** *hill* SE Belgium *50.22N 5.50E*

Frakštát *see* Hlohovec

207 S10 **Fram Basin** ***var.*** Amundsen Basin. *undersea feature* Arctic Ocean

101 F20 **Frameries** Hainaut, S Belgium *50.25N 3.40E*

21 O11 **Framingham** Massachusetts, NE USA *42.15N 71.24W*

62 L7 **Franca** São Paulo, S Brazil *20.33S 47.27W*

197 G4 **Français, Récif des** *reef* W New Caledonia

109 K14 **Francavilla al Mare** Abruzzo, C Italy *42.25N 14.16E*

109 P18 **Francavilla Fontana** Puglia, SE Italy *40.31N 17.34E*

104 M8 **France** ***off.*** French Republic, ***It./Sp.*** Francia; ***prev.*** Gaul, Gaule, ***Lat.*** Gallia. ◆ *republic* W Europe

47 O8 **Francés Viejo, Cabo** *headland* NE Dominican Republic *19.39N 69.57W*

81 F19 **Franceville** ***var.*** Massoukou, Masuku. Haut-Ogooué, E Gabon *1.40S 13.31E*

81 F19 **Franceville** ✕ Haut-Ogooué, E Gabon *1.38S 13.24E*

Francfort *see* Frankfurt am Main

105 T8 **Franche-Comté** ◐ *region* E France

Francia *see* France

31 O11 **Francis Case, Lake** ⊠ South Dakota, N USA

62 H12 **Francisco Beltrão** Paraná, S Brazil *26.04S 53.04W*

Francisco l. Madero *see* Villa Madero

63 A21 **Francisco Madero** Buenos Aires, E Argentina *35.52S 62.03W*

44 H6 **Francisco Morazán** ***prev.*** Tegucigalpa. ◐ *department* C Honduras

85 J18 **Francistown** North East, NE Botswana *21.08S 27.31E*

Franconian Forest *see* Frankenwald

Franconian Jura *see* Fränkische Alb

100 K6 **Franeker** ***Fris.*** Frjentsjer. Friesland, N Netherlands *53.10N 5.33E*

Frankenalb *see* Fränkische Alb

103 H16 **Frankenberg** Hessen, C Germany *51.04N 8.49E*

103 J20 **Frankenhöhe** *hill range* C Germany

33 R8 **Frankenmuth** Michigan, N USA *43.19N 83.44W*

103 F20 **Frankenstein** *hill* W Germany *49.24N 8.04E*

Frankenstein/Frankenstein in Schlesien *see* Ząbkowice Śląskie

103 G20 **Frankenthal** Rheinland-Pfalz, W Germany *49.33N 8.21E*

103 L18 **Frankenwald** ***Eng.*** Franconian Forest. ▲▲ C Germany

46 J12 **Frankfield** C Jamaica *18.07N 77.22W*

12 J14 **Frankford** Ontario, SE Canada *44.12N 77.36W*

33 O13 **Frankfort** Indiana, N USA *40.16N 86.30W*

29 O3 **Frankfort** Kansas, C USA *39.42N 96.25W*

22 L5 **Frankfort** *state capital* Kentucky, S USA *38.12N 84.52W*

Frankfort on the Main *see* Frankfurt am Main

Frankfurt *see* Słubice, Poland

Frankfurt *see* Frankfurt am Main, Germany

103 G18 **Frankfurt am Main** ***var.*** Frankfurt, ***Fr.*** Francfort; ***prev. Eng.*** Frankfort on the Main. Hessen, SW Germany *50.07N 8.40E*

102 Q12 **Frankfurt an der Oder** Brandenburg, E Germany *52.19N 14.31E*

103 L21 **Fränkische Alb** ***var.*** Frankenalb, ***Eng.*** Franconian Jura. ▲▲ S Germany

103 I18 **Fränkische Saale** ⇝ C Germany

103 L19 **Fränkische Schweiz** *hill range* C Germany

25 R4 **Franklin** Georgia, SE USA *33.15N 85.06W*

33 P14 **Franklin** Indiana, N USA *39.28N 86.01W*

22 J7 **Franklin** Kentucky, S USA *36.43N 86.34W*

24 I9 **Franklin** Louisiana, S USA *29.48N 91.30W*

31 O17 **Franklin** Nebraska, C USA *40.06N 98.57W*

23 N10 **Franklin** North Carolina, SE USA *35.07N 83.22W*

20 C13 **Franklin** Pennsylvania, NE USA *41.24N 79.49W*

22 J9 **Franklin** Tennessee, S USA *35.55N 86.52W*

27 U9 **Franklin** Texas, SW USA *31.01N 96.29W*

23 X7 **Franklin** Virginia, NE USA *36.40N 76.55W*

23 T4 **Franklin** West Virginia, NE USA *38.39N 79.19W*

32 M9 **Franklin** Wisconsin, N USA *42.53N 88.00W*

15 H2 **Franklin Bay** *inlet* Northwest Territories, N Canada

34 K7 **Franklin D.Roosevelt Lake** ⊠ Washington, NW USA

37 W4 **Franklin Lake** ◎ Nevada, W USA

193 B22 **Franklin Mountains** ▲▲ South Island, NZ

41 R5 **Franklin Mountains** ▲▲ Alaska, USA

41 N4 **Franklin, Point** *headland* Alaska, USA *70.54N 158.48W*

191 O17 **Franklin River** ⇝ Tasmania, SE Australia

15 K2 **Franklin Strait** *strait* Nunavut, N Canada

24 K8 **Franklinton** Louisiana, S USA *30.51N 90.09W*

23 U9 **Franklinton** North Carolina, SE USA *36.06N 78.27W*

Frankstadt *see* Frenštát pod Radhoštěm

27 V7 **Frankston** Texas, SW USA *32.03N 95.30W*

35 U12 **Frannie** Wyoming, C USA *44.57N 108.37W*

13 U5 **Franquelin** Québec, SE Canada *49.17N 67.52W*

13 U5 **Franquelin** ⇝ Québec, SE Canada

85 C18 **Fransfontein** Kunene, NW Namibia *20.10S 15.03E*

95 H17 **Fränsta** Västernorrland, C Sweden *62.30N 16.06E*

126 H1 **Frantsa-Iosifa, Zemlya** ***Eng.*** Franz Josef Land. *island group* N Russian Federation

193 E18 **Franz Josef Glacier** West Coast, South Island, NZ *43.22S 170.11E*

Franz Josef Land *see* Frantsa-Iosifa, Zemlya

Franz-Josef Spitze *see* Gerlachovský stít

103 L23 **Franz Josef Strauss** ***abbrev.*** F.J.S. ✕ (München) Bayern, SE Germany *48.07N 11.43E*

109 A19 **Frasca, Capo della** *headland* Sardegna, Italy, C Mediterranean Sea *39.46N 8.27E*

109 I15 **Frascati** Lazio, C Italy *41.48N 12.40E*

9 N14 **Fraser** ⇝ British Columbia, SW Canada

85 G24 **Fraserburg** Western Cape, SW South Africa *31.49S 21.29E*

98 L8 **Fraserburgh** NE Scotland, UK *57.41N 2.19W*

189 Z9 **Fraser Island** ***var.*** Great Sandy Island. *island* Queensland, E Australia

8 L14 **Fraser Lake** British Columbia, SW Canada *54.00N 124.45W*

8 L15 **Fraser Plateau** *plateau* British Columbia, SW Canada

192 P10 **Frasertown** Hawke's Bay, North Island, NZ *38.58S 177.25E*

101 E19 **Frasnes-lez-Buissenal** Hainaut, SW Belgium *50.40N 3.37E*

110 I7 **Frastanz** Vorarlberg, NW Austria *47.13N 9.37E*

12 B8 **Frater** Ontario, S Canada *47.19N 84.28W*

Frauenbach *see* Baia Mare

Frauenburg *see* Saldus, Latvia

Frauenburg *see* Frombork, Poland

110 H6 **Frauenfeld** Thurgau, NE Switzerland *47.34N 8.54E*

111 Z5 **Frauenkirchen** Burgenland, E Austria *47.49N 16.57E*

63 D19 **Fray Bentos** Río Negro, W Uruguay *33.09S 58.14W*

63 F19 **Fray Marcos** Florida, S Uruguay *34.13S 55.43W*

31 S6 **Frazee** Minnesota, N USA *46.42N 95.40W*

106 M5 **Frechilla** Castilla-León, N Spain *42.07N 4.49W*

32 I4 **Frederic** Wisconsin, N USA *45.42N 92.30W*

97 G23 **Fredericia** Vejle, C Denmark *55.34N 9.46E*

23 W3 **Frederick** Maryland, NE USA *39.24N 77.24W*

28 L12 **Frederick** Oklahoma, C USA *34.23N 99.01W*

31 P7 **Frederick** South Dakota, N USA *45.49N 98.31W*

31 X12 **Fredericksburg** Iowa, C USA *42.58N 92.12W*

27 R10 **Fredericksburg** Texas, SW USA *30.16N 98.52W*

23 W5 **Fredericksburg** Virginia, NE USA *38.16N 77.27W*

41 X13 **Frederick Sound** *sound* Alaska , USA

29 X6 **Fredericktown** Missouri, C USA *37.33N 90.17W*

62 H13 **Frederico Westphalen** Rio Grande do Sul, S Brazil *27.22S 53.20W*

11 O15 **Fredericton** New Brunswick, SE Canada *45.57N 66.40W*

97 I22 **Frederiksborg** ***off.*** Frederiksborgs Amt. ◐ *county* E Denmark

Frederikshåb *see* Paamiut

97 H19 **Frederikshavn** ***prev.*** Fladstrand. Nordjylland, N Denmark *57.28N 10.33E*

97 J22 **Frederikssund** Frederiksborg, E Denmark *55.51N 12.04E*

47 T9 **Frederiksted** Saint Croix, S Virgin Islands (US) *17.41N 64.51W*

97 I22 **Frederiksværk** ***var.*** Frederiksværk og Hanehoved. Frederiksborg, E Denmark *55.58N 12.01E*

Frederiksværk og Hanehoved *see* Frederiksværk

56 E9 **Fredonia** Antioquia, W Colombia *5.57N 75.42W*

38 K8 **Fredonia** Arizona, SW USA *36.57N 112.31W*

29 P7 **Fredonia** Kansas, C USA *37.31N 95.49W*

20 C11 **Fredonia** New York, NE USA *42.26N 79.19W*

37 P4 **Fredonyer Pass** *pass* California, W USA *40.21N 120.52W*

95 I15 **Fredrika** Västerbotten, N Sweden *64.03N 18.25E*

97 L14 **Fredriksberg** Dalarna, C Sweden *60.07N 14.22E*

Fredrikshald *see* Halden

Fredrikshamn *see* Hamina

97 H16 **Fredrikstad** Østfold, S Norway *59.12N 10.57E*

32 K16 **Freeburg** Illinois, N USA *38.25N 89.54W*

20 K15 **Freehold** New Jersey, NE USA *40.14N 74.14W*

20 H14 **Freeland** Pennsylvania, NE USA *41.01N 75.54W*

190 J5 **Freeling Heights** ▲ South Australia *30.09S 139.24E*

37 Q7 **Freel Peak** ▲ California, W USA *38.52N 119.52W*

16 T7 **Freels, Cape** *headland* Newfoundland and Labrador, E Canada *49.16N 53.30W*

31 Q11 **Freeman** South Dakota, N USA *43.21N 97.26W*

46 G1 **Freeport** Grand Bahama Island, N Bahamas *26.28N 78.43W*

32 L10 **Freeport** Illinois, N USA *42.18N 89.37W*

27 W12 **Freeport** Texas, SW USA *28.57N 95.21W*

46 G1 **Freeport** ✕ Grand Bahama Island, N Bahamas *26.31N 78.48W*

27 R14 **Freer** Texas, SW USA *27.52N 98.37W*

85 I22 **Free State** ***off.*** Free State Province; ***prev.*** Orange Free State, ***Afr.*** Oranje Vrystaat. ◐ *province* C South Africa

Free State *see* Maryland

78 G15 **Freetown** ● (Sierra Leone) W Sierra Leone *8.27N 13.16W*

180 J16 **Frégate** *island* Inner Islands, NE Seychelles

106 J12 **Fregenal de la Sierra** Extremadura, W Spain *38.10N 6.39W*

190 C2 **Fregon** South Australia *26.44S 132.03E*

104 H5 **Fréhel, Cap** *headland* NW France *48.41N 2.21W*

96 F8 **Frei** Møre og Romsdal, S Norway *63.02N 7.47E*

103 O16 **Freiberg** Sachsen, E Germany *50.55N 13.21E*

103 O16 **Freiberger Mulde** ⇝ E Germany

Freiburg *see* Fribourg, Switzerland

Freiburg *see* Freiburg im Breisgau, Germany

103 F23 **Freiburg im Breisgau** ***var.*** Freiburg, ***Fr.*** Fribourg-en-Brisgau. Baden-Württemberg, SW Germany *48.00N 7.52E*

Freiburg in Schlesien *see* Świebodzice

Freie Hansestadt Bremen *see* Bremen

Freie und Hansestadt Hamburg *see* Brandenburg

103 L22 **Freising** Bayern, SE Germany *48.24N 11.45E*

111 T3 **Freistadt** Oberösterreich, N Austria *48.30N 14.27E*

Freistadtl *see* Hlohovec

103 O16 **Freital** Sachsen, E Germany *51.00N 13.40E*

Freiwaldau *see* Jeseník

106 J6 **Freixo de Espada à Cinta** Bragança, N Portugal *41.04N 6.49W*

105 U15 **Fréjus** ***anc.*** Forum Julii. Var, SE France *43.25N 6.43E*

188 I13 **Fremantle** Western Australia *32.07S 115.43E*

37 N9 **Fremont** California, W USA *37.32N 121.56W*

33 Q11 **Fremont** Indiana, N USA *41.43N 84.54W*

31 W15 **Fremont** Iowa, C USA *41.12N 92.26W*

33 P8 **Fremont** Michigan, N USA *43.28N 85.56W*

31 R15 **Fremont** Nebraska, C USA *41.25N 96.30W*

33 S11 **Fremont** Ohio, N USA *41.21N 83.07W*

35 T14 **Fremont Peak** ▲ Wyoming, C USA *43.07N 109.37W*

38 M6 **Fremont River** ⇝ Utah, W USA

23 O9 **French Broad River** ⇝ Tennessee, S USA

23 N5 **Frenchburg** Kentucky, S USA *37.57N 83.41W*

20 C12 **French Creek** ⇝ Pennsylvania, NE USA

34 K15 **Frenchglen** Oregon, NW USA *42.49N 118.55W*

57 Y10 **French Guiana** ***var.*** Guiana, Guyane. ◇ *French overseas department* N South America

French Guinea *see* Guinea

33 O15 **French Lick** Indiana, N USA *38.33N 86.37W*

193 J14 **French Pass** Marlborough, South Island, NZ *40.57S 173.49E*

203 T11 **French Polynesia** ◇ *French overseas territory* C Polynesia

French Republic *see* France

12 F11 **French River** ⇝ Ontario, S Canada

French Somaliland *see* Djibouti

181 P12 **French Southern and Antarctic Territories** ***Fr.*** Terres Australes et Antarctiques Françaises. ◇ *French overseas territory* S Indian Ocean

French Sudan *see* Mali

French Territory of the Afars and Issas *see* Djibouti

French Togoland *see* Togo

76 J6 **Frenda** NW Algeria *35.06N 1.03E*

113 I18 **Frenštát pod Radhoštěm** ***Ger.*** Frankstadt. Moravskoslezský Kraj E Czech Republic *49.33N 18.10E*

78 M17 **Fresco** S Ivory Coast *5.05N 5.34W*

205 U16 **Freshfield, Cape** *headland* Antarctica

42 L10 **Fresnillo** ***var.*** Fresnillo de González Echeverría. Zacatecas, C Mexico *23.10N 102.52W*

Fresnillo de González Echeverría *see* Fresnillo

37 Q10 **Fresno** California, W USA *36.44N 119.48W*

Freu, Cabo del *see* Freu, Cap des

107 Y9 **Freu, Cap des** ***var.*** Cabo del Freu. *headland* Mallorca, Spain, W Mediterranean Sea *39.44N 3.28E*

103 G22 **Freudenstadt** Baden-Württemberg, SW Germany *48.28N 8.25E*

Freudenthal *see* Bruntál

191 Q17 **Freycinet Peninsula** *peninsula* Tasmania, SE Australia

78 H14 **Fria** Guinée-Maritime, W Guinea *10.27N 13.37W*

85 A17 **Fria, Cape** *headland* NW Namibia *18.32S 12.00E*

37 Q10 **Friant** California, W USA *36.56N 119.44W*

64 K8 **Frías** Catamarca , N Argentina *28.40S 65.00W*

110 D9 **Fribourg** ***Ger.*** Freiburg. Fribourg, W Switzerland *46.49N 7.10E*

110 C9 **Fribourg** ***Ger.*** Freiburg. ◐ *canton* W Switzerland

Fribourg-en-Brisgau *see* Freiburg im Breisgau

34 G7 **Friday Harbor** San Juan Islands, Washington, NW USA *48.31N 123.01W*

194 F11 **Frieda** ⇝ NW PNG

Friedau *see* Ormož

103 K23 **Friedberg** Bayern, S Germany *48.21N 10.58E*

103 H18 **Friedberg** Hessen, W Germany *50.19N 8.46E*

Friedeberg Neumark *see* Strzelce Krajeńskie

Friedek-Mistek *see* Frýdek-Místek

Friedland *see* Pravdinsk

103 I24 **Friedrichshafen** Baden-Württemberg, S Germany *47.39N 9.28E*

Friedrichstadt *see* Jaunjelgava

31 Q16 **Friend** Nebraska, C USA *40.37N 97.16W*

Friendly Islands *see* Tonga

57 V9 **Friendship** Coronie, N Suriname *5.49N 56.16W*

32 L7 **Friendship** Wisconsin, N USA *43.58N 89.48W*

111 T8 **Friesach** Kärnten, S Austria *46.58N 14.24E*

Friesche Eilanden *see* Frisian Islands

103 F22 **Friesenheim** Baden-Württemberg, SW Germany *48.27N 7.56E*

Friesische Inseln *see* Frisian Islands

100 K6 **Friesland** ◐ *province* N Netherlands

62 Q10 **Frio, Cabo** *headland* SE Brazil *23.01S 41.59W*

26 M3 **Friona** Texas, SW USA *34.38N 102.43W*

44 L12 **Frío, Río** ⇝ N Costa Rica

27 R13 **Frio River** ⇝ Texas, SW USA

101 M25 **Frisange** Luxembourg, S Luxembourg *49.31N 6.12E*

Frisches Haff *see* Vistula Lagoon

38 J6 **Frisco Peak** ▲ Utah, W USA *38.31N 113.17W*

86 F9 **Frisian Islands** ***Dut.*** Friesche Eilanden, ***Ger.*** Friesische Inseln. *island group* N Europe

20 L12 **Frissell, Mount** ▲ Connecticut, NE USA *42.01N 73.25W*

97 J19 **Fristad** Västra Götaland, S Sweden *57.49N 13.01E*

27 N2 **Fritch** Texas, SW USA *35.38N 101.36W*

97 J19 **Fritsla** Västra Götaland, S Sweden *57.33N 12.46E*

103 H16 **Fritzlar** Hessen, C Germany *51.09N 9.16E*

108 H6 **Friuli-Venezia Giulia** ◐ *region* NE Italy

Frjentsjer *see* Franeker

206 L13 **Frobisher Bay** *inlet* Baffin Island, Nunavut, NE Canada

Frobisher Bay *see* Iqaluit

9 S12 **Frobisher Lake** ◎ Saskatchewan, C Canada

96 G7 **Frohavet** *sound* C Norway

Frohenbruck *see* Veselí nad Lužnicí

111 V7 **Frohnleiten** Steiermark, SE Austria *47.16N 15.19E*

101 G22 **Froidchapelle** Hainaut, S Belgium *50.10N 4.18E*

131 O9 **Frolovo** Volgogradskaya Oblast', SW Russian Federation *49.46N 43.38E*

112 K7 **Frombork** ***Ger.*** Frauenburg. Warmińsko-Mazurskie, NE Poland *54.21N 19.40E*

99 L22 **Frome** SW England, UK *51.15N 2.21W*

190 I4 **Frome Creek** *seasonal river* South Australia

190 J6 **Frome Downs** South Australia *31.17S 139.48E*

◆ Country
● Country Capital
◇ Dependent Territory
○ Dependent Territory Capital
◐ Administrative Region
✕ International Airport
▲ Mountain
▲▲ Mountain Range
Volcano
⇝ River
◎ Lake
⊠ Reservoir

FROME, LAKE – GARDEN CITY

190 J5 **Frome, Lake** *salt lake* South Australia
Fronicken *see* Wronki
106 H10 **Fronteira** Portalegre, C Portugal 39.03N 7.39W
42 M7 **Frontera** Coahuila de Zaragoza, NE Mexico 26.55N 101.27W
43 U14 **Frontera** Tabasco, SE Mexico 18.32N 92.35W
42 G3 **Fronteras** Sonora, NW Mexico 30.51N 109.36W
105 Q16 **Frontignan** Hérault, S France 43.27N 3.45E
56 D8 **Frontino** Antioquia, NW Colombia 6.46N 76.10W
23 V4 **Front Royal** Virginia, NE USA 38.52N 78.09W
109 J16 **Frosinone** *anc.* Frusino. Lazio, C Italy 41.37N 13.19E
109 K16 **Frosolone** Molise, C Italy 41.34N 14.25E
27 U7 **Frost** Texas, SW USA 32.04N 96.48W
23 U2 **Frostburg** Maryland, NE USA 39.39N 78.55W
25 X13 **Frostproof** Florida, SE USA 27.45N 81.31W
Frostviken *see* Kvarnbergsvattnet
97 M15 **Frövi** Örebro, C Sweden 59.28N 15.24E
96 F7 **Frøya** *island* W Norway
39 P5 **Fruita** Colorado, C USA 39.10N 108.42W
30 J9 **Fruitdale** South Dakota, N USA 44.39N 103.38W
25 W11 **Fruitland Park** Florida, SE USA 28.51N 81.54W
Frumentum *see* Formentera
153 S11 **Frunze** Batkenskaya Oblast', SW Kyrgyzstan 40.07N 71.40E
Frunze *see* Bishkek
119 O9 **Frunzivka** Odes'ka Oblast', SW Ukraine 47.19N 29.46E
Frusino *see* Frosinone
110 E9 **Frutigen** Bern, W Switzerland 46.35N 7.38E
113 I17 **Frýdek-Místek** *Ger.* Friedek-Mistek. Moravskoslezský Kraj, E Czech Republic 49.40N 18.22E
200 Qq16 **Fua'amotu** Tongatapu, S Tonga 21.15S 175.08W
202 A9 **Fuafatu** *island* Funafuti Atoll, C Tuvalu
202 A9 **Fuagea** *island* Funafuti Atoll, C Tuvalu
202 B8 **Fualifeke** *atoll* C Tuvalu
202 A8 **Fualopa** *island* Funafuti Atoll, C Tuvalu
157 K22 **Fuammulah** *var.* Gnaviyani Atoll. *atoll* S Maldives
167 R11 **Fu'an** Fujian, SE China 27.11N 119.42E
Fu-chien *see* Fujian
Fu-chou *see* Fuzhou
170 F13 **Fuchū** *var.* Hutyû. Hiroshima, Honshū, SW Japan 34.33N 133.16E
166 M13 **Fuchuan** Guangxi Zhuangzu Zizhiqu, S China 24.56N 111.15E
172 N11 **Fudai** Iwate, Honshū, C Japan 39.59N 141.50E
167 S11 **Fuding** Fujian, SE China 27.21N 120.10E
83 J20 **Fudua** *spring/well* S Kenya 2.13S 39.43E
105 M16 **Fuengirola** Andalucía, S Spain 36.31N 4.37W
106 J12 **Fuente de Cantos** Extremadura, W Spain 38.15N 6.18W
106 J11 **Fuente del Maestre** Extremadura, W Spain 38.31N 6.26W
106 L12 **Fuente Obejuna** Andalucía, S Spain 38.15N 5.25W
106 L6 **Fuentesaúco** Castilla-León, N Spain 41.13N 5.30W
64 O3 **Fuerte Olimpo** *var.* Olimpo. Alto Paraguay, NE Paraguay 21.01S 57.51W
42 H8 **Fuerte, Río** ≈ C Mexico
66 Q11 **Fuerteventura** *island* Islas Canarias, Spain, NE Atlantic Ocean
147 S14 **Fughmah** *var.* Faghman, Fugma. C Yemen 16.07N 49.22E
94 M2 **Fuglehuken** *headland* W Svalbard 78.54N 10.30E
97 B18 **Fugloy** *Dan.* Fuglø *Island* Faeroe Islands 62.21N 6.16W
207 T15 **Fugløya Bank** *undersea feature* E Norwegian Sea
166 E11 **Fugong** Yunnang, SW China
Fugma *see* Fughmah
83 K16 **Fugugo** *spring/well* NE Kenya 3.19N 39.39E
164 L2 **Fuhai** *var.* Burultokay. Xinjiang Uygur Zizhiqu, NW China 47.15N 87.39E
167 P10 **Fu He** ≈ S China
Fuhkien *see* Fujian
102 J9 **Fuhlsbüttel** ✕ (Hamburg) Hamburg, N Germany 53.37N 9.57E
103 L14 **Fuhne** ≈ C Germany
Fu-hsin *see* Fuxin
Fujairah *see* Al Fujayrah
171 J17 **Fuji** *var.* Huzi. Shizuoka, Honshū, S Japan 35.08N 138.39E
167 Q12 **Fujian** *var.* Fu-chien, Fuhkien, Fujian Sheng, Fukien, Min. ◐ *province* SE China
166 I9 **Fu Jiang** ≈ C China
Fujian Sheng *see* Fujian
171 Ii17 **Fujieda** *var.* Huzieda. Shizuoka, Honshū, S Japan 34.54N 138.15E
Fuji, Mount/Fujiyama *see* Fuji-san
169 Y7 **Fujin** Heilongjiang, NE China 47.12N 132.01E
171 J16 **Fujinomiya** *var.* Huzinomiya. Shizuoka, Honshū, S Japan 35.19N 138.34E
171 J16 **Fuji-san** *var.* Fujiyama, *Eng.* Mount Fuji. ▲ Honshū, SE Japan 35.23N 138.44E
171 Jj17 **Fujisawa** *var.* Huzisawa. Kanagawa, Honshū, S Japan 35.22N 139.28E
171 J16 **Fuji-Yoshida** *var.* Huziyosida. Yamanashi, Honshū, S Japan 35.30N 138.48E
172 Oo4 **Fukagawa** *var.* Hukagawa. Hokkaidō, NE Japan 43.44N 142.01E
164 L5 **Fukang** Xinjiang Uygur Zizhiqu, W China 44.07N 87.55E
171 M8 **Fukaura** Aomori, Honshū, C Japan 40.38N 139.55E
200 R15 **Fukave** *island* Tongatapu Group, S Tonga
Fukien *see* Fujian
171 Gg14 **Fukuchiyama** *var.* Hukutiyama. Kyōto, Honshū, SW Japan 35.16N 135.07E
170 B12 **Fukue** *var.* Hukue. Nagasaki, Fukue-jima, SW Japan 32.40N 128.46E
170 B12 **Fukue-jima** *island* Gotō-rettō, SW Japan
171 Hh13 **Fukui** *var.* Hukui. Fukui, Honshū, SW Japan 36.03N 136.12E
171 Hh14 **Fukui** *off.* Fukui-ken, *var.* Hukui. ◐ *prefecture* Honshū, SW Japan
170 C12 **Fukuoka** *var.* Hukuoka; *hist.* Najima. Fukuoka, Kyūshū, SW Japan 33.36N 130.24E
170 Cc13 **Fukuoka** *off.* Fukuoka-ken, *var.* Hukuoka. ◐ *prefecture* Kyūshū, SW Japan
171 L13 **Fukushima** *var.* Hukusima. Fukushima, Honshū, C Japan 37.46N 140.27E
171 Mm7 **Fukushima** Hokkaidō, NE Japan 41.27N 140.14E
171 Kk14 **Fukushima** *off.* Fukushima-ken, *var.* Hukusima. ◐ *prefecture* Honshū, C Japan
170 F14 **Fukuyama** *var.* Hukuyama. Hiroshima, Honshū, SW Japan 34.28N 133.23E
78 G13 **Fulacunda** C Guinea-Bissau 11.46N 15.09W
133 P8 **Fūlādī, Kūh-e** ▲ E Afghanistan 34.37N 67.31E
197 K16 **Fulaga** *island* Lau Group, E Fiji
103 I17 **Fulda** Hessen, C Germany 50.33N 9.40E
31 S10 **Fulda** Minnesota, N USA 43.52N 95.36W
103 I16 **Fulda** ≈ C Germany
Fülek *see* Fil'akovo
Fulin *see* Hanyuan
166 K10 **Fuling** Chongqing Shi, C China 29.45N 107.23E
37 T15 **Fullerton** California, SE USA 33.52N 117.55W
31 P15 **Fullerton** Nebraska, C USA 41.21N 97.58W
110 M8 **Fulpmes** Tirol, W Austria 47.11N 11.22E
22 G8 **Fulton** Kentucky, S USA 36.31N 88.52W
25 N2 **Fulton** Mississippi, S USA 34.16N 88.24W
29 V4 **Fulton** Missouri, C USA 38.51N 91.57W
20 H9 **Fulton** New York, NE USA 43.18N 76.22W
Fuman/Fumen *see* Fowman
105 R3 **Fumay** Ardennes, N France 49.58N 4.42E
104 M13 **Fumel** Lot-et-Garonne, SW France 44.31N 0.58E
171 K17 **Funabashi** *var.* Hunabasi. Chiba, Honshū, S Japan 35.40N 139.57E
202 B10 **Funafara** *atoll* C Tuvalu
202 C9 **Funafuti** ✕ Funafuti Atoll, C Tuvalu 8.30S 179.12E
Funafuti *see* Fongafale
202 F8 **Funafuti Atoll** *atoll* C Tuvalu
202 B9 **Funangongo** *atoll* C Tuvalu
95 F17 **Funäsdalen** Jämtland, C Sweden 62.33N 12.33E
66 O6 **Funchal** Madeira, Portugal, NE Atlantic Ocean 32.40N 16.55W
66 P5 **Funchal** ✕ Madeira, Portugal, NE Atlantic Ocean 32.37N 16.52W
56 F5 **Fundación** Magdalena, N Colombia 10.28N 74.10W
106 I8 **Fundão** *var.* Fundáo. Castelo Branco, C Portugal 40.07N 7.30W
11 O16 **Fundy, Bay of** *bay* Canada/USA
Fünen *see* Fyn
56 C13 **Fúnes** Nariño, SW Colombia 0.58N 77.27W
Fünfkirchen *see* Pécs
85 M19 **Funhalouro** Inhambane, S Mozambique 23.04S 34.24E
167 R6 **Funing** Jiangsu, E China 33.43N 119.47E
166 I14 **Funing** *var.* Xinhua. Yunnan, SW China 23.39N 105.41E
166 M7 **Funiu Shan** ▲ C China
79 U13 **Funtua** Katsina, N Nigeria 11.31N 7.19E
167 R12 **Fuqing** Fujian, SE China 25.40N 119.23E
85 M14 **Furancungo** Tete, NW Mozambique 14.49S 33.32E
172 P5 **Furano** *var.* Hurano. Hokkaidō, NE Japan 43.22N 142.25E
118 I15 **Furculeşti** Teleorman, S Romania 43.51N 25.07E
Füred *see* Balatonfüred
172 Qq7 **Füren-ko** ◎ Hokkaidō, NE Japan
149 R12 **Fürg** Fārs, S Iran 28.16N 55.13E
Furluk *see* Fârliug
Fürmanov/Furmanovka *see* Moyynkum
Furmanovo *see* Zhalpaktal
61 L20 **Furnas, Represa de** ▣ SE Brazil
191 Q14 **Furneaux Group** *island group* Tasmania, SE Australia
Furnes *see* Veurne
166 J9 **Furong Jiang** ≈ S China
144 I5 **Furqlus** Ḩimş, W Syria 34.40N 37.02E
102 F12 **Fürstenau** Niedersachsen, NW Germany 52.30N 7.40E
111 X8 **Fürstenfeld** Steiermark, SE Austria 47.03N 16.01E
103 L23 **Fürstenfeldbruck** Bayern, S Germany 48.10N 11.16E
102 P12 **Fürstenwalde** Brandenburg, NE Germany 52.22N 14.04E
103 K20 **Fürth** Bayern, S Germany 49.28N 10.58E
111 W3 **Furth bei Göttweig** Niederösterreich, NW Austria 48.22N 15.33E
172 O4 **Furubira** Hokkaidō, NE Japan 43.14N 140.38E
96 L12 **Furudal** Dalarna, C Sweden 61.10N 15.07E
171 Ii14 **Furukawa** Gifu, Honshū, SW Japan 36.13N 137.11E
171 M12 **Furukawa** *var.* Hurukawa. Miyagi, Honshū, C Japan 38.36N 140.56E
56 F10 **Fusagasugá** Cundinamarca, C Colombia 4.22N 74.21W
Fusan *see* Pusan
Fushë-Arëzi/Fushë-Arrësi *see* Fushë-Arrëz
115 L18 **Fushë-Arrëz** *var.* Fushë-Arëzi, Fushë-Arrësi. Shkodër, N Albania 42.05N 20.01E
Fushë-Kruja *see* Fushë-Krujë
115 K19 **Fushë-Krujë** *var.* Fushë-Kruja. Durrës, C Albania 41.30N 19.43E
169 V12 **Fushun** *var.* Fou-shan, Fu-shun. Liaoning, NE China 41.49N 123.54E
Fusin *see* Fuxin
110 G10 **Fusio** Ticino, S Switzerland 46.27N 8.39E
169 X11 **Fusong** Jilin, NE China 42.19N 127.16E
103 K24 **Füssen** Bayern, S Germany 47.34N 10.42E
166 K15 **Fusui** *prev.* Funan. Guangxi Zhuangzu Zizhiqu, S China 22.39N 107.49E
Futa Jallon *see* Fouta Djallon
65 G18 **Futaleufú** Los Lagos, S Chile 43.12S 71.53W
114 K10 **Futog** Serbia, NW Serbia and Montenegro (Yugoslavia) 45.15N 19.43E
171 K17 **Futtsu** *var.* Huttu. Chiba, Honshū, S Japan 35.11N 139.52E
197 E16 **Futuna** *island* S Vanuatu
202 D12 **Futuna, Île** *island* S Wallis and Futuna
167 Q11 **Futun Xi** ≈ SE China
166 L5 **Fuxian** *var.* Fu Xian. Shaanxi, C China 36.03N 109.19E
Fuxian *see* Wafangdian
166 G13 **Fuxian Hu** ◎ SW China
169 U12 **Fuxin** *var.* Fou-hsin, Fu-hsin, Fusin. Liaoning, NE China 41.59N 121.39E
Fuxing *see* Wangmo
167 P7 **Fuyang** Anhui, E China 32.54N 115.47E
167 O4 **Fuyang He** ≈ E China
169 U7 **Fuyu** Heilongjiang, NE China 47.48N 124.25E
Fuyu/Fu-yü *see* Songyuan
169 Z6 **Fuyuan** Heilongjiang, NE China 48.20N 134.22E
164 M3 **Fuyun** *var.* Koktokay. Xinjiang Uygur Zizhiqu, NW China 46.57N 89.29E
113 L22 **Füzesabony** Heves, E Hungary 47.44N 20.23E
167 R12 **Fuzhou** *var.* Foochow, Fu-chou. Fujian, SE China 26.09N 119.16E
167 P11 **Fuzhou** *prev.* Linchuan. Jiangxi, S China 27.58N 116.19E
143 W13 **Füzuli** *Rus.* Fizuli. SW Azerbaijan 39.33N 47.09E
121 I20 **Fyadory** *Rus.* Fëdory. Brestskaya Voblasts', SW Belarus 51.56N 26.21E
97 G24 **Fyn** *off.* Fyns Amt, *var.* Fünen. ◐ *county* C Denmark
97 G23 **Fyn** *Ger.* Fünen. *island* C Denmark
98 H12 **Fyne, Loch** *inlet* W Scotland, UK
97 E16 **Fyresvatn** ◎ S Norway
FYR Macedonia/FYROM *see* Macedonia, FYR
Fyzabad *see* Feyẕābād

G

83 O14 **Gaalkacyo** *var.* Galka'yo, *It.* Galcaio. Mudug, C Somalia 6.42N 47.24E
152 J11 **Gabakly** *Rus.* Kabakly. Lebap Welaýaty, NE Turkmenistan 39.45N 62.30E
116 H8 **Gabare** Vratsa, NW Bulgaria 43.20N 23.57E
104 K15 **Gabas** ≈ SW France
Gabasumdo *see* Tongde
37 T7 **Gabbs** Nevada, W USA 38.51N 117.55W
84 B12 **Gabela** Cuanza Sul, W Angola 10.49S 14.21E
Gaberones *see* Gaborone
201 X14 **Gabert** *island* Caroline Islands, E Micronesia
76 M7 **Gabès** *var.* Qābis. E Tunisia 33.53N 10.03E
76 M6 **Gabès, Golfe de** *Ar.* Khalij Qābis. *gulf* E Tunisia
Gablonz an der Neisse *see* Jablonec nad Nisou
Gablös *see* Cavalese
81 E18 **Gabon** *off.* Gabonese Republic. ◆ *republic* C Africa
85 I20 **Gaborone** *prev.* Gaberones. ● (Botswana) South East, SE Botswana 24.42S 25.49E
85 I20 **Gaborone** ✕ South East, SE Botswana 24.45S 25.49E
106 K8 **Gabriel y Galán, Embalse de** ▣ W Spain
149 U15 **Gābrīk, Rūd-e** ≈ SE Iran
116 J9 **Gabrovo** Gabrovo, N Bulgaria 42.54N 25.19E
116 I9 **Gabrovo** ◐ *province* N Bulgaria
78 H12 **Gabú** *prev.* Nova Lamego. E Guinea-Bissau 12.16N 14.09W
31 O6 **Gackle** North Dakota, N USA 46.34N 99.07W
115 I15 **Gacko** Republika Srpska, Bosnia and Herzegovina 43.08N 18.29E
161 F17 **Gadag** Karnātaka, W India 15.25N 75.37E
95 G15 **Gäddede** Jämtland, C Sweden 64.30N 14.15E
165 S12 **Gadê** Qinghai, C China 33.56N 99.49E
Gades/Gadier/Gadir/Gadire *see* Cádiz
107 P15 **Gádor, Sierra de** ▲ S Spain
155 S15 **Gadra** Sind, SE Pakistan 25.39N 70.28E
25 Q3 **Gadsden** Alabama, S USA 34.00N 86.00W
38 H15 **Gadsden** Arizona, SW USA 32.33N 114.45W
Gadyach *see* Hadyach
81 H15 **Gadzi** Mambéré-Kadéï, SW Central African Republic 4.46N 16.42E
118 J13 **Găeşti** Dâmboviţa, S Romania 44.41N 25.18E
109 J17 **Gaeta** Lazio, C Italy 41.12N 13.34E
109 J17 **Gaeta, Golfo di** *var.* Gulf of Gaeta. *gulf* C Italy
196 L14 **Gaferut** *atoll* Caroline Islands, W Micronesia
23 Q10 **Gaffney** South Carolina, SE USA 35.04N 81.39W
Gäfle *see* Gävle
Gäfleborg *see* Gävleborg
76 M6 **Gafsa** *var.* Qafşah. W Tunisia 34.24N 8.51E
Gafurov *see* Ghafurov
153 O10 **Gagarin** Jizzax Viloyati, C Uzbekistan 40.40N 68.04E
103 G21 **Gaggenau** Baden-Württemberg, SW Germany 48.48N 8.19E
196 F16 **Gagil Tamil** *var.* Gagil-Tomil. *island* Caroline Islands, W Micronesia
Gagil-Tomil *see* Gagil Tamil
131 O4 **Gagino** Nizhegorodskaya Oblast', W Russian Federation 55.18N 45.01E
109 Q19 **Gagliano del Capo** Puglia, SE Italy 39.49N 18.22E
96 L13 **Gagnef** Dalarna, C Sweden 60.34N 15.04E
78 M17 **Gagnoa** C Ivory Coast 6.10N 5.56W
11 N10 **Gagnon** Québec, E Canada 51.55N 68.16W
Gago Coutinho *see* Lumbala N'Guimbo
175 Tt8 **Gag, Pulau** *island* E Indonesia
143 P8 **Gagra** NW Georgia 43.17N 40.17E
33 S13 **Gahanna** Ohio, N USA 40.01N 82.52W
149 R13 **Gahkom** Hormozgān, S Iran 28.14N 55.48E
Gahnpa *see* Ganta
59 Q19 **Gaíba, Laguna** ◎ E Bolivia
159 T13 **Gaibanda** *var.* Gaibandah. Rajshahi, NW Bangladesh 25.15N 89.32E
Gaibandah *see* Gaibanda
Gaibhlte, Cnoc Mór na n *see* Galtymore Mountain
111 R9 **Gail** ≈ S Austria
103 I21 **Gaildorf** Baden-Württemberg, S Germany 48.41N 10.08E
105 N15 **Gaillac** *var.* Gaillac-sur-Tarn. Tarn, S France 43.54N 1.54E
Gaillac-sur-Tarn *see* Gaillac
Gaillimh *see* Galway
Gaillimhe, Cuan na *see* Galway Bay
111 Q9 **Gailtaler Alpen** ▲ S Austria
65 J17 **Gaimán** Chaco, S Argentina 43.15S 65.30W
22 K8 **Gainesboro** Tennessee, S USA 36.21N 85.39W
25 V10 **Gainesville** Florida, SE USA 29.39N 82.19W
25 T2 **Gainesville** Georgia, SE USA 34.18N 83.49W
29 U8 **Gainesville** Missouri, C USA 36.36N 92.25W
27 T5 **Gainesville** Texas, SW USA 33.37N 97.09W
111 X5 **Gainfarn** Niederösterreich, NE Austria 47.59N 16.11E
99 N18 **Gainsborough** E England, UK 53.24N 0.48W
190 G6 **Gairdner, Lake** *salt lake* South Australia
Gaissane *see* Gáissát
94 L8 **Gáissát** *var.* Gaissane. ▲ N Norway
45 T15 **Gaital, Cerro** ▲ C Panama 8.37N 80.04W
23 W3 **Gaithersburg** Maryland, NE USA 39.07N 77.07W
169 U13 **Gaizhou** Liaoning, NE China 40.24N 122.16E
Gaizina Kalns *see* Gaiziņkalns
120 H7 **Gaiziņkalns** *var.* Gaizina Kalns. ▲ E Latvia 56.51N 25.58E
Gajac *see* Villeneuve-sur-Lot
174 L15 **Gajahmungkur, Danau** ◎ Jawa, S Indonesia
41 S10 **Gakona** Alaska, USA 62.21N 145.16W
Galaassiya *see* Galaosiyo
Galāğil *see* Jalājil
Galam, Pulau *see* Gelam, Pulau
64 J6 **Galán, Cerro** ▲ NW Argentina 25.54S 66.45W
113 H21 **Galanta** *Hung.* Galánta. Trnavský Kraj, W Slovakia 48.11N 17.45E
152 L11 **Galaosiyo** *Rus.* Galaassiya. Buxoro Viloyati, C Uzbekistan 39.53N 64.25E
59 B17 **Galápagos** *off.* Provincia de Galápagos. ◐ *province* Ecuador, E Pacific Ocean
199 M9 **Galapagos Fracture Zone** *tectonic feature* E Pacific Ocean
200 O10 **Galapagos Rise** *undersea feature* E Pacific Ocean
98 K13 **Galashiels** SE Scotland, UK 55.37N 2.49W
118 M12 **Galaţi** *Ger.* Galatz. Galaţi, E Romania 45.27N 28.00E
118 L12 **Galaţi** ◐ *county* E Romania
109 Q19 **Galatina** Puglia, SE Italy 40.10N 18.10E
109 Q19 **Galatone** Puglia, SE Italy 40.09N 18.04E
Galatz *see* Galaţi
23 R8 **Galax** Virginia, NE USA 36.39N 80.55W
152 J16 **Galaýmor** *Rus.* Kala-i-Mor. Mary Welaýaty, S Turkmenistan 35.40N 62.28E
Galcaio *see* Gaalkacyo
66 P11 **Gáldar** Gran Canaria, Islas Canarias, NE Atlantic Ocean 28.09N 15.40W
96 F11 **Galdhøpiggen** ▲ S Norway 61.30N 8.08E
42 I4 **Galeana** Chihuahua, N Mexico 30.07N 107.35W
43 O9 **Galeana** Nuevo León, NE Mexico 24.45N 99.59W
62 P9 **Galeão** ✕ (Rio de Janeiro) Rio de Janeiro, SE Brazil 22.48S 43.16W
175 T6 **Galela** Pulau Halmahera, E Indonesia 1.52N 127.48E
41 O9 **Galena** Alaska, USA 64.43N 156.55W
32 K10 **Galena** Illinois, N USA 42.25N 90.25W
29 R7 **Galena** Kansas, C USA 37.04N 94.38W
29 T8 **Galena** Missouri, C USA 36.45N 93.30W
47 V15 **Galeota Point** *headland* Trinidad, Trinidad and Tobago 10.07N 60.59W
107 P13 **Galera** Andalucía, S Spain 37.45N 2.33W
47 Y16 **Galera Point** *headland* Trinidad, Trinidad and Tobago 10.49N 60.54W
58 A5 **Galera, Punta** *headland* NW Ecuador 0.49N 80.03W
32 K12 **Galesburg** Illinois, N USA 40.57N 90.22W
32 J7 **Galesville** Wisconsin, N USA 44.04N 91.21W
20 F12 **Galeton** Pennsylvania, NE USA 41.43N 77.38W
118 H9 **Gălgău** *Hung.* Galgó; *prev.* Gîlgău. Sălaj, NW Romania 47.15N 23.44E
Galgó *see* Gălgău
Galgóc *see* Hlohovec
83 N15 **Galguduud** *off.* Gobolka Galguduud. ◐ *region* E Somalia
143 Q9 **Gali** W Georgia 42.40N 41.39E
129 N14 **Galich** Kostromskaya Oblast', NW Russian Federation 58.21N 42.21E
116 H7 **Galiche** Vratsa, NW Bulgaria 43.36N 23.53E
106 H3 **Galicia** *anc.* Gallaecia. ◐ *autonomous community* NW Spain
66 M8 **Galicia Bank** *undersea feature* E Atlantic Ocean
Galilee *see* HaGalil
189 W7 **Galilee, Lake** ◎ Queensland, NE Australia
Galilee, Sea of *see* Tiberias, Lake
108 E11 **Galileo Galilei** ✕ (Pisa) Toscana, C Italy 43.40N 10.22E
33 S12 **Galion** Ohio, N USA 40.43N 82.47W
Galka'yo *see* Gaalkacyo
152 K12 **Galkynyş** *prev. Rus.* Deynau, Dyanev, *Turkm.* Dänew. Lebap Welaýaty, NE Turkmenistan 39.16N 63.09E
82 H11 **Gallabat** Gedaref, E Sudan 12.56N 36.08E
Gallaecia *see* Galicia
153 O11 **G'allaorol** Jizzax Viloyati, C Uzbekistan 40.01N 67.30E
108 C7 **Gallarate** Lombardia, NW Italy 45.39N 8.46E
29 S2 **Gallatin** Missouri, C USA 39.54N 93.57W
22 J8 **Gallatin** Tennessee, S USA 36.23N 86.27W
35 R11 **Gallatin Peak** ▲ Montana, NW USA 45.22N 111.21W
35 R12 **Gallatin River** ≈ Montana/Wyoming, NW USA
161 J26 **Galle** *prev.* Point de Galle. Southern Province, SW Sri Lanka 6.04N 80.11E
107 S5 **Gállego** ≈ NE Spain
200 N9 **Gallego Rise** *undersea feature* E Pacific Ocean
Gallegos *see* Río Gallegos
65 H23 **Gallegos, Río** ≈ Argentina/Chile
Gallia *see* France
24 K10 **Galliano** Louisiana, S USA 29.26N 90.18W
116 G13 **Gallikós** ≈ N Greece
39 S12 **Gallinas Peak** ▲ New Mexico, SW USA 34.14N 105.47W
56 H3 **Gallinas, Punta** *headland* NE Colombia 12.27N 71.44W
39 T11 **Gallinas River** ≈ New Mexico, SW USA
109 Q19 **Gallipoli** Puglia, SE Italy 40.07N 18.00E
Gallipoli *see* Gelibolu
Gallipoli Peninsula *see* Gelibolu Yarımadası
33 T15 **Gallipolis** Ohio, N USA 38.45N 82.13W
94 J12 **Gällivare** *Lapp.* Váhtjer. Norrbotten, N Sweden 67.08N 20.39E
111 T4 **Gallneukirchen** Oberösterreich, N Austria 48.21N 14.22E
107 Q7 **Gallo** ≈ C Spain
95 G17 **Gällö** Jämtland, C Sweden 62.57N 15.15E
109 I23 **Gallo, Capo** *headland* Sicilia, Italy, C Mediterranean Sea 38.13N 13.18E
39 P13 **Gallo Mountains** ▲ New Mexico, SW USA
20 G8 **Galloo Island** *island* New York, NE USA
99 H15 **Galloway, Mull of** *headland* S Scotland, UK 54.37N 4.54W
39 P10 **Gallup** New Mexico, SW USA 35.31N 108.45W
107 R5 **Gallur** Aragón, NE Spain 41.51N 1.21W
Gálma *see* Guelma
37 O8 **Galt** California, W USA 38.13N 121.19W
76 C10 **Galtat-Zemmour** C Western Sahara 25.07N 12.21W
97 G22 **Galten** Århus, C Denmark 56.09N 9.54E
99 D20 **Galtymore Mountain** *Ir.* Cnoc Mór na nGaibhlte. ▲ S Ireland 52.21N 8.09W
99 D20 **Galty Mountains** *Ir.* Na Gaibhlte. ▲ S Ireland
32 K11 **Galva** Illinois, N USA 41.10N 90.02W
27 X12 **Galveston** Texas, SW USA 29.16N 94.48W
27 W11 **Galveston Bay** *inlet* Texas, SW USA
27 W12 **Galveston Island** *island* Texas, SW USA
63 B18 **Gálvez** Santa Fe, C Argentina 31.57S 61.13W
99 C18 **Galway** *Ir.* Gaillimh. W Ireland 53.16N 9.03W
99 B18 **Galway** *Ir.* Gaillimh. *cultural region* W Ireland
99 B18 **Galway Bay** *Ir.* Cuan na Gaillimhe. *bay* W Ireland
85 F18 **Gam** Otjozondjupa, NE Namibia 20.10S 20.51E
194 G14 **Gama** ≈ SW PNG
171 Hh16 **Gamagōri** Aichi, Honshū, SW Japan 34.49N 137.12E
56 F7 **Gamarra** Cesar, N Colombia 8.21N 73.46W
Gámas *see* Kaamanen
164 L17 **Gamba** Xizang Zizhiqu, W China 28.13N 88.31E
Gamba *see* Zamtang
79 P14 **Gambaga** NE Ghana 10.32N 0.28W
82 G13 **Gambēla** Gambēla, W Ethiopia 8.09N 34.15E
83 H14 **Gambēla** ◐ *region*, W Ethiopia 8.09N 34.15E
40 K10 **Gambell** Saint Lawrence Island, Alaska, USA 63.43N 171.40W
78 E12 **Gambia** *off.* Republic of The Gambia, The Gambia. ◆ *republic* W Africa
78 I12 **Gambia** *Fr.* Gambie. ≈ W Africa
66 K12 **Gambia Plain** *undersea feature* E Atlantic Ocean
Gambie *see* Gambia
33 T13 **Gambier** Ohio, N USA 40.22N 82.24W
203 Y13 **Gambier, Îles** *island group* E French Polynesia
190 G10 **Gambier Islands** *island group* South Australia
81 H19 **Gamboma** Plateaux, E Congo 1.52S 15.51E
81 G16 **Gamboula** Mambéré-Kadéï, SW Central African Republic 4.09N 15.12E
39 P10 **Gamerco** New Mexico, SW USA 35.34N 108.45W
143 V12 **Gamış Dağı** ▲ W Azerbaijan 40.18N 46.15E
Gamlakarleby *see* Kokkola
97 N18 **Gamleby** Kalmar, S Sweden 57.54N 16.25E
Gammelstad *see* Gammelstaden
95 J14 **Gammelstaden** *var.* Gammelstad. Norrbotten, N Sweden 65.37N 22.04E
Gammouda *see* Sidi Bouzid
161 J25 **Gampaha** Western Province, W Sri Lanka 07.05N 80.00E
161 K25 **Gampola** Central Province, C Sri Lanka 7.10N 80.34E
176 Uu8 **Gam, Pulau** *island* E Indonesia
178 Jj5 **Gâm, Sông** ≈ N Vietnam
94 L7 **Gamvik** Finnmark, N Norway 71.04N 28.08E
156 H13 **Gan** Addu Atoll, C Maldives
Gan *see* Gansu, China
Gan *see* Jiangxi, China
Ganaane *see* Juba
39 O10 **Ganado** Arizona, SW USA 35.42N 109.31W
27 U12 **Ganado** Texas, SW USA 29.02N 96.30W
12 L14 **Gananoque** Ontario, SE Canada 44.19N 76.10W
Ganāveh *see* Bandar-e Gonāveh
143 V11 **Gäncä** *Rus.* Gyandzha; *prev.* Kirovabad, Yelisavetpol. W Azerbaijan 40.41N 46.22E
Ganchi *see* Ghonchí
Gand *see* Gent
84 B13 **Ganda** *var.* Mariano Machado, *Port.* Vila Mariano Machado. Benguela, W Angola 12.59S 14.37E
81 L22 **Gandajika** Kasai Oriental, S Dem. Rep. Congo 6.42S 24.00E
159 O12 **Gandak** *Nep.* Nārāyāni. ≈ India/Nepal
11 U11 **Gander** Newfoundland and Labrador, SE Canada 48.55N 54.33W
11 U11 **Gander** ✕ Newfoundland and Labrador, E Canada 49.03N 54.49W
102 G11 **Ganderkesee** Niedersachsen, NW Germany 53.01N 8.33E
107 T7 **Gandesa** Cataluña, NE Spain 41.03N 0.25E
160 B10 **Gāndhīdhām** Gujarāt, W India 23.07N 70.05E
160 D10 **Gāndhīnagar** Gujarāt, W India 23.12N 72.37E
160 F9 **Gāndhi Sāgar** ◎ C India
107 T11 **Gandía** País Valenciano, E Spain 38.58N 0.10W
165 O10 **Gang** Qinghai, W China
158 G9 **Gangānagar** Rājasthān, NW India 29.54N 73.55E
158 I12 **Gangāpur** Rājasthān, N India 26.30N 76.49E
159 S17 **Ganga Sāgar** West Bengal, NE India 21.39N 88.04E
Gangavathi *see* Gangāwati
161 G17 **Gangāwati** *var.* Gangavathi. Karnātaka, C India 15.26N 76.35E
165 S9 **Gangca** *var.* Shaliuhe. Qinghai, C China 37.21N 100.09E
164 H14 **Gangdisê Shan** *Eng.* Kailas Range. ▲ W China
105 Q15 **Ganges** Hérault, S France 43.57N 3.42E
159 P13 **Ganges** *Ben.* Padma. ≈ Bangladesh/India *see also* Padma
Ganges Cone *see* Ganges Fan
181 S3 **Ganges Fan** *var.* Ganges Cone. *undersea feature* N Bay of Bengal
159 U17 **Ganges, Mouths of the** *delta* Bangladesh/India
109 K23 **Gangi** *anc.* Engyum. Sicilia, Italy, C Mediterranean Sea 37.48N 14.13E
158 K8 **Gangotri** Uttaranchal, N India 30.55N 79.01E
Gangra *see* Çankırı
159 S11 **Gangtok** Sikkim, N India 27.19N 88.39E
165 W11 **Gangu** Gansu, C China 34.46N 105.21E
169 U5 **Gan He** ≈ NE China
175 T9 **Gani** Pulau Halmahera, E Indonesia 0.45S 128.13E
167 O12 **Gan Jiang** ≈ S China
169 U11 **Ganjig** *var.* Horqin Zuoyi Houqi. Nei Mongol Zizhiqu, N China 42.53N 122.22E
152 H15 **Gannaly** Ahal Welaýaty, S Turkmenistan 37.02N 60.43E
169 U7 **Gannan** Heilongjiang, NE China 47.58N 123.36E
105 P10 **Gannat** Allier, C France 46.06N 3.12E
35 T14 **Gannett Peak** ▲ Wyoming, C USA 43.10N 109.39W
31 O10 **Gannvalley** South Dakota, N USA 44.01N 98.59W
Ganqu *see* Lhünzhub
111 Y3 **Gänserndorf** Niederösterreich, NE Austria 48.22N 16.43E
Gansos, Lago dos *see* Goose Lake
165 T9 **Gansu** *var.* Gan, Gansu Sheng, Kansu. ◐ *province* N China
Gansu Sheng *see* Gansu
78 K16 **Ganta** *var.* Gahnpa. NE Liberia 7.15N 8.58W
190 H11 **Gantheaume, Cape** *headland* South Australia 36.04S 137.28E
Gantsevichi *see* Hantsavichy
167 Q6 **Ganyu** *var.* Qingkou. Jiangsu, E China 34.55N 119.06E
150 D12 **Ganyushkino** Atyrau, SW Kazakhstan 46.35N 49.15E
167 O12 **Ganzhou** Jiangxi, S China 25.51N 114.58E
Ganzhou *see* Zhangye
79 Q10 **Gao** Gao, E Mali 16.15N 0.03E
79 R10 **Gao** ◐ *region* SE Mali
167 O10 **Gao'an** Jiangxi, S China 28.24N 115.27E
Gaocheng *see* Litang
Gaoleshan *see* Xianfeng
167 R5 **Gaomi** Shandong, E China 36.23N 119.44E
167 N5 **Gaoping** Shanxi, C China 35.51N 112.55E
165 S8 **Gaotai** Gansu, N China 39.22N 99.44E
Gaoth Dobhair *see* Gweedore
79 O14 **Gaoua** SW Burkina 10.18N 3.12W
78 I13 **Gaoual** Moyenne-Guinée, N Guinea 11.43N 13.13W
Gaoxiong *see* Kaohsiung
167 R7 **Gaoyou** *var.* Dayishan. Jiangsu, E China 32.45N 119.30E
167 R7 **Gaoyou Hu** ◎ E China
166 M15 **Gaozhou** Guangdong, S China 21.56N 110.49E
105 T13 **Gap** *anc.* Vapincum. Hautes-Alpes, SE France 44.33N 6.04E
152 E9 **Gaplaňgyr Platosy** *Rus.* Plato Kaplangky. *ridge* Turkmenistan/Uzbekistan
164 G13 **Gar** *var.* Gar Xincun. Xizang Zizhiqu, W China 32.04N 80.01E
Garabekevyul *see* Garabekewül
152 L13 **Garabekewül** *Rus.* Garabekevyul, Karabekaul. Lebap Welaýaty, E Turkmenistan 38.31N 64.04E
152 K15 **Garabil Belentligi** *Rus.* Vozvyshennost' Karabil'. ▲ S Turkmenistan
152 B9 **Garabogaz Aylagy** *Rus.* Zaliv Kara-Bogaz-Gol. *bay* NW Turkmenistan
152 A9 **Garabogazköl** *Rus.* Kara-Bogaz-Kol. Balkan Welaýaty, NW Turkmenistan 41.03N 52.52E
45 V16 **Garachiné** Darién, SE Panama 8.03N 78.22W
45 V16 **Garachiné, Punta** *headland* SE Panama 8.05N 78.23W
152 K12 **Garagan** *Rus.* Karagan. Ahal Welaýaty, C Turkmenistan 38.16N 57.34E
56 G10 **Garagoa** Boyacá, C Colombia 5.04N 73.19W
152 A11 **Garagöl** *Rus.* Karagel'. Balkan Welaýaty, W Turkmenistan 39.24N 53.13E
152 F12 **Garagum** *var.* Garagumy, Qara Qum, *Eng.* Black Sand Desert, Kara Kum; *prev.* Peski Karakumy. *desert* C Turkmenistan
152 E12 **Garagum Kanaly** *var.* Kara Kum Canal, *Rus.* Garagumskiy Kanal, Karakumskiy Kanal. *canal* C Turkmenistan
Garagumskiy Kanal *see* Garagum Kanaly
Garagumy *see* Garagum
191 S4 **Garah** New South Wales, SE Australia 29.07S 149.37E
66 O11 **Garajonay** ▲ Gomera, Islas Canarias, NE Atlantic Ocean 28.07N 17.13W
116 M8 **Gara Khitrino** Shumen, NE Bulgaria 43.26N 26.55E
78 L13 **Garalo** Sikasso, SW Mali 10.58N 7.26W
Garam *see* Hron
152 L14 **Garamätnyýaz** *Rus.* Karamet-Niyaz. Lebap Welaýaty, E Turkmenistan 37.45N 64.28E
Garamszentkereszt *see* Žiar nad Hronom
79 Q13 **Garango** S Burkina 11.45N 0.30W
61 Q15 **Garanhuns** Pernambuco, E Brazil 8.52S 36.28W
196 H5 **Garapan** Saipan, S Northern Mariana Islands 15.12S 145.43E
Gárasavvon *see* Karesuando
Gárassavon *see* Kaaresuvanto
80 J13 **Garba** Bamingui-Bangoran, N Central African Republic 9.09N 20.24E
Garba *see* Jiulong
83 L16 **Garbahaarrey** *It.* Garba Harre. Gedo, SW Somalia 3.14N 42.18E
Garba Harre *see* Garbahaarrey
83 J18 **Garba Tula** Eastern, C Kenya 0.31N 38.35E
29 N9 **Garber** Oklahoma, C USA 36.26N 97.35W
36 L4 **Garberville** California, W USA 40.07N 123.48W
Garbo *see* Lhozhag
102 I12 **Garbsen** Niedersachsen, N Germany 52.24N 9.36E
62 K9 **Garça** São Paulo, S Brazil 22.13S 49.36W
106 L10 **García de Solá, Embalse de** ▣ C Spain
105 Q14 **Gard** ◐ *department* S France
105 Q14 **Gard** ≈ S France
108 F7 **Garda, Lago di** *var.* Benaco, *Eng.* Lake Garda, *Ger.* Gardasee. ◎ NE Italy
Garda, Lake *see* Garda, Lago di
Gardan Divāl *see* Gardan Dīwāl
155 Q5 **Gardan Dīwāl** *var.* Gardan Divāl. Wardag, C Afghanistan 34.30N 68.15E
105 S15 **Gardanne** Bouches-du-Rhône, SE France 43.27N 5.28E
Gardasee *see* Garda, Lago di
102 L12 **Gardelegen** Sachsen-Anhalt, C Germany 52.31N 11.25E
12 B10 **Garden** ≈ Ontario, S Canada
25 X6 **Garden City** Georgia, SE USA 32.06N 81.09W
28 I6 **Garden City** Kansas, C USA 37.58N 100.52W
29 S5 **Garden City** Missouri, C USA 38.34N 94.12W

◆ Country ● Country Capital ◇ Dependent Territory ○ Dependent Territory Capital ◐ Administrative Region ✕ International Airport ▲ Mountain ▲ Mountain Range ⩕ Volcano ≈ River ◎ Lake ▣ Reservoir

GARDEN CITY – GHIZO

27 N8 Garden City Texas, SW USA 31.50N 101.29W
25 P3 Gardendale Alabama, S USA 33.39N 86.48W
33 P5 Garden Island island Michigan, N USA
24 M11 Garden Island Bay bay Louisiana, S USA
33 O5 Garden Peninsula peninsula Michigan, N USA
Garden State see New Jersey
97 I14 Gardermoen Akershus, S Norway 60.10N 11.04E
Gardeyz see Gardēz
155 Q6 Gardēz var. Gardeyz, Gordiaz. Paktiā, E Afghanistan 33.34N 69.14E
95 G14 Gardiken ◎ N Sweden
21 Q7 Gardiner Maine, NE USA 44.13N 69.46W
35 S12 Gardiner Montana, NW USA 45.02N 110.42W
21 N13 Gardiners Island island New York, NE USA
Gardner Island see Nikumaroro
21 T6 Gardner Lake ◎ Maine, NE USA
37 Q6 Gardnerville Nevada, W USA 38.55N 119.44W
Gardo see Qardho
108 F7 Gardone Val Trompia Lombardia, N Italy 45.40N 10.11E
Garegegasnjárga see Karigasniemi
40 F17 Gareloi Island island Aleutian Islands, Alaska, USA
Gares see Puente la Reina
108 B10 Garessio Piemonte, NE Italy 44.14N 8.01E
34 M9 Garfield Washington, NW USA 47.00N 117.07W
33 U11 Garfield Heights Ohio, N USA 41.25N 81.36W
Gargaliani see Gargaliánoi
117 D21 Gargaliánoi var. Gargaliani. Pelopónnisos, S Greece 37.04N 21.37E
109 N15 Gargano, Promontorio del headland SE Italy 41.51N 16.11E
110 I8 Gargellen Graubünden, W Switzerland 46.57N 9.55E
95 I14 Gargnäs Västerbotten, N Sweden 65.19N 18.00E
120 C11 Gargždai Klaipėda, W Lithuania 55.42N 21.24E
160 J13 Garhchiroli Mahārāshtra, C India 20.14N 79.58E
159 O15 Garhwa Jhārkhand, N India 24.07N 83.52E
176 Ww11 Gariau Papua, E Indonesia 3.43S 134.54E
85 E24 Garies Northern Cape, W South Africa 30.25S 17.55E
109 K17 Garigliano ≈ C Italy
83 K19 Garissa Coast, E Kenya 0.27S 39.39E
23 V11 Garland North Carolina, SE USA 34.45N 78.25W
27 T6 Garland Texas, SW USA 32.54N 96.36W
38 L1 Garland Utah, W USA 41.43N 112.07W
108 D8 Garlasco Lombardia, N Italy 45.12N 8.59E
121 F14 Garliava Kaunas, S Lithuania 54.49N 23.52E
Garm see Gharm
148 M9 Garm, Āb-e var. Rūd-e Khersān. ≈ SW Iran
103 K25 Garmisch-Partenkirchen Bayern, S Germany 47.30N 11.06E
149 O5 Garmsār prev. Qishlaq. Semnān, N Iran 35.18N 52.21E
Garmser see Darvishān
31 V12 Garner Iowa, C USA 43.06N 93.36W
23 U9 Garner North Carolina, SE USA 35.42N 78.36W
29 Q5 Garnett Kansas, C USA 38.16N 95.14W
101 M25 Garnich Luxembourg, SW Luxembourg 49.37N 5.57E
190 M8 Garnpung, Lake salt lake New South Wales, SE Australia
Garoe see Garoowe
Garoet see Garut
159 U13 Gāro Hills hill range NE India
104 K13 Garonne anc. Garumna. ≈ S France
82 P13 Garoowe var. Garoe. Nugaal, N Somalia 8.24N 48.29E
80 F12 Garoua var. Garua. Nord, N Cameroon 9.16N 13.22E
81 G14 Garoua Boulaï Est, E Cameroon 5.54N 14.33E
79 O10 Garou, Lac ◎ C Mali
194 M11 Garove Island island Witu Islands, C PNG
97 L16 Garphyttan Örebro, C Sweden 59.18N 14.54E
31 R11 Garretson South Dakota, N USA 43.43N 96.30W
33 Q11 Garrett Indiana, N USA 41.21N 85.08W
35 Q10 Garrison Montana, NW USA 46.32N 112.46W
30 M4 Garrison North Dakota, N USA 47.36N 101.25W
27 X8 Garrison Texas, SW USA 31.49N 94.29W
30 L4 Garrison Dam dam North Dakota, N USA 47.29N 101.24W
106 J9 Garrovillas Extremadura, W Spain 39.43N 6.33W
152 D12 Garrygala Rus. Kara-Kala. Balkan Welaýaty, W Turkmenistan 38.27N 56.15E
15 Jj6 Garry Lake ◎ Nunavut, N Canada
Gars see Gars am Kamp
111 W3 Gars am Kamp var. Gars. Niederösterreich, NE Austria 48.35N 15.40E
83 K20 Garsen Coast, S Kenya 2.16S 40.07E
Garshy see Garşy
12 F10 Garson Ontario, S Canada 46.33N 80.51W
111 T5 Garsten Oberösterreich, N Austria 48.00N 14.24E
152 A9 Garşy var. Garshy, Rus. Karshi. Balkan Welaýaty, NW Turkmenistan 40.45N 52.50E
Gartar see Qianning
104 M10 Gartempe ≈ C France
Gartog see Markam
Garua see Garoua
85 D21 Garub Karas, SW Namibia 26.33S 16.00E
Garumna see Garonne
174 Jj15 Garut prev. Garoet. Jawa, C Indonesia 7.15S 107.55E
193 C20 Garvie Mountains ▲▲ South Island, NZ
112 N12 Garwolin Mazowieckie, E Poland 51.53N 21.36E
27 U12 Garwood Texas, SW USA 29.25N 96.25W
Gar Xincun see Gar
33 N11 Gary Indiana, N USA 41.35N 87.21W
27 X7 Gary Texas, SW USA 32.00N 94.21W
170 E12 Garyū-san ▲ Kyūshū, SW Japan 34.40N 132.12E
164 G13 Gar Zangbo ≈ W China
166 F8 Garzê Sichuan, C China 31.40N 99.58E
56 E12 Garzón Huila, S Colombia 2.13N 75.37W
Gasan-Kuli see Esenguly
33 P13 Gas City Indiana, N USA 40.29N 85.36W
104 K15 Gascogne Eng. Gascony. cultural region S France
Gascogne, Golfe de see Gascony, Gulf of
28 V5 Gasconade River ≈ Missouri, C USA
Gascony see Gascogne
188 H9 Gascoyne Junction Western Australia 25.06S 115.10E
181 V8 Gascoyne Plain undersea feature E Indian Ocean
188 H9 Gascoyne River ≈ Western Australia
199 I12 Gascoyne Tablemount undersea feature N Tasman Sea 36.30S 156.30E
69 U6 Gash var. Nahr al Qāsh. ≈ W Sudan
155 X3 Gasherbrum ▲ NE Pakistan 35.39N 76.34E
Gas Hu see Gas Hure Hu
79 X12 Gashua Yobe, NE Nigeria 12.55N 11.10E
165 N9 Gas Hure Hu var. Gas Hu. ◎ C China
176 Uu9 Gasim Papua, E Indonesia 1.21S 131.27E
195 N12 Gasmata New Britain, E PNG 6.12S 150.25E
25 V14 Gasparilla Island island Florida, SE USA
174 Jj11 Gaspar, Selat strait W Indonesia
13 Y6 Gaspé Québec, SE Canada 48.50N 64.33W
13 Z6 Gaspé, Cap de headland Québec, SE Canada 48.45N 64.10W
13 X6 Gaspé, Péninsule de var. Péninsule de la Gaspésie. peninsula Québec, SE Canada
Gaspésie, Péninsule de la see Gaspé, Péninsule de
171 Ll12 Gas-san ▲ Honshū, C Japan 38.33N 140.02E
79 W15 Gassol Taraba, E Nigeria 8.28N 10.24E
Gastein see Badgastein
23 R10 Gastonia North Carolina, SE USA 35.15N 81.11W
23 V8 Gaston, Lake ⊠ North Carolina/Virginia, SE USA
117 D19 Gastoúni Dytikí Ellás, S Greece 37.51N 21.15E
65 I17 Gastre Chubut, S Argentina 42.20S 69.10W
Gat see Ghāt
107 P15 Gata, Cabo de headland S Spain 36.43N 2.11W
Gata, Cape see Gátas, Akrotíri
107 T11 Gata de Gorgos País Valenciano, E Spain 38.45N 0.06E
118 E12 Gătaia Ger. Gataja, Hung. Gátalja; prev. Gáttája. Timiş, W Romania 45.24N 21.25E
Gataja/Gátalja see Gătaia
124 Nn4 Gátas, Akrotíri var. Cape Gata. headland S Cyprus 34.34N 33.03E
106 J8 Gata, Sierra de ▲▲ W Spain
128 G13 Gatchina Leningradskaya Oblast', NW Russian Federation 59.33N 30.06E
23 P8 Gate City Virginia, NE USA 36.38N 82.34W
99 M14 Gateshead NE England, UK 54.57N 1.37W
15 Jj2 Gateshead Island island Nunavut, N Canada
23 X8 Gatesville North Carolina, SE USA 36.23N 76.43W
27 S8 Gatesville Texas, SW USA 31.26N 97.44W
12 L12 Gatineau Québec, SE Canada 45.28N 75.40W
12 L11 Gatineau ≈ Ontario/Québec, SE Canada
23 N9 Gatlinburg Tennessee, S USA 35.42N 83.30W
Gatooma see Kadoma
Gáttája see Gătaia
45 T14 Gatún, Lago ⊠ C Panama
61 N14 Gaturiano Piauí, NE Brazil 6.53S 41.45W
99 O22 Gatwick ✕ (London) SE England, UK 51.10N 0.12W
197 J15 Gau prev. Ngau. island C Fiji
197 C11 Gaua var Santa Maria, island Banks Islands, N Vanuatu
106 L16 Gaucín Andalucía, S Spain 36.31N 5.19W
Gauhāti see Guwāhāti
120 I8 Gauja Ger. Aa. ≈ Estonia/Latvia
120 I7 Gaujiena Alūksne, NE Latvia 57.31N 26.24E
Gaul/Gaule see France
96 H9 Gauldalen valley S Norway
23 R5 Gauley River ≈ West Virginia, NE USA
101 D19 Gaurain-Ramecroix Hainaut, SW Belgium 50.35N 3.31E
97 F15 Gaustatoppen ▲ S Norway 59.50N 8.39E
85 J21 Gauteng off. Gauteng Province; prev. Pretoria-Witwatersrand-Vereeniging. ◐ province NE South Africa
Gauteng see Germiston, South Africa
Gauteng see Johannesburg, South Africa
176 Y10 Gauttier, Pegunungan ▲▲ Papua, E Indonesia
149 P14 Gāvbandī Hormozgān, S Iran 27.07N 53.21E
117 H25 Gavdopoúla island SE Greece
117 H26 Gávdos island SE Greece
104 K16 Gave de Pau var. Gave-de-Pay. ≈ SW France
Gave-de-Pay see Gave de Pau
104 J16 Gave d'Oloron ≈ SW France
101 E18 Gavere Oost-Vlaanderen, NW Belgium 50.56N 3.40E
96 N13 Gävle var. Gäfle; prev. Gefle. Gävleborg, C Sweden 60.40N 17.09E
96 M11 Gävleborg var. Gäfleborg, Gefleborg. ◐ county C Sweden
96 O13 Gävlebukten bay C Sweden
128 L16 Gavrilov-Yam Yaroslavskaya Oblast', W Russian Federation 57.19N 39.52E
195 P15 Gawa Island island SE Papau New Guinea
190 I9 Gawler South Australia 34.37S 138.43E
190 G7 Gawler Ranges hill range South Australia
Gawso see Goaso
168 H11 Gaxun Nur ◎ N China
159 P14 Gaya Bihār, N India 24.48N 85.00E
79 S13 Gaya Dosso, SW Niger 11.54N 3.25E
Gaya see Kyjov
33 Q6 Gaylord Michigan, N USA 45.01N 84.40W
31 U9 Gaylord Minnesota, N USA 44.33N 94.13W
189 Y9 Gayndah Queensland, E Australia 25.37S 151.30E
129 T12 Gayny Komi-Permyatskiy Avtonomnyy Okrug, NW Russian Federation 60.19N 54.15E
Gaysin see Haysyn
Gayvorno see Hayvoron
144 E11 Gaza Ar. Ghazzah, Heb. 'Azza. NE Gaza Strip 31.30N 34.00E
85 L20 Gaza off. Província de Gaza. ◐ province SW Mozambique
Gaz-Achak see Gazojak
153 Q9 G'azalkent Rus. Gazalkent. Toshkent Viloyati, E Uzbekistan 41.30N 69.46E
Gazandzhyk/Gazanjyk see Bereket
79 V12 Gazaoua Maradi, S Niger 13.28N 7.54E
144 E11 Gaza Strip Ar. Qiţā' Ghazzah. disputed region SW Asia
195 P11 Gazelle Peninsula headland New Britain, E PNG 4.32S 151.56E
197 J5 Gazelle, Récif de la reef C New Caledonia
Gazgan see G'ozg'on
Gazi Antep see Gaziantep
142 M16 Gaziantep var. Gazi Antep; prev. Aintab, Antep. Gaziantep, S Turkey 37.04N 37.21E
142 M17 Gaziantep var. Gazi Antep. ◐ province S Turkey
116 M13 Gaziköy Tekirdağ, NW Turkey 40.45N 27.18E
124 O3 Gazimağusa var. Famagusta, Gk. Ammóchostos. E Cyprus 35.06N 33.57E
124 Nn2 Gazimağusa Körfezi var. Famagusta Bay, Gk. Kólpos Ammóchostos. bay E Cyprus
152 K11 Gazli Buxoro Viloyati, C Uzbekistan 40.09N 63.28E
152 I9 Gazojak Rus. Gaz-Achak. Lebap Welaýaty, NE Turkmenistan 41.12N 61.24E
81 K15 Gbadolite Equateur, NW Dem. Rep. Congo 4.18N 20.55E
78 K16 Gbanga var. Gbarnga. N Liberia 7.01N 9.30W
Gbarnga see Gbanga
79 S14 Gbéroubouè var. Béroubouay. N Benin 10.35N 2.47E
79 W16 Gboko Benue, S Nigeria 7.21N 8.57E
Gcuwa see Butterworth
112 I7 Gdańsk Fr. Dantzig, Ger. Danzig. Pomorskie, N Poland 54.21N 18.35E
Gdan'skaya Bukhta/Gdańsk, Gulf of see Danzig, Gulf of
Gdańska, Zakota see Danzig, Gulf of
Gdingen see Gdynia
128 F13 Gdov Pskovskaya Oblast', W Russian Federation 58.43N 27.51E
112 I6 Gdynia Ger. Gdingen. Pomorskie, N Poland 54.31N 18.30E
28 M10 Geary Oklahoma, C USA 35.37N 98.19W
Geavvú see Kevo
78 H12 Gêba, Rio ≈ C Guinea-Bissau
175 Tt8 Gebe, Pulau island E Indonesia
142 E11 Gebze Kocaeli, NW Turkey 40.48N 29.25E
124 O2 Geçitkale Gk. Lefkonico, Lefkónikon. NE Cyprus 35.16N 33.44E
82 H10 Gedaref var. Al Qaḑārif, El Gedaref. Gedaref, E Sudan 14.03N 35.24E
82 H10 Gedaref ◐ state E Sudan
82 B11 Gedid Ras el Fil Southern Darfur, W Sudan 12.48N 25.42E
101 I23 Gedinne Namur, SE Belgium 49.57N 4.55E
142 E13 Gediz Kütahya, W Turkey 39.04N 29.25E
142 C14 Gediz Nehri ≈ W Turkey
83 N14 Gedlegubē Somali, E Ethiopia 6.53N 45.08E
83 L17 Gedo off. Gobolka Gedo. ◐ region SW Somalia
97 I25 Gedser Storstrøm, SE Denmark 54.34N 11.57E
101 I16 Geel var. Gheel. Antwerpen, N Belgium 51.10N 4.58E
191 N13 Geelong Victoria, SE Australia 38.09S 144.20E
Ge'e'mu see Golmud
101 I14 Geertruidenberg Noord-Brabant, S Netherlands 51.43N 4.52E
102 H10 Geeste ≈ NW Germany
102 J10 Geesthacht Schleswig-Holstein, N Germany 53.25N 10.22E
191 P17 Geeveston Tasmania, SE Australia 43.12S 146.54E
Gefle see Gävle
Gefleborg see Gävleborg
164 G13 Gê'gyai Xizang Zizhiqu, W China 32.28N 81.03E
79 X12 Geidam Yobe, NE Nigeria 12.52N 11.55E
9 T11 Geikie ≈ Saskatchewan, C Canada
96 F13 Geilo Buskerud, S Norway 60.31N 8.13E
96 E10 Geiranger Møre og Romsdal, S Norway 62.07N 7.12E
103 I22 Geislingen var. Geislingen an der Steige. Baden-Württemberg, SW Germany 48.35N 9.52E
Geislingen an der Steige see Geislingen
83 F20 Geita Mwanza, NW Tanzania 2.52S 32.12E
97 G15 Geithus Buskerud, S Norway 59.55N 9.57E
166 H14 Gejiu var. Kochiu. Yunnan, S China 23.21N 103.07E
Gëkdepe see Gökdepe
152 E9 Geklengkui, Solonchak var. Solonchak Goklenkuy. salt marsh NW Turkmenistan
83 D14 Gel ≈ W Sudan
109 K25 Gela prev. Terranova di Sicilia. Sicilia, Italy, C Mediterranean Sea 37.04N 14.15E
165 N13 Gêladaindong ▲ C China 33.24N 91.00E
83 N14 Geladī Somali, E Ethiopia 6.58N 46.24E
174 Kk11 Gelam, Pulau var. Pulau Galam. island N Indonesia
Gelaozu Miaozu Zizhixian see Wuchuan
100 L11 Gelderland prev. Eng. Guelders. ◐ province E Netherlands
100 J13 Geldermalsen Gelderland, C Netherlands 51.52N 5.16E
103 D14 Geldern Nordrhein-Westfalen, W Germany 51.31N 6.19E
101 K15 Geldrop Noord-Brabant, SE Netherlands 51.25N 5.31E
101 L17 Geleen Limburg, SE Netherlands 50.57N 5.49E
130 K14 Gelendzhik Krasnodarskiy Kray, SW Russian Federation 44.34N 38.06E
Gelib see Jilib
142 B11 Gelibolu Eng. Gallipoli. Çanakkale, NW Turkey 40.25N 26.40E
117 L14 Gelibolu Yarımadası Eng. Gallipoli Peninsula. peninsula NW Turkey
Gelinting, Teluk see Geliting, Teluk
175 Qq16 Geliting, Teluk var. Teluk Gelinting. bay Nusa Tenggara, S Indonesia
83 O14 Gellinsor Mudug, C Somalia 6.25N 46.44E
103 H18 Gelnhausen Hessen, C Germany 50.12N 9.12E
103 E14 Gelsenkirchen Nordrhein-Westfalen, W Germany 51.33N 7.06E
85 C20 Geluk Hardap, SW Namibia 24.35S 15.48E
101 H20 Gembloux Namur, Belgium 50.34N 4.42E
194 I12 Gembogl Chimbu, C PNG 5.52S 145.06E
81 J16 Gemena Equateur, NW Dem. Rep. Congo 3.13N 19.49E
101 L14 Gemert Noord-Brabant, SE Netherlands 51.33N 5.40E
142 E11 Gemlik Bursa, NW Turkey 40.25N 29.10E
Gem of the Mountains see Idaho
108 J6 Gemona del Friuli Friuli-Venezia Giulia, NE Italy 46.18N 13.11E
Gem State see Idaho
Genalē Wenz see Juba
174 Ll7 Genali, Danau ◎ Borneo, N Indonesia
101 G19 Genappe Wallon Brabant, C Belgium 50.39N 4.27E
143 P14 Genç Bingöl, E Turkey 38.45N 40.31E
Genck see Genk
100 M9 Genemuiden Overijssel, E Netherlands 52.38N 6.03E
65 K14 General Acha La Pampa, C Argentina 37.24S 64.34W
63 C21 General Alvear Buenos Aires, E Argentina 36.03S 60.01W
64 I12 General Alvear Mendoza, W Argentina 34.58S 67.40W
63 B20 General Arenales Buenos Aires, E Argentina 34.21S 61.19W
63 D21 General Belgrano Buenos Aires, E Argentina 35.46S 58.30W
204 H3 General Bernardo O'Higgins Chilean research station Antarctica 63.09S 57.13W
43 O8 General Bravo Nuevo León, NE Mexico 25.47N 99.04W
64 M7 General Capdevila Chaco, N Argentina 27.25S 61.30W
General Carrera, Lago see Buenos Aires, Lago
43 N9 General Cepeda Coahuila de Zaragoza, NE Mexico 25.18N 101.24W
65 K15 General Conesa Río Negro, E Argentina 40.07S 64.32W
63 G18 General Enrique Martínez Treinta y Tres, E Uruguay 33.13S 53.46W
64 L3 General Eugenio A. Garay var. Fortín General Eugenio Garay; prev. Yrendagüé. Nueva Asunción, NW Paraguay 20.31S 62.09W
63 C18 General Galarza Entre Ríos, E Argentina 32.43S 59.24W
63 E22 General Guido Buenos Aires, E Argentina 36.36S 57.45W
General José F.Uriburu see Zárate
63 E22 General Juan Madariaga Buenos Aires, E Argentina 37.02S 57.06W
43 O16 General Juan N Alvarez ✕ (Acapulco) Guerrero, S Mexico 16.47N 99.47W
63 B22 General La Madrid Buenos Aires, E Argentina 37.13S 61.10W
63 E21 General Lavalle Buenos Aires, E Argentina 36.25S 56.55W
General Machado see Camacupa
64 I8 General Manuel Belgrano, Cerro ▲ W Argentina 29.05S 67.05W
43 O8 General Mariano Escobero ✕ (Monterrey) Nuevo León, NE Mexico 25.47N 100.00W
63 B20 General O'Brien Buenos Aires, E Argentina 34.54S 60.45W
64 K13 General Pico La Pampa, C Argentina 35.40S 63.44W
64 M7 General Pinedo Chaco, N Argentina 27.16S 61.19W
63 B20 General Pinto Buenos Aires, E Argentina 34.45S 61.49W
63 E22 General Pirán Buenos Aires, E Argentina 37.16S 57.46W
45 N15 General, Río ≈ S Costa Rica
65 I15 General Roca Río Negro, C Argentina 39.00S 67.35W
179 Rr17 General Santos off. General Santos City. Mindanao, S Philippines 6.09N 125.10E
43 O9 General Terán Nuevo León, NE Mexico 25.17N 99.37W
116 N7 General Toshevo Rom. I.G.Duca, prev. Casim, Kasimköj. Dobrich, NE Bulgaria 43.43N 28.04E
63 B20 General Viamonte Buenos Aires, E Argentina 35.01S 61.00W
63 A20 General Villegas Buenos Aires, E Argentina 35.01S 63.01W
Gênes see Genova
20 E11 Genesee River ≈ New York/Pennsylvania, NE USA
32 K11 Geneseo Illinois, N USA 41.27N 90.08W
20 F10 Geneseo New York, NE USA 42.48N 77.46W
59 L14 Geneshuaya, Río ≈ N Bolivia
25 Q8 Geneva Alabama, S USA 31.01N 85.51W
32 M10 Geneva Illinois, N USA 41.53N 88.18W
31 Q16 Geneva Nebraska, C USA 40.31N 97.36W
20 G10 Geneva New York, NE USA 42.52N 76.58W
33 U10 Geneva Ohio, NE USA 41.48N 80.53W
Geneva see Genève
110 B10 Geneva, Lake Fr. Lac de Genève, Lac Léman, le Léman, Ger. Genfer See. ◎ France/Switzerland
110 A10 Genève Eng. Geneva, Ger. Genf, It. Ginevra. Genève, SW Switzerland 46.13N 6.09E
110 A11 Genève Eng. Geneva, Ger. Genf, It. Ginevra. ◐ canton SW Switzerland
110 A10 Genève var. Geneva. ✕ Vaud, SW Switzerland 46.13N 6.06E
Genève, Lac de see Geneva, Lake
Genf see Genève
Genfer See see Geneva, Lake
169 T5 Genhe prev. Ergun Zuoqi. Nei Mongol Zizhiqu, N China 50.48N 121.30E
169 S5 Gen He ≈ NE China
Genichesk see Heniches'k
106 L14 Genil ≈ S Spain
101 K18 Genk var. Genck. Limburg, NE Belgium 50.58N 5.30E
170 Cc12 Genkai-nada gulf Kyūshū, SW Japan
109 C19 Gennargentu, Monti del ▲ Sardegna, Italy, C Mediterranean Sea 40.01N 9.14E
101 M14 Gennep Limburg, SE Netherlands 51.43N 5.58E
32 M10 Genoa Illinois, N USA 42.06N 88.41W
31 Q15 Genoa Nebraska, C USA 41.27N 97.43W
Genoa see Genova
Genoa, Gulf of see Genova, Golfo di
108 D10 Genova Eng. Genoa, Fr. Gênes; anc. Genua. Liguria, NW Italy 44.28N 9.00E
108 D10 Genova, Golfo di Eng. Gulf of Genoa. gulf NW Italy
59 C17 Genovesa, Isla var. Tower Island. island Galapagos Islands, Ecuador, E Pacific Ocean
Gensū see Wŏnju
101 E17 Gent Eng. Ghent, Fr. Gand. Oost-Vlaanderen, NW Belgium 51.01N 3.42E
174 J15 Genteng Jawa, C Indonesia 7.21S 106.19E
102 M12 Genthin Sachsen-Anhalt, E Germany 52.24N 12.10E
29 R9 Gentry Arkansas, C USA 36.16N 94.28W
Genua see Genova
109 I15 Genzano di Roma Lazio, C Italy 41.42N 12.42E
Geokchay see Göyçay
Geok-Tepe see Gökdepe
126 Gg1 Georga, Zemlya Eng. George Land. island Zemlya Frantsa-Iosifa, N Russian Federation
85 G26 George Western Cape, S South Africa 33.51S 22.28E
31 S11 George Iowa, C USA 43.20N 96.00W
11 O5 George ≈ Newfoundland and Labrador/Québec, E Canada
47 T11 George F L Charles prev. Vigie. ✕ (Castries). NE Saint Lucia 14.01N 60.59W
67 C25 George Island island S Falkland Islands
191 R10 George, Lake ◎ New South Wales, SE Australia
83 E18 George, Lake ◎ SW Uganda
25 W10 George, Lake ◎ Florida, SE USA
20 L8 George, Lake ⊠ New York, NE USA
George Land see George, Zemlya
Georgenburg see Jurbarkas
George River see Kangiqsualujjuaq
66 G8 Georges Bank undersea feature W Atlantic Ocean
193 A21 George Sound sound South Island, NZ
67 F15 Georgetown ○ (Ascension Island) NW Ascension Island 17.55S 14.25W
189 V5 Georgetown Queensland, NE Australia 18.17S 143.37E
191 P15 George Town Tasmania, SE Australia 41.07S 146.50E
46 I4 George Town Great Exuma Island, C Bahamas 23.28N 75.47W
46 D8 George Town var. Georgetown. ○ (Cayman Islands) Grand Cayman, SW Cayman Islands 19.15N 81.22W
78 H12 Georgetown E Gambia 13.33N 14.49W
57 T8 Georgetown ● (Guyana) N Guyana 6.46N 58.10W
173 Ff3 George Town var. Penang, Pinang. Pinang, Peninsular Malaysia 5.28N 100.19E
47 Y14 Georgetown Saint Vincent, Saint Vincent and the Grenadines 13.14N 61.07W
23 Y4 Georgetown Delaware, NE USA 38.39N 75.22W
25 R6 Georgetown Georgia, SE USA 31.52N 85.04W
22 M5 Georgetown Kentucky, S USA 38.13N 84.33W
23 T13 Georgetown South Carolina, SE USA 33.22N 79.17W
27 S10 Georgetown Texas, SW USA 30.37N 97.40W
57 T8 Georgetown ✕ N Guyana 6.46N 58.10W
205 U16 George V Coast physical region Antarctica
205 T15 George V Land physical region Antarctica
204 J7 George VI Ice Shelf ice shelf Antarctica
204 J6 George VI Sound sound Antarctica
27 S14 George West Texas, SW USA 28.19N 98.07W
143 R9 Georgia off. Republic of Georgia, Geor. Sak'art'velo, Rus. Gruzinskaya SSR, Gruziya; prev. Georgian SSR. ◆ republic SW Asia
25 S5 Georgia off. State of Georgia; also known as Empire State of the South, Peach State. ◐ state SE USA
12 F12 Georgian Bay lake bay Ontario, S Canada
8 L17 Georgia, Strait of strait British Columbia, W Canada
Georgi Dimitrov see Kostenets
Georgi Dimitrov, Yazovir see Koprinka, Yazovir
116 M9 Georgi Traykov, Yazovir ⊠ NE Bulgaria
Georgiu-Dezh see Liski
151 W10 Georgiyevka Vostochnyy Kazakhstan, E Kazakhstan 49.19N 81.34E
Georgiyevka see Korday
131 N15 Georgiyevsk Stavropol'skiy Kray, SW Russian Federation 44.07N 43.22E
102 G13 Georgsmarienhütte Niedersachsen, NW Germany 52.12N 8.04E
205 O1 Georg von Neumayer German research station Antarctica 70.41S 8.18W
103 M16 Gera Thüringen, E Germany 50.51N 12.13E
103 K16 Gera ≈ C Germany
101 E19 Geraardsbergen Oost-Vlaanderen, SW Belgium 50.46N 3.52E
117 F21 Geráki Pelopónnisos, S Greece 36.56N 22.46E
29 W5 Gerald Missouri, C USA 38.24N 91.20W
49 V8 Geral de Goiás, Serra ▲▲ E Brazil
193 G20 Geraldine Canterbury, South Island, NZ 44.06S 171.13E
188 H11 Geraldton Western Australia 28.47S 114.39E
10 E11 Geraldton Ontario, S Canada 49.43N 86.58W
62 J12 Geral, Serra ▲▲ S Brazil
175 P16 Gerampi Sumbawa, S Indonesia 8.47S 118.51E
105 U6 Gérardmer Vosges, NE France 48.05N 6.54E
Gerasa see Jarash
Gerdauen see Zheleznodorozhnyy
41 Q11 Gerdine, Mount ▲ Alaska, USA 61.40N 152.21W
142 H11 Gerede Bolu, N Turkey 40.48N 32.13E
142 H11 Gerede Çayı ≈ N Turkey
154 M8 Gereshk Helmand, SW Afghanistan 31.49N 64.31E
103 L24 Geretsried Bayern, S Germany 47.51N 11.28E
107 P14 Gérgal Andalucía, S Spain 37.07N 2.34W
194 K13 Gerhards, Cape headland C PNG 6.43S 147.31E
30 I14 Gering Nebraska, C USA 41.49N 103.39W
37 R3 Gerlach Nevada, W USA 40.38N 119.21W
Gerlachfalvi Csúcs/Gerlachovka see Gerlachovský štít
113 L18 Gerlachovský štít var. Gerlachovka, Ger. Gerlsdorfer Spitze, Hung. Gerlachfalvi Csúcs; prev. Stalinov Štít, Ger. Franz-Josef Spitze, Hung. Ferencz-József Csúcs. ▲ N Slovakia 49.12N 20.09E
110 E8 Gerlafingen Solothurn, NW Switzerland 47.10N 7.34E
Gerlsdorfer Spitze see Gerlachovský štít
145 V3 Germak E Iraq 35.49N 46.09E
German East Africa see Tanzania
Germanicopolis see Çankırı
Germanicum, Mare/German Ocean see North Sea
Germanovichi see Hyermanavichy
German Southwest Africa see Namibia
22 E10 Germantown Tennessee, S USA 35.06N 89.51W
103 I15 Germany off. Federal Republic of Germany, Ger. Bundesrepublik Deutschland, Deutschland. ◆ federal republic N Europe
103 L23 Germering Bayern, SE Germany 48.07N 11.22E
85 J21 Germiston var. Gauteng. Gauteng, NE South Africa 26.15S 28.10E
Gernika see Gernika-Lumo
107 P2 Gernika-Lumo var. Gernika, Guernica, Guernica y Lumo. País Vasco, N Spain 43.19N 2.40W
171 Ii15 Gero Gifu, Honshū, SW Japan 35.48N 137.15E
117 F22 Geroliménas Pelopónnisos, S Greece 36.28N 22.25E
Gerona see Girona
101 H21 Gerpinnes Hainaut, S Belgium 50.20N 4.38E
104 L15 Gers ◐ department S France
104 L14 Gers ≈ S France
Gerunda see Girona
142 K10 Gerze Sinop, N Turkey 41.48N 35.13E
164 I13 Gêrzê var. Luring. Xizang Zizhiqu, W China 32.19N 84.05E
Gesoriacum/Gessoriacum see Boulogne-sur-Mer
101 J21 Gesves Namur, SE Belgium 50.24N 5.04E
95 J20 Geta Åland, SW Finland 60.22N 19.49E
107 N8 Getafe Madrid, C Spain 40.18N 3.43W
97 J21 Getinge Halland, S Sweden 56.46N 12.42E
20 F16 Gettysburg Pennsylvania, NE USA 39.49N 77.13W
31 N8 Gettysburg South Dakota, N USA 45.00N 99.57W
204 K12 Getz Ice Shelf ice shelf Antarctica
143 S15 Gevaş Van, SE Turkey 38.16N 43.04E
Gevgeli see Gevgelija
115 Q20 Gevgelija var. Đevđelija, Djevdjelija, Turk. Gevgeli. SE FYR Macedonia 41.09N 22.30E
105 T10 Gex Ain, E France 46.21N 6.02E
94 I3 Geysir physical region SW Iceland
142 F11 Geyve Sakarya, NW Turkey 40.31N 30.18E
82 G10 Gezira ◐ state E Sudan
111 V3 Gföhl Niederösterreich, N Austria 48.30N 15.27E
85 H22 Ghaap Plateau Afr. Ghaapplato. plateau C South Africa
Ghaapplato see Ghaap Plateau
Ghaba see Al Ghābah
144 J8 Ghāb, Tall ▲ SE Syria 33.09N 37.48E
145 Q9 Ghadaf, Wādī al dry watercourse C Iraq
Ghadamès see Ghadāmis
76 M9 Ghadāmis var. Ghadamès, Rhadames. W Libya 30.07N 9.30E
147 Y10 Ghadan E Oman 20.20N 57.58E
77 O10 Ghaddūwah C Libya 26.36N 14.26E
153 Q11 Ghafurov Rus. Gafurov; prev. Sovetabad. NW Tajikistan 40.13N 69.42E
159 N12 Ghāghara ≈ S Asia
155 P13 Ghaibi Dero Sind, SE Pakistan 27.34N 67.42E
147 Y10 Ghalat E Oman 21.06N 58.51E
145 W11 Ghamūkah, Hawr ◎ S Iraq
79 P15 Ghana off. Republic of Ghana. ◆ republic W Africa
147 X12 Ghānah spring/well S Oman 18.35N 56.34E
Ghanongga see Ranongga
Ghansi/Ghansiland see Ghanzi
85 F18 Ghanzi var. Khanzi. Ghanzi, W Botswana 21.39S 21.38E
85 G19 Ghanzi var. Ghansi, Ghansiland, Khanzi. ◐ district C Botswana
69 T14 Ghanzi var. Knanzi. ≈ Botswana/South Africa
Ghap'an see Kapan
144 F13 Gharandal Ma'ān, SW Jordan 30.12N 35.18E
Gharbt, Jabal al see Liban, Jebel
76 K7 Ghardaïa N Algeria 32.29N 3.44E
145 U14 Gharibīyah, Sha'īb al ≈ S Iraq
153 R12 Gharm Rus. Garm. C Tajikistan 39.03N 70.25E
155 P17 Gharo Sind, SE Pakistan 24.43N 67.34E
145 W10 Gharrāf, Shaṭṭ al ≈ S Iraq
Gharvān see Gharyān
77 O7 Gharyān var. Gharvān. NW Libya 32.10N 13.01E
76 M11 Ghāt var. Gat. SW Libya 24.58N 10.10E
Ghawdex see Gozo
147 U8 Ghayathi Abū Ẓaby, W UAE 23.51N 53.01E
Ghazāl, Baḩr al see Ghazal, Bahr el
80 H9 Ghazal, Bahr el var. Soro. seasonal river C Chad
82 E13 Ghazal, Bahr el var. Baḩr al Ghazāl. ≈ S Sudan
76 H6 Ghazaouet NW Algeria 35.05N 1.52W
158 J10 Ghāziābād Uttar Pradesh, N India 28.42N 77.28E
159 O13 Ghāzīpur Uttar Pradesh, N India 25.38N 83.33E
155 Q6 Ghaznī var. Ghazni. Ghaznī, E Afghanistan 33.31N 68.24E
155 P7 Ghaznī ◐ province SE Afghanistan
Ghazzah see Gaza
Gheel see Geel
Ghelīzâne see Relizane
Ghent see Gent
Gheorghe Braţul see Sfântu Gheorghe, Braţul
Gheorghe Gheorghiu-Dej see Oneşti
118 J10 Gheorgheni prev. Gheorghieni, Sînt-Miclăuş, Ger. Niklasmarkt, Hung. Gyergyószentmiklós. Harghita, C Romania 46.43N 25.34E
Gheorghieni see Gheorgheni
118 H10 Gherla Ger. Neuschliss, Hung. Szamosújvár; prev. Armenierstadt. Cluj, NW Romania 47.02N 23.55E
Gheweifat see Ghuwayfāt
Ghilan see Gīlān
109 C18 Ghilarza Sardegna, Italy, C Mediterranean Sea 40.09N 8.50E
Ghilizane see Relizane
Ghimbi see Gīmbī
Ghiriş see Câmpia Turzii
105 Y15 Ghisonaccia Corse, France, C Mediterranean Sea 42.00N 9.25E
Ghizo see Gizo

GHONCHÍ – GONZALES

153 Q11 **Ghonchí** *Rus.* Ganchi. NW Tajikistan 39.57N 69.10E
Ghor *see* Ghowr
159 T13 **Ghoraghat** Rajshahi, NW Bangladesh 25.17N 89.16E
155 R13 **Ghotki** Sind, SE Pakistan 28.00N 69.21E
154 M5 **Ghowr** *var.* Ghor. ◈ *province* C Afghanistan
153 T13 **Ghŭdara** *var.* Gudara, *Rus.* Kudara. SE Tajikistan 38.28N 72.39E
159 R13 **Ghugri** ~ N India
153 S14 **Ghund** *Rus.* Gunt. ~ SE Tajikistan
Ghurdaqah *see* Hurghada
154 J5 **Ghūriān** Herāt, W Afghanistan 34.19N 61.25E
147 T8 **Ghuwayfāt** *var.* Gheweifat. Abū Ẓaby, W UAE 24.06N 51.40E
123 Mm17 **Ghuzayyil, Sabkhat** *salt lake* N Libya
117 G17 **Giáltra** Évvoia, C Greece 38.21N 22.58E
Giamame *see* Jamaame
178 K13 **Gia Nghia** *var.* Åak Nông. Đăc Lăc, S Vietnam 11.59N 107.42E
116 F13 **Giannitsá** *var.* Yiannitsá. Kentrikí Makedonía, N Greece 40.48N 22.24E
109 F14 **Giannutri, Isola di** *island* Archipelago Toscano, C Italy
98 F13 **Giant's Causeway** *Ir.* Clochán an Aifir. *lava flow* N Northern Ireland, UK
178 J15 **Gia Rai** Minh Hai, S Vietnam 9.16N 105.25E
109 L24 **Giarre** Sicilia, Italy, C Mediterranean Sea 37.43N 15.12E
46 I7 **Gibara** Holguín, E Cuba 21.05N 76.08W
31 O16 **Gibbon** Nebraska, C USA 40.45N 98.50W
34 K11 **Gibbon** Oregon, NW USA 45.40N 118.22W
35 P11 **Gibbonsville** Idaho, NW USA 45.33N 113.55W
66 A13 **Gibb's Hill** *hill* S Bermuda 32.15N 64.51W
94 I9 **Gibostad** Troms, N Norway 69.21N 18.01E
106 I14 **Gibraleón** Andalucía, S Spain 37.22N 6.58W
106 L16 **Gibraltar** ○ (Gibraltar) S Gibraltar 36.08N 5.21W
106 L16 **Gibraltar** ◇ *UK dependent territory* SW Europe
Gibraltar, Détroit de/ Gibraltar, Estrecho de *see* Gibraltar, Strait of
106 J17 **Gibraltar, Strait of** *Fr.* Détroit de Gibraltar, *Sp.* Estrecho de Gibraltar. *strait* Atlantic Ocean/Mediterranean Sea
33 S11 **Gibsonburg** Ohio, N USA 41.22N 83.19W
32 M13 **Gibson City** Illinois, N USA 40.27N 88.24W
188 L8 **Gibson Desert** *desert* Western Australia
8 L17 **Gibsons** British Columbia, SW Canada 49.24N 123.31W
155 N12 **Gīdār** Baluchistān, SW Pakistan 28.16N 66.00E
161 I17 **Giddalūr** Andhra Pradesh, E India 15.24N 78.54E
27 U10 **Giddings** Texas, SW USA 30.10N 96.56W
29 Y8 **Gideon** Missouri, C USA 36.27N 89.55W
83 J15 **Gīdolē** Southern, S Ethiopia 5.31N 37.26E
120 H13 **Giedraičiai** Utena, E Lithuania 55.05N 25.16E
105 O7 **Gien** Loiret, C France 47.40N 2.37E
103 G17 **Giessen** Hessen, W Germany 50.34N 8.40E
100 O6 **Gieten** Drenthe, NE Netherlands 53.00N 6.43E
25 Y13 **Gifford** Florida, SE USA 27.40N 80.24W
15 Ll1 **Gifford** ~ Baffin Island, Nunavut, NE Canada
102 J12 **Gifhorn** Niedersachsen, N Germany 52.28N 10.33E
9 P13 **Gift Lake** Alberta, W Canada 55.49N 115.57W
171 Hh15 **Gifu** *var.* Gihu. Gifu, Honshū, SW Japan 35.23N 136.46E
171 I14 **Gifu** *off.* Gifu-ken, *var.* Gihu. ◈ *prefecture* Honshū, SW Japan
130 M13 **Gigant** Rostovskaya Oblast', SW Russian Federation 46.29N 41.18E
42 E8 **Giganta, Sierra de la** ▲▲ W Mexico
56 E12 **Gigante** Huila, S Colombia 2.24N 75.34W
116 I7 **Gigen** Pleven, N Bulgaria 43.40N 24.31E
Giggiga *see* Jījiga
98 G12 **Gigha Island** *island* SW Scotland, UK
109 E14 **Giglio, Isola del** *island* Archipelago Toscano, C Italy
Gihu *see* Gifu
152 L11 **G'ijduvon** *Rus.* Gizhduvan. Buxoro Viloyati, C Uzbekistan 40.06N 64.38E
106 L2 **Gijón** *var.* Xixón. Asturias, NW Spain 43.31N 5.40W
83 D20 **Gikongoro** SW Rwanda 2.30S 29.32E
38 K14 **Gila Bend** Arizona, SW USA 32.57N 112.43W
38 J14 **Gila Bend Mountains** ▲▲ Arizona, SW USA
39 N14 **Gila Mountains** ▲▲ Arizona, SW USA
38 I15 **Gila Mountains** ▲▲ Arizona, SW USA
148 M4 **Gīlān** *off.* Ostān-e Gīlān; *var.* Ghilan, Guilan. ◈ *province* NW Iran
Gilani *see* Gnjilane
38 L14 **Gila River** ~ Arizona, SW USA
31 W4 **Gilbert** Minnesota, N USA 47.29N 92.27W
Gilbert Islands *see* Tungaru
8 L16 **Gilbert, Mount** ▲ British Columbia, SW Canada 50.49N 124.03W
189 U4 **Gilbert River** ~ Queensland, NE Australia
(0) C6 **Gilbert Seamounts** *undersea feature* NE Pacific Ocean
35 S7 **Gildford** Montana, NW USA 48.34N 110.21W
85 P15 **Gilé** Zambézia, NE Mozambique 16.04S 38.16E
32 K4 **Gile Flowage** ◎ Wisconsin, N USA
190 G7 **Giles, Lake** *salt lake* South Australia
77 U12 **Gilf Kebir Plateau** *Ar.* Haḍabat al Jilf al Kabīr. *plateau* SW Egypt
191 R6 **Gilgandra** New South Wales, SE Australia 31.43S 148.39E
Gilgău *see* Gâlgău
83 I19 **Gilgil** Rift Valley, SW Kenya 0.33S 36.18E
191 S4 **Gil Gil Creek** ~ New South Wales, SE Australia
155 V3 **Gilgit** Jammu and Kashmir, NE Pakistan 35.54N 74.19E
155 V3 **Gilgit** ~ N Pakistan
9 X11 **Gillam** Manitoba, C Canada 56.25N 94.45W
97 J22 **Gilleleje** Frederiksborg, E Denmark 56.05N 12.17E
32 K14 **Gillespie** Illinois, N USA 39.07N 89.49W
29 W13 **Gillett** Arkansas, C USA 34.07N 91.22W
35 X12 **Gillette** Wyoming, C USA 44.17N 105.30W
99 P22 **Gillingham** SE England, UK 51.24N 0.33E
205 X6 **Gillock Island** *island* Antarctica
181 O16 **Gillot** ✈ (St-Denis) N Réunion 20.52S 55.31E
67 H25 **Gill Point** *headland* E Saint Helena 15.58S 5.37W
32 M12 **Gilman** Illinois, N USA 40.44N 87.58W
27 W6 **Gilmer** Texas, SW USA 32.43N 94.56W
Gilolo *see* Halmahera, Pulau
83 G14 **Gilo Wenz** ~ SW Ethiopia
37 O10 **Gilroy** California, W USA 37.00N 121.34W
194 H12 **Giluwe, Mount** ▲ W PNG 6.03S 143.52E
126 M14 **Gilyuy** ~ SE Russian Federation
101 I14 **Gilze** Noord-Brabant, S Netherlands 51.33N 4.55E
172 O14 **Gima** Okinawa, Kume-jima, SW Japan
82 H13 **Gīmbī** *It.* Ghimbi. Oromo, C Ethiopia 9.13N 35.39E
47 T12 **Gimie, Mount** ▲ C Saint Lucia 13.51N 61.00W
9 X16 **Gimli** Manitoba, S Canada 50.39N 97.00W
Gimma *see* Jīma
97 O14 **Gimo** Uppsala, C Sweden 60.10N 18.12E
104 L15 **Gimone** ~ S France
Gimpoe *see* Gimpu
175 Pp9 **Gimpu** *prev.* Gimpoe. Sulawesi, C Indonesia 1.38S 120.00E
190 F5 **Gina** South Australia 29.56S 134.33E
Ginevra *see* Genève
101 J19 **Gingelom** Limburg, NE Belgium 50.46N 5.09E
188 I12 **Gingin** Western Australia 31.22S 115.51E
179 R14 **Gingoog** Mindanao, S Philippines 8.47N 125.05E
83 K14 **Gīnīr** Oromo, C Ethiopia 7.12N 40.43E
Giohar *see* Jawhar
109 O17 **Gioia del Colle** Puglia, SE Italy 40.46N 16.55E
109 M22 **Gioia, Golfo di** *gulf* S Italy
Giona *see* Gkióna
117 I16 **Gioúra** *island* Vóreioi Sporádes, Greece, Aegean Sea
109 O17 **Giovinazzo** Puglia, SE Italy 41.10N 16.40E
Gipeswic *see* Ipswich
Gipuzkoa *see* Guipúzcoa
Giran *see* Ilan
32 K14 **Girard** Illinois, N USA 39.27N 89.46W
29 R7 **Girard** Kansas, C USA 37.30N 94.50W
27 O6 **Girard** Texas, SW USA 33.18N 100.38W
56 E10 **Girardot** Cundinamarca, C Colombia 4.19N 74.46W
180 M7 **Giraud Seamount** *undersea feature* SW Indian Ocean 9.57S 46.55E
85 A15 **Giraul** ~ SW Angola
98 L9 **Girdle Ness** *headland* NE Scotland, UK 57.09N 2.04W
143 N11 **Giresun** *var.* Kerasunt; *anc.* Cerasus, Pharnacia. Giresun, NE Turkey 40.55N 38.34E
143 N12 **Giresun** *var.* Kerasunt. ◈ *province* NE Turkey
143 N12 **Giresun Dağları** ▲▲ N Turkey
77 X10 **Girga** *var.* Girgeh, Jirjā. C Egypt 26.19N 31.49E
Girgeh *see* Girga
Girgenti *see* Agrigento
194 H10 **Girgir, Cape** *headland* NW PNG 3.48S 144.29E
159 Q15 **Girīdīh** Jhārkhand, NE India 24.10N 86.19E
191 P6 **Girilambone** New South Wales, SE Australia 31.19S 146.57E
Girin *see* Jilin
124 R12 **Girne** *Gk.* Kerýneia, Kyrenia. N Cyprus 35.19N 33.19E
Giron *see* Kiruna
107 X5 **Girona** *var.* Gerona; *anc.* Gerunda. Cataluña, NE Spain 41.58N 2.49E
107 W5 **Girona** *var.* Gerona ◈ *province* Cataluña, NE Spain
104 J12 **Gironde** ◈ *department* SW France
104 J11 **Gironde** *estuary* SW France
107 V5 **Gironella** Cataluña, NE Spain 42.01N 1.52E
105 N15 **Girou** ~ S France
99 H14 **Girvan** W Scotland, UK 55.14N 4.53W
26 M9 **Girvin** Texas, SW USA 31.05N 102.24W
192 Q9 **Gisborne** Gisborne, North Island, NZ 38.41S 178.01E
192 P9 **Gisborne** *off.* Gisborne District. ◈ *unitary authority* North Island, NZ
Giseifu *see* Ŭijŏngbu
Gisenye *see* Gisenyi
83 D19 **Gisenyi** *var.* Gisenye. NW Rwanda 1.42S 29.18E
97 K20 **Gislaved** Jönköping, S Sweden 57.19N 13.30E
105 N4 **Gisors** Eure, N France 49.18N 1.46E
Gissar *see* Hisor
153 P12 **Gissar Range** *Rus.* Gissarskiy Khrebet. ▲▲ Tajikistan/Uzbekistan
Gissarskiy Khrebet *see* Gissar Range
101 B16 **Gistel** West-Vlaanderen, W Belgium 51.09N 2.58E
110 F9 **Giswil** Unterwalden, C Switzerland 46.49N 8.11E
117 B16 **Gitánes** *ancient monument* Ípeiros, W Greece 39.34N 20.19E
83 E20 **Gitarama** C Rwanda 2.05S 29.45E
83 E20 **Gitega** C Burundi 3.20S 29.56E
Githio *see* Gýtheio
110 H11 **Giubiasco** Ticino, S Switzerland 46.10N 9.01E
108 K13 **Giulianova** Abruzzo, C Italy 42.45N 13.58E
Giulie, Alpi *see* Julian Alps
Giumri *see* Gyumri
118 M13 **Giurgeni** Ialomiţa, SE Romania 44.46N 27.51E
118 J15 **Giurgiu** Giurgiu, S Romania 43.54N 25.58E
118 J14 **Giurgiu** ◈ *county* SE Romania
97 F22 **Give** Vejle, C Denmark 55.51N 9.15E
105 R2 **Givet** Ardennes, N France 50.08N 4.50E
105 R11 **Givors** Rhône, E France 45.36N 4.46E
85 K19 **Giyani** Limpopo, NE South Africa 23.19S 30.37E
82 I13 **Giyon** Oromo, C Ethiopia 8.31N 37.56E
Gîza/Gizeh *see* El Gîza
77 V8 **Giza, Pyramids of** *ancient monument* N Egypt 29.46N 31.03E
Gizhduvan *see* G'ijduvon
127 Oo8 **Gizhiga** Magadanskaya Oblast', E Russian Federation 61.57N 160.16E
127 Oo8 **Gizhiginskaya Guba** *bay* E Russian Federation
195 T14 **Gizo** Gizo, NW Solomon Islands 8.03S 156.49E
195 T14 **Gizo** *var.* Ghizo. *island* NW Solomon Islands
112 N7 **Giżycko** *Ger.* Warmińsko-Mazurskie, NE Poland 54.03N 21.48E
Giżymałów *see* Hrymayliv
Gjakovë *see* Đakovica
96 F12 **Gjende** ◎ S Norway
97 F17 **Gjerstad** Aust-Agder, S Norway 58.54N 9.03E
Gjilan *see* Gnjilane
Gjinokastër *see* Gjirokastër
115 L23 **Gjirokastër** *var.* Gjirokastra; *prev.* Gjinokastër, *Gk.* Argyrokastron, *It.* Argirocastro. Gjirokastër, S Albania 40.04N 20.09E
115 L22 **Gjirokastër** ◈ *district* S Albania
15 K3 **Gjoa Haven** King William Island, Nunavut, NW Canada 68.37N 95.57W
96 H13 **Gjøvik** Oppland, S Norway 60.46N 10.40E
115 J22 **Gjuhëzës, Kepi i** *headland* SW Albania 40.25N 19.19E
Gjurgjevac *see* Đurđevac
117 E18 **Gkióna** *var.* Giona. ▲▲ C Greece
124 Oo3 **Gkréko, Akrotíri** *var.* Cape Greco, Pidálion. *headland* E Cyprus 34.57N 34.06E
101 I18 **Glabbeek-Zuurbemde** Vlaams Brabant, C Belgium 50.54N 4.58E
11 R14 **Glace Bay** Cape Breton Island, Nova Scotia, SE Canada 46.12N 59.57W
9 O16 **Glacier** British Columbia, SW Canada 51.12N 117.33W
41 W12 **Glacier Bay** *inlet* Alaska, USA
34 I7 **Glacier Peak** ▲ Washington, NW USA 48.06N 121.06W
23 Q7 **Glade Spring** Virginia, NE USA 36.47N 81.46W
45 W7 **Gladewater** Texas, SW USA 32.32N 94.57W
189 Y8 **Gladstone** Queensland, E Australia 23.52S 151.16E
190 I8 **Gladstone** South Australia 33.16S 138.21E
9 X16 **Gladstone** Manitoba, S Canada 50.12N 98.56W
33 O5 **Gladstone** Michigan, N USA 45.51N 87.01W
29 R4 **Gladstone** Missouri, C USA 39.12N 94.33W
33 Q7 **Gladwin** Michigan, N USA 43.58N 84.29W
97 J15 **Glafsfjorden** ◎ C Sweden
96 E9 **Gláma** *physical region* NW Iceland
96 I12 **Glåma** *var.* Glommen, Glomma. ~ S Norway
114 F13 **Glamoč** Federacija Bosna I Hercegovina, NE Bosnia and Herzegovina 44.01N 16.51E
99 J22 **Glamorgan** *cultural region* S Wales, UK
97 G24 **Glamsbjerg** Fyn, C Denmark 55.16N 10.07E
179 Rr17 **Glan** Mindanao, S Philippines 5.49N 125.11E
97 M17 **Glan** ◎ S Sweden
111 T9 **Glan** ~ SE Austria
103 F19 **Glan** ~ W Germany
Glaris *see* Glarus
110 H9 **Glarner Alpen** *Eng.* Glarus Alps. ▲▲ E Switzerland
110 H8 **Glarus** Glarus, E Switzerland 47.03N 9.04E
110 H9 **Glarus** *Fr.* Glaris. ◈ *canton* C Switzerland
Glarus Alps *see* Glarner Alpen
29 N3 **Glasco** Kansas, C USA 39.21N 97.50W
98 I12 **Glasgow** S Scotland, UK 55.52N 4.15W
22 K7 **Glasgow** Kentucky, S USA 37.00N 85.54W
29 T4 **Glasgow** Missouri, C USA 39.13N 92.51W
35 W7 **Glasgow** Montana, NW USA 48.12N 106.37W
23 T6 **Glasgow** Virginia, NE USA 37.37N 79.27W
98 I12 **Glasgow** ✈ W Scotland, UK 55.52N 4.27W
9 S14 **Glaslyn** Saskatchewan, S Canada 53.20N 108.18W
20 I16 **Glassboro** New Jersey, NE USA 39.40N 75.05W
26 L10 **Glass Mountains** ▲▲ Texas, SW USA
99 K23 **Glastonbury** SW England, UK 51.09N 2.43W
Glatz *see* Kłodzko
103 N16 **Glauchau** Sachsen, E Germany 50.48N 12.31E
Glavn'a Morava *see* Velika Morava
115 N16 **Glavnik** Serbia, S Serbia and Montenegro (Yugoslavia) 42.53N 21.10E
131 T1 **Glazov** Udmurtskaya Respublika, NW Russian Federation 58.05N 52.38E
Głda *see* Gwda
111 U8 **Gleinalpe** ▲▲ SE Austria
111 W8 **Gleisdorf** Steiermark, SE Austria 47.07N 15.43E
Gleiwitz *see* Gliwice
41 S11 **Glenallen** Alaska, USA 62.06N 145.33W
104 F7 **Glénan, Îles** *island group* NW France
193 G21 **Glenavy** Canterbury, South Island, NZ 44.53S 171.04E
8 H5 **Glenboyle** Yukon Territory, NW Canada 63.55N 138.43W
23 X3 **Glen Burnie** Maryland, NE USA 39.09N 76.37W
38 L8 **Glen Canyon** *canyon* Utah, W USA
38 L8 **Glen Canyon Dam** *dam* Arizona, SW USA 36.56N 111.29W
32 K15 **Glen Carbon** Illinois, N USA 38.45N 89.58W
12 E17 **Glencoe** Ontario, S Canada 42.44N 81.42W
85 K22 **Glencoe** KwaZulu/Natal, E South Africa 28.09S 30.12E
31 U9 **Glencoe** Minnesota, N USA 44.46N 94.09W
98 H10 **Glen Coe** *valley* N Scotland, UK
38 K13 **Glendale** Arizona, SW USA 33.32N 112.11W
37 S15 **Glendale** California, W USA 34.09N 118.17W
190 G5 **Glendambo** South Australia 30.59S 135.45E
35 Y8 **Glendive** Montana, NW USA 47.07N 104.42W
35 Y15 **Glendo** Wyoming, C USA 42.27N 105.01W
57 S10 **Glendor Mountains** ▲▲ C Guyana
190 K12 **Glenelg River** ~ South Australia/Victoria, SE Australia
31 P4 **Glenfield** North Dakota, N USA 47.25N 98.33W
27 V12 **Glen Flora** Texas, SW USA 29.22N 96.12W
189 P7 **Glen Helen** Northern Territory, N Australia 23.45S 132.46E
191 U5 **Glen Innes** New South Wales, SE Australia 29.42S 151.45E
33 P6 **Glen Lake** ◎ Michigan, N USA
8 I7 **Glenlyon Peak** ▲ Yukon Territory, W Canada 62.32N 134.51W
39 N16 **Glenn, Mount** ▲ Arizona, SW USA 31.55N 110.00W
35 N15 **Glenns Ferry** Idaho, NW USA 42.57N 115.18W
25 W6 **Glennville** Georgia, SE USA 31.56N 81.55W
8 J10 **Glenora** British Columbia, W Canada 57.52N 131.16W
190 M11 **Glenorchy** Victoria, SE Australia 36.56S 142.39E
191 V5 **Glenreagh** New South Wales, SE Australia 30.04S 153.00E
35 X15 **Glenrock** Wyoming, C USA 42.51N 105.52W
98 K11 **Glenrothes** E Scotland, UK 56.11N 3.09W
20 L9 **Glens Falls** New York, NE USA 43.18N 73.38W
99 D14 **Glenties** *Ir.* Na Gleannta. NW Ireland 54.46N 8.16W
30 L5 **Glen Ullin** North Dakota, N USA 46.49N 101.49W
23 R4 **Glenville** West Virginia, NE USA 38.55N 80.50W
29 T12 **Glenwood** Arkansas, C USA 34.19N 93.33W
31 S15 **Glenwood** Iowa, C USA 41.03N 95.44W
31 T7 **Glenwood** Minnesota, N USA 45.39N 95.23W
38 L5 **Glenwood** Utah, W USA 38.45N 111.59W
32 I5 **Glenwood City** Wisconsin, N USA 45.04N 92.11W
39 Q4 **Glenwood Springs** Colorado, C USA 39.33N 107.21W
110 F10 **Gletsch** Valais, S Switzerland 46.34N 8.21E
Glevum *see* Gloucester
31 U14 **Glidden** Iowa, C USA 42.03N 94.43W
114 E9 **Glina** Sisak-Moslavina, NE Croatia 45.19N 16.07E
96 F11 **Glittertind** ▲ S Norway 61.24N 8.19E
113 J16 **Gliwice** *Ger.* Gleiwitz. Śląskie, S Poland 50.19N 18.49E
38 M14 **Globe** Arizona, SW USA 33.24N 110.47W
Globino *see* Hlobyne
110 L9 **Glockturm** ▲ SW Austria 46.54N 10.42E
118 L9 **Glodeni** *Rus.* Glodyany. N Moldova 47.47N 27.33E
111 S9 **Glödnitz** Kärnten, S Austria 46.57N 14.03E
Glodyany *see* Glodeni
Glogau *see* Głogów
111 W6 **Gloggnitz** Niederösterreich, E Austria 47.41N 15.57E
112 F13 **Głogów** *Ger.* Glogau, Glogow. Dolnośląskie, SW Poland 51.39N 16.04E
113 I16 **Głogówek** *Ger.* Oberglogau. Opolskie, S Poland 50.21N 17.51E
94 G12 **Glomfjord** Nordland, C Norway 66.48N 13.57E
Glommen *see* Glåma
95 I14 **Glommersträsk** Norrbotten, N Sweden 65.16N 19.40E
180 I1 **Glorieuses, Nosy** *island group* N Madagascar
67 C25 **Glorious Hill** *hill* East Falkland, Falkland Islands
40 J12 **Glory of Russia Cape** *headland* Saint Matthew Island, Alaska, USA 60.36N 172.57W
24 J7 **Gloster** Mississippi, S USA 31.12N 91.01W
191 U7 **Gloucester** New South Wales, SE Australia 32.01S 152.00E
194 L12 **Gloucester** New Britain, E PNG 5.28S 148.28E
99 L21 **Gloucester** *hist.* Caer Glou, *Lat.* Glevum. C England, UK 51.52N 2.13W
21 P10 **Gloucester** Massachusetts, NE USA 42.36N 70.36W
23 X6 **Gloucester** Virginia, NE USA 37.23N 76.30W
99 K21 **Gloucestershire** *cultural region* C England, UK
33 T14 **Glouster** Ohio, N USA 39.30N 82.04W
44 H3 **Glovers Reef** *reef* E Belize
20 K10 **Gloversville** New York, NE USA 43.03N 74.20W
112 K12 **Głowno** Łódź, C Poland 51.58N 19.43E
113 H16 **Głubczyce** *Ger.* Leobschütz. Opolskie, S Poland 50.11N 17.49E
130 L11 **Glubokiy** Rostovskaya Oblast', SW Russian Federation 48.34N 40.16E
151 W9 **Glubokoye** Vostochnyy Kazakhstan, E Kazakhstan 50.10N 82.16E
Glubokoye *see* Hlybokaye
113 H16 **Głuchołazy** *Ger.* Ziegenhais. Opolskie, S Poland 50.18N 17.22E
102 I9 **Glückstadt** Schleswig-Holstein, N Germany 53.47N 9.25E
Glukhov *see* Hlukhiv
Glushkevichi *see* Hlushkavichy
Glusk/Glussk *see* Hlusk
Glybokaya *see* Hlyboka
97 F21 **Glyngøre** Viborg, NW Denmark 56.45N 8.55E
131 Q9 **Gmelinka** Volgogradskaya Oblast', SW Russian Federation 50.50N 46.51E
111 R8 **Gmünd** Kärnten, S Austria 46.56N 13.32E
111 U2 **Gmünd** Niederösterreich, N Austria 48.45N 14.57E
Gmünd *see* Schwäbisch Gmünd
111 S5 **Gmunden** Oberösterreich, N Austria 47.54N 13.46E
Gmundner See *see* Traunsee
96 N10 **Gnarp** Gävleborg, C Sweden 62.03N 17.19E
111 W8 **Gnas** Steiermark, SE Austria 46.53N 15.48E
Gnesen *see* Gniezno
97 O16 **Gnesta** Södermanland, C Sweden 59.02N 17.19E
112 H11 **Gniezno** *Ger.* Gnesen. Wielkopolskie, C Poland 52.33N 17.35E
115 O17 **Gnjilane** *var.* Gilani, *Alb.* Gjilan. Serbia, S Serbia and Montenegro (Yugoslavia) 42.27N 21.28E
97 K20 **Gnosjö** Jönköping, S Sweden 57.22N 13.43E
161 E17 **Goa** *prev.* Old Goa, Vela Goa, Velha Goa. Goa, W India 15.31N 73.55E
161 E17 **Goa** *var.* Old Goa. ◈ *state* W India
Goabddális *see* Kåbdalis
44 H7 **Goascorán, Río** ~ El Salvador/Honduras
79 O16 **Goaso** *var.* Gawso. W Ghana 6.49N 2.27W
83 K14 **Goba** *It.* Oromo, C Ethiopia 7.02N 39.58E
85 C20 **Gobabed** Erongo, W Namibia 23.36S 15.03E
85 E19 **Gobabis** Omaheke, E Namibia 22.24S 18.58E
Gobannium *see* Abergavenny
66 M7 **Goban Spur** *undersea feature* NW Atlantic Ocean
Gobbà *see* Goba
65 H21 **Gobernador Gregores** Santa Cruz, S Argentina 48.43S 70.21W
63 F14 **Gobernador Ingeniero Virasoro** Corrientes, NE Argentina
168 L12 **Gobi** *desert* China/Mongolia
170 G16 **Gobō** Wakayama, Honshū, SW Japan 33.52N 135.09E
103 D14 **Goch** Nordrhein-Westfalen, W Germany 51.41N 6.10E
85 E20 **Gochas** Hardap, S Namibia 24.54S 18.43E
161 L14 **Godāvari** *var.* Godavari. ~ C India
161 L16 **Godāvari, Mouths of the** *delta* E India
13 V5 **Godbout** Québec, SE Canada 49.19N 67.37W
13 U5 **Godbout** ~ Québec, SE Canada
13 U5 **Godbout Est** ~ Québec, SE Canada
29 N6 **Goddard** Kansas, C USA 37.39N 97.34W
12 E15 **Goderich** Ontario, S Canada 43.45N 81.42W
Godhavn *see* Qeqertarsuaq
160 E10 **Godhra** Gujarāt, W India 22.49N 73.40E
Göding *see* Hodonín
113 K22 **Gödöllő** Pest, N Hungary 47.36N 19.19E
64 H11 **Godoy Cruz** Mendoza, W Argentina 32.58S 68.49W
9 Y11 **Gods** ~ Manitoba, C Canada
9 Y13 **Gods Lake** Manitoba, C Canada 54.29N 94.21W
9 X13 **Gods Lake** ◎ Manitoba, C Canada
Godthaab/Godthåb *see* Nuuk
Godwin Austen, Mount *see* K2
Goede Hoop, Kaap de *see* Good Hope, Cape of
Goedgegun *see* Nhlangano
Goeie Hoop, Kaap die *see* Good Hope, Cape of
11 O7 **Goélands, Lac aux** ◎ Québec, SE Canada
100 E13 **Goeree** *island* SW Netherlands
101 F15 **Goes** Zeeland, SW Netherlands 51.30N 3.55E
Goettingen *see* Göttingen
21 O10 **Goffstown** New Hampshire, NE USA 43.01N 71.34W
12 E8 **Gogama** Ontario, S Canada 47.42N 81.43W
170 Ee12 **Gō-gawa** ~ Honshū, SW Japan
32 L3 **Gogebic, Lake** ◎ Michigan, N USA
32 K3 **Gogebic Range** *hill range* Michigan/Wisconsin, N USA
143 V13 **Gogi, Mount** *Arm.* Gogi Lerr, *Az.* Küküdağ. ▲ Armenia/Azerbaijan 39.33N 45.35E
128 F12 **Gogland, Ostrov** *island* NW Russian Federation
113 I15 **Gogolin** Opolskie, S Poland 50.28N 18.04E
Gogonou *see* Gogounou
79 S14 **Gogounou** *var.* Gogonou. N Benin 10.49N 2.49E
158 I10 **Gohāna** Haryāna, N India 29.06N 76.43E
61 K18 **Goianésia** Goiás, C Brazil 15.21S 49.01W
61 K18 **Goiânia** *prev.* Goyania. *state capital* Goiás, C Brazil 16.43S 49.18W
61 K18 **Goiás** Goiás, C Brazil 15.57S 50.07W
61 J18 **Goiás** *off.* Estado de Goiás; *prev.* Goiaz, Goyaz. ◈ *state* C Brazil
Goiaz *see* Goiás
165 R14 **Goinsargoin** Xizang Zizhiqu, W China 31.55N 98.04E
62 H10 **Goio-Erê** Paraná, SW Brazil 24.08S 53.07W
101 I15 **Goirle** Noord-Brabant, S Netherlands 51.31N 5.04E
106 H8 **Góis** Coimbra, N Portugal 40.10N 8.06W
171 Gg16 **Gojō** *var.* Gozyô. Nara, Honshū, SW Japan 34.21N 135.42E
171 M10 **Gojōme** Akita, Honshū, NW Japan 39.55N 140.07E
155 U9 **Gojra** Punjab, E Pakistan 31.09N 72.39E
170 D15 **Gokase-gawa** ~ Kyūshū, SW Japan
142 A11 **Gökçeada** *var.* Imroz Adasi, *Gk.* Imbros. *island* NW Turkey
Gökçeada *see* İmroz
152 F13 **Gökdepe** *Rus.* Gëkdepe, Geok-Tepe. Ahal Welaýaty, C Turkmenistan 38.05N 58.07E
142 I10 **Gökırmak** ~ N Turkey
Goklenkuy, Solonchak *see* Geklengkui, Solonchak
142 C16 **Gökova Körfezi** *gulf* SW Turkey
142 K15 **Göksu** ~ S Turkey
142 L15 **Göksun** Kahramanmaraş, C Turkey 38.03N 36.30E
142 I17 **Göksu Nehri** ~ S Turkey
85 J16 **Gokwe** Midlands, NW Zimbabwe 18.10S 28.54E
96 F13 **Gol** Buskerud, S Norway 60.42N 8.57E
159 X12 **Golāghāt** Assam, NE India 26.31N 93.54E
112 H10 **Gołańcz** Wielkopolskie, C Poland 52.57N 17.17E
144 G8 **Golan Heights** *Ar.* Al Jawlān, *Heb.* HaGolan. ▲▲ SW Syria
Golārā *see* Ārān
Golaya Pristan *see* Hola Prystan'
149 T11 **Golbāf** Kermān, C Iran 29.51N 57.44E
142 M15 **Gölbaşı** Adıyaman, S Turkey 37.46N 37.40E
111 P9 **Gölbner** ▲ SW Austria 46.51N 12.31E
32 M17 **Golconda** Illinois, N USA 37.18N 88.30W
37 T3 **Golconda** Nevada, W USA 40.56N 117.29W
142 E11 **Gölcük** Kocaeli, NW Turkey 40.42N 29.50E
110 I7 **Goldach** Sankt Gallen, NE Switzerland 47.28N 9.28E
112 N7 **Gołdap** *Ger.* Goldap. Warmińsko-Mazurskie, NE Poland 54.18N 22.23E
34 E15 **Gold Beach** Oregon, NW USA 42.24N 124.25W
Goldberg *see* Złotoryja
70 D11 **Gold Coast** *coastal region* S Ghana
191 V3 **Gold Coast** *cultural region* Queensland, E Australia
41 R10 **Gold Creek** Alaska, USA 62.48N 149.40W
9 O16 **Golden** British Columbia, SW Canada 51.19N 116.58W
39 T4 **Golden** Colorado, C USA 39.40N 105.12W
192 I13 **Golden Bay** *bay* South Island, NZ
29 R7 **Golden City** Missouri, C USA 37.23N 94.05W
34 I11 **Goldendale** Washington, NW USA 45.49N 120.49W
Goldener Tisch *see* Zlatý Stôl
46 L13 **Golden Grove** E Jamaica 17.55N 76.16W
12 J12 **Golden Lake** ◎ Ontario, SE Canada
24 K10 **Golden Meadow** Louisiana, S USA 29.22N 90.15W
47 V10 **Golden Rock** ✈ (Basseterre) Saint Kitts, Saint Kitts and Nevis 17.16N 62.43W
Golden State, The *see* California
85 K16 **Golden Valley** Mashonaland West, N Zimbabwe 18.15S 29.46E
37 U9 **Goldfield** Nevada, W USA 37.40N 117.13W
Goldingen *see* Kuldīga
Goldmarkt *see* Zlatna
8 K17 **Gold River** Vancouver Island, British Columbia, SW Canada 49.48N 126.01W
23 V10 **Goldsboro** North Carolina, SE USA 35.22N 77.59W
26 M8 **Goldsmith** Texas, SW USA 31.58N 102.36W
27 R8 **Goldthwaite** Texas, SW USA 31.27N 98.34W
143 R11 **Göle** Ardahan, NE Turkey 40.46N 42.36E
Golema Ada *see* Ostrovo
116 H9 **Golema Planina** ▲▲ W Bulgaria
116 F9 **Golemi Vrŭkh** ▲ W Bulgaria 42.41N 22.38E
112 D8 **Goleniów** *Ger.* Gollnow. Zachodnio-pomorskie, NW Poland 53.33N 14.48E
149 R3 **Golestān** ◈ *province* N Iran
37 Q14 **Goleta** California, W USA 34.25N 119.51W
45 O16 **Golfito** Puntarenas, SE Costa Rica 8.37N 83.07W
27 T13 **Goliad** Texas, SW USA 28.40N 97.23W
115 L14 **Golija** ▲▲ SW Serbia and Montenegro (Yugoslavia)
Golinka *see* Gongbo'gyamda
115 O16 **Goljak** ▲▲ SE Serbia and Montenegro (Yugoslavia)
142 M12 **Gölköy** Ordu, N Turkey 40.42N 37.37E
Gollel *see* Lavumisa
111 X3 **Göllersbach** ~ NE Austria
Gollnow *see* Goleniów
Golmo *see* Golmud
165 P10 **Golmud** *var.* Ge'e'mu, Golmo, *Chin.* Ko-erh-mu. Qinghai, C China 36.22N 94.56E
105 Y14 **Golo** ~ Corse, France, C Mediterranean Sea
Golovanevsk *see* Holovanivs'k
Golovchin *see* Halowchyn
41 N9 **Golovin** Alaska, USA 64.33N 162.54W
148 M7 **Golpāyegān** *var.* Gulpaigan. Eşfahān, W Iran 33.22N 50.18E
Golshan *see* Ţabas
Gol'shany *see* Hal'shany
98 J7 **Golspie** N Scotland, UK 57.58N 3.55W
114 O11 **Golubac** Serbia, NE Serbia and Montenegro (Yugoslavia) 44.38N 21.36E
112 J9 **Golub-Dobrzyń** Kujawski-pomorskie, C Poland 53.06N 19.03E
151 S7 **Golubovka** Pavlodar, N Kazakhstan 53.07N 74.11E
84 B11 **Golungo Alto** Cuanza Norte, NW Angola 9.10S 14.45E
116 M8 **Golyama Kamchiya** ~ E Bulgaria
116 L8 **Golyama Reka** ~ N Bulgaria
116 H11 **Golyama Syutkya** ▲ SW Bulgaria 41.55N 24.03E
116 I12 **Golyam Perelik** ▲ S Bulgaria 41.37N 24.34E
116 I11 **Golyam Persenk** ▲ S Bulgaria 41.50N 24.33E
125 F12 **Golyshmanovo** Tyumenskaya Oblast', C Russian Federation 56.22N 68.25E
81 P19 **Goma** Nord Kivu, NE Dem. Rep. Congo 1.36S 29.07E
171 Gg16 **Gomadan-zan** ▲ Honshū, SW Japan 34.03N 135.34E
Gomati *see* Gumti
79 X14 **Gombe** Gombe, E Nigeria 10.19N 11.02E
69 U10 **Gombe** *var.* Igombe. ~ E Tanzania
79 Y14 **Gombi** Adamawa, E Nigeria 10.07N 12.45E
Gombroon *see* Bandar-e 'Abbās
Gomel' *see* Homyel'
Gomel'skaya Oblast' *see* Homyel'skaya Voblasts'
66 N11 **Gomera** *island* Islas Canarias, Spain, NE Atlantic Ocean
42 I5 **Gómez Farias** Chihuahua, N Mexico 29.25N 107.46W
42 L8 **Gómez Palacio** Durango, C Mexico 25.39N 103.30W
164 J13 **Gomo** Xizang Zizhiqu, W China 33.37N 86.40E
175 T11 **Gomumu, Pulau** *island* Maluku, E Indonesia
149 T6 **Gonābād** *var.* Gunabad. Khorāsān, NE Iran 36.21N 58.38E
46 L8 **Gonaïves** *var.* Les Gonaïves. N Haiti 19.26N 72.40W
126 M13 **Gonam** ~ NE Russian Federation
46 L9 **Gonâve, Canal de la** *var.* Canal de Sud. *channel* N Caribbean Sea
46 K9 **Gonâve, Golfe de la** *gulf* N Caribbean Sea
Gonāveh *see* Bandar-e Gonāveh
46 K9 **Gonâve, Île de la** *island* C Haiti
Gonbadān *see* Dow Gonbadān
149 Q3 **Gonbad-e Kāvūs** *var.* Gunbad-i-Qawus. Golestān, N Iran 37.15N 55.10E
158 M12 **Gonda** Uttar Pradesh, N India 27.07N 81.58E
Gondar *see* Gonder
82 I11 **Gonder** *var.* Gondar. Amhara, N Ethiopia 12.35N 37.27E
80 J13 **Gondey** Moyen-Chari, S Chad 9.07N 19.10E
160 J12 **Gondia** Mahārāshtra, C India 21.27N 80.12E
106 G6 **Gondomar** Porto, NW Portugal 41.10N 8.34W
142 C12 **Gönen** Balıkesir, W Turkey 40.06N 27.39E
142 C12 **Gönen Çayı** ~ NW Turkey
165 O15 **Gongbo'gyamda** *var.* Golinka. Xizang Zizhiqu, W China 30.03N 93.10E
165 N16 **Gonggar** *var.* Gyixong. Xizang Zizhiqu, W China 29.18N 90.56E
166 G9 **Gongga Shan** ▲ C China 29.49N 101.55E
165 T10 **Gonghe** *var.* Qabqa. Qinghai, C China 36.22N 100.44E
Gongjiang *see* Yudu
164 I5 **Gongliu** *var.* Tokkuztara. Xinjiang Uygur Zizhiqu, NW China 43.29N 82.16E
79 W14 **Gongola** ~ E Nigeria
Gongoleh State *see* Jonglei
191 P5 **Gongolgon** New South Wales, SE Australia 30.19S 146.57E
165 Q6 **Gongpoquan** Gansu, N China 41.45N 100.27E
Gongquan *see* Gongxian
Gongtang *see* Damxung
166 I10 **Gongxian** *var.* Gongquan, Gong Xian. Sichuan, C China 28.25N 104.51E
163 V10 **Gongzhuling** *prev.* Huaide. Jilin, NE China 43.30N 124.48E
165 S14 **Gonjo** Xizang Zizhiqu, W China 30.51N 98.16E
109 B20 **Gonnesa** Sardegna, Italy, C Mediterranean Sea 39.15N 8.27E
Gonni/Gónnos *see* Gónnoi
117 F15 **Gónnoi** *var.* Gonni, Gónnos; *prev.* Dereli. Thessalía, C Greece 39.52N 22.27E
172 N9 **Gonohe** Aomori, Honshū, C Japan 40.34N 141.18E
170 Cc11 **Gōnoura** Nagasaki, Iki, SW Japan 33.44N 129.41E
37 O11 **Gonzales** California, W USA 36.30N 121.26W

◆ Country ● Country Capital ◇ Dependent Territory ○ Dependent Territory Capital ◈ Administrative Region ✈ International Airport ▲ Mountain ▲▲ Mountain Range Volcano ~ River ◎ Lake Reservoir

GONZALES – GRAUDENZ

24 J9 **Gonzales** Louisiana, S USA *30.14N 90.55W*
27 T12 **Gonzales** Texas, SW USA *29.30N 97.27W*
43 P11 **González** Tamaulipas, C Mexico *22.52N 98.25W*
23 V6 **Goochland** Virginia, NE USA *37.40N 77.53W*
195 N16 **Goodenough Bay** *inlet* SE PNG
205 X14 **Goodenough, Cape** *headland* Antarctica *66.15S 126.34E*
195 N15 **Goodenough Island** *var.* Morata. *island* SE PNG
Good Hope *see* Fort Good Hope
41 N8 **Goodhope Bay** *bay* Alaska, USA
85 D26 **Good Hope, Cape of** *Afr.* Kaap de Goede Hoop, Kaap die Goeie Hoop. *headland* SW South Africa *34.19S 18.25E*
8 K10 **Good Hope Lake** British Columbia, W Canada *59.15N 129.18W*
85 E23 **Goodhouse** Northern Cape, W South Africa *28.54S 18.13E*
35 O15 **Gooding** Idaho, NW USA *42.56N 114.42W*
28 H3 **Goodland** Kansas, C USA *39.21N 101.42W*
181 Y15 **Goodlands** NW Mauritius *20.01S 57.39E*
22 J8 **Goodlettsville** Tennessee, S USA *36.19N 86.42W*
41 N13 **Goodnews** Alaska, USA *59.07N 161.35W*
27 O3 **Goodnight** Texas, SW USA *35.00N 101.07W*
191 Q4 **Goodooga** New South Wales, SE Australia *29.09S 147.30E*
31 N4 **Goodrich** North Dakota, N USA *47.24N 100.07W*
27 W10 **Goodrich** Texas, SW USA *30.36N 94.57W*
31 X10 **Goodview** Minnesota, N USA *44.04N 91.42W*
28 H8 **Goodwell** Oklahoma, C USA *36.36N 101.38W*
99 N17 **Goole** E England, UK *53.43N 0.46W*
191 O8 **Goolgowi** New South Wales, SE Australia *34.00S 145.43E*
190 I10 **Goolwa** South Australia *35.31S 138.43E*
189 Y11 **Goondiwindi** Queensland, E Australia *28.33S 150.22E*
100 O11 **Goor** Overijssel, E Netherlands *52.13N 6.33E*
Goose Bay *see* Happy Valley-Goose Bay
35 V13 **Gooseberry Creek** ~ Wyoming, C USA
23 S14 **Goose Creek** South Carolina, SE USA *32.58N 80.01W*
65 M23 **Goose Green** *var.* Prado del Ganso. East Falkland, Falkland Islands *51.52S 59.00W*
17 G6 **Goose Lake** *var.* Lago dos Gansos. ⊚ California/Oregon, W USA
31 Q4 **Goose River** ~ North Dakota, N USA
159 T16 **Gopalganj** Dhaka, S Bangladesh *23.03N 89.52E*
159 O12 **Gopālganj** Bihār, N India *26.28N 84.25E*
Gopher State *see* Minnesota
103 I22 **Göppingen** Baden-Württemberg, SW Germany *48.42N 9.39E*
112 G13 **Góra** *Ger.* Guhrau. Dolnośląskie, SW Poland *51.40N 16.30E*
112 M12 **Góra Kalwaria** Mazowieckie, C Poland *52.00N 21.14E*
159 O12 **Gorakhpur** Uttar Pradesh, N India *26.45N 83.22E*
Gorany *see* Harany
115 J14 **Goražde** Federacija Bosna I Hercegovina, Bosnia and Herzegovina *43.39N 18.58E*
Gorbovichi *see* Harbavichy
Gorče Petrov *see* Đorče Petrov
(0) E9 **Gorda Ridges** *undersea feature* NE Pacific Ocean
Gordiaz *see* Gardēz
80 K12 **Gordil** Vakaga, N Central African Republic *9.37N 21.42E*
25 U5 **Gordon** Georgia, SE USA *32.52N 83.19W*
30 K12 **Gordon** Nebraska, C USA *42.48N 102.12W*
27 R7 **Gordon** Texas, SW USA *32.32N 98.21W*
30 L13 **Gordon Creek** ~ Nebraska, C USA
65 I25 **Gordon, Isla** *island* S Chile
191 O17 **Gordon, Lake** ⊚ Tasmania, SE Australia
191 O17 **Gordon River** ~ Tasmania, SE Australia
23 V5 **Gordonsville** Virginia, NE USA *38.08N 78.11W*
82 H13 **Gorē** Oromo, C Ethiopia *8.08N 35.33E*
193 D24 **Gore** Southland, South Island, NZ *46.06S 168.58E*
80 H13 **Goré** Logone-Oriental, S Chad *7.55N 16.37E*
12 D11 **Gore Bay** Manitoulin Island, Ontario, S Canada *45.54N 82.28W*
27 Q5 **Goree** Texas, SW USA *33.28N 99.31W*
143 O11 **Görele** Giresun, NE Turkey *41.00N 39.00E*
21 N6 **Gore Mountain** ▲ Vermont, NE USA *44.55N 71.47W*
41 R13 **Gore Point** *headland* Alaska, USA *59.12N 150.57W*
39 R4 **Gore Range** ▲▲ Colorado, C USA
99 F19 **Gorey** *Ir.* Guaire. SE Ireland *52.40N 6.18W*
149 R12 **Gorgāb** Kermān, S Iran
149 Q4 **Gorgān** *var.* Astarabad, Astrabad, Gurgan; *prev.* Asterābād, *anc.* Hyrcania. Golestān, N Iran *36.53N 54.28E*
149 Q4 **Gorgān, Rūd-e** ~ N Iran
78 I10 **Gorgol** ◈ *region* S Mauritania
108 D12 **Gorgona, Isola di** *island* Archipelago Toscano, C Italy
21 P8 **Gorham** Maine, NE USA *43.41N 70.27W*
143 T10 **Gori** C Georgia *42.00N 44.07E*
100 I13 **Gorinchem** *var.* Gorkum. Zuid-Holland, C Netherlands *51.49N 4.58E*
143 V13 **Goris** SE Armenia *39.31N 46.20E*
128 K16 **Goritsy** Tverskaya Oblast', W Russian Federation *57.09N 36.44E*
108 J7 **Gorizia** *Ger.* Görz. Friuli-Venezia Giulia, NE Italy *45.55N 13.37E*
118 G13 **Gorj** ◈ *county* SW Romania
111 W12 **Gorjanci** *var.* Uskočke Planine, Žumberak, Žumberačko Gorje, *Ger.* Uskokengebirge; *prev.* Sichelburger Gerbirge. ▲▲ Croatia/Slovenia *see also* Žumberačko Gorje
Görkau *see* Jirkov
Gorki *see* Horki
Gor'kiy *see* Nizhniy Novgorod
Gor'kiy Reservoir *see* Gor'kovskoye Vodokhranilishche
125 D9 **Gor'kovskoye Vodokhranilishche** *Eng.* Gor'kiy Reservoir. ⊠ W Russian Federation
Gorkum *see* Gorinchem
97 I23 **Gørlev** Vestsjælland, E Denmark *55.33N 11.13E*
113 M17 **Gorlice** Małopolskie, S Poland *49.37N 21.08E*
103 Q15 **Görlitz** Sachsen, E Germany *51.09N 14.57E*
Görlitz *see* Zgorzelec
Gorlovka *see* Horlivka
27 R7 **Gorman** Texas, SW USA *32.12N 98.40W*
23 T3 **Gormania** West Virginia, NE USA *39.16N 79.18W*
Gorna Dzhumaya *see* Blagoevgrad
116 K8 **Gorna Oryakhovitsa** Veliko Tŭrnovo, N Bulgaria *43.12N 25.38E*
116 J8 **Gorna Studena** Veliko Tŭrnovo, N Bulgaria *43.26N 25.21E*
Gornja Mužlja *see* Mužlja
111 X9 **Gornja Radgona** *Ger.* Oberradkersburg. NE Slovenia *46.39N 16.00E*
114 M13 **Gornji Milanovac** Serbia, C Serbia and Montenegro (Yugoslavia) *44.01N 20.26E*
114 G13 **Gornji Vakuf** *var.* Uskoplje. Federacija Bosna I Hercegovina, W Bosnia and Herzegovina *43.55N 17.34E*
126 H15 **Gorno-Altaysk** Respublika Altay, S Russian Federation *51.58N 85.55E*
Gorno-Altayskaya Respublika *see* Altay, Respublika
126 K13 **Gorno-Chuyskiy** Irkutskaya Oblast', C Russian Federation *57.33N 111.38E*
129 V14 **Gornozavodsk** Permskaya Oblast', NW Russian Federation *58.21N 58.24E*
127 O16 **Gornozavodsk** Ostrov Sakhalin, Sakhalinskaya Oblast', SE Russian Federation *46.34N 141.52E*
126 Gg15 **Gornyak** Altayskiy Kray, S Russian Federation *50.58N 81.24E*
126 K15 **Gornyy** Chitinskaya Oblast', S Russian Federation *51.42N 48.26E*
131 R8 **Gornyy** Saratovskaya Oblast', W Russian Federation *51.42N 48.26E*
Gornyy Altay *see* Altay, Respublika
131 O10 **Gornyy Balykley** Volgogradskaya Oblast', SW Russian Federation *49.37N 45.03E*
82 I13 **Gorocb'an** ▲ W Ethiopia *9.09N 37.16E*
Gorodenka *see* Horodenka
131 O3 **Gorodets** Nizhegorodskaya Oblast', W Russian Federation *56.36N 43.27E*
Gorodets *see* Haradzyets
Gorodeya *see* Haradzyeya
131 P6 **Gorodishche** Penzenskaya Oblast', W Russian Federation *53.17N 45.39E*
Gorodishche *see* Horodyshche
Gorodnya *see* Horodnya
Gorodok *see* Haradok
Gorodok/Gorodok Yagellonski *see* Horodok
130 M13 **Gorodovikovsk** Respublika Kalmykiya, SW Russian Federation *46.07N 41.56E*
194 I12 **Goroka** Eastern Highlands, C PNG *6.03S 145.22E*
Gorokhov *see* Horokhiv
131 N3 **Gorokhovets** Vladimirskaya Oblast', W Russian Federation *56.12N 42.40E*
79 Q11 **Gorom-Gorom** NE Burkina *14.27N 0.13W*
176 V12 **Gorong, Kepulauan** *island group* E Indonesia
85 M17 **Gorongosa** Sofala, C Mozambique *18.40S 34.03E*
176 Uu12 **Gorong, Pulau** *island* Kepulauan Gorong, E Indonesia
175 R8 **Gorontalo** Sulawesi, C Indonesia *0.33N 123.04E*
175 Qq7 **Gorontalo** *off.* Propinsi Gorontalo. ◈ *province* N Indonesia
175 Qq8 **Gorontalo, Teluk** *bay* Sulawesi, C Indonesia
Gorontalo, Teluk *see* Tomini, Gulf of
112 L7 **Górowo Iławeckie** *Ger.* Landsberg. Warmińsko-Mazurskie, NE Poland, *54.18N 20.30E*
100 M7 **Gorredijk** *Fris.* De Gordyk. Friesland, N Netherlands *53.00N 6.04E*
86 C14 **Gorringe Ridge** *undersea feature* E Atlantic Ocean
100 M11 **Gorssel** Gelderland, E Netherlands *52.12N 6.13E*
111 T8 **Görtschitz** ~ S Austria
Goryn *see* Horyn'
Görz *see* Gorizia
112 E10 **Gorzów Wielkopolski** *Ger.* Landsberg, Landsberg an der Warthe. Lubuskie, W Poland *52.43N 15.12E*
110 G9 **Göschenen** Uri, C Switzerland *46.40N 8.36E*
195 N16 **Goschen Strait** *strait* SE PNG
171 Kk13 **Gosen** Niigata, Honshū, C Japan *37.43N 139.11E*
191 T8 **Gosford** New South Wales, SE Australia *33.25S 151.22E*
33 P11 **Goshen** Indiana, N USA *41.34N 85.49W*
20 K13 **Goshen** New York, NE USA *41.24N 74.17W*
Goshoba *see* Goşoba
171 Mm8 **Goshogawara** *var.* Gosyogawara. Aomori, Honshū, C Japan *40.46N 140.24E*
Goshquduq Qum *see* Tosquduq Qumlari
103 J14 **Goslar** Niedersachsen, C Germany *51.55N 10.25E*
29 Y9 **Gosnell** Arkansas, C USA *35.57N 89.58W*
152 B10 **Goşoba** *var.* Goshoba, *Rus.* Koshoba. Balkanskiy Velayat, NW Turkmenistan *40.28N 54.11E*
114 C11 **Gospić** Lika-Senj, C Croatia *44.32N 15.21E*
99 N23 **Gosport** S England, UK *50.48N 1.07W*
96 D9 **Gossa** *island* S Norway
110 H7 **Gossau** Sankt Gallen, NE Switzerland *47.25N 9.16E*
101 G20 **Gosselies** *var.* Goss'lies. Hainaut, S Belgium *50.28N 4.25E*
79 P10 **Gossi** Tombouctou, C Mali *15.44N 1.19W*
Goss'lies *see* Gosselies
115 N18 **Gostivar** W FYR Macedonia *41.48N 20.55E*
Gostomel' *see* Hostomel'
112 G12 **Gostyń** *var.* Gostyn. Wielkopolskie, C Poland *51.53N 16.59E*
112 K11 **Gostynin** Mazowieckie, C Poland *52.25N 19.27E*
Gosyogawara *see* Goshogawara
97 J18 **Göta Älv** ~ S Sweden
97 N17 **Göta kanal** *canal* S Sweden
97 K18 **Götaland** *cultural region* S Sweden
97 H17 **Göteborg** *Eng.* Gothenburg. Västra Götaland, S Sweden *57.43N 11.58E*
79 X16 **Gotel Mountains** ▲▲ E Nigeria
97 K17 **Götene** Västra Götaland, S Sweden *58.31N 13.28E*
Gotera *see* San Francisco
103 K16 **Gotha** Thüringen, C Germany *50.57N 10.43E*
31 N15 **Gothenburg** Nebraska, C USA *40.57N 100.09W*
Gothenburg *see* Göteborg
79 R12 **Gothèye** Tillabéri, SW Niger *13.52N 1.27E*
Gothland *see* Gotland
97 P19 **Gotland** *var.* Gothland, Gottland. ◈ *county* SE Sweden
97 O18 **Gotland** *island* SE Sweden
170 B12 **Gotō-rettō** *island group* SW Japan
116 H12 **Gotse Delchev** *prev.* Nevrokop. Blagoevgrad, SW Bulgaria *41.35N 23.43E*
97 P17 **Gotska Sandön** *island* SE Sweden
170 Ee12 **Gōtsu** *var.* Gôtu. Shimane, Honshū, SW Japan *35.00N 132.13E*
103 I15 **Göttingen** *var.* Goettingen. Niedersachsen, C Germany *51.33N 9.55E*
Gottland *see* Gotland
95 I16 **Gottne** Västernorrland, C Sweden *63.27N 18.25E*
Gottschee *see* Kočevje
Gottwaldov *see* Zlín
Gôtu *see* Gōtsu
152 B11 **Goturdepe** *Rus.* Koturdepe. Balkan Welaýaty, W Turkmenistan *39.32N 53.39E*
110 I7 **Götzis** Vorarlberg, NW Austria *47.21N 9.40E*
100 H12 **Gouda** Zuid-Holland, C Netherlands *52.01N 4.42E*
78 I11 **Goudiri** *var.* Goudiry. E Senegal *14.12N 12.40W*
Goudiry *see* Goudiri
79 X12 **Goudoumaria** Diffa, S Niger *13.28N 11.15E*
13 R9 **Gouffre, Rivière du** ~ Québec, SE Canada
67 M19 **Gough Fracture Zone** *tectonic feature* S Atlantic Ocean
67 M19 **Gough Island** *island* Tristan da Cunha, S Atlantic Ocean
13 N8 **Gouin, Réservoir** ⊠ Québec, SE Canada
12 B10 **Goulais River** Ontario, S Canada *46.41N 84.22W*
191 R9 **Goulburn** New South Wales, SE Australia *34.45S 149.43E*
191 O11 **Goulburn River** ~ Victoria, SE Australia
205 O10 **Gould Coast** *physical region* Antarctica
Goulimime *see* Guelmime
116 F13 **Gouménissa** Kentrikí Makedonía, N Greece *40.55N 22.27E*
79 O10 **Goundam** Tombouctou, NW Mali *16.25N 3.41W*
80 H12 **Goundi** Moyen-Chari, S Chad *9.18N 17.21E*
80 G12 **Gounou-Gaya** Mayo-Kébbi, SW Chad *9.37N 15.30E*
79 O12 **Gourci** *var.* Gourcy. NW Burkina *13.14N 2.22W*
Gourcy *see* Gourci
104 M13 **Gourdon** Lot, S France *44.45N 1.22E*
79 W11 **Gouré** Zinder, SE Niger *13.58N 10.16E*
104 G6 **Gourin** Morbihan, NW France *48.07N 3.37W*
79 P10 **Gourma-Rharous** Tombouctou, C Mali *16.54N 1.55W*
105 N4 **Gournay-en-Bray** Seine-Maritime, N France *49.29N 1.42E*
80 J6 **Gouro** Borkou-Ennedi-Tibesti, N Chad *19.26N 19.36E*
106 H8 **Gouveia** Guarda, N Portugal *40.28N 7.34W*
20 I7 **Gouverneur** New York, NE USA *44.20N 75.27W*
101 L21 **Gouvy** Luxembourg, E Belgium *50.10N 5.55E*
47 R14 **Gouyave** *var.* Charlotte Town. NW Grenada *12.10N 61.43W*
Goverla, Gora *see* Hoverla, Hora
61 N20 **Governador Valadares** Minas Gerais, SE Brazil *18.51S 41.57W*
179 Rr16 **Governor Generoso** Mindanao, S Philippines *6.36N 126.06E*
46 I2 **Governor's Harbour** Eleuthera Island, C Bahamas *25.11N 76.15W*
168 F9 **Govĭ-Altay** ◈ *province* SW Mongolia
168 I10 **Govĭ Altayn Nuruu** ▲▲ S Mongolia
160 L9 **Govind Ballabh Pant Sāgar** ⊠ C India
158 I7 **Govind Sāgar** ⊠ NE India
168 M8 **Govĭ-Sumber** ◈ *province* C Mongolia
Govurdak *see* Gowurdak
20 D11 **Gowanda** New York, NE USA *42.25N 78.55W*
154 J10 **Gowd-e Zereh, Dasht-e** *var.* Guad-i-Zirreh. *marsh* SW Afghanistan
12 F8 **Gowganda** Ontario, S Canada *47.39N 80.43W*
12 G8 **Gowganda Lake** ⊚ Ontario, S Canada
31 U13 **Gowrie** Iowa, C USA *42.16N 94.17W*
153 N14 **Gowurdak** *Rus.* Govurdak; *prev.* Guardak. Lebap Welaýaty, E Turkmenistan *37.50N 66.06E*
63 C15 **Goya** Corrientes, NE Argentina *29.10S 59.15W*
Goyania *see* Goiânia
143 X11 **Göyçay** *Rus.* Geokchay. C Azerbaijan *40.38N 47.44E*
152 D10 **Goymat** *Rus.* Koymat. Balkan Welaýaty, NW Turkmenistan *40.23N 55.45E*
152 D10 **Goymatdag** *Rus.* **Gory** Koymatdag. *hill range* NW Turkmenistan
142 F12 **Göynük** Bolu, NW Turkey *40.24N 30.45E*
172 N12 **Goyō-san** ▲ Honshū, C Japan *39.12N 141.40E*
80 K11 **Goz Beïda** Ouaddaï, SE Chad *12.06N 21.22E*
152 M10 **G'ozg'on** *Rus.* Gazgan. Navoiy Viloyati, C Uzbekistan *40.36N 65.29E*
164 H11 **Gozha Co** ⊚ W China
123 J15 **Gozo** *Malt.* Ghawdex. *island* N Malta
82 H9 **Gôz Regeb** Kassala, NE Sudan *16.03N 35.33E*
Gozyô *see* Gojō
85 H25 **Graaff-Reinet** Eastern Cape, S South Africa *32.16S 24.31E*
Graasten *see* Gråsten
78 L17 **Grabo** SW Ivory Coast *4.57N 7.30W*
114 P11 **Grabovica** Serbia, E Serbia and Montenegro (Yugoslavia) *44.30N 22.29E*
112 I13 **Grabów nad Prosną** Wielkopolskie, C Poland *51.30N 18.06E*
110 I8 **Grabs** Sankt Gallen, NE Switzerland *47.10N 9.27E*
114 D12 **Gračac** Zadar, C Croatia *44.18N 15.52E*
114 I11 **Gračanica** Federacija Bosna I Hercegovina, NE Bosnia and Herzegovina *44.41N 18.20E*
12 L11 **Gracefield** Québec, SE Canada *46.06N 76.03W*
101 K19 **Grâce-Hollogne** Liège, E Belgium *50.38N 5.30E*
25 R8 **Graceville** Florida, SE USA *30.57N 85.31W*
31 R8 **Graceville** Minnesota, N USA *45.34N 96.25W*
44 G6 **Gracias** Lempira, W Honduras *14.34N 88.34W*
Gracias *see* Lempira
44 L5 **Gracias a Dios** ◈ *department* E Honduras
45 O6 **Gracias a Dios, Cabo de** *headland* Honduras/Nicaragua *15.00N 83.10W*
66 O2 **Graciosa** *var.* Ilha Graciosa. *island* Azores, Portugal, NE Atlantic Ocean
66 Q11 **Graciosa** *island* Islas Canarias, Spain, NE Atlantic Ocean
Graciosa, Ilha *see* Graciosa
114 I11 **Gradačac** Federacija Bosna I Hercegovina, N Bosnia and Herzegovina *44.51N 18.24E*
61 J15 **Gradaús, Serra dos** ▲▲ C Brazil
106 L3 **Gradefes** Castilla-León, N Spain *42.37N 5.13W*
Gradiška *see* Bosanska Gradiška
Gradizhsk *see* Hradyz'k
108 J7 **Grado** Friuli-Venezia Giulia, NE Italy *45.41N 13.24E*
106 K2 **Grado** Asturias, N Spain *43.22N 6.04W*
115 P19 **Gradsko** C FYR Macedonia *41.34N 21.56E*
39 V11 **Grady** New Mexico, SW USA *34.49N 103.19W*
31 T12 **Graettinger** Iowa, C USA *43.14N 94.45W*
103 M23 **Grafing** Bayern, SE Germany *48.01N 11.57E*
27 S6 **Graford** Texas, SW USA *32.56N 98.15W*
191 V5 **Grafton** New South Wales, SE Australia *29.41S 152.55E*
31 Q3 **Grafton** North Dakota, N USA *48.24N 97.24W*
23 S3 **Grafton** West Virginia, NE USA *39.20N 80.01W*
23 T9 **Graham** North Carolina, SE USA *36.04N 79.24W*
27 R6 **Graham** Texas, SW USA *33.06N 98.34W*
Graham Bell Island *see* Greem-Bell, Ostrov
8 I13 **Graham Island** *island* Queen Charlotte Islands, British Columbia, SW Canada
21 S6 **Graham Lake** ⊚ Maine, NE USA
204 H4 **Graham Land** *physical region* Antarctica
39 N15 **Graham, Mount** ▲ Arizona, SW USA *32.42N 109.52W*
Grahamstad *see* Grahamstown
85 I25 **Grahamstown** *Afr.* Grahamstad. Eastern Cape, S South Africa *33.18S 26.31E*
Grahovo *see* Bosansko Grahovo
70 C11 **Grain Coast** *coastal region* S Liberia
174 Mm16 **Grajagan** Jawa, S Indonesia *8.33S 114.13E*
174 Mm16 **Grajagan, Teluk** *bay* Jawa, S Indonesia
61 L14 **Grajaú** Maranhão, E Brazil *5.49S 45.12W*
60 M13 **Grajaú, Rio** ~ NE Brazil
112 O8 **Grajewo** Podlaskie, NE Poland *53.38N 22.25E*
97 F24 **Gram** Sønderjylland, SW Denmark *55.18N 9.03E*
105 N13 **Gramat** Lot, S France *44.45N 1.45E*
24 H5 **Grambling** Louisiana, S USA *32.31N 92.43W*
117 C14 **Grámmos** ▲▲ Albania/Greece
98 I9 **Grampian Mountains** ▲▲ C Scotland, UK
190 L12 **Grampians, The** ▲▲ Victoria, SE Australia
100 O9 **Gramsbergen** Overijssel, E Netherlands *52.37N 6.39E*
115 L21 **Gramsh** *var.* Gramshi. Elbasan, C Albania *40.52N 20.12E*
Gramshi *see* Gramsh
Gran *see* Hron, Slovakia
Gran *see* Esztergom, N Hungary
56 F11 **Granada** Meta, C Colombia *3.36N 73.44W*
44 J10 **Granada** Granada, SW Nicaragua *11.55N 85.58W*
107 N14 **Granada** Andalucía, S Spain *37.13N 3.40W*
39 W6 **Granada** Colorado, C USA *38.00N 102.18W*
44 J11 **Granada** ◈ *department* SW Nicaragua
107 N14 **Granada** ◈ *province* Andalucía, S Spain
65 I21 **Gran Altiplanicie Central** *plain* S Argentina
99 E17 **Granard** *Ir.* Gránard. C Ireland *53.46N 7.30W*
65 J20 **Gran Bajo** *basin* S Argentina
65 J15 **Gran Bajo del Gualicho** *basin* E Argentina
65 I21 **Gran Bajo de San Julián** *basin* SE Argentina
27 S7 **Granbury** Texas, SW USA *32.26N 97.47W*
13 P12 **Granby** Québec, SE Canada *45.24N 72.40W*
29 S8 **Granby** Missouri, C USA *36.55N 94.14W*
39 S3 **Granby, Lake** ⊠ Colorado, C USA
66 O12 **Gran Canaria** *var.* Grand Canary. *island* Islas Canarias, Spain, NE Atlantic Ocean
49 T11 **Gran Chaco** *var.* Chaco. *lowland plain* South America
47 R14 **Grand Anse** SW Grenada *12.01N 61.45W*
Grand-Anse *see* Portsmouth
46 G1 **Grand Bahama Island** *island* N Bahamas
Grand Balé *see* Tui
105 U7 **Grand Ballon** *Ger.* Ballon de Guebwiller. ▲ NE France *47.53N 7.06E*
11 T13 **Grand Bank** Newfoundland and Labrador, SE Canada *47.04N 55.46W*
66 I7 **Grand Banks of Newfoundland** *undersea feature* NW Atlantic Ocean
Grand Bassa *see* Buchanan
79 N17 **Grand-Bassam** *var.* Bassam. SE Ivory Coast *5.13N 3.46W*
12 E16 **Grand Bend** Ontario, S Canada *43.17N 81.46W*
78 L17 **Grand-Bérébi** *var.* Grand-Béréby. SW Ivory Coast *4.37N 6.55W*
Grand-Béréby *see* Grand-Bérébi
47 X11 **Grand-Bourg** Marie-Galante, SE Guadeloupe *15.53N 61.18W*
46 M6 **Grand Caicos** *var.* Middle Caicos. *island* C Turks and Caicos Islands
12 K12 **Grand Calumet, Île du** *island* Québec, SE Canada
99 E18 **Grand Canal** *Ir.* An Chanáil Mhór. *canal* C Ireland
Grand Canary *see* Gran Canaria
38 K10 **Grand Canyon** Arizona, SW USA *36.01N 112.10W*
38 J9 **Grand Canyon** *canyon* Arizona, SW USA
Grand Canyon State *see* Arizona
46 D8 **Grand Cayman** *island* SW Cayman Islands
9 R14 **Grand Centre** Alberta, SW Canada *54.25N 110.13W*
78 L17 **Grand Cess** SE Liberia *4.36N 8.12W*
110 D12 **Grand Combin** ▲ S Switzerland *45.58N 7.27E*
34 K8 **Grand Coulee** Washington, NW USA *47.56N 119.00W*
34 J8 **Grand Coulee** *valley* Washington, NW USA
47 X5 **Grand Cul-de-Sac Marin** *bay* N Guadeloupe
Grand Duchy of Luxembourg *see* Luxembourg
65 I22 **Grande, Bahía** *bay* S Argentina
9 N14 **Grande Cache** Alberta, W Canada *53.52N 119.07W*
105 U12 **Grande Casse** ▲ E France *45.22N 6.50E*
180 G12 **Grande Comore** *var.* Njazidja, Great Comoro. *island* NW Comoros
63 G18 **Grande, Cuchilla** *hill range* E Uruguay
47 S5 **Grande de Añasco, Río** ~ W Puerto Rico
Grande de Chiloé, Isla *see* Chiloé, Isla de
60 J12 **Grande de Gurupá, Ilha** *river island* NE Brazil
59 K21 **Grande de Lipez, Río** ~ SW Bolivia
47 U6 **Grande de Loíza, Río** ~ E Puerto Rico
47 T5 **Grande de Manatí, Río** ~ C Puerto Rico
44 L9 **Grande de Matagalpa, Río** ~ C Nicaragua
42 K12 **Grande de Santiago, Río** *var.* Santiago. ~ C Mexico
45 O15 **Grande de Térraba, Río** *var.* Río Térraba. ~ SE Costa Rica
10 J9 **Grande, Deux, Réservoir la** ⊠ Québec, E Canada
62 O10 **Grande, Ilha** *island* SE Brazil
9 O13 **Grande Prairie** Alberta, W Canada *55.10N 118.52W*
76 I8 **Grand Erg Occidental** *desert* W Algeria
76 L9 **Grand Erg Oriental** *desert* Algeria/Tunisia
61 J20 **Grande, Rio** ~ S Brazil
2 F15 **Grande, Rio** *var.* Río Bravo, *Sp.* Río Bravo del Norte, Bravo del Norte. ~ Mexico/USA
59 M18 **Grande, Río** ~ C Bolivia
13 Y7 **Grande-Rivière** Québec, SE Canada *48.27N 64.37W*
13 Y6 **Grande Rivière** ~ Québec, SE Canada
46 M8 **Grande-Rivière-du-Nord** N Haiti *19.28N 72.07W*
64 K9 **Grande, Salina** *var.* Gran Salitral. *salt lake* C Argentina
13 S7 **Grandes-Bergeronnes** Québec, SE Canada *48.16N 69.32W*
49 W6 **Grande, Serra** ▲ W Brazil
42 K4 **Grande, Sierra** ▲▲ N Mexico
105 S12 **Grandes Rousses** ▲▲ E France
65 K17 **Grandes, Salinas** *salt lake* E Argentina
47 Y5 **Grande Terre** *island* E West Indies
13 X5 **Grande-Vallée** Québec, SE Canada *49.12N 65.08W*
47 Y5 **Grande Vigie, Pointe de la** *headland* Grande Terre, N Guadeloupe *16.31N 61.27W*
11 N14 **Grand Falls** New Brunswick, SE Canada *47.01N 67.46W*
11 T11 **Grand Falls** Newfoundland and Labrador, SE Canada *48.57N 55.48W*
26 L9 **Grandfalls** Texas, SW USA *31.20N 102.51W*
23 P9 **Grandfather Mountain** ▲ North Carolina, SE USA *36.06N 81.48W*
28 L13 **Grandfield** Oklahoma, C USA *34.15N 98.40W*
9 N17 **Grand Forks** British Columbia, SW Canada *49.01N 118.30W*
31 R4 **Grand Forks** North Dakota, N USA *47.54N 97.02W*
33 O9 **Grand Haven** Michigan, N USA *43.03N 86.13W*
Grandichi *see* Hrandzichy
31 P15 **Grand Island** Nebraska, C USA *40.55N 98.20W*
33 O3 **Grand Island** *island* Michigan, N USA
24 K10 **Grand Isle** Louisiana, S USA *29.12N 90.00W*
67 A23 **Grand Jason** *island* Jason Islands, NW Falkland Islands
39 P5 **Grand Junction** Colorado, C USA *39.03N 108.33W*
22 F10 **Grand Junction** Tennessee, S USA *35.03N 89.11W*
12 J9 **Grand-Lac-Victoria** Québec, SE Canada *47.33N 77.28W*
12 J9 **Grand lac Victoria** ⊚ Québec, SE Canada
79 N17 **Grand-Lahou** *var.* Grand Lahu. S Ivory Coast *5.09N 5.01W*
Grand Lahu *see* Grand-Lahou
39 S3 **Grand Lake** Colorado, C USA *40.15N 105.49W*
11 S11 **Grand Lake** ⊚ Newfoundland and Labrador, E Canada
24 G9 **Grand Lake** ⊚ Louisiana, S USA
33 R5 **Grand Lake** ⊚ Michigan, N USA
33 Q13 **Grand Lake** ⊠ Ohio, N USA
29 R9 **Grand Lake O' The Cherokees** *var.* Lake O' The Cherokees. ⊠ Oklahoma, C USA
33 Q9 **Grand Ledge** Michigan, N USA *42.45N 84.45W*
104 I8 **Grand-Lieu, Lac de** ⊚ NW France
21 U6 **Grand Manan Channel** *channel* Canada/USA
11 O15 **Grand Manan Island** *island* New Brunswick, SE Canada
31 Y4 **Grand Marais** Minnesota, N USA *47.45N 90.19W*
13 P10 **Grand-Mère** Quebec, SE Canada *46.36N 72.41W*
39 P5 **Grand Mesa** ▲ Colorado, C USA
110 C10 **Grand Muveran** ▲ W Switzerland *46.16N 7.12E*
106 G12 **Grândola** Setúbal, S Portugal *38.10N 8.34W*
Grand Paradis *see* Gran Paradiso
197 G4 **Grand Passage** *passage* N New Caledonia
79 R16 **Grand-Popo** S Benin *6.19N 1.49E*
31 Z3 **Grand Portage** Minnesota, N USA *48.00N 89.36W*
27 T6 **Grand Prairie** Texas, SW USA *32.45N 97.00W*
9 W14 **Grand Rapids** Manitoba, C Canada *53.12N 99.19W*
33 P9 **Grand Rapids** Michigan, N USA *42.57N 86.40W*
31 V5 **Grand Rapids** Minnesota, N USA *47.14N 93.31W*
197 G5 **Grand Récif de Koumac** *reef* W New Caledonia
197 J8 **Grand Récif Sud** *reef* S New Caledonia
12 L10 **Grand-Remous** Québec, SE Canada *46.36N 75.53W*
12 F15 **Grand River** ~ Ontario, S Canada
33 P9 **Grand River** ~ Michigan, N USA
29 T3 **Grand River** ~ Missouri, C USA
30 M7 **Grand River** ~ South Dakota, N USA
47 Q11 **Grand' Rivière** N Martinique *14.51N 61.12W*
34 F11 **Grand Ronde** Oregon, NW USA *45.03N 123.43W*
34 L11 **Grand Ronde River** ~ Oregon/Washington, NW USA
Grand-Saint-Bernard, Col du *see* Great Saint Bernard Pass
27 V6 **Grand Saline** Texas, SW USA *32.40N 95.42W*
57 X10 **Grand-Santi** W French Guiana *4.19N 54.24W*
Grandsee *see* Grandson
110 B9 **Grandson** *prev.* Grandsee. Vaud, W Switzerland *46.49N 6.39E*
180 J16 **Grand Sœur** *island* Les Sœurs, NE Seychelles
35 S14 **Grand Teton** ▲ Wyoming, C USA *43.44N 110.48W*
33 P5 **Grand Traverse Bay** *lake bay* Michigan, N USA
47 N6 **Grand Turk** O (Turks and Caicos Islands) Grand Turk Island, S Turks and Caicos Islands *21.24N 71.08W*
47 N6 **Grand Turk Island** *island* SE Turks and Caicos Islands
105 S13 **Grand Veymont** ▲ E France *44.51N 5.32E*
9 W15 **Grandview** Manitoba, S Canada *51.10N 100.40W*
29 R4 **Grandview** Missouri, C USA *38.53N 94.31W*
38 I10 **Grand Wash Cliffs** *cliff* Arizona, SW USA
12 J8 **Granet, Lac** ⊚ Québec, SE Canada
97 L14 **Grangärde** Dalarna, C Sweden *60.15N 15.00E*
46 H12 **Grange Hill** W Jamaica *18.18N 78.10W*
98 J12 **Grangemouth** C Scotland, UK *56.01N 3.43W*
27 T10 **Granger** Texas, SW USA *30.43N 97.26W*
34 J10 **Granger** Washington, NW USA *46.20N 120.11W*
35 T17 **Granger** Wyoming, C USA *41.37N 109.58W*
Granges *see* Grenchen
97 L14 **Grängesberg** Dalarna, C Sweden *60.06N 15.00E*
35 N11 **Grangeville** Idaho, NW USA *45.55N 116.07W*
8 K13 **Granisle** British Columbia, SW Canada *54.55N 126.13W*
32 K15 **Granite City** Illinois, N USA *38.42N 90.09W*
31 S9 **Granite Falls** Minnesota, N USA *44.48N 95.33W*
23 Q9 **Granite Falls** North Carolina, SE USA *35.48N 81.25W*
38 K12 **Granite Mountain** ▲ Arizona, SW USA *34.38N 112.34W*
35 T12 **Granite Peak** ▲ Montana, NW USA *45.09N 109.48W*
37 T2 **Granite Peak** ▲ Nevada, W USA *41.40N 117.35W*
38 J3 **Granite Peak** ▲ Utah, W USA *40.09N 113.18W*
Granite State *see* New Hampshire
109 H24 **Granitola, Capo** *headland* Sicilia, Italy, C Mediterranean Sea *37.33N 12.39E*
193 H15 **Granity** West Coast, South Island, NZ *41.37S 171.53E*
Gran Lago *see* Nicaragua, Lago de
65 J18 **Gran Laguna Salada** ⊚ S Argentina
Gran Malvina, Isla *see* West Falkland
97 L18 **Gränna** Jönköping, S Sweden *58.01N 14.30E*
107 W5 **Granollers** *var.* Granollérs. Cataluña, NE Spain *41.37N 2.18E*
108 A7 **Gran Paradiso** *Fr.* Grand Paradis. ▲ NW Italy *45.31N 7.13E*
Gran Pilastro *see* Hochfeiler
Gran Salitral *see* Grande, Salina
Gran San Bernardo, Passo di *see* Great Saint Bernard Pass
Gran Santiago *see* Santiago
109 J14 **Gran Sasso d'Italia** ▲▲ C Italy
102 N11 **Gransee** Brandenburg, NE Germany *53.00N 13.10E*
30 L15 **Grant** Nebraska, C USA *40.50N 101.43W*
29 R1 **Grant City** Missouri, C USA *40.29N 94.24W*
99 N19 **Grantham** E England, UK *52.55N 0.39W*
67 D24 **Grantham Sound** *sound* East Falkland, Falkland Islands
204 K13 **Grant Island** *island* Antarctica
47 Z14 **Grantley Adams** ✈ (Bridgetown) SE Barbados *13.04N 59.29W*
37 S7 **Grant, Mount** ▲ Nevada, W USA *38.34N 118.47W*
98 J9 **Grantown-on-Spey** N Scotland, UK *57.11N 3.52W*
37 W8 **Grant Range** ▲▲ Nevada, W USA
39 Q11 **Grants** New Mexico, SW USA *35.09N 107.50W*
32 I4 **Grantsburg** Wisconsin, N USA *45.46N 92.40W*
34 F15 **Grants Pass** Oregon, NW USA *42.26N 123.19W*
38 K3 **Grantsville** Utah, W USA *40.36N 112.27W*
23 R4 **Grantsville** West Virginia, NE USA *38.54N 81.04W*
104 I5 **Granville** Manche, N France *48.49N 1.34W*
9 V12 **Granville Lake** ⊚ Manitoba, C Canada
27 V8 **Grapeland** Texas, SW USA *31.29N 95.28W*
27 T6 **Grapevine** Texas, SW USA *32.55N 97.04W*
85 K20 **Graskop** Mpumalanga, NE South Africa *24.58S 30.49E*
97 P14 **Gräsö** Uppsala, C Sweden *60.22N 18.30E*
95 I19 **Gräsö** *island* C Sweden
105 U15 **Grasse** Alpes-Maritimes, SE France *43.42N 6.52E*
20 E14 **Grassflat** Pennsylvania, NE USA *41.00N 78.04W*
35 U9 **Grassrange** Montana, NW USA *47.02N 108.48W*
20 J6 **Grass River** ~ New York, NE USA
37 P6 **Grass Valley** California, W USA *39.12N 121.04W*
191 N14 **Grassy** Tasmania, SE Australia *40.03S 144.04E*
30 K4 **Grassy Butte** North Dakota, N USA *47.20N 103.13W*
23 R5 **Grassy Knob** ▲ West Virginia, NE USA *38.04N 80.31W*
97 G24 **Gråsten** *var.* Graasten. Sønderjylland, SW Denmark *54.55N 9.37E*
97 J18 **Grästorp** Västra Götaland, S Sweden *58.19N 12.45E*
Gratianopolis *see* Grenoble
111 V8 **Gratwein** Steiermark, SE Austria *47.06N 15.18E*
Gratz *see* Graz
110 I9 **Graubünden** *Fr.* Grisons, *It.* Grigioni. ◈ *canton* SE Switzerland
Graudenz *see* Grudziądz

◆ Country
● Country Capital
◇ Dependent Territory
○ Dependent Territory Capital
◈ Administrative Region
✈ International Airport
▲ Mountain
▲▲ Mountain Range
Volcano
~ River
⊚ Lake
⊠ Reservoir

GRAULHET – GUANACASTE

105 N15 **Graulhet** Tarn, S France 43.45N 1.58E
107 T4 **Graus** Aragón, NE Spain 42.11N 0.21E
63 I16 **Gravataí** Rio Grande do Sul, S Brazil 29.55S 51.00W
100 L13 **Grave** Noord-Brabant, SE Netherlands 51.45N 5.45E
9 T17 **Gravelbourg** Saskatchewan, S Canada 49.52N 106.33W
105 N1 **Gravelines** Nord, N France 51.00N 2.07E
Graven see Grez-Doiceau
12 H13 **Gravenhurst** Ontario, S Canada 44.55N 79.22W
35 O10 **Grave Peak** ▲ Idaho, NW USA 46.24N 114.43W
104 I11 **Grave, Pointe de** headland W France 45.33N 1.24W
191 S4 **Gravesend** New South Wales, SE Australia 29.37S 150.15E
99 P22 **Gravesend** SE England, UK 51.27N 0.24E
109 N17 **Gravina in Puglia** Puglia, SE Italy 40.48N 16.25E
105 S8 **Gray** Haute-Saône, E France 47.28N 5.34E
25 T4 **Gray** Georgia, SE USA 33.00N 83.31W
205 V16 **Gray, Cape** headland Antarctica, 67.30S 143.30E
34 F9 **Grayland** Washington, NW USA 46.46N 124.07W
41 N10 **Grayling** Alaska, USA 62.55N 160.07W
33 Q6 **Grayling** Michigan, N USA 44.40N 84.43W
34 F9 **Grays Harbor** inlet Washington, NW USA
23 O5 **Grayson** Kentucky, S USA 38.19N 82.57W
39 S4 **Grays Peak** ▲ Colorado, C USA 39.37N 105.49W
32 M16 **Grayville** Illinois, N USA 38.15N 87.59W
111 V8 **Graz** prev. Gratz. Steiermark, SE Austria 47.04N 15.23E
106 L15 **Grazalema** Andalucía, S Spain 36.46N 5.22W
115 P15 **Grdelica** Serbia, SE Serbia and Montenegro (Yugoslavia) 42.54N 22.05E
46 H1 **Great Abaco** var. Abaco Island. island N Bahamas
Great Admiralty Island see Manus Island
Great Alfold see Great Hungarian Plain
Great Ararat see Büyükağrı Dağı
189 U8 **Great Artesian Basin** lowlands Queensland, C Australia
197 I15 **Great Astrolabe Reef** reef Kadavu, SW Fiji
189 O12 **Great Australian Bight** bight S Australia
66 E11 **Great Bahama Bank** undersea feature E Gulf of Mexico
192 M4 **Great Barrier Island** island N NZ
189 X4 **Great Barrier Reef** reef Queensland, NE Australia
20 L11 **Great Barrington** Massachusetts, NE USA 42.11N 73.20W
(0) F10 **Great Basin** basin W USA
15 H5 **Great Bear Lake** Fr. Grand Lac de l'Ours. ◎ Northwest Territories, NW Canada
Great Belt see Storebælt
28 L5 **Great Bend** Kansas, C USA 38.21N 98.45W
Great Bermuda see Bermuda
99 A20 **Great Blasket Island** Ir. An Blascaod Mór. island SW Ireland
Great Britain see Britain
157 Q23 **Great Channel** channel Andaman Sea/Indian Ocean
177 F10 **Great Coco Island** island SW Myanmar
Great Crosby see Crosby
23 X7 **Great Dismal Swamp** wetland North Carolina/Virginia, SE USA
35 V16 **Great Divide Basin** basin Wyoming, C USA
189 W7 **Great Dividing Range** ▲▲ NE Australia
12 D12 **Great Duck Island** island Ontario, S Canada
Great Elder Reservoir see Waconda Lake
205 V8 **Greater Antarctica** var. East Antarctica. physical region Antarctica
46 G8 **Greater Antilles** island group West Indies
133 V16 **Greater Sunda Islands** var. Sunda Islands. island group Indonesia
192 I1 **Great Exhibition Bay** inlet North Island, NZ
46 H4 **Great Exuma Island** island C Bahamas
35 R8 **Great Falls** Montana, NW USA 47.30N 111.18W
23 R11 **Great Falls** South Carolina, SE USA 34.34N 80.54W
86 F9 **Great Fisher Bank** undersea feature C North Sea
Great Glen see Mor, Glen
Great Grimsby see Grimsby
46 I4 **Great Guana Cay** island C Bahamas
66 I5 **Great Hellefiske Bank** undersea feature N Atlantic Ocean
113 L24 **Great Hungarian Plain** var. Great Alfold, Plain of Hungary, Hung. Alföld. plain SE Europe
46 L7 **Great Inagua** var. Inagua Islands. island S Bahamas
Great Indian Desert see Thar Desert
85 G25 **Great Karoo** var. Great Karroo, High Veld, Afr. Groot Karoo, Hoë Karoo. plateau region S South Africa
Great Karroo see Great Karoo
Great Kei see Groot-Kei
Great Khingan Range see Da Hinggan Ling
12 E11 **Great La Cloche Island** island Ontario, S Canada
191 P16 **Great Lake** ◎ Tasmania, SE Australia
Great Lake see Tônlé Sap
16 O16 **Great Lakes** lakes Ontario, Canada/USA
Great Lakes State see Michigan
99 L20 **Great Malvern** W England, UK 52.07N 2.19W
192 M5 **Great Mercury Island** island N NZ
Great Meteor Seamount see Great Meteor Tablemount
66 K10 **Great Meteor Tablemount** var. Great Meteor Seamount. undersea feature E Atlantic Ocean 30.00N 28.30W
33 Q14 **Great Miami River** ≈ Ohio, N USA
157 Q24 **Great Nicobar** island Nicobar Islands, India, NE Indian Ocean
99 O19 **Great Ouse** var. Ouse. ≈ E England, UK
191 Q17 **Great Oyster Bay** bay Tasmania, SE Australia
46 I13 **Great Pedro Bluff** headland W Jamaica 17.51N 77.44W
23 T12 **Great Pee Dee River** ≈ North Carolina/South Carolina, SE USA
133 W9 **Great Plain of China** plain E China
(0) F12 **Great Plains** var. High Plains. plains Canada/USA
39 W6 **Great Plains Reservoirs** ⊡ Colorado, C USA
21 Q13 **Great Point** headland Nantucket Island, Massachusetts, NE USA 41.23N 70.03W
70 I13 **Great Rift Valley** var. Rift Valley. depression Asia/Africa
83 I23 **Great Ruaha** ≈ S Tanzania
20 K10 **Great Sacandaga Lake** ⊡ New York, NE USA
110 C12 **Great Saint Bernard Pass** Fr. Col du Grand-Saint-Bernard, It. Passo di Gran San Bernardo. pass Italy/Switzerland 45.52N 7.10E
46 F1 **Great Sale Cay** island N Bahamas
Great Salt Desert see Kavir, Dasht-e
38 K1 **Great Salt Lake** salt lake Utah, W USA
38 J3 **Great Salt Lake Desert** plain Utah, W USA
28 M8 **Great Salt Plains Lake** ⊡ Oklahoma, C USA
77 T9 **Great Sand Sea** desert Egypt/Libya
188 L6 **Great Sandy Desert** desert Western Australia
Great Sandy Desert see Ar Rub' al Khālī
Great Sandy Island see Fraser Island
197 I13 **Great Sea Reef** reef Vanua Levu, N Fiji
40 H17 **Great Sitkin Island** island Aleutian Islands, Alaska, USA
15 I8 **Great Slave Lake** Fr. Grand Lac des Esclaves. ◎ Northwest Territories, NW Canada
23 O10 **Great Smoky Mountains** ▲▲ North Carolina/Tennessee, SE USA
8 L11 **Great Snow Mountain** ▲ British Columbia, W Canada 57.22N 124.08W
66 A12 **Great Sound** bay Bermuda, NW Atlantic Ocean
188 M10 **Great Victoria Desert** desert South Australia/Western Australia
204 H2 **Great Wall** Chinese research station South Shetland Islands, Antarctica 61.57S 58.23W
21 T7 **Great Wass Island** island Maine, NE USA
99 Q19 **Great Yarmouth** var. Yarmouth. E England, UK 52.37N 1.43E
145 S1 **Great Zab** Ar. Az Zāb al Kabīr, Kurd. Zē-i Bādīnān, Turk. Büyükzap Suyu. ≈ Iraq/Turkey
97 I17 **Grebbestad** Västra Götaland, S Sweden 58.42N 11.15E
Grebenka see Hrebinka
44 M13 **Grecia** Alajuela, C Costa Rica 10.04N 84.19W
63 E18 **Greco** Río Negro, W Uruguay 32.49S 57.03W
Greco, Cape see Gkréko, Akrotíri
106 L8 **Gredos, Sierra de** ▲▲ W Spain
20 F9 **Greece** New York, NE USA 43.12N 77.41W
117 E17 **Greece** off. Hellenic Republic, Gk. Elláς; anc. Hellas. ◆ republic SE Europe
Greece Central see Stereá Ellás
Greece West see Dytikí Ellás
39 T3 **Greeley** Colorado, C USA 40.21N 104.41W
31 P14 **Greeley** Nebraska, C USA 41.33N 98.31W
126 Hh1 **Greem-Bell, Ostrov** Eng. Graham Bell Island. island Zemlya Frantsa-Iosifa, N Russian Federation
32 M6 **Green Bay** Wisconsin, N USA 44.32N 88.00W
33 N6 **Green Bay** lake bay Michigan/Wisconsin, N USA
23 S5 **Greenbrier River** ≈ West Virginia, NE USA
31 S2 **Greenbush** Minnesota, N USA 48.42N 96.10W
191 R12 **Green Cape** headland New South Wales, SE Australia 37.15S 150.03E
33 O14 **Greencastle** Indiana, N USA 39.38N 86.51W
20 F16 **Greencastle** Pennsylvania, NE USA 39.47N 77.43W
29 T2 **Green City** Missouri, C USA 40.16N 92.57W
23 O9 **Greeneville** Tennessee, S USA 36.09N 82.49W
37 O11 **Greenfield** California, W USA 36.19N 121.15W
33 P14 **Greenfield** Indiana, N USA 39.47N 85.46W
31 U15 **Greenfield** Iowa, C USA 41.18N 94.27W
20 M11 **Greenfield** Massachusetts, NE USA 42.33N 72.34W
29 S7 **Greenfield** Missouri, C USA 37.25N 93.50W
33 S14 **Greenfield** Ohio, N USA 39.21N 83.22W
22 G8 **Greenfield** Tennessee, S USA 36.09N 88.48W
32 M9 **Greenfield** Wisconsin, N USA 42.55N 87.59W
29 T9 **Green Forest** Arkansas, C USA 36.19N 93.24W
39 T7 **Greenhorn Mountain** ▲ Colorado, C USA 37.50N 104.59W
Green Island see Lü Tao
195 R10 **Green Islands** var. Nissan Islands. island group NE PNG
9 S14 **Green Lake** Saskatchewan, C Canada 54.15N 107.51W
32 L8 **Green Lake** ◎ Wisconsin, N USA
207 O14 **Greenland** Dan. Grønland, Inuit Kalaallit Nunaat. ◇ Danish external territory NE North America
86 D4 **Greenland** island NE North America
207 R13 **Greenland Plain** undersea feature N Greenland Sea
207 R14 **Greenland Sea** sea Arctic Ocean
39 R4 **Green Mountain Reservoir** ⊡ Colorado, C USA
20 M8 **Green Mountains** ▲▲ Vermont, NE USA
Green Mountain State see Vermont
98 H12 **Greenock** W Scotland, UK 55.57N 4.45W
41 T5 **Greenough, Mount** ▲ Alaska, USA 69.15N 141.37W
194 E10 **Green River** Sandaun, NW PNG 3.46S 141.10E
39 N5 **Green River** Utah, W USA 39.00N 110.07W
35 U17 **Green River** Wyoming, C USA 41.33N 109.27W
18 Ii7 **Green River** ≈ W USA
32 K11 **Green River** ≈ Illinois, N USA
22 J7 **Green River** ≈ Kentucky, S USA
30 K5 **Green River** ≈ North Dakota, N USA
39 N6 **Green River** ≈ Utah, W USA
35 T16 **Green River** ≈ Wyoming, C USA
22 L7 **Green River Lake** ⊡ Kentucky, S USA
25 O5 **Greensboro** Alabama, S USA 32.42N 87.36W
25 U3 **Greensboro** Georgia, SE USA 33.34N 83.10W
23 T9 **Greensboro** North Carolina, SE USA 36.04N 79.47W
33 P14 **Greensburg** Indiana, N USA 39.20N 85.28W
28 K6 **Greensburg** Kansas, C USA 37.36N 99.17W
22 L7 **Greensburg** Kentucky, S USA 37.15N 85.28W
20 C15 **Greensburg** Pennsylvania, NE USA 40.18N 79.32W
39 O13 **Greens Peak** ▲ Arizona, SW USA 34.06N 109.34W
23 V12 **Green Swamp** wetland North Carolina, SE USA
23 O4 **Greenup** Kentucky, S USA 38.34N 82.49W
38 M16 **Green Valley** Arizona, SW USA 31.49N 111.00W
78 K17 **Greenville** var. Sino, Sinoe. SE Liberia 5.01N 9.03W
25 P6 **Greenville** Alabama, S USA 31.49N 86.37W
25 T8 **Greenville** Florida, SE USA 30.28N 83.37W
25 S4 **Greenville** Georgia, SE USA 33.03N 84.42W
32 L15 **Greenville** Illinois, N USA 38.53N 89.24W
22 I7 **Greenville** Kentucky, S USA 37.12N 87.10W
21 Q5 **Greenville** Maine, NE USA 45.26N 69.36W
33 P9 **Greenville** Michigan, N USA 43.10N 85.15W
24 J4 **Greenville** Mississippi, S USA 33.24N 91.03W
23 W9 **Greenville** North Carolina, SE USA 35.36N 77.22W
33 Q13 **Greenville** Ohio, N USA 40.06N 84.37W
21 O12 **Greenville** Rhode Island, NE USA 41.52N 71.33W
23 P11 **Greenville** South Carolina, SE USA 34.51N 82.23W
27 U6 **Greenville** Texas, SW USA 33.08N 96.06W
33 T12 **Greenwich** Ohio, N USA 41.01N 82.31W
29 S11 **Greenwood** Arkansas, C USA 35.13N 94.15W
33 O14 **Greenwood** Indiana, N USA 39.37N 86.06W
24 K4 **Greenwood** Mississippi, S USA 33.30N 90.11W
23 P12 **Greenwood** South Carolina, SE USA 34.12N 82.09W
23 Q12 **Greenwood, Lake** ⊡ South Carolina, SE USA
23 P11 **Greer** South Carolina, SE USA 34.56N 82.13W
29 V10 **Greers Ferry Lake** ⊡ Arkansas, C USA
29 S13 **Greeson, Lake** ⊡ Arkansas, C USA
31 O12 **Gregory** South Dakota, N USA 43.11N 99.26W
190 J3 **Gregory, Lake** salt lake South Australia
188 J9 **Gregory Lake** ◎ Western Australia
189 V5 **Gregory Range** ▲▲ Queensland, E Australia
Greifenberg/Greifenberg in Pommern see Gryfice
Greifenhagen see Gryfino
102 O8 **Greifswald** Mecklenburg-Vorpommern, NE Germany 54.04N 13.24E
102 O8 **Greifswalder Bodden** bay NE Germany
111 U4 **Grein** Oberösterreich, N Austria 48.14N 14.50E
103 M17 **Greiz** Thüringen, C Germany 50.40N 12.10E
Gremicha/Gremiha see Gremikha
128 M4 **Gremikha** var. Gremicha, Gremiha. Murmanskaya Oblast', NW Russian Federation 68.01N 39.31E
129 V14 **Gremyachinsk** Permskaya Oblast', NW Russian Federation 58.33N 57.52E
97 H21 **Grenaa** var. Grenå. Århus, C Denmark 56.25N 10.52E
Grenå see Grenaa
24 L3 **Grenada** Mississippi, S USA 33.46N 89.48W
47 W15 **Grenada** ◆ commonwealth republic SE West Indies
49 S4 **Grenada** island Grenada
49 R4 **Grenada Basin** undersea feature W Atlantic Ocean
24 L3 **Grenada Lake** ⊡ Mississippi, S USA
47 Y14 **Grenadines, The** island group Grenada/St Vincent and the Grenadines
110 D7 **Grenchen** Fr. Granges. Solothurn, NW Switzerland 47.12N 7.30E
191 Q9 **Grenfell** New South Wales, SE Australia 33.54S 148.09E
9 V16 **Grenfell** Saskatchewan, S Canada 50.24N 102.56W
94 J1 **Grenivík** Nordhurland Eystra, N Iceland 65.57N 18.10W
105 S12 **Grenoble** anc. Cularo, Gratianopolis. Isère, E France 45.10N 5.41E
30 J2 **Grenora** North Dakota, N USA 48.36N 103.57W
94 N8 **Grense-Jakobselv** Finnmark, N Norway 69.46N 30.39E
47 S14 **Grenville** E Grenada 12.07N 61.37W
34 G11 **Gresham** Oregon, NW USA 45.30N 122.25W
Gresk see Hresk
108 B7 **Gressoney-St-Jean** Valle d'Aosta, NW Italy 45.48N 7.49E
24 K9 **Gretna** Louisiana, S USA 29.54N 90.03W
23 T7 **Gretna** Virginia, NE USA 36.57N 79.21W
100 F13 **Grevelingen** inlet S North Sea
102 F13 **Greven** Nordrhein-Westfalen, NW Germany 52.06N 7.37E
117 D15 **Grevená** Dytikí Makedonía, N Greece 40.06N 21.26E
103 D16 **Grevenbroich** Nordrhein-Westfalen, W Germany 51.06N 6.34E
101 N24 **Grevenmacher** Grevenmacher, E Luxembourg 49.40N 6.27E
101 M24 **Grevenmacher** ◈ district E Luxembourg
102 K9 **Grevesmühlen** Mecklenburg-Vorpommern, N Germany 53.52N 11.12E
193 H16 **Grey** ≈ South Island, NZ
35 V12 **Greybull** Wyoming, C USA 44.29N 108.03W
35 U13 **Greybull River** ≈ Wyoming, C USA
67 A24 **Grey Channel** sound Falkland Islands
Greyerzer See see Gruyère, Lac de la
11 T10 **Grey Islands** island group Newfoundland and Labrador, E Canada
20 L10 **Greylock, Mount** ▲ Massachusetts, NE USA 42.38N 73.09W
193 G17 **Greymouth** West Coast, South Island, NZ 42.28S 171.13E
189 U10 **Grey Range** ▲▲ New South Wales/Queensland, E Australia
99 G18 **Greystones** Ir. Na Clocha Liatha. E Ireland 53.07N 6.04W
193 M14 **Greytown** Wellington, North Island, NZ 41.05S 175.25E
85 K23 **Greytown** KwaZulu/Natal, E South Africa 29.04S 30.34E
Greytown see San Juan del Norte
101 H19 **Grez-Doiceau** Dut. Graven. Wallon Brabant, C Belgium 50.43N 4.41E
117 J19 **Griá, Akrotírio** headland Ándros, Kykládes, Greece, Aegean Sea 37.54N 24.57E
131 N8 **Gribanovskiy** Voronezhskaya Oblast', W Russian Federation 51.27N 41.53E
80 I13 **Gribingui** ≈ N Central African Republic
37 O6 **Gridley** California, W USA 39.21N 121.41W
85 G23 **Griekwastad** Northern Cape, C South Africa 28.50S 23.16E
25 S4 **Griffin** Georgia, SE USA 33.15N 84.16W
191 O9 **Griffith** New South Wales, SE Australia 34.16S 146.01E
12 F13 **Griffith Island** island Ontario, S Canada
23 W10 **Grifton** North Carolina, SE USA 35.22N 77.26W
Grigioni see Graubünden
121 H14 **Grigiškes** Vilnius, SE Lithuania 54.42N 25.00E
119 N10 **Grigoriopol** C Moldova 47.09N 29.18E
153 X7 **Grigor'yevka** Issyk-Kul'skaya Oblast', E Kyrgyzstan 42.43N 77.27E
200 Oo9 **Grijalva Ridge** undersea feature E Pacific Ocean
43 U15 **Grijalva, Río** var. Tabasco. ≈ Guatemala/Mexico
100 N5 **Grijpskerk** Groningen, NE Netherlands 53.15N 6.18E
85 C22 **Grillenthal** Karas, SW Namibia 26.55S 15.24E
81 J15 **Grimari** Ouaka, C Central African Republic 5.44N 20.02E
Grimaylov see Hrymayliv
101 G18 **Grimbergen** Vlaams Brabant, C Belgium 50.55N 4.22E
191 N15 **Grim, Cape** headland Tasmania, SE Australia 40.42S 144.42E
102 N8 **Grimmen** Mecklenburg-Vorpommern, NE Germany 54.06N 13.03E
12 G16 **Grimsby** Ontario, S Canada 43.10N 79.34W
99 O17 **Grimsby** prev. Great Grimsby. E England, UK 53.34N 0.04W
94 J1 **Grímsey** var. Grimsey. island N Iceland
9 O12 **Grimshaw** Alberta, W Canada 56.12N 117.37W
97 F18 **Grimstad** Aust-Agder, S Norway 58.19N 8.34E
94 H4 **Grindavík** Reykjanes, W Iceland 65.57N 18.10W
110 F9 **Grindelwald** Bern, S Switzerland 46.37N 8.04E
97 F23 **Grindsted** Ribe, W Denmark 55.46N 8.55E
31 W14 **Grinnell** Iowa, C USA 41.44N 92.43W
111 U10 **Grintovec** ▲ N Slovenia 46.21N 14.31E
190 H1 **Griselda, Lake** salt lake South Australia
Grisons see Graubünden
97 P14 **Grisslehamn** Stockholm, C Sweden 60.04N 18.49E
31 T15 **Griswold** Iowa, C USA 41.14N 95.08W
104 M1 **Griz Nez, Cap** headland N France 50.51N 1.34E
114 P13 **Grljan** Serbia, E Serbia and Montenegro (Yugoslavia) 43.52N 22.18E
114 E11 **Grmeč** ▲▲ NW Bosnia and Herzegovina
101 H16 **Grobbendonk** Antwerpen, N Belgium 51.12N 4.41E
Grobin see Grobiņa
120 C10 **Grobiņa** Ger. Grobin. Liepāja, W Latvia 56.32N 21.12E
85 K20 **Groblersdal** Mpumalanga, NE South Africa 25.15S 29.25E
85 G23 **Groblershoop** Northern Cape, W South Africa 28.51S 22.01E
Gródek Jagielloński see Horodok
111 Q6 **Grödig** Salzburg, W Austria 47.42N 13.06E
113 H15 **Grodków** Opolskie, S Poland 50.42N 17.23E
Grodnenskaya Oblast' see Hrodzyenskaya Voblasts'
Grodno see Hrodna
112 L12 **Grodzisk Mazowiecki** Mazowieckie, C Poland 52.07N 20.40E
112 F12 **Grodzisk Wielkopolski** Wielkopolskie, C Poland 52.13N 16.21E
Grodzyanka see Hradzyanka
100 O12 **Groenlo** Gelderland, E Netherlands 52.01N 6.36E
85 E22 **Groenrivier** Karas, SE Namibia 27.27S 18.52E
27 U8 **Groesbeck** Texas, SW USA 31.31N 96.34W
100 L13 **Groesbeek** Gelderland, SE Netherlands 51.46N 5.55E
104 G7 **Groix, Îles de** island group NW France
112 M12 **Grójec** Mazowieckie, C Poland 51.51N 20.52E
67 K15 **Gröll Seamount** undersea feature C Atlantic Ocean 12.54S 33.24W
102 E13 **Gronau** var. Gronau in Westfalen. Nordrhein-Westfalen, NW Germany 52.12N 7.01E
Gronau in Westfalen see Gronau
95 F15 **Grong** Nord-Trøndelag, C Norway 64.29N 12.19E
97 N22 **Grönhögen** Kalmar, S Sweden 56.16N 16.09E
100 N5 **Groningen** Groningen, NE Netherlands 53.13N 6.34E
57 W9 **Groningen** Saramacca, N Suriname 5.45N 55.31W
100 N5 **Groningen** ◈ province NE Netherlands
Grønland see Greenland
110 H11 **Grono** Graubünden, S Switzerland 46.15N 9.07E
97 M20 **Grönskåra** Kalmar, S Sweden 57.04N 15.45E
27 O2 **Groom** Texas, SW USA 35.12N 101.06W
37 W9 **Groom Lake** ◎ Nevada, W USA
85 H25 **Groot** ≈ S South Africa
189 S2 **Groote Eylandt** island Northern Territory, N Australia
100 M6 **Grootegast** Groningen, NE Netherlands 53.11N 6.12E
85 D17 **Grootfontein** Otjozondjupa, N Namibia 19.31S 18.04E
85 E22 **Groot Karasberge** ▲▲ S Namibia
Groot Karoo see Great Karoo
85 J25 **Groot-Kei** Eng. Great Kei. ≈ S South Africa
47 T10 **Gros Islet** N Saint Lucia 14.04N 60.57W
46 L8 **Gros-Morne** NW Haiti 19.37N 72.39W
11 S11 **Gros Morne** ▲ Newfoundland and Labrador, E Canada 49.38N 57.45W
105 R9 **Grosne** ≈ C France
47 S12 **Gros Piton** ▲ SW Saint Lucia 13.48N 61.04W
Grossa, Isola see Dugi Otok
Grossbetschkerek see Zrenjanin
Grosse Isper see Grosse Ysper
Grosse Kokel see Târnava Mare
103 M21 **Grosse Laaber** var. Grosse Laber. ≈ SE Germany
Grosse Laber see Grosse Laaber
Grosse Morava see Velika Morava
103 O15 **Grossenhain** Sachsen, E Germany 51.18N 13.31E
111 Y4 **Grossenzersdorf** Niederösterreich, NE Austria 48.11N 16.34E
103 O21 **Grosser Arber** ▲ SE Germany 49.07N 13.10E
103 K17 **Grosser Beerberg** ▲ C Germany 50.39N 10.45E
103 G18 **Grosser Feldberg** ▲ W Germany 50.13N 8.28E
111 O8 **Grosser Löffler** It. Monte Lovello. ▲ Austria/Italy 47.02N 11.56E
111 N8 **Grosser Möseler** var. Mesule. ▲ Austria/Italy 47.01N 11.52E
102 J8 **Grosser Plöner See** ◎ N Germany
103 O21 **Grosser Rachel** ▲ SE Germany 48.59N 13.23E
Grosser Sund see Suur Väin
13 V6 **Grosses-Roches** Québec, SE Canada 48.55N 67.06W
111 P8 **Grosses Weiesbachhorn** var. Wiesbachhorn. ▲ W Austria 47.09N 12.44E
108 F13 **Grosseto** Toscana, C Italy 42.45N 11.07E
103 M22 **Grosse Vils** ≈ SE Germany
111 U4 **Grosse Ysper** var. Grosse Isper. ≈ N Austria
103 G19 **Gross-Gerau** Hessen, W Germany 49.55N 8.28E
111 U3 **Gross Gerungs** Niederösterreich, N Austria 48.33N 14.58E
111 P8 **Grossglockner** ▲ W Austria 47.05N 12.39E
Grosskanizsa see Nagykanizsa
Gross-Karol see Carei
Grosskikinda see Kikinda
111 W9 **Grossklein** Steiermark, SE Austria 46.43N 15.24E
Grosskoppe see Velká Deštná
Grossmeseritsch see Velké Meziříčí
Grossmichel see Michalovce
103 H19 **Grossostheim** Bayern, C Germany 49.54N 9.03E
111 X7 **Grosspetersdorf** Burgenland, SE Austria 47.15N 16.19E
111 T5 **Grossraming** Oberösterreich, C Austria 47.54N 14.34E
103 P14 **Grossräschen** Brandenburg, E Germany 51.34N 14.00E
Grossrauschenbach see Revúca
Gross-Sankt-Johannis see Suure-Jaani
Gross-Schlatten see Abrud
111 V2 **Gross-Siegharts** Niederösterreich, N Austria 48.48N 15.25E
Gross-Skaisgirren see Bol'shakovo
Gross-Steffelsdorf see Rimavská Sobota
Gross Strehlitz see Strzelce Opolskie
111 O8 **Grossvenediger** ▲ W Austria 47.07N 12.19E
Grosswardein see Oradea
Gross Wartenberg see Syców
111 U11 **Grosuplje** C Slovenia 46.00N 14.36E
101 H17 **Grote Nete** ≈ N Belgium
96 E10 **Grotli** Oppland, S Norway 62.02N 7.36E
21 N13 **Groton** Connecticut, NE USA 41.20N 72.03W
31 P8 **Groton** South Dakota, N USA 45.27N 98.06W
109 P18 **Grottaglie** Puglia, SE Italy 40.31N 17.25E
109 L17 **Grottaminarda** Campania, S Italy 41.04N 15.02E
108 K13 **Grottammare** Marche, C Italy 43.00N 13.52E
23 U5 **Grottoes** Virginia, NE USA 38.16N 78.49W
Grou see Grouw
11 N10 **Groulx, Monts** ▲▲ Québec, E Canada
12 E7 **Groundhog** ≈ Ontario, S Canada
38 J1 **Grouse Creek** Utah, W USA 41.41N 113.52W
38 J1 **Grouse Creek Mountains** ▲▲ Utah, W USA
100 L6 **Grouw** Fris. Grou. Friesland, N Netherlands 53.07N 5.51E
29 R8 **Grove** Oklahoma, C USA 36.35N 94.46W
33 S13 **Grove City** Ohio, N USA 39.52N 83.05W
20 B13 **Grove City** Pennsylvania, NE USA 41.09N 80.02W
25 O6 **Grove Hill** Alabama, S USA 31.42N 87.46W
35 S15 **Grover** Wyoming, C USA 42.48N 110.57W
37 P13 **Grover City** California, W USA 35.08N 120.37W
27 Y11 **Groves** Texas, SW USA 29.57N 93.55W
21 O7 **Groveton** New Hampshire, NE USA 44.35N 71.28W
27 W9 **Groveton** Texas, SW USA 31.03N 95.07W
38 J15 **Growler Mountains** ▲▲ Arizona, SW USA
Grozdovo see Bratya Daskalovi
131 P16 **Groznyy** Chechenskaya Respublika, SW Russian Federation 43.20N 45.42E
Grubeshov see Hrubieszów
114 G9 **Grubišno Polje** Bjelovar-Bilogora, NE Croatia 45.42N 17.09E
Grudovo see Sredets
112 J9 **Grudziądz** Ger. Graudenz. Kujawsko-pomorskie, C Poland 53.28N 18.45E
27 R17 **Grulla** var. La Grulla. Texas, SW USA 26.15N 98.37W
42 K14 **Grullo** Jalisco, SW Mexico 19.45N 104.15W
69 V10 **Grumeti** ≈ N Tanzania
97 K16 **Grums** Värmland, C Sweden 59.22N 13.10E
111 S5 **Grünau im Almtal** Oberösterreich, N Austria 47.51N 13.56E
103 H17 **Grünberg** Hessen, W Germany 50.36N 8.57E
Grünberg/Grünberg in Schlesien see Zielona Góra
Grünberg in Schlesien see Zielona Góra
94 H3 **Grundarfjördhur** Vestfirdhir, W Iceland 64.55N 23.15W
23 P7 **Grundy** Virginia, NE USA 37.16N 82.06W
31 W13 **Grundy Center** Iowa, C USA 42.21N 92.46W
Grüneberg see Zielona Góra
27 N1 **Gruver** Texas, SW USA 36.16N 101.24W
110 C9 **Gruyère, Lac de la** Ger. Greyerzer See. ◎ SW Switzerland
110 C9 **Gruyères** Fribourg, W Switzerland 46.34N 7.04E
120 E11 **Gruzdžiai** Šiauliai, N Lithuania 56.06N 23.15E
Gruzinskaya SSR/Gruziya see Georgia
Gryada Akkyr see Akgyr Erezi
130 L7 **Gryazi** Lipetskaya Oblast', W Russian Federation 52.27N 39.56E
128 M14 **Gryazovets** Vologodskaya Oblast', NW Russian Federation 58.52N 40.12E
113 M17 **Grybów** Małopolskie, SE Poland 49.35N 20.54E
96 M13 **Grycksbo** Dalarna, C Sweden 60.40N 15.30E
112 E8 **Gryfice** Ger. Greifenberg, Greifenberg in Pommern. Zachodnio-pomorskie, NW Poland 53.55N 15.10E
112 D9 **Gryfino** Ger. Greifenhagen. Zachodnio-pomorskie, NW Poland 53.15N 14.30E
94 H9 **Gryllefjord** Troms, N Norway 69.21N 17.07E
97 L15 **Grythyttan** Örebro, C Sweden 59.52N 14.31E
110 D10 **Gstaad** Bern, W Switzerland 46.30N 7.16E
45 P14 **Guabito** Bocas del Toro, NW Panama 9.30N 82.35W
46 G7 **Guacanayabo, Golfo de** gulf S Cuba
42 I7 **Guachochi** Chihuahua, N Mexico
106 J11 **Guadajira** ≈ SW Spain
106 M13 **Guadajoz** ≈ S Spain
42 L13 **Guadalajara** Jalisco, C Mexico 20.43N 103.23W
107 O8 **Guadalajara** Ar. Wad Al-Hajarah; anc. Arriaca. Castilla-La Mancha, C Spain 40.37N 3.10W
107 O7 **Guadalajara** ◈ province Castilla-La Mancha, C Spain
106 K12 **Guadalcanal** Andalucía, S Spain 38.06N 5.49W
195 W16 **Guadalcanal** off. Guadalcanal Province. ◈ province C Solomon Islands
195 W16 **Guadalcanal** island C Solomon Islands
107 O12 **Guadalén** ≈ S Spain
107 R13 **Guadalentín** ≈ SE Spain
106 K15 **Guadalete** ≈ SW Spain
107 O13 **Guadalimar** ≈ S Spain
107 P12 **Guadalmena** ≈ S Spain
106 L11 **Guadalmez** ≈ W Spain
107 S7 **Guadalope** ≈ E Spain
106 K13 **Guadalquivir** ≈ W Spain
106 J14 **Guadalquivir, Marismas del** var. Las Marismas. wetland SW Spain
42 M11 **Guadalupe** Zacatecas, C Mexico 22.44N 102.27W
59 E16 **Guadalupe** Ica, W Peru 13.59S 75.49W
106 L10 **Guadalupe** Extremadura, W Spain 39.26N 5.18W
38 L14 **Guadalupe** Arizona, SW USA 33.20N 111.57W
37 P13 **Guadalupe** California, W USA 34.55N 120.34W
199 Mm5 **Guadalupe** island NW Mexico
Guadalupe see Canelones
42 J3 **Guadalupe Bravos** Chihuahua, N Mexico 31.22N 106.04W
40 A4 **Guadalupe, Isla** island NW Mexico
39 U15 **Guadalupe Mountains** ▲▲ New Mexico/Texas, SW USA
26 J8 **Guadalupe Peak** ▲ Texas, SW USA 31.53N 104.51W
27 R11 **Guadalupe River** ≈ SW USA
106 K10 **Guadalupe, Sierra de** ▲▲ W Spain
42 K9 **Guadalupe Victoria** Durango, C Mexico 24.30N 104.03W
42 I8 **Guadalupe y Calvo** Chihuahua, N Mexico 26.04N 106.58W
107 N7 **Guadarrama** Madrid, C Spain 40.40N 4.06W
107 N7 **Guadarrama** ≈ C Spain
106 M7 **Guadarrama, Puerto de** pass C Spain 40.41N 4.14W
107 N9 **Guadarrama, Sierra de** ▲▲ C Spain
107 Q9 **Guadazaón** ≈ C Spain
47 X10 **Guadeloupe** ◇ French overseas department E West Indies
49 S3 **Guadeloupe** island group E West Indies
47 W10 **Guadeloupe Passage** passage E Caribbean Sea
106 H13 **Guadiana** ≈ Portugal/Spain
107 O13 **Guadiana Menor** ≈ S Spain
107 Q8 **Guadiela** ≈ C Spain
107 O14 **Guadix** Andalucía, S Spain 37.19N 3.07W
Guad-i-Zirreh see Gowd-e Zereh, Dasht-e
200 O13 **Guafo Fracture Zone** tectonic feature SE Pacific Ocean
65 F18 **Guafo, Isla** island S Chile
44 I6 **Guaimaca** Francisco Morazán, C Honduras 14.33N 86.49W
56 J12 **Guainía** off. Comisaría del Guainía. ◈ province E Colombia
56 K12 **Guainía, Río** ≈ Colombia/Venezuela
57 O9 **Guaiquinima, Cerro** elevation SE Venezuela 5.45N 63.46W
64 O7 **Guairá** off. Departamento del Guairá. ◈ department S Paraguay
62 G10 **Guaíra** Paraná, S Brazil 24.04S 54.15W
62 L7 **Guaíra** São Paulo, S Brazil 20.17S 48.21W
Guaire see Gorey
65 F18 **Guaiteca, Isla** island S Chile
46 G6 **Guajaba, Cayo** headland C Cuba 21.50N 77.33W
61 D16 **Guajará-Mirim** Rondônia, W Brazil 10.49S 65.21W
Guajira see La Guajira
56 H3 **Guajira, Península de la** peninsula N Colombia
44 J6 **Gualaco** Olancho, C Honduras 15.00N 86.03W
36 L7 **Gualala** California, W USA 38.45N 123.33W
44 E5 **Gualán** Zacapa, C Guatemala 15.06N 89.20W
63 C19 **Gualeguay** Entre Ríos, E Argentina 33.09S 59.19W
63 D18 **Gualeguaychú** Entre Ríos, E Argentina 32.58S 58.30W
63 C18 **Gualeguay, Río** ≈ E Argentina
65 K16 **Gualicho, Salina del** salt lake E Argentina
196 B15 **Guam** ◇ US unincorporated territory W Pacific Ocean
65 F19 **Guamblin, Isla** island Archipiélago de los Chonos, S Chile
63 A22 **Guaminí** Buenos Aires, E Argentina 37.04S 62.22W
42 H8 **Guamúchil** Sinaloa, C Mexico 25.23N 108.00W
56 H4 **Guana** var. Misión de Guana. Zulia, NW Venezuela 11.07N 72.17W
46 C4 **Guanabacoa** La Habana, W Cuba 23.01N 82.12W
44 K13 **Guanacaste** off. Provincia de Guanacaste. ◈ province NW Costa Rica

◆ Country ◇ Dependent Territory ◈ Administrative Region ▲ Mountain ≈ Volcano ◎ Lake
● Country Capital ○ Dependent Territory Capital ✈ International Airport ▲▲ Mountain Range ≈ River ⊡ Reservoir

Guanacaste, Cordillera de – Hafun, Ras

44 K12 **Guanacaste, Cordillera de** ⛰ NW Costa Rica
42 J8 **Guanaceví** Durango, C Mexico 25.55N 105.51W
46 A5 **Guanahacabibes, Golfo de** *gulf* W Cuba
44 K4 **Guanaja, Isla de** *island* Islas de la Bahía, N Honduras
46 C4 **Guanajay** La Habana, W Cuba 22.52N 82.39W
43 N12 **Guanajuato** Guanajuato, C Mexico 21.00N 101.16W
42 M12 **Guanajuato** ◈ *state* C Mexico
56 J6 **Guanare** Portuguesa, N Venezuela 9.04N 69.45W
56 K7 **Guanare, Río** ≈ W Venezuela
56 J6 **Guanarito** Portuguesa, NW Venezuela 8.39N 69.12W
166 M3 **Guancen Shan** ⛰ C China
64 I9 **Guandacol** La Rioja, W Argentina 29.31S 68.30W
46 A5 **Guane** Pinar del Río, W Cuba 22.12N 84.05W
167 N14 **Guangdong** *var.* Guangdong Sheng, Kuang-tung, Kwangtung, Yue. ◈ *province* S China
Guangdong Sheng *see* Guangdong
Guanghua *see* Laohekou
Guangju *see* Kwangju
166 I13 **Guangnan** *var.* Liancheng. Yunnan, SW China 24.07N 104.54E
167 N8 **Guangshui** *prev.* Yingshan. Hubei, C China 31.41N 113.53E
Guangxi *see* Guangxi Zhuangzu Zizhiqu
166 K14 **Guangxi Zhuangzu Zizhiqu** *var.* Guangxi, Gui, Kuang-hsi, Kwangsi, *Eng.* Kwangsi Chuang Autonomous Region. ◈ *autonomous region* S China
166 J8 **Guangyuan** *var.* Kuang-yuan, Kwangyuan. Sichuan, C China 32.27N 105.49E
167 N14 **Guangzhou** *var.* Kuang-chou, Kwangchow, *Eng.* Canton. Guangdong, S China 23.10N 113.19E
61 N19 **Guanhães** Minas Gerais, SE Brazil 18.46S 42.58W
166 I12 **Guanling** *var.* Guanling Buyeizu Miaozu Zizhixian. Guizhou, S China 25.56N 105.36E
Guanling Buyeizu Miaozu Zizhixian *see* Guanling
57 N5 **Guanta** Anzoátegui, NE Venezuela 10.15N 64.37W
46 J8 **Guantánamo** Guantánamo, SE Cuba 20.06N 75.16W
46 J8 **Guantánamo, Bahia de** *Eng.* Guantánamo Bay. *US military installation*, SE Cuba 20.06N 75.16W
Guantánamo Bay *see* Bahia de Guantánamo
Guanxian *see* Dujiangyan
167 Q6 **Guanyun** Jiangsu, E China 34.19N 119.16E
56 C12 **Guapí** Cauca, SW Colombia 2.36N 77.54W
45 N13 **Guápiles** Limón, NE Costa Rica 10.11N 83.45W
63 I15 **Guaporé** Rio Grande do Sul, S Brazil 28.55S 51.53W
49 S8 **Guaporé, Rio** *var.* Río Iténez. ≈ Bolivia/Brazil *see also* Iténez, Río
58 B7 **Guaranda** Bolívar, C Ecuador 1.34S 78.58W
62 H11 **Guaraniaçu** Paraná, S Brazil 25.05S 52.52W
61 O20 **Guarapari** Espírito Santo, SE Brazil 20.39S 40.31W
62 I12 **Guarapuava** Paraná, S Brazil 25.22S 51.28W
62 J8 **Guararapes** São Paulo, S Brazil 21.16S 50.37W
107 S4 **Guara, Sierra de** ⛰ NE Spain
62 N10 **Guaratinguetá** São Paulo, S Brazil 22.44S 45.16W
106 I7 **Guarda** Guarda, N Portugal 40.31N 7.16W
106 I7 **Guarda** ◈ *district* N Portugal
Guardak *see* Gowurdak
106 M3 **Guardo** Castilla-León, N Spain 42.48N 4.49W
106 K11 **Guareña** Extremadura, W Spain 38.51N 6.06W
62 J11 **Guaricana, Pico** ▲ S Brazil 25.13S 48.50W
56 L6 **Guárico** *off.* Estado Guárico. ◈ *state* N Venezuela
46 J7 **Guarico, Punta** *headland* E Cuba 20.36N 74.43W
56 L7 **Guárico, Río** ≈ C Venezuela
62 M10 **Guarujá** São Paulo, SE Brazil 23.50S 46.27W
63 L22 **Guarulhos** ✈ (São Paulo) São Paulo, S Brazil 23.23S 46.32W
45 R17 **Guarumal** Veraguas, S Panama 7.48N 81.15W
Guasapa *see* Guasopa
42 H8 **Guasave** Sinaloa, C Mexico 25.33N 108.28W
56 I8 **Guasdualito** Apure, C Venezuela 7.13N 70.45W
57 Q7 **Guasipati** Bolívar, E Venezuela 7.29N 61.54W
195 Q15 **Guasopa** *var.* Guasapa. Woodlark Island, SE PNG 9.12S 152.55E
108 F9 **Guastalla** Emilia-Romagna, C Italy 44.54N 10.38E
44 D6 **Guastatoya** *var.* El Progreso. El Progreso, C Guatemala 14.51N 90.02W
44 D5 **Guatemala** *off.* Republic of Guatemala. ◆ *republic* Central America
44 A2 **Guatemala** *off.* Departamento de Guatemala. ◈ *department* S Guatemala
200 O7 **Guatemala Basin** *undersea feature* E Pacific Ocean
Guatemala City *see* Ciudad de Guatemala
47 V14 **Guatuaro Point** *headland* Trinidad, Trinidad and Tobago 10.19N 60.58W
194 G14 **Guavi** ≈ SW PNG
56 G13 **Guaviare** *off.* Comisaría Guaviare. ◈ *province* S Colombia
56 J11 **Guaviare, Río** ≈ E Colombia
63 E15 **Guaviravi** Corrientes, NE Argentina 29.19S 56.49W
56 G12 **Guayabero, Río** ≈ SW Colombia
47 U6 **Guayama** E Puerto Rico 17.58N 66.07W
44 J7 **Guayambre, Río** ≈ S Honduras
Guayanas, Macizo de las *see* Guiana Highlands
47 V6 **Guayanés, Punta** *headland* E Puerto Rico 18.03N 65.48W
44 J6 **Guayape, Río** ≈ C Honduras
58 B7 **Guayaquil** *var.* Santiago de Guayaquil. Guayas, SW Ecuador 2.13S 79.54W
Guayaquil *see* Simon Bolivar
58 A8 **Guayaquil, Golfo de** *var.* Gulf of Guayaquil. *gulf* SW Ecuador
Guayaquil, Gulf of *see* Guayaquil, Golfo de
58 A7 **Guayas** ◈ *province* W Ecuador
64 N7 **Guaycurú, Río** ≈ NE Argentina
42 F6 **Guaymas** Sonora, NW Mexico 27.56N 110.54W
47 U5 **Guaynabo** E Puerto Rico 18.19N 66.05W
82 H12 **Guba** Benishangul, W Ethiopia 11.11N 35.21E
152 H8 **Gubadag** *Turkm.* Tel'man; *prev.* Tel'mansk. Daşoguz Welaýaty, N Turkmenistan 42.07N 59.55E
129 T1 **Guba Dolgaya** Nenetskiy Avtonomnyy Okrug, NW Russian Federation 70.16N 58.45E
129 V13 **Gubakha** Permskaya Oblast', NW Russian Federation 58.52N 57.35E
108 I12 **Gubbio** Umbria, C Italy 43.27N 12.34E
102 Q13 **Guben** *var.* Wilhelm-Pieck-Stadt. Brandenburg, E Germany 51.58N 14.42E
Guben *see* Gubin
112 D12 **Gubin** *Ger.* Guben. Lubuskie, W Poland 51.58N 14.42E
130 K8 **Gubkin** Belgorodskaya Oblast', W Russian Federation 51.16N 37.32E
Gudara *see* Ghŭdara
107 S8 **Gúdar, Sierra de** ⛰ E Spain
143 P8 **Gudaut'a** NW Georgia 43.06N 40.35E
96 G12 **Gudbrandsdalen** *valley* S Norway
97 G21 **Gudenå** *var.* Gudenaa. ≈ C Denmark
Gudenaa *see* Gudenå
131 P16 **Gudermes** Chechenskaya Respublika, SW Russian Federation 43.23N 46.06E
161 J18 **Gūdūr** Andhra Pradesh, E India 14.10N 79.51E
152 B13 **Gudurolum** Balkan Welaýaty, W Turkmenistan 37.28N 54.30E
96 D13 **Gudvangen** Sogn og Fjordane, S Norway 60.54N 6.49E
105 U7 **Guebwiller** Haut-Rhin, NE France 47.55N 7.13E
Guéckédou *see* Guékédou
12 K8 **Guéguen, Lac** ◎ Québec, SE Canada
78 J15 **Guékédou** *var.* Guéckédou. Guinée-Forestière, S Guinea 8.33N 10.08W
43 R16 **Guelatao** Oaxaca, SE Mexico
Guelders *see* Gelderland
80 G11 **Guélengdeng** Mayo-Kébbi, W Chad 10.55N 15.31E
76 L5 **Guelma** *var.* Gâlma. NE Algeria 36.28N 7.25E
76 D8 **Guelmime** *var.* Goulimime. SW Morocco 28.59N 10.10W
12 G15 **Guelph** Ontario, S Canada 43.33N 80.12W
104 I7 **Gueméné-Penfao** Loire-Atlantique, NW France 47.37N 1.49W
104 I7 **Guer** Morbihan, NW France 47.54N 2.07W
80 I11 **Guéra** *off.* Préfecture du Guéra. ◈ *prefecture* S Chad
104 H8 **Guérande** Loire-Atlantique, NW France 47.19N 2.25W
80 K9 **Guéréda** Biltine, E Chad 14.30N 22.04E
105 N10 **Guéret** Creuse, C France 46.10N 1.52E
Guernica/Guernica y Lumo *see* Gernika-Lumo
35 Z15 **Guernsey** Wyoming, C USA 42.16N 104.44W
99 K25 **Guernsey** *island* Channel Islands, NW Europe
78 J10 **Guérou** Assaba, S Mauritania 16.48N 11.40W
27 R16 **Guerra** Texas, SW USA 26.54N 98.53W
43 O15 **Guerrero** ◈ *state* S Mexico
42 D6 **Guerrero Negro** Baja California Sur, NW Mexico 27.55N 114.04W
105 P9 **Gueugnon** Saône-et-Loire, C France 46.36N 4.03E
78 M17 **Guéyo** S Ivory Coast 5.25N 6.04W
109 L15 **Guglionesi** Molise, C Italy 41.54N 14.54E
196 K5 **Guguan** *island* C Northern Mariana Islands
Guhrau *see* Góra
Gui *see* Guangxi Zhuangzu Zizhiqu
Guiana *see* French Guiana
49 V4 **Guiana Basin** *undersea feature* W Atlantic Ocean
50 G6 **Guiana Highlands** *var.* Macizo de las Guayanas. ⛰ N South America
Guiba *see* Juba
104 I7 **Guichen** Ille-et-Vilaine, NW France 47.57N 1.47W
Guichi *see* Chizhou
63 E18 **Guichón** Paysandú, W Uruguay 32.21S 57.12W
79 U12 **Guidan-Roumji** Maradi, S Niger 13.40N 6.41E
Guidder *see* Guider
165 T10 **Guide** *var.* Heyin. Qinghai, C China 36.06N 101.25E
80 F12 **Guider** *var.* Guidder. Nord, N Cameroon 9.55N 13.58E
78 I11 **Guidimaka** ◈ *region* S Mauritania
79 W12 **Guidimouni** Zinder, S Niger 13.40N 9.31E
78 G10 **Guier, Lac de** *var.* Lac de Guiers. ◎ N Senegal
166 L14 **Guigang** *prev.* Guixian, Gui Xian. Guangxi Zhuangzu Zizhiqu, S China 23.06N 109.36E
78 L16 **Guiglo** W Ivory Coast 6.33N 7.28W
56 L5 **Güigüe** Carabobo, N Venezuela 10.04N 67.48W
85 M20 **Guijá** Gaza, S Mozambique 24.30S 33.07E
44 E7 **Güija, Lago de** ◎ El Salvador/Guatemala
166 L14 **Gui Jiang** *var.* Gui Shui. ≈ S China
106 K8 **Guijuelo** Castilla-León, N Spain 40.34N 5.40W
Guilan *see* Gīlān
99 N22 **Guildford** SE England, UK 51.13N 0.34W
21 R5 **Guildford** Maine, NE USA 45.10N 69.22W
21 O7 **Guildhall** Vermont, NE USA 44.34N 71.36W
105 R13 **Guilherand** Ardèche, E France 44.57N 4.49E
166 L13 **Guilin** *var.* Kuei-lin, Kweilin. Guangxi Zhuangzu Zizhiqu, S China 25.15N 110.16E
10 J6 **Guillaume-Delisle, Lac** ◎ Québec, NE Canada
105 U13 **Guillestre** Hautes-Alpes, SE France 44.41N 6.39E
106 H6 **Guimarães** *var.* Guimaráes. Braga, N Portugal 41.25N 8.19W
60 D11 **Guimarães Rosas, Pico** ▲ NW Brazil
25 N3 **Guin** Alabama, S USA 33.58N 87.54W
Güina *see* Wina
78 I14 **Guinea** *off.* Republic of Guinea, *var.* Guinée; *prev.* French Guinea, People's Revolutionary Republic of Guinea. ◆ *republic* W Africa
66 N13 **Guinea Basin** *undersea feature* E Atlantic Ocean
78 E12 **Guinea-Bissau** *off.* Republic of Guinea-Bissau, *Fr.* Guinée-Bissau, *Port.* Guiné-Bissau; *prev.* Portuguese Guinea. ◆ *republic* W Africa
68 K7 **Guinea Fracture Zone** *tectonic feature* E Atlantic Ocean
66 O13 **Guinea, Gulf of** *Fr.* Golfe de Guinée. *gulf* E Atlantic Ocean
Guiné-Bissau *see* Guinea-Bissau
Guinée *see* Guinea
Guinée-Bissau *see* Guinea-Bissau
78 K15 **Guinée-Forestière** ◈ *state* SE Guinea
Guinée, Golfe de *see* Guinea, Gulf of
78 H13 **Guinée-Maritime** ◈ *state* W Guinea
46 C4 **Güines** La Habana, W Cuba 22.50N 82.02W
104 G5 **Guingamp** Côtes d'Armor, NW France 48.34N 3.09W
107 P3 **Guipúzcoa** *Basq.* Gipuzkoa. ◈ *province* País Vasco, N Spain
46 C5 **Güira de Melena** La Habana, W Cuba 22.43N 82.31W
76 G8 **Guir, Hamada du** *desert* Algeria/Morocco
57 P5 **Güiria** Sucre, NE Venezuela 10.37N 62.21W
Gui Shui *see* Gui Jiang
106 H2 **Guitiriz** Galicia, NW Spain 43.10N 7.52W
79 N17 **Guitri** S Ivory Coast 5.31N 5.13W
179 R13 **Guiuan** Samar, C Philippines 11.02N 125.45E
Gui Xian/Guixian *see* Guigang
166 J12 **Guiyang** *var.* Kuei-Yang, Kuei-yang, Kueyang, Kweiyang; *prev.* Kweichu. Guizhou, S China 26.33N 106.44E
166 J12 **Guizhou** *var.* Guizhou Sheng, Kuei-chou, Kweichow, Qian. ◈ *province* S China
Guizhou Sheng *see* Guizhou
104 J13 **Gujan-Mestras** Gironde, SW France 44.39N 1.04W
160 B10 **Gujarāt** *var.* Gujerat. ◈ *state* W India
155 V6 **Gūjar Khān** Punjab, E Pakistan 33.15N 73.18E
Gujerat *see* Gujarāt
155 V7 **Gujrānwāla** Punjab, NE Pakistan 32.11N 74.08E
155 V7 **Gujrāt** Punjab, E Pakistan 32.33N 74.03E
152 B8 **Gulandag** *Rus.* Gory Kulandag. ⛰ W Turkmenistan
165 U9 **Gulang** Gansu, C China 37.31N 102.55E
191 R6 **Gulargambone** New South Wales, SE Australia 31.19S 148.31E
161 G15 **Gulbarga** Karnātaka, C India 17.22N 76.46E
120 J8 **Gulbene** *Ger.* Alt-Schwanenburg. Gulbene, NE Latvia 57.10N 26.44E
153 U10 **Gul'cha** *Kir.* Gülchö. Oshskaya Oblast', SW Kyrgyzstan 40.16N 73.27E
Gülchö *see* Gul'cha
181 T10 **Gulden Draak Seamount** *undersea feature* E Indian Ocean 33.45S 101.00E
142 J16 **Gülek Boğazı** *var.* Cilician Gates. *pass* S Turkey 37.19N 34.49E
194 I14 **Gulf** ◈ *province* S PNG
25 O9 **Gulf Breeze** Florida, SE USA 30.21N 87.09W
25 V13 **Gulfport** Florida, SE USA 27.45N 82.42W
24 M9 **Gulfport** Mississippi, S USA 30.22N 89.05W
25 O9 **Gulf Shores** Alabama, S USA 30.15N 87.40W
Gulf, The *see* Persian Gulf
191 R7 **Gulgong** New South Wales, SE Australia 32.22S 149.31E
166 I11 **Gulin** Sichuan, C China 28.06N 105.47E
176 V12 **Gulir** Pulau Kasiui, E Indonesia 4.27S 131.41E
Gulistan *see* Guliston
153 P10 **Guliston** *Rus.* Gulistan. Sirdaryo Viloyati, E Uzbekistan 40.28N 68.45E
169 T6 **Guliya Shan** ▲ NE China 49.42N 122.22E
Gulja *see* Yining
41 S11 **Gulkana** Alaska, USA 62.17N 145.25W
9 S17 **Gull Lake** Saskatchewan, S Canada 50.04N 108.30W
33 P10 **Gull Lake** ◎ Michigan, N USA
31 T6 **Gull Lake** ◎ Minnesota, N USA
97 L16 **Gullspång** Västra Götaland, S Sweden 58.58N 14.04E
142 B15 **Güllük Körfezi** *prev.* Akbük Limanı. *bay* W Turkey
158 H5 **Gulmarg** Jammu and Kashmir, NW India 34.04N 74.25E
Gulpaigan *see* Golpāyegān
101 L18 **Gulpen** Limburg, SE Netherlands 50.48N 5.53E
Gul'shad *see* Gul'shat
151 S13 **Gul'shat** *var.* Gul'shad. Karaganda, E Kazakhstan 46.37N 74.21E
83 F17 **Gulu** N Uganda 2.46N 32.21E
116 K10 **Gŭlŭbovo** Stara Zagora, C Bulgaria 42.10N 25.52E
116 I7 **Gulyantsi** Pleven, N Bulgaria 43.37N 24.40E
Gulyaypole *see* Hulyaypole
Guma *see* Pishan
Gümai *see* Darlag
81 K16 **Gumba** Equateur, NW Dem. Rep. Congo 2.58N 21.23E
Gumbinnen *see* Gusev
83 H24 **Gumbiro** Ruvuma, S Tanzania 10.19S 35.40E
152 B11 **Gumdag** *prev.* Kum-Dag. Balkan Welaýaty, W Turkmenistan 39.13N 54.35E
79 W12 **Gumel** Jigawa, N Nigeria 12.37N 9.23E
107 N5 **Gumiel de Hizán** Castilla-León, N Spain 41.46N 3.42W
194 I12 **Gumine** *var.* Gumire. Chimbu, C PNG 6.12S 144.53E
Gumire *see* Gumine
159 P16 **Gumla** Jhārkhand, N India 23.03N 84.36E
Gumma *see* Gunma
103 F16 **Gummersbach** Nordrhein-Westfalen, W Germany 51.01N 7.34E
79 T13 **Gummi** Zamfara, NW Nigeria 12.07N 5.07E
Gumpolds *see* Humpolec
159 N13 **Gumti** *var.* Gomati. ≈ N India
Gümülcine/Gümüljina *see* Komotiní
Gümüşane *see* Gümüşhane
143 O12 **Gümüşhane** *var.* Gümüşane, Gumushkhane. Gümüşhane, NE Turkey 40.30N 39.27E
143 O12 **Gümüşhane** *var.* Gümüşane, Gumushkhane. ◈ *province* NE Turkey
Gumushkhane *see* Gümüşhane
176 W13 **Gumzai** Pulau Kola, E Indonesia 5.27S 134.38E
160 H9 **Guna** Madhya Pradesh, C India 24.39N 77.21E
Gunabad *see* Gonābād
Gunan *see* Qijiang
Gunbad-i-Qawus *see* Gonbad-e Kāvūs
191 O9 **Gunbar** New South Wales, SE Australia 34.03S 145.32E
191 O9 **Gun Creek** *seasonal river* New South Wales, SE Australia
191 Q10 **Gundagai** New South Wales, SE Australia 35.06S 148.03E
81 K17 **Gundji** Equateur, N Dem. Rep. Congo 2.13N 21.31E
161 G20 **Gundlupet** Karnātaka, W India 11.48N 76.42E
142 G16 **Gündoğmuş** Antalya, S Turkey 36.52N 32.01E
143 O14 **Güney Doğu Toroslar** ⛰ SE Turkey
81 J21 **Gungu** Bandundu, SW Dem. Rep. Congo 5.43S 19.19E
131 P17 **Gunib** Respublika Dagestan, SW Russian Federation 42.24N 46.55E
114 J11 **Gunja** Vukovar-Srijem, E Croatia 44.53N 18.51E
33 P9 **Gun Lake** ◎ Michigan, N USA
171 Jj15 **Gunma** *off.* Gunma-ken, *var.* Gumma. ◈ *prefecture* Honshū, S Japan
207 P15 **Gunnbjørn Fjeld** *var.* Gunnbjörns Bjerge. ▲ C Greenland 69.03N 29.36W
191 S6 **Gunnedah** New South Wales, SE Australia 30.58S 150.15E
181 Y15 **Gunner's Quoin** *var.* Coin de Mire. *island* N Mauritius
39 R6 **Gunnison** Colorado, C USA 38.33N 106.55W
38 L5 **Gunnison** Utah, W USA 39.09N 111.49W
39 P5 **Gunnison River** ≈ Colorado, C USA
23 X2 **Gunpowder River** ≈ Maryland, NE USA
Güns *see* Kőszeg
Gunsan *see* Kunsan
111 S4 **Gunskirchen** Oberösterreich, N Austria 48.07N 13.54E
Gunt *see* Ghund
161 H17 **Guntakal** Andhra Pradesh, C India 15.10N 77.24E
25 Q2 **Guntersville** Alabama, S USA 34.21N 86.17W
25 Q2 **Guntersville Lake** ⊠ Alabama, S USA
111 X4 **Guntramsdorf** Niederösterreich, E Austria 48.03N 16.19E
161 J16 **Guntūr** *var.* Guntur. Andhra Pradesh, SE India 16.19N 80.27E
173 F7 **Gunungsitoli** Pulau Nias, W Indonesia 1.11N 97.35E
161 M14 **Gunupur** Orissa, E India 19.04N 83.52E
103 J23 **Günz** ≈ S Germany
Gunzan *see* Kunsan
103 J22 **Günzburg** Bayern, S Germany 48.26N 10.18E
103 K21 **Gunzenhausen** Bayern, S Germany 49.07N 10.45E
Guovdageaidnu *see* Kautokeino
167 P7 **Guoyang** Anhui, E China 33.29N 116.14E
118 G11 **Gurahonţ** *Hung.* Honctő. Arad, W Romania 46.16N 22.20E
Gurahumora *see* Gura Humorului
118 K9 **Gura Humorului** *Ger.* Gurahumora. Suceava, NE Romania 47.31N 26.00E
164 K4 **Gurbantünggüt Shamo** *desert* W China
158 H7 **Gurdāspur** Punjab, N India 32.02N 75.23E
29 T13 **Gurdon** Arkansas, C USA 33.55N 93.09W
Gurdzhaani *see* Gurjaani
Gurgan *see* Gorgān
158 I10 **Gurgaon** Haryāna, N India 28.24N 76.59E
61 M15 **Gurguéia, Rio** ≈ NE Brazil
57 Q7 **Guri, Embalse de** ⊠ E Venezuela
143 V10 **Gurjaani** *Rus.* Gurdzhaani. E Georgia 41.42N 45.47E
111 T8 **Gurk** Kärnten, S Austria 46.52N 14.17E
111 T9 **Gurk** *Slvn.* Krka. ≈ S Austria
Gurkfeld *see* Krško
116 K9 **Gurkovo** *prev.* Kolupchii. Stara Zagora, C Bulgaria 42.42N 25.46E
111 S9 **Gurktaler Alpen** ⛰ S Austria
152 H8 **Gurlan** *Rus.* Gurlen. Xorazm Viloyati, W Uzbekistan 41.54N 60.18E
Gurlen *see* Gurlan
85 M16 **Guro** Manica, C Mozambique 17.25S 33.23E
142 M14 **Gürün** Sivas, C Turkey 38.43N 37.15E
61 K16 **Gurupi** Tocantins, C Brazil 11.43S 49.01W
60 L12 **Gurupi, Rio** ≈ NE Brazil
158 E14 **Guru Sikhar** ▲ NW India 24.45N 72.51E
Gur'yev/Gur'yevskaya Oblast' *see* Atyrau
79 U13 **Gusau** Zamfara, NW Nigeria 12.18N 6.27E
130 C3 **Gusev** *Ger.* Gumbinnen. Kaliningradskaya Oblast', W Russian Federation 54.36N 22.13E
152 J17 **Gushgy** *Rus.* Kushka. ≈ S Turkmenistan
Gushgy *see* Serhetabat
Gushiago *see* Gushiegu
79 Q14 **Gushiegu** *var.* Gushiago. NE Ghana 9.54N 0.12W
172 P15 **Gushikawa** Okinawa, Okinawa, SW Japan 26.21N 127.49E
115 L16 **Gusinje** Montenegro, SW Serbia and Montenegro (Yugoslavia) 42.34N 19.51E
126 Jj16 **Gusinoozersk** Respublika Buryatiya, S Russian Federation 51.18N 106.28E
130 M4 **Gus'-Khrustal'nyy** Vladimirskaya Oblast', W Russian Federation 55.39N 40.42E
109 B19 **Guspini** Sardegna, Italy, C Mediterranean Sea 39.33N 8.39E
111 X8 **Güssing** Burgenland, SE Austria 47.04N 16.18E
111 V6 **Gusswerk** Steiermark, E Austria 47.43N 15.18E
94 O2 **Gustav Adolf Land** *physical region* NE Svalbard
205 X5 **Gustav Bull Mountains** ⛰ Antarctica
41 W13 **Gustavus** Alaska, USA 58.24N 135.44W
94 O1 **Gustav V Land** *physical region* NE Svalbard
37 P9 **Gustine** California, W USA 37.14N 121.00W
27 R8 **Gustine** Texas, SW USA 31.51N 98.24W
102 M9 **Güstrow** Mecklenburg-Vorpommern, NE Germany 53.48N 12.11E
97 N18 **Gusum** Östergötland, S Sweden 58.15N 16.30E
Guta/Gúta *see* Kolárovo
Gutenstein *see* Ravne na Koroškem
103 G14 **Gütersloh** Nordrhein-Westfalen, W Germany 51.54N 8.22E
29 N10 **Guthrie** Oklahoma, C USA 35.52N 97.25W
27 P5 **Guthrie** Texas, SW USA 33.37N 100.21W
31 U14 **Guthrie Center** Iowa, C USA 41.40N 94.30W
43 Q13 **Gutiérrez Zamora** Veracruz-Llave, E Mexico 20.29N 97.07W
Gutta *see* Kolárovo
31 Y12 **Guttenberg** Iowa, C USA 42.47N 91.06W
Guttentag *see* Dobrodzień
Guttstadt *see* Dobre Miasto
168 G8 **Guulin** Govĭ-Altay, C Mongolia 46.33N 97.21E
159 V12 **Guwāhāti** *prev.* Gauhāti. Assam, NE India 26.09N 91.42E
145 R3 **Guwēr** *var.* Al Kuwayr, Al Quwayr, Quwair. N Iraq 36.03N 43.30E
152 A10 **Guwlumaýak** *Rus.* Kuuli-Mayak. Balkan Welaýaty, NW Turkmenistan 40.14N 52.43E
57 R9 **Guyana** *off.* Cooperative Republic of Guyana; *prev.* British Guiana. ◆ *republic* N South America
23 P5 **Guyandotte River** ≈ West Virginia, NE USA
Guyane *see* French Guiana
Guyi *see* Sanjiang
28 H8 **Guymon** Oklahoma, C USA 36.40N 101.28W
152 K12 **Guynuk** Lebap Welaýaty, NE Turkmenistan 39.18N 63.00E
Guyong *see* Jiangle
23 O9 **Guyot, Mount** ▲ North Carolina/Tennessee, SE USA 35.42N 83.15W
191 U5 **Guyra** New South Wales, SE Australia 30.13S 151.42E
165 W10 **Guyuan** Ningxia, N China 35.57N 106.13E
Guzar *see* G'uzor
124 N3 **Güzelyurt** *Gk.* Mórfou, Morphou. W Cyprus 35.11N 33.00E
124 N2 **Güzelyurt Körfezi** *var.* Morfou Bay, Morphou Bay, *Gk.* Kólpos Mórfou. *bay* W Cyprus
Guzhou *see* Rongjiang
42 I3 **Guzmán** Chihuahua, N Mexico 31.13N 107.27W
153 N13 **G'uzor** *Rus.* Guzar. Qashqadaryo Viloyati, S Uzbekistan 38.41N 66.12E
121 B14 **Gvardeysk** *Ger.* Tapaiu. Kaliningradskaya Oblast', W Russian Federation 54.39N 21.02E
Gvardeyskoye *see* Hvardiys'ke
191 R5 **Gwabegar** New South Wales, SE Australia 30.34S 148.58E
154 J16 **Gwādar** *var.* Gwadur. Baluchistān, SW Pakistan 25.09N 62.21E
154 J16 **Gwādar East Bay** *bay* SW Pakistan
154 J16 **Gwādar West Bay** *bay* SW Pakistan
Gwadur *see* Gwādar
85 J17 **Gwai** Matabeleland North, W Zimbabwe 19.17S 27.37E
160 I7 **Gwalior** Madhya Pradesh, C India 26.15N 78.12E
85 J18 **Gwanda** Matabeleland South, SW Zimbabwe 20.56S 29.00E
81 N15 **Gwane** Orientale, N Dem. Rep. Congo 4.40N 25.51E
85 I17 **Gwayi** ≈ W Zimbabwe
112 G8 **Gwda** *var.* Głda, *Ger.* Küddow. ≈ NW Poland
99 C14 **Gweebarra Bay** *Ir.* Béal an Bheara. *inlet* W Ireland
99 D14 **Gweedore** *Ir.* Gaoth Dobhair. NW Ireland 55.03N 8.13W
Gwelo *see* Gweru
99 K21 **Gwent** *cultural region* S Wales, UK
85 K17 **Gweru** *prev.* Gwelo. Midlands, C Zimbabwe 19.27S 29.49E
31 Q7 **Gwinner** North Dakota, N USA 46.10N 97.42W
79 Y13 **Gwoza** Borno, NE Nigeria 11.07N 13.40E
Gwy *see* Wye
191 R4 **Gwydir River** ≈ New South Wales, SE Australia
99 I19 **Gwynedd** *var.* Gwyneth. *cultural region* NW Wales, UK
Gwyneth *see* Gwynedd
165 O16 **Gyaca** *var.* Ngarrab. Xizang Zizhiqu, W China 29.06N 92.37E
Gya'gya *see* Saga
Gyaijêpozhanggê *see* Zhidoi
Gyaisi *see* Jiulong
117 M22 **Gyalí** *var.* Yialí. *island* Dodekánisos, Greece, Aegean Sea
Gyamotang *see* Dêngqên
Gyandzha *see* Gäncä
Gyangkar *see* Dinggyê
164 M16 **Gyangzê** Xizang Zizhiqu, W China 28.49N 89.37E
164 L14 **Gyaring Co** ◎ W China
165 Q12 **Gyaring Hu** ◎ C China
117 I20 **Gyáros** *var.* Yioúra. *island* Kykládes, Greece, Aegean Sea
126 Hh7 **Gyda** Yamalo-Nenetskiy Avtonomnyy Okrug, N Russian Federation 70.55N 78.34E
126 H7 **Gydanskiy Poluostrov** *Eng.* Gyda Peninsula. *peninsula* N Russian Federation
Gyda Peninsula *see* Gydanskiy Poluostrov
Gyêgu *see* Yushu
Gyéres *see* Câmpia Turzii
Gyergyószentmiklós *see* Gheorgheni
Gyergyótölgyes *see* Tulgheş
Gyertyámos *see* Cărpiniş
Gyeva *see* Detva
Gyigang *see* Zayü
Gyixong *see* Gonggar
97 I23 **Gyldenløveshøj** *hill range* C Denmark
189 Z10 **Gympie** Queensland, E Australia 26.04S 152.40E
177 Ff7 **Gyobingauk** Pegu, SW Myanmar 18.13N 95.39E
113 M23 **Gyomaendrőd** Békés, SE Hungary 46.55N 20.49E
Gyömbér *see* Ďumbier
113 L22 **Gyöngyös** Heves, NE Hungary 47.43N 19.48E
113 H22 **Győr** *Ger.* Raab; *Lat.* Arrabona. Győr-Moson-Sopron, NW Hungary 47.40N 17.40E
113 G22 **Győr-Moson-Sopron** *off.* Győr-Moson-Sopron Megye. ◈ *county* NW Hungary
9 X15 **Gypsumville** Manitoba, S Canada 51.46N 98.37W
10 M4 **Gyrfalcon Islands** *island group* Nunavut, NE Canada
97 N14 **Gysinge** Gävleborg, C Sweden 60.16N 16.55E
117 F22 **Gýtheio** *var.* Githio; *prev.* Yíthion. Pelopónnisos, S Greece 36.46N 22.34E
152 L13 **Gyuichbirleshik** Lebap Welaýaty, E Turkmenistan 38.10N 64.33E
113 N24 **Gyula** *Rom.* Jula. Békés, SE Hungary 46.37N 21.19E
Gyulafehérvár *see* Alba Iulia
Gyulovo *see* Roza
143 T11 **Gyumri** *var.* Giumri, *Rus.* Kumayri; *prev.* Aleksandropol', Leninakan. W Armenia 40.48N 43.51E
152 D13 **Gyunuzyndag, Gora** ▲ W Turkmenistan 38.15N 56.25E
Gyzylarbat *see* Serdar
152 J15 **Gyzylbaýdak** *Rus.* Krasnoye Znamya. Mary Welaýaty, S Turkmenistan 36.51N 62.24E
Gyzyletrek *see* Etrek
152 D10 **Gyzylgaýa** *Rus.* Kizyl-Kaya. Balkan Welaýaty, NW Turkmenistan 40.37N 55.15E
152 K12 **Gyzylsuw** *Rus.* Kizyl-Su. Balkan Welaýaty, W Turkmenistan 39.49N 53.00E
130 J3 **Gzhatsk** Smolenskaya Oblast', W Russian Federation 55.33N 35.00E

H

159 T12 **Ha** W Bhutan 27.16N 89.22E
Haabai *see* Ha'apai Group
101 H17 **Haacht** Vlaams Brabant, C Belgium 50.58N 4.37E
111 T4 **Haag** Niederösterreich, NE Austria 48.07N 14.32E
204 L8 **Haag Nunataks** ⛰ Antarctica
94 N2 **Haakon VII Land** *physical region* NW Svalbard
100 O11 **Haaksbergen** Overijssel, E Netherlands 52.09N 6.45E
101 E14 **Haamstede** Zeeland, SW Netherlands 51.43N 3.45E
200 Ss13 **Ha'ano** *island* Ha'apai Group, C Tonga
200 Ss13 **Ha'apai Group** *var.* Haabai. *island group* C Tonga
95 L15 **Haapajärvi** Oulu, C Finland 63.45N 25.19E
95 L17 **Haapamäki** Länsi-Suomi, W Finland 62.11N 24.32E
95 L15 **Haapavesi** Oulu, C Finland 64.09N 25.25E
203 N7 **Haapiti** Moorea, W French Polynesia 17.33S 149.52W
120 F4 **Haapsalu** *Ger.* Hapsal. Läänemaa, W Estonia 58.57N 23.32E
Ha'Arava *see* 'Arabah, Wādī al
97 G24 **Haarby** *var.* Hårby. Fyn, C Denmark 55.13N 10.07E
100 H10 **Haarlem** *prev.* Harlem. Noord-Holland, W Netherlands 52.22N 4.39E
193 D19 **Haast** West Coast, South Island, NZ 43.53S 169.01E
193 C20 **Haast** ≈ South Island, NZ
193 D20 **Haast Pass** *pass* South Island, NZ 44.07S 169.18E
200 R16 **Ha'atua** 'Eau, E Tonga 21.23S 174.57W
155 P15 **Hab** ≈ SW Pakistan
147 W7 **Haba** *var.* Al Haba. Dubayy, NE UAE 25.01N 55.37E
164 K2 **Habahe** *var.* Kaba. Xinjiang Uygur Zizhiqu, NW China 48.04N 86.20E
147 U13 **Ḩabarūt** *var.* Habrut. SW Oman 17.19N 52.45E
83 J18 **Habaswein** North Eastern, NE Kenya 1.01N 39.27E
101 L24 **Habay-la-Neuve** Luxembourg, SE Belgium 49.43N 5.38E
145 S8 **Ḩabbānīyah, Buḩayrat** ◎ C Iraq
Habelschwerdt *see* Bystrzyca Kłodzka
159 V14 **Habiganj** Chittagong, NE Bangladesh 24.22N 91.25E
169 Q12 **Habirag** Nei Mongol Zizhiqu, N China 42.18N 115.40E
97 L19 **Habo** Västra Götaland, S Sweden 57.55N 14.04E
127 P16 **Habomai Islands** *island group* Kuril'skiye Ostrova, SE Russian Federation
172 P3 **Haboro** Hokkaidō, NE Japan 44.19N 141.42E
159 S16 **Habra** West Bengal, NE India 22.39N 88.17E
Habrut *see* Ḩabarūt
149 P17 **Ḩabshān** Abū Ẓaby, C UAE 23.51N 53.34E
56 E14 **Hacha** Putumayo, S Colombia 00.02S 75.30W
172 Ss13 **Hachijō** Tōkyō, Hachijō-jima, SE Japan 35.40N 139.19E
172 Ss13 **Hachijō-jima** *var.* Hatizyô Zima. *island* Izu-shotō, SE Japan
171 I14 **Hachiman** Gifu, Honshū, SW Japan 35.46N 136.57E
171 M9 **Hachimori** Akita, Honshū, C Japan 40.22N 139.59E
172 N10 **Hachinohe** Aomori, Honshū, C Japan 40.30N 141.28E
171 Jj16 **Hachiōji** *var.* Hatiôzi. Tōkyō, Honshū, S Japan 35.39N 139.17E
95 G17 **Hackås** Jämtland, C Sweden 62.55N 14.31E
20 K14 **Hackensack** New Jersey, NE USA 40.51N 73.57W
Hadama *see* Nazrēt
171 J16 **Hadano** Kanagawa, Honshū, S Japan 35.23N 139.13E
147 W13 **Ḩaḑbaram** S Oman 17.27N 55.13E
145 U13 **Ḩaddānīyah** *well* S Iraq 30.27N 44.40E
98 K12 **Haddington** SE Scotland, UK 55.59N 2.45W
147 Z8 **Ḩadd, Ra's al** *headland* NE Oman 22.28N 59.58E
Haded *see* Xadeed
79 W12 **Hadejia** Jigawa, N Nigeria 12.22N 10.02E
79 W12 **Hadejia** ≈ N Nigeria
144 F9 **Hadera** *var.* Khadera. Haifa, C Israel 32.25N 34.55E
Hadersleben *see* Haderslev
97 G24 **Haderslev** *Ger.* Hadersleben. Sønderjylland, SW Denmark 55.15N 9.30E
157 J21 **Hadhdhunmathi Atoll** *var.* Haddummati Atoll, Laamu Atoll. *atoll* S Maldives
Hadhramaut *see* Ḩaḑramawt
147 W17 **Hadībоh** Suquṭrā, SE Yemen 12.37N 54.04E
164 K9 **Hadilik** Xinjiang Uygur Zizhiqu, W China 37.51N 86.10E
142 H16 **Hadım** Konya, S Turkey 36.58N 32.27E
146 K7 **Hadīyah** Al Madīnah, W Saudi Arabia 25.36N 38.31E
15 J1 **Hadley Bay** *bay* Victoria Island, Nunavut, N Canada
178 Jj6 **Ha Đông** *var.* Hadong. Ha Tây, N Vietnam 20.58N 105.46E
147 R15 **Ḩaḑramawt** *Eng.* Hadhramaut. ⛰ S Yemen
Hadria *see* Adria
Hadrianopolis *see* Edirne
Hadria Picena *see* Apricena
97 G22 **Hadsten** Århus, C Denmark 56.19N 10.03E
97 G21 **Hadsund** Nordjylland, N Denmark 56.43N 10.07E
119 S4 **Hadyach** *Rus.* Gadyach. Poltavs'ka Oblast', NE Ukraine 50.21N 34.00E
114 I13 **Hadžići** Federacija Bosna I Hercegovina, SE Bosnia and Herzegovina 43.49N 18.12E
169 W14 **Haeju** S North Korea 38.04N 125.40E
Haerbin/Haerhpin/Ha-erh-pin *see* Harbin
147 P5 **Ḩafar al Bāţin** Ash Sharqīyah, N Saudi Arabia 28.25N 45.58E
9 T15 **Hafford** Saskatchewan, S Canada 52.43N 107.19W
142 M13 **Hafik** Sivas, N Turkey 39.52N 37.24E
155 V8 **Hāfizābād** Punjab, E Pakistan 32.05N 73.37E
94 H4 **Hafnarfjördhur** Reykjanes, W Iceland 64.03N 21.57W
Hafnia *see* København, Denmark
Hafnia *see* Denmark
Hafren *see* Severn
Hafun *see* Xaafuun
Hafun, Ras *see* Xaafuun, Raas

◆ Country
● Country Capital
◇ Dependent Territory
○ Dependent Territory Capital
◈ Administrative Region
✈ International Airport
▲ Mountain
⛰ Mountain Range
Volcano
≈ River
◎ Lake
⊠ Reservoir

HAG 'ABDULLAH – HARPER, MOUNT

82 G10 **Hag 'Abdullah** Sinnar, E Sudan *13.58N 33.34E*
83 K18 **Hagadera** North Eastern, E Kenya *0.06N 40.23E*
144 G8 **HaGalil** *Eng.* Galilee. ▲▲ N Israel
12 G10 **Hagar** Ontario, S Canada *46.27N 80.22W*
161 G18 **Hagari** *var.* Vedāvati. ~ W India
196 B16 **Hagåtña** *var.* Agana, Agaña. ○ (Guam) NW Guam *13.27N 144.45E*
102 M13 **Hagelberg** *hill* NE Germany *52.03N 12.33E*
41 N14 **Hagemeister Island** *island* Alaska, USA
103 F15 **Hagen** Nordrhein-Westfalen, W Germany *51.21N 7.27E*
102 K10 **Hagenow** Mecklenburg-Vorpommern, N Germany *53.27N 11.10E*
8 K15 **Hagensborg** British Columbia, SW Canada *52.24N 126.24W*
82 I13 **Hägere Hiywet** *var.* Agere Hiywet, Ambo. Oromo, C Ethiopia *9.00N 37.55E*
35 O15 **Hagerman** Idaho, NW USA *42.48N 114.53W*
39 U14 **Hagerman** New Mexico, SW USA *33.07N 104.19W*
23 V2 **Hagerstown** Maryland, NE USA *39.38N 77.43W*
12 G16 **Hagersville** Ontario, S Canada *42.58N 80.03W*
104 J15 **Hagetmau** Landes, SW France *43.40N 0.36W*
97 K14 **Hagfors** Värmland, C Sweden *60.03N 13.45E*
95 G16 **Häggenås** Jämtland, C Sweden *63.24N 14.53E*
170 Dd12 **Hagi** Yamaguchi, Honshū, SW Japan *34.24N 131.22E*
178 J5 **Ha Giang** Ha Giang, N Vietnam *22.49N 104.58E*
Hagios Evstrátios *see* Ágios Efstrátios
HaGolan *see* Golan Heights
105 T4 **Hagondange** Moselle, NE France *49.15N 6.06E*
99 B18 **Hag's Head** *Ir.* Ceann Caillí. *headland* W Ireland *52.56N 9.29W*
104 I3 **Hague, Cap de la** *headland* N France *49.43N 1.56W*
105 V5 **Haguenau** Bas-Rhin, NE France *48.49N 7.46E*
172 T16 **Hahajima-rettō** *island group* SE Japan
13 R8 **Ha! Ha!, Lac** ◎ Québec, SE Canada
180 H13 **Hahaya** ✈ (Moroni) Grande Comore, NW Comoros
24 K9 **Hahnville** Louisiana, S USA *29.58N 90.24W*
85 E22 **Haib** Karas, S Namibia *28.12S 18.19E*
Haibak *see* Āybak
155 N15 **Haibo** ~ SW Pakistan
Haibowan *see* Wuhai
169 U12 **Haicheng** Liaoning, NE China *40.52N 122.45E*
Haida *see* Nový Bor
Haidarabad *see* Hyderābād
Haidenschaft *see* Ajdovščina
178 Jj6 **Hai Dương** Hai Hưng, N Vietnam *20.55N 106.21E*
144 F9 **Haifa** ◈ *district* NW Israel
Haifa *see* Ḥefa
Haifa, Bay of *see* Ḥefa, Mifraẓ
167 P14 **Haifeng** Guangdong, S China *22.58N 115.16E*
Haifong *see* Hai Phong
167 P3 **Hai He** ~ E China
Haikang *see* Leizhou
166 L17 **Haikou** *var.* Hai-k'ou, Hoihow, *Fr.* Hoï-Hao. Hainan, S China *20.00N 110.16E*
146 M6 **Ḥā'il** Ḥā'il, NW Saudi Arabia *27.00N 42.50E*
147 N5 **Ḥā'il** *off.* Minṭaqah Ḥā'il. ◈ *province* N Saudi Arabia
Hai-la-erh *see* Hailar
169 S6 **Hailar** *var.* Hai-la-erh; *prev.* Hulun. Nei Mongol Zizhiqu, N China *49.15N 119.40E*
169 S6 **Hailar He** ~ NE China
35 P14 **Hailey** Idaho, NW USA *43.31N 114.18W*
12 H9 **Haileybury** Ontario, S Canada *47.27N 79.39W*
169 X9 **Hailin** Heilongjiang, NE China *44.37N 129.24E*
Ḥā'il, Minṭaqah *see* Ḥā'il
Hailong *see* Meihekou
95 K14 **Hailuoto** *Swe.* Karlö. *island* W Finland
Haima *see* Haymā'
Haimen *see* Taizhou
166 M17 **Hainan** *var.* Hainan Sheng, Qiong. ◈ *province* S China
166 K17 **Hainan Dao** *island* S China
Hainan Sheng *see* Hainan
Hainan Strait *see* Qiongzhou Haixia
Hainasch *see* Ainaži
Hainau *see* Chojnów
101 E20 **Hainaut** ◈ *province* SW Belgium
Hainburg *see* Hainburg an der Donau
111 Z4 **Hainburg an der Donau** *var.* Hainburg. Niederösterreich, NE Austria *48.08N 16.57E*
41 W12 **Haines** Alaska, USA *59.13N 135.27W*
34 L12 **Haines** Oregon, NW USA *44.53N 117.56W*
25 W12 **Haines City** Florida, SE USA *28.06N 81.37W*
8 H8 **Haines Junction** Yukon Territory, W Canada *60.45N 137.30W*
111 W4 **Hainfeld** Niederösterreich, NE Austria *48.01N 15.45E*
103 N16 **Hainichen** Sachsen, E Germany *50.58N 13.07E*
178 K6 **Hai Phong** *var.* Haifong, Haiphong. N Vietnam *20.49N 106.40E*
167 S12 **Haitan Dao** *island* SE China
46 K8 **Haiti** *off.* Republic of Haiti. ◆ *republic* C West Indies
37 T11 **Haiwee Reservoir** ▣ California, W USA
82 I7 **Haiya** Red Sea, NE Sudan *18.16N 36.21E*
165 T10 **Haiyan** *var.* Sanjiaocheng. Qinghai, W China *36.55N 100.54E*
166 M13 **Haiyang Shan** ▲▲ S China
165 V10 **Haiyuan** Ningxia, N China *36.32N 105.31E*
Hajda *see* Nový Bor
113 M22 **Hajdú-Bihar** *off.* Hajdú-Bihar Megye. ◈ *county* E Hungary
113 N22 **Hajdúböszörmény** Hajdú-Bihar, E Hungary *47.39N 21.32E*
113 N22 **Hajdúhadház** Hajdú-Bihar, E Hungary *47.40N 21.40E*
113 N21 **Hajdúnánás** Hajdú-Bihar, E Hungary *47.49N 21.25E*
113 N22 **Hajdúszoboszló** Hajdú-Bihar, E Hungary *47.27N 21.23E*
148 I3 **Ḥājī Ebrāhīm, Kūh-e** ▲ Iran/Iraq *36.53N 44.56E*
171 Kk11 **Hajiki-zaki** *headland* Sado, C Japan *38.19N 138.28E*
Hajine *see* Abū Ḥardān
159 P13 **Hājīpur** Bihār, N India *25.40N 85.13E*
147 N14 **Ḥajjah** W Yemen *15.43N 43.33E*
145 U11 **Ḥajjama** S Iraq *31.24N 45.20E*
149 R12 **Ḥājjīābād** Hormozgān, C Iran *28.19N 55.55E*
145 U14 **Ḥājj, Thaqb al** *well* S Iraq *29.58N 44.32E*
115 L16 **Hajla** ▲▲ SW Serbia and Montenegro (Yugoslavia)
112 P10 **Hajnówka** *Ger.* Hermhausen. Podlaskie, NE Poland *52.43N 23.37E*
177 Ff4 **Haka** Chin State, W Myanmar *22.42N 93.40E*
Hakapehi *see* Punaauia
Hakâri *see* Hakkâri
143 T16 **Hakkâri** *var.* Çölemerik, Hakâri. Hakkâri, SE Turkey *37.36N 43.45E*
143 T16 **Hakkâri** *var.* Hakkari. ◈ *province* SE Turkey
94 J12 **Hakkas** Norrbotten, N Sweden *66.52N 21.36E*
171 Gg16 **Hakken-zan** ▲ Honshū, SW Japan *34.11N 135.57E*
172 N9 **Hakkōda-san** ▲ Honshū, C Japan *40.40N 140.49E*
172 Pp3 **Hako-dake** ▲ Hokkaidō, NE Japan *44.40N 142.22E*
172 N7 **Hakodate** Hokkaidō, NE Japan *41.46N 140.42E*
171 Ii12 **Hakui** Ishikawa, Honshū, SW Japan *36.52N 136.45E*
202 B16 **Hakupu** SE Niue *19.06S 169.49E*
171 I14 **Haku-san** ▲ Honshū, SW Japan *36.07N 136.45E*
Hal *see* Halle
155 Q15 **Hāla** Sind, SE Pakistan *25.46N 68.28E*
144 J3 **Ḥalab** *Eng.* Aleppo, *Fr.* Alep; *anc.* Beroea. Ḥalab, NW Syria *36.13N 37.10E*
144 J3 **Ḥalab** *off.* Muḥāfaẓat Ḥalab, *var.* Aleppo, Halab. ◈ *governorate* NW Syria
144 J3 **Ḥalab** ✈ Ḥalab, NW Syria *36.12N 37.10E*
147 O8 **Ḥalabān** *var.* Halibān. Ar Riyāḍ, C Saudi Arabia *23.28N 44.19E*
145 V4 **Ḥalabja** NE Iraq *35.10N 45.58E*
152 L13 **Halaç** *Rus.* Khalach. Lebap Welaýaty, E Turkmenistan *38.05N 64.46E*
202 A16 **Halagigie Point** *headland* W Niue
77 Z11 **Halaib** SE Egypt *22.10N 36.33E*
202 G12 **Halalo** Île Uvea, N Wallis and Futuna *13.21S 176.10W*
Halandri *see* Chalándri
147 X13 **Ḥalāniyāt, Juzur al** *var.* Jazā'ir Bin Ghalfān, *Eng.* Kuria Muria Islands. *island group* S Oman
147 W13 **Ḥalāniyāt, Khalīj al** *Eng.* Kuria Muria Bay. *bay* S Oman
Halas *see* Kiskunhalas
40 G11 **Hālawa** *var.* Halawa. Hawai'i, USA, C Pacific Ocean *20.13N 155.46W*
40 F9 **Hālawa, Cape** *var.* Cape Halawa *headland* Moloka'i, Hawai'i, USA, C Pacific Ocean *21.09N 156.43W*
168 H6 **Halban** Hövsgöl, N Mongolia *49.30N 97.33E*
103 K14 **Halberstadt** Sachsen-Anhalt, C Germany *51.54N 11.04E*
192 M12 **Halcombe** Manawatu-Wanganui, North Island, NZ *40.09S 175.30E*
97 I16 **Halden** *prev.* Fredrikshald. Østfold, S Norway *59.07N 11.19E*
102 L13 **Haldensleben** Sachsen-Anhalt, C Germany *52.18N 11.25E*
Háldi *see* Halti
159 S17 **Haldia** West Bengal, NE India *22.07N 88.06E*
158 K10 **Haldwāni** Uttaranchal, N India *29.13N 79.31E*
40 F10 **Haleakalā** *var.* Haleakala. *crater* Maui, Hawai'i, USA, C Pacific Ocean *20.45N 156.12W*
27 N4 **Hale Center** Texas, SW USA *34.03N 101.50W*
101 J18 **Halen** Limburg, NE Belgium *50.35N 5.08E*
25 O2 **Haleyville** Alabama, S USA *34.13N 87.37W*
79 O17 **Half Assini** SW Ghana *5.03N 2.57W*
37 R8 **Half Dome** ▲ California, W USA *37.46N 119.27W*
193 C25 **Halfmoon Bay** *var.* Oban. Stewart Island, Southland, NZ *46.52S 168.08E*
190 E5 **Half Moon Lake** *salt lake* South Australia
169 R7 **Halhgol** Dornod, E Mongolia *47.57N 118.07E*
Haliacmon *see* Aliákmonas
Halibān *see* Ḥalabān
12 I13 **Haliburton** Ontario, SE Canada *45.03N 78.32W*
12 I12 **Haliburton Highlands** *var.* Madawaska Highlands. *hill range* Ontario, SE Canada
11 Q15 **Halifax** Nova Scotia, SE Canada *44.37N 63.34W*
99 L17 **Halifax** N England, UK *53.43N 1.52W*
23 W8 **Halifax** North Carolina, SE USA *36.18N 77.35W*
23 U7 **Halifax** Virginia, NE USA *36.46N 78.55W*
11 Q15 **Halifax** ✈ Nova Scotia, SE Canada *44.33N 63.48W*
149 T13 **Halīl Rūd** *seasonal river* SE Iran
144 I6 **Ḥalīmah** ▲ Lebanon/Syria *34.12N 36.37E*
168 G8 **Haliun** Govĭ-Altay, W Mongolia *45.55N 96.06E*
120 I3 **Haljala** *Ger.* Halljal. Lääne-Virumaa, N Estonia *59.25N 26.18E*
41 Q4 **Halkett, Cape** *headland* Alaska, USA *70.48N 152.11W*
Halkida *see* Chalkída
98 J6 **Halkirk** N Scotland, UK *58.30N 3.29W*
13 X7 **Hall** ~ Québec, SE Canada
Hall *see* Schwäbisch Hall
95 H15 **Hälla** Västerbotten, N Sweden *63.55N 17.19E*
98 J6 **Halladale** ~ N Scotland, UK
97 J21 **Halland** ◈ *county* S Sweden
25 Z15 **Hallandale** Florida, SE USA *25.58N 80.09W*
97 K22 **Hallandsås** *physical region* S Sweden
15 M2 **Hall Beach** Nunavut, N Canada *68.10N 81.55W*
101 G19 **Halle** *Fr.* Hal. Vlaams Brabant, C Belgium *50.43N 4.13E*
103 M15 **Halle** *var.* Halle an der Saale. Sachsen-Anhalt, C Germany *51.28N 11.58E*
Halle an der Saale *see* Halle
37 W3 **Halleck** Nevada, W USA *40.57N 115.27W*
97 L15 **Hällefors** Örebro, C Sweden *59.48N 14.27E*
97 N16 **Hälleforsnäs** Södermanland, C Sweden *59.10N 16.30E*
111 Q6 **Hallein** Salzburg, N Austria *47.40N 13.06E*
103 L15 **Halle-Neustadt** Sachsen-Anhalt, C Germany *51.28N 11.54E*
27 U12 **Hallettsville** Texas, SW USA *29.27N 96.57W*
205 N4 **Halley** *UK research station* Antarctica *75.42S 26.30W*
30 L4 **Halliday** North Dakota, N USA *47.19N 102.19W*
39 S2 **Halligan Reservoir** ▣ Colorado, C USA
102 G7 **Halligen** *island group* N Germany
96 G13 **Hallingdal** *valley* S Norway
40 J12 **Hall Island** *island* Alaska, USA
Hall Island *see* Maiana
201 P15 **Hall Islands** *island group* C Micronesia
120 H6 **Halliste** ~ S Estonia
Halljal *see* Haljala
95 I15 **Hällnäs** Västerbotten, N Sweden *64.19N 19.41E*
31 R2 **Hallock** Minnesota, N USA *48.47N 96.56W*
16 Oo3 **Hall Peninsula** *peninsula* Baffin Island, Nunavut, NE Canada
22 F9 **Halls** Tennessee, S USA *35.52N 89.24W*
97 M16 **Hallsberg** Örebro, C Sweden *59.04N 15.07E*
189 N5 **Halls Creek** Western Australia *18.17S 127.39E*
190 L12 **Halls Gap** Victoria, SE Australia *37.09S 142.30E*
97 N15 **Hallstahammar** Västmanland, C Sweden *59.25N 16.16E*
111 R6 **Hallstatt** Salzburg, W Austria *47.32N 13.39E*
111 R6 **Hallstatter See** ◎ C Austria
97 P14 **Hallstavik** Stockholm, C Sweden *60.12N 18.45E*
27 X7 **Hallsville** Texas, SW USA *32.31N 94.30W*
105 P1 **Halluin** Nord, N France *50.46N 3.07E*
Halmahera, Laut *see* Halmahera Sea
175 T7 **Halmahera, Pulau** *prev.* Djailolo, Gilolo, Jailolo. *island* E Indonesia
175 Tt8 **Halmahera Sea** *Ind.* Laut Halmahera. *sea* E Indonesia
97 J21 **Halmstad** Halland, S Sweden *56.41N 12.48E*
175 T11 **Halong** Pulau Ambon, E Indonesia *3.39S 128.13E*
121 N15 **Halowchyn** *Rus.* Golovchin. Mahilyowskaya Voblasts', E Belarus *54.03N 29.52E*
97 H20 **Hals** Nordjylland, N Denmark *57.00N 10.19E*
96 F8 **Halsa** Møre og Romsdal, S Norway *63.04N 8.13E*
121 I15 **Hal'shany** *Rus.* Gol'shany. Hrodzyenskaya Voblasts', W Belarus *54.15N 26.01E*
Hälsingborg *see* Helsingborg
31 R5 **Halstad** Minnesota, N USA *47.21N 96.49W*
29 N6 **Halstead** Kansas, C USA *38.00N 97.30W*
101 G15 **Halsteren** Noord-Brabant, S Netherlands *51.31N 4.16E*
95 L16 **Halsua** Länsi-Suomi, W Finland *63.28N 24.10E*
103 E14 **Haltern** Nordrhein-Westfalen, W Germany *51.45N 7.10E*
94 J9 **Halti** *var.* Haltiatunturi, *Lapp.* Háldi. ▲ Finland/Norway *69.18N 21.19E*
Haltiatunturi *see* Halti
118 J6 **Halych** Ivano-Frankivs'ka Oblast', W Ukraine *49.08N 24.44E*
Halycus *see* Platani
105 P3 **Ham** Somme, N France *49.46N 3.03E*
Hama *see* Ḥamāh
170 Ee12 **Hamada** Shimane, Honshū, SW Japan *34.54N 132.07E*
148 L6 **Hamadān** *anc.* Ecbatana. Hamadān, W Iran *34.50N 48.31E*
148 L6 **Hamadān** *off.* Ostān-e Hamadān. ◈ *province* W Iran
144 I5 **Ḥamāh** *var.* Hama; *anc.* Epiphania, *Bibl.* Hamath. Ḥamāh, W Syria *35.09N 36.43E*
144 I5 **Ḥamāh** *off.* Muḥāfaẓat Ḥamāh, *var.* Hama. ◈ *governorate* C Syria
171 I17 **Hamakita** Shizuoka, Honshū, S Japan *34.46N 137.46E*
172 O4 **Hamamasu** Hokkaidō, NE Japan *43.37N 141.24E*
171 I17 **Hamamatsu** *var.* Hamamatu. Shizuoka, Honshū, S Japan *34.43N 137.45E*
Hamamatu *see* Hamamatsu
172 Qq7 **Hamanaka** Hokkaidō, NE Japan *43.05N 145.05E*
171 I17 **Hamana-ko** ◎ Honshū, S Japan
96 I13 **Hamar** *prev.* Storhammer. Hedmark, S Norway *60.48N 11.04E*
147 U10 **Ḥamārīr al Kidan, Qalamat** *well* E Saudi Arabia *21.40N 53.13E*
170 G12 **Hamasaka** Hyōgo, Honshū, SW Japan *35.37N 134.27E*
Hamath *see* Ḥamāh
172 Pp2 **Hamatonbetsu** Hokkaidō, NE Japan *45.07N 142.21E*
161 K26 **Hambantota** Southern Province, SE Sri Lanka *6.11N 81.10E*
194 G10 **Hambili** ~ NW PNG
Hambourg *see* Hamburg
102 J9 **Hamburg** Hamburg, N Germany *53.33N 10.02E*
29 V14 **Hamburg** Arkansas, C USA *33.13N 91.48W*
31 S16 **Hamburg** Iowa, C USA *40.36N 95.39W*
20 D10 **Hamburg** New York, NE USA *42.40N 78.49W*
102 I10 **Hamburg** *Fr.* Hambourg. ◈ *state* N Germany
154 K5 **Hamdam Āb, Dasht-e** *Pash.* Dasht-i Hamdamab. ▲▲ W Afghanistan
Hamdamab, Dasht-i *see* Hamdam Āb, Dasht-e
20 M13 **Hamden** Connecticut, NE USA *41.22N 72.55W*
146 K6 **Ḥamḍ, Wādī al** *dry watercourse* W Saudi Arabia
95 K18 **Hämeenkyrö** Länsi-Suomi, W Finland *61.39N 23.10E*
95 L19 **Hämeenlinna** *Swe.* Tavastehus. Etelä-Suomi, S Finland *61.00N 24.25E*
HaMelah, Yam *see* Dead Sea
Hamelin *see* Hameln
102 I13 **Hameln** *Eng.* Hamelin. Niedersachsen, N Germany *52.05N 9.21E*
188 I8 **Hamersley Range** ▲▲ Western Australia
169 Y12 **Hamgyŏng-sanmaek** ▲▲ N North Korea
169 X13 **Hamhŭng** C North Korea *39.53N 127.31E*
165 O6 **Hami** *var.* Ha-mi, *Uigh.* Kumul, Qomul. Xinjiang Uygur Zizhiqu, NW China *42.48N 93.27E*
145 X10 **Ḥāmid Amīn** E Iraq *32.06N 46.53E*
147 W11 **Hamīdān, Khawr** *oasis* SE Saudi Arabia *20.25N 54.43E*
144 H5 **Ḥamīdīyah** *var.* Ḥamīdīyé. Tartūs, W Syria *34.43N 35.58E*
116 L12 **Hamidiye** Edirne, NW Turkey *41.09N 26.40E*
Hamīdīyé *see* Ḥamīdīyah
190 L12 **Hamilton** Victoria, SE Australia *37.45S 142.04E*
66 B12 **Hamilton** ○ (Bermuda) C Bermuda *32.18N 64.48W*
12 G16 **Hamilton** Ontario, S Canada *43.15N 79.49W*
192 M7 **Hamilton** Waikato, North Island, NZ *37.48S 175.15E*
98 I12 **Hamilton** S Scotland, UK *55.46N 4.03W*
25 N3 **Hamilton** Alabama, S USA *34.08N 87.59W*
40 M10 **Hamilton** Alaska, USA *62.54N 163.53W*
32 J13 **Hamilton** Illinois, N USA *40.24N 91.20W*
29 S3 **Hamilton** Missouri, C USA *39.44N 94.00W*
35 P10 **Hamilton** Montana, NW USA *46.15N 114.09W*
27 S8 **Hamilton** Texas, SW USA *31.42N 98.07W*
12 G16 **Hamilton** ✈ Ontario, SE Canada *43.12N 79.54W*
66 I6 **Hamilton Bank** *undersea feature* SE Labrador Sea
190 E1 **Hamilton Creek** *seasonal river* South Australia
11 R8 **Hamilton Inlet** *inlet* Newfoundland and Labrador, E Canada
29 T12 **Hamilton, Lake** ▣ Arkansas, C USA
37 W6 **Hamilton, Mount** ▲ Nevada, W USA *39.15N 115.30W*
77 S8 **Ḥamīm, Wādī al** ~ NE Libya
95 N19 **Hamina** *Swe.* Fredrikshamn. Etelä-Suomi, S Finland *60.33N 27.15E*
9 W16 **Hamiota** Manitoba, S Canada *50.13N 100.37W*
158 L13 **Hamīrpur** Uttar Pradesh, N India *25.57N 80.07E*
Hamīs Musait *see* Khamīs Mushayṭ
23 T11 **Hamlet** North Carolina, SE USA *34.52N 79.41W*
27 P6 **Hamlin** Texas, SW USA *32.52N 100.07W*
23 P5 **Hamlin** West Virginia, NE USA *38.16N 82.06W*
33 O7 **Hamlin Lake** ◎ Michigan, N USA
103 F14 **Hamm** *var.* Hamm in Westfalen. Nordrhein-Westfalen, W Germany *51.39N 7.49E*
Ḥammāmāt, Khalīj al *see* Hammamet, Golfe de
77 N5 **Hammamet, Golfe de** *Ar.* Khalīj al Ḥammāmāt. *gulf* NE Tunisia
145 R3 **Ḥammān al 'Alīl** N Iraq *36.07N 43.15E*
145 X12 **Ḥammār, Hawr al** ◎ SE Iraq
95 J20 **Hammarland** Åland, SW Finland *60.13N 19.45E*
95 H16 **Hammarstrand** Jämtland, C Sweden *63.07N 16.27E*
95 O17 **Hammaslahti** Itä-Suomi, E Finland *62.26N 29.58E*
101 F17 **Hamme** Oost-Vlaanderen, NW Belgium *51.06N 4.07E*
102 H10 **Hamme** ~ NW Germany
97 G22 **Hammel** Århus, C Denmark *56.15N 9.52E*
103 I18 **Hammelburg** Bayern, C Germany *50.06N 9.50E*
101 H18 **Hamme-Mille** Walloon Brabant, C Belgium *50.48N 4.42E*
102 H10 **Hamme-Oste-Kanal** *canal* NW Germany
95 G16 **Hammerdal** Jämtland, C Sweden *63.34N 15.19E*
94 K8 **Hammerfest** Finnmark, N Norway *70.40N 23.40E*
103 D14 **Hamminkeln** Nordrhein-Westfalen, W Germany *51.43N 6.36E*
Hamm in Westfalen *see* Hamm
28 K10 **Hammon** Oklahoma, C USA *35.37N 99.22W*
33 N11 **Hammond** Indiana, N USA *41.35N 87.30W*
24 K8 **Hammond** Louisiana, S USA *30.30N 90.27W*
101 K20 **Hamoir** Liège, E Belgium *50.28N 5.35E*
101 J21 **Hamois** Namur, SE Belgium *50.21N 5.09E*
101 K16 **Hamont** Limburg, NE Belgium *51.15N 5.33E*
193 F22 **Hampden** Otago, South Island, NZ *45.18S 170.49E*
21 R6 **Hampden** Maine, NE USA *44.44N 68.51W*
99 M23 **Hampshire** *cultural region* S England, UK
11 O15 **Hampton** New Brunswick, SE Canada *45.30N 65.49W*
29 U14 **Hampton** Arkansas, C USA *33.33N 92.28W*
31 V12 **Hampton** Iowa, C USA *42.44N 93.12W*
21 P10 **Hampton** New Hampshire, NE USA *42.55N 70.48W*
23 R14 **Hampton** South Carolina, SE USA *32.52N 81.06W*
23 P8 **Hampton** Tennessee, S USA *36.16N 82.10W*
23 X7 **Hampton** Virginia, NE USA *37.01N 76.21W*
96 L11 **Hamra** Gävleborg, C Sweden *61.40N 15.00E*
82 D10 **Hamrat esh Sheikh** Northern Kordofan, C Sudan *14.37N 27.55E*
145 S5 **Ḥamrīn, Jabal** ▲▲ N Iraq
123 Jj16 **Ḥamrun** C Malta *35.53N 14.28E*
178 K14 **Ham Thuận Nam** Bình Thuận, S Vietnam *10.49N 107.49E*
176 Ww11 **Hamuku** Papua, E Indonesia *3.18S 135.00E*
Hāmūn, Daryācheh-ye *see* Ṣāberī, Hāmūn-e/Sīstān, Daryācheh-ye
Hamwih *see* Southampton
40 G10 **Hāna** *var.* Hana. Maui, Hawai'i, USA, C Pacific Ocean *20.45N 155.59W*
23 S14 **Hanahan** South Carolina, SE USA *32.55N 80.01W*
40 B8 **Hanalei** Kaua'i, Hawai'i, USA, C Pacific Ocean *22.12N 159.30W*
178 Kk10 **Ha Nam** Quang Nam-Đa Nẵng, C Vietnam *15.42N 108.24E*
171 Mm11 **Hanamaki** Iwate, Honshū, C Japan *39.25N 141.04E*
40 F10 **Hanamanioa, Cape** *headland* Maui, Hawai'i, USA, C Pacific Ocean *20.34N 156.22W*
202 B16 **Hanan** ✈ (Alofi) SW Niue
103 H18 **Hanau** Hessen, W Germany *50.06N 8.56E*
15 J7 **Hanbury** ~ Northwest Territories, NW Canada
Hâncești *see* Hîncești
8 M15 **Hanceville** British Columbia, SW Canada *51.54N 122.56W*
25 P3 **Hanceville** Alabama, S USA *34.03N 86.46W*
Hancewicze *see* Hantsavichy
166 L6 **Hancheng** Shaanxi, C China *35.22N 110.27E*
23 V2 **Hancock** Maryland, NE USA *39.42N 78.10W*
32 M3 **Hancock** Michigan, N USA *47.07N 88.34W*
31 S8 **Hancock** Minnesota, N USA *45.30N 95.47W*
20 I12 **Hancock** New York, NE USA *41.57N 75.15W*
82 Q12 **Handa** Bari, NE Somalia *10.35N 51.09E*
167 O5 **Handan** *var.* Han-tan. Hebei, E China *36.34N 114.28E*
97 P16 **Handen** Stockholm, C Sweden *59.12N 18.09E*
83 J22 **Handeni** Tanga, E Tanzania *5.25S 38.04E*
39 Q7 **Handies Peak** ▲ Colorado, C USA *37.54N 107.30W*
113 J19 **Handlová** *Ger.* Krickerhäu, *Hung.* Nyitrabánya; *prev. Ger.* Kriegerhaj. Trenčiansky Kraj, W Slovakia *48.45N 18.45E*
171 K17 **Haneda** ✈ (Tōkyō) Tōkyō, Honshū, S Japan *35.33N 139.45E*
144 F13 **HaNegev** *Eng.* Negev. *desert* S Israel
37 Q11 **Hanford** California, W USA *36.19N 119.39W*
203 V16 **Hanga Roa** Easter Island, Chile, E Pacific Ocean *27.09S 109.25W*
168 H7 **Hangayn Nuruu** ▲▲ C Mongolia
Hang-chou/Hangchow *see* Hangzhou
97 K20 **Hånger** Jönköping, S Sweden *57.06N 13.58E*
Hangö *see* Hanko
167 R9 **Hangzhou** *var.* Hang-chou, Hangchow. Zhejiang, SE China *30.18N 120.07E*
168 F5 **Hanhöhiy Uul** ▲▲ NW Mongolia
152 I14 **Hanhowuz** *Rus.* Khauz-Khan. Ahal Welaýaty, S Turkmenistan *37.15N 61.12E*
152 I14 **Hanhowuz Suw Howdany** *Rus.* Khauzkhanskoye Vodokhranilishche. ▣ S Turkmenistan
143 P15 **Hani** Diyarbakır, SE Turkey *38.25N 40.22E*
Hania *see* Chaniá
147 R11 **Ḥanīsh al Kabīr, Jazīrat al** *island* SW Yemen
Hanka, Lake *see* Khanka, Lake
95 M17 **Hankasalmi** Länsi-Suomi, W Finland *62.25N 26.27E*
31 R7 **Hankinson** North Dakota, N USA *46.04N 96.54W*
95 K20 **Hanko** *Swe.* Hangö. Etelä-Suomi, SW Finland *59.50N 23.00E*
Han-kou/Han-k'ou/Hankow *see* Wuhan
38 M6 **Hanksville** Utah, W USA *38.21N 110.43W*
158 K6 **Hanle** Jammu and Kashmir, NW India *32.46N 79.01E*
193 I17 **Hanmer Springs** Canterbury, South Island, NZ *42.30S 172.48E*
9 R16 **Hanna** Alberta, SW Canada *51.37N 111.55W*
29 V3 **Hannibal** Missouri, C USA *39.42N 91.23W*
188 M3 **Hann, Mount** ▲ Western Australia *15.53S 125.46E*
102 I12 **Hannover** *Eng.* Hanover. Niedersachsen, NW Germany *52.23N 9.43E*
101 J19 **Hannut** Liège, C Belgium *50.40N 5.04E*
97 L22 **Hanöbukten** *bay* S Sweden
178 Jj6 **Ha Nôi** *Eng.* Hanoi, *Fr.* Ha noï. ● (Vietnam) N Vietnam *21.01N 105.52E*
12 F14 **Hanover** Ontario, S Canada *44.22N 81.01W*
33 P15 **Hanover** Indiana, N USA *38.42N 85.28W*
20 G16 **Hanover** Pennsylvania, NE USA *39.46N 76.57W*
23 W6 **Hanover** Virginia, NE USA *37.44N 77.21W*
Hanover *see* Hannover
65 G23 **Hanover, Isla** *island* S Chile
Hanselbeck *see* Érd
205 X5 **Hansen Mountains** ▲▲ Antarctica
166 M8 **Han Shui** ~ C China
158 H10 **Hānsi** Haryāna, NW India *29.07N 75.58E*
97 F20 **Hanstholm** Viborg, NW Denmark *57.05N 8.39E*
Han-tan *see* Handan
164 H6 **Hantengri Feng** *var.* Pik Khan-Tengri. ▲ China/Kazakhstan *see also* Khan-Tengri, Pik *42.17N 80.11E*
121 I18 **Hantsavichy** *Pol.* Hancewicze, *Rus.* Gantsevichi. Brestskaya Voblasts', SW Belarus *52.45N 26.27E*
16 N2 **Hantzsch** ~ Baffin Island, Nunavut, NE Canada
158 G9 **Hanumāngarh** Rājasthān, NW India *29.33N 74.21E*
191 O9 **Hanwood** New South Wales, SE Australia *34.19S 146.03E*
Hanyang *see* Caidian
Hanyang *see* Wuhan
166 H10 **Hanyuan** *var.* Fulin. Sichuan, C China *29.22N 102.39E*
Hanyuan *see* Xihe
166 J7 **Hanzhong** Shaanxi, C China *33.12N 106.59E*
203 W11 **Hao** *atoll* Îles Tuamotu, C French Polynesia
159 S16 **Hāora** *prev.* Howrah. West Bengal, NE India *22.34N 88.19E*
80 K8 **Haouach, Ouadi** *dry watercourse* E Chad
94 K13 **Haparanda** Norrbotten, N Sweden *65.49N 24.04E*
27 N3 **Happy** Texas, SW USA *34.44N 101.51W*
36 M1 **Happy Camp** California, W USA *41.48N 123.24W*
11 Q9 **Happy Valley-Goose Bay** *prev.* Goose Bay. Newfoundland and Labrador, E Canada *53.19N 60.24W*
Hapsal *see* Haapsalu
158 J10 **Hāpur** Uttar Pradesh, N India *28.43N 77.46E*
144 F12 **HaQatan, HaMakhtesh** ▲▲ S Israel
146 I4 **Ḥaql** Tabūk, NW Saudi Arabia *29.18N 34.58E*
176 Vv13 **Har** Pulau Kai Besar, E Indonesia *5.21S 133.09E*
168 M8 **Haraat** Dundgovĭ, C Mongolia *46.30N 107.39E*
147 R8 **Ḥaraḍ** *var.* Haradh. Ash Sharqīyah, E Saudi Arabia *24.08N 49.01E*
Haradh *see* Ḥaraḍ
120 N12 **Haradok** *Rus.* Gorodok. Vitsyebskaya Voblasts', N Belarus *55.27N 30.00E*
94 J13 **Harads** Norrbotten, N Sweden *66.04N 21.04E*
121 G19 **Haradzyets** *Rus.* Gorodets. Brestskaya Voblasts', SW Belarus *52.11N 24.41E*
121 J17 **Haradzyeya** *Rus.* Gorodeya. Minskaya Voblasts', C Belarus *53.18N 26.33E*
203 V10 **Haraiki** *atoll* Îles Tuamotu, C French Polynesia
171 Ll14 **Haramachi** Fukushima, Honshū, E Japan *37.39N 140.55E*
120 M12 **Harany** *Rus.* Gorany. Vitsyebskaya Voblasts', N Belarus *55.25N 29.03E*
85 L16 **Harare** *prev.* Salisbury. ● (Zimbabwe) Mashonaland East, NE Zimbabwe *17.47S 31.03E*
85 L16 **Harare** ✈ Mashonaland East, NE Zimbabwe *17.51S 31.06E*
80 J10 **Haraz-Djombo** Batha, C Chad *14.10N 19.35E*
121 O16 **Harbavichy** *Rus.* Gorbovichi. Mahilyowskaya Voblasts', E Belarus *53.51N 30.42E*
78 J16 **Harbel** W Liberia *6.19N 10.19W*
169 W8 **Harbin** *var.* Haerbin, Ha-erh-pin, Kharbin; *prev.* Haerhpin, Pingkiang, Pinkiang. Heilongjiang, NE China *45.45N 126.40E*
33 S7 **Harbor Beach** Michigan, N USA *43.50N 82.39W*
11 T13 **Harbour Breton** Newfoundland and Labrador, E Canada *47.28N 55.49W*
67 D25 **Harbours, Bay of** *bay* East Falkland, Falkland Islands
Hårby *see* Haarby
38 I13 **Harcuvar Mountains** ▲▲ Arizona, SW USA
110 I7 **Hard** Vorarlberg, NW Austria *47.28N 9.42E*
160 H11 **Harda Khās** Madhya Pradesh, C India *22.22N 77.06E*
97 D14 **Hardanger** *physical region* S Norway
97 D14 **Hardangerfjorden** *fjord* S Norway
96 E13 **Hardangerjøkulen** *glacier* S Norway
97 E14 **Hardangervidda** *plateau* S Norway
85 D20 **Hardap** ◈ *district* S Namibia
23 R15 **Hardeeville** South Carolina, SE USA *32.18N 81.04W*
100 L5 **Hardegarijp** *Fris.* Hurdegaryp. Friesland, N Netherlands *53.13N 5.57E*
100 O9 **Hardenberg** Overijssel, E Netherlands *52.34N 6.37E*
191 Q9 **Harden-Murrumburrah** New South Wales, SE Australia *34.33S 148.22E*
100 K10 **Harderwijk** Gelderland, C Netherlands *52.21N 5.36E*
32 J14 **Hardin** Illinois, N USA *39.10N 90.37W*
35 V11 **Hardin** Montana, NW USA *45.43N 107.34W*
25 R5 **Harding, Lake** ▣ Alabama/Georgia, SE USA
22 J6 **Hardinsburg** Kentucky, S USA *37.46N 86.27W*
100 I13 **Hardinxveld-Giessendam** Zuid-Holland, C Netherlands *51.52N 4.49E*
9 R15 **Hardisty** Alberta, SW Canada *52.42N 111.22W*
158 L12 **Hardoi** Uttar Pradesh, N India *27.22N 80.06E*
25 U4 **Hardwick** Georgia, SE USA *33.03N 83.13W*
29 W9 **Hardy** Arkansas, C USA *36.19N 91.28W*
96 D10 **Hareid** Møre og Romsdal, S Norway *62.22N 6.01E*
15 Gg5 **Hare Indian** ~ Northwest Territories, NW Canada
101 D18 **Harelbeke** *var.* Harlebeke. West-Vlaanderen, W Belgium *50.51N 3.19E*
Harem *see* Ḥārim
102 E11 **Haren** Niedersachsen, NW Germany *52.47N 7.16E*
100 N6 **Haren** Groningen, NE Netherlands *53.09N 6.36E*
82 L13 **Hārer** Hārer, E Ethiopia *9.17N 42.18E*
97 P14 **Harg** Uppsala, C Sweden *60.13N 18.25E*
Hargeisa *see* Hargeysa
82 M13 **Hargeysa** *var.* Hargeisa. Woqooyi Galbeed, NW Somalia *9.31N 44.06E*
118 J10 **Harghita** ◈ *county* NE Romania
27 S17 **Hargill** Texas, SW USA *26.26N 98.00W*
168 J8 **Harhorin** Övörhangay, C Mongolia *47.13N 102.48E*
165 Q9 **Har Hu** ◎ C China
Hariana *see* Haryāna
147 P15 **Ḥarīb** W Yemen *15.08N 45.35E*
174 I9 **Hari, Batang** *prev.* Djambi. ~ Sumatera, W Indonesia
158 J9 **Haridwār** *prev.* Hardwar. Uttaranchal, N India *29.58N 78.09E*
161 F18 **Harihar** Karnātaka, W India *14.33N 75.43E*
193 F18 **Harihari** West Coast, South Island, NZ *43.09S 170.35E*
144 I3 **Ḥārim** *var.* Harem. Idlib, W Syria *36.30N 36.30E*
170 G14 **Harima-nada** *sea* S Japan
100 G13 **Haringvliet** *channel* SW Netherlands
100 F13 **Haringvlietdam** *dam* SW Netherlands *51.49N 4.04E*
155 U5 **Haripur** North-West Frontier Province, NW Pakistan *34.00N 73.01E*
154 J4 **Harīrūd** *var.* Tedzhen, *Turkm.* Tejen. ~ Afghanistan/Iran *see also* Tejen
Hārjahågnen *see* Østrehogna
95 K18 **Harjavalta** Länsi-Suomi, W Finland *61.17N 22.04E*
Hārjehågna *see* Østrehogna
120 G4 **Harjumaa** *off.* Harju Maakond. ◈ *province* NW Estonia
23 X11 **Harkers Island** North Carolina, SE USA *34.42N 76.33W*
145 S1 **Harki** N Iraq *37.03N 43.39E*
31 T14 **Harlan** Iowa, C USA *41.40N 95.19W*
23 O7 **Harlan** Kentucky, S USA *36.50N 83.19W*
31 N17 **Harlan County Lake** ▣ Nebraska, C USA
118 L9 **Hârlău** *var.* Hîrlău. Iași, NE Romania *47.24N 26.56E*
Harlebeke *see* Harelbeke
35 U7 **Harlem** Montana, NW USA *48.31N 108.46W*
Harlem *see* Haarlem
97 G22 **Harlev** Århus, C Denmark *56.08N 10.00E*
100 K6 **Harlingen** *Fris.* Harns. Friesland, N Netherlands *53.10N 5.25E*
27 T17 **Harlingen** Texas, SW USA *26.12N 97.43W*
99 O21 **Harlow** E England, UK *51.46N 0.07E*
35 T10 **Harlowton** Montana, NW USA *46.26N 109.49W*
96 N11 **Harmånger** Gävleborg, C Sweden *61.55N 17.19E*
100 I11 **Harmelen** Utrecht, C Netherlands *52.06N 4.58E*
31 X11 **Harmony** Minnesota, N USA *43.33N 92.00W*
34 J14 **Harney Basin** *basin* Oregon, NW USA
(0) F9 **Harney Basin** ▲▲ Oregon, NW USA
34 J14 **Harney Lake** ◎ Oregon, NW USA
30 J10 **Harney Peak** ▲ South Dakota, N USA *43.52N 103.31W*
95 H17 **Härnösand** *var.* Hernösand. Västernorrland, C Sweden *62.37N 17.55E*
Harns *see* Harlingen
168 F6 **Har Nuur** ◎ NW Mongolia
107 P4 **Haro** La Rioja, N Spain *42.34N 2.52W*
42 F6 **Haro, Cabo** *headland* NW Mexico *27.50N 110.55W*
96 D9 **Harøy** *island* S Norway
99 N21 **Harpenden** E England, UK *51.49N 0.22W*
78 L18 **Harper** *var.* Cape Palmas. NE Liberia *4.25N 7.43W*
28 M7 **Harper** Kansas, C USA *37.17N 98.01W*
34 L13 **Harper** Oregon, NW USA *43.51N 117.37W*
27 Q10 **Harper** Texas, SW USA *30.18N 99.18W*
37 U13 **Harper Lake** *salt flat* California, W USA
41 T9 **Harper, Mount** ▲ Alaska, USA *64.18N 143.54W*

◆ Country ● Country Capital ◇ Dependent Territory ○ Dependent Territory Capital ◈ Administrative Region ✈ International Airport ▲ Mountain ▲▲ Mountain Range Volcano ~ River ◎ Lake ▣ Reservoir

97 J21 **Harplinge** Halland, S Sweden 56.45N 12.45E

38 J13 **Harquahala Mountains** ▲ Arizona, SW USA

147 T15 **Ḥarrah** SE Yemen 15.02N 50.22E

10 H11 **Harricana** ✦ Québec, SE Canada

22 M9 **Harriman** Tennessee, S USA 35.57N 84.33W

11 R11 **Harrington Harbour** Québec, E Canada 50.34N 59.29W

66 B12 **Harrington Sound** bay Bermuda, NW Atlantic Ocean

98 F8 **Harris** physical region NW Scotland, UK

29 X10 **Harrison** Arkansas, C USA 35.33N 90.43W

32 M17 **Harrisburg** Illinois, N USA 37.44N 88.32W

30 I14 **Harrisburg** Nebraska, C USA 41.31N 103.43W

34 F12 **Harrisburg** Oregon, NW USA 44.16N 123.10W

20 G15 **Harrisburg** state capital Pennsylvania, NE USA 40.16N 76.52W

190 F6 **Harris, Lake** ◎ South Australia

25 W11 **Harris, Lake** ◎ Florida, SE USA

85 J22 **Harrismith** Free State, E South Africa 28.16S 29.06E

29 T9 **Harrison** Arkansas, C USA 36.13N 93.06W

33 Q7 **Harrison** Michigan, N USA 44.01N 84.49W

30 I12 **Harrison** Nebraska, C USA 42.39N 103.53W

Q5 **Harrison Bay** inlet Alaska, USA

24 I6 **Harrisonburg** Louisiana, S USA 31.44N 91.51W

23 U4 **Harrisonburg** Virginia, NE USA 38.27N 78.52W

11 R7 **Harrison, Cape** headland Newfoundland and Labrador, E Canada 54.55N 57.48W

29 R5 **Harrisonville** Missouri, C USA 38.39N 94.21W

Harris Ridge see Lomonosov Ridge

199 K3 **Harris Seamount** undersea feature N Pacific Ocean 46.09N 161.25W

98 F8 **Harris, Sound of** strait NW Scotland, UK

33 N6 **Harrisville** Michigan, N USA 44.39N 83.19W

23 R3 **Harrisville** West Virginia, NE USA 39.12N 81.03W

22 M6 **Harrodsburg** Kentucky, S USA 37.45N 84.50W

99 M16 **Harrogate** N England, UK 54.00N 1.33W

27 Q4 **Harrold** Texas, SW USA 34.05N 99.02W

29 S5 **Harry S.Truman Reservoir** ◙ Missouri, C USA

102 G13 **Harsewinkel** Nordrhein-Westfalen, W Germany 51.58N 8.13E

118 M14 **Hârşova** prev. Hîrşova. Constanța, SE Romania 44.40N 27.58E

94 H10 **Harstad** Troms, N Norway 68.48N 16.31E

33 O8 **Hart** Michigan, N USA 43.43N 86.22W

26 M4 **Hart** Texas, SW USA 34.23N 102.07W

8 I5 **Hart** ✦ Yukon Territory, NW Canada

85 F23 **Hartbees** ✦ C South Africa

111 X7 **Hartberg** Steiermark, SE Austria 47.15N 15.55E

190 I10 **Hart, Cape** headland South Australia 35.54S 138.01E

97 E14 **Hårteigen** ▲ S Norway 60.11N 7.01E

25 U7 **Hartford** Alabama, S USA 31.06N 85.42W

29 R11 **Hartford** Arkansas, C USA 35.01N 94.22W

20 M12 **Hartford** state capital Connecticut, NE USA 41.45N 72.41W

22 J6 **Hartford** Kentucky, S USA 37.24N 86.52W

33 P10 **Hartford** Michigan, N USA 42.12N 85.54W

31 R11 **Hartford** South Dakota, N USA 43.37N 96.56W

32 M8 **Hartford** Wisconsin, N USA 43.19N 88.25W

33 P13 **Hartford City** Indiana, N USA 40.27N 85.22W

31 Q13 **Hartington** Nebraska, C USA 42.37N 97.15W

11 N14 **Hartland** New Brunswick, SE Canada 46.18N 67.31W

99 H23 **Hartland Point** headland SW England, UK 51.01N 4.33W

99 M15 **Hartlepool** N England, UK 54.40N 1.13W

31 T12 **Hartley** Iowa, C USA 43.10N 95.28W

26 M1 **Hartley** Texas, SW USA 35.52N 102.24W

34 J15 **Hart Mountain** ▲ Oregon, NW USA 42.24N 119.46W

181 U10 **Hartog Ridge** undersea feature W Indian Ocean

95 M18 **Hartola** Etelä-Suomi, S Finland 61.34N 26.02E

69 U14 **Harts** var. Hartz. ✦ N South Africa

25 P2 **Hartselle** Alabama, S USA 34.26N 86.56W

25 S3 **Hartsfield Atlanta** ✕ Georgia, SE USA 33.38N 84.24W

29 Q11 **Hartshorne** Oklahoma, C USA 34.51N 95.33W

23 S12 **Hartsville** South Carolina, SE USA 34.22N 80.04W

22 K8 **Hartsville** Tennessee, S USA 36.23N 86.10W

29 U7 **Hartville** Missouri, C USA 37.15N 92.30W

25 U2 **Hartwell** Georgia, SE USA 34.21N 82.55W

23 O11 **Hartwell Lake** ◙ Georgia/South Carolina, SE USA

Hartz see Harts

Harunabad see Eslāmābād

168 J2 **Har-Us** Hovd, W Mongolia 48.30N 91.25E

168 L6 **Har Us Nuur** ◎ NW Mongolia

32 M10 **Harvard** Illinois, N USA 42.25N 88.36W

---

31 P16 **Harvard** Nebraska, C USA 40.37N 98.06W

39 R5 **Harvard, Mount** ▲ Colorado, C USA 38.55N 106.19W

33 N11 **Harvey** Illinois, N USA 41.36N 87.39W

31 N4 **Harvey** North Dakota, N USA 47.43N 99.55W

99 Q2 **Harwich** E England, UK 51.55N 1.16E

158 H10 **Haryāna** var. Hariana. ✦ state N India

147 N19 **Ḥaryān, Ṭawī al** spring/well NE Oman 21.56N 58.33E

103 J14 **Harz** ▲ C Germany

171 M12 **Hasama** Miyagi, Honshū, C Japan 38.42N 141.03E

142 J15 **Hasan Dağı** ▲ C Turkey 38.09N 34.15E

145 T9 **Ḥasan Ibn Ḥassūn** C Iraq 32.24N 44.13E

155 R6 **Ḥasan Khēl** var. Ahmad Khel. Paktia, SE Afghanistan 33.46N 69.37E

102 F12 **Hase** ✦ NW Germany

102 F12 **Haselberg** see Krasnoznamensk

102 F12 **Haselünne** Niedersachsen, NW Germany 52.40N 7.28E

168 K9 **Hashaat** Dundgovĭ, C Mongolia 45.09N 104.51E

Hashemite Kingdom of Jordan see Jordan

145 V13 **Hāshimah** E Iraq 33.22N 45.56E

171 Gg16 **Hashimoto** var. Hasimoto. Wakayama, Honshū, SW Japan 34.18N 135.34E

147 W13 **Ḥāsik** S Oman 17.22N 55.18E

155 U10 **Hāsilpur** Punjab, E Pakistan 29.44N 72.33E

Hasimoto see Hashimoto

29 Q10 **Haskell** Oklahoma, C USA 35.49N 95.40W

27 Q4 **Haskell** Texas, SW USA 33.09N 99.44W

116 M11 **Hasköy** Edirne, NW Turkey 41.37N 26.51E

97 L24 **Hasle** Bornholm, E Denmark 55.12N 14.43E

99 N23 **Haslemere** SE England, UK 51.06N 0.45W

104 I16 **Hasparren** Pyrénées-Atlantiques, SW France 43.22N 1.18W

161 G19 **Hassan** Karnātaka, W India 13.01N 76.03E

38 J13 **Hassayampa River** ✦ Arizona, SW USA

103 J18 **Hassberge** hill range C Germany

96 N10 **Hässelby** Gävleborg, C Sweden 62.06N 16.45E

101 J18 **Hasselt** Limburg, NE Belgium 50.55N 5.19E

100 M9 **Hasselt** Overijssel, E Netherlands 52.36N 6.06E

Hassetché see Al Ḥasakah

103 J18 **Hassfurt** Bayern, C Germany 50.02N 10.32E

76 L9 **Hassi Bel Guebbour** E Algeria

76 L8 **Hassi Messaoud** E Algeria 31.41N 6.10E

97 K22 **Hässleholm** Skåne, S Sweden 56.09N 13.45E

Hasta Colonia/Hasta Pompeia see Asti

191 O13 **Hastings** Victoria, SE Australia 38.18S 145.12E

192 O11 **Hastings** Hawke's Bay, North Island, NZ 39.39S 176.51E

99 P23 **Hastings** SE England, UK 50.51N 0.36E

33 P9 **Hastings** Michigan, N USA 42.37N 85.16W

31 W9 **Hastings** Minnesota, N USA 44.44N 92.51W

31 P16 **Hastings** Nebraska, C USA 40.35N 98.23W

97 K22 **Hästveda** Skåne, S Sweden 56.16N 13.55E

94 J8 **Hasvik** Finnmark, N Norway 70.29N 22.08E

39 V6 **Haswell** Colorado, C USA 38.27N 103.09W

168 H10 **Hatansuudal** Bayanhongor, C Mongolia 44.34N 100.41E

169 P9 **Hatavch** Sühbaatar, E Mongolia 46.10N 112.57E

142 K17 **Hatay** ✦ province S Turkey

39 R15 **Hatch** New Mexico, SW USA 32.40N 107.10W

38 K7 **Hatch** Utah, W USA 37.39N 112.25W

22 F9 **Hatchie River** ✦ Tennessee, S USA

118 G12 **Hațeg** Ger. Wallenthal, Hung. Hátszeg; prev. Hatzeg, Hötzing. Hunedoara, SW Romania 45.35N 22.57E

172 Oo17 **Hateruma-jima** island Yaeyama-shotō, SW Japan

191 N8 **Hatfield** New South Wales, SE Australia 33.54S 143.43E

168 I5 **Hatgal** Hövsgöl, N Mongolia

159 V16 **Hathazari** Chittagong, SE Bangladesh 22.30N 91.46E

147 N13 **Hathūt, Ḥişā'** oasis NE Yemen

178 Ii14 **Ha Tiên** Kiên Giang, S Vietnam 10.24N 104.30E

178 J8 **Ha Tinh** Ha Tinh, N Vietnam 18.21N 105.55E

Hatiōzi see Hachiōji

143 R15 **Hatira, Haré** hill range S Israel

178 J6 **Hat Lot** Sơn La, N Vietnam 21.07N 104.10E

193 J14 **Hato Airport** ✕ (Willemstad) Curaçao, SW Netherlands Antilles 12.10N 68.56W

56 H9 **Hato Corozal** Casanare, C Colombia 6.07N 71.45W

45 P9 **Hato del Volcán** see Volcán

45 P9 **Hato Mayor** E Dominican Republic 18.44N 69.16W

29 N4 **Hatra** see Al Ḥaḍr

99 H21 **Haverfordwest** SW Wales, UK 51.49N 4.57W

149 P5 **Ḥattā** Dubayy, NE UAE 24.50N 56.06E

190 I3 **Hattah** Victoria, SE Australia 34.49S 142.18E

100 M9 **Hattem** Gelderland, E Netherlands 52.28N 6.04E

---

23 Z10 **Hatteras** Hatteras Island, North Carolina, SE USA 35.13N 75.39W

23 Rr10 **Hatteras, Cape** headland North Carolina, SE USA 35.29N 75.33W

23 Z9 **Hatteras Island** island North Carolina, SE USA

66 F10 **Hatteras Plain** undersea feature W Atlantic Ocean

95 G14 **Hattfjelldal** Troms, N Norway 65.37N 13.58E

24 M7 **Hattiesburg** Mississippi, S USA 31.19N 89.17W

31 U4 **Hatton** North Dakota, N USA 47.38N 97.27W

66 L6 **Hatton Bank** see Hatton Ridge

66 L6 **Hatton Ridge** var. Hatton Bank. undersea feature N Atlantic Ocean

203 W6 **Hatutu** island Îles Marquises, NE French Polynesia

113 K22 **Hatvan** Heves, NE Hungary 47.40N 19.38E

178 H17 **Hat Yai** var. Ban Hat Yai. Songkhla, SW Thailand 7.01N 100.27E

Hatzeg see Hațeg

Hatzfeld see Jimbolia

82 N13 **Haud** plateau Ethiopia/Somalia

97 D18 **Hauge** Rogaland, S Norway 58.19N 6.16E

97 C15 **Haugesund** Rogaland, S Norway 59.24N 5.16E

111 X2 **Haugsdorf** Niederösterreich, NE Austria 48.41N 16.04E

192 M9 **Hauhungaroa Range** ▲ North Island, NZ

97 L16 **Haukeligrend** Telemark, S Norway 59.45N 7.33E

95 M17 **Haukipudas** Oulu, C Finland 65.11N 25.21E

95 M17 **Haukivesi** ◎ SE Finland

95 M17 **Haukivuori** Isä-Suomi, E Finland 62.02N 27.11E

Hauptkanal see Havellånd Grosse

195 Z12 **Hauraha** San Cristobal, SE Solomon Islands 10.47S 162.00E

192 L5 **Hauraki Gulf** gulf North Island, NZ

193 B24 **Hauroko, Lake** ◎ South Island, NZ

178 Jj15 **Hâu, Sông** ✦ S Vietnam

94 N12 **Hautajärvi** Lappi, NE Finland 66.30N 29.01E

76 F7 **Haut Atlas** Eng. High Atlas. ▲ C Morocco

81 M17 **Haut-Congo** off. Région du Haut-Congo; prev. Haut-Zaïre. ✦ region NE Dem. Rep. Congo

105 Y14 **Haute-Corse** ✦ department Corse, France, C Mediterranean Sea

104 L16 **Haute-Garonne** ✦ department S France

78 J13 **Haute-Guinée** ✦ SE New Guinea

81 K14 **Haute-Kotto** ✦ prefecture E Central African Republic

105 P12 **Haute-Loire** ✦ department C France

105 R6 **Haute-Marne** ✦ department N France

104 M3 **Haute-Normandie** ✦ region N France

13 U6 **Hauterive** Québec, SE Canada 49.10N 68.16W

105 T13 **Hautes-Alpes** ✦ department SE France

105 S7 **Haute-Saône** ✦ department E France

105 T10 **Haute-Savoie** ✦ department E France

101 M20 **Hautes Fagnes** Ger. Hohes Venn. ▲ E Belgium

104 K16 **Hautes-Pyrénées** ✦ department S France

101 L23 **Haute Sûre, Lac de la** ◙ NW Luxembourg

104 M11 **Haute-Vienne** ✦ department C France

21 S8 **Haut, Isle au** island Maine, NE USA

81 M14 **Haut-Mbomou** ✦ prefecture SE Central African Republic

105 Q2 **Hautmont** Nord, N France 50.15N 3.55E

105 S4 **Hautrage** Moselle, NE France 49.19N 6.04E

HaŸarden see Jordan

Hayastani Hanrapetut'yun see Armenia

Hayasui-seto see Hōyo-kaikyō

41 N9 **Haycock** Alaska, USA 65.12N 161.10W

38 M14 **Hayden** Arizona, SW USA 33.00N 110.46W

39 Q3 **Hayden** Colorado, C USA 40.29N 107.15W

30 M10 **Hayes** South Dakota, N USA 44.20N 101.01W

9 X13 **Hayes** ✦ Manitoba, C Canada

15 Kk11 **Hayes** ✦ Nunavut, NE Canada

30 M16 **Hayes Center** Nebraska, C USA 40.28N 101.01W

41 S10 **Hayes, Mount** ▲ Alaska, USA 63.37N 146.43W

23 N11 **Hayesville** North Carolina, SE USA 35.15N 84.15W

37 X10 **Hayford Peak** ▲ Nevada, W USA 36.40N 115.10W

38 M3 **Hayfork** California, W USA 40.33N 123.10W

29 V10 **Heber Springs** Arkansas, C USA 35.30N 91.58W

176 U9 **Hebe** Papua, E Indonesia 1.08S 129.54E

38 M3 **Heber City** Utah, W USA 40.29N 111.24W

---

113 I17 **Havířov** Moravskoslezský Kraj, E Czech Republic 49.47N 18.30E

113 E17 **Havlíčkův Brod** Ger. Deutsch-Brod; prev. Německý Brod. Vysočina, C Czech Republic 49.41N 15.47E

94 K7 **Havøysund** Finnmark, N Norway 70.59N 24.39E

35 T7 **Havre** Montana, NW USA 48.33N 109.40W

Havre see le Havre

101 F20 **Havré** Hainaut, S Belgium 50.28N 4.03E

11 P11 **Havre-St-Pierre** Québec, SE Canada 50.16N 63.36W

142 B10 **Havran** Edirne, NW Turkey 41.33N 26.49E

40 D8 **Hawai'i** off. State of Hawai'i; also known as Aloha State, Paradise of the Pacific var. Hawaii. ✦ state USA, C Pacific Ocean

40 G12 **Hawai'i** var. Hawaii. island Hawaiian Islands, USA, C Pacific Ocean

199 K5 **Hawaiian Islands** prev. Sandwich Islands. island group USA, C Pacific Ocean

199 Jj6 **Hawaiian Ridge** undersea feature N Pacific Ocean

199 Kk6 **Hawaiian Trough** undersea feature N Pacific Ocean

31 X4 **Hawarden** Iowa, C USA 43.00N 96.29W

Hawash see Awash

145 P6 **Hawbayn al Gharbiyah** C Iraq 34.24N 42.06E

193 D21 **Hawea, Lake** ◎ South Island, NZ

192 K11 **Hawera** Taranaki, North Island, NZ 39.36S 174.16E

22 J5 **Hawesville** Kentucky, S USA 37.53N 86.44W

40 Q1 **Hāwī** var. Hawi. Hawai'i, USA, C Pacific Ocean 20.13N 155.49W

98 K13 **Hawick** SE Scotland, UK 55.24N 2.49W

145 S4 **Ḥawījah** C Iraq 35.15N 43.54E

145 Y10 **Ḥawīzah, Hawr al** ◎ S Iraq

193 E21 **Hawkdun Range** ▲ South Island, NZ

190 I6 **Hawker** South Australia 31.54S 138.25E

192 N11 **Hawke's Bay** off. Hawkes Bay ✦ region North Island, NZ

155 O16 **Hawkes Bay** bay SE Pakistan

13 N12 **Hawkesbury** Ontario, SE Canada 45.35N 74.37W

25 T5 **Hawkinsville** Georgia, SE USA 32.16N 83.28W

12 B9 **Hawk Junction** Ontario, S Canada 48.05N 84.34W

23 Q9 **Hawksbill Mountain** ▲ North Carolina, SE USA 35.54N 81.53W

35 Z16 **Hawk Springs** Wyoming, C USA 41.48N 104.17W

Hawkler see Arbil

31 S7 **Hawley** Minnesota, N USA 46.53N 96.18W

27 P7 **Hawley** Texas, SW USA 32.36N 99.49W

147 R14 **Ḥawrā'** C Yemen 15.39N 48.20E

145 P7 **Ḥawrān, Wādi** dry watercourse W Iraq

23 T9 **Haw River** ✦ North Carolina, SE USA

145 U5 **Ḥawshqūrah** E Iraq 34.34N 45.33E

37 S7 **Hawthorne** Nevada, W USA 38.30N 118.38W

39 W3 **Haxtun** Colorado, C USA 40.36N 102.38W

191 N9 **Hay** New South Wales, SE Australia 34.31S 144.50E

9 O10 **Hay** ✦ W Canada

176 U11 **Haya** Pulau Seram, E Indonesia 3.22S 129.31E

172 N11 **Hayachine-san** ▲ Honshū, C Japan 39.31N 141.28E

29 N4 **Hayate** Oklahoma, C USA 34.13N 97.29W

191 O12 **Healesville** Victoria, SE Australia 37.41S 145.31E

41 R10 **Healy** Alaska, USA 63.51N 148.58W

181 R13 **Heard and McDonald Islands** ◊ Australian external territory S Indian Ocean

181 R13 **Heard Island** island Heard and McDonald Islands, S Indian Ocean

27 U9 **Hearne** Texas, SW USA 30.52N 96.35W

12 F12 **Hearst** Ontario, S Canada 49.42N 83.40W

204 J5 **Heart River** ✦ North Dakota, N USA

33 T13 **Heath** Ohio, N USA 40.01N 82.26W

191 N11 **Heathcote** Victoria, SE Australia 36.57S 144.43E

99 N22 **Heathrow** ✕ (London)SE England, UK 51.28N 0.27W

23 X5 **Heathsville** Virginia, NE USA 37.54N 76.25W

29 R11 **Heavener** Oklahoma, C USA 34.53N 94.36W

25 R15 **Hebbronville** Texas, SW USA 27.18N 98.40W

41 S10 **Hayes, Mount** ▲ Alaska, USA

176 U9 **Hebe** Papua, E Indonesia 1.08S 129.54E

34 F11 **Hebo** Oregon, NW USA 45.10N 123.55W

Hebrides, Sea of the sea NW Scotland, UK

11 P5 **Hebron** Newfoundland and Labrador, E Canada 58.15N 62.45W

33 N13 **Hebron** Indiana, N USA 41.19N 87.12W

33 Q17 **Hebron** Kentucky, S USA 40.10N 97.35W

26 L6 **Hebron** Nebraska, C USA 40.10N 97.35W

31 N4 **Hebron** North Dakota, N USA 46.54N 102.03W

144 F11 **Hebron** var. Al Khalīl, El Khalil, Heb. Hevron; anc. Kiriath-Arba. S West Bank 31.30N 35.00E

8 I1 **Hecate Strait** strait British Columbia, W Canada

43 W12 **Hecelchakán** Campeche, SE Mexico 20.09N 90.04W

---

15 Hh9 **Hay River** Northwest Territories, W Canada 60.51N 115.42W

28 K4 **Hays** Kansas, C USA 38.52N 99.19W

30 K12 **Hay Springs** Nebraska, C USA 42.39N 102.39W

67 H25 **Haystack, The** ▲ NE Saint Helena 15.55S 5.40W

29 N7 **Haysville** Kansas, C USA 37.34N 97.21W

119 O7 **Haysyn** Rus. Gaysin. Vinnyts'ka Oblast', C Ukraine 48.49N 29.29E

29 Y9 **Hayti** Missouri, C USA 36.13N 89.45W

31 Q9 **Hayti** South Dakota, N USA 44.39N 97.11W

119 O8 **Hayvoron** Rus. Gayvorno. Kirovohrads'ka Oblast', C Ukraine 48.19N 29.54E

37 N9 **Hayward** California, W USA 37.40N 122.07W

32 J4 **Hayward** Wisconsin, N USA 46.01N 91.25W

99 O23 **Haywards Heath** SE England, UK 51.00N 0.06W

152 A11 **Hazar** prev. Rus. Cheleken. Balkan Welaýaty, W Turkmenistan 39.25N 53.07E

149 S11 **Hazār-e Shāh** var. Kūh-e Hazr. ▲ SE Iran 29.26N 57.15E

23 O7 **Hazard** Kentucky, S USA 37.16N 83.12W

143 O15 **Hazar Gölü** ◎ C Turkey

159 P15 **Hazārībāg** var. Hazārībāgh. Jhārkhand, N India 24.00N 85.23E

159 P15 **Hazārībāgh** see Hazārībāg

105 O1 **Hazebrouck** Nord, N France 50.43N 2.33E

32 A9 **Hazel Green** Wisconsin, N USA 37.53N 86.44W

199 Ii10 **Hazel Holme Bank** undersea feature S Pacific Ocean 12.49S 174.30E

8 K13 **Hazelton** British Columbia, SW Canada 55.15N 127.37W

31 N6 **Hazelton** North Dakota, N USA 46.27N 100.17W

37 S5 **Hazen** Nevada, W USA 39.33N 119.02W

31 N5 **Hazen** North Dakota, N USA 47.18N 101.37W

40 L12 **Hazen Bay** bay E Bering Sea

145 S5 **Hazm, Bi'r** well C Iraq 34.50N 43.25E

25 V6 **Hazlehurst** Georgia, SE USA 31.51N 82.35W

24 K6 **Hazlehurst** Mississippi, S USA 31.51N 90.24W

20 K15 **Hazlet** New Jersey, NE USA 40.24N 74.10W

152 I9 **Hazorasp** Rus. Khazarosp. Xorazm Viloyati, W Uzbekistan 41.21N 61.01E

153 R13 **Hazratishoh, Qatorkūhi** var. Khrebet Khazretishi, Rus. Khrebet Khozretishi. ▲ S Tajikistan

155 U6 **Hazro** Punjab, E Pakistan 33.55N 72.33E

25 R7 **Headland** Alabama, S USA 31.21N 85.20W

190 C6 **Headquarters** Idaho, NW USA 46.38N 115.52W

35 N10 **Healdsburg** California, W USA 38.36N 122.52W

29 N13 **Healdton** Oklahoma, C USA 34.13N 97.29W

41 R10 **Healy** Alaska, USA 63.51N 148.58W

Heart of Dixie see Alabama

Heart River ✦ North Dakota, N USA

33 T13 **Heath** Ohio, N USA 40.01N 82.26W

191 N11 **Heathcote** Victoria, SE Australia

99 N22 **Heathrow** ✕ (London) SE England

23 X5 **Heathsville** Virginia, NE USA

29 R11 **Heavener** Oklahoma, C USA

25 R15 **Hebbronville** Texas, SW USA

169 Q13 **Hebei** var. Hebei Sheng, Hopeh, Hopei, Ji; prev. Chihli. ✦ province E China

Hebei Sheng see Hebei

176 U9 **Hebe** Papua, E Indonesia

34 F11 **Hebo** Oregon, NW USA

169 U10 **Hechuan** Chongqing Shi, C China 30.01N 106.15E

31 P7 **Hecla** South Dakota, N USA 45.52N 98.09W

31 T9 **Hector** Minnesota, N USA 44.44N 94.43W

95 F17 **Hede** Jämtland, C Sweden 62.25N 13.33E

97 M14 **Hedemora** Dalarna, C Sweden 60.18N 15.58E

97 N14 **Hedensted** Vejle, C Denmark 55.46N 9.43E

97 G23 **Hedensted** Vejle, C Denmark 55.46N 9.43E

97 N14 **Hedesunda** Gävleborg, C Sweden 60.25N 17.00E

97 N14 **Hedesundafjord** ◎ C Sweden

27 O3 **Hedley** Texas, SW USA 34.52N 100.39W

31 X15 **Hedrick** Iowa, C USA 41.10N 92.18W

201 Y12 **Heel Point** point Wake Island 19.18N 166.39E

100 H9 **Heemskerk** Noord-Holland, W Netherlands 52.31N 4.40E

100 M10 **Heerde** Gelderland, E Netherlands 52.24N 6.15E

100 I8 **Heerenveen** Fris. It Hearrenfean. Friesland, N Netherlands 52.57N 5.55E

100 I8 **Heerhugowaard** Noord-Holland, NW Netherlands 52.40N 4.49E

94 O3 **Heer Land** physical region S Svalbard

101 M18 **Heerlen** Limburg, SE Netherlands 50.55N 6.00E

101 J19 **Hees** Limburg, NE Belgium 50.46N 5.17E

Heerwegen see Polkowice

100 N11 **Heesch** Noord-Brabant, S Netherlands 51.43N 5.31E

101 K15 **Heeze** Noord-Brabant, SE Netherlands 51.22N 5.34E

144 F8 **Hefa** var. Haifa; hist. Caiffa, Caiphas, anc. Sycaminum. Haifa, N Israel 32.49N 34.58E

144 F8 **Hefa, Mifraz** Eng. Bay of Haifa. bay N Israel

167 Q8 **Hefei** var. Hofei; hist. Luchow. Anhui, E China 31.51N 117.20E

25 R3 **Heflin** Alabama, S USA 33.39N 85.35W

169 X7 **Hegang** Heilongjiang, NE China 47.18N 130.15E

171 Ii11 **Hegura-jima** island SW Japan

102 H8 **Heide** Schleswig-Holstein, N Germany 54.12N 9.06E

103 G20 **Heidelberg** Baden-Württemberg, SW Germany 49.24N 8.40E

85 J21 **Heidelberg** Gauteng, NE South Africa 26.27S 28.21E

24 M6 **Heidelberg** Mississippi, S USA 31.53N 88.58W

103 J22 **Heidenheim an der Brenz** var. Heidenheim. Baden-Württemberg, S Germany 48.40N 10.09E

111 Q8 **Heidenreichstein** Niederösterreich, N Austria 48.53N 15.07E

170 E14 **Heigun-tō** var. Heguri-jima. island SW Japan

169 W5 **Heihe** prev. Ai-hun. Heilongjiang, NE China 50.13N 127.29E

Hei-ho see Nagqu

Hei-ho see Heilongjiang

165 S8 **Heilbron** Free State, N South Africa 27.16S 27.58E

103 H21 **Heilbronn** Baden-Württemberg, SW Germany 49.09N 9.14E

Heiligenbeil see Mamonovo

111 Q8 **Heiligenblut** Tirol, W Austria 47.04N 12.50E

102 K7 **Heiligenhafen** Schleswig-Holstein, N Germany 54.22N 10.57E

Heiligenkreuz see Žiar nad Hronom

103 K17 **Heiligenstadt** Thüringen, C Germany 51.22N 10.09E

Heilong Jiang see Amur

169 V6 **Heilongjiang** var. Hei, Heilongjiang Sheng, Hei-lung-chiang, Heilungkiang. ✦ province NE China

Heilongjiang Sheng see Heilongjiang

100 H6 **Heiloo** Noord-Holland, NW Netherlands 52.36N 4.43E

Heilsberg see Lidzbark Warmiński

Hei-lung-chiang/Heilungkiang see Heilongjiang

94 N **Heimaey** var. Heimaey. island S Iceland

96 H **Heimdal** Sør-Trøndelag, S Norway 63.21N 10.22E

95 N17 **Heinävesi** Itä-Suomi, E Finland 62.22N 28.42E

101 M22 **Heinerscheid** Diekirch, N Luxembourg 50.06N 6.04E

100 M10 **Heino** Overijssel, E Netherlands 52.26N 6.13E

95 M18 **Heinola** Etelä-Suomi, S Finland 61.13N 26.04E

103 C16 **Heinsberg** Nordrhein-Westfalen, W Germany 51.02N 6.01E

169 U12 **Heishan** Liaoning, NE China

166 H8 **Heishui** var. Luhua. Sichuan, C China 32.05N 102.03W

1 H17 **Heist-op-den-Berg** Antwerpen, C Belgium 51.04N 4.43E

Heitō see P'ingtung

---

166 K13 **Hechi** var. Jinchengjiang. Guangxi Zhuangzu Zizhiqu, S China 24.40N 108.05E

103 H23 **Hechingen** Baden-Württemberg, S Germany 48.20N 8.58E

101 K17 **Hechtel** Limburg, NE Belgium 51.07N 5.24E

166 J9 **Hechuan** Chongqing Shi, C China 30.01N 106.15E

31 P7 **Hecla** South Dakota, N USA 45.52N 98.09W

31 T9 **Hector** Minnesota, N USA 44.44N 94.43W

95 F17 **Hede** Jämtland, C Sweden 62.25N 13.33E

97 M14 **Hedemora** Dalarna, C Sweden 60.18N 15.58E

94 K13 **Hedenæset** Norrbotten, N Sweden 66.12N 23.40E

97 G23 **Hedensted** Vejle, C Denmark 55.46N 9.43E

97 N14 **Hedesunda** Gävleborg, C Sweden 60.25N 17.00E

97 N14 **Hedesundafjord** ◎ C Sweden

27 O3 **Hedley** Texas, SW USA 34.52N 100.39W

31 X15 **Hedrick** Iowa, C USA 41.10N 92.18W

201 Y12 **Heel Point** point Wake Island 19.18N 166.39E

100 H9 **Heemskerk** Noord-Holland, W Netherlands 52.31N 4.40E

100 M10 **Heerde** Gelderland, E Netherlands 52.24N 6.15E

100 I8 **Heerenveen** Fris. It Hearrenfean. Friesland, N Netherlands 52.57N 5.55E

100 I8 **Heerhugowaard** Noord-Holland, NW Netherlands 52.40N 4.49E

94 O3 **Heer Land** physical region S Svalbard

101 M18 **Heerlen** Limburg, SE Netherlands 50.55N 6.00E

101 J19 **Hees** Limburg, NE Belgium 50.46N 5.17E

Heerwegen see Polkowice

100 N11 **Heesch** Noord-Brabant, S Netherlands 51.43N 5.31E

101 K15 **Heeze** Noord-Brabant, SE Netherlands 51.22N 5.34E

144 F8 **Hefa** var. Haifa; hist. Caiffa, Caiphas, anc. Sycaminum. Haifa, N Israel 32.49N 34.58E

144 F8 **Hefa, Mifraz** Eng. Bay of Haifa. bay N Israel

167 Q8 **Hefei** var. Hofei; hist. Luchow. Anhui, E China 31.51N 117.20E

25 R3 **Heflin** Alabama, S USA 33.39N 85.35W

169 X7 **Hegang** Heilongjiang, NE China 47.18N 130.15E

171 Ii11 **Hegura-jima** island SW Japan

102 H8 **Heide** Schleswig-Holstein, N Germany 54.12N 9.06E

103 G20 **Heidelberg** Baden-Württemberg, SW Germany 49.24N 8.40E

85 J21 **Heidelberg** Gauteng, NE South Africa 26.27S 28.21E

24 M6 **Heidelberg** Mississippi, S USA 31.53N 88.58W

103 J22 **Heidenheim an der Brenz** var. Heidenheim. Baden-Württemberg, S Germany 48.40N 10.09E

111 Q8 **Heidenreichstein** Niederösterreich, N Austria 48.53N 15.07E

170 E14 **Heigun-tō** var. Heguri-jima. island SW Japan

169 W5 **Heihe** prev. Ai-hun. Heilongjiang, NE China 50.13N 127.29E

Hei-ho see Nagqu

Hei-ho see Heilongjiang

165 S8 **Heilbron** Free State, N South Africa 27.16S 27.58E

103 H21 **Heilbronn** Baden-Württemberg, SW Germany 49.09N 9.14E

Heiligenbeil see Mamonovo

111 Q8 **Heiligenblut** Tirol, W Austria 47.04N 12.50E

102 K7 **Heiligenhafen** Schleswig-Holstein, N Germany 54.22N 10.57E

Heiligenkreuz see Žiar nad Hronom

103 K17 **Heiligenstadt** Thüringen, C Germany 51.22N 10.09E

Heilong Jiang see Amur

169 V6 **Heilongjiang** var. Hei, Heilongjiang Sheng, Hei-lung-chiang, Heilungkiang. ✦ province NE China

Heilongjiang Sheng see Heilongjiang

100 H6 **Heiloo** Noord-Holland, NW Netherlands 52.36N 4.43E

Heilsberg see Lidzbark Warmiński

Hei-lung-chiang/Heilungkiang see Heilongjiang

94 N **Heimaey** var. Heimaey. island S Iceland

96 H **Heimdal** Sør-Trøndelag, S Norway 63.21N 10.22E

95 N17 **Heinävesi** Itä-Suomi, E Finland 62.22N 28.42E

101 M22 **Heinerscheid** Diekirch, N Luxembourg 50.06N 6.04E

100 M10 **Heino** Overijssel, E Netherlands 52.26N 6.13E

95 M18 **Heinola** Etelä-Suomi, S Finland 61.13N 26.04E

103 C16 **Heinsberg** Nordrhein-Westfalen, W Germany 51.02N 6.01E

169 U12 **Heishan** Liaoning, NE China

166 H8 **Heishui** var. Luhua. Sichuan, C China 32.05N 102.03W

1 H17 **Heist-op-den-Berg** Antwerpen, C Belgium 51.04N 4.43E

Heitō see P'ingtung

Hejaz see Al Ḥijāz

166 M14 **He Jiang** ✦ S China

Hejiayan see Lüeyang

164 K6 **Hejing** Xinjiang Uygur Zizhiqu, NW China 42.21N 86.19E

Héjjasfalva see Vânători

Heka see Hoika

143 N14 **Hekimhan** Malatya, C Turkey 38.49N 37.55E

94 J4 **Hekla** ▲ S Iceland 63.56N 19.42W

Hekou see Yajiang, Sichuan, China

Hekou see Yanshan, Jiangxi, China

112 J6 **Hel** Ger. Hela. Pomorskie, N Poland 54.35N 18.48E

Hela see Hel

95 F17 **Helagsfjället** ▲ C Sweden 62.57N 12.31E

165 W8 **Helan** var. Xigang, Ningxia, N China 38.33N 106.21E

168 K14 **Helan Shan** ▲ N China

101 M16 **Helden** Limburg, SE Netherlands 51.20N 6.00E

29 X12 **Helena** Arkansas, C USA 34.32N 90.34W

35 R10 **Helena** state capital Montana, NW USA 46.35N 112.02W

98 H12 **Helensburgh** W Scotland, UK 56.00N 4.45W

192 K5 **Helensville** Auckland, North Island, NZ 36.42S 174.25E

17 L20 **Helgasjön** ◎ S Sweden

102 G8 **Helgoland** Eng. Heligoland. island NW Germany

Helgoland Bay see Helgoländer Bucht

102 G8 **Helgoländer Bucht** var. Helgoland Bay, Heligoland Bight. bay NW Germany

Heligoland see Helgoland

Heligoland Bight see Helgoländer Bucht

Heliopolis see Baalbek

94 I4 **Hella** Suðurland, SW Iceland 63.51N 20.24W

Hellas see Greece

91 N11 **Helleh, Rūd-e** ✦ S Iran

100 N10 **Hellendoorn** Overijssel, E Netherlands 52.22N 6.27E

Hellenic Republic see Greece

123 Gg10 **Hellenic Trough** undersea feature Aegean Sea, C Mediterranean Sea

96 E10 **Hellesylt** Møre og Romsdal, S Norway 62.06N 6.51E

100 F13 **Hellevoetsluis** Zuid-Holland, SW Netherlands 51.49N 4.07E

107 Q12 **Hellín** Castilla-La Mancha, C Spain 38.31N 1.43W

117 H19 **Hellinikon ✕** (Athína) Attikí, C Greece 37.53S 23.44E

34 M12 **Hells Canyon** valley Idaho/Oregon, NW USA

154 L9 **Helmand** ✦ province S Afghanistan

154 K10 **Helmand, Daryā-ye** var. Rūd-e Hirmand. ✦ Afghanistan/Iran see also Hirmand, Rūd-e

Helmantica see Salamanca

103 K15 **Helme** ✦ C Germany

101 L15 **Helmond** Noord-Brabant, S Netherlands 51.28N 5.40E

98 J7 **Helmsdale** N Scotland, UK 58.06N 3.36W

102 K13 **Helmstedt** Niedersachsen, N Germany 52.13N 11.01E

169 Y10 **Helong** Jilin, NE China 42.38N 129.01E

38 M4 **Helper** Utah, W USA 39.40N 110.52W

102 O10 **Helpter Berge** hill NE Germany 53.29N 13.37E

97 J22 **Helsingborg** prev. Hälsingborg. Skåne, S Sweden 55.59N 12.48E

97 J23 **Helsingfors** see Helsinki

97 J22 **Helsingør** Eng. Elsinore. Frederiksborg, E Denmark 56.03N 12.37E

95 M20 **Helsinki** Swe. Helsingfors. ● (Finland) Etelä-Suomi, S Finland 60.18N 24.58E

99 G25 **Helston** SW England, UK 50.04N 5.16W

Heltau see Cisnădie

63 C17 **Helvecia** Santa Fe, C Argentina 31.09S 60.09W

99 G18 **Helvellyn** ▲ NW England, UK 54.31N 3.00W

Helvetia see Switzerland

77 W8 **Helwân** var. Hilwân, Hulwan, Hulwān. N Egypt 29.51N 31.19E

99 N21 **Hemel Hempstead** E England, UK 51.46N 0.28W

37 U16 **Hemet** California, W USA 33.45N 116.58W

30 I13 **Hemingford** Nebraska, C USA 42.18N 103.02W

23 T13 **Hemingway** South Carolina, SE USA 33.45N 79.25W

95 G13 **Hemnesberget** Nordland, C Norway 66.13N 13.33E

96 Y8 **Hemphill** Texas, SW USA 31.20N 93.51W

27 V11 **Hempstead** Texas, SW USA 30.06N 96.04W

97 P20 **Hemse** Gotland, SE Sweden 57.12N 18.22E

96 F13 **Hemsedal** valley S Norway

165 T11 **Hemu** var. Hongqiaogou. Zizhixian, Yégainnyin. Qinghai, C China 34.42N 101.36E

192 L4 **Hen and Chickens** island group N NZ

Henan Mongolzu Zizhixian/Henan Sheng see Henan

107 O7 **Henares** ✦ C Spain

171 M8 **Henashi-zaki** headland Honshū, C Japan 40.37N 139.51E

104 I16 **Hendaye** Pyrénées-Atlantiques, SW France 43.22N 1.46W

142 F11 **Hendek** Sakarya, NW Turkey 40.49N 30.40E

63 B21 **Henderson** Buenos Aires, E Argentina 36.18S 61.43W

22 I5 **Henderson** Kentucky, S USA 37.50N 87.35W

37 X11 **Henderson** Nevada, W USA 36.02N 114.58W

23 T8 **Henderson** North Carolina, SE USA 36.19N 78.24W

22 G10 **Henderson** Tennessee, S USA 35.25N 88.37W

HENDERSON – HÖGSBY

27 W7 **Henderson** Texas, SW USA *32.09N 94.48W*
32 J12 **Henderson Creek** ≈ Illinois, N USA
195 X16 **Henderson Field** ✕ (Honiara) Guadalcanal, C Solomon Islands *9.28S 160.02E*
203 O17 **Henderson Island** *atoll* N Pitcairn Islands
23 O10 **Hendersonville** North Carolina, SE USA *35.19N 82.27W*
22 J8 **Hendersonville** Tennessee, S USA *36.18N 86.37W*
149 O14 **Hendorābī, Jazīreh-ye** *island* S Iran
57 V10 **Hendrik Top** *var.* Hendriktop. *elevation* C Suriname *4.14N 56.07W*
Hendū Kosh *see* Hindu Kush
12 L12 **Heney, Lac** ◎ Québec, SE Canada
194 I12 **Henganofi** Eastern Highlands, C PNG *6.13S 145.31E*
Hengchow *see* Hengyang
167 S15 **Hengchun** S Taiwan *22.09N 120.43E*
165 R16 **Hengduan Shan** ▲▲ SW China
100 N12 **Hengelo** Gelderland, E Netherlands *52.02N 6.18E*
100 O10 **Hengelo** Overijssel, E Netherlands *52.15N 6.48E*
Hengnan *see* Hengyang
167 N11 **Hengshan** Hunan, S China *27.17N 112.51E*
166 L4 **Hengshan** Shaanxi, C China *37.57N 109.17E*
167 O4 **Hengshui** Hebei, E China *37.42N 115.39E*
167 N12 **Hengyang** *var.* Hengnan, Hengyang; *prev.* Hengchow. Hunan, S China *26.54N 112.33E*
119 U11 **Heniches'k** *Rus.* Genichesk. Khersons'ka Oblast', S Ukraine *46.10N 34.49E*
23 Z4 **Henlopen, Cape** *headland* Delaware, NE USA *38.48N 75.06W*
Henna *see* Enna
96 M10 **Hennan** Gävleborg, C Sweden *62.01N 15.55E*
104 G7 **Hennebont** Morbihan, NW France *47.48N 3.16W*
32 L11 **Hennepin** Illinois, N USA *41.13N 89.21W*
28 M9 **Hennessey** Oklahoma, C USA *36.06N 97.54W*
102 N12 **Hennigsdorf** *var.* Hennigsdorf bei Berlin. Brandenburg, NE Germany *52.37N 13.13E*
Hennigsdorf bei Berlin *see* Hennigsdorf
21 N9 **Henniker** New Hampshire, NE USA *43.10N 71.47W*
27 S5 **Henrietta** Texas, SW USA *33.49N 98.12W*
Henrique de Carvalho *see* Saurimo
32 L12 **Henry** Illinois, N USA *41.06N 89.21W*
23 Y7 **Henry, Cape** *headland* Virginia, NE USA *36.55N 76.01W*
29 P10 **Henryetta** Oklahoma, C USA *35.26N 95.58W*
204 M7 **Henry Ice Rise** *ice cap* Antarctica
16 N1 **Henry Kater, Cape** *headland* Baffin Island, Nunavut, NE Canada *69.09N 66.45W*
35 R13 **Henrys Fork** ≈ Idaho, NW USA
12 E15 **Hensall** Ontario, S Canada *43.25N 81.28W*
102 J9 **Henstedt-Ulzburg** Schleswig-Holstein, N Germany *53.45N 9.59E*
169 N7 **Hentiy** ◈ *province* N Mongolia
168 M7 **Hentiyn Nuruu** ▲▲ N Mongolia
191 P10 **Henty** New South Wales, SE Australia *35.33S 147.03E*
177 Ff8 **Henzada** Irrawaddy, SW Myanmar *17.36N 95.25E*
Heping *see* Huishui
103 G19 **Heppenheim** Hessen, W Germany *49.39N 8.38E*
34 J11 **Heppner** Oregon, NW USA *45.21N 119.33W*
166 L15 **Hepu** *var.* Lianzhou. Guangxi Zhuangzu Zizhiqu, S China *21.40N 109.12E*
94 J2 **Heradhsvötn** ≈ C Iceland
Herakleion *see* Irákleio
154 K5 **Herāt** *var.* Herat; *anc.* Aria. Herāt, W Afghanistan *34.22N 62.11E*
154 J5 **Herāt** ◈ *province* W Afghanistan
105 P14 **Hérault** ◈ *department* S France
105 P15 **Hérault** ≈ S France
9 T16 **Herbert** Saskatchewan, S Canada *50.27N 107.09W*
193 F22 **Herbert** Otago, South Island, NZ *45.14S 170.48E*
40 J17 **Herbert Island** *island* Aleutian Islands, Alaska, USA
194 I12 **Herbert, Mount** ▲ C PNG *5.44S 145.00E*
Herbertshöhe *see* Kokopo
13 Q7 **Hérbertville** Québec, SE Canada *48.22N 71.42W*
103 G17 **Herborn** Hessen, W Germany *50.40N 8.18E*
115 I17 **Herceg-Novi** *It.* Castelnuovo; *prev.* Ercegnovi. Montenegro, SW Serbia and Montenegro (Yugoslavia) *42.28N 18.35E*
9 X10 **Herchmer** Manitoba, C Canada *57.25N 94.12W*
194 K14 **Hercules Bay** *bay* E PNG
94 K2 **Herdhubreidh** ▲ C Iceland *65.12N 16.26W*
44 M13 **Heredia** Heredia, C Costa Rica *10.00N 84.06W*
44 M12 **Heredia** *off.* Provincia de Heredia. ◈ *province* N Costa Rica
99 K21 **Hereford** W England, UK *52.04N 2.43W*
26 M3 **Hereford** Texas, SW USA *34.49N 102.25W*
13 Q13 **Hereford, Mont** ▲ Québec, SE Canada *45.04N 71.38W*
99 K21 **Herefordshire** *cultural region* W England, UK
203 U11 **Hereheretue** *atoll* Îles Tuamotu, C French Polynesia
107 N10 **Herencia** Castilla-La Mancha, C Spain *39.19N 3.19W*
101 H18 **Herent** Vlaams Brabant, C Belgium *50.54N 4.40E*
101 I16 **Herentals** *var.* Herenthals. Antwerpen, N Belgium *51.10N 4.49E*
Herenthals *see* Herentals
101 H17 **Herenthout** Antwerpen, N Belgium *51.09N 4.45E*
97 J23 **Herfølge** Roskilde, E Denmark *55.25N 12.09E*
102 G13 **Herford** Nordrhein-Westfalen, NW Germany *52.07N 8.40E*
29 O5 **Herington** Kansas, C USA *38.37N 96.55W*
110 H7 **Herisau** *Fr.* Hérisau. Appenzell Ausser Rhoden, NE Switzerland *47.22N 9.16E*
Héristal *see* Herstal
101 J18 **Herk-de-Stad** Limburg, NE Belgium *50.57N 5.12E*
Herkulesbad/Herkulesfürdő *see* Bäile Herculane
Herlen Gol/Herlen He *see* Kerulen
37 Q4 **Herlong** California, W USA *40.07N 120.06W*
99 L26 **Herm** *island* Channel Islands
111 R9 **Hermagor** *Slvn.* Šmohor. Kärnten, S Austria *46.37N 13.24E*
31 S7 **Herman** Minnesota, N USA *45.49N 96.08W*
98 L1 **Herma Ness** *headland* NE Scotland, UK *60.51N 0.55W*
29 V4 **Hermann** Missouri, C USA *38.40N 91.25W*
189 Q8 **Hermannsburg** Northern Territory, N Australia *23.59S 132.55E*
Hermannstadt *see* Sibiu
96 E12 **Hermansverk** Sogn og Fjordane, S Norway *61.10N 6.52E*
144 H6 **Hermel** *var.* Hirmil. NE Lebanon *34.23N 36.19E*
Hermhausen *see* Hajnówka
191 P6 **Hermidale** New South Wales, SE Australia *31.36S 146.42E*
57 X9 **Herminadorp** Sipaliwini, NE Suriname *5.05N 54.22W*
34 K11 **Hermiston** Oregon, NW USA *45.50N 119.17W*
29 T6 **Hermitage** Missouri, C USA *37.57N 93.21W*
194 I8 **Hermit Islands** *island group* N PNG
27 O7 **Hermleigh** Texas, SW USA *32.37N 100.44W*
144 G7 **Hermon, Mount** *Ar.* Jabal ash Shaykh. ▲ S Syria *35.30N 33.30E*
Hermopolis Parva *see* Damanhûr
30 J10 **Hermosa** South Dakota, N USA *43.49N 103.12W*
42 F5 **Hermosillo** Sonora, NW Mexico *28.58N 110.53W*
Hermoupolis *see* Ermoúpoli
113 N20 **Hernád** *var.* Hornád, *Ger.* Kundert. ≈ Hungary/Slovakia
63 C18 **Hernández** Entre Ríos, E Argentina *32.21S 60.01W*
25 V11 **Hernando** Florida, SE USA *28.54N 82.22W*
24 L1 **Hernando** Mississippi, S USA *34.49N 89.59W*
107 Q2 **Hernani** País Vasco, N Spain *43.16N 1.58W*
101 F19 **Herne** Vlaams Brabant, C Belgium *50.45N 4.03E*
103 E14 **Herne** Nordrhein-Westfalen, W Germany *51.33N 7.13E*
97 F22 **Herning** Ringkøbing, W Denmark *56.07N 8.58E*
Hernösand *see* Härnösand
124 Q13 **Herodotus Basin** *undersea feature* E Mediterranean Sea
124 Nn14 **Herodotus Trough** *undersea feature* C Mediterranean Sea
31 T11 **Heron Lake** Minnesota, N USA *43.48N 95.18W*
Herowābād *see* Khalkhāl
97 G16 **Herre** Telemark, S Norway *59.06N 9.34E*
31 N7 **Herreid** South Dakota, N USA *45.49N 100.04W*
103 H22 **Herrenberg** Baden-Württemberg, S Germany *48.36N 8.52E*
106 L14 **Herrera** Andalucía, S Spain *37.22N 4.49W*
45 R17 **Herrera** *off.* Provincia de Herrera. ◈ *province* S Panama
106 L10 **Herrera del Duque** Extremadura, W Spain *39.10N 5.03W*
106 M4 **Herrera de Pisuerga** Castilla-León, N Spain *42.34N 4.19W*
43 Z13 **Herrero, Punta** *headland* SE Mexico *19.15N 87.28W*
191 P16 **Herrick** Tasmania, SE Australia *41.07S 147.53E*
32 L17 **Herrin** Illinois, N USA *37.48N 89.01W*
22 M6 **Herrington Lake** ▣ Kentucky, S USA
97 K18 **Herrljunga** Västra Götaland, S Sweden *58.04N 13.01E*
105 N16 **Hers** ≈ S France
8 I1 **Herschel Island** *island* Yukon Territory, NW Canada
101 I17 **Herselt** Antwerpen, C Belgium *51.03N 4.52E*
20 G15 **Hershey** Pennsylvania, NE USA *40.17N 76.39W*
101 K19 **Herstal** *Fr.* Héristal. Liège, E Belgium *50.40N 5.37E*
99 O21 **Hertford** E England, UK *51.48N 0.04W*
23 X8 **Hertford** North Carolina, SE USA *36.11N 76.28W*
99 O21 **Hertfordshire** *cultural region* E England, UK
189 Z9 **Hervey Bay** Queensland, E Australia *25.17S 152.48E*
103 O14 **Herzberg** Brandenburg, E Germany *51.42N 13.15E*
101 E18 **Herzele** Oost-Vlaanderen, NW Belgium *50.52N 3.52E*
103 K20 **Herzogenaurach** Bayern, SE Germany *49.34N 10.52E*
111 W4 **Herzogenburg** Niederösterreich, NE Austria *48.18N 15.43E*
Herzogenbusch *see* 's-Hertogenbosch
105 N2 **Hesdin** Pas-de-Calais, N France *50.21N 2.00E*
166 K14 **Heshan** Guangxi Zhuangzu Zizhiqu, S China *23.45N 108.58E*
165 X10 **Heshui** *var.* Xihuachi. Gansu, C China *35.42N 108.06E*
101 M25 **Hespérange** Luxembourg, SE Luxembourg *49.34N 6.10E*
37 U14 **Hesperia** California, W USA *34.25N 117.17W*
39 P7 **Hesperus Mountain** ▲ Colorado, C USA *37.27N 108.05W*
8 J6 **Hess** ≈ Yukon Territory, NW Canada
Hesse *see* Hessen
103 J21 **Hesselberg** ▲ S Germany *49.04N 10.32E*
97 I22 **Hesselo** *island* E Denmark
103 H17 **Hessen** *Eng./Fr.* Hesse. ◈ *state* C Germany
199 Jj6 **Hess Tablemount** *undersea feature* C Pacific Ocean *17.49N 174.15W*
29 N6 **Hesston** Kansas, C USA *38.08N 97.25W*
95 G15 **Hestskjøltoppen** ▲ C Norway *64.21N 13.57E*
99 K18 **Heswall** NW England, UK *53.19N 3.06W*
159 P12 **Hetauda** Central, C Nepal
Hétfalu *see* Săcele
30 K7 **Hettinger** North Dakota, N USA *46.00N 102.38W*
103 L14 **Hettstedt** Sachsen-Anhalt, C Germany *51.39N 11.31E*
94 P3 **Heuglin, Kapp** *headland* SE Svalbard *78.15N 22.49E*
195 Y16 **Heuru** San Cristobal, SE Solomon Islands *10.13S 161.25E*
101 J17 **Heusden** Limburg, NE Belgium *51.01N 5.16E*
100 J13 **Heusden** Noord-Brabant, S Netherlands *51.43N 5.05E*
104 K3 **Hève, Cap de la** *headland* N France *49.28N 0.13W*
101 H18 **Heverlee** Vlaams Brabant, C Belgium *50.52N 4.41E*
113 L22 **Heves** Heves, NE Hungary *47.37N 20.17E*
113 L22 **Heves** *off.* Heves Megye. ◈ *county* NE Hungary
Hevron *see* Hebron
47 Y13 **Hewanorra** ✕ (Saint Lucia) S Saint Lucia *13.44N 60.57W*
Hexian *see* Hezhou
166 L6 **Heyang** Shaanxi, C China *35.03N 109.55E*
Heydebrech *see* Kędzierzyn-Kozle
Heydekrug *see* Šilutė
Heyin *see* Guide
99 K16 **Heysham** NW England, UK *54.02N 2.54W*
167 O14 **Heyuan** Guangdong, S China *23.50N 114.43E*
190 L12 **Heywood** Victoria, SE Australia *38.09S 141.38E*
188 K3 **Heywood Islands** *island group* Western Australia
167 O6 **Heze** *var.* Caozhou. Shandong, E China *35.16N 115.27E*
165 U11 **Hezheng** Gansu, C China *35.24N 103.21E*
166 M13 **Hezhou** *var.* Babu; *prev.* Hexian. Guangxi Zhuangzu Zizhiqu, S China *24.25N 111.31E*
165 U11 **Hezuo** Gansu, C China *34.55N 102.49E*
25 Z16 **Hialeah** Florida, SE USA *25.51N 80.16W*
29 Q3 **Hiawatha** Kansas, C USA *39.48N 95.31W*
38 M4 **Hiawatha** Utah, W USA *39.28N 111.00W*
31 V4 **Hibbing** Minnesota, N USA *47.24N 92.55W*
191 N17 **Hibbs, Point** *headland* Tasmania, SE Australia *42.37S 145.15E*
Hibernia *see* Ireland
170 D12 **Hibiki-nada** *inlet* SW Japan
22 F8 **Hickman** Kentucky, S USA *36.34N 89.11W*
23 Q9 **Hickory** North Carolina, SE USA *35.44N 81.20W*
23 Q9 **Hickory, Lake** ◎ North Carolina, SE USA
192 Q7 **Hicks Bay** Gisborne, North Island, NZ *37.36S 178.18E*
27 S8 **Hico** Texas, SW USA *31.58N 98.01W*
172 Oo6 **Hidaka** Hokkaidō, NE Japan *42.53N 142.24E*
171 Gg13 **Hidaka** Hyōgo, Honshū, SW Japan *35.27N 134.43E*
172 P7 **Hidaka-sanmyaku** ▲▲ Hokkaidō, NE Japan
43 O6 **Hidalgo** *var.* Villa Hidalgo. Coahuila de Zaragoza, NE Mexico *27.46N 99.54W*
43 N8 **Hidalgo** Nuevo León, NE Mexico *29.58N 100.27W*
43 O10 **Hidalgo** Tamaulipas, C Mexico *24.17N 99.21W*
43 O13 **Hidalgo** ◈ *state* C Mexico
42 J7 **Hidalgo del Parral** *var.* Parral. Chihuahua, N Mexico *26.58N 105.40W*
171 J14 **Hida-sanmyaku** ▲▲ Honshū, S Japan
102 N7 **Hiddensee** *island* NE Germany
82 G6 **Hidiglib, Wadi** ≈ NE Sudan
111 U6 **Hieflau** Salzburg, E Austria *47.36N 14.34E*
197 H5 **Hienghène** Province Nord, C New Caledonia *20.43S 164.54E*
Hierosolyma *see* Jerusalem
66 N12 **Hierro** *var.* Ferro. *island* Islas Canarias, Spain, NE Atlantic Ocean
170 Ee13 **Higashi-Hiroshima** *var.* Higasihirosima. Hiroshima, Honshū, SW Japan *34.25N 132.45E*
171 J18 **Higashi-Izu** Shizuoka, Honshū, S Japan *34.43N 138.58E*
171 Ll12 **Higashine** *var.* Higasine. Yamagata, Honshū, C Japan *38.26N 140.23E*
170 C11 **Higashi-suidō** *strait* SW Japan
Higasihirosima *see* Higashi-Hiroshima
Higasine *see* Higashine
27 P1 **Higgins** Texas, SW USA *36.06N 100.01W*
33 P7 **Higgins Lake** ◎ Michigan, N USA
29 S4 **Higginsville** Missouri, C USA *39.04N 93.43W*
High Atlas *see* Haut Atlas
32 M5 **High Falls Reservoir** ▣ Wisconsin, N USA
46 K12 **Highgate** C Jamaica *18.15N 76.53W*
27 X11 **High Island** Texas, SW USA *29.35N 94.24W*
33 O5 **High Island** *island* Michigan, N USA
32 K15 **Highland** Illinois, N USA *38.44N 89.40W*
33 N10 **Highland Park** Illinois, N USA *42.10N 87.48W*
23 O10 **Highlands** North Carolina, SE USA *35.04N 83.10W*
9 O11 **High Level** Alberta, W Canada *58.31N 117.07W*
31 O9 **Highmore** South Dakota, N USA *44.29N 99.26W*
179 Oo10 **High Peak** ▲ Luzon, N Philippines *15.28N 120.07E*
High Plains *see* Great Plains
23 S9 **High Point** North Carolina, SE USA *35.58N 80.00W*
20 J13 **High Point** *hill* New Jersey, NE USA *41.19N 74.38W*
9 P13 **High Prairie** Alberta, W Canada *55.27N 116.28W*
9 Q16 **High River** Alberta, SW Canada *50.34N 113.49W*
23 S9 **High Rock Lake** ▣ North Carolina, SE USA
25 V9 **High Springs** Florida, SE USA *29.49N 82.36W*
High Veld *see* Great Karoo
99 J24 **High Willhays** ▲ SW England, UK *50.39N 3.58W*
99 N22 **High Wycombe** *prev.* Chepping Wycombe, Chipping Wycombe. SE England, UK *51.37N 0.46W*
43 P12 **Higos** *var.* El Higo. Veracruz-Llave, E Mexico *21.47N 98.28W*
104 I16 **Higuer, Cap** *headland* NE Spain *43.23N 1.46W*
47 R5 **Higüero, Punta** *headland* W Puerto Rico *18.21N 67.15W*
47 P9 **Higüey** *var.* Salvaleón de Higüey. E Dominican Republic *18.34N 68.43W*
202 G11 **Hihifo** ✕ (Matā'utu) Île Uvea, N Wallis and Futuna
83 N16 **Hiiraan** *off.* Gobolka Hiiraan. ◈ *region* C Somalia
120 E4 **Hiiumaa** *off.* Hiiumaa Maakond. ◈ *province* W Estonia
120 D4 **Hiiumaa** *Ger.* Dagden, *Swe.* Dagö. *island* W Estonia
Hijanah *see* Al Hījānah
107 S6 **Híjar** Aragón, NE Spain *41.10N 0.27W*
170 E13 **Hikari** Yamaguchi, Honshū, SW Japan *33.55N 131.58E*
170 Ff15 **Hiketa** Kagawa, Shikoku, SW Japan *34.15N 134.20E*
171 Hh15 **Hikone** Shiga, Honshū, SW Japan *35.15N 136.14E*
170 D13 **Hiko-san** ▲ Kyūshū, SW Japan *33.27N 130.55E*
203 V10 **Hikueru** *atoll* Îles Tuamotu, C French Polynesia
192 K3 **Hikurangi** Northland, North Island, NZ *35.37S 174.16E*
192 Q8 **Hikurangi** ▲ North Island, NZ *37.55S 177.59E*
199 J13 **Hikurangi Trench** *var.* Hikurangi Trough. *undersea feature* SW Pacific Ocean
Hikurangi Trough *see* Hikurangi Trench
202 B15 **Hikutavake** NW Niue
124 Nn14 **Hilāl, Ra's al** *headland* N Libya *32.55N 22.09E*
63 A24 **Hilario Ascasubi** Buenos Aires, E Argentina *39.22S 62.39W*
103 K17 **Hildburghausen** Thüringen, C Germany *50.26N 10.44E*
103 E15 **Hilden** Nordrhein-Westfalen, W Germany *51.10N 6.55E*
102 I13 **Hildesheim** Niedersachsen, N Germany *52.09N 9.57E*
35 T9 **Hilger** Montana, NW USA *47.15N 109.18W*
Hili *see* Hilli
Hilla *see* Al Ḥillah
47 O14 **Hillaby, Mount** ▲ N Barbados *13.12N 59.34W*
97 K19 **Hillared** Västra Götaland, S Sweden *57.37N 13.10E*
205 R12 **Hillary Coast** *physical region* Antarctica
44 G2 **Hill Bank** Orange Walk, N Belize *17.36N 88.43W*
35 O14 **Hill City** Idaho, NW USA *43.18N 115.03W*
28 K3 **Hill City** Kansas, C USA *39.21N 99.51W*
31 V5 **Hill City** Minnesota, N USA *46.59N 93.36W*
30 J10 **Hill City** South Dakota, N USA *43.54N 103.33W*
67 C24 **Hill Cove Settlement** West Falkland, Falkland Islands
100 H10 **Hillegom** Zuid-Holland, W Netherlands *52.18N 4.34E*
97 J22 **Hillerød** Frederiksborg, E Denmark *55.55N 12.19E*
38 M7 **Hillers, Mount** ▲ Utah, W USA *37.53N 110.42W*
159 S13 **Hilli** *var.* Hili. Rajshahi, NW Bangladesh *25.17N 89.02E*
31 R11 **Hills** Minnesota, N USA *43.31N 96.21W*
32 L14 **Hillsboro** Illinois, N USA *39.09N 89.29W*
29 N5 **Hillsboro** Kansas, C USA *38.21N 97.12W*
29 X5 **Hillsboro** Missouri, C USA *38.13N 90.33W*
21 N10 **Hillsboro** New Hampshire, NE USA *43.06N 71.52W*
39 Q14 **Hillsboro** New Mexico, SW USA *32.55N 107.33W*
31 R4 **Hillsboro** North Dakota, N USA *47.25N 97.03W*
33 R14 **Hillsboro** Ohio, N USA *39.12N 83.36W*
34 G11 **Hillsboro** Oregon, NW USA *45.31N 122.59W*
27 T8 **Hillsboro** Texas, SW USA *32.01N 97.08W*
32 K8 **Hillsboro** Wisconsin, N USA *43.40N 90.21W*
25 Y14 **Hillsboro Canal** *canal* Florida, SE USA
47 Y15 **Hillsborough** Carriacou, N Grenada *12.28N 61.28W*
99 G15 **Hillsborough** E Northern Ireland, UK *54.27N 6.06W*
23 U9 **Hillsborough** North Carolina, SE USA *36.04N 79.06W*
33 Q10 **Hillsdale** Michigan, N USA *41.55N 84.37W*
191 O8 **Hillston** New South Wales, SE Australia *33.30S 145.33E*
23 R7 **Hillsville** Virginia, NE USA *36.45N 80.44W*
98 L2 **Hillswick** NE Scotland, UK *60.28N 1.37W*
Hill Tippera *see* Tripura
40 H11 **Hilo** Hawai'i, USA, C Pacific Ocean *19.42N 155.04W*
20 F9 **Hilton** New York, NE USA *43.17N 77.47W*
12 C10 **Hilton Beach** Ontario, S Canada *46.14N 83.51W*
23 R16 **Hilton Head Island** South Carolina, SE USA *32.13N 80.45W*
23 R16 **Hilton Head Island** *island* South Carolina, SE USA
101 J15 **Hilvarenbeek** Noord-Brabant, S Netherlands *51.28N 5.07E*
100 J11 **Hilversum** Noord-Holland, C Netherlands *52.13N 5.10E*
Hilwân *see* Helwân
158 J7 **Himāchal Pradesh** ◈ *state* NW India
Himalaya/Himalaya Shan *see* Himalayas
158 M9 **Himalayas** *var.* Himalaya, *Chin.* Himalaya Shan. ▲▲ S Asia
179 Q14 **Himamaylan** Negros, C Philippines *10.04N 122.52E*
95 K15 **Himanka** Länsi-Suomi, W Finland *64.03N 24.40E*
Himara *see* Himarë
115 L23 **Himarë** *var.* Himara. Vlorë, S Albania *40.06N 19.45E*
144 M2 **Ḥimār, Wādī al** *dry watercourse* N Syria
160 D9 **Himatnagar** Gujarāt, W India *23.37N 73.01E*
111 Y4 **Himberg** Niederösterreich, E Austria *48.03N 16.27E*
171 J14 **Hime-gawa** ≈ Honshū, S Japan
170 G14 **Himeji** *var.* Himezi. Hyōgo, Honshū, SW Japan *34.47N 134.32E*
170 Dd13 **Hime-jima** *island* SW Japan
Himezi *see* Himeji
171 Ii13 **Himi** Toyama, Honshū, SW Japan *36.52N 136.59E*
111 S9 **Himmelberg** Kärnten, S Austria *46.45N 14.01E*
144 I5 **Ḥimş** *var.* Homs; *anc.* Emesa. Ḥimş, C Syria *34.43N 36.43E*
144 K6 **Ḥimş** *off.* Muḥāfaẓat Ḥimş, *var.* Homs. ◈ *governorate* C Syria
144 I5 **Ḥimş, Buḥayrat** *var.* Buḥayrat Qaṭṭīnah. ◎ W Syria
179 Rr15 **Hinatuan** Mindanao, S Philippines *8.21N 126.19E*
119 N10 **Hînceşti** *var.* Hânceşti; *prev.* Kotovsk. C Moldova *46.48N 28.33E*
46 M9 **Hinche** C Haiti *19.07N 72.00W*
189 X5 **Hinchinbrook Island** *island* Queensland, NE Australia
41 S12 **Hinchinbrook Island** *island* Alaska, USA
99 M19 **Hinckley** C England, UK *52.33N 1.21W*
31 V7 **Hinckley** Minnesota, N USA *46.01N 92.57W*
38 K5 **Hinckley** Utah, W USA *39.21N 112.39W*
20 J9 **Hinckley Reservoir** ▣ New York, NE USA
158 I12 **Hindaun** Rājasthān, N India *26.43N 77.01E*
Hindenburg/Hindenburg in Oberschlesien *see* Zabrze
Hindiya *see* Al Hindīyah
23 O6 **Hindman** Kentucky, S USA *37.20N 82.58W*
190 L10 **Hindmarsh, Lake** ◎ Victoria, SE Australia
193 G19 **Hinds** Canterbury, South Island, NZ *44.00S 171.33E*
193 G19 **Hinds** ≈ South Island, NZ
97 H23 **Hindsholm** *island* C Denmark
155 S4 **Hindu Kush** *Per.* Hendū Kosh. ▲▲ Afghanistan/Pakistan
161 H19 **Hindupur** Andhra Pradesh, E India *13.46N 77.33E*
9 O12 **Hines Creek** Alberta, W Canada *56.14N 118.36W*
25 W6 **Hinesville** Georgia, SE USA *31.51N 81.36W*
160 I12 **Hinganghāt** Mahārāshtra, C India *20.31N 78.52E*
155 N15 **Hingol** ≈ SW Pakistan
160 H13 **Hingoli** Mahārāshtra, C India *19.45N 77.08E*
143 R13 **Hınıs** Erzurum, E Turkey *39.22N 41.43E*
94 O2 **Hinlopenstretet** *strait* N Svalbard
94 G10 **Hinnøya** *Lapp.* Iinnasuolu. *island* C Norway
170 D15 **Hinokage** Miyazaki, Kyūshū, SW Japan *32.39N 131.20E*
170 F11 **Hino-misaki** *headland* Honshū, SW Japan *35.25N 132.37E*
110 H10 **Hinterrhein** ≈ SW Switzerland
9 O14 **Hinton** Alberta, SW Canada *53.24N 117.34W*
28 M10 **Hinton** Oklahoma, C USA *35.28N 98.21W*
23 R6 **Hinton** West Virginia, NE USA *37.40N 80.53W*
Hios *see* Chíos
43 N8 **Hipolito** Coahuila de Zaragoza, NE Mexico *25.42N 101.22W*
Hipponium *see* Vibo Valentia
170 C12 **Hirado** Nagasaki, Hirado-shima, SW Japan *33.22N 129.32E*
170 C12 **Hirado-shima** *island* SW Japan
171 Gg15 **Hirakata** Ōsaka, Honshū, SW Japan *34.48N 135.37E*
172 P17 **Hirakubo-saki** *headland* Ishigaki-jima, SW Japan *24.36N 124.19E*
160 M11 **Hīrākud Reservoir** ▣ E India
Hir al Gharbi, Qasr al *see* Ḥayr al Gharbī, Qaşr al
172 N9 **Hiranai** Aomori, Honshū, N Japan *40.56N 140.55E*
172 Pp16 **Hirara** Okinawa, Miyako-jima, SW Japan *24.48N 125.16E*
Qasr al Hir Ash Sharqī *see* Ḥayr ash Sharqī, Qaşr al
170 F12 **Hirata** Shimane, Honshū, SW Japan *35.26N 132.50E*
171 Jj17 **Hiratsuka** *var.* Hiratuka. Kanagawa, Honshū, S Japan *35.20N 139.20E*
Hiratuka *see* Hiratsuka
142 I13 **Hirfanlı Barajı** ▣ C Turkey
161 G18 **Hiriyūr** Karnātaka, W India *13.58N 76.33E*
Hîrlău *see* Hârlău
154 K10 **Hīrmand, Rūd-e** *var.* Daryā-ye Helmand. ≈ Afghanistan/Iran *see also* Helmand, Daryā-ye
Hirmil *see* Hermel
172 P8 **Hiroo** Hokkaidō, NE Japan *42.16N 143.16E*
171 Mm9 **Hirosaki** Aomori, Honshū, C Japan *40.34N 140.28E*
170 E13 **Hiroshima** *var.* Hirosima. Hiroshima, Honshū, SW Japan *34.22N 132.25E*
170 Ee13 **Hiroshima** *off.* Hiroshima-ken, *var.* Hirosima. ◈ *prefecture* Honshū, SW Japan
Hirosima *see* Hiroshima
Hirschberg/Hirschberg im Riesengebirge/Hirschberg in Schlesien *see* Jelenia Góra
105 Q3 **Hirson** Aisne, N France *49.55N 4.04E*
Hîrşova *see* Hârşova
97 G19 **Hirtshals** Nordjylland, N Denmark *57.34N 9.58E*
171 H16 **Hisai** Mie, Honshū, SW Japan *34.38N 136.27E*
158 H10 **Hisār** Haryāna, NW India *29.10N 75.45E*
194 J15 **Hisiu** Central, SW PNG *9.01S 146.49E*
153 P13 **Hisor** *Rus.* Gissar. W Tajikistan *38.34N 68.29E*
Hispalis *see* Sevilla
Hispana/Hispania *see* Spain
46 M7 **Hispaniola** *island* Dominion Republic/Haiti
66 F11 **Hispaniola Basin** *var.* Hispaniola Trough. *undersea feature* SW Atlantic Ocean
Hispaniola Trough *see* Hispaniola Basin
Histonium *see* Vasto
145 R7 **Hīt** SW Iraq *33.38N 42.50E*
170 D14 **Hita** Ōita, Kyūshū, SW Japan *33.20N 130.55E*
171 L16 **Hitachi** *var.* Hitati. Ibaraki, Honshū, S Japan *36.40N 140.42E*
171 L15 **Hitachi-Ōta** *var.* Hitatiôta. Ibaraki, Honshū, S Japan *36.31N 140.31E*
Hitati *see* Hitachi
Hitatiôta *see* Hitachi-Ōta
99 O21 **Hitchin** E England, UK *51.57N 0.16W*
203 Q7 **Hitiaa** Tahiti, W French Polynesia *17.34S 149.16W*
170 Cc15 **Hitoyoshi** *var.* Hitoyosi. Kumamoto, Kyūshū, SW Japan *32.12N 130.45E*
Hitoyosi *see* Hitoyoshi
96 F7 **Hitra** *prev.* Hitteren. *island* S Norway
Hitteren *see* Hitra
197 B10 **Hiu** *island* Torres Islands, N Vanuatu
171 K14 **Hiuchiga-take** ▲ Honshū, C Japan *36.57N 139.18E*
170 Ee14 **Hiuchi-nada** *gulf* S Japan
203 X7 **Hiva Oa** *island* Îles Marquises, N French Polynesia
22 M10 **Hiwassee Lake** ▣ North Carolina, SE USA
22 M10 **Hiwassee River** ≈ SE USA
97 H20 **Hjallerup** Nordjylland, N Denmark *57.10N 10.10E*
97 M16 **Hjälmaren** *Eng.* Lake Hjalmar. ◎ C Sweden
Hjalmar, Lake *see* Hjälmaren
97 C14 **Hjellestad** Hordaland, S Norway *60.15N 5.13E*
97 D16 **Hjelmeland** Rogaland, S Norway *59.12N 6.07E*
96 G10 **Hjerkinn** Oppland, S Norway *62.13N 9.37E*
97 L18 **Hjo** Västra Götaland, S Sweden *58.16N 14.07E*
97 G19 **Hjørring** Nordjylland, N Denmark *57.28N 9.58E*
178 H1 **Hkakabo Razi** ▲ Myanmar/China *28.17N 97.28E*
178 H1 **Hkring Bum** ▲ N Myanmar *27.05N 97.16E*
85 L21 **Hlathikulu** *var.* Hlatikulu. S Swaziland *26.57S 31.19E*
Hlatikulu *see* Hlathikulu
Hliboka *see* Hlyboka
113 F17 **Hlinsko** *var.* Hlinsko v Čechách. Pardubický Kraj, C Czech Republic *49.46N 15.54E*
Hlinsko v Čechách *see* Hlinsko
119 S6 **Hlobyne** *Rus.* Globino. Poltavs'ka Oblast', NE Ukraine *49.24N 33.16E*
113 H20 **Hlohovec** *Ger.* Freistadtl, *Hung.* Galgóc; *prev.* Frakštát. Trnavský Kraj, W Slovakia *48.27N 17.47E*
85 J23 **Hlotse** *var.* Leribe. NW Lesotho *28.55S 28.01E*
113 I17 **Hlučín** *Ger.* Hultschin, *Pol.* Hulczyn. Moravskoslezský Kraj, E Czech Republic *49.54N 18.10E*
119 S2 **Hlukhiv** *Rus.* Glukhov. Sums'ka Oblast', NE Ukraine *51.39N 33.52E*
121 K21 **Hlushkavichy** *Rus.* Glushkevichi. Homyel'skaya Voblasts', SE Belarus *51.33N 27.48E*
121 L18 **Hlusk** *Rus.* Glusk, Glussk. Mahilyowskaya Voblasts', E Belarus *52.54N 28.40E*
118 K8 **Hlyboka** *Ger.* Hliboka, *Rus.* Glybokaya. Chernivets'ka Oblast', W Ukraine *48.04N 25.55E*
120 K13 **Hlybokaye** *Rus.* Glubokoye. Vitsyebskaya Voblasts', N Belarus *55.08N 27.40E*
79 Q16 **Ho** SE Ghana *6.36N 0.28E*
178 Jj6 **Hoa Binh** Hoa Binh, N Vietnam *20.49N 105.19E*
85 E20 **Hoachanas** Hardap, C Namibia *23.52S 18.02E*
Hoai Nhơn *see* Bông Sơn
178 Jj8 **Hoa Lac** Quang Binh, C Vietnam *17.54N 106.24E*
178 J5 **Hoang Liên Sơn** ▲▲ N Vietnam
85 B17 **Hoanib** ≈ NW Namibia
35 S15 **Hoback Peak** ▲ Wyoming, C USA *43.04N 110.34W*
191 P17 **Hobart** *prev.* Hobarton, Hobart Town. *state capital* Tasmania, SE Australia *42.54S 147.18E*
28 L11 **Hobart** Oklahoma, C USA *35.01N 99.05W*
191 P17 **Hobart** ✕ Tasmania, SE Australia *42.52S 147.28E*
Hobarton/Hobart Town *see* Hobart
39 W14 **Hobbs** New Mexico, SW USA *32.42N 103.08W*
204 L12 **Hobbs Coast** *physical region* Antarctica
25 Z14 **Hobe Sound** Florida, SE USA *27.03N 80.08W*
Hobicaurikány *see* Uricani
56 E12 **Hobo** Huila, S Colombia *2.34N 75.28W*
101 G16 **Hoboken** Antwerpen, N Belgium *51.12N 4.22E*
164 K3 **Hoboksar** *var.* Hoboksar Mongol Zizhixian. Xinjiang Uygur Zizhiqu, NW China *46.48N 85.42E*
Hoboksar Mongol Zizhixian *see* Hoboksar
97 G21 **Hobro** Nordjylland, N Denmark *56.39N 9.51E*
23 X10 **Hobucken** North Carolina, SE USA *35.15N 76.31W*
97 O20 **Hoburgen** *headland* SE Sweden *56.54N 18.07E*
83 P15 **Hobyo** *It.* Obbia. Mudug, E Somalia *5.16N 48.24E*
111 R8 **Hochalmspitze** ▲ SW Austria *47.00N 13.19E*
111 Q4 **Hochburg** Oberösterreich, N Austria *48.10N 12.57E*
110 F8 **Hochdorf** Luzern, N Switzerland *47.10N 8.16E*
111 N8 **Hochfeiler** *It.* Gran Pilastro. ▲ Austria/Italy *46.59N 11.42E*
178 Jj14 **Hô Chi Minh** *var.* Ho Chi Minh City; *prev.* Saigon. S Vietnam *10.46N 106.43E*
Ho Chi Minh City *see* Hô Chi Minh
110 I7 **Höchst** Vorarlberg, NW Austria *47.28N 9.40E*
Höchstadt *see* Höchstadt an der Aisch
103 K19 **Höchstadt an der Aisch** *var.* Höchstadt. Bayern, C Germany *49.43N 10.48E*
110 L9 **Hochwilde** *It.* L'Altissima. ▲ Austria/Italy *46.45N 11.00E*
111 S7 **Hochwildstelle** ▲ C Austria *47.21N 13.53E*
33 T14 **Hocking River** ≈ Ohio, N USA
Hoctúm *see* Hoctún
43 X12 **Hoctún** *var.* Hoctúm. Yucatán, E Mexico *20.48N 89.13W*
Hodeida *see* Al Ḥudaydah
22 K6 **Hodgenville** Kentucky, S USA *37.34N 85.44W*
9 T17 **Hodgeville** Saskatchewan, S Canada *50.06N 106.55W*
78 L9 **Hodh ech Chargui** ◈ *region* E Mauritania
Hodh el Garbi *see* Hodh el Gharbi
78 J10 **Hodh el Gharbi** *var.* Hodh el Garbi. ◈ *region* S Mauritania
113 L25 **Hódmezővásárhely** Csongrád, SE Hungary *46.27N 20.17E*
76 J6 **Hodna, Chott El** *var.* Chott el-Hodna, *Ar.* Shatt al-Hodna. *salt lake* N Algeria
Hodna, Shatt al- *see* Hodna, Chott El
113 G19 **Hodonín** *Ger.* Göding. Jihomoravský Kraj, SE Czech Republic *48.51N 17.07E*
168 G6 **Hödrögö** Dzavhan, N Mongolia *48.51N 96.48E*
Hodság/Hodschag *see* Odžaci
41 R7 **Hodzana River** ≈ Alaska, USA
Hoei *see* Huy
101 H19 **Hoeilaart** Vlaams Brabant, C Belgium *50.46N 4.28E*
Hoë Karoo *see* Great Karoo
100 F12 **Hoek van Holland** *Eng.* Hook of Holland. Zuid-Holland, W Netherlands *52.00N 4.07E*
100 L11 **Hoenderloo** Gelderland, E Netherlands *52.08N 5.46E*
101 L18 **Hoensbroek** Limburg, SE Netherlands *50.55N 5.55E*
169 Y11 **Hoeryŏng** NE North Korea *42.23N 129.46E*
101 K18 **Hoeselt** Limburg, NE Belgium *50.49N 5.30E*
100 K11 **Hoevelaken** Gelderland, C Netherlands *52.10N 5.27E*
Hoey *see* Huy
103 M18 **Hof** Bayern, SE Germany *50.19N 11.55E*
Höfdhakaupstadhur *see* Skagaströnd
Hofei *see* Hefei
103 G18 **Hofheim am Taunus** Hessen, W Germany *50.04N 8.27E*
Hofmarkt *see* Odorheiu Secuiesc
94 L3 **Höfn** Austurland, SE Iceland *64.14N 15.17W*
96 N13 **Hofors** Gävleborg, C Sweden *60.33N 16.21E*
94 J6 **Hofsjökull** *glacier* C Iceland
94 J1 **Hofsós** Nordhurland Vestra, N Iceland *65.54N 19.25W*
170 Dd13 **Hōfu** Yamaguchi, Honshū, SW Japan *34.01N 131.34E*
Hofuf *see* Al Hufūf
97 J22 **Höganäs** Skåne, S Sweden *56.11N 12.39E*
191 P14 **Hogan Group** *island group* Tasmania, SE Australia
25 R4 **Hogansville** Georgia, SE USA *33.10N 84.55W*
41 P8 **Hogatza River** ≈ Alaska, USA
30 I14 **Hogback Mountain** ▲ Nebraska, C USA *41.40N 103.44W*
97 G14 **Høgevarde** ▲ S Norway *60.19N 9.27E*
Högfors *see* Karkkila
33 P5 **Hog Island** *island* Michigan, N USA
23 Y6 **Hog Island** *island* Virginia, NE USA
Hogoley Islands *see* Chuuk Islands
97 N20 **Högsby** Kalmar, S Sweden *57.10N 16.03E*

◆ Country
● Country Capital
◇ Dependent Territory
○ Dependent Territory Capital
◈ Administrative Region
✕ International Airport
▲ Mountain
▲▲ Mountain Range
Volcano
≈ River
◎ Lake
▣ Reservoir

Hogup Mountains – Huaihua

38 *K1* **Hogup Mountains** ▲▲ Utah, W USA
103 *E17* **Hohe Acht** ▲ W Germany *50.23N 7.00E*
Hohenelbe *see* Vrchlabí
110 *I7* **Hohenems** Vorarlberg, W Austria *47.22N 9.43E*
Hohenmauth *see* Vysoké Mýto
Hohensalza *see* Inowrocław
Hohenstadt *see* Zábřeh
Hohenstein in Ostpreussen *see* Olsztynek
22 *I9* **Hohenwald** Tennessee, S USA *35.33N 87.33W*
103 *L17* **Hohenwarte-Stausee** ⊠ C Germany
Hohes Venn *see* Hautes Fagnes
111 *Q8* **Hohe Tauern** ▲▲ W Austria
169 *O13* **Hohhot** ***var.*** Huhehot, Huhuohaote, ***Mong.*** Kukukhoto; ***prev.*** Kweisui, Kwesui. Nei Mongol Zizhiqu, N China *40.49N 111.37E*
105 *U6* **Hohneck** ▲ NE France *48.04N 7.01E*
79 *Q16* **Hohoe** E Ghana *7.07N 0.31E*
170 *D12* **Hōhoku** Yamaguchi, Honshū, SW Japan *34.15N 130.56E*
165 *O11* **Hoh Sai Hu** ◎ C China
165 *N11* **Hoh Xil Hu** ◎ C China
164 *L11* **Hoh Xil Shan** ▲▲ W China
178 *Kk10* **Hôi An** ***prev.*** Faifo. Quang Nam-Đa Năng, C Vietnam *15.54N 108.19E*
Hoï-Hao/Hoihow *see* Haikou
165 *S11* **Hoika** ***prev.*** Heka. Qinghai, W China *35.49N 99.49E*
83 *F17* **Hoima** W Uganda *1.25N 31.22E*
28 *L5* **Hoisington** Kansas, C USA *38.31N 98.46W*
152 *D12* **Hojagala** ***Rus.*** Khodzhalaka. Balkan Welaýaty, W Turkmenistan *38.46N 56.14E*
152 *M13* **Hojambaz** ***Rus.*** Khodzhambas. Lebap Welaýaty, E Turkmenistan *38.11N 64.33E*
97 *H23* **Højby** Fyn, C Denmark *55.19N 10.27E*
97 *F24* **Højer** Sønderjylland, SW Denmark *54.57N 8.43E*
170 *Ee14* **Hōjō** ***var.*** Hôzyô. Ehime, Shikoku, SW Japan *33.58N 132.47E*
192 *J3* **Hokianga Harbour** *inlet* SE Tasman Sea
193 *F17* **Hokitika** West Coast, South Island, NZ *42.43S 170.58E*
172 *P5* **Hokkai-dō** ⬖ *territory* Hokkaidō, NE Japan
172 *Oo5* **Hokkaidō** ***prev.*** Ezo, Yeso, Yezo. *island* NE Japan
97 *G15* **Hokksund** Buskerud, S Norway *59.46N 9.54E*
149 *S4* **Hokmābād** Khorāsān, N Iran *36.37N 57.34E*
Hokō *see* P'ohang
Hoko-guntō/Hoko-shotō *see* P'enghu Liehtao
Hoktemberyan *see* Armavir
96 *F13* **Hol** Buskerud, S Norway *60.36N 8.18E*
119 *R11* **Hola Prystan'** ***Rus.*** Golaya Pristan. Khersons'ka Oblast', S Ukraine *46.31N 32.31E*
97 *I23* **Holbæk** Vestsjælland, E Denmark *55.42N 11.42E*
168 *G6* **Holboo** Dzavhan, W Mongolia *48.35N 95.25E*
191 *P10* **Holbrook** New South Wales, SE Australia *35.45S 147.18E*
39 *N11* **Holbrook** Arizona, SW USA *34.54N 110.09W*
29 *S5* **Holden** Missouri, C USA *38.42N 93.59W*
38 *K5* **Holden** Utah, W USA *39.06N 112.16W*
29 *O11* **Holdenville** Oklahoma, C USA *35.04N 96.24W*
31 *O16* **Holdrege** Nebraska, C USA *40.28N 99.28W*
37 *X3* **Hole in the Mountain Peak** ▲ Nevada, W USA *40.54N 115.06W*
161 *G20* **Hole Narsipur** Karnātaka, W India *12.46N 76.13E*
113 *H18* **Holešov** ***Ger.*** Holleschau. Zlínský Kraj, E Czech Republic *49.19N 17.34E*
47 *N14* **Holetown** ***prev.*** Jamestown. W Barbados *13.09N 59.37W*
33 *Q12* **Holgate** Ohio, N USA *41.12N 84.06W*
46 *I7* **Holguín** Holguín, SE Cuba *20.51N 76.16W*
25 *V12* **Holiday** Florida, SE USA *28.11N 82.44W*
41 *O12* **Holitna River** ≈ Alaska, USA
96 *J13* **Höljes** Värmland, C Sweden *60.54N 12.34E*
111 *X3* **Hollabrunn** Niederösterreich, NE Austria *48.33N 16.06E*
38 *L3* **Holladay** Utah, W USA *40.39N 111.49W*
9 *X16* **Holland** Manitoba, S Canada *49.36N 98.52W*
33 *O9* **Holland** Michigan, N USA *42.47N 86.06W*
27 *T9* **Holland** Texas, SW USA *30.52N 97.24W*
Holland *see* Netherlands
24 *K4* **Hollandale** Mississippi, S USA *33.10N 90.51W*
Hollandia *see* Jayapura
Hollandsch Diep *see* Hollands Diep
101 *H14* **Hollands Diep** ***var.*** Hollandsch Diep. *channel* SW Netherlands
Holleschau *see* Holešov
27 *R5* **Holliday** Texas, SW USA *33.49N 98.41W*
20 *E15* **Hollidaysburg** Pennsylvania, NE USA *40.24N 78.22W*
23 *S6* **Hollins** Virginia, NE USA *37.20N 79.56W*
28 *J12* **Hollis** Oklahoma, C USA *34.42N 99.54W*
37 *O10* **Hollister** California, W USA *36.51N 121.25W*
29 *T8* **Hollister** Missouri, C USA *36.37N 93.13W*
95 *M19* **Hollola** Etelä-Suomi, S Finland *60.59N 25.31E*
100 *K4* **Hollum** Friesland, N Netherlands *53.27N 5.38E*
97 *J23* **Höllviksnäs** Skåne, S Sweden *55.25N 12.57E*
39 *W6* **Holly** Colorado, C USA *38.03N 102.07W*
33 *R9* **Holly** Michigan, N USA *42.47N 83.37W*
23 *S14* **Holly Hill** South Carolina, SE USA *33.19N 80.24W*
23 *W11* **Holly Ridge** North Carolina, SE USA *34.31N 77.31W*
24 *L1* **Holly Springs** Mississippi, S USA *34.46N 89.25W*
25 *Z15* **Hollywood** Florida, SE USA *26.00N 80.09W*
15 *I2* **Holman** Victoria Island, Northwest Territories, N Canada *70.42N 117.45W*
94 *I2* **Hólmavík** Vestfirdhir, NW Iceland *65.42N 21.43W*
32 *J7* **Holmen** Wisconsin, N USA *43.57N 91.14W*
25 *R8* **Holmes Creek** ≈ Alabama/Florida, SE USA
97 *H16* **Holmestrand** Vestfold, S Norway *59.28N 10.19E*
95 *J16* **Holmön** *island* N Sweden
97 *E22* **Holmsland Klit** *beach* W Denmark
95 *J16* **Holmsund** Västerbotten, N Sweden *63.42N 20.25E*
97 *Q18* **Holmudden** *headland* SE Sweden *57.59N 19.14E*
194 *L15* **Holnicote Bay** *headland* SW PNG *8.30S 148.18E*
144 *F10* **Holon** ***var.*** Kholon. Tel Aviv, C Israel *32.01N 34.46E*
119 *P8* **Holovanivs'k** ***Rus.*** Golovanevsk. Kirovohrads'ka Oblast', C Ukraine *48.21N 30.26E*
97 *F21* **Holstebro** Ringkøbing, W Denmark *56.22N 8.37E*
97 *F23* **Holsted** Ribe, W Denmark *55.30N 8.54E*
31 *T13* **Holstein** Iowa, C USA *42.29N 95.32W*
Holsteinborg/Holsteinsborg/Holstenborg/Holstensborg *see* Sisimiut
23 *O8* **Holston River** ≈ Tennessee, S USA
33 *Q9* **Holt** Michigan, N USA *42.38N 84.31W*
100 *N10* **Holten** Overijssel, E Netherlands *52.16N 6.25E*
29 *P3* **Holton** Kansas, C USA *39.28N 95.44W*
29 *U5* **Holts Summit** Missouri, C USA *38.38N 92.07W*
37 *X17* **Holtville** California, W USA *32.48N 115.22W*
100 *L5* **Holwerd** ***Fris.*** Holwert. Friesland, N Netherlands *53.22N 5.51E*
Holwert *see* Holwerd
41 *O11* **Holy Cross** Alaska, USA *62.12N 159.46W*
39 *R4* **Holy Cross, Mount Of The** ▲ Colorado, C USA *39.28N 106.28W*
99 *I18* **Holyhead** ***Wel.*** Caer Gybi. NW Wales, UK *53.19N 4.37W*
99 *H18* **Holy Island** *island* NW Wales, UK
98 *L12* **Holy Island** *island* NE England, UK
39 *W3* **Holyoke** Colorado, C USA *40.31N 102.18W*
20 *M11* **Holyoke** Massachusetts, NE USA *42.12N 72.37W*
103 *I14* **Holzminden** Niedersachsen, C Germany *51.49N 9.27E*
83 *G19* **Homa Bay** Nyanza, W Kenya *0.31S 34.30E*
Homāyūnshahr *see* Khomeynīshahr
79 *P11* **Hombori** Mopti, S Mali *15.13N 1.39W*
103 *E20* **Homburg** Saarland, SW Germany *49.19N 7.19E*
16 *Nn1* **Home Bay** *bay* Baffin Bay, Nunavut, NE Canada
Homenau *see* Humenné
41 *Q13* **Homer** Alaska, USA *59.38N 151.33W*
24 *H4* **Homer** Louisiana, S USA *32.47N 93.03W*
20 *H10* **Homer** New York, NE USA *42.38N 76.10W*
25 *V7* **Homerville** Georgia, SE USA *31.02N 82.45W*
25 *Y16* **Homestead** Florida, SE USA *25.28N 80.28W*
29 *O9* **Hominy** Oklahoma, C USA *36.24N 96.24W*
96 *H8* **Hommelvik** Sør-Trøndelag, S Norway *63.24N 10.46E*
97 *C16* **Hommersåk** Rogaland, S Norway *58.55N 5.51E*
161 *H15* **Homnābād** Karnātaka, C India *17.46N 77.08E*
24 *J7* **Homochitto River** ≈ Mississippi, S USA
85 *N20* **Homoine** Inhambane, SE Mozambique *23.51S 35.04E*
114 *O12* **Homoljske Planine** ▲▲ E Serbia and Montenegro (Yugoslavia)
Homonna *see* Humenné
Homs *see* Al Khums, Libya
Homs *see* Ḥimṣ, Syria
121 *P19* **Homyel'** ***Rus.*** Gomel'. Homyel'skaya Voblasts', SE Belarus *52.24N 31.00E*
120 *L12* **Homyel'** Vitsyebskaya Voblasts', N Belarus *55.20N 28.52E*
121 *L19* **Homyel'skaya Voblasts'** ***prev. Rus.*** Gomel'skaya Oblast'. ⬖ *province* SE Belarus
Honan *see* Henan, China
Honan *see* Luoyang, China
172 *Pp6* **Honbetsu** Hokkaidō, NE Japan *43.09N 143.46E*
Honctő *see* Gurahonț
56 *E9* **Honda** Tolima, C Colombia *5.12N 74.45W*
85 *D24* **Hondeklip** ***Afr.*** Hondeklipbaai. Northern Cape, W South Africa *30.15S 17.17E*
Hondeklipbaai *see* Hondeklip
9 *Q13* **Hondo** Alberta, W Canada *54.43N 113.14W*
170 *C14* **Hondo** Kumamoto, Shimo-jima, SW Japan *32.27N 130.10E*
27 *Q12* **Hondo** Texas, SW USA *29.21N 99.08W*
44 *G1* **Hondo** ≈ Central America
Hondo *see* Honshū
44 *G6* **Honduras** ***off.*** Republic of Honduras. ◆ *republic* Central America
Honduras, Golfo de *see* Honduras, Gulf of
44 *H4* **Honduras, Gulf of** ***Sp.*** Golfo de Honduras. *gulf* W Caribbean Sea
9 *V12* **Hone** Manitoba, C Canada *56.13N 101.12W*
23 *P12* **Honea Path** South Carolina, SE USA *34.27N 82.23W*
97 *H14* **Hønefoss** Buskerud, S Norway *60.10N 10.15E*
33 *S12* **Honey Creek** ≈ Ohio, N USA
27 *V5* **Honey Grove** Texas, SW USA *33.34N 95.54W*
37 *Q4* **Honey Lake** ◎ California, W USA
104 *L4* **Honfleur** Calvados, N France *49.25N 0.13E*
Hon Gai *see* Hông Gai
167 *O8* **Hong'an** ***prev.*** Huang'an. Hubei, C China *31.20N 114.43E*
Hongay *see* Hông Gai
178 *K6* **Hông Gai** ***var.*** Hon Gai, Hongay. Quang Ninh, N Vietnam *20.57N 107.06E*
167 *O15* **Honghai Wan** *bay* N South China Sea
Hông Hà, Sông *see* Red River
167 *O7* **Hong He** ≈ C China
167 *N9* **Hong Hu** ◎ C China
166 *L11* **Hongjiang** Hunan, S China *27.09N 109.58E*
Hongjiang *see* Wangcang
167 *O15* **Hong Kong** ***Chin.*** Xianggang. S China *22.16N 114.09E*
166 *L4* **Hongliu He** ≈ C China
165 *P8* **Hongliuwan** ***var.*** Aksay, Aksay Kazakzu Zizhixian. Gansu, N China *39.40N 94.16E*
165 *P7* **Hongliuyuan** Gansu, N China *41.01N 95.24E*
169 *O9* **Hongor** Dornogovĭ, SE Mongolia *45.49N 111.20E*
167 *S8* **Hongqiao** ✕ (Shanghai) Shanghai Shi, E China *31.28N 121.08E*
166 *K14* **Hongshui He** ≈ S China
166 *M5* **Hongtong** Shanxi, C China *36.30N 111.42E*
170 *G16* **Hongū** Wakayama, Honshū, SW Japan *33.50N 135.42E*
Honguedo, Détroit d' *see* Honguedo Passage
13 *Y5* **Honguedo Passage** ***var.*** Honguedo Strait, ***Fr.*** Détroit d'Honguedo. *strait* Québec, E Canada
Honguedo Strait *see* Honguedo Passage
Hongwan *see* Hongwansi
165 *S8* **Hongwansi** ***var.*** Sunan, Sunan Yugurzu Zizhixian ***prev.*** Hongwan. Gansu, N China *38.55N 99.29E*
169 *X13* **Hongwŏn** E North Korea *40.03N 127.54E*
166 *H7* **Hongyuan** ***var.*** Qiongxi, ***prev.*** Hurama. Sichuan, C China *32.49N 102.40E*
167 *Q7* **Hongze Hu** ***var.*** Hung-tse Hu. ◎ E China
195 *W16* **Honiara** ● (Solomon Islands) Guadalcanal, C Solomon Islands *9.27S 159.55E*
171 *Ll11* **Honjō** ***var.*** Honzyô. Akita, Honshū, C Japan *39.22N 140.03E*
95 *K18* **Honkajoki** Länsi-Suomi, W Finland *62.00N 22.15E*
171 *Ii16* **Honkawane** Shizuoka, Honshū, S Japan *35.07N 138.07E*
94 *K7* **Honningsvåg** Finnmark, N Norway *70.58N 25.58E*
97 *I19* **Hönö** Västra Götaland, S Sweden *57.42N 11.39E*
40 *G11* **Honoka'a** ***var.*** Honokaa. Hawai'i, USA, C Pacific Ocean *20.04N 155.27W*
40 *D9* **Honolulu** ◐ O'ahu, Hawai'i, USA, C Pacific Ocean *21.18N 157.51W*
40 *H11* **Honomū** ***var.*** Honomu. Hawai'i, USA, C Pacific Ocean *19.51N 155.06W*
107 *P10* **Honrubia** Castilla-La Mancha, C Spain *39.36N 2.16W*
171 *I15* **Honshū** ***var.*** Hondo, Honsyû. *island* SW Japan
Honsyû *see* Honshū
Honte *see* Westerschelde
Honzyô *see* Honjō
15 *Ii5* **Hood** ≈ Nunavut, NW Canada
Hood Island *see* Española, Isla
34 *H11* **Hood, Mount** ▲ Oregon, NW USA *45.22N 121.41W*
194 *K16* **Hood Point** *headland* S PNG *10.04S 147.42E*
34 *H11* **Hood River** Oregon, NW USA *45.42N 121.31W*
100 *H10* **Hoofddorp** Noord-Holland, W Netherlands *52.18N 4.40E*
101 *G15* **Hoogerheide** Noord-Brabant, S Netherlands *51.25N 4.19E*
100 *N8* **Hoogeveen** Drenthe, NE Netherlands *52.43N 6.30E*
100 *O6* **Hoogezand-Sappemeer** Groningen, NE Netherlands *53.10N 6.46E*
100 *J8* **Hoogkarspel** Noord-Holland, NW Netherlands *52.42N 4.59E*
100 *N5* **Hoogkerk** Groningen, NE Netherlands *53.13N 6.30E*
100 *G13* **Hoogvliet** Zuid-Holland, SW Netherlands *51.51N 4.23E*
28 *I8* **Hooker** Oklahoma, C USA *36.51N 101.12W*
99 *E21* **Hook Head** ***Ir.*** Rinn Duáin. *headland* SE Ireland *52.07N 6.55W*
Hook of Holland *see* Hoek van Holland
168 *J9* **Hoolt** Övörhangay, C Mongolia *45.31N 103.06E*
41 *W13* **Hoonah** Chichagof Island, Alaska, USA *58.05N 135.21W*
40 *L11* **Hooper Bay** Alaska, USA *61.31N 166.06W*
33 *N13* **Hoopeston** Illinois, N USA *40.28N 87.40W*
97 *K22* **Höör** Skåne, S Sweden *55.55N 13.33E*
100 *I9* **Hoorn** Noord-Holland, NW Netherlands *52.37N 5.04E*
20 *L10* **Hoosic River** ≈ New York, NE USA
Hoosier State *see* Indiana
37 *Y11* **Hoover Dam** *dam* Arizona/Nevada, W USA *36.01N 114.44W*
168 *I9* **Höövör** Övörhangay, C Mongolia *45.10N 101.19E*
143 *Q11* **Hopa** Artvin, NE Turkey *41.23N 41.27E*
20 *J14* **Hopatcong** New Jersey, NE USA *40.55N 74.39W*
8 *M17* **Hope** British Columbia, SW Canada *49.21N 121.28W*
41 *R12* **Hope** Alaska, USA *60.55N 149.38W*
29 *T14* **Hope** Arkansas, C USA *33.40N 93.35W*
33 *P14* **Hope** Indiana, N USA *39.18N 85.46W*
31 *Q5* **Hope** North Dakota, N USA *47.18N 97.42W*
11 *Q7* **Hopedale** Newfoundland and Labrador, NE Canada *55.25N 60.14W*
Hopeh/Hopei *see* Hebei
188 *K13* **Hope, Lake** *salt lake* Western Australia
43 *X13* **Hopelchén** Campeche, SE Mexico *19.44N 89.52W*
23 *U11* **Hope Mills** North Carolina, SE USA *34.58N 78.57W*
191 *O7* **Hope, Mount** New South Wales, SE Australia *32.49S 145.55E*
94 *P4* **Hopen** *island* SE Svalbard
207 *Q4* **Hope, Point** *headland* Alaska, USA
10 *M3* **Hopes Advance, Cap** *headland* Québec, NE Canada *61.07N 69.30W*
190 *L10* **Hopetoun** Victoria, SE Australia *35.46S 142.23E*
85 *H23* **Hopetown** Northern Cape, W South Africa *29.38S 24.06E*
23 *W6* **Hopewell** Virginia, NE USA *37.16N 77.15W*
111 *O7* **Hopfgarten-im-Brixental** Tirol, W Austria *47.28N 12.14E*
189 *N8* **Hopkins Lake** *salt lake* Western Australia
190 *M12* **Hopkins River** ≈ Victoria, SE Australia
22 *I7* **Hopkinsville** Kentucky, S USA *36.52N 87.29W*
36 *M6* **Hopland** California, W USA *38.58N 123.09W*
97 *G24* **Hoptrup** Sønderjylland, SW Denmark *55.09N 9.27E*
Hoqin Zuoyi Zhongji *see* Baokang
34 *F9* **Hoquiam** Washington, NW USA *46.58N 123.53W*
31 *R6* **Horace** North Dakota, N USA *46.44N 96.54W*
143 *R12* **Horasan** Erzurum, NE Turkey *40.03N 42.10E*
103 *G22* **Horb am Neckar** Baden-Württemberg, S Germany *48.27N 8.42E*
97 *K23* **Hörby** Skåne, S Sweden *55.50N 13.42E*
45 *P16* **Horconcitos** Chiriquí, W Panama *8.17N 82.10W*
97 *C14* **Hordaland** ⬖ *county* S Norway
118 *H13* **Horezu** Vâlcea, SW Romania *45.06N 24.00E*
110 *G7* **Horgen** Zürich, N Switzerland *47.16N 8.36E*
168 *I7* **Horgo** Arhangay, C Mongolia *48.06N 99.52E*
Hōrin *see* Fenglin
169 *O13* **Horinger** Nei Mongol Zizhiqu, N China *40.23N 111.48E*
168 *I9* **Horiult** Bayanhongor, C Mongolia *45.09N 100.50E*
9 *U17* **Horizon** Saskatchewan, S Canada *49.33N 105.05W*
199 *J10* **Horizon Bank** *undersea feature* S Pacific Ocean
199 *Jj11* **Horizon Deep** *undersea feature* W Pacific Ocean
97 *L14* **Hörken** Örebro, S Sweden *60.03N 14.55E*
121 *O15* **Horki** ***Rus.*** Gorki. Mahilyowskaya Voblasts', E Belarus *54.17N 30.59E*
205 *O10* **Horlick Mountains** ▲▲ Antarctica
119 *X7* **Horlivka** ***Rom.*** Adâncata, ***Rus.*** Gorlovka. Donets'ka Oblast', E Ukraine *48.19N 38.04E*
149 *V11* **Ḥormak** Sīstān va Balūchestān, SE Iran *30.00N 60.50E*
149 *R13* **Hormozgān** ***off.*** Ostān-e Hormozgān. ⬖ *province* S Iran
Hormoz, Tangeh-ye *see* Hormuz, Strait of
147 *W6* **Hormuz, Strait of** ***var.*** Strait of Ormuz, ***Per.*** Tangeh-ye Hormoz. *strait* Iran/Oman
111 *W2* **Horn** Niederösterreich, NE Austria *48.39N 15.37E*
97 *M18* **Horn** Östergötland, S Sweden *57.54N 15.49E*
15 *Hh8* **Horn** ≈ Northwest Territories, NW Canada
Hornád *see* Hernád
15 *H3* **Hornaday** ≈ Northwest Territories, NW Canada
94 *H13* **Hornavan** ◎ N Sweden
67 *C24* **Hornby Mountains** *hill range* West Falkland, Falkland Islands
Horn, Cape *see* Hornos, Cabo de
99 *O18* **Horncastle** E England, UK *53.12N 0.07W*
97 *N14* **Horndal** Dalarna, C Sweden *60.16N 16.25E*
95 *I16* **Hörnefors** Västerbotten, N Sweden *63.37N 19.54E*
20 *F11* **Hornell** New York, NE USA *42.19N 77.38W*
Horné Nové Mesto *see* Kysucké Nové Mesto
10 *F12* **Hornepayne** Ontario, S Canada *49.13N 84.48W*
96 *D10* **Hornindalsvatnet** ◎ S Norway
103 *G22* **Hornisgrinde** ▲ SW Germany *48.37N 8.13E*
24 *M9* **Horn Island** *island* Mississippi, S USA
Hornja Łužica *see* Oberlausitz
65 *J26* **Hornos, Cabo de** ***Eng.*** Cape Horn. *headland* S Chile *55.52S 67.00W*
119 *S10* **Hornostayivka** Khersons'ka Oblast', S Ukraine *47.00N 33.42E*
191 *T9* **Hornsby** New South Wales, SE Australia *33.44S 151.08E*
99 *O16* **Hornsea** E England, UK *53.54N 0.09W*
96 *O11* **Hornslandet** *peninsula* C Sweden
97 *H22* **Hornslet** Århus, C Denmark *56.19N 10.19E*
94 *O4* **Hornsundtind** ▲ S Svalbard *76.54N 16.07E*
Horochów *see* Horokhiv
118 *J7* **Horodenka** ***Rus.*** Gorodenka. Ivano-Frankivs'ka Oblast', W Ukraine *48.41N 25.28E*
119 *Q2* **Horodnya** ***Rus.*** Gorodnya. Chernihivs'ka Oblast', NE Ukraine *51.54N 31.30E*
118 *K6* **Horodok** Khmel'nyts'ka Oblast', W Ukraine *49.10N 26.34E*
118 *H5* **Horodok** ***Pol.*** Gródek Jagielloński, ***Rus.*** Gorodok, Gorodok Yagellonski. L'vivs'ka Oblast', NW Ukraine *49.48N 23.39E*
119 *Q6* **Horodyshche** ***Rus.*** Gorodishche. Cherkas'ka Oblast', C Ukraine *49.18N 31.27E*
172 *P4* **Horokanai** Hokkaidō, NE Japan *44.02N 142.08E*
118 *J4* **Horokhiv** ***Pol.*** Horochów, ***Rus.*** Gorokhov. Volyns'ka Oblast', NW Ukraine *50.31N 24.50E*
172 *P7* **Horoshiri-dake** ***var.*** Horosiri Dake. ▲ Hokkaidō, N Japan *42.43N 142.41E*
Horosiri Dake *see* Horoshiri-dake
113 *C17* **Hořovice** ***Ger.*** Horowitz. Středočeský Kraj, W Czech Republic *49.49N 13.53E*
Horowitz *see* Hořovice
Horqin Zuoyi Houqi *see* Ganjig
Horqin Zuoyi Zhongji *see* Bayan Huxu
64 *O5* **Horqueta** Concepción, C Paraguay *23.23S 57.04W*
57 *O12* **Horqueta Minas** Amazonas, S Venezuela *2.19N 63.31W*
97 *J20* **Horred** Västra Götaland, S Sweden *57.22N 12.25E*
157 *J19* **Horsburgh Atoll** *atoll* N Maldives
22 *K7* **Horse Cave** Kentucky, S USA *37.10N 85.54W*
39 *V6* **Horse Creek** ≈ Colorado, C USA
29 *S6* **Horse Creek** ≈ Missouri, C USA
20 *G11* **Horseheads** New York, NE USA *42.10N 76.49W*
39 *P13* **Horse Mount** ▲ New Mexico, SW USA *33.58N 108.10W*
97 *G22* **Horsens** Vejle, C Denmark *55.52N 9.52E*
67 *F25* **Horse Pasture Point** *headland* W Saint Helena *15.57S 5.46W*
35 *N13* **Horseshoe Bend** Idaho, NW USA *43.55N 116.11W*
38 *L13* **Horseshoe Reservoir** ⊠ Arizona, SW USA
66 *M9* **Horseshoe Seamounts** *undersea feature* E Atlantic Ocean
190 *L11* **Horsham** Victoria, SE Australia *36.44S 142.13E*
99 *O23* **Horsham** SE England, UK *51.01N 0.21W*
101 *M15* **Horst** Limburg, SE Netherlands *51.29N 6.04E*
66 *N2* **Horta** Faial, Azores, Portugal, NE Atlantic Ocean *38.31N 28.39W*
97 *H16* **Horten** Vestfold, S Norway *59.25N 10.24E*
113 *M23* **Hortobágy-Berettyó** ≈ E Hungary
29 *Q3* **Horton** Kansas, C USA *39.39N 95.31W*
15 *H3* **Horton** ≈ Northwest Territories, NW Canada
97 *I23* **Hørve** Vestsjælland, E Denmark *55.46N 11.28E*
97 *L22* **Hörvik** Blekinge, S Sweden *56.01N 14.45E*
144 *E11* **Horvot Haluza** ***var.*** Khorvot Khalutsa. *ruins* Southern, S Israel *30.49N 34.50E*
12 *E7* **Horwood Lake** ◎ Ontario, S Canada
118 *K4* **Horyn'** ***Rus.*** Goryn. ≈ NW Ukraine
83 *I14* **Hosa'ina** ***var.*** Hosseina, ***It.*** Hosanna. Southern, S Ethiopia *7.38N 37.58E*
Hosanna *see* Hosa'ina
103 *H18* **Hösbach** Bayern, C Germany *50.00N 9.12E*
Hose Mountains *see* Hose, Pegunungan
174 *Mm6* **Hose, Pegunungan** ***var.*** Hose Mountains. ▲▲ East Malaysia
154 *L15* **Hoshāb** Baluchistān, SW Pakistan *26.01N 63.51E*
160 *H10* **Hoshangābād** Madhya Pradesh, C India *22.43N 77.45E*
118 *L4* **Hoshcha** Rivnens'ka Oblast', NW Ukraine *50.37N 26.38E*
158 *I7* **Hoshiārpur** Punjab, NW India *31.35N 75.57E*
168 *J7* **Höshööt** Arhangay, C Mongolia *48.06N 102.34E*
101 *M23* **Hosingen** Diekirch, NE Luxembourg *50.01N 6.04E*
195 *N12* **Hoskins** New Britain, E PNG *5.28S 150.25E*
161 *G17* **Hospet** Karnātaka, C India *15.16N 76.19E*
106 *K4* **Hospital de Orbigo** Castilla-León, N Spain *42.27N 5.52W*
Hospitalet *see* L'Hospitalet de Llobregat
94 *N13* **Hossa** Oulu, E Finland *65.28N 29.36E*
Hosseina *see* Hosa'ina
Hosszúmezjő *see* Câmpulung Moldovenesc
65 *I25* **Hoste, Isla** *island* S Chile
119 *O4* **Hostomel'** ***Rus.*** Gostomel'. Kyyivs'ka Oblast', N Ukraine *50.40N 30.15E*
161 *H20* **Hosūr** Tamil Nādu, SE India *12.45N 77.51E*
178 *H8* **Hot** Chiang Mai, NW Thailand *18.14N 98.35E*
164 *G10* **Hotan** ***var.*** Khotan, ***Chin.*** Ho-t'ien. Xinjiang Uygur Zizhiqu, NW China *37.10N 79.51E*
164 *H9* **Hotan He** ≈ NW China
85 *G22* **Hotazel** Northern Cape, N South Africa *27.12S 22.58E*
39 *Q5* **Hotchkiss** Colorado, C USA *38.47N 107.43W*
37 *V7* **Hot Creek Range** ▲▲ Nevada, W USA
Hote *see* Hoti
176 *U11* **Hoti** ***var.*** Hote. Pulau Seram, E Indonesia *2.58S 130.19E*
Ho-t'ien *see* Hotan
Hotin *see* Khotyn
95 *H15* **Hoting** Jämtland, C Sweden *64.07N 16.14E*
168 *L14* **Hotong Qagan Nur** ◎ N China
168 *J8* **Hotont** Arhangay, C Mongolia *47.21N 102.27E*
29 *T12* **Hot Springs** Arkansas, C USA *34.30N 93.03W*
30 *J11* **Hot Springs** South Dakota, N USA *43.25N 103.28W*
23 *S5* **Hot Springs** Virginia, NE USA *38.00N 79.50W*
37 *Q4* **Hot Springs Peak** ▲ California, W USA *40.23N 120.06W*
29 *T12* **Hot Springs Village** Arkansas, C USA *34.39N 93.03W*
Hotspur Bank *see* Hotspur Seamount
67 *J16* **Hotspur Seamount** ***var.*** Hotspur Bank. *undersea feature* C Atlantic Ocean *18.00S 35.00W*
15 *Hh6* **Hottah Lake** ◎ Northwest Territories, NW Canada
46 *K9* **Hotte, Massif de la** ▲▲ SW Haiti
101 *K21* **Hotton** Luxembourg, SE Belgium *50.18N 5.25E*
Hötzing *see* Hațeg
197 *I6* **Houaïlou** Province Nord, C New Caledonia *21.17S 165.37E*
76 *K5* **Houari Boumediène** ✕ (Alger) N Algeria *36.38N 3.15E*
178 *Hh6* **Houayxay** ***var.*** Ban Houayxay, Ban Houei Sai. Bokèo, N Laos *20.16N 100.27E*
105 *N5* **Houdan** Yvelines, N France *48.48N 1.36E*
101 *F20* **Houdeng-Goegnies** ***var.*** Houdeng-Gœgnies. Hainaut, S Belgium *50.28N 4.10E*
104 *K14* **Houeillès** Lot-et-Garonne, SW France *44.15N 0.02E*
101 *L22* **Houffalize** Luxembourg, SE Belgium *50.08N 5.47E*
32 *M3* **Houghton** Michigan, N USA *41.55N 84.37W*
33 *Q7* **Houghton Lake** Michigan, N USA *44.18N 84.45W*
33 *Q7* **Houghton Lake** ◎ Michigan, N USA
21 *T3* **Houlton** Maine, NE USA *46.09N 67.49W*
166 *M5* **Houma** Shanxi, C China *35.33N 111.19E*
200 *Q15* **Houma** 'Eua, C Tonga *21.10S 175.17W*
200 *R16* **Houma** Tongatapu, S Tonga *21.18S 174.55W*
24 *J10* **Houma** Louisiana, S USA *29.34N 90.43W*
200 *Qq16* **Houma Taloa** *headland* Tongatapu, S Tonga *21.16S 175.07W*
79 *O13* **Houndé** SW Burkina *11.34N 3.31W*
104 *J12* **Hourtin-Carcans, Lac d'** ◎ SW France
38 *J5* **House Range** ▲▲ Utah, W USA
8 *K13* **Houston** British Columbia, SW Canada *54.24N 126.39W*
41 *R11* **Houston** Alaska, USA *61.37N 149.50W*
31 *X10* **Houston** Minnesota, N USA *43.45N 91.34W*
24 *M3* **Houston** Mississippi, S USA *33.54N 89.00W*
29 *V7* **Houston** Missouri, C USA *37.19N 91.57W*
27 *W11* **Houston** Texas, SW USA *29.45N 95.21W*
27 *W11* **Houston** ✕ Texas, SW USA *30.03N 95.18W*
100 *J12* **Houten** Utrecht, C Netherlands *52.01N 5.10E*
101 *K17* **Houthalen** Limburg, NE Belgium *51.01N 5.22E*
101 *I22* **Houyet** Namur, SE Belgium *50.10N 5.00E*
97 *H22* **Hov** Århus, C Denmark *55.54N 10.13E*
97 *L17* **Hova** Västra Götaland, S Sweden *58.52N 14.13E*
168 *E6* **Hovd** ***var.*** Khovd, Kobdo; ***prev.*** Jirgalanta. Hovd, W Mongolia *47.58N 91.40E*
168 *J10* **Hovd** Övörhangay, C Mongolia *44.43N 102.08E*
168 *E7* **Hovd** ⬖ *province* W Mongolia
168 *C5* **Hovd Gol** ≈ NW Mongolia
99 *O23* **Hove** SE England, UK *50.49N 0.10W*
31 *N8* **Hoven** South Dakota, N USA *45.12N 99.47W*
118 *I8* **Hoverla, Hora** ***Rus.*** Gora Goverla. ▲ W Ukraine *48.09N 24.30E*
168 *H8* **Höviyn Am** Bayanhongor, C Mongolia *47.08N 98.41E*
97 *M21* **Hovmantorp** Kronoberg, S Sweden *56.46N 15.07E*
169 *N11* **Hövsgöl** Dornogovĭ, SE Mongolia *43.35N 109.40E*
168 *I5* **Hövsgöl** ⬖ *province* N Mongolia
Hovsgol, Lake *see* Hövsgöl Nuur
168 *J5* **Hövsgöl Nuur** ***var.*** Lake Hovsgol. ◎ N Mongolia
80 *L9* **Howa, Ouadi** ***var.*** Wādi Howar. ≈ Chad/Sudan ***see also*** Howar, Wādi
29 *P7* **Howard** Kansas, C USA *37.28N 96.15W*
31 *Q10* **Howard** South Dakota, N USA *43.58N 97.31W*
27 *N10* **Howard Draw** *valley* Texas, SW USA
31 *U8* **Howard Lake** Minnesota, N USA *45.03N 94.03W*
82 *B8* **Howar, Wādi** ***var.*** Ouadi Howa. ≈ Chad/Sudan ***see also*** Howa, Ouadi
27 *U5* **Howe** Texas, SW USA *33.29N 96.38W*
191 *R12* **Howe, Cape** *headland* New South Wales/Victoria, SE Australia *37.30S 149.58E*
33 *R9* **Howell** Michigan, N USA *42.36N 83.55W*
30 *L9* **Howes** South Dakota, N USA *44.34N 102.03W*
85 *K23* **Howick** KwaZulu/Natal, E South Africa *29.29S 30.13E*
Howrah *see* Hāora
29 *W9* **Hoxie** Arkansas, C USA *36.03N 90.58W*
28 *J3* **Hoxie** Kansas, C USA *39.21N 100.26W*
103 *I14* **Höxter** Nordrhein-Westfalen, W Germany *51.46N 9.22E*
164 *K6* **Hoxud** Xinjiang Uygur Zizhiqu, NW China *42.18N 86.51E*
98 *J5* **Hoy** *island* N Scotland, UK
45 *S17* **Hoya, Cerro** ▲ S Panama *7.22N 80.38W*
96 *D12* **Høyanger** Sogn og Fjordane, S Norway *61.13N 6.04E*
103 *P15* **Hoyerswerda** ***Lus.*** Wojerecy. Sachsen, E Germany *51.27N 14.17E*
170 *Dd15* **Hōyo-kaikyō** ***var.*** Hayasui-seto. *strait* SW Japan
106 *J8* **Hoyos** Extremadura, W Spain *40.10N 6.43W*
31 *W4* **Hoyt Lakes** Minnesota, N USA *47.31N 92.08W*
89 *V2* **Hoyvík** Streymoy, N Faeroe Islands
143 *O14* **Hozat** Tunceli, E Turkey *39.09N 39.13E*
Hôzyô *see* Hōjō
113 *F16* **Hradec Králové** ***Ger.*** Königgrätz. Královéhradecký Kraj, N Czech Republic *50.13N 15.49E*
Hradecký Kraj *see* Královéhradecký Kraj
113 *B16* **Hradiště** ***Ger.*** Burgstadlberg. ▲ NW Czech Republic *50.12N 13.04E*
119 *R6* **Hradyz'k** ***Rus.*** Gradizhsk. Poltavs'ka Oblast', NE Ukraine *49.12N 33.08E*
121 *M16* **Hradzyanka** ***Rus.*** Grodzyanka. Mahilyowskaya Voblasts', E Belarus *53.36N 28.47E*
121 *F16* **Hrandzichy** ***Rus.*** Grandichi. Hrodzyenskaya Voblasts', W Belarus *53.43N 23.50E*
113 *H18* **Hranice** ***Ger.*** Mährisch-Weisskirchen. Olomoucký Kraj, E Czech Republic *49.34N 17.45E*
114 *I13* **Hrasnica** Federacija Bosna I Hercegovina, SE Bosnia and Herzegovina *43.48N 18.19E*
111 *V11* **Hrastnik** C Slovenia *46.09N 15.08E*
143 *U12* **Hrazdan** ***Rus.*** Razdan. C Armenia *40.30N 44.50E*
143 *T12* **Hrazdan** ***var.*** Zanga, ***Rus.*** Razdan. ≈ C Armenia
119 *R5* **Hrebinka** ***Rus.*** Grebenka. Poltavs'ka Oblast', NE Ukraine *50.08N 32.27E*
121 *K17* **Hresk** ***Rus.*** Gresk. Minskaya Voblasts', C Belarus *53.10N 27.28E*
Hrisoupoli *see* Chrysoúpoli
121 *F16* **Hrodna** ***Pol.*** Grodno. Hrodzyenskaya Voblasts', W Belarus *53.40N 23.50E*
121 *F16* **Hrodzyenskaya Voblasts'** ***prev. Rus.*** Grodnenskaya Oblast'. ⬖ *province* W Belarus
113 *J21* **Hron** ***Ger.*** Gran, ***Hung.*** Garam. ≈ C Slovakia
113 *Q14* **Hrubieszów** ***Rus.*** Grubeshov. Lubelskie, E Poland *50.48N 23.54E*
114 *F13* **Hrvace** Split-Dalmacija, SE Croatia *43.46N 16.35E*
Hrvatska *see* Croatia
114 *F10* **Hrvatska Kostajnica** ***var.*** Kostajnica. Sisak-Moslavina, C Croatia *45.14N 16.35E*
Hrvatsko Grahovo *see* Bosansko Grahovo
118 *K6* **Hrymayliv** ***Pol.*** Gízymałów, ***Rus.*** Grimaylov. Ternopil's'ka Oblast', W Ukraine *49.18N 26.02E*
178 *H4* **Hsenwi** Shan State, E Myanmar *23.20N 97.59E*
Hsia-men *see* Xiamen
Hsiang-t'an *see* Xiangtan
Hsi Chiang *see* Xi Jiang
178 *Gg6* **Hsihseng** Shan State, C Myanmar *20.07N 97.16E*
167 *S13* **Hsinchu** *municipality* N Taiwan *24.51N 121.01E*
Hsing-k'ai Hu *see* Khanka, Lake
Hsi-ning/Hsining *see* Xining
Hsinking *see* Changchun
Hsin-yang *see* Xinyang
167 *S14* **Hsinying** ***var.*** Sinying, ***Jap.*** Shinei. C Taiwan *23.12N 120.15E*
178 *Gg4* **Hsipaw** Shan State, C Myanmar *22.36N 97.16E*
Hsu-chou *see* Xuzhou
167 *S13* **Hsüeh Shan** ▲ N Taiwan
Hu *see* Shanghai Shi
85 *B18* **Huab** ≈ W Namibia
59 *M21* **Huacaya** Chuquisaca, S Bolivia *20.55S 63.24W*
59 *J19* **Huachacalla** Oruro, SW Bolivia *19.01S 68.22W*
165 *X9* **Huachi** ***var.*** Rouyuanchengzi. Gansu, C China *36.24N 107.58E*
59 *N16* **Huachi, Laguna** ◎ N Bolivia
59 *D14* **Huacho** Lima, W Peru *11.09S 77.37W*
169 *Y7* **Huachuan** Heilongjiang, NE China *46.57N 130.48E*
169 *P12* **Huade** Nei Mongol Zizhiqu, N China *41.52N 113.58E*
169 *W10* **Huadian** Jilin, NE China *42.58N 126.37E*
58 *E13* **Huagaruncho, Cordillera** ▲▲ C Peru
Hua Hin *see* Ban Hua Hin
203 *S10* **Huahine** *island* Îles Sous le Vent, W French Polynesia
Huahua, Rio *see* Wawa, Río
178 *Ii9* **Huai** ≈ E Thailand
167 *Q7* **Huai'an** ***var.*** Qingjiang; ***prev.*** Huaiyin. Jiangsu, E China *33.33N 119.03E*
167 *P6* **Huaibei** Anhui, E China *34.00N 116.48E*
Huaide *see* Gongzhuling
163 *T10* **Huai He** ≈ C China
166 *L11* **Huaihua** Hunan, S China *27.36N 109.56E*

◆ Country
● Country Capital
◇ Dependent Territory
○ Dependent Territory Capital
⬖ Administrative Region
✕ International Airport
▲ Mountain
▲▲ Mountain Range
Ж Volcano
≈ River
◎ Lake
⊠ Reservoir

HUAIJI – IFALIK ATOLL

167 N14 **Huaiji** Guangdong, S China *23.54N 112.12E*
167 O2 **Huailai** *var.* Shacheng. Hebei, E China *40.22N 115.34E*
167 P7 **Huainan** *var.* Huai-nan, Hwainan. Anhui, E China *32.36N 116.56E*
167 N2 **Huairen** Shanxi, C China *35.28N 110.29E*
167 O7 **Huaiyang** Henan, C China *33.39N 114.34E*
Huaiyin *see* Huai'an
178 Gg16 **Huai Yot** Trang, SW Thailand *7.45N 99.36E*
43 Q15 **Huajuapan** *var.* Huajuapan de León. Oaxaca, SE Mexico *17.49N 97.48W*
Huajuapan de León *see* Huajuapan
43 O9 **Hualahuises** Nuevo León, NE Mexico *24.55N 99.44W*
38 I11 **Hualapai Mountains** ▲▲ Arizona, SW USA
38 I11 **Hualapai Peak** ▲ Arizona, SW USA *35.04N 113.54W*
64 J7 **Hualfín** Catamarca, N Argentina *27.15S 66.52W*
167 T13 **Hualien** *var.* Hwalien, *Jap.* Karen. C Taiwan *23.58N 121.34E*
58 E10 **Huallaga, Río** ≈ N Peru
58 C11 **Huamachuco** La Libertad, C Peru *7.50S 78.03W*
43 Q14 **Huamantla** Tlaxcala, S Mexico *19.18N 97.57W*
84 C13 **Huambo** *Port.* Nova Lisboa. Huambo, C Angola *12.48S 15.45E*
84 B13 **Huambo** ◈ *province* C Angola
43 P15 **Huamuxtitlán** Guerrero, S Mexico *17.49N 98.34W*
169 Y8 **Huanan** Heilongjiang, NE China *46.21N 130.43E*
65 H17 **Huancache, Sierra** ▲▲ SW Argentina
59 I17 **Huancané** Puno, SE Peru *15.15S 69.47W*
59 F16 **Huancapi** Ayacucho, C Peru *13.36S 74.09W*
59 E15 **Huancavelica** Huancavelica, SW Peru *12.45S 75.03W*
59 E15 **Huancavelica** *off.* Departamento de Huancavelica. ◈ *department* W Peru
59 E14 **Huancayo** Junín, C Peru *12.03S 75.13W*
59 K20 **Huanchaca, Cerro** ▲ S Bolivia *20.12S 66.35W*
58 C12 **Huandoy, Nevado** ▲ W Peru *8.48S 77.33W*
167 O8 **Huangchuan** Henan, C China *32.08N 115.03E*
167 O9 **Huanggang** Hubei, C China *30.27N 114.48E*
Huang Hai *see* Yellow Sea
163 Q8 **Huang He** *var.* Yellow River. ≈ C China
167 Q4 **Huanghe Kou** *delta* E China
166 L5 **Huangling** Shaanxi, C China *35.34N 109.12E*
169 P13 **Huangqi Hai** ◎ N China
167 Q9 **Huang Shan** ▲ Anhui, E China *29.43N 118.19E*
167 Q9 **Huangshan** *var.* Tunxi. Anhui, E China *29.48N 118.17E*
167 O9 **Huangshi** *var.* Huang-shih, Hwangshih. Hubei, C China *30.14N 115.00E*
Huang-shih *see* Huangshi
166 L5 **Huangtu Gaoyuan** *plateau* C China
63 B22 **Huanguelén** Buenos Aires, E Argentina *37.01S 61.57W*
167 S10 **Huangyan** Zhejiang, SE China *28.42N 121.13E*
165 T10 **Huangyuan** Qinghai, C China *36.40N 101.12E*
165 T10 **Huangzhong** *var.* Lushar. Qinghai, C China *36.31N 101.32E*
169 W12 **Huanren** *var.* Huanren Manzu Zizhixian. Liaoning, NE China *41.16N 125.25E*
Huanren Manzu Zizhixian *see* Huanren
59 F15 **Huanta** Ayacucho, C Peru *12.54S 74.13W*
58 E13 **Huánuco** Huánuco, C Peru *9.57S 76.15W*
58 D13 **Huánuco** *off.* Departamento de Huánuco. ◈ *department* C Peru
59 K19 **Huanuni** Oruro, W Bolivia *18.15S 66.54W*
165 X9 **Huanxian** Gansu, C China *36.30N 107.20E*
167 S12 **Huap'ing Yu** *island* N Taiwan
64 H3 **Huara** Tarapacá, N Chile *19.59S 69.42W*
59 D14 **Huaral** Lima, W Peru *11.28S 77.12W*
Huarás *see* Huaraz
58 D13 **Huaraz** *var.* Huarás. Ancash, W Peru *9.30S 77.31W*
59 J16 **Huari Huari, Río** ≈ S Peru
58 C13 **Huarmey** Ancash, W Peru *10.03S 78.09W*
42 H4 **Huásabas** Sonora, NW Mexico *29.46N 109.18W*
58 D8 **Huasaga, Río** ≈ Ecuador/Peru
178 H16 **Hua Sai** Nakhon Si Thammarat, SW Thailand *8.01N 100.18E*
58 D12 **Huascarán, Nevado** ▲ W Peru *9.01S 77.27W*
64 G8 **Huasco** Atacama, N Chile *28.28S 71.12W*
64 G8 **Huasco, Río** ≈ C Chile
165 S11 **Huashikia** Qinghai, W China
42 G7 **Huatabampo** Sonora, NW Mexico *26.49N 109.40W*
165 W10 **Huating** Gansu, C China *35.13N 106.39E*
178 Jj7 **Huatt, Phou** ▲ N Vietnam *19.45N 104.48E*
43 Q14 **Huatusco** *var.* Huatusco de Chicuellar. Veracruz-Llave, C Mexico *19.13N 96.57W*
Huatusco de Chicuellar *see* Huatusco
43 P13 **Huauchinango** Puebla, S Mexico *20.12N 98.03W*
Huaunta *see* Wounta
43 R15 **Huautla** *var.* Huautla de Jiménez. Oaxaca, SE Mexico *18.10N 96.51W*
Huautla de Jiménez *see* Huautla
167 O5 **Huaxian** *var.* Daokou, Hua Xian. Henan, C China *35.33N 114.30E*
Huazangsi *see* Tianzhu
31 V13 **Hubbard** Iowa, C USA *42.18N 93.18W*
27 U8 **Hubbard** Texas, SW USA *31.52N 96.43W*
27 Q6 **Hubbard Creek Lake** ◎ Texas, SW USA
33 R6 **Hubbard Lake** ◎ Michigan, N USA
166 M9 **Hubei** *var.* E, Hubei Sheng, Hupeh, Hupei. ◈ *province* C China
Hubei Sheng *see* Hubei
111 P8 **Huben** Tirol, W Austria *46.55N 12.35E*
33 R13 **Huber Heights** Ohio, N USA *39.50N 84.07W*
161 F17 **Hubli** Karnātaka, SW India *15.19N 75.13E*
169 X12 **Huch'ang** N North Korea *41.24N 127.04E*
99 M18 **Hucknall** C England, UK *53.01N 1.10W*
99 L17 **Huddersfield** N England, UK *53.39N 1.46W*
97 O16 **Huddinge** Stockholm, C Sweden *59.15N 17.57E*
96 N11 **Hudiksvall** Gävleborg, C Sweden *61.45N 17.12E*
31 W13 **Hudson** Iowa, C USA *42.24N 92.27W*
21 O11 **Hudson** Massachusetts, NE USA *42.24N 71.34W*
33 Q11 **Hudson** Michigan, N USA *41.51N 84.21W*
32 H6 **Hudson** Wisconsin, N USA *44.58N 92.43W*
9 V14 **Hudson Bay** Saskatchewan, S Canada *58.13N 90.48W*
10 G6 **Hudson Bay** *bay* NE Canada
205 T16 **Hudson, Cape** *headland* Antarctica *68.15S 154.00E*
Hudson, Détroit d' *see* Hudson Strait
29 Q9 **Hudson, Lake** ⊠ Oklahoma, C USA
20 K9 **Hudson River** ≈ New Jersey/New York, NE USA
8 M12 **Hudson's Hope** British Columbia, W Canada *56.03N 121.58W*
10 L2 **Hudson Strait** *Fr.* Détroit d'Hudson. *strait* Nunavut/Québec, NE Canada
Hudūd ash Shamālīyah, Minṭaqat al *see* Al Ḥudūd ash Shamālīyah
Hudur *see* Xuddur
178 K9 **Huê** Thưa Thiên-Huê, C Vietnam *16.28N 107.34E*
106 J7 **Huebra** ≈ W Spain
26 H8 **Hueco Mountains** ▲▲ Texas, SW USA
118 G10 **Huedin** *Hung.* Bánffyhunyad. Cluj, NW Romania *46.51N 23.01E*
42 J10 **Huehuento, Cerro** ▲ C Mexico *24.04N 105.42W*
44 B5 **Huehuetenango** Huehuetenango, W Guatemala *15.19N 91.25W*
44 B4 **Huehuetenango** *off.* Departamento de Huehuetenango. ◈ *department* W Guatemala
42 L11 **Huejuquilla** Jalisco, SW Mexico *22.40N 103.52W*
43 P12 **Huejutla** *var.* Huejutla de Reyes. Hidalgo, C Mexico *21.08N 98.16W*
Huejutla de Reyes *see* Huejutla
104 G6 **Huelgoat** Finistère, NW France *48.22N 3.45W*
107 O13 **Huelma** Andalucía, S Spain *37.39N 3.28W*
106 I14 **Huelva** *anc.* Onuba. Andalucía, SW Spain *37.15N 6.55W*
106 I13 **Huelva** ◈ *province* Andalucía, SW Spain
106 J13 **Huelva** ≈ SW Spain
107 Q14 **Huércal-Overa** Andalucía, S Spain *37.22N 1.55W*
39 Q9 **Huerfano Mountain** ▲ New Mexico, SW USA *36.25N 107.50W*
39 T7 **Huerfano River** ≈ Colorado, C USA
107 S12 **Huertas, Cabo** *headland* SE Spain *38.21N 0.25W*
107 R6 **Huerva** ≈ N Spain
107 S4 **Huesca** *anc.* Osca. Aragón, NE Spain *42.07N 0.25W*
107 T4 **Huesca** ◈ *province* Aragón, NE Spain
107 P13 **Huéscar** Andalucía, S Spain *37.39N 2.31W*
43 N15 **Huetamo** *var.* Huetamo de Núñez. Michoacán de Ocampo, SW Mexico *18.37N 100.53W*
Huetamo de Núñez *see* Huetamo
107 P8 **Huete** Castilla-La Mancha, C Spain *40.07N 2.40W*
25 P4 **Hueytown** Alabama, S USA *33.27N 87.00W*
30 L16 **Hugh Butler Lake** ⊠ Nebraska, C USA
189 V6 **Hughenden** Queensland, NE Australia *20.56S 144.15E*
190 A6 **Hughes** South Australia *30.41S 129.31E*
41 P8 **Hughes** Alaska, USA *66.03N 154.15W*
29 X11 **Hughes** Arkansas, C USA *34.57N 90.28W*
27 W6 **Hughes Springs** Texas, SW USA *33.00N 94.37W*
39 V5 **Hugo** Colorado, C USA *39.08N 103.28W*
29 Q13 **Hugo** Oklahoma, C USA *34.01N 95.31W*
29 Q13 **Hugo Lake** ⊠ Oklahoma, C USA
28 H7 **Hugoton** Kansas, C USA *37.10N 101.21W*
Huhehot/Huhuohaote *see* Hohhot
Huhttán *see* Kvikkjokk
167 R13 **Hui'an** *var.* Luocheng. Fujian, SE China *25.06N 118.45E*
192 O9 **Huiarau Range** ▲▲ North Island, NZ
85 D22 **Huib-Hoch Plateau** *plateau* S Namibia
43 O13 **Huichapán** Hidalgo, C Mexico *20.22N 99.42W*
Huicheng *see* Shexian
169 W13 **Hŭich'ŏn** C North Korea *40.09N 126.17E*
56 E12 **Huila** *off.* Departamento del Huila. ◈ *province* S Colombia
85 B15 **Huila** ◈ *province* SW Angola
56 D11 **Huila, Nevado del** *elevation* C Colombia *2.56N 75.59W*
85 B15 **Huíla Plateau** *plateau* S Angola
166 G12 **Huili** Sichuan, C China *26.39N 102.13E*
167 P4 **Huimin** Shandong, E China *37.28N 117.30E*
169 W11 **Huinan** *var.* Chaoyang. Jilin, NE China *42.40N 126.03E*
64 K12 **Huinca Renancó** Córdoba, C Argentina *34.51S 64.22W*
165 V10 **Huining** *var.* Huishi. Gansu, C China *35.42N 105.01E*
Huishi *see* Huining
166 J12 **Huishui** *var.* Heping. Guizhou, S China *26.07N 106.39E*
104 L6 **Huisne** ≈ NW France
100 L12 **Huissen** Gelderland, SE Netherlands *51.57N 5.57E*
165 N11 **Huiten Nur** ◎ C China
95 K19 **Huittinen** Länsi-Suomi, W Finland *61.10N 22.40E*
43 O15 **Huitzuco** *var.* Huitzuco de los Figueroa. Guerrero, S Mexico *18.18N 99.22W*
Huitzuco de los Figueroa *see* Huitzuco
165 W11 **Huixian** *var.* Hui Xian. Gansu, C China *33.48N 106.02E*
43 V17 **Huixtla** Chiapas, SE Mexico *15.07N 92.29W*
166 H12 **Huize** *var.* Zhongping. Yunnan, SW China *26.28N 103.18E*
100 J10 **Huizen** Noord-Holland, C Netherlands *52.16N 5.15E*
167 O14 **Huizhou** Guangdong, S China *23.05N 114.22E*
168 J6 **Hujirt** Arhangay, C Mongolia *48.49N 101.20E*
168 J8 **Hujirt** Övörhangay, C Mongolia *46.50N 102.38E*
168 K8 **Hujirt** Töv, C Mongolia *46.41N 104.40E*
Hukagawa *see* Fukagawa
Hŭksan-chedo *see* Hŭksan-gundo
169 W17 **Hŭksan-gundo** *var.* Hŭksan-chedo. *island group* SW South Korea
Hukue *see* Fukue
Hukui *see* Fukui
85 G20 **Hukuntsi** Kgalagadi, SW Botswana *23.58S 21.43E*
Hukuoka *see* Fukuoka
Hukusima *see* Fukushima
Hukutiyama *see* Fukuchiyama
Hukuyama *see* Fukuyama
169 W8 **Hulan** Heilongjiang, NE China *45.58N 126.37E*
169 W8 **Hulan He** ≈ NE China
33 Q4 **Hulbert Lake** ◎ Michigan, N USA
Hulczyn *see* Hlučín
Huliao *see* Dabu
169 Z8 **Hulin** Heilongjiang, NE China *45.49N 133.06E*
169 S9 **Hulingol** *prev.* Huolin Gol. Nei Mongol Zizhiqu, N China *45.35N 119.53E*
12 L12 **Hull** Québec, SE Canada *45.25N 75.45W*
31 S12 **Hull** Iowa, C USA *43.11N 96.07W*
Hull *see* Kingston upon Hull
Hull Island *see* Orona
101 F16 **Hulst** Zeeland, SW Netherlands *51.16N 4.03E*
169 Q7 **Hulstay** Dornod, NE Mongolia *48.25N 114.56E*
Hultschin *see* Hlučín
97 M19 **Hultsfred** Kalmar, S Sweden *57.30N 15.49E*
169 T13 **Huludao** *prev.* Jinxi, Lianshan. Liaoning, NE China *40.42N 120.52E*
Hulun *see* Hailar
Hu-lun Ch'ih *see* Hulun Nur
169 Q6 **Hulun Nur** *var.* Hu-lun Ch'ih; *prev.* Dalai Nor. ◎ NE China
Hulwan/Hulwân *see* Helwân
119 V6 **Hulyaypole** *Rus.* Gulyaypole. Zaporiz'ka Oblast', SE Ukraine *47.41N 36.10E*
169 V4 **Huma** Heilongjiang, NE China *51.40N 126.38E*
47 V6 **Humacao** E Puerto Rico *18.09N 65.49W*
169 U4 **Huma He** ≈ NE China
64 J5 **Humahuaca** Jujuy, N Argentina *23.13S 65.19W*
61 E14 **Humaitá** Amazonas, N Brazil *7.33S 63.01W*
64 N7 **Humaitá** Ñeembucú, S Paraguay *27.06S 58.28W*
85 H26 **Humansdorp** Eastern Cape, S South Africa *34.01S 24.45E*
29 S6 **Humansville** Missouri, C USA *37.47N 93.34W*
42 I8 **Humaya, Río** ≈ C Mexico
85 C16 **Humbe** Cunene, SW Angola *16.37S 14.52E*
99 N17 **Humber** *estuary* E England, UK
99 N17 **Humberside** *cultural region* E England, UK
Humberto *see* Umberto
27 W11 **Humble** Texas, SW USA *29.58N 95.15W*
9 U15 **Humboldt** Saskatchewan, S Canada *52.13N 105.09W*
31 U12 **Humboldt** Iowa, C USA *42.42N 94.13W*
29 Q6 **Humboldt** Kansas, C USA *37.48N 95.26W*
31 S17 **Humboldt** Nebraska, C USA *40.09N 95.56W*
37 S3 **Humboldt** Nevada, W USA *40.36N 118.15W*
22 G9 **Humboldt** Tennessee, S USA *35.49N 88.55W*
36 K3 **Humboldt Bay** *bay* California, W USA
37 S4 **Humboldt Lake** ◎ Nevada, W USA
197 J7 **Humboldt, Mont** ▲ S New Caledonia *21.57S 166.24E*
37 S4 **Humboldt River** ≈ Nevada, W USA
37 T5 **Humboldt Salt Marsh** *wetland* Nevada, W USA
191 P11 **Hume, Lake** ◎ New South Wales/Victoria, SE Australia
113 N19 **Humenné** *Ger.* Homenau, *Hung.* Homonna. Prešovský Kraj, E Slovakia *48.57N 21.54E*
31 V15 **Humeston** Iowa, C USA *40.51N 93.30W*
56 J5 **Humocaro Bajo** Lara, N Venezuela *9.42N 70.02W*
31 Q14 **Humphrey** Nebraska, C USA *41.38N 97.29W*
37 S9 **Humphreys, Mount** ▲ California, W USA *37.11N 118.39W*
38 L11 **Humphreys Peak** ▲ Arizona, SW USA *35.18N 111.40W*
113 E17 **Humpolec** *Ger.* Gumpolds, Humpoletz. Vysočina, C Czech Republic *49.33N 15.22E*
Humpoletz *see* Humpolec
95 K19 **Humppila** Etelä-Suomi, S Finland *60.54N 23.21E*
34 F8 **Humptulips** Washington, NW USA *47.13N 123.57W*
44 H7 **Humuya, Río** ≈ W Honduras
77 P9 **Hūn** N Libya *29.06N 15.56E*
Hunabasi *see* Funabashi
94 I1 **Húnaflói** *bay* NW Iceland
166 M11 **Hunan** *var.* Hunan Sheng, Xiang. ◈ *province* S China
Hunan Sheng *see* Hunan
169 Y10 **Hunchun** Jilin, NE China *42.51N 130.21E*
97 I22 **Hundested** Frederiksborg, E Denmark *55.58N 11.52E*
Hundred Mile House *see* 100 Mile House
118 G12 **Hunedoara** *Ger.* Eisenmarkt, *Hung.* Vajdahunyad. Hunedoara, SW Romania *45.45N 22.54E*
118 G12 **Hunedoara** ◈ *county* W Romania
103 I17 **Hünfeld** Hessen, C Germany *50.40N 9.46E*
113 H23 **Hungary** *off.* Republic of Hungary, *Ger.* Ungarn, *Hung.* Magyarország, *Rom.* Ungaria, *SCr.* Madarska, *Ukr.* Uhorshchyna; *prev.* Hungarian People's Republic. ◆ *republic* C Europe
Hungary, Plain of *see* Great Hungarian Plain
168 F6 **Hungiy** Dzavhan, W Mongolia *48.31N 94.15E*
169 X13 **Hŭngnam** E North Korea *39.50N 127.36E*
35 P8 **Hungry Horse Reservoir** ⊠ Montana, NW USA
Hungt'ou *see* Lan Yü
Hung-tse Hu *see* Hongze Hu
178 Jj6 **Hưng Yên** Hai Hưng, N Vietnam *20.37N 106.04E*
Hunjiang *see* Baishan
97 I18 **Hunnebostrand** Västra Götaland, S Sweden *58.26N 11.19E*
103 E19 **Hunsrück** ▲▲ W Germany
99 P18 **Hunstanton** E England, UK *52.57N 0.28E*
161 G20 **Hunsūr** Karnātaka, E India *12.18N 76.15E*
168 I7 **Hunt** Arhangay, C Mongolia *47.49N 99.24E*
102 G12 **Hunte** ≈ NW Germany
31 Q5 **Hunter** North Dakota, N USA *47.10N 97.11W*
27 S11 **Hunter** Texas, SW USA *29.47N 98.01W*
193 D20 **Hunter** ≈ South Island, NZ
191 N15 **Hunter Island** *island* Tasmania, SE Australia
20 K11 **Hunter Mountain** ▲ New York, NE USA *42.10N 74.13W*
193 B23 **Hunter Mountains** ▲▲ South Island, NZ
191 S7 **Hunter River** ≈ New South Wales, SE Australia
34 L7 **Hunters** Washington, NW USA *48.07N 118.13W*
193 F20 **Hunters Hills, The** *hill range* South Island, NZ
192 M12 **Hunterville** Manawatu-Wanganui, North Island, NZ *39.55S 175.34E*
33 N16 **Huntingburg** Indiana, N USA *38.18N 86.57W*
99 O20 **Huntingdon** E England, UK *52.19N 0.12W*
20 E15 **Huntingdon** Pennsylvania, NE USA *40.28N 78.00W*
22 G9 **Huntingdon** Tennessee, S USA *36.00N 88.25W*
99 O20 **Huntingdonshire** *cultural region* C England, UK
33 P12 **Huntington** Indiana, N USA *40.52N 85.30W*
34 L13 **Huntington** Oregon, NW USA *44.22N 117.18W*
27 X9 **Huntington** Texas, SW USA *31.16N 94.34W*
38 M5 **Huntington** Utah, W USA *39.19N 110.57W*
23 P5 **Huntington** West Virginia, NE USA *38.24N 82.27W*
37 T16 **Huntington Beach** California, W USA *33.39N 118.00W*
37 W4 **Huntington Creek** ≈ Nevada, W USA
192 L7 **Huntly** Waikato, North Island, NZ *37.33S 175.09E*
98 K8 **Huntly** NE Scotland, UK *57.25N 2.48W*
8 K8 **Hunt, Mount** ▲ Yukon Territory, NW Canada *61.29N 129.10W*
12 H12 **Huntsville** Ontario, S Canada *45.18N 79.12W*
25 P2 **Huntsville** Alabama, S USA *34.43N 86.35W*
29 S9 **Huntsville** Arkansas, C USA *36.05N 93.43W*
29 U3 **Huntsville** Missouri, C USA *39.26N 92.33W*
22 M8 **Huntsville** Tennessee, S USA *36.25N 84.30W*
27 V10 **Huntsville** Texas, SW USA *30.43N 95.34W*
38 L2 **Huntsville** Utah, W USA *41.16N 111.47W*
43 W12 **Hunucmá** Yucatán, SE Mexico *20.59N 89.55W*
155 W3 **Hunza** *var.* Karīmābād. Jammu and Kashmir, NE Pakistan *36.22N 74.43E*
155 W3 **Hunza** ≈ NE Pakistan
Hunze *see* Oostermoers Vaart
164 H4 **Huocheng** *var.* Shuiding. Xinjiang Uygur Zizhiqu, NW China *44.03N 80.49E*
167 N6 **Huojia** Henan, C China *35.13N 113.37E*
Huolin Gol *see* Hulingol
197 F3 **Huon** *reef* N New Caledonia
194 K13 **Huon Gulf** *gulf* E PNG
194 K13 **Huon Peninsula** *headland* C PNG *6.24S 147.50E*
Huoshao Dao *see* Lü Tao
Huoshao Tao *see* Lan Yü
Hupeh/Hupei *see* Hubei
Hurama *see* Hongyuan
Hurano *see* Furano
97 H14 **Hurdalsjøen** ◎ S Norway
12 E13 **Hurd, Cape** *headland* Ontario, S Canada *45.12N 81.43W*
Hurdegaryp *see* Hardegarijp
31 N4 **Hurdsfield** North Dakota, N USA *47.24N 99.55W*
168 J7 **Hüremt** Bulgan, C Mongolia *48.40N 102.33E*
168 J8 **Hüremt** Övörhangay, C Mongolia *46.18N 102.27E*
77 X9 **Hurghada** *var.* Al Ghurdaqah, Ghurdaqah. E Egypt *27.16N 33.46E*
69 V9 **Huri Hills** ▲▲ NW Kenya
39 P15 **Hurley** New Mexico, SW USA *32.42N 108.07W*
32 K4 **Hurley** Wisconsin, N USA *46.25N 90.15W*
23 Y4 **Hurlock** Maryland, NE USA *38.37N 75.51W*
31 P10 **Huron** South Dakota, N USA *44.19N 98.13W*
33 S6 **Huron, Lake** ◎ Canada/USA
33 N3 **Huron Mountains** *hill range* Michigan, N USA
38 J8 **Hurricane** Utah, W USA *37.10N 113.18W*
23 P5 **Hurricane** West Virginia, NE USA *38.25N 82.01W*
38 J8 **Hurricane Cliffs** *cliff* Arizona, SW USA
25 V6 **Hurricane Creek** ≈ Georgia, SE USA
96 E12 **Hurrungane** ▲ S Norway *61.25N 7.48E*
103 E16 **Hürth** Nordrhein-Westfalen, W Germany *50.52N 6.52E*
Hurukawa *see* Furukawa
193 I17 **Hurunui** ≈ South Island, NZ
97 F21 **Hurup** Viborg, NW Denmark *56.46N 8.25E*
119 T14 **Hurzuf** Respublika Krym, S Ukraine *44.33N 34.18E*
Huş *see* Huşi
97 B19 **Húsavík** *Dan.* Husevig Faeroe Islands *61.19N 6.41W*
94 K1 **Húsavík** Nordhurland Eystra, NE Iceland *66.03N 17.19W*
118 M10 **Huşi** *var.* Huş. Vaslui, E Romania *46.40N 28.05E*
97 L19 **Huskvarna** Jönköping, S Sweden *57.46N 14.15E*
41 P8 **Huslia** Alaska, USA *65.42N 156.24W*
Husn *see* Al Ḥuṣn
97 C15 **Husnes** Hordaland, S Norway *59.52N 5.46E*
96 D8 **Hustadvika** *sea area* S Norway
Husté *see* Khust
102 H7 **Husum** Schleswig-Holstein, N Germany *54.28N 9.04E*
95 I16 **Husum** Västernorrland, C Sweden *63.21N 19.12E*
118 K6 **Husyatyn** Ternopil's'ka Oblast', W Ukraine *49.04N 26.10E*
Huszt *see* Khust
168 K6 **Hutag** Bulgan, N Mongolia *49.22N 102.50E*
28 M6 **Hutchinson** Kansas, C USA *38.03N 97.55W*
31 U9 **Hutchinson** Minnesota, N USA *44.53N 94.22W*
25 Y13 **Hutchinson Island** *island* Florida, SE USA
38 L11 **Hutch Mountain** ▲ Arizona, SW USA *34.49N 111.22W*
147 O14 **Ḥūth** NW Yemen *16.13N 44.00E*
195 R11 **Hutjena** Buka Island, NE PNG *5.19S 154.40E*
111 T8 **Hüttenberg** Kärnten, S Austria *46.58N 14.33E*
27 T10 **Hutto** Texas, SW USA *30.32N 97.33W*
Huttu *see* Futtsu
110 E8 **Huttwil** Bern, W Switzerland *47.06N 7.48E*
164 K5 **Hutubi** Xinjiang Uygur Zizhiqu, NW China *44.10N 86.51E*
167 N4 **Hutuo He** ≈ C China
Hutyû *see* Fuchū
193 E20 **Huxley, Mount** ▲ South Island, NZ *44.02S 169.42E*
101 J20 **Huy** *Dut.* Hoei, Hoey. Liège, E Belgium *50.31N 5.13E*
167 R8 **Huzhou** *var.* Wuxing. Zhejiang, SE China *30.54N 120.04E*
Huzi *see* Fuji
Huzieda *see* Fujieda
Huzinomiya *see* Fujinomiya
Huzisawa *see* Fujisawa
Huziyosida *see* Fuji-Yoshida
94 I2 **Hvammstangi** Nordhurland Vestra, N Iceland *65.22N 20.54W*
94 K4 **Hvannadalshnúkur** ▲ S Iceland *64.01N 16.39W*
115 E15 **Hvar** *It.* Lesina. Split-Dalmacija, S Croatia *43.10N 16.27E*
115 F15 **Hvar** *It.* Lesina; *anc.* Pharus. *island* S Croatia
119 T13 **Hvardiys'ke** *Rus.* Gvardeyskoye. Respublika Krym, S Ukraine *45.07N 34.01E*
94 I4 **Hveragerdhi** Sudhurland, SW Iceland *64.00N 21.13W*
97 E22 **Hvide Sande** Ringkøbing, W Denmark *56.00N 8.08E*
94 I3 **Hvítá** ≈ C Iceland
97 G15 **Hvittingfoss** Buskerud, S Norway *59.28N 10.00E*
94 I4 **Hvolsvöllur** Sudhurland, SW Iceland *63.44N 20.12W*
Hwach'ŏn-chŏsuji *see* P'aro-ho
Hwainan *see* Huainan
Hwalien *see* Hualien
85 I16 **Hwange** *prev.* Wankie. Matabeleland North, W Zimbabwe *18.18S 26.30E*
Hwang-Hae *see* Yellow Sea
Hwangshih *see* Huangshi
85 L17 **Hwedza** Mashonaland East, E Zimbabwe *18.15S 29.48E*
65 G20 **Hyades, Cerro** ▲ S Chile *46.57S 73.09W*
21 Q12 **Hyannis** Massachusetts, NE USA *41.38N 70.15W*
30 L13 **Hyannis** Nebraska, C USA *41.58N 101.45W*
168 F6 **Hyargas Nuur** ◎ NW Mongolia
Hybla/Hybla Major *see* Paternò
41 Y14 **Hydaburg** Prince of Wales Island, Alaska, USA *55.10N 132.44W*
193 F22 **Hyde** Otago, South Island, NZ *45.17S 170.17E*
23 O7 **Hyden** Kentucky, S USA *37.07N 83.22W*
20 K12 **Hyde Park** New York, NE USA *41.46N 73.52W*
41 Z14 **Hyder** Alaska, USA *55.55N 130.01W*
161 I15 **Hyderābād** *var.* Haidarabad. Andhra Pradesh, C India *17.22N 78.25E*
155 Q16 **Hyderābād** *var.* Haidarabad. Sind, SE Pakistan *25.25N 68.21E*
105 T16 **Hyères** Var, SE France *43.07N 6.07E*
105 T16 **Hyères, Îles d'** *island group* S France
120 K12 **Hyermanavichy** *Rus.* Germanovichi. Vitsyebskaya Voblasts', N Belarus *55.25N 27.43E*
169 X12 **Hyesan** NE North Korea *41.17N 128.13E*
8 K8 **Hyland** ≈ Yukon Territory, NW Canada
97 K20 **Hyltebruk** Halland, S Sweden *57.00N 13.14E*
20 D16 **Hyndman** Pennsylvania, NE USA *39.49N 78.42W*
35 P14 **Hyndman Peak** ▲ Idaho, NW USA *43.45N 114.07W*
170 G13 **Hyōgo** *off.* Hyōgo-ken. ◈ *prefecture* Honshū, SW Japan
170 G13 **Hyōno-sen** ▲ Kyūshū, SW Japan *35.21N 134.30E*
Hypanis *see* Kuban'
Hypsas *see* Belice
Hyrcania *see* Gorgān
38 L1 **Hyrum** Utah, W USA *41.37N 111.51W*
95 N14 **Hyrynsalmi** Oulu, C Finland *64.40N 28.30E*
35 V10 **Hysham** Montana, NW USA *46.16N 107.14W*
9 N13 **Hythe** Alberta, W Canada *55.18N 119.44W*
99 Q23 **Hythe** SE England, UK *51.04N 1.04E*
170 D15 **Hyūga** Miyazaki, Kyūshū, SW Japan *32.24N 131.34E*
Hyvinge *see* Hyvinkää
95 L19 **Hyvinkää** *Swe.* Hyvinge. Etelä-Suomi, S Finland *60.37N 24.49E*

I

118 J9 **Iacobeni** *Ger.* Jakobeny. Suceava, NE Romania *47.24N 25.19E*
Iader *see* Zadar
180 I7 **Iakora** Fianarantsoa, SE Madagascar *23.04S 46.40E*
194 H12 **Ialibu** Southern Highlands, W PNG *6.15S 143.55E*
118 K14 **Ialomiţa** *var.* Jalomitsa. ◈ *county* SE Romania
118 K14 **Ialomiţa** ≈ SE Romania
119 N10 **Ialoveni** *Rus.* Yaloveny. C Moldova *46.57N 28.47E*
119 N11 **Ialpug** *var.* Ialpugul Mare, *Rus.* Yalpug. ≈ Moldova/Ukraine
Ialpugul Mare *see* Ialpug
25 T8 **Iamonia, Lake** ◎ Florida, SE USA
118 L13 **Ianca** Brăila, SE Romania *45.06N 27.29E*
118 M10 **Iaşi** *Ger.* Jassy. Iaşi, NE Romania *47.08N 27.38E*
118 L9 **Iaşi** *Ger.* Jassy, Yassy. ◈ *county* NE Romania
116 J13 **Íasmos** Anatolikí Makedonía kai Thráki, NE Greece *41.07N 25.12E*
24 H6 **Iatt, Lake** ⊠ Louisiana, S USA
60 B11 **Iauaretê** Amazonas, NW Brazil *0.37N 69.10W*
179 Oo10 **Iba** Luzon, N Philippines *15.25N 119.55E*
79 S16 **Ibadan** Oyo, SW Nigeria *7.21N 4.01E*
56 E10 **Ibagué** Tolima, C Colombia *4.27N 75.13W*
62 J10 **Ibaiti** Paraná, S Brazil *23.52S 50.09W*
179 Pp12 **Ibajay** Panay Island, C Philippines *11.42N 122.17E*
38 J4 **Ibapah Peak** ▲ Utah, W USA *39.51N 113.55W*
115 M15 **Ibar** *Alb.* Ibër. ≈ C Serbia and Montenegro (Yugoslavia)
170 F14 **Ibara** Okayama, Honshū, SW Japan *34.36N 133.27E*
171 Kk16 **Ibaraki** *off.* Ibaraki-ken. ◈ *prefecture* Honshū, S Japan
58 C5 **Ibarra** *var.* San Miguel de Ibarra. Imbabura, N Ecuador *0.22S 78.07W*
Ibaşfalău *see* Dumbrăveni
147 O16 **Ibb** W Yemen *13.55N 44.10E*
102 F13 **Ibbenbüren** Nordrhein-Westfalen, NW Germany *52.17N 7.43E*
81 H16 **Ibenga** ≈ N Congo
Ibër *see* Ibar
59 I14 **Iberia** Madre de Dios, E Peru *11.21S 69.36W*
Iberia *see* Spain
68 M1 **Iberian Basin** *undersea feature* E Atlantic Ocean
Iberian Mountains *see* Ibérico, Sistema
86 D12 **Iberian Peninsula** *physical region* Portugal/Spain
66 M8 **Iberian Plain** *undersea feature* E Atlantic Ocean
Ibérica, Cordillera *see* Ibérico, Sistema
107 P6 **Ibérico, Sistema** *var.* Cordillera Ibérica, *Eng.* Iberian Mountains. ▲▲ NE Spain
10 K7 **Iberville, Lac d'** ◎ Québec, NE Canada
79 T14 **Ibeto** Niger, W Nigeria *10.30N 5.07E*
79 W15 **Ibi** Taraba, C Nigeria *8.13N 9.46E*
107 S11 **Ibi** País Valenciano, E Spain *38.37N 0.34W*
61 L20 **Ibiá** Minas Gerais, SE Brazil *19.30S 46.31W*
63 F15 **Ibicuí, Rio** ≈ S Brazil
63 C19 **Ibicuy** Entre Ríos, E Argentina *33.46S 59.07W*
63 F16 **Ibirapuitã** ≈ S Brazil
Ibiza *see* Eivissa
144 J4 **Ibn Wardān, Qaṣr** *ruins* Ḥamāh, C Syria *35.19N 37.13E*
Ibo *see* Sassandra
196 E9 **Ibobang** Babeldaob, N Palau
176 Vv11 **Ibonma** Papua, E Indonesia *3.27S 133.30E*
61 N17 **Ibotirama** Bahia, E Brazil *12.13S 43.12W*
147 Y8 **Ibrā** NE Oman *22.45N 58.30E*
131 Q4 **Ibresi** Chavash Respubliki, W Russian Federation *55.22N 47.04E*
147 X8 **'Ibrī** NW Oman *23.12N 56.28E*
170 Bb16 **Ibusuki** Kagoshima, Kyūshū, SW Japan *31.13N 130.37E*
59 E16 **Ica** Ica, SW Peru *14.01S 75.48W*
59 E16 **Ica** *off.* Departamento de Ica. ◈ *department* SW Peru
60 C11 **Içana** Amazonas, NW Brazil *0.22N 67.25W*
Icaria *see* Ikaría
60 B13 **Içá, Rio** *var.* Río Putumayo. ≈ NW South America *see also* Putumayo, Río
142 I17 **İçel** *var.* Ichili. ◈ *province* S Turkey
94 I3 **Iceland** *off.* Republic of Iceland, *Dan.* Island, *Icel.* Ísland. ◆ *republic* N Atlantic Ocean
88 B7 **Iceland** *island* N Atlantic Ocean
66 L5 **Iceland Basin** *undersea feature* N Atlantic Ocean
Icelandic Plateau *see* Iceland Plateau
207 Q15 **Iceland Plateau** *var.* Icelandic Plateau. *undersea feature* S Greenland Sea
161 E16 **Ichalkaranji** Mahārāshtra, W India *16.42N 74.28E*
170 Cc15 **Ichifusa-yama** ▲ Kyūshū, SW Japan *32.18N 131.05E*
171 K17 **Ichihara** *var.* Itihara. Chiba, Honshū, S Japan *35.30N 140.08E*
Ichili *see* İçel
171 I15 **Ichinomiya** *var.* Itinomiya. Aichi, Honshū, SW Japan *35.19N 136.47E*
171 Mm12 **Ichinoseki** *var.* Itinoseki. Iwate, Honshū, C Japan *38.25N 141.16E*
119 R3 **Ichnya** Chernihivs'ka Oblast', NE Ukraine *50.52N 32.24E*
59 L17 **Ichoa, Río** ≈ C Bolivia
I-ch'un *see* Yichun
Iconium *see* Konya
Iculisma *see* Angoulême
41 U12 **Icy Bay** *inlet* Alaska, USA
41 N5 **Icy Cape** *headland* Alaska, USA *70.19N 161.52W*
41 W13 **Icy Strait** *strait* Alaska, USA
29 R13 **Idabel** Oklahoma, C USA *33.54N 94.49W*
31 T13 **Ida Grove** Iowa, C USA *42.21N 95.28W*
79 U16 **Idah** Kogi, S Nigeria *7.06N 6.45E*
35 N13 **Idaho** *off.* State of Idaho; also known as Gem of the Mountains, Gem State. ◈ *state* NW USA
35 N14 **Idaho City** Idaho, NW USA *43.48N 115.51W*
35 R14 **Idaho Falls** Idaho, NW USA *43.28N 112.01W*
124 Nn3 **Idālion** *var.* Dali, Dhali. C Cyprus *35.00N 33.25E*
27 N5 **Idalou** Texas, SW USA *33.40N 101.40W*
106 I9 **Idanha-a-Nova** Castelo Branco, C Portugal *39.55N 7.15W*
103 E19 **Idar-Oberstein** Rheinland-Pfalz, SW Germany *49.43N 7.19E*
120 J3 **Ida-Virumaa** *off.* Ida-Viru Maakond. ◈ *province* NE Estonia
128 J8 **Idel'** Respublika Kareliya, NW Russian Federation *64.08N 34.12E*
81 C15 **Idenao** Sud-Ouest, SW Cameroon *4.04N 9.01E*
Idenburg-rivier *see* Taritatu, Sungai
Idensalmi *see* Iisalmi
168 I6 **Ider** Hövsgöl, C Mongolia *48.45N 99.52E*
77 X10 **Idfu** *var.* Edfu. SE Egypt *24.57N 32.51E*
Ídhi Óros *see* Ídi
Ídhra *see* Ýdra
173 F3 **Idi** Sumatera, W Indonesia *5.00N 98.00E*
117 I25 **Ídi** *var.* Ídhi Óros. ▲ Kríti, Greece, E Mediterranean Sea
Idi Amin, Lac *see* Edward, Lake
108 G10 **Idice** ≈ N Italy
78 G9 **Idini** Trarza, W Mauritania *17.58N 15.40W*
81 J21 **Idiofa** Bandundu, SW Dem. Rep. Congo *5.00S 19.38E*
41 O10 **Iditarod River** ≈ Alaska, USA
97 M14 **Idkerberget** Dalarna, C Sweden *60.22N 15.15E*
144 I3 **Idlib** Idlib, NW Syria *35.57N 36.37E*
144 I4 **Idlib** *off.* Muḥāfaẓat Idlib. ◈ *governorate* NW Syria
Idra *see* Ýdra
96 J11 **Idre** Dalarna, C Sweden *61.52N 12.45E*
Idria *see* Idrija
111 S11 **Idrija** *It.* Idria. W Slovenia *46.00N 14.59E*
103 G18 **Idstein** Hessen, W Germany *50.10N 8.16E*
85 J25 **Idutywa** Eastern Cape, SE South Africa *32.06S 28.19E*
Idzhevan *see* Ijevan
120 G9 **Iecava** Bauska, S Latvia *56.36N 24.10E*
172 P14 **Ie-jima** *var.* Ie-shima. *island* Nansei-shotō, SW Japan
101 B18 **Ieper** *Fr.* Ypres. West-Vlaanderen, W Belgium *50.51N 2.52E*
117 K25 **Ierápetra** Kríti, Greece, E Mediterranean Sea *35.00N 25.45E*
117 G22 **Iérax, Akrotírio** *headland* S Greece *36.45N 23.06E*
Ierisós *see* Ierissós
117 H14 **Ierissós** *var.* Ierisós. Kentrikí Makedonía, N Greece *40.24N 23.52E*
118 I11 **Iernut** *Hung.* Radnót. Mureş, C Romania *46.27N 24.18E*
108 J12 **Iesi** *var.* Jesi. Marche, C Italy *43.33N 13.16E*
94 K9 **Iešjávri** *var.* Jiesjavrre. ◎ N Norway
Iesolo *see* Jesolo
196 K16 **Ifalik Atoll** *atoll* Caroline Islands, C Micronesia

268

◆ COUNTRY ● COUNTRY CAPITAL ◇ DEPENDENT TERRITORY ○ DEPENDENT TERRITORY CAPITAL ◈ ADMINISTRATIVE REGION ✕ INTERNATIONAL AIRPORT ▲ MOUNTAIN ▲▲ MOUNTAIN RANGE VOLCANO ≈ RIVER ◎ LAKE ⊠ RESERVOIR

IFANADIANA – IOWA CITY

180 I6 **Ifanadiana** Fianarantsoa, SE Madagascar *21.19S 47.39E*
79 T16 **Ife** Osun, SW Nigeria *7.25N 4.31E*
79 V8 **Iferouâne** Agadez, N Niger *19.08N 8.21E*
Iferten *see* Yverdon
94 L8 **Ifjord** Finnmark, N Norway *70.27N 27.06E*
79 R8 **Ifôghas, Adrar des** *var.* Adrar des Iforas. ▲▲ NE Mali
Iforas, Adrar des *see* Ifôghas, Adrar des
190 D6 **Ifould lake** *salt lake* South Australia
76 G6 **Ifrane** C Morocco *33.31N 5.09W*
175 T7 **Iga** Pulau Halmahera, E Indonesia *1.23N 128.17E*
83 G18 **Iganga** SE Uganda *0.34N 33.27E*
62 L7 **Igarapava** São Paulo, S Brazil *20.01S 47.46W*
126 Hh9 **Igarka** Krasnoyarskiy Kray, N Russian Federation *67.31N 86.33E*
Igaunija *see* Estonia
I.G.Duca *see* General Toshevo
Igel *see* Jihlava
143 T12 **Igdır** ◐ *province* E Turkey
96 N11 **Iggesund** Gävleborg, C Sweden *61.37N 17.15E*
41 P7 **Igikpak, Mount** ▲ Alaska, USA *67.28N 154.55W*
41 P13 **Igiugig** Alaska, USA *59.19N 155.53W*
Iglau/Iglawa/Igława *see* Jihlava
109 B20 **Iglesias** Sardegna, Italy, C Mediterranean Sea *39.19N 8.33E*
131 V4 **Iglino** Respublika Bashkortostan, W Russian Federation *54.51N 56.29E*
Igló *see* Spišská Nová Ves
15 Ll2 **Igloolik** Nunavut, N Canada *69.24N 81.55W*
10 B11 **Ignace** Ontario, S Canada *49.25N 91.40W*
120 I12 **Ignalina** Utena, E Lithuania *55.20N 26.10E*
131 Q5 **Ignatovka** Ul'yanovskaya Oblast', W Russian Federation *53.56N 47.40E*
128 K12 **Ignatovo** Vologodskaya Oblast', NW Russian Federation *60.47N 37.51E*
116 N11 **İğneada** Kırklareli, NW Turkey *41.54N 27.58E*
124 P7 **İğneada Burnu** *headland* NW Turkey *41.54N 28.03E*
Igombe *see* Gombe
117 B16 **Igoumenítsa** Ípeiros, W Greece *39.30N 20.16E*
131 T2 **Igra** Udmurtskaya Respublika, NW Russian Federation *57.30N 53.01E*
125 Ff9 **Igrim** Khanty-Mansiyskiy Avtonomnyy Okrug, N Russian Federation *63.09N 64.33E*
62 G12 **Iguaçu, Rio** *Sp.* Río Iguazú. ≈ Argentina/Brazil *see also* Iguazú, Río
61 I22 **Iguaçu, Salto do** *Sp.* Cataratas del Iguazú; *prev.* Victoria Falls. *waterfall* Argentina/Brazil *25.37S 54.28W* *see also* Iguazú, Cataratas del
43 O15 **Iguala** *var.* Iguala de la Independencia. Guerrero, S Mexico *18.21N 99.33W*
107 V5 **Igualada** Cataluña, NE Spain *41.34N 1.37E*
Iguala de la Independencia *see* Iguala
62 G12 **Iguazú, Cataratas del** *Port.* Salto do Iguaçu, *prev.* Victoria Falls. *waterfall* Argentina/Brazil *25.40S 54.25W* *see also* Iguaçu, Salto do
64 Q6 **Iguazú, Río** *Port.* Rio Iguaçu. ≈ Argentina/Brazil *see also* Iguaçu, Rio
81 D19 **Iguéla** Ogooué-Maritime, SW Gabon *2.00S 9.23E*
Iguid, Erg *see* Iguîdi, 'Erg
69 M5 **Iguîdi, 'Erg** *var.* Erg Iguid. *desert* Algeria/Mauritania
180 K2 **Iharaña** *prev.* Vohémar. Antsirañana, NE Madagascar *13.22S 50.00E*
157 K18 **Ihavandippolhu Atoll** *var.* Ihavandiffulu Atoll. *atoll* N Maldives
168 M11 **Ih Bulag** Ömnögovĭ, S Mongolia *43.04N 107.43E*
172 Pp14 **Iheya-jima** *island* Nansei-shotō, SW Japan
168 L8 **Ihhayrhan** Töv, C Mongolia *46.57N 105.51E*
180 I6 **Ihosy** Fianarantsoa, S Madagascar *22.22S 46.09E*
168 L7 **Ihsüüj** Töv, C Mongolia *48.12N 106.23E*
95 L14 **Ii** Oulu, C Finland *65.18N 25.23E*
171 Ii16 **Iida** Nagano, Honshū, S Japan *35.30N 137.48E*
171 L13 **Iide-san** ▲ Honshū, C Japan *38.03N 139.39E*
95 M14 **Iijoki** ≈ C Finland
Iinnasuolu *see* Hinnøya
120 J4 **Iisaku** *Ger.* Isaak. Ida-Virumaa, NE Estonia *59.07N 27.18E*
95 M16 **Iisalmi** *var.* Idensalmi. Itä-Suomi, C Finland *63.31N 27.10E*
171 Jj14 **Iiyama** Nagano, Honshū, S Japan *36.52N 138.22E*
170 D13 **Iizuka** Fukuoka, Kyūshū, SW Japan *33.37N 130.40E*
79 S16 **Ijebu-Ode** Ogun, SW Nigeria *6.46N 3.57E*
143 U11 **Ijevan** *Rus.* Idzhevan. N Armenia *40.53N 45.07E*
100 H9 **IJmuiden** Noord-Holland, W Netherlands *52.28N 4.34E*
100 M12 **IJssel** *var.* Yssel. ≈ Netherlands/Germany
100 J8 **IJsselmeer** *prev.* Zuider Zee. ◎ N Netherlands
100 L9 **IJsselmuiden** Overijssel, E Netherlands *52.34N 5.55E*
100 I12 **IJsselstein** Utrecht, C Netherlands *52.01N 5.01E*
63 G14 **Ijuí** Rio Grande do Sul, S Brazil *28.22S 53.55W*
63 G14 **Ijuí, Rio** ≈ S Brazil
201 R8 **Ijuw** NE Nauru *0.30S 166.57E*
101 E16 **IJzendijke** Zeeland, SW Netherlands *51.20N 3.36E*
101 A18 **Ijzer** ≈ W Belgium
95 K18 **Ikaalinen** Länsi-Suomi, W Finland *61.46N 23.04E*
180 I6 **Ikalamavony** Fianarantsoa, SE Madagascar *21.10S 46.34E*
193 G16 **Ikamatua** West Coast, South Island, NZ *42.16S 171.42E*
79 U16 **Ikare** Ondo, SW Nigeria *7.36N 5.52E*
117 L20 **Ikaría** *var.* Kariot, Nicaria, Nikaria; *anc.* Icaria. *island* Dodekánisos, Greece, Aegean Sea
97 F22 **Ikast** Ringkøbing, W Denmark *56.09N 9.10E*
192 O9 **Ikawhenua Range** ▲▲ North Island, NZ
172 Pp7 **Ikeda** Hokkaidō, NE Japan *42.54N 143.25E*
170 F15 **Ikeda** Tokushima, Shikoku, SW Japan *34.00N 133.47E*
79 S16 **Ikeja** Lagos, SW Nigeria *6.36N 3.16E*
81 L19 **Ikela** Equateur, C Dem. Rep. Congo *1.10S 23.16E*
116 H10 **Ikhtiman** Sofiya, W Bulgaria *42.25N 23.49E*
170 Cc12 **Iki** *island* SW Japan
131 O13 **Iki Burul** Respublika Kalmykiya, SW Russian Federation *45.48N 44.44E*
170 C12 **Iki-suidō** *strait* SW Japan
170 Bb12 **Ikitsuki-shima** *island* SW Japan
143 P11 **İkizdere** Rize, NE Turkey *40.46N 40.34E*
41 P14 **Ikolik, Cape** *headland* Kodiak Island, Alaska, USA *57.12N 154.46W*
79 V17 **Ikom** Cross River, SE Nigeria *5.57N 8.43E*
180 I6 **Ikongo** *prev.* Fort-Carnot. Fianarantsoa, SE Madagascar *21.52S 47.27E*
41 P5 **Ikpikpuk River** ≈ Alaska, USA
202 H1 **Iku** *prev.* Lone Tree Islet. *atoll* Tungaru, W Kiribati
171 Gg14 **Ikuno** Hyōgo, Honshū, SW Japan *35.13N 134.48E*
202 H16 **Ikurangi** ▲ Rarotonga, S Cook Islands *21.12S 159.45W*
176 Xx12 **Ilaga** Papua, E Indonesia *3.54S 137.30E*
179 Pp8 **Ilagan** Luzon, N Philippines *17.07N 121.54E*
159 R12 **Ilam** Eastern, E Nepal *26.52N 87.58E*
148 J7 **Īlām** *var.* Elam. Īlām, W Iran *33.40N 46.24E*
148 J8 **Īlām** *off.* Ostān-e Īlām. ◐ *province* W Iran
167 T13 **Ilan** *Jap.* Giran. N Taiwan *24.46N 121.46E*
152 G9 **Ilanly Obvodnitel'nyy Kanal** *canal* N Turkmenistan
126 Ii14 **Ilanskiy** Krasnoyarskiy Kray, S Russian Federation *56.16N 95.59E*
110 H9 **Ilanz** Graubünden, S Switzerland *46.46N 9.10E*
79 S16 **Ilaro** Ogun, SW Nigeria *6.52N 3.01E*
59 I17 **Ilave** Puno, S Peru *16.07S 69.37W*
112 K8 **Iława** *Ger.* Deutsch-Eylau. Warmińsko-Mazurskie, NE Poland, *53.36N 19.34E*
126 Ll11 **Il'benge** Respublika Sakha (Yakutiya), NE Russian Federation *62.52N 124.13E*
133 R7 **Ile** *var.* Ili, *Chin.* Ili He, *Rus.* Reka Ili. ≈ China/Kazakhstan *see also* Ili He
9 S13 **Ile-à-la-Crosse** Saskatchewan, C Canada *55.29N 108.00W*
81 J21 **Ilebo** *prev.* Port-Francqui. Kasai Occidental, W Dem. Rep. Congo *4.19S 20.31E*
105 N5 **Île-de-France** ◐ *region* N France
150 I9 **Ilek** *Kaz.* Elek. ≈ Kazakhstan/Russian Federation
Ilerda *see* Lleida
79 T16 **Ilesha** Osun, SW Nigeria *7.35N 4.49E*
197 J5 **Îles Loyauté, Province des** ◐ *province* E New Caledonia
9 X12 **Ilford** Manitoba, C Canada *56.02N 95.48W*
99 I23 **Ilfracombe** SW England, UK *51.12N 4.09W*
142 I11 **Ilgaz Dağları** ▲▲ N Turkey
142 G15 **Ilgın** Konya, W Turkey *38.16N 31.57E*
62 I7 **Ilha Solteira** São Paulo, S Brazil *20.28S 51.19W*
106 G7 **Ílhavo** Aveiro, N Portugal *40.36N 8.40W*
61 O18 **Ilhéus** Bahia, E Brazil *14.49S 39.06W*
Ili *see* Ile/Ili He
118 G11 **Ilia** *Hung.* Marosillye. Hunedoara, SW Romania *45.57N 22.39E*
41 P13 **Iliamna** Alaska, USA *59.42N 154.49W*
41 P13 **Iliamna Lake** ◎ Alaska, USA
143 N13 **Iliç** Erzincan, C Turkey *39.27N 38.34E*
Il'ichevsk *see* Şärur, Azerbaijan
Il'ichevsk *see* Illichivs'k, Ukraine
Ilici *see* Elche
39 V2 **Iliff** Colorado, C USA *40.46N 103.04W*
179 R15 **Iligan** *off.* Iligan City. Mindanao, S Philippines *8.12N 124.15E*
179 R15 **Iligan Bay** *bay* S Philippines
164 I5 **Ili He** *var.* Ili, *Kaz.* Ile, *Rus.* Reka Ili. ≈ China/Kazakhstan *see also* Ile
58 C6 **Iliniza** ▲ N Ecuador *0.37S 78.41W*
Ilinski *see* Il'inskiy
129 U14 **Il'inskiy** *var.* Ilinski. Permskaya Oblast', NW Russian Federation *58.33N 55.31E*
127 Oo15 **Il'inskiy** Ostrov Sakhalin, Sakhalinskaya Oblast', SE Russian Federation *47.59N 142.14E*
20 I10 **Ilion** New York, NE USA *43.01N 75.02W*
40 E9 **'Īlio Point** *var.* Ilio Point *headland* Moloka'i, Hawai'i, USA, C Pacific Ocean *21.13N 157.15W*
111 T13 **Ilirska Bistrica** *prev.* Bistrica, *Ger.* Feistritz, Illyrisch-Feistritz, *It.* Villa del Nevoso. SW Slovenia *45.34N 14.12E*
143 Q16 **Ilisu Barajı** ⊠ SE Turkey
161 G17 **Ilkal** Karnātaka, C India *15.59N 76.08E*
99 M19 **Ilkeston** C England, UK *52.58N 1.18W*
123 Jj17 **Il-Kullana** *headland* SW Malta *35.49N 14.26E*
110 J8 **Ill** ≈ W Austria
105 U6 **Ill** ≈ NE France
64 G10 **Illapel** Coquimbo, C Chile *31.40S 71.13W*
Illaue Fartak Trench *see* Alula-Fartak Trench
190 C2 **Illbillee, Mount** ▲ South Australia *27.01S 132.13E*
104 I6 **Ille-et-Vilaine** ◐ *department* NW France
79 T11 **Illéla** Tahoua, SW Niger *14.25N 5.10E*
103 J24 **Iller** ≈ S Germany
103 J23 **Illertissen** Bayern, S Germany *48.13N 10.08E*
107 N8 **Illescas** Castilla-La Mancha, C Spain *40.07N 3.51W*
Ille-sur-la-Têt *see* Ille-sur-Têt
105 O17 **Ille-sur-Têt** *var.* Ille-sur-la-Têt. Pyrénées-Orientales, S France *42.40N 2.37E*
Illiberis *see* Elne
119 P11 **Illichivs'k** *Rus.* Il'ichevsk. Odes'ka Oblast', SW Ukraine *46.18N 30.36E*
Illicis *see* Elche
104 M6 **Illiers-Combray** Eure-et-Loir, C France *48.19N 1.14E*
32 K12 **Illinois** *off.* State of Illinois; also known as Prairie State, Sucker State. ◐ *state* C USA
32 J13 **Illinois River** ≈ Illinois, N USA
119 N6 **Illintsi** Vinnyts'ka Oblast', C Ukraine *49.07N 29.13E*
Illiturgis *see* Andújar
76 M10 **Illizi** SE Algeria *26.30N 8.28E*
29 Y7 **Illmo** Missouri, C USA *37.13N 89.30W*
Illur co *see* Lorca
Illuro *see* Mataró
Illyrisch-Feistritz *see* Ilirska Bistrica
103 K16 **Ilm** ≈ C Germany
103 K17 **Ilmenau** Thüringen, C Germany *50.40N 10.55E*
128 H14 **Il'men', Ozero** ◎ NW Russian Federation
59 H18 **Ilo** Moquegua, SW Peru *17.39S 71.22W*
179 Q13 **Iloilo** *off.* Iloilo City. Panay Island, C Philippines *10.42N 122.34E*
114 K10 **Ilok** *Hung.* Újlak. Serbia, NW Serbia and Montenegro (Yugoslavia) *45.12N 19.22E*
95 O16 **Ilomantsi** Itä-Suomi, E Finland *62.40N 30.55E*
44 F8 **Ilopango, Lago de** *volcanic lake* C El Salvador
79 T15 **Ilorin** Kwara, W Nigeria *8.32N 4.34E*
119 X8 **Ilovays'k** *Rus.* Ilovaysk. Donets'ka Oblast', SE Ukraine *47.54N 38.13E*
131 O10 **Ilovlya** Volgogradskaya Oblast', SW Russian Federation *49.45N 44.18E*
131 O10 **Ilovlya** ≈ SW Russian Federation
127 P8 **Il'pyrskoye** Koryakskiy Avtonomnyy Okrug, E Russian Federation *60.00N 164.16E*
130 K14 **Il'skiy** Krasnodarskiy Kray, SW Russian Federation *44.52N 38.26E*
190 B2 **Iltur** South Australia *27.33S 130.31E*
176 Y11 **Ilugwa** Papua, E Indonesia *3.42S 139.09E*
İluh *see* Batman
120 I11 **Ilūkste** Daugvapils, SE Latvia *55.58N 26.21E*
176 Uu12 **Ilur** Pulau Gorong, E Indonesia *4.00S 131.25E*
34 F10 **Ilwaco** Washington, NW USA *46.19N 124.03W*
Il'yaly *see* Ýylanly
İlyasbaba Burnu *see* Tekke Burnu
129 U9 **Ilych** ≈ NW Russian Federation
103 O21 **Ilz** ≈ SE Germany
113 M14 **Iłża** Radom, SE Poland *51.09N 21.15E*
170 Ee14 **Imabari** *var.* Imaharu. Ehime, Shikoku, SW Japan *34.04N 132.58E*
172 N5 **Imagane** Hokkaidō, NE Japan *42.26N 140.00E*
Imaharu *see* Imabari
171 K15 **Imaichi** *var.* Imaiti. Tochigi, Honshū, S Japan *36.43N 139.40E*
Imaiti *see* Imaichi
171 Hh14 **Imajō** Fukui, Honshū, SW Japan *35.45N 136.10E*
145 R9 **Imām Ibn Hāshim** C Iraq *32.46N 43.21E*
145 T11 **Imān 'Abd Allāh** S Iraq *31.36N 44.34E*
128 J4 **Imandra, Ozero** ◎ NW Russian Federation
170 E16 **Imano-yama** ▲ Shikoku, SW Japan *32.51N 132.48E*
170 C13 **Imari** Saga, Kyūshū, SW Japan *33.16N 129.51E*
Imarssuak Mid-Ocean Seachannel *see* Imarssuak Seachannel
66 J6 **Imarssuak Seachannel** *var.* Imarssuak Mid-Ocean Seachannel. *channel* N Atlantic Ocean
95 N18 **Imatra** Etelä-Suomi, S Finland *61.13N 28.49E*
171 H14 **Imazu** Shiga, Honshū, SW Japan *35.25N 136.00E*
58 C6 **Imbabura** ◐ *province* N Ecuador
57 R9 **Imbaimadai** W Guyana *5.44N 60.23W*
63 K14 **Imbituba** Santa Catarina, S Brazil *28.15S 48.43W*
29 W9 **Imboden** Arkansas, C USA *36.12N 91.10W*
Imbros *see* Gökçeada
Imeni 26 Bakinskikh Komissarov *see* 26 Bakı Komissarı/Uzboý
129 N13 **Imeni Babushkina** Vologodskaya Oblast', NW Russian Federation *59.40N 43.04E*
130 J7 **Imeni Karla Libknekhta** Kurskaya Oblast', W Russian Federation *51.36N 35.28E*
Imeni Mollanepesa *see* Mollanepes Adyndaky
127 N14 **Imeni Poliny Osipenko** Khabarovskiy Kray, SE Russian Federation *52.21N 136.17E*
Imeni S.A.Niyazova *see* S.A.Nyýazow Adyndaky
Imeni Sverdlova Rudnik *see* Sverdlovs'k
196 E9 **Imeong** Babeldaob, N Palau
83 L14 **Īmī** Somali, E Ethiopia *6.27N 42.10E*
117 M21 **Imia** *Turk.* Kardak. *island* Dodekánisos, Greece, Aegean Sea
Imishli *see* İmişli
143 X12 **İmişli** *Rus.* Imishli. C Azerbaijan *39.54N 48.04E*
169 X14 **Imjin-gang** ≈ North Korea/South Korea
37 S3 **Imlay** Nevada, W USA *40.39N 118.10W*
33 S9 **Imlay City** Michigan, N USA *43.01N 83.04W*
25 X15 **Immokalee** Florida, SE USA *26.24N 81.25W*
79 U17 **Imo** ◐ *state* SE Nigeria
108 G10 **Imola** Emilia-Romagna, N Italy *44.22N 11.43E*
194 E9 **Imonda** Sandaun, NW PNG *3.19S 141.10E*
Imoschi *see* Imotski
115 G14 **Imotski** *It.* Imoschi. Split-Dalmacija, SE Croatia *43.28N 17.13E*
61 L14 **Imperatriz** Maranhão, NE Brazil *5.31S 47.28W*
108 B10 **Imperia** Liguria, NW Italy *43.52N 8.03E*
59 E15 **Imperial** Lima, W Peru *13.04S 76.20W*
37 X17 **Imperial** California, W USA *32.51N 115.34W*
30 L16 **Imperial** Nebraska, C USA *40.30N 101.37W*
26 M9 **Imperial** Texas, SW USA *31.15N 102.40W*
37 Y17 **Imperial Dam** *dam* California, W USA *32.52N 114.27W*
81 I17 **Impfondo** La Likouala, NE Congo *1.40N 18.02E*
159 X14 **Imphāl** Manipur, NE India *24.46N 93.55E*
105 P9 **Imphy** Nièvre, C France *46.55N 3.16E*
108 G11 **Impruneta** Toscana, C Italy *43.42N 11.16E*
117 K15 **İmroz** *var.* Gökçeada. Çanakkale, NW Turkey *40.11N 25.53E*
Imroz Adası *see* Gökçeada
110 L7 **Imst** Tirol, W Austria *47.13N 10.40E*
42 F3 **Imuris** Sonora, NW Mexico *30.48N 110.52W*
179 P11 **Imus** Luzon, N Philippines *14.27N 120.55E*
171 J15 **Ina** Nagano, Honshū, S Japan *35.55N 137.59E*
67 M18 **Inaccessible Island** *island* W Tristan da Cunha
117 F20 **Ínachos** ≈ S Greece
196 H6 **I Naftan, Puntan** *headland* Saipan, S Northern Mariana Islands
Inagua Islands *see* Great Inagua/Little Inagua
193 H15 **Inangahua** West Coast, South Island, NZ *41.51S 171.58E*
176 V10 **Inanwatan** Papua, E Indonesia *2.06S 132.07E*
59 I14 **Iñapari** Madre de Dios, E Peru *11.00S 69.34W*
196 B17 **Inarajan** SE Guam *13.16N 144.45E*
94 L10 **Inari** *Lapp.* Anár, Aanaar. Lappi, N Finland *68.54N 27.06E*
94 L10 **Inarijärvi** *Lapp.* Aanaarjävri, *Swe.* Enareträsk. ◎ N Finland
94 L9 **Inarijoki** *Lapp.* Anárjohka. ≈ Finland/Norway
Inău *see* Ineu
171 L14 **Inawashiro-ko** *var.* Inawasiro Ko. ◎ Honshū, C Japan
Inawasiro Ko *see* Inawashiro-ko
64 H7 **Inca de Oro** Atacama, N Chile *26.45S 69.54W*
117 J15 **İnce Burnu** *headland* NW Turkey *40.08N 25.39E*
142 K9 **İnce Burnu** *headland* N Turkey *42.06N 34.57E*
142 I17 **İncekum Burnu** *headland* S Turkey *36.13N 33.57E*
78 G7 **Inchiri** ◐ *region* NW Mauritania
169 X15 **Inch'ŏn** *off.* Inch'ŏn-gwangyŏksi, *Jap.* Jinsen; *prev.* Chemulpo. NW South Korea *37.27N 126.40E*
169 X15 **Inch'on** ✈ (Sŏul) NW South Korea *37.37N 126.42E*
85 M17 **Inchope** Manica, C Mozambique *19.09S 33.54E*
Incoronata *see* Kornat
105 Y15 **Incudine, Monte** ▲ Corse, France, C Mediterranean Sea *41.52N 9.13E*
62 M10 **Indaiatuba** São Paulo, S Brazil *23.03S 47.14W*
95 H17 **Indal** Västernorrland, C Sweden *62.36N 17.06E*
95 H17 **Indalsälven** ≈ C Sweden
42 K8 **Inde** Durango, C Mexico *25.55N 105.10W*
Indefatigable Island *see* Santa Cruz, Isla
37 S10 **Independence** California, W USA *36.48N 118.12W*
31 X13 **Independence** Iowa, C USA *42.28N 91.42W*
29 P7 **Independence** Kansas, C USA *37.13N 95.42W*
22 M4 **Independence** Kentucky, S USA *38.56N 84.32W*
29 R4 **Independence** Missouri, C USA *39.05N 94.25W*
23 R8 **Independence** Virginia, NE USA *36.37N 81.09W*
32 J7 **Independence** Wisconsin, N USA *44.21N 91.25W*
207 R12 **Independence Fjord** *fjord* N Greenland
Independence Island *see* Malden Island
37 W2 **Independence Mountains** ▲▲ Nevada, W USA
59 K18 **Independencia** Cochabamba, C Bolivia *17.07S 66.52W*
59 E16 **Independencia, Bahía de la** *bay* W Peru
Independencia, Monte *see* Adam, Mount
118 M12 **Independența** Galați, SE Romania *45.27N 27.45E*
Inderagiri *see* Indragiri, Sungai
Īnderbor *see* Inderborskiy
150 F11 **Inderborskiy** *Kaz.* Īnderbor. Atyrau, W Kazakhstan *48.35N 51.45E*
157 I14 **India** *off.* Republic of India, *var.* Indian Union, Union of India, *Hind.* Bhārat. ◆ *republic* S Asia
India *see* Inđija
20 D14 **Indiana** Pennsylvania, NE USA *40.37N 79.09W*
33 N13 **Indiana** *off.* State of Indiana; also known as The Hoosier State. ◐ *state* N USA
33 O14 **Indianapolis** *state capital* Indiana, N USA *39.46N 86.09W*
9 O10 **Indian Cabins** Alberta, W Canada *59.51N 117.06W*
44 G1 **Indian Church** Orange Walk, N Belize *17.47N 88.39W*
Indian Desert *see* Thar Desert
9 U16 **Indian Head** Saskatchewan, S Canada *50.31N 103.40W*
33 O4 **Indian Lake** ◎ Michigan, N USA
20 K9 **Indian Lake** ◎ New York, NE USA
33 R13 **Indian Lake** ⊠ Ohio, N USA
180-181 **Indian Ocean** *ocean*
31 V15 **Indianola** Iowa, C USA *41.21N 93.33W*
24 K4 **Indianola** Mississippi, S USA *33.27N 90.39W*
38 J6 **Indian Peak** ▲ Utah, W USA *38.18N 113.52W*
25 Y13 **Indian River** *lagoon* Florida, SE USA
37 W10 **Indian Springs** Nevada, W USA *36.33N 115.40W*
25 Y14 **Indiantown** Florida, SE USA *27.01N 80.29W*
61 K19 **Indiara** Goiás, S Brazil *17.12S 50.09W*
129 Q4 **Indiga** Nenetskiy Avtonomnyy Okrug, NW Russian Federation *67.40N 49.01E*
126 Mm6 **Indigirka** ≈ NE Russian Federation
114 L10 **Inđija** *Hung.* India; *prev.* Indjija. Serbia, N Serbia and Montenegro (Yugoslavia) *45.03N 20.04E*
37 V16 **Indio** California, W USA *33.42N 116.13W*
44 M12 **Indio, Río** ≈ SE Nicaragua
158 I10 **Indira Gandhi International** ✈ (Delhi) Delhi, N India
157 Q23 **Indira Point** *headland* Andaman and Nicobar Islands, India, NE Indian Ocean *6.54N 93.54E*
195 X15 **Indispensable Strait** *strait* C Solomon Islands
Indjija *see* Inđija
133 Q13 **Indo-Australian Plate** *tectonic feature*
181 N11 **Indomed Fracture Zone** *tectonic feature* SW Indian Ocean
175 Nn12 **Indonesia** *off.* Republic of Indonesia, *Ind.* Republik Indonesia; *prev.* Dutch East Indies, Netherlands East Indies, United States of Indonesia. ◆ *republic* SE Asia
Indonesian Borneo *see* Kalimantan
160 G10 **Indore** Madhya Pradesh, C India *22.42N 75.50E*
174 Hh8 **Indragiri, Sungai** *var.* Batang Kuantan, Inderagiri. ≈ Sumatera, W Indonesia
Indramajoe/Indramaju *see* Indramayu
174 K14 **Indramayu** *prev.* Indramajoe, Indramaju. Jawa, C Indonesia *6.22S 108.19E*
161 K14 **Indrāvati** ≈ S India
105 N9 **Indre** ◐ *department* C France
104 M8 **Indre** ≈ C France
96 D13 **Indre Ålvik** Hordaland, S Norway *60.26N 6.27E*
104 L8 **Indre-et-Loire** ◐ *department* C France
Indreville *see* Châteauroux
158 G3 **Indus** *Chin.* Yindu He; *prev.* Yin-tu Ho. ≈ S Asia
Indus Cone *see* Indus Fan
181 P3 **Indus Fan** *var.* Indus Cone. *undersea feature* N Arabian Sea
155 P17 **Indus, Mouths of the** *delta* S Pakistan
85 I24 **Indwe** Eastern Cape, SE South Africa *31.28S 27.19E*
142 I10 **İnebolu** Kastamonu, N Turkey *41.57N 33.45E*
79 P8 **I-n-Échaï** *oasis* C Mali *20.04N 2.00W*
116 M13 **İnecik** Tekirdağ, NW Turkey *40.55N 27.16E*
142 E12 **İnegöl** Bursa, NW Turkey *40.06N 29.31E*
Inessa *see* Biancavilla
118 F10 **Ineu** *Hung.* Borosjenő; *prev.* Inău. Arad, W Romania *46.25N 21.50E*
Ineul/Ineu, Vîrful *see* Ineu, Vârful
118 J9 **Ineu, Vârful** *var.* Ineul; *prev.* Vîrful Ineu. ▲ N Romania *47.31N 24.52E*
23 P6 **Inez** Kentucky, S USA *37.53N 82.33W*
76 E8 **Inezgane** ✈ (Agadir) W Morocco *30.35N 9.27W*
43 T17 **Inferior, Laguna** *lagoon* S Mexico
42 M15 **Infiernillo, Presa del** ⊠ S Mexico
106 L2 **Infiesto** Asturias, N Spain *43.21N 5.21W*
95 L20 **Ingå** *Fin.* Inkoo. Etelä-Suomi, S Finland *60.01N 24.05E*
79 U10 **Ingal** *var.* I-n-Gall. Agadez, C Niger *16.52N 6.57E*
I-n-Gall *see* Ingal
101 C18 **Ingelmunster** West-Vlaanderen, W Belgium *50.12N 3.15E*
81 I18 **Ingende** Equateur, W Dem. Rep. Congo *0.15S 18.58E*
64 L5 **Ingeniero Guillermo Nueva Juárez** Formosa, N Argentina *23.55S 61.49W*
65 H16 **Ingeniero Jacobacci** Río Negro, C Argentina *41.21S 69.46W*
12 F16 **Ingersoll** Ontario, S Canada *43.03N 80.52W*
168 K6 **Ingettolgoy** Bulgan, N Mongolia *49.27N 103.59E*
189 W5 **Ingham** Queensland, NE Australia *18.34S 146.12E*
152 M11 **Ingichka** Samarqand Viloyati, C Uzbekistan *39.46N 65.56E*
99 L16 **Ingleborough** ▲ N England, UK *54.07N 2.22W*
27 T14 **Ingleside** Texas, SW USA *27.52N 97.12W*
192 K10 **Inglewood** Taranaki, North Island, NZ *39.10S 174.12E*
37 S15 **Inglewood** California, W USA *33.57N 118.21W*
126 Kk16 **Ingoda** ≈ S Russian Federation
103 L21 **Ingolstadt** Bayern, S Germany *48.46N 11.25E*
35 V9 **Ingomar** Montana, NW USA *46.34N 107.21W*
11 R14 **Ingonish Beach** Cape Breton Island, Nova Scotia, SE Canada *46.42N 60.22W*
159 S14 **Ingrāj Bāzār** *prev.* English Bazar. West Bengal, NE India *25.00N 88.10E*
27 Q11 **Ingram** Texas, SW USA *30.04N 99.14W*
205 X7 **Ingrid Christensen Coast** *physical region* Antarctica
76 K14 **I-n-Guezzam** S Algeria *19.35N 5.49E*
Ingulets *see* Inhulets'
Inguri *see* Enguri
Ingushetia/Ingushetiya, Respublika *see* Ingushskaya Respublika
131 O15 **Ingushskaya Respublika** *var.* Respublika Ingushetiya, *Eng.* Ingushetia. ◐ *autonomous republic* SW Russian Federation
85 N20 **Inhambane** Inhambane, SE Mozambique *23.52S 35.31E*
85 M20 **Inhambane** *off.* Província de Inhambane. ◐ *province* S Mozambique
85 N17 **Inhaminga** Sofala, C Mozambique *18.22S 35.02E*
85 N20 **Inharrime** Inhambane, SE Mozambique *24.28S 35.01E*
85 M18 **Inhassoro** Inhambane, E Mozambique *21.31S 35.13E*
119 S9 **Inhulets'** *Rus.* Ingulets. Dnipropetrovs'ka Oblast', E Ukraine *47.40N 33.15E*
119 R10 **Inhulets'** *Rus.* Ingulets. ≈ S Ukraine
107 Q10 **Iniesta** Castilla-La Mancha, C Spain *39.27N 1.45W*
I-ning *see* Yining
56 K11 **Inírida, Río** ≈ E Colombia
Inis *see* Ennis
Inis Ceithleann *see* Enniskillen
Inis Córthaidh *see* Enniscorthy
Inis Díomáin *see* Ennistimon
99 A17 **Inishbofin** *Ir.* Inis Bó Finne. *island* W Ireland
99 B18 **Inisheer** *var.* Inishere, *Ir.* Inis Oírr. *island* W Ireland
Inishere *see* Inisheer
99 B18 **Inishmaan** *Ir.* Inis Meáin. *island* W Ireland
99 A18 **Inishmore** *Ir.* Árainn. *island* W Ireland
98 E13 **Inishtrahull** *Ir.* Inis Trá Tholl. *island* NW Ireland
99 A17 **Inishturk** *Ir.* Inis Toirc. *island* W Ireland
Inkoo *see* Ingå
193 J16 **Inland Kaikoura Range** ▲▲ South Island, NZ
Inland Sea *see* Seto-naikai
23 P11 **Inman** South Carolina, SE USA *35.03N 82.05W*
110 L7 **Inn** ≈ C Europe
207 O11 **Innaanganeq** *var.* Kap York. *headland* NW Greenland *75.54N 66.27W*
190 K2 **Innamincka** South Australia *27.47S 140.45E*
94 G12 **Inndyr** Nordland, C Norway *67.01N 14.00E*
44 G3 **Inner Channel** *inlet* SE Belize
98 F11 **Inner Hebrides** *island group* W Scotland, UK
180 H15 **Inner Islands** *var.* Central Group. *island group* NE Seychelles
Inner Mongolia/Inner Mongolian Autonomous Region *see* Nei Mongol Zizhiqu
98 G8 **Inner Sound** *strait* NW Scotland, UK
102 J13 **Innerste** ≈ C Germany
189 W5 **Innisfail** Queensland, NE Australia *17.29S 146.03E*
9 Q15 **Innisfail** Alberta, SW Canada *52.01N 113.58W*
Inniskilling *see* Enniskillen
41 O11 **Innoko River** ≈ Alaska, USA
170 F14 **Innoshima** *var.* Innosima. Hiroshima, SW Japan *34.18N 133.09E*
Innosima *see* Innoshima
Innsbruch *see* Innsbruck
110 M7 **Innsbruck** *var.* Innsbruch. Tirol, W Austria *47.16N 11.25E*
81 I19 **Inongo** Bandundu, W Dem. Rep. Congo *1.55S 18.19E*
Inoucdjouac *see* Inukjuak
Inowrazlaw *see* Inowrocław
112 I10 **Inowrocław** *Ger.* Hohensalza; *prev.* Inowrazlaw. Kujawski-pomorskie, C Poland *52.47N 18.15E*
59 K18 **Inquisivi** La Paz, W Bolivia *17.01S 67.03W*
Inrin *see* Yüanlin
79 O8 **I-n-Sâkâne, 'Erg** *desert* N Mali
76 J10 **I-n-Salah** *var.* In Salah. C Algeria *27.10N 2.31E*
131 O5 **Insar** Respublika Mordoviya, W Russian Federation *53.52N 44.26E*
201 X15 **Insiaf** Kosrae, E Micronesia
96 L13 **Insjön** Dalarna, C Sweden *60.40N 15.05E*
Insterburg *see* Chernyakhovsk
Insula *see* Lille
118 L13 **Însurăţei** Brăila, SE Romania *44.55N 27.40E*
129 V6 **Inta** Respublika Komi, NW Russian Federation *66.00N 60.09E*
79 R9 **I-n-Tebezas** Kidal, E Mali *17.58N 1.51E*
Interamna *see* Teramo
Interamna Nahars *see* Terni
30 L11 **Interior** South Dakota, N USA *43.42N 101.57W*
110 E9 **Interlaken** Bern, SW Switzerland *46.40N 7.51E*
31 V2 **International Falls** Minnesota, N USA *48.37N 93.25W*
178 Gg7 **Inthanon, Doi** ▲ NW Thailand *18.33N 98.29E*
44 G7 **Intibucá** ◐ *department* SW Honduras
44 G8 **Intipucá** La Unión, SE El Salvador *13.10N 88.03W*
63 B15 **Intiyaco** Santa Fe, C Argentina *28.43S 60.04W*
118 K12 **Întorsura Buzăului** *Ger.* Bozau, *Hung.* Bodzafordulő. Covasna, E Romania *45.49N 26.10E*
24 H9 **Intracoastal Waterway** *inland waterway system* Louisiana, S USA
27 V13 **Intracoastal Waterway** *inland waterway system* Texas, SW USA
110 G11 **Intragna** Ticino, S Switzerland *46.12N 8.42E*
171 Kk17 **Inubō-zaki** *headland* Honshū, S Japan *35.42N 140.51E*
170 D14 **Inukai** Ōita, Kyūshū, SW Japan *33.05N 131.37E*
10 I5 **Inukjuak** *var.* Inoucdjouac; *prev.* Port Harrison. Québec, NE Canada *58.28N 77.58W*
65 I24 **Inútil, Bahía** *bay* S Chile
Inuuvik *see* Inuvik
14 G3 **Inuvik** *var.* Inuuvik. Northwest Territories, NW Canada *68.25N 133.34W*
171 I15 **Inuyama** Aichi, Honshū, SW Japan *35.22N 136.55E*
58 G13 **Inuya, Río** ≈ E Peru
129 U13 **In'va** ≈ NW Russian Federation
98 H11 **Inveraray** W Scotland, UK *56.13N 5.04W*
193 C24 **Invercargill** Southland, South Island, NZ *46.25S 168.22E*
191 T5 **Inverell** New South Wales, SE Australia *29.49S 151.07E*
98 I8 **Invergordon** N Scotland, UK *57.42N 4.01W*
9 P16 **Invermere** British Columbia, SW Canada *50.30N 116.00W*
11 R14 **Inverness** Cape Breton Island, Nova Scotia, SE Canada *46.13N 61.19W*
98 I8 **Inverness** N Scotland, UK *57.27N 4.15W*
25 V11 **Inverness** Florida, SE USA *28.50N 82.19W*
98 I9 **Inverness** *cultural region* NW Scotland, UK
98 K9 **Inverurie** NE Scotland, UK *57.13N 2.13W*
190 F8 **Investigator Group** *island group* South Australia
181 T7 **Investigator Ridge** *undersea feature* E Indian Ocean
190 H10 **Investigator Strait** *strait* South Australia
31 R11 **Inwood** Iowa, C USA *43.16N 96.25W*
126 H16 **Inya** Respublika Altay, S Russian Federation *50.27N 86.45E*
127 Nn10 **Inya** ≈ E Russian Federation
Inyanga *see* Nyanga
85 M16 **Inyangani** ▲ NE Zimbabwe *18.22S 32.57E*
85 J17 **Inyathi** Matabeleland North, SW Zimbabwe *19.36S 28.52E*
37 T12 **Inyokern** California, W USA *35.37N 117.48W*
37 T10 **Inyo Mountains** ▲▲ California, W USA
131 P6 **Inza** Ul'yanovskaya Oblast', W Russian Federation *53.51N 46.21E*
131 W5 **Inzer** Respublika Bashkortostan, W Russian Federation *54.11N 57.37E*
131 N7 **Inzhavino** Tambovskaya Oblast', W Russian Federation *52.18N 42.28E*
117 C16 **Ioánnina** *var.* Janina, Yannina. Ípeiros, W Greece *39.39N 20.52E*
170 B17 **Iō-jima** *var.* Iwojima. *island* Nansei-shotō, SW Japan
128 L4 **Iokan'ga** ≈ NW Russian Federation
29 Q6 **Iola** Kansas, C USA *37.55N 95.24W*
Iolcus *see* Iolkós
117 G16 **Iolkós** *anc.* Iolcus. *site of ancient city* Thessalía, C Greece *39.24N 22.56E*
Iolotan' *see* Ýolöten
85 A16 **Iona** Namibe, SW Angola *16.54S 12.39E*
98 F11 **Iona** *island* W Scotland, UK
118 M15 **Ion Corvin** Constanța, SE Romania *44.06N 27.49E*
37 P7 **Ione** California, W USA *38.21N 120.55W*
118 I13 **Ionești** Vâlcea, SW Romania *44.51N 24.12E*
33 Q9 **Ionia** Michigan, N USA *42.59N 85.04W*
Ionia Basin *see* Ionian Basin
123 Mm12 **Ionian Basin** *var.* Ionia Basin. *undersea feature* Ionian Sea, C Mediterranean Sea
Ionian Islands *see* Iónioi Nísoi
123 Mm11 **Ionian Sea** *Gk.* Iónio Pélagos, *It.* Mar Ionio. *sea* C Mediterranean Sea
117 B17 **Iónioi Nísoi** *Eng.* Ionian Islands. ◐ *region* W Greece
117 B17 **Iónioi Nísoi** *Eng.* Ionian Islands. *island group* W Greece
Ionio, Mar/Iónio Pélagos *see* Ionian Sea
Iordan *see* Yordan
143 U10 **Iori** *var.* Qabırrı. ≈ Azerbaijan/Georgia
Iorrais, Ceann *see* Erris Head
117 J22 **Íos** Íos, Kykládes, Greece, Aegean Sea *36.42N 25.16E*
117 J22 **Íos** *var.* Nio. *island* Kykládes, Greece, Aegean Sea
24 G9 **Iowa** Louisiana, S USA *30.12N 93.00W*
31 V13 **Iowa** *off.* State of Iowa; also known as The Hawkeye State. ◐ *state* C USA
31 Y14 **Iowa City** Iowa, C USA *41.39N 91.31W*

◆ Country
● Country Capital
◇ Dependent Territory
○ Dependent Territory Capital
◐ Administrative Region
✈ International Airport
▲ Mountain
▲▲ Mountain Range
Volcano
≈ River
◎ Lake
⊠ Reservoir
269

IOWA FALLS – JABĀLIYAH

31 V13 **Iowa Falls** Iowa, C USA 42.31N 93.15W
27 R4 **Iowa Park** Texas, SW USA 33.57N 98.40W
31 Y14 **Iowa River** ≈ Iowa, C USA
121 M19 **Ipa** *Rus.* Ipa. ≈ SE Belarus
61 N20 **Ipatinga** Minas Gerais, SE Brazil 19.31S 42.30W
131 N13 **Ipatovo** Stavropol'skiy Kray, SW Russian Federation 45.40N 42.51E
117 C16 **Ípeiros** *Eng.* Epirus. ◈ *region* W Greece
Ipek *see* Peć
113 J21 **Ipel'** *var.* Ipoly, *Ger.* Eipel. ≈ Hungary/Slovakia
56 C13 **Ipiales** Nariño, SW Colombia 0.50N 77.42W
201 V14 **Ipis** *atoll* Chuuk Islands, C Micronesia
61 A14 **Ipixuna** Amazonas, W Brazil 6.57S 71.42W
174 Gg4 **Ipoh** Perak, Peninsular Malaysia 4.36N 101.01E
Ipoly *see* Ipel'
197 D15 **Ipota** Erromango, S Vanuatu 18.54S 169.19E
81 K14 **Ippy** Ouaka, C Central African Republic 6.17N 21.13E
116 L13 **İpsala** Edirne, NW Turkey 40.55N 26.24E
Ipsario *see* Ypsário
191 V3 **Ipswich** Queensland, E Australia 27.36S 152.49E
99 Q20 **Ipswich** *hist.* Gipeswic. E England, UK 52.05N 1.08E
31 O8 **Ipswich** South Dakota, N USA 45.24N 99.00W
Iput' *see* Iputs'
121 P18 **Iputs'** *Rus.* Iput'. ≈ Belarus/Russian Federation
16 O3 **Iqaluit** *prev.* Frobisher Bay. Baffin Island, Nunavut, NE Canada 63.43N 68.28W
165 P9 **Iqe** Qinghai, W China 38.03N 94.45E
165 P9 **Iqe He** ≈ C China
Iqlid *see* Eqlīd
64 G3 **Iquique** Tarapacá, N Chile 20.15S 70.07W
58 G8 **Iquitos** Loreto, N Peru 3.51S 73.13W
27 N9 **Iraan** Texas, SW USA 30.52N 101.52W
81 K14 **Ira Banda** Haute-Kotto, E Central African Republic 5.57N 22.05E
172 Pp16 **Irabu-jima** *island* Miyako-shotō, SW Japan
57 Y9 **Iracoubo** N French Guiana 5.28N 53.15W
171 Hh17 **Irago-misaki** *headland* Honshū, SW Japan 34.35N 137.00E
62 H13 **Iraí** Rio Grande do Sul, S Brazil 27.15S 53.16W
116 G12 **Irákleia** Kentrikí Makedonía, N Greece 41.09N 23.16E
117 J21 **Irákleia** *island* Kykládes, Greece, Aegean Sea
117 J25 **Irákleio** *var.* Herakleion, *Eng.* Candia; *prev.* Iráklion. Kríti, Greece, E Mediterranean Sea 35.19N 25.07E
117 J25 **Irákleio** ✕ Kríti, Greece, E Mediterranean Sea 35.20N 25.10E
117 F15 **Irákleio** *anc.* Heracleum. *castle* Kentrikí Makedonía, N Greece 40.02N 22.34E
Iráklion *see* Irákleio
149 O7 **Iran** *off.* Islamic Republic of Iran; *prev.* Persia. ◆ *republic* SW Asia
60 F13 **Iranduba** Amazonas, NW Brazil 3.19S 60.09W
87 P13 **Iranian Plate** *tectonic feature*
149 Q9 **Iranian Plateau** *var.* Plateau of Iran. *plateau* N Iran
175 N6 **Iran, Pegunungan** *var.* Iran Mountains. ▲▲ Indonesia/Malaysia
Iran, Plateau of *see* Iranian Plateau
149 W13 **Īrānshahr** Sīstān va Balūchestān, SE Iran 27.14N 60.40E
57 P5 **Irapa** Sucre, NE Venezuela 10.33N 62.37W
43 N13 **Irapuato** Guanajuato, C Mexico 20.40N 101.22W
145 R7 **Iraq** *off.* Republic of Iraq, *Ar.* 'Irāq. ◆ *republic* SW Asia
62 J12 **Irati** Paraná, S Brazil 25.25S 50.37W
107 R3 **Irati** ≈ N Spain
129 T8 **Irayël'** Respublika Komi, NW Russian Federation 64.28N 55.20E
45 N13 **Irazú, Volcán** Ѧ C Costa Rica 9.57N 83.52W
Irbenskiy Zaliv/Irbes Šaurums *see* Irbe Strait
120 D7 **Irbe Strait** *Est.* Kura Kurk, *Latv.* Irbes Šaurums, *Rus.* Irbenskiy Zaliv; *prev. Est.* Irbe Väin. *strait* Estonia/Latvia
Irbe Väin *see* Irbe Strait
144 G9 **Irbid** Irbid, N Jordan 32.33N 35.51E
144 G9 **Irbid** *off.* Muḩāfaẓat Irbid. ◈ *governorate* N Jordan
Irbīl *see* Arbīl
125 F11 **Irbit** Sverdlovskaya Oblast', C Russian Federation 57.37N 63.10E
111 S6 **Irdning** Steiermark, SE Austria 47.29N 14.04E
81 I18 **Irebu** Equateur, W Dem. Rep. Congo 0.32S 17.44E
86 C9 **Ireland** *Lat.* Hibernia. *island* Ireland/UK
99 D17 **Ireland** *off.* Ireland, *var.* Republic of Ireland, *Ir.* Éire. ◆ *republic* NW Europe
66 A12 **Ireland Island North** *island* W Bermuda
66 A12 **Ireland Island South** *island* W Bermuda
Ireland, Republic of *see* Ireland
129 V15 **Iren'** ≈ NW Russian Federation
193 A22 **Irene, Mount** ▲ South Island, NZ 45.04S 167.24E
Irgalem *see* Yirga 'Alem
150 L11 **Irgiz** Aktyubinsk, C Kazakhstan 48.37N 61.12E
Irian *see* New Guinea
Irian Barat *see* Papua
Irian, Teluk *see* Cenderawasih, Teluk
80 K9 **Iriba** Biltine, NE Chad 15.10N 22.10E
179 Q11 **Iriga** Luzon, N Philippines 13.25N 123.24E
131 X7 **Iriklinskoye Vodokhranilishche** ▣ W Russian Federation
83 H23 **Iringa** Iringa, C Tanzania 7.49S 35.39E
83 H23 **Iringa** ◈ *region* S Tanzania
172 O17 **Iriomote-jima** *island* Sakishima-shotō, SW Japan
44 L4 **Iriona** Colón, NE Honduras 15.53N 85.08W
49 U7 **Iriri** ≈ N Brazil
60 I13 **Iriri, Rio** ≈ C Brazil
Iris *see* Yeşilırmak
37 W9 **Irish, Mount** ▲ Nevada, W USA 37.39N 115.22W
99 H17 **Irish Sea** *Ir.* Muir Éireann. *sea* C British Isles
145 U12 **Irjal ash Shaykhīyah** S Iraq 30.49N 44.58E
153 U11 **Irkeshtam** Oshskaya Oblast', SW Kyrgyzstan 39.39N 73.49E
126 J16 **Irkut** ≈ S Russian Federation
126 Jj16 **Irkutsk** Irkutskaya Oblast', S Russian Federation 52.18N 104.15E
126 Jj13 **Irkutskaya Oblast'** ◈ *province* S Russian Federation
Irlir, Gora *see* Irlir Toghi
152 K8 **Irlir Tog'i** *var.* Gora Irlir. ▲ N Uzbekistan 42.43N 63.24E
Irminger Basin *see* Reykjanes Basin
23 R12 **Irmo** South Carolina, SE USA 34.05N 81.10W
104 E6 **Iroise** *sea* NW France
201 X2 **Iroj** *var.* Eroj. *island* Ratak Chain, SE Marshall Islands
190 H7 **Iron Baron** South Australia 33.01S 137.13E
195 X15 **Iron Bottom Sound** *sound* C Solomon Islands
12 C10 **Iron Bridge** Ontario, S Canada 46.16N 83.12W
22 H10 **Iron City** Tennessee, S USA 35.01N 87.34W
12 I13 **Irondale** ≈ Ontario, SE Canada
190 H7 **Iron Knob** South Australia 32.46S 137.08E
32 M5 **Iron Mountain** Michigan, N USA 45.51N 88.03W
32 M4 **Iron River** Michigan, N USA 46.05N 88.38W
32 J3 **Iron River** Wisconsin, N USA 46.34N 91.22W
29 X6 **Ironton** Missouri, C USA 37.36N 90.37W
33 S15 **Ironton** Ohio, N USA 38.32N 82.40W
32 K4 **Ironwood** Michigan, N USA 46.27N 90.10W
10 H12 **Iroquois Falls** Ontario, S Canada 48.46N 80.40W
33 N12 **Iroquois River** ≈ Illinois/Indiana, N USA
171 Ii18 **Irō-zaki** *headland* Honshū, S Japan 34.36N 138.49E
Irpen' *see* Irpin'
119 O4 **Irpin'** *Rus.* Irpen'. Kyyivs'ka Oblast', N Ukraine 50.31N 30.15E
119 O4 **Irpin'** *Rus.* Irpen'. ≈ N Ukraine
147 Q16 **'Irqah** SW Yemen 13.42N 47.21E
177 Ff8 **Irrawaddy** *var.* Ayeyarwady. ◈ *division* SW Myanmar
177 G6 **Irrawaddy** *var.* Ayeyarwady. ≈ W Myanmar
177 Ff9 **Irrawaddy, Mouths of the** *delta* SW Myanmar
119 N4 **Irsha** ≈ N Ukraine
118 H7 **Irshava** Zakarpats'ka Oblast', W Ukraine 48.19N 23.03E
109 N18 **Irsina** Basilicata, S Italy 40.42N 16.18E
Irtish *see* Irtysh
133 R5 **Irtysh** *var.* Irtish, *Kaz.* Ertis. ≈ C Asia
151 S7 **Irtyshsk** *Kaz.* Ertis. Pavlodar, NE Kazakhstan 53.21N 75.27E
81 P17 **Irumu** Orientale, E Dem. Rep. Congo 1.27N 29.52E
107 Q2 **Irún** País Vasco, N Spain 43.19N 1.48W
Iruña *see* Pamplona
107 Q3 **Irurtzun** Navarra, N Spain 42.55N 1.49W
98 I13 **Irvine** W Scotland, UK 55.37N 4.40W
23 N6 **Irvine** Kentucky, S USA 37.42N 83.58W
27 T6 **Irving** Texas, SW USA 32.48N 96.57W
22 K5 **Irvington** Kentucky, S USA 37.52N 86.16W
Isaak *see* Iisaku
30 L8 **Isabel** South Dakota, N USA 45.21N 101.25W
195 W14 **Isabel** *off.* Isabel Province. ◈ *province* N Solomon Islands
179 Q17 **Isabela** Basilan Island, SW Philippines 6.41N 122.00E
47 S5 **Isabela** W Puerto Rico 18.30N 67.01W
47 N8 **Isabela, Cabo** *headland* NW Dominican Republic 19.54N 71.03W
59 A18 **Isabela, Isla** *var.* Albemarle Island. *island* Galapagos Islands, Ecuador, E Pacific Ocean
42 I12 **Isabela, Isla** *island* C Mexico
44 K9 **Isabella, Cordillera** ▲▲ NW Nicaragua
37 S12 **Isabella Lake** ▣ California, W USA
33 N2 **Isabelle, Point** *headland* Michigan, N USA 47.20N 87.56W
Isabel Segunda *see* Vieques
118 M13 **Isaccea** Tulcea, E Romania 45.16N 28.28E
94 H1 **Ísafjarðardjúp** *inlet* NW Iceland
94 H1 **Ísafjörður** Vestfirdhir, NW Iceland 66.04N 23.09W
170 C13 **Isahaya** Nagasaki, Kyūshū, SW Japan 32.51N 130.04E
155 S7 **Isa Khel** Punjab, E Pakistan 32.39N 71.12E
180 H7 **Isalo** *var.* Massif de L'Isalo. ▲▲ SW Madagascar
Isalo, Massif de L' *see* Isalo
81 K20 **Isandja** Kasai Occidental, C Dem. Rep. Congo 3.03S 21.57E
197 D16 **Isangel** Tanna, S Vanuatu 19.34S 169.17E
81 M18 **Isangi** Orientale, C Dem. Rep. Congo 0.46N 24.15E
103 L24 **Isar** ≈ Austria/Germany
103 M23 **Isar-Kanal** *canal* SE Germany
Isbarta *see* Isparta
Isca Damnoniorum *see* Exeter
109 K18 **Ischia** *var.* Isola d'Ischia; *anc.* Aenaria. Campania, S Italy 40.43N 13.57E
109 J18 **Ischia, Isola d'** *island* S Italy
56 B12 **Iscuandé** *var.* Santa Bárbara. Nariño, SW Colombia 2.31N 78.04W
171 Hh16 **Ise** Mie, Honshū, SW Japan 34.28N 136.42E
102 J12 **Ise** ≈ N Germany
97 I23 **Isefjord** *fjord* E Denmark
Iseghem *see* Izegem
199 Jj17 **Iselin Seamount** *undersea feature* S Pacific Ocean 72.30S 179.00W
Isenhof *see* Püssi
108 E7 **Iseo** Lombardia, N Italy 45.40N 10.03E
105 U12 **Iseran, Col de l'** *pass* E France 45.26N 7.00E
105 S11 **Isère** ◈ *department* E France
105 S12 **Isère** ≈ E France
103 F15 **Iserlohn** Nordrhein-Westfalen, W Germany 51.22N 7.42E
109 K16 **Isernia** *var.* Æsernia. Molise, C Italy 41.34N 14.13E
171 Jj15 **Isesaki** Gunma, Honshū, S Japan 36.19N 139.10E
133 Q5 **Iset'** ≈ C Russian Federation
171 Hh16 **Ise-wan** *bay* S Japan
79 S15 **Iseyin** Oyo, W Nigeria 7.56N 3.33E
Isfahan *see* Eşfahān
153 Q11 **Isfana** Batkenskaya Oblast', SW Kyrgyzstan 39.51N 69.31E
153 R11 **Isfara** N Tajikistan 40.06N 70.34E
155 O4 **Isfi Maidān** Ghowr, N Afghanistan 35.09N 66.16E
94 O3 **Isfjorden** *fjord* W Svalbard
Isha Baydhabo *see* Baydhabo
129 V11 **Isherim, Gora** ▲ NW Russian Federation 61.06N 59.09E
131 Q5 **Isheyevka** Ul'yanovskaya Oblast', W Russian Federation 54.27N 48.18E
172 Oo17 **Ishigaki** Okinawa, Ishigaki-jima, SW Japan 24.19N 124.09E
172 P17 **Ishigaki-jima** *var.* Isigaki Zima. *island* Sakishima-shotō, SW Japan
172 O5 **Ishikari** Hokkaidō, NE Japan 43.12N 141.21E
172 Oo5 **Ishikari-gawa** *var.* Isikari Gawa. ≈ Hokkaidō, NE Japan
172 O4 **Ishikari-wan** *bay* Hokkaidō, NE Japan
171 L14 **Ishikawa** Fukushima, Honshū, C Japan 37.08N 140.26E
172 Oo14 **Ishikawa** *var.* Isikawa. Okinawa, Okinawa, SW Japan 26.25N 127.46E
171 I13 **Ishikawa** *off.* Ishikawa-ken, *var.* Isikawa. ◈ *prefecture* Honshū, SW Japan
125 Ff12 **Ishim** Tyumenskaya Oblast', C Russian Federation 56.12N 69.25E
133 R6 **Ishim** *Kaz.* Esil. ≈ Kazakhstan/Russian Federation
131 V6 **Ishimbay** Respublika Bashkortostan, W Russian Federation 53.21N 56.03E
151 O9 **Ishimskoye** Akmola, C Kazakhstan 51.22N 67.07E
171 M13 **Ishinomaki** *var.* Isinomaki. Miyagi, Honshū, C Japan 38.25N 141.16E
171 Kk16 **Ishioka** *var.* Isioka. Ibaraki, Honshū, S Japan 36.12N 140.18E
170 Ee15 **Ishizuchi-san** ▲ Shikoku, SW Japan 33.44N 133.07E
Ishkashim *see* Ishkoshim
Ishkashimskiy Khrebet *see* Ishkoshim, Qatorkŭhi
153 S15 **Ishkoshim** *Rus.* Ishkashim. S Tajikistan 36.46N 71.35E
153 S15 **Ishkoshim, Qatorkŭhi** *Rus.* Ishkashimskiy Khrebet. ▲▲ SE Tajikistan
33 N4 **Ishpeming** Michigan, N USA 46.29N 87.40W
153 N11 **Ishtixon** *Rus.* Ishtykhan. Samarqand Viloyati, C Uzbekistan 39.59N 66.28E
Ishtykhan *see* Ishtixon
159 T15 **Ishurdi** *var.* Iswardi. Rajshahi, W Bangladesh 24.10N 89.04E
63 G17 **Isidoro Noblia** Cerro Largo, NE Uruguay 31.58S 54.09W
104 J4 **Isigny-sur-Mer** Calvados, N France 49.20N 1.06W
Isikari Gawa *see* Ishikari-gawa
Isikawa *see* Ishikawa
142 C11 **Işıklar Dağı** ▲▲ NW Turkey
109 C19 **Isili** Sardegna, Italy, C Mediterranean Sea 39.46N 9.06E
125 Ff13 **Isil'kul'** Omskaya Oblast', C Russian Federation 54.52N 71.07E
Isinomaki *see* Ishinomaki
Isioka *see* Ishioka
83 I18 **Isiolo** Eastern, C Kenya 0.21N 37.33E
81 O16 **Isiro** Orientale, NE Dem. Rep. Congo 2.51N 27.46E
94 P2 **Isispynten** *headland* NE Svalbard 79.51N 26.44E
126 Ll11 **Isit** Respublika Sakha (Yakutiya), NE Russian Federation 60.53N 125.32E
155 O2 **Iskabad Canal** *canal* N Afghanistan
153 Q9 **Iskandar** *Rus.* Iskander. Toshkent Viloyati, E Uzbekistan 41.32N 69.46E
Iskander *see* Iskandar
Iskăr *see* Iskŭr
124 O2 **İskele** *var.* Trikomo, *Gk.* Tríkomon. E Cyprus 35.16N 33.54E
142 K17 **İskenderun** *Eng.* Alexandretta. Hatay, S Turkey 36.34N 36.10E
144 H2 **İskenderun Körfezi** *Eng.* Gulf of Alexandretta. *gulf* S Turkey
142 J11 **İskilip** Çorum, N Turkey 40.45N 34.28E
Iski-Nauket *see* Eski-Nookat
126 Gg14 **Iskitim** Novosibirskaya Oblast', C Russian Federation 54.36N 83.05E
116 J11 **Iskra** *prev.* Popovo. Kŭrdzhali, S Bulgaria 41.55N 25.12E
116 G10 **Iskŭr** *var.* Iskăr. ≈ NW Bulgaria
116 H10 **Iskŭr, Yazovir** *prev.* Yazovir Stalin. ▣ W Bulgaria
43 S15 **Isla** Veracruz-Llave, SE Mexico 18.01N 95.30W
121 J15 **Islach** *Rus.* Isloch'. ≈ C Belarus
106 H14 **Isla Cristina** Andalucía, S Spain 37.12N 7.19W
Isla de León *see* San Fernando
155 U6 **Islāmābād** ● (Pakistan) Federal Capital Territory Islāmābād, NE Pakistan 33.40N 73.07E
155 V6 **Islāmābād** ✕ Federal Capital Territory Islāmābād, NE Pakistan 33.40N 73.07E
Islamabad *see* Anantnāg
155 R17 **Islāmkot** Sind, SE Pakistan 24.37N 70.04E
25 Y17 **Islamorada** Florida Keys, Florida, SE USA 24.55N 80.37W
159 P14 **Islāmpur** Bihār, N India 25.09N 85.13E
Islam Qala *see* Eslām Qal'eh
Island/Ísland *see* Iceland
20 K16 **Island Beach** *spit* New Jersey, NE USA
21 S4 **Island Falls** Maine, NE USA 45.59N 68.16W
190 H6 **Island Lagoon** ◎ South Australia
9 Y13 **Island Lake** ◎ Manitoba, C Canada
31 W5 **Island Lake Reservoir** ▣ Minnesota, N USA
35 R13 **Island Park** Idaho, NW USA 44.27N 111.21W
21 N6 **Island Pond** Vermont, NE USA 44.48N 71.51W
192 K2 **Islands, Bay of** *inlet* North Island, NZ
105 R7 **Is-sur-Tille** Côte d'Or, C France 47.34N 5.03E
44 J3 **Islas de la Bahía** ◈ *department* N Honduras
67 L20 **Islas Orcadas Rise** *undersea feature* S Atlantic Ocean
98 F12 **Islay** *island* SW Scotland, UK
118 I15 **Islaz** Teleorman, S Romania 43.43N 24.52E
31 V7 **Isle** Minnesota, N USA 46.08N 93.28W
104 M12 **Isle** ≈ W France
99 I16 **Isle of Man** ◇ *UK crown dependency* NW Europe
23 X7 **Isle of Wight** Virginia, NE USA 36.54N 76.41W
99 M24 **Isle of Wight** *cultural region* S England, UK
203 Y3 **Isles Lagoon** ◎ Kiritimati, E Kiribati
39 R11 **Isleta Pueblo** New Mexico, SW USA 34.54N 106.40W
Isloch' *see* Islach
63 E19 **Ismael Cortinas** Flores, S Uruguay 33.57S 57.04W
Ismailia *see* Ismâ'ilîya
77 W7 **Ismâ'ilîya** *var.* Ismailia. N Egypt 30.31N 32.13E
Ismailly *see* İsmayıllı
143 X11 **İsmayıllı** *Rus.* Ismailly. C Azerbaijan 40.47N 48.09E
Ismid *see* İzmit
77 X10 **Isna** *var.* Esna. SE Egypt 25.16N 32.24E
95 K18 **Isojoki** Länsi-Suomi, W Finland 62.07N 22.00E
84 M12 **Isoka** Northern, NE Zambia 10.07S 32.42E
Isola d'Ischia *see* Ischia
Isola d'Istria *see* Izola
Isonzo *see* Soča
13 U4 **Isoukustouc** ≈ Québec, SE Canada
142 F15 **Isparta** *var.* Isbarta. Isparta, SW Turkey 37.46N 30.31E
142 F15 **Isparta** *var.* Isbarta. ◈ *province* SW Turkey
116 M7 **Isperikh** *prev.* Kemanlar. Razgrad, N Bulgaria 43.43N 26.49E
109 L26 **Ispica** Sicilia, Italy, C Mediterranean Sea 36.46N 14.55E
154 J14 **Ispikān** Baluchistān, SW Pakistan 26.21N 62.15E
143 Q12 **İspir** Erzurum, NE Turkey 40.28N 41.01E
144 E12 **Israel** *off.* State of Israel, *var.* Medinat Israel, *Heb.* Yisrael, Yisra'el. ◆ *republic* SW Asia
Issa *see* Vis
57 S9 **Issano** C Guyana 5.49N 59.28W
78 M16 **Issia** SW Ivory Coast 6.33N 6.33W
Issiq Köl *see* Issyk-Kul', Ozero
105 P11 **Issoire** Puy-de-Dôme, C France 45.33N 3.15E
105 N9 **Issoudun** *anc.* Uxellodunum. Indre, C France 46.57N 1.58E
83 H22 **Issuna** Singida, C Tanzania 5.24S 34.48E
Issyk *see* Yesik
Issyk-Kul' *see* Balykchy
153 X7 **Issyk-Kul', Ozero** *var.* Issiq Köl, *Kir.* Ysyk-Köl. ◎ E Kyrgyzstan
153 X7 **Issyk-Kul'skaya Oblast'** *Kir.* Ysyk-Köl Oblasty. ◈ *province* E Kyrgyzstan
155 Q7 **Īstādeh-ye Moqor, Āb-e-** *var.* Āb-i-Istāda. ◎ SE Afghanistan
142 D11 **İstanbul** *Bul.* Tsarigrad, *Eng.* Istanbul; *prev.* Constantinople, *anc.* Byzantium. İstanbul, NW Turkey 41.01N 28.57E
116 P12 **İstanbul** ◈ *province* NW Turkey
116 P12 **İstanbul Boğazı** *var.* Bosporus Thracius, *Eng.* Bosphorus, Bosporus, *Turk.* Karadeniz Boğazı. *strait* NW Turkey
Istarska Županija *see* Istra
117 G19 **Isthmía** Pelopónnisos, S Greece 37.55N 23.02E
117 G17 **Istiaía** Évvoia, C Greece 38.57N 23.09E
56 D9 **Istmina** Chocó, W Colombia 5.09N 76.42W
25 W13 **Istokpoga, Lake** ◎ Florida, SE USA
114 A9 **Istra** *off.* Istarska županija. ◈ *province* NW Croatia
114 I10 **Istra** *Eng.* Istria, *Ger.* Istrien. *cultural region* NW Croatia
105 R15 **Istres** Bouches-du-Rhône, SE France 43.30N 4.58E
Istria/Istrien *see* Istra
179 R16 **Isulan** Mindanao, S Philippines 6.36N 124.36E
194 I11 **Isumrud Strait** *strait* NE PNG
Iswardi *see* Ishurdi
131 V7 **Isyangulovo** Respublika Bashkortostan, W Russian Federation 52.10N 56.38E
64 O6 **Itá** Central, S Paraguay 25.28S 57.21W
61 O17 **Itaberaba** Bahia, E Brazil 12.34S 40.21W
61 M20 **Itabira** *prev.* Presidente Vargas. Minas Gerais, SE Brazil 19.39S 43.13W
61 O18 **Itabuna** Bahia, E Brazil 14.48S 39.18W
61 J18 **Itacaiu** Mato Grosso, S Brazil 14.49S 51.21W
60 G12 **Itacoatiara** Amazonas, N Brazil 3.06S 58.22W
56 D9 **Itagüí** Antioquia, W Colombia 6.12N 75.40W
62 D13 **Itá Ibaté** Corrientes, NE Argentina 27.27S 57.24W
62 G11 **Itaipú, Represa de** ▣ Brazil/Paraguay
60 H13 **Itaituba** Pará, NE Brazil 4.15S 55.55W
62 K13 **Itajaí** Santa Catarina, S Brazil 26.49S 48.39W
Italia/Italiana, Republica/Italian Republic, The *see* Italy
Italian Somaliland *see* Somalia
27 T7 **Italy** Texas, SW USA 32.10N 96.52W
108 G12 **Italy** *off.* The Italian Republic, *It.* Italia, Republica Italiana. ◆ *republic* S Europe
61 O19 **Itamaraju** Bahia, E Brazil 16.58S 39.31W
61 C14 **Itamarati** Amazonas, W Brazil 6.12S 68.16W
61 M19 **Itambé, Pico de** ▲ SE Brazil 18.22S 43.21W
171 Gg15 **Itami** ✕ (Ōsaka) Ōsaka, Honshū, SW Japan 34.47N 135.24E
117 H15 **Ítamos** ▲ N Greece 40.06N 23.51E
159 W11 **Itānagar** Arunāchal Pradesh, NE India 27.09N 93.35E
Itany *see* Litani
61 N19 **Itaobim** Minas Gerais, SE Brazil 16.34S 41.27W
61 P15 **Itaparica, Represa de** ▣ E Brazil
60 M13 **Itapecuru-Mirim** Maranhão, E Brazil 3.24S 44.19W
62 Q8 **Itaperuna** Rio de Janeiro, SE Brazil 21.13S 41.51W
61 O18 **Itapetinga** Bahia, E Brazil 15.16S 40.16W
62 L10 **Itapetininga** São Paulo, S Brazil 23.33S 48.03W
62 K10 **Itapeva** São Paulo, S Brazil 23.58S 48.54W
49 W6 **Itapicuru, Rio** ≈ NE Brazil
60 O13 **Itapipoca** Ceará, E Brazil 3.28S 39.34W
62 M9 **Itapira** São Paulo, S Brazil 22.25S 46.46W
62 K8 **Itápolis** São Paulo, S Brazil 21.36S 48.43W
62 K10 **Itaporanga** São Paulo, S Brazil 23.43S 49.28W
64 P7 **Itapúa** *off.* Departamento de Itapúa. ◈ *department* SE Paraguay
61 E15 **Itapuã do Oeste** Rondônia, W Brazil 9.21S 63.07W
63 E15 **Itaqui** Rio Grande do Sul, S Brazil 29.10S 56.28W
62 K10 **Itararé** São Paulo, S Brazil 24.07S 49.16W
62 K10 **Itararé, Rio** ≈ S Brazil
160 H11 **Itārsi** Madhya Pradesh, C India 22.42N 77.55E
27 T7 **Itasca** Texas, SW USA 32.09N 97.09W
Itassi *see* Vieille Case
95 N17 **Itä-Suomi** ◈ *province* E Finland
62 D13 **Itatí** Corrientes, NE Argentina 27.16S 58.15W
62 K10 **Itatinga** São Paulo, S Brazil 23.08S 48.36W
117 F18 **Itéas, Kólpos** *gulf* C Greece
59 N15 **Iténez, Río** *var.* Rio Guaporé. ≈ Bolivia/Brazil *see also* Guaporé, Rio
56 H11 **Iteviate, Río** ≈ C Colombia
102 I13 **Ith** *hill range* C Germany
33 Q8 **Ithaca** Michigan, N USA 43.17N 84.36W
20 H11 **Ithaca** New York, NE USA 42.25N 76.30W
117 C18 **Itháki** Itháki, Iónioi Nísoi, Greece, C Mediterranean Sea 38.22N 20.43E
117 C18 **Itháki** *island* Iónioi Nísoi, Greece, C Mediterranean Sea
It Hearrenfean *see* Heerenveen
Ithara *see* Ichihara
81 L17 **Itimbiri** ≈ N Dem. Rep. Congo
Itinomiya *see* Ichinomiya
Itinoseki *see* Ichinoseki
41 Q5 **Itkilik River** ≈ Alaska, USA
171 J17 **Itō** Shizuoka, Honshū, S Japan 34.59N 139.03E
171 J13 **Itoigawa** Niigata, Honshū, C Japan 37.01N 137.52E
13 R6 **Itomamo, Lac** ◎ Québec, SE Canada
172 Oo15 **Itoman** Okinawa, SW Japan 26.04N 127.40E
104 M5 **Iton** ≈ N France
59 M16 **Itonamas Río** ≈ NE Bolivia
Itoupé, Mont *see* Sommet Tabulaire
Itseqqortoormiit *see* Ittoqqortoormiit
24 K4 **Itta Bena** Mississippi, S USA 33.30N 90.19W
109 B17 **Ittiri** Sardegna, Italy, C Mediterranean Sea 40.36N 8.34E
207 Q14 **Ittoqqortoormiit** *var.* Itseqqortoormiit, *Dan.* Scoresbysund, *Eng.* Scoresby Sound. Tunu, C Greenland 70.33N 21.52W
62 M10 **Itu** São Paulo, S Brazil 23.17S 47.16W
178 Mm14 **Itu Aba Island** *island* W Spratly Islands
56 D8 **Ituango** Antioquia, NW Colombia 7.06N 75.51W
61 A14 **Ituí, Rio** ≈ NW Brazil
81 O20 **Itula** Sud Kivu, E Dem. Rep. Congo 3.30S 27.49E
61 K19 **Itumbiara** Goiás, C Brazil 18.25S 49.15W
57 T9 **Ituni** E Guyana 5.24N 58.18W
43 X13 **Iturbide** Campeche, SE Mexico 19.41N 89.29W
Ituri *see* Aruwimi
127 Pp16 **Iturup, Ostrov** *island* Kuril'skiye Ostrova, SE Russian Federation
62 L7 **Ituverava** São Paulo, S Brazil 20.22S 47.48W
61 C15 **Ituxi, Rio** ≈ W Brazil
63 E14 **Ituzaingó** Corrientes, NE Argentina 27.34S 56.43W
103 K18 **Itz** ≈ C Germany
102 I9 **Itzehoe** Schleswig-Holstein, N Germany 53.55N 9.31E
25 N2 **Iuka** Mississippi, S USA 34.48N 88.11W
62 I11 **Ivaiporã** Paraná, S Brazil 24.16S 51.46W
62 I11 **Ivaí, Rio** ≈ S Brazil
94 L10 **Ivalo** *Lapp.* Avveel, Avvil. Lappi, N Finland 68.34N 27.29E
94 L10 **Ivalojoki** *Lapp.* Avreel. ≈ N Finland
121 H20 **Ivanava** *Pol.* Janów, Janów Poleski, *Rus.* Ivanovo. Brestskaya Voblasts', SW Belarus 52.07N 25.31E
Ivangorod *see* Dęblin
Ivangrad *see* Berane
191 N7 **Ivanhoe** New South Wales, SE Australia 32.54S 144.20E
31 S9 **Ivanhoe** Minnesota, N USA 44.27N 96.15W
12 D8 **Ivanhoe** ≈ Ontario, S Canada
114 E8 **Ivanić-Grad** Sisak-Moslavina, N Croatia 45.43N 16.23E
119 T10 **Ivanivka** Khersons'ka Oblast', S Ukraine 46.43N 34.28E
119 P10 **Ivanivka** Odes'ka Oblast', SW Ukraine 46.57N 30.26E
115 L14 **Ivanjica** Serbia, C Serbia and Montenegro (Yugoslavia) 43.36N 20.14E
114 G11 **Ivanjska** *var.* Potkozarje. Republika Srpska, NW Bosnia & Herzegovina 44.54N 17.04E
113 H21 **Ivanka** ✕ (Bratislava) Bratislavský Kraj, W Slovakia 48.10N 17.13E
119 O3 **Ivankiv** *Rus.* Ivankov. Kyyivs'ka Oblast', N Ukraine 50.55N 29.53E
Ivankov *see* Ivankiv
41 O15 **Ivanof Bay** Alaska, USA 55.55N 159.28W
118 J7 **Ivano-Frankivs'k** *Ger.* Stanislau, *Pol.* Stanisławów, *Rus.* Ivano-Frankovsk; *prev.* Stanislav. Ivano-Frankivs'ka Oblast', W Ukraine 48.55N 24.45E
Ivano-Frankivs'k *see* Ivano-Frankivs'ka Oblast'
118 I7 **Ivano-Frankivs'ka Oblast'** *var.* Ivano-Frankivs'k, *Rus.* Ivano-Frankovskaya Oblast'; *prev.* Stanislavskaya Oblast'. ◈ *province* W Ukraine
Ivano-Frankovsk *see* Ivano-Frankivs'k
Ivano-Frankovskaya Oblast' *see* Ivano-Frankivs'ka Oblast'
128 M16 **Ivanovo** Ivanovskaya Oblast', W Russian Federation 57.01N 40.58E
Ivanovo *see* Ivanava
125 A16 **Ivanovskaya Oblast'** ◈ *province* W Russian Federation
37 X12 **Ivanpah Lake** ◎ California, W USA
114 E7 **Ivanščica** ▲▲ NE Croatia
116 M8 **Ivanski** Shumen, NE Bulgaria 43.09N 27.02E
131 R7 **Ivanteyevka** Saratovskaya Oblast', W Russian Federation 52.13N 49.06E
Ivantsevichi/Ivatsevichi *see* Ivatsevichy
118 I4 **Ivanychi** Volyns'ka Oblast', NW Ukraine 50.37N 24.22E
121 H18 **Ivatsevichy** *Pol.* Iwacewicze, *Rus.* Ivantsevichi, Ivatsevichi. Brestskaya Voblasts', SW Belarus 52.43N 25.21E
116 L12 **Ivaylovgrad** Khaskovo, S Bulgaria 41.32N 26.06E
116 K11 **Ivaylovgrad, Yazovir** ▣ S Bulgaria
125 F10 **Ivdel'** Sverdlovskaya Oblast', C Russian Federation 60.42N 60.07E
Ivenets *see* Ivyanyets
118 L12 **Iveşti** Galaţi, E Romania 45.27N 28.00E
Ivgovuotna *see* Lyngen
Ivigtut *see* Ivittuut
81 F18 **Ivindo** ≈ Congo/Gabon
61 I21 **Ivinheima** Mato Grosso do Sul, SW Brazil 22.16S 53.52W
206 M15 **Ivittuut** *var.* Ivigtut. Kitaa, S Greenland 61.28N 48.33W
Iviza *see* Eivissa
180 I6 **Ivohibe** Fianarantsoa, SE Madagascar 22.28S 46.52E
Ivoire, Côte d' *see* Ivory Coast
194 I14 **Ivori** ≈ S PNG
78 L15 **Ivory Coast** *off.* Republic of the Ivory Coast, *Fr.* Côte d'Ivoire, République de la Côte d'Ivoire. ◆ *republic* W Africa
70 C11 **Ivory Coast** *Fr.* Côte d'Ivoire. *coastal region* S Ivory Coast
97 L22 **Ivösjön** ◎ S Sweden
108 B7 **Ivrea** *anc.* Eporedia. Piemonte, NW Italy 45.28N 7.52E
10 J2 **Ivujivik** Québec, NE Canada 62.25N 77.49W
121 J16 **Ivyanyets** *Rus.* Ivenets. Minskaya Voblasts', C Belarus 53.52N 26.45E
Iv'ye *see* Iwye
Iwacewicze *see* Ivatsevichy
172 N11 **Iwaizumi** Iwate, Honshū, NE Japan 39.48N 141.46E
171 Ll15 **Iwaki** Fukushima, Honshū, N Japan 37.01N 140.52E
171 Mm9 **Iwaki-san** ▲ Honshū, C Japan 40.39N 140.20E
170 E13 **Iwakuni** Yamaguchi, Honshū, SW Japan 34.07N 132.06E
172 Oo5 **Iwamizawa** Hokkaidō, NE Japan 43.11N 141.43E
172 Nn5 **Iwanai** Hokkaidō, NE Japan 42.51N 140.21E
171 Ll13 **Iwanuma** Miyagi, Honshū, C Japan 38.07N 140.49E
171 I17 **Iwata** Shizuoka, Honshū, S Japan 34.42N 137.49E
172 N10 **Iwate** Iwate, Honshū, N Japan 40.02N 141.12E
171 Mm11 **Iwate** *off.* Iwate-ken. ◈ *prefecture* Honshū, C Japan
171 Mm10 **Iwate-san** ▲ Honshū, C Japan 39.52N 140.59E
Iwje *see* Iwye
79 S16 **Iwo** Oyo, SW Nigeria 7.21N 3.58E
Iwojima *see* Iō-jima
121 I16 **Iwye** *Pol.* Iwje, *Rus.* Iv'ye. Hrodzyenskaya Voblasts', W Belarus 53.55N 25.46E
44 C4 **Ixcán, Río** ≈ Guatemala/Mexico
101 G18 **Ixelles** *Dut.* Elsene. Brussels, C Belgium 50.49N 4.21E
59 J16 **Ixiamas** La Paz, NW Bolivia 13.43S 68.10W
43 O13 **Ixmiquilpan** *var.* Ixmiquilpán. Hidalgo, C Mexico 20.28N 99.11W
85 K23 **Ixopo** KwaZulu/Natal, E South Africa 30.07S 30.03E
Ixtaccíhuatal, Volcán *see* Iztaccíhuati, Volcán
42 M16 **Ixtapa** Guerrero, S Mexico 17.37N 101.29W
43 S16 **Ixtepec** Oaxaca, SE Mexico 16.32N 95.03W
42 K12 **Ixtlán** *var.* Ixtlán del Río. Nayarit, C Mexico 21.03N 104.23W
Ixtlán del Río *see* Ixtlán
125 F12 **Iyevlevo** Tyumenskaya Oblast', C Russian Federation 57.36N 67.20E
170 E14 **Iyo** Ehime, Shikoku, SW Japan 33.44N 132.42E
170 F15 **Iyomishima** *var.* Iyomisima. Ehime, Shikoku, SW Japan 33.58N 133.31E
Iyomisima *see* Iyomishima
170 Dd14 **Iyo-nada** *sea* S Japan
44 E4 **Izabal** *off.* Departamento de Izabal. ◈ *department* E Guatemala
44 F5 **Izabal, Lago de** *prev.* Golfo Dulce. ◎ E Guatemala
149 O9 **Īzad Khvāst** Fārs, C Iran 31.31N 52.08E
43 X12 **Izamal** Yucatán, SE Mexico 20.58N 89.00W
131 Q16 **Izberbash** Respublika Dagestan, SW Russian Federation 42.32N 47.51E
101 C18 **Izegem** *prev.* Iseghem. West-Vlaanderen, W Belgium 50.55N 3.13E
148 M9 **Īzeh** Khūzestān, SW Iran 31.48N 49.52E
172 P14 **Izena-jima** *island* Nansei-shotō, SW Japan
116 N10 **Izgrev** Burgas, E Bulgaria 42.09N 27.49E
131 T2 **Izhevsk** *prev.* Ustinov. Udmurtskaya Respublika, NW Russian Federation 56.48N 53.12E
129 S7 **Izhma** Respublika Komi, NW Russian Federation 64.56N 53.52E
129 S7 **Izhma** ≈ NW Russian Federation
147 X8 **Izkī** NE Oman 22.45N 57.35E
Izmail *see* Izmayil
119 N13 **Izmayil** *Rus.* Izmail. Odes'ka Oblast', SW Ukraine 45.19N 28.48E
142 B14 **İzmir** *prev.* Smyrna. İzmir, W Turkey 38.25N 27.10E
142 C14 **İzmir** *prev.* Smyrna. ◈ *province* W Turkey
142 E11 **İzmit** *var.* Ismid; *anc.* Astacus. Kocaeli, NW Turkey 40.46N 29.55E
106 M14 **Iznájar** Andalucía, S Spain 37.17N 4.16W
106 M14 **Iznajar, Embalse de** ▣ S Spain
107 N14 **Iznalloz** Andalucía, S Spain 37.23N 3.31W
142 E11 **İznik** Bursa, NW Turkey 40.27N 29.43E
142 E12 **İznik Gölü** ◎ NW Turkey
130 M14 **Izobil'nyy** Stavropol'skiy Kray, SW Russian Federation 45.22N 41.40E
111 S13 **Izola** *It.* Isola d'Istria. SW Slovenia 45.31N 13.40E
144 H9 **Izra'** *var.* Ezra, Ezraa. Dar'ā, S Syria 32.52N 36.15E
43 P14 **Iztaccíhuatl, Volcán** *var.* Volcán Ixtaccíhuatal. Ѧ S Mexico 19.07N 98.37W
44 C7 **Iztapa** Escuintla, SE Guatemala 13.55N 90.45W
Izúcar de Matamoros *see* Matamoros
171 J17 **Izu-hantō** *peninsula* Honshū, S Japan
170 C11 **Izuhara** Nagasaki, Tsushima, SW Japan 34.11N 129.16E
170 C15 **Izumi** Kagoshima, Kyūshū, SW Japan 32.05N 130.22E
171 Gg15 **Izumiōtsu** Ōsaka, Honshū, SW Japan 34.29N 135.25E
171 Gg15 **Izumi-Sano** Ōsaka, Honshū, SW Japan 34.24N 135.19E
170 F12 **Izumo** Shimane, Honshū, SW Japan 35.22N 132.45E
Izu Shichito *see* Izu-shotō
172 Ss13 **Izu-shotō** *var.* Izu Shichito. *island group* S Japan
199 H4 **Izu Trench** *undersea feature* NW Pacific Ocean
126 I4 **Izvestiy TsIK, Ostrova** *island* N Russian Federation
116 G10 **Izvor** Pernik, W Bulgaria 42.27N 22.53E
118 L5 **Izyaslav** Khmel'nyts'ka Oblast', W Ukraine 50.08N 26.53E
119 W6 **Izyum** Kharkivs'ka Oblast', E Ukraine 49.12N 37.18E

J

95 M18 **Jaala** Etelä-Suomi, S Finland 61.04N 26.30E
146 J5 **Jabal ash Shifā** *desert* NW Saudi Arabia
147 U8 **Jabal az̧ Z̧annah** *var.* Jebel Dhanna. Abū Z̧aby, W UAE 24.10N 52.36E
144 E11 **Jabālīya** *var.* Jabāliyah. NE Gaza Strip 31.30N 34.25E
Jabāliyah *see* Jabālīya

◆ Country ● Country Capital ◇ Dependent Territory ○ Dependent Territory Capital ◈ Administrative Region ✕ International Airport ▲ Mountain ▲▲ Mountain Range Ѧ Volcano ≈ River ◎ Lake ▣ Reservoir

JABALÓN – JIANGJUNMIAO

107 N11 **Jabalón** ≈ C Spain
160 J10 **Jabalpur** *prev.* Jubbulpore. Madhya Pradesh, C India *23.10N 79.58E*
147 N15 **Jabal Zuqar, Jazīrat** *var.* Az Zuqur. *island* SW Yemen
Jabat *see* Jabwot
144 J3 **Jabbūl, Sabkhat al** *salt flat* NW Syria
189 P1 **Jabiru** Northern Territory, N Australia *12.44S 132.48E*
144 H4 **Jablah** *var.* Jeble, *Fr.* Djéblé. Al Lādhiqīyah, W Syria *35.00N 36.00E*
114 C11 **Jablanac** Lika-Senj, W Croatia *44.43N 14.54E*
115 H14 **Jablanica** Federacija Bosna I Hercegovina, SW Bosnia and Herzegovina *43.39N 17.43E*
115 M20 **Jablanica** *Alb.* Mali i Jabllanicës, *var.* Malet e Jabllanicës. ⛰ Albania/FYR Macedonia *see also* Jabllanicës, Mali i
Jabllanicës, Malet e *see* Jablanica/Jabllanicës, Mali i
115 M20 **Jabllanicës, Mali i** *var.* Malet e Jabllanicës, *Mac.* Jablanica. ⛰ Albania/FYR Macedonia *see also* Jablanica
113 E15 **Jablonec nad Nisou** *Ger.* Gablonz an der Neisse. Liberecký Kraj, N Czech Republic *50.43N 15.10E*
Jabłonków/Jablunkau *see* Jablunkov
112 J9 **Jabłonowo Pomorskie** Kujawski-pomorskie, C Poland *53.24N 19.08E*
113 J17 **Jablunkov** *Ger.* Jablunkau, *Pol.* Jabłonków. Moravskoslezský Kraj, E Czech Republic *49.34N 18.45E*
61 Q15 **Jaboatão** Pernambuco, E Brazil *08.05S 35.00W*
62 L8 **Jaboticabal** São Paulo, S Brazil *21.15S 48.16W*
201 U7 **Jabwot** *var.* Jabat, Jebat, Jōwat. *island* Ralik Chain, S Marshall Islands
107 S4 **Jaca** Aragón, NE Spain *42.34N 0.33W*
44 B4 **Jacaltenango** Huehuetenango, W Guatemala *15.39N 91.46W*
61 G14 **Jacaré-a-Canga** Pará, NE Brazil *5.58S 57.31W*
62 N10 **Jacareí** São Paulo, S Brazil *23.18S 45.55W*
61 I18 **Jaciara** Mato Grosso, W Brazil *15.58S 54.57W*
61 E15 **Jaciparaná** Rondônia, W Brazil *9.20S 64.27W*
21 P5 **Jackman** Maine, NE USA *45.35N 70.14W*
37 X1 **Jackpot** Nevada, W USA *41.57N 114.41W*
22 M8 **Jacksboro** Tennessee, S USA *36.19N 84.10W*
27 S6 **Jacksboro** Texas, SW USA *33.13N 98.10W*
25 N7 **Jackson** Alabama, S USA *31.30N 87.53W*
37 P7 **Jackson** California, W USA *38.19N 120.46W*
23 O6 **Jackson** Kentucky, S USA *37.30N 83.22W*
24 J8 **Jackson** Louisiana, S USA *30.50N 91.13W*
33 Q10 **Jackson** Michigan, N USA *42.15N 84.24W*
31 T11 **Jackson** Minnesota, N USA *43.38N 95.00W*
24 K5 **Jackson** *state capital* Mississippi, S USA *32.19N 90.12W*
29 Y7 **Jackson** Missouri, C USA *37.22N 89.40W*
23 W8 **Jackson** North Carolina, SE USA *36.24N 77.22W*
33 T15 **Jackson** Ohio, NE USA *39.03N 82.40W*
22 G9 **Jackson** Tennessee, S USA *35.37N 88.46W*
35 S14 **Jackson** Wyoming, C USA *43.28N 110.45W*
193 C19 **Jackson Bay** *bay* South Island, NZ
194 K16 **Jackson Field** ✕ (Port Moresby) Central/National Capital District, S PNG *9.28S 147.12E*
193 C20 **Jackson Head** *headland* South Island, NZ *43.57S 168.38E*
25 S8 **Jackson, Lake** ◎ Florida, SE USA
35 S13 **Jackson Lake** ◎ Wyoming, C USA
204 J6 **Jackson, Mount** ▲ Antarctica *71.43S 63.45W*
39 U3 **Jackson Reservoir** ◎ Colorado, C USA
25 Q3 **Jacksonville** Alabama, S USA *33.48N 85.45W*
29 V11 **Jacksonville** Arkansas, C USA *34.52N 92.06W*
25 W8 **Jacksonville** Florida, SE USA *30.19N 81.39W*
32 K14 **Jacksonville** Illinois, N USA *39.43N 90.13W*
23 W11 **Jacksonville** North Carolina, SE USA *34.45N 77.25W*
27 W7 **Jacksonville** Texas, SW USA *31.57N 95.16W*
25 X9 **Jacksonville Beach** Florida, SE USA *30.17N 81.23W*
46 L9 **Jacmel** *var.* Jaquemel. S Haiti *18.13N 72.33W*
Jacob *see* Nkayi
155 Q12 **Jacobābād** Sind, SE Pakistan *28.16N 68.30E*
57 T11 **Jacobs Ladder Falls** *waterfall* S Guyana *2.57N 58.06W*
47 O11 **Jaco, Pointe** *headland* N Dominica *15.38N 61.25W*
13 Q9 **Jacques-Cartier** ≈ Québec, SE Canada
11 P11 **Jacques-Cartier, Détroit de** *var.* Jacques-Cartier Passage. *strait* Gulf of St. Lawrence/St. Lawrence River
13 W6 **Jacques-Cartier, Mont** ▲ Québec, SE Canada *48.58N 66.00W*
Jacques-Cartier Passage *see* Jacques-Cartier, Détroit de
195 O12 **Jacquinot Bay** *inlet* New Britain, PNG
63 H16 **Jacuí, Rio** ≈ S Brazil
62 L11 **Jacupiranga** São Paulo, S Brazil *24.42S 48.00W*
102 G10 **Jade** ≈ NW Germany
102 G10 **Jadebusen** *bay* NW Germany
Jadotville *see* Likasi
Jadransko More/Jadransko Morje *see* Adriatic Sea
107 O7 **Jadraque** Castilla-La Mancha, C Spain *40.55N 2.55W*
58 C10 **Jaén** Cajamarca, N Peru *5.43S 78.46W*
107 N13 **Jaén** Andalucía, SW Spain *37.46N 3.48W*
107 N13 **Jaén** ◐ *province* Andalucía, S Spain
161 J23 **Jaffna** Northern Province, N Sri Lanka *9.42N 80.03E*
161 K23 **Jaffna Lagoon** *lagoon* N Sri Lanka
21 N10 **Jaffrey** New Hampshire, NE USA *42.46N 72.00W*
144 H13 **Jafr, Qāʿ al** *var.* El Jafr. *salt pan* S Jordan
158 J9 **Jagādhri** Haryāna, N India *30.10N 77.18E*
120 H4 **Jägala** *var.* Jägala Jõgi, *Ger.* Jaggowal. ≈ NW Estonia
Jägala Jõgi *see* Jägala
Jagannath *see* Puri
161 L14 **Jagdalpur** Chhattīsgarh, C India *19.07N 82.04E*
169 U5 **Jagdaqi** Nei Mongol Zizhiqu, N China *50.25N 124.02E*
Jägerndorf *see* Krnov
Jaggowal *see* Jägala
145 O2 **Jaghjaghah, Nahr** ≈ N Syria
179 Qq14 **Jagna** Bohol, C Philippines *9.37N 124.16E*
114 N13 **Jagodina** *prev.* Svetozarevo. Serbia, C Serbia and Montenegro (Yugoslavia) *43.59N 21.15E*
114 K12 **Jagodnja** ⛰ W Serbia and Montenegro (Yugoslavia)
103 I20 **Jagst** ≈ SW Germany
161 I14 **Jagtiāl** Andhra Pradesh, C India *18.49N 78.53E*
63 H18 **Jaguarão** Rio Grande do Sul, S Brazil *32.32S 53.20W*
63 H18 **Jaguarão, Rio** *var.* Río Yaguarón. ≈ Brazil/Uruguay
62 K11 **Jaguariaíva** Paraná, S Brazil *24.15S 49.43W*
46 D5 **Jagüey Grande** Matanzas, W Cuba *22.31N 81.09W*
159 P14 **Jahānābād** Bihār, N India *25.13N 84.58E*
Jahra *see* Al Jahrāʾ
149 P12 **Jahrom** *var.* Jahrum. Fārs, S Iran *28.34N 53.32E*
Jahrum *see* Jahrom
Jailolo *see* Halmahera, Pulau
175 Tt8 **Jailolo, Selat** *strait* E Indonesia
Jainat *see* Chai Nat
Jainti *see* Jayanti
158 H12 **Jaipur** *prev.* Jeypore. Rājasthān, N India *26.54N 75.46E*
159 T14 **Jaipur Hat** Rajshahi, NW Bangladesh *25.04N 89.03E*
158 D11 **Jaisalmer** Rājasthān, NW India *26.55N 70.56E*
160 O12 **Jājapur** Orissa, E India *18.54N 82.36E*
149 R4 **Jājarm** Khorāsān, NE Iran *36.58N 56.25E*
114 G12 **Jajce** Federacija Bosna I Hercegovina, W Bosnia and Herzegovina *44.20N 17.16E*
Jajı *see* ʿAlī Kheyl
85 D17 **Jakalsberg** Otjozondjupa, N Namibia *19.22S 17.28E*
174 J14 **Jakarta** *prev.* Djakarta, *Dut.* Batavia. ● (Indonesia) Jawa, C Indonesia *6.07S 106.45E*
8 I8 **Jakes Corner** Yukon Territory, W Canada *60.18N 134.00W*
158 H9 **Jākhal** Haryāna, NW India *29.46N 75.51E*
Jakobeny *see* Iacobeni
95 K16 **Jakobstad** *Fin.* Pietarsaari. Länsi-Suomi, W Finland *63.40N 22.40E*
Jakobstadt *see* Jēkabpils
115 O18 **Jakupica** ⛰ C FYR Macedonia
39 W15 **Jal** New Mexico, SW USA *32.07N 103.10W*
147 P7 **Jalājil** *var.* Ğalāğıl. Ar Riyāḍ, C Saudi Arabia *25.42N 45.22E*
Jalal-Abad *see* Dzhalal-Abad, Dzhalal-Abadskaya Oblast', W Kyrgyzstan
155 S5 **Jalālābād** *var.* Jalalabad, Jelalabad. Nangarhār, E Afghanistan *34.25N 70.28E*
Jalal-Abad Oblasty *see* Dzhalal-Abadskaya Oblast'
155 V7 **Jalālpur** Punjab, E Pakistan *32.39N 74.10E*
155 T11 **Jalālpur Pīrwāla** Punjab, E Pakistan *29.30N 71.19E*
158 H8 **Jalandhar** *prev.* Jullundur. Punjab, N India *31.19N 75.36E*
44 J7 **Jalán, Río** ≈ S Honduras
44 E6 **Jalapa** Jalapa, C Guatemala *14.39N 89.58W*
44 J7 **Jalapa** Nueva Segovia, NW Nicaragua *13.57N 86.09W*
44 A3 **Jalapa** *off.* Departamento de Jalapa. ◐ *department* SE Guatemala
44 E6 **Jalapa, Río** ≈ SE Guatemala
149 X13 **Jālaq** Sīstān va Balūchestān, SE Iran
95 K17 **Jalasjärvi** Länsi-Suomi, W Finland *62.30N 22.49E*
155 O8 **Jaldak** Zābul, SE Afghanistan *32.00N 66.45E*
62 J7 **Jales** São Paulo, S Brazil *20.15S 50.34W*
160 P11 **Jaleshwar** *var.* Jaleswar. Orissa, NE India *21.51N 87.15E*
Jaleswar *see* Jaleshwar
160 F12 **Jalgaon** Mahārāshtra, C India *21.01N 75.34E*
145 W12 **Jalībah** S Iraq *30.37N 46.31E*
145 W13 **Jalīb Shahāb** S Iraq *30.25N 46.08E*
79 X15 **Jalingo** Taraba, E Nigeria *8.54N 11.22E*
42 K13 **Jalisco** ◐ *state* SW Mexico
160 G13 **Jālna** Mahārāshtra, W India *19.52N 75.55E*
Jalomitsa *see* Ialomiţa
107 R5 **Jalón** ≈ N Spain
158 E13 **Jālor** Rājasthān, N India *25.21N 72.43E*
114 K11 **Jalovik** Serbia, W Serbia and Montenegro (Yugoslavia) *44.37N 19.48E*
42 L12 **Jalpa** Zacatecas, C Mexico *21.40N 103.00W*
159 S12 **Jalpāiguri** West Bengal, NE India *26.43N 88.24E*
43 O12 **Jalpán** *var.* Jalpan. Querétaro de Arteaga, C Mexico *21.13N 99.28W*
69 P2 **Jalta** *island* N Tunisia
77 S9 **Jālū** *var.* Jūlā. NE Libya *29.01N 21.33E*
201 U8 **Jaluit Atoll** *var.* Jālwōj. *atoll* Ralik Chain, S Marshall Islands
Jālwōj *see* Jaluit Atoll
83 L18 **Jamaame** *It.* Giamame; *prev.* Margherita. Jubbada Hoose, S Somalia *0.00N 42.43E*
79 W13 **Jamaare** ≈ NE Nigeria
46 G9 **Jamaica** ◆ *commonwealth republic* W West Indies
49 P3 **Jamaica** *island* W West Indies
46 I9 **Jamaica Channel** *channel* Haiti/Jamaica
159 T14 **Jamalpur** Dhaka, N Bangladesh *24.54N 89.57E*
159 Q14 **Jamālpur** Bihār, NE India *25.19N 86.30E*
174 I6 **Jamaluang** *var.* Jemaluang. Johor, Peninsular Malaysia *2.13N 103.48E*
61 I14 **Jamanxim, Rio** ≈ C Brazil
58 B8 **Jambeli, Canal de** *channel* S Ecuador
101 I20 **Jambes** Namur, SE Belgium *50.26N 4.51E*
174 Hh9 **Jambi** *var.* Telanaipura; *prev.* Djambi. Sumatera, W Indonesia *1.34S 103.37E*
174 H9 **Jambi** *off.* Propinsi Jambi, *var.* Djambi. ◐ *province* W Indonesia
Jamdena *see* Yamdena, Pulau
10 H8 **James Bay** *bay* Ontario/Québec, E Canada
65 F19 **James, Isla** *island* Archipiélago de los Chonos, S Chile
189 Q8 **James Ranges** ⛰ Northern Territory, C Australia
31 P8 **James River** ≈ North Dakota/South Dakota, N USA
23 X7 **James River** ≈ Virginia, NE USA
204 H4 **James Ross Island** *island* Antarctica
190 I8 **Jamestown** South Australia *33.13S 138.36E*
67 G25 **Jamestown** ○ (Saint Helena) NW Saint Helena *15.55S 5.43W*
37 P8 **Jamestown** California, W USA *37.57N 120.25W*
22 L7 **Jamestown** Kentucky, S USA *36.58N 85.03W*
20 D11 **Jamestown** New York, NE USA *42.04N 79.15W*
31 P5 **Jamestown** North Dakota, N USA *46.54N 98.42W*
22 L8 **Jamestown** Tennessee, S USA *36.25N 84.57W*
Jamestown *see* Holetown
13 N10 **Jamet** ≈ Québec, SE Canada
43 Q17 **Jamiltepec** *var.* Santiago Jamiltepec. Oaxaca, SE Mexico *16.16N 97.50W*
97 F20 **Jammerbugten** *bay* Skagerrak, E North Sea
158 H6 **Jammu** *prev.* Jummoo. Jammu and Kashmir, NW India *32.43N 74.54E*
158 I5 **Jammu and Kashmir** *var.* Jammu-Kashmir, Kashmir. ◐ *state* NW India
155 V4 **Jammu and Kashmir** *disputed region* India/Pakistan
160 B10 **Jāmnagar** *prev.* Navanagar. Gujarāt, W India *22.28N 70.06E*
155 S11 **Jāmpur** Punjab, E Pakistan *29.39N 70.34E*
95 L18 **Jämsä** Länsi-Suomi, W Finland *61.51N 25.10E*
95 L18 **Jämsänkoski** Länsi-Suomi, W Finland *61.54N 25.10E*
159 Q16 **Jamshedpur** Jhārkhand, NE India *22.46N 86.12E*
96 K9 **Jämtland** ◐ *county* C Sweden
159 Q14 **Jamūi** Bihār, NE India *24.57N 86.13E*
159 T14 **Jamuna** ≈ N Bangladesh
Jamuna *see* Brahmaputra
Jamundá *see* Nhamundá, Rio
56 D11 **Jamundí** Valle del Cauca, SW Colombia *3.16N 76.31W*
159 Q12 **Janakpur** Central, C Nepal *26.45N 85.55E*
61 N18 **Janaúba** Minas Gerais, SE Brazil *15.46S 43.16W*
60 K11 **Janaucu, Ilha** *island* NE Brazil
149 Q7 **Jandaq** Eşfahān, C Iran *34.04N 54.25E*
66 Q11 **Jandia, Punta de** *headland* Fuerteventura, Islas Canarias, Spain, NE Atlantic Ocean *28.03N 14.31W*
61 B14 **Jandiatuba, Rio** ≈ NW Brazil
107 N12 **Jándula** ≈ S Spain
31 V10 **Janesville** Minnesota, N USA *44.07N 93.43W*
32 L9 **Janesville** Wisconsin, N USA *42.42N 89.01W*
155 N13 **Jangal** Baluchistān, SW Pakistan *28.00N 65.48E*
85 N20 **Jangamo** Inhambane, SE Mozambique *24.04S 35.25E*
161 J14 **Jangaon** Andhra Pradesh, C India *18.47N 79.25E*
159 S14 **Jangīpur** West Bengal, NE India *24.31N 88.03E*
Janina *see* Ioánnina
Janischken *see* Joniškis
114 J11 **Janja** Republika Srpska, NE Bosnia and Herzegovina *44.40N 19.15E*
Jankovac *see* Jánoshalma
207 Q15 **Jan Mayen** ◇ *Norwegian dependency* N Atlantic Ocean
86 D5 **Jan Mayen** *island* N Atlantic Ocean
207 R15 **Jan Mayen Fracture Zone** *tectonic feature* Greenland Sea/Norwegian Sea
207 R15 **Jan Mayen Ridge** *undersea feature* Greenland Sea/Norwegian Sea
42 H3 **Janos** Chihuahua, N Mexico *30.45N 108.21W*
113 K25 **Jánoshalma** *SCr.* Jankovac. Bács-Kiskun, S Hungary *46.18N 19.16E*
Janow/Janów *see* Jonava, Lithuania
Janów *see* Ivanava, Belarus
112 H10 **Janowiec Wielkopolski** *Ger.* Janowitz. Kujawski-pomorskie, C Poland *52.47N 17.30E*
Janowitz *see* Janowiec Wielkopolski
113 O15 **Janów Lubelski** Lubelskie, E Poland *50.43N 22.24E*
Janów Poleski *see* Ivanava
85 H25 **Jansenville** Eastern Cape, S South Africa *32.55S 24.40E*
176 W12 **Jantan** Papua, E Indonesia *3.53S 134.20E*
61 M18 **Januária** Minas Gerais, SE Brazil *15.28S 44.22W*
Janūbīyah, Al Bādiyah al *see* Ash Shāmīyah
104 I7 **Janzé** Ille-et-Vilaine, NW France *47.55N 1.28W*
160 F10 **Jaora** Madhya Pradesh, C India *23.40N 75.10E*
171 H12 **Japan** *var.* Nippon, *Jap.* Nihon. ◆ *monarchy* E Asia
133 Y9 **Japan** *island group* E Asia
199 H3 **Japan Basin** *undersea feature* N Sea of Japan
133 Y8 **Japan, Sea of** *var.* East Sea, *Rus.* Yapanskoye More. *sea* NW Pacific Ocean *see also* East Sea
199 H4 **Japan Trench** *undersea feature* NW Pacific Ocean
Japen *see* Yapen, Pulau
61 A15 **Japiim** *var.* Máncio Lima. Acre, W Brazil *8.00S 73.39W*
60 D12 **Japurá** Amazonas, N Brazil *1.43S 66.14W*
60 C12 **Japurá, Rio** *var.* Río Caquetá, Yapurá. ≈ Brazil/Colombia *see also* Caquetá, Río
45 W17 **Jaqué** Darién, SE Panama *7.30N 78.09W*
Jaquemel *see* Jacmel
Jarablos *see* Jarābulus
144 K2 **Jarābulus** *var.* Jarablos, Jerablus, *Fr.* Djérablous. Ḥalab, N Syria *36.51N 38.02E*
62 K13 **Jaraguá do Sul** Santa Catarina, S Brazil *26.28S 49.07W*
106 K9 **Jaraicejo** Extremadura, W Spain *39.40N 5.49W*
106 K9 **Jaráiz de la Vera** Extremadura, W Spain *40.04N 5.45W*
107 O7 **Jarama** ≈ C Spain
65 J20 **Jaramillo** Santa Cruz, SE Argentina *47.10S 67.07W*
Jarandilla de la Vega *see* Jarandilla de la Vera
106 K8 **Jarandilla de la Vera** *var.* Jarandilla de la Vega. Extremadura, W Spain *40.07N 5.39W*
155 V9 **Jarānwāla** Punjab, E Pakistan *31.19N 73.25E*
144 G9 **Jarash** *var.* Jerash; *anc.* Gerasa. Irbid, NW Jordan *32.16N 35.54E*
Jarbah, Jazīrat *see* Jerba, Île de
96 N13 **Järbo** Gävleborg, C Sweden *60.43N 16.40E*
Jardan *see* Yordan
46 F7 **Jardines de la Reina, Archipiélago de los** *island group* C Cuba
168 J7 **Jargalant** Arhangay, C Mongolia *47.46N 101.56E*
168 I8 **Jargalant** Bayanhongor, C Mongolia *47.14N 99.43E*
168 D7 **Jargalant** Bayan-Ölgiy, W Mongolia *46.56N 91.07E*
168 K6 **Jargalant** Bulgan, N Mongolia *49.09N 104.19E*
168 G9 **Jargalant** Govĭ-Altay, W Mongolia *45.39N 97.10E*
Jarīd, Shaţţ al *see* Jerid, Chott el
60 I11 **Jari, Rio** *var.* Jary. ≈ N Brazil
147 N7 **Jarīr, Wādī al** *dry watercourse* C Saudi Arabia
Jarja *see* Yur'ya
96 L13 **Järna** *var.* Dala-Jarna. Dalarna, C Sweden *60.31N 14.22E*
97 O16 **Järna** Stockholm, C Sweden *59.04N 17.34E*
104 K11 **Jarnac** Charente, W France *45.41N 0.10W*
112 H12 **Jarocin** Wielkopolskie, C Poland *51.58N 17.30E*
113 F16 **Jaroměř** *Ger.* Jermer. Královéhradecký Kraj, N Czech Republic *50.22N 15.55E*
Jaroslau *see* Jarosław
113 O16 **Jarosław** *Ger.* Jaroslau, *Rus.* Yaroslav. Podkarpackie, SE Poland *50.01N 22.41E*
95 F16 **Järpen** Jämtland, C Sweden *63.21N 13.30E*
153 O14 **Jarqoʻrgʻon** *Rus.* Dzharkurgan. Surkhondaryo Viloyati, S Uzbekistan *37.31N 67.20E*
145 P2 **Jarrāh, Wadi** *dry watercourse* NE Syria
Jars, Plain of *see* Xiangkhoang, Plateau de
168 K14 **Jartai Yanchi** ◎ N China
61 E16 **Jaru** Rondônia, W Brazil *10.24S 62.45W*
Jarud Qi *see* Lubei
120 I4 **Järva-Jaani** *Ger.* Sankt-Johannis. Järvamaa, N Estonia *59.02N 25.52E*
120 G5 **Järvakandi** *Ger.* Jerwakant. Raplamaa, NW Estonia *58.47N 24.49E*
120 H4 **Järvamaa** *off.* Järva Maakond. ◐ *province* N Estonia
95 L19 **Järvenpää** Etelä-Suomi, S Finland *60.28N 25.03E*
12 G17 **Jarvis** Ontario, S Canada *42.53N 80.06W*
185 R8 **Jarvis Island** ◇ *US unincorporated territory* C Pacific Ocean
96 M11 **Järvsö** Gävleborg, C Sweden *61.43N 16.25E*
Jary *see* Jari, Rio
114 M9 **Jaša Tomić** Serbia, NE Serbia and Montenegro (Yugoslavia) *45.27N 20.51E*
114 D12 **Jasenice** Zadar, SW Croatia *44.15N 15.33E*
144 I11 **Jashshat al ʿAdlah, Wādī al** *dry watercourse* C Jordan
79 Q16 **Jasikan** E Ghana *7.24N 0.28E*
149 T15 **Jāsk** Hormozgān, SE Iran *25.35N 58.06E*
152 F6 **Jasliq** *Rus.* Zhaslyk. Qoraqalpogʻiston Respublikasi, NW Uzbekistan *43.57N 57.30E*
113 N17 **Jasło** Podkarpackie, SE Poland *49.45N 21.28E*
9 U16 **Jasmin** Saskatchewan, S Canada *51.11N 103.34W*
67 A23 **Jason Islands** *island group* NW Falkland Islands
204 I4 **Jason Peninsula** *peninsula* Antarctica
33 N15 **Jasonville** Indiana, N USA *39.09N 87.12W*
9 O15 **Jasper** Alberta, SW Canada *52.55N 118.04W*
12 L13 **Jasper** Ontario, SE Canada *44.50N 75.57W*
25 O3 **Jasper** Alabama, S USA *33.49N 87.16W*
29 T9 **Jasper** Arkansas, C USA *36.00N 93.11W*
25 U8 **Jasper** Florida, SE USA *30.31N 82.57W*
33 N16 **Jasper** Indiana, N USA *38.22N 86.57W*
31 R11 **Jasper** Minnesota, N USA *43.51N 96.24W*
29 S7 **Jasper** Missouri, C USA *37.20N 94.18W*
22 K10 **Jasper** Tennessee, S USA *35.04N 85.37W*
27 Y9 **Jasper** Texas, SW USA *30.55N 94.00W*
9 O15 **Jasper National Park** *national park* Alberta/British Columbia, SW Canada
Jassy *see* Iaşi
115 N14 **Jastrebac** ⛰ SE Serbia and Montenegro (Yugoslavia)
114 D9 **Jastrebarsko** Zagreb, N Croatia *45.40N 15.40E*
Jastrow *see* Jastrowie
112 G9 **Jastrowie** *Ger.* Jastrow. Wielkopolskie, C Poland *53.25N 16.48E*
113 J17 **Jastrzębie-Zdrój** Śląskie, S Poland *49.58N 18.34E*
113 L22 **Jászapáti** Jász-Nagykun-Szolnok, E Hungary *47.31N 20.09E*
113 L22 **Jászberény** Jász-Nagykun-Szolnok, E Hungary *47.30N 19.54E*
113 L23 **Jász-Nagykun-Szolnok** *off.* Jász-Nagykun-Szolnok Megye. ◐ *county* E Hungary
61 J19 **Jataí** Goiás, C Brazil *17.58S 51.45W*
60 G12 **Jatapu, Serra do** ⛰ N Brazil
43 W16 **Jatate, Río** ≈ SE Mexico
155 P17 **Jāti** Sind, SE Pakistan *24.19N 68.18E*
46 F6 **Jatibonico** Sancti Spíritus, C Cuba *21.55N 79.12W*
174 Jj14 **Jatiluhur, Danau** ◎ Jawa, S Indonesia
Jativa *see* Xátiva
174 K14 **Jatiwangi** *prev.* Djatiwangi. Jawa, C Indonesia *6.45S 108.12E*
155 S11 **Jattoi** Punjab, E Pakistan *29.22N 70.55E*
62 L9 **Jaú** São Paulo, S Brazil *22.17S 48.32W*
60 F11 **Jauaperi, Rio** ≈ N Brazil
101 I19 **Jauche** Wallon Brabant, C Belgium *50.42N 4.55E*
Jauer *see* Jawor
Jauf *see* Al Jawf
155 U7 **Jauharābād** Punjab, E Pakistan *32.19N 72.15E*
59 E14 **Jauja** Junín, C Peru *11.44S 75.30W*
43 O10 **Jaumave** Tamaulipas, C Mexico *23.28N 99.22W*
120 H10 **Jaunjelgava** *Ger.* Friedrichstadt. Aizkraukle, S Latvia *56.38N 25.03E*
Jaunlatgale *see* Pytalovo
120 I8 **Jaunpiebalga** Gulbene, NE Latvia *57.10N 26.02E*
120 E9 **Jaunpils** Tukums, C Latvia *56.45N 23.03E*
159 N13 **Jaunpur** Uttar Pradesh, N India *25.43N 82.40E*
31 N8 **Java** South Dakota, N USA *45.29N 99.54W*
Java *see* Jawa
107 R9 **Javalambre** ▲ E Spain *40.02N 1.06W*
181 V7 **Java Ridge** *undersea feature* E Indian Ocean
61 A14 **Javari, Rio** *var.* Yavarí. ≈ Brazil/Peru
169 O7 **Javarthushuu** Dornod, NE Mongolia *49.05N 112.40E*
174 Kk13 **Java Sea** *Ind.* Laut Jawa. *sea* W Indonesia
181 U7 **Java Trench** *var.* Sunda Trench. *undersea feature* E Indian Ocean
107 T11 **Jávea** *Cat.* Xàbia. País Valenciano, E Spain *38.48N 0.10E*
169 O7 **Javhlant** Hentiy, E Mongolia *47.46N 112.06E*
65 G20 **Javier, Isla** *island* S Chile
115 L14 **Javor** ⛰ Bosnia and Herzegovina/Serbia and Montenegro (Yugoslavia)
113 K20 **Javorie** *Hung.* Jávoros. ▲ S Slovakia *48.26N 19.16E*
Jávoros *see* Javorie
95 J14 **Jävre** Norrbotten, N Sweden *65.07N 21.31E*
174 K14 **Jawa** *Eng.* Java; *prev.* Djawa. *island* C Indonesia
174 J15 **Jawa Barat** *off.* Propinsi Jawa Barat, *Eng.* West Java. ◐ *province* S Indonesia
Jawa, Laut *see* Java Sea
145 R3 **Jawān** NW Iraq *35.57N 43.03E*
174 Kk15 **Jawa Tengah** *off.* Propinsi Jawa Tengah, *Eng.* Central Java. ◐ *province* S Indonesia
174 Ll15 **Jawa Timur** *off.* Propinsi Jawa Timur, *Eng.* East Java. ◐ *province* S Indonesia
83 N17 **Jawhar** *var.* Jowhar, *It.* Giohar. Shabeellaha Dhexe, S Somalia *2.36N 45.30E*
113 F14 **Jawor** *Ger.* Jauer. Dolnośląskie, SW Poland *51.01N 16.10E*
Jaworów *see* Yavoriv
113 J16 **Jaworzno** Śląskie, S Poland *50.13N 19.07E*
Jaxartes *see* Syr Darya
29 R9 **Jay** Oklahoma, C USA *36.25N 94.48W*
Jayabum *see* Chaiyaphum
Jayanath *see* Chai Nat
159 T12 **Jayanti** *prev.* Jainti. West Bengal, NE India *26.43N 89.43E*
176 Xx12 **Jaya, Puncak** *prev.* Puntjak Carstensz, Puntjak Sukarno. ▲ Papua, E Indonesia *4.00S 137.10E*
176 Z10 **Jayapura** *var.* Djajapura, *Dut.* Hollandia; *prev.* Kotabaru, Sukarnapura. Papua, E Indonesia *2.37S 140.39E*
176 Y12 **Jayawijaya, Pegunungan** ⛰ Papua, E Indonesia
Jay Dairen *see* Dalian
Jayhawker State *see* Kansas
153 S12 **Jayilgan** *Rus.* Dzhailgan, Dzhayilgan. C Tajikistan *39.17N 71.32E*
161 L14 **Jaypur** *var.* Jeypore, Jeypur. Orissa, E India *18.54N 82.36E*
27 O6 **Jayton** Texas, SW USA *33.15N 100.34W*
149 U13 **Jaz Murian, Hāmūn-e** ◎ SE Iran
144 M4 **Jazrah** Ar Raqqah, C Syria *35.56N 39.02E*
144 G6 **Jbaïl** *var.* Jebeil, Jubayl, Jubeil; *anc.* Biblical Gebal, Bybles. W Lebanon *34.00N 35.45E*
27 O7 **J.B.Thomas, Lake** ⊡ Texas, SW USA
Jdaïdé *see* Judaydah
37 X12 **Jean** Nevada, W USA *35.45N 115.20W*
24 I9 **Jeanerette** Louisiana, S USA *29.54N 91.39W*
46 L8 **Jean-Rabel** NW Haiti *19.49N 73.12W*
149 T12 **Jebāl Bārez, Kūh-e** ⛰ SE Iran
Jebat *see* Jabwot
79 T15 **Jebba** Kwara, W Nigeria *9.04N 4.50E*
Jebeil *see* Jbaïl
118 E12 **Jebel** *Hung.* Széphely; *prev. Hung.* Zsebely. Timiş, W Romania *45.33N 21.13E*
152 B11 **Jebel** *Rus.* Dzhebel. Balkan Welaýaty, W Turkmenistan *39.42N 54.10E*
Jebel, Bahr el *see* White Nile
Jebel Dhanna *see* Jabal az̧ Z̧annah
Jeble *see* Jablah
98 K13 **Jedburgh** SE Scotland, UK *55.28N 2.34W*
Jedda *see* Jiddah
113 L15 **Jędrzejów** *Ger.* Endersdorf. Świętokrzyskie, C Poland *50.39N 20.18E*
102 K12 **Jeetze** *var.* Jeetzel. ≈ C Germany
Jeetzel *see* Jeetze
31 U14 **Jefferson** Iowa, C USA *42.01N 94.22W*
23 Q8 **Jefferson** North Carolina, SE USA *36.24N 81.33W*
27 X6 **Jefferson** Texas, SW USA *32.45N 94.21W*
32 M9 **Jefferson** Wisconsin, N USA *43.01N 88.48W*
29 U5 **Jefferson City** *state capital* Missouri, C USA *38.33N 92.12W*
35 R10 **Jefferson City** Montana, NW USA *46.24N 112.01W*
23 N9 **Jefferson City** Tennessee, S USA *36.07N 83.29W*
37 U7 **Jefferson, Mount** ▲ Nevada, W USA *38.49N 116.54W*
34 H12 **Jefferson, Mount** ▲ Oregon, NW USA *44.40N 121.48W*
22 L5 **Jeffersontown** Kentucky, S USA *38.11N 85.33W*
33 P16 **Jeffersonville** Indiana, N USA *38.16N 85.45W*
35 V15 **Jeffrey City** Wyoming, C USA *42.29N 107.49W*
79 T13 **Jega** Kebbi, NW Nigeria *12.15N 4.21E*
Jehol *see* Chengde
64 P5 **Jejui-Guazú, Río** ≈ E Paraguay
120 I10 **Jēkabpils** *Ger.* Jakobstadt. Jēkabpils, S Latvia *56.30N 25.56E*
25 W7 **Jekyll Island** *island* Georgia, SE USA
174 L11 **Jelai, Sungai** ≈ Borneo, N Indonesia
Jelalabad *see* Jalālābād
113 H14 **Jelcz-Laskowice** Dolnośląskie, SW Poland *51.01N 17.24E*
113 E14 **Jelenia Góra** *Ger.* Hirschberg, Hirschberg im Riesengebirge, Hirschberg in Riesengebirge, Hirschberg in Schlesien. Dolnośląskie, SW Poland *50.54N 15.48E*
159 S11 **Jelep La** *pass* N India *27.24N 88.51E*
120 F9 **Jelgava** *Ger.* Mitau. Jelgava, C Latvia *56.38N 23.47E*
114 L13 **Jelica** ⛰ C Serbia and Montenegro (Yugoslavia)
22 M8 **Jellico** Tennessee, S USA *36.33N 84.06W*
97 G23 **Jelling** Vejle, C Denmark *55.45N 9.24E*
174 Ii5 **Jemaja, Pulau** *island* W Indonesia
Jemaluang *see* Jamaluang
101 E20 **Jemappes** Hainaut, S Belgium *50.27N 3.52E*
174 M16 **Jember** *prev.* Djember. Jawa, C Indonesia *8.07S 113.45E*
101 I20 **Jemeppe-sur-Sambre** Namur, S Belgium *50.27N 4.41E*
39 R10 **Jemez Pueblo** New Mexico, SW USA *35.36N 106.43W*
164 K2 **Jeminay** Xinjiang Uygur Zizhiqu, NW China *47.28N 85.49E*
201 U5 **Jemo Island** *atoll* Ratak Chain, C Marshall Islands
175 Nn8 **Jempang, Danau** ◎ Borneo, N Indonesia
103 L16 **Jena** Thüringen, C Germany *50.55N 11.34E*
24 I6 **Jena** Louisiana, S USA *31.40N 92.07W*
110 I8 **Jenaz** Graubünden, SE Switzerland *46.56N 9.43E*
111 N7 **Jenbach** Tirol, W Austria *47.23N 11.47E*
175 P13 **Jeneponto** *prev.* Djeneponto. Sulawesi, C Indonesia *5.40S 119.42E*
144 F9 **Jenīn** N West Bank *32.28N 35.17E*
23 P7 **Jenkins** Kentucky, S USA *37.10N 82.37W*
29 P9 **Jenks** Oklahoma, C USA *36.01N 95.58W*
Jenné *see* Djenné
111 X8 **Jennersdorf** Burgenland, SE Austria *46.57N 16.08E*
24 H9 **Jennings** Louisiana, S USA *30.13N 92.39W*
15 Jj4 **Jenny Lind Island** *island* Nunavut, N Canada
25 Y13 **Jensen Beach** Florida, SE USA *27.15N 80.13W*
15 M2 **Jens Munk Island** *island* Nunavut, NE Canada
61 O17 **Jequié** Bahia, E Brazil *13.52S 40.06W*
61 O18 **Jequitinhonha, Rio** ≈ E Brazil
Jerablus *see* Jarābulus
76 H6 **Jerada** NE Morocco *34.16N 2.07W*
Jerash *see* Jarash
77 N7 **Jerba, Île de** *var.* Djerba, Jazīrat Jarbah. *island* E Tunisia
46 K9 **Jérémie** SW Haiti *18.38N 74.10W*
Jerez *see* Jeréz de la Frontera, Spain
Jeréz *see* Jerez de García Salinas, Mexico
42 L11 **Jerez de García Salinas** *var.* Jeréz. Zacatecas, C Mexico *22.40N 103.00W*
106 J15 **Jeréz de la Frontera** *var.* Jerez; *prev.* Xeres. Andalucía, SW Spain *36.40N 6.07W*
106 I12 **Jeréz de los Caballeros** Extremadura, W Spain *38.19N 6.45W*
Jergucati *see* Jorgucat
144 G10 **Jericho** *Ar.* Arīḩā, *Heb.* Yeriḫo. E West Bank *31.51N 35.27E*
76 M7 **Jerid, Chott el** *var.* Shaţţ al Jarīd. *salt lake* SW Tunisia
191 O10 **Jerilderie** New South Wales, SE Australia *35.24S 145.43E*
Jerischmarkt *see* Câmpia Turzii
94 K11 **Jerisjärvi** ◎ NW Finland
Jermentau *see* Yereymentau
Jermer *see* Jaroměř
38 K11 **Jerome** Arizona, SW USA *34.45N 112.06W*
35 O15 **Jerome** Idaho, NW USA *42.43N 114.31W*
99 L26 **Jersey** *island* Channel Islands, NW Europe
20 K14 **Jersey City** New Jersey, NE USA *40.42N 74.01W*
20 F13 **Jersey Shore** Pennsylvania, NE USA *41.12N 77.13W*
32 K14 **Jerseyville** Illinois, N USA *39.07N 90.19W*
106 K8 **Jerte** ≈ W Spain
144 F10 **Jerusalem** *Ar.* Al Quds, Al Quds ash Sharīf, *Heb.* Yerushalayim; *anc.* Hierosolyma. ● (Israel) Jerusalem, NE Israel *31.46N 35.13E*
144 G10 **Jerusalem** ◐ *district* E Israel
191 S10 **Jervis Bay** New South Wales, SE Australia *35.09S 150.42E*
191 S10 **Jervis Bay Territory** ◐ *territory* SE Australia
Jerwakant *see* Järvakandi
111 S10 **Jesenice** *Ger.* Assling. NW Slovenia *46.26N 14.00E*
113 H16 **Jeseník** *Ger.* Freiwaldau. Olomoucký Kraj, E Czech Republic *50.14N 17.12E*
Jesi *see* Iesi
108 I8 **Jesolo** *var.* Iesolo. Veneto, NE Italy *45.32N 12.37E*
Jesselton *see* Kota Kinabalu
97 I14 **Jessheim** Akershus, S Norway *60.07N 11.10E*
159 T15 **Jessore** Khulna, W Bangladesh *23.10N 89.12E*
25 W6 **Jesup** Georgia, SE USA *31.36N 81.54W*
43 S15 **Jesús Carranza** Veracruz-Llave, SE Mexico *17.30N 95.01W*
64 K10 **Jesús María** Córdoba, C Argentina *30.58S 64.04W*
28 K6 **Jetmore** Kansas, C USA *38.04N 99.53W*
105 Q2 **Jeumont** Nord, N France *50.18N 4.06E*
97 H14 **Jevnaker** Oppland, S Norway *60.13N 10.22E*
Jewe *see* Jõhvi
27 V9 **Jewett** Texas, SW USA *31.21N 96.08W*
21 N12 **Jewett City** Connecticut, NE USA *41.36N 71.58W*
Jewish Autonomous Oblast *see* Yevreyskaya Avtonomnaya Oblast'
Jeypore/Jeypur *see* Jaypur, Orissa, India
Jeypore *see* Jaipur, Rājasthān, India
115 L17 **Jezercës, Maja e** ▲ N Albania *42.27N 19.49E*
113 B18 **Jezerní Hora** ▲ SW Czech Republic *49.10N 13.11E*
160 F10 **Jhābua** Madhya Pradesh, C India *22.47N 74.36E*
158 H14 **Jhālāwār** Rājasthān, N India *24.33N 76.10E*
Jhang/Jhang Sadar *see* Jhang Sadr
155 U9 **Jhang Sadr** *var.* Jhang, Jhang Sadar. Punjab, NE Pakistan *31.16N 72.19E*
158 J13 **Jhānsi** Uttar Pradesh, N India *25.27N 78.34E*
159 O16 **Jhārkhand** ◐ *state* NE India
160 M11 **Jhārsuguda** Orissa, E India *21.54N 84.09E*
155 V7 **Jhelum** Punjab, NE Pakistan *32.55N 73.42E*
133 P9 **Jhelum** ≈ E Pakistan
Jhenaidaha *see* Jhenida
159 T15 **Jhenida** *var.* Jhenaidaha. Dhaka, W Bangladesh *23.34N 89.39E*
155 P16 **Jhimpīr** Sind, SE Pakistan *25.01N 67.59E*
Jhind *see* Jīnd
155 R16 **Jhudo** Sind, SE Pakistan *24.58N 69.23E*
Jhumra *see* Chak Jhumra
158 H11 **Jhunjhunūn** Rājasthān, N India *28.07N 75.21E*
Ji *see* Hebei, China
Ji *see* Jilin, China
Jiading *see* Xinfeng
159 S14 **Jiāganj** West Bengal, NE India *24.18N 88.07E*
166 J7 **Jialing Jiang** ≈ C China
169 Y7 **Jiamusi** *var.* Chia-mu-ssu, Kiamusze. Heilongjiang, NE China *46.45N 130.19E*
167 O11 **Ji'an** Jiangxi, S China *27.06N 114.57E*
169 W12 **Ji'an** Jilin, NE China *41.04N 126.07E*
169 T13 **Jianchang** Liaoning, NE China *40.48N 119.51E*
Jianchang *see* Nancheng
166 F11 **Jianchuan** *var.* Jinhuan. Yunnan, SW China *26.28N 99.49E*
164 M4 **Jiangjunmiao** Xinjiang Uygur Zizhiqu, W China *44.42N 90.06E*

◆ Country ● Country Capital ◇ Dependent Territory ○ Dependent Territory Capital ◐ Administrative Region ✕ International Airport ▲ Mountain ⛰ Mountain Range Volcano ≈ River ◎ Lake ⊡ Reservoir

166 K11 **Jiangkou** *var.* Shuangjiang. Guizhou, S China 27.46N 108.53E
Jiangkou *see* Fengkai
167 Q12 **Jiangle** *var.* Guyong. Fujian, SE China 26.44N 117.26E
167 N15 **Jiangmen** Guangdong, S China 22.34N 113.01E
Jiangna *see* Yanshan
167 Q10 **Jiangshan** Zhejiang, SE China 28.41N 118.33E
167 Q7 **Jiangsu** *var.* Chiang-su, Jiangsu Sheng, Kiangsu, Su. ◈ *province* E China
Jiangsu Sheng *see* Jiangsu
167 O11 **Jiangxi** *var.* Chiang-hsi, Gan, Jiangxi Sheng, Kiangsi. ◈ *province* S China
Jiangxi Sheng *see* Jiangxi
166 I8 **Jiangyou** *prev.* Zhongba. Sichuan, C China 31.52N 104.52E
167 N9 **Jianli** *var.* Rongcheng. Hubei, C China 29.48N 112.45E
167 Q11 **Jian'ou** Fujian, SE China 27.04N 118.19E
169 S12 **Jianping** *var.* Yebaishou. Liaoning, NE China 41.13N 119.37E
Jianshe *see* Baiyü
166 L9 **Jianshi** *var.* Yezhou. Hubei, C China 30.37N 109.42E
133 V11 **Jian Xi** ∽ SE China
167 Q11 **Jianyang** Fujian, SE China 27.24N 118.06E
166 I9 **Jianyang** Sichuan, C China 30.22N 104.31E
169 X10 **Jiaohe** Jilin, NE China 43.41N 127.20E
Jiaojiang *see* Taizhou
Jiaoxian *see* Jiaozhou
167 R5 **Jiaozhou** *prev.* Jiaoxian. Shandong, E China 36.17N 120.00E
167 N6 **Jiaozuo** Henan, C China 35.13N 113.13E
Jiashan *see* Mingguang
164 F8 **Jiashi** *var.* Payzawat. Xinjiang Uygur Zizhiqu, NW China 39.27N 76.45E
160 L9 **Jiāwān** Madhya Pradesh, C India 24.19N 82.16E
167 S9 **Jiaxing** Zhejiang, SE China 30.43N 120.46E
Jiayi *see* Chiai
169 X6 **Jiayin** *var.* Chaoyang. Heilongjiang, NE China 48.51N 130.24E
165 R8 **Jiayuguan** Gansu, N China 39.49N 98.27E
Jibhalanta *see* Uliastay
144 M4 **Jibli** Ar Raqqah, C Syria 35.49N 39.23E
118 H9 **Jibou** *Hung.* Zsibó. Sălaj, NW Romania 47.13N 23.17E
147 Z9 **Jibsh, Ra's al** *headland* E Oman 21.20N 59.23E
Jibuti *see* Djibouti
113 E15 **Jičín** *Ger.* Jitschin. Královéhradecký Kraj, N Czech Republic 50.27N 15.20E
146 K10 **Jiddah** *Eng.* Jedda. ● (Saudi Arabia) Makkah, W Saudi Arabia 21.33N 39.13E
147 W11 **Jiddat al Ḩarāsīs** *desert* C Oman
Jiesjavrre *see* Iešjávri
166 M4 **Jiexiu** Shanxi, C China 37.00N 111.50E
167 P14 **Jieyang** Guangdong, S China 23.33N 116.21E
121 F14 **Jieznas** Kaunas, S Lithuania 54.37N 24.10E
Jīfa', Bi'r *see* Jif'īyah, Bi'r
147 P15 **Jif'īyah, Bi'r** *var.* Bi'r Jīfa'. *well* C Yemen 14.48N 46.00E
79 W13 **Jigawa** ◈ *state* N Nigeria
152 J10 **Jigerbent** *Rus.* Dzhigirbent. Lebap Welaýaty, NE Turkmenistan 40.44N 61.56E
46 I7 **Jiguaní** Granma, E Cuba 20.24N 76.25W
165 T12 **Jigzhi** *var.* Chugqênsumdo. Qinghai, C China 33.23N 101.25E
Jih-k'a-tse *see* Xigazê
113 E18 **Jihlava** *Ger.* Iglau, *Pol.* Igława. Vysočina, C Czech Republic 49.22N 15.36E
113 E18 **Jihlava** *var.* Igel, *Ger.* Iglawa. ∽ S Czech Republic
Jihlavský Kraj *see* Vysočina
113 C18 **Jihočeský Kraj** *prev.* Budějovický Kraj. ◈ *region* S Czech Republic
113 G19 **Jihomoravský Kraj** *prev.* Brněnský Kraj. ◈ *region* SE Czech Republic
76 L5 **Jijel** *var.* Djidjel; *prev.* Djidjelli. NE Algeria 36.49N 5.43E
118 L9 **Jijia** ∽ N Romania
82 L13 **Jijiga** *It.* Giggiga. Somali, E Ethiopia 9.21N 42.53E
107 S12 **Jijona** *var.* Xixona. País Valenciano, E Spain 38.34N 0.29W
Jilf al Kabīr, Haḑabat al *see* Gilf Kebir Plateau
83 L18 **Jilib** *It.* Gelib. Jubbada Dhexe, S Somalia 0.18N 42.48E
169 W10 **Jilin** *var.* Chi-lin, Girin, Kirin; *prev.* Yungki, Yunki. Jilin, NE China 43.46N 126.31E
169 W10 **Jilin** *var.* Chi-lin, Girin, Ji, Jilin Sheng, Kirin. ◈ *province* NE China
169 W11 **Jilin Hada Ling** ▲▲ NE China
Jilin Sheng *see* Jilin
169 S4 **Jiliu He** ∽ NE China
107 Q6 **Jiloca** ∽ N Spain
83 I14 **Jīma** *var.* Jimma, *It.* Gimma. Oromo, C Ethiopia 7.41N 36.51E
46 M9 **Jimaní** W Dominican Republic 18.27N 71.51W
118 E11 **Jimbolia** *Ger.* Hatzfeld, *Hung.* Zsombolya. Timiş, W Romania 45.47N 20.43E
106 K16 **Jimena de la Frontera** Andalucía, S Spain 36.27N 5.28W
42 K7 **Jiménez** Chihuahua, N Mexico 27.09N 104.54W
43 N5 **Jiménez** Coahuila de Zaragoza, NE Mexico 29.04N 100.43W
43 P9 **Jiménez** *var.* Santander Jiménez. Tamaulipas, C Mexico 24.11N 98.29W
42 L10 **Jiménez del Teul** Zacatecas, C Mexico 23.13N 103.46W
79 Y14 **Jimeta** Adamawa, E Nigeria 9.16N 12.25E
Jimma *see* Jīma
164 M5 **Jimsar** Xinjiang Uygur Zizhiqu, NW China 44.05N 88.48E
20 I14 **Jim Thorpe** Pennsylvania, NE USA 40.51N 75.43W
Jin *see* Shanxi, China
Jin *see* Tianjin Shi, China
167 P5 **Jinan** *var.* Chinan, Chi-nan, Tsinan. Shandong, E China 36.42N 116.57E
Jin'an *see* Songpan
Jinbi *see* Dayao
165 T8 **Jinchang** Gansu, N China 38.31N 102.07E
167 N5 **Jincheng** Shanxi, C China 35.33N 112.51E
Jincheng *see* Wuding
Jinchengjiang *see* Hechi
158 I9 **Jīnd** *prev.* Jhind. Haryāna, NW India 29.25N 76.14E
191 Q11 **Jindabyne** New South Wales, SE Australia 36.28S 148.36E
113 O18 **Jindřichův Hradec** *Ger.* Neuhaus. Jihočeský Kraj, S Czech Republic 49.09N 15.01E
Jing *see* Beijing Shi, China
Jing *see* Jinghe, China
165 X10 **Jingchuan** Gansu, C China 35.19N 107.23E
167 Q10 **Jingdezhen** Jiangxi, S China 29.18N 117.18E
167 O12 **Jinggangshan** Jiangxi, S China 26.36N 114.11E
167 P3 **Jinghai** Tianjin Shi, E China 38.53N 116.45E
166 K6 **Jing He** ∽ C China
164 I4 **Jinghe** *var.* Jing. Xinjiang Uygur Zizhiqu, NW China 44.35N 82.55E
166 F15 **Jinghong** *var.* Yunjinghong. Yunnan, SW China 22.03N 100.55E
166 M9 **Jingmen** Hubei, C China 30.58N 112.09E
169 X10 **Jingpo Hu** ◎ NE China
166 M8 **Jing Shan** ▲▲ C China
165 V9 **Jingtai** *var.* Yitiaoshan. Gansu, C China 37.12N 104.06E
166 J14 **Jingxi** *var.* Xinjing. Guangxi Zhuangzu Zizhiqu, S China 23.10N 106.22E
Jing Xian *see* Jingzhou, Hunan
169 W11 **Jingyu** Jilin, NE China 42.23N 126.48E
165 V10 **Jingyuan** Gansu, C China 36.34N 104.43E
166 M9 **Jingzhou** *prev.* Shashi, Sha-shih, Shasi. Hubei, C China 30.21N 112.09E
166 L12 **Jingzhou** *var.* Jing Xian, Jingzhou Miaozu Dongzu Zizhixian, Quyang. Hunan, S China 26.34N 109.40E
Jingzhou Miaozu Dongzu Zizhixian *see* Jingzhou, Hunan
167 R10 **Jinhua** Zhejiang, SE China 29.15N 119.36E
Jinhuan *see* Jianchuan
169 P13 **Jining** Nei Mongol Zizhiqu, N China 40.58N 113.08E
167 P5 **Jining** Shandong, E China 35.25N 116.35E
83 G18 **Jinja** S Uganda 0.27N 33.13E
167 R13 **Jinjiang** *var.* Qingyang. Fujian, SE China 24.45N 118.35E
167 O11 **Jin Jiang** ∽ S China
Jinjiang *see* Chengmai
176 W14 **Jin, Kepulauan** *island group* E Indonesia
Jinmen Dao *see* Chinmen Tao
44 J9 **Jinotega** Jinotega, NW Nicaragua 13.03N 85.59W
44 K7 **Jinotega** ◈ *department* N Nicaragua
44 J11 **Jinotepe** Carazo, SW Nicaragua 11.49N 86.11W
166 L13 **Jinping** *var.* Sanjiang. Guizhou, S China 26.42N 109.13E
166 H14 **Jinping** Yunnan, SW China 22.47N 103.12E
Jinsen *see* Inch'ŏn
166 J11 **Jinsha** Guizhou, S China 27.24N 106.16E
163 N12 **Jinsha Jiang** *Eng.* Yangtze. ∽ SW China
166 M10 **Jinshi** Hunan, S China 29.42N 111.46E
Jinshi *see* Xinning
165 R7 **Jinta** Gansu, N China 40.01N 98.57E
179 Q12 **Jintotolo Channel** *channel* C Philippines
167 Q12 **Jin Xi** ∽ SE China
Jinxi *see* Huludao
Jinxian *see* Jinzhou
167 P6 **Jinxiang** Shandong, E China 35.07N 116.19E
167 P8 **Jinzhai** *var.* Meishan. Anhui, E China 31.42N 115.47E
167 N4 **Jinzhong** *var.* Yuci. Shanxi, C China 37.34N 112.45E
169 U14 **Jinzhou** *prev.* Jinxian. Liaoning, NE China 39.04N 121.45E
169 T12 **Jinzhou** *var.* Chin-chou, Chinchow; *prev.* Chinhsien. Liaoning, NE China 41.07N 121.06E
Jinzhu *see* Daocheng
144 H12 **Jinz, Qā' al** ◎ C Jordan
49 S8 **Jiparaná, Rio** ∽ W Brazil
58 A7 **Jipijapa** Manabí, W Ecuador 1.22S 80.34W
44 F8 **Jiquilisco** Usulután, S El Salvador 13.19N 88.34W
Jirgalanta *see* Hovd
153 S12 **Jirgatol** *Rus.* Dzhirgatal'. C Tajikistan 39.13N 71.09E
Jirjā *see* Girga
113 B15 **Jirkov** *Ger.* Görkau. Ústecký Kraj, NW Czech Republic 50.30N 13.28E
Jiroft *see* Sabzvārān
166 L11 **Jishou** Hunan, S China 28.20N 109.43E
Jisr ash Shadadi *see* Ash Shadādah
118 I14 **Jitaru** Olt, S Romania 44.27N 24.32E
Jitschin *see* Jičín
118 H14 **Jiu** *Ger.* Schil, Schyl, *Hung.* Zsil, Zsily. ∽ S Romania
167 R11 **Jiufeng Shan** ▲▲ SE China
167 P9 **Jiujiang** Jiangxi, S China 29.45N 115.58E
167 O10 **Jiuling Shan** ▲▲ S China
166 G10 **Jiulong** *var.* Garba, *Tib.* Gyaisi. Sichuan, C China 29.00N 101.30E
167 Q13 **Jiulong Jiang** ∽ SE China
167 Q12 **Jiulong Xi** ∽ SE China
165 R8 **Jiuquan** *var.* Suzhou. Gansu, N China 39.42N 98.36E
166 K17 **Jiusuo** Hainan, S China 18.25N 109.55E
169 W10 **Jiutai** Jilin, NE China 44.01N 125.51E
166 K13 **Jiuwan Dashan** ▲▲ S China
166 I7 **Jiuzhaigou** *prev.* Nanping. Sichuan, C China 33.25N 104.05E
154 I16 **Jīwani** Baluchistān, SW Pakistan 25.05N 61.46E
169 Y8 **Jixi** Heilongjiang, NE China 45.16N 131.01E
169 Y7 **Jixian** Heilongjiang, NE China 46.43N 131.10E
166 M5 **Jixian** *var.* Ji Xian. Shanxi, C China 36.15N 110.41E
Jiza *see* Al Jīzah
147 N13 **Jīzān** *var.* Qīzān. Jīzān, SW Saudi Arabia 17.49N 42.49E
147 N13 **Jīzān** *var.* Minţaqat Jīzān. ◈ *province* SW Saudi Arabia
146 K6 **Jizl, Wādī al** *dry watercourse* W Saudi Arabia
170 Ff12 **Jizō-zaki** *headland* Honshū, SW Japan 35.34N 133.16E
147 U14 **Jiz', Wādī al** *dry watercourse* E Yemen
153 O11 **Jizzax** *Rus.* Dzhizak. Jizzax Viloyati, C Uzbekistan 40.07N 67.47E
153 N10 **Jizzax Viloyati** *Rus.* Dzhizakskaya Oblast'. ◈ *province* C Uzbekistan
62 I13 **Joaçaba** Santa Catarina, S Brazil 27.08S 51.30W
Joal *see* Joal-Fadiout
78 F11 **Joal-Fadiout** *prev.* Joal. W Senegal 14.16N 16.51W
78 E10 **João Barrosa** Boa Vista, E Cape Verde 16.01N 22.44W
João Belo *see* Xai-Xai
João de Almeida *see* Chibia
61 Q15 **João Pessoa** *prev.* Paraíba. *state capital* Paraíba, E Brazil 7.06S 34.52W
27 X7 **Joaquin** Texas, SW USA 31.58N 94.03W
64 K6 **Joaquín V.González** Salta, N Argentina 25.03S 64.06W
Joazeiro *see* Juazeiro
Jo'burg *see* Johannesburg
111 O7 **Jochberger Ache** ∽ W Austria
Jo-ch'iang *see* Ruoqiang
94 K12 **Jock** Norrbotten, N Sweden 66.40N 22.45E
44 I5 **Jocón** Yoro, N Honduras 15.17N 86.55W
107 O13 **Jódar** Andalucía, S Spain 37.51N 3.18W
158 F12 **Jodhpur** Rājasthān, NW India 26.16N 73.01E
101 I19 **Jodoigne** Wallon Brabant, C Belgium 50.43N 4.52E
97 I22 **Jægerspris** Frederiksborg, E Denmark 55.52N 11.58E
95 O16 **Joensuu** Itä-Suomi, E Finland 62.36N 29.45E
97 C17 **Jæren** *physical region* S Norway
39 W4 **Joes** Colorado, C USA 39.36N 102.40W
203 Z3 **Joe's Hill** *hill* Kiritimati, NE Kiribati 1.48N 157.19W
171 Jj13 **Jōetsu** *var.* Zyôetu. Niigata, Honshū, C Japan 37.09N 138.13E
85 M18 **Jofane** Inhambane, S Mozambique 21.16S 34.21E
159 R12 **Jogbani** Bihār, NE India 26.22N 87.16E
120 I5 **Jõgeva** *Ger.* Laisholm. Jõgevamaa, E Estonia 58.46N 26.23E
120 I4 **Jõgevamaa** *off.* Jõgeva Maakond. ◈ *province* E Estonia
161 E18 **Jog Falls** *waterfall* Karnātaka, W India 14.16N 74.44E
149 S4 **Joghatāy** Khorāsān, NE Iran 36.34N 57.00E
159 U12 **Jogīghopa** Assam, NE India 26.13N 90.34E
158 I7 **Jogindarnagar** Himāchal Pradesh, N India 31.55N 76.55E
Jogjakarta *see* Yogyakarta
171 Ii13 **Jōhana** Toyama, Honshū, SW Japan 36.30N 136.53E
85 J21 **Johannesburg** *var.* Egoli, Erautini, Gauteng, *abbrev.* Jo'burg. Gauteng, NE South Africa 26.10S 28.01E
37 T13 **Johannesburg** California, W USA 35.20N 117.37W
85 I21 **Johannesburg** ✕ Gauteng, NE South Africa 26.08S 28.01E
Johannisburg *see* Pisz
155 P14 **Johi** Sind, SE Pakistan 26.46N 67.28E
57 T13 **Johi Village** S Guyana 1.48N 58.33W
34 K13 **John Day** Oregon, NW USA 44.25N 118.57W
34 I11 **John Day River** ∽ Oregon, NW USA
20 L14 **John F Kennedy** ✕ (New York) Long Island, New York, NE USA 40.39N 73.45W
23 V8 **John H.Kerr Reservoir** *var.* Buggs Island Lake, Kerr Lake. ▣ North Carolina/Virginia, SE USA
39 V6 **John Martin Reservoir** ▣ Colorado, C USA
98 K6 **John o'Groats** N Scotland, UK 58.37N 3.03W
29 P5 **John Redmond Reservoir** ▣ Kansas, C USA
41 Q7 **John River** ∽ Alaska, USA
28 H6 **Johnson** Kansas, C USA 37.33N 101.46W
20 M7 **Johnson** Vermont, NE USA 44.39N 72.40W
20 D13 **Johnsonburg** Pennsylvania, NE USA 41.28N 78.37W
20 H11 **Johnson City** New York, NE USA 42.06N 75.54W
23 P8 **Johnson City** Tennessee, S USA 36.18N 82.21W
27 R10 **Johnson City** Texas, SW USA 30.16N 98.24W
37 S12 **Johnsondale** California, W USA 35.58N 118.32W
8 I8 **Johnsons Crossing** Yukon Territory, W Canada 60.30N 133.15W
23 T13 **Johnsonville** South Carolina, SE USA 33.50N 79.26W
23 Q13 **Johnston** South Carolina, SE USA 33.49N 81.48W
199 K6 **Johnston Atoll** ◇ *US unincorporated territory* C Pacific Ocean
183 Q3 **Johnston Atoll** *atoll* C Pacific Ocean
32 L17 **Johnston City** Illinois, N USA 37.49N 88.55W
188 K12 **Johnston, Lake** *salt lake* Western Australia
33 S13 **Johnstown** Ohio, N USA 40.08N 82.39W
20 D15 **Johnstown** Pennsylvania, NE USA 40.19N 78.55W
174 Hh6 **Johor** *var.* Johore. ◈ *state* Peninsular Malaysia
Johor Baharu *see* Johor Bahru
174 I6 **Johor Bahru** *var.* Johor Baharu, Johore Bahru. Johor, Peninsular Malaysia 1.28N 103.43E
Johore *see* Johor
Johore Bahru *see* Johor Bahru
120 K3 **Jõhvi** *Ger.* Jewe. Ida-Virumaa, NE Estonia 59.21N 27.25E
105 P7 **Joigny** Yonne, C France 47.58N 3.24E
Joinvile *see* Joinville
62 K12 **Joinville** *var.* Joinvile. Santa Catarina, S Brazil 26.19S 48.55W
105 R6 **Joinville** Haute-Marne, N France 48.26N 5.07E
204 H3 **Joinville Island** *island* Antarctica
43 O15 **Jojutla** *var.* Jojutla de Juárez. Morelos, S Mexico 18.36N 99.11W
Jojutla de Juárez *see* Jojutla
94 I12 **Jokkmokk** *Lapp.* Dálvvadis. Norrbotten, N Sweden 66.35N 19.56E
94 L2 **Jökulsá á Dal** ∽ E Iceland
94 K2 **Jökulsá á Fjöllum** ∽ NE Iceland
Jokyakarta *see* Yogyakarta
32 M11 **Joliet** Illinois, N USA 41.33N 88.04W
13 O11 **Joliette** Québec, SE Canada 46.01N 73.27W
179 Pp17 **Jolo** Jolo Island, SW Philippines 6.02N 121.00E
96 D11 **Jølstravatnet** ◎ S Norway
174 Ll15 **Jombang** *prev.* Djombang. Jawa, S Indonesia 7.33S 112.13E
165 R14 **Jomda** Xizang Zizhiqu, W China 31.26N 98.09E
120 G13 **Jonava** *Ger.* Janow, *Pol.* Janów. Kaunas, C Lithuania 55.04N 24.19E
152 L11 **Jondor** *Rus.* Zhondor. Buxoro Viloyati, C Uzbekistan 39.46N 64.11E
165 V11 **Jonê** Gansu, C China 34.36N 103.39E
152 K10 **Jongeldi** *Rus.* Dzhankel'dy. Buxoro Viloyati, C Uzbekistan 40.50N 63.16E
29 X9 **Jonesboro** Arkansas, C USA 35.50N 90.42W
25 S4 **Jonesboro** Georgia, SE USA 33.31N 84.21W
32 L17 **Jonesboro** Illinois, N USA 37.25N 89.19W
24 H5 **Jonesboro** Louisiana, S USA 32.14N 92.43W
23 P8 **Jonesboro** Tennessee, S USA 36.17N 82.28W
21 T6 **Jonesport** Maine, NE USA 44.33N 67.35W
(0) J4 **Jones Sound** *channel* Nunavut, N Canada
24 I6 **Jonesville** Louisiana, S USA 31.37N 91.49W
33 Q10 **Jonesville** Michigan, N USA 41.58N 84.39W
23 Q11 **Jonesville** South Carolina, SE USA 34.49N 81.38W
83 F14 **Jonglei** Jonglei, SE Sudan 6.54N 31.19E
83 F14 **Jonglei** *var.* Gongoleh State. ◈ *state* SE Sudan
83 F14 **Jonglei Canal** *canal* S Sudan
120 F11 **Joniškėlis** Panevėžys, N Lithuania 56.02N 24.10E
120 F10 **Joniškis** *Ger.* Janischken. Šiauliai, N Lithuania 56.15N 23.36E
97 L19 **Jönköping** Jönköping, S Sweden 57.45N 14.10E
97 K20 **Jönköping** ◈ *county* S Sweden
13 Q7 **Jonquière** Québec, SE Canada 48.25N 71.16W
43 V15 **Jonuta** Tabasco, SE Mexico 18.04N 92.03W
104 K12 **Jonzac** Charente-Maritime, W France 45.26N 0.25W
29 R7 **Joplin** Missouri, C USA 37.04N 94.30W
35 W8 **Jordan** Montana, NW USA 47.18N 106.54W
144 H12 **Jordan** *off.* Hashemite Kingdom of Jordan, *Ar.* Al Mamlakah al Urdunīyah al Hāshimīyah, Al Urdunn; *prev.* Transjordan. ◆ *monarchy* SW Asia
144 G9 **Jordan** *Ar.* Urdunn, *Heb.* HaYarden. ∽ SW Asia
Jordan Lake *see* B.Everett Jordan Reservoir
113 K17 **Jordanów** Małopolskie, S Poland 49.39N 19.51E
34 M15 **Jordan Valley** Oregon, NW USA 42.59N 117.03W
144 G9 **Jordan Valley** *valley* N Israel
59 D15 **Jorge Chávez International** *var.* Lima. ✕ (Lima) Lima, W Peru 12.07S 77.01W
115 L23 **Jorgucat** *var.* Jergucati, Jorgucati. Gjirokastër, S Albania 39.57N 20.14E
Jorgucati *see* Jorgucat
159 X12 **Jorhāt** Assam, NE India 26.45N 94.09E
95 J14 **Jörn** Västerbotten, N Sweden 65.02N 20.04E
39 R14 **Jornada Del Muerto** *valley* New Mexico, SW USA
95 N17 **Joroinen** Isä-Suomi, E Finland 62.10N 27.49E
97 C16 **Jørpeland** Rogaland, S Norway 59.01N 6.01E
79 W14 **Jos** Plateau, C Nigeria 9.58N 8.57E
179 Rr17 **Jose Abad Santos** *var.* Trinidad. Mindanao, S Philippines 5.51N 125.35E
63 F19 **José Batlle y Ordóñez** *var.* Batlle y Ordóñez. Florida, C Uruguay 33.28S 55.07W
65 H18 **José de San Martín** Chubut, S Argentina 44.03S 70.27W
63 E19 **José Enrique Rodó** *var.* Rodó, José E.Rodo; *prev.* Drabble, Drable. Soriano, SW Uruguay 33.43S 57.33W
José E.Rodo *see* José Enrique Rodó
Josefsdorf *see* Žabalj
46 C4 **José Martí** ✕ (La Habana) Cuidad de La Habana, N Cuba 23.03N 82.22W
63 F19 **José Pedro Varela** *var.* José P.Varela. Lavalleja, S Uruguay 33.30S 54.28W
189 N2 **Joseph Bonaparte Gulf** *gulf* N Australia
39 N11 **Joseph City** Arizona, SW USA 34.56N 110.18W
11 O9 **Joseph, Lake** ◎ Newfoundland and Labrador, E Canada
12 G13 **Joseph, Lake** ◎ Ontario, S Canada
194 I11 **Josephstaal** Madang, N PNG 4.42S 144.59E
José P.Varela *see* José Pedro Varela
61 J14 **José Rodrigues** Pará, N Brazil 5.45S 51.19W
158 K9 **Joshīmath** Uttaranchal, N India 30.33N 79.34E
27 T7 **Joshua** Texas, SW USA 32.27N 97.23W
37 V15 **Joshua Tree** California, W USA 34.07N 116.18W
79 V14 **Jos Plateau** *plateau* C Nigeria
104 H6 **Josselin** Morbihan, NW France 47.57N 2.35W
Jos Sudarso *see* Yos Sudarso, Pulau
96 E11 **Jostedalsbreen** *glacier* S Norway
96 F12 **Jotunheimen** ▲▲ S Norway
144 G7 **Joûnié** *var.* Junīyah. W Lebanon 33.54N 33.36E
27 R13 **Jourdanton** Texas, SW USA 28.55N 98.33W
100 L7 **Joure** *Fris.* De Jouwer. Friesland, N Netherlands 52.58N 5.48E
95 M18 **Joutsa** Länsi-Suomi, W Finland 61.46N 26.09E
95 N18 **Joutseno** Etelä-Suomi, S Finland 61.06N 28.30E
94 M12 **Joutsijärvi** Lappi, NE Finland 66.40N 28.00E
110 A9 **Joux, Lac de** ◎ W Switzerland
46 D5 **Jovellanos** Matanzas, W Cuba 22.49N 81.14W
159 V13 **Jowai** Meghālaya, NE India 25.25N 92.21E
Jōwat *see* Jabwot
Jowhar *see* Jawhar
149 O12 **Jowkān** Fārs, S Iran
149 Q10 **Jowzam** Kermān, C Iran
155 N2 **Jowzjān** ◈ *province* N Afghanistan
Józseffalva *see* Žabalj
J.Storm Thurmond Reservoir *see* Clark Hill Lake
47 T6 **Juana Díaz** C Puerto Rico 18.03N 66.30W
42 L9 **Juan Aldama** Zacatecas, C Mexico 24.18N 103.23W
(0) E9 **Juan de Fuca Plate** *tectonic feature*
34 F7 **Juan de Fuca, Strait of** *strait* Canada/USA
Juan Fernandez Islands *see* Juan Fernández, Islas
200 Oo12 **Juan Fernández, Islas** *Eng.* Juan Fernandez Islands. *island group* W Chile
57 O4 **Juangriego** Nueva Esparta, NE Venezuela 11.03N 63.58W
58 D11 **Juanjuí** *var.* Juanjuy. San Martín, N Peru 7.12S 76.45W
Juanjuy *see* Juanjuí
95 N16 **Juankoski** Itä-Suomi, C Finland 63.01N 28.24E
Juan Lacaze *see* Juan L.Lacaze
63 E20 **Juan L.Lacaze** *var.* Juan Lacaze, Puerto Sauce; *prev.* Sauce. Colonia, SW Uruguay 34.25S 57.25W
64 L5 **Juan Solá** Salta, N Argentina 23.30S 62.42W
65 F21 **Juan Stuven, Isla** *island* S Chile
61 H16 **Juará** Mato Grosso, W Brazil 11.10S 57.28W
43 N7 **Juárez** *var.* Villa Juárez. Coahuila de Zaragoza, NE Mexico 27.39N 100.43W
42 C2 **Juárez, Sierra de** ▲▲ NW Mexico
61 O15 **Juazeiro** *prev.* Joazeiro. Bahia, E Brazil 9.25S 40.30W
61 P14 **Juazeiro do Norte** Ceará, E Brazil 7.10S 39.18W
83 F15 **Juba** *var.* Jūbā. Bahr el Gabel, S Sudan 4.49N 31.34E
83 L17 **Juba** *Amh.* Genalē Wenz, *It.* Guiba, *Som.* Ganaane, Webi Jubba. ∽ Ethiopia/Somalia
204 H2 **Jubany** *Argentinian research station* Antarctica 61.57S 58.23W
Jubayl *see* Jbaïl
83 L18 **Jubbada Dhexe** *off.* Gobolka Jubbada Dhexe. ◈ *region* SW Somalia
83 K18 **Jubbada Hoose** ◈ *region* SW Somalia
Jubba, Webi *see* Juba
Jubbulpore *see* Jabalpur
Jubeil *see* Jbaïl
76 B9 **Juby, Cap** *headland* SW Morocco 27.58N 12.56W
107 R10 **Júcar** *var.* Jucar. ∽ C Spain
42 L12 **Juchipila** Zacatecas, C Mexico 21.25N 103.06W
43 S16 **Juchitán** *var.* Juchitán de Zaragosa. Oaxaca, SE Mexico 16.27N 95.00W
Juchitán de Zaragosa *see* Juchitán
144 G11 **Judaea** *cultural region* Israel/West Bank
144 F11 **Judaean Hills** *Heb.* Haré Yehuda. *hill range* E Israel
144 H8 **Judaydah** *Fr.* Jdaïdé. Dimashq, W Syria 33.17N 36.15E
145 P11 **Judayyidat Hāmir** S Iraq 31.29N 41.25E
111 U8 **Judenburg** Steiermark, C Austria 47.09N 14.42E
35 T8 **Judith River** ∽ Montana, NW USA
29 V11 **Judsonia** Arkansas, C USA 35.16N 91.38W
147 P14 **Jufrah, Wādī al** *dry watercourse* NW Yemen
Jugar *see* Sêrxü
Jugoslavija/Jugoslavija, Savezna Republika *see* Serbia and Montenegro (Yugoslavia)
44 K10 **Juigalpa** Chontales, S Nicaragua 12.04N 85.21W
167 T13 **Juishui** C Taiwan 23.43N 121.28E
102 E9 **Juist** *island* NW Germany
61 M21 **Juiz de Fora** Minas Gerais, SE Brazil 21.46S 43.22W
64 J5 **Jujuy** *off.* Provincia de Jujuy. ◈ *province* N Argentina
Jujuy *see* San Salvador de Jujuy
94 J11 **Jukkasjärvi** *Lapp.* Čohkkiras. Norrbotten, N Sweden 67.52N 20.39E
Jula *see* Gyula, Hungary
Jūlā *see* Jālū, Libya
39 W2 **Julesburg** Colorado, C USA 40.59N 102.15W
Julia Beterrae *see* Béziers
59 I17 **Juliaca** Puno, SE Peru 15.32S 70.10W
189 U6 **Julia Creek** Queensland, C Australia 20.40S 141.49E
37 V17 **Julian** California, W USA 33.04N 116.36W
100 H7 **Julianadorp** Noord-Holland, NW Netherlands 52.53N 4.43E
111 S11 **Julian Alps** *Ger.* Julische Alpen, *It.* Alpi Giulie, *Slvn.* Julijske Alpe. ▲▲ Italy/Slovenia
57 V11 **Juliana Top** ▲ C Suriname 3.39N 56.36W
Julianehåb *see* Qaqortoq
Julijske Alpe *see* Julian Alps
42 J6 **Julimes** Chihuahua, N Mexico 28.29N 105.21W
Julio Briga *see* Bragança, Portugal
Juliobriga *see* Logroño, Spain
63 G15 **Júlio de Castilhos** Rio Grande do Sul, S Brazil 29.14S 53.42W
Juliomagus *see* Angers
Julische Alpen *see* Julian Alps
Jullundur *see* Jalandhar
153 N11 **Juma** *Rus.* Dzhuma. Samarqand Viloyati, C Uzbekistan 39.43N 66.37E
167 O3 **Juma He** ∽ E China
83 L18 **Jumboo** Jubbada Hoose, S Somalia 0.12S 42.34E
37 Y11 **Jumbo Peak** ▲ Nevada, W USA 36.12N 114.09W
107 R12 **Jumilla** Murcia, SE Spain 38.28N 1.19W
159 N10 **Jumla** Mid Western, NW Nepal 29.22N 82.13E
Jummoo *see* Jammu
Jumna *see* Yamuna
Jumporn *see* Chumphon
32 K5 **Jump River** ∽ Wisconsin, N USA
160 B11 **Jūnāgadh** *var.* Junagarh. Gujarāt, W India 21.31N 70.31E
Junagarh *see* Jūnāgadh
167 Q6 **Junan** *var.* Shizilu. Shandong, E China 35.11N 118.47E
64 G11 **Juncal, Cerro** ▲ C Chile 33.03S 70.02W
27 Q10 **Junction** Texas, SW USA 30.29N 99.46W
38 K6 **Junction** Utah, W USA 38.14N 112.13W
29 O4 **Junction City** Kansas, C USA 39.01N 96.49W
34 F13 **Junction City** Oregon, NW USA 44.13N 123.12W
62 M10 **Jundiaí** São Paulo, S Brazil 23.10S 46.54W
194 E13 **June** ∽ W PNG
41 X12 **Juneau** *state capital* Alaska, USA 58.13N 134.11W
32 M8 **Juneau** Wisconsin, N USA 43.22N 88.42W
107 U6 **Juneda** Cataluña, NE Spain 41.33N 0.49E
191 Q9 **Junee** New South Wales, SE Australia 34.51S 147.33E
37 R8 **June Lake** California, W USA 37.46N 119.04W
Jungbunzlau *see* Mladá Boleslav
164 L4 **Junggar Pendi** *Eng.* Dzungarian Basin. *basin* NW China
101 N24 **Junglinster** Grevenmacher, C Luxembourg 49.43N 6.15E
20 F14 **Juniata River** ∽ Pennsylvania, NE USA
63 B20 **Junín** Buenos Aires, E Argentina 34.36S 61.01W
59 E14 **Junín** Junín, C Peru 11.13S 76.01W
59 F14 **Junín** *off.* Departamento de Junín. ◈ *department* C Peru
65 H15 **Junín de los Andes** Neuquén, W Argentina 39.57S 71.04W
59 D14 **Junín, Lago de** ◎ C Peru
Junīyah *see* Joûnié
Junkseylon *see* Phuket
166 I11 **Junlian** Sichuan, C China 28.11N 104.31E
27 O11 **Juno** Texas, SW USA 30.09N 101.07W
94 J11 **Junosuando** *Lapp.* Čunusavvon. Norrbotten, N Sweden 67.25N 22.28E
95 H16 **Junsele** Västernorrland, C Sweden 63.42N 16.54E
Junten *see* Sunch'ŏn
34 L14 **Juntura** Oregon, NW USA 43.43N 118.05W
95 N14 **Juntusranta** Oulu, E Finland 65.12N 29.30E
120 H11 **Juodupė** Panevėžys, NE Lithuania 56.07N 25.37E
121 H14 **Juozapinės Kalnas** ▲ SE Lithuania 54.29N 25.27E
101 K19 **Juprelle** Liège, E Belgium 50.43N 5.31E
82 D13 **Jur** ∽ C Sudan
105 S9 **Jura** ◈ *department* E France
110 C7 **Jura** ◈ *canton* NW Switzerland
110 B8 **Jura** *var.* Jura Mountains. ▲▲ France/Switzerland
98 G12 **Jura** *island* SW Scotland, UK
Juraciszki *see* Yuratsishki
56 C8 **Juradó** Chocó, NW Colombia 7.07N 77.45W
Jura Mountains *see* Jura
98 G12 **Jura, Sound of** *strait* W Scotland, UK
145 V15 **Juraybīyāt, Bi'r** *well* S Iraq 29.13N 45.28E
120 E13 **Jurbarkas** *Ger.* Georgenburg, Jurburg. Tauragė, W Lithuania 55.04N 22.45E
101 F20 **Jurbise** Hainaut, SW Belgium 50.33N 3.54E
Jurburg *see* Jurbarkas
120 F9 **Jūrmala** Rīga, C Latvia 56.56N 23.42E
176 Ww13 **Jursian, Pulau** *island* E Indonesia
60 D13 **Juruá** Amazonas, NW Brazil 3.08S 65.59W
50 F7 **Juruá, Rio** *var.* Río Yuruá. ∽ Brazil/Peru
61 G16 **Juruena** Mato Grosso, W Brazil 10.32S 58.38W
61 G16 **Juruena** ∽ W Brazil
171 Mm8 **Jūsan-ko** ◎ Honshū, C Japan
27 O6 **Justiceburg** Texas, SW USA 32.57N 101.07W
Justinianopolis *see* Kirşehir
64 K11 **Justo Daract** San Luis, C Argentina 33.52S 65.12W
61 C14 **Jutaí** Amazonas, W Brazil 5.10S 68.45W
60 C13 **Jutaí, Rio** ∽ NW Brazil
102 N13 **Jüterbog** Brandenburg, E Germany 51.58N 13.06E
44 E6 **Jutiapa** Jutiapa, S Guatemala 14.18N 89.52W
44 A3 **Jutiapa** *off.* Departamento de Jutiapa. ◈ *department* SE Guatemala
44 J6 **Juticalpa** Olancho, C Honduras 14.39N 86.12W
84 I13 **Jutila** North Western, NW Zambia 12.33S 26.09E
Jutland *see* Jylland
86 F8 **Jutland Bank** *undersea feature* SE North Sea
95 N16 **Juuka** Itä-Suomi, E Finland 63.12N 29.16E
95 N17 **Juva** Isä-Suomi, SE Finland 61.55N 27.54E
Juvavum *see* Salzburg
46 A6 **Juventud, Isla de la** *var.* Isla de Pinos, *Eng.* Isle of Youth; *prev.* The Isle of the Pines. *island* W Cuba
167 Q5 **Juxian** *var.* Chengyang, Ju Xian. Shandong, E China 35.33N 118.45E
167 P6 **Juye** Shandong, E China 35.25N 116.04E
115 O15 **Južna Morava** *Ger.* Südliche Morava. ∽ SE Serbia and Montenegro (Yugoslavia)
85 H20 **Jwaneng** Southern, S Botswana 24.35S 24.45E
97 I23 **Jyderup** Vestsjælland, E Denmark 55.40N 11.25E
97 F22 **Jylland** *Eng.* Jutland. *peninsula* W Denmark
Jyrgalan *see* Dzhergalan
95 M17 **Jyväskylä** Länsi-Suomi, W Finland 62.07N 25.47E

K

155 X3 **K2** *Chin.* Qogir Feng, *Eng.* Mount Godwin Austen. ▲ China/Pakistan 35.55N 76.30E
40 D9 **Ka'a'awa** *var.* Kaaawa. O'ahu, Hawai'i, USA, C Pacific Ocean 21.33N 157.51W
83 G16 **Kaabong** NE Uganda 3.30N 34.07E
Kaaden *see* Kadaň
57 V9 **Kaaimanston** Sipaliwini, N Suriname 5.06N 56.04W
Kaakhka *see* Kaka
Kaala *see* Caála
197 H5 **Kaala-Gomen** Province Nord, W New Caledonia 20.40S 164.24E
94 L9 **Kaamanen** *Lapp.* Gámas. Lappi, N Finland 69.04N 27.16E
Kaapstad *see* Cape Town
Kaarasjoki *see* Karasjok
Kaaresuanto *see* Karesuando
94 J10 **Kaaresuvanto** *Lapp.* Gárassavon. Lappi, N Finland 68.28N 22.29E
95 K19 **Kaarina** Länsi-Suomi, W Finland 60.24N 22.25E
101 I14 **Kaatsheuvel** Noord-Brabant, S Netherlands 51.39N 5.01E
95 N16 **Kaavi** Itä-Suomi, C Finland 62.58N 28.30E
Ka'a'wa *see* Kaaawa
176 Y15 **Kaba** Papua, E Indonesia 7.34S 138.27E
Kaba *see* Habahe
175 Q13 **Kabaena, Pulau** *island* C Indonesia
175 Q13 **Kabaena, Selat** *strait* Sulawesi, C Indonesia
Kabakly *see* Gabakly
78 J14 **Kabala** N Sierra Leone 9.40N 11.36W
83 E19 **Kabale** SW Uganda 1.15S 29.58E
57 U10 **Kabalebo Rivier** ∽ W Suriname
81 N22 **Kabalo** Katanga, SE Dem. Rep. Congo 6.01S 26.55E
151 W13 **Kabanbay** *Kaz.* Qabanbay *prev.* Andreyevka, *Kaz.* Andreevka. Almaty, SE Kazakhstan 45.49N 80.34E
81 O21 **Kabambare** Maniema, E Dem. Rep. Congo 4.40S 27.40E
197 K15 **Kabara** *prev.* Kambara. *island* Lau Group, E Fiji
Kabardino-Balkaria *see* Kabardino-Balkarskaya Respublika
130 M15 **Kabardino-Balkarskaya Respublika** *Eng.* Kabardino-Balkaria. ◈ *autonomous republic* SW Russian Federation
81 O19 **Kabare** Sud Kivu, E Dem. Rep. Congo 2.13S 28.40E
176 Uu8 **Kabarei** Papua, E Indonesia 0.01S 130.58E
179 Q16 **Kabasalan** Mindanao, S Philippines 7.46N 122.49E
79 U15 **Kabba** Kogi, S Nigeria 7.48N 6.07E
94 I13 **Kåbdalis** *Lapp.* Goabddális. Norrbotten, N Sweden 66.08N 20.03E
144 M6 **Kabd aş Şārim** *hill range* E Syria
12 B7 **Kabenung Lake** ◎ Ontario, S Canada
31 W3 **Kabetogama Lake** ◎ Minnesota, N USA
Kabia, Pulau *see* Kabin, Pulau
81 M22 **Kabinda** Kasai Oriental, SE Dem. Rep. Congo 6.09S 24.28E
Kabinda *see* Cabinda
175 P13 **Kabin, Pulau** *var.* Pulau Kabia. *island* W Indonesia
175 Rr16 **Kabir** Pulau Pantar, S Indonesia 8.15S 124.12E

◆ Country
● Country Capital
◇ Dependent Territory
○ Dependent Territory Capital
◈ Administrative Region
✕ International Airport
▲ Mountain
▲▲ Mountain Range
Volcano
∽ River
◎ Lake
▣ Reservoir

Kabīrwāla – Kampeska, Lake

155 T10 **Kabīrwāla** Punjab, E Pakistan *30.24N 71.51E*
176 U8 **Kable Bet** Papua, E Indonesia *0.24S 129.54E*
80 I13 **Kabo** Ouham, NW Central African Republic *7.43N 18.38E*
Kābol *see* Kābul
85 H14 **Kabompo** North Western, W Zambia *13.36S 24.10E*
85 H14 **Kabompo** ≈ W Zambia
81 M22 **Kabongo** Katanga, SE Dem. Rep. Congo *7.19S 25.34E*
123 Kk12 **Kaboudia, Rass** *headland* E Tunisia *35.13N 11.09E*
149 U4 **Kabūd Gonbad** Khorāsān, NE Iran *37.01N 59.46E*
148 L5 **Kabūd Rāhang** Hamadān, W Iran *35.12N 48.43E*
84 L12 **Kabuko** Northern, NE Zambia *11.31S 31.16E*
155 Q5 **Kābul** ***var.*** Kabul, ***Per.*** Kābol. ● (Afghanistan) Kābul, E Afghanistan *34.34N 69.07E*
155 Q5 **Kābul** ***Eng.*** Kabul, ***Per.*** Kābol. ⬖ *province* E Afghanistan
155 Q5 **Kābul** ✕ Kābul, E Afghanistan *34.31N 69.10E*
155 R5 **Kabul** ***var.*** Daryā-ye Kābul. ≈ Afghanistan/Pakistan ***see also*** Kābul, Daryā-ye
155 S5 **Kābul, Daryā-ye** ***var.*** Kabul. ≈ Afghanistan/Pakistan ***see also*** Kabul
81 O25 **Kabunda** Katanga, SE Dem. Rep. Congo *12.21S 29.14E*
175 Ss4 **Kaburuang, Pulau** *island* Kepulauan Talaud, N Indonesia
82 G8 **Kabushiya** River Nile, NE Sudan *16.54N 33.40E*
85 J14 **Kabwe** Central, C Zambia *14.28S 28.25E*
194 K12 **Kabwum** Morobe, C PNG *6.07S 147.11E*
115 N17 **Kačanik** Serbia, S Serbia and Montenegro (Yugoslavia) *42.13N 21.16E*
176 U8 **Kacepi** Pulau Gebe, E Indonesia *0.05S 129.30E*
120 F13 **Kačerginė** Kaunas, C Lithuania *54.55N 23.40E*
119 S13 **Kacha** Respublika Krym, S Ukraine *44.46N 33.33E*
160 A10 **Kachchh, Gulf of** ***var.*** Gulf of Cutch, Gulf of Kutch. *gulf* W India
160 I11 **Kachchhīdhāna** Madhya Pradesh, C India *21.33N 78.54E*
155 Q11 **Kachchh, Rann of** ***var.*** Rann of Kachh, Rann of Kutch. *salt marsh* India/Pakistan
41 Q13 **Kachemak Bay** *bay* Alaska, USA
Kachh, Rann of *see* Kachchh, Rann of
79 V14 **Kachia** Kaduna, C Nigeria *9.52N 8.00E*
178 Gg2 **Kachin State** ⬖ *state* N Myanmar
151 T7 **Kachiry** Pavlodar, NE Kazakhstan *53.04N 76.05E*
126 Jj15 **Kachug** Irkutskaya Oblast', S Russian Federation *53.52N 105.54E*
143 Q11 **Kaçkar Dağları** ▲▲ NE Turkey
161 C21 **Kadamatt Island** *island* Lakshadweep, India, N Indian Ocean
113 B15 **Kadaň** ***Ger.*** Kaaden.Ústecký Kraj, NW Czech Republic *50.22N 13.14E*
178 Gg12 **Kadan Kyun** ***prev.*** King Island. *island* Mergui Archipelago, S Myanmar
197 I16 **Kadavu** ***prev.*** Kandavu. *island* S Fiji
197 I15 **Kadavu Passage** *channel* S Fiji
81 G16 **Kadéï** ≈ Cameroon/Central African Republic
Kadhimain *see* Al Kāẓimīyah
Kadijica *see* Kadiytsa
116 M13 **Kadıköy Barajı** ▣ NW Turkey
190 I8 **Kadina** South Australia *33.59S 137.43E*
142 H15 **Kadınhanı** Konya, C Turkey *38.15N 32.13E*
78 M14 **Kadiolo** Sikasso, S Mali *10.30N 5.43W*
142 L16 **Kadirli** Osmaniye, S Turkey *37.22N 36.04E*
116 G11 **Kadiytsa** ***Mac.*** Kadijica. ▲ Bulgaria/FYR Macedonia *41.48N 22.58E*
30 L10 **Kadoka** South Dakota, N USA *43.49N 101.30W*
131 N5 **Kadom** Ryazanskaya Oblast', W Russian Federation *54.35N 42.27E*
85 K16 **Kadoma** ***prev.*** Gatooma. Mashonaland West, C Zimbabwe *18.18S 29.55E*
82 E12 **Kadugli** Southern Kordofan, S Sudan *11.00N 29.44E*
79 V14 **Kaduna** Kaduna, C Nigeria *10.32N 7.25E*
79 V14 **Kaduna** ⬖ *state* C Nigeria
79 V15 **Kaduna** ≈ N Nigeria
128 K14 **Kaduy** Vologodskaya Oblast', NW Russian Federation *59.10N 37.11E*
160 E13 **Kadwa** ≈ W India
127 Nn9 **Kadykchan** Magadanskaya Oblast', E Russian Federation *62.54N 146.53E*
Kadzharan *see* K'ajaran
129 T7 **Kadzherom** Respublika Komi, NW Russian Federation *64.42N 55.51E*
153 X8 **Kadzhi-Say** ***Kir.*** Kajisay. Issyk-Kul'skaya Oblast', NE Kyrgyzstan *42.07N 77.10E*
78 I10 **Kaédi** Gorgol, S Mauritania *16.12N 13.31W*
80 G12 **Kaélé** Extrême-Nord, N Cameroon *10.09N 14.25E*
40 C9 **Ka'ena Point** ***var.*** Kaena Point *headland* O'ahu, Hawai'i, USA, C Pacific Ocean *21.34N 158.16W*
192 J2 **Kaeo** Northland, North Island, NZ *35.03S 173.40E*
169 X14 **Kaesŏng** ***var.*** Kaesŏng-si. S North Korea *37.57N 126.30E*
Kaesŏng-si *see* Kaesŏng
Kaewieng *see* Kavieng
81 L24 **Kafakumba** Katanga, S Dem. Rep. Congo *9.39S 23.43E*
Kafan *see* Kapan
79 V14 **Kafanchan** Kaduna, C Nigeria *9.32N 8.18E*
Kaffa *see* Feodosiya
78 G11 **Kaffrine** C Senegal *14.07N 15.27W*
Kafiau *see* Kofiau, Pulau
117 I19 **Kafiréas, Akrotírio** *headland* Évvoia, C Greece *38.10N 24.35E*
117 I19 **Kafiréos, Stenó** *strait* Évvoia/Kykládes, Greece, Aegean Sea
Kafirnigan *see* Kofarnihon
Kafo *see* Kafu
Kafr ash Shaykh/Kafrel Sheik *see* Kafr el Sheikh
77 W7 **Kafr el Sheikh** ***var.*** Kafr ash Shaykh, Kafrel Sheik. N Egypt *31.08N 30.58E*
83 F17 **Kafu** ***var.*** Kafo. ≈ W Uganda
85 J15 **Kafue** Lusaka, SE Zambia *15.43S 28.10E*
85 I14 **Kafue** ≈ C Zambia
69 T13 **Kafue Flats** *plain* C Zambia
171 I13 **Kaga** Ishikawa, Honshū, SW Japan *36.18N 136.19E*
81 J14 **Kaga Bandoro** ***prev.*** Fort-Crampel. Nana-Grébizi, C Central African Republic *6.54N 19.09E*
83 E18 **Kagadi** W Uganda *0.57N 30.52E*
40 H17 **Kagalaska Island** *island* Aleutian Islands, Alaska, USA
Kagan *see* Kogon
Kaganovichabad *see* Kolkhozobod
Kagarlyk *see* Kaharlyk
170 F15 **Kagawa** ***off.*** Kagawa-ken. ⬖ *prefecture* Shikoku, SW Japan
160 J13 **Kagaznagar** Andhra Pradesh, C India *19.25N 79.30E*
95 J14 **Kåge** Västerbotten, N Sweden *64.49N 21.00E*
83 E19 **Kagera** ***var.*** Ziwa Magharibi, ***Eng.*** West Lake. ⬖ *region* NW Tanzania
83 E19 **Kagera** ***var.*** Akagera. ≈ Rwanda/Tanzania ***see also*** Akagera
78 L5 **Kâgheṭ** ***var.*** Karet. *physical region* N Mauritania
Kagi *see* Chiai
143 S12 **Kağızman** Kars, NE Turkey *40.08N 43.10E*
196 I6 **Kagman Point** *headland* Saipan, S Northern Mariana Islands
170 Bb15 **Kagoshima** ***var.*** Kagosima. Kagoshima, Kyūshū, SW Japan *31.36N 130.33E*
172 Qq14 **Kagoshima** ***off.*** Kagoshima-ken, ***var.*** Kagosima. ⬖ *prefecture* Kyūshū, SW Japan
170 Bb16 **Kagoshima-wan** *bay* SW Japan
Kagosima *see* Kagoshima
194 H12 **Kagua** Southern Highlands, W PNG *6.25S 143.48E*
Kagul *see* Cahul
Kagul, Ozero *see* Kahul, Ozero
40 B8 **Kahala Point** *headland* Kaua'i, Hawai'i, USA, C Pacific Ocean *22.08N 159.17W*
83 F21 **Kahama** Shinyanga, NW Tanzania *3.48S 32.36E*
119 P5 **Kaharlyk** ***Rus.*** Kagarlyk. Kyyivs'ka Oblast', N Ukraine *49.49N 30.49E*
174 Mm10 **Kahayan, Sungai** ≈ Borneo, C Indonesia
81 I22 **Kahemba** Bandundu, SW Dem. Rep. Congo *7.20S 19.00E*
193 A23 **Kaherekoau Mountains** ▲▲ South Island, NZ
149 W14 **Kahīrī** ***var.*** Kūhīrī. Sīstān va Balūchestān, SE Iran *26.55N 61.04E*
103 L16 **Kahla** Thüringen, C Germany *50.49N 11.33E*
103 G15 **Kahler Asten** ▲ W Germany *51.11N 8.32E*
155 Q4 **Kahmard, Daryā-ye** ***prev.*** Darya-i-Surkhab. ≈ NE Afghanistan
149 T13 **Kahnūj** Kermān, SE Iran *27.59N 57.40E*
29 V1 **Kahoka** Missouri, C USA *40.25N 91.43W*
40 E10 **Kaho'olawe** ***var.*** Kahoolawe *island* Hawai'i, USA, C Pacific Ocean
142 M16 **Kahramanmaraş** ***var.*** Kahraman Maraş, Maraş, Marash. Kahramanmaraş, S Turkey *37.34N 36.54E*
142 L15 **Kahramanmaraş** ***var.*** Kahraman Maraş, Maraş, Marash. ⬖ *province* C Turkey
Kahror/Kahror Pakka *see* Karor Pacca
143 N15 **Kâhta** Adıyaman, S Turkey *37.48N 38.34E*
40 D8 **Kahuku** O'ahu, Hawai'i, USA, C Pacific Ocean *21.40N 157.57W*
40 D8 **Kahuku Point** *headland* O'ahu, Hawai'i, USA, C Pacific Ocean *21.42N 157.59W*
118 M12 **Kahul, Ozero** ***var.*** Lacul Cahul, ***Rus.*** Ozero Kagul. ◎ Moldova/Ukraine
149 V11 **Kahūrak** Sīstān va Balūchestān, SE Iran *29.25N 59.37E*
192 G13 **Kahurangi Point** *headland* South Island, NZ *40.41S 171.57E*
155 V6 **Kahūta** Punjab, E Pakistan *33.34N 73.22E*
79 S14 **Kaiama** Kwara, W Nigeria *9.37N 3.58E*
194 J12 **Kaiapit** Morobe, C PNG *6.16S 146.13E*
193 I18 **Kaiapoi** Canterbury, South Island, NZ *43.22S 172.39E*
38 K9 **Kaibab Plateau** *plain* Arizona, SW USA
171 Gg14 **Kaibara** Hyōgo, Honshū, SW Japan *35.06N 135.03E*
176 Vv13 **Kai Besar, Pulau** *island* Kepulauan Kai, E Indonesia
38 L9 **Kaibito Plateau** *plain* Arizona, SW USA
164 K6 **Kaidu He** ***var.*** Karaxahar. ≈ NW China
57 S10 **Kaieteur Falls** *waterfall* C Guyana *5.04N 59.32W*
167 O6 **Kaifeng** Henan, C China *34.46N 114.19E*
192 J3 **Kaihu** Northland, North Island, NZ *35.47S 173.39E*
Kaihua *see* Wenshan
176 V13 **Kai Kecil, Pulau** *island* Kepulauan Kai, E Indonesia
176 V14 **Kai, Kepulauan** ***prev.*** Kei Islands. *island group* Maluku, SE Indonesia
192 J3 **Kaikohe** Northland, North Island, NZ *35.25S 173.48E*
193 J16 **Kaikoura** Canterbury, South Island, NZ *42.21S 173.40E*
193 J16 **Kaikoura Peninsula** *peninsula* South Island, NZ
Kailas Range *see* Gangdisê Shan
166 K12 **Kaili** Guizhou, S China *26.34N 107.58E*
40 F10 **Kailua** Maui, Hawai'i, USA, C Pacific Ocean *20.53N 156.13W*
Kailua *see* Kalaoa
40 G11 **Kailua-Kona** ***var.*** Kona. Hawai'i, USA, C Pacific Ocean *19.43N 155.58W*
194 E13 **Kaim** ≈ W PNG
176 Y13 **Kaima** Papua, E Indonesia *5.36S 138.39E*
192 M7 **Kaimai Range** ▲▲ North Island, NZ
116 E13 **Kaïmaktsalán** ▲ Greece/FYR Macedonia *40.57N 21.48E*
193 C20 **Kaimanawa Mountains** ▲▲ North Island, NZ
120 E4 **Käina** ***Ger.*** Keinis; ***prev.*** Keina. Hiiumaa, W Estonia *58.49N 22.45E*
111 V7 **Kainach** ≈ SE Austria
170 G16 **Kainan** Tokushima, Shikoku, SW Japan *33.36N 134.20E*
170 Ff16 **Kainan** Wakayama, Honshū, SW Japan *34.10N 135.11E*
194 J12 **Kainantu** Eastern Highlands, C PNG *6.16S 145.49E*
153 U7 **Kaindy** ***Kir.*** Kayyngdy. Chuyskaya Oblast', N Kyrgyzstan *42.48N 73.39E*
79 T14 **Kainji Dam** *dam* W Nigeria *9.52N 4.36E*
Kainji Lake *see* Kainji Reservoir
79 T14 **Kainji Reservoir** ***var.*** Kainji Lake. ▣ W Nigeria
194 J14 **Kaintiba** ***var.*** Kamina. Gulf, S PNG *7.29S 146.04E*
94 K12 **Kainulaisjärvi** Norrbotten, N Sweden *67.00N 22.31E*
192 K5 **Kaipara Harbour** *harbor* North Island, NZ
158 I10 **Kairāna** Uttar Pradesh, N India *29.24N 77.10E*
194 G9 **Kairiru Island** *island* NW PNG
76 M6 **Kairouan** ***var.*** Al Qayrawān. E Tunisia *35.45N 10.11E*
Kaisaria *see* Kayseri
103 F20 **Kaiserslautern** Rheinland-Pfalz, SW Germany *49.27N 7.46E*
120 G13 **Kaišiadorys** Kaunas, S Lithuania *54.51N 24.27E*
192 I2 **Kaitaia** Northland, North Island, NZ *35.07S 173.13E*
193 E24 **Kaitangata** Otago, South Island, NZ *46.15S 169.49E*
158 I9 **Kaithal** Haryāna, NW India *29.46N 76.20E*
Kaitong *see* Tongyu
174 J11 **Kait, Tanjung** *headland* Sumatera, W Indonesia *3.13S 106.03E*
40 E9 **Kaiwi Channel** *channel* Hawai'i, USA, C Pacific Ocean
166 K9 **Kaixian** ***var.*** Kai Xian. Sichuan, C China *31.13N 108.25E*
169 V11 **Kaiyuan** ***var.*** K'ai-yüan. Liaoning, NE China *42.36N 124.03E*
166 H14 **Kaiyuan** Yunnan, SW China *23.42N 103.13E*
41 O9 **Kaiyuh Mountains** ▲▲ Alaska, USA
95 M15 **Kajaani** ***Swe.*** Kajana. Oulu, C Finland *64.16N 27.46E*
155 N7 **Kajakī, Band-e** ◎ C Afghanistan
Kajan *see* Kayan, Sungai
Kajana *see* Kajaani
143 V13 **K'ajaran** ***Rus.*** Kadzharan. SE Armenia *39.10N 46.09E*
Kajisay *see* Kadzhi-Say
115 O20 **Kajmakčalan** ▲ S FYR Macedonia *40.57N 21.48E*
Kajnar *see* Kaynar
155 N6 **Kajrān** Urūzgān, C Afghanistan *33.12N 65.28E*
155 N5 **Kaj Rūd** ≈ C Afghanistan
152 G14 **Kaka** ***Rus.*** Kaakhka. Ahal Welaýaty, S Turkmenistan *37.19N 59.36E*
10 C12 **Kakabeka Falls** Ontario, S Canada *48.24N 89.40W*
85 F23 **Kakamas** Northern Cape, W South Africa *28.45S 20.33E*
83 H18 **Kakamega** Western, W Kenya *0.13N 34.43E*
114 H13 **Kakanj** Federacija Bosna I Hercegovina, Bosnia and Herzegovina *44.06N 18.07E*
193 F22 **Kakanui Mountains** ▲▲ South Island, NZ
192 K11 **Kakaramea** Taranaki, North Island, NZ *39.42S 174.27E*
78 J16 **Kakata** C Liberia *6.34N 10.19W*
192 M11 **Kakatahi** Manawatu-Wanganui, North Island, NZ *39.40S 175.20E*
115 M23 **Kakavi** Gjirokastër, S Albania *39.55N 20.19E*
153 O14 **Kakaydi** Surkhondaryo Viloyati, S Uzbekistan *37.37N 67.30E*
170 Ee13 **Kake** Hiroshima, Honshū, SW Japan *34.37N 132.17E*
41 X13 **Kake** Kupreanof Island, Alaska, USA *56.58N 133.57W*
175 R12 **Kakea** Pulau Wowoni, C Indonesia *4.09S 123.06E*
171 Ii17 **Kakegawa** Shizuoka, Honshū, S Japan *34.58N 138.21E*
172 Qq13 **Kakeromajima** Kagoshima, SW Japan
149 T6 **Kākhak** ***var.*** Kākhk. Khorāsān, E Iran
120 L11 **Kakhanavichy** ***Rus.*** Kokhanovichi. Vitsyebskaya Voblasts', N Belarus *55.57N 28.06E*
41 P13 **Kakhonak** Alaska, USA *59.26N 154.48W*
119 S10 **Kakhovka** Khersons'ka Oblast', S Ukraine *46.48N 33.30E*
119 U9 **Kakhovs'ka Vodoskhovyshche** ***Rus.*** Kakhovskoye Vodokhranilishche. ▣ SE Ukraine
Kakhovskoye Vodokhranilishche *see* Kakhovs'ka Vodoskhovyshche
119 T11 **Kakhovs'kyy Kanal** *canal* S Ukraine
Kakia *see* Khakhea
161 L16 **Kākināda** ***prev.*** Cocanada. Andhra Pradesh, E India *16.55N 82.13E*
Käkisalmi *see* Priozersk
170 G14 **Kakogawa** Hyōgo, Honshū, SW Japan *34.49N 134.52E*
83 F18 **Kakoge** C Uganda *1.03N 32.30E*
151 O7 **Kak, Ozero** ◎ N Kazakhstan
Ka-Krem *see* Malyy Yenisey
Kakshaal-Too, Khrebet *see* Kokshaal-Tau
41 S5 **Kaktovik** Alaska, USA *70.07N 143.37W*
171 Ll13 **Kakuda** Miyagi, Honshū, C Japan *37.59N 140.47E*
171 M11 **Kakunodate** Akita, Honshū, C Japan *39.36N 140.38E*
Kalaallit Nunaat *see* Greenland
155 T7 **Kālābāgh** Punjab, E Pakistan *32.58N 71.30E*
175 Rr16 **Kalabahi** Pulau Alor, S Indonesia *8.13S 124.31E*
196 I5 **Kalabera** Saipan, S Northern Mariana Islands
85 G14 **Kalabo** Western, W Zambia *14.52S 22.33E*
130 M9 **Kalach** Voronezhskaya Oblast', W Russian Federation *50.24N 41.00E*
125 G13 **Kalachinsk** Omskaya Oblast', C Russian Federation *55.03N 74.30E*
131 N10 **Kalach-na-Donu** Volgogradskaya Oblast', SW Russian Federation *48.45N 43.29E*
177 F5 **Kaladan** ≈ W Myanmar
12 K14 **Kaladar** Ontario, SE Canada *44.38N 77.06W*
40 G13 **Ka Lae** ***var.*** South Cape, South Point. *headland* Hawai'i, USA, C Pacific Ocean *18.54N 155.40W*
85 G19 **Kalahari Desert** *desert* Southern Africa
40 B8 **Kalāheo** ***var.*** Kalaheo. Kaua'i, Hawai'i, USA, C Pacific Ocean *21.55N 159.31W*
Kalaikhum *see* Qal'aikhum
Kala-i-Mor *see* Galaýmor
95 K15 **Kalajoki** Oulu, W Finland *64.15N 24.00E*
Kalak *see* Eski Kaļak
Kal al Sraghna *see* El Kelâa Srarhna
34 G10 **Kalama** Washington, NW USA *46.00N 122.50W*
Kalámai *see* Kalámata
117 G14 **Kalamariá** Kentrikí Makedonía, N Greece *40.36N 22.58E*
117 E21 **Kalámata** ***prev.*** Kalámai. Pelopónnisos, S Greece *37.01N 22.07E*
33 P10 **Kalamazoo** Michigan, N USA *42.17N 85.35W*
33 P9 **Kalamazoo River** ≈ Michigan, N USA
Kalambaka *see* Kalampáka
119 S13 **Kalamits'ka Zatoka** ***Rus.*** Kalamitskiy Zaliv. *gulf* S Ukraine
Kalamitskiy Zaliv *see* Kalamits'ka Zatoka
117 H18 **Kálamos** Attikí, C Greece *38.16N 23.51E*
117 C18 **Kálamos** *island* Iónioi Nísoi, Greece, C Mediterranean Sea
117 D15 **Kalampáka** ***var.*** Kalambaka. Thessalía, C Greece *39.43N 21.36E*
Kalan *see* Călan, Romania
Kalan *see* Tunceli, Turkey
119 S11 **Kalanchak** Khersons'ka Oblast', S Ukraine *46.14N 33.19E*
40 G11 **Kalaoa** ***var.*** Kailua. Hawai'i, USA, C Pacific Ocean *19.43N 155.58W*
175 Pp15 **Kalao, Pulau** *island* Kepulauan Bonerate, W Indonesia
175 Q15 **Kalaotoa, Pulau** *island* W Indonesia
161 J24 **Kala Oya** ≈ NW Sri Lanka
Kalarash *see* Călărași
95 H17 **Kälarne** Jämtland, C Sweden *63.00N 16.10E*
149 V15 **Kalar Rūd** ≈ SE Iran
178 Ii9 **Kalasin** ***var.*** Muang Kalasin. Kalasin, E Thailand *16.28N 103.31E*
155 O8 **Kalāt** ***Per.*** Qalāt. Zābul, S Afghanistan *32.10N 66.54E*
155 O11 **Kālat** ***var.*** Kelat, Khelat. Baluchistān, SW Pakistan *29.02N 66.34E*
117 J14 **Kalathriá, Akrotírio** *headland* Samothráki, NE Greece *40.24N 25.34E*
200 R17 **Kalau** *island* Tongatapu Group, SE Tonga
40 E9 **Kalaupapa** Moloka'i, Hawai'i, USA, C Pacific Ocean *21.11N 156.59W*
131 N13 **Kalaus** ≈ SW Russian Federation
Kalávrita *see* Kalávryta
117 E19 **Kalávryta** ***var.*** Kalávrita. Dytikí Ellás, S Greece *38.01N 22.06E*
147 Y10 **Kalbān** W Oman *20.19N 58.40E*
188 H11 **Kalbarri** Western Australia *27.43S 114.08E*
151 X10 **Kalbinskiy Khrebet** ***Kaz.*** Qalba Zhotasy. ▲▲ E Kazakhstan
150 G10 **Kaldygayty** ≈ W Kazakhstan
142 I12 **Kalecik** Ankara, N Turkey *40.08N 33.27E*
175 R13 **Kaledupa, Pulau** *island* Kepulauan Tukangbesi, C Indonesia
81 O19 **Kalehe** Sud Kivu, E Dem. Rep. Congo *2.04S 28.52E*
81 P22 **Kalemie** ***prev.*** Albertville. Katanga, SE Dem. Rep. Congo *5.55S 29.09E*
177 Ff3 **Kalemyo** Sagaing, W Myanmar *23.11N 94.03E*
84 H12 **Kalene Hill** North Western, NW Zambia *11.10S 24.12E*
Kale Sultanie *see* Çanakkale
128 I7 **Kalevala** Respublika Kareliya, NW Russian Federation *65.12N 31.16E*
177 Ff3 **Kalewa** Sagaing, C Myanmar *23.15N 94.19E*
Kalgan *see* Zhangjiakou
41 Q12 **Kalgin Island** *island* Alaska, USA
188 L12 **Kalgoorlie** Western Australia *30.51S 121.27E*
Kali *see* Sārda
117 E17 **Kaliakoúda** ▲ C Greece *38.47N 21.42E*
116 O8 **Kaliakra, Nos** *headland* NE Bulgaria *43.22N 28.28E*
117 F19 **Kaliánoi** Pelopónnisos, S Greece *37.55N 22.28E*
179 Q13 **Kalibo** Panay Island, C Philippines *11.40N 122.21E*
117 N24 **Kalí Límni** ▲ Kárpathos, SE Greece *35.34N 27.08E*
81 N20 **Kalima** Maniema, E Dem. Rep. Congo *2.33S 26.27E*
174 M8 **Kalimantan** ***Eng.*** Indonesian Borneo. *geopolitical region* Borneo, C Indonesia
174 L8 **Kalimantan Barat** ***off.*** Propinsi Kalimantan Barat, ***Eng.*** West Borneo, West Kalimantan. ⬖ *province* N Indonesia
174 Mm11 **Kalimantan Selatan** ***off.*** Propinsi Kalimantan Selatan, ***Eng.*** South Borneo, South Kalimantan. ⬖ *province* N Indonesia
174 M9 **Kalimantan Tengah** ***off.*** Propinsi Kalimantan Tengah, ***Eng.*** Central Borneo, Central Kalimantan. ⬖ *province* N Indonesia
175 N7 **Kalimantan Timur** ***off.*** Propinsi Kalimantan Timur, ***Eng.*** East Borneo, East Kalimantan. ⬖ *province* N Indonesia
Kálimnos *see* Kálymnos
159 S12 **Kālimpang** West Bengal, NE India *27.05N 88.25E*
Kalinin *see* Tver', Russian Federation
Kalinin *see* Boldumsaz, Turkmenistan
Kalininabad *see* Kalininobod
130 B3 **Kaliningrad** Kaliningradskaya Oblast', W Russian Federation *54.48N 21.33E*
Kaliningrad *see* Kaliningradskaya Oblast'
130 A3 **Kaliningradskaya Oblast'** ***var.*** Kaliningrad. ⬖ *province and enclave* W Russian Federation
Kalinino *see* Tashir
153 P14 **Kalininobod** ***Rus.*** Kalininabad. SW Tajikistan *37.49N 68.55E*
131 O8 **Kalininsk** Saratovskaya Oblast', W Russian Federation *51.31N 44.25E*
Kalininsk *see* Boldumsaz
Kalinisk *see* Cupcina
121 M19 **Kalinkavichy** ***Rus.*** Kalinkovichi. Homyel'skaya Voblasts', SE Belarus *52.07N 29.19E*
Kalinkovichi *see* Kalinkavichy
83 G18 **Kaliro** SE Uganda *0.54N 33.30E*
Kalisch/Kalish *see* Kalisz
35 O7 **Kalispell** Montana, NW USA *48.12N 114.18W*
112 I13 **Kalisz** ***Ger.*** Kalisch, ***Rus.*** Kalish; ***anc.*** Calisia. Wielkopolskie, C Poland *51.46N 18.04E*
112 F9 **Kalisz Pomorski** ***Ger.*** Kallies. Zachodnio-pomorskie, NW Poland *53.55N 15.55E*
130 M10 **Kalitva** ≈ SW Russian Federation
83 F21 **Kaliua** Tabora, C Tanzania *5.03S 31.48E*
94 K13 **Kalix** Norrbotten, N Sweden *65.51N 23.13E*
94 J11 **Kalixfors** Norrbotten, N Sweden *67.45N 20.20E*
151 T8 **Kalkaman** Pavlodar, NE Kazakhstan *51.57N 75.58E*
Kalkandelen *see* Tetovo
189 O4 **Kalkarindji** Northern Territory, N Australia *17.31S 130.40E*
33 P6 **Kalkaska** Michigan, N USA *44.43N 85.12W*
95 F16 **Kall** Jämtland, C Sweden *63.30N 13.15E*
201 X2 **Kallalen** ***var.*** Calalen. *island* Ratak Chain, SE Marshall Islands
120 J5 **Kallaste** ***Ger.*** Krasnogor. Tartumaa, SE Estonia *58.37N 27.12E*
95 N16 **Kallavesi** ◎ SE Finland
117 F17 **Kallídromo** ▲▲ C Greece
Kallies *see* Kalisz Pomorski
97 M22 **Kallinge** Blekinge, S Sweden *56.13N 15.16E*
117 L16 **Kalloní** Lésvos, E Greece *39.14N 26.15E*
95 F16 **Kallsjön** ◎ C Sweden
97 N21 **Kalmar** ***var.*** Calmar. Kalmar, S Sweden *56.40N 16.22E*
97 M19 **Kalmar** ***var.*** Calmar. ⬖ *county* S Sweden
97 N20 **Kalmarsund** *strait* S Sweden
154 L16 **Kalmat, Khor** ***Eng.*** Kalmat Lagoon. *lagoon* SW Pakistan
Kalmat Lagoon *see* Kalmat, Khor
119 X9 **Kal'mius** ≈ E Ukraine
101 H15 **Kalmthout** Antwerpen, N Belgium *51.24N 4.27E*
Kalmykia/Kalmykiya-Khal'mg Tangch, Respublika *see* Kalmykiya, Respublika
131 O12 **Kalmykiya, Respublika** ***var.*** Respublika Kalmykiya-Khal'mg Tangch, ***Eng.*** Kalmykia; ***prev.*** Kalmytskaya ASSR. ⬖ *autonomous republic* SW Russian Federation
Kalmytskaya ASSR *see* Kalmykiya, Respublika
120 F9 **Kalnciems** Jelgava, C Latvia *56.46N 23.37E*
116 L10 **Kalnitsa** ≈ SE Bulgaria
113 J24 **Kalocsa** Bács-Kiskun, S Hungary *46.31N 19.00E*
116 J9 **Kalofer** Plovdiv, C Bulgaria *42.36N 25.00E*
40 E10 **Kalohi Channel** *channel* Hawai'i, USA, C Pacific Ocean
85 I16 **Kalomo** Southern, S Zambia *17.04S 26.27E*
31 X14 **Kalona** Iowa, C USA *41.28N 91.42W*
117 K22 **Kalotási, Akrotírio** *headland* Amorgós, Kykládes, Greece, Aegean Sea *36.47N 25.45E*
158 J8 **Kalpa** Himāchal Pradesh, N India *31.33N 78.16E*
117 C15 **Kalpáki** Ípeiros, W Greece *39.53N 20.38E*
161 C22 **Kalpeni Island** *island* Lakshadweep, India, N Indian Ocean
158 K13 **Kālpi** Uttar Pradesh, N India *26.07N 79.43E*
164 G7 **Kalpin** Xinjiang Uygur Zizhiqu, NW China *40.35N 78.52E*
155 P16 **Kalri Lake** ◎ SE Pakistan
149 R5 **Kāl Shūr** N Iran
41 N11 **Kalskag** Alaska, USA *61.32N 160.15W*
97 B18 **Kalsoy** ***Dan.*** Kalsø *Island* Faeroe Islands *62.20N 6.46W*
41 O9 **Kaltag** Alaska, USA *64.19N 158.43W*
110 H7 **Kaltbrunn** Sankt Gallen, NE Switzerland *47.11N 9.00E*
Kaltdorf *see* Pruszków
79 X14 **Kaltungo** Gombe, E Nigeria *9.49N 11.22E*
130 K4 **Kaluga** Kaluzhskaya Oblast', W Russian Federation *54.31N 36.16E*
161 J26 **Kalu Ganga** ≈ S Sri Lanka
84 J13 **Kalulushi** Copperbelt, C Zambia *12.52S 28.06E*
188 M2 **Kalumburu** Western Australia *14.11S 126.40E*
97 H23 **Kalundborg** Vestsjælland, E Denmark *55.42N 11.06E*
84 K11 **Kalungwishi** ≈ N Zambia
155 T8 **Kalūr Kot** Punjab, E Pakistan *32.07N 71.19E*
118 I6 **Kalush** ***Pol.*** Kałusz. Ivano-Frankivs'ka Oblast', W Ukraine *49.01N 24.21E*
Kałusz *see* Kalush
112 N11 **Kałuszyn** Mazowieckie, C Poland *52.12N 21.43E*
161 J26 **Kalutara** Western Province, SW Sri Lanka *6.34N 79.58E*
Kaluwawa *see* Fergusson Island
130 I5 **Kaluzhskaya Oblast'** ⬖ *province* W Russian Federation
121 E14 **Kalvarija** ***Pol.*** Kalwaria. Marijampolė, S Lithuania *54.25N 23.13E*
95 K15 **Kälviä** Länsi-Suomi, W Finland *63.50N 23.31E*
111 U6 **Kalwang** Steiermark, E Austria *47.25N 14.48E*
Kalwaria *see* Kalvarija
160 D13 **Kalyān** Mahārāshtra, W India *19.16N 73.10E*
128 K16 **Kalyazin** Tverskaya Oblast', W Russian Federation *57.15N 37.53E*
117 D18 **Kalydón** ***anc.*** Calydon. *site of ancient city* Dytikí Ellás, C Greece *38.24N 21.31E*
117 M21 **Kálymnos** ***var.*** Kálimnos. Kálymnos, Dodekánisos, Greece, Aegean Sea *36.57N 26.58E*
117 M21 **Kálymnos** ***var.*** Kálimnos. *island* Dodekánisos, Greece, Aegean Sea
119 O5 **Kalynivka** Kyyivs'ka Oblast', N Ukraine *50.14N 30.16E*
119 N6 **Kalynivka** Vinnyts'ka Oblast', C Ukraine *49.27N 28.32E*
44 M10 **Kama** ***var.*** Cama. Región Autónoma Atlántico Sur, SE Nicaragua *12.06N 83.55W*
125 E9 **Kama** ≈ NW Russian Federation
172 N12 **Kamaishi** ***var.*** Kamaisi. Iwate, Honshū, C Japan *39.17N 141.51E*
Kamaisi *see* Kamaishi
120 H11 **Kamajai** Panevėžys, NE Lithuania *55.16N 25.30E*
120 H13 **Kamajai** Utena, E Lithuania *55.49N 25.30E*
171 Jj17 **Kamakura** Kanagawa, Honshū, S Japan *35.17N 139.31E*
155 U9 **Kamālia** Punjab, NE Pakistan *30.43N 72.39E*
85 I14 **Kamalondo** North Western, NW Zambia *13.42S 25.38E*
142 I13 **Kaman** Kirşehir, C Turkey *39.22N 33.43E*
81 O20 **Kamanyola** Sud Kivu, E Dem. Rep. Congo *2.54S 29.04E*
147 N14 **Kamarān** *island* W Yemen
57 R9 **Kamarang** W Guyana *5.49N 60.38W*
Kāmāreddi/Kamareddy *see* Rāmāreddi
Kama Reservoir *see* Kamskoye Vodokhranilishche
154 K13 **Kamarod** Baluchistān, SW Pakistan *27.34N 63.36E*
175 R13 **Kamaru** Pulau Buton, C Indonesia *5.10S 123.03E*
79 S13 **Kamba** Kebbi, NW Nigeria *11.50N 3.44E*
Kambaeng Petch *see* Kamphaeng Phet
188 L12 **Kambalda** Western Australia *31.15S 121.33E*
155 P13 **Kambar** ***var.*** Qambar. Sind, SE Pakistan *27.34N 68.03E*
Kambara *see* Kabara
78 I14 **Kambia** W Sierra Leone *9.09N 12.52W*
175 S16 **Kambing, Pulau** *island* W East Timor
Kambos *see* Kámpos
81 N25 **Kambove** Katanga, SE Dem. Rep. Congo *10.49S 26.39E*
Kambryk *see* Cambrai
127 Pp10 **Kamchatka** ≈ E Russian Federation
Kamchatka *see* Kamchatka, Poluostrov
Kamchatka Basin *see* Komandorskaya Basin
127 P11 **Kamchatka, Poluostrov** ***Eng.*** Kamchatka. *peninsula* E Russian Federation
127 Pp11 **Kamchatskaya Oblast'** ⬖ *province* E Russian Federation
127 Pp10 **Kamchatskiy Zaliv** *gulf* E Russian Federation
116 N9 **Kamchiya** ≈ E Bulgaria
116 L9 **Kamchiya, Yazovir** ◎ E Bulgaria
Kamdesh *see* Kāmdeysh
155 T4 **Kāmdeysh** ***var.*** Kamdesh. Kunar, E Afghanistan *35.25N 71.25E*
170 Ee14 **Kamega-mori** ▲ Shikoku, SW Japan *33.45N 133.12E*
120 M13 **Kamen'** ***Rus.*** Kamen'. Vitsyebskaya Voblasts', N Belarus *55.01N 28.52E*
Kamenets *see* Kamyanyets
Kamenets-Podol'skaya Oblast' *see* Khmel'nyts'ka Oblast'
Kamenets-Podol'skiy *see* Kam"yanets'-Podil's'kyy
115 Q18 **Kamenica** NE FYR Macedonia *42.03N 22.34E*
114 A11 **Kamenjak, Rt** *headland* NW Croatia
150 F8 **Kamenka** Zapadnyy Kazakhstan, NW Kazakhstan *51.06N 51.16E*
129 O6 **Kamenka** Arkhangel'skaya Oblast', NW Russian Federation *65.55N 44.01E*
130 06 **Kamenka** Penzenskaya Oblast', W Russian Federation *53.12N 44.00E*
131 L8 **Kamenka** Voronezhskaya Oblast', W Russian Federation *50.44N 39.31E*
Kamenka *see* Camenca, Moldova
Kamenka *see* Kam"yanka, Ukraine
Kamenka-Bugskaya *see* Kam"yanka-Buz'ka
Kamenka Dneprovskaya *see* Kam"yanka-Dniprovs'ka
Kamen Kashirskiy *see* Kamin'-Kashyrs'kyy
126 Gg14 **Kamen'-na-Obi** Altayskiy Kray, S Russian Federation *53.42N 81.04E*
130 L15 **Kamennomostskiy** Respublika Adygeya, SW Russian Federation *44.13N 40.12E*
130 L11 **Kamenolomni** Rostovskaya Oblast', SW Russian Federation *47.36N 40.18E*
131 P8 **Kamenskiy** Saratovskaya Oblast', W Russian Federation *50.56N 45.32E*
127 P7 **Kamenskoye** Koryakskiy Avtonomnyy Okrug, E Russian Federation *62.29N 166.16E*
Kamenskoye *see* Dniprodzerzhyns'k
130 L11 **Kamensk-Shakhtinskiy** Rostovskaya Oblast', SW Russian Federation *48.18N 40.16E*
125 Ee11 **Kamensk-Ural'skiy** Sverdlovskaya Oblast', C Russian Federation *56.30N 61.45E*
103 P15 **Kamenz** Sachsen, E Germany *51.15N 14.06E*
171 Gg14 **Kameoka** Kyōto, Honshū, SW Japan *35.02N 135.35E*
130 M3 **Kameshkovo** Vladimirskaya Oblast', W Russian Federation *56.21N 41.01E*
171 H15 **Kameyama** Mie, Honshū, SW Japan *34.52N 136.25E*
170 Cc10 **Kami-Agata** Nagasaki, Tsushima, SW Japan *34.40N 129.27E*
35 N10 **Kamiah** Idaho, NW USA *46.13N 116.01W*
Kamień Koszyrski *see* Kamin'-Kashyrs'kyy
112 H9 **Kamień Krajeński** ***Ger.*** Kamin in Westpreussen. Kujawsko-pomorskie, C Poland *53.31N 17.31E*
113 F15 **Kamienna Góra** ***Ger.*** Landeshut, Landeshut in Schlesien. Dolnośląskie, SW Poland *50.48N 16.00E*
112 D8 **Kamień Pomorski** ***Ger.*** Cummin in Pommern. Zachodnio-pomorskie, NW Poland *53.57N 14.44E*
172 N7 **Kamiiso** Hokkaidō, NE Japan *41.50N 140.38E*
81 L22 **Kamiji** Kasai Oriental, S Dem. Rep. Congo *6.35S 23.18E*
172 Pp5 **Kamikawa** Hokkaidō, NE Japan *43.51N 142.47E*
170 Bb15 **Kami-Koshiki-jima** *island* SW Japan
81 M23 **Kamina** Katanga, S Dem. Rep. Congo *8.42S 25.01E*
Kamina *see* Kaintiba
44 C6 **Kaminaljuyú** *ruins* Guatemala, C Guatemala *14.34N 90.36W*
Kamin in Westpreussen *see* Kamień Krajeński
118 J2 **Kamin'-Kashyrs'kyy** ***Pol.*** Kamień Koszyrski, ***Rus.*** Kamen Kashirskiy. Volyns'ka Oblast', NW Ukraine *51.39N 24.59E*
172 N6 **Kaminokuni** Hokkaidō, NE Japan *41.48N 140.05E*
171 Ll13 **Kaminoyama** Yamagata, Honshū, C Japan *38.09N 140.15E*
171 Ii14 **Kamioka** Gifu, Honshū, SW Japan *36.20N 137.18E*
41 Q13 **Kamishak Bay** *bay* Alaska, USA
172 Pp6 **Kami-Shihoro** Hokkaidō, NE Japan *43.14N 143.18E*
Kamishli *see* Al Qāmishlī
Kamissar *see* Kamsar
170 Cc10 **Kami-Tsushima** Nagasaki, Tsushima, SW Japan *34.40N 129.27E*
81 O20 **Kamituga** Sud Kivu, E Dem. Rep. Congo *3.07S 28.10E*
170 B17 **Kamiyaku** Kagoshima, Yaku-shima, SW Japan *30.24N 130.32E*
9 N16 **Kamloops** British Columbia, SW Canada *50.39N 120.24W*
109 G25 **Kamma** Sicilia, Italy, C Mediterranean Sea *36.46N 12.03E*
199 Ii4 **Kammu Seamount** *undersea feature* N Pacific Ocean *32.09N 173.00E*
111 U11 **Kamnik** ***Ger.*** Stein. C Slovenia *46.13N 14.34E*
Kamniške Alpe *see* Kamniško-Savinjske Alpe
111 T10 **Kamniško-Savinjske Alpe** ***var.*** Kamniške Alpe, Sanntaler Alpen, ***Ger.*** Steiner Alpen. ▲▲ N Slovenia
171 Kk13 **Kamo** Niigata, Honshū, C Japan *37.42N 139.03E*
171 K17 **Kamogawa** Chiba, Honshū, S Japan *35.05N 140.04E*
155 W8 **Kāmoke** Punjab, E Pakistan *31.58N 74.13E*
84 L13 **Kamoto** Eastern, E Zambia *13.16S 32.04E*
111 V3 **Kamp** ≈ N Austria
83 F18 **Kampala** ● (Uganda) S Uganda *0.21N 32.28E*
174 H8 **Kampar, Sungai** ≈ Sumatera, W Indonesia
174 Ii10 **Kampa, Teluk** *bay* Pulau Bangka, W Indonesia
100 L9 **Kampen** Overijssel, E Netherlands *52.33N 5.55E*
81 N20 **Kampene** Maniema, E Dem. Rep. Congo *3.34S 26.40E*
31 Q9 **Kampeska, Lake** ◎ South Dakota, N USA

◆ Country
● Country Capital
◇ Dependent Territory
○ Dependent Territory Capital
⬖ Administrative Region
✕ International Airport
▲ Mountain
▲▲ Mountain Range
Volcano
≈ River
◎ Lake
▣ Reservoir

KAMPHAENG PHET – KARLSTAD

178 Gg9 **Kamphaeng Phet** *var.* Kambaeng Petch. Kamphaeng Phet, W Thailand *16.28N 99.31E*
Kampo *see* Campo, Cameroon
Kampo *see* Ntem, Cameroon/Equatorial Guinea
178 J13 **Kâmpóng Cham** *prev.* Kompong Cham. Kâmpóng Cham, C Cambodia *12.00N 105.27E*
178 J13 **Kâmpóng Chhnăng** *prev.* Kompong. Kâmpóng Chhnăng, C Cambodia *12.15N 104.40E*
178 Ii12 **Kâmpóng Khleăng** *prev.* Kompong Kleang. Siĕmréab, NW Cambodia *13.04N 104.07E*
178 I14 **Kâmpóng Saôm** *prev.* Kompong Som, Sihanoukville. Kâmpóng Saôm, SW Cambodia *10.37N 103.30E*
178 J13 **Kâmpóng Spoe** *prev.* Kompong Speu. Kâmpóng Spœ, S Cambodia *11.28N 104.29E*
124 N3 **Kámpos** *var.* Kambos. NW Cyprus *35.03N 32.44E*
178 Ii14 **Kâmpôt** Kâmpôt, SW Cambodia *10.37N 104.10E*
Kamptee *see* Kāmthi
79 O14 **Kampti** SW Burkina *10.07N 3.22W*
Kampuchea *see* Cambodia
174 Ll5 **Kampung Sirik** Sarawak, East Malaysia *2.42N 111.28E*
176 Y13 **Kampung, Sungai** ⟿ Papua, E Indonesia
176 Vv12 **Kamrau, Teluk** *bay* Papua, E Indonesia
9 V15 **Kamsack** Saskatchewan, S Canada *51.34N 101.51W*
78 H13 **Kamsar** *var.* Kamissar. Guinée-Maritime, W Guinea *10.36N 14.34W*
131 R4 **Kamskoye Ust'ye** Respublika Tatarstan, W Russian Federation *55.13N 49.11E*
129 U14 **Kamskoye Vodokhranilishche** *var.* Kama Reservoir. ⊠ NW Russian Federation
160 I12 **Kāmthi** *prev.* Kamptee. Mahārāshtra, C India *21.19N 79.11E*
Kamuela *see* Waimea
172 Nn5 **Kamuenai** Hokkaidō, NE Japan *43.07N 140.25E*
172 P7 **Kamui-dake** ▲ Hokkaidō, NE Japan *42.24N 142.57E*
172 Nn4 **Kamui-misaki** *headland* Hokkaidō, NE Japan *43.20N 140.20E*
45 O15 **Kámuk, Cerro** ▲ SE Costa Rica *9.15N 83.01W*
176 Vv9 **Kamundan, Sungai** ⟿ Papua, E Indonesia
176 X12 **Kamura, Sungai** ⟿ Papua, E Indonesia
118 K7 **Kam"yanets'-Podil's'kyy** *Rus.* Kamenets-Podol'skiy. Khmel'nyts'ka Oblast', W Ukraine *48.42N 26.36E*
119 Q6 **Kam"yanka** *Rus.* Kamenka. Cherkas'ka Oblast', C Ukraine *49.03N 32.06E*
118 I5 **Kam"yanka-Buz'ka** *Rus.* Kamenka-Bugskaya. L'vivs'ka Oblast', NW Ukraine *50.03N 24.20E*
119 T9 **Kam"yanka-Dniprovs'ka** *Rus.* Kamenka Dneprovskaya. Zaporiz'ka Oblast', SE Ukraine *47.28N 34.24E*
121 F19 **Kamyanyets** *Rus.* Kamenets. Brestskaya Voblasts', SW Belarus *52.24N 23.50E*
131 P9 **Kamyshin** Volgogradskaya Oblast', SW Russian Federation *50.06N 45.20E*
125 Ee11 **Kamyshlov** Sverdlovskaya Oblast', C Russian Federation *56.55N 62.37E*
131 Q13 **Kamyzyak** Astrakhanskaya Oblast', SW Russian Federation *46.07N 48.03E*
10 K8 **Kanaaupscow** ⟿ Québec, C Canada
38 K8 **Kanab** Utah, W USA *37.03N 112.31W*
38 K9 **Kanab Creek** ⟿ Arizona/Utah, SW USA
197 J13 **Kanacea** *prev.* Kanathea. Taveuni, N Fiji *16.59S 179.54E*
197 K14 **Kanacea** *island* Lau Group, E Fiji
40 G17 **Kanaga Island** *island* Aleutian Islands, Alaska, USA
40 G17 **Kanaga Volcano** ▲ Kanaga Island, Alaska, USA *51.55N 177.09W*
171 J17 **Kanagawa** *off.* Kanagawa-ken. ◆ *prefecture* Honshū, S Japan
11 Q8 **Kanairiktok** ⟿ Newfoundland and Labrador, E Canada
Kanaky *see* New Caledonia
81 K22 **Kananga** *prev.* Luluabourg. Kasai Occidental, S Dem. Rep. Congo *5.51S 22.22E*
Kananur *see* Cannanore
Kanara *see* Karnātaka
38 J7 **Kanarraville** Utah, W USA *37.32N 113.10W*
131 Q4 **Kanash** Chuvashskaya Respubliki, W Russian Federation *55.30N 47.27E*
Kanathea *see* Kanacea
23 Q4 **Kanawha River** ⟿ West Virginia, NE USA
171 I15 **Kanayama** Gifu, Honshū, SW Japan *35.46N 137.15E*
171 I12 **Kanazawa** Ishikawa, Honshū, SW Japan *36.34N 136.40E*
177 G4 **Kanbalu** Sagaing, C Myanmar *23.10N 95.31E*
177 Ff8 **Kanbe** Yangon, SW Myanmar *16.40N 96.01E*
178 H11 **Kanchanaburi** Kanchanaburi, W Thailand *14.01N 99.31E*
Kānchenjunga *see* Kangchenjunga
151 V11 **Kanchingiz, Khrebet** ▲ E Kazakhstan
161 J19 **Kānchīpuram** *prev.* Conjeeveram. Tamil Nādu, SE India *12.49N 79.43E*
155 N8 **Kandahār** *Per.* Qandahār. Kandahār, S Afghanistan *31.36N 65.48E*
155 N9 **Kandahār** *Per.* Qandahār. ◆ *province* SE Afghanistan
Kandalakša *see* Kandalaksha
128 I5 **Kandalaksha** *var.* Kandalakša, *Fin.* Kantalahti. Murmanskaya Oblast', NW Russian Federation *67.09N 32.13E*
Kandalaksha Gulf/Kandalakshskaya Guba *see* Kandalakshskiy Zaliv
128 K6 **Kandalakshskiy Zaliv** *var.* Kandalakshskaya Guba, *Eng.* Kandalaksha Gulf. *bay* NW Russian Federation
Kandalangodi *see* Kandalangoti
85 G17 **Kandalangoti** *var.* Kandalangodi. Ngamiland, NW Botswana *19.25S 22.12E*
175 N10 **Kandangan** Borneo, C Indonesia *2.49S 115.15E*
Kandau *see* Kandava
120 E8 **Kandava** *Ger.* Kandau. Tukums, W Latvia *57.02N 22.48E*
Kandavu *see* Kadavu
79 R14 **Kandé** *var.* Kanté. NE Togo *9.55N 1.01E*
103 F23 **Kandel** ▲ SW Germany *48.03N 8.00E*
194 G12 **Kandep** Enga, W PNG *5.50S 143.26E*
155 R12 **Kandh Kot** Sind, SE Pakistan *28.15N 69.18E*
79 S13 **Kandi** N Benin *11.04N 2.58E*
155 P14 **Kandiāro** Sind, SE Pakistan *27.01N 68.16E*
142 F11 **Kandıra** Kocaeli, NW Turkey *41.04N 30.07E*
191 S8 **Kandos** New South Wales, SE Australia *32.52S 149.58E*
154 M16 **Kandrāch** *var.* Kanrach. Baluchistān, SW Pakistan *25.26N 65.28E*
180 I4 **Kandreho** Mahajanga, C Madagascar *17.27S 46.06E*
194 M12 **Kandrian** New Britain, E PNG *6.10S 149.33E*
Kandukur *see* Kondukūr
161 K25 **Kandy** Central Province, C Sri Lanka *7.16N 80.40E*
150 I10 **Kandyagash** *Kaz.* Qandyaghash; *prev.* Oktyabr'sk. Aktyubinsk, W Kazakhstan *49.25N 57.24E*
20 D12 **Kane** Pennsylvania, NE USA *41.39N 78.47W*
66 I11 **Kane Fracture Zone** *tectonic feature* NW Atlantic Ocean
Kanëka *see* Kanëvka
80 G9 **Kanem** *off.* Préfecture du Kanem. ◆ *prefecture* W Chad
40 D9 **Kāne'ohe** *var.* Kaneohe. O'ahu, Hawai'i, USA, C Pacific Ocean *21.25N 157.48W*
Kanestron, Akrotírio *see* Palioúri, Akrotírio
Kanëv *see* Kaniv
128 M5 **Kanëvka** *var.* Kanëka. Murmanskaya Oblast', NW Russian Federation *67.07N 39.43E*
130 K13 **Kanevskaya** Krasnodarskiy Kray, SW Russian Federation *46.07N 38.57E*
Kanevskoye Vodokhranilishche *see* Kanivs'ke Vodoskhovyshche
171 Ll12 **Kaneyama** Yamagata, Honshū, C Japan *38.54N 140.20E*
85 G20 **Kang** Kgalagadi, C Botswana *23.40S 22.49E*
78 L13 **Kangaba** Koulikoro, SW Mali *11.57N 8.24W*
142 M13 **Kangal** Sivas, C Turkey *39.15N 37.22E*
149 O13 **Kangān** Būshehr, S Iran *25.50N 57.30E*
149 S15 **Kangān** Hormozgān, SE Iran *27.49N 52.04E*
173 G2 **Kangar** Perlis, Peninsular Malaysia *6.28N 100.10E*
78 L13 **Kangaré** Sikasso, S Mali *11.39N 8.10W*
190 F10 **Kangaroo Island** *island* South Australia
95 M17 **Kangasniemi** Itä-Suomi, E Finland *61.58N 26.36E*
148 K6 **Kangāvar** *var.* Kangāwar. Kermānshāh, W Iran *34.30N 47.53E*
Kangāwar *see* Kangāvar
159 S11 **Kangchenjunga** *var.* Kānchenjunga. ▲ NE India *27.36N 88.06E*
166 G9 **Kangding** *var.* Lucheng, *Tib.* Dardo. Sichuan, C China *30.03N 101.56E*
175 Nn14 **Kangean, Kepulauan** *island group* S Indonesia
175 N14 **Kangean, Pulau** *island* Kepulauan Kangean, S Indonesia
69 U8 **Kangen** *var.* Kengen. ⟿ SE Sudan
207 N14 **Kangerlussuaq** *Dan.* Søndre Strømfjord ✕ Kitaa, W Greenland *66.59N 50.28W*
207 Q15 **Kangertittivaq** *Dan.* Scoresby Sund. *fjord* E Greenland
178 H2 **Kangfang** Kachin State, N Myanmar *26.09N 98.36E*
176 Z13 **Kanggup** Papua, E Indonesia *5.56S 140.49E*
169 X12 **Kanggye** N North Korea *40.57N 126.37E*
207 P15 **Kangikajik** *var.* Kap Brewster. *headland* E Greenland *70.10N 22.00W*
11 N5 **Kangiqsualujjuaq** *prev.* George River, Port-Nouveau-Québec. Quebec, E Canada *58.34N 65.58W*
10 L2 **Kangiqsujuaq** *prev.* Maricourt, Wakeham Bay. Québec, NE Canada *61.35N 72.00W*
10 M4 **Kangirsuk** *prev.* Bellin, Payne. Québec, E Canada *60.00N 70.01W*
Kangle *see* Wanzai
164 J15 **Kangmar** Xizang Zizhiqu, W China *30.45N 85.43E*
164 M16 **Kangmar** Xizang Zizhiqu, W China *28.34N 89.40E*
169 Y14 **Kangnŭng** *Jap.* Kōryō. NE South Korea *37.47N 128.51E*
81 D18 **Kango** Estuaire, NW Gabon *0.17N 10.00E*
158 I7 **Kāngra** Himāchal Pradesh, NW India *32.04N 76.16E*
159 Q16 **Kangsabati Reservoir** ⊠ N India
165 O17 **Kangto** ▲ China/India *27.54N 92.33E*
165 W12 **Kangxian** *var.* Kang Xian, Zuitai, Zuitaizi. Gansu, C China *33.21N 105.40E*
177 Ff4 **Kani** Sagaing, C Myanmar *22.24N 94.55E*
78 M15 **Kani** NW Ivory Coast *8.24N 6.38W*
81 M23 **Kaniama** Katanga, S Dem. Rep. Congo *7.31S 24.10E*
Kanibadam *see* Konibodom
175 O2 **Kanibongan** Sabah, East Malaysia *6.40N 117.12E*
193 F17 **Kaniere** West Coast, South Island, NZ *42.45S 171.00E*
193 G17 **Kaniere, Lake** ◎ South Island, NZ
196 E17 **Kanifaay** Yap, W Micronesia
129 O4 **Kanin Kamen'** ▲ NW Russian Federation
129 N3 **Kanin Nos** Nenetskiy Avtonomnyy Okrug, NW Russian Federation *68.38N 43.19E*
129 N3 **Kanin Nos, Mys** *headland* NW Russian Federation *68.39N 43.14E*
129 O5 **Kanin, Poluostrov** *peninsula* NW Russian Federation
145 V8 **Kānī Sakht** E Iraq *33.19N 46.04E*
145 T3 **Kānī Sulaymān** N Iraq *35.54N 44.35E*
172 N8 **Kanita** Aomori, Honshū, C Japan *41.04N 140.36E*
119 Q5 **Kaniv** *Rus.* Kanëv. Cherkas'ka Oblast', C Ukraine *49.46N 31.28E*
190 K11 **Kaniva** Victoria, SE Australia *36.25S 141.13E*
119 Q5 **Kanivs'ke Vodoskhovyshche** *Rus.* Kanevskoye Vodokhranilishche. ⊠ C Ukraine
114 L8 **Kanjiža** *Ger.* Altkanischa, *Hung.* Magyarkanizsa, Ókanizsa; *prev.* Stara Kanjiža. Serbia, N Serbia and Montenegro (Yugoslavia) *46.03N 20.03E*
95 K18 **Kankaanpää** Länsi-Suomi, W Finland *61.46N 22.25E*
32 M12 **Kankakee** Illinois, N USA *41.07N 87.51W*
33 O11 **Kankakee River** ⟿ Illinois/Indiana, N USA
78 K14 **Kankan** Haute-Guinée, E Guinea *10.25N 9.19W*
160 K13 **Kānker** Chhattisgarh, C India *20.19N 81.29E*
78 J10 **Kankossa** Assaba, S Mauritania *15.54N 11.31W*
178 Gg13 **Kanmaw Kyun** *var.* Kisseraing, Kithareng. *island* Mergui Archipelago, S Myanmar
170 E13 **Kanmuri-yama** ▲ Kyūshū, SW Japan *34.28N 132.03E*
23 R10 **Kannapolis** North Carolina, SE USA *35.29N 80.37W*
95 L16 **Kannonkoski** Länsi-Suomi, W Finland *62.58N 25.19E*
Kannur *see* Cannanore
95 K15 **Kannus** Länsi-Suomi, W Finland *63.51N 23.55E*
79 V13 **Kano** Kano, N Nigeria *11.56N 8.30E*
79 V13 **Kano** ◆ *state* N Nigeria
79 V13 **Kano** ✕ Kano, N Nigeria *11.56N 8.26E*
170 F14 **Kan'onji** *var.* Kanonzi. Kagawa, Shikoku, SW Japan *34.10N 133.38E*
Kanonzi *see* Kan'onji
28 M5 **Kanopolis Lake** ⊠ Kansas, C USA
38 K5 **Kanosh** Utah, W USA *38.48N 112.26W*
174 Ll6 **Kanowit** Sarawak, East Malaysia *2.03N 112.15E*
170 Bb17 **Kanoya** Kagoshima, Kyūshū, SW Japan *31.21N 130.49E*
158 L13 **Kānpur** *Eng.* Cawnpore. Uttar Pradesh, N India *26.28N 80.21E*
Kanrach *see* Kandrāch
171 Gg15 **Kansai** ✕ (Ōsaka) Ōsaka, Honshū, SW Japan *34.25N 135.13E*
29 R9 **Kansas** Oklahoma, C USA *36.14N 94.46W*
28 L5 **Kansas** *off.* State of Kansas; also known as Jayhawker State, Sunflower State. ◆ *state* C USA
29 R4 **Kansas City** Kansas, C USA *39.06N 94.37W*
29 R4 **Kansas City** Missouri, C USA *39.06N 94.34W*
29 R3 **Kansas City** ✕ Missouri, C USA *39.18N 94.45W*
29 P4 **Kansas River** ⟿ Kansas, C USA
126 I14 **Kansk** Krasnoyarskiy Kray, S Russian Federation *56.11N 95.32E*
Kansu *see* Gansu
153 V7 **Kant** Chuyskaya Oblast', N Kyrgyzstan *42.54N 74.47E*
Kantalahti *see* Kandalaksha
178 Gg16 **Kantang** *var.* Ban Kantang. Trang, SW Thailand *7.25N 99.30E*
117 H25 **Kántanos** Kríti, Greece, E Mediterranean Sea *35.20N 23.42E*
79 R12 **Kantchari** E Burkina *12.28N 1.31E*
Kanté *see* Kandé
Kantemir *see* Cantemir
130 L9 **Kantemirovka** Voronezhskaya Oblast', W Russian Federation *49.43N 39.53E*
178 J11 **Kantharalak** Si Sa Ket, E Thailand *14.32N 104.37E*
Kantipur *see* Kathmandu
41 Q9 **Kantishna River** ⟿ Alaska, USA
171 K16 **Kantō** *physical region* Honshū, SW Japan
203 S3 **Kanton** *var.* Abariringa, Canton Island; *prev.* Mary Island. *atoll* Phoenix Islands, C Kiribati
171 Jj15 **Kantō-sanchi** ▲ Honshū, S Japan
99 C20 **Kanturk** *Ir.* Ceann Toirc. SW Ireland *52.12N 8.54W*
57 T11 **Kanuku Mountains** ▲ S Guyana
171 Kk15 **Kanuma** Tochigi, Honshū, S Japan *36.36N 139.46E*
85 H20 **Kanye** Southern, SE Botswana *24.54S 25.14E*
85 H17 **Kanyu** Ngamiland, C Botswana *20.07S 24.36E*
177 G7 **Kanyutkwin** Pegu, C Myanmar *18.19N 96.30E*
81 M24 **Kanzenze** Katanga, SE Dem. Rep. Congo *10.33S 25.28E*
200 Ss13 **Kao** *island* Kotu Group, W Tonga
167 S14 **Kaohsiung** *var.* Gaoxiong, *Jap.* Takao, Takow. S Taiwan *22.36N 120.16E*
167 S14 **Kaohsiung** ✕ S Taiwan *22.26N 120.32E*
Kaokaona *see* Kirakira
85 B17 **Kaoko Veld** ▲ N Namibia
78 G11 **Kaolack** *var.* Kaolak. W Senegal *14.09N 16.07W*
Kaolak *see* Kaolack
Kaolan *see* Lanzhou
195 W15 **Kaolo** San Jorge, N Solomon Islands *8.24S 159.35E*
85 H14 **Kaoma** Western, W Zambia *14.43S 24.46E*
40 B8 **Kapa'a** *var.* Kapaa. Kaua'i, Hawai'i, USA, C Pacific Ocean *22.04N 159.19W*
115 J16 **Kapa Moračka** ▲ SW Serbia and Montenegro (Yugoslavia) *42.53N 19.01E*
143 V13 **Kapan** *Rus.* Kafan; *prev.* Ghap'an. SE Armenia *39.13N 46.25E*
84 L13 **Kapandashila** Northern, NE Zambia *12.43S 31.00E*
81 L23 **Kapanga** Katanga, S Dem. Rep. Congo *8.22S 22.37E*
151 U15 **Kapchagay** *Kaz.* Kapshaghay. Almaty, SE Kazakhstan *43.52N 77.05E*
151 V15 **Kapchagayskoye Vodokhranilishche** *Kaz.* Qapshagay Böyeni. ⊠ SE Kazakhstan
101 F15 **Kapelle** Zeeland, SW Netherlands *51.28N 3.58E*
101 G16 **Kapellen** Antwerpen, N Belgium *51.19N 4.25E*
97 P15 **Kapellskär** Stockholm, C Sweden *59.43N 19.03E*
83 H18 **Kapenguria** Rift Valley, W Kenya *1.13N 35.07E*
111 V6 **Kapfenberg** Steiermark, C Austria *47.27N 15.15E*
85 J14 **Kapiri Mposhi** Central, C Zambia *13.54S 28.40E*
155 R4 **Kāpīsā** ◆ *province* E Afghanistan
10 G10 **Kapiskau** ⟿ Ontario, C Canada
192 K13 **Kapiti Island** *island* C NZ
80 K9 **Kapka, Massif du** ▲ E Chad
Kaplamada *see* Kaubalatmada, Gunung
24 H9 **Kaplan** Louisiana, S USA *30.00N 92.16W*
Kaplangky, Plato *see* Gaplaňgyr Platosy
113 D19 **Kaplice** *Ger.* Kaplitz. Jihočeský Kraj , S Czech Republic *48.42N 14.27E*
Kaplitz *see* Kaplice
Kapoche *see* Capoche
176 U10 **Kapocol** Papua, E Indonesia *1.59S 130.11E*
178 Gg14 **Kapoe** Ranong, SW Thailand *9.33N 98.37E*
Kapoeas *see* Kapuas, Sungai
83 G15 **Kapoeta** Eastern Equatoria, SE Sudan *4.49N 33.34E*
113 I25 **Kapos** ⟿ S Hungary
113 H25 **Kaposvár** Somogy, SW Hungary *46.22N 17.54E*
96 H13 **Kapp** Oppland, S Norway *60.42N 10.49E*
102 I7 **Kappeln** Schleswig-Holstein, N Germany *54.40N 9.56E*
Kaproncza *see* Koprivnica
111 P7 **Kaprun** Salzburg, C Austria *47.15N 12.48E*
Kapshaghay *see* Kapchagay
Kapstad *see* Cape Town
Kapsukas *see* Marijampolė
176 Yy10 **Kaptiau** Papua, E Indonesia *2.23S 139.51E*
121 L19 **Kaptsevichy** *Rus.* Koptsevichi. Homyel'skaya Voblasts', SE Belarus *52.13N 28.19E*
Kapuas Hulu, Banjaran/Kapuas Hulu, Pegunungan *see* Kapuas Mountains
174 M7 **Kapuas Mountains** *Ind.* Banjaran Kapuas Hulu, Pegunungan Kapuas Hulu. ▲ Indonesia/Malaysia
174 Kk8 **Kapuas, Sungai** ⟿ Borneo, N Indonesia
175 N10 **Kapuas, Sungai** *prev.* Kapoeas. ⟿ Borneo, C Indonesia
190 J9 **Kapunda** South Australia *34.23S 138.51E*
158 H8 **Kapūrthala** Punjab, N India *31.22N 75.15E*
174 L14 **Kapur Utara, Pegunungan** ▲ Jawa, S Indonesia
10 G12 **Kapuskasing** Ontario, S Canada *49.25N 82.25W*
12 D6 **Kapuskasing** ⟿ Ontario, S Canada
131 P11 **Kapustin Yar** Astrakhanskaya Oblast', SW Russian Federation *48.36N 45.49E*
84 K11 **Kaputa** Northern, NE Zambia *8.27S 29.35E*
113 G22 **Kapuvár** Győr-Moson-Sopron, NW Hungary *47.35N 17.01E*
Kapydzhik, Gora *see* Qazangödağ
121 J17 **Kapyl'** *Rus.* Kopyl'. Minskaya Voblasts', C Belarus *53.09N 27.04E*
45 N9 **Kara** *var.* Cara. Región Autónoma Atlántico Sur, E Nicaragua *12.52N 83.35W*
79 R14 **Kara** *var.* Lama-Kara. NE Togo *9.36N 1.12E*
79 Q14 **Kara** ⟿ N Togo
153 U7 **Kara-Balta** Chuyskaya Oblast', N Kyrgyzstan *42.50N 73.51E*
150 L7 **Karabalyk** *prev.* Komsomol, Komsomolets. Kostanay, N Kazakhstan *53.48N 61.58E*
150 G11 **Karabau** Atyrau, W Kazakhstan *48.29N 53.05E*
152 E7 **Karabaur', Uval** *Kaz.* Korabavur Pastligi, *Uzb.* Qorabowur Kirlari. *physical region* Kazakhstan/Uzbekistan
Karabekaul *see* Garabekewül
Karabil', Vozvyshennost' *see* Garabil Belentligi
Kara-Bogaz-Gol *see* Garabogazköl
Kara-Bogaz-Gol, Zaliv *see* Garabogaz Aylagy
151 R15 **Karaboget** *Kaz.* Qaraböget. Zhambyl, S Kazakhstan *44.36N 72.03E*
142 H11 **Karabük** Karabük, NW Turkey *41.12N 32.36E*
142 H11 **Karabük** ◆ *province* NW Turkey
126 Ii13 **Karabula** Krasnoyarskiy Kray, C Russian Federation *58.01N 97.17E*
151 V14 **Karabulak** *Kaz.* Qarabulaq. Almaty, SE Kazakhstan *44.54N 78.29E*
151 Y11 **Karabulak** *Kaz.* Qarabulaq. Vostochnyy Kazakhstan, E Kazakhstan *47.33N 84.38E*
151 Q17 **Karabulak** *Kaz.* Qarabulaq. Yuzhnyy Kazakhstan, S Kazakhstan *42.31N 69.46E*
142 C17 **Kara Burnu** *headland* SW Turkey *36.34N 28.00E*
150 K10 **Karabutak** *Kaz.* Qarabutaq. Aktyubinsk, W Kazakhstan *49.58N 60.06E*
142 D12 **Karacabey** Bursa, NW Turkey *40.13N 28.22E*
116 O12 **Karacaköy** İstanbul, NW Turkey *41.24N 28.21E*
116 M12 **Karacaoğlan** Kırklareli, NW Turkey *41.30N 27.06E*
Karachay-Cherkessia *see* Karachayevo-Cherkesskaya Respublika
130 L15 **Karachayevo-Cherkesskaya Respublika** *Eng.* Karachay-Cherkessia. ◆ *autonomous republic* SW Russian Federation
130 M15 **Karachayevsk** Karachayevo-Cherkesskaya Respublika, SW Russian Federation *43.43N 41.53E*
130 J6 **Karachev** Bryanskaya Oblast', W Russian Federation *53.07N 35.56E*
155 O16 **Karāchi** Sind, SE Pakistan *24.51N 67.01E*
155 O16 **Karāchi** ✕ Sind, S Pakistan *24.51N 67.01E*
Karácsonkő *see* Piatra-Neamț
161 E15 **Karād** Mahārāshtra, W India *17.19N 74.15E*
142 H16 **Karadağ** ▲ S Turkey *37.00N 33.00E*
153 T10 **Karadar'ya** *Uzb.* Qoradaryo. ⟿ Kyrgyzstan/Uzbekistan
Karadeniz *see* Black Sea
Karadeniz Boğazı *see* İstanbul Boğazı
152 B13 **Karadepe** Balkan Welaýaty, W Turkmenistan *38.04N 54.01E*
Karadzhar *see* Qorajar
Karaferiye *see* Véroia
Karagan *see* Garagan
151 R10 **Karaganda** *Kaz.* Qaraghandy. Karaganda, C Kazakhstan *49.52N 73.07E*
151 R10 **Karaganda** *off.* Karagandinskaya Oblast', *Kaz.* Qaraghandy Oblysy. ◆ *province* C Kazakhstan
Karagandinskaya Oblast' *see* Karaganda
151 T10 **Karagayly** *Kaz.* Qaraghayly. Karaganda, C Kazakhstan *49.25N 75.31E*
Karagel' *see* Garagöl
127 Pp8 **Karaginskiy, Ostrov** *island* E Russian Federation
207 T1 **Karaginskiy Zaliv** *bay* E Russian Federation
143 P13 **Karagöl Dağları** ▲ NE Turkey
116 L13 **Karahisar** Edirne, NW Turkey *40.47N 26.34E*
131 V3 **Karaidel'** Respublika Bashkortostan, W Russian Federation *55.50N 56.55E*
131 V3 **Karaidel'skiy** Respublika Bashkortostan, W Russian Federation *55.51N 57.09E*
116 L13 **Karaidemir Barajı** ⊠ NW Turkey
161 J21 **Kāraikāl** Pondicherry, SE India *10.58N 79.49E*
161 I22 **Kāraikkudi** Tamil Nādu, SE India *10.04N 78.46E*
151 Y11 **Kara Irtysh** *Rus.* Chërnyy Irtysh. ⟿ NE Kazakhstan
149 N5 **Karaj** Tehrān, N Iran *35.43N 51.25E*
174 H5 **Karak** Pahang, Peninsular Malaysia *3.24N 101.58E*
Karak *see* Al Karak
153 T11 **Kara-Kabak** Oshskaya Oblast', SW Kyrgyzstan *39.40N 72.45E*
Kara-Kala *see* Garrygala
Karakala *see* Oqqal'a
Karakalpakstan, Respublika *see* Qoraqalpog'iston Respublikasi
Karakalpakya *see* Qoraqalpog'iston
Karakax *see* Moyu
164 G10 **Karakax He** ⟿ NW China
124 S9 **Karakaya Barajı** ⊠ C Turkey
175 Ss4 **Karakelang, Pulau** *island* N Indonesia
Karakılısse *see* Ağrı
Karak, Muḥāfaẓat al *see* Al Karak
Kara-Köl *see* Kara-Kul'
153 Y7 **Karakol** *prev.* Przheval'sk. Issyk-Kul'skaya Oblast', NE Kyrgyzstan *42.31N 78.20E*
153 X8 **Karakol** *var.* Karakolka. Issyk-Kul'skaya Oblast', NE Kyrgyzstan *41.30N 77.18E*
Karakolka *see* Karakol
155 W2 **Karakoram Highway** *road* China/Pakistan
155 Z3 **Karakoram Pass** *Chin.* Karakoram Shankou. *pass* C Asia *35.23N 77.45E*
158 I3 **Karakoram Range** ▲ C Asia
Karakoram Shankou *see* Karakoram Pass
Karaköse *see* Ağrı
151 P14 **Karakoyyn, Ozero** *Kaz.* Qaraqoyyn. ◎ C Kazakhstan
85 F19 **Karakubis** Ghanzi, W Botswana *22.03S 20.36E*
153 T9 **Kara-Kul'** *Kir.* Kara-Köl. Dzhalal-Abadskaya Oblast', W Kyrgyzstan *40.35N 73.36E*
Karakul' *see* Qorako'l, Uzbekistan
Karakul' *see* Qarokŭl, Tajikistan
153 U10 **Kara-Kul'dzha** Oshskaya Oblast', SW Kyrgyzstan *40.32N 73.50E*
131 T3 **Karakulino** Udmurtskaya Respublika, NW Russian Federation *56.02N 53.45E*
Karakul', Ozero *see* Qarokŭl
Kara Kum *see* Garagum
Kara Kum Canal/Karakumskiy Kanal *see* Garagum Kanaly
Karakumy, Peski *see* Garagum
85 E17 **Karakuwisa** Okavango, NE Namibia *18.55S 19.40E*
126 Jj14 **Karam** Irkutskaya Oblast', S Russian Federation *55.07N 107.21E*
Karamai *see* Karamay
175 N13 **Karamain, Pulau** *island* N Indonesia
142 I16 **Karaman** Karaman, S Turkey *37.10N 33.13E*
142 H16 **Karaman** ◆ *province* S Turkey
116 M8 **Karamandere** ⟿ NE Bulgaria
164 J4 **Karamay** *var.* Karamai, Kelamayi, *prev. Chin.* K'o-la-ma-i. Xinjiang Uygur Zizhiqu, NW China *45.33N 84.45E*
175 Nn11 **Karambu** Borneo, N Indonesia *3.48S 116.06E*
193 H14 **Karamea** West Coast, South Island, NZ *41.15S 172.07E*
193 H14 **Karamea** ⟿ South Island, NZ
193 G15 **Karamea Bight** *gulf* South Island, NZ
Karamet-Niyaz *see* Garamätnyýaz
164 K10 **Karamiran He** ⟿ NW China
176 Yy11 **Karamor, Pengunungan** ▲ Papua, E Indonesia
153 S11 **Karamyk** Oshskaya Oblast', SW Kyrgyzstan *39.28N 71.45E*
175 Nn16 **Karangasem** Bali, S Indonesia *8.24S 115.40E*
160 H12 **Kāranja** Mahārāshtra, C India *20.30N 77.26E*
Karanpur *see* Karanpura
158 F9 **Karanpura** *var.* Karanpur. Rājasthān, NW India *29.46N 73.30E*
Karánsebes/Karansebesch *see* Caransebeş
151 T14 **Karaoy** *Kaz.* Qaraoy. Almaty, SE Kazakhstan *45.52N 74.44E*
116 N7 **Karapelit** *Rom.* Stejarul. Dobrich, NE Bulgaria *43.40N 27.33E*
142 I15 **Karapınar** Konya, C Turkey *37.43N 33.34E*
85 D22 **Karas** ◆ *district* S Namibia
153 Y8 **Kara-Say** Issyk-Kul'skaya Oblast', NE Kyrgyzstan *41.34N 77.55E*
85 E22 **Karasburg** Karas, S Namibia *27.59S 18.45E*
Kara Sea *see* Karskoye More
94 K9 **Kárášjohka** *var.* Karasjokka. ⟿ N Norway
94 L9 **Karasjok** *Fin.* Kaarasjoki, *Lapp.* Kárášjohka. Finnmark, N Norway *69.27N 25.28S*
Kárášjohka *see* Karasjok
Karasjokka *see* Kárášjohka
Kara Strait *see* Karskiye Vorota, Proliv
Kara Su *see* Mesta/Néstos
151 N8 **Karasu** *Kaz.* Qarasū. Kostanay, N Kazakhstan *52.43N 65.28E*
142 F11 **Karasu** Sakarya, NW Turkey *41.03N 30.39E*
Karasubazar *see* Bilohirs'k
125 G14 **Karasuk** Novosibirskaya Oblast', C Russian Federation *53.41N 78.04E*
151 U13 **Karatal** *Kaz.* Qaratal. ⟿ SE Kazakhstan
142 K17 **Karataş** Adana, S Turkey *36.37N 35.24E*
151 Q16 **Karatau** *Kaz.* Qaratau. Zhambyl, S Kazakhstan *43.09N 70.28E*
Karatau *see* Karatau, Khrebet
151 P16 **Karatau, Khrebet** *var.* Karatau, *Kaz.* Qarataū. ▲ S Kazakhstan
150 G13 **Karaton** *Kaz.* Qaraton. Atyrau, W Kazakhstan *46.33N 53.31E*
170 C12 **Karatsu** *var.* Karatu. Saga, Kyūshū, SW Japan *33.27N 129.55E*
Karatu *see* Karatsu
126 Hh7 **Karaul** Taymyrskiy (Dolgano-Nenetskiy) Avtonomnyy Okrug, N Russian Federation *70.07N 83.12E*
Karaulbazar *see* Qorovulbozor
Karauzyak *see* Qorao'zak
117 D16 **Karáva** ▲ C Greece *39.19N 21.33E*
Karavanke *see* Karawanken
117 F22 **Karavás** Kýthira, S Greece *36.21N 22.57E*
115 J20 **Karavastasë, Laguna e** *var.* Kënet' e Karavastas, Kravasta Lagoon. *lagoon* W Albania
Karavastas, Kënet' e *see* Karavastasë, Laguna e
120 I5 **Karavere** Tartumaa, E Estonia *58.25N 26.29E*
117 L23 **Karavonísia** *island* Kykládes, Greece, Aegean Sea
174 Jj14 **Karawang** *prev.* Krawang. Jawa, C Indonesia *6.13S 107.16E*
111 T10 **Karawanken** *Slvn.* Karavanke. ▲ Austria/Serbia and Montenegro (Yugoslavia)
Karaxahar *see* Kaidu He
143 R13 **Karayazı** Erzurum, NE Turkey *39.40N 42.09E*
151 Q12 **Karazhal** Karaganda, C Kazakhstan *48.02N 70.52E*
145 S9 **Karbalā'** *var.* Kerbala, Kerbela. S Iraq *32.37N 44.03E*
96 L11 **Kärböle** Gävleborg, C Sweden *61.59N 15.16E*
113 M23 **Karcag** Jász-Nagykun-Szolnok, E Hungary *47.21N 20.51E*
Kardak *see* Imia
116 N7 **Kardam** Dobrich, NE Bulgaria *43.45N 28.06E*
117 M22 **Kardamaina** Kos, Dodekánisos, Greece, Aegean Sea *36.46N 27.08E*
Kardamila *see* Kardámyla
117 L18 **Kardámyla** *var.* Kardamila, Kardhámila. Chíos, E Greece *38.33N 26.04E*
Kardeljevo *see* Ploče
Kardh *see* Qardho
Kardhámila *see* Kardámyla
Kardhítsa *see* Kardítsa
117 E16 **Kardítsa** *var.* Kardhítsa. Thessalía, C Greece *39.22N 21.55E*
120 E4 **Kärdla** *Ger.* Kertel. Hiiumaa, W Estonia *59.00N 22.42E*
Karelia *see* Kareliya, Respublika
121 I16 **Karelichy** *Pol.* Korelicze, *Rus.* Korelichi. Hrodzyenskaya Voblasts', W Belarus *53.34N 26.07E*
128 I10 **Kareliya, Respublika** *prev.* Karel'skaya ASSR, *Eng.* Karelia. ◆ *autonomous republic* NW Russian Federation
Karel'skaya ASSR *see* Kareliya, Respublika
83 E22 **Karema** Rukwa, W Tanzania *6.49S 30.25E*
Karen *see* Hualien
85 I14 **Karenda** Central, C Zambia *14.42S 26.52E*
178 Gg8 **Karen State** *var.* Kawthule State, Kayin State. ◆ *state* S Myanmar
94 J10 **Karesuando** *Fin.* Kaaresuanto, *Lapp.* Gárasavvon. Norrbotten, N Sweden *68.25N 22.28E*
Karet *see* Kâghet
Kareyz-e-Elyās/Kārez Iliās *see* Kārīz-e Elyās
126 Gg12 **Kargasok** Tomskaya Oblast', C Russian Federation *59.01N 80.34E*
126 Gg14 **Kargat** Novosibirskaya Oblast', C Russian Federation *55.07N 80.19E*
142 J11 **Kargı** Çorum, N Turkey *41.09N 34.31E*
158 I5 **Kargil** Jammu and Kashmir, NW India *34.34N 76.06E*
Kargilik *see* Yecheng
128 L11 **Kargopol'** Arkhangel'skaya Oblast', NW Russian Federation *61.30N 38.53E*
112 F12 **Kargowa** *Ger.* Unruhstadt. Lubuskie, W Poland *52.05N 15.50E*
79 X13 **Kari** Bauchi, E Nigeria *11.13N 10.34E*
85 J15 **Kariba** Mashonaland West, N Zimbabwe *16.28S 28.47E*
85 J16 **Kariba, Lake** ⊠ Zambia/Zimbabwe
172 Nn5 **Kariba-yama** ▲ Hokkaidō, NE Japan *42.36N 139.55E*
85 C19 **Karibib** Erongo, C Namibia *21.56S 15.51E*
Karies *see* Karyés
94 L9 **Karigasniemi** *Lapp.* Garegegasnjárga. Lappi, N Finland *69.24N 25.52E*
172 P6 **Karikachi-tōge** *pass* Hokkaidō, NE Japan *43.08N 142.46E*
192 J2 **Karikari, Cape** *headland* North Island, NZ *34.47S 173.24E*
Karīmābād *see* Hunza
174 K10 **Karimata, Kepulauan** *island group* N Indonesia
174 K9 **Karimata, Pulau** *island* Kepulauan Karimata, N Indonesia
174 K10 **Karimata, Selat** *strait* W Indonesia
161 I14 **Karīmnagar** Andhra Pradesh, C India *18.28N 79.09E*
194 I13 **Karimui** Chimbu, C PNG *6.19S 144.48E*
174 L13 **Karimunjawa, Pulau** *island* S Indonesia
82 N12 **Karin** Woqooyi Galbeed, N Somalia *10.48N 45.46E*
Kariot *see* Ikaría
95 L20 **Karis** *Fin.* Karjaa. Etelä-Suomi, SW Finland *60.05N 23.39E*
Káristos *see* Kárystos
154 J4 **Kārīz-e Elyās** *var.* Kareyz-e-Elyās, Kārez Iliās. Herāt, NW Afghanistan *35.26N 61.24E*
Karjaa *see* Karis
151 T10 **Karkaralinsk** *Kaz.* Qarqaraly. Karaganda, E Kazakhstan *49.31N 75.53E*
194 J11 **Karkar Island** *island* N PNG
149 N7 **Karkas, Kūh-e** ▲ C Iran
148 K8 **Karkheh, Rūd-e** ⟿ SW Iran
117 L20 **Karkinágrio** Ikaría, Dodekánisos, Greece, Aegean Sea *37.31N 26.01E*
119 R12 **Karkinits'ka Zatoka** *Rus.* Karkinitskiy Zaliv. *gulf* S Ukraine
Karkinitskiy Zaliv *see* Karkinits'ka Zatoka
95 L19 **Karkkila** *Swe.* Högfors. Etelä-Suomi, S Finland *60.31N 24.10E*
95 M19 **Kärkölä** Etelä-Suomi, S Finland *60.52N 25.17E*
190 G9 **Karkoo** South Australia *34.03S 135.45E*
Karkūk *see* Kirkūk
120 D5 **Kärla** *Ger.* Kergel. Saaremaa, W Estonia *58.19N 22.15E*
Karleby *see* Kokkola
112 F7 **Karlino** *Ger.* Körlin an der Persante. Zachodnio-pomorskie, NW Poland *54.02N 15.52E*
143 Q13 **Karlıova** Bingöl, E Turkey *39.16N 41.01E*
119 U6 **Karlivka** Poltavs'ka Oblast', C Ukraine *49.27N 35.08E*
Karl-Marx-Stadt *see* Chemnitz
Karlö *see* Hailuoto
114 C11 **Karlobag** *It.* Carlopago. Lika-Senj, W Croatia *44.31N 15.06E*
114 D9 **Karlovac** *Ger.* Karlstadt, *Hung.* Károlyváros. Karlovac, C Croatia *45.28N 15.31E*
114 C10 **Karlovac** *off.* Karlovačka Županija. ◆ *province* C Croatia
Karlovačka Županija *see* Karlovac
113 A16 **Karlovarský Kraj** ◆ W Czech Republic
116 J9 **Karlovo** *prev.* Levskigrad. Plovdiv, C Bulgaria *42.39N 24.49E*
113 A16 **Karlovy Vary** *Ger.* Karlsbad; *prev. Eng.* Carlsbad. Karlovarský Kraj, W Czech Republic *50.13N 12.51E*
Karlsbad *see* Karlovy Vary
97 L17 **Karlsborg** Västra Götaland, S Sweden *58.31N 14.31E*
Karlsburg *see* Alba Iulia
97 L22 **Karlshamn** Blekinge, S Sweden *56.10N 14.49E*
97 L16 **Karlskoga** Örebro, C Sweden *59.19N 14.33E*
97 M22 **Karlskrona** Blekinge, S Sweden *56.11N 15.38E*
103 G21 **Karlsruhe** *var.* Carlsruhe. Baden-Württemberg, SW Germany *49.01N 8.24E*
97 K16 **Karlstad** Värmland, C Sweden *59.22N 13.36E*
31 R3 **Karlstad** Minnesota, N USA *48.34N 96.31W*

◆ Country ◇ Dependent Territory ◆ Administrative Region ▲ Mountain ▲ Volcano ◎ Lake
● Country Capital ○ Dependent Territory Capital ✕ International Airport ▲ Mountain Range ⟿ River ⊠ Reservoir

Karlstadt – Keltsy

103 I18 **Karlstadt** Bayern, C Germany 49.58N 9.46E
Karlstadt see Karlovac
41 Q14 **Karluk** Kodiak Island, Alaska, USA 57.34N 154.27W
Karluk see Qarluq
121 O17 **Karma** Rus. Korma. Homyel'skaya Voblasts', SE Belarus 53.07N 30.48E
161 F14 **Karmāla** Mahārāshtra, W India 18.26N 75.08E
152 M11 **Karmana** Navoiy Viloyati, C Uzbekistan 40.09N 65.18E
144 G8 **Karmi'él** var. Carmiel. Northern, N Israel 32.55N 35.21E
97 B16 **Karmøy** island S Norway
158 I9 **Karnāl** Haryāna, N India 29.40N 76.58E
159 W15 **Karnaphuli Reservoir** ⊠ NE India
161 F17 **Karnātaka** var. Kanara; prev. Maisur, Mysore. ◆ state W India
27 S13 **Karnes City** Texas, SW USA 28.52N 97.54W
111 P9 **Karnische Alpen** It. Alpi Carniche. ▲ Austria/Italy
116 M9 **Karnobat** Burgas, E Bulgaria 42.39N 26.58E
111 Q9 **Kärnten** off. Land Kärnten, Eng. Carinthi, Slvn. Koroška. ◆ state S Austria
Karnul see Kurnool
85 K16 **Karoi** Mashonaland West, N Zimbabwe 16.49S 29.40E
Karol see Carei
Károly-Fehérvár see Alba Iulia
Károlyváros see Karlovac
179 Qq15 **Karomatan** Mindanao, S Philippines 7.47N 123.48E
84 M12 **Karonga** Northern, N Malawi 9.56S 33.54E
153 W10 **Karool-Tëbë** Narynskaya Oblast', C Kyrgyzstan 40.33N 75.52E
190 J9 **Karoonda** South Australia 35.04S 139.58E
155 S9 **Karor Lāl Esan** Punjab, E Pakistan 31.15N 70.54E
155 T11 **Karor Pacca** var. Kahror, Kahror Pakka. Punjab, E Pakistan 29.37N 71.58E
175 P10 **Karosa** Sulawesi, C Indonesia 1.38S 119.21E
Karpasía/Karpas Peninsula see Kırpaşa
Karpaten see Carpathian Mountains
117 L22 **Karpáthio Pélagos** sea Dodekánisos, Greece, Aegean Sea
117 N24 **Kárpathos** Kárpathos, SE Greece 35.30N 27.13E
117 N24 **Kárpathos** It. Scarpanto; anc. Carpathos, Carpathus. island SE Greece
Karpathos Strait see Karpathou, Stenó
117 N24 **Karpathou, Stenó** var. Karpathos Strait, Scarpanto Strait. strait Dodekánisos, Greece, Aegean Sea
Karpaty see Carpathian Mountains
117 E17 **Karpenísi** prev. Karpenísion. Stereá Ellás, C Greece 38.55N 21.45E
Karpenísion see Karpenísi
Karpilovka see Aktsyabrski
129 O8 **Karpogory** Arkhangel'skaya Oblast', NW Russian Federation 64.01N 44.22E
188 I7 **Karratha** Western Australia 20.43S 116.52E
143 S12 **Kars** var. Qars. Kars, NE Turkey 40.34N 43.04E
143 S12 **Kars** var. Qars. ◆ province NE Turkey
151 O12 **Karsakpay** Kaz. Qarsaqbay. Karaganda, C Kazakhstan 47.51N 66.42E
95 L15 **Kärsämäki** Oulu, C Finland 63.58N 25.49E
Karsau see Kārsava
120 K9 **Kārsava** Ger. Karsau; prev. Rus. Korsovka. Ludza, E Latvia 56.46N 27.39E
Karshi see Garşy, Turkmenistan
Karshi see Qarshi, Uzbekistan
Karshinskaya Step see Qarshi Cho'li
Karshinskiy Kanal see Qarshi Kanali
86 I5 **Karskiye Vorota, Proliv** Eng. Kara Strait. strait N Russian Federation
126 Gg5 **Karskoye More** Eng. Kara Sea. sea Arctic Ocean
95 L17 **Karstula** Länsi-Suomi, W Finland 62.52N 24.48E
131 Q5 **Karsun** Ul'yanovskaya Oblast', W Russian Federation 54.12N 47.00E
125 E12 **Kartaly** Chelyabinskaya Oblast', C Russian Federation 53.02N 60.42E
20 E13 **Karthaus** Pennsylvania, NE USA 41.06N 78.03W
112 I7 **Kartuzy** Pomorskie, NW Poland 54.21N 18.10E
172 N10 **Karumai** Iwate, Honshū, C Japan 40.19N 141.27E
189 U4 **Karumba** Queensland, NE Australia 17.31S 140.51E
148 L10 **Kārūn** var. Rūd-e Kārūn. ⚓ SW Iran
94 K13 **Karungi** Norrbotten, N Sweden 66.03N 23.55E
94 K13 **Karunki** Lappi, N Finland 66.01N 24.06E
Kārūn, Rūd-e see Kārūn
161 H21 **Karūr** Tamil Nādu, SE India 10.58N 78.03E
95 K17 **Karvia** Länsi-Suomi, W Finland 62.07N 22.34E
113 J17 **Karviná** Ger. Karwin, Pol. Karwina; prev. Nová Karvinná. Moravskoslezský Kraj, E Czech Republic 49.51N 18.33E
161 E17 **Kārwār** Karnātaka, W India 14.49N 74.09E
110 M7 **Karwendelgebirge** ▲ Austria/Germany
Karwin/Karwina see Karviná
117 I14 **Karyés** var. Karies. Ágion Óros, N Greece 40.15N 24.15E
126 Kk16 **Karymskoye** Chitinskaya Oblast', S Russian Federation 51.36N 114.02E
117 I19 **Kárystos** var. Káristos. Évvoia, C Greece 38.01N 24.25E
142 E17 **Kaş** Antalya, SW Turkey 36.12N 29.37E
41 Y14 **Kasaan** Prince of Wales Island, Alaska, USA 55.32N 132.24W
170 G14 **Kasai** Hyōgo, Honshū, SW Japan 34.56N 134.49E
81 K21 **Kasai** var. Cassai, Kassai. ⚓ Angola/Dem. Rep. Congo
81 K22 **Kasai Occidental** off. Région Kasai Occidental. ◆ region S Dem. Rep. Congo
81 L21 **Kasai Oriental** off. Région Kasai Oriental. ◆ region C Dem. Rep. Congo
81 L24 **Kasaji** Katanga, S Dem. Rep. Congo 10.22S 23.29E
171 Kk16 **Kasama** Ibaraki, Honshū, S Japan 36.21N 140.15E
84 L12 **Kasama** Northern, N Zambia 10.13S 31.12E
Kasan see Koson
85 H16 **Kasane** Chobe, NE Botswana 17.48S 25.06E
83 E23 **Kasanga** Rukwa, W Tanzania 8.27S 31.10E
81 G21 **Kasangulu** Bas-Congo, W Dem. Rep. Congo 4.33S 15.12E
Kasansay see Kosonsoy
Kasargen see Kasari
161 E20 **Kāsaragod** Kerala, SW India 12.30N 75.01E
120 P13 **Kasari** var. Kasari Jõgi, Ger. Kasargen. ⚓ W Estonia
Kasari Jõgi see Kasari
15 K9 **Kasba Lake** ⊚ Northwest Territories/Nunavut, N Canada
Kaschau see Košice
170 Bb16 **Kaseda** Kagoshima, Kyūshū, SW Japan 31.23N 130.18E
85 I14 **Kasempa** North Western, NW Zambia 13.27S 25.49E
81 O24 **Kasenga** Katanga, SE Dem. Rep. Congo 10.22S 28.37E
81 P17 **Kasenye** var. Kasenyi. Orientale, NE Dem. Rep. Congo 1.22N 30.25E
Kasenyi see Kasenye
83 E18 **Kasese** SW Uganda 0.10N 30.06E
81 O19 **Kasese** Maniema, E Dem. Rep. Congo 1.36S 27.31E
158 J11 **Kāsganj** Uttar Pradesh, N India 27.48N 78.36E
149 U4 **Kashaf Rūd** ⚓ NE Iran
149 N7 **Kāshān** Eşfahān, C Iran 33.57N 51.30E
130 M10 **Kashary** Rostovskaya Oblast', SW Russian Federation 49.02N 40.58E
41 O12 **Kashegelok** Alaska, USA 60.57N 157.46W
Kashgar see Kashi
164 E7 **Kashi** Chin. Kaxgar, K'o-shih, Uigh. Kashgar. Xinjiang Uygur Zizhiqu, NW China 39.32N 75.58E
171 Gg16 **Kashihara** var. Kasihara. Nara, Honshū, SW Japan 34.31N 135.49E
171 Kk17 **Kashima** Ibaraki, Honshū, S Japan 35.59N 140.37E
170 C13 **Kashima** var. Kasima. Saga, Kyūshū, SW Japan 33.09N 130.07E
171 L16 **Kashima-nada** gulf S Japan
128 K15 **Kashin** Tverskaya Oblast', W Russian Federation 57.20N 37.34E
158 K10 **Kāshīpur** Uttaranchal, N India 29.13N 78.58E
130 L4 **Kashira** Moskovskaya Oblast', W Russian Federation 54.53N 38.13E
171 K17 **Kashiwa** var. Kasiwa. Chiba, Honshū, S Japan 35.50N 139.59E
171 Jj13 **Kashiwazaki** var. Kasiwazaki. Niigata, Honshū, C Japan 37.22N 138.33E
Kashkadar'inskaya Oblast' see Qashqadaryo Viloyati
149 T5 **Kāshmar** var. Turshiz; prev. Solţānābād, Torshiz. Khorāsān, NE Iran 35.15N 58.28E
Kashmir see Jammu and Kashmir
155 R12 **Kashmor** Sind, SE Pakistan 28.23N 69.43E
155 S5 **Kashmūnd Ghar** Eng. Kashmund Range. ▲ E Afghanistan
Kashmund Range see Kashmūnd Ghar
Kasi see Vārānasi
159 O12 **Kasia** Uttar Pradesh, N India 26.45N 83.55E
41 N12 **Kasigluk** Alaska, USA 60.54N 162.31W
Kasihara see Kashihara
41 R12 **Kasilof** Alaska, USA 60.20N 151.16W
Kasima see Kashima
Kasimköj see General Toshevo
130 M4 **Kasimov** Ryazanskaya Oblast', W Russian Federation 54.59N 41.22E
81 P18 **Kasindi** Nord Kivu, E Dem. Rep. Congo 0.07N 29.41E
175 Ss8 **Kasiruta, Pulau** island Kepulauan Bacan, E Indonesia
84 M12 **Kasitu** ⚓ N Malawi
176 V12 **Kasiui, Pulau** island Kepulauan Watubela, E Indonesia
Kasiwa see Kashiwa
Kasiwazaki see Kashiwazaki
32 L14 **Kaskaskia River** ⚓ Illinois, N USA
95 J17 **Kaskinen** Swe. Kaskö. Länsi-Suomi, W Finland 62.19N 21.15E
Kaskö see Kaskinen
Kas Kong see Kông, Kaôh
9 O17 **Kaslo** British Columbia, SW Canada 49.54N 116.57W
Kāsmark see Kežmarok
174 M10 **Kasongan** Borneo, C Indonesia 2.01S 113.21E
81 N21 **Kasongo** Maniema, E Dem. Rep. Congo 4.22S 26.42E
81 H22 **Kasongo-Lunda** Bandundu, SW Dem. Rep. Congo 6.30S 16.51E
117 M24 **Kásos** island S Greece
Kasos Strait see Kasou, Stenó
117 M25 **Kasou, Stenó** var. Kasos Strait. strait Dodekánisos/Kríti, Greece, Aegean Sea
143 T10 **Kaspi** C Georgia 41.54N 44.25E
116 M8 **Kaspichan** Shumen, NE Bulgaria 43.18N 27.09E
Kaspīy Mangy Oypaty see Caspian Depression
131 Q16 **Kaspiysk** Respublika Dagestan, SW Russian Federation 42.52N 47.40E
Kaspiyskiy see Lagan'
Kaspiyskoye More/Kaspiy Tengizi see Caspian Sea
Kassa see Košice
Kassai see Kasai
82 I9 **Kassala** Kassala, E Sudan 15.24N 36.25E
82 H9 **Kassala** ◆ state NE Sudan
117 G15 **Kassándra** prev. Pallíni; anc. Pallene. peninsula NE Greece
117 G15 **Kassándras, Akrotírio** headland N Greece 39.58N 23.22E
117 H15 **Kassándras, Kólpos** var. Kólpos Toronaíos. gulf N Greece
145 Y11 **Kassārah** E Iraq 31.21N 47.25E
103 I15 **Kassel** prev. Cassel. Hessen, C Germany 51.19N 9.30E
76 M6 **Kasserine** var. Al Qaşrayn. W Tunisia 35.15N 8.52E
12 J14 **Kasshabog Lake** ⊚ Ontario, SE Canada
145 O5 **Kassīr, Sabkhat al** ⊚ E Syria
31 W10 **Kasson** Minnesota, N USA 44.00N 92.42W
117 C17 **Kassópi** site of ancient city Ípeiros, W Greece 39.08N 20.38E
117 N24 **Kastállou, Akrotírio** headland Kárpathos, SE Greece 35.24N 27.08E
142 I11 **Kastamonu** var. Castamoni, Kastamuni. Kastamonu, N Turkey 41.22N 33.46E
142 I10 **Kastamonu** var. Kastamuni. ◆ province N Turkey
Kastamuni see Kastamonu
117 E14 **Kastaneá** Kentrikí Makedonía, N Greece 40.25N 22.09E
117 H24 **Kastélli** Kríti, Greece, E Mediterranean Sea 35.30N 23.39E
Kastellórizon see Megísti
97 N21 **Kastlösa** Kalmar, S Sweden 56.25N 16.25E
117 D14 **Kastoría** Dytikí Makedonía, N Greece 40.30N 21.16E
130 K7 **Kastornoye** Kurskaya Oblast', W Russian Federation 51.49N 38.07E
117 I21 **Kástro** Sífnos, Kykládes, Greece, Aegean Sea 36.58N 24.45E
97 J23 **Kastrup** ✕ (København) København, E Denmark 55.36N 12.39E
121 Q17 **Kastsyukovichy** Rus. Kostyukovichi. Mahilyowskaya Voblasts', E Belarus 53.19N 32.03E
121 O18 **Kastsyukowka** Rus. Kostyukovka. Homyel'skaya Voblasts', SE Belarus 52.32N 30.54E
170 Cc12 **Kasuga** Fukuoka, Kyūshū, SW Japan 33.31N 130.27E
171 I15 **Kasugai** Aichi, Honshū, SW Japan 35.15N 136.57E
83 E21 **Kasulu** Kigoma, W Tanzania 4.33S 30.06E
171 Gg13 **Kasumi** Hyōgo, Honshū, SW Japan 35.36N 134.37E
171 Kk16 **Kasumiga-ura** ⊚ Honshū, S Japan
131 R17 **Kasumkent** Respublika Dagestan, SW Russian Federation 41.39N 48.09E
84 M13 **Kasungu** Central, C Malawi 13.01S 33.30E
155 W9 **Kasūr** Punjab, E Pakistan 31.07N 74.30E
85 G15 **Kataba** Western, W Zambia 15.28S 23.25E
21 R4 **Katahdin, Mount** ▲ Maine, NE USA 45.55N 68.52W
81 M20 **Katako-Kombe** Kasai Oriental, C Dem. Rep. Congo 3.24S 24.25E
41 T12 **Katalla** Alaska, USA 60.12N 144.31W
Katana see Qaţanā
81 L24 **Katanga** off. Région du Katanga; prev. Shaba. ◆ region SE Dem. Rep. Congo
126 I12 **Katanga** ⚓ C Russian Federation
160 J11 **Katangi** Madhya Pradesh, C India 21.46N 79.49E
188 J13 **Katanning** Western Australia 33.44S 117.33E
189 P8 **Kata Tjuta** var. Mount Olga ▲ Northern Territory, C Australia 25.20S 130.47E
Katawaz see Zarghūn Shahr
157 Q22 **Katchall Island** island Nicobar Islands, India, NE Indian Ocean
117 F14 **Kateríni** Kentrikí Makedonía, N Greece 40.17N 22.30E
119 P7 **Kateryno̧pil'** Cherkas'ka Oblast', C Ukraine 49.00N 30.59E
178 Gg3 **Katha** Sagaing, N Myanmar 24.10N 96.19E
189 P2 **Katherine** Northern Territory, N Australia 14.28S 132.19E
160 B11 **Kāthiāwār Peninsula** peninsula W India
159 P11 **Kathmandu** prev. Kantipur. ● (Nepal) Central, C Nepal 27.46N 85.16E
158 H7 **Kathua** Jammu and Kashmir, NW India 32.24N 75.34E
78 L12 **Kati** Koulikoro, SW Mali 12.45N 8.06W
159 R13 **Katihār** Bihār, NE India 25.33N 87.34E
192 N7 **Katikati** Bay of Plenty, North Island, NZ 37.33S 175.55E
85 H16 **Katima Mulilo** Caprivi, NE Namibia 17.31S 24.19E
79 N15 **Katiola** C Ivory Coast 8.12N 5.04W
203 V10 **Katiu** atoll Îles Tuamotu, C French Polynesia
119 N12 **Katlabukh, Ozero** ⊚ SW Ukraine
41 P14 **Katmai, Mount** ▲ Alaska, USA 58.16N 154.57W
160 J9 **Katni** Madhya Pradesh, C India 23.46N 80.28E
117 D19 **Káto Achaïa** var. Kato Ahaia, Káto Akhaía. Dytikí Ellás, S Greece 38.08N 21.35E
Kato Ahaia/Káto Akhaía see Káto Achaïa
124 Nn3 **Kato Lakatámeia** var. Kato Lakatamia. C Cyprus 35.07N 33.20E
Kato Lakatamia see Kato Lakatámeia
81 N22 **Katompi** Katanga, SE Dem. Rep. Congo 6.10S 26.19E
85 K14 **Katondwe** Lusaka, C Zambia 15.08S 30.10E
116 H12 **Káto Nevrokópi** prev. Káto Nevrokópion. Anatolikí Makedonía kai Thráki, NE Greece 41.21N 23.52E
Káto Nevrokópion see Káto Nevrokópi
83 E18 **Katonga** ⚓ S Uganda
117 F15 **Káto Ólympos** ▲ C Greece
117 D17 **Katoúna** Dytikí Ellás, C Greece 38.46N 21.07E
117 E19 **Káto Vlasiá** Dytikí Makedonía, S Greece 38.02N 21.54E
113 J16 **Katowice** Ger. Kattowitz. Śląskie, S Poland 50.14N 19.00E
159 S15 **Kātoya** West Bengal, NE India 23.39N 88.10E
142 E16 **Katrançik Dağı** ▲ SW Turkey
97 N16 **Katrineholm** Södermanland, C Sweden 58.58N 16.15E
98 I11 **Katrine, Loch** ⊚ C Scotland, UK
79 V12 **Katsina** Katsina, N Nigeria 12.58N 7.33E
79 U12 **Katsina** ◆ state N Nigeria
69 P8 **Katsina Ala** ⚓ S Nigeria
170 C11 **Katsumoto** Nagasaki, Iki, SW Japan 33.49N 129.42E
171 L16 **Katsuta** var. Katuta. Ibaraki, Honshū, S Japan 36.24N 140.31E
171 K17 **Katsuura** var. Katuura. Chiba, Honshū, S Japan 35.09N 140.16E
171 I14 **Katsuyama** var. Katuyama. Fukui, Honshū, SW Japan 36.03N 136.28E
170 Ff13 **Katsuyama** Okayama, Honshū, SW Japan 35.06N 133.43E
Kattakurgan see Kattaqo'rg'on
153 N11 **Kattaqo'rg'on** Rus. Kattakurgan. Samarqand Viloyati, C Uzbekistan 39.55N 66.11E
117 O23 **Kattavía** Ródos, Dodekánisos, Greece, Aegean Sea 35.56N 27.47E
97 I21 **Kattegat** Dan. Kattegatt. strait N Europe
Kattegatt see Kattegat
97 P19 **Katthammarsvik** Gotland, SE Sweden 57.27N 18.54E
Kattowitz see Katowice
127 N17 **Katun'** ⚓ S Russian Federation
Katuta see Katsuta
Katuura see Katsuura
Katuyama see Katsuyama
Katwijk see Katwijk aan Zee
100 G11 **Katwijk aan Zee** var. Katwijk. Zuid-Holland, W Netherlands 52.12N 4.24E
40 B8 **Kaua'i** var. Kauai. island Hawaiian Islands, Hawai'i, USA, C Pacific Ocean
40 C8 **Kaua'i Channel** var. Kauai Channel channel Hawai'i, USA, C Pacific Ocean
175 Ss11 **Kaubalatmada, Gunung** var. Kaplamada. ▲ Pulau Buru, E Indonesia 3.16S 126.17E
203 U10 **Kauehi** atoll Îles Tuamotu, C French Polynesia
Kauen see Kaunas
103 K24 **Kaufbeuren** Bayern, S Germany 47.52N 10.37E
27 U7 **Kaufman** Texas, SW USA 32.35N 96.18W
103 I15 **Kaufungen** Hessen, C Germany 51.16N 9.39E
95 K17 **Kauhajoki** Länsi-Suomi, W Finland 62.24N 22.12E
95 K16 **Kauhava** Länsi-Suomi, W Finland 63.06N 23.07E
32 M7 **Kaukauna** Wisconsin, N USA 44.18N 88.18W
94 L11 **Kaukonen** Lappi, N Finland 67.28N 24.49E
40 A8 **Kaulakahi Channel** channel Hawai'i, USA, C Pacific Ocean
40 E9 **Kaunakakai** Moloka'i, Hawai'i, USA, C Pacific Ocean 21.05N 157.01W
40 F12 **Kaunā Point** var. Kauna Point headland Hawai'i, USA, C Pacific Ocean 19.02N 155.52W
120 F13 **Kaunas** Ger. Kauen, Pol. Kowno; prev. Rus. Kovno. Kaunas, C Lithuania 54.54N 23.57E
120 F13 **Kaunas** ◆ province C Lithuania
194 H10 **Kaup** East Sepik, NW PNG 3.48S 143.56E
79 U12 **Kaura Namoda** Zamfara, NW Nigeria 12.43N 6.17E
Kaushany see Căuşeni
95 K16 **Kaustinen** Länsi-Suomi, W Finland 63.33N 23.40E
175 T7 **Kau, Teluk** bay Pulau Halmahera, E Indonesia
101 M23 **Kautenbach** Diekirch, NE Luxembourg 49.57N 6.01E
94 K10 **Kautokeino** Lapp. Guovdageaidnu. Finnmark, N Norway 69.00N 23.01E
Kavadar see Kavadarci
115 P19 **Kavadarci** Turk. Kavadar. C FYR Macedonia 41.25N 22.00E
Kavaja see Kavajë
115 K20 **Kavajë** It. Cavaia, Kavaja. Tiranë, W Albania 41.11N 19.33E
116 M13 **Kavak Çayı** ⚓ NW Turkey
Kavakli see Topolovgrad
116 I13 **Kavála** prev. Kaválla. Anatolikí Makedonía kai Thráki, NE Greece 40.57N 24.25E
116 I13 **Kavála, Kólpos** gulf Aegean Sea, NE Mediterranean Sea
127 Nn17 **Kavalerovo** Primorskiy Kray, SE Russian Federation 44.17N 135.06E
161 J17 **Kāvali** Andhra Pradesh, E India 15.04N 80.02E
Kaválla see Kavála
Kavango see Cubango/Okavango
161 C21 **Kavaratti** Lakshadweep, SW India 10.33N 72.37E
116 O8 **Kavarna** Dobrich, NE Bulgaria 43.26N 28.21E
120 G12 **Kavarskas** Utena, E Lithuania 55.27N 24.55E
78 I13 **Kavendou** ▲ C Guinea 10.49N 12.14W
Kavengo see Cubango/Okavango
161 F20 **Kāveri** var. Cauvery. ⚓ S India
195 N9 **Kavieng** var. Kaewieng. NE PNG 2.34S 150.48E
85 H16 **Kavimba** Chobe, NE Botswana 18.03S 24.30E
85 I15 **Kavingu** Southern, S Zambia 15.39S 26.03E
149 Q6 **Kavīr, Dasht-e** var. Great Salt Desert. salt pan N Iran
Kavirondo Gulf see Winam Gulf
Kavkaz see Caucasus
97 K23 **Kävlinge** Skåne, S Sweden 55.46N 13.04E
197 I15 **Kavukavu Reef** var. Beqa Barrier Reef, Cakaubalavu Reef. reef Viti Levu, SW Fiji
84 G12 **Kavungo** Moxico, E Angola 11.31S 22.59E
171 M10 **Kawabe** Akita, Honshū, C Japan 39.39N 140.14E
171 K15 **Kawagoe** Saitama, Honshū, S Japan 35.55N 139.30E
171 K16 **Kawaguchi** var. Kawaguti. Saitama, Honshū, S Japan 35.49N 139.42E
Kawaguti see Kawaguchi
172 N11 **Kawai** Iwate, Honshū, C Japan 39.36N 141.40E
40 A8 **Kawaihoa Point** headland Ni'ihau, Hawai'i, USA, C Pacific Ocean 21.47N 160.12W
192 K3 **Kawakawa** Northland, North Island, NZ 35.23S 174.03E
84 I13 **Kawama** North Western, NW Zambia 13.04S 25.59E
84 K11 **Kawambwa** Luapula, N Zambia 9.48S 29.04E
170 F14 **Kawanoe** Ehime, Shikoku, SW Japan 34.01N 133.32E
160 K11 **Kawardha** Chhattīsgarh, C India 21.59N 81.12E
12 I14 **Kawartha Lakes** ⊚ Ontario, SE Canada
171 K17 **Kawasaki** Kanagawa, Honshū, S Japan 35.33N 139.40E
175 T9 **Kawassi** Pulau Obi, E Indonesia 1.32S 127.25E
172 N8 **Kawauchi** Aomori, Honshū, C Japan 41.11N 141.00E
192 L5 **Kawau Island** island N NZ
192 N10 **Kaweka Range** ▲ North Island, NZ
Kawelecht see Puhja
176 Z13 **Kawentinkim** Papua, E Indonesia 5.04S 140.55E
192 O8 **Kawerau** Bay of Plenty, North Island, NZ 38.06S 176.42E
192 L8 **Kawhia** Waikato, North Island, NZ 38.04S 174.49E
192 K8 **Kawhia Harbour** inlet North Island, NZ
37 V8 **Kawich Peak** ▲ Nevada, W USA 38.00N 116.27W
37 V9 **Kawich Range** ▲ Nevada, W USA
12 G12 **Kawigamog Lake** ⊚ Ontario, S Canada
175 Rr3 **Kawio, Kepulauan** island group N Indonesia
178 Gg9 **Kawkareik** Karen State, S Myanmar 16.34N 98.14E
29 O8 **Kaw Lake** ⊠ Oklahoma, C USA
177 G3 **Kawlin** Sagaing, N Myanmar 23.48N 95.40E
Kawm Umbū see Kôm Ombo
Kawthule State see Karen State
Kaxgar see Kashi
164 D7 **Kaxgar He** ⚓ NW China
164 J5 **Kax He** ⚓ NW China
79 P12 **Kaya** C Burkina 13.04N 1.09W
178 Gg7 **Kayah State** ◆ state C Myanmar
126 J7 **Kayak** Taymyrskiy (Dolgano-Nenetskiy) Avtonomnyy Okrug, N Russian Federation 71.27N 103.21E
41 T12 **Kayak Island** island Alaska, USA
116 M11 **Kayalıköy Barajı** ⊠ NW Turkey
161 G23 **Kāyamkulam** Kerala, SW India 9.10N 76.31E
177 G8 **Kayan** Yangon, SW Myanmar 16.54N 96.34E
175 N6 **Kayan, Sungai** prev. Kajan. ⚓ Borneo, C Indonesia
150 F14 **Kaydak, Sor** salt flat SW Kazakhstan
Kaydanovo see Dzyarzhynsk
39 N9 **Kayenta** Arizona, SW USA 36.43N 110.15W
78 J11 **Kayes** Kayes, W Mali 14.25N 11.21W
78 J11 **Kayes** ◆ region SW Mali
Kayin State see Karen State
151 U10 **Kaynar** var. Kajnar. Vostochnyy Kazakhstan, E Kazakhstan 49.13N 77.27E
Kaynary see Căinari
85 H15 **Kayoya** Western, W Zambia 16.13S 24.09E
Kayrakkum see Qayroqqum
Kayrakkumskoye Vodokhranilishche see Qayroqqum, Obanbori
142 K14 **Kayseri** var. Kaisaria; anc. Caesarea Mazaca, Mazaca. Kayseri, C Turkey 38.42N 35.28E
142 K14 **Kayseri** var. Kaisaria. ◆ province C Turkey
38 L2 **Kaysville** Utah, W USA 41.10N 111.55W
126 Hh8 **Kayyerkan** Taymyrskiy (Dolgano-Nenetskiy) Avtonomnyy Okrug, N Russian Federation 69.26N 87.31E
Kayyngdy see Kaindy
12 L11 **Kazabazua** Québec, SE Canada 45.58N 76.00W
12 L12 **Kazabazua** ⚓ Québec, SE Canada
126 M7 **Kazach'ye** Respublika Sakha (Yakutiya), NE Russian Federation 70.38N 135.54E
152 E9 **Kazakhlyshor, Solonchak** var. Solonchak Shorkazakhly. salt marsh NW Turkmenistan
Kazakhskaya SSR/Kazakh Soviet Socialist Republic see Kazakhstan
151 R9 **Kazakhskiy Melkosopochnik** Eng. Kazakh Uplands, Kirghiz Steppe, Kaz. Saryarqa. uplands C Kazakhstan
150 L12 **Kazakhstan** off. Republic of Kazakhstan, var. Kazakstan, Kaz. Qazaqstan, Qazaqstan Respublikasy; prev. Kazakh Soviet Socialist Republic, Rus. Kazakhskaya SSR. ◆ republic C Asia
Kazakh Uplands see Kazakhskiy Melkosopochnik
Kazakstan see Kazakhstan
150 L14 **Kazalinsk** Kzylorda, S Kazakhstan 45.51N 62.08E
131 R4 **Kazan'** Respublika Tatarstan, W Russian Federation 55.43N 49.07E
131 R4 **Kazan'** ✕ Respublika Tatarstan, W Russian Federation 55.46N 49.21E
15 K8 **Kazan** ⚓ Nunavut, NW Canada
Kazandzhik see Bereket
119 R8 **Kazanka** Mykolayivs'ka Oblast', S Ukraine 47.49N 32.50E
Kazanketken see Qozonketkan
Kazanlik see Kazanlŭk
116 J9 **Kazanlŭk** prev. Kazanlik. Stara Zagora, C Bulgaria 42.38N 25.24E
172 T17 **Kazan-rettō** Eng. Volcano Islands. island group SE Japan
125 F12 **Kazanskoye** Tyumenskaya Oblast', C Russian Federation 55.39N 69.06E
119 V12 **Kazantip, Mys** headland S Ukraine 45.27N 35.50E
153 U9 **Kazarman** Narynskaya Oblast', C Kyrgyzstan 41.21N 74.03E
Kazatin see Kozyatyn
Kazbegi see Kazbek
Kazbegi see Qazbegi
143 T9 **Kazbek** var. Kazbegi, Geor. Mqinvartsveri. ▲ N Georgia 42.43N 44.28E
84 M13 **Kazembe** Eastern, NE Zambia 12.06S 32.45E
149 N11 **Kāzerūn** Fārs, S Iran 29.40N 51.38E
129 R12 **Kazhym** Respublika Komi, NW Russian Federation 60.19N 51.26E
Kazi Ahmad see Qāzi Ahmad
Kazi Magomed see Qazimämmäd
142 H16 **Kâzımkarabekir** Karaman, S Turkey 37.13N 32.58E
113 M20 **Kazincbarcika** Borsod-Abaúj-Zemplén, NE Hungary 48.15N 20.40E
121 H17 **Kazlowshchyna** Pol. Kozłowszczyzna, Rus. Kozlovshchina. Hrodzyenskaya Voblasts', W Belarus 53.19N 25.18E
121 E14 **Kazlų Rūda** Marijampolė, S Lithuania 54.45N 23.28E
150 E9 **Kaztalovka** Zapadnyy Kazakhstan, W Kazakhstan 49.47N 48.40E
81 K22 **Kazumba** Kasai Occidental, S Dem. Rep. Congo 6.19S 21.57E
171 Mm10 **Kazuno** Akita, Honshū, C Japan 40.08N 140.47E
Kazvin see Qazvīn
120 J12 **Kaz'yany** Rus. Koz'yany. Vitsyebskaya Voblasts', NW Belarus 55.19N 26.52E
125 Ff9 **Kazym** ⚓ N Russian Federation
112 H10 **Kcynia** Ger. Exin. Kujawsko-pomorskie, C Poland 53.00N 17.29E
117 I20 **Kéa** Kéa, Kykládes, Greece, Aegean Sea 37.22N 24.21E
117 I20 **Kéa** prev. Kéos, anc. Ceos. island Kykládes, Greece, Aegean Sea
40 H11 **Kea'au** var. Keaau. Hawai'i, USA, C Pacific Ocean 19.36N 155.01W
40 F11 **Keāhole Point** var. Keahole Point headland Hawai'i, USA, C Pacific Ocean 19.43N 156.03W
40 G12 **Kealakekua** Hawai'i, USA, C Pacific Ocean 19.31N 155.55W
40 H11 **Kea, Mauna** ▲ Hawai'i, USA, C Pacific Ocean 19.50N 155.30W
39 N10 **Keams** Arizona, SW USA 35.47N 110.09W
Kéamu see Aneityum
31 O16 **Kearney** Nebraska, C USA 40.42N 99.06W
38 L3 **Kearns** Utah, W USA 40.39N 112.00W
117 H20 **Kéas, Stenó** strait SE Greece
143 O14 **Keban Barajı** dam C Turkey 38.49N 38.46E
143 O14 **Keban Barajı** ⊠ C Turkey
79 S13 **Kebbi** ◆ state NW Nigeria
78 G10 **Kébémèr** NW Senegal 15.24N 16.25W
76 M7 **Kebili** var. Qibilī. C Tunisia 33.42N 9.06E
144 H4 **Kebir, Nahr el** ⚓ NW Syria
82 A10 **Kebkabiya** Northern Darfur, W Sudan 13.39N 24.04E
94 I11 **Kebnekaise** ▲ N Sweden 68.01N 18.24E
83 M14 **K'ebrī Dehar** Somali, E Ethiopia 6.43N 44.15E
154 K15 **Kech** ⚓ SW Pakistan
8 K10 **Kechika** ⚓ British Columbia, W Canada
113 K23 **Kecskemét** Bács-Kiskun, C Hungary 46.54N 19.41E
174 Gg2 **Kedah** ◆ state Peninsular Malaysia
120 F12 **Kėdainiai** Kaunas, C Lithuania 55.19N 24.00E
Kedder see Kehra
11 N13 **Kedgwick** New Brunswick, SE Canada 47.37N 67.21W
174 Ll15 **Kediri** Jawa, C Indonesia 7.45S 112.01E
176 Y10 **Kedir Sarmi** Papua, E Indonesia 2.00S 139.01E
169 V7 **Kedong** Heilongjiang, NE China 48.00N 126.15E
78 I12 **Kédougou** SE Senegal 12.34N 12.09W
126 Gg13 **Kedrovyy** Tomskaya Oblast', C Russian Federation 57.31N 79.45E
113 H16 **Kędzierzyn-Koźle** Ger. Heydebrech. Opolskie, S Poland 50.20N 18.12E
14 G6 **Keele** ⚓ Northwest Territories, NW Canada
8 K6 **Keele Peak** ▲ Yukon Territory, NW Canada 63.31N 130.21W
Keelung see Chilung
21 N10 **Keene** New Hampshire, NE USA 42.56N 72.14W
101 H17 **Keerbergen** Vlaams Brabant, C Belgium 51.01N 4.39E
85 E21 **Keetmanshoop** Karas, S Namibia 26.36S 18.07E
10 A11 **Keewatin** Ontario, S Canada 49.46N 94.30W
31 V4 **Keewatin** Minnesota, N USA 47.24N 93.04W
117 B18 **Kefallinía** var. Kefallonía. island Iónioi Nísoi, Greece, C Mediterranean Sea
Kefallonía see Kefallinía
117 M22 **Kéfalos** Kos, Dodekánisos, Greece, Aegean Sea 36.44N 26.58E
175 Rr17 **Kefamenanu** Timor, C Indonesia 9.31S 124.28E
144 F10 **Kefar Sava** var. Kfar Saba. Central, C Israel 32.12N 34.58E
Kefe see Feodosiya
79 V15 **Keffi** Nassarawa, C Nigeria 8.52N 7.54E
94 H4 **Keflavík** ✕ (Reykjavík) Reykjanes, W Iceland 63.58N 22.37W
94 H4 **Keflavík** Reykjanes, W Iceland 64.01N 22.35W
Kegalee see Kegalla
161 J25 **Kegalla** var. Kegalee, Kegalle. Sabaragamuwa Province, C Sri Lanka 7.13N 80.21E
Kegalle see Kegalla
Kegayli see Kegeyli
Kegel see Keila
151 W16 **Kegen** Almaty, SE Kazakhstan 42.57N 79.15E
152 H7 **Kegeyli** prev. Kegayli. Qoraqalpog'iston Respublikasi, W Uzbekistan 42.46N 59.49E
103 F22 **Kehl** Baden-Württemberg, SW Germany 48.34N 7.49E
120 H3 **Kehra** Ger. Kedder. Harjumaa, NW Estonia 59.19N 25.22E
119 U6 **Kehychivka** Kharkivs'ka Oblast', E Ukraine 49.18N 35.46E
99 L17 **Keighley** N England, UK 53.51N 1.53W
Kei Islands see Kai, Kepulauan
Keijō see Sŏul
120 G3 **Keila** Ger. Kegel. Harjumaa, NW Estonia 59.19N 24.28E
Keilberg see Klínovec
85 F23 **Keimoes** Northern Cape, W South Africa 28.41S 20.57E
Keina/Keinis see Käina
176 Yy14 **Keisak** Papua, E Indonesia 7.01S 140.02E
Keishū see Kyŏngju
79 T11 **Keïta** Tahoua, C Niger 14.43N 5.45E
80 J12 **Kéita, Bahr** var. Doka. ⚓ S Chad
190 K10 **Keith** South Australia 36.01S 140.22E
98 K8 **Keith** NE Scotland, UK 57.33N 2.57W
28 K3 **Keith Sebelius Lake** ⊠ Kansas, C USA
34 G11 **Keizer** Oregon, NW USA 44.59N 123.01W
40 A8 **Kekaha** Kaua'i, Hawai'i, USA, C Pacific Ocean 21.58N 159.43W
153 U10 **Këk-Art** prev. Alaykel', Alay-Kuu. Oshskaya Oblast', SW Kyrgyzstan 40.15N 74.21E
153 W10 **Këk-Aygyr** var. Keyaygyr. Narynskaya Oblast', C Kyrgyzstan 40.42N 75.37E
153 V9 **Këk-Dzhar** Narynskaya Oblast', C Kyrgyzstan 41.28N 74.48E
12 L8 **Kekek** ⚓ Québec, SE Canada
193 K15 **Kekerengu** Canterbury, South Island, NZ 41.55S 174.05E
113 L21 **Kékes** ▲ N Hungary 47.53N 19.59E
175 Rr17 **Kekneno, Gunung** ▲ Timor, S Indonesia
153 S9 **Këk-Tash** Kir. Kök-Tash. Dzhalal-Abadskaya Oblast', W Kyrgyzstan 41.08N 72.25E
83 M15 **K'elafo** Somali, E Ethiopia 5.36N 44.12E
175 O6 **Kelai, Sungai** ⚓ Borneo, N Indonesia
Kelamayi see Karamay
Kelang see Klang
174 H3 **Kelantan** ◆ state Peninsular Malaysia
Kelantan see Kelantan, Sungai
174 H3 **Kelantan, Sungai** var. Kelantan. ⚓ Peninsular Malaysia
Kelat see Kālat
Kelcyra see Këlcyrë
115 L22 **Këlcyrë** var. Këlcyra. Gjirokastër, S Albania 40.19N 20.10E
Kelifskiy Uzboy see Kelif Uzboÿy
152 L14 **Kelif Uzboÿy** Rus. Kelifskiy Uzboy. salt marsh E Turkmenistan
143 O12 **Kelkit** Gümüşhane, NE Turkey 40.05N 39.25E
142 M12 **Kelkit Çayı** ⚓ N Turkey
79 W11 **Kellé** Zinder, S Niger 14.10N 10.10E
81 G18 **Kéllé** Cuvette, W Congo 0.04S 14.33E
151 P7 **Kellerovka** Severnyy Kazakhstan, N Kazakhstan 53.51N 69.15E
15 H1 **Kellett, Cape** headland Banks Island, Northwest Territories, NW Canada 71.57N 125.55W
33 S11 **Kelleys Island** island Ohio, N USA
35 N8 **Kellogg** Idaho, NW USA 47.30N 116.07W
94 M12 **Kelloselkä** Lappi, N Finland 66.55N 28.52E
99 F17 **Kells** Ir. Ceanannas. E Ireland 53.43N 6.52W
120 E12 **Kelmė** Šiauliai, C Lithuania 55.39N 22.57E
101 M19 **Kelmis** var. La Calamine. Liège, E Belgium 50.43N 6.01E
80 H12 **Kélo** Tandjilé, SW Chad 9.21N 15.49E
85 I14 **Kelongwa** North Western, NW Zambia 13.41S 26.19E
9 N17 **Kelowna** British Columbia, SW Canada 49.49N 119.28W
9 X12 **Kelsey** Manitoba, C Canada 56.02N 96.31W
36 M6 **Kelseyville** California, W USA 38.58N 122.51W
98 K13 **Kelso** SE Scotland, UK 55.36N 2.27W
34 G10 **Kelso** Washington, NW USA 46.09N 122.54W
205 W15 **Keltie, Cape** headland Antarctica
Keltsy see Kielce

◆ Country ● Country Capital ◇ Dependent Territory ○ Dependent Territory Capital ◆ Administrative Region ✕ International Airport ▲ Mountain ▲ Mountain Range ⛰ Volcano ⚓ River ⊚ Lake ⊠ Reservoir

KELUANG – KHOROG

174 Hh6 **Keluang** var. Kluang. Johor, Peninsular Malaysia 2.01N 103.18E
174 I8 **Kelume** Pulau Lingga, W Indonesia 0.12S 104.27E
9 U15 **Kelvington** Saskatchewan, S Canada 52.10N 103.30W
128 J7 **Kem'** Respublika Kareliya, NW Russian Federation 64.55N 34.17E
128 I7 **Kem'** ∽ NW Russian Federation
143 O13 **Kemah** Erzincan, E Turkey 39.34N 39.01E
143 N13 **Kemaliye** Erzincan, C Turkey 39.17N 38.30E
Kemaman see Cukai
Kemanlar see Isperikh
8 K14 **Kemano** British Columbia, SW Canada 53.39N 127.58W
Kemarat see Khemmarat
175 Qq9 **Kembani** Pulau Peleng, N Indonesia 1.32S 122.57E
142 F17 **Kemer** Antalya, SW Turkey 36.39N 30.33E
126 H14 **Kemerovo** prev. Shcheglovsk. Kemerovskaya Oblast', C Russian Federation 55.25N 86.04E
126 H14 **Kemerovskaya Oblast'** ⬖ province S Russian Federation
94 L13 **Kemi** Lappi, NW Finland 65.46N 24.34E
94 M12 **Kemijärvi** Swe. Kemiträsk. Lappi, N Finland 66.41N 27.24E
94 M12 **Kemijärvi** ◎ N Finland
94 L13 **Kemijoki** ∽ NW Finland
153 V7 **Kemin** prev. Bystrovka. Chuyskaya Oblast', N Kyrgyzstan 42.49N 75.42E
94 L13 **Keminmaa** Lappi, NW Finland 65.49N 24.34E
Kemins Island see Nikumaroro
Kemiö see Kimito
Kemiträsk see Kemijärvi
131 P5 **Kemlya** Respublika Mordoviya, W Russian Federation 54.42N 45.16E
101 B18 **Kemmel** West-Vlaanderen, W Belgium 50.42N 2.51E
35 S16 **Kemmerer** Wyoming, C USA 41.47N 110.32W
Kemmuna see Comino
81 I14 **Kémo** ⬖ prefecture S Central African Republic
27 U7 **Kemp** Texas, SW USA 32.26N 96.13W
95 L14 **Kempele** Oulu, C Finland 64.55N 25.25E
103 D15 **Kempen** Nordrhein-Westfalen, W Germany 51.22N 6.25E
27 Q5 **Kemp, Lake** ◎ Texas, SW USA
205 W5 **Kemp Land** physical region Antarctica
27 S9 **Kempner** Texas, SW USA 31.03N 98.01W
46 H3 **Kemp's Bay** Andros Island, W Bahamas 24.02N 77.32W
191 U6 **Kempsey** New South Wales, SE Australia 31.04S 152.49E
103 J24 **Kempten** Bayern, S Germany 47.43N 10.19E
13 N9 **Kempt, Lac** ◎ Québec, SE Canada
191 P17 **Kempton** Tasmania, SE Australia 42.34S 147.13E
160 J9 **Ken** ∽ C India
41 R12 **Kenai** Alaska, USA 60.33N 151.15W
(0) D5 **Kenai Mountains** ▲ Alaska, USA
41 R12 **Kenai Peninsula** peninsula Alaska, USA
23 V11 **Kenansville** North Carolina, SE USA 34.57N 77.54W
152 A10 **Kenar** prev. Rus. Ufra. Balkan Welaýaty, NW Turkmenistan 40.00N 53.05E
124 Pp15 **Kenäyis, Râs el-** headland N Egypt 31.13N 27.53E
99 K16 **Kendal** NW England, UK 54.19N 2.45W
25 Y16 **Kendall** Florida, SE USA 25.39N 80.18W
15 Ll6 **Kendall, Cape** headland Nunavut, E Canada 63.31N 87.09W
20 J15 **Kendall Park** New Jersey, NE USA 40.25N 74.33W
33 Q11 **Kendallville** Indiana, N USA 41.24N 85.10W
175 Qq12 **Kendari** Sulawesi, C Indonesia 3.57S 122.36E
174 L10 **Kendawangan** Borneo, C Indonesia 2.31S 110.13E
174 Ll15 **Kendeng, Pegunungan** ▲ Jawa, S Indonesia
160 O12 **Kendrāpāra** var. Kendrāparha. Orissa, E India 20.29N 86.25E
Kendrāparha see Kendrāpāra
160 O11 **Kendujhargarh** prev. Keonjhargarh. Orissa, E India 21.42N 85.36E
27 S13 **Kenedy** Texas, SW USA 28.49N 97.51W
Kënekesir see Könekesir
78 J15 **Kenema** SE Sierra Leone 7.55N 11.12W
31 P16 **Kenesaw** Nebraska, C USA 40.37N 98.39W
Këneurgench see Köneürgenç
81 H21 **Kenge** Bandundu, SW Dem. Rep. Congo 4.52S 16.58E
Kengen see Kangen
178 Hh5 **Keng Tung** var. Kentung. Shan State, E Myanmar 21.18N 99.36E
85 F23 **Kenhardt** Northern Cape, W South Africa 29.20S 21.10E
78 J12 **Kéniéba** Kayes, W Mali 12.47N 11.16W
Kenimekh see Konimex
175 Nn3 **Keningau** Sabah, East Malaysia 5.21N 116.10E
76 F6 **Kénitra** prev. Port-Lyautey. NW Morocco 34.19N 6.29W
23 V9 **Kenly** North Carolina, SE USA 35.39N 78.16W
99 B21 **Kenmare** Ir. Neidín. S Ireland 51.52N 9.34W
30 L2 **Kenmare** North Dakota, N USA 48.40N 102.04W
99 A21 **Kenmare River** Ir. An Ribhéar. inlet NE Atlantic Ocean
20 D10 **Kenmore** New York, NE USA 42.58N 78.52W
27 W8 **Kennard** Texas, SW USA 31.21N 95.10W
31 N10 **Kennebec** South Dakota, N USA 43.53N 99.52W
21 Q7 **Kennebec River** ∽ Maine, NE USA
21 P9 **Kennebunk** Maine, NE USA 43.22N 70.33W
41 R13 **Kennedy Entrance** strait Alaska, USA
177 Ff3 **Kennedy Peak** ▲ W Myanmar 23.18N 93.52E
24 K9 **Kenner** Louisiana, S USA 29.57N 90.15W
188 I8 **Kenneth Range** ▲ Western Australia
29 Y9 **Kennett** Missouri, C USA 36.14N 90.03W
20 I16 **Kennett Square** Pennsylvania, NE USA 39.50N 75.40W
34 K10 **Kennewick** Washington, NW USA 46.12N 119.08W
10 E11 **Kenogami** ∽ Ontario, S Canada
13 Q7 **Kénogami, Lac** ◎ Québec, SE Canada
12 G8 **Kenogami Lake** Ontario, S Canada 48.04N 80.10W
12 F7 **Kenogamissi Lake** ◎ Ontario, S Canada
8 I6 **Keno Hill** Yukon Territory, NW Canada 63.54N 135.18W
10 A11 **Kenora** Ontario, S Canada 49.46N 94.25W
33 N9 **Kenosha** Wisconsin, N USA 42.34N 87.49W
11 P14 **Kensington** Prince Edward Island, SE Canada 46.25N 63.39W
28 L3 **Kensington** Kansas, C USA 39.46N 99.01W
34 I11 **Kent** Oregon, NW USA 45.14N 120.43W
26 J9 **Kent** Texas, SW USA 31.03N 104.13W
34 H8 **Kent** Washington, NW USA 47.22N 122.13W
99 P22 **Kent** cultural region SE England, UK
151 P16 **Kentau** Yuzhnyy Kazakhstan, S Kazakhstan 43.28N 68.40E
191 P14 **Kent Group** island group Tasmania, SE Australia
33 N12 **Kentland** Indiana, N USA 40.46N 87.25W
33 R12 **Kenton** Ohio, N USA 40.39N 83.36W
15 J4 **Kent Peninsula** peninsula Nunavut, N Canada
117 F14 **Kentrikí Makedonía** Eng. Macedonia Central. ⬖ region N Greece
22 J6 **Kentucky** off. Commonwealth of Kentucky; also known as The Bluegrass State. ⬖ state C USA
22 H8 **Kentucky Lake** ⊠ Kentucky/Tennessee, S USA
Kentung see Keng Tung
11 P15 **Kentville** Nova Scotia, SE Canada 45.04N 64.30W
24 K8 **Kentwood** Louisiana, S USA 30.56N 90.30W
33 P9 **Kentwood** Michigan, N USA 42.52N 85.33W
83 H17 **Kenya** off. Republic of Kenya. ◆ republic E Africa
Kenya, Mount see Kirinyaga
174 Hh3 **Kenyir, Tasik** var. Tasek Kenyir. ◎ Peninsular Malaysia
31 W10 **Kenyon** Minnesota, N USA 44.16N 92.59W
31 Y16 **Keokuk** Iowa, C USA 40.24N 91.22W
Keonjihargarh see Kendujhargarh
Kéos see Kéa
31 X16 **Keosauqua** Iowa, C USA 40.43N 91.58W
31 X15 **Keota** Iowa, C USA 41.21N 91.57W
23 O11 **Keowee, Lake** ⊠ South Carolina, SE USA
128 I7 **Kepa** var. Kepe. Respublika Kareliya, NW Russian Federation 65.09N 32.15E
Kepe see Kepa
201 O13 **Kepirohi Falls** waterfall Pohnpei, E Micronesia
193 B22 **Kepler Mountains** ▲ South Island, NZ
113 I14 **Kępno** Wielkopolskie, C Poland 51.17N 17.56E
67 C24 **Keppel Island** island N Falkland Islands
Keppel Island see Niuatoputapu
67 C23 **Keppel Sound** sound N Falkland Islands
142 D12 **Kepsut** Balıkesir, NW Turkey 39.40N 28.09E
174 J6 **Kepulauan Riau** off. Propinsi Kepulauan Riau. ⬖ province NW Indonesia
176 W12 **Kerai** Papua, E Indonesia 3.53S 134.30E
Kerak see Al Karak
161 F22 **Kerala** ⬖ state S India
194 H10 **Keram** ∽ N PNG
172 O14 **Kerama-rettō** island group SW Japan
191 N10 **Kerang** Victoria, SE Australia 35.46S 144.01E
Kerasunt see Giresun
117 H19 **Keratéa** var. Keratea. Attikí, C Greece 37.48N 23.58E
95 M19 **Kerava** Swe. Kervo. Etelä-Suomi, S Finland 60.22N 25.01E
Kerbala/Kerbela see Karbalā'
34 F15 **Kerby** Oregon, NW USA 42.10N 123.39W
119 W12 **Kerch** Rus. Kerch'. Respublika Krym, SE Ukraine 45.22N 36.30E
Kerchens'ka Protska/ Kerchenskiy Proliv see Kerch Strait
119 V13 **Kerchens'kyy Pivostriv** peninsula S Ukraine
124 R4 **Kerch Strait** var. Bosporus Cimmerius, Enikale Strait, Rus. Kerchenskiy Proliv, Ukr. Kerchens'ka Protska. strait Black Sea/Sea of Azov
158 K8 **Kerdārnāth** Uttaranchal, N India 30.43N 79.03E
Kerdilio see Kerdýlio
116 H13 **Kerdýlio** var. Kerdilio. ▲ N Greece 40.46N 23.37E
194 J14 **Kerema** Gulf, S PNG 7.58S 145.46E
Keremitlik see Lyulyakovo
142 I9 **Kerempe Burnu** headland N Turkey 42.01N 33.20E
82 J9 **Keren** var. Cheren. C Eritrea 15.45N 38.22E
27 U7 **Kerens** Texas, SW USA 32.07N 96.13W
192 M6 **Kerepehi** Waikato, North Island, NZ 37.18S 175.33E
151 P10 **Kerey, Ozero** ◎ C Kazakhstan
Kergel see Kärla
181 Q12 **Kerguelen** island C French Southern and Antarctic Territories
181 Q13 **Kerguelen Plateau** undersea feature S Indian Ocean
117 C20 **Kerí** Zákynthos, Iónioi Nísoi, Greece, C Mediterranean Sea 37.40N 20.48E
83 H19 **Kericho** Rift Valley, W Kenya 0.21S 35.16E
192 K2 **Kerikeri** Northland, North Island, NZ 35.13S 173.57E
95 O17 **Kerimäki** Isä-Suomi, E Finland 61.55N 29.18E
174 Gg10 **Kerinci, Danau** ◎ Sumatera, W Indonesia
174 Gg9 **Kerinci, Gunung** ▲ Sumatera, W Indonesia 2.00S 101.40E
Keriya see Yutian
164 H9 **Keriya He** ∽ NW China
100 J9 **Kerkbuurt** Noord-Holland, C Netherlands 52.29N 5.08E
100 J13 **Kerkdriel** Gelderland, C Netherlands 51.46N 5.21E
77 N6 **Kerkenah, Îles de** var. Kerkenna Islands, Ar. Juzur Qarqannah. island group E Tunisia
Kerkenna Islands see Kerkenah, Îles de
117 M20 **Kerketévs** ▲ Sámos, Dodekánisos, Greece, Aegean Sea 37.44N 26.39E
31 T8 **Kerkhoven** Minnesota, N USA 45.12N 95.18W
Kerki see Atamyrat
Kerkichi see Kerkiçi
152 M14 **Kerkiçi** Rus. Kerkichi. Lebap Welaýaty, E Turkmenistan 37.46N 65.18E
117 F16 **Kerkíneo** prehistoric site Thessalía, C Greece 39.32N 22.42E
116 G12 **Kerkinitis, Límni** ◎ N Greece
Kérkira see Kérkyra
101 M18 **Kerkrade** Limburg, SE Netherlands 50.52N 6.04E
Kerkuk see Kirkūk
117 B16 **Kérkyra** ✕ Kérkyra, Iónioi Nísoi, Greece, C Mediterranean Sea 39.36N 19.55E
117 B16 **Kérkyra** var. Kérkira, Eng. Corfu. Kérkyra, Iónioi Nísoi, Greece, C Mediterranean Sea 39.36N 19.55E
117 A16 **Kérkyra** var. Kérkira, Eng. Corfu. island Iónioi Nísoi, Greece, C Mediterranean Sea
199 Jj12 **Kermadec Islands** island group NZ, SW Pacific Ocean
183 R10 **Kermadec Ridge** undersea feature SW Pacific Ocean
183 R11 **Kermadec Trench** undersea feature SW Pacific Ocean
149 S10 **Kermān** var. Kirman; anc. Carmana. Kermān, C Iran 30.18N 57.04E
149 R11 **Kermān** off. Ostān-e Kermān, var. Kirman; anc. Carmania. ⬖ province SE Iran
149 U12 **Kermān, Bīābān-e** var. Kerman Desert. desert SE Iran
148 K6 **Kermānshāh** var. Qahremānshahr, prev. Bākhtarān. Kermānshāh, W Iran 34.19N 47.04E
149 Q9 **Kermānshāh** Yazd, C Iran 34.19N 47.04E
148 J6 **Kermānshāh** off. Ostān-e Kermānshāh; prev. Bākhtarān, Kermānshāhān. ⬖ province W Iran
Kermānshāhān see Kermānshāh
116 L10 **Kermen** Sliven, C Bulgaria 42.30N 26.12E
26 L8 **Kermit** Texas, SW USA 31.51N 103.05W
23 P6 **Kermit** West Virginia, NE USA 37.51N 82.24W
23 S9 **Kernersville** North Carolina, SE USA 36.12N 80.13W
37 S12 **Kern River** ∽ California, W USA
37 S12 **Kernville** California, W USA 35.44N 118.25W
117 K21 **Kéros** island Kykládes, Greece, Aegean Sea
78 K14 **Kérouané** Haute-Guinée, SE Guinea 9.16N 9.00W
103 D16 **Kerpen** Nordrhein-Westfalen, W Germany 50.51N 6.40E
152 I11 **Kerpichli** Lebap Welaýaty, NE Turkmenistan 40.12N 61.09E
26 M1 **Kerrick** Texas, SW USA 36.29N 102.14W
Kerr Lake see John H.Kerr Reservoir
9 S15 **Kerrobert** Saskatchewan, S Canada 51.55N 109.09W
27 Q11 **Kerrville** Texas, SW USA 30.03N 99.09W
99 B20 **Kerry** Ir. Ciarraí. cultural region SW Ireland
23 S11 **Kershaw** South Carolina, SE USA 34.33N 80.34W
Kertel see Kärdla
97 H23 **Kerteminde** Fyn, C Denmark 55.27N 10.40E
169 Q7 **Kerulen** Chin. Herlen He, Mong. Herlen Gol. ∽ China/Mongolia
Kervo see Kerava
Kerýneia see Girne
10 H11 **Kesagami Lake** ◎ Ontario, SE Canada
95 O17 **Kesälahti** Itä-Suomi, E Finland 61.54N 29.49E
142 B11 **Keşan** Edirne, NW Turkey 40.52N 26.38E
171 Mm12 **Kesennuma** Miyagi, Honshū, C Japan 38.54N 141.34E
169 V7 **Keshan** Heilongjiang, NE China 48.00N 125.46E
32 M6 **Keshena** Wisconsin, N USA 44.54N 88.37W
142 I13 **Keskin** Kırıkkale, C Turkey 39.40N 33.36E
Késmárk see Kežmarok
128 I6 **Kesten'ga** var. Kest Enga. Respublika Kareliya, NW Russian Federation 65.53N 31.47E
100 K12 **Kesteren** Gelderland, C Netherlands 51.55N 5.34E
12 H14 **Keswick** Ontario, S Canada 44.15N 79.26W
99 K15 **Keswick** NW England, UK 54.30N 3.03W
113 H24 **Keszthely** Zala, SW Hungary 46.46N 17.16E
126 Hh13 **Ket'** ∽ C Russian Federation
79 R17 **Keta** SE Ghana 5.54N 1.02E
174 Kk10 **Ketapang** Borneo, C Indonesia 1.49S 109.58E
131 O12 **Ketchenery** prev. Sovetskoye. Respublika Kalmykiya, SW Russian Federation 47.18N 44.31E
41 Y14 **Ketchikan** Revillagigedo Island, Alaska, USA 55.20N 131.39W
35 O14 **Ketchum** Idaho, NW USA 43.40N 114.24W
Kete/Kete Krakye see Kete-Krachi
79 Q15 **Kete-Krachi** var. Kete, Kete Krakye. E Ghana 7.49N 0.03W
100 L9 **Ketelmeer** channel E Netherlands
155 P17 **Keti Bandar** Sind, SE Pakistan 23.55N 67.31E
151 W16 **Ketmen', Khrebet** ▲ SE Kazakhstan
79 S16 **Kétou** SE Benin 7.25N 2.36E
112 M7 **Kętrzyn** Ger. Rastenburg. Warmińsko-Mazurskie, NE Poland, 54.03N 21.22E
99 N20 **Kettering** C England, UK 52.24N 0.43W
33 R14 **Kettering** Ohio, N USA 39.41N 84.10W
20 F13 **Kettle Creek** ∽ Pennsylvania, NE USA
34 L7 **Kettle Falls** Washington, NW USA 48.36N 118.03W
12 D16 **Kettle Point** headland Ontario, S Canada 43.12N 82.01W
31 V6 **Kettle River** ∽ Minnesota, N USA
194 E12 **Ketu** ∽ W PNG
20 G10 **Keuka Lake** ◎ New York, NE USA
Keupriya see Primorsko
95 L17 **Keuruu** Länsi-Suomi, W Finland 62.15N 24.34E
Kevevára see Kovin
94 L9 **Kevo** Lapp. Geavvú. Lappi, N Finland 69.42N 27.08E
46 M6 **Kew** North Caicos, N Turks and Caicos Islands 21.52N 71.57W
32 K11 **Kewanee** Illinois, N USA 41.15N 89.55W
33 N7 **Kewaunee** Wisconsin, N USA 44.27N 87.31W
32 M3 **Keweenaw Bay** ◎ Michigan, N USA
33 N2 **Keweenaw Peninsula** peninsula Michigan, N USA 47.15N 88.19W
33 N2 **Keweenaw Point** headland Michigan, N USA 47.24N 87.42W
31 N12 **Keya Paha River** ∽ Nebraska/ South Dakota, N USA
Keyaygyr see Këk-Aygyr
25 Z16 **Key Biscayne** Florida, SE USA 25.41N 80.09W
28 G8 **Keyes** Oklahoma, C USA 36.48N 102.15W
25 Y17 **Key Largo** Key Largo, Florida, SE USA 25.06N 80.24W
23 U3 **Keyser** West Virginia, NE USA 39.26N 78.58W
29 O9 **Keystone Lake** ⊠ Oklahoma, C USA
38 L16 **Keystone Peak** ▲ Arizona, SW USA 31.52N 111.12W
Keystone State see Pennsylvania
23 U7 **Keysville** Virginia, NE USA 37.02N 78.28W
29 T3 **Keytesville** Missouri, C USA 39.25N 92.56W
25 W17 **Key West** Florida Keys, Florida, SE USA 24.34N 81.48W
131 T1 **Kez** Udmurtskaya Respublika, NW Russian Federation 57.55N 53.42E
Kezdivásárhely see Târgu Secuiesc
126 J13 **Kezhma** Krasnoyarskiy Kray, C Russian Federation 58.57N 101.00E
113 L18 **Kežmarok** Ger. Käsmark, Hung. Késmárk. Prešovský Kraj, E Slovakia 49.09N 20.25E
Kfar Saba see Kefar Sava
85 F20 **Kgalagadi** ⬖ district SW Botswana
85 I20 **Kgatleng** ⬖ district SE Botswana
196 F8 **Kgkeklau** Babeldaob, N Palau
129 R6 **Khabarikha** var. Chabaricha. Respublika Komi, NW Russian Federation 65.52N 52.19E
127 N16 **Khabarovsk** Khabarovskiy Kray, SE Russian Federation 48.31N 135.07E
126 Mm12 **Khabarovskiy Kray** ⬖ territory E Russian Federation
147 W7 **Khabb** Abū Ẓaby, E UAE 24.39N 55.43E
Khabour, Nahr al see Khābūr, Nahr al
Khabura see Al Khābūrah
145 N2 **Khābūr, Nahr al** var. Nahr al Khabour. ∽ Syria/Turkey
Khachmas see Xaçmaz
82 B12 **Khadari** ∽ W Sudan
Khadera see Hadera
147 X12 **Khādhil** var. Khudal. SE Oman 18.48N 56.48E
161 E14 **Khadki** prev. Kirkee. Mahārāshtra, W India 18.34N 73.52E
130 L14 **Khadyzhensk** Krasnodarskiy Kray, SW Russian Federation 44.26N 39.31E
116 N9 **Khadzhiyska Reka** ∽ E Bulgaria
119 P10 **Khadzhybeys'kyy Lyman** ◎ SW Ukraine
144 K3 **Khafsah** Ḥalab, N Syria 36.16N 38.03E
158 M13 **Khāga** Uttar Pradesh, N India 25.46N 81.04E
159 Q13 **Khagaria** Bihār, NE India 25.31N 86.27E
155 Q13 **Khairpur** Sind, SE Pakistan 27.30N 68.49E
126 Hh15 **Khakasiya, Respublika** prev. Khakasskaya Avtonomnaya Oblast', Eng. Khakassia. ⬖ autonomous republic C Russian Federation
Khakassia/Khakasskaya Avtonomnaya Oblast' see Khakasiya, Respublika
178 H9 **Kha Khaeng, Khao** ▲ W Thailand 16.13N 99.03E
85 G20 **Khakhea** var. Kakia. Southern, S Botswana 24.40S 23.28E
Khalach see Halaç
Khalándrion see Chalándri
131 W7 **Khalilovo** Orenburgskaya Oblast', W Russian Federation 51.25N 58.13E
Khalkabad see Xalqobod
148 L3 **Khalkhāl** prev. Herowābād. Ardabīl, NW Iran 37.40N 48.34E
Khalkidhikí see Chalkidikí
Khalkís see Chalkída
129 W3 **Khal'mer-Yu** Respublika Komi, NW Russian Federation 68.00N 64.45E
121 M14 **Khalopyenichy** Rus. Kholopenichi. Minskaya Voblasts', NE Belarus 54.31N 28.58E
Khalturin see Orlov
147 Y10 **Khalūf** var. Al Khaluf. E Oman 20.27N 57.58E
160 K10 **Khamaria** Madhya Pradesh, C India 23.07N 80.54E
160 D11 **Khambhāt** Gujarāt, W India 22.19N 72.39E
160 C12 **Khambhāt, Gulf of** Eng. Gulf of Cambay. gulf W India
178 K10 **Khâm Đưc** Quang Nam-Đa Nâng, C Vietnam 15.28N 107.49E
160 G12 **Khāmgaon** Mahārāshtra, C India 20.40N 76.34E
147 O14 **Khamir** var. Khamr. W Yemen 16.00N 43.56E
147 N12 **Khamīs Mushayṭ** var. Hamīs Musait. 'Asīr, SW Saudi Arabia 18.19N 42.41E
126 L10 **Khampa** Respublika Sakha (Yakutiya), NE Russian Federation 63.43N 123.02E
Khamr see Khamir
85 C19 **Khan** ∽ W Namibia
155 Q2 **Khānābād** Kunduz, NE Afghanistan 36.42N 69.07E
Khân Abou Châmâte/ Khan Abou Ech Cham see Khān Abū Shāmāt
144 I7 **Khān Abū Shāmāt** var. Khân Abou Châmâte, Khan Abou Ech Cham. Dimashq, W Syria 33.43N 36.56E
Khān al Baghdādī see Al Baghdādī
Khān al Maḥāwīl see Al Maḥāwīl
145 T7 **Khān al Mashāhidah** C Iraq 33.40N 44.15E
145 T10 **Khān al Muṣallá** S Iraq 32.09N 44.19E
145 U6 **Khānaqīn** E Iraq 34.22N 45.22E
145 T11 **Khān ar Ruḥbah** S Iraq 31.42N 44.18E
145 P2 **Khān as Sūr** N Iraq 36.28N 41.36E
145 T8 **Khān Āzād** C Iraq 33.07N 44.21E
160 N13 **Khandaparha** prev. Khandpara. Orissa, E India 20.15N 85.10E
Khandpara see Khandaparha
155 T2 **Khandūd** var. Khandud, Wakhan. Badakhshān, NE Afghanistan 36.57N 72.19E
160 G11 **Khandwa** Madhya Pradesh, C India 21.49N 76.22E
126 Mm10 **Khandyga** Respublika Sakha (Yakutiya), NE Russian Federation 62.39N 135.30E
155 T10 **Khānewāl** Punjab, NE Pakistan 30.18N 71.55E
155 S10 **Khāngarh** Punjab, E Pakistan 29.56N 71.10E
Khanh Hung see Soc Trăng
Khaniá see Chaniá
Khanka see Xonqa
169 Z8 **Khanka, Lake** var. Hsing-k'ai Hu, Lake Hanka, Chin. Xingkai Hu, Rus. Ozero Khanka. ◎ China/Russian Federation
Khanka, Ozero see Khanka, Lake
Khankendi see Xankändi
Khanlar see Xanlar
126 Kk10 **Khannya** ∽ NE Russian Federation
155 S12 **Khānpur** Punjab, SE Pakistan 23.37N 70.40E
155 S12 **Khānpur** Punjab, E Pakistan 28.31N 70.30E
144 I4 **Khān Shaykhūn** var. Khan Sheikhun. Idlib, NW Syria 35.27N 36.37E
Khan Sheikhun see Khān Shaykhūn
151 S15 **Khantau** Zhambyl, S Kazakhstan 44.13N 73.47E
151 W16 **Khan Tengri, Pik** ▲ SE Kazakhstan 42.13N 80.13E
178 J9 **Khanthabouli** prev. Savannakhét. Savannakhét, S Laos 16.37N 104.48E
125 Ff10 **Khanty-Mansiysk** prev. Ostyako-Voguls'k. Khanty-Mansiyskiy Avtonomnyy Okrug, C Russian Federation 61.01N 69.00E
129 V8 **Khanty-Mansiyskiy Avtonomnyy Okrug** ⬖ autonomous district C Russian Federation
145 R4 **Khānūqah** C Iraq 35.25N 43.15E
144 E11 **Khān Yūnis** var. Khān Yūnus. S Gaza Strip 31.23N 34.19E
Khān Yūnus see Khān Yūnis
Khanzi see Ghanzi
145 U5 **Khān Zūr** E Iraq 35.03N 45.08E
178 H10 **Khao Laem Reservoir** ⊠ W Thailand
126 Kk17 **Khapcheranga** Chitinskaya Oblast', S Russian Federation 49.46N 112.21E
131 Q12 **Kharabali** Astrakhanskaya Oblast', SW Russian Federation 47.28N 47.14E
159 R16 **Kharagpur** West Bengal, NE India 22.30N 87.19E
145 V11 **Kharā'ib 'Abd al Karīm** S Iraq 31.07N 45.33E
149 Q8 **Kharānaq** Yazd, C Iran 31.54N 54.21E
Kharbin see Harbin
152 H13 **Khardzhagaz** Ahal Welaýaty, C Turkmenistan 37.54N 60.10E
Khārga Oasis see Great Oasis, The
160 F11 **Khargon** Madhya Pradesh, C India 21.49N 75.39E
155 V7 **Khāriān** Punjab, NE Pakistan 32.52N 73.52E
119 X8 **Kharisyz'k** Donets'ka Oblast', E Ukraine 48.01N 38.10E
119 V5 **Kharkiv** Rus. Khar'kov. Kharkivs'ka Oblast', NE Ukraine 50.00N 36.14E
119 V5 **Kharkiv** ✕ Kharkivs'ka Oblast', E Ukraine 49.54N 36.20E
Kharkiv see Kharkivs'ka Oblast'
119 U5 **Kharkivs'ka Oblast'** var. Kharkiv, Rus. Khar'kovskaya Oblast'. ⬖ province E Ukraine
Khar'kov see Kharkiv
Khar'kovskaya Oblast' see Kharkivs'ka Oblast'
128 L3 **Kharlovka** Murmanskaya Oblast', NW Russian Federation 68.47N 37.09E
116 K11 **Kharmanli** Khaskovo, S Bulgaria 41.55N 25.54E
116 K11 **Kharmanliyska Reka** ∽ S Bulgaria
128 M13 **Kharovsk** Vologodskaya Oblast', NW Russian Federation 59.57N 40.05E
82 F9 **Khartoum** var. El Khartûm, Khartum. ● (Sudan) Khartoum, C Sudan 15.33N 32.31E
82 F9 **Khartoum** ⬖ state NE Sudan
82 F9 **Khartoum** ✕ Khartoum, C Sudan 15.36N 32.37E
82 F9 **Khartoum North** Khartoum, C Sudan 15.37N 32.33E
119 X8 **Khartsyz'k** Rus. Khartsyzsk. Donets'ka Oblast', SE Ukraine 48.01N 38.10E
Khartsyzsk see Khartsyz'k
Khartum see Khartoum
Khasab see Al Khaṣab
127 N18 **Khasan** Primorskiy Kray, SE Russian Federation 42.24N 130.45E
131 P16 **Khasavyurt** Respublika Dagestan, SW Russian Federation 43.16N 46.33E
149 W12 **Khāsh** prev. Vāsht. Sīstān va Balūchestān, SE Iran 28.15N 61.11E
154 K8 **Khāsh, Dasht-e** Eng. Khash Desert. desert SW Afghanistan
Khash Desert see Khāsh, Dasht-e
Khashim Al Qirba/Khashm al Qirbah see Khashm el Girba
82 H9 **Khashm el Girba** var. Khashim Al Qirba, Khashm al Qirbah. Kassala, E Sudan 15.00N 35.59E
144 G14 **Khashsh, Jabal al** ▲ S Jordan
143 S10 **Khashuri** C Georgia 41.59N 43.36E
159 V13 **Khāsi Hills** hill range NE India
116 K11 **Khaskovo** Khaskovo, S Bulgaria 41.56N 25.34E
116 K11 **Khaskovo** ⬖ province S Bulgaria
126 J7 **Khatanga** Taymyrskiy (Dolgano-Nenetskiy) Avtonomnyy Okrug, N Russian Federation 71.55N 102.17E
126 J7 **Khatanga** ∽ N Russian Federation
Khatanga, Gulf of see Khatangskiy Zaliv
126 Jj6 **Khatangskiy Zaliv** var. Gulf of Khatanga. bay N Russian Federation
147 W7 **Khatmat al Malāḥah** N Oman 24.56N 56.22E
149 S16 **Khaṭmat al Malāḥah** Ash Shāriqah, E UAE
127 Q6 **Khatyrka** Chukotskiy Avtonomnyy Okrug, NE Russian Federation 62.03N 175.09E
Khauz-Khan see Hanhowuz
Khauzkhanskoye Vodokhranilishche see Hanhowuz Suw Howdany
Khavaling see Khovaling
Khavast see Xovos
145 W10 **Khawrah, Nahr al** ∽ S Iraq
Khawr Barakah see Baraka
147 W7 **Khawr Fakkān** var. Khor Fakkan. Ash Shāriqah, NE UAE 25.21N 56.19E
146 L6 **Khaybar** Al Madīnah, NW Saudi Arabia 25.52N 39.15E
Khaybar, Kowtal-e see Khyber Pass
153 S11 **Khaydarkan** var. Khaydarken. Batkenskaya Oblast', SW Kyrgyzstan 39.56N 71.16E
Khaydarken see Khaydarkan
129 U2 **Khaypudyrskaya Guba** bay NW Russian Federation
145 S1 **Khayrūzuk** E Iraq 36.58N 44.19E
Khazar, Baḥr-e/Khazar, Daryā-ye see Caspian Sea
Khazarosp see Hazorasp
Khazretishi, Khrebet see Hazratishoh, Qatorkŭhi
Khelat see Kālat
76 F6 **Khemisset** NW Morocco 33.52N 6.04W
178 J10 **Khemmarat** var. Kemarat. Ubon Ratchathani, E Thailand 16.03N 105.10E
76 L6 **Khenchela** var. Khenchla. NE Algeria 35.22N 7.09E
Khenchla see Khenchela
76 G7 **Khénifra** C Morocco 32.59N 5.37W
Khersān, Rūd-e see Garm, Āb-e
119 R10 **Kherson** Khersons'ka Oblast', S Ukraine 46.39N 32.37E
Kherson see Khersons'ka Oblast'
119 S14 **Khersones, Mys** Rus. Mys Khersonesskiy. headland S Ukraine 44.34N 33.24E
Khersonesskiy, Mys see Khersones, Mys
119 R10 **Khersons'ka Oblast'** var. Kherson, Rus. Khersonskaya Oblast'. ⬖ province S Ukraine
Khersonskaya Oblast' see Khersons'ka Oblast'
126 J7 **Kheta** Taymyrskiy (Dolgano-Nenetskiy) Avtonomnyy Okrug, N Russian Federation 71.33N 99.40E
126 J7 **Kheta** ∽ N Russian Federation
178 Jj8 **Khe Ve** Quang Bình, C Vietnam 17.52N 105.49E
155 U7 **Khewra** Punjab, E Pakistan 32.40N 73.04E
Khiam see El Khiyam
128 J4 **Khibiny** ▲ NW Russian Federation
126 K16 **Khilok** Chitinskaya Oblast', S Russian Federation 51.26N 110.25E
126 K16 **Khilok** ∽ S Russian Federation
130 K3 **Khimki** Moskovskaya Oblast', W Russian Federation 55.57N 37.48E
153 S12 **Khingov** Rus. Obi-Khingou. ∽ C Tajikistan
Khíos see Chíos
155 R15 **Khipro** Sind, SE Pakistan 25.50N 69.18E
145 S10 **Khirr, Wādī al** dry watercourse S Iraq
116 I10 **Khisarya** Plovdiv, C Bulgaria 42.33N 24.43E
Khiva/Khiwa see Xiva
178 H9 **Khlong Khlung** Kamphaeng Phet, W Thailand 16.15N 99.41E
178 Gg16 **Khlong Thom** Krabi, SW Thailand 7.55N 99.09E
178 I12 **Khlung** Chantaburi, S Thailand 12.25N 102.12E
Khmel'nik see Khmil'nyk
Khmel'nitskaya Oblast' see Khmel'nyts'ka Oblast'
Khmel'nitskiy see Khmel'nyts'kyy
118 K5 **Khmel'nyts'ka Oblast'** var. Khmel'nyts'kyy, Rus. Khmel'nitskaya Oblast'; prev. Kamenets-Podol'skaya Oblast'. ⬖ province NW Ukraine
118 L6 **Khmel'nyts'kyy** Rus. Khmel'nitskiy; prev. Proskurov. Khmel'nyts'ka Oblast', W Ukraine 49.24N 26.59E
Khmel'nyts'kyy see Khmel'nyts'ka Oblast'
118 M6 **Khmil'nyk** Rus. Khmel'nik. Vinnyts'ka Oblast', C Ukraine 49.36N 27.59E
150 I10 **Khobda** prev. Novoalekseyevka. Aktyubinsk, W Kazakhstan 50.10N 55.39E
143 R9 **Khobi** W Georgia 42.20N 41.54E
121 P15 **Khodasy** Rus. Khodosy. Mahilyowskaya Voblasts', E Belarus 53.56N 31.28E
118 I6 **Khodoriv** Pol. Chodorów, Rus. Khodorov. L'vivs'ka Oblast', NW Ukraine 49.19N 24.19E
Khodorov see Khodoriv
Khodosy see Khodasy
Khodzhakala see Hojagala
Khodzhambas see Hojambaz
Khodzhent see Khŭjand
Khodzheyli see Xo'jayli
Khoi see Khvoy
Khojend see Khŭjand
Khokand see Qo'qon
130 L8 **Khokhol'skiy** Voronezhskaya Oblast', W Russian Federation 51.33N 38.43E
178 Hh10 **Khok Samrong** Lop Buri, C Thailand 15.03N 100.43E
155 P2 **Kholm** var. Tashqurghan, Pash. Khulm. Balkh, N Afghanistan 36.42N 67.40E
128 H15 **Kholm** Novgorodskaya Oblast', W Russian Federation 57.10N 31.06E
Kholm see Chełm
Kholmech' see Kholmyech
127 Oo16 **Kholmsk** Ostrov Sakhalin, Sakhalinskaya Oblast', SE Russian Federation 46.57N 142.10E
121 O19 **Kholmyech** Rus. Kholmech'. Homyel'skaya Voblasts', SE Belarus 52.09N 30.37E
Kholon see Holon
Kholopenichi see Khalopyenichy
85 D19 **Khomas** ⬖ district C Namibia
85 D19 **Khomas Hochland** var. Khomasplato. plateau C Namibia
Khomasplato see Khomas Hochland
Khomein see Khomeyn
148 M7 **Khomeyn** var. Khomein, Khumain. Markazī, W Iran 33.37N 50.03E
149 N8 **Khomeynīshahr** prev. Homāyūnshahr. Eşfahān, C Iran 32.39N 51.34E
Khoms see Al Khums
Khong Sedone see Muang Khôngxédôn
178 Ii9 **Khon Kaen** var. Muang Khon Kaen. Khon Kaen, E Thailand 16.25N 102.49E
Khonqa see Xonqa
178 I9 **Khon San** Khon Kaen, E Thailand 16.40N 101.51E
127 N8 **Khonuu** Respublika Sakha (Yakutiya), NE Russian Federation 66.24N 143.15E
131 N8 **Khopër** var. Khoper. ∽ SW Russian Federation
127 Nn16 **Khor** Khabarovskiy Kray, SE Russian Federation 47.43N 134.48E
127 Nn16 **Khor** ∽ SE Russian Federation
149 S6 **Khorāsān** off. Ostān-e Khorāsān, var. Khorassan, Khurasan. ⬖ province NE Iran
Khorassan see Khorāsān
Khorat see Nakhon Ratchasima
160 O13 **Khordha** prev. Khurda. Orissa, E India 20.13N 85.39E
129 U4 **Khorey-Ver** Nenetskiy Avtonomnyy Okrug, NW Russian Federation 67.25N 58.05E
Khorezmskaya Oblast' see Xorazm Viloyati
Khor Fakkan see Khawr Fakkān
151 W15 **Khorgos** Almaty, SE Kazakhstan 44.13N 80.22E
126 K16 **Khorinsk** Respublika Buryatiya, S Russian Federation 52.13N 109.52E
85 C18 **Khorixas** Kunene, NW Namibia 20.22S 14.55E
147 O17 **Khormaksar** var. Aden. ✕ ('Adan) SW Yemen 12.56N 45.00E
Khormal see Khurmāl
Khormuj see Khvormūj
Khorog see Khorugh

◆ Country ● Country Capital ◇ Dependent Territory ○ Dependent Territory Capital ⬖ Administrative Region ✕ International Airport ▲ Mountain ▲ Mountain Range Volcano ∽ River ◎ Lake ⊠ Reservoir

119 S5 **Khorol** Poltavs'ka Oblast', NE Ukraine 49.49N 33.16E
148 L7 **Khorramābād** *var.* Khurramabad. Lorestān, W Iran 33.28N 48.21E
148 K10 **Khorramshahr** *var.* Khurramshahr, Muhammerah; *prev.* Mohammerah. Khūzestān, SW Iran 30.29N 48.09E
153 S14 **Khorugh** *Rus.* Khorog. S Tajikistan 37.29N 71.31E
131 Q12 **Khosheutovo** Astrakhanskaya Oblast', SW Russian Federation 47.04N 47.49E
Khotan *see* Hotan
Khorvot Khalutsa *see* Horvot Haluza
Khotimsk *see* Khotsimsk
Khotin *see* Khotyn
121 R16 **Khotsimsk** *Rus.* Khotimsk. Mahilyowskaya Voblasts', E Belarus 53.24N 32.34E
118 K7 **Khotyn** *Rom.* Hotin, *Rus.* Khotin. Chernivets'ka Oblast', W Ukraine 48.29N 26.30E
76 F7 **Khouribga** C Morocco 32.54N 6.51W
153 Q13 **Khovaling** *Rus.* Khavaling. SW Tajikistan 38.22N 69.54E
Khovd *see* Hovd
155 R6 **Khowst** Paktīā, E Afghanistan 33.22N 69.57E
Khoy *see* Khvoy
121 N20 **Khoyniki** *Rus.* Khoyniki. Homyel'skaya Voblasts', SE Belarus 51.53N 29.58E
Khozretishi, Khrebet *see* Hazratishoh, Qatorkŭhi
Khrisoúpolis *see* Chrysoúpoli
126 Mm6 **Khroma** ≈ NE Russian Federation
150 J10 **Khromtau** *Kaz.* Khromtaū. Aktyubinsk, W Kazakhstan 50.14N 58.22E
Khrysokhou Bay *see* Chrysochoú, Kólpos
119 O7 **Khrystynivka** Cherkas'ka Oblast', C Ukraine 48.49N 29.55E
178 J10 **Khuang Nai** Ubon Ratchathani, E Thailand 15.22N 104.33E
Khudal *see* Khādhil
Khudat *see* Xudat
155 W9 **Khudiān** Punjab, E Pakistan 30.58N 74.19E
Khudzhand *see* Khŭjand
153 O13 **Khufar** Surkhondaryo Viloyati, S Uzbekistan 38.31N 67.45E
85 G21 **Khuis** Kgalagadi, SW Botswana 26.37S 21.50E
153 Q11 **Khŭjand** *var.* Khodzhent, Khojend, *Rus.* Khudzhand; *prev.* Leninabad, *Taj.* Leninobod. N Tajikistan 40.16N 69.37E
178 Ii11 **Khukhan** Si Sa Ket, E Thailand 14.38N 104.12E
Khulm *see* Kholm
159 T16 **Khulna** Khulna, SW Bangladesh 22.48N 89.31E
159 T16 **Khulna** ◆ *division* SW Bangladesh
Khumain *see* Khomeyn
Khums *see* Al Khums
155 W2 **Khunjerāb Pass** *Chin.* Kunjirap Daban. *pass* China/Pakistan *see also* Kunjirap Daban 36.46N 75.16E
159 P16 **Khunti** Jhārkhand, N India 23.01N 85.19E
178 Gg7 **Khun Yuam** Mae Hong Son, NW Thailand 18.54N 97.54E
Khurais *see* Khurayş
Khurasan *see* Khorāsān
147 R7 **Khurayş** *var.* Khurais. Ash Sharqīyah, C Saudi Arabia 25.06N 48.02E
Khurda *see* Khordha
158 J11 **Khurja** Uttar Pradesh, N India 28.15N 77.51E
145 V4 **Khurmāl** *var.* Khormal. NE Iraq 35.19N 46.06E
Khurramabad *see* Khorramābād
Khurramshahr *see* Khorramshahr
155 U7 **Khushāb** Punjab, NE Pakistan 32.16N 72.18E
118 H8 **Khust** *Cz.* Chust, Husté, *Hung.* Huszt. Zakarpats'ka Oblast', W Ukraine 48.10N 23.19E
82 D11 **Khuwei** Western Kordofan, C Sudan 13.01N 29.13E
155 O13 **Khuzdār** Baluchistān, SW Pakistan 27.49N 66.33E
148 L9 **Khūzestān** *off.* Ostān-e Khūzestān, *var.* Khuzistan; *prev.* Arabistan, *anc.* Susiana. ◆ *province* SW Iran
126 Jj15 **Khuzhir** Respublika Buryatiya, S Russian Federation 53.10N 107.18E
Khuzistan *see* Khūzestān
155 R2 **Khvājeh Ghār** *var.* Khwajaghar, Khwaja-i-Ghar. Takhār, NE Afghanistan 37.05N 69.28E
131 Q7 **Khvalynsk** Saratovskaya Oblast', W Russian Federation 52.30N 48.06E
149 N12 **Khvormūj** *var.* Khormuj. Būshehr, S Iran 28.32N 51.22E
148 I2 **Khvoy** *var.* Khoi, Khoy. Āžarbāyjān-e Bākhtarī, NW Iran 38.36N 45.03E
Khwajaghar/Khwaja-i-Ghar *see* Khvājeh Ghār
155 S5 **Khyber Pass** *var.* Kowtal-e Khaybar. *pass* Afghanistan/Pakistan 34.07N 71.05E
195 V14 **Kia** Santa Isabel, N Solomon Islands 7.34S 158.31E
191 S10 **Kiama** New South Wales, SE Australia 34.40S 150.49E
179 R17 **Kiamba** Mindanao, S Philippines 5.59N 124.36E
81 O22 **Kiambi** Katanga, SE Dem. Rep. Congo 7.15S 28.01E
29 Q12 **Kiamichi Mountains** ▲▲ Oklahoma, C USA
29 Q12 **Kiamichi River** ≈ Oklahoma, C USA
12 M10 **Kiamika, Réservoir** ▣ Québec, SE Canada
Kiamusze *see* Jiamusi
41 N7 **Kiana** Alaska, USA 66.58N 160.25W
Kiangmai *see* Chiang Mai
Kiang-ning *see* Nanjing
Kiangsi *see* Jiangxi
Kiangsu *see* Jiangsu
95 M14 **Kiantajärvi** ◎ E Finland
117 F19 **Kiáto** *prev.* Kiáton. Pelopónnisos, S Greece 38.01N 22.45E
Kiáton *see* Kiáto
Kiayi *see* Chiai
69 T9 **Kibali** *var.* Uele (upper course). ≈ NE Dem. Rep. Congo
81 E20 **Kibangou** Le Niari, SW Congo 3.27S 12.21E
Kibarty *see* Kybartai
94 M8 **Kiberg** Finnmark, N Norway 70.17N 30.47E
97 F22 **Kibæk** Ringkøbing, W Denmark 56.03N 8.52E
81 N20 **Kibombo** Maniema, E Dem. Rep. Congo 3.52S 25.59E
83 E20 **Kibondo** Kigoma, NW Tanzania 3.34S 30.40E
83 J15 **Kibre Mengist** *var.* Adola. Oromo, C Ethiopia 5.50N 39.06E
Kıbrıs/Kıbrıs Cumhuriyeti *see* Cyprus
83 E20 **Kibungo** *var.* Kibungu. SE Rwanda 2.09S 30.30E
Kibungu *see* Kibungo
115 N19 **Kičevo** SW FYR Macedonia 41.31N 20.57E
129 P13 **Kichmengskiy Gorodok** Vologodskaya Oblast', NW Russian Federation 60.00N 45.52E
32 J8 **Kickapoo River** ≈ Wisconsin, N USA
9 P16 **Kicking Horse Pass** *pass* Alberta/British Columbia, SW Canada 51.27N 116.13W
79 R9 **Kidal** Kidal, C Mali 18.22N 1.21E
79 Q8 **Kidal** ◆ *region* NE Mali
179 R16 **Kidapawan** Mindanao, S Philippines 7.02N 125.04E
99 L20 **Kidderminster** C England, UK 52.22N 2.13W
78 I11 **Kidira** E Senegal 14.27N 12.18W
192 O11 **Kidnappers, Cape** *headland* North Island, NZ 41.13S 175.15E
102 J8 **Kiel** Schleswig-Holstein, N Germany 54.21N 10.04E
113 L15 **Kielce** *Rus.* Keltsy. Świętokrzyskie, C Poland 50.52N 20.39E
102 K7 **Kieler Bucht** *bay* N Germany
102 J7 **Kieler Förde** *inlet* N Germany
178 K13 **Kiên Đưc** *var.* Đak Lap. Đăc Lăc, S Vietnam 11.59N 107.30E
81 N24 **Kienge** Katanga, SE Dem. Rep. Congo 10.33S 27.33E
195 S12 **Kieta** Bougainville Island, NE PNG 6.13S 155.39E
102 Q12 **Kietz** Brandenburg, NE Germany 52.33N 14.36E
Kiev *see* Kyyiv
Kiev Reservoir *see* Kyyivs'ke Vodoskhovyshche
78 J10 **Kiffa** Assaba, S Mauritania 16.37N 11.22W
117 H19 **Kifisiá** Attikí, C Greece 38.04N 23.49E
117 F18 **Kifisós** ≈ C Greece
145 U5 **Kifrī** N Iraq 34.43N 44.58E
83 D20 **Kigali** ● (Rwanda) C Rwanda 1.58S 30.02E
83 E20 **Kigali** ✕ C Rwanda 1.43S 30.01E
143 P13 **Kiğı** Bingöl, E Turkey 39.19N 40.19E
83 E21 **Kigoma** Kigoma, W Tanzania 4.52S 29.36E
83 E21 **Kigoma** ◆ *region* W Tanzania
40 F10 **Kīhei** *var.* Kihei. Maui, Hawai'i, USA, C Pacific Ocean 20.47N 156.28W
95 K17 **Kihniö** Länsi-Suomi, W Finland 62.10N 23.10E
120 F6 **Kihnu** *var.* Kihnu Saar, *Ger.* Kühnö. *island* SW Estonia
Kihnu Saar *see* Kihnu
40 A8 **Kii Landing** Ni'ihau, Hawai'i, USA, C Pacific Ocean 21.58N 160.03W
95 L14 **Kiiminki** Oulu, C Finland 65.05N 25.46E
171 H16 **Kii-Nagashima** *var.* Nagashima. Mie, Honshū, SW Japan 34.10N 136.18E
171 Gg16 **Kii-sanchi** ▲▲ Honshū, SW Japan
94 L11 **Kiistala** Lappi, N Finland 67.52N 25.19E
170 Ff16 **Kii-suidō** *strait* S Japan
172 R14 **Kikai-shima** *var.* Kikaiga-shima. *island* Nansei-shotō, SW Japan
114 M8 **Kikinda** *Ger.* Grosskikinda, *Hung.* Nagykikinda; *prev.* Velika Kikinda. Serbia, N Serbia and Montenegro (Yugoslavia) 45.48N 20.29E
Kikládhes *see* Kykládes
172 N7 **Kikonai** Hokkaidō, NE Japan 41.40N 140.25E
194 H14 **Kikori** Gulf, S PNG 7.31S 144.16E
194 G13 **Kikori** ≈ W PNG
170 Cc14 **Kikuchi** *var.* Kikuti. Kumamoto, Kyūshū, SW Japan 33.00N 130.49E
Kikuti *see* Kikuchi
131 N8 **Kikvidze** Volgogradskaya Oblast', SW Russian Federation 50.47N 42.58E
12 I10 **Kikwissi, Lac** ◎ Québec, SE Canada
81 I21 **Kikwit** Bandundu, W Dem. Rep. Congo 4.59S 18.53E
97 K15 **Kil** Värmland, C Sweden 59.30N 13.19E
96 N12 **Kilafors** Gävleborg, C Sweden 61.13N 16.34E
40 B8 **Kīlauea** *var.* Kilauea. Kaua'i, Hawai'i, USA, C Pacific Ocean 22.12N 159.24W
40 H12 **Kīlauea Caldera** *var.* Kilauea Caldera *crater* Hawai'i, USA, C Pacific Ocean 19.25N 155.16W
111 V4 **Kilb** Niederösterreich, C Austria 48.06N 15.21E
41 O12 **Kilbuck Mountains** ▲▲ Alaska, USA
169 Y12 **Kilchu** NE North Korea 40.57N 129.22E
99 F18 **Kilcock** *Ir.* Cill Choca. E Ireland 53.25N 6.40W
191 V2 **Kilcoy** Queensland, E Australia 26.58S 152.30E
99 F18 **Kildare** *Ir.* Cill Dara. E Ireland 53.10N 6.55W
99 F18 **Kildare** *Ir.* Cill Dara. *cultural region* E Ireland
128 K2 **Kil'din, Ostrov** *island* NW Russian Federation
27 W7 **Kilgore** Texas, SW USA 32.23N 94.52W
Kilien Mountains *see* Qilian Shan
116 K9 **Kilifarevo** Veliko Tŭrnovo, N Bulgaria 43.00N 25.36E
83 K20 **Kilifi** Coast, SE Kenya 3.37S 39.49E
201 U9 **Kili Island** *var.* Kōle. *island* Ralik Chain, S Marshall Islands
155 V2 **Kilik Pass** *pass* Afghanistan/China 37.03N 74.31E
Kilimane *see* Quelimane
83 I21 **Kilimanjaro** ◆ *region* E Tanzania
83 I20 **Kilimanjaro** *var.* Uhuru Peak. ▲ NE Tanzania 3.01S 37.14E
Kilimbangara *see* Kolombangara
Kilinailau Islands *see* Tulun Islands
83 K23 **Kilindoni** Pwani, E Tanzania 7.55S 39.40E
120 H6 **Kilingi-Nõmme** *Ger.* Kurkund. Pärnumaa, SW Estonia 58.07N 24.00E
142 M17 **Kilis** Kilis, S Turkey 36.43N 37.07E
142 M16 **Kilis** ◆ *province* S Turkey
119 N12 **Kiliya** *Rom.* Chilia-Nouă. Odes'ka Oblast', SW Ukraine 45.29N 29.16E
99 B19 **Kilkee** *Ir.* Cill Chaoi. W Ireland 52.40N 9.37W
99 E19 **Kilkenny** *Ir.* Cill Chainnigh. S Ireland 52.39N 7.15W
99 E19 **Kilkenny** *Ir.* Cill Chainnigh. *cultural region* S Ireland
99 B18 **Kilkieran Bay** *Ir.* Cuan Chill Chiaráin. *bay* W Ireland
116 G13 **Kilkís** Kentrikí Makedonía, N Greece 40.59N 22.54E
99 C15 **Killala Bay** *Ir.* Cuan Chill Ala. *inlet* NW Ireland
9 R15 **Killam** Alberta, SW Canada 52.45N 111.46W
191 U3 **Killarney** Queensland, E Australia 28.18S 152.15E
9 W17 **Killarney** Manitoba, S Canada 49.12N 99.40W
12 E11 **Killarney** Ontario, S Canada 45.58N 81.27W
99 B20 **Killarney** *Ir.* Cill Airne. SW Ireland 52.03N 9.30W
30 K4 **Killdeer** North Dakota, N USA 47.21N 102.45W
30 J4 **Killdeer Mountains** ▲▲ North Dakota, N USA
47 V15 **Killdeer River** ≈ Trinidad, Trinidad and Tobago
27 S9 **Killeen** Texas, SW USA 31.07N 97.43W
41 P6 **Killik River** ≈ Alaska, USA
16 P4 **Killinek Island** *island* Nunavut, NE Canada
Killini *see* Kyllíni
117 C19 **Killínis, Akrotírio** *headland* S Greece 37.55N 21.07E
99 D15 **Killybegs** *Ir.* Na Cealla Beaga. NW Ireland 54.37N 8.27W
Kilmain *see* Quelimane
98 I13 **Kilmarnock** W Scotland, UK 55.37N 4.30W
23 X6 **Kilmarnock** Virginia, NE USA 37.42N 76.22W
129 S16 **Kil'mez'** Kirovskaya Oblast', NW Russian Federation 56.55N 51.03E
131 S2 **Kil'mez'** Udmurtskaya Respublika, NW Russian Federation 57.04N 51.22E
129 R16 **Kil'mez'** ≈ NW Russian Federation
69 V11 **Kilombero** ≈ S Tanzania
94 J10 **Kilpisjarvi** Lappi, N Finland 69.03N 20.49E
99 B19 **Kilrush** *Ir.* Cill Rois. W Ireland 52.39N 9.28W
81 O24 **Kilwa** Katanga, SE Dem. Rep. Congo 9.22S 28.19E
Kilwa *see* Kilwa Kivinje
83 J24 **Kilwa Kivinje** *var.* Kilwa. Lindi, SE Tanzania 8.45S 39.21E
83 J24 **Kilwa Masoko** Lindi, SE Tanzania 8.55S 39.31E
176 Uu11 **Kilwo** Pulau Seram, E Indonesia 3.36S 130.48E
116 P12 **Kilyos** İstanbul, NW Turkey 41.15N 29.01E
39 V8 **Kim** Colorado, C USA 37.12N 103.22W
175 N3 **Kimanis, Teluk** *bay* Sabah, East Malaysia
190 H8 **Kimba** South Australia 33.09S 136.26E
30 I15 **Kimball** Nebraska, C USA 41.16N 103.40W
31 O11 **Kimball** South Dakota, N USA 43.45N 98.57W
81 I21 **Kimbao** Bandundu, SW Dem. Rep. Congo 5.27S 17.40E
195 N12 **Kimbe** New Britain, E PNG 5.36S 150.10E
195 N11 **Kimbe Bay** *inlet* New Britain, E PNG
9 P17 **Kimberley** British Columbia, SW Canada 49.40N 115.58W
85 H23 **Kimberley** Northern Cape, C South Africa 28.45S 24.46E
188 M4 **Kimberley Plateau** *plateau* Western Australia
35 P15 **Kimberly** Idaho, NW USA 42.31N 114.21W
169 Y12 **Kimch'aek** *prev.* Sŏngjin. E North Korea 40.42N 129.12E
169 Y15 **Kimch'ŏn** C South Korea 36.08N 128.06E
169 Z16 **Kim Hae** *var.* Pusan. ✕ (Pusan) SE South Korea 35.10N 128.57E
Kími *see* Kými
95 K20 **Kimito** *Swe.* Kemiö. Länsi-Suomi, W Finland 60.10N 22.45E
172 O6 **Kimobetsu** Hokkaidō, NE Japan 42.47N 140.55E
117 I21 **Kímolos** *island* Kykládes, Greece, Aegean Sea
117 I21 **Kímolou Sífnou, Stenó** *strait* Kykládes, Greece, Aegean Sea
130 L5 **Kimovsk** Tul'skaya Oblast', W Russian Federation 53.59N 38.34E
Kimpolung *see* Câmpulung Moldovenesc
128 K16 **Kimry** Tverskaya Oblast', W Russian Federation 56.52N 37.21E
81 H21 **Kimvula** Bas-Congo, SW Dem. Rep. Congo 5.38S 15.51E
175 Nn2 **Kinabalu, Gunung** ▲ East Malaysia 5.52N 116.08E
Kinabatangan *see* Kinabatangan, Sungai
175 Oo3 **Kinabatangan, Sungai** *var.* Kinabatangan. ≈ East Malaysia
117 L21 **Kínaros** *island* Kykládes, Greece, Aegean Sea
9 O15 **Kinbasket Lake** ▣ British Columbia, SW Canada
98 I7 **Kinbrace** N Scotland, UK 58.16N 2.59W
12 E14 **Kincardine** Ontario, S Canada 44.10N 81.35W
98 K10 **Kincardine** *cultural region* E Scotland, UK
81 K21 **Kinda** Kasai Occidental, SE Dem. Rep. Congo 4.48S 21.49E
81 M24 **Kinda** Katanga, SE Dem. Rep. Congo 9.19S 25.06E
177 Ff3 **Kindat** Sagaing, N Myanmar 23.42N 94.28E
111 V6 **Kindberg** Steiermark, C Austria 47.31N 15.27E
24 H8 **Kinder** Louisiana, S USA 30.29N 92.51W
100 H13 **Kinderdijk** Zuid-Holland, SW Netherlands 51.52N 4.37E
99 M17 **Kinder Scout** ▲ C England, UK 53.25N 1.52W
9 S16 **Kindersley** Saskatchewan, S Canada 51.28N 109.08W
78 I14 **Kindia** Guinée-Maritime, SW Guinea 10.12N 12.26W
66 B11 **Kindley Field** *air base* E Bermuda
31 R6 **Kindred** North Dakota, N USA 46.39N 97.01W
81 N20 **Kindu** *prev.* Kindu-Port-Empain. Maniema, C Dem. Rep. Congo 2.57S 25.54E
Kindu-Port-Empain *see* Kindu
131 S6 **Kinel'** Samarskaya Oblast', W Russian Federation 53.14N 50.40E
129 N15 **Kineshma** Ivanovskaya Oblast', W Russian Federation 57.28N 42.07E
King *see* King William's Town
146 K10 **King Abdul Aziz** ✕ (Makkah) Makkah, W Saudi Arabia 21.44N 39.08E
23 X6 **King and Queen Court House** Virginia, NE USA 37.40N 76.49W
King Charles Islands *see* Kong Karls Land
King Christian IX Land *see* Kong Christian IX Land
King Christian X Land *see* Kong Christian X Land
37 O11 **King City** California, W USA 36.12N 121.09W
29 R2 **King City** Missouri, C USA 40.03N 94.31W
40 M16 **King Cove** Alaska, USA 55.03N 162.19W
28 M10 **Kingfisher** Oklahoma, C USA 35.49N 97.56W
King Frederik VI Coast *see* Kong Frederik VI Kyst
King Frederik VIII Land *see* Kong Frederik VIII Land
67 B24 **King George Bay** *bay* West Falkland, Falkland Islands
204 G3 **King George Island** *var.* King George Land. *island* South Shetland Islands, Antarctica
10 I6 **King George Islands** *island group* Nunavut, C Canada
King George Land *see* King George Island
128 G13 **Kingisepp** Leningradskaya Oblast', NW Russian Federation 59.23N 28.37E
191 N14 **King Island** *island* Tasmania, SE Australia
8 J15 **King Island** *island* British Columbia, SW Canada
King Island *see* Kadan Kyun
Kingissepp *see* Kuressaare
147 Q7 **King Khalid** ✕ (Ar Riyāḍ) Ar Riyāḍ, C Saudi Arabia 25.00N 46.40E
37 S2 **King Lear Peak** ▲ Nevada, W USA 41.13N 118.30W
205 Y8 **King Leopold and Queen Astrid Land** *physical region* Antarctica
188 M4 **King Leopold Ranges** ▲▲ Western Australia
38 I11 **Kingman** Arizona, SW USA 35.12N 114.02W
28 M6 **Kingman** Kansas, C USA 37.39N 98.06W
199 K7 **Kingman Reef** ◇ *US territory* C Pacific Ocean
81 N20 **Kingombe** Maniema, E Dem. Rep. Congo 2.37S 26.39E
190 F5 **Kingoonya** South Australia 30.56S 135.20E
204 J10 **King Peninsula** *peninsula* Antarctica
41 P13 **King Salmon** Alaska, USA 58.41N 156.39W
37 Q6 **Kings Beach** California, W USA 39.13N 120.02W
37 R11 **Kingsburg** California, W USA 36.30N 119.33W
190 I10 **Kingscote** South Australia 35.41S 137.36E
King's County *see* Offaly
204 H2 **King Sejong** *South Korean research station* Antarctica 61.57S 58.23W
191 T9 **Kingsford Smith** ✕ (Sydney) New South Wales, SE Australia 33.58S 151.09E
9 P17 **Kingsgate** British Columbia, SW Canada 48.58N 116.09W
25 W8 **Kingsland** Georgia, SE USA 30.48N 81.41W
31 S13 **Kingsley** Iowa, C USA 42.35N 95.58W
99 O19 **King's Lynn** *var.* Bishop's Lynn, Kings Lynn, Lynn, Lynn Regis. E England, UK 52.45N 0.24E
23 Q10 **Kings Mountain** North Carolina, SE USA 35.15N 81.20W
188 K4 **King Sound** *sound* Western Australia
39 N2 **Kings Peak** ▲ Utah, W USA 40.43N 110.27W
23 O8 **Kingsport** Tennessee, S USA 36.32N 82.31W
37 R11 **Kings River** ≈ California, W USA
191 P17 **Kingston** Tasmania, SE Australia 42.58S 147.18E
12 K14 **Kingston** Ontario, SE Canada 44.13N 76.30W
46 K13 **Kingston** ● (Jamaica) E Jamaica 17.58N 76.48W
193 C22 **Kingston** Otago, South Island, NZ 45.20S 168.45E
21 P12 **Kingston** Massachusetts, NE USA 41.59N 70.43W
29 S3 **Kingston** Missouri, C USA 39.36N 94.02W
20 K12 **Kingston** New York, NE USA 41.55N 74.00W
33 S14 **Kingston** Ohio, N USA 39.28N 82.54W
21 O13 **Kingston** Rhode Island, NE USA 41.28N 71.31W
22 M9 **Kingston** Tennessee, S USA 35.52N 84.30W
37 W12 **Kingston Peak** ▲ California, W USA 35.43N 115.54W
190 J11 **Kingston Southeast** South Australia 36.51S 139.53E
99 N17 **Kingston upon Hull** *var.* Hull. E England, UK 53.45N 0.19W
99 N22 **Kingston upon Thames** SE England, UK 51.25N 0.18W
47 P14 **Kingstown** ● (Saint Vincent and the Grenadines) Saint Vincent, Saint Vincent and the Grenadines 13.09N 61.13W
Kingstown *see* Dún Laoghaire
23 T13 **Kingstree** South Carolina, SE USA 33.40N 79.49W
66 L8 **Kings Trough** *undersea feature* E Atlantic Ocean
12 C18 **Kingsville** Ontario, S Canada 42.03N 82.43W
27 S15 **Kingsville** Texas, SW USA 27.31N 97.52W
23 W6 **King William** Virginia, NE USA 37.42N 77.03W
15 K3 **King William Island** *island* Nunavut, N Canada Arctic Ocean
85 I25 **King William's Town** *var.* King, Kingwilliamstown. Eastern Cape, S South Africa 32.51S 27.20E
23 T3 **Kingwood** West Virginia, NE USA 39.28N 79.40W
142 C13 **Kınık** İzmir, W Turkey 39.04N 27.25E
81 G21 **Kinkala** Le Pool, S Congo 4.18S 14.49E
171 Mm14 **Kinka-san** *headland* Honshū, C Japan 38.17N 141.34E
192 M8 **Kinleith** Waikato, North Island, NZ 38.16S 175.53E
97 J19 **Kinna** Västra Götaland, S Sweden 57.31N 12.42E
98 L8 **Kinnaird Head** *var.* Kinnairds Head. *headland* NE Scotland, UK 58.39N 3.22W
97 K20 **Kinnared** Halland, S Sweden 57.01N 13.04E
Kinneret, Yam *see* Tiberias, Lake
161 K24 **Kinniyai** Eastern Province, NE Sri Lanka 8.30N 81.10E
95 L16 **Kinnula** Länsi-Suomi, W Finland 63.24N 25.00E
12 I8 **Kinojévis** ≈ Québec, SE Canada
170 G16 **Kino-kawa** ≈ Honshū, SW Japan
9 U11 **Kinoosao** Saskatchewan, C Canada 57.06N 101.01W
101 L17 **Kinrooi** Limburg, NE Belgium 51.09N 5.47E
98 J11 **Kinross** C Scotland, UK 56.13N 3.26W
98 J11 **Kinross** *cultural region* C Scotland, UK
99 C21 **Kinsale** *Ir.* Cionn tSáile. SW Ireland 51.42N 8.31W
97 D14 **Kinsarvik** Hordaland, S Norway 60.22N 6.43E
81 G21 **Kinshasa** *prev.* Léopoldville. ● (Zaire) Kinshasa, W Dem. Rep. Congo 4.21S 15.16E
81 G21 **Kinshasa** *off.* Ville de Kinshasa, *var.* Kinshasa City. ◆ *region* SW Dem. Rep. Congo
81 G21 **Kinshasa** ✕ Kinshasa, SW Dem. Rep. Congo 4.23S 15.30E
Kinshasa City *see* Kinshasa
119 U9 **Kins'ka** ≈ SE Ukraine
28 K6 **Kinsley** Kansas, C USA 37.52N 99.25W
23 W10 **Kinston** North Carolina, SE USA 35.15N 77.34W
79 P15 **Kintampo** W Ghana 6.36N 0.28E
190 B1 **Kintore, Mount** ▲ South Australia 26.30S 130.24E
98 G13 **Kintyre** *peninsula* W Scotland, UK
98 G13 **Kintyre, Mull of** *headland* W Scotland, UK 55.16N 5.46W
177 G4 **Kin-u** Sagaing, C Myanmar 22.46N 95.36E
10 G8 **Kinushseo** ≈ Ontario, C Canada
9 P13 **Kinuso** Alberta, W Canada 55.19N 115.23W
160 I13 **Kinwat** Mahārāshtra, C India 19.37N 78.12E
83 F16 **Kinyeti** ▲ S Sudan 3.56N 32.52E
103 I17 **Kinzig** ≈ SW Germany
197 J13 **Kioa** *island* N Fiji
Kioga, Lake *see* Kyoga, Lake
28 M8 **Kiowa** Kansas, C USA 37.01N 98.29W
29 P12 **Kiowa** Oklahoma, C USA 34.43N 95.54W
Kiparissía *see* Kyparissía
12 H10 **Kipawa, Lac** ◎ Québec, SE Canada
83 G24 **Kipengere Range** ▲▲ SW Tanzania
83 E23 **Kipili** Rukwa, W Tanzania 7.30S 30.39E
83 K20 **Kipini** Coast, SE Kenya 2.30S 40.30E
9 V16 **Kipling** Saskatchewan, S Canada 50.04N 102.45W
40 M13 **Kipnuk** Alaska, USA 59.56N 164.02W
99 F18 **Kippure** *Ir.* Cipiúr. ▲ E Ireland 53.10N 6.22W
81 N25 **Kipushi** Katanga, SE Dem. Rep. Congo 11.45S 27.19E
195 Y17 **Kirakira** *var.* Kaokaona. San Cristobal, SE Solomon Islands 10.28S 161.54E
161 K14 **Kirandul** *var.* Bailādila. Chhattīsgarh, C India 18.46N 81.18E
161 I21 **Kīranūr** Tamil Nādu, SE India 11.37N 79.10E
121 N21 **Kiraw** *Rus.* Kirovo. Homyel'skaya Voblasts', SE Belarus 51.30N 29.25E
121 M17 **Kirawsk** *Rus.* Kirovsk; *prev.* Startsy. Mahilyowskaya Voblasts', E Belarus 53.16N 29.28E
120 F5 **Kirbla** Läänemaa, W Estonia 58.45N 23.57E
27 Y9 **Kirbyville** Texas, SW USA 30.39N 93.53W
116 M12 **Kırcasalih** Edirne, NW Turkey 41.24N 26.48E
111 W8 **Kirchbach** *var.* Kirchbach in Steiermark. Steiermark, SE Austria 46.55N 15.40E
Kirchbach in Steiermark *see* Kirchbach
110 H7 **Kirchberg** Sankt Gallen, NE Switzerland 47.24N 9.03E
111 S5 **Kirchdorf an der Krems** Oberösterreich, N Austria 47.54N 14.06E
Kirchheim *see* Kirchheim unter Teck
103 I22 **Kirchheim unter Teck** *var.* Kirchheim. Baden-Württemberg, SW Germany 48.39N 9.27E
Kirdzhali *see* Kŭrdzhali
126 Jj14 **Kirenga** ≈ S Russian Federation
126 Jj13 **Kirensk** Irkutskaya Oblast', C Russian Federation 57.37N 107.54E
Kirghizia *see* Kyrgyzstan
151 S16 **Kirghiz Range** *Rus.* Kirgizskiy Khrebet; *prev.* Alexander Range. ▲▲ Kazakhstan/Kyrgyzstan
Kirghiz SSR *see* Kyrgyzstan
Kirghiz Steppe *see* Kazakhskiy Melkosopochnik
Kirgizskaya SSR *see* Kyrgyzstan
Kirgizskiy Khrebet *see* Kirghiz Range
81 I19 **Kiri** Bandundu, W Dem. Rep. Congo 1.29S 19.00E
Kiriath-Arba *see* Hebron
203 R3 **Kiribati** *off.* Republic of Kiribati. ◆ *republic* C Pacific Ocean
142 L17 **Kırıkhan** Hatay, S Turkey 36.30N 36.19E
142 I13 **Kırıkkale** Kırıkkale, C Turkey 39.50N 33.31E
142 C10 **Kırıkkale** ◆ *province* C Turkey
128 L13 **Kirillov** Vologodskaya Oblast', NW Russian Federation 59.52N 38.24E
Kirin *see* Jilin
83 I18 **Kirinyaga** *prev.* Mount Kenya. ☒ C Kenya 0.02S 37.19E
128 H13 **Kirishi** *var.* Kirisi. Leningradskaya Oblast', NW Russian Federation 59.28N 32.02E
170 C16 **Kirishima-yama** ▲ Kyūshū, SW Japan 31.58N 130.51E
Kirisi *see* Kirishi
203 Y2 **Kiritimati** ✕ Kiritimati, E Kiribati 2.00N 157.30W
203 Y2 **Kiritimati** *prev.* Christmas Island. *atoll* Line Islands, E Kiribati
195 O15 **Kiriwina Island** *Eng.* Trobriand Island. *island* SE PNG
195 O15 **Kiriwina Islands** *var.* Trobriand Islands. *island group* S PNG
98 K12 **Kirkcaldy** E Scotland, UK 56.07N 3.10W
99 I14 **Kirkcudbright** S Scotland, UK 54.49N 4.03W
99 I14 **Kirkcudbright** *cultural region* S Scotland, UK
Kirkee *see* Khadki
94 M8 **Kirkenes** *Fin.* Kirkkoniemi. Finnmark, N Norway 69.43N 30.01E
97 I14 **Kirkenær** Hedmark, S Norway 60.27N 12.04E
94 J4 **Kirkjubæjarklaustur** Sudhurland, S Iceland 63.46N 18.03W
Kirk-Kilissa *see* Kırklareli
Kirkkoniemi *see* Kirkenes
95 L20 **Kirkkonummi** *Swe.* Kyrkslätt. Etelä-Suomi, S Finland 60.06N 24.25E
12 G7 **Kirkland Lake** Ontario, S Canada 48.10N 80.01W
142 C9 **Kırklareli** *prev.* Kirk-Kilissa. Kırklareli, NW Turkey 41.45N 27.12E
142 I13 **Kırklareli** ◆ *province* NW Turkey
193 F20 **Kirkliston Range** ▲▲ South Island, NZ
12 D10 **Kirkpatrick Lake** ◎ Ontario, S Canada
205 Q11 **Kirkpatrick, Mount** ▲ Antarctica 84.37S 164.36E
29 U2 **Kirksville** Missouri, C USA 40.11N 92.34W
145 T4 **Kirkūk** *var.* Karkūk, Kerkuk. N Iraq 35.28N 44.25E
145 U7 **Kir Kush** E Iraq 33.42N 45.15E
98 K5 **Kirkwall** NE Scotland, UK
85 H25 **Kirkwood** Eastern Cape, S South Africa 33.23S 25.19E
29 X5 **Kirkwood** Missouri, C USA 38.34N 90.24W
Kirman *see* Kermān
Kir Moab/Kir of Moab *see* Al Karak
130 I5 **Kirov** Kaluzhskaya Oblast', W Russian Federation 54.01N 34.16E
129 R14 **Kirov** *prev.* Vyatka. Kirovskaya Oblast', NW Russian Federation 58.34N 49.38E
Kīrov *see* Balpyk Bi, Kazakhstan
Kīrov/Kirova *see* Kopbirlik, Kazakhstan
Kirovabad *see* Gäncä, Azerbaijan
Kirovabad *see* Panj, Tajikistan
Kirovakan *see* Vanadzor
Kirovo *see* Kiraw, Belarus
Kirovo/Kirovograd *see* Kirovohrad, Ukraine
Kirovo *see* Beshariq, Uzbekistan
129 R14 **Kirovo-Chepetsk** Kirovskaya Oblast', NW Russian Federation 58.33N 50.06E
Kirovogradskaya Oblast'/Kirovohrad *see* Kirovohrads'ka Oblast'
119 R7 **Kirovohrad** *Rus.* Kirovograd; *prev.* Kirovo, Yelizavetgrad, Zinov'yevsk. Kirovohrads'ka Oblast', C Ukraine 48.30N 31.17E
119 P7 **Kirovohrads'ka Oblast'** *var.* Kirovohrad, *Rus.* Kirovogradskaya Oblast'. ◆ *province* C Ukraine
128 J4 **Kirovsk** Murmanskaya Oblast', NW Russian Federation 67.37N 33.38E
Kirovsk *see* Babadaýhan, Turkmenistan
Kirovsk *see* Kirawsk, Belarus
119 X7 **Kirovs'k** Luhans'ka Oblast', E Ukraine 48.40N 38.39E
125 Dd9 **Kirovskaya Oblast'** ◆ *province* NW Russian Federation
119 X8 **Kirov'ske** Donets'ka Oblast', E Ukraine 48.12N 38.19E
119 U13 **Kirovs'ke** *Rus.* Kirovskoye. Respublika Krym, S Ukraine 45.13N 35.12E
Kirovskiy *see* Balpyk Bi/Ust'yevoye
Kirovskoye *see* Kyzyl-Adyr
Kirovskoye *see* Kirovs'ke
124 Oo2 **Kırpaşa** *var.* Karpas Peninsula, *Gk.* Karpasía. *peninsula* NE Cyprus
152 E11 **Kirpili** Ahal Welaýaty, C Turkmenistan 39.31N 57.13E
98 K10 **Kirriemuir** E Scotland, UK 56.37N 3.00W
129 S13 **Kirs** Kirovskaya Oblast', NW Russian Federation 59.22N 52.20E
131 N7 **Kirsanov** Tambovskaya Oblast', W Russian Federation 52.40N 42.48E
142 J14 **Kırşehir** *anc.* Justinianopolis. Kırşehir, C Turkey 39.09N 34.07E
142 I13 **Kırşehir** ◆ *province* C Turkey
155 P4 **Kīrthar Range** ▲▲ S Pakistan
39 P9 **Kirtland** New Mexico, SW USA 36.43N 108.21W
Kirun/Kirun' *see* Chilung
94 J11 **Kiruna** *Lapp.* Giron. Norrbotten, N Sweden 67.50N 20.16E
81 M18 **Kirundu** Orientale, NE Dem. Rep. Congo 0.45S 25.28E
28 L3 **Kirwin Reservoir** ▣ Kansas, C USA
131 Q4 **Kirya** Chavash Respubliki, W Russian Federation 55.04N 46.50E
Kiryat Gat *see* Qiryat Gat
171 K15 **Kiryū** Gunma, Honshū, S Japan 36.24N 139.19E
97 M18 **Kisa** Östergötland, S Sweden 58.00N 15.39E
171 Ll11 **Kisakata** Akita, Honshū, C Japan 39.12N 139.55E
Kisalföld *see* Little Alföld
81 L18 **Kisangani** *prev.* Stanleyville. Orientale, NE Dem. Rep. Congo 0.30N 25.13E
41 N12 **Kisaralik River** ≈ Alaska, USA
171 K17 **Kisarazu** Chiba, Honshū, S Japan 35.19N 139.51E
113 I22 **Kisbér** Komárom-Esztergom, NW Hungary 47.30N 18.00E
9 V17 **Kisbey** Saskatchewan, S Canada 49.41N 102.39W
126 H14 **Kiselevsk** Kemerovskaya Oblast', S Russian Federation 54.00N 86.38E
159 R13 **Kishanganj** Bihār, NE India 26.06N 87.57E
158 G12 **Kishangarh** Rājasthān, N India 26.33N 74.52E
Kishegyes *see* Mali Iđoš
79 S15 **Kishi** Oyo, W Nigeria 9.01N 3.53E
Kishinev *see* Chişinău
Kishiözen *see* Malyy Uzen'
171 Gg15 **Kishiwada** *var.* Kisiwada. Ōsaka, Honshū, SW Japan 34.28N 135.22E
149 P14 **Kīsh, Jazīreh-ye** *var.* Qeys. *island* S Iran
151 R7 **Kishkenekol'** *prev.* Kzyltu. *Kaz.* Qyzyltu; Severnyy Kazakhstan, N Kazakhstan 53.39N 72.22E
158 I6 **Kishtwār** Jammu and Kashmir, NW India 33.19N 75.49E
83 H19 **Kisii** Nyanza, SW Kenya 0.40S 34.46E
83 J23 **Kisiju** Pwani, E Tanzania 7.25S 39.19E
Kisiwada *see* Kishiwada
Kisjenő *see* Chişineu-Criş
40 E17 **Kiska Island** *island* Aleutian Islands, Alaska, USA
Kiskapus *see* Copşa Mică
113 M22 **Kiskörei-víztároló** ▣ E Hungary
Kis-Küküllo *see* Târnava Mică
113 L24 **Kiskunfélegyháza** *var.* Félegyháza. Bács-Kiskun, C Hungary 46.42N 19.52E
113 K25 **Kiskunhalas** *var.* Halas. Bács-Kiskun, S Hungary 46.25N 19.28E
113 K24 **Kiskunmajsa** Bács-Kiskun, S Hungary 46.31N 19.45E
131 N15 **Kislovodsk** Stavropol'skiy Kray, SW Russian Federation 43.55N 42.44E
83 L18 **Kismaayo** *var.* Chisimayu, Kismayu, *It.* Chisimaio. Jubbada Hoose, S Somalia 0.04S 42.34E
Kismayu *see* Kismaayo
171 Ii15 **Kiso-sanmyaku** ▲▲ Honshū, S Japan
Kisseraing *see* Kanmaw Kyun
78 K14 **Kissidougou** Guinée-Forestière, S Guinea 9.15N 10.07W
25 X12 **Kissimmee** Florida, SE USA 28.17N 81.24W
25 X12 **Kissimmee, Lake** ◎ Florida, SE USA
25 X13 **Kissimmee River** ≈ Florida, SE USA
9 V13 **Kississing Lake** ◎ Manitoba, C Canada
113 L24 **Kistelek** Csongrád, SE Hungary 46.27N 19.58E
Kistna *see* Krishna
113 M23 **Kisújszállás** Jász-Nagykun-Szolnok, E Hungary 47.13N 20.43E
170 F12 **Kisuki** Shimane, Honshū, SW Japan 35.25N 133.15E
83 H18 **Kisumu** *prev.* Port Florence. Nyanza, W Kenya 0.02N 34.42E
Kisutzaneustadtl *see* Kysucké Nové Mesto
113 O20 **Kisvárda** *Ger.* Kleinwardein. Szabolcs-Szatmár-Bereg, E Hungary 48.13N 22.03E
83 J24 **Kiswere** Lindi, SE Tanzania 9.24S 39.37E
Kiszucaújhely *see* Kysucké Nové Mesto
78 K12 **Kita** Kayes, W Mali 13.04N 9.29W

◆ Country
● Country Capital
◇ Dependent Territory
○ Dependent Territory Capital
◆ Administrative Region
✕ International Airport
▲ Mountain
▲▲ Mountain Range
☒ Volcano
≈ River
◎ Lake
▣ Reservoir

KITAA – KOMSOMOLOBOD

207 N14 **Kitaa** ◆ *province* W Greenland
Kitab *see* Kitob
172 *N5* **Kitahiyama** Hokkaidō, NE Japan *42.25N 139.55E*
171 *L15* **Kita-Ibaraki** Ibaraki, Honshū, S Japan *36.48N 140.43E*
172 *Ss17* **Kita-Iō-jima** ***Eng.*** San Alessandro. *island* SE Japan
171 *Mm11* **Kitakami** Iwate, Honshū, C Japan *39.16N 141.06E*
171 *M13* **Kitakami-gawa** ≈ Honshū, C Japan
172 *N11* **Kitakami-sanchi** ▲▲ Honshū, C Japan
171 *L13* **Kitakata** Fukushima, Honshū, C Japan *37.38N 139.51E*
170 *D12* **Kitakyūshū** ***var.*** Kitakyûsyû. Fukuoka, Kyūshū, SW Japan *33.51N 130.49E*
Kitakyûsyû *see* Kitakyūshū
83 *H18* **Kitale** Rift Valley, W Kenya *1.01N 35.01E*
172 *Q5* **Kitami** Hokkaidō, NE Japan *43.51N 143.50E*
172 *Pp4* **Kitami-sanchi** ▲▲ Hokkaidō, NE Japan
171 *Kk17* **Kita-ura** ◎ Honshū, S Japan
195 *O15* **Kitava Island** *island* Kiriwina Islands, SE PNG
39 *W5* **Kit Carson** Colorado, C USA *38.45N 102.47W*
188 *M12* **Kitchener** Western Australia *31.03S 124.00E*
12 *F16* **Kitchener** Ontario, S Canada *43.28N 80.27W*
95 *O17* **Kitee** Itä-Suomi, E Finland *62.06N 30.09E*
83 *G16* **Kitgum** N Uganda *3.16N 32.54E*
Kithareng *see* Kanmaw Kyun
Kíthira *see* Kýthira
Kíthnos *see* Kýthnos
8 *J13* **Kitimat** British Columbia, SW Canada *54.04N 128.37W*
94 *L11* **Kitinen** ≈ N Finland
153 *N12* **Kitob** ***Rus.*** Kitab. Qashqadaryo Viloyati, S Uzbekistan *39.06N 66.46E*
118 *K7* **Kitsman'** ***Ger.*** Kotzman, ***Rom.*** Cozmeni, ***Rus.*** Kitsman. Chernivets'ka Oblast', W Ukraine *48.27N 25.46E*
170 *Dd14* **Kitsuki** ***var.*** Kituki. Ōita, Kyūshū, SW Japan *33.25N 131.37E*
20 *C14* **Kittanning** Pennsylvania, NE USA *40.48N 79.28W*
21 *P10* **Kittery** Maine, NE USA *43.05N 70.44W*
94 *L11* **Kittilä** Lappi, N Finland *67.39N 24.52E*
111 *Z4* **Kittsee** Burgenland, E Austria *48.05N 17.05E*
83 *J19* **Kitui** Eastern, S Kenya *1.25S 38.00E*
Kituki *see* Kitsuki
83 *G22* **Kitunda** Tabora, C Tanzania *6.47S 33.13E*
8 *K13* **Kitwanga** British Columbia, SW Canada *55.07N 128.03W*
84 *J13* **Kitwe** ***var.*** Kitwe-Nkana. Copperbelt, C Zambia *12.48S 28.13E*
Kitwe-Nkana *see* Kitwe
111 *O7* **Kitzbühel** Tirol, W Austria *47.27N 12.22E*
111 *O7* **Kitzbüheler Alpen** ▲▲ W Austria
103 *J19* **Kitzingen** Bayern, SE Germany *49.43N 10.10E*
159 *Q14* **Kiul** Bihār, NE India *25.10N 86.06E*
194 *E12* **Kiunga** Western, SW PNG *6.06S 141.12E*
95 *M16* **Kiuruvesi** Itä-Suomi, C Finland *63.37N 26.40E*
40 *M7* **Kivalina** Alaska, USA *67.43N 164.31W*
94 *L13* **Kivalo** *ridge* C Finland
118 *J3* **Kivertsi** ***Pol.*** Kiwerce, ***Rus.*** Kivertsy. Volyns'ka Oblast', NW Ukraine *50.49N 25.31E*
Kivertsy *see* Kivertsi
95 *L16* **Kivijärvi** Länsi-Suomi, W Finland *63.09N 25.04E*
97 *L23* **Kivik** Skåne, S Sweden *55.40N 14.15E*
120 *J3* **Kiviõli** Ida-Virumaa, NE Estonia *59.20N 27.00E*
Kivu, Lac *see* Kivu, Lake
69 *U10* **Kivu, Lake** ***Fr.*** Lac Kivu. ◎ Rwanda/Dem. Rep. Congo
194 *G15* **Kiwai Island** *island* SW PNG
41 *N8* **Kiwalik** Alaska, USA *66.01N 161.50W*
Kiwerce *see* Kivertsi
Kiyev *see* Kyyiv
151 *R10* **Kiyevka** Karaganda, C Kazakhstan *50.15N 71.33E*
Kiyevskaya Oblast' *see* Kyyivs'ka Oblast'
Kiyevskoye Vodokhranilishche *see* Kyyivs'ke Vodoskhovyshche
142 *D10* **Kıyıköy** Kırklareli, NW Turkey *41.37N 28.07E*
151 *O9* **Kiyma** Akmola, C Kazakhstan *51.37N 67.31E*
129 *V13* **Kizel** Permskaya Oblast', NW Russian Federation *58.59N 57.37E*
129 *O12* **Kizema** ***var.*** Kizëma. Arkhangel'skaya Oblast', NW Russian Federation *61.06N 44.51E*
Kizilagach *see* Elkhovo
142 *H12* **Kızılcahamam** Ankara, N Turkey *40.28N 32.37E*
142 *J10* **Kızıl Irmak** ≈ C Turkey
Kızılkoca *see* Şefaatli
Kizil Kum *see* Kyzyl Kum
143 *P16* **Kızıltepe** Mardin, SE Turkey *37.12N 40.36E*
Ki Zil Uzen *see* Qezel Owzan, Rūd-e
131 *Q16* **Kizilyurt** Respublika Dagestan, SW Russian Federation *43.13N 46.54E*
131 *Q15* **Kizlyar** Respublika Dagestan, SW Russian Federation *43.51N 46.39E*
131 *S3* **Kizner** Udmurtskaya Respublika, NW Russian Federation *56.19N 51.37E*
Kizyl-Arvat *see* Serdar
Kizyl-Atrek *see* Etrek
Kizyl-Kaya *see* Gyzylgaya
Kizyl-Su *see* Gyzylsuw
97 *H16* **Kjerkøy** *island* S Norway
Kjølen *see* Kölen
94 *L7* **Kjøllefjord** Finnmark, N Norway *70.55N 27.19E*
94 *H11* **Kjøpsvik** Nordland, C Norway *68.07N 16.22E*
174 *Ii9* **Klabat, Teluk** *bay* Pulau Bangka, W Indonesia
114 *I12* **Kladanj** Federacija Bosan I Hercegovina, C Bosnia and Herzegovina *44.14N 18.42E*
176 *Xx16* **Kladar** Papua, E Indonesia *8.14S 137.46E*
113 *C16* **Kladno** Středočeský Kraj, NW Czech Republic *50.10N 14.04E*
114 *P11* **Kladovo** Serbia, E Serbia and Montenegro (Yugoslavia) *44.37N 22.36E*
178 *Hh12* **Klaeng** Rayong, S Thailand *12.48N 101.41E*
111 *T9* **Klagenfurt** ***Slvn.*** Celovec. Kärnten, S Austria *46.37N 14.19E*
120 *B11* **Klaipėda** ***Ger.*** Memel. Klaipėda, NW Lithuania *55.42N 21.09E*
120 *C11* **Klaipėda** ◆ *province* W Lithuania
174 *M15* **Klakah** Jawa, C Indonesia *7.55S 113.12E*
97 *B18* **Klaksvík** ***Dan.*** Klaksvig Faeroe Islands *62.13N 6.43W*
36 *L2* **Klamath** California, W USA *41.31N 124.02W*
34 *H16* **Klamath Falls** Oregon, NW USA *42.13N 121.46W*
36 *M1* **Klamath Mountains** ▲▲ California/Oregon, W USA
36 *L2* **Klamath River** ≈ California/Oregon, W USA
174 *Gg5* **Klang** ***var.*** Kelang; ***prev.*** Port Swettenham. Selangor, Peninsular Malaysia *3.01N 101.27E*
96 *J13* **Klarälven** ≈ Norway/Sweden
113 *B15* **Klášterec nad Ohří** ***Ger.*** Klösterle an der Eger. Ústecký Kraj, NW Czech Republic *50.24N 13.10E*
174 *L15* **Klaten** Jawa, C Indonesia *7.40S 110.31E*
113 *B18* **Klatovy** ***Ger.*** Klattau. Plzeňský Kraj, W Czech Republic *49.24N 13.16E*
Klattau *see* Klatovy
Klausenburg *see* Cluj-Napoca
41 *Y14* **Klawock** Prince of Wales Island, Alaska, USA *55.33N 133.06W*
100 *P8* **Klazienaveen** Drenthe, NE Netherlands *52.43N 7.00E*
Kleck *see* Klyetsk
112 *H11* **Kłecko** Wielkolpolskie, C Poland *52.37N 17.27E*
112 *I11* **Kleczew** Wielkopolskie, C Poland *52.22N 18.12E*
8 *L15* **Kleena Kleene** British Columbia, SW Canada *51.55N 124.54W*
85 *D20* **Klein Aub** Hardap, C Namibia *23.48S 16.39E*
Kleine Donau *see* Mosoni-Duna
103 *O14* **Kleine Elster** ≈ E Germany
Kleine Kokel *see* Târnava Mică
101 *I16* **Kleine Nete** ≈ N Belgium
Kleines Ungarisches Tiefland *see* Little Alföld
85 *E22* **Klein Karas** Karas, S Namibia *27.37S 18.05E*
Kleinkopisch *see* Copşa Mică
Klein-Marien *see* Väike-Maarja
Kleinschlatten *see* Zlatna
85 *D23* **Kleinsee** Northern Cape, W South Africa *29.43S 17.03E*
Kleinwardein *see* Kisvárda
117 *C16* **Kleisoúra** Ípeiros, W Greece *39.21N 20.52E*
97 *C17* **Klepp** Rogaland, S Norway *58.46N 5.39E*
85 *I22* **Klerksdorp** North-West, N South Africa *26.52S 26.39E*
130 *I5* **Kletnya** Bryanskaya Oblast', W Russian Federation *53.25N 32.58E*
Kletsk *see* Klyetsk
103 *D14* **Kleve** ***Eng.*** Cleves, ***Fr.*** Clèves; ***prev.*** Cleve. Nordrhein-Westfalen, W Germany *51.46N 6.07E*
115 *J16* **Kličevo** Montenegro, SW Serbia and Montenegro (Yugoslavia) *42.45N 18.58E*
121 *M16* **Klichaw** ***Rus.*** Klichev. Mahilyowskaya Voblasts', E Belarus *53.28N 29.21E*
Klichev *see* Klichaw
121 *Q16* **Klimavichy** ***Rus.*** Klimovichi. Mahilyowskaya Voblasts', E Belarus *53.37N 31.58E*
116 *M7* **Kliment** Shumen, NE Bulgaria *43.37N 27.00E*
Klimovichi *see* Klimavichy
95 *G14* **Klimpfjäll** Västerbotten, N Sweden *65.04N 14.49E*
130 *K3* **Klin** Moskovskaya Oblast', W Russian Federation *56.19N 36.45E*
115 *M16* **Klina** Serbia, S Serbia and Montenegro (Yugoslavia) *42.38N 20.35E*
113 *B15* **Klínovec** ***Ger.*** Keilberg. ▲ NW Czech Republic *50.23N 12.57E*
97 *P19* **Klintehamn** Gotland, SE Sweden *57.22N 18.15E*
131 *R8* **Klintsovka** Saratovskaya Oblast', W Russian Federation *51.42N 49.17E*
130 *H6* **Klintsy** Bryanskaya Oblast', W Russian Federation *52.46N 32.20E*
97 *K22* **Klippan** Skåne, S Sweden *56.07N 13.10E*
94 *G13* **Klippen** Västerbotten, N Sweden *65.50N 15.07E*
124 *Nn3* **Klírou** W Cyprus *35.01N 33.11E*
116 *I9* **Klisura** Plovdiv, C Bulgaria *42.42N 24.28E*
97 *F20* **Klitmøller** Viborg, NW Denmark *57.01N 8.29E*
114 *F11* **Ključ** Federacija Bosna I Hercegovina, NW Bosnia and Herzegovina *44.32N 16.46E*
113 *J14* **Kłobuck** Śląskie, S Poland *50.55N 18.54E*
112 *J11* **Kłodawa** Wielkopolskie, C Poland *52.14N 18.55E*
113 *G16* **Kłodzko** ***Ger.*** Glatz. Dolnośląskie, SW Poland *50.27N 16.37E*
97 *I14* **Kløfta** Akershus, S Norway *60.04N 11.09E*
114 *P12* **Klokočevac** Serbia, E Serbia and Montenegro (Yugoslavia) *44.19N 22.11E*
120 *G3* **Klooga** ***Ger.*** Lodensee. Harjumaa, NW Estonia *59.18N 24.15E*
101 *F15* **Kloosterzande** Zeeland, SW Netherlands *51.22N 4.01E*
115 *L19* **Klos** ***var.*** Klosi. Dibër, C Albania *41.30N 20.07E*
Klosi *see* Klos
Klösterle an der Eger *see* Klášterec nad Ohří
111 *X3* **Klosterneuburg** Niederösterreich, NE Austria *48.19N 16.19E*
110 *J9* **Klosters** Graubünden, SE Switzerland *46.54N 9.52E*
110 *G7* **Kloten** Zürich, N Switzerland *47.27N 8.34E*
110 *G7* **Kloten** ✕ (Zürich) Zürich, N Switzerland *47.25N 8.36E*
102 *K12* **Klötze** Sachsen-Anhalt, C Germany *52.37N 11.09E*
10 *K3* **Klotz, Lac** ◎ Québec, NE Canada
103 *O15* **Klotzsche** ✕ (Dresden) Sachsen, E Germany *51.06N 13.44E*
8 *H7* **Kluane Lake** ◎ Yukon Territory, W Canada
Kluang *see* Keluang
113 *I14* **Kluczbork** ***Ger.*** Kreuzburg, Kreuzburg in Oberschlesien. Opolskie, S Poland *50.59N 18.13E*
41 *W12* **Klukwan** Alaska, USA *59.24N 135.49W*
Klyastitsy *see* Klyastsitsy
120 *L11* **Klyastsitsy** ***Rus.*** Klyastitsy. Vitsyebskaya Voblasts', N Belarus *55.54N 28.38E*
131 *T5* **Klyavlino** Samarskaya Oblast', W Russian Federation *54.21N 52.12E*
86 *K9* **Klyaz'in** ≈ W Russian Federation
131 *N3* **Klyaz'ma** ≈ W Russian Federation
121 *J17* **Klyetsk** ***Pol.*** Kleck, ***Rus.*** Kletsk. Minskaya Voblasts', SW Belarus *53.04N 26.38E*
153 *S8* **Klyuchevka** Talasskaya Oblast', NW Kyrgyzstan *42.33N 71.45E*
127 *Pp10* **Klyuchevskaya Sopka, Vulkan** ⩚ E Russian Federation *56.03N 160.37E*
127 *Pp10* **Klyuchi** Kamchatskaya Oblast', E Russian Federation *56.18N 160.44E*
97 *D17* **Knaben** Vest-Agder, S Norway *58.46N 7.04E*
Knanzi *see* Ghanzi
97 *K21* **Knäred** Halland, S Sweden *56.30N 13.21E*
99 *M16* **Knaresborough** N England, UK *54.01N 1.35W*
116 *H8* **Knezha** Vratsa , NW Bulgaria *43.29N 24.04E*
27 *O9* **Knickerbocker** Texas, SW USA *31.18N 100.35W*
30 *K5* **Knife River** ≈ North Dakota, N USA
8 *K16* **Knight Inlet** *inlet* British Columbia, W Canada
41 *S12* **Knight Island** *island* Alaska, USA
99 *K20* **Knighton** E Wales, UK *52.20N 3.00W*
37 *O7* **Knights Landing** California, W USA *38.47N 121.43W*
114 *E13* **Knin** Šibenik-Knin, S Croatia *44.03N 16.12E*
27 *Q12* **Knippal** Texas, SW USA
111 *U7* **Knittelfeld** Steiermark, C Austria *47.13N 14.51E*
97 *O15* **Knivsta** Uppsala, C Sweden *59.43N 17.49E*
115 *P14* **Knjaževac** Serbia, E Serbia and Montenegro (Yugoslavia) *43.34N 22.16E*
29 *S4* **Knob Noster** Missouri, C USA *38.47N 93.33W*
101 *D15* **Knokke-Heist** West-Vlaanderen, NW Belgium *51.21N 3.19E*
97 *H20* **Knøsen** *hill* N Denmark *57.09N 10.15E*
Knosós *see* Knossos
117 *J25* **Knossos** ***Gk.*** Knosós. *prehistoric site* Kríti, Greece, E Mediterranean Sea *35.17N 25.10E*
27 *N7* **Knott** Texas, SW USA *32.21N 101.35W*
204 *K5* **Knowles, Cape** *headland* Antarctica *71.45S 60.19W*
33 *O11* **Knox** Indiana, N USA *41.16N 86.37W*
31 *O3* **Knox** North Dakota, N USA *48.19N 99.43W*
20 *C13* **Knox** Pennsylvania, NE USA *41.13N 79.33W*
201 *X8* **Knox Atoll** ***var.*** Ṇadikdik, Narikrik. *atoll* Ratak Chain, SE Marshall Islands
8 *H13* **Knox, Cape** *headland* Graham Island, British Columbia, SW Canada *54.05N 133.02W*
27 *P5* **Knox City** Texas, SW USA *33.25N 99.49W*
205 *Y11* **Knox Coast** *physical region* Antarctica
33 *T12* **Knox Lake** ▣ Ohio, N USA
25 *T5* **Knoxville** Georgia, SE USA *32.44N 83.58W*
32 *K12* **Knoxville** Illinois, N USA *40.54N 90.16W*
31 *W15* **Knoxville** Iowa, C USA *41.19N 93.06W*
23 *N9* **Knoxville** Tennessee, S USA *35.57N 83.55W*
207 *P11* **Knud Rasmussen Land** *physical region* N Greenland
Knüll *see* Knüllgebirge
103 *I16* **Knüllgebirge** ***var.*** Knüll. ▲▲ C Germany
Knyazhevo *see* Sredishte
Knyazhitsy *see* Knyazhytsy
121 *O15* **Knyazhytsy** ***Rus.*** Knyazhitsy. Mahilyowskaya Voblasts', E Belarus *54.10N 30.27E*
85 *G26* **Knysna** Western Cape, SW South Africa *34.01S 23.05E*
176 *V10* **Koagas** Papua, E Indonesia *2.40S 132.16E*
Koartac *see* Quaqtaq
174 *J10* **Koba** Pulau Bangka, W Indonesia *2.29S 106.22E*
170 *C16* **Kobayashi** ***var.*** Kobayasi. Miyazaki, Kyūshū, SW Japan *32.01N 130.55E*
Kobayasi *see* Kobayashi
Kobdo *see* Hovd
171 *Gg14* **Kōbe** Hyōgo, Honshū, SW Japan *34.39N 135.10E*
Kobelyaki *see* Kobelyaky
119 *T6* **Kobelyaky** ***Rus.*** Kobelyaki. Poltavs'ka Oblast', NE Ukraine *49.10N 34.13E*
97 *J22* **København** ***Eng.*** Copenhagen; ***anc.*** Hafnia. ● (Denmark) Sjælland, København, E Denmark *55.43N 12.34E*
97 *J23* **København** ***off.*** Københavns Amt. ◆ *county* E Denmark
78 *K10* **Kobenni** Hodh el Gharbi, S Mauritania *15.58N 9.24W*
176 *U11* **Kobi** Pulau Seram, E Indonesia *2.56S 129.53E*
103 *F17* **Koblenz** ***prev.*** Coblenz, ***Fr.*** Coblence, ***anc.*** Confluentes. Rheinland-Pfalz, W Germany *50.21N 7.36E*
110 *F6* **Koblenz** Aargau, N Switzerland *47.34N 8.16E*
176 *Ww11* **Kobowre, Pegunungan** ▲▲ Papua, E Indonesia
128 *J14* **Kobozha** Novgorodskaya Oblast', W Russian Federation *58.48N 35.00E*
Kobrin *see* Kobryn
176 *W14* **Kobroor, Pulau** *island* Kepulauan Aru, E Indonesia
121 *G19* **Kobryn** ***Pol.*** Kobryn, ***Rus.*** Kobrin. Brestskaya Voblasts', SW Belarus *52.13N 24.21E*
41 *O7* **Kobuk** Alaska, USA *66.54N 156.52W*
41 *O7* **Kobuk River** ≈ Alaska, USA
143 *Q10* **K'obulet'i** W Georgia *41.47N 41.46E*
126 *Ll10* **Kobyay** Respublika Sakha (Yakutiya), NE Russian Federation *63.36N 126.33E*
142 *E11* **Kocaeli** ◆ *province* NW Turkey
115 *P18* **Kočani** NE FYR Macedonia *41.55N 22.25E*
114 *K12* **Koceljevo** Serbia, W Serbia and Montenegro (Yugoslavia) *44.28N 19.49E*
111 *U12* **Kočevje** ***Ger.*** Gottschee. S Slovenia *45.41N 14.47E*
159 *T12* **Koch Bihār** West Bengal, NE India *26.19N 89.25E*
126 *J10* **Kochechum** ≈ N Russian Federation
103 *I20* **Kocher** ≈ SW Germany
129 *T13* **Kochevo** Komi-Permyatskiy Avtonomnyy Okrug, NW Russian Federation *59.37N 54.16E*
170 *Ee15* **Kōchi** ***var.*** Kôti. Kōchi, Shikoku, SW Japan *33.31N 133.30E*
170 *Ee15* **Kōchi** ***off.*** Kōchi-ken, ***var.*** Kôti. ◆ *prefecture* Shikoku, SW Japan
Kochi *see* Cochin
Kochiu *see* Gejiu
Kochkor *see* Kochkorka
153 *V8* **Kochkorka** ***Kir.*** Kochkor. Narynskaya Oblast', C Kyrgyzstan *42.09N 75.42E*
129 *V5* **Kochmes** Respublika Komi, NW Russian Federation *66.10N 60.46E*
131 *P15* **Kochubey** Respublika Dagestan, SW Russian Federation *44.25N 46.33E*
117 *I17* **Kochýlas** ▲ Skýros, Vóreioi Sporádes, Greece, Aegean Sea *38.50N 24.35E*
112 *O13* **Kock** Lubelskie, E Poland *51.39N 22.26E*
83 *J19* **Kodacho** *spring/well* S Kenya *1.52S 39.22E*
161 *K24* **Koddiyar Bay** *bay* NE Sri Lanka
41 *Q14* **Kodiak** Kodiak Island, Alaska, USA *57.47N 152.24W*
41 *Q14* **Kodiak Island** *island* Alaska, USA
160 *B12* **Kodīnār** Gujarāt, W India *20.43N 70.46E*
128 *M9* **Kodino** Arkhangel'skaya Oblast', NW Russian Federation *63.36N 39.54E*
126 *Ii13* **Kodinsk** Krasnoyarskiy Kray, C Russian Federation *58.37N 99.18E*
82 *F12* **Kodok** Upper Nile, SE Sudan *9.51N 32.07E*
119 *N8* **Kodyma** Odes'ka Oblast', SW Ukraine *48.05N 29.09E*
101 *B17* **Koekelare** West-Vlaanderen, W Belgium *51.07N 2.58E*
Koeln *see* Köln
Koepang *see* Kupang
Ko-erh-mu *see* Golmud
101 *J17* **Koersel** Limburg, NE Belgium *51.04N 5.17E*
85 *E21* **Koës** Karas, SE Namibia *25.57S 19.04E*
Koetai *see* Mahakam, Sungai
Koetaradja *see* Bandaaceh
38 *I14* **Kofa Mountains** ▲▲ Arizona, SW USA
176 *Z15* **Kofarau** Papua, E Indonesia *7.29S 140.28E*
153 *P13* **Kofarnihon** ***Rus.*** Kofarnikhon; ***prev.*** Ordzhonikidzeabad, ***Taj.*** Orjonikidzeobod, Yangi-Bazar. W Tajikistan *38.32N 68.56E*
153 *P14* **Kofarnihon** ***Rus.*** Kafirnigan. ≈ SW Tajikistan
Kofarnikhon *see* Kofarnihon
116 *M11* **Kofçaz** Kırklareli, NW Turkey *41.57N 27.07E*
176 *U9* **Kofiau, Pulau** ***var.*** Kafiau. *island* Kepulauan Raja Ampat, E Indonesia
117 *J25* **Kófinas** ▲ Kríti, Greece, E Mediterranean Sea *34.58N 25.03E*
124 *Nn4* **Kofínou** ***var.*** Kophinou. S Cyprus *34.49N 33.24E*
111 *V8* **Köflach** Steiermark, SE Austria *47.04N 15.04E*
79 *Q17* **Koforidua** SE Ghana *6.04N 0.17W*
170 *Ff12* **Kōfu** Tottori, Honshū, SW Japan *35.16N 133.31E*
171 *J15* **Kōfu** ***var.*** Kôhu. Yamanashi, Honshū, S Japan *35.40N 138.33E*
171 *K16* **Koga** Ibaraki, Honshū, S Japan *36.12N 139.42E*
83 *F22* **Koga** Tabora, C Tanzania *6.08S 32.20E*
Kogălniceanu *see* Mihail Kogălniceanu
11 *P6* **Kogaluk** ≈ Newfoundland and Labrador, E Canada
10 *J4* **Kogaluk** ≈ Québec, NE Canada
126 *Gg10* **Kogalym** Khanty-Mansiyskiy Avtonomnyy Okrug, C Russian Federation *62.13N 74.34E*
97 *J23* **Køge** Roskilde, E Denmark *55.28N 12.12E*
97 *J23* **Køge Bugt** *bay* E Denmark
79 *U16* **Kogi** ◆ *state* C Nigeria
152 *L11* **Kogon** ***Rus.*** Kagan. Buxoro Viloyati, C Uzbekistan *39.46N 64.28E*
169 *Y17* **Kŏgŭm-do** *island* S South Korea
Kőhalom *see* Rupea
155 *T6* **Kohāt** North-West Frontier Province, NW Pakistan *33.37N 71.30E*
120 *G4* **Kohila** ***Ger.*** Koil. Raplamaa, NW Estonia *59.07N 24.46E*
159 *X13* **Kohīma** Nāgāland, E India *25.40N 94.07E*
Koh I Noh *see* Büyükağrı Dağı
148 *L10* **Kohgīlūyeh va Būyer Aḩmad** ***off.*** Ostān-e Kohgīlūyeh va Būyer Aḩmad, ***var.*** Boyer Ahmadī va Kohkīlūyeh. ◆ *province* SW Iran
Kohsān *see* Kūhestān
120 *J3* **Kohtla-Järve** Ida-Virumaa, NE Estonia *59.22N 27.21E*
Kôhu *see* Kōfu
119 *N10* **Kohyl'nyk** ***Rom.*** Cogîlnic. ≈ Moldova/Ukraine
171 *K13* **Koide** Niigata, Honshū, C Japan *37.13N 138.58E*
8 *G7* **Koidern** Yukon Territory, W Canada *61.55N 140.22W*
78 *J15* **Koidu** E Sierra Leone *8.39N 11.01W*
120 *I4* **Koigi** Järvamaa, C Estonia *58.51N 25.45E*
Koil *see* Kohila
180 *H13* **Koimbani** Grande Comore, NW Comoros *11.37S 43.22E*
145 *T3* **Koi Sanjaq** ***var.*** Koysanjaq, Küysanjaq. N Iraq *36.04N 44.37E*
95 *O16* **Koitere** ◎ E Finland
Koivisto *see* Primorsk
169 *Z16* **Kŏje-do** ***Jap.*** Kyōsai-tō. *island* S South Korea
82 *J13* **K'ok'a Hāyk'** ◎ C Ethiopia
Kokand *see* Qo'qon
190 *F6* **Kokatha** South Australia *31.17S 135.16E*
Kokcha *see* Koʻkcha
152 *M10* **Koʻkcha** ***Rus.*** Kokcha. Buxoro Viloyati, C Uzbekistan *40.30N 64.58E*
Kokchetav *see* Kokshetau
95 *K18* **Kokemäenjoki** ≈ SW Finland
176 *X12* **Kokenau** ***var.*** Kokonau. Papua, E Indonesia *4.38S 136.24E*
85 *E22* **Kokerboom** Karas, SE Namibia *28.10S 19.25E*
121 *N14* **Kokhanava** ***Rus.*** Kokhanovo. Vitsyebskaya Voblasts', NE Belarus *54.28N 29.58E*
Kokhanovichi *see* Kakhanavichy
Kokhanovo *see* Kokhanava
Kök-Janggak *see* Kok-Yangak
95 *K16* **Kokkola** ***Swe.*** Karleby; ***prev. Swe.*** Gamlakarleby. Länsi-Suomi, W Finland *63.49N 23.10E*
164 *L3* **Kok Kuduk** *well* N China *46.03N 87.34E*
120 *H9* **Koknese** Aizkraukle, C Latvia *56.38N 25.27E*
79 *T13* **Koko** Kebbi, W Nigeria *11.25N 4.33E*
194 *K15* **Kokoda** Northern, S PNG *8.51S 147.37E*
78 *K12* **Kokofata** Kayes, W Mali *12.48N 9.56W*
41 *N6* **Kokolik River** ≈ Alaska, USA
33 *O13* **Kokomo** Indiana, N USA *40.29N 86.07W*
Kokonau *see* Kokenau
Koko Nor *see* Qinghai Hu, China
Koko Nor *see* Qinghai, China
195 *P10* **Kokopo** ***var.*** Kopopo; ***prev.*** Herbertshöhe. New Britain, E PNG *4.19S 152.13E*
151 *X10* **Kokpekti** ***Kaz.*** Kökpekti. Vostochnyy Kazakhstan, E Kazakhstan *48.45N 82.24E*
151 *X11* **Kokpekti** ≈ E Kazakhstan
41 *P9* **Kokrines** Alaska, USA *64.57N 154.42W*
41 *P9* **Kokrines Hills** ▲▲ Alaska, USA
151 *P17* **Koksaray** Yuzhnyy Kazakhstan, S Kazakhstan *42.40N 68.09E*
153 *X9* **Kokshaal-Tau** ***Rus.*** Khrebet Kakshaal-Too. ▲▲ China/Kyrgyzstan
151 *P7* **Kokshetau** ***Kaz.*** Kökshetaū; ***prev.*** Kokchetav. Akmola, N Kazakhstan *53.18N 69.25E*
101 *A17* **Koksijde** West-Vlaanderen, W Belgium *51.07N 2.39E*
10 *M5* **Koksoak** ≈ Québec, E Canada
85 *K24* **Kokstad** KwaZulu/Natal, E South Africa *30.23S 29.22E*
151 *W15* **Koktal** ***Kaz.*** Köktal. Almaty, SE Kazakhstan *44.04N 79.43E*
151 *Q12* **Koktas** ≈ C Kazakhstan
Kök-Tash *see* Këk-Tash
Koktokay *see* Fuyun
170 *C16* **Kokubu** Kagoshima, Kyūshū, SW Japan *31.44N 130.44E*
126 *L15* **Kokuy** Chitinskaya Oblast', S Russian Federation *52.13N 117.18E*
153 *T9* **Kok-Yangak** ***Kir.*** Kök-Janggak. Dzhalal-Abadskaya Oblast', W Kyrgyzstan *41.02N 73.11E*
164 *F9* **Kokyar** Xinjiang Uygur Zizhiqu, W China *37.24N 77.15E*
155 *O13* **Kolāchi** ***var.*** Kulachi. ≈ SW Pakistan
78 *J15* **Kolahun** N Liberia *8.24N 10.01W*
175 *Q12* **Kolaka** Sulawesi, C Indonesia *4.04S 121.37E*
Kolam *see* Quilon
K'o-la-ma-i *see* Karamay
Kola Peninsula *see* Kol'skiy Poluostrov
161 *H19* **Kolār** Karnātaka, E India *13.10N 78.10E*
161 *H19* **Kolār Gold Fields** Karnātaka, E India *12.56N 78.16E*
94 *K11* **Kolari** Lappi, NW Finland *67.19N 23.51E*
113 *I21* **Kolárovo** ***Ger.*** Gutta; ***prev.*** Guta, ***Hung.*** Gúta. Nitriansky Kraj, SW Slovakia *47.54N 18.00E*
115 *K16* **Kolašin** Montenegro, SW Serbia and Montenegro (Yugoslavia) *42.49N 19.32E*
158 *F11* **Kolāyat** Rājasthān, NW India *27.55N 73.01E*
97 *N15* **Kolbäck** Västmanland, C Sweden *59.33N 16.15E*
Kolbcha *see* Kowbcha
207 *Q15* **Kolbeinsey Ridge** *undersea feature* Denmark Strait/ Norwegian Sea
Kolberg *see* Kołobrzeg
97 *H15* **Kolbotn** Akershus, S Norway *62.15N 10.24E*
113 *N16* **Kolbuszowa** Podkarpackie, SE Poland *50.12N 22.07E*
130 *L3* **Kol'chugino** Vladimirskaya Oblast', W Russian Federation *56.19N 39.24E*
78 *H12* **Kolda** S Senegal *12.58N 14.58W*
97 *G23* **Kolding** Vejle, C Denmark *55.28N 9.30E*
81 *M17* **Kole** Orientale, N Dem. Rep. Congo *2.09N 25.17E*
81 *K20* **Kole** Kasai Oriental, SW Dem. Rep. Congo *3.27S 22.28E*
Kōle *see* Kili Island
86 *F6* **Kölen** ***Nor.*** Kjølen. ▲▲ Norway/Sweden
Kolepom, Pulau *see* Yos Sudarso, Pulau
120 *H3* **Kolga Laht** ***Ger.*** Kolko-Wiek. *bay* N Estonia
129 *Q3* **Kolguyev, Ostrov** *island* NW Russian Federation
161 *E16* **Kolhāpur** Mahārāshtra, SW India *16.42N 74.13E*
157 *K21* **Kolhumadulu Atoll** ***var.*** Kolumadulu Atoll, Thaa Atoll. *atoll* S Maldives
95 *O16* **Koli** ***var.*** Kolinkylä. Itä-Suomi, E Finland *63.06N 29.45E*
41 *O13* **Koliganek** Alaska, USA *59.43N 157.16W*
113 *E16* **Kolín** ***Ger.*** Kolin. Středočeský Kraj, C Czech Republic *50.01N 15.10E*
Kolinkylä *see* Koli
202 *E12* **Koliu** Île Futuna, W Wallis and Futuna
120 *E7* **Kolka** Talsi, NW Latvia *57.43N 22.33E*
120 *E7* **Kolkasrags** ***prev. Eng.*** Cape Domesnes. *headland* NW Latvia *57.45N 22.35E*
159 *S16* **Kolkata** ***var.*** Calcutta. West Bengal, NE India *22.30N 88.19E*
Kolkhozabad *see* Kolkhozobod
153 *P14* **Kolkhozobod** ***Rus.*** Kolkhozabad; ***prev.*** Kaganovichabad, Tugalan. SW Tajikistan *37.33N 68.34E*
Kolki/Kołki *see* Kolky
Kolko-Wiek *see* Kolga Laht
118 *K3* **Kolky** ***Pol.*** Kołki, ***Rus.*** Kolki. Volyns'ka Oblast', NW Ukraine *51.05N 25.40E*
Kollam *see* Quilon
161 *G20* **Kollegāl** Karnātaka, W India *12.07N 77.06E*
100 *M5* **Kollum** Friesland, N Netherlands *53.16N 6.09E*
Kolmar *see* Colmar
103 *E16* **Köln** ***var.*** Koeln, ***Eng./Fr.*** Cologne; ***prev.*** Cöln, ***anc.*** Colonia Agrippina, Oppidum Ubiorum. Nordrhein-Westfalen, W Germany *50.57N 6.57E*
112 *N9* **Kolno** Podlaskie, NE Poland *53.24N 21.57E*
112 *J12* **Koło** Wielkopolskie, C Poland *52.10N 18.39E*
40 *B8* **Kōloa** ***var.*** Koloa. Kaua'i, Hawai'i, USA, C Pacific Ocean *21.54N 159.28W*
112 *E7* **Kołobrzeg** ***Ger.*** Kolberg. Zachodnio-pomorskie, NW Poland *54.10N 15.33E*
130 *H4* **Kolodnya** Smolenskaya Oblast', W Russian Federation *54.57N 32.22E*
202 *E13* **Kolofau, Mont** ⩚ Île Alofi, S Wallis and Futuna *14.21S 178.01W*
129 *O14* **Kologriv** Kostromskaya Oblast', NW Russian Federation *58.49N 44.22E*
78 *L12* **Kolokani** Koulikoro, W Mali *13.34N 8.01W*
79 *N13* **Koloko** W Burkina *11.06N 5.18W*
195 *U14* **Kolombangara** ***var.*** Kilimbangara, Nduke. *island* New Georgia Islands, NW Solomon Islands
Kolomea *see* Kolomyya
130 *L4* **Kolomna** Moskovskaya Oblast', W Russian Federation *55.02N 38.52E*
118 *J7* **Kolomyya** ***Ger.*** Kolomea. Ivano-Frankivs'ka Oblast', W Ukraine *48.31N 25.00E*
78 *M13* **Kolondiéba** Sikasso, SW Mali *11.04N 6.55W*
200 *R15* **Kolonga** Tongatapu, S Tonga *21.07S 175.04W*
201 *U16* **Kolonia** ***var.*** Colonia. Pohnpei, E Micronesia *6.57N 158.12E*
Kolonja *see* Kolonjë
115 *K21* **Kolonjë** ***var.*** Kolonja. Fier, C Albania *40.49N 19.37E*
Kolonjë *see* Ersekë
Kolotambu *see* Avuavu
200 *Q15* **Kolovai** Tongatapu, S Tonga *21.05S 175.20W*
175 *R13* **Kolowanawatobo, Teluk** *bay* Pulau Buton, C Indonesia
Kolozsvár *see* Cluj-Napoca
114 *C9* **Kolpa** ***Ger.*** Kulpa, ***SCr.*** Kupa. ≈ Croatia/Slovenia
126 *H12* **Kolpashevo** Tomskaya Oblast', C Russian Federation *58.21N 82.44E*
128 *H13* **Kolpino** Leningradskaya Oblast', NW Russian Federation *59.43N 30.39E*
102 *M10* **Kölpinsee** ◎ NE Germany
152 *K8* **Koʻlquduq** ***Rus.*** Kulkuduk. Navoiy Viloyati, N Uzbekistan *42.36N 63.24E*
128 *K5* **Kol'skiy Poluostrov** ***Eng.*** Kola Peninsula. *peninsula* NW Russian Federation
131 *T6* **Koltubanovskiy** Orenburgskaya Oblast', W Russian Federation *53.00N 52.00E*
114 *L11* **Kolubara** ≈ C Serbia and Montenegro (Yugoslavia)
Kolupchii *see* Gurkovo
112 *K13* **Koluszki** Łodzkie, C Poland *51.43N 19.49E*
129 *T6* **Kolva** ≈ NW Russian Federation
95 *E14* **Kolvereid** Nord-Trøndelag, W Norway *64.47N 11.22E*
154 *L15* **Kolwa** Baluchistān, SW Pakistan *26.03N 64.00E*
81 *M24* **Kolwezi** Katanga, S Dem. Rep. Congo *10.43S 25.29E*
127 *Nn7* **Kolyma** ≈ NE Russian Federation
Kolyma Lowland *see* Kolymskaya Nizmennost'
Kolyma Range/Kolymskiy, Khrebet *see* Kolymskoye Nagor'ye
127 *Nn6* **Kolymskaya Nizmennost'** ***Eng.*** Kolyma Lowland. *lowlands* NE Russian Federation
127 *Nn6* **Kolymskoye** Respublika Sakha (Yakutiya), NE Russian Federation *68.42N 158.46E*
127 *N17* **Kolymskoye Nagor'ye** ***var.*** Khrebet Kolymskiy, ***Eng.*** Kolyma Range. ▲▲ E Russian Federation
127 *N17* **Kolyuchinskaya Guba** *bay* NE Russian Federation
151 *W15* **Kol'zhat** Almaty, SE Kazakhstan *43.30N 80.37E*
116 *G8* **Kom** ▲ NW Bulgaria *43.10N 23.02E*
82 *I13* **Koma** Oromo, C Ethiopia *8.19N 36.48E*
79 *X12* **Komadugu Gana** ≈ NE Nigeria
171 *Ii15* **Komagane** Nagano, Honshū, S Japan *35.46N 137.56E*
81 *P17* **Komanda** Orientale, NE Dem. Rep. Congo *1.23N 29.44E*
207 *U1* **Komandorskaya Basin** ***var.*** Kamchatka Basin. *undersea feature* SW Bering Sea
129 *Pp9* **Komandorskiye Ostrova** ***Eng.*** Commander Islands. *island group* E Russian Federation
Kománfalva *see* Comănești
113 *I22* **Komárno** ***Ger.*** Komorn, ***Hung.*** Komárom. Nitriansky Kraj, SW Slovakia *47.46N 18.07E*
113 *I22* **Komárom** Komárom-Esztergom, NW Hungary *47.44N 18.06E*
Komárom *see* Komárno
113 *I22* **Komárom-Esztergom** ***off.*** Komárom-Esztergom Megye. ◆ *county* N Hungary
171 *I13* **Komatsu** ***var.*** Komatu. Ishikawa, Honshū, SW Japan *36.24N 136.27E*
170 *Ff15* **Komatsushima** Tokushima, Shikoku, SW Japan *34.00N 134.36E*
Komatu *see* Komatsu
85 *D17* **Kombat** Otjozondjupa, N Namibia *19.42S 17.45E*
Kombissiguiri *see* Kombissiri
79 *P13* **Kombissiri** ***var.*** Kombissiguiri. C Burkina *12.03N 1.14W*
196 *E10* **Komebail Lagoon** *lagoon* N Palau
83 *F20* **Kome Island** *island* N Tanzania
Komeyo *see* Wandai
176 *W13* **Komfane** Pulau Wokam, E Indonesia *5.36S 134.42E*
119 *P10* **Kominternivs'ke** Odes'ka Oblast', SW Ukraine *46.52N 30.56E*
129 *R12* **Komi-Permyatskiy Avtonomnyy Okrug** ◆ *autonomous district* W Russian Federation
129 *R8* **Komi, Respublika** ◆ *autonomous republic* NW Russian Federation
113 *I25* **Komló** Baranya, SW Hungary *46.11N 18.19E*
Kommunarsk *see* Alchevs'k
153 *S12* **Kommunizm, Qullai** ▲ E Tajikistan
194 *G12* **Komo** Southern Highlands, W PNG *6.06S 142.52E*
175 *P16* **Komodo** Pulau Komodo, S Indonesia *8.35S 119.27E*
175 *P16* **Komodo, Pulau** *island* Nusa Tenggara, S Indonesia
79 *N15* **Komoé** ***var.*** Komoé Fleuve. ≈ E Ivory Coast
Komoé Fleuve *see* Komoé
77 *X11* **Kôm Ombo** ***var.*** Kawm Umbū. SE Egypt *24.23N 32.58E*
81 *F20* **Komono** La Lékoumou, SW Congo *3.15S 13.13E*
176 *Y16* **Komoran** Papua, E Indonesia *8.14S 138.51E*
176 *Y16* **Komoran, Pulau** *island* E Indonesia
Komorn *see* Komárno
Komornok *see* Comorâşte
171 *J14* **Komoro** Nagano, Honshū, S Japan *36.22N 138.25E*
Komosolabad *see* Komsomolobod
Komotau *see* Chomutov
116 *K13* **Komotiní** ***var.*** Gümüljina, ***Turk.*** Gümülcine. Anatolikí Makedonía kai Thráki, NE Greece *41.06N 25.27E*
115 *K16* **Komovi** ▲▲ SW Serbia and Montenegro (Yugoslavia)
119 *R8* **Kompaniyivka** Kirovohrads'ka Oblast', C Ukraine *48.16N 32.12E*
194 *H12* **Kompiam** Enga, W PNG *5.23S 143.54E*
Kompong *see* Kâmpóng Chhnăng
Kompong Cham *see* Kâmpóng Cham
Kompong Kleang *see* Kâmpóng Khleăng
Kompong Som *see* Kâmpóng Saôm
Kompong Speu *see* Kâmpóng Spoe
Komrat *see* Comrat
Komsomol *see* Komsomol'skiy, Atyrau, Kazakhstan
Komsomol/Komsomolets *see* Karabalyk, Kostanay, Kazakhstan
126 *Ii2* **Komsomolets, Ostrov** *island* Severnaya Zemlya, N Russian Federation
150 *F13* **Komsomolets, Zaliv** *lake gulf* SW Kazakhstan
153 *Q12* **Komsomolobod** ***Rus.*** Komosolabad. C Tajikistan *38.51N 69.54E*

◆ Country
● Country Capital
◇ Dependent Territory
○ Dependent Territory Capital
◆ Administrative Region
✕ International Airport
▲ Mountain
▲▲ Mountain Range
⩚ Volcano
≈ River
◎ Lake
▣ Reservoir

Komsomol'sk – Kralup an der Moldau

128 M16 **Komsomol'sk** Ivanovskaya Oblast', W Russian Federation 56.58N 40.15E
119 S6 **Komsomol's'k** Poltavs'ka Oblast', C Ukraine 49.01N 33.37E
152 M11 **Komsomol'sk** Navoiy Viloyati, N Uzbekistan 40.14N 65.10E
150 G12 **Komsomol'skiy** *Kaz.* Komsomol. Atyrau, W Kazakhstan 47.18N 53.37E
129 W4 **Komsomol'skiy** Respublika Komi, NW Russian Federation 67.33N 64.00E
127 Nn15 **Komsomol'sk-na-Amure** Khabarovskiy Kray, SE Russian Federation 50.31N 136.58E
Komsomol'sk-na-Ustyurte *see* Kubla-Ustyurt
150 K10 **Komsomol'skoye** Aktyubinsk, NW Kazakhstan
131 Q8 **Komsomol'skoye** Saratovskaya Oblast', W Russian Federation 50.45N 47.00E
151 P10 **Kon** ⁓ C Kazakhstan
Kona *see* Kailua-Kona
128 K16 **Konakovo** Tverskaya Oblast', W Russian Federation 56.42N 36.44E
149 V15 **Konārak** Sīstān va Balūchestān, SE Iran 25.26N 60.22E
Konarhā *see* Kunar
29 O11 **Konawa** Oklahoma, C USA 34.57N 96.45W
176 V9 **Konda** Papua, E Indonesia 1.34S 131.58E
125 Ff11 **Konda** ⁓ C Russian Federation
160 L13 **Kondagaon** Chhattīsgarh, C India 19.38N 81.41E
12 K10 **Kondiaronk, Lac** ◎ Québec, SE Canada
188 J13 **Kondinin** Western Australia 32.31S 118.15E
83 H21 **Kondoa** Dodoma, C Tanzania 4.54S 35.46E
131 P6 **Kondol'** Penzenskaya Oblast', W Russian Federation 52.49N 45.03E
116 N10 **Kondolovo** Burgas, E Bulgaria 42.07N 27.43E
176 Z16 **Kondomirat** Papua, E Indonesia 8.57S 140.55E
128 J10 **Kondopoga** Respublika Kareliya, NW Russian Federation 62.12N 34.16E
Kondoz *see* Kunduz
161 J17 **Kondukūr** *var.* Kandukur. Andhra Pradesh, E India 15.17N 79.49E
Kondūz *see* Kunduz
197 H6 **Koné** Province Nord, W New Caledonia 21.04S 164.51E
152 E13 **Könekesir** *Rus.* Kënekesir. Balkan Welaýaty, W Turkmenistan 38.16N 56.51E
152 G8 **Köneürgenç** *var.* Köneürgench, *Rus.* Këneurgench; *prev.* Kunya-Urgench. Daşoguz Welaýaty, N Turkmenistan 42.20N 59.09E
Köneürgench *see* Köneürgenç
79 N15 **Kong** N Ivory Coast 9.06N 4.34W
41 S5 **Kongakut River** ⁓ Alaska, USA
207 O14 **Kong Christian IX Land** *Eng.* King Christian IX Land. *physical region* SE Greenland
207 P13 **Kong Christian X Land** *Eng.* King Christian X Land. *physical region* E Greenland
207 N13 **Kong Frederik IX Land** *Eng.* King Frederik IX Land. *physical region* SW Greenland
207 Q12 **Kong Frederik VIII Land** *Eng.* Kingfrederik VIII Land. *physical region* NE Greenland
207 N15 **Kong Frederik VI Kyst** *Eng.* King Frederik VI Coast. *physical region* SE Greenland
178 I13 **Kông, Kaôh** *prev.* Kas Kong. *island* SW Cambodia
94 P2 **Kong Karls Land** *Eng.* King Charles Islands. *island group* SE Svalbard
83 G14 **Kong Kong** ⁓ SE Sudan
Kongo *see* Congo (river)
85 G16 **Kongola** Caprivi, NE Namibia 17.47S 23.24E
81 N21 **Kongolo** Katanga, E Dem. Rep. Congo 5.20S 26.57E
83 F14 **Kongor** Jonglei, SE Sudan 7.09N 31.44E
207 Q14 **Kong Oscar Fjord** *fjord* E Greenland
79 P12 **Kongoussi** N Burkina 13.19N 1.31W
97 G15 **Kongsberg** Buskerud, S Norway 59.39N 9.37E
94 Q2 **Kongsøya** *island* Kong Karls Land, E Svalbard
97 I14 **Kongsvinger** Hedmark, S Norway 60.10N 12.00E
Kongtong *see* Pingliang
178 Jj11 **Kông, Tônle** *Lao.* Xê Kong. ⁓ Cambodia/Laos
164 E8 **Kongur Shan** ▲ NW China 38.39N 75.21E
83 I22 **Kongwa** Dodoma, C Tanzania 6.13S 36.28E
Kong, Xê *see* Kông, Tônle
Konia *see* Konya
153 R11 **Konibodom** *Rus.* Kanibadam. N Tajikistan 40.16N 70.20E
113 K15 **Koniecpol** Śląskie, S Poland 50.47N 19.45E
Konich *see* Konya
Königgrätz *see* Hradec Králové
Königinhof an der Elbe *see* Dvůr Králové nad Labem
103 K23 **Königsbrunn** Bayern, S Germany 48.16N 10.52E
Königshütte *see* Chorzów
103 O24 **Königssee** ◎ SE Germany
111 S8 **Königstuhl** ▲ S Austria 46.57N 13.47E
111 U3 **Königswiesen** Oberösterreich, N Austria 48.25N 14.48E
103 E17 **Königswinter** Nordrhein-Westfalen, W Germany 50.40N 7.12E
152 M11 **Konimex** *Rus.* Kenimekh. Navoiy Viloyati, N Uzbekistan 40.14N 65.10E
112 I12 **Konin** *Ger.* Kuhnau. Wielkopolskie, C Poland 52.13N 18.16E
Koninkrijk der Nederlanden *see* Netherlands
115 L24 **Konispol** *var.* Konispoli. Vlorë, S Albania 39.40N 20.10E
Konispoli *see* Konispol
117 C15 **Kónitsa** Ípeiros, W Greece 40.04N 20.48E
Konitz *see* Chojnice
110 D8 **Köniz** Bern, W Switzerland 46.55N 7.26E
115 H14 **Konjic** Federacija Bosna I Hercegovina, C Bosnia and Herzegovina 43.39N 17.55E
94 J10 **Könkämäälven** ⁓ Finland/Sweden
161 D14 **Konkan** W India
85 D22 **Konkiep** ⁓ S Namibia
78 I14 **Konkouré** ⁓ W Guinea
79 O11 **Konna** Mopti, S Mali 14.58N 3.49W
195 P10 **Konogaiang, Mount** ▲ New Ireland, NE PNG 4.05S 152.43E
195 P10 **Konogogo** New Ireland, NE PNG 3.25S 152.09E
110 E9 **Konolfingen** Bern, W Switzerland 46.53N 7.36E
79 P16 **Kononogo** C Ghana 6.39N 1.06W
195 O9 **Konos** New Ireland, NE PNG 3.07S 151.43E
128 M12 **Konosha** Arkhangel'skaya Oblast', NW Russian Federation 60.58N 40.09E
119 R3 **Konotop** Sums'ka Oblast', NE Ukraine 51.15N 33.13E
164 L7 **Konqi He** ⁓ NW China
113 L14 **Końskie** Świętokrzyskie, C Poland 51.12N 20.26E
Konstantinovka *see* Kostyantynivka
130 M11 **Konstantinovsk** Rostovskaya Oblast', SW Russian Federation 47.37N 41.07E
103 H24 **Konstanz** *var.* Constanz, *Eng.* Constance; *hist.* Kostnitz, *anc.* Constantia. Baden-Württemberg, S Germany 47.40N 9.10E
Konstanza *see* Constanţa
79 T14 **Kontagora** Niger, W Nigeria 10.25N 5.29E
80 E13 **Kontcha** Nord, N Cameroon 8.00N 12.13E
101 G17 **Kontich** Antwerpen, N Belgium 51.07N 4.27E
95 O16 **Kontiolahti** Itä-Suomi, E Finland 62.46N 29.51E
95 M15 **Kontiomäki** Oulu, C Finland 64.20N 28.09E
178 K11 **Kon Tum** *var.* Kontum. Kon Tum, C Vietnam 14.23N 108.00E
Konur *see* Sulakyurt
142 H15 **Konya** *var.* Konieh; *prev.* Konia, *anc.* Iconium. Konya, C Turkey 37.51N 32.30E
142 H15 **Konya** *var.* Konieh. ◈ *province* C Turkey
151 T13 **Konyrat** *var.* Kounradskiy, *Kaz.* Qongyrat. Karaganda, C Kazakhstan 46.58N 74.54E
151 W15 **Konyrolen** Almaty, SE Kazakhstan 44.16N 79.18E
83 I19 **Konza** Eastern, S Kenya 1.44S 37.07E
100 I9 **Koog aan den Zaan** Noord-Holland, C Netherlands 52.28N 4.49E
190 F7 **Koonibba** South Australia 31.55S 133.23E
33 O11 **Koontz Lake** Indiana, N USA 41.25N 86.24W
176 V8 **Koor** Papua, E Indonesia 0.21S 132.28E
191 R9 **Koorawatha** New South Wales, SE Australia 34.03S 148.33E
120 J5 **Koosa** Tartumaa, E Estonia 58.31N 27.06E
35 N7 **Kootenai** *var.* Kootenay. ⁓ Canada/USA *see also* Kootenay
9 P17 **Kootenay** *var.* Kootenai. ⁓ Canada/USA *see also* Kootenai
85 F24 **Kootjieskolk** Northern Cape, W South Africa 31.16S 20.21E
115 M15 **Kopaonik** ▲▲ S Serbia and Montenegro (Yugoslavia)
Kopar *see* Koper
94 K1 **Kópasker** Nordhurland Eystra, N Iceland 66.15N 16.23W
94 H4 **Kópavogur** Reykjanes, W Iceland 64.06N 21.47W
151 U13 **Kopbirlik** *prev.* Kirov, Kirova. Almaty, SE Kazakhstan 46.24N 77.16E
111 S13 **Koper** *It.* Capodistria; *prev.* Kopar. SW Slovenia 45.32N 13.42E
97 C16 **Kopervik** Rogaland, S Norway 59.16N 5.18E
Köpetdag Gershi/Kopetdag, Khrebet *see* Koppeh Dāgh
125 Ee12 **Kopeysk** Kurganskaya Oblast', C Russian Federation 55.06N 61.31E
Kophinou *see* Kofínou
190 G8 **Kopi** South Australia 33.24S 135.40E
Kopiago *see* Lake Copiago
159 W12 **Kopili** ⁓ NE India
97 M15 **Köping** Västmanland, C Sweden 59.31N 16.00E
115 K17 **Koplik** *var.* Kopliku. Shkodër, NW Albania 42.12N 19.26E
Kopliku *see* Koplik
Kopopo *see* Kokopo
96 I11 **Koppang** Hedmark, S Norway 61.34N 11.01E
Kopparberg *see* Dalarna
149 S3 **Koppeh Dāgh** *Rus.* Khrebet Kopetdag, *Turkm.* Köpetdag Gershi. ▲▲ Iran/Turkmenistan
Koppename *see* Coppename Rivier
97 J15 **Koppom** Värmland, C Sweden 59.42N 12.07E
Kopreinitz *see* Koprivnica
116 K9 **Koprinka, Yazovir** *prev.* Yazovir Georgi Dimitrov. ⊠ C Bulgaria
114 F7 **Koprivnica** *Ger.* Kopreinitz, *Hung.* Kaproncza. Koprivnica-Križevci, N Croatia 46.10N 16.49E
114 F8 **Koprivnica-Križevci** *off.* Koprivničko-Križevačka Županija. ◈ *province* N Croatia
113 I17 **Kopřivnice** *Ger.* Nesselsdorf. Moravskoslezský Kraj, E Czech Republic 49.36N 18.09E
Köprülü *see* Veles
Koptsevichi *see* Kaptsevichy
Kopyl' *see* Kapyl'
121 O14 **Kopys'** *Rus.* Kopys'. Vitsyebskaya Voblasts', NE Belarus 54.21N 30.21E
115 M18 **Korab** ▲ Albania/FYR Macedonia 41.48N 20.33E
Korabavur Pastligi *see* Karabaur', Uval
83 M14 **K'orahē** Somali, E Ethiopia 6.36N 44.21E
117 L16 **Kórakas, Akrotírio** *headland* Lésvos, E Greece 39.20N 26.20E
114 D9 **Korana** ⁓ C Croatia
161 L14 **Korāput** Orissa, E India 18.49N 82.43E
Korat *see* Nakhon Ratchasima
178 Ii9 **Korat Plateau** *plateau* E Thailand
145 T1 **Korāwa, Sar-i** ▲ NE Iraq 37.07N 44.39E
160 L11 **Korba** Chhattīsgarh, C India 22.25N 82.43E
103 H15 **Korbach** Hessen, C Germany 51.16N 8.52E
Korça *see* Korçë
115 M21 **Korçë** *var.* Korça, *Gk.* Korytsa, *It.* Corriza; *prev.* Koritsa. Korçë, SE Albania 40.37N 20.46E
115 M21 **Korçë** ◈ *district* SE Albania
115 G15 **Korčula** *It.* Curzola. Dubrovnik-Neretva, S Croatia 42.57N 17.08E
115 F15 **Korčula** *It.* Curzola; *anc.* Corcyra Nigra. *island* S Croatia
115 F15 **Korčulanski Kanal** *channel* S Croatia
151 T6 **Korday** *prev.* Georgiyevka. Zhambyl, SE Kazakhstan 43.06N 74.42E
148 J5 **Kordestān** *off.* Ostān-e Kordestān, *var.* Kurdestan. ◈ *province* W Iran
149 P4 **Kord Kūy** *var.* Kurd Kui. Golestān, N Iran 36.49N 54.04E
169 V13 **Korea Bay** *bay* China/North Korea
Korea, Democratic People's Republic of *see* North Korea
176 Uu15 **Koreare** Pulau Yamdena, E Indonesia 7.33S 131.13E
Korea, Republic of *see* South Korea
169 Z17 **Korea Strait** *Jap.* Chōsen-kaikyō, *Kor.* Taehan-haehyōp. *channel* Japan/South Korea
Korelichi/Korelicze *see* Karelichy
82 J11 **Korem** Tigray, N Ethiopia 12.32N 39.29E
79 U11 **Korén Adoua** ⁓ C Niger
130 I7 **Korenevo** Kurskaya Oblast', W Russian Federation 51.21N 34.53E
130 L13 **Korenovsk** Krasnodarskiy Kray, SW Russian Federation 45.28N 39.25E
118 L4 **Korets'** *Pol.* Korzec, *Rus.* Korets. Rivnens'ka Oblast', NW Ukraine 50.38N 27.12E
127 Pp8 **Korf** Koryakskiy Avtonomnyy Okrug, E Russian Federation 60.20N 165.37E
204 L7 **Korff Ice Rise** *ice cap* Antarctica
151 Q10 **Korgalzhyn** *var.* Kurgal'dzhino, Kurgal'dzhinsky, *Kaz.* Qorgazhyn. Akmola, C Kazakhstan 50.33N 69.58E
94 G13 **Korgen** Troms, N Norway 66.04N 13.51E
153 R9 **Korgon-Dĕbĕ** Dzhalal-Abadskaya Oblast', W Kyrgyzstan 41.51N 70.52E
78 M14 **Korhogo** N Ivory Coast 9.28N 5.38W
117 F19 **Korinthiakós Kólpos** *Eng.* Gulf of Corinth; *anc.* Corinthiacus Sinus. *gulf* C Greece
117 F19 **Kórinthos** *Eng.* Corinth; *anc.* Corinthus. Pelopónnisos, S Greece 37.55N 22.55E
115 M18 **Koritnik** ▲ S Serbia and Montenegro (Yugoslavia) 42.06N 20.34E
Koritsa *see* Korçë
171 L14 **Kōriyama** Fukushima, Honshū, C Japan 37.25N 140.20E
142 E16 **Korkuteli** Antalya, SW Turkey 37.04N 30.12E
164 K6 **Korla** *Chin.* K'u-erh-lo. Xinjiang Uygur Zizhiqu, NW China 41.48N 86.10E
126 H11 **Korliki** Khanty-Mansiyskiy Avtonomnyy Okrug, C Russian Federation 61.28N 82.12E
Körlin an der Persante *see* Karlino
Korma *see* Karma
12 D8 **Kormak** Ontario, S Canada 47.38N 83.00W
Kormakiti, Akrotíri/Kormakiti, Cape/Kormakítis *see* Koruçam Burnu
113 G23 **Körmend** Vas, W Hungary 47.01N 16.34E
145 T5 **Körmör** E Iraq 35.06N 44.47E
114 C13 **Kornat** *It.* Incoronata. *island* W Croatia
Korneshty *see* Corneşti
111 X3 **Korneuburg** Niederösterreich, NE Austria 48.22N 16.20E
151 P7 **Korneyevka** Severnyy Kazakhstan, N Kazakhstan 54.01N 68.30E
97 I17 **Kornsjø** Østfold, S Norway 58.55N 11.40E
79 O11 **Koro** Mopti, S Mali 14.05N 3.06W
197 J14 **Koro** *island* C Fiji
194 F12 **Koroba** Southern Highlands, W PNG 5.46S 142.48E
130 K8 **Korocha** Belgorodskaya Oblast', W Russian Federation 50.49N 37.08E
142 H12 **Köroğlu Dağları** ▲▲ C Turkey
191 V6 **Korogoro Point** *headland* New South Wales, SE Australia 31.03S 153.04E
83 J21 **Korogwe** Tanga, E Tanzania 5.12S 38.26E
190 L13 **Koroit** Victoria, SE Australia 38.17S 142.22E
197 H15 **Korolevu** Viti Levu, W Fiji 18.12S 177.44E
202 I17 **Koromiri** *island* S Cook Islands
179 R16 **Koronadal** Mindanao, S Philippines 6.23N 124.54E
117 E22 **Koróni** Pelopónnisos, S Greece 36.46N 21.57E
116 G13 **Korónia, Límni** ◎ N Greece
112 I9 **Koronowo** *Ger.* Krone an der Brahe. Kujawski-pomorskie, C Poland 53.18N 17.56E
119 R2 **Korop** Chernihivs'ka Oblast', N Ukraine 51.35N 32.57E
117 H19 **Koropí** Attikí, C Greece 37.54N 23.52E
196 C8 **Koror** *var.* Oreor. ● (Palau) Oreor, N Palau 7.21N 134.28E
Koror *see* Oreor
Kőrös *see* Križevci
113 L23 **Körös** ⁓ E Hungary
Kőrösbánya *see* Baia de Criş
197 J14 **Koro Sea** *sea* C Fiji
Koroška *see* Kärnten
119 N3 **Korosten'** Zhytomyrs'ka Oblast', NW Ukraine 50.56N 28.39E
Korostyshev *see* Korostyshiv
119 N4 **Korostyshiv** *Rus.* Korostyshev. Zhytomyrs'ka Oblast', N Ukraine 50.18N 29.04E
129 V3 **Korotaikha** ⁓ NW Russian Federation
126 H9 **Korotchayevo** Yamalo-Nenetskiy Avtonomnyy Okrug, N Russian Federation 66.00N 78.11E
80 I8 **Koro Toro** Borkou-Ennedi-Tibesti, N Chad 16.01N 18.27E
41 N16 **Korovin Island** *island* Shumagin Islands, Alaska, USA
197 I14 **Korovou** Viti Levu, W Fiji 17.48S 178.32E
95 M17 **Korpilahti** Länsi-Suomi, W Finland 62.01N 25.34E
94 K12 **Korpilombolo** *Lapp.* Dállogilli. Norrbotten, N Sweden 66.51N 23.00E
127 Oo16 **Korsakov** Ostrov Sakhalin, Sakhalinskaya Oblast', SE Russian Federation 46.41N 142.45E
95 J16 **Korsholm** *Fin.* Mustasaari. Länsi-Suomi, W Finland 63.07N 21.45E
97 I23 **Korsør** Vestsjælland, E Denmark 55.19N 11.09E
Korsovka *see* Kārsava
119 P6 **Korsun'-Shevchenkivs'kyy** *Rus.* Korsun'-Shevchenkovskiy. Cherkas'ka Oblast', C Ukraine 49.25N 31.15E
Korsun'-Shevchenkovskiy *see* Korsun'-Shevchenkivs'kyy
101 C17 **Kortemark** West-Vlaanderen, W Belgium 51.03N 3.03E
101 H18 **Kortenberg** Vlaams Brabant, C Belgium 50.52N 4.33E
101 K18 **Kortessem** Limburg, NE Belgium 50.52N 5.22E
101 E14 **Kortgene** Zeeland, SW Netherlands 51.34N 3.48E
82 F8 **Korti** Northern, N Sudan 18.06N 31.33E
101 C18 **Kortrijk** *Fr.* Courtrai. West-Vlaanderen, W Belgium 50.49N 3.16E
124 N2 **Koruçam Burnu** *var.* Cape Kormakiti, Kormakítis, *Gk.* Akrotíri Kormakíti. *headland* N Cyprus 35.24N 32.55E
191 O13 **Korumburra** Victoria, SE Australia 38.27S 145.48E
Koryak Range *see* Koryakskoye Nagor'ye
127 P8 **Koryakskiy Avtonomnyy Okrug** ◈ *autonomous district* E Russian Federation
Koryakskiy Khrebet *see* Koryakskoye Nagor'ye
127 Pp7 **Koryakskoye Nagor'ye** *var.* Koryakskiy Khrebet, *Eng.* Koryak Range. ▲▲ NE Russian Federation
129 P11 **Koryazhma** Arkhangel'skaya Oblast', NW Russian Federation 61.16N 47.06E
Kōryŏ *see* Kangnŭng
Korytsa *see* Korçë
119 Q2 **Koryukivka** Chernihivs'ka Oblast', N Ukraine 51.45N 32.16E
Korzec *see* Korets'
117 N21 **Kos** Kos, Dodekánisos, Greece, Aegean Sea 36.53N 27.18E
117 M21 **Kos** *It.* Coo; *anc.* Cos. *island* Dodekánisos, Greece, Aegean Sea
129 T12 **Kosa** Komi-Permyatskiy Avtonomnyy Okrug, NW Russian Federation 59.55N 54.54E
129 T13 **Kosa** ⁓ NW Russian Federation
170 C11 **Kō-saki** *headland* Nagasaki, Tsushima, SW Japan 34.06N 129.13E
169 X13 **Kosan** SE North Korea 38.50N 127.26E
121 H18 **Kosava** *Rus.* Kosovo. Brestskaya Voblasts', SW Belarus 52.45N 25.16E
Kosch *see* Kose
150 G12 **Koschagyl** *Kaz.* Qosshaghyl. Atyrau, W Kazakhstan 46.52N 53.46E
112 G12 **Kościan** *Ger.* Kosten. Wielkopolskie, C Poland 52.04N 16.37E
112 I7 **Kościerzyna** Pomorskie, NW Poland 54.06N 17.55E
24 L4 **Kosciusko** Mississippi, S USA 33.03N 89.35W
Kosciusko, Mount *see* Kosciuszko, Mount
191 R11 **Kosciuszko, Mount** *prev.* Mount Kosciusko ▲ New South Wales, SE Australia 36.28S 148.15E
120 H4 **Kose** *Ger.* Kosch. Harjumaa, NW Estonia 59.10N 25.10E
116 G6 **Koshava** Vidin, NW Bulgaria 44.03N 23.00E
153 U9 **Kosh-Dĕbĕ** *var.* Koshtebë. Narynskaya Oblast', C Kyrgyzstan 41.03N 74.08E
171 K16 **Koshigaya** *var.* Kosigaya. Saitama, Honshū, S Japan 35.54N 139.46E
K'o-shih *see* Kashi
170 B15 **Koshikijima-rettō** *var.* Kosikizima Rettô. *island group* SW Japan
151 W13 **Koshkarkol', Ozero** ◎ SE Kazakhstan
32 L9 **Koshkonong, Lake** ◎ Wisconsin, N USA
Koshoba *see* Goşoba
171 J14 **Kōshoku** *var.* Kôsyoku. Nagano, Honshū, S Japan 36.31N 138.07E
Koshtebë *see* Kosh-Dĕbĕ
Kōshū *see* Kwangju
113 N19 **Košice** *Ger.* Kaschau, *Hung.* Kassa. Košický Kraj, E Slovakia 48.43N 21.15E
113 M20 **Košický Kraj** ◈ *region* E Slovakia
Kosigaya *see* Koshigaya
Kosikizima Rettô *see* Koshikijima-rettō
159 R12 **Kosi Reservoir** ⊠ E Nepal
118 J8 **Kosiv** Ivano-Frankivs'ka Oblast', W Ukraine 48.19N 25.04E
151 O11 **Koskol'** Karaganda, C Kazakhstan 49.34N 67.03E
129 Q9 **Koslan** Respublika Komi, NW Russian Federation 63.27N 48.52E
Köslin *see* Koszalin
152 M12 **Koson** *Rus.* Kasan. Qashqadaryo Viloyati, S Uzbekistan 39.03N 65.34E
169 Y13 **Kosŏng** SE North Korea 38.40N 128.13E
153 S9 **Kosonsoy** *Rus.* Kasansay. Namangan Viloyati, E Uzbekistan 41.15N 71.28E
115 M16 **Kosovo** *prev.* Autonomous Province of Kosovo and Metohija. *region* S Serbia and Montenegro (Yugoslavia)
Kosovo *see* Kosava
Kosovo and Metohija, Autonomous Province of *see* Kosovo
115 N16 **Kosovo Polje** Serbia, S Serbia and Montenegro (Yugoslavia) 42.40N 21.07E
115 O16 **Kosovska Kamenica** Serbia, SE Serbia and Montenegro (Yugoslavia) 42.37N 21.33E
115 M16 **Kosovska Mitrovica** *Alb.* Mitrovicë; *prev.* Mitrovica, Titova Mitrovica. Serbia, S Serbia and Montenegro (Yugoslavia) 42.54N 20.52E
201 X17 **Kosrae** ◈ *state* E Micronesia
201 Y14 **Kosrae** *prev.* Kusaie. *island* Caroline Islands, E Micronesia
27 U9 **Kosse** Texas, SW USA 31.16N 96.38W
111 P6 **Kössen** Tirol, W Austria 47.40N 12.24E
78 M16 **Kossou, Lac de** ◎ C Ivory Coast
Kossukavak *see* Krumovgrad
Kostajnica *see* Hrvatska Kostajnica
150 M7 **Kostanay** *var.* Kustanay, *Kaz.* Qostanay. N Kazakhstan 53.15N 63.34E
150 L8 **Kostanay** *var.* Kostanayskaya Oblast, *Kaz.* Qostanay Oblysy. ◈ *province* N Kazakhstan
Kostanayskaya Oblast *see* Kostanay
Kostamus *see* Kostomuksha
Kosten *see* Kościan
116 H10 **Kostenets** *prev.* Georgi Dimitrov. Sofiya, W Bulgaria 42.17N 23.52E
82 F10 **Kosti** White Nile, C Sudan 13.10N 32.37E
Kostnitz *see* Konstanz
128 H7 **Kostomuksha** *Fin.* Kostamus. Respublika Kareliya, NW Russian Federation 64.33N 30.28E
118 K3 **Kostopil'** *Rus.* Kostopol'. Rivnens'ka Oblast', NW Ukraine 50.20N 26.28E
Kostopol' *see* Kostopil'
128 M15 **Kostroma** Kostromskaya Oblast', NW Russian Federation 57.46N 40.59E
129 N14 **Kostroma** ⁓ NW Russian Federation
129 N14 **Kostromskaya Oblast'** ◈ *province* NW Russian Federation
112 D11 **Kostrzyn** *Ger.* Cüstrin, Küstrin. Lubuskie, W Poland 52.35N 14.39E
112 H11 **Kostrzyn** Wielkolpolskie, C Poland 52.23N 17.13E
119 X7 **Kostyantynivka** *Rus.* Konstantinovka. Donets'ka Oblast', SE Ukraine 48.30N 37.45E
Kostyukovichi *see* Kastsyukovichy
Kostyukovka *see* Kastsyukowka
Kôsyoku *see* Kōshoku
129 U6 **Kos'yu** Respublika Komi, NW Russian Federation 65.39N 59.01E
129 U6 **Kos'yu** ⁓ NW Russian Federation
112 F7 **Koszalin** *Ger.* Köslin. Zachodnio-pomorskie, NW Poland 54.11N 16.10E
113 F22 **Kőszeg** *Ger.* Güns. Vas, W Hungary 47.24N 16.33E
158 H13 **Kota** *prev.* Kotah. Rājasthān, N India 25.13N 75.51E
174 H9 **Kota Baru** Sumatera, W Indonesia 1.07S 101.43E
175 Nn11 **Kotabaru** Pulau Laut, C Indonesia 3.15S 116.15E
Kotabaru *see* Jayapura
174 H2 **Kota Bharu** *var.* Kota Baharu, Kota Bahru. Kelantan, Peninsular Malaysia 6.07N 102.15E
Kotaboemi *see* Kotabumi
174 Ii12 **Kotabumi** *prev.* Kotaboemi. Sumatera, W Indonesia 4.49S 104.54E
155 S10 **Kot Addu** Punjab, E Pakistan 30.25N 70.54E
Kotah *see* Kota
175 Nn2 **Kota Kinabalu** *prev.* Jesselton. Sabah, East Malaysia 5.58N 116.04E
175 Nn2 **Kota Kinabalu** ✕ Sabah, East Malaysia 5.58N 116.04E
94 M12 **Kotala** Lappi, N Finland 67.01N 29.00E
Kotamobagoe *see* Kotamobagu
175 Rr7 **Kotamobagu** *prev.* Kotamobagoe. Sulawesi, C Indonesia 0.46N 124.21E
161 L14 **Kotapad** *var.* Kotapārh. Orissa, E India 19.10N 82.23E
Kotapārh *see* Kotapad
178 Gg17 **Ko Ta Ru Tao** *island* SW Thailand
174 L11 **Kotawaringin, Teluk** *bay* Borneo, C Indonesia
155 Q13 **Kot Dīji** Sind, SE Pakistan 27.16N 68.43E
158 K9 **Kotdwāra** Uttaranchal, N India 29.43N 78.33E
129 Q14 **Kotel'nich** Kirovskaya Oblast', NW Russian Federation 58.19N 48.12E
131 N12 **Kotel'nikovo** Volgogradskaya Oblast', SW Russian Federation 47.37N 43.07E
126 Ll4 **Kotel'nyy, Ostrov** *island* Novosibirskiye Ostrova, N Russian Federation
119 T5 **Kotel'va** Poltavs'ka Oblast', C Ukraine 50.04N 34.46E
103 M14 **Köthen** *var.* Cöthen. Sachsen-Anhalt, C Germany 51.46N 11.58E
Kōti *see* Kōchi
83 G17 **Kotido** NE Uganda 3.03N 34.07E
95 N19 **Kotka** Etelä-Suomi, S Finland 60.28N 26.54E
129 P11 **Kotlas** Arkhangel'skaya Oblast', NW Russian Federation 61.13N 46.43E
40 M10 **Kotlik** Alaska, USA 63.01N 163.33W
79 Q17 **Kotoka** ✕ (Accra) S Ghana 5.41N 0.10W
Kotonu *see* Cotonou
115 J17 **Kotor** *It.* Cattaro. Montenegro, SW Serbia and Montenegro (Yugoslavia) 42.25N 18.47E
Kotor *see* Kotoriba
114 F7 **Kotoriba** *Hung.* Kotor. Međimurje, N Croatia 46.20N 16.47E
115 I17 **Kotorska, Boka** *It.* Bocche di Cattaro. *bay* Montenegro, SW Serbia and Montenegro (Yugoslavia)
114 H11 **Kotorsko** Republika Srpska, N Bosnia and Herzegovina 44.50N 18.03E
114 G11 **Kotor Varoš** Republika Srpska, N Bosnia and Herzegovina 44.37N 17.24E
Koto Sho/Kotosho *see* Lan Yü
130 M7 **Kotovsk** Tambovskaya Oblast', W Russian Federation 52.39N 41.31E
119 O9 **Kotovs'k** *Rus.* Kotovsk. Odes'ka Oblast', SW Ukraine 47.42N 29.30E
Kotovsk *see* Hînceşti
121 G16 **Kotra** *Rus.* Kotra. ⁓ W Belarus
155 P16 **Kotri** Sind, SE Pakistan 25.22N 68.16E
111 Q9 **Kötschach** Kärnten, S Austria 46.41N 12.57E
161 K15 **Kottagūdem** Andhra Pradesh, E India 17.36N 80.40E
161 F21 **Kottappadi** Kerala, SW India 11.38N 76.03E
161 G23 **Kottayam** Kerala, SW India 9.37N 76.31E
Kottbus *see* Cottbus
Kotte *see* Sri Jayawardanapura
81 K15 **Kotto** ⁓ Central African Republic/Dem. Rep. Congo
200 S13 **Kotu Group** *island group* W Tonga
Koturdepe *see* Goturdepe
126 J9 **Kotuy** ⁓ N Russian Federation
85 M16 **Kotwa** Mashonaland East, NE Zimbabwe 16.58S 32.46E
41 N7 **Kotzebue** Alaska, USA 66.54N 162.36W
40 M7 **Kotzebue Sound** *inlet* Alaska, USA
Kotzenan *see* Chocianów
Kotzman *see* Kitsman'
79 R14 **Kouandé** NW Benin 10.19N 1.42E
81 J15 **Kouango** Ouaka, S Central African Republic 5.00N 20.01E
79 O13 **Koudougou** C Burkina 12.15N 2.22W
100 K7 **Koudum** Friesland, N Netherlands 52.55N 5.26E
117 L25 **Koufonísi** *island* SE Greece
117 K21 **Koufonísi** *island* Kykládes, Greece, Aegean Sea
40 M8 **Kougarok Mountain** ▲ Alaska, USA 65.41N 165.29W
81 E20 **Kouilou** ⁓ S Congo
16 N3 **Koukdjuak** ⁓ Baffin Island, Nunavut, NE Canada
124 N4 **Koúklia** SW Cyprus 34.42N 32.35E
81 E19 **Koulamoutou** Ogooué-Lolo, C Gabon 1.06S 12.26E
78 L12 **Koulikoro** Koulikoro, SW Mali 12.55N 7.31W
78 L11 **Koulikoro** ◈ *region* SW Mali
197 H5 **Koumac** Province Nord, W New Caledonia 20.34S 164.18E
171 J15 **Koumi** Nagano, Honshū, S Japan 36.06N 138.27E
80 I13 **Koumra** Moyen-Chari, S Chad 8.55N 17.31E
Kounadougou *see* Koundougou
78 M15 **Kounahiri** C Ivory Coast 7.47N 5.51W
78 I12 **Koundâra** Moyenne-Guinée, NW Guinea 12.28N 13.15W
79 N13 **Koundougou** *var.* Kounadougou. C Burkina 11.43N 4.40W
78 H11 **Koungheul** C Senegal 14.00N 14.48W
Kounradskiy *see* Konyrat
27 X10 **Kountze** Texas, SW USA 30.22N 94.18W
79 Q13 **Koupéla** C Burkina 12.09N 0.23W
79 N13 **Kouri** Sikasso, SW Mali 12.09N 4.46W
57 Y9 **Kourou** N French Guiana 5.07N 52.37W
116 J12 **Kouroú** ⁓ NE Greece
78 K14 **Kouroussa** Haute-Guinée, C Guinea 10.40N 9.49W
Kousseir *see* Al Quşayr
80 G11 **Kousséri** *prev.* Fort-Foureau. Extrême-Nord, NE Cameroon 12.01N 15.03E
Kouteifé *see* Al Quţayfah
78 M13 **Koutiala** Sikasso, S Mali 12.24N 5.30W
78 M14 **Kouto** NW Ivory Coast 9.51N 6.25W
95 M19 **Kouvola** Etelä-Suomi, S Finland 60.50N 26.48E
81 G18 **Kouyou** ⁓ C Congo
114 M10 **Kovačica** *Hung.* Antafalva; *prev.* Kovacsicza. Serbia, N Serbia and Montenegro (Yugoslavia) 45.08N 20.36E
Kovacsicza *see* Kovačica
Kővárhosszúfalu *see* Satulung
Kovászna *see* Covasna
128 I4 **Kovdor** Murmanskaya Oblast', NW Russian Federation 67.32N 30.27E
128 I5 **Kovdozero, Ozero** ◎ NW Russian Federation
118 J3 **Kovel'** *Pol.* Kowel. Volyns'ka Oblast', NW Ukraine 51.13N 24.42E
114 M11 **Kovin** *Hung.* Kevevára; *prev.* Temes-Kubin. Serbia, NE Serbia and Montenegro (Yugoslavia) 44.45N 20.59E
Kovno *see* Kaunas
131 N3 **Kovrov** Vladimirskaya Oblast', W Russian Federation 56.24N 41.21E
131 O5 **Kovylkino** Respublika Mordoviya, W Russian Federation 54.03N 43.52E
112 J11 **Kowal** Kujawsko-pomorskie, C Poland 52.31N 19.08E
112 J9 **Kowalewo Pomorskie** *Ger.* Schönsee. Kujawsko-pomorskie, C Poland 53.07N 18.48E
Kowasna *see* Covasna
121 M16 **Kowbcha** *Rus.* Kolbcha. Mahilyowskaya Voblasts', E Belarus 53.40N 29.13E
Koweit *see* Kuwait
Kowel *see* Kovel'
193 F17 **Kowhitirangi** West Coast, South Island, NZ 42.54S 171.01E
167 O15 **Kowloon** *Chin.* Jiulong. Hong Kong, S China
Kowno *see* Kaunas
165 N7 **Kox Kuduk** *well* NW China 40.32N 92.30E
142 D16 **Köyceğiz** Muğla, SW Turkey 36.58N 28.38E
129 N6 **Koyda** Arkhangel'skaya Oblast', NW Russian Federation 66.22N 42.42E
Koymat *see* Goymat
Koymatdag, Gory *see* Goymatdag
Koyna Reservoir *see* Shivāji Sāgar
171 M11 **Koyoshi-gawa** ⁓ Honshū, C Japan
Koysanjaq *see* Koi Sanjaq
Koytash *see* Qo'ytosh
152 M14 **Köytendag** *prev. Rus.* Charshanga, Charshangy, *Turkm.* Charshangngy. Lebap Welaýaty, E Turkmenistan 37.31N 65.58E
41 N9 **Koyuk** Alaska, USA 64.55N 161.09W
41 N9 **Koyuk River** ⁓ Alaska, USA
41 O9 **Koyukuk** Alaska, USA 64.52N 157.42W
41 O9 **Koyukuk River** ⁓ Alaska, USA
142 J13 **Kozaklı** Nevşehir, C Turkey 39.13N 34.51E
170 F13 **Kōzan** Hiroshima, Honshū, SW Japan 34.35N 133.02E
142 K16 **Kozan** Adana, S Turkey 37.27N 35.46E
117 E14 **Kozáni** Dytikí Makedonía, N Greece 40.18N 21.48E
114 F10 **Kozara** ▲▲ NW Bosnia and Herzegovina
Kozarska Dubica *see* Bosanska Dubica
119 P3 **Kozelets'** *Rus.* Kozelets. Chernihivs'ka Oblast', NE Ukraine 50.54N 31.09E
119 S6 **Kozel'shchyna** Poltavs'ka Oblast', C Ukraine 49.13N 33.49E
130 J5 **Kozel'sk** Kaluzhskaya Oblast', W Russian Federation 54.04N 35.51E
Kozhikode *see* Calicut
129 V9 **Kozhimiz, Gora** ▲ NW Russian Federation 63.13N 58.54E
128 L9 **Kozhozero, Ozero** ◎ NW Russian Federation
129 T7 **Kozhva** *var.* Kozya. Respublika Komi, NW Russian Federation 65.06N 57.00E
129 T7 **Kozhva** ⁓ NW Russian Federation
129 U6 **Kozhim** Respublika Komi, NW Russian Federation 65.43N 59.25E
112 N13 **Kozienice** Mazowieckie, C Poland 51.37N 21.30E
111 S13 **Kozina** SW Slovenia 45.36N 13.56E
116 H7 **Kozloduy** Vratsa, NW Bulgaria 43.47N 23.42E
131 Q3 **Kozlovka** Chavash Respubliki, W Russian Federation 55.53N 48.07E
Kozlovshchina/Kozlowszczyzna *see* Kazlowshchyna
131 P3 **Koz'modem'yansk** Respublika Mariy El, W Russian Federation 56.19N 46.33E
118 J6 **Kozova** Ternopil's'ka Oblast', W Ukraine 49.25N 25.09E
115 P20 **Kožuf** ▲ S FYR Macedonia 41.10N 22.14E
172 S13 **Kōzu-shima** *island* E Japan
Kozya *see* Kozhva
Koz'yany *see* Kaz'yany
119 N5 **Kozyatyn** *Rus.* Kazatin. Vinnyts'ka Oblast', C Ukraine 49.40N 28.48E
79 Q16 **Kpalimé** *var.* Palimé. SW Togo 6.54N 0.37E
79 Q16 **Kpandu** E Ghana 7.00N 0.18E
101 F15 **Krabbendijke** Zeeland, SW Netherlands 51.25N 4.07E
178 Gg16 **Krabi** *var.* Muang Krabi. Krabi, SW Thailand 8.04N 98.52E
178 Gg14 **Kra Buri** Ranong, SW Thailand 10.25N 98.48E
178 Jj13 **Krâchéh** *prev.* Kratie. Krâchéh, E Cambodia 12.28N 106.01E
97 G17 **Kragerø** Telemark, S Norway 58.53N 9.22E
114 M13 **Kragujevac** Serbia, C Serbia and Montenegro (Yugoslavia) 44.01N 20.54E
Krainburg *see* Kranj
178 Gg14 **Kra, Isthmus of** *isthmus* Malaysia/Thailand
114 D12 **Krajina** *cultural region* SW Croatia
Krakatau, Pulau *see* Rakata, Pulau
Krakau *see* Małopolskie
113 K16 **Kraków** *Eng.* Cracow, *Ger.* Krakau; *anc.* Cracovia. Małopolskie, S Poland 50.03N 19.57E
102 L9 **Krakower See** ◎ NE Germany
178 Ii12 **Krâlănh** Siĕmréab, NW Cambodia 13.35N 103.27E
47 Q16 **Kralendijk** Bonaire, E Netherlands Antilles 12.07N 68.13W
114 B10 **Kraljevica** *It.* Porto Re. Primorje-Gorski Kotar, NW Croatia 45.15N 14.36E
114 M13 **Kraljevo** *prev.* Rankovićevo. Serbia, C Serbia and Montenegro (Yugoslavia) 43.44N 20.40E
113 E16 **Královéhradecký Kraj** *prev.* Hradecký Kraj. ◈ *region* N Czech Republic
Kralup an der Moldau *see* Kralupy nad Vltavou

♦ Country ● Country Capital ◇ Dependent Territory ○ Dependent Territory Capital ◈ Administrative Region ✕ International Airport ▲ Mountain ▲▲ Mountain Range Volcano ⁓ River ◎ Lake ⊠ Reservoir

279

KRALUPY NAD VLTAVOU – KUNDLA

113 C16 **Kralupy nad Vltavou** *Ger.* Kralup an der Moldau. Středočeský Kraj, NW Czech Republic 50.13N 14.17E
119 W7 **Kramators'k** *Rus.* Kramatorsk. Donets'ka Oblast', SE Ukraine 48.43N 37.34E
95 H17 **Kramfors** Västernorrland, C Sweden 62.55N 17.49E
117 D15 **Kranéa** Dytikí Makedonía, N Greece 39.54N 21.21E
110 M7 **Kranebitten** ✈ (Innsbruck) Tirol, W Austria 47.18N 11.21E
117 G20 **Kranídi** Pelopónnisos, S Greece 37.21N 23.09E
111 T11 **Kranj** *Ger.* Krainburg. NW Slovenia 46.16N 14.16E
117 F16 **Krannón** *battleground* Thessalía, C Greece 39.32N 22.20E
Kranz *see* Zelenogradsk
114 D7 **Krapina** Krapina-Zagorje, N Croatia 46.12N 15.52E
114 E8 **Krapina** ≈ N Croatia
114 D8 **Krapina-Zagorje** *off.* Krapinsko-Zagorska Županija. ◆ *province* N Croatia
116 L7 **Krapinets** ≈ NE Bulgaria
113 I15 **Krapkowice** *Ger.* Krappitz. Opolskie, S Poland 50.28N 17.55E
Krappitz *see* Krapkowice
129 O12 **Krasavino** Vologodskaya Oblast', NW Russian Federation 60.56N 46.27E
125 Ff5 **Krasino** Novaya Zemlya, Arkhangel'skaya Oblast', N Russian Federation 70.45N 54.16E
127 N18 **Kraskino** Primorskiy Kray, SE Russian Federation 42.40N 130.51E
120 J11 **Krāslava** Krāslava, SE Latvia 55.56N 27.08E
121 M14 **Krasnaluki** *Rus.* Krasnoluki. Vitsyebskaya Voblasts', N Belarus 54.37N 28.49E
121 P17 **Krasnapollye** *Rus.* Krasnopol'ye. Mahilyowskaya Voblasts', E Belarus 53.19N 31.24E
130 L15 **Krasnaya Polyana** Krasnodarskiy Kray, SW Russian Federation 43.40N 40.13E
121 J18 **Krasnaya Slabada** *var.* Chyrvonaya Slabada, *Rus.* Krasnaya Sloboda. Minskaya Voblasts', S Belarus 52.51N 27.10E
Krasnaya Sloboda *see* Krasnaya Slabada
121 J15 **Krasnaye** *Rus.* Krasnoye. Minskaya Voblasts', C Belarus 54.13N 27.04E
113 O14 **Kraśnik** *Ger.* Kratznick. Lubelskie, E Poland 50.55N 22.13E
119 O9 **Krasni Okny** Odes'ka Oblast', SW Ukraine 47.33N 29.28E
151 P7 **Krasnoarmeysk** Severnyy Kazakhstan, N Kazakhstan 53.52N 69.51E
131 P8 **Krasnoarmeysk** Saratovskaya Oblast', W Russian Federation 51.01N 45.42E
Krasnoarmeysk *see* Krasnoarmiys'k/Tayynsha
127 Oo4 **Krasnoarmeyskiy** Chukotskiy Avtonomnyy Okrug, NE Russian Federation 69.30N 171.44E
119 W7 **Krasnoarmiys'k** *Rus.* Krasnoarmeysk. Donets'ka Oblast', SE Ukraine 48.16N 37.13E
129 P11 **Krasnoborsk** Arkhangel'skaya Oblast', NW Russian Federation 61.31N 45.57E
130 K14 **Krasnodar** *prev.* Ekaterinodar, Yekaterinodar. Krasnodarskiy Kray, SW Russian Federation 45.02N 39.00E
130 K13 **Krasnodarskiy Kray** ◆ *territory* SW Russian Federation
119 Z7 **Krasnodon** Luhans'ka Oblast', E Ukraine 48.16N 39.45E
Krasnogor *see* Kallaste
131 T2 **Krasnogorskoye** *Latv.* Sarkaņi. Udmurtskaya Respublika, NW Russian Federation 57.42N 52.29E
Krasnograd *see* Krasnohrad
Krasnogvardeysk *see* Bulung'ur
130 M13 **Krasnogvardeyskoye** Stavropol'skiy Kray, SW Russian Federation 45.49N 41.31E
Krasnogvardeyskoye *see* Krasnohvardiys'ke
119 U6 **Krasnohrad** *Rus.* Krasnograd. Kharkivs'ka Oblast', E Ukraine 49.22N 35.27E
119 S12 **Krasnohvardiys'ke** *Rus.* Krasnogvardeyskoye. Respublika Krym, S Ukraine 45.30N 34.19E
126 L16 **Krasnokamensk** Chitinskaya Oblast', S Russian Federation 50.03N 118.01E
129 U14 **Krasnokamsk** Permskaya Oblast', W Russian Federation 58.07N 55.48E
131 U8 **Krasnokholm** Orenburgskaya Oblast', W Russian Federation 51.34N 54.11E
119 U5 **Krasnokuts'k** *Rus.* Krasnokutsk. Kharkivs'ka Oblast', E Ukraine 50.01N 35.03E
130 L7 **Krasnolesnyy** Voronezhskaya Oblast', W Russian Federation 51.53N 39.37E
Krasnoluki *see* Krasnaluki
Krasnoosol'skoye Vodokhranilishche *see* Chervonooskil's'ke Vodoskhovyshche
119 S11 **Krasnoperekops'k** *Rus.* Krasnoperekopsk. Respublika Krym, S Ukraine 45.56N 33.46E
119 U4 **Krasnopillya** Sums'ka Oblast', NE Ukraine 50.46N 35.17E
Krasnopol'ye *see* Krasnapollye
126 H9 **Krasnosel'kup** Yamalo-Nenetskiy Avtonomnyy Okrug, N Russian Federation 65.46N 82.11E
128 L5 **Krasnoshchel'ye** Murmanskaya Oblast', NW Russian Federation 67.22N 37.03E
131 O5 **Krasnoslobodsk** Respublika Mordoviya, W Russian Federation 54.24N 43.51E
131 T2 **Krasnoslobodsk** Volgogradskaya Oblast', SW Russian Federation 48.41N 44.34E
Krasnostav *see* Krasnystaw
125 F10 **Krasnotur'insk** Sverdlovskaya Oblast', C Russian Federation 59.45N 60.19E
125 E11 **Krasnoufimsk** Sverdlovskaya Oblast', C Russian Federation 56.43N 57.39E
125 Ee10 **Krasnoural'sk** Sverdlovskaya Oblast', C Russian Federation 58.24N 59.44E
131 V5 **Krasnousol'skiy** Respublika Bashkortostan, W Russian Federation 53.55N 56.22E
129 U12 **Krasnovishersk** Permskaya Oblast', NW Russian Federation 60.22N 57.04E
Krasnovodsk *see* Türkmenbaşy
Krasnovodskiy Zaliv *see* Türkmenbaşy Aylagy
152 B10 **Krasnovodskoye Plato** *Turkm.* Krasnowodsk Platosy. *plateau* NW Turkmenistan
Krasnowodsk Aylagy *see* Türkmenbaşy Aylagy
Krasnowodsk Platosy *see* Krasnovodskoye Plato
126 Hh14 **Krasnoyarsk** Krasnoyarskiy Kray, S Russian Federation 56.04N 92.46E
131 X7 **Krasnoyarskiy** Orenburgskaya Oblast', W Russian Federation 51.56N 59.54E
126 I12 **Krasnoyarskiy Kray** ◆ *territory* C Russian Federation
126 I14 **Krasnoyarskoye Vodokhranilishche** ⊠ S Russian Federation
Krasnoye *see* Krasnaye
Krasnoye Znamya *see* Gyzylbaýdak
129 R11 **Krasnozatonskiy** Respublika Komi, NW Russian Federation 61.39N 51.00E
120 D13 **Krasnoznamensk** *prev.* Lasdehnen, *Ger.* Haselberg. Kaliningradskaya Oblast', W Russian Federation 54.57N 22.28E
130 K3 **Krasnoznamensk** Moskovskaya Oblast', W Russian Federation 55.40N 37.05E
119 R11 **Krasnoznam"yans'kyy Kanal** *canal* S Ukraine
113 P14 **Krasnystaw** *Rus.* Krasnostav. Lubelskie, SE Poland 51.00N 23.10E
130 H4 **Krasnyy** Smolenskaya Oblast', W Russian Federation 54.36N 31.27E
131 P2 **Krasnyye Baki** Nizhegorodskaya Oblast', W Russian Federation 57.07N 45.12E
131 Q13 **Krasnyye Barrikady** Astrakhanskaya Oblast', SW Russian Federation 46.14N 47.48E
128 K15 **Krasnyy Kholm** Tverskaya Oblast', W Russian Federation 58.04N 37.05E
131 Q8 **Krasnyy Kut** Saratovskaya Oblast', W Russian Federation 50.54N 46.58E
Krasnyy Liman *see* Krasnyy Lyman
119 Y7 **Krasnyy Luch** *prev.* Krindachevka. Luhans'ka Oblast', E Ukraine 48.08N 38.52E
119 X6 **Krasnyy Lyman** *Rus.* Krasnyy Liman. Donets'ka Oblast', SE Ukraine 49.00N 37.50E
131 R3 **Krasnyy Steklovar** Respublika Mariy El, W Russian Federation 56.14N 48.49E
131 P8 **Krasnyy Tekstil'shchik** Saratovskaya Oblast', W Russian Federation 51.35N 45.49E
131 R13 **Krasnyy Yar** Astrakhanskaya Oblast', SW Russian Federation 46.33N 48.21E
Krassóvár *see* Caraşova
118 L5 **Krasyliv** Khmel'nyts'ka Oblast', W Ukraine 49.38N 26.59E
113 O21 **Kraszna** *Rom.* Crasna. ≈ Hungary/Romania
Kratie *see* Krâchéh
194 I13 **Kratke Range** ▲ C PNG
115 P17 **Kratovo** NE FYR Macedonia 42.04N 22.08E
Kratznick *see* Kraśnik
176 Yy11 **Krau** Papua, E Indonesia 3.15S 140.07E
178 Ii13 **Krâvanh, Chuŏr Phnum** *Eng.* Cardamom Mountains, *Fr.* Chaîne des Cardamomes. ▲ W Cambodia
Kravasta Lagoon *see* Karavastasë, Laguna e
Krawang *see* Karawang
Kraxatau *see* Rakata, Pulau
131 Q15 **Kraynovka** Respublika Dagestan, SW Russian Federation 43.58N 47.24E
120 D12 **Kražiai** Šiauliai, C Lithuania 55.36N 22.41E
29 P11 **Krebs** Oklahoma, C USA 34.55N 95.43W
103 D15 **Krefeld** Nordrhein-Westfalen, W Germany 51.19N 6.34E
Kreisstadt *see* Krosno Odrzańskie
117 D17 **Kremastón, Technití Límni** ⊠ C Greece
Kremenchug *see* Kremenchuk
Kremenchugskoye Vodokhranilishche/Kremenchuk Reservoir *see* Kremenchuts'ke Vodoskhovyshche
119 S6 **Kremenchuk** *Rus.* Kremenchug. Poltavs'ka Oblast', NE Ukraine 49.03N 33.27E
119 R6 **Kremenchuts'ke Vodoskhovyshche** *Eng.* Kremenchuk Reservoir, *Rus.* Kremenchugskoye Vodokhranilishche. ⊠ C Ukraine
118 K5 **Kremenets'** *Pol.* Krzemieniec, *Rus.* Kremenets. Ternopil's'ka Oblast', W Ukraine 50.05N 25.43E
Kremennaya *see* Kreminna
119 X6 **Kreminna** *Rus.* Kremennaya. Luhans'ka Oblast', E Ukraine 49.03N 38.14E
39 R4 **Kremmling** Colorado, C USA 40.03N 106.23W
111 V3 **Krems** ≈ NE Austria
Krems *see* Krems an der Donau
111 W3 **Krems an der Donau** *var.* Krems. Niederösterreich, N Austria 48.25N 15.34E
Kremsier *see* Kroměříž
111 S4 **Kremsmünster** Oberösterreich, N Austria 48.04N 14.08E
40 M17 **Krenitzin Islands** *island* Aleutian Islands, Alaska, USA
Kresena *see* Kresna
116 G11 **Kresna** *var.* Kresena. Blagoevgrad, SW Bulgaria 41.43N 23.12E
114 O12 **Krespoljin** Serbia, E Serbia and Montenegro (Yugoslavia) 44.37N 21.36E
27 N4 **Kress** Texas, SW USA 34.21N 101.43W
127 Pp4 **Kresta, Zaliv** *bay* E Russian Federation
117 D20 **Kréstena** *prev.* Selinoús. Dytikí Ellás, S Greece 37.36N 21.36E
128 H14 **Krestsy** Novgorodskaya Oblast', W Russian Federation 58.15N 32.28E
126 Kk11 **Krestyakh** Respublika Sakha (Yakutiya), NE Russian Federation 62.10N 116.24E
Kretikon Delagos *see* Kritikó Pélagos
120 C11 **Kretinga** *Ger.* Krottingen. Klaipėda, NW Lithuania 55.53N 21.13E
Kreutz *see* Cristuru Secuiesc
Kreuz *see* Križevci, Croatia
Kreuz *see* Risti, Estonia
Kreuzburg/Kreuzburg in Oberschlesien *see* Kluczbork
Kreuzingen *see* Bol'shakovo
110 H6 **Kreuzlingen** Thurgau, NE Switzerland 47.37N 9.10E
103 K25 **Kreuzspitze** ▲ S Germany 47.30N 10.55E
103 F16 **Kreuztal** Nordrhein-Westfalen, W Germany 50.58N 8.00E
121 I15 **Kreva** *Rus.* Krevo. Hrodzyenskaya Voblasts', W Belarus 54.19N 26.16E
Krevo *see* Kreva
Kría Vrísi *see* Krýa Vrýsi
81 D16 **Kribi** Sud, SW Cameroon 2.53N 9.57E
Krichëv *see* Krychaw
Krickerhäu/Kriegerhaj *see* Handlová
111 W6 **Krieglach** Steiermark, E Austria 47.33N 15.37E
110 F8 **Kriens** Luzern, W Switzerland 47.01N 8.16E
Krimmitschau *see* Crimmitschau
100 H12 **Krimpen aan den IJssel** Zuid-Holland, SW Netherlands 51.56N 4.39E
Krindachevka *see* Krasnyy Luch
117 G25 **Kriós, Akrotírio** *headland* Kríti, Greece, E Mediterranean Sea 35.17N 23.31E
161 J16 **Krishna** *prev.* Kistna. ≈ C India
161 H20 **Krishnagiri** Tamil Nādu, SE India 12.33N 78.10E
161 K17 **Krishna, Mouths of the** *delta* SE India
159 S15 **Krishnanagar** West Bengal, N India 23.22N 88.31E
161 G20 **Krishnarājāsāgara Reservoir** ⊠ W India
97 N19 **Kristdala** Kalmar, S Sweden 57.24N 16.12E
Kristiania *see* Oslo
97 E18 **Kristiansand** *var.* Christiansand. Vest-Agder, S Norway 58.07N 7.52E
97 L22 **Kristianstad** Skåne, S Sweden 56.01N 14.10E
96 F8 **Kristiansund** *var.* Christiansund. Møre og Romsdal, S Norway 63.07N 7.45E
Kristiinankaupunki *see* Kristinestad
95 I14 **Kristineberg** Västerbotten, N Sweden 65.07N 18.36E
97 L16 **Kristinehamn** Värmland, C Sweden 59.16N 14.09E
95 J17 **Kristinestad** *Fin.* Kristiinankaupunki. Länsi-Suomi, W Finland 62.15N 21.24E
Kristyor *see* Crişcior
117 J25 **Kriti** *Eng.* Crete. ◆ *region* Greece, Aegean Sea
117 J24 **Kriti** *Eng.* Crete. *island* Greece, Aegean Sea
117 J23 **Kritikó Pélagos** *var.* Kretikon Delagos, *Eng.* Sea of Crete; *anc.* Mare Creticum. *sea* Greece, Aegean Sea
Kriulyany *see* Criuleni
114 I12 **Krivaja** ≈ NE Bosnia and Herzegovina
Krivaja *see* Mali Iđoš
115 P17 **Kriva Palanka** *Turk.* Eğri Palanka. NE FYR Macedonia 42.13N 22.19E
Krivichi *see* Kryvychy
116 H8 **Krivodol** Vratsa, NW Bulgaria 43.23N 23.30E
130 M10 **Krivorozh'ye** Rostovskaya Oblast', SW Russian Federation 48.51N 40.49E
Krivoshin *see* Kryvoshyn
Krivoy Rog *see* Kryvyy Rih
114 F7 **Križevci** *Ger.* Kreuz, *Hung.* Kőrös. Varaždin, NE Croatia 46.02N 16.32E
114 B10 **Krk** *It.* Veglia. Primorje-Gorski Kotar, NW Croatia 45.01N 14.36E
114 B10 **Krk** *It.* Veglia; *anc.* Curieta. *island* NW Croatia
111 V12 **Krka** ≈ SE Slovenia
Krka *see* Gurk
111 R11 **Krn** ▲ NW Slovenia 46.15N 13.37E
113 H16 **Krnov** *Ger.* Jägerndorf. Moravskoslezský Kraj, E Czech Republic 50.05N 17.42E
Kroatien *see* Croatia
97 G14 **Krøderen** Buskerud, S Norway 60.06N 9.48E
97 G14 **Krøderen** ⊚ S Norway
Kroi *see* Krui
97 N17 **Krokek** Östergötland, S Sweden 58.40N 16.25E
Krokodil *see* Crocodile
95 G16 **Krokom** Jämtland, C Sweden 63.19N 14.30E
119 S2 **Krolevets'** *Rus.* Krolevets. Sums'ka Oblast', NE Ukraine 51.34N 33.24E
Królewska Huta *see* Chorzów
113 H18 **Kroměříž** *Ger.* Kremsier. Zlínský Kraj, E Czech Republic 49.18N 17.24E
100 I9 **Krommenie** Noord-Holland, C Netherlands 52.30N 4.46E
130 J6 **Kromy** Orlovskaya Oblast', W Russian Federation 52.41N 35.45E
103 L18 **Kronach** Bayern, E Germany 50.14N 11.19E
Krone an der Brahe *see* Koronowo
178 I13 **Krông Kaôh Kông** Kaôh Kông, SW Cambodia 11.37N 102.58E
97 K21 **Kronoberg** ◆ *county* S Sweden
127 Pp11 **Kronotskiy Zaliv** *bay* E Russian Federation
205 O2 **Kronprinsesse Märtha Kyst** *physical region* Antarctica
205 V3 **Kronprins Olav Kyst** *physical region* Antarctica
128 G12 **Kronshtadt** Leningradskaya Oblast', NW Russian Federation 60.01N 29.42E
Kronstadt *see* Braşov
85 I22 **Kroonstad** Free State, C South Africa 27.40S 27.15E
126 Kk13 **Kropotkin** Irkutskaya Oblast', C Russian Federation 58.30N 115.21E
130 L14 **Kropotkin** Krasnodarskiy Kray, SW Russian Federation 45.28N 40.30E
112 J11 **Krośniewice** Łódzkie, C Poland 52.14N 19.10E
113 N17 **Krosno** *Ger.* Krossen. Podkarpackie, SE Poland 49.40N 21.46E
112 E12 **Krosno Odrzańskie** *Ger.* Crossen, Kreisstadt. Lubuskie, W Poland 52.02N 15.06E
Krossen *see* Krosno
Krotoschin *see* Krotoszyn
112 H13 **Krotoszyn** *Ger.* Krotoschin. Wielkopolskie, C Poland 51.43N 17.24E
Krottingen *see* Kretinga
Krousón *see* Krousónas
117 J25 **Krousónas** *prev.* Krousón, Kroussón. Kríti, Greece, E Mediterranean Sea 35.13N 24.58E
Kroussón *see* Krousónas
Krraba *see* Krrabë
115 L20 **Krrabë** *var.* Krraba. Tiranë, C Albania 41.15N 19.56E
115 L17 **Krrabit, Mali i** ▲ N Albania
111 W12 **Krško** *Ger.* Gurkfeld; *prev.* Videm-Krško. E Slovenia 45.57N 15.31E
85 K19 **Kruger National Park** *national park* Northern, N South Africa
85 J21 **Krugersdorp** Gauteng, NE South Africa 26.04S 27.46E
40 D16 **Krugloi Point** *headland* Agattu Island, Alaska, USA 52.30N 173.46E
Krugloye *see* Kruhlaye
121 N15 **Kruhlaye** *Rus.* Krugloye. Mahilyowskaya Voblasts', E Belarus 54.15N 29.48E
174 I13 **Krui** *var.* Kroi. Sumatera, SW Indonesia 5.11S 103.55E
101 G16 **Kruibeke** Oost-Vlaanderen, N Belgium 51.10N 4.18E
85 G25 **Kruidfontein** Western Cape, SW South Africa 32.50S 21.59E
101 F15 **Kruiningen** Zeeland, SW Netherlands 51.28N 4.01E
Kruja *see* Krujë
115 L19 **Krujë** *var.* Kruja, *It.* Croia. Durrës, C Albania 41.30N 19.48E
Krulevshchina *see* Krulewshchyna
120 K13 **Krulewshchyna** *Rus.* Krulevshchina. Vitsyebskaya Voblasts', N Belarus 55.01N 27.46E
27 T6 **Krum** Texas, SW USA 33.15N 97.14W
103 J23 **Krumbach** Bayern, S Germany 48.12N 10.21E
115 M17 **Krumë** Kukës, NE Albania 42.11N 20.25E
Krummau *see* Český Krumlov
116 K12 **Krumovgrad** *prev.* Kossukavak. Kŭrdzhali, S Bulgaria 41.27N 25.40E
116 K12 **Krumovitsa** ≈ S Bulgaria
116 L10 **Krumovo** Yambol, E Bulgaria 42.16N 26.25E
178 Hh11 **Krung Thep** *var.* Krung Thep Mahanakhon, *Eng.* Bangkok. ● (Thailand) Bangkok, C Thailand 13.43N 100.30E
178 Hh12 **Krung Thep, Ao** *var.* Bight of Bangkok. *bay* S Thailand
Krung Thep Mahanakhon *see* Krung Thep
Krupa/Krupa na Uni *see* Bosanska Krupa
121 M15 **Krupki** *Rus.* Krupki. Minskaya Voblasts', C Belarus 54.19N 29.07E
97 G24 **Kruså** *var.* Krusaa. Sønderjylland, SW Denmark 54.49N 9.25E
Krusaa *see* Kruså
15 I4 **Krusenstern, Cape** *headland* Nunavut, NW Canada 68.17N 114.00W
115 N14 **Kruševac** Serbia, C Serbia and Montenegro (Yugoslavia) 43.36N 21.19E
115 N19 **Kruševo** SW FYR Macedonia 41.22N 21.15E
113 A15 **Krušné Hory** *Eng.* Ore Mountains, *Ger.* Erzgebirge. ▲ Czech Republic/Germany *see also* Erzgebirge
41 W13 **Kruzof Island** *island* Alexander Archipelago, Alaska, USA
116 F13 **Krýa Vrýsi** *var.* Kría Vrísi. Kentrikí Makedonía, N Greece 40.40N 22.18E
121 P16 **Krychaw** *Rus.* Krichëv. Mahilyowskaya Voblasts', E Belarus 53.42N 31.43E
66 K11 **Krylov Seamount** *undersea feature* E Atlantic Ocean 17.34N 30.07W
Krym *see* Krym, Respublika
119 S13 **Krym, Respublika** *var.* Krym, *Eng.* Crimea, Crimean Oblast; *prev. Rus.* Krymskaya ASSR, Krymskaya Oblast'. ◆ *province* SE Ukraine
130 K14 **Krymsk** Krasnodarskiy Kray, SW Russian Federation 44.56N 38.02E
Krymskaya ASSR/Krymskaya Oblast' *see* Krym, Respublika
119 T13 **Kryms'ki Hory** ▲ S Ukraine
119 T13 **Kryms'kyy Pivostriv** *peninsula* S Ukraine
113 M18 **Krynica** *Ger.* Tannenhof. Małopolskie, S Poland 49.26N 20.57E
119 P8 **Kryve Ozero** Odes'ka Oblast', SW Ukraine 47.54N 30.19E
121 I18 **Kryvoshyn** *Rus.* Krivoshin. Brestskaya Voblasts', SW Belarus 52.52N 26.07E
121 K14 **Kryvychy** *Rus.* Krivichi. Minskaya Voblasts', C Belarus 54.43N 27.16E
119 S8 **Kryvyy Rih** *Rus.* Krivoy Rog. Dnipropetrovs'ka Oblast', SE Ukraine 47.53N 33.24E
119 N8 **Kryzhopil'** Vinnyts'ka Oblast', C Ukraine 48.22N 28.51E
Krzemieniec *see* Kremenets'
113 J14 **Krzepice** Śląskie, S Poland 50.58N 18.42E
112 F10 **Krzyż Wielkopolski** Wielkopolskie, C Poland 52.52N 16.03E
Ksar al Kabir *see* Ksar-el-Kebir
Ksar al Soule *see* Er-Rachidia
76 J5 **Ksar El Boukhari** N Algeria 35.57N 2.49E
76 G5 **Ksar-el-Kebir** *var.* Alcázar, Ksar al Kabir, Ksar-el-Kébir, *Ar.* Al-Kasr al-Kebir, Al-Qsar al-Kbir, *Sp.* Alcazarquivir. NW Morocco 35.04N 5.55W
112 H12 **Książ Wielkopolski** *Ger.* Xions. Wielkolpolskie, C Poland 52.03N 17.10E
131 O3 **Kstovo** Nizhegorodskaya Oblast', W Russian Federation 56.07N 44.12E
174 Mm4 **Kuala Belait** W Brunei 4.48N 114.12E
Kuala Dungun *see* Dungun
174 M7 **Kualakerian** Borneo, C Indonesia
174 M10 **Kualakuayan** Borneo, C Indonesia 2.01S 112.34E
174 H4 **Kuala Lipis** Pahang, Peninsular Malaysia 04.11N 102.00E
174 H5 **Kuala Lumpur** ● (Malaysia) Kuala Lumpur, Peninsular Malaysia 3.07N 101.42E
174 H5 **Kuala Lumpur International** ✈ Selangor, Peninsular Malaysia 2.51N 101.45E
Kuala Pelabohan Kelang *see* Pelabuhan Klang
175 Nn3 **Kuala Penyu** Sabah, East Malaysia 5.37N 115.36E
40 E9 **Kualapu'u** *var.* Kualapuu. Moloka'i, Hawai'i, USA, C Pacific Ocean 21.09N 157.02W
173 G6 **Kuala, Sungai** ≈ Sumatera, W Indonesia
174 Hh3 **Kuala Terengganu** *var.* Kuala Trengganu. Terengganu, Peninsular Malaysia 5.19N 103.07E
174 Hh9 **Kualatungkal** Sumatera, W Indonesia 0.49S 103.22E
175 O3 **Kuamut, Sungai** ≈ East Malaysia
175 Qq7 **Kuandang** Sulawesi, N Indonesia 0.50N 122.55E
175 Qq7 **Kuandang, Teluk** *bay* Sulawesi, N Indonesia
169 V12 **Kuandian** *var.* Kuandian Manzu Zizhixian. Liaoning, NE China 40.41N 124.46E
Kuandian Manzu Zizhixian *see* Kuandian
Kuando-Kubango *see* Cuando Cubango
Kuang-chou *see* Guangzhou
Kuang-hsi *see* Guangxi Zhuangzu Zizhiqu
Kuang-tung *see* Guangdong
Kuang-yuan *see* Guangyuan
174 Hh4 **Kuantan** Pahang, Peninsular Malaysia 3.49N 103.19E
Kuantan, Batang *see* Indragiri, Sungai
Kuanza Norte *see* Cuanza Norte
Kuanza Sul *see* Cuanza Sul
Kuba *see* Quba
125 Aa12 **Kuban'** *var.* Hypanis. ≈ SW Russian Federation
Kubango *see* Cubango/Okavango
147 X8 **Kubārah** NW Oman 23.03N 56.52E
95 H16 **Kubbe** Västernorrland, C Sweden 63.31N 18.04E
82 A11 **Kubbum** Southern Darfur, W Sudan 11.46N 23.46E
128 L13 **Kubenskoye, Ozero** ⊚ NW Russian Federation
152 G6 **Kubla-Ustyurt** *Rus.* Komsomol'sk-na-Ustyurte. Qoraqalpog'iston Respublikasi, NW Uzbekistan 44.06N 58.14E
170 Ee16 **Kubokawa** Kōchi, Shikoku, SW Japan 33.22N 133.14E
116 L7 **Kubrat** *prev.* Balbunar. Razgrad, N Bulgaria 43.48N 26.31E
175 Oo15 **Kubu** Sumbawa, S Indonesia 8.15S 115.30E
114 O13 **Kučajske Planine** ▲ E Serbia and Montenegro (Yugoslavia)
172 Pp2 **Kuccharo-ko** ⊚ Hokkaidō, N Japan
114 O11 **Kučevo** Serbia, NE Serbia and Montenegro (Yugoslavia) 44.29N 21.42E
Kuchan *see* Qūchān
174 L6 **Kuching** *prev.* Sarawak. Sarawak, East Malaysia 1.31N 110.19E
174 L7 **Kuching** ✈ Sarawak, East Malaysia 1.31N 110.19E
170 Aa17 **Kuchinoerabu-jima** *island* Nansei-shotō, SW Japan
170 C13 **Kuchinotsu** Nagasaki, Kyūshū, SW Japan 32.36N 130.11E
111 Q6 **Kuchl** Salzburg, NW Austria 47.37N 13.12E
154 L9 **Kūchnay Darweyshān** Helmand, S Afghanistan 31.01N 64.09E
Kuchurgan *see* Kuchurhan
119 O9 **Kuchurhan** *Rus.* Kuchurgan. ≈ NE Ukraine
Kuçova *see* Kuçovë
115 L21 **Kuçovë** *var.* Kuçova; *prev.* Qyteti Stalin. Berat, C Albania 40.48N 19.55E
142 D11 **Küçük Çekmece** İstanbul, NW Turkey 41.01N 28.46E
170 Dd13 **Kudamatsu** *var.* Kudamatu. Yamaguchi, Honshū, SW Japan 34.00N 131.53E
Kudamatu *see* Kudamatsu
Kudara *see* Ghŭdara
175 O1 **Kudat** Sabah, East Malaysia 6.54N 116.46E
Küddow *see* Gwda
161 G17 **Kūdligi** Karnātaka, W India 14.58N 76.24E
Kudowa *see* Kudowa-Zdrój
113 F16 **Kudowa-Zdrój** *Ger.* Kudowa. Wałbrzych, SW Poland 50.27N 16.13E
119 P9 **Kudryavtsivka** Mykolayivs'ka Oblast', S Ukraine 47.18N 31.02E
174 L14 **Kudus** *prev.* Koedoes. Jawa, C Indonesia 6.46S 110.48E
129 T13 **Kudymkar** Komi-Permyatskiy Avtonomnyy Okrug, NW Russian Federation 59.01N 54.40E
Kudzsir *see* Cugir
Kuei-chou *see* Guizhou
Kuei-lin *see* Guilin
Kuei-yang *see* Guiyang
K'u-erh-lo *see* Korla
Kueyang *see* Guiyang
Kufa *see* Al Kūfah
142 E14 **Küfiçayı** ≈ C Turkey
111 O6 **Kufstein** Tirol, W Austria 47.36N 12.10E
151 V14 **Kugaly** *Kaz.* Qoghaly. Almaty, SE Kazakhstan 44.30N 78.40E
15 I4 **Kugluktuk** *var.* Qurlurtuuq *prev.* Coppermine. Nunavut, NW Canada 67.49N 115.12W
149 Y13 **Kūhak** Sīstān va Balūchestān, SE Iran 27.10N 63.15E
149 R9 **Kūhbonān** Kermān, C Iran 31.22N 56.16E
154 J5 **Kūhestān** *var.* Kohsān. Herāt, W Afghanistan 34.40N 61.10E
95 N15 **Kuhmo** Oulu, E Finland 64.04N 29.34E
95 L18 **Kuhmoinen** Länsi-Suomi, W Finland 61.32N 25.09E
Kuhnau *see* Konin
Kūhnö *see* Kihnu
149 O8 **Kūhpāyeh** Eşfahān, C Iran 32.42N 52.25E
178 H13 **Kui Buri** *var.* Ban Kui Nua. Prachuap Khiri Khan, SW Thailand 12.10N 99.49E
Kuibyshev *see* Kuybyshevskoye Vodokhranilishche
84 D13 **Kuito** *Port.* Silva Porto. Bié, C Angola 12.21S 16.54E
41 X14 **Kuiu Island** *island* Alexander Archipelago, Alaska, USA
94 L13 **Kuivaniemi** Oulu, C Finland 65.34N 25.13E
79 V14 **Kujama** Kaduna, C Nigeria 10.27N 7.39E
112 I10 **Kujawsko-pomorskie** ◆ *province*, C Poland
172 N10 **Kuji** *var.* Kuzi. Iwate, Honshū, C Japan 40.12N 141.47E
Kujto, Ozero *see* Kuyto, Ozero
Kujū-renzan *see* Kujū-san
170 D14 **Kujū-san** *var.* Kujū-renzan. ▲ Kyūshū, SW Japan 33.07N 131.13E
45 N7 **Kukalaya, Rio** *var.* Rio Cuculaya, Rio Kukulaya. ≈ NE Nicaragua
115 O16 **Kukavica** *var.* Vlajna. ▲ SE Serbia and Montenegro (Yugoslavia) 42.46N 21.58E
115 M18 **Kukës** *var.* Kukësi. Kukës, NE Albania 42.03N 20.25E
115 L18 **Kukës** ◆ *district* NE Albania
Kukësi *see* Kukës
194 J14 **Kukipi** Gulf, S PNG 8.10S 146.09E
131 S3 **Kukmor** Respublika Tatarstan, W Russian Federation 56.11N 50.56E
Kukong *see* Shaoguan
41 N6 **Kukpowruk River** ≈ Alaska, USA
40 M6 **Kukpuk River** ≈ Alaska, USA
Kukukhoto *see* Hohhot
Kukulaya, Rio *see* Kukalaya, Rio
174 Hh7 **Kukup** Johor, Peninsular Malaysia 1.18N 103.27E
201 W12 **Kuku Point** *headland* NW Wake Island 19.19N 166.36E
152 G11 **Kukurtli** Ahal Welaýaty, C Turkmenistan 39.58N 58.47E
Kül *see* Kül, Rūd-e
116 F7 **Kula** Vidin, NW Bulgaria 43.55N 22.32E
142 D14 **Kula** Manisa, W Turkey 38.33N 28.36E
114 K9 **Kula** Serbia, NW Serbia and Montenegro (Yugoslavia) 45.37N 19.31E
155 S8 **Kulāchi** North-West Frontier Province, NW Pakistan 31.58N 70.30E
Kulachi *see* Kolāchi
150 F11 **Kulagino** *Kaz.* Külagīno. Atyrau, W Kazakhstan 48.30N 51.33E
174 Hh6 **Kulai** Johor, Peninsular Malaysia 1.40N 103.33E
116 M7 **Kulak** ≈ NE Bulgaria
159 T11 **Kula Kangri** *var.* Kulhakangri. ▲ Bhutan/China 28.06N 90.19E
150 E13 **Kulaly, Ostrov** *island* SW Kazakhstan
151 S16 **Kulan** *Kaz.* Qulan; *prev.* Lugovoy, Lugovoye. Zhambyl, S Kazakhstan 42.55N 72.49E
153 V9 **Kulanak** Narynskaya Oblast', C Kyrgyzstan 41.18N 75.38E
Kulandag, Gory *see* Gulandag
159 V14 **Kulaura** Chittagong, NE Bangladesh 24.31N 92.01E
120 D9 **Kuldīga** *Ger.* Goldingen. Kuldīga, W Latvia 56.57N 21.59E
Kuldja *see* Yining
Kul'dzhuktau, Gory *see* Quljuqtov Tog'lari
131 N4 **Kulebaki** Nizhegorodskaya Oblast', W Russian Federation 55.25N 42.31E
114 E11 **Kulen Vakuf** *var.* Spasovo. Federacija Bosna I Hercegovina, NW Bosnia and Herzegovina 44.32N 16.05E
189 Q9 **Kulgera Roadhouse** Northern Territory, N Australia 25.49S 133.30E
Kulhakangri *see* Kula Kangri
131 T1 **Kuliga** Udmurtskaya Respublika, NW Russian Federation 58.14N 53.49E
Kulkuduk *see* Ko'lquduq
120 G4 **Kullamaa** Läänemaa, W Estonia 58.52N 24.05E
207 O12 **Kullorsuaq** *var.* Kuvdlorssuak. Kitaa, C Greenland 74.57N 57.07W
31 O6 **Kulm** North Dakota, N USA 46.18N 98.57W
Kulm *see* Chełmno
152 D12 **Kul'mach** *prev. Turkm.* Isgender. Balkan Welaýaty, W Turkmenistan 39.04N 55.49E
103 L18 **Kulmbach** Bayern, SE Germany 50.07N 11.27E
Kulmsee *see* Chełmża
153 Q14 **Kŭlob** *Rus.* Kulyab. SW Tajikistan 37.55N 68.46E
94 M13 **Kuloharju** Lappi, N Finland 65.51N 28.10E
129 N7 **Kuloy** Arkhangel'skaya Oblast', NW Russian Federation 64.55N 43.35E
129 N7 **Kuloy** ≈ NW Russian Federation
143 Q14 **Kulp** Dıyarbakır, SE Turkey 38.31N 41.01E
Kulpa *see* Kolpa
79 P14 **Kulpawn** ≈ N Ghana
149 R13 **Kūl, Rūd-e** *var.* Kül. ≈ S Iran
150 G12 **Kul'sary** *Kaz.* Qulsary. Atyrau, W Kazakhstan 46.58N 53.58E
159 R15 **Kulti** West Bengal, NE India 23.45N 86.49E
95 G14 **Kultsjön** ⊚ N Sweden
142 I14 **Kulu** Konya, W Turkey 39.06N 33.01E
127 Nn10 **Kulu** ≈ E Russian Federation
125 G14 **Kulunda** Altayskiy Kray, S Russian Federation 52.33N 79.04E
151 T7 **Kulunda Steppe** *Kaz.* Qulyndy Zhazyghy, *Rus.* Kulundinskaya Ravnina. *grassland* Kazakhstan/Russian Federation
Kulundinskaya Ravnina *see* Kulunda Steppe
190 M9 **Kulwin** Victoria, SE Australia 35.04S 142.37E
Kulyab *see* Kŭlob
119 Q3 **Kulykivka** Chernihivs'ka Oblast', N Ukraine 51.23N 31.39E
Kum *see* Qom
170 Ee15 **Kuma** Ehime, Shikoku, SW Japan 33.36N 132.53E
131 P14 **Kuma** ≈ SW Russian Federation
Kumafa *see* Kumawa, Pegunungan
171 K15 **Kumagaya** Saitama, Honshū, S Japan 36.10N 139.22E
172 N6 **Kumaishi** Hokkaidō, NE Japan 42.08N 139.57E
174 L11 **Kumai, Teluk** *bay* Borneo, C Indonesia
131 Y7 **Kumak** Orenburgskaya Oblast', W Russian Federation 51.16N 60.06E
176 Y9 **Kumamba, Kepulauan** *island group* E Indonesia
170 Cc14 **Kumamoto** Kumamoto, Kyūshū, SW Japan 32.49N 130.40E
170 C14 **Kumamoto** *off.* Kumamoto-ken. ◆ *prefecture* Kyūshū, SW Japan
171 Gg17 **Kumano** Mie, Honshū, SW Japan 33.54N 136.03E
Kumanova *see* Kumanovo
115 O17 **Kumanovo** *Turk.* Kumanova. N FYR Macedonia 42.08N 21.42E
193 G17 **Kumara** West Coast, South Island, NZ 42.39S 171.12E
188 J8 **Kumarina Roadhouse** Western Australia 24.46S 119.39E
159 T15 **Kumarkhali** Khulna, W Bangladesh 23.52N 89.13E
79 P16 **Kumasi** *prev.* Coomassie. C Ghana 6.40N 1.39W
176 Vv11 **Kumawa, Pegunungan** *var.* Kumafa. ▲ Papua, E Indonesia
Kumayri *see* Gyumri
81 D15 **Kumba** Sud-Ouest, W Cameroon 4.39N 9.25E
116 N13 **Kumbağ** Tekirdağ, NW Turkey 40.51N 27.26E
161 J21 **Kumbakonam** Tamil Nādu, SE India 10.58N 79.24E
176 Z16 **Kumbe, Sungai** ≈ Papua, E Indonesia
Kum-Dag *see* Gumdag
172 O14 **Kume-jima** *island* Nansei-shotō, SW Japan
131 V6 **Kumertau** Respublika Bashkortostan, W Russian Federation 52.48N 55.48E
125 F11 **Kuminskiy** Khanty-Mansiyskiy Avtonomnyy Okrug, C Russian Federation 58.42N 65.56E
37 R4 **Kumiva Peak** ▲ Nevada, W USA 40.24N 119.16W
165 N8 **Kum Kuduk** *well* NW China 40.21N 91.43E
165 N7 **Kumkuduk** Xinjiang Uygur Zizhiqu, W China 40.15N 91.55E
Kumkurgan *see* Qumqo'rg'on
97 M16 **Kumla** Örebro, C Sweden 59.51N 16.40E
142 E17 **Kumluca** Antalya, SW Turkey 36.22N 30.16E
102 N9 **Kummerower See** ⊚ NE Germany
79 X14 **Kumo** Gombe, E Nigeria 10.03N 11.13E
151 O13 **Kumola** ≈ C Kazakhstan
178 H1 **Kumon Range** ▲ N Myanmar
126 K14 **Kumora** Respublika Buryatiya, S Russian Federation 55.43N 110.47E
85 F22 **Kums** Karas, SE Namibia 28.07S 19.40E
161 E18 **Kumta** Karnātaka, W India 14.25N 74.24E
164 L6 **Kümük** Xinjiang Uygur Zizhiqu, W China
40 H12 **Kumukahi, Cape** *headland* Hawai'i, USA, C Pacific Ocean 19.31N 154.48W
131 Q17 **Kumukh** Respublika Dagestan, SW Russian Federation 42.10N 47.07E
Kumul *see* Hami
131 N9 **Kumylzhenskaya** Volgogradskaya Oblast', SW Russian Federation 49.54N 42.35E
147 W6 **Kumzār** N Oman 26.19N 56.26E
155 S4 **Kunar** *Per.* Konarhā. ◆ *province* E Afghanistan
Kunashiri *see* Kunashir, Ostrov
127 P16 **Kunashir, Ostrov** *var.* Kunashiri. *island* Kuril'skiye Ostrova, SE Russian Federation
120 I3 **Kunda** Lääne-Virumaa, NE Estonia 59.31N 26.32E
158 M13 **Kunda** Uttar Pradesh, N India 25.43N 81.31E
161 E19 **Kundāpura** *var.* Coondapoor. Karnātaka, W India 13.39N 74.41E
81 O24 **Kundelungu, Monts** ▲ S Dem. Rep. Congo
Kundert *see* Hernád
194 I12 **Kundiawa** Chimbu, W PNG 06.00S 144.57E
Kundla *see* Sāvarkundla

◆ Country ● Country Capital ◇ Dependent Territory ○ Dependent Territory Capital ◈ Administrative Region ✈ International Airport ▲ Mountain ▲ Mountain Range ▲ Volcano ≈ River ⊚ Lake ⊠ Reservoir

Kundur, Pulau – Lachanás

174 *Hh7* **Kundur, Pulau** *island* W Indonesia
155 *Q2* **Kunduz** *var.* Kondoz, Kundūz, Qondūz, *Per.* Kondūz. Kunduz, NE Afghanistan *36.48N 68.50E*
155 *Q2* **Kunduz** *Per.* Kondūz. ◈ *province* NE Afghanistan
Kuneitra *see* Al Qunayṭirah
85 *B18* **Kunene** ◈ *district* NE Namibia
85 *A16* **Kunene** *var.* Cunene. ⁓ Angola/Namibia *see also* Cunene
Künes *see* Xinyuan
164 *J5* **Künes He** ⁓ NW China
97 *I19* **Kungälv** Västra Götaland, S Sweden *57.54N 12.00E*
153 *W7* **Kungei Ala-Tau** *Rus.* Khrebet Kyungëy Ala-Too, *Kir.* Küngöy Ala-Too. ▲▲ Kazakhstan/Kyrgyzstan
Küngöy Ala-Too *see* Kungei Ala-Tau
Kungrad *see* Qo'ng'irot
97 *J19* **Kungsbacka** Halland, S Sweden *57.30N 12.04E*
97 *I18* **Kungshamn** Västra Götaland, S Sweden *58.21N 11.15E*
97 *M16* **Kungsör** Västmanland, C Sweden *59.25N 16.21E*
81 *J16* **Kungu** Equateur, NW Dem. Rep. Congo *2.46N 19.12E*
129 *V15* **Kungur** Permskaya Oblast', NW Russian Federation *57.24N 56.56E*
177 *G9* **Kungyangon** Yangon, SW Myanmar *16.27N 96.00E*
113 *M22* **Kunhegyes** Jász-Nagykun-Szolnok, E Hungary *47.23N 20.37E*
178 *H5* **Kunhing** Shan State, E Myanmar *21.17N 98.26E*
170 *Cc15* **Kunimi-dake** ▲ Kyūshū, SW Japan *32.31N 131.01E*
164 *D9* **Kunjirap Daban** *var.* Khūnjerāb Pass. *pass* China/Pakistan *36.46N 75.16E* *see also* Khūnjerāb Pass
Kunlun Mountains *see* Kunlun Shan
164 *H10* **Kunlun Shan** *Eng.* Kunlun Mountains. ▲▲ NW China
165 *P11* **Kunlun Shankou** *pass* C China *35.45N 93.59E*
166 *G13* **Kunming** *var.* K'un-ming; *prev.* Yunnan. Yunnan, SW China *25.04N 102.40E*
172 *N6* **Kunnui** Hokkaidō, NE Japan *42.26N 140.18E*
97 *B18* **Kunoy** *Dan.* Kunø *Island* Faeroe Islands *62.18N 6.40W*
169 *X16* **Kunsan** *var.* Gunsan, *Jap.* Gunzan. W South Korea *35.58N 126.42E*
113 *L24* **Kunszentmárton** Jász-Nagykun-Szolnok, E Hungary *46.49N 20.15E*
113 *J23* **Kunszentmiklós** Bács-Kiskun, C Hungary *47.02N 19.05E*
189 *N3* **Kununurra** Western Australia *15.49S 128.43E*
Kunyang *see* Pingyang
Kunya-Urgench *see* Köneürgenç
Kunyé *see* Pins, Île des
174 *Mm8* **Kunyi** Borneo, C Indonesia *3.22S 119.19E*
103 *I20* **Künzelsau** Baden-Württemberg, S Germany *49.22N 9.43E*
167 *S10* **Kuocang Shan** ▲▲ SE China
128 *H5* **Kuoloyarvi** *var.* Luolajarvi. Murmanskaya Oblast', NW Russian Federation *66.58N 29.13E*
95 *N16* **Kuopio** Itä-Suomi, C Finland *62.54N 27.41E*
95 *K17* **Kuortane** Länsi-Suomi, W Finland *62.48N 23.30E*
95 *M18* **Kuortti** Itä-Suomi, E Finland *61.25N 26.25E*
Kupa *see* Kolpa
175 *R17* **Kupang** *prev.* Koepang. Timor, C Indonesia *10.13S 123.37E*
41 *Q5* **Kuparuk River** ⁓ Alaska, USA
Kupchino *see* Cupcina
194 *L16* **Kupiano** Central, S PNG *10.04S 148.16E*
188 *M4* **Kupingarri** Western Australia *16.46S 125.57E*
125 *G14* **Kupino** Novosibirskaya Oblast', C Russian Federation *54.22N 77.09E*
120 *H11* **Kupiškis** Panevėžys, NE Lithuania *55.51N 24.58E*
116 *L13* **Küplü** Edirne, NW Turkey *41.06N 26.23E*
41 *X13* **Kupreanof Island** *island* Alexander Archipelago, Alaska, USA
41 *O16* **Kupreanof Point** *headland* Alaska, USA *55.34N 159.36W*
114 *G13* **Kupres** Federacija Bosna I Hercegovina, SW Bosnia and Herzegovina *44.00N 17.15E*
119 *W5* **Kup"yans'k** *Rus.* Kupyansk. Kharkivs'ka Oblast', E Ukraine *49.42N 37.36E*
119 *W5* **Kup"yans'k-Vuzlovyy** Kharkivs'ka Oblast', E Ukraine *49.40N 37.41E*
164 *I6* **Kuqa** Xinjiang Uygur Zizhiqu, NW China *41.43N 82.58E*
Kür *see* Kura
143 *W11* **Kura** *Az.* Kür, *Geor.* Mtkvari, *Turk.* Kura Nehri. ⁓ SW Asia
57 *R8* **Kuracki** NW Guyana *6.52N 60.13W*
170 *Ee13* **Kurahashi-jima** *island* SW Japan
Kura Kurk *see* Irbe Strait
153 *Q10* **Kurama Range** *Rus.* Kuraminskiy Khrebet. ▲▲ Tajikistan/Uzbekistan
Kuraminskiy Khrebet *see* Kurama Range
Kura Nehri *see* Kura
176 *Ww10* **Kuran, Kepulauan** *island group* E Indonesia
121 *J14* **Kuranyets** *Rus.* Kurenets. Minskaya Voblasts', C Belarus *54.34N 26.58E*
170 *Ff14* **Kurashiki** *var.* Kurasiki. Okayama, Honshū, SW Japan *34.35N 133.44E*
160 *L10* **Kurasia** Chhattīsgarh, C India *23.11N 82.16E*
Kurasiki *see* Kurashiki
170 *G12* **Kurayoshi** *var.* Kurayosi. Tottori, Honshū, SW Japan *35.25N 133.51E*
Kurayosi *see* Kurayoshi
169 *X6* **Kurbin He** ⁓ NE China
151 *X10* **Kurchum** *Kaz.* Kürshim. Vostochnyy Kazakhstan, E Kazakhstan *48.35N 83.37E*
151 *Y10* **Kurchum** ⁓ E Kazakhstan
143 *X11* **Kürdämir** *Rus.* Kyurdamir. C Azerbaijan *40.21N 48.08E*
Kurdestan *see* Kordestān
145 *S1* **Kurdistan** *cultural region* SW Asia
Kurd Kui *see* Kord Kūy
161 *F15* **Kurduvādi** Mahārāshtra, W India *18.06N 75.31E*
116 *J11* **Kŭrdzhali** *var.* Kirdzhali. Kŭrdzhali, S Bulgaria *41.39N 25.23E*
116 *K11* **Kŭrdzhali** ◈ *province* S Bulgaria
116 *J11* **Kŭrdzhali, Yazovir** ⊠ S Bulgaria
170 *Ee13* **Kure** Hiroshima, Honshū, SW Japan *34.15N 132.33E*
199 *J5* **Kure Atoll** *var.* Ocean Island. *atoll* Hawaiian Islands, Hawaii, USA, C Pacific Ocean
142 *J10* **Küre Dağları** ▲▲ N Turkey
152 *C11* **Kürendag** *Rus.* Gora Kyuren. ▲ W Turkmenistan *39.05N 55.09E*
Kurenets *see* Kuranyets
120 *E6* **Kuressaare** *Ger.* Arensburg; *prev.* Kingissepp. Saaremaa, W Estonia *58.14N 22.27E*
126 *I9* **Kureyka** Krasnoyarskiy Kray, N Russian Federation *66.22N 87.21E*
126 *I9* **Kureyka** ⁓ N Russian Federation
Kurgal'dzhino/Kurgal'dzhinskiy *see* Korgalzhyn
125 *F12* **Kurgan** Kurganskaya Oblast', C Russian Federation *55.30N 65.19E*
130 *L14* **Kurganinsk** Krasnodarskiy Kray, SW Russian Federation *44.55N 40.45E*
125 *Ee12* **Kurganskaya Oblast'** ◈ *province* C Russian Federation
Kurgan-Tyube *see* Qŭrghonteppa
203 *O2* **Kuria** *prev.* Woodle Island. *island* Tungaru, W Kiribati
Kuria Muria Bay *see* Ḥalāniyāt, Khalīj al
Kuria Muria Islands *see* Ḥalāniyāt, Juzur al
159 *T13* **Kurigram** Rajshahi, N Bangladesh *25.49N 89.37E*
176 *Yy16* **Kurik** Papua, E Indonesia *8.12S 140.15E*
95 *K17* **Kurikka** Länsi-Suomi, W Finland *62.36N 22.25E*
171 *M12* **Kurikoma-yama** ▲ Honshū, C Japan *38.57N 140.44E*
199 *Hh3* **Kurile Basin** *undersea feature* NW Pacific Ocean
Kurile Islands *see* Kuril'skiye Ostrova
Kurile-Kamchatka Depression *see* Kurile Trench
199 *Hh3* **Kurile Trench** *var.* Kurile-Kamchatka Depression. *undersea feature* NW Pacific Ocean
131 *Q9* **Kurilovka** Saratovskaya Oblast', W Russian Federation *50.39N 48.02E*
127 *P15* **Kuril'sk** Kuril'skiye Ostrova, Sakhalinskaya Oblats', SE Russian Federation *45.10N 147.51E*
127 *Pp15* **Kuril'skiye Ostrova** *Eng.* Kurile Islands. *island group* SE Russian Federation
44 *M9* **Kurinwas, Río** ⁓ E Nicaragua
Kurisches Haff *see* Courland Lagoon
Kurkund *see* Kilingi-Nõmme
130 *M4* **Kurlovskiy** Vladimirskaya Oblast', W Russian Federation *55.25N 40.39E*
82 *G12* **Kurmuk** Blue Nile, SE Sudan *10.36N 34.16E*
Kurna *see* Al Qurnah
161 *H17* **Kurnool** *var.* Karnul. Andhra Pradesh, S India *15.51N 78.01E*
171 *J13* **Kurobe** Toyama, Honshū, SW Japan *36.52N 137.26E*
170 *Cc13* **Kurogi** Fukuoka, Kyūshū, SW Japan *33.09N 130.45E*
171 *Mm9* **Kuroishi** *var.* Kuroisi. Aomori, Honshū, C Japan *40.40N 140.34E*
Kuroisi *see* Kuroishi
171 *Kk14* **Kuroiso** Tochigi, Honshū, S Japan *36.58N 140.01E*
172 *N5* **Kuromatsunai** Hokkaidō, NE Japan *42.40N 140.18E*
172 *Oo17* **Kuro-shima** *island* SW Japan
171 *H16* **Kuroso-yama** ▲ Honshū, SW Japan *34.31N 136.10E*
193 *F21* **Kurow** Canterbury, South Island, NZ *44.44S 170.29E*
176 *Uu13* **Kur, Pulau** *island* E Indonesia
131 *N15* **Kursavka** Stavropol'skiy Kray, SW Russian Federation *44.28N 42.31E*
120 *E11* **Kuršėnai** Šiauliai, N Lithuania *56.00N 22.56E*
Kürshim *see* Kurchum
Kurshskaya Kosa/Kuršių Nerija *see* Courland Spit
130 *J7* **Kursk** Kurskaya Oblast', W Russian Federation *51.43N 36.46E*
130 *I7* **Kurskaya Oblast'** ◈ *province* W Russian Federation
Kurskiy Zaliv *see* Courland Lagoon
115 *N15* **Kuršumlija** Serbia, S Serbia and Montenegro (Yugoslavia) *43.09N 21.16E*
143 *R15* **Kurtalan** Siirt, SE Turkey *37.56N 41.43E*
125 *Ee12* **Kurtamysh** Kurganskaya Oblast', C Russian Federation *54.51N 64.46E*
Kurtbunar *see* Tervel
Kurt-Dere *see* Vŭlchidol
Kurtitsch/Kürtös *see* Curtici
Kurtty *see* Kurty
151 *U15* **Kurty** *var.* Kurtty. ⁓ SE Kazakhstan
95 *L18* **Kuru** Länsi-Suomi, W Finland *61.51N 23.46E*
82 *C13* **Kuru** ⁓ W Sudan
116 *M13* **Kuru Dağı** ▲▲ NW Turkey
164 *L7* **Kuruktag** ▲▲ NW China
85 *G22* **Kuruman** Northern Cape, N South Africa *27.28S 23.27E*
69 *T14* **Kuruman** ⁓ W South Africa
170 *Cc13* **Kurume** Fukuoka, Kyūshū, SW Japan *33.15N 130.27E*
126 *K15* **Kurumkan** Respublika Buryatiya, S Russian Federation *54.13N 110.21E*
161 *J25* **Kurunegala** North Western Province, C Sri Lanka *7.28N 80.22E*
57 *T10* **Kurupukari** C Guyana *4.39N 58.39W*
129 *U10* **Kur"ya** Respublika Komi, NW Russian Federation *61.38N 57.12E*
150 *E15* **Kuryk** *prev.* Yeraliyev. Mangistau, SW Kazakhstan *43.12N 51.43E*
142 *B15* **Kuşadası** Aydın, SW Turkey *37.51N 27.15E*
117 *M19* **Kuşadası Körfezi** *gulf* SW Turkey
170 *Aa16* **Kusagaki-guntō** *island* SW Japan
Kusaie *see* Kosrae
151 *T12* **Kusak** ⁓ C Kazakhstan
Kusary *see* Qusar
178 *Hh8* **Ku Sathan, Doi** ▲ NW Thailand *18.22N 100.31E*
171 *H15* **Kusatsu** *var.* Kusatu. Shiga, Honshū, SW Japan *35.02N 135.58E*
Kusatu *see* Kusatsu
144 *F11* **Kuseifa** Southern, C Israel *31.15N 35.01E*
142 *C12* **Kuş Gölü** ◎ NW Turkey
130 *L12* **Kushchevskaya** Krasnodarskiy Kray, SW Russian Federation *46.35N 39.40E*
171 *H16* **Kushida-gawa** ⁓ Honshū, SW Japan
170 *Bb15* **Kushikino** *var.* Kusikino. Kagoshima, Kyūshū, SW Japan *31.42N 130.13E*
170 *C17* **Kushima** *var.* Kusima. Miyazaki, Kyūshū, SW Japan *31.27N 131.11E*
170 *G17* **Kushimoto** Wakayama, Honshū, SW Japan *33.28N 135.45E*
172 *Q7* **Kushiro** *var.* Kusiro. Hokkaidō, NE Japan *42.58N 144.24E*
154 *K4* **Küshk** Herāt, W Afghanistan *34.54N 62.09E*
Kushka *see* Gushgy/Serhetabat
151 *N8* **Kushmurun** *Kaz.* Qusmuryn. Kostanay, N Kazakhstan *52.27N 64.31E*
151 *N8* **Kushmurun, Ozero** *Kaz.* Qusmuryn. ◎ N Kazakhstan
131 *U4* **Kushnarenkovo** Respublika Bashkortostan, W Russian Federation *55.07N 55.24E*
Kushrabat *see* Qo'shrabot
159 *T15* **Kushtia** *var.* Kustia. Khulna, W Bangladesh *23.54N 89.07E*
125 *Ee10* **Kushva** Sverdlovskaya Oblast', C Russian Federation *58.14N 59.36E*
Kusikino *see* Kushikino
Kusima *see* Kushima
Kusiro *see* Kushiro
40 *M13* **Kuskokwim Bay** *bay* Alaska, USA
41 *P11* **Kuskokwim Mountains** ▲▲ Alaska, USA
41 *N12* **Kuskokwim River** ⁓ Alaska, USA
110 *G7* **Küsnacht** Zürich, N Switzerland *47.21N 8.32E*
172 *Qq6* **Kussharo-ko** *var.* Kussyaro. ◎ Hokkaidō, NE Japan
Küssnacht *see* Küssnacht am Rigi
110 *F8* **Küssnacht am Rigi** *var.* Küssnacht. Schwyz, C Switzerland *47.03N 8.25E*
Kussyaro *see* Kussharo-ko
Kustanay *see* Kostanay
Küstence/Küstendje *see* Constanța
102 *F11* **Küstenkanal** *var.* Ems-Hunte Canal. *canal* NW Germany
Küstrin *see* Kostrzyn
Kustia *see* Kushtia
175 *T7* **Kusu** Pulau Halmahera, E Indonesia *0.51N 127.41E*
175 *Nn16* **Kuta** Pulau Lombok, S Indonesia *8.52S 116.15E*
145 *T4* **Kutabān** N Iraq *35.21N 44.45E*
142 *E13* **Kütahya** *prev.* Kutaia. Kütahya, W Turkey *39.25N 29.55E*
142 *E13* **Kütahya** *var.* Kutaia. ◈ *province* W Turkey
Kutai *see* Mahakam, Sungai
Kutaia *see* Kütahya
143 *R9* **K'ut'aisi** W Georgia *42.15N 42.42E*
Kūt al 'Amārah *see* Al Kūt
Kut al Hai/Kūt al Ḥayy *see* Al Ḥayy
Kut al Imara *see* Al Kūt
126 *M12* **Kutana** Respublika Sakha (Yakutiya), NE Russian Federation *59.05N 131.43E*
Kutaradja/Kutaraja *see* Bandaaceh
172 *Nn5* **Kutchan** Hokkaidō, NE Japan *42.54N 140.46E*
Kutch, Gulf of *see* Kachchh, Gulf of
Kutch, Rann of *see* Kachchh, Rann of
114 *F9* **Kutina** Sisak-Moslavina, NE Croatia *45.29N 16.45E*
114 *H9* **Kutjevo** Požega-Slavonija, NE Croatia *45.26N 17.54E*
113 *E17* **Kutná Hora** *Ger.* Kuttenberg. Středočeský Kraj, C Czech Republic *49.57N 15.15E*
112 *K12* **Kutno** Łódzkie, C Poland *52.13N 19.23E*
Kuttenberg *see* Kutná Hora
81 *I20* **Kutu** Bandundu, W Dem. Rep. Congo *2.42S 18.07E*
159 *V17* **Kutubdia Island** *island* SE Bangladesh
82 *B10* **Kutum** Northern Darfur, W Sudan *14.10N 24.40E*
153 *Y7* **Kuturgu** Issyk-Kul'skaya Oblast', E Kyrgyzstan *42.45N 78.04E*
10 *M5* **Kuujjuaq** *prev.* Fort-Chimo. Québec, E Canada *58.10N 68.15W*
10 *I7* **Kuujjuarapik** Québec, C Canada *55.07N 78.09W*
Kuuli-Mayak *see* Guwlumaýak
120 *I6* **Kuulse magi** ▲ S Estonia
94 *N13* **Kuusamo** Oulu, E Finland *65.57N 29.15E*
95 *M19* **Kuusankoski** Etelä-Suomi, S Finland *60.51N 26.40E*
131 *W7* **Kuvandyk** Orenburgskaya Oblast', W Russian Federation *51.27N 57.18E*
Kuvango *see* Cubango
Kuvasay *see* Quwasoy
Kuvdlorssuak *see* Kullorsuaq
128 *I16* **Kuvshinovo** Tverskaya Oblast', W Russian Federation *57.03N 34.09E*
147 *Q4* **Kuwait** *off.* State of Kuwait, *var.* Dawlat al Kuwait, Koweit, Kuweit. ◆ *monarchy* SW Asia
Kuwait *see* Al Kuwayt
Kuwait Bay *see* Kuwayt, Jūn al
Kuwait City *see* Al Kuwayt
Kuwait, Dawlat al *see* Kuwait
Kuwajleen *see* Kwajalein Atoll
171 *H15* **Kuwana** Mie, Honshū, SW Japan *35.03N 136.40E*
176 *V9* **Kuwawin** Papua, E Indonesia *1.10S 132.40E*
145 *X9* **Kuwayt** E Iraq *32.26N 47.12E*
148 *K11* **Kuwayt, Jūn al** *var.* Kuwait Bay. *bay* E Kuwait
Kuweit *see* Kuwait
119 *P10* **Kuyal'nyts'kyy Lyman** ◎ SW Ukraine
125 *G13* **Kuybyshev** Novosibirskaya Oblast', C Russian Federation *55.28N 77.55E*
Kuybyshev *see* Bolgar, Respublika Tatarstan, Russian Federation
Kuybyshev *see* Samara
119 *W9* **Kuybysheve** *Rus.* Kuybyshevo. Zaporiz'ka Oblast', SE Ukraine *47.20N 36.41E*
Kuybyshevo *see* Kuybysheve
Kuybyshev Reservoir *see* Kuybyshevskoye Vodokhranilishche
Kuybyshevskaya Oblast' *see* Samarskaya Oblast'
Kuybyshevskiy *see* Novoishimskiy
131 *R4* **Kuybyshevskoye Vodokhranilishche** *var.* Kuibyshev, *Eng.* Kuybyshev Reservoir. ⊠ W Russian Federation
127 *N9* **Kuydusun** Respublika Sakha (Yakutiya), NE Russian Federation *63.15N 143.10E*
129 *U16* **Kuyeda** Permskaya Oblast', NW Russian Federation *56.23N 55.19E*
Kūysanjaq *see* Koi Sanjaq
128 *I7* **Kuyto, Ozero** *var.* Ozero Kujto. ◎ NW Russian Federation
164 *J4* **Kuytun** Xinjiang Uygur Zizhiqu, NW China *44.25N 84.55E*
126 *J15* **Kuytun** Irkutskaya Oblast', S Russian Federation *54.18N 101.28E*
126 *Ii12* **Kuyumba** Evenkiyskiy Avtonomnyy Okrug, C Russian Federation *61.00N 97.07E*
57 *S12* **Kuyuwini Landing** S Guyana *2.06N 59.14W*
Kuzi *see* Kuji
40 *M9* **Kuzitrin River** ⁓ Alaska, USA
131 *P6* **Kuznetsk** Penzenskaya Oblast', W Russian Federation *53.06N 46.27E*
118 *K3* **Kuznetsovs'k** Rivnens'ka Oblast', NW Ukraine *51.21N 25.51E*
128 *K6* **Kuzomen'** Murmanskaya Oblast', NW Russian Federation *66.16N 36.47E*
172 *N10* **Kuzumaki** Iwate, Honshū, C Japan *40.04N 141.26E*
94 *H9* **Kvaløya** *island* N Norway
94 *K8* **Kvalsund** Finnmark, N Norway *70.30N 23.56E*
96 *G11* **Kvam** Oppland, S Norway *61.42N 9.43E*
131 *X7* **Kvarkeno** Orenburgskaya Oblast', W Russian Federation *52.09N 59.44E*
95 *G15* **Kvarnbergsvattnet** *var.* Frostviken. ◎ N Sweden
114 *A11* **Kvarner** *var.* Carnaro, *It.* Quarnero. *gulf* W Croatia
114 *B11* **Kvarnerić** *channel* W Croatia
41 *O14* **Kvichak Bay** *bay* Alaska, USA
94 *H12* **Kvikkjokk** *Lapp.* Huhttán. Norrbotten, N Sweden *66.58N 17.45E*
97 *D17* **Kvina** ⁓ S Norway
94 *Q1* **Kvitøya** *island* NE Svalbard
97 *F16* **Kviteseid** Telemark, S Norway *59.23N 8.31E*
97 *H24* **Kværndrup** Fyn, C Denmark *55.10N 10.31E*
81 *H20* **Kwa** ⁓ W Dem. Rep. Congo
79 *Q15* **Kwadwokurom** C Ghana *7.49N 0.15W*
195 *X14* **Kwailibesi** Malaita, N Solomon Islands *8.25S 160.48E*
201 *S6* **Kwajalein Atoll** *var.* Kuwajleen. *atoll* Ralik Chain, C Marshall Islands
57 *W9* **Kwakoegron** Brokopondo, N Suriname *5.13N 55.19W*
83 *J21* **Kwale** Coast, S Kenya *4.11S 39.30E*
79 *U17* **Kwale** Delta, S Nigeria *5.51N 6.29E*
81 *H20* **Kwamouth** Bandundu, W Dem. Rep. Congo *3.10S 16.16E*
Kwando *see* Cuando
Kwangchow *see* Guangzhou
Kwangchu *see* Kwangju
169 *X16* **Kwangju** *off.* Kwangju-gwangyŏksi, *var.* Guangju, Kwangchu, *Jap.* Kōshū. SW South Korea *35.09N 126.52E*
81 *H20* **Kwango** *Port.* Cuango. ⁓ Angola/Dem. Rep. Congo *see also* Cuango
Kwangsi/Kwangsi Chuang Autonomous Region *see* Guangxi Zhuangzu Zizhiqu
Kwangtung *see* Guangdong
Kwangyuan *see* Guangyuan
83 *F17* **Kwania, Lake** ◎ C Uganda
Kwanza *see* Cuanza
79 *S15* **Kwara** ◈ *state* SW Nigeria
176 *Ww11* **Kwatisore** Papua, E Indonesia *3.14S 134.57E*
85 *K22* **KwaZulu/Natal** *off.* KwaZulu/Natal Province; *prev.* Natal. ◈ *province* E South Africa
Kweichow *see* Guizhou
Kweichu *see* Guiyang
Kweilin *see* Guilin
Kweisui *see* Hohhot
Kweiyang *see* Guiyang
85 *K17* **Kwekwe** *prev.* Que Que. Midlands, C Zimbabwe *18.55S 29.48E*
85 *G20* **Kweneng** ◈ *district* S Botswana
Kwesui *see* Hohhot
41 *N12* **Kwethluk** Alaska, USA *60.48N 161.26W*
41 *N12* **Kwethluk River** ⁓ Alaska, USA
112 *J8* **Kwidzyń** *Ger.* Marienwerder. Pomorskie, N Poland *53.44N 18.55E*
40 *M13* **Kwigillingok** Alaska, USA *59.51N 163.07W*
194 *K16* **Kwikila** Central, S PNG *9.48S 147.37E*
81 *I20* **Kwilu** ⁓ W Dem. Rep. Congo
Kwito *see* Cuito
176 *V8* **Kwoka, Gunung** ▲ Papua, E Indonesia *0.34S 132.25E*
80 *I12* **Kyabé** Moyen-Chari, S Chad *9.28N 18.54E*
191 *O11* **Kyabram** Victoria, SE Australia *36.21S 145.04E*
178 *Gg9* **Kyaikkami** *prev.* Amherst. Mon State, S Myanmar *16.02N 97.36E*
177 *Ff9* **Kyaiklat** Irrawaddy, SW Myanmar *16.25N 95.42E*
177 *G8* **Kyaikto** Mon State, S Myanmar *17.16N 97.01E*
126 *Jj16* **Kyakhta** Respublika Buryatiya, S Russian Federation *50.24N 106.12E*
190 *G8* **Kyancutta** South Australia *33.10S 135.33E*
177 *Ff7* **Kyangin** Irrawaddy, SW Myanmar *18.19N 95.15E*
178 *Jj8* **Ky Anh** Ha Tinh, N Vietnam *18.05N 106.16E*
177 *Ff5* **Kyaukpadaung** Mandalay, C Myanmar *20.49N 95.07E*
177 *F6* **Kyaukpyu** Arakan State, W Myanmar *19.27N 93.33E*
177 *G5* **Kyaukse** Mandalay, C Myanmar *21.34N 96.12E*
177 *Ff8* **Kyaunggon** Irrawaddy, SW Myanmar *17.04N 95.12E*
121 *E14* **Kybartai** *Pol.* Kibarty. Marijampolė, S Lithuania *54.37N 22.44E*
158 *I7* **Kyelang** Himāchal Pradesh, NW India *32.33N 77.03E*
113 *G19* **Kyjov** *Ger.* Gaya. Jihomoravský Kraj, SE Czech Republic *49.00N 17.07E*
117 *J21* **Kykládes** *var.* Kikládhes, *Eng.* Cyclades. *island group* SE Greece
27 *S11* **Kyle** Texas, SW USA *29.59N 97.52W*
98 *G9* **Kyle of Lochalsh** N Scotland, UK *57.17N 5.39W*
103 *D18* **Kyll** ⁓ W Germany
117 *F19* **Kyllíni** *var.* Killini. ▲▲ S Greece
95 *M19* **Kymijoki** ⁓ S Finland
117 *H18* **Kýmis, Akrotírio** *headland* Évvoia, C Greece *38.39N 24.08E*
129 *W14* **Kyn** Permskaya Oblast', NW Russian Federation *57.48N 58.38E*
191 *N12* **Kyneton** Victoria, SE Australia *37.14S 144.28E*
83 *G17* **Kyoga, Lake** *var.* Lake Kioga. ◎ C Uganda
171 *H13* **Kyōga-misaki** *headland* Honshū, SW Japan *35.46N 135.13E*
191 *V4* **Kyogle** New South Wales, SE Australia *28.37S 153.00E*
169 *W15* **Kyŏnggi-man** *bay* NW South Korea
169 *Z16* **Kyŏngju** *Jap.* Keishū. SE South Korea *35.49N 129.09E*
Kyŏngsŏng *see* Sŏul
Kyōsai-tō *see* Kŏje-do
83 *F19* **Kyotera** S Uganda *0.37S 31.34E*
171 *H15* **Kyōto** Kyōto, Honshū, SW Japan *35.01N 135.46E*
171 *H14* **Kyōto** *off.* Kyōto-fu, *var.* Kyōto Hu. ◈ *urban prefecture* Honshū, SW Japan
Kyōto-fu/Kyōto Hu *see* Kyōto
117 *D21* **Kyparissía** *var.* Kiparissía. Pelopónnisos, S Greece *37.13N 21.39E*
117 *D20* **Kyparissiakós Kólpos** *gulf* S Greece
Kyperounda *see* Kyperoúnta
124 *N3* **Kyperoúnta** *var.* Kyperounda. C Cyprus *34.57N 33.02E*
Kypros *see* Cyprus
117 *H16* **Kyrá Panagía** *island* Vóreioi Sporádes, Greece, Aegean Sea
Kyrenia *see* Girne
Kyrenia Mountains *see* Beşparmak Dağları
Kyrgyz Republic *see* Kyrgyzstan
153 *U9* **Kyrgyzstan** *off.* Kyrgyz Republic, *var.* Kirghizia; *prev.* Kirgizskaya SSR, Kirghiz SSR, Republic of Kyrgyzstan. ◆ *republic* C Asia
102 *M11* **Kyritz** Brandenburg, NE Germany *52.56N 12.24E*
Kyrkslätt *see* Kirkkonummi
96 *G8* **Kyrksæterøra** Sør-Trøndelag, S Norway *63.16N 9.04E*
129 *U8* **Kyrta** Respublika Komi, NW Russian Federation *64.03N 57.41E*
125 *Ee12* **Kyshtym** Chelyabinskaya Oblast', S Russian Federation *55.39N 60.31E*
113 *J18* **Kysucké Nové Mesto** *prev.* Horné Nové Mesto, *Ger.* Kisutzaneustadtl, Oberneustadtl, *Hung.* Kiszucaújhely. Žilinnský Kraj, N Slovakia *49.19N 18.47E*
119 *N12* **Kytay, Ozero** ◎ SW Ukraine
117 *F23* **Kýthira** *var.* Kíthira, *It.* Cerigo; *Lat.* Cythera. Kýthira, S Greece *36.09N 22.58E*
117 *F23* **Kýthira** *var.* Kíthira, *It.* Cerigo; *Lat.* Cythera. *island* S Greece
117 *I20* **Kýthnos** Kýthnos, Kykládes, Greece, Aegean Sea *37.24N 24.28E*
117 *I20* **Kýthnos** *var.* Kíthnos, Thermiá, *It.* Termia; *anc.* Cythnos. *island* Kykládes, Greece, Aegean Sea
117 *I20* **Kýthnou, Stenó** *strait* Kykládes, Greece, Aegean Sea
Kythréa *see* Değirmenlik
Kyungëy Ala-Too, Khrebet *see* Kungei Ala-Tau
Kyurdamir *see* Kürdämir
Kyuren, Gora *see* Kürendag
172 *C15* **Kyūshū** *var.* Kyûsyû. *island* SW Japan
199 *Gg6* **Kyushu-Palau Ridge** *var.* Kyusyu-Palau Ridge. *undersea feature* W Pacific Ocean
170 *Cc15* **Kyūshū-sanchi** ▲▲ Kyūshū, SW Japan
116 *F10* **Kyustendil** *anc.* Pautalia. Kyustendil, W Bulgaria *42.17N 22.42E*
116 *G11* **Kyustendil** ◈ *province* W Bulgaria
Kyûsyû *see* Kyūshū
Kyusyu-Palau Ridge *see* Kyushu-Palau Ridge
126 *L7* **Kyusyur** Respublika Sakha (Yakutiya), NE Russian Federation *70.36N 127.19E*
191 *P10* **Kywong** New South Wales, SE Australia *34.59S 146.42E*
119 *P4* **Kyyiv** *Eng.* Kiev, *Rus.* Kiyev. ● (Ukraine) Kyyivs'ka Oblast', N Ukraine *50.26N 30.31E*
Kyyiv *see* Kyyivs'ka Oblast'
119 *O4* **Kyyivs'ka Oblast'** *var.* Kyyiv, *Rus.* Kiyevskaya Oblast'. ◈ *province* N Ukraine
119 *P3* **Kyyivs'ke Vodoskhovyshche** *Eng.* Kiev Reservoir, *Rus.* Kiyevskoye Vodokhranilishche. ⊠ N Ukraine
95 *L16* **Kyyjärvi** Länsi-Suomi, W Finland *63.01N 24.34E*
126 *I16* **Kyzyl** Respublika Tyva, C Russian Federation *51.45N 94.28E*
153 *S8* **Kyzyl-Adyr** *prev.* Kirovskoye. Talasskaya Oblast', NW Kyrgyzstan *42.37N 71.34E*
151 *V14* **Kyzylagash** Almaty, SE Kazakhstan *45.19N 78.45E*
152 *C13* **Kyzylbair** Balkan Welaýaty, W Turkmenistan *38.13N 55.38E*
Kyzyl-Dzhiik, Pereval *see* Uzbel Shankou
151 *S7* **Kyzylkak, Ozero** ◎ NE Kazakhstan
151 *X11* **Kyzylkesek** Vostochnyy Kazakhstan, E Kazakhstan *47.55N 82.01E*
153 *S10* **Kyzyl-Kiya** *Kir.* Kyzyl-Kyya. Batkenskaya Oblast', SW Kyrgyzstan *40.15N 72.07E*
150 *L11* **Kyzylkol', Ozero** ◎ C Kazakhstan
151 *N15* **Kyzylorda** *var.* Kzyl-Orda, Qizil Orda *Kaz.* Qyzylorda; *prev.* Perovsk. Kyzylorda, S Kazakhstan *44.54N 65.30E*
150 *L14* **Kyzylorda** *off.* Kyzylordinskaya Oblast' *Kaz.* Qyzylorda Oblysy. ◈ *province* S Kazakhstan
138 *Ll9* **Kyzyl Kum** *var.* Kizil Kum, Qizil Qum, *Uzb.* Qizilqum. *desert* Kazakhstan/Uzbekistan
Kyzyl-Kyya *see* Kyzyl-Kiya
Kyzylrabat *see* Qizilravote
Kyzylrabot *see* Qizilrabot
Kyzylsu *see* Kyzyl-Suu
153 *X7* **Kyzyl-Suu** *prev.* Pokrovka. Issyk-Kul'skaya Oblast', NE Kyrgyzstan *42.19N 77.55E*
153 *S12* **Kyzyl-Suu** *var.* Kyzylsu. ⁓ Kyrgyzstan/Tajikistan
153 *X8* **Kyzyl-Tuu** Issyk-Kul'skaya Oblast', E Kyrgyzstan *42.06N 76.54E*
151 *Q12* **Kyzylzhar** *Kaz.* Qyzylzhar. Karaganda, C Kazakhstan *48.22N 70.00E*
Kzyl-Orda *see* Kyzylorda
Kyzylordinskaya Oblast' *see* Kyzylorda
Kzyltu *see* Kishkenekol'

L

111 *X2* **Laa an der Thaya** Niederösterreich, NE Austria *48.42N 16.22E*
65 *K15* **La Adela** La Pampa, SE Argentina *38.57S 64.02W*
Laagen *see* Numedalslågen
111 *S5* **Laakirchen** Oberösterreich, N Austria *47.59N 13.49E*
Laaland *see* Lolland
106 *I11* **La Albuera** Extremadura, W Spain *38.43N 6.49W*
107 *O7* **La Alcarria** *physical region* C Spain
106 *K14* **La Algaba** Andalucía, S Spain *37.27N 6.01W*
107 *P9* **La Almarcha** Castilla-La Mancha, C Spain *39.40N 2.22W*
107 *R6* **La Almunia de Doña Godina** Aragón, NE Spain *41.28N 1.22W*
43 *N5* **La Amistad, Presa** ⊠ NW Mexico
120 *F4* **Läänemaa** *off.* Lääne Maakond. ◈ *province* NW Estonia
120 *I3* **Lääne-Virumaa** *off.* Lääne-Viru Maakond. ◈ *province* NE Estonia
64 *J9* **La Antigua, Salina** *salt lake* W Argentina
101 *E17* **Laarne** Oost-Vlaanderen, NW Belgium *51.03N 3.49E*
82 *O13* **Laas Caanood** Nugaal, N Somalia *8.33N 47.44E*
43 *O9* **La Ascensión** Nuevo León, NE Mexico *24.15N 99.53W*
82 *N12* **Laas Dhaareed** Woqooyi Galbeed, N Somalia *10.12N 46.09E*
57 *O4* **La Asunción** Nueva Esparta, NE Venezuela *11.06N 63.53W*
Laatokka *see* Ladozhskoye Ozero
102 *I13* **Laatzen** Niedersachsen, NW Germany *52.19N 9.46E*
40 *E9* **Lā'au Point** *var.* Laau Point *headland* Moloka'i, Hawai'i, USA, C Pacific Ocean *21.06N 157.18W*
44 *D6* **La Aurora** ✕ (Ciudad de Guatemala) Guatemala, C Guatemala *14.33N 90.30W*
76 *C9* **Laâyoune** *var.* Aaiún. ○ (Western Sahara) NW Western Sahara *27.10N 13.10W*
130 *L14* **Laba** ⁓ SW Russian Federation
42 *M6* **La Babia** Coahuila de Zaragoza, NE Mexico *28.36N 102.04W*
13 *R7* **La Baie** Québec, SE Canada *48.20N 70.54W*
175 *R16* **Labala** Pulau Lomblen, S Indonesia *8.30S 123.27E*
64 *K8* **La Banda** Santiago del Estero, N Argentina *27.43S 64.13W*
La Banda Oriental *see* Uruguay
106 *K4* **La Bañeza** Castilla-León, N Spain *42.18N 5.54W*
42 *M13* **La Barca** Jalisco, SW Mexico *20.18N 102.30W*
42 *K14* **La Barra de Navidad** Jalisco, C Mexico *19.12N 104.38W*
197 *J13* **Labasa** *prev.* Lambasa. Vanua Levu, N Fiji *16.25S 179.24E*
179 *Q15* **Labason** Mindanao, S Philippines *8.03N 122.31E*
104 *H8* **la Baule-Escoublac** Loire-Atlantique, NW France *47.16N 2.24W*
Labe *see* Elbe
78 *I13* **Labé** Moyenne-Guinée, NW Guinea *11.19N 12.16W*
25 *X14* **La Belle** Florida, SE USA *26.45N 81.26W*
13 *N11* **Labelle** Québec, SE Canada *46.15N 74.43W*
8 *H7* **Laberge, Lake** ◎ Yukon Territory, W Canada
Labes *see* Łobez
Labiau *see* Polessk
114 *A10* **Labin** *It.* Albona. Istra, NW Croatia *45.05N 14.07E*
130 *L14* **Labinsk** Krasnodarskiy Kray, SW Russian Federation *44.39N 40.43E*
107 *X5* **La Bisbal d'Empordà** Cataluña, NE Spain *41.58N 3.01E*
121 *P16* **Labkovichy** *Rus.* Lobkovichi. Mahilyowskaya Voblasts', E Belarus *53.49N 31.43E*
13 *S4* **La Blache, Lac de** ◎ Québec, SE Canada
179 *Q11* **Labo** Luzon, N Philippines *14.10N 122.47E*
Laboehanbadjo *see* Labuhanbajo
Laborca *see* Laborec
113 *N18* **Laborec** *Hung.* Laborca. ⁓ E Slovakia
110 *D11* **La Borgne** ⁓ S Switzerland
47 *T12* **Laborie** SW Saint Lucia *13.45N 61.00W*
81 *F21* **La Bouenza** ◈ *province* S Congo
104 *J14* **Labouheyre** Landes, SW France *44.12N 0.55W*
64 *L12* **Laboulaye** Córdoba, C Argentina *34.05S 63.20W*
11 *Q7* **Labrador** *cultural region* Newfoundland and Labrador, SW Canada
66 *I6* **Labrador Basin** *var.* Labrador Sea Basin. *undersea feature* Labrador Sea
11 *N9* **Labrador City** Newfoundland and Labrador, E Canada *52.55N 66.52W*
11 *Q5* **Labrador Sea** *sea* NW Atlantic Ocean
Labrador Sea Basin *see* Labrador Basin
Labrang *see* Xiahe
56 *G9* **Labranzagrande** Boyacá, C Colombia *5.30N 72.33W*
47 *U15* **La Brea** Trinidad, Trinidad and Tobago *10.13N 61.36W*
61 *D14* **Lábrea** Amazonas, N Brazil *7.19S 64.46W*
13 *S6* **Labrieville** Québec, SE Canada *49.15N 69.31W*
104 *K14* **Labrit** Landes, SW France *44.03N 0.29W*
110 *C9* **La Broye** ⁓ SW Switzerland
105 *N15* **Labruguière** Tarn, S France *43.31N 2.15E*
174 *I8* **Labu** Pulau Singkep, W Indonesia *0.34S 104.24E*
175 *N3* **Labuan** *var.* Victoria. Labuan, East Malaysia *5.19N 115.13E*
175 *N3* **Labuan** ◈ *federal territory* East Malaysia
Labuan *see* Labuan, Pulau
175 *N3* **Labuan, Pulau** *var.* Labuan. *island* East Malaysia
Labudalin *see* Ergun
175 *Pp16* **Labuhanbajo** *prev.* Laboehanbadjo. Flores, S Indonesia *8.29S 119.54E*
173 *G6* **Labuhanbilik** Sumatera, N Indonesia *2.33N 100.09E*
173 *Ee5* **Labuhanhaji** Sumatera, W Indonesia *3.31N 97.00E*
Labuk *see* Labuk, Sungai
Labuk Bay *see* Labuk, Teluk
175 *O2* **Labuk, Sungai** *var.* Labuk. ⁓ East Malaysia
175 *Oo2* **Labuk, Teluk** *var.* Labuk Bay, Telukan Labuk. *bay* S Sulu Sea
Labuk, Telukan *see* Labuk, Teluk
177 *Ff9* **Labutta** Irrawaddy, SW Myanmar *16.07N 94.45E*
125 *G8* **Labytnangi** Yamalo-Nenetskiy Avtonomnyy Okrug, N Russian Federation *66.39N 66.26E*
80 *F10* **Lac** *off.* Préfecture du Lac. ◈ *prefecture* W Chad
115 *K19* **Laç** *var.* Laci. Lezhë, C Albania *41.37N 19.37E*
59 *K19* **Lacajahuira, Rio** ⁓ W Bolivia
La Calamine *see* Kelmis
64 *G11* **La Calera** Valparaíso, C Chile *32.48S 71.13W*
11 *P11* **Lac-Allard** Québec, E Canada *50.37N 63.26W*
106 *L13* **La Campana** Andalucía, S Spain *37.35N 5.24W*
104 *J12* **Lacanau** Gironde, SW France *44.59N 1.04W*
44 *C2* **Lacandón, Sierra del** ▲▲ Guatemala/Mexico
La Cañiza *see* A Cañiza
43 *W16* **Lacantún, Río** ⁓ SE Mexico
105 *Q3* **la Capelle** Aisne, N France *49.58N 3.55E*
114 *K10* **Laćarak** Serbia, NW Serbia and Montenegro (Yugoslavia) *45.00N 19.34E*
64 *L11* **La Carlota** Córdoba, C Argentina *33.27S 63.16W*
179 *Q13* **La Carlota** Negros, S Philippines *10.21N 122.55E*
106 *L13* **La Carlota** Andalucía, S Spain *37.40N 4.55W*
107 *N12* **La Carolina** Andalucía, S Spain *38.15N 3.37W*
105 *O15* **Lacaune** Tarn, S France *43.42N 2.42E*
13 *P7* **Lac-Bouchette** Québec, SE Canada *48.14N 72.11W*
Laccadive Islands/Laccadive Minicoy and Amindivi Islands, the *see* Lakshadweep
9 *Y16* **Lac du Bonnet** Manitoba, S Canada *50.13N 96.04W*
32 *L4* **Lac du Flambeau** Wisconsin, N USA *45.58N 89.51W*
13 *P8* **Lac-Édouard** Québec, SE Canada *47.39N 72.16W*
44 *I4* **La Ceiba** Atlántida, N Honduras *15.45N 86.28W*
56 *E9* **La Ceja** Antioquia, W Colombia *6.08N 75.21W*
190 *J11* **Lacepede Bay** *bay* South Australia
34 *G9* **Lacey** Washington, NW USA *47.01N 122.49W*
105 *P12* **la Chaise-Dieu** Haute-Loire, C France *45.19N 3.41E*
116 *G13* **Lachanás** Kentrikí Makedonía, N Greece *40.57N 23.15E*

◆ Country ● Country Capital ◇ Dependent Territory ○ Dependent Territory Capital ◈ Administrative Region ✕ International Airport ▲ Mountain ▲▲ Mountain Range ⋀ Volcano ⁓ River ◎ Lake ⊠ Reservoir

281

◆ COUNTRY   ◇ DEPENDENT TERRITORY   ◆ ADMINISTRATIVE REGION   ▲ MOUNTAIN   ◎ LAKE
● COUNTRY CAPITAL   ◇ DEPENDENT TERRITORY CAPITAL   ✕ INTERNATIONAL AIRPORT   ▲ MOUNTAIN RANGE   ⚄ RIVER   ◙ RESERVOIR

Langeb, Wadi – Lay Lake

82 I8 **Langeb, Wadi** ≈ NE Sudan
Långed see Dals Långed
97 G25 **Langeland** island S Denmark
101 B18 **Langemark** West-Vlaanderen, W Belgium 50.55N 2.55E
103 G18 **Langen** Hessen, W Germany 49.58N 8.40E
103 J22 **Langenau** Baden-Württemberg, S Germany 48.30N 10.08E
9 V16 **Langenburg** Saskatchewan, S Canada 50.49N 101.43W
103 E16 **Langenfeld** Nordrhein-Westfalen, W Germany 51.06N 6.57E
110 L8 **Längenfeld** Tirol, W Austria 47.04N 10.59E
102 I12 **Langenhagen** Niedersachsen, N Germany 52.25N 9.43E
102 I12 **Langenhagen** ✈ (Hannover) Niedersachsen, NW Germany 52.28N 9.40E
111 W3 **Langenlois** Niederösterreich, NE Austria 48.28N 15.42E
110 E7 **Langenthal** Bern, NW Switzerland 47.13N 7.46E
111 W6 **Langenwang** Steiermark, E Austria 47.34N 15.39E
111 X3 **Langenzersdorf** Niederösterreich, E Austria 48.19N 16.22E
102 F9 **Langeoog** island NW Germany
126 Gg11 **Langepas** Khanty-Mansiyskiy Avtonomnyy Okrug, C Russian Federation 61.12N 75.24E
97 H23 **Langeskov** Fyn, C Denmark 55.22N 10.36E
97 G16 **Langesund** Telemark, S Norway 59.00N 9.43E
97 G17 **Langesundsfjorden** fjord S Norway
96 D10 **Langevåg** Møre og Romsdal, S Norway 62.25N 6.13E
167 P3 **Langfang** Hebei, E China 39.30N 116.39E
96 E9 **Langfjorden** fjord S Norway
31 Q8 **Langford** South Dakota, N USA 45.36N 97.48W
173 G6 **Langgapayung** Sumatera, W Indonesia 1.42N 99.57E
108 E9 **Langhirano** Emilia-Romagna, C Italy 44.37N 10.16E
99 K14 **Langholm** S Scotland, UK 55.13N 3.11W
94 I3 **Langjökull** glacier C Iceland
173 Ff2 **Langkawi, Pulau** island Peninsular Malaysia
175 R13 **Langkesi, Kepulauan** island group C Indonesia
178 Gg15 **Langkha Tuk, Khao** ▲ SW Thailand 9.19N 98.39E
12 L8 **Langlade** Québec, SE Canada 48.13N 75.58W
8 M17 **Langley** British Columbia, SW Canada 49.07N 122.39W
178 Jj7 **Lang Mô** Thanh Hoa, N Vietnam 19.36N 105.30E
Langnau see Langnau im Emmental
110 E8 **Langnau im Emmental** var. Langnau. Bern, W Switzerland 46.57N 7.46E
105 Q13 **Langogne** Lozère, S France 44.40N 3.52E
104 K13 **Langon** Gironde, SW France 47.43N 1.49W
La Ngounié see Ngounié
94 G10 **Langøya** island C Norway
164 G14 **Langqên Zangbo** ≈ China/India
106 K2 **Langreo** var. Sama de Langreo. Asturias, N Spain 43.18N 5.40W
105 S7 **Langres** Haute-Marne, N France 47.52N 5.19E
105 R8 **Langres, Plateau de** plateau C France
173 F4 **Langsa** Sumatera, W Indonesia 4.29N 97.53E
95 H16 **Långsele** Västernorrland, C Sweden 63.10N 17.04E
168 L12 **Lang Shan** ▲▲ N China
97 M14 **Långshyttan** Dalarna, C Sweden 60.25N 16.01E
178 K5 **Lang Sơn** var. Langson. Lang Sơn, N Vietnam 21.49N 106.45E
178 Gg14 **Lang Suan** Chumphon, SW Thailand 9.52N 99.03E
95 J14 **Långträsk** Norrbotten, N Sweden 65.22N 20.19E
27 N11 **Langtry** Texas, SW USA 29.46N 101.25W
105 P16 **Languedoc** cultural region S France
105 P15 **Languedoc-Roussillon** ◐ region S France
29 X10 **L'Anguille River** ≈ Arkansas, C USA
95 I16 **Långviksmon** Västernorrland, N Sweden 63.39N 18.45E
103 K22 **Langweid** Bayern, S Germany 48.29N 10.50E
166 J8 **Langzhong** Sichuan, C China 31.46N 105.55E
Lan Hsü see Lan Yü
9 U15 **Lanigan** Saskatchewan, S Canada 51.49N 105.01W
118 K5 **Lanivtsi** Ternopil's'ka Oblast', W Ukraine 49.52N 26.05E
143 Y13 **Länkäran** Rus. Lenkoran'. S Azerbaijan 38.46N 48.50E
104 L16 **Lannemezan** Hautes-Pyrénées, S France 43.07N 0.22E
104 G5 **Lannion** Côtes d'Armor, NW France 48.43N 3.27W
12 M11 **L'Annonciation** Québec, SE Canada 46.22N 74.51W
107 V5 **L'Anoia** ≈ NE Spain
20 I15 **Lansdale** Pennsylvania, NE USA 40.14N 75.13W
12 L14 **Lansdowne** Ontario, SE Canada 44.25N 76.00W
158 K9 **Lansdowne** Uttaranchal, N India 29.49N 78.42E
32 M3 **L'Anse** Michigan, N USA 46.45N 88.27W
13 S7 **L'Anse-St-Jean** Québec, SE Canada 48.14N 70.13W
95 K18 **Länsi-Suomi** ◐ province W Finland
31 Y11 **Lansing** Iowa, C USA 43.22N 91.11W
29 R4 **Lansing** Kansas, C USA 39.15N 94.54W
33 Q9 **Lansing** state capital Michigan, N USA 42.43N 84.33W
94 J12 **Lansjärv** Norrbotten, N Sweden 66.39N 22.10E
113 G17 **Lanškroun** Ger. Landskron. Pardubický Kraj, C Czech Republic 49.53N 16.34E
178 Gg16 **Lanta, Ko** island S Thailand
167 O15 **Lantau Island** Cant. Tai Yue Shan, Chin. Landao. island Hong Kong, S China
Lan-ts'ang Chiang see Mekong
175 Q7 **Lanu** Sulawesi, N Indonesia 1.00N 121.33E
109 D19 **Lanusei** Sardegna, Italy, C Mediterranean Sea 39.55N 9.31E
104 H7 **Lanvaux, Landes de** physical region NW France
169 W8 **Lanxi** Heilongjiang, NE China 46.18N 126.49E
167 R10 **Lanxi** Zhejiang, SE China 29.13N 119.30E
La Nyanga see Nyanga
167 T15 **Lan Yü** var. Huoshao Tao, var. Hungt'ou, Lan Hsü, Lanyü, Eng. Orchid Island; prev. Kotosho, Koto Sho. island SE Taiwan
66 P11 **Lanzarote** island Islas Canarias, Spain, NE Atlantic Ocean
165 V10 **Lanzhou** var. Lan-chou, Lanchow, Lan-chow; prev. Kaolan. Gansu, C China 36.01N 103.52E
108 B8 **Lanzo Torinese** Piemonte, NE Italy 45.18N 7.26E
179 P8 **Laoag** Luzon, N Philippines 18.11N 120.34E
179 R12 **Laoang** Samar, C Philippines 12.29N 125.01E
178 J5 **Lao Cai** Lao Cai, N Vietnam 22.29N 104.00E
Laodicea/Laodicea ad Mare see Al Lādhiqīyah
Laoet see Laut, Pulau
169 T11 **Laoha He** ≈ NE China
166 M8 **Laohekou** prev. Guanghua. Hubei, C China 32.21N 111.40E
Laoi, An see Lee
99 E19 **Laois** prev. Leix, Queen's County. cultural region C Ireland
Laojunmiao see Yumen
169 W12 **Lao Ling** ▲▲ NE China
66 Q11 **La Oliva** var. Oliva. Fuerteventura, Islas Canarias, Spain, NE Atlantic Ocean 28.36N 13.52W
Lao, Loch see Belfast Lough
Laolong see Longchuan
Lao Mangnai see Mangnai
105 P3 **Laon** var. la Laon; anc. Laudunum. Aisne, N France 49.34N 3.37E
Lao People's Democratic Republic see Laos
56 M3 **La Orchila, Isla** island N Venezuela
66 O11 **La Orotava** Tenerife, Islas Canarias, Spain, NE Atlantic Ocean 28.22N 16.31W
59 E14 **La Oroya** Junín, C Peru 11.29S 75.57W
178 Ii7 **Laos** off. Lao People's Democratic Republic. ◆ republic SE Asia
167 R5 **Laoshan Wan** bay E China
169 Y10 **Laoye Ling** ▲▲ NE China
62 J12 **Lapa** Paraná, S Brazil 25.46S 49.43W
105 P10 **Lapalisse** Allier, C France 46.13N 3.39E
56 F9 **La Palma** Cundinamarca, C Colombia 5.22N 74.24W
44 F7 **La Palma** Chalatenango, N El Salvador 14.19N 89.10W
45 W16 **La Palma** Darién, SE Panama 8.24N 78.09W
66 N11 **La Palma** island Islas Canarias, Spain, NE Atlantic Ocean
106 J14 **La Palma del Condado** Andalucía, S Spain 37.22N 6.33W
63 F18 **La Paloma** Durazno, C Uruguay 34.37S 54.07W
63 G20 **La Paloma** Rocha, E Uruguay 34.37S 54.07W
63 A21 **La Pampa** off. Provincia de La Pampa. ◐ province C Argentina
57 P8 **La Paragua** Bolívar, E Venezuela 6.53N 63.16W
121 O16 **Lapatsichy** Rus. Lopatichi. Mahilyowskaya Voblasts', E Belarus 53.34N 30.53E
63 C16 **La Paz** Entre Ríos, E Argentina 30.45S 59.36W
64 I11 **La Paz** Mendoza, C Argentina 33.27S 67.35W
59 J18 **La Paz** var. La Paz de Ayacucho. ● (Bolivia-legislative and administrative capital) La Paz, W Bolivia 16.30S 68.12W
44 H6 **La Paz** La Paz, SW Honduras 14.27N 87.41W
42 F9 **La Paz** Baja California Sur, NW Mexico 24.06N 110.18W
63 F20 **La Paz** Canelones, S Uruguay 34.46S 56.13W
59 J16 **La Paz** ◐ department W Bolivia
44 B9 **La Paz** ◐ department S El Salvador
44 G7 **La Paz** ◐ department SW Honduras
La Paz see El Alto, Bolivia
La Paz see Robles, Colombia
La Paz see La Paz Centro, Nicaragua
42 F9 **La Paz, Bahía de** bay W Mexico
44 I10 **La Paz Centro** var. La Paz. León, W Nicaragua 12.19N 86.40W
La Paz de Ayacucho see La Paz
56 J15 **La Pedrera** Amazonas, SE Colombia 1.19S 69.31W
33 S9 **Lapeer** Michigan, N USA 43.03N 83.19W
42 K6 **La Perla** Chihuahua, N Mexico 28.11N 104.28W
172 Pp1 **La Perouse Strait** Jap. Sōya-kaikyō, Rus. Proliv Laperuza. strait Japan/Russian Federation
65 I14 **La Perra, Salitral de** salt lake C Argentina
Laperuza, Proliv see La Perouse Strait
43 Q10 **La Pesca** Tamaulipas, C Mexico 23.49N 97.45W
42 M13 **La Piedad Cavadas** Michoacán de Ocampo, C Mexico 20.19N 102.01W
Lapines see Lafnitz
95 M16 **Lapinlahti** Itä-Suomi, C Finland 63.21N 27.25E
Lápithos see Lapta
24 K9 **Laplace** Louisiana, S USA 30.04N 90.28W
47 X12 **La Plaine** SE Dominica 15.19N 61.15W
181 P16 **la Plaine-des-Palmistes** C Réunion
94 K11 **Lapland** Fin. Lappi, Swe. Lappland. cultural region N Europe
30 M8 **La Plant** South Dakota, N USA 45.06N 100.40W
63 D20 **La Plata** Buenos Aires, E Argentina 34.56S 57.55W
56 D12 **La Plata** Huila, SW Colombia 2.25N 75.47W
23 W4 **La Plata** Maryland, NE USA 38.28N 76.55W
La Plata see Sucre
47 U6 **la Plata, Río de** ≈ C Puerto Rico
107 W4 **La Pobla de Lillet** Cataluña, NE Spain 42.15N 1.57E
107 U4 **La Pobla de Segur** Cataluña, NE Spain 42.15N 0.58E
13 S9 **La Pocatière** Québec, SE Canada 47.17N 70.04W
106 L3 **La Pola de Gordón** Castilla-León, N Spain 42.50N 5.38W
33 O11 **La Porte** Indiana, N USA 41.36N 86.43W
20 H13 **Laporte** Pennsylvania, NE USA 41.25N 76.28W
31 X13 **La Porte City** Iowa, C USA 42.19N 92.11W
64 J8 **La Posta** Catamarca, C Argentina 27.59S 65.32W
42 E8 **La Poza Grande** Baja California Sur, W Mexico 25.45N 111.58W
95 K16 **Lappajärvi** Länsi-Suomi, W Finland 63.11N 23.37E
95 L16 **Lappajärvi** ◎ W Finland
95 N18 **Lappeenranta** Swe. Villmanstrand. Etelä-Suomi, S Finland 61.04N 28.15E
95 J17 **Lappfjärd** Fin. Lapväärtti. Länsi-Suomi, W Finland 62.13N 21.34E
94 L12 **Lappi** Swe. Lappland. ◐ province N Finland
Lappi/Lappland see Lapland
Lappo see Lapua
63 C23 **Laprida** Buenos Aires, E Argentina 37.33S 60.46W
27 P13 **La Pryor** Texas, SW USA 28.56N 99.51W
142 B11 **Lâpseki** Çanakkale, NW Turkey 40.17N 26.36E
124 Nn2 **Lapta** Gk. Lápithos. NW Cyprus 35.19N 33.11E
Laptev Sea see Laptevykh, More
126 Kk5 **Laptevykh, More** Eng. Laptev Sea. sea Arctic Ocean
95 K16 **Lapua** Swe. Lappo. Länsi-Suomi, W Finland 62.57N 23.00E
107 P3 **La Puebla de Arganzón** País Vasco, N Spain 42.45N 2.49W
106 L14 **La Puebla de Cazalla** Andalucía, S Spain 37.13N 5.18W
106 M9 **La Puebla de Montalbán** Castilla-La Mancha, C Spain 39.52N 4.22W
56 I6 **La Puerta** Trujillo, NW Venezuela 9.09N 70.44W
179 Qq13 **Lapu-Lapu** C Philippines 10.18N 123.58E
Lapurdum see Bayonne
42 E7 **La Purísima** Baja California Sur, W Mexico 26.10N 112.04W
Lapväärtti see Lappfjärd
112 O10 **Łapy** Podlaskie, NE Poland 53.00N 22.50E
82 D6 **Laqiya Arba'in** Northern, NW Sudan 20.01N 28.01E
64 J4 **La Quiaca** Jujuy, N Argentina 22.12S 65.36W
109 J14 **L'Aquila** var. Aquila, Aquila degli Abruzzo. Abruzzo, C Italy 42.21N 13.24E
149 Q13 **Lār** Fārs, S Iran 27.42N 54.19E
56 J5 **Lara** off. Estado Lara. ◐ state NW Venezuela
106 G2 **Laracha** Galicia, NW Spain 43.14N 8.34W
76 G5 **Larache** var. al Araïch, El Araïch, El Araïche, anc. Lixus. NW Morocco 35.16N 6.07W
105 T14 **Laragne-Montéglin** Hautes-Alpes, SE France 44.21N 5.46E
106 M13 **La Rambla** Andalucía, S Spain 37.37N 4.44W
35 Y17 **Laramie** Wyoming, C USA 41.18N 105.35W
35 X15 **Laramie Mountains** ▲▲ Wyoming, C USA
35 Y16 **Laramie River** ≈ Wyoming, C USA
62 H12 **Laranjeiras do Sul** Paraná, S Brazil 25.22S 52.22W
Larantoeka see Larantuka
175 Qq16 **Larantuka** prev. Larantoeka. Flores, C Indonesia 8.20S 123.00E
176 V15 **Larat** Pulau Larat, E Indonesia 7.07S 131.46E
176 V15 **Larat, Pulau** island Kepulauan Tanimbar, E Indonesia
97 P19 **Lärbro** Gotland, SE Sweden 57.46N 18.49E
108 A9 **Larche, Col de** pass France/Italy 44.26N 6.54E
12 H8 **Larder Lake** Ontario, S Canada 48.06N 79.43W
107 O2 **Laredo** Cantabria, N Spain 43.22N 3.22W
27 Q15 **Laredo** Texas, SW USA 27.30N 99.30W
42 H9 **La Reforma** Sinaloa, W Mexico 25.04N 108.03W
100 N11 **Laren** Gelderland, E Netherlands 52.12N 6.22E
100 J11 **Laren** Noord-Holland, C Netherlands 52.15N 5.13E
104 K13 **la Réole** Gironde, SW France 44.34N 0.00W
La Réunion see Réunion
Largeau see Faya
105 U13 **l'Argentière-la-Bessée** Hautes-Alpes, SE France 44.49N 6.34E
155 O4 **Lar Gerd** var. Largird. Balkh, N Afghanistan 35.36N 66.48E
Largird see Lar Gerd
25 V12 **Largo** Florida, SE USA 27.54N 82.47W
39 Q9 **Largo, Canon** valley New Mexico, SW USA
46 D6 **Largo, Cayo** island W Cuba
25 Z17 **Largo, Key** island Florida Keys, Florida, SE USA
98 H12 **Largs** W Scotland, UK 55.47N 4.50W
104 I16 **la Rhune** var. Larrún. ▲ France/Spain see also Larrún 43.19N 1.36W
la Riege see Ariège
31 Q4 **Larimore** North Dakota, N USA 47.54N 97.37W
109 L15 **Larino** Molise, C Italy 41.46N 14.50E
Lario see Como, Lago di
64 J9 **La Rioja** La Rioja, NW Argentina 29.25S 66.49W
64 I9 **La Rioja** off. Provincia de La Rioja. ◐ province NW Argentina
107 O4 **La Rioja** ◐ autonomous community N Spain
117 F16 **Lárisa** var. Larissa. Thessalía, C Greece 39.38N 22.27E
Larissa see Lárisa
155 Q13 **Lārkāna** var. Larkhana. Sind, SE Pakistan 27.31N 68.18E
Larkhana see Lārkāna
Larnaca see Lárnaka
124 Nn3 **Lárnaka** var. Larnaca, Larnax. SE Cyprus 34.54N 33.38E
124 Nn3 **Lárnaka** ✈ SE Cyprus 34.52N 33.38E
Larnax see Lárnaka
99 G14 **Larne** Ir. Latharna. E Northern Ireland, UK 54.51N 5.49W
28 L5 **Larned** Kansas, C USA 38.10N 99.06W
106 L3 **La Robla** Castilla-León, N Spain 42.48N 5.37W
106 J10 **La Roca de la Sierra** Extremadura, W Spain 39.06N 6.41W
101 K22 **La Roche-en-Ardenne** Luxembourg, SE Belgium 50.11N 5.35E
104 L11 **la Rochefoucauld** Charente, W France 45.43N 0.23E
104 J10 **la Rochelle** anc. Rupella. Charente-Maritime, W France 46.09N 1.07W
104 I9 **la Roche-sur-Yon** prev. Bourbon Vendée, Napoléon-Vendée. Vendée, NW France 46.40N 1.25W
107 Q10 **La Roda** Castilla-La Mancha, C Spain 39.13N 2.10W
106 L14 **La Roda de Andalucía** Andalucía, S Spain 37.12N 4.45W
47 P9 **La Romana** E Dominican Republic 18.25N 69.00W
9 T13 **La Ronge** Saskatchewan, C Canada 55.07N 105.18W
9 U13 **La Ronge, Lac** ◎ Saskatchewan, C Canada
24 K10 **Larose** Louisiana, S USA 29.34N 90.22W
44 M7 **La Rosita** Región Autónoma Atlántico Norte, NE Nicaragua 13.55N 84.23W
189 Q3 **Larrimah** Northern Territory, N Australia 15.30S 133.12E
64 N11 **Larroque** Entre Ríos, E Argentina 33.05S 59.06W
107 Q2 **Larrún** Fr. la Rhune. ▲ France/Spain see also la Rhune 43.18N 1.35W
205 X6 **Lars Christensen Coast** physical region Antarctica
41 Q14 **Larsen Bay** Kodiak Island, Alaska, USA 57.32N 153.58W
204 I5 **Larsen Ice Shelf** ice shelf Antarctica
15 K3 **Larsen Sound** sound Nunavut, N Canada
La Rúa see A Rúa de Valdeorras
104 K16 **Laruns** Pyrénées-Atlantiques, SW France 43.00N 0.25W
97 G16 **Larvik** Vestfold, S Norway 59.03N 10.01E
126 H11 **Lar'yak** Khanty-Mansiyskiy Avtonomnyy Okrug, C Russian Federation 61.09N 80.01E
La-sa see Lhasa
175 Tt11 **Lasahata** Pulau Seram, E Indonesia 2.52S 128.27E
Lasahau see Lasihao
39 O6 **La Sal** Utah, W USA 38.19N 109.14W
12 C17 **La Salle** Ontario, S Canada 42.13N 83.05W
32 L11 **La Salle** Illinois, N USA 41.19N 89.06W
47 O9 **Las Americas** ✈ (Santo Domingo) S Dominican Republic 18.24N 69.38W
81 G17 **La Sangha** ◐ province N Congo
39 V6 **Las Animas** Colorado, C USA 38.04N 103.13W
110 D10 **La Sarine** var. Sarine. ≈ SW Switzerland
110 B9 **La Sarraz** Vaud, W Switzerland 46.40N 6.32E
10 H12 **La Sarre** Québec, SE Canada 48.49N 79.12W
56 L3 **Las Aves, Islas** var. Islas de Aves. island group N Venezuela
57 N7 **Las Bonitas** Bolívar, C Venezuela 7.50N 65.40W
106 K15 **Las Cabezas de San Juan** Andalucía, S Spain 36.58N 5.55W
63 G19 **Lascano** Rocha, E Uruguay 33.40S 54.12W
64 I5 **Lascar, Volcán** ▲ N Chile 23.22S 67.33W
43 T15 **Las Choapas** var. Choapas. Veracruz-Llave, SE Mexico 17.51N 94.00W
39 R15 **Las Cruces** New Mexico, SW USA 32.19N 106.49W
Lasdehnen see Krasnoznamensk
107 V4 **La See d'Urgel** var. La Seu d'Urgell, Seo de Urgel. Cataluña, NE Spain 42.22N 1.27E
La Selle see Selle, Pic de la
64 G9 **La Serena** Coquimbo, C Chile 29.54S 71.18W
106 K11 **La Serena** physical region W Spain
La Seu d'Urgell see La See d'Urgel
105 T16 **la Seyne-sur-Mer** Var, SE France 43.07N 5.52E
63 D21 **Las Flores** Buenos Aires, E Argentina 36.03S 59.07W
64 H9 **Las Flores** San Juan, W Argentina 30.14S 69.10W
9 S14 **Lashburn** Saskatchewan, S Canada 53.09N 109.37W
64 I11 **Las Heras** Mendoza, W Argentina 32.46S 68.51W
178 Gg4 **Lashio** Shan State, E Myanmar 22.58N 97.48E
154 M8 **Lashkar Gāh** var. Lash-Kar-Gar'. Helmand, S Afghanistan 31.34N 64.21E
Lash-Kar-Gar' see Lashkar Gāh
175 Qq13 **Lasihao** var. Lasahau. Pulau Muna, C Indonesia 5.01S 122.23E
109 N21 **La Sila** ▲▲ SW Italy
65 H23 **La Silueta, Cerro** ▲ S Chile 52.22S 72.09W
44 L9 **La Sirena** Región Autónoma Atlántico Sur, E Nicaragua 12.58N 84.42W
112 J13 **Łask** Łódzkie, C Poland 51.36N 19.06E
111 V11 **Laško** Ger. Tüffer. C Slovenia 46.08N 15.13E
65 H14 **Las Lajas** Neuquén, W Argentina 38.31S 70.22W
65 H15 **Las Lajas, Cerro** ▲ W Argentina 38.49S 70.42W
64 M6 **Las Lomitas** Formosa, N Argentina 24.44S 60.34W
43 V16 **Las Margaritas** Chiapas, SE Mexico 16.15N 91.58W
Las Marismas see Guadalquivir, Marismas del
56 M6 **Las Mercedes** Guárico, N Venezuela 9.06N 66.22W
44 F6 **Las Minas, Cerro** ▲ W Honduras 14.33N 88.41W
107 O11 **La Solana** Castilla-La Mancha, C Spain 38.55N 3.13W
47 Q14 **La Soufrière** ⛰ Saint Vincent, Saint Vincent and the Grenadines 13.20N 61.11W
104 M10 **la Souterraine** Creuse, C France 46.15N 1.28E
64 N7 **Las Palmas** Chaco, N Argentina 27.07S 58.45W
45 Q16 **Las Palmas** Veraguas, W Panama 8.09N 81.28W
66 P12 **Las Palmas** var. Las Palmas de Gran Canaria. Gran Canaria, Islas Canarias, Spain, NE Atlantic Ocean 28.07N 15.27W
66 P12 **Las Palmas** ◐ province Islas Canarias, Spain, NE Atlantic Ocean
66 Q12 **Las Palmas** ✈ Gran Canaria, Islas Canarias, Spain, NE Atlantic Ocean
Las Palmas de Gran Canaria see Las Palmas
42 D6 **Las Palomas** Baja California Sur, W Mexico 31.43N 107.37W
107 P10 **Las Pedroñeras** Castilla-La Mancha, C Spain 39.27N 2.40W
108 E10 **La Spezia** Liguria, NW Italy 44.07N 9.49E
63 F20 **Las Piedras** Canelones, S Uruguay 34.42S 56.13W
65 J18 **Las Plumas** Chubut, S Argentina 43.46S 67.15W
63 B18 **Las Rosas** Santa Fe, C Argentina 32.27S 61.30W
Lassa see Lhasa
37 O4 **Lassen Peak** ▲ California, W USA 40.27N 121.28W
204 K6 **Lassiter Coast** physical region Antarctica
111 V9 **Lassnitz** ≈ SE Austria
13 O12 **L'Assomption** Québec, SE Canada 45.48N 73.27W
13 N11 **L'Assomption** ≈ Québec, SE Canada
45 S17 **Las Tablas** Los Santos, S Panama 7.45N 80.17W
Lastarria, Volcán see Azufre, Volcán
39 V4 **Last Chance** Colorado, C USA 39.41N 103.34W
Last Frontier, The see Alaska
9 U16 **Last Mountain Lake** ◎ Saskatchewan, S Canada
64 H9 **Las Tórtolas, Cerro** ▲ W Argentina 29.57S 69.49W
63 C14 **Las Toscas** Santa Fe, C Argentina 28.22S 59.19W
81 F19 **Lastoursville** Ogooué-Lolo, E Gabon 0.49S 12.43E
115 F16 **Lastovo** It. Lagosta. island SW Croatia
115 F16 **Lastovski Kanal** channel SW Croatia
42 E6 **Las Tres Vírgenes, Volcán** ⛰ W Mexico 27.27N 112.34W
42 F4 **Las Trincheras** Sonora, NW Mexico 30.21N 111.27W
57 N8 **Las Trincheras** Bolívar, E Venezuela 6.57N 64.49W
46 H7 **Las Tunas** var. Victoria de las Tunas. Las Tunas, E Cuba 20.58N 76.58W
La Suisse see Switzerland
42 I5 **Las Varas** Chihuahua, N Mexico 29.35N 108.01W
42 J12 **Las Varas** Nayarit, C Mexico 21.11N 105.09W
64 L10 **Las Varillas** Córdoba, E Argentina 31.54S 62.45W
37 X11 **Las Vegas** Nevada, W USA 36.09N 115.10W
39 T10 **Las Vegas** New Mexico, SW USA 35.35N 105.15W
195 W8 **Lata** Nendö, Solomon Islands 10.45S 165.43E
11 R10 **La Tabatière** Québec, E Canada 50.51N 58.58W
58 C6 **Latacunga** Cotopaxi, C Ecuador 0.58S 78.36W
204 I7 **Latady Island** island Antarctica
56 E14 **La Tagua** Putumayo, S Colombia 0.04S 74.39W
Latakia see Al Lādhiqīyah
94 J10 **Lätäseno** ≈ NW Finland
12 H9 **Latchford** Ontario, S Canada 47.20N 79.45W
12 J13 **Latchford Bridge** Ontario, SE Canada 45.16N 77.29W
200 Ss12 **Late** island Vava'u Group, N Tonga
159 P15 **Lātehār** Jhārkhand, N India 23.48N 84.28E
13 R7 **Laterrière** Québec, SE Canada 48.17N 71.10W
104 J13 **la Teste** Gironde, SW France 44.37N 1.04W
27 V8 **Latexo** Texas, SW USA 31.24N 95.28W
20 L10 **Latham** New York, NE USA 42.45N 73.45W
Latharna see Larne
110 B9 **La Thielle** var. Thièle. ≈ W Switzerland
29 R3 **Lathrop** Missouri, C USA 39.33N 94.19W
109 I16 **Latina** prev. Littoria. Lazio, C Italy 41.28N 12.52E
43 R14 **La Tinaja** Veracruz-Llave, S Mexico
108 J7 **Latisana** Friuli-Venezia Giulia, NE Italy 45.47N 13.01E
Latium see Lazio
117 K25 **Lató** site of ancient city Kríti, Greece, E Mediterranean Sea 35.09N 25.40E
197 J7 **La Tontouta** ✈ (Noumea) Province Sud, S New Caledonia 22.06S 166.12E
57 N4 **La Tortuga, Isla** var. Isla Tortuga. island N Venezuela
110 C10 **La Tour-de-Peilz** var. La Tour de Peilz. Vaud, SW Switzerland 46.28N 6.52E
105 S11 **la Tour-du-Pin** Isère, E France 45.34N 5.25E
104 J11 **la Tremblade** Charente-Maritime, W France 45.45N 1.07W
104 L10 **la Trimouille** Vienne, W France 46.27N 1.02E
44 J9 **La Trinidad** Estelí, NW Nicaragua 12.57N 86.13W
179 P9 **La Trinidad** Luzon, N Philippines 16.30N 120.39E
43 V16 **La Trinitaria** Chiapas, SE Mexico 16.02N 92.00W
47 Q11 **la Trinité** E Martinique 14.43N 60.57W
13 U7 **La Trinité-des-Monts** Québec, SE Canada 48.07N 68.31W
20 C15 **Latrobe** Pennsylvania, NE USA 40.18N 79.19W
191 P13 **La Trobe River** ≈ Victoria, SE Australia
Lattakia/Lattaquié see Al Lādhiqīyah
175 Tt11 **Latu** Pulau Seram, E Indonesia 3.24S 128.37E
13 P9 **La Tuque** Québec, SE Canada 47.25N 72.46W
161 G14 **Lātūr** Mahārāshtra, C India 18.24N 76.34E
120 G8 **Latvia** off. Republic of Latvia, Ger. Lettland, Latv. Latvija, Latvijas Republika; prev. Latvian SSR, Rus. Latviyskaya SSR. ◆ republic NE Europe
Latvian SSR/Latvija/Latvijas Republika/Latviyskaya SSR see Latvia
195 O12 **Lau** New Britain, E PNG 5.46S 151.21E
183 R9 **Lau Basin** undersea feature S Pacific Ocean
103 O15 **Lauchhammer** Brandenburg, E Germany 51.27N 13.32E
Laudunum see Laon
Laudus see St-Lô
Lauenburg/Lauenburg in Pommern see Lębork
103 L20 **Lauf an der Pegnitz** Bayern, SE Germany 49.31N 11.16E
110 D7 **Laufen** Basel, NW Switzerland 47.25N 7.31E
111 P5 **Lauffen** Salzburg, NW Austria 47.54N 12.57E
94 I2 **Laugarbakki** Nordhurland Vestra, N Iceland 65.18N 20.51W
94 I4 **Laugarvatn** Sudhurland, SW Iceland 64.09N 20.43W
33 O3 **Laughing Fish Point** headland Michigan, N USA 46.31N 87.01W
197 L14 **Lau Group** island group E Fiji
Lauis see Lugano
95 M17 **Laukaa** Länsi-Suomi, W Finland 62.27N 25.58E
120 D12 **Laukuva** Tauragė, W Lithuania 55.37N 22.12E
Laun see Louny
191 P16 **Launceston** Tasmania, SE Australia 41.25S 147.07E
99 I24 **Launceston** anc. Dunheved. SW England, UK 50.37N 4.21W
56 C13 **La Unión** Nariño, SW Colombia 1.34N 77.09W
44 H8 **La Unión** La Unión, SE El Salvador 13.19N 87.52W
44 I6 **La Unión** Olancho, C Honduras 15.02N 86.40W
42 M15 **La Unión** Guerrero, S Mexico 17.59N 101.48W
43 Y14 **La Unión** Quintana Roo, E Mexico 18.00N 101.48W
107 S13 **La Unión** Murcia, SE Spain 37.37N 0.53W
56 L7 **La Unión** Barinas, C Venezuela 8.12N 67.46W
44 B10 **La Unión** ◐ department E El Salvador
40 H11 **Laupāhoehoe** var. Laupahoehoe. Hawai'i, USA, C Pacific Ocean 20.00N 155.15W
103 I23 **Laupheim** Baden-Württemberg, S Germany 48.13N 9.54E
189 W3 **Laura** Queensland, NE Australia 15.37S 144.34E
201 X2 **Laura** atoll Majuro Atoll, SE Marshall Islands
Laurana see Lovran
56 L8 **La Urbana** Bolívar, C Venezuela 7.05N 66.58W
23 Y4 **Laurel** Delaware, NE USA 38.33N 75.34W
25 V14 **Laurel** Florida, SE USA 27.07N 82.27W
23 W3 **Laurel** Maryland, NE USA 39.06N 76.51W
24 M6 **Laurel** Mississippi, S USA 31.41N 89.10W
35 U11 **Laurel** Montana, NW USA 45.40N 108.46W
31 R13 **Laurel** Nebraska, C USA 42.25N 97.04W
20 H15 **Laureldale** Pennsylvania, NE USA 40.24N 75.52W
20 C16 **Laurel Hill** ridge Pennsylvania, NE USA
31 T12 **Laurens** Iowa, C USA 42.51N 94.51W
23 P11 **Laurens** South Carolina, SE USA 34.29N 82.01W
Laurentian Highlands see Laurentian Mountains
13 P10 **Laurentian Mountains** var. Laurentian Highlands, Fr. Les Laurentides. plateau Newfoundland and Labrador/Québec, Canada
13 O12 **Laurentides** Québec, SE Canada 45.51N 73.49W
Laurentides, Les see Laurentian Mountains
109 M19 **Lauria** Basilicata, S Italy 40.03N 15.49E
204 I1 **Laurie Island** island Antarctica
23 T11 **Laurinburg** North Carolina, SE USA 34.51N 79.40W
32 M2 **Laurium** Michigan, N USA 47.14N 88.26W
Lauru see Choiseul
110 B9 **Lausanne** It. Losanna. Vaud, SW Switzerland 46.31N 6.39E
103 Q16 **Lausche** Cz. Luže. ▲ Czech Republic/Germany see also Luže 50.52N 14.39E
103 Q16 **Lausitzer Bergland** var. Lausitzer Gebirge, Cz. Gory Lużyckie, Lužické Hory, Eng. Lusatian Mountains. ▲▲ E Germany
Lausitzer Gebirge see Lausitzer Bergland
Lausitzer Neisse see Neisse
105 T12 **Lautaret, Col du** pass SE France 45.03N 6.23E
65 G15 **Lautaro** Araucanía, C Chile 38.31S 72.27W
103 F21 **Lauter** ≈ W Germany
110 I7 **Lauterach** Vorarlberg, NW Austria 47.28N 9.43E
103 I17 **Lauterbach** Hessen, C Germany 50.37N 9.24E
110 E9 **Lauterbrunnen** Bern, C Switzerland 46.36N 7.52E
175 Nn12 **Laut Kecil, Kepulauan** island group N Indonesia
197 H14 **Lautoka** Viti Levu, W Fiji 17.40S 177.25E
175 Nn11 **Laut, Pulau** prev. Laoet. island Borneo, C Indonesia
174 Jj4 **Laut, Pulau** island Kepulauan Natuna, W Indonesia
175 Nn11 **Laut, Selat** strait Borneo, C Indonesia
173 F4 **Laut Tawar, Danau** ◎ Sumatera, NW Indonesia
201 V14 **Lauvergne Island** island Chuuk, C Micronesia
100 M5 **Lauwers Meer** ◎ N Netherlands
100 M4 **Lauwersoog** Groningen, NE Netherlands 53.25N 6.14E
104 M14 **Lauzerte** Tarn-et-Garonne, S France 44.15N 1.08E
27 U13 **Lavaca Bay** bay Texas, SW USA
27 U12 **Lavaca River** ≈ Texas, SW USA
13 O12 **Laval** Québec, SE Canada 45.32N 73.44W
104 J6 **Laval** Mayenne, NW France 48.04N 0.46W
13 T6 **Laval** ≈ Québec, SE Canada
63 F19 **Lavalleja** ◐ department S Uruguay
13 O12 **Lavaltrie** Québec, SE Canada 45.56N 73.14W
195 X17 **Lavanggu** Rennell, S Solomon Islands 11.39S 160.13E
149 O14 **Lāvān, Jazīreh-ye** island S Iran
111 U8 **Lavant** ≈ S Austria
120 G5 **Lavassaare** Ger. Lawassaar. Pärnumaa, SW Estonia 58.31N 24.22E
106 L3 **La Vecilla de Curueño** Castilla-León, N Spain 42.51N 5.24W
47 N8 **La Vega** var. Concepción de la Vega. C Dominican Republic 19.15N 70.32W
La Vela see La Vela de Coro
56 J4 **La Vela de Coro** var. La Vela. Falcón, N Venezuela 11.26N 69.35W
105 N17 **Lavelanet** Ariège, S France 42.55N 1.49E
109 M17 **Lavello** Basilicata, S Italy 41.03N 15.48E
38 J8 **La Verkin** Utah, W USA 37.12N 113.16W
28 J8 **Laverne** Oklahoma, C USA 36.42N 99.53W
27 S12 **La Vernia** Texas, SW USA 29.19N 98.07W
95 K18 **Lavia** Länsi-Suomi, W Finland 61.36N 22.34E
12 I12 **Lavieille, Lake** ◎ Ontario, SE Canada
96 C12 **Lavik** Sogn og Fjordane, S Norway 61.06N 5.25E
La Vila Joíosa see Villajoyosa
35 U10 **Lavina** Montana, NW USA 46.18N 108.55W
204 H5 **Lavoisier Island** island Antarctica
25 U2 **Lavonia** Georgia, SE USA 34.26N 83.06W
105 R13 **la Voulte-sur-Rhône** Ardèche, E France 44.49N 4.46E
127 Q3 **Lavrentiya** Chukotskiy Avtonomnyy Okrug, NE Russian Federation 65.33N 171.12W
117 H20 **Lávrio** prev. Lávrion. Attikí, C Greece 37.43N 24.03E
Lávrion see Lávrio
85 L22 **Lavumisa** prev. Gollel. SE Swaziland 27.20S 31.51E
155 T4 **Lawarai Pass** pass N Pakistan 35.22N 71.48E
Lawassaar see Lavassaare
147 P16 **Lawdar** SW Yemen 13.49N 45.54E
27 Q7 **Lawn** Texas, SW USA 32.07N 99.45W
205 Y4 **Law Promontory** headland Antarctica
79 O14 **Lawra** NW Ghana 10.40N 2.55W
193 E23 **Lawrence** Otago, South Island, NZ 45.53S 169.43E
33 P14 **Lawrence** Indiana, N USA 39.49N 86.01W
29 Q4 **Lawrence** Kansas, C USA 38.58N 95.14W
21 O10 **Lawrence** Massachusetts, NE USA 42.42N 71.09W
22 L5 **Lawrenceburg** Kentucky, S USA 38.02N 84.54W
22 I10 **Lawrenceburg** Tennessee, S USA 35.14N 87.19W
25 T3 **Lawrenceville** Georgia, SE USA 33.57N 83.59W
33 N15 **Lawrenceville** Illinois, N USA 38.43N 87.40W
23 V7 **Lawrenceville** Virginia, NE USA 36.45N 77.51W
29 S3 **Lawson** Missouri, C USA 39.26N 94.12W
28 L12 **Lawton** Oklahoma, C USA 34.35N 98.19W
146 I4 **Lawz, Jabal al** ▲ NW Saudi Arabia 28.45N 35.20E
97 L16 **Laxå** Örebro, C Sweden 59.00N 14.37E
129 T5 **Laya** ≈ NW Russian Federation
59 I19 **La Yarada** Tacna, SW Peru 18.14S 70.30W
147 S15 **Layjūn** C Yemen 15.27N 49.16E
147 Q9 **Laylā** var. Laila. Ar Riyāḍ, C Saudi Arabia 22.13N 46.39E
25 P4 **Lay Lake** ⊠ Alabama, S USA

◆ Country
● Country Capital
◇ Dependent Territory
○ Dependent Territory Capital
◐ Administrative Region
✈ International Airport
▲ Mountain
▲▲ Mountain Range
⛰ Volcano
≈ River
◎ Lake
⊠ Reservoir

Leuze-en-Hainaut – Listafjorden

101 E19 **Leuze-en-Hainaut** *var.* Leuze. Hainaut, SW Belgium 50.36N 3.37E
Léva *see* Levice
Levádhia *see* Leivádia
Levajok *see* Leavvajohka
38 L4 **Levan** Utah, W USA 39.33N 111.51W
95 E16 **Levanger** Nord-Trøndelag, C Norway 63.45N 11.18E
124 P14 **Levantine Basin** *undersea feature* E Mediterranean Sea
108 D10 **Levanto** Liguria, W Italy 44.12N 9.33E
109 H23 **Levanzo, Isola di** *island* Isole Egadi, S Italy
131 Q17 **Levashi** Respublika Dagestan, SW Russian Federation 42.27N 47.19E
26 M5 **Levelland** Texas, SW USA 33.35N 102.22W
41 P13 **Levelock** Alaska, USA 59.07N 156.51W
103 E16 **Leverkusen** Nordrhein-Westfalen, W Germany 51.01N 7.00E
113 J21 **Levice** *Ger.* Lewentz, Lewenz, *Hung.* Léva. Nitriansky Kraj, SW Slovakia 48.13N 18.37E
108 G6 **Levico Terme** Trentino-Alto Adige, N Italy 46.02N 11.19E
117 E20 **Levídi** Pelopónnisos, S Greece 37.39N 22.13E
105 P14 **le Vigan** Gard, S France 43.00N 3.36E
192 L13 **Levin** Manawatu-Wanganui, North Island, NZ 40.37S 175.17E
13 R10 **Lévis** *var.* Levis. Québec, SE Canada 46.46N 71.10W
23 P6 **Levisa Fork** Kentucky/Virginia, S USA
117 L21 **Levítha** *island* Kykládes, Greece, Aegean Sea
20 L14 **Levittown** Long Island, New York, NE USA 40.42N 73.29W
20 J15 **Levittown** Pennsylvania, NE USA 40.09N 74.50W
Levkás *see* Lefkáda
Levkímmi *see* Lefkímmi
113 L19 **Levoča** *Ger.* Leutschau, *Hung.* Locse. Prešovský Kraj, E Slovakia 49.01N 20.34E
Lévrier, Baie du *see* Nouâdhibou, Dakhlet
105 N9 **Levroux** Indre, C France 47.00N 1.37E
116 J8 **Levski** Pleven, N Bulgaria 43.22N 25.10E
Levskigrad *see* Karlovo
130 L6 **Lev Tolstoy** Lipetskaya Oblast', W Russian Federation 53.12N 39.28E
197 I14 **Levuka** Ovalau, C Fiji 17.42S 178.49E
177 G6 **Lewe** Mandalay, C Myanmar 19.40N 96.04E
Lewentz/Lewenz *see* Levice
99 O23 **Lewes** SE England, UK 50.52N 0.01E
23 Z4 **Lewes** Delaware, NE USA 38.46N 75.08W
31 Q12 **Lewis and Clark Lake** Nebraska/South Dakota, N USA
20 G14 **Lewisburg** Pennsylvania, NE USA 40.57N 76.52W
22 J10 **Lewisburg** Tennessee, S USA 35.27N 86.47W
23 S6 **Lewisburg** West Virginia, NE USA 37.48N 80.27W
98 F6 **Lewis, Butt of** *headland* NW Scotland, UK 58.31N 6.18W
98 F7 **Lewis, Isle of** *island* NW Scotland, UK
37 U4 **Lewis, Mount** ▲ Nevada, W USA 40.22N 116.50W
193 H16 **Lewis Pass** *pass* South Island, NZ 42.23S 172.21E
35 P7 **Lewis Range** ▲ Montana, NW USA
25 O3 **Lewis Smith Lake** Alabama, S USA
34 M10 **Lewiston** Idaho, NW USA 46.25N 117.01W
21 P7 **Lewiston** Maine, NE USA 44.07N 70.13W
31 X10 **Lewiston** Minnesota, N USA 43.58N 91.52W
20 D9 **Lewiston** New York, NE USA 43.10N 79.02W
38 L1 **Lewiston** Utah, W USA 41.58N 111.52W
32 K13 **Lewistown** Illinois, N USA 40.23N 90.09W
35 T9 **Lewistown** Montana, NW USA 47.04N 109.25W
29 T14 **Lewisville** Arkansas, C USA 33.21N 93.34W
27 T6 **Lewisville** Texas, SW USA 33.00N 96.57W
27 T6 **Lewisville, Lake** Texas, SW USA
Le Woleu-Ntem *see* Woleu-Ntem
25 U3 **Lexington** Georgia, SE USA 33.51N 83.04W
22 M5 **Lexington** Kentucky, S USA 38.03N 84.30W
24 L4 **Lexington** Mississippi, S USA 33.06N 90.03W
29 S4 **Lexington** Missouri, C USA 39.10N 93.52W
31 N16 **Lexington** Nebraska, C USA 40.46N 99.44W
22 S9 **Lexington** North Carolina, SE USA 35.49N 80.15W
29 N11 **Lexington** Oklahoma, C USA 35.00N 97.20W
23 R12 **Lexington** South Carolina, SE USA 33.58N 81.14W
22 G9 **Lexington** Tennessee, S USA 35.39N 88.23W
27 T10 **Lexington** Texas, SW USA 30.25N 97.00W
23 T6 **Lexington** Virginia, NE USA 37.46N 79.26W
23 X5 **Lexington Park** Maryland, NE USA 38.16N 76.27W
Leyden *see* Leiden
104 J14 **Leyre** SW France
179 R13 **Leyte** *island* C Philippines
179 R13 **Leyte Gulf** *gulf* E Philippines
113 O16 **Leżajsk** Podkarpackie, SE Poland 50.15N 22.24E
Lezha *see* Lezhë
115 K18 **Lezhë** *var.* Lezha; *prev.* Lesh, Leshi. Lezhë, NW Albania 41.46N 19.40E
115 K18 **Lezhë** ◆ *district* NW Albania
105 O16 **Lézignan-Corbières** Aude, S France 43.12N 2.46E
130 J7 **L'gov** Kurskaya Oblast', W Russian Federation 51.38N 35.17E
165 P15 **Lhari** Xizang Zizhiqu, W China 30.34N 93.40E
165 N16 **Lhasa** *var.* La-sa, Lassa. Xizang Zizhiqu, W China 29.40N 91.10E
165 O15 **Lhasa He** W China
164 K16 **Lhazê** *var.* Quxar. Xizang Zizhiqu, W China 29.07N 87.32E
164 K14 **Lhazhong** Xizang Zizhiqu, W China 31.58N 86.43E
173 F3 **Lhoksukon** Sumatera, W Indonesia 5.04N 97.19E
165 Q15 **Lhorong** *var.* Zito. Xizang Zizhiqu, W China 30.51N 95.41E
107 W6 **L'Hospitalet de Llobregat** *var.* Hospitalet. Cataluña, NE Spain 41.21N 2.06E
159 R11 **Lhotse** ▲ China/Nepal 28.00N 86.55E
165 N17 **Lhozhag** *var.* Garbo. Xizang Zizhiqu, W China 28.21N 90.47E
165 O16 **Lhünzê** *var.* Xingba. Xizang Zizhiqu, W China 28.25N 92.30E
165 N15 **Lhünzhub** *var.* Ganqu. Xizang Zizhiqu, W China 29.58N 91.20E
178 H8 **Li** Lamphun, NW Thailand 17.46N 98.54E
167 P12 **Liancheng** *var.* Lianfeng. Fujian, SE China 25.47N 116.42E
Liancheng *see* Qinglong, Guizhou, China
Liancheng *see* Guangnan, Yunnan, China
Lianfeng *see* Liancheng
179 Rr14 **Lianga** Mindanao, S Philippines 8.36N 126.04E
166 K9 **Liangping** *var.* Liangshan. Chongqing Shi, C China 30.40N 107.46E
Liangshan *see* Liangping
Liangzhou *see* Wuwei
167 O9 **Liangzi Hu** C China
167 R12 **Lianjiang** Fujian, SE China 26.13N 119.33E
166 L15 **Lianjiang** Guangdong, S China 21.41N 110.12E
Lianjiang *see* Xingguo
167 O13 **Lianping** *var.* Yuanshan. Guangdong, S China 24.22N 114.23E
Lianshan *see* Huludao
Lian Xian *see* Lianzhou
166 M11 **Lianyuan** *prev.* Lantian. Hunan, S China 27.51N 111.44E
167 Q6 **Lianyungang** *var.* Xinpu. Jiangsu, E China 34.37N 119.12E
167 N13 **Lianzhou** *var.* Linxian; *prev.* Lian Xian. Guangdong, S China 24.48N 112.20E
Lianzhou *see* Hepu
Liao *see* Liaoning
167 P5 **Liaocheng** Shandong, E China 36.31N 115.59E
169 U13 **Liaodong Bandao** *var.* Liaotung Peninsula. *peninsula* NE China
169 T13 **Liaodong Wan** *Eng.* Gulf of Lantung, Gulf of Liaotung. *gulf* NE China
169 U11 **Liao He** NE China
169 U12 **Liaoning** *var.* Liao, Liaoning Sheng, Shengking; *hist.* Fengtien, Shenking. ◆ *province* NE China
Liaoning Sheng *see* Liaoning
Liaotung, Gulf of *see* Liaodong Wan
Liaotung Peninsula *see* Liaodong Bandao
169 V12 **Liaoyang** *var.* Liao-yang. Liaoning, NE China 41.16N 123.12E
169 V11 **Liaoyuan** *var.* Dongliao, Shuang-liao, *Jap.* Chengchiatun. Jilin, NE China 42.51N 125.09E
169 U12 **Liaozhong** Liaoning, NE China 41.33N 122.54E
Liaqatabad *see* Piplān
8 M10 **Liard** W Canada
Liard *see* Fort Liard
8 L10 **Liard River** British Columbia, W Canada 59.22N 126.04W
155 O15 **Liāri** Baluchistān, SW Pakistan 25.43N 66.28E
Liatroim *see* Leitrim
201 S6 **Lib** *var.* Ellep. *island* Ralik Chain, C Marshall Islands
Liban *see* Lebanon
144 H6 **Liban, Jebel** *Ar.* Jabal al Gharbt, Jabal Lubnān, *Eng.* Mount Lebanon. ▲ C Lebanon
Libau *see* Liepāja
35 N7 **Libby** Montana, NW USA 48.25N 115.33W
81 I16 **Libenge** Equateur, NW Dem. Rep. Congo 3.39N 18.39E
28 I7 **Liberal** Kansas, C USA 37.01N 100.55W
29 R7 **Liberal** Missouri, C USA 37.33N 94.31W
Liberalitas Julia *see* Évora
113 D15 **Liberec** *Ger.* Reichenberg. Liberecký Kraj, N Czech Republic 50.44N 15.04E
113 D15 **Liberecký Kraj** ◆ *region* N Czech Republic
44 K12 **Liberia** Guanacaste, NW Costa Rica 10.36N 85.26W
78 K17 **Liberia** *off.* Republic of Liberia. ◆ *republic* W Africa
63 D16 **Libertad** Corrientes, NE Argentina 30.01S 57.51W
63 E20 **Libertad** San José, S Uruguay 34.37S 56.39W
56 I7 **Libertad** Barinas, NW Venezuela 8.21N 69.39W
56 K6 **Libertad** Cojedes, N Venezuela 9.19N 68.43W
64 G12 **Libertador** *off.* Región del Libertador General Bernardo O'Higgins. ◆ *region* C Chile
Libertador General San Martín *see* Ciudad de Libertador General San Martín
22 L6 **Liberty** Kentucky, S USA 37.19N 84.54W
24 J7 **Liberty** Mississippi, S USA 31.09N 90.49W
29 R4 **Liberty** Missouri, C USA 39.15N 94.22W
20 J12 **Liberty** New York, NE USA 41.48N 74.45W
23 T9 **Liberty** North Carolina, SE USA 35.49N 79.34W
Libian Desert *see* Libyan Desert
101 J23 **Libin** Luxembourg, SE Belgium 50.01N 5.13E
166 K13 **Libo** *var.* Yuping. Guizhou, S China 25.28N 107.52E
Libohova *see* Libohovë
115 L23 **Libohovë** *var.* Libohova. Gjirokastër, S Albania 40.03N 20.13E
83 K18 **Liboi** North Eastern, E Kenya 0.23N 40.55E
104 K13 **Libourne** Gironde, SW France 44.55N 0.13W
101 K23 **Libramont** Luxembourg, SE Belgium 49.55N 5.21E
115 M20 **Librazhd** *var.* Librazhdi. Elbasan, E Albania 41.10N 20.22E
Librazhdi *see* Librazhd
81 C18 **Libreville** ● (Gabon) Estuaire, NW Gabon 0.25N 9.29E
179 Rr15 **Libuganon** Mindanao, S Philippines
77 P10 **Libya** *off.* Socialist People's Libyan Arab Jamahiriya, *Ar.* Al Jamāhīrīyah al 'Arabīyah al Lībīyah ash Sha'bīyah al Ishtirākīyah; *prev.* Libyan Arab Republic. ◆ *Islamic state* N Africa
77 T11 **Libyan Desert** *var.* Libian Desert, *Ar.* Aş Şahrā' al Lībīyah. *desert* N Africa
77 T8 **Libyan Plateau** *var.* Aḍ Diffah. *plateau* Egypt/Libya
Lībīyah, Aş Şahrā' al *see* Libyan Desert
64 G12 **Licantén** Maule, C Chile 35.00S 72.00W
109 J25 **Licata** *anc.* Phintias. Sicilia, Italy, C Mediterranean Sea 37.07N 13.56E
143 P14 **Lice** Dıyarbakır, SE Turkey 38.28N 40.39E
99 L19 **Lichfield** C England, UK 52.42N 1.48W
85 N14 **Lichinga** Niassa, N Mozambique 13.17S 35.15E
111 V3 **Lichtenau** Niederösterreich, N Austria 48.29N 15.24E
85 I21 **Lichtenburg** North-West, N South Africa 26.06S 26.08E
103 K18 **Lichtenfels** Bayern, SE Germany 50.09N 11.03E
100 O12 **Lichtenvoorde** Gelderland, E Netherlands 51.58N 6.34E
Lichtenwald *see* Sevnica
101 C17 **Lichtervelde** West-Vlaanderen, W Belgium 51.01N 3.09E
166 L9 **Lichuan** Hubei, C China 30.19N 108.55E
29 V7 **Licking** Missouri, C USA 37.30N 91.51W
22 M4 **Licking River** Kentucky, S USA
114 C11 **Lički Osik** Lika-Senj, C Croatia 44.36N 15.24E
Ličko-Senjska Županija *see* Lika-Senj
109 K19 **Licosa, Punta** *headland* S Italy 40.15N 14.54E
121 H16 **Lida** *Rus.* Lida. Hrodzyenskaya Voblasts', W Belarus 53.53N 25.19E
95 H17 **Liden** Västernorrland, C Sweden 62.43N 16.49E
31 R7 **Lidgerwood** North Dakota, N USA 46.04N 97.09W
Lidhorikíon *see* Lidoríki
97 K21 **Lidhult** Kronoberg, S Sweden 56.49N 13.25E
97 P16 **Lidingö** Stockholm, C Sweden 59.22N 18.10E
97 K17 **Lidköping** Västra Götaland, S Sweden 58.30N 13.10E
Lido di Iesolo *see* Lido di Jesolo
108 I8 **Lido di Jesolo** *var.* Lido di Iesolo. Veneto, NE Italy 45.30N 12.37E
109 H15 **Lido di Ostia** Lazio, C Italy 41.42N 12.19E
Lidokhorikion *see* Lidoríki
117 E18 **Lidoríki** *prev.* Lidhorikíon, Lidokhorikion. Stereá Ellás, C Greece 38.31N 22.12E
112 K9 **Lidzbark** Warmińsko-Mazurskie, NE Poland 53.15N 19.49E
112 L7 **Lidzbark Warmiński** *Ger.* Heilsberg. Warmińsko-Mazurskie, NE Poland, 54.07N 20.34E
111 U3 **Liebenau** Oberösterreich, N Austria 48.33N 14.48E
189 P7 **Liebig, Mount** ▲ Northern Territory, C Australia 23.19S 131.30E
111 V8 **Lieboch** Steiermark, SE Austria 47.00N 15.21E
110 I8 **Liechtenstein** *off.* Principality of Liechtenstein. ◆ *principality* C Europe
101 F18 **Liedekerke** Vlaams Brabant, C Belgium 50.51N 4.05E
101 K19 **Liège** *Dut.* Luik, *Ger.* Lüttich. Liège, E Belgium 50.37N 5.34E
101 K20 **Liège** *Dut.* Luik. ◆ *province* E Belgium
Liegnitz *see* Legnica
95 O16 **Lieksa** Itä-Suomi, E Finland 63.20N 30.00E
120 F10 **Lielupe** Latvia/Lithuania
120 G9 **Lielvārde** Ogre, C Latvia 56.45N 24.48E
178 Kk14 **Liên Hương** *var.* Tuy Phong. Binh Thuận, S Vietnam 11.13N 108.40E
Liên Nghia *see* Đưc Trong
111 P9 **Lienz** Tirol, W Austria 46.49N 12.45E
120 B10 **Liepāja** *Ger.* Libau. Liepāja, W Latvia 56.31N 21.02E
101 H17 **Lier** *Fr.* Lierre. Antwerpen, N Belgium 51.07N 4.34E
97 H15 **Lierbyen** Buskerud, S Norway 59.46N 10.13E
101 L21 **Lierneux** Liège, E Belgium 50.12N 5.51E
Lierre *see* Lier
103 D18 **Lieser** W Germany
111 U7 **Liesing** E Austria
110 E6 **Liestal** Basel-Land, N Switzerland 47.28N 7.43E
Lietuva *see* Lithuania
Lievenhof *see* Līvāni
105 O2 **Liévin** Pas-de-Calais, N France 50.25N 2.48E
12 M9 **Lièvre, Rivière du** Québec, SE Canada
111 T6 **Liezen** Steiermark, C Austria 47.34N 14.12E
99 E14 **Lifford** *Ir.* Leifear. NW Ireland 54.49N 7.28W
197 K5 **Lifou** *island* Îles Loyauté, E New Caledonia
200 Ss13 **Lifuka** *island* Ha'apai Group, C Tonga
179 Q11 **Ligao** Luzon, N Philippines 13.16N 123.30E
Liger *see* Loire
44 H2 **Lighthouse Reef** *reef* E Belize
191 Q4 **Lightning Ridge** New South Wales, SE Australia 29.29S 148.00E
105 N9 **Lignières** Cher, C France 46.45N 2.10E
105 S5 **Ligny-en-Barrois** Meuse, NE France 48.42N 5.22E
85 P15 **Ligonha** NE Mozambique
33 P11 **Ligonier** Indiana, N USA 41.25N 85.33W
83 I25 **Ligunga** Ruvuma, S Tanzania 10.51S 37.10E
108 D9 **Ligure, Appennino** *Eng.* Ligurian Mountains. ▲ NW Italy
Ligure, Mar *see* Ligurian Sea
108 C9 **Liguria** ◆ *region* NW Italy
Ligurian Mountains *see* Ligure, Appennino
123 K6 **Ligurian Sea** *Fr.* Mer Ligurienne, *It.* Mar Ligure. *sea* N Mediterranean Sea
Ligurienne, Mer *see* Ligurian Sea
195 P9 **Lihir Group** *island group* NE PNG
195 P9 **Lihir Island** *island* Lihir Group, N PNG
40 B8 **Līhu'e** *var.* Lihue. Kaua'i, Hawai'i, USA, C Pacific Ocean 21.58N 159.22W
120 F5 **Lihula** *Ger.* Leal. Läänemaa, W Estonia 58.43N 23.52E
128 I2 **Liinakhamari** *var.* Linacmamari. Murmanskaya Oblast', NW Russian Federation 69.40N 31.27E
Liivi Laht *see* Riga, Gulf of
166 F11 **Lijiang** *var.* Dayan, Lijiang Naxizu Zizhixian. Yunnan, SW China 26.52N 100.10E
Lijiang Naxizu Zizhixian *see* Lijiang
114 C11 **Lika-Senj** *off.* Ličko-Senjska Županija. ◆ *province* W Croatia
81 N25 **Likasi** *prev.* Jadotville. Katanga, SE Dem. Rep. Congo 11.01S 26.51E
81 L16 **Likati** Orientale, N Dem. Rep. Congo 3.28N 23.45E
8 M15 **Likely** British Columbia, SW Canada 52.40N 121.34W
159 Y11 **Likhapāni** Assam, NE India 27.24N 95.51E
128 J16 **Likhoslavl'** Tverskaya Oblast', W Russian Federation 57.08N 35.27E
201 U5 **Likiep Atoll** *atoll* Ratak Chain, C Marshall Islands
97 D18 **Liknes** Vest-Agder, S Norway 58.19N 6.58E
81 H18 **Likouala** N Congo
81 H18 **Likouala aux Herbes** E Congo
202 B16 **Liku** E Niue 19.01S 169.46E
Likupang, Selat *see* Bangka, Selat
29 Y8 **Lilbourn** Missouri, C USA 36.35N 89.37W
105 X14 **l'Île-Rousse** Corse, France, C Mediterranean Sea 42.39N 8.59E
111 W5 **Lilienfeld** Niederösterreich, NE Austria 48.01N 15.36E
167 N11 **Liling** Hunan, S China 27.42N 113.49E
97 J18 **Lilla Edet** Västra Götaland, S Sweden 58.07N 12.07E
105 P1 **Lille** *var.* l'Isle, *Dut.* Rijssel, *Flem.* Ryssel; *prev. Lisle, anc.* Insula. Nord, N France 50.37N 3.04E
97 G24 **Lillebælt** *var.* Lille Bælt, *Eng.* Little Belt. *strait* S Denmark
104 L3 **Lillebonne** Seine-Maritime, N France 49.30N 0.34E
96 H12 **Lillehammer** Oppland, S Norway 61.07N 10.28E
105 O1 **Lillers** Pas-de-Calais, N France 50.34N 2.26E
97 F18 **Lillesand** Aust-Agder, S Norway 58.13N 8.22E
97 I15 **Lillestrøm** Akershus, S Norway 59.58N 11.04E
95 F18 **Lillhärdal** Jämtland, C Sweden 61.51N 14.04E
23 U10 **Lillington** North Carolina, SE USA 35.24N 78.49W
107 O9 **Lillo** Castilla-La Mancha, C Spain 39.43N 3.19W
8 M16 **Lillooet** British Columbia, SW Canada 50.40N 121.58W
85 M14 **Lilongwe** ● (Malawi) Central, W Malawi 13.58S 33.48E
85 M14 **Lilongwe** ✕ Central, W Malawi 13.46S 33.44E
85 M14 **Lilongwe** W Malawi
179 Q15 **Liloy** Mindanao, S Philippines 8.04N 122.42E
Lilybaeum *see* Marsala
190 J7 **Lilydale** South Australia 32.57S 140.00E
191 P16 **Lilydale** Tasmania, SE Australia 41.17S 147.13E
115 J14 **Lim** Bosnia and Herzegovina/Serbia and Montenegro (Yugoslavia)
59 D15 **Lima** ● (Peru) Lima, W Peru 12.05S 78.00W
96 K13 **Lima** Dalarna, C Sweden 60.55N 13.19E
33 R12 **Lima** Ohio, NE USA 40.43N 84.06W
59 D14 **Lima** ◆ *department* W Peru
Lima *see* Jorge Chávez International
106 G5 **Lima, Rio** *Sp.* Limia Portugal/Spain *see also* Limia
113 L17 **Limanowa** Małopolskie, S Poland 49.43N 20.25E
174 I8 **Limas** Pulau Sebangka, W Indonesia 0.09N 104.31E
Limassol *see* Lemesós
99 F14 **Limavady** *Ir.* Léim an Mhadaidh. NW Northern Ireland, UK 55.03N 6.57W
65 J14 **Limay Mahuida** La Pampa, C Argentina 37.09S 66.40W
65 H15 **Limay, Río** W Argentina
103 N16 **Limbach-Oberfrohna** Sachsen, E Germany 50.52N 12.46E
83 F22 **Limba Limba** C Tanzania
109 C17 **Limbara, Monte** ▲ Sardegna, Italy, C Mediterranean Sea 40.50N 9.10E
120 G7 **Limbaži** *Est.* Lemsalu. Limbaži, N Latvia 57.33N 24.46E
46 M8 **Limbé** N Haiti 19.40N 72.25W
175 Qq7 **Limboto, Danau** Sulawesi, N Indonesia
101 L19 **Limbourg** Liège, E Belgium 50.37N 5.55E
101 K17 **Limburg** ◆ *province* NE Belgium
101 L16 **Limburg** ◆ *province* SE Netherlands
103 F17 **Limburg an der Lahn** Hessen, W Germany 50.22N 8.04E
96 K13 **Limedsforsen** Dalarna, C Sweden 60.52N 13.25E
62 L9 **Limeira** São Paulo, S Brazil 22.34S 47.25W
99 C19 **Limerick** *Ir.* Luimneach. SW Ireland 52.40N 8.37W
99 C20 **Limerick** *Ir.* Luimneach. *cultural region* SW Ireland
21 S2 **Limestone** Maine, NE USA 46.52N 67.49W
27 U9 **Limestone, Lake** Texas, SW USA
41 P12 **Lime Village** Alaska, USA 61.21N 155.26W
97 F20 **Limfjorden** *fjord* N Denmark
97 J23 **Limhamn** Skåne, S Sweden 55.34N 12.57E
106 H5 **Limia** *Port.* Rio Lima. Portugal/Spain *see also* Lima, Rio
95 L14 **Liminka** Oulu, C Finland 64.48N 25.19E
Límin Vathéos *see* Sámos
117 G17 **Límni** Évvoia, C Greece 38.46N 23.20E
117 J15 **Límnos** *anc.* Lemnos. *island* E Greece
104 M11 **Limoges** *anc.* Augustoritum Lemovicensium, Lemovices. Haute-Vienne, C France 45.50N 1.16E
39 U5 **Limon** Colorado, C USA 39.15N 103.41W
45 O13 **Limón** *var.* Puerto Limón. Limón, E Costa Rica 9.59N 83.02W
44 K4 **Limón** Colón, NE Honduras 15.51N 85.30W
45 N13 **Limón** *off.* Provincia de Limón. ◆ *province* E Costa Rica
108 A10 **Limone Piemonte** Piemonte, NE Italy 44.12N 7.37E
Limones *see* Valdéz
Limonum *see* Poitiers
105 N11 **Limousin** ◆ *region* C France
105 N16 **Limoux** Aude, S France 43.03N 2.13E
85 L19 **Limpopo** *var.* Crocodile. S Africa
85 J20 **Limpopo** *off.* Limpopo Province; *prev.* Northern, Northern Transvaal. ◆ *province* NE South Africa
166 K17 **Limu Ling** ▲ S China
115 M20 **Lin** *var.* Lini. Elbasan, E Albania 41.03N 20.37E
Linacmamari *see* Liinakhamari
179 P13 **Linapacan Island** *island* W Philippines
64 G13 **Linares** Maule, C Chile 35.49S 71.37W
56 C13 **Linares** Nariño, SW Colombia 1.23N 77.33W
43 O9 **Linares** Nuevo León, NE Mexico 24.50N 99.33W
107 N12 **Linares** Andalucía, S Spain 38.04N 3.37W
109 G15 **Linaro, Capo** *headland* C Italy 42.01N 11.49E
108 D8 **Linate** ✕ (Milano) Lombardia, N Italy 45.27N 9.18E
178 Jj8 **Lin Camh** *prev.* Đưc Tho. Ha Tinh, N Vietnam 18.30N 105.36E
166 F13 **Lincang** Yunnan, SW China 23.55N 100.03E
Lincheng *see* Lingao
Linchuan *see* Fuzhou
63 B20 **Lincoln** Buenos Aires, E Argentina 34.50S 61.32W
193 H19 **Lincoln** Canterbury, South Island, NZ 43.37S 172.30E
99 N18 **Lincoln** *anc.* Lindum, Lindum Colonia. E England, UK 53.13N 0.33W
37 O6 **Lincoln** California, W USA 38.52N 121.18W
32 L13 **Lincoln** Illinois, N USA 40.09N 89.21W
28 M4 **Lincoln** Kansas, C USA 39.03N 98.09W
21 S5 **Lincoln** Maine, NE USA 45.22N 68.30W
29 T5 **Lincoln** Missouri, C USA 38.23N 93.19W
31 R16 **Lincoln** *state capital* Nebraska, C USA 40.46N 96.42W
34 F11 **Lincoln City** Oregon, NW USA 44.57N 124.01W
178 M10 **Lincoln Island** *island* E Paracel Islands
207 Q11 **Lincoln Sea** *sea* Arctic Ocean
99 N18 **Lincolnshire** *cultural region* E England, UK
23 R10 **Lincolnton** North Carolina, SE USA 35.28N 81.15W
27 V7 **Lindale** Texas, SW USA 32.31N 95.24W
103 I25 **Lindau** *var.* Lindau am Bodensee. Bayern, S Germany 47.33N 9.40E
Lindau am Bodensee *see* Lindau
126 J9 **Linde** NE Russian Federation
57 T9 **Linden** E Guyana 5.58N 58.11W
25 O6 **Linden** Alabama, S USA 32.18N 87.48W
22 H9 **Linden** Tennessee, S USA 35.37N 87.50W
27 X6 **Linden** Texas, SW USA 33.01N 94.22W
20 J16 **Lindenwold** New Jersey, NE USA 39.47N 74.58W
97 M15 **Lindesberg** Örebro, C Sweden 59.36N 15.15E
97 D18 **Lindesnes** *headland* S Norway 57.58N 7.03E
Líndhos *see* Líndos
83 K24 **Lindi** Lindi, SE Tanzania 10.00S 39.41E
83 J24 **Lindi** ◆ *region* SE Tanzania
81 N17 **Lindi** NE Dem. Rep. Congo
169 V7 **Lindian** Heilongjiang, NE China 47.10N 124.51E
193 E21 **Lindis Pass** *pass* South Island, NZ 44.33S 169.40E
85 J22 **Lindley** Free State, C South Africa 27.48S 27.57E
97 J19 **Lindome** Västra Götaland, S Sweden 57.34N 12.04E
169 S10 **Lindong** *var.* Bairin Zuoqi. Nei Mongol Zizhiqu, N China 43.59N 119.24E
117 O23 **Líndos** *var.* Líndhos. Ródos, Dodekánisos, Greece, Aegean Sea 36.04N 28.04E
12 I14 **Lindsay** Ontario, SE Canada 44.21N 78.43W
37 R11 **Lindsay** California, W USA 36.11N 119.06W
35 X8 **Lindsay** Montana, NW USA 47.13N 105.10W
29 N11 **Lindsay** Oklahoma, C USA 34.50N 97.37W
29 N5 **Lindsborg** Kansas, C USA 38.34N 97.39W
97 N21 **Lindsdal** Kalmar, S Sweden 56.43N 16.18E
175 Pp9 **Lindu, Danau** Sulawesi, N Indonesia
Lindum/Lindum Colonia *see* Lincoln
203 W3 **Line Islands** *island group* E Kiribati
Linëvo *see* Linova
166 M5 **Linfen** *var.* Lin-fen. Shanxi, C China 36.07N 111.34E
161 F18 **Linganamakki Reservoir** SW India
166 L17 **Lingao** *var.* Lincheng. Hainan, S China 19.44N 109.23E
179 Oo9 **Lingayen** Luzon, N Philippines 16.00N 120.12E
179 Oo9 **Lingayen Gulf** *gulf* Luzon, N Philippines
166 M6 **Lingbao** *var.* Guolüezhen. Henan, C China 34.34N 110.50E
96 N12 **Lingbo** Gävleborg, C Sweden 61.04N 16.45E
Lingeh *see* Bandar-e Langeh
102 E12 **Lingen** *var.* Lingen an der Ems. Niedersachsen, NW Germany 52.31N 7.19E
Lingen an der Ems *see* Lingen
174 Ii8 **Lingga, Kepulauan** *island group* W Indonesia
174 I8 **Lingga, Pulau** *island* Kepulauan Lingga, W Indonesia
12 J14 **Lingham Lake** Ontario, SE Canada
96 M13 **Linghed** Dalarna, C Sweden 60.48N 15.55E
35 Z15 **Lingle** Wyoming, C USA 42.07N 104.21W
20 G15 **Linglestown** Pennsylvania, NE USA 40.20N 76.46W
81 K18 **Lingomo** II Equateur, NW Dem. Rep. Congo 0.42N 21.59E
166 L15 **Lingshan** Guangxi Zhuangzu Zizhiqu, S China 22.28N 109.19E
166 L17 **Lingshui** *var.* Lingshui Lizu Zizhixian. Hainan, S China 18.35N 110.03E
Lingshui Lizu Zizhixian *see* Lingshui
161 G16 **Lingsugūr** Karnātaka, C India 16.13N 76.33E
109 L23 **Linguaglossa** Sicilia, Italy, C Mediterranean Sea 37.51N 15.06E
78 H10 **Linguère** N Senegal 15.24N 15.06W
165 W8 **Lingwu** Ningxia, N China 38.04N 106.21E
Lingxi *see* Yongshun, Hunan, China
Lingxi *see* Cangnan, Zhejiang, China
Lingxian/Ling Xian *see* Yanling
169 S12 **Lingyuan** Liaoning, NE China 41.09N 119.24E
169 U4 **Linhai** Heilongjiang, NE China 51.30N 124.18E
167 S10 **Linhai** *var.* Taizhou. Zhejiang, SE China 28.53N 121.10E
61 O20 **Linhares** Espírito Santo, SE Brazil 19.22S 40.04W
168 M13 **Linhe** Nei Mongol Zizhiqu, N China 40.46N 107.27E
Lini *see* Lin
145 S1 **Līnik, Chiyā-ē** ▲ N Iraq
97 M18 **Linköping** Östergötland, S Sweden 58.25N 15.37E
169 Y8 **Linkou** Heilongjiang, NE China 45.18N 130.16E
120 F11 **Linkuva** Šiauliai, N Lithuania 56.06N 23.58E
29 V5 **Linn** Missouri, C USA 38.29N 91.51W
27 S16 **Linn** Texas, SW USA 26.32N 98.06W
29 T2 **Linneus** Missouri, C USA 39.53N 93.10W
98 H10 **Linnhe, Loch** *inlet* W Scotland, UK
121 G19 **Linova** *Rus.* Linëvo. Brestskaya Voblasts', SW Belarus 52.28N 24.33E
167 O5 **Linqing** Shandong, E China 36.49N 115.39E
62 K8 **Lins** São Paulo, S Brazil 21.40S 49.43W
95 F17 **Linsell** Jämtland, C Sweden 62.10N 14.00E
166 J9 **Linshui** Sichuan, C China 30.24N 106.54E
46 K12 **Linstead** C Jamaica 18.07N 77.01W
165 U11 **Lintan** Gansu, N China 34.43N 101.27E
165 V11 **Lintao** Gansu, C China 35.23N 103.54E
13 S12 **Lintère** Québec, SE Canada
110 H8 **Linth** NW Switzerland
110 H8 **Linthal** Glarus, NE Switzerland 46.59N 8.57E
33 N15 **Linton** Indiana, N USA 39.01N 87.10W
31 N6 **Linton** North Dakota, N USA 46.16N 100.13W
169 R11 **Linxi** Nei Mongol Zizhiqu, N China 43.29N 117.59E
165 U11 **Linxia** *var.* Linxia Huizu Zizhizhou. Gansu, C China 35.33N 103.08E
Linxia Huizu Zizhizhou *see* Linxia
Linxian *see* Lianzhou
167 Q6 **Linyi** Shandong, S China 37.12N 116.54E
167 P4 **Linyi** Shandong, E China 37.13N 116.50E
166 M6 **Linyi** Shanxi, C China 35.10N 110.45E
111 T4 **Linz** *anc.* Lentia. Oberösterreich, N Austria 48.19N 14.18E
165 S8 **Linze** *var.* Shahepu. Gansu, N China 39.06N 100.03E
46 J13 **Lionel Town** C Jamaica 17.49N 77.13W
105 Q16 **Lion, Golfe du** *Eng.* Gulf of Lion, Gulf of Lions; *anc.* Sinus Gallicus. *gulf* S France
Lion, Gulf of/Lions, Gulf of *see* Lion, Golfe du
85 K16 **Lions Den** Mashonaland West, N Zimbabwe 17.16S 30.00E
12 F13 **Lion's Head** Ontario, S Canada 44.59N 81.16W
Lios Ceannúir, Bá *see* Liscannor Bay
Lios Mór *see* Lismore
Lios na gCearrbhach *see* Lisburn
Lios Tuathail *see* Listowel
81 G17 **Liouesso** La Sangha, N Congo 1.01N 15.43E
Liozno *see* Lyozna
179 P11 **Lipa** *off.* Lipa City. Luzon, N Philippines 13.57N 121.10E
27 S7 **Lipan** Texas, SW USA 32.31N 98.03W
Lipari Islands/Lipari, Isole *see* Eolie, Isole
109 L22 **Lipari, Isola** *island* Isole Eolie, S Italy
118 L8 **Lipcani** *Rus.* Lipkany. N Moldova 48.16N 26.47E
95 N17 **Liperi** Itä-Suomi, E Finland 62.30N 29.25E
130 L7 **Lipetsk** Lipetskaya Oblast', W Russian Federation 52.37N 39.37E
130 K6 **Lipetskaya Oblast'** ◆ *province* W Russian Federation
59 K22 **Lipez, Cordillera de** ▲ SW Bolivia
112 E10 **Lipiany** *Ger.* Lippehne. Zachodnio-pomorskie, W Poland 53.00N 14.58E
114 G9 **Lipik** Požega-Slavonija, NE Croatia 45.24N 17.08E
128 L12 **Lipin Bor** Vologodskaya Oblast', NW Russian Federation 60.12N 38.04E
166 L12 **Liping** *var.* Defeng. Guizhou, S China 26.16N 109.07E
Lipkany *see* Lipcani
121 H15 **Lipnishki** *Rus.* Lipnishki. Hrodzyenskaya Voblasts', W Belarus 54.01N 25.39E
112 J10 **Lipno** Kujawsko-pomorskie, C Poland 52.51N 19.11E
118 F11 **Lipova** *Hung.* Lippa. Arad, W Romania 46.06N 21.40E
Lipovets *see* Lypovets'
Lippa *see* Lipova
103 E14 **Lippe** W Germany
Lippehne *see* Lipiany
103 G14 **Lippstadt** Nordrhein-Westfalen, W Germany 51.40N 8.21E
27 P1 **Lipscomb** Texas, SW USA 36.12N 100.13W
Lipsia/Lipsk *see* Leipzig
Liptau-Sankt-Nikolaus/Liptószentmiklós *see* Liptovský Mikuláš
113 K19 **Liptovský Mikuláš** *Ger.* Liptau-Sankt-Nikolaus, *Hung.* Liptószentmiklós. Žilinský Kraj, N Slovakia 49.06N 19.36E
191 O13 **Liptrap, Cape** *headland* Victoria, SE Australia 38.55S 145.58E
166 L13 **Lipu** Guangxi Zhuangzu Zizhiqu, S China 24.29N 110.24E
147 X12 **Liqbi** S Oman 18.27N 56.37E
83 G17 **Lira** N Uganda 2.15N 32.55E
59 F15 **Lircay** Huancavelica, C Peru 12.58S 74.43W
109 J15 **Liri** C Italy
150 M8 **Lisakovsk** Kostanay, NW Kazakhstan 52.37N 62.34E
81 K17 **Lisala** Equateur, N Dem. Rep. Congo 2.10N 21.28E
106 F11 **Lisboa** *Eng.* Lisbon; *anc.* Felicitas Julia, Olisipo. ● (Portugal) Lisboa, W Portugal 38.43N 9.07W
106 F10 **Lisboa** ◆ *Eng.* Lisbon. *district* C Portugal
21 N7 **Lisbon** New Hampshire, NE USA 44.11N 71.52W
31 Q6 **Lisbon** North Dakota, N USA 46.27N 97.42W
Lisbon *see* Lisboa
21 Q8 **Lisbon Falls** Maine, NE USA 44.00N 70.03W
99 G15 **Lisburn** *Ir.* Lios na gCearrbhach. E Northern Ireland, UK 54.31N 6.03W
40 L6 **Lisburne, Cape** *headland* Alaska, USA 68.52N 166.13W
99 B19 **Liscannor Bay** *Ir.* Bá Lios Ceannúir. *inlet* W Ireland
115 Q18 **Lisec** ▲ E FYR Macedonia 41.46N 22.30E
166 F13 **Lishe Jiang** SW China
166 M4 **Lishi** Shanxi, C China 37.27N 111.05E
169 V10 **Lishu** Jilin, NE China 43.25N 124.19E
167 R10 **Lishui** Zhejiang, SE China 28.27N 119.25E
199 Jj5 **Lisianski Island** *island* Hawaiian Islands, Hawaii, USA, C Pacific Ocean
Lisichansk *see* Lysychans'k
104 L4 **Lisieux** *anc.* Noviomagus. Calvados, N France 49.09N 0.13E
130 L8 **Liski** *prev.* Georgiu-Dezh. Voronezhskaya Oblast', W Russian Federation 51.00N 39.36E
Lisle/l'Isle *see* Lille
105 N4 **l'Isle-Adam** Val-d'Oise, N France 49.07N 2.13E
105 R15 **l'Isle-sur-la-Sorgue** Vaucluse, SE France 43.55N 5.03E
13 S9 **L'Islet** Québec, SE Canada 47.07N 70.18W
190 M12 **Lismore** Victoria, SE Australia 37.59S 143.18E
99 D20 **Lismore** *Ir.* Lios Mór. S Ireland 52.10N 7.10W
Lissa *see* Vis, Croatia
Lissa *see* Leszno, Poland
100 H11 **Lisse** Zuid-Holland, W Netherlands 52.15N 4.33E
97 D18 **Lista** *peninsula* S Norway
97 D18 **Listafjorden** *fjord* S Norway

◆ Country ◇ Dependent Territory ◆ Administrative Region ▲ Mountain Volcano Lake
● Country Capital ○ Dependent Territory Capital ✕ International Airport ▲ Mountain Range River Reservoir

LISTER, MOUNT – LORA CREEK

205 R13 **Lister, Mount** ▲ Antarctica 78.12S 161.46E
130 M8 **Listopadovka** Voronezhskaya Oblast', W Russian Federation 51.54N 41.08E
12 F15 **Listowel** Ontario, S Canada 43.44N 80.57W
99 B20 **Listowel** *Ir.* Lios Tuathail. SW Ireland 52.27N 9.28W
166 L14 **Litang** Guangxi Zhuangzu Zizhiqu, S China 23.09N 109.07E
166 F9 **Litang** *var.* Gaocheng. Sichuan, C China 30.03N 100.12E
166 F10 **Litang Qu** C China
57 X12 **Litani** *var.* Itany. French Guiana/Suriname
144 G8 **Lītani, Nahr el** *var.* Nahr al Litant. C Lebanon
Litant, Nahr al *see* Lītani, Nahr el
Litauen *see* Lithuania
32 K14 **Litchfield** Illinois, N USA 39.17N 89.52W
31 U8 **Litchfield** Minnesota, N USA 45.09N 94.31W
38 K13 **Litchfield Park** Arizona, SW USA 33.29N 112.21W
191 S8 **Lithgow** New South Wales, SE Australia 33.30S 150.09E
117 I26 **Líthino, Akrotírio** *headland* Kríti, Greece, E Mediterranean Sea 34.55N 24.43E
120 D12 **Lithuania** *off.* Republic of Lithuania, *Ger.* Litauen, *Lith.* Lietuva, *Pol.* Litwa, *Rus.* Litva; *prev.* Lithuanian SSR, *Rus.* Litovskaya SSR. ◆ *republic* NE Europe
Lithuanian SSR *see* Lithuania
111 U11 **Litija** *Ger.* Littai. C Slovenia 46.03N 14.50E
20 H15 **Lititz** Pennsylvania, NE USA 40.09N 76.18W
117 F15 **Litóchoro** *var.* Litohoro, Litókhoron. Kentrikí Makedonía, N Greece 40.06N 22.30E
Litohoro/Litókhoron *see* Litóchoro
113 C15 **Litoměřice** *Ger.* Leitmeritz. Ústecký Kraj, NW Czech Republic 50.32N 14.09E
113 F17 **Litomyšl** *Ger.* Leitomischl. Pardubický Kraj, C Czech Republic 49.52N 16.16E
113 G17 **Litovel** *Ger.* Littau. Olomoucký Kraj, E Czech Republic 49.42N 17.04E
127 Nn15 **Litovko** Khabarovskiy Kray, SE Russian Federation 49.22N 135.10E
Litovskaya SSR *see* Lithuania
Littai *see* Litija
Littau *see* Litovel
46 G1 **Little Abaco** *var.* Abaco Island. *island* N Bahamas
113 I21 **Little Alföld** *Ger.* Kleines Ungarisches Tiefland, *Hung.* Kisalföld, *Slvk.* Podunajská Rovina. *plain* Hungary/Slovakia
157 Q20 **Little Andaman** *island* Andaman Islands, India, NE Indian Ocean
28 M5 **Little Arkansas River** Kansas, C USA
192 L4 **Little Barrier Island** *island* N NZ
Little Belt *see* Lillebælt
40 M11 **Little Black River** Alaska, USA
29 O2 **Little Blue River** Kansas/Nebraska, C USA
46 D8 **Little Cayman** *island* E Cayman Islands
9 X11 **Little Churchill** Manitoba, C Canada
177 Ee10 **Little Coco Island** *island* SW Myanmar
38 L10 **Little Colorado River** Arizona, SW USA
12 E11 **Little Current** Manitoulin Island, Ontario, S Canada 45.57N 81.55W
10 E11 **Little Current** Ontario, S Canada
40 L8 **Little Diomede Island** *island* Alaska, USA
46 J4 **Little Exuma** *island* C Bahamas
31 U7 **Little Falls** Minnesota, N USA 45.59N 94.21W
20 J10 **Little Falls** New York, NE USA 43.02N 74.51W
26 M5 **Littlefield** Texas, SW USA 33.55N 102.19W
31 V3 **Littlefork** Minnesota, N USA 48.24N 93.33W
31 V3 **Little Fork River** Minnesota, N USA
9 N16 **Little Fort** British Columbia, SW Canada 51.27N 120.15W
9 Y14 **Little Grand Rapids** Manitoba, C Canada 52.06N 95.29W
99 N23 **Littlehampton** SE England, UK 50.48N 0.33W
37 T2 **Little Humboldt River** Nevada, W USA
46 K6 **Little Inagua** *var.* Inagua Islands. *island* S Bahamas
23 Q4 **Little Kanawha River** West Virginia, NE USA
85 F25 **Little Karoo** *plateau* S South Africa
41 O16 **Little Koniuji Island** *island* Shumagin Islands, Alaska, USA
46 H12 **Little London** W Jamaica 18.14N 78.13W
11 R10 **Little Mecatina** *Fr.* Rivière du Petit Mécatina. Newfoundland and Labrador/Québec, E Canada
98 F8 **Little Minch, The** *strait* NW Scotland, UK
29 T13 **Little Missouri River** Arkansas, USA
30 J7 **Little Missouri River** NW USA
30 J3 **Little Muddy River** North Dakota, N USA
157 Q22 **Little Nicobar** *island* Nicobar Islands, India, NE Indian Ocean
29 R6 **Little Osage River** Missouri, C USA
99 P20 **Little Ouse** E England, UK
155 V2 **Little Pamir** *Pash.* Pāmīr-e Khord, *Rus.* Malyy Pamir. ▲▲ Afghanistan/Tajikistan
23 U12 **Little Pee Dee River** North Carolina/South Carolina, SE USA
29 V10 **Little Red River** Arkansas, C USA
Little Rhody *see* Rhode Island
193 I19 **Little River** Canterbury, South Island, NZ 43.45S 172.49E
23 U12 **Little River** South Carolina, SE USA 33.52N 78.36W
29 Y9 **Little River** Arkansas/Missouri, C USA
29 R13 **Little River** Arkansas/Oklahoma, USA
27 T7 **Little River** Georgia, SE USA
24 H6 **Little River** Louisiana, S USA
27 T10 **Little River** Texas, SW USA
29 V12 **Little Rock** *state capital* Arkansas, C USA 34.45N 92.17W
33 N8 **Little Sable Point** *headland* Michigan, N USA 43.38N 86.32W
105 U11 **Little Saint Bernard Pass** *Fr.* Col du Petit St-Bernard, *It.* Colle di Piccolo San Bernardo. *pass* France/Italy 45.41N 6.54E
38 K7 **Little Salt Lake** ⊙ Utah, W USA
188 K8 **Little Sandy Desert** *desert* Western Australia
31 S13 **Little Sioux River** Iowa, C USA
40 E17 **Little Sitkin Island** *island* Aleutian Islands, Alaska, USA
9 O13 **Little Smoky** Alberta, W Canada 54.35N 117.06W
9 O14 **Little Smoky** Alberta, W Canada
39 P3 **Little Snake River** Colorado, C USA
66 A12 **Little Sound** *bay* Bermuda, NW Atlantic Ocean
39 T4 **Littleton** Colorado, C USA 39.36N 105.01W
21 N7 **Littleton** New Hampshire, NE USA 44.18N 71.46W
20 D11 **Little Valley** New York, NE USA 42.15N 78.46W
32 M15 **Little Wabash River** Illinois, N USA
12 D10 **Little White River** Ontario, S Canada
30 M12 **Little White River** South Dakota, N USA
27 R5 **Little Wichita River** Texas, SW USA
148 J4 **Little Zab** *Ar.* Nahraz Zāb aş Şaghīr, *Kurd.* Zē-i Kōya, *Per.* Rūdkhāneh-ye Zāb-e Kūchek. Iran/Iraq
81 D15 **Littoral** ◐ *province* W Cameroon
Littoria *see* Latina
Litva/Litwa *see* Lithuania
113 B15 **Litvínov** *Ger.* Leutensdorf. Ústecký Kraj, NW Czech Republic 50.37N 13.37E
118 M6 **Lityn** Vinnyts'ka Oblast', C Ukraine 49.19N 28.06E
Liu-chou/Liuchow *see* Liuzhou
169 W11 **Liuhe** Jilin, NE China 42.15N 125.49E
Liukang Tenggaya, Kepulauan *see* Sabalana, Kepulauan
85 Q15 **Liúpo** Nampula, NE Mozambique 15.36S 39.57E
85 G14 **Liuwa Plain** *plain* W Zambia
166 L13 **Liuzhou** *var.* Liu-chou, Liuchow. Guangxi Zhuangzu Zizhiqu, S China 24.08N 108.54E
118 H8 **Livada** *Hung.* Sárköz. Satu Mare, NW Romania 47.52N 23.03E
117 J20 **Liváda, Akrotírio** *headland* Tínos, Kykládes, Greece, Aegean Sea 37.36N 25.15E
117 L21 **Livádi** *island* Kykládes, Greece, Aegean Sea
Livanátai *see* Livanátes
117 G18 **Livanátes** *prev.* Livanátai. Stereá Ellás, C Greece 38.43N 23.01E
120 I10 **Līvāni** *Ger.* Lievenhof. Preiļi, SE Latvia 56.22N 26.12E
67 E25 **Lively Island** *island* SE Falkland Islands
67 D25 **Lively Sound** *sound* SE Falkland Islands
41 R8 **Livengood** Alaska, USA 65.31N 148.32W
108 I7 **Livenza** NE Italy
37 O6 **Live Oak** California, W USA 39.17N 121.41W
25 U9 **Live Oak** Florida, SE USA 30.18N 82.59W
37 O9 **Livermore** California, W USA 37.40N 121.46W
22 I6 **Livermore** Kentucky, S USA 37.31N 87.08W
21 Q7 **Livermore Falls** Maine, NE USA 44.30N 70.09W
26 J10 **Livermore, Mount** ▲ Texas, SW USA 30.37N 104.10W
11 P16 **Liverpool** Nova Scotia, SE Canada 44.03N 64.43W
99 K17 **Liverpool** NW England, UK 53.25N 2.55W
191 S7 **Liverpool Range** ▲▲ New South Wales, SE Australia
98 J12 **Livingston** C Scotland, UK 55.51N 3.31W
25 N5 **Livingston** Alabama, S USA 32.34N 88.12W
37 P9 **Livingston** California, W USA 37.22N 120.45W
24 J8 **Livingston** Louisiana, S USA 30.30N 90.45W
35 S11 **Livingston** Montana, NW USA 45.40N 110.33W
22 L8 **Livingston** Tennessee, S USA 36.22N 85.19W
27 W9 **Livingston** Texas, SW USA 30.42N 94.55W
44 F4 **Lívingston** Izabal, E Guatemala 15.49N 88.46W
85 I16 **Livingstone** *var.* Maramba. Southern, S Zambia 17.51S 25.48E
193 B22 **Livingstone Mountains** ▲▲ South Island, NZ
82 K13 **Livingstone Mountains** ▲▲ S Tanzania
84 N12 **Livingstonia** Northern, N Malawi 10.29S 34.06E
204 G4 **Livingston Island** *island* Antarctica
27 W9 **Livingston, Lake** ⊡ Texas, SW USA
114 F13 **Livno** Federacija Bosna I Hercegovina, SW Bosnia and Herzegovina 43.49N 17.00E
130 K7 **Livny** Orlovskaya Oblast', W Russian Federation 52.25N 37.42E
95 M14 **Livojoki** C Finland
33 R10 **Livonia** Michigan, N USA 42.22N 83.22W
108 E11 **Livorno** *Eng.* Leghorn. Toscana, C Italy 43.31N 10.18E
Livramento *see* Santana do Livramento
147 U8 **Liwā** *var.* Al Liwā'. *oasis region* S UAE
83 I24 **Liwale** Lindi, SE Tanzania 9.46S 37.55E
165 W9 **Liwangbu** Ningxia, N China 36.42N 106.04E
85 N15 **Liwonde** Southern, S Malawi 15.04S 35.12E
165 V11 **Lixian** *var.* Li Xian. Gansu, C China 34.15N 105.07E
166 H8 **Lixian** *var.* Li Xian, Zagunao. Sichuan, C China 31.27N 103.06E
Lixian Jiang *see* Black River
117 B18 **Lixoúri** *prev.* Lixoúrion. Kefallinía, Iónioi Nísoi, Greece, C Mediterranean Sea 38.12N 20.25E
Lixoúrion *see* Lixoúri
Lixus *see* Larache
Lizarra *see* Estella
35 U15 **Lizard Head Peak** ▲ Wyoming, C USA 42.47N 109.12W
99 H25 **Lizard Point** *headland* SW England, UK 49.57N 5.12W
114 L12 **Ljig** Serbia, C Serbia and Montenegro (Yugoslavia) 44.14N 20.16E
Ljouwert *see* Leeuwarden
Ljubelj *see* Loibl Pass
111 U11 **Ljubljana** *Ger.* Laibach, *It.* Lubiana; *anc.* Aemona, Emona. ● (Slovenia) C Slovenia 46.03N 14.28E
111 T11 **Ljubljana** ✈ C Slovenia 46.14N 14.26E
115 N17 **Ljuboten** ▲ S Serbia and Montenegro (Yugoslavia) 42.12N 21.06E
97 P19 **Ljugarn** Gotland, SE Sweden 57.23N 18.45E
86 G7 **Ljungan** N Sweden
95 F17 **Ljungan** C Sweden
97 K21 **Ljungby** Kronoberg, S Sweden 56.49N 13.55E
97 M17 **Ljungsbro** Östergötland, S Sweden 58.31N 15.30E
97 I18 **Ljungskile** Västra Götaland, S Sweden 58.13N 11.55E
96 M11 **Ljusdal** Gävleborg, C Sweden 61.49N 16.10E
96 M11 **Ljusnan** C Sweden
96 N12 **Ljusne** Gävleborg, C Sweden 61.11N 17.07E
97 P15 **Ljusterö** Stockholm, C Sweden 59.31N 18.40E
111 X9 **Ljutomer** *Ger.* Luttenberg. NE Slovenia 46.31N 16.12E
65 G15 **Llaima, Volcán** ▲ S Chile 39.01S 71.38W
107 X4 **Llançà** *var.* Llansá. Cataluña, NE Spain 42.23N 3.08E
99 J21 **Llandovery** C Wales, UK 52.01N 3.47W
99 J20 **Llandrindod Wells** E Wales, UK 52.15N 3.22W
99 J18 **Llandudno** N Wales, UK 53.19N 3.49W
99 I21 **Llanelli** *prev.* Llanelly. SW Wales, UK 51.41N 4.11W
Llanelly *see* Llanelli
106 M2 **Llanes** Asturias, N Spain 43.24N 4.46W
99 K19 **Llangollen** NE Wales, UK 52.58N 3.10W
27 R10 **Llano** Texas, SW USA 30.45N 98.40W
27 Q10 **Llano River** Texas, SW USA
56 I9 **Llanos** *physical region* Colombia/Venezuela
65 G16 **Llanquihue, Lago** ⊙ S Chile
Llansá *see* Llançà
107 U5 **Lleida** *Cast.* Lérida; *anc.* Ilerda. Cataluña, NE Spain 41.37N 0.36E
107 U5 **Lleida** *Cast.* Lérida. ◐ *province* Cataluña, NE Spain
106 K12 **Llerena** Extremadura, W Spain 38.13N 6.00W
107 S9 **Llíria** País Valenciano, E Spain 39.37N 0.36W
107 W4 **Llivia** Cataluña, NE Spain 42.27N 2.00E
107 O3 **Llodio** País Vasco, N Spain 43.07N 2.58W
107 X5 **Lloret de Mar** Cataluña, NE Spain 41.42N 2.51E
Llorri *see* Tossal de l'Orri
8 L11 **Lloyd George, Mount** ▲ British Columbia, W Canada 57.46N 124.57W
9 R14 **Lloydminster** Alberta/Saskatchewan, SW Canada 53.18N 110.00W
38 L6 **Loa** Utah, W USA 38.24N 111.38W
174 Mm4 **Loagan Bunut** ⊙ East Malaysia
178 Mm14 **Loaita Island** *island* W Spratly Islands
40 G12 **Loa, Mauna** ▲ Hawai'i, USA, C Pacific Ocean 19.28N 155.39W
Loanda *see* Luanda
81 J22 **Loange** S Dem. Rep. Congo
81 E21 **Loango** Le Kouilou, S Congo 4.37S 11.49E
108 B10 **Loano** Liguria, NW Italy 44.07N 8.15E
64 H4 **Loa, Río** N Chile
85 I20 **Lobatse** *var.* Lobatsi. Kgatleng, SE Botswana 25.10S 25.40E
Lobatsi *see* Lobatse
103 Q15 **Löbau** Sachsen, E Germany 51.06N 14.39E
81 H16 **Lobaye** ◐ *prefecture* SW Central African Republic
81 I16 **Lobaye** SW Central African Republic
101 G21 **Lobbes** Hainaut, S Belgium 50.21N 4.16E
63 D23 **Lobería** Buenos Aires, E Argentina 38.07S 58.48W
112 F8 **Łobez** *Ger.* Labes. Zachodnio-pomorskie, NW Poland 53.29N 15.39E
84 A13 **Lobito** Benguela, W Angola 12.19S 13.34E
Lobkovichi *see* Labkovichy
Lob Nor *see* Lop Nur
176 W11 **Lobo** Papua, E Indonesia 3.41S 134.06E
106 J11 **Lobón** Extremadura, W Spain 38.51N 6.37W
63 D20 **Lobos** Buenos Aires, E Argentina 35.10S 59.07W
42 E4 **Lobos, Cabo** *headland* NW Mexico 29.53N 112.43W
42 F6 **Lobos, Isla** *island* NW Mexico
Lobositz *see* Lovosice
Lobsens *see* Łobżenica
Loburi *see* Lop Buri
112 H9 **Łobżenica** *Ger.* Lobsens. Wielkopolskie, C Poland 53.19N 17.11E
110 G11 **Locarno** *Ger.* Luggarus. Ticino, S Switzerland 46.10N 8.47E
98 E9 **Lochboisdale** NW Scotland, UK 57.08N 7.17W
100 N11 **Lochem** Gelderland, E Netherlands 52.10N 6.25E
104 M8 **Loches** Indre-et-Loire, C France 47.08N 1.00E
Loch Garman *see* Wexford
98 H12 **Lochgilphead** W Scotland, UK 56.02N 5.27W
98 H7 **Lochinver** N Scotland, UK 58.10N 5.14W
98 F8 **Lochmaddy** NW Scotland, UK 57.35N 7.10W
98 J10 **Lochnagar** ▲ C Scotland, UK 56.58N 3.09W
101 E17 **Lochristi** Oost-Vlaanderen, NW Belgium 51.07N 3.49E
98 H9 **Lochy, Loch** ⊙ N Scotland, UK
190 G8 **Lock** South Australia 33.37S 135.45E
99 J14 **Lockerbie** S Scotland, UK 55.10N 3.27W
29 S13 **Lockesburg** Arkansas, C USA 33.58N 94.10W
191 P10 **Lockhart** New South Wales, SE Australia 35.15S 146.43E
27 S11 **Lockhart** Texas, SW USA 29.52N 97.40W
20 F13 **Lock Haven** Pennsylvania, NE USA 41.08N 77.27W
27 N4 **Lockney** Texas, SW USA 34.06N 101.27W
102 O12 **Löcknitz** NE Germany
20 E9 **Lockport** New York, NE USA 43.09N 78.40W
178 Jj13 **Lôc Ninh** Sông Be, S Vietnam 11.51N 106.34E
109 N23 **Locri** Calabria, SW Italy 38.16N 16.16E
Locse *see* Levoča
29 T2 **Locust Creek** Missouri, C USA
25 P3 **Locust Fork** Alabama, S USA
29 Q9 **Locust Grove** Oklahoma, C USA 36.12N 95.10W
96 E11 **Lodalskåpa** ▲ S Norway 61.47N 7.10E
191 N10 **Loddon River** Victoria, SE Australia
Lodensee *see* Klooga
105 P15 **Lodève** *anc.* Luteva. Hérault, S France 43.43N 3.19E
128 I12 **Lodeynoye Pole** Leningradskaya Oblast', NW Russian Federation 60.41N 33.29E
35 V11 **Lodge Grass** Montana, NW USA 45.19N 107.20W
30 J15 **Lodgepole Creek** Nebraska/Wyoming, C USA
155 T11 **Lodhrān** Punjab, E Pakistan 29.36N 71.34E
108 D8 **Lodi** Lombardia, NW Italy 45.15N 9.36E
37 O8 **Lodi** California, W USA 38.07N 121.17W
33 T12 **Lodi** Ohio, N USA 41.00N 82.01W
94 H10 **Lødingen** Nordland, C Norway 68.24N 15.52E
81 L20 **Lodja** Kasai Oriental, C Dem. Rep. Congo 3.28S 23.24E
39 O3 **Lodore, Canyon of** *canyon* Colorado, C USA
107 Q4 **Lodosa** Navarra, N Spain 42.25N 2.04W
83 H16 **Lodwar** Rift Valley, NW Kenya 3.06N 35.38E
112 K13 **Łódź** *Rus.* Lodz. Łódź, C Poland 51.51N 19.26E
112 J13 **Łódzkie** ◐ *province* C Poland 51.51N 19.26E
178 I8 **Loei** *var.* Loey, Muang Loei. Loei, C Thailand 17.28N 101.42E
100 I11 **Loenen** Utrecht, C Netherlands 52.13N 5.01E
178 J9 **Loeng Nok Tha** Yasothon, E Thailand 16.12N 104.31E
85 F24 **Loeriesfontein** Northern Cape, W South Africa 30.55S 19.28E
97 H20 **Læsø** *island* N Denmark
Loewoek *see* Luwuk
Loey *see* Loei
78 J16 **Lofa** N Liberia
111 P6 **Lofer** Salzburg, C Austria 47.37N 12.42E
94 F11 **Lofoten** *var.* Lofoten Islands. *island group* C Norway
Lofoten Islands *see* Lofoten
97 N18 **Loftahammar** Kalmar, S Sweden 57.55N 16.45E
131 O10 **Log** Volgogradskaya Oblast', SW Russian Federation 49.32N 43.52E
79 S12 **Loga** Dosso, SW Niger 13.33N 3.18E
31 S14 **Logan** Iowa, C USA 41.38N 95.47W
28 K3 **Logan** Kansas, C USA 39.39N 99.34W
33 T14 **Logan** Ohio, N USA 39.32N 82.24W
38 L1 **Logan** Utah, W USA 41.45N 111.50W
23 P6 **Logan** West Virginia, NE USA 37.51N 81.59W
37 Y10 **Logandale** Nevada, W USA 36.36N 114.28W
21 O11 **Logan International** ✈ (Boston) Massachusetts, NE USA 42.22N 71.00W
9 N16 **Logan Lake** British Columbia, SW Canada 50.28N 120.42W
25 Q4 **Logan Martin Lake** ⊡ Alabama, S USA
8 G8 **Logan, Mount** ▲ Yukon Territory, W Canada 60.32N 140.34W
34 I7 **Logan, Mount** ▲ Washington, NW USA 48.32N 120.57W
35 P7 **Logan Pass** *pass* Montana, NW USA 48.43N 113.44W
33 O12 **Logansport** Indiana, N USA 40.44N 86.25W
24 F6 **Logansport** Louisiana, S USA 31.58N 94.00W
Logar *see* Lowgar
69 R11 **Loge** NW Angola
Logishin *see* Lahishyn
Log na Coille *see* Lugnaquillia Mountain
80 G11 **Logone** *var.* Lagone. Cameroon/Chad
80 G13 **Logone-Occidental** *off.* Préfecture du Logone-Occidental. ◐ *prefecture* SW Chad
80 H13 **Logone Occidental** SW Chad
80 G13 **Logone-Oriental** *off.* Préfecture du Logone-Oriental. ◐ *prefecture* SW Chad
80 H13 **Logone Oriental** SW Chad
Logone Oriental *see* Pendé
L'Ogooué-Ivindo *see* Ogooué-Ivindo
L'Ogooué-Lolo *see* Ogooué-Lolo
L'Ogooué-Maritime *see* Ogooué-Maritime
Logosyk *see* Lahoysk
107 P4 **Logroño** *anc.* Vareia, *Lat.* Juliobriga. La Rioja, N Spain 42.28N 2.25W
106 L10 **Logrosán** Extremadura, W Spain 39.21N 5.28W
97 G20 **Løgstør** Nordjylland, N Denmark 56.57N 9.19E
97 H22 **Løgten** Århus, C Denmark 56.16N 10.19E
97 F24 **Løgumkloster** Sønderjylland, SW Denmark 55.04N 8.58E
Lögurinn *see* Lagarfljót
197 B10 **Loh** *island* Torres Islands, N Vanuatu
159 P15 **Lohārdaga** Jhārkhand, N India 23.27N 84.42E
158 H10 **Lohāru** Haryāna, N India 28.27N 75.53E
103 D15 **Lohausen** ✈ (Düsseldorf) Nordrhein-Westfalen, W Germany 51.18N 6.51E
201 O14 **Lohd** Pohnpei, E Micronesia
194 I14 **Lohiki** S PNG
94 L12 **Lohiniva** Lappi, N Finland 67.09N 25.04E
Lohiszyn *see* Lahishyn
95 L20 **Lohja** *var.* Lojo. Etelä-Suomi, S Finland 60.14N 24.07E
175 O8 **Lohjanan** Borneo, C Indonesia
27 Q9 **Lohn** Texas, SW USA 31.15N 99.22W
102 G12 **Lohne** Niedersachsen, NW Germany 52.40N 8.13E
Lohr *see* Lohr am Main
103 I18 **Lohr am Main** *var.* Lohr. Bayern, C Germany 50.00N 9.30E
111 T10 **Loibl Pass** *Ger.* Loiblpass, *Slvn.* Ljubelj. *pass* Austria/Slovenia 46.25N 14.15E
178 Gg6 **Loi-Kaw** Kayah State, C Myanmar 19.40N 97.12E
95 K19 **Loimaa** Länsi-Suomi, W Finland 60.51N 23.03E
105 O6 **Loing** C France
178 Ii6 **Loi, Phou** ▲ N Laos 20.18N 103.14E
104 L7 **Loir** C France
105 Q11 **Loire** ◐ *department* E France
104 M7 **Loire** *var.* Liger. C France
104 I7 **Loire-Atlantique** ◐ *department* NW France
105 O7 **Loiret** ◐ *department* C France
104 M8 **Loir-et-Cher** ◐ *department* C France
103 L24 **Loisach** SE Germany
58 B9 **Loja** Loja, S Ecuador 3.58S 79.16W
106 M14 **Loja** Andalucía, S Spain 37.10N 4.09W
58 B9 **Loja** ◐ *province* S Ecuador
Lojo *see* Lohja
118 J4 **Lokachi** Volyns'ka Oblast', NW Ukraine 50.44N 24.39E
81 M20 **Lokandu** Maniema, C Dem. Rep. Congo 2.34S 25.43E
94 M11 **Lokan Tekojärvi** ⊙ NE Finland
143 Z11 **Lökbatan** *Rus.* Lokbatan. E Azerbaijan 40.21N 49.43E
101 F17 **Lokeren** Oost-Vlaanderen, NW Belgium 51.06N 3.58E
Lokhvitsa *see* Lokhvytsya
119 S4 **Lokhvytsya** *Rus.* Lokhvitsa. Poltavs'ka Oblast', NE Ukraine 50.21N 33.15E
83 H17 **Lokichar** Rift Valley, NW Kenya 2.22N 35.40E
83 G16 **Lokichokio** Rift Valley, NW Kenya 4.16N 34.22E
83 H16 **Lokitaung** Rift Valley, NW Kenya 4.15N 35.45E
94 M11 **Lokka** Lappi, N Finland 67.47N 27.40E
96 G8 **Løkken Verk** Sør-Trøndelag, S Norway 63.07N 9.40E
128 G16 **Loknya** Pskovskaya Oblast', W Russian Federation 56.48N 30.08E
79 V15 **Loko** Nassarawa, C Nigeria 8.00N 7.48E
79 U15 **Lokoja** Kogi, C Nigeria 7.47N 6.44E
125 E12 **Lokomotivnyy** Chelyabinskaya Oblast', C Russian Federation 53.00N 60.35E
83 H17 **Lokori** Rift Valley, W Kenya 1.55N 36.03E
79 R16 **Lokossa** S Benin 6.37N 1.43E
120 I3 **Loksa** *Ger.* Loxa. Harjumaa, NW Estonia 59.36N 25.43E
16 P3 **Loks Land** *island* Nunavut, NE Canada
82 C13 **Lol** S Sudan
78 K15 **Lola** Guinée-Forestière, SE Guinea 7.52N 8.28W
37 Q5 **Lola, Mount** ▲ California, W USA 39.27N 120.20W
83 H20 **Loliondo** Arusha, NE Tanzania 2.03S 35.46E
97 H25 **Lolland** *prev.* Laaland. *island* S Denmark
195 O11 **Lolobau Island** *island* E PNG
175 T6 **Loloda Utara, Kepulauan** *island group* E Indonesia
81 E16 **Lolodorf** Sud, SW Cameroon 3.16N 10.49E
116 G7 **Lom** *prev.* Lom-Palanka. Oblast Montana, NW Bulgaria 43.48N 23.16E
116 G7 **Lom** NW Bulgaria
81 M19 **Lomami** C Dem. Rep. Congo
59 F17 **Lomas** Arequipa, SW Peru 15.29S 74.54W
65 I23 **Lomas, Bahía** *bay* S Chile
63 D20 **Lomas de Zamora** Buenos Aires, E Argentina 34.52S 58.26W
63 D20 **Loma Verde** Buenos Aires, E Argentina 35.16S 58.24W
188 K4 **Lombadina** Western Australia 16.39S 122.54E
108 E6 **Lombardia** *Eng.* Lombardy. ◐ *region* N Italy
Lombardy *see* Lombardia
104 M15 **Lombez** Gers, S France 43.28N 0.54E
175 R15 **Lomblen, Pulau** *island* Nusa Tenggara, S Indonesia
181 W7 **Lombok Basin** *undersea feature* E Indian Ocean
175 Nn16 **Lombok, Pulau** *island* Nusa Tenggara, C Indonesia
175 Nn16 **Lombok, Selat** *strait* S Indonesia
79 Q16 **Lomé** ● (Togo) S Togo 6.08N 1.13E
79 Q16 **Lomé** ✈ S Togo 6.08N 1.13E
81 L19 **Lomela** Kasai Oriental, C Dem. Rep. Congo 2.19S 23.15E
27 R9 **Lometa** Texas, SW USA 31.13N 98.23W
81 F16 **Lomié** Est, SE Cameroon 3.09N 13.34E
32 M8 **Lomira** Wisconsin, N USA 43.36N 88.26W
97 K23 **Lomma** Skåne, S Sweden 55.40N 13.04E
101 J16 **Lommel** Limburg, N Belgium 51.13N 5.19E
98 I11 **Lomond, Loch** ⊙ C Scotland, UK
207 R9 **Lomonosov Ridge** *var.* Harris Ridge, *Rus.* Khrebet Lomonsova. *undersea feature* Arctic Ocean
Lomonsova, Khrebet *see* Lomonosov Ridge
Lom-Palanka *see* Lom
Lomphat *see* Lumphăt
37 P14 **Lompoc** California, W USA 34.39N 120.29W
178 Hh9 **Lom Sak** *var.* Muang Lom Sak. Phetchabun, C Thailand 16.45N 101.12E
112 N9 **Łomża** *Rus.* Lomzha. Podlaskie, NE Poland 53.10N 22.04E
Lomzha *see* Łomża
161 D14 **Lonāvale** *prev.* Lonauli. Mahārāshtra, W India 18.45N 73.27E
65 G15 **Loncoche** Araucanía, C Chile 39.21S 72.34W
65 H14 **Loncopue** Neuquén, W Argentina 38.06S 70.36W
101 G17 **Londerzeel** Vlaams Brabant, C Belgium 51.00N 4.19E
Londinium *see* London
12 E16 **London** Ontario, S Canada 42.59N 81.12W
203 Y2 **London** Kiritimati, E Kiribati 02.00N 157.28W
99 O22 **London** *anc.* Augusta, *Lat.* Londinium. ● (UK) SE England, UK 51.30N 0.10W
23 N7 **London** Kentucky, S USA 37.06N 84.03W
33 S13 **London** Ohio, NE USA 39.52N 83.27W
27 Q10 **London** Texas, SW USA 30.40N 99.33W
99 O22 **London City** ✈ SE England, UK 51.31N 0.07E
99 E14 **Londonderry** *var.* Derry, *Ir.* Doire. NW Northern Ireland, UK 55.00N 7.19W
99 F14 **Londonderry** *cultural region* NW Northern Ireland, UK
188 M2 **Londonderry, Cape** *headland* Western Australia 13.46S 126.55E
65 H25 **Londonderry, Isla** *island* S Chile
45 O7 **Londres, Cayos** *reef* NE Nicaragua
62 I10 **Londrina** Paraná, S Brazil 23.18S 51.13W
29 N13 **Lone Grove** Oklahoma, C USA 34.11N 97.15W
12 E12 **Lonely Island** *island* Ontario, S Canada
37 T8 **Lone Mountain** ▲ Nevada, W USA 38.01N 117.28W
27 V6 **Lone Oak** Texas, SW USA 33.02N 95.58W
37 T11 **Lone Pine** California, W USA 36.36N 118.04W
Lone Star State *see* Texas
85 D14 **Longa** Cuando Cubango, C Angola 14.37S 18.27E
84 B12 **Longa** W Angola
85 E15 **Longa** S Angola
Long'an *see* Pingwu
207 S4 **Longa, Proliv** *Eng.* Long Strait. *strait* NE Russian Federation
46 J13 **Long Bay** *bay* W Jamaica
23 V13 **Long Bay** *bay* North Carolina/South Carolina, E USA
37 T16 **Long Beach** California, W USA 33.46N 118.11W
24 M9 **Long Beach** Mississippi, S USA 30.21N 89.09W
20 L14 **Long Beach** Long Island, New York, NE USA 40.34N 73.38W
34 F9 **Long Beach** Washington, NW USA 46.21N 124.03W
20 K16 **Long Beach Island** *island* New Jersey, NE USA
67 M25 **Longbluff** *headland* SW Tristan da Cunha
25 U13 **Longboat Key** *island* Florida, SE USA
20 K15 **Long Branch** New Jersey, NE USA 40.18N 73.59W
46 J5 **Long Cay** *island* SE Bahamas
Longcheng *see* Xiaoxian
167 P14 **Longchuan** *var.* Laolong. Guangdong, S China 24.07N 115.10E
Longchuan *see* Nanhua
Longchuan Jiang *see* Shweli
34 K12 **Long Creek** Oregon, NW USA 44.40N 119.07W
165 W10 **Longde** Ningxia, N China 35.37N 106.07E
191 P16 **Longford** Tasmania, SE Australia 41.41S 147.03E
99 D17 **Longford** *Ir.* An Longfort. C Ireland 53.44N 7.49W
99 E17 **Longford** *Ir.* An Longfort. *cultural region* C Ireland
Longgang *see* Dazu
169 W11 **Longgang Shan** ▲▲ NE China
167 P1 **Longhua** Hebei, E China 41.18N 117.43E
175 Nn8 **Longiram** Borneo, C Indonesia 0.01S 115.36E
46 J4 **Long Island** *island* C Bahamas
10 H8 **Long Island** *island* Nunavut, C Canada
194 K11 **Long Island** *var.* Arop Island. *island* N PNG
20 L14 **Long Island** *island* New York, NE USA
Long Island *see* Bermuda
20 M14 **Long Island Sound** *sound* NE USA
166 K13 **Long Jiang** S China
169 U7 **Longjiang** Heilongjiang, NE China 47.20N 123.09E
169 Y10 **Longjing** *var.* Yanji. Jilin, NE China 42.48N 129.26E
167 R4 **Longkou** Shandong, E China 37.40N 120.21E
10 E11 **Longlac** Ontario, S Canada 49.46N 86.34W
21 S1 **Long Lake** ⊙ Maine, NE USA
33 O6 **Long Lake** ⊙ Michigan, N USA
33 R5 **Long Lake** ⊙ Michigan, N USA
31 N6 **Long Lake** ⊙ North Dakota, N USA
32 J4 **Long Lake** ⊡ Wisconsin, N USA
101 K23 **Longlier** Luxembourg, SE Belgium 49.51N 5.27E
166 I13 **Longlin** *var.* Longlin Gezu Zizhixian, Xinzhou. Guangxi Zhuangzu Zizhiqu, S China 24.46N 105.19E
39 T3 **Longmont** Colorado, C USA 40.09N 105.07W
31 N13 **Long Pine** Nebraska, C USA 42.32N 99.42W
Longping *see* Luodian
12 F17 **Long Point** *headland* Ontario, S Canada 42.33N 80.15W
12 K15 **Long Point** *headland* Ontario, SE Canada 43.56N 76.53W
192 P10 **Long Point** *headland* North Island, NZ 39.07S 177.41E
32 L2 **Long Point** *headland* Michigan, N USA 47.50N 89.09W
12 G17 **Long Point Bay** *lake bay* Ontario, S Canada
31 T7 **Long Prairie** Minnesota, N USA 45.58N 94.52W
Longquan *see* Fenggang
11 S11 **Long Range Mountains** *hill range* Newfoundland and Labrador, E Canada
67 H25 **Long Range Point** *headland* SE Saint Helena 16.00S 05.41W
189 V8 **Longreach** Queensland, E Australia 23.31S 144.18E
166 H7 **Longriba** Sichuan, C China 32.32N 102.20E
166 L10 **Longshan** *var.* Min'an. Hunan, S China 29.25N 109.28E
39 S3 **Longs Peak** ▲ Colorado, C USA 40.15N 105.37W
Long Strait *see* Longa, Proliv
104 K8 **Longué** Maine-et-Loire, NW France 47.23N 0.07W
11 P11 **Longue-Pointe** Québec, E Canada 50.20N 64.13W
105 S4 **Longuyon** Meurthe-et-Moselle, NE France 49.25N 5.37E
27 W7 **Longview** Texas, SW USA 32.30N 94.44W
34 G10 **Longview** Washington, NW USA 46.08N 122.56W
67 H25 **Longwood** C Saint Helena
27 P7 **Longworth** Texas, SW USA 32.37N 100.20W
105 S3 **Longwy** Meurthe-et-Moselle, NE France 49.31N 5.46E
165 V11 **Longxi** Gansu, C China 35.00N 104.34E
Longxian *see* Wengyuan
178 J14 **Long Xuyên** *var.* Longxuyen. An Giang, S Vietnam 10.22N 105.25E
167 Q13 **Longyan** Fujian, SE China 25.06N 117.01E
94 O3 **Longyearbyen** ○ (Svalbard) Spitsbergen, W Svalbard 78.12N 15.39E
166 J15 **Longzhou** Guangxi Zhuangzu Zizhiqu, S China 22.22N 106.46E
Longzhouping *see* Changyang
102 F12 **Löningen** Niedersachsen, NW Germany 52.43N 7.42E
29 V11 **Lonoke** Arkansas, C USA 34.46N 91.54W
97 L21 **Lönsboda** Skåne, S Sweden 56.24N 14.19E
105 S9 **Lons-le-Saunier** *anc.* Ledo Salinarius. Jura, E France 46.40N 5.31E
33 O15 **Loogootee** Indiana, N USA 38.40N 86.54W
33 Q9 **Looking Glass River** Michigan, N USA
23 X11 **Lookout, Cape** *headland* North Carolina, SE USA 34.36N 76.31W
41 O6 **Lookout Ridge** *ridge* Alaska, USA
189 N11 **Loongana** Western Australia 30.53S 127.15E
101 I14 **Loon op Zand** Noord-Brabant, S Netherlands 51.37N 5.04E
99 A19 **Loop Head** *Ir.* Ceann Léime. *headland* W Ireland 52.55N 10.33W
111 V4 **Loosdorf** Niederösterreich, NE Austria 48.13N 15.25E
164 G10 **Lop** Xinjiang Uygur Zizhiqu, NW China 37.06N 80.12E
114 J11 **Lopare** Republika Srpska, NE Bosnia and Herzegovina 44.39N 18.49E
Lopatichi *see* Lapatsichy
131 Q15 **Lopatin** Respublika Dagestan, SW Russian Federation 43.52N 47.40E
131 P7 **Lopatino** Penzenskaya Oblast', W Russian Federation 52.38N 45.46E
178 Hh10 **Lop Buri** *var.* Loburi. Lop Buri, C Thailand 14.46N 100.40E
27 R16 **Lopeno** Texas, SW USA 26.42N 99.06W
197 D13 **Lopevi** *var.* Ulveah. *island* C Vanuatu
81 C18 **Lopez, Cap** *headland* W Gabon 0.39S 8.44E
100 I12 **Lopik** Utrecht, C Netherlands 51.58N 4.57E
Lop Nor *see* Lop Nur
164 M7 **Lop Nur** *var.* Lob Nor, Lop Nor, Lo-p'u Po. *seasonal lake* NW China
Lopnur *see* Yuli
81 K17 **Lopori** NW Dem. Rep. Congo
100 O5 **Loppersum** Groningen, NE Netherlands 53.19N 6.45E
94 I8 **Lopphavet** *sound* N Norway
Lo-p'u Po *see* Lop Nur
Lora *see* Lowrah
190 F3 **Lora Creek** *seasonal river* South Australia

◆ Country
● Country Capital
◇ Dependent Territory
○ Dependent Territory Capital
◐ Administrative Region
✈ International Airport
▲ Mountain
▲▲ Mountain Range
Volcano
River
⊙ Lake
⊡ Reservoir

Lora del Río – Luninyets

106 K13 **Lora del Río** Andalucía, S Spain 37.39N 5.31W
154 M11 **Lora, Hāmūn-i** *wetland* SW Pakistan
33 T11 **Lorain** Ohio, N USA 41.27N 82.10W
27 O7 **Loraine** Texas, SW USA 32.24N 100.42W
33 R13 **Loramie, Lake** ⊠ Ohio, N USA
107 Q13 **Lorca** *Ar.* Lurka; *anc.* Eliocroca, *Lat.* Illur co. Murcia, S Spain 37.40N 1.40W
199 I12 **Lord Howe Island** *island* E Australia
Lord Howe Island *see* Ontong Java Atoll
183 O10 **Lord Howe Rise** *undersea feature* SW Pacific Ocean
199 I12 **Lord Howe Seamounts** *undersea feature* W Pacific Ocean
39 P15 **Lordsburg** New Mexico, SW USA 32.19N 108.42W
194 K8 **Lorengau** *var.* Lorungau. Manus Island, N PNG 2.03S 147.16E
27 N5 **Lorenzo** Texas, SW USA 33.40N 101.31W
148 K7 **Lorestān** *off.* Ostān-e Lorestān, *var.* Luristan. ◈ *province* W Iran
59 M17 **Loreto** Beni, N Bolivia 15.19S 64.40W
108 J12 **Loreto** Marche, C Italy 43.25N 13.37E
42 F8 **Loreto** Baja California Sur, W Mexico 25.59N 111.21W
42 M11 **Loreto** Zacatecas, C Mexico 22.15N 102.00W
58 E9 **Loreto** *off.* Departamento de Loreto. ◈ *department* NE Peru
18 K8 **Lorian Swamp** *swamp* E Kenya
56 E6 **Lorica** Córdoba, NW Colombia 9.13N 75.49W
104 G7 **Lorient** *prev.* l'Orient. Morbihan, NW France 47.45N 3.22W
113 K22 **Lőrinci** Heves, NE Hungary 47.43N 19.39E
12 G11 **Loring** Ontario, S Canada 45.55N 79.59W
35 V6 **Loring** Montana, NW USA 48.49N 107.48W
105 R13 **Loriol-sur-Drôme** Drôme, E France 44.46N 4.51E
23 U12 **Loris** South Carolina, SE USA 34.03N 78.53W
59 I18 **Loriscota, Laguna** ◎ S Peru
191 N13 **Lorne** Victoria, SE Australia 38.33S 143.57E
98 G11 **Lorn, Firth of** *inlet* W Scotland, UK
Loro Sae *see* East Timor
103 F24 **Lörrach** Baden-Württemberg, S Germany 47.37N 7.40E
105 T5 **Lorraine** ◈ *region* NE France
Lorungau *see* Lorengau
96 L11 **Los** Gävleborg, C Sweden 61.42N 15.15E
37 P14 **Los Alamos** California, W USA 34.44N 120.16W
39 S10 **Los Alamos** New Mexico, SW USA 35.52N 106.17W
44 F5 **Los Amates** Izabal, E Guatemala 15.16N 89.07W
37 S15 **Los Angeles** California, W USA 34.03N 118.14W
37 S15 **Los Angeles** ✕ California, W USA 33.54N 118.24W
65 G14 **Los Ángeles** Bío Bío, C Chile 37.29S 72.18W
37 T13 **Los Angeles Aqueduct** *aqueduct* California, W USA
Losanna *see* Lausanne
65 H20 **Los Antiguos** Santa Cruz, SW Argentina 46.36S 71.31W
201 Q16 **Losap Atoll** *atoll* C Micronesia
37 P10 **Los Banos** California, W USA 37.00N 120.39W
106 K16 **Los Barrios** Andalucía, S Spain 36.10N 5.30W
64 L5 **Los Blancos** Salta, N Argentina 23.39S 62.36W
44 L12 **Los Chiles** Alajuela, NW Costa Rica 11.00N 84.42W
107 O2 **Los Corrales de Buelna** Cantabria, N Spain 43.15N 4.04W
27 T17 **Los Fresnos** Texas, SW USA 26.03N 97.28W
37 N9 **Los Gatos** California, W USA 37.13N 121.58W
112 O11 **Łosice** Mazowieckie, E Poland 52.13N 22.42E
114 B11 **Lošinj** *Ger.* Lussin, *It.* Lussino. *island* W Croatia
Los Jardines *see* Ngetik Atoll
65 G15 **Los Lagos** Los Lagos, C Chile 39.52S 72.52W
65 F17 **Los Lagos** *off.* Región de los Lagos. ◈ *region* C Chile
Loslau *see* Wodzisław Śląski
66 N11 **Los Llanos** *var.* Los Llanos de Aridane. La Palma, Islas Canarias, Spain, NE Atlantic Ocean 28.39N 17.54W
Los Llanos de Aridane *see* Los Llanos
39 R11 **Los Lunas** New Mexico, SW USA 34.48N 106.43W
65 I16 **Los Menucos** Río Negro, C Argentina 40.52S 68.07W
42 H8 **Los Mochis** Sinaloa, C Mexico 25.48N 108.57W
37 N4 **Los Molinos** California, W USA 40.00N 122.05W
106 M9 **Los Navalmorales** Castilla-La Mancha, C Spain 39.43N 4.37W
27 S15 **Los Olmos Creek** ≈ Texas, SW USA
Losonc/Losontz *see* Lučenec
178 Jj5 **Lô, Sông** *Chin.* Panlong Jiang. ≈ China/Vietnam
46 B5 **Los Palacios** Pinar del Río, W Cuba 22.30N 83.19W
106 K14 **Los Palacios y Villafranca** Andalucía, S Spain 37.10N 5.55W
175 Ss16 **Lospalos** E East Timor 8.28S 126.56E
39 R12 **Los Pinos Mountains** ▲▲ New Mexico, SW USA
39 R11 **Los Ranchos De Albuquerque** New Mexico, SW USA 35.09N 106.37W
42 M14 **Los Reyes** Michoacán de Ocampo, SW Mexico 19.36N 102.29W
58 B7 **Los Ríos** ◈ *province* C Ecuador
66 O11 **Los Rodeos** ✕ (Santa Cruz de Tenerife) Tenerife, Islas Canarias, Spain, NE Atlantic Ocean 28.27N 16.19W
56 L4 **Los Roques, Islas** *island group* N Venezuela
45 S17 **Los Santos** Los Santos, S Panama 7.55N 80.25W
45 S17 **Los Santos** *off.* Provincia de Los Santos. ◈ *province* S Panama
Los Santos *see* Los Santos de Maimona
106 J12 **Los Santos de Maimona** *var.* Los Santos. Extremadura, W Spain 38.27N 6.22W
100 P10 **Losser** Overijssel, E Netherlands 52.16N 7.01E
98 J8 **Lossiemouth** NE Scotland, UK 57.43N 3.18W
63 B14 **Los Tábanos** Santa Fe, C Argentina 28.27S 59.57W
56 J4 **Los Taques** Falcón, N Venezuela 11.49N 70.16W
12 G11 **Lost Channel** Ontario, S Canada 45.54N 80.20W
56 L5 **Los Teques** Miranda, N Venezuela 10.23N 67.01W
37 Q12 **Lost Hills** California, W USA 35.35N 119.40W
38 I7 **Lost Peak** ▲ Utah, W USA 37.30N 113.57W
35 P11 **Lost Trail Pass** *pass* Montana, NW USA 45.40N 113.58W
195 N15 **Losuia** Kiriwina Island, SE PNG 8.30S 151.04E
64 G10 **Los Vilos** Coquimbo, C Chile 31.52S 71.28W
107 N10 **Los Yébenes** Castilla-La Mancha, C Spain 39.34N 3.52W
105 N13 **Lot** ◈ *department* S France
105 N13 **Lot** ≈ S France
65 F14 **Lota** Bío Bío, C Chile 37.07S 73.07W
83 G15 **Lotagipi Swamp** *wetland* Kenya/Sudan
104 K14 **Lot-et-Garonne** ◈ *department* SW France
85 K21 **Lothair** Mpumalanga, NE South Africa 26.22S 30.25E
35 R7 **Lothair** Montana, NW USA 48.28N 111.15W
81 L20 **Loto** Kasai Oriental, C Dem. Rep. Congo 2.48S 22.30E
198 B8 **Lotofagā** Upolu, SE Samoa 13.57S 171.51W
110 E10 **Lötschbergtunnel** *tunnel* Valais, SW Switzerland
27 T9 **Lott** Texas, SW USA 31.12N 97.02W
128 H3 **Lotta** *var.* Lutto. ≈ Finland/Russian Federation
192 Q7 **Lottin Point** *headland* North Island, NZ 37.26S 178.07E
Lötzen *see* Giżycko
Loualaba *see* Lualaba
178 I6 **Louangnamtha** *var.* Luong Nam Tha. Louang Namtha, N Laos 20.55N 101.24E
178 I7 **Louangphabang** *var.* Louangphabang, Luang Prabang. Louangphabang, N Laos 19.51N 102.08E
Louangphrabang *see* Louangphabang
204 H5 **Loubet Coast** *physical region* Antarctica
Loubomo *see* Dolisie
Louch *see* Loukhi
104 H6 **Loudéac** Côtes d'Armor, NW France 48.10N 2.45W
166 M11 **Loudi** Hunan, S China 27.51N 111.58E
81 F21 **Loudima** La Bouenza, S Congo 4.06S 13.04E
22 M9 **Loudon** Tennessee, S USA 35.43N 84.19W
33 T12 **Loudonville** Ohio, N USA 40.38N 82.13W
104 L8 **Loudun** Vienne, W France 47.01N 0.04E
104 L7 **Loué** Sarthe, NW France 48.00N 0.14W
78 G10 **Louga** NW Senegal 15.36N 16.14W
99 M19 **Loughborough** C England, UK 52.46N 1.10W
99 C18 **Loughrea** *Ir.* Baile Locha Riach. W Ireland 53.12N 8.34W
105 S9 **Louhans** Saône-et-Loire, C France 46.38N 5.12E
23 P5 **Louisa** Kentucky, S USA 38.06N 82.40W
23 V5 **Louisa** Virginia, NE USA 38.02N 78.00W
23 V9 **Louisburg** North Carolina, SE USA 36.05N 78.18W
27 U12 **Louise** Texas, SW USA 29.07N 96.22W
13 P11 **Louiseville** Québec, SE Canada 46.15N 72.54W
195 Q17 **Louisiade Archipelago** *island group* SE PNG
29 W3 **Louisiana** Missouri, C USA 39.25N 91.03W
24 G8 **Louisiana** *off.* State of Louisiana; *also known as* Creole State, Pelican State. ◈ *state* S USA
194 K9 **Lou Island** *island* N PNG
85 K19 **Louis Trichardt** Limpopo, NE South Africa 23.06S 29.55E
25 V4 **Louisville** Georgia, SE USA 33.00N 82.24W
32 M15 **Louisville** Illinois, N USA 38.46N 88.32W
22 K5 **Louisville** Kentucky, S USA 38.15N 85.45W
24 M4 **Louisville** Mississippi, S USA 33.07N 89.03W
31 S15 **Louisville** Nebraska, C USA 41.00N 96.09W
199 Jj12 **Louisville Ridge** *undersea feature* S Pacific Ocean
128 J6 **Loukhi** *var.* Louch. Respublika Kareliya, NW Russian Federation 66.05N 33.04E
81 H19 **Loukoléla** Cuvette, E Congo 1.04S 17.10E
106 G14 **Loulé** Faro, S Portugal 37.08N 8.01W
113 C16 **Louny** *Ger.* Laun. Ústecký kraj NW Czech Republic 50.22N 13.49E
31 O15 **Loup City** Nebraska, C USA 41.16N 98.58W
31 P15 **Loup River** ≈ Nebraska, C USA
13 S9 **Loup, Rivière du** ≈ Québec, SE Canada
10 K7 **Loups Marins, Lacs des** *lakes* Québec, NE Canada
104 K16 **Lourdes** Hautes-Pyrénées, S France 43.06N 0.03W
Lourenço Marques *see* Maputo
106 F11 **Loures** Lisboa, C Portugal 38.49N 9.10W
106 F10 **Lourinhã** Lisboa, C Portugal 39.13N 9.19W
117 C16 **Loúros** ≈ W Greece
106 G8 **Lousã** Coimbra, N Portugal 40.07N 8.15W
166 M10 **Lou Shui** ≈ C China
191 O5 **Louth** New South Wales, SE Australia 30.34S 145.07E
99 O18 **Louth** E England, UK 53.18N 0.00W
99 F17 **Louth** *Ir.* Lú. *cultural region* NE Ireland
117 H15 **Loutrá** Kentrikí Makedonía, N Greece 39.55N 23.37E
117 G19 **Loutráki** Pelopónnisos, S Greece 37.55N 22.55E
Louvain *see* Leuven
101 H19 **Louvain-la Neuve** Wallon Brabant, C Belgium 50.39N 4.36E
12 J8 **Louvicourt** Québec, SE Canada 48.04N 77.22W
104 M4 **Louviers** Eure, N France 49.13N 1.10E
32 K14 **Lou Yaeger, Lake** ⊠ Illinois, N USA
95 J15 **Lövånger** Västerbotten, N Sweden 64.22N 21.19E
128 J14 **Lovat'** ≈ NW Russian Federation
115 J17 **Lovćen** ▲ S Serbia and Montenegro (Yugoslavia) 42.22N 18.49E
116 I8 **Lovech** Lovech, N Bulgaria 43.09N 24.42E
116 I9 **Lovech** ◈ *province* N Bulgaria
27 V9 **Lovelady** Texas, SW USA 31.07N 95.27W
39 T3 **Loveland** Colorado, C USA 40.24N 105.04W
35 U12 **Lovell** Wyoming, C USA 44.50N 108.23W
Lovello, Monte *see* Grosser Löffler
37 S4 **Lovelock** Nevada, W USA 40.11N 118.30W
108 E7 **Lovere** Lombardia, N Italy 45.51N 10.06E
32 L10 **Loves Park** Illinois, N USA 42.19N 89.03W
28 M2 **Lovewell Reservoir** ⊠ Kansas, C USA
95 M19 **Loviisa** *Swe.* Lovisa. Etelä-Suomi, S Finland 60.27N 26.15E
39 V15 **Loving** New Mexico, SW USA 32.17N 104.06W
23 U6 **Lovingston** Virginia, NE USA 37.45N 78.47W
39 V14 **Lovington** New Mexico, SW USA 32.56N 103.21W
Lovisa *see* Loviisa
113 C15 **Lovosice** *Ger.* Lobositz. Ústecký Kraj, NW Czech Republic 50.29N 14.01E
128 K4 **Lovozero** Murmanskaya Oblast', NW Russian Federation 68.00N 35.03E
128 K4 **Lovozero, Ozero** ◎ NW Russian Federation
114 B9 **Lovran** *It.* Laurana. Primorje-Gorski Kotar, NW Croatia 45.16N 14.15E
118 E11 **Lovrin** *Ger.* Lowrin. Timiș, W Romania 45.58N 20.48E
84 E10 **Lóvua** Lunda Norte, NE Angola 7.21S 20.09E
84 G12 **Lóvua** Moxico, E Angola 11.33S 23.35E
67 D25 **Low Bay** *bay* East Falkland, Falkland Islands
15 M6 **Low, Cape** *headland* Nunavut, E Canada 63.05N 85.27W
35 N10 **Lowell** Idaho, NW USA 46.07N 115.36W
21 O10 **Lowell** Massachusetts, NE USA 42.37N 71.19W
Löwen *see* Leuven
Löwenberg in Schlesien *see* Lwówek Śląski
Lower Austria *see* Niederösterreich
Lower Bann *see* Bann
Lower California *see* Baja California
Lower Danube *see* Niederösterreich
193 L14 **Lower Hutt** Wellington, North Island, NZ 41.13S 174.51E
41 N11 **Lower Kalskag** Alaska, USA 61.30N 160.28W
37 O1 **Lower Klamath Lake** ◎ California, W USA
37 Q2 **Lower Lake** ◎ California/Nevada, W USA
99 E15 **Lower Lough Erne** ◎ SW Northern Ireland, UK
Lower Lusatia *see* Niederlausitz
Lower Normandy *see* Basse-Normandie, France
8 K9 **Lower Post** British Columbia, W Canada 59.53N 128.19W
31 T4 **Lower Red Lake** ◎ Minnesota, N USA
Lower Rhine *see* Neder Rijn
Lower Saxony *see* Niedersachsen
Lower Tunguska *see* Nizhnyaya Tunguska
99 Q19 **Lowestoft** E England, UK 52.28N 1.45E
155 Q5 **Lowgar** *var.* Logar. ◈ *province* E Afghanistan
190 H7 **Low Hill** South Australia 32.17S 136.46E
112 K12 **Łowicz** Łódzkie, C Poland 52.06N 19.55E
35 N13 **Lowman** Idaho, NW USA 44.04N 115.37W
155 P8 **Lowrah** *var.* Lora. ≈ SE Afghanistan
Lowrin *see* Lovrin
191 N17 **Low Rocky Point** *headland* Tasmania, SE Australia 42.59S 145.28E
20 I8 **Lowville** New York, NE USA 43.47N 75.29W
Loxa *see* Loksa
190 K9 **Loxton** South Australia 34.30S 140.36E
83 G21 **Loya** Tabora, C Tanzania 4.57S 33.53E
32 K6 **Loyal** Wisconsin, N USA 44.45N 90.30W
20 G13 **Loyalsock Creek** ≈ Pennsylvania, NE USA
37 Q5 **Loyalton** California, W USA 39.39N 120.16W
Lo-yang *see* Luoyang
197 J6 **Loyauté, Îles** *island group* S New Caledonia
Loyev *see* Loyew
121 O20 **Loyew** *Rus.* Loyev. Homyel'skaya Voblasts', SE Belarus 51.55N 30.48E
129 S13 **Loyno** Kirovskaya Oblast', NW Russian Federation 59.44N 52.42E
105 P13 **Lozère** ◈ *department* S France
105 Q14 **Lozère, Mont** ▲ S France 44.27N 3.44E
114 J11 **Loznica** Serbia, W Serbia and Montenegro (Yugoslavia) 44.32N 19.13E
119 V7 **Lozova** *Rus.* Lozovaya. Kharkivs'ka Oblast', E Ukraine 48.54N 36.22E
Lozovaya *see* Lozova
107 N7 **Lozoyuela** Madrid, C Spain 40.55N 3.36W
Lœvvajok *see* Leavvajohka
Lu *see* Shandong, China
Lú *see* Louth, Ireland
84 F12 **Luacano** Moxico, E Angola 11.19S 21.30E
81 N21 **Lualaba** *Fr.* Loualaba. ≈ SE Dem. Rep. Congo
85 H14 **Luampa** Western, NW Zambia 15.02S 24.27E
85 H15 **Luampa Kuta** Western, W Zambia 15.22S 24.40E
167 P8 **Lu'an** Anhui, E China 31.46N 116.31E
106 K2 **Luanco** Asturias, N Spain 43.36N 5.48W
84 A11 **Luanda** *var.* Loanda, *Port.* São Paulo de Loanda. ● (Angola) Luanda, NW Angola 8.48S 13.17E
84 A11 **Luanda** ◈ *province* NW Angola
84 A11 **Luanda** ✕ Luanda, NW Angola 8.49S 13.16E
84 D12 **Luando** ≈ C Angola
Luang *see* Tapi, Mae Nam
85 G14 **Luanginga** *var.* Luanguinga. ≈ Angola/Zambia
178 Gg15 **Luang, Khao** ▲ SW Thailand 8.21N 99.46E
Luang Prabang *see* Louangphabang
178 I8 **Luang Prabang Range** *Th.* Thiukhaoluang Phrahang. ▲▲ Laos/Thailand
178 H16 **Luang, Thale** *lagoon* S Thailand
Luangua, Rio *see* Luangwa
84 E11 **Luangue** ≈ NE Angola
Luanguinga *see* Luanginga
85 K15 **Luangwa** *var.* Aruângua. Lusaka, C Zambia 15.34S 30.23E
85 K14 **Luangwa** *var.* Aruângua, Rio Luangua. ≈ Mozambique/Zambia
167 Q2 **Luan He** ≈ E China
202 G11 **Luaniva, Île** *island* E Wallis and Futuna
167 P2 **Luanping** *var.* Anjiangying. Hebei, E China 40.55N 117.19E
84 J13 **Luanshya** Copperbelt, C Zambia 13.09S 28.24E
64 K13 **Luan Toro** La Pampa, C Argentina 36.14S 65.08W
167 Q2 **Luanxian** *var.* Luan Xian. Hebei, E China 39.47N 118.46E
84 J12 **Luapula** ◈ *province* N Zambia
81 O25 **Luapula** ≈ Dem. Rep. Congo/Zambia
106 J2 **Luarca** Asturias, N Spain 43.33N 6.31W
174 Ll7 **Luar, Danau** ◎ Borneo, N Indonesia
81 L25 **Luashi** Katanga, S Dem. Rep. Congo 10.54S 23.55E
84 G12 **Luau** *Port.* Vila Teixeira de Sousa. Moxico, NE Angola 10.43S 22.07E
81 C16 **Luba** *prev.* San Carlos. Isla de Bioco, NW Equatorial Guinea 3.26N 8.36E
44 F4 **Lubaantun** *ruins* Toledo, S Belize 16.18N 88.57W
113 P16 **Lubaczów** *var.* Lúbaczów. Podkarpackie, SE Poland 50.09N 23.08E
Lubale *see* Lubalo
84 E11 **Lubalo** Lunda Norte, NE Angola 9.02S 19.11E
84 E11 **Lubalo** *var.* Lubale. ≈ Angola/Zaire
120 J9 **Lubāna** Madona, E Latvia 56.55N 29.43E
Lubānas Ezers *see* Lubāns
179 P11 **Lubang Island** *island* N Philippines
85 B15 **Lubango** *Port.* Sá da Bandeira. Huíla, SW Angola 14.54S 13.33E
120 J9 **Lubāns** *var.* Lubānas Ezers. ◎ E Latvia
81 M21 **Lubao** Kasai Oriental, C Dem. Rep. Congo 5.21S 25.42E
112 O13 **Lubartów** *Ger.* Qumälisch. Lubelskie, E Poland 51.26N 22.36E
102 G13 **Lübbecke** Nordrhein-Westfalen, NW Germany 52.18N 8.37E
102 O13 **Lübben** Brandenburg, E Germany 51.56N 13.52E
103 P14 **Lübbenau** Brandenburg, E Germany 51.52N 13.57E
27 N5 **Lubbock** Texas, SW USA 33.34N 101.51W
Lubcz *see* Lyubcha
21 U6 **Lubec** Maine, NE USA 44.49N 67.00W
102 K9 **Lübeck** Schleswig-Holstein, N Germany 53.52N 10.40E
102 K8 **Lübecker Bucht** *bay* N Germany
81 M21 **Lubefu** Kasai Oriental, C Dem. Rep. Congo 4.43S 24.25E
169 T10 **Lubei** *var.* Jarud Qi. Nei Mongol Zizhiqu, N China 44.25N 121.12E
113 O14 **Lubelska, Wyżyna** *plateau* SE Poland
113 O14 **Lubelskie** ◈ *province* E Poland
Lubembe *see* Luembe
Lüben *see* Lubin
150 H9 **Lubenka** Zapadnyy Kazakhstan, W Kazakhstan 50.27N 54.07E
81 P18 **Lubero** Nord Kivu, E Dem. Rep. Congo 0.10S 29.12E
81 L22 **Lubi** ≈ S Dem. Rep. Congo
Lubiana *see* Ljubljana
112 J11 **Lubień Kujawski** Kujawsko-pomorskie, C Poland 52.25N 19.10E
69 T11 **Lubilandji** ≈ S Dem. Rep. Congo
112 F13 **Lubin** *Ger.* Lüben. Dolnośląskie, SW Poland 51.22N 16.12E
113 O14 **Lublin** *Rus.* Lyublin. Lubelskie, E Poland 51.15N 22.33E
113 J15 **Lubliniec** Śląskie, S Poland 50.40N 18.40E
Lubnān, Jabal *see* Liban, Jebel
119 R5 **Lubny** Poltavs'ka Oblast', NE Ukraine 50.00N 33.00E
Luboml *see* Lyuboml'
112 G11 **Luboń** *Ger.* Peterhof. Wielkolpolskie, C Poland 52.22N 16.54E
112 D12 **Lubsko** *Ger.* Sommerfeld. Lubuskie, W Poland 51.46N 14.56E
81 N24 **Lubudi** Katanga, SE Dem. Rep. Congo 9.57S 25.58E
174 Hh11 **Lubuklinggau** Sumatera, W Indonesia 3.15S 102.51E
81 N25 **Lubumbashi** *prev.* Élisabethville. Katanga, SE Dem. Rep. Congo 11.39S 27.31E
85 I14 **Lubungu** Central, C Zambia 14.28S 26.30E
112 E12 **Lubuskie** ◈ *province* W Poland
81 N18 **Lubutu** Maniema, E Dem. Rep. Congo 0.42S 26.31E
Luca *see* Lucca
84 C11 **Lucala** ≈ W Angola
12 E16 **Lucan** Ontario, S Canada 43.10N 81.22W
99 F18 **Lucan** *Ir.* Leamhcán. E Ireland 53.22N 6.27W
Lucanian Mountains *see* Lucano, Appennino
109 M18 **Lucano, Appennino** *Eng.* Lucanian Mountains. ▲▲ S Italy
84 F11 **Lucapa** *var.* Lukapa. Lunda Norte, NE Angola 8.23S 20.42E
31 V15 **Lucas** Iowa, C USA 41.01N 93.26W
63 C18 **Lucas González** Entre Ríos, E Argentina 32.25S 59.33W
67 C25 **Lucas Point** *headland* West Falkland, Falkland Islands 52.10S 60.22W
33 S15 **Lucasville** Ohio, N USA 38.52N 83.00W
108 F11 **Lucca** *anc.* Luca. Toscana, C Italy 43.49N 10.30E
46 H12 **Lucea** W Jamaica 18.26N 78.10W
99 H15 **Luce Bay** *inlet* SW Scotland, UK
24 M8 **Lucedale** Mississippi, S USA 30.55N 88.35W
179 Pp11 **Lucena** *off.* Lucena City. Luzon, N Philippines 13.57N 121.38E
106 M14 **Lucena** Andalucía, S Spain 37.25N 4.28W
107 S8 **Lucena del Cid** País Valenciano, E Spain 40.07N 0.15W
113 D15 **Lučenec** *Ger.* Losontz, *Hung.* Losonc. Banskobystrický Kraj, C Slovakia 48.21N 19.36E
Lucentum *see* Alicante
Luceria *see* Lucera
109 M16 **Lucera** Puglia, SE Italy 41.30N 15.19E
Lucerna/Lucerne *see* Luzern
Lucerne, Lake of *see* Vierwaldstätter See
42 J4 **Lucero** Chihuahua, N Mexico 30.51N 106.27W
127 Nn17 **Luchegorsk** Primorskiy Kray, SE Russian Federation 46.26N 134.10E
107 Q13 **Luchena** ≈ SE Spain
Lucheng *see* Kangding
84 N13 **Lucheringo** *var.* Luchulingo. ≈ N Mozambique
Luchesa *see* Luchosa
Luchin *see* Luchyn
120 N13 **Luchosa** *Rus.* Luchesa. ≈ N Belarus
Luchow *see* Hefei
102 K11 **Lüchow** Mecklenburg-Vorpommern, N Germany 52.57N 11.10E
Luchulingo *see* Lucheringo
121 N17 **Luchyn** *Rus.* Luchin. Homyel'skaya Voblasts', SE Belarus 53.01N 30.01E
57 U11 **Lucie Rivier** ≈ W Suriname
190 K11 **Lucindale** South Australia 36.57S 140.20E
175 T13 **Lucipara, Kepulauan** *island group* E Indonesia
85 A14 **Lucira** Namibe, SW Angola 13.51S 12.35E
Łuck *see* Luts'k
103 O14 **Luckau** Brandenburg, E Germany 51.50N 13.42E
102 N13 **Luckenwalde** Brandenburg, E Germany 52.06N 13.11E
12 E15 **Lucknow** Ontario, S Canada 43.58N 81.30W
158 L12 **Lucknow** *var.* Lakhnau. Uttar Pradesh, N India 26.49N 80.54E
104 J10 **Luçon** Vendée, NW France 46.27N 1.10W
46 I7 **Lucrecia, Cabo** *headland* E Cuba 21.00N 75.34W
84 F13 **Lucusse** Moxico, E Angola 12.32S 20.46E
Lüda *see* Dalian
116 M9 **Luda Kamchiya** ≈ E Bulgaria
Ludasch *see* Luduș
116 I10 **Luda Yana** ≈ C Bulgaria
114 F7 **Ludbreg** Varaždin, N Croatia 46.15N 16.36E
31 P7 **Ludden** North Dakota, N USA 45.58N 98.07W
103 F15 **Lüdenscheid** Nordrhein-Westfalen, W Germany 51.13N 7.37E
85 C21 **Lüderitz** *prev.* Angra Pequena. Karas, SW Namibia 26.37S 15.10E
158 H8 **Ludhiāna** Punjab, N India 30.55N 75.52E
33 O7 **Ludington** Michigan, N USA 43.58N 86.27W
99 K20 **Ludlow** W England, UK 52.19N 2.27W
37 W14 **Ludlow** California, W USA 34.43N 116.07W
30 J7 **Ludlow** South Dakota, N USA 45.48N 103.21W
20 M9 **Ludlow** Vermont, NE USA 43.24N 72.39W
116 L7 **Ludogorie** *physical region* NE Bulgaria
25 W6 **Ludowici** Georgia, SE USA 31.42N 81.44W
Ludsan *see* Ludza
118 I10 **Luduș** *Ger.* Ludasch, *Hung.* Marosludas. Mureș, C Romania 46.27N 24.04E
97 M14 **Ludvika** Dalarna, C Sweden 60.07N 15.14E
103 H21 **Ludwigsburg** Baden-Württemberg, S Germany 48.54N 9.12E
102 O13 **Ludwigsfelde** Brandenburg, NE Germany 52.17N 13.15E
103 G20 **Ludwigshafen** *var.* Ludwigshafen am Rhein. Rheinland-Pfalz, W Germany 49.29N 8.24E
Ludwigshafen am Rhein *see* Ludwigshafen
103 L20 **Ludwigskanal** *canal* SE Germany
102 L10 **Ludwigslust** Mecklenburg-Vorpommern, N Germany 53.19N 11.28E
120 K10 **Ludza** *Ger.* Ludsan. Ludza, E Latvia 56.32N 27.41E
81 K21 **Luebo** Kasai Occidental, SW Dem. Rep. Congo 5.19S 21.21E
27 Q6 **Lueders** Texas, SW USA 32.46N 99.38W
81 N20 **Lueki** Maniema, C Dem. Rep. Congo 3.25S 25.49E
84 F10 **Luembe** *var.* Lubembe. ≈ Angola/Dem. Rep. Congo
84 E13 **Luena** *var.* Lwena, *Port.* Luso. Moxico, E Angola 11.46S 19.52E
81 M24 **Luena** Katanga, SE Dem. Rep. Congo 9.28S 25.45E
84 K12 **Luena** Northern, NE Zambia 10.31S 30.12E
84 F13 **Luena** ≈ E Angola
85 F16 **Luengue** ≈ SE Angola
69 V13 **Luenha** ≈ W Mozambique
85 G15 **Lueti** ≈ Angola/Zambia
166 J7 **Lüeyang** *var.* Hejiayan. Shaanxi, C China 33.12N 106.31E
167 P14 **Lufeng** Guangdong, S China 22.58N 115.36E
81 N24 **Lufira** ≈ SE Dem. Rep. Congo
81 N25 **Lufira, Lac de Retenue de la** *var.* Lac Tshangalele. ◎ SE Dem. Rep. Congo
27 W8 **Lufkin** Texas, SW USA 31.20N 94.43W
84 L11 **Lufubu** ≈ N Zambia
128 G14 **Luga** Leningradskaya Oblast', NW Russian Federation 58.43N 29.46E
128 G13 **Luga** ≈ NW Russian Federation
Luganer See *see* Lugano, Lago di
110 H11 **Lugano** *Ger.* Lauis. Ticino, S Switzerland 46.01N 8.57E
110 H12 **Lugano, Lago di** *var.* Ceresio, *Ger.* Luganer See. ◎ S Switzerland
Lugansk *see* Luhans'k
197 B12 **Luganville** Espiritu Santo, C Vanuatu 15.31S 167.12E
Lugdunum *see* Lyon
Lugdunum Batavorum *see* Leiden
85 O15 **Lugela** Zambézia, NE Mozambique 16.27S 36.47E
85 O16 **Lugela** ≈ C Mozambique
84 P13 **Lugenda, Rio** ≈ N Mozambique
Luggarus *see* Locarno
Lugh Ganana *see* Luuq
99 G19 **Lugnaquillia Mountain** *Ir.* Log na Coille. ▲ E Ireland 52.58N 6.27W
108 H10 **Lugo** Emilia-Romagna, N Italy 44.25N 11.52E
106 I3 **Lugo** *anc.* Lugus Augusti. Galicia, NW Spain 43.00N 7.33W
106 I3 **Lugo** ◈ *province* Galicia, NW Spain
23 R12 **Lugoff** South Carolina, SE USA 34.13N 80.41W
118 F12 **Lugoj** *Ger.* Lugosch, *Hung.* Lugos. Timiș, W Romania 45.40N 21.56E
Lugos/Lugosch *see* Lugoj
Lugovoy/Lugovoye *see* Kulan
164 I13 **Lugu** Xizang Zizhiqu, W China 33.26N 84.10E
Lugus Augusti *see* Lugo
Luguvallium/Luguvallum *see* Carlisle
119 Y7 **Luhans'k** *Rus.* Lugansk; *prev.* Voroshilovgrad. Luhans'ka Oblast', E Ukraine 48.32N 39.21E
119 Y7 **Luhans'k** ✕ Luhans'ka Oblast', E Ukraine 48.25N 39.24E
119 X6 **Luhans'ka Oblast'** *var.* Luhans'k; *prev.* Voroshilovgrad, *Rus.* Voroshilovgradskaya Oblast'. ◈ *province* E Ukraine
167 Q7 **Luhe** Jiangsu, E China 32.22N 118.51E
175 T11 **Luhu** Pulau Seram, E Indonesia 3.20S 127.58E
Luhua *see* Heishui
166 G8 **Luhuo** *var.* Xindu, *Tib.* Zhaggo. Sichuan, C China 31.25N 100.39E
118 M3 **Luhyny** Zhytomyrs'ka Oblast', N Ukraine 51.06N 28.24E
85 G15 **Lui** ≈ W Zambia
85 G16 **Luiana** ≈ SE Angola
85 L15 **Luia, Rio** *var.* Ruya. ≈ Mozambique/Zimbabwe
Luichow Peninsula *see* Leizhou Bandao
Luik *see* Liège
84 C13 **Luimbale** Huambo, C Angola 12.15S 15.19E
Luimneach *see* Limerick
108 D6 **Luino** Lombardia, N Italy 46.00N 8.45E
84 E13 **Luio** ≈ E Angola
94 L11 **Luiro** ≈ NE Finland
81 N25 **Luishia** Katanga, SE Dem. Rep. Congo 11.18S 27.08E
61 M19 **Luislândia do Oeste** Minas Gerais, SE Brazil 17.59S 45.35W
42 K5 **Luis L.León, Presa** ⊠ N Mexico
Luis Muñoz Marin *see* San Juan
205 N5 **Luitpold Coast** *physical region* Antarctica
81 K22 **Luiza** Kasai Occidental, S Dem. Rep. Congo 7.10S 22.27E
63 D20 **Luján** Buenos Aires, E Argentina 34.34S 59.07W
81 N24 **Lukafu** Katanga, SE Dem. Rep. Congo 10.28S 27.31E
Lukapa *see* Lucapa
114 I11 **Lukavac** Federacija Bosna I Hercegovina, NE Bosnia and Herzegovina 44.33N 18.31E
81 I20 **Lukenie** ≈ C Dem. Rep. Congo
81 H19 **Lukolela** Equateur, W Dem. Rep. Congo 1.10S 17.11E
121 M14 **Lukoml'skaye, Vozyera** *Rus.* Ozero Lukoml'skoye. ◎ N Belarus
Lukoml'skoye, Ozero *see* Lukoml'skaye, Vozyera
116 I8 **Lukovit** Lovech, N Bulgaria 43.13N 24.10E
112 O12 **Łuków** *Ger.* Bogendorf. Lubelskie, E Poland 51.57N 22.22E
131 O4 **Lukoyanov** Nizhegorodskaya Oblast', W Russian Federation 55.02N 44.26E
81 N22 **Lukuga** ≈ SE Dem. Rep. Congo
81 F21 **Lukula** Bas-Congo, SW Dem. Rep. Congo 5.22S 12.57E
85 G14 **Lukulu** Western, NW Zambia 14.24S 23.12E
201 R17 **Lukunor Atoll** *atoll* Mortlock Islands, C Micronesia
84 J12 **Lukwesa** Luapula, NE Zambia 10.03S 28.42E
95 K14 **Luleå** Norrbotten, N Sweden 65.34N 22.10E
94 J13 **Luleälven** ≈ N Sweden
142 C10 **Lüleburgaz** Kırklareli, NW Turkey 41.25N 27.22E
166 M4 **Lüliang Shan** ▲▲ C China
81 O21 **Lulimba** Maniema, E Dem. Rep. Congo 4.42S 28.37E
24 K9 **Luling** Louisiana, S USA 29.55N 90.22W
27 T11 **Luling** Texas, SW USA 29.40N 97.39W
81 I18 **Lulonga** ≈ NW Dem. Rep. Congo
81 K22 **Lulua** ≈ S Dem. Rep. Congo
Luluabourg *see* Kananga
198 Dd8 **Luma** Ta'ū, E American Samoa 14.15S 169.30W
174 M16 **Lumajang** Jawa, C Indonesia 8.06S 113.13E
164 G12 **Lumajangdong Co** ◎ W China
84 G13 **Lumbala Kaquengue** Moxico, E Angola 12.40S 22.34E
85 F14 **Lumbala N'Guimbo** *var.* Nguimbo, *Port.* Gago Coutinho, Vila Gago Coutinho. Moxico, E Angola 14.04S 21.25E
23 T11 **Lumber River** ≈ North Carolina/South Carolina, SE USA
Lumber State *see* Maine
24 L8 **Lumberton** Mississippi, S USA 31.00N 89.27W
23 U11 **Lumberton** North Carolina, SE USA 34.37N 79.00W
107 R4 **Lumbier** Navarra, N Spain 42.39N 1.19W
85 Q15 **Lumbo** Nampula, NE Mozambique 15.00S 40.40E
128 M4 **Lumbovka** Murmanskaya Oblast', NW Russian Federation 67.41N 40.31E
106 J7 **Lumbrales** Castilla-León, N Spain 40.57N 6.43W
159 W13 **Lumding** Assam, NE India 25.46N 93.10E
84 F12 **Lumege** *var.* Lumeje. Moxico, E Angola 11.30S 20.57E
Lumeje *see* Lumege
194 F10 **Lumi** Sandaun, NW PNG 3.30S 142.04E
101 J17 **Lummen** Limburg, NE Belgium 50.58N 5.12E
95 J20 **Lumparland** Åland, SW Finland 60.06N 20.15E
178 K12 **Lumphăt** *prev.* Lomphat. Rôtânôkiri, NE Cambodia 13.32N 106.57E
9 U16 **Lumsden** Saskatchewan, S Canada 50.39N 104.52W
193 C23 **Lumsden** Southland, South Island, NZ 45.43S 168.26E
174 J11 **Lumut, Tanjung** *headland* Sumatera, W Indonesia 3.47S 105.55E
163 P4 **Lün** Töv, C Mongolia 47.51N 105.11E
118 I13 **Lunca Corbului** Argeș, S Romania 44.41N 24.46E
97 K23 **Lund** Skåne, S Sweden 55.42N 13.10E
37 X6 **Lund** Nevada, W USA 38.50N 115.00W
84 D11 **Lunda Norte** ◈ *province* NE Angola
84 E12 **Lunda Sul** ◈ *province* NE Angola
84 M13 **Lundazi** Eastern, NE Zambia 12.19S 33.10E
97 G16 **Lunde** Telemark, S Norway 61.31N 6.37E
Lundenburg *see* Břeclav
97 C17 **Lundevatnet** ◎ S Norway
Lundi *see* Runde
99 I23 **Lundy** *island* SW England, UK
102 J10 **Lüneburg** Niedersachsen, N Germany 53.15N 10.25E
102 J11 **Lüneburger Heide** *heathland* NW Germany
105 Q15 **Lunel** Hérault, S France 43.40N 4.08E
103 F14 **Lünen** Nordrhein-Westfalen, W Germany 51.37N 7.31E
11 P16 **Lunenburg** Nova Scotia, SE Canada 44.22N 64.21W
23 V7 **Lunenburg** Virginia, NE USA 36.56N 78.15W
105 T5 **Lunéville** Meurthe-et-Moselle, NE France 48.34N 6.30E
85 I14 **Lunga** ≈ C Zambia
Lunga, Isola *see* Dugi Otok
164 H12 **Lungdo** Xizang Zizhiqu, W China 33.45N 82.09E
164 I14 **Lunggar** Xizang Zizhiqu, W China 31.10N 84.01E
78 I15 **Lungi** ✕ (Freetown) W Sierra Leone 8.36N 13.10W
Lungkiang *see* Qiqihar
Lungleh *see* Lunglei
159 W15 **Lunglei** *prev.* Lungleh. Mizoram, NE India 22.55N 92.49E
164 L15 **Lungsang** Xizang Zizhiqu, W China 29.49N 88.27E
84 E13 **Lungué-Bungo** *var.* Lungwebungu. ≈ Angola/Zambia *see also* Lungwebungu
85 G14 **Lungwebungu** *var.* Lungué-Bungo. ≈ Angola/Zambia *see also* Lungué-Bungo
158 F12 **Lūni** Rājasthān, N India 26.03N 73.00E
158 F12 **Lūni** ≈ N India
Luninets *see* Luninyets
37 S7 **Luning** Nevada, W USA 38.29N 118.10W
Łuniniec *see* Luninyets
131 P6 **Lunino** Penzenskaya Oblast', W Russian Federation 53.35N 45.12E
121 J19 **Luninyets** *Pol.* Łuniniec, *Rus.* Luninets. Brestskaya Voblasts', SW Belarus 52.15N 26.49E

◆ Country ● Country Capital ◇ Dependent Territory ○ Dependent Territory Capital ◈ Administrative Region ✕ International Airport ▲ Mountain ▲▲ Mountain Range Volcano ≈ River ◎ Lake ⊠ Reservoir

Lūnkaransar – Mae Tho, Doi

158 F10 **Lūnkaransar** Rājasthān, NW India 28.31N 73.49E
121 G17 **Luninyets** *Pol.* Łunna, *Rus.* Lunnna. Hrodzyenskaya Voblasts', W Belarus 53.27N 24.16E
78 I15 **Lunsar** W Sierra Leone 8.40N 12.31W
85 K14 **Lunsemfwa** ⩳ C Zambia
164 J6 **Luntai** *var.* Bügür. Xinjiang Uygur Zizhiqu, NW China 41.48N 84.14E
100 K11 **Lunteren** Gelderland, C Netherlands 52.04N 5.37E
175 O16 **Lunyuk** Sumbawa, S Indonesia 8.56S 117.15E
111 U5 **Lunz am See** Niederösterreich, C Austria 47.54N 15.01E
169 Y7 **Luobei** *var.* Fengxiang. Heilongjiang, NE China 47.35N 130.51E
Luocheng *see* Hui'an
166 J13 **Luodian** *var.* Longping. Guizhou, S China 25.25N 106.49E
166 M15 **Luoding** Guangdong, S China 22.44N 111.28E
166 M6 **Luo He** ⩳ C China
166 L5 **Luo He** ⩳ C China
167 N7 **Luohe** Henan, C China 33.37N 114.00E
Luolajarvi *see* Kuoloyarvi
Luong Nam Tha *see* Louangnamtha
166 L13 **Luoqing Jiang** ⩳ S China
167 O8 **Luoshan** Henan, C China 32.12N 114.30E
167 O12 **Luoxiao Shan** ▲ S China
167 N6 **Luoyang** *var.* Honan, Lo-yang. Henan, C China 34.40N 112.25E
167 R12 **Luoyuan** *var.* Fengshan. Fujian, SE China 26.29N 119.32E
81 F21 **Luozi** Bas-Congo, W Dem. Rep. Congo 4.57S 14.07E
85 J17 **Lupane** Matabeleland North, W Zimbabwe 18.46S 27.47E
166 I12 **Lupanshui** *prev.* Shuicheng. Guizhou, S China 26.38N 104.49E
174 Ll7 **Lupar, Batang** ⩳ East Malaysia
Lupatia *see* Altamura
118 G12 **Lupeni** *Hung.* Lupény. Hunedoara, SW Romania 45.20N 23.07E
Lupény *see* Lupeni
84 N13 **Lupiliche** Niassa, N Mozambique 11.36S 35.15E
85 E14 **Lupire** Cuando Cubango, E Angola 14.39S 19.39E
179 Rr16 **Lupon** Mindanao, S Philippines 6.53N 126.00E
81 L22 **Luputa** Kasai Oriental, S Dem. Rep. Congo 7.07S 23.43E
123 Jj17 **Luqa** ✕ (Valletta) S Malta 35.53N 14.27E
165 U11 **Luqu** *var.* Ma'ai. Gansu, C China 34.34N 102.27E
47 U5 **Luquillo, Sierra de** ▲ E Puerto Rico
28 L4 **Luray** Kansas, C USA 39.06N 98.41W
23 U4 **Luray** Virginia, NE USA 38.40N 78.27W
105 T7 **Lure** Haute-Saône, E France 47.42N 6.30E
84 D11 **Luremo** Lunda Norte, NE Angola 8.32S 17.55E
99 F15 **Lurgan** *Ir.* An Lorgain. S Northern Ireland, UK 54.28N 6.19W
59 K18 **Luribay** La Paz, W Bolivia 17.09S 67.39W
Luring *see* Gêrzê
85 Q14 **Lúrio** Nampula, NE Mozambique 13.32S 40.33E
85 P14 **Lúrio, Rio** ⩳ NE Mozambique
Luristan *see* Lorestān
Lurka *see* Lorca
85 J15 **Lusaka** ● (Zambia) Lusaka, SE Zambia 15.23S 28.16E
85 J15 **Lusaka** ◆ *province* C Zambia
85 J15 **Lusaka** ✕ Lusaka, C Zambia 15.10S 28.22E
81 L21 **Lusambo** Kasai Oriental, C Dem. Rep. Congo 4.54S 23.25E
195 N14 **Lusancay Islands and Reefs** *island group* SE PNG
81 I21 **Lusanga** Bandundu, SW Dem. Rep. Congo 4.55S 18.40E
81 N21 **Lusangi** Maniema, E Dem. Rep. Congo 4.39S 27.10E
Lusatian Mountains *see* Lausitzer Bergland
Lushar *see* Huangzhong
Lushnja *see* Lushnjë
115 K21 **Lushnjë** *var.* Lushnja. Fier, C Albania 40.54N 19.43E
83 J21 **Lushoto** Tanga, E Tanzania 4.48S 38.19E
104 L10 **Lusignan** Vienne, W France 46.25N 0.06E
35 Z15 **Lusk** Wyoming, C USA 42.45N 104.27W
Luso *see* Luena
104 L10 **Lussac-les-Châteaux** Vienne, W France 46.23N 0.44E
Lussin/Lussino *see* Lošinj
Lussinpiccolo *see* Mali Lošinj
110 I7 **Lustenau** Vorarlberg, W Austria 47.26N 9.39E
167 T14 **Lü Tao** *var.* Huoshao Dao, Lütao, *Eng.* Green Island. *island* SE Taiwan
Lūt, Baḩrat/Lut, Bahret *see* Dead Sea
24 K9 **Lutcher** Louisiana, S USA 30.02N 90.42W
149 T9 **Lūt, Dasht-e** *var.* Kavīr-e Lūt. *desert* E Iran
85 F14 **Lutembo** Moxico, E Angola 13.30S 21.21E
Lutetia/Lutetia Parisiorum *see* Paris
Luteva *see* Lodève
12 G15 **Luther Lake** ⊚ Ontario, S Canada
195 U13 **Luti** Choiseul Island, NW Solomon Islands 7.13S 157.01E
Lūt, Kavīr-e *see* Lūt, Dasht-e
99 N21 **Luton** SE England, UK 51.52N 0.25W
99 N21 **Luton** ✕ (London) SE England, UK 51.54N 0.24W
110 B10 **Lutry** Vaud, SW Switzerland 46.31N 6.31E
15 Ii8 **Łutselk'e** *prev.* Snowdrift. Northwest Territories, W Canada 62.24N 110.42W
31 Y4 **Lutsen** Minnesota, N USA 47.39N 90.37W
118 J4 **Luts'k** *Pol.* Łuck, *Rus.* Lutsk. Volyns'ka Oblast', NW Ukraine 50.45N 25.22E
Luttenberg *see* Ljutomer
Lüttich *see* Liège
85 G25 **Luttig** Western Cape, SW South Africa 32.33S 22.13E
Lutto *see* Lotta
84 E13 **Lutuai** Moxico, E Angola 12.38S 20.06E
119 Y7 **Lutuhyne** Luhans'ka Oblast', E Ukraine 48.24N 39.12E
176 Ww13 **Lutur, Pulau** *island* Kepulauan Aru, E Indonesia
25 V12 **Lutz** Florida, SE USA 28.09N 82.27W
Lutzow-Holm Bay *see* Lützow Holmbukta
205 V2 **Lützow Holmbukta** *var.* Lutzow-Holm Bay. *bay* Antarctica
83 L16 **Luuq** *It.* Lugh Ganana. Gedo, SW Somalia 3.42N 42.34E
94 M12 **Luusua** Lappi, NE Finland 66.28N 27.16E
25 Q6 **Luverne** Alabama, S USA 31.43N 86.15W
31 S11 **Luverne** Minnesota, N USA 43.39N 96.12W
81 O22 **Luvua** ⩳ SE Dem. Rep. Congo
84 F13 **Luvuei** Moxico, E Angola 13.08S 21.09E
83 H24 **Luwego** ⩳ S Tanzania
84 K12 **Luwingu** Northern, NE Zambia 10.13S 29.55E
175 Qq9 **Luwuk** *prev.* Loewoek. Sulawesi, C Indonesia 0.55S 122.46E
25 N3 **Luxapallila Creek** ⩳ Alabama/Mississippi, S USA
101 M25 **Luxembourg** ● (Luxembourg) Luxembourg, S Luxembourg 49.37N 6.07E
101 M25 **Luxembourg** *off.* Grand Duchy of Luxembourg, *var.* Lëtzebuerg, Luxemburg. ◆ *monarchy* NW Europe
101 J23 **Luxembourg** ◆ *province* SE Belgium
101 L24 **Luxembourg** ◆ *district* S Luxembourg
33 N6 **Luxemburg** Wisconsin, N USA 44.32N 87.42W
Luxemburg *see* Luxembourg
105 U7 **Luxeuil-les-Bains** Haute-Saône, E France 47.49N 6.22E
166 E13 **Luxi** *prev.* Mangshi. Yunnan, SW China 24.27N 98.31E
84 E10 **Luxico** ⩳ Angola/Dem. Rep. Congo
77 X10 **Luxor** *Ar.* Al Uqṣur. E Egypt 25.39N 32.39E
77 X10 **Luxor** ✕ C Egypt 25.39N 32.48E
166 M4 **Luya Shan** ▲ C China
104 J15 **Luy de Béarn** ⩳ SW France
104 J15 **Luy de France** ⩳ SW France
129 P12 **Luza** Kirovskaya Oblast', NW Russian Federation 60.37N 47.13E
129 Q12 **Luza** ⩳ NW Russian Federation
106 I16 **Luz, Costa de la** *coastal region* SW Spain
113 K20 **Luže** *var.* Lausche. ▲ Czech Republic/Germany *see also* Lausche 50.51N 14.40E
110 F8 **Luzern** *Fr.* Lucerne, *It.* Lucerna. Luzern, C Switzerland 47.03N 8.16E
110 E8 **Luzern** *Fr.* Lucerne. ◆ *canton* C Switzerland
166 L13 **Luzhai** Guangxi Zhuangzu Zizhiqu, S China 24.33N 109.46E
120 K12 **Luzhki** *Rus.* Luzhki. Vitsyebskaya Voblasts', N Belarus 55.20N 27.54E
166 I10 **Luzhou** Sichuan, C China 28.55N 105.28E
Lužická Nisa *see* Neisse
Lužické Hory *see* Lausitzer Bergland
Lužnice *see* Lainsitz
179 Pp9 **Luzon** *island* N Philippines
179 Oo6 **Luzon Strait** *strait* Philippines/Taiwan
118 I5 **L'viv** *Ger.* Lemberg, *Pol.* Lwów, *Rus.* L'vov. L'vivs'ka Oblast', W Ukraine 49.49N 24.04E
L'viv *see* L'vivs'ka Oblast'
118 I4 **L'vivs'ka Oblast'** *var.* L'viv, *Rus.* L'vovskaya Oblast'. ◆ *province* NW Ukraine
L'vov *see* L'viv
L'vovskaya Oblast' *see* L'vivs'ka Oblast'
Lwena *see* Luena
Lwów *see* L'viv
112 F11 **Lwówek** *Ger.* Neustadt bei Pinne. Wielkolpolskie, C Poland 52.27N 16.10E
113 E14 **Lwówek Śląski** *Ger.* Löwenberg in Schlesien. Dolnośląskie, SW Poland 51.06N 15.35E
121 I18 **Lyakhavichy** *Rus.* Lyakhovichi. Brestskaya Voblasts', SW Belarus 53.01N 26.15E
Lyakhovichi *see* Lyakhavichy
193 B22 **Lyall, Mount** ▲ South Island, NZ 45.14S 167.31E
Lyallpur *see* Faisalābād
125 G10 **Lyamin** ⩳ C Russian Federation
Lyangar *see* Langar
125 G10 **Lyantor** Khanty-Mansiyskiy Avtonomnyy Okrug, C Russian Federation 61.40N 72.21E
128 H11 **Lyaskelya** Respublika Kareliya, NW Russian Federation 61.42N 31.06E
121 I18 **Lyasnaya** *Rus.* Lesnaya. Brestskaya Voblasts', SW Belarus 52.58N 25.46E
121 F19 **Lyasnaya** *Pol.* Leśna, *Rus.* Lesnaya. ⩳ SW Belarus
128 H15 **Lychkovo** Novgorodskaya Oblast', W Russian Federation 57.55N 32.24E
Lyck *see* Ełk
95 I15 **Lycksele** Västerbotten, N Sweden 64.34N 18.40E
20 G13 **Lycoming Creek** ⩳ Pennsylvania, NE USA
Lycopolis *see* Asyūt
205 N3 **Lyddan Island** *island* Antarctica
85 K20 **Lydenburg** Mpumalanga, NE South Africa 25.01S 30.27E
121 L20 **Lyel'chytsy** *Rus.* Lel'chitsy. Homyel'skaya Voblasts', SE Belarus 51.46N 28.19E
121 P14 **Lyenina** *Rus.* Lenino. Mahilyowskaya Voblasts', E Belarus 54.26N 31.07E
120 L13 **Lyepyel'** *Rus.* Lepel'. Vitsyebskaya Voblasts', N Belarus 54.54N 28.43E
27 S17 **Lyford** Texas, SW USA 26.24N 97.47W
97 E17 **Lygna** ⩳ S Norway
20 G14 **Lykens** Pennsylvania, NE USA 40.33N 76.42W
117 E21 **Lykódimo** ▲ S Greece 36.56N 21.49E
99 K24 **Lyme Bay** *bay* S England, UK
99 K24 **Lyme Regis** S England, UK 50.44N 2.55W
112 L7 **Łyna** *Ger.* Alle. ⩳ N Poland
31 P12 **Lynch** Nebraska, C USA 42.49N 98.27W
22 J10 **Lynchburg** Tennessee, S USA 35.15N 86.22W
23 T6 **Lynchburg** Virginia, NE USA 37.24N 79.08W
23 T12 **Lynches River** ⩳ South Carolina, SE USA
34 H6 **Lynden** Washington, NW USA 48.57N 122.27W
190 I5 **Lyndhurst** South Australia 30.19S 138.20E
29 Q5 **Lyndon** Kansas, C USA 38.37N 95.40W
21 N7 **Lyndonville** Vermont, NE USA 44.31N 71.58W
97 D18 **Lyngdal** Vest-Agder, S Norway 58.07N 7.04E
94 I9 **Lyngen** *Lapp.* Ivgovuotna. *inlet* Arctic Ocean
97 G17 **Lyngør** Aust-Agder, S Norway 58.38N 9.05E
94 I9 **Lyngseidet** Troms, N Norway 69.36N 20.07E
21 P11 **Lynn** Massachusetts, NE USA 42.28N 70.57W
Lynn *see* King's Lynn
25 R9 **Lynn Haven** Florida, SE USA 30.15N 85.39W
9 V11 **Lynn Lake** Manitoba, C Canada 56.51N 101.01W
Lynn Regis *see* King's Lynn
120 I13 **Lyntupy** *Rus.* Lyntupy. Vitsyebskaya Voblasts', NW Belarus 55.03N 26.19E
105 R11 **Lyon** *Eng.* Lyons; *anc.* Lugdunum. Rhône, E France 45.46N 4.49E
15 H3 **Lyon, Cape** *headland* Northwest Territories, NW Canada 69.47N 123.10W
20 K6 **Lyon Mountain** ▲ New York, NE USA 44.42N 73.52W
105 Q11 **Lyonnais, Monts du** ▲ C France
67 N25 **Lyon Point** *headland* SE Tristan da Cunha 37.06S 12.13W
190 E5 **Lyons** South Australia 30.40S 133.50E
39 T3 **Lyons** Colorado, C USA 40.13N 105.16W
25 V6 **Lyons** Georgia, SE USA 32.12N 82.19W
28 M5 **Lyons** Kansas, C USA 38.21N 98.12W
31 R14 **Lyons** Nebraska, C USA 41.56N 96.28W
20 G10 **Lyons** New York, NE USA 43.03N 76.58W
Lyons *see* Lyon
120 O13 **Lyozna** *Rus.* Liozno. Vitsyebskaya Voblasts', NE Belarus 55.01N 30.48E
119 S4 **Lypova Dolyna** Sums'ka Oblast', NE Ukraine 50.36N 33.50E
119 N6 **Lypovets'** *Rus.* Lipovets. Vinnyts'ka Oblast', C Ukraine 49.13N 29.06E
Lys *see* Leie
113 I18 **Lysá Hora** ▲ E Czech Republic 49.31N 18.27E
97 D16 **Lysefjorden** *fjord* S Norway
97 I18 **Lysekil** Västra Götaland, S Sweden 58.16N 11.25E
Lyser *see* Akdoğan
35 V14 **Lysite** Wyoming, C USA 43.16N 107.42W
131 P3 **Lyskovo** Nizhegorodskaya Oblast', W Russian Federation 56.04N 45.01E
110 D8 **Lyss** Bern, W Switzerland 47.04N 7.19E
97 H22 **Lystrup** Århus, C Denmark 56.13N 10.13E
129 V14 **Lys'va** Permskaya Oblast', NW Russian Federation 58.04N 57.48E
119 P6 **Lysyanka** Cherkas'ka Oblast', C Ukraine 49.15N 30.50E
119 X6 **Lysychans'k** *Rus.* Lisichansk. Luhans'ka Oblast', E Ukraine 48.52N 38.27E
99 K17 **Lytham St Anne's** NW England, UK 53.45N 3.01W
193 I19 **Lyttelton** Canterbury, South Island, NZ 43.35S 172.44E
8 M17 **Lytton** British Columbia, SW Canada 50.12N 121.34W
121 L18 **Lyuban'** *Rus.* Lyuban'. Minskaya Voblasts', S Belarus 52.48N 28.00E
121 L18 **Lyubanskaye Vodaskhovishcha** ⊞ C Belarus
118 M5 **Lyubar** Zhytomyrs'ka Oblast', N Ukraine 49.54N 27.48E
Lyubashëvka *see* Lyubashivka
119 O8 **Lyubashivka** *Rus.* Lyubashëvka. Odes'ka Oblast', SW Ukraine 47.49N 30.18E
121 I16 **Lyubcha** *Pol.* Lubcz, *Rus.* Lyubcha. Hrodzyenskaya Voblasts', W Belarus 53.46N 26.04E
130 L4 **Lyubertsy** Moskovskaya Oblast', W Russian Federation 55.37N 38.02E
118 K2 **Lyubeshiv** Volyns'ka Oblast', NW Ukraine 51.46N 25.33E
128 M14 **Lyubim** Yaroslavskaya Oblast', NW Russian Federation 58.21N 40.46E
116 K11 **Lyubimets** Khaskovo, S Bulgaria 41.51N 26.03E
Lyublin *see* Lublin
118 I3 **Lyuboml'** *Pol.* Luboml. Volyns'ka Oblast', NW Ukraine 51.12N 24.01E
Lyubotin *see* Lyubotyn
119 U5 **Lyubotyn** *Rus.* Lyubotin. Kharkivs'ka Oblast', E Ukraine 49.57N 35.57E
130 I5 **Lyudinovo** Kaluzhskaya Oblast', W Russian Federation 53.52N 34.28E
131 T2 **Lyuk** Udmurtskaya Respublika, NW Russian Federation 56.55N 52.45E
116 M9 **Lyulyakovo** *prev.* Keremitlik. Burgas, E Bulgaria 42.53N 27.05E
121 I18 **Lyusina** *Rus.* Lyusino. Brestskaya Voblasts', SW Belarus 52.37N 26.31E
Lyusino *see* Lyusina

M

144 G9 **Ma'ād** Irbid, N Jordan 32.37N 35.36E
Ma'ai *see* Luqu
Maalahti *see* Malax
Maale *see* Male'
144 G13 **Ma'ān** Ma'ān, SW Jordan 30.10N 35.45E
144 H13 **Ma'ān** *off.* Muḩāfaẓat Ma'ān, *var.* Ma'an, Ma'ān. ◆ *governorate* S Jordan
95 M16 **Maaninka** Itä-Suomi, C Finland 63.10N 27.19E
168 K7 **Maanīt** Bulgan, C Mongolia 48.17N 103.29E
168 M8 **Maanīt** Töv, C Mongolia 47.14N 107.34E
95 N15 **Maanselkä** Oulu, C Finland 63.53N 28.27E
167 Q8 **Ma'anshan** Anhui, E China 31.45N 118.31E
196 F16 **Maap** *island* Caroline Islands, W Micronesia
120 H3 **Maardu** *Ger.* Maart. Harjumaa, NW Estonia 59.28N 25.01E
Ma'aret-en-Nu'man *see* Ma'arrat an Nu'mān
101 K16 **Maarheeze** Noord-Brabant, SE Netherlands 51.19N 5.37E
Maarianhamina *see* Mariehamn
144 I4 **Ma'arrat an Nu'mān** *var.* Ma'aret-en-Nu'man, *Fr.* Maarret enn Naamâne. Idlib, NW Syria 35.40N 36.40E
Maarret enn Naamâne *see* Ma'arrat an Nu'mān
100 I11 **Maarssen** Utrecht, C Netherlands 52.07N 5.03E
Maart *see* Maardu
101 L17 **Maas** *Fr.* Meuse. ⩳ W Europe *see also* Meuse
101 M15 **Maasbree** Limburg, SE Netherlands 51.22N 6.03E
101 L17 **Maaseik** *prev.* Maeseyck. Limburg, NE Belgium 51.04N 5.48E
179 R13 **Maasin** Leyte, C Philippines 10.10N 124.55E
101 L17 **Maasmechelen** Limburg, NE Belgium 50.58N 5.42E
100 G12 **Maassluis** Zuid-Holland, SW Netherlands 51.55N 4.15E
101 L18 **Maastricht** *var.* Maestricht; *anc.* Traietum ad Mosam, Traiectum Tungorum. Limburg, SE Netherlands 50.51N 5.42E
191 N18 **Maatsuyker Group** *island group* Tasmania, SE Australia
Maba *see* Qujiang
85 L20 **Mabalane** Gaza, S Mozambique 23.43S 32.37E
27 V7 **Mabank** Texas, SW USA 32.22N 96.06W
172 N10 **Mabechi-gawa** *var.* Mabuchi-gawa. ⩳ Honshū, C Japan
99 O18 **Mablethorpe** E England, UK 53.20N 0.14E
176 W9 **Maboi** Papua, E Indonesia 1.00S 134.02E
85 M19 **Mabote** Inhambane, S Mozambique 22.03S 34.09E
34 J10 **Mabton** Washington, NW USA 46.13N 120.00W
Mabuchi-gawa *see* Mabechi-gawa
85 H20 **Mabutsane** Southern, S Botswana 24.22S 23.34E
65 G19 **Macá, Cerro** ▲ S Chile 45.07S 73.11W
62 Q9 **Macaé** Rio de Janeiro, SE Brazil 22.21S 41.48W
84 N13 **Macaloge** Niassa, N Mozambique 12.30S 35.25E
Macan *see* Bonerate, Kepulauan
167 N15 **Macao** *Chin.* Aomen, *Port.* Macau. S China
106 H9 **Mação** Santarém, C Portugal 39.33N 8.00W
60 J11 **Macapá** *state capital* Amapá, N Brazil 0.04N 51.04W
45 S17 **Macaracas** Los Santos, S Panama 7.43N 80.33W
57 P6 **Macare, Caño** ⩳ NE Venezuela
57 Q6 **Macareo, Caño** ⩳ NE Venezuela
Macarsca *see* Makarska
MacArthur *see* Ormoc
190 L12 **Macarthur** Victoria, SE Australia 38.04S 142.02E
58 C7 **Macas** Morona Santiago, SE Ecuador 2.22S 78.07W
Macassar *see* Makassar
61 Q14 **Macau** Rio Grande do Norte, E Brazil 5.04S 36.37W
Macau *see* Macao
Macău *see* Makó, Hungary
67 E24 **Macbride Head** *headland* East Falkland, Falkland Islands 51.25S 57.55W
25 V9 **Macclenny** Florida, SE USA 30.16N 82.07W
99 L18 **Macclesfield** C England, UK 53.16N 2.07W
198 F6 **Macclesfield Bank** *undersea feature* N South China Sea
MacCluer Gulf *see* Berau, Teluk
189 N7 **Macdonald, Lake** *salt lake* Western Australia
189 Q7 **Macdonnell Ranges** ▲ Northern Territory, C Australia
98 K8 **Macduff** NE Scotland, UK 57.39N 2.28W
106 I6 **Macedo de Cavaleiros** Bragança, N Portugal 41.31N 6.57W
Macedonia Central *see* Kentrikí Makedonía
Macedonia East and Thrace *see* Anatolikí Makedonía kai Thráki
115 O19 **Macedonia, FYR** *off.* the Former Yugoslav Republic of Macedonia, *var.* Macedonia, *Mac.* Makedonija, *abbrev.* FYR Macedonia, FYROM. ◆ *republic* SE Europe
Macedonia West *see* Dytikí Makedonía
61 Q16 **Maceió** *state capital* Alagoas, E Brazil 9.40S 35.43W
78 K15 **Macenta** Guinée-Forestière, SE Guinea 8.31N 9.31W
108 J12 **Macerata** Marche, C Italy 43.19N 13.28E
9 S11 **MacFarlane** ⩳ Saskatchewan, C Canada
190 H7 **Macfarlane, Lake** *var.* Lake Mcfarlane. ⊚ South Australia
Macgillicuddy's Reeks Mountains *see* Macgillycuddy's Reeks
99 B21 **Macgillycuddy's Reeks** *var.* Macgillicuddy's Reeks Mountains, *Ir.* Na Cruacha Dubha. ▲ SW Ireland
9 X16 **MacGregor** Manitoba, S Canada 49.58N 98.49W
155 O10 **Mach** Baluchistān, SW Pakistan 29.52N 67.19E
58 C6 **Machachi** Pichincha, C Ecuador 0.33S 78.34W
85 M19 **Machaila** Gaza, S Mozambique 22.15S 32.57E
Machaire Fíolta *see* Magherafelt
Machaire Rátha *see* Maghera
83 I19 **Machakos** Eastern, S Kenya 1.33S 37.17E
58 B8 **Machala** El Oro, SW Ecuador 3.19S 79.57W
Machali *see* Madoi
85 J19 **Machaneng** Central, SE Botswana 23.12S 27.28E
85 M18 **Machanga** Sofala, E Mozambique 20.55S 35.03E
82 G13 **Machar Marshes** *wetland* SE Sudan
104 I8 **Machecoul** Loire-Atlantique, NW France 46.59N 1.51W
167 O8 **Macheng** Hubei, C China 31.10N 115.00E
161 J16 **Mācherla** Andhra Pradesh, C India 16.28N 79.25E
159 O11 **Machhapuchhre** ▲ C Nepal 28.30N 83.57E
21 T6 **Machias** Maine, NE USA 44.43N 67.28W
21 R3 **Machias River** ⩳ Maine, NE USA
21 T6 **Machias River** ⩳ Maine, NE USA
66 P5 **Machico** Madeira, Portugal, NE Atlantic Ocean 32.43N 16.46W
161 K16 **Machilīpatnam** *var.* Bandar Masulipatnam. Andhra Pradesh, E India 16.12N 81.10E
56 G5 **Machiques** Zulia, NW Venezuela 10.01N 72.40W
59 G15 **Machupicchu** Cusco, C Peru 13.07S 72.30W
85 M20 **Macia** *var.* Vila de Macia. Gaza, S Mozambique 25.01S 33.05E
Macías Nguema Biyogo *see* Bioco, Isla de
118 M13 **Măcin** Tulcea, SE Romania 45.15N 28.09E
191 T4 **Macintyre River** ⩳ New South Wales/Queensland, SE Australia
189 Y7 **Mackay** Queensland, NE Australia 21.10S 149.10E
189 O7 **Mackay, Lake** *salt lake* Northern Territory/Western Australia
8 M13 **Mackenzie** British Columbia, W Canada 55.18N 123.09W
15 Gg6 **Mackenzie** ⩳ Northwest Territories, NW Canada
205 Y6 **Mackenzie Bay** *bay* Antarctica
8 J1 **Mackenzie Bay** *bay* NW Canada
2 D9 **Mackenzie Delta** *delta* Northwest Territories, NW Canada
207 P8 **Mackenzie King Island** *island* Queen Elizabeth Islands, Northwest Territories, N Canada
14 G5 **Mackenzie Mountains** ▲ Northwest Territories, NW Canada
33 Q5 **Mackinac, Straits of** ⊚ Michigan, N USA
204 K5 **Mackintosh, Cape** *headland* Antarctica 72.52S 60.00W
9 R15 **Macklin** Saskatchewan, S Canada 52.19N 109.51W
191 V6 **Macksville** New South Wales, SE Australia 30.39S 152.54E
191 V5 **Maclean** New South Wales, SE Australia 29.30S 153.15E
85 J24 **Maclear** Eastern Cape, SE South Africa 31.04S 28.22E
191 U6 **Macleay River** ⩳ New South Wales, SE Australia
MacLeod *see* Fort Macleod
188 G9 **Macleod, Lake** ⊚ Western Australia
8 I6 **Macmillan** ⩳ Yukon Territory, NW Canada
32 J12 **Macomb** Illinois, N USA 40.27N 90.40W
109 B18 **Macomer** Sardegna, Italy, C Mediterranean Sea 40.14N 8.46E
84 Q13 **Macomia** Cabo Delgado, NE Mozambique 12.15S 40.06E
25 T5 **Macon** Georgia, SE USA 32.48N 83.41W
25 N4 **Macon** Mississippi, S USA 33.06N 88.33W
29 U3 **Macon** Missouri, C USA 39.44N 92.28W
105 R10 **Mâcon** *anc.* Matisco, Matisco Ædourum. Saône-et-Loire, C France 46.19N 4.48E
24 J6 **Macon, Bayou** ⩳ Arkansas/Louisiana, S USA
84 G13 **Macondo** Moxico, E Angola 12.31S 23.45E
85 M16 **Macossa** Manica, C Mozambique 17.51S 33.54E
9 T12 **Macoun Lake** ⊚ Saskatchewan, C Canada
32 K14 **Macoupin Creek** ⩳ Illinois, N USA
Macouria *see* Tonate
85 N18 **Macovane** Inhambane, SE Mozambique 21.30S 35.07E
191 N17 **Macquarie Harbour** *inlet* Tasmania, SE Australia
199 Ii15 **Macquarie Island** *island* NZ, SW Pacific Ocean
191 T8 **Macquarie, Lake** *lagoon* New South Wales, SE Australia
191 Q6 **Macquarie Marshes** *wetland* New South Wales, SE Australia
183 O13 **Macquarie Ridge** *undersea feature* SW Pacific Ocean
191 Q6 **Macquarie River** ⩳ New South Wales, SE Australia
191 P17 **Macquarie River** ⩳ Tasmania, SE Australia
205 V5 **Mac. Robertson Land** *physical region* Antarctica
99 C21 **Macroom** *Ir.* Maigh Chromtha. SW Ireland 51.54N 8.57W
44 G5 **Macuelizo** Santa Bárbara, NW Honduras 15.21N 88.31W
190 G2 **Macumba River** ⩳ South Australia
59 I16 **Macusani** Puno, S Peru 14.07S 70.27W
58 E8 **Macusari, Río** ⩳ N Peru
43 U15 **Macuspana** Tabasco, SE Mexico 17.43N 92.36W
144 G10 **Ma'dabā** *var.* Mādabā, Madeba; *anc.* Medeba. Al 'Āṣimah NW Jordan 31.43N 35.48E
180 G2 **Madagascar** *off.* Democratic Republic of Madagascar, *Malg.* Madagasikara; *prev.* Malagasy Republic. ◆ *republic* W Indian Ocean
180 I5 **Madagascar** *island* W Indian Ocean
132 L17 **Madagascar Basin** *undersea feature* W Indian Ocean
132 L16 **Madagascar Plain** *undersea feature* W Indian Ocean
69 Y14 **Madagascar Plateau** *var.* Madagascar Ridge, Madagascar Rise, *Rus.* Madagaskarskiy Khrebet. *undersea feature* W Indian Ocean
Madagascar Ridge/ Madagascar Rise *see* Madagascar Plateau
Madagasikara *see* Madagascar
Madagaskarskiy Khrebet *see* Madagascar Plateau
66 N2 **Madalena** Pico, Azores, Portugal, NE Atlantic Ocean 38.31N 28.15W
79 Y6 **Madama** Agadez, NE Niger 21.54N 13.43E
116 J12 **Madan** Smolyan, S Bulgaria 41.30N 24.58E
161 I19 **Madanapalle** Andhra Pradesh, E India 13.33N 78.31E
194 I11 **Madang** Madang, N PNG 5.09S 145.48E
194 I11 **Madang** ◆ *province* N PNG
152 G7 **Madaniyat** *Rus.* Madeniyet. Qoraqalpog'iston Respublikasi, W Uzbekistan 42.48N 59.00E
Madanīyīn *see* Médenine
79 U11 **Madaoua** Tahoua, SW Niger 14.06N 6.01E
Madaras *see* Vtáčnik
159 U15 **Madaripur** Dhaka, C Bangladesh 23.09N 90.10E
79 U12 **Madarounfa** Maradi, S Niger 13.16N 7.07E
Mad'arska *see* Hungary
Madau *see* Madaw
195 P15 **Madau Island** *island* SE PNG
152 B13 **Madaw** *Rus.* Madau. Balkan Welaýaty, W Turkmenistan 38.11N 54.46E
21 S1 **Madawaska** Maine, NE USA 47.19N 68.19W
12 J13 **Madawaska** ⩳ Ontario, SE Canada
Madawaska Highlands *see* Haliburton Highlands
177 G4 **Madaya** Mandalay, C Myanmar 22.12N 96.04E
109 K17 **Maddaloni** Campania, S Italy 41.03N 14.22E
31 O3 **Maddock** North Dakota, N USA 47.57N 99.31W
101 I14 **Made** Noord-Brabant, S Netherlands 51.40N 4.48E
Madeba *see* Ma'dabā
66 L9 **Madeira** *var.* Ilha de Madeira. *island* Madeira, Portugal, NE Atlantic Ocean
Madeira, Ilha de *see* Madeira
66 O5 **Madeira Islands** *Port.* Região Autoónoma da Madeira. ◆ *autonomous region* Madeira, Portugal, NE Atlantic Ocean
66 L9 **Madeira Plain** *undersea feature* E Atlantic Ocean
66 L9 **Madeira Ridge** *undersea feature* E Atlantic Ocean
61 F14 **Madeira, Rio** *Sp.* Río Madera. ⩳ Bolivia/Brazil *see also* Madera, Río
103 J25 **Madelegabel** ▲ Austria/Germany 47.18N 10.19E
13 X6 **Madeleine** ⩳ Québec, SE Canada
13 X5 **Madeleine, Cap de la** *headland* Québec, SE Canada 49.13N 65.20W
11 Q13 **Madeleine, Îles de la** *Eng.* Magdalen Islands. *island group* Québec, E Canada
31 U10 **Madelia** Minnesota, N USA 44.03N 94.26W
37 P3 **Madeline** California, W USA 41.02N 120.28W
32 K3 **Madeline Island** *island* Apostle Islands, Wisconsin, N USA
143 O15 **Maden** Elazığ, SE Turkey 38.24N 39.42E
151 V12 **Madeniyet** Vostochnyy Kazakhstan, E Kazakhstan 47.51N 78.37E
Madeniyet *see* Madaniyat
42 H5 **Madera** Chihuahua, N Mexico 29.10N 108.10W
37 Q10 **Madera** California, W USA 36.57N 120.02W
58 L13 **Madera, Río** *Port.* Rio Madeira. ⩳ Bolivia/Brazil *see also* Madeira, Rio
108 D6 **Madesimo** Lombardia, N Italy 46.20N 9.26E
147 O14 **Madhāb, Wādī** *dry watercourse* NW Yemen
159 R13 **Madhepura** *prev.* Madhipure. Bihār, NE India 25.55N 86.48E
Madhipure *see* Madhepura
159 Q13 **Madhubani** Bihār, N India 26.21N 86.04E
159 Q15 **Madhupur** Jhārkhand, NE India 24.16N 86.37E
160 I10 **Madhya Pradesh** *prev.* Central Provinces and Berar. ◆ *state* C India
59 K15 **Madidi, Río** ⩳ W Bolivia
161 F20 **Madikeri** *prev.* Mercara. Karnātaka, W India 12.28N 75.40E
29 O13 **Madill** Oklahoma, C USA 34.05N 96.46W
81 G21 **Madimba** Bas-Congo, SW Dem. Rep. Congo 4.58S 15.07E
144 M4 **Ma'dīn** Ar Raqqah, C Syria 35.45N 39.36E
Madīnah, Minṭaqat al *see* Al Madīnah
78 M14 **Madinani** NW Ivory Coast 9.37N 6.57W
147 O17 **Madīnat ash Sha'b** *prev.* Al Ittiḩād. SW Yemen 12.52N 44.55E
144 K3 **Madīnat ath Thawrah** *var.* Ath Thawrah. Ar Raqqah, N Syria Asia 35.36N 39.00E
181 O6 **Madingley Rise** *undersea feature* W Indian Ocean
81 E21 **Madingo-Kayes** Le Kouilou, S Congo 4.25S 11.40E
81 F21 **Madingou** La Bouenza, S Congo 4.10S 13.33E
Madioen *see* Madiun
25 U8 **Madison** Florida, SE USA 30.27N 83.24W
25 T3 **Madison** Georgia, SE USA 33.37N 83.28W
33 P15 **Madison** Indiana, N USA 38.44N 85.22W
29 P6 **Madison** Kansas, C USA 38.08N 96.08W
21 Q6 **Madison** Maine, NE USA 44.48N 69.52W
31 S9 **Madison** Minnesota, N USA 45.00N 96.12W
24 K5 **Madison** Mississippi, S USA 32.27N 90.07W
31 Q14 **Madison** Nebraska, C USA 41.49N 97.27W
31 R10 **Madison** South Dakota, N USA 44.00N 97.06W
23 V5 **Madison** Virginia, NE USA 38.24N 78.12W
23 Q5 **Madison** West Virginia, NE USA 38.04N 81.49W
32 L9 **Madison** *state capital* Wisconsin, N USA 43.04N 89.22W
23 T6 **Madison Heights** Virginia, NE USA 37.25N 79.07W
22 I6 **Madisonville** Kentucky, S USA 37.19N 87.30W
22 M10 **Madisonville** Tennessee, S USA 35.31N 84.21W
27 V9 **Madisonville** Texas, SW USA 30.57N 95.54W
174 Ll15 **Madiun** *prev.* Madioen. Jawa, C Indonesia 7.37S 111.33E
Madjene *see* Majene
12 J14 **Madoc** Ontario, SE Canada 44.31N 77.27W
Madoera *see* Madura, Pulau
83 J18 **Mado Gashi** North Eastern, E Kenya 0.40N 39.09E
165 R11 **Madoi** *var.* Machali. Qinghai, C China 34.53N 98.07E
201 O13 **Madolenihmw** Pohnpei, E Micronesia
120 I9 **Madona** *Ger.* Modohn. Madona, E Latvia 56.51N 26.10E
109 J23 **Madonie** ▲ Sicilia, Italy, C Mediterranean Sea
147 Y11 **Madrakah, Ra's** *headland* E Oman 18.56N 57.54E
34 I12 **Madras** Oregon, NW USA 44.37N 121.07W
Madras *see* Chennai
59 H14 **Madre de Dios** *off.* Departamento de Madre de Dios. ◆ *department* E Peru
65 F22 **Madre de Dios, Isla** *island* S Chile
59 J14 **Madre de Dios, Río** ⩳ Bolivia/Peru
27 T16 **Madre, Laguna** ⊚ Texas, SW USA
43 Q9 **Madre, Laguna** *lagoon* NE Mexico
39 Q12 **Madre Mount** ▲ New Mexico, SW USA 34.18N 107.54W
107 N8 **Madrid** ● (Spain) Madrid, C Spain 40.25N 3.43W
31 V14 **Madrid** Iowa, C USA 41.52N 93.49W
107 N7 **Madrid** ◆ *autonomous community* C Spain
107 N10 **Madridejos** Castilla-La Mancha, C Spain 39.28N 3.31W
106 L7 **Madrigal de las Altas Torres** Castilla-León, N Spain 41.05N 5.00W
106 K10 **Madrigalejo** Extremadura, W Spain 39.08N 5.36W
36 L3 **Mad River** ⩳ California, W USA
44 J8 **Madriz** ◆ *department* NW Nicaragua
106 K10 **Madroñera** Extremadura, W Spain 39.25N 5.46W
189 N12 **Madura** Western Australia 31.52S 127.01E
Madura *see* Madurai
161 H22 **Madurai** *prev.* Madura, Mathurai. Tamil Nādu, S India 9.55N 78.07E
174 M15 **Madura, Pulau** *prev.* Madoera. *island* C Indonesia
174 Mm15 **Madura, Selat** *strait* C Indonesia
131 Q17 **Madzhalis** Respublika Dagestan, SW Russian Federation 42.12N 47.46E
116 K12 **Madzharovo** Khaskovo, S Bulgaria 41.36N 25.52E
85 M14 **Madzimoyo** Eastern, E Zambia 13.39S 32.31E
171 K15 **Maebashi** *var.* Maebasi, Mayebashi. Gunma, Honshū, S Japan 36.24N 139.01E
Maebasi *see* Maebashi
178 Hh6 **Mae Chan** Chiang Rai, NW Thailand 20.13N 99.52E
178 Gg7 **Mae Hong Son** *var.* Maehongson, Muai To. Mae Hong Son, NW Thailand 19.16N 97.55E
Mae Nam Khong *see* Mekong
178 Hh7 **Mae Nam Nan** ⩳ NW Thailand
178 H10 **Mae Nam Tha Chin** ⩳ W Thailand
178 Hh7 **Mae Nam Yom** ⩳ W Thailand
178 H7 **Mae Sariang** Mae Hong Son, NW Thailand 18.07N 97.57E
39 O3 **Maeser** Utah, W USA 40.28N 109.35W
Maeseyck *see* Maaseik
178 Gg9 **Mae Sot** *var.* Ban Mae Sot. Tak, W Thailand 16.43N 98.31E
Maestricht *see* Maastricht
178 H7 **Mae Suai** *var.* Ban Mae Suai. Chiang Rai, NW Thailand 19.36N 99.32E
178 H7 **Mae Tho, Doi** ▲ NW Thailand 18.56N 99.20E

◆ Country ● Country Capital ◇ Dependent Territory ○ Dependent Territory Capital ◆ Administrative Region ✕ International Airport ▲ Mountain ▲ Mountain Range ⛰ Volcano ⩳ River ⊚ Lake ⊞ Reservoir

MAEVATANANA – MALTA

180 I4 **Maevatanana** Mahajanga, C Madagascar 16.57S 46.49E
197 C12 **Maéwo** prev. Aurora. island C Vanuatu
175 T8 **Mafa** Pulau Halmahera, E Indonesia 0.01N 127.49E
85 I23 **Mafeteng** W Lesotho 29.48S 27.15E
101 J21 **Maffe** Namur, SE Belgium 50.21N 5.19E
176 Y10 **Maffin** Papua, E Indonesia 1.57S 138.48E
191 P12 **Maffra** Victoria, SE Australia 37.59S 147.03E
83 K23 **Mafia** island E Tanzania
83 J23 **Mafia Channel** sea waterway E Tanzania
85 I21 **Mafikeng** North-West, N South Africa 25.52S 25.39E
62 J12 **Mafra** Santa Catarina, S Brazil 26.07S 49.46W
106 F10 **Mafra** Lisboa, C Portugal 38.57N 9.19W
149 Q17 **Mafraq** Abū Ẓaby, C UAE 24.21N 54.33E
Mafraq/Mafraq, Muḥāfaẓat al see Al Mafraq
127 O10 **Magadan** Magadanskaya Oblast', E Russian Federation 59.37N 150.49E
127 Nn8 **Magadanskaya Oblast'** ◈ province E Russian Federation
110 G11 **Magadino** Ticino, S Switzerland 46.09N 8.50E
65 G23 **Magallanes** off. Región de Magallanes y de la Antártica Chilena. ◈ region S Chile
Magallanes see Punta Arenas
Magallanes, Estrecho de see Magellan, Strait of
12 I10 **Maganasipi, Lac** ◎ Québec, SE Canada
56 F6 **Magangué** Bolívar, N Colombia 9.13N 74.46W
Magareva see Mangareva
79 V12 **Magaria** Zinder, S Niger 13.00N 8.55E
194 M16 **Magarida** Central, SW PNG 10.13S 149.17E
179 Pp9 **Magat** ≈ Luzon, N Philippines
29 T11 **Magazine Mountain** ▲ Arkansas, C USA 35.10N 93.38W
78 I15 **Magburaka** C Sierra Leone 8.43N 11.57W
126 M14 **Magdagachi** Amurskaya Oblast', SE Russian Federation 53.25N 125.41E
64 O12 **Magdalena** Buenos Aires, E Argentina 35.04S 57.30W
59 M15 **Magdalena** Beni, N Bolivia 13.22S 64.07W
42 F4 **Magdalena** Sonora, NW Mexico 30.37N 110.58W
39 Q13 **Magdalena** New Mexico, SW USA 34.07N 107.14W
56 F5 **Magdalena** off. Departamento del Magdalena. ◈ province N Colombia
42 E9 **Magdalena, Bahía** bay W Mexico
65 G19 **Magdalena, Isla** island Archipiélago de los Chonos, S Chile
42 D8 **Magdalena, Isla** island W Mexico
49 P6 **Magdalena, Río** ≈ C Colombia
42 F4 **Magdalena, Río** ≈ NW Mexico
Magdalen Islands see Madeleine, Îles de la
102 L13 **Magdeburg** Sachsen-Anhalt, C Germany 52.07N 11.39E
24 L6 **Magee** Mississippi, S USA 31.52N 89.43W
174 Kk15 **Magelang** Jawa, C Indonesia 7.28S 110.10E
199 J7 **Magellan Rise** undersea feature C Pacific Ocean
65 H24 **Magellan, Strait of** Sp. Estrecho de Magallanes. strait Argentina/Chile
108 D7 **Magenta** Lombardia, NW Italy 45.28N 8.52E
Magerøy see Magerøya
94 K7 **Magerøya** var. Magerøy, Lapp. Máhkarávju. island N Norway
170 B17 **Mage-shima** island Nansei-shotō, SW Japan
110 G11 **Maggia** Ticino, S Switzerland 46.15N 8.42E
110 G10 **Maggia** ≈ SW Switzerland
Maggiore, Lago see Maggiore, Lake
108 C6 **Maggiore, Lake** It. Lago Maggiore. ◎ Italy/Switzerland
46 I12 **Maggotty** W Jamaica 18.09N 77.46W
78 I10 **Maghama** Gorgol, S Mauritania 15.31N 12.49W
99 F14 **Maghera** Ir. Machaire Rátha. C Northern Ireland, UK 54.51N 6.40W
99 F15 **Magherafelt** Ir. Machaire Fíolta. C Northern Ireland, UK 54.45N 6.36W
196 H6 **Magicienne Bay** bay Saipan, S Northern Mariana Islands
107 O13 **Magina** ▲ S Spain 37.43N 3.24W
83 H24 **Magingo** Ruvuma, S Tanzania 9.57S 35.23E
126 Jj14 **Magistral'nyy** Irkutskaya Oblast', S Russian Federation 56.18N 107.27E
114 H11 **Maglaj** Federacija Bosna I Hercegovina, N Bosnia and Herzegovina 44.32N 18.03E
109 Q19 **Maglie** Puglia, SE Italy 40.07N 18.18E
38 L2 **Magna** Utah, W USA 40.42N 112.06W
Magnesia see Manisa
12 G12 **Magnetawan** ≈ Ontario, S Canada
125 Dd12 **Magnitogorsk** Chelyabinskaya Oblast', C Russian Federation 53.28N 59.06E
29 T14 **Magnolia** Arkansas, C USA 33.16N 93.14W
24 K7 **Magnolia** Mississippi, S USA 31.08N 90.27W
27 V10 **Magnolia** Texas, SW USA 30.12N 95.46W
Magnolia State see Mississippi
97 J15 **Magnor** Hedmark, S Norway 59.57N 12.14E
197 K14 **Mago** prev. Mango. island Lau Group, E Fiji
85 L15 **Màgoé** Tete, NW Mozambique 15.51S 31.49E
13 Q13 **Magog** Québec, SE Canada 45.16N 72.09W
85 J15 **Magoye** Southern, S Zambia 16.01S 27.37E
43 Q12 **Magozal** Veracruz-Llave, C Mexico 21.33N 97.57W
12 B7 **Magpie** ≈ Ontario, S Canada
9 Q17 **Magrath** Alberta, SW Canada 49.27N 112.52W
107 R10 **Magro** ≈ E Spain
78 I9 **Magta' Lahjar** var. Magta Lahjar, Magta' Lahjar, Magtá Lahjar. Brakna, SW Mauritania 17.27N 13.07W
85 L20 **Magude** Maputo, S Mozambique 25.01S 32.40E
79 Y12 **Magumeri** Borno, NE Nigeria 12.07N 12.48E
201 O14 **Magur Islands** island group Caroline Islands, C Micronesia
Magway see Magwe
177 Ff6 **Magwe** var. Magway. Magwe, W Myanmar 20.07N 94.59E
177 Ff6 **Magwe** var. Magway. ◈ division C Myanmar
Magyar-Becse see Bečej
Magyarkanizsa see Kanjiža
Magyarország see Hungary
Magyarzsombor see Zimbor
148 J4 **Mahābād** var. Mehabad; prev. Sāūjbulāgh. Āžarbāyjān-e Bākhtarī, NW Iran 36.43N 45.43E
180 H5 **Mahabo** Toliara, W Madagascar 20.22S 44.39E
Maha Chai see Samut Sakhon
161 D14 **Mahād** Mahārāshtra, W India 18.04N 73.21E
83 N17 **Mahadday Weyne** Shabeellaha Dhexe, C Somalia 2.55N 45.30E
81 Q17 **Mahagi** Orientale, NE Dem. Rep. Congo 2.16N 30.58E
Mahāil see Muhāyil
180 I4 **Mahajamba** seasonal river NW Madagascar
158 G10 **Mahājan** Rājasthān, NW India 28.46N 73.49E
180 I3 **Mahajanga** var. Majunga. Mahajanga, NW Madagascar 15.40S 46.19E
180 I3 **Mahajanga** ◈ province W Madagascar
180 I3 **Mahajanga** ✈ Mahajanga, NW Madagascar 15.40S 46.19E
175 N7 **Mahakam, Sungai** var. Koetai, Kutai. ≈ Borneo, C Indonesia
85 I19 **Mahalapye** var. Mahalatswe. Central, SE Botswana 23.01S 26.52E
Mahalatswe see Mahalapye
Mahalla el Kubra see El Maḥalla el Kubra
175 Q10 **Mahalona** Sulawesi, C Indonesia 2.37S 121.26E
Mahameru see Semeru, Gunung
149 S11 **Mahān** Kermān, E Iran 30.07N 57.15E
160 N12 **Mahānadi** ≈ E India
180 J5 **Mahanoro** Toamasina, E Madagascar 19.52S 48.48E
159 P13 **Mahārājganj** Bihār, N India 26.07N 84.31E
160 G13 **Mahārāshtra** ◈ state W India
180 I4 **Mahavavy** seasonal river N Madagascar
161 K24 **Mahaweli Ganga** ≈ C Sri Lanka
Mahbés see El Mahbas
161 J15 **Mahbūbābād** Andhra Pradesh, E India 17.35N 80.00E
161 H16 **Mahbūbnagar** Andhra Pradesh, C India 16.45N 78.01E
146 M8 **Mahd adh Dhahab** Al Madīnah, W Saudi Arabia 23.33N 40.56E
57 S9 **Mahdia** C Guyana 5.16N 59.08W
77 N6 **Mahdia** var. Al Mahdīyah, Mehdia. NE Tunisia 35.14N 11.06E
161 F20 **Mahe** Fr. Mahé; prev. Mayyali. Pondicherry, SW India 11.44N 75.33E
180 I16 **Mahé** ✈ Mahé, NE Seychelles 4.37S 55.27E
180 H16 **Mahé** island Inner Islands, NE Seychelles
181 Y17 **Mahebourg** SE Mauritius 20.24S 57.42E
158 L10 **Mahendranagar** Far Western, W Nepal 28.58N 80.13E
83 I23 **Mahenge** Morogoro, SE Tanzania 8.40S 36.40E
193 F22 **Maheno** Otago, South Island, NZ 45.10S 170.51E
160 D9 **Mahesāna** Gujarāt, W India 23.37N 72.28E
160 F11 **Maheshwar** Madhya Pradesh, C India 22.12N 75.40E
157 F14 **Mahi** ≈ N India
192 Q10 **Mahia Peninsula** peninsula North Island, NZ
121 O16 **Mahilyow** Rus. Mogilëv. Mahilyowskaya Voblasts', E Belarus 53.54N 30.23E
121 M16 **Mahilyowskaya Voblasts'** prev. Rus. Mogilëvskaya Oblast'. ◈ province E Belarus
203 P7 **Mahina** Tahiti, W French Polynesia 17.28S 149.27W
193 E23 **Mahinerangi, Lake** ◎ South Island, NZ
Máhkarávju see Magerøya
85 L22 **Mahlabatini** KwaZulu/Natal, E South Africa 28.10S 31.27E
177 G5 **Mahlaing** Mandalay, C Myanmar 21.03N 95.43E
111 X8 **Mahldorf** Steiermark, SE Austria 46.54N 15.55E
Mahmūd-e 'Erāqī see Maḥmūd-e Rāqī
155 R4 **Maḥmūd-e Rāqī** var. Mahmūd-e 'Erāqī. Kāpīsā, NE Afghanistan 35.01N 69.19E
Mahmudiya see Al Maḥmūdīyah
31 S5 **Mahnomen** Minnesota, N USA 47.19N 95.58W
158 K14 **Mahoba** Uttar Pradesh, N India 25.18N 79.52E
107 Z9 **Mahón** Cat. Maó, Eng. Port Mahon; anc. Portus Magonis. Menorca, Spain, W Mediterranean Sea 39.54N 4.15E
20 D14 **Mahoning Creek Lake** ▣ Pennsylvania, NE USA
107 Q10 **Mahora** Castilla-La Mancha, C Spain 39.13N 1.43W
Mähren see Moravia
Mährisch-Budwitz see Moravské Budějovice
Mährisch-Kromau see Moravský Krumlov
Mährisch-Neustadt see Uničov
Mährisch-Schönberg see Šumperk
Mährisch-Trübau see Moravská Třebová
Mährisch-Weisskirchen see Hranice
Māh-Shahr see Bandar-e Māhshahr
81 N19 **Mahulu** Maniema, E Dem. Rep. Congo 1.04S 27.10E
160 C12 **Mahuva** Gujarāt, W India 21.06N 71.46E
116 N11 **Mahya Dağı** ▲ NW Turkey 41.47N 27.34E
107 T6 **Maials** var. Mayals. Cataluña, NE Spain 41.22N 0.30E
203 O2 **Maiana** prev. Hall Island. atoll Tungaru, W Kiribati
203 S11 **Maiao** var. Tapuaemanu, Tubuai-Manu. island Îles du Vent, W French Polynesia
56 H4 **Maicao** La Guajira, N Colombia 11.25N 72.15W
Mai Ceu/Mai Chio see Maych'ew
105 U8 **Maîche** Doubs, E France 47.15N 6.43E
99 N22 **Maidenhead** S England, UK 51.31N 0.43W
9 S15 **Maidstone** Saskatchewan, S Canada 53.06N 109.21W
99 P22 **Maidstone** SE England, UK 51.16N 0.31E
79 Y13 **Maiduguri** Borno, NE Nigeria 11.51N 13.09E
110 I8 **Maienfeld** Sankt Gallen, NE Switzerland 47.01N 9.30E
118 J12 **Măieruş** Hung. Szászmagyarós. Braşov, C Romania 45.55N 25.30E
Maigh Chromtha see Macroom
Maigh Eo see Mayo
57 N9 **Maigualida, Sierra** ▲▲ S Venezuela
160 K9 **Maihar** Madhya Pradesh, C India 24.18N 80.46E
160 K11 **Maikala Range** ▲▲ C India
69 T10 **Maiko** ≈ W Dem. Rep. Congo
Mailand see Milano
158 L11 **Mailāni** Uttar Pradesh, N India 28.16N 80.19E
155 U10 **Māilsi** Punjab, E Pakistan 29.46N 72.15E
153 R8 **Maimak** Talasskaya Oblast', NW Kyrgyzstan 42.40N 71.12E
Maimāna see Meymaneh
Maimansingh see Mymensingh
176 Vv11 **Maimawa** Papua, E Indonesia 3.21S 133.36E
Maimuna see Al Maymūnah
103 G18 **Main** ≈ C Germany
117 F22 **Maïna** ancient monument Pelopónnisos, S Greece 36.24N 22.28E
117 E20 **Maínalo** ▲▲ S Greece
103 L22 **Mainburg** Bayern, SE Germany 48.40N 11.48E
Main Camp see Banana
12 E12 **Main Channel** lake channel Ontario, S Canada
81 I20 **Mai-Ndombe, Lac** prev. Lac Léopold II. ◎ W Dem. Rep. Congo
103 K20 **Main-Donau-Kanal** canal SE Germany
21 R6 **Maine** off. State of Maine; also known as Lumber State, Pine Tree State. ◈ state NE USA
104 K6 **Maine** cultural region NW France
104 J7 **Maine-et-Loire** ◈ department NW France
21 Q9 **Maine, Gulf of** gulf NE USA
79 X12 **Maïné-Soroa** Diffa, SE Niger 13.13N 12.05E
178 Gg1 **Maingkwan** var. Mungkawn. Kachin State, N Myanmar 26.19N 96.37E
Main Island see Bermuda
Mainistir Fhear Maí see Fermoy
Mainistir na Búille see Boyle
Mainistir na Corann see Midleton
Mainistir na Féile see Abbeyfeale
98 J5 **Mainland** island Orkney, N Scotland, UK
98 L2 **Mainland** island Shetland, NE Scotland, UK
165 P16 **Mainling** var. Tungdor. Xizang Zizhiqu, W China 29.12N 94.06E
158 K12 **Mainpuri** Uttar Pradesh, N India 27.13N 79.01E
105 N5 **Maintenon** Eure-et-Loir, C France 48.35N 1.34E
180 H4 **Maintirano** Mahajanga, W Madagascar 18.01S 44.03E
95 M15 **Mainua** Oulu, C Finland 64.05N 27.28E
103 G18 **Mainz** Fr. Mayence. Rheinland-Pfalz, SW Germany 50.00N 8.16E
78 I9 **Maio** var. Vila do Maio. Maio, S Cape Verde 15.07N 23.12W
78 E10 **Maio** var. Mayo. island Ilhas de Sotavento, SE Cape Verde
64 G12 **Maipo, Río** ≈ C Chile
64 H12 **Maipo, Volcán** ▲ W Argentina 34.09S 69.51W
63 E22 **Maipú** Buenos Aires, E Argentina 36.52S 57.52W
64 I11 **Maipú** Mendoza, E Argentina 33.00S 68.46W
64 H11 **Maipú** Santiago, C Chile 33.30S 70.52W
56 L5 **Maiquetía** Distrito Federal, N Venezuela 10.36N 66.57W
110 I10 **Maira** It. Mera. ≈ Italy/Switzerland
108 A9 **Maira** ≈ NW Italy
159 V12 **Mairābari** Assam, NE India 26.28N 92.22E
46 K7 **Maisí** Guantánamo, E Cuba 20.13N 74.08W
120 H13 **Maišiagala** Vilnius, SE Lithuania 54.52N 25.03E
159 V17 **Maiskhal Island** island SE Bangladesh
178 Gg13 **Mai Sombun** Chumphon, SW Thailand 10.49N 99.13E
Maisur see Karnātaka, India
Maisur see Mysore, India
191 T8 **Maitland** New South Wales, SE Australia 32.47S 151.31E
190 I9 **Maitland** South Australia 34.21S 137.42E
12 F15 **Maitland** ≈ Ontario, S Canada
205 R1 **Maitri** Indian research station Antarctica 70.03S 8.59E
165 N15 **Maizhokunggar** Xizang Zizhiqu, W China 29.49N 91.40E
45 O10 **Maíz, Islas del** var. Corn Islands. island group SE Nicaragua
171 H14 **Maizuru** Kyōto, Honshū, SW Japan 35.28N 135.21E
56 F6 **Majagual** Sucre, N Colombia 8.36N 74.30W
43 Z13 **Majahual** Quintana Roo, E Mexico 18.43N 87.43W
Majardah, Wādī see Medjerda, Oued/Mejerda
Mājeej see Mejit Island
175 P11 **Majene** prev. Madjene. Sulawesi, C Indonesia 3.33S 118.58E
45 V15 **Majé, Serranía de** ▲▲ E Panama
114 I11 **Majevica** ▲▲ NE Bosnia and Herzegovina
83 H15 **Maji** Southern, S Ethiopia 6.11N 35.32E
147 X7 **Majīs** NW Oman 24.25N 56.34E
Majorca see Mallorca
Mājro see Majuro Atoll
Majunga see Mahajanga
201 Y3 **Majuro** ✈ Majuro Atoll, SE Marshall Islands 7.04N 171.07E
201 Y2 **Majuro Atoll** var. Mājro. atoll Ratak Chain, SE Marshall Islands
201 X2 **Majuro Lagoon** lagoon Majuro Atoll, SE Marshall Islands
78 H11 **Maka** C Senegal 13.39N 14.25W
81 F20 **Makabana** Le Niari, SW Congo 3.28S 12.36E
40 D9 **Mākaha** var. Makaha. O'ahu, Hawai'i, USA, C Pacific Ocean 21.28N 158.13W
40 B8 **Makahū'ena Point** var. Makahuena Point headland Kaua'i, Hawai'i, USA, C Pacific Ocean 21.52N 159.28W
40 D9 **Makakilo City** O'ahu, Hawai'i, USA, C Pacific Ocean 21.21N 158.05W
85 H18 **Makalamabedi** Central, C Botswana 20.18S 23.52E
Makale see Mek'elē
164 K17 **Makalu** Chin. Makaru Shan. ▲ China/Nepal 27.53N 87.09E
83 G23 **Makampi** Mbeya, S Tanzania 8.00S 33.17E
151 X12 **Makanchi** Kaz. Maqanshy. Vostochnyy Kazakhstan, E Kazakhstan 46.47N 82.00E
44 M8 **Makantaka** Región Autónoma Atlántico Norte, NE Nicaragua 13.13N 84.04W
202 B16 **Makapu Point** headland W Niue 18.58S 169.55E
193 C24 **Makarewa** Southland, South Island, NZ 46.17S 168.16E
119 O4 **Makariv** Kyyivs'ka Oblast', N Ukraine 50.28N 29.49E
193 D20 **Makarora** ≈ South Island, NZ
127 Oo15 **Makarov** Ostrov Sakhalin, Sakhalinskaya Oblast', SE Russian Federation 48.24N 142.37E
207 R9 **Makarov Basin** undersea feature Arctic Ocean
199 Hh4 **Makarov Seamount** undersea feature W Pacific Ocean 29.30N 153.30E
115 F15 **Makarska** It. Macarsca. Split-Dalmacija, SE Croatia 43.18N 17.00E
Makaru Shan see Makalu
129 O15 **Makar'yev** Kostromskaya Oblast', NW Russian Federation 57.52N 43.46E
84 L11 **Makasa** Northern, NE Zambia 9.42S 31.54E
Makasar see Makassar
Makasar, Selat see Makassar Straits
175 P13 **Makassar** var. Macassar, Makasar; prev. Ujungpandang. Sulawesi, C Indonesia 5.09S 119.28E
198 Ff8 **Makassar Straits** Ind. Selat Makasar. strait C Indonesia
150 G12 **Makat** Kaz. Maqat. Atyrau, SW Kazakhstan 47.41N 53.24E
203 T10 **Makatea** island Îles Tuamotu, C French Polynesia
145 U7 **Makātū** E Iraq 33.55N 45.25E
180 H6 **Makay** var. Massif du Makay. ▲▲ SW Madagascar
116 J12 **Makaza** pass Bulgaria/Greece 41.16N 25.26E
176 Uu9 **Makbon** Papua, E Indonesia 0.43S 131.30E
Makedonija see Macedonia, FYR
202 B16 **Makefu** W Niue 18.58S 169.55W
203 V10 **Makemo** atoll Îles Tuamotu, C French Polynesia
78 I15 **Makeni** C Sierra Leone 8.57N 12.01W
Makenzen see Orlyak
Makeyevka see Makiyivka
131 Q16 **Makhachkala** prev. Petrovsk-Port. Respublika Dagestan, SW Russian Federation 42.58N 47.30E
150 F11 **Makhambet** Atyrau, W Kazakhstan 47.35N 51.35E
Makharadze see Ozurget'i
145 W13 **Makhfar Al Buşayyah** S Iraq 30.09N 46.09E
145 R4 **Makhmūr** N Iraq 35.46N 43.31E
144 I11 **Makhrūq, Wadi al** dry watercourse E Jordan
145 R4 **Makḥūl, Jabal** ▲ C Iraq
147 R13 **Makhyah, Wādī** dry watercourse N Yemen
176 W11 **Maki** Papua, E Indonesia 3.00S 134.10E
175 Ss8 **Makian, Pulau** island Maluku, E Indonesia
193 G21 **Makikihi** Canterbury, South Island, NZ 44.36S 171.09E
203 O2 **Makin** prev. Pitt Island. atoll Tungaru, W Kiribati
83 I20 **Makindu** Eastern, S Kenya 2.15S 37.49E
151 Q8 **Makinsk** Akmola, N Kazakhstan 52.37N 70.26E
195 Y17 **Makira** off. Makira Province. ◈ province SE Solomon Islands
Makira see San Cristobal
119 X8 **Makiyivka** Rus. Makeyevka; prev. Dmitriyevsk. Donets'ka Oblast', E Ukraine 47.57N 37.47E
146 L10 **Makkah** Eng. Mecca. Makkah, W Saudi Arabia 21.27N 39.50E
146 M10 **Makkah** var. Mintaqat Makkah. ◈ province W Saudi Arabia
11 R7 **Makkovik** Newfoundland and Labrador, NE Canada 55.06N 59.06W
100 K6 **Makkum** Friesland, N Netherlands 53.03N 5.25E
Mako see Makung
113 M25 **Makó** Rom. Macău. Csongrád, SE Hungary 46.14N 20.28E
12 G9 **Makobe Lake** ◎ Ontario, S Canada
197 I14 **Makogai** island C Fiji
81 F18 **Makokou** Ogooué-Ivindo, NE Gabon 0.37N 12.46E
83 G23 **Makongolosi** Mbeya, S Tanzania 8.24S 33.09E
83 E19 **Makota** SW Uganda 0.37S 30.12E
81 G18 **Makoua** Cuvette, C Congo 0.01S 15.40E
112 M10 **Maków Mazowiecki** Mazowieckie, C Poland 52.51N 21.06E
113 K17 **Maków Podhalański** Małopolskie, S Poland 49.43N 19.40E
149 V14 **Makran** cultural region Iran/Pakistan
158 G12 **Makrāna** Rājasthān, N India 27.01N 74.43E
149 U15 **Makran Coast** coastal region SE Iran
121 F20 **Makrany** Rus. Mokrany. Brestskaya Voblasts', SW Belarus 51.49N 24.15E
Makrinoros see Makrynóros
117 H20 **Makrónisosi** island Kykládes, Greece, Aegean Sea
117 D17 **Makrynóros** var. Makrinoros. ▲▲ C Greece
117 G19 **Makryplági** ▲ C Greece 38.00N 23.06E
Maksamaa see Maxmo
128 J15 **Maksatikha** var. Maksatha, Maksaticha. Tverskaya Oblast', W Russian Federation 57.49N 35.46E
160 G10 **Maksi** Madhya Pradesh, C India 23.18N 76.09E
148 I1 **Mākū** Āżarbāyjān-e Bākhtarī, NW Iran 39.16N 44.33E
159 Y11 **Mākum** Assam, NE India 27.28N 95.28E
Makun see Makung
167 R14 **Makung** prev. Mako, Makun. W Taiwan 23.34N 119.34E
170 Bb16 **Makurazaki** Kagoshima, Kyūshū, SW Japan 31.15N 130.15E
79 V15 **Makurdi** Benue, C Nigeria 7.41N 8.35E
125 F12 **Makushino** Kurganskaya Oblast', C Russian Federation 55.11N 67.16E
40 L17 **Makushin Volcano** ▲ Unalaska Island, Alaska, USA 53.53N 166.55W
85 K16 **Makwiro** Mashonaland West, N Zimbabwe 17.52S 30.24E
59 D15 **Mala** Lima, W Peru 12.45S 76.38W
Mala see Mallow, Ireland
Mala see Malaita, Solomon Islands
95 I14 **Malå** Västerbotten, N Sweden 65.12N 18.45E
202 G12 **Mala'atoli** Île Uvea, E Wallis and Futuna
179 Qq15 **Malabang** Mindanao, S Philippines 7.37N 124.04E
161 E21 **Malabār Coast** coast SW India
81 C16 **Malabo** prev. Santa Isabel. ● (Equatorial Guinea) Isla de Bioco, NW Equatorial Guinea 3.43N 8.51E
81 C16 **Malabo** ✈ Isla de Bioco, N Equatorial Guinea 3.44N 8.51E
Malaca see Málaga
Malacca see Melaka
173 G4 **Malacca, Strait of** Ind. Selat Malaka. strait Indonesia/Malaysia
Malacka see Malacky
113 G20 **Malacky** Hung. Malacka. Bratislavský Kraj, W Slovakia 48.25N 17.01E
35 R16 **Malad City** Idaho, NW USA 42.10N 112.16W
119 Q4 **Mala Divytsya** Chernihivs'ka Oblast', N Ukraine 50.40N 32.13E
121 J15 **Maladzyechna** Pol. Molodeczno, Rus. Molodechno. Minskaya Voblasts', C Belarus 54.19N 26.51E
202 D12 **Malaee** Île Futuna, N Wallis and Futuna
39 V15 **Malaga** New Mexico, SW USA 32.10N 104.04W
56 G8 **Málaga** Santander, C Colombia 6.42N 72.43W
106 M15 **Málaga** anc. Malaca. Andalucía, S Spain 36.43N 4.25W
106 L15 **Málaga** ◈ province Andalucía, S Spain
106 M15 **Málaga** ✈ Andalucía, S Spain 36.38N 4.36W
Malagasy Republic see Madagascar
107 N10 **Malagón** Castilla-La Mancha, C Spain 39.10N 3.51W
99 G18 **Malahide** Ir. Mullach Íde. E Ireland 53.27N 6.09W
195 Y14 **Malaita** off. Malaita Province. ◈ province N Solomon Islands
195 Y15 **Malaita** var. Mala. island N Solomon Islands
82 F13 **Malakal** Upper Nile, S Sudan 9.31N 31.40E
114 C10 **Mala Kapela** ▲▲ NW Croatia
27 V7 **Malakoff** Texas, SW USA 32.10N 96.00W
Malakula see Malekula
155 V7 **Malakwāl** var. Mālikwāla. Punjab, E Pakistan 32.31N 73.18E
194 J12 **Malalamai** Madang, W PNG 5.47S 146.40E
194 J14 **Malalaua** Gulf, S PNG 8.04S 146.09E
175 Q11 **Malamala** Sulawesi, C Indonesia 3.21S 120.58E
174 M15 **Malang** Jawa, C Indonesia 7.58S 112.45E
85 O14 **Malanga** Niassa, N Mozambique 13.27S 36.05E
Malange see Malanje
94 I9 **Malangen** sound N Norway
84 C11 **Malanje** var. Malange. Malanje, NW Angola 9.33S 16.25E
84 C11 **Malanje** var. Malange. ◈ province N Angola
154 M16 **Malān, Rās** headland SW Pakistan 25.13N 63.31E
79 S13 **Malanville** NE Benin 11.49N 3.22E
Malapane see Ozimek
161 F21 **Malappuram** Kerala, SW India 11.00N 76.02E
45 T17 **Mala, Punta** headland S Panama 7.28N 79.58W
97 N16 **Mälaren** ◎ C Sweden
64 H13 **Malargüe** Mendoza, W Argentina 35.31S 69.34W
12 J8 **Malartic** Québec, SE Canada 48.09N 78.09W
121 F20 **Malaryta** Pol. Maloryta, Rus. Malorita. Brestskaya Voblasts', SW Belarus 51.46N 24.04E
65 J19 **Malaspina** Chubut, SE Argentina 44.56S 66.52W
41 U12 **Malaspina Glacier** glacier Alaska, USA
143 N15 **Malatya** anc. Melitene. Malatya, SE Turkey 38.22N 38.18E
142 M14 **Malatya** ◈ province C Turkey
119 Q7 **Mala Vyska** Rus. Malaya Viska. Kirovohrads'ka Oblast', S Ukraine 48.37N 31.36E
85 M14 **Malawi** off. Republic of Malaŵi; prev. Nyasaland, Nyasaland Protectorate. ◆ republic S Africa
Malawi, Lake see Nyasa, Lake
95 J17 **Malax** Fin. Maalahti. Länsi-Suomi, W Finland 62.55N 21.30E
128 H14 **Malaya Vishera** Novgorodskaya Oblast', W Russian Federation 58.52N 32.12E
Malaya Viska see Mala Vyska
179 R15 **Malaybalay** Mindanao, S Philippines 8.10N 125.08E
148 L6 **Malāyer** prev. Daulatabad. Hamadān, W Iran 34.19N 48.46E
174 Gg3 **Malay Peninsula** peninsula Malaysia/Thailand
174 I3 **Malaysia** var. Federation of Malaysia; prev. the separate territories of Federation of Malaya, Sarawak and Sabah (North Borneo) and Singapore. ◆ monarchy SE Asia
143 R14 **Malazgirt** Muş, E Turkey 39.09N 42.30E
13 R8 **Malbaie** ≈ Québec, SE Canada
79 T12 **Malbaza** Tahoua, S Niger 13.57N 5.32E
112 J7 **Malbork** Ger. Marienburg, Marienburg in Westpreussen. Pomorskie, N Poland 54.01N 19.02E
102 N9 **Malchin** Mecklenburg-Vorpommern, N Germany 53.43N 12.46E
102 M9 **Malchiner See** ◎ NE Germany
101 D16 **Maldegem** Oost-Vlaanderen, NW Belgium 51.12N 3.27E
100 L13 **Malden** Gelderland, SE Netherlands 51.46N 5.51E
21 O11 **Malden** Massachusetts, NE USA 42.25N 71.04W
29 Y8 **Malden** Missouri, C USA 36.33N 89.58W
203 X4 **Malden Island** prev. Independence Island. atoll E Kiribati
181 Q6 **Maldives** off. Maldivian Divehi, Republic of Maldives. ◆ republic N Indian Ocean
Maldivian Divehi see Maldives
99 P21 **Maldon** E England, UK 51.43N 0.40E
63 G20 **Maldonado** Maldonado, S Uruguay 34.57S 54.58W
63 G20 **Maldonado** ◈ department S Uruguay
43 P17 **Maldonado, Punta** headland S Mexico 16.18N 98.31W
157 K19 **Male'** Div. Maale ● (Maldives) Male' Atoll, C Maldives 4.10N 73.29E
108 G6 **Malè** Trentino-Alto Adige, N Italy 46.21N 10.51E
78 K13 **Maléa** var. Maléya. Haute-Guinée, NE Guinea 11.46N 9.43W
117 G22 **Maléas, Akrotírio** headland S Greece 36.25N 23.11E
117 L17 **Maléas, Akrotírio** headland Lésvos, E Greece 39.01N 26.36E
157 K19 **Male' Atoll** var. Kaafu Atoll. atoll C Maldives
Malebo, Pool see Stanley Pool
160 E12 **Mālegaon** Mahārāshtra, W India 20.33N 74.31E
83 F15 **Malek** Jonglei, S Sudan 6.04N 31.36E
197 B13 **Malekula** var. Malakula; prev. Mallicolo. island W Vanuatu
201 Y15 **Malem** Kosrae, E Micronesia 5.16N 163.01E
85 O15 **Malema** Nampula, N Mozambique 14.57S 37.28E
81 N23 **Malemba-Nkulu** Katanga, SE Dem. Rep. Congo 8.01S 26.48E
195 Q10 **Malendok Island** island Tanga Islands, NE PNG
128 K9 **Malen'ga** Respublika Kareliya, NW Russian Federation 63.50N 36.21E
97 M20 **Målerås** Kalmar, S Sweden 56.55N 15.34E
105 O6 **Malesherbes** Loiret, C France 48.18N 2.25E
117 G18 **Malesína** Stereá Ellás, E Greece 38.37N 23.15E
Maléya see Maléa
131 O15 **Malgobek** Chechenskaya Respublika, SW Russian Federation 43.34N 44.34E
107 X5 **Malgrat de Mar** Cataluña, NE Spain 41.39N 2.45E
82 C9 **Malha** Northern Darfur, W Sudan 15.07N 26.00E
145 Q5 **Malḥāt** C Iraq 34.44N 42.41E
34 K14 **Malheur Lake** ◎ Oregon, NW USA
34 L14 **Malheur River** ≈ Oregon, NW USA
78 I13 **Mali** Moyenne-Guinée, NW Guinea 12.07N 12.28W
79 O9 **Mali** off. Republic of Mali, Fr. République du Mali; prev. French Sudan, Sudanese Republic. ◆ republic W Africa
175 S16 **Maliana** W East Timor 8.57S 125.25E
178 H1 **Mali Hka** ≈ N Myanmar
Mali Idjoš see Mali Idoš
114 K8 **Mali Idoš** var. Mali Idjoš, Hung. Kishegyes; prev. Krivaja. Serbia, N Serbia and Montenegro (Yugoslavia) 45.43N 19.40E
114 K9 **Mali Kanal** canal N Serbia and Montenegro (Yugoslavia)
175 R8 **Maliku** Sulawesi, N Indonesia 0.36S 123.13E
Malik, Wadi al see Milk, Wadi el
Mālikwāla see Malakwāl
178 Gg12 **Mali Kyun** var. Tavoy Island. island Mergui Archipelago, S Myanmar
97 M19 **Målilla** Kalmar, S Sweden 57.24N 15.49E
114 B11 **Mali Lošinj** It. Lussinpiccolo. Primorje-Gorski Kotar, W Croatia 44.31N 14.28E
Malin see Malyn
179 Q15 **Malindang, Mount** ▲ Mindanao, S Philippines 8.12N 123.37E
83 K20 **Malindi** Coast, SE Kenya 3.13S 40.04E
Malines see Mechelen
98 E13 **Malin Head** Ir. Cionn Mhálanna. headland NW Ireland 55.37N 7.37W
175 Pp7 **Malino, Gunung** ▲ Sulawesi, N Indonesia 0.44N 120.45E
115 M21 **Maliq** var. Maliqi. Korçë, SE Albania 40.45N 20.45E
Maliqi see Maliq
179 Rr16 **Malita** Mindanao, S Philippines 6.13N 125.39E
160 G12 **Malkāpur** Mahārāshtra, C India 20.52N 76.18E
142 B10 **Malkara** Tekirdağ, NW Turkey 40.55N 26.56E
121 J19 **Mal'kavichy** Rus. Mal'kovichi. Brestskaya Voblasts', SW Belarus 52.28N 26.39E
Malkiye see Al Mālikīyah
116 L11 **Malko Sharkovo, Yazovir** ▣ SE Bulgaria
116 N11 **Malko Tŭrnovo** Burgas, E Bulgaria 42.00N 27.33E
Mal'kovichi see Mal'kavichy
191 R12 **Mallacoota** Victoria, SE Australia 37.34S 149.45E
98 G10 **Mallaig** N Scotland, UK 57.03N 5.48W
190 I9 **Mallala** South Australia 34.29S 138.30E
77 W9 **Mallawi** C Egypt 27.49N 30.43E
107 R5 **Mallén** Aragón, NE Spain 41.52N 1.25W
108 F5 **Malles Venosta** Ger. Mals im Vinschgau. Trentino-Alto Adige, N Italy 46.40N 10.37E
Mallicolo see Malekula
111 Q8 **Mallnitz** Salzburg, S Austria 46.58N 13.09E
107 W9 **Mallorca** Eng. Majorca; anc. Baleares Major. island Islas Baleares, Spain, W Mediterranean Sea
99 C20 **Mallow** Ir. Mala. SW Ireland 52.07N 8.39W
95 E15 **Malm** Nord-Trøndelag, C Norway 64.04N 11.12E
97 L19 **Malmbäck** Jönköping, S Sweden 57.34N 14.30E
94 J12 **Malmberget** Lapp. Malmivaara. Norrbotten, N Sweden 67.09N 20.39E
101 M20 **Malmédy** Liège, E Belgium 50.25N 6.01E
85 E25 **Malmesbury** Western Cape, SW South Africa 33.28S 18.43E
Malmivaara see Malmberget
97 N16 **Malmköping** Södermanland, C Sweden 59.07N 16.49E
97 K23 **Malmö** Skåne, S Sweden 55.36N 13.00E
97 K23 **Malmo** ✈ Skåne, S Sweden 55.33N 13.23E
47 Q16 **Malmok** headland Bonaire, S Netherlands Antilles 12.16N 68.21W
97 M18 **Malmslätt** Östergötland, S Sweden 58.25N 15.30E
129 R16 **Malmyzh** Kirovskaya Oblast', NW Russian Federation 56.30N 50.37E
197 B12 **Malo** island W Vanuatu
130 J7 **Maloarkhangel'sk** Orlovskaya Oblast', W Russian Federation 52.25N 36.37E
Maloelap see Maloelap Atoll
201 V6 **Maloelap Atoll** var. Maļoeļap. atoll E Marshall Islands
Maloenda see Malunda
110 I10 **Maloja** Graubünden, S Switzerland 46.25N 9.42E
84 L12 **Malole** Northern, NE Zambia 10.05S 31.37E
197 H13 **Malolo** island Mamanuca Group, W Fiji
197 H13 **Malolo Barrier Reef** var. Ro Ro Reef. reef W Fiji
179 P10 **Malolos** Luzon, N Philippines 14.51N 120.49E
20 K6 **Malone** New York, NE USA 44.51N 74.18W
81 K25 **Malonga** Katanga, S Dem. Rep. Congo 10.30S 23.06E
113 L15 **Małopolska** plateau S Poland
113 K17 **Małopolskie** ◈ province S Poland
Malorita/Maloryta see Malaryta
128 K9 **Maloshuyka** Arkhangel'skaya Oblast', NW Russian Federation 63.43N 37.20E
116 G10 **Mal'ovitsa** ▲ W Bulgaria 42.12N 23.19E
151 V15 **Malovodnoye** Almaty, SE Kazakhstan 43.31N 77.42E
96 C10 **Måløy** Sogn og Fjordane, S Norway 61.55N 5.06E
130 K4 **Maloyaroslavets** Kaluzhskaya Oblast', W Russian Federation 55.03N 36.31E
125 F6 **Malozemel'skaya Tundra** physical region NW Russian Federation
106 J10 **Malpartida de Cáceres** Extremadura, W Spain 39.25N 6.30W
106 K9 **Malpartida de Plasencia** Extremadura, W Spain 39.58N 6.03W
108 C7 **Malpensa** ✈ (Milano) Lombardia, N Italy 45.41N 8.40E
78 J6 **Malqteïr** desert N Mauritania
Mals im Vinschgau see Malles Venosta
120 J10 **Malta** Rēzekne, SE Latvia 56.19N 27.11E
35 V7 **Malta** Montana, NW USA 48.21N 107.52W

◆ Country
● Country Capital
◇ Dependent Territory
○ Dependent Territory Capital
◈ Administrative Region
✈ International Airport
▲ Mountain
▲▲ Mountain Range
▲ Volcano
≈ River
◎ Lake
▣ Reservoir

123 Jj14 **Malta** *off.* Republic of Malta. ◆ *republic* C Mediterranean Sea
111 R8 **Malta** *var.* Maltabach. ≈ S Austria
123 L11 **Malta** *island* Malta, C Mediterranean Sea
Maltabach *see* Malta
Malta, Canale di *see* Malta Channel
123 L12 **Malta Channel** *It.* Canale di Malta. *strait* Italy/Malta
85 D20 **Maltahöhe** Hardap, SW Namibia 24.49S 16.58E
99 N16 **Malton** N England, UK 54.07N 0.49W
175 T11 **Maluku** *off.* Propinsi Maluku, *Dut.* Molukken, *Eng.* Moluccas. ⬖ *province* E Indonesia
175 Ss9 **Maluku** *Dut.* Molukken, *Eng.* Moluccas; *prev.* Spice Islands. *island group* E Indonesia
Maluku, Laut *see* Molucca Sea
175 Ss8 **Maluku Utara** *off.* Propinsi Maluku Utara. ⬖ *province* E Indonesia
79 V13 **Malumfashi** Katsina, N Nigeria 11.51N 7.39E
175 P11 **Malunda** *prev.* Maloenda. Sulawesi, C Indonesia 2.58S 118.52E
96 K13 **Malung** Dalarna, C Sweden 60.40N 13.45E
96 K13 **Malungsfors** Dalarna, C Sweden 60.43N 13.34E
195 X14 **Maluu** *var.* Malu'u. Malaita, N Solomon Islands 8.22S 160.39E
161 D16 **Mālvan** Mahārāshtra, W India 16.05N 73.28E
Malventum *see* Benevento
29 U12 **Malvern** Arkansas, C USA 34.21N 92.48W
31 S15 **Malvern** Iowa, C USA 40.59N 95.36W
46 I13 **Malvern** ▲ W Jamaica 17.59N 77.42W
Malvinas, Islas *see* Falkland Islands
119 N4 **Malyn** *Rus.* Malin. Zhytomyrs'ka Oblast', N Ukraine 50.46N 29.14E
127 O5 **Malyy Anyuy** ≈ NE Russian Federation
131 O11 **Malyye Derbety** Respublika Kalmykiya, SW Russian Federation 47.57N 44.39E
Malyy Kavkaz *see* Lesser Caucasus
126 M5 **Malyy Lyakhovskiy, Ostrov** *island* NE Russian Federation
Malyy Pamir *see* Little Pamir
126 Jj4 **Malyy Taymyr, Ostrov** *island* Severnaya Zemlya, N Russian Federation
150 E10 **Malyy Uzen'** *Kaz.* Kishiözen. ≈ Kazakhstan/Russian Federation
126 I16 **Malyy Yenisey** *var.* Ka-Krem. ≈ S Russian Federation
126 K13 **Mama** Irkutskaya Oblast', C Russian Federation 58.13N 112.45E
131 S3 **Mamadysh** Respublika Tatarstan, W Russian Federation 55.46N 51.22E
119 N14 **Mamaia** Constanța, E Romania 44.13N 28.37E
197 G14 **Mamanuca Group** *island group* Yasawa Group, W Fiji
152 L13 **Mamash** Lebap Welaýaty, E Turkmenistan 38.24N 64.12E
176 W11 **Mamasiware** Papua, E Indonesia 2.46S 134.26E
194 L14 **Mambare** ≈ S PNG
81 O17 **Mambasa** Orientale, NE Dem. Rep. Congo 1.22N 29.02E
176 Xx10 **Mamberamo, Sungai** ≈ Papua, E Indonesia
81 G15 **Mambéré** ≈ SW Central African Republic
81 G15 **Mambéré-Kadéï** ⬖ *prefecture* SW Central African Republic
176 X9 **Mambetaloi** Papua, E Indonesia 1.38S 136.12E
Mambij *see* Manbij
81 H18 **Mambili** ≈ W Congo
85 N18 **Mambone** *var.* Nova Mambone. Inhambane, E Mozambique 20.59S 35.04E
179 P11 **Mamburao** Mindoro, N Philippines 13.16N 120.36E
180 I16 **Mamelles** *island* Inner Islands, NE Seychelles
101 M25 **Mamer** Luxembourg, SW Luxembourg 49.37N 6.01E
104 L6 **Mamers** Sarthe, NW France 48.21N 0.22E
81 D15 **Mamfe** Sud-Ouest, W Cameroon 5.46N 9.18E
151 P6 **Mamlyutka** Severnyy Kazakhstan, N Kazakhstan 54.55N 68.31E
38 M15 **Mammoth** Arizona, SW USA 32.43N 110.38W
35 S12 **Mammoth Hot Springs** Wyoming, C USA 44.57N 110.40W
Mamoedjoe *see* Mamuju
121 A14 **Mamonovo** *Ger.* Heiligenbeil. Kaliningradskaya Oblast', W Russian Federation 54.28N 19.57E
59 L14 **Mamoré, Rio** ≈ Bolivia/Brazil
78 I14 **Mamou** Moyenne-Guinée, W Guinea 10.34N 12.45W
24 H8 **Mamou** Louisiana, S USA 30.37N 92.25W
180 I14 **Mamoudzou** ○ (Mayotte) C Mayotte 12.48S 45.00E
180 I3 **Mampikony** Mahajanga, N Madagascar 16.03S 47.39E
79 P16 **Mampong** C Ghana 7.01N 1.36W
112 M7 **Mamry, Jezioro** *Ger.* Mauersee. ⊚ NE Poland
175 P10 **Mamuju** *prev.* Mamoedjoe. Sulawesi, S Indonesia 2.40S 118.51E
175 Oo10 **Mamuju, Teluk** *bay* Sulawesi, C Indonesia
85 F19 **Mamuno** Ghanzi, W Botswana 22.15S 20.01E
115 K19 **Mamuras** *var.* Mamurasi, Mamurras. Lezhë, C Albania 41.34N 19.42E
Mamurasi/Mamurras *see* Mamuras
78 L16 **Man** W Ivory Coast 7.24N 7.33W
57 X9 **Mana** NW French Guiana 5.40N 53.49W
58 A6 **Manabí** ⬖ *province* W Ecuador
44 G4 **Manabique, Punta** *var.* Cabo Tres Puntas. *headland* E Guatemala 15.57N 88.37W
56 G11 **Manacacías, Río** ≈ C Colombia
60 F13 **Manacapuru** Amazonas, N Brazil 3.16S 60.37W
175 Rr6 **Manado** *prev.* Menado. Sulawesi, C Indonesia 1.31N 124.55E
196 H5 **Managaha** *island* S Northern Mariana Islands
101 G20 **Manage** Hainaut, S Belgium 50.30N 4.13E
44 J10 **Managua** ● (Nicaragua) Managua, W Nicaragua 12.07N 86.15W
44 J10 **Managua** ⬖ *department* W Nicaragua
44 J10 **Managua** ✕ Managua, W Nicaragua 12.07N 86.11W
44 J10 **Managua, Lago de** *var.* Xolotlán. ⊚ W Nicaragua
Manaḩ *see* Bilād Manaḩ
20 K16 **Manahawkin** New Jersey, NE USA 39.39N 74.12W
192 K11 **Manaia** Taranaki, North Island, NZ 39.32S 174.04E
180 J6 **Manakara** Fianarantsoa, SE Madagascar 22.09S 48.00E
158 J7 **Manāli** Himāchal Pradesh, NW India 32.18N 77.12E
133 U12 **Ma, Nam** *Vtn.* Sông Mã. ≈ Laos/Vietnam
Manama *see* Al Manāmah
194 I10 **Manam Island** *island* N PNG
69 Y13 **Mananara** ≈ SE Madagascar
190 M9 **Manangatang** Victoria, SE Australia 35.04S 142.53E
180 J6 **Mananjary** Fianarantsoa, SE Madagascar 21.13S 48.19E
78 L14 **Manankoro** Sikasso, SW Mali 10.33N 7.25W
78 J12 **Manantali, Lac de** ⊡ W Mali
Manáos *see* Manaus
193 B23 **Manapouri** Southland, South Island, NZ 45.33S 167.38E
193 B23 **Manapouri, Lake** ⊚ South Island, NZ
60 F13 **Manaquiri** Amazonas, NW Brazil 3.27S 60.37W
Manar *see* Mannar
164 K5 **Manas** Xinjiang Uygur Zizhiqu, NW China 44.16N 86.12E
159 U12 **Manās** *var.* Dangme Chu. ≈ Bhutan/India
153 R8 **Manas, Gora** ▲ Kyrgyzstan/Uzbekistan 42.17N 71.04E
164 K3 **Manas Hu** ⊚ NW China
159 P10 **Manaslu** ▲ C Nepal 28.33N 84.33E
39 S8 **Manassa** Colorado, C USA 37.10N 105.56W
23 W4 **Manassas** Virginia, NE USA 38.45N 77.28W
47 T5 **Manatí** C Puerto Rico 18.26N 66.29W
175 S16 **Manatuto** N East Timor 8.31S 126.00E
194 L14 **Manau** Northern, S PNG 8.05S 147.57E
56 H4 **Manaure** La Guajira, N Colombia 11.46N 72.28W
60 F12 **Manaus** *prev.* Manáos. *state capital* Amazonas, NW Brazil 03.06S 60.00W
142 G17 **Manavgat** Antalya, SW Turkey 36.46N 31.28E
192 M13 **Manawatu** ≈ North Island, NZ
192 L11 **Manawatu-Wanganui** *off.* Manawatu-Wanganui Region. ⬖ *region* North Island, NZ
176 Uu12 **Manawoka, Pulau** *island* Kepulauan Gorong, E Indonesia
179 Rr16 **Manay** Mindanao, S Philippines 7.12N 126.29E
144 K2 **Manbij** *var.* Mambij, *Fr.* Membidj. Ḩalab, N Syria 36.31N 37.55E
107 N13 **Mancha Real** Andalucía, S Spain 37.46N 3.37W
104 I4 **Manche** ⬖ *department* N France
99 L17 **Manchester** *Lat.* Mancunium. NW England, UK 53.30N 2.15W
25 S5 **Manchester** Georgia, SE USA 32.51N 84.37W
31 Y13 **Manchester** Iowa, C USA 42.28N 91.27W
23 N7 **Manchester** Kentucky, S USA 37.10N 83.40W
21 O10 **Manchester** New Hampshire, NE USA 42.58N 71.25W
22 K10 **Manchester** Tennessee, S USA 35.28N 86.05W
20 M9 **Manchester** Vermont, NE USA 43.09N 73.03W
99 L18 **Manchester** ✕ NW England, UK 53.21N 2.16W
155 P15 **Manchhar Lake** ⊚ SE Pakistan
Man-chou-li *see* Manzhouli
133 X7 **Manchurian Plain** *plain* NE China
Máncio Lima *see* Japiim
Mancunium *see* Manchester
154 J15 **Mand** Baluchistān, SW Pakistan 26.06N 61.58E
Mand *see* Mand, Rūd-e
83 H25 **Manda** Iringa, SW Tanzania 10.25S 34.38E
180 H6 **Mandabe** Toliara, W Madagascar 21.01S 44.55E
168 I5 **Mandal** Hövsgöl, N Mongolia 49.55N 99.21E
168 L7 **Mandal** Töv, C Mongolia 48.24N 106.47E
97 E18 **Mandal** Vest-Agder, S Norway 58.01N 7.27E
177 G5 **Mandalay** Mandalay, C Myanmar 21.57N 96.04E
177 G6 **Mandalay** ⬖ *division* C Myanmar
168 L9 **Mandalgovĭ** Dundgovĭ, C Mongolia 45.47N 106.18E
145 V7 **Mandalī** E Iraq 33.43N 45.33E
97 E18 **Mandalselva** ≈ S Norway
169 P11 **Mandalt** *var.* Sonid Zuoqi. Nei Mongol Zizhiqu, N China 43.49N 113.36E
30 M5 **Mandan** North Dakota, N USA 46.49N 100.53W
Mandargiri Hill *see* Mandār Hill
159 R14 **Mandār Hill** *prev.* Mandargiri Hill. Bihār, NE India 24.51N 87.03E
175 P11 **Mandar, Teluk** *bay* Sulawesi, C Indonesia
109 C19 **Mandas** Sardegna, Italy, C Mediterranean Sea 39.40N 9.07E
Mandasor *see* Mandsaur
83 L16 **Mandera** North Eastern, NE Kenya 3.55N 41.52E
35 V13 **Manderson** Wyoming, C USA 44.13N 107.55W
46 J12 **Mandeville** C Jamaica 18.01N 77.31W
24 K9 **Mandeville** Louisiana, S USA 30.21N 90.04W
158 I7 **Mandi** Himāchal Pradesh, NW India 31.40N 76.58E
78 K14 **Mandiana** Haute-Guinée, E Guinea 10.37N 8.39W
155 U10 **Mandi Būrewāla** *var.* Būrewāla. Punjab, E Pakistan 30.04N 72.46E
158 G9 **Mandi Dabwāli** Haryāna, NW India 29.55N 74.40E
Mandidzudzure *see* Chimanimani
85 M15 **Mandié** Manica, NW Mozambique 16.27S 33.28E
85 N14 **Mandimba** Niassa, N Mozambique 14.21S 35.40E
175 Ss9 **Mandioli, Pulau** *island* Kepulauan Bacan, E Indonesia
59 Q19 **Mandioré, Laguna** ⊚ E Bolivia
160 J10 **Mandla** Madhya Pradesh, C India 22.39N 80.21E
85 M20 **Mandlakazi** *var.* Manjacaze. Gaza, S Mozambique 24.43S 33.57E
97 E24 **Mandø** *var.* Manø. *island* W Denmark
176 Ww9 **Mandori** Papua, E Indonesia 1.01S 134.58E
Mandoúdhion/Mandoudi *see* Mantoúdi
117 G19 **Mándra** Attikí, C Greece 38.04N 23.31E
180 I7 **Mandrare** ≈ S Madagascar
116 M10 **Mandra, Yazovir** *salt lake* SE Bulgaria
109 L23 **Mandrazzi, Portella** *pass* Sicilia, Italy, C Mediterranean Sea 37.57N 15.02E
180 J3 **Mandritsara** Mahajanga, N Madagascar 15.49S 48.49E
149 O13 **Mand, Rūd-e** *var.* Mand. ≈ S Iran
160 F9 **Mandsaur** *prev.* Mandasor. Madhya Pradesh, C India 24.05N 75.04E
160 F11 **Māndu** Madhya Pradesh, C India 22.22N 75.24E
175 Oo5 **Mandul, Pulau** *island* N Indonesia
85 G15 **Mandundu** Western, W Zambia 16.34S 22.18E
188 I13 **Mandurah** Western Australia 32.31S 115.40E
109 P18 **Manduria** Puglia, SE Italy 40.24N 17.37E
161 G20 **Mandya** Karnātaka, C India 12.34N 76.55E
79 P12 **Mané** C Burkina 12.59N 1.21W
108 E8 **Manerbio** Lombardia, NW Italy 45.22N 10.09E
Manevichi *see* Manevychi
118 K3 **Manevychi** *Pol.* Maniewicze, *Rus.* Manevichi. Volyns'ka Oblast', NW Ukraine 51.18N 25.29E
109 N16 **Manfredonia** Puglia, SE Italy 41.38N 15.54E
109 N16 **Manfredonia, Golfo di** *gulf* Adriatic Sea, N Mediterranean Sea
79 P13 **Manga** C Burkina 11.40N 1.04W
61 L16 **Mangabeiras, Chapada das** ⛰ E Brazil
81 J20 **Mangai** Bandundu, W Dem. Rep. Congo 3.57S 19.32E
202 L17 **Mangaia** *island group* S Cook Islands
192 M9 **Mangakino** Waikato, North Island, NZ 38.22S 175.45E
118 M15 **Mangalia** *anc.* Callatis. Constanța, SE Romania 43.46N 28.34E
80 J11 **Mangalmé** Guéra, SE Chad 12.25N 19.37E
161 E19 **Mangalore** Karnātaka, W India 12.54N 74.51E
203 Y13 **Mangareva** *var.* Magareva. *island* Îles Tuamotu, SE French Polynesia
85 I23 **Mangaung** Free State, C South Africa 29.10S 26.19E
Mangaung *see* Bloemfontein
160 K9 **Mangawān** Madhya Pradesh, C India 24.39N 81.33E
192 M11 **Mangaweka** Manawatu-Wanganui, North Island, NZ 39.49S 175.47E
192 N11 **Mangaweka** ▲ North Island, NZ 39.51S 176.06E
81 P17 **Mangbwalu** Orientale, NE Dem. Rep. Congo 2.06N 30.04E
103 L24 **Mangfall** ≈ SE Germany
174 K11 **Manggar** Pulau Belitung, W Indonesia 2.51S 108.14E
176 Vv12 **Manggawitu** Papua, E Indonesia 4.11S 133.28E
177 G2 **Mangin Range** ⛰ N Myanmar
145 R1 **Mangish** N Iraq 37.03N 43.04E
150 F15 **Mangistau** *Kaz.* Mangqystaū Oblysy; *prev.* Mangyshlaskaya. ⬖ *province* SW Kazakhstan
Mangit *see* Mang'it
152 H8 **Mang'it** *Rus.* Mangit. Qoraqalpog'iston Respublikasi, W Uzbekistan 42.06N 60.02E
56 A13 **Manglares, Cabo** *headland* SW Colombia 1.36N 79.01W
155 V6 **Mangla Reservoir** ⊡ NE Pakistan
165 N9 **Mangnai** *var.* Lao Mangnai. Qinghai, C China 37.52N 91.39E
Mango *see* Mago, Fiji
Mango *see* Sansanné-Mango, Togo
Mangoche *see* Mangochi
85 N14 **Mangochi** *var.* Mangoche; *prev.* Fort Johnston. Southern, SE Malawi 14.27S 35.15E
79 N14 **Mangodara** SW Burkina 9.49N 4.22W
180 H6 **Mangoky** ≈ W Madagascar
175 S10 **Mangole, Pulau** *island* Kepulauan Sula, E Indonesia
192 J2 **Mangonui** Northland, North Island, NZ 35.00S 173.30E
Mangqystaū Oblysy *see* Mangistau
Mangqystaū Shyghanaghy *see* Mangyshlakskiy Zaliv
106 H7 **Mangualde** Viseu, N Portugal 40.36N 7.46W
63 H18 **Mangueira, Lagoa** ⊚ S Brazil
79 X6 **Manguéni, Plateau du** ⛰ NE Niger
169 T4 **Mangui** Nei Mongol Zizhiqu, N China 52.02N 122.13E
28 K11 **Mangum** Oklahoma, C USA 34.52N 99.30W
81 O18 **Manguredjipa** Nord Kivu, E Dem. Rep. Congo 0.28N 28.33E
85 L16 **Mangwendi** Mashonaland East, E Zimbabwe 18.22S 31.24E
150 F15 **Mangyshlak, Plato** *plateau* SW Kazakhstan
150 E14 **Mangyshlakskiy Zaliv** *Kaz.* Mangqystaū Shyghanaghy. *gulf* SW Kazakhstan
Mangyshlaskaya *see* Mangistau
168 I5 **Manhan** Hövsgöl, N Mongolia 50.05N 100.01E
29 O4 **Manhattan** Kansas, C USA 39.11N 96.33W
101 L21 **Manhay** Luxembourg, SE Belgium 50.13N 5.43E
85 L21 **Manhiça** *prev.* Vila de Manhiça. Maputo, S Mozambique 25.20S 32.49E
85 L21 **Manhoca** Maputo, S Mozambique 26.47S 32.37E
61 N20 **Manhuaçu** Minas Gerais, SE Brazil 20.16S 42.01W
149 R11 **Mānī** Kermān, C Iran
56 H10 **Maní** Casanare, C Colombia 4.49N 72.15W
85 M17 **Manica** *var.* Vila de Manica. Manica, W Mozambique 18.51S 32.50E
85 M17 **Manica** *off.* Província de Manica. ⬖ *province* W Mozambique
85 L17 **Manicaland** ⬖ *province* E Zimbabwe
13 U5 **Manic Deux, Réservoir** ⊡ Québec, SE Canada
Manich *see* Manych
61 F14 **Manicoré** Amazonas, N Brazil 5.48S 61.16W
11 N11 **Manicouagan** Québec, SE Canada 50.40N 68.46W
11 N11 **Manicouagan** ≈ Québec, SE Canada
13 U6 **Manicouagan, Péninsule de** *peninsula* Québec, SE Canada
11 N11 **Manicouagan, Réservoir** ⊚ Québec, E Canada
13 T4 **Manic Trois, Réservoir** ⊡ Québec, SE Canada
81 M20 **Maniema** *off.* Région du Maniema. ⬖ *region* E Dem. Rep. Congo
Maniewicze *see* Manevychi
166 F8 **Maniganggo** Sichuan, C China 32.01N 99.04E
9 Y15 **Manigotagan** Manitoba, S Canada 51.06N 96.18W
159 R13 **Manihāri** Bihār, N India 25.21N 87.37E
203 U9 **Manihi** *island* Îles Tuamotu, C French Polynesia
202 L13 **Manihiki** *atoll* N Cook Islands
183 U8 **Manihiki Plateau** *undersea feature* C Pacific Ocean
206 M14 **Maniitsoq** *var.* Manîtsoq, *Dan.* Sukkertoppen. Kita, S Greenland 65.12N 52.05W
159 T15 **Manikganj** Dhaka, C Bangladesh 23.52N 90.00E
158 M14 **Mānikpur** Uttar Pradesh, N India 25.04N 81.06E
179 P11 **Manila** *off.* City of Manila. ● (Philippines) Luzon, N Philippines 14.34N 120.58E
29 Y9 **Manila** Arkansas, C USA 35.52N 90.10W
201 N16 **Manila Reef** *reef* W Micronesia
191 T6 **Manilla** New South Wales, SE Australia 30.44S 150.43E
200 Qq14 **Maniloa** *island* Tongatapu Group, S Tonga
127 P7 **Manily** Koryakskiy Avtonomnyy Okrug, E Russian Federation 62.33N 165.03E
176 Ww9 **Manim, Pulau** *island* E Indonesia
173 Ff8 **Maninjau, Danau** ⊚ Sumatera, W Indonesia
159 W13 **Manipur** ⬖ *state* NE India
159 X14 **Manipur Hills** *hill range* E India
142 C14 **Manisa** *var.* Manissa; *prev.* Saruhan, *anc.* Magnesia. Manisa, W Turkey 38.36N 27.28E
142 C13 **Manisa** *var.* Manissa. ⬖ *province* W Turkey
Manissa *see* Manisa
33 O7 **Manistee** Michigan, N USA 44.14N 86.19W
33 P7 **Manistee River** ≈ Michigan, N USA
33 O4 **Manistique** Michigan, N USA 45.57N 86.15W
33 P4 **Manistique Lake** ⊚ Michigan, N USA
9 W13 **Manitoba** ⬖ *province* S Canada
9 X16 **Manitoba, Lake** ⊚ Manitoba, S Canada
9 X17 **Manitou** Manitoba, S Canada 49.12N 98.28W
33 N2 **Manitou Island** *island* Michigan, N USA
12 H11 **Manitou Lake** ⊚ Ontario, SE Canada
10 G15 **Manitoulin Island** *island* Ontario, S Canada
39 T5 **Manitou Springs** Colorado, C USA 38.51N 104.56W
12 G12 **Manitouwabing Lake** ⊚ Ontario, S Canada
10 E12 **Manitouwadge** Ontario, S Canada 49.13N 85.51W
10 G15 **Manitowaning** Manitoulin Island, Ontario, S Canada 45.43N 81.49W
12 B7 **Manitowik Lake** ⊚ Ontario, S Canada
33 N7 **Manitowoc** Wisconsin, N USA 44.04N 87.40W
Manîtsoq *see* Maniitsoq
145 O7 **Mānī', Wādī al** *dry watercourse* W Iraq
10 J14 **Maniwaki** Québec, SE Canada 46.24N 75.58W
176 X11 **Maniwori** Papua, E Indonesia 2.49S 136.00E
56 E10 **Manizales** Caldas, W Colombia 5.03N 73.52W
114 F11 **Manjača** ⛰ NW Bosnia and Herzegovina
Manjacaze *see* Mandlakazi
188 J14 **Manjimup** Western Australia 34.18S 116.14E
111 V4 **Mank** Niederösterreich, C Austria 48.06N 15.13E
81 I17 **Mankanza** Equateur, NW Dem. Rep. Congo 1.40N 19.08E
159 N12 **Mankāpur** Uttar Pradesh, N India 27.03N 82.12E
28 M3 **Mankato** Kansas, C USA 39.45N 98.10W
31 U10 **Mankato** Minnesota, N USA 44.10N 94.00W
119 O7 **Man'kivka** Cherkas'ka Oblast', C Ukraine 48.58N 30.10E
78 M15 **Mankono** C Ivory Coast 8.06N 6.07W
9 T17 **Mankota** Saskatchewan, S Canada 49.25N 107.04W
161 K23 **Mankulam** Northern Province, N Sri Lanka 9.09N 80.27E
41 Q9 **Manley Hot Springs** Alaska, USA 65.00N 150.37W
20 H10 **Manlius** New York, NE USA 43.00N 75.58W
107 W5 **Manlleu** Cataluña, NE Spain 41.58N 2.16E
31 V11 **Manly** Iowa, C USA 43.17N 93.12W
160 E13 **Manmād** Mahārāshtra, W India 20.15N 74.28E
190 J7 **Mannahill** South Australia 32.29S 139.58E
161 J23 **Mannar** *var.* Manar. Northern Province, NW Sri Lanka 9.01N 79.53E
161 I24 **Mannar, Gulf of** *gulf* India/Sri Lanka
161 J23 **Mannar Island** *island* N Sri Lanka
Mannersdorf *see* Mannersdorf am Leithagebirge
111 Y5 **Mannersdorf am Leithagebirge** *var.* Mannersdorf. Niederösterreich, E Austria 47.58N 16.36E
111 Y6 **Mannersdorf an der Rabnitz** Burgenland, E Austria 47.25N 16.32E
103 G20 **Mannheim** Baden-Württemberg, SW Germany 49.28N 8.29E
9 O12 **Manning** Alberta, W Canada 56.52N 117.39W
31 T14 **Manning** Iowa, C USA 41.54N 95.03W
30 K5 **Manning** North Dakota, N USA 47.13N 102.46W
23 S13 **Manning** South Carolina, SE USA 33.42N 80.12W
203 Y2 **Manning, Cape** *headland* Kiritimati, NE Kiribati 2.01N 157.25W
195 V13 **Manning Strait** *strait* NW Solomon Islands
23 S3 **Mannington** West Virginia, NE USA 39.31N 80.20W
190 A1 **Mann Ranges** ⛰ South Australia
109 C19 **Mannu** ≈ Sardegna, Italy, C Mediterranean Sea
9 R14 **Mannville** Alberta, SW Canada 53.19N 111.08W
78 J15 **Mano** ≈ Liberia/Sierra Leone
Manø *see* Mandø
41 O13 **Manokotak** Alaska, USA 59.00N 158.58W
176 W9 **Manokwari** Papua, E Indonesia 0.49S 134.04E
81 N22 **Manono** Shabo, SE Dem. Rep. Congo 7.18S 27.25E
27 T10 **Manor** Texas, SW USA 30.20N 97.33W
99 D16 **Manorhamilton** *Ir.* Cluainín. NW Ireland 54.18N 8.10W
105 S15 **Manosque** Alpes-de-Haute-Provence, SE France 43.49N 5.46E
10 L11 **Manouane, Lac** ⊚ Québec, SE Canada
169 W12 **Manp'o** *var.* Manp'ojin. NW North Korea 41.10N 126.24E
Manp'ojin *see* Manp'o
203 T4 **Manra** *prev.* Sydney Island. *atoll* Phoenix Islands, C Kiribati
107 V5 **Manresa** Cataluña, NE Spain 41.44N 1.52E
158 H9 **Mānsa** Punjab, NW India 30.00N 75.25E
84 J12 **Mansa** *prev.* Fort Rosebery. Luapula, N Zambia 11.13S 28.55E
78 G12 **Mansa Konko** C Gambia 13.26N 15.29W
13 Q11 **Manseau** Québec, SE Canada 46.23N 71.59W
155 U5 **Mānsehra** North-West Frontier Province, NW Pakistan 34.22N 73.18E
15 Mm6 **Mansel Island** *island* Nunavut, NE Canada
191 O12 **Mansfield** Victoria, SE Australia 37.04S 146.06E
99 M18 **Mansfield** C England, UK 53.09N 1.10W
29 S11 **Mansfield** Arkansas, C USA 35.03N 94.15W
24 G6 **Mansfield** Louisiana, S USA 32.02N 93.42W
21 O12 **Mansfield** Massachusetts, NE USA 42.00N 71.11W
33 T12 **Mansfield** Ohio, N USA 40.45N 82.31W
20 G12 **Mansfield** Pennsylvania, NE USA 41.46N 77.02W
20 M7 **Mansfield, Mount** ▲ Vermont, NE USA 44.31N 72.49W
61 M16 **Mansidão** Bahia, E Brazil 10.46S 44.03W
104 L11 **Mansle** Charente, W France 45.52N 0.11E
78 G12 **Mansôa** C Guinea-Bissau 12.07N 15.18W
49 V8 **Manso, Rio** ≈ C Brazil
Manṣûra *see* El Manṣûra
Mansurabad *see* Mehrān, Rūd-e
58 A6 **Manta** Manabí, W Ecuador 0.57S 80.39W
58 A6 **Manta, Bahía de** *bay* W Ecuador
59 F14 **Mantaro, Río** ≈ C Peru
37 O8 **Manteca** California, W USA 37.48N 121.13W
56 J7 **Mantecal** Apure, C Venezuela 7.34N 69.07W
33 N11 **Manteno** Illinois, N USA 41.15N 87.49W
23 Y9 **Manteo** Roanoke Island, North Carolina, SE USA 35.53N 75.39W
Mantes-Gassicourt *see* Mantes-la-Jolie
105 N5 **Mantes-la-Jolie** *prev.* Mantes-Gassicourt, Mantes-sur-Seine, *anc.* Medunta. Yvelines, N France 48.58N 1.42E
Mantes-sur-Seine *see* Mantes-la-Jolie
38 L5 **Manti** Utah, W USA 39.16N 111.38W
Mantinea *see* Mantíneia
117 F20 **Mantíneia** *anc.* Mantinea. *site of ancient city* Pelopónnisos, S Greece 37.36N 22.22E
61 M21 **Mantiqueira, Serra da** ⛰ S Brazil
31 W10 **Mantorville** Minnesota, N USA 44.04N 92.45W
117 G17 **Mantoúdi** *var.* Mandoudi; *prev.* Mandoúdhion. Évvoia, C Greece 38.46N 23.28E
Mantoue *see* Mantova
108 F8 **Mantova** *Eng.* Mantua, *Fr.* Mantoue. Lombardia, NW Italy 45.10N 10.46E
95 M19 **Mäntsälä** Etelä-Suomi, S Finland 60.38N 25.21E
95 L17 **Mänttä** Länsi-Suomi, W Finland 62.00N 24.36E
Mantua *see* Mantova
129 O14 **Manturovo** Kostromskaya Oblast', NW Russian Federation 58.19N 44.42E
95 M18 **Mäntyharju** Ita-Suomi, SE Finland 61.25N 26.52E
94 M13 **Mäntyjärvi** Lappi, N Finland 66.00N 27.35E
202 L16 **Manuae** *island* S Cook Islands
203 Q10 **Manuae** *atoll* Îles Sous le Vent, W French Polynesia
198 Dd8 **Manua Islands** *island group* E American Samoa
42 L5 **Manuel Benavides** Chihuahua, N Mexico 29.07N 103.52W
63 D21 **Manuel J.Cobo** Buenos Aires, E Argentina 35.49S 57.54W
60 M12 **Manuel Luís, Recife** *reef* E Brazil
63 F15 **Manuel Viana** Rio Grande do Sul, S Brazil 29.33S 55.28W
61 I14 **Manuel Zinho** Pará, N Brazil 7.21S 54.47W
203 V11 **Manuhangi** *atoll* Îles Tuamotu, C French Polynesia
193 E22 **Manuherikia** ≈ South Island, NZ
175 R11 **Manui, Pulau** *island* N Indonesia
Manukau *see* Manurewa
192 L6 **Manukau Harbour** *harbor* North Island, NZ
174 K14 **Manuk, Ci** ≈ Jawa, S Indonesia
176 U12 **Manuk, Pulau** *island* Maluku, E Indonesia
203 Z2 **Manulu Lagoon** ⊚ Kiritimati, E Kiribati
190 J7 **Manunda Creek** *seasonal river* South Australia
59 K15 **Manupari, Río** ≈ N Bolivia
192 L6 **Manurewa** *var.* Manukau. Auckland, North Island, NZ 37.03S 174.55E
59 K15 **Manurimi, Río** ≈ NW Bolivia
194 I8 **Manus** ⬖ *province* N PNG
194 J8 **Manus Island** *var.* Great Admiralty Island. *island* N PNG
176 U15 **Manuwui** Pulau Babar, E Indonesia 7.47S 129.39E
31 Q3 **Manvel** North Dakota, N USA 48.07N 97.15W
35 Z14 **Manville** Wyoming, C USA 42.45N 104.38W
24 G6 **Many** Louisiana, S USA 31.34N 93.28W
83 H21 **Manyara, Lake** ⊚ NE Tanzania
130 L12 **Manych** *var.* Manich. ≈ SW Russian Federation
131 N13 **Manych-Gudilo, Ozero** *salt lake* SW Russian Federation
85 H14 **Manyinga** North Western, NW Zambia 13.28S 24.18E
107 O11 **Manzanares** Castilla-La Mancha, C Spain 39.00N 3.23W
46 H7 **Manzanillo** Granma, E Cuba 20.21N 77.07W
42 K14 **Manzanillo** Colima, SW Mexico 19.00N 104.18W
42 K14 **Manzanillo, Bahía** *bay* SW Mexico
39 S11 **Manzano Mountains** ⛰ New Mexico, SW USA
39 R12 **Manzano Peak** ▲ New Mexico, SW USA 34.35N 106.27W
169 R6 **Manzhouli** *var.* Man-chou-li. Nei Mongol Zizhiqu, N China 49.36N 117.28E
Manzil Bū Ruqaybah *see* Menzel Bourguiba
145 X9 **Manzilīyah** E Iraq 32.26N 47.01E
85 L21 **Manzini** *prev.* Bremersdorp. C Swaziland 26.30S 31.33E
85 L21 **Manzini** ✕ (Mbabane) C Swaziland 26.36S 31.25E
80 G10 **Mao** Kanem, W Chad 14.06N 15.16E
47 N8 **Mao** NW Dominican Republic 19.33N 71.09W
Maó *see* Mahón
Maoemere *see* Maumere
165 W9 **Maojing** Gansu, N China 36.25N 106.36E
176 Xx12 **Maoke, Pegunungan** *Dut.* Sneeuw-gebergte, *Eng.* Snow Mountains. ⛰ Papua, E Indonesia
Maol Réidh, Caoc *see* Mweelrea
166 M15 **Maoming** Guangdong, S China 21.45N 110.50E
166 H8 **Maoxian** *var.* Mao Xian; *prev.* Fengyizhen. Sichuan, C China 31.42N 103.48E
85 L19 **Mapai** Gaza, SW Mozambique 22.52S 32.00E
164 H15 **Mapam Yumco** ⊚ W China
85 I15 **Mapanza** Southern, S Zambia 16.16S 26.54E
56 J4 **Mapararí** Falcón, N Venezuela 10.47N 69.26W
43 U17 **Mapastepec** Chiapas, SE Mexico 15.24N 92.55W
175 O5 **Mapat, Pulau** *island* N Indonesia
176 Yy14 **Mapi** Papua, E Indonesia 7.02S 139.24E
176 Vv7 **Mapia, Kepulauan** *island group* E Indonesia
42 L8 **Mapimí** Durango, C Mexico 25.50N 103.50W
85 N19 **Mapinhane** Inhambane, SE Mozambique 22.14S 35.07E
57 N7 **Mapire** Monagas, NE Venezuela 7.48N 64.40W
9 S17 **Maple Creek** Saskatchewan, S Canada 49.55N 109.28W
33 Q9 **Maple River** ≈ Michigan, N USA
31 P7 **Maple River** ≈ North Dakota/South Dakota, N USA
31 S13 **Mapleton** Iowa, C USA 42.10N 95.47W
31 U10 **Mapleton** Minnesota, N USA 43.55N 93.57W
31 R5 **Mapleton** North Dakota, N USA 46.51N 97.04W
34 F13 **Mapleton** Oregon, NW USA 44.01N 123.56W
38 L3 **Mapleton** Utah, W USA 40.07N 111.37W
199 Ii5 **Mapmaker Seamounts** *undersea feature* N Pacific Ocean
194 G10 **Maprik** East Sepik, NW PNG 3.35S 143.03E
85 L21 **Maputo** *prev.* Lourenço Marques. ● (Mozambique) Maputo, S Mozambique 25.58S 32.34E
85 L21 **Maputo** ⬖ *province* S Mozambique
85 L21 **Maputo** ✕ Maputo, S Mozambique 25.47S 32.36E
69 V14 **Maputo** ≈ S Mozambique
Maqanshy *see* Makanchi
Maqat *see* Makat
115 K19 **Maqë** ≈ NW Albania
115 M19 **Maqellarë** Dibër, C Albania 41.36N 20.29E
165 S12 **Maqên** *var.* Dawo; *prev.* Dawu. Qinghai, C China 34.32N 100.17E
165 S11 **Maqen Kangri** ▲ C China 34.44N 99.25E
165 U12 **Maqu** *var.* Nyinma. Gansu, C China 34.02N 102.00E
106 M9 **Maqueda** Castilla-La Mancha, C Spain 40.04N 4.22W
84 B9 **Maquela do Zombo** Uíge, NW Angola 6.03S 15.05E
65 I16 **Maquinchao** Río Negro, C Argentina 41.19S 68.46W
31 Z13 **Maquoketa** Iowa, C USA 42.03N 90.42W
31 Y13 **Maquoketa River** ≈ Iowa, C USA
12 F13 **Mar** Ontario, S Canada 44.48N 81.12W
97 F14 **Mår** ⊚ S Norway
83 G19 **Mara** ⬖ *region* N Tanzania
203 P8 **Maraa** Tahiti, W French Polynesia 17.43S 149.34W
60 D12 **Maraã** Amazonas, NW Brazil 1.48S 65.21W
203 O8 **Maraa, Pointe** *headland* Tahiti, W French Polynesia 17.43S 149.34W
61 K14 **Marabá** Pará, NE Brazil 5.22S 49.10W
56 H5 **Maracaibo** Zulia, NW Venezuela 10.39N 71.39W
Maracaibo, Gulf of *see* Venezuela, Golfo de
56 H5 **Maracaibo, Lago de** *var.* Lake Maracaibo. *inlet* NW Venezuela
Maracaibo, Lake *see* Maracaibo, Lago de
60 K10 **Maracá, Ilha de** *island* NE Brazil
61 H20 **Maracaju, Serra de** ⛰ S Brazil
60 I11 **Maracanaquará, Planalto** ⛰ NE Brazil
56 L5 **Maracay** Aragua, N Venezuela 10.15N 67.36W
Marada *see* Marādah
77 R9 **Marādah** *var.* Marada. N Libya 29.15N 19.28E
79 U12 **Maradi** Maradi, S Niger 13.30N 7.05E
79 U11 **Maradi** ⬖ *department* S Niger
83 E21 **Maragarazi** *var.* Muragarazi. ≈ Burundi/Tanzania
Maragha *see* Marāgheh
148 J3 **Marāgheh** *var.* Maragha. Āžarbāyjān-e Khāvarī, NW Iran 37.21N 46.13E
147 P7 **Marāh** *var.* Marrāt. Ar Riyāḑ, C Saudi Arabia 25.04N 45.30E
57 N11 **Marahuaca, Cerro** ▲ S Venezuela 3.37N 65.25W
29 R5 **Marais des Cygnes River** ≈ Kansas/Missouri, C USA
60 L11 **Marajó, Baía de** *bay* N Brazil
61 K12 **Marajó, Ilha de** *island* N Brazil
203 O2 **Marakei** *atoll* Tungaru, W Kiribati
Marakesh *see* Marrakech
83 I18 **Maralal** Rift Valley, C Kenya 1.04N 36.42E
85 G21 **Maralaleng** Kgalagadi, S Botswana 25.42S 22.39E
151 U8 **Maraldy, Ozero** ⊚ NE Kazakhstan
190 C5 **Maralinga** South Australia 30.16S 131.35E
179 R15 **Maramag** Mindanao, S Philippines 7.45N 124.58E
Máramarossziget *see* Sighetu Marmației
195 Y16 **Maramasike** *var.* Small Malaita. *island* N Solomon Islands
Maramba *see* Livingstone
204 H3 **Marambio** *Argentinian research station* Antarctica 64.22S 57.18W
118 H9 **Maramureș** ⬖ *county* NW Romania
38 L15 **Marana** Arizona, SW USA 32.24N 111.12W
107 P7 **Maranchón** Castilla-La Mancha, C Spain 41.01N 2.10W
148 J2 **Marand** *var.* Merend. Āžarbāyjān-e Khāvarī, NW Iran 38.23N 45.48E
Marandellas *see* Marondera
60 L13 **Maranhão** *off.* Estado do Maranhão. ⬖ *state* E Brazil
106 H10 **Maranhão, Barragem do** ⊡ C Portugal
155 O11 **Mārān, Koh-i** ▲ SW Pakistan 29.24N 66.50E
108 J7 **Marano, Laguna di** *lagoon* NE Italy
58 E9 **Marañón, Río** ≈ N Peru
104 J10 **Marans** Charente-Maritime, W France 46.19N 0.58W
85 M20 **Marão** Inhambane, S Mozambique 24.15S 34.09E
193 B23 **Mararoa** ≈ South Island, NZ
Maraş/Marash *see* Kahramanmaraş
109 M19 **Maratea** Basilicata, S Italy 39.57N 15.44E
106 G11 **Marateca** Setúbal, S Portugal 38.34N 8.40W
117 B20 **Marathiá, Akrotírio** *headland* Zákynthos, Iónioi Nísoi, Greece, C Mediterranean Sea 37.39N 20.49E
10 E12 **Marathon** Ontario, S Canada 48.43N 86.22W
25 Y17 **Marathon** Florida Keys, Florida, SE USA 24.42N 81.05W
26 L10 **Marathon** Texas, SW USA 30.10N 103.14W
Marathón *see* Marathónas

◆ Country
● Country Capital
◇ Dependent Territory
○ Dependent Territory Capital
⬖ Administrative Region
✕ International Airport
▲ Mountain
⛰ Mountain Range
Volcano
≈ River
⊚ Lake
⊡ Reservoir

◆ COUNTRY   ◇ DEPENDENT TERRITORY   ◆ ADMINISTRATIVE REGION   ▲ MOUNTAIN   ▲ VOLCANO   ⊚ LAKE
● COUNTRY CAPITAL   ○ DEPENDENT TERRITORY CAPITAL   ✕ INTERNATIONAL AIRPORT   ▲ MOUNTAIN RANGE   ⟶ RIVER   ⊚ RESERVOIR

291

Massakory – Meaux

80 G10 **Massakory** *var.* Massakori; *prev.* Dagana. Chari-Baguirmi, W Chad *13.01N 15.43E*
80 H11 **Massalassef** Chari-Baguirmi, SW Chad *11.37N 17.09E*
108 F13 **Massa Marittima** Toscana, C Italy *43.03N 10.55E*
84 B11 **Massangano** Cuanza Norte, NW Angola *9.36S 14.19E*
85 M18 **Massangena** Gaza, S Mozambique *21.34S 32.57E*
82 J9 **Massawa** *var.* Masawa, *Amh.* Mits'iwa. E Eritrea *15.37N 39.27E*
82 K9 **Massawa Channel** *channel* E Eritrea
20 J6 **Massena** New York, NE USA *44.55N 74.53W*
80 H11 **Massenya** Chari-Baguirmi, SW Chad *11.21N 16.09E*
8 I13 **Masset** Graham Island, British Columbia, SW Canada *54.00N 132.09W*
104 L16 **Masseube** Gers, S France *43.26N 0.33E*
12 E11 **Massey** Ontario, S Canada *46.13N 82.06W*
105 P12 **Massiac** Cantal, C France *45.16N 3.13E*
105 P12 **Massif Central** *plateau* C France
Massilia *see* Marseille
33 U12 **Massillon** Ohio, N USA *40.48N 81.31W*
79 N12 **Massina** Ségou, W Mali *13.58N 5.24W*
85 N19 **Massinga** Inhambane, SE Mozambique *23.16S 35.23E*
85 L20 **Massingir** Gaza, SW Mozambique *23.57S 32.12E*
205 Z10 **Masson Island** *island* Antarctica
Massoukou *see* Franceville
143 Z11 **Maştağa** *Rus.* Mashtagi, Mastaga. E Azerbaijan *40.31N 50.01E*
Mastanli *see* Momchilgrad
192 M13 **Masterton** Wellington, North Island, NZ *40.56S 175.39E*
20 M14 **Mastic** Long Island, New York, NE USA *40.48N 72.50W*
155 O10 **Mastung** Baluchistān, SW Pakistan *29.46N 66.48E*
121 J20 **Mastva** *Rus.* Mostva. ≈ SW Belarus
121 G17 **Masty** *Rus.* Mosty. Hrodzyenskaya Voblasts', W Belarus *53.25N 24.30E*
170 E12 **Masuda** Shimane, Honshū, SW Japan *34.40N 131.50E*
94 J11 **Masugnsbyn** Norrbotten, N Sweden *67.28N 22.01E*
Masuku *see* Franceville
85 K17 **Masvingo** *prev.* Fort Victoria, Nyanda, Victoria. Masvingo, SE Zimbabwe *20.04S 30.49E*
85 K18 **Masvingo** *prev.* Victoria. ◈ *province* SE Zimbabwe
176 W10 **Maswaar, Pulau** *island* Irian Jaya, E Indonesia
144 H5 **Maşyāf** *Fr.* Misiaf. Ḥamāh, C Syria *35.04N 36.21E*
Masyû Ko *see* Mashū-ko
112 E9 **Maszewo** Zachodniopomorskie, NW Poland *53.29N 15.01E*
85 I17 **Matabeleland North** ◈ *province* W Zimbabwe
85 J18 **Matabeleland South** ◈ *province* S Zimbabwe
84 O13 **Mataca** Niassa, N Mozambique *12.27S 36.13E*
197 G13 **Matacawa Levu** *island* Yasawa Group, NW Fiji
12 G8 **Matachewan** Ontario, S Canada *47.57N 80.39W*
81 F22 **Matadi** Bas-Congo, W Dem. Rep. Congo *5.49S 13.31E*
27 O4 **Matador** Texas, SW USA *34.01N 100.50W*
44 J9 **Matagalpa** Matagalpa, C Nicaragua *12.53N 85.55W*
44 K9 **Matagalpa** ◈ *department* W Nicaragua
10 I12 **Matagami** Québec, S Canada *49.46N 77.37W*
27 U13 **Matagorda** Texas, SW USA *28.40N 96.57W*
27 U13 **Matagorda Bay** *inlet* Texas, SW USA
27 U14 **Matagorda Island** *island* Texas, SW USA
27 V13 **Matagorda Peninsula** *headland* Texas, SW USA *28.34N 96.01W*
203 Q8 **Mataiea** Tahiti, W French Polynesia *17.46S 149.25W*
203 T9 **Mataiva** *atoll* Îles Tuamotu, C French Polynesia
191 O7 **Matakana** New South Wales, SE Australia *32.59S 145.53E*
192 N7 **Matakana Island** *island* NE NZ
85 C15 **Matala** Huíla, SW Angola *14.45S 15.01E*
202 G12 **Matala'a Pointe** *headland* Île Uvea, N Wallis and Futuna *13.19S 176.07W*
161 K25 **Matale** Central Province, C Sri Lanka *7.28N 80.37E*
202 E12 **Matalesina, Pointe** *headland* Île Alofi, W Wallis and Futuna
78 I10 **Matam** NE Senegal *15.40N 13.18W*
192 M8 **Matamata** Waikato, North Island, NZ *37.49S 175.45E*
79 V12 **Matamey** Zinder, S Niger *13.27N 8.27E*
42 L8 **Matamoros** Coahuila de Zaragoza, NE Mexico *25.34N 103.12W*
43 P15 **Matamoros** *var.* Izúcar de Matamoros. Puebla, S Mexico *18.36N 98.30W*
43 Q8 **Matamoros** Tamaulipas, C Mexico *25.49N 97.31W*
175 Q10 **Matana, Danau** ⊚ Sulawesi, C Indonesia
77 S13 **Ma'ṭan as Sārah** SE Libya *21.45N 21.55E*
84 J12 **Matanda** Luapula, N Zambia *11.24S 28.25E*
83 J24 **Matandu** ≈ S Tanzania
13 V6 **Matane** Québec, SE Canada *48.48N 67.31W*
13 V6 **Matane** ≈ Québec, SE Canada
79 S12 **Matankari** Dosso, SW Niger *13.39N 4.03E*
41 R11 **Matanuska River** ≈ Alaska, USA
56 G7 **Matanza** Santander, N Colombia *7.22N 73.01W*
46 D4 **Matanzas** Matanzas, NW Cuba *23.00N 81.32W*
13 V7 **Matapédia** ≈ Québec, SE Canada
13 V6 **Matapédia, Lac** ⊚ Québec, SE Canada
202 B17 **Mata Point** *headland* SE Niue *19.07S 169.51E*
202 D12 **Matapu, Pointe** *headland* Île Futuna, W Wallis and Futuna
64 G12 **Mataquito, Río** ≈ C Chile
161 K26 **Matara** Southern Province, S Sri Lanka *5.57N 80.33E*
117 D18 **Matarágka** *var.* Mataránga. Dytikí Ellás, C Greece *38.31N 21.32E*
175 Nn16 **Mataram** Pulau Lombok, C Indonesia *8.36S 116.07E*
Mataránga *see* Matarágka
189 Q3 **Mataranka** Northern Territory, N Australia *14.55S 133.03E*
107 W6 **Mataró** *anc.* Illuro. Cataluña, E Spain *41.31N 2.27E*
192 O8 **Matata** Bay of Plenty, North Island, NZ *37.54S 176.45E*
198 Cc8 **Matātula, Cape** *headland* Tutuila, W American Samoa *14.15S 170.34W*
193 D24 **Mataura** Southland, South Island, NZ *46.11S 168.53E*
193 D24 **Mataura** ≈ South Island, NZ
Mata Uta *see* Matā'utu
202 G11 **Matā'utu** *var.* Mata Uta. ○ (Wallis and Futuna) Île Uvea, Wallis and Futuna *13.22S 176.12W*
198 B8 **Matāutu** Upolu, C Samoa *13.57S 171.55W*
202 G12 **Matā'utu, Baie de** *bay* Île Uvea, Wallis and Futuna
203 P7 **Mataval, Baie de** *bay* Tahiti, W French Polynesia
202 I16 **Matavera** Rarotonga, S Cook Islands *21.13S 159.43W*
203 V16 **Mataveri** Easter Island, Chile, E Pacific Ocean *27.10S 109.27W*
203 V17 **Mataveri** ✕ (Easter Island) Easter Island, Chile, E Pacific Ocean *27.10S 109.27W*
192 P9 **Matawai** Gisborne, North Island, NZ *38.23S 177.31E*
13 O10 **Matawin** ≈ Québec, SE Canada
151 V13 **Matay** Almaty, SE Kazakhstan *45.52N 78.45E*
12 K8 **Matchi-Manitou, Lac** ⊚ Québec, SE Canada
43 O10 **Matehuala** San Luis Potosí, C Mexico *23.40N 100.37W*
47 V13 **Matelot** Trinidad, Trinidad and Tobago *10.48N 61.06W*
85 M15 **Matenge** Tete, NW Mozambique *15.22S 33.47E*
109 O18 **Matera** Basilicata, S Italy *40.39N 16.34E*
113 O21 **Mátészalka** Szabolcs-Szatmár-Bereg, E Hungary *47.57N 22.16E*
176 Y10 **Matewar** Papua, E Indonesia *1.44S 138.26E*
95 H17 **Matfors** Västernorrland, C Sweden *62.22N 16.59E*
104 K11 **Matha** Charente-Maritime, W France *45.50N 0.13W*
(0) F15 **Mathematicians Seamounts** *undersea feature* E Pacific Ocean
23 X6 **Mathews** Virginia, NE USA *37.24N 76.17W*
27 S14 **Mathis** Texas, SW USA *28.05N 97.49W*
158 J11 **Mathura** *prev.* Muttra. Uttar Pradesh, N India *27.30N 77.42E*
Mathurai *see* Madurai
179 Rr16 **Mati** Mindanao, S Philippines *6.58N 126.11E*
Matianus *see* Orūmīyeh, Daryācheh-ye
Matiara *see* Matiāri
155 Q15 **Matiāri** *var.* Matiara. Sind, SE Pakistan *25.37N 68.28E*
43 S16 **Matías Romero** Oaxaca, SE Mexico *16.52N 94.57W*
45 O13 **Matina** Limón, E Costa Rica *10.02N 83.15W*
12 D10 **Matinenda Lake** ⊚ Ontario, S Canada
21 R8 **Matinicus Island** *island* Maine, NE USA
Matisco/Matisco Ædourum *see* Mâcon
155 Q16 **Mātli** Sind, SE Pakistan *25.06N 68.37E*
99 M18 **Matlock** C England, UK *53.07N 1.31W*
61 F18 **Mato Grosso** *prev.* Vila Bela da Santissima Trindade. Mato Grosso, W Brazil *14.52S 59.58W*
61 G17 **Mato Grosso** *off.* Estado de Mato Grosso; *prev.* Matto Grosso. ◈ *state* W Brazil
62 H8 **Mato Grosso do Sul** *off.* Estado de Mato Grosso do Sul. ◈ *state* S Brazil
61 I18 **Mato Grosso, Planalto de** *plateau* C Brazil
106 G6 **Matosinhos** *prev.* Matozinhos. Porto, NW Portugal *41.10N 8.42W*
Matou *see* Pingguo
57 Z10 **Matoury** NE French Guiana *4.49N 52.17W*
Matozinhos *see* Matosinhos
113 L21 **Mátra** ▲▲ N Hungary
147 Y8 **Maṭraḥ** *var.* Mutrah. NE Oman *23.35N 58.30E*
118 L12 **Mătrașești** Vrancea, E Romania *45.52N 27.13E*
110 M8 **Matrei Am Brenner** Tirol, W Austria *47.09N 11.28E*
111 P8 **Matrei in Osttirol** Tirol, W Austria *47.04N 12.31E*
78 I15 **Matru** SW Sierra Leone *7.37N 12.07W*
77 U7 **Maṭrûḥ** *var.* Mersa Maṭrûḥ; *anc.* Paraetonium. NW Egypt *31.20N 27.15E*
172 Q13 **Matsubara** *var.* Matubara. Kagoshima, Tokuno-shima, SW Japan *32.58N 129.55E*
171 K16 **Matsudo** *var.* Matudo. Chiba, Honshū, S Japan *35.45N 139.49E*
170 F11 **Matsue** *var.* Matsuye, Matue. Shimane, Honshū, SW Japan *35.27N 133.03E*
171 Mm7 **Matsumae** Hokkaidō, NE Japan *41.27N 140.04E*
171 J14 **Matsumoto** *var.* Matumoto. Nagano, Honshū, S Japan *36.18N 137.58E*
171 H16 **Matsusaka** *var.* Matsuzaka, Matusaka. Mie, Honshū, SW Japan *34.34N 136.30E*
167 S12 **Matsu Tao** *Chin.* Mazu Dao. *island* NW Taiwan
Matsutō *see* Mattō
170 C12 **Matsuura** *var.* Matuura. Nagasaki, Kyūshū, SW Japan *33.21N 129.40E*
170 Ee14 **Matsuyama** *var.* Matuyama. Ehime, Shikoku, SW Japan *33.49N 132.46E*
Matsuye *see* Matsue
Matsuzaka *see* Matsusaka
171 J17 **Matsuzaki** Shizuoka, Honshū, S Japan *34.43N 138.45E*
12 F8 **Mattagami** ≈ Ontario, S Canada
12 F8 **Mattagami Lake** ⊚ Ontario, S Canada
64 K12 **Mattaldi** Córdoba, C Argentina *34.32S 64.18W*
23 Y9 **Mattamuskeet, Lake** ⊚ North Carolina, SE USA
23 W6 **Mattaponi River** ≈ Virginia, NE USA
12 I11 **Mattawa** Ontario, SE Canada *46.19N 78.42W*
12 I11 **Mattawa** ≈ Ontario, SE Canada
21 S5 **Mattawamkeag** Maine, NE USA *45.30N 68.20W*
21 S4 **Mattawamkeag Lake** ⊚ Maine, NE USA
110 D11 **Matterhorn** *It.* Monte Cervino. ▲ Italy/Switzerland *45.58N 7.36E* *see also* Cervino, Monte
37 W1 **Matterhorn** ▲ Nevada, W USA *41.48N 115.22W*
34 L12 **Matterhorn** *var.* Sacajawea Peak. ▲ Oregon, NW USA *45.12N 117.18W*
37 R8 **Matterhorn Peak** ▲ California, W USA *38.06N 119.19W*
111 Y5 **Mattersburg** Burgenland, E Austria *47.44N 16.23E*
110 E11 **Matter Vispa** ≈ S Switzerland
57 R7 **Matthews Ridge** N Guyana *7.30N 60.07W*
46 K7 **Matthew Town** Great Inagua, S Bahamas *20.56N 73.40W*
111 Q4 **Mattighofen** Oberösterreich, NW Austria *48.07N 13.09E*
109 N16 **Mattinata** Puglia, SE Italy *41.41N 16.01E*
147 T9 **Maṭṭī, Sabkhat** *salt flat* Saudi Arabia/UAE
20 M14 **Mattituck** Long Island, New York, NE USA *40.59N 72.31W*
171 I13 **Mattō** *var.* Matsutō. Ishikawa, Honshū, SW Japan *36.31N 136.34E*
Matto Grosso *see* Mato Grosso
32 M14 **Mattoon** Illinois, N USA *39.28N 88.22W*
59 L16 **Mattos, Río** ≈ C Bolivia
Mattu *see* Metu
174 Ll5 **Matu** Sarawak, East Malaysia *2.39N 111.31E*
59 E14 **Matucana** Lima, W Peru *11.53S 76.23W*
Matudo *see* Matsudo
Matue *see* Matsue
197 J16 **Matuku** *island* S Fiji
114 B9 **Matulji** Primorje-Gorski Kotar, NW Croatia *45.21N 14.18E*
Matumoto *see* Matsumoto
57 P5 **Maturín** Monagas, NE Venezuela *9.45N 63.10W*
Matusaka *see* Matsusaka
Matuura *see* Matsuura
Matuyama *see* Matsuyama
130 K11 **Matveyev Kurgan** Rostovskaya Oblast', SW Russian Federation *47.31N 38.55E*
131 O8 **Matyshevo** Volgogradskaya Oblast', SW Russian Federation *50.53N 44.09E*
159 O13 **Mau** *var.* Maunāth Bhanjan. Uttar Pradesh, N India *25.57N 83.33E*
85 O14 **Maúa** Niassa, N Mozambique *13.54S 37.13E*
104 M17 **Maubermé, Pic de** *var.* Tuc de Moubermé, *Sp.* Pico Mauberme; *prev.* Tuc de Maubermé. ▲ France/Spain *42.48N 0.54E* *see also* Moubermé, Tuc de
Mauberme, Pico *see* Maubermé, Pic de/Moubermé, Tuc de
Maubermé, Tuc de *see* Maubermé, Pic de/ Moubermé, Tuc de
105 Q2 **Maubeuge** Nord, N France *50.16N 4.00E*
177 Ff8 **Maubin** Irrawaddy, SW Myanmar *16.43N 95.37E*
158 L13 **Maudaha** Uttar Pradesh, N India *25.40N 80.07E*
191 N9 **Maude** New South Wales, SE Australia *34.30S 144.20E*
205 P3 **Maudheimvidda** *physical region* Antarctica
67 N22 **Maud Rise** *undersea feature* S Atlantic Ocean
111 Q4 **Mauerkirchen** Oberösterreich, NW Austria *48.10N 13.07E*
Mauersee *see* Mamry, Jezioro
196 K2 **Maug Islands** *island group* N Northern Mariana Islands
105 Q15 **Mauguio** Hérault, S France *43.37N 4.01E*
199 Kk6 **Maui** *island* Hawai'i, USA, C Pacific Ocean
202 M16 **Mauke** *atoll* S Cook Islands
64 G13 **Maule** *off.* Región del Maule. ◈ *region* C Chile
104 J9 **Mauléon** Deux-Sèvres, W France *46.55N 0.45W*
104 J16 **Mauléon-Licharre** Pyrénées-Atlantiques, SW France *43.14N 0.51W*
64 G13 **Maule, Río** ≈ C Chile
65 G17 **Maullín** Los Lagos, S Chile *41.37S 73.34W*
Maulmain *see* Moulmein
33 R11 **Maumee** Ohio, N USA *41.34N 83.40W*
33 Q12 **Maumee River** ≈ Indiana/Ohio, N USA
29 U11 **Maumelle** Arkansas, C USA *34.51N 92.24W*
29 T11 **Maumelle, Lake** ⊞ Arkansas, C USA
175 Qq16 **Maumere** *prev.* Maoemere. Flores, S Indonesia *8.34S 122.13E*
85 G17 **Maun** Ngamiland, C Botswana *20.00S 23.25E*
Maunāth Bhanjan *see* Mau
Maunawai *see* Waimea
202 H16 **Maungaroa** ▲ Rarotonga, S Cook Islands *21.13S 159.48W*
192 K3 **Maungatapere** Northland, North Island, NZ *35.46S 174.10E*
192 K4 **Maungaturoto** Northland, North Island, NZ *36.06S 174.21E*
203 R10 **Maupiti** *var.* Maurua. *island* Îles Sous le Vent, W French Polynesia
158 K14 **Mau Rānīpur** Uttar Pradesh, N India *25.13N 79.07E*
24 K9 **Maurepas, Lake** ⊚ Louisiana, S USA
105 T16 **Maures** ▲▲ SE France
105 O12 **Mauriac** Cantal, C France *45.13N 2.21E*
Maurice *see* Mauritius
67 J20 **Maurice Ewing Bank** *undersea feature* SW Atlantic Ocean
190 C4 **Maurice, Lake** *salt lake* South Australia
20 I17 **Maurice River** ≈ New Jersey, NE USA
27 Y10 **Mauriceville** Texas, SW USA *30.13N 93.52W*
100 K12 **Maurik** Gelderland, C Netherlands *51.57N 5.25E*
78 H8 **Mauritania** *off.* Islamic Republic of Mauritania, *Ar.* Mūrītānīyah. ◆ *republic* W Africa
181 W15 **Mauritius** *off.* Republic of Mauritius, *Fr.* Maurice. ◆ *republic* W Indian Ocean
132 M17 **Mauritius** *island* W Indian Ocean
181 N9 **Mauritius Trench** *undersea feature* W Indian Ocean
104 H6 **Mauron** Morbihan, NW France *48.06N 2.16W*
105 N13 **Maurs** Cantal, C France *44.45N 2.12E*
Maurua *see* Maupiti
Maury Mid-Ocean Channel *see* Maury Seachannel
66 L6 **Maury Seachannel** *var.* Maury Mid-Ocean Channel. *undersea feature* N Atlantic Ocean
32 K8 **Mauston** Wisconsin, N USA *43.45N 90.01W*
111 R8 **Mauterndorf** Salzburg, NW Austria *47.09N 13.39E*
111 T4 **Mauthausen** Oberösterreich, N Austria *48.13N 14.30E*
111 Q9 **Mauthen** Kärnten, S Austria *46.39N 12.58E*
85 F15 **Mavinga** Cuando Cubango, SE Angola *15.49S 20.23E*
85 M17 **Mavita** Manica, W Mozambique *19.31S 33.09E*
117 K22 **Mavrópetra, Akrotírio** *headland* Thíra, Kykládes, Greece, Aegean Sea *36.28N 25.22E*
117 F16 **Mavrovoúni** ▲ C Greece *39.37N 22.45E*
192 Q8 **Mawhai Point** *headland* North Island, NZ *38.08S 178.24E*
177 Ff3 **Mawlaik** Sagaing, C Myanmar *23.40N 94.25E*
Mawlamyine *see* Moulmein
147 N14 **Mawr, Wādī** *dry watercourse* NW Yemen
205 X5 **Mawson** *Australian research station* Antarctica *67.24S 63.16E*
205 X5 **Mawson Coast** *physical region* Antarctica
30 M4 **Max** North Dakota, N USA *47.48N 101.18W*
43 W12 **Maxcanú** Yucatán, SE Mexico *20.35N 90.00W*
Maxesibebi *see* Mount Ayliff
111 Q5 **Maxglan** ✕ (Salzburg) Salzburg, W Austria *47.46N 13.00E*
95 K16 **Maxmo** *Fin.* Maksamaa. Länsi-Suomi, W Finland *63.13N 22.04E*
23 T11 **Maxton** North Carolina, SE USA *34.47N 79.34W*
27 R8 **May** Texas, SW USA *31.58N 98.54W*
194 E10 **May** ≈ NW PNG
127 N17 **Maya** ≈ E Russian Federation
157 Q19 **Māyābandar** Andaman and Nicobar Islands, India, E Indian Ocean *12.43N 92.52E*
Mayadin *see* Al Mayādīn
46 L5 **Mayaguana** *island* SE Bahamas
46 L5 **Mayaguana Passage** *passage* SE Bahamas
47 S6 **Mayagüez** W Puerto Rico *18.12N 67.08W*
47 R6 **Mayagüez, Bahía de** *bay* W Puerto Rico
Mayals *see* Maials
81 G20 **Mayama** Le Pool, SE Congo *3.49S 14.52E*
39 V8 **Maya, Mesa De** ▲ Colorado, C USA *37.06N 103.30W*
149 R4 **Mayamey** Semnān, N Iran *36.26N 55.49E*
44 F3 **Maya Mountains** *Sp.* Montañas Mayas. ▲▲ Belize/Guatemala
46 I7 **Mayarí** Holguín, E Cuba *20.40N 75.42W*
Mayas, Montañas *see* Maya Mountains
20 I17 **May, Cape** *headland* New Jersey, NE USA *38.55N 74.57W*
82 J11 **Maych'ew** *var.* Mai Chio, *It.* Mai Ceu, Tigray, N Ethiopia *12.55N 39.30E*
144 I2 **Maydān Ikbiz** Ḥalab, N Syria *36.51N 36.40E*
155 Q5 **Maydān Shahr** Wardag, E Afghanistan *34.27N 68.48E*
82 O12 **Maydh** Sanaag, N Somalia *10.57N 47.07E*
Maydī *see* Mīdī
Mayebashi *see* Maebashi
Mayence *see* Mainz
104 K6 **Mayenne** Mayenne, NW France *48.18N 0.37W*
104 J6 **Mayenne** ◈ *department* NW France
104 J7 **Mayenne** ≈ N France
38 K12 **Mayer** Arizona, SW USA *34.25N 112.15W*
24 J4 **Mayersville** Mississippi, S USA *32.54N 91.04W*
9 P14 **Mayerthorpe** Alberta, SW Canada *53.58N 115.06W*
23 S12 **Mayesville** South Carolina, SE USA *34.00N 80.10W*
193 G19 **Mayfield** Canterbury, South Island, NZ *43.50S 171.24E*
35 N14 **Mayfield** Idaho, NW USA *43.24N 115.56W*
22 G7 **Mayfield** Kentucky, S USA *36.44N 88.38W*
38 L5 **Mayfield** Utah, W USA *39.06N 111.42W*
168 K9 **Mayhan** Övörhangay, C Mongolia *46.02N 104.00E*
39 T14 **Mayhill** New Mexico, SW USA *32.52N 105.28W*
151 T9 **Maykain** *Kaz.* Mayqayyng. Pavlodar, NE Kazakhstan *51.24N 75.46E*
130 L14 **Maykop** Respublika Adygeya, SW Russian Federation *44.36N 40.06E*
Maylibash *see* Maylybas
Mayli-Say *see* Mayluu-Suu
153 T9 **Mayluu-Suu** *prev.* Mayli-Say, *Kir.* Mayly-Say. Dzhalal-Abadskaya Oblast', W Kyrgyzstan *41.16N 72.27E*
150 L14 **Maylybas** *prev.* Maylibash. Kyzylorda, S Kazakhstan *45.51N 62.37E*
Mayly-Say *see* Mayluu-Suu
Maymana *see* Meymaneh
178 Gg5 **Maymyo** Mandalay, C Myanmar *22.03N 96.30E*
127 P6 **Mayn** ≈ NE Russian Federation
131 Q5 **Mayna** Ul'yanovskaya Oblast', W Russian Federation *54.04N 47.20E*
23 N8 **Maynardville** Tennessee, S USA *36.15N 83.48W*
12 J13 **Maynooth** Ontario, SE Canada *45.14N 77.54W*
8 I6 **Mayo** Yukon Territory, NW Canada *63.37N 135.48W*
25 U9 **Mayo** Florida, SE USA *30.03N 83.10W*
99 B16 **Mayo** *Ir.* Maigh Eo. *cultural region* W Ireland
Mayo *see* Maio
80 G12 **Mayo-Kébbi** *off.* Préfecture du Mayo-Kébbu, *var.* Mayo-Kébi. ◈ *prefecture* SW Chad
Mayo-Kébi *see* Mayo-Kébbi
81 F19 **Mayoko** Le Niari, SW Congo *2.18S 12.45E*
179 Q11 **Mayon Volcano** ※ Luzon, N Philippines *13.15N 123.40E*
63 A24 **Mayor Buratovich** Buenos Aires, E Argentina *39.12S 62.41W*
106 L4 **Mayorga** Castilla-León, N Spain *42.10N 5.16W*
192 N6 **Mayor Island** *island* NE NZ
Mayor Pablo Lagerenza *see* Capitán Pablo Lagerenza
181 I14 **Mayotte** ◇ *French territorial collectivity* E Africa
Mayoumba *see* Mayumba
46 J13 **May Pen** C Jamaica *17.58N 77.15W*
Mayqayyng *see* Maykain
179 P7 **Mayraira Point** *headland* Luzon, N Philippines *18.36N 120.47E*
111 N8 **Mayrhofen** Tirol, W Austria *47.09N 11.52E*
194 F10 **May River** East Sepik, NW PNG *4.10S 141.51E*
126 Mm15 **Mayskiy** Amurskaya Oblast', SE Russian Federation *52.13N 129.30E*
131 O15 **Mayskiy** Kabardino-Balkarskaya Respublika, SW Russian Federation *43.37N 44.04E*
151 U9 **Mayskoye** Pavlodar, NE Kazakhstan *50.55N 78.11E*
20 J17 **Mays Landing** New Jersey, NE USA *39.27N 74.43W*
23 N4 **Maysville** Kentucky, S USA *38.39N 83.44W*
29 R2 **Maysville** Missouri, C USA *39.53N 94.21W*
176 Y14 **Mayu** *channel* Papua, E Indonesia
81 D20 **Mayumba** *var.* Mayoumba. Nyanga, S Gabon *3.22S 10.37E*
175 Ss7 **Mayu, Pulau** *island* Maluku, E Indonesia
33 S8 **Mayville** Michigan, N USA *43.18N 83.16W*
20 C11 **Mayville** New York, NE USA *42.15N 79.31W*
31 Q4 **Mayville** North Dakota, N USA *47.27N 97.17W*
126 M11 **Mayya** Respublika Sakha (Yakutiya), NE Russian Federation *61.45N 130.16E*
Mayyali *see* Mahe
Mayyit, Al Baḥr al *see* Dead Sea
85 J15 **Mazabuka** Southern, S Zambia *15.52S 27.46E*
Mazaca *see* Kayseri
Mazagan *see* El-Jadida
34 J7 **Mazama** Washington, NW USA *48.34N 120.26W*
105 O15 **Mazamet** Tarn, S France *43.30N 2.21E*
149 O4 **Māzandarān** *off.* Ostān-e Māzandarān. ◈ *province* N Iran
162 F7 **Mazar** Xinjiang Uygur Zizhiqu, NW China *36.31N 76.59E*
109 H24 **Mazara del Vallo** Sicilia, Italy, C Mediterranean Sea *37.39N 12.36E*
155 O2 **Mazār-e Sharīf** *var.* Mazār-i Sharif. Balkh, N Afghanistan *36.44N 67.06E*
Mazār-i Sharif *see* Mazār-e Sharīf
107 R13 **Mazarrón** Murcia, SE Spain *37.36N 1.19W*
107 R14 **Mazarrón, Golfo de** *gulf* SE Spain
57 S9 **Mazaruni River** ≈ N Guyana
44 B6 **Mazatenango** Suchitepéquez, SW Guatemala *14.31N 91.28W*
42 I10 **Mazatlán** Sinaloa, C Mexico *23.15N 106.24W*
38 L12 **Mazatzal Mountains** ▲▲ Arizona, SW USA
120 D10 **Mažeikiai** Telšiai, NW Lithuania *56.19N 22.21E*
120 D7 **Mazirbe** Talsi, NW Latvia *57.39N 22.16E*
42 G5 **Mazocahui** Sonora, NW Mexico *29.34N 110.07W*
59 I18 **Mazocruz** Puno, S Peru *16.41S 69.42W*
Mazoe, Rio *see* Mazowe
81 N21 **Mazomeno** Maniema, E Dem. Rep. Congo *4.54S 27.13E*
165 Q6 **Mazong Shan** ▲ N China *41.40N 97.10E*
85 L16 **Mazowe** *var.* Rio Mazoe. ≈ Mozambique/Zimbabwe
112 L11 **Mazowieckie** ◈ *province* C Poland
Mazra'a *see* Al Mazra'ah
144 G6 **Mazraat Kfar Debiâne** C Lebanon *34.00N 35.51E*
120 H7 **Mazsalaca** *Est.* Väike-Salatsi, *Ger.* Salisburg. Valmiera, N Latvia *57.52N 25.03E*
112 L9 **Mazury** *physical region* NE Poland
121 M20 **Mazyr** *Rus.* Mozyr'. Homyel'skaya Voblasts', SE Belarus *52.03N 29.14E*
109 K25 **Mazzarino** Sicilia, Italy, C Mediterranean Sea *37.18N 14.13E*
Mba *see* Ba
85 L21 **Mbabane** ● (Swaziland) NW Swaziland *26.24S 31.13E*
Mbacké *see* Mbaké
79 N16 **Mbahiakro** E Ivory Coast *7.25N 4.18W*
81 I16 **Mbaïki** *var.* M'Baiki. Lobaye, SW Central African Republic *3.52N 17.58E*
81 F14 **Mbakaou, Lac de** ⊚ C Cameroon
78 G11 **Mbaké** *var.* Mbacké. W Senegal *14.50N 15.52W*
84 L11 **Mbala** *prev.* Abercorn. Northern, NE Zambia *8.49S 31.22E*
85 J18 **Mbalabala** *prev.* Balla Balla. Matabeleland South, SW Zimbabwe *20.27S 29.03E*
83 G18 **Mbale** E Uganda *1.04N 34.12E*
81 E16 **Mbalmayo** *var.* M'Balmayo. Centre, S Cameroon *3.30N 11.31E*
83 H25 **Mbamba Bay** Ruvuma, S Tanzania *11.15S 34.44E*
81 I18 **Mbandaka** *prev.* Coquilhatville. Equateur, NW Dem. Rep. Congo *0.07N 18.11E*
84 B9 **M'Banza Congo** *var.* Mbanza Congo; *prev.* São Salvador, São Salvador do Congo. Zaire, NW Angola *6.10S 14.16E*
81 G21 **Mbanza-Ngungu** Bas-Congo, W Dem. Rep. Congo *5.19S 14.45E*
69 V11 **Mbarangandu** ≈ E Tanzania
83 E19 **Mbarara** SW Uganda *0.36S 30.40E*
81 L15 **Mbari** ≈ SE Central African Republic
83 I24 **Mbarika Mountains** ▲▲ S Tanzania
85 J24 **Mbashe** ≈ S South Africa
Mbatiki *see* Batiki
80 F13 **Mbé** Nord, N Cameroon *7.51N 13.36E*
83 J24 **Mbemkuru** *var.* Mbwemkuru. ≈ S Tanzania
Mbengga *see* Beqa
180 H13 **Mbéni** Grande Comore, NW Comoros
85 K18 **Mberengwa** Midlands, S Zimbabwe *20.25S 29.57E*
83 G24 **Mbeya** Mbeya, SW Tanzania *8.54S 33.28E*
83 G23 **Mbeya** ◈ *region* S Tanzania
81 E19 **Mbigou** Ngounié, C Gabon *01.54S 12.00E*
Mbilua *see* Vella Lavella
81 F19 **Mbinda** Le Niari, SW Congo *2.07S 12.52E*
81 D17 **Mbini** W Equatorial Guinea *1.34N 9.39E*
Mbini *see* Uolo, Río
85 L18 **Mbizi** Masvingo, SE Zimbabwe *21.21S 30.58E*
83 G23 **Mbogo** Mbeya, W Tanzania *7.24S 33.26E*
81 N15 **Mboki** Haut-Mbomou, SE Central African Republic *5.18N 25.52E*
81 G18 **Mbomo** Cuvette, NW Congo *0.25N 14.42E*
81 L15 **Mbomou** ◈ *prefecture* SE Central African Republic
Mbomou/M'Bomu/Mbomu *see* Bomu
78 F11 **Mbour** W Senegal *14.24N 16.58W*
78 I10 **Mbout** Gorgol, S Mauritania *16.01N 12.37W*
81 J14 **Mbrès** *var.* Mbrés. Nana-Grébizi, C Central African Republic *6.40N 19.46E*
81 L22 **Mbuji-Mayi** *prev.* Bakwanga. Kasai Oriental, S Dem. Rep. Congo *6.04S 23.30E*
194 J9 **M'buke Islands** *island group* N PNG
83 H21 **Mbulu** Arusha, N Tanzania *3.45S 35.33E*
194 K8 **M'bunai** *var.* Bunai. Manus Island, N PNG *2.09S 147.11E*
64 N8 **Mburucuyá** Corrientes, NE Argentina *28.03S 58.15W*
Mbutha *see* Buca
Mbwemkuru *see* Mbemkuru
83 G21 **Mbwikwe** Singida, C Tanzania *5.19S 34.09E*
11 O15 **McAdam** New Brunswick, SE Canada *45.34N 67.19W*
27 O5 **McAdoo** Texas, SW USA *33.41N 100.58W*
37 V2 **McAfee Peak** ▲ Nevada, W USA *41.31N 115.57W*
29 P11 **McAlester** Oklahoma, C USA *34.55N 95.46W*
27 S17 **McAllen** Texas, SW USA *26.12N 98.13W*
23 S11 **McBee** South Carolina, SE USA *34.30N 80.12W*
9 N14 **McBride** British Columbia, SW Canada *53.21N 120.19W*
26 M9 **McCamey** Texas, SW USA *31.08N 102.13W*
35 R15 **McCammon** Idaho, NW USA *42.38N 112.10W*
37 X11 **McCarran** ✕ (Las Vegas) Nevada, W USA *36.04N 115.07W*
41 T11 **McCarthy** Alaska, USA *61.25N 142.55W*
32 M5 **McCaslin Mountain** *hill* Wisconsin, N USA *45.24N 88.24W*
27 O2 **McClellan Creek** ≈ Texas, SW USA
23 T14 **McClellanville** South Carolina, SE USA *33.07N 79.27W*
15 Jj2 **McClintock Channel** *channel* Nunavut, N Canada
205 R12 **McClintock, Mount** ▲ Antarctica *80.09S 156.42E*
37 N2 **McCloud** California, W USA *41.15N 122.09W*
37 N3 **McCloud River** ≈ California, W USA
37 Q9 **McClure, Lake** ⊞ California, W USA
207 O8 **McClure Strait** *strait* Northwest Territories, N Canada
31 N4 **McClusky** North Dakota, N USA *47.27N 100.25W*
23 T11 **McColl** South Carolina, SE USA *34.40N 79.33W*
24 K7 **McComb** Mississippi, S USA *31.14N 90.27W*
20 E16 **McConnellsburg** Pennsylvania, NE USA *39.56N 78.00W*
33 T14 **McConnelsville** Ohio, N USA *39.39N 81.51W*
30 M17 **McCook** Nebraska, C USA *40.12N 100.37W*
23 P13 **McCormick** South Carolina, SE USA *33.54N 82.17W*
9 W16 **McCreary** Manitoba, S Canada *50.48N 99.34W*
29 W11 **McCrory** Arkansas, C USA *35.15N 91.12W*
27 T10 **McDade** Texas, SW USA *30.15N 97.15W*
25 O8 **McDavid** Florida, SE USA *30.51N 87.18W*
37 T1 **McDermitt** Nevada, W USA *41.57N 117.43W*
25 S4 **McDonough** Georgia, SE USA *33.27N 84.09W*
38 L12 **McDowell Mountains** ▲▲ Arizona, SW USA
22 H8 **McEwen** Tennessee, S USA *36.06N 87.37W*
37 R12 **McFarland** California, W USA *35.41N 119.14W*
Mcfarlane, Lake *see* Macfarlane, Lake
29 P12 **McGee Creek Lake** ⊞ Oklahoma, C USA
29 W13 **McGehee** Arkansas, C USA *33.37N 91.24W*
37 X5 **Mcgill** Nevada, W USA *39.24N 114.46W*
12 K11 **McGillivray, Lac** ⊚ Québec, SE Canada
41 P10 **Mcgrath** Alaska, USA *62.57N 155.36W*
27 T8 **McGregor** Texas, SW USA *31.26N 97.24W*
35 O12 **McGuire, Mount** ▲ Idaho, NW USA *45.10N 114.36W*
85 M14 **Mchinji** *prev.* Fort Manning. Central, W Malawi *13.47S 32.51E*
30 M7 **McIntosh** South Dakota, N USA *45.52N 101.19W*
16 O3 **McKeand** ≈ Baffin Island, Nunavut, NE Canada
203 R4 **McKean Island** *island* Phoenix Islands, C Kiribati
32 J13 **McKee Creek** ≈ Illinois, N USA
20 C15 **Mckeesport** Pennsylvania, NE USA *40.18N 79.48W*
23 V7 **McKenney** Virginia, NE USA *36.57N 77.42W*
22 G8 **McKenzie** Tennessee, S USA *36.07N 88.31W*
193 B20 **McKerrow, Lake** ⊚ South Island, NZ
41 Q10 **McKinley, Mount** *var.* Denali. ▲ Alaska, USA *63.04N 151.00W*
41 R10 **McKinley Park** Alaska, USA *63.42N 149.01W*
36 K3 **McKinleyville** California, W USA *40.56N 124.06W*
27 U6 **McKinney** Texas, SW USA *33.12N 96.37W*
28 I5 **McKinney, Lake** ⊚ Kansas, C USA
30 M7 **McLaughlin** South Dakota, N USA *45.48N 100.48W*
27 O2 **McLean** Texas, SW USA *35.13N 100.36W*
32 M16 **Mcleansboro** Illinois, N USA *38.05N 88.32W*
9 O13 **McLennan** Alberta, W Canada *55.42N 116.49W*
12 L9 **McLennan, Lac** ⊚ Québec, SE Canada
8 M13 **McLeod Lake** British Columbia, W Canada *55.03N 123.02W*
29 N10 **McLoud** Oklahoma, C USA *35.26N 97.05W*
34 G15 **McLoughlin, Mount** ▲ Oregon, NW USA *42.27N 122.18W*
39 U15 **McMillan, Lake** ⊞ New Mexico, SW USA
34 G11 **McMinnville** Oregon, NW USA *45.13N 123.12W*
22 K9 **McMinnville** Tennessee, S USA *35.42N 85.46W*
205 R13 **McMurdo** *US research station* Antarctica *77.40S 167.16E*
26 H9 **McNary** Texas, SW USA *31.15N 105.46W*
39 N13 **Mcnary** Arizona, SW USA *34.04N 109.51W*
29 N5 **McPherson** Kansas, C USA *38.22N 97.39W*
McPherson *see* Fort McPherson
25 U6 **McRae** Georgia, SE USA *32.04N 82.54W*
31 P4 **McVille** North Dakota, N USA *47.45N 98.10W*
85 J25 **Mdantsane** Eastern Cape, SE South Africa *32.54S 27.39E*
178 Jj6 **Me** Ninh Binh, N Vietnam *20.21N 105.49E*
28 J7 **Meade** Kansas, C USA *37.14N 100.20W*
41 O5 **Meade River** ≈ Alaska, USA
37 Y11 **Mead, Lake** ⊞ Arizona/Nevada, W USA
26 M5 **Meadow** Texas, SW USA *33.20N 102.12W*
9 S14 **Meadow Lake** Saskatchewan, C Canada *55.08N 108.25W*
37 Y10 **Meadow Valley Wash** ≈ Nevada, W USA
24 J7 **Meadville** Mississippi, S USA *31.28N 90.51W*
20 B12 **Meadville** Pennsylvania, NE USA *41.38N 80.09W*
12 F14 **Meaford** Ontario, S Canada *44.35N 80.35W*
Meáin, Inis *see* Inishmaan
106 G8 **Mealhada** Aveiro, N Portugal *40.22N 8.27W*
11 R8 **Mealy Mountains** ▲▲ Newfoundland and Labrador, E Canada
9 O10 **Meander River** Alberta, W Canada *59.01N 117.42W*
34 E11 **Meares, Cape** *headland* Oregon, NW USA *45.29N 123.59W*
49 V6 **Mearim, Rio** ≈ NE Brazil
Measca, Loch *see* Mask, Lough
99 F17 **Meath** *Ir.* An Mhí. *cultural region* E Ireland
9 T14 **Meath Park** Saskatchewan, S Canada *53.25N 105.18W*
105 O5 **Meaux** Seine-et-Marne, N France *48.58N 2.54E*

◆ Country
● Country Capital
◇ Dependent Territory
○ Dependent Territory Capital
◈ Administrative Region
✕ International Airport
▲ Mountain
▲▲ Mountain Range
※ Volcano
≈ River
⊚ Lake
⊞ Reservoir

MEBANE – MESHED

23 T9 **Mebane** North Carolina, SE USA *36.06N 79.16W*
176 W9 **Mebo, Gunung** ▲ Papua, E Indonesia *1.10S 133.53E*
96 I8 **Mebonden** Sør-Trøndelag, S Norway *63.13N 11.00E*
84 A10 **Mebridege** ≈ NW Angola
37 W16 **Mecca** California, W USA *33.34N 116.04W*
Mecca *see* Makkah
31 Y14 **Mechanicsville** Iowa, C USA *41.54N 91.15W*
20 L10 **Mechanicville** New York, NE USA *42.54N 73.41W*
101 H17 **Mechelen** *Eng.* Mechlin, *Fr.* Malines. Antwerpen, C Belgium *51.01N 4.28E*
196 C8 **Mecherchar** *var.* Eil Malk. *island* Palau Islands, Palau
103 D17 **Mechernich** Nordrhein-Westfalen, W Germany *50.36N 6.39E*
130 L12 **Mechetinskaya** Rostovskaya Oblast', SW Russian Federation *46.46N 40.30E*
116 J11 **Mechka** ≈ S Bulgaria
Mechlin *see* Mechelen
63 D23 **Mechongué** Buenos Aires, E Argentina *38.09S 58.13W*
117 L14 **Mecidiye** Edirne, NW Turkey *40.39N 26.33E*
103 I24 **Meckenbeuren** Baden-Württemberg, S Germany *47.42N 9.34E*
102 L8 **Mecklenburger Bucht** *bay* N Germany
102 M10 **Mecklenburgische Seenplatte** *wetland* NE Germany
102 L9 **Mecklenburg-Vorpommern** ◆ *state* NE Germany
85 Q15 **Meconta** Nampula, NE Mozambique *15.01S 39.52E*
113 I25 **Mecsek** ▲ SW Hungary
85 P14 **Mecubúri** ≈ N Mozambique
85 Q14 **Mecúfi** Cabo Delgado, NE Mozambique *13.18S 40.33E*
84 O13 **Mecula** Niassa, N Mozambique *12.03S 37.37E*
173 Ff5 **Medan** Sumatera, E Indonesia *3.34N 98.39E*
63 A24 **Médanos** *var.* Medanos. Buenos Aires, E Argentina *38.51S 62.44W*
63 C19 **Médanos** Entre Ríos, E Argentina *33.25S 59.03W*
161 K24 **Medawachchiya** North Central Province, N Sri Lanka *8.32N 80.30E*
108 C8 **Mede** Lombardia, N Italy *45.06N 8.43E*
76 J5 **Médéa** *var.* El Mediyya, Lemdiyya. N Algeria *36.24N 2.42E*
Medeba *see* Ma'dabā
56 E8 **Medellín** Antioquia, NW Colombia *6.15N 75.36W*
102 H9 **Medem** ≈ NW Germany
100 J8 **Medemblik** Noord-Holland, NW Netherlands *52.46N 5.06E*
77 N7 **Médenine** *var.* Madanīyīn. SE Tunisia *33.23N 10.30E*
78 G9 **Mederdra** Trarza, SW Mauritania *16.55N 15.40W*
Medeshamstede *see* Peterborough
44 F4 **Medesto Mendez** Izabal, NE Guatemala *15.54N 89.13W*
21 O11 **Medford** Massachusetts, NE USA *42.25N 71.08W*
29 N8 **Medford** Oklahoma, C USA *36.49N 97.45W*
34 G15 **Medford** Oregon, NW USA *42.19N 122.52W*
32 K6 **Medford** Wisconsin, N USA *45.07N 90.22W*
41 P10 **Medfra** Alaska, USA *63.06N 154.42W*
118 M14 **Medgidia** Constanţa, SE Romania *44.16N 28.13E*
Medgyes *see* Mediaş
45 O5 **Media Luna, Arrecifes de la** *reef* E Honduras
62 G11 **Medianeira** Paraná, S Brazil *25.15S 54.07W*
31 Y15 **Mediapolis** Iowa, C USA *41.00N 91.09W*
118 I11 **Mediaş** *Ger.* Mediasch, *Hung.* Medgyes. Sibiu, C Romania *46.09N 24.20E*
43 S15 **Medias Aguas** Veracruz-Llave, SE Mexico *17.40N 95.01W*
Mediasch *see* Mediaş
108 G10 **Medicina** Emilia-Romagna, C Italy *44.29N 11.41E*
35 X16 **Medicine Bow** Wyoming, C USA *41.52N 106.11W*
39 S2 **Medicine Bow Mountains** ▲ Colorado/Wyoming, C USA
35 X16 **Medicine Bow River** ≈ Wyoming, C USA
9 R17 **Medicine Hat** Alberta, SW Canada *50.03N 110.40W*
28 L7 **Medicine Lodge** Kansas, C USA *37.14N 98.33W*
28 L7 **Medicine Lodge River** ≈ Kansas/Oklahoma, C USA
114 E7 **Međimurje** *off.* Međimurska Županija. ◆ *province* N Croatia
Međimurska Županija *see* Međimurje
56 G10 **Medina** Cundinamarca, C Colombia *4.31N 73.21W*
20 E9 **Medina** New York, NE USA *43.13N 78.23W*
31 O5 **Medina** North Dakota, N USA *46.53N 99.18W*
33 T11 **Medina** Ohio, N USA *41.08N 81.51W*
27 Q11 **Medina** Texas, SW USA *29.46N 99.14W*
Medina *see* Al Madīnah
123 Ll12 **Medina Bank** *undersea feature* C Mediterranean Sea
107 P6 **Medinaceli** Castilla-León, N Spain *41.10N 2.25W*
106 L6 **Medina del Campo** Castilla-León, N Spain *41.18N 4.55W*
106 L5 **Medina de Ríoseco** Castilla-León, N Spain *41.52N 5.03W*
Médina Gonassé *see* Médina Gounas
78 H12 **Médina Gounas** *var.* Médina Gonassé. S Senegal *13.06N 13.49W*
27 S12 **Medina River** ≈ Texas, SW USA
106 K16 **Medina Sidonia** Andalucía, S Spain *36.28N 5.55W*
Medinat Israel *see* Israel
121 H14 **Medininkai** Vilnius, SE Lithuania *54.32N 25.39E*
159 R16 **Medinīpur** West Bengal, NE India *22.27N 87.19E*
Mediolanum *see* Saintes, France
Mediolanum *see* Milano, Italy
Mediomatrica *see* Metz
124 O13 **Mediterranean Ridge** *undersea feature* C Mediterranean Sea
123 L11 **Mediterranean Sea** *Fr.* Mer Méditerranée. *sea* Africa/Asia/Europe
Méditerranée, Mer *see* Mediterranean Sea
81 N17 **Medje** Orientale, NE Dem. Rep. Congo *2.27N 27.14E*
123 K11 **Medjerda, Oued** *var.* Mejerda, Wādī Majardah. ≈ Algeria/Tunisia *see also* Mejerda
116 G7 **Medkovets** Montana, NW Bulgaria *43.39N 23.22E*
95 J15 **Medle** Västerbotten, N Sweden *64.45N 20.45E*
131 W7 **Mednogorsk** Orenburgskaya Oblast', W Russian Federation *51.24N 57.37E*
127 Qq9 **Mednyy, Ostrov** *island* E Russian Federation
104 J12 **Médoc** *cultural region* SW France
165 Q16 **Mêdog** Xizang Zizhiqu, W China *29.25N 95.25E*
30 J5 **Medora** North Dakota, N USA *46.52N 103.32W*
81 E17 **Médouneu** Woleu-Ntem, N Gabon *0.58N 10.49E*
108 I7 **Meduna** ≈ NE Italy
Medunta *see* Mantes-la-Jolie
Medvedica *see* Medveditsa
128 J16 **Medveditsa** *var.* Medvedica. ≈ W Russian Federation
131 O9 **Medveditsa** ≈ SW Russian Federation
114 E8 **Medvednica** ▲ NE Croatia
129 R15 **Medvedok** Kirovskaya Oblast', NW Russian Federation *57.23N 50.01E*
127 Nn5 **Medvezh'i, Ostrova** *island group* NE Russian Federation
128 J9 **Medvezh'yegorsk** Respublika Kareliya, NW Russian Federation *62.56N 34.26E*
111 T11 **Medvode** *Ger.* Zwischenwässern. NW Slovenia *46.09N 14.21E*
130 J4 **Medyn'** Kaluzhskaya Oblast', W Russian Federation *54.59N 35.52E*
188 J10 **Meekatharra** Western Australia *26.36S 118.34E*
39 Q4 **Meeker** Colorado, C USA *40.02N 107.54W*
11 T12 **Meelpaeg Lake** ◎ Newfoundland and Labrador, E Canada
Meenen *see* Menen
103 M16 **Meerane** Sachsen, E Germany *50.49N 12.28E*
103 D15 **Meerbusch** Nordrhein-Westfalen, W Germany *51.19N 6.43E*
100 I12 **Meerkerk** Zuid-Holland, C Netherlands *51.55N 5.00E*
101 L18 **Meerssen** *var.* Mersen. Limburg, SE Netherlands *50.52N 5.45E*
158 J10 **Meerut** Uttar Pradesh, N India *29.01N 77.40E*
35 U13 **Meeteetse** Wyoming, C USA *44.10N 108.53W*
101 K17 **Meeuwen** Limburg, NE Belgium *51.04N 5.36E*
83 J16 **Mēga** Oromo, C Ethiopia *4.03N 38.15E*
83 J16 **Mēga Escarpment** *escarpment* S Ethiopia
Megála Kalívia *see* Megála Kalývia
117 E16 **Megála Kalývia** *var.* Megála Kalívia. Thessalía, C Greece *39.30N 21.48E*
117 H14 **Megáli Panagiá** *var.* Megáli Panayía. Kentrikí Makedonía, N Greece *40.24N 23.42E*
Megáli Panayía *see* Megáli Panagiá
Megáli Préspa, Límni *see* Prespa, Lake
116 K12 **Megálo Livádi** ▲ Bulgaria/Greece *41.18N 25.51E*
117 E20 **Megalópoli** *prev.* Megalópolis. Pelopónnisos, S Greece *37.23N 22.08E*
Megalópolis *see* Megalópoli
176 V9 **Megamo** Papua, E Indonesia *0.55S 131.46E*
117 C18 **Meganísi** *island* Iónioi Nísoi, Greece, C Mediterranean Sea
Meganom, Mys *see* Mehanom, Mys
Mégantic *see* Lac-Mégantic
13 R12 **Mégantic, Mont** ▲ Québec, SE Canada *45.27N 71.09W*
117 G19 **Mégara** Attikí, C Greece *38.00N 23.20E*
27 R5 **Megargel** Texas, SW USA *33.27N 98.55W*
100 K13 **Megen** Noord-Brabant, S Netherlands *51.49N 5.34E*
159 U13 **Meghālaya** ◆ *state* NE India
159 U16 **Meghna** ≈ S Bangladesh
143 V14 **Meghri** *Rus.* Megri. SE Armenia *38.57N 46.15E*
126 Gg11 **Megion** Khanty-Mansiyskiy Avtonomnyy Okrug, C Russian Federation *61.01N 76.15E*
117 Q23 **Megísti** *var.* Kastellórizon. *island* SE Greece
Megri *see* Meghri
Mehabad *see* Mahābād
118 F13 **Mehadia** *Hung.* Mehádia. Caraş-Severin, SW Romania *44.53N 22.20E*
94 L7 **Mehamn** Finnmark, N Norway *71.01N 27.46E*
119 U13 **Mehanom, Mys** *Rus.* Mys Meganom. *headland* S Ukraine *44.48N 35.04E*
155 P14 **Mehar** Sind, SE Pakistan *27.10N 67.56E*
188 J8 **Meharry, Mount** ▲ Western Australia *23.17S 118.48E*
Mehdia *see* Mahdia
118 G14 **Mehedinţi** ◆ *county* SW Romania
159 S15 **Meherpur** Khulna, W Bangladesh *23.46N 88.40E*
23 W8 **Meherrin River** ≈ North Carolina/Virginia, SE USA
Meheso *see* Mī'ēso
203 T11 **Mehetia** *island* Îles du Vent, W French Polynesia
120 K6 **Mehikoorma** Tartumaa, E Estonia *58.14N 27.29E*
Me Hka *see* Nmai Hka
149 N5 **Mehrabad** ✈ (Tehrān) Tehrān, N Iran *35.46N 51.07E*
148 J7 **Mehrān** Īlām, W Iran *33.07N 46.10E*
149 Q14 **Mehrān, Rūd-e** *prev.* Mansurabad. ≈ W Iran
149 Q9 **Mehrīz** Yazd, C Iran *31.31N 54.28E*
155 R5 **Mehtarlām** *var.* Mehtar Lām, Meterlam, Methariam, Metharlam. Laghmān, E Afghanistan *34.39N 70.10E*
105 N8 **Mehun-sur-Yèvre** Cher, C France *47.09N 2.15E*
81 G14 **Meiganga** Adamaoua, NE Cameroon *6.31N 14.07E*
166 H10 **Meigu** *var.* Bapu. Sichuan, C China *28.22N 103.07E*
169 W11 **Meihekou** *var.* Hailong. Jilin, NE China *42.31N 125.40E*
101 L15 **Meijel** Limburg, SE Netherlands *51.22N 5.52E*
Meijiang *see* Ningdu
177 G5 **Meiktila** Mandalay, C Myanmar *20.52N 95.54E*
Meilbhe, Loch *see* Melvin, Lough
110 G7 **Meilen** Zürich, N Switzerland *47.16N 8.39E*
Meilu *see* Wuchuan
167 T12 **Meinhua Yu** *island* N Taiwan
103 J17 **Meiningen** Thüringen, C Germany *50.34N 10.25E*
110 F9 **Meiringen** Bern, S Switzerland *46.42N 8.13E*
Meishan *see* Jinzhai
103 O15 **Meissen** *var.* Meißen. Sachsen, E Germany *51.10N 13.28E*
103 I15 **Meissner** ▲ C Germany *51.13N 9.52E*
101 K25 **Meix-devant-Virton** Luxembourg, SE Belgium *49.36N 5.27E*
Mei Xian *see* Meizhou
Meixing *see* Xinjin
167 P13 **Meizhou** *var.* Meixian, Mei Xian. Guangdong, S China *24.21N 116.05E*
69 P2 **Mejerda** *var.* Oued Medjerda, Wādī Majardah. ≈ Algeria/Tunisia *see also* Medjerda, Oued
44 F7 **Mejicanos** San Salvador, C El Salvador *13.50N 89.13W*
Méjico *see* Mexico
64 G5 **Mejillones** Antofagasta, N Chile *23.03S 70.25W*
201 V5 **Mejit Island** *var.* Mājeej. *island* Ratak Chain, NE Marshall Islands
81 F17 **Mékambo** Ogooué-Ivindo, NE Gabon *1.03N 13.49E*
82 J10 **Mek'elē** *var.* Makale. Tigray, N Ethiopia *13.36N 39.28E*
76 I10 **Mekerrhane, Sebkha** *var.* Sebkha Meqerghane, Sebkra Mekerrhane. *salt flat* C Algeria
Mekerrhane, Sebkra *see* Mekerrhane, Sebkha
78 G10 **Mékhé** NW Senegal *15.08N 16.42W*
152 G14 **Mekhinli** Ahal Welaýaty, C Turkmenistan *37.28N 59.20E*
13 P9 **Mékinac, Lac** ◎ Québec, SE Canada
Meklong *see* Samut Songhram
76 G6 **Meknès** N Morocco *33.54N 5.27W*
133 U12 **Mekong** *var.* Lan-ts'ang Chiang, *Cam.* Mékôngk, *Chin.* Lancang Jiang, *Lao.* Mènam Khong, *Th.* Mae Nam Khong, *Tib.* Dza Chu, *Vtn.* Sông Tiên Giang. ≈ SE Asia
Mekongga, Pegunungan *see* Mengkoka, Pegunungan
Mékôngk *see* Mekong
178 K15 **Mekong, Mouths of the** *delta* S Vietnam
40 L12 **Mekoryuk** Nunivak Island, Alaska, USA *60.23N 166.11W*
79 R14 **Mékrou** ≈ N Benin
174 H6 **Melaka** *var.* Malacca. Melaka, Peninsular Malaysia *2.13N 102.13E*
174 H6 **Melaka** *var.* Malacca. ◆ *state* Peninsular Malaysia
Melaka, Selat *see* Malacca, Strait of
183 O6 **Melanesia** *island group* W Pacific Ocean
183 P5 **Melanesian Basin** *undersea feature* W Pacific Ocean
175 Ss4 **Melanguane** Pulau Karakelang, N Indonesia *4.02N 126.43E*
174 Ll8 **Melawi, Sungai** ≈ Borneo, N Indonesia
191 N12 **Melbourne** *state capital* Victoria, SE Australia *37.51S 144.56E*
29 V9 **Melbourne** Arkansas, C USA *36.03N 91.54W*
25 Y12 **Melbourne** Florida, SE USA *28.04N 80.36W*
31 W14 **Melbourne** Iowa, C USA *41.57N 93.07W*
94 G10 **Melbu** Nordland, C Norway *68.30N 14.46E*
Melchor de Mencos *see* Ciudad Melchor de Mencos
65 F19 **Melchor, Isla** *island* Archipiélago de los Chonos, S Chile
42 M9 **Melchor Ocampo** Zacatecas, C Mexico *24.45N 101.38W*
12 C11 **Meldrum Bay** Manitoulin Island, Ontario, S Canada *45.55N 83.06W*
Meleda *see* Mljet
108 D8 **Melegnano** *prev.* Marignano. Lombardia, N Italy *45.22N 9.19E*
196 F9 **Melekeok** *var.* Melekeiok. Babeldaob, N Palau *7.30N 134.39E*
114 L9 **Melenci** *Hung.* Melencze. Serbia, N Serbia and Montenegro (Yugoslavia) *45.32N 20.18E*
Melencze *see* Melenci
131 N4 **Melenki** Vladimirskaya Oblast', W Russian Federation *55.21N 41.37E*
131 V6 **Meleuz** Respublika Bashkortostan, W Russian Federation *52.55N 55.54E*
10 L6 **Mélèzes, Rivière aux** ≈ Québec, C Canada
80 I11 **Melfi** Guéra, S Chad *11.04N 17.57E*
109 M17 **Melfi** Basilicata, S Italy *41.00N 15.33E*
9 U14 **Melfort** Saskatchewan, S Canada *52.52N 104.37W*
106 H4 **Melgaço** Viana do Castelo, N Portugal *42.07N 8.15W*
107 N4 **Melgar de Fernamental** Castilla-León, N Spain *42.24N 4.15W*
76 L6 **Melghir, Chott** *var.* Chott Melrhir. *salt lake* E Algeria
96 H8 **Melhus** Sør-Trøndelag, S Norway *63.16N 10.16E*
106 H3 **Melide** Galicia, NW Spain *42.54N 8.01W*
Meligalá *see* Meligalás
117 E21 **Meligalás** *prev.* Meligalá. Pelopónnisos, S Greece *37.13N 21.58E*
62 L12 **Mel, Ilha do** *island* S Brazil
122 G11 **Melilla** *anc.* Rusaddir, Russadir. Melilla, Spain, N Africa *35.18N 2.55W*
73 N1 **Melilla** *enclave* Spain, N Africa
65 G18 **Melimoyu, Monte** ▲ S Chile *44.06S 72.49W*
175 N8 **Melintang, Danau** ◎ Borneo, N Indonesia
119 U7 **Melioratyvne** Dnipropetrovs'ka Oblast', E Ukraine *48.35N 35.18E*
64 G11 **Melipilla** Santiago, C Chile *33.33S 71.34W*
117 I25 **Mélissa, Akrotírio** *headland* Kríti, Greece, E Mediterranean Sea *35.06N 24.33E*
15 Kk16 **Melita** Manitoba, S Canada *49.16N 100.58W*
Melita *see* Mljet
Melitene *see* Malatya
109 M23 **Melito di Porto Salvo** Calabria, SW Italy *37.55N 15.48E*
119 U10 **Melitopol'** Zaporiz'ka Oblast', SE Ukraine *46.49N 35.22E*
111 V4 **Melk** Niederösterreich, NE Austria *48.12N 15.20E*
97 K15 **Mellan-Fryken** ◎ C Sweden
101 E17 **Melle** Oost-Vlaanderen, NW Belgium *51.00N 3.48E*
102 G13 **Melle** Niedersachsen, NW Germany *52.12N 8.19E*
97 J17 **Mellerud** Västra Götaland, S Sweden *58.42N 12.27E*
104 K10 **Melle-sur-Bretonne** Deux-Sèvres, W France *46.13N 0.07W*
31 P8 **Mellette** South Dakota, N USA *45.07N 98.29W*
123 J16 **Mellieha** E Malta *35.58N 14.21E*
82 B10 **Mellit** Northern Darfur, W Sudan *14.07N 25.34E*
77 N7 **Mellita** ✈ SE Tunisia *33.47N 10.51E*
65 G21 **Mellizo Sur, Cerro** ▲ S Chile *48.27S 73.10W*
102 G9 **Mellum** *island* NW Germany
85 L22 **Melmoth** KwaZulu/Natal, E South Africa *28.35S 31.23E*
113 D16 **Mělník** *Ger.* Melnik. Středočeský Kraj, NW Czech Republic *50.21N 14.30E*
126 H13 **Mel'nikovo** Tomskaya Oblast', C Russian Federation *56.35N 84.11E*
63 G18 **Melo** Cerro Largo, NE Uruguay *32.22S 54.10W*
Melodunum *see* Melun
Melrhir, Chott *see* Melghir, Chott
191 P7 **Melrose** New South Wales, SE Australia *32.41S 146.58E*
190 I7 **Melrose** South Australia *32.52S 138.16E*
31 T7 **Melrose** Minnesota, N USA *45.40N 94.46W*
35 Q11 **Melrose** Montana, NW USA *45.33N 112.41W*
39 V12 **Melrose** New Mexico, SW USA *34.25N 103.37W*
110 I8 **Mels** Sankt Gallen, NE Switzerland *47.03N 9.25E*
Melsetter *see* Chimanimani
35 V9 **Melstone** Montana, NW USA *46.37N 107.49W*
103 I16 **Melsungen** Hessen, C Germany *51.07N 9.33E*
94 L12 **Meltaus** Lappi, NW Finland *66.54N 25.18E*
99 N19 **Melton Mowbray** C England, UK *52.46N 1.03W*
84 Q13 **Meluco** Cabo Delgado, NE Mozambique *12.39S 39.35E*
105 O5 **Melun** *anc.* Melodunum. Seine-et-Marne, N France *48.31N 2.40E*
82 F12 **Melut** Upper Nile, SE Sudan *10.27N 32.13E*
29 P5 **Melvern Lake** ⊠ Kansas, C USA
9 V16 **Melville** Saskatchewan, S Canada *50.57N 102.49W*
Melville Bay/Melville Bugt *see* Qimusseriarsuaq
47 O11 **Melville Hall** ✈ (Dominica) NE Dominica *15.33N 61.19W*
189 O1 **Melville Island** *island* Northern Territory, N Australia
207 O8 **Melville Island** *island* Parry Islands, Northwest Territories, NW Canada
16 R7 **Melville, Lake** ◎ Newfoundland and Labrador, E Canada
15 Ll2 **Melville Peninsula** *peninsula* Nunavut, NE Canada
Melville Sound *see* Viscount Melville Sound
27 Q9 **Melvin** Texas, SW USA *31.12N 99.34W*
99 D15 **Melvin, Lough** *Ir.* Loch Meilbhe. ◎ S Northern Ireland, UK/Ireland
174 M9 **Memala** Borneo, C Indonesia *1.43S 112.36E*
115 L22 **Memaliaj** Gjirokastër, S Albania *40.21N 19.56E*
85 Q14 **Memba** Nampula, NE Mozambique *14.07S 40.33E*
85 Q14 **Memba, Baia de** *inlet* NE Mozambique
Membidj *see* Manbij
Memel *see* Neman, NE Europe
Memel *see* Klaipėda, Lithuania
103 J23 **Memmingen** Bayern, S Germany *47.58N 10.10E*
29 U1 **Memphis** Missouri, C USA *40.27N 92.10W*
22 E10 **Memphis** Tennessee, S USA *35.09N 90.03W*
27 P3 **Memphis** Texas, SW USA *34.43N 100.31W*
22 E10 **Memphis** ✈ Tennessee, S USA *35.02N 89.57W*
13 Q13 **Memphrémagog, Lac** *var.* Lake Memphremagog. ◎ Canada/USA *see also* Memphremagog, Lake
21 N6 **Memphremagog, Lake** *var.* Lac Memphrémagog. ◎ Canada/USA *see also* Memphrémagog, Lac
119 Q2 **Mena** Chernihivs'ka Oblast', NE Ukraine *51.30N 32.15E*
29 S12 **Mena** Arkansas, C USA *34.35N 94.14W*
Menaam *see* Menaldum
Menado *see* Manado
108 D6 **Menaggio** Lombardia, N Italy *46.03N 9.14E*
31 T6 **Menahga** Minnesota, N USA *46.45N 95.06W*
79 R10 **Ménaka** Goa, E Mali *15.54N 2.25E*
100 K5 **Menaldum** *Fris.* Menaam. Friesland, N Netherlands *53.13N 5.37E*
Mènam Khong *see* Mekong
76 E7 **Menara** ✈ (Marrakech) C Morocco *31.36N 8.00W*
27 Q9 **Menard** Texas, SW USA *30.55N 99.47W*
199 M14 **Menard Fracture Zone** *tectonic feature* E Pacific Ocean
32 M7 **Menasha** Wisconsin, N USA *44.13N 88.25W*
Mencezi Garagum *see* Merkezi Garagumy
200 O10 **Mendaña Fracture Zone** *tectonic feature* E Pacific Ocean
174 M10 **Mendawai, Sungai** ≈ Borneo, C Indonesia
105 P13 **Mende** *anc.* Mimatum. Lozère, S France *44.31N 3.30E*
83 J14 **Mendebo** ▲ C Ethiopia
82 J9 **Mendefera** *prev.* Adi Ugri. S Eritrea *14.53N 38.51E*
207 S7 **Mendeleyev Ridge** *undersea feature* Arctic Ocean
131 T3 **Mendeleyevsk** Respublika Tatarstan, W Russian Federation *55.54N 52.19E*
103 F15 **Menden** Nordrhein-Westfalen, W Germany *51.25N 7.48E*
24 L6 **Mendenhall** Mississippi, S USA *31.57N 89.52W*
40 L13 **Mendenhall, Cape** *headland* Nunivak Island, Alaska, USA *59.45N 166.10W*
43 P9 **Méndez** *var.* Villa de Méndez. Tamaulipas, C Mexico *25.06N 98.32W*
82 H13 **Mendī** Oromo, C Ethiopia *9.43N 35.07E*
194 G12 **Mendi** Southern Highlands, W PNG *6.07S 143.39E*
99 K22 **Mendip Hills** *var.* Mendips. *hill range* S England, UK
Mendips *see* Mendip Hills
36 L6 **Mendocino** California, W USA *39.18N 123.48W*
36 J3 **Mendocino, Cape** *headland* California, W USA *40.26N 124.24W*
(0) B8 **Mendocino Fracture Zone** *tectonic feature* NE Pacific Ocean
37 P10 **Mendota** California, W USA *36.44N 120.24W*
32 L11 **Mendota** Illinois, N USA *41.32N 89.04W*
32 K8 **Mendota, Lake** ◎ Wisconsin, N USA
64 I11 **Mendoza** Mendoza, W Argentina *33.00S 68.47W*
64 I12 **Mendoza** *off.* Provincia de Mendoza. ◆ *province* W Argentina
110 H12 **Mendrisio** Ticino, S Switzerland *45.52N 8.58E*
174 Hh7 **Mendung** Pulau Mendol, W Indonesia *0.33N 103.09E*
56 I5 **Mene de Mauroa** Falcón, NW Venezuela *10.39N 71.04W*
56 I5 **Mene Grande** Zulia, NW Venezuela *9.51N 70.57W*
142 B14 **Menemen** İzmir, W Turkey *38.34N 27.03E*
101 C18 **Menen** *var.* Meenen, *Fr.* Menin. West-Vlaanderen, W Belgium *50.48N 3.07E*
169 Q8 **Menengiyn Tal** *plain* E Mongolia
201 R9 **Meneng Point** *headland* SW Nauru *0.33S 166.57E*
94 L10 **Menesjärvi** *Lapp.* Menešjávri. Lappi, N Finland *68.39N 26.22E*
Menešjávri *see* Menesjärvi
109 I24 **Menfi** Sicilia, Italy, C Mediterranean Sea *37.34N 12.58E*
167 P7 **Mengcheng** Anhui, E China *33.17N 116.31E*
166 F15 **Menghai** Yunnan, SW China *22.02N 100.18E*
175 Q11 **Mengkoka, Pegunungan** *var.* Pegunungan Mekongga. ▲ Sulawesi, C Indonesia
166 F15 **Mengla** Yunnan, SW China *21.30N 101.33E*
67 F24 **Menguera Point** *headland* East Falkland, Falkland Islands
166 M13 **Mengzhu Ling** ▲ S China
166 H14 **Mengzi** Yunnan, SW China *23.20N 103.32E*
Menin *see* Menen
190 L7 **Menindee** New South Wales, SE Australia *32.24S 142.25E*
190 L7 **Menindee Lake** ◎ New South Wales, SE Australia
190 J10 **Meningie** South Australia *35.43S 139.20E*
105 O5 **Mennecy** Essonne, N France *48.34N 2.25E*
31 Q12 **Menno** South Dakota, N USA *43.14N 97.34W*
116 H13 **Menoíkio** ▲ NE Greece
33 N5 **Menominee** Michigan, N USA *45.06N 87.36W*
32 M5 **Menominee River** ≈ Michigan/Wisconsin, N USA
32 M8 **Menomonee Falls** Wisconsin, N USA *43.11N 88.09W*
32 I6 **Menomonie** Wisconsin, N USA *44.52N 91.55W*
85 D14 **Menongue** *var.* Vila Serpa Pinto, *Port.* Serpa Pinto. Cuando Cubango, C Angola *14.38S 17.38E*
123 Ii8 **Menorca** *Eng.* Minorca; *anc.* Balearis Minor. *island* Islas Baleares, Spain, W Mediterranean Sea
107 S13 **Menor, Mar** *lagoon* SE Spain
41 S10 **Mentasta Lake** ◎ Alaska, USA
41 S10 **Mentasta Mountains** ▲ Alaska, USA
173 Ff10 **Mentawai, Kepulauan** *island group* W Indonesia
173 G10 **Mentawai, Selat** *strait* W Indonesia
174 Ii10 **Mentok** Pulau Bangka, W Indonesia *2.01S 105.10E*
105 V15 **Menton** *It.* Mentone. Alpes-Maritimes, SE France *43.46N 7.30E*
26 K8 **Mentone** Texas, SW USA *31.42N 103.36W*
Mentone *see* Menton
33 U11 **Mentor** Ohio, N USA *41.40N 81.20W*
175 Nn7 **Menyapa, Gunung** ▲ Borneo, N Indonesia *1.04N 116.01E*
165 T9 **Menyuan** *var.* Menyuan Huizu Zizhixian. Qinghai, C China *37.27N 101.33E*
Menyuan Huizu Zizhixian *see* Menyuan
76 M5 **Menzel Bourguiba** *var.* Manzil Bū Ruqaybah; *prev.* Ferryville. N Tunisia *37.09N 9.51E*
142 M15 **Menzelet Barajı** ⊠ C Turkey
131 T4 **Menzelinsk** Respublika Tatarstan, W Russian Federation *55.44N 53.00E*
188 K11 **Menzies** Western Australia *29.42S 121.04E*
205 V6 **Menzies, Mount** ▲ Antarctica *73.32S 61.02E*
42 J6 **Meoqui** Chihuahua, N Mexico *28.19N 105.30W*
85 N14 **Meponda** Niassa, NE Mozambique *13.19S 34.52E*
100 M8 **Meppel** Drenthe, NE Netherlands *52.42N 6.12E*
102 E12 **Meppen** Niedersachsen, NW Germany *52.42N 7.18E*
Meqerghane, Sebkha *see* Mekerrhane, Sebkha
107 T6 **Mequinenza, Embalse de** ⊠ NE Spain
32 M8 **Mequon** Wisconsin, N USA *43.13N 87.57W*
Mera *see* Maira
190 D3 **Meramangye, Lake** *salt lake* South Australia
29 W5 **Meramec River** ≈ Missouri, C USA
Meran *see* Merano
174 H10 **Merangin** ≈ Sumatera, W Indonesia
108 G5 **Merano** *Ger.* Meran. Trentino-Alto Adige, N Italy *46.40N 11.10E*
174 H4 **Meraph Lama** Pahang, Peninsular Malaysia *4.37N 101.58E*
108 D7 **Merate** Lombardia, N Italy *45.42N 9.26E*
175 Nn11 **Meratus, Pegunungan** ▲ Borneo, N Indonesia
176 Z16 **Merauke** Papua, E Indonesia *8.28S 140.28E*
176 Z16 **Merauke, Sungai** ≈ Papua, E Indonesia
190 L9 **Merbein** Victoria, SE Australia *34.11S 142.03E*
101 F21 **Merbes-le-Château** Hainaut, S Belgium *50.19N 4.09E*
Merca *see* Marka
56 C13 **Mercaderes** Cauca, SW Colombia *1.47N 77.10W*
Mercara *see* Madikeri
37 P9 **Merced** California, W USA *37.17N 120.30W*
63 C20 **Mercedes** Buenos Aires, E Argentina *34.42S 59.30W*
63 D15 **Mercedes** Corrientes, NE Argentina *29.09S 58.04W*
64 J11 **Mercedes** *prev.* Villa Mercedes. San Luis, C Argentina *33.40S 65.24W*
63 D19 **Mercedes** Soriano, SW Uruguay *33.16S 58.01W*
27 S17 **Mercedes** Texas, SW USA *26.09N 97.54W*
37 R9 **Merced Peak** ▲ California, W USA *37.34N 119.30W*
37 P9 **Merced River** ≈ California, W USA
20 B13 **Mercer** Pennsylvania, NE USA *41.13N 80.13W*
101 G18 **Merchtem** Vlaams Brabant, C Belgium *50.57N 4.13E*
13 O13 **Mercier** Québec, SE Canada *45.15N 73.45W*
27 Q9 **Mercury** Texas, SW USA *31.23N 99.09W*
192 M5 **Mercury Islands** *island group* N NZ
21 O9 **Meredith** New Hampshire, NE USA *43.36N 71.28W*
67 B25 **Meredith, Cape** *var.* Cabo Belgrano *headland* West Falkland, Falkland Islands *52.15S 60.40W*
39 V6 **Meredith, Lake** ◎ Colorado, C USA
27 N2 **Meredith, Lake** ⊠ Texas, SW USA
83 O16 **Mereeg** *var.* Mareeq, *It.* Meregh. Galguduud, E Somalia *3.47N 47.19E*
119 V5 **Merefa** Kharkivs'ka Oblast', E Ukraine *49.48N 36.04E*
Meregh *see* Mereeg
197 C11 **Mere Lava** *island* Banks Islands, N Vanuatu
101 E17 **Merelbeke** Oost-Vlaanderen, NW Belgium *51.00N 3.45E*
Merend *see* Marand
127 Oo9 **Merenga** Magadanskaya Oblast', E Russian Federation *61.43N 156.02E*
178 K12 **Mereuch** Môndól Kiri, E Cambodia *13.01N 107.26E*
Mergate *see* Margate
178 Gg12 **Mergui** Tenasserim, S Myanmar *12.25N 98.34E*
177 G12 **Mergui Archipelago** *island group* S Myanmar
116 L12 **Meriç** Edirne, NW Turkey *41.12N 26.24E*
116 L12 **Meriç** *Bul.* Maritsa, *Gk.* Évros; *anc.* Hebrus. ≈ SE Europe *see also* Évros/Maritsa
43 X12 **Mérida** Yucatán, SW Mexico *20.58N 89.35W*
106 J11 **Mérida** *anc.* Augusta Emerita. Extremadura, W Spain *38.55N 6.19W*
56 I6 **Mérida** Mérida, W Venezuela *8.36N 71.07W*
56 H7 **Mérida** *off.* Estado Mérida. ◆ *state* W Venezuela
20 M13 **Meriden** Connecticut, NE USA *41.32N 72.48W*
24 M5 **Meridian** Mississippi, S USA *32.24N 88.43W*
27 S8 **Meridian** Texas, SW USA *31.55N 97.39W*
104 J13 **Mérignac** Gironde, SW France *44.50N 0.39W*
104 J13 **Mérignac** ✈ (Bordeaux) Gironde, SW France *44.51N 0.44W*
95 J18 **Merikarvia** Länsi-Suomi, W Finland *61.51N 21.30E*
191 R12 **Merimbula** New South Wales, SE Australia *36.52S 149.51E*
190 L9 **Meringur** Victoria, SE Australia *34.26S 141.19E*
Merín, Laguna *see* Mirim Lagoon
99 I19 **Merioneth** *cultural region* W Wales, UK
196 A11 **Merir** *island* Palau Islands, N Palau
196 B17 **Merizo** SW Guam *13.15N 144.40E*
Merjama *see* Märjamaa
151 S16 **Merke** Zhambyl, S Kazakhstan *42.52N 73.09E*
27 P7 **Merkel** Texas, SW USA *32.28N 100.00W*
152 E12 **Merkezi Garagumy** *var.* Mencezi Garagum, *Rus.* Tsentral'nyye Nizmennyye Garagumy. *desert* C Turkmenistan
121 F15 **Merkinė** Alytus, S Lithuania *54.09N 24.11E*
101 G16 **Merksem** Antwerpen, N Belgium *51.17N 4.26E*
101 I15 **Merksplas** Antwerpen, N Belgium *51.22N 4.54E*
Merkulovichi *see* Myerkulavichy
121 G15 **Merkys** ≈ S Lithuania
34 F15 **Merlin** Oregon, NW USA *42.34N 123.23W*
63 C20 **Merlo** Buenos Aires, E Argentina *34.39S 58.45W*
144 G8 **Meron, Haré** ▲ N Israel *35.06N 33.00E*
76 K6 **Merouane, Chott** *salt lake* NE Algeria
82 F7 **Merowe** Northern, N Sudan *18.28N 31.49E*
188 J12 **Merredin** Western Australia *31.31S 118.18E*
99 I14 **Merrick** ▲ S Scotland, UK *55.09N 4.28W*
34 H16 **Merrill** Oregon, NW USA *42.00N 121.37W*
32 L5 **Merrill** Wisconsin, N USA *45.12N 89.43W*
33 N11 **Merrillville** Indiana, N USA *41.28N 87.19W*
21 O10 **Merrimack River** ≈ Massachusetts/New Hampshire, NE USA
30 L12 **Merriman** Nebraska, C USA *42.54N 101.42W*
9 N17 **Merritt** British Columbia, SW Canada *50.09N 120.49W*
25 Y12 **Merritt Island** Florida, SE USA *28.21N 80.42W*
25 Y11 **Merritt Island** *island* Florida, SE USA
30 M12 **Merritt Reservoir** ⊠ Nebraska, C USA
191 S7 **Merriwa** New South Wales, SE Australia *32.09S 150.24E*
191 O8 **Merriwagga** New South Wales, SE Australia *33.51S 145.38E*
24 G8 **Merryville** Louisiana, S USA *30.45N 93.32W*
82 K9 **Mersa Fatma** E Eritrea *14.52N 40.16E*
104 M7 **Mer St-Aubin** Loir-et-Cher, C France *47.42N 1.31E*
Mersa Maṭrûḥ *see* Maṭrūḥ
101 M24 **Mersch** Luxembourg, C Luxembourg *49.45N 6.06E*
103 M15 **Merseburg** Sachsen-Anhalt, C Germany *51.22N 12.00E*
Mersen *see* Meerssen
99 K18 **Mersey** ≈ NW England, UK
142 J17 **Mersin** İçel, S Turkey *36.49N 34.39E*
174 I6 **Mersing** Johor, Peninsular Malaysia *2.25N 103.49E*
120 E8 **Mērsrags** Talsi, NW Latvia *57.21N 23.05E*
158 G12 **Merta** *var.* Merta City. Rājasthān, N India *26.40N 74.04E*
Merta City *see* Merta
158 F12 **Merta Road** Rājasthān, N India *26.45N 73.59E*
99 J21 **Merthyr Tydfil** S Wales, UK *51.46N 3.22W*
106 H13 **Mértola** Beja, S Portugal *37.37N 7.40W*
150 G14 **Mertvyy Kultuk, Sor** *salt flat* SW Kazakhstan
205 V16 **Mertz Glacier** *glacier* Antarctica
101 M24 **Mertzig** Diekirch, C Luxembourg *49.50N 6.00E*
27 O9 **Mertzon** Texas, SW USA *31.15N 100.49W*
83 I18 **Meru** Eastern, C Kenya *0.03N 37.37E*
105 N4 **Méru** Oise, N France *49.15N 2.07E*
83 I20 **Meru, Mount** ▲ NE Tanzania *3.12S 36.45E*
Merv *see* Mary
Mervdasht *see* Marv Dasht
142 K11 **Merzifon** Amasya, N Turkey *40.52N 35.28E*
103 D20 **Merzig** Saarland, SW Germany *49.27N 6.39E*
38 L14 **Mesa** Arizona, SW USA *33.25N 111.49W*
31 V4 **Mesabi Range** ▲ Minnesota, N USA
56 H6 **Mesa Bolívar** Mérida, NW Venezuela *8.30N 71.37W*
109 Q18 **Mesagne** Puglia, SE Italy *40.33N 17.49E*
41 P12 **Mesa Mountain** ▲ Alaska, USA *60.26N 155.14W*
117 J25 **Mesará** *lowland* Kríti, Greece, E Mediterranean Sea
39 S14 **Mescalero** New Mexico, SW USA *33.09N 105.46W*
103 G15 **Meschede** Nordrhein-Westfalen, W Germany *51.21N 8.16E*
143 Q12 **Mescit Dağları** ▲ NE Turkey
201 V13 **Mesegon** *island* Chuuk, C Micronesia
Meseritz *see* Międzyrzecz
56 F11 **Mesetas** Meta, C Colombia *3.14N 74.09W*
Meshchera Lowland *see* Meshcherskaya Nizina
130 M4 **Meshcherskaya Nizina** *Eng.* Meshchera Lowland. *basin* W Russian Federation
130 J5 **Meshchovsk** Kaluzhskaya Oblast', W Russian Federation *54.21N 35.23E*
129 R9 **Meshchura** Respublika Komi, NW Russian Federation *63.18N 50.56E*
Meshed *see* Mashhad

◆ Country ◇ Dependent Territory ◆ Administrative Region ▲ Mountain ⚲ Volcano ◎ Lake
● Country Capital ○ Dependent Territory Capital ✈ International Airport ▲ Mountain Range ≈ River ⊠ Reservoir

MESHED-I-SAR – MINGECHAURSKOYE VODOKHRANILISHCHE/MINGECHEVIRSKOYE VODOKHRANILISHCHE

Meshed-i-Sar see Bābolsar
82 E13 Meshra'er Req Warab, S Sudan 8.30N 29.27E
39 R15 Mesilla New Mexico, SW USA 32.15N 106.49W
110 H10 Mesocco Ger. Misox. Ticino, S Switzerland 46.18N 9.13E
117 D18 Mesológgi prev. Mesolóngion. Dytikí Elláς, W Greece 38.22N 21.26E
Mesolóngion see Mesológgi
12 E8 Mesomikenda Lake Ontario, S Canada
63 D15 Mesopotamia var. Mesopotamia Argentina. physical region NE Argentina
Mesopotamia Argentina see Mesopotamia
37 Y10 Mesquite Nevada, SW USA 36.47N 114.04W
84 Q13 Messalo, Rio var. Muâlo. NE Mozambique
Messana/Messene see Messina
101 L25 Messancy Luxembourg, SE Belgium 49.36N 5.49E
109 M23 Messina var. Messana, Messene; anc. Zancle. Sicilia, Italy, C Mediterranean Sea 38.11N 15.33E
Messina see Musina
Messina, Strait of see Messina, Stretto di
109 M23 Messina, Stretto di Eng. Strait of Messina. strait SW Italy
117 E21 Messíni Pelopónnisos, S Greece 37.03N 22.00E
117 E21 Messinía peninsula S Greece
117 E22 Messiniakós Kólpos gulf S Greece
126 H8 Messoyakha N Russian Federation
116 H11 Mesta Gk. Néstos, Turk. Kara Su. Bulgaria/Greece see also Néstos
Mestghanem see Mostaganem
143 R8 Mestia var. Mestiya. N Georgia 43.03N 42.49E
Mestiya see Mestia
117 K18 Mestón, Akrotírio headland Chíos, E Greece 38.15N 25.52E
108 H8 Mestre Veneto, NE Italy 45.30N 12.13E
61 M16 Mestre, Espigão ▲ E Brazil
174 Ii11 Mesuji Sumatera, W Indonesia
Mesule see Grosser Möseler
8 J10 Meszah Peak ▲ British Columbia, W Canada 58.31N 131.28W
56 G11 Meta off. Departamento del Meta. ◆ province C Colombia
13 Q8 Metabetchouane Québec, SE Canada
16 O4 Meta Incognita Peninsula peninsula Baffin Island, Nunavut, NE Canada
24 K9 Metairie Louisiana, S USA 29.58N 90.09W
34 M6 Metaline Falls Washington, NW USA 48.51N 117.21W
64 K6 Metán Salta, N Argentina 25.25S 64.52W
84 N13 Metangula Niassa, N Mozambique 12.40S 34.49E
44 E7 Metapán Santa Ana, NW El Salvador 14.19N 89.30W
56 K9 Meta, Río Colombia/Venezuela
108 I11 Metauro C Italy
82 H11 Metema Amhara, N Ethiopia 12.53N 36.10E
117 D15 Metéora religious building Thessalía, C Greece 39.45N 21.37E
67 O20 Meteor Rise undersea feature SW Indian Ocean
195 N9 Meteran New Hanover, NE PNG 2.36S 150.09E
Meterlam/Methariam/Metharlam see Mehtarlām
117 G20 Methanon peninsula S Greece
34 J6 Methow River Washington, NW USA
21 O10 Methuen Massachusetts, NE USA 42.43N 71.10W
193 G19 Methven Canterbury, South Island, NZ 43.37S 171.38E
Metis see Metz
115 G15 Metković Dubrovnik-Neretva, SE Croatia 43.02N 17.37E
41 Y14 Metlakatla Annette Island, Alaska, USA 55.07N 131.34W
111 V13 Metlika Ger. Möttling. SE Slovenia 45.38N 15.18E
111 T8 Metnitz Kärnten, S Austria 46.58N 14.09E
29 W12 Meto, Bayou Arkansas, C USA
174 Ii13 Metro Sumatera, W Indonesia 5.05S 105.17E
32 M17 Metropolis Illinois, N USA 37.09N 88.43W
Metropolitan see Santiago
37 N8 Metropolitan Oakland ✈ California, W USA 37.42N 122.13W
117 D15 Métsovo prev. Métsovon. Ípeiros, C Greece 39.47N 21.12E
Métsovon see Métsovo
25 V5 Metter Georgia, SE USA 32.24N 82.03W
101 H21 Mettet Namur, S Belgium 50.19N 4.43E
103 D20 Mettlach Saarland, SW Germany 49.28N 6.37E
Mettu see Metu
82 H13 Metu var. Mattu, Mettu. Oromo, C Ethiopia 8.18N 35.39E
175 N7 Metulang Borneo, N Indonesia 1.28N 114.40E
144 G8 Metulla Northern, N Israel 33.16N 35.35E
105 T4 Metz anc. Divodurum Mediomatricum, Mediomatrica, Metis. Moselle, NE France 49.07N 6.09E
103 H22 Metzingen Baden-Württemberg, S Germany 48.31N 9.16E
173 E4 Meulaboh Sumatera, W Indonesia 4.10N 96.09E
101 D18 Meulebeke West-Vlaanderen, W Belgium 50.57N 3.18E
105 U6 Meurthe NE France
105 S5 Meurthe-et-Moselle ◆ department NE France
105 S4 Meuse ◆ department NE France
86 F10 Meuse Dut. Maas. W Europe see also Maas
195 O11 Mevelo New Britain, C Papau New Guinea
Mexcala, Río see Balsas, Río
27 U8 Mexia Texas, SW USA 31.40N 96.28W
60 K11 Mexiana, Ilha island NE Brazil
42 C1 Mexicali Baja California, NW Mexico 32.34N 115.26W
29 V4 Mexico Missouri, C USA 39.10N 91.52W
20 H9 Mexico New York, NE USA 43.27N 76.14W
42 L7 Mexico off. United Mexican States, var. Méjico, México, Sp. Estados Unidos Mexicanos. ◆ federal republic N Central America
43 O14 México var. Ciudad de México, Eng. Mexico City. ● (Mexico) México, C Mexico 19.24N 99.04W
43 O13 México ◆ state S Mexico
(0) J13 Mexico Basin var. Sigsbee Deep. undersea feature C Gulf of Mexico
Mexico City see México
México, Golfo de see Mexico, Gulf of
46 B4 Mexico, Gulf of Sp. Golfo de México. gulf W Atlantic Ocean
Meyadine see Al Mayādīn
41 Y14 Meyers Chuck Etolin Island, Alaska, USA 55.44N 132.15W
154 M3 Meymaneh var. Maimāna, Maymana. Fāryāb, NW Afghanistan 35.57N 64.48E
149 N7 Meymeh Eşfahān, C Iran 33.28N 51.09E
127 Pp6 Meynypil'gyno Chukotskiy Avtonomnyy Okrug, NE Russian Federation 62.33N 177.00E
110 A10 Meyrin Genève, SW Switzerland 46.13N 6.04E
177 Ff8 Mezaligon Irrawaddy, SW Myanmar 17.53N 95.12E
43 O15 Mezcala Guerrero, S Mexico 17.55N 99.34W
116 H8 Mezdra Vratsa, NW Bulgaria 43.09N 23.44E
105 P16 Mèze Hérault, S France 43.25N 3.37E
129 O6 Mezen' Arkhangel'skaya Oblast', NW Russian Federation 65.54N 44.10E
129 P8 Mezen' NW Russian Federation
Mezen, Bay of see Mezenskaya Guba
105 Q13 Mézenc, Mont ▲ C France 44.57N 4.15E
129 O8 Mezenskaya Guba var. Bay of Mezen. bay NW Russian Federation
125 Bb7 Mezha W Russian Federation
Mezha see Myazha
126 Hh15 Mezhdurechensk Kemerovskaya Oblast', S Russian Federation 53.37N 87.59E
125 F4 Mezhdusharskiy, Ostrov island Novaya Zemlya, N Russian Federation
Mezhëvo see Myezhava
Mezhgor'ye see Mizhhir"ya
131 W5 Mezhgor'ye Respublika Bashkortostan, W Russian Federation 54.10N 57.55E
119 V8 Mezhova Dnipropetrovs'ka Oblast', E Ukraine 48.15N 36.44E
8 J12 Meziadin Junction British Columbia, W Canada 56.06N 129.15W
113 G16 Mezileské sedlo var. Przełęcz Międzyleska. pass Czech Republic/Poland 50.10N 16.40E
104 L14 Mézin Lot-et-Garonne, SW France 44.03N 0.16E
113 M24 Mezőberény Békés, SE Hungary 46.49N 21.00E
113 M25 Mezőhegyes Békés, SE Hungary 46.19N 20.51E
113 M25 Mezőkovácsháza Békés, SE Hungary 46.25N 20.52E
113 M21 Mezőkövesd Borsod-Abaúj-Zemplén, NE Hungary 47.48N 20.34E
Mezőtelegd see Tileagd
113 M23 Mezőtúr Jász-Nagykun-Szolnok, E Hungary 47.00N 20.37E
42 K10 Mezquital Durango, C Mexico 23.29N 104.24W
108 G6 Mezzolombardo Trentino-Alto Adige, N Italy 46.13N 11.08E
84 L13 Mfuwe Northern, N Zambia 13.00S 31.45E
123 J16 Mgarr Gozo, N Malta 36.01N 14.18E
130 H6 Mglin Bryanskaya Oblast', W Russian Federation 53.01N 32.54E
Mhálanna, Cionn see Malin Head
160 G10 Mhow Madhya Pradesh, C India 22.36N 75.47E
Miadzioł Nowy see Myadzyel
179 Q13 Miagao Panay Island, C Philippines 10.40N 122.15E
43 R17 Miahuatlán var. Miahuatlán de Porfirio Díaz. Oaxaca, SE Mexico 16.21N 96.36W
Miahuatlán de Porfirio Díaz see Miahuatlán
106 K10 Miajadas Extremadura, W Spain 39.10N 5.54W
Miajlar see Myājlār
38 M14 Miami Arizona, SW USA 33.23N 110.53W
25 Z16 Miami Florida, SE USA 25.46N 80.11W
29 R8 Miami Oklahoma, C USA 36.52N 94.52W
27 O2 Miami Texas, SW USA 35.41N 100.38W
25 Z16 Miami ✈ Florida, SE USA 25.47N 80.16W
25 Z16 Miami Beach Florida, SE USA 25.47N 80.07W
25 Y15 Miami Canal canal Florida, SE USA
33 R14 Miamisburg Ohio, N USA 39.38N 84.17W
155 U10 Miān Channūn Punjab, E Pakistan 30.27N 72.24E
148 J4 Miāndowāb var. Miandowab, Miyāndoāb. Āzarbāyjān-e Bākhtarī, NW Iran 36.58N 46.06E
180 H5 Miandrivazo Toliara, C Madagascar 19.31S 45.28E
Miandowab see Miāndowāb
148 K3 Miāneh var. Miyāneh. Āzarbāyjān-e Khāvarī, NW Iran 37.25N 47.43E
155 O16 Miāni Hōr lagoon S Pakistan
166 G10 Mianning Sichuan, C China 28.34N 102.12E
155 T7 Miānwāli Punjab, NE Pakistan 32.31N 71.33E
166 J7 Mianxian var. Mian Xian. Shaanxi, C China 33.12N 106.36E
166 I8 Mianyang Sichuan, C China 31.28N 104.43E
Mianyang see Xiantao
167 R3 Miaodao Qundao island group E China
167 S13 Miaoli N Taiwan 24.33N 120.48E
125 E12 Miass Chelyabinskaya Oblast', C Russian Federation 55.00N 59.55E
112 G8 Miastko Ger. Rummelsburg in Pommern. Pomorskie, N Poland 54.00N 16.58E
Miava see Myjava
9 O15 Mica Creek British Columbia, SW Canada 51.58N 118.29W
166 J7 Micang Shan ▲ C China
194 I12 Michael, Mount ▲ C PNG 6.24S 145.18E
Mi Chai see Nong Khai
113 O19 Michalovce Ger. Grossmichel, Hung. Nagymihály. Košický Kraj, E Slovakia 48.46N 21.54E
101 M20 Michel, Baraque hill E Belgium 50.38N 6.09E
41 S5 Michelson, Mount ▲ Alaska, USA 69.19N 144.16W
47 P9 Miches E Dominican Republic 18.56N 69.04W
32 M4 Michigamme, Lake Michigan, USA
32 M4 Michigamme Reservoir Michigan, N USA
33 N4 Michigamme River Michigan, N USA
33 O7 Michigan off. State of Michigan; also known as Great Lakes State, Lake State, Wolverine State. ◆ state N USA
33 O11 Michigan City Indiana, N USA 41.43N 86.52W
33 O8 Michigan, Lake N USA
33 P2 Michipicoten Bay lake bay Ontario, N Canada
12 A8 Michipicoten Island island Ontario, S Canada
12 B7 Michipicoten River Ontario, S Canada 47.56N 84.48W
Michurin see Tsarevo
130 M6 Michurinsk Tambovskaya Oblast', W Russian Federation 52.56N 40.30E
Mico, Punta/Mico, Punto see Monkey Point
44 L10 Mico, Río SE Nicaragua
47 T12 Micoud SE Saint Lucia 13.49N 60.54W
201 N16 Micronesia off. Federated States of Micronesia. ◆ federation W Pacific Ocean
183 P4 Micronesia island group W Pacific Ocean
174 Jj5 Midai, Pulau island Kepulauan Natuna, W Indonesia
Mid-Atlantic Cordillera see Mid-Atlantic Ridge
67 M17 Mid-Atlantic Ridge var. Mid-Atlantic Cordillera, Mid-Atlantic Rise, Mid-Atlantic Swell. undersea feature Atlantic Ocean
Mid-Atlantic Rise/Mid-Atlantic Swell see Mid-Atlantic Ridge
101 E15 Middelburg Zeeland, SW Netherlands 51.30N 3.36E
85 H24 Middelburg Eastern Cape, S South Africa 31.28S 25.01E
85 K21 Middelburg Mpumalanga, NE South Africa 25.46S 29.28E
97 G23 Middelfart Fyn, C Denmark 55.30N 9.43E
100 G13 Middelharnis Zuid-Holland, SW Netherlands 51.45N 4.10E
101 B16 Middelkerke West-Vlaanderen, W Belgium 51.11N 2.51E
100 I9 Middenbeemster Noord-Holland, C Netherlands 52.33N 4.55E
100 I8 Middenmeer Noord-Holland, NW Netherlands 52.48N 4.58E
37 Q2 Middle Alkali Lake California, W USA
200 Nn6 Middle America Trench undersea feature E Pacific Ocean
157 P19 Middle Andaman island Andaman Islands, India, NE Indian Ocean
Middle Atlas see Moyen Atlas
23 R3 Middlebourne West Virginia, NE USA 39.29N 80.54W
25 W9 Middleburg Florida, SE USA 30.03N 81.55W
Middleburg Island see 'Eua
Middle Caicos see Grand Caicos
27 N8 Middle Concho River Texas, SW USA
Middle Congo see Congo (Republic of)
41 R6 Middle Fork Chandalar River Alaska, USA
41 Q7 Middle Fork Koyukuk River Alaska, USA
35 O12 Middle Fork Salmon River Idaho, NW USA
9 T15 Middle Lake Saskatchewan, S Canada 52.31N 105.16W
30 L13 Middle Loup River Nebraska, C USA
193 E22 Middlemarch Otago, South Island, NZ 45.30S 170.07E
33 T15 Middleport Ohio, N USA 39.00N 82.03W
31 U14 Middle Raccoon River Iowa, C USA
31 R3 Middle River Minnesota, N USA
23 N8 Middlesboro Kentucky, S USA 36.37N 83.42W
99 M15 Middlesbrough N England, UK 54.34N 1.13W
44 G3 Middlesex Stann Creek, C Belize 17.00N 88.31W
99 N22 Middlesex cultural region SE England, UK
11 P15 Middleton Nova Scotia, SE Canada 44.54N 65.01W
22 F10 Middleton Tennessee, S USA 35.05N 88.57W
32 L9 Middleton Wisconsin, N USA 43.06N 89.30W
41 S13 Middleton Island island Alaska, USA
36 M7 Middletown California, W USA 38.44N 122.39W
23 Y2 Middletown Delaware, NE USA 39.25N 75.39W
20 K15 Middletown New Jersey, NE USA 40.22N 74.07W
20 K13 Middletown New York, NE USA 41.27N 74.25W
33 R14 Middletown Ohio, N USA 39.33N 84.19W
20 G15 Middletown Pennsylvania, NE USA 40.11N 76.42W
147 N14 Mīdī var. Maydī. NW Yemen 16.18N 42.51E
105 O16 Midi, Canal du canal S France
104 K17 Midi de Bigorre, Pic du ▲ S France 42.57N 0.08E
104 K17 Midi d'Ossau, Pic du ▲ SW France 42.51N 0.27W
181 R7 Mid-Indian Basin undersea feature N Indian Ocean
181 P7 Mid-Indian Ridge var. Central Indian Ridge. undersea feature C Indian Ocean
105 N14 Midi-Pyrénées ◆ region S France
27 N8 Midkiff Texas, SW USA 31.35N 101.51W
12 G13 Midland Ontario, S Canada 44.43N 79.51W
33 R8 Midland Michigan, N USA 43.37N 84.15W
30 M10 Midland South Dakota, N USA 44.04N 101.07W
26 M8 Midland Texas, SW USA 32.00N 102.04W
85 K17 Midlands ◆ province C Zimbabwe
99 D21 Midleton Ir. Mainistir na Corann. SW Ireland 51.55N 8.10W
27 T7 Midlothian Texas, SW USA 32.28N 96.59W
98 K12 Midlothian cultural region S Scotland, UK
180 I7 Midongy Fianarantsoa, S Madagascar 21.58S 47.46E
104 K15 Midou SW France
199 Ii6 Mid-Pacific Mountains var. Mid-Pacific Seamounts. undersea feature NW Pacific Ocean
Mid-Pacific Seamounts see Mid-Pacific Mountains
179 R16 Midsayap Mindanao, S Philippines 7.12N 124.31E
38 L3 Midway Utah, W USA 40.30N 111.28W
199 Jj5 Midway Islands ◇ US territory C Pacific Ocean
35 X14 Midwest Wyoming, C USA 43.24N 106.15W
29 N10 Midwest City Oklahoma, C USA 35.27N 97.24W
158 M10 Mid Western ◆ zone W Nepal
100 P5 Midwolda Groningen, NE Netherlands 53.12N 7.00E
143 Q16 Midyat Mardin, SE Turkey 37.25N 41.19E
116 F8 Midzhur SCr. Midžor. ▲ Bulgaria/Serbia and Montenegro (Yugoslavia) 43.24N 22.41E see also Midžor
115 Q14 Midžor Bul. Midzhur. ▲ Bulgaria/Serbia and Montenegro (Yugoslavia) 43.24N 22.40E see also Midzhur
171 H16 Mie off. Mie-ken. ◆ prefecture Honshū, SW Japan
113 L16 Miechów Małopolskie, S Poland 50.20N 20.00E
112 F11 Międzychód Ger. Mitteldorf. Wielkopolskie, C Poland 52.36N 15.52E
Międzyleska, Przełęcz see Mezileské Sedlo
112 O12 Międzyrzec Podlaski Lubelskie, E Poland 52.00N 22.47E
112 E11 Międzyrzecz Ger. Meseritz. Lubelskie, W Poland 52.26N 15.33E
Mie-ken see Mie
104 L16 Miélan Gers, S France 43.25N 0.18E
113 N16 Mielec Podkarpackie, SE Poland 50.18N 21.27E
97 L21 Mien S Sweden
43 O8 Mier Tamaulipas, C Mexico 26.25N 99.10W
118 J11 Miercurea-Ciuc Ger. Szeklerburg, Hung. Csíkszereda. Harghita, C Romania 46.23N 25.47E
Mieresch see Maros/Mureş
Mieres del Camín see Mieres del Camino
106 K2 Mieres del Camino var. Mieres del Camín. Asturias, NW Spain 43.15N 5.46W
101 K15 Mierlo Noord-Brabant, SE Netherlands 51.27N 5.37E
43 O10 Mier y Noriega Nuevo León, NE Mexico 23.24N 100.06W
Mies see Stříbro
82 K13 Mī'ēso var. Meheso, Miesso. Oromo, C Ethiopia 9.13N 40.47E
Miesso see Mī'ēso
112 D10 Mieszkowice Ger. Bärwalde Neumark. Zachodnio-pomorskie, W Poland 52.45N 14.24E
20 G14 Mifflinburg Pennsylvania, NE USA 40.55N 77.03W
20 F14 Mifflintown Pennsylvania, NE USA 40.34N 77.24W
43 R15 Miguel Alemán, Presa SE Mexico
42 L9 Miguel Asua var. Miguel Auza. Zacatecas, C Mexico 24.16N 103.28W
Miguel Auza see Miguel Asua
45 S15 Miguel de la Borda var. Donoso. Colón, C Panama 9.06N 80.19W
43 N13 Miguel Hidalgo ✈ (Guadalajara) Jalisco, SW Mexico 20.52N 101.09W
42 H7 Miguel Hidalgo, Presa W Mexico
118 J14 Mihăileşti Giurgiu, S Romania 44.19N 25.54E
118 M14 Mihail Kogălniceanu var. Kogălniceanu; prev. Caramurat, Ferdinand. Constanţa, SE Romania 44.23N 28.24E
119 N14 Mihai Viteazu Constanţa, SE Romania 44.37N 28.41E
142 G12 Mihalıççık Eskişehir, NW Turkey 39.52N 31.30E
170 Ee13 Mihara Hiroshima, Honshū, SW Japan 34.24N 133.03E
171 Jj17 Mihara-yama Miyako-jima, SE Japan 34.43N 139.22E
107 S8 Mijares E Spain
100 I11 Mijdrecht Utrecht, C Netherlands 52.12N 4.52E
172 Oo5 Mikasa Hokkaidō, NE Japan 43.19N 141.54E
Mikashevichi see Mikashevichy
121 K19 Mikashevichy Pol. Mikaszewicze, Rus. Mikashevichi. Brestskaya Voblasts', SW Belarus 52.13N 27.28E
Mikaszewicze see Mikashevichy
171 Hh16 Mikawa-wan bay S Japan
130 L5 Mikhaylov Ryazanskaya Oblast', W Russian Federation 54.12N 39.03E
Mikhaylovgrad see Montana
205 Z8 Mikhaylov Island island Antarctica
151 T6 Mikhaylovka Pavlodar, N Kazakhstan 53.49N 76.31E
131 N9 Mikhaylovka Volgogradskaya Oblast', SW Russian Federation 50.06N 43.17E
Mikhaylovka see Mykhaylivka
170 G14 Miki Hyōgo, Honshū, SW Japan 34.46N 135.00E
83 K24 Mikindani Mtwara, SE Tanzania 10.16S 40.04E
95 N18 Mikkeli Swe. Sankt Michel. Itä-Suomi, E Finland 61.41N 27.14E
112 M8 Mikołajki Ger. Nikolaiken. Warmińsko-Mazurskie, NE Poland 53.49N 21.31E
Míkonos see Mýkonos
116 I9 Mikre Lovech, N Bulgaria 43.02N 24.32E
116 C13 Mikrí Préspa, Límni N Greece
129 P4 Mikulkin, Mys headland NW Russian Federation 67.50N 46.36E
83 I23 Mikumi Morogoro, SE Tanzania 7.22S 37.00E
129 R10 Mikun' Respublika Komi, NW Russian Federation 62.20N 50.02E
171 Hh13 Mikuni Fukui, Honshū, SW Japan 36.12N 136.09E
171 Jj14 Mikuni-tōge pass Honshū, C Japan 36.48N 138.47E
172 Ss13 Mikura-jima island E Japan
31 V7 Milaca Minnesota, N USA 45.45N 93.40W
64 J10 Milagro La Rioja, C Argentina 31.00S 66.01W
58 B7 Milagro Guayas, SW Ecuador 2.08S 79.34W
33 P4 Milakokia Lake Michigan, N USA
32 J1 Milan Illinois, N USA 41.27N 90.33W
33 R10 Milan Michigan, N USA 42.05N 83.40W
29 T2 Milan Missouri, C USA 40.12N 93.07W
39 Q11 Milan New Mexico, SW USA 35.10N 107.53W
22 G9 Milan Tennessee, S USA 35.55N 88.45W
Milan see Milano
97 F15 Miland Telemark, S Norway 59.57N 8.48E
85 N15 Milange Zambézia, NE Mozambique 16.08S 35.51E
108 D8 Milano Eng. Milan, Ger. Mailand; anc. Mediolanum. Lombardia, N Italy 45.28N 9.10E
27 U10 Milano Texas, SW USA 30.42N 96.51W
142 C15 Milas Muğla, SW Turkey 37.16N 27.46E
121 K21 Milashavichy Rus. Milashevichi. Homyel'skaya Voblasts', SE Belarus 51.38N 27.54E
Milashevichi see Milashavichy
121 I18 Milavidy Rus. Milovidy. Brestskaya Voblasts', SW Belarus 52.54N 25.51E
109 L23 Milazzo anc. Mylae. Sicilia, Italy, C Mediterranean Sea 38.13N 15.15E
31 R8 Milbank South Dakota, N USA 45.12N 96.36W
21 T7 Milbridge Maine, NE USA 44.31N 67.55W
102 L11 Milde C Germany
12 F14 Mildmay Ontario, S Canada 44.03N 81.07W
190 L9 Mildura Victoria, SE Australia 34.13S 142.09E
143 X12 Mil Düzü Rus. Mil'skaya Ravnina, Mil'skaya Step'. physical region C Azerbaijan
166 H13 Mile var. Miyang. Yunnan, SW China 24.28N 103.25E
Mile see Mili Atoll
189 Y10 Miles Queensland, E Australia 26.41S 150.15E
27 P8 Miles Texas, SW USA 31.36N 100.10W
35 X9 Miles City Montana, NW USA 46.24N 105.48W
9 U17 Milestone Saskatchewan, S Canada 50.00N 104.24W
109 N22 Mileto Calabria, SW Italy 38.35N 16.03E
109 K16 Miletto, Monte ▲ C Italy 41.28N 14.21E
20 M13 Milford Connecticut, NE USA 41.12N 73.01W
23 Y3 Milford var. Milford City. Delaware, NE USA 38.54N 75.25W
31 T11 Milford Iowa, C USA 43.19N 95.09W
21 S6 Milford Maine, NE USA 44.57N 68.37W
31 R16 Milford Nebraska, C USA 40.46N 97.03W
21 O10 Milford New Hampshire, NE USA 42.49N 71.38W
20 J13 Milford Pennsylvania, NE USA 41.19N 74.48W
27 T7 Milford Texas, SW USA 32.07N 96.57W
38 K6 Milford Utah, W USA 38.22N 112.57W
Milford see Milford Haven
Milford City see Milford
99 H21 Milford Haven prev. Milford. SW Wales, UK 51.43N 5.01W
29 O4 Milford Lake Kansas, C USA
193 B21 Milford Sound Southland, South Island, NZ 44.40S 167.57E
193 B21 Milford Sound inlet South Island, NZ
Milhau see Millau
Milḩ, Baḩr al see Razāzah, Buḩayrat ar
145 T10 Milḩ, Wādī al dry watercourse S Iraq
201 W8 Mili Atoll var. Mile. atoll Ratak Chain, SE Marshall Islands
112 H13 Milicz Dolnośląskie, SW Poland 51.31N 17.18E
109 L25 Militello in Val di Catania Sicilia, Italy, C Mediterranean Sea 37.16N 14.46E
127 Pp11 Mil'kovo Kamchatskaya Oblast', E Russian Federation 54.39N 158.35E
9 R17 Milk River Alberta, SW Canada 49.10N 112.06W
46 J13 Milk River C Jamaica
35 W7 Milk River Montana, NW USA
82 D9 Milk, Wadi el var. Wadi al Malik. C Sudan
101 L14 Mill Noord-Brabant, SE Netherlands 51.42N 5.46E
105 P14 Millau var. Milhau; anc. Æmilianum. Aveyron, S France 44.06N 3.04E
12 I14 Millbrook Ontario, SE Canada 44.09N 78.26W
25 U4 Milledgeville Georgia, SE USA 33.04N 83.13W
10 C12 Mille Lacs, Lac des Ontario, S Canada
31 V6 Mille Lacs Lake Minnesota, N USA
25 V4 Millen Georgia, SE USA 32.50N 81.56W
203 Y5 Millennium Island prev. Caroline Island, Thornton Island. atoll Line Islands, E Kiribati
31 O9 Miller South Dakota, N USA 44.31N 98.59W
32 K5 Miller Dam Flowage Wisconsin, N USA
41 U12 Miller, Mount ▲ Alaska, USA 60.29N 142.16W
130 L10 Millerovo Rostovskaya Oblast', SW Russian Federation 48.57N 40.25E
39 N17 Miller Peak ▲ Arizona, SW USA 31.23N 110.17W
33 T12 Millersburg Ohio, N USA 40.33N 81.55W
20 G15 Millersburg Pennsylvania, NE USA 40.31N 76.56W
193 D23 Millers Flat Otago, South Island, NZ 45.42S 169.25E
27 Q8 Millersview Texas, SW USA 31.26N 99.44W
108 B10 Millesimo Piemonte, NE Italy 44.24N 8.09E
15 Mm15 Milles Lacs, Lac des Ontario, SW Canada
27 Q13 Millett Texas, SW USA 28.33N 99.10W
105 N11 Millevaches, Plateau de plateau C France
190 K12 Millicent South Australia 37.37S 140.21E
100 M13 Millingen aan den Rijn Gelderland, SE Netherlands 51.52N 6.02E
22 E10 Millington Tennessee, S USA 35.20N 89.54W
21 R4 Millinocket Maine, NE USA 45.38N 68.45W
21 R4 Millinocket Lake Maine, NE USA
205 Z11 Mill Island island Antarctica
191 T3 Millmerran Queensland, E Australia 27.52S 151.15E
111 R9 Millstatt Kärnten, S Austria 46.45N 13.36E
99 B19 Milltown Malbay Ir. Sráid na Cathrach. W Ireland 52.51N 9.23W
20 J17 Millville New Jersey, NE USA 39.24N 75.01W
29 S13 Millwood Lake Arkansas, C USA
Milne Bank see Milne Seamounts
195 O17 Milne Bay ◆ province SE PNG
195 N17 Milne Bay bay SE PNG
66 J8 Milne Seamounts var. Milne Bank. undersea feature N Atlantic Ocean
31 Q6 Milnor North Dakota, N USA 46.15N 97.27W
21 R5 Milo Maine, NE USA 45.15N 69.01W
117 I22 Mílos Mílos, Kykládes, Greece, Aegean Sea 36.45N 24.26E
117 I22 Mílos island Kykládes, Greece, Aegean Sea
112 H11 Miłosław Wielkopolskie, C Poland 52.13N 17.28E
115 K19 Milot var. Miloti. Lezhë, C Albania 41.42N 19.43E
Miloti see Milot
119 Z5 Milove Luhans'ka Oblast', E Ukraine 49.22N 40.09E
Milovidy see Milavidy
190 L4 Milparinka New South Wales, SE Australia 29.48S 141.57E
37 N9 Milpitas California, W USA 37.25N 121.54W
Mil'skaya Ravnina/Mil'skaya Step' see Mil Düzü
12 G15 Milton Ontario, S Canada 43.31N 79.52W
193 E24 Milton Otago, South Island, NZ 46.07S 169.59E
23 Y4 Milton Delaware, NE USA 38.48N 75.21W
25 P8 Milton Florida, SE USA 30.37N 87.02W
20 G14 Milton Pennsylvania, NE USA 41.01N 76.49W
20 L7 Milton Vermont, NE USA 44.37N 73.04W
34 K11 Milton-Freewater Oregon, NW USA 45.54N 118.24W
99 N21 Milton Keynes SE England, UK 52.00N 0.43W
29 N3 Miltonvale Kansas, C USA 39.21N 97.27W
167 N10 Miluo Hunan, S China 28.52N 113.00E
32 M9 Milwaukee Wisconsin, N USA 43.03N 87.55W
Milyang see Miryang
Mimatum see Mende
39 Q15 Mimbres Mountains ▲ New Mexico, SW USA
190 D2 Mimili South Australia 27.01S 132.33E
104 J14 Mimizan Landes, SW France 44.12N 1.12W
Mimmaya see Minmaya
81 E19 Mimongo Ngounié, C Gabon 1.36S 11.43E
Min see Fujian
37 T7 Mina Nevada, W USA 38.23N 118.07W
149 S14 Mīnāb Hormozgān, SE Iran 27.08N 57.02E
Minā Baranīs see Berenice
155 R9 Mīna Bāzār Baluchistān, SW Pakistan 30.58N 69.11E
170 C15 Minamata Kumamoto, Kyūshū, SW Japan 32.12N 130.23E
172 Ss17 Minami-Iō-jima Eng. San Augustine. island SE Japan
172 Nn7 Minami-Kayabe Hokkaidō, NE Japan 41.54N 140.58E
170 B17 Minamitane Kagoshima, Tanega-shima, SW Japan 30.23N 130.54E
Minami Tori Shima see Marcus Island
Min'an see Longshan
64 J4 Mina Pirquitas Jujuy, NW Argentina 22.48S 66.24W
181 O3 Mīnā' Qābūs NE Oman
63 F19 Minas Lavalleja, S Uruguay 34.19S 55.19W
11 P15 Minas Basin bay Nova Scotia, SE Canada
63 F17 Minas de Corrales Rivera, NE Uruguay 31.34S 55.19W
46 A5 Minas de Matahambre Pinar del Río, W Cuba 22.34N 83.57W
106 J13 Minas de Ríotinto Andalucía, S Spain 37.40N 6.36W
62 K7 Minas Gerais off. Estado de Minas Gerais. ◆ state E Brazil
44 E5 Minas, Sierra de las ▲ E Guatemala
43 T15 Minatitlán Veracruz-Llave, E Mexico 17.58N 94.31W
177 Ff6 Minbu Magwe, W Myanmar 20.09N 94.52E
155 V10 Minchinābād Punjab, E Pakistan 30.10N 73.40E
65 G17 Minchinmávida, Volcán ▲ S Chile 42.51S 72.23W
98 G7 Minch, The var. North Minch. strait NW Scotland, UK
108 F8 Mincio anc. Mincius. N Italy
Mincius see Mincio
28 M11 Minco Oklahoma, C USA 35.18N 97.56W
179 Rr16 Mindanao island S Philippines
Mindanao Sea see Bohol Sea
103 J23 Mindel S Germany
103 J23 Mindelheim Bayern, S Germany 48.03N 10.29E
Mindello see Mindelo
78 C9 Mindelo var. Mindello; prev. Porto Grande. São Vicente, N Cape Verde 16.54N 25.01W
12 I13 Minden Ontario, SE Canada 44.54N 78.41W
102 H13 Minden anc. Minthun. Nordrhein-Westfalen, NW Germany 52.18N 8.55E
24 G5 Minden Louisiana, S USA 32.37N 93.17W
31 O16 Minden Nebraska, C USA 40.30N 98.57W
37 Q6 Minden Nevada, W USA 38.58N 119.46W
190 L8 Mindona Lake seasonal lake New South Wales, SE Australia
179 Pp12 Mindoro island N Philippines
179 P12 Mindoro Strait strait W Philippines
165 S9 Mine Gansu, N China
170 Dd12 Mine Yamaguchi, Honshū, SW Japan 34.10N 131.12E
99 E21 Mine Head Ir. Mionn Ard. headland S Ireland 51.58N 7.36W
99 J23 Minehead SW England, UK 51.13N 3.28W
61 J19 Mineiros Goiás, C Brazil 17.34S 52.33W
27 V6 Mineola Texas, SW USA 32.39N 95.29W
27 S13 Mineral Texas, SW USA 28.32N 97.54W
131 N15 Mineral'nyye Vody Stavropol'skiy Kray, SW Russian Federation 44.13N 43.06E
32 K9 Mineral Point Wisconsin, N USA 42.54N 90.09W
27 S6 Mineral Wells Texas, SW USA 32.48N 98.06W
38 K6 Minersville Utah, W USA 38.12N 112.56W
33 U12 Minerva Ohio, N USA 40.43N 81.06W
109 N17 Minervino Murge Puglia, SE Italy 41.06N 16.04E
105 O16 Minervois physical region S France
164 I10 Minfeng var. Niya. Xinjiang Uygur Zizhiqu, NW China 37.07N 82.43E
81 O25 Minga Katanga, SE Dem. Rep. Congo 11.06S 27.57E
143 W11 Mingäçevir Rus. Mingechaur, Mingechevir. C Azerbaijan 40.46N 47.02E
143 W11 Mingäçevir Su Anbarı Rus. Mingechaurskoye Vodokhranilishche, Mingechevirskoye Vodokhranilishche. NW Azerbaijan
177 G8 Mingaladon ✈ (Yangon) Yangon, SW Myanmar 16.55N 96.11E
11 P11 Mingan Québec, E Canada 50.19N 64.01W
155 U5 Mingāora var. Mingora, Mongora. North-West Frontier Province, N Pakistan 34.46N 72.22E
152 K8 Mingbuloq Rus. Mynbulak. Navoiy Viloyati, N Uzbekistan 42.18N 62.53E
152 K9 Mingbuloq Botig'I Rus. Vpadina Mynbulak. depression N Uzbekistan
Mingechaur/Mingechevir see Mingäçevir
Mingechaurskoye Vodokhranilishche/Mingechevirskoye Vodokhranilishche see Mingäçevir Su Anbarı

294

◆ Country ● Country Capital ◇ Dependent Territory ○ Dependent Territory Capital ◆ Administrative Region ✈ International Airport ▲ Mountain ▲ Mountain Range Volcano River Lake Reservoir

MINGGUANG – MÖLNLYCKE

167 Q7 **Mingguang** *prev.* Jiashan. Anhui, S China *32.45N 117.58E*
177 Ff4 **Mingin** Sagaing, C Myanmar *22.51N 94.30E*
107 Q10 **Minglanilla** Castilla-La Mancha, C Spain *39.31N 1.36W*
33 V13 **Mingo Junction** Ohio, N USA *40.19N 80.36W*
Mingora *see* Mingāora
169 V7 **Mingshui** Heilongjiang, NE China *47.10N 125.52E*
Mingteke Daban *see* Mintaka Pass
85 Q14 **Minguri** Nampula, NE Mozambique *14.30S 40.37E*
165 U10 **Minhe** *var.* Shangchuankou. Qinghai, C China *36.21N 102.40E*
177 Ff6 **Minhla** Magwe, W Myanmar *19.57N 94.58E*
178 J15 **Minh Lương** Kiên Giang, S Vietnam *9.52N 105.10E*
106 G5 **Minho, Rio** *Sp.* Miño. ≈ Portugal/Spain *see also* Miño
106 G5 **Minho** *former province* N Portugal
161 C24 **Minicoy Island** *island* SW India
35 P15 **Minidoka** Idaho, NW USA *42.45N 113.29W*
120 C11 **Minija** ≈ W Lithuania
188 G9 **Minilya** Western Australia *23.45S 114.03E*
12 E8 **Minisinakwa Lake** ◎ Ontario, S Canada
47 T12 **Ministre Point** *headland* S Saint Lucia *13.42N 60.57W*
9 V15 **Minitonas** Manitoba, S Canada *52.07N 101.02W*
Minius *see* Miño
167 R12 **Min Jiang** ≈ SE China
166 H10 **Min Jiang** ≈ C China
190 H9 **Minlaton** South Australia *34.52S 137.33E*
172 N8 **Minmaya** *var.* Mimmaya. Aomori, Honshū, C Japan *41.10N 140.24E*
79 U14 **Minna** Niger, C Nigeria *9.33N 6.33E*
172 Pp16 **Minna-jima** *island* Sakishima-shotō, SW Japan
29 N4 **Minneapolis** Kansas, C USA *39.07N 97.42W*
31 U9 **Minneapolis** Minnesota, N USA *44.58N 93.15W*
31 V8 **Minneapolis-Saint Paul** ✈ Minnesota, N USA *44.53N 93.13W*
15 Kk15 **Minnedosa** Manitoba, S Canada *50.13N 99.49W*
28 J7 **Minneola** Kansas, C USA *37.26N 100.00W*
31 S7 **Minnesota** *off.* State of Minnesota; also known as Gopher State, New England of the West, North Star State. ◆ *state* N USA
31 S9 **Minnesota River** ≈ Minnesota/South Dakota, N USA
31 V9 **Minnetonka** Minnesota, N USA *44.55N 93.28W*
31 O3 **Minnewaukan** North Dakota, N USA *48.03N 99.15W*
190 F7 **Minnipa** South Australia *32.52S 135.07E*
106 H2 **Miño** Galicia, NW Spain *43.21N 8.12W*
106 G5 **Miño** *var.* Mino, Minius, *Port.* Rio Minho. ≈ Portugal/Spain see also Minho, Rio
171 Ii16 **Minobu** Yamanashi, Honshū, S Japan *35.22N 138.30E*
32 L4 **Minocqua** Wisconsin, N USA *45.53N 89.42W*
171 I15 **Minokamo** Gifu, Honshū, SW Japan *35.24N 136.57E*
32 L12 **Minonk** Illinois, N USA *40.54N 89.01W*
Minorca *see* Menorca
30 M3 **Minot** North Dakota, N USA *48.15N 101.19W*
165 U8 **Minqin** Gansu, N China *38.35N 103.07E*
121 J16 **Minsk** ● (Belarus) Minskaya Voblasts', C Belarus *53.52N 27.34E*
121 L16 **Minsk** ✈ Minskaya Voblasts', C Belarus *53.52N 27.58E*
Minskaya Oblast' *see* Minskaya Voblasts'
121 K16 **Minskaya Voblasts'** *prev. Rus.* Minskaya Oblast'. ◐ *province* C Belarus
121 J16 **Minskaya Wzvyshsha** ▲ C Belarus
112 N12 **Mińsk Mazowiecki** *var.* Nowo-Minsk. Mazowieckie, C Poland *52.11N 21.33E*
33 Q13 **Minster** Ohio, N USA *40.23N 84.22W*
81 F15 **Minta** Centre, C Cameroon *4.34N 12.54E*
155 W2 **Mintaka Pass** *Chin.* Mingteke Daban. *pass* China/Pakistan *36.59N 75.04E*
117 D20 **Mínthi** ▲▲ S Greece
Minthun *see* Minden
11 O14 **Minto** New Brunswick, SE Canada *46.04N 66.04W*
8 H6 **Minto** Yukon Territory, W Canada *62.33N 136.45W*
41 R9 **Minto** Alaska, USA *65.07N 149.22W*
31 Q3 **Minto** North Dakota, N USA *48.17N 97.22W*
10 K6 **Minto, Lac** ◎ Québec, C Canada
205 R16 **Minto, Mount** ▲ Antarctica *71.38S 169.11E*
9 U17 **Minton** Saskatchewan, S Canada *49.12N 104.33W*
201 R15 **Minto Reef** *atoll* Caroline Islands, C Micronesia
39 R4 **Minturn** Colorado, C USA *39.34N 106.21W*
109 J16 **Minturno** Lazio, C Italy *41.15N 13.47E*
126 Hh15 **Minusinsk** Krasnoyarskiy Kray, S Russian Federation *53.37N 91.49E*
110 G11 **Minusio** Ticino, S Switzerland *46.11N 8.47E*
81 E17 **Minvoul** Woleu-Ntem, N Gabon *2.07N 12.12E*
147 R13 **Minwakh** N Yemen *16.54N 48.04E*
165 V11 **Minxian** *var.* Min Xian. Gansu, C China *34.22N 104.02E*
Minya *see* El Minya
33 R6 **Mio** Michigan, N USA *44.40N 84.09W*
Mionn Ard *see* Mine Head
176 Ww9 **Mios Num, Selat** *strait* Papua, E Indonesia
164 L5 **Miquan** Xinjiang Uygur Zizhiqu, NW China *44.04N 87.40E*
121 I17 **Mir** Hrodzyenskaya Voblasts', W Belarus *53.25N 26.28E*
108 H8 **Mira** Veneto, NE Italy *45.25N 12.07E*
106 G13 **Mira, Rio** ≈ S Portugal
10 K15 **Mirabel** *var.* Montreal. ✈ (Montréal) Québec, SE Canada *45.27N 73.47W*
62 Q8 **Miracema** Rio de Janeiro, SE Brazil *21.24S 42.10W*
56 G9 **Miraflores** Boyacá, C Colombia *5.07N 73.09W*
42 G10 **Miraflores** Baja California Sur, W Mexico *23.24N 109.45W*
46 L9 **Miragoâne** S Haiti *18.25N 73.07W*
161 E16 **Miraj** Mahārāshtra, W India *16.51N 74.42E*
63 E23 **Miramar** Buenos Aires, E Argentina *38.15S 57.49W*
105 R15 **Miramas** Bouches-du-Rhône, SE France *43.34N 4.58E*
104 K12 **Mirambeau** Charente-Maritime, W France *45.23N 0.33W*
104 L13 **Miramont-de-Guyenne** Lot-et-Garonne, SW France *44.34N 0.20E*
117 L25 **Mirampéllou Kólpos** *gulf* Kríti, Greece, E Mediterranean Sea
164 L8 **Miran** Xinjiang Uygur Zizhiqu, NW China *39.13N 88.58E*
56 M5 **Miranda** *off.* Estado Miranda. ◐ *state* N Venezuela
Miranda de Corvo *see* Miranda do Corvo
107 O3 **Miranda de Ebro** La Rioja, N Spain *42.40N 2.57W*
106 G8 **Miranda do Corvo** *var.* Miranda de Corvo. Coimbra, N Portugal *40.04N 8.19W*
106 J6 **Miranda do Douro** Bragança, N Portugal *41.30N 6.16W*
104 L15 **Mirande** Gers, S France *43.31N 0.25E*
106 I6 **Mirandela** Bragança, N Portugal *41.28N 7.10W*
27 R15 **Mirando City** Texas, SW USA *27.24N 99.00W*
108 G9 **Mirandola** Emilia-Romagna, N Italy *44.52N 11.04E*
62 I8 **Mirandópolis** São Paulo, S Brazil *21.10S 51.03W*
62 K8 **Mirassol** São Paulo, S Brazil *20.50S 49.30W*
106 J3 **Miravalles** ▲ NW Spain *42.52N 6.45W*
44 L12 **Miravalles, Volcán** (volcano) NW Costa Rica *10.43N 85.07W*
147 W13 **Mirbāṭ** *var.* Marbat. S Oman *17.03N 54.44E*
46 M9 **Mirebalais** C Haiti *18.46N 72.03W*
105 T6 **Mirecourt** Vosges, NE France *48.19N 6.04E*
105 N16 **Mirepoix** Ariège, S France *43.04N 1.52E*
Mirgorod *see* Myrhorod
145 W10 **Mīr Ḥājī Khalīl** E Iraq *32.11N 46.19E*
174 Mm4 **Miri** Sarawak, East Malaysia *4.22N 113.58E*
79 W12 **Miria** Zinder, S Niger *13.39N 9.15E*
190 F5 **Mirikata** South Australia *29.56S 135.13E*
56 K4 **Mirimire** Falcón, N Venezuela *11.07N 68.36W*
63 H18 **Mirim Lagoon** *var.* Lake Mirim, *Sp.* Laguna Merín. *lagoon* Brazil/Uruguay
Mirim, Lake *see* Mirim Lagoon
Mírina *see* Mýrina
180 H14 **Miringoni** Mohéli, S Comoros *12.16S 93.39E*
149 W11 **Mīrjāveh** Sīstān va Balūchestān, SE Iran *29.04N 61.24E*
205 Z9 **Mirny** *Russian research station* Antarctica *66.25S 93.09E*
128 M10 **Mirnyy** Arkhangel'skaya Oblast', NW Russian Federation *62.50N 40.20E*
126 Kk11 **Mirnyy** Respublika Sakha (Yakutiya), NE Russian Federation *62.30N 113.58E*
Mironovka *see* Myronivka
112 F9 **Mirosławiec** Zachodnio-pomorskie, NW Poland *53.21N 16.04E*
Mirovo *see* Vrattsa
102 N10 **Mirow** Mecklenburg-Vorpommern, N Germany *53.16N 12.48E*
158 G6 **Mīrpur** Jammu and Kashmir, NW India *33.06N 73.49E*
Mīrpur *see* New Mirpur
155 P17 **Mīrpur Batoro** Sind, SE Pakistan *24.40N 68.15E*
155 Q16 **Mīrpur Khās** Sind, SE Pakistan *25.31N 69.00E*
155 P17 **Mīrpur Sakro** Sind, SE Pakistan *24.31N 67.37E*
149 T14 **Mīr Shahdād** Hormozgān, S Iran *26.15N 58.28E*
Mirtoan Sea *see* Mirtóo Pélagos
117 G21 **Mirtóo Pélagos** *Eng.* Mirtoan Sea; *anc.* Myrtoum Mare. *sea* S Greece
169 Z16 **Miryang** *var.* Milyang, *Jap.* Mitsuō. SE South Korea *35.30N 128.46E*
Mirzachirla *see* Murzechirla
170 Dd14 **Misaki** Ehime, Shikoku, SW Japan *33.22N 132.04E*
43 Q13 **Misantla** Veracruz-Llave, E Mexico *19.54N 96.51W*
172 N9 **Misawa** Aomori, Honshū, C Japan *40.41N 141.22E*
59 G14 **Mishagua, Río** ≈ C Peru
169 Z8 **Mishan** Heilongjiang, NE China *45.30N 131.53E*
33 O11 **Mishawaka** Indiana, N USA *41.40N 86.10W*
41 N6 **Misheguk Mountain** ▲ Alaska, USA *68.13N 161.11W*
171 Jj17 **Mishima** *var.* Misima. Shizuoka, Honshū, S Japan *35.07N 138.55E*
170 Dd11 **Mi-shima** *island* SW Japan
131 V4 **Mishkino** Respublika Bashkortostan, W Russian Federation *55.31N 55.57E*
159 Y10 **Mishmi Hills** *hill range* NE India
167 N11 **Mi Shui** ≈ S China
Misiaf *see* Maşyāf
109 J23 **Misilmeri** Sicilia, Italy, C Mediterranean Sea *38.03N 13.27E*
Misima *see* Mishima
195 P17 **Misima Island** *island* SE PNG
Misión de Guana *see* Guana
62 F13 **Misiones** *off.* Provincia de Misiones. ◐ *province* NE Argentina
64 P8 **Misiones** *off.* Departamento de las Misiones. ◐ *department* S Paraguay
Misión San Fernando *see* San Fernando
Miskin *see* Maskin
Miskito Coast *see* La Mosquitia
45 O7 **Miskitos, Cayos** *island group* NE Nicaragua
113 M21 **Miskolc** Borsod-Abaúj-Zemplén, NE Hungary *48.04N 20.46E*
175 Tt10 **Misool, Pulau** *island* Maluku, E Indonesia
Misox *see* Mesocco
31 Y3 **Misquah Hills** *hill range* Minnesota, N USA
77 P7 **Miṣrātah** *var.* Misurata. NW Libya *32.22N 15.04E*
123 Ll15 **Miṣrātah, Râs** *headland* N Libya *32.22N 15.16E*
12 C7 **Missanabie** Ontario, S Canada *48.18N 84.04W*
60 E10 **Missão Catrimani** Roraima, N Brazil *1.25N 62.05W*
12 D6 **Missinaibi** ≈ Ontario, S Canada
12 C7 **Missinaibi Lake** ◎ Ontario, S Canada
9 T13 **Missinipe** Saskatchewan, C Canada *55.36N 104.45W*
30 M11 **Mission** South Dakota, N USA *43.16N 100.38W*
27 S17 **Mission** Texas, SW USA *26.13N 98.19W*
10 F10 **Missisa Lake** ◎ Ontario, C Canada
20 M6 **Missisquoi Bay** *lake bay* Canada/USA
12 C10 **Mississagi** ≈ Ontario, S Canada
12 G15 **Mississauga** Ontario, S Canada *43.36N 79.34W*
33 P12 **Mississinewa Lake** ⊠ Indiana, N USA
33 P12 **Mississinewa River** ≈ Indiana/Ohio, N USA
24 K4 **Mississippi** *off.* State of Mississippi; also known as Bayou State, Magnolia State. ◆ *state* SE USA
12 K13 **Mississippi** ≈ Ontario, SE Canada
24 M10 **Mississippi Delta** *delta* Louisiana, S USA
49 N1 **Mississippi Fan** *undersea feature* N Gulf of Mexico
12 L13 **Mississippi Lake** ◎ Ontario, SE Canada
(0) J11 **Mississippi River** ≈ C USA
24 M9 **Mississippi Sound** *sound* Alabama/Mississippi, S USA
35 P9 **Missoula** Montana, NW USA *46.54N 114.03W*
29 T5 **Missouri** *off.* State of Missouri; also known as Bullion State, Show Me State. ◆ *state* C USA
27 V11 **Missouri City** Texas, SW USA *29.37N 95.32W*
(0) J10 **Missouri River** ≈ C USA
13 Q6 **Mistassibi** ≈ Québec, SE Canada
13 P6 **Mistassini** Québec, SE Canada *48.54N 72.13W*
13 P6 **Mistassini** ≈ Québec, SE Canada
10 J11 **Mistassini, Lac** ◎ Québec, SE Canada
111 Y3 **Mistelbach an der Zaya** Niederösterreich, NE Austria *48.33N 16.33E*
109 L24 **Misterbianco** Sicilia, Italy, C Mediterranean Sea *37.31N 15.01E*
97 N19 **Misterhult** Kalmar, S Sweden *57.28N 16.34E*
59 H17 **Misti, Volcán** ▲ S Peru *16.20S 71.22W*
Mistras *see* Mystrás
109 K23 **Mistretta** *anc.* Amestratus. Sicilia, Italy, C Mediterranean Sea *37.55N 14.22E*
170 C14 **Misumi** Kumamoto, Kyūshū, SW Japan *32.37N 130.29E*
170 Ee12 **Misumi** Shimane, Honshū, SW Japan *34.47N 132.00E*
Misurata *see* Miṣrātah
85 O14 **Mitande** Niassa, N Mozambique *14.06S 36.03E*
42 J13 **Mita, Punta de** *headland* C Mexico *20.46N 105.31W*
57 W12 **Mitaraka, Massif du** ▲ NE South America *2.18N 54.31W*
Mitau *see* Jelgava
189 X9 **Mitchell** Queensland, E Australia *26.29S 148.00E*
12 E15 **Mitchell** Ontario, S Canada *43.28N 81.11W*
30 J13 **Mitchell** Nebraska, C USA *41.56N 103.48W*
34 J12 **Mitchell** Oregon, NW USA *44.34N 120.09W*
31 P11 **Mitchell** South Dakota, N USA *43.42N 98.01W*
25 P5 **Mitchell Lake** ⊠ Alabama, S USA
33 P7 **Mitchell, Lake** ◎ Michigan, N USA
23 P9 **Mitchell, Mount** ▲ North Carolina, SE USA *35.46N 82.16W*
189 V3 **Mitchell River** ≈ Queensland, NE Australia
99 D20 **Mitchelstown** *Ir.* Baile Mhistéala. SW Ireland *52.19N 8.16W*
12 M9 **Mitchinamécus, Lac** ◎ Québec, SE Canada
Mitèmboni *see* Mitemele, Río
81 D17 **Mitemele, Río** *var.* Mitèmboni, Temboni, Utamboni. ≈ S Equatorial Guinea
155 S12 **Mithānkot** Punjab, E Pakistan *28.57N 70.21E*
155 T7 **Mitha Tiwāna** Punjab, E Pakistan *32.16N 72.07E*
155 R17 **Mithi** Sind, SE Pakistan *24.43N 69.52E*
Míthimna *see* Míthymna
Mi Tho *see* My Tho
117 L16 **Míthymna** *var.* Míthimna. Lésvos, E Greece *39.22N 26.11E*
202 L16 **Mitiaro** *island* S Cook Islands
Mitilíni *see* Mytilíni
13 U7 **Mitis** ≈ Québec, SE Canada
43 R16 **Mitla** Oaxaca, SE Mexico *16.55N 96.19W*
171 Kk16 **Mito** Ibaraki, Honshū, S Japan *36.21N 140.25E*
94 N2 **Mitra, Kapp** *headland* W Svalbard *79.07N 11.11E*
192 M13 **Mitre** ▲ North Island, NZ *40.46S 175.27E*
193 B21 **Mitre Peak** ▲ South Island, NZ *44.37S 167.45E*
41 O15 **Mitrofania Island** *island* Alaska, USA
Mitrovica/Mitrowitz *see* Sremska Mitrovica, Serbia, Serbia and Montenegro (Yugoslavia)
Mitrovica/Mitrovicë *see* Kosovska Mitrovica, Serbia, Serbia and Montenegro (Yugoslavia)
180 H12 **Mitsamiouli** Grande Comore, NW Comoros *11.22S 43.19E*
180 I3 **Mitsinjo** Mahajanga, NW Madagascar *16.00S 45.52E*
Mits'iwa *see* Massawa
180 H13 **Mitsoudjé** Grande Comore, NW Comoros
Mitspe Ramon *see* Mizpé Ramon
172 Oo7 **Mitsuishi** Hokkaidō, NE Japan *42.12N 142.40E*
171 K13 **Mitsuke** *var.* Mituke. Niigata, Honshū, C Japan *37.33N 138.57E*
Mitsuō *see* Miryang
170 Cc10 **Mitsushima** Nagasaki, Tsushima, SW Japan *34.16N 129.18E*
102 G12 **Mittellandkanal** *canal* NW Germany
110 J7 **Mittelberg** Vorarlberg, NW Austria *47.19N 10.09E*
Mitteldorf *see* Międzychód
Mittelstadt *see* Baia Sprie
Mitterburg *see* Pazin
111 P7 **Mittersill** Salzburg, NW Austria *47.16N 12.27E*
103 N16 **Mittweida** Sachsen, E Germany *50.59N 12.57E*
56 J13 **Mitú** Vaupés, SE Colombia *1.07N 70.04W*
Mituke *see* Mitsuke
Mitumba, Chaîne des/ Mitumba Range *see* Mitumba, Monts
81 O22 **Mitumba, Monts** *var.* Chaîne des Mitumba, Mitumba Range. ▲▲ E Dem. Rep. Congo
81 N23 **Mitwaba** Katanga, SE Dem. Rep. Congo *8.37S 27.19E*
81 E18 **Mitzic** Woleu-Ntem, N Gabon *0.48N 11.30E*
84 K11 **Miueru Wantipa, Lake** ◎ N Zambia
171 Jj17 **Miura** Kanagawa, Honshū, S Japan *35.07N 139.37E*
171 M13 **Miyagi** *off.* Miyagi-ken. ◐ *prefecture* Honshū, C Japan
144 M7 **Miyāh, Wādī al** *dry watercourse* E Syria
172 Ss13 **Miyake** Tōkyō, Miyako-jima, SE Japan *34.34N 135.33E*
172 N11 **Miyako** Iwate, Honshū, C Japan *39.39N 141.57E*
172 Q16 **Miyako-jima** *island* Sakishima-shotō, SW Japan
170 C16 **Miyakonojō** *var.* Miyakonzyô. Miyazaki, Kyūshū, SW Japan *31.42N 131.03E*
Miyakonzyô *see* Miyakonojō
172 Pp16 **Miyako-shotō** *island group* SW Japan
150 G11 **Miyaly** Atyrau, W Kazakhstan *48.52N 53.55E*
Miyāndoāb *see* Miāndowāb
Miyāneh *see* Mīāneh
Miyang *see* Mile
170 C15 **Miyanojō** Kagoshima, Kyūshū, SW Japan *31.55N 130.29E*
170 Cc16 **Miyazaki** Miyazaki, Kyūshū, SW Japan *31.55N 131.23E*
170 C15 **Miyazaki** *off.* Miyazaki-ken. ◐ *prefecture* Kyūshū, SW Japan
171 H13 **Miyazu** Kyōto, Honshū, SW Japan *35.28N 135.21E*
Miyory *see* Myory
170 F13 **Miyoshi** *var.* Miyosi. Hiroshima, Honshū, SW Japan *34.48N 132.51E*
Miyosi *see* Miyoshi
Miza *see* Mizë
83 H14 **Mīzan Teferī** Southern, S Ethiopia *6.57N 35.30E*
Mizda *see* Mizdah
77 O8 **Mizdah** *var.* Mizda. NW Libya *31.25N 12.58E*
115 K20 **Mizë** *var.* Miza. Fier, W Albania *40.58N 19.32E*
99 A22 **Mizen Head** *Ir.* Carn Uí Néid. *headland* SW Ireland *51.26N 9.50W*
118 H7 **Mizhhir"ya** *Rus.* Mezhgor'ye. Zakarpats'ka Oblast', W Ukraine *48.28N 23.31E*
166 L4 **Mizhi** Shaanxi, C China *37.43N 110.13E*
118 K13 **Mizil** Prahova, SE Romania *45.00N 26.29E*
116 J7 **Miziya** Vratsa, NW Bulgaria *43.42N 23.52E*
159 W15 **Mizo Hills** *hill range* E India
159 W15 **Mizoram** ◐ *state* NE India
144 F12 **Mizpé Ramon** *var.* Mitspe Ramon. Southern, S Israel *30.37N 34.46E*
59 L19 **Mizque** Cochabamba, C Bolivia *17.58S 65.18W*
59 M19 **Mizque, Río** ≈ C Bolivia
171 I15 **Mizunami** Gifu, Honshū, SW Japan *35.19N 137.12E*
171 Mm12 **Mizusawa** Iwate, Honshū, C Japan *39.09N 141.07E*
97 M18 **Mjölby** Östergötland, S Sweden *58.19N 15.10E*
97 G15 **Mjøndalen** Buskerud, S Norway *59.45N 9.58E*
97 J19 **Mjörn** ◎ S Sweden
96 I13 **Mjøsa** *var.* Mjøsen. ◎ S Norway
Mjøsen *see* Mjøsa
83 G21 **Mkalama** Singida, C Tanzania *4.09S 34.34E*
82 K13 **Mkata** ≈ C Tanzania
85 K14 **Mkushi** Central, C Zambia *13.37S 29.27E*
85 L22 **Mkuze** KwaZulu/Natal, E South Africa *27.40S 32.05E*
83 J22 **Mkwaja** Tanga, E Tanzania *5.45S 38.48E*
113 D16 **Mladá Boleslav** *Ger.* Jungbunzlau. Středočeský Kraj, N Czech Republic *50.24N 14.55E*
114 M12 **Mladenovac** Serbia, C Serbia and Montenegro (Yugoslavia) *44.27N 20.42E*
116 L11 **Mladinovo** Khaskovo, S Bulgaria *41.57N 26.13E*
115 O17 **Mlado Nagoričane** N FYR Macedonia *42.11N 21.49E*
Mlanje *see* Mulanje
114 N12 **Mlava** ≈ E Serbia and Montenegro (Yugoslavia)
112 L9 **Mława** Mazowieckie, C Poland *53.07N 20.23E*
115 G16 **Mljet** *It.* Meleda; *anc.* Melita. *island* S Croatia
118 K4 **Mlyniv** Rivnens'ka Oblast', NW Ukraine *50.31N 25.36E*
85 I21 **Mmabatho** North-West, N South Africa *25.51S 25.37E*
85 I19 **Mmashoro** Central, E Botswana *21.56S 26.39E*
46 J7 **Moa** Holguín, E Cuba *20.38N 74.56W*
78 J15 **Moa** ≈ Guinea/Sierra Leone
39 O6 **Moab** Utah, W USA *38.34N 109.34W*
189 V1 **Moa Island** *island* Queensland, NE Australia
197 J15 **Moala** *island* S Fiji
85 L21 **Moamba** Maputo, SW Mozambique *25.33S 32.15E*
81 F19 **Moanda** *var.* Mouanda. Haut-Ogooué, SE Gabon *1.31S 13.07E*
175 T16 **Moa, Pulau** *island* Kepulauan Leti, E Indonesia
85 M15 **Moatize** Tete, NW Mozambique *16.03S 33.49E*
81 P22 **Moba** Katanga, E Dem. Rep. Congo *7.03S 29.51E*
171 K17 **Mobara** Chiba, Honshū, S Japan *35.25N 140.19E*
Mobay *see* Montego Bay
81 K15 **Mobaye** Basse-Kotto, S Central African Republic *4.19N 21.17E*
81 K15 **Mobayi-Mbongo** Equateur, NW Dem. Rep. Congo *4.19N 21.18E*
27 P2 **Mobeetie** Texas, SW USA *35.33N 100.25W*
29 U3 **Moberly** Missouri, C USA *39.25N 92.26W*
25 N8 **Mobile** Alabama, S USA *30.41N 88.02W*
25 N9 **Mobile Bay** *bay* Alabama, S USA
25 N8 **Mobile River** ≈ Alabama, S USA
31 N8 **Mobridge** South Dakota, N USA *45.32N 100.25W*
Mobutu Sese Seko, Lac *see* Albert, Lake
47 N8 **Moca** N Dominican Republic *19.23N 70.31W*
Moçâmedes *see* Namibe
178 J6 **Môc Châu** Sơn La, N Vietnam *20.52N 104.38E*
197 L15 **Moce** *island* Lau Group, E Fiji
85 Q15 **Moçambique** Nampula, NE Mozambique *15.00S 40.44E*
Mocha *see* Al Mukhā
200 Oo13 **Mocha Fracture Zone** *tectonic feature* SE Pacific Ocean
65 F14 **Mocha, Isla** *island* C Chile
58 C12 **Moche, Río** ≈ W Peru
178 J14 **Môc Hoa** Long An, S Vietnam *10.46N 105.55E*
85 I20 **Mochudi** Kgatleng, SE Botswana *24.25S 26.07E*
84 Q13 **Mocímboa da Praia** *var.* Vila de Mocímboa da Praia. Cabo Delgado, N Mozambique *11.16S 40.21E*
96 L13 **Mockfjärd** Dalarna, C Sweden *60.30N 14.57E*
23 R9 **Mocksville** North Carolina, SE USA *35.53N 80.33W*
34 F8 **Moclips** Washington, NW USA *47.11N 124.13W*
84 C13 **Môco** *var.* Morro de Môco. ▲ W Angola *12.36S 15.09E*
56 D13 **Mocoa** Putumayo, SW Colombia *1.07N 76.37W*
62 M8 **Mococa** São Paulo, S Brazil *21.30S 47.00W*
Môco, Morro de *see* Môco
42 H8 **Mocorito** Sinaloa, C Mexico *25.24N 107.55W*
42 J4 **Moctezuma** Chihuahua, N Mexico *30.10N 106.24W*
43 N11 **Moctezuma** San Luis Potosí, C Mexico *22.44N 101.04W*
42 G4 **Moctezuma** Sonora, NW Mexico *29.49N 109.40W*
43 P12 **Moctezuma, Río** ≈ C Mexico
Mó, Cuan *see* Clew Bay
85 O16 **Mocuba** Zambézia, NE Mozambique *16.49S 37.01E*
105 U12 **Modane** Savoie, E France *45.14N 6.41E*
108 F9 **Modena** *anc.* Mutina. Emilia-Romagna, N Italy *44.39N 10.55E*
38 I7 **Modena** Utah, W USA *37.46N 113.54W*
37 O9 **Modesto** California, W USA *37.38N 121.01W*
109 L25 **Modica** *anc.* Motyca. Sicilia, Italy, C Mediterranean Sea *36.52N 14.45E*
85 J20 **Modimolle** prev. Nylstroom. Limpopo, NE South Africa *24.39S 28.23E*
81 K17 **Modjamboli** Equateur, N Dem. Rep. Congo *2.27N 22.03E*
111 X4 **Mödling** Niederösterreich, NE Austria *48.07N 16.15E*
Modohn *see* Madona
169 N8 **Modot** Hentiy, C Mongolia *47.45N 109.03E*
176 W12 **Modowi** Papua, E Indonesia *4.05S 134.39E*
114 I12 **Modračko Jezero** ⊠ NE Bosnia and Herzegovina
114 I10 **Modriča** Republika Srpska, N Bosnia and Herzegovina *44.57N 18.17E*
191 O13 **Moe** Victoria, SE Australia *38.10S 146.18E*
Moearatewe *see* Muaratewe
Moei, Mae Nam *see* Thaungyin
96 H13 **Moelv** Hedmark, S Norway *60.55N 10.47E*
94 I10 **Moen** Troms, N Norway *69.08N 18.35E*
Moen *see* Weno, Micronesia
Möen *see* Møn, Denmark
Moena *see* Muna, Pulau
38 M10 **Moenkopi Wash** ≈ Arizona, SW USA
193 F22 **Moeraki Point** *headland* South Island, NZ *45.23S 170.52E*
101 F16 **Moerbeke** Oost-Vlaanderen, NW Belgium *51.11N 3.57E*
101 H14 **Moerdijk** Noord-Brabant, S Netherlands *51.42N 4.37E*
Moero, Lac *see* Mweru, Lake
103 D15 **Moers** *var.* Mörs. Nordrhein-Westfalen, W Germany *51.27N 6.37E*
Moesi *see* Musi, Air
Moeskroen *see* Mouscron
98 J13 **Moffat** S Scotland, UK *55.28N 3.36W*
193 C22 **Moffat Peak** ▲ South Island, NZ *44.57S 168.10E*
158 H8 **Moga** Punjab, N India *30.49N 75.13E*
81 N19 **Moga** Sud Kivu, E Dem. Rep. Congo *2.16S 26.54E*
Mogadiscio/Mogadishu *see* Muqdisho
Mogador *see* Essaouira
106 J6 **Mogadouro** Bragança, N Portugal *41.19N 6.43W*
171 Ll12 **Mogami-gawa** ≈ Honshū, C Japan
178 Gg2 **Mogaung** Kachin State, N Myanmar *25.19N 96.54E*
112 L13 **Mogielnica** Mazowieckie, C Poland *51.40N 20.42E*
Mogilëv *see* Mahilyow
Mogilev-Podol'skiy *see* Mohyliv-Podil's'kyy
Mogilëvskaya Oblast' *see* Mahilyowskaya Voblasts'
112 I11 **Mogilno** Kujawsko-pomorskie, C Poland *52.39N 17.58E*
62 L9 **Mogi-Mirim** *var.* Moji-Mirim. São Paulo, S Brazil *22.26S 46.55W*
85 Q15 **Mogincual** Nampula, NE Mozambique *15.33S 40.28E*
116 E13 **Moglenítsas** ≈ N Greece
108 H8 **Mogliano Veneto** Veneto, NE Italy *45.34N 12.13E*
115 M21 **Mogliçë** Korçë, SE Albania *40.43N 20.22E*
126 L15 **Mogocha** Chitinskaya Oblast', S Russian Federation *53.39N 119.47E*
126 H13 **Mogochin** Tomskaya Oblast', C Russian Federation *57.42N 83.24E*
82 F13 **Mogogh** Jonglei, SE Sudan *8.25N 31.19E*
176 Vv10 **Mogoi** Papua, E Indonesia *1.44S 133.13E*
178 Gg4 **Mogok** Mandalay, C Myanmar *22.55N 96.28E*
39 P14 **Mogollon Mountains** ▲▲ New Mexico, SW USA
38 M12 **Mogollon Rim** *cliff* Arizona, SW USA
63 E23 **Mogotes, Punta** *headland* E Argentina *38.03S 57.31W*
44 J8 **Mogotón** ▲ NW Nicaragua *13.45N 86.22W*
106 I14 **Moguer** Andalucía, S Spain *37.15N 6.52W*
113 J26 **Mohács** Baranya, SW Hungary *46.00N 18.40E*
193 C20 **Mohaka** ≈ North Island, NZ
30 M2 **Mohall** North Dakota, N USA *48.45N 101.30W*
Moḥammadābād *see* Dargaz
76 F6 **Mohammedia** *prev.* Fédala. NW Morocco *33.46N 7.16W*
76 F6 **Mohammed V** ✈ (Casablanca) W Morocco *33.07N 8.28W*
Mohammerah *see* Khorramshahr
38 H10 **Mohave, Lake** ⊠ Arizona/Nevada, W USA
38 I12 **Mohave Mountains** ▲▲ Arizona, SW USA
38 I15 **Mohawk Mountains** ▲▲ Arizona, SW USA
20 J10 **Mohawk River** ≈ New York, NE USA
169 T3 **Mohe** *var.* Xilinji. Heilongjiang, NE China *53.00N 122.33E*
97 L20 **Moheda** Kronoberg, S Sweden *57.00N 14.34E*
180 H13 **Mohéli** *var.* Mwali, Mohilla, Mohila, *Fr.* Moili. *island* S Comoros
158 I11 **Mohendergarh** Haryāna, N India *28.16N 76.13E*
40 K12 **Mohican, Cape** *headland* Nunivak Island, Alaska, USA *60.12N 167.25W*
Mohn *see* Muhu
103 G15 **Möhne** ≈ W Germany
103 G15 **Möhne-Stausee** ⊠ W Germany
94 P2 **Mohn, Kapp** *headland* NW Svalbard *79.26N 25.44E*
207 S14 **Mohns Ridge** *undersea feature* Greenland Sea/Norwegian Sea
59 I17 **Moho** Puno, SW Peru *15.21S 69.32W*
Mohokare *see* Caledon
97 L17 **Moholm** Västra Götaland, S Sweden *58.37N 14.04E*
38 J11 **Mohon Peak** ▲ Arizona, SW USA *34.55N 113.07W*
83 J23 **Mohoro** Pwani, E Tanzania *8.09S 39.10E*
Mohra *see* Moravice
Mohrungen *see* Morąg
118 M7 **Mohyliv-Podil's'kyy** *Rus.* Mogilev-Podol'skiy. Vinnyts'ka Oblast', C Ukraine *48.28N 27.49E*
97 D17 **Moi** Rogaland, S Norway *58.27N 6.31E*
197 I6 **Moindou** Province Sud, C New Caledonia *21.42S 165.40E*
118 K11 **Moinești** *Hung.* Mojnest. Bacău, E Romania *46.27N 26.31E*
Móinteach Mílic *see* Mountmellick
12 J14 **Moira** ≈ Ontario, SE Canada
94 G13 **Mo i Rana** Nordland, C Norway *66.19N 14.10E*
159 X14 **Moirāng** Manipur, NE India *24.28N 93.45E*
117 J25 **Moíres** Kríti, Greece, E Mediterranean Sea *35.03N 24.51E*
120 H6 **Mõisaküla** *Ger.* Moiseküll. Viljandimaa, S Estonia *58.05N 25.11E*
Moiseküll *see* Mõisaküla
13 W4 **Moisie** Québec, E Canada *50.12N 66.06W*
13 W3 **Moisie** ≈ Québec, SE Canada
104 M14 **Moissac** Tarn-et-Garonne, S France *44.07N 1.04E*
80 I13 **Moïssala** Moyen-Chari, S Chad *8.21N 17.46E*
57 O7 **Moitaco** Bolívar, E Venezuela *8.00N 64.22W*
97 P15 **Möja** Stockholm, C Sweden *59.25N 18.55E*
107 Q14 **Mojácar** Andalucía, S Spain *37.09N 1.49W*
37 T13 **Mojave** California, W USA *35.03N 118.10W*
37 V13 **Mojave Desert** *plain* California, W USA
37 V13 **Mojave River** ≈ California, W USA
Moji-Mirim *see* Mogi-Mirim
115 K15 **Mojkovac** Montenegro, SW Serbia and Montenegro (Yugoslavia) *42.57N 19.34E*
Mojnest *see* Moinești
174 Ll15 **Mojokerto** *prev.* Modjokerto. Jawa, C Indonesia *7.25S 112.31E*
Mōka *see* Mooka
159 Q13 **Mokāma** *prev.* Mokameh, Mukama. Bihār, N India *25.24N 85.55E*
81 O25 **Mokambo** Katanga, SE Dem. Rep. Congo *12.23S 28.21E*
Mokameh *see* Mokāma
40 D9 **Mōkapu Point** *var.* Mokapu Point *headland* Oʻahu, Hawaiʻi, USA, C Pacific Ocean *21.27N 157.43W*
192 L9 **Mokau** Waikato, North Island, NZ *38.42S 174.37E*
192 L9 **Mokau** ≈ North Island, NZ
37 P7 **Mokelumne River** ≈ California, W USA
85 J23 **Mokhotlong** NE Lesotho *29.19S 29.06E*
Mokil Atoll *see* Mwokil Atoll
97 N14 **Möklinta** Västmanland, C Sweden *60.04N 16.34E*
192 L4 **Mokohinau Islands** *island group* N NZ
159 X12 **Mokokchūng** Nāgāland, NE India *26.19N 94.30E*
80 F12 **Mokolo** Extrême-Nord, N Cameroon *10.49N 13.54E*
193 D24 **Mokoreta** ≈ South Island, NZ
85 J20 **Mokopane** *prev.* Potgietersrus. Limpopo, NE South Africa *24.09S 28.58E*
169 X17 **Mokp'o** *Jap.* Moppo. SW South Korea *34.49N 126.26E*
115 L16 **Mokra Gora** ▲ S Serbia and Montenegro (Yugoslavia)
Mokrany *see* Makrany
131 O5 **Moksha** ≈ W Russian Federation
Moktama *see* Martaban
79 T14 **Mokwa** Niger, W Nigeria *9.19N 5.01E*
101 J16 **Mol** *prev.* Moll. Antwerpen, N Belgium *51.10N 5.07E*
109 O17 **Mola di Bari** Puglia, SE Italy *41.03N 17.04E*
Molai *see* Moláoi
43 P13 **Molango** Hidalgo, C Mexico *20.48N 98.43W*
117 F22 **Moláoi** *var.* Molai. Pelopónnisos, S Greece *36.47N 22.50E*
43 Z12 **Molas del Norte, Punta** *var.* Punta Molas. *headland* SE Mexico *20.34N 86.43W*
Molas, Punta *see* Molas del Norte, Punta
107 R11 **Molatón** ▲ C Spain *38.58N 1.19W*
99 K18 **Mold** NE Wales, UK *53.10N 3.07W*
Moldau *see* Moldova
Moldau *see* Vltava, Czech Republic
Moldavia *see* Moldova
Moldavian SSR/Moldavskaya SSR *see* Moldova
96 E9 **Molde** Møre og Romsdal, S Norway *62.43N 7.07E*
Moldotau, Khrebet *see* Moldo-Too, Khrebet
153 V9 **Moldo-Too, Khrebet** *prev.* Khrebet Moldotau. ▲▲ C Kyrgyzstan
118 K9 **Moldova** ≈ N Romania
118 K9 **Moldova** *Eng.* Moldavia, *Ger.* Moldau. *former province* NE Romania
118 L9 **Moldova** *off.* Republic of Moldova, *var.* Moldavia; *prev.* Moldavian SSR, *Rus.* Moldavskaya SSR. ◆ *republic* SE Europe
118 F13 **Moldova Nouă** *Ger.* Neumoldowa, *Hung.* Újmoldova. Caraş-Severin, SW Romania *44.45N 21.39E*
118 F13 **Moldova Veche** *Ger.* Altmoldowa, *Hung.* Ómoldova. Caraş-Severin, SW Romania *44.45N 21.13E*
Moldoveanul *see* Vârful Moldoveanu
85 I20 **Molepolole** Kweneng, SE Botswana *24.25S 25.30E*
46 L8 **Môle-St-Nicolas** NW Haiti *19.46N 73.19W*
120 H13 **Molėtai** Utena, E Lithuania *55.14N 25.25E*
109 O17 **Molfetta** Puglia, SE Italy *41.12N 16.34E*
175 R8 **Molibagu** Sulawesi, N Indonesia *0.25N 123.57E*
64 G12 **Molina** Maule, C Chile *35.06S 71.18W*
107 Q7 **Molina de Aragón** Castilla-La Mancha, C Spain *40.49N 1.54W*
107 R13 **Molina de Segura** Murcia, SE Spain *38.03N 1.10W*
32 J11 **Moline** Illinois, N USA *41.30N 90.31W*
29 P7 **Moline** Kansas, C USA *37.21N 96.18W*
81 P23 **Moliro** Katanga, SE Dem. Rep. Congo *8.10S 30.31E*
109 K16 **Molise** ◐ *region* S Italy
97 K15 **Molkom** Värmland, C Sweden *59.36N 13.43E*
Moll *see* Mol
111 Q9 **Möll** ≈ S Austria
152 I14 **Mollanepes Adyndaky** *Rus.* Imeni Mollanepesa. Mary Welaýaty, S Turkmenistan *37.36N 61.54E*
97 J22 **Mölle** Skåne, S Sweden *56.15N 12.19E*
59 H18 **Mollendo** Arequipa, SW Peru *17.01S 72.01W*
107 U5 **Mollerussa** Cataluña, NE Spain *41.37N 0.52E*
110 H8 **Mollis** Glarus, NE Switzerland *47.05N 9.03E*
97 J19 **Mölndal** Västra Götaland, S Sweden *57.39N 12.05E*
97 J19 **Mölnlycke** Västra Götaland, S Sweden *57.42N 12.19E*

◆ Country ● Country Capital ◇ Dependent Territory ○ Dependent Territory Capital ◐ Administrative Region ✈ International Airport ▲ Mountain ▲▲ Mountain Range Volcano ≈ River ◎ Lake ⊠ Reservoir
295

MOLOCHANS'K – MORENA, SIERRA

119 U9 Molochans'k Rus. Molochansk. Zaporiz'ka Oblast', SE Ukraine 47.10N 35.38E
119 U10 Molochna Rus. Molochnaya. ≈ S Ukraine
Molochnaya see Molochna
119 U10 Molochnyy Lyman bay N Black Sea
Molodechno/Molodeczno see Maladzyechna
205 V3 Molodezhnaya Russian research station Antarctica 67.33S 46.12E
128 J14 Mologa ≈ NW Russian Federation
40 E9 Moloka'i var. Molokai. island Hawai'i, USA, C Pacific Ocean
183 X3 Molokai Fracture Zone tectonic feature NE Pacific Ocean
128 K15 Molokovo Tverskaya Oblast', W Russian Federation 58.10N 36.43E
129 Q14 Moloma ≈ NW Russian Federation
191 R8 Molong New South Wales, SE Australia 33.07S 148.52E
85 H21 Molopo seasonal river Botswana/South Africa
117 F17 Mólos Stereá Ellás, C Greece 38.48N 22.40E
175 Q7 Molosipat Sulawesi, N Indonesia 0.28N 121.08E
Molotov see Severodvinsk, Arkhangel'skaya Oblast', Russian Federation
Molotov see Perm', Permskaya Oblast', Russian Federation
81 G17 Moloundou Est, SE Cameroon 2.03N 15.13E
105 U5 Molsheim Bas-Rhin, NE France 48.33N 7.30E
15 L12 Molson Lake ◎ Manitoba, C Canada
Moluccas see Maluku
175 Rr8 Molucca Sea Ind. Laut Maluku. sea E Indonesia
Molukken see Maluku
85 O15 Molumbo Zambézia, N Mozambique 15.33S 36.19E
176 Uu14 Molu, Pulau island Maluku, E Indonesia
85 P16 Moma Nampula, NE Mozambique 16.42S 39.12E
176 Xx13 Momats ≈ Papua, E Indonesia
44 J11 Mombacho, Volcán ▲ SW Nicaragua 11.49N 85.58W
83 K21 Mombasa Coast, SE Kenya 4.04N 39.40E
83 J21 Mombasa ✕ Coast, SE Kenya 4.01S 39.31E
Mombetsu see Monbetsu
176 Y16 Mombum Papua, E Indonesia 8.16S 138.51E
116 J12 Momchilgrad prev. Mastanli. Kŭrdzhali, S Bulgaria 41.33N 25.25E
101 F23 Momignies Hainaut, S Belgium 50.02N 4.10E
56 E6 Momil Córdoba, NW Colombia 9.15N 75.40W
44 I10 Momotombo, Volcán ▲ W Nicaragua 12.25N 86.33W
58 B5 Mompiche, Ensenada de bay NW Ecuador
81 K18 Mompono Equateur, NW Dem. Rep. Congo 0.11N 21.31E
56 F6 Mompós Bolívar, NW Colombia 9.10N 74.21W
97 J24 Møn prev. Möen. island SE Denmark
38 L4 Mona Utah, W USA 39.49N 111.52W
Mona, Canal de la see Mona Passage
98 E8 Monach Islands island group NW Scotland, UK
105 V14 Monaco var. Monaco-Ville; anc. Monoecus. ● (Monaco) S Monaco 43.46N 7.22E
105 V14 Monaco off. Principality of Monaco. ◆ monarchy W Europe
Monaco see München
Monaco Basin see Canary Basin
Monaco-Ville see Monaco
98 I9 Monadhliath Mountains ▲ N Scotland, UK
57 O6 Monagas off. Estado Monagas. ◐ state NE Venezuela
99 F16 Monaghan Ir. Muineachán. N Ireland 54.15N 6.58W
99 E16 Monaghan Ir. Muineachán. cultural region N Ireland
45 S16 Monagrillo Herrera, S Panama 7.58N 80.23W
26 L8 Monahans Texas, SW USA 31.33N 102.52W
47 Q9 Mona, Isla island W Puerto Rico
47 Q9 Mona Passage Sp. Canal de la Mona. channel Dominican Republic/Puerto Rico
45 O14 Mona, Punta headland E Costa Rica 9.44N 82.48W
161 K25 Monaragala Uva Province, SE Sri Lanka 6.52N 81.22E
35 S9 Monarch Montana, NW USA 47.04N 110.51W
14 Ff14 Monarch Mountain ▲ British Columbia, SW Canada 51.59N 125.56W
Monasterio see Monesterio
Monasterzyska see Monastyrys'ka
Monastir see Bitola
Monastyriska see Monastyrys'ka
119 O7 Monastyryshche Cherkas'ka Oblast', C Ukraine 48.59N 29.47E
118 J6 Monastyrys'ka Pol. Monasterzyska, Rus. Monastyriska. Ternopil's'ka Oblast', W Ukraine 49.04N 25.10E
81 E15 Monatélé Centre, SW Cameroon 4.16N 11.12E
172 Q4 Monbetsu var. Mombetsu, Monbetu. Hokkaidō, NE Japan 44.22N 143.22E
Monbetu see Monbetsu
108 B8 Moncalieri Piemonte, NW Italy 45.00N 7.41E
106 G4 Monção Viana do Castelo, N Portugal 42.03N 8.29W
107 Q5 Moncayo ▲ N Spain 41.43N 1.51W
107 Q5 Moncayo, Sierra del ▲▲ N Spain
128 J4 Monchegorsk Murmanskaya Oblast', NW Russian Federation 67.55N 32.46E
103 D15 Mönchengladbach prev. München-Gladbach. Nordrhein-Westfalen, W Germany 51.12N 6.25E
106 F14 Monchique Faro, S Portugal 37.19N 8.33W
106 G14 Monchique, Serra de ▲▲ S Portugal
23 S14 Moncks Corner South Carolina, SE USA 33.12N 80.00W
43 N7 Monclova Coahuila de Zaragoza, NE Mexico 26.55N 101.25W
Moncorvo see Torre de Moncorvo
11 P14 Moncton New Brunswick, SE Canada 46.04N 64.49W
106 F8 Mondego, Cabo headland N Portugal 40.10N 8.58W
106 G8 Mondego, Rio ≈ N Portugal
106 I2 Mondoñedo Galicia, NW Spain 43.25N 7.22W
101 N25 Mondorf-les-Bains Grevenmacher, SE Luxembourg 49.30N 6.16E
104 M7 Mondoubleau Loir-et-Cher, C France 48.00N 0.49E
32 J6 Mondovi Wisconsin, N USA 44.34N 91.40W
108 B9 Mondovì Piemonte, NW Italy 44.22N 7.55E
107 P3 Mondragón var. Arrasate. País Vasco, N Spain 43.04N 2.30W
109 J17 Mondragone Campania, S Italy 41.07N 13.52E
111 R5 Mondsee ◎ N Austria
126 J16 Mondy Respublika Buryatiya, S Russian Federation 51.41N 101.03E
117 G22 Monemvasía Pelopónnisos, S Greece 36.22N 23.03E
20 B15 Monessen Pennsylvania, NE USA 40.07N 79.51W
106 J12 Monesterio var. Monasterio. Extremadura, W Spain 38.04N 6.16W
12 L8 Monet Québec, SE Canada 48.09N 75.37W
29 S8 Monett Missouri, C USA 36.55N 93.55W
29 X9 Monette Arkansas, C USA 35.53N 90.20W
12 G11 Monetville Ontario, S Canada 46.08N 80.24W
108 J7 Monfalcone Friuli-Venezia Giulia, NE Italy 45.49N 13.31E
106 H10 Monforte Portalegre, C Portugal 39.03N 7.25W
106 I4 Monforte de Lemos Galicia, NW Spain 42.31N 7.30W
83 I24 Monga Lindi, SE Tanzania 9.05S 37.51E
81 L16 Monga Orientale, N Dem. Rep. Congo 4.12N 22.49E
83 F15 Mongalla Bahr el Gabel, S Sudan 5.12N 31.42E
159 U11 Mongar E Bhutan 27.16N 91.07E
178 K6 Mong Cai Quang Ninh, N Vietnam 21.33N 107.56E
188 I11 Mongers Lake salt lake Western Australia
195 U14 Mongga Kolombangara, NW Solomon Islands 7.51S 157.00E
178 Hh6 Möng Hpayak Shan State, E Myanmar 20.56N 100.00E
Monghyr see Munger
108 B10 Mongioie ▲ NW Italy 44.13N 7.46E
178 Gg5 Möng Küng Shan State, E Myanmar 21.39N 97.31E
Mongla see Mungla
196 C15 Mongmong C Guam
178 Gg6 Möng Nai Shan State, E Myanmar 20.28N 97.51E
80 I11 Mongo Guéra, C Chad 12.11N 18.39E
78 I14 Mongo ≈ N Sierra Leone
169 I8 Mongolia Mong. Mongol Uls. ◆ republic E Asia
133 V8 Mongolia, Plateau of plateau E Mongolia
Mongolküre see Zhaosu
Mongol Uls see Mongolia
81 E17 Mongomo E Equatorial Guinea 1.39N 11.18E
79 Y12 Mongonu var. Monguno. Borno, NE Nigeria 12.42N 13.37E
Mongora see Mingãora
80 K11 Mongororo Ouaddaï, SE Chad 12.03N 22.26E
Mongos, Chaîne des see Bongo, Massif des
81 I16 Mongoumba Lobaye, SW Central African Republic 3.39N 18.30E
Mongrove, Punta see Cayacal, Punta
85 G15 Mongu Western, W Zambia 15.13S 23.09E
78 I10 Mônguel Gorgol, SW Mauritania 16.25N 13.07W
Monguno see Mongonu
178 H4 Möng Yai Shan State, E Myanmar 22.25N 98.02E
178 Hh5 Möng Yang Shan State, E Myanmar 21.52N 99.31E
178 H3 Möng Yu Shan State, E Myanmar 24.00N 97.57E
168 K8 Mönhbulag Övörhangay, C Mongolia 46.48N 103.25E
Mönh Sarĭdag see Munku-Sardyk, Gora
194 L15 Moni ≈ S Papau New Guinea
117 I15 Moní Megístis Lávras monastery Kentrikí Makedonía, N Greece 40.10N 24.22E
117 F18 Moní Osíou Loúkas monastery Stereá Ellás, C Greece 38.22N 22.42E
56 F9 Moniquirá Boyacá, C Colombia 5.57N 73.35W
105 Q12 Monistrol-sur-Loire Haute-Loire, C France 45.19N 4.12E
37 V7 Monitor Range ▲▲ Nevada, W USA
117 I14 Moní Vatopedíou monastery Kentrikí Makedonía, N Greece 40.19N 24.13E
179 Rr15 Monkayo Mindanao, S Philippines 7.45N 125.58E
Monkchester see Newcastle upon Tyne
85 N14 Monkey Bay Southern, SE Malawi 14.09S 34.53E
45 N11 Monkey Point var. Punta Mico, Punte Mono, Punto Mico. headland SE Nicaragua 11.37N 83.39W
Monkey River see Monkey River Town
44 G3 Monkey River Town var. Monkey River. Toledo, SE Belize 16.22N 88.28W
12 M13 Monkland Ontario, SE Canada 45.11N 74.51W
81 J19 Monkoto Equateur, NW Dem. Rep. Congo 1.35S 20.43E
99 K21 Monmouth Wel. Trefynwy. SE Wales, UK 51.49N 2.43W
32 J12 Monmouth Illinois, N USA 40.54N 90.39W
34 F12 Monmouth Oregon, NW USA 44.51N 123.13W
99 K21 Monmouth cultural region SE Wales, UK
100 I10 Monnickendam Noord-Holland, C Netherlands 52.28N 5.01E
79 R15 Mono ≈ C Togo
Monoecus see Monaco
37 R8 Mono Lake ◎ California, W USA
117 O23 Monólithos Ródos, Dodekánisos, Greece, Aegean Sea 36.08N 27.45E
21 Q12 Monomoy Island island Massachusetts, NE USA
33 O12 Monon Indiana, N USA 40.52N 86.54W
31 Y12 Monona Iowa, C USA 43.03N 91.23W
32 L9 Monona Wisconsin, N USA 43.03N 89.18W
20 B15 Monongahela Pennsylvania, NE USA 40.10N 79.54W
20 B16 Monongahela River ≈ NE USA
109 P17 Monopoli Puglia, SE Italy 40.57N 17.18E
Mono, Punte see Monkey Point
113 K23 Monor Pest, C Hungary 47.19N 19.28E
Monostor see Beli Manastir
80 K8 Monou Borkou-Ennedi-Tibesti, NE Chad 16.22N 22.15E
107 S12 Monovar Cat. Monover. País Valenciano, E Spain 38.25N 0.49W
Monover see Monovar
107 R7 Monreal del Campo Aragón, NE Spain 40.46N 1.19W
109 I23 Monreale Sicilia, Italy, C Mediterranean Sea 38.04N 13.16E
25 T3 Monroe Georgia, SE USA 33.47N 83.42W
31 W14 Monroe Iowa, C USA 41.31N 93.06W
24 I5 Monroe Louisiana, S USA 32.31N 92.06W
33 S10 Monroe Michigan, N USA 41.55N 83.24W
20 K13 Monroe New York, NE USA 41.18N 74.09W
23 S11 Monroe North Carolina, SE USA 34.59N 80.33W
38 L6 Monroe Utah, W USA 38.37N 112.07W
34 H7 Monroe Washington, NW USA 47.51N 121.58W
32 L9 Monroe Wisconsin, N USA 42.34N 89.39W
29 V3 Monroe City Missouri, C USA 39.39N 91.43W
33 O15 Monroe Lake ⊡ Indiana, N USA
25 O7 Monroeville Alabama, S USA 31.31N 87.19W
20 C15 Monroeville Pennsylvania, NE USA 40.24N 79.44W
78 J16 Monrovia ● (Liberia) W Liberia 6.18N 10.48W
78 J16 Monrovia ✕ W Liberia 6.22N 10.50W
107 T7 Monroyo Aragón, NE Spain 40.46N 0.03W
101 F20 Mons Dut. Bergen. Hainaut, S Belgium 50.28N 3.58E
106 I8 Monsanto Castelo Branco, C Portugal 40.01N 7.07W
108 H8 Monselice Veneto, NE Italy 45.15N 11.47E
178 Gg9 Mon State ◐ state S Myanmar
100 G12 Monster Zuid-Holland, W Netherlands 52.01N 4.10E
97 N20 Mönsterås Kalmar, S Sweden 57.03N 16.27E
103 F17 Montabaur Rheinland-Pfalz, W Germany 50.25N 7.48E
108 G8 Montagnana Veneto, NE Italy 45.14N 11.31E
37 N1 Montague California, W USA 41.43N 122.31W
27 S5 Montague Texas, SW USA 33.39N 97.41W
191 S11 Montague Island island New South Wales, SE Australia
41 S12 Montague Island island Alaska, USA
41 S13 Montague Strait strait N Gulf of Alaska
104 J8 Montaigu Vendée, NW France 46.58N 1.18W
Montaigu see Scherpenheuvel
107 S7 Montalbán Aragón, NE Spain 40.49N 0.48W
108 G13 Montalcino Toscana, C Italy 43.01N 11.34E
106 H5 Montalegre Vila Real, N Portugal 41.49N 7.48W
116 G8 Montana prev. Ferdinand, Mikhaylovgrad. Montana, NW Bulgaria 43.25N 23.14E
110 D10 Montana Valais, SW Switzerland 46.23N 7.29E
41 R11 Montana Alaska, USA 62.06N 150.03W
116 G8 Montana ◐ province NW Bulgaria
35 T9 Montana off. State of Montana; also known as Mountain State, Treasure State. ◐ state NW USA
106 J10 Montánchez Extremadura, W Spain 39.15N 6.07W
Montañita see La Montañita
13 Q8 Mont-Apica Québec, SE Canada 47.57N 71.24W
106 G10 Montargil Portalegre, C Portugal 39.04N 8.10W
106 G10 Montargil, Barragem de ⊡ C Portugal
105 O7 Montargis Loiret, C France 48.00N 2.43E
105 O4 Montataire Oise, N France 49.16N 2.24E
104 M14 Montauban Tarn-et-Garonne, S France 44.01N 1.19E
21 N14 Montauk Long Island, New York, NE USA 41.01N 71.58W
21 N14 Montauk Point headland Long Island, New York, NE USA 41.04N 71.51W
105 Q7 Montbard Côte d'Or, C France 47.35N 4.25E
105 U7 Montbéliard Doubs, E France 47.31N 6.49E
27 W11 Mont Belvieu Texas, SW USA 29.51N 94.53W
107 U6 Montblanc var. Montblanch. Cataluña, NE Spain 41.22N 1.10E
Montblanch see Montblanc
105 Q11 Montbrison Loire, E France 45.37N 4.04E
Montcalm, Lake see Dogai Coring
105 Q9 Montceau-les-Mines Saône-et-Loire, C France 46.40N 4.19E
105 U12 Mont Cenis, Col du pass E France 45.16N 6.54E
104 K15 Mont-de-Marsan Landes, SW France 43.54N 0.30W
105 O3 Montdidier Somme, N France 49.39N 2.34E
197 J7 Mont-Dore Province Sud, S New Caledonia 22.18S 166.34E
22 K10 Monteagle Tennessee, S USA 35.15N 85.47W
59 M20 Monteagudo Chuquisaca, S Bolivia 19.48S 63.57W
43 R16 Monte Albán ruins Oaxaca, S Mexico 17.01N 96.46W
107 R11 Montealegre del Castillo Castilla-La Mancha, C Spain 38.48N 1.18W
61 N18 Monte Azul Minas Gerais, SE Brazil 15.13S 42.52W
12 M12 Montebello Québec, SE Canada 45.40N 74.55W
108 H7 Montebelluna Veneto, NE Italy 45.46N 12.03E
62 G13 Montecarlo Misiones, NE Argentina 26.37S 54.45W
63 D16 Monte Caseros Corrientes, NE Argentina 30.15S 57.39W
62 J13 Monte Castelo Santa Catarina, S Brazil 26.34S 50.12W
108 F11 Montecatini Terme Toscana, C Italy 43.52N 10.46E
44 H7 Montecillos, Cordillera de ▲▲ W Honduras
64 I12 Monte Comén Mendoza, W Argentina 34.34S 67.52W
46 M8 Monte Cristi var. San Fernando de Monte Cristi. NW Dominican Republic 19.52N 71.39W
60 C13 Monte Cristo Amazonas, W Brazil 3.13S 68.00W
109 E14 Montecristo, Isola di island Archipelago Toscano, C Italy
Monte Croce Carnico, Passo di see Plöcken Pass
60 J12 Monte Dourado Pará, NE Brazil 0.48S 52.32W
42 L11 Monte Escobedo Zacatecas, C Mexico 22.19N 103.30W
108 I13 Montefalco Umbria, C Italy 42.54N 12.40E
109 H14 Montefiascone Lazio, C Italy 42.33N 12.01E
107 N14 Montefrío Andalucía, S Spain 37.19N 4.00W
46 I11 Montego Bay var. Mobay. W Jamaica 18.28N 77.55W
Montego Bay see Sangster
106 J8 Montehermoso Extremadura, W Spain 40.04N 6.19W
106 F10 Montejunto, Serra de ▲ C Portugal 39.10N 9.01W
Monteleone di Calabria see Vibo Valentia
56 E7 Montelíbano Córdoba, NW Colombia 7.58N 75.24W
105 R13 Montélimar anc. Acunum Acusio, Montilium Adhemari. Drôme, E France 44.33N 4.45E
107 L15 Montellano Andalucía, S Spain 37.00N 5.34W
37 Y2 Montello Nevada, W USA 41.18N 114.10W
32 L8 Montello Wisconsin, N USA 43.46N 89.19W
65 J18 Montemayor, Meseta de plain SE Argentina
43 O9 Montemorelos Nuevo León, NE Mexico 25.10N 99.51W
106 G11 Montemor-o-Novo Évora, S Portugal 38.37N 8.13W
106 G8 Montemor-o-Velho var. Montemor-o-Vélho. Coimbra, N Portugal 40.10N 8.40W
106 H7 Montemuro, Serra de ▲ N Portugal 40.59N 7.59W
104 K12 Montendre Charente-Maritime, W France 45.17N 0.24W
63 I15 Montenegro Rio Grande do Sul, S Brazil 29.40S 51.32W
115 J16 Montenegro Serb. Crna Gora. ◐ republic SW Serbia and Montenegro (Yugoslavia)
64 G10 Monte Patria Coquimbo, N Chile 30.40S 71.00W
47 O9 Monte Plata E Dominican Republic 18.46N 69.43W
85 P14 Montepuez Cabo Delgado, N Mozambique 13.11S 38.59E
85 P14 Montepuez ≈ N Mozambique
108 G13 Montepulciano Toscana, C Italy 43.02N 11.51E
64 L6 Monte Quemado Santiago del Estero, N Argentina 25.46S 62.51W
105 O6 Montereau-Faut-Yonne anc. Condate. Seine-St-Denis, N France 48.22N 2.57E
37 N11 Monterey California, W USA 36.36N 121.53W
22 L9 Monterey Tennessee, S USA 36.09N 85.16W
23 T5 Monterey Virginia, NE USA 38.24N 79.33W
Monterey see Monterrey
37 N10 Monterey Bay bay California, W USA
56 D6 Montería Córdoba, NW Colombia 8.45N 75.54W
59 N18 Montero Santa Cruz, C Bolivia 17.19S 63.15W
64 J7 Monteros Tucumán, C Argentina 27.12S 65.30W
106 I5 Monterrei Galicia, NW Spain 41.55N 7.27W
43 O8 Monterrey var. Monterey. Nuevo León, NE Mexico 25.40N 100.16W
34 F9 Montesano Washington, NW USA 46.58N 123.37W
109 M19 Montesano sulla Marcellana Campania, S Italy 40.15N 15.41E
109 N16 Monte Sant' Angelo Puglia, SE Italy 41.43N 15.58E
61 O16 Monte Santo Bahia, E Brazil 10.25S 39.18W
109 D18 Monte Santu, Capo di headland Sardegna, Italy, C Mediterranean Sea 40.05N 9.43E
61 M19 Montes Claros Minas Gerais, SE Brazil 16.45S 43.52W
109 K14 Montesilvano Marina Abruzzo, C Italy 42.28N 14.07E
25 P4 Montevallo Alabama, S USA 33.06N 86.51W
108 G12 Montevarchi Toscana, C Italy 43.31N 11.34E
31 S9 Montevideo Minnesota, N USA 44.56N 95.43W
63 F20 Montevideo ● (Uruguay) Montevideo, S Uruguay 34.55S 56.10W
39 S7 Monte Vista Colorado, C USA 37.33N 106.08W
25 T5 Montezuma Georgia, SE USA 32.18N 84.01W
31 W14 Montezuma Iowa, C USA 41.35N 92.31W
28 J6 Montezuma Kansas, C USA 37.33N 100.25W
105 U12 Montgenèvre, Col de pass France/Italy 44.56N 6.45E
99 K20 Montgomery E Wales, UK 52.37N 3.05W
25 Q5 Montgomery state capital Alabama, S USA 32.22N 86.18W
31 V9 Montgomery Minnesota, N USA 44.26N 93.34W
20 G13 Montgomery Pennsylvania, NE USA 41.08N 76.52W
23 Q5 Montgomery West Virginia, NE USA 38.07N 81.19W
99 K19 Montgomery cultural region E Wales, UK
Montgomery see Sāhīwāl
29 V4 Montgomery City Missouri, C USA 38.58N 91.30W
37 S8 Montgomery Pass pass Nevada, W USA 37.57N 118.21W
104 K12 Montguyon Charente-Maritime, W France 45.12N 0.13W
110 C10 Monthey Valais, SW Switzerland 46.15N 6.55E
29 V13 Monticello Arkansas, C USA 33.37N 91.44W
25 T4 Monticello Florida, SE USA 30.33N 83.52W
25 T8 Monticello Georgia, SE USA 33.18N 83.40W
32 M13 Monticello Illinois, N USA 40.01N 88.34W
33 O12 Monticello Indiana, N USA 40.45N 86.46W
31 Y13 Monticello Iowa, C USA 42.14N 91.11W
22 L7 Monticello Kentucky, S USA 36.51N 84.51W
31 V8 Monticello Minnesota, N USA 45.19N 93.45W
24 K7 Monticello Mississippi, S USA 31.33N 90.06W
29 V2 Monticello Missouri, C USA 40.07N 91.42W
20 J12 Monticello New York, NE USA 41.39N 74.41W
39 O7 Monticello Utah, W USA 37.52N 109.20W
108 F8 Montichiari Lombardia, N Italy 45.24N 10.27E
104 M12 Montignac Dordogne, SW France 45.24N 0.54E
101 G21 Montignies-le-Tilleul var. Montigny-le-Tilleul. Hainaut, S Belgium 50.22N 4.22E
12 J8 Montigny, Lac de ◎ Québec, SE Canada
105 S6 Montigny-le-Roi Haute-Marne, N France 48.02N 5.28E
Montigny-le-Tilleul see Montignies-le-Tilleul
45 R16 Montijo Veraguas, S Panama 7.58N 81.12W
106 F11 Montijo Setúbal, W Portugal 38.42N 8.58W
106 J11 Montijo Extremadura, W Spain 38.55N 6.37W
Montilium Adhemari see Montélimar
106 M13 Montilla Andalucía, S Spain 37.36N 4.39W
104 L3 Montivilliers Seine-Maritime, N France 49.31N 0.10E
13 U7 Mont-Joli Québec, SE Canada 48.33N 68.12W
12 M10 Mont-Laurier Québec, SE Canada 46.33N 75.31W
13 X5 Mont-Louis Québec, SE Canada 49.13N 65.44W
105 N17 Mont-Louis var. Mont Louis. Pyrénées-Orientales, S France 42.30N 2.07E
105 O10 Montluçon Allier, C France 46.21N 2.37E
13 R10 Montmagny Québec, SE Canada 47.00N 70.31W
105 S3 Montmédy Meuse, NE France 49.31N 5.21E
105 P5 Montmirail Marne, N France 48.53N 3.31E
13 R9 Montmorency ≈ Québec, SE Canada
104 M10 Montmorillon Vienne, W France 46.25N 0.52E
109 J14 Montorio al Vomano Abruzzo, C Italy 42.31N 13.39E
106 M13 Montoro Andalucía, S Spain 38.00N 4.21W
35 S16 Montpelier Idaho, NW USA 42.19N 111.18W
31 P6 Montpelier North Dakota, N USA 46.40N 98.34W
20 M7 Montpelier state capital Vermont, NE USA 44.15N 72.32W
105 Q15 Montpellier Hérault, S France 43.37N 3.52E
104 L12 Montpon-Ménestérol Dordogne, SW France 45.01N 0.10E
10 K15 Montréal Eng. Montreal. Québec, SE Canada 45.30N 73.36W
12 C8 Montreal ≈ Ontario, S Canada
12 G8 Montreal ≈ Ontario, S Canada
Montreal see Mirabel
9 T14 Montreal Lake ◎ Saskatchewan, C Canada
12 B9 Montreal River Ontario, S Canada 47.13N 84.36W
105 N2 Montreuil Pas-de-Calais, N France 50.28N 1.46E
104 K8 Montreuil-Bellay Maine-et-Loire, NW France 47.07N 0.10W
110 C10 Montreux Vaud, SW Switzerland 46.27N 6.55E
110 B9 Montricher Vaud, W Switzerland 46.37N 6.24E
98 K10 Montrose E Scotland, UK 56.43N 2.28W
29 W14 Montrose Arkansas, C USA 33.18N 91.29W
39 Q6 Montrose Colorado, C USA 38.28N 107.52W
31 Y16 Montrose Iowa, C USA 40.31N 91.24W
20 H12 Montrose Pennsylvania, NE USA 41.49N 75.52W
23 X5 Montross Virginia, NE USA 38.04N 76.50W
13 O12 Mont-St-Hilaire Québec, SE Canada 45.34N 73.10W
105 S3 Mont-St-Martin Meurthe-et-Moselle, NE France 49.31N 5.51E
47 V10 Montserrat var. Emerald Isle. ◇ UK dependent territory E West Indies
107 V5 Montserrat ▲ NE Spain 41.39N 1.44E
106 M7 Montuenga Castilla-León, N Spain 41.04N 4.37W
101 M19 Montzen Liège, E Belgium 50.42N 5.59E
39 N8 Monument Valley valley Arizona/Utah, SW USA
177 G4 Monywa Sagaing, C Myanmar 22.04N 95.12E
108 D7 Monza Lombardia, N Italy 45.34N 9.16E
85 J15 Monze Southern, S Zambia 16.19S 27.29E
107 T5 Monzón Aragón, NE Spain 41.54N 0.12E
27 T9 Moody Texas, SW USA 31.18N 97.21W
100 L13 Mook Limburg, SE Netherlands 51.45N 5.52E
171 Kk15 Mooka var. Mōka. Tochigi, Honshū, S Japan 36.28N 140.01E
190 K3 Moomba South Australia 28.07S 140.12E
12 G13 Moon ≈ Ontario, S Canada
Moon see Muhu
189 Y10 Moonie Queensland, E Australia 27.45S 150.22E
198 B10 Moonless Mountains undersea feature E Pacific Ocean
190 L13 Moonlight Head headland Victoria, SE Australia 38.47S 143.12E
Moon-Sund see Väinameri
190 H8 Moonta South Australia 34.03S 137.36E
Moor see Mór
188 I12 Moora Western Australia 30.22S 116.04E
100 H12 Moordrecht Zuid-Holland, C Netherlands 51.58N 4.40E
35 T9 Moore Montana, NW USA 47.00N 109.40W
29 N11 Moore Oklahoma, C USA 35.20N 97.29W
27 R12 Moore Texas, SW USA 29.03N 99.01W
203 S10 Moorea island Îles du Vent, W French Polynesia
23 U3 Moorefield West Virginia, NE USA 39.03N 78.58W
25 X14 Moore Haven Florida, SE USA 26.49N 81.05W
188 J11 Moore, Lake ◎ Western Australia
21 N7 Moore Reservoir ⊡ New Hampshire/Vermont, NE USA
46 G1 Moores Island island N Bahamas
23 R10 Mooresville North Carolina, SE USA 35.34N 80.48W
31 R5 Moorhead Minnesota, N USA 46.51N 96.43W
24 K4 Moorhead Mississippi, S USA 33.27N 90.30W
176 Ww10 Moor, Kepulauan island group E Indonesia
101 F18 Moorsel Oost-Vlaanderen, C Belgium 50.58N 4.06E
101 C18 Moorslede West-Vlaanderen, W Belgium 50.53N 3.03E
20 L8 Moosalamoo, Mount ▲ Vermont, NE USA 43.55N 73.03W
103 M22 Moosburg an der Isar Bayern, SE Germany 48.28N 11.55E
35 S14 Moose Wyoming, C USA 43.38N 110.42W
10 H11 Moose ≈ Ontario, S Canada
10 H10 Moose Factory Ontario, S Canada 51.16N 80.31W
21 Q4 Moosehead Lake ◎ Maine, NE USA
9 U16 Moose Jaw Saskatchewan, S Canada 50.25N 105.29W
9 V14 Moose Lake Manitoba, C Canada 53.42N 100.22W
31 W6 Moose Lake Minnesota, N USA 46.28N 92.46W
21 P6 Mooselookmeguntic Lake ◎ Maine, NE USA
41 R12 Moose Pass Alaska, USA 60.28N 149.21W
21 P5 Moose River ≈ Maine, NE USA
20 J9 Moose River ≈ New York, NE USA
9 V16 Moosomin Saskatchewan, S Canada 50.09N 101.40W
10 H10 Moosonee Ontario, SE Canada 51.18N 80.40W
21 N12 Moosup Connecticut, NE USA 41.42N 71.51W
85 N16 Mopeia Zambézia, NE Mozambique 17.58S 35.43E
85 H18 Mopipi Central, C Botswana 21.10S 24.54E
Moppo see Mokp'o
79 N11 Mopti Mopti, C Mali 14.30N 4.15W
79 O11 Mopti ◐ region S Mali
59 H18 Moquegua Moquegua, SE Peru 17.12S 70.55W
59 H18 Moquegua off. Departamento de Moquegua. ◐ department S Peru
113 I23 Mór Ger. Moor. Fejér, C Hungary 47.21N 18.13E
80 G11 Mora Extrême-Nord, N Cameroon 11.01N 14.07E
106 G11 Mora Évora, S Portugal 38.55N 8.10W
107 N9 Mora Castilla-La Mancha, C Spain 39.40N 3.46W
96 L12 Mora Dalarna, C Sweden 61.00N 14.30E
31 V7 Mora Minnesota, N USA 45.52N 93.18W
39 T10 Mora New Mexico, SW USA 35.56N 105.16W
115 J17 Morača ≈ SW Serbia and Montenegro (Yugoslavia)
158 K10 Morādābād Uttar Pradesh, N India 28.49N 78.45E
107 U6 Móra d'Ebre var. Mora de Ebro. Cataluña, NE Spain 41.04N 0.37E
Mora de Ebro see Móra d'Ebre
107 S8 Mora de Rubielos Aragón, NE Spain 40.15N 0.45W
180 H4 Morafenobe Mahajanga, W Madagascar 17.49S 44.54E
112 K8 Morąg Ger. Mohrungen. Warmińsko-Mazurskie, NE Poland 53.55N 19.55E
113 L25 Mórahalom Csongrád, S Hungary 46.13N 19.51E
107 N11 Moral de Calatrava Castilla-La Mancha, C Spain 38.49N 3.34W
65 G19 Moraleda, Canal strait SE Pacific Ocean
56 J3 Morales Bolívar, N Colombia 8.16N 73.52W
56 D12 Morales Cauca, SW Colombia 2.43N 76.36W
44 F5 Morales Izabal, E Guatemala 15.29N 88.46W
180 J5 Moramanga Toamasina, E Madagascar 18.57S 48.13E
29 Q6 Moran Kansas, C USA 37.55N 95.10W
27 Q7 Moran Texas, SW USA 32.33N 99.10W
189 X7 Moranbah Queensland, NE Australia 22.01S 148.07E
46 L13 Morant Bay E Jamaica 17.52N 76.24W
98 G10 Morar, Loch ◎ N Scotland, UK
Morata see Goodenough Island
107 Q12 Moratalla Murcia, SE Spain 38.10N 1.52W
110 C8 Morat, Lac de Ger. Murtensee. ◎ W Switzerland
86 I11 Morava var. March. ≈ C Europe see also March
Morava see Moravia, Czech Republic
Morava see Velika Morava, Serbia and Montenegro (Yugoslavia)
31 W15 Moravia Iowa, C USA 40.53N 92.49W
113 F18 Moravia Cz. Morava, Ger. Mähren. cultural region E Czech Republic
113 H17 Moravice Ger. Mohra. ≈ NE Czech Republic
118 E12 Moravița Timiș, SW Romania 45.15N 21.17E
113 G17 Moravská Třebová Ger. Mährisch-Trübau. Pardubický Kraj, C Czech Republic 49.45N 16.40E
113 E19 Moravské Budějovice Ger. Mährisch-Budwitz. Vysočina, C Czech Republic 49.03N 15.48E
113 H17 Moravskoslezský Kraj prev. Ostravský Kraj. ◐ region E Czech Republic
113 F19 Moravský Krumlov Ger. Mährisch-Kromau. Jihomoravský Kraj, SE Czech Republic 48.58N 16.30E
98 J8 Moray cultural region N Scotland, UK
98 J8 Moray Firth inlet N Scotland, UK
44 B10 Morazán ◐ department NE El Salvador
160 C10 Morbi Gujarāt, W India 22.51N 70.49E
104 G7 Morbihan ◐ department NW France
Mörbisch see Mörbisch am See
111 Y5 Mörbisch am See var. Mörbisch. Burgenland, E Austria 47.43N 16.40E
97 N21 Mörbylånga Kalmar, S Sweden 56.31N 16.25E
104 J14 Morcenx Landes, SW France 44.04N 0.55W
Morcheh Khort see Mürcheh Khvort
169 T5 Mordaga Nei Mongol Zizhiqu, N China 51.15N 120.47E
15 L16 Morden Manitoba, S Canada 49.12N 98.04W
Mordovskaya ASSR/Mordvinia see Mordoviya, Respublika
131 N5 Mordoviya, Respublika prev. Mordovskaya ASSR, Eng. Mordovia, Mordvinia. ◐ autonomous republic W Russian Federation
130 M7 Mordovo Tambovskaya Oblast', W Russian Federation 52.05N 40.49E
Morea see Pelopónnisos
30 K8 Moreau River ≈ South Dakota, N USA
99 K16 Morecambe NW England, UK 54.04N 2.52W
99 K16 Morecambe Bay inlet NW England, UK
191 S4 Moree New South Wales, SE Australia 29.28S 149.52E
194 E15 Morehead Western, SW PNG 8.42S 141.37E
23 N5 Morehead Kentucky, S USA 38.13N 83.25W
194 E15 Morehead ≈ SW PNG
23 X11 Morehead City North Carolina, SE USA 34.43N 76.43W
29 Y8 Morehouse Missouri, C USA 36.51N 89.41W
110 E10 Mörel Valais, SW Switzerland 46.22N 8.03E
56 D13 Morelia Caquetá, S Colombia 1.27N 75.46W
43 N14 Morelia Michoacán de Ocampo, S Mexico 19.40N 101.10W
107 T7 Morella País Valenciano, E Spain 40.37N 0.06W
42 I7 Morelos Chihuahua, N Mexico 26.37N 107.37W
43 O15 Morelos ◐ state S Mexico
160 H7 Morena Madhya Pradesh, C India 26.35N 77.59E
106 L12 Morena, Sierra ▲▲ S Spain

◆ Country ● Country Capital ◇ Dependent Territory ○ Dependent Territory Capital ◐ Administrative Region ✕ International Airport ▲ Mountain ▲▲ Mountain Range ▲ Volcano ≈ River ◎ Lake ⊡ Reservoir

Morenci – Muddebihāl

39 O14 **Morenci** Arizona, SW USA 33.05N 109.21W
33 R11 **Morenci** Michigan, N USA 41.43N 84.13W
118 J13 **Moreni** Dâmbovița, S Romania 44.58N 25.39E
96 D9 **Møre og Romsdal** ◈ county S Norway
14 Ee12 **Moresby Island** island Queen Charlotte Islands, British Columbia, SW Canada
191 W2 **Moreton Island** island Queensland, E Australia
105 O3 **Moreuil** Somme, N France 49.47N 2.28E
37 V7 **Morey Peak** ▲ Nevada, W USA 38.40N 116.16W
129 U4 **More-Yu** ~ NW Russian Federation
105 T9 **Morez** Jura, E France 46.33N 6.01E
Mórfou see Güzelyurt
Morfou Bay/Mórfou, Kólpos see Güzelyurt Körfezi
190 J8 **Morgan** South Australia 34.02S 139.39E
25 S7 **Morgan** Georgia, SE USA 31.31N 84.34W
27 S8 **Morgan** Texas, SW USA 32.01N 97.36W
24 J10 **Morgan City** Louisiana, S USA 29.42N 91.12W
22 H6 **Morganfield** Kentucky, S USA 37.40N 87.55W
37 O10 **Morgan Hill** California, W USA 37.05N 121.38W
23 Q9 **Morganton** North Carolina, SE USA 35.45N 81.41W
22 J7 **Morgantown** Kentucky, S USA 37.13N 86.40W
23 S2 **Morgantown** West Virginia, NE USA 39.37N 79.57W
110 B10 **Morges** Vaud, SW Switzerland 46.30N 6.24E
154 M4 **Morghāb, Daryā-ye** Rus. Murgab, Murghab, Turkm. Murgap, Murgap Deryasy. ~ Afghanistan/Turkmenistan see also Murgap
98 I9 **Mor, Glen** var. Glen Albyn, Great Glen. valley N Scotland, UK
105 T5 **Morhange** Moselle, NE France 48.56N 6.37E
164 M5 **Mori** var. Mori Kazak Zizhixian. Xinjiang Uygur Zizhiqu, NW China 43.48N 90.21E
172 Nn6 **Mori** Hokkaidō, NE Japan 42.04N 140.35E
37 Y6 **Moriah, Mount** ▲ Nevada, W USA 39.16N 114.10W
39 S11 **Moriarty** New Mexico, SW USA 34.59N 106.03W
56 J12 **Morichal** Guaviare, E Colombia 2.18N 69.54W
194 H14 **Morigio Island** island S PNG
Mori Kazak Zizhixian see Mori
Morin Dawa Daurzu Zizhiqi see Nirji
15 I13 **Morinville** Alberta, SW Canada 53.48N 113.37W
171 Mm11 **Morioka** Iwate, Honshū, C Japan 39.42N 141.08E
191 T8 **Morisset** New South Wales, SE Australia 33.07S 151.32E
171 Mm10 **Moriyoshi-yama** ▲ Honshū, C Japan 39.58N 140.32E
94 K13 **Morjärv** Norrbotten, N Sweden 66.03N 22.45E
131 R3 **Morki** Respublika Mariy El, W Russian Federation 56.27N 49.01E
126 K10 **Morkoka** ~ NE Russian Federation
104 F5 **Morlaix** Finistère, NW France 48.34N 3.49W
97 M20 **Mörlunda** Kalmar, S Sweden 57.19N 15.52E
109 N19 **Mormanno** Calabria, SW Italy 39.54N 15.58E
38 L11 **Mormon Lake** ◎ Arizona, SW USA
37 Y10 **Mormon Peak** ▲ Nevada, W USA 36.59N 114.25W
Mormon State see Utah
47 Y5 **Morne-à-l'Eau** Grande Terre, N Guadeloupe 16.20N 61.28W
31 Y15 **Morning Sun** Iowa, C USA 41.06N 91.15W
200 O14 **Mornington Abyssal Plain** undersea feature SE Pacific Ocean
65 F22 **Mornington, Isla** island S Chile
189 T4 **Mornington Island** island Wellesley Islands, Queensland, N Australia
117 E18 **Mórnos** ~ C Greece
155 P14 **Moro** Sind, SE Pakistan 26.36N 67.58E
34 I11 **Moro** Oregon, NW USA 45.28N 120.44W
194 K14 **Morobe** Morobe, C PNG 7.46S 147.35E
194 J14 **Morobe** ◈ province C PNG
33 N12 **Morocco** Indiana, N USA 40.57N 87.27W
76 E8 **Morocco** off. Kingdom of Morocco, Ar. Al Mamlakah. ◆ monarchy N Africa
Morocco see Marrakech
83 I22 **Morogoro** Morogoro, E Tanzania 6.49S 37.40E
83 H24 **Morogoro** ◈ region SE Tanzania
179 Qq16 **Moro Gulf** gulf S Philippines
43 N13 **Moroleón** Guanajuato, C Mexico 20.00N 101.13W
180 H6 **Morombe** Toliara, W Madagascar 21.46S 43.21E
46 G5 **Morón** Ciego de Ávila, C Cuba 22.04N 78.39W
56 K5 **Morón** Carabobo, N Venezuela 10.28N 68.10W
Morón see Morón de la Frontera
169 N8 **Mörön** Hentiy, C Mongolia 47.21N 110.21E
168 I6 **Mörön** Hövsgöl, N Mongolia 49.38N 100.07E
58 D8 **Morona, Río** ~ N Peru
58 C8 **Morona Santiago** ◈ province E Ecuador
180 H5 **Morondava** Toliara, W Madagascar 20.19S 44.16E
106 K14 **Morón de la Frontera** var. Morón. Andalucía, S Spain 37.07N 5.27W
180 G13 **Moroni** ● (Comoros) Grande Comore, NW Comoros 11.40S 43.16E
175 Tt6 **Morotai, Pulau** island Maluku, E Indonesia
175 T6 **Morotai, Selat** strait Maluku, E Indonesia
Morotiri see Marotiri
83 H17 **Moroto** NE Uganda 2.31N 34.40E
Morozov see Bratan
130 M11 **Morozovsk** Rostovskaya Oblast', SW Russian Federation 48.21N 41.54E
99 L14 **Morpeth** N England, UK 55.10N 1.40W
Morphou see Güzelyurt
Morphou Bay see Güzelyurt Körfezi
30 I13 **Morrill** Nebraska, C USA 41.57N 103.55W
29 U11 **Morrilton** Arkansas, C USA 35.09N 92.44W
9 Q16 **Morrin** Alberta, SW Canada 51.40N 112.45W
192 M7 **Morrinsville** Waikato, North Island, NZ 37.40S 175.32E
9 X16 **Morris** Manitoba, S Canada 49.21N 97.21W
32 M11 **Morris** Illinois, N USA 41.21N 88.25W
31 S8 **Morris** Minnesota, N USA 45.31N 95.52W
12 M13 **Morrisburg** Ontario, SE Canada 44.55N 75.07W
207 R11 **Morris Jesup, Kap** headland N Greenland 83.33N 32.40W
190 B1 **Morris, Mount** ▲ South Australia 26.04S 131.03E
32 K10 **Morrison** Illinois, N USA 41.48N 89.58W
38 K13 **Morristown** Arizona, SW USA 33.48N 112.34W
20 J14 **Morristown** New Jersey, NE USA 40.48N 74.28W
23 O8 **Morristown** Tennessee, S USA 36.12N 83.18W
44 L11 **Morrito** Río San Juan, SW Nicaragua 11.37N 85.03W
37 P13 **Morro Bay** California, W USA 35.21N 120.51W
97 L22 **Mörrum** Blekinge, S Sweden 56.10N 14.45E
85 N16 **Morrumbala** Zambézia, NE Mozambique 17.16S 35.34E
85 N20 **Morrumbene** Inhambane, SE Mozambique 23.38S 35.22E
97 F21 **Mors** island NW Denmark
Mörs see Moers
27 N1 **Morse** Texas, SW USA 36.03N 101.28W
131 N6 **Morshansk** Tambovskaya Oblast', W Russian Federation 53.27N 41.46E
104 L5 **Mortagne-au-Perche** Orne, N France 48.32N 0.31E
104 J8 **Mortagne-sur-Sèvre** Vendée, NW France 47.00N 0.57W
106 G8 **Mortágua** Viseu, N Portugal 40.24N 8.13W
104 J5 **Mortain** Manche, N France 48.39N 0.51W
108 C8 **Mortara** Lombardia, N Italy 45.15N 8.43E
61 J17 **Mortes, Rio das** ~ C Brazil
190 M12 **Mortlake** Victoria, SE Australia 38.06S 142.48E
Mortlock Group see Takuu Islands
201 Q17 **Mortlock Islands** prev. Nomoi Islands. island group C Micronesia
31 T9 **Morton** Minnesota, N USA 44.33N 94.58W
24 L5 **Morton** Mississippi, S USA 32.21N 89.39W
26 M5 **Morton** Texas, SW USA 33.40N 102.45W
34 H9 **Morton** Washington, NW USA 46.33N 122.16W
(0) D7 **Morton Seamount** undersea feature NE Pacific Ocean 50.15N 142.45W
47 U15 **Moruga** Trinidad, Trinidad and Tobago 10.04N 61.16W
191 P9 **Morundah** New South Wales, SE Australia 34.57S 146.18E
Moruroa see Mururoa
191 S11 **Moruya** New South Wales, SE Australia 35.55S 150.04E
105 Q8 **Morvan** physical region C France
193 G21 **Morven** Canterbury, South Island, NZ 44.51S 171.07E
191 O13 **Morwell** Victoria, SE Australia 38.13S 146.25E
129 N6 **Morzhovets, Ostrov** island NW Russian Federation
130 J4 **Mosal'sk** Kaluzhskaya Oblast', W Russian Federation 54.30N 34.55E
103 H20 **Mosbach** Baden-Württemberg, SW Germany 49.21N 9.06E
97 E18 **Mosby** Vest-Agder, S Norway 58.12N 7.55E
35 V9 **Mosby** Montana, NW USA 46.58N 107.53W
34 M9 **Moscow** Idaho, NW USA 46.43N 117.00W
22 F10 **Moscow** Tennessee, S USA 35.04N 89.27W
Moscow see Moskva
103 D19 **Mosel** Fr. Moselle. ~ W Europe see also Moselle
105 T4 **Moselle** ◈ department NE France
105 T6 **Moselle** Ger. Mosel. ~ W Europe see also Mosel
34 K9 **Moses Lake** ◎ Washington, NW USA
85 I18 **Mosetse** Central, E Botswana 20.40S 26.39E
94 H4 **Mosfellsbær** Sudhurland, SW Iceland 65.09N 21.43W
193 F23 **Mosgiel** Otago, South Island, NZ 45.51S 170.21E
128 M11 **Mosha** ~ NW Russian Federation
83 I20 **Moshi** Kilimanjaro, NE Tanzania 3.21S 37.19E
112 G12 **Mosina** Wielkolpolskie, C Poland 52.13N 16.48E
32 L6 **Mosinee** Wisconsin, N USA 44.45N 89.39W
94 F13 **Mosjøen** Nordland, C Norway 65.49N 13.12E
127 Nn13 **Moskal'vo** Ostrov Sakhalin, Sakhalinskaya Oblast', SE Russian Federation 53.36N 142.31E
94 I13 **Moskosel** Norrbotten, N Sweden 65.52N 19.30E
130 K4 **Moskovskaya Oblast'** ◈ province W Russian Federation
Moskovskiy see Moskva
130 J3 **Moskva** Eng. Moscow. ● (Russian Federation) Gorod Moskva, W Russian Federation 55.45N 37.42E
153 Q14 **Moskva** Rus. Moskovskiy; prev. Chubek. SW Tajikistan 37.41N 69.33E
130 L4 **Moskva** ~ W Russian Federation
85 I20 **Mosomane** Kgatleng, SE Botswana 24.03S 26.16E
Moson and Magyaróvár see Mosonmagyaróvár
113 H21 **Mosoni-Duna** Ger. Kleine Donau. ~ NW Hungary
113 H21 **Mosonmagyaróvár** Ger. Wieselburg-Ungarisch-Altenburg; prev. Moson and Magyaróvár, Ger. Wieselburg and Ungarisch-Altenburg. Győr-Moson-Sopron, NW Hungary 47.51N 17.15E
Mospino see Mospyne
119 X8 **Mospyne** Rus. Mospino. Donets'ka Oblast', E Ukraine 47.53N 38.03E
56 B12 **Mosquera** Nariño, SW Colombia 2.31N 78.24W
39 U10 **Mosquero** New Mexico, SW USA 35.46N 103.57W
Mosquito Coast see La Mosquitia
33 U11 **Mosquito Creek Lake** ⊡ Ohio, N USA
Mosquito Gulf see Mosquitos, Golfo de los
25 X11 **Mosquito Lagoon** wetland Florida, SE USA
45 N10 **Mosquito, Punta** headland E Nicaragua 12.18N 83.38W
45 W14 **Mosquito, Punta** headland NE Panama 9.06N 77.52W
45 Q15 **Mosquitos, Golfo de los** Eng. Mosquito Gulf. gulf N Panama
97 H16 **Moss** Østfold, S Norway 59.25N 10.40E
Mossâmedes see Namibe
24 G8 **Moss Bluff** Louisiana, S USA 30.18N 93.11W
193 C23 **Mossburn** Southland, South Island, NZ 45.40S 168.15E
85 G26 **Mosselbaai** var. Mosselbai, Eng. Mossel Bay. Western Cape, SW South Africa 34.10S 22.07E
Mosselbai/Mossel Bay see Mosselbaai
81 F20 **Mossendjo** Le Niari, SW Congo 2.57S 12.39E
191 N8 **Mossgiel** New South Wales, SE Australia 33.16S 144.34E
103 H22 **Mössingen** Baden-Württemberg, S Germany 48.22N 9.01E
189 W4 **Mossman** Queensland, NE Australia 16.34S 145.27E
61 P14 **Mossoró** Rio Grande do Norte, NE Brazil 5.10S 37.19W
25 N9 **Moss Point** Mississippi, S USA 30.24N 88.31W
191 S9 **Moss Vale** New South Wales, SE Australia 34.33S 150.22E
34 G9 **Mossyrock** Washington, NW USA 46.32N 122.30W
113 B15 **Most** Ger. Brüx. Ústecký Kraj, NW Czech Republic 50.30N 13.37E
123 Jj16 **Mosta** var. Musta. C Malta 35.54N 14.25E
76 I5 **Mostaganem** var. Mestghanem. NW Algeria 35.55N 0.08E
115 H14 **Mostar** Federacija Bosna I Hercegovina, S Bosnia and Herzegovina 43.20N 17.47E
63 J17 **Mostardas** Rio Grande do Sul, S Brazil 31.06S 50.52W
118 K14 **Moștiștea** ~ S Romania
Mostva see Mastva
Mosty see Masty
118 H5 **Mostys'ka** L'vivs'ka Oblast', W Ukraine 49.47N 23.09E
Mosul see Al Mawşil
97 F15 **Møsvatnet** ◎ S Norway
82 J12 **Mot'a** Amhara, N Ethiopia 11.03N 38.03E
197 C10 **Mota** island Banks Islands, N Vanuatu
81 H16 **Motaba** ~ N Congo
107 O10 **Mota del Cuervo** Castilla-La Mancha, C Spain 39.30N 2.52W
106 L5 **Mota del Marqués** Castilla-León, N Spain 41.37N 5.10W
44 F5 **Motagua, Río** ~ Guatemala/Honduras
121 H19 **Motal'** Brestskaya Voblasts', SW Belarus 52.13N 25.34E
97 L17 **Motala** Östergötland, S Sweden 58.33N 15.05E
197 C10 **Mota Lava** island Banks Islands, N Vanuatu
203 X7 **Motane** var. Mohotani. island Îles Marquises, NE French Polynesia
158 K13 **Moth** Uttar Pradesh, N India 25.43N 78.55E
Mother of Presidents/Mother of States see Virginia
98 I12 **Motherwell** C Scotland, UK 55.48N 4.00W
159 P12 **Motīhāri** Bihār, N India 26.40N 84.55E
107 Q10 **Motilla del Palancar** Castilla-La Mancha, C Spain 39.34N 1.55W
192 N7 **Motiti Island** island NE NZ
67 E25 **Motley Island** island SE Falkland Islands
85 I19 **Motloutse** ~ E Botswana
43 V17 **Motozintla de Mendoza** Chiapas, SE Mexico 15.22N 92.11W
107 N15 **Motril** Andalucía, S Spain 36.45N 3.29W
118 G13 **Motru** Gorj, SW Romania 44.49N 22.56E
171 Mm5 **Motsuta-misaki** headland Hokkaidō, NE Japan 42.36N 139.48E
30 L6 **Mott** North Dakota, N USA 46.21N 102.17W
Möttling see Metlika
109 O18 **Mottola** Puglia, SE Italy 40.37N 17.01E
192 P8 **Motu** ~ North Island, NZ
193 I14 **Motueka** Tasman, South Island, NZ 41.08S 173.01E
193 I14 **Motueka** ~ South Island, NZ
Motu Iti see Tupai
43 X12 **Motul** var. Motul de Felipe Carrillo Puerto. Yucatán, SE Mexico 21.06N 89.16W
Motul de Felipe Carrillo Puerto see Motul
203 U17 **Motu Nui** island Easter Island, Chile, E Pacific Ocean
203 Q10 **Motu One** var. Bellingshausen. atoll Îles Sous le Vent, W French Polynesia
202 I16 **Motutapu** island E Cook Islands
200 R15 **Motu Tapu** island Tongatapu Group, S Tonga
192 L5 **Motutapu Island** island N NZ
Motyca see Modica
126 I13 **Motygino** Krasnoyarskiy Kray, C Russian Federation 58.09N 94.35E
Mouanda see Moanda
Mouaskar see Mascara
107 U3 **Moubermé, Tuc de** Fr. Pic de Maubermé, Sp. Pico Mauberme; prev. Tuc de Maubermé. ▲ France/Spain 42.48N 0.57E see also Maubermé, Pic de
47 N7 **Mouchoir Passage** passage SE Turks and Caicos Islands
78 I9 **Moudjéria** Tagant, SW Mauritania 17.52N 12.19W
110 C9 **Moudon** Vaud, W Switzerland 46.41N 6.49E
Mouhoun see Black Volta
81 E19 **Mouila** Ngounié, C Gabon 1.49S 11.01E
81 K14 **Mouka** Haute-Kotto, C Central African Republic 7.12N 21.52E
Moukden see Shenyang
191 N10 **Moulamein** New South Wales, SE Australia 35.06S 144.03E
Moulamein Creek see Billabong Creek
76 F6 **Moulay-Bousselham** NW Morocco 34.54N 6.15W
Moule see le Moule
82 M11 **Moulhoulé** N Djibouti 12.34N 43.06E
105 P9 **Moulins** Allier, C France 46.34N 3.19E
178 Gg9 **Moulmein** var. Maulmain, Mawlamyine. Mon State, S Myanmar 16.30N 97.39E
177 F9 **Moulmeingyun** Irrawaddy, SW Myanmar 16.24N 95.15E
76 G6 **Moulouya** var. Mulucha, Muluya, Mulwiya. seasonal river NE Morocco
25 O2 **Moulton** Alabama, S USA 34.28N 87.16W
31 W16 **Moulton** Iowa, C USA 40.41N 92.40W
27 T11 **Moulton** Texas, SW USA 29.34N 97.08W
25 T7 **Moultrie** Georgia, SE USA 31.10N 83.47W
23 S14 **Moultrie, Lake** ⊡ South Carolina, SE USA
24 K3 **Mound Bayou** Mississippi, S USA 33.52N 90.43W
32 L17 **Mound City** Illinois, N USA 37.06N 89.09W
29 R6 **Mound City** Kansas, C USA 38.08N 94.48W
29 Q2 **Mound City** Missouri, C USA 40.07N 95.13W
31 N7 **Mound City** South Dakota, N USA 45.42N 100.04W
80 H13 **Moundou** Logone-Occidental, SW Chad 8.34N 16.01E
29 P10 **Mounds** Oklahoma, C USA 35.52N 96.03W
23 R2 **Moundsville** West Virginia, NE USA 39.55N 80.44W
178 Ii12 **Moŭng Roessei** Bătdâmbâng, W Cambodia 12.46N 103.28E
Moun Hou see Black Volta
14 G5 **Mountain** ~ Northwest Territories, NW Canada
39 S12 **Mountainair** New Mexico, SW USA 34.31N 106.14W
37 V1 **Mountain City** Nevada, W USA 41.48N 115.58W
23 Q8 **Mountain City** Tennessee, S USA 36.28N 81.48W
29 U7 **Mountain Grove** Missouri, C USA 37.07N 92.15W
29 U9 **Mountain Home** Arkansas, C USA 36.19N 92.24W
35 N15 **Mountain Home** Idaho, NW USA 43.07N 115.42W
27 Q11 **Mountain Home** Texas, SW USA 30.11N 99.19W
31 W4 **Mountain Iron** Minnesota, N USA 47.31N 92.37W
31 T10 **Mountain Lake** Minnesota, N USA 43.57N 94.54W
25 S3 **Mountain Park** Georgia, SE USA 34.04N 84.24W
37 W12 **Mountain Pass** pass California, W USA 35.28N 115.31W
29 T12 **Mountain Pine** Arkansas, C USA 34.34N 93.10W
41 Y14 **Mountain Point** Annette Island, Alaska, USA 55.17N 131.31W
Mountain State see Montana, USA
Mountain State see West Virginia, USA
29 V7 **Mountain View** Arkansas, C USA 35.52N 92.07W
40 H12 **Mountain View** Hawai'i, USA, C Pacific Ocean 19.31N 155.03W
29 V10 **Mountain View** Missouri, C USA 37.00N 91.42W
40 M11 **Mountain Village** Alaska, USA 62.06N 163.42W
23 R8 **Mount Airy** North Carolina, SE USA 36.30N 80.36W
85 K24 **Mount Ayliff** Xh. Maxesibebi. Eastern Cape, SE South Africa 30.48S 29.22E
31 U16 **Mount Ayr** Iowa, C USA 40.42N 94.14W
190 J9 **Mount Barker** South Australia 35.06S 138.52E
188 J14 **Mount Barker** Western Australia 34.42S 117.40E
191 P11 **Mount Beauty** Victoria, SE Australia 36.47S 147.12E
12 E16 **Mount Brydges** Ontario, S Canada 42.54N 81.29W
33 N16 **Mount Carmel** Illinois, N USA 38.23N 87.46W
32 K10 **Mount Carroll** Illinois, N USA 42.04N 89.58W
33 S9 **Mount Clemens** Michigan, N USA 42.36N 82.52W
193 E19 **Mount Cook** Canterbury, South Island, NZ 43.46S 170.06E
85 L16 **Mount Darwin** Mashonaland Central, NE Zimbabwe 16.45S 31.32E
21 S7 **Mount Desert Island** island Maine, NE USA
25 W11 **Mount Dora** Florida, SE USA 28.48N 81.38W
190 G5 **Mount Eba** South Australia 30.11S 135.40E
27 W8 **Mount Enterprise** Texas, SW USA 31.53N 94.40W
190 J4 **Mount Fitton** South Australia 29.55S 139.26E
85 J24 **Mount Fletcher** Eastern Cape, SE South Africa 30.40S 28.30E
12 F15 **Mount Forest** Ontario, S Canada 43.58N 80.43W
190 K12 **Mount Gambier** South Australia 37.47S 140.48E
189 W5 **Mount Garnet** Queensland, NE Australia 17.41S 145.07E
23 P6 **Mount Gay** West Virginia, NE USA 37.49N 82.00W
33 S12 **Mount Gilead** Ohio, N USA 40.33N 82.49W
194 H12 **Mount Hagen** Western Highlands, C PNG 5.53S 144.12E
20 J16 **Mount Holly** New Jersey, NE USA 39.59N 74.46W
23 R10 **Mount Holly** North Carolina, SE USA 35.18N 81.01W
29 T12 **Mount Ida** Arkansas, C USA 34.33N 93.37W
189 T6 **Mount Isa** Queensland, C Australia 20.48S 139.32E
23 U4 **Mount Jackson** Virginia, NE USA 38.45N 78.38W
20 D12 **Mount Jewett** Pennsylvania, NE USA 41.43N 78.37W
20 L13 **Mount Kisco** New York, NE USA 41.12N 73.42W
20 B15 **Mount Lebanon** Pennsylvania, NE USA 40.21N 80.03W
190 J8 **Mount Lofty Ranges** ▲▲ South Australia
188 J10 **Mount Magnet** Western Australia 28.09S 117.52E
192 N7 **Mount Maunganui** Bay of Plenty, North Island, NZ 37.39S 176.11E
99 E18 **Mountmellick** Ir. Móinteach Mílic. C Ireland 53.07N 7.19W
32 L10 **Mount Morris** Illinois, N USA 42.03N 89.25W
33 R9 **Mount Morris** Michigan, N USA 43.07N 83.42W
20 F10 **Mount Morris** New York, NE USA 42.43N 77.51W
20 B16 **Mount Morris** Pennsylvania, NE USA 39.43N 80.06W
32 K15 **Mount Olive** Illinois, N USA 39.04N 89.43W
23 V10 **Mount Olive** North Carolina, SE USA 35.12N 78.03W
23 N4 **Mount Olivet** Kentucky, S USA 38.32N 84.01W
31 Y15 **Mount Pleasant** Iowa, C USA 40.57N 91.33W
33 Q8 **Mount Pleasant** Michigan, N USA 43.36N 84.46W
20 C15 **Mount Pleasant** Pennsylvania, NE USA 40.07N 79.33W
23 T14 **Mount Pleasant** South Carolina, SE USA 32.47N 79.51W
22 I9 **Mount Pleasant** Tennessee, S USA 35.32N 87.11W
27 W6 **Mount Pleasant** Texas, SW USA 33.10N 94.49W
38 L4 **Mount Pleasant** Utah, W USA 39.33N 111.27W
65 N23 **Mount Pleasant** ✖ (Stanley) East Falkland, Falkland Islands
99 G25 **Mount's Bay** inlet SW England, UK
37 N2 **Mount Shasta** California, W USA 41.18N 122.19W
32 J13 **Mount Sterling** Illinois, N USA 39.59N 90.44W
23 N5 **Mount Sterling** Kentucky, S USA 38.03N 83.56W
20 E15 **Mount Union** Pennsylvania, NE USA 40.21N 77.51W
25 V6 **Mount Vernon** Georgia, SE USA 32.10N 82.35W
32 L16 **Mount Vernon** Illinois, N USA 38.19N 88.54W
22 M6 **Mount Vernon** Kentucky, S USA 37.22N 84.22W
29 S7 **Mount Vernon** Missouri, C USA 37.06N 93.49W
33 T13 **Mount Vernon** Ohio, N USA 40.23N 82.29W
34 K13 **Mount Vernon** Oregon, NW USA 44.22N 119.07W
27 W6 **Mount Vernon** Texas, SW USA 33.11N 95.13W
34 H7 **Mount Vernon** Washington, NW USA 48.25N 122.19W
22 L5 **Mount Washington** Kentucky, S USA 38.03N 85.33W
190 F8 **Mount Wedge** South Australia 33.29S 135.08E
32 L14 **Mount Zion** Illinois, N USA 39.46N 88.52W
189 Y9 **Moura** Queensland, NE Australia 24.34S 149.57E
60 F12 **Moura** Amazonas, NW Brazil 1.32S 61.43W
106 H12 **Moura** Beja, S Portugal 38.07N 7.27W
106 I12 **Mourão** Évora, S Portugal 38.22N 7.19W
78 L11 **Mourdiah** Koulikoro, W Mali 14.28N 7.31W
80 K7 **Mourdi, Dépression du** desert lowland Chad/Sudan
104 J16 **Mourenx** Pyrénées-Atlantiques, SW France 43.24N 0.37W
Mourgana see Mourgkána
117 C15 **Mourgkána** var. Mourgana. ▲ Albania/Greece 39.48N 20.24E
99 G16 **Mourne Mountains** Ir. Beanna Boirche. ▲▲ SE Northern Ireland, UK
117 I15 **Moúrtzeflos, Akrotírio** headland Límnos, E Greece 40.00N 25.02E
101 C19 **Mouscron** Dut. Moeskroen. Hainaut, W Belgium 50.43N 3.13E
Mouse River see Souris River
80 H10 **Moussoro** Kanem, W Chad 13.40N 16.31E
105 T11 **Moûtiers** Savoie, E France 45.28N 6.31E
180 J14 **Moutsamoudou** var. Mutsamudu. Anjouan, SE Comoros 12.10S 44.25E
76 K11 **Mouydir, Monts de** ▲ S Algeria
81 F20 **Mouyondzi** La Bouenza, S Congo 3.58S 13.57E
117 E16 **Mouzáki** prev. Mouzákion. Thessalía, C Greece 39.25N 21.40E
Mouzákion see Mouzáki
31 S13 **Moville** Iowa, C USA 42.30N 96.04W
84 E13 **Moxico** ◈ province E Angola
180 I14 **Moya** Anjouan, SE Comoros 12.18S 44.27E
42 L12 **Moyahua** Zacatecas, C Mexico 21.19N 103.10W
83 J16 **Moyalē** Oromo, C Ethiopia 3.34N 38.58E
78 I15 **Moyamba** W Sierra Leone 8.04N 12.30W
76 G7 **Moyen Atlas** Eng. Middle Atlas. ▲▲ N Morocco
80 H13 **Moyen-Chari** off. Préfecture du Moyen-Chari. ◈ prefecture S Chad
Moyen-Congo see Congo (Republic of)
85 J24 **Moyeni** var. Quthing. SW Lesotho 30.25S 27.43E
78 H13 **Moyenne-Guinée** ◈ state NW Guinea
81 D18 **Moyen-Ogooué** off. Province du Moyen-Ogooué, var. Le Moyen-Ogooué. ◈ province C Gabon
105 S4 **Moyeuvre-Grande** Moselle, NE France 49.15N 6.03E
35 N7 **Moyie Springs** Idaho, NW USA 48.43N 116.15W
152 G6 **Mo'ynoq** Rus. Muynak. Qoraqalpog'iston Respublikasi, NW Uzbekistan 43.45N 59.03E
83 F16 **Moyo** NW Uganda 3.37N 31.43E
58 D10 **Moyobamba** San Martín, NW Peru 6.04S 76.55W
175 O16 **Moyo, Pulau** island S Indonesia
80 H10 **Moyto** Chari-Baguirmi, W Chad 12.34N 16.33E
164 G9 **Moyu** var. Karakax. Xinjiang Uygur Zizhiqu, NW China 37.16N 79.39E
126 Jj9 **Moyyero** ~ N Russian Federation
151 S15 **Moyynkum** var. Furmanovka, Kaz. Fürmanov. Zhambyl, S Kazakhstan 44.15N 72.55E
151 Q15 **Moyynkum, Peski** Kaz. Moyynqum. desert S Kazakhstan
Moyynqum see Moyynkum, Peski
151 S12 **Moyynty** Karaganda, C Kazakhstan 47.10N 73.24E
151 S12 **Moyynty** ~ C Kazakhstan
Mozambika, Lakandranon' i see Mozambique Channel
85 M18 **Mozambique** off. Republic of Mozambique; prev. People's Republic of Mozambique, Portuguese East Africa. ◆ republic S Africa
Mozambique Basin see Natal Basin
Mozambique, Canal de see Mozambique Channel
85 P17 **Mozambique Channel** Fr. Canal de Mozambique, Mal. Lakandranon' i Mozambika. strait W Indian Ocean
180 L11 **Mozambique Escarpment** var. Mozambique Scarp. undersea feature SW Indian Ocean
180 L10 **Mozambique Plateau** var. Mozambique Rise. undersea feature SW Indian Ocean
Mozambique Rise see Mozambique Plateau
Mozambique Scarp see Mozambique Escarpment
131 O15 **Mozdok** Respublika Severnaya Osetiya, SW Russian Federation 43.48N 44.42E
59 K17 **Mozetenes, Serranías de** ▲▲ C Bolivia
130 J4 **Mozhaysk** Moskovskaya Oblast', W Russian Federation 55.31N 36.01E
131 T3 **Mozhga** Udmurtskaya Respublika, NW Russian Federation 56.24N 52.13E
Mozyr' see Mazyr
81 P22 **Mpala** Katanga, E Dem. Rep. Congo 6.43S 29.28E
81 G19 **Mpama** ~ C Congo
83 E22 **Mpanda** Rukwa, W Tanzania 6.21S 31.01E
84 L11 **Mpande** Northern, NE Zambia 9.13S 31.42E
85 J18 **Mphoengs** Matabeleland South, SW Zimbabwe 21.04S 27.56E
83 F18 **Mpigi** S Uganda 0.13N 32.19E
84 L13 **Mpika** Northern, NE Zambia 11.49S 31.27E
85 J14 **Mpima** Central, C Zambia 14.25S 28.34E
84 J13 **Mpongwe** Copperbelt, C Zambia 13.25S 28.13E
84 K11 **Mporokoso** Northern, N Zambia 9.22S 30.06E
81 H20 **Mpouya** Plateaux, SE Congo 2.38S 16.12E
79 P16 **Mpraeso** C Ghana 6.46N 0.41W
84 L11 **Mpulungu** Northern, N Zambia 8.47S 31.09E
85 K21 **Mpumalanga** prev. Eastern Transvaal, Afr. Oos-Transvaal. ◈ province NE South Africa
85 D16 **Mpungu** Okavango, N Namibia 17.36S 18.16E
83 I22 **Mpwapwa** Dodoma, C Tanzania 6.21S 36.28E
Mqinvartsveri see Kazbek
112 M8 **Mrągowo** Ger. Sensburg. Warmińsko-Mazurskie, NE Poland 53.52N 21.19E
131 V6 **Mrakovo** Respublika Bashkortostan, W Russian Federation 52.43N 56.36E
180 I13 **Mramani** Anjouan, E Comoros 12.18S 44.39E
114 F12 **Mrkonjić Grad** Republika Srpska, W Bosnia and Herzegovina 44.25N 17.04E
112 H9 **Mrocza** Kujawsko-pomorskie, NW Poland 53.15N 17.38E
128 I14 **Msta** ~ NW Russian Federation
Mtkvari see Kura
Mtoko see Mutoko
130 K6 **Mtsensk** Orlovskaya Oblast', W Russian Federation 53.17N 36.34E
83 K24 **Mtwara** Mtwara, SE Tanzania 10.16S 40.10E
83 J25 **Mtwara** ◈ region SE Tanzania
106 G14 **Mu** ▲ S Portugal 37.24N 8.04W
200 Qq15 **Mu'a** Tongatapu, S Tonga 21.11S 175.07W
Muai To see Mae Hong Son
85 P16 **Mualama** Zambézia, NE Mozambique 16.51S 38.21E
Mualo see Messalo, Rio
81 E22 **Muanda** Bas-Congo, SW Dem. Rep. Congo 5.53S 12.17E
Muang Chiang Rai see Chiang Rai
178 J6 **Muang Ham** Houaphan, N Laos 20.19N 104.00E
178 J9 **Muang Hinboun** Khammouan, C Laos 17.37N 104.37E
Muang Kalasin see Kalasin
Muang Khammouan see Thakhèk
178 Jj11 **Muang Không** Champasak, S Laos 14.08N 105.48E
178 Jj10 **Muang Khôngxédôn** var. Khong Sedone. Salavan, S Laos 15.34N 105.46E
Muang Khon Kaen see Khon Kaen
178 Ii6 **Muang Khoua** Phôngsali, N Laos 21.07N 102.31E
Muang Krabi see Krabi
Muang Lampang see Lampang
Muang Lamphun see Lamphun
Muang Loei see Loei
Muang Lom Sak see Lom Sak
Muang Nakhon Sawan see Nakhon Sawan
178 I6 **Muang Namo** Oudômxai, N Laos 20.58N 101.46E
Muang Nan see Nan
178 Ii6 **Muang Ngoy** Louangphabang, N Laos 20.43N 102.42E
178 I5 **Muang Ou Tai** Phôngsali, N Laos 22.06N 101.59E
Muang Pak Lay see Pak Lay
Muang Pakxan see Pakxan
178 Jj10 **Muang Pakxong** Champasak, S Laos 15.10N 106.17E
178 Jj9 **Muang Phalan** var. Muang Phalane. Savannakhét, S Laos 16.40N 105.33E
Muang Phalane see Muang Phalan
Muang Phan see Phan
Muang Phayao see Phayao
Muang Phichit see Phichit
178 Jj9 **Muang Phin** Savannakhét, S Laos 16.31N 106.01E
Muang Phitsanulok see Phitsanulok
Muang Phrae see Phrae
Muang Roi Et see Roi Et
Muang Sakon Nakhon see Sakon Nakhon
Muang Samut Prakan see Samut Prakan
178 I6 **Muang Sing** Louang Namtha, N Laos 21.12N 101.09E
Muang Ubon see Ubon Ratchathani
Muang Uthai Thani see Uthai Thani
178 I7 **Muang Vangviang** Viangchan, C Laos 18.53N 102.27E
Muang Xaignabouri see Xaignabouli
Muang Xay see Xai
178 Jj9 **Muang Xépôn** var. Sepone. Savannakhét, S Laos 16.40N 106.15E
174 H6 **Muar** var. Bandar Maharani. Johor, Peninsular Malaysia 2.01N 102.34E
173 Ff6 **Muara** Sumatera, W Indonesia 2.18N 98.54E
174 Hh11 **Muarabeliti** Sumatera, W Indonesia 3.13S 103.00E
174 H9 **Muarabungo** Sumatera, W Indonesia 1.36S 103.37E
174 I11 **Muaraenim** Sumatera, W Indonesia 3.36S 103.43E
174 Mm8 **Muarajuloi** Borneo, C Indonesia 0.12S 114.03E
175 Nn9 **Muarakaman** Borneo, C Indonesia 0.09S 116.43E
173 Ff9 **Muarasigep** Pulau Siberut, W Indonesia 1.01S 98.48E
174 Hh9 **Muaratembesi** Sumatera, W Indonesia 1.42S 103.07E
175 N9 **Muaratewe** var. Muarateweh; prev. Moearatewe. Borneo, C Indonesia 0.58S 114.52E
Muarateweh see Muaratewe
175 O7 **Muarawahau** Borneo, N Indonesia 1.03N 116.48E
144 G13 **Mubārak, Jabal** ▲ S Jordan 29.19N 35.13E
159 N13 **Mubārakpur** Uttar Pradesh, N India 26.05N 83.19E
Mubarek see Muborak
83 F18 **Mubende** SW Uganda 0.34N 31.24E
79 Y14 **Mubi** Adamawa, NE Nigeria 10.15N 13.18E
152 M12 **Muborak** Rus. Mubarek. Qashqadaryo Viloyati, S Uzbekistan 39.17N 65.10E
176 Vv9 **Mubrani** Papua, E Indonesia 0.42S 133.25E
69 U12 **Muchinga Escarpment** escarpment NE Zambia
131 N7 **Muchkapskiy** Tambovskaya Oblast', W Russian Federation 51.51N 42.25E
98 G10 **Muck** island W Scotland, UK
84 Q13 **Mucojo** Cabo Delgado, N Mozambique 12.04S 40.30E
84 F12 **Muconda** Lunda Sul, NE Angola 10.37S 21.19E
56 I10 **Muco, Río** ~ E Colombia
85 O16 **Mucubela** Zambézia, NE Mozambique 16.51S 37.48E
44 J5 **Mucupina, Monte** ▲ N Honduras 15.07N 86.36W
142 J14 **Mucur** Kırşehir, C Turkey 39.04N 34.25E
149 U8 **Mūd** Khorāsān, E Iran 32.40N 59.30E
169 Y9 **Mudanjiang** var. Mu-tan-chiang. Heilongjiang, NE China 44.33N 129.40E
169 Y9 **Mudan Jiang** ~ NE China
142 D11 **Mudanya** Bursa, NW Turkey 40.22N 28.52E
30 K8 **Mud Butte** South Dakota, N USA 45.00N 102.51W
161 G16 **Muddebihāl** Karnātaka, C India 16.26N 76.07E

◆ Country ● Country Capital ◇ Dependent Territory ○ Dependent Territory Capital ◈ Administrative Region ✖ International Airport ▲ Mountain ▲▲ Mountain Range △ Volcano ~ River ◎ Lake ⊡ Reservoir

MUDDY BOGGY CREEK – MYNBULAK

29 P12 **Muddy Boggy Creek** ≈ Oklahoma, C USA
38 M6 **Muddy Creek** ≈ Utah, W USA
39 V7 **Muddy Creek Reservoir** ⊠ Colorado, C USA
35 W15 **Muddy Gap** Wyoming, C USA 42.21N 107.27W
37 Y11 **Muddy Peak** ▲ Nevada, W USA 36.17N 114.40W
191 R7 **Mudgee** New South Wales, SE Australia 32.37S 149.34E
31 S3 **Mud Lake** ◎ Minnesota, N USA
31 P7 **Mud Lake Reservoir** ⊠ South Dakota, N USA
178 Gg9 **Mudon** Mon State, S Myanmar 16.14N 97.46E
83 O14 **Mudug** *off.* Gobolka Mudug. ◈ *region* NE Somalia
83 O14 **Mudug** *var.* Mudugh. *plain* N Somalia
Mudugh *see* Mudug
85 Q15 **Muecate** Nampula, NE Mozambique 14.56S 39.38E
84 Q13 **Mueda** Cabo Delgado, NE Mozambique 11.40S 39.36E
44 L10 **Muelle de los Bueyes** Región Autónoma Atlántico Sur, SE Nicaragua 12.03N 84.34W
Muenchen *see* München
85 M14 **Muende** Tete, NW Mozambique 14.22S 33.00E
27 T5 **Muenster** Texas, SW USA 33.39N 97.22W
Muenster *see* Münster
45 O6 **Muerto, Cayo** *reef* NE Nicaragua
43 T17 **Muerto, Mar** *lagoon* SE Mexico
66 F11 **Muertos Trough** *undersea feature* N Caribbean Sea
85 H14 **Mufaya Kuta** Western, NW Zambia 14.30S 24.18E
84 J13 **Mufulira** Copperbelt, C Zambia 12.33S 28.15E
167 O10 **Mufu Shan** ⛰ C China
Mugalzhar Taūlary *see* Mugodzhary, Gory
143 Y12 **Muğan Düzü** *Rus.* Muganskaya Ravnina, Muganskaya Step'. *physical region* S Azerbaijan
Muganskaya Ravnina/Muganskaya Step' *see* Muğan Düzü
108 K8 **Muggia** Friuli-Venezia Giulia, NE Italy 45.36N 13.48E
159 N14 **Mughal Sarāi** Uttar Pradesh, N India 25.18N 83.07E
Mughla *see* Muğla
147 W11 **Mughshin** *var.* Muqshin. S Oman 19.25N 54.38E
153 S12 **Mughsu** *Rus.* Muksu. ≈ C Tajikistan
170 Ff16 **Mugi** Tokushima, Shikoku, SW Japan 33.39N 134.24E
142 C16 **Muğla** *var.* Mughla. Muğla, SW Turkey 37.13N 28.22E
142 C16 **Muğla** *var.* Mughla. ◈ *province* SW Turkey
150 J11 **Mugodzhary, Gory** *Kaz.* Mugalzhar Taūlary. ⛰ W Kazakhstan
85 O15 **Mugulama** Zambézia, NE Mozambique 16.01S 37.33E
145 U9 **Muḩammad** E Iraq 32.46N 45.14E
145 R8 **Muḩammadīyah** C Iraq 33.22N 42.48E
82 I6 **Muhammad Qol** Red Sea, NE Sudan 20.52N 37.09E
77 Y9 **Muhammad, Râs** *headland* E Egypt 27.45N 34.18E
Muhammerah *see* Khorramshahr
146 M12 **Muḩāyil** *var.* Mahāil. 'Asīr, SW Saudi Arabia 18.34N 42.01E
145 O7 **Muḩaywīr** W Iraq 33.34N 41.06E
103 H21 **Mühlacker** Baden-Württemberg, SW Germany 48.57N 8.51E
Mühlbach *see* Sebeş
Mühldorf *see* Mühldorf am Inn
103 N23 **Mühldorf am Inn** *var.* Mühldorf. Bayern, SE Germany 48.14N 12.32E
103 J15 **Mühlhausen** *var.* Mühlhausen in Thüringen. Thüringen, C Germany 51.13N 10.28E
Mühlhausen in Thüringen *see* Mühlhausen
205 Q2 **Mühlig-Hofmann Mountains** ⛰ Antarctica
95 L14 **Muhos** Oulu, C Finland 64.48N 26.00E
144 K6 **Mūḩ, Sabkhat al** ◎ C Syria
120 E5 **Muhu** *Ger.* Mohn, Moon. *island* W Estonia
83 F19 **Muhutwe** Kagera, NW Tanzania 1.31S 31.40E
Muhu Väin *see* Väinameri
100 J10 **Muiden** Noord-Holland, C Netherlands 52.19N 5.04E
200 R15 **Mui Hopohoponga** *headland* Tongatapu, S Tonga 21.09S 175.01W
171 K14 **Muika** *var.* Muikamachi. Niigata, Honshū, C Japan 37.04N 138.53E
Muikamachi *see* Muika
Muinchille *see* Cootehill
Muineachán *see* Monaghan
99 F19 **Muine Bheag** *Eng.* Bagenalstown. SE Ireland 52.42N 6.57W
58 B5 **Muisne** Esmeraldas, NW Ecuador 0.34N 79.58W
85 P14 **Muite** Nampula, NE Mozambique 14.02S 39.06E
43 Z11 **Mujeres, Isla** *island* E Mexico
118 G7 **Mukacheve** *Hung.* Munkács, *Rus.* Mukachevo. Zakarpats'ka Oblast', W Ukraine 48.26N 22.44E
Mukachevo *see* Mukacheve
174 Ll5 **Mukah** Sarawak, East Malaysia 2.55N 112.01E
Mukalla *see* Al Mukallā
Mukama *see* Mokāma
Mukāshafa/Mukashshafah *see* Mukayshīfah
172 Oo6 **Mu-kawa** ≈ Hokkaidō, NE Japan
145 S6 **Mukayshīfah** *var.* Mukāshafa, Mukashshafah. N Iraq 34.24N 43.44E
178 J9 **Mukdahan** Mukdahan, E Thailand 16.31N 104.43E
Mukden *see* Shenyang
172 Ss16 **Mukojima-rettō** *Eng.* Parry group. *island group* SE Japan
152 M14 **Mukry** Lebap Welaýaty, E Turkmenistan 37.39N 65.37E
Muksu *see* Mughsu
159 U14 **Muktagacha** *var.* Muktagachha Dhaka, N Bangladesh 24.46N 90.16E
Muktagachha *see* Muktagacha
84 K13 **Mukuku** Central, C Zambia 12.10S 29.50E
84 K11 **Mukupa Kaoma** Northern, NE Zambia 9.55S 30.19E
83 J18 **Mukutan** Rift Valley, W Kenya 1.06N 36.16E
85 F16 **Mukwe** Caprivi, NE Namibia 18.01S 21.24E
107 R13 **Mula** Murcia, SE Spain 38.01N 1.28W
157 K20 **Mulaku Atoll** *var.* Meemu Atoll. *atoll* C Maldives
85 J15 **Mulalika** Lusaka, C Zambia 15.37S 28.48E
169 X8 **Mulan** Heilongjiang, NE China 45.57N 128.00E
85 N15 **Mulanje** *var.* Mlanje. Southern, S Malawi 16.04S 35.35E
42 H5 **Mulatos** Sonora, NW Mexico 28.42N 108.44W
25 P3 **Mulberry Fork** ≈ Alabama, S USA
41 P12 **Mulchatna River** ≈ Alaska, USA
129 W4 **Mul'da** Respublika Komi, NW Russian Federation 67.29N 63.55E
103 M14 **Mulde** ≈ E Germany
29 R10 **Muldrow** Oklahoma, C USA 35.25N 94.34W
42 E7 **Mulegé** Baja California Sur, W Mexico 26.54N 112.00W
110 I10 **Mulegns** Graubünden, S Switzerland 46.30N 9.36E
81 M21 **Mulenda** Kasai Oriental, C Dem. Rep. Congo 4.19S 24.55E
26 M4 **Muleshoe** Texas, SW USA 34.13N 102.43W
85 O15 **Mulevala** Zambézia, NE Mozambique 16.18S 37.40E
191 P5 **Mulgoa Creek** *seasonal river* New South Wales, SE Australia
107 O15 **Mulhacén** *var.* Cerro de Mulhacén. ▲ S Spain 37.07N 3.11W
Mulhacén, Cerro de *see* Mulhacén
Mülhausen *see* Mulhouse
103 E24 **Mülheim** Baden-Württemberg, SW Germany 47.49N 7.36E
103 E15 **Mülheim** *var.* Mulheim an der Ruhr. Nordrhein-Westfalen, W Germany 51.25N 6.52E
Mulheim an der Ruhr *see* Mülheim
105 U7 **Mulhouse** *Ger.* Mülhausen. Haut-Rhin, NE France 47.45N 7.19E
166 G11 **Muli** *var.* Qiaowa, Muli Zangzu Zizhixian. Sichuan, C China 27.49N 101.10E
176 Y15 **Muli** *channel* Papua, E Indonesia
169 Y9 **Muling** Heilongjiang, NE China 44.54N 130.35E
Mullach Íde *see* Malahide
Mullaitivu *see* Mullaittivu
161 K23 **Mullaittivu** *var.* Mullaitivu. Northern Province, N Sri Lanka 9.15N 80.48E
35 N8 **Mullan** Idaho, NW USA 47.28N 115.48W
30 M13 **Mullen** Nebraska, C USA 42.02N 101.01W
191 Q6 **Mullengudgery** New South Wales, SE Australia 31.42S 147.24E
23 Q6 **Mullens** West Virginia, NE USA 37.34N 81.22W
Müller-gerbergte *see* Muller, Pegunungan
174 Mm7 **Muller, Pegunungan** *Dut.* Müller-gerbergte. ⛰ Borneo, C Indonesia
194 F12 **Muller Range** ⛰ W PNG
33 Q5 **Mullett Lake** ◎ Michigan, N USA
20 J16 **Mullica River** ≈ New Jersey, NE USA
27 R8 **Mullin** Texas, SW USA 31.33N 98.40W
99 E17 **Mullingar** *Ir.* An Muileann gCearr. C Ireland 53.31N 7.19W
23 T12 **Mullins** South Carolina, SE USA 34.12N 79.15W
98 G11 **Mull, Isle of** *island* W Scotland, UK
131 R5 **Mullovka** Ul'yanovskaya Oblast', W Russian Federation 54.13N 49.19E
97 K19 **Mullsjö** Västra Götaland, S Sweden 57.55N 13.55E
191 V4 **Mullumbimby** New South Wales, SE Australia 28.34S 153.28E
85 H15 **Mulobezi** Western, SW Zambia 16.48S 25.10E
85 C15 **Mulondo** Huíla, SW Angola 15.41S 15.09E
85 G15 **Mulonga Plain** *plain* W Zambia
81 N23 **Mulongo** Katanga, SE Dem. Rep. Congo 7.44S 26.57E
155 T10 **Multān** Punjab, E Pakistan 30.12N 71.29E
95 L17 **Multia** Länsi-Suomi, W Finland 62.27N 24.49E
Mulucha *see* Moulouya
85 J14 **Mulungushi** Central, C Zambia 14.15S 28.27E
85 K14 **Mulungwe** Central, C Zambia 13.57S 29.51E
Muluya *see* Moulouya
29 N7 **Mulvane** Kansas, C USA 37.28N 97.14W
191 O10 **Mulwala** New South Wales, SE Australia 35.59S 146.00E
Mulwiya *see* Moulouya
190 K6 **Mulyungarie** South Australia 31.29S 140.45E
160 D13 **Mumbai** *prev.* Bombay. Mahārāshtra, W India 18.55N 72.51E
160 D13 **Mumbai** ✕ Mahārāshtra, W India 19.10N 72.51E
85 D14 **Mumbué** Bié, C Angola 13.52S 17.15E
194 J13 **Mumeng** Morobe, C PNG 6.57S 146.37E
176 W9 **Mumi** Papua, E Indonesia 1.33S 134.09E
Muminabad/Mū'minobod *see* Leningrad
131 Q13 **Mumra** Astrakhanskaya Oblast', SW Russian Federation 45.46N 47.46E
43 X12 **Muna** Yucatán, SE Mexico 20.28N 89.45W
126 Kk9 **Muna** ≈ NE Russian Federation
158 C12 **Munābāo** Rājasthān, NW India 25.46N 70.19E
Munamägi *see* Suur Munamägi
175 Qq13 **Muna, Pulau** *prev.* Moena. *island* C Indonesia
175 Qq13 **Muna, Selat** *strait* Sulawesi, C Indonesia
103 L18 **Münchberg** Bayern, E Germany 50.10N 11.49E
103 L23 **München** *var.* Muenchen, *Eng.* Munich, *It.* Monaco. Bayern, SE Germany 48.08N 11.34E
München-Gladbach *see* Mönchengladbach
110 E6 **Münchenstein** Basel-Land, NW Switzerland 47.31N 7.37E
8 L10 **Muncho Lake** British Columbia, W Canada 58.52N 125.40W
33 P13 **Muncie** Indiana, N USA 40.10N 85.22W
20 G13 **Muncy** Pennsylvania, NE USA 41.10N 76.46W
195 U14 **Munda** New Georgia, NW Solomon Islands 8.15S 157.15E
9 Q14 **Mundare** Alberta, SW Canada 53.34N 112.20W
27 Q5 **Munday** Texas, SW USA 33.27N 99.37W
33 N10 **Mundelein** Illinois, N USA 42.15N 88.00W
103 I15 **Münden** Niedersachsen, C Germany 52.16N 8.54E
107 Q12 **Mundo** ≈ S Spain
194 L11 **Mundua Island** *island* Witu Islands, C PNG
84 B12 **Munenga** Cuanza Sul, NW Angola 10.05S 14.35E
107 P11 **Munera** Castilla-La Mancha, C Spain 39.03N 2.28W
22 E9 **Munford** Tennessee, S USA 35.27N 89.49W
22 K7 **Munfordville** Kentucky, S USA 37.15N 85.53W
190 D5 **Mungala** South Australia 30.36S 132.57E
85 M16 **Mungári** Manica, C Mozambique 17.09S 33.33E
81 O16 **Mungbere** Orientale, NE Dem. Rep. Congo 2.37N 28.30E
159 Q13 **Munger** *prev.* Monghyr. Bihār, NE India 25.22N 86.28E
190 I2 **Mungeranie** South Australia 28.02S 138.42E
Mu Nggava *see* Rennell
174 K6 **Mungguresak, Tanjung** *headland* Borneo, N Indonesia 1.57N 109.19E
Mungiki *see* Bellona
191 R4 **Mungindi** New South Wales, SE Australia 28.59S 149.00E
Mungkawn *see* Maingkwan
159 T16 **Mungla** *var.* Mongla. Khulna, S Bangladesh 22.18N 89.34E
84 C13 **Mungo** Huambo, W Angola 11.46S 16.13E
196 F16 **Munguuy Bay** *bay* Yap, W Micronesia
84 E13 **Munhango** Bié, C Angola 12.12S 18.34E
197 L14 **Munia** *island* Lau Group, E Fiji
Munich *see* München
107 S7 **Muniesa** Aragón, NE Spain 41.01N 0.49W
33 O4 **Munising** Michigan, N USA 46.24N 86.39W
Munkács *see* Mukacheve
97 I17 **Munkedal** Västra Götaland, S Sweden 58.28N 11.37E
97 K15 **Munkfors** Värmland, C Sweden 59.49N 13.34E
126 J16 **Munku-Sardyk, Gora** *var.* Mönh Sarīdag. ▲ Mongolia/Russian Federation 51.45N 100.22E
101 E18 **Munkzwalm** Oost-Vlaanderen, NW Belgium 50.53N 3.44E
178 I10 **Mun, Mae Nam** ≈ E Thailand
159 U15 **Munshiganj** Dhaka, C Bangladesh 23.31N 90.31E
110 D8 **Münsingen** Bern, W Switzerland 46.52N 7.36E
105 U6 **Munster** Haut-Rhin, NE France 48.03N 7.09E
102 J11 **Munster** Niedersachsen, NW Germany 52.58N 10.06E
99 B20 **Munster** *Ir.* Cúige Mumhan. *cultural region* S Ireland
102 F13 **Münster** *var.* Muenster, Münster in Westfalen. Nordrhein-Westfalen, W Germany 51.58N 7.37E
110 F10 **Münster** Valais, S Switzerland 46.31N 8.18E
Münsterberg in Schlesien *see* Ziębice
Münster in Westfalen *see* Münster
102 E13 **Münsterland** *cultural region* NW Germany
102 F13 **Münster-Osnabruck** ✕ Nordrhein-Westfalen, NW Germany 52.08N 7.41E
33 R4 **Munuscong Lake** ◎ Michigan, N USA
85 K17 **Munyati** ≈ C Zimbabwe
111 R3 **Münzkirchen** Oberösterreich, N Austria 48.29N 13.37E
94 K11 **Muodoslompolo** Norrbotten, N Sweden 67.57N 23.31E
94 M13 **Muojärvi** ◎ NE Finland
178 J6 **Mương Khên** Hoa Binh, N Vietnam 20.34N 105.18E
Muong Sai *see* Xai
178 I7 **Muong Xiang Ngeun** *var.* Xieng Ngeun. Louangphabang, N Laos 19.43N 102.09E
94 K11 **Muonio** Lappi, N Finland 67.58N 23.40E
Muonioälv/Muoniojoki *see* Muonionjoki
94 K11 **Muonionjoki** *var.* Muoniojoki, *Swe.* Muonioälv. ≈ Finland/Sweden
85 N17 **Mupa** ≈ C Mozambique
85 E16 **Mupini** Okavango, NE Namibia 17.55S 19.34E
82 F8 **Muqaddam, Wadi** ≈ N Sudan
144 K9 **Muqāţ** Al Mafraq, E Jordan 32.28N 38.04E
147 X7 **Muqaz** N Oman 24.13N 56.48E
83 N17 **Muqdisho** *Eng.* Mogadishu, *It.* Mogadiscio. ● (Somalia) Banaadir, S Somalia 2.06N 45.27E
83 N17 **Muqdisho** ✕ Banaadir, E Somalia 1.58N 45.18E
Muqshin *see* Mughshin
111 T8 **Mur** *SCr.* Mura. ≈ C Europe
Mura *see* Mur
111 X9 **Mura** ≈ NE Slovenia
143 T14 **Muradiye** Van, E Turkey 39.00N 43.44E
Muragarazi *see* Maragarazi
171 L12 **Murakami** Niigata, Honshū, C Japan 38.13N 139.28E
65 G22 **Murallón, Cerro** ▲ S Argentina 49.49S 73.25W
83 E20 **Muramvya** C Burundi 3.18S 29.41E
83 I19 **Murang'a** *prev.* Fort Hall. Central, SW Kenya 0.43S 37.10E
83 H16 **Murangering** Rift Valley, NW Kenya 3.48N 35.29E
146 M5 **Murār, Bi'r al** *well* NW Saudi Arabia 27.20N 40.21E
129 Q13 **Murashi** Kirovskaya Oblast', NW Russian Federation 59.27N 48.02E
105 O12 **Murat** Cantal, C France 45.07N 2.52E
116 N12 **Muratlı** Tekirdağ, NW Turkey 41.12N 27.30E
143 R14 **Murat Nehri** *var.* Eastern Euphrates; *anc.* Arsanias. ≈ NE Turkey
109 D20 **Muravera** Sardegna, Italy, C Mediterranean Sea 39.24N 9.34E
171 Ll12 **Murayama** Yamagata, Honshū, C Japan 38.29N 140.21E
124 Oo15 **Muraysah, Ra's al** *headland* N Libya 31.58N 25.00E
106 I6 **Murça** Vila Real, N Portugal 41.24N 7.28W
82 Q11 **Murcanyo** Bari, NE Somalia 11.39N 50.27E
149 N8 **Mūrcheh Khvort** *var.* Morcheh Khort. Eşfahān, C Iran 33.07N 51.26E
193 H15 **Murchison** Tasman, South Island, NZ 41.48S 172.19E
193 B22 **Murchison Mountains** ⛰ South Island, NZ
188 I10 **Murchison River** ≈ Western Australia
107 R13 **Murcia** Murcia, SE Spain 37.58N 1.07W
107 Q13 **Murcia** ◈ *autonomous community* SE Spain
105 O13 **Mur-de-Barrez** Aveyron, S France 44.48N 2.39E
190 G8 **Murdinga** South Australia 33.46S 135.46E
30 M10 **Murdo** South Dakota, N USA 43.53N 100.42W
13 X6 **Murdochville** Québec, SE Canada 48.57N 65.30W
111 W9 **Mureck** Steiermark, SE Austria 46.42N 15.46E
116 M13 **Mürefte** Tekirdağ, NW Turkey 40.40N 27.15E
118 I10 **Mureş** ◈ *county* N Romania
86 J11 **Mureş** *var.* Maros, Mureşul, *Ger.* Marosch, Mieresch. ≈ Hungary/Romania *see also* Maros
Mureşul *see* Maros/Mureş
104 M16 **Muret** Haute-Garonne, S France 43.28N 1.19E
29 T13 **Murfreesboro** Arkansas, C USA 34.03N 93.41W
23 W8 **Murfreesboro** North Carolina, SE USA 36.26N 77.06W
22 J9 **Murfreesboro** Tennessee, S USA 35.51N 86.23W
Murgab *see* Morghāb, Daryā-ye/Murgap/Murghob
152 I14 **Murgap** *Rus.* Murgab. Mary Welaýaty, S Turkmenistan 37.19N 61.48E
152 J16 **Murgap** *var.* Murgap Deryasy, Murghab, *Pash.* Daryā-ye Morghāb, *Rus.* Murgab. ≈ Afghanistan/Turkmenistan *see also* Morghāb, Daryā-ye
Murgap Deryasy *see* Morghāb, Daryā-ye/Murgap
116 H9 **Murgash** ▲ W Bulgaria 42.51N 23.58E
Murghab *see* Morghāb, Daryā-ye/Murgap
153 U13 **Murghob** *Rus.* Murgab. SE Tajikistan 38.11N 73.59E
153 U13 **Murghob** *Rus.* Murgab. ≈ SE Tajikistan
189 Z10 **Murgon** Queensland, E Australia 26.07S 152.03E
202 I16 **Muri** Rarotonga, S Cook Islands 21.15S 159.43W
110 F7 **Muri** Aargau, W Switzerland 47.16N 8.21E
110 D8 **Muri** *var.* Muri bei Bern. Bern, W Switzerland 46.55N 7.30E
106 K3 **Murias de Paredes** Castilla-León, N Spain 42.51N 6.11W
Muri bei Bern *see* Muri
84 F11 **Muriege** Lunda Sul, NE Angola 9.55S 21.12E
201 P14 **Murilo Atoll** *atoll* Hall Islands, C Micronesia
Mūrītānīyah *see* Mauritania
102 N10 **Müritz** *var.* Müritzee. ◎ NE Germany
Müritzee *see* Müritz
102 L10 **Müritz-Elde-Kanal** *canal* N Germany
192 K6 **Muriwai Beach** Auckland, North Island, NZ 36.56S 174.28E
94 J13 **Murjek** Norrbotten, N Sweden 66.27N 20.54E
128 J3 **Murmansk** Murmanskaya Oblast', NW Russian Federation 68.58N 33.07E
128 I4 **Murmanskaya Oblast'** ◈ *province* NW Russian Federation
207 V14 **Murmansk Rise** *undersea feature* SW Barents Sea
128 J3 **Murmashi** Murmanskaya Oblast', NW Russian Federation 68.49N 32.42E
130 M5 **Murmino** Ryazanskaya Oblast', W Russian Federation 54.31N 40.01E
103 K24 **Murnau** Bayern, SE Germany 47.41N 11.12E
105 X16 **Muro, Capo di** *headland* Corse, France, C Mediterranean Sea 41.45N 8.40E
109 M18 **Muro Lucano** Basilicata, S Italy 40.48N 15.33E
131 N4 **Murom** Vladimirskaya Oblast', W Russian Federation 55.33N 42.03E
125 G13 **Muromtsevo** Omskaya Oblast', C Russian Federation 56.18N 75.15E
172 Nn6 **Muroran** Hokkaidō, NE Japan 42.19N 140.58E
106 G3 **Muros** Galicia, NW Spain 42.46N 9.03W
106 F3 **Muros e Noia, Ría de** *estuary* NW Spain
170 F16 **Muroto** Kōchi, Shikoku, SW Japan 33.18N 134.07E
170 F16 **Muroto-zaki** *headland* Shikoku, SW Japan 33.15N 134.09E
118 L7 **Murovani Kurylivtsi** Vinnyts'ka Oblast', C Ukraine 48.43N 27.31E
112 G11 **Murowana Goślina** Wielkolpolskie, C Poland 52.33N 16.59E
34 M14 **Murphy** Idaho, NW USA 43.14N 116.36W
23 N10 **Murphy** North Carolina, SE USA 35.05N 84.01W
37 P8 **Murphys** California, W USA 38.07N 120.27W
32 L17 **Murphysboro** Illinois, N USA 37.45N 89.20W
31 V15 **Murray** Iowa, C USA 41.03N 93.56W
22 H8 **Murray** Kentucky, S USA 36.36N 88.18W
190 J10 **Murray Bridge** South Australia 35.06S 139.15E
183 X2 **Murray Fracture Zone** *tectonic feature* NE Pacific Ocean
194 E13 **Murray, Lake** ◎ SW PNG
23 P12 **Murray, Lake** ⊠ South Carolina, SE USA
8 K8 **Murray, Mount** ▲ Yukon Territory, NW Canada 60.49N 128.57W
194 H13 **Murray Range** *var.* Leonard Murray Mountains. ⛰ W PNG
Murray Range *see* Murray Ridge
181 O3 **Murray Ridge** *var.* Murray Range. *undersea feature* N Arabian Sea
191 N10 **Murray River** ≈ SE Australia
190 K10 **Murrayville** Victoria, SE Australia 35.17S 141.12E
155 U5 **Murree** Punjab, E Pakistan 33.55N 73.25E
103 I21 **Murrhardt** Baden-Württemberg, S Germany 49.00N 9.34E
191 O9 **Murrumbidgee River** ≈ New South Wales, SE Australia
85 P15 **Murrupula** Nampula, NE Mozambique 15.26S 38.46E
191 T7 **Murrurundi** New South Wales, SE Australia 31.47S 150.51E
111 X9 **Murska Sobota** *Ger.* Olsnitz. NE Slovenia 46.40N 16.09E
160 G12 **Murtajāpur** *prev.* Murtazapur. Mahārāshtra, C India 20.43N 77.28E
79 S16 **Murtala Muhammed** ✕ (Lagos) Ogun, SW Nigeria 6.31N 3.12E
Murtazapur *see* Murtajāpur
110 C8 **Murten** Neuchâtel, W Switzerland 46.55N 7.06E
Murtensee *see* Morat, Lac de
190 L11 **Murtoa** Victoria, SE Australia 36.39S 142.27E
94 N13 **Murtovaara** Oulu, E Finland 65.40N 29.25E
Murua Island *see* Woodlark Island
161 D14 **Murud** Mahārāshtra, W India 18.27N 72.56E
192 O9 **Murupara** *var.* Murapara. Bay of Plenty, North Island, NZ 38.27S 176.40E
203 X12 **Mururoa** *var.* Moruroa. *atoll* Îles Tuamotu, SE French Polynesia
Murviedro *see* Sagunto
160 J9 **Murwāra** Madhya Pradesh, N India 23.50N 80.23E
191 V4 **Murwillumbah** New South Wales, SE Australia 28.19S 153.24E
152 H11 **Murzechirla** *prev.* Mirzachirla. Ahal Welaýaty, C Turkmenistan 39.33N 60.02E
Murzuk *see* Murzuq
77 O11 **Murzuq** *var.* Marzūq, Murzuk. SW Libya 25.55N 13.55E
Murzuq, Edeyin *see* Murzuq, Idhān
77 N11 **Murzuq, Ḩamādat** *plateau* W Libya
77 O11 **Murzuq, Idhān** *var.* Edeyin Murzuq. *desert* SW Libya
111 W6 **Mürzzuschlag** Steiermark, E Austria 47.34N 15.40E
143 Q14 **Muş** *var.* Mush. Muş, E Turkey 38.45N 41.30E
143 Q14 **Muş** *var.* Mush. ◈ *prov.* E Turkey
194 L16 **Musa** ≈ S PNG
120 G11 **Mūša** ≈ Latvia/Lithuania
77 X8 **Mûsa, Gebel** ▲ NE Egypt 28.33N 33.51E
Musaiyib *see* Al Musayyib
Musa Khel *see* Mūsā Khel Bazār
155 R9 **Mūsā Khel Bazār** *var.* Musa Khel. Baluchistān, SW Pakistan 30.52N 69.46E
116 H10 **Musala** ▲ W Bulgaria 42.12N 23.36E
173 F6 **Musala, Pulau** *island* W Indonesia
85 I15 **Musale** Southern, S Zambia 15.27S 26.50E
147 Y9 **Muşalla** NE Oman 22.19N 58.03E
147 W6 **Musandam Peninsula** *Ar.* Masandam Peninsula. *peninsula* N Oman
Musay'īd *see* Umm Sa'īd
Muscat *see* Masqaţ
Muscat and Oman *see* Oman
31 Y14 **Muscatine** Iowa, C USA 41.25N 91.03W
Muscat Sīb Airport *see* Seeb
33 O15 **Muscatuck River** ≈ Indiana, N USA
194 G10 **Muschu Island** *island* NW PNG
32 K8 **Muscoda** Wisconsin, N USA 43.11N 90.27W
193 F19 **Musgrave, Mount** ▲ South Island, NZ 43.48S 170.43E
189 P9 **Musgrave Ranges** ⛰ South Australia
Mush *see* Muş
144 H12 **Mushayyish, Qaşr al** *castle* Ma'ān, C Jordan 30.58N 36.41E
81 H20 **Mushie** Bandundu, W Dem. Rep. Congo 3.00S 16.55E
174 I11 **Musi, Air** *prev.* Moesi. ≈ Sumatera, W Indonesia
199 K5 **Musicians Seamounts** *undersea feature* N Pacific Ocean
85 K19 **Musina** *prev.* Messina. Limpopo, NE South Africa 22.18S 30.02E
56 D8 **Musinga, Alto** ▲ NW Colombia 6.49N 76.24W
31 T2 **Muskeg Bay** *lake bay* Minnesota, N USA
33 O8 **Muskegon** Michigan, N USA 43.13N 86.15W
33 O8 **Muskegon Heights** Michigan, N USA 43.12N 86.14W
33 P8 **Muskegon River** ≈ Michigan, N USA
33 T14 **Muskingum River** ≈ Ohio, N USA
97 P16 **Muskö** Stockholm, C Sweden 58.58N 18.10E
Muskogean *see* Tallahassee
29 Q10 **Muskogee** Oklahoma, C USA 35.45N 95.22W
12 H13 **Muskoka, Lake** ◎ Ontario, S Canada
82 H8 **Musmar** Red Sea, NE Sudan 18.13N 35.40E
85 K14 **Musofu** Central, C Zambia 13.31S 29.03E
83 G19 **Musoma** Mara, N Tanzania 1.31S 33.49E
84 L13 **Musonoi** Central, C Zambia 13.21S 31.04E
194 M8 **Mussau Island** *island* NE PNG
100 P7 **Musselkanaal** Groningen, NE Netherlands 52.55N 7.01E
35 V9 **Musselshell River** ≈ Montana, NW USA
84 C12 **Mussende** Cuanza Sul, NW Angola 10.33S 16.01E
104 L12 **Mussidan** Dordogne, SW France 45.03N 0.22E
101 L25 **Musson** Luxembourg, SE Belgium 49.33N 5.42E
158 J9 **Mussoorie** Uttaranchal, N India 30.25N 78.04E
Musta *see* Mosta
158 M13 **Mustafābād** Uttar Pradesh, N India 25.54N 81.16E
142 D12 **Mustafakemalpaşa** Bursa, NW Turkey 40.03N 28.25E
Mustafa-Pasha *see* Svilengrad
83 M15 **Mustahīl** Somali, E Ethiopia 5.18N 44.34E
26 M7 **Mustang Draw** *valley* Texas, SW USA
27 T14 **Mustang Island** *island* Texas, SW USA
Mustasaari *see* Korsholm
Muster *see* Disentis
65 I19 **Musters, Lago** ◎ S Argentina
47 Y14 **Mustique** *island* C Saint Vincent and the Grenadines
120 I6 **Mustla** Viljandimaa, S Estonia 58.12N 25.51E
120 J4 **Mustvee** *Ger.* Tschorna. Jõgevamaa, E Estonia 58.51N 26.57E
44 L9 **Musún, Cerro** ▲ NE Nicaragua 13.01N 85.02W
191 T7 **Muswellbrook** New South Wales, SE Australia 32.16S 150.55E
113 M18 **Muszyna** Małopolskie, SE Poland 49.21N 20.54E
142 I17 **Mut** İçel, S Turkey 36.37N 33.27E
77 V10 **Mût** *var.* Mut. C Egypt 25.34N 28.58E
111 V9 **Muta** N Slovenia 46.37N 15.09E
202 B15 **Mutalau** N Niue 18.55S 169.49E
Mu-tan-chiang *see* Mudanjiang
84 I13 **Mutanda** North Western, NW Zambia 12.22S 26.15E
61 O17 **Mutá, Ponta do** *headland* E Brazil 13.54S 38.54W
85 L17 **Mutare** *var.* Mutari; *prev.* Umtali. Manicaland, E Zimbabwe 18.54S 32.36E
Mutari *see* Mutare
56 D8 **Mutatá** Antioquia, NW Colombia 7.16N 76.31W
Mutina *see* Modena
176 Z15 **Muting** Papua, E Indonesia 7.10S 140.41E
85 L16 **Mutoko** *prev.* Mtoko. Mashonaland East, NE Zimbabwe 17.24S 32.13E
83 J20 **Mutomo** Eastern, S Kenya 1.49S 38.13E
126 J12 **Mutoray** Evenkiyskiy Avtonomnyy Okrug, C Russian Federation 61.30N 101.00E
Mutrah *see* Maţraḩ
81 M24 **Mutshatsha** Katanga, S Dem. Rep. Congo 10.40S 24.25E
172 Nn8 **Mutsu** *var.* Mutu. Aomori, Honshū, N Japan 41.18N 141.11E
172 N8 **Mutsu-wan** *bay* N Japan
110 E6 **Muttenz** Basel-Land, NW Switzerland 47.31N 7.39E
193 A26 **Muttonbird Islands** *island group* SW NZ
Mutu *see* Mutsu
85 O15 **Mutuáli** Nampula, N Mozambique 14.51S 37.01E
84 D13 **Mutumbo** Bié, C Angola 13.10S 17.22E
201 Y14 **Mutunte, Mount** *var.* Mount Buache. ▲ Kosrae, E Micronesia 5.21N 163.00E
161 K24 **Mutur** Eastern Province, E Sri Lanka 8.27N 81.15E
94 L13 **Muurola** Lappi, NW Finland 66.21N 25.19E
168 M14 **Mu Us Shadi** *var.* Ordos Desert, *prev.* Mu Us Shamo. *desert* N China
Mu Us Shamo *see* Mu Us Shadi
84 B11 **Muxima** Bengo, NW Angola 9.27S 13.58E
128 I8 **Muyezerskiy** Respublika Kareliya, NW Russian Federation 63.54N 32.00E
83 E20 **Muyinga** NE Burundi 2.54S 30.19E
44 K9 **Muy Muy** Matagalpa, C Nicaragua 12.43N 85.37W
Muynak *see* Mo'ynoq
81 N22 **Muyumba** Katanga, SE Dem. Rep. Congo 7.13S 27.02E
155 V5 **Muzaffarābād** Jammu and Kashmir, NE Pakistan 34.24N 73.30E
155 S10 **Muzaffargarh** Punjab, E Pakistan 30.04N 71.10E
158 J9 **Muzaffarnagar** Uttar Pradesh, N India 29.28N 77.42E
159 P13 **Muzaffarpur** Bihār, N India 26.07N 85.22E
164 H6 **Muzat He** ≈ W China
85 L15 **Muze** Tete, NW Mozambique 15.05S 31.16E
125 Ff8 **Muzhi** Yamalo-Nenetskiy Avtonomnyy Okrug, N Russian Federation 65.25N 64.28E
104 H7 **Muzillac** Morbihan, NW France 47.34N 2.30W
Muzkol, Khrebet *see* Muzqŭl, Qatorkŭhi
114 L9 **Mužlja** *Hung.* Felsőmuzslya; *prev.* Gornja Mužlja. Serbia, N Serbia and Montenegro (Yugoslavia) 45.21N 20.25E
56 F9 **Muzo** Boyacá, C Colombia 5.34N 74.07W
85 J15 **Muzoka** Southern, S Zambia 16.39S 27.21E
41 Y15 **Muzon, Cape** *headland* Dall Island, Alaska, USA 54.39N 132.41W
42 M6 **Múzquiz** Coahuila de Zaragoza, NE Mexico 27.52N 101.31W
153 U13 **Muzqŭl, Qatorkŭhi** *Rus.* Khrebet Muzkol. ⛰ SE Tajikistan
164 G10 **Muztag** ▲ NW China 36.02N 80.13E
164 K10 **Muz Tag** ▲ W China 36.26N 87.15E
164 D8 **Muztagata** ▲ NW China 38.16N 75.03E
85 K17 **Mvuma** *prev.* Umvuma. Midlands, C Zimbabwe 19.16S 30.31E
84 L13 **Mwanya** Eastern, E Zambia 12.40S 32.15E
83 G20 **Mwanza** Mwanza, NW Tanzania 2.31S 32.55E
81 N23 **Mwanza** Katanga, SE Dem. Rep. Congo 7.49S 26.49E
83 F20 **Mwanza** ◈ *region* N Tanzania
84 M13 **Mwase Lundazi** Eastern, E Zambia 12.26S 33.20E
99 B17 **Mweelrea** *Ir.* Caoc Maol Réidh. ▲ W Ireland 53.37N 9.47W
81 K21 **Mweka** Kasai Occidental, C Dem. Rep. Congo 4.51S 21.37E
84 K12 **Mwenda** Luapula, N Zambia 10.25S 29.10E
81 L22 **Mwene-Ditu** Kasai Oriental, S Dem. Rep. Congo 7.05S 23.33E
85 L18 **Mwenezi** ≈ S Zimbabwe
81 O20 **Mwenga** Sud Kivu, E Dem. Rep. Congo 3.00S 28.28E
84 K11 **Mweru, Lake** *var.* Lac Moero. ◎ Dem. Rep. Congo/Zambia
84 H13 **Mwinilunga** North Western, NW Zambia 11.43S 24.24E
201 V16 **Mwokil Atoll** *var.* Mokil Atoll. *atoll* Caroline Islands, E Micronesia
Myadel' *see* Myadzyel
120 J13 **Myadzyel** *Pol.* Miadziol Nowy, *Rus.* Myadel'. Minskaya Voblasts', N Belarus 54.51N 26.51E
158 C12 **Myājlār** *var.* Miajlar. Rājasthān, NW India 26.16N 70.21E
127 O9 **Myakit** Magadanskaya Oblast', E Russian Federation 61.23N 151.58E
25 W13 **Myakka River** ≈ Florida, SE USA
128 L14 **Myaksa** Vologodskaya Oblast', NW Russian Federation 58.54N 38.15E
191 U8 **Myall Lake** ◎ New South Wales, SE Australia
177 Ff7 **Myanaung** Irrawaddy, SW Myanmar 18.16N 95.19E
178 Gg4 **Myanmar** *off.* Union of Myanmar, *var.* Burma. ◆ *military dictatorship* SE Asia
177 F9 **Myaungmya** Irrawaddy, SW Myanmar 16.33N 94.55E
120 N11 **Myazha** *Rus.* Mezha. Vitsyebskaya Voblasts', NE Belarus 55.40N 30.25E
121 O18 **Myerkulavichy** *Rus.* Merkulovichi. Homyel'skaya Voblasts', SE Belarus 52.57N 30.33E
121 N14 **Myezhava** *Rus.* Mezhëvo. Vitsyebskaya Voblasts', NE Belarus 54.39N 30.18E
177 Ff5 **Myingyan** Mandalay, C Myanmar 21.25N 95.19E
177 G5 **Myinmu** Sagaing, C Myanmar 21.58N 95.34E
178 Gg2 **Myitkyina** Kachin State, N Myanmar 25.24N 97.25E
177 G5 **Myittha** Mandalay, C Myanmar 21.21N 96.06E
113 H19 **Myjava** *Hung.* Miava. Trenčiansky Kraj, W Slovakia 48.48N 17.31E
Myjeldino *see* Myyëldino
119 U9 **Mykhaylivka** *Rus.* Mikhaylovka. Zaporiz'ka Oblast', SE Ukraine 47.16N 35.14E
97 A18 **Mykines** *Dan.* Myggenaes Island Faeroe Islands 62.07N 7.38W
118 I5 **Mykolayiv** L'vivs'ka Oblast', W Ukraine 49.34N 23.58E
119 Q10 **Mykolayiv** *Rus.* Nikolayev. Mykolayivs'ka Oblast', S Ukraine 46.57N 31.58E
119 Q10 **Mykolayiv** ✕ Mykolayivs'ka Oblast', S Ukraine 47.02N 31.54E
Mykolayiv *see* Mykolayivs'ka Oblast'
119 P9 **Mykolayivka** Odes'ka Oblast', SW Ukraine 47.34N 30.48E
119 S13 **Mykolayivka** Respublika Krym, S Ukraine 44.58N 33.37E
119 P9 **Mykolayivs'ka Oblast'** *var.* Mykolayiv, *Rus.* Nikolayevskaya Oblast'. ◈ *province* S Ukraine
117 J20 **Mýkonos** Mýkonos, Kykládes, Greece, Aegean Sea 37.27N 25.20E
117 K20 **Mýkonos** *var.* Míkonos. *island* Kykládes, Greece, Aegean Sea
129 R7 **Myla** Respublika Komi, NW Russian Federation 65.24N 50.51E
Mylae *see* Milazzo
95 M19 **Myllykoski** Etelä-Suomi, S Finland 60.45N 26.52E
Mymensing *see* Mymensingh
159 U14 **Mymensingh** *var.* Maimansingh, Mymensing; *prev.* Nasirābād. Dhaka, N Bangladesh 24.45N 90.22E
95 K19 **Mynämäki** Länsi-Suomi, W Finland 60.41N 22.00E
151 S14 **Mynaral** *Kaz.* Myngaral. Zhambyl, S Kazakhstan 45.25N 73.37E
Mynbulak *see* Mingbuloq

◆ Country ● Country Capital ◇ Dependent Territory ○ Dependent Territory Capital ◈ Administrative Region ✕ International Airport ▲ Mountain ⛰ Mountain Range Volcano ≈ River ◎ Lake ⊠ Reservoir

Mynbulak, Vpadina – Nares Abyssal Plain

Mynbulak, Vpadina see Mingbuloq Botig'I
Myngaral see Mynaral
177 F5 **Myohaung** Arakan State, W Myanmar 20.34N 93.12E
169 W13 **Myohyang-sanmaek** ▲▲ C North Korea
171 Jj13 **Myōkō-san** ▲ Honshū, S Japan 36.54N 138.05E
85 J15 **Myooye** Central, C Zambia 15.10S 27.24E
120 K12 **Myory** prev. Miyory. Vitsyebskaya Voblasts', N Belarus 55.39N 27.39E
94 J4 **Mýrdalsjökull** glacier S Iceland
94 G10 **Myre** Nordland, C Norway 68.54N 15.04E
119 S5 **Myrhorod** Rus. Mirgorod. Poltavs'ka Oblast', NE Ukraine 49.57N 33.36E
117 J15 **Mýrina** var. Mírina. Límnos, SE Greece 39.52N 25.04E
119 P5 **Myronivka** Rus. Mironovka. Kyyivs'ka Oblast', N Ukraine 49.40N 30.58E
23 U13 **Myrtle Beach** South Carolina, SE USA 33.41N 78.53W
34 F14 **Myrtle Creek** Oregon, NW USA 43.01N 123.19W
191 P11 **Myrtleford** Victoria, SE Australia 36.34S 146.45E
34 E14 **Myrtle Point** Oregon, NW USA 43.04N 124.08W
117 K25 **Mýrtos** Kríti, Greece, E Mediterranean Sea 35.00N 25.34E
Myrtoum Mare see Mirtóo Pélagos
95 G17 **Myrviken** Jämtland, C Sweden 62.59N 14.19E
97 I15 **Mysen** Østfold, S Norway 59.33N 11.19E
128 L15 **Myshkin** Yaroslavskaya Oblast', NW Russian Federation 57.47N 38.28E
113 K17 **Myślenice** Małopolskie, S Poland 49.49N 19.55E
112 D10 **Myślibórz** Zachodnio-pomorskie, NW Poland 52.55N 14.51E
161 G20 **Mysore** var. Maisur. Karnātaka, W India 12.18N 76.37E
Mysore see Karnātaka
117 F21 **Mystrás** var. Mistras. Pelopónnisos, S Greece 37.03N 22.22E
129 T12 **Mysy** Komi-Permyatskiy Avtonomnyy Okrug, NW Russian Federation 60.40N 53.59E
113 K15 **Myszków** Śląskie, S Poland 50.35N 19.16E
178 Jj14 **My Tho** var. Mi Tho. Tiên Giang, S Vietnam 10.21N 106.21E
Mytilene see Mytilíni
117 L17 **Mytilíni** var. Mitilíni; anc. Mytilene. Lésvos, E Greece 39.05N 26.33E
130 K3 **Mytishchi** Moskovskaya Oblast', W Russian Federation 56.00N 37.51E
39 N3 **Myton** Utah, W USA 40.11N 110.03W
94 K2 **Mývatn** ◎ C Iceland
129 T11 **Myyëldino** var. Myjeldino. Respublika Komi, NW Russian Federation 61.46N 54.48E
84 M13 **Mzimba** Northern, NW Malawi 11.56S 33.36E
84 M12 **Mzuzu** Northern, N Malawi 11.23S 34.03E

N

103 M19 **Naab** ≈ SE Germany
100 G12 **Naaldwijk** Zuid-Holland, W Netherlands 52.00N 4.13E
40 G12 **Nā'ālehu** var. Naalehu. Hawai'i, USA, C Pacific Ocean 19.04N 155.36W
95 K19 **Naantali** Swe. Nådendal. Länsi-Suomi, W Finland 60.25N 22.10E
100 J10 **Naarden** Noord-Holland, C Netherlands 52.18N 5.10E
111 U4 **Naarn** ≈ N Austria
99 F18 **Naas** Ir. An Nás, Nás na Ríogh. C Ireland 53.13N 6.39W
94 M9 **Näätämöjoki** Lapp. Njávdám. ≈ NE Finland
85 E23 **Nababeep** var. Nababiep. Northern Cape, W South Africa 29.36S 17.46E
Nababiep see Nababeep
Nabadwip see Navadwīp
171 H16 **Nabari** Mie, Honshū, SW Japan 34.37N 136.06E
Nabatié see Nabatîyé
144 G8 **Nabatîyé** var. An Nabatīyah at Taḥtā, Nabatié, Nabatiyet et Tahta. SW Lebanon 33.18N 35.36E
Nabatiyet et Tahta see Nabatîyé
197 I13 **Nabavatu** Vanua Levu, N Fiji 16.35S 178.55E
202 I2 **Nabeina** island Tungaru, W Kiribati
131 T4 **Naberezhnyye Chelny** prev. Brezhnev. Respublika Tatarstan, W Russian Federation 55.43N 52.21E
41 T10 **Nabesna** Alaska, USA 62.22N 143.00W
41 T10 **Nabesna River** ≈ Alaska, USA
77 N5 **Nabeul** var. Nābul. NE Tunisia 36.32N 10.45E
158 I9 **Nābha** Punjab, NW India 30.22N 76.12E
176 Ww11 **Nabire** Papua, E Indonesia 3.22S 135.31E
147 O15 **Nabī Shu'ayb, Jabal an** ▲ W Yemen 15.24N 44.04E
197 I13 **Nabiti** Vanua Levu, N Fiji 16.37S 178.54E
144 F10 **Nablus** var. Nāblus, Heb. Shekhem; anc. Neapolis, Bibl. Shechem. N West Bank 32.14N 35.16E
197 I13 **Nabouwalu** Vanua Levu, N Fiji 17.00S 178.43E
Nābul see Nabeul
Nābulus see Nablus
197 J13 **Nabuna** Vanua Levu, N Fiji 16.13S 179.46E
179 Rr15 **Nabunturan** Mindanao, S Philippines 7.34N 125.54E
85 Q14 **Nacala** Nampula, NE Mozambique 14.30S 40.37E
44 H8 **Nacaome** Valle, S Honduras 13.30N 87.31W
Na Cealla Beaga see Killybegs
Na-ch'ii see Nagqu
171 Gg17 **Nachikatsuura** var. Nachi-Katsuura. Wakayama, Honshū, SE Japan 33.37N 135.54E
83 J24 **Nachingwea** Lindi, SE Tanzania 10.21S 38.46E
113 F16 **Náchod** Královéhradecký Kraj, N Czech Republic 50.25N 16.09E
Na Clocha Liatha see Greystones
42 G3 **Naco** Sonora, NW Mexico 31.16N 109.56W
27 X8 **Nacogdoches** Texas, SW USA 31.36N 94.40W
42 G4 **Nacozari de García** Sonora, NW Mexico 30.27N 109.43W
197 H13 **Nacula** prev. Nathula. island Yasawa Group, NW Fiji
Nada see Danzhou
79 O14 **Nadawli** NW Ghana 10.30N 2.40W
106 I3 **Nadela** Galicia, NW Spain 42.58N 7.33W
Nådendal see Naantali
150 M7 **Nadezhdinka** prev. Nadezhdinskiy. Kostanay, N Kazakhstan 53.46N 63.43E
Nadezhdinskiy see Nadezhdinka
Nadgan see Nadqān, Qalamat
197 H14 **Nadi** prev. Nandi. Viti Levu, W Fiji 17.48S 177.25E
197 H14 **Nadi** prev. Nandi. ✕ Viti Levu, W Fiji 17.46S 177.28E
160 D10 **Nadiād** Gujarāt, W India 22.42N 72.54E
Ņadikdik see Knox Atoll
118 E11 **Nădlac** Ger. Nadlak, Hung. Nagylak. Arad, W Romania 46.10N 20.47E
Nadlak see Nădlac
76 H6 **Nador** prev. Villa Nador. NE Morocco 35.15N 2.56W
147 S9 **Nadqān, Qalamat** var. Nadgan. well E Saudi Arabia 23.10N 50.08E
113 N22 **Nádudvar** Hajdú-Bihar, E Hungary 47.26N 21.09E
123 J16 **Nadur** Gozo, N Malta 36.03N 14.18E
197 J13 **Naduri** prev. Nanduri. Vanua Levu, N Fiji 16.27S 179.10E
118 I7 **Nadvirna** Pol. Nadwórna, Rus. Nadvornaya. Ivano-Frankivs'ka Oblast', W Ukraine 48.27N 24.30E
128 J8 **Nadvoitsy** Respublika Kareliya, NW Russian Federation 63.52N 34.17E
Nadvornaya/Nadwórna see Nadvirna
126 Gg9 **Nadym** Yamalo-Nenetskiy Avtonomnyy Okrug, N Russian Federation 65.25N 72.40E
126 Gg9 **Nadym** ≈ C Russian Federation
194 J13 **Nadzab** Morobe, C PNG 6.36S 146.45E
79 X13 **Nafada** Gombe, E Nigeria 11.02N 11.18E
110 H8 **Näfels** Glarus, NE Switzerland 47.06N 9.04E
117 E18 **Náfpaktos** var. Návpaktos. Dytikí Ellás, C Greece 38.22N 21.49E
117 F20 **Náfplio** prev. Návplion. Pelopónnisos, S Greece 37.33N 22.50E
145 U6 **Nafṭ Khāneh** E Iraq 34.01N 45.26E
155 N13 **Nāg** Baluchistān, SW Pakistan 27.43N 65.31E
179 Q11 **Naga** off. Naga City; prev. Nueva Caceres. Luzon, N Philippines 13.36N 123.10E
Nagaarzê see Nagarzê
10 F11 **Nagagami** ≈ Ontario, S Canada
170 E14 **Nagahama** Ehime, Shikoku, SW Japan 33.36N 132.29E
171 Hh14 **Nagahama** Shiga, Honshū, SW Japan 35.22N 136.16E
159 X12 **Nāga Hills** ▲▲ NE India
171 Ll13 **Nagai** Yamagata, Honshū, C Japan 38.07N 140.02E
Na Gaibhlte see Galty Mountains
41 N16 **Nagai Island** island Shumagin Islands, Alaska, USA
159 X12 **Nāgāland** ⬖ state NE India
171 Jj13 **Nagano** Nagano, Honshū, S Japan 36.39N 138.10E
171 J14 **Nagano** off. Nagano-ken. ⬖ prefecture Honshū, S Japan
171 K13 **Nagaoka** Niigata, Honshū, C Japan 37.26N 138.48E
159 W12 **Nagaon** prev. Nowgong. Assam, NE India 26.21N 92.41E
161 J21 **Nāgappattinam** var. Negapatam, Negapattinam. Tamil Nādu, SE India 10.45N 79.49E
Nagara Nayok see Nakhon Nayok
Nagara Panom see Nakhon Phanom
Nagara Pathom see Nakhon Pathom
Nagara Sridharmaraj see Nakhon Si Thammarat
Nagara Svarga see Nakhon Sawan
161 H16 **Nāgārjuna Sāgar** ⊠ E India
44 I10 **Nagarote** León, SW Nicaragua 12.16N 86.33W
164 M16 **Nagarzê** var. Nagaarzê. Xizang Zizhiqu, W China 28.57N 90.25E
170 Bb13 **Nagasaki** Nagasaki, Kyūshū, SW Japan 32.45N 129.52E
170 Bb12 **Nagasaki** off. Nagasaki-ken. ⬖ prefecture Kyūshū, SW Japan
170 Bb14 **Naga-shima** island SW Japan
170 Dd13 **Naga-shima** island SW Japan
Nagashima see Kii-Nagashima
170 Dd12 **Nagato** Yamaguchi, Honshū, SW Japan 34.22N 131.10E
158 F11 **Nāgaur** Rājasthān, NW India 27.12N 73.43E
160 F10 **Nāgda** Madhya Pradesh, C India 23.28N 75.27E
100 L8 **Nagele** Flevoland, N Netherlands 52.39N 5.43E
161 H24 **Nāgercoil** Tamil Nādu, SE India 8.10N 77.30E
159 X12 **Nāginimāra** Nāgāland, NE India 26.43N 94.51E
Na Gleannta see Glenties
172 P14 **Nago** Okinawa, Okinawa, SW Japan 26.36N 127.58E
160 K9 **Nāgod** Madhya Pradesh, C India 24.36N 80.35E
161 J26 **Nagoda** Southern Province, S Sri Lanka 6.13N 80.13E
103 G22 **Nagold** Baden-Württemberg, SW Germany 48.33N 8.43E
Nagorno-Karabakhskaya Avtonomnaya Oblast see Nagorno-Karabakh
126 Ll13 **Nagornyy** Respublika Sakha (Yakutiya), NE Russian Federation 55.53N 124.58E
143 V12 **Nagorno-Karabakh** var. Nagorno-Karabakhskaya Avtonomnaya Oblast , Arm. Lerrnayin Gharabakh, Az. Dağliq Qarabağ, Rus. Nagornyy Karabakh. former autonomous region SW Azerbaijan
Nagornyy Karabakh see Nagorno-Karabakh
129 R13 **Nagorsk** Kirovskaya Oblast', NW Russian Federation 59.18N 50.49E
171 Hh15 **Nagoya** Aichi, Honshū, SW Japan 35.10N 136.52E
160 I12 **Nāgpur** Mahārāshtra, C India 21.09N 79.06E
162 K10 **Nagqu** Chin. Na-ch'ii; prev. Hei-ho. Xizang Zizhiqu, W China 31.30N 91.57E
158 J8 **Nāg Tibba Range** ▲▲ N India
47 O8 **Nagua** NE Dominican Republic 19.18N 69.48W
113 H25 **Nagyatád** Somogy, SW Hungary 46.14N 17.19E
Nagybánya see Baia Mare
Nagybecskerek see Zrenjanin
Nagydisznód see Cisnădie
Nagyenyed see Aiud
113 N21 **Nagykálló** Szabolcs-Szatmár-Bereg, E Hungary 47.49N 21.47E
113 G25 **Nagykanizsa** Ger. Grosskanizsa. Zala, SW Hungary 46.27N 17.00E
Nagykároly see Carei
113 K22 **Nagykáta** Pest, C Hungary 47.24N 19.43E
Nagykikinda see Kikinda
113 K23 **Nagykőrös** Pest, C Hungary 47.04N 19.45E
Nagy-Küküllő see Târnava Mare
Nagylak see Nădlac
Nagymihály see Michalovce
Nagyrőce see Revúca
Nagysomkút see Şomcuta Mare
Nagysurány see Šurany
Nagyszalonta see Salonta
Nagyszeben see Sibiu
Nagyszentmiklós see Sânnicolau Mare
Nagyszöllös see Vynohradiv
Nagyszombat see Trnava
Nagytapolcsány see Topoľčany
Nagyvárad see Oradea
172 Oo15 **Naha** Okinawa, Okinawa, SW Japan 26.10N 127.40E
158 J8 **Nāhan** Himāchal Pradesh, NW India 30.33N 77.18E
Nahang, Rūd-e see Nihing
Nahariya see Nahariyya
144 F8 **Nahariyya** var. Nahariya. Northern, N Israel 33.01N 35.04E
148 L6 **Nahāvand** var. Nehavend. Hamadān, W Iran 34.13N 48.21E
103 F19 **Nahe** ≈ SW Germany
Na h-Iarmhidhe see Westmeath
201 O13 **Nahnalaud** ▲ Pohnpei, E Micronesia
Nahoi, Cape see Cumberland, Cape
Nahtavárr see Nattavaara
65 H16 **Nahuel Huapi, Lago** ◎ W Argentina
25 W7 **Nahunta** Georgia, SE USA 31.11N 81.58W
42 J6 **Naica** Chihuahua, N Mexico 27.53N 105.30W
9 U15 **Naicam** Saskatchewan, S Canada 52.26N 104.30W
Naiman Qi see Daqin Tal
164 M4 **Naimin Bulak** spring NW China 44.57N 90.29E
11 P6 **Nain** Newfoundland and Labrador, NE Canada 56.33N 61.45W
149 P8 **Nā'īn** Eşfahān, C Iran 32.52N 53.04E
158 K10 **Naini Tāl** Uttaranchal, N India 29.22N 79.25E
160 J11 **Nainpur** Madhya Pradesh, C India 22.25N 80.10E
197 J14 **Nairai** island C Fiji
98 J8 **Nairn** N Scotland, UK 57.36N 3.51W
98 I8 **Nairn** cultural region NE Scotland, UK
83 I19 **Nairobi** ● (Kenya) Nairobi Area, S Kenya 1.16S 36.49E
83 I19 **Nairobi** ✕ Nairobi Area, S Kenya 1.21S 37.01E
84 P13 **Nairoto** Cabo Delgado, NE Mozambique 12.22S 39.05E
120 G3 **Naissaar** island N Estonia
Naissus see Niš
197 K13 **Naitaba** var. Naitauba; prev. Naitamba. island Lau Group, E Fiji
Naitamba/Naitauba see Naitaba
83 I19 **Naivasha** Rift Valley, SW Kenya 0.43S 36.25E
83 H19 **Naivasha, Lake** ◎ SW Kenya
Najaf see An Najaf
149 N8 **Najafābād** var. Nejafabad. Eşfahān, C Iran 32.37N 51.22E
147 N7 **Najd** var. Nejd. cultural region C Saudi Arabia
107 O4 **Nájera** La Rioja, N Spain 42.25N 2.45W
107 P4 **Najerilla** ≈ N Spain
169 U7 **Naji** var. Arun Qi. Nei Mongol Zizhiqu, N China 48.05N 123.28E
158 J9 **Najībābād** Uttar Pradesh, N India 29.37N 78.19E
Najima see Fukuoka
169 Y11 **Najin** NE North Korea 42.13N 130.15E
145 T9 **Najm al Ḥassūn** C Iraq 32.24N 44.13E
147 O13 **Najrān** var. Abā as Su'ūd. Najrān, S Saudi Arabia 17.31N 44.08E
147 P12 **Najrān** off. Minṭaqat al Najrān. ⬖ province S Saudi Arabia
170 Bb12 **Nakadōri-jima** island Gotō-rettō, SW Japan
172 Pp3 **Nakagawa** Hokkaidō, NE Japan 44.49N 142.04E
171 Kk15 **Naka-gawa** ≈ Honshū, S Japan
40 F9 **Nākālele Point** var. Nakalele Point headland Maui, Hawai'i, USA, C Pacific Ocean 21.01N 156.35W
170 D12 **Nakama** Fukuoka, Kyūshū, SW Japan 33.49N 130.42E
Nakambé see White Volta
Nakamti see Nek'emtē
170 E15 **Nakamura** Kōchi, Shikoku, SW Japan 33.00N 132.54E
195 O12 **Nakanai Mountains** ▲▲ New Britain, E PNG
171 Jj14 **Nakano** Nagano, Honshū, S Japan 36.43N 138.22E
170 Ff11 **Nakano-shima** island Oki-shotō, SW Japan
170 Ff12 **Nakano-umi** var. Naka-umi. ◎ Honshū, SW Japan
171 Mm8 **Nakasato** Aomori, Honshū, C Japan 40.58N 140.26E
172 P7 **Nakasatsunai** Hokkaidō, NE Japan 42.42N 143.09E
172 Qq7 **Nakashibetsu** Hokkaidō, NE Japan 43.31N 144.58E
83 F18 **Nakasongola** C Uganda 1.19N 32.28E
172 Pp3 **Nakatonbetsu** Hokkaidō, NE Japan 44.58N 142.18E
170 D13 **Nakatsu** var. Nakatu. Ōita, Kyūshū, SW Japan 33.34N 131.12E
171 I15 **Nakatsugawa** var. Nakatugawa. Gifu, Honshū, SW Japan 35.30N 137.29E
Nakatu see Nakatsu
Nakatugawa see Nakatsugawa
Naka-umi see Nakano-umi
172 O5 **Nakayama-tōge** pass Hokkaidō, NE Japan 42.51N 141.05E
Nakdong see Naktong-gang
Nakel see Nakło nad Notecią
82 J8 **Nakfa** N Eritrea 16.38N 38.26E
Nakhichevan' see Naxçıvan
127 Nn18 **Nakhodka** Primorskiy Kray, SE Russian Federation 42.46N 132.47E
126 H8 **Nakhodka** Yamalo-Nenetskiy Avtonomnyy Okrug, N Russian Federation 67.48N 77.48E
Nakhon Navok see Nakhon Nayok
178 Hh11 **Nakhon Nayok** var. Nagara Nayok, Nakhon Navok. Nakhon Nayok, C Thailand 14.12N 101.08E
178 H11 **Nakhon Pathom** var. Nagara Pathom, Nakorn Pathom. Nakhon Pathom, W Thailand 13.49N 100.06E
178 J9 **Nakhon Phanom** var. Nagara Panom. Nakhon Phanom, E Thailand 17.22N 104.46E
178 Hh10 **Nakhon Ratchasima** var. Khorat, Korat. Nakhon Ratchasima, E Thailand 15.00N 102.06E
178 H10 **Nakhon Sawan** var. Muang Nakhon Sawan, Nagara Svarga. Nakhon Sawan, W Thailand 15.42N 100.06E
178 H15 **Nakhon Si Thammarat** var. Nagara Sridharmaraj, Nakhon Sithamnaraj. Nakhon Si Thammarat, SW Thailand 8.24N 99.58E
Nakhon Sithamnaraj see Nakhon Si Thammarat
145 Y11 **Nakhrash** SE Iraq 31.13N 47.24E
8 I9 **Nakina** British Columbia, W Canada 59.12N 132.48W
112 H9 **Nakło nad Notecią** Ger. Nakel. Kujawsko-pomorskie, C Poland 53.07N 17.34E
41 P13 **Naknek** Alaska, USA 58.45N 157.01W
158 H8 **Nakodar** Punjab, NW India 31.06N 75.31E
84 M11 **Nakonde** Northern, NE Zambia 9.22S 32.45E
Nakorn Pathom see Nakhon Pathom
97 H24 **Nakskov** Storstrøm, SE Denmark 54.50N 11.05E
169 Y15 **Naktong-gang** var. Nakdong, Jap. Rakutō-kō. ≈ C South Korea
83 H18 **Nakuru** Rift Valley, SW Kenya 0.16S 36.04E
83 H19 **Nakuru, Lake** ◎ Rift Valley, C Kenya
9 O17 **Nakusp** British Columbia, SW Canada 50.13N 117.48W
155 N15 **Nāl** ≈ W Pakistan
168 M7 **Nalayh** Töv, C Mongolia 47.48N 107.17E
159 V12 **Nalbāri** Assam, NE India 26.36N 91.49E
65 G19 **Nalcayec, Isla** island Archipiélago de los Chonos, S Chile
131 N15 **Nal'chik** Kabardino-Balkarskaya Respublika, SW Russian Federation 43.29N 43.39E
161 I16 **Nalgonda** Andhra Pradesh, C India 17.04N 79.15E
159 S14 **Nalhāti** West Bengal, NE India 24.19N 87.52E
159 U14 **Nalitabari** Dhaka, N Bangladesh 25.06N 90.10E
161 I17 **Nallamala Hills** ▲▲ E India
142 G12 **Nallıhan** Ankara, NW Turkey 40.12N 31.22E
106 K2 **Nalón** ≈ NW Spain
178 Gg3 **Nalong** Kachin State, N Myanmar 24.42N 97.27E
77 N8 **Nālūt** NW Libya 31.52N 10.58E
176 Uu12 **Nama** Pulau Manawoka, E Indonesia 4.07S 131.22E
201 Q16 **Nama** island C Micronesia
85 O16 **Namacurra** Zambézia, NE Mozambique 17.31S 37.03E
196 F9 **Namai Bay** bay Babeldaob, N Palau
31 W2 **Namakan Lake** ◎ Canada/USA
149 O6 **Namak, Daryācheh-ye** marsh N Iran
149 T6 **Namak, Kavīr-e** salt pan NE Iran
178 H6 **Namaklwe** Shan State, E Myanmar 19.45N 99.01E
Namaksār, Kowl-e/Namakzār, Daryācheh-ye see Namakzar
154 I5 **Namakzar** Pash. Daryācheh-ye Namakzār, Kowl-e Namaksār. marsh Afghanistan/Iran
176 W13 **Namalau** Pulau Jursian, E Indonesia 5.50S 134.43E
83 I20 **Namanga** Rift Valley, S Kenya 2.33S 36.48E
153 S10 **Namangan** Namangan Viloyati, E Uzbekistan 40.59N 71.33E
Namanganskaya Oblast' see Namangan Viloyati
153 R10 **Namangan Viloyati** Rus. Namanganskaya Oblast'. ⬖ province E Uzbekistan
85 Q14 **Namapa** Nampula, NE Mozambique 13.43S 39.48E
85 C21 **Namaqualand** physical region S Namibia
83 G18 **Namasagali** C Uganda 1.01N 32.58E
195 P10 **Namatanai** New Ireland, NE PNG 3.42S 152.28E
85 I14 **Nambala** Central, C Zambia 15.06S 27.03E
83 J23 **Nambanje** Lindi, SE Tanzania 8.37S 38.21E
176 Ww9 **Namber** Papua, E Indonesia 0.58S 134.51E
85 G16 **Nambiya** Ngamiland, N Botswana 18.09S 23.08E
191 V2 **Nambour** Queensland, E Australia 26.43S 152.54E
191 V6 **Nambucca Heads** New South Wales, SE Australia 30.37S 153.00E
165 N15 **Nam Co** ◎ W China
178 Ii5 **Nậm Cum** Lai Châu, N Vietnam 22.37N 103.12E
Namdik see Namorik Atoll
178 Jj6 **Nam Định** Nam Ha, N Vietnam 20.25N 106.12E
175 Tt11 **Namea, Tanjung** headland Pulau Seram, SE Indonesia
101 I20 **Namêche** Namur, SE Belgium 50.29N 5.02E
32 J4 **Namekagon Lake** ◎ Wisconsin, N USA
196 F10 **Namekakl Passage** passage Babeldaob, N Palau
Namen see Namur
85 P15 **Nametil** Nampula, NE Mozambique 15.46S 39.21E
169 X14 **Nam-gang** ≈ C North Korea
169 Y16 **Nam-gang** ≈ S South Korea
169 Y17 **Namhae-do** Jap. Nankai-tō. island S South Korea
Namhoi see Foshan
85 C19 **Namib Desert** desert W Namibia
85 A15 **Namibe** Port. Moçâmedes, Mossâmedes. Namibe, SW Angola 15.10S 12.09E
85 A15 **Namibe** ⬖ province SE Angola
85 C18 **Namibia** off. Republic of Namibia, var. South West Africa, Afr. Suidwes-Afrika, Ger. Deutsch-Südwestafrika; prev. German Southwest Africa, South-West Africa. ◆ republic S Africa
67 O17 **Namibia Plain** undersea feature S Atlantic Ocean
171 Ll14 **Namie** Fukushima, Honshū, C Japan 37.29N 140.58E
171 Mm8 **Namioka** Aomori, Honshū, C Japan 40.43N 140.34E
42 I5 **Namiquipa** Chihuahua, N Mexico 29.15N 107.25W
165 P15 **Namjagbarwa Feng** ▲ W China 29.39N 95.00E
Namka see Doilungdêqên
175 Ss11 **Namlea** Pulau Buru, E Indonesia 3.12S 127.06E
164 L16 **Namling** Xizang Zizhiqu, W China 29.40N 88.58E
Namnetes see Nantes
178 Ii8 **Nam Ngum** ≈ C Laos
Namo see Namu Atoll
191 R5 **Namoi River** ≈ New South Wales, SE Australia
201 Q17 **Namoluk Atoll** atoll Mortlock Islands, C Micronesia
201 O15 **Namonuito Atoll** atoll Caroline Islands, C Micronesia
201 T9 **Namorik Atoll** var. Namdik. atoll Ralik Chain, S Marshall Islands
178 Ii6 **Nam Ou** ≈ N Laos
34 M14 **Nampa** Idaho, NW USA 43.32N 116.33W
78 M11 **Nampala** Ségou, W Mali 15.21N 5.32W
169 W14 **Namp'o** SW North Korea 38.45N 125.25E
85 P15 **Nampula** Nampula, NE Mozambique 15.09S 39.13E
85 P15 **Nampula** off. Província de Nampula. ⬖ province NE Mozambique
169 W13 **Namsan-ni** NW North Korea 40.25N 125.01E
Namslau see Namysłów
95 E15 **Namsos** Nord-Trøndelag, C Norway 64.28N 11.31E
95 F14 **Namsskogan** Nord-Trøndelag, C Norway 64.57N 13.04E
178 H6 **Nam Teng** ≈ E Myanmar
178 I6 **Nam Tha** ≈ N Laos
126 M10 **Namtsy** Respublika Sakha (Yakutiya), NE Russian Federation 62.42N 129.30E
178 Gg4 **Namtu** Shan State, E Myanmar 23.04N 97.25E
8 J15 **Namu** British Columbia, SW Canada 51.46N 127.49W
201 T7 **Namu Atoll** var. Namo. atoll Ralik Chain, C Marshall Islands
197 K15 **Namuka-i-lau** island Lau Group, E Fiji
85 O15 **Namuli, Mont** ▲ NE Mozambique 15.15S 37.33E
85 P14 **Namuno** Cabo Delgado, N Mozambique 13.36S 38.52E
101 I20 **Namur** Dut. Namen. Namur, SE Belgium 50.28N 4.52E
101 H21 **Namur** Dut. Namen. ⬖ province S Belgium
85 D17 **Namutoni** Kunene, N Namibia 18.47S 16.48E
169 Y16 **Namwŏn** Jap. Nangen. S South Korea 35.24N 127.20E
178 Mm14 **Namyit Island** island S Spratly Islands
113 H14 **Namysłów** Ger. Namslau. Opolskie, S Poland 51.05N 17.41E
178 Hh7 **Nan** var. Muang Nan. Nan, NW Thailand 18.47N 100.46E
81 G15 **Nana** ≈ W Central African Republic
172 Nn7 **Nanae** Hokkaidō, NE Japan 41.55N 140.40E
81 I14 **Nana-Grébizi** ⬖ prefecture N Central African Republic
8 L17 **Nanaimo** Vancouver Island, British Columbia, SW Canada 49.07N 123.58W
40 C9 **Nānākuli** var. Nanakuli. O'ahu, Hawai'i, USA, C Pacific Ocean 21.23N 158.09W
81 G15 **Nana-Mambéré** ⬖ prefecture W Central African Republic
167 R13 **Nan'an** Fujian, SE China 24.57N 118.22E
191 U2 **Nanango** Queensland, E Australia 26.42S 151.58E
171 Ii12 **Nanao** Ishikawa, Honshū, SW Japan 37.02N 136.57E
167 Q14 **Nan'ao Dao** island S China
171 Ii11 **Nanatsu-shima** island SW Japan
58 F8 **Nanay, Río** ≈ NE Peru
166 J8 **Nanbu** Sichuan, C China 31.19N 106.02E
169 X7 **Nancha** Heilongjiang, NE China 47.09N 129.16E
167 P10 **Nanchang** var. Nan-ch'ang, Nanch'ang-hsien. Jiangxi, S China 28.38N 115.57E
Nanch'ang-hsien see Nanchang
167 P11 **Nancheng** var. Jianchang. Jiangxi, S China 27.37N 116.37E
Nan-ching see Nanjing
166 J9 **Nanchong** Sichuan, C China 30.46N 106.03E
166 J10 **Nanchuan** Chongqing Shi, C China 29.06N 107.13E
105 T5 **Nancy** Meurthe-et-Moselle, NE France 48.40N 6.10E
193 A22 **Nancy Sound** sound South Island, NZ
158 L9 **Nanda Devi** ▲ NW India 30.27N 80.00E
44 J11 **Nandaime** Granada, SW Nicaragua 11.46N 86.03W
166 K13 **Nandan** Guangxi Zhuangzu Zizhiqu, S China 25.03N 107.31E
161 H14 **Nānded** Mahārāshtra, C India 19.10N 77.21E
170 G15 **Nanden** Hyōgo, Awaji-shima, SW Japan 34.19N 134.53E
191 S5 **Nandewar Range** ▲▲ New South Wales, SE Australia
Nandi see Nadi
166 E13 **Nanding He** ≈ China/Vietnam
Nándorhgy see Oţelu Roşu
160 E11 **Nandurbār** Mahārāshtra, W India 21.22N 74.18E
Nanduri see Naduri
161 I17 **Nandyāl** Andhra Pradesh, E India 15.30N 78.28E
167 P11 **Nanfeng** var. Qincheng. Jiangxi, S China 27.15N 116.30E
Nang see Nangxian
81 E15 **Nanga Eboko** Centre, C Cameroon 4.37N 12.21E
155 W4 **Nanga Parbat** ▲ India/Pakistan 35.15N 74.36E
174 L8 **Nangapinoh** Borneo, C Indonesia 0.21S 111.43E
155 R5 **Nangarhār** ⬖ province E Afghanistan
174 M8 **Nangaserawai** var. Nangah Serawai. Borneo, C Indonesia 0.19S 112.25E
174 L9 **Nangatayap** Borneo, C Indonesia 1.30S 110.33E
Nangen see Namwŏn
105 P5 **Nangis** Seine-et-Marne, N France 48.36N 3.02E
169 X13 **Nangnim-sanmaek** ▲▲ C North Korea
167 O4 **Nangong** Hebei, E China 37.24N 115.24E
165 Q14 **Nangqên** var. Xangda. Qinghai, C China 32.05N 96.28E
178 I11 **Nang Rong** Buri Ram, E Thailand 14.37N 102.48E
165 O16 **Nangxian** var. Nang. Xizang Zizhiqu, W China 29.04N 93.03E
Nan Hai see South China Sea
166 L8 **Nan He** ≈ C China
166 F12 **Nanhua** var. Longchuan. Yunnan, SW China 25.15N 101.15E
Naniwa see Ōsaka
161 G20 **Nanjangūd** Karnātaka, W India 12.07N 76.40E
167 Q8 **Nanjing** var. Nan-ching, Nanking; prev. Chianning, Chian-ning, Kiang-ning. Jiangsu, E China 32.03N 118.46E
Nankai-tō see Namhae-do
167 O12 **Nankang** var. Rongjiang. Jiangxi, S China 25.40N 114.40E
Nanking see Nanjing
170 F15 **Nankoku** Kōchi, Shikoku, SW Japan 33.34N 133.37E
167 N13 **Nan Ling** ▲▲ S China
166 L15 **Nanliu Jiang** ≈ S China
201 P13 **Nan Madol** ruins Temwen Island, E Micronesia
166 K15 **Nanning** var. Nan-ning; prev. Yung-ning. Guangxi Zhuangzu Zizhiqu, S China 22.49N 108.19E
206 M15 **Nanortalik** Kitaa, S Greenland 60.12N 44.53W
Nanouki see Aranuka
166 H13 **Nanpan Jiang** ≈ S China
158 M11 **Nānpāra** Uttar Pradesh, N India 27.51N 81.30E
167 Q12 **Nanping** var. Nan-p'ing; prev. Yenping. Fujian, SE China 26.40N 118.07E
Nanping see Jiuzhaigou
Nanpu see Pucheng
167 R12 **Nanri Dao** island SE China
172 Q13 **Nansei-shotō** Eng. Ryukyu Islands. island group SW Japan
Nansei Syotō Trench see Ryukyu Trench
207 T10 **Nansen Basin** undersea feature Arctic Ocean
207 T10 **Nansen Cordillera** var. Arctic-Mid Oceanic Ridge, Nansen Ridge. undersea feature Arctic Ocean
Nansen Ridge see Nansen Cordillera
133 T9 **Nan Shan** ▲▲ C China
179 Nn14 **Nanshan Island** island E Spratly Islands
Nansha Qundao see Spratly Islands
10 K3 **Nantais, Lac** ◎ Québec, NE Canada
105 N5 **Nanterre** Hauts-de-Seine, N France 48.52N 2.13E
104 I8 **Nantes** Bret. Naoned; anc. Condivincum, Namnetes. Loire-Atlantique, NW France 47.12N 1.31W
12 G17 **Nanticoke** Ontario, S Canada 42.49N 80.04W
20 H13 **Nanticoke** Pennsylvania, NE USA 41.12N 76.00W
23 Y4 **Nanticoke River** ≈ Delaware/Maryland, NE USA
9 Q17 **Nanton** Alberta, SW Canada 50.21N 113.46W
167 S8 **Nantong** Jiangsu, E China 32.00N 120.52E
167 S13 **Nant'ou** W Taiwan 23.54N 120.33E
105 S10 **Nantua** Ain, E France 46.10N 5.34E
21 Q13 **Nantucket** Nantucket Island, Massachusetts, NE USA 41.15N 70.05W
21 Q13 **Nantucket Island** island Massachusetts, NE USA
21 Q13 **Nantucket Sound** sound Massachusetts, NE USA
84 P13 **Nantulo** Cabo Delgado, N Mozambique 12.30S 39.03E
201 O12 **Nanuh** Pohnpei, E Micronesia
197 K13 **Nanuku Passage** channel NE Fiji
202 D6 **Nanumaga** var. Nanumanga. atoll NW Tuvalu
Nanumanga see Nanumaga
202 D5 **Nanumea Atoll** atoll NW Tuvalu
61 O19 **Nanuque** Minas Gerais, SE Brazil 17.49S 40.21W
175 Ss4 **Nanusa, Kepulauan** island group N Indonesia
169 U4 **Nanweng He** ≈ NE China
166 I10 **Nanxi** Sichuan, C China 28.54N 104.58E
167 N10 **Nanxian** var. Nan Xian, Nanzhou. Hunan, S China 29.23N 112.18E
167 N7 **Nanyang** var. Nan-yang. Henan, C China 32.58N 112.29E
167 P6 **Nanyang Hu** ◎ E China
171 L13 **Nan'yō** Yamagata, Honshū, C Japan 38.05N 140.07E
83 I18 **Nanyuki** Central, C Kenya 0.01N 37.04E
166 M8 **Nanzhang** Hubei, C China 31.47N 111.48E
Nanzhou see Nanxian
107 T11 **Nao, Cabo de La** headland E Spain 38.43N 0.13E
10 M9 **Naococane, Lac** ◎ Québec, E Canada
159 S14 **Naogaon** Rajshahi, NW Bangladesh 24.49N 88.58E
Naokot see Naukot
197 C12 **Naone** Maewo, C Vanuatu 15.03S 168.06E
Naoned see Nantes
117 E14 **Náousa** Kentrikí Makedonía, N Greece 40.38N 22.06E
37 N8 **Napa** California, W USA 38.15N 122.17W
41 O11 **Napaimiut** Alaska, USA 61.32N 158.46W
41 N12 **Napakiak** Alaska, USA 60.42N 161.57W
126 H7 **Napalkovo** Yamalo-Nenetskiy Avtonomnyy Okrug, N Russian Federation 70.06N 73.43E
10 I16 **Napanee** Ontario, SE Canada 44.13N 76.57W
176 Ww11 **Napanwainami** Papua, E Indonesia 3.01S 135.51E
176 W11 **Napan-Yaur** Papua, E Indonesia 2.55S 134.50E
41 N12 **Napaskiak** Alaska, USA 60.42N 161.46W
178 Jj5 **Na Phac** Cao Băng, N Vietnam 22.24N 105.54E
176 Ww9 **Napido** Papua, E Indonesia 0.41S 135.27E
192 O11 **Napier** Hawke's Bay, North Island, NZ 39.30S 176.55E
205 X3 **Napier Mountains** ▲▲ Antarctica
13 O13 **Napierville** Québec, SE Canada 45.12N 73.25W
25 W15 **Naples** Florida, SE USA 26.08N 81.48W
27 W5 **Naples** Texas, SW USA 33.12N 94.40W
Naples see Napoli
166 I14 **Napo** Guangxi Zhuangzu Zizhiqu, S China 23.21N 105.47E
58 C6 **Napo** ⬖ province NE Ecuador
31 O6 **Napoleon** North Dakota, N USA 46.30N 99.46W
33 R11 **Napoleon** Ohio, N USA 41.23N 84.07W
Napoléon-Vendée see la Roche-sur-Yon
24 J9 **Napoleonville** Louisiana, S USA 29.55N 91.01W
109 K17 **Napoli** Eng. Naples, Ger. Neapel; anc. Neapolis. Campania, S Italy 40.52N 14.15E
109 J18 **Napoli, Golfo di** gulf S Italy
59 F7 **Napo, Río** ≈ Ecuador/Peru
203 W9 **Napuka** island Îles Tuamotu, C French Polynesia
148 J3 **Naqadeh** Āẕarbāyjān-e Bākhtarī, NW Iran 36.57N 45.24E
145 U6 **Naqnah** E Iraq 34.13N 45.33E
Nar see Nera
171 H15 **Nara** Nara, Honshū, SW Japan 34.40N 135.49E
78 L11 **Nara** Koulikoro, W Mali 15.04N 7.19W
171 Gg16 **Nara** off. Nara-ken. ⬖ prefecture Honshū, SW Japan
155 R14 **Nāra Canal** irrigation canal S Pakistan
190 K11 **Naracoorte** South Australia 37.01S 140.45E
191 P8 **Naradhan** New South Wales, SE Australia 33.37S 146.19E
Naradhivas see Narathiwat
58 B8 **Naranjal** Guayas, W Ecuador 2.39S 79.34W
59 Q19 **Naranjos** Santa Cruz, E Bolivia
43 Q12 **Naranjos** Veracruz-Llave, E Mexico 21.20N 97.42W
165 Q6 **Naran Sebstein Bulag** spring NW China 42.40N 96.58E
149 X12 **Narānū** Sīstān va Balūchestān, SE Iran
170 Bb12 **Narao** Nagasaki, Nakadōri-jima, SW Japan 32.40N 129.03E
161 J16 **Narasaraopet** Andhra Pradesh, E India 16.16N 80.06E
164 J5 **Narat** Xinjiang Uygur Zizhiqu, W China 43.19N 84.01E
178 Hh17 **Narathiwat** var. Naradhivas. Narathiwat, SW Thailand 6.25N 101.48E
39 V10 **Nara Visa** New Mexico, SW USA 35.35N 103.06W
Nārāyāni see Gandak
Narbada see Narmada
Narbo Martius see Narbonne
105 P16 **Narbonne** anc. Narbo Martius. Aude, S France 43.11N 3.00E
Narborough Island see Fernandina, Isla
106 J2 **Narcea** ≈ NW Spain
158 J9 **Narendranagar** Uttaranchal, N India 30.10N 78.21E
Nares Abyssal Plain see Nares Plain

◆ Country
● Country Capital
◇ Dependent Territory
○ Dependent Territory Capital
⬖ Administrative Region
✕ International Airport
▲ Mountain
▲▲ Mountain Range
Volcano
≈ River
◎ Lake
⊠ Reservoir

NARES PLAIN – NESSELSDORF

66 G11 **Nares Plain** *var.* Nares Abyssal Plain. *undersea feature* NW Atlantic Ocean
207 P10 **Nares Strait** *Dan.* Nares Stræde. *strait* Canada/Greenland
Nares Stræde *see* Nares Strait
112 O9 **Narew** ≈ E Poland
161 F17 **Nargund** Karnātaka, W India 15.43N 75.23E
85 D20 **Narib** Hardap, S Namibia 24.10S 17.46E
Narikrik *see* Knox Atoll
Narin Gol *see* Dong He
56 B13 **Nariño** *off.* Departamento de Nariño. ◐ *province* SW Colombia
171 Kk17 **Narita** Chiba, Honshū, S Japan 35.46N 140.17E
171 Kk17 **Narita** ✈ (Tōkyō) Chiba, Honshū, S Japan 35.45N 140.23E
Narıya *see* An Nu'ayrīyah
168 F5 **Nariyn Gol** ≈ Mongolia/Russian Federation
158 J8 **Nārkanda** Himāchal Pradesh, NW India 31.13N 77.27E
94 L13 **Narkaus** Lappi, NW Finland 66.13N 26.09E
160 E11 **Narmada** *var.* Narbada. ≈ C India
158 H11 **Narnaul** *var.* Nārnaul. Haryāna, N India 28.05N 76.12E
109 I14 **Narni** Umbria, C Italy 42.31N 12.31E
109 J24 **Naro** Sicilia, Italy, C Mediterranean Sea 37.18N 13.48E
Narodichi *see* Narodychi
129 V7 **Narodnaya, Gora** ▲ NW Russian Federation 65.04N 60.12E
119 N3 **Narodychi** *Rus.* Narodichi. Zhytomyrs'ka Oblast', N Ukraine 51.11N 29.01E
130 J4 **Naro-Fominsk** Moskovskaya Oblast', W Russian Federation 55.25N 36.41E
83 H19 **Narok** Rift Valley, SW Kenya 1.04S 35.54E
106 H2 **Narón** Galicia, NW Spain 43.31N 8.08W
191 S11 **Narooma** New South Wales, SE Australia 36.16S 150.08E
Narova *see* Narva
Narovlya *see* Narowlya
155 W8 **Nārowāl** Punjab, E Pakistan 32.04N 74.54E
121 N20 **Narowlya** *Rus.* Narovlya. Homyel'skaya Voblasts', SE Belarus 51.49N 29.30E
95 J17 **Närpes** *Fin.* Närpiö. Länsi-Suomi, W Finland 62.28N 21.19E
Närpiö *see* Närpes
191 S5 **Narrabri** New South Wales, SE Australia 30.21S 149.48E
191 P9 **Narrandera** New South Wales, SE Australia 34.46S 146.32E
191 Q4 **Narran Lake** ◎ New South Wales, SE Australia
191 Q4 **Narran River** ≈ New South Wales/Queensland, SE Australia
188 J13 **Narrogin** Western Australia 32.52S 117.16E
191 Q7 **Narromine** New South Wales, SE Australia 32.16S 148.15E
23 R6 **Narrows** Virginia, NE USA 37.19N 80.48W
206 M15 **Narsarsuaq** ✈ Kitaa, S Greenland 61.07N 45.03W
160 I10 **Narsimhapur** Madhya Pradesh, C India 22.58N 79.15E
Narsingdi *see* Narsinghdi
159 U15 **Narsinghdi** *var.* Narsingdi. Dhaka, C Bangladesh 23.55N 90.40E
160 H9 **Narsinghgarh** Madhya Pradesh, C India 23.45N 77.04E
169 Q11 **Nart** Nei Mongol Zizhiqu, N China 42.54N 115.55E
Nartës, Gjol i/Nartës, Laguna e *see* Nartës, Liqeni i
115 J22 **Nartës, Liqeni i** *var.* Gjol i Nartës, Laguna e Nartës. ◎ SW Albania
117 F17 **Nartháki** ▲ C Greece 39.12N 22.24E
131 O15 **Nartkala** Kabardino-Balkarskaya Respublika, SW Russian Federation 43.34N 43.55E
170 Ff15 **Naruto** Tokushima, Shikoku, SW Japan 34.09N 134.34E
120 K3 **Narva** Ida-Virumaa, NE Estonia 59.22N 28.12E
120 K4 **Narva** *prev.* Narova. ≈ Estonia/Russian Federation
120 J3 **Narva Bay** *Est.* Narva Laht, *Ger.* Narwa-Bucht, *Rus.* Narvskiy Zaliv. *bay* Estonia/Russian Federation
Narva Laht *see* Narva Bay
128 F13 **Narva Reservoir** *Est.* Narva Veehoidla, *Rus.* Narvskoye Vodokhranilishche. ⊞ Estonia/Russian Federation
Narva Veehoidla *see* Narva Reservoir
94 H10 **Narvik** Nordland, C Norway 68.25N 17.24E
Narvskiy Zaliv *see* Narva Bay
Narvskoye Vodokhranilishche *see* Narva Reservoir
Narwa-Bucht *see* Narva Bay
158 I9 **Narwāna** Haryāna, NW India 29.40N 76.10E
129 R4 **Nar'yan-Mar** *prev.* Beloshchel'ye, Dzerzhinskiy. Nenetskiy Avtonomnyy Okrug, NW Russian Federation 67.38N 53.00E
126 H12 **Narym** Tomskaya Oblast', C Russian Federation 58.59N 81.20E
151 Y10 **Narymskiy Khrebet** *Kaz.* Naryn Zhotasy. ▲▲ E Kazakhstan
153 W9 **Naryn** Narynskaya Oblast', C Kyrgyzstan 41.24N 75.59E
153 U8 **Naryn** ≈ Kyrgyzstan/Uzbekistan
151 W16 **Narynkol** *Kaz.* Naryngol. Almaty, SE Kazakhstan 42.41N 80.10E
Naryn Oblasty *see* Narynskaya Oblast'
Narynqol *see* Narynkol
153 V9 **Narynskaya Oblast'** *Kir.* Naryn Oblasty. ◐ *province* C Kyrgyzstan
Naryn Zhotasy *see* Narymskiy Khrebet
130 J6 **Naryshkino** Orlovskaya Oblast', W Russian Federation 53.00N 35.41E
97 L14 **Nås** Dalarna, C Sweden 60.28N 14.30E
94 G13 **Nasafjellet** *Lapp.* Násávárre. ▲ C Norway 66.29N 15.23E
95 H16 **Näsåker** Västernorrland, C Sweden 63.27N 16.55E
197 J14 **Nasau** Koro, C Fiji 17.20S 179.26E
118 I9 **Năsăud** *Ger.* Nussdorf, *Hung.* Naszód. Bistriţa-Năsăud, N Romania 47.16N 24.24E
Násávárre *see* Nasafjellet
105 P13 **Nasbinals** Lozère, S France 44.40N 3.03E
Na Sceirí *see* Skerries
Nase *see* Naze
193 E22 **Naseby** Otago, South Island, NZ 45.02S 170.09E
149 R10 **Nāşerīyeh** Kermān, C Iran
27 X5 **Nash** Texas, SW USA 33.26N 94.04W
160 E13 **Nāshik** *prev.* Nāsik. Mahārāshtra, W India 20.04N 73.48E
58 E7 **Nashiño, Río** ≈ Ecuador/Peru
31 W12 **Nashua** Iowa, C USA 42.57N 92.32W
35 W7 **Nashua** Montana, NW USA 48.06N 106.16W
21 O10 **Nashua** New Hampshire, NE USA 42.45N 71.26W
29 S13 **Nashville** Arkansas, C USA 33.57N 93.51W
25 U7 **Nashville** Georgia, SE USA 31.12N 83.15W
32 L16 **Nashville** Illinois, N USA 38.20N 89.22W
33 O14 **Nashville** Indiana, N USA 39.13N 86.15W
23 V9 **Nashville** North Carolina, SE USA 35.58N 77.58W
22 J8 **Nashville** *state capital* Tennessee, S USA 36.10N 86.48W
22 J9 **Nashville** ✈ Tennessee, S USA 36.06N 86.44W
66 H10 **Nashville Seamount** *undersea feature* NW Atlantic Ocean 30.00N 57.20W
114 H9 **Našice** Osijek-Baranja, E Croatia 45.29N 18.05E
112 M11 **Nasielsk** Mazowieckie, C Poland 52.33N 20.46E
95 K18 **Näsijärvi** ◎ SW Finland
Nāsik *see* Nāshik
82 G13 **Nasir** Upper Nile, SE Sudan 8.37N 33.06E
155 Q12 **Nasīrābād** Baluchistān, SW Pakistan 28.29N 68.24E
154 K15 **Nasīrābād** Baluchistān, SW Pakistan 28.25N 68.28E
Nasīrābād *see* Mymensingh
Nasir, Buhayrat/Nasîr, Buheiret *see* Nasser, Lake
Nāsiri *see* Ahvāz
Nasiriya *see* An Nāşirīyah
Nás na Ríogh *see* Naas
109 L23 **Naso** Sicilia, Italy, C Mediterranean Sea 38.07N 14.46E
Nasratabad *see* Zābol
8 J11 **Nass** ≈ British Columbia, SW Canada
79 V15 **Nassarawa** Nassarawa, C Nigeria 8.33N 7.42E
46 H2 **Nassau** ● (Bahamas) New Providence, N Bahamas 25.03N 77.20W
46 H2 **Nassau** ✈ New Providence, C Bahamas 25.00N 77.26W
202 J13 **Nassau** *island* N Cook Islands
25 W8 **Nassau Sound** *sound* Florida, SE USA
110 L7 **Nassereith** Tirol, W Austria 47.19N 10.51E
97 L19 **Nässjö** Jönköping, S Sweden 57.39N 14.40E
101 K22 **Nassogne** Luxembourg, SE Belgium 50.08N 5.19E
10 J6 **Nastapoka Islands** *island group* Nunavut, C Canada
95 M19 **Nastola** Etelä-Suomi, S Finland 60.57N 25.55E
171 L14 **Nasu-dake** ▲ Honshū, S Japan 37.07N 139.57E
179 P11 **Nasugbu** Luzon, N Philippines 14.03N 120.39E
96 N11 **Näsviken** Gävleborg, C Sweden 61.46N 16.55E
Naszód *see* Năsăud
85 I17 **Nata** Central, NE Botswana 20.10S 26.10E
56 E11 **Natagaima** Tolima, C Colombia 3.30N 75.06W
61 Q14 **Natal** Rio Grande do Norte, E Brazil 5.46S 35.15W
173 Ff8 **Natal** Sumatera, N Indonesia 0.25N 99.09E
Natal *see* KwaZulu/Natal
181 L10 **Natal Basin** *var.* Mozambique Basin. *undersea feature* W Indian Ocean
27 R12 **Natalia** Texas, SW USA 29.11N 98.51W
69 W15 **Natal Valley** *undersea feature* SW Indian Ocean
Natanya *see* Netanya
149 O7 **Naţanz** Eşfahān, C Iran 33.31N 51.55E
11 Q11 **Natashquan** Québec, E Canada 50.10N 61.49W
11 Q10 **Natashquan** ≈ Newfoundland and Labrador/Québec, E Canada
24 J7 **Natchez** Mississippi, S USA 31.33N 91.24W
24 G6 **Natchitoches** Louisiana, S USA 31.45N 93.05W
110 E10 **Naters** Valais, S Switzerland 46.22N 8.00E
Nathanya *see* Netanya
94 O3 **Nathorst Land** *physical region* W Svalbard
Nathula *see* Nacula
194 J15 **National Capital District** ◐ *province* S PNG
37 U17 **National City** California, W USA 32.40N 117.06W
190 M10 **National Park** Manawatu-Wanganui, North Island, NZ 39.11S 175.22E
79 R14 **Natitingou** NW Benin 10.21N 1.25E
42 B5 **Natividad, Isla** *island* W Mexico
171 M13 **Natori** Miyagi, Honshū, C Japan 38.11N 140.52E
20 C14 **Natrona Heights** Pennsylvania, NE USA 40.37N 79.42W
83 H20 **Natron, Lake** ◎ Kenya/Tanzania
Natsrat *see* Nazerat
177 Ff7 **Nattalin** Pegu, C Myanmar 18.25N 95.34E
94 J12 **Nattavaara** *Lapp.* Nahtavárr. Norrbotten, N Sweden 66.45N 20.58E
111 S3 **Natternbach** Oberösterreich, N Austria 48.26N 13.44E
97 M22 **Nättraby** Blekinge, S Sweden 56.12N 15.30E
174 K4 **Natuna Besar, Pulau** *island* Kepulauan Natuna, W Indonesia
174 **Natuna Islands** *see* Natuna, Kepulauan
174 Jj5 **Natuna, Kepulauan** *var.* Natuna Islands. *island group* W Indonesia
174 J6 **Natuna, Laut** *sea* W Indonesia
23 N6 **Natural Bridge** *tourist site* Kentucky, C USA 37.44N 83.37W
181 V11 **Naturaliste Fracture Zone** *tectonic feature* E Indian Ocean
182 J10 **Naturaliste Plateau** *undersea feature* E Indian Ocean
Nau *see* Nov
105 O14 **Naucelle** Aveyron, S France 44.10N 2.19E
85 D20 **Nauchas** Hardap, C Namibia 23.36S 16.21E
110 K9 **Nauders** Tirol, W Austria 46.52N 10.31E
Naugard *see* Nowogard
120 F12 **Naujamiestis** Panevėžys, C Lithuania 55.42N 24.10E
120 E10 **Naujoji Akmenė** Šiauliai, NW Lithuania 56.20N 22.57E
155 R16 **Naukot** *var.* Naokot. Sind, SE Pakistan 24.52N 69.27E
103 L16 **Naumburg** *var.* Naumburg an der Saale. Sachsen-Anhalt, C Germany 51.09N 11.48E
Naumburg am Queis *see* Nowogrodziec
Naumburg an der Saale *see* Naumburg
203 W15 **Naunau** *ancient monument* Easter Island, Chile, E Pacific Ocean
144 G10 **Nā'ūr** Al 'Āşimah, W Jordan 31.52N 35.49E
201 Q8 **Nauru** *off.* Republic of Nauru; *prev.* Pleasant Island. ◆ *republic* W Pacific Ocean
183 P5 **Nauru** *island* W Pacific Ocean
201 Q9 **Nauru International** ✈ S Nauru
Nausari *see* Navsāri
21 Q12 **Nauset Beach** *beach* Massachusetts, NE USA
Naushahra *see* Nowshera
155 P14 **Naushahro Firoz** Sind, SE Pakistan 26.53N 68.12E
Naushara *see* Nowshera
197 I14 **Nausori** Viti Levu, W Fiji 17.48S 177.35E
59 F9 **Nauta** Loreto, N Peru 4.31S 73.35W
159 O12 **Nautanwa** Uttar Pradesh, N India 27.25N 83.25E
43 R13 **Nautla** Veracruz-Llave, E Mexico 20.12N 96.46W
Nauzad *see* Now Zād
43 N6 **Nava** Coahuila de Zaragoza, NE Mexico 28.28N 100.45W
Navabad *see* Navobod
106 L6 **Nava del Rey** Castilla-León, N Spain 41.19N 5.04W
159 S15 **Navadwīp** *prev.* Nabadwip. West Bengal, NE India 23.24N 88.22E
197 J14 **Navaga** Koro, W Fiji 17.21S 179.22E
106 M9 **Navahermosa** Castilla-La Mancha, C Spain 39.39N 4.25W
121 I16 **Navahrudak** *Pol.* Nowogródek, *Rus.* Novogrudok. Hrodzyenskaya Voblasts', W Belarus 53.34N 25.54E
121 I16 **Navahrudskaye Wzvyshsha** ▲ W Belarus
38 M8 **Navajo Mount** ▲ Utah, W USA 37.00N 110.52W
39 Q9 **Navajo Reservoir** ⊞ New Mexico, SW USA
179 Qq12 **Naval** Biliran Island, C Philippines 11.32N 124.26E
106 K9 **Navalmoral de la Mata** Extremadura, W Spain 39.54N 5.33W
106 K10 **Navalvillar de Pelea** Extremadura, W Spain 39.05N 5.27W
99 F17 **Navan** *Ir.* An Uaimh. E Ireland 53.39N 6.40W
Navanagar *see* Jāmnagar
120 L12 **Navapolatsk** *Rus.* Novopolotsk. Vitsyebskaya Voblasts', N Belarus 55.33N 28.34E
155 P6 **Nāvar, Dasht-e** *Pash.* Dasht-i-Nawar. *desert* C Afghanistan
127 Q5 **Navarin, Mys** *headland* NE Russian Federation 62.18N 179.06E
65 I25 **Navarino, Isla** *island* S Chile
107 Q4 **Navarra** *Eng./Fr.* Navarre. ◐ *autonomous community* N Spain
Navarre *see* Navarra
107 P4 **Navarrete** La Rioja, N Spain 42.25N 2.34W
63 C20 **Navarro** Buenos Aires, E Argentina 35.01S 59.18W
107 O12 **Navas de San Juan** Andalucía, S Spain 38.10N 3.19W
27 V10 **Navasota** Texas, SW USA 30.23N 96.05W
27 U9 **Navasota River** ≈ Texas, SW USA
46 I9 **Navassa Island** ◇ *US unincorporated territory* C West Indies
121 L19 **Navasyolki** *Rus.* Novosëlki. Homyel'skaya Voblasts', SE Belarus 52.24N 28.27E
121 H17 **Navayel'nya** *Pol.* Nowojelnia, *Rus.* Novoyel'nya. Hrodzyenskaya Voblasts', W Belarus 53.26N 25.36E
176 Yy11 **Naver** Papua, E Indonesia 3.27S 139.45E
120 H5 **Navesti** ≈ C Estonia
106 J2 **Navia** Asturias, N Spain 43.33N 6.43W
106 J2 **Navia** ≈ NW Spain
61 I21 **Naviraí** Mato Grosso do Sul, SW Brazil 23.01S 54.09W
197 G14 **Naviti** *island* Yasawa Group, NW Fiji
130 I6 **Navlya** Bryanskaya Oblast', W Russian Federation 52.47N 34.28E
197 J13 **Navoalevu** Vanua Levu, N Fiji 16.22S 179.28E
153 R12 **Navobod** *Rus.* Navabad, Novabad. C Tajikistan 39.00N 70.06E
153 P13 **Navobod** *Rus.* Navabad. W Tajikistan 38.37N 68.42E
Navoi *see* Navoiy
152 M11 **Navoiy** *Rus.* Navoi. Navoiy Viloyati, C Uzbekistan 40.05N 65.22E
Navoiyskaya Oblast' *see* Navoiy Viloyati
152 K8 **Navoiy Viloyati** *Rus.* Navoiyskaya Oblast'. ◐ *province* N Uzbekistan
42 G7 **Navojoa** Sonora, NW Mexico 27.04N 109.28W
Navolat *see* Navolato
42 H9 **Navolato** *var.* Navolat. Sinaloa, C Mexico 24.46N 167.42W
197 C12 **Navonda** Ambae, C Vanuatu 15.21S 167.58E
Návpaktos *see* Náfpaktos
Návplion *see* Náfplio
79 P14 **Navrongo** N Ghana 10.54N 1.03W
160 D12 **Navsāri** *var.* Nausari. Gujarāt, W India 20.55N 72.55E
197 I15 **Navua** Viti Levu, W Fiji 18.13S 178.10E
144 H8 **Nawá** Dar'ā, S Syria 32.52N 36.03E
Nawabashah *see* Nawābshāh
159 S14 **Nawābganj** Rajshahi, NW Bangladesh 24.36N 88.17E
159 S14 **Nawābganj** Uttar Pradesh, N India 26.52N 82.09E
155 Q15 **Nawābshāh** *var.* Nawabashah. Sind, S Pakistan 26.15N 68.25E
159 P14 **Nawāda** Bihār, N India 24.54N 85.33E
158 H11 **Nawalgarh** Rājasthān, N India 27.51N 75.16E
Nawāl, Sabkhat an *see* Noual, Sebkhet en
Nawar, Dasht-i- *see* Nāvar, Dasht-e
178 Gg4 **Nawnghkio** *var.* Nawngkio. Shan State, C Myanmar 22.21N 96.48E
Nawngkio *see* Nawnghkio
143 U13 **Naxçıvan** *Rus.* Nakhichevan'. SW Azerbaijan 39.13N 45.24E
166 I10 **Naxi** Sichuan, C China 28.48N 105.25E
117 K21 **Náxos** *var.* Naxos. Náxos, Kykládes, Greece, Aegean Sea 37.06N 25.22E
117 K21 **Náxos** *island* Kykládes, Greece, Aegean Sea
42 J11 **Nayarit** ◐ *state* C Mexico
197 K14 **Nayau** *island* Lau Group, E Fiji
149 S8 **Nāy Band** Yazd, E Iran 32.26N 57.30E
172 Pp4 **Nayoro** Hokkaidō, NE Japan 44.21N 142.27E
106 F9 **Nazaré** *var.* Nazare. Leiria, C Portugal 39.36N 9.04W
26 M4 **Nazareth** Texas, SW USA 34.32N 102.06W
Nazareth *see* Nazerat
181 O8 **Nazareth Bank** *undersea feature* W Indian Ocean
126 Hh14 **Nazarovo** Krasnoyarskiy Kray, S Russian Federation 56.00N 89.33E
42 K9 **Nazas** Durango, C Mexico 25.16N 104.04W
59 F16 **Nazca** Ica, S Peru 14.52S 75.01W
(0) L17 **Nazca Plate** *tectonic feature*
200 Oo11 **Nazca Ridge** *undersea feature* E Pacific Ocean
172 R13 **Naze** *var.* Nase. Kagoshima, Amami-ōshima, SW Japan 28.21N 129.30E
144 G9 **Nazerat** *var.* Natsrat, *Ar.* En Nazira, *Eng.* Nazareth. Northern, N Israel 32.42N 35.18E
143 R14 **Nazik Gölü** ◎ E Turkey
142 C15 **Nazilli** Aydın, SW Turkey 37.55N 28.19E
143 P14 **Nazimiye** Tunceli, E Turkey 39.12N 39.51E
126 Gg11 **Nazino** Tomskaya Oblast', C Russian Federation 60.02N 78.51E
Nazinon *see* Red Volta
8 L15 **Nazko** British Columbia, SW Canada 52.57N 123.44W
131 O16 **Nazran'** Ingushskaya Respublika, SW Russian Federation 43.15N 44.52E
82 J13 **Nazrēt** *var.* Adama, Hadama. Oromo, C Ethiopia 8.31N 39.20E
Nazwāh *see* Nizwá
125 Ff13 **Nazyvayevsk** Omskaya Oblast', C Russian Federation 55.35N 71.13E
84 J13 **Nchanga** Copperbelt, C Zambia 12.30S 27.52E
84 K11 **Nchelenge** Luapula, N Zambia 9.24S 28.45E
Ncheu *see* Ntcheu
Ndaghamcha, Sebkra de *see* Te-n-Dghâmcha, Sebkhet
83 G21 **Ndala** Tabora, C Tanzania 4.45S 33.15E
84 B11 **N'Dalatando** *Port.* Salazar, Vila Salazar. Cuanza Norte, NW Angola 9.18S 14.48E
79 S14 **Ndali** C Benin 9.52N 2.44E
83 E18 **Ndeke** SW Uganda 0.11S 30.04E
80 J13 **Ndélé** Bamingui-Bangoran, N Central African Republic 8.24N 20.40E
81 E19 **Ndendé** Ngounié, S Gabon 2.21S 11.19E
81 E20 **Ndindi** Nyanga, S Gabon 3.46S 11.06E
80 G11 **Ndjamena** *var.* N'Djamena; *prev.* Fort-Lamy. ● (Chad) Chari-Baguirmi, W Chad 12.08N 15.01E
80 G11 **Ndjamena** ✈ Chari-Baguirmi, W Chad 12.09N 15.00E
81 D18 **Ndjolé** Moyen-Ogooué, W Gabon 0.07S 10.45E
84 J13 **Ndola** Copperbelt, C Zambia 12.58S 28.35E
Ndrhamcha, Sebkha de *see* Te-n-Dghâmcha, Sebkhet
81 L15 **Ndu** Orientale, N Dem. Rep. Congo 4.46N 22.54E
83 H21 **Nduguti** Singida, C Tanzania 4.19S 34.40E
195 X16 **Nduindui** Guadalcanal, C Solomon Islands 9.46S 159.54E
Nea Anchialos *see* Néa Anchíalos
117 F16 **Néa Anchiálos** *var.* Nea Anhialos, Néa Ankhíalos. Thessalía, C Greece 39.18N 22.49E
Nea Anhialos/Nea Ankhíalos *see* Néa Anchiálos
117 H18 **Néa Artáki** Évvoia, C Greece 38.31N 23.39E
99 F15 **Neagh, Lough** ◎ E Northern Ireland, UK
34 F7 **Neah Bay** Washington, NW USA 48.21N 124.39W
117 J22 **Nea Kaméni** *island* Kykládes, Greece, Aegean Sea
189 O8 **Neale, Lake** ◎ Northern Territory, C Australia
190 G2 **Neales River** *seasonal river* South Australia
117 G14 **Néa Moudanía** *var.* Néa Moudhaniá. Kentrikí Makedonía, N Greece 40.15N 23.19E
Néa Moudhaniá *see* Néa Moudanía
118 K10 **Neamţ** ◐ *county* NE Romania
Neapel *see* Napoli
117 D14 **Neápoli** *prev.* Neápolis. Dytikí Makedonía, N Greece 40.18N 21.23E
117 K25 **Neápoli** Kríti, Greece, E Mediterranean Sea 35.15N 25.37E
117 G22 **Neápoli** Pelopónnisos, S Greece 36.29N 23.05E
Neapolis *see* Napoli, Italy
Neapolis *see* Nablus, West Bank
Neápolis *see* Neápoli, Greece
40 D16 **Near Islands** *island group* Aleutian Islands, Alaska, USA
99 J21 **Neath** S Wales, UK 51.39N 3.48W
116 H13 **Néa Zíchni** *var.* Néa Zíkhni; *prev.* Néa Zíkhna. Kentrikí Makedonía, NE Greece 41.02N 23.51E
Néa Zíkhna/Néa Zíkhni *see* Néa Zíchni
44 C5 **Nebaj** Quiché, W Guatemala 15.25N 91.05W
79 P13 **Nebbou** S Burkina 11.22N 1.49W
Nebitdag *see* Balkanabat
56 M13 **Neblina, Pico da** ▲ NW Brazil 0.49N 66.31W
128 I13 **Nebolchi** Novgorodskaya Oblast', W Russian Federation 59.08N 33.19E
38 L4 **Nebo, Mount** ▲ Utah, W USA 39.47N 111.46W
30 L14 **Nebraska** *off.* State of Nebraska; also known as Blackwater State, Cornhusker State, Tree Planters State. ◐ *state* C USA
31 S16 **Nebraska City** Nebraska, C USA 40.38N 95.52W
109 K23 **Nebrodi, Monti** *var.* Monti Caronie. ▲▲ Sicilia, Italy, C Mediterranean Sea
8 L14 **Nechako** ≈ British Columbia, SW Canada
31 Q2 **Neche** North Dakota, N USA 48.57N 97.33W
27 V8 **Neches** Texas, SW USA 31.51N 95.28W
27 W8 **Neches River** ≈ Texas, SW USA
103 H20 **Neckar** ≈ SW Germany
103 H20 **Neckarsulm** Baden-Württemberg, SW Germany 49.12N 9.13E
199 K5 **Necker Island** *island* C British Virgin Islands
183 U3 **Necker Ridge** *undersea feature* N Pacific Ocean
63 D23 **Necochea** Buenos Aires, E Argentina 38.33S 58.42W
106 H2 **Neda** Galicia, NW Spain 43.28N 8.09W
117 E20 **Nédas** ≈ S Greece
27 Y11 **Nederland** Texas, SW USA 29.58N 93.59W
Nederland *see* Netherlands
100 K12 **Neder Rijn** *Eng.* Lower Rhine. ≈ C Netherlands
101 L16 **Nederweert** Limburg, SE Netherlands 51.16N 5.45E
97 G16 **Nedre Tokke** ◎ S Norway
Nedrigaylov *see* Nedryhayliv
119 S3 **Nedryhayliv** *Rus.* Nedrigaylov. Sums'ka Oblast', NE Ukraine 50.51N 33.52E
100 O11 **Neede** Gelderland, E Netherlands 52.07N 6.36E
35 T13 **Needle Mountain** ▲ Wyoming, C USA 44.03N 109.33W
37 Y14 **Needles** California, W USA 34.50N 114.37W
99 M24 **Needles, The** *rocks* Isle of Wight, S England, UK
64 O7 **Ñeembucú** *off.* Departamento de Ñeembucú. ◐ *department* SW Paraguay
32 M7 **Neenah** Wisconsin, N USA 44.09N 88.26W
9 W16 **Neepawa** Manitoba, S Canada 50.13N 99.28W
101 J16 **Neerpelt** Limburg, NE Belgium 51.13N 5.25E
76 M6 **Nefta** ✈ W Tunisia 34.03N 8.05E
130 L15 **Neftegorsk** Krasnodarskiy Kray, SW Russian Federation 44.21N 39.40E
131 U3 **Neftekamsk** Respublika Bashkortostan, W Russian Federation 56.06N 54.12E
131 O14 **Neftekumsk** Stavropol'skiy Kray, SW Russian Federation 44.45N 45.00E
125 G11 **Nefteyugansk** Khanty-Mansiyskiy Avtonomnyy Okrug, C Russian Federation 61.07N 72.18E
Neftezavodsk *see* Seýdi
84 C10 **Negage** *var.* N'Gage. Uíge, NW Angola 7.46S 15.27E
Negapatam/Negapattinam *see* Nāgappattinam
175 N16 **Negara** Bali, Indonesia 8.21S 114.34E
175 N10 **Negara** Borneo, C Indonesia 2.40S 115.04E
Negara Brunei Darussalam *see* Brunei
33 N4 **Negaunee** Michigan, N USA 46.30N 87.36W
83 J15 **Negēlē** *var.* Negelli, *It.* Neghelli. Oromo, C Ethiopia 5.13N 39.43E
Negelli *see* Negēlē
Negeri Pahang Darul Makmur *see* Pahang
Negeri Selangor Darul Ehsan *see* Selangor
174 H5 **Negeri Sembilan** *var.* Negri Sembilan. ◐ *state* Peninsular Malaysia
94 P3 **Negerpynten** *headland* S Svalbard 77.15N 22.40E
Negev *see* HaNegev
Neghelli *see* Negēlē
118 I12 **Negoiu** *var.* Negoiul. ▲ S Romania 45.34N 24.34E
Negoiul *see* Negoiu
84 P13 **Negomane** *var.* Negomano. Cabo Delgado, N Mozambique 11.22S 38.32E
Negomano *see* Negomane
161 J25 **Negombo** Western Province, SW Sri Lanka 7.13N 79.51E
Negoreloye *see* Nyeharelaye
114 P12 **Negotin** Serbia, E Serbia and Montenegro (Serbia and Montenegro (Yugoslavia)) 44.13N 22.31E
115 P19 **Negotino** C FYR Macedonia 41.29N 22.04E
58 A10 **Negra, Punta** *headland* NW Peru 6.03S 81.08W
106 G3 **Negreira** Galicia, NW Spain 42.54N 8.46W
118 L10 **Negreşti** Vaslui, E Romania 46.49N 27.28E
Negreşti *see* Negreşti-Oaş
118 H8 **Negreşti-Oaş** *Hung.* Avasfelsőfalu; *prev.* Negreşti. Satu Mare, NE Romania 47.56N 23.21E
46 H12 **Negril** W Jamaica 18.16N 78.21W
Negri Sembilan *see* Negeri Sembilan
65 K15 **Negro, Río** ≈ E Argentina
64 N7 **Negro, Río** ≈ NE Argentina
59 N17 **Negro, Río** ≈ E Bolivia
64 O5 **Negro, Río** ≈ C Paraguay
50 F6 **Negro, Río** ≈ N South America
63 E18 **Negro, Río** ≈ Brazil/Uruguay
Negro, Río *see* Sico Tinto, Río, Honduras
Negro, Río *see* Chixoy, Río, Guatemala/Mexico
179 Q14 **Negros** *island* C Philippines
118 M15 **Negru Vodă** Constanţa, SE Romania 43.47N 28.10E
11 P13 **Neguac** New Brunswick, SE Canada 47.16N 65.04W
12 B7 **Negwazu, Lake** ◎ Ontario, S Canada
Négyfalu *see* Săcele
34 F10 **Nehalem** Oregon, NW USA 45.42N 123.55W
34 F10 **Nehalem River** ≈ Oregon, NW USA
Nehavend *see* Nahāvand
149 V9 **Nehbandān** Khorāsān, E Iran 31.33N 60.01E
169 V6 **Nehe** Heilongjiang, NE China 48.28N 124.52E
200 Ss12 **Neiafu** 'Uta Vava'u, N Tonga 18.36S 173.58W
47 N9 **Neiba** *var.* Neyba. SW Dominican Republic 18.27N 71.28W
Néid, Carn Uí *see* Mizen Head
94 M9 **Neiden** Finnmark, N Norway 69.40N 29.22E
Neidín *see* Kenmare
Néifinn *see* Nephin
105 S10 **Neige, Crêt de la** ▲ E France 46.18N 5.58E
181 O16 **Neiges, Piton des** ▲ C Réunion 21.04S 55.28E
13 R9 **Neiges, Rivière des** ≈ Québec, SE Canada
166 I10 **Neijiang** Sichuan, C China 29.31N 105.03E
32 K6 **Neillsville** Wisconsin, N USA 44.34N 90.36W
Nei Monggol Zizhiqu/Nei Mongol *see* Nei Mongol Zizhiqu
169 Q10 **Nei Mongol Gaoyuan** *plateau* NE China
169 O12 **Nei Mongol Zizhiqu** *var.* Nei Mongol, *Eng.* Inner Mongolia, Inner Mongolian Autonomous Region; *prev.* Nei Monggol Zizhiqu. ◐ *autonomous region* N China
167 O4 **Neiqiu** Hebei, E China 37.22N 114.34E
Neiriz *see* Neyrīz
103 Q16 **Neisse** *Cz.* Lužická Nisa, *Ger.* Lausitzer Neisse, *Pol.* Nisa, Nysa Łużycka. ≈ C Europe
Neisse *see* Nysa
56 E11 **Neiva** Huila, S Colombia 2.58N 75.15W
166 M7 **Neixiang** Henan, C China 33.07N 111.49E
Nejafabad *see* Najafābād
9 V9 **Nejanilini Lake** ◎ Manitoba, C Canada
Nejd *see* Najd
82 I13 **Nek'emtē** *var.* Lakemti, Nakamti. Oromo, C Ethiopia 9.06N 36.31E
130 M9 **Nekhayevskiy** Volgogradskaya Oblast', SW Russian Federation 50.25N 41.44E
32 K7 **Nekoosa** Wisconsin, N USA 44.19N 89.54W
Neksø *see* Nexø
117 C16 **Nekyomanteío** *ancient monument* Ípeiros, W Greece 39.13N 20.31E
106 H7 **Nelas** Viseu, N Portugal 40.31N 7.52W
128 H16 **Nelidovo** Tverskaya Oblast', W Russian Federation 56.13N 32.45E
31 P13 **Neligh** Nebraska, C USA 42.07N 98.01W
127 N12 **Nel'kan** Khabarovskiy Kray, E Russian Federation 57.44N 136.09E
94 M10 **Nellim** *var.* Nellimö, *Lapp.* Njellim. Lappi, N Finland 68.49N 28.18E
Nellimö *see* Nellim
161 J18 **Nellore** Andhra Pradesh, E India 14.29N 80.00E
127 O16 **Nel'ma** Khabarovskiy Kray, SE Russian Federation 47.43N 139.08E
63 B17 **Nelson** Santa Fe, C Argentina 31.16S 60.45W
9 O17 **Nelson** British Columbia, SW Canada 49.29N 117.13W
193 I14 **Nelson** Nelson, South Island, NZ 41.16S 173.16E
99 L17 **Nelson** NW England, UK 53.51N 2.13W
31 P17 **Nelson** Nebraska, C USA 40.12N 98.04W
193 J14 **Nelson** ◐ *unitary authority* South Island, NZ
9 X12 **Nelson** ≈ Manitoba, C Canada
191 U8 **Nelson Bay** New South Wales, SE Australia 32.45S 152.09E
190 K13 **Nelson, Cape** *headland* Victoria, SE Australia 38.25S 141.33E
194 M15 **Nelson, Cape** *headland* S PNG 8.57S 149.19E
65 G23 **Nelson, Estrecho** *strait* SE Pacific Ocean
9 W12 **Nelson House** Manitoba, C Canada 55.49N 98.51W
32 J4 **Nelson Lake** ◎ Wisconsin, N USA
33 T14 **Nelsonville** Ohio, N USA 39.27N 82.13W
29 S2 **Nelson River** ≈ Iowa/Missouri, C USA
85 K21 **Nelspruit** Mpumalanga, NE South Africa 25.28S 30.58E
78 L10 **Néma** Hodh ech Chargui, SE Mauritania 16.31N 7.12W
120 D13 **Neman** *Ger.* Ragnit. Kaliningradskaya Oblast', W Russian Federation 55.01N 22.00E
86 I9 **Neman** *Bel.* Nyoman, *Ger.* Memel, *Lith.* Nemunas, *Pol.* Niemen, *Rus.* Neman. ≈ NE Europe
Nemausus *see* Nîmes
117 F19 **Neméa** Pelopónnisos, S Greece 37.49N 22.40E
Německý Brod *see* Havlíčkův Brod
12 D7 **Nemegosenda** ≈ Ontario, S Canada
12 D8 **Nemegosenda Lake** ◎ Ontario, S Canada
121 H14 **Nemencinė** Vilnius, SE Lithuania 54.50N 25.29E
Nemetocenna *see* Arras
Nemirov *see* Nemyriv
105 O6 **Nemours** Seine-et-Marne, N France 48.16N 2.40E
Nemunas *see* Neman
172 R7 **Nemuro** Hokkaidō, NE Japan 43.19N 145.34E
172 R7 **Nemuro-hantō** *peninsula* Hokkaidō, NE Japan
172 R6 **Nemuro-kaikyō** *strait* Japan/Russian Federation
172 R7 **Nemuro-wan** *bay* N Japan
118 H5 **Nemyriv** *Rus.* Nemirov. L'vivs'ka Oblast', NW Ukraine 50.07N 23.27E
119 N7 **Nemyriv** *Rus.* Nemirov. Vinnyts'ka Oblast', C Ukraine 48.57N 28.51E
99 D19 **Nenagh** *Ir.* An tAonach. C Ireland 52.52N 8.12W
41 R9 **Nenana** Alaska, USA 64.33N 149.05W
41 R9 **Nenana River** ≈ Alaska, USA
195 W8 **Nendö** *var.* Swallow Island. *island* Santa Cruz Islands, E Solomon Islands
99 O19 **Nene** ≈ E England, UK
129 R4 **Nenetskiy Avtonomnyy Okrug** ◐ *autonomous district* NW Russian Federation
203 W11 **Nengonengo** *atoll* Îles Tuamotu, C French Polynesia
169 U6 **Nen Jiang** *var.* Nonni. ≈ NE China
169 V6 **Nenjiang** Heilongjiang, NE China 49.10N 125.18E
201 P16 **Neoch** *atoll* Caroline Islands, C Micronesia
117 D18 **Neochóri** Dytikí Ellás, C Greece 38.23N 21.14E
29 Q7 **Neodesha** Kansas, C USA 37.25N 95.40W
31 S14 **Neola** Iowa, C USA 41.27N 95.40W
117 M19 **Néon Karlovási** *var.* Néon Karlovásion. Sámos, Dodekánisos, Greece, Aegean Sea 37.48N 26.42E
Néon Karlovásion *see* Néon Karlovási
117 E16 **Néon Monastíri** Thessalía, C Greece 39.22N 21.55E
29 R8 **Neosho** Missouri, C USA 36.52N 94.22W
29 Q7 **Neosho River** ≈ Kansas/Oklahoma, C USA
127 N17 **Nepa** ≈ C Russian Federation
159 N10 **Nepal** *off.* Kingdom of Nepal. ◆ *monarchy* S Asia
158 M11 **Nepalganj** Mid Western, SW Nepal 28.04N 81.37E
12 L13 **Nepean** Ontario, SE Canada 45.19N 75.53W
38 L4 **Nephi** Utah, W USA 39.43N 111.49W
99 B16 **Nephin** *Ir.* Néifinn. ▲ W Ireland 54.00N 9.21W
69 T9 **Nepoko** ≈ NE Dem. Rep. Congo
20 K15 **Neptune** New Jersey, NE USA 40.10N 74.03W
190 G10 **Neptune Islands** *island group* South Australia
109 I14 **Nera** *anc.* Nar. ≈ C Italy
104 L14 **Nérac** Lot-et-Garonne, SW France 44.07N 0.21E
113 D16 **Neratovice** *Ger.* Neratowitz. Středočeský Kraj, C Czech Republic 50.16N 14.31E
Neratowitz *see* Neratovice
126 L15 **Nercha** ≈ S Russian Federation
126 L15 **Nerchinsk** Chitinskaya Oblast', S Russian Federation 52.01N 116.25E
126 L16 **Nerchinskiy Zavod** Chitinskaya Oblast', S Russian Federation 51.13N 119.25E
128 M15 **Nerekhta** Kostromskaya Oblast', NW Russian Federation 57.27N 40.33E
120 H10 **Nereta** Aizkraukle, S Latvia 56.12N 25.18E
108 K13 **Nereto** Abruzzo, C Italy 42.49N 13.50E
115 H15 **Neretva** ≈ Bosnia and Herzegovina/Croatia
117 C17 **Nerikós** *ruins* Lefkáda, Iónioi Nísoi, Greece, C Mediterranean Sea 38.48N 20.43E
85 F15 **Neriquinha** Cuando Cubango, SE Angola 15.44S 21.34E
120 I13 **Neris** *Bel.* Viliya, *Pol.* Wilia; *prev. Pol.* Wilja. ≈ Belarus/Lithuania
Neris *see* Viliya
107 N15 **Nerja** Andalucía, S Spain 36.45N 3.34W
128 L16 **Nerl'** ≈ W Russian Federation
176 Vv13 **Nerong, Selat** *strait* Kepulauan Kai, E Indonesia
107 P12 **Nerpio** Castilla-La Mancha, C Spain 38.08N 2.18W
106 J13 **Nerva** Andalucía, S Spain 37.39N 6.31W
126 Ll13 **Neryungri** Respublika Sakha (Yakutiya), NE Russian Federation 56.37N 124.19E
100 L4 **Nes** Friesland, N Netherlands 53.28N 5.46E
96 G13 **Nesbyen** Buskerud, S Norway 60.34N 9.34E
94 L2 **Neskaupstadhur** Austurland, E Iceland 65.08N 13.45W
94 F13 **Nesna** Nordland, C Norway 66.11N 12.54E
28 K5 **Ness City** Kansas, C USA 38.27N 99.54W
Nesselsdorf *see* Kopřivnice

◆ Country ● Country Capital ◇ Dependent Territory ○ Dependent Territory Capital ◐ Administrative Region ✈ International Airport ▲ Mountain ▲▲ Mountain Range Volcano ≈ River ◎ Lake ⊞ Reservoir

NIĞDE – NORTH BRANCH NEALES

142 J15 **Niğde** ◈ province C Turkey
85 J21 **Nigel** Gauteng, NE South Africa 26.25S 28.28E
79 V10 **Niger** off. Republic of Niger. ◆ republic W Africa
79 T14 **Niger** ◈ state C Nigeria
69 P8 **Niger** ≈ W Africa
Niger Cone see Niger Fan
69 P9 **Niger Delta** delta S Nigeria
69 P9 **Niger Fan** var. Niger Cone. undersea feature E Atlantic Ocean
79 T13 **Nigeria** off. Federal Republic of Nigeria. ◆ federal republic W Africa
79 T17 **Niger, Mouths of the** delta S Nigeria
193 C24 **Nightcaps** Southland, South Island, NZ 45.58S 168.03E
12 F7 **Night Hawk Lake** ◎ Ontario, S Canada
67 M19 **Nightingale Island** island S Tristan da Cunha, S Atlantic Ocean
40 M12 **Nightmute** Alaska, USA 60.28N 164.43W
116 G13 **Nigrita** Kentrikí Makedonía, NE Greece 40.54N 23.28E
154 J15 **Nihing** Per. Rūd-e Nahang. ≈ Iran/Pakistan
203 V10 **Nihiru** atoll Îles Tuamotu, C French Polynesia
Nihommatsu see Nihonmatsu
Nihon see Japan
171 L13 **Nihonmatsu** var. Nihommatsu, Nihonmatu. Fukushima, Honshū, C Japan 37.35N 140.22E
Nihonmatu see Nihonmatsu
64 I12 **Nihuil, Embalse del** ⊡ W Argentina
171 K12 **Niigata** Niigata, Honshū, C Japan 37.55N 139.01E
171 K13 **Niigata** off. Niigata-ken. ◈ prefecture Honshū, C Japan
170 F15 **Niihama** Ehime, Shikoku, SW Japan 33.57N 133.15E
40 A8 **Ni'ihau** var. Niihau. island Hawai'i, USA, C Pacific Ocean
172 Ss13 **Nii-jima** island E Japan
170 Ff13 **Niimi** Okayama, Honshū, SW Japan 35.00N 133.27E
171 Kk13 **Niitsu** var. Niitu. Niigata, Honshū, C Japan 37.48N 139.06E
Niitu see Niitsu
107 P15 **Níjar** Andalucía, S Spain 36.57N 2.13W
100 K11 **Nijkerk** Gelderland, C Netherlands 52.13N 5.30E
101 H16 **Nijlen** Antwerpen, N Belgium 51.10N 4.40E
100 L13 **Nijmegen** Ger. Nimwegen; anc. Noviomagus. Gelderland, SE Netherlands 51.49N 5.52E
100 N10 **Nijverdal** Overijssel, E Netherlands 52.22N 6.28E
202 G16 **Nikao** Rarotonga, S Cook Islands
Nikaria see Ikaría
128 I2 **Nikel'** Murmanskaya Oblast', NW Russian Federation 69.24N 30.12E
175 Rr17 **Nikiniki** Timor, S Indonesia 10.00S 124.30E
133 Q15 **Nikitin Seamount** undersea feature E Indian Ocean 5.48S 84.48E
79 S14 **Nikki** E Benin 9.55N 3.12E
171 Kk15 **Nikkō** var. Nikko. Tochigi, Honshū, S Japan 36.45N 139.37E
Niklasmarkt see Gheorgheni
41 P10 **Nikolai** Alaska, USA 63.00N 154.22W
Nikolaiken see Mikołajki
Nikolainkaupunki see Länsi-Suomi
Nikolayev see Mykolayiv
151 O6 **Nikolayevka** Severnyy Kazakhstan, N Kazakhstan
Nikolayevka see Zhetigen
131 P9 **Nikolayevsk** Volgogradskaya Oblast', SW Russian Federation 50.03N 45.30E
Nikolayevskaya Oblast' see Mykolayivs'ka Oblast'
127 Nn14 **Nikolayevsk-na-Amure** Khabarovskiy Kray, SE Russian Federation 53.04N 140.39E
131 P6 **Nikol'sk** Penzenskaya Oblast', W Russian Federation 53.46N 46.03E
129 O13 **Nikol'sk** Vologodskaya Oblast', NW Russian Federation 59.35N 45.31E
Nikol'sk see Ussuriysk
40 K17 **Nikolski** Umnak Island, Alaska, USA 52.56N 168.52W
Nikol'skiy see Satpayev
131 V7 **Nikol'skoye** Orenburgskaya Oblast', W Russian Federation 52.01N 55.48E
Nikol'sk-Ussuriyskiy see Ussuriysk
116 J7 **Nikopol** anc. Nicopolis. Pleven, N Bulgaria 43.43N 24.55E
119 S9 **Nikopol'** Dnipropetrovs'ka Oblast', SE Ukraine 47.34N 34.23E
117 C17 **Nikópoli** anc. Nicopolis. site of ancient city Ípeiros, W Greece 39.01N 20.43E
142 M12 **Niksar** Tokat, N Turkey 40.36N 36.54E
149 V14 **Nīkshahr** Sīstān va Balūchestān, SE Iran 26.15N 60.10E
115 J16 **Nikšić** Montenegro, SW Serbia and Montenegro (Yugoslavia) 42.46N 18.56E
203 R4 **Nikumaroro** prev. Gardner Island, Kemins Island. atoll Phoenix Islands, C Kiribati
203 P3 **Nikunau** var. Nukunau; prev. Byron Island. atoll Tungaru, W Kiribati
161 G21 **Nilambūr** Kerala, SW India 11.16N 76.15E
37 X16 **Niland** California, W USA 33.14N 115.31W
69 T3 **Nile** Ar. Nahr an Nil. ≈ N Africa
82 G8 **Nile** former province NW Uganda
77 W7 **Nile Delta** delta N Egypt
69 T3 **Nile Fan** undersea feature E Mediterranean Sea
33 O11 **Niles** Michigan, N USA 41.49N 86.15W
33 V11 **Niles** Ohio, N USA 41.10N 80.46W
161 F20 **Nileswaram** Kerala, SW India 12.18N 75.07E
12 K10 **Nilgaut, Lac** ◎ Québec, SE Canada
164 I5 **Nilka** Xinjiang Uygur Zizhiqu, NW China 43.46N 82.33E
Nil, Nahr an see Nile
95 N16 **Nilsiä** Itä-Suomi, C Finland 63.13N 28.00E
160 F9 **Nīmach** Madhya Pradesh, C India 24.30N 74.51E
158 G14 **Nimbāhera** Rājasthān, N India 24.37N 74.45E
78 L15 **Nimba, Monts** var. Nimba Mountains. ▲▲ W Africa
Nimba Mountains see Nimba, Monts
Nimburg see Nymburk
105 Q15 **Nîmes** anc. Nemausus, Nismes. Gard, S France 43.49N 4.19E
158 H11 **Nīm ka Thāna** Rājasthān, N India 27.44N 75.44E
191 R11 **Nimmitabel** New South Wales, SE Australia 36.34S 149.18E
Nimptsch see Niemcza
205 R11 **Nimrod Glacier** glacier Antarctica
Nimroze see Nīmrūz
154 K8 **Nīmrūz** var. Nimroze; prev. Chakhānsūr. ◈ province SW Afghanistan
83 F16 **Nimule** Eastern Equatoria, S Sudan 3.33N 32.06E
Nimwegen see Nijmegen
161 C23 **Nine Degree Channel** channel India/Maldives
20 G9 **Ninemile Point** headland New York, NE USA 43.31N 76.22W
181 S8 **Ninetyeast Ridge** undersea feature E Indian Ocean
191 P13 **Ninety Mile Beach** beach Victoria, SE Australia
192 I2 **Ninety Mile Beach** beach North Island, NZ
23 P12 **Ninety Six** South Carolina, SE USA 34.10N 82.01W
169 Y9 **Ning'an** Heilongjiang, NE China 44.20N 129.28E
167 S9 **Ningbo** var. Ning-po, Yin-hsien; prev. Ninghsien. Zhejiang, SE China 29.54N 121.33E
167 U12 **Ningde** Fujian, SE China 26.48N 119.33E
167 P12 **Ningdu** var. Meijiang. Jiangxi, S China 26.28N 115.58E
Ning'er see Pu'er
194 E12 **Ningerum** Western, SW PNG 5.43S 141.09E
167 R9 **Ningguo** Anhui, E China 30.33N 118.58E
167 S9 **Ninghai** Zhejiang, SE China 29.19N 121.22E
Ning-hsia see Ningxia
Ninghsien see Ningbo
166 J15 **Ningming** var. Chengzhong. Guangxi Zhuangzu Zizhiqu, S China 22.07N 106.43E
166 H11 **Ningnan** var. Pisha. Sichuan, C China 26.59N 102.49E
Ning-po see Ningbo
Ningsia/Ningsia Hui/Ningsia Hui Autonomous Region see Ningxia
166 J5 **Ningxia** off. Ningxia Huizu Zizhiqu, var. Ning-hsia, Ningsia, Eng. Ningsia Hui, Ningsia Hui Autonomous Region. ◈ autonomous region N China
165 X10 **Ningxian** Gansu, N China 35.30N 108.04E
178 Jj7 **Ninh Binh** Ninh Binh, N Vietnam 20.12N 105.58E
178 Kk13 **Ninh Hoa** Khanh Hoa, S Vietnam 12.28N 109.07E
194 H7 **Ninigo Group** island group N PNG
41 Q12 **Ninilchik** Alaska, USA 60.03N 151.40W
29 N7 **Ninnescah River** ≈ Kansas, C USA
205 U16 **Ninnis Glacier** glacier Antarctica
172 N10 **Ninohe** Iwate, Honshū, C Japan 40.17N 141.18E
101 F18 **Ninove** Oost-Vlaanderen, C Belgium 50.49N 4.01E
179 P11 **Ninoy Aquino** ✈ (Manila) Luzon, N Philippines 14.26N 121.00E
Nio see Íos
31 P12 **Niobrara** Nebraska, C USA 42.43N 97.59W
30 M12 **Niobrara River** ≈ Nebraska/Wyoming, C USA
81 I20 **Nioki** Bandundu, W Dem. Rep. Congo 2.44S 17.42E
78 M11 **Niono** Ségou, C Mali 14.15N 5.57W
78 K11 **Nioro** var. Nioro du Sahel. Kayes, W Mali 15.13N 9.38W
78 G11 **Nioro du Rip** SW Senegal 13.44N 15.48W
Nioro du Sahel see Nioro
104 K10 **Niort** Deux-Sèvres, W France 46.21N 0.24W
180 H14 **Nioumachoua** Mohéli, S Comoros 12.21S 43.43E
194 G12 **Nipa** Southern Highlands, W PNG 6.12S 143.29E
9 U14 **Nipawin** Saskatchewan, S Canada 53.21N 103.55W
10 D12 **Nipigon** Ontario, S Canada 49.01N 88.15W
10 D11 **Nipigon, Lake** ◎ Ontario, S Canada
9 S13 **Nipin** ≈ Saskatchewan, C Canada
12 G11 **Nipissing, Lake** ◎ Ontario, S Canada
37 P13 **Nipomo** California, W USA 35.02N 120.28W
Nippon see Japan
144 K6 **Niqniqīyah, Jabal an** ▲ C Syria
64 I9 **Niquivil** San Juan, W Argentina 30.25S 68.42W
176 Yy10 **Nirabotong** Papua, E Indonesia 2.35S 140.08E
171 J16 **Nirasaki** Yamanashi, Honshū, S Japan 35.43N 138.24E
Niriz see Neyrīz
169 U7 **Nirji** var. Morin Dawa Daurzu Zizhiqu. Nei Mongol Zizhiqu, N China 48.21N 124.32E
161 I14 **Nirmal** Andhra Pradesh, C India 19.04N 78.21E
159 Q13 **Nirmāli** Bihār, NE India 26.18N 86.34E
115 O14 **Niš** Eng. Nish, Ger. Nisch; anc. Naissus. Serbia, SE Serbia and Montenegro (Yugoslavia) 43.20N 21.52E
106 H9 **Nisa** Portalegre, C Portugal 39.31N 7.39W
Nisa see Neisse
147 P4 **Nişab** Al Ḥudūd ash Shamālīyah, N Saudi Arabia 29.10N 44.43E
147 Q15 **Nişāb** var. Anşāb. SW Yemen 14.24N 46.47E
115 P14 **Nišava** Bul. Nishava. ≈ Bulgaria/Serbia and Montenegro (Yugoslavia) see also Nishava
109 K25 **Niscemi** Sicilia, Italy, C Mediterranean Sea 37.09N 14.22E
Nisch/Nish see Niš
172 Nn5 **Niseko** Hokkaidō, NE Japan 42.50N 140.43E
Nishapur see Neyshābūr
116 G9 **Nishava** var. Nišava. ≈ Bulgaria/Serbia and Montenegro (Yugoslavia) see also Nišava
120 L11 **Nishcha** Rus. Nishcha. ≈ N Belarus
172 Qq7 **Nishibetsu-gawa** ≈ Hokkaidō, NE Japan
170 E13 **Nishi-gawa** ≈ Honshū, SW Japan
170 Ee13 **Nishi-Nōmi-jima** var. Nōmi-jima. island SW Japan
170 Bb17 **Nishinoomote** Kagoshima, Tanega-shima, SW Japan 30.42N 130.59E
172 Ss16 **Nishino-shima** Eng. Rosario. island Ogasawara-shotō, SE Japan
171 Hh16 **Nishio** var. Nisio. Aichi, Honshū, SW Japan 34.52N 137.01E
170 C13 **Nishi-Sonogi-hantō** peninsula Kyūshū, SW Japan
171 Gg14 **Nishiwaki** var. Nisiwaki. Hyōgo, Honshū, SW Japan 35.02N 134.57E
147 U14 **Nishtūn** SE Yemen 15.47N 52.08E
Nisiros see Nísyros
Nisiwaki see Nishiwaki
Niska see Niesky
115 O14 **Niška Banja** Serbia, SE Serbia and Montenegro (Yugoslavia) 43.18N 22.01E
10 D6 **Niskibi** ≈ Ontario, C Canada
113 O15 **Nisko** Podkarpackie, SE Poland 50.31N 22.09E
8 H7 **Nisling** ≈ Yukon Territory, W Canada
101 H22 **Nismes** Namur, S Belgium 50.04N 4.31E
Nismes see Nîmes
118 M10 **Nisporeni** Rus. Nisporeny. W Moldova 47.04N 28.10E
Nisporeny see Nisporeni
97 K20 **Nissan** ≈ S Sweden
195 R11 **Nissan Island** island Green Islands, NE PNG
Nissan Islands see Green Islands
97 F16 **Nisser** ◎ S Norway
97 E21 **Nissum Bredning** inlet NW Denmark
31 U6 **Nisswa** Minnesota, N USA 46.31N 94.17W
Nistru see Dniester
117 M22 **Nísyros** var. Nisiros. island Dodekánisos, Greece, Aegean Sea
120 H8 **Nītaure** Cēsis, C Latvia 57.05N 25.12E
62 P10 **Niterói** prev. Nictheroy. Rio de Janeiro, SE Brazil 22.54S 43.06W
12 F16 **Nith** ≈ Ontario, S Canada
98 J13 **Nith** ≈ S Scotland, UK
Nitinan see Nichinan
113 I21 **Nitra** Ger. Neutra, Hung. Nyitra. Nitriansky Kraj, SW Slovakia 48.19N 18.04E
113 I20 **Nitra** Ger. Neutra, Hung. Nyitra. ≈ W Slovakia
113 I21 **Nitriansky Kraj** ◈ region SW Slovakia
23 Q5 **Nitro** West Virginia, NE USA 38.24N 81.50W
125 F11 **Nitsa** ≈ C Russian Federation
97 H14 **Nittedal** Akershus, S Norway 60.08N 10.45E
Niuatobutabu see Niuatoputapu
200 S11 **Niuatoputapu** var. Niuatobutabu; prev. Keppel Island. island N Tonga
200 Q15 **Niu'Aunofa** headland Tongatapu, S Tonga 21.03S 175.19W
Niuchwang see Yingkou
202 B16 **Niue** ◇ self-governing territory in free association with NZ S Pacific Ocean
202 F10 **Niulakita** var. Nurakita. atoll S Tuvalu
202 E6 **Niutao** atoll NW Tuvalu
95 L15 **Nivala** Oulu, C Finland 63.56N 25.00E
104 I15 **Nive** ≈ SW France
101 G19 **Nivelles** Wallon Brabant, C Belgium 50.36N 4.04E
105 P8 **Nivernais** cultural region C France
13 N8 **Niverville, Lac** ◎ Québec, SE Canada
29 T7 **Nixa** Missouri, C USA 37.02N 93.17W
37 R5 **Nixon** Nevada, W USA 39.48N 119.24W
27 S12 **Nixon** Texas, SW USA 29.16N 97.45W
Niya see Minfeng
Niyazov see Nyýazow
161 H14 **Nizāmābād** Andhra Pradesh, C India 18.40N 78.04E
161 H15 **Nizām Sāgar** ◎ C India
129 N16 **Nizhegorodskaya Oblast'** ◈ province W Russian Federation
126 K14 **Nizhneangarsk** Respublika Buryatiya, S Russian Federation 55.47N 109.39E
Nizhnegorskiy see Nyzhn'ohirs'kyy
131 S4 **Nizhnekamsk** Respublika Tatarstan, W Russian Federation 55.36N 51.45E
131 U3 **Nizhnekamskoye Vodokhranilishche** ⊡ W Russian Federation
127 O5 **Nizhnekolymsk** Respublika Sakha (Yakutiya), NE Russian Federation 68.32N 161.00E
127 N16 **Nizhneleninskoye** Yevreyskaya Avtonomnaya Oblast', SE Russian Federation 47.50N 132.30E
126 I14 **Nizhneudinsk** Irkutskaya Oblast', S Russian Federation 54.48N 98.51E
126 Gg11 **Nizhnevartovsk** Khanty-Mansiyskiy Avtonomnyy Okrug, C Russian Federation 60.57N 76.40E
126 Ll6 **Nizhneyansk** Respublika Sakha (Yakutiya), NE Russian Federation 71.25N 135.59E
131 Q11 **Nizhniy Baskunchak** Astrakhanskaya Oblast', SW Russian Federation 48.15N 46.49E
126 M11 **Nizhniy Bestyakh** Respublika Sakha (Yakutiya), NE Russian Federation 61.55N 130.07E
131 O6 **Nizhniy Lomov** Penzenskaya Oblast', W Russian Federation 53.32N 43.39E
131 P3 **Nizhniy Novgorod** prev. Gor'kiy. Nizhegorodskaya Oblast', W Russian Federation 56.17N 43.59E
129 T8 **Nizhniy Odes** Respublika Komi, NW Russian Federation 63.42N 54.58E
Nizhniy Pyandzh see Panji Poyon
125 Ee11 **Nizhniy Tagil** Sverdlovskaya Oblast', C Russian Federation 57.57N 59.51E
129 T9 **Nizhnyaya-Omra** Respublika Komi, NW Russian Federation 62.46N 55.54E
129 P5 **Nizhnyaya Pesha** Nenetskiy Avtonomnyy Okrug, NW Russian Federation 66.54N 47.37E
125 F11 **Nizhnyaya Tavda** Tyumenskaya Oblast', C Russian Federation 57.41N 65.54E
126 Jj12 **Nizhnyaya Tunguska** Eng. Lower Tunguska. ≈ N Russian Federation
119 Q3 **Nizhyn** Rus. Nezhin. Chernihivs'ka Oblast', NE Ukraine 51.03N 31.54E
142 M17 **Nizip** Gaziantep, S Turkey 37.01N 37.46E
147 X8 **Nizwá** var. Nazwāh. NE Oman 22.50N 57.27E
Nizza see Nice
108 C9 **Nizza Monferrato** Piemonte, NE Italy 44.47N 8.22E
Njávdám see Näätämöjoki
Njellim see Nellim
83 H24 **Njombe** Iringa, S Tanzania 9.19S 34.46E
83 G23 **Njombe** ≈ C Tanzania
94 I10 **Njunis** ▲ N Norway 68.47N 19.24E
95 H17 **Njurunda** Västernorrland, C Sweden 62.15N 17.24E
96 N11 **Njutånger** Gävleborg, C Sweden 61.37N 17.04E
81 D14 **Nkambe** Nord-Ouest, NW Cameroon 6.34N 10.43E
Nkata Bay see Nkhata Bay
81 F21 **Nkayi** prev. Jacob. La Bouenza, S Congo 4.10S 13.17E
85 J17 **Nkayi** Matabeleland North, W Zimbabwe 19.02S 28.55E
84 N13 **Nkhata Bay** var. Nkata Bay. Northern, N Malawi 11.36S 34.16E
83 E22 **Nkonde** Kigoma, N Tanzania 6.16S 30.17E
81 D15 **Nkongsamba** var. N'Kongsamba. Littoral, W Cameroon 4.58N 9.52E
85 E16 **Nkurenkuru** Okavango, N Namibia 17.39S 18.37E
79 Q15 **Nkwanta** E Ghana 8.18N 0.27E
178 H1 **Nmai Hka** var. Me Hka. ≈ N Myanmar
Noardwâlde see Noordwolde
41 N7 **Noatak** Alaska, USA 67.34N 162.58W
41 N7 **Noatak River** ≈ Alaska, USA
Nobeji see Noheji
170 D15 **Nobeoka** Miyazaki, Kyūshū, SW Japan 32.34N 131.37E
29 N11 **Noble** Oklahoma, C USA 35.08N 97.23W
33 P13 **Noblesville** Indiana, N USA 40.03N 86.00W
172 O6 **Noboribetsu** var. Noboribetu. Hokkaidō, NE Japan 42.27N 141.08E
Noboribetu see Noboribetsu
61 H18 **Nobres** Mato Grosso, W Brazil 14.43S 56.15W
109 N21 **Nocera Terinese** Calabria, S Italy 39.03N 16.10E
43 Q16 **Nochixtlán** var. Asunción Nochixtlán. Oaxaca, SE Mexico 17.28N 97.18W
27 S5 **Nocona** Texas, SW USA 33.47N 97.43W
65 K21 **Nodales, Bahía de los** bay S Argentina
29 Q2 **Nodaway River** ≈ Iowa/Missouri, C USA
29 R8 **Noel** Missouri, C USA 36.33N 94.29W
97 C17 **Nærbø** Rogaland, S Norway 58.40N 5.39E
97 I24 **Næstved** Storstrøm, SE Denmark 55.12N 11.47E
42 H3 **Nogales** Chihuahua, NW Mexico 18.49N 97.12W
42 F3 **Nogales** Sonora, NW Mexico 31.16N 110.52W
38 M17 **Nogales** Arizona, SW USA 31.20N 110.55W
Nogal Valley see Dooxo Nugaaleed
104 K15 **Nogaro** Gers, S France 43.46N 0.01W
112 J7 **Nogat** ≈ N Poland
170 D12 **Nōgata** Fukuoka, Kyūshū, SW Japan 33.42N 130.43E
131 P15 **Nogayskaya Step'** steppe SW Russian Federation
104 M6 **Nogent-le-Rotrou** Eure-et-Loir, C France 48.19N 0.49E
105 O4 **Nogent-sur-Oise** Oise, N France 49.16N 2.28E
105 P6 **Nogent-sur-Seine** Aube, N France 48.30N 3.31E
126 I10 **Noginsk** Evenkiyskiy Avtonomnyy Okrug, N Russian Federation 64.28N 91.09E
130 L3 **Noginsk** Moskovskaya Oblast', W Russian Federation 55.51N 38.23E
127 O14 **Nogliki** Ostrov Sakhalin, Sakhalinskaya Oblast', SE Russian Federation 51.44N 143.14E
171 I14 **Nōgōhaku-san** ▲ Honshū, SW Japan 35.46N 136.30E
168 D5 **Nogoonnuur** Bayan-Ölgiy, NW Mongolia 49.31N 89.48E
63 C18 **Nogoyá** Entre Ríos, E Argentina 32.25S 59.49W
113 K21 **Nógrád** off. Nógrád Megye. ◈ county N Hungary
107 U5 **Noguera Pallaresa** ≈ NE Spain
107 U4 **Noguera Ribagorçana** ≈ NE Spain
172 N9 **Noheji** var. Nobeji. Aomori, Honshū, C Japan 40.51N 141.07E
103 E19 **Nohfelden** Saarland, SW Germany 49.35N 7.08E
40 A8 **Nohili Point** headland Kaua'i, Hawai'i, USA, C Pacific Ocean 22.03N 159.48W
106 G3 **Noia** Galicia, NW Spain 42.48N 8.52W
105 N16 **Noire, Montagne** ▲▲ S France
13 P12 **Noire, Rivière** ≈ Québec, SE Canada
12 J10 **Noire, Rivière** ≈ Québec, SE Canada
Noire, Rivière see Black River
104 G6 **Noires, Montagnes** ▲▲ NW France
104 H8 **Noirmoutier-en-l'Île** Vendée, NW France 47.00N 2.15W
104 H8 **Noirmoutier, Île de** island NW France
171 Jj17 **Nojima-zaki** headland Honshū, S Japan 34.54N 139.54E
195 W8 **Noka** Nendō, E Solomon Islands 10.42S 165.57E
85 G17 **Nokaneng** Ngamiland, NW Botswana 19.40S 22.12E
95 L18 **Nokia** Länsi-Suomi, W Finland 61.28N 23.30E
154 K11 **Nok Kundi** Baluchistān, SW Pakistan 28.49N 62.39E
32 L14 **Nokomis** Illinois, N USA 39.18N 89.17W
32 K5 **Nokomis, Lake** ⊡ Wisconsin, N USA
80 G9 **Nokou** Kanem, W Chad 14.36N 14.45E
197 B12 **Nokuku** Espiritu Santo, W Vanuatu 14.56S 166.34E
97 J18 **Nol** Västra Götaland, S Sweden 57.55N 12.03E
81 H16 **Nola** Sangha-Mbaéré, SW Central African Republic 3.28N 16.05E
27 P7 **Nolan** Texas, SW USA 32.15N 100.15W
129 R15 **Nolinsk** Kirovskaya Oblast', NW Russian Federation 57.34N 49.54E
97 B19 **Nólsoy** Dan. Nolsø Island Faeroe Islands 61.59N 6.39W
194 F12 **Nomad** Western, SW Papau New Guinea 6.11S 142.13E
170 B15 **Noma-zaki** headland Kyūshū, SW Japan 31.24N 130.07E
42 K10 **Nombre de Dios** Durango, C Mexico 23.51N 104.13W
44 I5 **Nombre de Dios, Cordillera** ▲▲ N Honduras
40 M9 **Nome** Alaska, USA 64.30N 165.24W
31 Q6 **Nome** North Dakota, N USA 46.39N 97.49W
40 M9 **Nome, Cape** headland Alaska, USA 64.25N 165.00W
Nōmi-jima see Nishi-Nōmi-jima
12 M11 **Nominingue, Lac** ◎ Québec, SE Canada
Nomoi Islands see Mortlock Islands
170 Bb13 **Nomo-zaki** headland Kyūshū, SW Japan 32.34N 129.45E
200 S13 **Nomuka** island Nomuka Group, C Tonga
200 S14 **Nomuka Group** island group W Tonga
201 Q15 **Nomwin Atoll** atoll Hall Islands, C Micronesia
15 Ii8 **Nonacho Lake** ◎ Northwest Territories, NW Canada
Nondaburi see Nonthaburi
41 P12 **Nondalton** Alaska, USA 59.58N 154.51W
169 V10 **Nong'an** Jilin, NE China 44.25N 125.10E
178 I10 **Nong Bua Khok** Nakhon Ratchasima, C Thailand 15.23N 101.51E
178 I9 **Nong Bua Lamphu** Udon Thani, E Thailand 17.11N 102.27E
178 J7 **Nông Hèt** Xiangkhoang, N Laos 19.27N 104.02E
Nongkaya see Nong Khai
178 I8 **Nong Khai** var. Mi Chai, Nongkaya. Nong Khai, E Thailand 17.52N 102.43E
178 Gg15 **Nong Met** Surat Thani, SW Thailand 9.27N 99.09E
85 L22 **Nongoma** KwaZulu/Natal, E South Africa 27.54S 31.40E
178 Hh10 **Nong Phai** Phetchabun, C Thailand 15.58N 101.02E
159 U13 **Nongstoin** Meghālaya, NE India 25.24N 91.19E
85 C19 **Nonidas** Erongo, N Namibia 22.36S 14.40E
Nonni see Nen Jiang
42 J7 **Nonoava** Chihuahua, N Mexico 27.24N 106.18W
203 O3 **Nonouti** prev. Sydenham Island. atoll Tungaru, W Kiribati
178 Hh11 **Nonthaburi** var. Nondaburi, Nontha Buri. Nonthaburi, C Thailand 13.55N 100.33E
104 L11 **Nontron** Dordogne, SW France 45.34N 0.41E
189 P1 **Noonamah** Northern Territory, N Australia 12.46S 131.08E
30 K2 **Noonan** North Dakota, N USA 48.51N 102.57W
101 E14 **Noord-Beveland** var. North Beveland. island SW Netherlands
101 J14 **Noord-Brabant** Eng. North Brabant. ◈ province S Netherlands
100 H7 **Noorder Haaks** spit NW Netherlands
100 H9 **Noord-Holland** Eng. North Holland. ◈ province NW Netherlands
Noordhollandsch Kanaal see Noordhollands Kanaal
100 H8 **Noordhollands Kanaal** var. Noordhollandsch Kanaal. canal NW Netherlands
Noord-Kaap see Northern Cape
100 L8 **Noordoostpolder** island N Netherlands
47 P16 **Noordpunt** headland Curaçao, C Netherlands Antilles 12.21N 69.08W
100 I8 **Noord-Scharwoude** Noord-Holland, NW Netherlands 52.42N 4.48E
Noordwes see North-West
100 G11 **Noordwijk aan Zee** Zuid-Holland, W Netherlands 52.15N 4.25E
100 H11 **Noordwijkerhout** Zuid-Holland, W Netherlands 52.16N 4.30E
100 M7 **Noordwolde** Fris. Noardwâlde. Friesland, N Netherlands 52.54N 6.10E
Noordzee see North Sea
100 H10 **Noordzee-Kanaal** canal NW Netherlands
95 K18 **Noormarkku** Swe. Norrmark. Länsi-Suomi, W Finland 61.34N 21.54E
41 N8 **Noorvik** Alaska, USA 66.50N 161.01W
8 J17 **Nootka Sound** inlet British Columbia, W Canada
84 A9 **Nóqui** Zaire, NW Angola 5.53S 13.26E
97 L15 **Nora** Örebro, C Sweden 59.31N 15.01E
153 Q13 **Norak** Rus. Nurek. W Tajikistan 38.23N 69.13E
16 P14 **Noranda** Quebec, SE Canada 48.16N 79.03W
31 W12 **Nora Springs** Iowa, C USA 43.08N 93.00W
97 M14 **Norberg** Västmanland, C Sweden 60.04N 15.34E
12 K13 **Norcan Lake** ◎ Ontario, SE Canada
207 R12 **Nord** Avannaarsua, N Greenland 81.38N 12.51W
80 F13 **Nord** Eng. North. ◈ province N Cameroon
105 P2 **Nord** ◈ department N France
94 P1 **Nordaustlandet** island NE Svalbard
97 G24 **Nordborg** Ger. Nordburg. Sønderjylland, SW Denmark 55.04N 9.40E
Nordburg see Nordborg
97 F23 **Nordby** Ribe, W Denmark 55.27N 8.25E
9 P15 **Nordegg** Alberta, SW Canada 52.27N 116.06W
102 E9 **Norden** Niedersachsen, NW Germany 53.36N 7.12E
102 G10 **Nordenham** Niedersachsen, NW Germany 53.28N 8.27E
126 Ii4 **Nordenshel'da, Arkhipelag** island group N Russian Federation
94 O3 **Nordenskiold Land** physical region W Svalbard
102 E9 **Norderney** island NW Germany
102 J9 **Norderstedt** Schleswig-Holstein, N Germany 53.42N 9.58E
96 C11 **Nordfjord** physical region S Norway
96 D11 **Nordfjord** fjord S Norway
96 D11 **Nordfjordeid** Sogn og Fjordane, S Norway 61.54N 6.01E
94 G11 **Nordfold** Nordland, C Norway 67.48N 15.16E
Nordfriesische Inseln see North Frisian Islands
102 H7 **Nordfriesland** cultural region N Germany
103 K15 **Nordhausen** Thüringen, C Germany 51.31N 10.48E
27 T13 **Nordheim** Texas, SW USA 28.55N 97.36W
96 C13 **Nordhordland** physical region S Norway
102 E12 **Nordhorn** Niedersachsen, NW Germany 52.25N 7.04E
94 I1 **Nordhurfjördhur** Vestfirdhir, NW Iceland 66.01N 21.33W
94 J1 **Nordhurland Eystra** ◈ region N Iceland
94 I2 **Nordhurland Vestra** ◈ region N Iceland
180 H16 **Nord, Île du** island Inner Islands, NE Seychelles
97 F20 **Nordjylland** off. Nordjyllands Amt. ◈ county N Denmark
94 K7 **Nordkapp** Eng. North Cape. headland N Norway 71.10N 25.42E
94 O1 **Nordkapp** headland N Svalbard 80.31N 19.58E
94 L7 **Nordkinn** headland N Norway 71.07N 27.40E
81 N19 **Nord Kivu** off. Région du Nord Kivu. ◈ region E Dem. Rep. Congo
96 G12 **Nordland** ◈ county C Norway
103 J21 **Nördlingen** Bayern, S Germany 48.49N 10.28E
95 I16 **Nordmaling** Västerbotten, N Sweden 63.34N 19.30E
97 K15 **Nordmark** Värmland, C Sweden 59.52N 14.04E
Nord, Mer du see North Sea
96 F8 **Nordmøre** physical region S Norway
102 I8 **Nord-Ostee-Kanal** canal N Germany
(0) J3 **Nordostrundingen** headland NE Greenland 83.00N 10.00W
81 D14 **Nord-Ouest** Eng. North-West. ◈ province NW Cameroon
Nord-Ouest, Territoires du see Northwest Territories
105 N2 **Nord-Pas-de-Calais** ◈ region N France
103 F19 **Nordpfälzer Bergland** ▲ W Germany
Nord, Pointe see Fatua, Pointe
197 H5 **Nord, Province** ◈ province C New Caledonia
103 D14 **Nordrhein-Westfalen** Eng. North Rhine-Westphalia, Fr. Rhénanie du Nord-Westphalie. ◈ state W Germany
Nordsee/Nordsjøen/Nordsøen see North Sea
102 H7 **Nordstrand** island N Germany
95 E15 **Nord-Trøndelag** ◈ county C Norway
99 E19 **Nore** Ir. An Fheoir. ≈ S Ireland
31 Q14 **Norfolk** Nebraska, C USA 42.01N 97.25W
23 X7 **Norfolk** Virginia, NE USA 36.51N 76.17W
99 P19 **Norfolk** cultural region E England, UK
199 I11 **Norfolk Island** ◇ Australian external territory SW Pacific Ocean
183 P9 **Norfolk Ridge** undersea feature W Pacific Ocean
29 U8 **Norfork Lake** ⊡ Arkansas/Missouri, C USA
100 N6 **Norg** Drenthe, NE Netherlands 53.04N 6.28E
Norge see Norway
97 D14 **Norheimsund** Hordaland, S Norway 60.22N 6.09E
27 S16 **Norias** Texas, SW USA 26.47N 97.45W
171 J14 **Norikura-dake** ▲ Honshū, S Japan 36.06N 137.33E
126 I8 **Noril'sk** Taymyrskiy (Dolgano-Nenetskiy) Avtonomnyy Okrug, N Russian Federation 69.21N 88.01E
12 I13 **Norland** Ontario, SE Canada 44.46N 78.48W
23 V8 **Norlina** North Carolina, SE USA 36.26N 78.11W
32 L13 **Normal** Illinois, N USA 40.30N 88.59W
29 N11 **Norman** Oklahoma, C USA 35.13N 97.27W
Norman see Tulita
195 O16 **Normanby Island** island SE PNG
Normandes, Îles see Channel Islands
60 G9 **Normandia** Roraima, N Brazil 3.57N 59.39W
104 L5 **Normandie** Eng. Normandy. cultural region N France
104 J5 **Normandie, Collines de** hill range NW France
Normandy see Normandie
27 V9 **Normangee** Texas, SW USA 31.01N 96.06W
23 Q10 **Norman, Lake** ⊡ North Carolina, SE USA
46 K13 **Norman Manley** ✈ (Kingston) E Jamaica 17.55N 76.46W
189 U5 **Norman River** ≈ Queensland, NE Australia
189 U4 **Normanton** Queensland, NE Australia 17.48S 141.07E
15 Gg5 **Norman Wells** Northwest Territories, NW Canada 65.18N 126.42W
10 H12 **Normétal** Québec, S Canada 48.58N 79.22W
9 V15 **Norquay** Saskatchewan, S Canada 51.51N 102.04W
96 N11 **Norra Dellen** ◎ C Sweden
95 G15 **Norråker** Jämtland, C Sweden 64.25N 15.40E
96 N12 **Norrala** Gävleborg, C Sweden 61.22N 17.04E
Norra Ny see Stöllet
94 G13 **Norra Storjfjället** ▲ N Sweden 65.57N 15.15E
94 I13 **Norrbotten** ◈ county N Sweden
97 G23 **Nørre Aaby** var. Nørre Åby. Fyn, C Denmark 55.28N 9.52E
Nørre Åby see Nørre Aaby
97 I24 **Nørre Alslev** Storstrøm, SE Denmark 54.54N 11.52E
97 E23 **Nørre Nebel** Ribe, W Denmark 55.45N 8.16E
97 G20 **Nørresundby** Nordjylland, N Denmark 57.05N 9.55E
23 N8 **Norris Lake** ⊡ Tennessee, S USA
20 I15 **Norristown** Pennsylvania, NE USA 40.07N 75.20W
97 N17 **Norrköping** Östergötland, S Sweden 58.34N 16.10E
Norrmark see Noormarkku
96 N13 **Norrsundet** Gävleborg, C Sweden 60.55N 17.09E
97 P15 **Norrtälje** Stockholm, C Sweden 59.45N 18.42E
188 L12 **Norseman** Western Australia 32.16S 121.45E
95 I14 **Norsjö** Västerbotten, N Sweden 64.55N 19.30E
97 G16 **Norsjø** ◎ S Norway
126 Mm15 **Norsk** Amurskaya Oblast', SE Russian Federation 52.20N 129.57E
Norske Havet see Norwegian Sea
197 C13 **Norsup** Malekula, C Vanuatu 16.05S 167.24E
203 V15 **Norte, Cabo** headland Easter Island, Chile, E Pacific Ocean 27.03S 109.24W
56 F7 **Norte de Santander** off. Departamento de Norte de Santander. ◈ province N Colombia
63 E21 **Norte, Punta** headland E Argentina 36.17S 56.46W
23 R13 **North** South Carolina, SE USA 33.37N 81.06W
North see Nord
20 L10 **North Adams** Massachusetts, NE USA 42.40N 73.06W
115 L17 **North Albanian Alps** Alb. Bjeshkët e Namuna, SCr. Prokletije. ▲▲ Albania/Serbia and Montenegro (Yugoslavia)
99 M15 **Northallerton** N England, UK 54.19N 1.25W
188 J12 **Northam** Western Australia 31.40S 116.40E
85 J20 **Northam** Northern, N South Africa 24.56S 27.18E
1 **North America** continent
1 N12 **North American Basin** undersea feature W Sargasso Sea
(0) C5 **North American Plate** tectonic feature
20 M11 **North Amherst** Massachusetts, NE USA 42.24N 72.31W
99 N20 **Northampton** C England, UK 52.13N 0.54W
99 M20 **Northamptonshire** cultural region C England, UK
157 P18 **North Andaman** island Andaman Islands, India, NE Indian Ocean
67 D25 **North Arm** East Falkland, Falkland Islands 52.06S 59.21W
23 Q13 **North Augusta** South Carolina, SE USA 33.30N 81.58W
181 W8 **North Australian Basin** Fr. Bassin Nord de l' Australie. undersea feature E Indian Ocean
33 R11 **North Baltimore** Ohio, N USA 41.10N 83.40W
9 T15 **North Battleford** Saskatchewan, S Canada 52.46N 108.19W
12 H11 **North Bay** Ontario, S Canada 46.19N 79.28W
10 H6 **North Belcher Islands** island group Belcher Islands, Nunavut, C Canada
31 R15 **North Bend** Nebraska, C USA 41.27N 96.46W
34 E14 **North Bend** Oregon, NW USA 43.24N 124.13W
98 K12 **North Berwick** SE Scotland, UK 56.03N 2.44W
North Beveland see Noord-Beveland
North Borneo see Sabah
191 P5 **North Bourke** New South Wales, SE Australia 30.03S 145.56E
North Brabant see Noord-Brabant
190 F2 **North Branch Neales** seasonal river South Australia

◆ Country ● Country Capital ◇ Dependent Territory ○ Dependent Territory Capital ◈ Administrative Region ✈ International Airport ▲ Mountain ▲▲ Mountain Range Volcano ≈ River ◎ Lake ⊡ Reservoir

North Caicos – Nowa Ruda

46 M6 **North Caicos** *island* NW Turks and Caicos Islands
28 L10 **North Canadian River** ≈ Oklahoma, C USA
33 U12 **North Canton** Ohio, N USA *40.52N 81.24W*
11 R13 **North, Cape** *headland* Cape Breton Island, Nova Scotia, SE Canada *47.06N 60.24W*
192 I1 **North Cape** *headland* North Island, NZ *34.23S 173.02E*
195 N9 **North Cape** *headland* New Ireland, NE PNG *2.33S 150.48E*
North Cape *see* Nordkapp
20 J17 **North Cape May** New Jersey, NE USA *38.59N 74.55W*
10 C9 **North Caribou Lake** ◎ Ontario, C Canada
23 U10 **North Carolina** *off.* State of North Carolina; also known as Old North State, Tar Heel State, Turpentine State. ◈ *state* SE USA
North Celebes *see* Sulawesi Utara
161 J24 **North Central Province** ◈ *province* N Sri Lanka
33 S4 **North Channel** *lake channel* Canada/USA
99 G14 **North Channel** *strait* Northern Ireland/Scotland, UK
23 S14 **North Charleston** South Carolina, SE USA *32.51N 79.58W*
33 N10 **North Chicago** Illinois, N USA *42.19N 87.50W*
205 Y10 **Northcliffe Glacier** *glacier* Antarctica
33 Q14 **North College Hill** Ohio, N USA *39.13N 84.33W*
27 O8 **North Concho River** ≈ Texas, SW USA
21 O8 **North Conway** New Hampshire, NE USA *44.03N 71.06W*
29 V14 **North Crossett** Arkansas, C USA *33.10N 91.56W*
30 L4 **North Dakota** *off.* State of North Dakota; also known as Flickertail State, Peace Garden State, Sioux State. ◈ *state* N USA
North Devon Island *see* Devon Island
99 O22 **North Downs** *hill range* SE England, UK
20 C11 **North East** Pennsylvania, NE USA *42.13N 79.49W*
85 I18 **North East** ◈ *district* NE Botswana
67 G15 **North East Bay** *bay* Ascension Island, C Atlantic Ocean
40 L10 **Northeast Cape** *headland* Saint Lawrence Island, Alaska, USA *63.16N 168.50W*
178 Mm13 **Northeast Cay** *island* NW Spratly Islands
83 J17 **North Eastern** ◈ *province* Kenya
North East Frontier Agency/ North East Frontier Agency of Assam *see* Arunāchal Pradesh
67 E25 **North East Island** *island* E Falkland Islands
201 V11 **Northeast Island** *island* Chuuk, C Micronesia
46 L12 **North East Point** *headland* E Jamaica *18.09N 76.19W*
46 L6 **Northeast Point** *headland* Great Inagua, S Bahamas *21.18N 73.01W*
46 K5 **Northeast Point** *headland* Acklins Island, SE Bahamas *22.43N 73.50W*
203 Z2 **Northeast Point** *headland* Kiritimati, E Kiribati *10.22S 105.45E*
46 H2 **Northeast Providence Channel** *channel* N Bahamas
103 J14 **Northeim** Niedersachsen, C Germany *51.42N 10.00E*
31 X14 **North English** Iowa, C USA *41.30N 92.04W*
144 G8 **Northern** ◈ *district* N Israel
84 M12 **Northern** ◈ *region* N Malawi
195 L15 **Northern** ◈ *province* S PNG
82 D7 **Northern** ◈ *state* N Sudan
84 K12 **Northern** ◈ *province* NE Zambia
Northern *see* Limpopo
82 B13 **Northern Bahr el Ghazal** ◈ *state* SW Sudan
Northern Border Region *see* Al Ḥudūd ash Shamālīyah
85 F24 **Northern Cape** *off.* Northern Cape Province, *Afr.* Noord-Kaap. ◈ *province* W South Africa
202 K14 **Northern Cook Islands** *island group* N Cook Islands
82 B8 **Northern Darfur** ◈ *state* NW Sudan
Northern Dvina *see* Severnaya Dvina
99 F14 **Northern Ireland** *var.* The Six Counties. *political division* UK
82 D9 **Northern Kordofan** ◈ *state* C Sudan
197 K14 **Northern Lau Group** *island group* Lau Group, NE Fiji
196 K3 **Northern Mariana Islands** ◇ *US commonwealth territory* W Pacific Ocean
161 J23 **Northern Province** ◈ *province* N Sri Lanka
Northern Rhodesia *see* Zambia
Northern Sporades *see* Vóreioi Sporádes
190 D1 **Northern Territory** ◈ *territory* N Australia
Northern Transvaal *see* Limpopo
Northern Ural Hills *see* Severnyye Uvaly
86 I9 **North European Plain** *plain* N Europe
29 V2 **North Fabius River** ≈ Missouri, C USA
67 D24 **North Falkland Sound** *sound* N Falkland Islands
31 V9 **Northfield** Minnesota, N USA *44.27N 93.10W*
21 O9 **Northfield** New Hampshire, NE USA *43.26N 71.34W*
183 Q8 **North Fiji Basin** *undersea feature* N Coral Sea
99 Q22 **North Foreland** *headland* SE England, UK *51.22N 1.26E*
37 P6 **North Fork American River** ≈ California, W USA
41 R7 **North Fork Chandalar River** ≈ Alaska, USA
30 K7 **North Fork Grand River** ≈ North Dakota/South Dakota, N USA
23 O6 **North Fork Kentucky River** ≈ Kentucky, S USA
41 Q7 **North Fork Koyukuk River** ≈ Alaska, USA
41 Q10 **North Fork Kuskokwim River** ≈ Alaska, USA
28 K11 **North Fork Red River** ≈ Oklahoma/Texas, SW USA
28 K3 **North Fork Solomon River** ≈ Kansas, C USA
25 W14 **North Fort Myers** Florida, SE USA *26.40N 81.52W*
33 P5 **North Fox Island** *island* Michigan, N USA
102 G6 **North Frisian Islands** *var.* Nordfriesische Inseln. *island group* N Germany
207 N9 **North Geomagnetic Pole** *pole* Arctic Ocean *78.30N 69.00W*
20 M13 **North Haven** Connecticut, NE USA *41.25N 72.51W*
192 J5 **North Head** *headland* North Island, NZ *36.23S 174.01E*
20 L6 **North Hero** Vermont, NE USA *44.49N 73.14W*
37 O7 **North Highlands** California, W USA *38.40N 121.25W*
North Holland *see* Noord-Holland
83 I16 **North Horr** Eastern, N Kenya *3.17N 37.08E*
157 K21 **North Huvadhu Atoll** *var.* Gaafu Alifu Atoll. *atoll* S Maldives
67 A24 **North Island** *island* W Falkland Islands
192 N9 **North Island** *island* N NZ
23 U14 **North Island** *island* South Carolina, SE USA
33 O11 **North Judson** Indiana, N USA *41.12N 86.44W*
North Kazakhstan *see* Severnyy Kazakhstan
33 V10 **North Kingsville** Ohio, N USA *41.54N 80.41W*
169 Y13 **North Korea** *off.* Democratic People's Republic of Korea, *Kor.* Chosŏn-minjujuŭi-inmin-kanghwaguk. ◆ *republic* E Asia
159 X11 **North Lakhimpur** Assam, NE India *27.10N 94.00E*
192 J3 **Northland** *off.* Northland Region. ◈ *region* North Island, NZ
199 J12 **Northland Plateau** *undersea feature* S Pacific Ocean
37 X11 **North Las Vegas** Nevada, W USA *36.12N 115.07W*
33 O11 **North Liberty** Indiana, N USA *41.36N 86.22W*
31 X14 **North Liberty** Iowa, C USA *41.45N 91.36W*
29 V12 **North Little Rock** Arkansas, C USA *34.46N 92.15W*
30 M13 **North Loup River** ≈ Nebraska, C USA
157 K18 **North Maalhosmadulu Atoll** *var.* North Malosmadulu Atoll, Raa Atoll. *atoll* N Maldives
33 U10 **North Madison** Ohio, N USA *41.48N 81.03W*
33 P12 **North Manchester** Indiana, N USA *41.00N 85.45W*
33 P6 **North Manitou Island** *island* Michigan, N USA
31 U10 **North Mankato** Minnesota, N USA *44.11N 94.03W*
25 Z15 **North Miami** Florida, SE USA *25.54N 80.11W*
157 K18 **North Miladummadulu Atoll** *atoll* N Maldives
North Minch *see* Minch, The
25 W15 **North Naples** Florida, SE USA *26.13N 81.47W*
183 P8 **North New Hebrides Trench** *undersea feature* N Coral Sea
25 Y15 **North New River Canal** ≈ Florida, SE USA
157 K20 **North Nilandhe Atoll** *var.* Faafu Atoll. *atoll* C Maldives
38 L2 **North Ogden** Utah, W USA *41.18N 111.57W*
North Ossetia *see* Severnaya Osetiya-Alaniya, Respublika
37 S10 **North Palisade** ▲ California, W USA *37.06N 118.31W*
201 U11 **North Pass** *passage* Chuuk Islands, C Micronesia
30 M15 **North Platte** Nebraska, C USA *41.07N 100.46W*
35 X17 **North Platte River** ≈ C USA
67 G14 **North Point** *headland* Ascension Island, C Atlantic Ocean
180 I16 **North Point** *headland* Mahé, NE Seychelles *4.22S 55.28E*
33 S6 **North Point** *headland* Michigan, N USA *45.01N 83.16W*
33 R5 **North Point** *headland* Michigan, N USA *45.21N 83.30W*
41 S9 **North Pole** Alaska, USA *64.42N 147.09W*
207 R9 **North Pole** *pole* Arctic Ocean *90.00N 0.00W*
25 O4 **Northport** Alabama, S USA *33.13N 87.34W*
25 W14 **North Port** Florida, SE USA *27.03N 82.15W*
34 L6 **Northport** Washington, NW USA *48.54N 117.48W*
34 L12 **North Powder** Oregon, NW USA *45.00N 117.56W*
31 U13 **North Raccoon River** ≈ Iowa, C USA
North Rhine-Westphalia *see* Nordrhein-Westfalen
99 M16 **North Riding** *cultural region* N England, UK
98 G5 **North Rona** *island* NW Scotland, UK
98 K4 **North Ronaldsay** *island* NE Scotland, UK
38 L2 **North Salt Lake** Utah, W USA *40.51N 111.54W*
9 P15 **North Saskatchewan** ≈ Alberta/Saskatchewan, S Canada
37 X5 **North Schell Peak** ▲ Nevada, W USA *39.25N 114.34W*
North Scotia Ridge *see* South Georgia Ridge
88 D10 **North Sea** *Dan.* Nordsøen, *Dut.* Noordzee, *Fr.* Mer du Nord, *Ger.* Nordsee, *Nor.* Nordsjøen; *prev.* German Ocean, *Lat.* Mare Germanicum. *sea* NW Europe
37 T6 **North Shoshone Peak** ▲ Nevada, W USA *39.08N 117.28W*
North Siberian Lowland/ North Siberian Plain *see* Severo-Sibirskaya Nizmennost'
31 R13 **North Sioux City** South Dakota, N USA *42.31N 96.28W*
98 K4 **North Sound, The** *sound* N Scotland, UK
191 T4 **North Star** New South Wales, SE Australia *28.55S 150.25E*
North Star State *see* Minnesota
191 V3 **North Stradbroke Island** *island* Queensland, E Australia
North Sulawesi *see* Sulawesi Utara
North Sumatra *see* Sumatera Utara
12 D17 **North Sydenham** ≈ Ontario, S Canada
20 H9 **North Syracuse** New York, NE USA *43.07N 76.07W*
192 K9 **North Taranaki Bight** *gulf* North Island, NZ
10 H9 **North Twin Island** *island* Nunavut, C Canada
98 E8 **North Uist** *island* NW Scotland, UK
99 L14 **Northumberland** *cultural region* N England, UK
189 Y7 **Northumberland Isles** *island group* Queensland, NE Australia
11 Q14 **Northumberland Strait** *strait* SE Canada
34 G14 **North Umpqua River** ≈ Oregon, NW USA
47 Q13 **North Union** Saint Vincent, Saint Vincent and the Grenadines *13.15N 61.07W*
8 L17 **North Vancouver** British Columbia, SW Canada *49.21N 123.04W*
20 K9 **Northville** New York, NE USA *43.13N 74.08W*
99 Q19 **North Walsham** E England, UK *52.49N 1.22E*
41 T10 **Northway** Alaska, USA *62.57N 141.56W*
85 G21 **North-West** *off.* North-West Province, *Afr.* Noordwes. ◈ *province* N South Africa
North-West *see* Nord-Ouest
66 I6 **Northwest Atlantic Mid-Ocean Canyon** *undersea feature* N Atlantic Ocean
188 G8 **North West Cape** *headland* Western Australia *21.48S 114.10E*
40 J9 **Northwest Cape** *headland* Saint Lawrence Island, Alaska, USA *63.46N 171.45W*
84 H13 **North Western** ◈ *province* W Zambia
161 J24 **North Western Province** ◈ *province* W Sri Lanka
155 U4 **North-West Frontier Province** ◈ *province* NW Pakistan
98 H8 **North West Highlands** ▲▲ N Scotland, UK
199 Hh4 **Northwest Pacific Basin** *undersea feature* NW Pacific Ocean
203 Y2 **Northwest Point** *headland* Kiritimati, E Kiribati *10.25S 105.34E*
46 G1 **Northwest Providence Channel** *channel* N Bahamas
11 Q8 **North West River** Newfoundland and Labrador, E Canada *53.30N 60.10W*
15 Ii5 **Northwest Territories** *Fr.* Territoires du Nord-Ouest. ◈ *territory* NW Canada
99 K18 **Northwich** C England, UK *53.16N 2.31W*
27 Q5 **North Wichita River** ≈ Texas, SW USA
20 J17 **North Wildwood** New Jersey, NE USA *39.00N 74.45W*
23 R9 **North Wilkesboro** North Carolina, SE USA *36.09N 81.09W*
21 P8 **North Windham** Maine, NE USA *43.51N 70.25W*
207 Q6 **Northwind Plain** *undersea feature* Arctic Ocean
31 V11 **Northwood** Iowa, C USA *43.26N 93.13W*
31 Q4 **Northwood** North Dakota, N USA *47.43N 97.34W*
99 M15 **North York Moors** *moorland* N England, UK
27 V9 **North Zulch** Texas, SW USA *30.54N 96.06W*
28 K2 **Norton** Kansas, C USA *39.49N 99.53W*
33 S13 **Norton** Ohio, N USA *40.25N 83.04W*
23 P7 **Norton** Virginia, NE USA *36.55N 82.37W*
41 N9 **Norton Bay** *bay* Alaska, USA
Norton de Matos *see* Balombo
33 O9 **Norton Shores** Michigan, N USA *43.10N 86.15W*
40 M10 **Norton Sound** *inlet* Alaska, USA
29 Q3 **Nortonville** Kansas, C USA *39.25N 95.19W*
104 I8 **Nort-sur-Erdre** Loire-Atlantique, NW France *47.27N 1.30W*
205 N2 **Norvegia, Cape** *headland* Antarctica *71.16S 12.25W*
20 L13 **Norwalk** Connecticut, NE USA *41.08N 73.28W*
31 V14 **Norwalk** Iowa, C USA *41.28N 93.40W*
33 S11 **Norwalk** Ohio, N USA *41.14N 82.37W*
21 P7 **Norway** Maine, NE USA *44.13N 70.30W*
33 N5 **Norway** Michigan, N USA *45.47N 87.54W*
95 E17 **Norway** *off.* Kingdom of Norway, *Nor.* Norge. ◆ *monarchy* N Europe
9 X13 **Norway House** Manitoba, C Canada *53.58N 97.49W*
207 R16 **Norwegian Basin** *undersea feature* NW Norwegian Sea
86 D6 **Norwegian Sea** *Nor.* Norske Havet. *sea* NE Atlantic Ocean
207 S17 **Norwegian Trench** *undersea feature* NE North Sea
12 F16 **Norwich** Ontario, S Canada *42.57N 80.37W*
99 Q19 **Norwich** E England, UK *52.37N 1.18E*
21 N13 **Norwich** Connecticut, NE USA *41.30N 72.02W*
20 I11 **Norwich** New York, NE USA *42.31N 75.31W*
31 U9 **Norwood** Minnesota, N USA *44.46N 93.55W*
33 Q15 **Norwood** Ohio, N USA *39.07N 84.27W*
12 H11 **Nosbonsing, Lake** ◎ Ontario, S Canada
Nösen *see* Bistriţa
172 P1 **Noshappu-misaki** *headland* Hokkaidō, NE Japan *45.26N 141.38E*
171 M9 **Noshiro** *var.* Nosiro; *prev.* Noshirominato. Akita, Honshū, C Japan *40.10N 140.01E*
Noshirominato/Nosiro *see* Noshiro
119 Q3 **Nosivka** *Rus.* Nosovka. Chernihivs'ka Oblast', NE Ukraine *50.55N 31.37E*
69 T14 **Nosop** *var.* Nossob, Nossop. ≈ Botswana/Namibia
129 S4 **Nosovaya** Nenetskiy Avtonomnyy Okrug, NW Russian Federation *68.12N 54.33E*
Nosovka *see* Nosivka
149 V11 **Noşratābād** Sīstān va Balūchestān, E Iran *29.53N 59.57E*
97 J18 **Nossebro** Västra Götaland, S Sweden *58.12N 12.42E*
98 K6 **Noss Head** *headland* N Scotland, UK *58.29N 3.03W*
Nossi-Bé *see* Be, Nosy
85 E20 **Nossob** ≈ E Namibia
Nossob/Nossop *see* Nosop
180 J2 **Nosy Be** ✕ Antsiraňana, N Madagascar *23.36S 47.36E*
180 J6 **Nosy Varika** Fianarantsoa, SE Madagascar *20.36S 48.31E*
12 L10 **Notawassi** ≈ Québec, SE Canada
12 M9 **Notawassi, Lac** ◎ Québec, SE Canada
38 J5 **Notch Peak** ▲ Utah, W USA *39.08N 113.24W*
112 G10 **Noteć** *Ger.* Netze. ≈ NW Poland
Nóties Sporádes *see* Dodekánisos
117 J22 **Nótion Aigaíon** *Eng.* Aegean South. ◈ *region* E Greece
117 H18 **Nótios Evvoïkós Kólpos** *gulf* E Greece
117 B16 **Nótio Stenó Kérkyras** *strait* W Greece
109 L25 **Noto** *anc.* Netum. Sicilia, Italy, C Mediterranean Sea *36.52N 15.04E*
171 J12 **Noto** Ishikawa, Honshū, SW Japan *37.18N 137.11E*
97 G15 **Notodden** Telemark, S Norway *59.33N 9.15E*
109 L25 **Noto, Golfo di** *gulf* Sicilia, Italy, C Mediterranean Sea
171 J12 **Noto-hantō** *peninsula* Honshū, SW Japan
171 J12 **Noto-jima** *island* SW Japan
172 Qq5 **Notoro-ko** ◎ Hokkaidō, NE Japan
11 T11 **Notre Dame Bay** *bay* Newfoundland, E Canada
13 P6 **Notre-Dame-de-Lorette** Québec, SE Canada *49.05N 72.24W*
12 L11 **Notre-Dame-de-Pontmain** Québec, SE Canada *46.18N 75.37W*
13 T8 **Notre-Dame-du-Lac** Québec, SE Canada *47.36N 68.48W*
13 Q6 **Notre-Dame-du-Rosaire** Québec, SE Canada *48.48N 71.27W*
13 U8 **Notre-Dame, Monts** ▲▲ Québec, S Canada
79 R16 **Notsé** S Togo *6.53N 1.09E*
172 R7 **Notsuke-suidō** *strait* Japan/Russian Federation
172 R7 **Notsuke-zaki** *headland* Hokkaidō, NE Japan *43.33N 145.18E*
12 G14 **Nottawasaga** ≈ Ontario, S Canada
12 G14 **Nottawasaga Bay** *lake bay* Ontario, S Canada
10 I11 **Nottaway** ≈ Québec, SE Canada
25 S1 **Nottely Lake** ◎ Georgia, SE USA
97 H16 **Nøtterøy** *island* S Norway
99 M19 **Nottingham** C England, UK *52.58N 1.10W*
16 N5 **Nottingham Island** *island* Nunavut, NE Canada
99 N18 **Nottinghamshire** *cultural region* C England, UK
23 V7 **Nottoway** Virginia, NE USA *37.07N 78.03W*
23 V7 **Nottoway River** ≈ Virginia, NE USA
78 G7 **Nouâdhibou** *prev.* Port-Étienne. Dakhlet Nouâdhibou, W Mauritania *20.54N 17.01W*
78 G7 **Nouâdhibou** ✕ Dakhlet Nouâdhibou, W Mauritania *20.59N 17.02W*
78 F7 **Nouâdhibou, Dakhlet** *prev.* Baie du Lévrier. *bay* W Mauritania
78 F7 **Nouâdhibou, Râs** *prev.* Cap Blanc. *headland* NW Mauritania *20.48N 17.03W*
78 G9 **Nouakchott** ● (Mauritania) Nouakchott District, SW Mauritania *18.09N 15.58W*
78 G9 **Nouakchott** ✕ Trarza, SW Mauritania *18.18N 15.54W*
123 K13 **Noual, Sebkhet en** *var.* Sabkhat an Nawāl. *salt flat* C Tunisia
78 G8 **Nouâmghâr** *var.* Nouamrhar. Dakhlet Nouâdhibou, W Mauritania *19.22N 16.31W*
Nouamrhar *see* Nouâmghâr
Nouă Sulița *see* Novoselytsya
197 I7 **Nouméa** ○ (New Caledonia) Province Sud, S New Caledonia *22.13S 166.29E*
81 E15 **Noun** ≈ C Cameroon
79 N12 **Nouna** W Burkina *12.43N 3.54W*
85 H24 **Noupoort** Northern Cape, C South Africa *31.10S 24.57E*
Nouveau-Brunswick *see* New Brunswick
Nouveau-Comptoir *see* Wemindji
13 T4 **Nouvel, Lacs** ◎ Québec, SE Canada
13 W7 **Nouvelle** Québec, SE Canada *48.07N 66.16W*
13 W7 **Nouvelle** ≈ Québec, SE Canada
Nouvelle-Calédonie *see* New Caledonia
Nouvelle Écosse *see* Nova Scotia
105 R3 **Nouzonville** Ardennes, N France *49.49N 4.45E*
153 Q11 **Nov** *Rus.* Nau. NW Tajikistan *40.10N 69.16E*
61 I21 **Nova Alvorada** Mato Grosso do Sul, SW Brazil *21.25S 54.19W*
Novabad *see* Navobod
113 D19 **Nová Bystřice** *Ger.* Neubistritz. Jihočeský Kraj, S Czech Republic *48.59N 15.05E*
118 H13 **Novaci** Gorj, SW Romania *45.08N 23.39E*
Nova Civitas *see* Neustadt an der Weinstrasse
Novaesium *see* Neuss
62 H10 **Nova Esperança** Paraná, S Brazil *23.09S 52.13W*
108 H11 **Novafeltria** Marche, C Italy *43.54N 12.18E*
62 Q9 **Nova Friburgo** Rio de Janeiro, SE Brazil *22.16S 42.34W*
84 D12 **Nova Gaia** *var.* Cambundi-Catembo. Malanje, NE Angola *10.03S 17.31E*
111 S12 **Nova Gorica** W Slovenia *45.57N 13.40E*
114 G10 **Nova Gradiška** *Ger.* Neugradisk, *Hung.* Újgradiska. Brod-Posavina, NE Croatia *45.15N 17.23E*
62 K7 **Nova Granada** São Paulo, S Brazil *20.33S 49.19W*
62 O10 **Nova Iguaçu** Rio de Janeiro, SE Brazil *22.31S 44.04W*
119 S10 **Nova Kakhovka** *Rus.* Novaya Kakhovka. Khersons'ka Oblast', SE Ukraine *46.45N 33.19E*
Nová Karvinná *see* Karviná
Nova Lamego *see* Gabú
Nova Lisboa *see* Huambo
114 C11 **Novalja** Lika-Senj, W Croatia *44.33N 14.53E*
121 M14 **Novalukoml'** *Rus.* Novolukoml'. Vitsyebskaya Voblasts', N Belarus *54.40N 29.09E*
Nova Mambone *see* Mambone
85 P16 **Nova Nabúri** Zambézia, NE Mozambique *16.47S 38.55E*
119 Q9 **Nova Odesa** *var.* Novaya Odessa. Mykolayivs'ka Oblast', S Ukraine *47.18N 31.45E*
62 H10 **Nova Olímpia** Paraná, S Brazil *23.28S 53.12W*
63 I15 **Nova Prata** Rio Grande do Sul, S Brazil *28.45S 51.37W*
12 H12 **Novar** Ontario, S Canada *45.26N 79.14W*
108 C7 **Novara** *anc.* Novaria. Piemonte, NW Italy *45.27N 8.36E*
Novaria *see* Novara
119 P7 **Novarkanels'k** Kirovohrads'ka Oblast', C Ukraine *48.39N 30.48E*
11 P15 **Nova Scotia** *Fr.* Nouvelle Écosse. ◈ *province* SE Canada
(0) M9 **Nova Scotia** *physical region* SE Canada
36 M8 **Novato** California, W USA *38.06N 122.35W*
199 Jj8 **Nova Trough** *undersea feature* W Pacific Ocean
118 L7 **Nova Ushtsya** Khmel'nyts'ka Oblast', W Ukraine *48.50N 27.16E*
85 M17 **Nova Vanduzi** Manica, C Mozambique *18.54S 33.18E*
119 U5 **Nova Vodolaha** *Rus.* Novaya Vodolaga. Kharkivs'ka Oblast', E Ukraine *49.42N 35.48E*
126 L13 **Novaya Chara** Chitinskaya Oblast', S Russian Federation *56.45N 117.58E*
126 J14 **Novaya Igirma** Irkutskaya Oblast', C Russian Federation *57.08N 103.52E*
Novaya Kakhovka *see* Nova Kakhovka
150 E10 **Novaya Kazanka** Zapadnyy Kazakhstan, W Kazakhstan *48.57N 49.34E*
128 I12 **Novaya Ladoga** Leningradskaya Oblast', NW Russian Federation *60.03N 32.15E*
125 Ee10 **Novaya Lyalya** Sverdlovskaya Oblast, C Russian Federation *59.01N 60.37E*
131 R5 **Novaya Malykla** Ul'yanovskaya Oblast', W Russian Federation *54.13N 49.55E*
Novaya Odessa *see* Nova Odesa
126 M4 **Novaya Sibir', Ostrov** *island* Novosibirskiye Ostrova, NE Russian Federation
Novaya Vodolaga *see* Nova Vodolaha
121 P17 **Novaya Yel'nya** *Rus.* Novaya Yel'nya. Mahilyowskaya Voblasts', E Belarus *53.16N 31.13E*
125 G4 **Novaya Zemlya** *island group* N Russian Federation
Novaya Zemlya Trough *see* East Novaya Zemlya Trough
116 K10 **Nova Zagora** Sliven, C Bulgaria *42.29N 26.00E*
107 S12 **Novelda** País Valenciano, E Spain *38.24N 0.45W*
113 H19 **Nové Mesto nad Váhom** *Ger.* Waagneustadtl, *Hung.* Vágújhely. Trenčiansky Kraj, W Slovakia *48.48N 17.50E*
113 F17 **Nové Město na Moravě** *Ger.* Neustadtl in Mähren. Vysočina, C Czech Republic *49.34N 16.04E*
Novesium *see* Neuss
113 I21 **Nové Zámky** *Ger.* Neuhäusel, *Hung.* Érsekújvár. Nitriansky Kraj, SW Slovakia *49.00N 18.10E*
Novgorod *see* Velikiy Novgorod
Novgorod-Severskiy *see* Novhorod-Sivers'kyy
125 C6 **Novgorodskaya Oblast'** ◈ *province* W Russian Federation
119 R8 **Novhorodka** Kirovohrads'ka Oblast', C Ukraine *48.21N 32.38E*
119 R2 **Novhorod-Sivers'kyy** *Rus.* Novgorod-Severskiy. Chernihivs'ka Oblast', NE Ukraine *52.00N 33.15E*
33 R10 **Novi** Michigan, N USA *42.28N 83.28W*
Novi *see* Novi Vinodolski
114 L9 **Novi Bečej** *prev.* Új-Becse, Vološinovo, *Ger.* Neubetsche, *Hung.* Törökbecse. Serbia, N Serbia and Montenegro (Yugoslavia) *45.36N 20.09E*
27 Q8 **Novice** Texas, SW USA *32.00N 99.38W*
114 A9 **Novigrad** Istra, NW Croatia *45.19N 13.33E*
Novi Grad *see* Bosanski Novi
116 G9 **Novi Iskŭr** Sofiya-Grad, W Bulgaria *42.46N 23.19E*
108 C9 **Novi Ligure** Piemonte, NW Italy *44.46N 8.46E*
101 L22 **Noville** Luxembourg, SE Belgium *50.04N 5.46E*
204 I10 **Noville Peninsula** *peninsula* Thurston Island, Antarctica
Noviodunum *see* Soissons, Aisne, France
Noviodunum *see* Nevers, Nièvre, France
Noviodunum *see* Nyon, Vaud, Switzerland
Noviomagus *see* Lisieux, France
Noviomagus *see* Nijmegen, Netherlands
116 M8 **Novi Pazar** Shumen, NE Bulgaria *43.21N 27.13E*
115 M15 **Novi Pazar** *Turk.* Yenipazar. Serbia, S Serbia and Montenegro (Yugoslavia) *43.09N 20.31E*
114 K10 **Novi Sad** *Ger.* Neusatz, *Hung.* Újvidék. Serbia, N Serbia and Montenegro (Yugoslavia) *45.16N 19.49E*
119 T6 **Novi Sanzhary** Poltavs'ka Oblast', C Ukraine *49.21N 34.18E*
114 H12 **Novi Travnik** *prev.* Pučarevo. Federacija Bosna I Hercegovina, C Bosnia and Herzegovina *44.12N 17.39E*
114 B10 **Novi Vinodolski** *var.* Novi. Primorje-Gorski Kotar, NW Croatia *45.08N 14.46E*
60 F12 **Novo Airão** Amazonas, N Brazil *2.06S 61.19W*
131 N14 **Novoaleksandrovsk** Stavropol'skiy Kray, SW Russian Federation *44.41N 43.01E*
Novoalekseyevka *see* Khobda
126 H14 **Novoaltaysk** Altayskiy Kray, S Russian Federation *53.22N 83.58E*
131 N9 **Novoanninskiy** Volgogradskaya Oblast', SW Russian Federation *50.31N 42.43E*
60 F13 **Novo Aripuanã** Amazonas, N Brazil *5.04S 60.19W*
119 Y6 **Novoaydar** Luhans'ka Oblast', E Ukraine *49.00N 39.00E*
119 X9 **Novoazovs'k** *Rus.* Novoazovsk. Donets'ka Oblast', E Ukraine *47.07N 38.06E*
126 Mm16 **Novobureyskiy** Amurskaya Oblast', SE Russian Federation *49.42N 129.46E*
131 Q3 **Novocheboksarsk** Chavash Respubliki, W Russian Federation *56.07N 47.32E*
131 R5 **Novocheremshansk** Ul'yanovskaya Oblast', W Russian Federation *54.23N 50.08E*
130 L12 **Novocherkassk** Rostovskaya Oblast', SW Russian Federation *47.23N 40.00E*
131 R6 **Novodevich'ye** Samarskaya Oblast', W Russian Federation *53.33N 48.51E*
128 M8 **Novodvinsk** Arkhangel'skaya Oblast', NW Russian Federation *64.22N 40.48E*
Novograd-Volynskiy *see* Novohrad-Volyns'kyy
Novogrudok *see* Navahrudak
63 I15 **Novo Hamburgo** Rio Grande do Sul, S Brazil *29.42S 51.07W*
61 H16 **Novo Horizonte** Mato Grosso, W Brazil *11.19S 57.11W*
62 K8 **Novo Horizonte** São Paulo, S Brazil *21.27S 49.14W*
118 M4 **Novohrad-Volyns'kyy** *Rus.* Novograd-Volynskiy. Zhytomyrs'ka Oblast', N Ukraine *50.33N 27.31E*
151 O7 **Novoishimskiy** *prev.* Kuybyshevskiy. Severnyy Kazakhstan, N Kazakhstan *53.16N 66.53E*
150 L14 **Novokazalinsk** *see* Ayteke Bi
130 M8 **Novokhopersk** Voronezhskaya Oblast', W Russian Federation *51.09N 41.34E*
131 R6 **Novokuybyshevsk** Samarskaya Oblast', W Russian Federation *53.06N 49.56E*
126 H14 **Novokuznetsk** *prev.* Stalinsk. Kemerovskaya Oblast', S Russian Federation *53.45N 87.12E*
205 R1 **Novolazarevskaya** *Russian research station* Antarctica *70.42S 11.31E*
Novolukoml' *see* Novalukoml'
111 V12 **Novo mesto** *Ger.* Rudolfswert; *prev. Ger.* Neustadtl. SE Slovenia *45.48N 15.09E*
130 K15 **Novomikhaylovskiy** Krasnodarskiy Kray, SW Russian Federation *44.18N 38.49E*
114 L8 **Novo Miloševo** Serbia, N Serbia and Montenegro (Yugoslavia) *45.43N 20.20E*
Novomirgorod *see* Novomyrhorod
130 L5 **Novomoskovsk** Tul'skaya Oblast', W Russian Federation *54.04N 38.23E*
119 U7 **Novomoskovs'k** *Rus.* Novomoskovsk. Dnipropetrovs'ka Oblast', E Ukraine *48.37N 35.13E*
119 V8 **Novomykolayivka** Zaporiz'ka Oblast', SE Ukraine *47.58N 35.54E*
119 Q7 **Novomyrhorod** *Rus.* Novomirgorod. Kirovohrads'ka Oblast', S Ukraine *48.46N 31.39E*
126 I12 **Novonazimovo** Krasnoyarskiy Kray, C Russian Federation *59.30N 90.45E*
131 N8 **Novonikolayevskiy** Volgogradskaya Oblast', SW Russian Federation *50.55N 42.24E*
131 P10 **Novonikol'skoye** Volgogradskaya Oblast', SW Russian Federation *49.23N 45.06E*
131 X7 **Novoorsk** Orenburgskaya Oblast', W Russian Federation *51.21N 59.03E*
130 M13 **Novopokrovskaya** Krasnodarskiy Kray, SW Russian Federation *45.58N 40.43E*
Novopolotsk *see* Navapolatsk
119 Y5 **Novopskov** Luhans'ka Oblast', E Ukraine *49.33N 39.07E*
Novoradomsk *see* Radomsko
Novo Redondo *see* Sumbe
131 R8 **Novorepnoye** Saratovskaya Oblast', W Russian Federation *51.04N 48.34E*
130 K14 **Novorossiysk** Krasnodarskiy Kray, SW Russian Federation *44.49N 37.37E*
Novorossiyskiy/ Novorossiyskoye *see* Akzhar
126 Jj6 **Novorybnaya** Taymyrskiy (Dolgano-Nenetskiy) Avtonomnyy Okrug, N Russian Federation *72.48N 105.49E*
128 F15 **Novorzhev** Pskovskaya Oblast', W Russian Federation *57.01N 29.19E*
Novoselitsa *see* Novoselytsya
119 S12 **Novoselivs'ke** Respublika Krym, S Ukraine *45.26N 33.37E*
Novosëlki *see* Navasyolki
116 G6 **Novo Selo** Vidin, NW Bulgaria *44.08N 22.48E*
115 M14 **Novo Selo** Serbia, C Serbia and Montenegro (Yugoslavia) *43.39N 20.54E*
118 K8 **Novoselytsya** *Rom.* Nouă Sulița, *Rus.* Novoselitsa. Chernivets'ka Oblast', W Ukraine *48.13N 26.18E*
131 U7 **Novosergiyevka** Orenburgskaya Oblast', W Russian Federation *52.04N 53.40E*
130 L11 **Novoshakhtinsk** Rostovskaya Oblast', SW Russian Federation *47.48N 39.51E*
126 Gg14 **Novosibirsk** Novosibirskaya Oblast', C Russian Federation *55.04N 83.04E*
125 G13 **Novosibirskaya Oblast'** ◈ *province* C Russian Federation
126 M4 **Novosibirskiye Ostrova** *Eng.* New Siberian Islands. *island group* N Russian Federation
130 K6 **Novosil'** Orlovskaya Oblast', W Russian Federation *53.00N 37.59E*
128 G16 **Novosokol'niki** Pskovskaya Oblast', W Russian Federation *56.21N 30.07E*
131 Q6 **Novospasskoye** Ul'yanovskaya Oblast', W Russian Federation *53.08N 47.48E*
131 X8 **Novotroitsk** Orenburgskaya Oblast', W Russian Federation *51.09N 58.18E*
Novotroitskoye *see* Brlik, Kazakhstan
Novotroitskoye *see* Novotroyits'ke, Ukraine
119 T11 **Novotroyits'ke** *Rus.* Novotroitskoye. Khersons'ka Oblast', S Ukraine *46.21N 34.21E*
Novoukrainka *see* Novoukrayinka
119 Q8 **Novoukrayinka** *Rus.* Novoukrainka. Kirovohrads'ka Oblast', C Ukraine *48.19N 31.33E*
131 Q5 **Novoul'yanovsk** Ul'yanovskaya Oblast', W Russian Federation *54.10N 48.19E*
125 Ee10 **Novoural'sk** Sverdlovskaya Oblast', C Russian Federation *56.58N 59.50E*
131 W8 **Novouralets** Orenburgskaya Oblast', W Russian Federation *51.19N 56.57E*
Novo-Urgench *see* Urganch
118 I4 **Novovolyns'k** *Rus.* Novovolynsk. Volyns'ka Oblast', NW Ukraine *50.46N 24.09E*
119 S9 **Novovorontsovka** Khersons'ka Oblast', S Ukraine *47.28N 33.55E*
153 Y7 **Novovoznesenovka** Issyk-Kul'skaya Oblast', E Kyrgyzstan *42.36N 78.44E*
129 R14 **Novovyatsk** Kirovskaya Oblast', NW Russian Federation *58.30N 49.42E*
Novoyel'nya *see* Navayel'nya
128 I7 **Novoye Yushkozero** Respublika Kareliya, NW Russian Federation *64.46N 32.13E*
119 O6 **Novozhyvotiv** Vinnyts'ka Oblast', C Ukraine *49.16N 29.31E*
130 H6 **Novozybkov** Bryanskaya Oblast', W Russian Federation *52.36N 31.58E*
114 F9 **Novska** Sisak-Moslavina, NE Croatia *45.20N 16.58E*
Nový Bohumín *see* Bohumín
113 D15 **Nový Bor** *Ger.* Haida; *prev.* Bor u České Lípy, Hajda. Liberecký Kraj, N Czech Republic *50.46N 14.32E*
113 E16 **Nový Bydžov** *Ger.* Neubidschow. Královéhradecký Kraj, N Czech Republic *50.15N 15.27E*
121 G18 **Novy Dvor** *Rus.* Novyy Dvor. Hrodzyenskaya Voblasts', W Belarus *52.49N 24.22E*
113 I17 **Nový Jičín** *Ger.* Neutitschein. Moravskoslezský Kraj, E Czech Republic *49.36N 18.00E*
120 K12 **Novy Pahost** *Rus.* Novyy Pogost. Vitsyebskaya Voblasts', NW Belarus *55.30N 27.28E*
Novyy Bug *see* Novyy Buh
119 R9 **Novyy Buh** *Rus.* Novyy Bug. Mykolayivs'ka Oblast', S Ukraine *47.39N 32.31E*
119 Q4 **Novyy Bykiv** Chernihivs'ka Oblast', N Ukraine *50.36N 31.39E*
Novyy Dvor *see* Novy Dvor
Novyye Aneny *see* Anenii Noi
131 P7 **Novyye Burasy** Saratovskaya Oblast', W Russian Federation *52.10N 46.00E*
Novyy Margilan *see* Farghona
130 K8 **Novyy Oskol** Belgorodskaya Oblast', W Russian Federation *50.43N 37.55E*
Novyy Pogost *see* Novy Pahost
131 R2 **Novyy Tor"yal** Respublika Mariy El, W Russian Federation *56.59N 48.53E*
126 K14 **Novyy Uoyan** Respublika Buryatiya, S Russian Federation *56.06N 111.27E*
126 Gg9 **Novyy Urengoy** Yamalo-Nenetskiy Avtonomnyy Okrug, N Russian Federation *66.06N 76.25E*
127 N15 **Novyy Urgal** Khabarovskiy Kray, E Russian Federation *51.02N 132.45E*
Novyy Uzen' *see* Zhanaozen
125 G12 **Novyy Vasyugan** Tomskaya Oblast', C Russian Federation *58.28N 76.19E*
110 N16 **Nowa Dęba** Podkarpackie, SE Poland *50.31N 21.53E*
113 G15 **Nowa Ruda** *Ger.* Neurode. Dolnośląskie, SW Poland *50.34N 16.30E*

◆ Country ● Country Capital ◇ Dependent Territory ○ Dependent Territory Capital ◈ Administrative Region ✕ International Airport ▲ Mountain ▲▲ Mountain Range ✸ Volcano ≈ River ◎ Lake ⊡ Reservoir

304

ODRA – ONHAYE

Odra *see* Oder
114 J9 **Odžaci** *Ger.* Hodschag, *Hung.* Hodság. Serbia, NW Serbia and Montenegro (Yugoslavia) 45.31N 19.15E
61 N14 **Oeiras** Piauí, E Brazil 07.00S 42.07W
106 F11 **Oeiras** Lisboa, C Portugal 38.40N 9.18W
103 G14 **Oelde** Nordrhein-Westfalen, W Germany 51.49N 8.09E
30 J11 **Oelrichs** South Dakota, N USA 43.08N 103.13W
Oels/Oels in Schlesien *see* Oleśnica
103 M17 **Oelsnitz** Sachsen, E Germany 50.22N 12.12E
31 X12 **Oelwein** Iowa, C USA 42.40N 91.54W
Oeniadae *see* Oiniádes
203 N17 **Oeno Island** *atoll* Pitcairn Islands, C Pacific Ocean
Oesel *see* Saaremaa
110 L7 **Oetz** *var.* Ötz. Tirol, W Austria 47.15N 10.56E
143 P11 **Of** Trabzon, NE Turkey 40.57N 40.16E
32 K15 **O'Fallon** Illinois, N USA 38.35N 89.54W
29 W4 **O'Fallon** Missouri, C USA 38.54N 90.31W
109 N16 **Ofanto** ≈ S Italy
99 D18 **Offaly** *Ir.* Ua Uíbh Fhailí; *prev.* King's County. *cultural region* C Ireland
103 H18 **Offenbach** *var.* Offenbach am Main. Hessen, W Germany 50.06N 8.46E
Offenbach am Main *see* Offenbach
103 F22 **Offenburg** Baden-Württemberg, SW Germany 48.28N 7.57E
190 C2 **Officer Creek** *seasonal river* South Australia
Oficina María Elena *see* María Elena
Oficina Pedro de Valdivia *see* Pedro de Valdivia
117 K22 **Ofidoússa** *island* Kykládes, Greece, Aegean Sea
Ofiral *see* Sharm el Sheikh
94 H10 **Ofotfjorden** *fjord* N Norway
198 D8 **Ofu** *island* Manua Islands, E American Samoa
171 Mm12 **Ōfunato** Iwate, Honshū, C Japan 39.04N 141.41E
171 M10 **Oga** Akita, Honshū, C Japan 39.54N 139.48E
Ogaadeen *see* Ogadēn
171 M11 **Ogachi** Akita, Honshū, C Japan 39.03N 140.26E
171 M11 **Ogachi-tōge** *pass* Honshū, C Japan 39.00N 140.20E
83 N14 **Ogadēn** *Som.* Ogaadeen. *plateau* Ethiopia/Somalia
171 M10 **Oga-hantō** *peninsula* Honshū, C Japan
171 Hh14 **Ōgaki** Gifu, Honshū, SW Japan 35.21N 136.35E
30 L15 **Ogallala** Nebraska, C USA 41.09N 101.43W
174 I12 **Ogan, Air** ≈ Sumatera, W Indonesia
172 T16 **Ogasawara-shotō** *Eng.* Bonin Islands. *island group* SE Japan
12 I9 **Ogascanane, Lac** ◎ Québec, SE Canada
172 N9 **Ogawara-ko** ◎ Honshū, C Japan
79 T15 **Ogbomosho** *var.* Ogmoboso. Oyo, W Nigeria 8.10N 4.16E
Ogbomoso *see* Ogbomosho
31 U13 **Ogden** Iowa, C USA 42.03N 94.01W
38 L2 **Ogden** Utah, W USA 41.09N 111.58W
20 I6 **Ogdensburg** New York, NE USA 44.42N 75.25W
197 L16 **Ogea Driki** *island* Lau Group, E Fiji
197 L16 **Ogea Levu** *island* Lau Group, E Fiji
25 W5 **Ogeechee River** ≈ Georgia, SE USA
Oger *see* Ogre
171 K12 **Ogi** Niigata, Sado, C Japan 37.49N 138.16E
8 H5 **Ogilvie** Yukon Territory, NW Canada 63.34N 139.43W
8 H4 **Ogilvie** ≈ Yukon Territory, NW Canada
8 H5 **Ogilvie Mountains** ▲▲ Yukon Territory, NW Canada
Oginskiy Kanal *see* Ahinski Kanal
152 F6 **Og'iyon Sho'rxogi** *wetland* NW Uzbekistan
152 B10 **Oglanly** Balkan Welaýaty, W Turkmenistan 39.56N 54.25E
25 T5 **Oglethorpe** Georgia, SE USA 32.17N 84.03W
25 T2 **Oglethorpe, Mount** ▲ Georgia, SE USA 34.29N 84.19W
108 F7 **Oglio** *anc.* Ollius. ≈ N Italy
105 T8 **Ognon** ≈ E France
175 Pp7 **Ogoamas, Pegunungan** ▲▲ Sulawesi, N Indonesia
127 N14 **Ogodzha** Amurskaya Oblast', S Russian Federation 52.51N 132.49E
79 W16 **Ogoja** Cross River, S Nigeria 6.37N 8.48E
10 C10 **Ogoki** ≈ Ontario, S Canada
10 D11 **Ogoki Lake** ◎ Ontario, C Canada
168 K10 **Ögöömör** Ömnögovĭ, S Mongolia 43.47N 104.31E
81 F19 **Ogooué** ≈ Congo/Gabon
81 E18 **Ogooué-Ivindo** *off.* Province de l'Ogooué-Ivindo, *var.* L'Ogooué-Ivindo. ◈ *province* N Gabon
81 E19 **Ogooué-Lolo** *off.* Province de l'Ogooué-Lolo, *var.* L'Ogooué-Lolo. ◈ *province* C Gabon
81 C19 **Ogooué-Maritime** *off.* Province de l'Ogooué-Maritime, *var.* L'Ogooué-Maritime. ◈ *province* W Gabon
170 Cc13 **Ogōri** Fukuoka, Kyūshū, SW Japan 33.25N 130.30E
170 Dd13 **Ogōri** Yamaguchi, Honshū, SW Japan 34.05N 131.20E
116 H7 **Ogosta** ≈ NW Bulgaria
114 Q9 **Ograzden** *Bul.* Ograzhden. ▲▲ Bulgaria/FYR Macedonia *see also* Ograzhden
116 G12 **Ograzhden** | Mac. Orgraždèn. ▲▲ Bulgaria/FYR Macedonia *see also* Ogražden
120 G9 **Ogre** *Ger.* Oger. Ogre, C Latvia 56.49N 24.36E
120 H9 **Ogre** ≈ C Latvia
114 C10 **Ogulin** Karlovac, NW Croatia 45.15N 15.13E
79 S16 **Ogun** ◈ *state* SW Nigeria
Ogurdzhaly, Ostrov *see* Ogurjaly Adasy
152 A12 **Ogurjaly Adasy** *Rus.* Ogurdzhaly, Ostrov. *island* W Turkmenistan
79 U16 **Ogwashi-Uku** Delta, S Nigeria 6.08N 6.38E
193 B23 **Ohai** Southland, South Island, NZ 45.56S 167.59E
153 Q10 **Ohangaron** *Rus.* Akhangaran. Toshkent Viloyati, E Uzbekistan 40.56N 69.37E
153 Q10 **Ohangaron** *Rus.* Akhangaran. ≈ E Uzbekistan
85 C16 **Ohangwena** ◈ *district* N Namibia
171 K17 **Ōhara** Chiba, Honshū, S Japan 35.14N 140.19E
32 M10 **O'Hare** ✈ (Chicago) Illinois, N USA 41.59N 87.56W
172 Nn8 **Ōhata** Aomori, Honshū, C Japan 41.23N 141.09E
192 L13 **Ohau** Manawatu-Wanganui, North Island, NZ 40.40S 175.15E
193 E20 **Ohau, Lake** ◎ South Island, NZ
Ohcejohka *see* Utsjoki
101 J20 **Ohey** Namur, SE Belgium 50.26N 5.07E
203 X15 **O'Higgins, Cabo** *headland* Easter Island, Chile, E Pacific Ocean 27.04S 109.15W
O'Higgins, Lago *see* San Martín, Lago
33 S12 **Ohio** *off.* State of Ohio; also known as The Buckeye State. ◈ *state* N USA
(0) L10 **Ohio River** ≈ N USA
Ohlau *see* Oława
103 H16 **Ohm** ≈ C Germany
200 R16 **Ohonua** 'Eua, E Tonga 21.20S 174.57W
25 V5 **Ohoopee River** ≈ Georgia, SE USA
102 L12 **Ohre** *Ger.* Eger. ≈ Czech Republic/Germany
Ohri *see* Ohrid
115 M20 **Ohrid** *Turk.* Ochrida, Ohri. SW FYR Macedonia 41.07N 20.48E
115 M20 **Ohrid, Lake** *var.* Lake Ochrida, *Alb.* Liqeni i Ohrit, *Mac.* Ohridsko Ezero. ◎ Albania/FYR Macedonia
Ohridsko Ezero/Ohrit, Liqeni i *see* Ohrid, Lake
192 L9 **Ohura** Manawatu-Wanganui, North Island, NZ 38.51S 174.58E
60 J9 **Oiapoque** Amapá, E Brazil 3.54N 51.46W
60 J10 **Oiapoque, Rio** *var.* Fleuve l'Oyapok, Oyapock. ≈ Brazil/French Guiana *see also* Oyapok, Fleuve l'
13 O9 **Oies, Île aux** *island* Québec, SE Canada
94 L13 **Oijärvi** Oulu, C Finland 65.37N 26.04E
94 L12 **Oikarainen** Lappi, N Finland 66.30N 25.46E
196 F10 **Oikuul** Babeldaob, N Palau
20 C13 **Oil City** Pennsylvania, NE USA 41.25N 79.42W
20 C12 **Oil Creek** ≈ Pennsylvania, NE USA
37 R13 **Oildale** California, W USA 35.25N 119.01W
Oileán Ciarral *see* Castleisland
Oil Islands *see* Chagos Archipelago
117 D18 **Oiniádes** *anc.* Oeniadae. *site of ancient city* Dytikí Ellás, W Greece 38.23N 21.13E
117 L18 **Oinoússes** *island* E Greece
Oírr, Inis *see* Inisheer
101 J15 **Oirschot** Noord-Brabant, S Netherlands 51.30N 5.18E
105 N4 **Oise** ◈ *department* N France
105 P3 **Oise** ≈ N France
101 J14 **Oisterwijk** Noord-Brabant, S Netherlands 51.34N 5.12E
47 O14 **Oistins** S Barbados 13.04N 59.33W
170 D14 **Ōita** Ōita, Kyūshū, SW Japan 33.15N 131.34E
170 D14 **Ōita** *off.* Ōita-ken. ◈ *prefecture* Kyūshū, SW Japan
117 E17 **Oíti** ▲ C Greece 38.48N 22.12E
172 Oo6 **Oiwake** Hokkaidō, NE Japan 42.54N 141.49E
37 R14 **Ojai** California, W USA 34.25N 119.15W
96 K13 **Öje** Dalarna, C Sweden 60.49N 13.54E
95 J14 **Öjebyn** Norrbotten, N Sweden 65.20N 21.26E
170 Bb12 **Ojika-jima** *island* SW Japan
42 K5 **Ojinaga** Chihuahua, N Mexico 29.30N 104.25W
171 K13 **Ojiya** *var.* Oziya. Niigata, Honshū, C Japan 37.18N 138.47E
42 M11 **Ojo Caliente** *var.* Ojocaliente. Zacatecas, C Mexico 22.39N 102.17W
42 D6 **Ojo de Liebre, Laguna** *var.* Laguna Scammon, Scammon Lagoon. *lagoon* W Mexico
64 I7 **Ojos del Salado, Cerro** ▲ W Argentina 27.04S 68.34W
107 R7 **Ojos Negros** Aragón, NE Spain 40.43N 1.30W
42 M12 **Ojuelos de Jalisco** Aguascalientes, C Mexico 21.52N 101.40W
131 N4 **Oka** ≈ W Russian Federation
85 D19 **Okahandja** Otjozondjupa, C Namibia 21.58S 16.55E
192 L9 **Okahukura** Manawatu-Wanganui, North Island, NZ 38.48S 175.13E
192 J3 **Okaihau** Northland, North Island, NZ 35.18S 173.44E
85 D18 **Okakarara** Otjozondjupa, N Namibia 20.34S 17.24E
11 P5 **Okak Islands** *island group* Newfoundland and Labrador, E Canada
8 M17 **Okanagan** ≈ British Columbia, SW Canada
9 N17 **Okanagan Lake** ◎ British Columbia, SW Canada
Ókanizsa *see* Kanjiža
85 C16 **Okankolo** Otjikoto, N Namibia 17.57S 16.28E
34 K6 **Okanogan River** ≈ Washington, NW USA
194 I13 **Okapa** Eastern Highlands, C PNG 6.22S 145.29E
85 D18 **Okaputa** Otjozondjupa, N Namibia 20.09S 16.55E
155 V9 **Okāra** Punjab, E Pakistan 30.49N 73.31E
28 M10 **Okarche** Oklahoma, C USA 35.43N 97.58W
Okarem *see* Ekerem
201 X14 **Okat Harbor** *harbor* Kosrae, E Micronesia
24 M5 **Okatibbee Creek** ≈ Mississippi, S USA
85 C17 **Okaukuejo** Kunene, N Namibia 19.09S 15.57E
Okavanggo *see* Cubango/Okavango
85 E17 **Okavango** ◈ *district* NW Namibia
85 G17 **Okavango** *var.* Cubango, Kavango, Kavengo, Kubango, Okavanggo, *Port.* Ocavango. ≈ S Africa *see also* Cubango
85 G17 **Okavango Delta** *wetland* N Botswana
171 J15 **Okaya** Nagano, Honshū, S Japan 36.04N 138.02E
170 Ff14 **Okayama** Okayama, Honshū, SW Japan 34.40N 133.54E
170 F13 **Okayama** *off.* Okayama-ken. ◈ *prefecture* Honshū, SW Japan
171 I16 **Okazaki** Aichi, Honshū, C Japan 34.58N 137.10E
112 M12 **Okęcie** ✈ (Warszawa) Mazowieckie, C Poland 52.08N 20.57E
25 Y13 **Okeechobee** Florida, SE USA 27.14N 80.49W
25 Y14 **Okeechobee, Lake** ◎ Florida, SE USA
28 M9 **Okeene** Oklahoma, C USA 36.07N 98.19W
25 V8 **Okefenokee Swamp** *wetland* Georgia, SE USA
99 J24 **Okehampton** SW England, UK 50.44N 4.00W
29 P10 **Okemah** Oklahoma, C USA 35.25N 96.18W
79 U16 **Okene** Kogi, S Nigeria 7.31N 6.15E
102 K13 **Oker** *var.* Ocker. ≈ NW Germany
103 J14 **Oker-Stausee** ◎ C Germany
127 O13 **Okha** Ostrov Sakhalin, Sakhalinskaya Oblast', SE Russian Federation 53.33N 142.55E
129 U15 **Okhansk** *var.* Ochansk. Permskaya Oblast', NW Russian Federation 57.44N 55.20E
127 N10 **Okhota** ≈ E Russian Federation
127 Nn11 **Okhotsk** Khabarovskiy Kray, E Russian Federation 59.21N 143.14E
199 I2 **Okhotsk, Sea of** *sea* NW Pacific Ocean
119 T4 **Okhtyrka** *Rus.* Akhtyrka. Sums'ka Oblast', NE Ukraine 50.19N 34.54E
199 Gg6 **Oki-Daitō Ridge** *undersea feature* W Pacific Ocean
85 E23 **Okiep** Northern Cape, W South Africa 29.39S 17.53E
Oki-guntō *see* Oki-shotō
170 Ff11 **Oki-kaikyō** *strait* SW Japan
172 P15 **Okinawa** Okinawa, SW Japan 26.19N 127.46E
172 Oo14 **Okinawa** *off.* Okinawa-ken. ◈ *prefecture* Okinawa, SW Japan
172 Oo14 **Okinawa** *island* SW Japan
172 Q14 **Okinoerabu-jima** *island* Nansei-shotō, SW Japan
170 Dd15 **Okino-shima** *island* SW Japan
170 Ff11 **Oki-shotō** *var.* Oki-guntō. *island group* SW Japan
79 T16 **Okitipupa** Ondo, SW Nigeria 6.33N 4.43E
177 G8 **Okkan** Pegu, SW Myanmar 17.31N 95.51E
29 N10 **Oklahoma** *off.* State of Oklahoma; also known as The Sooner State. ◈ *state* C USA
29 N11 **Oklahoma City** *state capital* Oklahoma, C USA 35.28N 97.31W
27 Q4 **Oklaunion** Texas, SW USA 34.07N 99.07W
25 W10 **Oklawaha River** ≈ Florida, SE USA
29 P10 **Okmulgee** Oklahoma, C USA 35.37N 95.57W
Oknitsa *see* Ocnița
24 M3 **Okolona** Mississippi, S USA 34.00N 88.45W
172 Q4 **Okoppe** Hokkaidō, NE Japan 44.27N 143.06E
9 Q16 **Okotoks** Alberta, SW Canada 50.46N 113.57W
82 H6 **Oko, Wadi** ≈ NE Sudan
81 G19 **Okoyo** Cuvette, W Congo 1.28S 15.04E
79 S15 **Okpara** ≈ Benin/Nigeria
94 J8 **Øksfjord** Finnmark, N Norway 70.13N 22.22E
176 Z12 **Oksibil** Papua, E Indonesia 4.52S 140.32E
129 R4 **Oksino** Nenetskiy Avtonomnyy Okrug, NW Russian Federation 67.33N 52.15E
94 G13 **Oksskolten** ▲ C Norway 66.00N 14.18E
Oksu *see* Oqsu
150 M8 **Oktaybr'skiy** Kostanay, N Kazakhstan
194 E11 **Ok Tedi** Western, W PNG
Oktemberyan *see* Armavir
177 G7 **Oktwin** Pegu, C Myanmar 18.46N 96.21E
131 R6 **Oktyabr'sk** Samarskaya Oblast', W Russian Federation 53.13N 48.36E
Oktyabr'sk *see* Kandyagash
129 N12 **Oktyabr'skiy** Arkhangel'skaya Oblast', NW Russian Federation 61.03N 43.16E
127 Pp12 **Oktyabr'skiy** Kamchatskaya Oblast', E Russian Federation 52.35N 94.18E
131 T5 **Oktyabr'skiy** Respublika Bashkortostan, W Russian Federation 54.28N 53.29E
131 O11 **Oktyabr'skiy** Volgogradskaya Oblast', SW Russian Federation 48.00N 43.35E
Oktyabr'skiy *see* Aktsyabrski
131 V7 **Oktyabr'skoye** Orenburgskaya Oblast', W Russian Federation 52.22N 55.39E
126 J3 **Oktyabr'skoy Revolyutsii, Ostrov** *Eng.* October Revolution Island. *island* Severnaya Zemlya, N Russian Federation
170 C15 **Ōkuchi** *var.* Ôkuti. Kagoshima, Kyūshū, SW Japan 32.03N 130.36E
Okulovka *see* Uglovka
171 Mm5 **Okushiri-tō** *var.* Okusiri Tô. *island* NE Japan
Okusiri Tô *see* Okushiri-tō
79 S15 **Okuta** Kwara, W Nigeria 9.18N 3.09E
Ôkuti *see* Ōkuchi
85 F19 **Okwa** *var.* Chapman's. ≈ Botswana/Namibia
127 O10 **Ola** Magadanskaya Oblast', E Russian Federation 59.36N 151.18E
29 T11 **Ola** Arkansas, C USA 35.01N 93.13W
Ola *see* Ala
37 T11 **Olacha Peak** ▲ California, W USA 36.15N 118.07W
94 J1 **Ólafsfjördhur** Nordhurland Eystra, N Iceland 66.04N 18.36W
94 H3 **Ólafsvík** Vesturland, W Iceland 64.52N 23.45W
Oláhbrettye *see* Bretea-Română
Oláhszentgyőrgy *see* Sângeorz-Băi
Oláh-Toplicza *see* Toplița
37 T11 **Olancha** California, W USA 36.16N 118.00W
44 J5 **Olanchito** Yoro, C Honduras 15.27N 86.37W
44 J6 **Olancho** ◈ *department* E Honduras
97 O20 **Öland** *island* S Sweden
97 O19 **Ölands norra udde** *headland* S Sweden 57.21N 17.06E
97 N22 **Ölands södra udde** *headland* S Sweden 56.12N 16.26E
190 K7 **Olary** South Australia 32.18S 140.16E
29 R4 **Olathe** Kansas, C USA 38.52N 94.49W
63 C22 **Olavarría** Buenos Aires, E Argentina 36.57S 60.19W
94 O2 **Olav V Land** *physical region* C Svalbard
113 H14 **Oława** *Ger.* Ohlau. Dolnośląskie, SW Poland 50.57N 17.18E
109 D17 **Olbia** *prev.* Terranova Pausania. Sardegna, Italy, C Mediterranean Sea 40.55N 9.30E
46 G5 **Old Bahama Channel** *channel* Bahamas/Cuba
Old Bay State/Old Colony State *see* Massachusetts
8 H2 **Old Crow** Yukon Territory, NW Canada 67.34N 139.55W
Old Dominion *see* Virginia
Oldeberkeap *see* Oldeberkoop
100 M7 **Oldeberkoop** *Fris.* Oldeberkeap. Friesland, N Netherlands 52.55N 6.07E
100 L10 **Oldebroek** Gelderland, E Netherlands 52.27N 5.54E
100 L8 **Oldemarkt** Overijssel, N Netherlands 52.49N 5.58E
96 E11 **Olden** Sogn og Fjordane, C Norway 61.52N 6.44E
102 G10 **Oldenburg** Niedersachsen, NW Germany 53.09N 8.13E
102 K8 **Oldenburg** *var.* Oldenburg in Holstein. Schleswig-Holstein, N Germany 54.17N 10.55E
Oldenburg in Holstein *see* Oldenburg
100 P10 **Oldenzaal** Overijssel, E Netherlands 52.19N 6.52E
Olderfjord *see* Leaibevuotna
20 J8 **Old Forge** New York, NE USA 43.42N 74.59W
Old Goa *see* Goa
99 L17 **Oldham** NW England, UK 53.36N 2.00W
41 Q14 **Old Harbor** Kodiak Island, Alaska, USA 57.12N 153.18W
46 J13 **Old Harbour** C Jamaica 17.55N 77.06W
99 C22 **Old Head of Kinsale** *Ir.* An Seancheann. *headland* SW Ireland 51.37N 8.33W
22 J8 **Old Hickory Lake** ⊠ Tennessee, S USA
Old Line State *see* Maryland
Old North State *see* North Carolina
83 I17 **Ol Doinyo Lengeyo** ▲▲ C Kenya
9 Q16 **Olds** Alberta, SW Canada 51.49N 114.06W
21 O7 **Old Speck Mountain** ▲ Maine, NE USA 44.34N 70.55W
21 S6 **Old Town** Maine, NE USA 44.55N 68.39W
9 T17 **Old Wives Lake** ◎ Saskatchewan, S Canada
168 J7 **Öldziyt** Arhangay, C Mongolia 48.30N 101.25E
169 N10 **Öldziyt** Dornogovĭ, SE Mongolia 44.42N 109.10E
196 H6 **Oleai** *var.* San Jose. Saipan, S Northern Mariana Islands
20 E11 **Olean** New York, NE USA 42.04N 78.24W
112 O7 **Olecko** *Ger.* Treuburg. Warmińsko-Mazurskie, NE Poland 54.01N 22.28E
108 C7 **Oleggio** Piemonte, NE Italy 45.36N 8.37E
126 L13 **Olëkma** Amurskaya Oblast', SE Russian Federation 57.00N 120.27E
126 L13 **Olëkma** ≈ C Russian Federation
126 L12 **Olëkminsk** Respublika Sakha (Yakutiya), NE Russian Federation 60.25N 120.25E
119 W7 **Oleksandrivka** Donets'ka Oblast', E Ukraine 48.42N 36.56E
119 R7 **Oleksandrivka** *Rus.* Aleksandrovka. Kirovohrads'ka Oblast', C Ukraine 48.58N 32.13E
119 Q9 **Oleksandrivka** Mykolayivs'ka Oblast', S Ukraine 47.42N 31.17E
119 S7 **Oleksandriya** *Rus.* Aleksandriya. Kirovohrads'ka Oblast', C Ukraine 48.42N 33.07E
95 B20 **Ølen** Hordaland, S Norway 59.36N 5.48E
128 J4 **Olenegorsk** Murmanskaya Oblast', NW Russian Federation 68.06N 33.15E
126 K8 **Olenëk** Respublika Sakha (Yakutiya), NE Russian Federation 68.28N 112.18E
126 Jj9 **Olenëk** ≈ NE Russian Federation
126 Kk6 **Olenëkskiy Zaliv** *bay* N Russian Federation
128 K6 **Olenitsa** Murmanskaya Oblast', NW Russian Federation 66.27N 35.21E
104 I11 **Oléron, Île d'** *island* W France
113 H14 **Oleśnica** *Ger.* Oels, Oels in Schlesien. Dolnośląskie, SW Poland 51.13N 17.19E
113 I15 **Olesno** *Ger.* Rosenberg. Opolskie, S Poland 50.53N 18.23E
118 M3 **Olevs'k** *Rus.* Olevsk. Zhytomyrs'ka Oblast', N Ukraine 51.12N 27.38E
127 Nn18 **Ol'ga** Primorskiy Kray, SE Russian Federation 43.41N 135.06E
Olga, Mount *see* Kata Tjuta
94 P2 **Olgastretet** *strait* E Svalbard
168 D5 **Ölgiy** Bayan-Ölgiy, W Mongolia 48.57N 89.59E
97 F23 **Ølgod** Ribe, W Denmark 55.43N 8.37E
106 H14 **Olhão** Faro, S Portugal 37.01N 7.49W
95 L14 **Olhava** Oulu, C Finland 65.28N 25.25E
114 B12 **Olib** *It.* Ulbo. *island* W Croatia
85 B16 **Olifa** Kunene, NW Namibia 17.25S 14.27E
85 E20 **Olifants** *var.* Elephant River. ≈ E Namibia
85 E25 **Olifants** *var.* Elefantes. ≈ SW South Africa
85 G22 **Olifantshoek** Northern Cape, N South Africa 27.52S 22.46E
196 L15 **Olimarao Atoll** *atoll* Caroline Islands, C Micronesia
Ólimbos *see* Ólympos
Olimpo *see* Fuerte Olimpo
61 Q15 **Olinda** Pernambuco, E Brazil 08.00S 34.51W
Olinthos *see* Ólynthos
85 I20 **Oliphants Drift** Kgatleng, SE Botswana 24.13S 26.52E
Olisipo *see* Lisboa
Olita *see* Alytus
107 Q4 **Olite** Navarra, N Spain 42.28N 1.40W
64 K10 **Oliva** Córdoba, C Argentina 32.03S 63.34W
107 T11 **Oliva** País Valenciano, E Spain 38.55N 0.09W
106 I12 **Oliva de la Frontera** Extremadura, W Spain 38.16N 6.54W
Olivares *see* Olivares de Júcar
64 H9 **Olivares, Cerro de** ▲ N Chile 30.25S 69.52W
107 P9 **Olivares de Júcar** *var.* Olivares. Castilla-La Mancha, C Spain 39.45N 2.21W
24 L1 **Olive Branch** Mississippi, S USA 34.58N 89.49W
23 O5 **Olive Hill** Kentucky, S USA 38.18N 83.10W
37 O6 **Olivehurst** California, W USA 39.05N 121.33W
106 G7 **Oliveira de Azeméis** Aveiro, N Portugal 40.49N 8.28W
106 I11 **Olivenza** Extremadura, W Spain 38.40N 7.06W
9 N17 **Oliver** British Columbia, SW Canada 49.10N 119.37W
105 N7 **Olivet** Loiret, C France 47.52N 1.53E
31 Q12 **Olivet** South Dakota, N USA 43.13N 97.40W
31 T9 **Olivia** Minnesota, N USA 44.46N 94.59W
193 C20 **Olivine Range** ▲▲ South Island, NZ
110 H10 **Olivone** Ticino, S Switzerland 46.32N 8.55E
Ölkeyek *see* Ul'kayak
131 O9 **Ol'khovka** Volgogradskaya Oblast', SW Russian Federation 49.54N 44.36E
113 K16 **Olkusz** Małopolskie, S Poland 50.16N 19.31E
24 I6 **Olla** Louisiana, S USA 31.54N 92.14W
64 I4 **Ollagüe, Volcán** *var.* Oyahue, Volcán Oyahue. ▲ N Chile 21.25S 68.10W
201 U13 **Ollan** *island* Chuuk, C Micronesia
196 F7 **Ollei** Babeldaob, N Palau 7.43N 134.37E
Ollius *see* Oglio
110 C10 **Ollon** Vaud, W Switzerland 46.19N 7.00E
153 Q10 **Olmaliq** *Rus.* Almalyk. Toshkent Viloyati, E Uzbekistan 40.51N 69.39E
106 M6 **Olmedo** Castilla-León, N Spain 41.16N 4.40W
58 B10 **Olmos** Lambayeque, W Peru 6.00S 79.43W
Olmütz *see* Olomouc
32 M15 **Olney** Illinois, N USA 38.43N 88.05W
27 R5 **Olney** Texas, SW USA 33.22N 98.45W
97 L22 **Olofström** Blekinge, S Sweden 56.16N 14.33E
195 Y15 **Olomburi** Malaita, N Solomon Islands 9.00S 161.09E
113 H17 **Olomouc** *Ger.* Olmütz, *Pol.* Ołomuniec. Olomoucký Kraj, E Czech Republic 49.36N 17.13E
113 H18 **Olomoucký Kraj** ◈ region E Czech Republic
Ołomuniec *see* Olomouc
125 Cc6 **Olonets** Respublika Kareliya, NW Russian Federation 60.58N 33.01E
179 P10 **Olongapo** *off.* Olongapo City. Luzon, N Philippines 14.52N 120.16E
104 J16 **Oloron-Ste-Marie** Pyrénées-Atlantiques, SW France 43.12N 0.34W
198 Dd8 **Olosega** *island* Manua Islands, E American Samoa
107 W4 **Olot** Cataluña, NE Spain 42.10N 2.30E
152 K12 **Olot** *Rus.* Alat. Buxoro Viloyati, C Uzbekistan 39.22N 63.42E
114 I12 **Olovo** Federacija Bosna I Hercegovina, E Bosnia and Herzegovina 44.08N 18.35E
126 Kk16 **Olovyannaya** Chitinskaya Oblast', S Russian Federation 50.58N 115.24E
127 Oo6 **Oloy** ≈ NE Russian Federation
103 F16 **Olpe** Nordrhein-Westfalen, W Germany 51.01N 7.51E
111 N8 **Olperer** ▲ SW Austria 47.03N 11.36E
Olshanka *see* Vil'shanka
Ol'shany *see* Al'shany
Olsnitz *see* Murska Sobota
100 M10 **Olst** Overijssel, E Netherlands 52.19N 6.06E
112 L8 **Olsztyn** *Ger.* Allenstein. Warmińsko-Mazurskie, NE Poland, 53.46N 20.28E
112 L8 **Olsztynek** *Ger.* Hohenstein in Ostpreussen. Warmińsko-Mazurskie, NE Poland, 53.34N 20.16E
118 I14 **Olt** ◈ *county* SW Romania
118 I14 **Olt** *var.* Oltul, *Ger.* Alt. ≈ S Romania
110 E7 **Olten** Solothurn, NW Switzerland 47.20N 7.51E
118 K14 **Oltenița** *prev. Eng.* Oltenitsa, *anc.* Constantiola. Călărași, SE Romania 44.04N 26.40E
Oltenitsa *see* Oltenița
118 H14 **Olteț** ≈ S Romania
26 M4 **Olton** Texas, SW USA 34.10N 102.07W
143 R12 **Oltu** Erzurum, NE Turkey 40.34N 41.58E
Oltul *see* Olt
152 G7 **Oltynko'l** Qoraqalpog'iston Respublikasi, NW Uzbekistan 43.04N 58.51E
167 S15 **Oluan Pi** *Eng.* Cape Olwanpi. *headland* S Taiwan 21.57N 120.48E
Ólubló *see* Stará L'ubovňa
143 R11 **Olur** Erzurum, NE Turkey 40.49N 42.07E
106 L15 **Olvera** Andalucía, S Spain 36.55N 5.15W
Ol'viopol' *see* Pervomays'k
Olwanpi, Cape *see* Oluan Pi
17 G2 **Olympia** *state capital* Washington, NW USA 47.02N 122.54W
117 D20 **Olympía** Dytikí Ellás, S Greece 37.39N 21.36E
190 H5 **Olympic Dam** South Australia 30.25S 136.56E
34 F7 **Olympic Mountains** ▲▲ Washington, NW USA
124 R12 **Ólympos** *var.* Troodos, *Eng.* Mount Olympus. ▲ C Cyprus 34.55N 32.49E
117 F15 **Ólympos** *var.* Ólimbos, *Eng.* Mount Olympus. ▲ N Greece 40.04N 22.24E
117 L17 **Ólympos** ▲ Lésvos, E Greece 39.03N 26.20E
17 G1 **Olympus, Mount** ▲ Washington, NW USA 47.48N 123.42W
Olympus, Mount *see* Ólympos
117 G14 **Ólynthos** *var.* Olinthos; *anc.* Olynthus. *site of ancient city* Kentrikí Makedonía, N Greece 40.16N 23.21E
Olynthus *see* Ólynthos
119 Q3 **Olyshivka** Chernihivs'ka Oblast', N Ukraine 51.13N 31.19E
127 Q7 **Olyutorskiy, Mys** *headland* E Russian Federation 59.56N 170.22E
127 Pp8 **Olyutorskiy Zaliv** *bay* E Russian Federation
194 F11 **Om** ≈ W PNG
133 S6 **Om'** ≈ N Russian Federation
164 I13 **Oma** Xizang Zizhiqu, W China 32.30N 83.13E
172 N8 **Ōma** Aomori, Honshū, C Japan 41.31N 140.54E
129 P6 **Oma** ≈ NW Russian Federation
171 J14 **Ōmachi** *var.* Ômati. Nagano, Honshū, S Japan 36.33N 137.49E
171 Ii17 **Omae-zaki** *headland* Honshū, S Japan 34.36N 138.12E
171 M11 **Ōmagari** Akita, Honshū, C Japan 39.27N 140.28E
99 E15 **Omagh** *Ir.* An Ómaigh. W Northern Ireland, UK 54.36N 7.18W
31 S15 **Omaha** Nebraska, C USA 41.14N 95.57W
85 E19 **Omaheke** ◈ *district* W Namibia
147 W10 **Oman** *off.* Sultanate of Oman, *Ar.* Salṭanat 'Umān; *prev.* Muscat and Oman. ◆ *monarchy* SW Asia
133 O10 **Oman Basin** *var.* Bassin d'Oman. *undersea feature* N Indian Ocean
Oman, Bassin d' *see* Oman Basin
133 N10 **Oman, Gulf of** *Ar.* Khalīj 'Umān. *gulf* N Arabian Sea
192 J3 **Omapere** Northland, North Island, NZ 35.32S 173.24E
193 E20 **Omarama** Canterbury, South Island, NZ 44.29S 169.57E
114 F11 **Omarska** Republika Srpska, NW Bosnia and Herzegovina 44.53N 16.52E
85 C18 **Omaruru** Erongo, NW Namibia 21.25S 15.57E
85 C19 **Omaruru** ≈ W Namibia
85 E17 **Omatako** ≈ NE Namibia
Ômati *see* Ōmachi
85 E18 **Omawewozonyanda** Omaheke, E Namibia 21.30S 19.34E
172 N7 **Oma-zaki** *headland* Honshū, C Japan 41.32N 140.53E
Omba *see* Ambae
Ombai *see* Alor, Pulau
175 Rr16 **Ombai, Selat** *strait* Nusa Tenggara, S Indonesia
85 C16 **Ombalantu** Omusati, N Namibia 17.33S 14.58E
81 H15 **Ombella-Mpoko** ◈ *prefecture* S Central African Republic
Ombetsu *see* Onbetsu
85 B17 **Ombombo** Kunene, NW Namibia 18.43S 13.55E
81 D19 **Omboué** Ogooué-Maritime, W Gabon 1.37S 9.19E
108 G13 **Ombrone** ≈ C Italy
82 F9 **Omdurman** *var.* Umm Durmān. Khartoum, C Sudan 15.37N 32.28E
171 Jj16 **Ōme** Tōkyō, Honshū, S Japan 35.48N 139.10E
108 C6 **Omegna** Piemonte, NE Italy 45.54N 8.25E
191 P12 **Omeo** Victoria, SE Australia 37.09S 147.36E
144 F11 **'Omer** Southern, C Israel 31.16N 34.51E
43 P16 **Ometepec** Guerrero, S Mexico 16.39N 98.22W
44 K11 **Ometepe, Isla de** *island* S Nicaragua
Om Hager *see* Om Hajer
82 I10 **Om Hajer** *var.* Om Hager. SW Eritrea 14.19N 36.46E
171 H14 **Ōmi-Hachiman** *var.* Ômihachiman. Shiga, Honshū, SW Japan 35.09N 136.04E
8 L12 **Omineca Mountains** ▲▲ British Columbia, W Canada
115 F14 **Omiš** *It.* Almissa. Split-Dalmacija, S Croatia 43.27N 16.41E
114 B10 **Omišalj** Primorje-Gorski Kotar, NW Croatia 45.10N 14.33E
170 Dd12 **Ōmi-shima** *island* SW Japan
85 D19 **Omitara** Khomas, C Namibia 22.18S 18.01E
43 O16 **Omitlán, Río** ≈ S Mexico
41 X14 **Ommaney, Cape** *headland* Baranof Island, Alaska, USA 56.10N 134.40W
100 N9 **Ommen** Overijssel, E Netherlands 52.31N 6.25E
168 K11 **Ömnögovĭ** ◈ *province* S Mongolia
203 X7 **Omoa** Fatu Hira, NE French Polynesia 10.30S 138.40E
Omo Botego *see* Omo Wenz
Ómoldova *see* Moldova Veche
127 O6 **Omolon** Chukotskiy Avtonomnyy Okrug, NE Russian Federation 65.11N 96.33E
127 O7 **Omolon** ≈ NE Russian Federation
126 Ll8 **Omoloy** ≈ NE Russian Federation
171 M10 **Omono-gawa** ≈ Honshū, C Japan
83 I14 **Omo Wenz** *var.* Omo Botego. ≈ Ethiopia/Kenya
125 Ff13 **Omsk** Omskaya Oblast', C Russian Federation 55.00N 73.22E
125 Ff12 **Omskaya Oblast'** ◈ *province* C Russian Federation
127 O8 **Omsukchan** Magadanskaya Oblast', E Russian Federation 62.25N 155.22E
172 Q4 **Ōmu** Hokkaidō, NE Japan 44.36N 142.55E
112 M9 **Omulew** ≈ NE Poland
118 J12 **Omul, Vârful** *prev.* Vîrful Omu. ▲ C Romania 45.24N 25.26E
85 D16 **Omundaungilo** Ohangwena, N Namibia 17.28S 16.39E
170 C13 **Ōmura** Nagasaki, Kyūshū, SW Japan 32.55N 129.54E
85 B17 **Omusati** ◈ *district* N Namibia
170 Cc13 **Ōmuta** Fukuoka, Kyūshū, SW Japan 33.02N 130.26E
129 S14 **Omutninsk** Kirovskaya Oblast', NW Russian Federation 58.37N 52.08E
Omu, Vîrful *see* Omul, Vârful
31 V7 **Onamia** Minnesota, N USA 46.04N 93.40W
23 Y5 **Onancock** Virginia, NE USA 37.42N 75.45W
12 E10 **Onaping Lake** ◎ Ontario, S Canada
32 M12 **Onarga** Illinois, N USA 40.39N 88.00W
13 R6 **Onatchiway, Lac** ◎ Québec, SE Canada
31 S14 **Onawa** Iowa, C USA 42.01N 96.06W
172 Pp7 **Onbetsu** *var.* Ombetsu. Hokkaidō, NE Japan 42.52N 143.54E
85 B16 **Oncócua** Cunene, SW Angola 16.37S 13.23E
107 S9 **Onda** País Valenciano, E Spain 39.58N 0.17W
113 N18 **Ondava** ≈ NE Slovakia
Ondjiva *see* N'Giva
79 T16 **Ondo** Ondo, SW Nigeria 7.07N 4.50E
79 T16 **Ondo** ◈ *state* SW Nigeria
169 N8 **Öndörhaan** *var.* Undur Khan; *prev.* Tsetsen Khan. Hentiy, E Mongolia 47.20N 110.42E
85 D18 **Ondundazongonda** Otjozondjupa, N Namibia 20.28S 18.00E
157 K21 **One and Half Degree Channel** *channel* S Maldives
197 L15 **Oneata** *island* Lau Group, E Fiji
128 L9 **Onega** Arkhangel'skaya Oblast', NW Russian Federation 63.54N 37.58E
125 Dd6 **Onega** ≈ NW Russian Federation
Onega Bay *see* Onezhskaya Guba
Onega, Lake *see* Onezhskoye Ozero
20 I10 **Oneida** New York, NE USA 43.05N 75.39W
22 M8 **Oneida** Tennessee, S USA 36.30N 84.30W
20 H9 **Oneida Lake** ◎ New York, NE USA
31 P13 **O'Neill** Nebraska, C USA 42.28N 98.37W
127 Pp13 **Onekotan, Ostrov** *island* Kuril'skiye Ostrova, SE Russian Federation
25 P3 **Oneonta** Alabama, S USA 33.57N 86.28W
20 J11 **Oneonta** New York, NE USA 42.27N 75.03W
202 I16 **Oneroa** *island* S Cook Islands
118 K11 **Onești** *Hung.* Onyest; *prev.* Gheorghe Gheorghiu-Dej. Bacău, E Romania 46.13N 26.46E
200 Qq15 **Onevai** *island* Tongatapu Group, S Tonga
110 A11 **Onex** Genève, SW Switzerland 46.11N 6.04E
128 K8 **Onezhskaya Guba** *Eng.* Onega Bay. *bay* NW Russian Federation
125 D6 **Onezhskoye Ozero** *Eng.* Lake Onega. ◎ NW Russian Federation
85 C16 **Ongandjera** Omusati, N Namibia 17.49S 15.06E
192 N12 **Ongaonga** Hawke's Bay, North Island, NZ 39.57S 176.21E
168 K9 **Ongi** Dundgovĭ, C Mongolia 45.27N 103.58E
168 J8 **Ongi** Övörhangay, C Mongolia 46.30N 102.18E
169 W14 **Ongjin** SW North Korea 37.55N 125.21E
161 J17 **Ongole** Andhra Pradesh, E India 15.33N 80.03E
168 K8 **Ongon** Övörhangay, C Mongolia 46.58N 103.45E
Ongtüstik Qazaqstan Oblysy *see* Yuzhnyy Kazakhstan
101 I21 **Onhaye** Namur, S Belgium 50.15N 4.51E

◆ Country
● Country Capital
◇ Dependent Territory
○ Dependent Territory Capital
◈ Administrative Region
✈ International Airport
▲ Mountain
▲▲ Mountain Range
Volcano
≈ River
◎ Lake
⊠ Reservoir

ONHNE – ÖSTERMYRA

177 G8 **Onhne** Pegu, SW Myanmar 17.02N 96.28E
143 S9 **Oni** N Georgia 42.36N 43.13E
31 N9 **Onida** South Dakota, N USA 44.42N 100.03W
170 E15 **Onigajō-yama** ▲ Shikoku, SW Japan 33.10N 132.37E
180 H7 **Onilahy** ⚡ S Madagascar
79 U16 **Onitsha** Anambra, S Nigeria 6.09N 6.48E
171 Gg14 **Ono** Hyōgo, Honshū, SW Japan 34.51N 134.56E
197 I15 **Ono** island SW Fiji
171 I14 **Ōno** Fukui, Honshū, SW Japan 35.59N 136.29E
170 D12 **Onoda** Yamaguchi, Honshū, SW Japan 33.59N 131.10E
197 L17 **Ono-i-lau** island SE Fiji
170 Cc13 **Ōnojō** var. Ōnozyô. Fukuoka, Kyūshū, SW Japan 33.30N 130.30E
126 K16 **Onokhoy** Respublika Buryatiya, S Russian Federation 51.51N 108.17E
170 F14 **Onomichi** var. Onomiti. Hiroshima, Honshū, SW Japan 34.25N 133.13E
Onomiti see Onomichi
169 O7 **Onon Gol** ⚡ N Mongolia
Ononte see Orontes
57 N6 **Onoto** Anzoátegui, NE Venezuela 9.36N 65.10W
203 O3 **Onotoa** prev. Clerk Island. atoll Tungaru, W Kiribati
Ōnozyô see Ōnojō
97 I19 **Onsala** Halland, S Sweden 57.25N 12.00E
85 E23 **Onseepkans** Northern Cape, W South Africa 28.44S 19.18E
106 F4 **Ons, Illa de** island NW Spain
188 H7 **Onslow** Western Australia 21.42S 115.07E
23 W11 **Onslow Bay** bay North Carolina, E USA
100 P6 **Onstwedde** Groningen, NE Netherlands 53.01N 7.04E
170 Bb16 **On-take** ▲ Kyūshū, SW Japan 31.35N 130.39E
171 Ii15 **Ontake-san** ▲ Honshū, S Japan 35.54N 137.28E
37 T15 **Ontario** California, W USA 34.03N 117.39W
34 M13 **Ontario** Oregon, NW USA 44.01N 116.57W
10 D10 **Ontario** ◆ province S Canada
15 Gg2 **Ontario, Lake** ⊚ Canada/USA
(0) L9 **Ontario Peninsula** peninsula Canada/USA
Onteniente see Ontinyent
107 S11 **Ontinyent** var. Onteniente. País Valenciano, E Spain 38.49N 0.37W
95 N15 **Ontojärvi** ⊚ E Finland
32 L3 **Ontonagon** Michigan, N USA 46.52N 89.18W
32 L3 **Ontonagon River** ⚡ Michigan, N USA
195 W11 **Ontong Java Atoll** prev. Lord Howe Island. atoll N Solomon Islands
183 N5 **Ontong Java Rise** undersea feature W Pacific Ocean
Onuba see Huelva
57 W9 **Onverwacht** Para, N Suriname 5.36N 55.12W
Onyest see Onești
190 J7 **Oodla Wirra** South Australia 32.52S 139.05E
190 F2 **Oodnadatta** South Australia 27.34S 135.27E
190 C5 **Ooldea** South Australia 30.29S 131.50E
29 Q8 **Oologah Lake** ⊠ Oklahoma, C USA
Oos-Kaap see Eastern Cape
Oos-Londen see East London
101 E17 **Oostakker** Oost-Vlaanderen, NW Belgium 51.06N 3.46E
101 D15 **Oostburg** Zeeland, SW Netherlands 51.19N 3.30E
100 K9 **Oostelijk-Flevoland** polder C Netherlands
101 B16 **Oostende** Eng. Ostend, Fr. Ostende. West-Vlaanderen, NW Belgium 51.13N 2.55E
101 B16 **Oostende** ✕ West-Vlaanderen, NW Belgium 51.12N 2.55E
100 L12 **Oosterbeek** Gelderland, SE Netherlands 51.58N 5.51E
101 I14 **Oosterhout** Noord-Brabant, S Netherlands 51.37N 4.51E
100 O6 **Oostermoers Vaart** var. Hunze. ⚡ NE Netherlands
101 F14 **Oosterschelde** Eng. Eastern Scheldt. inlet SW Netherlands
101 E14 **Oosterscheldedam** dam SW Netherlands 51.38N 3.45E
100 M7 **Oosterwolde** Fris. Easterwâlde. Friesland, N Netherlands 53.00N 6.15E
100 I9 **Oosthuizen** Noord-Holland, NW Netherlands 52.34N 5.00E
101 H16 **Oostmalle** Antwerpen, N Belgium 51.18N 4.44E
Oos-Transvaal see Mpumalanga
101 E15 **Oost-Souburg** Zeeland, SW Netherlands 51.28N 3.36E
101 E17 **Oost-Vlaanderen** Eng. East Flanders. ◆ province NW Belgium
100 J5 **Oost-Vlieland** Friesland, N Netherlands 53.19N 5.02E
100 F12 **Oostvoorne** Zuid-Holland, SW Netherlands 51.55N 4.06E
Ootacamund see Udagamandalam
100 O10 **Ootmarsum** Overijssel, E Netherlands 52.25N 6.55E
8 K14 **Ootsa Lake** ⊠ British Columbia, SW Canada
116 L8 **Opaka** Tŭrgovishte, N Bulgaria 43.26N 26.12E
81 M18 **Opala** Orientale, C Dem. Rep. Congo 0.40S 24.19E
129 Q13 **Oparino** Kirovskaya Oblast', NW Russian Federation 59.52N 48.14E
12 H8 **Opasatica, Lac** ⊚ Québec, SE Canada
114 B9 **Opatija** It. Abbazia. Primorje-Gorski Kotar, NW Croatia 45.18N 14.15E
113 N15 **Opatów** Świętokrzyskie, C Poland 50.45N 21.27E
113 I17 **Opava** Ger. Troppau. Moravskoslezský Kraj, E Czech Republic 49.55N 17.53E
113 H16 **Opava** Ger. Oppa. ⚡ NE Czech Republic
Ópazova see Stara Pazova
194 L14 **Ope** ⚡ S PNG
Ópécska see Pecica
12 E8 **Opeepeesway Lake** ⊚ Ontario, S Canada
25 R5 **Opelika** Alabama, S USA 32.39N 85.22W
24 I8 **Opelousas** Louisiana, S USA 30.31N 92.04W
195 O11 **Open Bay** bay New Britain, E PNG
12 I12 **Opeongo Lake** ⊚ Ontario, SE Canada
101 K17 **Opglabbeek** Limburg, NE Belgium 51.04N 5.39E
35 W6 **Opheim** Montana, NW USA 48.50N 106.24W
41 P10 **Ophir** Alaska, USA 63.08N 94.31W
Ophiusa see Formentera
81 N18 **Opienge** Orientale, E Dem. Rep. Congo 0.15N 27.25E
193 G20 **Opihi** ⚡ South Island, NZ
10 J9 **Opinaca** ⚡ Québec, C Canada
10 J10 **Opinaca, Réservoir** ⊠ Québec, E Canada
119 T5 **Opishnya** Rus. Oposhnya. Poltavs'ka Oblast', NE Ukraine 49.56N 34.36E
100 I8 **Opmeer** Noord-Holland, NW Netherlands 52.43N 4.55E
79 V17 **Opobo** Akwa Ibom, S Nigeria 4.36N 7.37E
128 F16 **Opochka** Pskovskaya Oblast', W Russian Federation 56.42N 28.39E
112 L13 **Opoczno** Łodzkie, C Poland 51.24N 20.18E
113 I15 **Opole** Ger. Oppeln. Opolskie, S Poland 50.40N 17.55E
113 H15 **Opolskie** ◆ province S Poland
Opornyy see Borankul
106 G4 **O Porriño** var. Porriño. Galicia, NW Spain 42.10N 8.37W
Oporto see Porto
Oposhnya see Opishnya
192 P8 **Opotiki** Bay of Plenty, North Island, NZ 38.02S 177.18E
25 Q7 **Opp** Alabama, S USA 31.16N 86.14W
Oppa see Opava
96 G9 **Oppdal** Sør-Trøndelag, S Norway 62.36N 9.41E
Oppeln see Opole
109 N23 **Oppido Mamertina** Calabria, SW Italy 38.17N 15.58E
Oppidum Ubiorum see Köln
96 F12 **Oppland** ◆ county S Norway
120 J12 **Opsa** Rus. Opsa. Vitsyebskaya Voblasts', NW Belarus 55.31N 26.49E
28 I8 **Optima Lake** ⊠ Oklahoma, C USA
192 J11 **Opunake** Taranaki, North Island, NZ 39.27S 173.51E
203 N6 **Opunohu, Baie d'** bay Moorea, W French Polynesia
85 B17 **Opuwo** Kunene, NW Namibia 18.06S 13.52E
152 H6 **Oqqal'a** var. Akkala, Rus. Karakala. Qoraqalpog'iston Respublikasi, NW Uzbekistan 43.43N 59.25E
153 V13 **Oqsu** Rus. Oksu. ⚡ SE Tajikistan
153 P14 **Oqtogh, Qatorkŭhi** Rus. Khrebet Aktau. ▲ SW Tajikistan
152 M11 **Oqtosh** Rus. Aktash. Samarqand Viloyati, C Uzbekistan 39.23N 65.45E
153 N11 **Oqtov Tizmasi** Rus. Khrebet Aktau. ▲ C Uzbekistan
32 J12 **Oquawka** Illinois, N USA 40.55N 90.55W
150 J10 **Or'** Kaz. Or. ⚡ Kazakhstan/Russian Federation
38 M15 **Oracle** Arizona, SW USA 32.36N 110.46W
153 N13 **O'radaryo** Rus. Uradar'ya. ⚡ S Uzbekistan
118 F9 **Oradea** prev. Oradea Mare, Ger. Grosswardein, Hung. Nagyvárad. Bihor, NW Romania 47.02N 21.55E
Oradea Mare see Oradea
115 M17 **Orahovac** Alb. Rahovec. Serbia, S Serbia and Montenegro (Yugoslavia) 42.24N 20.40E
114 H9 **Orahovica** Virovitica-Podravina, NE Croatia 45.33N 17.54E
158 K13 **Orai** Uttar Pradesh, N India 26.00N 79.26E
94 K12 **Orajärvi** Lappi, NW Finland 66.54N 24.04E
Or Akiva see Or 'Aqiva
Oral see Ural'sk
76 I5 **Oran** var. Ouahran, Wahran. NW Algeria 35.42N 0.37W
191 R8 **Orange** New South Wales, SE Australia 33.16S 149.06E
105 R14 **Orange** anc. Arausio. Vaucluse, SE France 44.06N 4.52E
27 Y10 **Orange** Texas, SW USA 30.05N 93.44W
23 V5 **Orange** Virginia, NE USA 38.15N 78.06W
23 R13 **Orangeburg** South Carolina, SE USA 33.29N 80.51W
60 J9 **Orange, Cabo** headland NE Brazil 4.24N 51.33W
31 S12 **Orange City** Iowa, C USA 43.00N 96.03W
Orange Cone see Orange Fan
180 J10 **Orange Fan** var. Orange Cone. undersea feature SW Indian Ocean
Orange Free State see Free State
27 S14 **Orange Grove** Texas, SW USA 27.57N 97.56W
20 K13 **Orange Lake** New York, NE USA 41.32N 74.06W
25 V10 **Orange Lake** ⊠ Florida, SE USA
Orange Mouth/Orangemund see Oranjemund
25 W9 **Orange Park** Florida, SE USA 30.10N 81.42W
194 M17 **Orangerie Bay** bay SE PNG
85 E23 **Orange River** Afr. Oranjerivier. ⚡ S Africa
12 G15 **Orangeville** Ontario, S Canada 43.55N 80.06W
38 M5 **Orangeville** Utah, W USA 39.14N 111.03W
44 G1 **Orange Walk** Orange Walk, N Belize 18.06N 88.30W
44 F1 **Orange Walk** ◆ district NW Belize
102 N11 **Oranienburg** Brandenburg, NE Germany 52.46N 13.15E
100 O7 **Oranjekanaal** canal NE Netherlands
85 D23 **Oranjemund** var. Orangemund; prev. Orange Mouth. Karas, SW Namibia 28.33S 16.27E
Oranjerivier see Orange River
47 N16 **Oranjestad** ○ (Aruba) W Aruba 12.31N 70.00W
Oranje Vrystaat see Free State
176 W9 **Oransbari** Papua, E Indonesia 1.18S 134.16E
Orany see Varėna
85 H18 **Orapa** Central, C Botswana 21.18S 25.22E
144 F9 **Or 'Aqiva** var. Or Akiva. Haifa, W Israel 32.40N 34.58E
114 I10 **Orašje** Federacija Bosna I Hercegovina, N Bosnia and Herzegovina 45.01N 18.42E
118 G11 **Orăștie** Ger. Broos, Hung. Szászváros. Hunedoara, W Romania 45.49N 23.10E
Orașul Stalin see Brașov
113 K18 **Orava** Hung. Árva, Pol. Orawa. ⚡ N Slovakia
Oravainen see Oravais
95 K16 **Oravais** Fin. Oravainen. Länsi-Suomi, W Finland 63.18N 22.25E
Oravicabánya see Oravița
118 F13 **Oravița** Ger. Orawitza, Hung. Oravicabánya. Caraș-Severin, SW Romania 45.01N 21.43E
Orawa see Orava
193 B24 **Orawia** Southland, South Island, NZ 46.03S 167.49E
Orawitza see Oravița
105 P16 **Orb** ⚡ S France
108 C9 **Orba** ⚡ NW Italy
164 H12 **Orba Co** ⊚ W China
110 B9 **Orbe** Vaud, W Switzerland 46.42N 6.28E
109 G14 **Orbetello** Toscana, C Italy 42.27N 11.14E
106 K3 **Órbigo** ⚡ NW Spain
191 Q12 **Orbost** Victoria, SE Australia 37.44S 148.28E
97 O14 **Örbyhus** Uppsala, C Sweden 60.15N 17.43E
204 I1 **Orcadas** Argentinian research station South Orkney Islands, Antarctica 60.37S 44.48W
107 P12 **Orcera** Andalucía, S Spain 38.20N 2.36W
35 P9 **Orchard Homes** Montana, NW USA 46.52N 114.01W
39 P5 **Orchard Mesa** Colorado, C USA 39.02N 108.33W
20 D10 **Orchard Park** New York, NE USA 42.46N 78.44W
Orchid Island see Lan Yü
117 G18 **Orchómenos** var. Orhomenos, Orkhómenos; prev. Skripón, anc. Orchomenus. Stereá Ellás, C Greece 38.29N 22.58E
Orchomenus see Orchómenos
108 B7 **Orco** ⚡ NW Italy
105 R8 **Or, Côte d'** physical region C France
31 O14 **Ord** Nebraska, C USA 41.36N 98.55W
Ordat' see Ordats'
121 O15 **Ordats'** Rus. Ordat'. Mahilyowskaya Voblasts', E Belarus 54.09N 30.42E
38 K8 **Orderville** Utah, W USA 37.16N 112.38W
106 H2 **Ordes** Galicia, NW Spain 43.04N 8.25W
37 V14 **Ord Mountain** ▲ California, W USA 34.41N 116.46W
169 N14 **Ordos** prev. Dongsheng. Nei Mongol Zizhiqu, N China 39.51N 110.00E
Ordos Desert see Mu Us Shadi
196 B16 **Ordot** C Guam
143 N11 **Ordu** anc. Cotyora. Ordu, N Turkey 41.00N 37.52E
142 M11 **Ordu** ◆ province N Turkey
143 V14 **Ordubad** SW Azerbaijan 38.55N 46.00E
107 O3 **Orduña** País Vasco, N Spain 43.00N 3.00W
39 U6 **Ordway** Colorado, C USA 38.13N 103.45W
119 T9 **Ordzhonikidze** Dnipropetrovs'ka Oblast', E Ukraine 47.39N 34.09E
Ordzhonikidze see Denisovka, Kazakhstan
Ordzhonikidze see Vladikavkaz, Russian Federation
Ordzhonikidze see Yenakiyeve, Ukraine
Ordzhonikidzeabad see Kofarnihon
57 U9 **Orealla** E Guyana 5.13N 57.17W
115 G15 **Orebić** It. Sabbioncello. Dubrovnik-Neretva, S Croatia 42.58N 17.12E
97 M16 **Örebro** Örebro, C Sweden 59.18N 15.12E
97 L16 **Örebro** ◆ county C Sweden
27 W6 **Ore City** Texas, SW USA 32.48N 94.43W
32 L10 **Oregon** Illinois, N USA 42.00N 89.19W
29 Q2 **Oregon** Missouri, C USA 39.59N 95.08W
33 R11 **Oregon** Ohio, N USA 41.38N 83.29W
34 H13 **Oregon** off. State of Oregon; also known as Beaver State, Sunset State, Valentine State, Webfoot State. ◆ state NW USA
34 G11 **Oregon City** Oregon, NW USA 45.21N 122.36W
97 P14 **Öregrund** Uppsala, C Sweden 60.19N 18.30E
Orekhov see Orikhiv
130 L3 **Orekhovo-Zuyevo** Moskovskaya Oblast', W Russian Federation 55.46N 39.01E
Orekhovsk see Arekhawsk
Orel see Oril'
130 J6 **Orël** Orlovskaya Oblast', W Russian Federation 52.57N 36.06E
58 E11 **Orellana** Loreto, N Peru 6.55S 75.10W
58 E6 **Orellana** ◆ province NE Ecuador
106 L11 **Orellana, Embalse de** ⊠ W Spain
38 L3 **Orem** Utah, W USA 40.18N 111.41W
Ore Mountains see Erzgebirge/Krušné Hory
131 V7 **Orenburg** prev. Chkalov. Orenburgskaya Oblast', W Russian Federation 51.45N 55.11E
131 V7 **Orenburg** ✕ Orenburgskaya Oblast', W Russian Federation 51.54N 55.15E
131 T7 **Orenburgskaya Oblast'** ◆ province W Russian Federation
Orense see Ourense
196 C8 **Oreor** var. Koror. island N Palau
Oreor see Koror
193 B24 **Orepuki** Southland, South Island, NZ 46.17S 167.45E
116 L12 **Orestiáda** prev. Orestiás. Anatolikí Makedonía kai Thráki, NE Greece 41.30N 26.31E
Orestiás see Orestiáda
Öresund/Øresund see Sound, The
193 C23 **Oreti** ⚡ South Island, NZ
192 L5 **Orewa** Auckland, North Island, NZ 36.36S 174.42E
176 Y14 **Oreyabo** Papua, E Indonesia 6.57S 139.05E
67 A25 **Orford, Cape** headland West Falkland, Falkland Islands 52.00S 61.04W
46 B5 **Órganos, Sierra de los** ▲ W Cuba
39 R15 **Organ Peak** ▲ New Mexico, SW USA 32.17N 106.35W
107 N9 **Orgaz** Castilla-La Mancha, C Spain 39.39N 3.52W
Orgeyev see Orhei
168 I6 **Orgil** Hövsgöl, C Mongolia 48.31N 99.19E
107 O15 **Órgiva** var. Orjiva. Andalucía, S Spain 36.54N 3.25W
168 I9 **Örgön** Bayanhongor, C Mongolia 44.43N 100.23E
119 N9 **Orhei** var. Orheiu, Rus. Orgeyev. N Moldova 47.25N 28.48E
Orheiu see Orhei
107 R3 **Orhi** var. Orhy, Pico de Orhy, Pic d'Orhy. ▲ France/Spain 42.55N 1.01W see also Orhy
Orhomenos see Orchómenos
168 K6 **Orhon** ◆ province N Mongolia
168 L6 **Orhon Gol** ⚡ N Mongolia
104 J16 **Orhy** var. Orhi, Pico de Orhy, Pic d'Orhy. ▲ France/Spain 42.55N 1.01W see also Orhi
Orhy, Pic d'/Orhy, Pico de see Orhi/Orhy
36 L2 **Orick** California, W USA 41.16N 124.03W
34 L6 **Orient** Washington, NW USA 48.51N 118.14W
50 D6 **Oriental, Cordillera** ▲ Bolivia/Peru
50 D6 **Oriental, Cordillera** ▲ C Colombia
59 H16 **Oriental, Cordillera** ▲ C Peru
65 M15 **Oriente** Buenos Aires, E Argentina 38.45S 60.37W
107 R12 **Orihuela** País Valenciano, E Spain 38.04N 0.55W
119 V9 **Orikhiv** Rus. Orekhov. Zaporiz'ka Oblast', SE Ukraine 47.32N 35.48E
115 K22 **Orikum** var. Orikumi. Vlorë, SW Albania 40.20N 19.28E
Orikumi see Orikum
119 V6 **Oril'** Rus. Orel. ⚡ E Ukraine
12 H14 **Orillia** Ontario, S Canada 44.36N 79.25W
95 M19 **Orimattila** Etelä-Suomi, S Finland 60.51N 25.46E
35 Y15 **Orin** Wyoming, C USA 42.39N 105.10W
49 R4 **Orinoco, Río** ⚡ Colombia/Venezuela
194 G15 **Oriomo** Western, SW PNG 8.53S 143.13E
32 K11 **Orion** Illinois, N USA 41.21N 90.22W
31 Q5 **Oriska** North Dakota, N USA 46.54N 97.46W
159 P17 **Orissa** ◆ state NE India
Orissaar see Orissaare
120 E5 **Orissaare** Ger. Orissaar. Saaremaa, W Estonia 58.33N 23.05E
109 B19 **Oristano** Sardegna, Italy, C Mediterranean Sea 39.54N 8.34E
109 A19 **Oristano, Golfo di** gulf Sardegna, Italy, C Mediterranean Sea
56 D13 **Orito** Putumayo, SW Colombia 0.41N 76.48W
95 L18 **Orivesi** Häme, SW Finland 61.39N 24.21E
95 N17 **Orivesi** ⊚ Länsi-Suomi, SE Finland
60 H12 **Oriximiná** Pará, NE Brazil 1.45S 55.49W
43 Q14 **Orizaba** Veracruz-Llave, E Mexico 18.55N 97.57W
43 Q14 **Orizaba, Volcán Pico de** var. Citlaltépetl. ▲ S Mexico 19.00N 97.15W
97 I16 **Ørje** Østfold, S Norway 59.28N 11.39E
115 I16 **Orjen** ▲ Bosnia and Herzegovina/Serbia and Montenegro (Yugoslavia)
Orjiva see Órgiva
96 G8 **Orkanger** Sør-Trøndelag, S Norway 63.18N 9.51E
96 G8 **Orkdalen** valley S Norway
97 K22 **Örkelljunga** Skåne, S Sweden 56.16N 13.19E
Orkhaniye see Botevgrad
Orkhómenos see Orchómenos
96 H9 **Orkla** ⚡ S Norway
Orkney see Orkney Islands
67 J22 **Orkney Deep** undersea feature Scotia Sea/Weddell Sea
98 J4 **Orkney Islands** var. Orkney, Orkneys. island group N Scotland, UK
Orkneys see Orkney Islands
26 K8 **Orla** Texas, SW USA 31.48N 103.55W
37 N5 **Orland** California, W USA 39.43N 122.12W
25 X11 **Orlando** Florida, SE USA 28.32N 81.22W
25 X12 **Orlando** ✕ Florida, SE USA 28.24N 81.16W
109 K23 **Orlando, Capo d'** headland Sicilia, Italy, C Mediterranean Sea 38.10N 14.44E
Orlau see Orlová
105 N6 **Orléanais** cultural region C France
36 L2 **Orleans** California, W USA 41.16N 123.36W
21 Q12 **Orleans** Massachusetts, NE USA 41.48N 69.57W
105 N7 **Orléans** anc. Aurelianum. Loiret, C France 47.54N 1.52E
13 R10 **Orléans, Île d'** island Québec, SE Canada
Orléansville see Chlef
113 F16 **Orlice** Ger. Adler. ⚡ NE Czech Republic
126 Ii15 **Orlik** Respublika Buryatiya, S Russian Federation 52.32N 99.36E
129 Q14 **Orlov** prev. Khalturin. Kirovskaya Oblast', NW Russian Federation 58.34N 48.57E
113 I17 **Orlová** Ger. Orlau, Pol. Orłowa. Moravskoslezský Kraj, E Czech Republic 49.52N 18.25E
Orlov, Mys see Orlovskiy, Mys
130 I6 **Orlovskaya Oblast'** ◆ province W Russian Federation
128 M5 **Orlovskiy, Mys** var. Mys Orlov. headland NW Russian Federation 67.14N 41.17E
Orlowa see Orlová
105 O5 **Orly** ✕ (Paris) Essonne, N France 48.43N 2.24E
121 G16 **Orlya** Rus. Orlya. Hrodzyenskaya Voblasts', W Belarus 53.30N 24.58E
116 M7 **Orlyak** prev. Makenzen, Trubchular, Rom. Trupcilar. Dobrich, NE Bulgaria 43.39N 27.21E
154 L16 **Ormāra** Baluchistān, SW Pakistan 25.14N 64.36E
179 Qq13 **Ormoc** off. Ormoc City, var. MacArthur. Leyte, C Philippines 11.02N 124.35E
25 X10 **Ormond Beach** Florida, SE USA 29.16N 81.04W
111 X10 **Ormož** Ger. Friedau. NE Slovenia 46.24N 16.09E
12 J13 **Ormsby** Ontario, SE Canada 44.52N 77.45W
99 K17 **Ormskirk** NW England, UK 53.34N 2.54W
Ormsö see Vormsi
13 N13 **Ormstown** Québec, SE Canada 45.08N 73.57W
Ormuz, Strait of see Hormuz, Strait of
105 T8 **Ornans** Doubs, E France 47.06N 6.06E
104 K5 **Orne** ◆ department N France
104 K5 **Orne** ⚡ N France
94 G12 **Ørnes** Nordland, C Norway 66.51N 13.43E
112 L7 **Orneta** Warmińsko-Mazurskie, NE Poland 54.07N 20.10E
97 P16 **Ornö** Stockholm, C Sweden 59.03N 18.28E
39 Q3 **Orno Peak** ▲ Colorado, C USA 40.06N 107.06W
95 I16 **Örnsköldsvik** Västernorrland, C Sweden 63.16N 18.45E
169 X13 **Oro** E North Korea 39.59N 127.27E
47 T6 **Orocovis** C Puerto Rico 18.13N 66.22W
56 H10 **Orocué** Casanare, E Colombia 4.46N 71.22W
79 N13 **Orodara** SW Burkina 11.00N 4.54W
107 S4 **Orol, Peña de** ▲ N Spain 42.30N 0.31W
35 N10 **Orofino** Idaho, NW USA 46.28N 116.15W
168 I9 **Orog Nuur** ⊚ S Mongolia
37 U14 **Oro Grande** California, W USA 34.36N 117.19W
39 S15 **Orogrande** New Mexico, SW USA 32.24N 106.04W
203 Q7 **Orohena, Mont** ⛰ Tahiti, W French Polynesia 17.37S 149.27W
Orolaunum see Arlon
Orol Dengizi see Aral Sea
201 S15 **Oroluk Atoll** atoll Caroline Islands, C Micronesia
82 J13 **Oromo** ◆ region C Ethiopia
11 O15 **Oromocto** New Brunswick, SE Canada 45.49N 66.28W
203 S4 **Orona** prev. Hull Island. atoll Phoenix Islands, C Kiribati
203 V17 **Orongo** ancient monument Easter Island, Chile, E Pacific Ocean 27.10S 109.27W
144 I3 **Orontes** var. Ononte, Ar. Nahr el Aassi, Nahr al 'Āṣī. ⚡ SW Asia
106 L9 **Oropesa** Castilla-La Mancha, C Spain 39.55N 5.10W
107 T8 **Oropesa** País Valenciano, E Spain 40.06N 0.07E
Oropeza see Cochabamba
Oroqen Zizhiqi see Alihe
179 Qq15 **Oroquieta** var. Oroquieta City. Mindanao, S Philippines 8.27N 123.46E
42 J8 **Oro, Río del** ⚡ C Mexico
61 O14 **Orós, Açude** ⊠ E Brazil
109 D18 **Orosei, Golfo di** gulf Tyrrhenian Sea, C Mediterranean Sea
113 M24 **Orosháza** Békés, SE Hungary 46.33N 20.40E
Orosirá Rodhópis see Rhodope Mountains
113 I22 **Oroszlány** Komárom-Esztergom, W Hungary 47.31N 18.19E
196 B16 **Orote Peninsula** peninsula W Guam
127 O9 **Orotukan** Magadanskaya Oblast', E Russian Federation 62.18N 150.46E
37 O5 **Oroville** California, W USA 39.29N 121.35W
34 K6 **Oroville** Washington, NW USA 48.56N 119.25W
37 O5 **Oroville, Lake** ⊠ California, W USA
(0) G15 **Orozco Fracture Zone** tectonic feature E Pacific Ocean
66 I7 **Orphan Knoll** undersea feature NW Atlantic Ocean 51.00N 47.00W
31 V3 **Orr** Minnesota, N USA 48.03N 92.48W
97 M21 **Orrefors** Kalmar, S Sweden 56.48N 15.45E
190 I7 **Orroroo** South Australia 32.46S 138.38E
33 T12 **Orrville** Ohio, N USA 40.50N 81.45W
96 L12 **Orsa** Dalarna, C Sweden 61.07N 14.40E
Orschowa see Orşova
Orschütz see Orzyc
121 O14 **Orsha** Rus. Orsha. Vitsyebskaya Voblasts', NE Belarus 54.30N 30.25E
131 Q2 **Orshanka** Respublika Mariy El, W Russian Federation 56.54N 47.54E
110 C11 **Orsières** Valais, SW Switzerland 46.00N 7.09E
125 Dd13 **Orsk** Orenburgskaya Oblast', W Russian Federation 51.13N 58.34E
118 F13 **Orşova** Ger. Orschowa, Hung. Orsova. Mehedinți, SW Romania 44.42N 22.22E
96 D10 **Ørsta** Møre og Romsdal, S Norway 62.12N 6.07E
97 O15 **Örsundsbro** Uppsala, C Sweden 59.45N 17.19E
142 D16 **Ortaca** Muğla, SW Turkey 36.49N 28.43E
109 M16 **Orta Nova** Puglia, SE Italy 41.19N 15.43E
142 I17 **Orta Toroslar** ▲ S Turkey
56 E11 **Orteguaza** Tolima, W Colombia 3.57N 75.10W
106 H1 **Ortegal, Cabo** headland NW Spain 43.46N 7.54W
Ortelsburg see Szczytno
104 J15 **Orthez** Pyrénées-Atlantiques, SW France 43.28N 0.46W
59 K14 **Orthon, Río** ⚡ N Bolivia
62 J10 **Ortigueira** Paraná, S Brazil 24.10S 50.55W
106 H1 **Ortigueira** Galicia, NW Spain 43.40N 7.50W
108 H5 **Ortisei** Ger. Sankt-Ulrich. Trentino-Alto Adige, N Italy 46.35N 11.42E
42 F6 **Ortiz** Sonora, NW Mexico 28.18N 110.40W
56 L5 **Ortiz** Guárico, N Venezuela 9.37N 67.17W
Ortler see Ortles
108 F5 **Ortles** Ger. Ortler. ▲ N Italy 46.29N 10.33E
109 K14 **Ortona** Abruzzo, C Italy 42.21N 14.24E
31 R8 **Ortonville** Minnesota, N USA 45.18N 96.26W
153 W8 **Orto-Tokoy** Issyk-Kul'skaya Oblast', NE Kyrgyzstan 42.20N 76.03E
95 I15 **Örträsk** Västerbotten, N Sweden 64.10N 19.00E
102 J12 **Örtze** ⚡ NW Germany
Oruba see Aruba
148 I3 **Orūmīyeh** var. Rizaiyeh, Urmia, Urmiyeh; prev. Reẓā'īyeh. Āžarbāyjān-e Bākhtarī, NW Iran 37.33N 45.06E
148 J3 **Orūmīyeh, Daryācheh-ye** var. Matianus, Sha Hi, Urumi Yeh, Eng. Lake Urmia; prev. Daryācheh-ye Reẓā'īyeh. ⊚ NW Iran
59 K19 **Oruro** Oruro, W Bolivia 17.57S 67.05W
59 J19 **Oruro** ◆ department W Bolivia
97 I18 **Orust** island S Sweden
Oruzgān/Orūzgān see Ūrūzgān
108 H13 **Orvieto** anc. Velsuna. Umbria, C Italy 42.43N 12.07E
204 K7 **Orville Coast** physical region Antarctica
116 H7 **Oryakhovo** Vratsa, NW Bulgaria 43.43N 23.58E
Oryokko see Yalu
119 R5 **Orzhytsya** Poltavs'ka Oblast', C Ukraine 49.48N 32.40E
112 M9 **Orzyc** Ger. Orschütz. ⚡ NE Poland
112 N8 **Orzysz** Ger. Arys. Warmińsko-Mazurskie, NE Poland 53.49N 21.54E
96 I10 **Os** Hedmark, S Norway 62.29N 11.14E
129 U15 **Osa** Permskaya Oblast', NW Russian Federation 57.16N 55.22E
31 W11 **Osage** Iowa, C USA 43.16N 92.48W
29 U5 **Osage Beach** Missouri, C USA 38.09N 92.37W
29 P5 **Osage City** Kansas, C USA 38.37N 95.49W
29 U7 **Osage Fork River** ⚡ Missouri, C USA
29 U5 **Osage River** ⚡ Missouri, C USA
171 Gg15 **Ōsaka** hist. Naniwa. Ōsaka, Honshū, SW Japan 34.38N 135.27E
171 Gg15 **Ōsaka** off. Ōsaka-fu, var. Ōsaka Hu. ◆ urban prefecture Honshū, SW Japan
Ōsaka-fu/Ōsaka Hu see Ōsaka
151 R10 **Osakarovka** Karaganda, C Kazakhstan 50.27N 72.43E
170 G15 **Ōsaka-wan** bay SW Japan
31 T7 **Osakis** Minnesota, N USA 45.51N 95.08W
45 N16 **Osa, Península de** peninsula S Costa Rica
62 M10 **Osasco** São Paulo, S Brazil 23.31S 46.46W
29 R5 **Osawatomie** Kansas, C USA 38.30N 94.57W
28 L3 **Osborne** Kansas, C USA 39.26N 98.41W
181 S8 **Osborn Plateau** undersea feature E Indian Ocean
97 L21 **Osby** Skåne, S Sweden 56.24N 14.00E
Osca see Huesca
94 N2 **Oscar II Land** physical region W Svalbard
29 Y10 **Osceola** Arkansas, C USA 35.40N 89.58W
31 V15 **Osceola** Iowa, C USA 41.01N 93.45W
29 S6 **Osceola** Missouri, C USA 38.03N 93.42W
31 Q15 **Osceola** Nebraska, C USA 41.09N 97.28W
103 N15 **Oschatz** Sachsen, E Germany 51.17N 13.10E
102 K13 **Oschersleben** Sachsen-Anhalt, C Germany 52.02N 11.14E
33 R7 **Oscoda** Michigan, N USA 44.25N 83.19W
Ösel see Saaremaa
96 H6 **Osen** Sør-Trøndelag, S Norway 64.17N 10.29E
96 I12 **Osensjøen** ⊚ S Norway
170 Aa12 **Ōse-zaki** headland Fukue-jima, SW Japan 32.36N 128.37E
153 T10 **Osh** Oshskaya Oblast', SW Kyrgyzstan 40.34N 72.46E
85 C16 **Oshakati** Oshana, N Namibia 17.45S 15.42E
172 Nn6 **Oshamanbe** Hokkaidō, NE Japan 42.31N 140.22E
85 C16 **Oshana** ◆ district N Namibia
126 Ii12 **Osharovo** Evenkiyskiy Avtonomnyy Okrug, N Russian Federation 60.16N 98.20E
12 H15 **Oshawa** Ontario, SE Canada 43.54N 78.50W
171 Mm13 **Oshika-hantō** peninsula Honshū, C Japan
85 C16 **Oshikango** Ohangwena, N Namibia 17.28S 15.54E
Oshikoto see Otjikoto
170 Cc12 **Ō-shima** island SW Japan
171 M7 **Ō-shima** island NE Japan
171 Jj17 **Ō-shima** island S Japan
170 G17 **Ō-shima** island SW Japan
172 N6 **Oshima-hantō** ▲ Hokkaidō, NE Japan
85 D17 **Oshivelo** Otjikoto, N Namibia 18.37S 17.10E
30 K14 **Oshkosh** Nebraska, C USA 41.25N 102.21W
32 M7 **Oshkosh** Wisconsin, N USA 44.01N 88.31W
Oshmyany see Ashmyany
Osh Oblasty see Oshskaya Oblast'
79 T16 **Oshogbo** var. Osogbo. Osun, W Nigeria 7.42N 4.31E
153 T11 **Oshskaya Oblast'** Kir. Osh Oblasty. ◆ province SW Kyrgyzstan
Oshun see Osun
81 J20 **Oshwe** Bandundu, C Dem. Rep. Congo 3.24S 19.31E
Osiek see Osijek
114 I9 **Osijek** prev. Osiek, Osjek, Ger. Esseg, Hung. Eszék. Osijek-Baranja, E Croatia 45.33N 18.40E
114 I9 **Osijek-Baranja** off. Osječko-Baranjska Županija. ◆ province E Croatia
108 J12 **Osimo** Marche, C Italy 43.28N 13.28E
126 H15 **Osinniki** Kemerovskaya Oblast', S Russian Federation 53.30N 87.25E
126 J14 **Osinovka** Irkutskaya Oblast', C Russian Federation 56.19N 101.55E
Osintorf see Asintorf
114 N11 **Osipaonica** Serbia, NE Serbia and Montenegro (Yugoslavia) 44.34N 21.00E
Osipenko see Berdyans'k
Osipovichi see Asipovichy
Osječko-Baranjska Županija see Osijek-Baranja
Osjek see Osijek
31 W15 **Oskaloosa** Iowa, C USA 41.17N 92.38W
29 Q4 **Oskaloosa** Kansas, C USA 39.13N 95.18W
97 N20 **Oskarshamn** Kalmar, S Sweden 57.16N 16.25E
97 J21 **Oskarström** Halland, S Sweden 56.48N 13.00E
12 M8 **Oskélanéo** Québec, SE Canada 48.06N 75.12W
Öskemen see Ust'-Kamenogorsk
Oskil see Oskol
119 W5 **Oskol** Ukr. Oskil. ⚡ Russian Federation/Ukraine
95 D20 **Oslo** prev. Christiania, Kristiania. ● (Norway) Oslo, S Norway 59.54N 10.43E
95 D20 **Oslo** ◆ county S Norway
95 D21 **Oslofjorden** fjord S Norway
161 G15 **Osmānābād** Mahārāshtra, C India 18.09N 76.06E
142 J11 **Osmancık** Çorum, N Turkey 40.58N 34.49E
142 L16 **Osmaniye** Osmaniye, S Turkey 37.04N 36.15E
142 L16 **Osmaniye** ◆ province S Turkey
97 O16 **Ösmo** Stockholm, C Sweden 58.58N 17.55E
120 E3 **Osmussaar** island W Estonia
102 G13 **Osnabrück** Niedersachsen, NW Germany 52.08N 7.42E
112 D11 **Ośno Lubuskie** Ger. Drossen. Lubuskie, W Poland 52.28N 14.51E
Osogbo see Oshogbo
115 P19 **Osogov Mountains** var. Osogovske Planine, Osogovski Planina, Mac. Osogovski Planini. ▲ Bulgaria/FYR Macedonia
Osogovske Planine/ Osogovski Planina/ Osogovski Planini see Osogov Mountains
172 N8 **Osore-yama** ▲ Honshū, C Japan 41.18N 141.06E
Oşorhei see Târgu Mureş
63 J16 **Osório** Rio Grande do Sul, S Brazil 29.52S 50.16W
65 G16 **Osorno** Los Lagos, C Chile 40.38S 73.04W
106 M4 **Osorno** Castilla-León, N Spain 42.24N 4.22W
9 N17 **Osoyoos** British Columbia, SW Canada 49.01N 119.31W
97 C14 **Osøyro** Hordaland, S Norway 60.10N 5.30E
56 J6 **Ospino** Portuguesa, N Venezuela 9.16N 69.25W
100 K13 **Oss** Noord-Brabant, S Netherlands 51.46N 5.31E
106 H11 **Ossa** ▲ S Portugal 38.43N 7.33W
117 F15 **Óssa** ▲ C Greece
25 X6 **Ossabaw Island** island Georgia, SE USA
25 X6 **Ossabaw Sound** sound Georgia, SE USA
191 O16 **Ossa, Mount** ▲ Tasmania, SE Australia 41.55S 146.03E
106 H11 **Ossa, Serra d'** ▲ SE Portugal
79 U16 **Osse** ⚡ S Nigeria
32 J6 **Osseo** Wisconsin, N USA 44.33N 91.13W
111 S9 **Ossiacher See** ⊚ S Austria
20 K13 **Ossining** New York, NE USA 41.10N 73.50W
127 P9 **Ossora** Koryakskiy Avtonomnyy Okrug, E Russian Federation 59.16N 163.01E
128 I15 **Ostashkov** Tverskaya Oblast', W Russian Federation 57.08N 33.10E
102 H9 **Oste** ⚡ NW Germany
Ostee see Baltic Sea
Ostend/Ostende see Oostende
119 P3 **Oster** Chernihivs'ka Oblast', N Ukraine 50.57N 30.55E
97 O14 **Österbybruk** Uppsala, C Sweden 60.13N 17.55E
97 M19 **Österbymo** Östergotland, S Sweden 57.49N 15.15E
96 K12 **Österdalälven** ⚡ C Sweden
96 I12 **Østerdalen** valley S Norway
97 L18 **Östergötland** ◆ county S Sweden
102 H10 **Osterholz-Scharmbeck** Niedersachsen, NW Germany 53.13N 8.46E
Östermark see Teuva
Östermyra see Seinäjoki

◆ Country ● Country Capital ◇ Dependent Territory ○ Dependent Territory Capital ◆ Administrative Region ✕ International Airport ▲ Mountain ▲ Mountain Range ⛰ Volcano ⚡ River ⊚ Lake ⊠ Reservoir

OSTERODE/OSTERODE IN OSTPREUSSEN – PAINAN

Osterode/Osterode in Ostpreussen *see* Ostróda
103 J14 **Osterode am Harz** Niedersachsen, C Germany 51.43N 10.15E
96 C13 **Osterøy** *island* S Norway
Österreich *see* Austria
95 G16 **Östersund** Jämtland, C Sweden 63.10N 14.43E
97 N14 **Östervåla** Västmanland, C Sweden 60.10N 17.13E
103 H22 **Ostfildern** Baden-Württemberg, SW Germany 48.43N 9.16E
97 H16 **Østfold** ◈ *county* S Norway
102 E9 **Ostfriesische Inseln** *Eng.* East Frisian Islands. *island group* NW Germany
102 F10 **Ostfriesland** *historical region* NW Germany
97 P14 **Östhammar** Uppsala, C Sweden 60.16N 18.25E
Ostia Aterni *see* Pescara
108 G8 **Ostiglia** Lombardia, N Italy 45.03N 11.09E
97 J14 **Östmark** Värmland, C Sweden 60.15N 12.45E
97 K22 **Östra Ringsjön** ◎ S Sweden
113 I17 **Ostrava** Moravskoslezský Kraj, E Czech Republic 49.49N 18.15E
Ostravský Kraj *see* Moravskoslezský Kraj
96 J11 **Østrehogna** *Swe.* Härjahågnen, Härjehågna. ▲ Norway/Sweden 61.43N 12.07E
112 K8 **Ostróda** *Ger.* Osterode, Osterode in Ostpreussen. Warmińsko-Mazurskie, NE Poland 53.42N 19.58E
Ostrog/Ostróg *see* Ostroh
130 L8 **Ostrogozhsk** Voronezhskaya Oblast', W Russian Federation 50.52N 39.00E
118 L4 **Ostroh** *Pol.* Ostróg, *Rus.* Ostrog. Rivnens'ka Oblast', NW Ukraine 50.19N 26.30E
112 N9 **Ostrołęka** *Ger.* Wiesenhof, *Rus.* Ostrolenka. Mazowieckie, C Poland 53.06N 21.33E
113 A16 **Ostrov** *Ger.* Schlackenwerth. Karlovarský Kraj, W Czech Republic 50.18N 12.53E
128 F15 **Ostrov** *Latv.* Austrava. Pskovskaya Oblast', W Russian Federation 57.21N 28.18E
Ostrovets *see* Ostrowiec Świętokrzyski
115 M21 **Ostrovicës, Mali i** ▲ SE Albania 40.36N 20.25E
172 T6 **Ostrov Iturup** *island* NE Russian Federation
128 M4 **Ostrovnoy** Murmanskaya Oblast', NW Russian Federation 68.00N 39.40E
116 L7 **Ostrovo** *prev.* Golema Ada. Razgrad, N Bulgaria 43.40N 26.37E
129 N15 **Ostrovskoye** Kostromskaya Oblast', NW Russian Federation 57.46N 42.18E
Ostrów *see* Ostrów Wielkopolski
Ostrowiec *see* Ostrowiec Świętokrzyski
113 M14 **Ostrowiec Świętokrzyski** *var.* Ostrowiec, *Rus.* Ostrovets. Świętokrzyskie, C Poland 50.54N 21.22E
112 P13 **Ostrów Lubelski** Lubelskie, E Poland 51.29N 22.57E
112 N10 **Ostrów Mazowiecka** *var.* Ostrów Mazowiecki. Mazowieckie, C Poland 52.48N 21.53E
Ostrów Mazowiecki *see* Ostrów Mazowiecka
Ostrowo *see* Ostrów Wielkopolski
112 H13 **Ostrów Wielkopolski** *var.* Ostrów, *Ger.* Ostrowo. Wielkopolskie, C Poland 51.40N 17.47E
Ostryna *see* Astryna
112 I13 **Ostrzeszów** Wielkopolskie, C Poland 51.26N 17.54E
109 P18 **Ostuni** Puglia, SE Italy 40.43N 17.34E
Ostyako-Voguls'k *see* Khanty-Mansiysk
Osum *see* Osumit, Lumi i
116 I9 **Osŭm** ≈ N Bulgaria
170 Bb17 **Ōsumi-hantō** ▲▲ Kyūshū, SW Japan
170 Bb17 **Ōsumi-kaikyō** *strait* SW Japan
115 L22 **Osumit, Lumi i** *var.* Osum. ≈ SE Albania
79 T16 **Osun** *var.* Oshun. ◈ *state* SW Nigeria
106 L14 **Osuna** Andalucía, S Spain 37.13N 5.06W
62 J8 **Osvaldo Cruz** São Paulo, S Brazil 21.49S 50.52W
Osveya *see* Asvyeya
20 J7 **Oswegatchie River** ≈ New York, NE USA
29 Q7 **Oswego** Kansas, C USA 37.08N 95.07W
20 H9 **Oswego** New York, NE USA 43.27N 76.13W
99 K19 **Oswestry** W England, UK 52.50N 3.06W
113 J16 **Oświęcim** *Ger.* Auschwitz. Małopolskie, S Poland 50.02N 19.11E
171 K15 **Ōta** Gunma, Honshū, S Japan 36.17N 139.20E
193 E22 **Otago** *off.* Otago Region. ◈ *region* South Island, NZ
193 F23 **Otago Peninsula** *peninsula* South Island, NZ
170 E13 **Ōtake** Hiroshima, Honshū, SW Japan 34.13N 132.13E
192 L13 **Otaki** Wellington, North Island, NZ 40.46S 175.08E
171 L14 **Ōtakine-yama** ▲ Honshū, C Japan 37.23N 140.42E
95 M15 **Otanmäki** Oulu, C Finland 64.07N 27.04E
151 T15 **Otar** Zhambyl, SE Kazakhstan 43.34N 75.13E
172 O5 **Otaru** Hokkaidō, NE Japan 43.13N 140.58E
193 C24 **Otatara** Southland, South Island, NZ 46.26S 168.18E
193 C24 **Otautau** Southland, South Island, NZ 46.10S 168.01E
95 M18 **Otava** Isä-Suomi, E Finland 61.37N 27.07E
113 B18 **Otava** *Ger.* Wottawa. ≈ SW Czech Republic
58 C6 **Otavalo** Imbabura, N Ecuador 0.13N 78.15W
85 D17 **Otavi** Otjozondjupa, N Namibia 19.34S 17.25E
171 Kk15 **Ōtawara** Tochigi, Honshū, S Japan 36.52N 140.01E
85 B16 **Otchinjau** Cunene, SW Angola 16.31S 13.54E
118 F12 **Oțelu Roșu** *Ger.* Ferdinandsberg, *Hung.* Nándorhgy. Caras-Severin, SW Romania 45.30N 22.22E
193 E21 **Otematata** Canterbury, South Island, NZ 44.37S 170.12E
120 I6 **Otepää** *Ger.* Odenpäh. Valgamaa, SE Estonia 58.04N 26.31E
34 K9 **Othello** Washington, NW USA 46.49N 119.10W
117 A15 **Othonoí** *island* Iónioi Nísoi, Greece, C Mediterranean Sea
Othris *see* Óthrys
117 F17 **Óthrys** *var.* Othris. ▲▲ C Greece
79 Q14 **Oti** ≈ N Togo
42 K10 **Otinapa** Durango, C Mexico 24.01N 104.58W
193 G17 **Otira** West Coast, South Island, NZ 42.51S 171.32E
39 V3 **Otis** Colorado, C USA 40.09N 102.57W
10 L10 **Otish, Monts** ▲▲ Québec, E Canada
85 C17 **Otjikondo** Kunene, N Namibia 19.48S 15.28E
85 C17 **Otjikoto** *var.* Oshikoto. ◈ *district* N Namibia
85 E18 **Otjinene** Omaheke, NE Namibia 21.10S 18.43E
85 D18 **Otjiwarongo** Otjozondjupa, N Namibia 20.28S 16.36E
85 D18 **Otjosondu** *var.* Otjosundu. Otjozondjupa, C Namibia 21.19S 17.51E
Otjosundu *see* Otjosondu
85 D18 **Otjozondjupa** ◈ *district* C Namibia
114 C11 **Otočac** Lika-Senj, W Croatia 44.52N 15.13E
172 Pp6 **Otofuke-gawa** ≈ Hokkaidō, NE Japan
Otog Qi *see* Ulan
172 Pp3 **Otoineppu** Hokkaidō, NE Japan 44.43N 142.13E
114 J10 **Otok** Vukovar-Srijem, E Croatia 45.10N 18.52E
118 K14 **Otopeni** ✕ (București) București, S Romania 44.34N 26.09E
192 L8 **Otorohanga** Waikato, North Island, NZ 38.10S 175.13E
10 D9 **Otoskwin** ≈ Ontario, C Canada
170 F15 **Ōtoyo** Kōchi, Shikoku, SW Japan 33.45N 133.42E
97 E16 **Otra** ≈ S Norway
109 R19 **Otranto** Puglia, SE Italy 40.08N 18.28E
Otranto, Canale d' *see* Otranto, Strait of
109 Q18 **Otranto, Strait of** *It.* Canale d'Otranto. *strait* Albania/Italy
113 H18 **Otrokovice** *Ger.* Otrokowitz. Zlínský Kraj, E Czech Republic 49.13N 17.32E
Otrokowitz *see* Otrokovice
33 P10 **Otsego** Michigan, N USA 42.27N 85.42W
33 Q6 **Otsego Lake** ◎ Michigan, N USA
20 I11 **Otselic River** ≈ New York, NE USA
171 H15 **Ōtsu** *var.* Ôtu. Shiga, Honshū, SW Japan 35.03N 135.49E
171 Jj16 **Ōtsuki** *var.* Otuki. Yamanashi, Honshū, S Japan 35.35N 138.53E
96 G11 **Otta** Oppland, S Norway 61.46N 9.31E
201 U13 **Otta** *island* Chuuk, C Micronesia
96 F11 **Otta** ≈ S Norway
201 U13 **Otta Pass** *passage* Chuuk Islands, C Micronesia
97 J22 **Ottarp** Skåne, S Sweden 55.55N 12.55E
12 L12 **Ottawa** ● (Canada) Ontario, SE Canada 45.24N 75.40W
32 L11 **Ottawa** Illinois, N USA 41.21N 88.50W
29 Q5 **Ottawa** Kansas, C USA 38.37N 95.16W
33 R12 **Ottawa** Ohio, N USA 41.01N 84.03W
12 L12 **Ottawa** *var.* Uplands. ✕ Ontario, SE Canada 45.19N 75.39W
12 M12 **Ottawa** *Fr.* Outaouais. ≈ Ontario/Québec, SE Canada
10 I4 **Ottawa Islands** *island group* Nunavut, C Canada
20 L8 **Otter Creek** ≈ Vermont, NE USA
38 L6 **Otter Creek Reservoir** ▣ Utah, W USA
100 L11 **Otterlo** Gelderland, E Netherlands 52.06N 5.46E
96 D9 **Otterøya** *island* S Norway
31 S6 **Otter Tail Lake** ◎ Minnesota, N USA
31 R7 **Otter Tail River** ≈ Minnesota, C USA
97 H23 **Otterup** Fyn, C Denmark 55.31N 10.25E
101 H19 **Ottignies** Wallon Brabant, C Belgium 50.40N 4.34E
103 L23 **Ottobrunn** Bayern, SE Germany 48.02N 11.40E
194 I12 **Otto, Mount** ▲ C PNG 5.54S 145.24E
31 X15 **Ottumwa** Iowa, C USA 41.00N 92.24W
Ôtu *see* Ōtsu
85 B16 **Otuazuma** Kunene, NW Namibia 17.52S 13.16E
Otuki *see* Ōtsuki
79 V16 **Oturkpo** Benue, S Nigeria 7.12N 8.06E
200 Ss14 **Otu Tolu Group** *island group* SE Tonga
190 M13 **Otway, Cape** *headland* Victoria, SE Australia 38.52S 143.31E
65 H24 **Otway, Seno** *inlet* S Chile
Ötz *see* Oetz
110 L8 **Ötztaler Ache** ≈ W Austria
110 L9 **Ötztaler Alpen** *It.* Alpi Venoste. ▲▲ SW Austria
29 T12 **Ouachita, Lake** ▣ Arkansas, C USA
29 R11 **Ouachita Mountains** ▲▲ Arkansas/Oklahoma, C USA
29 U13 **Ouachita River** ≈ Arkansas/Louisiana, C USA
Ouadaï *see* Ouaddaï
78 J7 **Ouadâne** *var.* Ouadane. Adrar, C Mauritania 20.57N 11.34W
80 K13 **Ouadda** Haute-Kotto, N Central African Republic 8.02N 22.22E
80 J10 **Ouaddaï** *off.* Préfecture du Ouaddaï, *var.* Ouadaï, Wadai. ◈ *prefecture* SE Chad
79 P13 **Ouagadougou** *var.* Wagadugu. ● (Burkina) C Burkina 12.20N 1.31W
79 P13 **Ouagadougou** ✕ C Burkina 12.21N 1.27W
79 O12 **Ouahigouya** NW Burkina 13.31N 2.19W
Ouahran *see* Oran
81 J14 **Ouaka** ◈ *prefecture* C Central African Republic
81 J15 **Ouaka** ≈ S Central African Republic
Oualam *see* Ouallam
78 M9 **Oualâta** *var.* Oualata. Hodh ech Chargui, SE Mauritania 17.18N 7.00W
79 R11 **Ouallam** *var.* Oualam. Tillabéri, W Niger 14.13N 2.07E
180 H14 **Ouanani** Mohéli, S Comoros 12.19S 94.37E
57 Z10 **Ouanary** E French Guiana 4.10N 51.40W
80 L13 **Ouanda Djallé** Vakaga, NE Central African Republic 8.53N 22.47E
81 N14 **Ouando** Haut-Mbomou, SE Central African Republic 5.57N 25.57E
81 L15 **Ouango** Mbomou, S Central African Republic 4.19N 22.30E
79 N14 **Ouangolodougou** *var.* Wangolodougou. N Ivory Coast 9.58N 5.09W
180 I13 **Ouani** Anjouan, SE Comoros
81 M15 **Ouara** ≈ E Central African Republic
78 K7 **Ouarâne** *desert* C Mauritania
13 O11 **Ouareau** ≈ Québec, SE Canada
76 K7 **Ouargla** *var.* Wargla. NE Algeria 32.00N 5.16E
76 F8 **Ouarzazate** S Morocco 30.54N 6.55W
79 Q11 **Ouatagouna** Gao, E Mali 15.06N 0.41E
76 G6 **Ouazzane** *var.* Ouezzane, *Ar.* Wazan, Wazzan. N Morocco 34.52N 5.34W
Oubangui *see* Ubangi
Oubangui-Chari *see* Central African Republic
Oubari, Edeyen d' *see* Awbāri, Idhān
100 G13 **Oud-Beijerland** Zuid-Holland, SW Netherlands 51.49N 4.25E
100 F13 **Ouddorp** Zuid-Holland, SW Netherlands 51.49N 3.55E
79 P9 **Oudeïka** *oasis* C Mali 17.16N 1.42W
100 G13 **Oude Maas** ≈ SW Netherlands
101 E18 **Oudenaarde** *Fr.* Audenarde. Oost-Vlaanderen, SW Belgium 50.49N 3.37E
101 H14 **Oudenbosch** Noord-Brabant, S Netherlands 51.34N 4.31E
100 P6 **Oude Pekela** Groningen, NE Netherlands 53.06N 7.00E
Ouderkerk *see* Ouderkerk aan den Amstel
100 I10 **Ouderkerk aan den Amstel** *var.* Ouderkerk. Noord-Holland, C Netherlands 52.18N 4.54E
100 I6 **Oudeschild** Noord-Holland, NW Netherlands 53.01N 4.51E
101 G14 **Oude-Tonge** Zuid-Holland, SW Netherlands 51.40N 4.13E
100 I12 **Oudewater** Utrecht, C Netherlands 52.01N 4.54E
Oudjda *see* Oujda
100 L5 **Oudkerk** Friesland, N Netherlands 53.16N 5.52E
104 J7 **Oudon** ≈ NW France
100 I9 **Oudorp** Noord-Holland, NW Netherlands 52.39N 4.46E
85 G25 **Oudtshoorn** Western Cape, SW South Africa 33.32S 22.12E
101 I16 **Oud-Turnhout** Antwerpen, N Belgium 51.19N 5.01E
76 F7 **Oued-Zem** C Morocco 32.53N 6.30W
197 H5 **Ouégoa** Province Nord, C New Caledonia 20.22S 164.25E
78 L13 **Ouéléssébougou** *var.* Ouolossébougou. Koulikoro, SW Mali 11.58N 7.51W
79 N16 **Ouellé** E Ivory Coast 7.18N 4.01W
79 R16 **Ouémé** ≈ C Benin
197 J7 **Ouen, Île** *island* S New Caledonia
79 O13 **Ouessa** S Burkina 11.02N 2.44W
104 D5 **Ouessant, Île d'** *Eng.* Ushant. *island* NW France
81 H17 **Ouésso** La Sangha, NW Congo 1.37N 16.03E
81 D15 **Ouest** *Eng.* West. ◈ *province* W Cameroon
202 G11 **Ouest, Baie de l'** *bay* Îles Wallis, Wallis and Futuna
13 Y7 **Ouest, Pointe de l'** *headland* Québec, SE Canada 48.08N 64.57W
Ouezzane *see* Ouazzane
101 K20 **Ouffet** Liège, E Belgium 50.30N 5.31E
81 H14 **Ouham** ◈ *prefecture* NW Central African Republic
80 I13 **Ouham** ≈ Central African Republic/Chad
81 G14 **Ouham-Pendé** ◈ *prefecture* W Central African Republic
79 R16 **Ouidah** *Eng.* Whydah, Wida. S Benin 6.22N 2.07E
76 H6 **Oujda** *Ar.* Oudjda, Ujda. NE Morocco 34.45N 1.53W
78 I7 **Oujeft** Adrar, C Mauritania 20.05N 13.00W
95 L15 **Oulainen** Oulu, C Finland 64.14N 24.50E
Ould Yanja *see* Ould Yenjé
78 J10 **Ould Yenjé** *var.* Ould Yanja. Guidimaka, S Mauritania 15.33N 11.43W
95 L14 **Oulu** *Swe.* Uleåborg. Oulu, C Finland 65.01N 25.28E
95 M14 **Oulu** *Swe.* Uleåborg. ◈ *province* N Finland
95 L15 **Oulujärvi** *Swe.* Uleträsk. ◎ C Finland
95 M14 **Oulujoki** *Swe.* Uleälv. ≈ C Finland
95 L14 **Oulunsalo** Oulu, C Finland 64.55N 25.19E
108 A8 **Oulx** Piemonte, NE Italy 45.05N 6.41E
80 J9 **Oum-Chalouba** Borkou-Ennedi-Tibesti, NE Chad 15.48N 20.46E
78 M16 **Oumé** C Ivory Coast 6.23N 5.25W
76 F7 **Oum er Rbia** ≈ C Morocco
80 J10 **Oum-Hadjer** Batha, E Chad 13.18N 19.40E
94 K10 **Ounasjoki** ≈ N Finland
80 J7 **Ounianga Kébir** Borkou-Ennedi-Tibesti, N Chad 19.06N 20.28E
Ouolossébougou *see* Ouéléssébougou
Oup *see* Auob
101 K19 **Oupeye** Liège, E Belgium 50.42N 5.37E
101 N21 **Our** ≈ NW Europe
39 Q7 **Ouray** Colorado, C USA 38.01N 107.40W
105 R7 **Ource** ≈ C France
106 G9 **Ourém** Santarém, C Portugal 39.40N 8.32W
106 H4 **Ourense** *Cast.* Orense; *Lat.* Aurium. Galicia, NW Spain 42.19N 7.52W
106 I4 **Ourense** *Cast.* Orense ◈ *province* Galicia, NW Spain
61 O15 **Ouricuri** Pernambuco, E Brazil 7.51S 40.04W
62 J9 **Ourinhos** São Paulo, S Brazil 22.58S 49.52W
106 G13 **Ourique** Beja, S Portugal 37.37N 8.13W
61 M20 **Ouro Preto** Minas Gerais, NE Brazil 20.25S 43.30W
Ours, Grand Lac de l' *see* Great Bear Lake
101 K20 **Ourthe** ≈ E Belgium
171 Mm11 **Ōu-sanmyaku** ▲▲ Honshū, C Japan
99 M17 **Ouse** ≈ N England, UK
Ouse *see* Great Ouse
104 H7 **Oust** ≈ NW France
Outaouais *see* Ottawa
13 T4 **Outardes Quatre, Réservoir** ▣ Québec, SE Canada
13 T5 **Outardes, Rivière aux** ≈ Québec, SE Canada
98 E8 **Outer Hebrides** *var.* Western Isles. *island group* NW Scotland, UK
32 K3 **Outer Island** *island* Apostle Islands, Wisconsin, N USA
37 S16 **Outer Santa Barbara Passage** *passage* California, SW USA
106 G3 **Outes** Galicia, NW Spain 42.50N 8.54W
85 C18 **Outjo** Kunene, N Namibia 20.06S 16.06E
9 T16 **Outlook** Saskatchewan, S Canada 51.30N 107.03W
95 N16 **Outokumpu** Itä-Suomi, E Finland 62.43N 29.04E
98 M2 **Out Skerries** *island group* NE Scotland, UK
197 J5 **Ouvéa** *island* Îles Loyauté, NE New Caledonia
105 S14 **Ouvèze** ≈ SE France
190 L9 **Ouyen** Victoria, SE Australia 35.06S 142.18E
41 Q14 **Ouzinkie** Kodiak Island, Alaska, USA 57.54N 152.27W
143 O13 **Ovacık** Tunceli, E Turkey 39.22N 39.13E
108 C9 **Ovada** Piemonte, NE Italy 44.41N 8.39E
197 I14 **Ovalau** *island* C Fiji
64 G9 **Ovalle** Coquimbo, N Chile 30.33S 71.16W
85 C17 **Ovamboland** *physical region* N Namibia
56 L10 **Ovana, Cerro** ▲ S Venezuela 4.41N 66.54W
106 G7 **Ovar** Aveiro, N Portugal 40.52N 8.37W
116 L10 **Ovcharitsa, Yazovir** ▣ SE Bulgaria
56 E6 **Ovejas** Sucre, NW Colombia 9.30N 75.15W
103 E16 **Overath** Nordrhein-Westfalen, W Germany 50.55N 7.16E
100 F13 **Overflakkee** *island* SW Netherlands
101 H19 **Overijse** Vlaams Brabant, C Belgium 50.46N 4.31E
100 N10 **Overijssel** ◈ *province* E Netherlands
100 M9 **Overijssels Kanaal** *canal* E Netherlands
94 K13 **Överkalix** Norrbotten, N Sweden 66.19N 22.49E
29 R4 **Overland Park** Kansas, C USA 38.57N 94.40W
101 L14 **Overloon** Noord-Brabant, SE Netherlands 51.35N 5.54E
101 K16 **Overpelt** Limburg, NE Belgium 51.13N 5.24E
37 Y10 **Overton** Nevada, W USA 36.32N 114.25W
27 W7 **Overton** Texas, SW USA 32.16N 94.58W
94 K13 **Övertorneå** Norrbotten, N Sweden 66.22N 23.38E
97 N18 **Överum** Kalmar, S Sweden 57.58N 16.19E
94 G13 **Överuman** ◎ N Sweden
119 P11 **Ovidiopol'** Odes'ka Oblast', SW Ukraine 46.15N 30.27E
118 M14 **Ovidiu** Constanța, SE Romania 44.16N 28.34E
47 N10 **Oviedo** SW Dominican Republic 17.46N 71.22W
106 K2 **Oviedo** *anc.* Asturias. Asturias, NW Spain 43.21N 5.49W
106 K2 **Oviedo** ✕ Asturias, N Spain 43.21N 5.49W
Ovilava *see* Wels
120 D7 **Oviši** Ventspils, W Latvia 57.34N 21.43E
152 K10 **Ovminzatovo Tog'lari** *Rus.* Gory Auminzatau. ▲▲ N Uzbekistan
168 H6 **Övögdiy** Dzavhan, C Mongolia 48.38N 97.39E
169 P10 **Ovoot** Sühbaatar, SE Mongolia 45.08N 113.51E
163 O4 **Övörhangay** ◈ *province* C Mongolia
96 E12 **Øvre Årdal** Sogn og Fjordane, S Norway 61.17N 7.44E
97 J14 **Övre Fryken** ◎ C Sweden
94 J11 **Övre Soppero** *Lapp.* Badje-Sohppar. Norrbotten, N Sweden 68.07N 21.40E
119 N3 **Ovruch** Zhytomyrs'ka Oblast', N Ukraine 51.19N 28.50E
168 J8 **Övt** Övörhangay, C Mongolia 46.50N 102.15E
193 E24 **Owaka** Otago, South Island, NZ 46.27S 169.42E
81 H18 **Owando** *prev.* Fort-Rousset. Cuvette, C Congo 0.28S 15.55E
171 Gg17 **Owase** Mie, Honshū, SW Japan 34.04N 136.10E
29 P9 **Owasso** Oklahoma, C USA 36.16N 95.51W
31 V10 **Owatonna** Minnesota, N USA 44.04N 93.13W
181 O4 **Owen Fracture Zone** *tectonic feature* W Arabian Sea
193 H15 **Owen, Mount** ▲ South Island, NZ 41.32S 172.33E
193 H15 **Owen River** Tasman, South Island, NZ 41.40S 172.28E
46 D8 **Owen Roberts** ✕ Grand Cayman, Cayman Islands 19.15N 81.22W
22 I6 **Owensboro** Kentucky, S USA 37.46N 87.06W
37 T11 **Owens Lake** *salt flat* California, W USA
12 F14 **Owen Sound** Ontario, S Canada 44.34N 80.55W
12 F13 **Owen Sound** ◎ Ontario, S Canada
37 T10 **Owens River** ≈ California, W USA
194 K15 **Owen Stanley Range** ▲▲ S PNG
29 V5 **Owensville** Missouri, C USA 38.21N 91.30W
22 M4 **Owenton** Kentucky, S USA 38.33N 84.51W
79 U17 **Owerri** Imo, S Nigeria 5.19N 7.07E
192 M10 **Owhango** Manawatu-Wanganui, North Island, NZ 39.01S 175.22E
23 N5 **Owingsville** Kentucky, S USA 38.10N 83.42W
79 T16 **Owo** Ondo, SW Nigeria 7.10N 5.31E
33 R9 **Owosso** Michigan, N USA 43.00N 84.10W
37 V1 **Owyhee** Nevada, W USA 41.57N 116.07W
34 L14 **Owyhee, Lake** ◎ Oregon, NW USA
34 L15 **Owyhee River** ≈ Idaho/Oregon, NW USA
94 K1 **Öxarfjördhur** *var.* Axarfjördhur. *fjord* N Iceland
96 K12 **Oxberg** Dalarna, C Sweden 61.07N 14.10E
9 V17 **Oxbow** Saskatchewan, S Canada 49.16N 102.12W
97 O17 **Oxelösund** Södermanland, S Sweden 58.40N 17.10E
193 H18 **Oxford** Canterbury, South Island, NZ 43.18S 172.10E
99 M21 **Oxford** *Lat.* Oxonia. S England, UK 51.46N 1.15W
25 Q3 **Oxford** Alabama, S USA 33.36N 85.50W
24 L2 **Oxford** Mississippi, S USA 34.23N 89.30W
31 N16 **Oxford** Nebraska, C USA 40.15N 99.37W
20 I11 **Oxford** New York, NE USA 42.21N 75.39W
23 U8 **Oxford** North Carolina, SE USA 36.18N 78.35W
33 Q14 **Oxford** Ohio, N USA 39.30N 84.45W
20 H16 **Oxford** Pennsylvania, NE USA 39.46N 75.57W
9 X12 **Oxford House** Manitoba, C Canada 54.55N 95.13W
31 Y13 **Oxford Junction** Iowa, C USA 41.58N 90.57W
9 X12 **Oxford Lake** ◎ Manitoba, C Canada
99 M21 **Oxfordshire** *cultural region* S England, UK
Oxia *see* Oxyá
43 X12 **Oxkutzcab** Yucatán, SE Mexico 20.14N 89.20W
37 R15 **Oxnard** California, W USA 34.12N 119.10W
Oxonia *see* Oxford
12 I12 **Oxtongue** ≈ Ontario, SE Canada
Oxus *see* Amu Darya
117 E15 **Oxyá** *var.* Oxia. ▲ C Greece 39.46N 21.56E
171 Ii13 **Oyabe** Toyama, Honshū, SW Japan 36.41N 136.53E
Oyahue/Oyahue, Volcán *see* Ollagüe, Volcán
171 K16 **Oyama** Tochigi, Honshū, S Japan 36.19N 139.46E
49 U5 **Oyapock** ≈ E French Guiana
Oyapock *see* Oiapoque, Rio
57 Z10 **Oyapok, Baie de L'** *bay* Brazil/French Guiana
57 Z11 **Oyapok, Fleuve l'** *var.* Oyapock, Rio Oiapoque. ≈ Brazil/French Guiana *see also* Oiapoque, Rio
81 E17 **Oyem** Woleu-Ntem, N Gabon 1.34N 11.31E
9 R16 **Oyen** Alberta, SW Canada 51.19N 110.28W
97 I15 **Øyeren** ◎ S Norway
168 G6 **Oygon** Dzavhan, N Mongolia 48.57N 96.33E
98 I7 **Oykel** ≈ N Scotland, UK
127 N9 **Oymyakon** Respublika Sakha (Yakutiya), NE Russian Federation 63.28N 142.22E
81 H19 **Oyo** Cuvette, C Congo 1.05S 15.55E
79 S15 **Oyo** Oyo, W Nigeria 7.51N 3.57E
79 S15 **Oyo** ◈ *state* SW Nigeria
58 D13 **Oyón** Lima, C Peru 10.39S 76.46W
105 S10 **Oyonnax** Ain, E France 46.16N 5.39E
152 L10 **Oyoqog'itma** *Rus.* Ayakagytma. Buxoro Viloyati, C Uzbekistan 40.37N 64.26E
152 M9 **Oyoqquduq** *Rus.* Ayakkuduk. Navoiy Viloyati, N Uzbekistan 41.16N 65.12E
34 F9 **Oysterville** Washington, NW USA 46.33N 124.03W
97 D14 **Øystese** Hordaland, S Norway 60.22N 6.13E
153 U10 **Oy-Tal** Oshskaya Oblast', SW Kyrgyzstan 40.23N 74.04E
153 T10 **Oy-Tal** ≈ SW Kyrgyzstan
151 S16 **Oytal** Zhambyl, S Kazakhstan 42.50N 73.21E
Oyyl *see* Uil
179 Qq15 **Ozamiz** Mindanao, S Philippines 8.09N 123.51E
Ozarichi *see* Azarychy
25 R7 **Ozark** Alabama, S USA 31.27N 85.38W
29 S10 **Ozark** Arkansas, C USA 35.29N 93.49W
29 T8 **Ozark** Missouri, C USA 37.01N 93.12W
29 T8 **Ozark Plateau** *plain* Arkansas/Missouri, C USA
29 T6 **Ozarks, Lake of the** ▣ Missouri, C USA
199 Jj11 **Ozbourn Seamount** *undersea feature* W Pacific Ocean 26.00S 174.49W
113 L20 **Ózd** Borsod-Abaúj-Zemplén, NE Hungary 48.14N 20.18E
114 D11 **Ozeblin** ▲ C Croatia 44.37N 15.52E
127 Pp12 **Ozernovskiy** Kamchatskaya Oblast', E Russian Federation 51.28N 94.32E
150 M7 **Ozërnoye** *var.* Ozërnyy. Kostanay, N Kazakhstan 53.27N 63.10E
Ozërnyy *see* Ozërnoye
128 I15 **Ozërnyy** Tverskaya Oblast', W Russian Federation 57.55N 33.45E
117 D18 **Ozerós, Límni** ◎ W Greece
121 D14 **Ozersk** *prev.* Darkehnen, *Ger.* Angerapp. Kaliningradskaya Oblast', W Russian Federation 54.23N 21.59E
124 Ee11 **Ozërsk** Chelyabinskaya Oblast', C Russian Federation 55.44N 60.59E
130 L4 **Ozery** Moskovskaya Oblast', W Russian Federation 54.51N 38.37E
Özgön *see* Uzgen
109 C17 **Ozieri** Sardegna, Italy, C Mediterranean Sea 40.34N 9.01E
113 I15 **Ozimek** *Ger.* Malapane. Opolskie, S Poland 50.41N 18.16E
131 R8 **Ozinki** Saratovskaya Oblast', W Russian Federation 51.16N 49.45E
Oziya *see* Ojiya
27 O10 **Ozona** Texas, SW USA 30.42N 101.12W
Ozorkov *see* Ozorków
112 J12 **Ozorków** *Rus.* Ozorkov. Łódź, C Poland 51.58N 19.16E
170 E14 **Ōzu** Ehime, Shikoku, SW Japan 33.31N 132.31E
143 R10 **Ozurget'i** *prev.* Makharadze. W Georgia 41.57N 42.01E

P

101 J17 **Paal** Limburg, NE Belgium 51.03N 5.08E
197 C13 **Paama** *island* C Vanuatu
206 M14 **Paamiut** *var.* Pâmiut, *Dan.* Frederikshåb. Kitaa, S Greenland 62.22N 49.52W
178 Gg9 **Pa-an** Karen State, S Myanmar 16.51N 97.37E
103 L22 **Paar** ≈ SE Germany
85 E26 **Paarl** Western Cape, SW South Africa 33.45S 18.58E
95 L15 **Paavola** Oulu, C Finland 64.34N 25.15E
98 E8 **Pabbay** *island* NW Scotland, UK
175 P12 **Pabbiring, Kepulauan** *island group* C Indonesia
159 T15 **Pabna** Rajshahi, W Bangladesh 24.02N 89.15E
111 U4 **Pabneukirchen** Oberösterreich, N Austria 48.19N 14.49E
120 H13 **Pabradė** *Pol.* Podbrodzie. Vilnius, SE Lithuania 54.58N 25.43E
58 L13 **Pacahuaras, Río** ≈ N Bolivia
Pacaraima, Sierra/Pacaraim, Serra *see* Pakaraima Mountains
58 B11 **Pacasmayo** La Libertad, W Peru 7.27S 79.34W
44 D6 **Pacaya, Volcán de** Ѧ S Guatemala 14.19N 90.36W
117 K23 **Pachía** *island* Kykládes, Greece, Aegean Sea
109 L26 **Pachino** Sicilia, Italy, C Mediterranean Sea 36.43N 15.06E
58 F12 **Pachitea, Río** ≈ C Peru
160 I11 **Pachmarhi** Madhya Pradesh, C India 22.36N 78.18E
124 N4 **Páchna** *var.* Pakhna. SW Cyprus 34.47N 32.48E
117 H25 **Páchnes** ▲ Kríti, Greece, E Mediterranean Sea 35.19N 24.00E
56 F9 **Pacho** Cundinamarca, C Colombia 5.07N 74.11W
160 F12 **Pāchora** Mahārāshtra, C India 20.52N 75.28E
43 P13 **Pachuca** *var.* Pachuca de Soto. Hidalgo, C Mexico 20.05N 98.46W
Pachuca de Soto *see* Pachuca
29 W5 **Pacific** Missouri, C USA 38.28N 90.44W
199 Jj15 **Pacific-Antarctic Ridge** *undersea feature* S Pacific Ocean
34 F8 **Pacific Beach** Washington, NW USA 47.09N 124.12W
37 N10 **Pacific Grove** California, W USA 36.35N 121.54W
31 S15 **Pacific Junction** Iowa, C USA 41.01N 95.48W
198-199 **Pacific Ocean** *ocean*
133 Z10 **Pacific Plate** *tectonic feature*
115 J15 **Pačir** ▲ SW Serbia and Montenegro (Yugoslavia) 43.19N 19.07E
190 L5 **Packsaddle** New South Wales, SE Australia 30.42S 141.55E
34 H9 **Packwood** Washington, NW USA 46.37N 121.38W
Padalung *see* Phatthalung
175 Q12 **Padamarang, Pulau** *island* C Indonesia
173 G9 **Padang** Sumatera, W Indonesia 01.00S 100.21E
174 Hh5 **Padang Endau** Pahang, Peninsular Malaysia 2.38N 103.37E
Padangpandjang *see* Padangpanjang
173 G8 **Padangpanjang** *prev.* Padangpandjang. Sumatera, W Indonesia 0.30S 100.25E
173 Ff7 **Padangsidempuan** *prev.* Padangsidimpoean. Sumatera, W Indonesia 1.22N 99.14E
Padangsidimpoean *see* Padangsidempuan
128 I9 **Padany** Respublika Kareliya, NW Russian Federation 63.18N 33.20E
95 M18 **Padasjoki** Etelä-Suomi, S Finland 61.20N 25.20E
59 M22 **Padcaya** Tarija, S Bolivia 21.52S 64.46W
103 H14 **Paderborn** Nordrhein-Westfalen, NW Germany 51.43N 8.45E
Padeşul/Padeş, Vîrful *see* Padeş, Vârful
118 F12 **Padeş, Vârful** *var.* Padeşul; *prev.* Vîrful Padeş. ▲ W Romania 45.39N 22.19E
114 L10 **Padinska Skela** Serbia, N Serbia and Montenegro (Yugoslavia) 44.58N 20.25E
Padma *see* Brahmaputra
159 S14 **Padma** *var.* Ganges. ≈ Bangladesh/India *see also* Ganges
108 H8 **Padova** *Eng.* Padua; *anc.* Patavium. Veneto, NE Italy 45.24N 11.52E
84 A10 **Padrão, Ponta do** *headland* NW Angola 6.06S 12.18E
27 T16 **Padre Island** *island* Texas, SW USA
106 G3 **Padrón** Galicia, NW Spain 42.43N 8.40W
120 K13 **Padsvillye** *Rus.* Podsvil'ye. Vitsyebskaya Voblasts', N Belarus 55.10N 27.58E
190 K11 **Padthaway** South Australia 36.39S 140.30E
Padua *see* Padova
22 G7 **Paducah** Kentucky, S USA 37.09N 88.52W
27 P4 **Paducah** Texas, SW USA 33.59N 100.19W
107 N15 **Padul** Andalucía, S Spain 37.01N 3.37W
203 P8 **Paea** Tahiti, W French Polynesia 17.40S 149.34W
193 L14 **Paekakariki** Wellington, North Island, NZ 41.00S 174.58E
169 X11 **Paektu-san** *var.* Baitou Shan. ▲ China/North Korea 42.00N 128.03W
169 V15 **Paengnyŏng-do** *island* NW South Korea
192 M7 **Paeroa** Waikato, North Island, NZ 37.22S 175.39E
56 D12 **Páez** Cauca, SW Colombia 2.37N 76.00W
123 Mm4 **Páfos** *var.* Paphos. W Cyprus 34.46N 32.25E
123 Mm4 **Páfos** ✕ SW Cyprus 34.46N 32.25E
85 L19 **Pafúri** Gaza, SW Mozambique 22.24S 31.27E
114 C12 **Pag** *It.* Pago. Lika-Senj, W Croatia 44.26N 15.01E
114 B11 **Pag** *It.* Pago. *island* Zadar, SW Croatia
179 Qq16 **Pagadian** Mindanao, S Philippines 7.47N 123.22E
173 G11 **Pagai Selatan, Pulau** *island* Kepulauan Mentawai, W Indonesia
173 Ff10 **Pagai Utara, Pulau** *island* Kepulauan Mentawai, W Indonesia
196 K4 **Pagan** *island* C Northern Mariana Islands
117 G16 **Pagasitikós Kólpos** *gulf* E Greece
38 L8 **Page** Arizona, SW USA 36.54N 111.28W
31 Q5 **Page** North Dakota, N USA 47.09N 97.33W
120 D13 **Pagėgiai** *Ger.* Pogegen. Tauragė, SW Lithuania 55.08N 21.54E
23 S11 **Pageland** South Carolina, SE USA 34.46N 80.23W
83 G16 **Pager** ≈ NE Uganda
155 Q5 **Paghmān** Kābul, E Afghanistan 34.33N 68.55E
Pago *see* Pag
196 C16 **Pago Bay** *bay* E Guam, W Pacific Ocean
117 M20 **Pagóndas** *var.* Pagóndhas. Sámos, Dodekánisos, Greece, Aegean Sea 37.40N 26.49E
Pagóndhas *see* Pagóndas
198 C8 **Pago Pago** ○ (American Samoa) Tutuila, W American Samoa 14.16S 170.43W
39 R8 **Pagosa Springs** Colorado, C USA 37.13N 107.01W
40 H12 **Pāhala** *var.* Pahala. Hawai'i, USA, C Pacific Ocean 19.12N 155.28W
174 H4 **Pahang** *off.* Negeri Pahang Darul Makmur. ◈ *state* Peninsular Malaysia
Pahang *see* Pahang, Sungai
174 Hh5 **Pahang, Sungai** *var.* Pahang, Sungei Pahang. ≈ Peninsular Malaysia
155 S8 **Pahārpur** North-West Frontier Province, NW Pakistan 32.06N 71.00E
193 B24 **Pahia Point** *headland* South Island, NZ 46.19S 167.42E
192 M13 **Pahiatua** Manawatu-Wanganui, North Island, NZ 40.30S 175.48E
40 H12 **Pāhoa** *var.* Pahoa. Hawai'i, USA, C Pacific Ocean 19.28N 154.55W
25 Y14 **Pahokee** Florida, SE USA 26.49N 80.40W
37 X9 **Pahranagat Range** ▲▲ Nevada, W USA
37 W11 **Pahrump** Nevada, W USA 36.11N 115.58W
Pahsien *see* Chongqing
37 V9 **Pahute Mesa** ▲▲ Nevada, W USA
178 H7 **Pai** Mae Hong Son, NW Thailand 19.24N 98.25E
40 F10 **Pā'ia** *var.* Paia. Maui, Hawai'i, USA, C Pacific Ocean 20.54N 94.22W
Pai-ch'eng *see* Baicheng
120 H4 **Paide** *Ger.* Weissenstein. Järvamaa, N Estonia 58.54N 25.36E
99 J24 **Paignton** SW England, UK 50.25N 3.34W
192 K3 **Paihia** Northland, North Island, NZ 35.18S 174.06E
95 M18 **Päijänne** ◎ S Finland
116 F13 **Páïko** ▲▲ N Greece
59 M17 **Paila, Río** ≈ C Bolivia
178 I12 **Pailĭn** Bătdâmbâng, W Cambodia 12.51N 102.34E
56 F6 **Pailitas** Cesar, N Colombia 8.58N 73.37W
40 F9 **Pailolo Channel** *channel* Hawai'i, USA, C Pacific Ocean
95 K19 **Paimio** *Swe.* Pemar. Länsi-Suomi, W Finland 60.27N 22.42E
172 O17 **Paimi-saki** *var.* Yaeme-saki. *headland* Iriomote-jima, SW Japan 24.18N 123.40E
104 G5 **Paimpol** Côtes d'Armor, NW France 48.46N 3.03W
174 Gg9 **Painan** Sumatera, W Indonesia 1.22S 100.33E

◆ Country ● Country Capital ◇ Dependent Territory ○ Dependent Territory Capital ◈ Administrative Region ✕ International Airport ▲ Mountain ▲▲ Mountain Range Ѧ Volcano ≈ River ◎ Lake ▣ Reservoir

PAINE, CERRO – PARIÑAS, PUNTA

65 G23 **Paine, Cerro** ▲ S Chile *51.01S 72.57W*
33 U11 **Painesville** Ohio, N USA *41.43N 81.15W*
33 S14 **Paint Creek** ≈ Ohio, N USA
38 L10 **Painted Desert** *desert* Arizona, SW USA
Paint Hills *see* Wemindji
32 M4 **Paint River** ≈ Michigan, N USA
27 P8 **Paint Rock** Texas, SW USA *31.30N 99.55W*
23 O6 **Paintsville** Kentucky, S USA *37.48N 82.48W*
Paisance *see* Piacenza
98 I12 **Paisley** W Scotland, UK *55.49N 4.25W*
34 I15 **Paisley** Oregon, NW USA *42.40N 120.31W*
107 R10 **País Valenciano** ***var.*** Valencia, ***Cat.*** València; ***anc.*** Valentia. ◐ *autonomous community* NE Spain
107 O3 **País Vasco** ***Basq.*** Euskadi, ***Eng.*** The Basque Country, ***Sp.*** Provincias Vascongadas. ◐ *autonomous community* N Spain
58 A9 **Paita** Piura, NW Peru *5.07S 81.07W*
197 J7 **Païta** Province Sud, S New Caledonia *22.06S 166.18E*
175 O1 **Paitan, Teluk** *bay* Sabah, East Malaysia
106 H7 **Paiva, Rio** ≈ N Portugal
94 K12 **Pajala** Norrbotten, N Sweden *67.12N 23.19E*
106 K3 **Pajares, Puerto de** *pass* NW Spain *43.00N 5.53W*
56 G9 **Pajárito** Boyacá, C Colombia *5.18N 72.43W*
56 G4 **Pajaro** La Guajira, S Colombia *11.41N 72.37W*
Pakanbaru *see* Pekanbaru
57 Q10 **Pakaraima Mountains** ***var.*** Serra Pacaraim, Sierra Pacaraima. ⛰ N South America
178 Hh11 **Pak Chong** Nakhon Ratchasima, C Thailand *14.38N 101.22E*
127 Pp7 **Pakhachi** Koryakskiy Avtonomnyy Okrug, E Russian Federation *60.36N 168.59E*
Pakhna *see* Páchna
201 U16 **Pakin Atoll** *atoll* Caroline Islands, E Micronesia
155 Q12 **Pakistan** ***off.*** Islamic Republic of Pakistan, ***var.*** Islami Jamhuriya e Pakistan. ◆ *republic* S Asia
Pakistan, Islami Jamhuriya e *see* Pakistan
178 I8 **Pak Lay** ***var.*** Muang Pak Lay. Xaignabouli, C Laos *18.06N 101.21E*
Paknam *see* Samut Prakan
177 Ff5 **Pakokku** Magwe, C Myanmar *21.19N 95.04E*
112 I10 **Pakość** ***Ger.*** Pakosch. Kujawski-pomorskie, C Poland *52.47N 18.03E*
Pakosch *see* Pakość
155 V10 **Pākpattan** Punjab, E Pakistan *30.19N 73.27E*
178 H16 **Pak Phanang** ***var.*** Ban Pak Phanang. Nakhon Si Thammarat, SW Thailand *8.19N 100.10E*
114 G9 **Pakrac** ***Hung.*** Pakrácz. Požega-Slavonija, NE Croatia *45.26N 17.09E*
Pakrácz *see* Pakrac
120 F11 **Pakruojis** Šiauliai, N Lithuania *55.59N 23.50E*
113 J24 **Paks** Tolna, S Hungary *46.37N 18.51E*
Pak Sane *see* Pakxan
Paksé *see* Pakxé
178 I11 **Pak Thong Chai** Nakhon Ratchasima, C Thailand *14.43N 102.01E*
155 R6 **Paktīā** ◐ *province* SE Afghanistan
155 Q7 **Paktīkā** ◐ *province* SE Afghanistan
175 Pp9 **Pakuli** Sulawesi, C Indonesia *1.14S 119.55E*
83 F17 **Pakwach** NW Uganda *2.28N 31.28E*
178 Ii8 **Pakxan** ***var.*** Muang Pakxan, Pak Sane. Bolikhamxai, C Laos *18.27N 103.38E*
178 Jj10 **Pakxé** ***var.*** Paksé. Champasak, S Laos *15.09N 105.49E*
80 G12 **Pala** Mayo-Kébbi, SW Chad *9.22N 14.54E*
63 A17 **Palacios** Santa Fe, C Argentina *30.43S 61.37W*
27 V13 **Palacios** Texas, SW USA *28.42N 96.13W*
107 X5 **Palafrugell** Cataluña, NE Spain *41.55N 3.10E*
109 L24 **Palagonia** Sicilia, Italy, C Mediterranean Sea *37.19N 14.45E*
115 E17 **Palagruža** ***It.*** Pelagosa. *island* SW Croatia
117 G20 **Palaiá Epídavros** Pelopónnisos, S Greece *37.38N 23.09E*
124 Nn3 **Palaichóri** ***var.*** Palekhori. C Cyprus *34.55N 33.06E*
117 H25 **Palaiochóra** Kríti, Greece, E Mediterranean Sea *35.14N 23.37E*
117 A15 **Palaiolastrítsa** *religious building* Kérkyra, Iónioi Nísoi, Greece, C Mediterranean Sea *39.41N 19.42E*
117 J19 **Palaiópoli** Ándros, Kykládes, Greece, Aegean Sea *37.49N 24.49E*
105 N5 **Palaiseau** Essonne, N France *48.40N 2.13E*
Palakkad *see* Pālghāt
160 N11 **Pāla Laharha** Orissa, E India *21.27N 85.14E*
85 G19 **Palamakoloi** Ghanzi, C Botswana *23.10S 22.22E*
117 E16 **Palamás** Thessalía, C Greece *39.28N 22.04E*
107 X5 **Palamós** Cataluña, NE Spain *41.51N 3.06E*
120 J5 **Palamuse** ***Ger.*** Sankt-Bartholomäi. Jõgevamaa, E Estonia *58.40N 26.34E*
191 Q14 **Palana** Tasmania, SE Australia *39.48S 147.54E*
127 P9 **Palana** Koryakskiy Avtonomnyy Okrug, E Russian Federation *59.04N 159.58E*
120 C11 **Palanga** ***Ger.*** Polangen. Klaipėda, NW Lithuania *5.54N 21.05E*
149 V10 **Palangān, Kūh-e** ⛰ E Iran
Palangkaraja *see* Palangkaraya
174 Mm10 **Palangkaraya** ***prev.*** Palangkaraja. Borneo, C Indonesia *2.16S 113.55E*
161 H22 **Palani** Tamil Nādu, SE India *10.30N 77.24E*
Palanka *see* Bačka Palanka
160 D9 **Pālanpur** Gujarāt, W India *24.12N 72.28E*
Palantia *see* Palencia
85 I19 **Palapye** Central, SE Botswana *22.37S 27.06E*
161 J19 **Pālār** ≈ SE India
106 H3 **Palas de Rei** Galicia, NW Spain *42.52N 7.51W*
127 O10 **Palatka** Magadanskaya Oblast', E Russian Federation *60.09N 150.33E*
25 W10 **Palatka** Florida, SE USA *29.39N 81.38W*
196 B9 **Palau** ***var.*** Belau. ◆ *republic* W Pacific Ocean
133 Y14 **Palau Islands** ***var.*** Palau. *island group* N Palau
198 Aa8 **Palauli Bay** *bay* Savai'i, Samoa, C Pacific Ocean
178 Gg12 **Palaw** Tenasserim, S Myanmar *12.57N 98.39E*
179 Oo15 **Palawan** *island* W Philippines
179 Oo15 **Palawan Passage** *passage* W Philippines
198 F7 **Palawan Trough** *undersea feature* S South China Sea
179 P10 **Palayan City** Luzon, N Philippines *15.34N 121.34E*
161 H23 **Pālayankottai** Tamil Nādu, SE India *8.44N 77.45E*
109 L25 **Palazzolo Acreide** ***anc.*** Acrae. Sicilia, Italy, C Mediterranean Sea *37.04N 14.54E*
120 G3 **Paldiski** ***prev.*** Baltiski, ***Eng.*** Baltic Port, ***Ger.*** Baltischport. Harjumaa, NW Estonia *59.20N 24.04E*
114 I13 **Pale** Republika Srpska, E Bosnia and Herzegovina *43.49N 18.35E*
Palekhori *see* Palaichóri
175 Q7 **Paleleh, Pegunungan** ⛰ Sulawesi, N Indonesia
175 Qq7 **Paleleh, Teluk** *bay* Sulawesi, N Indonesia
174 I11 **Palembang** Sumatera, W Indonesia *2.58S 104.45E*
65 G18 **Palena** Los Lagos, S Chile *43.40S 71.49W*
65 G18 **Palena, Río** ≈ S Chile
106 M5 **Palencia** ***anc.*** Palantia, Pallantia. Castilla-León, NW Spain *41.01N 4.31W*
106 M3 **Palencia** ◐ *province* Castilla-León, N Spain
37 X15 **Palen Dry Lake** ◎ California, W USA
43 V15 **Palenque** Chiapas, SE Mexico *17.37N 92.03W*
43 V15 **Palenque** ***var.*** Ruinas de Palenque. *ruins* Chiapas, SE Mexico *17.31N 91.58W*
47 O9 **Palenque, Punta** *headland* S Dominican Republic *18.13N 70.08W*
Palenque, Ruinas de *see* Palenque
Palerme *see* Palermo
109 I23 **Palermo** ***Fr.*** Palerme; ***anc.*** Panhormus, Panormus. Sicilia, Italy, C Mediterranean Sea *38.07N 13.22E*
27 V8 **Palestine** Texas, SW USA *31.44N 95.38W*
27 V7 **Palestine, Lake** ⊠ Texas, SW USA
109 I15 **Palestrina** Lazio, C Italy *41.49N 12.53E*
177 F5 **Paletwa** Chin State, W Myanmar *21.21N 92.51E*
161 G21 **Pālghāt** ***var.*** Palakkad; ***prev.*** Pulicat. Kerala, SW India *10.46N 76.42E*
158 F13 **Pāli** Rājasthān, N India *25.48N 73.21E*
178 Gg16 **Palian** Trang, SW Thailand
201 O12 **Palikir** ● (Micronesia) Pohnpei, E Micronesia *6.58N 158.13E*
179 R17 **Palimbang** Mindanao, S Philippines *6.16N 124.10E*
Palimé *see* Kpalimé
109 L19 **Palinuro, Capo** *headland* S Italy *40.02N 15.16E*
117 H15 **Palioúri, Akrotírio** ***var.*** Akra Kanestron. *headland* N Greece *39.55N 23.45E*
35 R14 **Palisades Reservoir** ⊠ Idaho, NW USA
101 J23 **Paliseul** Luxembourg, SE Belgium *49.55N 5.09E*
160 C11 **Pālitāna** Gujarāt, W India *21.30N 71.49E*
120 F4 **Palivere** Läänemaa, W Estonia *58.59N 23.58E*
43 V14 **Palizada** Campeche, SE Mexico *18.15N 92.03W*
95 L18 **Pälkäne** Länsi-Suomi, W Finland *61.21N 24.15E*
161 J22 **Palk Strait** *strait* India/Sri Lanka
161 J23 **Pallai** Northern Province, NW Sri Lanka *9.34N 80.19E*
Pallantia *see* Palencia
108 C6 **Pallanza** Piemonte, NE Italy *45.57N 8.32E*
131 Q9 **Pallasovka** Volgogradskaya Oblast', SW Russian Federation *50.06N 46.52E*
Pallene/Pallíni *see* Kassándra
193 L15 **Palliser Bay** *bay* North Island, NZ
193 L15 **Palliser, Cape** *headland* North Island, NZ *41.37S 175.16E*
203 U9 **Palliser, Îles** *island group* Îles Tuamotu, C French Polynesia
107 X9 **Palma** ***var.*** Palma de Mallorca. Mallorca, Spain, W Mediterranean Sea *39.34N 2.39E*
107 X9 **Palma** ✕ Mallorca, Spain, W Mediterranean Sea
84 Q12 **Palma** Cabo Delgado, N Mozambique *10.46S 40.30E*
107 X10 **Palma, Badia de** *bay* Mallorca, Spain, W Mediterranean Sea
106 L13 **Palma del Río** Andalucía, S Spain *37.42N 5.16W*
Palma de Mallorca *see* Palma
109 J25 **Palma di Montechiaro** Sicilia, Italy, C Mediterranean Sea *37.12N 13.46E*
108 J7 **Palmanova** Friuli-Venezia Giulia, NE Italy *45.54N 13.20E*
56 J7 **Palmarito** Apure, C Venezuela *7.36N 70.11W*
45 N15 **Palmar Sur** Puntarenas, SE Costa Rica *8.54N 83.27W*
62 I12 **Palmas** Paraná, S Brazil *26.29S 52.00W*
61 K16 **Palmas** ***var.*** Palmas do Tocantins, C Brazil *10.24S 48.19W*
78 L18 **Palmas, Cape** ***Fr.*** Cap des Palmès *headland* SW Ivory Coast *4.18N 7.31W*
Palmas do Tocantins *see* Palmas
56 D11 **Palmaseca** ✕ (Cali) Valle del Cauca, SW Colombia *3.31N 76.27W*
109 B21 **Palmas, Golfo di** *gulf* Sardegna, Italy, C Mediterranean Sea
46 I7 **Palma Soriano** Santiago de Cuba, E Cuba *20.10N 76.00W*
25 Y12 **Palm Bay** Florida, SE USA *28.01N 80.35W*
37 T14 **Palmdale** California, W USA *34.34N 118.07W*
63 H14 **Palmeira das Missões** Rio Grande do Sul, S Brazil *27.54S 53.19W*
84 A11 **Palmeirinhas, Ponta das** *headland* NW Angola *9.04S 13.02E*
41 R11 **Palmer** Alaska, USA *61.36N 149.06W*
21 N11 **Palmer** Massachusetts, NE USA *42.09N 72.19W*
27 U7 **Palmer** Texas, SW USA *32.25N 96.40W*
204 H4 **Palmer** *US research station* Antarctica *64.37S 64.01W*
13 R11 **Palmer** ≈ Québec, SE Canada
39 T5 **Palmer Lake** Colorado, C USA *39.07N 104.55W*
204 J6 **Palmer Land** *physical region* Antarctica
12 F15 **Palmerston** Ontario, SE Canada *43.51N 80.49W*
193 F22 **Palmerston** Otago, South Island, NZ *45.27S 170.42E*
202 K15 **Palmerston** *island* S Cook Islands
Palmerston *see* Darwin
192 M12 **Palmerston North** Manawatu-Wanganui, North Island, NZ *40.19S 175.52E*
Palmés, Cap des *see* Palmas, Cape
25 V13 **Palmetto** Florida, SE USA *27.31N 82.34W*
Palmetto State *see* South Carolina
109 M22 **Palmi** Calabria, SW Italy *38.21N 15.51E*
56 D11 **Palmira** Valle del Cauca, W Colombia *3.33N 76.16W*
58 F8 **Palmira, Río** ≈ N Peru
63 D19 **Palmitas** Soriano, SW Uruguay *33.27S 57.48W*
Palmnicken *see* Yantarnyy
37 V15 **Palm Springs** California, W USA *33.48N 116.33W*
29 V2 **Palmyra** Missouri, C USA *39.47N 91.31W*
20 G10 **Palmyra** New York, NE USA *43.02N 77.13W*
20 G15 **Palmyra** Pennsylvania, NE USA *40.18N 76.35W*
23 V5 **Palmyra** Virginia, NE USA *37.53N 78.15W*
Palmyra *see* Tudmur
199 K7 **Palmyra Atoll** ◇ *US privately owned unincorporated territory* C Pacific Ocean
160 P12 **Palmyras Point** *headland* E India *20.46N 87.00E*
37 N9 **Palo Alto** California, W USA *37.26N 122.08W*
27 O1 **Palo Duro Creek** ≈ Texas, SW USA
Paloe *see* Palu
Paloe *see* Denpasar, Bali, C Indonesia
174 Hh6 **Paloh** Johor, Peninsular Malaysia *2.10N 103.10E*
82 F12 **Paloich** Upper Nile, SE Sudan *10.28N 32.31E*
42 I3 **Palomas** Chihuahua, N Mexico *31.45N 107.38W*
109 I15 **Palombara Sabina** Lazio, C Italy *42.04N 12.45E*
107 S13 **Palos, Cabo de** *headland* SE Spain *37.38N 0.42W*
106 I14 **Palos de la Frontera** Andalucía, S Spain *37.13N 6.52W*
62 G11 **Palotina** Paraná, S Brazil *24.16S 53.49W*
34 M9 **Palouse** Washington, NW USA *46.54N 117.04W*
34 L9 **Palouse River** ≈ Washington, NW USA
37 Y16 **Palo Verde** California, W USA *33.25N 114.43W*
59 E16 **Palpa** Ica, W Peru *14.33S 75.09W*
97 M16 **Pålsboda** Örebro, C Sweden *59.04N 15.21E*
95 M15 **Paltamo** Oulu, C Finland *64.25N 27.49E*
175 Pp9 **Palu** ***prev.*** Paloe. Sulawesi, C Indonesia *0.54S 119.52E*
143 P14 **Palu** Elazığ, E Turkey *38.43N 39.55E*
175 Q16 **Palu, Pulau** *island* S Indonesia
175 P8 **Palu, Teluk** *bay* Sulawesi, C Indonesia
158 I11 **Palwal** Haryāna, N India *28.15N 77.18E*
127 Oo4 **Palyavaam** ≈ NE Russian Federation
79 Q13 **Pama** SE Burkina *11.13N 0.46E*
180 J14 **Pamandzi** ✕ (Mamoudzou) Petite-Terre, E Mayotte
Pamangkat *see* Pemangkat
149 R11 **Pā Mazār** Kermān, C Iran
85 N19 **Pambarra** Inhambane, SE Mozambique *21.57S 35.06E*
176 Xx10 **Pamdai** Papua, E Indonesia *1.58S 137.19E*
176 X10 **Pami** Papua, E Indonesia *2.45S 136.02E*
105 N16 **Pamiers** Ariège, S France *43.07N 1.36E*
153 T14 **Pamir** ***var.*** Daryā-ye Pāmīr, ***Taj.*** Dar"yoi Pomir. ≈ Afghanistan/Tajikistan ***see also*** Pāmīr, Daryā-ye
Pamir/Pāmīr, Daryā-ye *see* Pamirs
155 U1 **Pāmīr, Daryā-ye** ***var.*** Pamir, ***Taj.*** Dar"yoi Pomir. ≈ Afghanistan/Tajikistan ***see also*** Pamir
Pāmīr-e Khord *see* Little Pamir
133 Q8 **Pamirs** ***Pash.*** Daryā-ye Pāmīr, ***Rus.*** Pamir. ⛰ C Asia
Pâmiut *see* Paamiut
23 X10 **Pamlico River** ≈ North Carolina, SE USA
23 Y10 **Pamlico Sound** *sound* North Carolina, SE USA
27 O2 **Pampa** Texas, SW USA *35.31N 100.58W*
Pampa Aullagas, Lago *see* Poopó, Lago
63 B21 **Pampa Húmeda** *grassland* E Argentina
58 A10 **Pampa las Salinas** *salt lake* NW Peru
59 F15 **Pampas** Huancavelica, C Peru *12.22S 74.52W*
64 K13 **Pampas** *plain* C Argentina
57 O4 **Pampatar** Nueva Esparta, NE Venezuela *10.58N 63.49W*
Pampeluna *see* Pamplona
106 H8 **Pampilhosa da Serra** ***var.*** Pampilhosa de Serra. Coimbra, N Portugal *40.03N 7.58W*
181 Y15 **Pamplemousses** N Mauritius *20.06S 57.34E*
56 G7 **Pamplona** Norte de Santander, N Colombia *7.24N 72.37W*
107 Q3 **Pamplona** ***Basq.*** Iruña; ***prev.*** Pampeluna, ***anc.*** Pompaelo. Navarra, N Spain *42.49N 1.39W*
116 I11 **Pamporovo** ***prev.*** Vasil Kolarov. Smolyan, S Bulgaria *41.39N 24.45E*
142 D15 **Pamukkale** Denizli, W Turkey *37.51N 29.13E*
23 W5 **Pamunkey River** ≈ Virginia, NE USA
158 K5 **Pamzal** Jammu and Kashmir, NW India *34.16N 78.49E*
32 L14 **Pana** Illinois, N USA *39.23N 89.04W*
43 Y11 **Panabá** Yucatán, SE Mexico *21.18N 88.15W*
37 Y8 **Panaca** Nevada, W USA *37.47N 114.24W*
117 E19 **Panachaikó** ⛰ S Greece
12 F11 **Panache Lake** ◎ Ontario, S Canada
116 I10 **Panagyurishte** Pazardzhik, C Bulgaria *42.30N 24.10E*
174 I14 **Panaitan, Pulau** *island* S Indonesia
174 Ii14 **Panaitan, Selat** *strait* Jawa, SW Indonesia
117 D18 **Panaitolikó** ⛰ C Greece
161 E17 **Panaji** ***var.*** Pangim, Panjim, New Goa. Goa, W India *15.31N 73.52E*
45 T14 **Panama** ***off.*** Republic of Panama. ◆ *republic* Central America
45 T15 **Panamá** ***var.*** Ciudad de Panamá, ***Eng.*** Panama City. ● (Panama) Panamá, C Panama *8.57N 79.33W*
45 U14 **Panamá** ***off.*** Provincia de Panamá. ◐ *province* E Panama
45 U15 **Panamá, Bahía de** *bay* N Gulf of Panama
200 Oo8 **Panama Basin** *undersea feature* E Pacific Ocean
45 T15 **Panama Canal** *canal* E Panama
25 R9 **Panama City** Florida, SE USA *30.09N 85.39W*
45 T14 **Panama City** ✕ Panamá, C Panama *9.02N 79.24W*
Panama City *see* Panamá
25 Q9 **Panama City Beach** Florida, SE USA *30.10N 85.48W*
45 T17 **Panamá, Golfo de** ***var.*** Gulf of Panama. *gulf* S Panama
Panama, Gulf of *see* Panamá, Golfo de
Panama, Isthmus of *see* Panamá, Istmo de
45 T15 **Panamá, Istmo de** ***Eng.*** Isthmus of Panama; ***prev.*** Isthmus of Darien. *isthmus* E Panama
37 U11 **Panamint Range** ⛰ California, W USA
109 L22 **Panarea, Isola** *island* Isole Eolie, S Italy
108 G9 **Panaro** ≈ N Italy
179 Q14 **Panay Gulf** *gulf* C Philippines
179 Pp13 **Panay Island** *island* C Philippines
37 W7 **Pancake Range** ⛰ Nevada, W USA
114 M11 **Pančevo** ***Ger.*** Pantschowa, ***Hung.*** Pancsova. Serbia, N Serbia and Montenegro (Yugoslavia) *44.52N 20.39E*
115 M15 **Pančićev Vrh** ▲ SW Serbia and Montenegro (Yugoslavia) *43.16N 20.49E*
118 L12 **Panciu** Vrancea, E Romania *45.54N 27.07E*
118 F10 **Pâncota** ***Hung.*** Pankota; ***prev.*** Pîncota. Arad, W Romania *46.19N 21.45E*
Pancsova *see* Pančevo
85 N20 **Panda** Inhambane, SE Mozambique *24.04S 34.44E*
176 X9 **Pandaidori, Kepulauan** *island group* E Indonesia
27 N11 **Pandale** Texas, SW USA *30.09N 101.34W*
174 H7 **Pandang, Pulau** *island* W Indonesia
174 Kk9 **Pandang Tikar, Pulau** *island* N Indonesia
63 F20 **Pan de Azúcar** Maldonado, S Uruguay *34.45S 55.13W*
120 H11 **Pandėlys** Panevėžys, NE Lithuania *56.04N 25.18E*
161 F15 **Pandharpur** Mahārāshtra, W India *17.42N 75.24E*
190 J1 **Pandie Pandie** South Australia *26.06S 139.26E*
175 Pp9 **Pandiri** Sulawesi, C Indonesia *1.32S 120.47E*
63 F20 **Pando** Canelones, S Uruguay *34.43S 55.58W*
59 J14 **Pando** ◐ *department* N Bolivia
199 Ii10 **Pandora Bank** *undersea feature* W Pacific Ocean
97 G20 **Pandrup** Nordjylland, N Denmark *57.13N 9.42E*
159 V12 **Pandu** Assam, NE India *26.08N 91.37E*
81 J15 **Pandu** Equateur, NW Dem. Rep. Congo *5.03N 19.14E*
Paneas *see* Bāniyās
61 F15 **Panelas** Mato Grosso, W Brazil *9.06S 60.41W*
120 G12 **Panevėžys** Panevėžys, C Lithuania *55.44N 24.21E*
120 G11 **Panevėžys** ◐ *province* NE Lithuania
Panfilov *see* Zharkent
131 N9 **Panfilovo** Volgogradskaya Oblast', SW Russian Federation *50.25N 42.55E*
81 N17 **Panga** Orientale, N Dem. Rep. Congo *1.52N 26.18E*
200 Ss13 **Pangai** Lifuka, C Tonga *19.49S 174.22W*
116 H13 **Pangaío** ⛰ N Greece
81 G20 **Pangala** Le Pool, S Congo *3.26S 14.38E*
83 J22 **Pangani** Tanga, E Tanzania *5.27S 39.00E*
83 I21 **Pangani** ≈ NE Tanzania
195 U13 **Panggoe** Choiseul Island, NW Solomon Islands *7.00S 95.05E*
81 N20 **Pangi** Maniema, E Dem. Rep. Congo *3.12S 26.39E*
194 H12 **Pangia** Southern Highlands, W PNG *6.18S 144.12E*
Pangim *see* Panaji
173 F4 **Pangkalanbrandan** Sumatera, W Indonesia *4.00N 98.15E*
Pangkalanbun *see* Pangkalanbuun
174 Ll10 **Pangkalanbuun** ***var.*** Pangkalanbun. Borneo, C Indonesia *2.43S 111.37E*
174 J10 **Pangkalpinang** Pulau Bangka, W Indonesia *2.04S 106.09E*
9 U17 **Pangman** Saskatchewan, S Canada *49.37N 104.33W*
Pang-Nga *see* Phang-Nga
16 Nn2 **Pangnirtung** Baffin Island, Nunavut, NE Canada *66.04N 65.45W*
158 K6 **Pangong Tso** ***var.*** Bangong Co. ◎ China/India ***see also*** Bangong Co
38 K7 **Panguitch** Utah, W USA *37.49N 112.26W*
195 S12 **Panguna** Bougainville Island, NE PNG *6.22S 155.19E*
179 Pp17 **Pangutaran Group** *island group* Sulu Archipelago, SW Philippines
27 N2 **Panhandle** Texas, SW USA *35.18N 101.23W*
Panhormus *see* Palermo
176 X12 **Paniai, Danau** ◎ Papua, E Indonesia
81 L21 **Pania-Mutombo** Kasai Oriental, C Dem. Rep. Congo *5.09S 23.49E*
Panicherevo *see* Dolno Panicherevo
197 H5 **Panié, Mont** ▲ C New Caledonia *20.33S 164.41E*
158 I10 **Pānīpat** Haryāna, N India *29.18N 77.00E*
153 Q14 **Panj** ***Rus.*** Pyandzh; ***prev.*** Kirovabad. SW Tajikistan *37.39N 69.55E*
153 P15 **Panj** ***Rus.*** Pyandzh. ≈ Afghanistan/Tajikistan
155 O5 **Panjāb** Bāmīān, C Afghanistan *34.21N 67.00E*
153 O12 **Panjakent** ***Rus.*** Pendzhikent. W Tajikistan *39.28N 67.33E*
154 L14 **Panjgūr** Baluchistān, SW Pakistan *26.58N 64.05E*
Panjim *see* Panaji
169 U12 **Panjin** Liaoning, NE China *41.11N 122.05E*
153 P14 **Panji Poyon** ***Rus.*** Nizhniy Pyandzh. SW Tajikistan *37.14N 68.32E*
155 Q4 **Panjshīr** ≈ E Afghanistan
Pankota *see* Pâncota
79 W14 **Pankshin** Plateau, C Nigeria *9.21N 9.27E*
169 Y10 **Pan Ling** ⛰ N China
Panlong Jiang *see* Lô, Sông
160 J9 **Panna** Madhya Pradesh, C India *24.43N 80.10E*
101 M16 **Panningen** Limburg, SE Netherlands *51.19N 5.58E*
155 R13 **Pāno Āqil** Sind, SE Pakistan *27.56N 69.16E*
124 Nn3 **Páno Léfkara** S Cyprus *34.52N 33.18E*
124 N3 **Páno Panagiá** ***var.*** Pano Panayia. W Cyprus *34.55N 32.38E*
Pano Panayia *see* Páno Panagiá
Panopolis *see* Akhmīm
31 U14 **Panora** Iowa, C USA *41.41N 94.21W*
62 I8 **Panorama** São Paulo, S Brazil *21.22S 51.51W*
117 I24 **Pánormos** Kríti, Greece, E Mediterranean Sea *35.24N 24.42E*
Panormus *see* Palermo
169 W11 **Panshi** Jilin, NE China *42.50N 126.06E*
61 H19 **Pantanal** ***var.*** Pantanalmato-Grossense. *swamp* SW Brazil
Pantanalmato-Grossense *see* Pantanal
63 H16 **Pântano Grande** Rio Grande do Sul, S Brazil *30.12S 52.24W*
175 R16 **Pantar, Pulau** *island* Kepulauan Alor, S Indonesia
23 X9 **Pantego** North Carolina, SE USA *35.34N 76.39E*
109 G25 **Pantelleria** ***anc.*** Cossyra, Cosyra. Sicilia, Italy, C Mediterranean Sea *36.47N 12.00E*
109 G25 **Pantelleria, Isola di** *island* SW Italy
Pante Macassar/Pante Makassar *see* Pante Makasar
175 Rr17 **Pante Makasar** ***var.*** Pante Macassar, Pante Makassar. W East Timor *9.10S 124.27E*
158 K10 **Pantnagar** Uttaranchal, N India *29.00N 79.28E*
117 A15 **Pantokrátoras** ▲ Kérkyra, Iónioi Nísoi, Greece, C Mediterranean Sea *39.45N 19.51E*
Pantschowa *see* Pančevo
179 Rr16 **Pantukan** Mindanao, S Philippines *7.10N 125.55E*
43 P11 **Pánuco** Veracruz-Llave, E Mexico *22.01N 98.10W*
43 P11 **Pánuco, Río** ≈ C Mexico
166 I12 **Panxian** Guizhou, S China *25.45N 104.28E*
173 G7 **Panyabungan** Sumatera, N Indonesia *0.55N 99.30E*
79 W14 **Panyam** Plateau, C Nigeria *9.28N 9.13E*
163 N13 **Panzhihua** ***prev.*** Dukou, Tu-k'ou. Sichuan, C China *26.35N 101.41E*
81 I22 **Panzi** Bandundu, SW Dem. Rep. Congo *7.10S 17.55E*
44 E5 **Panzós** Alta Verapaz, E Guatemala *15.21N 89.40W*
Pao-chi/Paoki *see* Baoji
Pao-king *see* Shaoyang
109 N20 **Paola** Calabria, SW Italy *39.21N 16.03E*
123 Jj17 **Paola** E Malta *35.52N 14.30E*
29 R5 **Paola** Kansas, C USA *38.34N 94.52W*
33 O15 **Paoli** Indiana, N USA *38.31N 86.26W*
197 D14 **Paonangisu** Éfaté, C Vanuatu *17.33S 168.23E*
175 Tt11 **Paoni** ***var.*** Pauni. Pulau Seram, E Indonesia *2.48S 129.03E*
39 Q5 **Paonia** Colorado, C USA *38.52N 107.35W*
203 O7 **Paopao** Moorea, W French Polynesia *17.28S 149.48W*
Pao-shan *see* Baoshan
Pao-ting *see* Baoding
Pao-t'ou/Paotow *see* Baotou
81 H14 **Paoua** Ouham-Pendé, W Central African Republic *7.22N 16.25E*
Pap *see* Pop
113 H23 **Pápa** Veszprém, W Hungary *47.19N 17.27E*
44 J12 **Papagayo, Golfo de** *gulf* NW Costa Rica
40 H11 **Pāpa'ikou** ***var.*** Papaikou. Hawai'i, USA, C Pacific Ocean *19.45N 155.06W*
43 R15 **Papaloapan, Río** ≈ S Mexico
192 L6 **Papakura** Auckland, North Island, NZ *37.03S 174.57E*
43 Q13 **Papantla** ***var.*** Papantla de Olarte. Veracruz-Llave, E Mexico *20.27N 97.21W*
Papantla de Olarte *see* Papantla
203 P8 **Papara** Tahiti, W French Polynesia *17.45S 149.33W*
192 K4 **Paparoa** Northland, North Island, NZ *36.06S 174.12E*
193 G16 **Paparoa Range** ⛰ South Island, NZ
117 K20 **Pápas, Akrotírio** *headland* Ikaría, Dodekánisos, Greece, Aegean Sea *37.31N 25.58E*
98 L2 **Papa Stour** *island* NE Scotland, UK
192 L6 **Papatoetoe** Auckland, North Island, NZ *36.58S 174.52E*
193 E25 **Papatowai** Otago, South Island, NZ *46.33S 169.33E*
98 K4 **Papa Westray** *island* NE Scotland, UK
203 T10 **Papeete** ○ (French Polynesia) Tahiti, W French Polynesia *17.31S 149.34W*
102 F11 **Papenburg** Niedersachsen, NW Germany *53.04N 7.24E*
100 H13 **Papendrecht** Zuid-Holland, SW Netherlands *51.49N 4.42E*
203 Q7 **Papenoo** Tahiti, W French Polynesia *17.28S 149.25W*
203 Q7 **Papenoo Rivière** ≈ Tahiti, W French Polynesia
203 N7 **Papetoai** Moorea, W French Polynesia *17.28S 149.52W*
94 L3 **Papey** *island* E Iceland
Paphos *see* Páfos
42 H5 **Papigochic, Río** ≈ NW Mexico
120 E10 **Papilė** Šiauliai, NW Lithuania *56.08N 22.51E*
31 S15 **Papillion** Nebraska, C USA *41.09N 96.02W*
13 T5 **Papinachois** ≈ Québec, SE Canada
176 Y13 **Papua** ***var.*** Irian Barat, West Irian, West New Guinea, West Papua ; ***prev.*** Dutch New Guinea, Irian Jaya, Netherlands New Guinea. ◐ *province* E Indonesia
194 I15 **Papua, Gulf of** *gulf* S PNG
194 H13 **Papua New Guinea** ***off.*** Independent State of Papua New Guinea; ***prev.*** Territory of Papua and New Guinea, ***abbrev.*** PNG. ◆ *commonwealth republic* NW Melanesia
199 H10 **Papua Plateau** *undersea feature* N Coral Sea
114 G9 **Papuk** ⛰ NE Croatia
177 G8 **Papun** Karen State, S Myanmar *18.04N 97.25E*
44 L14 **Paquera** Puntarenas, W Costa Rica *9.52N 84.55W*
57 V9 **Para** ◐ *district* N Suriname
60 I13 **Pará** ***off.*** Estado do Pará. ◐ *state* NE Brazil
Pará *see* Belém
126 H12 **Parabel'** Tomskaya Oblast', C Russian Federation *58.54N 80.45E*
188 I8 **Paraburdoo** Western Australia *23.07S 117.40E*
59 E16 **Paracas, Península de** *peninsula* W Peru
61 L19 **Paracatu** Minas Gerais, NE Brazil *17.13S 46.52W*
198 F7 **Paracel Islands** ◇ *disputed territory* SE Asia
190 I6 **Parachilna** South Australia *31.09S 138.23E*
155 R6 **Pārachinār** North-West Frontier Province, NW Pakistan *33.55N 70.04E*
114 N13 **Paraćin** Serbia, C Serbia and Montenegro (Yugoslavia) *43.51N 21.25E*
12 K8 **Paradis** Québec, SE Canada *48.13N 76.36W*
41 N11 **Paradise** ***var.*** Paradise Hill. Alaska, USA *62.28N 96.09W*
37 O5 **Paradise** California, W USA *39.42N 121.39W*
37 X11 **Paradise** Nevada, W USA *36.05N 115.10W*
Paradise Hill *see* Paradise
39 R11 **Paradise Hills** New Mexico, SW USA *35.12N 106.42W*
Paradise of the Pacific *see* Hawaii
38 L13 **Paradise Valley** Arizona, SW USA *33.31N 111.56W*
37 T2 **Paradise Valley** Nevada, W USA *41.30N 117.30W*
117 O22 **Paradisi** ✕ (Ródos) Ródos, Dodekánisos, Greece, Aegean Sea *36.24N 28.08E*
176 X10 **Paradoi** Papua, E Indonesia *2.10S 136.25E*
160 P12 **Pārādwīp** Orissa, E India *20.18N 86.39E*
Paraetonium *see* Matrūḥ
119 R4 **Parafiyivka** Chernihivs'ka Oblast', N Ukraine *50.53N 32.40E*
38 K7 **Paragonah** Utah, W USA *37.53N 112.46W*
29 X9 **Paragould** Arkansas, C USA *36.03N 90.30W*
49 X8 **Paraguaçu** ***var.*** Paraguassú. ≈ E Brazil
62 J9 **Paraguaçu Paulista** São Paulo, S Brazil *22.22S 50.35W*
56 H4 **Paraguaipoa** Zulia, NW Venezuela *11.21N 71.58W*
64 O6 **Paraguarí** Paraguarí, S Paraguay *25.38S 57.09W*
64 O7 **Paraguarí** ***off.*** Departamento de Paraguarí. ◐ *department* S Paraguay
57 O8 **Paragua, Río** ≈ SE Venezuela
59 O16 **Paraguá, Río** ≈ NE Bolivia
Paraguassú *see* Paraguaçu
64 N5 **Paraguay** ◆ *republic* C South America
49 U10 **Paraguay** ***var.*** Río Paraguay. ≈ C South America
Parahiba/Parahyba *see* Paraíba
61 P15 **Paraíba** ***off.*** Estado da Paraíba; ***prev.*** Parahiba, Parahyba. ◐ *state* E Brazil
Paraíba *see* João Pessoa
62 P9 **Paraíba do Sul, Rio** ≈ SE Brazil
Parainen *see* Pargas
45 N14 **Paraíso** Cartago, C Costa Rica *9.50N 83.51W*
43 U14 **Paraíso** Tabasco, SE Mexico *18.23N 93.03W*
59 O17 **Paraiso, Río** ≈ E Bolivia
Parajd *see* Praid
79 S14 **Parakou** C Benin *9.22N 2.40E*
124 O3 **Paralimni** E Cyprus *35.01N 34.01E*
117 G18 **Paralímni, Límni** ◎ C Greece
194 G15 **Parama Island** *island* SW PNG
57 W8 **Paramaribo** ● (Suriname) Paramaribo, N Suriname *5.52N 55.13W*
57 W9 **Paramaribo** ◐ *dist.* N Suriname
57 W9 **Paramaribo** ✕ Paramaribo, N Suriname *5.52N 55.13W*
Paramithiá *see* Paramythiá
58 C13 **Paramonga** Lima, W Peru *10.40S 77.51W*
127 Pp13 **Paramushir, Ostrov** *island* SE Russian Federation
117 C16 **Paramythiá** ***var.*** Paramithiá. Ípeiros, W Greece *39.28N 20.31E*
64 M10 **Paraná** Entre Ríos, E Argentina *31.48S 60.29W*
62 H11 **Paraná** ***off.*** Estado do Paraná. ◐ *state* S Brazil
49 U11 **Paraná** ***var.*** Alto Paraná. ≈ C South America
62 K12 **Paranaguá** Paraná, S Brazil *25.31S 48.36W*
61 J20 **Paranaíba, Rio** ≈ E Brazil
63 C19 **Paraná Ibicuy, Río** ≈ E Argentina
61 H15 **Paranaíta** Mato Grosso, W Brazil *9.35S 57.01W*
62 H9 **Paranapanema, Rio** ≈ S Brazil
62 K11 **Paranapiacaba, Serra do** ⛰ S Brazil
62 H9 **Paranavaí** Paraná, S Brazil *23.03S 52.25W*
149 N5 **Parandak** Markazī, W Iran *35.19N 50.40E*
116 I12 **Paranéstio** Anatolikí Makedonía kai Thráki, NE Greece *41.16N 24.31E*
203 W11 **Paraoa** *atoll* Îles Tuamotu, C French Polynesia
192 L13 **Paraparaumu** Wellington, North Island, NZ *40.55S 175.01E*
59 N20 **Parapetí, Río** ≈ SE Bolivia
56 L10 **Paraque, Cerro** ▲ W Venezuela *6.00S 67.00W*
160 I11 **Parasiya** Madhya Pradesh, C India *22.11N 78.47E*
117 M23 **Paraspóri, Akrotírio** *headland* Kárpathos, SE Greece *35.54N 27.15E*
62 O10 **Parati** Rio de Janeiro, SE Brazil *23.15S 44.42W*
61 K14 **Parauapebas** Pará, N Brazil *6.03S 49.48W*
105 Q10 **Paray-le-Monial** Saône-et-Loire, C France *46.27N 4.07E*
Parbatsar *see* Parvatsar
160 G13 **Parbhani** Mahārāshtra, C India *19.16N 76.51E*
102 L10 **Parchim** Mecklenburg-Vorpommern, N Germany *53.25N 11.51E*
Parchwitz *see* Prochowice
112 P13 **Parczew** Lubelskie, E Poland *51.39N 22.59E*
62 L8 **Pardo, Rio** ≈ S Brazil
113 E16 **Pardubice** ***Ger.*** Pardubitz. Pardubický Kraj, C Czech Republic *50.01N 15.46E*
113 E17 **Pardubický Kraj** ◐ *region* C Czech Republic
Pardubitz *see* Pardubice
121 F16 **Parechcha** ***Pol.*** Porzecze, ***Rus.*** Porech'ye. Hrodzyenskaya Voblasts', W Belarus *53.51N 24.07E*
61 F17 **Parecis, Chapada dos** ***var.*** Serra dos Parecis. ⛰ W Brazil
Parecis, Serra dos *see* Parecis, Chapada dos
106 M4 **Paredes de Nava** Castilla-León, N Spain *42.09N 4.42W*
201 U12 **Parem** *island* Chuuk, C Micronesia
201 O12 **Parem Island** *island* E Micronesia
192 I1 **Parengarenga Harbour** *inlet* North Island, NZ
13 N8 **Parent** Québec, SE Canada *47.55N 74.36W*
104 J14 **Parentis-en-Born** Landes, SW France *44.22N 1.04W*
Parenzo *see* Poreč
193 G20 **Pareora** Canterbury, South Island, NZ *44.28S 171.12E*
175 P12 **Parepare** Sulawesi, C Indonesia *4.00S 119.40E*
117 B16 **Párga** Ípeiros, W Greece *39.18N 20.19E*
95 K20 **Pargas** ***Swe.*** Parainen. Länsi-Suomi, W Finland *60.18N 22.19E*
66 O5 **Pargo, Ponta do** *headland* Madeira, Portugal, NE Atlantic Ocean *32.48N 17.16W*
Paria, Golfo de *see* Paria, Gulf of
57 N6 **Pariaguán** Anzoátegui, NE Venezuela *8.51N 64.43W*
47 X17 **Paria, Gulf of** ***var.*** Golfo de Paria. *gulf* Trinidad and Tobago/Venezuela
59 I15 **Pariamanu, Río** ≈ E Peru
38 L8 **Paria River** ≈ Utah, W USA
Parichi *see* Parychy
42 M14 **Paricutín, Volcán** ⚲ C Mexico *19.25N 102.20W*
45 P16 **Parida, Isla** *island* SW Panama
57 T8 **Parika** NE Guyana *6.51N 58.25W*
95 O18 **Parikkala** Etelä-Suomi, S Finland *61.33N 29.33E*
60 E10 **Parima, Serra** ***var.*** Sierra Parima. ⛰ Brazil/Venezuela ***see also*** Parima, Sierra
57 N11 **Parima, Sierra** ***var.*** Serra Parima. ⛰ Brazil/Venezuela ***see also*** Parima, Serra
59 F17 **Parinacochas, Laguna** ◎ SW Peru
58 A9 **Pariñas, Punta** *headland* NW Peru *4.45S 81.22W*

◆ Country
● Country Capital
◇ Dependent Territory
○ Dependent Territory Capital
◐ Administrative Region
✕ International Airport
▲ Mountain
⛰ Mountain Range
⚲ Volcano
≈ River
◎ Lake
⊠ Reservoir

PARINTINS – PEMBINA

60 *H12* **Parintins** Amazonas, N Brazil *2.37S 56.45W*
105 *O5* **Paris** *anc.* Lutetia, Lutetia Parisiorum, Parisii. ● (France) Paris, N France *48.52N 2.19E*
203 *Y2* **Paris** Kiritimati, E Kiribati *1.55N 95.30W*
29 *S11* **Paris** Arkansas, C USA *35.17N 93.43W*
35 *S16* **Paris** Idaho, NW USA *42.14N 111.24W*
33 *N14* **Paris** Illinois, N USA *39.36N 87.42W*
22 *M5* **Paris** Kentucky, S USA *38.12N 84.15W*
29 *V3* **Paris** Missouri, C USA *39.28N 92.00W*
22 *H8* **Paris** Tennessee, S USA *36.18N 88.19W*
27 *V5* **Paris** Texas, SW USA *33.40N 95.33W*
Parisii *see* Paris
45 *S16* **Parita** Herrera, S Panama *7.59N 80.31W*
45 *S16* **Parita, Bahía de** *bay* S Panama
Parkan/Párkány *see* Štúrovo
95 *K18* **Parkano** Länsi-Suomi, W Finland *62.03N 23.00E*
29 *N6* **Park City** Kansas, C USA *37.48N 97.19W*
38 *L3* **Park City** Utah, W USA *40.39N 111.30W*
38 *I12* **Parker** Arizona, SW USA *34.07N 114.16W*
25 *R9* **Parker** Florida, SE USA *30.07N 85.36W*
31 *R11* **Parker** South Dakota, N USA *43.24N 97.08W*
37 *Z14* **Parker Dam** California, W USA *34.17N 114.08W*
31 *W13* **Parkersburg** Iowa, C USA *42.34N 92.47W*
23 *Q3* **Parkersburg** West Virginia, NE USA *39.15N 81.33W*
31 *T7* **Parkers Prairie** Minnesota, N USA *46.09N 95.19W*
179 *R17* **Parker Volcano** ⩓ Mindanao, S Philippines *6.09N 124.52E*
189 *W13* **Parkes** New South Wales, SE Australia *33.09S 148.10E*
32 *K4* **Park Falls** Wisconsin, N USA *45.57N 90.25W*
Parkhar *see* Farkhor
12 *E16* **Parkhill** Ontario, S Canada *43.11N 81.39W*
31 *T5* **Park Rapids** Minnesota, N USA *46.55N 95.03W*
31 *Q3* **Park River** North Dakota, N USA *48.24N 97.44W*
31 *Q11* **Parkston** South Dakota, N USA *43.24N 97.58W*
8 *L17* **Parksville** Vancouver Island, British Columbia, SW Canada *49.13N 124.13W*
39 *S3* **Parkview Mountain** ▲ Colorado, C USA *40.19N 106.08W*
107 *N8* **Parla** Madrid, C Spain *40.13N 3.48W*
31 *S8* **Parle, Lac qui** ⊠ Minnesota, N USA
117 *F20* **Parlía Tyroú** Pelopónnisos, S Greece *37.17N 22.50E*
161 *G14* **Parli Vaijnāth** Mahārāshtra, C India *18.52N 76.36E*
108 *F9* **Parma** Emilia-Romagna, N Italy *44.49N 10.19E*
33 *T11* **Parma** Ohio, N USA *41.24N 81.43W*
Parnahyba *see* Parnaíba
60 *N13* **Parnaíba** *var.* Parnahyba. Piauí, E Brazil *2.58S 41.46W*
67 *J14* **Parnaíba Ridge** *undersea feature* C Atlantic Ocean
60 *N13* **Parnaíba, Rio** ≈ NE Brazil
117 *F18* **Parnassós** ▲▲ C Greece
193 *J17* **Parnassus** Canterbury, South Island, NZ *42.41S 173.18E*
190 *H10* **Parndana** South Australia *35.48S 137.13E*
117 *H19* **Párnitha** ▲▲ C Greece
117 *F21* **Párnon** ▲▲ S Greece
120 *G5* **Pärnu** *Ger.* Pernau, *Latv.* Pērnava; *prev. Rus.* Pernov. Pärnumaa, SW Estonia *58.23N 24.31E*
120 *G6* **Pärnu** *var.* Parnu Jõgi, *Ger.* Pernau. ≈ SW Estonia
120 *G5* **Pärnu-Jaagupi** *Ger.* Sankt-Jakobi. Pärnumaa, SW Estonia *58.36N 24.30E*
Parnu Jõgi *see* Pärnu
120 *G5* **Pärnu Laht** *Ger.* Pernauer Bucht. *bay* SW Estonia
120 *F5* **Pärnumaa** *off.* Pärnu Maakond. ◈ *province* SW Estonia
159 *T11* **Paro** W Bhutan *27.22N 89.31E*
159 *T11* **Paro** ✕ (Thimphu) W Bhutan *27.22N 89.31E*
193 *G17* **Paroa** West Coast, South Island, NZ *42.31S 171.10E*
169 *X14* **P'aro-ho** *var.* Hwach'ŏn-chŏsuji. ⊠ N South Korea
191 *N6* **Paroo River** *seasonal river* New South Wales/Queensland, SE Australia
Paropamisus Range *see* Sefīdkūh, Selseleh-ye
117 *J21* **Páros** Páros, Kykládes, Greece, Aegean Sea *37.04N 25.09E*
117 *J21* **Páros** *island* Kykládes, Greece, Aegean Sea
38 *K7* **Parowan** Utah, W USA *37.50N 112.49W*
105 *U13* **Parpaillon** ▲▲ SE France
110 *I9* **Parpan** Graubünden, S Switzerland *46.46N 9.32E*
64 *G13* **Parral** Maule, C Chile *36.07S 71.47W*
Parral *see* Hidalgo del Parral
191 *T9* **Parramatta** New South Wales, SE Australia *33.49S 150.58E*
23 *Y6* **Parramore Island** *island* Virginia, NE USA
42 *M8* **Parras** *var.* Parras de la Fuente. Coahuila de Zaragoza, NE Mexico *25.26N 102.07W*
Parras de la Fuente *see* Parras
44 *M14* **Parrita** Puntarenas, S Costa Rica *9.33N 84.20W*
12 *G13* **Parry Island** *island* Ontario, S Canada
207 *O9* **Parry Islands** *island group* Nunavut, NW Canada
12 *G12* **Parry Sound** Ontario, S Canada *45.21N 80.03W*
112 *F7* **Parsęta** *Ger.* Persante. ≈ NW Poland
30 *L3* **Parshall** North Dakota, N USA *47.57N 102.07W*
29 *Q7* **Parsons** Kansas, C USA *37.20N 95.15W*
22 *H9* **Parsons** Tennessee, S USA *35.39N 88.07W*
23 *T3* **Parsons** West Virginia, NE USA *39.06N 79.40W*
Parsonstown *see* Birr
102 *P11* **Parsteiner See** ◎ NE Germany
109 *I24* **Partanna** Sicilia, Italy, C Mediterranean Sea *37.43N 12.54E*
110 *J8* **Partenen** Graubünden, E Switzerland *46.58N 10.01E*
104 *K9* **Parthenay** Deux-Sèvres, W France *46.39N 0.13W*
97 *J19* **Partille** Västra Götaland, S Sweden *57.43N 12.12E*
109 *I23* **Partinico** Sicilia, Italy, C Mediterranean Sea *38.03N 13.07E*
113 *I20* **Partizánske** *prev.* Šimonovany; *Hung.* Simony. Trenčiansky Kraj, W Slovakia *48.39N 18.22E*
60 *H11* **Paru de Oeste, Rio** ≈ N Brazil
190 *K9* **Paruna** South Australia *34.45S 140.43E*
60 *I11* **Paru, Rio** ≈ N Brazil
Parvān *see* Parwān
161 *M14* **Pārvatipuram** Andhra Pradesh, E India *17.01N 81.47E*
158 *G12* **Parvatsar** *prev.* Parbatsar. Rājasthān, N India *26.52N 74.49E*
155 *Q5* **Parwān** *Per.* Parvān. ◈ *province* E Afghanistan
164 *I15* **Paryang** Xizang Zizhiqu, W China *30.04N 83.28E*
121 *M18* **Parychy** *Rus.* Parichi. Homyel'skaya Voblasts', SE Belarus *52.48N 29.25E*
85 *J21* **Parys** Free State, C South Africa *26.51S 27.28E*
37 *T15* **Pasadena** California, W USA *34.09N 118.08W*
27 *W11* **Pasadena** Texas, SW USA *29.41N 95.12W*
58 *B8* **Pasaje** El Oro, SW Ecuador *3.17S 79.45W*
143 *T9* **P'asanauri** N Georgia *42.21N 44.40E*
173 *G10* **Pasapuat** Pulau Pagai Utara, W Indonesia *2.36S 99.58E*
178 *Gg7* **Pasawng** Kayah State, C Myanmar *18.50N 97.16E*
116 *L13* **Paşayiğit** Edirne, NW Turkey *40.58N 26.38E*
25 *N9* **Pascagoula** Mississippi, S USA *30.21N 88.31W*
24 *M8* **Pascagoula River** ≈ Mississippi, S USA
118 *F12* **Paşcani** *Hung.* Páskán. Iaşi, NE Romania *47.13N 26.46E*
111 *T4* **Pasching** Oberösterreich, N Austria *48.16N 14.10E*
34 *K10* **Pasco** Washington, NW USA *46.13N 119.06W*
58 *E13* **Pasco** *off.* Departamento de Pasco. ◈ *department* C Peru
203 *N11* **Pascua, Isla de** *var.* Rapa Nui, *Eng.* Easter Island. *island* E Pacific Ocean
65 *G21* **Pascua, Río** ≈ S Chile
105 *N1* **Pas-de-Calais** ◈ *department* N France
102 *P10* **Pasewalk** Mecklenburg-Vorpommern, NE Germany *53.30N 13.58E*
9 *T10* **Pasfield Lake** ◎ Saskatchewan, C Canada
Pa-shih Hai-hsia *see* Bashi Channel
Pashkeni *see* Bolyarovo
Pashmakli *see* Smolyan
179 *P10* **Pasig** Luzon, N Philippines *14.34N 121.04E*
159 *X10* **Pāsighāt** Arunāchal Pradesh, NE India *28.08N 95.13E*
143 *Q12* **Pasinler** Erzurum, NE Turkey *39.58N 41.40E*
Pasi Oloy, Qatorkŭhi *see* Zaalayskiy Khrebet
44 *E3* **Pasión, Río de la** ≈ N Guatemala
174 *Gg10* **Pasirganting** Sumatera, W Indonesia *2.04S 100.51E*
Pasirpangarayan *see* Bagansiapiapi
174 *H2* **Pasir Puteh** *var.* Pasir Putih. Kelantan, Peninsular Malaysia *5.49N 102.24E*
174 *L6* **Pasir, Tanjung** *headland* East Malaysia *2.24N 111.12E*
97 *N20* **Påskallavik** Kalmar, S Sweden *57.10N 16.25E*
Páskán *see* Paşcani
Paskevicha, Zaliv *see* Tushchybas, Zaliv
112 *K7* **Pasłęk** *Ger.* Preußisch Holland. Warmińsko-Mazurskie, NE Poland *54.03N 19.39E*
112 *K7* **Pasłęka** *Ger.* Passarge. ≈ N Poland
154 *K16* **Pasni** Baluchistān, SW Pakistan *25.13N 63.30E*
65 *I18* **Paso de Indios** Chubut, S Argentina *43.52S 69.06W*
56 *L7* **Paso del Caballo** Guárico, N Venezuela *8.19N 67.07W*
63 *E15* **Paso de los Libres** Corrientes, NE Argentina *29.39S 57.04W*
63 *E18* **Paso de los Toros** Tacuarembó, C Uruguay *32.45S 56.30W*
37 *P12* **Paso Robles** California, W USA *35.37N 120.42W*
13 *Y7* **Paspébiac** Québec, SE Canada *48.03N 65.10W*
9 *U14* **Pasquia Hills** ▲▲ Saskatchewan, S Canada
155 *W7* **Pasrūr** Punjab, E Pakistan *32.12N 74.42E*
32 *M1* **Passage Island** *island* Michigan, N USA
67 *B24* **Passage Islands** *island group* W Falkland Islands
15 *I1* **Passage Point** *headland* Banks Island, Northwest Territories, NW Canada *73.31N 115.12W*
Passarge *see* Pasłęka
117 *C15* **Passarón** *ancient monument* Ípeiros, W Greece *39.41N 20.43E*
Passarowitz *see* Požarevac
103 *O22* **Passau** Bayern, SE Germany *48.34N 13.28E*
24 *M9* **Pass Christian** Mississippi, S USA *30.19N 89.15W*
109 *L26* **Passero, Capo** *headland* Sicilia, Italy, C Mediterranean Sea *36.40N 15.09E*
179 *Q13* **Passi** Panay Island, C Philippines *11.05N 122.37E*
63 *H14* **Passo Fundo** Rio Grande do Sul, S Brazil *28.16S 52.19W*
62 *H13* **Passo Fundo, Barragem de** ⊠ S Brazil
63 *H15* **Passo Real, Barragem de** ⊠ S Brazil
61 *L20* **Passos** Minas Gerais, NE Brazil *20.45S 46.37W*
178 *M11* **Passu Keah** *island* S Paracel Islands
120 *J13* **Pastavy** *Pol.* Postawy, *Rus.* Postavy. Vitsyebskaya Voblasts', NW Belarus *55.07N 26.50E*
58 *D7* **Pastaza** ◈ *province* E Ecuador
58 *D9* **Pastaza, Río** ≈ Ecuador/Peru
63 *A21* **Pasteur** Buenos Aires, E Argentina *35.10S 62.13W*
13 *V3* **Pasteur** ≈ Québec, SE Canada
153 *Q12* **Pastigav** *Rus.* Pastigov. W Tajikistan *39.27N 69.16E*
Pastigov *see* Pastigav
56 *C13* **Pasto** Nariño, SW Colombia *1.12N 77.16W*
40 *M10* **Pastol Bay** *bay* Alaska, USA
39 *O8* **Pastora Peak** ▲ Arizona, SW USA *36.48N 109.10W*
107 *O8* **Pastrana** Castilla-La Mancha, C Spain *40.24N 2.55W*
174 *M15* **Pasuruan** *prev.* Pasoeroean. Jawa, C Indonesia *7.37S 112.43E*
120 *F11* **Pasvalys** Panevėžys, N Lithuania *56.03N 24.24E*
113 *K21* **Pásztó** Nógrád, N Hungary *47.57N 19.41E*
201 *U12* **Pata** *var.* Patta. *atoll* Chuuk Islands, C Micronesia
38 *M16* **Patagonia** Arizona, SW USA *31.32N 110.45W*
65 *H20* **Patagonia** *physical region* Argentina/Chile
Patalung *see* Phatthalung
160 *D9* **Pātan** Gujarāt, W India *23.51N 72.10E*
160 *J10* **Pātan** Madhya Pradesh, C India *23.19N 79.41E*
175 *Tt8* **Patani** Pulau Halmahera, E Indonesia *0.19N 128.46E*
Patani *see* Pattani
13 *V7* **Patapédia Est** ≈ Québec, SE Canada
118 *K13* **Pătârlagele** *prev.* Pătîriagele. Buzău, SE Romania *45.19N 26.21E*
Patavium *see* Padova
190 *I5* **Patawarta Hill** ▲ South Australia *30.57S 138.42E*
190 *L10* **Patchewollock** Victoria, SE Australia *35.24S 142.11E*
192 *K11* **Patea** Taranaki, North Island, NZ *39.48S 174.35E*
192 *K11* **Patea** ≈ North Island, NZ
79 *U15* **Pategi** Kwara, C Nigeria *8.39N 5.46E*
83 *K20* **Pate Island** *var.* Patta Island. *island* SE Kenya
107 *S10* **Paterna** País Valenciano, E Spain *39.30N 0.24W*
111 *R9* **Paternion** *Slvn.* Špatrjan. Kärnten, S Austria *46.40N 13.43E*
109 *L24* **Paternò** *anc.* Hybla, Hybla Major. Sicilia, Italy, C Mediterranean Sea *37.34N 14.55E*
34 *J7* **Pateros** Washington, NW USA *48.01N 119.55W*
20 *J14* **Paterson** New Jersey, NE USA *40.54N 74.11W*
34 *J10* **Paterson** Washington, NW USA *45.56N 119.37W*
193 *C25* **Paterson Inlet** *inlet* Stewart Island, NZ
100 *N6* **Paterswolde** Drenthe, NE Netherlands *53.07N 6.32E*
158 *H7* **Pathānkot** Himāchal Pradesh, N India *32.16N 75.43E*
Pathein *see* Bassein
35 *W15* **Pathfinder Reservoir** ⊠ Wyoming, C USA
178 *Hh11* **Pathum Thani** *var.* Patumdhani, Prathum Thani. Pathum Thani, C Thailand *14.03N 100.28E*
174 *L14* **Pati** Jawa, C Indonesia *6.45S 111.00E*
56 *C12* **Patía** *var.* El Bordo. Cauca, SW Colombia *2.06N 77.02W*
158 *I9* **Patiāla** *var.* Puttiala. Punjab, NW India *30.21N 76.27E*
56 *B12* **Patía, Río** ≈ SW Colombia
175 *T8* **Patinti, Selat** *strait* Maluku, E Indonesia
196 *D15* **Pati Point** *headland* NE Guam *13.36N 144.39E*
Pătîriagele *see* Pătârlagele
58 *C13* **Pativilca** Lima, W Peru *10.40S 77.52W*
178 *Gg1* **Pātkai Bum** *var.* Patkai Range. ▲▲ Myanmar/India
Patkai Range *see* Pātkai Bum
117 *L20* **Pátmos** Pátmos, Dodekánisos, Greece, Aegean Sea *37.18N 26.32E*
117 *L20* **Pátmos** *island* Dodekánisos, Greece, Aegean Sea
159 *P13* **Patna** *var.* Azimabad. Bihār, N India *25.36N 85.11E*
160 *M12* **Patnāgarh** Orissa, E India *20.42N 83.12E*
179 *Pp13* **Patnongon** Panay Island, C Philippines *10.56N 122.03E*
143 *S13* **Patnos** Ağrı, E Turkey *39.13N 42.52E*
62 *H12* **Pato Branco** Paraná, S Brazil *26.15S 52.40W*
33 *O16* **Patoka Lake** ◎ Indiana, N USA
94 *L9* **Patoniva** *Lapp.* Buoddobohki. Lappi, N Finland *69.44N 27.01E*
115 *K21* **Patos** *var.* Patosi. Fier, SW Albania *40.40N 19.37E*
Patos *see* Patos de Minas
61 *K19* **Patos de Minas** *var.* Patos. Minas Gerais, NE Brazil *18.34S 46.31W*
Patosi *see* Patos
63 *I17* **Patos, Lagoa dos** *lagoon* S Brazil
64 *J9* **Patquía** La Rioja, C Argentina *30.01S 66.54W*
117 *E19* **Pátra** *Eng.* Patras; *prev.* Pátrai. Dytikí Ellás, S Greece *38.13N 21.45E*
Pátrai/Patras *see* Pátra
117 *D18* **Patraïkós Kólpos** *gulf* S Greece
94 *G2* **Patreksfjördhur** Vestfirdhir, W Iceland *65.33N 23.54W*
26 *M7* **Patricia** Texas, SW USA *32.34N 102.00W*
65 *F21* **Patricio Lynch, Isla** *island* S Chile
Patta *see* Pata
Patta Island *see* Pate Island
178 *Hh17* **Pattani** *var.* Patani. Pattani, SW Thailand *6.50N 101.18E*
178 *Hh12* **Pattaya** Chon Buri, S Thailand *12.55N 100.55E*
21 *S4* **Patten** Maine, NE USA *45.58N 68.27W*
37 *O9* **Patterson** California, W USA *37.27N 121.07W*
24 *J10* **Patterson** Louisiana, S USA *29.41N 91.18W*
37 *R7* **Patterson, Mount** ▲ California, W USA *38.27N 119.16W*
33 *P4* **Patterson, Point** *headland* Michigan, N USA *45.58N 85.39W*
109 *L23* **Patti** Sicilia, Italy, C Mediterranean Sea *38.07N 14.59E*
109 *L23* **Patti, Golfo di** *gulf* Sicilia, Italy, C Mediterranean Sea
95 *L14* **Pattijoki** Oulu, W Finland *64.41N 24.40E*
199 *Mm5* **Patton Escarpment** *undersea feature* E Pacific Ocean
29 *S2* **Pattonsburg** Missouri, C USA *40.03N 94.08W*
(0) *D6* **Patton Seamount** *undersea feature* NE Pacific Ocean *54.40N 150.30W*
8 *J12* **Pattullo, Mount** ▲ British Columbia, W Canada *56.18N 129.43W*
Patuakhali *see* Patukhali
44 *M5* **Patuca, Río** ≈ E Honduras
159 *U16* **Patukhali** *var.* Patuakhali. Khulna, S Bangladesh *22.19N 90.19E*
Patumdhani *see* Pathum Thani
42 *M14* **Pátzcuaro** Michoacán de Ocampo, SW Mexico *19.30N 101.36W*
44 *C6* **Patzicía** Chimaltenango, S Guatemala *14.37N 90.54W*
104 *K16* **Pau** Pyrénées-Atlantiques, SW France *43.18N 0.22W*
104 *J12* **Pauillac** Gironde, SW France *45.12N 0.44W*
177 *Ff5* **Pauk** Magwe, W Myanmar *21.25N 94.30E*
15 *H3* **Paulatuk** Northwest Territories, NW Canada *69.23N 124.00W*
44 *K5* **Paulayá, Río** ≈ NE Honduras
24 *M6* **Paulding** Mississippi, S USA *32.01N 89.01W*
33 *Q12* **Paulding** Ohio, N USA *41.08N 84.34W*
31 *S12* **Paullina** Iowa, C USA *42.58N 95.41W*
61 *P15* **Paulo Afonso** Bahia, E Brazil *9.21S 38.13W*
40 *M16* **Pauloff Harbor** *var.* Pavlor Harbour. Sanak Island, Alaska, USA *54.26N 162.43W*
29 *N12* **Pauls Valley** Oklahoma, C USA *34.44N 97.13W*
177 *Ff7* **Paungde** Pegu, C Myanmar *18.30N 95.30E*
Pauni *see* Paoni
158 *K9* **Pauri** Uttaranchal, N India *30.07N 78.48E*
Pautalia *see* Kyustendil
176 *Z11* **Pauwasi** ≈ Papua, E Indonesia
148 *J5* **Pāveh** Kermānshāh, NW Iran *35.01N 46.15E*
130 *L5* **Pavelets** Ryazanskaya Oblast', W Russian Federation *53.47N 39.22E*
108 *D8* **Pavia** *anc.* Ticinum. Lombardia, N Italy *45.10N 9.10E*
120 *C9* **Pāvilosta** Liepāja, W Latvia *56.52N 21.12E*
129 *P14* **Pavino** Kostromskaya Oblast', NW Russian Federation *59.10N 46.09E*
116 *J8* **Pavlikeni** Veliko Tŭrnovo, N Bulgaria *43.15N 25.20E*
151 *T8* **Pavlodar** Pavlodar, NE Kazakhstan *52.21N 76.58E*
151 *S9* **Pavlodar** *off.* Pavlodarskaya Oblast', *Kaz.* Pavlodar Oblysy. ◈ *province* NE Kazakhstan
Pavlodar Oblysy/Pavlodarskaya Oblast' *see* Pavlodar
Pavlograd *see* Pavlohrad
119 *U7* **Pavlohrad** *Rus.* Pavlograd. Dnipropetrovs'ka Oblast', E Ukraine *48.32N 35.50E*
Pavlor Harbour *see* Pauloff Harbor
151 *R9* **Pavlovka** Akmola, C Kazakhstan *51.22N 72.35E*
131 *V4* **Pavlovka** Respublika Bashkortostan, W Russian Federation *55.28N 56.36E*
131 *Q7* **Pavlovka** Ul'yanovskaya Oblast', W Russian Federation *52.40N 47.08E*
131 *N3* **Pavlovo** Nizhegorodskaya Oblast', W Russian Federation *55.59N 43.03E*
130 *L9* **Pavlovsk** Voronezhskaya Oblast', W Russian Federation *50.26N 40.08E*
130 *L13* **Pavlovskaya** Krasnodarskiy Kray, SW Russian Federation *46.06N 39.52E*
119 *S7* **Pavlysh** Kirovohrads'ka Oblast', C Ukraine *48.54N 33.20E*
108 *F10* **Pavullo nel Frignano** Emilia-Romagna, C Italy *44.19N 10.52E*
29 *P8* **Pawhuska** Oklahoma, C USA *36.40N 96.20W*
23 *U13* **Pawleys Island** South Carolina, SE USA *33.27N 79.07W*
178 *Gg6* **Pawn** ≈ C Myanmar
32 *K14* **Pawnee** Illinois, N USA *39.35N 89.34W*
29 *O9* **Pawnee** Oklahoma, C USA *36.18N 96.47W*
39 *U2* **Pawnee Buttes** ▲ Colorado, C USA *40.49N 103.58W*
31 *S17* **Pawnee City** Nebraska, C USA *40.06N 96.09W*
28 *K5* **Pawnee River** ≈ Kansas, C USA
33 *O10* **Paw Paw** Michigan, N USA *42.12N 86.09W*
33 *O10* **Paw Paw Lake** Michigan, N USA *42.12N 86.16W*
21 *O12* **Pawtucket** Rhode Island, NE USA *41.52N 71.22W*
Pax Augusta *see* Badajoz
117 *I25* **Paximádia** *island* SE Greece
Pax Julia *see* Beja
117 *B16* **Paxoí** *island* Iónioi Nísoi, Greece, C Mediterranean Sea
41 *S10* **Paxson** Alaska, USA *62.58N 145.27W*
153 *O11* **Paxtakor** Jizzax Viloyati, C Uzbekistan *40.21N 67.54E*
32 *M13* **Paxton** Illinois, N USA *40.27N 88.06W*
128 *J11* **Pay** Respublika Kareliya, NW Russian Federation *61.10N 34.24E*
177 *G8* **Payagyi** Pegu, SW Myanmar *17.28N 96.31E*
110 *C9* **Payerne** *Ger.* Peterlingen. Vaud, W Switzerland *46.49N 6.57E*
34 *M13* **Payette** Idaho, NW USA *44.04N 116.55W*
34 *M13* **Payette River** ≈ Idaho, NW USA
129 *V2* **Pay-Khoy, Khrebet** ▲▲ NW Russian Federation
Payne *see* Kangirsuk
10 *K4* **Payne, Lac** ◎ Québec, NE Canada
31 *T8* **Paynesville** Minnesota, N USA *45.22N 94.42W*
174 *M4* **Payong, Tanjung** *headland* East Malaysia *3.46N 113.27E*
Payo Obispo *see* Chetumal
63 *D18* **Paysandú** Paysandú, W Uruguay *32.21S 58.04W*
63 *D17* **Paysandú** ◈ *department* W Uruguay
104 *I7* **Pays de la Loire** ◈ *region* NW France
38 *L12* **Payson** Arizona, SW USA *34.13N 111.19W*
38 *L4* **Payson** Utah, W USA *40.02N 111.43W*
129 *W4* **Payyer, Gora** ▲ NW Russian Federation *66.49N 64.33E*
Payzawat *see* Jiashi
143 *Q11* **Pazar** Rize, NE Turkey *41.10N 40.52E*
142 *F10* **Pazarbaşı Burnu** *headland* NW Turkey *41.12N 30.18E*
142 *M16* **Pazarcık** Kahramanmaraş, S Turkey *37.31N 37.19E*
116 *I10* **Pazardzhik** *prev.* Tatar Pazardzhik. Pazardzhik, C Bulgaria *42.11N 24.21E*
66 *H11* **Pazardzhik** ◈ *province* C Bulgaria *42.11N 24.21E*
56 *H9* **Paz de Ariporo** Casanare, E Colombia *5.51N 71.52W*
114 *A10* **Pazin** *Ger.* Mitterburg, *It.* Pisino. Istra, NW Croatia *45.14N 13.56E*
44 *D7* **Paz, Río** ≈ El Salvador/Guatemala
115 *O18* **Pčinja** ≈ N FYR Macedonia
200 *Qq15* **Pea** Tongatapu, S Tonga *21.10S 175.14W*
29 *O6* **Peabody** Kansas, C USA *38.10N 97.06W*
9 *O12* **Peace** ≈ Alberta/British Columbia, W Canada
Peace Garden State *see* North Dakota
9 *Q10* **Peace Point** Alberta, C Canada *59.11N 112.12W*
9 *O12* **Peace River** Alberta, W Canada *56.15N 117.18W*
25 *W13* **Peace River** ≈ Florida, SE USA
9 *N17* **Peachland** British Columbia, SW Canada *49.49N 119.48W*
38 *J10* **Peach Springs** Arizona, SW USA *35.33N 113.27W*
Peach State *see* Georgia
25 *S4* **Peachtree City** Georgia, SE USA *33.24N 84.36W*
201 *Y13* **Peacock Point** *point* SE Wake Island *19.16N 166.39E*
99 *M18* **Peak District** *physical region* C England, UK
191 *Q7* **Peak Hill** New South Wales, SE Australia *32.39S 148.12E*
67 *G15* **Peak, The** ▲ C Ascension Island
107 *O13* **Peal de Becerro** Andalucía, S Spain *37.55N 3.07W*
201 *X11* **Peale Island** *island* N Wake Island
39 *O6* **Peale, Mount** ▲ Utah, W USA *38.26N 109.13W*
41 *O4* **Peard Bay** *bay* Alaska, USA
25 *Q7* **Pea River** ≈ Alabama/Florida, S USA
27 *W11* **Pearland** Texas, SW USA *29.33N 95.17W*
40 *D9* **Pearl City** O'ahu, Hawai'i, USA, C Pacific Ocean *21.24N 95.58W*
40 *D9* **Pearl Harbor** *inlet* O'ahu, Hawai'i, USA, C Pacific Ocean
Pearl Islands *see* Perlas, Archipiélago de las
Pearl Lagoon *see* Perlas, Laguna de
24 *M5* **Pearl River** ≈ Louisiana/Mississippi, S USA
27 *Q13* **Pearsall** Texas, SW USA *28.53N 99.05W*
25 *U7* **Pearson** Georgia, SE USA *31.18N 82.51W*
27 *P4* **Pease River** ≈ Texas, SW USA
10 *F7* **Peawanuk** Ontario, C Canada *54.55N 85.31W*
85 *P16* **Pebane** Zambézia, NE Mozambique *17.13S 38.10E*
67 *C23* **Pebble Island** *island* N Falkland Islands
67 *C23* **Pebble Island Settlement** Pebble Island, N Falkland Islands *51.19S 59.40W*
115 *L16* **Peć** *Alb.* Pejë, *Turk.* Ipek. Serbia, S Serbia and Montenegro (Yugoslavia) *42.40N 20.19E*
27 *R8* **Pecan Bayou** ≈ Texas, SW USA
24 *H10* **Pecan Island** Louisiana, S USA *29.39N 92.26W*
62 *L12* **Peças, Ilha das** *island* S Brazil
32 *L10* **Pecatonica River** ≈ Illinois/Wisconsin, N USA
110 *G10* **Peccia** Ticino, S Switzerland *46.24N 8.39E*
Pechenegi *see* Pechenihy
Pechenezhskoye Vodokhranilishche *see* Pecheniz'ke Vodoskhovyshche
128 *I2* **Pechenga** *Fin.* Petsamo. Murmanskaya Oblast', NW Russian Federation *69.34N 31.14E*
119 *V5* **Pechenihy** *Rus.* Pechenegi. Kharkivs'ka Oblast', E Ukraine *49.49N 36.57E*
119 *V5* **Pecheniz'ke Vodoskhovyshche** *Rus.* Pechenezhskoye Vodokhranilishche. ⊠ E Ukraine
129 *U7* **Pechora** Respublika Komi, NW Russian Federation *65.08N 57.09E*
129 *R6* **Pechora** ≈ NW Russian Federation
Pechora Bay *see* Pechorskaya Guba
Pechora Sea *see* Pechorskoye More
129 *S3* **Pechorskaya Guba** *Eng.* Pechora Bay. *bay* NW Russian Federation
125 *Ff6* **Pechorskoye More** *Eng.* Pechora Sea. *sea* NW Russian Federation
118 *E11* **Pecica** *Ger.* Petschka, *Hung.* Ópécska. Arad, W Romania *46.09N 21.06E*
26 *K8* **Pecos** Texas, SW USA *31.25N 103.30W*
27 *N11* **Pecos River** ≈ New Mexico/Texas, SW USA
113 *I25* **Pécs** *Ger.* Fünfkirchen; *Lat.* Sopianae. Baranya, SW Hungary *46.04N 18.11E*
45 *T17* **Pedasí** Los Santos, S Panama *7.30N 80.02W*
Pedde *see* Pedja
191 *O17* **Pedder, Lake** ◎ Tasmania, SE Australia
46 *M10* **Pedernales** SW Dominican Republic *17.59N 71.42W*
57 *Q5* **Pedernales** Delta Amacuro, NE Venezuela *9.58N 62.15W*
27 *R10* **Pedernales River** ≈ Texas, SW USA
64 *H6* **Pedernales, Salar de** *salt lake* N Chile
Pedhoulas *see* Pedoulás
57 *X11* **Pédima** *var.* Malavate. SW French Guiana *3.15N 54.07W*
190 *F1* **Pedirka** South Australia *26.41S 135.11E*
175 *T7* **Pediwang** Pulau Halmahera, E Indonesia *1.29N 127.57E*
120 *I5* **Pedja** *var.* Pedja Jõgi, *Ger.* Pedde. ≈ E Estonia
Pedja Jõgi *see* Pedja
124 *N3* **Pedoulás** *var.* Pedhoulas. W Cyprus *34.58N 32.51E*
61 *N18* **Pedra Azul** Minas Gerais, NE Brazil *16.01S 41.16W*
106 *I3* **Pedrafita, Porto de** *var.* Puerto de Piedrafita. *pass* NW Spain *42.43N 7.01W*
78 *E9* **Pedra Lume** Sal, NE Cape Verde *16.46N 22.54W*
45 *P16* **Pedregal** Chiriquí, W Panama *8.21N 82.26W*
56 *J4* **Pedregal** Falcón, N Venezuela *11.01N 70.06W*
42 *L9* **Pedriceña** Durango, C Mexico *25.08N 103.46W*
62 *L11* **Pedro Barros** São Paulo, S Brazil *24.12S 47.22W*
41 *Q13* **Pedro Bay** Alaska, USA *59.47N 154.06W*
64 *H4* **Pedro de Valdivia** *var.* Oficina Pedro de Valdivia. Antofagasta, N Chile *22.33S 69.37W*
64 *P4* **Pedro Juan Caballero** Amambay, E Paraguay *22.33S 55.40W*
65 *L15* **Pedro Luro** Buenos Aires, E Argentina *39.26S 62.40W*
107 *O10* **Pedro Muñoz** Castilla-La Mancha, C Spain *39.25N 2.55W*
161 *J22* **Pedro, Point** *headland* NW Sri Lanka *9.54N 80.08E*
190 *K9* **Peebinga** South Australia *34.56S 140.56E*
98 *J13* **Peebles** SE Scotland, UK *55.39N 3.14W*
33 *S15* **Peebles** Ohio, N USA *38.57N 83.23W*
98 *J12* **Peebles** *cultural region* SE Scotland, UK
20 *K13* **Peekskill** New York, NE USA *41.17N 73.54W*
99 *I16* **Peel** W Isle of Man *54.13N 4.04W*
14 *Ff4* **Peel** ≈ Northwest Territories/Yukon Territory, NW Canada
15 *I1* **Peel Point** *headland* Victoria Island, Northwest Territories, NW Canada *73.22N 114.33W*
15 *K1* **Peel Sound** *passage* Nunavut, N Canada
102 *N9* **Peene** ≈ NE Germany
101 *K17* **Peer** Limburg, NE Belgium *51.08N 5.28E*
12 *H14* **Pefferlaw** Ontario, S Canada *44.18N 79.11W*
193 *I18* **Pegasus Bay** *bay* South Island, NZ
123 *Mm3* **Pégeia** *var.* Peyia. SW Cyprus *34.52N 32.24E*
111 *V7* **Peggau** Steiermark, SE Austria *47.10N 15.20E*
103 *L19* **Pegnitz** Bayern, SE Germany *49.45N 11.33E*
103 *L19* **Pegnitz** ≈ SE Germany
107 *T11* **Pego** País Valenciano, E Spain *38.51N 0.07W*
177 *G8* **Pegu** *var.* Bago. Pegu, SW Myanmar *17.18N 96.31E*
177 *G7* **Pegu** ◈ *division* S Myanmar
176 *W7* **Pegun, Pulau** *island* Kepulauan Mapia, E Indonesia
201 *N13* **Pehleng** Pohnpei, E Micronesia
116 *M12* **Pehlivanköy** Kırklareli, NW Turkey *41.21N 26.56E*
79 *R14* **Péhonko** C Benin *10.14N 1.57E*
63 *B21* **Pehuajó** Buenos Aires, E Argentina *35.48S 61.52W*
Pei-ching *see* Beijing/Beijing Shi
102 *J13* **Peine** Niedersachsen, C Germany *52.19N 10.13E*
Pei-p'ing *see* Beijing/Beijing Shi
Peipsi Järv/Peipus-See *see* Peipus, Lake
120 *J5* **Peipus, Lake** *Est.* Peipsi Järv, *Ger.* Peipus-See, *Rus.* Chudskoye Ozero. ◎ Estonia/Russian Federation
117 *H19* **Peiraías** *prev.* Piraiévs, *Eng.* Piraeus. Attikí, C Greece *37.56N 23.39E*
Peisern *see* Pyzdry
62 *I8* **Peixe, Rio do** ≈ S Brazil
61 *I16* **Peixoto de Azevedo** Mato Grosso, W Brazil *10.18S 55.03W*
174 *J8* **Pejantan, Pulau** *island* W Indonesia
Pejë *see* Peć
114 *N11* **Pek** ≈ E Serbia and Montenegro (Yugoslavia)
178 *Ii7* **Pèk** *var.* Xieng Khouang; *prev.* Xiangkhoang. Xiangkhoang, N Laos *19.19N 103.23E*
174 *Kk14* **Pekalongan** Jawa, C Indonesia *6.54S 109.37E*
174 *Gg7* **Pekanbaru** *var.* Pakanbaru. Sumatera, W Indonesia *0.31N 101.27E*
32 *L12* **Pekin** Illinois, N USA *40.34N 89.38W*
Peking *see* Beijing/Beijing Shi
Pelabohan Kelang/Pelabuhan Kelang *see* Pelabuhan Klang
173 *G5* **Pelabuhan Klang** *var.* Kuala Pelabohan Kelang, Pelabohan Kelang, Pelabuhan Kelang, Port Klang, Port Swettenham. Selangor, Peninsular Malaysia *2.57N 101.24E*
174 *J15* **Pelabuhan Ratu, Teluk** *bay* Jawa, SW Indonesia
123 *L12* **Pelagie, Isole** *island group* SW Italy
Pelagosa *see* Palagruža
24 *L5* **Pelahatchie** Mississippi, S USA *32.19N 89.48W*
175 *N11* **Pelaihari** *var.* Pleihari. Borneo, C Indonesia *3.48S 114.45E*
105 *U14* **Pelat, Mont** ▲ SE France *44.16N 6.46E*
118 *F12* **Peleaga, Vârful** *prev.* Vîrful Peleaga. ▲ W Romania *45.23N 22.52E*
Peleaga, Vîrful *see* Peleaga, Vârful
126 *K12* **Peleduy** Respublika Sakha (Yakutiya), NE Russian Federation *59.39N 112.36E*
12 *C18* **Pelee Island** *island* Ontario, S Canada
47 *Q11* **Pelée, Montagne** ⩓ N Martinique *14.47N 61.10W*
12 *D18* **Pelee, Point** *headland* Ontario, S Canada *41.56N 82.30W*
175 *R9* **Pelei** Pulau Peleng, N Indonesia *1.26S 123.27E*
Peleliu *see* Beliliou
175 *R9* **Peleng, Pulau** *island* Kepulauan Banggai, N Indonesia
175 *Qq9* **Peleng, Selat** *strait* Sulawesi, C Indonesia
25 *T7* **Pelham** Georgia, SE USA *31.07N 84.09W*
113 *E18* **Pelhřimov** *Ger.* Pilgram. Vysočina, C Czech Republic *49.25N 15.13E*
41 *W13* **Pelican** Chichagof Island, Alaska, USA *57.52N 136.05W*
203 *Z3* **Pelican Lagoon** ◎ Kiritimati, E Kiribati
31 *U6* **Pelican Lake** ◎ Minnesota, N USA
31 *V3* **Pelican Lake** ◎ Minnesota, N USA
32 *L5* **Pelican Lake** ◎ Wisconsin, N USA
46 *G1* **Pelican Point** Grand Bahama Island, N Bahamas *26.39N 78.09W*
85 *B19* **Pelican Point** *headland* W Namibia *22.55S 14.25E*
31 *S6* **Pelican Rapids** Minnesota, N USA *46.34N 96.04W*
Pelican State *see* Louisiana
9 *U13* **Pelikan Narrows** Saskatchewan, C Canada *55.11N 102.51W*
117 *L18* **Pelinaío** ▲ Chíos, E Greece *38.31N 26.01E*
Pelinnaeum *see* Pelinnaío
117 *E16* **Pelinnaío** *anc.* Pelinnaeum. *ruins* Thessalía, C Greece *39.33N 21.45E*
115 *N20* **Pelister** ▲ SW FYR Macedonia *41.00N 21.12E*
115 *G15* **Pelješac** *peninsula* S Croatia
94 *M12* **Pelkosenniemi** Lappi, NE Finland *67.06N 27.30E*
31 *W15* **Pella** Iowa, C USA *41.24N 92.55W*
116 *F13* **Pélla** *site of ancient city* Kentrikí Makedonía, N Greece *40.46N 22.35E*
25 *Q3* **Pell City** Alabama, S USA *33.35N 86.17W*
63 *A22* **Pellegrini** Buenos Aires, E Argentina *36.16S 63.07W*
94 *K12* **Pello** Lappi, NW Finland *66.47N 24.00E*
102 *G7* **Pellworm** *island* N Germany
8 *H6* **Pelly** ≈ Yukon Territory, NW Canada
15 *L3* **Pelly Bay** Nunavut, N Canada *68.37N 89.45W*
8 *I8* **Pelly Mountains** ▲▲ Yukon Territory, W Canada
Pélmonostor *see* Beli Manastir
39 *P13* **Pelona Mountain** ▲ New Mexico, SW USA *33.40N 108.06W*
Peloponnese/Peloponnesus *see* Pelopónnisos
117 *E20* **Pelopónnisos** *Eng.* Peloponnese. ◈ *region* S Greece
117 *E20* **Pelopónnisos** *var.* Morea, *Eng.* Peloponnese; *anc.* Peloponnesus. *peninsula* S Greece
109 *L23* **Peloritani, Monti** *anc.* Pelorus and Neptunius. ▲▲ Sicilia, Italy, C Mediterranean Sea
109 *M22* **Peloro, Capo** *var.* Punta del Faro. *headland* S Italy *38.15N 15.39E*
Pelorus and Neptunius *see* Peloritani, Monti
63 *H17* **Pelotas** Rio Grande do Sul, S Brazil *31.45S 52.19W*
63 *I14* **Pelotas, Rio** ≈ S Brazil
94 *K10* **Peltovuoma** *Lapp.* Bealdovuopmi. Lappi, N Finland *68.23N 24.11E*
125 *F10* **Pelym** ≈ C Russian Federation
21 *R4* **Pemadumcook Lake** ◎ Maine, NE USA
174 *Kk14* **Pemalang** Jawa, C Indonesia *6.52S 109.07E*
174 *K7* **Pemangkat** *var.* Pamangkat. Borneo, C Indonesia *1.11N 109.00E*
Pemar *see* Paimio
173 *Ff5* **Pematangsiantar** Sumatera, W Indonesia *2.58N 99.01E*
85 *Q14* **Pemba** *prev.* Port Amelia, Porto Amélia. Cabo Delgado, NE Mozambique *13.00S 40.30E*
83 *J22* **Pemba** ◈ *region* E Tanzania
83 *K21* **Pemba** *island* E Tanzania
85 *Q14* **Pemba, Baia de** *inlet* NE Mozambique
83 *J21* **Pemba Channel** *channel* E Tanzania
188 *J14* **Pemberton** Western Australia *34.27S 116.09E*
8 *M16* **Pemberton** British Columbia, SW Canada *50.19N 122.49W*
31 *Q2* **Pembina** North Dakota, N USA *48.58N 97.14W*
31 *Q2* **Pembina** ≈ Canada/USA
9 *P15* **Pembina** ≈ Alberta, SW Canada

◆ Country
● Country Capital
◇ Dependent Territory
○ Dependent Territory Capital
◈ Administrative Region
✕ International Airport
▲ Mountain
▲▲ Mountain Range
⩓ Volcano
≈ River
◎ Lake
⊠ Reservoir

PEMBRE – PHUMĬ YEAY SÊN

176 *Xx15* **Pembre** Papua, E Indonesia *7.49S 138.01E*
12 *K12* **Pembroke** Ontario, SE Canada *45.49N 77.07W*
99 *H21* **Pembroke** SW Wales, UK *51.40N 4.55W*
25 *W6* **Pembroke** Georgia, SE USA *32.09N 81.35W*
23 *U11* **Pembroke** North Carolina, SE USA *34.40N 79.12W*
23 *R7* **Pembroke** Virginia, NE USA *37.19N 80.38W*
99 *H21* **Pembroke** *cultural region* SW Wales, UK
Pembuang, Sungai *see* Seruyan, Sungai
45 *S15* **Peña Blanca, Cerro** ▲ C Panama *8.39N 80.39W*
106 *K8* **Peña de Francia, Sierra de la** ▲ W Spain
106 *G6* **Penafiel** *var.* Peñafiel. Porto, N Portugal *41.12N 8.16W*
107 *N6* **Peñafiel** Castilla-León, N Spain *41.36N 4.07W*
107 *S8* **Peñagolosa** ▲ E Spain *40.10N 0.15W*
107 *N7* **Peñalara, Pico de** ▲ C Spain *40.52N 3.55W*
175 *Nn5* **Penambo, Banjaran** *var.* Banjaran Tama Abu, Penambo Range. ▲ Indonesia/Malaysia
Penambo Range *see* Penambo, Banjaran
43 *O10* **Peña Nevada, Cerro** ▲ C Mexico *23.46N 99.52W*
Penang *see* Pinang, Pulau, Peninsular Malaysia
Penang *see* Pinang
Penang *see* George Town
62 *J8* **Penápolis** São Paulo, S Brazil *21.23S 50.02W*
106 *L7* **Peñaranda de Bracamonte** Castilla-León, N Spain *40.54N 5.13W*
107 *S8* **Peñarroya** ▲ E Spain *40.24N 0.42W*
106 *L12* **Peñarroya-Pueblonuevo** Andalucía, S Spain *38.21N 5.18W*
99 *K22* **Penarth** S Wales, UK *51.27N 3.10W*
106 *K1* **Peñas, Cabo de** *headland* N Spain *43.39N 5.52W*
65 *F20* **Penas, Golfo de** *gulf* S Chile
Pen-ch'i *see* Benxi
81 *H14* **Pendé** *var.* Logone Oriental. ≈ Central African Republic/Chad
78 *I14* **Pendembu** E Sierra Leone *9.06N 12.12W*
31 *R13* **Pender** Nebraska, C USA *42.06N 96.42W*
Penderma *see* Bandırma
34 *K11* **Pendleton** Oregon, NW USA *45.40N 118.47W*
34 *M7* **Pend Oreille, Lake** ◎ Idaho, NW USA
34 *M7* **Pend Oreille River** ≈ Idaho/Washington, NW USA
Pendzhikent *see* Panjakent
Peneius *see* Pineiós
106 *G8* **Penela** Coimbra, N Portugal *40.01N 8.22W*
12 *G13* **Penetanguishene** Ontario, S Canada *44.45N 79.55W*
157 *H15* **Penganga** ≈ C India
167 *T12* **P'engchia Yu** *island* N Taiwan
81 *M21* **Penge** Kasai Oriental, C Dem. Rep. Congo *5.29S 24.38E*
Penghu Archipelago/P'enghu Ch'üntao/Penghu Islands *see* P'enghu Liehtao
167 *R14* **P'enghu Liehtao** *var.* P'enghu Ch'üntao, Penghu Islands, *Eng.* Penghu Archipelago, Pescadores, *Jap.* Hoko-guntō, Hoko-shotō. *island group* W Taiwan
Penghu Shuidao/P'enghu Shuitao *see* Pescadores Channel
167 *R4* **Penglai** *var.* Dengzhou. Shandong, E China *37.48N 120.43E*
Peng-pu *see* Bengbu
Penhsihu *see* Benxi
Penibético, Sistema *see* Béticos, Sistemas
106 *F10* **Peniche** Leiria, W Portugal *39.21N 9.22W*
175 *Nn16* **Penida, Nusa** *island* S Indonesia
Peninsular State *see* Florida
107 *T8* **Peñíscola** País Valenciano, E Spain *40.22N 0.24E*
42 *M13* **Pénjamo** Guanajuato, C Mexico *20.20N 101.35W*
Penki *see* Benxi
104 *F7* **Penmarch, Pointe de** *headland* NW France *47.46N 4.34W*
109 *L15* **Penna, Punta della** *headland* C Italy *42.10N 14.43E*
109 *K14* **Penne** Abruzzo, C Italy *42.28N 13.57E*
Penner *see* Penneru
161 *J18* **Penneru** *var.* Penner. ≈ C India
190 *I10* **Penneshaw** South Australia *35.45S 137.57E*
20 *C14* **Penn Hills** Pennsylvania, NE USA *40.28N 79.52W*
Penninae, Alpes/Pennine, Alpi *see* Pennine Alps
110 *D11* **Pennine Alps** *Fr.* Alpes Pennines, *It.* Alpi Pennine; *Lat.* Alpes Penninae. ▲ Italy/Switzerland
Pennine Chain *see* Pennines
99 *L15* **Pennines** *var.* Pennine Chain. ▲ N England, UK
Pennines, Alpes *see* Pennine Alps
23 *O8* **Pennington Gap** Virginia, NE USA *36.45N 83.01W*
20 *I16* **Penns Grove** New Jersey, NE USA *39.42N 75.27W*
20 *I16* **Pennsville** New Jersey, NE USA *39.37N 75.29W*
20 *E14* **Pennsylvania** *off.* Commonwealth of Pennsylvania; *also known as* The Keystone State. ◆ *state* NE USA
20 *G10* **Penn Yan** New York, NE USA *42.39N 77.02W*
128 *H16* **Peno** Tverskaya Oblast', W Russian Federation *56.55N 32.44E*
21 *R7* **Penobscot Bay** *bay* Maine, NE USA
21 *S5* **Penobscot River** ≈ Maine, NE USA
190 *K12* **Penola** South Australia *37.24S 140.50E*
42 *K9* **Peñón Blanco** Durango, C Mexico *25.12N 100.50W*
190 *E7* **Penong** South Australia *31.57S 133.01E*
45 *S16* **Penonomé** Coclé, C Panama *8.29N 80.21W*
202 *L13* **Penrhyn** *atoll* N Cook Islands
199 *Kk10* **Penrhyn Basin** *undersea feature* C Pacific Ocean
191 *S9* **Penrith** New South Wales, SE Australia *33.45S 150.48E*
99 *K15* **Penrith** NW England, UK *54.40N 2.43W*
25 *O9* **Pensacola** Florida, SE USA *30.25N 87.13W*
25 *O9* **Pensacola Bay** *bay* Florida, SE USA
205 *N7* **Pensacola Mountains** ▲ Antarctica
190 *L12* **Penshurst** Victoria, SE Australia *37.54S 142.19E*
197 *C12* **Pentecost** *Fr.* Pentecôte. *island* C Vanuatu
13 *V4* **Pentecôte** ≈ Québec, SE Canada
Pentecôte *see* Pentecost
13 *V4* **Pentecôte, Lac** ◎ Québec, SE Canada
15 *Gg16* **Penticton** British Columbia, SW Canada *49.29N 119.37W*
98 *J6* **Pentland Firth** *strait* N Scotland, UK
98 *J12* **Pentland Hills** *hill range* S Scotland, UK
175 *Rr10* **Penu** Pulau Taliabu, E Indonesia *1.43S 125.09E*
161 *H18* **Penukonda** Andhra Pradesh, E India *14.04N 77.38E*
177 *G7* **Penwegon** Pegu, C Myanmar *18.13N 96.34E*
26 *M8* **Penwell** Texas, SW USA *31.45N 102.32W*
99 *J21* **Pen y Fan** ▲ SE Wales, UK *51.52N 3.25W*
99 *L16* **Pen-y-ghent** ▲ N England, UK *54.11N 2.15W*
175 *T12* **Penyu, Kepulauan** *island group* E Indonesia
131 *O6* **Penza** Penzenskaya Oblast', W Russian Federation *53.11N 45.00E*
99 *G25* **Penzance** SW England, UK *50.07N 5.33W*
131 *N6* **Penzenskaya Oblast'** ◆ *province* W Russian Federation
127 *P7* **Penzhina** ≈ E Russian Federation
127 *N17* **Penzhinskaya Guba** *bay* E Russian Federation
Penzig *see* Pieńsk
38 *K13* **Peoria** Arizona, SW USA *33.34N 112.14W*
32 *L12* **Peoria** Illinois, N USA *40.41N 89.35W*
32 *L12* **Peoria Heights** Illinois, N USA *40.45N 89.34W*
33 *N11* **Peotone** Illinois, N USA *41.19N 87.47W*
20 *J11* **Pepacton Reservoir** ▣ New York, NE USA
78 *I15* **Pepel** W Sierra Leone *8.39N 13.04W*
32 *I6* **Pepin, Lake** ▣ Minnesota/Wisconsin, N USA
101 *L20* **Pepinster** Liège, E Belgium *50.34N 5.49E*
115 *L20* **Peqin** *var.* Peqini. Elbasan, C Albania *41.03N 19.46E*
Peqini *see* Peqin
42 *D7* **Pequeña, Punta** *headland* W Mexico *26.13N 112.34W*
174 *I11* **Perabumulih** *var.* Prabumulih. Sumatera, W Indonesia *3.27S 104.15E*
174 *Gg4* **Perak** ◆ *state* Peninsular Malaysia
174 *Gg4* **Perak, Sungai** ≈ Peninsular Malaysia
107 *R7* **Perales del Alfambra** Aragón, NE Spain *40.38N 1.00W*
117 *C15* **Pérama** *var.* Perama. Ípeiros, W Greece *39.42N 20.51E*
94 *M13* **Perä-Posio** Lappi, NE Finland *66.10N 27.56E*
13 *Z6* **Percé** Québec, SE Canada *48.31N 64.15W*
13 *Z6* **Percé, Rocher** *island* Québec, S Canada
104 *L5* **Perche, Collines de** ▲ N France
111 *X4* **Perchtoldsdorf** Niederösterreich, NE Austria *48.06N 16.16E*
188 *L6* **Percival Lakes** *lakes* Western Australia
107 *T3* **Perdido, Monte** ▲ NE Spain *42.41N 0.01E*
25 *O8* **Perdido River** ≈ Alabama/Florida, S USA
Perece Vela Basin *see* West Mariana Basin
118 *G7* **Perechyn** Zakarpats'ka Oblast', W Ukraine *48.45N 22.28E*
56 *E10* **Pereira** Risaralda, W Colombia *4.52N 75.48W*
62 *I7* **Pereira Barreto** São Paulo, S Brazil *20.37S 51.07W*
61 *G15* **Pereirinha** Pará, N Brazil *8.18S 57.30W*
131 *N10* **Perelazovskiy** Volgogradskaya Oblast', SW Russian Federation *49.10N 42.30E*
131 *S7* **Perelyub** Saratovskaya Oblast', W Russian Federation *51.52N 50.19E*
33 *P7* **Pere Marquette River** ≈ Michigan, N USA
Peremyshl *see* Przemyśl
118 *I5* **Peremyshlyany** L'vivs'ka Oblast', W Ukraine *49.42N 24.33E*
Pereshchepino *see* Pereshchepyne
118 *L9* **Pereshchepyne** *Rus.* Pereshchepino. Dnipropetrovs'ka Oblast', E Ukraine *48.59N 35.21E*
128 *L16* **Pereslavl'-Zalesskiy** Yaroslavskaya Oblast', W Russian Federation *56.42N 38.45E*
119 *Y7* **Pereval's'k** Luhans'ka Oblast', E Ukraine *48.28N 38.54E*
131 *U7* **Perevolotskiy** Orenburgskaya Oblast', W Russian Federation *51.54N 54.05E*
127 *Nn16* **Pereyaslavka** Khabarovskiy Kray, SE Russian Federation *47.49N 134.56E*
Pereyaslav-Khmel'nitskiy *see* Pereyaslav-Khmel'nyts'kyy
119 *Q5* **Pereyaslav-Khmel'nyts'kyy** *Rus.* Pereyaslav-Khmel'nitskiy. Kyyivs'ka Oblast', N Ukraine *50.04N 31.28E*
111 *U4* **Perg** Oberösterreich, N Austria *48.15N 14.39E*
63 *B19* **Pergamino** Buenos Aires, E Argentina *33.55S 60.37W*
108 *G6* **Pergine Valsugana** *Ger.* Persen. Trentino-Alto Adige, N Italy *46.04N 11.13E*
31 *S6* **Perham** Minnesota, N USA *46.35N 95.34W*
95 *L16* **Perho** Länsi-Suomi, W Finland *63.15N 24.25E*
118 *E11* **Periam** *Ger.* Perjamosch, *Hung.* Perjámos. Timiş, W Romania *46.01N 20.54E*
13 *Q6* **Péribonca** ≈ Québec, SE Canada
10 *L11* **Péribonca, Lac** ◎ Québec, SE Canada
13 *Q6* **Péribonca, Petite Rivière** ≈ Québec, SE Canada
13 *Q7* **Péribonka** Québec, SE Canada *48.45N 72.01W*
42 *I9* **Pericos** Sinaloa, C Mexico *25.04N 107.40W*
174 *Kk7* **Perigi** Borneo, C Indonesia
104 *L12* **Périgueux** *anc.* Vesuna. Dordogne, SW France *45.12N 0.41E*
56 *G5* **Perijá, Serranía de** ▲ Columbia/Venezuela
117 *H17* **Peristéra** *island* Vóreioi Sporádes, Greece, Aegean Sea
65 *H20* **Perito Moreno** Santa Cruz, S Argentina *46.35S 71.00W*
161 *G22* **Periyal** *var.* Periyār. ≈ SW India
Periyār *see* Periyal
161 *G23* **Periyār Lake** ◎ S India
Perjámos/Perjamosch *see* Periam
29 *O9* **Perkins** Oklahoma, C USA *35.58N 97.01W*
118 *L7* **Perkivtsi** Chernivets'ka Oblast', W Ukraine *48.28N 26.48E*
45 *U15* **Perlas, Archipiélago de las** *Eng.* Pearl Islands. *island group* SE Panama
45 *O10* **Perlas, Cayos de** *reef* SE Nicaragua
45 *N9* **Perlas, Laguna de** *Eng.* Pearl Lagoon. *lagoon* E Nicaragua
45 *N10* **Perlas, Punta de** *headland* E Nicaragua *12.22N 83.30W*
102 *L11* **Perleberg** Brandenburg, N Germany *53.04N 11.51E*
Perlepe *see* Prilep
173 *G2* **Perlis** ◆ *state* Peninsular Malaysia
129 *U14* **Perm'** *prev.* Molotov. Permskaya Oblast', NW Russian Federation *58.01N 56.10E*
115 *M22* **Përmet** *var.* Përmeti, Prëmet. Gjirokastër, S Albania *40.12N 20.24E*
Përmeti *see* Përmet
129 *U15* **Permskaya Oblast'** ◆ *province* NW Russian Federation
61 *P15* **Pernambuco** *off.* Estado de Pernambuco. ◆ *state* E Brazil
Pernambuco *see* Recife
Pernambuco Abyssal Plain *see* Pernambuco Plain
49 *Y6* **Pernambuco Plain** *var.* Pernambuco Abyssal Plain. *undersea feature* E Atlantic Ocean
67 *K15* **Pernambuco Seamounts** *undersea feature* C Atlantic Ocean
190 *H6* **Pernatty Lagoon** *salt lake* South Australia
Pernau *see* Pärnu
Pernauer Bucht *see* Pärnu Laht
Pērnava *see* Pärnu
116 *G9* **Pernik** *prev.* Dimitrovo. Pernik, W Bulgaria *42.36N 23.01E*
116 *G10* **Pernik** ◆ *province* W Bulgaria
95 *K20* **Perniö** *Swe.* Bjärnå. Länsi-Suomi, W Finland *60.13N 23.10E*
111 *X5* **Pernitz** Niederösterreich, E Austria *47.54N 15.58E*
Pernov *see* Pärnu
105 *O3* **Péronne** Somme, N France *49.55N 2.57E*
12 *L8* **Péronne, Lac** ◎ Québec, SE Canada
108 *A8* **Perosa Argentina** Piemonte, NE Italy *45.02N 7.10E*
43 *Q14* **Perote** Veracruz-Llave, E Mexico *19.31N 97.16W*
Pérouse *see* Perugia
203 *W15* **Pérouse, Bahía de la** *bay* Easter Island, Chile, E Pacific Ocean
Perovsk *see* Kyzylorda
105 *O17* **Perpignan** Pyrénées-Orientales, S France *42.40N 2.52E*
115 *M20* **Përrenjas** *var.* Përrenjasi, Prenjas, Prenjasi. Elbasan, E Albania *41.04N 20.34E*
Përrenjasi *see* Përrenjas
94 *O2* **Perriertoppen** ▲ C Svalbard *79.10N 17.01E*
27 *S6* **Perrin** Texas, SW USA *32.59N 98.03W*
25 *Y16* **Perrine** Florida, SE USA *25.36N 80.21W*
39 *S12* **Perro, Laguna del** ◎ New Mexico, SW USA
104 *G5* **Perros-Guirec** Côtes d'Armor, NW France *48.49N 3.28W*
25 *T9* **Perry** Florida, SE USA *30.07N 83.34W*
25 *T5* **Perry** Georgia, SE USA *32.27N 83.43W*
31 *U14* **Perry** Iowa, C USA *41.50N 94.06W*
20 *E10* **Perry** New York, NE USA *42.43N 78.00W*
29 *N9* **Perry** Oklahoma, C USA *36.17N 97.17W*
29 *Q3* **Perry Lake** ▣ Kansas, C USA
33 *R11* **Perrysburg** Ohio, N USA *41.33N 83.37W*
27 *O1* **Perryton** Texas, SW USA *36.24N 100.48W*
41 *O15* **Perryville** Alaska, USA *55.55N 159.08W*
29 *U11* **Perryville** Arkansas, C USA *35.00N 92.48W*
29 *Y6* **Perryville** Missouri, C USA *37.43N 89.51W*
Persante *see* Parsęta
Persen *see* Pergine Valsugana
Pershay *see* Pyarshai
119 *V7* **Pershotravens'k** Dnipropetrovs'ka Oblast', E Ukraine *48.19N 36.22E*
119 *W9* **Pershotravneve** Donets'ka Oblast', E Ukraine *47.03N 37.20E*
Persia *see* Iran
147 *T5* **Persian Gulf** *var.* The Gulf, *Ar.* Khalīj al 'Arabī, *Per.* Khalīj-e Fars. *gulf* SW Asia
Persis *see* Fārs
97 *K22* **Perstorp** Skåne, S Sweden *56.07N 13.22E*
143 *O14* **Pertek** Tunceli, C Turkey *38.52N 39.19E*
191 *P16* **Perth** Tasmania, SE Australia *41.39S 147.11E*
188 *I13* **Perth** *state capital* Western Australia *31.58S 115.49E*
12 *L13* **Perth** Ontario, SE Canada *44.54N 76.15W*
98 *J11* **Perth** C Scotland, UK *56.24N 3.28W*
188 *I12* **Perth** ✕ Western Australia *31.51S 116.06E*
98 *J10* **Perth** *cultural region* C Scotland, UK
181 *V10* **Perth Basin** *undersea feature* SE Indian Ocean
105 *S15* **Pertuis** Vaucluse, SE France *43.42N 5.30E*
105 *Y16* **Pertusato, Capo** *headland* Corse, France, C Mediterranean Sea *41.22N 9.10E*
32 *L11* **Peru** Illinois, N USA *41.18N 89.09W*
33 *P12* **Peru** Indiana, N USA *40.45N 86.04W*
59 *E13* **Peru** *off.* Republic of Peru. ◆ *republic* W South America
Peru *see* Beru
200 *Oo10* **Peru Basin** *undersea feature* E Pacific Ocean
200 *Oo9* **Peru-Chile Trench** *undersea feature* E Pacific Ocean
114 *F13* **Perućko Jezero** ◎ S Croatia
108 *H13* **Perugia** *Fr.* Pérouse; *anc.* Perusia. Umbria, C Italy *43.06N 12.24E*
Perugia, Lake of *see* Trasimeno, Lago
63 *D15* **Perugorría** Corrientes, NE Argentina *29.21S 58.34W*
62 *M11* **Peruíbe** São Paulo, S Brazil *24.18S 47.01W*
161 *B21* **Perumalpār** *reef* India, N Indian Ocean
Perusia *see* Perugia
101 *D20* **Péruwelz** Hainaut, SW Belgium *50.30N 3.34E*
143 *R15* **Pervari** Siirt, SE Turkey *37.58N 42.30E*
131 *O4* **Pervomaysk** Nizhegorodskaya Oblast', W Russian Federation *54.52N 43.49E*
119 *X7* **Pervomays'k** Luhans'ka Oblast', E Ukraine *48.37N 38.36E*
119 *P8* **Pervomays'k** *prev.* Ol'viopol'. Mykolayivs'ka Oblast', S Ukraine *48.01N 30.51E*
119 *S12* **Pervomays'ke** Respublika Krym, S Ukraine *45.43N 33.49E*
129 *R14* **Pervomayskiy** Kirovskaya Oblast', NW Russian Federation *59.15N 49.20E*
131 *V7* **Pervomayskiy** Orenburgskaya Oblast', W Russian Federation *51.32N 54.58E*
130 *M6* **Pervomayskiy** Tambovskaya Oblast', W Russian Federation *53.15N 40.20E*
119 *V6* **Pervomays'kyy** Kharkivs'ka Oblast', E Ukraine *49.24N 36.12E*
125 *E10* **Pervoural'sk** Sverdlovskaya Oblast', C Russian Federation *56.58N 59.50E*
127 *Pp12* **Pervyy Kuril'skiy Proliv** *strait* E Russian Federation
101 *I19* **Perwez** Walloon Brabant, C Belgium *50.39N 4.49E*
108 *I11* **Pesaro** *anc.* Pisaurum. Marche, C Italy *43.55N 12.52E*
37 *N9* **Pescadero** California, W USA *37.15N 122.23W*
Pescadores *see* P'enghu Liehtao
167 *S14* **Pescadores Channel** *var.* Penghu Shuidao, P'enghu Shuitao. *channel* W Taiwan
109 *K14* **Pescara** *anc.* Aternum, Ostia Aterni. Abruzzo, C Italy *42.28N 14.13E*
109 *K15* **Pescara** ≈ C Italy
108 *F11* **Pescia** Toscana, C Italy *43.54N 10.40E*
110 *C8* **Peseux** Neuchâtel, W Switzerland *46.58N 6.52E*
129 *P6* **Pesha** ≈ NW Russian Federation
155 *T5* **Peshāwar** North-West Frontier Province, N Pakistan *34.00N 71.33E*
155 *T6* **Peshāwar** ✕ North-West Frontier Province, N Pakistan *34.01N 71.40E*
115 *M19* **Peshkopi** *var.* Peshkopia, Peshkopija. Dibër, NE Albania *41.40N 20.25E*
Peshkopia/Peshkopija *see* Peshkopi
116 *I11* **Peshtera** Pazardzhik, C Bulgaria *42.01N 24.18E*
33 *N6* **Peshtigo** Wisconsin, N USA *45.04N 87.43W*
33 *N6* **Peshtigo River** ≈ Wisconsin, N USA
Peski *see* Pyeski
129 *S13* **Peskovka** Kirovskaya Oblast', NW Russian Federation *59.04N 52.17E*
105 *S8* **Pesmes** Haute-Saône, E France *47.17N 5.33E*
106 *H6* **Peso da Régua** *var.* Pêso da Regua. Vila Real, N Portugal *41.10N 7.46W*
42 *F5* **Pesqueira** Sonora, NW Mexico *29.22N 110.52W*
104 *J13* **Pessac** Gironde, SW France *44.46N 0.42W*
113 *J23* **Pest** *off.* Pest Megye. ◆ *county* C Hungary
128 *J14* **Pestovo** Novgorodskaya Oblast', W Russian Federation *58.37N 35.48E*
42 *M15* **Petacalco, Bahía** *bay* W Mexico
Petach-Tikva/Petah Tiqva *see* Petah Tiqwa
144 *F10* **Petah Tiqwa** *var.* Petach-Tikva, Petah Tiqva, Petakh Tikva. Tel Aviv, C Israel *32.04N 34.52E*
Petakh Tikva *see* Petah Tiqwa
95 *L17* **Petäjävesi** Länsi-Suomi, W Finland *62.16N 25.10E*
24 *M7* **Petal** Mississippi, S USA *31.21N 89.15W*
117 *I19* **Petalioí** *island* C Greece
117 *H19* **Petalión, Kólpos** *gulf* E Greece
117 *J19* **Pétalo** ▲ Ándros, Kykládes, Greece, Aegean Sea *37.51N 24.50E*
36 *M8* **Petaluma** California, W USA *38.15N 122.37W*
101 *L25* **Pétange** Luxembourg, SW Luxembourg *49.33N 5.52E*
56 *M5* **Petare** Miranda, N Venezuela *10.29N 66.47W*
43 *N16* **Petatlán** Guerrero, S Mexico *17.31N 101.16W*
85 *L14* **Petauke** Eastern, E Zambia *14.12S 31.16E*
12 *J12* **Petawawa** Ontario, SE Canada *45.53N 77.16W*
12 *J11* **Petawawa** ≈ Ontario, SE Canada
Petchaburi *see* Phetchaburi
44 *D2* **Petén** *off.* Departamento del Petén. ◆ *department* N Guatemala
44 *D2* **Petén Itzá, Lago** *var.* Lago de Flores. ◎ N Guatemala
32 *K7* **Petenwell Lake** ▣ Wisconsin, N USA
12 *D6* **Peterbell** Ontario, S Canada *48.34N 83.19W*
190 *I7* **Peterborough** South Australia *32.59S 138.50E*
12 *I14* **Peterborough** Ontario, SE Canada *44.19N 78.19W*
99 *N20* **Peterborough** *prev.* Medeshamstede. E England, UK *52.34N 0.15W*
21 *N10* **Peterborough** New Hampshire, NE USA *42.51N 71.54W*
98 *L8* **Peterhead** NE Scotland, UK *57.30N 1.46W*
Peterhof *see* Luboń
199 *Mm16* **Peter I Island** ◇ *Norwegian dependency* Antarctica
204 *H9* **Peter I Island** *var.* Peter I øy. *island* Antarctica
Peter I øy *see* Peter I Island
99 *M14* **Peterlee** N England, UK *54.45N 1.18W*
Peterlingen *see* Payerne
207 *P14* **Petermann Bjerg** ▲ C Greenland *73.16N 27.59W*
9 *S12* **Peter Pond Lake** ◎ Saskatchewan, C Canada
41 *X13* **Petersburg** Mytkof Island, Alaska, USA *56.43N 132.51W*
32 *K13* **Petersburg** Illinois, N USA *40.01N 89.52W*
33 *N16* **Petersburg** Indiana, N USA *38.30N 87.16W*
31 *Q3* **Petersburg** North Dakota, N USA *47.59N 97.59W*
27 *N5* **Petersburg** Texas, SW USA *33.52N 101.36W*
23 *V7* **Petersburg** Virginia, NE USA *37.13N 77.24W*
23 *T4* **Petersburg** West Virginia, NE USA *38.59N 79.07W*
102 *H12* **Petershagen** Nordrhein-Westfalen, NW Germany *52.22N 8.58E*
57 *S9* **Peters Mine** *var.* Peter's Mine. N Guyana *6.13N 59.18W*
109 *O21* **Petilia Policastro** Calabria, SW Italy *39.07N 16.48E*
46 *M9* **Pétionville** S Haiti *18.29N 72.16W*
47 *X6* **Petit-Bourg** Basse Terre, C Guadeloupe *16.11N 61.34W*
13 *Y5* **Petit-Cap** Québec, SE Canada *49.00N 64.26W*
47 *Y6* **Petit Cul-de-Sac Marin** *bay* C Guadeloupe
46 *M9* **Petite-Rivière-de-l'Artibonite** C Haiti *19.06N 72.28W*
181 *X16* **Petite Rivière Noire, Piton de la** ▲ C Mauritius
13 *R9* **Petite-Rivière-St-François** Québec, SE Canada *47.18N 70.34W*
46 *L9* **Petit-Goâve** S Haiti *18.23N 72.51W*
Petitjean *see* Sidi-Kacem
11 *N10* **Petit Lac Manicouagan** ◎ Québec, E Canada
21 *T7* **Petit Manan Point** *headland* Maine, NE USA *44.23N 67.54W*
Petit Mécatina, Rivière du *see* Little Mecatina
9 *N10* **Petitot** ≈ Alberta/British Columbia, W Canada
47 *S12* **Petit Piton** ▲ SW Saint Lucia *13.49N 61.03W*
Petit-Popo *see* Aného
Petit St-Bernard, Col du *see* Little Saint Bernard Pass
11 *O8* **Petitsikapau Lake** ◎ Newfoundland and Labrador, E Canada
94 *L11* **Petkula** Lappi, N Finland *67.40N 26.43E*
43 *X12* **Peto** Yucatán, SE Mexico *20.09N 88.55W*
64 *G10* **Petorca** Valparaíso, C Chile *32.13S 70.49W*
33 *Q5* **Petoskey** Michigan, N USA *45.51N 88.03W*
144 *G14* **Petra** *archaeological site* Ma'ān, W Jordan *30.19N 35.25E*
Petra *see* Wādī Mūsā
117 *F14* **Pétras, Sténa** *pass* N Greece *40.12N 22.15E*
127 *Nn18* **Petra Velikogo, Zaliv** *bay* SE Russian Federation
Petrel *see* Petrer
12 *K15* **Petre, Point** *headland* Ontario, SE Canada *43.49N 77.07W*
107 *S12* **Petrer** *var.* Petrel. País Valenciano, E Spain *38.28N 0.46W*
129 *U11* **Petretsovo** Permskaya Oblast', NW Russian Federation *61.22N 57.21E*
116 *G12* **Petrich** Blagoevgrad, SW Bulgaria *41.24N 23.12E*
197 *H3* **Petrie, Récif** *reef* N New Caledonia
39 *N11* **Petrified Forest** *prehistoric site* Arizona, SW USA *35.10N 109.49W*
Petrikau *see* Piotrków Trybunalski
Petrikov *see* Pyetrykaw
118 *H12* **Petrila** *Hung.* Petrilla. Hunedoara, W Romania *45.27N 23.25E*
Petrilla *see* Petrila
114 *E9* **Petrinja** Sisak-Moslavina, C Croatia *45.27N 16.14E*
Petroaleksandrovsk *see* To'rtkok'l
Petrőcz *see* Bački Petrovac
128 *G12* **Petrodvorets** *Fin.* Pietarhovi. Leningradskaya Oblast', NW Russian Federation *59.52N 29.52E*
Petrograd *see* Sankt-Peterburg
Petrokov *see* Piotrków Trybunalski
56 *G6* **Petrólea** Norte de Santander, NE Colombia *8.30N 72.34W*
12 *D16* **Petrolia** Ontario, S Canada *42.54N 82.07W*
27 *S4* **Petrolia** Texas, SW USA *34.00N 98.13W*
61 *O15* **Petrolina** Pernambuco, E Brazil *9.22S 40.30W*
47 *T6* **Petrona, Punta** *headland* C Puerto Rico *17.57N 66.23W*
Petropavl *see* Petropavlovsk
119 *V7* **Petropavlivka** Dnipropetrovs'ka Oblast', E Ukraine *48.28N 36.28E*
151 *P6* **Petropavlovsk** *Kaz.* Petropavl. Severnyy Kazakhstan, N Kazakhstan *54.46N 69.06E*
127 *Pp11* **Petropavlovsk-Kamchatskiy** Kamchatskaya Oblast', E Russian Federation *53.03N 158.43E*
62 *P9* **Petrópolis** Rio de Janeiro, SE Brazil *22.30S 43.28W*
118 *H12* **Petroşani** *var.* Petroşeni, *Ger.* Petroschen, *Hung.* Petrozsény. Hunedoara, W Romania *45.25N 23.22E*
Petroschen/Petroşeni *see* Petroşani
Petroskoi *see* Petrozavodsk
Petrovac/Petrovácz *see* Bački Petrovac
115 *J17* **Petrovac na Moru** Montenegro, SW Serbia and Montenegro (Yugoslavia) *42.11N 19.00E*
119 *S8* **Petrove** Kirovohrads'ka Oblast', C Ukraine *48.22N 33.12E*
115 *O18* **Petrovec** C FYR Macedonia *41.57N 21.37E*
Petrovgrad *see* Zrenjanin
131 *P7* **Petrovsk** Saratovskaya Oblast', W Russian Federation *52.20N 45.23E*
128 *J9* **Petrovskiy Yam** Respublika Kareliya, NW Russian Federation *63.19N 35.14E*
Petrovsk-Port *see* Makhachkala
126 *K16* **Petrovsk-Zabaykal'skiy** Chitinskaya Oblast', S Russian Federation *51.15N 108.36E*
131 *P9* **Petrov Val** Volgogradskaya Oblast', SW Russian Federation *50.10N 45.16E*
128 *J11* **Petrozavodsk** *Fin.* Petroskoi. Respublika Kareliya, NW Russian Federation *61.46N 34.19E*
Petrozsény *see* Petroşani
85 *D20* **Petrusdal** Hardap, C Namibia *23.42S 17.23E*
119 *T7* **Petrykivka** Dnipropetrovs'ka Oblast', E Ukraine *48.44N 34.42E*
Petsamo *see* Pechenga
Petschka *see* Pecica
Pettau *see* Ptuj
111 *S5* **Pettenbach** Oberösterreich, C Austria *47.58N 14.03E*
27 *S13* **Pettus** Texas, SW USA *28.34N 97.49W*
125 *F13* **Petukhovo** Kurganskaya Oblast', C Russian Federation *55.04N 67.49E*
Petuna *see* Songyuan
111 *R4* **Peuerbach** Oberösterreich, N Austria *48.19N 13.45E*
64 *G12* **Peumo** Libertador, C Chile *34.22S 71.58W*
173 *Ee3* **Peusangan, Krueng** ≈ Sumatera, NW Indonesia
127 *O4* **Pevek** Chukotskiy Avtonomnyy Okrug, NE Russian Federation *69.40N 170.19E*
29 *X5* **Pevely** Missouri, C USA *38.16N 90.24W*
Peyia *see* Pégeia
104 *J15* **Peyrehorade** Landes, SW France *43.33N 1.04W*
128 *J14* **Peza** ≈ NW Russian Federation
105 *P16* **Pézenas** Hérault, S France *43.28N 3.25E*
113 *H20* **Pezinok** *Ger.* Bösing, *Hung.* Bazin. Bratislavský Kraj, W Slovakia *48.18N 17.15E*
103 *L22* **Pfaffenhofen an der Ilm** Bayern, SE Germany *48.31N 11.30E*
110 *G7* **Pfäffikon** Schwyz, C Switzerland *47.11N 8.46E*
103 *F20* **Pfälzer Wald** *hill range* W Germany
103 *N22* **Pfarrkirchen** Bayern, SE Germany *48.25N 12.56E*
103 *G21* **Pforzheim** Baden-Württemberg, SW Germany *48.52N 8.42E*
103 *H24* **Pfullendorf** Baden-Württemberg, S Germany *47.55N 9.16E*
110 *K8* **Pfunds** Tirol, W Austria *46.56N 10.30E*
103 *G19* **Pfungstadt** Hessen, W Germany *49.48N 8.36E*
85 *L20* **Phalaborwa** Limpopo, NE South Africa *23.50S 31.08E*
158 *E11* **Phalodi** Rājasthān, NW India *27.06N 72.22E*
158 *E12* **Phalsund** Rājasthān, NW India *26.22N 71.55E*
161 *E15* **Phaltan** Mahārāshtra, W India *18.01N 74.31E*
178 *Hh7* **Phan** *var.* Muang Phan. Chiang Rai, NW Thailand *19.34N 99.43E*
178 *H14* **Phangan, Ko** *island* SW Thailand
178 *Gg15* **Phang-Nga** *var.* Pang-Nga, Phangnga. Phangnga, SW Thailand *8.28N 98.31E*
Phan Rang/Phanrang *see* Phan Rang-Thap Cham
178 *Kk13* **Phan Rang-Thap Cham** *var.* Phanrang, Phan Rang, Phan Rang Thap Cham. Ninh Thuân, S Vietnam *11.34N 109.00E*
178 *Kk14* **Phan Ri** Binh Thuân, S Vietnam *11.11N 108.31E*
178 *K14* **Phan Thiêt** Binh Thuân, S Vietnam *10.55N 108.06E*
Pharnacia *see* Giresun
27 *S17* **Pharr** Texas, SW USA *26.11N 98.10W*
Pharus *see* Hvar
178 *H16* **Phatthalung** *var.* Padalung, Patalung. Phatthalung, SW Thailand *7.37N 100.04E*
178 *Hh7* **Phayao** *var.* Muang Phayao. Phayao, N Thailand *19.10N 99.55E*
9 *U10* **Phelps Lake** ◎ Saskatchewan, C Canada
23 *X9* **Phelps Lake** ◎ North Carolina, SE USA
25 *R5* **Phenix City** Alabama, S USA *32.28N 85.00W*
178 *Jj8* **Pheo** Quang Binh, C Vietnam *17.42N 105.58E*
Phet Buri *see* Phetchaburi
178 *H12* **Phetchaburi** *var.* Bejraburi, Petchaburi, Phet Buri. Phetchaburi, SW Thailand *13.04N 99.58E*
178 *Hh9* **Phichit** *var.* Bichitra, Muang Phichit, Pichit. Phichit, C Thailand *16.28N 100.21E*
24 *M5* **Philadelphia** Mississippi, S USA *32.45N 89.06W*
20 *I7* **Philadelphia** New York, NE USA *44.10N 75.40W*
20 *I16* **Philadelphia** Pennsylvania, NE USA *40.00N 75.10W*
20 *I16* **Philadelphia** ✕ Pennsylvania, NE USA *39.51N 75.13W*
Philadelphia *see* 'Ammān
30 *L10* **Philip** South Dakota, N USA *44.02N 101.39W*
101 *H22* **Philippeville** Namur, S Belgium *50.12N 4.33E*
Philippeville *see* Skikda
23 *S3* **Philippi** West Virginia, NE USA *39.09N 80.02W*
Philippi *see* Fílippoi
205 *Y9* **Philippi Glacier** *glacier* Antarctica
198 *G7* **Philippine Basin** *undersea feature* W Pacific Ocean
133 *X12* **Philippine Plate** *tectonic feature*
179 *Q13* **Philippines** *off.* Republic of the Philippines. ◆ *republic* SE Asia
133 *X13* **Philippines** *island group* W Pacific Ocean
179 *S12* **Philippine Sea** *sea* W Pacific Ocean
198 *G7* **Philippine Trench** *undersea feature* W Philippine Sea
85 *H23* **Philippolis** Free State, C South Africa *30.16S 25.16E*
Philippopolis *see* Plovdiv, Bulgaria
Philippopolis *see* Shahbā', Syria
47 *V9* **Philipsburg** Sint Maarten, N Netherlands Antilles *17.58N 63.02W*
35 *P10* **Philipsburg** Montana, NW USA *46.19N 113.17W*
41 *R6* **Philip Smith Mountains** ▲ Alaska, USA
158 *H8* **Phillaur** Punjab, N India *31.01N 75.49E*
191 *N13* **Phillip Island** *island* Victoria, SE Australia
27 *N2* **Phillips** Texas, SW USA *35.39N 101.21W*
32 *K5* **Phillips** Wisconsin, N USA *45.42N 90.22W*
28 *K3* **Phillipsburg** Kansas, C USA *39.45N 99.19W*
20 *I14* **Phillipsburg** New Jersey, NE USA *40.39N 75.09W*
23 *S7* **Philpott Lake** ▣ Virginia, NE USA
Phintias *see* Licata
178 *Hh9* **Phitsanulok** *var.* Bisnulok, Muang Phitsanulok, Pitsanulok. Phitsanulok, C Thailand *16.49N 100.15E*
Phlórina *see* Flórina
Phnom Penh *see* Phnum Penh
178 *Ii13* **Phnum Penh** *var.* Phnom Penh. ● (Cambodia) Phnum Penh, S Cambodia *11.34N 104.55E*
178 *Jj12* **Phnum Tbêng Meanchey** Preăh Vihéar, N Cambodia *13.45N 104.58E*
38 *K13* **Phoenix** *state capital* Arizona, SW USA *33.27N 112.04W*
Phoenix Island *see* Rawaki
203 *R3* **Phoenix Islands** *island group* C Kiribati
20 *I15* **Phoenixville** Pennsylvania, NE USA *40.07N 75.31W*
85 *K22* **Phofung** *var.* Mont-aux-Sources. ▲ N Lesotho *28.47S 28.52E*
178 *I10* **Phon** Khon Kaen, E Thailand *15.47N 102.35E*
178 *I5* **Phôngsali** *var.* Phong Saly. Phôngsali, N Laos *21.40N 102.04E*
Phong Saly *see* Phôngsali
178 *I8* **Phônhông** C Laos *18.29N 102.26E*
178 *J5* **Phô Rang** Lao Cai, N Vietnam *22.12N 104.27E*
Phort Láirge, Cuan *see* Waterford Harbour
178 *Gg10* **Phra Chedi Sam Ong** Kanchanaburi, W Thailand *15.18N 98.26E*
178 *Hh8* **Phrae** *var.* Muang Phrae, Prae. Phrae, NW Thailand *18.07N 100.09E*
Phra Nakhon Si Ayutthaya *see* Ayutthaya
177 *G15* **Phra Thong, Ko** *island* SW Thailand
Phu Cuong *see* Thu Dâu Môt
177 *G16* **Phuket** *var.* Bhuket, Puket, *Mal.* Ujung Salang; *prev.* Junkseylon, Salang. Phuket, SW Thailand *7.52N 98.22E*
177 *G16* **Phuket** ✕ Phuket, SW Thailand *8.03N 98.16E*
177 *G16* **Phuket, Ko** *island* SW Thailand
160 *N12* **Phulabāni** *prev.* Phulbani. Orissa, E India *20.30N 84.18E*
Phulbani *see* Phulabāni
178 *K10* **Phu Lôc** Th,a Thiên-Huê, C Vietnam *16.13N 107.53E*
178 *J14* **Phumĭ Banam** Prey Vêng, S Cambodia *11.14N 105.18E*
178 *Ii13* **Phumĭ Chŏâm** Kâmpóng Spœ, SW Cambodia *11.42N 103.58E*
178 *Jj11* **Phumĭ Kalêng** Stœng Trêng, NE Cambodia *13.57N 106.17E*
178 *J12* **Phumĭ Kâmpóng Trâbêk** *prev.* Phum Kompong Trabek. Kâmpóng Thum, C Cambodia *13.06N 105.16E*
178 *Ii12* **Phumĭ Koŭk Kduŏch** Bătdâmbâng, NW Cambodia *13.16N 103.08E*
178 *K12* **Phumĭ Labăng** Rôtânôkiri, NE Cambodia *13.51N 107.01E*
178 *J11* **Phumĭ Mlu Prey** Preăh Vihéar, N Cambodia *13.48N 105.16E*
178 *Ii11* **Phumĭ Moŭng** Siĕmréab, NW Cambodia *13.45N 103.35E*
178 *Ii13* **Phumĭ Prâmaôy** Poŭthĭsăt, W Cambodia *12.13N 103.05E*
178 *I14* **Phumĭ Samĭt** Kaôh Kông, SW Cambodia *10.54N 103.09E*
178 *Ii11* **Phumĭ Sâmraông** *prev.* Phum Samrong. Siĕmréab, NW Cambodia *14.09N 103.30E*
178 *Jj12* **Phumĭ Siĕmbok** Stœng Trêng, N Cambodia *13.28N 105.59E*
178 *Jj12* **Phumĭ Thalabârĭvăt** Stœng Trêng, N Cambodia *13.34N 105.57E*
178 *Ii14* **Phumĭ Veal Renh** Kâmpôt, SW Cambodia *10.43N 103.49E*
178 *I13* **Phumĭ Yeay Sên** Kaôh Kông, SW Cambodia *11.09N 103.09E*

◆ Country ● Country Capital ◇ Dependent Territory ○ Dependent Territory Capital ◆ Administrative Region ✕ International Airport ▲ Mountain ▲ Mountain Range ▲ Volcano ≈ River ◎ Lake ▣ Reservoir

Phum Kompong Trabek – Plessisville

Phum Kompong Trabek see Phumĭ Kâmpóng Trâbêk
Phum Samrong see Phumĭ Sâmraông
178 Kk11 **Phu My** Binh Đinh, C Vietnam 14.07N 109.05E
178 J15 **Phung Hiêp** Cân Thơ, S Vietnam 9.49N 105.48E
159 T12 **Phuntsholing** SW Bhutan 26.52N 89.25E
178 J15 **Phươc Long** Minh Hai, S Vietnam 9.27N 105.25E
178 Ii14 **Phu Quôc, Đao** var. Phu Quoc Island. island S Vietnam
Phu Quoc Island see Phu Quôc, Đao
178 J6 **Phu Tho** Vinh Phu, N Vietnam 21.22N 105.13E
Phu Vinh see Tra Vinh
201 T13 **Piaanu Pass** passage Chuuk Islands, C Micronesia
108 E8 **Piacenza** Fr. Paisance; anc. Placentia. Emilia-Romagna, N Italy 45.01N 9.42E
109 K14 **Pianella** Abruzzo, C Italy 42.23N 14.04E
109 M15 **Pianosa, Isola** island Archipelago Toscano, C Italy
176 Vv11 **Piar** Papua, E Indonesia 2.49S 132.46E
47 U14 **Piarco** var. Port of Spain. ✕ (Port-of-Spain) Trinidad, Trinidad and Tobago 10.36N 61.21W
112 M12 **Piaseczno** Mazowieckie, C Poland 52.04N 21.05E
118 I15 **Piatra** Teleorman, S Romania 43.49N 25.10E
118 L10 **Piatra-Neamţ** Hung. Karácsonkő. Neamţ, NE Romania 46.54N 26.23E
Piauhy see Piauí
61 N15 **Piauí** off. Estado do Piauí; prev. Piauhy. ◐ state E Brazil
108 I7 **Piave** ≈ NE Italy
109 K24 **Piazza Armerina** var. Chiazza. Sicilia, Italy, C Mediterranean Sea 37.22N 14.22E
83 G14 **Pibor** Amh. Pībor Wenz. ≈ Ethiopia/Sudan
83 G14 **Pibor Post** Jonglei, SE Sudan 6.49N 33.06E
Pībor Wenz see Pibor
Píbram see Příbram
38 K11 **Picacho Butte** ▲ Arizona, SW USA 35.12N 112.44W
42 D4 **Picachos, Cerro** ▲ NW Mexico 29.15N 114.04W
105 O4 **Picardie** Eng. Picardy. ◐ region N France
Picardy see Picardie
24 L8 **Picayune** Mississippi, S USA 30.31N 89.40W
Piccolo San Bernardo, Colle di see Little Saint Bernard Pass
64 K5 **Pichanal** Salta, N Argentina 23.22S 64.11W
153 P12 **Pichandar** W Tajikistan 38.44N 68.51E
29 R8 **Picher** Oklahoma, C USA 36.59N 94.49W
64 G12 **Pichilemu** Libertador, C Chile 34.25S 72.00W
42 F9 **Pichilingue** Baja California Sur, W Mexico 24.19N 110.16W
58 B6 **Pichincha** ◐ province N Ecuador
58 C6 **Pichincha** ▲ N Ecuador 0.12S 78.39W
Pichit see Phichit
43 U15 **Pichucalco** Chiapas, SE Mexico 17.32N 93.07W
24 L5 **Pickens** Mississippi, S USA 32.52N 89.58W
23 O11 **Pickens** South Carolina, SE USA 34.52N 82.42W
12 G11 **Pickerel** ≈ Ontario, S Canada
12 H15 **Pickering** Ontario, S Canada 43.50N 79.03W
99 N16 **Pickering** N England, UK 54.14N 0.46W
33 S13 **Pickerington** Ohio, N USA 39.52N 82.45W
10 C10 **Pickle Lake** Ontario, C Canada 51.30N 90.10W
31 P12 **Pickstown** South Dakota, N USA 43.02N 98.31W
27 V6 **Pickton** Texas, SW USA 33.01N 95.19W
25 N1 **Pickwick Lake** ▣ S USA
66 N2 **Pico** var. Ilha do Pico. island Azores, Portugal, NE Atlantic Ocean
65 J19 **Pico de Salamanca** Chubut, SE Argentina 45.26S 67.26W
1 P9 **Pico Fracture Zone** tectonic feature NW Atlantic Ocean
Pico, Ilha do see Pico
61 O14 **Picos** Piauí, E Brazil 7.04S 41.24W
65 I20 **Pico Truncado** Santa Cruz, SE Argentina 46.49S 68.01W
191 S9 **Picton** New South Wales, SE Australia 34.12S 150.36E
12 K15 **Picton** Ontario, SE Canada 43.59N 77.09W
193 K14 **Picton** Marlborough, South Island, NZ 41.18S 174.00E
65 H15 **Picún Leufú, Arroyo** ≈ SW Argentina
Pidálion see Gkréko, Akrotíri
161 K25 **Pidurutalagala** ▲ S Sri Lanka 7.03N 80.47E
118 K6 **Pidvolochys'k** Ternopil's'ka Oblast', W Ukraine 49.31N 26.09E
109 K16 **Piedimonte Matese** Campania, S Italy 41.20N 14.30E
29 X7 **Piedmont** Missouri, C USA 37.09N 90.42W
23 P11 **Piedmont** South Carolina, SE USA 34.42N 82.27W
19 Q12 **Piedmont** escarpment E USA
Piedmont see Piemonte
33 U13 **Piedmont Lake** ▣ Ohio, N USA
106 M11 **Piedrabuena** Castilla-La Mancha, C Spain 39.01N 4.10W
Piedrafita, Puerto de see Pedrafita, Porto de
106 L8 **Piedrahita** Castilla-León, N Spain 40.27N 5.19W
43 N6 **Piedras Negras** var. Ciudad Porfirio Díaz. Coahuila de Zaragoza, NE Mexico 28.40N 100.31W
63 E21 **Piedras, Punta** headland E Argentina 35.27S 57.04W
59 I14 **Piedras, Río de las** ≈ E Peru
113 J16 **Piekary Śląskie** Śląskie, S Poland 50.23N 19.01E
95 M17 **Pieksämäki** Isä-Suomi, E Finland 62.18N 27.10E
111 V5 **Pielach** ≈ NE Austria
95 M16 **Pielavesi** Itä-Suomi, C Finland 63.13N 26.45E
95 M16 **Pielavesi** ◎ C Finland
95 N16 **Pielinen** var. Pielisjärvi. ◎ E Finland
Pielisjärvi see Pielinen
108 A8 **Piemonte** Eng. Piedmont. ◐ region NW Italy
113 L18 **Pieniny** ▲▲ Poland/Slovakia
113 E14 **Pieńsk** Ger. Penzig. Dolnośląskie, SW Poland 51.14N 15.03E
31 Q13 **Pierce** Nebraska, C USA 42.12N 97.31W
9 R14 **Pierceland** Saskatchewan, C Canada
117 E14 **Piéria** ▲▲ N Greece
31 N10 **Pierre** state capital South Dakota, N USA 44.22N 100.21W
104 K16 **Pierrefitte-Nestalas** Hautes-Pyrénées, S France 42.58N 0.04W
105 R14 **Pierrelatte** Drôme, E France 44.22N 4.40E
13 P11 **Pierreville** Québec, SE Canada 46.05N 72.48W
13 O7 **Pierriche** ≈ Québec, SE Canada
113 H20 **Piešťany** Ger. Pistyan, Hung. Pöstyén. Trnavský, W Slovakia 48.36N 17.48E
111 X5 **Piesting** ≈ E Austria
Pietarhovi see Petrodvorets
Pietari see Sankt-Peterburg
Pietarsaari see Jakobstad
85 K23 **Pietermaritzburg** var. Maritzburg. KwaZulu/Natal, E South Africa 29.34S 30.23E
Pietersburg see Polokwane
109 K24 **Pietraperzia** Sicilia, Italy, C Mediterranean Sea 37.25N 14.07E
109 N22 **Pietra Spada, Passo della** pass SW Italy 38.30N 16.20E
85 K22 **Piet Retief** Mpumalanga, E South Africa 27.00S 30.49E
118 I9 **Pietrosul, Vârful** prev. Vîrful Pietrosu. ▲ N Romania 47.36N 24.39E
118 J10 **Pietrosul, Vârful** prev. Vîrful Pietrosu. ▲ N Romania 47.06N 25.09E
Pietrosu, Vîrful see Pietrosul, Vârful
108 I6 **Pieve di Cadore** Veneto, NE Italy 46.27N 12.22E
12 C18 **Pigeon Bay** lake bay Ontario, S Canada
29 X8 **Piggott** Arkansas, C USA 36.22N 90.11W
85 L21 **Piggs Peak** NW Swaziland 25.58S 31.16E
Pigs, Bay of see Cochinos, Bahía de
63 A23 **Pigüé** Buenos Aires, E Argentina 37.37S 62.24W
43 O12 **Piguícas** ▲ C Mexico 21.08N 99.37W
200 Qq15 **Piha Passage** passage S Tonga
Pihkva Järv see Pskov, Lake
95 N18 **Pihlajavesi** ◎ SE Finland
95 J18 **Pihlava** Länsi-Suomi, W Finland 61.33N 21.36E
95 L16 **Pihtipudas** Länsi-Suomi, W Finland 63.20N 25.37E
42 L14 **Pihuamo** Jalisco, SW Mexico 19.16N 103.21W
201 U11 **Piis Moen** var. Pis. atoll Chuuk Islands, C Micronesia
43 U17 **Pijijiapán** Chiapas, SE Mexico 15.39N 93.13W
100 G12 **Pijnacker** Zuid-Holland, W Netherlands 52.01N 4.25E
44 H5 **Pijol, Pico** ▲ NW Honduras 15.07N 87.39W
Pikaar see Bikar Atoll
128 I13 **Pikalevo** Leningradskaya Oblast', NW Russian Federation 59.33N 34.04E
196 M15 **Pikelot** island Caroline Islands, C Micronesia
32 M5 **Pike River** ≈ Wisconsin, N USA
39 T5 **Pikes Peak** ▲ Colorado, C USA 38.51N 105.06W
23 P6 **Pikeville** Kentucky, S USA 37.28N 82.31W
22 L9 **Pikeville** Tennessee, S USA 35.36N 85.11W
Pikinni see Bikini Atoll
81 H18 **Pikounda** La Sangha, C Congo 0.30N 16.43E
112 G9 **Piła** Ger. Schneidemühl. Wielkopolskie, C Poland 53.09N 16.43E
64 N6 **Pilagá, Riacho** ≈ NE Argentina
63 D20 **Pilar** Buenos Aires, E Argentina 34.28S 58.55W
64 N7 **Pilar** var. Villa del Pilar. Ñeembucú, S Paraguay 26.55S 58.19W
64 N6 **Pilcomayo, Río** ≈ C South America
153 R12 **Pildon** Rus. Pil'don. C Tajikistan 39.10N 71.00E
Piles see Pylés
Pilgram see Pelhřimov
179 Q11 **Pili** Luzon, N Philippines 13.31N 123.15E
158 L10 **Pīlībhīt** Uttar Pradesh, N India 28.37N 79.48E
112 M13 **Pilica** ≈ C Poland
117 G16 **Pílio** ▲ C Greece
113 J22 **Pilisvörösvár** Pest, N Hungary 47.37N 18.55E
67 G15 **Pillar Bay** bay Ascension Island, C Atlantic Ocean
191 P17 **Pillar, Cape** headland Tasmania, SE Australia 43.13S 147.58E
Pillau see Baltiysk
191 R5 **Pilliga** New South Wales, SE Australia 30.22S 148.53E
46 H8 **Pilón** Granma, E Cuba 19.54N 77.20W
Pilos see Pýlos
9 W17 **Pilot Mound** Manitoba, S Canada 49.12N 98.49W
23 S8 **Pilot Mountain** North Carolina, SE USA 36.23N 80.28W
41 O14 **Pilot Point** Alaska, USA 57.33N 95.34W
27 T5 **Pilot Point** Texas, SW USA 33.24N 96.57W
34 K11 **Pilot Rock** Oregon, NW USA 45.28N 118.49W
40 M11 **Pilot Station** Alaska, USA 61.56N 162.52W
Pilsen see Plzeň
113 K18 **Pilsko** ▲ N Slovakia 49.31N 19.21E
Pilten see Piltene
120 D8 **Piltene** Ger. Pilten. Ventspils, W Latvia 57.14N 21.41E
113 M16 **Pilzno** Podkarpackie, SE Poland 49.58N 21.18E
Pilzno see Plzeň
39 N14 **Pima** Arizona, SW USA 32.49N 109.50W
60 H13 **Pimenta** Pará, N Brazil 4.32S 56.17W
61 F16 **Pimenta Bueno** Rondônia, W Brazil 11.40S 61.13W
58 B11 **Pimentel** Lambayeque, W Peru 6.51S 79.52W
107 S6 **Pina** Aragón, NE Spain 41.28N 0.31W
121 I20 **Pina** Rus. Pina. ≈ SW Belarus
42 E2 **Pinacate, Sierra del** ▲ NW Mexico 31.49N 113.30W
65 H22 **Pináculo, Cerro** ▲ S Argentina 50.46S 72.07W
203 X11 **Pinaki** atoll Îles Tuamotu, E French Polynesia
39 N15 **Pinaleno Mountains** ▲▲ Arizona, SW USA
179 Pp12 **Pinamalayan** Mindoro, N Philippines 13.00N 121.30E
174 Kk8 **Pinang** Borneo, C Indonesia 0.36N 109.10W
173 G3 **Pinang** var. Penang. ◐ state Peninsular Malaysia
Pinang see Pinang, Pulau, Peninsular Malaysia
Pinang see George Town
173 G3 **Pinang, Pulau** var. Penang, Pinang; prev. Prince of Wales Island. island Peninsular Malaysia
46 B5 **Pinar del Río** Pinar del Río, W Cuba 22.23N 83.42W
116 N11 **Pınarhisar** Kırklareli, NW Turkey 41.37N 27.30E
179 P10 **Pinatubo, Mount** ⚠ Luzon, N Philippines 15.07N 120.21E
9 Y16 **Pinawa** Manitoba, S Canada 50.09N 95.52W
9 Q17 **Pincher Creek** Alberta, SW Canada 49.31N 113.52W
32 L16 **Pinckneyville** Illinois, N USA 38.04N 89.22W
Pincota see Pâncota
113 L15 **Pińczów** Świętokrzyskie, C Poland 50.30N 20.31E
155 U7 **Pind Dādan Khān** Punjab, E Pakistan 32.36N 73.07E
Píndhos/Píndhos Óros see Píndos
155 V8 **Pindi Bhattiān** Punjab, E Pakistan 31.54N 73.19E
155 U6 **Pindi Gheb** Punjab, E Pakistan 33.15N 72.16E
117 D15 **Píndos** var. Píndhos Óros, Eng. Pindus Mountains; prev. Píndhos. ▲▲ C Greece
Pindus Mountains see Píndos
20 J16 **Pine Barrens** physical region New Jersey, NE USA
29 V12 **Pine Bluff** Arkansas, C USA 34.13N 92.01W
25 X11 **Pine Castle** Florida, SE USA 28.28N 81.22W
31 V7 **Pine City** Minnesota, N USA 45.49N 92.55W
189 P2 **Pine Creek** Northern Territory, N Australia 13.51S 131.51E
37 V4 **Pine Creek** ≈ Nevada, W USA
20 F13 **Pine Creek** ≈ Pennsylvania, NE USA
29 Q13 **Pine Creek Lake** ▣ Oklahoma, C USA
35 T15 **Pinedale** Wyoming, C USA 42.52N 109.51W
9 X15 **Pine Dock** Manitoba, S Canada 51.34N 96.47W
9 Y16 **Pine Falls** Manitoba, S Canada 50.29N 96.12W
37 R10 **Pine Flat Lake** ▣ California, W USA
129 N8 **Pinega** Arkhangel'skaya Oblast', NW Russian Federation 64.40N 43.24E
129 N8 **Pinega** ≈ NW Russian Federation
13 N12 **Pine Hill** Québec, SE Canada 45.44N 74.30W
9 T12 **Pinehouse Lake** ◎ Saskatchewan, C Canada
23 T10 **Pinehurst** North Carolina, SE USA 35.12N 79.28W
117 D19 **Pineiós** ≈ S Greece
117 E16 **Pineiós** var. Piniós; anc. Peneius. ≈ C Greece
31 W10 **Pine Island** Minnesota, N USA 44.12N 92.39W
25 V15 **Pine Island** island Florida, SE USA
204 K10 **Pine Island Glacier** glacier Antarctica
27 X9 **Pineland** Texas, SW USA 31.15N 93.58W
25 V13 **Pinellas Park** Florida, SE USA 27.50N 82.42W
8 M13 **Pine Pass** pass British Columbia, W Canada 55.21N 122.43W
15 I9 **Pine Point** Northwest Territories, W Canada 60.52N 114.30W
30 K12 **Pine Ridge** South Dakota, N USA 43.01N 102.33W
31 U6 **Pine River** Minnesota, N USA 46.43N 94.24W
33 Q8 **Pine River** ≈ Michigan, N USA
32 M4 **Pine River** ≈ Wisconsin, N USA
108 A8 **Pinerolo** Piemonte, NE Italy 44.56N 7.21E
27 W6 **Pines, Lake O' the** ▣ Texas, SW USA
Pines, The Isle of the see Juventud, Isla de la
Pine Tree State see Maine
23 N7 **Pineville** Kentucky, S USA 36.45N 83.42W
24 H7 **Pineville** Louisiana, S USA 31.19N 92.25W
29 R8 **Pineville** Missouri, C USA 36.35N 94.22W
23 R10 **Pineville** North Carolina, SE USA 35.04N 80.53W
23 Q6 **Pineville** West Virginia, NE USA 37.34N 81.32W
35 Y8 **Piney Buttes** physical region Montana, NW USA
166 H14 **Pingbian** var. Pingbian Miaozu Zizhixian, Yuping. Yunnan, SW China 22.51N 103.28E
Pingbian Miaozu Zizhixian see Pingbian
163 S9 **Pingdingshan** Henan, C China 33.52N 113.19E
167 R4 **Pingdu** Shandong, E China 36.48N 119.56E
201 W16 **Pingelap Atoll** atoll Caroline Islands, E Micronesia
166 K14 **Pingguo** var. Matou. Guangxi Zhuangzu Zizhiqu, S China 23.22N 107.34E
167 Q13 **Pinghe** var. Xiaoxi. Fujian, SE China 24.30N 117.19E
P'ing-hsiang see Pingxiang
167 N10 **Pingjiang** Hunan, S China 28.44N 113.33E
Pingkiang see Harbin
166 L8 **Pingli** Shaanxi, C China 32.24N 109.17E
165 W10 **Pingliang** var. Kongtong, P'ing-liang. Gansu, C China 35.31N 106.46E
165 W8 **Pingluo** Ningxia, N China 38.55N 106.31E
Pingma see Tiandong
178 H9 **Ping, Mae Nam** ≈ W Thailand
167 Q1 **Pingquan** Hebei, E China 41.01N 118.34E
31 P5 **Pingree** North Dakota, N USA 47.07N 98.54W
169 W9 **Pingshan** Jilin, NE China 44.36N 127.13E
Pingsiang see Pingxiang
167 S14 **P'ingtung** Jap. Heitō. S Taiwan 22.43N 120.26E
166 I8 **Pingwu** var. Long'an. Sichuan, C China 32.33N 104.32E
166 J15 **Pingxiang** Guangxi Zhuangzu Zizhiqu, S China 22.03N 106.43E
167 O11 **Pingxiang** var. P'ing-hsiang; prev. Pingsiang. Jiangxi, S China 27.42N 113.49E
167 S11 **Pingyang** var. Kunyang. Zhejiang, SE China 27.46N 120.37E
167 P5 **Pingyi** Shandong, E China 35.30N 117.37E
167 P5 **Pingyin** Shandong, E China 36.18N 116.24E
62 H13 **Pinhalzinho** Santa Catarina, S Brazil 26.53S 52.57W
62 I12 **Pinhão** Paraná, S Brazil 25.46S 51.32W
63 H17 **Pinheiro Machado** Rio Grande do Sul, S Brazil 31.34S 53.22W
106 I7 **Pinhel** Guarda, N Portugal 40.46N 7.03W
Piniós see Pineiós
195 R10 **Pinipel Island** island Green Islands, NE PNG
173 Ff8 **Pini, Pulau** island Kepulauan Batu, W Indonesia
111 Y7 **Pinka** ≈ SE Austria
111 X7 **Pinkafeld** Burgenland, SE Austria 47.18N 16.09E
Pinkiang see Harbin
8 M12 **Pink Mountain** British Columbia, W Canada 57.01N 122.26W
177 G3 **Pinlebu** Sagaing, N Myanmar 24.02N 95.21E
40 J12 **Pinnacle Island** island Alaska, USA
188 I12 **Pinnacles, The** tourist site Western Australia
190 K10 **Pinnaroo** South Australia 35.17S 140.54E
Pinne see Pniewy
102 I9 **Pinneberg** Schleswig-Holstein, N Germany 53.40N 9.48E
117 I15 **Pínnes, Akrotírio** headland N Greece 40.06N 24.19E
Pinos, Isla de see Juventud, Isla de la
37 R14 **Pinos, Mount** ▲ California, W USA 34.48N 119.09W
107 R12 **Pinoso** País Valenciano, E Spain 38.25N 1.01W
107 N14 **Pinos-Puente** Andalucía, S Spain 37.16N 3.46W
43 Q17 **Pinotepa Nacional** var. Santiago Pinotepa Nacional. Oaxaca, SE Mexico 16.19N 98.02W
116 F13 **Pínovo** ▲ N Greece 41.06N 22.19E
197 K7 **Pins, Île des** var. Kunyé. island E New Caledonia
121 I20 **Pinsk** Pol. Pińsk. Brestskaya Voblasts', SW Belarus 52.07N 26.07E
12 D18 **Pins, Pointe aux** headland Ontario, S Canada 42.14N 81.53W
59 B16 **Pinta, Isla** var. Abingdon. island Galapagos Islands, Ecuador, E Pacific Ocean
129 Q12 **Pinyug** Kirovskaya Oblast', NW Russian Federation 60.12N 47.45E
59 B17 **Pinzón, Isla** var. Duncan Island. island Galapagos Islands, Ecuador, E Pacific Ocean
37 Y8 **Pioche** Nevada, W USA 37.54N 114.27W
108 F13 **Piombino** Toscana, C Italy 42.54N 10.30E
(0) C9 **Pioneer Fracture Zone** tectonic feature NE Pacific Ocean
126 Ii2 **Pioner, Ostrov** island Severnaya Zemlya, N Russian Federation
120 A13 **Pionerskiy** Ger. Neukuhren. Kaliningradskaya Oblast', W Russian Federation 54.57N 20.16E
112 N13 **Pionki** Mazowieckie, C Poland 51.28N 21.27E
192 L9 **Piopio** Waikato, North Island, NZ 38.27S 175.00E
112 K13 **Piotrków Trybunalski** Ger. Petrikau, Rus. Petrokov. Łodzkie, C Poland 51.25N 19.42E
158 F12 **Pīpār Road** Rājasthān, N India 26.25N 73.28E
117 I16 **Pipéri** island Vóreioi Sporádes, Greece, Aegean Sea
31 S10 **Pipestone** Minnesota, N USA 44.00N 96.19W
10 C9 **Pipestone** ≈ Ontario, C Canada
63 E21 **Pipinas** Buenos Aires, E Argentina 35.31S 57.19W
155 T7 **Piplān** prev. Liaqatabad. Punjab, E Pakistan 32.19N 71.21E
13 R5 **Pipmuacan, Réservoir** ▣ Québec, SE Canada
Piqan see Shanshan
33 R13 **Piqua** Ohio, N USA 40.08N 84.14W
107 P5 **Piqueras, Puerto de** pass N Spain 42.04N 2.35W
62 H11 **Piquiri, Rio** ≈ S Brazil
62 L9 **Piracicaba** São Paulo, S Brazil 22.44S 47.33W
Piraeus/Piraiévs see Peiraías
62 K10 **Piraju** São Paulo, S Brazil 23.12S 49.24W
62 K9 **Pirajuí** São Paulo, S Brazil 21.58S 49.27W
65 G21 **Pirámide, Cerro** ▲ S Chile 49.06S 73.32W
Piramiva see Pyramíva
111 R13 **Piran** It. Pirano. SW Slovenia 45.31N 13.36E
64 N6 **Pirané** Formosa, N Argentina 25.42S 59.06W
61 J18 **Piranhas** Goiás, S Brazil 16.24S 51.51W
Pirano see Piran
148 I4 **Pīrānshahr** Āzarbāyjān-e Bākhtarī, NW Iran 36.46N 45.10E
61 M19 **Pirapora** Minas Gerais, NE Brazil 17.19S 44.54W
62 I9 **Pirapòzinho** São Paulo, S Brazil 22.17S 51.31W
63 G19 **Piraraja** Lavalleja, S Uruguay 33.43S 54.45W
62 L9 **Pirassununga** São Paulo, S Brazil 21.58S 47.23W
47 V6 **Pirata, Monte** ▲ E Puerto Rico 18.06N 65.33W
62 I13 **Piratuba** Santa Catarina, S Brazil 27.26S 51.47W
116 I9 **Pirdop** prev. Srednogorie. Sofiya, W Bulgaria 42.44N 24.09E
203 P7 **Pirea** Tahiti, W French Polynesia
61 K18 **Pirenópolis** Goiás, S Brazil 15.48S 49.00W
159 S13 **Pirganj** Rajshahi, NW Bangladesh 25.51N 88.25E
Pirgi see Pyrgí
Pírgos see Pýrgos
63 F20 **Piriápolis** Maldonado, S Uruguay 34.51S 55.15W
116 G11 **Pirin** ▲▲ SW Bulgaria
Pirineos see Pyrenees
60 N13 **Piripiri** Piauí, E Brazil 4.15S 41.46W
120 H4 **Pirita** var. Pirita Jõgi. ≈ NW Estonia
Pirita Jõgi see Pirita
56 J6 **Píritu** Portuguesa, N Venezuela 9.21N 69.16W
95 L18 **Pirkkala** Länsi-Suomi, W Finland 61.27N 23.47E
103 F20 **Pirmasens** Rheinland-Pfalz, SW Germany 49.12N 7.36E
103 P16 **Pirna** Sachsen, E Germany 50.57N 13.56E
Piroe see Piru
115 Q15 **Pirot** Serbia, SE Serbia and Montenegro (Yugoslavia) 43.12N 22.34E
158 H6 **Pīr Panjāl Range** ▲▲ NE India
45 W16 **Pirre, Cerro** ▲ SE Panama 7.54N 77.42W
143 Y11 **Pirsaat** Rus. Pirsagat. ≈ E Azerbaijan
Pirsagat see Pirsaat
149 V11 **Pīr Shūrān, Selseleh-ye** ▲▲ SE Iran
94 M12 **Pirttikoski** Lappi, N Finland 66.20N 27.08E
Pirttikylä see Pörtom
175 T11 **Piru** prev. Piroe. Pulau Seram, E Indonesia 3.01S 128.10E
Piryatin see Pyryatyn
Pis see Piis Moen
108 F11 **Pisa** var. Pisae. Toscana, C Italy 43.43N 10.22E
Pisae see Pisa
176 Uu10 **Pisang, Kepulauan** island group E Indonesia
176 Xx11 **Pisapa** Papua, E Indonesia 3.25S 137.04E
201 V12 **Pisar** atoll Chuuk Islands, C Micronesia
Pisaurum see Pesaro
12 M10 **Piscatosine, Lac** ◎ Québec, SE Canada
111 W7 **Pischeldorf** Steiermark, SE Austria 47.11N 15.48E
Pischk see Simeria
109 L19 **Pisciotta** Campania, S Italy 40.07N 15.13E
59 E16 **Pisco** Ica, SW Peru 13.46S 76.12W
118 G9 **Pişcolt** Hung. Piskolt. Satu Mare, NW Romania 47.34N 22.18E
59 E16 **Pisco, Río** ≈ E Peru
113 C18 **Písek** Budějovický Kraj, S Czech Republic 49.18N 14.07E
33 R14 **Pisgah** Ohio, N USA 39.19N 84.22W
Pisha see Ningnan
164 F9 **Pishan** var. Guma. Xinjiang Uygur Zizhiqu, NW China 37.36N 78.45E
119 N8 **Pishchanka** Vinnyts'ka Oblast', C Ukraine 48.12N 28.52E
115 K21 **Pishë** Fier, SW Albania 40.40N 19.22E
149 X14 **Pīshīn** Sīstān va Balūchestān, SE Iran 26.05N 61.46E
155 O9 **Pishin** North-West Frontier Province, NW Pakistan 30.39N 66.52E
155 N11 **Pishin Lora** var. Psein Lora, Pash. Pseyn Bowr. ≈ SW Pakistan
Pishma see Pizhma
Pishpek see Bishkek
175 Q13 **Pising** Pulau Kabaena, C Indonesia 5.07S 121.50E
Pisino see Pazin
Piski see Simeria
Piskolt see Pişcolt
153 Q9 **Piskom** Rus. Pskem. ≈ E Uzbekistan
Piskom Tizmasi see Pskemskiy Khrebet
37 P13 **Pismo Beach** California, W USA 35.08N 120.38W
79 P12 **Pissila** C Burkina 13.07N 0.51W
64 H8 **Pissis, Monte** ▲ N Argentina 27.45S 68.43W
43 X12 **Piste** Yucatán, E Mexico 20.40N 88.34W
109 O18 **Pisticci** Basilicata, S Italy 40.23N 16.33E
108 F11 **Pistoia** anc. Pistoria, Pistoriæ. Toscana, C Italy 43.57N 10.53E
34 E15 **Pistol River** Oregon, NW USA 42.13N 124.23W
Pistoria/Pistoriæ see Pistoia
13 U5 **Pistuacanis** ≈ Québec, SE Canada
Pistyan see Piešťany
106 M5 **Pisuerga** ≈ N Spain
112 N8 **Pisz** Ger. Johannisburg. Warmińsko-Mazurskie, NE Poland 53.37N 21.49E
78 I13 **Pita** Moyenne-Guinée, NW Guinea 11.04N 12.15W
56 D12 **Pitalito** Huila, S Colombia 1.51N 76.01W
62 I11 **Pitanga** Paraná, S Brazil 24.45S 51.43W
190 M9 **Pitarpunga Lake** salt lake New South Wales, SE Australia
199 M11 **Pitcairn Island** island S Pitcairn Islands
199 M11 **Pitcairn Islands** ◇ UK dependent territory C Pacific Ocean
95 J14 **Piteå** Norrbotten, N Sweden 65.19N 21.30E
94 I13 **Piteälven** ≈ N Sweden
118 I13 **Piteşti** Argeş, S Romania 44.53N 24.49E
Pithagorio see Pythagóreio
188 I12 **Pithara** Western Australia 30.31S 116.38E
105 N6 **Pithiviers** Loiret, C France 48.10N 2.15E
158 L9 **Pithorāgarh** Uttaranchal, N India 29.34N 80.12E
196 B16 **Piti** W Guam 13.28N 144.42E
108 G13 **Pitigliano** Toscana, C Italy 42.38N 11.40E
42 F3 **Pitiquito** Sonora, NW Mexico 30.39N 112.00W
Pitkäranta see Pitkyaranta
40 M11 **Pitkas Point** Alaska, USA 62.01N 163.17W
128 H11 **Pitkyaranta** Fin. Pitkäranta. Respublika Kareliya, NW Russian Federation 61.34N 31.27E
98 J10 **Pitlochry** C Scotland, UK 56.46N 3.48W
20 I16 **Pitman** New Jersey, NE USA 39.43N 75.06W
152 I9 **Pitnak** Var. Drujba, Rus. Druzhba. Xorazm Viloyati, W Uzbekistan 41.14N 61.13E
114 G8 **Pitomača** Virovitica-Podravina, NE Croatia 45.57N 17.14E
37 O2 **Pit River** ≈ California, W USA
65 G15 **Pitrufquén** Araucanía, S Chile 38.58S 72.40W
Pitsanulok see Phitsanulok
Pitschen see Byczyna
Pitsunda see Bichvint'a
111 X6 **Pitten** ≈ E Austria
8 J14 **Pitt Island** island British Columbia, W Canada
Pitt Island see Makin
24 M3 **Pittsboro** Mississippi, S USA 33.55N 89.20W
23 T9 **Pittsboro** North Carolina, SE USA 35.46N 79.21W
29 R7 **Pittsburg** Kansas, C USA 37.24N 94.42W
27 W6 **Pittsburg** Texas, SW USA 33.00N 94.58W
20 B14 **Pittsburgh** Pennsylvania, NE USA 40.26N 80.00W
32 J14 **Pittsfield** Illinois, N USA 39.36N 90.48W
21 R6 **Pittsfield** Maine, NE USA 44.46N 69.22W
20 L11 **Pittsfield** Massachusetts, NE USA 42.27N 73.15W
191 U3 **Pittsworth** Queensland, E Australia 27.43S 151.36E
64 I8 **Pituil** La Rioja, NW Argentina 28.33S 67.24W
58 A10 **Piura** Piura, NW Peru 5.11S 80.41W
58 A9 **Piura** off. Departamento de Piura. ◐ department NW Peru
37 S13 **Piute Peak** ▲ California, W USA 35.27N 118.24W
115 J15 **Piva** ≈ SW Serbia and Montenegro (Yugoslavia)
119 V5 **Pivdenne** Kharkivs'ka Oblast', E Ukraine 49.52N 36.04E
119 P8 **Pivdennyy Buh** Rus. Yuzhnyy Bug. ≈ S Ukraine
56 F5 **Pivijay** Magdalena, N Colombia 10.28N 74.37W
111 T13 **Pivka** prev. Šent Peter, Ger. Sankt Peter, It. San Pietro del Carso. SW Slovenia 45.41N 14.12E
119 U13 **Pivnichno-Kryms'kyy Kanal** canal S Ukraine
115 J15 **Pivsko Jezero** ▣ SW Serbia and Montenegro (Yugoslavia)
113 M18 **Piwniczna** Małopolskie, S Poland 49.26N 20.43E
37 R12 **Pixley** California, W USA 35.58N 119.18W
129 Q15 **Pizhma** var. Pishma. ≈ NW Russian Federation
11 U13 **Placentia** Newfoundland and Labrador, SE Canada 47.12N 53.58W
Placentia see Piacenza
11 U13 **Placentia Bay** inlet Newfoundland and Labrador, SE Canada
179 Qq12 **Placer** Masbate, N Philippines 11.54N 123.54E
37 P7 **Placerville** California, W USA 38.42N 120.48W
46 F5 **Placetas** Villa Clara, C Cuba 22.18N 79.40W
115 Q18 **Plačkovica** ▲ E FYR Macedonia
38 L2 **Plain City** Utah, W USA 41.18N 112.05W
24 G4 **Plain Dealing** Louisiana, S USA 32.54N 93.42W
33 O14 **Plainfield** Indiana, N USA 39.42N 86.18W
20 K14 **Plainfield** New Jersey, NE USA 40.37N 74.25W
35 O8 **Plains** Montana, NW USA 47.27N 114.52W
26 L6 **Plains** Texas, SW USA 33.11N 102.49W
31 X10 **Plainview** Minnesota, N USA 44.10N 92.10W
31 Q13 **Plainview** Nebraska, C USA 42.21N 97.47W
27 N4 **Plainview** Texas, SW USA 34.12N 101.43W
28 K4 **Plainville** Kansas, C USA 39.13N 99.18W
117 L25 **Pláka, Akrotírio** headland Kríti, Greece, E Mediterranean Sea 35.10N 26.19E
117 J15 **Pláka, Akrotírio** headland Límnos, E Greece 40.02N 25.25E
115 N19 **Plakenska Planina** ▲▲ SW FYR Macedonia
46 K5 **Plana Cays** islets SE Bahamas
107 S12 **Plana, Isla** var. Nueva Tabarca. island E Spain
61 L18 **Planaltina** Goiás, S Brazil 15.34S 47.27W
85 O14 **Planalto Moçambicano** plateau N Mozambique
114 N10 **Plandište** Serbia, NE Serbia and Montenegro (Yugoslavia) 45.13N 21.07E
102 N13 **Plane** ≈ NE Germany
56 E6 **Planeta Rica** Córdoba, NW Colombia 8.24N 75.39W
31 P11 **Plankinton** South Dakota, N USA 43.43N 98.28W
32 M11 **Plano** Illinois, N USA 41.39N 88.32W
27 U6 **Plano** Texas, SW USA 33.01N 96.42W
25 W12 **Plant City** Florida, SE USA 28.01N 82.06W
24 J9 **Plaquemine** Louisiana, S USA 30.17N 91.13W
106 K9 **Plasencia** Extremadura, W Spain 40.01N 6.04W
112 P7 **Płaska** Podlaskie, NE Poland 53.55N 23.18E
114 C10 **Plaški** Karlovac, C Croatia 45.04N 15.21E
115 N19 **Plasnica** SW FYR Macedonia 41.28N 21.07E
125 E12 **Plast** Chelyabinskaya Oblast', C Russian Federation 54.24N 60.51E
11 N14 **Plaster Rock** New Brunswick, SE Canada 46.55N 67.24W
109 J24 **Platani** anc. Halycus. ≈ Sicilia, Italy, C Mediterranean Sea
117 G17 **Plataniá** Thessalía, C Greece 39.09N 23.15E
117 G24 **Plátanos** Kríti, Greece, E Mediterranean Sea 35.27N 23.34E
67 H18 **Plata, Río de la** var. River Plate. estuary Argentina/Uruguay
79 V15 **Plateau** ◐ state C Nigeria
81 G19 **Plateaux** var. Région des Plateaux. ◐ province C Congo
94 P1 **Platen, Kapp** headland NE Svalbard 80.30N 22.46E
Plate, River see Plata, Río de la
101 G22 **Plate Taille, Lac de la** var. L'Eau d'Heure. ◎ SE Belgium
Plathe see Płoty
41 N13 **Platinum** Alaska, USA 59.00N 161.49W
56 F5 **Plato** Magdalena, N Colombia 9.47N 74.46W
31 O11 **Platte** South Dakota, N USA 43.20N 98.51W
29 R3 **Platte City** Missouri, C USA 39.22N 94.46W
Plattensee see Balaton
29 R3 **Platte River** ≈ Iowa/Missouri, USA
31 Q15 **Platte River** ≈ Nebraska, C USA
39 T3 **Platteville** Colorado, C USA 40.13N 104.49W
32 K9 **Platteville** Wisconsin, N USA 42.44N 90.27W
103 N21 **Plattling** Bayern, SE Germany 48.45N 12.52E
29 R3 **Plattsburg** Missouri, C USA 39.34N 94.27W
20 L6 **Plattsburgh** New York, NE USA 44.42N 73.28W
31 S15 **Plattsmouth** Nebraska, C USA 41.00N 95.52W
103 M17 **Plauen** var. Plauen im Vogtland. Sachsen, E Germany 50.30N 12.08E
Plauen im Vogtland see Plauen
102 M10 **Plauer See** ◎ NE Germany
115 L16 **Plav** Montenegro, SW Serbia and Montenegro (Yugoslavia) 42.36N 19.57E
120 I10 **Pļaviņas** Ger. Stockmannshof. Aizkraukle, S Latvia 56.37N 25.40E
130 K5 **Plavsk** Tul'skaya Oblast', W Russian Federation 53.42N 37.21E
43 Z12 **Playa del Carmen** Quintana Roo, E Mexico 20.37N 87.04W
42 J12 **Playa Los Corchos** Nayarit, SW Mexico 22.31N 105.28W
39 P16 **Playas Lake** ◎ New Mexico, SW USA
43 S15 **Playa Vicenté** Veracruz-Llave, SE Mexico 17.42N 95.01W
178 K11 **Plây Cu** var. Pleiku. Gia Lai, C Vietnam 13.57N 108.01E
30 L3 **Plaza** North Dakota, N USA 48.00N 102.00W
65 I15 **Plaza Huincul** Neuquén, C Argentina 38.54S 69.10W
38 L3 **Pleasant Grove** Utah, W USA 40.21N 111.44W
31 V14 **Pleasant Hill** Iowa, C USA 41.34N 93.31W
29 R4 **Pleasant Hill** Missouri, C USA 38.47N 94.16W
Pleasant Island see Nauru
38 K13 **Pleasant, Lake** ▣ Arizona, SW USA
21 P8 **Pleasant Mountain** ▲ Maine, NE USA 44.01N 70.47W
29 R5 **Pleasanton** Kansas, C USA 38.09N 94.43W
27 R12 **Pleasanton** Texas, SW USA 28.58N 98.28W
193 G20 **Pleasant Point** Canterbury, South Island, NZ 44.16S 171.09E
21 R5 **Pleasant River** ≈ Maine, NE USA
20 J17 **Pleasantville** New Jersey, NE USA 39.22N 74.31W
105 N12 **Pléaux** Cantal, C France 45.08N 2.10E
113 B19 **Plechý** Ger. Plöckenstein. ▲ Austria/Czech Republic 48.45N 13.50E
Pleebo see Plibo
Pleihari see Pelaihari
Pleiku see Plây Cu
103 M16 **Pleisse** ≈ E Germany
Plencia see Plentzia
192 O7 **Plenty, Bay of** bay North Island, NZ
35 Y6 **Plentywood** Montana, NW USA 48.46N 104.33W
107 O2 **Plentzia** var. Plencia. País Vasco, N Spain 43.25N 2.56W
104 H5 **Plérin** Côtes d'Armor, NW France 48.33N 2.46W
128 M10 **Plesetsk** Arkhangel'skaya Oblast', NW Russian Federation 62.40N 40.14E
Pleshchenitsy see Plyeshchanitsy
Pleskau see Pskov
Pleskauer See see Pskov, Lake
Pleskava see Pskov
114 E8 **Pleso International** ✕ (Zagreb) Zagreb, NW Croatia 45.45N 16.00E
Pless see Pszczyna
13 Q11 **Plessisville** Québec, SE Canada 46.14N 71.45W

◆ Country
● Country Capital
◇ Dependent Territory
○ Dependent Territory Capital
◐ Administrative Region
✕ International Airport
▲ Mountain
▲▲ Mountain Range
⚠ Volcano
≈ River
◎ Lake
▣ Reservoir

Pleszew – Port Blair

112 H12 **Pleszew** Wielkopolskie, C Poland *51.54N 17.46E*
10 L10 **Plétipi, Lac** ◎ Québec, SE Canada
103 F15 **Plettenberg** Nordrhein-Westfalen, W Germany *51.13N 7.52E*
116 I8 **Pleven** *prev.* Plevna. Pleven, N Bulgaria *43.25N 24.36E*
116 I8 **Pleven** ◐ *province* N Bulgaria
Plevlja/Plevlje *see* Pljevlja
Plevna *see* Pleven
Plezzo *see* Bovec
Pliberk *see* Bleiburg
78 L17 **Plibo** *var.* Pleebo. SE Liberia *4.37N 7.40W*
124 Oo13 **Pliny Trench** *undersea feature* C Mediterranean Sea
120 K13 **Plisa** *Rus.* Plissa. Vitsyebskaya Voblasts', N Belarus *55.12N 27.58E*
Plissa *see* Plisa
114 D11 **Plitvica Selo** Lika-Senj, W Croatia *44.53N 15.36E*
114 D11 **Pljesevica** ▲▲ C Croatia
115 K14 **Pljevlja** *prev.* Plevlja, Plevlje. Montenegro, N Serbia and Montenegro (Yugoslavia) *43.21N 19.21E*
Ploça *see* Ploçë
Plocce *see* Ploče
115 G15 **Ploče** *It.* Plocce; *prev.* Kardeljevo. Dubrovnik-Neretva, SE Croatia *43.02N 17.25E*
115 K22 **Ploçë** *var.* Ploça. Vlorë, SW Albania *40.24N 19.41E*
112 K11 **Płock** *Ger.* Plozk. Mazowieckie, C Poland *52.31N 19.40E*
111 Q10 **Plöcken Pass** *Ger.* Plöckenpass, *It.* Passo di Monte Croce Carnico. *pass* SW Austria *46.36N 12.55E*
Plöckenstein *see* Plechý
101 B19 **Ploegsteert** Hainaut, W Belgium *50.45N 2.52E*
104 H6 **Ploërmel** Morbihan, NW France *47.57N 2.24W*
Ploești *see* Ploiești
118 K13 **Ploiești** *prev.* Ploești. Prahova, SE Romania *44.56N 26.03E*
117 L17 **Plomári** *prev.* Plomárion. Lésvos, E Greece *38.58N 26.24E*
Plomárion *see* Plomári
105 O12 **Plomb du Cantal** ▲ C France *45.03N 2.48E*
191 V6 **Plomer, Point** *headland* New South Wales, SE Australia *31.19S 153.00E*
102 J8 **Plön** Schleswig-Holstein, N Germany *54.10N 10.25E*
112 L11 **Płońsk** Mazowieckie, C Poland *52.37N 20.22E*
121 J20 **Plotnitsa** *Rus.* Plotnitsa. Brestskaya Voblasts', SW Belarus *52.03N 26.39E*
112 E8 **Płoty** *Ger.* Plathe. Zachodnio-pomorskie, NW Poland *53.48N 15.16E*
104 G7 **Plouay** Morbihan, NW France *47.54N 3.14W*
113 D15 **Ploučnice** *Ger.* Polzen. ≈ NE Czech Republic
116 I10 **Plovdiv** *prev.* Eumolpias, *anc.* Evmolpia, Philippopolis, *Lat.* Trimontium. Plovdiv, C Bulgaria *42.08N 24.47*
116 J11 **Plovdiv** ◐ *province* C Bulgaria
32 L6 **Plover** Wisconsin, N USA *44.30N 89.33W*
Plozk *see* Płock
29 U11 **Plumerville** Arkansas, C USA *35.09N 92.38W*
21 P10 **Plum Island** *island* Massachusetts, NE USA
34 M9 **Plummer** Idaho, NW USA *47.19N 116.54W*
85 J18 **Plumtree** Matabeleland South, SW Zimbabwe *20.27S 27.49E*
120 D11 **Plungė** Telšiai, W Lithuania *55.55N 21.53E*
115 J15 **Plužine** Montenegro, SW Serbia and Montenegro (Yugoslavia) *43.08N 18.49E*
121 K14 **Plyeshchanitsy** *Rus.* Pleshchenitsy. Minskaya Voblasts', N Belarus *54.25N 27.49E*
47 V10 **Plymouth** ○ (Montserrat) SW Montserrat *16.39N 62.11W*
99 I24 **Plymouth** SW England, UK *50.22N 4.10W*
33 O11 **Plymouth** Indiana, N USA *41.19N 86.19W*
21 P12 **Plymouth** Massachusetts, NE USA *41.57N 70.40W*
21 N8 **Plymouth** New Hampshire, NE USA *43.43N 71.39W*
23 X9 **Plymouth** North Carolina, SE USA *35.52N 76.45W*
32 M8 **Plymouth** Wisconsin, N USA *43.48N 87.58W*
99 J20 **Plynlimon** ▲ C Wales, UK *52.27N 3.48W*
128 G14 **Plyussa** Pskovskaya Oblast', W Russian Federation *58.27N 29.21E*
113 B17 **Plzeň** *Ger.* Pilsen, *Pol.* Pilzno. Plzeňský Kraj, W Czech Republic *49.44N 13.22E*
113 B17 **Plzeňský Kraj** ◐ *region* W Czech Republic
112 F11 **Pniewy** *Ger.* Pinne. Wielkopolskie, C Poland *52.31N 16.14E*
108 D8 **Po** ≈ N Italy
79 P13 **Pô** S Burkina *11.10N 1.10W*
44 M13 **Poás, Volcán** ⛰ NW Costa Rica *10.12N 84.12W*
79 S16 **Pobè** S Benin *7.00N 2.41E*
127 N8 **Pobeda, Gora** ▲ NE Russian Federation *65.28N 145.44E*
Pobeda Peak *see* Pobedy, Pik/Tomür Feng
153 Z7 **Pobedy, Pik** *Chin.* Tomür Feng. ▲ China/Kazakhstan *42.02N 80.02E* *see also* Tomür Feng
112 H11 **Pobiedziska** *Ger.* Pudewitz. Wielkolpolskie, C Poland *52.30N 17.19E*
Po, Bocche del *see* Po, Foci del
29 W9 **Pocahontas** Arkansas, C USA *36.15N 90.58W*
31 U12 **Pocahontas** Iowa, C USA *42.44N 94.40W*
35 Q15 **Pocatello** Idaho, NW USA *42.52N 112.27W*
178 J13 **Pochentong** ✕ (Phnum Penh) Phnum Penh, S Cambodia *11.24N 104.52E*
130 I6 **Pochep** Bryanskaya Oblast', W Russian Federation *52.56N 33.20E*
130 H4 **Pochinok** Smolenskaya Oblast', W Russian Federation *54.20N 32.29E*
43 R17 **Pochutla** *var.* San Pedro Pochutla. Oaxaca, SE Mexico *15.44N 96.27W*
64 I6 **Pocitos, Salar** *var.* Salar Quiróm. *salt lake* NW Argentina
103 O22 **Pocking** Bayern, SE Germany *48.22N 13.17E*
195 R17 **Pocklington Reef** *reef* PNG
199 Hh9 **Pocklington Trough** *undersea feature* W Pacific Ocean
61 P15 **Poço da Cruz, Açude** ⊠ E Brazil
29 R11 **Pocola** Oklahoma, C USA *35.13N 94.28W*
23 Y5 **Pocomoke City** Maryland, NE USA *38.04N 75.34W*
61 L21 **Poços de Caldas** Minas Gerais, NE Brazil *21.48S 46.33W*
128 H14 **Podberez'ye** Novgorodskaya Oblast', NW Russian Federation *58.42N 31.22E*
Podbrodzie *see* Pabradė
129 U8 **Podcher'ye** Respublika Komi, NW Russian Federation *63.55N 57.34E*
113 E16 **Poděbrady** *Ger.* Podiebrad. Středočeský Kraj, C Czech Republic *50.09N 15.06E*
176 Yy10 **Podena, Kepulauan** *island group* E Indonesia
130 L9 **Podgorenskiy** Voronezhskaya Oblast', W Russian Federation *50.22N 39.43E*
115 J17 **Podgorica** *prev.* Titograd. Montenegro, SW Serbia and Montenegro (Yugoslavia) *42.25N 19.16E*
115 K17 **Podgorica** ✕ Montenegro, SW Serbia and Montenegro (Yugoslavia) *42.22N 19.16E*
111 T13 **Podgrad** SW Slovenia *45.31N 14.09E*
Podiebrad *see* Poděbrady
118 M5 **Podil's'ka Vysochina** *plateau* W Ukraine
Podium Anicensis *see* le Puy
126 Ii11 **Podkamennaya Tunguska** *Eng.* Stony Tunguska. ≈ C Russian Federation
113 N17 **Podkarpackie** ◐ *province* SE Poland
Pod Klošter *see* Arnoldstein
112 O9 **Podlaskie** ◐ *province* NE Poland
131 Q8 **Podlesnoye** Saratovskaya Oblast', W Russian Federation *51.51N 47.03E*
130 K4 **Podol'sk** Moskovskaya Oblast', W Russian Federation *55.24N 37.30E*
78 H10 **Podor** N Senegal *16.40N 14.57W*
129 P12 **Podosinovets** Kirovskaya Oblast', NW Russian Federation *60.15N 47.06E*
128 I12 **Podporozh'ye** Leningradskaya Oblast', NW Russian Federation *60.52N 34.00E*
Podravska Slatina *see* Slatina, Croatia
114 J13 **Podromanlja** Republika Srpska, SE Bosnia & Herzegovina *43.55N 18.46E*
Podsvil'ye *see* Padsvillye
118 L9 **Podu Iloaiei** *prev.* Podul Iloaiei. Iași, NE Romania *47.13N 27.16E*
115 N15 **Podujevo** Serbia, S Serbia and Montenegro (Yugoslavia) *42.56N 21.13E*
Podul Iloaiei *see* Podu Iloaiei
Podunajská Rovina *see* Little Alföld
128 M12 **Podyuga** Arkhangel'skaya Oblast', NW Russian Federation *61.04N 40.46E*
58 A9 **Poechos, Embalse** ⊠ NW Peru
57 W10 **Poeketi** Sipaliwini, E Suriname *4.25N 54.24W*
102 L8 **Poel** *island* N Germany
85 M20 **Poelela, Lagoa** ◎ S Mozambique
Poerwodadi *see* Purwodadi
Poetovio *see* Ptuj
85 E23 **Pofadder** Northern Cape, W South Africa *29.03S 19.25E*
108 I9 **Po, Foci del** *var.* Bocche del Po. ≈ NE Italy
118 E12 **Pogăniș** ≈ W Romania
Pogegen *see* Pagėgiai
108 G12 **Poggibonsi** Toscana, C Italy *43.28N 11.09E*
109 I14 **Poggio Mirteto** Lazio, C Italy *42.17N 12.42E*
111 V4 **Pöggstall** Niederösterreich, N Austria *48.19N 15.10E*
118 L13 **Pogoanele** Buzău, SE Romania *44.55N 27.00E*
Pogónion *see* Delvináki
115 M21 **Pogradec** *var.* Pogradeci. Korçë, SE Albania *40.54N 20.40E*
Pogradeci *see* Pogradec
127 N18 **Pogranichnyy** Primorskiy Kray, SE Russian Federation *44.18N 131.33E*
40 M16 **Pogromni Volcano** ▲ Unimak Island, Alaska, USA *54.34N 164.41W*
169 Z15 **P'ohang** *Jap.* Hokō. E South Korea *36.01N 129.20E*
13 T9 **Pohénégamook, Lac** ◎ Québec, SE Canada
95 L20 **Pohja** *Swe.* Pojo. Etelä-Suomi, SW Finland *60.07N 23.30E*
Pohjanlahti *see* Bothnia, Gulf of
201 U16 **Pohnpei** ◐ *state* E Micronesia
201 O12 **Pohnpei** ✕ Pohnpei, E Micronesia
201 O12 **Pohnpei** *prev.* Ponape Ascension Island. *island* E Micronesia
113 F19 **Pohořelice** *Ger.* Pohrlitz. Jihomoravský Kraj, SE Czech Republic *48.58N 16.30E*
111 V10 **Pohorje** *Ger.* Bacher. ▲▲ N Slovenia
119 N6 **Pohrebyshche** Vinnyts'ka Oblast', C Ukraine *49.31N 29.16E*
Pohrlitz *see* Pohořelice
175 Qq9 **Poh, Teluk** *bay* Sulawesi, C Indonesia
167 P9 **Po Hu** ⊠ E China
118 G15 **Poiana Mare** Dolj, S Romania *43.55N 23.01E*
Poictiers *see* Poitiers
131 N6 **Poim** Penzenskaya Oblast', W Russian Federation *53.03N 43.11E*
197 I6 **Poindimié** Province Nord, C New Caledonia *20.55S 165.18E*
165 N15 **Poindo** Xizang Zizhiqu, W China *29.58N 91.20E*
205 Y13 **Poinsett, Cape** *headland* Antarctica *65.35S 113.00E*
31 R9 **Poinsett, Lake** ◎ South Dakota, N USA
24 I10 **Point Au Fer Island** *island* Louisiana, S USA
41 X14 **Point Baker** Prince of Wales Island, Alaska, USA *56.19N 133.31W*
27 U13 **Point Comfort** Texas, SW USA *28.40N 96.33W*
Point de Galle *see* Galle
46 K10 **Pointe à Gravois** *headland* SW Haiti *18.00N 73.53W*
24 L10 **Pointe a la Hache** Louisiana, S USA *29.34N 89.48W*
47 Y6 **Pointe-à-Pitre** Grande Terre, C Guadeloupe *16.15N 61.31W*
13 U7 **Pointe-au-Père** Québec, SE Canada *48.31N 68.27W*
13 V5 **Pointe-aux-Anglais** Québec, SE Canada *49.40N 67.09W*
47 T10 **Pointe du Cap** *headland* N Saint Lucia *14.06N 60.56W*
81 E21 **Pointe-Noire** Le Kouilou, S Congo *4.46S 11.52E*
47 X6 **Pointe Noire** Basse Terre, W Guadeloupe *16.13N 61.47W*
81 E21 **Pointe-Noire** ✕ Le Kouilou, S Congo *4.45S 11.55E*
47 U15 **Point Fortin** Trinidad, Trinidad and Tobago *10.09N 61.41W*
40 M6 **Point Hope** Alaska, USA *68.21N 166.48W*
41 N5 **Point Lay** Alaska, USA *69.42N 162.57W*
20 B16 **Point Marion** Pennsylvania, NE USA *39.44N 79.53W*
20 K16 **Point Pleasant** New Jersey, NE USA *40.04N 74.00W*
23 P4 **Point Pleasant** West Virginia, NE USA *38.50N 82.08W*
47 R14 **Point Salines** ✕ (St.George's) SW Grenada *12.00N 61.47W*
104 L9 **Poitiers** *prev.* Poictiers, *anc.* Limonum. Vienne, W France *46.34N 0.19E*
104 K9 **Poitou** *cultural region* W France
104 K10 **Poitou-Charentes** ◐ *region* W France
105 N3 **Poix-de-Picardie** Somme, N France *49.47N 1.58E*
Pojo *see* Pohja
39 S10 **Pojoaque** New Mexico, SW USA *35.52N 106.01W*
158 E11 **Pokaran** Rājasthān, NW India *26.55N 71.55E*
191 R4 **Pokataroo** New South Wales, SE Australia *29.37S 148.43E*
121 P18 **Pokats'** *Rus.* Pokot'. ≈ SE Belarus
31 V5 **Pokegama Lake** ◎ Minnesota, N USA
192 L6 **Pokeno** Waikato, North Island, NZ *37.15S 175.01E*
159 O11 **Pokhara** Western, C Nepal *28.13N 84.00E*
131 T6 **Pokhvistnevo** Samarskaya Oblast', W Russian Federation *53.38N 52.07E*
57 W10 **Pokigron** Sipaliwini, C Suriname *4.25N 55.24W*
94 L10 **Pokka** *Lapp.* Bohkká. Lappi, N Finland *68.10N 25.45E*
81 N16 **Poko** Orientale, NE Dem. Rep. Congo *3.07N 26.51E*
Pokot' *see* Pokats'
Po-ko-to Shan *see* Bogda Shan
153 S7 **Pokrovka** Talasskaya Oblast', NW Kyrgyzstan *42.45N 71.33E*
Pokrovka *see* Kyzyl-Suu
126 M11 **Pokrovsk** Respublika Sakha (Yakutiya), NE Russian Federation *61.40N 129.25E*
119 V8 **Pokrovs'ke** *Rus.* Pokrovskoye. Dnipropetrovs'ka Oblast', E Ukraine *47.58N 36.15E*
Pokrovskoye *see* Pokrovs'ke
Pola *see* Pula
39 N10 **Polacca** Arizona, SW USA *35.49N 110.21W*
106 L2 **Pola de Laviana** Asturias, N Spain *43.15N 5.33W*
106 K2 **Pola de Lena** Asturias, N Spain *43.10N 5.49W*
106 L2 **Pola de Siero** Asturias, N Spain *43.24N 5.39W*
203 Y3 **Poland** Kiritimati, E Kiribati *1.52N 95.33W*
112 H12 **Poland** *off.* Republic of Poland, *var.* Polish Republic, *Pol.* Polska, Rzeczpospolita Polska; *prev. Pol.* Polska Rzeczpospolita Ludowa, Polish People's Republic. ◆ *republic* C Europe
Polangen *see* Palanga
112 G7 **Polanów** *Ger.* Pollnow. Zachodnio-pomorskie, NW Poland *54.07N 16.38E*
142 H13 **Polatlı** Ankara, C Turkey *39.34N 32.07E*
120 L12 **Polatsk** *Rus.* Polotsk. Vitsyebskaya Voblasts', N Belarus *55.28N 28.46E*
112 F8 **Połczyn-Zdrój** *Ger.* Bad Polzin. Zachodnio-pomorskie, NW Poland *53.43N 16.02E*
Polekhatum *see* Pulhatyn
155 Q3 **Pol-e Khomrī** *var.* Pul-i-Khumri. Baghlān, NE Afghanistan *35.55N 68.45E*
207 S10 **Pole Plain** *undersea feature* Arctic Ocean
149 P5 **Pol-e Safīd** *var.* Pol-e-Sefid, Pul-i-Sefid. Māzandarān, N Iran *36.10N 53.03E*
Pol-e-Sefid *see* Pol-e Safīd
120 B13 **Polessk** *Ger.* Labiau. Kaliningradskaya Oblast', W Russian Federation *54.52N 21.06E*
Polesskoye *see* Polis'ke
175 P11 **Polewali** Sulawesi, C Indonesia *3.25S 119.22E*
116 G11 **Polezhan** ▲ SW Bulgaria *41.42N 23.28E*
80 F13 **Poli** Nord, N Cameroon *8.42N 13.09E*
Poli *see* Pólis
109 M19 **Policastro, Golfo di** *gulf* S Italy
112 D8 **Police** *Ger.* Politz. Zachodniopomorskie, NW Poland *53.34N 14.34E*
180 I17 **Police, Pointe** *headland* Mahé, NE Seychelles *4.48S 55.31E*
117 L17 **Polichnitos** *var.* Polihnitos, Políkhnitos. Lésvos, E Greece *39.04N 26.10E*
Poligiros *see* Polýgyros
109 P17 **Polignano a Mare** Puglia, SE Italy *40.58N 17.13E*
105 S9 **Poligny** Jura, E France *46.51N 5.42E*
Polihnitos *see* Polichnitos
Polikastro/Políkastron *see* Polýkastro
Políkhnitos *see* Polichnitos
116 K8 **Polikrayshte** Veliko Tŭrnovo, N Bulgaria *43.12N 25.38E*
179 Pp10 **Polillo Islands** *island group* N Philippines
111 Q9 **Polinik** ▲ SW Austria *46.54N 13.10E*
123 Mm3 **Pólis** *var.* Poli. W Cyprus *35.02N 32.27E*
Polish People's Republic *see* Poland
Polish Republic *see* Poland
119 O3 **Polis'ke** *Rus.* Polesskoye. Kyyivs'ka Oblast', N Ukraine *51.15N 29.27E*
109 N22 **Polistena** Calabria, SW Italy *38.25N 16.04E*
Politz *see* Police
Políyiros *see* Polýgyros
31 V14 **Polk City** Iowa, C USA *41.46N 93.42W*
112 F13 **Polkowice** *Ger.* Heerwegen. Dolnośląskie, SW Poland *51.31N 16.04E*
161 G22 **Pollāchi** Tamil Nādu, SE India *10.38N 77.00E*
111 W7 **Pöllau** Steiermark, SE Austria *47.18N 15.46E*
201 T13 **Polle** *atoll* Chuuk Islands, C Micronesia
Pollnow *see* Polanów
31 N7 **Pollock** South Dakota, N USA *45.53N 100.15W*
94 L8 **Polmak** Finnmark, N Norway *70.01N 28.04E*
32 L10 **Polo** Illinois, N USA *41.59N 89.34W*
200 Qq15 **Poloa** *island* Tongatapu Group, N Tonga
44 E5 **Polochic, Río** ≈ C Guatemala
Pologi *see* Polohy
119 V9 **Polohy** *Rus.* Pologi. Zaporiz'ka Oblast', SE Ukraine *47.29N 36.18E*
85 K20 **Polokwane** *prev.* Pietersburg. Limpopo, NE South Africa *23.54S 29.22E*
12 M10 **Polonais, Lac des** ◎ Québec, SE Canada
63 G20 **Polonio, Cabo** *headland* E Uruguay *34.22S 53.46W*
161 K24 **Polonnaruwa** North Central Province, C Sri Lanka *7.55N 81.01E*
118 L5 **Polonne** *Rus.* Polonnoye. Khmel'nyts'ka Oblast', NW Ukraine *50.10N 27.30E*
Polonnoye *see* Polonne
Polotsk *see* Polatsk
111 T7 **Pöls** *var.* Pölsbach. ≈ E Austria
Pölsbach *see* Pöls
Polska/Polska, Rzeczpospolita/Polska Rzeczpospolita Ludowa *see* Poland
116 L10 **Polski Gradets** Stara Zagora, C Bulgaria *42.12N 26.06E*
116 K8 **Polsko Kosovo** Ruse, N Bulgaria *43.26N 25.40E*
35 P8 **Polson** Montana, NW USA *47.41N 114.09W*
119 T6 **Poltava** Poltavs'ka Oblast', NE Ukraine *49.33N 34.32E*
Poltava *see* Poltavs'ka Oblast'
119 R5 **Poltavs'ka Oblast'** *var.* Poltava, *Rus.* Poltavskaya Oblast'. ◐ *province* NE Ukraine
Poltavskaya Oblast' *see* Poltavs'ka Oblast'
Poltoratsk *see* Aşgabat
120 I5 **Põltsamaa** *Ger.* Oberpahlen. Jõgevamaa, E Estonia *58.40N 25.58E*
120 I4 **Põltsamaa** *var.* Põltsamaa Jõgi. ≈ C Estonia
Põltsamaa Jõgi *see* Põltsamaa
125 F10 **Polunochnoye** Sverdlovskaya Oblast', C Russian Federation *60.56N 60.15E*
125 G8 **Poluy** ≈ N Russian Federation
120 I6 **Põlva** *Ger.* Põlwe. Põlvamaa, SE Estonia *58.03N 27.05E*
95 N16 **Polvijärvi** Itä-Suomi, E Finland *62.52N 29.19E*
Põlwe *see* Põlva
117 I22 **Polyaigos** *island* Kykládes, Greece, Aegean Sea
117 I22 **Polyaígou Folégandrou, Stenó** *strait* Kykládes, Greece, Aegean Sea
128 J3 **Polyarnyy** Murmanskaya Oblast', NW Russian Federation *69.10N 33.21E*
129 W5 **Polyarnyy Ural** ▲▲ NW Russian Federation
117 G14 **Polýgyros** *var.* Poligiros, Políyiros. Kentrikí Makedonía, N Greece *40.21N 23.27E*
116 F13 **Polýkastro** *var.* Polikastro; *prev.* Políkastron. Kentrikí Makedonía, N Greece *41.01N 22.33E*
199 Kk9 **Polynesia** *island group* C Pacific Ocean
117 J15 **Polýochni** *site of ancient city* Límnos, E Greece *39.51N 25.21E*
43 Y13 **Polyuc** Quintana Roo, E Mexico *18.15N 88.55W*
111 V10 **Polzela** C Slovenia *46.18N 15.04E*
Polzen *see* Ploučnice
176 Ww9 **Pom** Papua, E Indonesia *1.34S 135.39E*
58 D12 **Pomabamba** Ancash, C Peru *8.51S 77.13W*
193 D23 **Pomahaka** ≈ South Island, NZ
108 F12 **Pomarance** Toscana, C Italy *43.19N 10.53E*
106 G9 **Pombal** Leiria, C Portugal *39.55N 8.37W*
78 D9 **Pombas** Santo Antão, NW Cape Verde *17.09N 25.02W*
85 N19 **Pomene** Inhambane, SE Mozambique *22.57S 35.34E*
112 G8 **Pomerania** *cultural region* Germany/Poland
112 D7 **Pomeranian Bay** *Ger.* Pommersche Bucht, *Pol.* Zatoka Pomorska. *bay* Germany/Poland
33 T15 **Pomeroy** Ohio, N USA *39.01N 82.01W*
34 L10 **Pomeroy** Washington, NW USA *46.28N 117.36W*
119 Q8 **Pomichna** Kirovohrads'ka Oblast', C Ukraine *48.07N 31.25E*
195 O12 **Pomio** New Britain, E PNG *5.28S 151.29E*
Pomir, Dar"yoi *see* Pamir/Pāmīr, Daryā-ye
29 T6 **Pomme de Terre Lake** ⊠ Missouri, C USA
31 S8 **Pomme de Terre River** ≈ Minnesota, N USA
Pommersche Bucht *see* Pomeranian Bay
37 T15 **Pomona** California, W USA *34.03N 117.45W*
116 N9 **Pomorie** Burgas, E Bulgaria *42.31N 27.39E*
Pomorska, Zatoka *see* Pomeranian Bay
112 H8 **Pomorskie** ◐ *province* N Poland
129 Q4 **Pomorskiy Proliv** *strait* NW Russian Federation
129 T10 **Pomozdino** Respublika Komi, NW Russian Federation *62.11N 54.13E*
Pompaelo *see* Pamplona
175 Q9 **Pompangeo, Pegunungan** ▲▲ Sulawesi, C Indonesia
25 Z15 **Pompano Beach** Florida, SE USA *26.14N 80.06W*
109 K18 **Pompei** Campania, S Italy *40.45N 14.27E*
35 V10 **Pompeys Pillar** Montana, NW USA *45.58N 107.55W*
Ponape Ascension Island *see* Pohnpei
31 R13 **Ponca** Nebraska, C USA *42.34N 96.42W*
29 O8 **Ponca City** Oklahoma, C USA *36.42N 97.05W*
47 T6 **Ponce** C Puerto Rico *18.01N 66.36W*
25 X10 **Ponce de Leon Inlet** *inlet* Florida, SE USA
24 K8 **Ponchatoula** Louisiana, S USA *30.26N 90.26W*
28 M8 **Pond Creek** Oklahoma, C USA *36.40N 97.48W*
161 J20 **Pondicherry** *var.* Puduchcheri, *Fr.* Pondichéry. Pondicherry, SE India *11.58N 79.49E*
157 I20 **Pondicherry** *var.* Puduchcheri, *Fr.* Pondichéry. ◐ *union territory* India
Pondichéry *see* Pondicherry
Pondo *see* Pune
207 N11 **Pond Inlet** Baffin Island, Nunavut, NE Canada *72.37N 77.56W*
197 I6 **Ponérihouen** Province Nord, C New Caledonia *21.04S 165.24E*
106 J4 **Ponferrada** Castilla-León, NW Spain *42.33N 6.34W*
192 N13 **Pongaroa** Manawatu-Wanganui, North Island, NZ *40.36S 176.08E*
178 I12 **Pong Nam Ron** Chantaburi, S Thailand *12.55N 102.15E*
83 C14 **Pongo** ≈ S Sudan
158 I7 **Pong Reservoir** ⊠ N India
113 N14 **Poniatowa** Lubelskie, E Poland *51.10N 22.04E*
178 J13 **Pônley** Kâmpóng Chhnăng, C Cambodia *12.26N 104.25E*
161 I20 **Ponnaiyār** ≈ SE India
9 Q15 **Ponoka** Alberta, SW Canada *52.42N 113.33W*
131 U6 **Ponomarevka** Orenburgskaya Oblast', W Russian Federation *53.16N 54.10E*
174 L15 **Ponorogo** Jawa, C Indonesia *7.51S 111.30E*
128 M5 **Ponoy** Murmanskaya Oblast', NW Russian Federation *67.00N 41.06E*
125 E5 **Ponoy** ≈ NW Russian Federation
104 K11 **Pons** Charente-Maritime, W France *45.31N 0.31W*
Pons *see* Ponts
Pons Aelii *see* Newcastle upon Tyne
Pons Vetus *see* Pontevedra
101 G20 **Pont-à-Celles** Hainaut, S Belgium *50.31N 4.21E*
104 K16 **Pontacq** Pyrénées-Atlantiques, SW France *43.10N 0.07W*
66 P3 **Ponta Delgada** São Miguel, Azores, Portugal, NE Atlantic Ocean *37.28N 25.40W*
66 P3 **Ponta Delgado** ✕ São Miguel, Azores, Portugal, NE Atlantic Ocean
66 N2 **Ponta do Pico** ▲ Pico, Azores, Portugal, NE Atlantic Ocean *38.28N 28.25W*
62 J11 **Ponta Grossa** Paraná, S Brazil *25.07S 50.09W*
105 S5 **Pont-à-Mousson** Meurthe-et-Moselle, NE France *48.55N 6.03E*
105 T9 **Pontarlier** Doubs, E France *46.54N 6.19E*
108 G11 **Pontassieve** Toscana, C Italy *43.46N 11.28E*
104 L4 **Pont-Audemer** Eure, N France *49.22N 0.31E*
24 K9 **Pontchartrain, Lake** ◎ Louisiana, S USA
104 I8 **Pontchâteau** Loire-Atlantique, NW France *47.26N 2.04W*
105 R10 **Pont-de-Vaux** Ain, E France *46.25N 4.57E*
106 G4 **Ponteareas** Galicia, NW Spain *42.10N 8.29W*
108 J6 **Pontebba** Friuli-Venezia Giulia, NE Italy *46.32N 13.18E*
106 G4 **Ponte Caldelas** Galicia, NW Spain *42.22N 8.30W*
109 J16 **Pontecorvo** Lazio, C Italy *41.27N 13.40E*
106 G5 **Ponte da Barca** Viana do Castelo, N Portugal *41.48N 8.25W*
106 G5 **Ponte de Lima** Viana do Castelo, N Portugal *41.46N 8.34W*
108 F11 **Pontedera** Toscana, C Italy *43.40N 10.37E*
106 H10 **Ponte de Sor** Portalegre, C Portugal *39.15N 8.01W*
106 H2 **Pontedeume** Galicia, NW Spain *43.22N 8.09W*
108 F6 **Ponte di Legno** Lombardia, N Italy *46.16N 10.31E*
9 T17 **Ponteix** Saskatchewan, S Canada *49.43N 107.22W*
61 N20 **Ponte Nova** Minas Gerais, NE Brazil *20.25S 42.54W*
61 G18 **Pontes e Lacerda** Mato Grosso, W Brazil *15.13S 59.21W*
106 G4 **Pontevedra** *anc.* Pons Vetus. Galicia, NW Spain *42.25N 8.39W*
106 G3 **Pontevedra** ◐ *province* Galicia, NW Spain
106 G4 **Pontevedra, Ría de** *estuary* NW Spain
32 M12 **Pontiac** Illinois, N USA *40.51N 88.37W*
33 R9 **Pontiac** Michigan, N USA *42.38N 83.17W*
174 Kk8 **Pontianak** Borneo, C Indonesia *0.04S 109.16E*
109 I16 **Pontino, Agro** *plain* C Italy
Pontisarae *see* Pontoise
104 H6 **Pontivy** Morbihan, NW France *48.04N 2.58W*
104 F6 **Pont-l'Abbé** Finistère, NW France *47.52N 4.13W*
105 N4 **Pontoise** *anc.* Briva Isarae, Cergy-Pontoise, Pontisarae. Val-d'Oise, N France *49.03N 2.04E*
9 W13 **Ponton** Manitoba, C Canada *54.36N 99.02W*
104 J5 **Pontorson** Manche, N France *48.33N 1.31W*
24 M2 **Pontotoc** Mississippi, S USA *34.15N 89.00W*
27 R9 **Pontotoc** Texas, SW USA *30.52N 98.57W*
108 E10 **Pontremoli** Toscana, C Italy *44.24N 9.55E*
110 J10 **Pontresina** Graubünden, S Switzerland *46.29N 9.52E*
107 U5 **Ponts** *var.* Pons. Cataluña, NE Spain *41.55N 1.12E*
105 R14 **Pont-St-Esprit** Gard, S France *44.15N 4.37E*
99 K21 **Pontypool** *Wel.* Pontypŵl. SE Wales, UK *51.43N 3.01W*
99 J22 **Pontypridd** S Wales, UK *51.37N 3.22W*
Pontypŵl *see* Pontypool
45 R17 **Ponuga** Veraguas, SE Panama *7.50N 80.58W*
192 L6 **Ponui Island** *island* N NZ
121 K14 **Ponya** *Rus.* Ponya. ≈ N Belarus
109 I17 **Ponza, Isola di** *island* Isole Ponziane, S Italy
109 I17 **Ponziane, Isole** *island* C Italy
190 F7 **Poochera** South Australia *32.45S 134.51E*
99 L24 **Poole** S England, UK *50.43N 1.58W*
27 S6 **Poolville** Texas, SW USA *33.00N 97.55W*
Poona *see* Pune
190 M8 **Pooncarie** New South Wales, SE Australia *33.26S 142.37E*
191 N6 **Poopelloe Lake** *seasonal lake* New South Wales, SE Australia
59 K19 **Poopó** Oruro, C Bolivia *18.23S 66.58W*
59 K19 **Poopó, Lago** *var.* Lago Pampa Aullagas. ◎ W Bolivia
192 L3 **Poor Knights Islands** *island* N NZ
41 P10 **Poorman** Alaska, USA *64.05N 155.34W*
190 E3 **Pootnoura** South Australia *28.31S 134.09E*
153 R10 **Pop** *Rus.* Pap. Namangan Viloyati, E Uzbekistan *40.49N 71.06E*
119 X7 **Popasna** *Rus.* Popasnaya. Luhans'ka Oblast', E Ukraine *48.37N 38.24E*
Popasnaya *see* Popasna
56 D12 **Popayán** Cauca, SW Colombia *2.27N 76.31W*
101 B18 **Poperinge** West-Vlaanderen, W Belgium *50.52N 2.43E*
126 K7 **Popigay** Taymyrskiy (Dolgano-Nenetskiy) Avtonomnyy Okrug, N Russian Federation *71.54N 110.45E*
126 Jj7 **Popigay** ≈ N Russian Federation
119 O5 **Popil'nya** Zhytomyrs'ka Oblast', N Ukraine *49.57N 29.24E*
190 K8 **Popiltah Lake** *seasonal lake* New South Wales, SE Australia
35 X7 **Poplar** Montana, NW USA *48.06N 105.12W*
9 Y14 **Poplar** ≈ Manitoba, C Canada
29 X8 **Poplar Bluff** Missouri, C USA *36.45N 90.23W*
35 X6 **Poplar River** ≈ Montana, NW USA
43 P14 **Popocatépetl** ⛰ S Mexico *18.59N 98.37W*
174 L116 **Popoh** Jawa, S Indonesia *8.13S 111.50E*
81 H21 **Popokabaka** Bandundu, SW Dem. Rep. Congo *5.43S 16.35E*
109 J15 **Popoli** Abruzzo, C Italy *42.09N 13.51E*
195 X16 **Popomanaseu, Mount** ▲ Guadalcanal, C Solomon Islands *9.40S 96.01E*
194 L15 **Popondetta** Northern, S PNG *8.45S 148.15E*
114 F9 **Popovača** Sisak-Moslavina, NE Croatia *45.35N 16.37E*
116 J10 **Popovitsa** Tŭrgovishte, C Bulgaria *42.08N 25.04E*
116 L8 **Popovo** Tŭrgovishte, N Bulgaria *43.19N 26.13E*
Popovo *see* Iskra
Popper *see* Poprad
32 M5 **Popple River** ≈ Wisconsin, N USA
113 L19 **Poprad** *Ger.* Deutschendorf, *Hung.* Poprád. Prešovský Kraj, E Slovakia *49.03N 20.16E*
113 L18 **Poprad** *Ger.* Popper, *Hung.* Poprád. ≈ Poland/Slovakia
113 L19 **Poprad-Tatry** ✕ (Poprad) Prešovský Kraj, E Slovakia *49.04N 20.21E*
23 X7 **Poquoson** Virginia, NE USA *37.07N 76.21W*
155 O15 **Porāli** ≈ SW Pakistan
192 N12 **Porangahau** Hawke's Bay, North Island, NZ *40.19S 176.36E*
61 K17 **Porangatu** Goiás, C Brazil *13.28S 49.13W*
121 G18 **Porazava** *Pol.* Porozow, *Rus.* Porozovo. Hrodzyenskaya Voblasts', W Belarus *52.57N 24.24E*
160 A11 **Porbandar** Gujarāt, W India *21.40N 69.40E*
8 I13 **Porcher Island** *island* British Columbia, SW Canada
106 M13 **Porcuna** Andalucía, S Spain *37.52N 4.12W*
12 F7 **Porcupine** Ontario, S Canada *48.31N 81.07W*
66 M6 **Porcupine Bank** *undersea feature* N Atlantic Ocean
9 V15 **Porcupine Hills** ▲▲ Manitoba/Saskatchewan, S Canada
32 L3 **Porcupine Mountains** *hill range* Michigan, N USA
66 M7 **Porcupine Plain** *undersea feature* E Atlantic Ocean
14 F4 **Porcupine River** ≈ Canada/USA
108 I7 **Pordenone** *anc.* Portenau. Friuli-Venezia Giulia, NE Italy *45.58N 12.39E*
56 H9 **Pore** Casanare, E Colombia *5.42N 71.58W*
114 A9 **Poreč** *It.* Parenzo. Istra, NW Croatia *45.16N 13.36E*
62 I9 **Porecatu** Paraná, S Brazil *22.46S 51.22W*
Porech'ye *see* Parechcha
131 P4 **Poretskoye** Chavash Respubliki, W Russian Federation *55.12N 46.20E*
79 Q13 **Porga** N Benin *11.04N 0.58E*
194 G12 **Porgera** Enga, W PNG *5.27S 143.09E*
95 K18 **Pori** *Swe.* Björneborg. Länsi-Suomi, W Finland *61.28N 21.49E*
193 L14 **Porirua** Wellington, North Island, NZ *41.08S 174.50E*
94 I12 **Porjus** *Lapp.* Bårjås. Norrbotten, N Sweden *66.55N 19.55E*
128 G14 **Porkhov** Pskovskaya Oblast', W Russian Federation *57.46N 29.26E*
57 O4 **Porlamar** Nueva Esparta, NE Venezuela *10.56N 63.53W*
104 I8 **Pornic** Loire-Atlantique, NW France *47.07N 2.07W*
194 G12 **Poroma** Southern Highlands, W PNG *6.15S 143.34E*
127 Oo15 **Poronaysk** Ostrov Sakhalin, Sakhalinskaya Oblast', SE Russian Federation *49.15N 143.00E*
117 G20 **Póros** Póros, S Greece *37.30N 23.29E*
117 C19 **Póros** Kefallinía, Iónioi Nísoi, Greece, C Mediterranean Sea *38.09N 20.45E*
117 G20 **Póros** *island* S Greece
83 G24 **Poroto Mountains** ▲▲ SW Tanzania
114 B10 **Porozina** Primorje-Gorski Kotar, NW Croatia *45.07N 14.17E*
Porozovo/Porozow *see* Porazava
205 X15 **Porpoise Bay** *bay* Antarctica
67 G15 **Porpoise Point** *headland* NE Ascension Island *7.54S 14.22W*
67 C25 **Porpoise Point** *headland* East Falkland, Falkland Islands *52.19S 59.18W*
110 C6 **Porrentruy** Jura, NW Switzerland *47.25N 7.06E*
108 F10 **Porretta Terme** Emilia-Romagna, C Italy *44.10N 11.01E*
Porriño *see* O Porriño
94 L7 **Porsangerfjorden** *Lapp.* Porsángguvuotna. *fjord* N Norway
94 K8 **Porsangerhalvøya** *peninsula* N Norway
Porsángguvuotna *see* Porsangerfjorden
97 G16 **Porsgrunn** Telemark, S Norway *59.07N 9.37E*
142 E13 **Porsuk Çayı** ≈ C Turkey
Porsy *see* Boldumsaz
59 N18 **Portachuelo** Santa Cruz, C Bolivia *17.20S 63.24W*
190 I9 **Port Adelaide** South Australia *34.49S 138.31E*
99 F15 **Portadown** *Ir.* Port An Dúnáin. S Northern Ireland, UK *54.25N 6.27W*
33 P10 **Portage** Michigan, N USA *42.12N 85.34W*
20 D15 **Portage** Pennsylvania, NE USA *40.23N 78.40W*
32 K8 **Portage** Wisconsin, N USA *43.33N 89.28W*
32 M3 **Portage Lake** ◎ Michigan, N USA
9 X16 **Portage la Prairie** Manitoba, S Canada *49.58N 98.19W*
33 R11 **Portage River** ≈ Ohio, N USA
29 Y8 **Portageville** Missouri, C USA *36.25N 89.42W*
30 L2 **Portal** North Dakota, N USA *48.57N 102.33W*
8 L17 **Port Alberni** Vancouver Island, British Columbia, SW Canada *49.11N 124.49W*
12 E15 **Port Albert** Ontario, S Canada *43.51N 81.42W*
106 I10 **Portalegre** *anc.* Ammaia, Amoea. Portalegre, E Portugal *39.16N 7.25W*
106 I10 **Portalegre** ◐ *district* C Portugal
39 V12 **Portales** New Mexico, SW USA *34.11N 103.19W*
41 X14 **Port Alexander** Baranof Island, Alaska, USA *56.15N 134.38W*
85 I25 **Port Alfred** Eastern Cape, S South Africa *33.30S 26.55E*
8 J16 **Port Alice** Vancouver Island, British Columbia, SW Canada *50.22N 127.24W*
24 J8 **Port Allen** Louisiana, S USA *30.27N 91.12W*
Port Amelia *see* Pemba
Port An Dúnáin *see* Portadown
34 G7 **Port Angeles** Washington, NW USA *48.07N 123.25W*
46 L12 **Port Antonio** NE Jamaica *18.10N 76.27W*
117 D16 **Pórta Panagiá** *religious building* Thessalía, C Greece *39.28N 21.37E*
27 T14 **Port Aransas** Texas, SW USA *27.49N 97.03W*
99 E18 **Portarlington** *Ir.* Cúil an tSúdaire. C Ireland *53.10N 7.10W*
191 P17 **Port Arthur** Tasmania, SE Australia *43.09S 147.51E*
27 Y11 **Port Arthur** Texas, SW USA *29.55N 93.55W*
98 G12 **Port Askaig** W Scotland, UK *55.51N 6.06W*
190 I7 **Port Augusta** South Australia *32.29S 137.43E*
46 M9 **Port-au-Prince** ● (Haiti) C Haiti *18.33N 72.19W*
46 M9 **Port-au-Prince** ✕ E Haiti *18.38N 72.13W*
24 I8 **Port Barre** Louisiana, S USA *30.33N 91.57W*
157 Q19 **Port Blair** Andaman and Nicobar Islands, SE India *11.40N 92.43E*

◆ Country ● Country Capital ◇ Dependent Territory ○ Dependent Territory Capital ◐ Administrative Region ✕ International Airport ▲ Mountain ▲▲ Mountain Range ⛰ Volcano ≈ River ◎ Lake ⊠ Reservoir

Port Bolivar – Prince Albert Peninsula

27 X12 **Port Bolivar** Texas, SW USA 29.21N 94.45W
107 X4 **Portbou** Cataluña, NE Spain 42.26N 3.10E
79 N17 **Port Bouet** ✈ (Abidjan) SE Ivory Coast 5.17N 3.55W
190 I8 **Port Broughton** South Australia 33.39S 137.55E
12 F17 **Port Burwell** Ontario, S Canada 42.37N 80.47W
10 G17 **Port Burwell** Québec, NE Canada 60.25N 64.49W
190 M13 **Port Campbell** Victoria, SE Australia 38.37S 143.00E
13 V4 **Port-Cartier** Québec, SE Canada 50.00N 66.55W
193 F23 **Port Chalmers** Otago, South Island, NZ 45.46S 170.37E
25 W14 **Port Charlotte** Florida, SE USA 27.00N 82.07W
40 L9 **Port Clarence** Alaska, USA 65.15N 166.51W
8 I13 **Port Clements** Graham Island, British Columbia, SW Canada 53.37N 132.12W
33 S11 **Port Clinton** Ohio, N USA 41.30N 82.56W
12 H17 **Port Colborne** Ontario, S Canada 42.51N 79.16W
13 Y7 **Port-Daniel** Québec, SE Canada 48.10N 64.58W
Port Darwin *see* Darwin
191 O17 **Port Davey** *headland* Tasmania, SE Australia 43.19S 145.54E
46 K8 **Port-de-Paix** NW Haiti 19.53N 72.50W
189 W4 **Port Douglas** Queensland, NE Australia 16.32S 145.27E
8 J13 **Port Edward** British Columbia, SW Canada 54.10N 130.16W
85 K24 **Port Edward** KwaZulu/Natal, SE South Africa 31.03S 30.13E
60 J12 **Portel** Pará, NE Brazil 1.58S 50.45W
106 H12 **Portel** Évora, S Portugal 38.18N 7.42W
12 E14 **Port Elgin** Ontario, S Canada 44.26N 81.22W
47 Y14 **Port Elizabeth** Bequia, Saint Vincent and the Grenadines 13.01N 61.15W
85 I26 **Port Elizabeth** Eastern Cape, S South Africa 33.58S 25.36E
98 G13 **Port Ellen** W Scotland, UK 55.37N 6.12W
Portenau *see* Pordenone
99 H16 **Port Erin** SW Isle of Man 54.05N 4.47W
47 Q13 **Porter Point** *headland* Saint Vincent, Saint Vincent and the Grenadines 13.22N 61.10W
193 G18 **Porters Pass** *pass* South Island, NZ 43.18S 171.45E
85 E25 **Porterville** Western Cape, SW South Africa 33.03S 19.00E
37 R12 **Porterville** California, W USA 36.03N 119.03W
Port-Étienne *see* Nouâdhibou
190 L13 **Port Fairy** Victoria, SE Australia 38.24S 142.13E
192 M4 **Port Fitzroy** Great Barrier Island, Auckland, NE NZ 36.10S 175.21E
Port Florence *see* Kisumu
Port-Francqui *see* Ilebo
81 C18 **Port-Gentil** Ogooué-Maritime, W Gabon 0.40S 8.49E
190 I7 **Port Germein** South Australia 33.02S 138.01E
24 J6 **Port Gibson** Mississippi, S USA 31.57N 90.58W
41 Q13 **Port Graham** Alaska, USA 59.21N 151.49W
79 U17 **Port Harcourt** Rivers, S Nigeria 4.43N 7.02E
8 J16 **Port Hardy** Vancouver Island, British Columbia, SW Canada 50.40N 127.30W
Port Harrison *see* Inukjuak
11 R14 **Port Hawkesbury** Cape Breton Island, Nova Scotia, SE Canada 45.36N 61.22W
188 I6 **Port Hedland** Western Australia 20.22S 118.40E
41 O15 **Port Heiden** Alaska, USA 56.54N 158.40W
99 I19 **Porthmadog** *var.* Portmadoc. NW Wales, UK 52.55N 4.07W
12 I15 **Port Hope** Ontario, SE Canada 43.56N 78.16W
11 S9 **Port Hope Simpson** Newfoundland and Labrador, E Canada 52.30N 56.18W
67 C24 **Port Howard Settlement** West Falkland, Falkland Islands
33 T9 **Port Huron** Michigan, N USA 42.58N 82.25W
109 K17 **Portici** Campania, S Italy 40.48N 14.19E
143 Y13 **Port-İliç** *Rus.* Port Il'ich. SE Azerbaijan 38.54N 48.49E
Port Il'ich *see* Port-İliç
106 G14 **Portimão** *var.* Vila Nova de Portimão. Faro, S Portugal 37.07N 8.31W
27 T17 **Port Isabel** Texas, SW USA 26.04N 97.13W
20 J13 **Port Jervis** New York, NE USA 41.22N 74.39W
57 S7 **Port Kaituma** NW Guyana 7.42N 59.52W
130 K12 **Port-Katon** Rostovskaya Oblast', SW Russian Federation 46.52N 38.46E
191 S9 **Port Kembla** New South Wales, SE Australia 34.29S 150.53E
190 F8 **Port Kenny** South Australia 33.09S 134.38E
Port Klang *see* Pelabuhan Klang
Port Láirge *see* Waterford
191 S8 **Portland** New South Wales, SE Australia 33.24S 150.00E
190 L13 **Portland** Victoria, SE Australia 38.21S 141.37E
192 K4 **Portland** Northland, North Island, NZ 35.48S 174.19E
33 Q13 **Portland** Indiana, N USA 40.25N 84.58W
21 P8 **Portland** Maine, NE USA 43.40N 70.16W
33 Q9 **Portland** Michigan, N USA 42.51N 84.52W
31 Q4 **Portland** North Dakota, N USA 47.28N 97.22W
34 G11 **Portland** Oregon, NW USA 45.31N 122.40W
22 J8 **Portland** Tennessee, S USA 36.34N 86.31W
27 T14 **Portland** Texas, SW USA 27.52N 97.19W
34 G11 **Portland** ✈ Oregon, NW USA 45.36N 122.34W
190 L13 **Portland Bay** *bay* Victoria, SE Australia
46 K13 **Portland Bight** *bay* S Jamaica
99 L24 **Portland Bill** *var.* Bill of Portland. *headland* S England, UK 50.31N 2.28W
Portland, Bill of *see* Portland Bill
191 P15 **Portland, Cape** *headland* Tasmania, SE Australia 40.46S 147.58E
8 J12 **Portland Inlet** *inlet* British Columbia, W Canada
192 P11 **Portland Island** *island* E NZ
67 F15 **Portland Point** *headland* SW Ascension Island
46 J13 **Portland Point** *headland* C Jamaica 17.42N 77.10W
105 P16 **Port-la-Nouvelle** Aude, S France 43.01N 3.04E
Portlaoighise *see* Port Laoise
99 E18 **Port Laoise** *var.* Portlaoise, *Ir.* Portlaoighise; *prev.* Maryborough. C Ireland 53.01N 7.16W
27 U13 **Port Lavaca** Texas, SW USA 28.36N 96.39W
190 G9 **Port Lincoln** South Australia 34.43S 135.49E
41 Q14 **Port Lions** Kodiak Island, Alaska, USA 57.55N 152.48W
78 I15 **Port Loko** W Sierra Leone 8.49N 12.49W
67 E24 **Port Louis** East Falkland, Falkland Islands 51.31S 58.07W
47 Y5 **Port-Louis** Grande Terre, N Guadeloupe 16.25N 61.31W
181 X16 **Port Louis** ● (Mauritius) NW Mauritius 20.10S 57.30E
Port Louis *see* Scarborough
Port-Lyautey *see* Kénitra
190 K12 **Port MacDonnell** South Australia 38.04S 140.40E
191 U7 **Port Macquarie** New South Wales, SE Australia 31.25S 152.55E
Portmadoc *see* Porthmadog
Port Mahon *see* Mahón
46 K12 **Port Maria** C Jamaica 18.21N 76.53W
8 K16 **Port McNeill** Vancouver Island, British Columbia, SW Canada 50.34N 127.06W
11 P11 **Port-Menier** Île d'Anticosti, Québec, E Canada 49.49N 64.19W
41 N15 **Port Moller** Alaska, USA 56.00N 96.31W
46 L13 **Port Morant** E Jamaica 17.52N 76.19W
46 K13 **Portmore** C Jamaica 17.58N 76.52W
194 I16 **Port Moresby** ● (PNG) Central/National Capital District, SW PNG 9.28S 147.11E
Port Natal *see* Durban
27 Y11 **Port Neches** Texas, SW USA 29.59N 93.57W
190 G9 **Port Neill** South Australia 34.06S 136.19E
13 S6 **Portneuf** ≈ Québec, SE Canada
13 R6 **Portneuf, Lac** ◎ Québec, SE Canada
85 D23 **Port Nolloth** Northern Cape, W South Africa 29.18S 16.58E
20 J17 **Port Norris** New Jersey, NE USA 39.13N 75.00W
Port-Nouveau-Québec *see* Kangiqsualujjuaq
106 G6 **Porto** *Eng.* Oporto; *anc.* Portus Cale. Porto, NW Portugal 41.09N 8.37W
106 G6 **Porto** *var.* Pôrto. ◆ *district* N Portugal
106 G6 **Porto** ✈ Porto, W Portugal 41.15N 8.45W
63 I16 **Porto Alegre** *var.* Pôrto Alegre. *state capital* Rio Grande do Sul, S Brazil 30.03S 51.10W
Porto Alexandre *see* Tombua
84 B12 **Porto Amboim** Cuanza Sul, NW Angola 10.43S 13.49E
Porto Amélia *see* Pemba
Porto Bello *see* Portobelo
45 T14 **Portobelo** *var.* Porto Bello, Puerto Bello. Colón, N Panama 9.32N 79.40W
62 G10 **Pôrto Camargo** Paraná, S Brazil 23.23S 53.47W
27 U13 **Port O'Connor** Texas, SW USA 28.26N 96.26W
Pôrto de Mós *see* Porto de Moz
60 J12 **Porto de Moz** *var.* Pôrto de Mós. Pará, NE Brazil 1.45S 52.15W
66 O5 **Porto do Moniz** Madeira, Portugal, NE Atlantic Ocean
61 H16 **Porto dos Gaúchos** Mato Grosso, W Brazil 11.31S 57.16W
Porto Edda *see* Sarandë
109 J24 **Porto Empedocle** Sicilia, Italy, C Mediterranean Sea 37.16N 13.31E
61 H20 **Porto Esperança** Mato Grosso do Sul, SW Brazil 19.36S 57.24W
108 E13 **Portoferraio** Toscana, C Italy 42.48N 10.18E
98 G6 **Port of Ness** NW Scotland, UK 58.29N 6.15W
47 U14 **Port-of-Spain** ● (Trinidad and Tobago) Trinidad, Trinidad and Tobago 10.39N 61.30W
Port of Spain *see* Piarco
105 X15 **Porto, Golfe de** *gulf* Corse, France, C Mediterranean Sea
Porto Grande *see* Mindelo
108 I7 **Portogruaro** Veneto, NE Italy 45.46N 12.49E
37 P5 **Portola** California, W USA 39.48N 120.28W
197 B12 **Port-Olry** Espiritu Santo, C Vanuatu 15.03S 167.04E
95 J17 **Pörtom** *Fin.* Pirttikylä. Länsi-Suomi, W Finland 62.42N 21.40E
Port Omna *see* Portumna
61 G21 **Porto Murtinho** Mato Grosso do Sul, SW Brazil 21.42S 57.52W
61 K16 **Porto Nacional** Tocantins, C Brazil 10.40S 48.19W
79 S16 **Porto-Novo** ● (Benin) S Benin 6.28N 2.27E
25 X10 **Port Orange** Florida, SE USA 29.06N 80.59W
34 G8 **Port Orchard** Washington, NW USA 47.32N 122.38W
Porto Re *see* Kraljevica
34 E15 **Port Orford** Oregon, NW USA 42.45N 124.30W
Porto Rico *see* Puerto Rico
108 J13 **Porto San Giorgio** Marche, C Italy 43.10N 13.47E
109 F14 **Porto San Stefano** Toscana, C Italy 42.26N 11.09E
66 P5 **Porto Santo** *var.* Vila Baleira. Porto Santo, Madeira, Portugal, NE Atlantic Ocean 33.04N 16.19W
66 Q5 **Porto Santo** ✈ Porto Santo, Madeira, Portugal, NE Atlantic Ocean 33.04N 16.19W
66 P5 **Porto Santo** *var.* Ilha do Porto Santo. *island* Madeira, Portugal, NE Atlantic Ocean
62 H9 **Porto São José** Paraná, S Brazil 22.43S 53.10W
61 O19 **Porto Seguro** Bahia, E Brazil 16.25S 39.07W
109 B17 **Porto Torres** Sardegna, Italy, C Mediterranean Sea 40.49N 8.22E
61 J23 **Porto União** Santa Catarina, S Brazil 26.15S 51.04W
105 Y16 **Porto-Vecchio** Corse, France, C Mediterranean Sea 41.35N 9.17E
61 E15 **Porto Velho** *var.* Velho. *state capital* Rondônia, W Brazil 8.45S 63.54W
58 A6 **Portoviejo** *var.* Puertoviejo. Manabí, W Ecuador 1.02S 80.31W
193 B26 **Port Pegasus** *bay* Stewart Island, NZ
12 H15 **Port Perry** Ontario, SE Canada 44.08N 78.57W
191 N12 **Port Phillip Bay** *harbor* Victoria, SE Australia
190 I8 **Port Pirie** South Australia 33.10S 138.01E
98 G9 **Portree** N Scotland, UK 57.25N 6.11W
Port Rex *see* East London
Port Rois *see* Portrush
46 K13 **Port Royal** E Jamaica 17.56N 76.49W
23 R15 **Port Royal** South Carolina, SE USA 32.22N 80.41W
23 R15 **Port Royal Sound** *inlet* South Carolina, SE USA
99 F14 **Portrush** *Ir.* Port Rois. N Northern Ireland, UK 55.12N 6.40W
77 W7 **Port Said** *Ar.* Būr Saʻīd. N Egypt 31.16N 32.18E
25 R9 **Port Saint Joe** Florida, SE USA 29.49N 85.18W
25 Y11 **Port Saint John** Florida, SE USA 28.28N 80.46W
85 K24 **Port St.Johns** Eastern Cape, SE South Africa 31.35S 29.30E
105 R16 **Port-St-Louis-du-Rhône** Bouches-du-Rhône, SE France 43.22N 4.48E
46 K10 **Port Salut** SW Haiti 18.04N 73.55W
67 E24 **Port Salvador** *inlet* East Falkland, Falkland Islands
67 D24 **Port San Carlos** East Falkland, Falkland Islands 51.30S 58.58W
11 S10 **Port Saunders** Newfoundland and Labrador, SE Canada 50.40N 57.17W
85 K24 **Port Shepstone** KwaZulu/Natal, E South Africa 30.40S 30.24E
47 O11 **Portsmouth** *var.* Grand-Anse. NW Dominica 15.33N 61.27W
99 N24 **Portsmouth** S England, UK 50.48N 1.04W
21 P10 **Portsmouth** New Hampshire, NE USA 43.04N 70.46W
33 S15 **Portsmouth** Ohio, N USA 38.43N 83.00W
23 X7 **Portsmouth** Virginia, NE USA 36.50N 76.18W
12 E17 **Port Stanley** Ontario, S Canada 42.39N 81.12W
67 B25 **Port Stephens** *inlet* West Falkland, Falkland Islands
67 B25 **Port Stephens Settlement** West Falkland, Falkland Islands
99 F14 **Portstewart** *Ir.* Port Stíobhaird. N Northern Ireland, UK 55.10N 6.43W
Port Stíobhaird *see* Portstewart
82 I7 **Port Sudan** Red Sea, NE Sudan 19.37N 37.13E
24 L10 **Port Sulphur** Louisiana, S USA 29.28N 89.41W
Port Swettenham *see* Klang/Pelabuhan Klang
99 J22 **Port Talbot** S Wales, UK 51.36N 3.46W
94 L11 **Porttipahdan Tekojärvi** ◎ N Finland
34 G7 **Port Townsend** Washington, NW USA 48.07N 122.45W
106 H9 **Portugal** *off.* Republic of Portugal. ◆ *republic* SW Europe
107 O2 **Portugalete** País Vasco, N Spain 43.19N 3.01W
56 J6 **Portuguesa** *off.* Estado Portuguesa. ◆ *state* N Venezuela
Portuguese East Africa *see* Mozambique
Portuguese Guinea *see* Guinea-Bissau
Portuguese Timor *see* East Timor
Portuguese West Africa *see* Angola
99 D18 **Portumna** *Ir.* Port Omna. W Ireland 53.06N 8.13W
Portus Cale *see* Porto
Portus Magnus *see* Almería
Portus Magonis *see* Mahón
105 P17 **Port-Vendres** *var.* Port Vendres. Pyrénées-Orientales, S France 42.31N 3.06E
190 H9 **Port Victoria** South Australia 34.34S 137.31E
197 C14 **Port-Vila** *var.* Vila. ● (Vanuatu) Éfaté, C Vanuatu 17.45S 168.21E
190 I9 **Port Wakefield** South Australia 34.13S 138.10E
33 N8 **Port Washington** Wisconsin, N USA 43.22N 87.54W
59 J14 **Porvenir** Pando, NW Bolivia 11.15S 68.43W
65 I24 **Porvenir** Magallanes, S Chile 53.18S 70.22W
63 D18 **Porvenir** Paysandú, W Uruguay 32.22S 57.58W
95 M19 **Porvoo** *Swe.* Borgå. Etelä-Suomi, S Finland 60.25N 25.40E
Porzecze *see* Parechcha
106 M10 **Porzuna** Castilla-La Mancha, C Spain 39.10N 4.10W
63 E14 **Posadas** Misiones, NE Argentina 27.27S 55.52W
106 L13 **Posadas** Andalucía, S Spain 37.48N 5.06W
Poschega *see* Požega
110 J11 **Poschiavino** ≈ Italy/Switzerland
110 J10 **Poschiavo** *Ger.* Puschlav. Graubünden, S Switzerland 46.19N 10.02E
114 D12 **Posedarje** Zadar, SW Croatia 44.12N 15.27E
Posen *see* Poznań
128 L14 **Poshekhon'ye** Yaroslavskaya Oblast', W Russian Federation 58.31N 39.07E
94 M13 **Posio** Lappi, NE Finland 66.06N 28.16E
Poskam *see* Zepu
Posnania *see* Poznań
175 Pp9 **Poso** Sulawesi, C Indonesia 1.22S 120.45E
175 Pp10 **Poso, Danau** ◎ Sulawesi, C Indonesia
143 R10 **Posof** Ardahan, NE Turkey 41.31N 42.44E
175 Pp9 **Poso, Sungai** ≈ Sulawesi, C Indonesia
27 R6 **Possum Kingdom Lake** ▣ Texas, SW USA
27 N6 **Post** Texas, SW USA 33.11N 101.22W
Postavy/Postawy *see* Pastavy
10 I7 **Poste-de-la-Baleine** Québec, NE Canada 55.13N 77.54W
101 M17 **Posterholt** Limburg, SE Netherlands 51.07N 6.01E
85 G22 **Postmasburg** Northern Cape, N South Africa 28.19S 23.04E
Pôsto Diuarum *see* Campo de Diauarum
61 I16 **Pôsto Jacaré** Mato Grosso, W Brazil 11.59S 53.27W
111 T12 **Postojna** *Ger.* Adelsberg, *It.* Postumia. SW Slovenia 45.48N 14.12E
Postumia *see* Postojna
31 X12 **Postville** Iowa, C USA 43.04N 91.34W
Pöstyén *see* Piešťany
115 G14 **Posušje** Federacija Bosna I Hercegovina, SE Bosnia & Herzegovina 43.28N 17.20E
175 Pp16 **Pota** Flores, C Indonesia 8.21S 120.49E
117 G23 **Potamós** Antikýthira, S Greece 35.53N 23.17E
57 S9 **Potaru River** ≈ C Guyana
85 I21 **Potchefstroom** North-West, N South Africa 26.42S 27.06E
29 R11 **Poteau** Oklahoma, C USA 35.03N 94.37W
27 R12 **Poteet** Texas, SW USA 29.02N 98.34W
117 G14 **Poteídaia** *site of ancient city* Kentrikí Makedonía, N Greece 40.12N 23.21E
Potentia *see* Potenza
109 M18 **Potenza** *anc.* Potentia. Basilicata, S Italy 40.40N 15.49E
193 A24 **Poteriteri, Lake** ◎ South Island, NZ
106 M2 **Potes** Cantabria, N Spain 43.10N 4.40W
Potgietersrus *see* Mokopane
27 S12 **Poth** Texas, SW USA 29.04N 98.04W
34 J9 **Potholes Reservoir** ▣ Washington, NW USA
143 Q9 **P'ot'i** W Georgia 42.10N 41.42E
79 X13 **Potiskum** Yobe, NE Nigeria 11.38N 11.07E
Potkozarje *see* Ivanjska
34 M9 **Potlatch** Idaho, NW USA 46.55N 116.51W
35 N9 **Pot Mountain** ▲ Idaho, NW USA 46.44N 115.24W
115 H14 **Potoci** Federacija Bosna I Hercegovina, SE Bosnia & Herzegovina 43.24N 17.52E
23 V3 **Potomac River** ≈ NE USA
29 W6 **Potosi** Missouri, C USA 37.56N 90.47W
59 L20 **Potosí** Potosí, S Bolivia 19.34S 65.51W
44 H9 **Potosí** Chinandega, NW Nicaragua 12.58N 87.30W
59 K21 **Potosí** ◆ *department* SW Bolivia
64 H7 **Potrerillos** Atacama, N Chile 26.25S 70.09W
44 H5 **Potrerillos** Cortés, NW Honduras 15.12N 87.57W
64 H8 **Potro, Cerro del** ▲ N Chile 28.22S 69.34W
102 N12 **Potsdam** Brandenburg, NE Germany 52.24N 13.04E
20 J7 **Potsdam** New York, NE USA 44.40N 74.58W
111 X5 **Pottendorf** Niederösterreich, E Austria 47.53N 16.22E
111 X5 **Pottenstein** Niederösterreich, E Austria 47.55N 16.06E
197 G4 **Pott, Île** *island* Îles Belep, W New Caledonia
20 I15 **Pottstown** Pennsylvania, NE USA 40.15N 75.39W
20 H14 **Pottsville** Pennsylvania, NE USA 40.40N 76.10W
161 L25 **Pottuvil** Eastern Province, SE Sri Lanka 6.52N 81.49E
155 U6 **Potwar Plateau** *plateau* NE Pakistan
104 J7 **Pouancé** Maine-et-Loire, W France 47.46N 1.11W
197 H5 **Pouébo** Province Nord, C New Caledonia 20.40S 164.02E
197 H6 **Pouembout** Province Nord, W New Caledonia 21.09S 164.52E
13 R6 **Poulin de Courval, Lac** ◎ Québec, SE Canada
20 L9 **Poultney** Vermont, NE USA 43.31N 73.12W
197 H5 **Poum** Province Nord, W New Caledonia 20.15S 164.03E
61 L21 **Pouso Alegre** Minas Gerais, NE Brazil 22.13S 45.55W
198 Bb8 **Poutasi** Upolu, SE Samoa 14.00S 171.43W
178 Ii12 **Poŭthĭsăt** *prev.* Pursat. Poŭthĭsăt, W Cambodia 12.31N 103.55E
178 Ii13 **Poŭthĭsăt, Stœng** *prev.* Pursat. ≈ W Cambodia
104 J9 **Pouzauges** Vendée, NW France 46.47N 0.54W
Po, Valle del *see* Po Valley
108 F8 **Po Valley** *It.* Valle del Po. *valley* N Italy
113 I19 **Považská Bystrica** *Ger.* Waagbistritz, *Hung.* Vágbeszterce. Trenčiansky Kraj, W Slovakia 49.07N 18.26E
128 J10 **Povenets** Respublika Kareliya, NW Russian Federation 62.50N 34.47E
192 Q9 **Poverty Bay** *inlet* North Island, NZ
114 K12 **Povlen** ▲ W Serbia and Montenegro (Yugoslavia)
106 G6 **Póvoa de Varzim** Porto, NW Portugal 41.22N 8.46W
131 N8 **Povorino** Voronezhskaya Oblast', W Russian Federation 51.10N 42.16E
Povungnituk *see* Puvirnituq
10 J3 **Povungnituk, Rivière de** ≈ Québec, NE Canada
12 H11 **Powassan** Ontario, S Canada 46.04N 79.21W
37 U17 **Poway** California, W USA 32.57N 117.02W
35 W14 **Powder River** Wyoming, C USA 43.01N 106.57W
35 Y10 **Powder River** ≈ Montana/Wyoming, NW USA
34 L12 **Powder River** ≈ Oregon, NW USA
35 W13 **Powder River Pass** *pass* Wyoming, C USA 44.08N 107.03W
35 U12 **Powell** Wyoming, C USA 44.45N 108.45W
67 I22 **Powell Basin** *undersea feature* NW Weddell Sea
38 M8 **Powell, Lake** ◎ Utah, W USA
39 R4 **Powell, Mount** ▲ Colorado, C USA 39.25N 106.20W
8 L17 **Powell River** British Columbia, SW Canada 49.54N 124.34W
33 N5 **Powers** Michigan, N USA 45.40N 87.29W
30 K2 **Powers Lake** North Dakota, N USA 48.33N 102.37W
23 V6 **Powhatan** Virginia, NE USA 37.32N 77.55W
33 V13 **Powhatan Point** Ohio, N USA 39.49N 80.49W
99 J20 **Powys** *cultural region* E Wales, UK
197 I6 **Poya** Province Nord, C New Caledonia 21.19S 165.07E
167 P10 **Poyang Hu** ◎ S China
126 Mm16 **Poyarkovo** Amurskaya Oblast', SE Russian Federation 49.37N 128.40E
32 L7 **Poygan, Lake** ◎ Wisconsin, N USA
111 Y2 **Poysdorf** Niederösterreich, NE Austria 48.40N 16.37E
114 N11 **Požarevac** *Ger.* Passarowitz. Serbia, NE Serbia and Montenegro (Yugoslavia) 44.37N 21.11E
43 Q13 **Poza Rica** *var.* Poza Rica de Hidalgo. Veracruz-Llave, E Mexico 20.33N 97.27W
Poza Rica de Hidalgo *see* Poza Rica
114 L13 **Požega** *Prev.* Slavonska Požega; *Ger.* Poschega, *Hung.* Pozsega. Požega-Slavonija, NE Croatia 43.19N 17.42E
114 H9 **Požega-Slavonija** *off.* Požeško-Slavonska Županija. ◆ *province* NE Croatia
129 U13 **Pozhva** Komi-Permyatskiy Avtonomnyy Okrug, NW Russian Federation 59.07N 56.04E
112 G11 **Poznań** *Ger.* Posen, Posnania. Wielkopolskie, C Poland 52.24N 16.56E
107 O13 **Pozo Alcón** Andalucía, S Spain 37.43N 2.55W
64 H3 **Pozo Almonte** Tarapacá, N Chile 20.13S 69.48W
106 L12 **Pozoblanco** Andalucía, S Spain 38.22N 4.47W
107 Q11 **Pozo Cañada** Castilla-La Mancha, C Spain 38.49N 1.45W
64 N5 **Pozo Colorado** Presidente Hayes, C Paraguay 23.25S 58.51W
65 J20 **Pozos, Punta** *headland* S Argentina 47.55S 65.46W
Pozsega *see* Požega
Pozsony *see* Bratislava
57 N5 **Pozuelos** Anzoátegui, NE Venezuela 10.10N 64.39W
109 L26 **Pozzallo** Sicilia, Italy, C Mediterranean Sea 36.43N 14.51E
109 K17 **Pozzuoli** *anc.* Puteoli. Campania, S Italy 40.49N 14.07E
79 P17 **Pra** ≈ S Ghana
Prabumulih *see* Perabumulih
113 C19 **Prachatice** *Ger.* Prachatitz. Jihočeský Kraj, S Czech Republic 49.01N 14.00E
Prachatitz *see* Prachatice
178 Hh11 **Prachin Buri** *var.* Prachinburi. Prachin Buri, C Thailand 14.05N 101.19E
Prachuab Girikhand *see* Prachuap Khiri Khan
178 H13 **Prachuap Khiri Khan** *var.* Prachuab Girikhand. Prachuap Khiri Khan, SW Thailand 11.50N 99.45E
113 H16 **Praděd** *Ger.* Altvater. ▲ NE Czech Republic 50.06N 17.14E
56 D11 **Pradera** Valle del Cauca, SW Colombia 3.24N 76.19W
105 O17 **Prades** Pyrénées-Orientales, S France 42.36N 2.22E
61 O19 **Prado** Bahia, SE Brazil 17.13S 39.15W
56 E11 **Prado** Tolima, C Colombia 3.38N 74.57W
Prado del Ganso *see* Goose Green
Prae *see* Phrae
Prag/Praga/Prague *see* Praha
29 O10 **Prague** Oklahoma, C USA 35.29N 96.40W
113 D16 **Praha** *Eng.* Prague, *Ger.* Prag, *Pol.* Praga. ● (Czech Republic) Středočeský Kraj, NW Czech Republic 50.06N 14.25E
118 J13 **Prahova** ◆ *county* SE Romania
118 J13 **Prahova** ≈ S Romania
78 E10 **Praia** ● (Cape Verde) Santiago, S Cape Verde 14.55N 23.31W
85 M21 **Praia do Bilene** Gaza, S Mozambique 25.18S 33.10E
85 M20 **Praia do Xai-Xai** Gaza, S Mozambique 25.04S 33.43E
118 J10 **Praid** *Hung.* Parajd. Harghita, C Romania 46.33N 25.06E
28 J3 **Prairie Dog Creek** ≈ Kansas/Nebraska, C USA
32 J9 **Prairie du Chien** Wisconsin, N USA 43.01N 91.07W
29 S9 **Prairie Grove** Arkansas, C USA 35.58N 94.19W
33 P10 **Prairie River** ≈ Michigan, N USA
Prairie State *see* Illinois
27 V11 **Prairie View** Texas, SW USA 30.05N 95.59W
178 Ii11 **Prakhon Chai** Buri Ram, E Thailand 14.36N 103.04E
111 R4 **Pram** ≈ N Austria
111 S4 **Prambachkirchen** Oberösterreich, N Austria 48.18N 13.50E
120 H2 **Prangli** *island* N Estonia
160 J13 **Prānhita** ≈ C India
180 I15 **Praslin** *island* Inner Islands, NE Seychelles
117 O23 **Prasonísi, Akrotírio** *headland* Ródos, Dodekánisos, Greece, Aegean Sea 35.53N 27.46E
113 I14 **Praszka** Opolskie, S Poland 51.05N 18.29E
121 M18 **Pratasy** *Rus.* Protasy. Homyel'skaya Voblasts', SE Belarus 52.48N 29.04E
178 I10 **Prathai** Nakhon Ratchasima, E Thailand 15.31N 102.42E
Prathet Thai *see* Thailand
Prathum Thani *see* Pathum Thani
65 F21 **Prat, Isla** *island* S Chile
108 G11 **Prato** Toscana, C Italy 43.52N 11.04E
105 O17 **Prats-de-Mollo-la-Preste** Pyrénées-Orientales, S France 42.25N 2.28E
28 L6 **Pratt** Kansas, C USA 37.38N 98.44W
110 E6 **Pratteln** Basel-Land, NW Switzerland 47.31N 7.42E
199 L2 **Pratt Seamount** *undersea feature* N Pacific Ocean 56.09N 142.30W
25 P5 **Prattville** Alabama, S USA 32.27N 86.27W
Praust *see* Pruszcz Gdański
116 M7 **Pravda** *prev.* Dogrular. Silistra, NE Bulgaria 43.53N 26.58E
121 B14 **Pravdinsk** *Ger.* Friedland. Kaliningradskaya Oblast', W Russian Federation 54.26N 21.01E
106 K2 **Pravia** Asturias, N Spain 43.29N 6.06W
120 L12 **Prazaroki** *Rus.* Prozoroki. Vitsyebskaya Voblasts', N Belarus 55.16N 28.11E
Prázsmár *see* Prejmer
178 J11 **Preăh Vihéar** Preăh Vihéar, N Cambodia 13.57N 104.48E
118 J12 **Predeal** *Hung.* Predeál. Brașov, C Romania 45.30N 25.31E
111 S8 **Predlitz** Steiermark, SE Austria 47.04N 13.54E
9 V15 **Preeceville** Saskatchewan, S Canada 51.58N 102.40W
Preenkuln *see* Priekule
104 K6 **Pré-en-Pail** Mayenne, NW France 48.27N 0.15W
111 T4 **Pregarten** Oberösterreich, N Austria 48.21N 14.31E
56 H7 **Pregonero** Táchira, NW Venezuela 8.01N 71.45W
120 J10 **Preiļi** *Ger.* Preli. Preiļi, SE Latvia 56.17N 26.52E
118 J12 **Prejmer** *Ger.* Tartlau, *Hung.* Prázsmár. Brașov, S Romania 45.42N 25.49E
115 J16 **Prekornica** ▲ SW Serbia and Montenegro (Yugoslavia)
Preli *see* Preiļi
Prëmet *see* Përmet
102 M12 **Premnitz** Brandenburg, NE Germany 52.33N 12.22E
27 S15 **Premont** Texas, SW USA 27.21N 98.07W
115 H14 **Prenj** ▲ S Bosnia and Herzegovina
Prenjas/Prenjasi *see* Përrenjas
24 L7 **Prentiss** Mississippi, S USA 31.36N 89.52W
Preny *see* Prienai
102 O10 **Prenzlau** Brandenburg, NE Germany 53.19N 13.52E
126 Jj12 **Preobrazhenka** Irkutskaya Oblast', C Russian Federation 60.01N 108.00E
177 Ee9 **Preparis Island** *island* SW Myanmar
Prerau *see* Přerov
113 H18 **Přerov** *Ger.* Prerau. Olomoucký Kraj, E Czech Republic 49.27N 17.27E
Preschau *see* Prešov
12 M14 **Prescott** Ontario, SE Canada 44.43N 75.33W
38 K12 **Prescott** Arizona, SW USA 34.33N 112.26W
29 T13 **Prescott** Arkansas, C USA 33.48N 93.22W
34 L10 **Prescott** Washington, NW USA 46.17N 118.21W
32 H6 **Prescott** Wisconsin, N USA 44.46N 92.45W
193 A24 **Preservation Inlet** *inlet* South Island, NZ
114 O7 **Preševo** Serbia, SE Serbia and Montenegro (Yugoslavia) 42.20N 21.38E
31 N10 **Presho** South Dakota, N USA 43.54N 100.03W
60 M13 **Presidente Dutra** Maranhão, E Brazil 5.16S 44.30W
62 I8 **Presidente Epitácio** São Paulo, S Brazil 21.45S 52.07W
64 N5 **Presidente Hayes** *off.* Departamento de Presidente Hayes. ◆ *department* C Paraguay
62 I9 **Presidente Prudente** São Paulo, S Brazil 22.09S 51.24W
Presidente Stroessner *see* Ciudad del Este
Presidente Vargas *see* Itabira
62 I8 **Presidente Venceslau** São Paulo, S Brazil 21.52S 51.51W
199 L11 **President Thiers Seamount** *undersea feature* C Pacific Ocean 24.39S 145.50W
26 J11 **Presidio** Texas, SW USA 29.33N 104.22W
Preslav *see* Veliki Preslav
113 M19 **Prešov** *var.* Preschau, *Ger.* Eperies, *Hung.* Eperjes. Prešovský Kraj, E Slovakia 49.00N 21.13E
113 M19 **Prešovský Kraj** ◆ *region* E Slovakia
115 N20 **Prespa, Lake** *Alb.* Liqen i Prespës, *Gk.* Límni Megáli Préspa, Límni Prespa, *Mac.* Prespansko Ezero, *Serb.* Prespansko Jezero. ◎ SE Europe
Prespa, Limni/Prespansko Ezero/Prespansko Jezero/Prespës, Liqen i *see* Prespa, Lake
21 S2 **Presque Isle** Maine, NE USA 46.40N 68.01W
20 B11 **Presque Isle** *headland* Pennsylvania, NE USA 42.09N 80.06W
Pressburg *see* Bratislava
79 P17 **Prestea** SW Ghana 5.22N 2.07W
113 B17 **Přeštice** *Ger.* Pschestitz. Plzeňský Kraj, W Czech Republic 49.36N 13.19E
99 K17 **Preston** NW England, UK 53.46N 2.42W
25 S6 **Preston** Georgia, SE USA 32.08N 84.35W
35 R16 **Preston** Idaho, NW USA 42.06N 111.52W
31 Z13 **Preston** Iowa, C USA 42.03N 90.24W
31 X11 **Preston** Minnesota, N USA 43.41N 92.06W
23 O6 **Prestonsburg** Kentucky, S USA 37.40N 82.46W
98 I13 **Prestwick** W Scotland, UK 55.30N 4.39W
85 J21 **Pretoria** *var.* Epitoli, Tshwane. ● (South Africa-administrative capital) Gauteng, NE South Africa 25.40S 28.11E
Pretoria-Witwatersrand-Vereeniging *see* Gauteng
Pretusha *see* Pretushë
115 M21 **Pretushë** *var.* Pretusha. Korçë, SE Albania 40.50N 20.45E
Preussisch Eylau *see* Bagrationovsk
Preussisch-Stargard *see* Starogard Gdański
Preußisch Holland *see* Pasłęk
117 C17 **Préveza** Ípeiros, W Greece 38.58N 20.43E
39 V3 **Prewitt Reservoir** ▣ Colorado, C USA
178 J13 **Prey Vêng** Prey Vêng, S Cambodia 11.30N 105.19E
150 M12 **Priaral'skiye Karakumy, Peski** *desert* SW Kazakhstan
126 L16 **Priargunsk** Chitinskaya Oblast', S Russian Federation 50.25N 119.12E
40 K14 **Pribilof Islands** *island group* Alaska, USA
115 K14 **Priboj** Serbia, W Serbia and Montenegro (Yugoslavia) 43.34N 19.33E
113 C17 **Příbram** *Ger.* Pibrans. Středočeský Kraj, W Czech Republic 49.40N 14.01E
38 M4 **Price** Utah, W USA 39.34N 110.48W
39 N5 **Price River** ≈ Utah, W USA
25 N8 **Prichard** Alabama, S USA 30.44N 88.04W
27 R8 **Priddy** Texas, SW USA 31.39N 98.30W
107 P8 **Priego** Castilla-La Mancha, C Spain 40.25N 2.19W
106 M14 **Priego de Córdoba** Andalucía, S Spain 37.27N 4.12W
120 C10 **Priekule** *Ger.* Preenkuln. Liepāja, SW Latvia 56.26N 21.36E
120 C12 **Priekulė** *Ger.* Prökuls. Klaipėda, W Lithuania 55.36N 21.16E
121 F14 **Prienai** *Pol.* Preny. Kaunas, S Lithuania 54.37N 23.56E
85 G23 **Prieska** Northern Cape, C South Africa 29.40S 22.45E
34 M7 **Priest Lake** ▣ Idaho, NW USA
34 M7 **Priest River** Idaho, NW USA 48.10N 117.02W
106 M3 **Prieta, Peña** ▲ N Spain 43.01N 4.42W
42 J10 **Prieto, Cerro** ▲ C Mexico 24.10N 105.21W
113 J19 **Prievidza** *var.* Priewitz, *Ger.* Priwitz, *Hung.* Privigye. Trenčiansky Kraj, C Slovakia 48.48N 18.37E
Priewitz *see* Prievidza
114 F10 **Prijedor** Republika Srpska, NW Bosnia & Herzegovina 45.00N 16.43E
115 K14 **Prijepolje** Serbia, W Serbia and Montenegro (Yugoslavia) 43.24N 19.39E
Prikaspiyskaya Nizmennost' *see* Caspian Depression
115 O19 **Prilep** *Turk.* Perlepe. S FYR Macedonia 41.21N 21.33E
110 B9 **Prilly** Vaud, SW Switzerland 46.32N 6.36E
Priluki *see* Pryluky
64 L10 **Primero, Río** ≈ C Argentina
31 S12 **Primghar** Iowa, C USA 43.05N 95.37W
114 B9 **Primorje-Gorski Kotar** *off.* Primorsko-Goranska Županija. ◆ *province* NW Croatia
120 A13 **Primorsk** *Ger.* Fischhausen. Kaliningradskaya Oblast', W Russian Federation 54.45N 20.00E
128 G12 **Primorsk** *Fin.* Koivisto. Leningradskaya Oblast', NW Russian Federation 60.20N 28.39E
Primorsk/Primorskoye *see* Prymors'k
127 Nn17 **Primorskiy Kray** *prev. Eng.* Maritime Territory. ◆ *territory* SE Russian Federation
116 N10 **Primorsko** *prev.* Keupriya. Burgas, E Bulgaria 42.15N 27.45E
130 K13 **Primorsko-Akhtarsk** Krasnodarskiy Kray, SW Russian Federation 46.03N 38.44E
119 U13 **Primors'kyy** Respublika Krym, S Ukraine 45.09N 35.33E
115 D14 **Primošten** Šibenik-Knin, S Croatia 43.34N 15.57E
9 R13 **Primrose Lake** ◎ Saskatchewan, C Canada
9 T14 **Prince Albert** Saskatchewan, S Canada 53.08N 105.43W
85 G25 **Prince Albert** Western Cape, SW South Africa 33.13S 22.03E
15 I1 **Prince Albert Peninsula** *peninsula* Victoria Island, Northwest Territories, NW Canada

◆ Country ● Country Capital ◇ Dependent Territory ○ Dependent Territory Capital ◆ Administrative Region ✈ International Airport ▲ Mountain ▲ Mountain Range ⚠ Volcano ≈ River ◎ Lake ▣ Reservoir

Prince Albert Sound – Putumayo, Río

15 I3 **Prince Albert Sound** *inlet* Northwest Territories, N Canada
15 Mm2 **Prince Charles Island** *island* Nunavut, NE Canada
205 W6 **Prince Charles Mountains** ▲ Antarctica
Prince-Édouard, Île-du *see* Prince Edward Island
180 M13 **Prince Edward Fracture Zone** *tectonic feature* SW Indian Ocean
11 P14 **Prince Edward Island** *Fr.* Île-du Prince-Édouard. ◆ *province* SE Canada
11 Q14 **Prince Edward Island** *Fr.* Île-du Prince-Édouard. *island* SE Canada
181 M12 **Prince Edward Islands** *island group* S South Africa
23 X4 **Prince Frederick** Maryland, NE USA *38.32N 76.33W*
8 M14 **Prince George** British Columbia, SW Canada *53.55N 122.49W*
23 W6 **Prince George** Virginia, NE USA *37.13N 77.13W*
207 O8 **Prince Gustaf Adolf Sea** *sea* Nunavut, N Canada
207 Q3 **Prince of Wales, Cape** *headland* Alaska, USA *65.39N 168.12W*
189 V1 **Prince of Wales Island** *island* Queensland, E Australia
15 Jj1 **Prince of Wales Island** *island* Queen Elizabeth Islands, Nunavut, NW Canada
41 Y14 **Prince of Wales Island** *island* Alexander Archipelago, Alaska, USA
Prince of Wales Island *see* Pinang, Pulau
15 I1 **Prince of Wales Strait** *strait* Northwest Territories, N Canada
207 O8 **Prince Patrick Island** *island* Parry Islands, Northwest Territories, NW Canada
15 Kk1 **Prince Regent Inlet** *channel* Nunavut, N Canada
8 J13 **Prince Rupert** British Columbia, SW Canada *54.18N 130.16W*
Prince's Island *see* Príncipe
23 Y5 **Princess Anne** Maryland, NE USA *38.12N 75.48W*
205 R1 **Princess Astrid Kyst** *physical region* Antarctica
189 W2 **Princess Charlotte Bay** *bay* Queensland, NE Australia
205 W7 **Princess Elizabeth Land** *physical region* Antarctica
8 J14 **Princess Royal Island** *island* British Columbia, SW Canada
47 U15 **Princes Town** Trinidad, Trinidad and Tobago *10.16N 61.22W*
9 N17 **Princeton** British Columbia, SW Canada *49.25N 120.34W*
32 L11 **Princeton** Illinois, N USA *41.22N 89.27W*
33 N16 **Princeton** Indiana, N USA *38.21N 87.33W*
31 Z14 **Princeton** Iowa, C USA *41.40N 90.21W*
22 H7 **Princeton** Kentucky, S USA *37.06N 87.52W*
31 V8 **Princeton** Minnesota, N USA *45.34N 93.34W*
29 S1 **Princeton** Missouri, C USA *40.24N 93.34W*
20 J15 **Princeton** New Jersey, NE USA *40.21N 74.39W*
23 R6 **Princeton** West Virginia, NE USA *37.22N 81.06W*
41 S12 **Prince William Sound** *inlet* Alaska, USA
69 P9 **Príncipe** *var.* Príncipe Island, *Eng.* Prince's Island. *island* N Sao Tome and Principe
Príncipe Island *see* Príncipe
34 I13 **Prineville** Oregon, NW USA *44.18N 120.50W*
30 J11 **Pringle** South Dakota, N USA *43.34N 103.34W*
27 N1 **Pringle** Texas, SW USA *35.55N 101.28W*
101 H14 **Prinsenbeek** Noord-Brabant, S Netherlands *51.36N 4.42E*
100 L6 **Prinses Margriet Kanaal** *canal* N Netherlands
205 T2 **Prinsesse Ragnhild Kyst** *physical region* Antarctica
205 U2 **Prins Harald Kyst** *physical region* Antarctica
94 N2 **Prins Karls Forland** *island* W Svalbard
45 N8 **Prinzapolka** Región Autónoma Atlántico Norte, NE Nicaragua *13.19N 83.34W*
44 L8 **Prinzapolka, Río** ≈ NE Nicaragua
125 Ff9 **Priob'ye** Khanty-Mansiyskiy Avtonomnyy Okrug, N Russian Federation *62.25N 65.36E*
106 H1 **Prior, Cabo** *headland* NW Spain *43.33N 8.21W*
31 V9 **Prior Lake** Minnesota, N USA *44.42N 93.25W*
128 H11 **Priozersk** *Fin.* Käkisalmi. Leningradskaya Oblast', NW Russian Federation *61.02N 30.07E*
121 J20 **Pripet** *Bel.* Prypyats', *Ukr.* Pryp"yat'. ≈ Belarus/Ukraine
121 J20 **Pripet Marshes** *wetland* Belarus/Ukraine
Prishtinë *see* Priština
130 J8 **Pristen'** Kurskaya Oblast', W Russian Federation *51.15N 36.47E*
115 N16 **Priština** *Alb.* Prishtinë. Serbia, S Serbia and Montenegro (Yugoslavia) *42.39N 21.09E*
102 M10 **Pritzwalk** Brandenburg, NE Germany *53.10N 12.11E*
105 R13 **Privas** Ardèche, E France *44.45N 4.34E*
109 I16 **Priverno** Lazio, C Italy *41.28N 13.10E*
Privigye *see* Prievidza
114 C12 **Privlaka** Zadar, SW Croatia *44.15N 15.07E*
128 M15 **Privolzhsk** Ivanovskaya Oblast', NW Russian Federation *57.24N 41.16E*
131 P7 **Privolzhskaya Vozvyshennost'** *var.* Volga Uplands. ▲ W Russian Federation
131 P8 **Privolzhskoye** Saratovskaya Oblast', W Russian Federation *51.08N 45.57E*
Priwitz *see* Prievidza
131 N13 **Priyutnoye** Respublika Kalmykiya, SW Russian Federation *46.08N 43.33E*
115 M17 **Prizren** *Alb.* Prizreni. Serbia, S Serbia and Montenegro (Yugoslavia) *42.13N 20.46E*
Prizreni *see* Prizren
109 I24 **Prizzi** Sicilia, Italy, C Mediterranean Sea *37.43N 13.25E*
115 P18 **Probištip** NE FYR Macedonia *42.00N 22.06E*
174 M15 **Probolinggo** Jawa, C Indonesia *7.45S 113.12E*
Probstberg *see* Wyszków
113 F14 **Prochowice** *Ger.* Parchwitz. Dolnośląskie, SW Poland *51.15N 16.22E*
31 W5 **Proctor** Minnesota, N USA *46.46N 92.13W*
27 R8 **Proctor** Texas, SW USA *31.57N 98.25W*
27 R8 **Proctor Lake** ▣ Texas, SW USA
161 I18 **Proddatūr** Andhra Pradesh, E India *14.46N 78.39E*
106 H9 **Proença-a-Nova** Castelo Branco, C Portugal *39.45N 7.55W*
97 I24 **Præstø** Storstrøm, SE Denmark *55.07N 12.03E*
101 I21 **Profondeville** Namur, SE Belgium *50.22N 4.52E*
43 W11 **Progreso** Yucatán, SE Mexico *21.14N 89.40W*
126 Mm16 **Progress** Amurskaya Oblast', SE Russian Federation *49.40N 129.30E*
131 O15 **Prokhladnyy** Kabardino-Balkarskaya Respublika, SW Russian Federation *43.48N 44.02E*
Prokletije *see* North Albanian Alps
126 H14 **Prokop'yevsk** Kemerovskaya Oblast', S Russian Federation *53.56N 86.48E*
Prökuls *see* Priekulė
115 O15 **Prokuplje** Serbia, SE Serbia and Montenegro (Yugoslavia) *43.15N 21.35E*
128 H14 **Proletariy** Novgorodskaya Oblast', W Russian Federation *58.24N 31.40E*
130 M12 **Proletarsk** Rostovskaya Oblast', SW Russian Federation *46.42N 41.48E*
130 J8 **Proletarskiy** Belgorodskaya Oblast', W Russian Federation *50.48N 35.46E*
177 Ff7 **Prome** *var.* Pyè. Pegu, C Myanmar *18.49N 95.13E*
62 J8 **Promissão** São Paulo, S Brazil *21.33S 49.51W*
62 J8 **Promissão, Represa de** ▣ S Brazil
129 V4 **Promyshlennyy** Respublika Komi, NW Russian Federation *67.36N 63.59E*
121 O16 **Pronya** *Rus.* Pronya. ≈ E Belarus
8 M11 **Prophet River** British Columbia, W Canada *58.07N 122.39W*
32 K11 **Prophetstown** Illinois, N USA *41.40N 89.56W*
61 P16 **Propriá** Sergipe, E Brazil *10.15S 36.51W*
105 X16 **Propriano** Corse, France, C Mediterranean Sea *41.41N 8.54E*
Prościejów *see* Prostějov
Proskurov *see* Khmel 'nyts'kyy
116 H12 **Prosotsáni** Anatolikí Makedonía kai Thráki, NE Greece *41.10N 23.58E*
179 Rr15 **Prosperidad** Mindanao, S Philippines *8.36N 125.54E*
34 J10 **Prosser** Washington, NW USA *46.12N 119.46W*
Prossnitz *see* Prostějov
113 G18 **Prostějov** *Ger.* Prossnitz, *Pol.* Prościejów. Olomoucký Kraj, E Czech Republic *49.28N 17.07E*
119 V8 **Prosyana** Dnipropetrovs'ka Oblast', E Ukraine *48.07N 36.22E*
113 L16 **Proszowice** Małopolskie, S Poland *50.12N 20.15E*
Protasy *see* Pratasy
180 J11 **Protea Seamount** *undersea feature* SW Indian Ocean *36.49S 18.04E*
117 D21 **Próti** *island* S Greece
116 N8 **Provadiya** Varna, E Bulgaria *43.10N 27.28E*
105 S15 **Provence** *prev.* Marseille-Marignane. ✕ (Marseille) Bouches-du-Rhône, SE France *43.25N 5.15E*
105 T14 **Provence** *cultural region* SE France
105 T14 **Provence-Alpes-Côte d'Azur** ◆ *region* SE France
22 H6 **Providence** Kentucky, S USA *37.23N 87.47W*
21 N12 **Providence** *state capital* Rhode Island, NE USA *41.50N 71.26W*
38 L1 **Providence** Utah, W USA *41.42N 111.49W*
Providence *see* Fort Providence
69 X10 **Providence Atoll** *var.* Providence. *atoll* S Seychelles
12 D12 **Providence Bay** Manitoulin Island, Ontario, S Canada *45.39N 82.16W*
25 R6 **Providence Canyon** *valley* Alabama/Georgia, S USA
24 I5 **Providence, Lake** ◎ Louisiana, S USA
37 X13 **Providence Mountains** ▲ California, W USA
46 L6 **Providenciales** *island* W Turks and Caicos Islands
127 Q4 **Provideniya** Chukotskiy Avtonomnyy Okrug, NE Russian Federation *64.22N 173.14W*
21 Q12 **Provincetown** Massachusetts, NE USA *42.01N 70.10W*
105 P5 **Provins** Seine-et-Marne, N France *48.34N 3.18E*
38 L3 **Provo** Utah, W USA *40.13N 111.39W*
9 R15 **Provost** Alberta, SW Canada *52.24N 110.16W*
114 G13 **Prozor** Federacija Bosna I Hercegovina, SW Bosnia & Herzegovina *43.46N 17.38E*
Prozoroki *see* Prazaroki
62 I11 **Prudentópolis** Paraná, S Brazil *25.12S 50.58W*
41 R5 **Prudhoe Bay** Alaska, USA *70.16N 148.18W*
41 R4 **Prudhoe Bay** *bay* Alaska, USA
113 H16 **Prudnik** *Ger.* Neustadt, Neustadt in Oberschlesien. Opolskie, S Poland *50.19N 17.34E*
121 J16 **Prudy** *Rus.* Prudy. Minskaya Voblasts', C Belarus *53.48N 26.32E*
103 D18 **Prüm** Rheinland-Pfalz, W Germany *50.15N 6.27E*
103 D18 **Prüm** ≈ W Germany
Prusa *see* Bursa
112 J7 **Pruszcz Gdański** *Ger.* Praust. Pomorskie, N Poland *54.16N 18.36E*
112 M12 **Pruszków** *Ger.* Kaltdorf. Mazowieckie, C Poland *52.09N 20.49E*
118 K8 **Prut** *Ger.* Pruth. ≈ E Europe
Pruth *see* Prut
110 L8 **Prutz** Tirol, W Austria *47.07N 10.42E*
Pružana *see* Pruzhany
121 G19 **Pruzhany** *Pol.* Prużana. Brestskaya Voblasts', SW Belarus *52.33N 24.28E*
128 I11 **Pryazha** Respublika Kareliya, NW Russian Federation *61.42N 33.39E*
119 U10 **Pryazovs'ke** Zaporiz'ka Oblast', SE Ukraine *46.43N 35.39E*
Prychornomors'ka Nyzovyna *see* Black Sea Lowland
Prydniprovs'ka Nyzovyna/Prydnyaprowskaya Nizina *see* Dnieper Lowland
205 Y7 **Prydz Bay** *bay* Antarctica
119 R4 **Pryluky** *Rus.* Priluki. Chernihivs'ka Oblast', NE Ukraine *50.34N 32.23E*
119 V10 **Prymors'k** *Rus.* Primorsk; *prev.* Primorskoye. Zaporiz'ka Oblast', SE Ukraine *46.43N 36.19E*
29 Q9 **Pryor** Oklahoma, C USA *36.18N 95.18W*
35 U11 **Pryor Creek** ≈ Montana, NW USA
Pryp"yat'/Prypyats' *see* Pripet
112 M10 **Przasnysz** Mazowieckie, C Poland *53.01N 20.53E*
113 K14 **Przedbórz** Łodzkie, S Poland *51.04N 19.51E*
113 P17 **Przemyśl** *Rus.* Peremyshl. Podkarpackie, SE Poland *49.46N 22.46E*
113 O16 **Przeworsk** Podkarpackie, SE Poland *50.04N 22.30E*
Przheval'sk *see* Karakol
112 L13 **Przysucha** Mazowieckie, SE Poland *51.22N 20.36E*
117 H18 **Psachná** *var.* Psahna, Psakhná. Évvoia, C Greece *38.34N 23.40E*
Psahna/Psakhná *see* Psachná
117 K18 **Psará** *island* E Greece
117 I16 **Psathoúra** *island* Vóreioi Sporádes, Greece, Aegean Sea
Pschestitz *see* Přeštice
Psein Lora *see* Pishin Lora
119 S5 **Psël** ≈ Russian Federation/Ukraine
117 M21 **Psérimos** *island* Dodekánisos, Greece, Aegean Sea
Pseyn Bowr *see* Pishin Lora
Pskem *see* Piskom
153 R8 **Pskemskiy Khrebet** *Uzb.* Piskom Tizmasi. ▲ Kyrgyzstan/Uzbekistan
128 F14 **Pskov** *Ger.* Pleskau, *Latv.* Pleskava. Pskovskaya Oblast', W Russian Federation *58.31N 31.15E*
120 K6 **Pskov, Lake** *Est.* Pihkva Järv, *Ger.* Pleskauer See, *Rus.* Pskovskoye Ozero. ◎ Estonia/Russian Federation
128 F15 **Pskovskaya Oblast'** ◆ *province* W Russian Federation
Pskovskoye Ozero *see* Pskov, Lake
114 G9 **Psunj** ▲ NE Croatia
113 J17 **Pszczyna** *Ger.* Pless. Śląskie, S Poland *49.58N 18.56E*
Ptačnik/Ptacsnik *see* Vtáčnik
117 D17 **Ptéri** ▲ C Greece *39.08N 21.32E*
Ptich' *see* Ptsich
117 E14 **Ptolemaïda** *prev.* Ptolemaïs. Dytikí Makedonía, N Greece *40.31N 21.40E*
Ptolemaïs *see* Ptolemaïda, Greece
Ptolemaïs *see* 'Akko, Israel
123 Gg10 **Ptolemy Seamounts** *undersea feature* C Mediterranean Sea
121 M19 **Ptsich** *Rus.* Ptich'. Homyel'skaya Voblasts', SE Belarus *52.10N 28.49E*
121 M18 **Ptsich** *Rus.* Ptich'. ≈ SE Belarus
111 X10 **Ptuj** *Ger.* Pettau; *anc.* Poetovio. NE Slovenia *46.26N 15.53E*
194 E9 **Pua** ≈ NW PNG
63 A23 **Puán** Buenos Aires, E Argentina *37.34S 62.45W*
198 B7 **Pu'apu'a** Savai'i, C Samoa *13.31S 172.09W*
198 A7 **Puava, Cape** *headland* Savai'i, NW Samoa
58 F12 **Pucallpa** Ucayali, C Peru *8.21S 74.33W*
59 J17 **Pucarani** La Paz, NW Bolivia *16.18S 68.28W*
Pučarevo *see* Novi Travnik
163 U12 **Pucheng** *var.* Nanpu. Fujian, SE China *27.54N 118.34E*
166 L6 **Pucheng** Shaanxi, C China *34.55N 109.28E*
129 N16 **Puchezh** Ivanovskaya Oblast', W Russian Federation *56.58N 41.08E*
113 I19 **Púchov** *Hung.* Puhó. Trenčiansky Kraj, W Slovakia *49.06N 18.19E*
118 J13 **Pucioasa** Dâmbovița, S Romania *45.04N 25.22E*
112 I6 **Puck** Pomorskie, N Poland *54.43N 18.24E*
32 L8 **Puckaway Lake** ◎ Wisconsin, N USA
65 G15 **Pucón** Araucanía, S Chile *39.18S 71.52W*
95 M14 **Pudasjärvi** Oulu, C Finland *65.19N 27.01E*
154 L8 **Pūdeh Tal, Shelleh-ye** ≈ SW Afghanistan
131 S1 **Pudem** Udmurtskaya Respublika, NW Russian Federation *58.18N 52.08E*
Pudewitz *see* Pobiedziska
128 K11 **Pudozh** Respublika Kareliya, NW Russian Federation *61.48N 36.30E*
99 M17 **Pudsey** N England, UK *53.48N 1.40W*
Puduchcheri *see* Pondicherry
157 H21 **Pudukkottai** Tamil Nādu, SE India *10.22N 78.46E*
176 Z10 **Pue** Papua, E Indonesia *2.42S 140.36E*
43 P14 **Puebla** *var.* Puebla de Zaragoza. Puebla, S Mexico *19.02N 98.12W*
43 P15 **Puebla** ◆ *state* S Mexico
106 L11 **Puebla de Alcocer** Extremadura, W Spain *38.58N 5.13W*
Puebla de Don Fabrique *see* Puebla de Don Fadrique
107 P13 **Puebla de Don Fadrique** *var.* Puebla de Don Fabrique. Andalucía, S Spain *37.58N 2.25W*
106 J11 **Puebla de la Calzada** Extremadura, W Spain *38.54N 6.37W*
106 J5 **Puebla de Sanabria** Castilla-León, N Spain *42.04N 6.37W*
Puebla de Trives *see* A Pobla de Trives
Puebla de Zaragoza *see* Puebla
39 T6 **Pueblo** Colorado, C USA *38.15N 104.36W*
39 N10 **Pueblo Colorado Wash** *valley* Arizona, SW USA
63 C16 **Pueblo Libertador** Corrientes, NE Argentina *30.13S 59.22W*
42 J10 **Pueblo Nuevo** Durango, C Mexico *23.24N 105.21W*
44 J8 **Pueblo Nuevo** Estelí, NW Nicaragua *13.24N 86.26W*
56 J3 **Pueblo Nuevo** Falcón, N Venezuela *11.58N 69.57W*
44 B6 **Pueblo Nuevo Tiquisate** *var.* Tiquisate. Escuintla, SW Guatemala *14.16N 91.21W*
43 Q11 **Pueblo Viejo, Laguna de** *lagoon* E Mexico
65 J14 **Puelches** La Pampa, C Argentina *38.08S 65.56W*
106 L14 **Puente-Genil** Andalucía, S Spain *37.23N 4.45W*
107 Q3 **Puente la Reina** *Bas.* Gares. Navarra, N Spain *42.40N 1.49W*
106 L12 **Puente Nuevo, Embalse de** ▣ S Spain
59 D14 **Puente Piedra** Lima, W Peru *11.49S 77.01W*
166 F14 **Pu'er** *var.* Ning'er. Yunnan, SW China *23.09N 100.57E*
47 V6 **Puerca, Punta** *headland* E Puerto Rico *18.13N 65.36W*
39 R12 **Puerco, Rio** ≈ New Mexico, SW USA
59 J17 **Puerto Acosta** La Paz, W Bolivia *15.33S 69.15W*
65 G19 **Puerto Aisén** Aisén, S Chile *45.24S 72.42W*
43 R17 **Puerto Ángel** Oaxaca, SE Mexico *15.39N 96.29W*
Puerto Argentino *see* Stanley
43 T17 **Puerto Arista** Chiapas, SE Mexico *15.55N 93.47W*
45 O16 **Puerto Armuelles** Chiriquí, SW Panama *8.16N 82.51W*
Puerto Arrecife *see* Arrecife
56 D14 **Puerto Asís** Putumayo, SW Colombia *0.27N 76.27W*
56 L9 **Puerto Ayacucho** Amazonas, SW Venezuela *5.44N 67.36W*
59 C18 **Puerto Ayora** Galapagos Islands, Ecuador, E Pacific Ocean *0.45S 90.19W*
59 C18 **Puerto Baquerizo Moreno** *var.* Baquerizo Moreno. Galapagos Islands, Ecuador, E Pacific Ocean *0.54S 89.37W*
44 G4 **Puerto Barrios** Izabal, E Guatemala *15.42N 88.34W*
Puerto Bello *see* Portobelo
56 F8 **Puerto Berrío** Antioquia, C Colombia *6.25N 74.27W*
56 F9 **Puerto Boyaca** Boyacá, C Colombia *5.58N 74.36W*
56 K4 **Puerto Cabello** Carabobo, N Venezuela *10.27N 68.02W*
45 N7 **Puerto Cabezas** *var.* Bilwi. Región Autónoma Atlántico Norte, NE Nicaragua *14.04N 83.22W*
56 L9 **Puerto Carreño** Vichada, E Colombia *6.08N 67.30W*
56 E4 **Puerto Colombia** Atlántico, N Colombia *10.58N 74.57W*
44 H4 **Puerto Cortés** Cortés, NW Honduras *15.49N 87.55W*
56 J4 **Puerto Cumarebo** Falcón, N Venezuela *11.28N 69.21W*
Puerto de Cabras *see* Puerto del Rosario
57 Q5 **Puerto de Hierro** Sucre, NE Venezuela *10.40N 62.03W*
66 O11 **Puerto de la Cruz** Tenerife, Islas Canarias, Spain, NE Atlantic Ocean *28.24N 16.33W*
66 Q11 **Puerto del Rosario** *var.* Puerto de Cabras. Fuerteventura, Islas Canarias, Spain, NE Atlantic Ocean *28.28N 13.52W*
65 J20 **Puerto Deseado** Santa Cruz, SE Argentina *47.46S 65.52W*
42 F8 **Puerto Escondido** Baja California Sur, W Mexico *25.49N 111.20W*
43 R17 **Puerto Escondido** Oaxaca, SE Mexico *15.48N 96.57W*
62 G12 **Puerto Esperanza** Misiones, NE Argentina *26.01S 54.39W*
58 D6 **Puerto Francisco de Orellana** *var.* Coca. Orellana, N Ecuador *0.27S 76.57W*
56 H10 **Puerto Gaitán** Meta, C Colombia *4.19N 72.07W*
Puerto Gallegos *see* Río Gallegos
62 G12 **Puerto Iguazú** Misiones, NE Argentina *25.39S 54.34W*
58 F12 **Puerto Inca** Huánuco, N Peru *9.21S 74.55W*
56 L11 **Puerto Inírida** *var.* Obando. Guainía, E Colombia *3.48N 67.54W*
44 K13 **Puerto Jesús** Guanacaste, NW Costa Rica *10.08N 85.26W*
43 Z11 **Puerto Juárez** Quintana Roo, SE Mexico *21.06N 86.46W*
57 N5 **Puerto La Cruz** Anzoátegui, NE Venezuela *10.13N 64.40W*
56 E14 **Puerto Leguízamo** Putumayo, S Colombia *0.07S 74.51W*
45 N5 **Puerto Lempira** Gracias a Dios, E Honduras *15.13N 83.48W*
Puerto Libertad *see* La Libertad
56 I11 **Puerto Limón** Meta, E Colombia *4.00N 71.09W*
56 D13 **Puerto Limón** Putumayo, SW Colombia *1.01N 76.30W*
Puerto Limón *see* Limón
107 N11 **Puertollano** Castilla-La Mancha, C Spain *38.40N 4.07W*
65 K17 **Puerto Lobos** Chubut, SE Argentina *42.00S 64.58W*
56 I3 **Puerto López** La Guajira, N Colombia *11.54N 71.21W*
107 Q14 **Puerto Lumbreras** Murcia, SE Spain *37.34N 1.49W*
43 V17 **Puerto Madero** Chiapas, SE Mexico *14.43N 92.25W*
65 K17 **Puerto Madryn** Chubut, S Argentina *42.45S 65.01W*
Puerto Magdalena *see* Bahía Magdalena
59 J15 **Puerto Maldonado** Madre de Dios, E Peru *12.37S 69.10W*
Puerto Masachapa *see* Masachapa
Puerto México *see* Coatzacoalcos
65 G17 **Puerto Montt** Los Lagos, C Chile *41.28S 72.57W*
43 Z12 **Puerto Morelos** Quintana Roo, SE Mexico *20.47N 86.54W*
56 L10 **Puerto Nariño** Vichada, E Colombia *4.57N 67.51W*
65 H23 **Puerto Natales** Magallanes, S Chile *51.42S 72.28W*
45 X15 **Puerto Obaldía** San Blas, NE Panama *8.37N 77.25W*
46 H6 **Puerto Padre** Las Tunas, E Cuba *21.13N 76.34W*
56 L9 **Puerto Páez** Apure, C Venezuela *6.10N 67.30W*
42 E3 **Puerto Peñasco** Sonora, NW Mexico *31.21N 113.32W*
57 N5 **Puerto Píritu** Anzoátegui, NE Venezuela *10.02N 65.02W*
47 N8 **Puerto Plata** *var.* San Felipe de Puerto Plata. N Dominican Republic *19.46N 70.42W*
47 N8 **Puerto Plata** ✕ N Dominican Republic *19.43N 70.43W*
Puerto Presidente Stroessner *see* Ciudad del Este
179 Oo14 **Puerto Princesa** *off.* Puerto Princesa City. Palawan, W Philippines *9.48N 118.43E*
Puerto Princesa City *see* Puerto Princesa
Puerto Príncipe *see* Camagüey
Puerto Quellón *see* Quellón
62 F13 **Puerto Rico** Misiones, NE Argentina *26.48S 54.59W*
59 K14 **Puerto Rico** Pando, N Bolivia *11.09S 67.28W*
56 E12 **Puerto Rico** Caquetá, S Colombia *1.53N 75.08W*
47 U5 **Puerto Rico** *off.* Commonwealth of Puerto Rico; *prev.* Porto Rico. ◇ *US commonwealth territory* C West Indies
66 F11 **Puerto Rico** *island* C West Indies
66 G11 **Puerto Rico Trench** *undersea feature* NE Caribbean Sea
56 I8 **Puerto Rondón** Arauca, E Colombia *6.16N 71.05W*
Puerto San José *see* San José
65 J21 **Puerto San Julián** *var.* San Julián. Santa Cruz, SE Argentina *49.14S 67.40W*
65 I22 **Puerto Santa Cruz** *var.* Santa Cruz. Santa Cruz, SE Argentina *50.05S 68.31W*
Puerto Sauce *see* Juan L.Lacaze
59 Q20 **Puerto Suárez** Santa Cruz, E Bolivia *18.58S 57.47W*
56 D13 **Puerto Umbría** Putumayo, SW Colombia *0.52N 76.31W*
42 J13 **Puerto Vallarta** Jalisco, SW Mexico *20.36N 105.15W*
65 G16 **Puerto Varas** Los Lagos, C Chile *41.24S 72.55W*
44 M13 **Puerto Viejo** Heredia, NE Costa Rica *10.27N 84.00W*
Puertoviejo *see* Portoviejo
59 B18 **Puerto Villamil** *var.* Villamil. Galapagos Islands, Ecuador, E Pacific Ocean *0.57S 91.00W*
56 F8 **Puerto Wilches** Santander, N Colombia *7.19N 73.55W*
65 H20 **Pueyrredón, Lago** *var.* Lago Cochrane. ◎ S Argentina
131 R7 **Pugachëv** Saratovskaya Oblast', W Russian Federation *52.06N 48.50E*
131 T3 **Pugachëvo** Udmurtskaya Respublika, NW Russian Federation *56.38N 53.03E*
34 H8 **Puget Sound** *sound* Washington, NW USA
109 O17 **Puglia** *var.* Le Puglie, *Eng.* Apulia. ◆ *region* SE Italy
109 N17 **Puglia, Canosa di** *anc.* Canusium. Puglia, SE Italy *41.13N 16.04E*
120 I6 **Puhja** *Ger.* Kawelecht. Tartumaa, SE Estonia *58.19N 26.19E*
Puhó *see* Púchov
107 V4 **Puigcerdà** Cataluña, NE Spain *42.25N 1.53E*
Puigmal *see* Puigmal d'Err
105 N17 **Puigmal d'Err** *var.* Puigmal. ▲ S France *42.24N 2.07E*
78 I16 **Pujehun** S Sierra Leone *7.22N 11.43W*
Puka *see* Pukë
193 E20 **Pukaki, Lake** ◎ South Island, NZ
40 F10 **Pukalani** Maui, Hawai'i, USA, C Pacific Ocean *20.50N 94.20W*
202 J13 **Pukapuka** *atoll* N Cook Islands
203 X9 **Pukapuka** *atoll* Îles Tuamotu, E French Polynesia
Pukari Neem *see* Purekkari Neem
203 X11 **Pukarua** *var.* Pukaruha. *atoll* Îles Tuamotu, E French Polynesia
Pukaruha *see* Pukarua
12 A7 **Pukaskwa** ≈ Ontario, S Canada
9 V12 **Pukatawagan** Manitoba, C Canada *55.46N 101.13W*
203 X16 **Pukatikei, Maunga** ▲ Easter Island, Chile, E Pacific Ocean
190 C1 **Pukatja** *var.* Ernabella. South Australia *26.18S 132.13E*
169 Y12 **Pukch'ŏng** E North Korea *40.13N 128.19E*
115 L18 **Pukë** *var.* Puka. Shkodër, N Albania *42.03N 19.53E*
192 L6 **Pukekohe** Auckland, North Island, NZ *37.12S 174.54E*
192 L7 **Pukemiro** Waikato, North Island, NZ *37.37S 175.02E*
202 D12 **Puke, Mont** ▲ Île Futuna, W Wallis and Futuna
Puket *see* Phuket
193 C20 **Puketeraki Range** ▲ South Island, NZ
192 N13 **Puketoi Range** ▲ North Island, NZ
193 F21 **Pukeuri Junction** Otago, South Island, NZ *45.01S 171.01E*
121 L16 **Pukhavichy** *Rus.* Pukhovichi. Minskaya Voblasts', C Belarus *53.30N 28.15E*
Pukhovichi *see* Pukhavichy
128 M10 **Puksoozero** Arkhangel'skaya Oblast', NW Russian Federation *62.37N 40.29E*
114 A10 **Pula** *It.* Pola; *prev.* Pulj. Istra, NW Croatia *44.53N 13.51E*
Pula *see* Nyingchi
169 U14 **Pulandian** *var.* Xinjin. Liaoning, NE China *39.25N 121.58E*
169 T14 **Pulandian Wan** *bay* NE China
179 Rr15 **Pulangi** ≈ Mindanao, S Philippines
201 O15 **Pulap Atoll** *atoll* Caroline Islands, C Micronesia
20 H9 **Pulaski** New York, NE USA *43.34N 76.06W*
22 I10 **Pulaski** Tennessee, S USA *35.11N 87.00W*
23 R7 **Pulaski** Virginia, NE USA *37.03N 80.46W*
176 Yy13 **Pulau, Sungai** ≈ Papua, E Indonesia
112 N13 **Puławy** *Ger.* Neu Amerika. Lubelskie, E Poland *51.25N 21.56E*
152 I16 **Pulhatyn** *Rus.* Polekhatum; *prev.* Pul'-I-Khatum. Ahal Welaýaty, S Turkmenistan *36.01N 61.08E*
103 E16 **Pulheim** Nordrhein-Westfalen, W Germany *51.00N 6.48E*
Pulicat *see* Pālghāt
161 J19 **Pulicat Lake** *lagoon* SE India
194 M12 **Pulie** ≈ New Britain, C PNG
Pul'-I-Khatum *see* Pulhatyn
Pul-i-Khumri *see* Pol-e Khomrī
Pul-i-Sefid *see* Pol-e Safid
Pulj *see* Pula
111 W2 **Pulkau** ≈ NE Austria
95 L15 **Pulkkila** Oulu, C Finland *64.14N 25.52E*
125 Cc6 **Pul'kovo** ✕ (Sankt-Peterburg) Leningradskaya Oblast', NW Russian Federation *60.06N 30.23E*
34 M9 **Pullman** Washington, NW USA *46.43N 117.10W*
110 B10 **Pully** Vaud, SW Switzerland *46.31N 6.40E*
42 F7 **Púlpita, Punta** *headland* W Mexico *26.30N 111.28W*
112 M10 **Pułtusk** Mazowieckie, C Poland *52.41N 21.04E*
164 H10 **Pulu** Xinjiang Uygur Zizhiqu, W China *36.10N 81.28E*
143 P13 **Pülümür** Tunceli, E Turkey *39.30N 39.54E*
201 N16 **Pulusuk** *island* Caroline Islands, C Micronesia
201 N16 **Puluwat Atoll** *atoll* Caroline Islands, C Micronesia
27 N11 **Pumpville** Texas, SW USA *29.55N 101.43W*
203 P7 **Punaauia** *var.* Hakapehi. Tahiti, W French Polynesia *17.37S 149.37W*
58 B8 **Puná, Isla** *island* SW Ecuador
193 G16 **Punakaiki** West Coast, South Island, NZ *42.07S 171.21E*
159 T11 **Punakha** C Bhutan *27.37N 89.49E*
59 L18 **Punata** Cochabamba, C Bolivia *17.33S 65.52W*
161 E14 **Pune** *prev.* Poona. Mahārāshtra, W India *18.31N 73.52E*
85 M17 **Pungoè, Rio** *var.* Púnguè, Pungwe. ≈ C Mozambique
23 X10 **Pungo River** ≈ North Carolina, SE USA
Púnguè/Pungwe *see* Pungoè, Rio
81 N19 **Punia** Maniema, E Dem. Rep. Congo *1.28S 26.25E*
64 H8 **Punilla, Sierra de la** ▲ W Argentina
167 P14 **Puning** Guangdong, S China *23.18N 116.12E*
64 G10 **Punitaqui** Coquimbo, C Chile *30.49S 71.13W*
158 H8 **Punjab** ◆ *state* NW India
155 T9 **Punjab** *prev.* West Punjab, Western Punjab. ◆ *province* E Pakistan
133 Q9 **Punjab Plains** *plain* N India
95 O17 **Punkaharju** *var.* Punkasalmi. Isä-Suomi, E Finland *61.45N 29.21E*
Punkasalmi *see* Punkaharju
59 I17 **Puno** Puno, SE Peru *15.52S 70.03W*
59 H17 **Puno** *off.* Departamento de Puno. ◆ *department* S Peru
63 B24 **Punta Alta** Buenos Aires, E Argentina *38.53S 62.00W*
65 H24 **Punta Arenas** *prev.* Magallanes. Magallanes, S Chile *53.10S 70.55W*
47 T6 **Punta, Cerro de** ▲ C Puerto Rico *18.10N 66.36W*
45 T15 **Punta Chame** Panamá, C Panama *8.39N 79.42W*
59 G17 **Punta Colorada** Arequipa, SW Peru *16.17S 72.31W*
42 F9 **Punta Coyote** Baja California Sur, W Mexico
64 G8 **Punta de Díaz** Atacama, N Chile *28.03S 70.36W*
63 G20 **Punta del Este** Maldonado, S Uruguay *34.58S 54.58W*
65 K17 **Punta Delgada** Chubut, SE Argentina *42.46S 63.40W*
57 O5 **Punta de Mata** Monagas, NE Venezuela *9.43N 63.39W*
57 O4 **Punta de Piedras** Nueva Esparta, NE Venezuela *10.54N 64.06W*
44 F4 **Punta Gorda** Toledo, SE Belize *16.07N 88.47W*
45 N11 **Punta Gorda** Región Autónoma Atlántico Sur, SE Nicaragua *11.31N 83.46W*
25 W14 **Punta Gorda** Florida, SE USA *26.55N 82.03W*
44 M11 **Punta Gorda, Río** ≈ SE Nicaragua
64 H6 **Punta Negra, Salar de** *salt lake* N Chile
42 D5 **Punta Prieta** Baja California, NW Mexico *28.55N 114.10W*
44 L13 **Puntarenas** Puntarenas, W Costa Rica *9.57N 84.49W*
44 L13 **Puntarenas** *off.* Provincia de Puntarenas. ◆ *province* W Costa Rica
56 J4 **Punto Fijo** Falcón, N Venezuela *11.42N 70.13W*
107 S4 **Puntón de Guara** ▲ N Spain *42.18N 0.13W*
20 D14 **Punxsutawney** Pennsylvania, NE USA *40.55N 78.57W*
95 M14 **Puolanka** Oulu, C Finland *64.51N 27.42E*
59 J17 **Pupuya, Nevado** ▲ W Bolivia *15.04S 69.01W*
Puqi *see* Chibi
59 F16 **Puquio** Ayacucho, S Peru *14.43S 74.06W*
126 H9 **Pur** ≈ N Russian Federation
194 I13 **Purari** ≈ S PNG
29 N11 **Purcell** Oklahoma, C USA *35.00N 97.21W*
9 O16 **Purcell Mountains** ▲ British Columbia, SW Canada
107 P14 **Purchena** Andalucía, S Spain *37.21N 2.21W*
29 S8 **Purdy** Missouri, C USA *36.49N 93.55W*
120 I2 **Purekkari Neem** *prev.* Pukari Neem. *headland* N Estonia *59.33N 24.49E*
39 U7 **Purgatoire River** ≈ Colorado, C USA
Purgstall *see* Purgstall an der Erlauf
111 V5 **Purgstall an der Erlauf** *var.* Purgstall. Niederösterreich, NE Austria *48.01N 15.08E*
160 O13 **Puri** *var.* Jagannath. Orissa, E India *19.52N 85.49E*
Puriramya *see* Buriram
111 X4 **Purkersdorf** Niederösterreich, NE Austria *48.13N 16.12E*
100 I9 **Purmerend** Noord-Holland, C Netherlands *52.30N 4.55E*
157 G16 **Pūrna** ≈ C India
Purnea *see* Pūrnia
159 R13 **Pūrnia** *prev.* Purnea. Bihār, NE India *25.46N 87.28E*
Pursat *see* Poŭthĭsăt, Poŭthĭsăt, W Cambodia
Pursat *see* Poŭthĭsăt, Stœng, W Cambodia
Purulia *see* Puruliya
156 L13 **Puruliya** *prev.* Purulia. West Bengal, NE India *23.19N 86.24E*
49 G7 **Purus, Rio** *Sp.* Río Purús. ≈ Brazil/Peru
194 G15 **Purutu Island** *island* SW PNG
95 N17 **Puruvesi** ◎ SE Finland
24 L7 **Purvis** Mississippi, S USA *31.08N 89.24W*
116 J11 **Pŭrvomay** *prev.* Borisovgrad. Plovdiv, C Bulgaria *42.06N 25.14E*
174 J14 **Purwakarta** *prev.* Poerwakarta. Jawa, C Indonesia *6.30S 107.25E*
174 L15 **Purwodadi** *prev.* Poerwodadi. Jawa, C Indonesia *7.04S 110.52E*
174 K15 **Purwokerto** *prev.* Poerwokerto. Jawa, C Indonesia *7.25S 109.13E*
174 Kk15 **Purworejo** *prev.* Poerworedjo. Jawa, C Indonesia *7.45S 110.04E*
22 H8 **Puryear** Tennessee, S USA *36.25N 88.21W*
160 H13 **Pusad** Mahārāshtra, C India *19.56N 77.40E*
169 Z16 **Pusan** *off.* Pusan-gwangyŏksi, *var.* Busan, *Jap.* Fusan. SE South Korea *35.11N 129.04E*
173 Ee4 **Pusatgajo, Pegunungan** ▲ Sumatera, NW Indonesia
Puschlav *see* Poschiavo
Pushkin *see* Tsarskoye Selo
131 Q8 **Pushkino** Saratovskaya Oblast', W Russian Federation *51.09N 47.00E*
Pushkino *see* Biläsuvar
113 M22 **Püspökladány** Hajdú-Bihar, E Hungary *47.19N 21.04E*
120 J3 **Püssi** *Ger.* Isenhof. Ida-Virumaa, NE Estonia *59.21N 27.05E*
118 I5 **Pustomyty** L'vivs'ka Oblast', W Ukraine *49.43N 23.55E*
128 F16 **Pustoshka** Pskovskaya Oblast', W Russian Federation *56.21N 29.16E*
Pusztakalán *see* Călan
178 H1 **Putao** *prev.* Fort Hertz. Kachin State, N Myanmar *27.22N 97.24E*
192 M8 **Putaruru** Waikato, North Island, NZ *38.02S 175.46E*
Puteoli *see* Pozzuoli
167 R12 **Putian** Fujian, SE China *25.28N 119.01E*
109 O17 **Putignano** Puglia, SE Italy *40.51N 17.07E*
Puting *see* De'an
Putivl' *see* Putyvl'
43 Q16 **Putla** *var.* Putla de Guerrero. Oaxaca, SE Mexico *16.54N 97.55W*
Putla de Guerrero *see* Putla
21 N12 **Putnam** Connecticut, NE USA *41.56N 71.52W*
27 Q7 **Putnam** Texas, SW USA *32.22N 99.11W*
20 M10 **Putney** Vermont, NE USA *42.59N 72.30W*
113 L20 **Putnok** Borsod-Abaúj-Zemplén, NE Hungary *48.18N 20.25E*
Putorana, Gory/Putorana Mountains *see* Putorana, Plato
126 Ii8 **Putorana, Plato** *var.* Gory Putorana, *Eng.* Putorana Mountains. ▲ N Russian Federation
174 H5 **Putrajaya** ● (Malaysia), Kuala Lumpur, Peninsular Malaysia *2.57N 101.42E*
64 H2 **Putre** Tarapacá, N Chile *18.11S 69.30W*
161 J24 **Puttalam** North Western Province, W Sri Lanka *8.01N 79.54E*
161 J24 **Puttalam Lagoon** *lagoon* W Sri Lanka
101 H17 **Putte** Antwerpen, C Belgium *51.04N 4.39E*
96 E10 **Puttegga** ▲ S Norway *62.13N 7.40E*
100 K11 **Putten** Gelderland, C Netherlands *52.15N 5.36E*
102 K7 **Puttgarden** Schleswig-Holstein, N Germany *54.30N 11.12E*
Puttiala *see* Patiāla
103 D20 **Püttlingen** Saarland, SW Germany *49.16N 6.52E*
56 D14 **Putumayo** *off.* Intendencia del Putumayo. ◆ *province* S Colombia
50 E7 **Putumayo, Río** *var.* Rio Içá. ≈ NW South America *see also* Içá, Rio

◆ Country ● Country Capital ◇ Dependent Territory ○ Dependent Territory Capital ◆ Administrative Region ✕ International Airport ▲ Mountain ▲ Mountain Range Volcano ≈ River ◎ Lake ▣ Reservoir

PUTUS, TANJUNG – QYTETI STALIN

174 K8 **Putus, Tanjung** headland Borneo, N Indonesia 0.27S 109.04E
118 J8 **Putyla** Chernivets'ka Oblast', W Ukraine 47.59N 25.04E
119 S3 **Putyvl'** Rus. Putivl'. Sums'ka Oblast', NE Ukraine 51.21N 33.52E
95 M18 **Puula** ◎ SE Finland
95 N18 **Puumala** Isä-Suomi, E Finland 61.31N 28.12E
120 I5 **Puurmani** Ger. Talkhof. Jõgevamaa, E Estonia 58.36N 26.17E
101 G17 **Puurs** Antwerpen, N Belgium 51.04N 4.16E
40 F10 **Pu'u 'Ula'ula** var. Red Hill. ▲ Maui, Hawai'i, USA, C Pacific Ocean 20.42N 94.16W
40 A8 **Pu'uwai** var. Puuwai. Ni'ihau, Hawai'i, USA, C Pacific Ocean 21.54N 96.11W
10 J4 **Puvirnituq** prev. Povungnituk. Québec, NE Canada 60.10N 77.19W
34 H8 **Puyallup** Washington, NW USA 47.11N 122.17W
167 O5 **Puyang** Henan, C China 35.42N 115.03E
167 R9 **Puyang Jiang** var. Tsien Tang. ∻ SE China
105 O11 **Puy-de-Dôme** ◆ department C France
105 N15 **Puylaurens** Tarn, S France 43.33N 2.01E
104 M13 **Puy-l'Evêque** Lot, S France 44.31N 1.10E
105 N17 **Puymorens, Col de** pass S France 42.33N 1.50E
58 C7 **Puyo** Pastaza, C Ecuador 1.30S 77.58W
193 A24 **Puysegur Point** headland South Island, NZ 46.09S 166.38E
154 J8 **Pūzak, Hāmūn-e** Pash. Hāmūn-i-Puzak. ◎ SW Afghanistan
Puzak, Hāmūn-i- see Pūzak, Hāmūn-e
83 J23 **Pwani** Eng. Coast. ◆ region E Tanzania
81 O23 **Pweto** Katanga, SE Dem. Rep. Congo 8.29S 28.57E
99 I19 **Pwllheli** NW Wales, UK 52.53N 4.22W
201 O14 **Pwok** Pohnpei, E Micronesia
126 Gg10 **Pyakupur** ∻ N Russian Federation
128 M6 **Pyalitsa** Murmanskaya Oblast', NW Russian Federation 66.16N 39.55E
128 K10 **Pyal'ma** Respublika Kareliya, NW Russian Federation 62.24N 35.56E
Pyandzh see Panj
128 I6 **Pyaozero, Ozero** ◎ NW Russian Federation
177 Ff9 **Pyapon** Irrawaddy, SW Myanmar 16.15N 95.40E
121 J15 **Pyarshai** Rus. Pershay. Minskaya Voblasts', C Belarus 54.02N 26.44E
126 I6 **Pyasina** ∻ N Russian Federation
116 I10 **Pyasŭchnik, Yazovir** ▣ C Bulgaria
125 B13 **Pyatigorsk** Stavropol'skiy Kray, SW Russian Federation 44.01N 43.06E
Pyatikhatki see P"yatykhatky
119 S7 **P"yatykhatky** Rus. Pyatikhatki. Dnipropetrovs'ka Oblast', E Ukraine 48.22N 33.43E
177 G6 **Pyawbwe** Mandalay, C Myanmar 20.39N 96.04E
131 T3 **Pychas** Udmurtskaya Respublika, NW Russian Federation 56.30N 52.33E
Pyè see Prome
177 F6 **Pyechin** Chin State, W Myanmar 20.01N 93.36E
121 G17 **Pyeski** Rus. Peski. Hrodzyenskaya Voblasts', W Belarus 53.22N 24.37E
121 L19 **Pyetrykaw** Rus. Petrikov. Homyel'skaya Voblasts', SE Belarus 52.07N 28.30E
95 M16 **Pyhäjärvi** ◎ C Finland
95 O17 **Pyhäjärvi** ◎ SE Finland
95 L15 **Pyhäjoki** Oulu, W Finland 64.28N 24.15E
95 L15 **Pyhäjoki** ∻ W Finland
95 M15 **Pyhäntä** Oulu, C Finland 64.07N 26.19E
95 M16 **Pyhäsalmi** Oulu, C Finland 63.38N 26.00E
95 O17 **Pyhäselkä** ◎ SE Finland
95 M19 **Pyhtää** Swe. Pyttis. Etelä-Suomi, S Finland 60.29N 26.40E
177 G6 **Pyinmana** Mandalay, C Myanmar 19.45N 96.12E
117 N24 **Pylés** var. Piles. Kárpathos, SE Greece 35.31N 27.08E
117 D21 **Pýlos** var. Pilos. Pelopónnisos, S Greece 36.55N 21.42E
20 B12 **Pymatuning Reservoir** ▣ Ohio/Pennsylvania, NE USA
169 X15 **P'yŏngt'aek** NW South Korea 37.00N 127.04E
169 V14 **P'yŏngyang** var. P'yŏngyang-si, Eng. Pyongyang. ● (North Korea) SW North Korea 39.04N 125.46E
P'yŏngyang-si see P'yŏngyang
37 Q4 **Pyramid Lake** ◎ Nevada, W USA
39 P15 **Pyramid Mountains** ▲ New Mexico, SW USA
39 R5 **Pyramid Peak** ▲ Colorado, C USA 39.04N 106.57W
117 D17 **Pyramíva** var. Piramiva. ▲ C Greece 39.08N 21.18E
Pyrenaei Montes see Pyrenees
88 B12 **Pyrenees** Fr. Pyrénées, Sp. Pirineos; anc. Pyrenaei Montes. ▲ SW Europe
104 J16 **Pyrénées-Atlantiques** ◆ department SW France
105 N17 **Pyrénées-Orientales** ◆ department S France
117 L19 **Pyrgí** var. Pirgi. Chíos, E Greece 38.13N 26.01E
117 D20 **Pýrgos** var. Pírgos. Dytikí Ellás, S Greece 37.40N 21.27E
Pyritz see Pyrzyce
117 E19 **Pýrros** ∻ S Greece
119 R4 **Pyryatyn** Rus. Piryatin. Poltavs'ka Oblast', NE Ukraine 50.13N 32.31E
112 D9 **Pyrzyce** Ger. Pyritz. Zachodnio-pomorskie, NW Poland 53.09N 14.52E
128 F15 **Pytalovo** Latv. Abrene; prev. Jaunlatgale. Pskovskaya Oblast', W Russian Federation 57.06N 27.55E
117 M20 **Pythagóreio** var. Pithagorio. Sámos, Dodekánisos, Greece, Aegean Sea 37.42N 26.57E
12 L11 **Pythonga, Lac** ◎ Québec, SE Canada
Pyttis see Pyhtää
177 G7 **Pyu** Pegu, C Myanmar 18.28N 96.25E
177 G8 **Pyuntaza** Pegu, SW Myanmar 17.51N 96.43E
159 N11 **Pyuthan** Mid Western, W Nepal 28.09N 82.50E
112 H12 **Pyzdry** Ger. Peisern. Wielkopolskie, C Poland 52.10N 17.42E

Q

144 H13 **Qā' al Jafr** ◎ S Jordan
207 O11 **Qaanaaq** var. Qânâq, Dan. Thule. Avannaarsua, N Greenland 77.34N 69.44W
144 G7 **Qabb Eliâs** E Lebanon 33.46N 35.49E
Qabil see Al Qābil
Qabırrı see Iori
Qābis see Gabès
Qābis, Khalīj see Gabès, Golfe de
Qabqa see Gonghe
147 S14 **Qabr Hūd** C Yemen 16.02N 49.36E
Qacentina see Constantine
154 L4 **Qādes** Bādghīs, NW Afghanistan 34.52N 63.25E
145 T11 **Qādisīyah** S Iraq 31.43N 44.28E
149 O4 **Qā'emshahr** prev. 'Alīābad, Shāhī. Māzandarān, N Iran 36.31N 52.49E
149 U7 **Qā'en** var. Qain, Qāyen. Khorāsān, E Iran 33.43N 59.07E
147 U13 **Qafa** spring/well SW Oman 17.46N 52.55E
Qafşah see Gafsa
169 Q12 **Qagan Nur** var. Xulun Hobot Qagan, Zhengxiangbai Qi. Nei Mongol Zizhiqu, N China 42.10N 114.57E
169 V9 **Qagan Nur** ◎ NE China
169 Q11 **Qagan Nur** ◎ N China
Qagan Us see Dulan
164 H13 **Qagcaka** Xizang Zizhiqu, W China 32.31N 81.52E
Qagcheng see Xiangcheng
Qahremānshahr see Kermānshāh
165 Q10 **Qaidam He** ∻ C China
162 L8 **Qaidam Pendi** basin C China
Qain see Qā'en
Qala Āhangarān see Chaghcharān
145 U3 **Qalā Diza** var. Qal 'at Dīzah. NE Iraq 36.10N 45.07E
Qal'ah Sālih see Qal'at Şāliḩ
153 R13 **Qal'aikhum** Rus. Kalaikhum. S Tajikistan 38.28N 70.49E
Qala Nau see Qal'eh-ye Now
147 V17 **Qalansīyah** Suquţrā, W Yemen 12.40N 53.30E
Qala Panja see Qal'eh-ye Panjeh
Qala Shāhar see Qal'eh Shahr
Qalāt see Kalāt
145 W9 **Qal'at Aḩmad** E Iraq 32.24N 46.46E
147 N11 **Qal'at Bīshah** 'Asīr, SW Saudi Arabia 19.59N 42.38E
144 H4 **Qal'at Burzay** Ḩamāh, W Syria 35.37N 36.16E
Qal 'at Dīzah see Qalā Diza
145 W9 **Qal'at Ḩusayh** E Iraq 32.19N 46.46E
145 V10 **Qal'at Majnūnah** S Iraq 31.39N 45.44E
145 W11 **Qal'at Şāliḩ** var. Qal'ah Sālih. E Iraq 31.30N 47.24E
145 V10 **Qal'at Sukkar** SE Iraq 31.52N 46.04E
Qalba Zhotasy see Kalbinskiy Khrebet
149 Q12 **Qal'eh Biābān** Fārs, S Iran
155 N4 **Qal'eh Shahr** Pash. Qala Shāhar. Sar-e Pol, N Afghanistan 35.34N 65.38E
154 L4 **Qal'eh-ye Now** var. Qala Nau. Bādghīs, NW Afghanistan 34.59N 63.07E
155 T2 **Qal'eh-ye Panjeh** var. Qala Panja. Badakhshān, NE Afghanistan 36.56N 72.15E
Qamar Bay see Qamar, Ghubbat al
147 U14 **Qamar, Ghubbat al** Eng. Qamar Bay. bay Oman/Yemen
147 V13 **Qamar, Jabal al** ▲ SW Oman
153 N12 **Qamashi** Qashqadaryo Viloyati, S Uzbekistan 38.52N 66.30E
Qambar see Kambar
165 R14 **Qamdo** Xizang Zizhiqu, W China 31.09N 97.09E
197 K13 **Qamea** prev. Nggamea. island Fiji
77 R7 **Qamīnis** NE Libya 31.48N 20.04E
Qamishly see Al Qāmishlī
Qânâq see Qaanaaq
Qandahār see Kandahār
82 Q11 **Qandala** Bari, NE Somalia 11.30N 50.00E
Qandyaghash see Kandyagash
144 L2 **Qanţarī** Ar Raqqah, N Syria 36.24N 39.16E
Qapiciğ Dağı see Qazangödağ
164 H5 **Qapqal** var. Qapqal Xibe Zizhixian. Xinjiang Uygur Zizhiqu, NW China 43.46N 81.09E
Qapqal Xibe Zizhixian see Qapqal
Qapshagay Böyeni see Kapchagayskoye Vodokhranilishche
Qapugtang see Zadoi
206 M15 **Qaqortoq** Dan. Julianehåb. Kitaa, S Greenland 60.51N 46.01W
77 U8 **Qāra** var. Qārah. NW Egypt 29.34N 26.28E
145 T4 **Qara Anjīr** N Iraq 35.30N 44.37E
Qarabāgh see Qarah Bāgh
Qaraböget see Karaboget
Qarabulaq see Karabulak
Qarabutaq see Karabutak
Qaraghandy/Qaraghandy Oblysy see Karaganda
Qaraghayly see Karagayly
145 U4 **Qara Gol** NE Iraq 35.21N 45.38E
Qārah see Qāra
154 J4 **Qarah Bāgh** var. Qarabāgh. Herāt, NW Afghanistan 35.06N 61.33E
144 G7 **Qaraoun, Lac de** var. Buḩayrat al Qir'awn. ◎ S Lebanon
Qaraoy see Karaoy
Qaraqoyyn see Karakoyyn, Ozero
Qara Qum see Garagum
Qarasū see Karasu
Qaratal see Karatal
Qarataū see Karatau, Khrebet, Kazakhstan
Qarataū see Karatau, Zhambyl, Kazakhstan
Qaraton see Karaton
82 P13 **Qardho** var. Kardh, It. Gardo. Bari, N Somalia 9.34N 49.30E
148 M6 **Qareh Chāy** ∻ N Iran
148 K2 **Qareh Sū** ∻ NW Iran
Qariateïne see Al Qaryatayn
Qarkilik see Ruoqiang
153 O13 **Qarluq** Rus. Karluk. Surkhondaryo Viloyati, S Uzbekistan 38.17N 67.39E
153 U12 **Qarokŭl** Rus. Karakul'. E Tajikistan 39.07N 73.33E
153 T12 **Qarokŭl** Rus. Ozero Karakul'. ◎ E Tajikistan
Qarqan see Qiemo
164 K9 **Qarqan He** ∻ NW China
Qarqannah, Juzur see Kerkenah, Îles de
Qarqaraly see Karkaralinsk
155 O1 **Qarqīn** Jowzjān, N Afghanistan 37.25N 66.03E
Qars see Kars
Qarsaqbay see Karsakpay
152 M12 **Qarshi** Rus. Karshi; prev. Bek-Budi. Qashqadaryo Viloyati, S Uzbekistan 38.54N 65.48E
152 L12 **Qarshi Cho'li** Rus. Karshinskaya Step. grassland S Uzbekistan
152 M13 **Qarshi Kanali** Rus. Karshinskiy Kanal. canal Turkmenistan/Uzbekistan
Qaryatayn see Al Qaryatayn
152 M12 **Qashqadaryo Viloyati** Rus. Kashkadar'inskaya Oblast'. ◆ province S Uzbekistan
Qasigianguit see Qasigiannguit
207 N13 **Qasigiannguit** var. Qasigianguit, Dan. Christianshåb. Kitaa, C Greenland 68.42N 50.49W
Qaşīm, Minţaqat see Al Qaşīm
145 P8 **Qaşr 'Amīj** C Iraq 33.30N 41.52E
145 M9 **Qaşr Darwīshāh** C Iraq 32.36N 43.27E
148 J6 **Qaşr-e Shīrīn** Kermānshāh, W Iran 34.33N 45.37E
77 V10 **Qaşr Farâfra** W Egypt 27.00N 27.58E
Qassim see Al Qaşīm
147 O16 **Qa'ṭabah** SW Yemen 13.51N 44.42E
144 H7 **Qaţanā** var. Katana. Dimashq, S Syria 33.27N 36.04E
149 N15 **Qatar** off. State of Qatar, Ar. Dawlat Qaţar. ◆ monarchy SW Asia
Qatrana see Al Qaţrānah
149 Q12 **Qaţrūyeh** Fārs, S Iran
Qattara Depression/Qaţţārah, Munkhafaḑ al see Qaţţâra, Monkhafad el
77 U8 **Qaţţâra, Monkhafad el** var. Munkhafaḑ al Qaţţārah, Eng. Qattara Depression. desert NW Egypt
Qaţţīnah, Buḩayrat see Ḩimş, Buḩayrat
Qaydār see Qeydār
Qāyen see Qā'en
153 Q11 **Qayroqqum** Rus. Kayrakkum. NW Tajikistan 40.16N 69.46E
153 Q10 **Qayroqqum, Obanbori** Rus. Kayrakkumskoye Vodokhranilishche. ▣ NW Tajikistan
143 V13 **Qazangödağ** Rus. Gora Kapydzhik, Turk. Qapiciğ Dağı. ▲ SW Azerbaijan 39.18N 46.00E
145 U7 **Qazānīyah** var. Dhū Shaykh. E Iraq 33.39N 45.33E
Qazaqstan/Qazaqstan Respublikasy see Kazakhstan
143 T9 **Qazbegi** Rus. Kazbegi. NE Georgia 42.39N 44.36E
155 P15 **Qāzi Ahmad** var. Kazi Ahmad. Sind, SE Pakistan 26.19N 68.06E
143 Y12 **Qazimämmäd** Rus. Kazi Magomed. SE Azerbaijan 40.03N 48.56E
Qazris see Cáceres
148 M4 **Qazvīn** var. Kazvin. Qazvīn, N Iran 36.16N 50.00E
148 M5 **Qazvīn** ◆ province N Iran
197 K12 **Qelelevu Lagoon** lagoon NE Fiji
77 X10 **Qena** var. Qinā; anc. Caene, Caenepolis. E Egypt 26.12N 32.49E
115 L23 **Qeparo** Vlorë, S Albania 40.04N 19.49E
Qeqertarssuaq see Qeqertarsuaq
207 N13 **Qeqertarsuaq** var. Qeqertarssuaq, Dan. Godhavn. Kitaa, Greenland 69.27N 52.54W
206 M13 **Qeqertarsuaq** island W Greenland
207 N13 **Qeqertarsuup Tunua** Dan. Disko Bugt. inlet W Greenland
Qerveh see Qorveh
149 S14 **Qeshm** Hormozgān, S Iran 26.58N 56.16E
149 R14 **Qeshm** var. Jazīreh-ye Qeshm, Qeshm Island. island S Iran
Qeshm Island/Qeshm, Jazīreh-ye see Qeshm
148 L4 **Qeydār** var. Qaydār. Zanjān, NW Iran 36.50N 47.40E
148 K5 **Qezel Owzan, Rūd-e** var. Ki Zil Uzen, Qi Zil Uzun. ∻ NW Iran
Qian see Guizhou
167 O2 **Qian'an** Hebei, E China 40.01N 118.43E
Qian Gorlo/ Qian Gorlos/ Qian Gorlos Mongolzu Zizhixian/Qianguozhen see Qianguo
169 V9 **Qianguo** var. Qian Gorlo, Qian Gorlos, Qian Gorlos Mongolzu Zizhixian, Qianguozhen. Jilin, NE China 45.06N 124.48E
167 N9 **Qianjiang** Hubei, C China 30.26N 112.55E
166 K10 **Qianjiang** Sichuan, C China 29.30N 108.45E
166 L14 **Qian Jiang** ∻ S China
166 G9 **Qianning** var. Gartar. Sichuan, C China 30.33N 101.22E
169 U13 **Qian Shan** ▲ NE China
166 H10 **Qianwei** var. Yujin. Sichuan, C China 29.15N 103.52E
166 J11 **Qianxi** Guizhou, S China 27.00N 106.01E
Qiaotou see Datong
Qiaowa see Muli
165 Q7 **Qiaowan** Gansu, N China 40.37N 96.43E
Qibili see Kebili
164 K9 **Qiemo** var. Qarqan. Xinjiang Uygur Zizhiqu, NW China 38.09N 85.30E
166 J10 **Qijiang** var. Gunan. Chongqing Shi, C China 29.06N 106.35E
165 N5 **Qijiaojing** Xinjiang Uygur Zizhiqu, NW China 43.28N 91.34E
Qike see Xunke
155 P9 **Qila Saifullāh** Baluchistān, SW Pakistan 30.45N 68.08E
165 S9 **Qilian** var. Babao. Qinghai, C China 38.09N 100.08E
139 Nn10 **Qilian Shan** var. Kilien Mountains. ▲ N China
207 O11 **Qimusseriarsuaq** Dan. Melville Bugt, Eng. Melville Bay. bay NW Greenland
Qinā see Qena
165 W11 **Qin'an** Gansu, C China 34.49N 105.50E
Qincheng see Nanfeng
Qing see Qinghai
169 W7 **Qing'an** Heilongjiang, NE China 46.53N 127.29E
167 R5 **Qingdao** var. Ching-Tao, Ch'ing-tao, Tsingtao, Tsintao, Ger. Tsingtau. Shandong, E China 36.30N 120.55E
169 V8 **Qinggang** Heilongjiang, NE China 46.40N 126.04E
Qinggil see Qinghe
165 P11 **Qinghai** var. Chinghai, Koko Nor, Qing, Qinghai Sheng, Tsinghai. ◆ province C China
165 S10 **Qinghai Hu** var. Ch'ing Hai, Tsing Hai, Mong. Koko Nor. ◎ C China
Qinghai Sheng see Qinghai
164 M3 **Qinghe** var. Qinggil. Xinjiang Uygur Zizhiqu, NW China 46.42N 90.19E
166 L4 **Qingjian** Shaanxi, C China 37.10N 110.09E
166 L9 **Qing Jiang** ∻ C China
Qingjiang see Huai'an
Qingkou see Ganyu
166 I12 **Qinglong** var. Liancheng. Guizhou, S China 25.49N 105.10E
167 Q2 **Qinglong** Hebei, E China 40.24N 118.57E
Qingshan see Wudalianchi
165 R12 **Qingshuihe** Qinghai, C China 33.08N 97.19E
165 X10 **Qingyang** var. Xifeng. Gansu, C China 35.46N 107.35E
Qingyang see Jinjiang
167 N14 **Qingyuan** Guangdong, S China 23.42N 113.02E
169 V11 **Qingyuan** var. Qingyuan Manzu Zizhixian. Liaoning, NE China 42.08N 124.55E
Qingyuan Manzu Zizhixian see Qingyuan
164 L13 **Qingzang Gaoyuan** var. Xizang Gaoyuan, Eng. Plateau of Tibet. plateau W China
167 Q4 **Qingzhou** prev. Yidu. Shandong, E China 36.46N 118.23E
166 J13 **Qin He** ∻ C China
167 Q2 **Qinhuangdao** Hebei, E China 39.57N 119.31E
166 K7 **Qin Ling** ▲ C China
Qin Xian see Qinxian
167 N5 **Qinxian** var. Qin Xian. Shanxi, C China 36.46N 112.42E
167 N6 **Qinyang** Henan, C China 35.04N 112.55E
166 K15 **Qinzhou** Guangxi Zhuangzu Zizhiqu, S China 22.09N 108.36E
Qiong see Hainan
166 L17 **Qionghai** prev. Jiaji. Hainan, S China 19.12N 110.26E
166 H9 **Qionglai** Sichuan, C China 30.24N 103.28E
166 H8 **Qionglai Shan** ▲ C China
Qiongxi see Hongyuan
166 L17 **Qiongzhou Haixia** var. Hainan Strait. strait S China
169 U7 **Qiqihar** var. Ch'i-ch'i-ha-erh, Tsitsihar; prev. Lungkiang. Heilongjiang, NE China 47.23N 124.00E
149 P12 **Qīr** Fārs, S Iran 28.27N 53.04E
164 H10 **Qira** Xinjiang Uygur Zizhiqu, NW China 37.04N 80.45E
Qir'awn, Buḩayrat al see Qaraoun, Lac de
144 F11 **Qiryat Gat** var. Kiryat Gat. Southern, C Israel 31.37N 34.46E
144 G8 **Qiryat Shemona** Northern, N Israel 33.13N 35.34E
Qishlaq see Garmsār
147 U14 **Qishn** SE Yemen 15.28N 51.43E
144 G9 **Qishon, Naḩal** ∻ N Israel
Qita Ghazzah see Gaza Strip
162 K5 **Qitai** Xinjiang Uygur Zizhiqu, NW China 44.00N 89.33E
169 Y8 **Qitaihe** Heilongjiang, NE China 45.45N 130.53E
147 W12 **Qitbīt, Wādī** dry watercourse S Oman
167 O5 **Qixian** var. Qi Xian, Zhaoge. Henan, C China 35.34N 114.10E
Qīzān see Jīzān
Qizil Orda see Kyzylorda
Qizil Qum/Qizilqum see Kyzyl Kum
153 V14 **Qizilrabot** Rus. Kyzylrabot. SE Tajikistan 37.28N 74.43E
152 J10 **Qizilravot** Rus. Kyzylrabat. Buxoro Viloyati, C Uzbekistan 40.35N 62.09E
Qi Zil Uzun see Qezel Owzan, Rūd-e
145 S4 **Qizil Yār** N Iraq 35.26N 44.12E
Qoghaly see Kugaly
Qogir Feng see K2
149 N6 **Qom** var. Kum, Qum. Qom, N Iran 34.43N 50.53E
149 N6 **Qom** ◆ province N Iran
Qomisheh see Shahreẕā
Qomolangma Feng see Everest, Mount
148 M7 **Qom, Rūd-e** ∻ C Iran
Qomsheh see Shahreẕā
Qomul see Hami
Qondūz see Kunduz
152 G7 **Qo'ng'irot** Rus. Kungrad. Qoraqalpog'iston Respublikasi, NW Uzbekistan 43.01N 58.49E
Qongyrat see Konyrat
Qoqek see Tacheng
153 R10 **Qo'qon** var. Khokand, Rus. Kokand. Farg'ona Viloyati, E Uzbekistan 40.34N 70.55E
Qorabowur Kirlari see Karabaur', Uval
Qoradaryo see Karadar'ya
152 G6 **Qorajar** Rus. Karadzhar. Qoraqalpog'iston Respublikasi, NW Uzbekistan 43.34N 58.35E
152 K12 **Qorako'l** Rus. Karakul'. Buxoro Viloyati, C Uzbekistan 39.27N 63.45E
152 E5 **Qoraqalpog'iston** Rus. Karakalpakya. Qoraqalpog'iston Respublikasi, NW Uzbekistan 44.45N 56.06E
152 G7 **Qoraqalpog'iston Respublikasi** Rus. Respublika Karakalpakstan. ◆ autonomous republic NW Uzbekistan
152 H7 **Qorao'zak** Rus. Karauzyak. Qoraqalpog'iston Respublikasi, NW Uzbekistan 43.07N 60.03E
Qorgazhyn see Korgalzhyn
144 H6 **Qornet es Saouda** ▲ NE Lebanon 36.06N 34.06E
152 L12 **Qorovulbozor** Rus. Karaulbazar. Buxoro Viloyati, C Uzbekistan 39.28N 64.49E
148 K5 **Qorveh** var. Qerveh, Qurveh. Kordestān, W Iran 35.13N 47.46E
153 N11 **Qo'shrabot** Rus. Kushrabat. Samarqand Viloyati, C Uzbekistan 40.15N 66.40E
Qosshaghyl see Koschagyl
Qostanay/Qostanay Oblysy see Kostanay
149 P12 **Qoţbābād** Fārs, S Iran 28.52N 53.40E
149 R13 **Qoţbābād** Hormozgān, S Iran 27.49N 56.00E
144 H6 **Qoubaïyât** var. Al Qubayyāt. N Lebanon 37.00N 34.30E
Qoussantina see Constantine
164 K16 **Qowowuyag** see Cho Oyu
153 O11 **Qo'ytosh** Rus. Koytash. Jizzax Viloyati, C Uzbekistan 40.13N 67.19E
152 G7 **Qozonketkan** Rus. Kazanketken. Qoraqalpog'iston Respublikasi, W Uzbekistan 42.59N 59.21E
152 H6 **Qozoqdaryo** Rus. Kazakdar'ya. Qoraqalpog'iston Respublikasi, NW Uzbekistan 43.26N 59.47E
21 N11 **Quabbin Reservoir** ▣ Massachusetts, NE USA
102 F12 **Quakenbrück** Niedersachsen, NW Germany 52.41N 7.57E
20 I15 **Quakertown** Pennsylvania, NE USA 40.26N 75.17W
190 M10 **Quambatook** Victoria, SE Australia 35.52S 143.28E
27 Q4 **Quanah** Texas, SW USA 34.19N 99.45W
178 Kk11 **Quang Ngai** var. Quangngai, Quang Nghia. Quang Ngai, C Vietnam 15.09N 108.49E
Quang Nghia see Quang Ngai
178 K9 **Quang Tri** Quang Tri, C Vietnam 16.42N 107.15E
Quanjiang see Suichuan
Quan Long see Ca Mau
158 L4 **Quanshuigou** China/India 35.40N 79.28E
167 R13 **Quanzhou** var. Ch'uan-chou, Tsinkiang; prev. Chin-chiang. Fujian, SE China 24.56N 118.31E
166 M12 **Quanzhou** Guangxi Zhuangzu Zizhiqu, S China 25.59N 111.01E
9 V16 **Qu'Appelle** ∻ Saskatchewan, S Canada
10 M3 **Quaqtaq** prev. Koartac. Québec, NE Canada 60.49N 69.30W
63 E16 **Quaraí** Rio Grande do Sul, S Brazil 30.24S 56.24W
61 H24 **Quaraí, Rio** Sp. Río Cuareim. ∻ Brazil/Uruguay see also Cuareim, Río
175 P10 **Quarles, Pegunungan** ▲ Sulawesi, C Indonesia
Quarnero see Kvarner
109 C20 **Quartu Sant' Elena** Sardegna, Italy, C Mediterranean Sea 39.15N 9.12E
31 X13 **Quasqueton** Iowa, C USA 42.23N 91.45W
181 X16 **Quatre Bornes** W Mauritius 20.15S 57.28E
180 I17 **Quatre Bornes** Mahé, NE Seychelles
143 X10 **Quba** Rus. Kuba. N Azerbaijan 41.22N 48.30E
Qubba see Ba'qūbah
149 T3 **Qūchān** var. Kuchan. Khorāsān, NE Iran 37.12N 58.28E
191 R10 **Queanbeyan** New South Wales, SE Australia 35.24S 149.16E
13 Q10 **Québec** var. Quebec. Québec, SE Canada 46.49N 71.15W
12 K10 **Québec** var. Quebec. ◆ province SE Canada
63 D17 **Quebracho** Paysandú, W Uruguay 31.58S 57.52W
103 K14 **Quedlinburg** Sachsen-Anhalt, C Germany 51.48N 11.09E
144 H10 **Queen Alia** ✕ ('Ammān) Al 'Āşimah, C Jordan
8 L16 **Queen Bess, Mount** ▲ British Columbia, SW Canada 51.15N 124.29W
8 I14 **Queen Charlotte** British Columbia, SW Canada 53.18N 132.04W
67 B24 **Queen Charlotte Bay** bay West Falkland, Falkland Islands
8 H14 **Queen Charlotte Islands** Fr. Îles de la Reine-Charlotte. island group British Columbia, SW Canada
8 I15 **Queen Charlotte Sound** sea area British Columbia, W Canada
8 J16 **Queen Charlotte Strait** strait British Columbia, W Canada
29 U1 **Queen City** Missouri, C USA 40.24N 92.34W
27 X5 **Queen City** Texas, SW USA 33.09N 94.09W
207 O9 **Queen Elizabeth Islands** Fr. Îles de la Reine-Élisabeth. island group Nunavut, N Canada
205 Y10 **Queen Mary Coast** physical region Antarctica
67 N24 **Queen Mary's Peak** ▲ C Tristan da Cunha
206 M8 **Queen Maud Gulf** gulf Arctic Ocean
205 P11 **Queen Maud Mountains** ▲ Antarctica
Queen's County see Laois
189 U7 **Queensland** ◆ state N Australia
199 Hh10 **Queensland Plateau** undersea feature N Coral Sea
191 O16 **Queenstown** Tasmania, SE Australia 42.06S 145.33E
193 C22 **Queenstown** Otago, South Island, NZ 45.03S 168.41E
85 I24 **Queenstown** Eastern Cape, S South Africa 31.52S 26.50E
Queenstown see Cobh
34 F8 **Queets** Washington, NW USA 47.31N 124.19W
63 D18 **Queguay Grande, Río** ∻ W Uruguay
61 O16 **Queimadas** Bahia, E Brazil 10.58S 39.37W
84 D11 **Quela** Malanje, NW Angola 9.18S 17.07E
85 O15 **Quelimane** var. Kilimane, Kilmain, Quilimane. Zambézia, NE Mozambique 17.53S 36.51E
65 G18 **Quellón** var. Puerto Quellón. Los Lagos, S Chile 43.05S 73.38W
Quelpart see Cheju-do
39 P12 **Quemado** New Mexico, SW USA 34.18N 108.29W
27 O12 **Quemado** Texas, SW USA 28.58N 100.36W
46 K7 **Quemado, Punta de** headland E Cuba 20.13N 74.07W
Quemoy see Chinmen Tao
64 K13 **Quemú Quemú** La Pampa, E Argentina 36.03S 63.30W
161 E17 **Quepem** Goa, W India 15.13N 74.03E
44 M14 **Quepos** Puntarenas, S Costa Rica 9.28N 84.10W
Que Que see Kwekwe
63 D23 **Quequén** Buenos Aires, E Argentina 38.30S 58.43W
63 D23 **Quequén Grande, Río** ∻ E Argentina
63 C23 **Quequén Salado, Río** ∻ E Argentina
Quera see Chur
43 N13 **Querétaro** Querétaro de Arteaga, C Mexico 20.36N 100.24W
42 F4 **Querobabi** Sonora, NW Mexico 30.03N 111.02W
44 M13 **Quesada** var. Ciudad Quesada, San Carlos. Alajuela, N Costa Rica 10.17N 84.24W
107 O13 **Quesada** Andalucía, S Spain 37.52N 3.05W
167 O7 **Queshan** Henan, C China 32.48N 114.03E
8 M15 **Quesnel** British Columbia, SW Canada 52.58N 122.30W
39 S9 **Questa** New Mexico, SW USA 36.41N 105.37W
104 H7 **Questembert** Morbihan, NW France 47.39N 2.24W
59 K22 **Quetena, Río** ∻ SW Bolivia
155 O10 **Quetta** Baluchistān, SW Pakistan 30.15N 67.00E
Quetzalcoalco see Coatzacoalcos
Quetzaltenango see Quezaltenango
58 B6 **Quevedo** Los Ríos, C Ecuador 1.01S 79.27W
44 B6 **Quezaltenango** var. Quetzaltenango. Quezaltenango, W Guatemala 14.48N 91.27W
44 A2 **Quezaltenango** off. Departamento de Quezaltenango, var. Quetzaltenango. ◆ department SW Guatemala
44 E6 **Quezaltepeque** Chiquimula, SE Guatemala 14.38N 89.25W
179 O15 **Quezon** Palawan, W Philippines 9.13N 118.01E
179 P10 **Quezon City** Luzon, N Philippines 14.39N 121.01E
167 P5 **Qufu** Shandong, E China 35.37N 117.05E
84 B12 **Quibala** Cuanza Sul, NW Angola 10.44S 14.58E
84 B11 **Quibaxe** var. Quibaxi. Cuanza Norte, NW Angola 8.30S 14.36E
Quibaxi see Quibaxe
56 D9 **Quibdó** Chocó, W Colombia 5.40N 76.37W
104 G7 **Quiberon** Morbihan, NW France 47.30N 3.07W
104 G7 **Quiberon, Baie de** bay NW France
56 J5 **Quíbor** Lara, N Venezuela 9.55N 69.34W
44 C4 **Quiché** off. Departamento del Quiché. ◆ department W Guatemala
101 E21 **Quiévrain** Hainaut, S Belgium 50.25N 3.40E
42 I9 **Quila** Sinaloa, C Mexico 24.24N 107.11W
85 B14 **Quilengues** Huíla, SW Angola 14.03S 14.03E
Quilimane see Quelimane
59 G15 **Quillabamba** Cusco, C Peru 12.48S 72.42W
59 L18 **Quillacollo** Cochabamba, C Bolivia 17.23S 66.15W
64 H4 **Quillagua** Antofagasta, N Chile 21.33S 69.32W
105 N17 **Quillan** Aude, S France 42.52N 2.10E
9 U15 **Quill Lakes** ◎ Saskatchewan, S Canada
64 G11 **Quillota** Valparaíso, C Chile 32.54S 71.16W
161 G23 **Quilon** var. Kolam, Kollam. Kerala, SW India 8.57N 76.36E
189 V9 **Quilpie** Queensland, C Australia 26.39S 144.15E
155 O4 **Quil-Qala** Bāmīān, N Afghanistan 35.13N 67.02E
64 L7 **Quimilí** Santiago del Estero, C Argentina 27.38S 62.25W
59 O19 **Quimome** Santa Cruz, E Bolivia 17.45S 61.15W
104 F6 **Quimper** anc. Quimper Corentin. Finistère, NW France 48.00N 4.05W
Quimper Corentin see Quimper
104 G7 **Quimperlé** Finistère, NW France 47.52N 3.33W
34 F8 **Quinault** Washington, NW USA 47.27N 123.53W
34 F8 **Quinault River** ∻ Washington, NW USA
37 P5 **Quincy** California, W USA 39.55N 120.57W
25 S8 **Quincy** Florida, SE USA 30.35N 84.34W
32 I13 **Quincy** Illinois, N USA 39.56N 91.24W
21 O11 **Quincy** Massachusetts, NE USA 42.15N 71.00W
34 J9 **Quincy** Washington, NW USA 47.13N 119.51W
56 E10 **Quindío** off. Departamento del Quindío. ◆ province C Colombia
56 E10 **Quindío, Nevado del** ▲ C Colombia 4.42N 75.25W
64 J10 **Quines** San Luis, C Argentina 32.15S 65.46W
41 N13 **Quinhagak** Alaska, USA 59.45N 161.55W
78 G13 **Quinhámel** W Guinea-Bissau 11.52N 15.52W
Qui Nhon/Quinhon see Quy Nhơn
Quinindé see Rosa Zárate
27 U6 **Quinlan** Texas, SW USA 32.54N 96.08W
63 H17 **Quinta** Rio Grande do Sul, S Brazil 32.05S 52.18W
107 O10 **Quintanar de la Orden** Castilla-La Mancha, C Spain 39.36N 3.03W
43 X13 **Quintana Roo** ◆ state SE Mexico
107 S6 **Quinto** Aragón, NE Spain 41.25N 0.31W
110 G10 **Quinto** Ticino, S Switzerland 46.32N 8.44E
29 Q11 **Quinton** Oklahoma, C USA 35.07N 95.22W
64 K12 **Quinto, Río** ∻ C Argentina
84 A10 **Quinzau** Zaire, NW Angola 6.50S 12.48E
12 H8 **Quinze, Lac des** ◎ Québec, SE Canada
85 B15 **Quipungo** Huíla, C Angola 14.49S 14.29E
64 G13 **Quirihue** Bío Bío, C Chile 36.15S 72.34W
84 D12 **Quirima** Malanje, NW Angola 10.51S 18.06E
191 T6 **Quirindi** New South Wales, SE Australia 31.29S 150.40E
57 P5 **Quiriquire** Monagas, NE Venezuela 9.58N 63.13W
12 D10 **Quirke Lake** ◎ Ontario, S Canada
63 B21 **Quiroga** Buenos Aires, E Argentina 35.18S 61.22W
106 I4 **Quiroga** Galicia, NW Spain 42.28N 7.15W
Quirom, Salar see Pocitos, Salar
58 B9 **Quiroz, Río** ∻ NW Peru
84 Q13 **Quissanga** Cabo Delgado, NE Mozambique 12.21S 40.31E
85 M20 **Quissico** Inhambane, S Mozambique 24.42S 34.43E
27 O4 **Quitaque** Texas, SW USA 34.22N 101.03W
84 Q13 **Quiterajo** Cabo Delgado, NE Mozambique 11.37S 40.22E
25 T6 **Quitman** Georgia, SE USA 30.46N 83.33W
24 M6 **Quitman** Mississippi, S USA 32.02N 88.43W
27 V6 **Quitman** Texas, SW USA 32.48N 95.27W
58 C6 **Quito** ● (Ecuador) Pichincha, N Ecuador 0.13S 78.30W
Quito see Mariscal Sucre
60 P13 **Quixadá** Ceará, E Brazil 4.57S 39.04W
85 Q15 **Quixaxe** Nampula, NE Mozambique 15.15S 40.07E
166 J9 **Qu Jiang** ∻ C China
167 R10 **Qu Jiang** ∻ SE China
167 N13 **Qujiang** var. Maba. Guangdong, S China 24.47N 113.34E
166 H12 **Qujing** Yunnan, SW China 25.39N 103.52E
Qulan see Kulan
169 T8 **Qulin Gol** prev. Chaor He. ∻ N China
152 L10 **Quljuqtov Tog'lari** Rus. Gory Kul'dzhuktau. ▲ C Uzbekistan
Qulsary see Kul'sary
Qulyndy Zhazyghy see Kulunda Steppe
Qum see Qom
Qumälisch see Lubartów
165 P11 **Qumar He** ∻ C China
165 Q12 **Qumarlêb** var. Yuegaitan. Qinghai, C China 34.06N 95.54E
Qumisheh see Shahreẕā
153 O14 **Qumqo'rg'on** Rus. Kumkurgan. Surkhondaryo Viloyati, S Uzbekistan 37.54N 67.31E
Qunaytirah/Qunayţirah, Muḩāfaẓat al/Qunaytra see Al Qunayţirah
201 V12 **Quoi** island Chuuk, C Micronesia
15 Kk6 **Quoich** ∻ Nunavut, NE Canada
85 E26 **Quoin Point** headland SW South Africa 34.48S 19.39E
190 I7 **Quorn** South Australia 32.22S 138.03E
Qurein see Al Kuwayt
153 P14 **Qŭrghonteppa** Rus. Kurgan-Tyube. SW Tajikistan 37.51N 68.42E
Qurlurtuuq see Kugluktuk
Qurveh see Qorveh
Qusair see Quseir
143 X10 **Qusar** Rus. Kusary. NE Azerbaijan 41.26N 48.27E
Quşayr see Al Quşayr
77 Y10 **Quseir** var. Al Quşayr, Qusair. E Egypt 26.05N 34.16E
148 I2 **Qūshchī** Āzarbāyjān-e Bākhtarī, N Iran 37.58N 45.04E
Qusmuryn see Kushmurun, Kostanay, Kazakhstan
Qusmuryn see Kushmurun, Ozero, Kazakhstan
Quţayfah/Qutayfe/Quteife see Al Quţayfah
Quthing see Moyeni
153 S10 **Quvasoy** Rus. Kuvasay. Farg'ona Viloyati, E Uzbekistan 40.17N 71.53E
Quwair see Guwēr
Quxar see Lhazê
Qu Xian see Quzhou
165 N16 **Qüxü** var. Xoi. Xizang Zizhiqu, W China 29.25N 90.48E
Quyang see Jingzhou, Hunan
178 Kk13 **Quy Chanh** Ninh Thuận, S Vietnam 11.28N 108.53E
178 Kk12 **Quy Nhơn** var. Quinhon, Qui Nhon. Binh Đinh, C Vietnam 13.46N 109.10E
167 R10 **Quzhou** var. Qu Xian. Zhejiang, SE China 28.55N 118.54E
Qyteti Stalin see Kuçovë

◆ Country ● Country Capital ◇ Dependent Territory ○ Dependent Territory Capital ◆ Administrative Region ✕ International Airport ▲ Mountain ▲ Mountain Range ▲ Volcano ∻ River ◎ Lake ▣ Reservoir

QYZYLORDA/QYZYLORDA OBLYSY – RAZGRAD

Qyzylorda/Qyzylorda Oblysy see Kyzylorda
Qyztū see Kishkenekol'
Qyzylzhar see Kyzylzhar

R

111 R4 **Raab** Oberösterreich, N Austria 48.19N 13.40E
111 X8 **Raab** Hung. Rába. ≈ Austria/Hungary see also Rába
Raab see Győr
111 V2 **Raabs an der Thaya** Niederösterreich, E Austria 48.51N 15.28E
95 L14 **Raahe** Swe. Brahestad. Oulu, W Finland 64.42N 24.30E
100 M10 **Raalte** Overijssel, E Netherlands 52.22N 6.16E
101 I14 **Raamsdonksveer** Noord-Brabant, S Netherlands 51.42N 4.54E
94 L12 **Raanujärvi** Lappi, NW Finland 66.39N 24.40E
98 G9 **Raasay** island NW Scotland, UK
120 H3 **Raasiku** Ger. Rasik. Harjumaa, NW Estonia 59.22N 25.12E
114 B11 **Rab** It. Arbe. Primorje-Gorski Kotar, NW Croatia 44.46N 14.46E
114 B11 **Rab** It. Arbe. island NW Croatia
175 P16 **Raba** Sumbawa, S Indonesia 8.30S 118.46E
113 G22 **Rába** Ger. Raab. ≈ Austria/Hungary see also Raab
114 A10 **Rabac** Istra, NW Croatia 45.03N 14.09E
106 I2 **Rábade** Galicia, NW Spain 42.07N 7.37W
82 F10 **Rabak** White Nile, C Sudan 13.12N 32.43E
194 M16 **Rabaraba** Milne Bay, SE PNG 10.02S 149.53E
104 K16 **Rabastens-de-Bigorre** Hautes-Pyrénées, S France 43.22N 0.10E
123 Jj17 **Rabat** W Malta 35.51N 14.25E
76 F6 **Rabat** var. al Dar al Baida. ● (Morocco) NW Morocco 34.01N 6.51W
Rabat see Victoria
195 P10 **Rabaul** New Britain, E PNG 4.13S 152.10E
Rabbah Ammon/Rabbath Ammon see 'Ammān
30 K8 **Rabbit Creek** ≈ South Dakota, N USA
12 H10 **Rabbit Lake** ◎ Ontario, S Canada
197 K13 **Rabi** prev. Rambi. island N Fiji
146 K9 **Rābigh** Makkah, W Saudi Arabia 22.51N 39.00E
44 D5 **Rabinal** Baja Verapaz, C Guatemala 15.05N 90.23W
173 Ee6 **Rabi, Pulau** island NW Indonesia, East Indies
113 L17 **Rabka** Małopolskie, S Poland 49.37N 20.00E
161 F16 **Rabkavi** Karnātaka, W India 16.40N 75.03E
Râbniţa see Rîbniţa
111 Y6 **Rabnitz** ≈ E Austria
128 J7 **Rabocheostrovsk** Respublika Kareliya, NW Russian Federation 64.58N 34.46E
25 U1 **Rabun Bald** ▲ Georgia, SE USA 34.58N 83.18W
77 S11 **Rabyānah** SE Libya 24.07N 21.58E
77 S11 **Rabyānah, Ramlat** var. Rebiana Sand Sea, Şaḩrā' Rabyānah. desert SE Libya
Rabyānah, Şaḩrā' see Rabyānah, Ramlat
118 L11 **Răcăciuni** Bacău, E Romania 46.20N 27.00E
Racaka see Riwoqê
109 J24 **Racalmuto** Sicilia, Italy, C Mediterranean Sea 37.25N 13.43E
118 J14 **Răcari** Dâmboviţa, SE Romania 44.37N 25.43E
Răcari see Durankulak
118 F13 **Răcăşdia** Hung. Rakasd. Caraş-Severin, SW Romania 44.58N 21.36E
108 B9 **Racconigi** Piemonte, NE Italy 44.45N 7.41E
33 T15 **Raccoon Creek** ≈ Ohio, N USA
11 V13 **Race, Cape** headland Newfoundland and Labrador, E Canada 46.40N 53.05W
24 K10 **Raceland** Louisiana, S USA 29.43N 90.36W
21 Q12 **Race Point** headland Massachusetts, NE USA 42.03N 70.14W
178 J15 **Rach Gia** Kiên Giang, S Vietnam 10.01N 105.04E
178 J14 **Rach Gia, Vinh** bay S Vietnam
78 J8 **Rachid** Tagant, C Mauritania 18.48N 11.40W
112 L10 **Raciąż** Mazowieckie, C Poland 52.46N 20.04E
113 I16 **Racibórz** Ger. Ratibor. Śląskie, S Poland 50.06N 18.13E
33 N9 **Racine** Wisconsin, N USA 42.42N 87.49W
12 D7 **Racine Lake** ◎ Ontario, S Canada
113 J23 **Ráckeve** Pest, C Hungary 47.07N 18.57E
Rácz-Becse see Bečej
147 O15 **Radā'** var. Ridā'. W Yemen 14.24N 44.49E
115 O15 **Radan** ▲ SE Serbia and Montenegro (Yugoslavia) 42.59N 21.31E
65 J19 **Rada Tilly** Chubut, SE Argentina 45.54S 67.33W
118 K8 **Rădăuţi** Ger. Radautz, Hung. Rádóc. Suceava, N Romania 47.49N 25.58E
118 L8 **Rădăuţi-Prut** Botoşani, NE Romania 48.14N 26.47E
Radautz see Rădăuţi
Radbusa see Radbuza
113 A17 **Radbuza** Ger. Radbusa. ≈ SE Czech Republic
22 K6 **Radcliff** Kentucky, S USA 37.50N 85.57W
145 O2 **Radd, Wādī ar** dry watercourse N Syria
97 H16 **Råde** Østfold, S Norway 59.21N 10.52E
111 V11 **Radeče** Ger. Ratschach. C Slovenia 46.01N 15.10E
Radein see Radenci
118 J4 **Radekhiv** Pol. Radziechów, Rus. Radekhov. L'vivs'ka Oblast', W Ukraine 50.17N 24.39E
Radekhov see Radekhiv
111 X9 **Radenci** Ger. Radein; prev. Radinci. NE Slovenia 46.36N 16.02E
111 S9 **Radenthein** Kärnten, S Austria 46.48N 13.42E
23 R7 **Radford** Virginia, NE USA 37.07N 80.34W
160 C9 **Rādhanpur** Gujarāt, W India 23.52N 71.49E
Radinci see Radenci
131 Q6 **Radishchevo** Ul'yanovskaya Oblast', W Russian Federation 52.49N 47.54E
10 I9 **Radisson** Québec, E Canada 53.47N 77.35W
9 P16 **Radium Hot Springs** British Columbia, SW Canada 50.39N 116.09W
118 F11 **Radna** Hung. Máriaradna. Arad, W Romania 46.04N 21.40E
116 K10 **Radnevo** Stara Zagora, C Bulgaria 42.18N 25.57E
99 J20 **Radnor** cultural region E Wales, UK
Radnót see Iernut
Rádóc see Rădăuţi
103 H24 **Radolfzell am Bodensee** Baden-Württemberg, S Germany 47.43N 8.58E
112 M13 **Radom** Mazowieckie, C Poland 51.23N 21.07E
118 I14 **Radomireşti** Olt, S Romania 44.06N 25.00E
113 K14 **Radomsko** Rus. Novoradomsk. Łodzkie, C Poland 51.04N 19.25E
119 N4 **Radomyshl'** Zhytomyrs'ka Oblast', N Ukraine 50.30N 29.16E
115 P19 **Radoviš** prev. Radovište. E FYR Macedonia 41.39N 22.26E
Radovište see Radoviš
96 B13 **Radøy** island S Norway
111 R7 **Radstadt** Salzburg, NW Austria 47.24N 13.31E
190 E8 **Radstock, Cape** headland South Australia 33.11S 134.18E
121 G15 **Radun'** Rus. Radun'. Hrodzyenskaya Voblasts', W Belarus 54.03N 25.00E
126 Gg11 **Raduzhnyy** Khanty-Mansiyskiy Avtonomnyy Okrug, C Russian Federation 62.03N 77.28E
130 M3 **Raduzhnyy** Vladimirskaya Oblast', W Russian Federation 55.59N 40.15E
120 F11 **Radviliškis** Šiauliai, N Lithuania 55.48N 23.32E
9 U17 **Radville** Saskatchewan, S Canada 49.28N 104.19W
146 K7 **Radwá, Jabal** ▲ W Saudi Arabia 24.31N 38.21E
113 P16 **Radymno** Podkarpackie, SE Poland 49.57N 22.49E
118 J5 **Radyvyliv** Rivnens'ka Oblast', NW Ukraine 50.07N 25.12E
Radziechów see Radekhiv
112 I11 **Radziejów** Kujawskio-pomorskie, C Poland 52.36N 18.33E
112 O12 **Radzyń Podlaski** Lubelskie, E Poland 51.48N 22.36E
15 Hh4 **Rae** ≈ Nunavut, NW Canada
158 M13 **Rāe Bareli** Uttar Pradesh, N India 26.13N 81.13E
Rae-Edzo see Edzo
23 T11 **Raeford** North Carolina, SE USA 34.58N 79.13W
101 M19 **Raeren** Liège, E Belgium 50.42N 6.06E
15 Kk3 **Rae Strait** strait Nunavut, N Canada
192 L11 **Raetihi** Manawatu-Wanganui, North Island, NZ 39.28S 175.16E
203 U13 **Raevavae** var. Raivavae. island Îles Australes, SW French Polynesia
Rafa see Rafah
64 M10 **Rafaela** Santa Fe, E Argentina 31.16S 61.25W
144 E11 **Rafah** var. Rafa, Rafaḩ, Heb. Rafiaḩ, Raphiah. SW Gaza Strip 31.17N 34.18E
81 L15 **Rafaï** Mbomou, SE Central African Republic 5.01N 23.51E
147 O4 **Rafḩah** Al Ḩudūd ash Shamālīyah, N Saudi Arabia 29.40N 43.28E
Rafiaḩ see Rafah
149 R10 **Rafsanjān** Kermān, C Iran 30.25N 56.00E
82 B13 **Raga** Western Bahr el Ghazal, SW Sudan 8.28N 25.40E
21 S8 **Ragged Island** island Maine, NE USA
46 I5 **Ragged Island Range** island group S Bahamas
192 L7 **Raglan** Waikato, North Island, NZ 37.49S 174.52E
24 G8 **Ragley** Louisiana, S USA 30.31N 93.13W
Ragnit see Neman
109 K25 **Ragusa** Sicilia, Italy, C Mediterranean Sea 36.55N 14.42E
Ragusa see Dubrovnik
Ragusavecchia see Cavtat
175 Qq12 **Raha** Pulau Muna, C Indonesia 4.49S 122.43E
121 N17 **Rahachow** Rus. Rogachëv. Homyel'skaya Voblasts', SE Belarus 53.03N 30.04E
69 U6 **Rahad** var. Nahr ar Rahad. ≈ W Sudan
Rahad, Nahr ar see Rahad
Rahaeng see Tak
144 F11 **Rahat** Southern, C Israel 31.20N 34.43E
146 L8 **Rahaţ, Ḩarrat** lavaflow W Saudi Arabia
155 S12 **Rahīmyār Khān** Punjab, SE Pakistan 28.27N 70.21E
97 I14 **Råholt** Akershus, S Norway 60.16N 11.10E
Rahovec see Orahovac
203 S10 **Raiatea** island Îles Sous le Vent, W French Polynesia
161 H16 **Rāichūr** Karnātaka, C India 16.15N 77.19E
Raidestos see Tekirdağ
159 S13 **Rāiganj** West Bengal, NE India 25.37N 88.10E
160 M11 **Raigarh** Chhattīsgarh, C India 21.55N 83.24E
175 Q18 **Raijua, Selat** strait Nusa Tenggara, S Indonesia
191 O16 **Railton** Tasmania, SE Australia 41.24S 146.28E
38 L8 **Rainbow Bridge** natural arch Utah, W USA
25 Q3 **Rainbow City** Alabama, S USA 33.57N 86.02W
9 N11 **Rainbow Lake** Alberta, W Canada 58.30N 119.24W
23 R5 **Rainelle** West Virginia, NE USA 37.57N 80.46W
34 G10 **Rainier** Oregon, NW USA 46.05N 122.55W
34 H9 **Rainier, Mount** ⛰ Washington, NW USA 46.51N 121.45W
25 Q2 **Rainsville** Alabama, S USA 34.29N 85.51W
10 B11 **Rainy Lake** ◎ Canada/USA
10 A11 **Rainy River** Ontario, C Canada 48.43N 94.33W
Raippaluoto see Replot
160 K12 **Raipur** Chhattīsgarh, C India 21.16N 81.42E
160 H10 **Raisen** Madhya Pradesh, C India 23.21N 77.49E
13 N13 **Raisin** ≈ Ontario, SE Canada
33 R11 **Raisin, River** ≈ Michigan, N USA
Raivavae see Raevavae
155 W9 **Rāiwind** Punjab, E Pakistan 31.13N 74.10E
176 U9 **Raja Ampat, Kepulauan** island group E Indonesia
161 L16 **Rājahmundry** Andhra Pradesh, E India 17.05N 81.42E
161 I18 **Rājampet** Andhra Pradesh, E India 14.09N 79.10E
Rajang see Rajang, Batang
174 Mm6 **Rajang, Batang** var. Rajang. ≈ East Malaysia
155 S11 **Rājanpur** Punjab, E Pakistan 29.07N 70.19E
161 H23 **Rājapālaiyam** Tamil Nādu, SE India 9.25N 77.36E
158 E12 **Rājasthān** ◐ state NW India
159 T15 **Rajbari** Dhaka, C Bangladesh 23.46N 89.39E
159 R12 **Rajbiraj** Eastern, E Nepal 26.34N 86.52E
160 G9 **Rājgarh** Madhya Pradesh, C India 24.01N 76.42E
158 H10 **Rājgarh** Rājasthān, NW India 28.37N 75.25E
159 P14 **Rājgīr** Bihār, N India 25.01N 85.25E
112 O8 **Rajgród** Podlaskie, NE Poland 53.43N 22.40E
160 L12 **Rājim** Chhattīsgarh, C India 20.57N 81.58E
114 C11 **Rajinac, Mali** ▲ W Croatia 44.47N 15.04E
160 B10 **Rājkot** Gujarāt, W India 22.18N 70.46E
159 R14 **Rājmahal** Jhārkhand, NE India 25.03N 87.49E
159 Q14 **Rājmahāl Hills** hill range N India
160 K12 **Rāj Nāndgaon** Chhattīsgarh, C India 21.06N 81.01E
158 I8 **Rājpura** Punjab, NW India 30.30N 76.36E
159 S14 **Rajshahi** prev. Rampur Boalia. Rajshahi, W Bangladesh 24.24N 88.40E
159 S13 **Rajshahi** ◐ division NW Bangladesh
202 K13 **Rakahanga** atoll N Cook Islands
193 H19 **Rakaia** Canterbury, South Island, NZ 43.45S 172.02E
193 G19 **Rakaia** ≈ South Island, NZ
158 H3 **Rakaposhi** ▲ N India 36.06N 74.31E
Rakasd see Răcăşdia
174 Ii14 **Rakata, Pulau** var. Pulau Krakatau. island S Indonesia
147 U10 **Rakbah, Qalamat ar** well SE Saudi Arabia 20.37N 52.45E
Rakhine State see Arakan State
118 I8 **Rakhiv** Zakarpats'ka Oblast', W Ukraine 48.05N 24.15E
147 V13 **Rakhyūt** SW Oman 16.41N 53.09E
197 I14 **Rakiraki** Viti Levu, W Fiji 17.21S 178.11E
Rakka see Ar Raqqah
120 I4 **Rakke** Lääne-Virumaa, NE Estonia 58.58N 26.14E
97 I16 **Rakkestad** Østfold, S Norway 59.25N 11.19E
112 F12 **Rakoniewice** Ger. Rakwitz. Wielkolpolskie, C Poland 52.09N 16.10E
Rakonitz see Rakovník
85 H18 **Rakops** Central, C Botswana 21.01S 24.23E
113 C16 **Rakovník** Ger. Rakonitz. Středočeský Kraj, W Czech Republic 50.07N 13.43E
116 J10 **Rakovski** Plovdiv, C Bulgaria 42.16N 24.58E
Rakutō-kō see Naktong-gang
120 I3 **Rakvere** Ger. Wesenberg. Lääne-Virumaa, N Estonia 59.21N 26.19E
Rakwitz see Rakoniewice
24 L6 **Raleigh** Mississippi, S USA 32.01N 89.30W
23 U9 **Raleigh** state capital North Carolina, SE USA 35.46N 78.38W
23 Y11 **Raleigh Bay** bay North Carolina, SE USA
23 U9 **Raleigh-Durham** ✕ North Carolina, SE USA 35.54N 78.45W
201 S6 **Ralik Chain** island group Ralik Chain, W Marshall Islands
27 N5 **Ralls** Texas, SW USA 33.40N 101.23W
20 G13 **Ralston** Pennsylvania, NE USA 41.29N 76.57W
147 O16 **Ramādah** W Yemen 13.35N 43.50E
Ramadi see Ar Ramādī
107 N2 **Ramales de la Victoria** Cantabria, N Spain 43.15N 3.28W
144 F10 **Ramallah** C West Bank 31.53N 34.49E
63 C19 **Ramallo** Buenos Aires, E Argentina 33.30S 60.01W
161 H20 **Rāmanagaram** Karnātaka, E India 12.45N 77.16E
161 I23 **Rāmanāthapuram** Tamil Nādu, SE India 9.22N 78.52E
160 N12 **Rāmapur** Orissa, E India 21.48N 84.00E
161 I14 **Rāmāreddi** var. Kāmāreddi, Kamareddy. Andhra Pradesh, C India 18.19N 78.23E
144 F10 **Ramat Gan** Tel Aviv, W Israel 32.04N 34.48E
105 T6 **Rambervillers** Vosges, NE France 48.15N 6.50E
Rambi see Rabi
105 N5 **Rambouillet** Yvelines, N France 48.39N 1.49E
194 L8 **Rambutyo Island** island N PNG
159 Q12 **Ramechhap** Central, C Nepal 27.19N 86.04E
191 R12 **Rame Head** headland Victoria, SE Australia 37.48S 149.30E
130 L4 **Ramenskoye** Moskovskaya Oblast', W Russian Federation 55.31N 38.24E
128 J15 **Rameshki** Tverskaya Oblast', W Russian Federation 57.21N 36.05E
159 P14 **Rāmgarh** Jhārkhand, N India 23.37N 85.31E
158 D11 **Rāmgarh** Rājasthān, NW India 27.26N 70.35E
148 M9 **Rāmhormoz** var. Ram Hormuz, Ramuz. Khūzestān, SW Iran 31.17N 49.37E
Ram Hormuz see Rāmhormoz
Ram, Jebel see Ramm, Jabal
144 F10 **Ramla** var. Ramle, Ramleh, Ar. Er Ramle. Central, C Israel 31.55N 34.52E
Ramle/Ramleh see Ramla
144 F14 **Ramm, Jabal** var. Jebel Ram. ▲ SW Jordan 29.34N 35.24E
158 K10 **Rāmnagar** Uttaranchal, N India 29.22N 79.07E
97 N15 **Ramnäs** Västmanland, C Sweden 59.46N 16.16E
Râmnicul-Sărat see Râmnicu Sărat
118 L12 **Râmnicu Sărat** prev. Râmnicul-Sărat, Rîmnicu-Sărat. Buzău, E Romania 45.24N 27.06E
118 I13 **Râmnicu Vâlcea** prev. Rîmnicu Vîlcea. Vâlcea, C Romania 45.04N 24.32E
Ramokgwebana see Ramokgwebane
85 J18 **Ramokgwebane** var. Ramokgwebana. Central, NE Botswana 20.36S 27.39E
130 L7 **Ramon'** Voronezhskaya Oblast', W Russian Federation 51.51N 39.18E
37 V17 **Ramona** California, W USA 33.02N 116.52W
58 A10 **Ramón, Laguna** ◎ NW Peru
12 G7 **Ramore** Ontario, S Canada 48.26N 80.19W
42 M11 **Ramos** San Luis Potosí, C Mexico 22.48N 101.55W
43 N8 **Ramos Arizpe** Coahuila de Zaragoza, NE Mexico 25.34N 100.58W
42 J9 **Ramos, Río de** ≈ C Mexico
85 I21 **Ramotswa** South East, S Botswana 24.51S 25.51E
41 R8 **Rampart** Alaska, USA 65.30N 150.10W
14 G5 **Ramparts** ≈ Northwest Territories, NW Canada
158 K10 **Rāmpur** Uttar Pradesh, N India 28.48N 79.03E
160 F9 **Rāmpura** Madhya Pradesh, C India 24.34N 75.25E
Rampur Boalia see Rajshahi
177 F6 **Ramree Island** island Myanmar
147 W6 **Rams** var. Ar Rams. Ra's al Khaymah, NE UAE 25.52N 56.01E
149 N4 **Rāmsar** prev. Sakhtsar. Māzandarān, N Iran 36.55N 50.39E
95 H16 **Ramsele** Västernorrland, N Sweden 63.33N 16.35E
23 T9 **Ramseur** North Carolina, SE USA 35.43N 79.39W
99 I16 **Ramsey** NE Isle of Man 54.19N 4.24W
99 I16 **Ramsey Bay** bay NE Isle of Man
12 E9 **Ramsey Lake** ◎ Ontario, S Canada
99 Q22 **Ramsgate** SE England, UK 51.19N 1.25E
96 M10 **Ramsjö** Gävleborg, C Sweden 62.10N 15.40E
160 I12 **Rāmtek** Mahārāshtra, C India 21.28N 79.28E
Ramtha see Ar Ramthā
194 H11 **Ramu** ≈ N PNG
Ramuz see Rāmhormoz
120 G12 **Ramygala** Panevėžys, C Lithuania 55.30N 24.18E
158 H14 **Rāna Pratāp Sāgar** ◎ N India
175 O2 **Ranau** Sabah, East Malaysia 5.55N 116.43E
174 I12 **Ranau, Danau** ◎ Sumatera, W Indonesia
64 H12 **Rancagua** Libertador, C Chile 34.10S 70.45W
101 G22 **Rance** Hainaut, S Belgium 50.09N 4.16E
104 H6 **Rance** ≈ NW France
62 J9 **Rancharia** São Paulo, S Brazil 22.13S 50.53W
159 P15 **Rānchi** Jhārkhand, N India 23.22N 85.19E
63 D21 **Ranchos** Buenos Aires, E Argentina 35.31S 58.22W
39 S9 **Ranchos De Taos** New Mexico, SW USA 36.21N 105.36W
65 G16 **Ranco, Lago** ◎ C Chile
97 C16 **Randaberg** Rogaland, S Norway 59.00N 5.38E
31 U7 **Randall** Minnesota, N USA 46.05N 94.30W
109 L23 **Randazzo** Sicilia, Italy, C Mediterranean Sea 37.52N 14.57E
97 G21 **Randers** Århus, C Denmark 56.28N 10.03E
94 I12 **Randijaure** ◎ N Sweden
23 T9 **Randleman** North Carolina, SE USA 35.49N 79.48W
21 O11 **Randolph** Massachusetts, NE USA 42.09N 71.02W
31 Q13 **Randolph** Nebraska, C USA 42.25N 97.05W
38 M1 **Randolph** Utah, W USA 41.40N 111.10W
102 P9 **Randow** ≈ NE Germany
97 H14 **Randsfjorden** ◎ S Norway
94 K13 **Råneå** Norrbotten, N Sweden 65.52N 22.17E
94 G12 **Ranelva** ≈ C Norway
95 F15 **Ranemsletta** Nord-Trøndelag, C Norway 64.36N 11.55E
78 H10 **Ranérou** C Senegal 15.17N 14.00W
Ráneš see Ringvassøya
193 E22 **Ranfurly** Otago, South Island, NZ 45.07S 170.06E
178 Hh17 **Rangae** Narathiwat, SW Thailand 6.19N 101.45E
159 V16 **Rangamati** Chittagong, SE Bangladesh 22.40N 92.10E
192 I2 **Rangaunu Bay** bay North Island, NZ
21 P6 **Rangeley** Maine, NE USA 44.58N 70.37W
39 O4 **Rangely** Colorado, C USA 40.05N 108.48W
27 R7 **Ranger** Texas, SW USA 32.28N 98.40W
12 C9 **Ranger Lake** Ontario, S Canada 46.51N 83.34W
12 C9 **Ranger Lake** ◎ Ontario, S Canada
159 V12 **Rangia** Assam, NE India 26.27N 91.34E
193 I18 **Rangiora** Canterbury, South Island, NZ 43.19S 172.33E
203 T9 **Rangiroa** atoll Îles Tuamotu, W French Polynesia
192 N9 **Rangitaiki** ≈ North Island, NZ
193 F19 **Rangitata** ≈ South Island, NZ
192 M12 **Rangitikei** ≈ North Island, NZ
192 L6 **Rangitoto Island** island N NZ
Rangkasbitoeng see Rangkasbitung
174 Ii14 **Rangkasbitung** prev. Rangkasbitoeng. Jawa, SW Indonesia 6.21S 106.12E
178 Hh9 **Rang, Khao** ▲ C Thailand 16.13N 99.03E
153 V13 **Rangkŭl** Rus. Rangkul'. SE Tajikistan 38.30N 74.24E
Rangkul' see Rangkŭl
Rangoon see Yangon
159 T13 **Rangpur** Rajshahi, N Bangladesh 25.46N 89.20E
174 Hh7 **Rangsang, Pulau** island W Indonesia
161 F18 **Rānibennur** Karnātaka, W India 14.36N 75.39E
159 R15 **Rāniganj** West Bengal, NE India 23.34N 87.13E
155 Q13 **Rānīpur** Sind, SE Pakistan 27.16N 68.34E
Rāniyah see Ŗānya
27 N9 **Rankin** Texas, SW USA 31.12N 101.56W
15 L7 **Rankin Inlet** Nunavut, C Canada 62.52N 92.13W
191 P8 **Rankins Springs** New South Wales, SE Australia 33.51S 146.16E
Rankovićevo see Kraljevo
110 I7 **Rankweil** Vorarlberg, W Austria 47.16N 9.40E
Rann see Brežice
131 T8 **Ranneye** Orenburgskaya Oblast', W Russian Federation 51.28N 52.29E
98 I10 **Rannoch, Loch** ◎ C Scotland, UK
203 U17 **Rano Kau** var. Rano Kao. crater Easter Island, Chile, E Pacific Ocean 27.10S 109.25W
178 Gg14 **Ranong** Ranong, SW Thailand 9.58N 98.40E
195 T14 **Ranongga** var. Ghanongga. island NW Solomon Islands
203 W16 **Rano Raraku** ancient monument Easter Island, Chile, E Pacific Ocean 27.07S 109.18W
176 W9 **Ransiki** Papua, E Indonesia 1.27S 134.12E
94 K12 **Rantajärvi** Norrbotten, N Sweden 66.45N 23.39E
95 N17 **Rantasalmi** Isä-Suomi, SE Finland 62.02N 28.22E
175 N11 **Rantau** Borneo, C Indonesia 2.55S 115.09E
174 Hh7 **Rantau, Pulau** var. Pulau Tebingtinggi. island W Indonesia
175 Pp11 **Rantepao** Sulawesi, C Indonesia 2.58S 119.58E
32 M13 **Rantoul** Illinois, N USA 40.19N 88.08W
95 L15 **Rantsila** Oulu, C Finland 64.31N 25.40E
94 L13 **Ranua** Lappi, NW Finland 65.55N 26.34E
145 T3 **Ŗānya** var. Rāniyah. NE Iraq 36.15N 44.52E
163 X3 **Raohe** Heilongjiang, NE China 46.49N 134.00E
76 H9 **Raoui, Erg er** desert W Algeria
199 L11 **Rapa** island Îles Australes, S French Polynesia
203 V14 **Rapa Iti** island Îles Australes, SW French Polynesia
108 D10 **Rapallo** Liguria, NW Italy 44.21N 9.13E
Rapa Nui see Pascua, Isla de
Raphiah see Rafah
23 V5 **Rapidan River** ≈ Virginia, NE USA
30 J10 **Rapid City** South Dakota, N USA 44.04N 103.13W
13 P8 **Rapide-Blanc** Québec, SE Canada 47.48N 72.57W
12 I8 **Rapide-Deux** Québec, SE Canada 47.56N 78.33W
120 K6 **Räpina** Ger. Rappin. Põlvamaa, SE Estonia 58.06N 27.27E
120 G4 **Rapla** Ger. Rappel. Raplamaa, NW Estonia 59.00N 24.46E
120 G4 **Raplamaa** off. Rapla Maakond. ◐ province NW Estonia
23 X6 **Rappahonnock River** ≈ Virginia, NE USA
Rappel see Rapla
110 G7 **Rapperswil** Sankt Gallen, NE Switzerland 47.13N 8.49E
Rappin see Räpina
159 N12 **Rāpti** ≈ N India
59 K16 **Rapulo, Río** ≈ E Bolivia
Raqqah/Raqqah, Muḩāfaẓat al see Ar Raqqah
20 J8 **Raquette Lake** ◎ New York, NE USA
20 J6 **Raquette River** ≈ New York, NE USA
203 V10 **Raraka** atoll Îles Tuamotu, C French Polynesia
203 V10 **Raroia** atoll Îles Tuamotu, C French Polynesia
202 H15 **Rarotonga** ✕ Rarotonga, S Cook Islands, C Pacific Ocean 21.15S 159.45W
202 H16 **Rarotonga** island S Cook Islands, C Pacific Ocean
153 P12 **Rarz** W Tajikistan 39.23N 68.43E
Ras al 'Ain see Ra's al 'Ayn
145 N2 **Ra's al 'Ayn** var. Ras al 'Ain. Al Ḩasakah, N Syria 36.52N 40.04E
144 H3 **Ra's al Basīţ** Al Lādhiqīyah, W Syria 35.57N 35.55E
Ra's al-Hafgī see Ra's al Khafjī
147 R5 **Ra's al Khafjī** var. Ra's al-Hafgī. Ash Sharqīyah, NE Saudi Arabia 28.22N 48.29E
Ras al-Khaimah/Ras al Khaimah see Ra's al Khaymah
149 R15 **Ra's al Khaymah** var. Ras al Khaimah. Ra's al Khaymah, NE UAE 25.44N 55.54E
149 R15 **Ra's al Khaymah** var. Ras al-Khaimah. ✕ Ra's al Khaymah, NE UAE 25.37N 55.51E
144 G13 **Ra's an Naqb** Ma'ān, S Jordan 30.00N 35.29E
63 B26 **Rasa, Punta** headland E Argentina 40.50S 62.15W
176 W10 **Rasawi** Papua, E Indonesia 2.04S 134.02E
Râşcani see Rîşcani
82 J10 **Ras Dashen Terara** ▲ N Ethiopia 13.12N 38.09E
157 K19 **Rasdu Atoll** atoll C Maldives
120 E12 **Raseiniai** Kaunas, C Lithuania 55.23N 23.06E
77 X8 **Râs Ghârib** E Egypt 28.16N 33.01E
168 D6 **Rashaant** Bayan-Ölgiy, W Mongolia 47.48N 90.45E
168 L10 **Rashaant** Dundgovĭ, C Mongolia 44.54N 106.32E
168 J6 **Rashaant** Hövsgöl, N Mongolia 49.08N 101.27E
145 Y11 **Rashīd** E Iraq 31.15N 47.31E
77 V7 **Rashîd** Eng. Rosetta. N Egypt 31.24N 30.25E
148 M3 **Rasht** var. Resht. Gīlān, NW Iran 37.18N 49.37E
145 S2 **Rashwān** N Iraq 36.28N 43.54E
Rasik see Raasiku
115 M15 **Raška** Serbia, C Serbia and Montenegro (Yugoslavia) 43.18N 20.37E
121 P15 **Rasna** Rus. Ryasna. Mahilyowskaya Voblasts', E Belarus 54.01N 31.12E
118 J12 **Râşnov** prev. Rîşno, Rozsnyó, Hung. Barcarozsnyó. Braşov, C Romania 45.34N 25.27E
120 L11 **Rasony** Rus. Rossony. Vitsyebskaya Voblasts', N Belarus 55.55N 28.51E
Ra's Shamrah see Ugarit
131 N7 **Rasskazovo** Tambovskaya Oblast', W Russian Federation 52.42N 41.45E
121 O16 **Rasta** ≈ E Belarus
Rastadt see Rastatt
Rastâne see Ar Rastān
147 S6 **Ra's Tannūrah** Eng. Ras Tanura. Ash Sharqīyah, NE Saudi Arabia 26.44N 50.04E
Ras Tanura see Ra's Tannūrah
103 G21 **Rastatt** var. Rastadt. Baden-Württemberg, SW Germany 48.52N 8.12E
Rastenburg see Kętrzyn
155 V7 **Rasūlnagar** Punjab, E Pakistan 32.19N 73.51E
201 U6 **Ratak Chain** island group Ratak Chain, E Marshall Islands
121 K15 **Ratamka** Rus. Ratomka. Minskaya Voblasts', C Belarus 53.57N 27.23E
95 G17 **Rätan** Jämtland, C Sweden 62.28N 14.34E
158 G11 **Ratangarh** Rājasthān, NW India 28.01N 74.39E
Rat Buri see Ratchaburi
178 H11 **Ratchaburi** var. Rat Buri. Ratchaburi, W Thailand 13.30N 99.49E
31 W15 **Rathbun Lake** ▣ Iowa, C USA
Ráth Caola see Rathkeale
177 F5 **Rathedaung** Arakan State, W Myanmar 20.30N 92.48E
102 M12 **Rathenow** Brandenburg, NE Germany 52.34N 12.20E
99 C19 **Rathkeale** Ir. Ráth Caola. SW Ireland 52.31N 8.55W
98 F13 **Rathlin Island** Ir. Reachlainn. island N Northern Ireland, UK
99 C20 **Ráthluirc** Ir. An Ráth. SW Ireland 52.22N 8.44W
Ratibor see Racibórz
Ratisbon/Ratisbona/Ratisbonne see Regensburg
Rätische Alpen see Rhaetian Alps
40 E17 **Rat Island** island Aleutian Islands, Alaska, USA
40 E17 **Rat Islands** island group Aleutian Islands, Alaska, USA
160 F10 **Ratlām** prev. Rutlam. Madhya Pradesh, C India 23.23N 75.03E
161 D15 **Ratnāgiri** Mahārāshtra, W India 17.00N 73.20E
161 K26 **Ratnapura** Sabaragamuwa Province, S Sri Lanka 6.40N 80.25E
118 J2 **Ratne** Rus. Ratno. Volyns'ka Oblast', NW Ukraine 51.40N 24.33E
Ratno see Ratne
Ratomka see Ratamka
39 U8 **Raton** New Mexico, SW USA 36.54N 104.27W
145 O7 **Ratqah, Wādī ar** dry watercourse W Iraq
Ratschach see Radeče
178 H17 **Rattaphum** Songkhla, SW Thailand 7.07N 100.16E
28 L6 **Rattlesnake Creek** ≈ Kansas, C USA
96 L13 **Rättvik** Dalarna, C Sweden 60.53N 15.12E
102 K9 **Ratzeburg** Mecklenburg-Vorpommern, N Germany 53.41N 10.48E
102 K9 **Ratzeburger See** ◎ N Germany
8 J10 **Ratz, Mount** ▲ British Columbia, SW Canada 57.22N 132.17W
63 D22 **Rauch** Buenos Aires, E Argentina 36.47S 59.06W
43 U16 **Raudales** Chiapas, SE Mexico
Raudhatain see Ar Rawḑatayn
Raudnitz an der Elbe see Roudnice nad Labem
94 K1 **Raufarhöfn** Nordhurland Eystra, NE Iceland 66.26N 15.57W
96 H13 **Raufoss** Oppland, S Norway 60.43N 10.36E
Raukawa see Cook Strait
192 Q8 **Raukumara** ▲ North Island, NZ 37.46S 178.07E
199 J12 **Raukumara Plain** undersea feature N Coral Sea
192 P8 **Raukumara Range** ▲▲ North Island, NZ
160 N11 **Rāulakela** var. Raurkela; prev. Rourkela. Orissa, E. India 22.13N 84.52E
97 F15 **Rauland** Telemark, S Norway 59.41N 7.57E
95 J19 **Rauma** Swe. Raumo. Länsi-Suomi, W Finland 61.09N 21.30E
96 F10 **Rauma** ≈ S Norway
Raumo see Rauma
120 H8 **Rauna** Cēsis, C Latvia 57.19N 25.34E
174 Mm16 **Raung, Gunung** ▲ Jawa, S Indonesia 8.00S 114.07E
Rāurkela see Rāulakela
97 J22 **Raus** Skåne, S Sweden 56.01N 12.48E
172 R6 **Rausu** Hokkaidō, NE Japan 44.00N 145.06E
172 R6 **Rausu-dake** ▲ Hokkaidō, NE Japan 44.06N 145.04E
95 M17 **Rautalampi** Itä-Suomi, C Finland 62.37N 26.48E
95 N16 **Rautavaara** Itä-Suomi, C Finland 63.30N 28.19E
118 M9 **Raŭtel** ≈ C Moldova
95 O18 **Rautjärvi** Etelä-Suomi, S Finland 61.21N 29.20E
Rautu see Sosnovo
203 V11 **Ravahere** atoll Îles Tuamotu, C French Polynesia
109 J25 **Ravanusa** Sicilia, Italy, C Mediterranean Sea 37.16N 13.57E
149 S9 **Rāvar** Kermān, C Iran 31.15N 56.51E
153 Q11 **Ravat** Batkenskaya Oblast', SW Kyrgyzstan 39.54N 70.06E
20 K11 **Ravena** New York, NE USA 42.28N 73.49W
108 H10 **Ravenna** Emilia-Romagna, N Italy 44.28N 12.15E
31 O15 **Ravenna** Nebraska, C USA 41.01N 98.54W
33 U11 **Ravenna** Ohio, N USA 41.09N 81.14W
103 I24 **Ravensburg** Baden-Württemberg, S Germany 47.46N 9.37E
189 W4 **Ravenshoe** Queensland, NE Australia 17.29S 145.28E
188 K13 **Ravensthorpe** Western Australia 33.37S 120.03E
23 Q4 **Ravenswood** West Virginia, NE USA 38.57N 81.45W
155 U9 **Rāvi** ≈ India/Pakistan
114 C9 **Ravna Gora** Primorje-Gorski Kotar, NW Croatia 45.20N 14.54E
111 U10 **Ravne na Koroškem** Ger. Gutenstein. N Slovenia 46.33N 14.57E
145 P6 **Rāwah** W Iraq 34.32N 41.54E
203 T4 **Rawaki** prev. Phoenix Island. atoll Phoenix Islands, C Kiribati
155 U6 **Rāwalpindi** Punjab, NE Pakistan 33.38N 73.06E
112 L13 **Rawa Mazowiecka** Łódzkie, C Poland 51.46N 20.15E
145 T2 **Ŗawāndiz** var. Rawandoz, Rawāndūz. N Iraq 36.37N 44.31E
Rawandoz/Rawāndūz see Ŗawāndiz
176 Vv9 **Rawarra** ≈ Papua, E Indonesia
176 V9 **Rawas** Papua, E Indonesia 1.07S 132.12E
145 O4 **Rawḑah** ◎ E Syria
112 G13 **Rawicz** Ger. Rawitsch. Wielkopolskie, C Poland 51.37N 16.51E
Rawitsch see Rawicz
188 M11 **Rawlinna** Western Australia 31.00S 125.35E
35 W16 **Rawlins** Wyoming, C USA 41.47N 107.14W
65 K17 **Rawson** Chubut, SE Argentina 43.22S 65.01W
165 R16 **Rawu** Xizang Zizhiqu, W China 29.30N 96.42E
159 P12 **Raxaul** Bihār, N India 26.58N 84.51E
30 K3 **Ray** North Dakota, N USA 48.19N 103.11W
174 M9 **Raya, Bukit** ▲ Borneo, C Indonesia 0.40S 112.40E
161 I18 **Rāyachoti** Andhra Pradesh, E India 14.03N 78.43E
Rāyadrug see Rāyagarha
161 M14 **Rāyagarha** prev. Rāyadrug. Orissa, E India 19.11N 83.22E
144 H7 **Rayak** var. Rayaq, Riyāq. E Lebanon 33.51N 36.03E
Rayaq see Rayak
145 T2 **Ŗāyat** E Iraq 36.39N 44.56E
174 J10 **Raya, Tanjung** headland Pulau Bangka, W Indonesia 1.49S 106.04E
11 R13 **Ray, Cape** headland Newfoundland and Labrador, E Canada 47.38N 59.15W
126 Mm16 **Raychikhinsk** Amurskaya Oblast', SE Russian Federation 49.47N 129.19E
131 U5 **Rayevskiy** Respublika Bashkortostan, W Russian Federation 54.04N 54.58E
9 Q17 **Raymond** Alberta, SW Canada 49.30N 112.40W
24 K6 **Raymond** Mississippi, S USA 32.15N 90.25W
34 F9 **Raymond** Washington, NW USA 46.41N 123.43W
191 T8 **Raymond Terrace** New South Wales, SE Australia 32.46S 151.45E
27 T17 **Raymondville** Texas, SW USA 26.27N 97.45W
9 U16 **Raymore** Saskatchewan, S Canada 51.24N 104.34W
41 Q8 **Ray Mountains** ▲▲ Alaska, USA
24 H9 **Rayne** Louisiana, S USA 30.13N 92.15W
43 O12 **Rayón** San Luis Potosí, C Mexico 21.54N 99.33W
42 G4 **Rayón** Sonora, NW Mexico 29.45N 110.33W
178 Hh12 **Rayong** Rayong, S Thailand 12.42N 101.16E
27 T5 **Ray Roberts, Lake** ◎ Texas, SW USA
20 E15 **Raystown Lake** ▣ Pennsylvania, NE USA
147 V13 **Raysūt** SW Oman 16.58N 54.01E
29 R4 **Raytown** Missouri, C USA 39.00N 94.27W
24 I5 **Rayville** Louisiana, S USA 32.29N 91.45W
148 L5 **Razan** Hamadān, W Iran 35.22N 48.58E
145 S9 **Razāzah, Buḩayrat ar** var. Baḩr al Milḩ. ◎ C Iraq
116 L9 **Razboyna** ▲ E Bulgaria 42.54N 26.31E
Razdan see Hrazdan
Razdolnoye see Rozdol'ne
Razelm, Lacul see Razim, Lacul
145 U2 **Ŗazga** E Iraq 36.25N 45.06E
116 L8 **Razgrad** Razgrad, N Bulgaria 43.33N 26.31E

316

◆ COUNTRY ● COUNTRY CAPITAL ◇ DEPENDENT TERRITORY ○ DEPENDENT TERRITORY CAPITAL ◐ ADMINISTRATIVE REGION ✕ INTERNATIONAL AIRPORT ▲ MOUNTAIN ▲▲ MOUNTAIN RANGE ⛰ VOLCANO ≈ RIVER ◎ LAKE ▣ RESERVOIR

Razgrad – Riiser-Larsen Sea

116 L8 **Razgrad** ◈ province N Bulgaria
119 N13 **Razim, Lacul** prev. Lacul Razelm. lagoon NW Black Sea
116 G11 **Razlog** Blagoevgrad, SW Bulgaria 41.52N 23.28E
118 K10 **Rāznas Ezers** ◎ SE Latvia
104 E6 **Raz, Pointe du** headland NW France 48.06N 4.52W
Reachlaim see Rathlin Island
Reachrainn see Lambay Island
99 N22 **Reading** S England, UK 51.28N 0.58W
20 H15 **Reading** Pennsylvania, NE USA 40.19N 75.55W
50 C7 **Real, Cordillera** ▲▲ C Ecuador
64 K12 **Realicó** La Pampa, C Argentina 35.01S 64.13W
27 R15 **Realitos** Texas, SW USA 27.26N 98.31W
110 G9 **Realp** Uri, C Switzerland 46.36N 8.32E
178 I12 **Reăng Kesei** Bătdâmbâng, W Cambodia 12.57N 103.15E
203 Y11 **Reao** atoll Îles Tuamotu, E French Polynesia
Reate see Rieti
188 L11 **Rebecca, Lake** ◎ Western Australia
Rebiana Sand Sea see Rabyānah, Ramlat
128 H8 **Reboly** Respublika Kareliya, NW Russian Federation 63.51N 30.49E
172 P1 **Rebun** Rebun-tō, NE Japan 45.19N 141.02E
172 P1 **Rebun-suidō** strait E Sea of Japan
172 P1 **Rebun-tō** island NE Japan
108 J12 **Recanati** Marche, C Italy 43.23N 13.34E
Rechitsa see Rechytsa
111 Y7 **Rechnitz** Burgenland, SE Austria 47.18N 16.26E
121 J20 **Rechytsa** Rus. Rechitsa. Brestskaya Voblasts', SW Belarus 51.51N 26.49E
121 O19 **Rechytsa** Rus. Rechitsa. Homyel'skaya Voblasts', SE Belarus 52.22N 30.22E
61 Q15 **Recife** prev. Pernambuco. state capital Pernambuco, E Brazil 8.06S 34.52W
85 I26 **Recife, Cape** Afr. Kaap Recife. headland S South Africa 34.03S 25.37E
Recife, Kaap see Recife, Cape
180 I16 **Récifs, Îles aux** island Inner Islands, NE Seychelles
103 E14 **Recklinghausen** Nordrhein-Westfalen, W Germany 51.37N 7.12E
102 M8 **Recknitz** ≈ NE Germany
101 K23 **Recogne** Luxembourg, SE Belgium 49.56N 5.20E
63 C15 **Reconquista** Santa Fe, C Argentina 29.10S 59.41W
205 O6 **Recovery Glacier** glacier Antarctica
61 G15 **Recreio** Mato Grosso, W Brazil 8.13S 58.15W
29 X9 **Rector** Arkansas, C USA 36.15N 90.17W
112 E9 **Recz** Ger. Reetz Neumark. Zachodnio-pomorskie, NW Poland 53.16N 15.32E
101 L24 **Redange** var. Redange-sur-Attert. Diekirch, W Luxembourg 49.46N 5.52E
Redange-sur-Attert see Redange
20 C13 **Redbank Creek** ≈ Pennsylvania, NE USA
11 S9 **Red Bay** Quebec, E Canada 51.40N 56.37W
25 N2 **Red Bay** Alabama, S USA 34.26N 88.08W
37 N4 **Red Bluff** California, W USA 40.09N 122.14W
26 J8 **Red Bluff Reservoir** ⊠ New Mexico/Texas, SW USA
32 K16 **Red Bud** Illinois, N USA 38.12N 89.59W
32 J5 **Red Cedar River** ≈ Wisconsin, N USA
9 R17 **Redcliff** Alberta, SW Canada 50.06N 110.48W
85 K17 **Redcliff** Midlands, C Zimbabwe 19.01S 29.43E
190 L9 **Red Cliffs** Victoria, SE Australia 34.21S 142.12E
31 P17 **Red Cloud** Nebraska, C USA 40.05N 98.31W
24 L8 **Red Creek** ≈ Mississippi, S USA
9 P15 **Red Deer** Alberta, SW Canada 52.15N 113.48W
9 Q16 **Red Deer** ≈ Alberta, SW Canada
41 O11 **Red Devil** Alaska, USA 61.45N 95.18W
37 N3 **Redding** California, W USA 40.33N 122.26W
99 L20 **Redditch** W England, UK 52.19N 1.55W
31 P9 **Redfield** South Dakota, N USA 44.51N 98.31W
26 J12 **Redford** Texas, SW USA 29.31N 104.19W
47 V13 **Redhead** Trinidad, Trinidad and Tobago 10.48N 60.56W
190 I8 **Red Hill** South Australia 33.34S 138.13E
Red Hill see Pu'u 'Ula'ula
28 K7 **Red Hills** hill range Kansas, C USA
11 T12 **Red Indian Lake** ◎ Newfoundland and Labrador, E Canada
128 J16 **Redkino** Tverskaya Oblast', W Russian Federation 56.41N 36.07E
10 A10 **Red Lake** Ontario, C Canada 51.00N 93.55W
38 I10 **Red Lake** salt flat Arizona, SW USA
31 S4 **Red Lake Falls** Minnesota, N USA 47.52N 96.16W
31 R4 **Red Lake River** ≈ Minnesota, N USA
37 U15 **Redlands** California, W USA 34.03N 117.10W
20 G16 **Red Lion** Pennsylvania, NE USA 39.53N 76.36W
35 U11 **Red Lodge** Montana, NW USA 45.11N 109.15W
34 H13 **Redmond** Oregon, NW USA 44.16N 121.10W
38 L5 **Redmond** Utah, W USA 39.00N 111.51W
34 H8 **Redmond** Washington, NW USA 47.40N 122.07W
Rednitz see Regnitz
31 T15 **Red Oak** Iowa, C USA 41.00N 95.10W
20 K12 **Red Oaks Mill** New York, NE USA 41.39N 73.52W
104 I7 **Redon** Ille-et-Vilaine, NW France 47.39N 2.04W
47 W10 **Redonda** island SW Antigua and Barbuda
106 G4 **Redondela** Galicia, NW Spain 42.16N 8.36W
106 H11 **Redondo** Évora, S Portugal 38.37N 7.31W
41 Q12 **Redoubt Volcano** ▲ Alaska, USA 60.29N 152.44W
9 Y16 **Red River** ≈ Canada/USA
133 U12 **Red River** var. Yuan, Chin. Yuan Jiang, Vtn. Sông Hông Hà. ≈ China/Vietnam
27 W4 **Red River** ≈ S USA
24 H7 **Red River** ≈ Louisiana, S USA
32 M6 **Red River** ≈ Wisconsin, N USA
Red Rock, Lake see Red Rock Reservoir
31 W14 **Red Rock Reservoir** var. Lake Red Rock. ⊠ Iowa, C USA
194 J15 **Redscar Bay** bay S PNG
82 H7 **Red Sea** ◈ state NE Sudan
77 Y9 **Red Sea** anc. Sinus Arabicus. sea Africa/Asia
23 T11 **Red Springs** North Carolina, SE USA 34.49N 79.10W
15 Gg6 **Redstone** ≈ Northwest Territories, NW Canada
9 V17 **Redvers** Saskatchewan, S Canada 49.31N 101.33W
79 P13 **Red Volta** var. Nazinon, Fr. Volta Rouge. ≈ Burkina/Ghana
9 Q14 **Redwater** Alberta, SW Canada 53.57N 113.06W
30 M16 **Red Willow Creek** ≈ Nebraska, C USA
31 W9 **Red Wing** Minnesota, N USA 44.33N 92.31W
37 N9 **Redwood City** California, W USA 37.29N 122.13W
31 T9 **Redwood Falls** Minnesota, N USA 44.33N 95.07W
198 Ff7 **Reed Bank** undersea feature C South China Sea
33 P7 **Reed City** Michigan, N USA 43.52N 85.30W
30 K6 **Reeder** North Dakota, N USA 46.03N 102.55W
37 R11 **Reedley** California, W USA 36.35N 119.27W
35 T11 **Reedpoint** Montana, NW USA 45.41N 109.33W
32 K8 **Reedsburg** Wisconsin, N USA 43.33N 90.03W
34 E13 **Reedsport** Oregon, NW USA 43.42N 124.06W
195 X8 **Reef Islands** island group Santa Cruz Islands, E Solomon Islands
193 H16 **Reefton** West Coast, South Island, NZ 42.07S 171.52E
22 F8 **Reelfoot Lake** ◎ Tennessee, S USA
99 D17 **Ree, Lough** Ir. Loch Rí. ◎ C Ireland
Reengus see Ringas
37 U4 **Reese River** ≈ Nevada, W USA
100 M8 **Reest** ≈ E Netherlands
Reetz Neumark see Recz
Reevhtse see Rossvatnet
143 N13 **Refahiye** Erzincan, C Turkey 39.54N 38.45E
25 N4 **Reform** Alabama, S USA 33.22N 88.01W
97 K20 **Reftele** Jönköping, S Sweden 57.10N 13.34E
27 T14 **Refugio** Texas, SW USA 28.18N 97.16W
112 E8 **Rega** ≈ NW Poland
Regar see Tursunzoda
103 O21 **Regen** Bayern, SE Germany 48.57N 13.10E
103 M20 **Regen** ≈ SE Germany
103 M21 **Regensburg** Eng. Ratisbon, Fr. Ratisbonne; hist. Ratisbona, anc. Castra Regina, Reginum. Bayern, SE Germany 49.01N 12.06E
103 M21 **Regenstauf** Bayern, SE Germany 49.06N 12.07E
76 I10 **Reggane** C Algeria 26.45N 0.10E
100 N9 **Regge** ≈ E Netherlands
Reggio see Reggio nell' Emilia
Reggio Calabria see Reggio di Calabria
109 M23 **Reggio di Calabria** var. Reggio Calabria, Gk. Rhegion; anc. Regium, Rhegium. Calabria, SW Italy 38.06N 15.39E
Reggio Emilia see Reggio nell' Emilia
108 F9 **Reggio nell' Emilia** var. Reggio Emilia, abbrev. Reggio; anc. Regium Lepidum. Emilia-Romagna, N Italy 44.42N 10.37E
118 I10 **Reghin** Ger. Sächsisch-Reen, Hung. Szászrégen; prev. Reghinul Săsesc, Ger. Sächsisch-Regen. Mureş, C Romania 46.46N 24.40E
Reghinul Săsesc see Reghin
9 U16 **Regina** Saskatchewan, S Canada 50.25N 104.39W
9 U16 **Regina** ✈ Saskatchewan, S Canada 50.21N 104.43W
57 Z10 **Régina** E French Guiana 4.19N 52.07W
9 U16 **Regina Beach** Saskatchewan, S Canada 50.44N 105.03W
Reginum see Regensburg
Registan see Rīgestān
62 L11 **Registro** São Paulo, S Brazil 24.30S 47.49W
Regium see Reggio di Calabria
Regium Lepidum see Reggio nell' Emilia
103 K19 **Regnitz** var. Rednitz. ≈ SE Germany
42 K10 **Regocijo** Durango, W Mexico 23.34N 105.10W
106 H12 **Reguengos de Monsaraz** Évora, S Portugal 38.25N 7.31W
103 M18 **Rehau** Bayern, E Germany 50.15N 12.03E
85 D19 **Rehoboth** Hardap, C Namibia 23.18S 17.03E
Rehoboth/Rehovoth see Reḥovot
23 Z4 **Rehoboth Beach** Delaware, NE USA 38.42N 75.03W
144 F10 **Reḥovot** var. Rehoboth, Rekhovot, Rehovoth. Central, C Israel 31.54N 34.49E
83 J20 **Rei** spring/well S Kenya 3.24S 39.18E
Reichenau see Rychnov nad Kněžnou, Czech Republic
Reichenau see Bogatynia, Poland
103 M17 **Reichenbach** var. Reichenbach im Vogtland. Sachsen, E Germany 50.36N 12.18E
Reichenbach see Dzierżoniów
Reichenbach im Vogtland see Reichenbach
Reichenberg see Liberec
189 O11 **Reid** Western Australia 30.48S 128.24E
25 V6 **Reidsville** Georgia, SE USA 32.05N 82.07W
23 T8 **Reidsville** North Carolina, SE USA 36.21N 79.39W
Reifnitz see Ribnica
99 O22 **Reigate** SE England, UK 51.13N 0.13W
Reikjavik see Reykjavík
104 I10 **Ré, Île de** island W France
39 N15 **Reiley Peak** ▲ Arizona, SW USA 32.24N 110.09W
105 Q4 **Reims** Eng. Rheims; anc. Durocortorum, Remi. Marne, N France 49.16N 4.01E
65 G23 **Reina Adelaida, Archipiélago** island group S Chile
47 O16 **Reina Beatrix** ✈ (Oranjestad) C Aruba 12.30N 69.57W
110 F7 **Reinach** Aargau, W Switzerland 47.15N 8.12E
110 E6 **Reinach** Basel-Land, NW Switzerland 47.30N 7.36E
66 O11 **Reina Sofía** ✈ (Tenerife) Tenerife, Islas Canarias, Spain, NE Atlantic Ocean
31 W13 **Reinbeck** Iowa, C USA 42.19N 92.36W
102 J10 **Reinbek** Schleswig-Holstein, N Germany 53.31N 10.15E
9 U12 **Reindeer** ≈ Saskatchewan, C Canada
9 U11 **Reindeer Lake** ◎ Manitoba/Saskatchewan, C Canada
Reine-Charlotte, Îles de la see Queen Charlotte Islands
Reine-Élisabeth, Îles de la see Queen Elizabeth Islands
96 F13 **Reineskarvet** ▲ S Norway 60.38N 7.48E
192 H1 **Reinga, Cape** headland North Island, NZ 34.24S 172.40E
107 N3 **Reinosa** Cantabria, N Spain 43.01N 4.09W
111 R8 **Reisseck** ▲ S Austria 46.57N 13.21E
23 W3 **Reisterstown** Maryland, NE USA 39.27N 76.46W
Reisui see Yŏsu
100 N5 **Reitdiep** ≈ NE Netherlands
203 V10 **Reitoru** atoll Îles Tuamotu, C French Polynesia
97 M17 **Rejmyre** Östergötland, S Sweden 58.49N 15.55E
Reka see Rijeka
Reka Ili see Ile/Ili He
97 N16 **Rekarne** Västmanland, C Sweden 59.25N 16.04
Rekhovot see Reḥovot
15 Ii7 **Reliance** Northwest Territories, C Canada 62.45N 109.07W
35 U16 **Reliance** Wyoming, C USA 41.42N 109.13W
76 J5 **Relizane** var. Ghelîzâne, Ghilizane. NW Algeria 35.45N 0.39E
190 J7 **Remarkable, Mount** ▲ South Australia 32.46S 138.08E
56 E8 **Remedios** Antioquia, N Colombia 7.01N 74.42W
45 Q16 **Remedios** Veraguas, W Panama 8.12N 81.49W
44 D8 **Remedios, Punta** headland SW El Salvador 13.31N 89.48W
Remi see Reims
101 N25 **Remich** Grevenmacher, SE Luxembourg 49.33N 6.22E
101 J19 **Remicourt** Liège, E Belgium 50.40N 5.19E
12 H8 **Rémigny, Lac** ◎ Québec, SE Canada
57 Z10 **Rémire** NE French Guiana 4.52N 52.16W
131 N13 **Remontnoye** Rostovskaya Oblast', SW Russian Federation 46.35N 43.38E
176 V13 **Remoon** Pulau Kur, E Indonesia 5.18S 131.59E
101 L20 **Remouchamps** Liège, E Belgium 50.29N 5.43E
105 R15 **Remoulins** Gard, S France 43.56N 4.34E
181 X16 **Rempart, Mont du** var. Mount Rempart. hill W Mauritius
103 E15 **Remscheid** Nordrhein-Westfalen, W Germany 51.10N 7.10E
31 S12 **Remsen** Iowa, C USA 42.48N 95.58W
96 I12 **Rena** Hedmark, S Norway 61.07N 11.21E
96 I11 **Renåa** ≈ S Norway
Renaix see Ronse
118 H7 **Rencēni** Valmiera, N Latvia 57.43N 25.25E
120 D9 **Renda** Kuldīga, W Latvia 57.04N 22.18E
109 N20 **Rende** Calabria, SW Italy 39.19N 16.10E
101 K21 **Rendeux** Luxembourg, SE Belgium 50.15N 5.28E
Rendina see Rentína
32 L16 **Rend Lake** ◎ Illinois, N USA
195 U15 **Rendova** island New Georgia Islands, NW Solomon Islands
102 I8 **Rendsburg** Schleswig-Holstein, N Germany 54.18N 9.40E
110 B9 **Renens** Vaud, SW Switzerland 46.31N 6.36E
12 K12 **Renfrew** Ontario, SE Canada 45.28N 76.42W
98 I12 **Renfrew** cultural region SW Scotland, UK
174 H8 **Rengat** Sumatera, W Indonesia 0.25S 102.38E
159 W12 **Rengma Hills** ▲▲ NE India
64 H12 **Rengo** Libertador, C Chile 34.24S 70.52W
118 M12 **Reni** Odes'ka Oblast', SW Ukraine 45.30N 28.24E
82 F11 **Renk** Upper Nile, E Sudan 11.48N 32.49E
95 L19 **Renko** Etelä-Suomi, S Finland 60.52N 24.16E
100 L12 **Renkum** Gelderland, SE Netherlands 51.58N 5.43E
190 K9 **Renmark** South Australia 34.12S 140.43E
195 W17 **Rennell** var. Mu Nggava. island S Solomon Islands
189 Q4 **Renner Springs Roadhouse** Northern Territory, N Australia 18.12S 133.48E
104 I6 **Rennes** Bret. Roazon; anc. Condate. Ille-et-Vilaine, NW France 48.07N 1.40W
205 S16 **Rennick Glacier** glacier Antarctica
9 Y16 **Rennie** Manitoba, S Canada 49.51N 95.28W
37 Q5 **Reno** Nevada, W USA 39.31N 119.48W
108 H10 **Reno** ≈ N Italy
37 Q5 **Reno-Cannon** ✈ Nevada, W USA 39.26N 119.42W
85 F24 **Renoster** ≈ SW South Africa
13 T5 **Renouard, Lac** ◎ Québec, SE Canada
20 F13 **Renovo** Pennsylvania, NE USA 41.19N 77.42W
167 O3 **Renqiu** Hebei, E China 38.49N 116.02E
166 I9 **Renshou** Sichuan, C China 29.58N 104.06E
33 N12 **Rensselaer** Indiana, N USA 40.55N 87.10W
20 L11 **Rensselaer** New York, NE USA 42.38N 73.44W
107 Q2 **Rentería** Basq. Errenteria. País Vasco, N Spain 43.17N 1.54W
117 E17 **Rentína** var. Rendina. Thessalía, C Greece 39.04N 21.58E
31 T9 **Renville** Minnesota, N USA 44.48N 95.13W
79 O13 **Réo** W Burkina 12.19N 2.28W
13 O12 **Repentigny** Québec, SE Canada 45.42N 73.28W
152 K13 **Repetek** Lebap Welaýaty, E Turkmenistan 38.40N 63.12E
95 J16 **Replot** Fin. Raippaluoto. island W Finland
Reppen see Rzepin
Reps see Rupea
29 T7 **Republic** Missouri, C USA 37.07N 93.28W
34 K7 **Republic** Washington, NW USA 48.39N 118.44W
29 N3 **Republican River** ≈ Kansas/Nebraska, C USA
15 Ll4 **Repulse Bay** Northwest Territories, N Canada 66.34N 86.19W
58 F9 **Requena** Loreto, NE Peru 5.02S 73.47W
107 R10 **Requena** País Valenciano, E Spain 39.28N 1.07W
105 O14 **Réquista** Aveyron, S France 44.00N 2.31E
142 M12 **Reşadiye** Tokat, N Turkey 40.24N 37.19E
Reschenpass see Resia, Passo di
Reschitza see Reşiţa
115 N20 **Resen** Turk. Resne. SW FYR Macedonia 41.07N 21.00E
62 J11 **Reserva** Paraná, S Brazil 24.40S 50.52W
9 V15 **Reserve** Saskatchewan, S Canada 52.24N 102.37W
39 P13 **Reserve** New Mexico, SW USA 33.42N 108.45W
Reshetilovka see Reshetylivka
119 S6 **Reshetylivka** Rus. Reshetilovka. Poltavs'ka Oblast', NE Ukraine 49.34N 34.04E
Resht see Rasht
108 F5 **Resia, Passo di** Ger. Reschenpass. pass Austria/Italy 46.51N 10.32E
Resicabánya see Reşiţa
64 N7 **Resistencia** Chaco, NE Argentina 27.27S 58.55W
118 F12 **Reşiţa** Ger. Reschitza, Hung. Resicabánya. Caraş-Severin, W Romania 45.13N 21.58E
Resne see Resen
207 N9 **Resolute** Cornwallis Island, Nunavut, N Canada 74.40N 94.54W
Resolution see Fort Resolution
Resolution Island island Nunavut, NE Canada
193 A23 **Resolution Island** island SW NZ
13 W7 **Restigouche** Québec, SE Canada 48.01N 66.42W
9 W17 **Reston** Manitoba, S Canada 49.33N 101.03W
12 H11 **Restoule Lake** ◎ Ontario, S Canada
56 F10 **Restrepo** Meta, C Colombia 4.20N 73.29W
44 B6 **Retalhuleu** Retalhuleu, SW Guatemala 14.30N 91.41W
44 A1 **Retalhuleu** off. Departamento de Retalhuleu. ◈ department SW Guatemala
99 N18 **Retford** C England, UK 53.18N 0.52W
105 Q3 **Rethel** Ardennes, N France 49.31N 4.22E
Rethimno/Réthimnon see Réthymno
117 I25 **Réthymno** var. Rethimno; prev. Réthimnon. Kríti, Greece, E Mediterranean Sea 35.21N 24.28E
Retiche, Alpi see Rhaetian Alps
101 J16 **Retie** Antwerpen, N Belgium 51.18N 5.05E
113 J21 **Rétság** Nógrád, N Hungary 47.57N 19.07E
111 W2 **Retz** Niederösterreich, NE Austria 48.46N 15.58E
181 N15 **Réunion** off. La Réunion. ◇ French overseas department W Indian Ocean
132 L17 **Réunion** island W Indian Ocean
107 U6 **Reus** Cataluña, E Spain 41.10N 1.06E
101 J15 **Reusel** Noord-Brabant, S Netherlands 51.21N 5.10E
110 F7 **Reuss** ≈ NW Switzerland
Reuţel see Ciuhuru
103 H22 **Reutlingen** Baden-Württemberg, S Germany 48.30N 9.13E
110 L7 **Reutte** Tirol, W Austria 47.30N 10.43E
101 M16 **Reuver** Limburg, SE Netherlands 51.16N 6.04E
30 K7 **Reva** South Dakota, N USA 45.30N 103.03W
Reval/Revel' see Tallinn
128 J4 **Revda** Murmanskaya Oblast', NW Russian Federation 67.57N 34.29E
125 Ee11 **Revda** Sverdlovskaya Oblast', C Russian Federation 56.48N 59.42E
105 N16 **Revel** Haute-Garonne, S France 43.27N 1.58E
9 O16 **Revelstoke** British Columbia, SW Canada 51.01N 118.12W
45 N13 **Reventazón, Río** ≈ E Costa Rica
108 G9 **Revere** Lombardia, N Italy 45.03N 11.07E
41 Y14 **Revillagigedo Island** island Alexander Archipelago, Alaska, USA
199 Mm7 **Revillagigedo Islands** island group NW Mexico
105 R3 **Revin** Ardennes, N France 49.57N 4.39E
94 O3 **Revnosa** headland C Svalbard 78.03N 18.52E
Revolyutsii, Pik see Revolyutsiya, Qullai
153 T13 **Revolyutsiya, Qullai** Rus. Pik Revolyutsii. ▲ SE Tajikistan 38.40N 72.26E
113 L19 **Revúca** Ger. Grossrauschenbach, Hung. Nagyrőce. Banskobystrický Kraj, C Slovakia 48.40N 20.10E
160 K9 **Rewa** Madhya Pradesh, C India 24.31N 81.18E
158 I11 **Rewāri** Haryāna, N India 28.13N 76.37E
35 R14 **Rexburg** Idaho, NW USA 43.49N 111.47W
80 G13 **Rey Bouba** Nord, NE Cameroon 8.40N 14.10E
94 L3 **Reydharfjördhur** Austurland, E Iceland 65.02N 14.12W
59 K16 **Reyes** Beni, NW Bolivia 14.17S 67.18W
36 L8 **Reyes, Point** headland California, W USA 37.58N 123.01W
56 B12 **Reyes, Punta** headland SW Colombia 2.43N 78.07W
142 L17 **Reyhanlı** Hatay, S Turkey 36.16N 36.33E
45 U16 **Rey, Isla del** island Archipiélago de las Perlas, SE Panama
94 H2 **Reykhólar** Vestfirdhir, W Iceland 65.28N 22.12W
94 K2 **Reykjahlídh** Nordhurland Eystra, NE Iceland 65.37N 16.54W
94 I4 **Reykjanes** ◈ region SW Iceland
207 O16 **Reykjanes Basin** var. Irminger Basin. undersea feature N Atlantic Ocean
207 N17 **Reykjanes Ridge** undersea feature N Atlantic Ocean
94 H4 **Reykjavík** var. Reikjavik. ● (Iceland) Höfudhborgarsvaedhi, W Iceland 64.07N 21.54W
20 D13 **Reynoldsville** Pennsylvania, NE USA 41.04N 78.51W
43 P8 **Reynosa** Tamaulipas, C Mexico 26.03N 98.19W
Reẓā'īyeh see Orūmīyeh
Reẓā'īyeh, Daryācheh-ye see Orūmīyeh, Daryācheh-ye
104 I8 **Rezé** Loire-Atlantique, NW France 47.10N 1.36W
120 K10 **Rēzekne** Ger. Rositten; prev. Rus. Rezhitsa. Rēzekne, SE Latvia 56.31N 27.22E
Rezhitsa see Rēzekne
119 N9 **Rezina** NE Moldova 47.44N 28.58E
116 N11 **Rezovo** Turk. Rezve. Burgas, E Bulgaria 42.00N 28.00E
116 N11 **Rezovska Reka** Turk. Rezve Deresi. ≈ Bulgaria/Turkey see also Rezve Deresi
Rezve see Rezovo
116 N11 **Rezve Deresi** Bul. Rezovska Reka. ≈ Bulgaria/Turkey see also Rezovska Reka
Rhadames see Ghadāmis
Rhaedestus see Tekirdağ
110 J10 **Rhaetian Alps** Fr. Alpes Rhétiques, Ger. Rätische Alpen, It. Alpi Retiche. ▲▲ C Europe
110 I8 **Rhätikon** ▲▲ C Europe
103 G14 **Rheda-Wiedenbrück** Nordrhein-Westfalen, W Germany 51.51N 8.19E
100 M12 **Rheden** Gelderland, E Netherlands 52.01N 6.03E
Rhegion/Rhegium see Reggio di Calabria
Rheims see Reims
Rhein see Rhine
103 E17 **Rheinbach** Nordrhein-Westfalen, W Germany 50.37N 6.57E
102 F13 **Rheine** var. Rheine in Westfalen. Nordrhein-Westfalen, NW Germany 52.16N 7.27E
Rheine in Westfalen see Rheine
Rheinfeld see Rheinfelden
103 F24 **Rheinfelden** Baden-Württemberg, S Germany 47.34N 7.46E
110 E6 **Rheinfelden** var. Rheinfeld. Aargau, N Switzerland 47.33N 7.46E
103 E17 **Rheinisches Schiefergebirge** var. Rhine State Uplands, Eng. Rhenish Slate Mountains. ▲▲ W Germany
103 D18 **Rheinland-Pfalz** Eng. Rhineland-Palatinate, Fr. Rhénanie-Palatinat. ◈ state W Germany
103 G18 **Rhein/Main** ✈ (Frankfurt am Main) Hessen, W Germany 50.03N 8.33E
Rhénanie du Nord-Westphalie see Nordrhein-Westfalen
Rhénanie-Palatinat see Rheinland-Pfalz
100 K12 **Rhenen** Utrecht, C Netherlands 51.57N 5.34E
Rhenish Slate Mountains see Rheinisches Schiefergebirge
Rhétiques, Alpes see Rhaetian Alps
102 N10 **Rhin** ≈ NE Germany
Rhin see Rhine
86 F10 **Rhine** Dut. Rijn, Fr. Rhin, Ger. Rhein. ≈ W Europe
32 L5 **Rhinelander** Wisconsin, N USA 45.39N 89.22W
Rhineland-Palatinate see Rheinland-Pfalz
Rhine State Uplands see Rheinisches Schiefergebirge
102 N11 **Rhinkanal** canal NE Germany
83 F17 **Rhino Camp** NW Uganda 2.58N 31.24E
76 D7 **Rhir, Cap** headland W Morocco 30.40N 9.54W
108 D7 **Rho** Lombardia, N Italy 45.31N 9.01E
21 N12 **Rhode Island** off. State of Rhode Island and Providence Plantations; also known as Little Rhody, Ocean State. ◈ state NE USA
21 O13 **Rhode Island** island Rhode Island, NE USA
21 O13 **Rhode Island Sound** sound Maine/Rhode Island, NE USA
Rhodes see Ródos
Rhode-Saint-Genèse see Sint-Genesius-Rode
86 L14 **Rhodes Basin** undersea feature E Mediterranean Sea
Rhodesia see Zimbabwe
116 I12 **Rhodope Mountains** var. Rodhópi Óri, Bul. Rhodope Planina, Rodopi, Gk. Orosirá Rodhópis, Turk. Dospad Dagh. ▲▲ Bulgaria/Greece
Rhodope Planina see Rhodope Mountains
Rhodos see Ródos
103 I18 **Rhön** ▲▲ C Germany
105 Q10 **Rhône** ◈ department E France
88 C12 **Rhône** ≈ France/Switzerland
105 R12 **Rhône-Alpes** ◈ region E France
123 J6 **Rhône Fan** undersea feature W Mediterranean Sea
100 G13 **Rhoon** Zuid-Holland, SW Netherlands 51.52N 4.25E
98 G9 **Rhum** var. Rum. island W Scotland, UK
Rhuthun see Ruthin
99 J18 **Rhyl** NE Wales, UK 53.19N 3.28W
61 K18 **Rialma** Goiás, S Brazil 15.22S 49.35W
106 L3 **Riaño** Castilla-León, N Spain 42.59N 5.00W
107 O9 **Riansáres** ≈ C Spain
158 H6 **Riāsi** Jammu and Kashmir, NW India 33.03N 74.51E
174 Gg7 **Riau** off. Propinsi Riau. ◈ province W Indonesia
Riau Archipelago see Riau, Kepulauan
174 I8 **Riau, Kepulauan** var. Riau Archipelago, Dut. Riouw-Archipel. island group W Indonesia
107 O6 **Riaza** Castilla-León, N Spain 41.17N 3.29W
107 N6 **Riaza** ≈ N Spain
83 K17 **Riba** spring/well NE Kenya 1.56N 40.38E
106 H4 **Ribadavia** Galicia, NW Spain 42.16N 8.07W
106 J2 **Ribadeo** Galicia, NW Spain 43.31N 7.04W
106 L2 **Ribadesella** Asturias, N Spain 43.27N 5.04W
106 G10 **Ribatejo** former province C Portugal
85 P15 **Ribáuè** Nampula, N Mozambique 14.56S 38.19E
99 K17 **Ribble** ≈ NW England, UK
97 F23 **Ribe** Ribe, W Denmark 55.19N 8.46E
97 F23 **Ribe** off. Ribe Amt, var. Ripen. ◈ county W Denmark
106 G3 **Ribeira** Galicia, NW Spain 42.33N 9.01W
66 O5 **Ribeira Brava** Madeira, Portugal, NE Atlantic Ocean 32.39N 17.04W
66 P3 **Ribeira Grande** São Miguel, Azores, Portugal, NE Atlantic Ocean 37.34N 25.31W
62 L8 **Ribeirão Preto** São Paulo, S Brazil 21.09S 47.48W
62 L11 **Ribeira, Rio** ≈ S Brazil
109 I24 **Ribera** Sicilia, Italy, C Mediterranean Sea 37.31N 13.16E
59 L14 **Riberalta** Beni, N Bolivia 11.00S 66.04W
107 W4 **Ribes de Freser** Cataluña, NE Spain 42.18N 2.11E
32 L6 **Rib Mountain** ▲ Wisconsin, N USA 44.55N 89.41W
111 U12 **Ribnica** Ger. Reifnitz. S Slovenia 45.46N 14.40E
119 N9 **Ribniţa** var. Râbniţa, Rus. Rybnitsa. NE Moldova 47.46N 29.01E
102 M8 **Ribnitz-Damgarten** Mecklenburg-Vorpommern, NE Germany 54.14N 12.25E
113 D16 **Říčany** Ger. Ritschan. Středočeský Kraj, W Czech Republic 49.58N 14.39E
31 U7 **Rice** Minnesota, N USA 45.42N 94.10W
32 J5 **Rice Lake** Wisconsin, N USA 45.33N 91.43W
12 I15 **Rice Lake** ◎ Ontario, SE Canada
12 E8 **Rice Lake** ◎ Ontario, S Canada
25 V3 **Richard B.Russell Lake** ⊠ Georgia, SE USA
27 U6 **Richardson** Texas, SW USA 32.57N 96.43W
9 R11 **Richardson** ≈ Alberta, C Canada
8 I3 **Richardson Mountains** ▲▲ Yukon Territory, NW Canada
193 C21 **Richardson Mountains** ▲▲ South Island, NZ
44 F3 **Richardson Peak** ▲ SE Belize 16.34N 88.46W
78 G10 **Richard Toll** N Senegal 16.27N 15.44W
30 L5 **Richardton** North Dakota, N USA 46.52N 102.19W
12 F13 **Rich, Cape** headland Ontario, S Canada 44.42N 80.37W
104 L8 **Richelieu** Indre-et-Loire, C France 47.01N 0.18E
35 P15 **Richfield** Idaho, NW USA 43.03N 114.11W
38 K5 **Richfield** Utah, W USA 38.46N 112.05W
20 J10 **Richfield Springs** New York, NE USA 42.52N 74.57W
20 M6 **Richford** Vermont, NE USA 44.59N 72.37W
29 R6 **Rich Hill** Missouri, C USA 38.06N 94.22W
11 P14 **Richibucto** New Brunswick, SE Canada 46.42N 64.54W
110 G8 **Richisau** Glarus, NE Switzerland 47.00N 8.54E
25 S6 **Richland** Georgia, SE USA 32.05N 84.40W
29 U6 **Richland** Missouri, C USA 37.51N 92.24W
27 U8 **Richland** Texas, SW USA 31.55N 96.25W
34 K10 **Richland** Washington, NW USA 46.17N 119.16W
32 K8 **Richland Center** Wisconsin, N USA 43.18N 90.22W
23 W11 **Richlands** North Carolina, SE USA 34.52N 77.33W
23 Q7 **Richlands** Virginia, NE USA 37.05N 81.47W
27 R9 **Richland Springs** Texas, SW USA 31.16N 98.56W
191 S8 **Richmond** New South Wales, SE Australia 33.36S 150.43E
8 L17 **Richmond** British Columbia, SW Canada 49.07N 123.09W
12 L13 **Richmond** Ontario, SE Canada 45.12N 75.49W
13 Q12 **Richmond** Québec, SE Canada 45.39N 72.07W
193 I14 **Richmond** Tasman, South Island, NZ 41.24S 173.04E
37 N8 **Richmond** California, W USA 37.57N 122.22W
33 Q14 **Richmond** Indiana, N USA 39.48N 84.52W
22 M6 **Richmond** Kentucky, S USA 37.45N 84.17W
29 S4 **Richmond** Missouri, C USA 39.16N 93.58W
27 V11 **Richmond** Texas, SW USA 29.34N 95.45W
38 L1 **Richmond** Utah, W USA 41.55N 111.51W
23 W6 **Richmond** state capital Virginia, NE USA 37.33N 77.27W
12 H15 **Richmond Hill** Ontario, S Canada 43.51N 79.24W
193 J15 **Richmond Range** ▲ South Island, NZ
29 S12 **Rich Mountain** ▲ Arkansas, C USA 34.37N 94.17W
33 S13 **Richwood** Ohio, N USA 40.25N 83.18W
23 R5 **Richwood** West Virginia, NE USA 38.13N 80.31W
106 K5 **Ricobayo, Embalse de** ⊠ NW Spain
Ricomagus see Riom
Ridā' see Radā'
100 H13 **Ridderkerk** Zuid-Holland, SW Netherlands 51.52N 4.34E
35 N16 **Riddle** Idaho, NW USA 42.07N 116.09W
34 F14 **Riddle** Oregon, NW USA 42.57N 123.21W
12 L13 **Rideau** ≈ Ontario, SE Canada
37 T12 **Ridgecrest** California, W USA 35.37N 117.40W
20 L13 **Ridgefield** Connecticut, NE USA 41.16N 73.30W
24 K5 **Ridgeland** Mississippi, S USA 32.25N 90.07W
23 R15 **Ridgeland** South Carolina, SE USA 32.28N 80.58W
22 F8 **Ridgely** Tennessee, S USA 36.15N 89.29W
12 D17 **Ridgetown** Ontario, S Canada 42.27N 81.52W
Ridgeway see Ridgway
23 R12 **Ridgeway** South Carolina, SE USA 34.17N 80.56W
20 D13 **Ridgway** var. Ridgeway. Pennsylvania, NE USA 41.24N 78.40W
9 W16 **Riding Mountain** ▲▲ Manitoba, S Canada
Ried see Ried im Innkreis
111 R4 **Ried im Innkreis** var. Ried. Oberösterreich, NW Austria 48.13N 13.28E
111 X8 **Riegersburg** Steiermark, SE Austria 47.03N 15.52E
110 E6 **Riehen** Basel-Stadt, NW Switzerland 47.34N 7.39E
94 J9 **Riehppegáisá** var. Rieppe. ▲ N Norway 69.38N 21.31E
101 K18 **Riemst** Limburg, NE Belgium 50.49N 5.35E
Rieppe see Riehppegáisá
103 O15 **Riesa** Sachsen, E Germany 51.18N 13.18E
65 H24 **Riesco, Isla** island S Chile
109 K25 **Riesi** Sicilia, Italy, C Mediterranean Sea 37.16N 14.04E
85 F25 **Riet** ≈ SW South Africa
85 I23 **Riet** ≈ SW South Africa
120 D11 **Rietavas** Telšiai, W Lithuania 55.43N 21.56E
85 F19 **Rietfontein** Omaheke, E Namibia 21.54S 20.57E
109 I14 **Rieti** anc. Reate. Lazio, C Italy 42.22N 12.49E
86 D14 **Rif** var. Er Rif, Er Riff, Riff. ▲▲ N Morocco
Riff see Rif
39 Q4 **Rifle** Colorado, C USA 39.30N 107.46W
33 R7 **Rifle River** ≈ Michigan, N USA
83 H18 **Rift Valley** ◈ province Kenya
Rift Valley see Great Rift Valley
120 F9 **Rīga** Eng. Riga. ● (Latvia) Rīga, C Latvia 56.57N 24.07E
Rigaer Bucht see Riga, Gulf of
120 F6 **Riga, Gulf of** Est. Liivi Laht, Ger. Rigaer Bucht, Latv. Rīgas Jūras Līcis, Rus. Rizhskiy Zaliv; prev. Est. Riia Laht. gulf Estonia/Latvia
149 U12 **Rīgān** Kermān, SE Iran 28.39N 59.01E
Rīgas Jūras Līcis see Riga, Gulf of
13 N12 **Rigaud** ≈ Ontario/Québec, SE Canada
35 R14 **Rigby** Idaho, NW USA 43.40N 111.54W
154 M10 **Rīgestān** var. Registan. desert region S Afghanistan
34 M11 **Riggins** Idaho, NW USA 45.24N 116.18W
11 R8 **Rigolet** Newfoundland and Labrador, NE Canada 54.10N 58.25W
80 G9 **Rig-Rig** Kanem, W Chad 14.19N 14.19E
120 F4 **Riguldi** Läänemaa, W Estonia 59.07N 23.34E
Riia Laht see Riga, Gulf of
95 L19 **Riihimäki** Etelä-Suomi, S Finland 60.45N 24.45E
205 O2 **Riiser-Larsen Ice Shelf** ice shelf Antarctica
205 U2 **Riiser-Larsen Peninsula** peninsula Antarctica
67 P22 **Riiser-Larsen Sea** sea Antarctica

◆ Country ● Country Capital ◇ Dependent Territory ○ Dependent Territory Capital ◈ Administrative Region ✈ International Airport ▲ Mountain ▲▲ Mountain Range ▲ Volcano ≈ River ◎ Lake ⊠ Reservoir
317

Riíto – Rondane

42 D2 **Riíto** Sonora, NW Mexico 32.06N 114.57W
114 B9 **Rijeka** Ger. Sankt Veit am Flaum, It. Fiume, Slvn. Reka; anc. Tarsatica. Primorje-Gorski Kotar, NW Croatia 45.20N 14.25E
101 I14 **Rijen** Noord-Brabant, S Netherlands 51.34N 4.55E
101 H15 **Rijkevorsel** Antwerpen, N Belgium 51.23N 4.43E
Rijn see Rhine
100 G11 **Rijnsburg** Zuid-Holland, W Netherlands 52.12N 4.27E
Rijssel see Lille
100 N10 **Rijssen** Overijssel, E Netherlands 52.19N 6.30E
100 G12 **Rijswijk** Eng. Ryswick. Zuid-Holland, W Netherlands 52.04N 4.22E
94 I10 **Riksgränsen** Norrbotten, N Sweden 68.24N 18.15E
172 Q6 **Rikubetsu** Hokkaidō, NE Japan 43.30N 143.43E
171 Mm12 **Rikuzen-Takata** Iwate, Honshū, C Japan 39.01N 141.37E
29 O4 **Riley** Kansas, C USA 39.18N 96.49W
101 I17 **Rillaar** Vlaams Brabant, C Belgium 50.58N 4.58E
Ri, Loch see Ree, Lough
116 G11 **Rilska Reka** ≈ W Bulgaria
79 T12 **Rima** ≈ N Nigeria
147 N7 **Rimah, Wādī ar** var. Wādī ar Rummah. dry watercourse C Saudi Arabia
Rimaszombat see Rimavská Sobota
203 R12 **Rimatara** island Îles Australes, SW French Polynesia
113 L20 **Rimavská Sobota** Ger. Gross-Steffelsdorf, Hung. Rimaszombat. Banskobystrický Kraj, C Slovakia 48.24N 20.01E
9 Q15 **Rimbey** Alberta, SW Canada 52.39N 114.10W
97 P15 **Rimbo** Stockholm, C Sweden 59.43N 18.21E
97 M18 **Rimforsa** Östergötland, S Sweden 58.06N 15.40E
108 I11 **Rimini** anc. Ariminum. Emilia-Romagna, N Italy 44.03N 12.33E
Rîmnicu-Sărat see Râmnicu Sărat
Rîmnicu Vîlcea see Râmnicu Vâlcea
155 Y3 **Rimo Muztāgh** ▲ India/Pakistan
13 U7 **Rimouski** Québec, SE Canada 48.25N 68.31W
164 M16 **Rinbung** Xizang Zizhiqu, W China 29.15N 89.40E
168 I5 **Rinchinlhümbe** Hövsgöl, N Mongolia 51.06N 99.40E
64 I5 **Rincón, Cerro** ▲ N Chile 24.01S 67.19W
106 M15 **Rincón de la Victoria** Andalucía, S Spain 36.43N 4.18W
Rincón del Bonete, Lago Artificial de see Río Negro, Embalse del
107 Q4 **Rincón de Soto** La Rioja, N Spain 42.15N 1.49W
96 G8 **Rindal** Møre og Romsdal, S Norway 63.02N 9.09E
117 J20 **Ríneia** island Kykládes, Greece, Aegean Sea
158 H11 **Ringas** prev. Reengus, Ringus. Rājasthān, N India 27.18N 75.27E
97 H24 **Ringe** Fyn, C Denmark 55.13N 10.30E
96 H11 **Ringebu** Oppland, S Norway 61.31N 10.09E
Ringen see Rõngu
195 U14 **Ringgi** Kolombangara, NW Solomon Islands 8.03S 95.08E
25 R1 **Ringgold** Georgia, SE USA 34.55N 85.06W
24 G5 **Ringgold** Louisiana, S USA 32.19N 93.16W
27 S5 **Ringgold** Texas, SW USA 33.47N 97.56W
97 E22 **Ringkøbing** Ringkøbing, W Denmark 56.04N 8.22E
97 E21 **Ringkøbing** off. Ringkøbing Amt. ◆ county W Denmark
97 E22 **Ringkøbing Fjord** fjord W Denmark
35 S10 **Ringling** Montana, NW USA 46.15N 110.48W
29 N13 **Ringling** Oklahoma, C USA 34.12N 97.35W
96 H13 **Ringsaker** Hedmark, S Norway 60.54N 10.45E
97 I23 **Ringsted** Vestsjælland, E Denmark 55.28N 11.48E
Ringus see Ringas
94 I9 **Ringvassøya** Lapp. Ráneš. island N Norway
20 K13 **Ringwood** New Jersey, NE USA 41.06N 74.15W
Rinn Duáin see Hook Head
102 H13 **Rinteln** Niedersachsen, NW Germany 52.10N 9.04E
Rio see Rio de Janeiro
117 E18 **Río** Dytikí Ellás, S Greece 38.18N 21.48E
58 C7 **Riobamba** Chimborazo, C Ecuador 1.38S 78.40W
62 P9 **Rio Bonito** Rio de Janeiro, SE Brazil 22.42S 42.38W
61 C16 **Rio Branco** state capital Acre, W Brazil 9.58S 67.49W
63 H18 **Río Branco** Cerro Largo, NE Uruguay 32.34S 53.21W
Rio Branco, Território de see Roraima
43 P8 **Río Bravo** Tamaulipas, C Mexico 25.57N 98.03W
65 G16 **Río Bueno** Los Lagos, C Chile 40.19S 72.55W
57 P5 **Río Caribe** Sucre, NE Venezuela 10.40N 63.07W
56 M5 **Río Chico** Miranda, N Venezuela 10.18N 66.00W
65 H18 **Río Cisnes** Aisén, S Chile 44.29S 71.15W
62 L9 **Rio Claro** São Paulo, S Brazil 22.22S 47.31W
47 V14 **Rio Claro** Trinidad, Trinidad and Tobago 10.18N 61.10W
56 J5 **Río Claro** Lara, N Venezuela 9.54N 69.22W
65 K15 **Río Colorado** Río Negro, E Argentina 39.04S 64.04W
64 K11 **Río Cuarto** Córdoba, C Argentina 33.06S 64.20W
62 P10 **Rio de Janeiro** var. Rio. state capital Rio de Janeiro, SE Brazil 22.52S 43.16W
62 P9 **Rio de Janeiro** off. Estado do Rio de Janeiro. ◆ state SE Brazil
45 R17 **Río de Jesús** Veraguas, S Panama 7.57N 81.09W
36 K3 **Rio Dell** California, W USA 40.30N 124.07W
62 K13 **Rio do Sul** Santa Catarina, S Brazil 27.15S 49.37W
65 I23 **Río Gallegos** var. Gallegos, Puerto Gallegos. Santa Cruz, S Argentina 51.39S 69.21W
63 I18 **Rio Grande** var. São Pedro do Rio Grande do Sul. Rio Grande do Sul, S Brazil 32.03S 52.07W
26 I9 **Rio Grande** ≈ Texas, SW USA
65 J24 **Río Grande** Tierra del Fuego, S Argentina 53.45S 67.46W
42 L10 **Río Grande** Zacatecas, C Mexico 23.48N 103.03W
44 J9 **Río Grande** León, NW Nicaragua 12.57N 86.31W
47 V5 **Río Grande** E Puerto Rico 18.22N 65.49W
27 R17 **Rio Grande City** Texas, SW USA 26.22N 98.49W
61 P14 **Rio Grande do Norte** off. Estado do Rio Grande do Norte. ◆ state E Brazil
63 G15 **Rio Grande do Sul** off. Estado do Rio Grande do Sul. ◆ state S Brazil
67 M17 **Rio Grande Fracture Zone** tectonic feature C Atlantic Ocean
67 J18 **Rio Grande Gap** undersea feature S Atlantic Ocean
Rio Grande Plateau see Rio Grande Rise
67 J18 **Rio Grande Rise** var. Rio Grande Plateau. undersea feature SW Atlantic Ocean
56 G4 **Ríohacha** La Guajira, N Colombia 11.22N 72.46W
45 S16 **Río Hato** Coclé, C Panama 8.22N 80.09W
27 T17 **Rio Hondo** Texas, SW USA 26.14N 97.34W
58 D10 **Rioja** San Martín, N Peru 6.03S 77.05W
43 Y11 **Río Lagartos** Yucatán, SE Mexico 21.34N 88.07W
105 P11 **Riom** anc. Ricomagus. Puy-de-Dôme, C France 45.54N 3.06E
106 F10 **Rio Maior** Santarém, C Portugal 39.19N 8.55W
105 O12 **Riom-ès-Montagnes** Cantal, C France 45.15N 2.39E
62 J12 **Rio Negro** Paraná, S Brazil 26.06S 49.46W
65 I15 **Río Negro** off. Provincia de Río Negro. ◆ province C Argentina
63 D18 **Río Negro** ◆ department W Uruguay
49 V12 **Río Negro, Embalse del** var. Lago Artificial de Rincón del Bonete. ⊠ C Uruguay
109 M17 **Rionero in Vulture** Basilicata, S Italy 40.55N 15.40E
143 S9 **Rioni** ≈ W Georgia
107 P12 **Riópar** Castilla-La Mancha, C Spain 38.31N 2.27W
63 H16 **Rio Pardo** Rio Grande do Sul, S Brazil 29.41S 52.25W
39 R11 **Rio Rancho Estates** New Mexico, SW USA 35.14N 106.40W
44 L11 **Río San Juan** ◆ department S Nicaragua
56 E9 **Riosucio** Caldas, W Colombia 5.25N 75.43W
56 C7 **Ríosucio** Chocó, NW Colombia 7.24N 77.09W
64 K10 **Río Tercero** Córdoba, C Argentina 32.12S 64.03W
56 J5 **Río Tocuyo** Lara, N Venezuela 10.12N 69.58W
Riouw-Archipel see Riau, Kepulauan
61 J19 **Rio Verde** Goiás, C Brazil 17.49S 50.55W
43 O12 **Río Verde** var. Rioverde. San Luis Potosí, C Mexico 21.58N 100.00W
37 O8 **Rio Vista** California, W USA 38.09N 121.42W
114 M11 **Ripanj** Serbia, N Serbia and Montenegro (Yugoslavia) 44.37N 20.30E
108 J13 **Ripatransone** Marche, C Italy 43.00N 13.45E
Ripen see Ribe
24 M2 **Ripley** Mississippi, S USA 34.43N 88.57W
33 R15 **Ripley** Ohio, N USA 38.45N 83.51W
22 F9 **Ripley** Tennessee, S USA 35.45N 89.31W
23 Q4 **Ripley** West Virginia, NE USA 38.49N 81.42W
107 W4 **Ripoll** Cataluña, NE Spain 42.12N 2.12E
99 M16 **Ripon** N England, UK 54.07N 1.31W
32 M7 **Ripon** Wisconsin, N USA 43.52N 88.48W
109 L24 **Riposto** Sicilia, Italy, C Mediterranean Sea 37.43N 15.13E
101 L14 **Rips** Noord-Brabant, SE Netherlands 51.31N 5.49E
56 D9 **Risaralda** off. Departamento de Risaralda. ◆ province C Colombia
118 L8 **Rişcani** var. Râşcani, Rus. Ryshkany. NW Moldova 47.55N 27.31E
158 J9 **Rishikesh** Uttaranchal, N India 30.06N 78.16E
172 P2 **Rishiri-suidō** strait E Sea of Japan
172 Oo2 **Rishiri-tō** var. Risiri Tô. island NE Japan
172 P2 **Rishiri-yama** ▲ Rishiri-tō, NE Japan 45.11N 141.11E
27 R7 **Rising Star** Texas, SW USA 32.06N 98.57W
33 Q15 **Rising Sun** Indiana, N USA 38.58N 84.52W
Risiri Tô see Rishiri-tō
104 L4 **Risle** ≈ N France
Rîşno see Râşnov
29 V13 **Rison** Arkansas, C USA 33.57N 92.11W
97 G17 **Risør** Aust-Agder, S Norway 58.43N 9.13E
94 H10 **Risøyhamn** Nordland, C Norway 69.00N 15.37E
103 I23 **Riss** ≈ S Germany
120 G4 **Risti** Ger. Kreuz. Läänemaa, W Estonia 59.03N 24.11E
13 V8 **Ristigouche** ≈ Québec, SE Canada
95 N18 **Ristiina** Isä-Suomi, E Finland 61.31N 27.15E
95 N14 **Ristijärvi** Oulu, C Finland 64.30N 28.15E
196 C14 **Ritidian Point** headland N Guam 13.39N 144.51E
Ritschan see Říčany
37 R9 **Ritter, Mount** ▲ California, W USA 37.40N 119.10W
33 T12 **Rittman** Ohio, N USA 40.58N 81.46W
34 L9 **Ritzville** Washington, NW USA 47.07N 118.22W
Riva see Riva del Garda
63 A21 **Rivadavia** Buenos Aires, E Argentina 35.28S 62.58W
108 F7 **Riva del Garda** var. Riva. Trentino-Alto Adige, N Italy 45.54N 10.50E
108 B8 **Rivarolo Canavese** Piemonte, W Italy 45.21N 7.42E
44 K11 **Rivas** Rivas, SW Nicaragua 11.25N 85.49W
44 J11 **Rivas** ◆ department SW Nicaragua
105 R11 **Rive-de-Gier** Loire, E France 45.31N 4.36E
63 A22 **Rivera** Buenos Aires, E Argentina 37.13S 63.13W
63 F16 **Rivera** Rivera, NE Uruguay 30.54S 55.31W
63 F17 **Rivera** ◆ department NE Uruguay
37 P9 **Riverbank** California, W USA 37.43N 120.59W
78 K17 **River Cess** SW Liberia 5.28N 9.31W
30 M4 **Riverdale** North Dakota, N USA 47.29N 101.22W
32 I6 **River Falls** Wisconsin, N USA 44.52N 92.38W
9 T16 **Riverhurst** Saskatchewan, S Canada 50.52N 106.49W
191 O10 **Riverina** physical region New South Wales, SE Australia
82 G8 **River Nile** ◆ state NE Sudan
65 F19 **Rivero, Isla** island Archipiélago de los Chonos, S Chile
9 W16 **Rivers** Manitoba, S Canada 50.01N 100.13W
79 U17 **Rivers** ◆ state S Nigeria
193 D23 **Riversdale** Southland, South Island, NZ 45.54S 168.44E
85 F26 **Riversdale** Western Cape, SW South Africa 34.04S 21.15E
37 U15 **Riverside** California, W USA 33.57N 117.24W
27 W9 **Riverside** Texas, SW USA 30.51N 95.24W
39 U3 **Riverside Reservoir** ⊠ Colorado, C USA
8 K15 **Rivers Inlet** British Columbia, SW Canada 51.43N 127.19W
8 K15 **Rivers Inlet** inlet British Columbia, SW Canada
9 X15 **Riverton** Manitoba, S Canada 51.00N 97.00W
193 C24 **Riverton** Southland, South Island, NZ 46.19S 168.02E
32 L13 **Riverton** Illinois, N USA 39.50N 89.31W
38 L3 **Riverton** Utah, W USA 40.32N 111.57W
35 V15 **Riverton** Wyoming, C USA 43.01N 108.22W
12 G10 **River Valley** Ontario, S Canada 46.36N 80.09W
11 P14 **Riverview** New Brunswick, SE Canada 46.03N 64.46W
105 O17 **Rivesaltes** Pyrénées-Orientales, S France 42.46N 2.48E
38 H11 **Riviera** Arizona, SW USA 35.06N 114.36W
27 S15 **Riviera** Texas, SW USA 27.15N 97.48W
25 Z14 **Riviera Beach** Florida, SE USA 26.46N 80.03W
13 Q10 **Rivière-à-Pierre** Québec, SE Canada 46.59N 72.12W
13 T9 **Rivière-Bleue** Québec, SE Canada 47.25N 69.01W
13 T8 **Rivière-du-Loup** Québec, SE Canada 47.49N 69.31W
181 Y15 **Rivière du Rempart** NE Mauritius 20.06S 57.40E
47 R12 **Rivière-Pilote** S Martinique 14.29N 60.54W
181 O17 **Rivière St-Etienne, Point de la** headland SW Réunion
11 S10 **Rivière-St-Paul** Québec, E Canada 51.26N 57.52W
Rivière Sèche see Bel Air
118 K4 **Rivne** Pol. Równe, Rus. Rovno. Rivnens'ka Oblast', NW Ukraine 50.37N 26.15E
Rivne see Rivnens'ka Oblast'
118 K3 **Rivnens'ka Oblast'** var. Rivne, Rus. Rovenskaya Oblast'. ◆ province NW Ukraine
108 B8 **Rivoli** Piemonte, NW Italy 45.04N 7.31E
165 Q14 **Riwoqê** var. Racaka. Xizang Zizhiqu, W China 31.10N 96.25E
101 H19 **Rixensart** Wallon Brabant, C Belgium 50.43N 4.31E
Riyadh/Riyāḍ, Minṭaqat ar see Ar Riyāḍ
Riyāq see Rayak
Rizaiyeh see Orūmīyeh
143 P11 **Rize** Rize, NE Turkey 41.02N 40.33E
143 P11 **Rize** prev. Çoruh. ◆ province NE Turkey
167 R5 **Rizhao** Shandong, E China 35.23N 119.31E
Rizhskiy Zaliv see Riga, Gulf of
Rizokarpaso/Rizokárpason see Dipkarpaz
109 O21 **Rizzuto, Capo** headland S Italy 38.54N 17.05E
97 F15 **Rjukan** Telemark, S Norway 59.52N 8.37E
97 D16 **Rjuven** ▲ S Norway
78 H9 **Rkiz** Trarza, W Mauritania 16.49N 15.19W
97 H14 **Roa** Oppland, S Norway 60.16N 10.38E
107 N5 **Roa** Castilla-León, N Spain 41.42N 3.55W
47 T9 **Road Town** ○ (British Virgin Islands) Tortola, C British Virgin Islands 18.24N 64.38W
98 F6 **Roag, Loch** inlet NW Scotland, UK
39 O5 **Roan Cliffs** cliff Colorado/Utah, W USA
23 P9 **Roan High Knob** var. Roan Mountain. ▲ North Carolina/Tennessee, SE USA 36.09N 82.07W
Roan Mountain see Roan High Knob
105 Q10 **Roanne** anc. Rodunma. Loire, E France 46.03N 4.04E
25 R4 **Roanoke** Alabama, S USA 33.09N 85.22W
23 S7 **Roanoke** Virginia, NE USA 37.16N 79.56W
23 Z9 **Roanoke Island** island North Carolina, SE USA
23 W8 **Roanoke Rapids** North Carolina, SE USA 36.27N 77.39W
23 X9 **Roanoke River** ≈ North Carolina/Virginia, SE USA
39 O4 **Roan Plateau** plain Utah, W USA
39 R5 **Roaring Fork River** ≈ Colorado, C USA
27 O5 **Roaring Springs** Texas, SW USA 33.54N 100.51W
44 J4 **Roatán** var. Coxen Hole, Coxin Hole. Islas de la Bahía, N Honduras 16.18N 86.32W
44 I4 **Roatán, Isla de** island Islas de la Bahía, N Honduras
Roat Kampuchea see Cambodia
Roazon see Rennes
149 T7 **Robāț-e Chāh Gonbad** Yazd, E Iran
149 R7 **Robāț-e Khān** Yazd, C Iran 33.24N 56.04E
149 T7 **Robāț-e Khvosh Āb** Yazd, E Iran
149 R8 **Robāț-e Posht-e Bādām** Yazd, NE Iran 33.01N 55.34E
149 Q8 **Robāț-e Rīzāb** Yazd, C Iran
183 S8 **Robbie Ridge** undersea feature W Pacific Ocean
23 T10 **Robbins** North Carolina, SE USA 35.25N 79.35W
191 N15 **Robbins Island** island Tasmania, SE Australia
23 N10 **Robbinsville** North Carolina, SE USA 35.19N 83.48W
190 J12 **Robe** South Australia 37.11S 139.48E
23 W9 **Robersonville** North Carolina, SE USA 35.49N 77.15W
27 P8 **Robert Lee** Texas, SW USA 31.54N 100.26W
37 V5 **Roberts Creek Mountain** ▲ Nevada, W USA 39.52N 116.16W
95 J15 **Robertsfors** Västerbotten, N Sweden 64.12N 20.49E
29 R11 **Robert S.Kerr Reservoir** ⊠ Oklahoma, C USA
40 L12 **Roberts Mountain** ▲ Nunivak Island, Alaska, USA 60.01N 166.15W
85 F26 **Robertson** Western Cape, SW South Africa 33.48S 19.52E
204 H4 **Robertson Island** island Antarctica
78 J16 **Robertsport** W Liberia 6.45N 11.15W
190 J8 **Robertstown** South Australia 34.00S 139.04E
Robert Williams see Caála
13 P7 **Roberval** Québec, SE Canada 48.31N 72.16W
33 N15 **Robinson** Illinois, N USA 39.00N 87.44W
200 Oo12 **Róbinson Crusoe, Isla** island Islas Juan Fernández, Chile, E Pacific Ocean
188 J9 **Robinson Range** ▲ Western Australia
194 L16 **Robinson River** Central, S PNG 10.06S 148.51E
190 M9 **Robinvale** Victoria, SE Australia 34.37S 142.45E
107 P11 **Robledo** Castilla-La Mancha, C Spain 38.45N 2.27W
56 G5 **Robles** var. La Paz, Robles La Paz. Cesar, N Colombia 10.24N 73.10W
Robles La Paz see Robles
9 V15 **Roblin** Manitoba, S Canada 51.15N 101.19W
195 U13 **Rob Roy** island NW Solomon Islands
9 S17 **Robsart** Saskatchewan, S Canada 49.22N 109.15W
9 N15 **Robson, Mount** ▲ British Columbia, SW Canada 53.09N 119.16W
27 T14 **Robstown** Texas, SW USA 27.47N 97.40W
27 P6 **Roby** Texas, SW USA 32.43N 100.22W
106 E11 **Roca, Cabo da** headland C Portugal 38.47N 9.32W
Rocadas see Xangongo
43 S14 **Roca Partida, Punta** headland C Mexico 18.43N 95.11W
49 X6 **Rocas, Atol das** island E Brazil
109 L18 **Roccadaspide** var. Rocca d'Aspide. Campania, S Italy 40.25N 15.12E
109 K15 **Roccaraso** Abruzzo, C Italy 41.49N 14.01E
108 H10 **Rocca San Casciano** Emilia-Romagna, C Italy 44.06N 11.51E
108 G13 **Roccastrada** Toscana, C Italy 43.00N 11.09E
63 G20 **Rocha** Rocha, E Uruguay 34.30S 54.22W
63 G19 **Rocha** ◆ department E Uruguay
99 L17 **Rochdale** NW England, UK 53.37N 2.09W
104 L11 **Rochechouart** Haute-Vienne, C France 45.49N 0.49E
101 J22 **Rochefort** Namur, SE Belgium 50.10N 5.13E
104 J11 **Rochefort** var. Rochefort sur Mer. Charente-Maritime, W France 45.57N 0.58W
Rochefort sur Mer see Rochefort
129 N10 **Rochegda** Arkhangel'skaya Oblast', NW Russian Federation 62.37N 43.21E
32 L10 **Rochelle** Illinois, N USA 41.54N 89.03W
27 Q9 **Rochelle** Texas, SW USA 31.13N 99.10W
13 V3 **Rochers Ouest, Rivière aux** ≈ Québec, SE Canada
99 O22 **Rochester** anc. Durobrivae. SE England, UK 51.24N 0.30E
33 O12 **Rochester** Indiana, N USA 41.03N 86.13W
31 W10 **Rochester** Minnesota, N USA 44.01N 92.28W
21 O9 **Rochester** New Hampshire, NE USA 43.18N 70.58W
20 F9 **Rochester** New York, NE USA 43.09N 77.37W
27 P5 **Rochester** Texas, SW USA 33.19N 99.51W
33 S9 **Rochester Hills** Michigan, N USA 42.39N 83.04W
Rocheuses, Montagnes/Rockies see Rocky Mountains
66 M6 **Rockall** island UK, N Atlantic Ocean
66 L6 **Rockall Bank** undersea feature N Atlantic Ocean
86 B8 **Rockall Rise** undersea feature N Atlantic Ocean
86 C9 **Rockall Trough** undersea feature N Atlantic Ocean
37 U2 **Rock Creek** ≈ Nevada, W USA
27 T10 **Rockdale** Texas, SW USA 30.39N 96.58W
205 N12 **Rockefeller Plateau** plateau Antarctica
32 K11 **Rock Falls** Illinois, N USA 41.46N 89.41W
25 Q5 **Rockford** Alabama, S USA 32.53N 86.11W
32 L10 **Rockford** Illinois, N USA 42.16N 89.05W
13 Q12 **Rock Forest** Québec, SE Canada 45.21N 71.58W
9 T17 **Rockglen** Saskatchewan, S Canada 49.10N 105.57W
189 Y8 **Rockhampton** Queensland, E Australia 23.31S 150.31E
23 R11 **Rock Hill** South Carolina, SE USA 34.55N 80.59W
188 I13 **Rockingham** Western Australia 32.16S 115.21E
23 T11 **Rockingham** North Carolina, SE USA 34.56N 79.46W
32 J11 **Rock Island** Illinois, N USA 41.30N 90.34W
27 U12 **Rock Island** Texas, SW USA 29.31N 96.33W
12 C10 **Rock Lake** Ontario, S Canada 46.25N 83.49W
31 O2 **Rock Lake** North Dakota, N USA 48.45N 99.12W
12 I12 **Rock Lake** ⊚ Ontario, SE Canada
12 M12 **Rockland** Ontario, SE Canada 45.33N 75.16W
21 R7 **Rockland** Maine, NE USA 44.08N 69.06W
190 L11 **Rocklands Reservoir** ⊠ Victoria, SE Australia
37 O7 **Rocklin** California, W USA 38.48N 121.13W
25 R3 **Rockmart** Georgia, SE USA 34.00N 85.02W
33 N16 **Rockport** Indiana, N USA 37.52N 87.04W
29 Q1 **Rock Port** Missouri, C USA 40.26N 95.30W
27 T14 **Rockport** Texas, SW USA 28.01N 97.03W
34 I7 **Rockport** Washington, NW USA 48.28N 121.36W
31 S11 **Rock Rapids** Iowa, C USA 43.25N 96.10W
32 K11 **Rock River** ≈ Illinois/Wisconsin, N USA
46 I3 **Rock Sound** Eleuthera Island, C Bahamas 24.51N 76.09W
35 U17 **Rock Springs** Wyoming, C USA 41.35N 109.12W
27 P11 **Rocksprings** Texas, SW USA 30.01N 100.12W
57 T9 **Rockstone** C Guyana 5.58N 58.33W
31 S12 **Rock Valley** Iowa, C USA 43.12N 96.17W
33 N14 **Rockville** Indiana, N USA 39.45N 87.13W
23 W3 **Rockville** Maryland, NE USA 39.04N 77.04W
27 U6 **Rockwall** Texas, SW USA 32.55N 96.27W
31 U13 **Rockwell City** Iowa, C USA 42.24N 94.37W
33 S10 **Rockwood** Michigan, N USA 42.04N 83.15W
22 M9 **Rockwood** Tennessee, S USA 35.52N 84.41W
27 Q8 **Rockwood** Texas, SW USA 31.29N 99.23W
39 U6 **Rocky Ford** Colorado, C USA 38.03N 103.45W
12 D9 **Rocky Island Lake** ⊚ Ontario, S Canada
23 V9 **Rocky Mount** North Carolina, SE USA 35.56N 77.47W
23 S7 **Rocky Mount** Virginia, NE USA 37.00N 79.53W
35 Q8 **Rocky Mountain** ▲ Montana, NW USA 47.45N 112.46W
9 P15 **Rocky Mountain House** Alberta, SW Canada 52.24N 114.52W
39 T3 **Rocky Mountain National Park** national park Colorado, C USA
2 E12 **Rocky Mountains** var. Rockies, Fr. Montagnes Rocheuses. ▲ Canada/USA
44 H1 **Rocky Point** headland NE Belize 18.21N 88.04W
85 A17 **Rocky Point** headland NW Namibia 19.01S 12.27E
97 F14 **Rødberg** Buskerud, S Norway 60.16N 9.00E
97 I25 **Rødby** Storstrøm, SE Denmark 54.42N 11.24E
97 I25 **Rødbyhavn** Storstrøm, SE Denmark 54.39N 11.24E
11 T10 **Roddickton** Newfoundland and Labrador, SE Canada 50.51N 56.03W
97 F23 **Rødding** Sønderjylland, SW Denmark 55.22N 9.04E
97 M22 **Rödeby** Blekinge, S Sweden 56.16N 15.34E
100 N6 **Roden** Drenthe, NE Netherlands 53.07N 6.25E
64 H9 **Rodeo** San Juan, W Argentina 30.12S 69.06W
105 O14 **Rodez** anc. Segodunum. Aveyron, S France 44.21N 2.34E
Rodholívos see Rodolívos
Rodhópi Óri see Rhodope Mountains
Ródhos/Rodi see Ródos
109 N15 **Rodi Garganico** Puglia, SE Italy 41.54N 15.51E
103 N20 **Roding** Bayern, SE Germany 49.12N 12.30E
115 J19 **Rodinit, Kepi i** headland W Albania 41.35N 19.27E
118 I9 **Rodnei, Munții** ▲ N Romania
192 L4 **Rodney, Cape** headland North Island, NZ 36.16S 174.48E
40 L9 **Rodney, Cape** headland Alaska, USA 64.39N 166.24W
128 M16 **Rodniki** Ivanovskaya Oblast', W Russian Federation 57.04N 41.45E
121 Q16 **Rodnya** Rus. Rodnya. Mahilyowskaya Voblasts', E Belarus 53.30N 32.12E
Rodó see José Enrique Rodó
116 H13 **Rodolívos** var. Rodholívos. Kentrikí Makedonía, NE Greece 40.55N 23.59E
Rodopi see Rhodope Mountains
117 O22 **Ródos** var. Ródhos, Eng. Rhodes, It. Rodi. Ródos, Dodekánisos, Greece, Aegean Sea 36.25N 28.13E
117 O22 **Ródos** var. Ródhos, Eng. Rhodes, It. Rodi; anc. Rhodos. island Dodekánisos, Greece, Aegean Sea
Rodosto see Tekirdağ
61 A14 **Rodrigues** Amazonas, W Brazil 6.50S 73.45W
181 P8 **Rodrigues** var. Rodriquez. island E Mauritius
Rodriquez see Rodrigues
Rodunma see Roanne
188 I7 **Roebourne** Western Australia 20.49S 117.04E
85 J20 **Roedtan** Limpopo, NE South Africa 24.37S 29.04E
100 H11 **Roelofarendsveen** Zuid-Holland, W Netherlands 52.12N 4.37E
Roepat see Rupat, Pulau
Roer see Rur
101 M16 **Roermond** Limburg, SE Netherlands 51.12N 6.00E
101 C18 **Roeselare** Fr. Roulers; prev. Rousselaere. West-Vlaanderen, W Belgium 50.57N 3.07E
15 Li5 **Roes Welcome Sound** strait Nunavut, N Canada
Roeteng see Ruteng
Rofreit see Rovereto
Rogachëv see Rahachow
59 L15 **Rogagua, Laguna** ⊚ NW Bolivia
97 C16 **Rogaland** ◆ county S Norway
27 Y9 **Roganville** Texas, SW USA 30.49N 93.54W
111 W11 **Rogaška Slatina** Ger. Rohitsch-Sauerbrunn; prev. Rogatec-Slatina. E Slovenia 46.13N 15.38E
Rogatec-Slatina see Rogaška Slatina
114 J13 **Rogatica** Republica Srpska, SE Bosnia & Herzegovina 43.50N 18.55E
Rogatin see Rohatyn
95 F17 **Rogen** ⊚ C Sweden
29 S9 **Rogers** Arkansas, C USA 36.19N 94.07W
31 P5 **Rogers** North Dakota, N USA 47.03N 98.12W
27 T9 **Rogers** Texas, SW USA 30.53N 97.10W
33 R5 **Rogers City** Michigan, N USA 45.25N 83.49W
Roger Simpson Island see Abemama
37 T14 **Rogers Lake** salt flat California, W USA
23 Q8 **Rogers, Mount** ▲ Virginia, NE USA 36.39N 81.32W
35 O16 **Rogerson** Idaho, NW USA 42.11N 114.36W
9 O16 **Rogers Pass** pass British Columbia, SW Canada 51.18N 117.36W
23 O8 **Rogersville** Tennessee, S USA 36.26N 83.01W
101 L16 **Roggel** Limburg, SE Netherlands 51.16N 5.55E
Roggeveen see Roggewein, Cabo
200 Nn12 **Roggeveen Basin** undersea feature E Pacific Ocean
203 X16 **Roggewein, Cabo** var. Roggeveen. headland Easter Island, Chile, E Pacific Ocean 27.07S 109.15W
105 Y13 **Rogliano** Corse, France, C Mediterranean Sea 42.58N 9.25E
109 N21 **Rogliano** Calabria, SW Italy 39.09N 16.18E
94 G12 **Rognan** Nordland, C Norway 67.04N 15.21E
102 K10 **Rögnitz** ≈ N Germany
Rogozhina/Rogozhinë see Rrogozhinë
112 G10 **Rogoźno** Wielkopolskie, C Poland 52.46N 16.57E
34 E15 **Rogue River** ≈ Oregon, NW USA
118 I6 **Rohatyn** Rus. Rogatin. Ivano-Frankivs'ka Oblast', W Ukraine 49.25N 24.35E
201 O14 **Rohi** Pohnpei, E Micronesia
Rohitsch-Sauerbrunn see Rogaška Slatina
155 Q13 **Rohri** Sind, SE Pakistan 27.40N 68.52E
158 I10 **Rohtak** Haryāna, N India 28.55N 76.32E
Roi Ed see Roi Et
178 Ii10 **Roi Et** var. Muang Roi Et, Roi Ed. Roi Et, E Thailand 16.04N 103.37E
203 U9 **Roi Georges, Îles du** island group Îles Tuamotu, C French Polynesia
159 Y10 **Roing** Arunāchal Pradesh, NE India 28.06N 95.46E
120 E7 **Roja** Talsi, NW Latvia 57.31N 22.44E
63 B20 **Rojas** Buenos Aires, E Argentina 34.13S 60.41W
155 R12 **Rojhān** Punjab, E Pakistan 28.44N 70.01E
43 Q12 **Rojo, Cabo** headland C Mexico 21.33N 97.19W
47 Q10 **Rojo, Cabo** headland W Puerto Rico 17.57N 67.10W
173 G7 **Rokan Kanan, Sungai** ≈ Sumatera, W Indonesia
173 G7 **Rokan Kiri, Sungai** ≈ Sumatera, W Indonesia
Rokha see Rokhah
155 R4 **Rokhah** var. Rokha. Kāpīsā, E Afghanistan 35.16N 69.28E
120 I11 **Rokiškis** Panevėžys, NE Lithuania 55.58N 25.34E
172 Nn9 **Rokkasho** Aomori, Honshū, C Japan 40.59N 141.22E
113 B17 **Rokycany** Ger. Rokytzan. Plzeňský Kraj, NW Czech Republic 49.45N 13.36E
119 P6 **Rokytne** Kyyivs'ka Oblast', N Ukraine 49.40N 30.29E
118 L3 **Rokytne** Rivnens'ka Oblast', NW Ukraine 51.19N 27.09E
Rokytzan see Rokycany
164 L11 **Rola Co** ⊚ W China
31 V13 **Roland** Iowa, C USA 42.10N 93.30W
97 D15 **Røldal** Hordaland, S Norway 59.52N 6.49E
100 O7 **Rolde** Drenthe, NE Netherlands 52.58N 6.39E
31 O2 **Rolette** North Dakota, N USA 48.39N 99.50W
29 V6 **Rolla** Missouri, C USA 37.57N 91.46W
31 O2 **Rolla** North Dakota, N USA 48.51N 99.37W
110 A10 **Rolle** Vaud, W Switzerland 46.27N 6.19E
189 X8 **Rolleston** Queensland, E Australia 24.30S 148.36E
193 H19 **Rolleston** Canterbury, South Island, NZ 43.34S 172.24E
193 G18 **Rolleston Range** ▲ South Island, NZ
12 H8 **Rollet** Québec, SE Canada 47.56N 79.14W
24 J4 **Rolling Fork** Mississippi, S USA 32.54N 90.52W
22 L6 **Rolling Fork** ≈ Kentucky, S USA
12 J11 **Rolphton** Ontario, SE Canada 46.09N 77.43W
Röm see Rømø
189 X10 **Roma** Queensland, E Australia 26.36S 148.53E
109 I15 **Roma** Eng. Rome. ● (Italy) Lazio, C Italy 41.52N 12.30E
97 P19 **Roma** Gotland, SE Sweden 57.31N 18.28E
23 T14 **Romain, Cape** headland South Carolina, SE USA 33.00N 79.21W
11 P11 **Romaine** ≈ Newfoundland and Labrador/Québec, E Canada
27 R17 **Roma Los Saenz** Texas, SW USA 26.24N 99.01W
116 H8 **Roman** Vratsa, NW Bulgaria 43.09N 23.56E
118 L10 **Roman** Hung. Románvásár. Neamț, NE Romania 46.46N 26.55E
66 M13 **Romanche Fracture Zone** tectonic feature E Atlantic Ocean
63 C15 **Romang** Santa Fe, C Argentina 29.30S 59.46W
175 T15 **Romang, Pulau** var. Pulau Roma. island Kepulauan Damar, E Indonesia
175 Ss15 **Romang, Selat** strait Nusa Tenggara, S Indonesia
118 J11 **Romania** Bul. Rumŭniya, Ger. Rumänien, Hung. Románia, Rom. România, SCr. Rumunjska, Ukr. Rumuniya; prev. Republica Socialistă România, Roumania, Rumania, Socialist Republic of Romania, Rom. Romînia. ◆ republic SE Europe
119 T14 **Roman-Kash** ▲ S Ukraine 44.37N 34.13E
25 W16 **Romano, Cape** headland Florida, SE USA 25.51N 81.40W
46 G5 **Romano, Cayo** island C Cuba
126 Kk15 **Romanovka** Respublika Buryatiya, S Russian Federation 53.10N 112.34E
131 N8 **Romanovka** Saratovskaya Oblast', W Russian Federation 51.45N 42.45E
110 I6 **Romanshorn** Thurgau, NE Switzerland 47.33N 9.21E
105 R12 **Romans-sur-Isère** Drôme, E France 45.03N 5.03E
201 U12 **Romanum** island Chuuk, C Micronesia
Románvásár see Roman
41 S5 **Romanzof Mountains** ▲ Alaska, USA
Roma, Pulau see Romang, Pulau
105 S4 **Rombas** Moselle, NE France 49.15N 6.04E
176 Xx10 **Rombebai, Danau** ⊚ Papua, E Indonesia
25 R2 **Rome** Georgia, SE USA 34.01N 85.01W
20 I9 **Rome** New York, NE USA 43.13N 75.28W
Rome see Roma
33 S9 **Romeo** Michigan, N USA 42.48N 83.00W
Römerstadt see Rýmařov
Rometan see Romiton
105 P5 **Romilly-sur-Seine** Aube, N France 48.31N 3.43E
Romînia see Romania
152 L11 **Romiton** Rus. Rometan. Buxoro Viloyati, C Uzbekistan 39.56N 64.21E
23 U3 **Romney** West Virginia, NE USA 39.20N 78.45W
119 S4 **Romny** Sums'ka Oblast', NE Ukraine 50.45N 33.30E
97 E24 **Rømø** Ger. Röm. island SW Denmark
119 S5 **Romodan** Poltavs'ka Oblast', NE Ukraine 50.00N 33.20E
131 P5 **Romodanovo** Respublika Mordoviya, W Russian Federation 54.25N 45.24E
Romorantin see Romorantin-Lanthenay
105 N8 **Romorantin-Lanthenay** var. Romorantin. Loir-et-Cher, C France 47.22N 1.43E
174 Hh5 **Rompin, Sungai** ≈ Peninsular Malaysia
96 F9 **Romsdal** physical region S Norway
96 F10 **Romsdalen** valley S Norway
96 E9 **Romsdalsfjorden** fjord S Norway
35 P8 **Ronan** Montana, NW USA 47.31N 114.06W
61 M14 **Roncador** Maranhão, E Brazil 5.48S 45.08W
195 W12 **Roncador Reef** reef N Solomon Islands
61 J17 **Roncador, Serra do** ▲ C Brazil
23 S6 **Ronceverte** West Virginia, NE USA 37.45N 80.27W
109 H14 **Ronciglione** Lazio, C Italy 42.16N 12.15E
106 L15 **Ronda** Andalucía, S Spain 36.45N 5.10W
96 G11 **Rondane** ▲ S Norway

◆ Country ● Country Capital ◇ Dependent Territory ○ Dependent Territory Capital ◆ Administrative Region ✈ International Airport ▲ Mountain ▲ Mountain Range ▲ Volcano ≈ River ⊚ Lake ⊠ Reservoir

RONDA, SERRANÍA DE – RUTLEDGE

106 L15 **Ronda, Serranía de** ▲▲ S Spain
97 H22 **Rønde** Århus, C Denmark 56.18N 10.28E
Rōŋdik *see* Rongrik Atoll
61 E16 **Rondônia** *off.* Estado de Rondônia; *prev.* Território de Rondônia. ◐ *state* W Brazil
61 I18 **Rondonópolis** Mato Grosso, W Brazil 16.28S 54.37W
96 G11 **Rondslottet** ▲ S Norway 61.54N 9.48E
97 P20 **Ronehamn** Gotland, SE Sweden 57.10N 18.30E
166 L13 **Rong'an** *var.* Chang'an, Rongan. Guangxi Zhuangzu Zizhiqu, S China 25.13N 109.19E
Rongcheng *see* Jianli
201 R4 **Rongelap Atoll** *var.* Rōnļap. *atoll* Ralik Chain, NW Marshall Islands
Rongerik *see* Rongrik Atoll
166 K12 **Rongjiang** *var.* Guzhou. Guizhou, S China 25.59N 108.27E
166 L13 **Rong Jiang** ≈ S China
Rongjiang *see* Nankang
Rong, Kas *see* Rŭng, Kaôh
178 Hh8 **Rong Kwang** Phrae, NW Thailand 18.19N 100.18E
201 T4 **Rongrik Atoll** *var.* Rōŋdik, Rongerik. *atoll* Ralik Chain, N Marshall Islands
201 X2 **Rongrong** *island* SE Marshall Islands
166 L13 **Rongshui** *var.* Rongshui Miaozu Zizhixian. Guangxi Zhuangzu Zizhiqu, S China 25.08N 109.15E
Rongshui Miaozu Zizhixian *see* Rongshui
120 I6 **Rõngu** *Ger.* Ringen. Tartumaa, SE Estonia 58.10N 26.17E
Rongwo *see* Tongren
166 L15 **Rongxian** *var.* Rong Xian. Guangxi Zhuangzu Zizhiqu, S China 22.52N 110.33E
Rongzhag *see* Danba
Roniu *see* Ronui, Mont
201 N13 **Ronkiti** Pohnpei, E Micronesia 6.48N 158.10E
Rōnļap *see* Rongelap Atoll
97 L24 **Rønne** Bornholm, E Denmark 55.07N 14.43E
97 M22 **Ronneby** Blekinge, S Sweden 56.12N 15.18E
204 J7 **Ronne Entrance** *inlet* Antarctica
204 L6 **Ronne Ice Shelf** *ice shelf* Antarctica
101 E19 **Ronse** *Fr.* Renaix. Oost-Vlaanderen, SW Belgium 50.45N 3.36E
203 R8 **Ronui, Mont** *var.* Roniu. ▲ Tahiti, W French Polynesia 17.49S 149.12W
32 K14 **Roodhouse** Illinois, N USA 39.28N 90.22W
85 C19 **Rooibank** Erongo, W Namibia 23.04S 14.34E
Rooke Island *see* Umboi Island
67 N24 **Rookery Point** *headland* NE Tristan da Cunha 37.03S 12.15W
176 W10 **Roon, Pulau** *island* E Indonesia
181 V7 **Roo Rise** *undersea feature* E Indian Ocean
158 J9 **Roorkee** Uttaranchal, N India 29.51N 77.54E
101 H15 **Roosendaal** Noord-Brabant, S Netherlands 51.31N 4.28E
27 P10 **Roosevelt** Texas, SW USA 30.28N 100.06W
39 N3 **Roosevelt** Utah, W USA 40.18N 109.59W
49 T8 **Roosevelt** ≈ W Brazil
205 O13 **Roosevelt Island** *island* Antarctica
8 L10 **Roosevelt, Mount** ▲ British Columbia, W Canada 58.28N 125.22W
9 P17 **Roosville** British Columbia, SW Canada 48.59N 115.03W
31 X10 **Root River** ≈ Minnesota, N USA
113 N16 **Ropczyce** Podkarpackie, SE Poland 50.03N 21.36E
189 Q3 **Roper Bar** Northern Territory, N Australia 14.45S 134.30E
26 M5 **Ropesville** Texas, SW USA 33.24N 102.09W
104 K14 **Roquefort** Landes, SW France 44.01N 0.18W
63 C21 **Roque Pérez** Buenos Aires, E Argentina 35.25S 59.24W
60 E10 **Roraima** *off.* Estado de Roraima; *prev.* Território de Rio Branco, Território de Roraima. ◐ *state* N Brazil
60 F9 **Roraima, Mount** ▲ N South America 5.10N 60.36W
176 X10 **Rori** Papua, E Indonesia 1.44S 136.49E
Ro Ro Reef *see* Malolo Barrier Reef
96 I9 **Røros** Sør-Trøndelag, S Norway 62.37N 11.25E
110 I7 **Rorschach** Sankt Gallen, NE Switzerland 47.28N 9.30E
95 E14 **Rørvik** Nord-Trøndelag, C Norway 64.52N 11.13E
121 G17 **Ros'** *Rus.* Ross'. Hrodzyenskaya Voblasts', W Belarus 53.20N 24.25E
121 G17 **Ros'** *Rus.* Ross'. ≈ W Belarus
119 O6 **Ros'** ≈ N Ukraine
46 K7 **Rosa, Lake** ◎ Great Inagua, S Bahamas
34 M9 **Rosalia** Washington, NW USA 47.14N 117.22W
203 W15 **Rosalia, Punta** *headland* Easter Island, Chile, E Pacific Ocean 27.04S 109.19W
47 P12 **Rosalie** E Dominica 15.22N 61.15W
37 T14 **Rosamond** California, W USA 34.51N 118.09W
37 S14 **Rosamond Lake** *salt flat* California, W USA
63 B18 **Rosario** Santa Fe, C Argentina 32.56S 60.38W
42 J11 **Rosario** Sinaloa, C Mexico 23.00N 105.51W
42 G6 **Rosario** Sonora, NW Mexico 27.53N 109.18W
64 O6 **Rosario** San Pedro, C Paraguay 24.26S 57.06W
63 E20 **Rosario** Colonia, SW Uruguay 34.19S 57.18W
56 H5 **Rosario** Zulia, NW Venezuela 10.18N 72.19W
Rosario *see* Rosarito
42 B4 **Rosario, Bahía del** *bay* NW Mexico
64 K6 **Rosario de la Frontera** Salta, N Argentina 25.50S 65.00W
63 C18 **Rosario del Tala** Entre Ríos, E Argentina 32.19S 59.10W
63 F16 **Rosário do Sul** Rio Grande do Sul, S Brazil 30.15S 54.55W
61 H18 **Rosário Oeste** Mato Grosso, W Brazil 14.49S 56.25W
42 E7 **Rosarito** Baja California, NW Mexico 26.27N 111.37W
42 B1 **Rosarito** *var.* Rosario. Baja California, NW Mexico 32.25N 117.03W
42 E7 **Rosarito** Baja California Sur, W Mexico 26.28N 111.40W
106 L9 **Rosarito, Embalse del** ⊠ W Spain
109 N22 **Rosarno** Calabria, SW Italy 38.28N 15.58E
58 B5 **Rosa Zárate** *var.* Quinindé. Esmeraldas, SW Ecuador 0.18N 79.28W
Roscianum *see* Rossano
31 O8 **Roscoe** South Dakota, N USA 45.24N 99.19W
27 P7 **Roscoe** Texas, SW USA 32.27N 100.32W
104 F5 **Roscoff** Finistère, NW France 48.43N 4.00W
Ros Comáin *see* Roscommon
99 C17 **Roscommon** *Ir.* Ros Comáin. C Ireland 53.37N 8.10W
33 Q7 **Roscommon** Michigan, N USA 44.30N 84.34W
99 C17 **Roscommon** *Ir.* Ros Comáin. *cultural region* C Ireland
Ros. Cré *see* Roscrea
99 D19 **Roscrea** *Ir.* Ros. Cré. C Ireland 52.57N 7.46W
47 X12 **Roseau** *prev.* Charlotte Town. ● (Dominica) SW Dominica 15.16N 61.22W
31 S2 **Roseau** Minnesota, N USA 48.51N 95.45W
181 Y16 **Rose Belle** SE Mauritius 20.24S 57.36E
191 O16 **Rosebery** Tasmania, SE Australia 41.51S 145.33E
23 U11 **Roseboro** North Carolina, SE USA 34.58N 78.31W
27 T9 **Rosebud** Texas, SW USA 31.04N 96.58W
35 W10 **Rosebud Creek** ≈ Montana, NW USA
34 F14 **Roseburg** Oregon, NW USA 43.13N 123.20W
24 J3 **Rosedale** Mississippi, S USA 33.51N 91.01W
101 H21 **Rosée** Namur, S Belgium 50.15N 4.43E
57 U8 **Rose Hall** E Guyana 6.14N 57.30W
181 X16 **Rose Hill** W Mauritius 20.13S 57.28E
82 H12 **Roseires, Reservoir** *var.* Lake Rusayris. ⊠ E Sudan
Rosenau *see* Rožnov pod Radhoštěm, Czech Republic
Rosenau *see* Rožňava, Slovakia
27 V11 **Rosenberg** Texas, SW USA 29.33N 95.48W
Rosenberg *see* Olesno, Poland
Rosenberg *see* Ružomberok, Slovakia
102 I10 **Rosengarten** Niedersachsen, N Germany 53.24N 9.53E
103 M24 **Rosenheim** Bayern, S Germany 47.51N 12.07E
Rosenhof *see* Zilupe
107 X4 **Roses** Cataluña, NE Spain 42.15N 3.10E
107 X4 **Roses, Golf de** *gulf* NE Spain
109 K14 **Roseto degli Abruzzi** Abruzzo, C Italy 42.39N 14.01E
9 S16 **Rosetown** Saskatchewan, S Canada 51.34N 107.58W
Rosetta *see* Rashīd
37 O7 **Roseville** California, W USA 38.44N 121.16W
32 J12 **Roseville** Illinois, N USA 40.42N 90.40W
31 V8 **Roseville** Minnesota, N USA 45.00N 93.09W
31 R7 **Rosholt** South Dakota, N USA 45.51N 96.42W
108 F12 **Rosignano Marittimo** Toscana, C Italy 43.24N 10.28E
118 I14 **Roşiori de Vede** Teleorman, S Romania 44.06N 25.00E
116 K8 **Rositsa** ≈ N Bulgaria
Rositten *see* Rēzekne
97 J23 **Roskilde** Roskilde, E Denmark 55.39N 12.07E
97 I23 **Roskilde** *off.* Roskilde Amt. ◐ *county* E Denmark
Ros Láir *see* Rosslare
130 H5 **Roslavl'** Smolenskaya Oblast', W Russian Federation 53.59N 32.57E
34 I8 **Roslyn** Washington, NW USA 47.13N 120.52W
101 K14 **Rosmalen** Noord-Brabant, S Netherlands 51.43N 5.21E
Ros Mhic Thriúin *see* New Ross
115 P19 **Rosoman** C FYR Macedonia 41.31N 21.55E
104 F6 **Rosporden** Finistère, NW France 47.58N 3.54W
193 F17 **Ross** West Coast, South Island, NZ 42.54S 170.51E
8 J7 **Ross** ≈ Yukon Territory, W Canada
Ross' *see* Ros'
98 H8 **Ross and Cromarty** *cultural region* N Scotland, UK
109 O20 **Rossano** *anc.* Roscianum. Calabria, SW Italy 39.34N 16.37E
24 L5 **Ross Barnett Reservoir** ⊠ Mississippi, S USA
9 W16 **Rossburn** Manitoba, S Canada 50.42N 100.49W
12 H13 **Rosseau** Ontario, S Canada 45.15N 79.38W
12 H13 **Rosseau, Lake** ◎ Ontario, S Canada
195 R17 **Rossel Island** *prev.* Yela Island. *island* SE PNG
205 P12 **Ross Ice Shelf** *ice shelf* Antarctica
11 P16 **Rossignol, Lake** ◎ Nova Scotia, SE Canada
85 C19 **Rössing** Erongo, W Namibia 22.27S 14.52E
205 Q14 **Ross Island** *island* Antarctica
Rossitten *see* Rybachiy
Rossiyskaya Federatsiya *see* Russian Federation
9 N17 **Rossland** British Columbia, SW Canada 49.03N 117.49W
99 F20 **Rosslare** *Ir.* Ros Láir. SE Ireland 52.15N 6.22W
99 F20 **Rosslare Harbour** Wexford, SE Ireland 52.15N 6.19W
103 M14 **Rosslau** Sachsen-Anhalt, E Germany 51.52N 12.15E
78 G10 **Rosso** Trarza, SW Mauritania 16.36N 15.49W
105 X14 **Rosso, Cap** *headland* Corse, France, C Mediterranean Sea 42.25N 8.22E
95 H16 **Rossön** Jämtland, C Sweden 63.54N 16.21E
99 K21 **Ross-on-Wye** W England, UK 51.55N 2.34W
Rossony *see* Rasony
130 L9 **Rossosh'** Voronezhskaya Oblast', W Russian Federation 50.09N 39.34E
189 Q7 **Ross River** Northern Territory, N Australia 23.36S 134.30E
8 J7 **Ross River** Yukon Territory, W Canada 61.57N 132.26W
205 O15 **Ross Sea** *sea* Antarctica
94 G13 **Røssvatnet** *Lapp.* Reevhtse. ◎ C Norway
25 R1 **Rossville** Georgia, SE USA 34.59N 85.22W
Rostak *see* Ar Rustāq
149 P14 **Rostāq** Hormozgān, S Iran 26.48N 53.50E
119 N5 **Rostavytsya** ≈ N Ukraine
9 T15 **Rosthern** Saskatchewan, S Canada 52.40N 106.19W
102 M8 **Rostock** Mecklenburg-Vorpommern, NE Germany 54.04N 12.07E
128 L16 **Rostov** Yaroslavskaya Oblast', W Russian Federation 57.11N 39.19E
Rostov *see* Rostov-na-Donu
130 L12 **Rostov-na-Donu** *var.* Rostov, *Eng.* Rostov-on-Don. Rostovskaya Oblast', SW Russian Federation 47.16N 39.45E
Rostov-on-Don *see* Rostov-na-Donu
130 L10 **Rostovskaya Oblast'** ◐ *province* SW Russian Federation
95 J14 **Rosvik** Norrbotten, N Sweden 65.26N 21.48E
25 S3 **Roswell** Georgia, SE USA 34.01N 84.21W
39 U14 **Roswell** New Mexico, SW USA 33.23N 104.31W
96 K12 **Rot** Dalarna, C Sweden 61.16N 14.04E
103 I23 **Rot** ≈ S Germany
106 J15 **Rota** Andalucía, S Spain 36.39N 6.20W
196 K9 **Rota** *island* S Northern Mariana Islands
27 P6 **Rotan** Texas, SW USA 32.51N 100.28W
Rotcher Island *see* Tamana
102 I11 **Rotenburg** Niedersachsen, NW Germany 53.06N 9.25E
Rotenburg *see* Rotenburg an der Fulda
103 I16 **Rotenburg an der Fulda** *var.* Rotenburg. Thüringen, C Germany 51.00N 9.43E
103 L18 **Roter Main** ≈ E Germany
103 K20 **Roth** Bayern, SE Germany 49.15N 11.06E
103 G16 **Rothaargebirge** ▲▲ W Germany
Rothenburg *see* Rothenburg ob der Tauber
103 J20 **Rothenburg ob der Tauber** *var.* Rothenburg. Bayern, S Germany 49.23N 10.10E
204 H6 **Rothera** *UK research station* Antarctica 67.28S 68.31W
193 I17 **Rotherham** Canterbury, South Island, NZ 42.42S 172.56E
99 M17 **Rotherham** N England, UK 53.25N 1.19W
98 H12 **Rothesay** W Scotland, UK 55.49N 5.03W
110 E7 **Rothrist** Aargau, N Switzerland 47.18N 7.54E
204 H6 **Rothschild Island** *island* Antarctica
175 Qq18 **Roti, Pulau** *island* S Indonesia
175 R18 **Roti, Selat** *strait* Nusa Tenggara, S Indonesia
191 O8 **Roto** New South Wales, SE Australia 33.04S 145.27E
192 N8 **Rotoiti, Lake** ◎ North Island, NZ
Rotomagus *see* Rouen
109 N19 **Rotondella** Basilicata, S Italy 40.12N 16.30E
105 X15 **Rotondo, Monte** ▲ Corse, France, C Mediterranean Sea 42.15N 9.03E
193 I15 **Rotoroa, Lake** ◎ South Island, NZ
192 N8 **Rotorua** Bay of Plenty, North Island, NZ 38.09S 176.13E
192 N8 **Rotorua, Lake** ◎ North Island, NZ
103 N22 **Rott** ≈ SE Germany
110 F10 **Rotten** ≈ S Switzerland
111 T6 **Rottenmann** Steiermark, E Austria 47.31N 14.18E
100 H12 **Rotterdam** Zuid-Holland, SW Netherlands 51.55N 4.30E
20 K10 **Rotterdam** New York, NE USA 42.46N 73.57W
97 M21 **Rottnen** ◎ S Sweden
100 N4 **Rottumeroog** *island* Waddeneilanden, NE Netherlands
100 N4 **Rottumerplaat** *island* Waddeneilanden, NE Netherlands
103 G23 **Rottweil** Baden-Württemberg, S Germany 48.10N 8.37E
203 O7 **Rotui, Mont** ▲ Moorea, W French Polynesia 17.30S 149.49W
105 P1 **Roubaix** Nord, N France 50.42N 3.10E
113 C15 **Roudnice nad Labem** *Ger.* Raudnitz an der Elbe. Ústecký Kraj, NW Czech Republic 50.25N 14.13E
104 M4 **Rouen** *anc.* Rotomagus. Seine-Maritime, N France 49.25N 1.04E
176 Y11 **Rouffaer Reserves** *reserve* Papua, E Indonesia
13 N10 **Rouge, Rivière** ≈ Québec, SE Canada
22 J6 **Rough River** ≈ Kentucky, S USA
22 J6 **Rough River Lake** ◎ Kentucky, S USA
Rouhaïbé *see* Ar Ruḩaybah
104 K11 **Rouillac** Charente, W France 45.46N 0.04W
Roulers *see* Roeselare
Roumania *see* Romania
181 Y15 **Round Island** *var.* Île Ronde. *island* NE Mauritius
12 J12 **Round Lake** ◎ Ontario, SE Canada
37 U7 **Round Mountain** Nevada, W USA 38.42N 117.04W
27 R10 **Round Mountain** Texas, SW USA 30.25N 98.20W
191 U5 **Round Mountain** ▲ New South Wales, SE Australia 30.22S 152.13E
27 S10 **Round Rock** Texas, SW USA 30.30N 97.40W
35 U10 **Roundup** Montana, NW USA 46.27N 108.32W
57 Y10 **Roura** NE French Guiana 4.45N 52.18W
Rourkela *see* Rāulakela
98 J4 **Rousay** *island* N Scotland, UK
Rousselaere *see* Roeselare
105 O17 **Roussillon** *cultural region* S France
13 V7 **Routhierville** Québec, SE Canada 48.09N 67.07W
101 K25 **Rouvroy** Luxembourg, SE Belgium 49.33N 5.28E
12 I7 **Rouyn-Noranda** Québec, SE Canada 48.16N 79.01W
Rouyuanchengzi *see* Huachi
94 L12 **Rovaniemi** Lappi, N Finland 66.28N 25.40E
108 E7 **Rovato** Lombardia, N Italy 45.34N 10.03E
129 N11 **Rovdino** Arkhangel'skaya Oblast', NW Russian Federation 61.36N 42.28E
Roven'ki *see* Roven'ky
119 Y8 **Roven'ky** *var.* Roven'ki. Luhans'ka Oblast', E Ukraine 48.04N 39.19E
Rovenskaya Oblast' *see* Rivnens'ka Oblast'
Rovenskaya Sloboda *see* Rovyenskaya Slabada
108 G7 **Rovereto** *Ger.* Rofreit. Trentino-Alto Adige, N Italy 45.52N 11.03E
178 J12 **Rôviĕng Tbong** Preăh Vihéar, N Cambodia 13.18N 105.06E
Rovigno *see* Rovinj
108 H8 **Rovigo** Veneto, NE Italy 45.04N 11.48E
114 A10 **Rovinj** *It.* Rovigno. Istra, NW Croatia 45.06N 13.39E
56 E10 **Rovira** Tolima, C Colombia 4.15N 75.15W
Rovno *see* Rivne
131 P9 **Rovnoye** Saratovskaya Oblast', W Russian Federation 50.43N 46.03E
84 Q12 **Rovuma, Rio** *var.* Ruvuma. ≈ Mozambique/Tanzania *see also* Ruvuma
121 O19 **Rovyenskaya Slabada** *Rus.* Rovenskaya Sloboda. Homyel'skaya Voblasts', SE Belarus 52.12N 30.19E
191 R5 **Rowena** New South Wales, SE Australia 29.51S 148.55E
23 T11 **Rowland** North Carolina, SE USA 34.32N 79.17W
15 M1 **Rowley** ≈ Baffin Island, Nunavut, NE Canada
15 M2 **Rowley Island** *island* Nunavut, NE Canada
181 W8 **Rowley Shoals** *reef* NW Australia
179 Pp12 **Roxas** Mindoro, N Philippines 12.36N 121.29E
179 Q13 **Roxas City** Panay Island, C Philippines 11.33N 122.43E
23 U8 **Roxboro** North Carolina, SE USA 36.23N 78.58W
193 D23 **Roxburgh** Otago, South Island, NZ 45.32S 169.18E
98 K13 **Roxburgh** *cultural region* SE Scotland, UK
190 H5 **Roxby Downs** South Australia 30.29S 136.56E
97 M17 **Roxen** ◎ S Sweden
27 V5 **Roxton** Texas, SW USA 33.33N 95.43W
13 P12 **Roxton-Sud** Québec, SE Canada 45.30N 72.35W
35 U8 **Roy** Montana, NW USA 47.19N 108.55W
39 U10 **Roy** New Mexico, SW USA 35.56N 104.12W
99 E17 **Royal Canal** *Ir.* An Chanáil Ríoga. *canal* C Ireland
32 L1 **Royale, Isle** *island* Michigan, N USA
39 S6 **Royal Gorge** *valley* Colorado, C USA
99 M20 **Royal Leamington Spa** *var.* Leamington, Leamington Spa. C England, UK 52.18N 1.31W
99 O23 **Royal Tunbridge Wells** *var.* Tunbridge Wells. SE England, UK 51.07N 0.16E
26 L9 **Royalty** Texas, SW USA 31.21N 102.51W
104 J11 **Royan** Charente-Maritime, W France 45.37N 1.01W
67 B24 **Roy Cove Settlement** West Falkland, Falkland Islands 51.51S 60.22W
105 O3 **Roye** Somme, N France 49.42N 2.46E
97 H15 **Røyken** Buskerud, S Norway 59.47N 10.21E
95 F14 **Røyrvik** Nord-Trøndelag, C Norway 64.53N 13.30E
27 U6 **Royse City** Texas, SW USA 32.58N 96.19W
99 O21 **Royston** E England, UK 52.05N 0.01W
25 U2 **Royston** Georgia, SE USA 34.17N 83.06W
116 L10 **Roza** *prev.* Gyulovo. Yambol, E Bulgaria 42.29N 26.30E
115 L16 **Rožaje** Montenegro, SW Serbia and Montenegro (Yugoslavia) 42.51N 20.11E
112 M10 **Różan** Mazowieckie, C Poland 52.36N 21.27E
119 O10 **Rozdil'na** Odes'ka Oblast', SW Ukraine 46.51N 30.03E
119 S12 **Rozdol'ne** *Rus.* Razdolnoye. Respublika Krym, S Ukraine 45.45N 33.27E
151 Q9 **Rozhdestvenka** Akmola, C Kazakhstan 50.51N 71.25E
118 I6 **Rozhnyativ** Ivano-Frankivs'ka Oblast', W Ukraine 48.58N 24.07E
118 J3 **Rozhyshche** Volyns'ka Oblast', NW Ukraine 50.54N 25.16E
Roznau am Radhost *see* Rožnov pod Radhoštěm
113 L19 **Rožňava** *Ger.* Rosenau, *Hung.* Rozsnyó. Košický Kraj, E Slovakia 48.40N 20.31E
118 K10 **Roznov** Neamţ, NE Romania 46.46N 26.33E
113 I18 **Rožnov pod Radhoštěm** *Ger.* Rosenau, Roznau am Radhost. Zlínský Kraj, E Czech Republic 49.28N 18.09E
Rózsahegy *see* Ružomberok
Rozsnyó *see* Râşnov, Romania
Rozsnyó *see* Rožňava, Slovakia
115 K18 **Rranxë** Shkodër, NW Albania 41.58N 19.27E
115 L18 **Rrëshen** *var.* Rresheni, Rrshen. Lezhë, C Albania 41.46N 19.54E
Rresheni *see* Rrëshen
Rrogozhina *see* Rrogozhinë
115 K20 **Rrogozhinë** *var.* Rogozhina, Rogozhinë, Rrogozhina. Tiranë, W Albania 41.04N 19.40E
Rrshen *see* Rrëshen
114 O13 **Rtanj** ▲ E Serbia and Montenegro (Yugoslavia) 43.45N 21.54E
131 O7 **Rtishchevo** Saratovskaya Oblast', W Russian Federation 52.16N 43.46E
192 N12 **Ruahine Range** *var.* Ruarine. ▲▲ North Island, NZ
193 L14 **Ruamahanga** ≈ North Island, NZ
Ruanda *see* Rwanda
192 M10 **Ruapehu, Mount** ▲ North Island, NZ 39.15S 175.33E
193 C25 **Ruapuke Island** *island* SW NZ
Ruarine *see* Ruahine Range
192 O9 **Ruatahuna** Bay of Plenty, North Island, NZ 38.38S 176.56E
192 Q8 **Ruatoria** Gisborne, North Island, NZ 37.54S 178.18E
192 K4 **Ruawai** Northland, North Island, NZ 36.08S 174.03E
13 N8 **Ruban** ≈ Québec, SE Canada
83 I22 **Rubeho Mountains** ▲▲ C Tanzania
172 Q5 **Rubeshibe** Hokkaidō, NE Japan 43.49N 143.37E
Rubezhnoye *see* Rubizhne
115 L18 **Rubik** Lezhë, C Albania 41.46N 19.48E
56 H7 **Rubio** Táchira, W Venezuela 7.42N 72.22W
119 X6 **Rubizhne** *Rus.* Rubezhnoye. Luhans'ka Oblast', E Ukraine 49.01N 38.22E
83 F20 **Rubondo Island** *island* N Tanzania
126 Gg15 **Rubtsovsk** Altayskiy Kray, S Russian Federation 51.34N 81.10E
41 P9 **Ruby** Alaska, USA 64.44N 155.29W
37 W3 **Ruby Dome** ▲ Nevada, W USA 40.35N 115.25W
37 W4 **Ruby Lake** ◎ Nevada, W USA
37 W4 **Ruby Mountains** ▲▲ Nevada, W USA
35 Q12 **Ruby Range** ▲▲ Montana, NW USA
120 C10 **Rucava** Liepāja, SW Latvia 56.09N 21.10E
Rūdān *see* Dehbārez
Rudelstadt *see* Ciechanowiec
Rudensk *see* Rudzyensk
121 G14 **Rūdiškės** Vilnius, S Lithuania 54.31N 24.49E
97 H24 **Rudkøbing** Fyn, C Denmark 54.57N 10.43E
127 Nn17 **Rudnaya Pristan'** Primorskiy Kray, SE Russian Federation 44.19N 135.42E
151 V14 **Rudnichnyy** *Kaz.* Rūdnīchnyy. Almaty, SE Kazakhstan 44.39N 78.57E
129 S13 **Rudnichnyy** Kirovskaya Oblast', NW Russian Federation 59.37N 52.28E
116 N9 **Rudnik** Varna, E Bulgaria 42.57N 27.46E
Rudny *see* Rudnyy
130 H4 **Rudnya** Smolenskaya Oblast', W Russian Federation 54.55N 31.10E
131 O8 **Rudnya** Volgogradskaya Oblast', SW Russian Federation 50.54N 44.27E
150 M7 **Rudnyy** *var.* Rudny. Kostanay, N Kazakhstan 53.00N 63.05E
126 Hh1 **Rudol'fa, Ostrov** *island* Zemlya Frantsa-Iosifa, NW Russian Federation
Rudolf, Lake *see* Lake Turkana
Rudolfswert *see* Novo mesto
103 L17 **Rudolstadt** Thüringen, C Germany 50.43N 11.19E
33 Q4 **Rudyard** Michigan, N USA 46.15N 84.36W
35 S7 **Rudyard** Montana, NW USA 48.33N 110.37W
121 K16 **Rudzyensk** *Rus.* Rudensk. Minskaya Voblasts', C Belarus 53.36N 27.52E
106 L6 **Rueda** Castilla-León, N Spain 41.24N 4.58W
116 F10 **Ruen** ▲ Bulgaria/FYR Macedonia 42.10N 22.31E
82 G10 **Rufa'a** Gezira, C Sudan 14.49N 33.21E
104 L10 **Ruffec** Charente, W France 46.01N 0.10E
23 R14 **Ruffin** South Carolina, SE USA 33.00N 80.48W
83 J23 **Rufiji** ≈ E Tanzania
63 A20 **Rufino** Santa Fe, C Argentina 34.15S 62.40W
78 F11 **Rufisque** W Senegal 14.44N 17.18W
85 K14 **Rufunsa** Lusaka, C Zambia 15.03S 29.36E
120 J9 **Rugāji** Balvi, E Latvia 57.01N 27.07E
167 R7 **Rugao** Jiangsu, E China 32.25N 120.39E
99 M20 **Rugby** C England, UK 52.22N 1.18W
31 N3 **Rugby** North Dakota, N USA 48.24N 100.00W
102 N7 **Rügen** *headland* NE Germany 54.25N 13.21E
Ruhaybeh *see* Ar Ruḩaybah
83 E19 **Ruhengeri** NW Rwanda 1.39S 29.16E
Ruhja *see* Rūjiena
102 M10 **Ruhner Berg** *hill* N Germany 53.17N 12.00E
120 F7 **Ruhnu** *var.* Ruhnu Saar, *Swe.* Runö. *island* SW Estonia
Ruhnu Saar *see* Ruhnu
103 G15 **Ruhr** ≈ W Germany
93 W6 **Ruhr Valley** *industrial region* W Germany
167 S11 **Rui'an** *var.* Rui an. Zhejiang, SE China 27.48N 120.36E
167 P10 **Ruichang** Jiangxi, S China 29.46N 115.37E
26 J11 **Ruidosa** Texas, SW USA 30.00N 104.40W
39 S14 **Ruidoso** New Mexico, SW USA 33.19N 105.40W
167 P12 **Ruijin** Jiangxi, S China 25.52N 116.01E
166 D13 **Ruili** Yunnan, SW China 24.04N 97.49E
100 N8 **Ruinen** Drenthe, NE Netherlands 52.46N 6.19E
101 D17 **Ruiselede** West-Vlaanderen, W Belgium 51.03N 3.21E
66 P5 **Ruivo de Santana, Pico** ▲ Madeira, Portugal, NE Atlantic Ocean 32.46N 16.57W
42 J12 **Ruiz** Nayarit, SW Mexico 22.00N 105.09W
56 E10 **Ruiz, Nevado del** ⩘ W Colombia 4.52N 75.22W
144 J9 **Rujaylah, Ḩarrat ar** *salt lake* N Jordan
Rujen *see* Rūjiena
120 H7 **Rūjiena** *Est.* Ruhja, *Ger.* Rujen. Valmiera, N Latvia 57.54N 25.22E
81 I18 **Ruki** ≈ W Dem. Rep. Congo (Zaire)
83 E22 **Rukwa** ◐ *region* SW Tanzania
83 F23 **Rukwa, Lake** ◎ SE Tanzania
27 P6 **Rule** Texas, SW USA 33.10N 99.53W
24 K3 **Ruleville** Mississippi, S USA 33.43N 90.33W
Rum *see* Rhum
114 K10 **Ruma** Serbia, N Yugoslavia 45.02N 19.51E
Rumadiya *see* Ar Ramādī
147 Q7 **Rumāḩ** Ar Riyāḑ, C Saudi Arabia 25.35N 47.09E
Rumaitha *see* Ar Rumaythah
Rumania/Rumänien *see* Romania
Rumänisch-Sankt-Georgen *see* Sângeorz-Băi
145 Y13 **Rumaylah** SE Iraq 30.16N 47.22E
145 P2 **Rumaylah, Wādī** *dry watercourse* NE Syria
176 V10 **Rumbati** Papua, E Indonesia 2.44S 132.04E
83 E14 **Rumbek** El Buhayrat, S Sudan 6.49N 29.42E
176 W10 **Rumberpon, Pulau** *island* E Indonesia
Rumburg *see* Rumburk
113 D14 **Rumburk** *Ger.* Rumburg. Ústecký Kraj, NW Czech Republic 50.59N 14.31E
46 J4 **Rum Cay** *island* C Bahamas
101 M26 **Rumelange** Luxembourg, S Luxembourg 49.28N 6.01E
101 D20 **Rumes** Hainaut, SW Belgium 50.33N 3.19E
21 P7 **Rumford** Maine, NE USA 44.31N 70.31W
112 I6 **Rumia** Pomorskie, N Poland 54.35N 18.21E
115 J17 **Rumija** ▲▲ SW Yugoslavia
105 T11 **Rumilly** Haute-Savoie, E France 45.52N 5.57E
145 O6 **Rūmīyah** W Iraq 34.28N 41.17E
Rummah, Wādī ar *see* Rimah, Wādī ar
Rummelsburg in Pommern *see* Miastko
172 Oo4 **Rumoi** Hokkaidō, NE Japan 43.55N 141.37E
84 M12 **Rumphi** *var.* Rumpi. Northern, N Malawi 11.00S 33.51E
Rumpi *see* Rumphi
31 V7 **Rum River** ≈ Minnesota, N USA
196 F16 **Rumung** *island* Caroline Islands, W Micronesia
Rumuniya/Rumŭniya/Rumunjska *see* Romania
193 G16 **Runanga** West Coast, South Island, NZ 42.24S 171.15E
192 P7 **Runaway, Cape** *headland* North Island, NZ 37.33S 177.59E
99 K18 **Runcorn** C England, UK 53.19N 2.43W
120 K10 **Rundāni** Ludza, E Latvia 56.19N 27.51E
85 L18 **Runde** *var.* Lundi. ≈ SE Zimbabwe
85 E16 **Rundu** *var.* Runtu. Okavango, NE Namibia 17.55S 19.45E
95 I16 **Rundvik** Västerbotten, N Sweden 63.31N 19.22E
83 G20 **Runere** Mwanza, N Tanzania 3.06S 33.18E
27 S13 **Runge** Texas, SW USA 28.52N 97.42W
178 I14 **Rŭng, Kaôh** *prev.* Kas Rong. *island* SW Cambodia
81 O16 **Rungu** Orientale, NE Dem. Rep. Congo (Zaire) 3.09N 27.58E
83 F23 **Rungwa** Rukwa, W Tanzania 7.18S 31.40E
83 G22 **Rungwa** Singida, C Tanzania 6.54S 33.33E
96 M13 **Runn** ◎ C Sweden
26 M4 **Running Water Draw** *valley* New Mexico/Texas, SW USA
Runö *see* Ruhnu
Runtu *see* Rundu
201 V12 **Ruo** *island* Caroline Islands, C Micronesia
164 L9 **Ruoqiang** *var.* Jo-ch'iang, *Uigh.* Charkhlik, Charkhliq, Qarkilik. Xinjiang Uygur Zizhiqu, NW China 38.59N 88.07E
165 S7 **Ruo Shui** ≈ N China
94 L8 **Ruostekfielbmá** *var.* Rustefjelbma Finnmark, N Norway 70.25N 28.10E
95 L18 **Ruovesi** Länsi-Suomi, W Finland 61.58N 24.04E
114 B9 **Rupa** Primorje-Gorski Kotar, NW Croatia 45.29N 14.15E
190 M11 **Rupanyup** Victoria, SE Australia 36.38S 142.37E
174 H6 **Rupat, Pulau** *prev.* Roepat. *island* W Indonesia
174 Gg6 **Rupat, Selat** *strait* Sumatera, W Indonesia
118 J11 **Rupea** *Ger.* Reps, *Hung.* Kőhalom; *prev.* Cohalm. Braşov, C Romania 46.01N 25.13E
101 G17 **Rupel** ≈ N Belgium
Rupella *see* la Rochelle
35 P15 **Rupert** Idaho, NW USA 42.37N 113.40W
23 R5 **Rupert** West Virginia, NE USA 37.57N 80.40W
Rupert House *see* Fort Rupert
10 J10 **Rupert, Rivière de** ≈ Québec, C Canada
204 M13 **Ruppert Coast** *physical region* Antarctica
102 N11 **Ruppiner Kanal** *canal* NE Germany
57 S11 **Rupununi River** ≈ S Guyana
103 D16 **Rur** *Dut.* Roer. ≈ Germany/Netherlands
60 H13 **Rurópolis Presidente Medici** Pará, N Brazil 4.05S 55.26W
203 S12 **Rurutu** *island* Îles Australes, SW French Polynesia
Rusaddir *see* Melilla
85 L17 **Rusape** Manicaland, E Zimbabwe 18.31S 32.07E
Rusayris, Lake *see* Roseires, Reservoir
Ruschuk/Rusçuk *see* Ruse
116 K7 **Ruse** *var.* Ruschuk, Rustchuk, *Turk.* Rusçuk. Ruse, N Bulgaria 43.49N 25.58E
116 L7 **Ruse** ◐ *province* N Bulgaria
111 W10 **Ruše** NE Slovenia 46.31N 15.30E
116 K7 **Rusenski Lom** ≈ N Bulgaria
99 G17 **Rush** *Ir.* An Ros. E Ireland 53.31N 6.06W
167 S4 **Rushan** *var.* Xiacun. Shandong, E China 36.57N 121.33E
Rushan *see* Rŭshon
Rushanskiy Khrebet *see* Rushon, Qatorkŭhi
31 V7 **Rush City** Minnesota, N USA 45.41N 92.56W
39 V5 **Rush Creek** ≈ Colorado, C USA
31 X10 **Rushford** Minnesota, N USA 43.48N 91.45W
160 N13 **Rushikulya** ≈ E India
12 D8 **Rush Lake** ◎ Ontario, S Canada
32 M7 **Rush Lake** ◎ Wisconsin, N USA
30 J10 **Rushmore, Mount** ▲ South Dakota, N USA 43.52N 103.27W
153 S13 **Rŭshon** *Rus.* Rushan. S Tajikistan 37.58N 71.31E
153 S14 **Rushon, Qatorkŭhi** *Rus.* Rushanskiy Khrebet. ▲▲ SE Tajikistan
28 M12 **Rush Springs** Oklahoma, C USA 34.46N 97.57W
47 V15 **Rushville** Trinidad, Trinidad and Tobago 10.07N 61.03W
32 J13 **Rushville** Illinois, N USA 40.07N 90.33W
30 K12 **Rushville** Nebraska, C USA 42.41N 102.28W
191 O11 **Rushworth** Victoria, SE Australia 36.36S 145.03E
27 W8 **Rusk** Texas, SW USA 31.48N 95.09W
95 I14 **Rusksele** Västerbotten, N Sweden 64.49N 18.55E
120 C12 **Rusnė** Klaipėda, W Lithuania 55.18N 21.19E
116 M10 **Rusokastrenska Reka** ≈ E Bulgaria
Russadir *see* Melilla
111 X3 **Russbach** ≈ NE Austria
9 V16 **Russell** Manitoba, S Canada 50.46N 101.16W
192 K2 **Russell** Northland, North Island, NZ 35.17S 174.07E
28 L4 **Russell** Kansas, C USA 38.54N 98.51W
23 O4 **Russell** Kentucky, S USA 38.30N 82.43W
195 W15 **Russell Islands** *island group* C Solomon Islands
22 L7 **Russell Springs** Kentucky, S USA 37.02N 85.03W
25 O2 **Russellville** Alabama, S USA 34.30N 87.43W
29 T11 **Russellville** Arkansas, C USA 35.16N 93.07W
22 J7 **Russellville** Kentucky, S USA 36.51N 86.53W
103 G18 **Rüsselsheim** Hessen, W Germany 50.00N 8.25E
Russia *see* Russian Federation
Russian America *see* Alaska
127 N17 **Russian Federation** *off.* Russian Federation, *var.* Russia, *Latv.* Krievija, *Rus.* Rossiyskaya Federatsiya. ◆ *republic* Asia/Europe
41 N11 **Russian Mission** Alaska, USA 61.48N 161.23W
36 M7 **Russian River** ≈ California, W USA
204 L13 **Russkaya** *Russian research station* Antarctica 74.45S 135.24W
126 H3 **Russkaya Gavan'** Novaya Zemlya, Arkhangel'skaya Oblast', N Russian Federation 76.13N 62.48E
126 J4 **Russkiy, Ostrov** *island* N Russian Federation
111 Y5 **Rust** Burgenland, E Austria 47.48N 16.42E
Rustaq *see* Ar Rustāq
143 U10 **Rust'avi** SE Georgia 41.36N 45.00E
23 T7 **Rustburg** Virginia, NE USA 37.16N 79.04W
Rustchuk *see* Ruse
Rustefjelbma *see* Ruostekfielbmá
85 I21 **Rustenburg** North-West, N South Africa 25.40S 27.15E
24 H5 **Ruston** Louisiana, S USA 32.31N 92.38W
83 E21 **Rutana** SE Burundi 4.01S 30.01E
64 I4 **Rutana, Volcán** ⩘ N Chile 22.43S 67.52W
Rutanzige, Lake *see* Edward, Lake
Rutba *see* Ar Ruṭbah
106 M14 **Rute** Andalucía, S Spain 37.19N 4.22W
175 Pp16 **Ruteng** *prev.* Roeteng. Flores, C Indonesia 8.34S 120.28E
204 L8 **Rutford Ice Stream** *ice feature* Antarctica
37 X6 **Ruth** Nevada, W USA 39.15N 115.00W
103 G15 **Rüthen** Nordrhein-Westfalen, W Germany 51.30N 8.28E
12 D17 **Rutherford** Ontario, S Canada 42.39N 82.06W
23 Q10 **Rutherfordton** North Carolina, SE USA 35.22N 81.57W
99 J18 **Ruthin** *Wel.* Rhuthun. NE Wales, UK 53.05N 3.18W
110 G7 **Rüti** Zürich, N Switzerland 47.16N 8.51E
Rutlam *see* Ratlām
20 M9 **Rutland** Vermont, NE USA 43.37N 72.58W
99 N19 **Rutland** *cultural region* C England, UK
23 N8 **Rutledge** Tennessee, S USA 36.16N 83.31W

◆ Country ● Country Capital ◇ Dependent Territory ○ Dependent Territory Capital ◐ Administrative Region ✕ International Airport ▲ Mountain ▲▲ Mountain Range ⩘ Volcano ≈ River ◎ Lake ⊠ Reservoir
319

RUTÖG – ST-JEAN-DE-MONTS

164 *G12* **Rutög** *var.* Rutog, Rutok. Xizang Zizhiqu, W China *33.27N 79.43E*
Rutok *see* Rutög
81 *P19* **Rutshuru** Nord Kivu, E Dem. Rep. Congo (Zaire) *1.13S 29.27E*
100 *L8* **Rutten** Flevoland, N Netherlands *52.49N 5.44E*
131 *Q17* **Rutul** Respublika Dagestan, SW Russian Federation *41.35N 47.30E*
95 *L14* **Ruukki** Oulu, C Finland *64.40N 25.35E*
100 *N11* **Ruurlo** Gelderland, E Netherlands *52.04N 6.27E*
149 *S15* **Ru'ūs al Jibāl** *headland* Oman/UAE *26.13N 56.23E*
144 *I7* **Ru'ūs aṭ Ṭiwāl, Jabal** ⛰ W Syria
83 *H23* **Ruvuma** ◈ *region* SE Tanzania
83 *I25* **Ruvuma** *var.* Rio Rovuma. 〰 Mozambique/Tanzania *see also* Rovuma, Rio
Ruwais *see* Ar Ruways
144 *L9* **Ruwayshid, Wadi ar** *dry watercourse* NE Jordan
147 *Z10* **Ruways, Ra's ar** *headland* E Oman *20.58N 59.00E*
81 *P18* **Ruwenzori** ⛰ Uganda/Dem. Rep. Congo (Zaire)
147 *Y8* **Ruwī** NE Oman *23.33N 58.31E*
116 *F9* **Ruy** ▲ Bulgaria/Yugoslavia *42.52N 22.35E*
Ruya *see* Luia, Rio
83 *E20* **Ruyigi** E Burundi *3.28S 30.19E*
131 *P5* **Ruzayevka** Respublika Mordoviya, W Russian Federation *54.04N 44.56E*
121 *G18* **Ruzhany** *Rus.* Ruzhany. Brestskaya Voblasts', SW Belarus *52.52N 24.52E*
116 *I10* **Rŭzhevo Konare** *var.* Rŭzhevo Konare. Plovdiv, C Bulgaria *42.16N 24.58E*
Ruzhin *see* Ruzhyn
116 *G7* **Ruzhintsi** Vidin, NW Bulgaria *43.38N 22.50E*
167 *N6* **Ruzhou** Henan, C China *34.12N 112.45E*
119 *N5* **Ruzhyn** *Rus.* Ruzhin. Zhytomyrs'ka Oblast', N Ukraine *49.42N 29.01E*
113 *K19* **Ružomberok** *Ger.* Rosenberg, *Hung.* Rózsahegy. Žilínský Kraj, N Slovakia *49.03N 19.18E*
113 *C16* **Ruzyně** ✈ (Praha) Praha, C Czech Republic *50.06N 14.16E*
83 *D19* **Rwanda** *off.* Rwandese Republic; *prev.* Ruanda. ◆ *republic* C Africa
Rwandese Republic *see* Rwanda
97 *G22* **Ry** Århus, C Denmark *56.06N 9.46E*
Ryasna *see* Rasna
130 *L5* **Ryazan'** Ryazanskaya Oblast', W Russian Federation *54.37N 39.37E*
130 *L5* **Ryazanskaya Oblast'** ◈ *province* W Russian Federation
130 *M6* **Ryazhsk** Ryazanskaya Oblast', W Russian Federation *53.42N 40.09E*
120 *B13* **Rybachiy** *Ger.* Rossitten. Kaliningradskaya Oblast', W Russian Federation *55.09N 20.49E*
128 *J2* **Rybachiy, Poluostrov** *peninsula* NW Russian Federation
Rybach'ye *see* Balykchy
128 *L15* **Rybinsk** *prev.* Andropov. Yaroslavskaya Oblast', W Russian Federation *58.03N 38.52E*
128 *K14* **Rybinskoye Vodokhranilishche** *Eng.* Rybinsk Reservoir, Rybinsk Sea. ▣ W Russian Federation
Rybinsk Reservoir/Rybinsk Sea *see* Rybinskoye Vodokhranilishche
113 *I16* **Rybnik** Śląskie, S Poland *50.05N 18.30E*
Rybnitsa *see* Rîbnița
113 *F16* **Rychnov nad Kněžnou** *Ger.* Reichenau. Královéhradecký Kraj, N Czech Republic *50.09N 16.15E*
112 *I12* **Rychwał** Wielkolpolskie, C Poland *52.04N 18.09E*
9 *O13* **Rycroft** Alberta, W Canada *55.45N 118.42W*
97 *L21* **Ryd** Kronoberg, S Sweden *56.27N 14.44E*
97 *L20* **Rydaholm** Jönköping, S Sweden *56.57N 14.19E*
204 *I8* **Rydberg Peninsula** *peninsula* Antarctica
99 *P23* **Rye** SE England, UK *50.57N 0.42E*
35 *T10* **Ryegate** Montana, NW USA *46.21N 109.12W*
37 *S3* **Rye Patch Reservoir** ▣ Nevada, W USA
97 *D15* **Ryfylke** *physical region* S Norway
97 *H16* **Rygge** Østfold, S Norway *59.22N 10.45E*
112 *N13* **Ryki** Lubelskie, E Poland *51.37N 21.57E*
Rykovo *see* Yenakiyeve
130 *I7* **Ryl'sk** Kurskaya Oblast', W Russian Federation *51.34N 34.41E*
191 *S8* **Rylstone** New South Wales, SE Australia *32.48S 149.58E*
113 *H17* **Rýmařov** *Ger.* Römerstadt. Moravskoslezský Kraj, E Czech Republic *49.57N 17.13E*
150 *E11* **Ryn-Peski** *desert* W Kazakhstan
171 *K12* **Ryōtsu** *var.* Ryôtu. Niigata, Sado, C Japan *38.02N 138.23E*
Ryôtu *see* Ryōtsu
112 *K10* **Rypin** Kujawsko-pomorskie, C Poland *53.03N 19.25E*
Ryshkany *see* Rîșcani
Ryssel *see* Lille
Ryswick *see* Rijswijk
97 *M24* **Rytterknægten** *hill* E Denmark *55.07N 14.53E*
171 *Kk16* **Ryūgasaki** Ibaraki, Honshū, S Japan *35.54N 140.11E*
198 *G5* **Ryukyu Trench** *var.* Nansei Syotō Trench. *undersea feature* S East China Sea
112 *D11* **Rzepin** *Ger.* Reppen. Lubuskie, W Poland *52.20N 14.48E*
113 *N16* **Rzeszów** Podkarpackie, SE Poland *50.04N 22.00E*
128 *I16* **Rzhev** Tverskaya Oblast', W Russian Federation *56.16N 34.21E*
Rzhishchev *see* Rzhyshchiv
119 *P5* **Rzhyshchiv** *Rus.* Rzhishchev. Kyyivs'ka Oblast', N Ukraine *49.58N 31.01E*

S

144 *E11* **Sa'ad** Southern, W Israel *31.27N 34.31E*
111 *P7* **Saalach** 〰 W Austria
103 *L14* **Saale** 〰 C Germany
103 *L17* **Saalfeld** *var.* Saalfeld an der Saale. Thüringen, C Germany *50.39N 11.22E*
Saalfeld *see* Zalewo
Saalfeld an der Saale *see* Saalfeld
110 *C8* **Saane** 〰 W Switzerland
103 *D19* **Saar** *Fr.* Sarre. 〰 France/Germany
103 *E20* **Saarbrücken** *Fr.* Sarrebruck. Saarland, SW Germany *49.13N 7.01E*
Saarburg *see* Sarrebourg
Saare *see* Saaremaa
120 *D6* **Sääre** *var.* Sjar. Saaremaa, W Estonia *57.55N 22.03E*
120 *D5* **Saaremaa** *off.* Saare Maakond. ◈ *province* W Estonia
120 *E6* **Saaremaa** *Ger.* Oesel, Ösel; *prev.* Saare. *island* W Estonia
94 *L12* **Saarenkylä** Lappi, N Finland *66.31N 25.51E*
Saargemund *see* Sarreguemines
95 *L17* **Saarijärvi** Länsi-Suomi, W Finland *62.42N 25.16E*
Saar in Mähren *see* Žďár nad Sázavou
94 *M10* **Saariselkä** *Lapp.* Suoločielgi. Lappi, N Finland *68.26N 27.28E*
94 *L10* **Saariselkä** *hill range* NE Finland
103 *D20* **Saarland** *Fr.* Sarre. ◈ *state* SW Germany
Saarlautern *see* Saarlouis
103 *D20* **Saarlouis** *prev.* Saarlautern. Saarland, SW Germany *49.18N 6.49E*
110 *E11* **Saaser Vispa** 〰 S Switzerland
143 *X12* **Saatlı** *Rus.* Saatly. C Azerbaijan *39.57N 48.24E*
Saatly *see* Saatlı
Saaz *see* Žatec
176 *X9* **Saba** Papua, E Indonesia *1.04S 136.15E*
47 *V9* **Saba** *island* N Netherlands Antilles
144 *J7* **Sab' Ābār** *var.* Sab'a Biyar, Sa'b Bi'ār. Ḥimṣ, C Syria *33.46N 37.40E*
Sab'a Biyar *see* Sab' Ābār
114 *K11* **Šabac** Serbia, W Yugoslavia *44.45N 19.42E*
107 *W5* **Sabadell** Cataluña, E Spain *41.33N 2.07E*
171 *Hh13* **Sabae** Fukui, Honshū, SW Japan *36.00N 136.12E*
175 *O3* **Sabah** *prev.* British North Borneo, North Borneo. ◈ *state* East Malaysia
174 *Gg4* **Sabak** *var.* Sabak Bernam. Selangor, Peninsular Malaysia *3.45N 100.58E*
Sabak Bernam *see* Sabak
40 *D16* **Sabak, Cape** *headland* Agattu Island, Alaska, USA *52.21N 173.43E*
83 *J20* **Sabaki** 〰 S Kenya
175 *P14* **Sabalana, Kepulauan** *var.* Kepulauan Liukang Tenggaya. *island group* C Indonesia
148 *L2* **Sabalān, Kuhhā-ye** ▲ NW Iran *38.21N 47.47E*
160 *H7* **Sabalgarh** Madhya Pradesh, C India *26.18N 77.28E*
46 *E4* **Sabana, Archipiélago de** *island group* C Cuba
44 *H7* **Sabanagrande** *var.* Sabana Grande. Francisco Morazán, S Honduras *13.48N 87.15W*
56 *E5* **Sabanalarga** Atlántico, N Colombia *10.37N 74.55W*
43 *W14* **Sabancuy** Campeche, SE Mexico *18.56N 91.08W*
47 *N8* **Sabaneta** NW Dominican Republic *19.27N 71.22W*
56 *J4* **Sabaneta** Falcón, N Venezuela *11.15N 70.04W*
196 *H4* **Sabaneta, Puntan** *prev.* Ushi Point. *headland* Saipan, S Northern Mariana Islands *15.17N 145.49E*
176 *Y12* **Sabang** Papua, E Indonesia *4.33S 138.42E*
118 *L10* **Săbăoani** Neamț, NE Romania *47.01N 26.51E*
161 *J26* **Sabaragamuwa Province** ◈ *province* C Sri Lanka
Sabaria *see* Szombathely
160 *D10* **Sābarmati** 〰 NW India
175 *T6* **Sabatai** Pulau Morotai, E Indonesia *2.04N 128.23E*
147 *Q15* **Sab'atayn, Ramlat as** *desert* C Yemen
109 *I16* **Sabaudia** Lazio, C Italy *41.17N 13.02E*
59 *J19* **Sabaya** Oruro, S Bolivia *19.09S 68.20W*
Sa'b Bi'ār *see* Sab' Ābār
Sabbioncello *see* Orebić
154 *I8* **Şāberī, Hāmūn-e** *var.* Daryācheh-ye Hāmūn, Daryācheh-ye Sīstān. ◎ Afghanistan/Iran *see also* Sīstān, Daryācheh-ye
29 *P2* **Sabetha** Kansas, C USA *39.54N 95.48W*
77 *P10* **Sabhā** C Libya *27.01N 14.25E*
69 *V13* **Sabi** *var.* Rio Save. 〰 Mozambique/Zimbabwe *see also* Save, Rio
120 *E8* **Sabile** *Ger.* Zabeln. Talsi, NW Latvia *57.03N 22.33E*
33 *R14* **Sabina** Ohio, N USA *39.29N 83.38W*
42 *I3* **Sabinal** Chihuahua, N Mexico *30.59N 107.29W*
27 *Q12* **Sabinal** Texas, SW USA *29.19N 99.28W*
27 *Q11* **Sabinal River** 〰 Texas, SW USA
107 *S4* **Sabiñánigo** Aragón, NE Spain *42.31N 0.22W*
43 *N6* **Sabinas** Coahuila de Zaragoza, NE Mexico *27.52N 101.04W*
43 *O8* **Sabinas Hidalgo** Nuevo León, NE Mexico *26.28N 100.08W*
43 *N6* **Sabinas, Río** 〰 NE Mexico
24 *F9* **Sabine Lake** ◎ Louisiana/Texas, S USA
94 *O3* **Sabine Land** *physical region* C Svalbard
27 *W7* **Sabine River** 〰 Louisiana/Texas, SW USA
143 *X12* **Sabirabad** C Azerbaijan *40.00N 48.27E*
Sabkha *see* As Sabkhah
179 *P12* **Sablayan** Mindoro, N Philippines *12.48N 120.48E*
11 *P16* **Sable, Cape** *headland* Newfoundland and Labrador, SE Canada *43.21N 65.40W*
25 *X17* **Sable, Cape** *headland* Florida, SE USA *25.12N 81.06W*
11 *R16* **Sable Island** *island* Nova Scotia, SE Canada
12 *L11* **Sables, Lac des** ◎ Québec, SE Canada
12 *E10* **Sables, Rivière aux** 〰 Ontario, S Canada
104 *K7* **Sable-sur-Sarthe** Sarthe, NW France *47.49N 0.19W*
129 *U7* **Sablya, Gora** ▲ NW Russian Federation *64.46N 58.52E*
79 *U14* **Sabon Birnin Gwari** Kaduna, C Nigeria *10.43N 6.39E*
79 *V11* **Sabon Kafi** Zinder, C Niger *14.37N 8.46E*
106 *I6* **Sabor, Rio** 〰 N Portugal
12 *J8* **Sabourin, Lac** ◎ Québec, SE Canada
104 *J14* **Sabres** Landes, SW France *44.07N 0.46W*
205 *X13* **Sabrina Coast** *physical region* Antarctica
146 *M11* **Sabt al Ulayā** 'Asīr, SW Saudi Arabia *19.33N 41.58E*
106 *I8* **Sabugal** Guarda, N Portugal *40.19N 7.04W*
31 *Z13* **Sabula** Iowa, C USA *42.04N 90.10W*
147 *N13* **Şabyā** Jīzān, SW Saudi Arabia *17.49N 42.49E*
Sabzawar *see* Sabzevār
Sabzawaran *see* Sabzvārān
149 *S4* **Sabzevār** *var.* Sabzawar. Khorāsān, NE Iran *36.13N 57.37E*
149 *T12* **Sabzvārān** *var.* Sabzawaran; *prev.* Jiroft. Kermān, SE Iran *28.40N 57.40E*
Sacajawea Peak *see* Matterhorn
84 *C9* **Sacandica** Uíge, NW Angola *6.01S 15.57E*
44 *A2* **Sacatepéquez** *off.* Departamento de Sacatepéquez. ◈ *department* S Guatemala
106 *F11* **Sacavém** Lisboa, W Portugal *38.46N 9.06W*
31 *T13* **Sac City** Iowa, C USA *42.25N 94.59W*
107 *P8* **Sacedón** Castilla-La Mancha, C Spain *40.28N 2.43W*
118 *J12* **Săcele** *Ger.* Vierdörfer, *Hung.* Négyfalu; *prev. Ger.* Sieben Dörfer, *Hung.* Hétfalu. Brașov, C Romania *45.36N 25.40E*
10 *C8* **Sachigo** Ontario, C Canada *53.52N 92.16W*
10 *C7* **Sachigo** 〰 Ontario, C Canada
10 *C8* **Sachigo Lake** ◎ Ontario, C Canada
169 *Y16* **Sach'ŏn** *Jap.* Sansenhō; *prev.* Samch'ŏnpŏ. S South Korea *34.55N 128.07E*
103 *O15* **Sachsen** *Eng.* Saxony, *Fr.* Saxe. ◈ *state* E Germany
103 *K14* **Sachsen-Anhalt** *Eng.* Saxony-Anhalt. ◈ *state* C Germany
111 *R9* **Sachsenburg** Salzburg, S Austria *46.49N 13.23E*
Sachsenfeld *see* Žalec
15 *H1* **Sachs Harbour** Banks Island, Northwest Territories, N Canada *72.00N 125.13W*
Sächsisch-Reen/Sächsisch-Regen *see* Reghin
20 *H8* **Sackets Harbor** New York, NE USA *43.57N 76.06W*
11 *P14* **Sackville** New Brunswick, SE Canada *45.54N 64.22W*
21 *P9* **Saco** Maine, NE USA *43.32N 70.25W*
21 *P8* **Saco River** 〰 Maine/New Hampshire, NE USA
37 *O7* **Sacramento** *state capital* California, W USA *38.34N 121.29W*
39 *T14* **Sacramento Mountains** ⛰ New Mexico, SW USA
37 *N6* **Sacramento River** 〰 California, W USA
37 *N5* **Sacramento Valley** *valley* California, W USA
38 *I10* **Sacramento Wash** *valley* Arizona, SW USA
107 *N15* **Sacratif, Cabo** *headland* S Spain *36.41N 3.30W*
118 *F9* **Săcueni** *prev.* Săcuieni, *Hung.* Székelyhid. Bihor, W Romania *47.19N 22.04E*
Săcuieni *see* Săcueni
107 *R4* **Sádaba** Aragón, NE Spain *42.15N 1.16W*
Sá da Bandeira *see* Lubango
144 *I6* **Şadad** Ḥimṣ, W Syria *34.19N 36.52E*
147 *O13* **Şa'dah** NW Yemen *16.59N 43.45E*
170 *Dd14* **Sadamisaki-hantō** *peninsula* Shikoku, SW Japan
175 *P12* **Sadang, Sungai** 〰 Sulawesi, C Indonesia
178 *H17* **Sadao** Songkhla, SW Thailand *6.34N 100.22E*
148 *L8* **Sadd-e Dez, Daryācheh-ye** ◎ W Iran
21 *S3* **Saddleback Mountain** *hill* Maine, NE USA *46.25N 68.00W*
21 *P6* **Saddleback Mountain** ▲ Maine, NE USA *44.57N 70.27W*
178 *J114* **Sa Đec** Đông Thap, S Vietnam *10.19N 105.45E*
147 *W13* **Sadḥ** S Oman *17.10N 55.07E*
78 *J11* **Sadiola** Kayes, W Mali *13.48N 11.47W*
155 *R12* **Sādiqābād** Punjab, E Pakistan *28.16N 70.10E*
159 *Y10* **Sadiya** Assam, NE India *27.49N 95.37E*
145 *W9* **Sa'dīyah, Hawr as** ◎ E Iraq
171 *K12* **Sado** *var.* Sadoga-shima. *island* C Japan
Sadoga-shima *see* Sado
106 *F12* **Sado, Rio** 〰 S Portugal
116 *I8* **Sadovets** Pleven, N Bulgaria *43.19N 24.21E*
131 *O11* **Sadovoye** Respublika Kalmykiya, SW Russian Federation *47.51N 44.34E*
107 *W9* **Sa Dragonera** *var.* Isla Dragonera. *island* Islas Baleares, Spain, W Mediterranean Sea
97 *H20* **Sæby** Nordjylland, N Denmark *57.19N 10.33E*
107 *P9* **Saelices** Castilla-La Mancha, C Spain *39.55N 2.49W*
Saena Julia *see* Siena
Saetabicula *see* Alzira
116 *O12* **Safaalan** Tekirdağ, NW Turkey *41.26N 28.07E*
Safad *see* Ẕefat
Şafāqis *see* Sfax
198 *B8* **Safata Bay** *bay* Upolo, Samoa, C Pacific Ocean
Safed *see* Ẕefat
Safed, Āb-i- *see* Sefīd, Darya-ye
145 *X11* **Şaffāf, Ḥawr aş** *wetland* S Iraq
97 *J16* **Säffle** Värmland, C Sweden *59.07N 12.55E*
39 *N15* **Safford** Arizona, SW USA *32.46N 109.41W*
76 *E7* **Safi** W Morocco *32.19N 9.14W*
149 *V9* **Safīdābeh** Khorāsān, E Iran *31.04N 60.30E*
148 *M4* **Safīd, Rūd-e** 〰 NW Iran
130 *I4* **Safonovo** Smolenskaya Oblast', W Russian Federation *55.05N 33.12E*
142 *H11* **Safranbolu** Karabük, N Turkey *41.16N 32.40E*
145 *Y13* **Safwān** SE Iraq *30.06N 47.43E*
164 *J16* **Saga** *var.* Gya'gya. Xizang Zizhiqu, W China *29.22N 85.19E*
170 *Cc13* **Saga** Saga, Kyūshū, SW Japan *33.14N 130.16E*
170 *Cc13* **Saga** *off.* Saga-ken. ◈ *prefecture* Kyūshū, SW Japan
171 *Ll12* **Sagae** Yamagata, Honshū, C Japan *38.22N 140.13E*
177 *G5* **Sagaing** Sagaing, C Myanmar *21.55N 95.55E*
177 *G3* **Sagaing** ◈ *division* N Myanmar
171 *Jj16* **Sagamihara** Kanagawa, Honshū, S Japan *35.32N 139.23E*
171 *Jj17* **Sagami-nada** *inlet* SW Japan
171 *Jj17* **Sagami-wan** *bay* SW Japan
Sagan *see* Żagań
31 *Y3* **Saganaga Lake** ◎ Minnesota, N USA
161 *F18* **Sāgar** Karnātaka, W India *14.09N 75.02E*
160 *I9* **Sāgar** *prev.* Saugor. Madhya Pradesh, C India *23.52N 78.46E*
13 *S8* **Sagard** Québec, SE Canada *48.01N 70.03W*
Sagarmatha *see* Everest, Mount
179 *Qq13* **Sagay** Negros, C Philippines *10.54N 123.26E*
Sagebrush State *see* Nevada
149 *V11* **Sāghand** Yazd, C Iran *32.33N 55.12E*
21 *N14* **Sag Harbor** Long Island, New York, NE USA *40.59N 72.15W*
Saghez *see* Saqqez
33 *R8* **Saginaw** Michigan, N USA *43.25N 83.57W*
33 *R8* **Saginaw Bay** *lake bay* Michigan, N USA
150 *H11* **Sagiz** Atyrau, W Kazakhstan *48.12N 54.55E*
66 *H6* **Saglek Bank** *undersea feature* W Labrador Sea
11 *P5* **Saglek Bay** *bay* SW Labrador Sea
Saglouc/Sagluk *see* Salluit
105 *X15* **Sagonne, Golfe de** *gulf* Corse, France, C Mediterranean Sea
107 *P13* **Sagra** ▲ S Spain *37.59N 2.33W*
106 *F14* **Sagres** Faro, S Portugal *37.01N 8.55W*
39 *S7* **Saguache** Colorado, C USA *38.05N 106.05W*
46 *J7* **Sagua de Tánamo** Holguín, E Cuba *20.34N 75.14W*
46 *E5* **Sagua la Grande** Villa Clara, C Cuba *22.48N 80.06W*
13 *R7* **Saguenay** 〰 Québec, SE Canada
76 *C9* **Saguia al Hamra** *var.* As Saqia al Hamra. 〰 N Western Sahara
Sagunt/Saguntum *see* Sagunto
107 *S9* **Sagunto** *Cat.* Sagunt, *Ar.* Murviedro; *anc.* Saguntum. País Valenciano, E Spain *39.40N 0.16W*
144 *H10* **Saḥāb** Al 'Āṣimah, NW Jordan *31.52N 36.00E*
56 *E6* **Sahagún** Córdoba, NW Colombia *8.57N 75.26W*
106 *L4* **Sahagún** Castilla-León, N Spain *42.22N 5.01W*
147 *X8* **Saḥam** N Oman *24.06N 56.52E*
70 *F9* **Sahara** *desert* Libya/Algeria
77 *U9* **Sahara el Gharbîya** *var.* Aş Şaḥrā' al Gharbīyah, *Eng.* Western Desert. *desert* C Egypt
77 *X9* **Sahara el Sharqîya** *var.* Aş Şaḥrā' ash Sharqīyah, *Eng.* Arabian Desert, Eastern Desert. *desert* E Egypt
Saharan Atlas *see* Atlas Saharien
158 *J9* **Sahāranpur** Uttar Pradesh, N India *29.58N 77.33E*
66 *L10* **Saharan Seamounts** *var.* Saharian Seamounts. *undersea feature* E Atlantic Ocean *25.00N 20.00W*
159 *Q13* **Saharsa** Bihār, NE India *25.54N 86.36E*
69 *O7* **Sahel** *physical region* C Africa
159 *R14* **Sāhibganj** Jhārkhand, NE India *25.15N 87.40E*
145 *Q7* **Sahīlīyah** C Iraq *33.43N 42.42E*
144 *H4* **Sāḥilīyah, Jibāl as** ⛰ NW Syria
116 *M13* **Şahin** Tekirdağ, NW Turkey *41.01N 26.51E*
155 *U8* **Sāhīwāl** Punjab, E Pakistan *31.57N 72.22E*
155 *U9* **Sāhīwāl** *prev.* Montgomery. Punjab, E Pakistan *30.40N 73.04E*
147 *W11* **Saḥmah, Ramlat as** *desert* C Oman
145 *T13* **Şaḥrā' al Ḥijārah** *desert* S Iraq
42 *H5* **Sahuaripa** Sonora, NW Mexico *29.02N 109.14W*
38 *M16* **Sahuarita** Arizona, SW USA *31.24N 110.55W*
42 *L13* **Sahuayo** *var.* Sahuayo de José Mariá Morelos; *prev.* Sahuayo de Díaz, Sahuayo de Porfirio Díaz. Michoacán de Ocampo, SW Mexico *20.04N 102.44W*
Sahuayo de Díaz/Sahuayo de José Mariá Morelos/Sahuayo de Porfirio Díaz *see* Sahuayo
181 *W8* **Sahul Shelf** *undersea feature* N Timor Sea
178 *Hh17* **Sai Buri** Pattani, SW Thailand *6.42N 101.37E*
76 *I6* **Saïda** NW Algeria *34.49N 0.10E*
144 *G7* **Saïda** *var.* Şaydā, Sayida; *anc.* Sidon. W Lebanon *33.20N 35.24E*
Sa'īdābād *see* Sīrjān
82 *B13* **Sa'id Bundas** Western Bahr el Ghazal, SW Sudan *8.24N 24.53E*
194 *J12* **Saidor** Madang, N PNG *5.37S 146.28E*
159 *S13* **Saidpur** *var.* Syedpur. Rajshahi, NW Bangladesh *25.48N 89.00E*
110 *C7* **Saignelégier** Jura, NW Switzerland *47.18N 7.03E*
170 *G11* **Saigō** Shimane, Dōgo, SW Japan *36.12N 133.18E*
Saigon *see* Hô Chi Minh
169 *P11* **Saihan Tal** *var.* Sonid Youqi. Nei Mongol Zizhiqu, N China *42.45N 112.36E*
168 *I12* **Saihan Toroi** Nei Mongol Zizhiqu, N China *41.44N 100.29E*
Sai Hun *see* Syr Darya
94 *M11* **Saija** Lappi, NE Finland *67.07N 28.46E*
170 *Ee14* **Saijō** Ehime, Shikoku, SW Japan *33.55N 133.10E*
170 *Dd15* **Saiki** Ōita, Kyūshū, SW Japan *32.57N 131.52E*
176 *Uu9* **Saileen** Papua, E Indonesia *1.14S 130.56E*
95 *N18* **Saimaa** ◎ SE Finland
95 *N18* **Saimaa Canal** *Fin.* Saimaan Kanava, *Rus.* Saymenskiy Kanal. *canal* Finland/Russian Federation
Saimaan Kanava *see* Saimaa Canal
42 *L10* **Saín Alto** Zacatecas, C Mexico *23.38N 103.13W*
98 *L12* **St Abb's Head** *headland* SE Scotland, UK *55.54N 2.07W*
9 *Y16* **St.Adolphe** Manitoba, S Canada *49.39N 96.55W*
105 *O15* **St-Affrique** Aveyron, S France *43.57N 2.52E*
13 *Q10* **St-Agapit** Québec, SE Canada *46.33N 71.25W*
99 *O21* **St Albans** *anc.* Verulamium. E England, UK *51.46N 0.21W*
20 *L6* **Saint Albans** Vermont, NE USA *44.49N 73.07W*
23 *Q5* **Saint Albans** West Virginia, NE USA *38.21N 81.47W*
St Alban's Head *see* St.Aldhelm's Head
9 *Q14* **St.Albert** Alberta, SW Canada *53.37N 113.37W*
99 *M24* **St. Aldhelm's Head** *var.* St.Alban's Head. *headland* S England, UK *50.34N 2.04W*
13 *S8* **St-Alexandre** Québec, SE Canada *47.39N 69.36W*
13 *O11* **St-Alexis-des-Monts** Québec, SE Canada *46.30N 73.08W*
105 *P2* **St-Amand-les-Eaux** Nord, N France *50.27N 3.25E*
105 *O9* **St-Amand-Montrond** *var.* St-Amand-Mont-Rond. Cher, C France *46.43N 2.28E*
13 *Q7* **St-Ambroise** Québec, SE Canada *48.35N 71.19W*
181 *P16* **St-André** NE Réunion
12 *M12* **St-André-Avellin** Québec, SE Canada *45.45N 75.04W*
104 *K12* **St-André-de-Cubzac** Gironde, SW France *45.01N 0.26W*
98 *K11* **St Andrews** E Scotland, UK *56.20N 2.48W*
25 *Q9* **Saint Andrews Bay** *bay* Florida, SE USA
25 *W7* **Saint Andrew Sound** *sound* Georgia, SE USA
Saint Anna Trough *see* Svyataya Anna Trough
46 *J11* **St.Ann's Bay** C Jamaica *18.25N 77.12W*
11 *T10* **St.Anthony** Newfoundland and Labrador, SE Canada *51.21N 55.34W*
35 *R13* **Saint Anthony** Idaho, NW USA *43.56N 111.38W*
190 *M11* **Saint Arnaud** Victoria, SE Australia *36.39S 143.15E*
193 *I15* **St.Arnaud Range** ⛰ South Island, NZ
13 *T8* **St-Arsène** Québec, SE Canada *47.55N 69.21W*
11 *R10* **St-Augustin** Québec, E Canada *51.13N 58.39W*
25 *X9* **Saint Augustine** Florida, SE USA *29.54N 81.19W*
99 *H24* **St Austell** SW England, UK *50.21N 4.46W*
105 *T4* **St-Avold** Moselle, NE France *49.06N 6.43E*
105 *N17* **St-Barthélemy** ⛰ S France
104 *L17* **St-Béat** Haute-Garonne, S France *42.55N 0.39E*
99 *I15* **St Bees Head** *headland* NW England, UK *54.30N 3.39W*
181 *P16* **St-Benoit** E Réunion
105 *T13* **St-Bonnet** Hautes-Alpes, SE France *44.41N 6.04E*
St.Botolph's Town *see* Boston
99 *G21* **St Brides Bay** *inlet* SW Wales, UK
104 *H5* **St-Brieuc** Côtes d'Armor, NW France *48.31N 2.45W*
104 *H5* **St-Brieuc, Baie de** *bay* NW France
104 *L7* **St-Calais** Sarthe, NW France *47.55N 0.48E*
13 *Q10* **St-Casimir** Québec, SE Canada *46.40N 72.05W*
12 *H16* **St.Catharines** Ontario, S Canada *43.10N 79.15W*
47 *S14* **St.Catherine, Mount** ▲ N Grenada *12.10N 61.41W*
66 *C11* **St Catherine Point** *headland* E Bermuda
25 *X6* **Saint Catherines Island** *island* Georgia, SE USA
99 *M24* **St Catherine's Point** *headland* S England, UK *50.34N 1.17W*
105 *N13* **St-Céré** Lot, S France *44.52N 1.53E*
110 *A10* **St.Cergue** Vaud, W Switzerland *46.25N 6.10E*
105 *R11* **St-Chamond** Loire, E France *45.28N 4.31E*
35 *S16* **Saint Charles** Idaho, NW USA *42.05N 111.23W*
29 *X4* **Saint Charles** Missouri, C USA *38.48N 90.28W*
105 *P13* **St-Chély-d'Apcher** Lozère, S France *44.51N 3.16E*
Saint Christopher-Nevis *see* Saint Kitts and Nevis
33 *S9* **Saint Clair** Michigan, N USA *42.49N 82.29W*
12 *D17* **St.Clair** 〰 Canada/USA
191 *O17* **St.Clair, Lake** ◎ Tasmania, SE Australia
12 *C17* **St.Clair, Lake** *var.* Lac à L'eau Claire. ◎ Canada/USA
33 *S10* **Saint Clair Shores** Michigan, N USA *42.30N 82.53W*
105 *S10* **St-Claude** *anc.* Condate. Jura, E France *46.22N 5.52E*
47 *X6* **St-Claude** Basse Terre, SW Guadeloupe *16.01N 61.41W*
25 *X12* **Saint Cloud** Florida, SE USA *28.15N 81.15W*
31 *U8* **Saint Cloud** Minnesota, N USA *45.33N 94.09W*
47 *T9* **Saint Croix** *island* S Virgin Islands (US)
32 *J4* **Saint Croix Flowage** ▣ Wisconsin, N USA
21 *T5* **Saint Croix River** 〰 Canada/USA
31 *W7* **Saint Croix River** 〰 Minnesota/Wisconsin, N USA
47 *S14* **St.David's** SE Grenada *12.01N 61.40W*
99 *H21* **St David's** SW Wales, UK *51.53N 5.16W*
99 *G21* **St David's Head** *headland* SW Wales, UK *51.54N 5.19W*
66 *C12* **St David's Island** *island* E Bermuda
181 *O16* **St-Denis** ○ (Réunion) NW Réunion *20.55S 14.33E*
105 *U6* **St-Dié** Vosges, NE France *48.16N 6.57E*
105 *R5* **St-Dizier** *anc.* Desiderii Fanum. Haute-Marne, N France *48.39N 5.00E*
13 *N11* **St-Donat** Québec, SE Canada *46.16N 74.12W*
13 *N11* **Ste-Adèle** Québec, SE Canada *45.58N 74.10W*
13 *N11* **Ste-Agathe-des-Monts** Québec, SE Canada *46.03N 74.19W*
180 *I16* **Sainte Anne** *island* Inner Islands, NE Seychelles
9 *Y16* **Ste.Anne** Manitoba, S Canada *49.40N 96.40W*
47 *R12* **Ste-Anne** Grande Terre, E Guadeloupe *16.13N 61.22W*
47 *Y6* **Ste-Anne** SE Martinique *14.25N 60.53W*
13 *Q10* **Ste-Anne** 〰 Québec, SE Canada
13 *W6* **Ste-Anne-des-Monts** Québec, SE Canada *49.07N 66.28W*
12 *M10* **Ste-Anne-du-Lac** Québec, SE Canada *46.51N 75.20W*
13 *U4* **Ste-Anne, Lac** ◎ Québec, SE Canada
13 *S10* **Ste-Apolline** Québec, SE Canada *46.47N 70.15W*
13 *U7* **Ste-Blandine** Québec, SE Canada *48.22N 68.27W*
13 *R10* **Ste-Claire** Québec, SE Canada *46.30N 70.40W*
13 *Q10* **Ste-Croix** Québec, SE Canada *46.36N 71.42W*
110 *B8* **Ste.Croix** Vaud, SW Switzerland *46.49N 6.31E*
105 *P14* **Ste-Énimie** Lozère, S France *44.21N 3.26E*
29 *Y6* **Sainte Genevieve** Missouri, C USA *37.57N 90.01W*
105 *S12* **St-Egrève** Isère, E France *45.15N 5.40E*
41 *T12* **Saint Elias, Cape** *headland* Kayak Island, Alaska, USA *59.48N 144.36W*
41 *U11* **Saint Elias, Mount** ▲ Alaska, USA *60.18N 140.57W*
8 *G8* **Saint Elias Mountains** ⛰ Canada/USA
57 *Y10* **St-Élie** N French Guiana *4.49N 53.21W*
105 *O10* **St-Eloy-les-Mines** Puy-de-Dôme, C France *46.07N 2.50E*
13 *R7* **Ste-Marguerite** 〰 Québec, SE Canada
13 *S7* **Ste-Marguerite-Nord-Est** 〰 Québec, SE Canada
13 *V4* **Ste-Marguerite, Pointe** *headland* Québec, SE Canada *50.01N 66.43W*
13 *R10* **Ste-Marie** Québec, SE Canada *46.28N 71.00W*
47 *Q11* **Ste-Marie** NE Martinique *14.48N 61.01W*
181 *P16* **Ste-Marie** NE Réunion
105 *U6* **Ste-Marie-aux-Mines** Haut-Rhin, NE France *48.16N 7.12E*
10 *J14* **Ste-Marie, Lac** ▣ Quebec, S Canada
180 *K4* **Sainte Marie, Nosy** *island* E Madagascar
104 *L8* **Ste-Maure-de-Touraine** Indre-et-Loire, C France *47.06N 0.38E*
105 *R4* **Ste-Menehould** Marne, NE France *49.06N 4.54E*
Ste-Perpétue *see* Ste-Perpétue-de-l'Islet
13 *S9* **Ste-Perpétue-de-l'Islet** *var.* Ste-Perpétue. Québec, SE Canada *47.02N 69.54W*
47 *X11* **Ste-Rose** Basse Terre, N Guadeloupe *16.20N 61.41W*
181 *P16* **Ste-Rose** E Réunion
9 *W15* **Ste.Rose du Lac** Manitoba, S Canada *51.04N 99.31W*
104 *J11* **Saintes** *anc.* Mediolanum. Charente-Maritime, W France *45.45N 0.37W*
47 *X7* **Saintes, Canal des** *channel* SW Guadeloupe
Saintes, Îles des *see* les Saintes
181 *P16* **Ste-Suzanne** N Réunion
13 *P10* **Ste-Thècle** Québec, SE Canada *46.48N 72.31W*
105 *Q12* **St-Étienne** Loire, E France *45.25N 4.22E*
104 *M4* **St-Étienne-du-Rouvray** Seine-Maritime, N France *49.22N 1.07E*
Saint Eustatius *see* Sint Eustatius
12 *M11* **Ste-Véronique** Québec, SE Canada *46.30N 74.58W*
13 *T7* **St-Fabien** Québec, SE Canada *48.19N 68.51W*
13 *P7* **St-Félicien** Québec, SE Canada *48.39N 72.28W*
13 *O11* **St-Félix-de-Valois** Québec, SE Canada *46.10N 73.25W*
105 *Y14* **St-Florent** Corse, France, C Mediterranean Sea *42.41N 9.19E*
105 *Y14* **St-Florent, Golfe de** *gulf* Corse, France, C Mediterranean Sea
105 *P6* **St-Florentin** Yonne, C France *48.00N 3.46E*
105 *N9* **St-Florent-sur-Cher** Cher, C France *47.00N 2.13E*
105 *P12* **St-Flour** Cantal, C France *45.01N 3.04E*
28 *H2* **Saint Francis** Kansas, C USA *39.45N 101.31W*
85 *H26* **St.Francis, Cape** *headland* S South Africa *34.11S 24.45E*
29 *X10* **Saint Francis River** 〰 Arkansas/Missouri, C USA
24 *J8* **Saint Francisville** Louisiana, S USA *30.46N 91.22W*
13 *Q12* **St-François** 〰 Québec, SE Canada
47 *Y6* **St-François** Grande Terre, E Guadeloupe *16.15N 61.16W*
13 *R11* **St-François, Lac** ◎ Québec, SE Canada
29 *X7* **Saint Francois Mountains** ⛰ Missouri, C USA
St-Gall/Saint Gall/St.Gallen *see* Sankt Gallen
104 *L16* **St-Gaudens** Haute-Garonne, S France *43.07N 0.43E*
13 *R12* **St-Gédéon** Québec, SE Canada *45.51N 70.36W*
189 *X10* **Saint George** Queensland, E Australia *28.04S 148.39E*
66 *B12* **St George** N Bermuda *32.24N 64.42W*
40 *K15* **Saint George** Saint George Island, Alaska, USA *56.34N 169.30W*
23 *S14* **Saint George** South Carolina, SE USA *33.10N 80.34W*
38 *J8* **Saint George** Utah, W USA *37.06N 113.35W*
11 *R12* **St.George, Cape** *headland* Newfoundland and Labrador, E Canada *48.26N 59.17W*
195 *P11* **St.George, Cape** *headland* New Ireland, NE PNG *4.49S 152.52E*
40 *J15* **Saint George Island** *island* Pribilof Islands, Alaska, USA
25 *S10* **Saint George Island** *island* Florida, SE USA
101 *J19* **Saint-Georges** Liège, E Belgium *50.36N 5.20E*
13 *R11* **St-Georges** Québec, SE Canada *46.07N 70.40W*
57 *Z11* **St-Georges** E French Guiana *3.55N 51.49W*
47 *R14* **St.George's** ● (Grenada) SW Grenada *12.03N 61.45W*
11 *R12* **St.George's Bay** *inlet* Newfoundland and Labrador, E Canada
99 *G21* **Saint George's Channel** *channel* Ireland/Wales, UK
195 *P10* **St.George's Channel** *channel* NE PNG
66 *B11* **St George's Island** *island* E Bermuda
101 *I21* **Saint-Gérard** Namur, S Belgium *50.20N 4.47E*
St-Germain *see* St-Germain-en-Laye
13 *P12* **St-Germain-de-Grantham** Québec, SE Canada *45.49N 72.32W*
105 *N5* **St-Germain-en-Laye** *var.* St-Germain. Yvelines, N France *48.52N 2.04E*
104 *H8* **St-Gildas, Pointe du** *headland* NW France *47.09N 2.25W*
105 *R15* **St-Gilles** Gard, S France *43.41N 4.24E*
104 *I9* **St-Gilles-Croix-de-Vie** Vendée, NW France *46.41N 1.55W*
181 *O16* **St-Gilles-les-Bains** W Réunion *21.01S 55.13E*
104 *M16* **St-Girons** Ariège, S France *42.58N 1.07E*
Saint Gotthard *see* Szentgotthárd
110 *G9* **St.Gotthard Tunnel** *tunnel* Ticino, S Switzerland
99 *H22* **St Govan's Head** *headland* SW Wales, UK *51.35N 4.55W*
36 *M7* **Saint Helena** California, W USA *38.29N 122.30W*
67 *F24* **Saint Helena** ◇ *UK dependent territory* C Atlantic Ocean
69 *O12* **Saint Helena** *island* C Atlantic Ocean
85 *E25* **St.Helena Bay** *bay* SW South Africa
67 *M16* **Saint Helena Fracture Zone** *tectonic feature* C Atlantic Ocean
36 *M7* **Saint Helena, Mount** ▲ California, W USA *38.40N 122.39W*
23 *S15* **Saint Helena Sound** *inlet* South Carolina, SE USA
33 *Q7* **Saint Helen, Lake** ◎ Michigan, N USA
191 *Q16* **Saint Helens** Tasmania, SE Australia *41.21S 148.15E*
99 *K18* **St Helens** NW England, UK *53.28N 2.43W*
34 *G10* **Saint Helens** Oregon, NW USA *45.55N 122.51W*
34 *H10* **Saint Helens, Mount** ♨ Washington, NW USA *46.24N 121.49W*
99 *L26* **St Helier** ○ (Jersey) S Jersey, Channel Islands *49.12N 2.07W*
13 *S9* **St-Hilarion** Québec, SE Canada *47.34N 70.24W*
101 *K22* **Saint-Hubert** Luxembourg, SE Belgium *50.02N 5.23E*
13 *T8* **St-Hubert** Québec, SE Canada *47.46N 69.15W*
13 *P12* **St-Hyacinthe** Québec, SE Canada *45.37N 72.57W*
St.Iago de la Vega *see* Spanish Town
33 *Q4* **Saint Ignace** Michigan, N USA *45.52N 84.43W*
13 *O10* **St-Ignace-du-Lac** Québec, SE Canada *46.43N 73.49W*
10 *D12* **St.Ignace Island** *island* Ontario, S Canada
110 *C7* **St.Imier** Bern, W Switzerland *47.09N 6.55E*
99 *G25* **St Ives** SW England, UK *50.12N 5.28W*
31 *U10* **Saint James** Minnesota, N USA *43.58N 94.40W*
8 *I15* **St.James, Cape** *headland* Graham Island, British Columbia, SW Canada *51.57N 131.04W*
13 *O13* **St-Jean** *var.* St-Jean-sur-Richelieu. Québec, SE Canada *45.15N 73.16W*
57 *X9* **St-Jean** NW French Guiana *5.21N 54.09W*
13 *R8* **St-Jean** 〰 Québec, SE Canada
Saint-Jean-d'Acre *see* 'Akko
104 *K11* **St-Jean-d'Angély** Charente-Maritime, W France *45.57N 0.31W*
105 *N7* **St-Jean-de-Braye** Loiret, C France *47.54N 1.58E*
104 *I16* **St-Jean-de-Luz** Pyrénées-Atlantiques, SW France *43.24N 1.40W*
105 *T12* **St-Jean-de-Maurienne** Savoie, E France *45.16N 6.21E*
104 *I9* **St-Jean-de-Monts** Vendée, NW France *46.45N 2.00W*

◆ Country
● Country Capital
◇ Dependent Territory
○ Dependent Territory Capital
◈ Administrative Region
✈ International Airport
▲ Mountain
⛰ Mountain Range
♨ Volcano
〰 River
◎ Lake
▣ Reservoir

St-Jean-du-Gard – Samarkand

105 *Q14* **St-Jean-du-Gard** Gard, S France *44.06N 3.49E*
13 *Q7* **St-Jean, Lac** ◎ Québec, SE Canada
104 *I16* **St-Jean-Pied-de-Port** Pyrénées-Atlantiques, SW France *43.10N 1.13W*
13 *S9* **St-Jean-Port-Joli** Québec, SE Canada *47.13N 70.16W*
St-Jean-sur-Richelieu *see* St-Jean
13 *N12* **St-Jérôme** Québec, SE Canada *45.46N 74.01W*
27 *T5* **Saint Jo** Texas, SW USA *33.42N 97.33W*
11 *O15* **St.John** New Brunswick, SE Canada *45.16N 66.03W*
28 *L6* **Saint John** Kansas, C USA *37.59N 98.44W*
78 *K16* **Saint John** ≈ C Liberia
47 *T9* **Saint John** *island* C Virgin Islands (US)
24 *I6* **Saint John, Lake** ◎ Louisiana, S USA
21 *Q2* **Saint John** *Fr.* Saint-John. ≈ Canada/USA
47 *W10* **St John's** ● (Antigua and Barbuda) Antigua, Antigua and Barbuda *17.06N 61.50W*
11 *V12* **St.John's** Newfoundland and Labrador, E Canada *47.34N 52.40W*
39 *O12* **Saint Johns** Arizona, SW USA *34.28N 109.22W*
33 *Q9* **Saint Johns** Michigan, N USA *42.58N 84.31W*
11 *V12* **St.John's** ✈ Newfoundland and Labrador, E Canada *47.22N 52.45W*
25 *X11* **Saint Johns River** ≈ Florida, SE USA
47 *N12* **St.Joseph** W Dominica *15.24N 61.25W*
181 *P17* **St-Joseph** S Réunion
24 *J6* **Saint Joseph** Louisiana, S USA *31.56N 91.14W*
33 *O10* **Saint Joseph** Michigan, N USA *42.04N 86.30W*
29 *R3* **Saint Joseph** Missouri, C USA *39.45N 94.49W*
22 *I10* **Saint Joseph** Tennessee, S USA *35.02N 87.29W*
24 *R9* **Saint Joseph Bay** *bay* Florida, SE USA
13 *R11* **St-Joseph-de-Beauce** Québec, SE Canada *46.20N 70.52W*
10 *C10* **St.Joseph, Lake** ◎ Ontario, C Canada
33 *Q11* **Saint Joseph River** ≈ N USA
12 *C11* **Saint Joseph's Island** *island* Ontario, S Canada
13 *N11* **St-Jovite** Québec, SE Canada *46.07N 74.35W*
123 *Jj16* **St Julian's** N Malta *35.55N 14.29E*
St-Julien *see* St-Julien-en-Genevois
105 *T10* **St-Julien-en-Genevois** *var.* St-Julien. Haute-Savoie, E France *46.07N 6.06E*
104 *M11* **St-Junien** Haute-Vienne, C France *45.52N 0.54E*
105 *Q11* **St-Just-St-Rambert** Loire, E France *45.30N 4.13E*
98 *D8* **St Kilda** *island* NW Scotland, UK
47 *V10* **Saint Kitts** *island* Saint Kitts and Nevis
47 *U10* **Saint Kitts and Nevis** *off.* Federation of Saint Christopher and Nevis, *var.* Saint Christopher-Nevis. ◆ *commonwealth republic* E West Indies
9 *X16* **St.Laurent** Manitoba, S Canada *50.20N 97.55W*
St-Laurent *see* St-Laurent-du-Maroni
57 *X9* **St-Laurent-du-Maroni** *var.* St-Laurent. NW French Guiana *5.28N 54.03W*
St-Laurent, Fleuve *see* St.Lawrence
104 *J12* **St-Laurent-Médoc** Gironde, SW France *45.11N 0.50W*
11 *N12* **St.Lawrence** *Fr.* Fleuve St-Laurent. ≈ Canada/USA
11 *Q12* **St.Lawrence, Gulf of** *gulf* NW Atlantic Ocean
40 *K10* **Saint Lawrence Island** *island* Alaska, USA
12 *M14* **Saint Lawrence River** ≈ Canada/USA
101 *L25* **Saint-Léger** Luxembourg, SE Belgium *49.36N 5.39E*
11 *N14* **St.Léonard** New Brunswick, SE Canada *47.10N 67.55W*
13 *P11* **St-Léonard** Québec, SE Canada *46.06N 72.18W*
181 *O17* **St-Leu** W Réunion *21.09S 55.16E*
104 *J4* **St-Lô** *anc.* Briovera, Laudus. Manche, N France *49.07N 1.08W*
9 *T15* **St.Louis** Saskatchewan, S Canada *52.50N 105.43W*
105 *V7* **St-Louis** Haut-Rhin, NE France *47.34N 7.34E*
181 *O17* **St-Louis** S Réunion
78 *G10* **Saint Louis** NW Senegal *15.58N 16.30W*
29 *X4* **Saint Louis** Missouri, C USA *38.38N 90.15W*
31 *W5* **Saint Louis River** ≈ Minnesota, N USA
105 *T7* **St-Loup-sur-Semouse** Haute-Saône, E France *47.53N 6.15E*
13 *O12* **St-Luc** Québec, SE Canada *45.19N 73.18W*
85 *L22* **St.Lucia** KwaZulu/Natal, E South Africa *28.22S 32.25E*
47 *X13* **Saint Lucia** ◆ *commonwealth republic* SE West Indies
49 *S3* **Saint Lucia** *island* SE West Indies
85 *L22* **St.Lucia, Cape** *headland* E South Africa *28.29S 32.26E*
47 *Y13* **Saint Lucia Channel** *channel* Martinique/Saint Lucia
25 *Y14* **Saint Lucie Canal** *canal* Florida, SE USA
25 *Z13* **Saint Lucie Inlet** *inlet* Florida, SE USA
98 *L2* **St Magnus Bay** *bay* N Scotland, UK
104 *K10* **St-Maixent-l'École** Deux-Sèvres, W France *46.24N 0.13W*
9 *Y16* **St.Malo** Manitoba, S Canada *49.16N 96.58W*
104 *I5* **St-Malo** Ille-et-Vilaine, NW France *48.39N 2.00W*
104 *H4* **St-Malo, Golfe de** *gulf* NW France
46 *L9* **St-Marc** C Haiti *19.05N 72.42W*
46 *L9* **St-Marc, Canal de** *channel* W Haiti
57 *Y12* **Saint-Marcel, Mont** ▲ S French Guiana *2.32N 53.00W*
105 *S12* **St-Marcellin-le-Mollard** Isère, E France *45.12N 5.18E*
98 *K5* **St Margaret's Hope** NE Scotland, UK *58.49N 2.57W*
34 *M9* **Saint Maries** Idaho, NW USA *47.19N 116.37W*
25 *T9* **Saint Marks** Florida, SE USA *30.09N 84.12W*
110 *D11* **St.Martin** Valais, SW Switzerland *46.09N 7.27E*
Saint Martin *see* Sint Maarten
33 *O5* **Saint Martin Island** *island* Michigan, N USA
24 *I9* **Saint Martinville** Louisiana, S USA *30.09N 91.51W*
193 *E20* **St.Mary, Mount** ▲ South Island, NZ *44.16S 169.42E*
194 *K14* **St.Mary, Mount** ▲ S PNG *8.06S 147.00E*
190 *I6* **Saint Mary Peak** ▲ South Australia *31.25S 138.39E*
191 *Q16* **Saint Marys** Tasmania, SE Australia *41.34S 148.13E*
12 *E16* **St.Marys** Ontario, S Canada *43.15N 81.08W*
40 *M11* **Saint Marys** Alaska, USA *62.03N 163.10W*
25 *W8* **Saint Marys** Georgia, SE USA *30.44N 81.30W*
29 *P4* **Saint Marys** Kansas, C USA *39.09N 96.00W*
33 *Q4* **Saint Marys** Ohio, N USA *40.31N 84.22W*
23 *R3* **Saint Marys** West Virginia, NE USA *39.23N 81.11W*
25 *W8* **Saint Marys River** ≈ Florida/Georgia, SE USA
33 *Q4* **Saint Marys River** ≈ Michigan, N USA
104 *D6* **St-Mathieu, Pointe** *headland* NW France *48.17N 4.56W*
40 *J12* **Saint Matthew Island** *island* Alaska, USA
23 *R13* **Saint Matthews** South Carolina, SE USA *33.40N 80.46W*
St.Matthew's Island *see* Zadetkyi Kyun
194 *M8* **St.Matthias Group** *island group* NE PNG
110 *C11* **St.Maurice** Valais, SW Switzerland *46.09N 7.28E*
13 *P9* **St-Maurice** ≈ Québec, SE Canada
104 *J13* **St-Médard-en-Jalles** Gironde, SW France *44.54N 0.43W*
41 *N10* **Saint Michael** Alaska, USA *63.28N 162.02W*
St.Michel *see* Mikkeli
13 *N10* **St-Michel-des-Saints** Québec, SE Canada *46.39N 73.54W*
105 *S5* **St-Mihiel** Meuse, NE France *48.57N 5.33E*
110 *J10* **St.Moritz** *Ger.* Sankt Moritz, *Rmsch.* San Murezzan. Graubünden, SE Switzerland *46.30N 9.50E*
104 *H8* **St-Nazaire** Loire-Atlantique, NW France *47.16N 2.12W*
Saint Nicholas *see* São Nicolau
Saint-Nicolas *see* Sint-Niklaas
105 *N1* **St-Omer** Pas-de-Calais, N France *50.45N 2.15E*
104 *J11* **Saintonge** *cultural region* W France
13 *S9* **St-Pacôme** Québec, SE Canada *47.22N 69.56W*
13 *S10* **St-Pamphile** Québec, SE Canada *46.57N 69.46W*
13 *S9* **St-Pascal** Québec, SE Canada *47.25N 69.51W*
12 *J11* **St-Patrice, Lac** ◎ Québec, SE Canada
9 *R14* **St.Paul** Alberta, SW Canada *54.00N 111.18W*
181 *O16* **St-Paul** NW Réunion
40 *K14* **Saint Paul** Saint Paul Island, Alaska, USA *57.08N 170.13W*
31 *V8* **Saint Paul** *state capital* Minnesota, N USA *45.00N 93.10W*
31 *P15* **Saint Paul** Nebraska, C USA *41.12N 98.26W*
23 *P7* **Saint Paul** Virginia, NE USA *36.53N 82.18W*
79 *Q17* **Saint Paul, Cape** *headland* S Ghana *5.44N 0.55E*
105 *O17* **St-Paul-de-Fenouillet** Pyrénées-Orientales, S France *42.49N 2.28E*
67 *K14* **Saint Paul Fracture Zone** *tectonic feature* E Atlantic Ocean
40 *J14* **Saint Paul Island** *island* Pribilof Islands, Alaska, USA
104 *J15* **St-Paul-les-Dax** Landes, SW France *43.45N 1.01W*
23 *U11* **Saint Pauls** North Carolina, SE USA *34.45N 78.56W*
Saint Paul's Bay *see* San Pawl il-Bahar
203 *R16* **St Paul's Point** *headland* Pitcairn Island, Pitcairn Islands
31 *U10* **Saint Peter** Minnesota, N USA *44.18N 93.59W*
99 *L26* **St Peter Port** ○ (Guernsey) C Guernsey, Channel Islands *49.28N 2.33W*
25 *V13* **Saint Petersburg** Florida, SE USA *27.46N 82.37W*
Saint Petersburg *see* Sankt-Peterburg
25 *V13* **Saint Petersburg Beach** Florida, SE USA *27.43N 82.43W*
181 *P17* **St-Philippe** SE Réunion *21.21S 55.46E*
47 *Q11* **St-Pierre** NW Martinique *14.44N 61.10W*
181 *O17* **St-Pierre** SW Réunion
11 *S13* **St-Pierre and Miquelon** *Fr.* Îles St-Pierre et Miquelon. ◇ *French territorial collectivity* NE North America
13 *P11* **St-Pierre, Lac** ◎ Québec, SE Canada
104 *F5* **St-Pol-de-Léon** Finistère, NW France *48.42N 4.00W*
105 *O2* **St-Pol-sur-Ternoise** Pas-de-Calais, N France *50.22N 2.21E*
St. Pons *see* St-Pons-de-Thomières
105 *O16* **St-Pons-de-Thomières** *var.* St.Pons. Hérault, S France *43.28N 2.48E*
105 *P10* **St-Pourçain-sur-Sioule** Allier, C France *46.19N 3.16E*
13 *S11* **St-Prosper** Québec, SE Canada *46.14N 70.28W*
105 *P3* **St-Quentin** Aisne, N France *49.51N 3.16E*
13 *R10* **St-Raphaël** Québec, SE Canada *46.47N 70.46W*
105 *U15* **St-Raphaël** Var, SE France *43.25N 6.46E*
13 *Q10* **St-Raymond** Québec, SE Canada *46.53N 71.49W*
35 *O9* **Saint Regis** Montana, NW USA *47.18N 115.06W*
20 *J7* **Saint Regis River** ≈ New York, NE USA
105 *R15* **St-Rémy-de-Provence** Bouches-du-Rhône, SE France *43.48N 4.49E*
13 *V6* **St-René-de-Matane** Québec, SE Canada *48.42N 67.22W*
104 *M9* **St-Savin** Vienne, W France *46.34N 0.53E*
13 *S8* **St-Siméon** Québec, SE Canada *47.49N 69.55W*
25 *X7* **Saint Simons Island** *island* Georgia, SE USA
203 *Y2* **Saint Stanislas Bay** *bay* Kiritimati, E Kiribati
11 *O15* **St.Stephen** New Brunswick, SE Canada *45.12N 67.18W*
41 *X12* **Saint Terese** Alaska, USA *58.28N 134.46W*
12 *E17* **St.Thomas** Ontario, S Canada *42.46N 81.12W*
31 *Q2* **Saint Thomas** North Dakota, N USA *48.37N 97.28W*
47 *T9* **Saint Thomas** *island* W Virgin Islands (US)
Saint Thomas *see* São Tomé, Sao Tome and Principe
Saint Thomas *see* Charlotte Amalie, Virgin Islands (US)
13 *P10* **St-Tite** Québec, SE Canada *46.42N 72.32W*
Saint-Trond *see* Sint-Truiden
105 *U16* **St-Tropez** Var, SE France *43.16N 6.39E*
Saint Ubes *see* Setúbal
104 *L3* **St-Valéry-en-Caux** Seine-Maritime, N France *49.53N 0.42E*
105 *Q9* **St-Vallier** Saône-et-Loire, C France *46.39N 4.19E*
108 *B7* **St-Vincent** Valle d'Aosta, NW Italy *45.47N 7.42E*
47 *Q14* **Saint Vincent** *island* N Saint Vincent and the Grenadines
Saint Vincent *see* São Vicente
47 *W14* **Saint Vincent and the Grenadines** ◆ *commonwealth republic* SE West Indies
Saint Vincent, Cape *see* São Vicente, Cabo de
104 *I15* **St-Vincent-de-Tyrosse** Landes, SW France *43.39N 1.16W*
190 *I9* **Saint Vincent, Gulf** *gulf* South Australia
25 *R10* **Saint Vincent Island** *island* Florida, SE USA
47 *T12* **Saint Vincent Passage** *passage* Saint Lucia/Saint Vincent and the Grenadines
191 *N18* **Saint Vincent, Point** *headland* Tasmania, SE Australia *43.19S 145.50E*
Saint-Vith *see* Sankt-Vith
9 *S14* **St.Walburg** Saskatchewan, S Canada *53.37N 109.12W*
St Wolfgangsee *see* Wolfgangsee
104 *M11* **St-Yrieix-la-Perche** Haute-Vienne, C France *45.31N 1.12E*
Saint Yves *see* Setúbal
13 *Y5* **St-Yvon** Québec, SE Canada *49.09N 64.51W*
196 *H5* **Saipan** *island* ● (Northern Mariana Islands) S Northern Mariana Islands
196 *H6* **Saipan Channel** *channel* S Northern Mariana Islands
196 *H6* **Saipan International Airport** ✈ Saipan, S Northern Mariana Islands
76 *G6* **Sais** ✈ (Fès) C Morocco *33.58N 4.48W*
Saishū *see* Cheju
Saishū *see* Cheju-do
104 *J16* **Saison** ≈ SW France
174 *L7* **Sai, Sungai** ≈ Borneo, N Indonesia
171 *Jj16* **Saitama** *off.* Saitama-ken. ◈ *prefecture* Honshū, S Japan
170 *Cc16* **Saito** Miyazaki, Kyūshū, SW Japan *32.07N 131.22E*
Saiyid Abid *see* Sayyid 'Abīd
59 *J19* **Sajama, Nevado** ▲ W Bolivia *17.57S 68.51W*
147 *V13* **Sājir, Ras** *headland* S Oman *16.42N 53.40E*
113 *M20* **Sajószentpéter** Borsod-Abaúj-Zemplén, NE Hungary *48.13N 20.43E*
85 *F24* **Sak** ≈ SW South Africa
83 *J18* **Saka** Coast, E Kenya *0.11S 39.27E*
178 *I11* **Sa Kaeo** Prachin Buri, C Thailand *13.47N 102.03E*
171 *Gg15* **Sakai** Ōsaka, Honshū, SW Japan *34.34N 135.28E*
170 *F14* **Sakaide** Kagawa, Shikoku, SW Japan *34.19N 133.49E*
170 *Ff12* **Sakaiminato** Tottori, Honshū, SW Japan *35.34N 133.12E*
146 *M3* **Sakākah** Al Jawf, NW Saudi Arabia *29.55N 40.10E*
30 *L4* **Sakakawea, Lake** ▣ North Dakota, N USA
10 *J9* **Sakami, Lac** ◎ Québec, C Canada
81 *O26* **Sakania** Katanga, SE Dem. Rep. Congo (Zaire) *12.43S 28.34E*
152 *K12* **Sakar** Lebap Welaýaty, E Turkmenistan *38.57N 63.46E*
180 *H7* **Sakaraha** Toliara, SW Madagascar *22.54S 44.31E*
152 *I14* **Sakarçäge** *var.* Sakarchäge, *Rus.* Sakar-Chaga. Mary Welaýaty, C Turkmenistan *37.40N 61.33E*
Sakar-Chaga/Sakarchäge *see* Sakarçäge
Sak'art'velo *see* Georgia
142 *F11* **Sakarya** ◈ *province* NW Turkey
142 *F12* **Sakarya Nehri** ≈ NW Turkey
150 *K13* **Sakasaul'skiy** *var.* Saksaul'skoye *Kaz.* Sekseüil. Kyzylorda, S Kazakhstan *47.07N 61.06E*
Saksaul'skoye *see* Sakasaul'skiy
171 *Ll11* **Sakata** Yamagata, Honshū, C Japan *38.54N 139.51E*
126 *L9* **Sakha (Yakutiya), Respublika** *var.* Respublika Yakutiya, Yakutiya, *Eng.* Yakutia. ◈ *autonomous republic* NE Russian Federation
Sakhalin *see* Sakhalin, Ostrov
127 *Oo14* **Sakhalin, Ostrov** *var.* Sakhalin. *island* SE Russian Federation
127 *P14* **Sakhalinskaya Oblast'** ◈ *province* SE Russian Federation
127 *Nn13* **Sakhalinskiy Zaliv** *gulf* E Russian Federation
Sakhnovshchina *see* Sakhnovshchyna
119 *U6* **Sakhnovshchyna** *Rus.* Sakhnovshchina. Kharkivs'ka Oblast', E Ukraine *49.08N 35.51E*
Sakhon Nakhon *see* Sakon Nakhon
Sakhtsar *see* Rāmsar
Saki *see* Saky
143 *W10* **Şäki** *Rus.* Sheki; *prev.* Nukha. NW Azerbaijan *41.09N 47.10E*
120 *E13* **Šakiai** *Ger.* Schaken. Marijampolė, S Lithuania *54.57N 23.04E*
176 *Z16* **Sakiramke** Papua, E Indonesia *8.36S 140.55E*
172 *Oo16* **Sakishima-shotō** *var.* Sakisima Syotô. *island group* SW Japan
Sakiz *see* Saqqez
Sakiz-Adasi *see* Chíos
161 *F19* **Sakleshpur** Karnātaka, E India *12.58N 75.45E*
178 *J9* **Sakon Nakhon** *var.* Muang Sakon Nakhon, Sakhon Nakhon. Sakon Nakhon, E Thailand *17.10N 104.07E*
155 *P15* **Sakrand** Sind, SE Pakistan *26.10N 68.13E*
85 *F24* **Sak River** *Afr.* Sakrivier. Northern Cape, W South Africa *30.49S 20.24E*
Sakrivier *see* Sak River
Saksaul'skiy *see* Saksaul'skoye
150 *K13* **Saksaul'skoye** *prev.* Saksaul'skiy, *Kaz.* Sekseüil. Kzylorda, S Kazakhstan *47.07N 61.06E*
97 *I25* **Sakskøbing** Storstrøm, SE Denmark *54.48N 11.39E*
171 *Jj15* **Saku** Nagano, Honshū, S Japan *36.15N 138.28E*
171 *K16* **Sakura** Chiba, Honshū, S Japan *35.42N 140.10E*
119 *S13* **Saky** *Rus.* Saki. Respublika Krym, S Ukraine *45.08N 33.36E*
78 *E9* **Sal** *island* Ilhas de Barlavento, NE Cape Verde
131 *N12* **Sal** ≈ SW Russian Federation
113 *I21* **Sal'a** *Hung.* Sellye, Vágsellye. Nitriansky Kraj, SW Slovakia *48.08N 17.55E*
97 *N15* **Sala** Västmanland, C Sweden *59.55N 16.37E*
175 *Qq11* **Salabangka, Kepulauan** *island group* N Indonesia
13 *N13* **Salaberry-de-Valleyfield** *var.* Valleyfield. Québec, SE Canada *45.15N 74.07W*
120 *G7* **Salacgrīva** *Est.* Salatsi. Limbaži, N Latvia *57.45N 24.21E*
109 *M18* **Sala Consilina** Campania, S Italy *40.22N 15.34E*
42 *C2* **Salada, Laguna** ◎ NW Mexico
63 *D14* **Saladas** Corrientes, NE Argentina *28.15S 58.40W*
63 *C21* **Saladillo** Buenos Aires, E Argentina *35.40S 59.49W*
63 *B16* **Saladillo, Río** ≈ C Argentina
27 *T9* **Salado** Texas, SW USA *30.57N 97.32W*
65 *J16* **Salado, Arroyo** ≈ SE Argentina
39 *Q12* **Salado, Rio** ≈ New Mexico, SW USA
63 *D21* **Salado, Río** ≈ E Argentina
64 *J12* **Salado, Río** ≈ C Argentina
43 *N7* **Salado, Río** ≈ NE Mexico
149 *N6* **Salafchegān** *var.* Sarafjagān. Qom, N Iran *34.28N 50.28E*
79 *Q15* **Salaga** C Ghana *8.31N 0.37W*
198 *Aa7* **Sala'ilua** Savai'i, W Samoa *13.39S 172.33W*
118 *G9* **Sălaj** ◈ *county* NW Romania
85 *H20* **Salajwe** Kweneng, SE Botswana *23.40S 24.46E*
80 *H9* **Salal** Kanem, W Chad *14.48N 17.12E*
82 *I6* **Salala** Red Sea, NE Sudan *21.16N 36.16E*
147 *V13* **Şalālah** SW Oman *17.01N 54.03E*
44 *D5* **Salamá** Baja Verapaz, C Guatemala *15.06N 90.18W*
44 *J6* **Salamá** Olancho, C Honduras *14.48N 86.34W*
64 *G10* **Salamanca** Coquimbo, C Chile *31.49S 70.58W*
43 *N13* **Salamanca** Guanajuato, C Mexico *20.33N 101.06W*
106 *K7* **Salamanca** *anc.* Helmantica, Salmantica. Castilla-León, NW Spain *40.58N 5.40W*
20 *D11* **Salamanca** New York, NE USA *42.09N 78.43W*
106 *J7* **Salamanca** ◈ *province* Castilla-León, W Spain
65 *J19* **Salamanca, Pampa de** *plain* S Argentina
80 *J12* **Salamat** *off.* Préfecture du Salamat. ◈ *prefecture* SE Chad
80 *I12* **Salamat, Bahr** ≈ S Chad
56 *F5* **Salamina** Magdalena, N Colombia *10.28N 74.46W*
117 *G19* **Salamína** *var.* Salamís. Salamína, C Greece *37.58N 23.28E*
117 *G19* **Salamína** *island* C Greece
Salamís *see* Salamína
144 *I5* **Salamīyah** *var.* As Salamīyah. Ḥamāh, W Syria *35.01N 37.01E*
33 *P12* **Salamonie Lake** ▣ Indiana, N USA
33 *P12* **Salamonie River** ≈ Indiana, N USA
Salang *see* Phuket
198 *Bb8* **Salani** Upolu, SE Samoa *14.00S 171.35W*
120 *C11* **Salantai** Klaipėda, NW Lithuania *56.05N 21.36E*
106 *K2* **Salas** Asturias, N Spain *43.25N 6.15W*
107 *O5* **Salas de los Infantes** Castilla-León, N Spain *42.01N 3.16W*
104 *M16* **Salat** ≈ S France
201 *V13* **Salat** *island* Chuuk, C Micronesia
174 *L15* **Salatiga** Jawa, C Indonesia *7.15S 110.34E*
201 *V13* **Salat Pass** *passage* W Pacific Ocean
Salatsi *see* Salacgrīva
178 *Jj10* **Salavan** *var.* Saravan, Saravane. Salavan, S Laos *15.43N 106.26E*
131 *V6* **Salavat** Respublika Bashkortostan, W Russian Federation *53.20N 55.54E*
58 *C12* **Salaverry** La Libertad, N Peru *8.15S 78.57W*
176 *Uu9* **Salawati, Pulau** *island* E Indonesia
200 *Nn11* **Sala y Gomez** *island* Chile, E Pacific Ocean
Sala y Gomez Fracture Zone *see* Sala y Gomez Ridge
200 *O11* **Sala y Gomez Ridge** *var.* Sala y Gomez Fracture Zone. *tectonic feature* SE Pacific Ocean
63 *A22* **Salazar** Buenos Aires, E Argentina *36.19S 62.10W*
56 *G7* **Salazar** Norte de Santander, N Colombia *7.46N 72.46W*
Salazar *see* N'Dalatando
181 *P16* **Salazie** C Réunion *21.01S 55.33E*
105 *N8* **Salbris** Loir-et-Cher, C France *47.25N 2.02E*
59 *G15* **Salcantay, Nevado** ▲ C Peru *13.21S 72.31W*
47 *O8* **Salcedo** N Dominican Republic *19.21N 70.23W*
41 *S9* **Salcha River** ≈ Alaska, USA
121 *H15* **Šalčininkai** Vilnius, SE Lithuania *54.19N 25.26E*
Saldae *see* Béjaïa
56 *E11* **Saldaña** Tolima, C Colombia *3.57N 75.01W*
106 *M4* **Saldaña** Castilla-León, N Spain *42.31N 4.43W*
85 *E25* **Saldanha** Western Cape, SW South Africa *33.00S 17.56E*
Salduba *see* Zaragoza
63 *B23* **Saldungaray** Buenos Aires, E Argentina *38.15S 61.45W*
120 *D9* **Saldus** *Ger.* Frauenburg. Saldus, W Latvia *56.40N 22.29E*
191 *P13* **Sale** Victoria, SE Australia *38.06S 147.06E*
76 *F6* **Salé** NW Morocco *34.07N 6.40W*
76 *F6* **Salé** ✈ (Rabat) W Morocco *34.09N 6.30W*
Salehābād *see* Andīmeshk
174 *Ii10* **Saleh, Air** ≈ Sumatera, W Indonesia
175 *Oo16* **Saleh, Teluk** *bay* Nusa Tenggara, S Indonesia
125 *G8* **Salekhard** *prev.* Obdorsk. Yamalo-Nenetskiy Avtonomnyy Okrug, N Russian Federation *66.33N 66.34E*
198 *B7* **Sālelologa** Savai'i, C Samoa *13.42S 172.10W*
161 *H21* **Salem** Tamil Nādu, SE India *11.37N 78.07E*
29 *V9* **Salem** Arkansas, C USA *36.21N 91.49W*
32 *L15* **Salem** Illinois, N USA *38.37N 88.57W*
33 *P15* **Salem** Indiana, N USA *38.37N 86.06W*
21 *P11* **Salem** Massachusetts, NE USA *42.30N 70.51W*
29 *V6* **Salem** Missouri, C USA *37.39N 91.32W*
20 *I16* **Salem** New Jersey, NE USA *39.33N 75.26W*
33 *U12* **Salem** Ohio, N USA *40.52N 80.51W*
34 *G12* **Salem** *state capital* Oregon, NW USA *44.57N 123.01W*
31 *Q11* **Salem** South Dakota, N USA *43.43N 97.23W*
38 *L4* **Salem** Utah, W USA *40.03N 111.40W*
23 *S7* **Salem** Virginia, NE USA *37.16N 80.00W*
23 *R3* **Salem** West Virginia, NE USA *39.15N 80.32W*
109 *H23* **Salemi** Sicilia, Italy, C Mediterranean Sea *37.48N 12.48E*
Salemy *see* As Sālimī
96 *K12* **Sälen** Dalarna, C Sweden *61.11N 13.14E*
109 *Q18* **Salentina, Campi** Puglia, SE Italy *40.22N 18.01E*
109 *Q18* **Salentina, Penisola** *peninsula* SE Italy
109 *L18* **Salerno** *anc.* Salernum. Campania, S Italy *40.40N 14.43E*
109 *L18* **Salerno, Golfo di** *Eng.* Gulf of Salerno. *gulf* S Italy
Salerno, Gulf of *see* Salerno, Golfo di
Salernum *see* Salerno
99 *K17* **Salford** NW England, UK *53.30N 2.16W*
Salgir *see* Salhyr
113 *K21* **Salgótarján** Nógrád, N Hungary *48.06N 19.46E*
61 *O15* **Salgueiro** Pernambuco, E Brazil *8.04S 39.04W*
96 *C13* **Salhus** Hordaland, S Norway *60.30N 5.15E*
119 *T12* **Salhyr** *Rus.* Salgir. ≈ S Ukraine
175 *S4* **Salibabu, Pulau** *island* N Indonesia
39 *S6* **Salida** Colorado, C USA *38.29N 105.57W*
104 *J15* **Salies-de-Béarn** Pyrénées-Atlantiques, SW France *43.28N 0.55W*
142 *C14* **Salihli** Manisa, W Turkey *38.28N 28.07E*
121 *K18* **Salihorsk** *Rus.* Soligorsk. Minskaya Voblasts', S Belarus *52.48N 27.31E*
121 *K18* **Salihorskaye Vodaskhovishcha** ▣ C Belarus
85 *N14* **Salima** Central, C Malawi *13.44S 34.21E*
177 *Ff5* **Salin** Magwe, W Myanmar *20.30N 94.40E*
29 *N4* **Salina** Kansas, C USA *38.50N 97.36W*
38 *L5* **Salina** Utah, W USA *38.57N 111.54W*
43 *S17* **Salina Cruz** Oaxaca, SE Mexico *16.10N 95.12W*
109 *L22* **Salina, Isola** *island* Isole Eolie, S Italy
46 *J5* **Salina Point** *headland* Acklins Island, SE Bahamas *22.10N 74.16W*
58 *A7* **Salinas** Guayas, W Ecuador *2.15S 80.54W*
42 *M11* **Salinas** *var.* Salinas de Hidalgo. San Luis Potosí, C Mexico *22.36N 101.41W*
47 *T6* **Salinas** C Puerto Rico *17.58N 66.18W*
37 *O10* **Salinas** California, W USA *36.40N 121.40W*
Salinas, Cabo de *see* Salines, Cap de ses
Salinas de Hidalgo *see* Salinas
84 *A13* **Salinas, Ponta das** *headland* W Angola *12.50S 12.57E*
47 *O10* **Salinas, Punta** *headland* S Dominican Republic *18.11N 70.32W*
Salinas, Río *see* Chixoy, Río
37 *O11* **Salinas River** ≈ California, W USA
24 *H6* **Saline Lake** ◎ Louisiana, S USA
27 *R17* **Salineno** Texas, SW USA *26.29N 99.06W*
29 *V14* **Saline River** ≈ Arkansas, C USA
32 *M17* **Saline River** ≈ Illinois, N USA
107 *X10* **Salines, Cap de ses** *var.* Cabo de Salinas. *headland* Mallorca, Spain, W Mediterranean Sea *39.15N 3.03E*
Salisburg *see* Mazsalaca
47 *O12* **Salisbury** *var.* Baroui. W Dominica *15.25N 61.27W*
99 *M23* **Salisbury** *var.* New Sarum. S England, UK *51.04N 1.48W*
23 *Y4* **Salisbury** Maryland, NE USA *38.21N 75.36W*
29 *T3* **Salisbury** Missouri, C USA *39.25N 92.48W*
23 *S9* **Salisbury** North Carolina, SE USA *35.40N 80.28W*
Salisbury *see* Harare
16 *N5* **Salisbury Island** *island* Nunavut, NE Canada
Salisbury, Lake *see* Bisina, Lake
99 *L23* **Salisbury Plain** *plain* S England, UK
23 *R14* **Salkehatchie River** ≈ South Carolina, SE USA
144 *I9* **Şalkhad** As Suwaydā', SW Syria *32.28N 36.42E*
94 *M12* **Salla** Lappi, NE Finland *66.49N 28.40E*
Sállan *see* Sørøya
105 *U11* **Sallanches** Haute-Savoie, E France *45.55N 6.37E*
107 *V5* **Sallent** Cataluña, NE Spain *41.48N 1.52E*
63 *A22* **Salliqueló** Buenos Aires, E Argentina *36.42S 62.52W*
29 *R10* **Sallisaw** Oklahoma, C USA *35.29N 94.47W*
82 *I7* **Sallom** Red Sea, NE Sudan *19.30N 37.11E*
10 *J2* **Salluit** *prev.* Saglouc, Sagluk. Québec, NE Canada *62.10N 75.40W*
Sallūm, Khalīj as *see* Salûm, Gulf of
11 *S11* **Sally's Cove** Newfoundland and Labrador, E Canada *49.43N 58.00W*
145 *W9* **Salmān Bin 'Arāzah** E Iraq *32.33N 46.36E*
Salmantica *see* Salamanca
148 *I2* **Salmās** *prev.* Dilman, Shāpūr. Āžarbāyjān-e Bākhtarī, NW Iran *38.13N 44.49E*
128 *I11* **Salmi** Respublika Kareliya, NW Russian Federation *61.21N 31.55E*
35 *P12* **Salmon** Idaho, NW USA *45.10N 113.54W*
9 *N16* **Salmon Arm** British Columbia, SW Canada *50.40N 119.18W*
199 *Jj5* **Salmon Bank** *undersea feature* N Pacific Ocean *26.55N 176.28W*
Salmon Leap *see* Leixlip
36 *L2* **Salmon Mountains** ⛰ California, W USA
12 *J15* **Salmon Point** *headland* Ontario, SE Canada *43.51N 77.15W*
35 *N11* **Salmon River** ≈ Idaho, NW USA
20 *K6* **Salmon River** ≈ New York, NE USA
35 *N12* **Salmon River Mountains** ⛰ Idaho, NW USA
20 *I9* **Salmon River Reservoir** ▣ New York, NE USA
95 *K19* **Salo** Länsi-Suomi, W Finland *60.22N 23.10E*
108 *F7* **Salò** Lombardia, N Italy *45.37N 10.30E*
Salona/Salonae *see* Solin
105 *S15* **Salon-de-Provence** Bouches-du-Rhône, SE France *43.39N 5.04E*
Salonica/Salonika *see* Thessaloníki
117 *I14* **Salonikós, Akrotírio** *headland* Thásos, E Greece *40.34N 24.39E*
118 *F10* **Salonta** *Hung.* Nagyszalonta. Bihor, W Romania *46.47N 21.37E*
106 *I9* **Salor** ≈ W Spain
107 *U6* **Salou** Cataluña, NE Spain *41.04N 1.07E*
78 *H11* **Saloum** ≈ C Senegal
44 *H4* **Sal, Punta** *headland* NW Honduras *15.55N 87.36W*
94 *N3* **Salpynten** *headland* W Svalbard *78.12N 12.11E*
144 *I3* **Salqīn** Idlib, W Syria *36.09N 36.27E*
95 *F14* **Salsbruket** Nord-Trøndelag, C Norway *64.49N 11.48E*
130 *M13* **Sal'sk** Rostovskaya Oblast', SW Russian Federation *46.30N 41.30E*
109 *K25* **Salso** ≈ Sicilia, Italy, C Mediterranean Sea
109 *J25* **Salso** ≈ Sicilia, Italy, C Mediterranean Sea
108 *E9* **Salsomaggiore Terme** Emilia-Romagna, N Italy *44.49N 9.58E*
Salt *see* As Salṭ
64 *J6* **Salta** Salta, NW Argentina *24.47S 65.23W*
64 *K6* **Salta** *off.* Provincia de Salta. ◈ *province* N Argentina
99 *I24* **Saltash** SW England, UK *50.26N 4.13W*
26 *I8* **Salt Basin** *basin* Texas, SW USA
9 *V16* **Saltcoats** Saskatchewan, S Canada *51.06N 102.12W*
32 *L13* **Salt Creek** ≈ Illinois, N USA
26 *J9* **Salt Draw** ≈ Texas, SW USA
99 *F21* **Saltee Islands** *island group* SE Ireland
94 *G12* **Saltfjorden** *inlet* C Norway
26 *I8* **Salt Flat** Texas, SW USA *31.43N 105.05W*
29 *N8* **Salt Fork Arkansas River** ≈ Oklahoma, C USA
33 *T13* **Salt Fork Lake** ▣ Ohio, N USA
28 *J11* **Salt Fork Red River** ≈ Oklahoma/Texas, C USA
97 *J23* **Saltholm** *island* E Denmark
43 *N8* **Saltillo** Coahuila de Zaragoza, NE Mexico *25.30N 101.00W*
190 *L5* **Salt Lake** *salt lake* New South Wales, SE Australia
39 *V15* **Salt Lake** ◎ New Mexico, SW USA
38 *K2* **Salt Lake City** *state capital* Utah, W USA *40.44N 111.54W*
63 *C20* **Salto** Buenos Aires, E Argentina *34.18S 60.17W*
63 *D17* **Salto** Salto, N Uruguay *31.22S 57.58W*
63 *E17* **Salto** ◈ *department* N Uruguay
109 *I14* **Salto** ≈ C Italy
64 *Q6* **Salto del Guairá** Canindeyú, E Paraguay *24.06S 54.22W*
63 *D17* **Salto Grande, Embalse de** *var.* Lago de Salto Grande. ▣ Argentina/Uruguay
Salto Grande, Lago de *see* Salto Grande, Embalse de
37 *W16* **Salton Sea** ◎ California, W USA
62 *I12* **Salto Santiago, Represa de** ▣ S Brazil
155 *U7* **Salt Range** ⛰ E Pakistan
38 *M13* **Salt River** ≈ Arizona, SW USA
22 *L5* **Salt River** ≈ Kentucky, S USA
29 *V3* **Salt River** ≈ Missouri, C USA
97 *F17* **Saltrød** Aust-Agder, S Norway *58.28N 8.49E*
97 *P16* **Saltsjöbaden** Stockholm, C Sweden *59.15N 18.19E*
94 *G12* **Saltstraumen** Nordland, C Norway *67.16N 14.42E*
23 *Q7* **Saltville** Virginia, NE USA *36.52N 81.48W*
Saluces/Saluciae *see* Saluzzo
23 *Q12* **Saluda** South Carolina, SE USA *34.00N 81.47W*
23 *X6* **Saluda** Virginia, NE USA *37.36N 76.36W*
23 *Q12* **Saluda River** ≈ South Carolina, SE USA
175 *R10* **Salue Timpuas, Selat** *var.* Selat Banggai. *strait* N Banda Sea
77 *T7* **Salûm** *var.* As Sallūm. NW Egypt *31.31N 25.09E*
158 *F14* **Sālūmbar** Rājasthān, N India *24.16N 74.04E*
77 *T7* **Salûm, Gulf of** *Ar.* Khalīj as Sallūm. *gulf* Egypt/Libya
175 *Q7* **Salumpaga** Sulawesi, N Indonesia *1.18N 120.58E*
161 *M14* **Sālūr** Andhra Pradesh, E India *18.31N 83.16E*
57 *Y9* **Salut, Îles du** *island group* N French Guiana
108 *A9* **Saluzzo** *Fr.* Saluces; *anc.* Saluciae. Piemonte, NW Italy *44.39N 7.28E*
65 *F23* **Salvación, Bahía** *bay* S Chile
61 *P17* **Salvador** *prev.* São Salvador. Bahia, E Brazil *12.58S 38.28W*
67 *E24* **Salvador** East Falkland, Falkland Islands *51.28S 58.22W*
24 *K10* **Salvador, Lake** ◎ Louisiana, S USA
Salvaleón de Higüey *see* Higüey
106 *F10* **Salvaterra de Magos** Santarém, C Portugal *39.01N 8.46W*
43 *N13* **Salvatierra** Guanajuato, C Mexico *20.13N 100.52W*
107 *P3* **Salvatierra** *Basq.* Agurain. País Vasco, N Spain *42.52N 2.22W*
Salwa/Salwah *see* As Salwā
178 *H5* **Salween** *Bur.* Thanlwin, *Chin.* Nu Chiang, Nu Jiang. ≈ SE Asia
143 *Y12* **Salyan** *Rus.* Sal'yany. SE Azerbaijan *39.36N 48.57E*
159 *N11* **Salyan** *var.* Sallyana. Mid Western, W Nepal *28.22N 82.10E*
Sal'yany *see* Salyan
23 *O6* **Salyersville** Kentucky, S USA *37.44N 83.01W*
111 *V6* **Salza** ≈ E Austria
111 *Q7* **Salzach** ≈ Austria/Germany
111 *Q6* **Salzburg** *anc.* Juvavum. Salzburg, N Austria *47.48N 13.03E*
111 *O8* **Salzburg** *off.* Land Salzburg. ◈ *state* C Austria
Salzburg *see* Ocna Sibiului
Salzburg Alps *see* Salzburger Kalkalpen
111 *Q7* **Salzburger Kalkalpen** *Eng.* Salzburg Alps. ⛰ C Austria
102 *J13* **Salzgitter** *prev.* Watenstedt-Salzgitter. Niedersachsen, C Germany *52.06N 10.24E*
103 *G14* **Salzkotten** Nordrhein-Westfalen, W Germany *51.40N 8.36E*
102 *K11* **Salzwedel** Sachsen-Anhalt, N Germany *52.51N 11.10E*
158 *D11* **Sām** Rājasthān, NW India *26.49N 70.30E*
Šamac *see* Bosanski Šamac
56 *G9* **Samacá** Boyacá, C Colombia *5.26N 73.30W*
42 *I7* **Samachique** Chihuahua, N Mexico *27.16N 107.28W*
147 *Y8* **Şamad** NE Oman *22.45N 58.07E*
Sama de Langreo *see* Sama
Samaden *see* Samedan
59 *M19* **Samaipata** Santa Cruz, C Bolivia *18.09S 63.49W*
178 *Jj11* **Samakhixai** *var.* Attapu, Attopeu. Attapu, S Laos *14.48N 106.51E*
Samakov *see* Samokov
44 *B6* **Samalá, Río** ≈ SW Guatemala
42 *J3* **Samalayuca** Chihuahua, N Mexico *31.14N 106.28W*
179 *Q17* **Samales Group** *island group* Sulu Archipelago, SW Philippines
161 *L16* **Sāmalkot** Andhra Pradesh, E India *17.03N 82.15E*
47 *P8* **Samaná** *var.* Santa Bárbara de Samaná. E Dominican Republic *19.11N 69.19W*
47 *P8* **Samaná, Bahía de** *bay* E Dominican Republic
46 *K4* **Samana Cay** *island* SE Bahamas
142 *K17* **Samandağı** Hatay, S Turkey *36.06N 35.56E*
155 *P3* **Samangān** ◈ *province* N Afghanistan
Samangān *see* Āybak
172 *P8* **Samani** Hokkaidō, NE Japan *42.07N 142.57E*
56 *C13* **Samaniego** Nariño, SW Colombia *1.22N 77.34W*
179 *R12* **Samar** *island* C Philippines
131 *S6* **Samara** *prev.* Kuybyshev. Samarskaya Oblast', W Russian Federation *53.14N 50.15E*
131 *S6* **Samara** ✈ Samarskaya Oblast', W Russian Federation *53.11N 50.27E*
131 *T7* **Samara** ≈ W Russian Federation
119 *V7* **Samara** ≈ E Ukraine
195 *N17* **Samarai** Milne Bay, SE PNG *10.37S 150.39E*
Samarang *see* Semarang
144 *G9* **Samarian Hills** *hill range* N Israel
56 *L9* **Samariapo** Amazonas, C Venezuela *5.13N 67.47W*
175 *O8* **Samarinda** Borneo, C Indonesia *0.30S 117.09E*
Samarkand *see* Samarqand

◆ Country
● Country Capital
◇ Dependent Territory
○ Dependent Territory Capital
◈ Administrative Region
✈ International Airport
▲ Mountain
⛰ Mountain Range
Volcano
≈ River
◎ Lake
▣ Reservoir

Samarkandskaya Oblast' – San Justo

Samarkandskaya Oblast' *see* Samarqand Viloyati
Samarkandski/Samarkandskoye *see* Temirtau
Samarobriva *see* Amiens
153 N11 **Samarqand** *Rus.* Samarkand. Samarqand Viloyati, C Uzbekistan 39.39N 66.55E
152 M11 **Samarqand Viloyati** *Rus.* Samarkandskaya Oblast'. ◈ *province* C Uzbekistan
145 S6 **Sāmarrā'** C Iraq 34.13N 43.52E
131 R7 **Samarskaya Oblast'** *prev.* Kuybyshevskaya Oblast'. ◈ *province* W Russian Federation
159 Q13 **Samastīpur** Bihār, N India 25.52N 85.46E
78 L14 **Samatiguila** NW Ivory Coast 9.51N 7.36W
121 Q17 **Samatsevichy** *Rus.* Samotevichi. Mahilyowskaya Voblasts', E Belarus 53.12N 31.49E
Samawa *see* As Samāwah
143 Y11 **Şamaxı** *Rus.* Shemakha. E Azerbaijan 40.38N 48.34E
158 H6 **Samba** Jammu and Kashmir, NW India 32.31N 75.07E
81 K18 **Samba** Equateur, NW Dem. Rep. Congo (Zaire) 0.13N 21.16E
81 N21 **Samba** Maniema, E Dem. Rep. Congo (Zaire) 4.40S 26.22E
175 Oo6 **Sambaliung, Pegunungan** ▲ Borneo, N Indonesia
160 M11 **Sambalpur** Orissa, E India 21.28N 83.04E
69 X12 **Sambao** ~ W Madagascar
174 Kk7 **Sambas, Sungai** ~ Borneo, N Indonesia
180 K2 **Sambava** Antsiraňana, NE Madagascar 14.16S 50.10E
176 Ww9 **Samberi** Papua, E Indonesia 1.07S 135.54E
158 J10 **Sambhal** Uttar Pradesh, N India 28.34N 78.34E
158 H12 **Sāmbhar Salt Lake** ◎ N India
109 N21 **Sambiase** Calabria, SW Italy 38.58N 16.16E
118 H5 **Sambir** *Rus.* Sambor. L'vivs'ka Oblast', NW Ukraine 49.29N 23.09E
84 C13 **Sambo** Huambo, C Angola 13.07S 16.06E
Sambor *see* Sambir
63 E21 **Samborombón, Bahía** *bay* NE Argentina
101 H20 **Sambre** ~ Belgium/France
45 V16 **Sambú, Río** ~ SE Panama
169 Z14 **Samch'ŏk** *Jap.* Sanchoku. NE South Korea 37.21N 129.12E
Samch'ŏnpŏ *see* Sach'ŏn
83 I21 **Same** Kilimanjaro, NE Tanzania 4.02S 37.46E
110 J10 **Samedan** *Ger.* Samaden. Graubünden, S Switzerland 46.31N 9.51E
84 K12 **Samfya** Luapula, N Zambia 11.25S 29.30E
147 W13 **Samḥān, Jabal** ▲ SW Oman
117 C18 **Sámi** Kefallinía, Iónioi Nísoi, Greece, C Mediterranean Sea 38.15N 20.39E
58 F10 **Samiria, Río** ~ N Peru
Samirum *see* Semīrom
143 V11 **Şämkir** *Rus.* Shamkhor. NW Azerbaijan 40.51N 46.03E
178 J7 **Sam, Nam** *Vtn.* Sông Chu. ~ Laos/Vietnam
Samnan *see* Semnān
Sam Neua *see* Xam Nua
77 P10 **Samnū** C Libya 27.19N 15.01E
198 Bb7 **Samoa** *off.* Independent State of Samoa, *var.* Sāmoa; *prev.* Western Samoa ◆ *monarchy* W Polynesia
198 C8 **Samoa** *island group* American Samoa
183 T9 **Samoa Basin** *undersea feature* W Pacific Ocean
Sāmoa-i-Sisifo *see* Samoa
114 D8 **Samobor** Zagreb, N Croatia 45.48N 15.38E
116 H10 **Samokov** *var.* Samakov. Sofiya, W Bulgaria 42.19N 23.34E
113 H21 **Šamorín** *Ger.* Sommerein, *Hung.* Somorja. Trnavský Kraj, W Slovakia 48.01N 17.18E
117 M19 **Sámos** *prev.* Limín Vathéos. Sámos, Dodekánisos, Greece, Aegean Sea 37.46N 26.58E
117 M20 **Sámos** *island* Dodekánisos, Greece, Aegean Sea
Samosch *see* Szamos
173 Ff5 **Samosir, Pulau** *island* W Indonesia
Samotevichi *see* Samatsevichy
Samothrace *see* Samothráki
117 K14 **Samothráki** Samothráki, NE Greece 40.28N 25.31E
117 J14 **Samothráki** *anc.* Samothrace. *island* NE Greece
117 A15 **Samothráki** *island* Iónioi Nísoi, Greece, C Mediterranean Sea
Samotschin *see* Szamocin
Sampê *see* Xiangcheng
174 M10 **Sampit** Borneo, C Indonesia 2.30S 112.30E
174 M10 **Sampit, Sungai** ~ Borneo, N Indonesia
Sampoku *see* Sanpoku
195 P11 **Sampun** New Britain, E PNG 5.19S 152.06E
81 N24 **Sampwe** Katanga, SE Dem. Rep. Congo (Zaire) 9.17S 27.22E
27 X8 **Sam Rayburn Reservoir** ▣ Texas, SW USA
178 Ii6 **Sam Sao, Phou** ▲ Laos/Thailand
97 H22 **Samsø** *island* E Denmark
97 H23 **Samsø Bælt** *channel* E Denmark
178 Jj7 **Sâm Sơn** Thanh Hoa, N Vietnam 19.43N 105.52E
142 L11 **Samsun** *anc.* Amisus. Samsun, N Turkey 41.16N 36.22E
142 K11 **Samsun** ◈ *province* N Turkey
143 R9 **Samtredia** W Georgia 42.09N 42.20E
61 E15 **Samuel, Represa de** ▣ W Brazil
178 H15 **Samui, Ko** *island* SW Thailand
Samundari *see* Samundri
155 U9 **Samundri** *var.* Samundari. Punjab, E Pakistan 31.04N 72.58E
143 X10 **Samur** ~ Azerbaijan/Russian Federation
143 Y11 **Samur-Abşeron Kanalı** *Rus.* Samur-Apsheronskiy Kanal. *canal* E Azerbaijan
Samur-Apsheronskiy Kanal *see* Samur-Abşeron Kanalı
178 Hh11 **Samut Prakan** *var.* Muang Samut Prakan, Paknam. Samut Prakan, C Thailand 13.33N 100.13E
178 H11 **Samut Sakhon** *var.* Maha Chai, Samut Sakorn, *Tha Chin.* Samut Sakhon, C Thailand 13.31N 100.15E
Samut Sakorn *see* Samut Sakhon
178 H11 **Samut Songhram** *prev.* Meklong. Samut Songkhram, SW Thailand 13.25N 100.01E
79 N12 **San** Ségou, C Mali 13.18N 4.51W
113 O15 **San** ~ SE Poland
147 O15 **Şan'ā'** *Eng.* Sana. ● (Yemen) W Yemen 15.24N 44.13E
114 F11 **Sana** ~ NW Bosnia and Herzegovina
82 O12 **Sanaag** *off.* Gobolka Sanaag. ◈ *region* N Somalia
116 J8 **Sanadinovo** Pleven, N Bulgaria 43.33N 25.00E
205 P1 **Sanae** *South African research station* Antarctica 70.19S 1.31W
145 Y10 **Sanāf, Hawr as** ◎ S Iraq
81 E15 **Sanaga** ~ C Cameroon
56 D12 **San Agustín** Huila, SW Colombia 1.52N 76.13W
179 S16 **San Agustin, Cape** *headland* Mindanao, S Philippines 6.17N 126.12E
39 Q13 **San Agustin, Plains of** *plain* New Mexico, SW USA
40 M16 **Sanak Islands** *island group* Aleutian Islands, Alaska, USA
200 P11 **San Ambrosio, Isla** *Eng.* San Ambrosio Island. *island* W Chile
San Ambrosio Island *see* San Ambrosio, Isla
175 S10 **Sanana** Pulau Sanana, E Indonesia 2.04S 125.58E
175 S10 **Sanana, Pulau** *island* Maluku, E Indonesia
148 K5 **Sanandaj** *prev.* Sinneh. Kordestān, W Iran 35.18N 47.01E
37 P8 **San Andreas** California, W USA 38.10N 120.40W
2 C13 **San Andreas Fault** *fault* W USA
56 G8 **San Andrés** Santander, C Colombia 6.52N 72.52W
63 C20 **San Andrés de Giles** Buenos Aires, E Argentina 34.27S 59.27W
39 R14 **San Andres Mountains** ▲ New Mexico, SW USA
43 S15 **San Andrés Tuxtla** *var.* Tuxtla. Veracruz-Llave, E Mexico 18.27N 95.18W
27 P8 **San Angelo** Texas, SW USA 31.27N 100.26W
109 A20 **San Antioco, Isola di** *island* W Italy
44 F4 **San Antonio** Toledo, S Belize 16.13N 89.02W
64 G11 **San Antonio** Valparaíso, C Chile 33.35S 71.34W
196 H6 **San Antonio** Saipan, S Northern Mariana Islands
39 R13 **San Antonio** New Mexico, SW USA 33.53N 106.52W
27 R12 **San Antonio** Texas, SW USA 29.25N 98.29W
56 M11 **San Antonio** Amazonas, S Venezuela 3.31N 66.46W
56 I7 **San Antonio** Barinas, C Venezuela 7.24N 71.28W
57 O5 **San Antonio** Monagas, NE Venezuela 10.03N 63.45W
27 S12 **San Antonio** ✕ Texas, SW USA 29.31N 98.11W
San Antonio *see* San Antonio del Táchira
San Antonio Abad *see* Sant Antoni de Portmany
27 U13 **San Antonio Bay** *inlet* Texas, SW USA
63 E22 **San Antonio, Cabo** *headland* E Argentina 36.45S 56.40W
46 A5 **San Antonio, Cabo de** *headland* W Cuba 21.51N 84.58W
107 T11 **San Antonio, Cabo de** *headland* E Spain 38.50N 0.09E
56 H7 **San Antonio de Caparo** Táchira, W Venezuela 7.34N 71.28W
64 J5 **San Antonio de los Cobres** Salta, NE Argentina 24.14S 66.17W
56 H7 **San Antonio del Táchira** *var.* San Antonio. Táchira, W Venezuela 7.49N 72.27W
37 T15 **San Antonio, Mount** ▲ California, W USA 34.18N 117.37W
65 K16 **San Antonio Oeste** Río Negro, E Argentina 40.45S 64.58W
27 T13 **San Antonio River** ~ Texas, SW USA
56 J5 **Sanare** Lara, N Venezuela 9.45N 69.39W
105 T16 **Sanary-sur-Mer** Var, SE France 43.07N 5.48E
27 X8 **San Augustine** Texas, SW USA 31.31N 94.06W
147 T13 **Sanāw** *var.* Sanaw. NE Yemen 18.00N 51.00E
43 O11 **San Bartolo** San Luis Potosí, C Mexico 22.19N 100.04W
109 L16 **San Bartolomeo in Galdo** Campania, S Italy 41.24N 15.01E
108 K13 **San Benedetto del Tronto** Marche, C Italy 42.57N 13.52E
44 E3 **San Benito** Petén, N Guatemala 16.55N 89.58W
27 T17 **San Benito** Texas, SW USA 26.07N 97.37W
56 E6 **San Benito Abad** Sucre, N Colombia 8.55N 75.01W
37 P11 **San Benito Mountain** ▲ California, W USA 36.21N 120.37W
37 O10 **San Benito River** ~ California, W USA
110 H10 **San Bernardino** Graubünden, S Switzerland 46.21N 9.13E
37 U15 **San Bernardino** California, W USA 34.06N 117.15W
64 H11 **San Bernardo** Santiago, C Chile 33.36S 70.40W
42 J8 **San Bernardo** Durango, C Mexico 25.58N 105.27W
170 F12 **Sanbe-san** ▲ Kyūshū, SW Japan 35.09N 132.36E
42 J12 **San Blas** Nayarit, C Mexico 21.33N 105.17W
42 H8 **San Blas** Sinaloa, C Mexico 26.05N 108.44W
45 V14 **San Blas** *off.* Comarca de San Blas. ◈ *special territory* NE Panama
45 U14 **San Blas, Archipiélago de** *island group* NE Panama
25 Q10 **San Blas, Cape** *headland* Florida, SE USA 29.39N 85.21W
45 V14 **San Blas, Cordillera de** ▲ NE Panama
64 J8 **San Blas de los Sauces** Catamarca, NW Argentina 28.18S 67.12W
108 G8 **San Bonifacio** Veneto, NE Italy 45.22N 11.14E
31 S12 **Sanborn** Iowa, C USA 43.10N 95.39W
42 M7 **San Buenaventura** Coahuila de Zaragoza, NE Mexico 27.03N 101.33W
107 S5 **San Caprasio** ▲ N Spain 41.45N 0.26W
64 G13 **San Carlos** Bío Bío, C Chile 36.25S 71.58W
42 E9 **San Carlos** Baja California Sur, W Mexico 24.52N 112.15W
43 N5 **San Carlos** Coahuila de Zaragoza, NE Mexico 29.00N 100.51W
San Carlos, Estrecho de *see* Falkland Sound
43 P9 **San Carlos** Tamaulipas, C Mexico 24.36N 98.42W
44 L12 **San Carlos** Río San Juan, S Nicaragua 11.06N 84.46W
45 T16 **San Carlos** Panamá, C Panama 8.28N 79.58W
179 P9 **San Carlos** *off.* San Carlos City. Luzon, N Philippines 15.57N 120.18E
38 M14 **San Carlos** Arizona, SW USA 33.21N 110.27W
63 G20 **San Carlos** Maldonado, S Uruguay 34.46S 54.58W
56 K5 **San Carlos** Cojedes, N Venezuela 9.39N 68.34W
San Carlos *see* Quesada, Costa Rica
San Carlos *see* Luba, Equatorial Guinea
63 B17 **San Carlos Centro** Santa Fe, C Argentina 31.45S 61.04W
179 Q13 **San Carlos City** Negros, C Philippines 10.34N 123.24E
San Carlos de Ancud *see* Ancud
65 H16 **San Carlos de Bariloche** Río Negro, SW Argentina 41.07S 71.15W
63 B21 **San Carlos de Bolívar** Buenos Aires, E Argentina 36.15S 61.06W
56 H6 **San Carlos del Zulia** Zulia, W Venezuela 9.01N 71.58W
56 L12 **San Carlos de Río Negro** Amazonas, S Venezuela 1.54N 67.54W
San Carlos, Estrecho de *see* Falkland Sound
38 M14 **San Carlos Reservoir** ▣ Arizona, SW USA
44 M12 **San Carlos, Río** ~ N Costa Rica
67 D24 **San Carlos Settlement** East Falkland, Falkland Islands
63 C23 **San Cayetano** Buenos Aires, E Argentina 38.19S 59.37W
105 O8 **Sancerre** Cher, C France 47.19N 2.53E
164 G7 **Sanchakou** Xinjiang Uygur Zizhiqu, NW China 39.58N 78.26E
Sanchoku *see* Samch'ŏk
43 O12 **San Ciro** San Luis Potosí, C Mexico 21.40N 99.49W
107 P10 **San Clemente** Castilla-La Mancha, C Spain 39.24N 2.25W
37 T16 **San Clemente** California, W USA 33.25N 117.36W
63 E21 **San Clemente del Tuyú** Buenos Aires, E Argentina 36.25S 56.45W
37 S17 **San Clemente Island** *island* Channel Islands, California, W USA
105 O9 **Sancoins** Cher, C France 46.49N 3.00E
195 Z17 **San Cristobal** *var.* Makira. *island* SE Solomon Islands
63 B16 **San Cristóbal** Santa Fe, C Argentina 30.19S 61.13W
46 B4 **San Cristóbal** Pinar del Río, W Cuba 22.43N 83.03W
47 O9 **San Cristóbal** *var.* Benemérita de San Cristóbal. S Dominican Republic 18.26N 70.07W
56 H7 **San Cristóbal** Táchira, W Venezuela 7.46N 72.15W
San Cristóbal *see* San Cristóbal de las Casas
43 U16 **San Cristóbal de Las Casas** *var.* San Cristóbal. Chiapas, SE Mexico 16.43N 92.40W
200 Oo8 **San Cristóbal, Isla** *var.* Chatham Island. *island* Galapagos Islands, Ecuador, E Pacific Ocean
44 D5 **San Cristóbal Verapaz** Alta Verapaz, C Guatemala 15.22N 90.25W
46 F6 **Sancti Spíritus** Sancti Spíritus, C Cuba 21.54N 79.27W
105 O11 **Sancy, Puy de** ▲ C France 45.33N 2.48E
97 D15 **Sand** Rogaland, S Norway 59.28N 6.16E
175 Oo2 **Sandakan** Sabah, East Malaysia 5.52N 118.04E
190 K9 **Sandalwood** South Australia 34.51S 140.13E
Sandalwood Island *see* Sumba, Pulau
96 D11 **Sandane** Sogn og Fjordane, S Norway 61.46N 6.13E
116 G12 **Sandanski** *prev.* Sveti Vrach. Blagoevgrad, SW Bulgaria 41.36N 23.18E
78 J11 **Sandaré** Kayes, W Mali 14.36N 10.22W
97 J19 **Sandared** Västra Götaland, S Sweden 57.43N 12.46E
96 N12 **Sandarne** Gävleborg, C Sweden 61.15N 17.15E
194 E10 **Sandaun** *prev.* West Sepik. ◈ *province* NW PNG
98 K4 **Sanday** *island* NE Scotland, UK
179 N14 **Sand Cay** *island* W Spratly Islands
33 P15 **Sand Creek** ~ Indiana, N USA
97 H15 **Sande** Vestfold, S Norway 59.34N 10.13E
97 H16 **Sandefjord** Vestfold, S Norway 59.10N 10.15E
79 O15 **Sandégué** E Ivory Coast 7.58N 3.33W
79 P14 **Sandema** N Ghana 10.42N 1.17W
39 O11 **Sanders** Arizona, SW USA 35.13N 109.21W
26 M11 **Sanderson** Texas, SW USA 30.08N 102.23W
25 U4 **Sandersville** Georgia, SE USA 32.58N 82.48W
94 H4 **Sandgerdhi** Sudhurland, SW Iceland 64.01N 22.42W
30 K14 **Sand Hills** ▲ Nebraska, C USA
27 S14 **Sandia** Texas, SW USA 27.59N 97.52W
37 T17 **San Diego** California, W USA 32.43N 117.09W
27 S14 **San Diego** Texas, SW USA 27.45N 98.14W
142 F14 **Sandıklı** Afyon, W Turkey 38.28N 30.16E
158 L12 **Sandila** Uttar Pradesh, N India 27.05N 80.37E
123 J15 **San Dimitri, Ras** *var.* San Dimitri Point. *headland* Gozo, NW Malta 36.04N 14.12E
174 Gg11 **Sanding, Selat** *strait* W Indonesia
32 J3 **Sand Island** *island* Apostle Islands, Wisconsin, N USA
97 C16 **Sandnes** Rogaland, S Norway 58.51N 5.45E
94 F13 **Sandnessjøen** Nordland, C Norway 66.00N 12.37E
81 L24 **Sandoa** Katanga, S Dem. Rep. Congo (Zaire) 9.39S 22.58E
113 N15 **Sandomierz** *Rus.* Sandomir. Świętokrzyskie, C Poland 50.42N 21.44E
Sandomir *see* Sandomierz
56 C13 **Sandoná** Nariño, SW Colombia 1.13N 77.29W
108 I7 **San Donà di Piave** Veneto, NE Italy 45.37N 12.34E
128 K14 **Sandovo** Tverskaya Oblast', W Russian Federation 58.26N 36.30E
177 Ff7 **Sandoway** Arakan State, W Myanmar 18.28N 94.19E
99 M24 **Sandown** S England, UK 50.39N 1.11W
97 B19 **Sandoy** *Dan.* Sandø *Island* Faeroe Islands 61.52N 6.51W
41 N16 **Sand Point** Popof Island, Alaska, USA 55.20N 160.30W
67 N24 **Sand Point** *headland* E Tristan da Cunha
33 R7 **Sand Point** *headland* Michigan, N USA 43.54N 83.24W
34 M7 **Sandpoint** Idaho, NW USA 48.16N 116.33W
95 H14 **Sandsele** Västerbotten, N Sweden 65.16N 17.40E
8 I14 **Sandspit** Moresby Island, British Columbia, SW Canada 53.13N 131.49W
29 P9 **Sand Springs** Oklahoma, C USA 36.08N 96.06W
31 W7 **Sandstone** Minnesota, N USA 46.07N 92.51W
38 K15 **Sand Tank Mountains** ▲ Arizona, SW USA
33 S8 **Sandusky** Michigan, N USA 43.24N 82.47W
33 S11 **Sandusky** Ohio, N USA 41.27N 82.42W
33 S12 **Sandusky River** ~ Ohio, N USA
85 D22 **Sandverhaar** Karas, S Namibia 26.49S 17.25E
97 L24 **Sandvig** Bornholm, E Denmark 55.15N 14.45E
97 H15 **Sandvika** Akershus, S Norway 59.54N 10.28E
96 N13 **Sandviken** Gävleborg, C Sweden 60.37N 16.49E
32 M11 **Sandwich** Illinois, N USA 41.39N 88.37W
Sandwich Island *see* Éfaté
Sandwich Islands *see* Hawaiian Islands
159 V16 **Sandwip Island** *island* SE Bangladesh
9 U12 **Sandy Bay** Saskatchewan, C Canada 55.31N 102.14W
191 N16 **Sandy Cape** *headland* Tasmania, SE Australia 41.27S 144.43E
178 Mm14 **Sandy Cay** *island* NW Spratly Islands
38 L3 **Sandy City** Utah, W USA 40.36N 111.53W
33 U12 **Sandy Creek** ~ Ohio, N USA
23 O5 **Sandy Hook** Kentucky, S USA 38.09N 83.05W
20 K15 **Sandy Hook** *headland* New Jersey, NE USA 40.27N 73.59W
Sandykachi/Sandykgachy *see* Sandykgaçy
152 J15 **Sandykgaçy** *var.* Sandykgachy, *Rus.* Sandykachi. Mary Welaýaty, S Turkmenistan 36.34N 62.28E
152 L13 **Sandykly Gumy** *Rus.* Peski Sandykly. *desert* E Turkmenistan
Sandykly, Peski *see* Sandykly Gumy
9 Q13 **Sandy Lake** Alberta, W Canada 55.50N 113.30W
10 B8 **Sandy Lake** Ontario, C Canada 53.00N 93.25W
10 B8 **Sandy Lake** ◎ Ontario, C Canada
25 S3 **Sandy Springs** Georgia, SE USA 33.57N 84.23W
26 H8 **San Elizario** Texas, SW USA 31.35N 106.16W
101 L25 **Sanem** Luxembourg, SW Luxembourg 49.33N 5.55E
44 K5 **San Esteban** Olancho, C Honduras 15.18N 85.45W
107 O6 **San Esteban de Gormaz** Castilla-León, N Spain 41.34N 3.13W
42 E5 **San Esteban, Isla** *island* NW Mexico
San Eugenio/San Eugenio del Cuareim *see* Artigas
64 H11 **San Felipe** *var.* San Felipe de Aconcagua. Valparaíso, C Chile 32.45S 70.42W
42 D3 **San Felipe** Baja California, NW Mexico 31.02N 114.55W
42 N12 **San Felipe** Guanajuato, C Mexico 21.27N 101.12W
56 K5 **San Felipe** Yaracuy, NW Venezuela 10.25N 68.40W
46 B5 **San Felipe, Cayos de** *island group* W Cuba
San Felipe de Aconcagua *see* San Felipe
San Felipe de Puerto Plata *see* Puerto Plata
39 R11 **San Felipe Pueblo** New Mexico, SW USA 35.25N 106.27W
San Feliú de Guixols *see* Sant Feliu de Guíxols
200 Oo11 **San Félix, Isla** *Eng.* San Felix Island. *island* W Chile
San Felix Island *see* San Félix, Isla
56 L11 **San Fernando de Atabapo** Amazonas, S Venezuela 4.00N 67.42W
42 C4 **San Fernando** *var.* Misión San Fernando. Baja California, NW Mexico 29.58N 115.14W
43 P9 **San Fernando** Tamaulipas, C Mexico 24.51N 98.09W
179 P9 **San Fernando** Luzon, N Philippines 16.45N 120.21E
179 P10 **San Fernando** Luzon, N Philippines 15.01N 120.41E
106 J16 **San Fernando** *prev.* Isla de León. Andalucía, S Spain 36.28N 6.12W
47 U14 **San Fernando** Trinidad, Trinidad and Tobago 10.16N 61.27W
37 S15 **San Fernando** California, W USA 34.16N 118.26W
56 L7 **San Fernando** *var.* San Fernando de Apure. Apure, C Venezuela 7.54N 67.28W
San Fernando de Apure *see* San Fernando
64 L8 **San Fernando del Valle de Catamarca** *var.* Catamarca. Catamarca, NW Argentina 28.28S 65.46W
San Fernando de Monte Cristi *see* Monte Cristi
43 P9 **San Fernando, Río** ~ C Mexico
25 X11 **Sanford** Florida, SE USA 28.48N 81.16W
21 P9 **Sanford** Maine, NE USA 43.26N 70.46W
23 T10 **Sanford** North Carolina, SE USA 35.28N 79.10W
27 N2 **Sanford** Texas, SW USA 35.42N 101.31W
41 T10 **Sanford, Mount** ▲ Alaska, USA 62.21N 144.12W
44 G8 **San Francisco** *var.* Gotera, San Francisco Gotera. Morazán, E El Salvador 13.40N 88.06W
45 R16 **San Francisco** Veraguas, C Panama 8.14N 80.58W
179 Pp11 **San Francisco** *var.* Aurora. Luzon, N Philippines 13.22N 122.31E
37 L8 **San Francisco** California, W USA 37.46N 122.25W
56 H5 **San Francisco** Zulia, NW Venezuela 10.36N 71.39W
36 M8 **San Francisco** ✕ California, W USA 37.37N 122.23W
37 N9 **San Francisco Bay** *bay* California, W USA
63 C24 **San Francisco de Bellocq** Buenos Aires, E Argentina 38.42S 60.01W
42 I6 **San Francisco de Borja** Chihuahua, N Mexico 27.57N 106.42W
44 J6 **San Francisco de la Paz** Olancho, C Honduras 14.55N 86.13W
42 J7 **San Francisco del Oro** Chihuahua, N Mexico 26.52N 105.49W
42 M12 **San Francisco del Rincón** Jalisco, SW Mexico 20.57N 101.54W
47 O8 **San Francisco de Macorís** C Dominican Republic 19.19N 70.15W
San Francisco de Satipo *see* Satipo
San Francisco Gotera *see* San Francisco
San Francisco Telixtlahuaca *see* Telixtlahuaca
109 K23 **San Fratello** Sicilia, Italy, C Mediterranean Sea 38.00N 14.35E
San Fructuoso *see* Tacuarembó
84 C12 **Sanga** Cuanza Sul, NW Angola 11.10S 15.27E
58 C5 **San Gabriel** Carchi, N Ecuador 0.37N 77.49W
165 S15 **Sa'ngain** Xizang Zizhiqu, W China 30.46N 98.45E
160 E13 **Sangamner** Mahārāshtra, W India 19.37N 74.18E
158 H12 **Sāngāner** Rājasthān, N India 26.48N 75.48E
Sangān, Koh-i- *see* Sangān, Kūh-e
155 N6 **Sangān, Kūh-e** *Pash.* Koh-i-Sangan. ▲ C Afghanistan
126 Ll10 **Sangar** Respublika Sakha (Yakutiya), NE Russian Federation 63.48N 127.37E
175 O8 **Sangasanga** Borneo, C Indonesia 0.36S 117.12E
105 N1 **Sangatte** Pas-de-Calais, N France 50.56N 1.41E
109 B19 **San Gavino Monreale** Sardegna, Italy, C Mediterranean Sea 39.33N 8.47E
59 D16 **Sangayan, Isla** *island* W Peru
32 L14 **Sangchris Lake** ◎ Illinois, N USA
175 P15 **Sangeang, Pulau** *island* S Indonesia
118 I10 **Sângeorgiu de Pădure** *prev.* Erdăt-Sângeorz, Sîngeorgiu de Pădure, *Hung.* Erdőszentgyörgy. Mureş, C Romania 46.27N 24.49E
118 I9 **Sângeorz-Băi** *var.* Singeroz Băi, *Ger.* Rumänisch-Sankt-Georgen, *Hung.* Oláhszentgyőrgy; *prev.* Sîngeorz-Băi. Bistriţa-Năsăud, N Romania 47.24N 24.40E
37 R10 **Sanger** California, W USA 36.42N 119.33W
27 T5 **Sanger** Texas, SW USA 33.21N 97.10W
Sângerei *see* Sîngerei
103 L15 **Sangerhausen** Sachsen-Anhalt, C Germany 51.28N 11.18E
47 S6 **San Germán** W Puerto Rico 18.05N 67.02W
San Germano *see* Cassino
167 N2 **Sanggan He** ~ E China
175 Oo16 **Sanggar, Teluk** *bay* Nusa Tenggara, S Indonesia
174 L8 **Sanggau** Borneo, C Indonesia 0.07N 110.34E
81 H16 **Sangha** ◈ Central African Republic/Congo
81 G16 **Sangha-Mbaéré** ◈ *prefecture* SW Central African Republic
155 Q15 **Sānghar** Sind, SE Pakistan 26.10N 68.58E
117 F22 **Sangiás** ▲ S Greece 36.39N 22.24E
Sangihe, Kepulauan *see* Sangir, Kepulauan
175 S4 **Sangihe, Pulau** *var.* Sangir. *island* N Indonesia
56 G8 **San Gil** Santander, C Colombia 6.34N 73.07W
108 F12 **San Gimignano** Toscana, C Italy 43.30N 11.00E
154 M8 **Sangīn** *var.* Sangin. Helmand, S Afghanistan 32.03N 64.49E
109 O21 **San Giovanni in Fiore** Calabria, SW Italy 39.16N 16.42E
109 M16 **San Giovanni Rotondo** Puglia, SE Italy 41.43N 15.43E
108 G12 **San Giovanni Valdarno** Toscana, C Italy 43.34N 11.31E
Sangir *see* Sangihe, Pulau
175 Rr6 **Sangir, Kepulauan** *var.* Kepulauan Sangihe. *island group* N Indonesia
168 K9 **Sangiyn Dalay** Dundgovĭ, C Mongolia 45.59N 104.58E
168 H9 **Sangiyn Dalay** Govĭ-Altay, C Mongolia 45.12N 97.51E
168 K11 **Sangiyn Dalay** Ömnögovĭ, S Mongolia 42.50N 105.04E
168 K8 **Sangiyn Dalay** Övörhangay, C Mongolia 46.35N 103.18E
169 Y15 **Sangju** *Jap.* Shōshū. C South Korea 36.26N 128.09E
178 Ii11 **Sangkha** Surin, E Thailand 14.36N 103.43E
175 Oo7 **Sangkulirang** Borneo, N Indonesia 1.00N 117.56E
175 Oo7 **Sangkulirang, Teluk** *bay* Borneo, N Indonesia
161 E16 **Sāngli** Mahārāshtra, W India 16.55N 74.37E
81 E16 **Sangmélima** Sud, S Cameroon 2.57N 11.55E
37 V15 **San Gorgonio Mountain** ▲ California, W USA 34.06N 116.50W
39 T8 **Sangre de Cristo Mountains** ▲ Colorado/New Mexico, C USA
63 A20 **San Gregorio** Santa Fe, C Argentina 34.18S 62.01W
63 F18 **San Gregorio de Polanco** Tacuarembó, C Uruguay 32.37S 55.49W
47 V14 **Sangre Grande** Trinidad, Trinidad and Tobago 10.35N 61.07W
165 N16 **Sangri** Xizang Zizhiqu, W China 29.17N 92.01E
158 H9 **Sangrūr** Punjab, NW India 30.16N 75.52E
46 I11 **Sangster** *off.* Sir Donald Sangster International Airport, *var.* Montego Bay. ✕ (Montego Bay) W Jamaica 18.30N 77.54W
61 G17 **Sangue, Rio do** ~ W Brazil
107 R4 **Sangüesa** Navarra, N Spain 42.34N 1.16W
63 C16 **San Gustavo** Entre Ríos, E Argentina 30.40S 59.22W
Sangyuan *see* Wuqiao
42 C6 **San Hipólito, Punta** *headland* W Mexico 26.57N 114.00W
25 W15 **Sanibel** Sanibel Island, Florida, SE USA 26.27N 82.01W
25 V15 **Sanibel Island** *island* Florida, SE USA
62 F13 **San Ignacio** Misiones, NE Argentina 27.13S 55.29W
44 F2 **San Ignacio** *prev.* Cayo, El Cayo. Cayo, W Belize 17.09N 89.02W
59 L16 **San Ignacio** Beni, N Bolivia 14.54S 65.34W
59 O18 **San Ignacio** Santa Cruz, E Bolivia 16.27S 60.57W
44 M14 **San Ignacio** *var.* San Ignacio de Acosta. San José, W Costa Rica 9.46N 84.10W
42 E6 **San Ignacio** Baja California Sur, W Mexico 27.18N 112.51W
42 J10 **San Ignacio** Sinaloa, W Mexico 23.55N 106.25W
58 B9 **San Ignacio** Cajamarca, N Peru 5.03S 79.03W
San Ignacio de Acosta *see* San Ignacio
42 D7 **San Ignacio, Laguna** *lagoon* W Mexico
10 I6 **Sanikiluaq** Belcher Islands, Nunavut, C Canada 55.16N 77.44W
179 Pp9 **San Ildefonso Peninsula** *peninsula* Luzon, N Philippines
Saniquillie *see* Sanniquellie
63 D20 **San Isidro** Buenos Aires, E Argentina 34.28S 58.31W
45 N14 **San Isidro** *var.* San Isidro de El General. San José, SE Costa Rica 9.21N 83.42W
San Isidro de El General *see* San Isidro
56 E5 **San Jacinto** Bolívar, N Colombia 9.52N 75.10W
37 U16 **San Jacinto** California, W USA 33.47N 116.58W
37 V15 **San Jacinto Peak** ▲ California, W USA 33.48N 116.40W
63 F14 **San Javier** Misiones, NE Argentina 27.49S 55.06W
63 C16 **San Javier** Santa Fe, C Argentina 30.34S 59.58W
107 S13 **San Javier** Murcia, SE Spain 37.49N 0.49W
63 D18 **San Javier** Río Negro, W Uruguay 32.40S 58.07W
63 C16 **San Javier, Río** ~ C Argentina
Sanjiang *see* Jinping, Guizhou
166 L12 **Sanjiang** *var.* Guyi, Sanjiang Dongzu Zizhixian. Guangxi Zhuangzu Zizhiqu, S China 25.49N 109.31E
Sanjiang Dongzu Zizhixian *see* Sanjiang
Sanjiaocheng *see* Haiyan
171 Kk13 **Sanjō** *var.* Sanzyô. Niigata, Honshū, C Japan 37.39N 139.00E
59 M15 **San Joaquín** Beni, N Bolivia 13.03S 64.47W
57 O6 **San Joaquín** Anzoátegui, NE Venezuela 9.21N 64.30W
37 O9 **San Joaquin River** ~ California, W USA
37 P10 **San Joaquin Valley** *valley* California, W USA
63 A18 **San Jorge** Santa Fe, C Argentina 31.49S 61.49W
195 W15 **San Jorge** *island* N Solomon Islands
42 D3 **San Jorge, Bahía de** *bay* NW Mexico
San Jorge, Isla de *see* Weddell Island
65 J19 **San Jorge, Golfo** *var.* Gulf of San Jorge. *gulf* S Argentina
San Jorge, Gulf of *see* San Jorge, Golfo
196 K8 **San Jose** Tinian, S Northern Mariana Islands 15.00S 145.38E
179 Pp12 **San Jose** Mindoro, N Philippines 12.20N 121.07E
37 N9 **San Jose** California, W USA 37.18N 121.53W
63 F14 **San José** Misiones, NE Argentina 27.46S 55.46W
59 P19 **San José** *var.* San José de Chiquitos. Santa Cruz, E Bolivia 14.13S 68.04W
44 M14 **San José** ● (Costa Rica) San José, C Costa Rica 9.55N 84.05W
44 C7 **San José** *var.* Puerto San José. Escuintla, S Guatemala 13.55N 90.48W
42 G6 **San José** Sonora, NW Mexico 27.31N 110.09W
107 U11 **San José** Eivissa, Spain, W Mediterranean Sea 38.55N 1.18E
56 H5 **San José** Zulia, NW Venezuela 9.58N 72.22W
44 M14 **San José** *off.* Provincia de San José. ◈ *province* W Costa Rica
63 E19 **San José** ◈ *department* S Uruguay
44 M13 **San José** ✕ Alajuela, C Costa Rica 10.03N 84.12W
San José *see* San José del Guaviare, Colombia
San José *see* San José de Mayo, S Uruguay
179 P9 **San Jose City** Luzon, N Philippines 15.49N 120.57E
179 Pp13 **San Jose de Buenavista** Panay Island, C Philippines 10.44N 122.00E
San José de Cúcuta *see* Cúcuta
63 D16 **San José de Feliciano** Entre Ríos, E Argentina 30.21S 58.47W
57 O6 **San José de Guanipa** *var.* El Tigrito. Anzoátegui, NE Venezuela 8.54N 64.10W
64 I9 **San José de Jáchal** San Juan, W Argentina 30.15S 68.46W
42 G10 **San José del Cabo** Baja California Sur, W Mexico 23.01N 109.40W
56 G12 **San José del Guaviare** *var.* San José. Guaviare, S Colombia 2.34N 72.37W
63 E20 **San José de Mayo** *var.* San José. San José, S Uruguay 34.19S 56.42W
56 I10 **San José de Ocuné** Vichada, E Colombia 4.10N 70.21W
43 O9 **San José de Raíces** Nuevo León, NE Mexico 24.32N 100.15W
65 K17 **San José, Golfo** *gulf* E Argentina
42 F9 **San José, Isla** *island* W Mexico
45 U16 **San José, Isla** *island* SE Panama
27 U14 **San Jose Island** *island* Texas, SW USA
64 I10 **San Juan** San Juan, W Argentina 31.36S 68.26W
47 N9 **San Juan** *var.* San Juan de la Maguana. C Dominican Republic 18.46N 71.13W
59 E17 **San Juan** Ica, S Peru 15.22S 75.08W
47 U5 **San Juan** ○ (Puerto Rico) NE Puerto Rico 18.28N 66.06W
64 H10 **San Juan** *off.* Provincia de San Juan. ◈ *province* W Argentina
47 U5 **San Juan** *var.* Luis Muñoz Marín. ✕ NE Puerto Rico 18.27N 66.05W
San Juan *see* San Juan de los Morros
64 O7 **San Juan Bautista** Misiones, S Paraguay 26.39S 57.08W
37 O10 **San Juan Bautista** California, W USA 36.50N 121.34W
San Juan Bautista *see* Villahermosa
San Juan Bautista Cuicatlán *see* Cuicatlán
San Juan Bautista Tuxtepec *see* Tuxtepec
81 C17 **San Juan, Cabo** *headland* S Equatorial Guinea 1.09N 9.25E
107 S12 **San Juan de Alicante** País Valenciano, E Spain 38.25N 0.27W
56 H7 **San Juan de Colón** Táchira, NW Venezuela 8.01N 72.16W
42 L9 **San Juan de Guadalupe** Durango, C Mexico 25.12N 100.50W
San Juan de la Maguana *see* San Juan
56 G4 **San Juan del Cesar** La Guajira, N Colombia 10.45N 73.00W
42 L15 **San Juan de Lima, Punta** *headland* SW Mexico 18.34N 103.40W
44 I8 **San Juan de Limay** Estelí, NW Nicaragua 13.10N 86.36W
45 N12 **San Juan del Norte** *var.* Greytown. Río San Juan, SE Nicaragua 10.54N 83.42W
56 K4 **San Juan de los Cayos** Falcón, N Venezuela 11.06N 68.25W
42 M12 **San Juan de los Lagos** Jalisco, C Mexico 21.15N 102.15W
56 L5 **San Juan de los Morros** *var.* San Juan. Guárico, N Venezuela 9.52N 67.22W
42 K9 **San Juan del Río** Durango, C Mexico 25.12N 100.50W
43 O13 **San Juan del Río** Querétaro de Arteaga, C Mexico 20.21N 100.01W
44 J11 **San Juan del Sur** Rivas, SW Nicaragua 11.14N 85.52W
56 M9 **San Juan de Manapiare** Amazonas, S Venezuela 5.15N 66.04W
42 E7 **San Juanico** Baja California Sur, W Mexico
42 D7 **San Juanico, Punta** *headland* W Mexico 26.01N 112.17W
34 G6 **San Juan Islands** *island group* Washington, NW USA
42 I6 **San Juanito** Chihuahua, N Mexico
42 I12 **San Juanito, Isla** *island* C Mexico
39 R8 **San Juan Mountains** ▲ Colorado, C USA
56 E5 **San Juan Nepomuceno** Bolívar, NW Colombia 9.57N 75.06W
46 E5 **San Juan, Pico** ▲ C Cuba 21.58N 80.10W
203 W15 **San Juan, Punta** *headland* Easter Island, Chile, E Pacific Ocean 27.03S 109.22W
44 M12 **San Juan, Río** ~ Costa Rica/Nicaragua
43 S15 **San Juan, Río** ~ SE Mexico
39 O8 **San Juan River** ~ Colorado/Utah, W USA
San Julián *see* Puerto San Julián
63 B17 **San Justo** Santa Fe, C Argentina 30.46S 60.31W

◆ Country ● Country Capital ◇ Dependent Territory ○ Dependent Territory Capital ◈ Administrative Region ✕ International Airport ▲ Mountain ▲ Mountain Range Volcano ~ River ◎ Lake ▣ Reservoir

Sankt Aegyd-am-Neuwalde – Santo

111 W5 **Sankt Aegyd-am-Neuwalde** Niederösterreich, E Austria 47.51N 15.34E
111 U9 **Sankt Andrä** *Slvn.* Šent Andraž. Kärnten, S Austria 46.46N 14.49E
Sankt Andrä *see* Szentendre
Sankt Anna *see* Sântana
110 K8 **Sankt Anton-am-Arlberg** Vorarlberg, W Austria 47.08N 10.11E
103 E16 **Sankt Augustin** Nordrhein-Westfalen, W Germany 50.46N 7.10E
Sankt-Bartholomäi *see* Palamuse
103 F24 **Sankt Blasien** Baden-Württemberg, SW Germany 47.43N 8.09E
111 R3 **Sankt Florian am Inn** Oberösterreich, N Austria 48.24N 13.27E
110 I7 **Sankt Gallen** *var.* St.Gallen, *Eng.* Saint Gall, *Fr.* St-Gall. Sankt Gallen, NE Switzerland 47.25N 9.22E
110 H8 **Sankt Gallen** *var.* St.Gallen, Eng. Saint Gall, *Fr.* St-Gall. ◈ *canton* NE Switzerland
110 J8 **Sankt Gallenkirch** Vorarlberg, W Austria 47.00N 10.59E
111 Q5 **Sankt Georgen** Salzburg, N Austria 47.59N 12.57E
Sankt Georgen *see* Đurđevac, Croatia
Sankt-Georgen *see* Sfântu Gheorghe, Romania
111 R6 **Sankt Gilgen** Salzburg, NW Austria 47.46N 13.21E
Sankt Gotthard *see* Szentgotthárd
103 E20 **Sankt Ingbert** Saarland, SW Germany 49.16N 7.07E
Sankt-Jakobi *see* Viru-Jaagupi, Lääne-Virumaa, Estonia
Sankt-Jakobi *see* Pärnu-Jaagupi, Pärnumaa, Estonia
Sankt Johann *see* Sankt Johann in Tirol
111 T7 **Sankt Johann am Tauern** Steiermark, E Austria 47.20N 14.27E
111 Q7 **Sankt Johann im Pongau** Salzburg, NW Austria 47.22N 13.13E
111 P6 **Sankt Johann in Tirol** *var.* Sankt Johann. Tirol, W Austria 47.31N 12.25E
Sankt-Johannis *see* Järva-Jaani
110 L8 **Sankt Leonhard** Tirol, W Austria 47.05N 10.53E
Sankt Margarethen *see* Sankt Margarethen im Burgenland
111 Y5 **Sankt Margarethen im Burgenland** *var.* Sankt Margarethen. Burgenland, E Austria 47.49N 16.37E
Sankt Martin *see* Martin
111 X8 **Sankt Martin an der Raab** Burgenland, SE Austria 46.59N 16.12E
111 U7 **Sankt Michael in Obersteiermark** Steiermark, SE Austria 47.21N 14.59E
Sankt Michel *see* Mikkeli
Sankt Moritz *see* St.Moritz
110 E11 **Sankt Niklaus** Valais, S Switzerland 46.09N 7.48E
111 S7 **Sankt Nikolai** *var.* Sankt Nikolai im Sölktal. Steiermark, SE Austria 47.18N 14.04E
Sankt Nikolai im Sölktal *see* Sankt Nikolai
111 U9 **Sankt Paul** *var.* Sankt Paul im Lavanttal. Kärnten, S Austria 46.42N 14.53E
Sankt Paul im Lavanttal *see* Sankt Paul
Sankt Peter *see* Pivka
111 W9 **Sankt Peter am Ottersbach** Steiermark, SE Austria 46.49N 15.48E
128 J13 **Sankt-Peterburg** *prev.* Leningrad, Petrograd, *Eng.* Saint Petersburg, *Fin.* Pietari. Leningradskaya Oblast', NW Russian Federation 59.55N 30.25E
102 H8 **Sankt Peter-Ording** Schleswig-Holstein, N Germany 54.18N 8.37E
111 V4 **Sankt Pölten** Niederösterreich, N Austria 48.14N 15.37E
111 W7 **Sankt Ruprecht** *var.* Sankt Ruprecht an der Raab. Steiermark, SE Austria 47.10N 15.41E
Sankt Ruprecht an der Raab *see* Sankt Ruprecht
Sankt-Ulrich *see* Ortisei
111 T4 **Sankt Valentin** Niederösterreich, C Austria 48.09N 14.30E
Sankt Veit am Flaum *see* Rijeka
111 T9 **Sankt Veit an der Glan** *Slvn.* Šent Vid. Kärnten, S Austria 46.46N 14.22E
101 M21 **Sankt-Vith** *var.* Saint-Vith. Liège, E Belgium 50.16N 6.07E
103 E20 **Sankt Wendel** Saarland, SW Germany 49.28N 7.10E
111 R6 **Sankt Wolfgang** Salzburg, NW Austria 47.43N 13.30E
81 K21 **Sankuru** ≈ C Dem. Rep. Congo
42 D8 **San Lázaro, Cabo** *headland* W Mexico 24.46N 112.15W
143 O16 **Şanlıurfa** *prev.* Sanli Urfa, Urfa, *anc.* Edessa. Şanlıurfa, S Turkey 37.07N 38.45E
143 O16 **Şanlıurfa** *prev.* Urfa. ◈ *province* SE Turkey
143 O16 **Şanlıurfa Yaylası** *plateau* SE Turkey
63 B18 **San Lorenzo** Santa Fe, C Argentina 32.37S 60.48W
59 M21 **San Lorenzo** Tarija, S Bolivia 21.27S 64.47W
58 C5 **San Lorenzo** Esmeraldas, N Ecuador 1.15N 78.51W
44 H8 **San Lorenzo** Valle, S Honduras 13.25N 87.27W
58 A6 **San Lorenzo, Cabo** *headland* W Ecuador 0.57S 80.49W
107 N8 **San Lorenzo de El Escorial** *var.* El Escorial. Madrid, C Spain 40.36N 4.07W
42 E5 **San Lorenzo, Isla** *island* NW Mexico
59 C14 **San Lorenzo, Isla** *island* W Peru
65 G20 **San Lorenzo, Monte** ▲ S Argentina 47.40S 72.12W
42 I9 **San Lorenzo, Río** ≈ C Mexico
106 J15 **Sanlúcar de Barrameda** Andalucía, S Spain 36.46N 6.21W
106 J14 **Sanlúcar la Mayor** Andalucía, S Spain 37.24N 6.13W
42 F11 **San Lucas** Baja California Sur, NW Mexico 22.49N 109.52W
42 E6 **San Lucas** *var.* Cabo San Lucas. Baja California Sur, W Mexico 27.13N 112.15W
42 G11 **San Lucas, Cabo** *var.* San Lucas Cape. *headland* W Mexico 22.52N 109.55W
San Lucas Cape *see* San Lucas, Cabo
64 J11 **San Luis** San Luis, C Argentina 33.18S 66.18W
44 E4 **San Luis** Petén, NE Guatemala 16.16N 89.27W
42 D2 **San Luis** *var.* San Luis Río Colorado. Sonora, NW Mexico 32.25N 114.48W
44 M7 **San Luis** Región Autónoma Atlántico Norte, NE Nicaragua 13.58N 84.10W
38 H15 **San Luis** Arizona, SW USA 32.27N 114.45W
39 T8 **San Luis** Colorado, C USA 37.09N 105.24W
56 J4 **San Luis** Falcón, N Venezuela 11.08N 69.36W
64 J11 **San Luis** *off.* Provincia de San Luis. ◈ *province* C Argentina
43 N12 **San Luis de la Paz** Guanajuato, C Mexico 21.15N 100.33W
42 K8 **San Luis del Cordero** Durango, C Mexico 25.25N 104.09W
42 D4 **San Luis, Isla** *island* NW Mexico
44 E6 **San Luis Jilotepeque** Jalapa, SE Guatemala 14.36N 89.40W
59 M16 **San Luis, Laguna de** ◎ NW Bolivia
37 P13 **San Luis Obispo** California, W USA 35.16N 120.39W
39 R7 **San Luis Peak** ▲ Colorado, C USA 37.59N 106.55W
43 N11 **San Luis Potosí** San Luis Potosí, C Mexico 22.09N 100.57W
43 N11 **San Luis Potosí** ◈ *state* C Mexico
37 O10 **San Luis Reservoir** ▣ California, W USA
San Luis Río Colorado *see* San Luis
39 S8 **San Luis Valley** *basin* Colorado, C USA
109 C19 **Sanluri** Sardegna, Italy, C Mediterranean Sea 39.34N 8.54E
63 D23 **San Manuel** Buenos Aires, E Argentina 37.46S 58.49W
38 M15 **San Manuel** Arizona, SW USA 32.36N 110.37W
108 F11 **San Marcello Pistoiese** Toscana, C Italy 44.03N 10.46E
109 N20 **San Marco Argentano** Calabria, SW Italy 39.31N 16.07E
56 E6 **San Marcos** Sucre, N Colombia 8.37N 75.12W
44 M14 **San Marcos** San José, C Costa Rica 9.39N 84.00W
44 B5 **San Marcos** San Marcos, W Guatemala 14.57N 91.46W
44 F6 **San Marcos** Ocotepeque, SW Honduras 14.23N 88.57W
43 O16 **San Marcos** Guerrero, S Mexico 16.47N 99.29W
27 S11 **San Marcos** Texas, SW USA 29.52N 97.56W
44 A5 **San Marcos** *off.* Departamento de San Marcos. ◈ *department* W Guatemala
San Marcos de Arica *see* Arica
42 E6 **San Marcos, Isla** *island* W Mexico
108 H11 **San Marino** ● (San Marino) C San Marino 43.53N 12.27E
108 I11 **San Marino** *off.* Republic of San Marino. ◆ *republic* S Europe
64 I11 **San Martín** Mendoza, C Argentina 33.04S 68.28W
56 F11 **San Martín** Meta, C Colombia 3.43N 73.42W
58 D11 **San Martín** *off.* Departamento de San Martín. ◈ *department* C Peru
204 I5 **San Martín** *Argentinian research station* Antarctica 68.18S 67.03W
65 H16 **San Martín de los Andes** Neuquén, W Argentina 40.10S 71.22W
106 M8 **San Martín de Valdeiglesias** Madrid, C Spain 40.21N 4.24W
65 G21 **San Martín, Lago** *var.* Lago O'Higgins. ◎ S Argentina
108 H6 **San Martino di Castrozza** Trentino-Alto Adige, N Italy 46.16N 11.50E
59 N16 **San Martín, Río** ≈ N Bolivia
San Martín Texmelucan *see* Texmelucan
37 N9 **San Mateo** California, W USA 37.33N 122.19W
57 O6 **San Mateo** Anzoátegui, NE Venezuela 9.34N 64.30W
44 B4 **San Mateo Ixtatán** Huehuetenango, W Guatemala 15.48N 91.30W
59 Q18 **San Matías** Santa Cruz, E Bolivia 16.19S 58.23W
65 K16 **San Matías, Golfo** *var.* Gulf of San Matías. *gulf* E Argentina
San Matías, Gulf of *see* San Matías
13 O8 **Sanmaur** Québec, SE Canada 47.52N 73.47W
167 T10 **Sanmen Wan** *bay* E China
166 M6 **Sanmenxia** *var.* Shan Xian. Henan, C China 34.46N 111.16E
Sânmiclăuş Mare *see* Sânnicolau Mare
63 D14 **San Miguel** Corrientes, NE Argentina 28.02S 57.38W
59 L16 **San Miguel** Beni, N Bolivia 16.43S 61.06W
44 G8 **San Miguel** San Miguel, SE El Salvador 13.27N 88.10W
42 L6 **San Miguel** Coahuila de Zaragoza, N Mexico 29.10N 101.28W
42 J9 **San Miguel** *var.* San Miguel de Cruces. Durango, C Mexico 24.25N 105.55W
45 U16 **San Miguel** Panamá, SE Panama 8.26N 78.57W
37 P12 **San Miguel** California, W USA 35.45N 120.42W
44 B9 **San Miguel** ◈ *department* E El Salvador
43 N13 **San Miguel de Allende** Guanajuato, C Mexico 20.54N 100.46W
San Miguel de Cruces *see* San Miguel
San Miguel de Ibarra *see* Ibarra
63 D21 **San Miguel del Monte** Buenos Aires, E Argentina 35.25S 58.49W
64 J7 **San Miguel de Tucumán** *var.* Tucumán. Tucumán, N Argentina 26.46S 65.15W
45 V16 **San Miguel, Golfo de** *gulf* S Panama
37 P15 **San Miguel Island** *island* California, W USA
44 L11 **San Miguelito** Río San Juan, S Nicaragua 11.22N 84.52W
45 T15 **San Miguelito** Panamá, C Panama 8.58N 79.31W
59 N18 **San Miguel, Río** ≈ E Bolivia
58 D6 **San Miguel, Río** ≈ Colombia/Ecuador
42 I7 **San Miguel, Río** ≈ N Mexico
44 G8 **San Miguel, Volcán de** △ SE El Salvador 13.27N 88.18W
167 Q12 **Sanming** Fujian, SE China 26.10N 117.37E
108 F11 **San Miniato** Toscana, C Italy 43.40N 10.53E
San Murezzan *see* St.Moritz
Sannār *see* Sennar
109 M15 **Sannicandro Garganico** Puglia, SE Italy 41.49N 15.31E
42 H6 **San Nicolás** Sonora, NW Mexico 28.31N 109.24W
63 C19 **San Nicolás de los Arroyos** Buenos Aires, E Argentina 33.17S 60.12W
37 R16 **San Nicolas Island** *island* Channel Islands, California, W USA
Sânnicolaul-Mare *see* Sânnicolau Mare
118 E11 **Sânnicolau Mare** *var.* Sânnicolaul-Mare, *Hung.* Nagyszentmiklós; *prev.* Sânmiclăuş Mare, Sînnicolau Mare. Timiş, W Romania 46.05N 20.37E
126 L15 **Sannikova, Proliv** *strait* NE Russian Federation
78 K16 **Sanniquellie** *var.* Saniquillie. NE Liberia 7.24N 8.45W
172 N9 **Sannohe** Aomori, Honshū, C Japan 40.23N 141.16E
Sanntaler Alpen *see* Kamniško-Savinjske Alpe
171 K15 **Sano** Tochigi, Honshū, S Japan 36.19N 139.26E
113 O17 **Sanok** Podkarpackie, SE Poland 49.31N 22.14E
56 E5 **San Onofre** Sucre, NW Colombia 9.45N 75.33W
59 K21 **San Pablo** Potosí, S Bolivia 21.43S 66.37W
179 P11 **San Pablo** *off.* San Pablo City. Luzon, N Philippines 14.04N 121.16E
San Pablo Balleza *see* Balleza
37 N8 **San Pablo Bay** *bay* California, W USA
42 C6 **San Pablo, Punta** *headland* W Mexico 27.12N 114.30W
45 R16 **San Pablo, Río** ≈ C Panama
179 Q11 **San Pascual** Burias Island, C Philippines 13.06N 122.59E
123 Jj16 **San Pawl il-Bahar** *Eng.* Saint Paul's Bay. E Malta 35.57N 14.24E
63 C19 **San Pedro** Buenos Aires, E Argentina 33.37S 59.42W
64 K5 **San Pedro** Jujuy, N Argentina 24.13S 64.51W
62 G13 **San Pedro** Misiones, NE Argentina 26.37S 54.12W
44 H1 **San Pedro** Corozal, NE Belize 17.58N 87.55W
42 L8 **San Pedro** *var.* San Pedro de las Colonias. Coahuila de Zaragoza, NE Mexico 25.47N 102.57W
64 O5 **San Pedro** San Pedro, SE Paraguay 24.04S 57.03W
64 O6 **San Pedro** *off.* Departamento de San Pedro. ◈ *department* C Paraguay
79 N16 **San Pedro** ✈ (Yamoussoukro) C Ivory Coast 6.49N 5.14W
46 G6 **San Pedro** ≈ C Cuba
San Pedro *see* San Pedro del Pinatar
78 M17 **San-Pédro** S Ivory Coast 4.45N 6.37W
44 D5 **San Pedro Carchá** Alta Verapaz, C Guatemala 15.30N 90.12W
37 S16 **San Pedro Channel** *channel* California, W USA
64 I5 **San Pedro de Atacama** Antofagasta, N Chile 22.52S 68.10W
San Pedro de Durazno *see* Durazno
42 G5 **San Pedro de la Cueva** Sonora, NW Mexico 29.16N 109.46W
San Pedro de las Colonias *see* San Pedro
58 B11 **San Pedro de Lloc** La Libertad, NW Peru 7.27S 79.34W
107 S13 **San Pedro del Pinatar** *var.* San Pedro. Murcia, SE Spain 37.49N 0.46W
47 P9 **San Pedro de Macorís** SE Dominican Republic 18.28N 69.19W
42 C3 **San Pedro Mártir, Sierra** ⛰ NW Mexico
San Pedro Pochutla *see* Pochutla
44 D2 **San Pedro, Río** ≈ Guatemala/Mexico
42 K10 **San Pedro, Río** ≈ C Mexico
106 I10 **San Pedro, Sierra de** ⛰ W Spain
44 G5 **San Pedro Sula** Cortés, NW Honduras 15.25N 88.01W
San Pedro Tapanatepec *see* Tapanatepec
64 I4 **San Pedro, Volcán** ▲ N Chile 21.46S 68.13W
108 E7 **San Pellegrino Terme** Lombardia, N Italy 45.53N 9.42E
27 T16 **San Perlita** Texas, SW USA 26.30N 97.38W
San Pietro *see* Supetar
San Pietro del Carso *see* Pivka
109 A20 **San Pietro, Isola di** *island* W Italy
34 K7 **Sanpoil River** ≈ Washington, NW USA
171 L12 **Sanpoku** *var.* Sampoku. Niigata, Honshū, C Japan 38.32N 139.33E
42 C3 **San Quintín** Baja California, NW Mexico 30.21N 115.58W
42 B3 **San Quintín, Bahía de** *bay* NW Mexico
42 B3 **San Quintín, Cabo** *headland* NW Mexico 30.22N 116.01W
64 I12 **San Rafael** Mendoza, W Argentina 34.43S 68.15W
43 N9 **San Rafael** Nuevo León, NE Mexico 25.01N 100.33W
36 M8 **San Rafael** California, W USA 37.58N 122.31W
39 Q11 **San Rafael** New Mexico, SW USA 35.03N 107.52W
56 H4 **San Rafael** *var.* El Moján. Zulia, NW Venezuela 10.58N 71.45W
44 J8 **San Rafael del Norte** Jinotega, NW Nicaragua 13.10N 86.10W
44 J10 **San Rafael del Sur** Managua, SW Nicaragua 11.51N 86.24W
38 M5 **San Rafael Knob** ▲ Utah, W USA 38.46N 110.45W
37 Q14 **San Rafael Mountains** ⛰ California, W USA
44 M13 **San Ramón** Alajuela, C Costa Rica 10.04N 84.27W
59 E14 **San Ramón** Junín, C Peru 11.08S 75.19W
63 F19 **San Ramón** Canelones, S Uruguay 34.18S 55.55W
64 K5 **San Ramón de la Nueva Orán** Salta, N Argentina 23.07S 64.19W
59 O16 **San Ramón, Río** ≈ E Bolivia
108 B11 **San Remo** Liguria, NW Italy 43.48N 7.46E
56 J3 **San Román, Cabo** *headland* NW Venezuela 12.10N 70.01W
63 C15 **San Roque** Corrientes, NE Argentina 28.34S 58.45W
196 I4 **San Roque** Saipan, S Northern Mariana Islands 15.15S 145.46E
106 K16 **San Roque** Andalucía, S Spain 36.13N 5.22W
27 R9 **San Saba** Texas, SW USA 31.12N 98.43W
27 Q9 **San Saba River** ≈ Texas, SW USA
63 D17 **San Salvador** Entre Ríos, E Argentina 31.37S 58.30W
44 F7 **San Salvador** ● (El Salvador) San Salvador, SW El Salvador 13.42N 89.12W
44 A10 **San Salvador** ◈ *department* C El Salvador
44 F8 **San Salvador** ✈ La Paz, S El Salvador 13.27N 89.04W
46 K4 **San Salvador** *prev.* Watlings Island. *island* E Bahamas
64 J5 **San Salvador de Jujuy** *var.* Jujuy. Jujuy, N Argentina 24.10S 65.19W
44 F7 **San Salvador, Volcán de** △ C El Salvador 13.58N 89.14W
79 Q14 **Sansanné-Mango** *var.* Mango. N Togo 10.21N 0.28E
47 S5 **San Sebastián** W Puerto Rico 18.21N 67.00W
65 J24 **San Sebastián, Bahía** *bay* S Argentina
Sansenhō *see* Sach'ŏn
108 H12 **Sansepolcro** Toscana, C Italy 43.34N 12.12E
109 M16 **San Severo** Puglia, SE Italy 41.40N 15.22E
114 F11 **Sanski Most** Federacija Bosna I Hercegovina, NW Bosnia & Herzegovina 44.43N 16.40E
176 Ww9 **Sansundi** Papua, E Indonesia 0.42S 135.48E
106 K11 **Santa Amalia** Extremadura, W Spain 39.00N 6.01W
62 F13 **Santa Ana** Misiones, NE Argentina 27.22S 55.34W
59 L16 **Santa Ana** Beni, N Bolivia 13.43S 65.37W
44 E7 **Santa Ana** Santa Ana, NW El Salvador 13.58N 89.34W
42 F4 **Santa Ana** Sonora, NW Mexico 30.33N 111.07W
37 T16 **Santa Ana** California, W USA 33.45N 117.52W
57 N6 **Santa Ana** Nueva Esparta, NE Venezuela 9.15N 64.39W
44 A9 **Santa Ana** ◈ *department* NW El Salvador
Santa Ana de Coro *see* Coro
44 E7 **Santa Ana, Volcán de** *var.* La Matepec. △ W El Salvador 13.49N 89.36W
42 J7 **Santa Barbara** Chihuahua, N Mexico 26.46N 105.46W
37 Q14 **Santa Barbara** California, W USA 34.24N 119.40W
44 G6 **Santa Bárbara** Santa Bárbara, W Honduras 14.57N 88.15W
56 L11 **Santa Bárbara** Amazonas, S Venezuela 3.55N 67.06W
56 I7 **Santa Bárbara** Barinas, W Venezuela 7.48N 71.10W
44 F5 **Santa Bárbara** ◈ *department* NW Honduras
Santa Bárbara *see* Iscuandé
37 Q15 **Santa Barbara Channel** *channel* California, W USA
Santa Bárbara de Samaná *see* Samaná
37 R16 **Santa Barbara Island** *island* Channel Islands, California, W USA
56 E5 **Santa Catalina** Bolívar, N Colombia 10.34N 75.22W
45 R15 **Santa Catalina** Bocas del Toro, W Panama 8.46N 81.18W
37 T17 **Santa Catalina, Gulf of** *gulf* California, W USA
42 F8 **Santa Catalina, Isla** *island* W Mexico
37 S16 **Santa Catalina Island** *island* Channel Islands, California, W USA
43 N8 **Santa Catarina** Nuevo León, NE Mexico 25.39N 100.30W
62 H13 **Santa Catarina** *off.* Estado de Santa Catarina. ◈ *state* S Brazil
Santa Catarina de Tepehuanes *see* Tepehuanes
62 L13 **Santa Catarina, Ilha de** *island* S Brazil
47 Q16 **Santa Catherina** Curaçao, C Netherlands Antilles 12.07N 68.46W
46 E5 **Santa Clara** Villa Clara, C Cuba 22.25N 78.00W
37 N9 **Santa Clara** California, W USA 37.20N 121.57W
38 J8 **Santa Clara** Utah, W USA 37.07N 113.39W
Santa Clara *see* Santa Clara de Olimar
63 F18 **Santa Clara de Olimar** *var.* Santa Clara. Cerro Largo, NE Uruguay 32.54S 54.55W
63 A17 **Santa Clara de Saguier** Santa Fe, C Argentina 31.21S 61.49W
Santa Coloma *see* Santa Coloma de Gramanet
107 X5 **Santa Coloma de Farners** *var.* Santa Coloma de Farnés. Cataluña, NE Spain 41.52N 2.39E
Santa Coloma de Farnés *see* Santa Coloma de Farners
107 W6 **Santa Coloma de Gramanet** *var.* Santa Coloma. Cataluña, NE Spain 41.28N 2.13E
106 G2 **Santa Comba** Galicia, NW Spain 43.01N 8.49W
Santa Comba *see* Uaco Cungo
106 H8 **Santa Comba Dão** Viseu, N Portugal 40.22N 8.07W
84 C10 **Santa Cruz** Uíge, NW Angola 6.56S 16.25E
59 N19 **Santa Cruz** *var.* Santa Cruz de la Sierra. Santa Cruz, C Bolivia 17.49S 63.10W
64 G12 **Santa Cruz** Libertador, C Chile 34.39S 71.16W
44 K13 **Santa Cruz** Guanacaste, W Costa Rica 10.15N 85.34W
46 I12 **Santa Cruz** W Jamaica 18.03N 77.41W
66 P6 **Santa Cruz** Madeira, Portugal, NE Atlantic Ocean 32.43N 16.46W
37 N10 **Santa Cruz** California, W USA 36.58N 122.01W
65 H20 **Santa Cruz** *off.* Provincia de Santa Cruz. ◈ *province* S Argentina
59 O18 **Santa Cruz** ◈ *department* E Bolivia
Santa Cruz *see* Viru-Viru
Santa Cruz *see* Puerto Santa Cruz
Santa Cruz Barillas *see* Barillas
61 O18 **Santa Cruz Cabrália** Bahia, E Brazil 16.16S 39.03W
Santa Cruz de El Seibo *see* El Seibo
66 N11 **Santa Cruz de la Palma** La Palma, Islas Canarias, Spain, NE Atlantic Ocean 28.40N 17.46W
Santa Cruz de la Sierra *see* Santa Cruz
107 O9 **Santa Cruz de la Zarza** Castilla-La Mancha, C Spain 39.59N 3.10W
44 C5 **Santa Cruz del Quiché** Quiché, W Guatemala 15.01N 91.08W
107 N8 **Santa Cruz del Retamar** Castilla-La Mancha, C Spain 40.07N 4.13W
Santa Cruz del Seibo *see* El Seibo
46 G7 **Santa Cruz del Sur** Camagüey, C Cuba 20.44N 78.00W
107 O11 **Santa Cruz de Mudela** Castilla-La Mancha, C Spain 38.37N 3.27W
66 Q11 **Santa Cruz de Tenerife** Tenerife, Islas Canarias, Spain, NE Atlantic Ocean 28.28N 16.15W
66 P11 **Santa Cruz de Tenerife** ◈ *province* Islas Canarias, Spain, NE Atlantic Ocean
62 K9 **Santa Cruz do Rio Pardo** São Paulo, S Brazil 22.52S 49.37W
63 H15 **Santa Cruz do Sul** Rio Grande do Sul, S Brazil 29.42S 52.25W
59 C17 **Santa Cruz, Isla** *var.* Indefatigable Island, Isla Chávez. *island* Galapagos Islands, Ecuador, E Pacific Ocean
42 F8 **Santa Cruz, Isla** *island* W Mexico
37 Q15 **Santa Cruz Island** *island* California, W USA
195 X8 **Santa Cruz Islands** *island group* E Solomon Islands
65 I22 **Santa Cruz, Río** ≈ S Argentina
38 L15 **Santa Cruz River** ≈ Arizona, SW USA
63 C17 **Santa Elena** Entre Ríos, E Argentina 30.58S 59.46W
44 F2 **Santa Elena** Cayo, W Belize 17.08N 89.04W
27 R16 **Santa Elena** Texas, SW USA 26.43N 98.30W
58 A7 **Santa Elena, Bahía de** *bay* W Ecuador
57 R10 **Santa Elena de Uairén** Bolívar, E Venezuela 4.40N 61.03W
44 K12 **Santa Elena, Península** *peninsula* NW Costa Rica
58 A7 **Santa Elena, Punta** *headland* W Ecuador 2.11S 81.00W
106 L11 **Santa Eufemia** Andalucía, S Spain 38.36N 4.54W
109 N21 **Santa Eufemia, Golfo di** *gulf* S Italy
107 S4 **Santa Eulalia de Gállego** Aragón, NE Spain 42.16N 0.46W
107 V11 **Santa Eulalia del Río** Eivissa, Spain, W Mediterranean Sea 39.00N 1.33E
63 B17 **Santa Fe** Santa Fe, C Argentina 31.36S 60.46W
107 N14 **Santa Fe** Andalucía, S Spain 37.10N 3.43W
39 S10 **Santa Fe** *state capital* New Mexico, SW USA 35.41N 105.56W
63 B15 **Santa Fe** *off.* Provincia de Santa Fe. ◈ *province* C Argentina
Santa Fe *see* Bogotá
46 C6 **Santa Fé** *var.* La Fe. Isla de la Juventud, W Cuba 21.39N 82.45W
45 R16 **Santa Fé** Veraguas, C Panama 8.28N 81.03W
Santa Fe de Bogotá *see* Bogotá
62 J7 **Santa Fé do Sul** São Paulo, S Brazil 20.13S 50.55W
59 B18 **Santa Fe, Isla** *var.* Barrington Island. *island* Galapagos Islands, Ecuador, E Pacific Ocean
25 V9 **Santa Fe River** ≈ Florida, SE USA
61 M15 **Santa Filomena** Piauí, E Brazil 9.06S 45.52W
42 G10 **Santa Genoveva** ▲ W Mexico 23.07N 109.56W
159 S14 **Santahar** Rajshahi, NW Bangladesh 24.45N 89.03E
62 G11 **Santa Helena** Paraná, S Brazil 24.53S 54.19W
56 J5 **Santa Inés** Lara, N Venezuela 10.37N 69.18W
65 G24 **Santa Inés, Isla** *island* S Chile
64 J13 **Santa Isabel** La Pampa, C Argentina 36.11S 66.59W
45 U14 **Santa Isabel** Colón, N Panama 9.31N 79.12W
195 W14 **Santa Isabel** *var.* Bughotu. *island* N Solomon Islands
Santa Isabel *see* Malabo
60 D11 **Santa Isabel do Rio Negro** Amazonas, NW Brazil 0.40S 64.55W
63 C15 **Santa Lucia** Corrientes, NE Argentina 28.58S 59.05W
59 I17 **Santa Lucía** Puno, S Peru 15.45S 70.34W
63 F20 **Santa Lucía** *var.* Santa Lucia. Canelones, S Uruguay 34.25S 56.25W
44 B6 **Santa Lucía Cotzumalguapa** Escuintla, SW Guatemala 14.20N 91.00W
109 L23 **Santa Lucia del Mela** Sicilia, Italy, C Mediterranean Sea 38.07N 15.16E
37 O11 **Santa Lucia Range** ⛰ California, W USA
42 D9 **Santa Margarita, Isla** *island* W Mexico
63 G15 **Santa Maria** Rio Grande do Sul, S Brazil 29.40S 53.48W
37 P13 **Santa Maria** California, W USA 34.56N 120.25W
66 Q4 **Santa Maria** ✈ Santa Maria, Azores, Portugal, NE Atlantic Ocean
66 P3 **Santa Maria** *island* Azores, Portugal, NE Atlantic Ocean
Santa Maria *see* Gaua.
64 J7 **Santa María** Catamarca, N Argentina 26.38S 66.01W
Santa María Asunción Tlaxiaco *see* Tlaxiaco
42 G9 **Santa María, Bahía** *bay* W Mexico
85 L21 **Santa Maria, Cabo de** *headland* S Mozambique 26.05S 32.58E
106 G15 **Santa Maria, Cabo de** *headland* S Portugal 36.57N 7.55W
46 J4 **Santa Maria, Cape** *headland* Long Island, C Bahamas 23.40N 75.20W
109 J17 **Santa Maria Capua Vetere** Campania, S Italy 41.04N 14.15E
61 M17 **Santa Maria da Vitória** Bahia, E Brazil 13.25S 44.09W
57 N9 **Santa María de Erebato** Bolívar, SE Venezuela 5.09N 64.49W
106 G7 **Santa Maria da Feira** Aveiro, N Portugal 40.55N 8.31W
57 N6 **Santa María de Ipire** Guárico, C Venezuela 8.51N 65.21W
Santa Maria del Buen Aire *see* Buenos Aires
42 J8 **Santa María del Oro** Durango, C Mexico 25.57N 105.22W
43 N12 **Santa María del Río** San Luis Potosí, C Mexico 21.48N 100.42W
Santa Maria di Castellabate *see* Castellabate
109 Q20 **Santa Maria di Leuca, Capo** *headland* SE Italy 39.48N 18.21E
110 K10 **Santa Maria-im-Münstertal** Graubünden, SE Switzerland 46.36N 10.25E
59 B18 **Santa María, Isla** *var.* Isla Floreana, Charles Island. *island* Galapagos Islands, Ecuador, E Pacific Ocean
42 J3 **Santa María, Laguna de** ◎ N Mexico
63 G16 **Santa Maria, Rio** ≈ S Brazil
45 R16 **Santa María, Río** ≈ C Panama
38 J12 **Santa Maria River** ≈ Arizona, SW USA
109 G15 **Santa Marinella** Lazio, C Italy 42.01N 11.51E
56 F4 **Santa Marta** Magdalena, N Colombia 11.13N 74.13W
106 J11 **Santa Marta** Extremadura, W Spain 38.37N 6.39W
Santa Maura *see* Lefkáda
37 S15 **Santa Monica** California, W USA 34.01N 118.29W
118 F10 **Sântana** *Ger.* Sankt Anna, *Hung.* Újszentanna; *prev.* Sîntana. Arad, W Romania 46.19N 21.30E
63 F16 **Santana, Coxilha de** *hill range* S Brazil
63 H16 **Santana da Boa Vista** Rio Grande do Sul, S Brazil 30.52S 53.03W
63 F16 **Santana do Livramento** *prev.* Livramento. Rio Grande do Sul, S Brazil 30.52S 55.30W
107 N2 **Santander** Cantabria, N Spain 43.28N 3.48W
56 F8 **Santander** *off.* Departamento de Santander. ◈ *province* C Colombia
Santander Jiménez *see* Jiménez
Sant'Andrea *see* Svetac
109 B20 **Sant'Antioco** Sardegna, Italy, C Mediterranean Sea 39.03N 8.28E
107 V11 **Sant Antoni de Portmany** *Cas.* San Antonio Abad. Eivissa, Spain, W Mediterranean Sea 35.58N 1.18E
106 J13 **Santa Olalla del Cala** Andalucía, S Spain 37.54N 6.13W
37 R15 **Santa Paula** California, W USA 34.21N 119.03W
38 L4 **Santaquin** Utah, W USA 39.58N 111.46W
60 I12 **Santarém** Pará, N Brazil 2.25S 54.40W
106 G10 **Santarém** *anc.* Scalabis. Santarém, W Portugal 39.13N 8.40W
106 G10 **Santarém** ◈ *district* C Portugal
46 F4 **Santaren Channel** *channel* W Bahamas
56 K10 **Santa Rita** Vichada, E Colombia 4.51N 68.27W
196 B16 **Santa Rita** SW Guam
44 H5 **Santa Rita** Cortés, NW Honduras 15.10N 87.54W
42 E9 **Santa Rita** Baja California Sur, W Mexico 27.28N 100.33W
56 H5 **Santa Rita** Zulia, NW Venezuela 10.33N 71.31W
61 I19 **Santa Rita de Araguaia** Goiás, S Brazil 17.17S 53.13W
Santa Rita de Cassia *see* Cássia
63 D14 **Santa Rosa** Corrientes, NE Argentina 28.18S 58.04W
64 K13 **Santa Rosa** La Pampa, C Argentina 36.37S 64.15W
63 G14 **Santa Rosa** Rio Grande do Sul, S Brazil 27.49S 54.28W
60 E10 **Santa Rosa** Roraima, N Brazil 3.41N 62.29W
58 B8 **Santa Rosa** El Oro, SW Ecuador 3.27S 79.57W
59 I16 **Santa Rosa** Puno, S Peru 14.38S 70.48W
36 M7 **Santa Rosa** California, W USA 38.26N 122.42W
39 U11 **Santa Rosa** New Mexico, SW USA 34.54N 104.43W
57 O6 **Santa Rosa** Anzoátegui, NE Venezuela 9.36N 64.16W
44 A3 **Santa Rosa** *off.* Departamento de Santa Rosa. ◈ *department* SE Guatemala
Santa Rosa *see* Santa Rosa de Copán
65 J15 **Santa Rosa, Bajo de** *basin* E Argentina
44 F6 **Santa Rosa de Copán** *var.* Santa Rosa. Copán, W Honduras 14.46N 88.48W
56 E8 **Santa Rosa de Osos** Antioquia, C Colombia 6.40N 75.27W
37 Q15 **Santa Rosa Island** *island* California, W USA
25 O9 **Santa Rosa Island** *island* Florida, SE USA
42 E6 **Santa Rosalía** Baja California Sur, W Mexico 27.19N 112.16W
56 K6 **Santa Rosalía** Portuguesa, NW Venezuela 9.01N 69.02W
196 C15 **Santa Rosa, Mount** ▲ NE Guam
37 V16 **Santa Rosa Mountains** ⛰ California, W USA
37 T2 **Santa Rosa Range** ⛰ Nevada, W USA
64 M8 **Santa Sylvina** Chaco, N Argentina 27.49S 61.07W
Santa Tecla *see* Nueva San Salvador
63 B19 **Santa Teresa** Santa Fe, C Argentina 33.30S 60.45W
61 O20 **Santa Teresa** Espírito Santo, SE Brazil 19.51S 40.49W
109 M23 **Santa Teresa di Riva** Sicilia, Italy, C Mediterranean Sea 38.00N 15.25E
63 E21 **Santa Teresita** Buenos Aires, E Argentina 36.34S 56.43W
63 H19 **Santa Vitória do Palmar** Rio Grande do Sul, S Brazil 33.31S 53.25W
37 Q14 **Santa Ynez River** ≈ California, W USA
Sant Carles de la Rápida *see* Sant Carles de la Ràpita
107 U7 **Sant Carles de la Ràpita** *var.* Sant Carles de la Rápida. Cataluña, NE Spain 40.37N 0.36E
107 W5 **Sant Celoni** Cataluña, NE Spain 41.39N 2.25E
37 U17 **Santee** California, W USA 32.50N 116.58W
23 T13 **Santee River** ≈ South Carolina, SE USA
42 K15 **San Telmo, Punta** *headland* SW Mexico 18.19N 103.30W
109 O17 **Santeramo in Colle** Puglia, SE Italy 40.46N 16.45E
107 X5 **Sant Feliu de Guíxols** *var.* San Feliú de Guixols. Cataluña, NE Spain 41.46N 3.01E
107 W6 **Sant Feliu de Llobregat** Cataluña, NE Spain 41.22N 2.00E
108 C7 **Santhià** Piemonte, NE Italy 45.21N 8.11E
63 F15 **Santiago** Rio Grande do Sul, S Brazil 29.10S 54.52W
64 H11 **Santiago** *var.* Gran Santiago. ● (Chile) Santiago, C Chile 33.30S 70.40W
47 N8 **Santiago** *var.* Santiago de los Caballeros. N Dominican Republic 19.27N 70.42W
42 G10 **Santiago** Baja California Sur, W Mexico 23.32N 109.45W
43 O8 **Santiago** Nuevo León, NE Mexico 25.22N 100.09W
45 R16 **Santiago** Veraguas, S Panama 8.06N 80.58W
59 E16 **Santiago** Ica, SW Peru 14.13S 75.43W
106 G3 **Santiago** *var.* Santiago de Compostela, *Eng.* Compostella; *anc.* Campus Stellae. Galicia, NW Spain 42.52N 8.33W
64 H11 **Santiago** *off.* Región Metropolitana de Santiago, *var.* Metropolitan. ◈ *region* C Chile
64 H11 **Santiago** ✈ Santiago, C Chile 33.27S 70.40W
106 G3 **Santiago** ✈ Galicia, NW Spain
78 D10 **Santiago** *var.* São Tiago. *island* Ilhas de Sotavento, S Cape Verde
Santiago *see* Santiago de Cuba, Cuba
Santiago *see* Grande de Santiago, Río, Mexico
44 B6 **Santiago Atitlán** Sololá, SW Guatemala 14.36N 91.13W
45 Q16 **Santiago, Cerro** ▲ W Panama 8.27N 81.42W
Santiago de Compostela *see* Santiago
46 I8 **Santiago de Cuba** *var.* Santiago. Santiago de Cuba, E Cuba 20.01N 75.50W
Santiago de Guayaquil *see* Guayaquil
64 K8 **Santiago del Estero** Santiago del Estero, C Argentina 27.51S 64.15W
63 A15 **Santiago del Estero** *off.* Provincia de Santiago del Estero. ◈ *province* N Argentina
42 I8 **Santiago de los Caballeros** Sinaloa, W Mexico 25.33N 107.22W
Santiago de los Caballeros *see* Santiago, Dominican Republic
Santiago de los Caballeros *see* Guatemala, Guatemala
44 F8 **Santiago de María** Usulután, SE El Salvador 13.28N 88.28W
106 F12 **Santiago do Cacém** Setúbal, S Portugal 38.01N 8.42W
42 J12 **Santiago Ixcuintla** Nayarit, C Mexico 21.49N 105.07W
Santiago Jamiltepec *see* Jamiltepec
26 L11 **Santiago Mountains** ⛰ Texas, SW USA
42 J9 **Santiago Papasquiaro** Durango, C Mexico 25.03N 105.25W
Santiago Pinotepa Nacional *see* Pinotepa Nacional
58 C8 **Santiago, Río** ≈ N Peru
42 M10 **San Tiburcio** Zacatecas, C Mexico 24.07N 101.28W
107 N2 **Santillana** Cantabria, N Spain 43.24N 4.06W
56 I5 **San Timoteo** Zulia, NW Venezuela 9.49N 71.04W
Santi Quaranta *see* Sarandë
Santissima Trinidad *see* Chilung
107 O12 **Santisteban del Puerto** Andalucía, S Spain 38.15N 3.10W
107 U7 **Sant Jordi, Golf de** *gulf* NE Spain
107 T8 **Sant Mateu** País Valenciano, E Spain 40.28N 0.10E
27 S7 **Santo** Texas, SW USA 32.35N 98.06W
Santo *see* Espiritu Santo

◆ Country
● Country Capital
◇ Dependent Territory
○ Dependent Territory Capital
◈ Administrative Region
✈ International Airport
▲ Mountain
⛰ Mountain Range
△ Volcano
≈ River
◎ Lake
▣ Reservoir

◆ COUNTRY ◇ DEPENDENT TERRITORY ◇ ADMINISTRATIVE REGION ⩙ MOUNTAIN ⩙ VOLCANO ⊟ LAKE
● COUNTRY CAPITAL ○ DEPENDENT TERRITORY CAPITAL ✕ INTERNATIONAL AIRPORT ⩙ MOUNTAIN RANGE ⤳ RIVER ⊟ RESERVOIR

SAVUSAVU – SEMPACHER SEE

197 J13 **Savusavu** Vanua Levu, N Fiji *16.47S 179.21E*
175 Q17 **Savu Sea** *Ind.* Laut Sawu. *sea* S Indonesia
85 H17 **Savute** Chobe, N Botswana *18.33S 24.06E*
145 N7 **Şawāb 'Uqlat** *well* W Iraq *33.57N 40.04E*
144 M7 **Sawāb, Wādī as** *dry watercourse* W Iraq
158 H13 **Sawāi Mādhopur** Rājasthān, N India *26.00N 76.22E*
175 Tt10 **Sawai, Teluk** *bay* Pulau Seram, E Indonesia
Sawakin *see* Suakin
178 Ii9 **Sawang Daen Din** Sakon Nakhon, E Thailand *17.28N 103.27E*
178 H8 **Sawankhalok** *var.* Swankalok. Sukhothai, NW Thailand *17.19N 99.49E*
171 Kk17 **Sawara** Chiba, Honshū, S Japan *35.52N 140.29E*
171 Jj12 **Sawasaki-bana** *headland* Sado, C Japan *37.48N 138.11E*
39 R5 **Sawatch Range** ▲ Colorado, C USA
147 N12 **Sawdā', Jabal** ▲ SW Saudi Arabia *18.15N 42.26E*
77 P9 **Sawdā', Jabal as** ▲ C Libya
Sawdirī *see* Sodiri
176 W9 **Saweba, Tanjung** *headland* Papua, E Indonesia *0.41S 133.59E*
99 F14 **Sawel Mountain** ▲ C Northern Ireland, UK *54.49N 7.04W*
Sawhāj *see* Sohâg
79 O15 **Sawla** N Ghana *9.14N 2.26W*
147 X12 **Şawqirah** *var.* Suqrah. S Oman *18.16N 56.34E*
147 X12 **Şawqirah, Dawḩat** *var.* Ghubbat Sawqirah, Sukra Bay, Suqrah Bay. *bay* S Oman
Sawqirah, Ghubbat *see* Şawqirah, Dawḩat
191 V5 **Sawtell** New South Wales, SE Australia *30.22S 153.04E*
144 K7 **Şawt, Wādī aş** *dry watercourse* S Syria
175 Q18 **Sawu, Kepulauan** *var.* Kepulauan Savu. *island group* S Indonesia
Sawu, Laut *see* Savu Sea
175 Qq18 **Sawu, Pulau** *var.* Pulau Savu. *island* Kepulauan Sawu, S Indonesia
107 S12 **Sax** País Valenciano, E Spain *38.33N 0.49W*
Saxe *see* Sachsen
110 C11 **Saxon** Valais, SW Switzerland *46.07N 7.09E*
Saxony *see* Sachsen
Saxony-Anhalt *see* Sachsen-Anhalt
79 R12 **Say** Niamey, SW Niger *13.02N 2.22E*
13 V7 **Sayabec** Québec, SE Canada *48.33N 67.42W*
Sayaboury *see* Xaignabouli
151 U12 **Sayak** *Kaz.* Sayaq. Karaganda, E Kazakhstan *46.54N 77.17E*
59 D14 **Sayán** Lima, W Peru *11.06S 77.09W*
126 Hh15 **Sayanogorsk** Respublika Khakasiya, S Russian Federation *53.07N 91.08E*
126 J15 **Sayansk** Irkutskaya Oblast', S Russian Federation *54.06N 102.10E*
133 T6 **Sayanskiy Khrebet** ▲ S Russian Federation
Sayaq *see* Sayak
152 K13 **Saýat** *Rus.* Sayat. Lebap Welaýaty, E Turkmenistan *38.44N 63.51E*
44 D3 **Sayaxché** Petén, N Guatemala *16.31N 90.10W*
Şaydā/Sayida *see* Saïda
147 T15 **Sayḩūt** E Yemen *15.18N 51.15E*
31 U14 **Saylorville Lake** ⊠ Iowa, C USA
Saymenskiy Kanal *see* Saimaa Canal
169 N10 **Saynshand** Dornogovĭ, SE Mongolia *44.51N 110.07E*
168 J11 **Saynshand** Ömnögovĭ, S Mongolia *43.30N 102.08E*
168 F7 **Sayn-Ust** Govĭ-Altay, W Mongolia *47.23N 94.19E*
Say-Ötesh *see* Say-Utës
144 J7 **Şayqal, Baḩr** ⊚ S Syria
Sayrab *see* Sayrob
164 H4 **Sayram Hu** ⊚ NW China
28 K11 **Sayre** Oklahoma, C USA *35.17N 99.38W*
20 H12 **Sayre** Pennsylvania, NE USA *41.57N 76.30W*
20 K15 **Sayreville** New Jersey, NE USA *40.27N 74.19W*
153 N13 **Sayrob** *Rus.* Sayrab. Surkhondaryo Viloyati, S Uzbekistan *38.03N 66.54E*
42 L13 **Sayula** Jalisco, SW Mexico *19.52N 103.36W*
147 R14 **Say' 'ūn** *var.* Saywūn. C Yemen *15.52N 48.31E*
150 G14 **Say-Utës** *Kaz.* Say-Ötesh. Mangistau, SW Kazakhstan *44.20N 53.32E*
8 K16 **Sayward** Vancouver Island, British Columbia, SW Canada *50.20N 126.01W*
Saywūn *see* Say 'ūn
Sayyāl *see* As Sayyāl
145 U8 **Sayyid 'Abīd** *var.* Saiyid Abid. E Iraq *32.51N 45.07E*
115 J22 **Sazan** *var.* Ishulli i Sazanit, *It.* Saseno. *island* SW Albania
Sazanit, Ishulli i *see* Sazan
Sazau/Sazawa *see* Sázava
113 E17 **Sázava** *var.* Sazau, *Ger.* Sazawa. ⚘ C Czech Republic
128 J14 **Sazonovo** Vologodskaya Oblast', NW Russian Federation *59.04N 35.10E*
104 G6 **Scaër** Finistère, NW France *48.00N 3.40W*
99 J15 **Scafell Pike** ▲ NW England, UK *54.26N 3.10W*
Scalabis *see* Santarém
98 M2 **Scalloway** N Scotland, UK *60.10N 1.17W*
40 M11 **Scammon Bay** Alaska, USA *61.50N 165.34W*
Scammon Lagoon/ Scammon, Laguna *see* Ojo de Liebre, Laguna
86 F7 **Scandinavia** *geophysical region* NW Europe
Scania *see* Skåne
98 K5 **Scapa Flow** *sea basin* N Scotland, UK
109 K26 **Scaramia, Capo** *headland* Sicilia, Italy, C Mediterranean Sea *36.46N 14.29E*
12 H15 **Scarborough** Ontario, SE Canada *43.46N 79.14W*
47 Z16 **Scarborough** *prev.* Port Louis. Tobago, Trinidad and Tobago *11.10N 60.45W*
99 N16 **Scarborough** N England, UK *54.16N 0.24W*
193 I17 **Scargill** Canterbury, South Island, NZ *42.57S 172.57E*
98 E7 **Scarp** *island* NW Scotland, UK
Scarpanto *see* Kárpathos
Scarpanto Strait *see* Karpathou, Stenó
109 G25 **Scauri** Sicilia, Italy, C Mediterranean Sea *36.45N 12.06E*
Scealg, Bá na *see* Ballinskelligs Bay
Scebeli *see* Shebeli
102 K10 **Schaale** ⚘ N Germany
102 K9 **Schaalsee** ⊚ N Germany
101 G18 **Schaerbeek** Brussels, C Belgium *50.51N 4.21E*
110 G6 **Schaffhausen** *Fr.* Schaffhouse. Schaffhausen, N Switzerland *47.42N 8.37E*
110 G6 **Schaffhausen** *Fr.* Schaffhouse. ◆ *canton* N Switzerland
Schaffhouse *see* Schaffhausen
100 I8 **Schagen** Noord-Holland, NW Netherlands *52.46N 4.46E*
Schaken *see* Šakiai
100 M10 **Schalkhaar** Overijssel, E Netherlands *52.16N 6.10E*
111 R3 **Schärding** Oberösterreich, N Austria *48.27N 13.26E*
102 G9 **Scharhörn** *island* NW Germany
Schässburg *see* Sighişoara
Schaulen *see* Šiauliai
32 M10 **Schaumburg** Illinois, N USA *42.01N 88.04W*
Schebschi Mountains *see* Shebshi Mountains
100 P6 **Scheemda** Groningen, NE Netherlands *53.10N 6.58E*
102 I10 **Scheessel** Niedersachsen, NW Germany *53.11N 9.32E*
11 N8 **Schefferville** Québec, E Canada *54.50N 67.00W*
Schelde *see* Scheldt
101 D18 **Scheldt** *Dut.* Schelde, *Fr.* Escaut. ⚘ W Europe
37 X5 **Schell Creek Range** ▲ Nevada, W USA
20 K10 **Schenectady** New York, NE USA *42.48N 73.57W*
101 I17 **Scherpenheuvel** *Fr.* Montaigu. Vlaams Brabant, C Belgium *51.00N 4.57E*
100 K11 **Scherpenzeel** Gelderland, C Netherlands *52.07N 5.30E*
27 S12 **Schertz** Texas, SW USA *29.33N 98.16W*
100 G11 **Scheveningen** Zuid-Holland, W Netherlands *52.07N 4.18E*
100 G12 **Schiedam** Zuid-Holland, SW Netherlands *51.55N 4.25E*
101 M24 **Schieren** Diekirch, NE Luxembourg *49.49N 6.06E*
100 M4 **Schiermonnikoog** *Fris.* Skiermûntseach. Friesland, N Netherlands *53.28N 6.09E*
100 M4 **Schiermonnikoog** *Fris.* Skiermûntseach. *island* Waddeneilanden, N Netherlands
101 K14 **Schijndel** Noord-Brabant, S Netherlands *51.37N 5.27E*
Schil *see* Jiu
101 H16 **Schilde** Antwerpen, N Belgium *51.13N 4.34E*
Schillen *see* Zhilino
105 V5 **Schiltigheim** Bas-Rhin, NE France *48.37N 7.46E*
108 G7 **Schio** Veneto, NE Italy *45.42N 11.21E*
100 H10 **Schiphol** ✕ (Amsterdam) Noord-Holland, C Netherlands *52.18N 4.48E*
Schippenbeil *see* Sępopol
Schiria *see* Şiria
Schivelbein *see* Świdwin
117 D22 **Schiza** *island* S Greece
183 U3 **Schjetman Reef** *reef* Antarctica
Schlackenwerth *see* Ostrov
111 R7 **Schladming** Steiermark, SE Austria *47.23N 13.37E*
Schlan *see* Slaný
Schlanders *see* Silandro
102 I7 **Schlei** *inlet* N Germany
103 D17 **Schleiden** Nordrhein-Westfalen, W Germany *50.31N 6.30E*
195 P9 **Schleinitz Range** ▲ New Ireland, N PNG
Schlelau *see* Szydłowiec
102 I7 **Schleswig** Schleswig-Holstein, N Germany *54.31N 9.34E*
31 T13 **Schleswig** Iowa, C USA *42.10N 95.27W*
102 H8 **Schleswig-Holstein** ◆ *state* N Germany
Schlettstadt *see* Sélestat
110 F7 **Schlieren** Zürich, N Switzerland *47.22N 8.27E*
Schlochau *see* Człuchów
Schloppe *see* Człopa
103 I18 **Schlüchtern** Hessen, C Germany *50.19N 9.27E*
103 J17 **Schmalkalden** Thüringen, C Germany *50.42N 10.26E*
111 W2 **Schmida** ⚘ NE Austria
67 P19 **Schmidt-Ott Seamount** *var.* Schmitt-Ott Seamount, Schmitt-Ott Tablemount. *undersea feature* SW Indian Ocean *39.37S 13.00E*
Schmiegel *see* Śmigiel
Schmitt-Ott Seamount/ Schmitt-Ott Tablemount *see* Schmidt-Ott Seamount
13 V3 **Schmon** ⚘ Québec, SE Canada
103 M18 **Schneeberg** ▲ W Germany *50.03N 11.51E*
Schneeberg *see* Veliki Snežnik
Schnee-Eifel *see* Schneifel
Schneekoppe *see* Sněžka
Schneidemühl *see* Piła
103 D18 **Schneifel** *var.* Schnee-Eifel. *plateau* W Germany
Schnelle Körös/Schnelle Kreisch *see* Crişul Repede
102 I11 **Schneverdingen** *var.* Schneverdingen (Wümme). Niedersachsen, NW Germany *53.07N 9.48E*
Schneverdingen (Wümme) *see* Schneverdingen
Schoden *see* Skuodas
20 K10 **Schoharie** New York, NE USA *42.40N 74.19W*
20 K11 **Schoharie Creek** ⚘ New York, NE USA
117 J21 **Schoinoússa** *island* Kykládes, Greece, Aegean Sea
102 L13 **Schönebeck** Sachsen-Anhalt, C Germany *52.01N 11.45E*
Schöneck *see* Skarszewy
102 O12 **Schönefeld** ✕ (Berlin) Berlin, NE Germany *52.23N 13.29E*
103 K24 **Schongau** Bayern, S Germany *47.49N 10.54E*
102 K13 **Schöningen** Niedersachsen, C Germany *52.07N 10.58E*
Schönlanke *see* Trzcianka
Schönsee *see* Kowalewo Pomorskie
33 P10 **Schoolcraft** Michigan, N USA *42.05N 85.39W*
100 O8 **Schoonebeek** Drenthe, NE Netherlands *52.39N 6.57E*
100 I12 **Schoonhoven** Zuid-Holland, C Netherlands *51.57N 4.51E*
100 H8 **Schoorl** Noord-Holland, NW Netherlands *52.42N 4.40E*
Schooten *see* Schoten
103 F24 **Schopfheim** Baden-Württemberg, SW Germany *47.39N 7.49E*
103 I21 **Schorndorf** Baden-Württemberg, S Germany *48.48N 9.31E*
102 F10 **Schortens** Niedersachsen, NW Germany *53.31N 7.57E*
101 H16 **Schoten** *var.* Schooten. Antwerpen, N Belgium *51.15N 4.30E*
191 Q17 **Schouten Island** *island* Tasmania, SE Australia
194 H9 **Schouten Islands** *island group* NW PNG
100 E13 **Schouwen** *island* SW Netherlands
47 Q12 **Schœlcher** W Martinique *14.37N 61.06W*
Schreiberhau *see* Szklarska Poręba
111 U2 **Schrems** Niederösterreich, E Austria *48.49N 15.01E*
103 L22 **Schrobenhausen** Bayern, SE Germany *48.33N 11.14E*
20 L8 **Schroon Lake** ⊚ New York, NE USA
110 J8 **Schruns** Vorarlberg, W Austria *47.04N 9.54E*
Schubin *see* Szubin
27 U11 **Schulenburg** Texas, SW USA *29.40N 96.54W*
Schuls *see* Scuol
110 F8 **Schüpfheim** Luzern, C Switzerland *47.02N 7.23E*
37 S6 **Schurz** Nevada, W USA *38.55N 118.48W*
103 I24 **Schussen** ⚘ S Germany
Schüttenhofen *see* Sušice
31 R15 **Schuyler** Nebraska, C USA *41.25N 97.04W*
20 L10 **Schuylerville** New York, NE USA *43.05N 73.34W*
103 K20 **Schwabach** Bayern, SE Germany *49.19N 11.02E*
Schwabenalb *see* Schwäbische Alb
103 I23 **Schwäbische Alb** *var.* Schwabenalb, *Eng.* Swabian Jura. ▲ S Germany
103 I22 **Schwäbisch Gmünd** *var.* Gmünd. Baden-Württemberg, SW Germany *48.49N 9.48E*
103 I21 **Schwäbisch Hall** *var.* Hall. Baden-Württemberg, SW Germany *49.07N 9.43E*
103 H16 **Schwalm** ⚘ C Germany
111 V9 **Schwanberg** Steiermark, SE Austria *46.46N 15.12E*
110 H8 **Schwanden** Glarus, E Switzerland *47.02N 9.04E*
103 M20 **Schwandorf** Bayern, SE Germany *49.19N 12.07E*
111 S5 **Schwanenstadt** Oberösterreich, NW Austria *48.03N 13.45E*
174 M9 **Schwaner, Pegunungan** ▲ Borneo, N Indonesia
111 W5 **Schwarza** ⚘ E Austria
111 P9 **Schwarzach** ⚘ S Austria
103 M20 **Schwarzach** *Cz.* Černice. ⚘ Czech Republic/Germany
Schwarzach *see* Schwarzach im Pongau, Austria
Schwarzach *see* Svratka, Czech Republic
111 Q7 **Schwarzach im Pongau** *var.* Schwarzach. Salzburg, NW Austria *47.19N 13.09E*
Schwarzawa *see* Svratka
103 N14 **Schwarze Elster** ⚘ E Germany
Schwarze Körös *see* Crişul Negru
110 D9 **Schwarzenburg** Bern, W Switzerland *46.51N 7.28E*
85 D21 **Schwarzrand** ▲ S Namibia
103 G23 **Schwarzwald** *Eng.* Black Forest. ▲ SW Germany
Schwarzwasser *see* Wda
41 P7 **Schwatka Mountains** ▲ Alaska, USA
111 N7 **Schwaz** Tirol, W Austria *47.21N 11.43E*
111 X4 **Schwechat** Niederösterreich, NE Austria *48.09N 16.28E*
111 Y4 **Schwechat** ✕ (Wien) Wien, E Austria *48.04N 16.31E*
102 P11 **Schwedt** Brandenburg, NE Germany *53.04N 14.16E*
103 D19 **Schweich** Rheinland-Pfalz, SW Germany *49.49N 6.44E*
Schweidnitz *see* Świdnica
103 J18 **Schweinfurt** Bayern, SE Germany *50.03N 10.13E*
Schweiz *see* Switzerland
102 L9 **Schwerin** Mecklenburg-Vorpommern, N Germany *53.37N 11.25E*
Schwerin *see* Skwierzyna
102 L9 **Schweriner See** ⊚ N Germany
Schwertberg *see* Świecie
103 F15 **Schwerte** Nordrhein-Westfalen, W Germany *51.27N 7.34E*
Schwiebus *see* Świebodzin
102 P13 **Schwielochsee** ⊚ NE Germany
Schwihau *see* Švihov
Schwiz *see* Schwyz
110 G8 **Schwyz** *var.* Schwiz. Schwyz, C Switzerland *47.01N 8.39E*
110 G8 **Schwyz** *var.* Schwiz. ◆ *canton* C Switzerland
12 J11 **Schyan** ⚘ Québec, SE Canada
Schyl *see* Jiu
109 I24 **Sciacca** Sicilia, Italy, C Mediterranean Sea *37.30N 13.05E*
Sciasciamana *see* Shashemenē
109 L26 **Scicli** Sicilia, Italy, C Mediterranean Sea *36.48N 14.43E*
99 F25 **Scilly, Isles of** *island group* SW England, UK
113 H17 **Ščinawa** *Ger.* Steinau an der Elbe. Dolnośląskie, SW Poland *51.22N 16.27E*
Scio *see* Chíos
33 S14 **Scioto River** ⚘ Ohio, N USA
38 L5 **Scipio** Utah, W USA *39.15N 112.06W*
35 X6 **Scobey** Montana, NW USA *48.47N 105.25W*
191 T7 **Scone** New South Wales, SE Australia *32.02S 150.51E*
Scoresby Sound/Scoresbysund *see* Ittoqqortoormiit
Scoresby Sund *see* Kangertittivaq
Scorno, Punta dello *see* Caprara, Punta
36 K3 **Scotia** California, W USA *40.04N 124.07W*
49 Y14 **Scotia Plate** *tectonic feature*
49 V15 **Scotia Ridge** *undersea feature* S Atlantic Ocean
204 H2 **Scotia Sea** *sea* SW Atlantic Ocean
31 Q12 **Scotland** South Dakota, N USA *43.09N 97.43W*
27 R5 **Scotland** Texas, SW USA *33.37N 98.27W*
98 H11 **Scotland** *national region* UK
23 W8 **Scotland Neck** North Carolina, SE USA *36.07N 77.25W*
205 R13 **Scott Base** *NZ research station* Antarctica *77.52S 167.18E*
8 J16 **Scott, Cape** *headland* Vancouver Island, British Columbia, SW Canada *50.43N 128.24W*
28 I5 **Scott City** Kansas, C USA *38.28N 100.54W*
29 Y7 **Scott City** Missouri, C USA *37.13N 89.31W*
205 R14 **Scott Coast** *physical region* Antarctica
20 C15 **Scottdale** Pennsylvania, NE USA *40.05N 79.35W*
205 Y11 **Scott Glacier** *glacier* Antarctica
205 Q17 **Scott Island** *island* Antarctica
28 L11 **Scott, Mount** ▲ Oklahoma, USA *34.52N 98.34W*
34 G15 **Scott, Mount** ▲ Oregon, NW USA *42.53N 122.06W*
36 M1 **Scott River** ⚘ California, W USA
30 I13 **Scottsbluff** Nebraska, C USA *41.52N 103.40W*
25 Q2 **Scottsboro** Alabama, S USA *34.40N 86.01W*
33 P15 **Scottsburg** Indiana, N USA *38.42N 85.46W*
191 P16 **Scottsdale** Tasmania, SE Australia *41.13S 147.30E*
38 L13 **Scottsdale** Arizona, SW USA *33.30N 111.54W*
47 O12 **Scotts Head Village** *var.* Cachacrou. S Dominica *15.12N 61.22W*
199 Jj17 **Scott Shoal** *undersea feature* S Pacific Ocean
22 K7 **Scottsville** Kentucky, S USA *36.45N 86.11W*
31 U14 **Scranton** Iowa, C USA *42.01N 94.33W*
20 I13 **Scranton** Pennsylvania, NE USA *41.25N 75.40W*
194 G10 **Screw** ⚘ NW PNG
31 R14 **Scribner** Nebraska, C USA *41.40N 96.40W*
Scrobesbyrig' *see* Shrewsbury
12 I14 **Scugog** ⚘ Ontario, SE Canada
12 I14 **Scugog, Lake** ⊚ Ontario, SE Canada
99 N17 **Scunthorpe** E England, UK *53.34N 0.39W*
110 K9 **Scuol** *Ger.* Schuls. Graubünden, E Switzerland *46.51N 10.21E*
Scupi *see* Skopje
Scutari *see* Shkodër
115 K17 **Scutari, Lake** *Alb.* Liqeni i Shkodrës, *SCr.* Skadarsko Jezero. ⊚ Albania/Serbia and Montenegro (Yugoslavia)
Scyros *see* Skýros
Scythopolis *see* Bet She'an
27 U13 **Seadrift** Texas, SW USA *28.25N 96.42W*
23 Y4 **Seaford** *var.* Seaford City. Delaware, NE USA *38.38N 75.36W*
Seaford City *see* Seaford
12 E15 **Seaforth** Ontario, S Canada *43.33N 81.25W*
26 M6 **Seagraves** Texas, SW USA *32.56N 102.33W*
9 X9 **Seal** ⚘ Manitoba, C Canada
190 M10 **Sea Lake** Victoria, SE Australia *35.34S 142.51E*
85 G26 **Seal, Cape** *headland* S South Africa *34.06S 23.18E*
67 D26 **Sea Lion Islands** *island group* SE Falkland Islands
21 S8 **Seal Island** *island* Maine, NE USA
27 V11 **Sealy** Texas, SW USA *29.46N 96.09W*
37 X12 **Searchlight** Nevada, W USA *35.27N 114.54W*
29 V11 **Searcy** Arkansas, C USA *35.15N 91.44W*
21 R7 **Searsport** Maine, NE USA *44.28N 68.54W*
37 N10 **Seaside** California, W USA *36.36N 121.51W*
34 F10 **Seaside** Oregon, NW USA *45.57N 123.55W*
20 K16 **Seaside Heights** New Jersey, NE USA *39.56N 74.03W*
34 H8 **Seattle** Washington, NW USA *47.34N 122.19W*
34 H9 **Seattle-Tacoma** ✕ Washington, NW USA *47.04N 122.27W*
193 J16 **Seaward Kaikoura Range** ▲ South Island, NZ
44 J9 **Sébaco** Matagalpa, W Nicaragua *12.50N 86.04W*
21 P8 **Sebago Lake** ⊚ Maine, NE USA
176 V11 **Sebakor, Teluk** *bay* Papua, E Indonesia
Sebangan, Sungai *see* Sebangau Besar, Sungai
174 M11 **Sebangan, Teluk** *bay* Borneo, C Indonesia
174 Mm11 **Sebanganu, Teluk** *bay* Borneo, C Indonesia
174 Mm11 **Sebangau Besar, Sungai** *var.* Sungai Sebangan. ⚘ Borneo, N Indonesia
174 I8 **Sebanglea, Pulau** *island* W Indonesia
Sebaste/Sebastia *see* Sivas
25 Y12 **Sebastian** Florida, SE USA *27.55N 80.31W*
42 C5 **Sebastián Vizcaíno, Bahía** *bay* NW Mexico
21 R6 **Sebasticook Lake** ⊚ Maine, NE USA
36 M7 **Sebastopol** California, W USA *38.22N 122.50W*
Sebastopol *see* Sevastopol'
175 Oo4 **Sebatik, Pulau** *island* N Indonesia
21 R5 **Sebec Lake** ⊚ Maine, NE USA
78 K12 **Sébékoro** Kayes, W Mali *13.00N 9.03W*
Sebenico *see* Šibenik
42 G6 **Seberi, Cerro** ▲ NW Mexico *27.49N 110.18W*
118 H11 **Sebeş** *Ger.* Mühlbach, *Hung.* Szászsebes; *prev.* Sebeşu Săsesc. Alba, W Romania *45.57N 23.34E*
Sebes-Körös *see* Crişul Repede
Sebeşu Săsesc *see* Sebeş
33 R8 **Sebewaing** Michigan, N USA *43.43N 83.27W*
128 F16 **Sebezh** Pskovskaya Oblast', W Russian Federation *56.19N 28.31E*
143 N12 **Şebinkarahisar** Giresun, N Turkey *40.19N 38.25E*
118 F11 **Sebiş** *Hung.* Borossebes. Arad, W Romania *46.21N 22.09E*
Sebkra Azz el Matti *see* Azzel Matti, Sebkha
21 Q4 **Seboomook Lake** ⊚ Maine, NE USA
76 G6 **Sebou** *var.* Sebu. ⚘ N Morocco
22 I6 **Sebree** Kentucky, S USA *37.34N 87.30W*
25 X13 **Sebring** Florida, SE USA *27.30N 81.26W*
Sebta *see* Ceuta
Sebu *see* Sebou
175 Nn11 **Sebuku, Pulau** *island* N Indonesia
175 Oo4 **Sebuku, Teluk** *bay* Borneo, N Indonesia
176 Vv10 **Sebyar** ⚘ Papua, E Indonesia
108 F10 **Secchia** ⚘ N Italy
8 L17 **Sechelt** British Columbia, SW Canada *49.25N 123.37W*
58 C12 **Sechin, Río** ⚘ W Peru
58 A10 **Sechura, Bahía de** *bay* NW Peru
193 A22 **Secretary Island** *island* SW NZ
161 I15 **Secunderābād** *var.* Sikandarabad. Andhra Pradesh, C India *17.30N 78.33E*
59 L17 **Sécure, Río** ⚘ C Bolivia
120 D10 **Seda** Telšiai, NW Lithuania *56.10N 22.04E*
29 T5 **Sedalia** Missouri, C USA *38.42N 93.13W*
105 R3 **Sedan** Ardennes, N France *49.42N 4.55E*
29 P7 **Sedan** Kansas, C USA *37.07N 96.11W*
107 N3 **Sedano** Castilla-León, N Spain *42.43N 3.43W*
106 H10 **Seda, Ribeira de** *stream* C Portugal
193 K15 **Seddon** Marlborough, South Island, NZ *41.41S 174.04E*
193 H15 **Seddonville** West Coast, South Island, NZ *41.34S 171.59E*
149 U7 **Sedeh** Khorāsān, E Iran *33.18N 59.12E*
125 G12 **Sedel'nikovo** Omskaya Oblast', C Russian Federation *56.54N 75.24E*
144 E11 **Sederot** Southern, S Israel *31.31N 34.34E*
67 B23 **Sedge Island** *island* NW Falkland Islands
78 G12 **Sédhiou** SW Senegal *12.39N 15.33W*
9 U16 **Sedley** Saskatchewan, S Canada *50.06N 103.51W*
Sedlez *see* Siedlce
119 Q2 **Sedniv** Chernihivs'ka Oblast', N Ukraine *51.39N 31.34E*
38 L11 **Sedona** Arizona, SW USA *34.52N 111.45W*
Sedunum *see* Sion
120 F12 **Šeduva** Šiauliai, N Lithuania *55.45N 23.46E*
147 Y8 **Seeb** *var.* Muscat Sīb Airport. ✕ (Masqaṭ) NE Oman *23.36N 58.27E*
Seeb *see* As Sīb
110 M7 **Seefeld-in-Tirol** Tirol, W Austria *47.19N 11.16E*
85 E22 **Seeheim Noord** Karas, S Namibia *26.49S 17.50E*
Seeland *see* Sjælland
205 N9 **Seelig, Mount** ▲ Antarctica *81.45S 102.15W*
Seeonee *see* Seoni
168 E6 **Seer** Hovd, W Mongolia *48.18N 92.37E*
104 L5 **Sées** Orne, N France *48.36N 0.11E*
103 J14 **Seesen** Niedersachsen, C Germany *51.54N 10.10E*
Seesker Höhe *see* Szeska Góra
102 J10 **Seevetal** Niedersachsen, N Germany *53.24N 10.01E*
111 V6 **Seewiesen** Steiermark, E Austria *47.37N 15.16E*
142 J13 **Şefaatli** *var.* Kızılkoca. Yozgat, C Turkey *39.31N 34.45E*
155 N3 **Sefid, Darya-ye** *Pash.* Āb-i-Safed. ⚘ N Afghanistan
154 K5 **Sefīd Kūh, Selseleh-ye** *Eng.* Paropamisus Range. ▲ W Afghanistan
76 G6 **Sefrou** N Morocco *33.51N 4.49W*
193 E19 **Sefton, Mount** ▲ South Island, NZ *43.43S 169.58E*
176 U10 **Segaf, Kepulauan** *island group* E Indonesia
175 Oo3 **Segama, Sungai** ⚘ East Malaysia
174 Hh6 **Segamat** Johor, Peninsular Malaysia *2.30N 102.48E*
79 S13 **Ségbana** NE Benin *10.55N 3.42E*
Segestica *see* Sisak
Segesvár *see* Sighişoara
176 Uu9 **Seget** Papua, E Indonesia *1.21S 131.04E*
Segewold *see* Sigulda
128 J9 **Segezha** Respublika Kareliya, NW Russian Federation *63.39N 34.24E*
Seghedin *see* Szeged
Segna *see* Senj
109 I16 **Segni** Lazio, C Italy *41.41N 13.02E*
Segodunum *see* Rodez
107 S9 **Segorbe** País Valenciano, E Spain *39.51N 0.30W*
78 M12 **Ségou** *var.* Segu. Ségou, C Mali *13.25N 6.12W*
78 M12 **Ségou** ◆ *region* SW Mali
56 E8 **Segovia** Antioquia, N Colombia *7.06N 74.42W*
107 N7 **Segovia** Castilla-León, C Spain *40.57N 4.07W*
106 M6 **Segovia** ◆ *province* Castilla-León, N Spain
Segoviao Wangkí *see* Coco, Río
128 J9 **Segozero, Ozero** ⊚ NW Russian Federation
107 U5 **Segre** ⚘ NE Spain
104 J7 **Segré** Maine-et-Loire, NW France *47.40N 0.51W*
Segu *see* Ségou
40 I17 **Seguam Island** *island* Aleutian Islands, Alaska, USA
40 I17 **Seguam Pass** *strait* Aleutian Islands, Alaska, USA
79 Y7 **Séguédine** Agadez, NE Niger *20.12N 13.03E*
78 M15 **Séguéla** W Ivory Coast *8.01N 6.38W*
27 S11 **Seguin** Texas, SW USA *29.34N 97.58W*
40 E17 **Segula Island** *island* Aleutian Islands, Alaska, USA
64 K10 **Segundo, Río** ⚘ C Argentina
107 Q12 **Segura** ⚘ S Spain
107 P13 **Segura, Sierra de** ▲ S Spain
85 G18 **Sehithwa** Ngamiland, N Botswana *20.28S 22.43E*
160 H10 **Sehore** Madhya Pradesh, C India *23.12N 77.07E*
195 O16 **Sehulea** Normanby Island, S PNG *9.55S 151.10E*
155 P15 **Sehwān** Sind, SE Pakistan *26.27N 67.46E*
111 V8 **Seiersberg** Steiermark, SE Austria *47.01N 15.22E*
28 L9 **Seiling** Oklahoma, C USA *36.09N 98.55W*
105 S9 **Seille** ⚘ E France
101 J20 **Seilles** Namur, SE Belgium *50.31N 5.12E*
95 K17 **Seinäjoki** *Swe.* Östermyra. Länsi-Suomi, W Finland *62.45N 22.54E*
10 B12 **Seine** ⚘ Ontario, S Canada
104 M4 **Seine** ⚘ N France
104 K4 **Seine, Baie de la** *bay* N France
Seine, Banc de la *see* Seine Seamount
105 O5 **Seine-et-Marne** ◆ *department* N France
104 L3 **Seine-Maritime** ◆ *department* N France
86 B14 **Seine Plain** *undersea feature* E Atlantic Ocean
86 B15 **Seine Seamount** *var.* Banc de la Seine. *undersea feature* E Atlantic Ocean *33.45N 14.25W*
104 E6 **Sein, Île de** *island* NW France
176 Y12 **Seinma** Papua, E Indonesia *4.10S 138.54E*
Seisbierrum *see* Sexbierum
111 U5 **Seitenstetten Markt** Niederösterreich, C Austria *48.03N 14.41E*
Seiyu *see* Chŏnju
97 H22 **Sejerø** *island* E Denmark
112 P7 **Sejny** Podlaskie, NE Poland *54.09N 23.21E*
174 Ii13 **Sekampung, Way** ⚘ Sumatera, SW Indonesia
83 G20 **Seke** Shinyanga, N Tanzania *3.16S 33.31E*
171 I15 **Seki** Gifu, Honshū, SW Japan *35.25N 136.51E*
167 U12 **Sekibi-sho** *island* China/Japan/Taiwan
172 Pp5 **Sekihoku-tōge** *pass* Hokkaidō, NE Japan *43.40N 143.10E*
Sekondi *see* Sekondi-Takoradi
79 P17 **Sekondi-Takoradi** *var.* Sekondi. S Ghana *4.55N 1.45W*
82 J11 **Sek'ot'a** Amhara, N Ethiopia *12.41N 39.05E*
Seksëuïl *see* Saksaul'skiy
34 I9 **Selah** Washington, NW USA *46.39N 120.31W*
174 Gg5 **Selangor** *var.* Negeri Selangor Darul Ehsan. ◆ *state* Peninsular Malaysia
Selânik *see* Thessaloníki
174 Hh7 **Selapanjang** Pulau Rantau, W Indonesia *1.00N 102.44E*
178 Ii10 **Selaphum** Roi Et, E Thailand *16.00N 103.54E*
176 Uu16 **Selaru, Pulau** *island* Kepulauan Tanimbar, E Indonesia
176 Vv11 **Selassi** Papua, E Indonesia *3.16S 132.50E*
173 G3 **Selatan, Selat** *strait* Peninsular Malaysia
41 N8 **Selawik** Alaska, USA *66.36N 160.00W*
41 N8 **Selawik Lake** ⊚ Alaska, USA
175 Pp13 **Selayar, Selat** *strait* Sulawesi, C Indonesia
97 C14 **Selbjørnsfjorden** *fjord* S Norway
96 H8 **Selbusjøen** ⊚ S Norway
99 M17 **Selby** N England, UK *53.49N 1.06W*
31 N8 **Selby** South Dakota, N USA *45.30N 100.01W*
23 Z4 **Selbyville** Delaware, NE USA *38.28N 75.12W*
142 B15 **Selçuk** *var.* Akıncılar. İzmir, SW Turkey *37.55N 27.21E*
41 Q13 **Seldovia** Alaska, USA *59.26N 151.42W*
109 M18 **Sele** *anc.* Silarus. ⚘ S Italy
85 J19 **Selebi-Phikwe** Central, E Botswana *21.58S 27.47E*
44 B5 **Selegua, Río** ⚘ W Guatemala
133 X7 **Selemdzha** ⚘ SE Russian Federation
133 U7 **Selenga** *Mong.* Selenge Mörön. ⚘ Mongolia/Russian Federation
168 K6 **Selenge** Bulgan, N Mongolia *49.34N 104.18E*
168 J6 **Selenge** Hövsgöl, N Mongolia *49.25N 101.30E*
81 I19 **Selenge** Bandundu, W Dem. Rep. Congo *1.58S 18.10E*
168 L6 **Selenge** ◆ *province* N Mongolia
Selenge Mörön *see* Selenga
126 Jj16 **Selenginsk** Respublika Buryatiya, S Russian Federation *52.00N 106.40E*
Selenica *see* Selenicë
115 K22 **Selenicë** *var.* Selenica. Vlorë, SW Albania *40.32N 19.38E*
126 M7 **Selennyakh** ⚘ NE Russian Federation
102 J8 **Selenter See** ⊚ N Germany
Sele Sound *see* Soela Väin
105 U6 **Sélestat** *Ger.* Schlettstadt. Bas-Rhin, NE France *48.16N 7.28E*
Selety *see* Sileti
Seleucia *see* Silifke
94 I4 **Selfoss** Sudhurland, SW Iceland *63.56N 20.59W*
30 M7 **Selfridge** North Dakota, N USA *46.01N 100.52W*
78 I15 **Seli** ⚘ N Sierra Leone
78 I11 **Sélibabi** *var.* Sélibaby. Guidimaka, S Mauritania *15.13N 12.10W*
Sélibaby *see* Sélibabi
Selidovka/Selidovo *see* Selydove
128 I15 **Seliger, Ozero** ⊚ W Russian Federation
38 J11 **Seligman** Arizona, SW USA *35.20N 112.56W*
29 S8 **Seligman** Missouri, C USA *36.31N 93.56W*
82 E6 **Selima Oasis** *oasis* N Sudan *21.22N 29.19E*
78 L13 **Sélingué, Lac de** ⊠ S Mali
Selinoús *see* Kréstena
20 G14 **Selinsgrove** Pennsylvania, NE USA *40.47N 76.51W*
Selishche *see* Syelishcha
128 I16 **Selizharovo** Tverskaya Oblast', W Russian Federation *56.50N 33.24E*
96 C10 **Selje** Sogn og Fjordane, S Norway *62.02N 5.22E*
9 X16 **Selkirk** Manitoba, S Canada *50.10N 96.52W*
98 K13 **Selkirk** SE Scotland, UK *55.35N 2.48W*
98 K13 **Selkirk** *cultural region* SE Scotland, UK
9 O16 **Selkirk Mountains** ▲ British Columbia, SW Canada
200 Oo12 **Selkirk Rise** *undersea feature* SE Pacific Ocean
117 F21 **Sellasía** Pelopónnisos, S Greece *37.14N 22.24E*
46 M9 **Selle, Pic de la** *var.* La Selle. ▲ SE Haiti *18.18N 71.55W*
104 M8 **Selles-sur-Cher** Loir-et-Cher, C France *47.16N 1.31E*
38 K16 **Sells** Arizona, SW USA *31.54N 111.52W*
Sellye *see* Sal'a
25 P5 **Selma** Alabama, S USA *32.24N 87.01W*
37 Q11 **Selma** California, W USA *36.33N 119.37W*
22 G10 **Selmer** Tennessee, S USA *35.10N 88.35W*
181 N17 **Sel, Pointe au** *headland* W Réunion
Selseleh-ye Kūh-e Vākhān *see* Nicholas Range
131 S2 **Selty** Udmurtskaya Respublika, NW Russian Federation *57.19N 52.09E*
Selukwe *see* Shurugwi
64 L9 **Selva** Santiago del Estero, N Argentina *29.46S 62.01W*
9 T9 **Selwyn Lake** ⊚ Northwest Territories/Saskatchewan, C Canada
8 K6 **Selwyn Mountains** ▲ Yukon Territory, NW Canada
189 T6 **Selwyn Range** ▲ Queensland, C Australia
119 W8 **Selydove** *var.* Selidovka, *Rus.* Selidovo. Donets'ka Oblast', SE Ukraine *48.06N 37.16E*
Selzaete *see* Zelzate
Seman *see* Semanit, Lumi i
174 Ii13 **Semangka, Teluk** *bay* Sumatera, SW Indonesia
174 I13 **Semangka, Way** ⚘ Sumatera, SW Indonesia
115 D22 **Semanit, Lumi i** *var.* Seman. ⚘ W Albania
174 Kk14 **Semarang** *var.* Samarang. Jawa, C Indonesia *6.58S 110.28E*
174 Kk6 **Sematan** Sarawak, East Malaysia *1.49N 109.43E*
175 Qq17 **Semau, Pulau** *island* S Indonesia
175 Nn8 **Semayang, Danau** ⊚ Borneo, N Indonesia
175 O4 **Sembakung, Sungai** ⚘ Borneo, N Indonesia
81 G17 **Sembé** La Sangha, NW Congo *1.37N 14.34E*
Semberong *see* Semberong, Sungai
174 Hh6 **Semberong, Sungai** *var.* Semberong. ⚘ Peninsular Malaysia
174 M10 **Sembulu, Danau** ⊚ Borneo, N Indonesia
Semendria *see* Smederevo
119 R1 **Semenivka** Chernihivs'ka Oblast', N Ukraine *52.10N 32.37E*
119 S6 **Semenivka** *Rus.* Semenovka. Poltavs'ka Oblast', NE Ukraine *49.36N 33.11E*
131 O3 **Semenov** Nizhegorodskaya Oblast', W Russian Federation *56.47N 44.27E*
Semenovka *see* Semenivka
174 M16 **Semeru, Gunung** *var.* Mahameru. ▲ Jawa, S Indonesia *8.01S 112.53E*
Semey *see* Semipalatinsk
Semezhevo *see* Syemyezhava
130 L7 **Semiluki** Voronezhskaya Oblast', W Russian Federation *51.46N 39.00E*
35 W16 **Seminoe Reservoir** ⊠ Wyoming, C USA
29 O11 **Seminole** Oklahoma, C USA *35.13N 96.40W*
26 M6 **Seminole** Texas, SW USA *32.43N 102.39W*
25 S8 **Seminole, Lake** ⊠ Florida/Georgia, SE USA
Semiozernoye *see* Auliyekol'
151 V9 **Semipalatinsk** *Kaz.* Semey. Vostochnyy Kazakhstan, E Kazakhstan *50.25N 80.16E*
149 O9 **Semīrom** *var.* Samirum. Eşfahān, C Iran *31.19N 51.49E*
40 F17 **Semisopochnoi Island** *island* Aleutian Islands, Alaska, USA
174 Ll7 **Semitau** Borneo, C Indonesia *0.30N 111.58E*
83 E18 **Semliki** ⚘ Uganda/Dem. Rep. Congo
149 P5 **Semnān** *var.* Samnān. Semnān, N Iran *35.37N 53.21E*
149 Q5 **Semnān** *off.* Ostān-e Semnān. ◆ *province* N Iran
101 K24 **Semois** ⚘ SE Belgium
110 E8 **Sempacher See** ⊚ C Switzerland

◆ Country ● Country Capital ◇ Dependent Territory ○ Dependent Territory Capital ◆ Administrative Region ✕ International Airport ▲ Mountain ▲ Mountain Range ⛰ Volcano ⚘ River ⊚ Lake ⊠ Reservoir

SENA – SHASHE

Sena see Vila de Sena
32 L12 Senachwine Lake ◎ Illinois, N USA
61 O14 Senador Pompeu Ceará, E Brazil 5.30S 39.25W
Sena Gallica see Senigallia
61 C15 Sena Madureira Acre, W Brazil 9.04S 68.40W
161 L25 Senanayake Samudra ◎ E Sri Lanka
85 G15 Senanga Western, SW Zambia 16.09S 23.16E
29 Y9 Senath Missouri, C USA 36.07N 90.09W
24 L2 Senatobia Mississippi, S USA 34.37N 89.58W
170 C15 Sendai Kagoshima, Kyūshū, SW Japan 31.48N 130.16E
171 M13 Sendai Miyagi, Honshū, C Japan 38.16N 140.52E
170 Bb15 Sendai-gawa ≈ Kyūshū, SW Japan
171 M14 Sendai-wan bay E Japan
103 J23 Senden Bayern, S Germany 48.18N 10.04E
160 F11 Sendhwa Madhya Pradesh, C India 21.38N 75.04E
113 H21 Senec Ger. Wartberg, Hung. Szenc; prev. Szempcz. Bratislavský Kraj, W Slovakia 48.14N 17.24E
29 P3 Seneca Kansas, C USA 39.47N 96.04W
29 R8 Seneca Missouri, C USA 36.50N 94.36W
34 K13 Seneca Oregon, NW USA 44.06N 118.57W
23 O11 Seneca South Carolina, SE USA 34.41N 82.57W
20 G11 Seneca Lake ◎ New York, NE USA
33 U13 Senecaville Lake ⊠ Ohio, N USA
78 G11 Senegal off. Republic of Senegal, Fr. Sénégal. ◆ republic W Africa
78 H9 Senegal Fr. Sénégal. ≈ W Africa
33 O4 Seney Marsh wetland Michigan, N USA
103 P14 Senftenberg Brandenburg, E Germany 51.31N 14.01E
84 L11 Senga Hill Northern, NE Zambia 9.26S 31.12E
164 G13 Sênggê Zangbo ≈ W China
176 Z11 Senggi Papua, E Indonesia 3.26S 140.46E
131 R5 Sengiley Ul'yanovskaya Oblast', W Russian Federation 53.54N 48.51E
65 I19 Senguerr, Río ≈ S Argentina
85 J16 Sengwa ≈ C Zimbabwe
Senia see Senj
113 H19 Senica Ger. Senitz, Hung. Szenice. Trnavský Kraj, W Slovakia 48.40N 17.22E
Seniça see Sjenica
108 J11 Senigallia anc. Sena Gallica. Marche, C Italy 43.43N 13.13E
142 F15 Senirkent Isparta, SW Turkey 38.07N 30.34E
Senitz see Senica
114 C10 Senj Ger. Zengg, It. Segna; anc. Senia. Lika-Senj, NW Croatia 44.58N 14.55E
169 O10 Senj Dornogovĭ, SE Mongolia 44.34N 110.58E
94 H9 Senja prev. Senjen. island N Norway
Senjen see Senja
167 U12 Senkaku-shotō island group SW Japan
143 R12 Şenkaya Erzurum, NE Turkey 40.33N 42.16E
85 I16 Senkobo Southern, S Zambia 17.34S 25.57E
105 O4 Senlis Oise, N France 49.13N 2.33E
178 K13 Senmonorom Môndól Kiri, E Cambodia 12.27N 107.12E
82 G10 Sennar var. Sannār. Sinnar, C Sudan 13.31N 33.37E
Senno see Syanno
Senones see Sens
111 W11 Senovo E Slovenia 46.01N 15.24E
105 P6 Sens anc. Agendicum, Senones. Yonne, C France 48.12N 3.16E
Sensburg see Mrągowo
178 J12 Sên, Stœng ≈ C Cambodia
44 F7 Sensuntepeque Cabañas, NE El Salvador 13.52N 88.37W
114 L8 Senta Hung. Zenta. Serbia, N Serbia and Montenegro (Yugoslavia) 45.57N 20.04E
Šent Andraž see Sankt Andrä
176 Z10 Sentani, Danau ◎ Papua, E Indonesia
30 J5 Sentinel Butte ▲ North Dakota, N USA 46.52N 103.50W
8 M13 Sentinel Peak ▲ British Columbia, W Canada 54.51N 122.02W
61 N16 Sento Sé Bahia, E Brazil 9.51S 41.56W
Šent Peter see Pivka
Šent Vid see Sankt Veit an der Glan
194 E10 Senu ≈ NW PNG
Seo de Urgel see La Seu d'Urgell
160 I7 Seondha Madhya Pradesh, C India 26.09N 78.46E
160 J11 Seoni prev. Seonee. Madhya Pradesh, C India 22.07N 79.33E
Seoul see Sŏul
192 I13 Separation Point headland South Island, NZ 40.46S 172.58E
175 O7 Sepasu Borneo, N Indonesia 0.44N 117.38E
194 F10 Sepik ≈ Indonesia/PNG
Sepone see Muang Xépôn
112 M7 Sępopol Ger. Schippenbeil. Warmińsko-Mazurskie, NE Poland, 54.16N 21.09E
118 F10 Şepreuş Hung. Seprős. Arad, W Romania 46.34N 21.44E
Seprős see Şepreuş
Şepşi-Sângeorz/Sepsiszentgyörgy see Sfântu Gheorghe
13 W4 Sept-Îles Québec, SE Canada 50.11N 66.18W
107 N6 Sepúlveda Castilla-León, N Spain 41.18N 3.45W
174 Ii12 Seputih, Way ≈ Sumatera, SW Indonesia
106 K8 Sequeros Castilla-León, N Spain 40.31N 6.04W
106 L5 Sequillo ≈ NW Spain
34 G7 Sequim Washington, NW USA 48.04N 123.06W
37 S11 Sequoia National Park national park California, W USA
143 Q14 Şerafettin Dağları ▲ E Turkey
131 N10 Serafimovich Volgogradskaya Oblast', SW Russian Federation 49.34N 42.43E
175 Rr6 Serai Sulawesi, N Indonesia 1.45N 124.58E
101 K19 Seraing Liège, E Belgium 50.37N 5.31E
Sêraitang see Baima
Serajgonj see Shirajganj Ghat
Serakhs see Sarahs
176 X10 Serami Papua, E Indonesia 2.11S 136.46E
Seram, Laut see Ceram Sea
Serampore/Serampur see Shrīrāmpur
175 Tt11 Seram, Pulau var. Serang, Eng. Ceram. island Maluku, E Indonesia
174 J14 Serang Jawa, C Indonesia 6.07S 106.09E
Serang see Seram, Pulau
174 Kk6 Serasan, Pulau island Kepulauan Natuna, W Indonesia
174 Kk6 Serasan, Selat strait Indonesia/Malaysia
114 M12 Serbia Ger. Serbien, Serb. Srbija. ◆ republic Serbia and Montenegro (Yugoslavia)
114 M13 Serbia and Montenegro (Yugoslavia) off. Federal Republic of Serbia and Montenegro, Prev. Yugoslavia, SCr. Jugoslavija, Savezna Republika Jugoslavija. ◆ federal republic SE Europe
Serbien see Serbia
Sercq see Sark
152 D12 Serdar prev. Rus. Gyzylarbat, Kizyl-Arvat. Balkan Welaýaty, W Turkmenistan 39.01N 56.14E
Serdica see Sofiya
131 O7 Serdobsk Penzenskaya Oblast', W Russian Federation 52.30N 44.16E
151 X9 Serebryansk Vostochnyy Kazakhstan, E Kazakhstan 49.43N 83.16E
126 Ll13 Serebryanyy Bor Respublika Sakha (Yakutiya), NE Russian Federation 56.40N 124.46E
113 H20 Sered' Hung. Szered. Trnavský Kraj, SW Slovakia 48.17N 17.44E
119 S1 Seredyna-Buda Sums'ka Oblast', NE Ukraine 52.09N 34.00E
120 E13 Seredžius Tauragė, C Lithuania 55.04N 23.24E
142 I14 Şereflikoçhisar Ankara, C Turkey 38.55N 33.31E
108 D7 Seregno Lombardia, N Italy 45.39N 9.12E
105 P7 Serein ≈ C France
174 H5 Seremban Negeri Sembilan, Peninsular Malaysia 2.42N 101.54E
83 H20 Serengeti Plain plain N Tanzania
84 K13 Serenje Central, E Zambia 13.12S 30.15E
Seres see Sérres
118 J5 Seret ≈ W Ukraine
Seret/Sereth see Siret
117 I21 Serfopoúla island Kykládes, Greece, Aegean Sea
131 P4 Sergach Nizhegorodskaya Oblast', W Russian Federation 55.31N 45.29E
31 S13 Sergeant Bluff Iowa, C USA 42.24N 96.19W
169 P7 Sergelen Dornod, NE Mongolia 48.31N 114.01E
169 O9 Sergelen Sühbaatar, E Mongolia 46.12N 111.48E
173 F4 Sergeulangit, Pegunungan ▲ Sumatera, NW Indonesia
126 J4 Sergeya Kirova, Ostrova island N Russian Federation
Sergeyevichi see Syarhyeyevichy
151 O7 Sergeyevka Severnyy Kazakhstan, N Kazakhstan 53.51N 67.17E
Sergiopol see Ayagoz
61 P16 Sergipe off. Estado de Sergipe. ◆ state E Brazil
130 L3 Sergiyev Posad Moskovskaya Oblast', W Russian Federation 56.21N 38.10E
128 K5 Sergozero, Ozero ◎ NW Russian Federation
152 J17 Serhetabat prev. Rus. Gushgy, Kushka. Mary Welaýaty, S Turkmenistan 35.18N 62.17E
174 L7 Serian Sarawak, East Malaysia 1.10N 110.34E
174 J13 Seribu, Kepulauan island group S Indonesia
117 I21 Sérifos anc. Seriphos. island Kykládes, Greece, Aegean Sea
117 I21 Sérifou, Stenó strait SE Greece
142 F16 Serik Antalya, SW Turkey 36.55N 31.06E
108 E7 Serio ≈ N Italy
Seriphos see Sérifos
Serir Tibesti see Sarīr Tibistī
Sêrkog see Sêrtar
131 S5 Sernovodsk Samarskaya Oblast', W Russian Federation 53.56N 51.16E
131 R2 Sernur Respublika Mariy El, W Russian Federation 56.55N 49.09E
112 M11 Serock Mazowieckie, C Poland 52.30N 21.03E
63 B18 Serodino Santa Fe, C Argentina 32.33S 60.52W
Seroei see Serui
107 P14 Serón Andalucía, S Spain 37.20N 2.28W
100 I7 Serooskerke Zeeland, SW Netherlands 51.42N 3.52E
107 T6 Seròs Cataluña, NE Spain 41.27N 0.24E
125 F10 Serov Sverdlovskaya Oblast', C Russian Federation 59.42N 60.31E
85 I19 Serowe Central, SE Botswana 22.25S 26.43E
106 H13 Serpa Beja, S Portugal 37.55N 7.36W
Serpa Pinto see Menongue
190 A4 Serpentine Lakes salt lake South Australia
47 T15 Serpent's Mouth, The Sp. Boca de la Serpiente. strait Trinidad and Tobago/Venezuela
Serpiente, Boca de la see Serpent's Mouth, The
130 K4 Serpukhov Moskovskaya Oblast', W Russian Federation 54.54N 37.25E
62 K13 Serra do Mar ▲ S Brazil
Sérrai see Sérres
109 N22 Serra San Bruno Calabria, SW Italy 38.32N 16.18E
105 S14 Serres Hautes-Alpes, SE France 44.26N 5.42E
116 H13 Sérres var. Seres; prev. Sérrai. Kentrikí Makedonía, NE Greece 41.04N 23.34E
64 J9 Serrezuela Córdoba, C Argentina 30.37S 65.25W
61 O16 Serrinha Bahia, E Brazil 11.37S 38.55W
61 M19 Serro var. Sêrro. Minas Gerais, NE Brazil 18.37S 43.22W
Sêrro see Serro
Sert see Siirt
Sertá see Sertã
106 H9 Sertã var. Sertá. Castelo Branco, C Portugal 39.48N 8.04W
62 L8 Sertãozinho São Paulo, S Brazil 21.04S 47.55W
166 F7 Sêrtar var. Sêrkog. Sichuan, C China 32.18N 100.18E
176 X10 Serui prev. Seroei. Papua, E Indonesia 1.52S 136.15E
85 J19 Serule Central, E Botswana 21.58S 27.18E
174 Ll10 Seruyan, Sungai var. Sungai Pembuang. ≈ Borneo, N Indonesia
117 E14 Sérvia Dytikí Makedonía, N Greece 40.12N 22.01E
166 E7 Sêrxü var. Jugar. Sichuan, C China 32.54N 98.06E
126 Mm15 Seryshevo Amurskaya Oblast', SE Russian Federation 51.03N 128.16E
Sesana see Sežana
175 Nn5 Sesayap, Sungai ≈ Borneo, N Indonesia
Sesdlets see Siedlce
81 N17 Sese Orientale, N Dem. Rep. Congo 2.13N 25.52E
83 F18 Sese Islands island group S Uganda
175 T9 Sesepe Pulau Obi, E Indonesia 1.26S 127.55E
85 H16 Sesheke var. Sesheko. Western, SE Zambia 17.27S 24.19E
Sesheko see Sesheke
108 C8 Sesia anc. Sessites. ≈ NW Italy
106 F11 Sesimbra Setúbal, S Portugal 38.25N 9.06W
117 N22 Seskliό island Dodekánisos, Greece, Aegean Sea
32 L16 Sesser Illinois, N USA 38.05N 89.03W
Sessites see Sesia
108 G11 Sesto Fiorentino Toscana, C Italy 43.49N 11.12E
108 E7 Sesto San Giovanni Lombardia, N Italy 45.31N 9.13E
108 A8 Sestriere Piemonte, NE Italy 45.00N 6.54E
108 D10 Sestri Levante Liguria, NW Italy 44.16N 9.22E
109 C20 Sestu Sardegna, Italy, C Mediterranean Sea 39.15N 9.06E
114 E8 Sesvete Zagreb, N Croatia 45.50N 16.03E
120 G12 Šeta Kaunas, C Lithuania 55.17N 24.16E
Setabis see Xàtiva
172 N5 Setana Hokkaidō, NE Japan 42.27N 139.52E
105 Q16 Sète prev. Cette. Hérault, S France 43.24N 3.42E
60 J11 Sete Ilhas Amapá, NE Brazil 1.06N 52.06W
61 L20 Sete Lagoas Minas Gerais, NE Brazil 19.28S 44.15W
62 G10 Sete Quedas, Ilha das island S Brazil
94 I10 Setermoen Troms, N Norway 68.51N 18.19E
97 E17 Setesdal valley S Norway
45 W16 Setetule, Cerro ▲ SE Panama 7.51N 77.37W
23 Q5 Seth West Virginia, NE USA 38.06N 81.40W
Setia see Sezze
76 K5 Sétif var. Stif. N Algeria 36.10N 5.24E
171 I15 Seto Aichi, Honshū, SW Japan 35.13N 137.03E
170 F14 Seto-naikai Eng. Inland Sea. sea S Japan
172 Qq13 Setouchi var. Setoushi. Kagoshima, Amami-Ō-shima, SW Japan 44.19N 142.58E
76 F6 Settat W Morocco 33.03N 7.37W
81 D20 Setté Cama Ogooué-Maritime, SW Gabon 2.31S 9.46E
9 W13 Setting Lake ◎ Manitoba, C Canada
99 L16 Settle N England, UK 54.04N 2.17W
201 Y12 Settlement E Wake Island 19.16N 166.37E
106 F11 Setúbal Eng. Saint Ubes, Saint Yves. Setúbal, W Portugal 38.31N 8.54W
106 F11 Setúbal ◆ district S Portugal
106 F12 Setúbal, Baía de bay W Portugal
Setul see Satun
10 B10 Seul, Lac ◎ Ontario, S Canada
105 R8 Seurre Côte d'Or, C France 47.00N 5.09E
143 U11 Sevan C Armenia 40.31N 44.55E
143 V12 Sevana Lich Eng. Lake Sevan, Rus. Ozero Sevan. ◎ E Armenia
Sevan, Lake/Sevan, Ozero see Sevana Lich
79 N11 Sévaré Mopti, C Mali 14.30N 4.08W
119 S14 Sevastopol' Eng. Sebastopol. Respublika Krym, S Ukraine 44.36N 33.33E
27 R14 Seven Sisters Texas, SW USA 27.57N 98.34W
8 K13 Seven Sisters Peaks ▲ British Columbia, SW Canada 54.57N 128.10W
101 M15 Sevenum Limburg, SE Netherlands 51.25N 6.01E
105 P14 Séverac-le-Château Aveyron, S France 44.18N 3.03E
12 H13 Severn ≈ Ontario, S Canada
99 L21 Severn Wel. Hafren. ≈ England/Wales, UK
129 O11 Severnaya Dvina var. Northern Dvina. ≈ NW Russian Federation
131 N16 Severnaya Osetiya-Alaniya, Respublika Eng. North Ossetia; prev. Respublika Severnaya Osetiya, Severo-Osetinskaya SSR. ◆ autonomous republic SW Russian Federation
Severnaya Osetiya, Respublika see Severnaya Osetiya-Alaniya, Respublika
125 F9 Severnaya Sos'va ≈ N Russian Federation
126 J2 Severnaya Zemlya var. Nicholas II Land. island group N Russian Federation
131 T5 Severnoye Orenburgskaya Oblast', W Russian Federation 54.03N 52.31E
37 S3 Severn Troughs Range ▲ Nevada, W USA
129 W3 Severnyy Respublika Komi, NW Russian Federation 67.37N 64.12E
150 I13 Severnyy Chink Ustyurta ▲ W Kazakhstan
129 Q13 Severnyye Uvaly var. Northern Ural Hills. hill range NW Russian Federation
151 O6 Severnyy Kazakhstan off. Severo-Kazakhstanskaya Oblast', var. North Kazakhstan, Kaz. Soltüstik Qazaqstan Oblysy. ◆ province N Kazakhstan
129 V9 Severnyy Ural ▲ NW Russian Federation
Severo-Alichurskiy Khrebet see Alichuri Shimolí, Qatorkŭhi
126 K14 Severobaykal'sk Respublika Buryatiya, S Russian Federation 55.39N 109.17E
Severodonetsk see Syeverodonets'k
128 M8 Severodvinsk prev. Molotov, Sudostroy. Arkhangel'skaya Oblast', NW Russian Federation 64.31N 39.50E
Severo-Kazakhstanskaya Oblast' see Severnyy Kazakhstan
127 Pp13 Severo-Kuril'sk Sakhalinskaya Oblast', SE Russian Federation 50.38N 155.57E
128 J3 Severomorsk Murmanskaya Oblast', NW Russian Federation 69.00N 33.15E
Severo-Osetinskaya SSR see Severnaya Osetiya-Alaniya, Respublika
126 J6 Severo-Sibirskaya Nizmennost' var. North Siberian Plain, Eng. North Siberian Lowland. lowlands N Russian Federation
125 Ee10 Severoural'sk Sverdlovskaya Oblast', C Russian Federation 60.09N 59.58E
126 I12 Severo-Yeniseyskiy Krasnoyarskiy Kray, C Russian Federation 60.29N 93.13E
126 H13 Seversk Tomskaya Oblast', C Russian Federation 53.37N 84.47E
130 M11 Severskiy Donets Ukr. Sivers'kyy Donets'. ≈ Russian Federation/Ukraine see also Sivers'kyy Donets'
94 M9 Sevettijärvi Lappi, N Finland 69.31N 28.40E
38 M5 Sevier Bridge Reservoir ⊠ Utah, W USA
38 J4 Sevier Desert plain Utah, W USA
38 J5 Sevier Lake ◎ Utah, W USA
23 N9 Sevierville Tennessee, S USA 35.52N 83.33W
106 J14 Sevilla Eng. Seville; anc. Hispalis. Andalucía, SW Spain 37.24N 5.58W
106 J13 Sevilla ◆ province Andalucía, SW Spain
Sevilla de Niefang see Niefang
45 O16 Sevilla, Isla island SW Panama
Seville see Sevilla
116 J9 Sevlievo Gabrovo, N Bulgaria 43.01N 25.07E
Sevluš/Sevlyush see Vynohradiv
111 V11 Sevnica Ger. Lichtenwald. E Slovenia 46.00N 15.20E
130 I7 Sevsk Bryanskaya Oblast', W Russian Federation 52.03N 34.31E
78 J15 Sewa ≈ E Sierra Leone
41 R12 Seward Alaska, USA 60.06N 149.26W
31 R15 Seward Nebraska, C USA 40.52N 97.06W
8 G8 Seward Glacier glacier Yukon Territory, W Canada
207 Q3 Seward Peninsula peninsula Alaska, USA
Seward's Folly see Alaska
64 H12 Sewell Libertador, C Chile 34.03S 70.16W
100 K5 Sexbierum Fris. Seisbierrum. Friesland, N Netherlands 53.13N 5.28E
9 O13 Sexsmith Alberta, W Canada 55.18N 118.45W
43 W13 Seybaplaya Campeche, SE Mexico 19.39N 90.36W
181 N6 Seychelles off. Republic of Seychelles. ◆ republic W Indian Ocean
69 Z9 Seychelles island group NE Seychelles
181 N6 Seychelles Bank var. Le Banc des Seychelles. undersea feature W Indian Ocean
Seychelles, Le Banc des see Seychelles Bank
180 H17 Seychellois, Morne ▲ Mahé, NE Seychelles
94 L2 Seydhisfjördhur Austurland, E Iceland 65.15N 14.00W
152 J12 Seýdi Rus. Seydi; prev. Neftezavodsk. Lebap Welaýaty, E Turkmenistan 39.30N 62.52E
142 G16 Seydişehir Konya, SW Turkey 37.25N 31.51E
142 J13 Seyfe Gölü ◎ C Turkey
Seyhan see Adana
142 K16 Seyhan Barajı ⊠ S Turkey
142 K17 Seyhan Nehri ≈ S Turkey
142 F13 Seyitgazi Eskişehir, W Turkey 39.27N 30.42E
130 J7 Seym ≈ W Russian Federation
119 S3 Seym ≈ N Ukraine
127 O9 Seymchan Magadanskaya Oblast', E Russian Federation 62.54N 152.27E
116 N12 Seymen Tekirdağ, NW Turkey 41.06N 27.56E
191 O11 Seymour Victoria, SE Australia 37.01S 145.10E
85 I25 Seymour Eastern Cape, S South Africa 32.31S 26.48E
31 W16 Seymour Iowa, C USA 40.40N 93.07W
29 U7 Seymour Missouri, C USA 37.09N 92.46W
27 Q5 Seymour Texas, SW USA 33.35N 99.15W
116 M12 Şeytan Deresi ≈ NW Turkey
111 S12 Sežana It. Sesana. SW Slovenia 45.42N 13.52E
105 P5 Sézanne Marne, N France 48.43N 3.41E
109 I16 Sezze anc. Setia. Lazio, C Italy 41.28N 13.04E
117 H25 Sfákia Kríti, Greece, E Mediterranean Sea 35.12N 24.05E
117 D21 Sfaktiría island S Greece
118 J11 Sfântu Gheorghe Ger. Sankt-Georgen, Hung. Sepsiszentgyőrgy; prev. Şepşi-Sângeorz, Sfîntu Gheorghe. Covasna, C Romania 45.52N 25.49E
119 N13 Sfântu Gheorghe, Braţul var. Gheorghe Braţul. ≈ E Romania
77 N6 Sfax Ar. Şafāqis. E Tunisia 34.45N 10.45E
77 N6 Sfax ✕ E Tunisia 34.43N 10.37E
Sfîntu Gheorghe see Sfântu Gheorghe
100 H13 's-Gravendeel Zuid-Holland, SW Netherlands 51.48N 4.36E
100 F11 's-Gravenhage var. Den Haag, Eng. The Hague, Fr. La Haye. ● (Netherlands-seat of government) Zuid-Holland, W Netherlands 52.07N 4.16E
100 G12 's-Gravenzande Zuid-Holland, W Netherlands 52.00N 4.10E
Shaan/Shaanxi Sheng see Shaanxi
165 X11 Shaanxi var. Shaan, Shaanxi Sheng, Shan-hsi, Shenshi, Shensi. ◆ province C China
Shaartuz see Shahrtuz
Shabani see Zvishavane
83 N17 Shabeellaha Dhexe off. Gobolka Shabeellaha Dhexe. ◆ region E Somalia
83 L17 Shabeellaha Hoose off. Gobolka Shabeellaha Hoose. ◆ region S Somalia
Shabeelle, Webi see Shebeli
116 O7 Shabla Dobrich, NE Bulgaria 43.33N 28.31E
116 O7 Shabla, Nos headland NE Bulgaria 43.30N 28.36E
11 N9 Shabogama Lake ◎ Newfoundland and Labrador, E Canada
81 N20 Shabunda Sud Kivu, E Dem. Rep. Congo 2.42S 27.19E
147 Q15 Shabwah C Yemen 15.09N 46.46E
164 F8 Shache var. Yarkant. Xinjiang Uygur Zizhiqu, NW China 38.27N 77.16E
Shacheng see Huailai
205 R12 Shackleton Coast physical region Antarctica
205 Z10 Shackleton Ice Shelf ice shelf Antarctica
Shaddādī see Ash Shadādah
30 K7 Shadehill Reservoir ⊠ South Dakota, N USA
125 Ee12 Shadrinsk Kurganskaya Oblast', C Russian Federation 56.08N 63.18E
33 O12 Shafer, Lake ⊠ Indiana, N USA
37 R13 Shafter California, W USA 35.27N 119.15W
26 J11 Shafter Texas, SW USA 29.49N 104.18W
99 L23 Shaftesbury S England, UK 51.01N 2.12W
193 F22 Shag ≈ South Island, NZ
151 V9 Shagan ≈ E Kazakhstan
41 O11 Shageluk Alaska, USA 62.40N 159.33W
126 I16 Shagonar Respublika Tyva, S Russian Federation 51.31N 93.06E
193 F22 Shag Point headland South Island, NZ 45.28S 170.50E
150 J12 Shagyray, Plato plain SW Kazakhstan
Shāhābād see Eslāmābād
174 H5 Shah Alam Selangor, Peninsular Malaysia 3.01N 101.31E
119 O12 Shahany, Ozero ◎ SW Ukraine
144 H9 Shahbā' anc. Philippopolis. As Suwaydā', S Syria 32.49N 36.37E
Shahbān see Ad Dayr
155 P17 Shāhbandar Sind, SE Pakistan 23.59N 67.54E
155 P13 Shāhdād Kot Sind, SW Pakistan 27.49N 67.49E
149 T10 Shāhdād, Namakzār-e salt pan E Iran
155 Q15 Shāhdādpur Sind, SE Pakistan 25.55N 68.40E
160 K10 Shahdol Madhya Pradesh, C India 23.19N 81.25E
167 N7 Sha He ≈ C China
Shahepu see Linze
159 N13 Shāhganj Uttar Pradesh, N India 26.03N 82.40E
158 C11 Shāhgarh Rājasthān, NW India 27.07N 69.55E
Sha Hi see Orūmīyeh, Daryācheh-ye, Iran
Shāhī see Qā'emshahr, Māzandarān, Iran
145 Q6 Shāhimah var. Shahma. C Iraq 34.21N 42.19E
Shahjahanabad see Delhi
158 L11 Shāhjahānpur Uttar Pradesh, N India 27.52N 79.55E
Shahma see Shāhimah
155 U7 Shāhpur Punjab, E Pakistan 32.15N 72.31E
Shāhpur see Shāhpur Chākar
158 G13 Shāhpura Rājasthān, N India 25.37N 75.01E
155 Q15 Shāhpur Chākar var. Shāhpur. Sind, SE Pakistan 26.09N 68.40E
154 M5 Shahrak Ghowr, C Afghanistan 34.09N 64.16E
149 Q11 Shahr-e Bābak Kermān, C Iran 30.07N 55.04E
149 N8 Shahr-e Kord var. Shahr Kord. Chahār Maḩall va Bakhtīārī, C Iran 32.19N 50.52E
149 O9 Shahreẓā var. Qomisheh, Qumisheh, Shahriza; prev. Qomsheh. Eşfahān, C Iran 32.01N 51.51E
153 S10 Shahrikhon Rus. Shakhrikhan. Andijon Viloyati, E Uzbekistan 40.42N 72.03E
153 P11 Shahriston Rus. Shakhristan. NW Tajikistan 39.45N 68.47E
Shahriza see Shahreẓā
Shahr-i-Zabul see Zābol
Shahr Kord see Shahr-e Kord
153 P14 Shahrtuz Rus. Shaartuz. SW Tajikistan 37.13N 68.05E
149 Q4 Shāhrūd prev. Emāmrūd, Emāmshahr. Semnān, N Iran 36.30N 54.59E
Shahsavār/Shahsawar see Tonekābon
Shaidara see Step' Nardara
Shaikh Ābid see Shaykh 'Ābid
Shaikh Fāris see Shaykh Fāris
Shaikh Najm see Shaykh Najm
144 K5 Shā'īr, Jabal ▲ C Syria 34.51N 37.49E
160 G10 Shājāpur Madhya Pradesh, C India 23.27N 76.21E
82 J8 Shakal, Ras headland NE Sudan 18.04N 38.34E
85 G17 Shakawe Ngamiland, N Botswana 18.25S 21.53E
Shakhdarinskiy Khrebet see Shokhdara, Qatorkŭhi
Shakhrikhan see Shahrikhon
Shakhrisabz see Sharixon
Shakhristan see Shahriston
119 X8 Shakhtars'k Rus. Shakhtërsk. Donets'ka Oblast', SE Ukraine 48.02N 38.18E
127 O15 Shakhtersk Ostrov Sakhalin, Sakhalinskaya Oblast', SE Russian Federation 49.10N 142.09E
Shakhtërsk see Shakhtars'k
151 R10 Shakhtinsk Karaganda, C Kazakhstan 49.40N 72.37E
130 L11 Shakhty Rostovskaya Oblast', SW Russian Federation 47.45N 40.14E
131 P2 Shakhun'ya Nizhegorodskaya Oblast', W Russian Federation 57.42N 46.36E
79 S15 Shaki Oyo, W Nigeria 8.37N 3.25E
83 J15 Shakīso Oromo, C Ethiopia 5.33N 38.48E
119 X8 Shakmars'k Donets'ka Oblast', E Ukraine 48.04N 38.22E
31 V9 Shakopee Minnesota, N USA 44.48N 93.31W
172 Nn5 Shakotan-hantō peninsula Hokkaidō, NE Japan
172 O4 Shakotan-misaki headland Hokkaidō, NE Japan 43.22N 140.28E
41 N9 Shaktoolik Alaska, USA 64.19N 161.05W
83 J14 Shala Hāyk' ◎ C Ethiopia
128 M10 Shalakusha Arkhangel'skaya Oblast', NW Russian Federation 62.16N 40.16E
151 U8 Shalday Pavlodar, NE Kazakhstan 51.57N 78.51E
131 P16 Shali Chechenskaya Respublika, SW Russian Federation 43.03N 45.55E
147 W12 Shalim var. Shelim. S Oman 18.07N 55.39E
Shaliuhe see Gangca
150 K12 Shalkar var. Chelkar. Aktyubinsk, W Kazakhstan 47.49N 59.28E
150 F9 Shalkar, Ozero prev. Chelkar, Ozero. ◎ W Kazakhstan
23 V12 Shallotte North Carolina, SE USA 33.58N 78.21W
27 N5 Shallowater Texas, SW USA 33.41N 102.00W
128 K11 Shal'skiy Respublika Kareliya, NW Russian Federation 61.45N 36.02E
166 F9 Shaluli Shan ▲ C China
83 F22 Shama ≈ C Tanzania
9 Z11 Shamattawa Manitoba, C Canada 55.52N 92.04W
10 F8 Shamattawa ≈ Ontario, C Canada
Shām, Bādiyat ash see Syrian Desert
Shamiya see Ash Shāmīyah
147 X8 Shām, Jabal ash var. Jebel Sham. ▲ NW Oman 23.21N 57.08E
Sham, Jebel see Shām, Jabal ash
Shamkhor see Şämkir
20 G14 Shamokin Pennsylvania, NE USA 40.47N 76.33W
27 P2 Shamrock Texas, SW USA 35.12N 100.15W
Sha'nabi, Jabal ash see Chambi, Jebel
145 Y12 Shanāwah E Iraq 30.57N 47.25E
Shancheng see Taining
165 T8 Shandan Gansu, N China 38.43N 101.12E
Shandī see Shendi
167 Q5 Shandong var. Lu, Shandong Sheng, Shantung. ◆ province E China
167 R4 Shandong Bandao var. Shantung Peninsula. peninsula E China
Shandong Peninsula see Shandong Bandao
Shandong Sheng see Shandong
145 U8 Shandrūkh E Iraq 33.20N 45.19E
85 J17 Shangani ≈ W Zimbabwe
167 O15 Shangchuan Dao island S China
Shangchuankou see Minhe
169 P12 Shangdu Nei Mongol Zizhiqu, N China 41.32N 113.33E
167 O11 Shanggao var. Aoyang. Jiangxi, S China 28.16N 114.52E
167 S8 Shanghai var. Shang-hai. Shanghai Shi, E China 31.13N 121.28E
Shanghai see Shanghai Shi
167 S8 Shanghai Shi var. Hu, Shanghai. ◆ municipality E China
167 P13 Shanghang Fujian, SE China 25.02N 116.21E
166 K14 Shanglin var. Dafeng. Guangxi Zhuangzu Zizhiqu, S China 23.25N 108.31E
85 G15 Shangombo Western, W Zambia 16.21S 22.12E
Shangpai see Feixi
167 O6 Shangqiu var. Zhuji. Henan, C China 34.29N 115.39E
167 Q10 Shangrao Jiangxi, S China 28.27N 117.57E
167 S9 Shangyu var. Baiguan. Zhejiang, SE China 30.03N 120.52E
169 X9 Shangzhi Heilongjiang, NE China 45.11N 127.58E
166 L7 Shangzhou var. Shang Xian. Shaanxi, C China 33.51N 109.55E
169 W9 Shanhetun Heilongjiang, NE China 44.42N 127.12E
Shan-hsi see Shaanxi, China
Shan-hsi see Shanxi, China
165 O6 Shankou Xinjiang Uygur Zizhiqu, W China 42.01N 94.07E
192 M13 Shannon Manawatu-Wanganui, North Island, NZ 40.33S 175.25E
99 B19 Shannon ✕ W Ireland 52.42N 8.57W
99 C17 Shannon Ir. An tSionainn. ≈ W Ireland
178 H6 Shan Plateau plateau E Myanmar
164 M6 Shanshan var. Piqan. Xinjiang Uygur Zizhiqu, NW China 42.53N 90.18E
Shansi see Shanxi
178 Gg5 Shan State ◆ state E Myanmar
Shantar Islands see Shantarskiye Ostrova
127 N13 Shantarskiye Ostrova Eng. Shantar Islands. island group E Russian Federation
167 Q14 Shantou var. Shan-t'ou, Swatow. Guangdong, S China 23.22N 116.39E
Shantung see Shandong
Shantung Peninsula see Shandong Bandao
169 O14 Shanxi var. Jin, Shan-hsi, Shansi, Shanxi Sheng. ◆ province C China
Shan Xian see Sanmenxia
167 P6 Shanxian var. Shan Xian. Shandong, E China 34.51N 116.05E
Shanxi Sheng see Shanxi
166 L7 Shanyang Shaanxi, C China 33.35N 109.48E
167 N13 Shanyin var. Daiyue. Shanxi, China 39.27N 112.58E
167 O13 Shaoguan var. Shao-kuan, Cant. Kukong; prev. Ch'u-chiang. Guangdong, S China 24.56N 113.37E
Shao-kuan see Shaoguan
167 Q11 Shaowu Fujian, SE China 27.24N 117.26E
167 S9 Shaoxing Zhejiang, SE China 30.01N 120.34E
166 M12 Shaoyang var. Tangdukou. Hunan, S China 26.54N 111.14E
166 M11 Shaoyang var. Baoqing, Shao-yang; prev. Pao-king. Hunan, S China 27.18N 111.33E
98 K5 Shapinsay island NE Scotland, UK
129 S4 Shapkina ≈ NW Russian Federation
Shāpūr see Salmās
164 M4 Shaqiuhe Xinjiang Uygur Zizhiqu, W China 45.00N 88.52E
145 T2 Shaqlāwa var. Shaqlāwah. E Iraq 36.24N 44.21E
Shaqlāwah see Shaqlāwa
144 I8 Shaqqā As Suwaydā', S Syria 32.53N 36.42E
147 P7 Shaqrā' Ar Riyāḑ, C Saudi Arabia 25.10N 45.08E
Shaqrā see Shuqrah
151 W10 Shar var. Charsk. Vostochnyy Kazakhstan, E Kazakhstan 49.33N 81.03E
155 O6 Sharan Urūzgān, SE Afghanistan 33.28N 66.19E
Sharaqpur see Sharqpur
Sharbaqty see Shcherbakty
147 X12 Sharbatāt S Oman 17.57N 56.14E
147 X12 Sharbithāt, Ras var. Ras Sharbatāt. headland S Oman 17.55N 56.30E
12 K14 Sharbot Lake Ontario, SE Canada 44.45N 76.46W
151 P17 Shardara var. Chardara. Yuzhnyy Kazakhstan, S Kazakhstan 41.17N 68.03E
Shardara Dalasy see Step' Nardara
168 F8 Sharga Govĭ-Altay, W Mongolia 46.16N 95.32E
168 H6 Sharga Hövsgöl, N Mongolia 49.33N 98.36E
118 M7 Sharhorod Vinnyts'ka Oblast', C Ukraine 48.46N 28.05E
168 K10 Sharhulsan Ömnögovĭ, S Mongolia 44.43N 104.06E
172 Qq6 Shari Hokkaidō, NE Japan 43.54N 144.42E
Shari see Chari
145 T6 Shārī, Buḩayrat ◎ C Iraq
153 N12 Sharixon Rus. Shakhrisabz. Qashqadaryo Viloyati, S Uzbekistan 39.01N 66.45E
Sharjah see Ash Shāriqah
120 K12 Sharkawshchyna var. Sharkowshchyna, Pol. Szarkowszczyzna, Rus. Sharkovshchina. Vitsyebskaya Voblasts', NW Belarus 55.21N 27.27E
188 G9 Shark Bay bay Western Australia
147 Y9 Sharkh E Oman 21.19N 59.04E
Sharkovshchina/Sharkowshchyna see Sharkawshchyna
131 U6 Sharlyk Orenburgskaya Oblast', W Russian Federation 52.52N 54.45E
Sharm ash Shaykh see Sharm el Sheikh
77 Y9 Sharm el Sheikh var. Ofiral, Sharm ash Shaykh. E Egypt 27.51N 34.16E
20 B13 Sharon Pennsylvania, NE USA 41.12N 80.28W
28 H4 Sharon Springs Kansas, C USA 38.54N 101.45W
33 Q14 Sharonville Ohio, N USA 39.16N 84.24W
Sharourah see Sharūrah
31 O10 Sharpe, Lake ⊠ South Dakota, N USA
Sharqī, Al Jabal ash/Sharqi, Jebel esh see Anti-Lebanon
Sharqīyah, Al Minṭaqah ash see Ash Sharqīyah
144 I6 Sharqīyat an Nabk, Jabal ▲ W Syria
155 W8 Sharqpur var. Sharaqpur. Punjab, E Pakistan 31.27N 74.10E
147 Q13 Sharūrah var. Sharourah. Najrān, S Saudi Arabia 17.29N 47.04E
129 O14 Shar'ya Kostromskaya Oblast', NW Russian Federation 58.22N 45.30E
151 V15 Sharyn var. Charyn. ≈ SE Kazakhstan
Sharyn see Charyn
85 J18 Shashe Central, NE Botswana 21.25S 27.28E
85 J18 Shashe var. Shashi. ≈ Botswana/Zimbabwe

◆ Country ● Country Capital ◇ Dependent Territory ○ Dependent Territory Capital ◆ Administrative Region ✕ International Airport ▲ Mountain ▲ Mountain Range Volcano ≈ River ◎ Lake ⊠ Reservoir

SHASHEMENĒ – SIBOLGA

83 J14 **Shashemenē** *var.* Shashemenne, Shashhamana, *It.* Sciasciamana. Oromo, C Ethiopia *7.16N 38.38E*
Shashemenne/Shashhamana *see* Shashemenē
Shashi *see* Shashe
Shashi/Sha-shih/Shasi *see* Jingzhou, Hubei
37 N3 **Shasta Lake** ⊠ California, W USA
37 N2 **Shasta, Mount** ▲ California, W USA *41.24N 122.11W*
131 O4 **Shatki** Nizhegorodskaya Oblast', W Russian Federation *55.09N 44.04E*
Shatlyk *see* Şatlyk
Shatra *see* Ash Shaṭrah
121 K17 **Shatsk** *Rus.* Shatsk. Minskaya Voblasts', C Belarus *53.25N 27.44E*
131 N5 **Shatsk** Ryazanskaya Oblast', W Russian Federation *54.02N 41.38E*
28 J9 **Shattuck** Oklahoma, C USA *36.16N 99.52W*
151 P16 **Shaul'der** Yuzhnyy Kazakhstan, S Kazakhstan *42.49N 68.22E*
9 S17 **Shaunavon** Saskatchewan, S Canada *49.37N 108.22W*
Shavat *see* Shovot
164 K4 **Shawan** Xinjiang Uygur Zizhiqu, NW China *44.19N 85.34E*
12 G12 **Shawanaga** Ontario, S Canada *45.29N 80.16W*
32 M6 **Shawano** Wisconsin, N USA *44.46N 88.36W*
32 M6 **Shawano Lake** ◎ Wisconsin, N USA
13 P10 **Shawinigan** *prev.* Shawinigan Falls. Québec, SE Canada *46.35N 72.45W*
Shawinigan Falls *see* Shawinigan
13 P10 **Shawinigan-Sud** Québec, SE Canada *46.30N 72.43W*
144 J5 **Shawmarīyah, Jabal ash** ▲ C Syria
29 O11 **Shawnee** Oklahoma, C USA *35.19N 96.55W*
12 K12 **Shawville** Québec, SE Canada *45.37N 76.31W*
151 Q16 **Shayan** *var.* Chayan. Yuzhnyy Kazakhstan, S Kazakhstan *42.55N 69.32E*
Shaykh *see* Ash Shakk
145 W9 **Shaykh 'Ābid** *var.* Shaikh Ābid. E Iraq *32.40N 46.09E*
145 Y10 **Shaykh Fāris** *var.* Shaikh Fāris. E Iraq *32.06N 47.39E*
145 T7 **Shaykh Ḥātim** E Iraq *33.28N 44.15E*
Shaykh, Jabal ash *see* Hermon, Mount
145 X10 **Shaykh Najm** *var.* Shaikh Najm. E Iraq *32.04N 46.54E*
145 W9 **Shaykh Sa'd** E Iraq *32.35N 46.16E*
153 T14 **Shazud** SE Tajikistan *37.45N 72.22E*
121 N18 **Shchadryn** *Rus.* Shchedrin. Homyel'skaya Voblasts', SE Belarus *52.55N 29.32E*
121 H18 **Shchara** ≈ SW Belarus
Shchedrin *see* Shchadryn
Shcheglovsk *see* Kemerovo
130 K5 **Shchëkino** Tul'skaya Oblast', W Russian Federation *53.57N 37.33E*
129 S7 **Shchel'yayur** Respublika Komi, NW Russian Federation *65.19N 53.27E*
151 U8 **Shcherbakty** *Kaz.* Sharbaqty. Pavlodar, E Kazakhstan *52.28N 78.00E*
130 K7 **Shchigry** Kurskaya Oblast', W Russian Federation *51.53N 36.49E*
Shchitkovichi *see* Shchytkavichy
119 Q2 **Shchors** Chernihivs'ka Oblast', N Ukraine *51.49N 31.58E*
119 T8 **Shchors'k** Dnipropetrovs'ka Oblast', E Ukraine *48.20N 34.10E*
Shchuchin *see* Shchuchyn
151 Q7 **Shchuchinsk** *prev.* Shchuchye. Akmola, N Kazakhstan *52.56N 70.09E*
Shchuchye *see* Shchuchinsk
121 G16 **Shchuchyn** *Pol.* Szczuczyn Nowogródzki, *Rus.* Shchuchin. Hrodzyenskaya Voblasts', W Belarus *53.38N 24.48E*
121 K17 **Shchytkavichy** *Rus.* Shchitkovichi. Minskaya Voblasts', C Belarus *53.13N 27.58E*
126 H15 **Shebalino** Respublika Altay, S Russian Federation *51.16N 85.41E*
130 J9 **Shebekino** Belgorodskaya Oblast', W Russian Federation *50.25N 36.54E*
Shebelē Wenz, Wabē *see* Shebeli
83 L14 **Shebeli** *Amh.* Wabē Shebelē Wenz, *It.* Scebeli, *Som.* Webi Shabeelle. ≈ Ethiopia/Somalia
115 M20 **Shebenikut, Maja e** ▲ E Albania *41.13N 20.27E*
155 N2 **Sheberghān** *var.* Shibarghān, Shiberghan, Shiberghān. Jowzjān, N Afghanistan *36.40N 65.45E*
150 F14 **Shebir** Mangistau, SW Kazakhstan *44.52N 52.01E*
33 N8 **Sheboygan** Wisconsin, N USA *43.46N 87.43W*
79 X15 **Shebshi Mountains** *var.* Schebschi Mountains. ▲▲ E Nigeria
Shechem *see* Nablus
Shedadi *see* Ash Shadādah
11 P14 **Shediac** New Brunswick, SE Canada *46.13N 64.34W*
130 L15 **Shedok** Krasnodarskiy Kray, SW Russian Federation *44.12N 40.49E*
82 N12 **Sheekh** Woqooyi Galbeed, N Somalia *10.01N 45.21E*
40 M11 **Sheenjek River** ≈ Alaska, USA
98 D13 **Sheep Haven** *Ir.* Cuan na gCaorach. *inlet* N Ireland
37 X10 **Sheep Range** ▲▲ Nevada, W USA
100 M13 **'s-Heerenberg** Gelderland, E Netherlands *51.52N 6.15E*
99 P22 **Sheerness** SE England, UK *51.27N 0.45E*
11 Q15 **Sheet Harbour** Nova Scotia, SE Canada *44.55N 62.31W*
193 H18 **Sheffield** Canterbury, South Island, NZ *43.22S 172.01E*
99 M18 **Sheffield** N England, UK *53.22N 1.30W*
25 O2 **Sheffield** Alabama, S USA *34.46N 87.42W*
31 V12 **Sheffield** Iowa, C USA *42.53N 93.13W*
27 N10 **Sheffield** Texas, SW USA *30.42N 101.49W*
65 H22 **Shehuen, Río** ≈ S Argentina
Shekhem *see* Nablus
155 V8 **Shekhūpura** Punjab, NE Pakistan *31.43N 73.58E*
Sheki *see* Şäki
128 L14 **Sheksna** Vologodskaya Oblast', NW Russian Federation *59.11N 38.32E*
127 O4 **Shelagskiy, Mys** *headland* NE Russian Federation *70.04N 170.39E*
29 V3 **Shelbina** Missouri, C USA *39.41N 92.02W*
11 P16 **Shelburne** Nova Scotia, SE Canada *43.46N 65.19W*
12 G14 **Shelburne** Ontario, S Canada *44.04N 80.12W*
35 R7 **Shelby** Montana, NW USA *48.30N 111.52W*
23 Q10 **Shelby** North Carolina, SE USA *35.17N 81.32W*
33 S12 **Shelby** Ohio, N USA *40.52N 82.39W*
32 L14 **Shelbyville** Illinois, N USA *39.24N 88.47W*
33 P14 **Shelbyville** Indiana, N USA *39.31N 85.46W*
22 L5 **Shelbyville** Kentucky, S USA *38.12N 85.13W*
29 V2 **Shelbyville** Missouri, C USA *39.48N 92.02W*
22 J10 **Shelbyville** Tennessee, S USA *35.28N 86.27W*
27 X8 **Shelbyville** Texas, SW USA *31.42N 94.03W*
32 L14 **Shelbyville, Lake** ⊠ Illinois, N USA
31 S12 **Sheldon** Iowa, C USA *43.10N 95.51W*
40 M11 **Sheldons Point** Alaska, USA *62.31N 165.03W*
126 J16 **Shelekhov** Irkutskaya Oblast', C Russian Federation *52.04N 104.03E*
Shelekhov Gulf *see* Shelikhova, Zaliv
127 Oo9 **Shelikhova, Zaliv** *Eng.* Shelekhov Gulf. *gulf* E Russian Federation
41 P14 **Shelikof Strait** *strait* Alaska, USA
Shelim *see* Shalīm
9 T14 **Shellbrook** Saskatchewan, S Canada *53.13N 106.24W*
30 L3 **Shell Creek** ≈ North Dakota, N USA
Shellif *see* Chelif, Oued
24 I10 **Shell Keys** *island group* Louisiana, S USA
32 I4 **Shell Lake** Wisconsin, N USA *45.43N 91.55W*
31 W12 **Shell Rock** Iowa, C USA *42.42N 92.34W*
193 C26 **Shelter Point** *headland* Stewart Island, NZ *47.04S 168.13E*
20 L13 **Shelton** Connecticut, NE USA *41.19N 73.06W*
34 G8 **Shelton** Washington, NW USA *47.13N 123.06W*
Shemakha *see* Şamaxı
151 W9 **Shemonaikha** Vostochnyy Kazakhstan, E Kazakhstan *50.39N 81.51E*
131 Q4 **Shemursha** Chavash Respubliki, W Russian Federation *54.57N 47.27E*
40 D16 **Shemya Island** *island* Aleutian Islands, Alaska, USA
31 T16 **Shenandoah** Iowa, C USA *40.46N 95.23W*
23 U4 **Shenandoah** Virginia, NE USA *38.26N 78.34W*
23 U4 **Shenandoah Mountains** *ridge* West Virginia, NE USA
23 V3 **Shenandoah River** ≈ West Virginia, NE USA
79 W15 **Shendam** Plateau, C Nigeria *8.52N 9.30E*
82 G8 **Shendi** *var.* Shandī. River Nile, NE Sudan *16.40N 33.22E*
78 I15 **Shenge** SW Sierra Leone *7.54N 12.54W*
152 L10 **Shengeldi** *Rus.* Chingildi. Navoiy Viloyati, N Uzbekistan *40.59N 64.13E*
151 U15 **Shengel'dy** Almaty, SE Kazakhstan *44.04N 77.31E*
115 K18 **Shëngjin** *var.* Shëngjini. Lezhë, NW Albania *41.49N 19.34E*
Shëngjini *see* Shëngjin
Shengking *see* Liaoning
Sheng Xian/Shengxian *see* Shengzhou
167 S9 **Shengzhou** *var.* Shengxian, Sheng Xian. Zhejiang, SE China *29.36N 120.47E*
Shenking *see* Liaoning
129 N11 **Shenkursk** Arkhangel'skaya Oblast', NW Russian Federation *62.10N 42.58E*
166 L3 **Shenmu** Shaanxi, C China *38.49N 110.27E*
115 L19 **Shën Noj i Madh** ▲ C Albania *41.23N 20.07E*
166 L8 **Shennong Ding** *var.* Dashennongjia. ▲ C China *31.24N 110.16E*
Shenshi/Shensi *see* Shaanxi
169 V12 **Shenyang** *Chin.* Shen-yang, *Eng.* Moukden, Mukden; *prev.* Fengtien. Liaoning, NE China *41.49N 123.25E*
167 O15 **Shenzhen** Guangdong, S China *22.39N 114.02E*
160 G8 **Sheopur** Madhya Pradesh, C India *25.40N 76.42E*
118 L5 **Shepetivka** *Rus.* Shepetovka. Khmel'nyts'ka Oblast', NW Ukraine *50.12N 27.01E*
Shepetovka *see* Shepetivka
27 W10 **Shepherd** Texas, SW USA *30.30N 95.00W*
197 D14 **Shepherd Islands** *island group* C Vanuatu
22 K5 **Shepherdsville** Kentucky, S USA *37.59N 85.43W*
191 O11 **Shepparton** Victoria, SE Australia *36.25S 145.25E*
99 P22 **Sheppey, Isle of** *island* SE England, UK
Sherabad *see* Sherobod
99 L23 **Sherborne** S England, UK *50.57N 2.30W*
78 H16 **Sherbro Island** *island* SW Sierra Leone
13 Q12 **Sherbrooke** Québec, SE Canada *45.23N 71.54W*
31 T11 **Sherburn** Minnesota, N USA *43.39N 94.43W*
80 H6 **Sherda** Borkou-Ennedi-Tibesti, N Chad *20.04N 16.48E*
82 G7 **Shereik** River Nile, N Sudan *18.43N 33.37E*
130 K3 **Sheremet'yevo** ✈ (Moskva) Moskovskaya Oblast', W Russian Federation *56.05N 37.10E*
159 P14 **Shergāti** Bihār, N India *24.35N 84.51E*
29 U12 **Sheridan** Arkansas, C USA *34.18N 92.24W*
35 W12 **Sheridan** Wyoming, C USA *44.47N 106.59W*
190 G8 **Sheringa** South Australia *33.51S 135.13E*
126 L16 **Sherlovaya Gora** Chitinskaya Oblast', S Russian Federation *50.26N 116.09E*
27 U5 **Sherman** Texas, SW USA *33.39N 96.34W*
204 J10 **Sherman Island** *island* Antarctica
21 S4 **Sherman Mills** Maine, NE USA *45.51N 68.23W*
31 O15 **Sherman Reservoir** ⊠ Nebraska, C USA
153 N14 **Sherobod** *Rus.* Sherabad. Surkhondaryo Viloyati, S Uzbekistan *37.43N 66.59E*
153 O13 **Sherobod** *Rus.* Sherabad. ≈ S Uzbekistan
159 T14 **Sherpur** Dhaka, N Bangladesh *25.00N 90.01E*
39 T4 **Sherrelwood** Colorado, C USA *39.49N 105.00W*
101 J14 **'s-Hertogenbosch** *Fr.* Bois-le-Duc, *Ger.* Herzogenbusch. Noord-Brabant, S Netherlands *51.40N 5.19E*
30 M2 **Sherwood** North Dakota, N USA *48.55N 101.36W*
9 Q14 **Sherwood Park** Alberta, SW Canada *53.34N 113.04W*
58 F13 **Sheshea, Río** ≈ E Peru
149 T5 **Sheshtamad** Khorāsān, NE Iran *36.03N 57.45E*
31 S10 **Shetek, Lake** ◎ Minnesota, N USA
98 M2 **Shetland Islands** *island group* NE Scotland, UK
150 F14 **Shetpe** Mangistau, SW Kazakhstan *44.06N 52.03E*
160 C11 **Shetrunji** ≈ W India
Shevchenko *see* Aktau
119 W5 **Shevchenkove** Kharkivs'ka Oblast', E Ukraine *49.40N 37.13E*
83 H14 **Shewa Gimira** Southern, S Ethiopia *7.12N 35.49E*
167 Q9 **Shexian** *var.* Huicheng, She Xian. Anhui, E China *29.52N 118.27E*
167 R6 **Sheyang** *prev.* Hede. Jiangsu, E China *33.49N 120.13E*
31 O4 **Sheyenne** North Dakota, N USA *47.49N 99.08W*
31 P4 **Sheyenne River** ≈ North Dakota, N USA
98 G7 **Shiant Islands** *island group* NW Scotland, UK
127 Pp14 **Shiashkotan, Ostrov** *island* Kuril'skiye Ostrova, SE Russian Federation
33 R9 **Shiawassee River** ≈ Michigan, N USA
147 R14 **Shibām** C Yemen *15.49N 48.24E*
Shibarghān *see* Sheberghān
171 Kk12 **Shibata** *var.* Sibata. Niigata, Honshū, C Japan *37.57N 139.19E*
172 Qq7 **Shibecha** Hokkaidō, NE Japan *43.19N 144.34E*
Shiberghan/Shiberghān *see* Sheberghān
172 Qq6 **Shibetsu** Hokkaidō, NE Japan *43.40N 145.10E*
172 Pp4 **Shibetsu** *var.* Sibetu. Hokkaidō, NE Japan *44.12N 142.23E*
172 P5 **Shibetsu** *var.* Sibetu. Hokkaidō, NE Japan *43.57N 142.15E*
Shibh Jazīrat Sīnā' *see* Sinai
Shibīn al Kawm *see* Shibîn el Kôm
77 W8 **Shibîn el Kôm** *var.* Shibīn al Kawm. N Egypt *30.33N 30.59E*
149 O13 **Shīb, Kūh-e** ▲ S Iran
10 D8 **Shibogama Lake** ◎ Ontario, C Canada
Shibotsu-jima *see* Zelënyy, Ostrov
171 K14 **Shibukawa** *var.* Sibukawa. Gunma, Honshū, S Japan *36.31N 138.58E*
170 Bb16 **Shibushi** Kagoshima, Kyūshū, SW Japan *31.27N 131.05E*
170 C17 **Shibushi-wan** *bay* SW Japan
172 N9 **Shichinohe** Aomori, Honshū, C Japan *40.40N 141.07E*
201 U13 **Shichiyo Islands** *island group* Chuuk, C Micronesia
Shickshock Mountains *see* Chic-Chocs, Monts
151 S8 **Shiderti** *var.* Shiderty. Pavlodar, NE Kazakhstan *51.43N 74.34E*
151 S9 **Shiderti** ≈ N Kazakhstan
Shiderty *see* Shiderti
98 G10 **Shiel, Loch** ◎ N Scotland, UK
171 H15 **Shiga** *off.* Shiga-ken, *var.* Siga. ◈ *prefecture* Honshū, SW Japan
Shigatse *see* Xigazê
147 U13 **Shiḥan** *oasis* NE Yemen *17.46N 52.25E*
Shih-chia-chuang/Shihmen *see* Shijiazhuang
164 K4 **Shihezi** Xinjiang Uygur Zizhiqu, NW China *44.20N 85.59E*
Shiichi *see* Shyichy
115 K19 **Shijak** *var.* Shijaku. Durrës, W Albania *41.21N 19.34E*
Shijaku *see* Shijak
167 O4 **Shijiazhuang** *var.* Shih-chia-chuang; *prev.* Shihmen. Hebei, E China *38.04N 114.28E*
172 Nn7 **Shikabe** Hokkaidō, NE Japan *42.03N 140.45E*
155 Q13 **Shikārpur** Sind, S Pakistan *27.59N 68.39E*
131 Q7 **Shikhany** Saratovskaya Oblast', W Russian Federation *52.07N 47.13E*
201 V12 **Shiki Islands** *island group* Chuuk, C Micronesia
170 Ee15 **Shikoku** *var.* Sikoku. *island* SW Japan
199 Gg6 **Shikoku Basin** *var.* Sikoku Basin. *undersea feature* N Philippine Sea
170 Ee15 **Shikoku-sanchi** ▲▲ Shikoku, SW Japan
172 S7 **Shikotan, Ostrov** *Jap.* Shikotan-tō. *island* NE Russian Federation
Shikotan-tō *see* Shikotan, Ostrov
172 O6 **Shikotsu-ko** *var.* Sikotu Ko. ◎ Hokkaidō, NE Japan
83 N15 **Shilabo** Somali, E Ethiopia *6.05N 44.48E*
131 X7 **Shil'da** Orenburgskaya Oblast', W Russian Federation *51.46N 59.48E*
145 V3 **Shilēr, Āw-e** ≈ E Iraq
159 S12 **Shiliguri** *prev.* Siliguri. West Bengal, NE India *26.45N 88.24E*
Shiliu *see* Changjiang
126 Kk16 **Shilka** Chitinskaya Oblast', S Russian Federation *51.52N 115.49E*
133 V7 **Shilka** ≈ S Russian Federation
20 H15 **Shillington** Pennsylvania, NE USA *40.18N 75.57W*
159 V13 **Shillong** Meghālaya, NE India *25.36N 91.54E*
130 M5 **Shilovo** Ryazanskaya Oblast', W Russian Federation *54.18N 40.53E*
170 C14 **Shimabara** *var.* Simabara. Nagasaki, Kyūshū, SW Japan *32.48N 130.19E*
170 C14 **Shimabara-wan** *bay* SW Japan
171 Ii17 **Shimada** *var.* Simada. Shizuoka, Honshū, S Japan *34.49N 138.10E*
170 Ee12 **Shimane** *off.* Shimane-ken, *var.* Simane. ◈ *prefecture* Honshū, SW Japan
170 F11 **Shimane-hantō** *peninsula* Honshū, SW Japan
126 M15 **Shimanovsk** Amurskaya Oblast', SE Russian Federation *52.00N 127.36E*
Shimbir Berris *see* Shimbiris
82 O12 **Shimbiris** *var.* Shimbir Berris. ▲ N Somalia *10.43N 47.10E*
172 P6 **Shimizu** Hokkaidō, NE Japan *42.58N 142.54E*
171 Ii16 **Shimizu** *var.* Simizu. Shizuoka, Honshū, S Japan *35.01N 138.28E*
158 I8 **Shimla** *prev.* Simla. Himāchal Pradesh, N India *31.07N 77.09E*
Shimminato *see* Shinminato
171 J18 **Shimoda** *var.* Simoda. Shizuoka, Honshū, S Japan *34.49N 138.09E*
171 Kk16 **Shimodate** *var.* Simodate. Ibaraki, Honshū, S Japan *36.18N 139.57E*
161 F18 **Shimoga** Karnātaka, W India *13.55N 75.31E*
170 Bb14 **Shimo-jima** *island* SW Japan
170 B15 **Shimo-Koshiki-jima** *island* SW Japan
83 J21 **Shimoni** Coast, S Kenya *4.40S 39.22E*
170 D12 **Shimonoseki** *var.* Simonoseki; *hist.* Akamagaseki, Bakan. Yamaguchi, Honshū, SW Japan *33.57N 130.54E*
171 Kk16 **Shimotsuma** *var.* Simotuma. Ibaraki, Honshū, S Japan *36.10N 139.58E*
128 G14 **Shimsk** Novgorodskaya Oblast', NW Russian Federation *58.12N 30.43E*
171 Jj14 **Shinano-gawa** *var.* Sinano Gawa. ≈ Honshū, C Japan
147 W7 **Shināṣ** N Oman *24.45N 56.24E*
154 J6 **Shīndand** Farāh, W Afghanistan *33.19N 62.09E*
Shinei *see* Hsinying
27 T12 **Shiner** Texas, SW USA *29.25N 97.10W*
178 Gg1 **Shingbwiyang** Kachin State, N Myanmar *26.40N 96.14E*
151 W11 **Shingozha** Vostochnyy Kazakhstan, E Kazakhstan *47.46N 80.38E*
171 Gg17 **Shingū** *var.* Singû. Wakayama, Honshū, SW Japan *33.40N 135.57E*
12 F8 **Shining Tree** Ontario, S Canada *47.36N 81.12W*
170 F12 **Shinji-ko** *var.* Sinzi-ko. ◎ Honshū, SW Japan
171 Ll12 **Shinjō** *var.* Sinzyô. Yamagata, Honshū, C Japan *38.46N 140.16E*
98 I7 **Shin, Loch** ◎ N Scotland, UK
171 Ii13 **Shinminato** *var.* Shimminato, Sinminato. Toyama, Honshū, SW Japan *36.46N 137.04E*
170 Dd12 **Shinnanyō** *var.* Shin-Nan'yō, Sinn'anyô. Yamaguchi, Honshū, SW Japan *34.04N 131.43E*
23 S3 **Shinnston** West Virginia, NE USA *39.22N 80.19W*
144 I6 **Shinshār** *Fr.* Chinnchâr. Ḥimṣ, W Syria *34.36N 36.45E*
171 I16 **Shinshiro** *var.* Sinsiro. Aichi, Honshū, SW Japan *34.52N 137.29E*
Shinshū *see* Chinju
172 P6 **Shintoku** Hokkaidō, NE Japan *43.03N 142.50E*
83 G20 **Shinyanga** Shinyanga, NW Tanzania *3.40S 33.25E*
83 G20 **Shinyanga** ◈ *region* N Tanzania
171 M13 **Shiogama** *var.* Siogama. Miyagi, Honshū, C Japan *38.19N 140.59E*
171 J15 **Shiojiri** *var.* Sioziri. Nagano, Honshū, S Japan *36.07N 137.57E*
170 G17 **Shiono-misaki** *headland* Honshū, SW Japan *33.25N 135.45E*
171 Ll15 **Shioya-zaki** *headland* Honshū, C Japan *37.00N 140.57E*
116 J9 **Shipchenski Prokhod** *pass* C Bulgaria *42.46N 25.21E*
166 G14 **Shiping** Yunnan, SW China *23.45N 102.23E*
11 P13 **Shippagan** *var.* Shippegan. New Brunswick, SE Canada *47.45N 64.43W*
Shippegan *see* Shippagan
20 F15 **Shippensburg** Pennsylvania, NE USA *40.03N 77.31W*
39 O9 **Ship Rock** ▲ New Mexico, SW USA *36.41N 108.50W*
39 P9 **Shiprock** New Mexico, SW USA *36.47N 108.41W*
13 R6 **Shipshaw** ≈ Québec, SE Canada
127 Pp11 **Shipunskiy, Mys** *headland* E Russian Federation *53.04N 159.57E*
166 K7 **Shiquan** Shaanxi, C China *33.06N 108.10E*
126 Hh14 **Shira** Respublika Khakasiya, S Russian Federation *54.35N 89.58E*
170 G16 **Shirahama** Wakayama, Honshū, SW Japan *33.40N 135.21E*
159 T14 **Shirajganj Ghat** *var.* Serajgonj, Sirajganj. Rajshahi, C Bangladesh *24.25N 89.40E*
171 Mm7 **Shirakami-misaki** *headland* Hokkaidō, NE Japan *41.26N 140.10E*
171 L14 **Shirakawa** *var.* Sirakawa. Fukushima, Honshū, C Japan *37.07N 140.11E*
171 Ii13 **Shirakawa** Gifu, Honshū, SW Japan *36.17N 136.52E*
171 K14 **Shirane-san** ▲ Honshū, S Japan *36.44N 139.21E*
171 J16 **Shirane-san** ▲ Honshū, S Japan *35.39N 138.13E*
172 Pp7 **Shiranuka** Hokkaidō, NE Japan *42.57N 144.01E*
172 O6 **Shiraoi** Hokkaidō, NE Japan *42.34N 141.24E*
205 N12 **Shirase Coast** *physical region* Antarctica
172 Pp5 **Shirataki** Hokkaidō, NE Japan *43.55N 143.14E*
149 O11 **Shīrāz** *var.* Shīrāz. Fārs, S Iran *29.37N 52.34E*
85 N15 **Shire** *var.* Chire. ≈ Malawi/Mozambique
168 G7 **Shiree** Dzavhan, W Mongolia *47.30N 96.48E*
169 O9 **Shireet** Sühbaatar, SE Mongolia *45.33N 112.19E*
172 R6 **Shiretoko-hantō** *headland* Hokkaidō, NE Japan *44.06N 145.07E*
172 R5 **Shiretoko-misaki** *headland* Hokkaidō, NE Japan *44.20N 145.19E*
131 N5 **Shiringushi** Respublika Mordoviya, W Russian Federation *53.50N 42.49E*
154 M3 **Shīrīn Tagāb** Fāryāb, N Afghanistan *36.49N 65.01E*
155 N2 **Shīrīn Tagāb** ≈ N Afghanistan
172 Nn8 **Shiriya-zaki** *headland* Honshū, C Japan *41.24N 141.27E*
150 I12 **Shirkala, Gryada** *plain* W Kazakhstan
171 Ll13 **Shiroishi** *var.* Siroisi. Miyagi, Honshū, C Japan *38.01N 140.37E*
Shirokoye *see* Shyroke
171 K12 **Shirone** *var.* Sirone. Niigata, Honshū, C Japan *37.46N 139.00E*
171 I14 **Shirotori** Gifu, Honshū, SW Japan *35.53N 136.52E*
171 J13 **Shirouma-dake** ▲ Honshū, S Japan *36.46N 137.46E*
207 T1 **Shirshov Ridge** *undersea feature* W Bering Sea
Shirshütür/Shirshyutyur, Peski *see* Şirşütür Gumy
149 T3 **Shīrvān** *var.* Shirwān. Khorāsān, NE Iran *37.25N 57.55E*
Shirwa, Lake *see* Chilwa, Lake
Shirwān *see* Shīrvān
165 N5 **Shisanjianfang** Xinjiang Uygur Zizhiqu, W China *43.10N 91.15E*
40 M16 **Shishaldin Volcano** Ж Unimak Island, Alaska, USA *54.45N 163.58W*
Shishchitsy *see* Shyshchytsy
40 M8 **Shishmaref** Alaska, USA *66.15N 166.04W*
Shisur *see* Ash Shişar
171 I16 **Shitara** Aichi, Honshū, SW Japan *35.06N 137.33E*
158 D12 **Shiv** Rājasthān, NW India *26.10N 71.13E*
157 E15 **Shivāji Sāgar** *prev.* Konya Reservoir ⊠ W India
160 H8 **Shivpuri** Madhya Pradesh, C India *25.28N 77.41E*
38 J9 **Shivwits Plateau** *plain* Arizona, SW USA
Shiwālik Range *see* Siwalik Range
166 M8 **Shiyan** Hubei, C China *32.39N 110.48E*
Shizilu *see* Junan
166 H13 **Shizong** *var.* Danfeng. Yunnan, SW China *24.49N 103.59E*
171 Mm13 **Shizugawa** Miyagi, Honshū, NE Japan *38.40N 141.26E*
165 W8 **Shizuishan** *var.* Dawukou. Ningxia, N China *39.04N 106.22E*
172 Oo7 **Shizunai** Hokkaidō, NE Japan *42.20N 142.24E*
171 Ii16 **Shizuoka** *var.* Sizuoka. Shizuoka, Honshū, S Japan *34.58N 138.20E*
171 Ii16 **Shizuoka** *off.* Shizuoka-ken, *var.* Sizuoka. ◈ *prefecture* Honshū, S Japan
Shklov *see* Shklow
121 N15 **Shklow** *Rus.* Shklov. Mahilyowskaya Voblasts', E Belarus *54.13N 30.16E*
115 K18 **Shkodër** *var.* Shkodra, *It.* Scutari, *SCr.* Skadar. Shkodër, NW Albania *42.03N 19.31E*
115 K17 **Shkodër** ◈ *district* NW Albania
Shkodra *see* Shkodër
Shkodrës, Liqeni i *see* Scutari, Lake
Shkumbî/Shkumbin *see* Shkumbinit, Lumi i
115 L20 **Shkumbinit, Lumi i** *var.* Shkumbî, Shkumbin. ≈ C Albania
Shligigh, Cuan *see* Sligo Bay
126 Ii2 **Shmidta, Ostrov** *island* Severnaya Zemlya, N Russian Federation
191 S10 **Shoalhaven River** ≈ New South Wales, SE Australia
9 W16 **Shoal Lake** Manitoba, S Canada *50.28N 100.36W*
33 O15 **Shoals** Indiana, N USA *38.40N 86.46W*
170 F13 **Shōbara** *var.* Syôbara. Hiroshima, Honshū, SW Japan *34.50N 132.58E*
170 Ff14 **Shōdo-shima** *island* SW Japan
171 Ii13 **Shō-gawa** ≈ Honshū, SW Japan
Shōka *see* Changhua
126 J3 **Shokal'skogo, Proliv** *strait* N Russian Federation
172 Oo4 **Shokanbetsu-dake** Ж Hokkaidō, NE Japan *43.43N 141.33E*
153 T14 **Shokhdara, Qatorkŭhi** *Rus.* Shakhdarinskiy Khrebet. ▲▲ SE Tajikistan
151 P17 **Sholakkorgan** *var.* Chulakkurgan. Yuzhnyy Kazakhstan, S Kazakhstan *43.45N 69.10E*
151 N9 **Sholaksay** Kostanay, N Kazakhstan *51.45N 64.45E*
Sholāpur *see* Solāpur
Sholdaneshty *see* Şoldăneşti
Shoqpar *see* Chokpar
161 G21 **Shoranūr** Kerala, SW India *10.53N 76.06E*
161 G16 **Shorāpur** Karnātaka, C India *16.34N 76.48E*
153 O14 **Sho'rchi** *Rus.* Shurchi. Surkhondaryo Viloyati, S Uzbekistan *37.58N 67.40E*
32 M11 **Shorewood** Illinois, N USA *41.31N 88.12W*
Shorkazakhly, Solonchak *see* Kazakhlyshor, Solonchak
151 Q9 **Shortandy** Akmola, C Kazakhstan *51.47N 70.55E*
Shortepa/Shor Tepe *see* Shūr Tappeh
195 S13 **Shortland Island** *var.* Alu. *island* Shortland Islands, NW Solomon Islands
195 T13 **Shortland Islands** *island group* NW Solomon Islands
Shosambetsu *see* Shosanbetsu
172 P3 **Shosanbetsu** *var.* Shosambetsu. Hokkaidō, NE Japan *44.31N 141.47E*
35 O15 **Shoshone** Idaho, NW USA *42.56N 114.24W*
37 T6 **Shoshone Mountains** ▲▲ Nevada, W USA
35 U12 **Shoshone River** ≈ Wyoming, C USA
85 I19 **Shoshong** Central, SE Botswana *23.03S 26.33E*
35 V14 **Shoshoni** Wyoming, C USA *43.13N 108.06W*
Shōshū *see* Sangju
119 S2 **Shostka** Sums'ka Oblast', NE Ukraine *51.51N 33.30E*
193 C21 **Shotover** ≈ South Island, NZ
152 H9 **Shovot** *Rus.* Shavat. Xorazm Viloyati, W Uzbekistan *41.41N 60.13E*
39 N12 **Show Low** Arizona, SW USA *34.15N 110.01W*
Show Me State *see* Missouri
129 O4 **Shoyna** Nenetskiy Avtonomnyy Okrug, NW Russian Federation *67.50N 44.09E*
128 M11 **Shozhma** Arkhangel'skaya Oblast', NW Russian Federation *61.57N 40.10E*
119 Q7 **Shpola** Cherkas'ka Oblast', N Ukraine *49.00N 31.27E*
Shqipëria/Shqipërisë, Republika e *see* Albania
24 G5 **Shreveport** Louisiana, S USA *32.31N 93.45W*
99 K19 **Shrewsbury** *hist.* Scrobesbyrig'. W England, UK *52.43N 2.45W*
158 D11 **Shri Mohangarh** *prev.* Sri Mohangorh. Rājasthān, NW India *27.16N 71.18E*
159 S16 **Shrīrāmpur** *prev.* Serampore, Serampur. West Bengal, NE India *22.43N 88.19E*
99 K19 **Shropshire** *cultural region* W England, UK
151 S16 **Shu** *Kaz.* Shū. Zhambyl, SE Kazakhstan *43.34N 73.40E*
Shū *see* Chu
166 G13 **Shuangbai** *var.* Tuodian. Yunnan, SW China *24.45N 101.38E*
169 W9 **Shuangcheng** Heilongjiang, NE China *45.20N 126.21E*
Shuangcheng *see* Zherong
166 E14 **Shuangjiang** *var.* Weiyuan. Yunnan, SW China *23.28N 99.43E*
Shuangjiang *see* Jiangkou
169 U10 **Shuangliao** *var.* Zhengjiatun. Jilin, NE China *43.31N 123.32E*
Shuang-liao *see* Liaoyuan
169 Y7 **Shuangyashan** *var.* Shuang-ya-shan. Heilongjiang, NE China *46.37N 131.10E*
147 W12 **Shu'aymiah** *var.* Shu'aymiah. S Oman *17.55N 55.39E*
150 I10 **Shubarkuduk** *Kaz.* Shubarqudyq. Aktyubinsk, W Kazakhstan *49.10N 56.28E*
Shubarqudyq *see* Shubarkuduk
151 N12 **Shubar-Tengiz, Ozero** ◎ C Kazakhstan
41 S5 **Shublik Mountains** ▲▲ Alaska, USA
Shubrā al Khaymah *see* Shubrâ el Kheima
124 Qq16 **Shubrâ el Kheima** *var.* Shubrā al Khaymah. N Egypt *30.06N 31.15E*
164 E8 **Shufu** Xinjiang Uygur Zizhiqu, NW China *39.18N 75.43E*
153 S14 **Shughnon, Qatorkŭhi** *Rus.* Shugnanskiy Khrebet. ▲▲ SE Tajikistan
Shugnanskiy Khrebet *see* Shughnon, Qatorkŭhi
167 Q6 **Shu He** ≈ E China
Shuiding *see* Huocheng
Shuidong *see* Dianbai
Shuiji *see* Laixi
Shū-Ile Taūlary *see* Chu-Iliyskiye Gory
Shuiluocheng *see* Zhuanglang
155 T10 **Shujāābād** Punjab, E Pakistan *29.52N 71.22E*
169 W9 **Shulan** Jilin, NE China *44.28N 126.57E*
164 E8 **Shule** Xinjiang Uygur Zizhiqu, NW China *39.19N 76.06E*
Shuleh *see* Shule He
165 Q8 **Shule He** *var.* Shuleh, Sulo. ≈ C China
32 K9 **Shullsburg** Wisconsin, N USA *42.37N 90.12W*
41 N16 **Shumagin Islands** *island group* Alaska, USA
152 G7 **Shumanay** Qoraqalpog'iston Respublikasi, W Uzbekistan *42.42N 58.56E*
116 M8 **Shumen** Shumen, NE Bulgaria *43.17N 26.57E*
116 M8 **Shumen** ◈ *province* NE Bulgaria
131 P4 **Shumerlya** Chavash Respubliki, W Russian Federation *55.31N 46.24E*
125 Ee12 **Shumikha** Kurganskaya Oblast', C Russian Federation *55.12N 63.09E*
120 M12 **Shumilina** *Rus.* Shumilino. Vitsyebskaya Voblasts', NE Belarus *55.19N 29.33E*
Shumilino *see* Shumilina
127 Pp12 **Shumshu, Ostrov** *island* SE Russian Federation
118 K5 **Shums'k** Ternopil's'ka Oblast', W Ukraine *50.06N 26.04E*
41 O7 **Shungnak** Alaska, USA *66.53N 157.08W*
Shunsen *see* Ch'unch'ŏn
Shuoxian *see* Shuozhou
167 N3 **Shuozhou** *var.* Shuoxian. Shanxi, C China *39.19N 112.25E*
147 P16 **Shuqrah** *var.* Shaqrā. SW Yemen *13.25N 45.43E*
Shurab *see* Shūrob
153 R11 **Shūrob** *Rus.* Shurab. NW Tajikistan *40.02N 70.31E*
149 T10 **Shūr, Rūd-e** ≈ E Iran
155 O2 **Shūr Tappeh** *var.* Shortepa, Shor Tepe. Balkh, N Afghanistan *37.22N 66.49E*
85 K17 **Shurugwi** *prev.* Selukwe. Midlands, C Zimbabwe *19.40S 30.00E*
148 L8 **Shūsh** *anc.* Susa, *Bibl.* Shushan. Khūzestān, SW Iran *32.11N 48.13E*
Shushan *see* Shūsh
148 L9 **Shūshtar** *var.* Shustar, Shushter. Khūzestān, SW Iran *32.03N 48.51E*
Shushter/Shustar *see* Shūshtar
147 T9 **Shuṭfah, Qalamat** *well* E Saudi Arabia *22.46N 52.50E*
145 V9 **Shuwayjah, Hawr ash** *var.* Hawr as Suwayqiyah. ◎ E Iraq
128 M16 **Shuya** Ivanovskaya Oblast', W Russian Federation *56.51N 41.24E*
41 Q14 **Shuyak Island** *island* Alaska, USA
177 G4 **Shwebo** Sagaing, C Myanmar *22.34N 95.42E*
177 Ff7 **Shwedaung** Pegu, W Myanmar *18.43N 95.15E*
177 G8 **Shwegyin** Pegu, SW Myanmar *17.55N 96.58E*
178 Gg4 **Shweli** *Chin.* Longchuan Jiang. ≈ Myanmar/China
177 G6 **Shwemyo** Mandalay, C Myanmar *20.04N 96.13E*
Shyghys Qazagastan Oblysy *see* Vostochnyy Kazakhstan
Shyghys Qongyrat *see* Shygys Konyrat
151 T12 **Shygys Konyrat** *var.* Vostochno-Kounradskiy, *Kaz.* Shyghys Qongyrat. Karaganda, C Kazakhstan *47.01N 75.05E*
121 M19 **Shyichy** *Rus.* Shiichi. Homyel'skaya Voblasts', SE Belarus *52.15N 29.13E*
151 Q17 **Shymkent** *prev.* Chimkent. Yuzhnyy Kazakhstan, S Kazakhstan *42.19N 69.36E*
Shyngghyrlaū *see* Chingirlau
158 J5 **Shyok** Jammu and Kashmir, NW India *34.13N 78.12E*
119 S9 **Shyroke** *Rus.* Shirokoye. Dnipropetrovs'ka Oblast', E Ukraine *47.37N 33.15E*
119 O9 **Shyryayeve** Odes'ka Oblast', SW Ukraine *47.21N 30.11E*
119 S5 **Shyshaky** Poltavs'ka Oblast', C Ukraine *49.54N 34.00E*
121 K17 **Shyshchytsy** *Rus.* Shishchitsy. Minskaya Voblasts', C Belarus *53.12N 27.33E*
155 Y3 **Siachen Muztāgh** ▲▲ NE Pakistan
Siadehan *see* Tākestān
154 M13 **Siāhān Range** ▲▲ W Pakistan
148 I1 **Sīāh Chashmeh** Āzarbāyjān-e Bākhtarī, N Iran *39.01N 44.22E*
155 W7 **Siālkot** Punjab, NE Pakistan *32.31N 74.33E*
194 K12 **Sialum** Morobe, C PNG *6.05S 147.33E*
Siam *see* Thailand
Siam, Gulf of *see* Thailand, Gulf of
Sian *see* Xi'an
Siang *see* Brahmaputra
Siangtan *see* Xiangtan
174 J5 **Siantan, Pulau** *island* Kepulauan Anambas, W Indonesia
56 H11 **Siare, Río** ≈ C Colombia
179 Rr13 **Siargao Island** *island* S Philippines
194 K12 **Siassi** Umboi Island, C PNG *5.34S 147.50E*
117 D14 **Siátista** Dytikí Makedonía, N Greece *40.16N 21.34E*
177 Ff4 **Siatlai** Chin State, W Myanmar *22.05N 93.36E*
179 Q15 **Siaton** Negros, C Philippines *9.03N 123.03E*
179 Q15 **Siaton Point** *headland* Negros, C Philippines *9.03N 123.00E*
120 F11 **Šiauliai** *Ger.* Schaulen. Šiauliai, N Lithuania *55.54N 23.21E*
120 E11 **Šiauliai** ◈ *province* N Lithuania
175 S5 **Siau, Pulau** *island* N Indonesia
85 J15 **Siavonga** Southern, SE Zambia *16.28S 28.45E*
Siazan' *see* Siyäzän
Sibah *see* As Sibah
109 N20 **Sibari** Calabria, S Italy *39.45N 16.26E*
Sibata *see* Shibata
131 X6 **Sibay** Respublika Bashkortostan, W Russian Federation *52.39N 58.39E*
95 M19 **Sibbo** *Fin.* Sipoo. Etelä-Suomi, S Finland *60.22N 25.19E*
114 D13 **Šibenik** *It.* Sebenico. Šibenik-Knin, S Croatia *43.43N 15.54E*
Šibenik *see* Šibenik-Knin
114 E13 **Šibenik-Knin** *off.* Šibenska Županija. *var.* Šibenik ◈ *province* S Croatia
Šibenska Županija *see* Šibenik-Knin
Siberia *see* Sibir'
Siberoet *see* Siberut, Pulau
173 Ff9 **Siberut, Pulau** *prev.* Siberoet. *island* Kepulauan Mentawai, W Indonesia
173 Ff9 **Siberut, Selat** *strait* W Indonesia
Sibetu *see* Shibetsu
155 P11 **Sibi** Baluchistān, SW Pakistan *29.31N 67.54E*
194 F15 **Sibidiri** Western, SW PNG *8.58S 142.14E*
126 K10 **Sibir'** *var.* Siberia. *physical region* NE Russian Federation
126 H14 **Sibirskiy** Altayskiy Oblast', S Russian Federation *53.45N 84.00E*
81 F20 **Sibiti** La Lékoumou, S Congo *3.40S 13.19E*
83 G21 **Sibiti** ≈ C Tanzania
118 I12 **Sibiu** *Ger.* Hermannstadt, *Hung.* Nagyszeben. Sibiu, C Romania *45.48N 24.08E*
118 I11 **Sibiu** ◈ *county* C Romania
31 S11 **Sibley** Iowa, C USA *43.24N 95.45W*
173 Ff6 **Sibolga** Sumatera, W Indonesia *1.42N 98.48E*

◆ COUNTRY ● COUNTRY CAPITAL ◇ DEPENDENT TERRITORY ○ DEPENDENT TERRITORY CAPITAL ◈ ADMINISTRATIVE REGION ✈ INTERNATIONAL AIRPORT ▲ MOUNTAIN ▲▲ MOUNTAIN RANGE Ж VOLCANO ≈ RIVER ◎ LAKE ⊠ RESERVOIR

327

SIBOLGA, TELUK – SITTWE

173 Ff6 **Sibolga, Teluk** *var.* Teluk Tapanuli. *bay* Sumatera, W Indonesia
174 Ll6 **Sibu** Sarawak, East Malaysia 2.18N 111.49E
Sibukawa *see* Shibukawa
44 G2 **Sibun** ≈ E Belize
81 I15 **Sibut** *prev.* Fort-Sibut. Kémo, S Central African Republic 5.44N 19.07E
179 P17 **Sibutu** *island* SW Philippines
179 P17 **Sibutu Passage** *passage* SW Philippines
179 Q12 **Sibuyan Island** *island* C Philippines
179 Q12 **Sibuyan Sea** *sea* C Philippines
201 U1 **Sibylla Island** *island* N Marshall Islands
9 N16 **Sicamous** British Columbia, SW Canada 50.49N 118.52W
Sichelburger Gebirge *see* Gorjanci/Žumberačko Gorje
178 H15 **Sichon** *var.* Ban Sichon, Si Chon. Nakhon Si Thammarat, SW Thailand 9.03N 99.51E
166 H9 **Sichuan** *var.* Chuan, Sichuan Sheng, Ssu-ch'uan, Szechuan, Szechwan. ◈ *province* C China
166 I9 **Sichuan Pendi** *basin* C China
Sichuan Sheng *see* Sichuan
105 S16 **Sicie, Cap** *headland* SE France 43.03N 5.50E
109 J24 **Sicilia** *Eng.* Sicily; *anc.* Trinacria. ◈ *region* Italy, C Mediterranean Sea
109 M24 **Sicilia** *Eng.* Sicily; *anc.* Trinacria. *island* Italy, C Mediterranean Sea
Sicilian Channel *see* Sicily, Strait of
Sicily *see* Sicilia
109 H24 **Sicily, Strait of** *var.* Sicilian Channel. *strait* C Mediterranean Sea
44 K5 **Sico Tinto, Río** *var.* Río Negro. ≈ NE Honduras
59 H16 **Sicuani** Cusco, S Peru 14.18S 71.16W
114 J10 **Šid** Serbia, NW Serbia and Montenegro (Yugoslavia) 45.07N 19.13E
117 A15 **Sidári** Kérkyra, Iónioi Nísoi, Greece, C Mediterranean Sea 39.47N 19.43E
174 Kk8 **Sidas** Borneo, C Indonesia 0.24N 109.46E
100 O5 **Siddeburen** Groningen, NE Netherlands 53.15N 6.52E
160 D9 **Siddhapur** *prev.* Siddhpur, Sidhpur. Gujarāt, W India 23.57N 72.28E
Siddhpur *see* Siddhapur
161 I15 **Siddipet** Andhra Pradesh, C India 18.10N 78.54E
195 O17 **Sideia Island** *island* SE PNG
175 Pp12 **Sidenreng, Danau** ◎ Sulawesi, C Indonesia
79 N14 **Sidéradougou** SW Burkina 10.39N 4.16W
109 N23 **Siderno** Calabria, SW Italy 38.17N 16.19E
Siders *see* Sierre
160 L9 **Sidhi** Madhya Pradesh, C India 24.24N 81.54E
Sidhirókastron *see* Sidirókastro
Sidhpur *see* Siddhapur
Sīdī al Hānī', Sabkhat *see* Sidi el Hani, Sebkhet de
77 U7 **Sîdi Barrâni** NW Egypt 31.33N 25.54E
76 I6 **Sidi Bel Abbès** *var.* Sidi bel Abbès, Sidi-Bel-Abbès. NW Algeria 35.12N 0.42W
76 E7 **Sidi-Bennour** W Morocco 32.39N 8.28W
76 M6 **Sidi Bouzid** *var.* Gammouda, Sīdī Bu Zayd. C Tunisia 35.05N 9.20E
123 K12 **Sidi el Hani, Sebkhet de** *var.* Sabkhat Sīdī al Hānī'. *salt flat* NE Tunisia
76 D8 **Sidi-Ifni** SW Morocco 29.33N 10.04W
76 G6 **Sidi-Kacem** *prev.* Petitjean. N Morocco 34.21N 5.46W
116 G12 **Sidirókastro** *prev.* Sidhirókastron. Kentrikí Makedonía, NE Greece 41.13N 23.24E
204 L12 **Sidley, Mount** ▲ Antarctica 76.39S 124.48W
31 S16 **Sidney** Iowa, C USA 40.45N 95.39W
35 Y7 **Sidney** Montana, NW USA 47.42N 104.10W
30 J15 **Sidney** Nebraska, C USA 41.09N 102.57W
20 I11 **Sidney** New York, NE USA 42.18N 75.21W
33 R13 **Sidney** Ohio, N USA 40.16N 84.09W
25 T2 **Sidney Lanier, Lake** ⊠ Georgia, SE USA
Sidon *see* Saïda
126 Hh9 **Sidorovsk** Yamalo-Nenetskiy Avtonomnyy Okrug, N Russian Federation 66.34N 82.12E
Sidra/Sidra, Gulf of *see* Surt, Khalīj, N Libya
Sidra *see* Surt, N Libya
Sīdī Bu Zayd *see* Sidi Bouzid
Siebenbürgen *see* Transylvania
Sieben Dörfer *see* Săcele
112 O12 **Siedlce** *Ger.* Sedlez, *Rus.* Sesdlets. Mazowieckie, C Poland 52.10N 22.18E
103 E16 **Sieg** ≈ W Germany
103 F16 **Siegen** Nordrhein-Westfalen, W Germany 50.52N 8.01E
111 X4 **Sieghartskirchen** Niederösterreich, E Austria 48.13N 16.01E
112 O11 **Siemiatycze** Podlaskie, NE Poland 52.27N 22.51E
178 Jj11 **Siĕmpang** Stœng Trêng, NE Cambodia 14.07N 106.24E
178 Ii12 **Siĕmréab** *prev.* Siemreap. Siĕmréab, NW Cambodia 13.21N 103.49E
Siemreap *see* Siĕmréab
108 G12 **Siena** *Fr.* Sienne; *anc.* Saena Julia. Toscana, C Italy 43.19N 11.19E
Sienne *see* Siena
94 K12 **Sieppijärvi** Lappi, NW Finland 67.09N 23.58E
112 J13 **Sieradz** Sieradz, C Poland 51.36N 18.42E
112 K10 **Sierpc** Mazowieckie, C Poland 52.51N 19.43E
26 I9 **Sierra Blanca** Texas, SW USA 31.10N 105.21W
39 S14 **Sierra Blanca Peak** ▲ New Mexico, SW USA 33.22N 105.48W
37 P5 **Sierra City** California, W USA 39.34N 120.35W
65 I16 **Sierra Colorada** Río Negro, S Argentina 40.37S 67.48W
64 I13 **Sierra del Nevado** ▲▲ W Argentina
65 J16 **Sierra Grande** Río Negro, E Argentina 41.40S 65.22W
78 G15 **Sierra Leone** *off.* Republic of Sierra Leone. ◆ *republic* W Africa
66 M13 **Sierra Leone Basin** *undersea feature* E Atlantic Ocean
68 K8 **Sierra Leone Fracture Zone** *tectonic feature* E Atlantic Ocean
Sierra Leone Ridge *see* Sierra Leone Rise
66 L13 **Sierra Leone Rise** *var.* Sierra Leone Ridge, Sierra Leone Schwelle. *undersea feature* E Atlantic Ocean
Sierra Leone Schwelle *see* Sierra Leone Rise
43 U17 **Sierra Madre** *var.* Sierra de Soconusco. ▲▲ Guatemala/Mexico
179 Pp9 **Sierra Madre** ▲▲ Luzon, N Philippines
39 R2 **Sierra Madre** ▲▲ Colorado/Wyoming, C USA
(0) H15 **Sierra Madre del Sur** ▲▲ S Mexico
(0) G13 **Sierra Madre Occidental** *var.* Western Sierra Madre. ▲▲ C Mexico
(0) H13 **Sierra Madre Oriental** *var.* Eastern Sierra Madre. ▲▲ C Mexico
46 H8 **Sierra Maestra** ▲▲ E Cuba
42 L7 **Sierra Mojada** Coahuila de Zaragoza, NE Mexico 27.13N 103.42W
107 O14 **Sierra Nevada** ▲▲ S Spain
37 P6 **Sierra Nevada** ▲▲ W USA
56 F4 **Sierra Nevada de Santa Marta** ▲▲ NE Colombia
44 K5 **Sierra Río Tinto** ▲▲ NE Honduras
26 J10 **Sierra Vieja** ▲▲ Texas, SW USA
39 N16 **Sierra Vista** Arizona, SW USA 31.33N 110.18W
110 D10 **Sierre** *Ger.* Siders. Valais, SW Switzerland 46.18N 7.33E
38 L16 **Sierrita Mountains** ▲▲ Arizona, SW USA
Siete Moai *see* Ahu Akivi
78 M15 **Sifié** W Ivory Coast 7.58N 6.55W
117 I21 **Sífnos** *anc.* Siphnos. *island* Kykládes, Greece, Aegean Sea
117 I21 **Sífnou, Stenó** *strait* SE Greece
Siga *see* Shiga
197 H15 **Sigatoka** *prev.* Singatoka. Viti Levu, W Fiji 18.10S 105.30E
105 P16 **Sigean** Aude, S France 43.01N 2.58E
Sighet *see* Sighetu Marmației
Sighetul Marmației *see* Sighetu Marmației
118 I8 **Sighetu Marmației** *var.* Sighet, Sighetul Marmației, *Hung.* Máramarossziget. Maramureș, N Romania 47.55N 23.52E
118 I11 **Sighișoara** *Ger.* Schässburg, *Hung.* Segesvár. Mureș, C Romania 46.12N 24.48E
173 E3 **Sigli** Sumatera, W Indonesia 5.21N 95.55E
94 J1 **Siglufjördhur** Nordhurland Vestra, N Iceland 66.09N 18.55W
103 H23 **Sigmaringen** Baden-Württemberg, S Germany 48.04N 9.12E
103 N20 **Signalberg** ▲ SE Germany 49.30N 12.34E
38 I13 **Signal Peak** ▲ Arizona, SW USA 33.20N 114.03W
Signan *see* Xi'an
204 H1 **Signy** *UK research station* South Orkney Islands, Antarctica 60.27S 45.35W
31 X15 **Sigourney** Iowa, C USA 41.19N 92.12W
117 K17 **Sígri, Akrotírio** *headland* Lésvos, E Greece 39.12N 25.49E
Sigsbee Deep *see* Mexico Basin
49 N2 **Sigsbee Escarpment** *undersea feature* N Gulf of Mexico
58 C8 **Sigsig** Azuay, S Ecuador 3.04S 78.49W
97 O15 **Sigtuna** Stockholm, C Sweden 59.36N 17.43E
44 H6 **Siguatepeque** Comayagua, W Honduras 14.38N 87.52W
107 P7 **Sigüenza** Castilla-La Mancha, C Spain 41.04N 2.37W
107 R4 **Sigües** Aragón, NE Spain 42.39N 1.01W
78 K13 **Siguiri** Haute-Guinée, NE Guinea 11.25N 9.07W
120 G8 **Sigulda** *Ger.* Segewold. Rīga, C Latvia 57.08N 24.51E
Sihanoukville *see* Kâmpóng Saôm
110 G8 **Sihlsee** ◎ NW Switzerland
95 K18 **Siikainen** Länsi-Suomi, W Finland 61.52N 21.49E
95 M16 **Siilinjärvi** Itä-Suomi, C Finland 63.04N 27.40E
143 R15 **Siirt** *var.* Sert; *anc.* Tigranocerta. Siirt, SE Turkey 37.55N 41.55E
143 R15 **Siirt** *var.* Sert. ◈ *province* SE Turkey
195 Z15 **Sikaiana** *var.* Stewert Islands. *island group* W Solomon Islands
Sikandarabad *see* Secunderābād
158 J11 **Sikandra Rao** Uttar Pradesh, N India 27.42N 78.22E
8 M11 **Sikanni Chief** British Columbia, W Canada 57.16N 122.44W
8 M11 **Sikanni Chief** ≈ British Columbia, W Canada
158 H11 **Sīkar** Rājasthān, N India 27.39N 75.09E
78 M13 **Sikasso** Sikasso, S Mali 11.21N 5.42W
78 L13 **Sikasso** ◈ *region* SW Mali
178 Gg3 **Sikaw** Kachin State, C Myanmar 23.50N 97.04E
85 H14 **Sikelenge** Western, W Zambia 14.51S 24.13E
29 Y7 **Sikeston** Missouri, C USA 36.52N 89.35W
95 J14 **Sikfors** Norrbotten, N Sweden 65.29N 21.17E
127 O16 **Sikhote-Alin', Khrebet** ▲▲ SE Russian Federation
Siking *see* Xi'an
117 J22 **Síkinos** *island* Kykládes, Greece, Aegean Sea
159 S11 **Sikkim** *Tib.* Denjong. ◈ *state* N India
113 I26 **Siklós** Baranya, SW Hungary 45.51N 18.18E
Sikoku *see* Shikoku
Sikoku Basin *see* Shikoku Basin
85 G14 **Sikongo** Western, W Zambia 15.03S 22.07E
Sikotu Ko *see* Shikotsu-ko
Sikouri/Sikoúrion *see* Sykoúri
126 L7 **Siktyakh** Respublika Sakha (Yakutiya), NE Russian Federation 69.45N 124.42E
120 D12 **Šilalė** Tauragė, W Lithuania 55.29N 22.10E
108 G5 **Silandro** *Ger.* Schlanders. Trentino-Alto Adige, N Italy 46.39N 10.55E
43 N12 **Silao** Guanajuato, C Mexico 20.55N 101.24W
Silarius *see* Sele
179 Q13 **Silay** *off.* Silay City. Negros, C Philippines 10.49N 122.58E
159 W14 **Silchar** Assam, NE India 24.49N 92.48E
110 G9 **Silenen** Uri, C Switzerland 46.49N 8.39E
23 T9 **Siler City** North Carolina, SE USA 35.43N 79.27W
35 U11 **Silesia** Montana, NW USA 45.32N 108.52W
112 F13 **Silesia** *physical region* SW Poland
76 K12 **Silet** S Algeria 22.45N 4.51E
151 R8 **Sileti** *var.* Selety. ≈ N Kazakhstan
Siletitengiz *see* Siletiteniz, Ozero
151 R7 **Siletiteniz, Ozero** *Kaz.* Siletitengiz. ◎ N Kazakhstan
180 H16 **Silhouette** *island* Inner Islands, SE Seychelles
142 I17 **Silifke** *anc.* Seleucia. İçel, S Turkey 36.22N 33.57E
Siliguri *see* Shiliguri
162 J10 **Siling Co** ◎ W China
Silinhot *see* Xilinhot
198 Aa7 **Silisili** ▲ Savai'i, C Samoa 13.37S 172.26W
116 M6 **Silistra** *var.* Silistria; *anc.* Durostorum. Silistra, NE Bulgaria 44.07N 27.16E
116 M7 **Silistra** ◈ *province* NE Bulgaria
Silistria *see* Silistra
142 D10 **Silivri** İstanbul, NW Turkey 41.04N 28.15E
96 L13 **Siljan** ◎ C Sweden
97 G22 **Silkeborg** Århus, C Denmark 56.10N 9.34E
110 M8 **Sill** ≈ W Austria
107 S10 **Silla** País Valenciano, E Spain 39.22N 0.25W
64 H3 **Sillajguay, Cordillera** ▲ N Chile 19.45S 68.39W
120 K3 **Sillamäe** *Ger.* Sillamäggi. Ida-Virumaa, NE Estonia 59.23N 27.45E
Sillamäggi *see* Sillamäe
Sillein *see* Žilina
111 P9 **Sillian** Tirol, W Austria 46.45N 12.25E
114 B10 **Šilo** Primorje-Gorski Kotar, NW Croatia 45.09N 14.39E
29 R9 **Siloam Springs** Arkansas, C USA 36.11N 94.32W
27 X10 **Silsbee** Texas, SW USA 30.21N 94.10W
149 W15 **Sīlūp, Rūd-e** ≈ SE Iran
120 C12 **Šilutė** *Ger.* Heydekrug. Klaipėda, W Lithuania 55.20N 21.29E
143 Q15 **Silvan** Dıyarbakır, SE Turkey 38.08N 41.00E
110 J10 **Silvaplana** Graubünden, S Switzerland 46.27N 9.45E
Silva Porto *see* Kuito
60 M12 **Silva, Recife do** *reef* E Brazil
160 D12 **Silvassa** Dādra and Nagar Haveli, W India 20.13N 73.03E
31 X4 **Silver Bay** Minnesota, N USA 47.17N 91.15W
39 P15 **Silver City** New Mexico, SW USA 32.46N 108.16W
20 D10 **Silver Creek** New York, NE USA 42.32N 79.10W
39 N12 **Silver Creek** ≈ Arizona, SW USA
29 P4 **Silver Lake** Kansas, C USA 39.06N 95.51W
34 I14 **Silver Lake** Oregon, NW USA 43.07N 121.04W
37 T9 **Silver Peak Range** ▲▲ Nevada, W USA
23 W3 **Silver Spring** Maryland, NE USA 38.59N 77.01W
Silver State *see* Nevada
Silver State *see* Colorado
39 Q7 **Silverton** Colorado, C USA 37.48N 107.39W
20 K16 **Silverton** New Jersey, NE USA 40.00N 74.09W
34 G11 **Silverton** Oregon, NW USA 45.00N 122.46W
27 N4 **Silverton** Texas, SW USA 34.26N 101.19W
106 G14 **Silves** Faro, S Portugal 37.10N 8.25W
56 D12 **Silvia** Cauca, SW Colombia 2.36N 76.20W
110 J9 **Silvrettagruppe** ▲▲ Austria/Switzerland
Sily-Vajdej *see* Vulcan
110 L7 **Silz** Tirol, W Austria 47.17N 11.00E
180 I13 **Sima** Anjouan, SE Comoros 12.10S 44.18E
Simabara *see* Shimabara
Simada *see* Shimada
85 H15 **Simakando** Western, W Zambia 16.43S 24.46E
Simane *see* Shimane
121 L20 **Simanichy** *Rus.* Simonichi. Homyel'skaya Voblasts', SE Belarus 51.53N 28.04E
166 F14 **Simao** Yunnan, SW China 22.30N 101.06E
159 P12 **Simara** Central, C Nepal 27.14N 85.00E
12 I8 **Simard, Lac** ◎ Québec, SE Canada
142 D13 **Simav** Kütahya, W Turkey 39.04N 28.58E
142 D13 **Simav Çayı** ≈ NW Turkey
81 L18 **Simba** Orientale, N Dem. Rep. Congo 0.46N 22.54E
194 H11 **Simbai** Madang, N PNG 5.12S 144.33E
195 O9 **Simberi Island** *island* Tabar Islands, N PNG
Simbirsk *see* Ul'yanovsk
12 F17 **Simcoe** Ontario, S Canada 42.50N 80.16W
12 H14 **Simcoe, Lake** ◎ Ontario, S Canada
82 J11 **Sīmēn** ▲▲ N Ethiopia
116 K11 **Simeonovgrad** *prev.* Maritsa. Khaskovo, S Bulgaria 42.03N 25.36E
118 G11 **Simeria** *Ger.* Pischk, *Hung.* Piski. Hunedoara, W Romania 45.51N 23.00E
109 L24 **Simeto** ≈ Sicilia, Italy, C Mediterranean Sea
173 E5 **Simeulue, Pulau** *island* NW Indonesia
119 T13 **Simferopol'** Respublika Krym, S Ukraine 44.55N 33.05E
119 T13 **Simferopol'** ✕ Respublika Krym, S Ukraine 44.55N 34.04E
Simi *see* Sými
158 M9 **Simikot** Far Western, NW Nepal 30.02N 81.49E
56 F7 **Simití** Bolívar, N Colombia 7.57N 73.57W
116 G11 **Simitla** Blagoevgrad, SW Bulgaria 41.57N 23.06E
37 S15 **Simi Valley** California, W USA 34.17N 118.52W
Simizu *see* Shimizu
Simla *see* Shimla
Şimlăul Silvaniei/Şimleul Silvaniei *see* Şimleu Silvaniei
118 G9 **Şimleu Silvaniei** *Hung.* Szilágsomlyó; *prev.* Şimlăul Silvaniei, Şimleul Silvaniei. Sălaj, NW Romania 47.12N 22.49E
Simmer *see* Simmerbach
103 E19 **Simmerbach** *var.* Simmer. ≈ W Germany
103 F18 **Simmern** Rheinland-Pfalz, W Germany 50.00N 7.30E
24 I7 **Simmesport** Louisiana, S USA 30.58N 91.48W
121 F14 **Simnas** Alytus, S Lithuania 54.23N 23.40E
94 L13 **Simo** Lappi, NW Finland 65.40N 25.04E
Simoda *see* Shimoda
Simodate *see* Shimodate
94 M13 **Simojärvi** ◎ N Finland
94 L13 **Simojoki** ≈ NW Finland
43 U15 **Simojovel** *var.* Simojovel de Allende. Chiapas, SE Mexico 17.12N 92.42W
Simojovel de Allende *see* Simojovel
58 B7 **Simon Bolivar** *var.* Guayaquil. ✕ (Quayaquil) Guayas, W Ecuador 2.16S 79.54W
56 L5 **Simon Bolívar** ✕ (Caracas) Distrito Federal, N Venezuela
Simonichi *see* Simanichy
12 M12 **Simon, Lac** ◎ Québec, SE Canada
Simonoseki *see* Shimonoseki
Šimonovany *see* Partizánske
Simonstad *see* Simon's Town
85 E26 **Simon's Town** *var.* Simonstad. Western Cape, SW South Africa 34.12S 18.25E
Simony *see* Partizánske
Simotuma *see* Shimotsuma
173 F6 **Simpangkaman, Sungai** ≈ Sumatera, NW Indonesia
173 F5 **Simpangkiri, Sungai** ≈ Sumatera, NW Indonesia
Simpeln *see* Simplon
101 M18 **Simpelveld** Limburg, SE Netherlands 50.49N 5.58E
110 E11 **Simplon** *var.* Simpeln. Valais, SW Switzerland 46.13N 8.01E
110 E11 **Simplon Pass** *pass* S Switzerland 46.18N 8.01E
108 C6 **Simplon Tunnel** *tunnel* Italy/Switzerland
Simpson *see* Fort Simpson
190 G1 **Simpson Desert** *desert* Northern Territory/South Australia
8 J9 **Simpson Peak** ▲ British Columbia, W Canada 59.43N 131.29W
15 L3 **Simpson Peninsula** *peninsula* Nunavut, NE Canada
23 P11 **Simpsonville** South Carolina, SE USA 34.44N 82.15W
97 L23 **Simrishamn** Skåne, S Sweden 55.34N 14.20E
127 Pp15 **Simushir, Ostrov** *island* Kuril'skiye Ostrova, SE Russian Federation
Sīnā'/Sinai Peninsula *see* Sinai
173 Ee6 **Sinabang** Sumatera, W Indonesia 2.27N 96.24E
83 N15 **Sina Dhaqa** Galguduud, C Somalia 5.21N 46.21E
77 X8 **Sinai** *var.* Sinai Peninsula, *Ar.* Shibh Jazīrat Sīnā', Sīnā'. *physical region* NE Egypt
118 J12 **Sinaia** Prahova, SE Romania 45.19N 25.33E
196 B16 **Sinajana** C Guam 13.28N 144.45E
42 H8 **Sinaloa** ◈ *state* C Mexico
56 H4 **Sinamaica** Zulia, NW Venezuela 11.06N 71.52W
169 X14 **Sinan-ni** SE North Korea 38.37N 127.43E
Sinano Gawa *see* Shinano-gawa
Sīnāwan *see* Sīnāwin
77 N8 **Sīnāwin** *var.* Sīnāwan. NW Libya 31.00N 10.37E
85 J16 **Sinazongwe** Southern, S Zambia 17.11S 27.20E
177 Ff6 **Sinbaungwe** Magwe, W Myanmar 19.43N 95.10E
177 Ff5 **Sinbyugyun** Magwe, W Myanmar 20.37N 94.40E
56 E6 **Since** Sucre, NW Colombia 9.15N 75.12W
56 E6 **Sincelejo** Sucre, NW Colombia 9.16N 75.22W
177 F5 **Sinchaingbyin** *var.* Zullapara. Arakan State, W Myanmar 20.51N 92.23E
25 U4 **Sinclair, Lake** ⊠ Georgia, SE USA
8 M14 **Sinclair Mills** British Columbia, SW Canada 54.03N 121.37W
178 Mm15 **Sin Cowe East Island** *island* S Spratly Islands
178 Mm15 **Sin Cowe Island** *island* SW Spratly Islands
155 Q14 **Sind** *var.* Sindh. ◈ *province* SE Pakistan
160 I8 **Sind** ≈ N India
97 H19 **Sindal** Nordjylland, N Denmark 57.28N 10.13E
179 Q15 **Sindañgan** Mindanao, S Philippines 8.09N 122.59E
81 D19 **Sindara** Ngounié, W Gabon 1.07S 10.40E
158 E13 **Sindari** *prev.* Sindri. Rājasthān, N India 25.34N 71.57E
175 Q16 **Sindeh, Teluk** *bay* Nusa Tenggara, C Indonesia
116 N8 **Sindel** Varna, E Bulgaria 43.07N 27.35E
103 H22 **Sindelfingen** Baden-Württemberg, SW Germany 48.43N 9.01E
161 G16 **Sindgi** Karnātaka, C India 17.01N 76.22E
Sindh *see* Sind
120 G5 **Sindi** *Ger.* Zintenhof. Pärnumaa, SW Estonia 58.25N 24.40E
142 C13 **Sındırgı** Balıkesir, W Turkey 39.15N 28.10E
79 N14 **Sindou** SW Burkina 10.34N 5.04W
Sindri *see* Sindari
155 T9 **Sind Sāgar Doāb** *desert* E Pakistan
130 M11 **Sinegorskiy** Rostovskaya Oblast', SW Russian Federation 48.01N 40.52E
127 O9 **Sinegor'ye** Magadanskaya Oblast', E Russian Federation 62.04N 150.33E
116 O12 **Sinekli** İstanbul, NW Turkey 41.13N 28.13E
106 F12 **Sines** Setúbal, S Portugal 37.58N 8.52W
106 F12 **Sines, Cabo de** *headland* S Portugal 37.57N 8.55W
94 L12 **Sinettä** Lappi, NW Finland 66.39N 25.25E
195 P11 **Sinewit, Mount** ▲ New Britain, C PNG 4.42S 151.58E
82 G11 **Singa** *var.* Sinja, Sinjah. Sinnar, E Sudan 13.07N 33.54E
80 J12 **Singako** Moyen-Chari, S Chad 9.52N 19.31E
Singan *see* Xi'an
174 I7 **Singapore** ● (Singapore) S Singapore 1.17N 103.48E
174 I7 **Singapore** *off.* Republic of Singapore. ◆ *republic* SE Asia
174 I7 **Singapore Strait** *var.* Strait of Singapore, *Mal.* Selat Singapura. *strait* Indonesia/Singapore
Singapore, Strait of/Singapura, Selat *see* Singapore Strait
175 N16 **Singaraja** Bali, C Indonesia 8.06S 115.04E
Singatoka *see* Sigatoka
178 H10 **Sing Buri** *var.* Singhaburi. Sing Buri, C Thailand 14.55N 100.21E
103 H24 **Singen** Baden-Württemberg, S Germany 47.46N 8.49E
Sîngeorgiu de Pădure *see* Sângeorgiu de Pădure
Sîngeorz-Băi/Singeroz Băi *see* Sângeorz-Băi
118 M9 **Sîngerei** *var.* Sângerei; *prev.* Lazovsk. N Moldova 47.38N 28.08E
Singhaburi *see* Sing Buri
83 H21 **Singida** Singida, C Tanzania 4.45S 34.48E
83 G22 **Singida** ◈ *region* C Tanzania
Singidunum *see* Beograd
177 G2 **Singkaling Hkamti** Sagaing, N Myanmar 26.00N 95.43E
175 Pp12 **Singkang** Sulawesi, C Indonesia 4.09S 119.58E
174 Gg8 **Singkarak, Danau** ◎ Sumatera, W Indonesia
174 K7 **Singkawang** Borneo, C Indonesia 0.57N 108.57E
174 I8 **Singkep, Pulau** *island* Kepulauan Lingga, W Indonesia
173 F6 **Singkilbaru** Sumatera, W Indonesia 2.18N 97.47E
191 T7 **Singleton** New South Wales, SE Australia 32.36S 151.10E
Singora *see* Songkhla
Singû *see* Shingū
Sining *see* Xining
109 D17 **Siniscola** Sardegna, Italy, C Mediterranean Sea 40.34N 9.42E
115 F14 **Sinj** Split-Dalmacija, SE Croatia 43.41N 16.37E
Sinja/Sinjah *see* Singa
Sinjajevina *see* Sinjavina
145 P3 **Sinjār** NW Iraq 36.19N 41.51E
145 P2 **Sinjār, Jabal** ▲▲ N Iraq
115 K15 **Sinjavina** *var.* Sinjajevina. ▲▲ SW Serbia and Montenegro (Yugoslavia)
82 I7 **Sinkat** Red Sea, NE Sudan 18.52N 36.51E
Sinkiang/Sinkiang Uighur Autonomous Region *see* Xinjiang Uygur Zizhiqu
Sînmartin *see* Târnăveni
169 V13 **Sinmi-do** *island* NW North Korea
Sinminato *see* Shinminato
103 I18 **Sinn** ≈ C Germany
Sinnamarie *see* Sinnamary
57 Y9 **Sinnamary** *var.* Sinnamarie. N French Guiana 5.23N 52.57W
Sinn'anyô *see* Shinnanyō
82 G11 **Sinnar** ◈ *state* E Sudan
Sinneh *see* Sanandaj
20 E13 **Sinnemahoning Creek** ≈ Pennsylvania, NE USA
Sînnicolau Mare *see* Sânnicolau Mare
Sino/Sinoe *see* Greenville
Sinoe, Lacul *see* Sinoie, Lacul
Sinoia *see* Chinhoyi
119 N14 **Sinoie, Lacul** *prev.* Lacul Sinoe. *lagoon* SE Romania
61 H16 **Sinop** Mato Grosso, W Brazil 11.38S 55.27W
142 K10 **Sinop** *anc.* Sinope. Sinop, N Turkey 42.01N 35.09E
142 J10 **Sinop** ◈ *province* N Turkey
142 K10 **Sinop Burnu** *headland* N Turkey 42.02N 35.12E
Sinope *see* Sinop
169 Y12 **Sinp'o** E North Korea 40.01N 128.09E
103 H20 **Sinsheim** Baden-Württemberg, SW Germany 49.15N 8.52E
Sinsiro *see* Shinshiro
Sîntana *see* Sântana
174 L8 **Sintang** Borneo, C Indonesia 0.03N 111.31E
101 F14 **Sint Annaland** Zeeland, SW Netherlands 51.36N 4.07E
100 L5 **Sint Annaparochie** Friesland, N Netherlands 53.20N 5.46E
47 V9 **Sint Eustatius** *Eng.* Saint Eustatius. *island* N Netherlands Antilles
101 G19 **Sint-Genesius-Rode** *Fr.* Rhode-Saint-Genèse. Vlaams Brabant, C Belgium 50.45N 4.21E
101 F16 **Sint-Gillis-Waas** Oost-Vlaanderen, N Belgium 51.14N 4.08E
101 H17 **Sint-Katelijne-Waver** Antwerpen, C Belgium 51.05N 4.31E
101 E18 **Sint-Lievens-Houtem** Oost-Vlaanderen, NW Belgium 50.55N 3.52E
47 V9 **Sint Maarten** *Eng.* Saint Martin. *island* N Netherlands Antilles
101 F14 **Sint Maartensdijk** Zeeland, SW Netherlands 51.33N 4.05E
101 L19 **Sint-Martens-Voeren** *Fr.* Fouron-Saint-Martin. Limburg, NE Belgium 50.46N 5.49E
101 J14 **Sint-Michielsgestel** Noord-Brabant, S Netherlands 51.37N 5.21E
Sînt-Miclăuş *see* Gheorgheni
47 O16 **Sint Nicholaas** S Aruba 12.25N 69.52W
101 F16 **Sint-Niklaas** *Fr.* Saint-Nicolas. Oost-Vlaanderen, N Belgium 51.10N 4.09E
101 K14 **Sint-Oedenrode** Noord-Brabant, S Netherlands 51.34N 5.28E
27 T14 **Sinton** Texas, SW USA 28.02N 97.30W
101 G14 **Sint Philipsland** Zeeland, SW Netherlands 51.37N 4.11E
101 G19 **Sint-Pieters-Leeuw** Vlaams Brabant, C Belgium 50.46N 4.16E
106 E11 **Sintra** *prev.* Cintra. Lisboa, W Portugal 38.48N 9.22W
101 J18 **Sint-Truiden** *Fr.* Saint-Trond. Limburg, NE Belgium 50.48N 5.13E
101 H14 **Sint Willebrord** Noord-Brabant, S Netherlands 51.33N 4.34E
169 V13 **Sinŭiju** W North Korea 40.08N 124.33E
82 P13 **Sinujiif** Nugaal, NE Somalia 8.33N 49.05E
Sinus Aelaniticus *see* Aqaba, Gulf of
Sinus Gallicus *see* Lion, Golfe du
Sinyang *see* Xinyang
Sinyavka *see* Sinyawka
121 I18 **Sinyawka** *Rus.* Sinyavka. Minskaya Voblasts', SW Belarus 52.57N 26.29E
126 Ll11 **Sinyaya** ≈ NE Russian Federation
Sinying *see* Hsinying
Sinyukha *see* Synyukha
Sinzi-ko *see* Shinji-ko
Sinzyô *see* Shinjō
113 I24 **Sió** ≈ W Hungary
179 Q16 **Siocon** Mindanao, S Philippines 7.37N 122.09E
113 I24 **Siófok** Somogy, C Hungary 46.54N 18.03E
Siogama *see* Shiogama
85 G15 **Sioma** Western, SW Zambia 16.41S 23.34E
110 D11 **Sion** *Ger.* Sitten; *anc.* Sedunum. Valais, SW Switzerland 46.15N 7.23E
105 O11 **Sioule** ≈ C France
31 S12 **Sioux Center** Iowa, C USA 43.04N 96.10W
31 R13 **Sioux City** Iowa, C USA 42.30N 96.24W
31 R11 **Sioux Falls** South Dakota, N USA 43.33N 96.45W
10 B11 **Sioux Lookout** Ontario, S Canada 49.27N 94.06W
31 T12 **Sioux Rapids** Iowa, C USA 42.53N 95.09W
Sioux State *see* North Dakota
Sioziri *see* Shiojiri
179 Q14 **Sipalay** Negros, C Philippines 9.46N 122.25E
57 V11 **Sipaliwini** ◈ *district* S Suriname
47 U15 **Siparia** Trinidad, Trinidad and Tobago 10.07N 61.33W
Siphnos *see* Sífnos
169 V11 **Siping** *var.* Ssu-p'ing, Szeping; *prev.* Ssu-p'ing-chieh. Jilin, NE China 43.09N 124.22E
9 X12 **Sipiwesk** Manitoba, C Canada 55.28N 97.16W
9 W13 **Sipiwesk Lake** ◎ Manitoba, C Canada
205 O11 **Siple Coast** *physical region* Antarctica
204 K12 **Siple Island** *island* Antarctica
204 K13 **Siple, Mount** ▲ Siple Island, Antarctica 73.25S 126.24W
Sipoo *see* Sibbo
114 G12 **Šipovo** Republika Srpska, W Bosnia and Herzegovina 44.16N 17.05E
25 O4 **Sipsey River** ≈ Alabama, S USA
173 Ff10 **Sipura, Pulau** *island* W Indonesia
(0) G16 **Siqueiros Fracture Zone** *tectonic feature* E Pacific Ocean
44 L10 **Siquia, Río** ≈ SE Nicaragua
179 Qq14 **Siquijor Island** *island* C Philippines
45 N13 **Siquirres** Limón, E Costa Rica 10.06N 83.33W
56 J5 **Siquisique** Lara, N Venezuela 10.36N 69.38W
161 G19 **Sīra** Karnātaka, W India 13.46N 76.54E
97 D16 **Sira** ≈ S Norway
178 Hh12 **Siracha** *var.* Ban Si Racha, Si Racha. Chon Buri, S Thailand 13.10N 100.57E
109 L25 **Siracusa** *Eng.* Syracuse. Sicilia, Italy, C Mediterranean Sea 37.04N 15.16E
Sirajganj *see* Shirajganj Ghat
Sirakawa *see* Shirakawa
9 N14 **Sir Alexander, Mount** ▲ British Columbia, W Canada 54.00N 120.33W
143 O12 **Şiran** Gümüşhane, NE Turkey 40.12N 39.07E
79 Q12 **Sirba** ≈ E Burkina
149 O17 **Şīr Banī Yās** *island* W UAE
97 D17 **Sirdalsvannet** ◎ S Norway
Sir Darya/Sirdaryo *see* Syr Darya
153 P10 **Sirdaryo** Sirdaryo Viloyati, E Uzbekistan 40.46N 68.34E
153 O11 **Sirdaryo Viloyati** *Rus.* Syrdar'inskaya Oblast'. ◈ *province* E Uzbekistan
Sir Donald Sangster International Airport *see* Sangster
194 H13 **Sirebi** ≈ S PNG
189 S3 **Sir Edward Pellew Group** *island group* Northern Territory, NE Australia
118 K8 **Siret** *Ger.* Sereth, *Hung.* Szeret. Suceava, N Romania 47.55N 26.04E
118 K8 **Siret** *var.* Siretul, *Ger.* Sereth, *Rus.* Seret, *Ukr.* Siret. ≈ Romania/Ukraine
Siretul *see* Siret
146 K3 **Sirḩān, Wādī as** *dry watercourse* Jordan/Saudi Arabia
158 I8 **Sirhind** Punjab, N India 30.39N 76.28E
118 F11 **Şiria** *Ger.* Schiria. Arad, W Romania 46.16N 21.37E
Siria *see* Syria
149 S14 **Sīrīk** Hormozgān, SE Iran 26.31N 57.06E
178 Hh8 **Sirikit Reservoir** ◎ N Thailand
60 K12 **Sirituba, Ilha** *island* NE Brazil
176 Ww11 **Siriwo** ≈ Papua, E Indonesia
149 R11 **Sīrjān** *prev.* Sa'īdābād. Kermān, S Iran 29.28N 55.39E
190 H9 **Sir Joseph Banks Group** *island group* South Australia
94 K11 **Sirkka** Lappi, N Finland 67.49N 24.48E
Sirna *see* Sýrna
143 R16 **Şırnak** Şırnak, SE Turkey 37.33N 42.27E
143 S16 **Şırnak** ◈ *province* SE Turkey
Siroisi *see* Shiroishi
161 J14 **Sironcha** Mahārāshtra, C India 18.51N 80.03E
Sirone *see* Shirone
Síros *see* Sýros
Sirotino *see* Sirotsina
120 M12 **Sirotsina** *Rus.* Sirotino. Vitsyebskaya Voblasts', N Belarus 55.22N 29.34E
158 H9 **Sirsa** Haryāna, NW India 29.31N 75.04E
181 Y17 **Sir Seewoosagur Ramgoolam** ✕ (Port Louis) SE Mauritius
161 E18 **Sirsi** Karnātaka, W India 14.46N 74.49E
152 K12 **Şirşütür Gumy** *var.* Shirshütür, *Rus.* Peski Shirshyutyur. *desert* E Turkmenistan
Sirte *see* Surt
190 A2 **Sir Thomas, Mount** ▲ South Australia 27.09S 129.49E
Sirti, Gulf of *see* Surt, Khalīj
148 J5 **Sīrvān, Rūdkhāneh-ye** *var.* Nahr Diyālá, Sirwan. ≈ Iran/Iraq *see also* Diyālá, Nahr
120 H13 **Širvintos** Vilnius, SE Lithuania 55.01N 24.58E
Sirwan *see* Diyālá, Nahr/Sīrvān, Rūdkhāneh-ye
9 N15 **Sir Wilfrid Laurier, Mount** ▲ British Columbia, SW Canada 52.45N 119.51W
12 M10 **Sir-Wilfrid, Mont** ▲ Québec, SE Canada 46.57N 75.33W
Sisačko-Moslavačka Županija *see* Sisak-Moslavina
114 E9 **Sisak** *var.* Siscia, *Ger.* Sissek, *Hung.* Sziszek; *anc.* Segestica. Sisak-Moslavina, C Croatia 45.28N 16.21E
178 J10 **Si Sa Ket** *var.* Sisaket, Sri Saket. Si Sa Ket, E Thailand 15.07N 104.18E
114 E9 **Sisak-Moslavina** *off.* Sisačko-Moslavačka Županija. ◈ *province* C Croatia
178 H8 **Si Satchanala** Sukhothai, NW Thailand
Siscia *see* Sisak
176 W10 **Sisember** Papua, E Indonesia 1.51S 134.09E
85 G22 **Sishen** Northern Cape, NW South Africa 27.46S 22.58E
143 V13 **Sisian** SE Armenia 39.31N 46.03E
207 N13 **Sisimiut** *var.* Holsteinborg, Holsteinsborg, Holstenborg, Holstensborg. Kitaa, S Greenland 67.07N 53.42W
32 M1 **Siskiwit Bay** *bay* Michigan, USA
36 L1 **Siskiyou Mountains** ▲▲ California/Oregon, W USA
178 I12 **Sisŏphŏn** Bătdâmbâng, NW Cambodia 13.37N 102.58E
110 E7 **Sissach** Basel-Land, NW Switzerland 47.27N 7.48E
194 F9 **Sissano** Sandaun, NW PNG 3.01S 142.01E
Sissek *see* Sisak
31 R7 **Sisseton** South Dakota, N USA 45.39N 97.03W
149 W9 **Sīstān, Daryācheh-ye** *var.* Daryācheh-ye Hāmūn, Hāmūn-e Şāberī. ◎ Afghanistan/Iran *see also* Şāberī, Hāmūn-e
149 V12 **Sīstān va Balūchestān** *off.* Ostān-e Sīstān va Balūchestān, *var.* Balūchestān va Sīstān. ◈ *province* SE Iran
105 T14 **Sisteron** Alpes-de-Haute-Provence, SE France 44.12N 5.55E
34 H13 **Sisters** Oregon, NW USA 44.17N 121.33W
67 G15 **Sisters Peak** ▲ N Ascension Island 7.55S 14.22W
23 R3 **Sistersville** West Virginia, NE USA 39.33N 81.00W
Sistova *see* Svishtov
Sitakund *see* Sitakunda
159 V16 **Sitakunda** *var.* Sitakund. Chittagong, SE Bangladesh 22.35N 91.40E
159 P12 **Sītāmarhi** Bihār, N India 26.36N 85.30E
158 L11 **Sītāpur** Uttar Pradesh, N India 27.33N 80.40E
Sitaş Cristuru *see* Cristuru Secuiesc
117 L25 **Siteía** *var.* Sitía. Kríti, Greece, E Mediterranean Sea 35.13N 26.06E
107 V6 **Sitges** Cataluña, NE Spain 41.13N 1.49E
117 H15 **Sithoniá** *peninsula* NE Greece
Sitía *see* Siteía
56 F4 **Sitionuevo** Magdalena, N Colombia 10.41N 74.42W
41 X13 **Sitka** Baranof Island, Alaska, USA 57.03N 135.19W
41 Q15 **Sitkinak Island** *island* Trinity Islands, Alaska, USA
177 G7 **Sittang** *var.* Sittoung. ≈ S Myanmar
101 L17 **Sittard** Limburg, SE Netherlands 51.00N 5.52E
Sitten *see* Sion
110 H7 **Sitter** ≈ NW Switzerland
111 U10 **Sittersdorf** Kärnten, S Austria 46.31N 14.34E
Sittoung *see* Sittang
177 F6 **Sittwe** *var.* Akyab. Arakan State, W Myanmar 22.09N 92.51E

◆ Country
● Country Capital
◇ Dependent Territory
○ Dependent Territory Capital
◈ Administrative Region
✕ International Airport
▲ Mountain
▲▲ Mountain Range
Volcano
≈ River
◎ Lake
⊠ Reservoir

SITUBONDO – SOKOTO

174 Mm15 Situbondo prev. Sitoebondo. Jawa, C Indonesia 7.40S 114.01E
44 L8 Siuna Región Autónoma Atlántico Norte, NE Nicaragua 13.43N 84.46W
159 R15 Siuri West Bengal, NE India 23.54N 87.31E
Siut see Asyūt
126 M15 Sivaki Amurskaya Oblast', SE Russian Federation 52.39N 126.43E
142 M13 Sivas anc. Sebastia, Sebaste. Sivas, C Turkey 39.43N 37.01E
142 M13 Sivas ◆ province C Turkey
143 O15 Siverek Şanlıurfa, S Turkey 37.46N 39.19E
119 X6 Sivers'k Donets'ka Oblast', E Ukraine 48.52N 38.07E
128 G13 Siverskiy Leningradskaya Oblast', NW Russian Federation 59.21N 30.01E
119 X6 Sivers'kyy Donets' Rus. Severskiy Donets. Russian Federation/Ukraine see also Severskiy Donets
129 W5 Sivomaskinskiy Respublika Komi, NW Russian Federation 66.42N 62.33E
142 G13 Sivrihisar Eskişehir, W Turkey 39.28N 31.29E
101 F22 Sivry Hainaut, S Belgium 50.10N 4.11E
127 Pp9 Sivuchiy, Mys headland E Russian Federation 56.45N 163.13E
77 U9 Siwa var. Sīwah. NW Egypt 29.11N 25.32E
Sīwah see Siwa
158 J9 Siwalik Range var. Shiwālik Range. India/Nepal
159 O13 Siwān Bihār, N India 26.13N 84.21E
45 O14 Sixaola, Río Costa Rica/Panama
Six Counties, The see Northern Ireland
105 T16 Six-Fours-les-Plages Var, SE France 43.04N 5.49E
167 Q7 Sixian var. Si Xian. Anhui, E China 33.28N 117.52E
24 J9 Six Mile Lake Louisiana, S USA
145 V3 Siyāh Gūz E Iraq 35.49N 45.45E
161 L25 Siyambalanduwa Uva Province, SE Sri Lanka 6.54N 81.31E
143 Y10 Siyäzän Rus. Siazan'. NE Azerbaijan 41.04N 49.04E
Sizebolu see Sozopol
Sizuoka see Shizuoka
Sjar see Sääre
115 L15 Sjenica Turk. Seniça. Serbia, SW Serbia and Montenegro (Yugoslavia) 43.16N 20.01E
96 G11 Sjoa S Norway
97 K23 Sjöbo Skåne, S Sweden 55.37N 13.45E
97 I24 Sjælland Eng. Zealand, Ger. Seeland. island E Denmark
96 E9 Sjøholt Møre og Romsdal, S Norway 62.28N 6.49E
94 O1 Sjuøyane island group N Svalbard
Skadar see Shkodër
Skadarsko Jezero see Scutari, Lake
119 R11 Skadovs'k Khersons'ka Oblast', S Ukraine 46.07N 32.53E
94 I2 Skagaströnd prev. Höfdhakaupstadhur. Nordhurland Vestra, N Iceland 65.49N 20.18W
97 H19 Skagen Nordjylland, N Denmark 57.43N 11.36E
Skagerak see Skagerrak
97 L16 Skagern C Sweden
207 T17 Skagerrak var. Skagerak. channel N Europe
96 G12 Skaget ▲ S Norway 61.19N 9.07E
34 H7 Skagit River Washington, NW USA
41 W12 Skagway Alaska, USA 59.27N 135.18W
94 K8 Skáidi Finnmark, N Norway 70.26N 24.31E
117 F21 Skála Pelopónnisos, S Greece 36.51N 22.39E
118 K6 Skalat Pol. Skałat. Ternopil's'ka Oblast', W Ukraine 49.27N 25.59E
97 J22 Skälderviken inlet Denmark/Sweden
128 J3 Skalistyy Murmanskaya Oblast', NW Russian Federation 69.16N 33.20E
94 I12 Skalka N Sweden
116 I12 Skalotí Anatolikí Makedonía kai Thráki, NE Greece 41.24N 24.16E
97 G22 Skanderborg Århus, C Denmark 56.01N 9.57E
97 K22 Skåne prev. Eng. Scania. ◆ county S Sweden
77 N6 Skanès ✕ (Sousse) E Tunisia 35.36N 10.56E
97 C15 Skånevik Hordaland, S Norway 59.43N 6.35E
97 M18 Skänninge Östergötland, S Sweden 58.24N 15.04E
97 J23 Skanör med Falsterbo Skåne, S Sweden 55.24N 12.48E
117 H17 Skantzoúra island Vóreioi Sporádes, Greece, Aegean Sea
97 K18 Skara Västra Götaland, S Sweden 58.22N 13.25E
97 M17 Skärblacka Östergötland, S Sweden 58.34N 15.54E
97 I18 Skärhamn Västra Götaland, S Sweden 57.58N 11.33E
97 I14 Skarnes Hedmark, S Norway 60.13N 11.40E
121 M21 Skarodnaye Rus. Skorodnoye. Homyel'skaya Voblasts', SE Belarus 51.38N 28.50E
112 I8 Skarszewy Ger. Schöneck. Pomorskie, NW Poland 54.04N 18.25E
113 M14 Skarżysko-Kamienna Świętokrzyskie, C Poland 51.07N 20.52E
97 K16 Skattkärr Värmland, C Sweden 59.25N 13.42E
120 D12 Skaudvilė Tauragė, SW Lithuania 55.25N 22.33E
94 J12 Skaulo Lapp. Sávdijári. Norrbotten, N Sweden 67.21N 21.03E
113 K17 Skawina Małopolskie, S Poland 49.56N 19.49E
8 K12 Skeena British Columbia, SW Canada
8 J11 Skeena Mountains ▲ British Columbia, W Canada
99 O18 Skegness E England, UK 53.10N 0.21E
94 J4 Skeidharársandur coast S Iceland
95 J15 Skellefteå Västerbotten, N Sweden 64.45N 20.57E
95 I14 Skellefteälven N Sweden
95 J15 Skelleftehamn Västerbotten, N Sweden 64.41N 21.13E
27 O2 Skellytown Texas, SW USA 35.34N 101.10W
97 J19 Skene Västra Götaland, S Sweden 57.30N 12.34E
99 G17 Skerries Ir. Na Sceirí. E Ireland 53.34N 6.07W
97 H15 Ski Akershus, S Norway 59.43N 10.49E
117 G17 Skíathos Skíathos, Vóreioi Sporádes, Greece, Aegean Sea 39.10N 23.30E
117 G17 Skíathos island Vóreioi Sporádes, Greece, Aegean Sea
29 P9 Skiatook Oklahoma, C USA 36.22N 96.00W
29 P9 Skiatook Lake Oklahoma, C USA
99 B22 Skibbereen Ir. An Sciobairín. SW Ireland 51.33N 9.15W
94 I9 Skibotn Troms, N Norway 69.22N 20.18E
121 F16 Skidal' Rus. Skidel'. Hrodzyenskaya Voblasts', W Belarus 53.34N 24.12E
99 K15 Skiddaw ▲ NW England, UK 54.37N 3.07W
Skidel' see Skidal'
27 T14 Skidmore Texas, SW USA 28.13N 97.40W
97 G16 Skien Telemark, S Norway 59.12N 9.36E
Skiermûntseach see Schiermonnikoog
112 L12 Skierniewice Łodzkie, C Poland 51.58N 20.10E
76 L5 Skikda prev. Philippeville. NE Algeria 36.51N 7.00E
32 M16 Skillet Fork Illinois, N USA
97 L19 Skillingaryd Jönköping, S Sweden 57.27N 14.04E
117 B19 Skinári, Akrotírio headland Zákynthos, Iónioi Nísoi, Greece, C Mediterranean Sea 37.55N 20.57E
97 M15 Skinnskatteberg Västmanland, C Sweden 59.49N 15.40E
190 M12 Skipton Victoria, SE Australia 37.44S 143.21E
99 L16 Skipton N England, UK 53.56N 1.59W
Skiropoula see Skyropoúla
Skíros see Skýros
97 F21 Skive Viborg, NW Denmark 56.34N 9.01E
96 F11 Skjåk Oppland, S Norway 61.52N 8.21E
94 K2 Skjálfandafljót C Iceland
97 F22 Skjern Ringkøbing, W Denmark 55.55N 8.30E
97 F22 Skjern Å var. Skjern Aa. W Denmark
Skjern Aa see Skjern Å
94 G12 Skjerstad Nordland, C Norway 67.14N 15.00E
94 J8 Skjervøy Troms, N Norway 70.01N 20.57E
94 I10 Skjold Troms, N Norway 69.03N 19.18E
113 I17 Skoczów Śląskie, S Poland 49.47N 18.46E
97 I24 Skælskør Vestsjælland, E Denmark 55.16N 11.18E
111 T11 Škofja Loka Ger. Bischoflack. NW Slovenia 46.12N 14.16E
96 N12 Skog Gävleborg, C Sweden 61.10N 16.49E
97 K16 Skoghall Värmland, C Sweden 59.19N 13.30E
33 N10 Skokie Illinois, N USA 42.01N 87.43W
118 H6 Skole L'vivs'ka Oblast', W Ukraine 49.04N 23.29E
117 D19 Skóllis ▲ S Greece 37.58N 21.33E
178 J13 Skon Kâmpóng Cham, C Cambodia 12.56N 104.36E
117 H17 Skópelos Skópelos, Vóreioi Sporádes, Greece, Aegean Sea 39.07N 23.44E
117 H17 Skópelos island Vóreioi Sporádes, Greece, Aegean Sea
130 L5 Skopin Ryazanskaya Oblast', W Russian Federation 53.46N 39.37E
115 N18 Skopje var. Üsküb, Turk. Üsküp; prev. Skoplje, anc. Scupi. ● (FYR Macedonia) N FYR Macedonia 42.01N 21.27E
115 O18 Skopje ✕ N FYR Macedonia 41.58N 21.35E
Skoplje see Skopje
112 I8 Skórcz Ger. Skurz. Pomorskie, N Poland 53.46N 18.43E
Skorodnoye see Skarodnaye
95 H16 Skorped Västernorrland, C Sweden 63.22N 17.55E
97 G21 Skørping Nordjylland, N Denmark 56.49N 9.55E
97 K18 Skövde Västra Götaland, S Sweden 58.24N 13.52E
126 Ll14 Skovorodino Amurskaya Oblast', SE Russian Federation 54.02N 123.47E
21 Q6 Skowhegan Maine, NE USA 44.46N 69.41W
9 W15 Skownan Manitoba, S Canada 51.55N 99.34W
96 H13 Skreia Oppland, S Norway 60.37N 11.00E
Skripón see Orchómenos
120 H9 Skrīveri Aizkraukle, S Latvia 56.39N 25.07E
120 J11 Skrudaliena Daugavpils, SE Latvia 55.50N 26.42E
120 D9 Skrunda Kuldīga, W Latvia 56.39N 22.01E
97 C16 Skudeneshavn Rogaland, S Norway 59.09N 5.16E
85 L20 Skukuza Mpumalanga, NE South Africa 24.54S 31.33E
99 B22 Skull Ir. An Scoil. SW Ireland 51.32N 9.33W
24 L3 Skuna River Mississippi, S USA
31 X15 Skunk River Iowa, C USA
120 C10 Skuodas Ger. Schoden, Pol. Szkudy. Klaipėda, NW Lithuania 56.16N 21.30E
97 K23 Skurup Skåne, S Sweden 55.28N 13.30E
Skurz see Skórcz
116 H8 Skŭt NW Bulgaria
96 O13 Skutskär Uppsala, C Sweden 60.38N 17.29E
97 B19 Skúvoy Dan. Skuø Island Faeroe Islands 61.46N 6.49W
Skvira see Skvyra
119 O5 Skvyra Rus. Skvira. Kyyivs'ka Oblast', N Ukraine 49.44N 29.40E
41 Q11 Skwentna Alaska, USA 61.56N 151.03W
112 E11 Skwierzyna Ger. Schwerin. Lubuskie, W Poland 52.36N 15.27E
38 K13 Sky Harbour ✕ (Phoenix) Arizona, SW USA 33.26N 112.00W
98 G9 Skye, Isle of island NW Scotland, UK
34 I8 Skykomish Washington, NW USA 47.40N 121.20W
Skylge see Terschelling
65 F19 Skyring, Peninsula peninsula S Chile
65 H24 Skyring, Seno inlet S Chile
117 H17 Skyropoúla var. Skiropoula. island Vóreioi Sporádes, Greece, Aegean Sea
117 I17 Skýros var. Skíros. Skýros, Vóreioi Sporádes, Greece, Aegean Sea 38.55N 24.34E
117 I17 Skýros var. Skíros; anc. Scyros. island Vóreioi Sporádes, Greece, Aegean Sea
120 J12 Slabodka Rus. Slobodka. Vitsyebskaya Voblasts', NW Belarus 55.42N 27.10E
97 I23 Slagelse Vestsjælland, E Denmark 55.25N 11.21E
95 I14 Slagnäs Norrbotten, N Sweden 65.36N 18.10E
174 Kk15 Slamet, Gunung ▲ Jawa, S Indonesia 7.12S 109.13E
41 T10 Slana Alaska, USA 62.46N 144.00W
99 F20 Slaney Ir. An tSláine. SE Ireland
118 J13 Slănic Prahova, SE Romania 45.13N 25.58E
118 K11 Slănic Moldova Bacău, E Romania 46.12N 26.23E
115 H16 Slano Dubrovnik-Neretva, SE Croatia 42.47N 17.54E
128 F13 Slantsy Leningradskaya Oblast', NW Russian Federation 59.06N 28.00E
113 C16 Slaný Ger. Schlan. Střední Čechy, NW Czech Republic 50.13N 14.04E
113 I16 Śląskie ◆ province S Poland
10 C10 Slate Falls Ontario, S Canada 51.11N 91.32W
29 T4 Slater Missouri, C USA 39.13N 93.04W
114 H9 Slatina Hung. Szlatina prev. Podravska Slatina. Virovitica-Podravina, NE Croatia 45.40N 17.46E
118 I14 Slatina Olt, S Romania 44.27N 24.21E
27 N5 Slaton Texas, SW USA 33.26N 101.38W
97 H14 Slattum Akershus, S Norway 60.00N 10.55E
9 R10 Slave Alberta/Northwest Territories, C Canada
70 E11 Slave Coast coastal region W Africa
9 P13 Slave Lake Alberta, SW Canada 55.16N 114.46W
125 G14 Slavgorod Altayskiy Kray, S Russian Federation 52.55N 78.46E
Slavgorod see Slawharad
Slavonia see Slavonija
114 G9 Slavonija Eng. Slavonia, Ger. Slawonien, Hung. Szlavonia, Szlavonorszag. cultural region NE Croatia
Slavonska Požega see Požega
114 H10 Slavonski Brod Ger. Brod, Hung. Bród; prev. Brod, Brod na Savi. Brod-Posavina, NE Croatia 45.09N 18.00E
118 L4 Slavuta Khmel'nyts'ka Oblast', NW Ukraine 50.17N 26.52E
119 P2 Slavutych Chernihivs'ka Oblast', N Ukraine 51.31N 30.47E
127 N18 Slavyanka Primorskiy Kray, SE Russian Federation 42.46N 131.19E
116 J8 Slavyanovo Pleven, N Bulgaria 43.28N 24.52E
Slavyansk see Slov"yans'k
130 K14 Slavyansk-na-Kubani Krasnodarskiy Kray, SW Russian Federation 45.16N 38.09E
121 N20 Slavyechna Rus. Slovechna. Belarus/Ukraine
121 O16 Slawharad Rus. Slavgorod. Mahilyowskaya Voblasts', E Belarus 53.27N 31.00E
112 G7 Sławno Zachodnio-pomorskie, NW Poland 54.22N 16.43E
Slawonien see Slavonija
31 S10 Slayton Minnesota, N USA 43.59N 95.45W
99 N18 Sleaford E England, UK 52.58N 0.27W
99 A20 Slea Head Ir. Ceann Sléibhe. headland SW Ireland 52.05N 10.25W
98 G9 Sleat, Sound of strait NW Scotland, UK
Sledyuki see Slyedzyuki
10 I5 Sleeper Islands island group Nunavut, C Canada
33 O6 Sleeping Bear Point headland Michigan, N USA 44.54N 86.02W
31 T10 Sleepy Eye Minnesota, N USA 44.18N 94.43W
41 O11 Sleetmute Alaska, USA 61.42N 157.10W
Sléibhe, Ceann see Slea Head
Slemāni see As Sulaymānīyah
205 O5 Slessor Glacier glacier Antarctica
24 L9 Slidell Louisiana, S USA 30.16N 89.46W
20 K12 Slide Mountain ▲ New York, NE USA 42.00N 74.23W
100 I13 Sliedrecht Zuid-Holland, C Netherlands 51.49N 4.45E
123 Jj16 Sliema N Malta 35.54N 14.31E
99 G16 Slieve Donard ▲ SE Northern Ireland, UK 54.10N 5.57W
Sligeach see Sligo
99 D16 Sligo Ir. Sligeach. NW Ireland 54.16N 8.28W
99 C16 Sligo Ir. Sligeach. cultural region NW Ireland
99 C15 Sligo Bay Ir. Cuan Shligigh. inlet NW Ireland
20 B13 Slippery Rock Pennsylvania, NE USA 41.02N 80.02W
97 P19 Slite Gotland, SE Sweden 57.37N 18.46E
116 L9 Sliven var. Slivno. Sliven, C Bulgaria 42.42N 26.20E
116 L10 Sliven ◆ province C Bulgaria
116 G9 Slivnitsa Sofiya, W Bulgaria 42.51N 23.01E
Slivno see Sliven
116 L7 Slivo Pole Ruse, N Bulgaria 43.57N 26.15E
31 S13 Sloan Iowa, C USA 42.13N 96.13W
37 X12 Sloan Nevada, W USA 35.56N 115.13W
Slobodka see Slabodka
129 R14 Slobodskoy Kirovskaya Oblast', NW Russian Federation 58.43N 50.12E
Slobodzeya see Slobozia
119 O10 Slobozia Rus. Slobodzeya. E Moldova 46.45N 29.42E
118 L14 Slobozia Ialomiţa, SE Romania 44.34N 27.22E
100 O5 Slochteren Groningen, NE Netherlands 53.13N 6.48E
121 H17 Slonim Pol. Słonim, Rus. Slonim. Hrodzyenskaya Voblasts', W Belarus 53.04N 25.21E
100 K7 Sloter Meer N Netherlands
Slot, The see New Georgia Sound
99 N22 Slough S England, UK 51.31N 0.36W
113 J20 Slovakia off. Slovenská Republika, Ger. Slowakei, Hung. Szlovákia, Slvk. Slovensko. ◆ republic C Europe
Slovak Ore Mountains see Slovenské rudohorie
Slovechna see Slavyechna
111 S12 Slovenia off. Republic of Slovenia, Ger. Slowenien, Slvn. Slovenija. ◆ republic SE Europe
Slovenija see Slovenia
111 V10 Slovenj Gradec Ger. Windischgraz. N Slovenia 46.29N 15.05E
111 W10 Slovenska Bistrica Ger. Windischfeistritz. NE Slovenia 46.21N 15.27E
Slovenská Republika see Slovakia
111 W10 Slovenske Konjice E Slovenia 46.21N 15.28E
113 K20 Slovenské rudohorie Eng. Slovak Ore Mountains, Ger. Slowakisches Erzgebirge, Ungarisches Erzgebirge. ▲ C Slovakia
Slovensko see Slovakia
119 Y7 Slov"yanoserbs'k Luhans'ka Oblast', E Ukraine 48.41N 39.00E
119 W6 Slov"yans'k Rus. Slavyansk. Donets'ka Oblast', E Ukraine 48.51N 37.38E
Slowakei see Slovakia
Slowakisches Erzgebirge see Slovenské rudohorie
Slowenien see Slovenia
112 D11 Słubice Ger. Frankfurt. Lubuskie, W Poland 52.19N 14.34E
121 K19 Sluch Rus. Sluch'. C Belarus
118 L4 Sluch NW Ukraine
101 D16 Sluis Zeeland, SW Netherlands 51.18N 3.22E
114 D10 Slunj Hung. Szluin. Karlovac, C Croatia 45.06N 15.35E
112 I11 Słupca Wielkopolskie, C Poland 52.16N 17.54E
112 G6 Słupia Ger. Stolpe. NW Poland
112 G6 Słupsk Ger. Stolp. Pomorskie, N Poland 54.27N 17.01E
121 K18 Slutsk Rus. Slutsk. Minskaya Voblasts', S Belarus 53.01N 27.31E
121 O16 Slyedzyuki Rus. Sledyuki. Mahilyowskaya Voblasts', E Belarus 53.34N 30.19E
99 A17 Slyne Head Ir. Ceann Léime. headland W Ireland 53.25N 10.11W
126 J16 Slyudyanka Irkutskaya Oblast', S Russian Federation 51.36N 103.28E
29 U14 Smackover Arkansas, C USA 33.21N 92.43W
97 L20 Småland cultural region S Sweden
97 K20 Smålandsstenar Jönköping, S Sweden 57.10N 13.24E
Small Malaita see Maramasike
11 O8 Smallwood Reservoir Newfoundland and Labrador, S Canada
121 N14 Smalyany Rus. Smolyany. Vitsyebskaya Voblasts', NE Belarus 54.36N 30.04E
121 L15 Smalyavichy Rus. Smolevichi. Minskaya Voblasts', C Belarus 54.01N 28.09E
76 C9 Smara var. Es Semara. N Western Sahara 26.45N 11.43W
121 I14 Smarhon' Pol. Smorgonie, Rus. Smorgon'. Hrodzyenskaya Voblasts', W Belarus 54.28N 26.24E
114 M11 Smederevo Ger. Semendria. Serbia, N Serbia and Montenegro (Yugoslavia) 44.40N 20.55E
114 M12 Smederevska Palanka Serbia, C Serbia and Montenegro (Yugoslavia) 44.23N 20.55E
97 M14 Smedjebacken Dalarna, C Sweden 60.07N 15.25E
118 L13 Smeeni Buzău, SE Romania 45.00N 26.52E
Smela see Smila
109 D16 Smeralda, Costa cultural region Sardegna, Italy, C Mediterranean Sea
113 J22 Šmigiel Ger. Schmiegel. Wielkolpolskie, C Poland 52.02N 16.33E
119 Q6 Smila Rus. Smela. Cherkas'ka Oblast', C Ukraine 49.15N 31.54E
100 N7 Smilde Drenthe, NE Netherlands 52.57N 6.28E
9 S16 Smiley Saskatchewan, S Canada 51.40N 109.24W
27 T12 Smiley Texas, SW USA 29.16N 97.38W
Smiltene see Smiltene
120 I8 Smiltene Ger. Smilten. Valka, N Latvia 57.25N 25.53E
127 O14 Smirnykh Ostrov Sakhalin, Sakhalinskaya Oblast', SE Russian Federation 49.43N 142.48E
9 Q13 Smith Alberta, W Canada 55.06N 113.57W
41 P4 Smith Bay bay Alaska, USA
10 I3 Smith, Cape headland Québec, NE Canada 60.50N 78.06W
28 L3 Smith Center Kansas, C USA 39.46N 98.46W
8 K13 Smithers British Columbia, SW Canada 54.45N 127.10W
23 V10 Smithfield North Carolina, SE USA 35.30N 78.20W
38 L1 Smithfield Utah, W USA 41.50N 111.49W
23 X7 Smithfield Virginia, NE USA 36.41N 76.38W
10 I3 Smith Island island Nunavut, C Canada
Smith Island see Sumisu-jima
22 H7 Smithland Kentucky, S USA 37.06N 88.24W
23 T7 Smith Mountain Lake var. Leesville Lake. Virginia, NE USA
36 L1 Smith River California, W USA 41.54N 124.09W
35 R9 Smith River Montana, NW USA
12 L13 Smiths Falls Ontario, SE Canada 44.54N 76.01W
35 N13 Smiths Ferry Idaho, NW USA 44.19N 116.04W
22 K7 Smiths Grove Kentucky, S USA 37.01N 86.14W
191 N15 Smithton Tasmania, SE Australia 40.54S 145.06E
20 L14 Smithtown Long Island, New York, NE USA 40.52N 73.13W
22 K9 Smithville Tennessee, S USA 35.57N 85.48W
27 T11 Smithville Texas, SW USA 30.04N 97.32W
Śmohor see Hermagor
37 Q4 Smoke Creek Desert desert Nevada, W USA
9 O14 Smoky Alberta, W Canada
190 E7 Smoky Bay South Australia 32.22S 133.57E
191 V6 Smoky Cape headland New South Wales, SE Australia 30.54S 153.06E
28 L4 Smoky Hill River Kansas, C USA
28 L4 Smoky Hills hill range Kansas, C USA
9 Q14 Smoky Lake Alberta, SW Canada 54.07N 112.25W
96 E8 Smøla island W Norway
130 H4 Smolensk Smolenskaya Oblast', W Russian Federation 54.48N 32.07E
130 H4 Smolenskaya Oblast' ◆ province W Russian Federation
Smolensk-Moscow Upland see Smolensko-Moskovskaya Vozvyshennost'
130 J3 Smolensko-Moskovskaya Vozvyshennost' var. Smolensk-Moscow Upland. ▲ W Russian Federation
Smolevichi see Smalyavichy
117 C15 Smolikás ▲ W Greece 40.06N 20.54E
116 I12 Smolyan prev. Pashmakli. Smolyan, S Bulgaria 41.33N 24.46E
116 I12 Smolyan ◆ province S Bulgaria
Smolyany see Smalyany
35 S15 Smoot Wyoming, C USA 42.37N 110.55W
10 G12 Smooth Rock Falls Ontario, S Canada 49.16N 81.37W
Smorgon'/Smorgonie see Smarhon'
97 K23 Smygehamn Skåne, S Sweden 55.19N 13.25E
204 I7 Smyley Island island Antarctica
23 Y3 Smyrna Delaware, NE USA 39.18N 75.36W
25 S3 Smyrna Georgia, SE USA 33.52N 84.30W
22 J9 Smyrna Tennessee, S USA 36.00N 86.30W
Smyrna see İzmir
176 W10 Snabai Papua, E Indonesia 1.45S 134.14E
99 I16 Snaefell ▲ C Isle of Man 54.15N 4.29W
94 H3 Snaefellsjökull ▲ W Iceland 64.51N 23.51W
8 J4 Snake Yukon Territory, NW Canada
31 O8 Snake Creek South Dakota, N USA
191 P13 Snake Island island Victoria, SE Australia
37 Y6 Snake Range ▲ Nevada, W USA
34 K10 Snake River NW USA
31 V6 Snake River Minnesota, N USA
30 L12 Snake River Nebraska, C USA
35 Q14 Snake River Plain plain Idaho, NW USA
15 I7 Snare Northwest Territories, NW Canada
95 F15 Snåsa Nord-Trøndelag, C Norway 64.16N 12.25E
23 O8 Sneedville Tennessee, S USA 36.31N 83.13W
100 K6 Sneek Friesland, N Netherlands 53.01N 5.40E
Sneeuw-gebergte see Maoke, Pegunungan
97 F22 Snejbjerg Ringkøbing, C Denmark 56.07N 8.55E
128 J3 Snezhnogorsk Murmanskaya Oblast', NW Russian Federation 69.12N 33.20E
126 I8 Snezhnogorsk Taymyrskiy (Dolgano-Nenetskiy) Avtonomnyy Okrug, N Russian Federation 68.06N 87.37E
Snezhnoye see Snizhne
113 G15 Sněžka Ger. Schneekoppe, Pol. Śnieżka. ▲ Czech Republic/Poland 50.42N 15.55E
112 N8 Śniardwy, Jezioro Ger. Spirdingsee. NE Poland
Sniečkus see Visaginas
Śnieżka see Sněžka
119 R10 Snihurivka Mykolayivs'ka Oblast', S Ukraine 47.05N 32.48E
118 I5 Snilov ✕ (L'viv) L'vivs'ka Oblast', W Ukraine 49.45N 23.59E
113 O19 Snina Hung. Szinna. Prešovský Kraj, E Slovakia 49.00N 22.10E
119 Y8 Snizhne Rus. Snezhnoye. Donets'ka Oblast', SE Ukraine 48.01N 38.46E
94 J3 Snækollur ▲ C Iceland 64.38N 19.18W
96 G10 Snøhetta var. Snøhetta. ▲ S Norway 62.22N 9.08E
94 G12 Snøtinden ▲ C Norway 66.39N 13.50E
99 I18 Snowdon ▲ NW Wales, UK 53.04N 4.04W
99 I18 Snowdonia ▲ NW Wales, UK
15 Ii8 Snowdrift Northwest Territories, NW Canada
Snowdrift see Łutselk'e
39 N12 Snowflake Arizona, SW USA 34.30N 110.04W
23 Y5 Snow Hill Maryland, NE USA 38.10N 75.23W
23 W10 Snow Hill North Carolina, SE USA 35.25N 77.40W
204 H3 Snowhill Island island Antarctica
9 V13 Snow Lake Manitoba, C Canada 54.55N 100.01W
39 R5 Snowmass Mountain ▲ Colorado, C USA 39.07N 107.04W
20 M10 Snow, Mount ▲ Vermont, NE USA 42.56N 72.52W
36 M5 Snow Mountain ▲ California, W USA 39.44N 123.01W
Snow Mountains see Maoke, Pegunungan
35 N7 Snowshoe Peak ▲ Montana, NW USA 48.15N 115.44W
190 I8 Snowtown South Australia 33.49S 138.13E
38 K1 Snowville Utah, W USA 41.59N 112.42W
37 X3 Snow Water Lake Nevada, W USA
191 Q11 Snowy Mountains ▲ New South Wales/Victoria, SE Australia
191 Q12 Snowy River New South Wales/Victoria, SE Australia
46 K5 Snug Corner Acklins Island, SE Bahamas 22.31N 73.51W
178 Jj13 Snuŏl Krâchéh, E Cambodia 12.04N 106.25E
118 J7 Snyatyn Rus. Snyatyn. Ivano-Frankivs'ka Oblast', W Ukraine 48.28N 25.33E
28 L12 Snyder Oklahoma, C USA 34.37N 98.56W
27 O6 Snyder Texas, SW USA 32.43N 100.54W
180 H3 Soalala Mahajanga, W Madagascar 16.04S 45.21E
180 J4 Soanierana-Ivongo Toamasina, E Madagascar 16.52S 49.34E
175 Ss7 Soasiu var. Tidore. Pulau Tidore, E Indonesia 0.40N 127.25E
56 G8 Soatá Boyacá, C Colombia 6.14N 72.42W
180 I5 Soavinandriana Antananarivo, C Madagascar 19.09S 46.43E
176 Yy12 Soba Papua, E Indonesia 4.18S 139.11E
79 V13 Soba Kaduna, C Nigeria 10.58N 8.06E
169 Y16 Sobaek-sanmaek ▲ S South Korea
82 F13 Sobat E Sudan
176 Z12 Sobger, Sungai Papua, E Indonesia
176 W10 Sobiei Papua, E Indonesia 2.31S 134.30E
130 M3 Sobinka Vladimirskaya Oblast', W Russian Federation 56.00N 39.55E
131 S7 Sobolevo Orenburgskaya Oblast', W Russian Federation 51.57N 51.42E
Soborsin see Săvârşin
170 D15 Sobo-san ▲ Kyūshū, SW Japan 32.50N 131.16E
113 G14 Sobótka Dolnośląskie, SW Poland 50.53N 16.48E
61 O15 Sobradinho Bahia, E Brazil 9.33S 40.56W
Sobradinho, Barragem de see Sobradinho, Represa de
61 O16 Sobradinho, Represa de var. Barragem de Sobradinho. E Brazil
60 O13 Sobral Ceará, E Brazil 3.45S 40.19W
107 T4 Sobrarbe physical region NE Spain
111 R10 Soča It. Isonzo. Italy/Slovenia
112 L11 Sochaczew Mazowieckie, C Poland 52.15N 20.15E
130 L15 Sochi Krasnodarskiy Kray, SW Russian Federation 43.34N 39.46E
116 G13 Sochós var. Sohos, Sokhós. Kentrikí Makedonía, N Greece 40.49N 23.22E
203 R11 Société, Archipel de la var. Archipel de Tahiti, Îles de la Société, Eng. Society Islands. island group W French Polynesia
Société, Îles de la/Society Islands see Société, Archipel de la
23 T11 Society Hill South Carolina, SE USA 34.28N 79.54W
183 W9 Society Ridge undersea feature C Pacific Ocean
64 I5 Socompa, Volcán ▲ N Chile 24.18S 68.03W
Soconusco, Sierra de see Sierra Madre
56 G8 Socorro Santander, C Colombia 6.25N 73.13W
39 R13 Socorro New Mexico, SW USA 33.58N 106.55W
Socotra see Suquţrā
178 Jj15 Soc Trăng var. Khanh Hung. Soc Trăng, S Vietnam 9.36N 105.58E
107 P10 Socuéllamos Castilla-La Mancha, C Spain 39.18N 2.48W
37 W13 Soda Lake salt flat California, W USA
94 L11 Sodankylä Lappi, N Finland 67.25N 26.34E
Sodari see Sodiri
35 R15 Soda Springs Idaho, NW USA 42.39N 111.36W
Soddo/Soddu see Sodo
22 L10 Soddy Daisy Tennessee, S USA 35.14N 85.11W
97 N14 Söderfors Uppsala, C Sweden 60.22N 17.19E
96 N12 Söderhamn Gävleborg, C Sweden 61.19N 17.10E
97 N17 Söderköping Östergötland, S Sweden 58.28N 16.19E
97 N17 Södermanland ◆ county C Sweden
97 O16 Södertälje Stockholm, C Sweden 59.10N 17.39E
82 D10 Sodiri var. Sawdirī, Sodari. Northern Kordofan, C Sudan 14.22N 29.06E
83 I14 Sodo var. Soddo, Soddu. Southern, S Ethiopia 6.49N 37.43E
96 N11 Södra Dellen C Sweden
97 M19 Södra Vi Kalmar, S Sweden 57.45N 15.45E
20 G9 Sodus Point headland New York, NE USA 43.16N 76.59W
175 Rr17 Soe prev. Soë. Timor, C Indonesia 9.51S 124.28E
174 J14 Soekarno-Hatta ✕ (Jakarta) Jawa, S Indonesia
Soëla-Sund see Soela Väin
120 E5 Soela Väin prev. Eng. Sele Sound, Ger. Dagden-Sund, Soëla-Sund. strait W Estonia
Soemba see Sumba, Pulau
Soembawa see Sumbawa
Soemenep see Sumenep
Soengaipenoeh see Sungaipenuh
Soerabaja see Surabaya
103 G14 Soest Nordrhein-Westfalen, W Germany 51.34N 8.07E
100 J11 Soest Utrecht, C Netherlands 52.10N 5.19E
102 F11 Soeste NW Germany
100 J11 Soesterberg Utrecht, C Netherlands 52.07N 5.16E
117 E16 Sofádes var. Sofádhes. Thessalía, C Greece 39.19N 22.06E
Sofádhes see Sofádes
85 N18 Sofala Sofala, C Mozambique 20.04S 34.43E
85 N17 Sofala ◆ province C Mozambique
85 N18 Sofala, Baia de bay E Mozambique
180 J3 Sofia seasonal river NW Madagascar
Sofia see Sofiya
117 G19 Sofikó Pelopónnisos, S Greece 37.46N 23.04E
Sofi-Kurgan see Sopu-Korgon
116 G10 Sofiya var. Sophia, Eng. Sofia; Lat. Serdica. ● (Bulgaria) Sofiya-Grad, W Bulgaria 42.42N 23.20E
116 G9 Sofiya ✕ Sofiya-Grad, W Bulgaria 42.42N 23.26E
116 H9 Sofiya ◆ province W Bulgaria
116 G9 Sofiya-Grad ◆ municipality W Bulgaria
Sofiyevka see Sofiyivka
119 S8 Sofiyivka Rus. Sofiyevka. Dnipropetrovs'ka Oblast', E Ukraine 48.03N 33.52E
127 Nn14 Sofiysk Khabarovskiy Kray, SE Russian Federation 51.31N 139.46E
127 N14 Sofiysk Khabarovskiy Kray, SE Russian Federation 52.20N 133.37E
128 I6 Sofporog Respublika Kareliya, NW Russian Federation 65.48N 31.30E
172 Ss15 Sōfu-gan island Izu-shotō, SE Japan
162 K10 Sog Xizang Zizhiqu, W China 31.52N 93.40E
56 G9 Sogamoso Boyacá, C Colombia 5.43N 72.55W
142 I11 Soğanlı Çayı N Turkey
96 E12 Sogn physical region S Norway
Sogndal see Sogndalsfjøra
96 E12 Sogndalsfjøra var. Sogndal. Sogn og Fjordane, S Norway 61.13N 7.06E
97 E18 Søgne Vest-Agder, S Norway 58.04N 7.48E
96 D12 Sognefjorden fjord NE North Sea
96 C12 Sogn Og Fjordane ◆ county S Norway
179 R13 Sogod Leyte, C Philippines 10.25N 125.00E
168 I11 Sogo Nur N China
165 T12 Sogruma Qinghai, W China 32.31N 100.52E
169 X17 Sŏgwip'o S South Korea 33.13N 126.33E
77 X10 Sohâg var. Sawhāj, Suliag. C Egypt 26.27N 31.43E
Sohar see Şuḩār
66 H9 Sohm Plain undersea feature NW Atlantic Ocean
102 H7 Soholmer Au N Germany
Sohos see Sochós
Sohrau see Żory
101 F20 Soignies Hainaut, SW Belgium 50.34N 4.04E
165 R15 Soila Xizang Zizhiqu, W China 30.40N 97.07E
105 P4 Soissons anc. Augusta Suessionum, Noviodunum. Aisne, N France 49.22N 3.19E
170 Ff14 Sōja Okayama, Honshū, SW Japan 34.41N 133.45E
158 F13 Sojat Rājasthān, N India 25.55N 73.43E
169 W13 Sŏjosŏn-man inlet W North Korea
118 I4 Sokal' Rus. Sokal. L'vivs'ka Oblast', NW Ukraine 50.28N 24.16E
169 Y14 Sokch'o N South Korea 38.07N 128.33E
142 B15 Söke Aydın, SW Turkey 37.45N 27.24E
201 N12 Sokehs Island island E Micronesia
81 M24 Sokele Katanga, SE Dem. Rep. Congo 9.54S 24.38E
153 R11 Sokh Uzb. Sŭkh. Kyrgyzstan/Uzbekistan
Sokh see So'x
Sokhós see Sochós
143 Q8 Sokhumi Rus. Sukhumi. NW Georgia 43.01N 41.01E
115 O14 Sokobanja Serbia, E Serbia and Montenegro (Yugoslavia) 43.39N 21.51E
79 R15 Sokodé C Togo 8.58N 1.10E
127 O10 Sokol Magadanskaya Oblast', E Russian Federation 59.51N 150.56E
128 M13 Sokol Vologodskaya Oblast', NW Russian Federation 59.26N 40.09E
112 P9 Sokółka Podlaskie, NE Poland 53.24N 23.30E
78 M11 Sokolo Ségou, W Mali 14.43N 6.02W
113 A16 Sokolov Ger. Falkenau an der Eger; prev. Falknov nad Ohří. Karlovarský Kraj, W Czech Republic 50.10N 12.38E
113 O16 Sokołów Małopolski Podkarpackie, SE Poland 50.12N 22.07E
112 O11 Sokołów Podlaski Mazowieckie, E Poland 52.25N 22.14E
78 G11 Sokone W Senegal 13.52N 16.22W
79 T12 Sokoto Sokoto, NW Nigeria 13.05N 5.15E
79 T12 Sokoto ◆ state NW Nigeria

◆ Country ● Country Capital ◇ Dependent Territory ○ Dependent Territory Capital ◆ Administrative Region ✕ International Airport ▲ Mountain ▲ Mountain Range Volcano River Lake Reservoir

SOKOTO – SOVETSK

79 S12 **Sokoto** ≈ NW Nigeria
Sokotra *see* Suquṭrā
153 U7 **Sokuluk** Chuyskaya Oblast', N Kyrgyzstan 42.53N 74.19E
118 L7 **Sokyryany** Chernivets'ka Oblast', W Ukraine 48.28N 27.25E
97 C16 **Sola** Rogaland, S Norway 58.52N 5.37E
197 C10 **Sola** Vanua Lava, N Vanuatu 13.51S 167.34E
97 C17 **Sola** ✈ (Stavanger) Rogaland, S Norway 58.54N 5.36E
83 H18 **Solai** Rift Valley, W Kenya 0.02N 36.03E
176 Y15 **Solaka** Papua, E Indonesia 7.52S 138.45E
158 I8 **Solan** Himāchal Pradesh, N India 30.54N 77.06E
193 A25 **Solander Island** *island* SW NZ
Solano *see* Bahía Solano
161 F15 **Solāpur** *var.* Sholāpur. Mahārāshtra, W India 17.42N 75.54E
95 H16 **Solberg** Västernorrland, C Sweden 63.48N 17.40E
118 K9 **Solca** *Ger.* Solka. Suceava, N Romania 47.40N 25.49E
107 O16 **Sol, Costa del** *coastal region* S Spain
108 F5 **Solda** *Ger.* Sulden. Trentino-Alto Adige, N Italy 46.33N 10.35E
119 N9 **Şoldăneşti** *Rus.* Sholdaneshty. N Moldova 47.49N 28.45E
Soldau *see* Wkra
110 L8 **Sölden** Tirol, W Austria 46.58N 11.01E
29 P3 **Soldier Creek** ≈ Kansas, C USA
41 R12 **Soldotna** Alaska, USA 60.29N 151.03W
112 I10 **Solec Kujawski** Kujawsko-pomorskie, C Poland 53.04N 18.09E
63 B16 **Soledad** Santa Fe, C Argentina 30.37S 60.52W
57 E4 **Soledad** Atlántico, N Colombia 10.54N 74.48W
37 O11 **Soledad** California, W USA 36.25N 121.19W
57 O7 **Soledad** Anzoátegui, NE Venezuela 8.10N 63.31W
Soledad *see* East Falkland
Soledad, Isla *see* East Falkland
63 H15 **Soledade** Rio Grande do Sul, S Brazil 28.49S 52.30W
105 Y15 **Solenzara** Corse, France, C Mediterranean Sea 41.55N 9.24E
Soleure *see* Solothurn
96 C12 **Solheim** Hordaland, S Norway 60.54N 5.30E
129 N14 **Soligalich** Kostromskaya Oblast', NW Russian Federation 59.05N 42.15E
Soligorsk *see* Salihorsk
99 L20 **Solihull** C England, UK 52.25N 1.45W
129 U13 **Solikamsk** Permskaya Oblast', NW Russian Federation 59.37N 56.46E
131 V8 **Sol'-Iletsk** Orenburgskaya Oblast', W Russian Federation 51.08N 55.05E
59 G17 **Solimana, Nevado** ▲ S Peru 15.24S 72.49W
60 E13 **Solimões, Rio** ≈ C Brazil
115 E14 **Solin** *It.* Salona; *anc.* Salonae. Split-Dalmacija, S Croatia 43.33N 16.29E
103 E15 **Solingen** Nordrhein-Westfalen, W Germany 51.10N 7.04E
Solka *see* Solca
95 H16 **Sollefteå** Västernorrland, C Sweden 63.09N 17.15E
97 O15 **Sollentuna** Stockholm, C Sweden 59.25N 17.55E
96 L13 **Sollerön** Dalarna, C Sweden 60.55N 14.34E
103 I14 **Solling** *hill range* C Germany
97 O16 **Solna** Stockholm, C Sweden 59.22N 17.58E
130 K3 **Solnechnogorsk** Moskovskaya Oblast', W Russian Federation 56.07N 37.04E
127 Nn15 **Solnechnyy** Khabarovskiy Kray, SE Russian Federation 50.41N 136.42E
126 Hh13 **Solnechnyy** Krasnoyarskiy Kray, C Russian Federation 55.15N 89.48E
127 N11 **Solnechnyy** Respublika Sakha (Yakutiya), NE Russian Federation 60.13N 137.42E
109 L17 **Solofra** Campania, S Italy 40.49N 14.48E
174 Gg9 **Solok** Sumatera, W Indonesia 0.45S 100.42E
44 C6 **Sololá** Sololá, W Guatemala 14.46N 91.09W
44 A2 **Sololá** *off.* Departamento de Sololá. ◐ *department* SW Guatemala
83 J16 **Sololo** Eastern, N Kenya 3.31N 38.39E
44 C4 **Soloma** Huehuetenango, W Guatemala 15.38N 91.25W
40 M9 **Solomon** Alaska, USA 64.33N 164.26W
29 N4 **Solomon** Kansas, C USA 38.55N 97.22W
195 U16 **Solomon Islands** *prev.* British Solomon Islands Protectorate. ◆ *commonwealth republic* W Pacific Ocean
195 T12 **Solomon Islands** *island group* PNG/Solomon Islands
28 M3 **Solomon River** ≈ Kansas, C USA
199 Hh9 **Solomon Sea** *sea* W Pacific Ocean
33 U11 **Solon** Ohio, N USA 41.23N 81.26W
119 T8 **Solone** Dnipropetrovs'ka Oblast', E Ukraine 48.12N 34.49E
175 R16 **Solor, Kepulauan** *island group* S Indonesia
130 M4 **Solotcha** Ryazanskaya Oblast', W Russian Federation 54.43N 39.50E
110 D7 **Solothurn** *Fr.* Soleure. Solothurn, NW Switzerland 47.12N 7.28E
110 D7 **Solothurn** *Fr.* Soleure. ◐ *canton* NW Switzerland
128 J7 **Solovetskiye Ostrova** *island group* NW Russian Federation
107 V5 **Solsona** Cataluña, NE Spain 42.00N 1.31E
115 E14 **Šolta** *It.* Solta. *island* S Croatia
Solṭānābād *see* Kāshmar
148 L4 **Solṭānīyeh** Zanjān, NW Iran 36.24N 48.49E
102 I11 **Soltau** Niedersachsen, NW Germany 52.58N 9.49E
128 G14 **Sol'tsy** Novgorodskaya Oblast', W Russian Federation 58.09N 30.22E
Soltūstik Qazaqstan Oblysy *see* Severnyy Kazakhstan
Solun *see* Thessaloníki
115 O19 **Solunska Glava** ▲ C FYR Macedonia 41.43N 21.24E
97 L22 **Sölvesborg** Blekinge, S Sweden 56.04N 14.34E
99 J15 **Solway Firth** *inlet* England/Scotland, UK
84 I13 **Solwezi** North Western, NW Zambia 12.10S 26.22E
171 Ll14 **Sōma** Fukushima, Honshū, C Japan 37.49N 140.52E
142 C13 **Soma** Manisa, W Turkey 39.11N 27.34E
83 M14 **Somali** ◐ *region* E Ethiopia
83 O15 **Somalia** *off.* Somali Democratic Republic, *Som.* Jamuuriyada Demuqraadiga Soomaaliyeed, Soomaaliya; *prev.* Italian Somaliland, Somaliland Protectorate. ◆ *republic* E Africa
181 N6 **Somali Basin** *undersea feature* W Indian Ocean
69 Y8 **Somali Plain** *undersea feature* W Indian Ocean
114 J8 **Sombor** *Hung.* Zombor. Serbia, NW Serbia and Montenegro (Yugoslavia) 45.46N 19.07E
101 H20 **Sombreffe** Namur, S Belgium 50.32N 4.39E
42 L10 **Sombrerete** Zacatecas, C Mexico 23.36N 103.46W
47 V8 **Sombrero** *island* N Anguilla
157 Q21 **Sombrero Channel** *channel* Nicobar Islands, India
118 H9 **Şomcuta Mare** *Hung.* Nagysomkút; *prev.* Somcuţa Mare. Maramureş, N Romania 47.28N 23.30E
178 Ii9 **Somdet** Kalasin, E Thailand 16.41N 103.44E
101 L15 **Someren** Noord-Brabant, SE Netherlands 51.22N 5.42E
95 L19 **Somero** Länsi-Suomi, W Finland 60.37N 23.30E
35 P7 **Somers** Montana, NW USA 48.04N 114.16W
66 A12 **Somerset** *var.* Somerset Village. W Bermuda 32.18N 64.52W
39 Q5 **Somerset** Colorado, C USA 38.55N 107.27W
22 M7 **Somerset** Kentucky, S USA 37.05N 84.36W
21 O12 **Somerset** Massachusetts, NE USA 41.46N 71.07W
99 K23 **Somerset** *cultural region* SW England, UK
Somerset East *see* Somerset-Oos
66 A12 **Somerset Island** *island* W Bermuda
207 N9 **Somerset Island** *island* Queen Elizabeth Islands, Nunavut, NW Canada
Somerset Nile *see* Victoria Nile
85 I25 **Somerset-Oos** *Eng.* Somerset East. Eastern Cape, S South Africa 32.43S 25.34E
85 E26 **Somerset-Wes** *Eng.* Somerset West. Western Cape, SW South Africa 34.01S 18.51E
Somerset West *see* Somerset-Wes
Somers Islands *see* Bermuda
20 J17 **Somers Point** New Jersey, NE USA 39.18N 74.34W
21 P9 **Somersworth** New Hampshire, NE USA 43.15N 70.52W
38 H15 **Somerton** Arizona, SW USA 32.36N 114.42W
20 J14 **Somerville** New Jersey, NE USA 40.34N 74.36W
22 F10 **Somerville** Tennessee, S USA 35.14N 89.21W
27 U10 **Somerville** Texas, SW USA 30.21N 96.31W
27 T10 **Somerville Lake** ⊠ Texas, SW USA
Someş/Somesch/Someşul *see* Szamos
105 N2 **Somme** ◐ *department* N France
105 N2 **Somme** ≈ N France
97 L18 **Sommen** Jönköping, S Sweden 58.07N 14.58E
97 M18 **Sommen** ◎ S Sweden
103 K16 **Sömmerda** Thüringen, C Germany 51.10N 11.07E
Sommerein *see* Šamorín
Sommerfeld *see* Lubsko
57 Y11 **Sommet Tabulaire** *var.* Mont Itoupé. ▲▲ S French Guiana
113 H25 **Somogy** *off.* Somogy Megye. ◐ *county* SW Hungary
Somorja *see* Šamorín
107 N7 **Somosierra, Puerto de** *pass* N Spain 41.07N 3.36W
197 J13 **Somosomo** Taveuni, N Fiji 16.46S 179.57W
44 I9 **Somotillo** Chinandega, NW Nicaragua 13.01N 86.54W
44 I8 **Somoto** Madriz, NW Nicaragua 13.28N 86.36W
112 I11 **Sompolno** Wielkolpolskie, C Poland 52.24N 18.30E
107 S3 **Somport** *var.* Puerto de Somport, *Fr.* Col du Somport; *anc.* Summus Portus. *pass* France/Spain *see also* Somport, Col du 42.48N 0.33W
104 J17 **Somport, Col du** *var.* Puerto de Somport, *Sp.* Somport; *anc.* Summus Portus. *pass* France/Spain *see also* Somport 42.47N 0.33W
Somport, Puerto de *see* Somport/Somport, Col du
101 K15 **Son** Noord-Brabant, S Netherlands 51.32N 5.34E
97 H15 **Son** Akershus, S Norway 59.31N 10.42E
160 L9 **Son** *var.* Sone. ≈ C India
45 R16 **Soná** Veraguas, W Panama 08.00N 81.20W
Sonag *see* Zêkog
160 M12 **Sonapur** *prev.* Sonepur. Orissa, E India 20.49N 83.58E
176 Vv10 **Sonar** Papua, E Indonesia 2.31S 133.01E
97 G24 **Sønderborg** *Ger.* Sonderburg. Sønderjylland, SW Denmark 54.55N 9.48E
Sonderburg *see* Sønderborg
97 F24 **Sønderjylland** *off.* Sønderjyllands Amt. ◐ *county* SW Denmark
103 K15 **Sondershausen** Thüringen, C Germany 51.22N 10.52E
Søndre Strømfjord *see* Kangerlussuaq
108 E6 **Sondrio** Lombardia, N Italy 46.10N 9.52E
Sone *see* Son
Sonepur *see* Sonapur
59 K22 **Sonequera** ▲ S Bolivia 22.06S 67.10W
178 Kk12 **Sông Câu** Phu Yên, C Vietnam 13.25N 109.12E
178 J15 **Sông Đôc** Minh Hai, S Vietnam 9.03N 104.51E
83 H25 **Songea** Ruvuma, S Tanzania 10.42S 35.39E
176 Z11 **Songgato, Sungai** ≈ Papua, E Indonesia
169 X10 **Songhua Hu** ◎ NE China
169 Y7 **Songhua Jiang** *var.* Sungari. ≈ NE China
167 S8 **Songjiang** Shanghai Shi, E China 31.01N 121.13E
Sŏngjin *see* Kimch'aek
178 H17 **Songkhla** *var.* Songkla, *Mal.* Singora. Songkhla, SW Thailand 7.12N 100.34E
Songkla *see* Songkhla
169 T13 **Song Ling** ▲▲ NE China
169 W14 **Songnim** SW North Korea 38.43N 125.40E
84 B10 **Songo** Uíge, NW Angola 7.30S 14.55E
85 M15 **Songo** Tete, NW Mozambique 15.35S 32.43E
81 F21 **Songololo** Bas-Congo, SW Dem. Rep. Congo 5.40S 14.04E
166 H7 **Songpan** *var.* Jin'an, *Tib.* Sungpu. Sichuan, C China 32.49N 103.39E
169 Y17 **Sŏngsan** S South Korea
167 R11 **Songxi** Fujian, SE China 27.33N 118.46E
166 M6 **Songxian** *var.* Song Xian. Henan, C China 34.11N 112.04E
167 R10 **Songyang** *var.* Xiping. Zhejiang, SE China 28.29N 119.27E
169 V9 **Songyuan** *var.* Fu-yü, Petuna; *prev.* Fuyu. Jilin, NE China 45.10N 124.52E
Sonid Youqi *see* Saihan Tal
Sonid Zuoqi *see* Mandalt
158 I10 **Sonīpat** Haryāna, N India 29.00N 77.01E
95 M15 **Sonkajärvi** Itä-Suomi, C Finland 63.40N 27.30E
178 J6 **Sơn La** Sơn La, N Vietnam 21.19N 103.55E
155 O16 **Sonmiāni** Baluchistān, S Pakistan 25.24N 66.37E
155 O16 **Sonmiāni Bay** *bay* S Pakistan
103 K18 **Sonneberg** Thüringen, C Germany 50.22N 11.10E
103 N24 **Sonntagshorn** ▲ Austria/Germany 47.40N 12.42E
Sonoita *see* Sonoyta
42 E3 **Sonoita, Rio** *var.* Río Sonoyta. ≈ Mexico/USA
37 N7 **Sonoma** California, W USA 38.16N 122.28W
37 T3 **Sonoma Peak** ▲ Nevada, W USA 40.50N 117.34W
37 P8 **Sonora** California, W USA 37.58N 120.22W
27 O10 **Sonora** Texas, SW USA 30.31N 100.40W
42 F5 **Sonora** ◐ *state* NW Mexico
37 X17 **Sonoran Desert** *var.* Desierto de Altar. *desert* Mexico/USA ***see also*** Altar, Desierto de
42 G5 **Sonora, Río** ≈ NW Mexico
42 E2 **Sonoyta** *var.* Sonoita. Sonora, NW Mexico 31.49N 112.50W
Sonoyta, Río *see* Sonoita, Rio
148 K6 **Sonqor** *var.* Sunqur. Kermānshāh, W Iran 34.45N 47.39E
107 N9 **Sonseca** *var.* Sonseca con Casalgordo. Castilla-La Mancha, C Spain 39.40N 3.58W
Sonseca con Casalgordo *see* Sonseca
56 E9 **Sonsón** Antioquia, W Colombia 5.41N 75.15W
44 E7 **Sonsonate** Sonsonate, W El Salvador 13.43N 89.43W
44 A9 **Sonsonate** ◐ *department* SW El Salvador
196 A10 **Sonsorol Islands** *island group* S Palau
114 J9 **Sonta** *Hung.* Szond; *prev.* Szonta. Serbia, NW Serbia and Montenegro (Yugoslavia) 45.34N 19.06E
178 Jj6 **Sơn Tây** *var.* Sontay. Ha Tây, N Vietnam 21.06N 105.31E
103 J25 **Sonthofen** Bayern, S Germany 47.31N 10.16E
Soochow *see* Suzhou
Soomaaliya/Soomaaliyeed, Jamuuriyada Demuqraadiga *see* Somalia
Soome Laht *see* Finland, Gulf of
Sooner State *see* Oklahoma
25 V5 **Soperton** Georgia, SE USA 32.22N 82.35W
178 J6 **Sop Hao** Houaphan, N Laos 20.33N 104.25E
Sophia *see* Sofiya
175 Tt5 **Sopi** Pulau Morotai, E Indonesia 2.36N 128.32E
Sopianae *see* Pécs
176 Vv11 **Sopinusa** Papua, E Indonesia 3.31S 132.55E
175 Tt5 **Sopi, Tanjung** *headland* Pulau Morotai, N Indonesia 2.39N 128.34E
83 B14 **Sopo** ≈ W Sudan
Sopockinie/Sopotskin *see* Sapotskino
116 I9 **Sopot** Plovdiv, C Bulgaria 42.40N 24.45E
112 I7 **Sopot** *Ger.* Zoppot. Pomorskie, N Poland 54.25N 18.33E
178 H8 **Sop Prap** *var.* Ban Sop Prap. Lampang, NW Thailand 17.55N 99.19E
113 G22 **Sopron** *Ger.* Ödenburg. Győr-Moson-Sopron, NW Hungary 47.40N 16.34E
153 U11 **Sopu-Korgon** *var.* Sofi-Kurgan. Oshskaya Oblast', SW Kyrgyzstan 40.03N 73.30E
158 H5 **Sopur** Jammu and Kashmir, NW India 34.19N 74.28E
109 J15 **Sora** Lazio, C Italy 41.43N 13.37E
160 N13 **Sorada** Orissa, E India 19.46N 84.28E
95 H17 **Söråker** Västernorrland, C Sweden 62.31N 17.31E
59 J17 **Sorata** La Paz, W Bolivia 15.49S 68.39W
Sorau/Sorau in der Niederlausitz *see* Żary
107 Q14 **Sorbas** Andalucía, S Spain 37.06N 2.06W
Sord/Sórd Choluim Chille *see* Swords
13 O11 **Sorel** Québec, SE Canada 46.02N 73.06W
191 P17 **Sorell** Tasmania, SE Australia 42.49S 147.34E
191 O17 **Sorell, Lake** ◎ Tasmania, SE Australia
108 E8 **Soresina** Lombardia, N Italy 45.16N 9.51E
97 D14 **Sørfjorden** *fjord* S Norway
96 N11 **Sörforsa** Gävleborg, C Sweden 61.45N 17.00E
105 R14 **Sorgues** Vaucluse, SE France 44.00N 4.52E
142 K13 **Sorgun** Yozgat, C Turkey 39.49N 35.10E
107 P5 **Soria** Castilla-León, N Spain 41.46N 2.26W
107 P6 **Soria** ◐ *province* Castilla-León, N Spain
63 D19 **Soriano** Soriano, SW Uruguay 33.25S 58.21W
63 D19 **Soriano** ◐ *department* SW Uruguay
94 O4 **Sørkapp** *headland* SW Svalbard 76.34N 16.33E
149 T5 **Sorkh, Kūh-e** ▲▲ NE Iran
Soro *see* Ghazal, Bahr el
97 I23 **Sorø** Vestsjælland, E Denmark 55.25N 11.34E
118 M8 **Soroca** *Rus.* Soroki. N Moldova 48.10N 28.18E
62 L10 **Sorocaba** São Paulo, S Brazil 23.28S 47.27W
Sorochino *see* Sarochyna
131 T7 **Sorochinsk** Orenburgskaya Oblast', W Russian Federation 52.26N 53.10E
Soroki *see* Soroca
196 H15 **Sorol** *atoll* Caroline Islands, W Micronesia
176 Uu9 **Sorong** Papua, E Indonesia 0.49S 131.16E
83 G17 **Soroti** C Uganda 1.42N 33.37E
Sørøy *see* Sørøya
94 J8 **Sørøya** *var.* Sørøy, *Lapp.* Sállan. *island* N Norway
106 G11 **Sorraia, Rio** ≈ C Portugal
94 I10 **Sørreisa** Troms, N Norway 69.08N 18.09E
109 K18 **Sorrento** *anc.* Surrentum. Campania, S Italy 40.37N 14.22E
106 H10 **Sor, Ribeira de** *stream* C Portugal
205 T3 **Sør Rondane Mountains** ▲▲ Antarctica
95 H14 **Sorsele** Västerbotten, N Sweden 65.31N 17.34E
109 B17 **Sorso** Sardegna, Italy, C Mediterranean Sea 40.46N 8.33E
179 Qq11 **Sorsogon** Luzon, N Philippines 12.57N 124.04E
107 U4 **Sort** Cataluña, NE Spain 42.25N 1.07E
128 H11 **Sortavala** Respublika Kareliya, NW Russian Federation 61.45N 30.36E
109 L25 **Sortino** Sicilia, Italy, C Mediterranean Sea 37.10N 15.01E
94 G10 **Sortland** Nordland, C Norway 68.40N 15.22E
96 G9 **Sør-Trøndelag** ◐ *county* S Norway
97 I15 **Sørumsand** Akershus, S Norway 59.58N 11.13E
120 D6 **Sõrve Säär** *headland* SW Estonia 57.54N 22.02E
97 K22 **Sösdala** Skåne, S Sweden 56.00N 13.36E
107 R4 **Sos del Rey Católico** Aragón, NE Spain 42.30N 1.13W
95 F15 **Sösjöfjällen** ▲ C Sweden 63.51N 13.15E
130 K7 **Sosna** ≈ W Russian Federation
64 H12 **Sosneado, Cerro** ▲ W Argentina 34.44S 69.52W
129 S9 **Sosnogorsk** Respublika Komi, NW Russian Federation 63.33N 53.55E
128 J8 **Sosnovets** Respublika Kareliya, NW Russian Federation 64.25N 34.23E
Sosnovets *see* Sosnowiec
131 Q3 **Sosnovka** Chavash Respubliki, W Russian Federation 56.18N 47.14E
129 S16 **Sosnovka** Kirovskaya Oblast', NW Russian Federation 56.15N 51.20E
128 M6 **Sosnovka** Murmanskaya Oblast', NW Russian Federation 66.28N 40.31E
130 M6 **Sosnovka** Tambovskaya Oblast', W Russian Federation 53.14N 41.19E
128 H12 **Sosnovo** *Fin.* Rautu. Leningradskaya Oblast', NW Russian Federation 60.30N 30.13E
126 K15 **Sosnovo-Ozerskoye** Respublika Buryatiya, S Russian Federation 52.34N 111.36E
Sosnovyy Bor *see* Sasnovy Bor
113 J16 **Sosnowiec** *Ger.* Sosnowitz, *Rus.* Sosnovets. Śląskie, S Poland 50.16N 19.07E
Sosnowitz *see* Sosnowiec
119 R2 **Sosnytsya** Chernihivs'ka Oblast', N Ukraine 51.31N 32.30E
111 V10 **Šoštanj** N Slovenia 46.23N 15.03E
125 F10 **Sos'va** Sverdlovskaya Oblast', C Russian Federation 59.13N 61.58E
56 D12 **Sotará, Volcán** ⩚ S Colombia 2.04N 76.40W
78 D10 **Sotavento, Ilhas de** *var.* Leeward Islands. *island group* S Cape Verde
95 N15 **Sotkamo** Oulu, C Finland 64.05N 28.30E
111 W11 **Sotla** ≈ E Slovenia
43 P10 **Soto la Marina** Tamaulipas, C Mexico 23.46N 98.12W
43 P10 **Soto la Marina, Río** ≈ C Mexico
97 B14 **Sotra** *island* S Norway
43 X12 **Sotuta** Yucatán, SE Mexico 20.34N 89.00W
81 F17 **Souanké** La Sangha, NW Congo 2.03N 14.01E
78 M17 **Soubré** S Ivory Coast 5.49N 6.34W
117 H24 **Soúda** *var.* Soúdha, *Eng.* Suda. Kríti, Greece, E Mediterranean Sea 35.28N 24.04E
Soúdha *see* Soúda
Soueida *see* As Suwaydā'
116 L12 **Souflí** *prev.* Souflíon. Anatolikí Makedonía kai Thráki, NE Greece 41.12N 26.17E
Souflíon *see* Souflí
47 S11 **Soufrière** W Saint Lucia 13.51N 61.03W
47 X6 **Soufrière** ⩚ Basse Terre, S Guadeloupe 16.03N 61.39W
104 M13 **Souillac** Lot, S France 44.53N 1.29E
181 Y17 **Souillac** S Mauritius 20.31S 57.31E
76 M5 **Souk Ahras** NE Algeria 36.14N 8.00E
76 E6 **Souk-el-Arba-Rharb** *var.* Souk el Arba du Rharb, Souk-el-Arba-du-Rharb, Souk-el-Arba-el-Rhab. NW Morocco 34.38N 6.00W
Soukhné *see* As Sukhnah
169 X14 **Sŏul** *off.* Sŏul-t'ŭkpyŏlsi, *Eng.* Seoul, *Jap.* Keijō; *prev.* Kyŏngsŏng. ● (South Korea) NW South Korea 37.30N 126.57E
104 J11 **Soulac-sur-Mer** Gironde, SW France 45.31N 1.06W
101 L19 **Soumagne** Liège, E Belgium 50.36N 5.48E
20 M14 **Sound Beach** Long Island, New York, NE USA 40.56N 72.58W
97 J22 **Sound, The** *Dan.* Øresund, *Swe.* Öresund. *strait* Denmark/Sweden
117 H20 **Soúnio, Akrotírio** *headland* C Greece 37.39N 24.01E
144 F8 **Soûr** *var.* Şūr; *anc.* Tyre. SW Lebanon 33.18N 35.30E
Sources, Mont-aux- *see* Phofung
106 G8 **Soure** Coimbra, N Portugal 40.04N 8.37W
9 W17 **Souris** Manitoba, S Canada 49.37N 100.16W
11 Q14 **Souris** Prince Edward Island, SE Canada 46.22N 62.16W
30 L2 **Souris River** *var.* Mouse River. ≈ Canada/USA
27 X10 **Sour Lake** Texas, SW USA 30.08N 94.24W
117 F17 **Sourpi** Thessalía, C Greece 39.07N 22.54E
106 H11 **Sousel** Portalegre, C Portugal 38.57N 7.40W
77 N6 **Sousse** *var.* Sūsah. NE Tunisia 35.45N 10.37E
12 H11 **South** ≈ Ontario, S Canada
South *see* Sud
85 G23 **South Africa** *off.* Republic of South Africa, *Afr.* Suid-Afrika. ◆ *republic* S Africa
48-49 **South America** *continent*
2 J17 **South American Plate** *tectonic feature*
99 M23 **Southampton** *hist.* Hamwih, *Lat.* Clausentum. S England, UK 50.54N 1.22W
21 N14 **Southampton** Long Island, New York, NE USA 40.52N 72.22W
15 M5 **Southampton Island** *island* Nunavut, NE Canada
157 P20 **South Andaman** *island* Andaman Islands, India, NE Indian Ocean
11 Q6 **South Aulatsivik Island** *island* Newfoundland and Labrador, E Canada
190 E4 **South Australia** ◐ *state* S Australia
South Australian Abyssal Plain *see* South Australian Plain
199 Gg13 **South Australian Basin** *undersea feature* SW Indian Ocean
181 X12 **South Australian Plain** *var.* South Australian Abyssal Plain. *undersea feature* SE Indian Ocean
39 R13 **South Baldy** ▲ New Mexico, SW USA 33.59N 107.11W
25 Y14 **South Bay** Florida, SE USA 26.39N 80.43W
12 E12 **South Baymouth** Manitoulin Island, Ontario, S Canada 45.33N 82.01W
32 L10 **South Beloit** Illinois, N USA 42.29N 89.02W
33 O11 **South Bend** Indiana, N USA 41.40N 86.15W
27 R6 **South Bend** Texas, SW USA 32.58N 98.39W
34 F9 **South Bend** Washington, NW USA 46.38N 123.48W
South Beveland *see* Zuid-Beveland
South Borneo *see* Kalimantan Selatan
23 U7 **South Boston** Virginia, NE USA 36.42N 78.54W
190 F2 **South Branch Neales** *seasonal river* South Australia
23 U3 **South Branch Potomac River** ≈ West Virginia, NE USA
193 H19 **Southbridge** Canterbury, South Island, NZ 43.49S 172.17E
21 N12 **Southbridge** Massachusetts, NE USA 42.03N 72.00W
191 P17 **South Bruny Island** *island* Tasmania, SE Australia
20 L7 **South Burlington** Vermont, NE USA 44.27N 73.08W
46 M6 **South Caicos** *island* S Turks and Caicos Islands
South Cape *see* Ka Lae
25 V3 **South Carolina** *off.* State of South Carolina; also known as The Palmetto State. ◐ *state* SE USA
South Carpathians *see* Carpaţii Meridionali
South Celebes *see* Sulawesi Selatan
23 Q5 **South Charleston** West Virginia, NE USA 38.22N 81.42W
198 F7 **South China Basin** *undersea feature* SE South China Sea
198 F7 **South China Sea** *Chin.* Nan Hai, *Ind.* Laut Cina Selatan, *Vtn.* Biên Đông. *sea* SE Asia
35 Z10 **South Dakota** *off.* State of South Dakota; also known as The Coyote State, Sunshine State. ◐ *state* N USA
25 X10 **South Daytona** Florida, SE USA 29.09N 81.01W
39 R10 **South Domingo Pueblo** New Mexico, SW USA 35.28N 106.24W
99 N23 **South Downs** *hill range* SE England, UK
85 I21 **South East** ◐ *district* SE Botswana
67 H15 **South East Bay** *bay* Ascension Island, C Atlantic Ocean
191 O17 **South East Cape** *headland* Tasmania, SE Australia 43.36S 146.52E
40 K10 **Southeast Cape** *headland* Saint Lawrence Island, Alaska, USA 62.56N 169.39W
South-East Celebes *see* Sulawesi Tenggara
198 G14 **Southeast Indian Ridge** *undersea feature* Indian Ocean/Pacific Ocean
Southeast Island *see* Tagula Island
199 Mm16 **Southeast Pacific Basin** *var.* Belling Hausen Mulde. *undersea feature* SE Pacific Ocean
67 H15 **South East Point** *headland* SE Ascension Island
191 O14 **South East Point** *headland* Victoria, S Australia 39.10S 146.21E
203 Z3 **South East Point** *headland* Kiritimati, NE Kiribati 1.42N 157.10W
46 L5 **Southeast Point** *headland* Mayaguana, SE Bahamas 22.15N 72.44W
South-East Sulawesi *see* Sulawesi Tenggara
9 U12 **Southend** Saskatchewan, C Canada 56.19N 103.13W
99 P22 **Southend-on-Sea** E England, UK 51.33N 0.43E
85 H20 **Southern** *var.* Bangwaketse, Ngwaketze. ◐ *district* SE Botswana
83 I15 **Southern** ◐ *region* S Ethiopia
144 E13 **Southern** ◐ *district* S Israel
85 N15 **Southern** ◐ *region* S Malawi
85 I15 **Southern** ◐ *province* S Zambia
193 E19 **Southern Alps** ▲▲ South Island, NZ
202 K15 **Southern Cook Islands** *island group* S Cook Islands
188 K12 **Southern Cross** Western Australia 31.17S 119.15E
82 A12 **Southern Darfur** ◐ *state* W Sudan
194 F13 **Southern Highlands** ◐ *province* W PNG
9 V11 **Southern Indian Lake** ◎ Manitoba, C Canada
82 E11 **Southern Kordofan** ◐ *state* C Sudan
197 L15 **Southern Lau Group** *island group* Lau Group, SE Fiji
181 S13 **Southern Ocean** *ocean*
23 T10 **Southern Pines** North Carolina, SE USA 35.10N 79.23W
161 J26 **Southern Province** ◐ *province* S Sri Lanka
98 I13 **Southern Uplands** ▲▲ S Scotland, UK
Southern Urals *see* Yuzhnyy Ural
191 P16 **South Esk River** ≈ Tasmania, SE Australia
9 U16 **Southey** Saskatchewan, S Canada 50.53N 104.27W
29 V2 **South Fabius River** ≈ Missouri, C USA
33 S10 **Southfield** Michigan, N USA 42.28N 83.12W
199 J11 **South Fiji Basin** *undersea feature* S Pacific Ocean
99 Q22 **South Foreland** *headland* SE England, UK 51.08N 1.22E
37 P7 **South Fork American River** ≈ California, W USA
30 K7 **South Fork Grand River** ≈ South Dakota, N USA
37 T12 **South Fork Kern River** ≈ California, W USA
41 Q7 **South Fork Koyukuk River** ≈ Alaska, USA
41 Q11 **South Fork Kuskokwim River** ≈ Alaska, USA
28 H2 **South Fork Republican River** ≈ C USA
28 L3 **South Fork Solomon River** ≈ Kansas, C USA
33 P5 **South Fox Island** *island* Michigan, N USA
22 G8 **South Fulton** Tennessee, S USA 36.28N 88.53W
205 U10 **South Geomagnetic Pole** *pole* Antarctica 78.30S 111.00E
67 J20 **South Georgia** *island* South Georgia and the South Sandwich Islands, SW Atlantic Ocean
67 K21 **South Georgia and the South Sandwich Islands** ◇ *UK dependent territory* SW Atlantic Ocean
49 Y14 **South Georgia Ridge** *var.* North Scotia Ridge. *undersea feature* SW Atlantic Ocean
189 Q1 **South Goulburn Island** *island* Northern Territory, N Australia
159 U16 **South Hatia Island** *island* SE Bangladesh
33 O10 **South Haven** Michigan, N USA 42.24N 86.16W
23 V7 **South Hill** Virginia, NE USA 36.43N 78.07W
South Holland *see* Zuid-Holland
23 P8 **South Holston Lake** ⊠ Tennessee/Virginia, S USA
183 N1 **South Honshu Ridge** *undersea feature* W Pacific Ocean
28 M6 **South Hutchinson** Kansas, C USA 38.01N 97.56W
157 K21 **South Huvadhu Atoll** *var.* Gaafu Dhaalu Atoll. *atoll* S Maldives
181 U14 **South Indian Basin** *undersea feature* Indian Ocean/Pacific Ocean
9 W11 **South Indian Lake** Manitoba, C Canada 56.48N 98.55W
83 I17 **South Island** *island* NW Kenya
193 C20 **South Island** *island* S NZ
67 B23 **South Jason** *island* Jason Islands, NW Falkland Islands
South Kalimantan *see* Kalimantan Selatan
South Kazakhstan *see* Yuzhnyy Kazakhstan
169 X15 **South Korea** *off.* Republic of Korea, *Kor.* Taehan Min'guk. ◆ *republic* E Asia
37 Q6 **South Lake Tahoe** California, W USA 38.56N 119.57W
27 N6 **Southland** Texas, SW USA 33.16N 101.31W
193 B23 **Southland** *off.* Southland Region. ◐ *region* South Island, NZ
31 N15 **South Loup River** ≈ Nebraska, C USA
157 K19 **South Maalhosmadulu Atoll** *var.* Baa Atoll. *atoll* N Maldives
12 E15 **South Maitland** ≈ Ontario, S Canada
198 Ff9 **South Makassar Basin** *undersea feature* E Java Sea
33 O6 **South Manitou Island** *island* Michigan, N USA
157 K18 **South Miladummadulu Atoll** *atoll* N Maldives
23 X8 **South Mills** North Carolina, SE USA 36.28N 76.18W
14 G7 **South Nahanni** ≈ Northwest Territories, NW Canada
41 P13 **South Naknek** Alaska, USA 58.39N 157.01W
12 M13 **South Nation** ≈ Ontario, SE Canada
46 F9 **South Negril Point** *headland* W Jamaica 18.14N 78.21W
157 K20 **South Nilandhe Atoll** *var.* Dhaalu Atoll. *atoll* C Maldives
38 L2 **South Ogden** Utah, W USA 41.09N 111.58W
20 M14 **Southold** Long Island, New York, NE USA 41.03N 72.24W
204 H1 **South Orkney Islands** *island group* Antarctica
143 S9 **South Ossetia** *former autonomous region* SW Georgia
South Pacific Basin *see* Southwest Pacific Basin
21 P7 **South Paris** Maine, NE USA 44.14N 70.29W
35 U15 **South Pass** *pass* Wyoming, C USA 42.20N 108.55W
201 U13 **South Pass** *passage* Chuuk Islands, C Micronesia
22 K10 **South Pittsburg** Tennessee, S USA 35.00N 85.42W
30 K15 **South Platte River** ≈ Colorado/Nebraska, C USA
33 T16 **South Point** Ohio, N USA 38.25N 82.35W
67 G15 **South Point** *headland* S Ascension Island
33 R6 **South Point** *headland* Michigan, N USA 44.51N 83.17W
South Point *see* Ka Lae
205 P9 **South Pole** *pole* Antarctica 90.00S 0.00E
191 P17 **Southport** Tasmania, SE Australia 43.26S 146.57E
99 K17 **Southport** NW England, UK 53.39N 3.01W
23 V12 **Southport** North Carolina, SE USA 33.55N 78.01W
21 P8 **South Portland** Maine, NE USA 43.38N 70.14W
12 H12 **South River** Ontario, S Canada 45.48N 79.21W
23 U11 **South River** ≈ North Carolina, SE USA
98 K5 **South Ronaldsay** *island* NE Scotland, UK
38 L2 **South Salt Lake** Utah, W USA 40.42N 111.52W
67 L21 **South Sandwich Islands** *island group* SE South Georgia and South Sandwich Islands
67 K21 **South Sandwich Trench** *undersea feature* SW Atlantic Ocean
9 S16 **South Saskatchewan** ≈ Alberta/Saskatchewan, S Canada
67 I21 **South Scotia Ridge** *undersea feature* S Scotia Sea
9 V10 **South Seal** ≈ Manitoba, C Canada
204 G4 **South Shetland Islands** *island group* Antarctica
67 H22 **South Shetland Trough** *undersea feature* Atlantic Ocean/Pacific Ocean
99 M14 **South Shields** NE England, UK 55.00N 1.25W
31 R13 **South Sioux City** Nebraska, C USA 42.28N 96.24W
199 I10 **South Solomon Trench** *undersea feature* W Pacific Ocean
191 V3 **South Stradbroke Island** *island* Queensland, E Australia
South Sulawesi *see* Sulawesi Selatan
South Sumatra *see* Sumatera Selatan
192 K11 **South Taranaki Bight** *bight* SE Tasman Sea
South Tasmania Plateau *see* Tasman Plateau
38 M15 **South Tucson** Arizona, SW USA 32.11N 110.56W
10 H9 **South Twin Island** *island* Nunavut, C Canada
98 E9 **South Uist** *island* NW Scotland, UK
South-West *see* Sud-Ouest
South-West Africa/South West Africa *see* Namibia
67 F15 **South West Bay** *bay* Ascension Island, C Atlantic Ocean
191 N18 **South West Cape** *headland* Tasmania, SE Australia 43.34S 146.01E
193 B26 **South West Cape** *headland* Stewart Island, NZ 47.15S 167.28E
40 J10 **Southwest Cape** *headland* Saint Lawrence Island, Alaska, USA 63.19N 171.27W
178 Mm13 **Southwest Cay** *island* NW Spratly Islands
Southwest Indian Ocean Ridge *see* Southwest Indian Ridge
181 N11 **Southwest Indian Ridge** *var.* Southwest Indian Ocean Ridge. *undersea feature* SW Indian Ocean
199 Kk13 **Southwest Pacific Basin** *var.* South Pacific Basin. *undersea feature* SE Pacific Ocean
46 H2 **Southwest Point** *headland* Great Abaco, N Bahamas 25.50N 77.12W
203 X3 **South West Point** *headland* Kiritimati, NE Kiribati 1.52N 157.34E
67 G25 **South West Point** *headland* SW Saint Helena 16.00S 5.48W
27 P5 **South Wichita River** ≈ Texas, SW USA
99 Q20 **Southwold** E England, UK 52.15N 1.36E
21 Q12 **South Yarmouth** Massachusetts, NE USA 41.38N 70.09W
118 J10 **Sovata** *Hung.* Szováta. Mureş, C Romania 46.36N 25.04E
109 N22 **Soverato** Calabria, SW Italy 38.40N 16.31E
Sovetabad *see* Ghafurov
130 C2 **Sovetsk** *Ger.* Tilsit. Kaliningradskaya Oblast', W Russian Federation 53.04N 21.52E

◆ COUNTRY
● COUNTRY CAPITAL
◇ DEPENDENT TERRITORY
○ DEPENDENT TERRITORY CAPITAL
◐ ADMINISTRATIVE REGION
✈ INTERNATIONAL AIRPORT
▲ MOUNTAIN
▲▲ MOUNTAIN RANGE
⩚ VOLCANO
≈ RIVER
◎ LAKE
⊠ RESERVOIR

SOVETSK – STERNBERG

129 Q15 **Sovetsk** Kirovskaya Oblast', NW Russian Federation 57.37N 49.02E
131 N10 **Sovetskaya** Rostovskaya Oblast', SW Russian Federation 49.00N 42.09E
127 O15 **Sovetskaya Gavan'** Khabarovskiy Kray, SE Russian Federation 48.54N 140.19E
125 F10 **Sovetskiy** Khanty-Mansiyskiy Avtonomnyy Okrug, C Russian Federation 61.20N 63.34E
Sovetskoye *see* Ketchenery
152 I15 **Sovet"yab** *prev.* Sovet"yap. Ahal Welaýaty, S Turkmenistan 36.29N 61.13E
Sovet"yap *see* Sovet"yab
119 U12 **Sovyets'kyy** Respublika Krym, S Ukraine 45.20N 34.54E
85 I18 **Sowa** *var.* Sua. Central, NE Botswana 20.33S 26.18E
Sowa Pan *see* Sua Pan
176 Ww9 **Sowek** Papua, E Indonesia 0.46S 135.31E
85 J21 **Soweto** Gauteng, NE South Africa 26.08S 27.53E
153 R11 **So'x** *Rus.* Sokh. Farg'ona Viloyati, E Uzbekistan 39.56N 71.10E
Sōya-kaikyō *see* La Perouse Strait
172 Pp1 **Sōya-misaki** *headland* Hokkaidō, NE Japan 45.31N 141.55E
129 N7 **Soyana** ≈ NW Russian Federation
152 A8 **Soye, Mys** *var.* Mys Suz. *headland* NW Turkmenistan 41.47N 52.27E
84 A10 **Soyo** Zaire, NW Angola 6.07S 12.19E
82 J10 **Soyra** ▲ C Eritrea 14.46N 39.29E
Sozaq *see* Suzak
121 P16 **Sozh** *Rus.* Sozh. ≈ NE Europe
116 N10 **Sozopol** *prev.* Sizebolu *anc.* Apollonia. Burgas, E Bulgaria
180 J15 **Sœurs, Les** *island group* Inner Islands, W Seychelles
101 L20 **Spa** Liège, E Belgium 50.28N 5.52E
204 I7 **Spaatz Island** *island* Antarctica
150 M14 **Space Launching Centre** *space station* Kzylorda, S Kazakhstan 45.50N 63.20E
107 O7 **Spain** *off.* Kingdom of Spain, *Sp.* España; *anc.* Hispania, Iberia, *Lat.* Hispana. ◆ *monarchy* SW Europe
Spalato *see* Split
99 O19 **Spalding** E England, UK 52.48N 0.06W
12 D11 **Spanish** Ontario, S Canada 46.12N 82.21W
38 L3 **Spanish Fork** Utah, W USA 40.09N 111.40W
66 B12 **Spanish Point** *headland* C Bermuda 32.18N 64.49W
12 E9 **Spanish River** ≈ Ontario, S Canada
46 K13 **Spanish Town** *hist.* St.Iago de la Vega. C Jamaica 18.00N 76.57W
117 H24 **Spánta, Akrotírio** *headland* Kríti, Greece, E Mediterranean Sea 35.40N 23.44E
37 Q5 **Sparks** Nevada, W USA 39.32N 119.45W
Sparnacum *see* Épernay
97 N16 **Sparreholm** Södermanland, C Sweden 59.04N 16.51E
25 U4 **Sparta** Georgia, SE USA 33.16N 82.58W
32 K16 **Sparta** Illinois, N USA 38.07N 89.42W
33 P9 **Sparta** Michigan, N USA 43.09N 85.42W
23 R8 **Sparta** North Carolina, SE USA 36.34N 81.21W
22 L9 **Sparta** Tennessee, S USA 35.55N 85.27W
32 I7 **Sparta** Wisconsin, N USA 43.57N 90.49W
Sparta *see* Spárti
23 Q11 **Spartanburg** South Carolina, SE USA 34.57N 81.55W
122 F10 **Spartel, Cap** *headland* N Morocco 35.49N 5.55W
117 F21 **Spárti** *Eng.* Sparta. Pelopónnisos, S Greece 37.04N 22.25E
109 B21 **Spartivento, Capo** *headland* Sardegna, Italy, C Mediterranean Sea 38.52N 8.50E
9 P17 **Sparwood** British Columbia, SW Canada 49.45N 114.45W
130 I4 **Spas-Demensk** Kaluzhskaya Oblast', W Russian Federation 54.22N 34.16E
130 M4 **Spas-Klepiki** Ryazanskaya Oblast', W Russian Federation 55.08N 40.15E
Spasovo *see* Kulen Vakuf
127 N17 **Spassk-Dal'niy** Primorskiy Kray, SE Russian Federation 44.34N 132.52E
130 M5 **Spassk-Ryazanskiy** Ryazanskaya Oblast', W Russian Federation 54.25N 40.21E
117 H19 **Spáta** Attikí, C Greece 37.58N 23.55E
124 O12 **Spátha, Akrotírio** *headland* Kríti, Greece, E Mediterranean Sea 35.42N 23.43E
Špatrjan *see* Paternion
30 I9 **Spearfish** South Dakota, N USA 44.29N 103.51W
27 O1 **Spearman** Texas, SW USA 36.12N 101.11W
67 C25 **Speedwell Island** *island* S Falkland Islands
67 C25 **Speedwell Island Settlement** S Falkland Islands 52.13S 59.40W
67 G25 **Speery Island** *island* S Saint Helena
47 N14 **Speightstown** NW Barbados 13.13N 59.37W
108 I13 **Spello** Umbria, C Italy 43.00N 12.41E
41 R12 **Spenard** Alaska, USA 61.09N 150.03W
Spence Bay *see* Taloyoak
33 O14 **Spencer** Indiana, N USA 39.18N 86.46W
31 T12 **Spencer** Iowa, C USA 43.09N 95.07W
31 P12 **Spencer** Nebraska, C USA 42.52N 98.42W
23 S9 **Spencer** North Carolina, SE USA 35.41N 80.26W
22 L9 **Spencer** Tennessee, S USA 35.46N 85.27W
23 Q4 **Spencer** West Virginia, NE USA 38.48N 81.21W
32 K6 **Spencer** Wisconsin, N USA 44.46N 90.17W
190 G10 **Spencer, Cape** *headland* South Australia 35.17S 136.52E
41 V13 **Spencer, Cape** *headland* Alaska, USA 58.12N 136.39W
190 H9 **Spencer Gulf** *gulf* South Australia
20 F9 **Spencerport** New York, NE USA 43.11N 77.48W
33 Q12 **Spencerville** Ohio, N USA 40.42N 84.21W
117 E17 **Spercheiáda** *var.* Sperhiada, Sperkhiás. Stereá Ellás, C Greece 38.54N 22.07E
117 E17 **Spercheiós** ≈ C Greece
Sperhiada *see* Spercheiáda
97 G14 **Sperillen** ◎ S Norway
Sperkhiás *see* Spercheiáda
103 I18 **Spessart** *hill range* C Germany
Spétsai *see* Spétses
117 G21 **Spétses** *prev.* Spétsai. Spétses, S Greece 37.16N 23.09E
117 G21 **Spétses** *island* S Greece
98 J8 **Spey** ≈ NE Scotland, UK
103 G20 **Speyer** *Eng.* Spires; *anc.* Civitas Nemetum, Spira. Rheinland-Pfalz, SW Germany 49.19N 8.25E
103 G20 **Speyerbach** ≈ W Germany
109 N20 **Spezzano Albanese** Calabria, SW Italy 39.40N 16.17E
Spice Islands *see* Maluku
102 F9 **Spiekeroog** *island* NW Germany
111 W9 **Spielfeld** Steiermark, SE Austria 46.43N 15.36E
67 N21 **Spiess Seamount** *undersea feature* S Atlantic Ocean 53.00S 2.00W
110 E9 **Spiez** Bern, W Switzerland 46.42N 7.40E
100 G13 **Spijkenisse** Zuid-Holland, SW Netherlands 51.52N 4.19E
41 T6 **Spike Mountain** ▲ Alaska, USA 67.42N 141.39W
117 I25 **Spíli** Kríti, Greece, E Mediterranean Sea 35.12N 24.33E
110 D10 **Spillgerten** ▲ W Switzerland 46.34N 7.25E
120 F9 **Spilva** ✕ (Rīga) Rīga, C Latvia 56.55N 24.03E
109 N17 **Spinazzola** Puglia, SE Italy 40.58N 16.06E
155 O9 **Spīn Būldak** Kandahār, S Afghanistan 31.01N 66.22E
Spira *see* Speyer
Spirdingsee *see* Śniardwy, Jezioro
Spires *see* Speyer
31 T11 **Spirit Lake** Iowa, C USA 43.25N 95.06W
31 T11 **Spirit Lake** ◎ Iowa, C USA
9 N13 **Spirit River** Alberta, W Canada 55.46N 118.51W
9 S14 **Spiritwood** Saskatchewan, S Canada 53.18N 107.33W
29 R11 **Spiro** Oklahoma, C USA 35.14N 94.37W
113 L19 **Spišská Nová Ves** *Ger.* Neudorf, Zipser Neudorf, *Hung.* Igló. Košický Kraj, E Slovakia 48.58N 20.34E
143 T11 **Spitak** NW Armenia 40.51N 44.17E
94 O2 **Spitsbergen** *island* NW Svalbard
Spittal *see* Spittal an der Drau
111 R9 **Spittal an der Drau** *var.* Spittal. Kärnten, S Austria 46.48N 13.30E
111 V3 **Spitz** Niederösterreich, NE Austria 48.24N 15.22E
96 D9 **Spjelkavik** Møre og Romsdal, S Norway 62.28N 6.22E
27 W10 **Splendora** Texas, SW USA 30.13N 95.09W
115 E14 **Split** *It.* Spalato. Split-Dalmacija, S Croatia 43.31N 16.27E
115 E14 **Split** ✕ Split-Dalmacija, S Croatia 43.33N 16.19E
115 E14 **Split-Dalmacija** *off.* Splitsko-Dalmatinska Županija. ◐ *province* S Croatia
9 X12 **Split Lake** ◎ Manitoba, C Canada
Splitsko-Dalmatinska Županija *see* Split-Dalmacija
110 H10 **Splügen** Graubünden, S Switzerland 46.33N 9.18E
Spodnji Dravograd *see* Dravograd
27 P12 **Spofford** Texas, SW USA 29.10N 100.24W
120 J11 **Špoģi** Daugvapils, SE Latvia 56.03N 26.47E
34 L8 **Spokane** Washington, NW USA 47.39N 117.25W
34 L8 **Spokane River** ≈ Washington, NW USA
108 I13 **Spoleto** Umbria, C Italy 42.43N 12.43E
32 I4 **Spooner** Wisconsin, N USA 45.51N 91.49W
32 K12 **Spoon River** ≈ Illinois, N USA
23 W5 **Spotsylvania** Virginia, NE USA 38.13N 77.31W
34 L8 **Sprague** Washington, NW USA 47.19N 117.55W
178 Ll16 **Spratly Island** *island* SW Spratly Islands
198 Ff7 **Spratly Islands** *Chin.* Nansha Qundao. ◇ *disputed territory* SE Asia
34 J12 **Spray** Oregon, NW USA 44.30N 119.38W
114 I11 **Spreča** ≈ N Bosnia and Herzegovina
102 P13 **Spree** ≈ E Germany
102 P13 **Spreewald** *wetland* NE Germany
103 P14 **Spremberg** Brandenburg, E Germany 51.34N 14.22E
27 W11 **Spring** Texas, SW USA 30.03N 95.24W
33 Q10 **Spring Arbor** Michigan, N USA 42.12N 84.33W
85 E23 **Springbok** Northern Cape, W South Africa 29.38S 17.56E
20 I15 **Spring City** Pennsylvania, NE USA 40.10N 75.33W
22 L9 **Spring City** Tennessee, S USA 35.41N 84.51W
38 L4 **Spring City** Utah, W USA 39.28N 111.30W
37 W3 **Spring Creek** Nevada, W USA 40.45N 115.40W
29 S9 **Springdale** Arkansas, C USA 36.11N 94.07W
33 Q14 **Springdale** Ohio, N USA 39.17N 84.29W
102 I13 **Springe** Niedersachsen, N Germany 52.13N 9.33E
39 U9 **Springer** New Mexico, SW USA 36.21N 104.35W
39 W7 **Springfield** Colorado, C USA 37.24N 102.36W
25 W5 **Springfield** Georgia, SE USA 32.21N 81.20W
32 K14 **Springfield** *state capital* Illinois, N USA 39.48N 89.38W
22 L6 **Springfield** Kentucky, S USA 37.41N 85.13W
20 M12 **Springfield** Massachusetts, NE USA 42.06N 72.32W
31 T10 **Springfield** Minnesota, N USA 44.15N 94.58W
29 T7 **Springfield** Missouri, C USA 37.13N 93.18W
33 R13 **Springfield** Ohio, N USA 39.55N 83.48W
34 G13 **Springfield** Oregon, NW USA 44.03N 123.01W
31 Q12 **Springfield** South Dakota, N USA 42.51N 97.54W
22 J8 **Springfield** Tennessee, S USA 36.30N 86.53W
20 M9 **Springfield** Vermont, NE USA 43.18N 72.27W
32 K14 **Springfield, Lake** ▣ Illinois, N USA
57 T8 **Spring Garden** NE Guyana 6.58N 58.34W
32 K8 **Spring Green** Wisconsin, N USA 43.10N 90.02W
31 X11 **Spring Grove** Minnesota, N USA 43.33N 91.38W
24 G4 **Springhill** Louisiana, S USA 33.01N 93.27W
25 V12 **Spring Hill** Florida, SE USA 28.28N 82.36W
29 R4 **Spring Hill** Kansas, C USA 38.44N 94.49W
11 P15 **Springhill** Nova Scotia, SE Canada 45.40N 64.04W
22 I9 **Spring Hill** Tennessee, S USA 35.46N 86.55W
23 U10 **Spring Lake** North Carolina, SE USA 35.10N 78.58W
26 M4 **Springlake** Texas, SW USA 34.13N 102.18W
37 W11 **Spring Mountains** ⛰ Nevada, W USA
67 B24 **Spring Point** West Falkland, Falkland Islands 51.49S 60.27W
29 W9 **Spring River** ≈ Arkansas/Missouri, C USA
29 S7 **Spring River** ≈ Missouri/Oklahoma, C USA
85 J21 **Springs** Gauteng, NE South Africa 26.13S 28.32E
193 H16 **Springs Junction** West Coast, South Island, NZ 42.20S 172.10E
189 X8 **Springsure** Queensland, E Australia 24.09S 148.06E
31 W11 **Spring Valley** Minnesota, N USA 43.41N 92.23W
20 K13 **Spring Valley** New York, NE USA 41.10N 73.58W
31 N12 **Springview** Nebraska, C USA 42.48N 99.45W
20 D11 **Springville** New York, NE USA 42.27N 78.52W
38 L3 **Springville** Utah, W USA 40.10N 111.36W
Sprottau *see* Szprotawa
13 V4 **Sproule, Pointe** *headland* Québec, SE Canada 49.47N 67.02W
9 Q14 **Spruce Grove** Alberta, SW Canada 53.36N 113.55W
23 T4 **Spruce Knob** ▲ West Virginia, NE USA 38.40N 79.37W
37 X3 **Spruce Mountain** ▲ Nevada, W USA 40.33N 114.46W
23 P9 **Spruce Pine** North Carolina, SE USA 35.55N 82.03W
100 G13 **Spui** ≈ SW Netherlands
109 O19 **Spulico, Capo** *headland* S Italy 39.57N 16.38E
27 O5 **Spur** Texas, SW USA 33.28N 100.51W
99 O17 **Spurn Head** *headland* E England, UK 53.34N 0.06E
101 H20 **Spy** Namur, S Belgium 50.29N 4.43E
97 I15 **Spydeberg** Østfold, S Norway 59.36N 11.04E
193 J17 **Spy Glass Point** *headland* South Island, NZ 42.33S 173.31E
8 L17 **Squamish** British Columbia, SW Canada 49.40N 123.10W
21 O8 **Squam Lake** ◎ New Hampshire, NE USA
21 S2 **Squa Pan Mountain** ▲ Maine, NE USA 46.36N 68.09W
41 N16 **Squaw Harbor** Unga Island, Alaska, USA 55.12N 160.41W
12 E11 **Squaw Island** *island* Ontario, S Canada
109 O22 **Squillace, Golfo di** *gulf* S Italy
109 Q18 **Squinzano** Puglia, SE Italy 40.25N 18.03E
174 L15 **Sragen** Jawa, C Indonesia 7.24S 111.00E
Sráid na Cathrach *see* Milltown Malbay
178 Jj11 **Srâlau** Stœ̆ng Trêng, N Cambodia 14.03N 105.46E
Srath an Urláir *see* Stranorlar
114 G10 **Srbac** Republika Srpska, N Bosnia & Herzegovina 45.06N 17.33E
Srbinje *see* Foča
Srbija *see* Serbia
Srbobran *see* Donji Vakuf
114 K9 **Srbobran** *var.* Bácsszenttamás, *Hung.* Szenttamás. Serbia, N Serbia and Montenegro (Yugoslavia) 45.33N 19.46E
178 Ii14 **Srê Âmbĕl** Kaôh Kông, SW Cambodia 11.07N 103.46E
114 K13 **Srebrenica** Republika Srpska, E Bosnia & Herzegovina 44.04N 19.18E
114 I11 **Srebrenik** Federacija Bosna I Hercegovina, E Bosnia & Herzegovina 44.42N 18.30E
116 M10 **Sredets** *prev.* Grudovo. Burgas, E Bulgaria 42.21N 27.13E
116 K10 **Sredets** *prev.* Syulemeshlii. Stara Zagora, C Bulgaria 42.16N 25.40E
116 M10 **Sredetska Reka** ≈ SE Bulgaria
127 P9 **Sredinnyy Khrebet** ⛰ E Russian Federation
116 N7 **Sredishte** *Rom.* Beibunar; *prev.* Knyazhevo. Dobrich, NE Bulgaria 43.51N 27.30E
116 I10 **Sredna Gora** ⛰ C Bulgaria
127 N7 **Srednekolymsk** Respublika Sakha (Yakutiya), NE Russian Federation 67.28N 153.52E
130 K7 **Srednerusskaya Vozvyshennost'** *Eng.* Central Russian Upland. ⛰ W Russian Federation
126 Ii9 **Srednesibirskoye Ploskogor'ye** *var.* Central Siberian Uplands, *Eng.* Central Siberian Plateau. ⛰ N Russian Federation
129 V13 **Sredniy Ural** ⛰ NW Russian Federation
178 Jj13 **Srê Khtŭm** Môndól Kiri, E Cambodia 12.10N 106.52E
112 G12 **Śrem** Wielkolpolskie, C Poland 52.07N 17.00E
114 K10 **Sremska Mitrovica** *prev.* Mitrovica, *Ger.* Mitrowitz. Serbia, NW Serbia and Montenegro (Yugoslavia) 44.58N 19.37E
178 Ii11 **Srêng, Stœ̆ng** ≈ NW Cambodia
178 Ii11 **Srê Noy** Siĕmréab, NW Cambodia 13.47N 104.03E
Srepok, Sông *see* Srêpôk, Tônle
178 K12 **Srêpôk, Tônle** *var.* Sông Srepok. ≈ Cambodia/Vietnam
126 L15 **Sretensk** Chitinskaya Oblast', S Russian Federation 52.14N 117.33E
174 Ll7 **Sri Aman** Sarawak, East Malaysia 1.13N 111.25E
119 R4 **Sribne** Chernihivs'ka Oblast', N Ukraine 50.40N 32.55E
161 I25 **Sri Jayawardanapura** *var.* Sri Jayawardenepura; *prev.* Kotte. Western Province, W Sri Lanka 6.54N 79.58E
161 M14 **Srīkākulam** Andhra Pradesh, E India 18.18N 83.54E
161 I25 **Sri Lanka** *off.* Democratic Socialist Republic of Sri Lanka; *prev.* Ceylon. ◆ *republic* S Asia
138 Mm15 **Sri Lanka** *island* S Asia
159 V14 **Srimangal** Chittagong, E Bangladesh 24.19N 91.40E
Sri Mohangorh *see* Shri Mohangarh
158 H5 **Srīnagar** Jammu and Kashmir, N India 34.06N 74.50E
178 H10 **Srinagarind Reservoir** ◎ W Thailand
161 F19 **Sringeri** Karnātaka, W India 13.25N 75.13E
161 K25 **Sri Pada** *Eng.* Adam's Peak. ▲ S Sri Lanka 6.49N 80.25E
Sri Saket *see* Si Sa Ket
113 G14 **Środa Śląska** *Ger.* Neumarkt. Dolnośląskie, SW Poland 51.10N 16.30E
112 H12 **Środa Wielkopolska** Wielkolpolskie, C Poland 52.13N 17.16E
Srpska Kostajnica *see* Bosanska Kostajnica
115 G14 **Srpska, Republika** ◐ *republic* Bosnia & Herzegovina
Srpski Brod *see* Bosanski Brod
Ssu-ch'uan *see* Sichuan
Ssu-p'ing/Ssu-p'ing-chieh *see* Siping
Stablo *see* Stavelot
101 G15 **Stabroek** Antwerpen, N Belgium 51.21N 4.22E
Stackeln *see* Strenči
98 I5 **Stack Skerry** *island* N Scotland, UK
102 I9 **Stade** Niedersachsen, NW Germany 53.36N 9.28E
96 C10 **Stadlandet** *peninsula* S Norway
111 R5 **Stadl-Paura** Oberösterreich, NW Austria 48.04N 13.52E
121 L20 **Stadolichy** *Rus.* Stodolichi. Homyel'skaya Voblasts', SE Belarus 51.43N 28.30E
100 P7 **Stadskanaal** Groningen, NE Netherlands 53.00N 6.55E
103 H16 **Stadtallendorf** Hessen, C Germany 50.49N 9.01E
103 K23 **Stadtbergen** Bayern, S Germany 48.21N 10.50E
110 G7 **Stäfa** Zürich, NE Switzerland 47.14N 8.42E
97 K23 **Staffanstorp** Skåne, S Sweden 55.37N 13.13E
103 K18 **Staffelstein** Bayern, C Germany 50.05N 11.00E
99 L19 **Stafford** C England, UK 52.48N 2.07W
28 L6 **Stafford** Kansas, C USA 37.57N 98.36W
23 W4 **Stafford** Virginia, NE USA 38.24N 77.22W
99 L19 **Staffordshire** *cultural region* C England, UK
21 N12 **Stafford Springs** Connecticut, NE USA 41.57N 72.18W
117 H14 **Stágira** Kentrikí Makedonía, N Greece 40.31N 23.46E
120 G7 **Staicele** Limbaži, N Latvia 57.52N 24.48E
Ştaierdorf-Anina *see* Anina
111 V8 **Stainz** Steiermark, SE Austria 46.55N 15.18E
Stájerlakanina *see* Anina
119 Y7 **Stakhanov** Luhans'ka Oblast', E Ukraine 48.30N 38.42E
110 E11 **Stalden** Valais, SW Switzerland 46.12N 7.55E
Stalin *see* Varna
Stalinabad *see* Dushanbe
Stalingrad *see* Volgograd
Staliniri *see* Ts'khinvali
Stalino *see* Donets'k
Stalinobod *see* Dushanbe
Stalinov Štít *see* Gerlachovský štít
Stalinsk *see* Novokuznetsk
Stalinskaya Oblast' *see* Donets'ka Oblast'
Stalinski Zaliv *see* Varnenski Zaliv
Stalin, Yazovir *see* Iskŭr, Yazovir
113 N15 **Stalowa Wola** Podkarpackie, SE Poland 50.34N 22.01E
116 I11 **Stamboliyski** Plovdiv, C Bulgaria 42.08N 24.36E
116 J8 **Stamboliyski, Yazovir** ▣ N Bulgaria
99 N19 **Stamford** E England, UK 52.39N 0.32W
20 L14 **Stamford** Connecticut, NE USA 41.03N 73.31W
27 P6 **Stamford** Texas, SW USA 32.55N 99.49W
27 Q6 **Stamford, Lake** ▣ Texas, SW USA
110 I10 **Stampa** Graubünden, SE Switzerland 46.21N 9.35E
Stampalia *see* Astypálaia
29 T14 **Stamps** Arkansas, C USA 33.22N 93.30W
94 G11 **Stamsund** Nordland, C Norway 68.07N 13.49E
29 R2 **Stanberry** Missouri, C USA 40.12N 94.33W
205 O3 **Stancomb-Wills Glacier** *glacier* Antarctica
85 K21 **Standerton** Mpumalanga, E South Africa 26.54S 29.15E
33 R7 **Standish** Michigan, N USA 43.58N 83.58W
22 M6 **Stanford** Kentucky, S USA 37.30N 84.39W
35 S9 **Stanford** Montana, NW USA 47.08N 110.15W
97 P19 **Stånga** Gotland, SE Sweden 57.16N 18.30E
96 I13 **Stange** Hedmark, S Norway 60.43N 11.12E
85 L23 **Stanger** KwaZulu/Natal, E South Africa 29.18S 31.17E
Stanimaka *see* Asenovgrad
Stanislau *see* Ivano-Frankivs'k
37 P8 **Stanislaus River** ≈ California, W USA
Stanislav *see* Ivano-Frankivs'k
Stanislavskaya Oblast' *see* Ivano-Frankivs'ka Oblast'
Stanisławów *see* Ivano-Frankivs'k
Stanke Dimitrov *see* Dupnitsa
191 O15 **Stanley** Tasmania, SE Australia 40.48S 145.18E
67 E24 **Stanley** *var.* Port Stanley, Puerto Argentino ○ (Falkland Islands) East Falkland, Falkland Islands 51.45S 57.55W
35 O13 **Stanley** Idaho, NW USA 44.12N 114.58W
30 L3 **Stanley** North Dakota, N USA 48.19N 102.23W
23 U4 **Stanley** Virginia, NE USA 38.34N 78.30W
32 J6 **Stanley** Wisconsin, N USA 44.58N 90.54W
81 G21 **Stanley Pool** *var.* Pool Malebo. ◎ Congo/Dem. Rep. Congo
161 H20 **Stanley Reservoir** ▣ S India
Stanleyville *see* Kisangani
44 G3 **Stann Creek** ◐ *district* SE Belize
Stann Creek *see* Dangriga
127 N17 **Stanovoy Khrebet** ⛰ SE Russian Federation
110 F8 **Stans** Unterwalden, C Switzerland 46.57N 8.22E
99 O21 **Stansted** ✕ (London) Essex, E England, UK 51.53N 0.16E
191 U4 **Stanthorpe** Queensland, E Australia 28.35S 151.52E
23 N6 **Stanton** Kentucky, S USA 37.51N 83.51W
33 Q8 **Stanton** Michigan, N USA 43.17N 85.01W
31 Q14 **Stanton** Nebraska, C USA 41.57N 97.13W
30 L5 **Stanton** North Dakota, N USA 47.19N 101.22W
27 N7 **Stanton** Texas, SW USA 32.07N 101.47W
34 H7 **Stanwood** Washington, NW USA 48.14N 122.22W
119 Y7 **Stanychno-Luhans'ke** Luhans'ka Oblast', E Ukraine 48.39N 39.30E
110 K7 **Stanzach** Tirol, W Austria 47.24N 10.36E
100 M9 **Staphorst** Overijssel, E Netherlands 52.37N 6.12E
12 D18 **Staples** Ontario, S Canada 42.09N 82.34W
31 T6 **Staples** Minnesota, N USA 46.21N 94.47W
30 M14 **Stapleton** Nebraska, C USA 41.28N 100.30W
27 S8 **Star** Texas, SW USA 31.27N 98.16W
113 M14 **Starachowice** Świętokrzyskie, C Poland 51.04N 21.02E
Stara Kanjiža *see* Kanjiža
113 M18 **Stará L'ubovňa** *Ger.* Altlublau, *Hung.* Prešovský Kraj, E Slovakia 49.18N 20.40E
114 L10 **Stara Pazova** *Ger.* Altpasua, *Hung.* Ópazova. Serbia, N Serbia and Montenegro (Yugoslavia) 44.59N 20.10E
Stara Planina *see* Balkan Mountains
116 L9 **Stara Reka** ≈ C Bulgaria
118 M5 **Stara Synyava** Khmel'nyts'ka Oblast', W Ukraine 49.39N 27.39E
118 I2 **Stara Vyzhivka** Volyns'ka Oblast', NW Ukraine 51.27N 24.25E
Staraya Belitsa *see* Staraya Byelitsa
121 M14 **Staraya Byelitsa** *Rus.* Staraya Belitsa. Vitsyebskaya Voblasts', NE Belarus 54.42N 29.37E
131 R5 **Staraya Mayna** Ul'yanovskaya Oblast', W Russian Federation 54.36N 48.57E
121 O18 **Staraya Rudnya** *Rus.* Staraya Rudnya. Homyel'skaya Voblasts', SE Belarus 52.50N 30.15E
128 H14 **Staraya Russa** Novgorodskaya Oblast', W Russian Federation 57.59N 31.18E
116 K10 **Stara Zagora** *Lat.* Augusta Trajana. Stara Zagora, C Bulgaria 42.26N 25.39E
116 K10 **Stara Zagora** ◐ *province* C Bulgaria
31 S8 **Starbuck** Minnesota, N USA 45.36N 95.31W
203 W4 **Starbuck Island** *prev.* Volunteer Island. *island* E Kiribati
29 V13 **Star City** Arkansas, C USA 33.56N 91.50W
114 F13 **Staretina** ⛰ W Bosnia and Herzegovina
Stargard in Pommern *see* Stargard Szczeciński
112 E9 **Stargard Szczeciński** *Ger.* Stargard in Pommern. Zachodnio-pomorskie, NW Poland 53.19N 15.01E
195 Z17 **Star Harbour** *harbor* San Cristobal, SE Solomon Islands
Stari Bečej *see* Bečej
115 F15 **Stari Grad** *It.* Cittavecchia. Split-Dalmacija, S Croatia 43.11N 16.36E
175 Qq12 **Staring, Teluk** *var.* Teluk Wawosungu. *bay* Sulawesi, C Indonesia
128 J16 **Staritsa** Tverskaya Oblast', W Russian Federation 56.28N 34.51E
25 V9 **Starke** Florida, SE USA 29.56N 82.07W
24 M4 **Starkville** Mississippi, S USA 33.27N 88.49W
194 E11 **Star Mountains** *Ind.* Pegunungan Sterren. ⛰ Indonesia/PNG
103 L23 **Starnberg** Bayern, SE Germany 48.00N 11.19E
103 L24 **Starnberger See** ◎ SE Germany
Starobel'sk *see* Starobil's'k
119 X8 **Starobesheve** Donets'ka Oblast', E Ukraine 47.45N 38.01E
119 Y6 **Starobil's'k** *Rus.* Starobel'sk. Luhans'ka Oblast', E Ukraine 49.16N 38.55E
Starobin *see* Starobyn
121 K18 **Starobyn** *Rus.* Starobin. Minskaya Voblasts', S Belarus 52.43N 27.28E
130 H6 **Starodub** Bryanskaya Oblast', W Russian Federation 52.30N 32.56E
112 I8 **Starogard Gdański** *Ger.* Preussisch-Stargard. Pomorskie, N Poland 53.57N 18.29E
151 P16 **Staroikan** Yuzhnyy Kazakhstan, S Kazakhstan 43.09N 68.34E
Starokonstantinov *see* Starokostyantyniv
118 L5 **Starokostyantyniv** *Rus.* Starokonstantinov. Khmel'nyts'ka Oblast', NW Ukraine 49.43N 27.12E
130 K12 **Starominskaya** Krasnodarskiy Kray, SW Russian Federation 46.31N 39.03E
116 L7 **Staro Selo** *Rom.* Satul-Vechi; *prev.* Star-Smil. Silistra, NE Bulgaria 43.58N 26.32E
130 K12 **Staroshcherbinovskaya** Krasnodarskiy Kray, SW Russian Federation 46.36N 38.42E
131 V6 **Starosubkhangulovo** Respublika Bashkortostan, W Russian Federation 53.05N 57.22E
37 S4 **Star Peak** ▲ Nevada, W USA 40.31N 118.09W
Star-Smil *see* Staro Selo
99 J25 **Start Point** *headland* SW England, UK 50.13N 3.38W
Startsy *see* Kirawsk
Starum *see* Stavoren
121 L18 **Staryya Darohi** *Rus.* Staryye Dorogi. Minskaya Voblasts', S Belarus 53.01N 28.12E
Staryye Dorogi *see* Staryya Darohi
131 T2 **Staryye Zyattsy** Udmurtskaya Respublika, NW Russian Federation 57.22N 52.42E
119 U13 **Staryy Krym** Respublika Krym, S Ukraine 45.03N 35.06E
130 K8 **Staryy Oskol** Belgorodskaya Oblast', W Russian Federation 51.21N 37.52E
118 H6 **Staryy Sambir** L'vivs'ka Oblast', W Ukraine 49.27N 23.00E
103 L14 **Stassfurt** *var.* Staßfurt. Sachsen-Anhalt, C Germany 51.51N 11.34E
113 M15 **Staszów** Świętokrzyskie, C Poland 50.34N 21.08E
31 W13 **State Center** Iowa, C USA 42.01N 93.09W
20 E14 **State College** Pennsylvania, NE USA 40.48N 77.52W
20 K15 **Staten Island** *island* New York, NE USA
Staten Island *see* Estados, Isla de los
25 U8 **Statenville** Georgia, SE USA 30.42N 83.00W
25 W5 **Statesboro** Georgia, SE USA 32.28N 81.46W
States, The *see* United States of America
23 R9 **Statesville** North Carolina, SE USA 35.46N 80.53W
97 G16 **Stathelle** Telemark, S Norway 59.01N 9.40E
32 K15 **Staunton** Illinois, N USA 39.00N 89.47W
23 T5 **Staunton** Virginia, NE USA 38.09N 79.04W
97 C16 **Stavanger** Rogaland, S Norway 58.58N 5.43E
101 L21 **Stavelot** *Dut.* Stablo. Liège, E Belgium 50.24N 5.55E
97 G16 **Stavern** Vestfold, S Norway 58.58N 10.01E
Stavers Island *see* Vostok Island
100 J7 **Stavoren** *Fris.* Starum. Friesland, N Netherlands 52.52N 5.22E
130 M14 **Stavropol'** *prev.* Voroshilovsk. Stavropol'skiy Kray, SW Russian Federation 45.02N 41.57E
Stavropol' *see* Tol'yatti
130 M14 **Stavropol'skaya Vozvyshennost'** ⛰ SW Russian Federation
130 M14 **Stavropol'skiy Kray** ◐ *territory* SW Russian Federation
117 H14 **Stavrós** Kentrikí Makedonía, N Greece 40.39N 23.43E
117 J24 **Stavrós, Akrotírio** *headland* Kríti, Greece, E Mediterranean Sea 35.25N 24.57E
117 K21 **Stavrós, Akrotírio** *headland* Náxos, Kykládes, Greece, Aegean Sea 37.12N 25.32E
116 I12 **Stavroúpoli** *prev.* Stavroúpolis. Anatolikí Makedonía kai Thráki, NE Greece 41.12N 24.42E
Stavroúpolis *see* Stavroúpoli
119 O6 **Stavyshche** Kyyivs'ka Oblast', N Ukraine 49.23N 30.10E
190 M11 **Stawell** Victoria, SE Australia 37.03S 142.47E
112 N9 **Stawiski** Podlaskie, NE Poland 53.22N 22.08E
12 G14 **Stayner** Ontario, S Canada 44.25N 80.05W
39 R3 **Steamboat Springs** Colorado, C USA 40.28N 106.51W
22 M8 **Stearns** Kentucky, S USA 36.39N 84.27W
41 N10 **Stebbins** Alaska, USA 63.30N 162.15W
110 K7 **Steeg** Tirol, W Austria 47.15N 10.18E
29 Y9 **Steele** Missouri, C USA 36.04N 89.49W
31 N5 **Steele** North Dakota, N USA 46.51N 99.55W
204 J5 **Steele Island** *island* Antarctica
32 K16 **Steeleville** Illinois, N USA 38.00N 89.39W
29 W6 **Steelville** Missouri, C USA 37.58N 91.21W
101 G14 **Steenbergen** Noord-Brabant, S Netherlands 51.34N 4.13E
Steenkool *see* Bintuni
9 O10 **Steen River** Alberta, W Canada 59.37N 117.16W
100 M8 **Steenwijk** Overijssel, N Netherlands 52.46N 6.07E
67 A23 **Steeple Jason** *island* Jason Islands, NW Falkland Islands
182 J8 **Steep Point** *headland* Western Australia 26.09S 113.10E
118 L9 **Ştefăneşti** Botoşani, NE Romania 47.43N 27.15E
Stefanie, Lake *see* Ch'ew Bahir
15 J1 **Stefansson Island** *island* Nunavut, N Canada
119 O10 **Ştefan Vodă** *Rus.* Suvorovo. SE Moldova 46.33N 29.39E
65 H18 **Steffen, Cerro** ▲ S Chile 44.27S 71.42W
110 D9 **Steffisburg** Bern, C Switzerland 46.46N 7.37E
97 J24 **Stege** Storstrøm, SE Denmark 54.58N 12.18E
118 G10 **Ştei** *Hung.* Vaskohsziklás. Bihor, W Romania 46.33N 22.28E
Steier *see* Steyr
Steierdorf/Steierdorf-Anina *see* Anina
111 T7 **Steiermark** *off.* Land Steiermark, *Eng.* Styria. ◐ *state* C Austria
103 J19 **Steigerwald** *hill range* C Germany
101 L17 **Stein** Limburg, SE Netherlands 50.58N 5.45E
Stein *see* Stein an der Donau, Austria
Stein *see* Kamnik, Slovenia
110 M8 **Steinach** Tirol, W Austria 47.07N 11.30E
Steinamanger *see* Szombathely
111 W3 **Stein an der Donau** *var.* Stein. Niederösterreich, NE Austria 48.24N 15.35E
Steinau an der Elbe *see* Ścinawa
9 Y16 **Steinbach** Manitoba, S Canada 49.31N 96.40W
Steiner Alpen *see* Kamniško-Savinjske Alpe
101 L24 **Steinfort** Luxembourg, W Luxembourg 49.39N 5.55E
102 H12 **Steinhuder Meer** ◎ NW Germany
95 E15 **Steinkjer** Nord-Trøndelag, C Norway 64.01N 11.28E
Stejarul *see* Karapelit
101 F16 **Stekene** Oost-Vlaanderen, NW Belgium 51.13N 4.04E
85 E26 **Stellenbosch** Western Cape, SW South Africa 33.48S 18.49E
100 F13 **Stellendam** Zuid-Holland, SW Netherlands 51.48N 4.01E
41 T12 **Steller, Mount** ▲ Alaska, USA 60.36N 142.49W
105 Y14 **Stello, Monte** ▲ Corse, France, C Mediterranean Sea 42.49N 9.24E
108 F5 **Stelvio, Passo dello** *pass* Italy/Switzerland 46.32N 10.27E
105 R3 **Stenay** Meuse, NE France 49.29N 5.12E
102 L12 **Stendal** Sachsen-Anhalt, C Germany 52.36N 11.52E
120 E8 **Stende** Talsi, NW Latvia 57.09N 22.33E
190 H10 **Stenhouse Bay** South Australia 35.15S 136.58E
97 J23 **Stenløse** Frederiksborg, E Denmark 55.46N 12.13E
97 L19 **Stensjön** Jönköping, S Sweden 57.36N 14.42E
97 K18 **Stenstorp** Västra Götaland, S Sweden 58.15N 13.45E
97 I18 **Stenungsund** Västra Götaland, S Sweden 58.04N 11.55E
Stepanakert *see* Xankändi
143 T11 **Step'anavan** N Armenia 41.00N 44.27E
102 K9 **Stepenitz** ≈ N Germany
31 O10 **Stephan** South Dakota, N USA 44.12N 99.25W
31 R3 **Stephen** Minnesota, N USA 48.27N 96.54W
29 T14 **Stephens** Arkansas, C USA 33.25N 93.04W
192 J13 **Stephens, Cape** *headland* D'Urville Island, Marlborough, SW NZ 40.42S 173.56E
23 V3 **Stephens City** Virginia, NE USA 39.03N 78.10W
190 L6 **Stephens Creek** New South Wales, SE Australia 31.51S 141.30E
192 K13 **Stephens Island** *island* C NZ
33 N5 **Stephenson** Michigan, N USA 45.27N 87.36W
11 S12 **Stephenville** Newfoundland and Labrador, SE Canada 48.33N 58.29W
27 S7 **Stephenville** Texas, SW USA 32.12N 98.13W
151 P17 **Step' Nardara** *Kaz.* Shardara Dalasy; *prev.* Shaidara. *grassland* S Kazakhstan
151 R8 **Stepnogorsk** Akmola, C Kazakhstan 52.04N 72.18E
131 O15 **Stepnoye** Stavropol'skiy Kray, SW Russian Federation 44.18N 44.34E
151 Q8 **Stepnyak** Akmola, N Kazakhstan 52.52N 70.49E
198 C9 **Steps Point** *headland* Tutuila, W American Samoa 14.22S 170.46W
117 F17 **Stereá Ellás** *Eng.* Greece Central. ◐ *region* C Greece
85 J24 **Sterkspruit** Eastern Cape, SE South Africa 30.28S 27.24E
131 U6 **Sterlibashevo** Respublika Bashkortostan, W Russian Federation 53.19N 55.12E
41 R12 **Sterling** Alaska, USA 60.32N 150.51W
39 V3 **Sterling** Colorado, C USA 40.37N 103.12W
32 K11 **Sterling** Illinois, N USA 41.47N 89.42W
28 M5 **Sterling** Kansas, C USA 38.12N 98.12W
27 O8 **Sterling City** Texas, SW USA 31.50N 100.58W
33 S9 **Sterling Heights** Michigan, N USA 42.34N 83.01W
23 W3 **Sterling Park** Virginia, NE USA 39.00N 77.24W
39 V2 **Sterling Reservoir** ▣ Colorado, C USA
24 I5 **Sterlington** Louisiana, S USA 32.42N 92.05W
131 U6 **Sterlitamak** Respublika Bashkortostan, W Russian Federation 53.39N 56.00E
Sternberg *see* Šternberk

◆ Country
● Country Capital
◇ Dependent Territory
○ Dependent Territory Capital
◐ Administrative Region
✕ International Airport
▲ Mountain
⛰ Mountain Range
Volcano
≈ River
◎ Lake
▣ Reservoir

Šternberk – Sumail

113 H17 **Šternberk** *Ger.* Sternberg. Olomoucký Kraj, E Czech Republic *49.45N 17.19E*
147 V17 **Stēroh** Suquṭrā, S Yemen *12.21N 53.50E*
112 G11 **Stęszew** Wielkolpolskie, C Poland *52.16N 16.41E*
Stettin *see* Szczecin
Stettiner Haff *see* Szczeciński, Zalew
9 Q15 **Stettler** Alberta, SW Canada *52.21N 112.40W*
33 V13 **Steubenville** Ohio, N USA *40.21N 80.37W*
99 O21 **Stevenage** E England, UK *51.55N 0.13W*
25 Q1 **Stevenson** Alabama, S USA *34.52N 85.50W*
34 H11 **Stevenson** Washington, NW USA *45.43N 121.54W*
190 E1 **Stevenson Creek** *seasonal river* South Australia
41 Q13 **Stevenson Entrance** *strait* Alaska, USA
32 L6 **Stevens Point** Wisconsin, N USA *44.31N 89.33W*
41 R8 **Stevens Village** Alaska, USA *66.01N 149.02W*
35 P10 **Stevensville** Montana, NW USA *46.30N 114.05W*
95 E25 **Stevns Klint** *headland* E Denmark *55.15N 12.25E*
8 J12 **Stewart** British Columbia, W Canada *55.58N 129.52W*
8 J6 **Stewart** ≈ Yukon Territory, NW Canada
8 I6 **Stewart Crossing** Yukon Territory, NW Canada *63.22N 136.37W*
65 H25 **Stewart, Isla** *island* S Chile
193 B25 **Stewart Island** *island* S NZ
189 W6 **Stewart, Mount** ▲ Queensland, E Australia *20.11S 145.29E*
8 H6 **Stewart River** Yukon Territory, NW Canada *63.17N 139.24W*
29 R3 **Stewartsville** Missouri, C USA *39.45N 94.30W*
9 S16 **Stewart Valley** Saskatchewan, S Canada *50.34N 107.47W*
31 W10 **Stewartville** Minnesota, N USA *43.51N 92.29W*
Steyerlak-Anina *see* Anina
111 T5 **Steyr** *var.* Steier. Oberösterreich, N Austria *48.02N 14.26E*
111 T5 **Steyr** ≈ NW Austria
31 P11 **Stickney** South Dakota, N USA *43.24N 98.23W*
100 L5 **Stiens** Friesland, N Netherlands *53.15N 5.45E*
Stif *see* Sétif
29 Q11 **Stigler** Oklahoma, C USA *35.15N 95.07W*
109 N18 **Stigliano** Basilicata, S Italy *40.24N 16.13E*
97 N17 **Stigtomta** Södermanland, C Sweden *58.48N 16.46E*
8 I11 **Stikine** ≈ British Columbia, W Canada
Stilida/Stilís *see* Stylída
97 G22 **Stilling** Århus, C Denmark *56.04N 10.00E*
31 W8 **Stillwater** Minnesota, N USA *45.03N 92.48W*
29 O9 **Stillwater** Oklahoma, C USA *36.07N 97.02W*
37 S5 **Stillwater Range** ▲▲ Nevada, W USA
20 I8 **Stillwater Reservoir** ▣ New York, NE USA
109 O22 **Stilo, Punta** *headland* S Italy *38.27N 16.36E*
29 R10 **Stilwell** Oklahoma, C USA *35.48N 94.37W*
115 N17 **Štimlje** Serbia, S Serbia and Montenegro (Yugoslavia) *42.27N 21.03E*
27 N1 **Stinnett** Texas, SW USA *35.49N 101.26W*
115 P18 **Štip** E FYR Macedonia *41.45N 22.10E*
Stira *see* Stýra
98 J12 **Stirling** C Scotland, UK *56.07N 3.57W*
98 I12 **Stirling** *cultural region* C Scotland, UK
188 J14 **Stirling Range** ▲▲ Western Australia
95 E16 **Stjørdalshalsen** Nord-Trøndelag, C Norway *63.27N 10.57E*
Stochód *see* Stokhid
103 H24 **Stockach** Baden-Württemberg, S Germany *47.51N 9.01E*
27 S12 **Stockdale** Texas, SW USA *29.14N 97.57W*
111 X3 **Stockerau** Niederösterreich, NE Austria *48.24N 16.13E*
95 H20 **Stockholm** ● (Sweden) Stockholm, C Sweden *59.16N 18.03E*
97 O15 **Stockholm** ◈ *county* C Sweden
Stockmannshof *see* Pļaviņas
99 L18 **Stockport** NW England, UK *53.25N 2.10W*
67 K15 **Stocks Seamount** *undersea feature* C Atlantic Ocean *11.42S 33.48W*
37 O8 **Stockton** California, W USA *37.55N 121.19W*
28 L3 **Stockton** Kansas, C USA *39.25N 99.17W*
29 S6 **Stockton** Missouri, C USA *37.42N 93.48W*
32 K3 **Stockton Island** *island* Apostle Islands, Wisconsin, N USA
29 S7 **Stockton Lake** ▣ Missouri, C USA
99 M15 **Stockton-on-Tees** *var.* Stockton on Tees. N England, UK *54.34N 1.19W*
26 M10 **Stockton Plateau** *plain* Texas, SW USA
30 M16 **Stockville** Nebraska, C USA *40.30N 100.21W*
95 H17 **Stöde** Västernorrland, C Sweden *62.27N 16.34E*
Stodolichi *see* Stadolichy
178 Jj12 **Stœng Trêng** *prev.* Stung Treng. Stœng Trêng, NE Cambodia *13.31N 105.58E*
115 M19 **Stogovo Karaorman** ▲▲ W FYR Macedonia
Stoke *see* Stoke-on-Trent
99 L19 **Stoke-on-Trent** *var.* Stoke. C England, UK *53.00N 2.10W*
190 M15 **Stokes Point** *headland* Tasmania, SE Australia *40.09S 143.55E*
118 J2 **Stokhid** *Pol.* Stochód, *Rus.* Stokhod. ≈ NW Ukraine
Stokhod *see* Stokhid
94 I4 **Stokkseyri** Sudhurland, SW Iceland *63.49N 21.00W*
94 G10 **Stokmarknes** Nordland, C Norway *68.33N 14.54E*
Stol *see* Veliki Krš
115 H15 **Stolac** Federacija Bosna I Hercegovina, S Bosnia and Herzegovina *43.04N 17.58E*
Stolbce *see* Stowbtsy
103 D16 **Stolberg** *var.* Stolberg im Rheinland. Nordrhein-Westfalen, W Germany *50.46N 6.13E*
Stolberg im Rheinland *see* Stolberg
126 L5 **Stolbovoy, Ostrov** *island* NE Russian Federation
Stolbtsy *see* Stowbtsy
121 J20 **Stolin** *Rus.* Stolin. Brestskaya Voblasts', SW Belarus *51.52N 26.51E*
97 K14 **Stöllet** *var.* Norra Ny. Värmland, C Sweden *60.24N 13.15E*
Stolp *see* Słupsk
Stolpe *see* Słupia
Stolpmünde *see* Ustka
117 F15 **Stómio** Thessalía, C Greece *39.51N 22.45E*
12 J11 **Stonecliffe** Ontario, SE Canada *46.12N 77.58W*
98 L10 **Stonehaven** NE Scotland, UK *56.58N 2.13W*
99 M23 **Stonehenge** *ancient monument* Wiltshire, S England, UK *51.12N 1.54W*
25 T3 **Stone Mountain** ▲ Georgia, SE USA *33.48N 84.10W*
9 X16 **Stonewall** Manitoba, S Canada *50.07N 97.19W*
23 S3 **Stonewood** West Virginia, NE USA *39.15N 80.18W*
12 D17 **Stoney Point** Ontario, S Canada *42.18N 82.32W*
94 H10 **Stonglandseidet** Troms, N Norway *69.03N 17.06E*
67 N25 **Stonybeach Bay** *bay* Tristan da Cunha, SE Atlantic Ocean
37 N5 **Stony Creek** ≈ California, W USA
67 N25 **Stonyhill Point** *headland* S Tristan da Cunha
12 I14 **Stony Lake** ◎ Ontario, SE Canada
9 Q14 **Stony Plain** Alberta, SW Canada *53.31N 114.04W*
23 R9 **Stony Point** North Carolina, SE USA *35.51N 81.04W*
20 G8 **Stony Point** *headland* New York, NE USA *43.50N 76.18W*
9 T10 **Stony Rapids** Saskatchewan, C Canada *59.13N 105.48W*
41 P11 **Stony River** Alaska, USA *61.48N 156.37W*
Stony Tunguska *see* Podkamennaya Tunguska
10 G10 **Stooping** ≈ Ontario, C Canada
102 I9 **Stör** ≈ N Germany
97 M15 **Storå** Örebro, S Sweden *59.43N 15.10E*
97 J16 **Stora Gla** ◎ C Sweden
97 I16 **Stora Le** *Nor.* Store Le. ◎ Norway/Sweden
94 I12 **Stora Lulevatten** ◎ N Sweden
94 H13 **Storavan** ◎ N Sweden
95 I20 **Storby** Åland, SW Finland *60.12N 19.33E*
96 E10 **Stordalen** Møre og Romsdal, S Norway *62.22N 7.00E*
Storebelt *see* Storebælt
97 H23 **Storebælt** *var.* Store Bælt, *Eng.* Great Belt, Storebelt. *channel* Baltic Sea/Kattegat
97 M19 **Storebro** Kalmar, S Sweden *57.36N 15.30E*
97 J24 **Store Heddinge** Storstrøm, SE Denmark *55.19N 12.24E*
Store Le *see* Stora Le
95 E16 **Støren** Sør-Trøndelag, S Norway *63.01N 10.16E*
94 O4 **Storfjorden** *fjord* S Norway
97 L15 **Storfors** Värmland, C Sweden *59.33N 14.16E*
94 G13 **Storforshei** Nordland, C Norway *66.25N 14.25E*
Storhammer *see* Hamar
102 L10 **Störkanal** *canal* N Germany
95 F16 **Storlien** Jämtland, C Sweden *63.18N 12.10E*
191 P17 **Storm Bay** *inlet* Tasmania, SE Australia
31 T12 **Storm Lake** Iowa, C USA *42.38N 95.12W*
31 S13 **Storm Lake** ◎ Iowa, C USA
98 G7 **Stornoway** NW Scotland, UK *58.13N 6.22W*
Storojineţ *see* Storozhynets'
94 P1 **Storøya** *island* NE Svalbard
129 S10 **Storozhevsk** Respublika Komi, NW Russian Federation *61.56N 52.18E*
Storozhinets *see* Storozhynets'
118 K8 **Storozhynets'** *Ger.* Storozynetz, *Rom.* Storojineţ, *Rus.* Storozhinets. Chernivets'ka Oblast', W Ukraine *48.09N 25.40E*
Storozynetz *see* Storozhynets'
94 H11 **Storriten** ▲ C Norway *68.09N 17.12E*
21 N12 **Storrs** Connecticut, NE USA *41.48N 72.15W*
96 I11 **Storsjøen** ◎ S Norway
96 N13 **Storsjön** ◎ C Sweden
95 F16 **Storsjön** ◎ C Sweden
94 J9 **Storslett** Troms, N Norway *69.45N 21.03E*
96 H11 **Storsølnkletten** ▲ S Norway *61.52N 11.32E*
94 I9 **Storsteinnes** Troms, N Norway *69.13N 19.14E*
97 I24 **Storstrøm** *off.* Storstrøms Amt. ◈ *county* SE Denmark
95 J14 **Storsund** Norrbotten, N Sweden *65.36N 20.40E*
96 J9 **Storsylen** *Swe.* Sylarna. ▲ Norway/Sweden *63.07N 12.10E*
94 H11 **Stortoppen** ▲ N Sweden *67.33N 17.27E*
95 H14 **Storuman** Västerbotten, N Sweden *65.04N 17.10E*
95 H14 **Storuman** ◎ N Sweden
96 N13 **Storvik** Gävleborg, C Sweden *60.37N 16.30E*
97 O14 **Storvreta** Uppsala, C Sweden *59.58N 17.42E*
31 V13 **Story City** Iowa, C USA *42.10N 93.36W*
9 V17 **Stoughton** Saskatchewan, S Canada *49.40N 103.01W*
21 O11 **Stoughton** Massachusetts, NE USA *42.07N 71.06W*
32 L9 **Stoughton** Wisconsin, N USA *42.56N 89.12W*
99 L23 **Stour** ≈ E England, UK
99 P21 **Stour** ≈ S England, UK
29 T5 **Stover** Missouri, C USA *38.26N 92.59W*
97 G21 **Støvring** Nordjylland, N Denmark *56.52N 9.52E*
121 J17 **Stowbtsy** *Pol.* Stolbce, *Rus.* Stolbtsy. Minskaya Voblasts', C Belarus *53.27N 26.44E*
27 X11 **Stowell** Texas, SW USA *29.47N 94.22W*
99 P20 **Stowmarket** E England, UK *52.04N 0.54E*
116 N8 **Stozher** Dobrich, NE Bulgaria *43.27N 27.49E*
99 E14 **Strabane** *Ir.* An Srath Bán. W Northern Ireland, UK *54.49N 7.27W*
123 Gg10 **Strabo Trench** *undersea feature* C Mediterranean Sea
29 T7 **Strafford** Missouri, C USA *37.16N 93.07W*
191 N17 **Strahan** Tasmania, SE Australia *42.10S 145.18E*
113 C18 **Strakonice** *Ger.* Strakonitz. Jihočeský Kraj, S Czech Republic *49.13N 13.55E*
Strakonitz *see* Strakonice
102 N8 **Stralsund** Mecklenburg-Vorpommern, NE Germany *54.18N 13.06E*
101 L16 **Stramproy** Limburg, SE Netherlands *51.12N 5.43E*
85 E26 **Strand** Western Cape, SW South Africa *34.06S 18.49E*
96 E10 **Stranda** Møre og Romsdal, S Norway *62.18N 6.55E*
99 G15 **Strangford Lough** *Ir.* Loch Cuan. *inlet* E Northern Ireland, UK
97 N16 **Strängnäs** Södermanland, C Sweden *59.22N 17.01E*
99 E14 **Stranorlar** *Ir.* Srath an Urláir. NW Ireland *54.48N 7.46W*
99 H14 **Stranraer** S Scotland, UK *54.54N 5.01W*
9 U16 **Strasbourg** Saskatchewan, S Canada *51.04N 104.58W*
105 V5 **Strasbourg** *Ger.* Strassburg; *anc.* Argentoratum. Bas-Rhin, NE France *48.34N 7.45E*
39 U4 **Strasburg** Colorado, C USA *39.42N 104.13W*
31 N7 **Strasburg** North Dakota, N USA *46.07N 100.10W*
33 U12 **Strasburg** Ohio, N USA *40.35N 81.31W*
23 U3 **Strasburg** Virginia, NE USA *38.59N 78.21W*
119 N10 **Străşeni** *var.* Strasheny. C Moldova *47.07N 28.37E*
Strasheny *see* Străşeni
111 T8 **Strassburg** Kärnten, S Austria *46.54N 14.21E*
Strassburg *see* Strasbourg, France
Strassburg *see* Aiud, Romania
101 M25 **Strassen** Luxembourg, S Luxembourg *49.37N 6.04E*
111 R5 **Strasswalchen** Salzburg, C Austria *47.59N 13.19E*
12 F16 **Stratford** Ontario, S Canada *43.22N 81.00W*
192 K10 **Stratford** Taranaki, North Island, NZ *39.20S 174.15E*
37 Q11 **Stratford** California, W USA *36.10N 119.47W*
31 V13 **Stratford** Iowa, C USA *42.16N 93.55W*
29 O12 **Stratford** Oklahoma, C USA *34.48N 96.57W*
27 N1 **Stratford** Texas, SW USA *36.20N 102.04W*
32 K6 **Stratford** Wisconsin, N USA *44.53N 90.13W*
Stratford *see* Stratford-upon-Avon
99 M20 **Stratford-upon-Avon** *var.* Stratford. C England, UK *52.12N 1.40W*
191 O17 **Strathgordon** Tasmania, SE Australia *42.49S 146.04E*
9 Q16 **Strathmore** Alberta, SW Canada *51.04N 113.19W*
37 R11 **Strathmore** California, W USA *36.07N 119.04W*
12 E16 **Strathroy** Ontario, S Canada *42.57N 81.40W*
98 I6 **Strathy Point** *headland* N Scotland, UK *58.36N 4.04W*
39 W4 **Stratton** Colorado, C USA *39.16N 102.34W*
21 P6 **Stratton** Maine, NE USA *45.08N 70.25W*
20 M10 **Stratton Mountain** ▲ Vermont, NE USA *43.05N 72.55W*
103 N21 **Straubing** Bayern, SE Germany *48.52N 12.34E*
102 O12 **Strausberg** Brandenburg, E Germany *52.34N 13.52E*
34 K13 **Strawberry Mountain** ▲ Oregon, NW USA *44.18N 118.43W*
31 X12 **Strawberry Point** Iowa, C USA *42.40N 91.31W*
38 M3 **Strawberry Reservoir** ▣ Utah, W USA
38 M4 **Strawberry River** ≈ Utah, W USA
27 R7 **Strawn** Texas, SW USA *32.33N 98.30W*
115 P17 **Straža** ▲ Bulgaria/FYR Macedonia *42.16N 22.13E*
113 I19 **Strážov** *Hung.* Sztrazsó. ▲ NW Slovakia *48.59N 18.29E*
190 F7 **Streaky Bay** South Australia *32.49S 134.13E*
190 E7 **Streaky Bay** *bay* South Australia
32 L12 **Streator** Illinois, N USA *41.07N 88.50W*
Streckenbach *see* Świdnik
113 C17 **Středočeský kraj** ◈ *region* C Czech Republic
Strednogorie *see* Pirdop
31 O6 **Streeter** North Dakota, N USA *46.37N 99.23W*
27 U8 **Streetman** Texas, SW USA *31.52N 96.19W*
118 G13 **Strehaia** Mehedinţi, SW Romania *44.37N 23.10E*
Strehlen *see* Strzelin
116 I10 **Strelcha** Pazardzhik, C Bulgaria *42.28N 24.21E*
126 I13 **Strelka** Krasnoyarskiy Kray, C Russian Federation *58.04N 92.54E*
128 L6 **Strel'na** ≈ NW Russian Federation
120 H7 **Strenči** *Ger.* Stackeln. Valka, N Latvia *57.38N 25.42E*
110 K8 **Strengen** Tirol, W Austria *47.07N 10.25E*
108 C6 **Stresa** Piemonte, NE Italy *45.52N 8.32E*
Streshin *see* Streshyn
121 N18 **Streshyn** *Rus.* Streshin. Homyel'skaya Voblasts', SE Belarus *52.42N 30.08E*
97 B18 **Streymoy** *Dan.* Strømø *Island* Faeroe Islands *62.10N 7.05W*
126 Gg11 **Strezhevoy** Tomskaya Oblast', C Russian Federation *60.39N 77.37E*
97 G23 **Strib** Fyn, C Denmark *55.33N 9.46E*
113 A17 **Stříbro** *Ger.* Mies. Plzeňský Kraj, W Czech Republic *49.44N 12.55E*
194 E13 **Strickland** ≈ SW PNG
Striegau *see* Strzegom
Strigonium *see* Esztergom
100 H13 **Strijen** Zuid-Holland, SW Netherlands *51.45N 4.34E*
65 H21 **Strobel, Lago** ◎ S Argentina
63 B25 **Stroeder** Buenos Aires, E Argentina *40.10S 62.34W*
117 C20 **Strofádes** *island* Iónioi Nísoi, Greece, C Mediterranean Sea
Strofilia *see* Strofyliá
117 G17 **Strofyliá** *var.* Strofilia. Évvoia, C Greece *38.49N 23.25E*
102 O10 **Strom** ≈ NE Germany
109 L22 **Stromboli** Ѫ Isola Stromboli, SW Italy *38.48N 15.13E*
109 L22 **Stromboli, Isola** *island* Isole Eolie, S Italy
98 H9 **Stromeferry** N Scotland, UK *57.20N 5.34W*
98 J5 **Stromness** N Scotland, UK *58.57N 3.18W*
96 N11 **Strömsbruk** Gävleborg, C Sweden *61.52N 17.19E*
31 Q15 **Stromsburg** Nebraska, C USA *41.06N 97.36W*
97 K21 **Strömsnäsbruk** Kronoberg, S Sweden *56.34N 13.45E*
97 I17 **Strömstad** Västra Götaland, S Sweden *58.55N 11.10E*
95 G16 **Strömsund** Jämtland, C Sweden *63.51N 15.34E*
95 G15 **Ströms Vattudal** *valley* N Sweden
29 V14 **Strong** Arkansas, C USA *33.06N 92.19W*
Strongilí *see* Strongylí
109 O21 **Strongoli** Calabria, SW Italy *39.17N 17.03E*
33 T11 **Strongsville** Ohio, N USA *41.18N 81.50W*
117 Q23 **Strongylí** *var.* Strongilí. *island* SE Greece
98 K5 **Stronsay** *island* NE Scotland, UK
99 L21 **Stroud** C England, UK *51.45N 2.15W*
29 O10 **Stroud** Oklahoma, C USA *35.45N 96.39W*
20 I14 **Stroudsburg** Pennsylvania, NE USA *40.59N 75.12W*
97 F21 **Struer** Ringkøbing, W Denmark *56.28N 8.37E*
115 M20 **Struga** SW FYR Macedonia *41.11N 20.40E*
Strugi-Kranyse *see* Strugi-Krasnyye
128 G14 **Strugi-Krasnyye** *var.* Strugi-Kranyse. Pskovskaya Oblast', W Russian Federation *58.19N 29.09E*
116 G11 **Struma** *Gk.* Strymónas. ≈ Bulgaria/Greece *see also* Strymónas
99 G21 **Strumble Head** *headland* SW Wales, UK *52.01N 5.05W*
115 Q19 **Strumeshnitsa** | Mac. Strumica. ≈ Bulgaria/FYR Macedonia
115 Q19 **Strumica** E FYR Macedonia *41.27N 22.39E*
Strumica *see* Strumeshnitsa
116 G11 **Strumyani** Blagoevgrad, SW Bulgaria *41.41N 23.13E*
33 V12 **Struthers** Ohio, N USA *41.03N 80.36W*
116 I10 **Stryama** ≈ C Bulgaria
116 G13 **Strymónas** *Bul.* Struma. ≈ Bulgaria/Greece *see also* Struma
117 H14 **Strymonikós Kólpos** *gulf* N Greece
118 I6 **Stryy** L'vivs'ka Oblast', NW Ukraine *49.16N 23.51E*
118 H6 **Stryy** ≈ W Ukraine
113 F14 **Strzegom** *Ger.* Striegau. Wałbrzych, SW Poland *50.58N 16.19E*
112 E10 **Strzelce Krajeńskie** *Ger.* Friedeberg Neumark. Lubuskie, W Poland *52.52N 15.30E*
113 I15 **Strzelce Opolskie** *Ger.* Gross Strehlitz. Opolskie, S Poland *50.31N 18.19E*
190 K3 **Strzelecki Creek** *seasonal river* South Australia
190 J3 **Strzelecki Desert** *desert* South Australia
113 G15 **Strzelin** *Ger.* Strehlen. Dolnośląskie, SW Poland *50.46N 17.03E*
112 I11 **Strzelno** Kujawsko-pomorskie, C Poland *52.38N 18.11E*
113 N17 **Strzyżów** Podkarpackie, SE Poland *49.52N 21.46E*
Stua Laighean *see* Leinster, Mount
25 Y13 **Stuart** Florida, SE USA *27.12N 80.15W*
31 U14 **Stuart** Iowa, C USA *41.30N 94.19W*
31 O13 **Stuart** Nebraska, C USA *42.36N 99.08W*
23 S8 **Stuart** Virginia, NE USA *36.38N 80.16W*
8 L13 **Stuart** ≈ British Columbia, SW Canada
41 N10 **Stuart Island** *island* Alaska, USA
8 L13 **Stuart Lake** ◎ British Columbia, SW Canada
193 B22 **Stuart Mountains** ▲▲ South Island, NZ
190 F3 **Stuart Range** *hill range* South Australia
Stubaital *see* Neustift im Stubaital
97 I24 **Stubbekøbing** Storstrøm, SE Denmark *54.52N 12.04E*
47 P14 **Stubbs** Saint Vincent, Saint Vincent and the Grenadines *13.08N 61.09W*
111 V6 **Stübming** ≈ E Austria
116 J11 **Studen Kladenets, Yazovir** ▣ S Bulgaria
193 G21 **Studholme** Canterbury, South Island, NZ *44.44S 171.07E*
Stuhlweissenberg *see* Székesfehérvár
Stuhm *see* Sztum
10 C7 **Stull Lake** ◎ Ontario, C Canada
Stung Treng *see* Stœng Trêng
130 L4 **Stupino** Moskovskaya Oblast', W Russian Federation *54.54N 38.06E*
29 U4 **Sturgeon** Missouri, C USA *39.13N 92.16W*
12 G10 **Sturgeon** ≈ Ontario, S Canada
33 N6 **Sturgeon Bay** Wisconsin, N USA *44.51N 87.21W*
12 G11 **Sturgeon Falls** Ontario, S Canada *46.22N 79.57W*
10 C11 **Sturgeon Lake** ◎ Ontario, S Canada
32 M3 **Sturgeon River** ≈ Michigan, N USA
22 H6 **Sturgis** Kentucky, S USA *37.33N 87.58W*
33 P11 **Sturgis** Michigan, N USA *41.48N 85.25W*
30 J9 **Sturgis** South Dakota, N USA *44.24N 103.30W*
114 D10 **Šturlić** Federacija Bosna I Hercegovina, NW Bosnia and Herzegovina *45.03N 15.47E*
113 J22 **Štúrovo** *Hung.* Párkány; *prev.* Parkan. Nitriansky Kraj, W Slovakia *47.49N 18.44E*
190 L4 **Sturt, Mount** *hill* New South Wales, SE Australia *29.30S 141.41E*
189 P4 **Sturt Plain** *plain* Northern Territory, N Australia
189 T9 **Sturt Stony Desert** *desert* South Australia
85 J25 **Stutterheim** Eastern Cape, S South Africa *32.34S 27.25E*
103 H21 **Stuttgart** Baden-Württemberg, SW Germany *48.47N 9.12E*
29 W12 **Stuttgart** Arkansas, C USA *34.30N 91.33W*
94 H2 **Stykkishólmur** Vesturland, W Iceland *65.03N 22.43W*
117 F17 **Stylída** *var.* Stilida, Stilís. Stereá Ellás, C Greece *38.55N 22.37E*
118 K2 **Styr** *Rus.* Styr'. ≈ Belarus/Ukraine
117 I19 **Stýra** *var.* Stira. Évvoia, C Greece *38.10N 24.13E*
Styria *see* Steiermark
Su *see* Jiangsu
Sua *see* Sowa
175 S17 **Suai** W East Timor *9.19S 125.16E*
56 G9 **Suaita** Santander, C Colombia *6.07N 73.30W*
82 I7 **Suakin** *var.* Sawakin. Red Sea, NE Sudan *19.06N 37.17E*
167 T13 **Suao** *Jap.* Suō. N Taiwan *24.33N 121.48E*
Suao *see* Suau
85 I18 **Sua Pan** *var.* Sowa Pan. *salt lake* NE Botswana *20.42N 94.16W*
42 G6 **Suaqui Grande** Sonora, NW Mexico *28.22N 109.52W*
63 A16 **Suardi** Santa Fe, C Argentina *30.31S 61.58W*
56 D11 **Suárez** Cauca, SW Colombia *2.55N 76.40W*
195 N17 **Suau** *var.* Suao. Suaul Island, SE PNG *10.44S 150.18E*
120 G12 **Subačius** Panevėžys, NE Lithuania *55.46N 24.45E*
174 Jj14 **Subang** *prev.* Soebang. Jawa, C Indonesia *6.31S 107.45E*
174 Gg5 **Subang** ✕ (Kuala Lumpur) Pahang, Peninsular Malaysia
133 S10 **Subansiri** ≈ NE India
120 I11 **Subate** Daugvapils, SE Latvia *56.00N 25.54E*
145 N5 **Subaykhān** Dayr az Zawr, E Syria *34.47N 40.38E*
Subei/Subei Mongolzu Zizhixian *see* Dangchengwan
174 K5 **Subi Besar, Pulau** *island* Kepulauan Natuna, W Indonesia
Subiyah *see* Aş Şubayḩīyah
28 I7 **Sublette** Kansas, C USA *37.26N 100.48W*
114 K8 **Subotica** *Ger.* Maria-Theresiopel, *Hung.* Szabadka. Serbia, N Serbia and Montenegro (Yugoslavia) *46.06N 19.40E*
118 K9 **Suceava** *Ger.* Suczawa, *Hung.* Szucsava. Suceava, NE Romania *47.40N 26.15E*
118 J9 **Suceava** ◈ *county* NE Romania
118 K9 **Suceava** *Ger.* Suczawa. ≈ N Romania
114 E12 **Sučevići** Zadar, SW Croatia *44.13N 16.04E*
113 K17 **Sucha Beskidzka** Małopolskie, S Poland *49.39N 19.11E*
113 M14 **Suchedniów** Świętokrzyskie, C Poland *51.01N 20.49E*
44 A2 **Suchitepéquez** *off.* Departamento de Suchitepéquez. ◈ *department* SW Guatemala
Su-chou *see* Suzhou
Suchow *see* Suzhou, Jiangsu, China
Suchow *see* Xuzhou, Jiangsu, China
99 D17 **Suck** ≈ C Ireland
Sucker State *see* Illinois
194 M16 **Suckling, Mount** ▲ S PNG *9.36S 149.00E*
59 L19 **Sucre** *hist.* Chuquisaca, La Plata. ● (Bolivia-legal capital) Chuquisaca, S Bolivia *18.52S 65.24W*
56 E6 **Sucre** Santander, N Colombia *8.50N 74.22W*
58 A7 **Sucre** Manabí, W Ecuador *1.21S 80.27W*
56 E6 **Sucre** *off.* Departamento de Sucre. ◈ *province* N Colombia
57 O5 **Sucre** *off.* Estado Sucre. ◈ *state* NE Venezuela
58 D6 **Sucumbíos** ◈ *province* NE Ecuador
115 G15 **Sućuraj** Split-Dalmacija, S Croatia *43.07N 17.10E*
60 K10 **Sucuriju** Amapá, NE Brazil *1.30N 50.00W*
Suczawa *see* Suceava
81 E16 **Sud** *Eng.* South. ◈ *province* S Cameroon
128 K13 **Suda** ≈ NW Russian Federation
Suda *see* Soúda
119 U13 **Sudak** Respublika Krym, S Ukraine *44.51N 34.55E*
26 M4 **Sudan** Texas, SW USA *34.04N 102.31W*
82 C10 **Sudan** *off.* Republic of Sudan, *Ar.* Jumhuriyat as-Sudan; *prev.* Anglo-Egyptian *Sudan.* ◆ *republic* N Africa
Sudanese Republic *see* Mali
Sudan, Jumhuriyat as- *see* Sudan
12 F10 **Sudbury** Ontario, S Canada *46.29N 80.59W*
99 P20 **Sudbury** E England, UK *52.04N 0.43E*
Sud, Canal de *see* Gonâve, Canal de la
82 E13 **Sudd** *swamp region* S Sudan
102 K10 **Sude** ≈ N Germany
Sudest Island *see* Tagula Island
113 E15 **Sudeten** *var.* Sudetes, Sudetic Mountains, *Cz./Pol.* Sudety. ▲▲ Czech Republic/Poland
Sudetes/Sudetic Mountains/Sudety *see* Sudeten
94 G1 **Sudhureyri** Vestfirdhir, NW Iceland *66.08N 23.31W*
94 J4 **Sudhurland** ◈ *region* S Iceland
97 B19 **Sudhuroy** *Dan.* Suderø *Island* Faeroe Islands *61.60N 6.29W*
176 Xx12 **Sudirman, Pegunungan** ▲▲ Papua, E Indonesia
128 M15 **Sudislavl'** Kostromskaya Oblast', NW Russian Federation *57.55N 41.45E*
Südkarpaten *see* Carpaţii Meridionali
81 N20 **Sud Kivu** *off.* Région Sud Kivu. ◈ *region* E Dem. Rep. Congo
Südliche Morava *see* Južna Morava
102 E12 **Süd-Nord-Kanal** *canal* NW Germany
130 M3 **Sudogda** Vladimirskaya Oblast', W Russian Federation *55.58N 40.57E*
Sudostroy *see* Severodvinsk
81 C15 **Sud-Ouest** *Eng.* South-West. ◈ *province* W Cameroon
181 X17 **Sud Ouest, Pointe** *headland* SW Mauritius *20.27S 57.18E*
197 J7 **Sud, Province** ◈ *province* S New Caledonia
130 J8 **Sudzha** Kurskaya Oblast', W Russian Federation *51.12N 35.19E*
83 D15 **Sue** ≈ S Sudan
107 S10 **Sueca** País Valenciano, E Spain *39.13N 0.19W*
116 I10 **Sŭedinenie** Plovdiv, C Bulgaria *42.14N 24.36E*
Suero *see* Alzira
77 X8 **Suez** *Ar.* As Suways, El Suweis. NE Egypt *29.58N 32.33E*
77 W7 **Suez Canal** *Ar.* Qanāt as Suways. *canal* NE Egypt
77 X8 **Suez, Gulf of** *Ar.* Khalīj as Suways. *gulf* NE Egypt
9 R17 **Suffield** Alberta, SW Canada *50.15N 111.05W*
23 X7 **Suffolk** Virginia, NE USA *36.43N 76.34W*
99 P20 **Suffolk** *cultural region* E England, UK
148 J2 **Şūfīān** Āzarbāyjān-e Khāvarī, N Iran *38.15N 45.58E*
33 N12 **Sugar Creek** ≈ Illinois, N USA
32 L13 **Sugar Creek** ≈ Illinois, N USA
33 R3 **Sugar Island** *island* Michigan, N USA
27 V11 **Sugar Land** Texas, SW USA *29.37N 95.37W*
21 P6 **Sugarloaf Mountain** ▲ Maine, NE USA *45.01N 70.18W*
67 G24 **Sugar Loaf Point** *headland* N Saint Helena *15.54S 5.43W*
142 G16 **Suğla Gölü** ◎ SW Turkey
127 O8 **Sugoy** ≈ E Russian Federation
164 F7 **Sugun** Xinjiang Uygur Zizhiqu, W China *39.46N 76.45E*
153 U11 **Sugut, Gora** ▲ SW Kyrgyzstan *39.52N 73.36E*
175 O2 **Sugut, Sungai** ≈ East Malaysia
165 O9 **Suhai Hu** ◎ C China
168 K14 **Suhait** Nei Mongol Zizhiqu, N China *39.29N 105.11E*
147 X7 **Şuḩār** *var.* Sohar. N Oman *24.20N 56.43E*
168 L6 **Sühbaatar** Selenge, N Mongolia *50.11N 106.14E*
169 P9 **Sühbaatar** ◈ *province* E Mongolia
103 K17 **Suhl** Thüringen, C Germany *50.37N 10.43E*
110 F7 **Suhr** Aargau, N Switzerland *47.22N 8.04E*
Sui'an *see* Zhangpu
167 O12 **Suichuan** *var.* Quanjiang. Jiangxi, S China *26.18N 114.31E*
Suid-Afrika *see* South Africa
166 L4 **Suide** Shaanxi, C China *37.30N 110.10E*
Suidwes-Afrika *see* Namibia
169 Y9 **Suifenhe** Heilongjiang, NE China *44.22N 131.12E*
Suigen *see* Suwŏn
169 W8 **Suihua** Heilongjiang, NE China *46.40N 127.00E*
Súilí, Loch *see* Swilly, Lough
167 Q6 **Suining** Jiangsu, E China *33.54N 117.58E*
166 I9 **Suining** Sichuan, C China *30.31N 105.33E*
105 Q4 **Suippes** Marne, N France *49.08N 4.31E*
99 E20 **Suir** *Ir.* An tSiúir. ≈ S Ireland
171 Gg15 **Suita** Ōsaka, Honshū, SW Japan *34.39N 135.27E*
166 L16 **Suixi** Guangdong, S China *21.22N 110.13E*
Sui Xian *see* Suizhou
169 T13 **Suizhong** Liaoning, NE China *40.19N 120.20E*
167 N8 **Suizhou** *prev.* Sui Xian. Hubei, C China *31.46N 113.20E*
155 P17 **Sujāwal** Sind, SE Pakistan *24.36N 68.06E*
174 Jj14 **Sukabumi** *prev.* Soekaboemi. Jawa, C Indonesia *6.55S 106.55E*
174 Kk9 **Sukadana, Teluk** *bay* Borneo, W Indonesia
171 Ll14 **Sukagawa** Fukushima, Honshū, C Japan *37.16N 140.19E*
Sukarnapura *see* Jayapura
Sukarno, Puntjak *see* Jaya, Puncak
Sŭkh *see* Sokh
116 N8 **Sukha Reka** ≈ NE Bulgaria
130 J5 **Sukhinichi** Kaluzhskaya Oblast', W Russian Federation *54.06N 35.22E*
Sukhne *see* As Sukhnah
133 Q4 **Sukhona** *var.* Tot'ma. ≈ NW Russian Federation
178 H9 **Sukhothai** *var.* Sukotai. Sukhothai, W Thailand *17.00N 99.51E*
Sukhumi *see* Sokhumi
Sukkertoppen *see* Maniitsoq
155 Q13 **Sukkur** Sind, SE Pakistan *27.44N 68.46E*
Sukotai *see* Sukhothai
Sukra Bay *see* Şawqirah, Dawḩat
129 V15 **Suksun** Permskaya Oblast', NW Russian Federation *57.10N 57.27E*
170 E16 **Sukumo** Kōchi, Shikoku, SW Japan *32.55N 132.42E*
96 B12 **Sula** *island* S Norway
129 Q5 **Sula** ≈ NW Russian Federation
119 R5 **Sula** ≈ N Ukraine
44 H6 **Sulaco, Río** ≈ NW Honduras
Sulaimaniya *see* As Sulaymānīyah
155 S10 **Sulaimān Range** ▲▲ C Pakistan
131 Q16 **Sulak** Respublika Dagestan, SW Russian Federation *43.19N 47.28E*
131 Q16 **Sulak** ≈ SW Russian Federation
175 Rr10 **Sula, Kepulauan** *island group* C Indonesia
142 I12 **Sulakyurt** *var.* Konur. Kırıkkale, N Turkey *40.10N 33.42E*
175 R17 **Sulamu** Timor, S Indonesia *9.57S 123.33E*
98 F5 **Sula Sgeir** *island* NW Scotland, UK
175 Pp10 **Sulawesi** *Eng.* Celebes. *island* C Indonesia
Sulawesi, Laut *see* Celebes Sea
175 P11 **Sulawesi Selatan** *off.* Propinsi Sulawesi Selatan, *Eng.* South Celebes, South Sulawesi. ◈ *province* C Indonesia
175 Q9 **Sulawesi Tengah** *off.* Propinsi Sulawesi Tengah, *Eng.* Central Celebes, Central Sulawesi. ◈ *province* N Indonesia
175 Q11 **Sulawesi Tenggara** *off.* Propinsi Sulawesi Tenggara, *Eng.* South-East Celebes, South-East Sulawesi. ◈ *province* C Indonesia
175 Qq7 **Sulawesi Utara** *off.* Propinsi Sulawesi Utara, *Eng.* North Celebes, North Sulawesi. ◈ *province* N Indonesia
145 T5 **Sulaymān Beg** N Iraq
97 D15 **Suldalsvatnet** ◎ S Norway
Sulden *see* Solda
112 E12 **Sulechów** *Ger.* Züllichau. Lubuskie, W Poland *52.04N 15.37E*
112 E11 **Sulęcin** Lubuskie, W Poland *52.29N 15.06E*
79 U14 **Suleja** Niger, C Nigeria *9.15N 7.10E*
113 K14 **Sulejów** Łodzkie, S Poland *51.21N 19.57E*
98 I5 **Sule Skerry** *island* N Scotland, UK
Suliag *see* Sohâg
78 J16 **Sulima** S Sierra Leone *6.58N 11.34W*
119 O13 **Sulina** Tulcea, SE Romania *45.07N 29.40E*
119 N13 **Sulina Braţul** ≈ SE Romania
102 H12 **Sulingen** Niedersachsen, NW Germany *52.40N 8.48E*
Sulisjielmmá *see* Sulitjelma
94 H12 **Suliskongen** ▲ C Norway *67.10N 16.16E*
94 H12 **Sulitjelma** *Lapp.* Sulisjielmmá. Nordland, C Norway *67.09N 15.59E*
58 A9 **Sullana** Piura, NW Peru *4.54S 80.42W*
25 N3 **Sulligent** Alabama, S USA *33.54N 88.07W*
32 M14 **Sullivan** Illinois, N USA *39.36N 88.36W*
33 N15 **Sullivan** Indiana, N USA *39.04N 87.24W*
29 W5 **Sullivan** Missouri, C USA *38.12N 91.09W*
Sullivan Island *see* Lanbi Kyun
98 M1 **Sullom Voe** NE Scotland, UK *60.24N 1.09W*
105 O7 **Sully-sur-Loire** Loiret, C France *47.46N 2.21E*
Sulmo *see* Sulmona
109 K15 **Sulmona** *anc.* Sulmo. Abruzzo, C Italy *42.03N 13.55E*
Sulo *see* Shule He
116 M11 **Süloğlu** Edirne, NW Turkey *41.46N 26.55E*
24 G9 **Sulphur** Louisiana, S USA *30.14N 93.22W*
29 O12 **Sulphur** Oklahoma, C USA *34.30N 96.58W*
30 K9 **Sulphur Creek** ≈ South Dakota, N USA
26 M5 **Sulphur Draw** ≈ Texas, SW USA
27 W5 **Sulphur River** ≈ Arkansas/Texas, SW USA
27 V6 **Sulphur Springs** Texas, SW USA *33.09N 95.36W*
26 M6 **Sulphur Springs Draw** ≈ Texas, SW USA
12 D8 **Sultan** Ontario, S Canada *47.34N 82.45W*
Sultānābād *see* Arāk
Sultan Alonto, Lake *see* Lanao, Lake
142 G15 **Sultan Dağları** ▲▲ C Turkey
116 N13 **Sultanköy** Tekirdağ, NW Turkey *41.01N 27.58E*
179 R16 **Sultan Kudarat** *var.* Nuling. Mindanao, S Philippines *7.20N 124.16E*
158 M13 **Sultānpur** Uttar Pradesh, N India *26.15N 82.04E*
179 Pp17 **Sulu Archipelago** *island group* SW Philippines
198 Ff7 **Sulu Basin** *undersea feature* SE South China Sea
Sülüktü *see* Sulyukta
Sulu, Laut *see* Sulu Sea
175 Pp1 **Sulu Sea** *Ind.* Laut Sulu. *sea* SW Philippines
151 O15 **Sulutobe** *Kaz.* Sulūtōbe. Kzylorda, S Kazakhstan *44.31N 66.17E*
153 Q11 **Sulyukta** *Kir.* Sülüktü. Batkenskaya Oblast', SW Kyrgyzstan *39.57N 69.30E*
Sulz *see* Sulz am Neckar
103 G22 **Sulz am Neckar** *var.* Sulz. Baden-Württemberg, SW Germany *48.22N 8.37E*
103 L20 **Sulzbach-Rosenberg** Bayern, SE Germany *49.30N 11.43E*
205 N13 **Sulzberger Bay** *bay* Antarctica
Sumail *see* Summēl

◆ Country ● Country Capital ◇ Dependent Territory ○ Dependent Territory Capital ◈ Administrative Region ✕ International Airport ▲ Mountain ▲▲ Mountain Range Ѫ Volcano ≈ River ◎ Lake ▣ Reservoir

SUMARTIN – SYNYUKHA

115 F15 **Sumartin** Split-Dalmacija, S Croatia *43.17N 16.52E*
34 H6 **Sumas** Washington, NW USA *49.00N 122.15W*
174 Gg7 **Sumatera** *Eng.* Sumatra. *island* W Indonesia
173 G9 **Sumatera Barat** *off.* Propinsi Sumatera Barat, *Eng.* West Sumatra. ◆ *province* W Indonesia
174 Hh11 **Sumatera Selatan** *off.* Propinsi Sumatera Selatan, *Eng.* South Sumatra. ◆ *province* W Indonesia
173 Ff6 **Sumatera Utara** *off.* Propinsi Sumatera Utara, *Eng.* North Sumatra. ◆ *province* W Indonesia
Sumatra *see* Sumatera
Šumava *see* Bohemian Forest
Sumayl *see* Summēl
145 U7 **Sumayr al Muḩammad** E Iraq *33.34N 45.06E*
175 P17 **Sumba, Pulau** *Eng.* Sandalwood Island; *prev.* Soemba. *island* Nusa Tenggara, C Indonesia
152 D12 **Sumbar** ≈ W Turkmenistan
175 P16 **Sumba, Selat** *strait* Nusa Tenggara, S Indonesia
175 Oo16 **Sumbawa** *prev.* Soembawa. *island* Nusa Tenggara, C Indonesia
175 O16 **Sumbawabesar** Sumbawa, S Indonesia *8.30S 117.25E*
83 F23 **Sumbawanga** Rukwa, W Tanzania *7.57S 31.36E*
84 B12 **Sumbe** *prev.* N'Gunza, *Port.* Novo Redondo. Cuanza Sul, W Angola *11.13S 13.52E*
98 M3 **Sumburgh Head** *headland* NE Scotland, UK *59.51N 1.16W*
113 H23 **Sümeg** Veszprém, W Hungary *47.00N 17.13E*
82 C12 **Sumeih** Southern Darfur, S Sudan *9.49N 27.39E*
174 Mm14 **Sumenep** *prev.* Soemenep. Pulau Madura, C Indonesia *7.01S 113.51E*
Sumgait *see* Sumqayıt, Azerbaijan
Sumgait *see* Sumqayıtçay, Azerbaijan
172 Ss14 **Sumisu-jima** *Eng.* Smith Island. *island* SE Japan
145 Q2 **Summēl** *var.* Sumail, Sumayl. N Iraq *36.52N 42.51E*
33 O5 **Summer Island** *island* Michigan, N USA
34 H15 **Summer Lake** ◎ Oregon, NW USA
9 N17 **Summerland** British Columbia, SW Canada *49.34N 119.45W*
11 P14 **Summerside** Prince Edward Island, SE Canada *46.24N 63.46W*
23 R5 **Summersville** West Virginia, NE USA *38.16N 80.51W*
23 R5 **Summersville Lake** ▣ West Virginia, NE USA
23 S13 **Summerton** South Carolina, SE USA *33.36N 80.21W*
25 R2 **Summerville** Georgia, SE USA *34.28N 85.21W*
23 S14 **Summerville** South Carolina, SE USA *33.01N 80.10W*
41 R10 **Summit** Alaska, USA *63.21N 148.50W*
37 V6 **Summit Mountain** ▲ Nevada, W USA *39.23N 116.25W*
39 R8 **Summit Peak** ▲ Colorado, C USA *37.21N 106.42W*
Summus Portus *see* Somport, Col du
31 X12 **Sumner** Iowa, C USA *42.51N 92.05W*
24 K3 **Sumner** Mississippi, S USA *33.58N 90.22W*
193 H17 **Sumner, Lake** ◎ South Island, NZ
39 U12 **Sumner, Lake** ▣ New Mexico, SW USA
171 Kk13 **Sumon-dake** ▲ Honshū, C Japan *37.24N 139.07E*
170 G15 **Sumoto** Hyōgo, Awaji-shima, SW Japan *34.18N 134.52E*
113 G17 **Šumperk** *Ger.* Mährisch-Schönberg. Olomoucký Kraj, E Czech Republic *49.59N 16.58E*
44 F7 **Sumpul, Río** ≈ El Salvador/Honduras
143 Z11 **Sumqayıt** *Rus.* Sumgait. E Azerbaijan *40.33N 49.41E*
143 Y11 **Sumqayıtçay** *Rus.* Sumgait. ≈ E Azerbaijan
153 R9 **Sumsar** Dzhalal-Abadskaya Oblast', W Kyrgyzstan *41.12N 71.16E*
119 S3 **Sums'ka Oblast'** *var.* Sumy, *Rus.* Sumskaya Oblast'. ◆ *province* NE Ukraine
Sumskaya Oblast' *see* Sums'ka Oblast'
128 J8 **Sumskiy Posad** Respublika Kareliya, NW Russian Federation *64.12N 35.22E*
23 S12 **Sumter** South Carolina, SE USA *33.55N 80.20W*
119 T3 **Sumy** Sums'ka Oblast', NE Ukraine *50.54N 34.48E*
Sumy *see* Sums'ka Oblast'
165 Q15 **Sumzom** Xizang Zizhiqu, W China *29.45N 96.13E*
129 R15 **Suna** Kirovskaya Oblast', NW Russian Federation *57.53N 50.04E*
128 I10 **Suna** ≈ NW Russian Federation
172 Oo5 **Sunagawa** Hokkaidō, NE Japan *43.30N 141.55E*
159 V13 **Sunamganj** Chittagong, NE Bangladesh *25.04N 91.24E*
169 W14 **Sunan** ✈ (P'yŏngyang) SW North Korea *39.12N 125.40E*
Sunan/Sunan Yugurzu Zizhixian *see* Hongwansi
21 N9 **Sunapee Lake** ◎ New Hampshire, NE USA
145 P4 **Sunaysilah** *salt marsh* N Iraq
22 M8 **Sunbright** Tennessee, S USA *36.12N 84.39W*
35 R6 **Sunburst** Montana, NW USA *48.51N 111.54W*
191 N12 **Sunbury** Victoria, SE Australia *37.36S 144.42E*
23 X8 **Sunbury** North Carolina, SE USA *36.27N 76.34W*
20 G14 **Sunbury** Pennsylvania, NE USA *40.51N 76.47W*
63 A17 **Sunchales** Santa Fe, C Argentina *30.58S 61.34W*
169 W13 **Sunch'ŏn** SW North Korea *39.28N 125.58E*
169 Y16 **Sunch'ŏn** *Jap.* Junten. S South Korea *34.56N 127.28E*
38 K13 **Sun City** Arizona, SW USA *33.36N 112.16W*
21 O9 **Suncook** New Hampshire, NE USA *43.07N 71.25W*
167 P5 **Suncun** *prev.* Xinwen. Shandong, E China *35.49N 117.36E*
Sunda Islands *see* Greater Sunda Islands
35 Z12 **Sundance** Wyoming, C USA *44.24N 104.22W*
159 T17 **Sundarbans** *wetland* Bangladesh/India
160 M11 **Sundargarh** Orissa, E India *22.07N 84.01E*
174 Ii14 **Sunda, Selat** *strait* Jawa/Sumatera, SW Indonesia
133 U15 **Sunda Shelf** *undersea feature* S South China Sea
Sunda Trench *see* Java Trench
133 U17 **Sunda Trough** *undersea feature* E Indian Ocean
97 O16 **Sundbyberg** Stockholm, C Sweden *59.22N 17.58E*
99 M14 **Sunderland** *var.* Wearmouth. NE England, UK *54.55N 1.22W*
103 F15 **Sundern** Nordrhein-Westfalen, W Germany *51.19N 8.00E*
142 F12 **Sündiken Dağları** ▲ C Turkey
26 M5 **Sundown** Texas, SW USA *33.27N 102.29W*
9 P16 **Sundre** Alberta, SW Canada *51.49N 114.46W*
12 H12 **Sundridge** Ontario, S Canada *45.45N 79.25W*
95 H17 **Sundsvall** Västernorrland, C Sweden *62.22N 17.19E*
28 H4 **Sunflower, Mount** ▲ Kansas, C USA *39.01N 102.02W*
Sunflower State *see* Kansas
174 Gg4 **Sungai Bernam** ≈ Peninsular Malaysia
174 Ii12 **Sungaibuntu** Sumatera, SW Indonesia *4.04S 105.37E*
174 Gg9 **Sungaidareh** Sumatera, W Indonesia *0.58S 101.30E*
178 Hh17 **Sungai Kolok** *var.* Sungai Ko-Lok. Narathiwat, SW Thailand *6.01N 101.58E*
174 Gg10 **Sungaipenuh** *prev.* Soengaipenoeh. Sumatera, W Indonesia *2.00S 101.28E*
174 Kk8 **Sungaipinyuh** Borneo, C Indonesia *0.16N 109.06E*
Sungari *see* Songhua Jiang
Sungaria *see* Dzungaria
Sungei Pahang *see* Pahang, Sungai
178 Hh8 **Sung Men** Phrae, NW Thailand *17.59N 100.07E*
85 M15 **Sungo** Tete, NW Mozambique *16.31S 33.58E*
Sungpu *see* Songpan
174 Ii10 **Sungsang** Sumatera, W Indonesia *2.22S 104.50E*
116 M9 **Sungurlare** Burgas, E Bulgaria *42.47N 26.46E*
142 J12 **Sungurlu** Çorum, N Turkey *40.10N 34.22E*
114 F9 **Sunja** Sisak-Moslavina, C Croatia *45.21N 16.33E*
159 Q12 **Sun Koshi** ≈ E Nepal
96 F9 **Sunndalen** *valley* S Norway
96 F9 **Sunndalsøra** Møre og Romsdal, S Norway *62.40N 8.34E*
97 K15 **Sunne** Värmland, C Sweden *59.52N 13.10E*
97 O15 **Sunnersta** Uppsala, C Sweden *59.46N 17.40E*
96 C11 **Sunnfjord** *physical region* S Norway
97 C15 **Sunnhordland** *physical region* S Norway
96 D10 **Sunnmøre** *physical region* S Norway
39 N4 **Sunnyside** Utah, W USA *39.33N 110.23W*
34 J10 **Sunnyside** Washington, NW USA *46.01N 119.58W*
37 N9 **Sunnyvale** California, W USA *37.22N 122.02W*
32 L8 **Sun Prairie** Wisconsin, N USA *43.12N 89.12W*
Sunqur *see* Sonqor
27 N1 **Sunray** Texas, SW USA *36.01N 101.49W*
24 I8 **Sunset** Louisiana, S USA *30.24N 92.04W*
27 S5 **Sunset** Texas, SW USA *33.24N 97.45W*
Sunset State *see* Oregon
189 Z10 **Sunshine Coast** *cultural region* Queensland, E Australia
Sunshine State *see* Florida, USA
Sunshine State *see* New Mexico, USA
Sunshine State *see* South Dakota, USA
126 Kk11 **Suntar** Respublika Sakha (Yakutiya), NE Russian Federation *62.09N 117.34E*
41 R10 **Suntrana** Alaska, USA *63.51N 148.51W*
154 J15 **Suntsar** Baluchistān, SW Pakistan *25.30N 62.03E*
169 W15 **Sunwi-do** *island* SW North Korea
169 W6 **Sunwu** Heilongjiang, NE China *49.23N 127.17E*
79 O16 **Sunyani** W Ghana *7.22N 2.18W*
Suō *see* Suao
95 M17 **Suolahti** Länsi-Suomi, W Finland *62.32N 25.51E*
Suoločielgi *see* Saariselkä
Suomenlahti *see* Finland, Gulf of
Suomen Tasavalta/Suomi *see* Finland
95 N14 **Suomussalmi** Oulu, E Finland *64.54N 29.05E*
170 D13 **Suō-nada** *sea* SW Japan
95 M17 **Suonenjoki** Itä-Suomi, C Finland *62.36N 27.06E*
178 Jj13 **Suŏng** Kâmpóng Cham, C Cambodia *11.53N 105.41E*
128 I10 **Suoyarvi** Respublika Kareliya, NW Russian Federation *62.01N 32.24E*
Supanburi *see* Suphan Buri
59 D14 **Supe** Lima, W Peru *10.49S 77.42W*
13 V7 **Supérieur, Lac** ◎ Québec, SE Canada
Supérieur, Lac *see* Superior, Lake
38 M14 **Superior** Arizona, SW USA *33.17N 111.06W*
35 O9 **Superior** Montana, NW USA *47.11N 114.53W*
31 P17 **Superior** Nebraska, C USA *40.01N 98.04W*
32 I3 **Superior** Wisconsin, N USA *46.41N 92.03W*
43 S17 **Superior, Laguna** *lagoon* S Mexico
33 N2 **Superior, Lake** *Fr.* Lac Supérieur. ◎ Canada/USA
38 L13 **Superstition Mountains** ▲ Arizona, SW USA
115 F14 **Supetar** *It.* San Pietro. Split-Dalmacija, S Croatia *43.22N 16.34E*
178 H11 **Suphan Buri** *var.* Supanburi. Suphan Buri, W Thailand *14.28N 100.10E*
176 W9 **Supiori, Pulau** *island* E Indonesia
196 K2 **Supply Reef** *reef* N Northern Mariana Islands
205 O7 **Support Force Glacier** *glacier* Antarctica
143 R10 **Sup'sa** *var.* Supsa. ≈ W Georgia
Sūq 'Abs *see* 'Abs
145 W12 **Sūq ash Shuyūkh** SE Iraq *30.52N 46.28E*
144 H4 **Şuqaylibīyah** Ḩamāh, W Syria *35.21N 36.24E*
167 Q6 **Suqian** Jiangsu, E China *33.57N 118.18E*
Suqrah *see* Şawqirah
Suqrah Bay *see* Şawqirah, Dawḩat
147 V16 **Suquṭrā** *var.* Sokotra, *Eng.* Socotra. *island* SE Yemen
147 Z8 **Şūr** NE Oman *22.32N 59.33E*
Şūr *see* Soûr
131 P5 **Sura** Penzenskaya Oblast', W Russian Federation *53.23N 45.03E*
131 P4 **Sura** ≈ W Russian Federation
155 N12 **Sūrāb** Baluchistān, SW Pakistan *28.28N 66.15E*
Surabaja *see* Surabaya
174 M15 **Surabaya** *prev.* Soerabaja, Surabaja. Jawa, C Indonesia *7.13S 112.45E*
97 N15 **Surahammar** Västmanland, C Sweden *59.43N 16.13E*
174 L15 **Surakarta** *Eng.* Solo; *prev.* Soerakarta. Jawa, S Indonesia *7.31S 110.49E*
Surakhany *see* Suraxanı
179 R17 **Surallah** Mindanao, S Philippines *6.16N 124.46E*
143 S10 **Surami** C Georgia *41.59N 43.36E*
149 X13 **Sūrān** Sīstān va Balūchestān, SE Iran *27.18N 61.58E*
113 I21 **Šurany** *Hung.* Nagysurány. Nitriansky Kraj, SW Slovakia *48.05N 18.10E*
160 D12 **Sūrat** Gujarāt, W India *21.10N 72.54E*
Suratdhani *see* Surat Thani
158 G9 **Sūratgarh** Rājasthān, NW India *29.19N 73.58E*
178 Gg15 **Surat Thani** *var.* Suratdhani. Surat Thani, SW Thailand *9.09N 99.19E*
121 Q16 **Suraw** *Rus.* Surov. ≈ E Belarus
143 Z11 **Suraxanı** *Rus.* Surakhany. E Azerbaijan *40.25N 49.59E*
147 Y11 **Surayr** E Oman *19.55N 57.46E*
144 K2 **Suraysāt** Ḩalab, N Syria *36.42N 38.01E*
122 O12 **Surazh** *Rus.* Surazh. Vitsyebskaya Voblasts', NE Belarus *55.24N 30.46E*
130 H6 **Surazh** Bryanskaya Oblast', W Russian Federation *53.04N 32.29E*
203 V17 **Sur, Cabo** *headland* Easter Island, Chile, E Pacific Ocean *27.10S 109.25W*
114 L11 **Surčin** Serbia, N Serbia and Montenegro (Yugoslavia) *44.48N 20.19E*
118 H9 **Surduc** *Hung.* Szurduk. Sălaj, NW Romania *47.13N 23.19E*
115 P16 **Surdulica** Serbia, SE Serbia and Montenegro (Yugoslavia) *42.43N 22.10E*
101 L24 **Sûre** *var.* Sauer. ≈ W Europe *see also* Sauer
160 C10 **Surendranagar** Gujarāt, W India *22.43N 71.43E*
20 K16 **Surf City** New Jersey, NE USA *39.21N 74.24W*
191 V3 **Surfers Paradise** Queensland, E Australia *27.54S 153.18E*
23 U13 **Surfside Beach** South Carolina, SE USA *33.36N 78.58W*
104 J10 **Surgères** Charente-Maritime, W France *46.07N 0.44W*
125 G11 **Surgut** Khanty-Mansiyskiy Avtonomnyy Okrug, C Russian Federation *61.13N 73.28E*
126 Hh10 **Surgutikha** Krasnoyarskiy Kray, N Russian Federation *64.44N 87.13E*
100 M6 **Surhuisterveen** Friesland, N Netherlands *53.10N 6.10E*
107 V5 **Súria** Cataluña, NE Spain *41.49N 1.45E*
149 P10 **Sūrīān** Fārs, S Iran
161 J15 **Suriāpet** Andhra Pradesh, C India *17.10N 79.42E*
179 R14 **Surigao** Mindanao, S Philippines *9.43N 125.31E*
178 Ii11 **Surin** Surin, E Thailand *14.52N 103.28E*
Surinam *see* Suriname
57 U11 **Suriname** *off.* Republic of Suriname, *var.* Surinam; *prev.* Dutch Guiana, Netherlands Guiana. ◆ *republic* N South America
Sūrīya/Sūrīyah, Al-Jumhūrīyah al-'Arabīyah as- *see* Syria
Surkhab, Darya-i- *see* Kahmard, Daryā-ye
Surkhandar'inskaya Oblast' *see* Surkhondaryo Viloyati
Surkhandar'ya *see* Surxondaryo
Surkhet *see* Birendranagar
153 R12 **Surkhob** ≈ C Tajikistan
153 N13 **Surkhondaryo Viloyati** *Rus.* Surkhandar'inskaya Oblast'. ◆ *province* S Uzbekistan
143 P11 **Sürmene** Trabzon, NE Turkey *40.55N 40.03E*
Surov *see* Suraw
131 N11 **Surovikino** Volgogradskaya Oblast', SW Russian Federation *48.39N 42.46E*
126 Jj14 **Surovo** Irkutskaya Oblast', S Russian Federation *55.45N 105.31E*
37 N11 **Sur, Point** *headland* California, W USA *36.18N 121.54W*
197 F3 **Surprise, Île** *island* N New Caledonia
63 E22 **Sur, Punta** *headland* E Argentina *50.58S 69.10W*
Surrentum *see* Sorrento
30 M3 **Surrey** North Dakota, N USA *48.13N 101.05W*
99 O22 **Surrey** *cultural region* SE England, UK
23 X7 **Surry** Virginia, NE USA *37.08N 76.48W*
110 F8 **Sursee** Luzern, W Switzerland *47.10N 8.07E*
131 P6 **Sursk** Penzenskaya Oblast', W Russian Federation *53.06N 45.46E*
131 P5 **Surskoye** Ul'yanovskaya Oblast', W Russian Federation *54.28N 46.47E*
77 P8 **Surt** *var.* Sidra, Sirte. N Libya *31.13N 16.34E*
97 I19 **Surte** Västra Götaland, S Sweden *57.49N 12.01E*
77 Q8 **Surt, Khalīj** *Eng.* Gulf of Sidra, Gulf of Sirti, Sidra. *gulf* N Libya
94 I5 **Surtsey** *island* S Iceland
143 N17 **Suruç** Şanlıurfa, S Turkey *36.58N 38.24E*
171 Ii17 **Suruga-wan** *bay* SE Japan
174 Hh10 **Surulangun** Sumatera, W Indonesia *2.36S 102.43E*
153 P13 **Surxondaryo** *Rus.* Surkhandar'ya. ≈ Tajikistan/Uzbekistan
Süs *see* Susch
108 A8 **Susa** Piemonte, NE Italy *45.09N 7.01E*
170 E12 **Susa** Yamaguchi, Honshū, SW Japan *34.35N 131.34E*
Susa *see* Shūsh
115 E16 **Sušac** *It.* Cazza. *island* SW Croatia
Sūsah *see* Sousse
170 Ee15 **Susaki** Kōchi, Shikoku, SW Japan *33.22N 133.13E*
170 G17 **Susami** Wakayama, Honshū, SW Japan *33.32N 135.32E*
148 K9 **Sūsangerd** *var.* Susangird. Khūzestān, SW Iran *31.40N 48.06E*
Susangird *see* Sūsangerd
37 P4 **Susanville** California, W USA *40.25N 120.39W*
110 J9 **Susch** *var.* Süs. Graubünden, SE Switzerland *46.45N 10.04E*
143 N12 **Suşehri** Sivas, N Turkey *40.10N 38.06E*
Susiana *see* Khūzestān
113 B18 **Sušice** *Ger.* Schüttenhofen. Plzeňský Kraj, W Czech Republic *49.13N 13.31E*
41 R11 **Susitna** Alaska, USA *61.32N 150.30W*
41 R11 **Susitna River** ≈ Alaska, USA
131 Q3 **Suslonger** Respublika Mariy El, W Russian Federation *56.18N 48.16E*
107 N14 **Suspiro del Moro, Puerto del** *pass* S Spain *37.04N 3.39W*
20 H16 **Susquehanna River** ≈ New York/Pennsylvania, NE USA
11 O15 **Sussex** New Brunswick, SE Canada *45.43N 65.31W*
20 J13 **Sussex** New Jersey, NE USA *41.12N 74.34W*
23 W7 **Sussex** Virginia, NE USA *36.54N 77.16W*
99 O23 **Sussex** *cultural region* S England, UK
191 S10 **Sussex Inlet** New South Wales, SE Australia *35.10S 150.35E*
101 L17 **Susteren** Limburg, SE Netherlands *51.04N 5.49E*
8 K12 **Sustut Peak** ▲ British Columbia, W Canada *56.25N 126.34W*
127 Nn9 **Susuman** Magadanskaya Oblast', E Russian Federation *62.46N 148.07E*
196 H6 **Susupe** Saipan, S Northern Mariana Islands
142 D12 **Susurluk** Balıkesir, NW Turkey *39.55N 28.10E*
116 M13 **Susuzmüsellim** Tekirdağ, NW Turkey *41.04N 27.03E*
142 F15 **Sütçüler** Isparta, SW Turkey *37.31N 31.00E*
118 L13 **Şuţeşti** Brăila, SE Romania *45.13N 27.26E*
85 F25 **Sutherland** Western Cape, SW South Africa *32.22S 20.42E*
30 L15 **Sutherland** Nebraska, C USA *41.09N 101.07W*
98 I7 **Sutherland** *cultural region* N Scotland, UK
193 B21 **Sutherland Falls** *waterfall* South Island, NZ *44.49S 167.32E*
34 F14 **Sutherlin** Oregon, NW USA *43.23N 123.18W*
155 V10 **Sutlej** ≈ India/Pakistan
Sutna *see* Satna
37 P7 **Sutter Creek** California, W USA *38.22N 120.49W*
41 R11 **Sutton** Alaska, USA *61.42N 148.53W*
31 Q16 **Sutton** Nebraska, C USA *40.36N 97.52W*
23 R4 **Sutton** West Virginia, NE USA *38.39N 80.42W*
10 F8 **Sutton** ≈ Ontario, C Canada
99 M19 **Sutton Coldfield** C England, UK *52.34N 1.48W*
23 R4 **Sutton Lake** ▣ West Virginia, NE USA
13 P13 **Sutton, Monts** *hill range* Québec, SE Canada
10 F8 **Sutton Ridges** ▲ Ontario, C Canada
172 Nn5 **Suttsu** Hokkaidō, NE Japan *42.46N 140.12E*
41 P15 **Sutwik Island** *island* Alaska, USA
168 K7 **Süüj** Bulgan, C Mongolia *47.49N 104.06E*
120 H5 **Suure-Jaani** *Ger.* Gross-Sankt-Johannis. Viljandimaa, S Estonia *58.34N 25.28E*
120 J7 **Suur Munamägi** *var.* Munamägi, *Ger.* Eier-Berg. ▲ SE Estonia *57.42N 27.03E*
120 F5 **Suur Väin** *Ger.* Grosser Sund. *strait* W Estonia
153 U8 **Suusamyr** Chuyskaya Oblast', C Kyrgyzstan *42.07N 73.55E*
197 I13 **Suva** ● (Fiji) Viti Levu, W Fiji *18.07S 178.26E*
197 I13 **Suva** ✈ Viti Levu, C Fiji *18.01S 178.30E*
115 N18 **Suva Gora** ▲ W FYR Macedonia
120 H11 **Suvainiškis** Panevėžys, NE Lithuania *56.09N 25.15E*
Suvalkai/Suvalki *see* Suwałki
115 P15 **Suva Planina** ▲ SE Serbia and Montenegro (Yugoslavia)
115 M17 **Suva Reka** Serbia, S Serbia and Montenegro (Yugoslavia) *42.23N 20.50E*
130 K5 **Suvorov** Tul'skaya Oblast', W Russian Federation *54.08N 36.33E*
119 N12 **Suvorove** Odes'ka Oblast', SW Ukraine *45.35N 28.58E*
Suvorovo *see* Ştefan Vodă
171 J15 **Suwa** Nagano, Honshū, S Japan *36.01N 138.07E*
Suwaik *see* As Suwayq
Suwaira *see* Aş Şuwayrah
112 O7 **Suwałki** *Lith.* Suvalkai, *Rus.* Suvalki. Podlaskie, NE Poland *54.06N 22.55E*
178 Ii10 **Suwannaphum** Roi Et, E Thailand *15.36N 103.46E*
25 V8 **Suwannee River** ≈ Florida/Georgia, SE USA
Şuwār *see* Aş Şuwār
202 K14 **Suwarrow** *atoll* N Cook Islands
Suwaydá/Suwaydā', Muḩāfaẓat as *see* As Suwaydā'
149 R16 **Suwaydān** *var.* Sweihan. Abū Ẓaby, E UAE *24.30N 55.18E*
Suwayqiyah, Hawr as *see* Shuwayjah, Hawr ash
Suways, Khalīj as *see* Suez, Gulf of
Suways, Qanāt as *see* Suez Canal
Suweida *see* As Suwaydā'
Suweon *see* Suwŏn
169 X15 **Suwŏn** *var.* Suweon, *Jap.* Suigen. NW South Korea *37.17N 127.03E*
Su Xian *see* Suzhou
149 R14 **Sūzā** Hormozgān, S Iran *26.49N 56.04E*
151 P15 **Suzak** *Kaz.* Sozaq. Yuzhnyy Kazakhstan, S Kazakhstan *44.09N 68.28E*
Suzaka *see* Suzuka
130 M3 **Suzdal'** Vladimirskaya Oblast', W Russian Federation *56.27N 40.29E*
167 P7 **Suzhou** *var.* Su Xian. Anhui, E China *33.39N 116.56E*
167 R8 **Suzhou** *var.* Soochow, Su-chou, Suchow; *prev.* Wuhsien. Jiangsu, E China *31.22N 120.34E*
Suzhou *see* Jiuquan
169 V12 **Suzi He** ≈ NE China
Suz, Mys *see* Soye, Mys
171 J12 **Suzu** Ishikawa, Honshū, SW Japan *37.24N 137.12E*
171 Hh16 **Suzuka** Mie, Honshū, SW Japan *34.51N 136.31E*
171 Jj14 **Suzuka** *var.* Suzaka. Nagano, Honshū, S Japan *36.39N 138.16E*
171 J12 **Suzu-misaki** *headland* Honshū, SW Japan *37.31N 137.19E*
Svågälv *see* Svågan
96 M10 **Svågan** *var.* Svågälv. ≈ C Sweden
Svalava/Svaljava *see* Svalyava
94 O2 **Svalbard** ◇ *Norwegian dependency* Arctic Ocean
94 J2 **Svalbardhseyri** Nordhurland Eystra, N Iceland *65.43N 18.03W*
97 K22 **Svalöv** Skåne, S Sweden *55.55N 13.06E*
118 H7 **Svalyava** *Cz.* Svalava, Svaljava, *Hung.* Szolyva. Zakarpats'ka Oblast', W Ukraine *48.33N 23.00E*
94 O2 **Svanbergfjellet** ▲ C Svalbard *78.40N 18.10E*
97 M24 **Svaneke** Bornholm, E Denmark *55.07N 15.08E*
97 L22 **Svängsta** Blekinge, S Sweden *56.16N 14.46E*
97 J16 **Svanskog** Värmland, C Sweden *59.10N 12.34E*
97 L16 **Svartå** Örebro, C Sweden *59.13N 14.07E*
97 L15 **Svartälven** ≈ C Sweden
94 G12 **Svartisen** *glacier* C Norway
119 X6 **Svatove** *Rus.* Svatovo. Luhans'ka Oblast', E Ukraine *49.24N 38.10E*
Svatovo *see* Svatove
Sväty Kríž nad Hronom *see* Žiar nad Hronom
178 Ii12 **Svay Chék, Stœng** ≈ Cambodia/Thailand
178 Jj14 **Svay Riĕng** Svay Riĕng, S Cambodia *11.04N 105.48E*
94 O3 **Sveagruva** Spitsbergen, W Svalbard *77.53N 16.42E*
97 K23 **Svedala** Skåne, S Sweden *55.30N 13.15E*
120 H12 **Svėdesai** Utena, NE Lithuania *55.42N 25.22E*
95 G18 **Sveg** Jämtland, C Sweden *62.01N 14.19E*
120 C12 **Švėkšna** Klaipėda, W Lithuania *55.31N 21.37E*
96 C11 **Svelgen** Sogn og Fjordane, S Norway *61.46N 5.18E*
97 H15 **Svelvik** Vestfold, S Norway *59.36N 10.22E*
120 I13 **Švenčionėliai** *Pol.* Nowo-Święciany. Vilnius, SE Lithuania *55.10N 26.00E*
120 I13 **Švenčionys** *Pol.* Swięciany. Vilnius, SE Lithuania *55.08N 26.08E*
97 H24 **Svendborg** Fyn, C Denmark *55.04N 10.37E*
97 K19 **Svenljunga** Västra Götaland, S Sweden *57.30N 13.04E*
94 P2 **Svenskøya** *island* E Svalbard
95 G17 **Svenstavik** Jämtland, C Sweden *62.39N 14.24E*
97 G20 **Svenstrup** Nordjylland, N Denmark *56.58N 9.52E*
120 H12 **Šventoji** ≈ C Lithuania
119 Z8 **Sverdlovs'k** *Rus.* Sverdlovsk; *prev.* Imeni Sverdlova Rudnik. Luhans'ka Oblast', E Ukraine *48.05N 39.37E*
Sverdlovsk *see* Yekaterinburg
131 W2 **Sverdlovskaya Oblast'** ◆ *province* C Russian Federation
126 Hh5 **Sverdrup, Ostrov** *island* N Russian Federation
Sverige *see* Sweden
115 D15 **Svetac** *prev.* Sveti Andrea, *It.* Sant'Andrea. *island* SW Croatia
Sveti Andrea *see* Svetac
Sveti Nikola *see* Sveti Nikole
115 O18 **Sveti Nikole** *prev.* Sveti Nikola. C FYR Macedonia *41.54N 21.55E*
Sveti Vrach *see* Sandanski
127 O16 **Svetlaya** Primorskiy Kray, SE Russian Federation *46.33N 138.20E*
130 B2 **Svetlogorsk** Kaliningradskaya Oblast', W Russian Federation *54.56N 20.09E*
126 I9 **Svetlogorsk** Krasnoyarskiy Kray, N Russian Federation *66.51N 88.29E*
Svetlogorsk *see* Svyetlahorsk
131 N14 **Svetlograd** Stavropol'skiy Kray, SW Russian Federation *45.19N 42.52E*
Svetlovodsk *see* Svitlovods'k
121 A14 **Svetlyy** *Ger.* Zimmerbude. Kaliningradskaya Oblast', W Russian Federation *54.42N 20.07E*
131 Y8 **Svetlyy** Orenburgskaya Oblast', W Russian Federation *50.34N 60.42E*
131 P7 **Svetlyy** Saratovskaya Oblast', W Russian Federation *51.42N 45.40E*
128 G11 **Svetogorsk** *Fin.* Enso. Leningradskaya Oblast', NW Russian Federation *61.06N 28.52E*
Svetozarevo *see* Jagodina
113 B18 **Švihov** *Ger.* Schwihau. Plzeňský Kraj, W Czech Republic *49.31N 13.18E*
114 E13 **Svilaja** ▲ SE Croatia
114 N12 **Svilajnac** Serbia, C Serbia and Montenegro (Yugoslavia) *44.15N 21.12E*
116 L11 **Svilengrad** *prev.* Mustafa-Pasha. Khaskovo, S Bulgaria *41.46N 26.13E*
Svinecea Mare, Munte *see* Svinecea Mare, Vârful
118 F13 **Svinecea Mare, Vârful** *var.* Munte Svinecea Mare. ▲ SW Romania *44.47N 22.10E*
97 B18 **Svínoy** *Dan.* Svinø. *Island* Faeroe Islands *62.17N 6.17W*
153 N14 **Svintsovyy Rudnik** *Turkm.* Swintsowyy Rudnik. Lebap Welaýaty, E Turkmenistan *37.54N 66.25E*
120 I13 **Svir** *Rus.* Svir'. Minskaya Voblasts', NW Belarus *54.51N 26.24E*
128 I12 **Svir'** *canal* NW Russian Federation
Svir', Ozero *see* Svir, Vozyera
121 I14 **Svir, Vozyera** *Rus.* Ozero Svir'. ◎ C Belarus
116 J7 **Svishtov** *prev.* Sistova. Veliko Tŭrnovo, N Bulgaria *43.37N 25.22E*
121 F18 **Svislach** *Pol.* Swisłocz, *Rus.* Svisloch'. Hrodzyenskaya Voblasts', W Belarus *53.01N 24.06E*
121 M17 **Svislach** *Rus.* Svisloch'. Mahilyowskaya Voblasts', E Belarus *53.25N 28.56E*
121 L17 **Svislach** *Rus.* Svisloch'. ≈ E Belarus
Svisloch' *see* Svislach
113 F17 **Svitavy** *Ger.* Zwittau. Pardubický Kraj, C Czech Republic *49.45N 16.27E*
119 S6 **Svitlovods'k** *Rus.* Svetlovodsk. Kirovohrads'ka Oblast', C Ukraine *49.04N 33.15E*
Svizzera *see* Switzerland
127 Mm15 **Svobodnyy** Amurskaya Oblast', SE Russian Federation *51.24N 128.05E*
116 G9 **Svoge** Sofiya, W Bulgaria *42.58N 23.20E*
94 G11 **Svolvær** Nordland, C Norway *68.15N 14.29E*
113 F18 **Svratka** *Ger.* Schwarzach, Schwarzawa. ≈ SE Czech Republic
115 P14 **Svrljig** Serbia, E Serbia and Montenegro (Yugoslavia) *43.26N 22.07E*
207 U10 **Svyataya Anna Trough** *var.* Saint Anna Trough. *undersea feature* N Kara Sea
128 M4 **Svyatoy Nos, Mys** *headland* NW Russian Federation *68.07N 39.49E*
126 M5 **Svyatoy Nos, Mys** *headland* NE Russian Federation *72.49N 140.45E*
121 N18 **Svyetlahorsk** *Rus.* Svetlogorsk. Homyel'skaya Voblasts', SE Belarus *52.39N 29.43E*
Swabian Jura *see* Schwäbische Alb
99 P19 **Swaffham** E England, UK *52.38N 0.40E*
25 V5 **Swainsboro** Georgia, SE USA *32.36N 82.19W*
85 C19 **Swakop** ≈ W Namibia
85 C19 **Swakopmund** Erongo, W Namibia *22.40S 14.34E*
99 M15 **Swale** ≈ N England, UK
Swallow Island *see* Nendö
101 M16 **Swalmen** Limburg, SE Netherlands *51.13N 6.01E*
10 G8 **Swan** ≈ Ontario, C Canada
99 L24 **Swanage** S England, UK *50.37N 1.59W*
190 M10 **Swan Hill** Victoria, SE Australia *35.21S 143.34E*
9 P13 **Swan Hills** Alberta, W Canada *54.40N 116.19W*
67 D24 **Swan Island** *island* C Falkland Islands
Swankalok *see* Sawankhalok
31 U10 **Swan Lake** ◎ Minnesota, N USA
23 Y10 **Swanquarter** North Carolina, SE USA *35.23N 76.17W*
190 J9 **Swan Reach** South Australia *34.39S 139.35E*
9 V15 **Swan River** Manitoba, S Canada *52.06N 101.16W*
191 P17 **Swansea** Tasmania, SE Australia *42.09S 148.03E*
99 J22 **Swansea** *Wel.* Abertawe. S Wales, UK *51.37N 3.57W*
23 R13 **Swansea** South Carolina, SE USA *33.47N 81.06W*
21 S7 **Swans Island** *island* Maine, NE USA
30 L17 **Swanson Lake** ▣ Nebraska, C USA
33 R11 **Swanton** Ohio, N USA *41.35N 83.53W*
112 G11 **Swarzędz** Poznań, C Poland *52.24N 17.05E*
Swatow *see* Shantou
85 L22 **Swaziland** *off.* Kingdom of Swaziland. ◆ *monarchy* S Africa
95 G18 **Sweden** *off.* Kingdom of Sweden, *Swe.* Sverige. ◆ *monarchy* N Europe
Swedru *see* Agona Swedru
27 V12 **Sweeny** Texas, SW USA *29.02N 95.42W*
35 R6 **Sweetgrass** Montana, NW USA *48.58N 111.58W*
34 G12 **Sweet Home** Oregon, NW USA *44.24N 122.44W*
27 T12 **Sweet Home** Texas, SW USA *29.21N 97.04W*
29 T4 **Sweet Springs** Missouri, C USA *38.57N 93.24W*
22 M10 **Sweetwater** Tennessee, S USA *35.36N 84.27W*
27 P7 **Sweetwater** Texas, SW USA *32.28N 100.24W*
35 V15 **Sweetwater River** ≈ Wyoming, C USA
Sweiham *see* Suwaydān
85 F26 **Swellendam** Western Cape, SW South Africa *34.01S 20.25E*
113 G15 **Świdnica** *Ger.* Schweidnitz. Wałbrzych, SW Poland *50.51N 16.28E*
113 O14 **Świdnik** *Ger.* Streckenbach. Lubelskie, E Poland *51.13N 22.39E*
112 F8 **Świdwin** *Ger.* Schivelbein. Zachodnio-pomorskie, NW Poland *53.46N 15.43E*
113 F15 **Świebodzice** *Ger.* Freiburg in Schlesien, Swiebodzice. Wałbrzych, SW Poland *50.54N 16.22E*
112 E11 **Świebodzin** *Ger.* Schwiebus. Lubuskie, W Poland *52.15N 15.30E*
Swięciany *see* Švenčionys
112 I9 **Świecie** *Ger.* Schwertberg. Kujawsko-pomorskie, N Poland *53.24N 18.24E*
113 L15 **Świętokrzyskie** ◆ *province* C Poland
9 T16 **Swift Current** Saskatchewan, S Canada *50.16N 107.49W*
100 K9 **Swifterbant** Flevoland, C Netherlands *52.36N 5.33E*
191 Q12 **Swifts Creek** Victoria, SE Australia *37.17S 147.41E*
98 E13 **Swilly, Lough** *Ir.* Loch Súilí. *inlet* N Ireland
99 M22 **Swindon** S England, UK *51.34N 1.46W*
Swinemünde *see* Świnoujście
112 D8 **Świnoujście** *Ger.* Swinemünde. Zachodnio-pomorskie, NW Poland *53.54N 14.12E*
Swintsowyy Rudnik *see* Svintsovyy Rudnik
Świsłocz *see* Svislach
Swiss Confederation *see* Switzerland
110 E9 **Switzerland** *off.* Swiss Confederation, *Fr.* La Suisse, *Ger.* Schweiz, *It.* Svizzera; *anc.* Helvetia. ◆ *federal republic* C Europe
99 F17 **Swords** *Ir.* Sord, Sórd Choluim Chille. E Ireland *53.28N 6.13W*
20 H13 **Swoyersville** Pennsylvania, NE USA *41.18N 75.48W*
128 I10 **Syamozero, Ozero** ◎ NW Russian Federation
128 M13 **Syamzha** Vologodskaya Oblast', NW Russian Federation *60.02N 41.09E*
120 N13 **Syanno** *Rus.* Senno. Vitsyebskaya Voblasts', NE Belarus *54.48N 29.44E*
121 K16 **Syarhyeyevichy** *Rus.* Sergeyevichi. Minskaya Voblasts', C Belarus *53.30N 27.45E*
128 I12 **Syas'stroy** Leningradskaya Oblast', NW Russian Federation *60.05N 32.37E*
Sycaminum *see* Ḩefa
32 M10 **Sycamore** Illinois, N USA *41.59N 88.41W*
130 J3 **Sychëvka** Smolenskaya Oblast', W Russian Federation *55.52N 34.19E*
113 H14 **Syców** *Ger.* Gross Wartenberg. Dolnośląskie, SW Poland *51.18N 17.42E*
12 E17 **Sydenham** ≈ Ontario, S Canada
Sydenham Island *see* Nonouti
191 T9 **Sydney** *state capital* New South Wales, SE Australia *33.55S 151.10E*
11 R14 **Sydney** Cape Breton Island, Nova Scotia, SE Canada *46.10N 60.10W*
Sydney Island *see* Manra
11 R14 **Sydney Mines** Cape Breton Island, Nova Scotia, SE Canada *46.14N 60.19W*
Syedpur *see* Saidpur
121 K18 **Syelishcha** *Rus.* Selishche. Minskaya Voblasts', C Belarus *53.01N 27.25E*
121 J18 **Syemyezhava** *Rus.* Semezhevo. Minskaya Voblasts', C Belarus *52.57N 27.01E*
Syene *see* Aswān
119 X6 **Syeverodonets'k** *Rus.* Severodonetsk. Luhans'ka Oblast', E Ukraine *48.58N 38.28E*
167 T6 **Syīao Shan** *island* SE China
102 H11 **Syke** Niedersachsen, NW Germany *52.55N 8.49E*
96 D10 **Sykkylven** Møre og Romsdal, S Norway *62.22N 6.34E*
117 F15 **Sykoúri** *var.* Sikouri; *prev.* Sikoúrion. Thessalía, C Greece *39.46N 22.34E*
129 R11 **Syktyvkar** *prev.* Ust'-Sysol'sk. Respublika Komi, NW Russian Federation *61.42N 50.45E*
25 Q4 **Sylacauga** Alabama, S USA *33.10N 86.15W*
Sylarna *see* Storsylen
159 V14 **Sylhet** Chittagong, NE Bangladesh *24.53N 91.51E*
102 G6 **Sylt** *island* NW Germany
23 O10 **Sylva** North Carolina, SE USA *35.22N 83.13W*
129 V15 **Sylva** ≈ NW Russian Federation
25 W5 **Sylvania** Georgia, SE USA *32.45N 81.38W*
33 R11 **Sylvania** Ohio, N USA *41.43N 83.42W*
9 Q15 **Sylvan Lake** Alberta, SW Canada *52.18N 114.02W*
35 T13 **Sylvan Pass** *pass* Wyoming, C USA *44.29N 110.03W*
25 T7 **Sylvester** Georgia, SE USA *31.31N 83.50W*
27 P6 **Sylvester** Texas, SW USA *32.42N 100.15W*
8 L11 **Sylvia, Mount** ▲ British Columbia, W Canada *58.03N 124.26W*
126 Hh12 **Sym** ≈ C Russian Federation
117 N22 **Sými** *var.* Simi. *island* Dodekánisos, Greece, Aegean Sea
119 U8 **Synel'nykove** Dnipropetrovs'ka Oblast', E Ukraine *48.18N 35.31E*
129 U6 **Synya** Respublika Komi, NW Russian Federation *65.21N 58.01E*
119 P7 **Synyukha** *Rus.* Synyukha. ≈ S Ukraine

◆ COUNTRY ● COUNTRY CAPITAL ◇ DEPENDENT TERRITORY ○ DEPENDENT TERRITORY CAPITAL ◆ ADMINISTRATIVE REGION ✈ INTERNATIONAL AIRPORT ▲ MOUNTAIN ▲ MOUNTAIN RANGE VOLCANO ≈ RIVER ◎ LAKE ▣ RESERVOIR

Syôbara – Tâmega, Rio

Syôbara see Shōbara
205 V2 **Syowa** Japanese research station Antarctica 68.58S 40.07E
28 H6 **Syracuse** Kansas, C USA 38.00N 101.43W
31 S16 **Syracuse** Nebraska, C USA 40.39N 96.11W
20 H10 **Syracuse** New York, NE USA 43.03N 76.09W
Syracuse see Siracusa
Syrdar'inskaya Oblast' see Sirdaryo Viloyati
Syrdariya see Syr Darya
150 L14 **Syr Darya** var. Sai Hun, Sir Darya, Syrdarya, Kaz. Syrdariya, Rus. Syrdar'ya, Uzb. Sirdaryo; anc. Jaxartes. ⟿ C Asia
144 J6 **Syria** off. Syrian Arab Republic, var. Siria, Syrie, Ar. Al-Jumhūrīyah al-'Arabīyah as-Sūrīyah, Sūrīya. ◆ republic SW Asia
144 L9 **Syrian Desert** Ar. Al Hamad, Bādiyat ash Shām. desert SW Asia
Syrie see Syria
117 L22 **Sýrna** var. Sirna. island Kykládes, Greece, Aegean Sea
117 I20 **Sýros** var. Síros. island Kykládes, Greece, Aegean Sea
95 M18 **Sysmä** Etelä-Suomi, S Finland 61.28N 25.37E
129 R12 **Sysola** ⟿ NW Russian Federation
Syulemeshlii see Sredets
131 S2 **Syumsi** Udmurtskaya Respublika, NW Russian Federation 57.07N 51.35E
116 K10 **Syuyutliyka** ⟿ C Bulgaria
Syvash, Zaliv see Syvash, Zatoka
119 U12 **Syvash, Zatoka** Rus. Zaliv Syvash. inlet S Ukraine
131 Q6 **Syzran'** Samarskaya Oblast', W Russian Federation 53.10N 48.22E
Szabadka see Subotica
113 N21 **Szabolcs-Szatmár-Bereg** off. Szabolcs-Szatmár-Bereg Megye. ◐ county E Hungary
112 G10 **Szamocin** Ger. Samotschin. Wielkopolskie, C Poland 53.02N 17.04E
118 H8 **Szamos** var. Someş, Someşul, Ger. Samosch, Somesch. ⟿ Hungary/Romania
Szamosújvár see Gherla
112 G11 **Szamotuły** Poznań, C Poland 52.35N 16.35E
Szarkowszczyzna see Sharkawshchyna
113 M24 **Szarvas** Békés, SE Hungary 46.52N 20.32E
Szászmagyarós see Măieruş
Szászrégen see Reghin
Szászsebes see Sebeş
Szászváros see Orăştie
Szatmárrnémeti see Satu Mare
Száva see Sava
113 P15 **Szczebrzeszyn** Lubelskie, E Poland 50.43N 23.00E
112 D9 **Szczecin** Eng./Ger. Stettin. Zachodnio-pomorskie, NW Poland 53.25N 14.31E
112 G8 **Szczecinek** Ger. Neustettin. Zachodnio-pomorskie, NW Poland 53.42N 16.39E
112 D8 **Szczeciński, Zalew** var. Stettiner Haff, Ger. Oderhaff. bay Germany/Poland
113 K15 **Szczekociny** Śląskie, S Poland 50.38N 19.46E
112 N8 **Szczuczyn** Podlaskie, NE Poland 53.34N 22.17E
Szczuczyn Nowogródzki see Shchuchyn
112 M8 **Szczytno** Ger. Ortelsburg. Warmińsko-Mazurskie, NE Poland 53.33N 21.00E
Szechuan/Szechwan see Sichuan
113 K21 **Szécsény** Nógrád, N Hungary 48.04N 19.31E
113 L25 **Szeged** Ger. Szegedin, Rom. Seghedin. Csongrád, SE Hungary 46.16N 20.06E
Szegedin see Szeged
113 N23 **Szeghalom** Békés, SE Hungary 47.02N 21.09E
Székelyhid see Săcueni
Székelykeresztúr see Cristuru Secuiesc
113 I23 **Székesfehérvár** Ger. Stuhlweissenberg; anc. Alba Regia. Fejér, W Hungary 47.13N 18.24E
Szeklerburg see Miercurea-Ciuc
Szekler Neumarkt see Târgu Secuiesc
113 J25 **Szekszárd** Tolna, S Hungary 46.21N 18.40E
Szempcz/Szenc see Senec
Szenice see Senica
Szentágota see Agnita
113 J22 **Szentendre** Ger. Sankt Andrä. Pest, N Hungary 47.40N 19.04E
113 L24 **Szentes** Csongrád, SE Hungary 46.40N 20.16E
113 F23 **Szentgotthárd** Eng. Saint Gotthard, Ger. Sankt Gotthard. Vas, W Hungary 46.57N 16.18E
Szentgyörgy see Đurđevac
Szenttamás see Srbobran
Széphely see Jebel
Szeping see Siping
Szered see Sereď
113 N21 **Szerencs** Borsod-Abaúj-Zemplén, NE Hungary 48.10N 21.10E
Szeret see Siret
Szeretfalva see Sărăţel
112 N7 **Szeska Góra** var. Szeskie Wygórza, Ger. Seesker Höhe. hill NE Poland 54.15N 22.19E
Szeskie Wygórza see Szeska Góra
113 H25 **Szigetvár** Baranya, SW Hungary 46.03N 17.47E
Szilágysomlyó see Şimleu Silvaniei
Szinna see Snina
Sziszek see Sisak
Szitás-Keresztúr see Cristuru Secuiesc
113 E15 **Szklarska Poręba** Ger. Schreiberhau. Dolnośląskie, SW Poland 50.50N 15.30E
Szkudy see Skuodas
Szlatina see Slatina, Croatia
Szlavonia/Szlavonország see Slavonija
Szlovákia see Slovakia
Szluin see Slunj
113 L23 **Szolnok** Jász-Nagykun-Szolnok, C Hungary 47.10N 20.12E
Szolyva see Svalyava
113 G23 **Szombathely** Ger. Steinamanger; anc. Sabaria, Savaria. Vas, W Hungary 47.13N 16.37E
Szond/Szonta see Sonta
Szováta see Sovata
112 F13 **Szprotawa** Ger. Sprottau. Lubuskie, W Poland 51.33N 15.31E
Sztálinváros see Dunaújváros
Sztrazsó see Strážov
112 J8 **Sztum** Ger. Stuhm. Pomorskie, N Poland 53.54N 19.01E
112 H10 **Szubin** Ger. Schubin. Kujawsko-pomorskie, W Poland 53.04N 17.49E
Szucsava see Suceava
Szurduk see Surduc
113 M14 **Szydłowiec** Ger. Schlelau. Mazowieckie, C Poland 51.15N 20.51E

T

Taalintehdas see Dalsbruk
179 P11 **Taal, Lake** ◎ Luzon, NW Philippines
97 J23 **Taastrup** var. Tåstrup. København, E Denmark 55.39N 12.19E
113 I24 **Tab** Somogy, W Hungary 46.40N 18.01E
179 Q11 **Tabaco** Luzon, N Philippines 13.22N 123.42E
194 M7 **Tabalo** Mussau Island, NE PNG 1.22S 149.37E
106 K5 **Tábara** Castilla-León, N Spain 41.49N 5.57W
195 P9 **Tabar Island** island Tabar Islands, N PNG
195 P9 **Tabar Islands** island group NE PNG
Tabariya, Bahrat see Tiberias, Lake
149 S7 **Tabas** var. Golshan. Yazd, C Iran 33.37N 56.54E
45 P15 **Tabasará, Serranía de** ▲▲ W Panama
43 U15 **Tabasco** ◐ state SE Mexico
Tabasco see Grijalva, Río
131 Q2 **Tabashino** Respublika Mariy El, W Russian Federation 57.00N 47.47E
60 B13 **Tabatinga** Amazonas, N Brazil 4.13S 69.43W
76 G9 **Tabelbala** W Algeria 29.22N 3.01W
9 Q17 **Taber** Alberta, SW Canada 49.48N 112.09W
176 W14 **Taberfane** Pulau Trangan, E Indonesia 6.14S 134.08E
97 L19 **Taberg** Jönköping, S Sweden 57.42N 14.04E
Tabibug see Tabibuga
194 H12 **Tabibuga** var. Tabibug. Western Highlands, C PNG 5.32S 144.37E
203 O3 **Tabiteuea** prev. Drummond Island. atoll Tungaru, W Kiribati
179 Q12 **Tablas Island** island C Philippines
179 Pp12 **Tablas Strait** strait C Philippines
192 M16 **Table Bay** bay SE PNG
192 Q10 **Table Cape** headland North Island, NZ 39.07S 178.00E
11 S13 **Table Mountain** ▲ Newfoundland and Labrador, E Canada 47.39N 59.15W
181 P17 **Table, Pointe de la** headland SE Réunion 21.19S 55.49E
29 S8 **Table Rock Lake** ▣ Arkansas/Missouri, C USA
38 K14 **Table Top** ▲ Arizona, SW USA 32.45N 112.07W
194 J13 **Tabletop, Mount** ▲ C PNG 6.51S 146.00E
126 Mm5 **Tabor** Respublika Sakha (Yakutiya), NE Russian Federation 71.14N 150.23E
31 S15 **Tabor** Iowa, C USA 40.54N 95.40W
113 D18 **Tábor** Jihočeský Kraj, S Czech Republic 49.25N 14.40E
83 F21 **Tabora** Tabora, W Tanzania 5.04S 32.49E
83 F21 **Tabora** ◐ region C Tanzania
23 U12 **Tabor City** North Carolina, SE USA 34.09N 78.52W
153 Q10 **Taboshar** NW Tajikistan 40.37N 69.33E
78 L18 **Tabou** var. Tabu. S Ivory Coast 4.28N 7.19W
148 J2 **Tabrīz** var. Tebriz; anc. Tauris. Āžarbāyjān-e Khāvarī, NW Iran 38.04N 46.18E
Tabu see Tabou
203 W1 **Tabuaeran** prev. Fanning Island. atoll Line Islands, E Kiribati
194 E11 **Tabubil** Western, SW PNG 5.13S 141.13E
179 P8 **Tabuk** Luzon, N Philippines 17.26N 121.25E
146 J4 **Tabūk** Tabūk, NW Saudi Arabia 28.25N 36.33E
146 J5 **Tabūk** off. Minṭaqat Tabūk. ◐ province NW Saudi Arabia
197 B12 **Tabwemasana, Mount** ▲ Espiritu Santo, W Vanuatu 15.22S 166.44E
97 O15 **Täby** Stockholm, C Sweden 59.28N 18.04E
43 N14 **Tacámbaro** Michoacán de Ocampo, SW Mexico 19.12N 101.27W
44 A5 **Tacaná, Volcán** ☒ Guatemala/Mexico 15.07N 92.06W
45 X16 **Tacarcuna, Cerro** ▲ SE Panama 8.08N 77.15W
Tachau see Tachov
164 J3 **Tacheng** var. Qoqek. Xinjiang Uygur Zizhiqu, NW China 46.45N 82.55E
56 H7 **Táchira** off. Estado Táchira. ◐ state W Venezuela
167 T13 **Tachoshui** N Taiwan 24.26N 121.43E
113 A17 **Tachov** Ger. Tachau. Plzeňský Kraj, W Czech Republic 49.48N 12.37E
179 R13 **Tacloban** off. Tacloban City. Leyte, C Philippines 11.15N 124.59E
59 I19 **Tacna** Tacna, SE Peru 18.00S 70.15W
59 H18 **Tacna** off. Departamento de Tacna. ◐ department S Peru
34 H8 **Tacoma** Washington, NW USA 47.15N 122.26W
20 L11 **Taconic Range** ▲▲ NE USA
64 L6 **Taco Pozo** Formosa, N Argentina 25.35S 63.15W
59 M20 **Tacsara, Cordillera de** ▲▲ S Bolivia
63 F17 **Tacuarembó** prev. San Fructuoso. Tacuarembó, C Uruguay 31.42S 56.00W
63 E18 **Tacuarembó** ◐ department C Uruguay
63 F17 **Tacuarembó, Río** ⟿ C Uruguay
85 I14 **Tacuili** North Western, NW Zambia 14.17S 26.51E
179 R16 **Tacurong** Mindanao, S Philippines 6.42N 124.40E
171 Kk13 **Tadamu-gawa** ⟿ Honshū, C Japan
79 V8 **Tadek** ⟿ NW Niger
76 J9 **Tademaït, Plateau du** plateau C Algeria
197 K6 **Tadine** Province des Îles Loyauté, E New Caledonia 21.33S 167.54E
82 L11 **Tadjoura** E Djibouti 11.47N 42.51E
82 M11 **Tadjoura, Golfe de** Eng. Gulf of Tajura. inlet E Djibouti
Tadmor/Tadmur see Tudmur
9 W10 **Tadoule Lake** ◎ Manitoba, C Canada
13 S8 **Tadoussac** Québec, SE Canada 48.07N 69.55W
161 H18 **Tādpatri** Andhra Pradesh, E India 14.55N 77.58E
Tadzhikabad see Tojikobod
Tadzhikistan see Tajikistan
169 Y14 **T'aebaek-sanmaek** ▲▲ E South Korea
169 V15 **Taechŏng-do** island NW South Korea
169 X13 **Taedong-gang** ⟿ C North Korea
169 Y16 **Taegu** off. Taegu-gwangyŏksi, var. Daegu, Jap. Taikyū. SE South Korea 35.55N 128.32E
Taehan-haehyŏp see Korea Strait
Taehan Min'guk see South Korea
169 Y15 **Taejŏn** off. Taejŏn-gwangyŏksi, Jap. Taiden. C South Korea 36.19N 127.28E
200 T11 **Tafahi** island N Tonga
107 Q4 **Tafalla** Navarra, N Spain 42.31N 1.40W
77 M12 **Tafassâsset, Oued** ⟿ SE Algeria
79 W7 **Tafassâsset, Ténéré du** desert N Niger
57 U11 **Tafelberg** ▲ S Suriname 3.55N 56.09W
99 J21 **Taff** ⟿ SE Wales, UK
Tafila/Ṭafīlah, Muḥāfaẓat aṭ see Aṭ Ṭafīlah
79 N15 **Tafiré** N Ivory Coast 9.04N 5.10W
148 M6 **Tafresh** Markazī, W Iran 34.40N 50.00E
149 Q9 **Taft** Yazd, C Iran 31.48N 54.10E
37 R13 **Taft** California, W USA 35.08N 119.27W
27 T14 **Taft** Texas, SW USA 27.58N 97.24W
149 W12 **Taftān, Kūh-e** ▲ SE Iran 28.38N 61.06E
37 R13 **Taft Heights** California, W USA 35.06N 119.29W
201 Y14 **Tafunsak** Kosrae, E Micronesia 5.21N 162.58E
198 Aa8 **Tāga** Savai'i, SW Samoa 13.46S 172.31W
155 O6 **Tagāb** Kāpīsā, E Afghanistan 33.52N 66.22E
41 O8 **Tagagawik River** ⟿ Alaska, USA
171 M13 **Tagajō** var. Tagayō. Miyagi, Honshū, C Japan 38.21N 141.02E
130 K12 **Taganrog** Rostovskaya Oblast', SW Russian Federation 47.10N 38.54E
130 K12 **Taganrog, Gulf of** Rus. Taganrogskiy Zaliv, Ukr. Tahanroz'ka Zatoka. gulf Russian Federation/Ukraine
Taganrogskiy Zaliv see Taganrog, Gulf of
78 J8 **Tagant** ◐ region C Mauritania
154 M14 **Tagas** Baluchistān, SW Pakistan 27.09N 64.36E
170 D13 **Tagawa** Fukuoka, Kyūshū, SW Japan 33.37N 130.46E
179 P11 **Tagaytay** Luzon, N Philippines 14.04N 120.55E
Tagazyō see Tagajō
179 Qq14 **Tagbilaran** var. Tagbilaran City. Bohol, C Philippines 9.41N 123.54E
108 B10 **Taggia** Liguria, NW Italy 43.51N 7.48E
79 V9 **Taghouaji, Massif de** ▲ C Niger 17.13N 8.37E
109 J15 **Tagliacozzo** Lazio, C Italy 42.03N 13.15E
108 J7 **Tagliamento** ⟿ NE Italy
179 R15 **Tagoloan** Mindanao, S Philippines 8.30N 124.45E
155 N3 **Tagow Bāy** var. Bai. Sar-e Pol, N Afghanistan 35.41N 66.01E
152 H9 **Tagta** var. Tahta, Rus. Takhta. Daşoguz Welaýaty, N Turkmenistan 41.40N 59.51E
152 J16 **Tagtabazar** Rus. Takhtabazar. Mary Welaýaty, S Turkmenistan 35.57N 62.49E
61 L17 **Taguatinga** Tocantins, C Brazil 12.16S 46.25W
195 Q17 **Tagula** Tagula Island, SE PNG 11.21S 153.13E
195 P17 **Tagula Island** prev. Southeast Island, Sudest Island. island SE PNG
179 Rr15 **Tagum** Mindanao, S Philippines 7.22N 125.51E
56 C7 **Tagún, Cerro** elevation Colombia/Panama 7.57N 77.13W
107 P7 **Tagus** Port. Rio Tejo, Sp. Río Tajo. ⟿ Portugal/Spain
66 M9 **Tagus Plain** undersea feature E Atlantic Ocean
203 S10 **Tahaa** island Îles Sous le Vent, W French Polynesia
203 U10 **Tahanea** atoll Îles Tuamotu, C French Polynesia
Tahanroz'ka Zatoka see Taganrog, Gulf of
171 I16 **Tahara** Aichi, Honshū, SW Japan 34.40N 137.15E
76 K12 **Tahat** ▲ SE Algeria 23.15N 5.34E
169 U4 **Tahe** Heilongjiang, NE China 52.21N 124.42E
168 G9 **Tahilt** Govĭ-Altay, W Mongolia 45.20N 96.42E
203 T10 **Tahiti** island Îles du Vent, W French Polynesia
Tahiti, Archipel de see Société, Archipel de la
120 E4 **Tahkuna nina** headland W Estonia 59.06N 22.35E
154 K12 **Tāhlāb** ⟿ W Pakistan
154 K12 **Tāhlāb, Dasht-i** desert SW Pakistan
29 R10 **Tahlequah** Oklahoma, C USA 35.55N 94.58W
37 Q6 **Tahoe City** California, W USA 39.09N 120.09W
37 P6 **Tahoe, Lake** ◎ California/Nevada, W USA
Tahoena see Tahuna
27 N6 **Tahoka** Texas, SW USA 33.10N 101.47W
34 F8 **Taholah** Washington, NW USA 47.19N 124.17W
79 T11 **Tahoua** Tahoua, W Niger 14.52N 5.18E
79 T11 **Tahoua** ◐ department W Niger
33 P3 **Tahquamenon Falls** waterfall Michigan, N USA 46.34N 85.14W
33 P4 **Tahquamenon River** ⟿ Michigan, N USA
145 V10 **Taḥrīr** S Iraq 31.58N 45.34E
8 K17 **Tahsis** Vancouver Island, British Columbia, SW Canada 49.42N 126.31W
Tahta see Tagta
77 W9 **Ṭahta** C Egypt 26.40N 31.27E
142 L15 **Tahtalı Dağları** ▲▲ C Turkey
59 I14 **Tahuamanu, Río** ⟿ Bolivia/Peru
58 F13 **Tahuanía, Río** ⟿ E Peru
203 X7 **Tahuata** island Îles Marquises, NE French Polynesia
175 S6 **Tahulandang, Pulau** island N Indonesia
175 S5 **Tahuna** prev. Tahoena. Pulau Sangihe, N Indonesia 3.33N 125.33E
176 Yy10 **Tahun, Danau** see Tahun, Danau
78 L17 **Taï** SW Ivory Coast 5.53N 7.28W
167 P5 **Tai'an** Shandong, E China 36.13N 117.12E
203 R8 **Taiarapu, Presqu'île de** peninsula Tahiti, W French Polynesia
Taibad see Tāybād
166 K7 **Taibai Shan** ▲ C China 33.57N 107.31E
107 Q12 **Taibilla, Sierra de** ▲▲ S Spain
Taibus Qi see Baochang
Taichū see T'aichung
167 S13 **T'aichung** Jap. Taichū; prev. Taiwan. C Taiwan 24.09N 120.40E
Taiden see Taejŏn
193 E23 **Taieri** ⟿ South Island, NZ
117 E21 **Taígetos** ▲▲ S Greece
167 N4 **Taihang Shan** ▲▲ C China
192 M11 **Taihape** Manawatu-Wanganui, North Island, NZ 39.41S 175.46E
167 O7 **Taihe** Anhui, E China 33.14N 115.35E
167 O12 **Taihe** var. Chengjiang. Jiangxi, S China 26.50N 114.49E
Taihoku see T'aipei
167 R8 **Tai Hu** ◎ E China
167 P9 **Taihu** Anhui, E China 30.26N 116.13E
165 O9 **Taikang** var. Dorbod, Dorbod Mongolzu Zizhixian. Heilongjiang, NE China 46.50N 124.25E
167 O6 **Taikang** Henan, C China 34.06N 114.53E
172 P7 **Taiki** Hokkaidō, NE Japan 42.29N 143.15E
177 Ff8 **Taikkyi** Yangon, SW Myanmar 17.16N 95.55E
Taikyū see Taegu
169 U8 **Tailai** Heilongjiang, NE China 46.25N 123.25E
173 Ff10 **Taileleo** Pulau Siberut, W Indonesia 1.45S 99.06E
190 J10 **Tailem Bend** South Australia 35.20S 139.33E
98 I8 **Tain** N Scotland, UK 57.49N 4.04W
167 S14 **T'ainan** Jap. Tainan; prev. Dainan. S Taiwan 23.00N 120.05E
117 E22 **Taínaro, Akrotírio** headland S Greece 36.41N 22.28E
167 Q11 **Taining** var. Shancheng. Fujian, SE China 26.55N 117.13E
203 W7 **Taiohae** prev. Madisonville. Nuku Hiva, NE French Polynesia 8.55S 140.04W
167 T13 **T'aipei** Jap. Taihoku; prev. Daihoku. ● (Taiwan) N Taiwan 25.01N 121.28E
174 Gg3 **Taiping** Perak, Peninsular Malaysia 4.54N 100.42E
169 S8 **Taiping Ling** ▲ NE China 47.27N 120.27E
172 N6 **Taisei** Hokkaidō, NE Japan 42.13N 139.52E
170 F12 **Taisha** Shimane, Honshū, SW Japan 35.23N 132.40E
111 R4 **Taiskirchen** Oberösterreich, NW Austria 48.15N 13.33E
65 F20 **Taitao, Peninsula de** peninsula S Chile
Taitō see T'aitung
167 T14 **T'aitung** Jap. Taitō. S Taiwan 22.49N 121.04E
94 M13 **Taivalkoski** Oulu, E Finland 65.34N 28.19E
95 K19 **Taivassalo** Länsi-Suomi, W Finland 60.35N 21.36E
167 T14 **Taiwan** off. Republic of China, var. Formosa, Formo'sa. ◆ republic E Asia
139 Q11 **Taiwan** var. Formosa. island E Asia
Taiwan see T'aichung
T'aiwan Haihsia/Taiwan Haixia see Taiwan Strait
Taiwan Shan see Chungyang Shanmo
167 R13 **Taiwan Strait** var. Formosa Strait, Chin. T'aiwan Haihsia, Taiwan Haixia. strait China/Taiwan
167 N4 **Taiyuan** prev. T'ai-yuan, T'ai-yüan, Yangku. Shanxi, C China 37.48N 112.33E
167 R7 **Taizhou** Jiangsu, E China 32.36N 119.52E
167 S10 **Taizhou** var. Jiaojiang; prev. Haimen. Zhejiang, SE China 28.36N 121.19E
Taizhou see Linhai
147 O16 **Ta'izz** SW Yemen 13.36N 44.04E
147 O16 **Ta'izz** ✈ SW Yemen 13.40N 44.10E
77 P12 **Tajarhi** SW Libya 24.21N 14.28E
153 P13 **Tajikistan** off. Republic of Tajikistan, Rus. Tadzhikistan, Taj. Jumhurii Tojikiston; prev. Tajik S.S.R. ◆ republic C Asia
Tajik S.S.R see Tajikistan
171 Kk14 **Tajima** Fukushima, Honshū, C Japan 37.10N 139.46E
Tajoe see Tayu
Tajo, Río see Tagus
44 B5 **Tajumulco, Volcán** ▲ W Guatemala 15.04N 91.50W
107 P7 **Tajuña** ⟿ C Spain
Tajura, Gulf of see Tadjoura, Golfe de
178 H9 **Tak** var. Rahaeng. Tak, W Thailand 16.51N 99.07E
201 U4 **Taka Atoll** var. Tōke. atoll Ratak Chain, N Marshall Islands
171 L16 **Takahagi** Ibaraki, Honshū, S Japan 36.43N 140.40E
170 Ff13 **Takahashi** var. Takahasi. Okayama, Honshū, SW Japan 34.48N 133.37E
170 F13 **Takahashi-gawa** ⟿ Honshū, SW Japan
Takahasi see Takahashi
201 P12 **Takaieu Island** island E Micronesia
192 I13 **Takaka** Tasman, South Island, NZ 40.52S 172.49E
175 P13 **Takalar** Sulawesi, C Indonesia 5.28S 119.24E
170 Ff14 **Takamatsu** var. Takamatu. Kagawa, Shikoku, SW Japan 34.18N 133.58E
Takamatu see Takamatsu
170 Cc14 **Takamori** Kumamoto, Kyūshū, SW Japan 32.50N 131.08E
170 Cc16 **Takanabe** Miyazaki, Kyūshū, SW Japan 32.13N 131.31E
175 O16 **Takan, Gunung** ▲ Pulau Sumba, S Indonesia 8.52S 117.32E
171 M9 **Takanosu** Akita, Honshū, C Japan 40.13N 140.23E
Takao see Kaohsiung
171 I13 **Takaoka** Toyama, Honshū, SW Japan 36.43N 137.01E
192 N12 **Takapau** Hawke's Bay, North Island, NZ 40.01S 176.21E
203 U9 **Takapoto** atoll Îles Tuamotu, C French Polynesia
192 L5 **Takapuna** Auckland, North Island, NZ 36.48S 174.45E
171 Gg14 **Takarazuka** Hyōgo, Honshū, SW Japan 34.48N 135.18E
203 U9 **Takaroa** atoll Îles Tuamotu, C French Polynesia
171 Jj15 **Takasaki** Gunma, Honshū, S Japan 36.20N 139.00E
171 Gg15 **Takatsuki** var. Takatuki. Ōsaka, Honshū, SW Japan 34.50N 135.36E
Takatuki see Takatsuki
171 Ii14 **Takayama** Gifu, Honshū, SW Japan 36.09N 137.17E
171 Hh13 **Takefu** var. Takehu. Fukui, Honshū, SW Japan 35.55N 136.11E
170 F14 **Takehara** Hiroshima, Honshū, SW Japan 34.19N 132.52E
Takehu see Takefu
170 C13 **Takeo** Saga, Kyūshū, SW Japan 33.12N 130.01E
Takeo see Takêv
170 B17 **Take-shima** island Nansei-shotō, SW Japan
148 M5 **Tākestān** var. Takistan; prev. Siadehan. Qazvin, N Iran 36.02N 49.36E
170 D14 **Taketa** Ōita, Kyūshū, SW Japan 32.58N 131.21E
178 J14 **Takêv** prev. Takeo. Takêv, S Cambodia 10.58N 104.46E
178 Hh10 **Tak Fah** Nakhon Sawan, C Thailand
145 T13 **Takhādīd** well S Iraq 29.56N 44.33E
155 R3 **Takhār** ◐ province NE Afghanistan
Takhiatash see Taxiatosh
178 J13 **Ta Khmau** Kândal, S Cambodia 11.30N 104.59E
Takhta see Tagta
Takhtabazar see Tagtabazar
151 O8 **Takhtabrod** Severnyy Kazakhstan, N Kazakhstan 52.35N 67.37E
Takhtakupyr see Taxtako'pir
148 M8 **Takht-e Shāh, Kūh-e** ▲ C Iran
79 V12 **Takiéta** Zinder, S Niger 13.43N 8.33E
15 I5 **Takijuq Lake** ◎ Nunavut, NW Canada
172 P4 **Takikawa** Hokkaidō, NE Japan 43.34N 141.54E
172 Pp4 **Takinoue** Hokkaidō, NE Japan 44.10N 143.09E
Takistan see Tākestān
193 B23 **Takitimu Mountains** ▲▲ South Island, NZ
Takkaze see Tekezē
172 N10 **Takko** Aomori, Honshū, C Japan 40.19N 141.11E
8 L13 **Takla Lake** ◎ British Columbia, SW Canada
Takla Makan Desert see Taklimakan Shamo
164 H9 **Taklimakan Shamo** Eng. Takla Makan Desert. desert NW China
178 Jj12 **Takôk** Môndól Kiri, E Cambodia 12.37N 106.30E
175 P9 **Takolekaju, Pegunungan** ▲▲ Sulawesi, N Indonesia
41 P10 **Takotna** Alaska, USA 62.59N 156.03W
Takow see Kaohsiung
126 Kk14 **Taksimo** Respublika Buryatiya, S Russian Federation 56.18N 114.53E
170 Cc13 **Taku** Saga, Kyūshū, SW Japan 33.17N 130.07E
8 I10 **Taku** ⟿ British Columbia, W Canada
177 G15 **Takua Pa** var. Ban Takua Pa. Phangnga, SW Thailand 8.47N 98.16E
79 W16 **Takum** Taraba, E Nigeria 7.16N 10.00E
203 V10 **Takume** atoll Îles Tuamotu, C French Polynesia
202 L16 **Takutea** island S Cook Islands
195 U11 **Takuu Islands** prev. Mortlock Group. island group NE PNG
121 L18 **Tal'** Rus. Tal'. Minskaya Voblasts', S Belarus 52.52N 27.59E
42 L13 **Tala** Jalisco, C Mexico 20.39N 103.45W
63 F19 **Tala** Canelones, S Uruguay 34.24S 55.45W
Talabriga see Aveiro, Portugal
Talabriga see Talavera de la Reina, Spain
121 N14 **Talachyn** Rus. Tolochin. Vitsyebskaya Voblasts', NE Belarus 54.25N 29.42E
155 U7 **Talagang** Punjab, E Pakistan 32.55N 72.25E
161 J23 **Talaimannar** Northern Province, NW Sri Lanka 9.07N 79.45E
119 R3 **Talalayivka** Chernihivs'ka Oblast', N Ukraine 50.51N 33.09E
45 O15 **Talamanca, Cordillera de** ▲▲ S Costa Rica
58 A9 **Talara** Piura, NW Peru 4.31S 81.17W
106 L11 **Talarrubias** Extremadura, W Spain 39.03N 5.13W
153 S8 **Talas** Talasskaya Oblast', NW Kyrgyzstan 42.29N 72.21E
153 S8 **Talas** ⟿ NW Kyrgyzstan
195 N11 **Talasea** New Britain, E PNG 5.19S 150.02E
Talas Oblasty see Talasskaya Oblast'
153 S8 **Talasskaya Oblast'** Kir. Talas Oblasty. ◐ province NW Kyrgyzstan
153 S8 **Talasskiy Alatau, Khrebet** ▲▲ Kazakhstan/Kyrgyzstan
79 U12 **Talata Mafara** Zamfara, NW Nigeria 12.33N 6.01E
175 Ss4 **Talaud, Kepulauan** island group E Indonesia
106 M9 **Talavera de la Reina** anc. Caesarobriga, Talabriga. Castilla-La Mancha, C Spain 39.58N 4.49W
106 J11 **Talavera la Real** Extremadura, W Spain 38.52N 6.46W
194 L12 **Talawe, Mount** ▲ New Britain, C PNG 5.30S 148.24E
25 S5 **Talbotton** Georgia, SE USA 32.40N 84.32W
191 R7 **Talbragar River** ⟿ New South Wales, SE Australia
64 G13 **Talca** Maule, C Chile 35.28S 71.42W
64 F13 **Talcahuano** Bío Bío, C Chile 36.43S 73.07W
160 N12 **Tālcher** Orissa, E India 20.57N 85.13E
27 W5 **Talco** Texas, SW USA 33.21N 95.06W
151 V14 **Taldykorgan** Kaz. Taldyqorghan; prev. Taldy-Kurgan. Almaty, SE Kazakhstan 45.00N 78.23E
Taldy-Kurgan/Taldyqorghan see Taldykorgan
153 Y7 **Taldy-Suu** Issyk-Kul'skaya Oblast', E Kyrgyzstan 42.49N 78.33E
153 U10 **Taldy-Suu** Oshskaya Oblast', SW Kyrgyzstan 40.33N 73.52E
Tal-e Khosravī see Yāsūj
200 Ss14 **Taleki Tonga** island Otu Tolu Group, C Tonga
200 Ss13 **Taleki Vavu'u** island Otu Tolu Group, C Tonga
104 J13 **Talence** Gironde, SW France 44.49N 0.35W
151 U16 **Talgar** Kaz. Talghar. Almaty, SE Kazakhstan 43.25N 77.07E
Talghar see Talgar
175 Rr10 **Taliabu, Pulau** island Kepulauan Sula, C Indonesia
117 L22 **Taliarós, Akrotírio** headland Astypálaia, Kykládes, Greece, Aegean Sea 36.31N 26.18E
Ta-lien see Dalian
29 Q12 **Talihina** Oklahoma, C USA 34.45N 95.03W
Talimardzhan see Tollimarjon
Talin see T'alin
143 T12 **T'alin** Rus. Talin; prev. Verin T'alin. W Armenia 40.23N 43.51E
83 E15 **Tali Post** Bahr el Gabel, S Sudan 5.55N 30.43E
Taliq-an see Tāloqān
Talış Dağları see Talish Mountains
148 L2 **Talish Mountains** Az. Talış Dağları, Per. Kūhhā-ye Ṭavālesh, Rus. Talyshskiye Gory. ▲▲ Azerbaijan/Iran
125 F11 **Talitsa** Sverdlovskaya Oblast', C Russian Federation 56.58N 63.34E
175 O16 **Taliwang** Sumbawa, C Indonesia 8.45S 116.55E
121 L17 **Tal'ka** Rus. Tal'ka. Minskaya Voblasts', C Belarus 53.22N 28.22E
41 R11 **Talkeetna** Alaska, USA 62.19N 150.06W
41 R11 **Talkeetna Mountains** ▲▲ Alaska, USA
Talkhof see Puurmani
94 H2 **Tálknafjördhur** Vestfirdhir, W Iceland 65.38N 23.51W
145 Q3 **Tall 'Abṭah** N Iraq 35.52N 42.40E
144 M2 **Tall Abyaḍ** var. Tell Abiad. Ar Raqqah, N Syria 36.42N 38.56E
25 Q4 **Talladega** Alabama, S USA 33.26N 86.06W
145 Q2 **Tall 'Afar** N Iraq 36.22N 42.27E
25 S8 **Tallahassee** prev. Muskogean. state capital Florida, SE USA 30.26N 84.16W
24 L2 **Tallahatchie River** ⟿ Mississippi, S USA
Tall al Abyaḍ see Tall Abyaḍ
145 W12 **Tall al Laḥm** S Iraq 30.46N 46.22E
191 P11 **Tallangatta** Victoria, SE Australia 36.15S 147.13E
25 R4 **Tallapoosa River** ⟿ Alabama/Georgia, S USA
105 T13 **Tallard** Hautes-Alpes, SE France 44.30N 6.04E
145 Q3 **Tall ash Sha'īr** N Iraq 36.11N 42.26E
25 Q5 **Tallassee** Alabama, S USA 32.32N 85.53W
145 R4 **Tall 'Azbah** NW Iraq 35.47N 43.13E
144 I5 **Tall Bīsah** Ḥimṣ, W Syria 34.49N 36.43E
145 R3 **Tall Ḥassūnah** N Iraq 36.05N 43.10E
145 Q2 **Tall Ḥuqnah** var. Tell Ḥuqnah. N Iraq 36.33N 42.34E
Tallin see Tallinn
120 G3 **Tallinn** Ger. Reval, Rus. Tallin; prev. Revel. ● (Estonia) Harjumaa, NW Estonia 59.25N 24.42E
120 H3 **Tallinn** ✈ Harjumaa, NW Estonia 59.23N 24.52E
144 H5 **Tall Kalakh** var. Tell Kalakh. Ḥimṣ, C Syria 34.40N 36.18E
145 R2 **Tall Kayf** NW Iraq 36.30N 43.07E
Tall Kūchak see Tall Kūshik
145 P2 **Tall Kūshik** var. Tall Kūchak. Al Ḥasakah, E Syria 36.48N 42.01E
33 U12 **Tallmadge** Ohio, N USA 41.06N 81.26W
24 J5 **Tallulah** Louisiana, S USA 32.22N 91.12W
145 Q2 **Tall 'Uwaynāt** NW Iraq 36.43N 42.18E
145 Q2 **Tall Ẓāhir** N Iraq 36.51N 42.29E
126 H14 **Tal'menka** Altayskiy Kray, S Russian Federation 53.55N 83.26E
126 I8 **Talnakh** Taymyrskiy (Dolgano-Nenetskiy) Avtonomnyy Okrug, N Russian Federation 69.26N 88.26E
119 P7 **Tal'ne** Rus. Tal'noye. Cherkas'ka Oblast', C Ukraine 48.54N 30.39E
Tal'noye see Tal'ne
82 E12 **Talodi** Southern Kordofan, C Sudan 10.40N 30.25E
196 B16 **Talofofo** SE Guam 13.21N 144.45E
196 B16 **Talofofo Bay** bay SE Guam
28 L9 **Taloga** Oklahoma, C USA 36.01N 98.58W
127 O10 **Talon** Magadanskaya Oblast', E Russian Federation 59.47N 148.46E
12 H11 **Talon, Lake** ◎ Ontario, S Canada
155 R2 **Tāloqān** var. Taliq-an. Takhār, NE Afghanistan 36.43N 69.33E
130 M8 **Talovaya** Voronezhskaya Oblast', W Russian Federation 51.07N 40.46E
175 Qq10 **Talowa, Teluk** bay Sulawesi, C Indonesia
15 Kk3 **Taloyoak** prev. Spence Bay. Nunavut, N Canada 69.30N 93.25W
27 Q8 **Talpa** Texas, SW USA 31.46N 99.42W
42 K13 **Talpa de Allende** Jalisco, C Mexico 20.22N 104.51W
25 S9 **Talquin, Lake** ◎ Florida, SE USA
Talsen see Talsi
168 H9 **Talshand** Govĭ-Altay, C Mongolia 45.21N 98.00E
120 E8 **Talsi** Ger. Talsen. Talsi, NW Latvia 57.14N 22.34E
149 V11 **Tal Sīāh** Sīstān va Balūchestān, SE Iran 28.19N 57.43E
64 G6 **Taltal** Antofagasta, N Chile 25.22S 70.27W
15 I8 **Taltson** ⟿ Northwest Territories, NW Canada
174 H8 **Taluk** Sumatera, W Indonesia 0.30S 101.36E
94 J8 **Talvik** Finnmark, N Norway 70.02N 22.58E
190 M7 **Talyawalka Creek** ⟿ New South Wales, SE Australia
Talyshskiye Gory see Talish Mountains
31 W14 **Tama** Iowa, C USA 41.58N 92.34W
Tama Abu, Banjaran see Penambo, Banjaran
175 N5 **Tamabo, Banjaran** ▲▲ East Malaysia
202 B16 **Tamakautoga** SW Niue 19.04S 169.55W
131 N7 **Tamala** Penzenskaya Oblast', W Russian Federation 52.32N 43.18E
79 P15 **Tamale** C Ghana 9.21N 0.54W
170 Cc13 **Tamana** Kumamoto, Kyūshū, SW Japan 32.54N 130.34E
203 P3 **Tamana** prev. Rotcher Island. atoll Tungaru, W Kiribati
170 Ff14 **Tamano** Okayama, Honshū, SW Japan 34.28N 133.53E
76 K12 **Tamanrasset** var. Tamenghest. S Algeria 22.49N 5.31E
76 J13 **Tamanrasset** wadi Algeria/Mali
177 G2 **Tamanthi** Sagaing, N Myanmar 25.17N 95.18E
99 I24 **Tamar** ⟿ SW England, UK
Tamar see Tudmur
56 H9 **Támara** Casanare, C Colombia 5.51N 72.10W
56 F7 **Tamar, Alto de** ▲ C Colombia 7.25N 74.28W
181 X16 **Tamarin** E Mauritius 20.19S 57.22E
107 T5 **Tamarite de Litera** var. Tararite de Llitera. Aragón, NE Spain 41.52N 0.25E
113 I24 **Tamási** Tolna, S Hungary 46.39N 18.16E
Tamatave see Toamasina
43 O9 **Tamaulipas** ◐ state C Mexico
43 P10 **Tamaulipas, Sierra de** ▲ C Mexico
58 F12 **Tamaya, Río** ⟿ E Peru
42 I9 **Tamazula** Durango, C Mexico 24.43N 106.33W
42 L14 **Tamazula** Jalisco, C Mexico 19.41N 103.18W
Tamazulápam see Tamazulapán
43 Q15 **Tamazulapán** var. Tamazulápam. Oaxaca, SE Mexico 17.40N 97.33W
43 P12 **Tamazunchale** San Luis Potosí, C Mexico 21.17N 98.45W
78 H11 **Tambacounda** SE Senegal 13.43N 13.43W
85 M16 **Tambara** Manica, C Mozambique 16.45S 34.14E
175 Pp9 **Tambarana** Sulawesi, N Indonesia 1.09S 120.30E
79 T13 **Tambawel** Sokoto, NW Nigeria 12.24N 4.42E
195 W15 **Tambea** Guadalcanal, C Solomon Islands 9.19S 159.42E
174 Jj7 **Tambelan, Kepulauan** island group W Indonesia
59 E15 **Tambo de Mora** Ica, W Peru 13.43S 76.12W
175 Oo15 **Tambora, Gunung** ☒ Sumbawa, S Indonesia 8.16S 117.59E
63 E17 **Tambores** Paysandú, W Uruguay 31.49S 56.16W
59 F14 **Tambo, Río** ⟿ C Peru
58 F7 **Tamboryacu, Río** ⟿ N Peru
130 M7 **Tambov** Tambovskaya Oblast', W Russian Federation 52.43N 41.28E
130 L6 **Tambovskaya Oblast'** ◐ province W Russian Federation
106 H3 **Tambre** ⟿ NW Spain
175 Nn3 **Tambunan** Sabah, East Malaysia 5.40N 116.22E
83 C15 **Tambura** Western Equatoria, SW Sudan 5.37N 27.30E
175 P8 **Tambu, Teluk** bay Sulawesi, C Indonesia
Tamchaket see Tâmchekkeṭ
78 J9 **Tâmchekkeṭ** var. Tamchaket. Hodh el Gharbi, S Mauritania 17.12N 10.36W
178 Jj7 **Tam Điệp** Ninh Binh, N Vietnam 20.09N 105.54E
Tamdybulak see Tomdibuloq
56 H8 **Tame** Arauca, C Colombia 6.27N 71.44W
106 H6 **Tâmega, Rio** Sp. Río Támega. ⟿ Portugal/Spain

◆ Country ● Country Capital ◇ Dependent Territory ○ Dependent Territory Capital ◐ Administrative Region ✈ International Airport ▲ Mountain ▲▲ Mountain Range ☒ Volcano ⟿ River ◎ Lake ▣ Reservoir

TAMÉLOS, AKROTÍRIO – TAXTAKO'PIR

117 H20 **Tamélos, Akrotírio** *headland* Kéa, Kykládes, Greece, Aegean Sea *37.31N 24.16E*
Tamenghest *see* Tamanrasset
79 V8 **Tamgak, Adrar** ▲ C Niger *19.10N 8.39E*
78 I13 **Tamgue** ▲ NW Guinea *12.14N 12.18W*
43 Q12 **Tamiahua** Veracruz-Llave, E Mexico *21.15N 97.27W*
43 Q12 **Tamiahua, Laguna de** *lagoon* E Mexico
25 Y16 **Tamiami Canal** *canal* Florida, SE USA
196 F17 **Tamil Harbor** *harbor* Yap, W Micronesia
161 H21 **Tamil Nādu** *prev.* Madras. ◐ *state* SE India
101 H20 **Tamines** Namur, S Belgium *50.27N 4.37E*
118 E12 **Tamiš** *Ger.* Temesch, *Hung.* Temes, *SCr.* Tamiš. ≈ Romania/Serbia and Montenegro (Yugoslavia)
178 Kk10 **Tam Ky** Quang Nam-Đa Nâng, C Vietnam *15.31N 108.30E*
Tammerfors *see* Tampere
Tammisaari *see* Ekenäs
97 N14 **Tämnaren** ◎ C Sweden
203 Q7 **Tamotoe, Passe** *passage* Tahiti, W French Polynesia
25 V12 **Tampa** Florida, SE USA *27.57N 82.27W*
25 V12 **Tampa** ✕ Florida, SE USA *27.57N 82.29W*
25 V13 **Tampa Bay** *bay* Florida, SE USA
95 L18 **Tampere** *Swe.* Tammerfors. Länsi-Suomi, W Finland *61.30N 23.45E*
43 Q11 **Tampico** Tamaulipas, C Mexico *22.18N 97.52W*
175 Qq12 **Tampo** Pulau Muna, C Indonesia *4.38S 122.40E*
178 Kk11 **Tam Quan** Binh Đinh, C Vietnam *14.34N 109.00E*
176 V9 **Tamrau, Pegunungan** ▲▲ Papua, E Indonesia
168 J13 **Tamsag Muchang** Nei Mongol Zizhiqu, N China *40.28N 102.34E*
Tamsal *see* Tamsalu
120 I4 **Tamsalu** *Ger.* Tamsal. Lääne-Virumaa, NE Estonia *59.10N 26.07E*
111 S8 **Tamsweg** Salzburg, SW Austria *47.07N 13.49E*
177 Ff3 **Tamu** Sagaing, N Myanmar *24.11N 94.21E*
43 P12 **Tamuín** San Luis Potosí, C Mexico *21.57N 98.46W*
196 C15 **Tamuning** NW Guam *13.29N 144.47E*
191 T6 **Tamworth** New South Wales, SE Australia *31.07S 150.54E*
99 M19 **Tamworth** C England, UK *52.39N 1.40W*
83 K19 **Tana** ≈ SE Kenya
Tana *see* Deatnu/Tenojoki
170 G17 **Tanabe** Wakayama, Honshū, SW Japan *33.43N 135.22E*
94 L8 **Tana Bru** Finnmark, N Norway *70.10N 28.06E*
41 T10 **Tanacross** Alaska, USA *63.30N 143.21W*
94 L7 **Tanafjorden** *Lapp.* Deanuvuotna. *fjord* N Norway
40 G17 **Tanaga Island** *island* Aleutian Islands, Alaska, USA
40 G17 **Tanaga Volcano** ✱ Tanaga Island, Alaska, USA *51.53N 178.08W*
109 M18 **Tanagro** ≈ S Italy
82 H11 **T'ana Hāyk'** *Eng.* Lake Tana. ◎ NW Ethiopia
173 F8 **Tanahbela, Pulau** *island* Kepulauan Batu, W Indonesia
175 Pp15 **Tanahjampea, Pulau** *island* W Indonesia
173 Ff8 **Tanahmasa, Pulau** *island* Kepulauan Batu, W Indonesia
Tanais *see* Don
158 L10 **Tanakpur** Uttaranchal, N India *29.04N 80.06E*
Tana, Lake *see* T'ana Hāyk'
189 P5 **Tanami Desert** *desert* Northern Territory, N Australia
178 Jj14 **Tân An** Long An, S Vietnam *10.31N 106.24E*
41 Q9 **Tanana** Alaska, USA *65.12N 152.00W*
Tananarive *see* Antananarivo
41 Q9 **Tanana River** ≈ Alaska, USA
97 C16 **Tananger** Rogaland, S Norway *58.55N 5.34E*
196 H5 **Tanapag** Saipan, S Northern Mariana Islands *15.13S 145.45E*
196 H5 **Tanapag, Puetton** *bay* Saipan, S Northern Mariana Islands
108 C9 **Tanaro** ≈ N Italy
169 Y12 **Tanch'ŏn** E North Korea *40.22N 128.49E*
42 M14 **Tancítaro, Cerro** ✱ C Mexico *19.16N 102.25W*
159 N12 **Tānda** Uttar Pradesh, N India *26.36N 82.39E*
79 O15 **Tanda** E Ivory Coast *7.48N 3.10W*
179 Rr14 **Tandag** Mindanao, S Philippines *9.00N 126.13E*
118 L14 **Ţăndărei** Ialomiţa, SE Romania *44.39N 27.40E*
65 N14 **Tandil** Buenos Aires, E Argentina *37.18S 59.10W*
80 H12 **Tandjilé** *off.* Préfecture du Tandjilé. ◐ *prefecture* SW Chad
Tandjoeng *see* Tanjung
Tandjoengpandan *see* Tanjungpandan
Tandjoengpinang *see* Tanjungpinang
Tandjoengredeb *see* Tanjungredeb
155 Q16 **Tando Allāhyār** Sind, SE Pakistan *25.30N 68.43E*
155 Q17 **Tando Bāgo** Sind, SE Pakistan *24.48N 68.58E*
155 Q16 **Tando Muhammad Khān** Sind, SE Pakistan *25.07N 68.34E*
190 L7 **Tandou Lake** *seasonal lake* New South Wales, SE Australia
96 L11 **Tandsjöborg** Gävleborg, C Sweden *61.40N 14.40E*
161 H15 **Tāndūr** Andhra Pradesh, C India *17.16N 77.37E*
170 Bb17 **Tanega-shima** *island* Nansei-shotō, SW Japan
172 N10 **Taneichi** Iwate, Honshū, C Japan *40.23N 141.42E*
Tanen Taunggyi *see* Tane Range
178 H8 **Tane Range** *Bur.* Tanen Taunggyi. ▲▲ W Thailand
113 P15 **Tanew** ≈ SE Poland
23 W2 **Taneytown** Maryland, NE USA *39.39N 77.10W*
76 H12 **Tanezrouft** *desert* Algeria/Mali
144 L7 **Ţanf, Jabal aţ** ▲ SE Syria *33.31N 38.43E*
83 J21 **Tanga** Tanga, E Tanzania *5.07S 39.04E*
83 J22 **Tanga** ◐ *region* E Tanzania
159 T14 **Tangail** Dhaka, C Bangladesh *24.15N 89.55E*
195 Q9 **Tanga Islands** *island group* NE PNG
161 K26 **Tangalla** Southern Province, S Sri Lanka *6.01N 80.46E*
Tanganyika and Zanzibar *see* Tanzania
70 I13 **Tanganyika, Lake** ◎ E Africa
58 E7 **Tangarana, Río** ≈ N Peru
195 W16 **Tangarare** Guadalcanal, C Solomon Islands *9.37S 159.40E*
203 V16 **Tangaroa, Maunga** ✱ Easter Island, Chile, E Pacific Ocean
Tangdukou *see* Shaoyang
76 G5 **Tanger** *var.* Tangiers, Tangier, *Fr./Ger.* Tangerk, *Sp.* Tánger; *anc.* Tingis. NW Morocco *35.49N 5.48W*
174 J14 **Tangerang** Jawa, C Indonesia *6.13S 106.36E*
Tangerk *see* Tanger
102 M12 **Tangermünde** Sachsen-Anhalt, C Germany *52.35N 11.57E*
165 O12 **Tanggulashan** *var.* Togton Heyan, *var.* Tuotuoheyan. Qinghai, C China *34.13N 92.25E*
162 K10 **Tanggula Shan** *var.* Dangla, Tangla Range. ▲▲ W China
165 N13 **Tanggula Shan** ▲ W China *33.18N 91.10E*
162 K10 **Tanggula Shankou** *Tib.* Dang La. *pass* W China *32.52N 91.59E*
167 N7 **Tanghe** Henan, C China *32.40N 112.49E*
155 T5 **Tāngi** North-West Frontier Province, NW Pakistan *34.18N 71.42E*
Tangier *see* Tanger
23 Y5 **Tangier Island** *island* Virginia, NE USA
Tangiers *see* Tanger
24 K8 **Tangipahoa River** ≈ Louisiana, S USA
Tangla Range *see* Tanggula Shan
171 H13 **Tango-hantō** *peninsula* Honshū, SW Japan
162 I10 **Tangra Yumco** *var.* Tangro Tso. ◎ W China
Tangro Tso *see* Tangra Yumco
163 T7 **Tangshan** *var.* T'ang-shan. Hebei, E China *39.38N 118.14E*
179 Qq15 **Tangub** *var.* Tangub City. Mindanao, S Philippines *8.07N 123.42E*
79 R14 **Tanguiéta** NW Benin *10.34N 1.19E*
169 X7 **Tangwang He** ≈ NE China
169 X7 **Tangyuan** Heilongjiang, NE China *46.45N 129.52E*
94 M11 **Tanhua** Lappi, N Finland *67.31N 27.30E*
176 Uu16 **Tanimbar, Kepulauan** *island group* Maluku, E Indonesia
Tanintharyi *see* Tenasserim
145 U4 **Tānjarō** ≈ E Iraq
133 T15 **Tanjong Piai** *headland* Peninsular Malaysia
Tanjore *see* Thanjāvūr
175 N10 **Tanjung** *prev.* Tandjoeng. Borneo, C Indonesia *2.07S 115.22E*
175 Oo6 **Tanjungbatu** Borneo, N Indonesia *2.19N 118.03E*
Tanjungkarang *see* Bandarlampung
174 J11 **Tanjunglabu** Pulau Lepar, W Indonesia *2.57S 106.51E*
174 J10 **Tanjungpandan** *prev.* Tandjoengpandan. Pulau Belitung, W Indonesia *2.43S 107.36E*
174 I7 **Tanjungpinang** *prev.* Tandjoengpinang. Pulau Bintan, W Indonesia *0.55N 104.28E*
175 O6 **Tanjungredeb** *var.* Tanjungredep; *prev.* Tandjoengredeb. Borneo, C Indonesia *2.09N 117.28E*
Tanjungredep *see* Tanjungredeb
155 S8 **Tānk** North-West Frontier Province, NW Pakistan *32.13N 70.28E*
197 D16 **Tanna** *island* S Vanuatu
95 F17 **Tännäs** Jämtland, C Sweden *62.27N 12.40E*
Tannenhof *see* Krynica
110 K7 **Tannheim** Tirol, W Austria *47.30N 10.32E*
Tannu-Tuva *see* Tyva, Respublika
175 Rr10 **Tano** Pulau Taliabu, E Indonesia *1.51S 124.55E*
79 O17 **Tano** ≈ S Ghana
158 D10 **Tanot** Rājasthān, NW India *27.49N 70.21E*
79 V11 **Tanout** Zinder, C Niger *14.58N 8.54E*
43 P12 **Tanquián** San Luis Potosí, C Mexico *21.38N 98.39W*
79 R13 **Tansarga** E Burkina *11.51N 1.51E*
178 Jj14 **Tân Son Nhat** ✕ (Hô Chi Minh) Tây Ninh, S Vietnam *10.52N 106.38E*
77 V8 **Tanta** *var.* Tantā. Tantā. N Egypt *30.42N 31.00E*
76 D9 **Tan-Tan** SW Morocco *28.30N 11.10W*
43 P12 **Tantoyuca** Veracruz-Llave, E Mexico *21.18N 98.12W*
158 J12 **Tāntpur** Uttar Pradesh, N India *26.51N 77.28E*
Tan-tung *see* Dandong
40 M12 **Tanunak** Alaska, USA *60.35N 165.15W*
177 Ff5 **Ta-nyaung** Magwe, W Myanmar *20.49N 94.40E*
178 J5 **Tân Yên** Tuyên Quang, N Vietnam *22.08N 104.58E*
83 F22 **Tanzania** *off.* United Republic of Tanzania, *Swa.* Jamhuri ya Muungano wa Tanzania; *prev.* German East Africa, Tanganyika and Zanzibar. ◆ *republic* E Africa
Tanzania, Jamhuri ya Muungano wa *see* Tanzania
Taoan/Tao'an *see* Taonan
169 T8 **Tao'er He** ≈ NE China
165 U11 **Tao He** ≈ C China
169 U9 **Taonan** *var.* Taoan, Tao'an. Jilin, NE China *45.19N 122.46E*
T'aon-an *see* Baicheng
Taongi *see* Bokaak Atoll
109 M23 **Taormina** *anc.* Tauromenium. Sicilia, Italy, C Mediterranean Sea *37.54N 15.18E*
39 S9 **Taos** New Mexico, SW USA *36.24N 105.34W*
Taoudenit *see* Taoudenni
79 O6 **Taoudenni** *var.* Taoudenit. Tombouctou, N Mali *22.46N 3.54W*
76 G6 **Taounate** N Morocco *34.34N 4.35W*
167 S13 **T'aoyüan** *Jap.* Tōen. N Taiwan *25.00N 121.15E*
120 I3 **Tapa** *Ger.* Taps. Lääne-Virumaa, NE Estonia *59.15N 26.00E*
43 V17 **Tapachula** Chiapas, SE Mexico *14.53N 92.18W*
Tapaiu *see* Gvardeysk
61 H14 **Tapajós, Rio** *var.* Tapajóz. ≈ NW Brazil
Tapajóz *see* Tapajós, Rio
63 C21 **Tapalqué** *var.* Tapalquén. Buenos Aires, E Argentina *36.21S 60.01W*
Tapalquén *see* Tapalqué
Tapanahoni *see* Tapanahony Rivier
57 W11 **Tapanahony Rivier** *var.* Tapanahoni. ≈ E Suriname
43 T16 **Tapanatepec** *var.* San Pedro Tapanatepec. Oaxaca, SE Mexico *16.23N 94.09W*
193 D23 **Tapanui** Otago, South Island, NZ *45.55S 169.16E*
Tapanuli, Teluk *see* Sibolga, Teluk
61 E14 **Tapauá** Amazonas, N Brazil *5.42S 64.15W*
49 R7 **Tapauá, Rio** ≈ W Brazil
193 I14 **Tapawera** Tasman, South Island, NZ *41.24S 172.50E*
63 I16 **Tapes** Rio Grande do Sul, S Brazil *30.40S 51.25W*
78 K16 **Tapeta** C Liberia *6.30N 8.53W*
160 H11 **Tāpi** *prev.* Tāpti. ≈ W India
106 J2 **Tapia de Casariego** Asturias, N Spain *43.34N 6.55W*
58 F10 **Tapiche, Río** ≈ N Peru
178 Gg15 **Tapi, Mae Nam** *var.* Luang. ≈ SW Thailand
194 K14 **Tapini** Central, S PNG *8.20S 146.57E*
Tapirapecó, Serra *see* Tapirapecó, Sierra
57 N13 **Tapirapecó, Sierra** *Port.* Serra Tapirapecó. ▲▲ Brazil/Venezuela
79 R13 **Tapoa** ≈ Benin/Niger
196 H5 **Tapochau, Mount** ▲ Saipan, S Northern Mariana Islands
113 H24 **Tapolca** Veszprém, W Hungary *46.54N 17.28E*
23 X5 **Tappahannock** Virginia, NE USA *37.55N 76.51W*
33 U13 **Tappan Lake** ⊠ Ohio, N USA
171 Mm7 **Tappi-zaki** *headland* Honshū, C Japan *41.15N 140.19E*
Taps *see* Tapa
Tāpti *see* Tāpi
193 J16 **Tapuaenuku** ▲ South Island, NZ *42.00S 173.39E*
179 Pp17 **Tapul Group** *island group* Sulu Archipelago, SW Philippines
60 E11 **Tapurucuará** *var.* Tapuruquara. Amazonas, NW Brazil *0.17S 65.00W*
Tapuruquara *see* Tapurucuará
198 C9 **Taputapu, Cape** *headland* Tutuila, W American Samoa *14.19S 170.51W*
147 W13 **Ţāqah** S Oman *17.04N 54.24E*
145 T3 **Taqtaq** N Iraq *35.54N 44.36E*
63 J15 **Taquara** Rio Grande do Sul, S Brazil *29.40S 50.46W*
61 H19 **Taquari, Rio** ≈ C Brazil
62 L8 **Taquaritinga** São Paulo, S Brazil *21.22S 48.29W*
125 G12 **Tara** Omskaya Oblast', C Russian Federation *56.54N 74.17E*
85 I16 **Tara** Southern, S Zambia *16.54S 26.47E*
115 J15 **Tara** ≈ SW Serbia and Montenegro (Yugoslavia)
114 K13 **Tara** ▲▲ W Serbia and Montenegro (Yugoslavia)
79 W15 **Taraba** ◐ *state* E Nigeria
79 X15 **Taraba** ≈ E Nigeria
77 O7 **Ţarābulus** *var.* Ţarābulus al Gharb, *Eng.* Tripoli. ● (Libya) NW Libya *32.54N 13.10E*
77 O7 **Ţarābulus** ✕ NW Libya *32.37N 13.07E*
Ţarābulus/Ţarābulus ash Shām *see* Tripoli
Ţarābulus al Gharb *see* Ţarābulus
107 O7 **Taracena** Castilla-La Mancha, C Spain *40.39N 3.07W*
119 N12 **Taraclia** *Rus.* Tarakilya. S Moldova *45.55N 28.40E*
145 V10 **Tarād al Kahf** SE Iraq *31.58N 45.58E*
191 R10 **Tarago** New South Wales, SE Australia *35.04S 149.40E*
174 Jj15 **Taraju** Jawa, S Indonesia *7.27S 107.58E*
176 Vv11 **Tarak** Papua, E Indonesia *3.21S 132.43E*
175 O5 **Tarakan** Borneo, C Indonesia *3.19N 117.37E*
175 O5 **Tarakan, Pulau** *island* N Indonesia
Tarakilya *see* Taraclia
172 Pp16 **Tarama-jima** *island* Sakishima-shotō, SW Japan
192 K10 **Taranaki** *off.* Taranaki Region. ◐ *region* North Island, NZ
192 K10 **Taranaki, Mount** *var.* Egmont. ▲ North Island, NZ *39.16S 174.04E*
107 O9 **Tarancón** Castilla-La Mancha, C Spain *40.01N 3.01W*
196 M15 **Tarang Reef** *reef* C Micronesia
98 E7 **Taransay** *island* NW Scotland, UK
109 P18 **Taranto** *var.* Tarentum. Puglia, SE Italy *40.30N 17.10E*
109 O19 **Taranto, Golfo di** *Eng.* Gulf of Taranto. *gulf* S Italy
Taranto, Gulf of *see* Taranto, Golfo di
64 G3 **Tarapacá** *off.* Región de Tarapacá. ◐ *region* N Chile
195 Y16 **Tarapaina** Maramasike Island, N Solomon Islands *9.28S 161.24E*
58 D10 **Tarapoto** San Martín, N Peru *6.31S 76.24W*
144 M6 **Ţaraq an Na'jah** *hill range* E Syria
144 M6 **Ţaraq Sidāwī** *hill range* E Syria
105 Q11 **Tarare** Rhône, E France *45.54N 4.25E*
Tararite de Llitera *see* Tamarite de Litera
192 M13 **Tararua Range** ▲▲ North Island, NZ
157 Q22 **Tarāsa Dwīp** *island* Nicobar Islands, India, NE Indian Ocean
105 Q15 **Tarascon** Bouches-du-Rhône, SE France *43.48N 4.39E*
104 M17 **Tarascon-sur-Ariège** Ariège, S France *42.51N 1.36E*
119 P6 **Tarashcha** Kyyivs'ka Oblast', N Ukraine *49.34N 30.31E*
59 L18 **Tarata** Cochabamba, C Bolivia *17.34S 66.04W*
59 I18 **Tarata** Tacna, SW Peru *17.30S 70.00W*
202 H2 **Taratai** *atoll* Tungaru, W Kiribati
61 B15 **Tarauacá** Acre, W Brazil *8.06S 70.45W*
61 B15 **Tarauacá, Rio** ≈ NW Brazil
203 Q8 **Taravao** Tahiti, W French Polynesia *17.43S 149.19W*
203 R8 **Taravao, Baie de** *bay* Tahiti, W French Polynesia
203 Q8 **Taravao, Isthme de** *isthmus* Tahiti, W French Polynesia
105 X16 **Taravo** ≈ Corse, France, C Mediterranean Sea
202 J3 **Tarawa** ✕ Tarawa, W Kiribati *0.52S 169.31E*
202 H2 **Tarawa** *atoll* Tungaru, W Kiribati
192 N10 **Tarawera** Hawke's Bay, North Island, NZ *39.03S 176.34E*
192 N8 **Tarawera, Lake** ◎ North Island, NZ
192 N8 **Tarawera, Mount** ▲ North Island, NZ *38.13S 176.29E*
107 S8 **Tarayuela** ▲ N Spain *40.28N 0.22W*
151 R16 **Taraz** *prev.* Aulie Ata, Auliye-Ata, Dzhambul, Zhambyl. Zhambyl, S Kazakhstan. *42.55N 71.27E*
107 Q5 **Tarazona** Aragón, NE Spain *41.54N 1.43W*
107 Q10 **Tarazona de la Mancha** Castilla-La Mancha, C Spain *39.16N 1.55W*
151 X12 **Tarbagatay, Khrebet** ▲▲ China/Kazakhstan
98 J8 **Tarbat Ness** *headland* N Scotland, UK *57.51N 3.48W*
155 U5 **Tarbela Reservoir** ⊠ N Pakistan
98 H12 **Tarbert** W Scotland, UK *55.52N 5.25W*
98 F7 **Tarbert** Western Isles, NW Scotland, UK *57.53N 6.48W*
104 K16 **Tarbes** *anc.* Bigorra. Hautes-Pyrénées, S France *43.13N 0.04E*
23 W9 **Tarboro** North Carolina, SE USA *35.54N 77.32W*
Tarca *see* Torysa
108 J6 **Tarcento** Friuli-Venezia Giulia, NE Italy *46.13N 13.13E*
190 F5 **Tarcoola** South Australia *30.44S 134.33E*
107 S5 **Tardienta** Aragón, NE Spain *41.58N 0.31W*
104 L11 **Tardoire** ≈ W France
191 U7 **Taree** New South Wales, SE Australia *31.55S 152.28E*
94 K12 **Tärendö** *Lapp.* Deargget. Norrbotten, N Sweden *67.10N 22.40E*
Tarentum *see* Taranto
76 C9 **Tarfaya** SW Morocco *27.56N 12.55W*
118 J13 **Târgoviște** *prev.* Tîrgoviște. Dâmbovița, S Romania *44.54N 25.28E*
118 M12 **Târgu Bujor** *prev.* Tîrgu Bujor. Galați, E Romania *45.52N 27.55E*
118 H13 **Târgu Cărbunești** *prev.* Tîrgu. Gorj, SW Romania *44.57N 23.31E*
118 L9 **Târgu Frumos** *prev.* Tîrgu Frumos. Iași, NE Romania *47.12N 27.00E*
118 H13 **Târgu Jiu** *prev.* Tîrgu Jiu. Gorj, W Romania *45.02N 23.19E*
118 H9 **Târgu Lăpuș** *prev.* Tîrgu Lăpuș. Maramureș, N Romania *47.28N 23.54E*
Târgul-Neamț *see* Târgu-Neamț
Târgul-Săcuiesc *see* Târgu Secuiesc
118 I10 **Târgu Mureș** *prev.* Oșorhei, Tîrgu Mures, *Ger.* Neumarkt, *Hung.* Marosvásárhely. Mureș, C Romania *46.33N 24.36E*
118 K9 **Târgu-Neamț** *var.* Târgul-Neamț; *prev.* Tîrgu-Neamț. Neamț, NE Romania *47.12N 26.25E*
118 K11 **Târgu Ocna** *Hung.* Aknavásár; *prev.* Tîrgu Ocna. Bacău, E Romania *46.16N 26.37E*
118 K11 **Târgu Secuiesc** *Ger.* Neumarkt, Szekler Neumarkt, *Hung.* Kezdivásárhely; *prev.* Chezdi-Oșorheiu, Târgul-Săcuiesc, Tîrgu Secuiesc. Covasna, E Romania *46.00N 26.08E*
151 X10 **Targyn** Vostochnyy Kazakhstan, E Kazakhstan *49.31N 82.46E*
Tar Heel State *see* North Carolina
194 G12 **Tari** Southern Highlands, W PNG *5.52S 142.58E*
149 P17 **Ţarif** Abū Ẓaby, C UAE *24.01N 53.46E*
106 K16 **Tarifa** Andalucía, S Spain *36.01N 5.36W*
86 C14 **Tarifa, Punta de** *headland* SW Spain *36.01N 5.39W*
59 M21 **Tarija** Tarija, S Bolivia *21.33S 64.42W*
59 M21 **Tarija** ◐ *department* S Bolivia
147 R14 **Tarim** C Yemen *16.00N 48.50E*
Tarim Basin *see* Tarim Pendi
83 G19 **Tarime** Mara, N Tanzania *1.19S 34.24E*
133 S8 **Tarim He** ≈ NW China
165 H8 **Tarim Pendi** *Eng.* Tarim Basin. *basin* NW China
155 N7 **Tarin Kowt** *var.* Terinkot. Urūzgān, C Afghanistan *32.37N 65.52E*
175 Pp10 **Taripa** Sulawesi, C Indonesia *1.51S 120.46E*
176 Z11 **Taritatu, Sungai** *prev.* Idenburg-rivier. ≈ Papua, E Indonesia
119 Q12 **Tarkhankut, Mys** *headland* S Ukraine *45.20N 32.32E*
29 Q1 **Tarkio** Missouri, C USA *40.25N 95.24W*
126 H9 **Tarko-Sale** Yamalo-Nenetskiy Avtonomnyy Okrug, N Russian Federation *64.55N 77.34E*
79 P17 **Tarkwa** S Ghana *5.16N 1.58W*
179 P10 **Tarlac** Luzon, N Philippines *15.29N 120.34E*
97 F22 **Tarm** Ringkøbing, W Denmark *55.55N 8.31E*
59 E14 **Tarma** Junín, C Peru *11.25S 75.43W*
105 N15 **Tarn** ◐ *department* S France
104 M15 **Tarn** ≈ S France
113 L22 **Tarna** ≈ C Hungary
94 G13 **Tärnaby** Västerbotten, N Sweden *65.43N 15.19E*
155 P8 **Tarnak Rūd** ≈ SE Afghanistan
118 J11 **Târnava Mare** *Ger.* Grosse Kokel, *Hung.* Nagy-Küküllő; *prev.* Tîrnava Mare. ≈ S Romania
118 I11 **Târnava Mică** *Ger.* Kleine Kokel, *Hung.* Kis-Küküllo; *prev.* Tîrnava Mică. ≈ C Romania
118 I11 **Târnăveni** *Ger.* Marteskirch, Martinskirch, *Hung.* Dicsőszentmárton; *prev.* Sînmartin, Tîrnăveni. Mureș, C Romania *46.19N 24.16E*
104 L14 **Tarn-et-Garonne** ◐ *department* S France
113 P18 **Tarnica** ▲ SE Poland *49.05N 22.43E*
113 N15 **Tarnobrzeg** Podkarpackie, SE Poland *50.34N 21.40E*
129 N12 **Tarnogskiy Gorodok** Vologodskaya Oblast', NW Russian Federation *60.28N 43.45E*
Tarnopol *see* Ternopil'
113 M16 **Tarnów** Małopolskie, SE Poland *50.01N 20.58E*
Tarnowice/Tarnowitz *see* Tarnowskie Góry
113 J16 **Tarnowskie Góry** *var.* Tarnowice, Tarnowskie Gory, *Ger.* Tarnowitz. Śląskie, S Poland *50.27N 18.52E*
97 N14 **Tärnsjö** Västmanland, C Sweden *60.10N 16.57E*
108 E9 **Taro** ≈ NW Italy
195 Q10 **Taron** New Ireland, NE PNG *4.22S 153.04E*
76 E8 **Taroudannt** *var.* Taroudant. SW Morocco *30.31N 8.50W*
Taroudant *see* Taroudannt
25 V12 **Tarpon, Lake** ◎ Florida, SE USA
25 V12 **Tarpon Springs** Florida, SE USA *28.09N 82.45W*
109 G14 **Tarquinia** *anc.* Tarquinii; *hist.* Corneto. Lazio, C Italy *42.22N 11.45E*
Tarquinii *see* Tarquinia
Tarraco *see* Tarragona
78 D10 **Tarrafal** Santiago, S Cape Verde *15.16N 23.45W*
107 V6 **Tarragona** *anc.* Tarraco. Cataluña, E Spain *41.07N 1.15E*
107 T7 **Tarragona** ◐ *province* Cataluña, NE Spain
191 O17 **Tarraleah** Tasmania, SE Australia *42.11S 146.29E*
25 P3 **Tarrant City** Alabama, S USA *33.34N 86.45W*
193 D21 **Tarras** Otago, South Island, NZ *44.48S 169.25E*
Tarrasa *see* Terrassa
107 U5 **Tàrrega** *var.* Tarrega. Cataluña, NE Spain *41.39N 1.09E*
23 W9 **Tar River** ≈ North Carolina, SE USA
Tarsatica *see* Rijeka
142 J17 **Tarsus** İçel, S Turkey *36.52N 34.52E*
64 K4 **Tartagal** Salta, N Argentina *22.33S 63.49W*
143 V12 **Tärtär** *Rus.* Terter. ≈ SW Azerbaijan
104 J15 **Tartas** Landes, SW France *43.52N 0.45W*
145 Q6 **Tärtasah** C Iraq *34.18N 42.21E*
Tartlau *see* Prejmer
Tartous/Tartouss *see* Ţarţūs
120 J5 **Tartu** *Ger.* Dorpat; *prev. Rus.* Yurev, Yur'yev. Tartumaa, SE Estonia *58.19N 26.43E*
120 I5 **Tartumaa** *off.* Tartu Maakond. ◐ *province* E Estonia
144 H5 **Ţarţūs** *Fr.* Tartouss; *anc.* Tortosa. Ţarţūs, W Syria *34.55N 35.52E*
144 H5 **Ţarţūs** *off.* Muḩāfaẓat Ţarţūs, *var.* Tartous, Tartus. ◐ *governorate* W Syria
170 Bb16 **Tarumizu** Kagoshima, Kyūshū, SW Japan *31.30N 130.40E*
130 K4 **Tarusa** Kaluzhskaya Oblast', W Russian Federation *54.45N 37.10E*
173 G9 **Tarusan** Sumatera, W Indonesia *1.13S 100.22E*
119 N11 **Tarutyne** Odes'ka Oblast', SW Ukraine *46.11N 29.09E*
168 I7 **Tarvagatyn Nuruu** ▲▲ N Mongolia
108 J6 **Tarvisio** Friuli-Venezia Giulia, NE Italy *46.31N 13.33E*
Tarvisium *see* Treviso
59 O16 **Tarvo, Río** ≈ E Bolivia
12 G8 **Tarzwell** Ontario, S Canada *48.00N 79.58W*
42 K5 **Tasajera, Sierra de la** ▲▲ N Mexico
151 S13 **Tasaral** Karaganda, C Kazakhstan *46.17N 73.54E*
Tasböget *see* Tasbuget
151 N15 **Tasbuget** *Kaz.* Tasböget. Kzylorda, S Kazakhstan *44.49N 65.34E*
110 E11 **Tasch** Valais, SW Switzerland *46.04N 7.43E*
Tasek Kenyir *see* Kenyir, Tasik
126 Hh16 **Tashanta** Respublika Altay, S Russian Federation *49.42N 89.15E*
Tashauz *see* Daşoguz
Tashi Chho Dzong *see* Thimphu
159 U11 **Tashigang** E Bhutan *27.19N 91.33E*
143 T11 **Tashir** *prev.* Kalinino. N Armenia *41.07N 44.16E*
149 Q11 **Ţashk, Daryācheh-ye** ◎ C Iran
Tashkent *see* Toshkent
Tashkentskaya Oblast' *see* Toshkent Viloyati
Tashkepri *see* Daşköpri
Tash-Kömür *see* Tash-Kumyr
153 S9 **Tash-Kumyr** *Kir.* Tash-Kömür. Dzhalal-Abadskaya Oblast', W Kyrgyzstan *41.22N 72.08E*
131 T7 **Tashla** Orenburgskaya Oblast', W Russian Federation *51.42N 52.33E*
Tashqurghan *see* Kholm
126 H15 **Tashtagol** Kemerovskaya Oblast', S Russian Federation *52.49N 88.00E*
174 Jj15 **Tasikmalaya** *prev.* Tasikmalaja. Jawa, C Indonesia *7.19S 108.16E*
97 H24 **Tåsinge** *island* C Denmark
10 M5 **Tasiujaq** Québec, E Canada *58.43N 69.58W*
127 Nn9 **Taskan** Magadanskaya Oblast', E Russian Federation *63.00N 150.03E*
79 W11 **Tasker** Zinder, C Niger *15.06N 10.42E*
151 W12 **Taskesken** Vostochnyy Kazakhstan, E Kazakhstan *47.15N 80.46E*
142 J10 **Taşköprü** Kastamonu, N Turkey *41.30N 34.12E*
Taskuduk, Peski *see* Tosquduq Qumlari
195 N9 **Taskul** New Ireland, NE PNG *2.30S 150.22E*
143 S13 **Taşlıçay** Ağrı, E Turkey *39.37N 43.22E*
193 H14 **Tasman** *off.* Tasman District. ◐ *unitary authority* South Island, NZ
199 I14 **Tasman Basin** *var.* East Australian Basin. *undersea feature* S Tasman Sea
193 I14 **Tasman Bay** *inlet* South Island, NZ
199 Hh14 **Tasman Fracture Zone** *tectonic feature* S Indian Ocean
193 E19 **Tasman Glacier** *glacier* South Island, NZ
Tasman Group *see* Nukumanu Islands
191 N15 **Tasmania** *prev.* Van Diemen's Land. ◐ *state* SE Australia
191 Q16 **Tasmania** *island* SE Australia
193 H14 **Tasman Mountains** ▲▲ South Island, NZ
191 P17 **Tasman Peninsula** *peninsula* Tasmania, SE Australia
199 Hh13 **Tasman Plain** *undersea feature* W Tasman Sea
199 Hh14 **Tasman Plateau** *var.* South Tasmania Plateau. *undersea feature* SW Tasman Sea
199 Ii14 **Tasman Sea** *sea* SW Pacific Ocean
118 G9 **Tășnad** *Ger.* Trestenberg, Trestendorf, *Hung.* Tasnád. Satu Mare, NW Romania *47.30N 22.33E*
142 L11 **Taşova** Amasya, N Turkey *40.45N 36.19E*
79 T10 **Tassara** Tahoua, W Niger *16.40N 5.34E*
10 K4 **Tassialouc, Lac** ◎ Québec, C Canada
Tassili du Hoggar *see* Tassili ta-n-Ahaggar
76 L11 **Tassili-n-Ajjer** *plateau* E Algeria
76 K14 **Tassili ta-n-Ahaggar** *var.* Tassili du Hoggar. *plateau* S Algeria
61 M15 **Tasso Fragoso** Maranhão, E Brazil *8.22S 45.53W*
Tåstrup *see* Taastrup
151 O9 **Tasty-Taldy** Akmola, C Kazakhstan *50.45N 66.35E*
149 W10 **Tāsūkī** Sīstān va Balūchestān, SE Iran
113 I22 **Tata** *Ger.* Totis. Komárom-Esztergom, NW Hungary *47.39N 18.19E*
76 E8 **Tata** SW Morocco *29.38N 8.04W*
Tataaihoa, Pointe *see* Vénus, Pointe
113 I22 **Tatabánya** Komárom-Esztergom, NW Hungary *47.33N 18.22E*
203 X10 **Tatakoto** *atoll* Îles Tuamotu, E French Polynesia
77 N7 **Tataouine** *var.* Taţāwīn. SE Tunisia *32.48N 10.27E*
57 O5 **Tataracual, Cerro** ▲ NE Venezuela *10.13N 64.20W*
119 O12 **Tatarbunary** Odes'ka Oblast', SW Ukraine *45.50N 29.37E*
121 M17 **Tatarka** *Rus.* Tatarka. Mahilyowskaya Voblasts', E Belarus *53.15N 28.49E*
Tatar Pazardzhik *see* Pazardzhik
125 G13 **Tatarsk** Novosibirskaya Oblast', C Russian Federation *55.08N 75.58E*
Tatarskaya ASSR *see* Tatarstan, Respublika
127 O15 **Tatarskiy Proliv** *Eng.* Tatar Strait. *strait* SE Russian Federation
131 R4 **Tatarstan, Respublika** *prev.* Tatarskaya ASSR. ◐ *autonomous republic* W Russian Federation
Tatar Strait *see* Tatarskiy Proliv
195 O9 **Tatau Island** *island* Tabar Islands, N PNG
Taţāwīn *see* Tataouine
175 P8 **Tate** Sulawesi, N Indonesia *0.12S 119.44E*
171 Jj17 **Tateyama** Chiba, Honshū, S Japan *35.00N 139.51E*
171 J14 **Tate-yama** ▲ Honshū, S Japan *36.27N 137.32E*
147 N11 **Tathlīth** 'Asīr, S Saudi Arabia *19.37N 43.31E*
147 O11 **Tathlīth, Wādī** *dry watercourse* S Saudi Arabia
191 R11 **Tathra** New South Wales, SE Australia *36.46S 149.58E*
131 P8 **Tatishchevo** Saratovskaya Oblast', W Russian Federation *51.43N 45.35E*
41 S12 **Tatitlek** Alaska, USA *60.49N 146.29W*
8 L15 **Tatla Lake** British Columbia, SW Canada *51.54N 124.39W*
124 O2 **Tatlısu** *Gk.* Akanthoú. N Cyprus *35.21N 33.45E*
9 Z10 **Tatnam, Cape** *headland* Manitoba, C Canada *57.16N 91.03W*
Tatra/Tátra *see* Tatra Mountains
113 K18 **Tatra Mountains** *Ger.* Tatra, *Hung.* Tátra, *Pol./Slvk.* Tatry. ▲▲ Poland/Slovakia
Tatry *see* Tatra Mountains
170 G14 **Tatsuno** *var.* Tatuno. Hyōgo, Honshū, SW Japan *34.51N 134.33E*
151 S16 **Tatti** *var.* Tatty. Zhambyl, S Kazakhstan *43.10N 73.22E*
Tatty *see* Tatti
62 L10 **Tatuí** São Paulo, S Brazil *23.21S 47.49W*
39 V14 **Tatum** New Mexico, SW USA *33.15N 103.19W*
27 X7 **Tatum** Texas, SW USA *32.19N 94.31W*
Ta-t'ung/Tatung *see* Datong
Tatuno *see* Tatsuno
143 R14 **Tatvan** Bitlis, SE Turkey *38.31N 42.15E*
97 C16 **Tau** Rogaland, S Norway *59.04N 5.55E*
198 Dd8 **Ta'ū** *var.* Tau. *island* Manua Islands, E American Samoa
200 R14 **Tau** *island* Tongatapu Group, N Tonga
61 O14 **Tauá** Ceará, E Brazil *6.04S 40.25W*
62 N10 **Taubaté** São Paulo, S Brazil *23.00S 45.36W*
103 I19 **Tauber** ≈ SW Germany
103 I19 **Tauberbischofsheim** Baden-Württemberg, C Germany *49.37N 9.39E*
150 E14 **Tauchik** *Kaz.* Taūshyq. Mangistau, SW Kazakhstan *44.17N 51.22E*
203 W10 **Tauere** *atoll* Îles Tuamotu, C French Polynesia
103 H17 **Taufstein** ▲ C Germany *50.31N 9.18E*
202 I17 **Taukoka** *island* SE Cook Islands
151 T15 **Taukum, Peski** *desert* SE Kazakhstan
192 L10 **Taumarunui** Manawatu-Wanganui, North Island, NZ *38.52S 175.14E*
61 A15 **Taumaturgo** Acre, W Brazil *8.54S 72.48W*
29 X6 **Taum Sauk Mountain** ▲ Missouri, C USA *37.34N 90.43W*
85 H22 **Taung** North-West, N South Africa *27.31S 24.47E*
177 G6 **Taungdwingyi** Magwe, C Myanmar *20.01N 95.34E*
178 Gg6 **Taunggyi** Shan State, C Myanmar *20.46N 97.00E*
177 G5 **Taungtha** Mandalay, C Myanmar *21.16N 95.25E*
177 F7 **Taungup** Arakan State, W Myanmar *18.49N 94.13E*
155 S9 **Taunsa** Punjab, E Pakistan *30.43N 70.40E*
99 K23 **Taunton** SW England, UK *51.01N 3.06W*
21 O12 **Taunton** Massachusetts, NE USA *41.54N 71.03W*
103 F18 **Taunus** ▲▲ W Germany
103 G18 **Taunusstein** Hessen, W Germany *50.09N 8.09E*
192 N9 **Taupo** Waikato, North Island, NZ *38.42S 176.05E*
192 M9 **Taupo, Lake** ◎ North Island, NZ
111 R8 **Taurach** *var.* Taurachbach. ≈ E Austria
Taurachbach *see* Taurach
120 D12 **Tauragė** *Ger.* Tauroggen. Tauragė, SW Lithuania *55.15N 22.17E*
120 D13 **Tauragė** ◐ *province* SW Lithuania
56 G10 **Tauramena** Casanare, C Colombia *5.01N 72.48W*
192 N7 **Tauranga** Bay of Plenty, North Island, NZ *37.41S 176.09E*
13 O10 **Taureau, Réservoir** ⊠ Québec, SE Canada
109 N22 **Taurianova** Calabria, SW Italy *38.22N 16.01E*
Tauris *see* Tabrīz
192 I2 **Tauroa Point** *headland* North Island, NZ *35.09S 173.02E*
Tauroggen *see* Tauragė
Tauromenium *see* Taormina
Taurus Mountains *see* Toros Dağları
Taus *see* Domažlice
Taūshyq *see* Tauchik
107 R5 **Tauste** Aragón, NE Spain *41.55N 1.15W*
203 V16 **Tautara, Motu** *island* Easter Island, Chile, E Pacific Ocean
203 R8 **Tautira** Tahiti, W French Polynesia *17.45S 149.10W*
Tauz *see* Tovuz
Ţavālesh, Kūhhā-ye *see* Talish Mountains
142 D15 **Tavas** Denizli, SW Turkey *37.33N 29.04E*
Tavastehus *see* Hämeenlinna
Tavau *see* Davos
125 F11 **Tavda** Sverdlovskaya Oblast', C Russian Federation *58.01N 65.07E*
125 F11 **Tavda** ≈ C Russian Federation
107 T11 **Tavernes de la Valldigna** País Valenciano, E Spain *39.03N 0.13W*
83 I20 **Taveta** Coast, S Kenya *3.24S 37.46E*
197 J13 **Taveuni** *island* N Fiji
153 R13 **Tavildara** *Rus.* Tavil'dara, Tovil'-Dora. C Tajikistan *38.42N 70.27E*
168 L8 **Tavin** Dundgovĭ, C Mongolia *46.27N 105.43E*
106 H14 **Tavira** Faro, S Portugal *37.07N 7.39W*
99 I24 **Tavistock** SW England, UK *50.33N 4.07W*
178 Gg11 **Tavoy** *var.* Dawei. Tenasserim, S Myanmar *14.01N 98.12E*
Tavoy Island *see* Mali Kyun
125 Ff13 **Tavricheskoye** Omskaya Oblast', C Russian Federation *54.34N 73.33E*
117 E16 **Tavropoú, Techníti Límni** ⊠ C Greece
142 E13 **Tavşanlı** Kütahya, NW Turkey *39.34N 29.28E*
197 H14 **Tavua** Viti Levu, W Fiji *17.26S 105.53E*
197 I16 **Tavuki** Kadavu, SW Fiji *19.05S 178.06E*
99 J23 **Taw** ≈ SW England, UK
193 L14 **Tawa** Wellington, North Island, NZ *41.11S 174.48E*
27 V6 **Tawakoni, Lake** ⊠ Texas, SW USA
159 V11 **Tawang** Arunāchal Pradesh, NE India *27.34N 91.54E*
174 L16 **Tawang, Teluk** *bay* Jawa, S Indonesia
33 R7 **Tawas Bay** ◎ Michigan, N USA
33 R7 **Tawas City** Michigan, N USA *44.16N 83.33W*
175 Oo4 **Tawau** Sabah, East Malaysia *4.16N 117.54E*
147 U10 **Ţawīl, Qalamat aţ** *well* SE Saudi Arabia *21.07N 52.11E*
179 P17 **Tawitawi** *island* Tawitawi Group, SW Philippines
179 Pp17 **Tawitawi Group** *island group* Sulu Archipelago, SW Philippines
Ţawkar *see* Tokar
Tawūq *see* Dāqūq
Tawzar *see* Tozeur
43 O15 **Taxco** *var.* Taxco de Alarcón. Guerrero, S Mexico *18.32N 99.37W*
Taxco de Alarcón *see* Taxco
152 H8 **Taxiatosh** *Rus.* Takhiatash. Qoraqalpog'iston Respublikasi, W Uzbekistan *42.27N 59.26E*
164 D9 **Taxkorgan** *var.* Taxkorgan Tajik Zizhixian. Xinjiang Uygur Zizhiqu, NW China *37.43N 75.13E*
Taxkorgan Tajik Zizhixian *see* Taxkorgan
152 H7 **Taxtako'pir** *Rus.* Takhtakupyr. Qoraqalpog'iston Respublikasi, NW Uzbekistan *43.04N 60.23E*

◆ Country ● Country Capital ◇ Dependent Territory ○ Dependent Territory Capital ◐ Administrative Region ✕ International Airport ▲ Mountain ▲▲ Mountain Range ✱ Volcano ≈ River ◎ Lake ⊠ Reservoir
335

Tetovo – Tingri

115 N18 **Tetovo** *Alb.* Tetova, Tetovë, *Turk.* Kalkandelen. NW FYR Macedonia 42.01N 20.58E
117 E20 **Tetrázio** ▲▲ S Greece
Tetschen *see* Děčín
Tetuán *see* Tétouan
203 Q8 **Tetufera, Mont** ▲ Tahiti, W French Polynesia 17.40S 149.25W
131 R4 **Tetyushi** Respublika Tatarstan, W Russian Federation 54.55N 48.46E
110 I7 **Teufen** Sankt Gallen, NE Switzerland 47.24N 9.24E
42 L12 **Teul** *var.* Teul de Gonzáles Ortega. Zacatecas, C Mexico 21.30N 103.28W
109 B21 **Teulada** Sardegna, Italy, C Mediterranean Sea 38.58N 8.46E
Teul de Gonzáles Ortega *see* Teul
9 X16 **Teulon** Manitoba, S Canada 50.20N 97.14W
44 I7 **Teupasenti** El Paraíso, S Honduras 14.14N 86.43W
172 Oo3 **Teuri-tō** *island* NE Japan
102 G13 **Teutoburger Wald** *Eng.* Teutoburg Forest. *hill range* NW Germany
Teutoburg Forest *see* Teutoburger Wald
95 K17 **Teuva** *Swe.* Östermark. Länsi-Suomi, W Finland 62.28N 21.45E
109 H15 **Tevere** *Eng.* Tiber. ≈ C Italy
144 G9 **Teverya** *var.* Tiberias, Tverya. Northern, N Israel 32.48N 35.31E
98 K13 **Teviot** ≈ SE Scotland, UK
Tevli *see* Tewli
125 Ff12 **Tevriz** Omskaya Oblast', C Russian Federation 57.30N 72.13E
193 B24 **Te Waewae Bay** *bay* South Island, NZ
99 L21 **Tewkesbury** C England, UK 51.58N 2.09W
121 F19 **Tewli** *Rus.* Tevli. Brestskaya Voblasts', SW Belarus 52.20N 24.13E
165 U12 **Têwo** *var.* Dêngkagoin. Gansu, C China 34.05N 103.15E
27 U12 **Texana, Lake** ◎ Texas, SW USA
29 S14 **Texarkana** Arkansas, C USA 33.26N 94.02W
27 X5 **Texarkana** Texas, SW USA 33.25N 94.03W
27 N9 **Texas** *off.* State of Texas; also known as The Lone Star State. ⬖ *state* S USA
27 W12 **Texas City** Texas, SW USA 29.22N 94.54W
43 P14 **Texcoco** México, C Mexico 19.31N 98.52W
100 I6 **Texel** *island* Waddeneilanden, NW Netherlands
28 H8 **Texhoma** Oklahoma, C USA 36.30N 101.46W
27 N1 **Texhoma** Texas, SW USA 36.30N 101.46W
39 W12 **Texico** New Mexico, SW USA 34.23N 103.03W
26 L1 **Texline** Texas, SW USA 36.22N 103.01W
43 P14 **Texmelucan** *var.* San Martín Texmelucan. Puebla, S Mexico 19.13N 98.25W
29 O13 **Texoma, Lake** ⊠ Oklahoma/Texas, C USA
27 N9 **Texon** Texas, SW USA 31.13N 101.42W
126 I12 **Teya** Krasnoyarskiy Kray, C Russian Federation 60.27N 92.46E
85 J23 **Teyateyaneng** NW Lesotho 29.04S 27.51E
128 M16 **Teykovo** Ivanovskaya Oblast', W Russian Federation 56.49N 40.31E
128 M16 **Teza** ≈ W Russian Federation
43 Q13 **Teziutlán** Puebla, S Mexico 19.49N 97.22W
159 W12 **Tezpur** Assam, NE India 26.39N 92.47E
15 L8 **Tha-Anne** ≈ Nunavut, NE Canada
85 K23 **Thabana Ntlenyana** *var.* Thabantshonyana, Mount Ntlenyana. ▲ E Lesotho 29.26S 29.16E
Thabantshonyana *see* Thabana Ntlenyana
85 J23 **Thaba Putsoa** ▲ C Lesotho 29.48S 27.46E
178 I8 **Tha Bo** Nong Khai, E Thailand 17.52N 102.34E
105 T12 **Thabor, Pic du** ▲ E France 45.07N 6.34E
Tha Chin *see* Samut Sakhon
177 G7 **Thagaya** Pegu, C Myanmar 19.19N 96.16E
Thai, Ao *see* Thailand, Gulf of
178 Jj6 **Thai Binh** Thai Binh, N Vietnam 20.27N 106.19E
178 Jj7 **Thai Hoa** Nghê An, N Vietnam 19.21N 105.26E
178 Hh10 **Thailand** *off.* Kingdom of Thailand, *Th.* Prathet Thai; *prev.* Siam. ◆ *monarchy* SE Asia
178 Hh13 **Thailand, Gulf of** *var.* Gulf of Siam, *Th.* Ao Thai, *Vtn.* Vinh Thai Lan. *gulf* SE Asia
Thai Lan, Vinh *see* Thailand, Gulf of
178 Jj6 **Thai Nguyên** Băc Thai, N Vietnam 21.36N 105.49E
178 J9 **Thakhèk** *prev.* Muang Khammouan. Khammouan, C Laos 17.24N 104.50E
159 S13 **Thakurgaon** Rajshahi, NW Bangladesh 26.04N 88.34E
155 S6 **Thal** North-West Frontier Province, NW Pakistan 33.24N 70.31E
177 G16 **Thalang** Phuket, SW Thailand 08.00N 98.21E
Thalassery *see* Tellicherry
178 I10 **Thalat Khae** Nakhon Ratchasima, C Thailand 15.15N 102.24E
111 Q5 **Thalgau** Salzburg, NW Austria 47.49N 13.19E
110 G7 **Thalwil** Zürich, NW Switzerland 47.16N 8.34E
85 I20 **Thamaga** Kweneng, SE Botswana 24.40S 25.31E
Thamarīd *see* Thamarīt
147 V13 **Thamarīt** *var.* Thamarīd, Thumrayt. SW Oman 17.39N 54.01E
147 P16 **Thamar, Jabal** ▲ SW Yemen 13.46N 45.32E
192 M6 **Thames** Waikato, North Island, NZ 37.10S 175.33E
12 D17 **Thames** ≈ Ontario, S Canada
99 O22 **Thames** ≈ S England, UK
192 M6 **Thames, Firth of** *gulf* North Island, NZ
12 D17 **Thamesville** Ontario, S Canada 42.33N 81.58W
147 S13 **Thamūd** N Yemen 17.17N 49.57E
178 Gg9 **Thanbyuzayat** Mon State, S Myanmar 15.58N 97.43E
158 I9 **Thānesar** Haryāna, NW India 29.58N 76.51E
178 Jj7 **Thanh Hoa** Thanh Hoa, N Vietnam 19.49N 105.48E
Thanintari Taungdan *see* Bilauktaung Range
161 I21 **Thanjāvūr** *prev.* Tanjore. Tamil Nādu, SE India 10.46N 79.09E
Thanlwin *see* Salween
105 U7 **Thann** Haut-Rhin, NE France 47.51N 7.04E
178 H16 **Tha Nong Phrom** Phatthalung, SW Thailand 7.24N 100.04E
178 H13 **Thap Sakae** *var.* Thap Sakau. Prachuap Khiri Khan, SW Thailand 11.30N 99.34E
Thap Sakau *see* Thap Sakae
100 L10 **'t Harde** Gelderland, E Netherlands 52.25N 5.52E
158 D11 **Thar Desert** *var.* Great Indian Desert, Indian Desert. *desert* India/Pakistan
189 V10 **Thargomindah** Queensland, C Australia 28.00S 143.47E
156 D11 **Thar Pārkar** *desert* SE Pakistan
145 S7 **Tharthār al Furāt, Qanāt ath** *canal* C Iraq
145 R7 **Tharthār, Buḩayrat ath** ◎ C Iraq
145 R5 **Tharthār, Wādī ath** *dry watercourse* N Iraq
178 Gg14 **Tha Sae** Chumphon, SW Thailand
178 H15 **Tha Sala** Nakhon Si Thammarat, SW Thailand 8.43N 99.54E
116 I13 **Thásos** Thásos, E Greece 40.46N 24.43E
117 I14 **Thásos** *island* E Greece
39 N14 **Thatcher** Arizona, SW USA 32.47N 109.46W
178 Jj5 **Thât Khê** *var.* Trâng Dinh. Lang Sơn, N Vietnam 22.15N 106.26E
178 Gg9 **Thaton** Mon State, S Myanmar 16.55N 97.19E
178 J9 **That Phanom** Nakhon Phanom, E Thailand 16.52N 104.41E
178 Ii10 **Tha Tum** Surin, E Thailand 15.18N 103.39E
105 P16 **Thau, Bassin de** *var.* Étang de Thau. ◎ S France
Thau, Étang de *see* Thau, Bassin de
177 G3 **Thaungdut** Sagaing, N Myanmar 24.25N 94.45E
178 Gg8 **Thaungyin** *Th.* Mae Nam Moei. ≈ Myanmar/Thailand
178 J9 **Tha Uthen** Nakhon Phanom, E Thailand 17.31N 104.34E
111 W2 **Thaya** *var.* Dyje. ≈ Austria/Czech Republic *see also* Dyje
29 V8 **Thayer** Missouri, C USA 36.31N 91.34W
177 Ff7 **Thayetmyo** Magwe, C Myanmar 19.19N 95.10E
35 S15 **Thayne** Wyoming, C USA 42.54N 111.01W
177 G6 **Thazi** Mandalay, C Myanmar 20.49N 96.04E
Thebes *see* Thíva
46 L5 **The Carlton** *var.* Abraham Bay. Mayaguana, SE Bahamas 22.21N 72.56W
47 O14 **The Crane** *var.* Crane. S Barbados 13.06N 59.26W
34 I11 **The Dalles** Oregon, NW USA 45.36N 121.10W
30 M14 **Thedford** Nebraska, C USA 41.58N 100.34W
The Hague *see* 's-Gravenhage
Theiss *see* Tisa/Tisza
15 Jj6 **Thelon** ≈ Northwest Territories/ Nunavut, N Canada
9 V15 **Theodore** Saskatchewan, S Canada 51.25N 103.01W
25 N8 **Theodore** Alabama, S USA 30.33N 88.10W
38 L13 **Theodore Roosevelt Lake** ⊠ Arizona, SW USA
Theodosia *see* Feodosiya
Theophilo Ottoni *see* Teófilo Otoni
15 K13 **The Pas** Manitoba, C Canada 53.49N 101.09W
33 T14 **The Plains** Ohio, N USA 39.22N 82.07W
Thera *see* Thíra
180 H17 **Thérèse, Île** *island* Inner Islands, NE Seychelles
Therezina *see* Teresina
117 L20 **Thérma** Ikaría, Dodekánisos, Greece, Aegean Sea 37.37N 26.18E
Thermae Himerenses *see* Termini Imerese
Thermae Pannonicae *see* Baden
Thermaic Gulf/Thermaicus Sinus *see* Thermaïkós Kólpos
123 Gg10 **Thermaïkós Kólpos** *Eng.* Thermaic Gulf; *anc.* Thermaicus Sinus. *gulf* N Greece
Thermiá *see* Kýthnos
117 L17 **Thermís** Lésvos, E Greece 39.08N 26.32E
117 E18 **Thérmo** Dytikí Ellás, C Greece 38.32N 21.42E
35 V14 **Thermopolis** Wyoming, C USA 43.39N 108.12W
191 P10 **The Rock** New South Wales, SE Australia 35.18S 147.07E
205 O5 **Theron Mountains** ▲▲ Antarctica
117 G18 **Thespiés** Stereá Ellás, C Greece 38.18N 23.08E
117 E16 **Thessalía** *Eng.* Thessaly. ⬖ *region* C Greece
12 C10 **Thessalon** Ontario, S Canada 46.15N 83.32W
117 G14 **Thessaloníki** *Eng.* Salonica, Salonika, *SCr.* Solun, *Turk.* Selânik. Kentrikí Makedonía, N Greece 40.37N 22.58E
117 G14 **Thessaloníki** ✕ Kentrikí Makedonía, N Greece 40.30N 22.58E
Thessaly *see* Thessalía
86 B12 **Theta Gap** *undersea feature* E Atlantic Ocean
99 P20 **Thetford** E England, UK 52.25N 0.45E
13 R11 **Thetford-Mines** Québec, SE Canada 46.07N 71.16W
115 K17 **Theth** *var.* Thethi. Shkodër, N Albania 42.25N 19.45E
Thethi *see* Theth
101 L20 **Theux** Liège, E Belgium 50.33N 5.48E
47 V9 **The Valley** ○ (Anguilla) E Anguilla 18.12N 63.00W
29 N10 **The Village** Oklahoma, C USA 35.33N 97.33W
27 W10 **The Woodlands** Texas, SW USA 30.09N 95.27E
Thiamis *see* Thýamis
Thian Shan *see* Tien Shan
24 J9 **Thibodaux** Louisiana, S USA 29.48N 90.49W
31 S3 **Thief Lake** ◎ Minnesota, N USA
31 S3 **Thief River** ≈ Minnesota, C USA
31 S3 **Thief River Falls** Minnesota, N USA 48.07N 96.10W
Thièle *see* La Thielle
34 G14 **Thielsen, Mount** ▲ Oregon, NW USA 43.09N 122.04W
Thielt *see* Tielt
108 G7 **Thiene** Veneto, NE Italy 45.43N 11.28E
Thienen *see* Tienen
105 P11 **Thiers** Puy-de-Dôme, C France 45.51N 3.33E
78 F11 **Thiès** W Senegal 14.51N 16.51W
83 I19 **Thika** Central, S Kenya 1.03S 37.04E
Thikombia *see* Cikobia
157 K18 **Thiladhunmathi Atoll** *var.* Tiladummati Atoll. *atoll* N Maldives
Thimbu *see* Thimphu
159 T11 **Thimphu** *var.* Thimbu; *prev.* Tashi Chho Dzong. ● (Bhutan) W Bhutan 27.28N 89.37E
94 H2 **Thingeyri** Vestfirdhir, NW Iceland 65.52N 23.28W
94 I3 **Thingvellir** Sudhurland, SW Iceland 64.15N 21.06W
197 J6 **Thio** Province Sud, C New Caledonia 21.37S 166.13E
105 T4 **Thionville** *Ger.* Diedenhofen. Moselle, NE France 49.22N 6.10E
117 K22 **Thíra** Thíra, Kykládes, Greece, Aegean Sea 36.25N 25.26E
117 K22 **Thíra** *prev.* Santorin, Santoríni, *anc.* Thera. *island* Kykládes, Greece, Aegean Sea
117 J22 **Thirasía** *island* Kykládes, Greece, Aegean Sea
99 M16 **Thirsk** N England, UK 54.06N 1.16W
12 F12 **Thirty Thousand Islands** *island group* Ontario, S Canada
Thiruvanathapuram *see* Trivandrum
97 F20 **Thisted** Viborg, NW Denmark 56.58N 8.42E
Thistil Fjord *see* Thistilfjördhur
94 L1 **Thistilfjördhur** *var.* Thistil Fjord. *fjord* NE Iceland
190 G9 **Thistle Island** *island* South Australia
Thithia *see* Cicia
179 N14 **Thitu Island** *island* NW Spratly Islands
Thiukhaoluang Phrahang *see* Luang Prabang Range
117 G18 **Thíva** *Eng.* Thebes; *prev.* Thívai. Stereá Ellás, C Greece 38.19N 23.19E
Thívai *see* Thíva
104 M12 **Thiviers** Dordogne, SW France 45.24N 0.54E
94 J4 **Thjórsá** ≈ C Iceland
15 L9 **Thlewiaza** ≈ Nunavut, NE Canada
15 J9 **Thoa** ≈ Northwest Territories, NW Canada
101 G14 **Tholen** Zeeland, SW Netherlands 51.31N 4.13E
101 F14 **Tholen** *island* SW Netherlands
28 L10 **Thomas** Oklahoma, C USA 35.44N 98.45W
23 T3 **Thomas** West Virginia, NE USA 39.09N 79.28W
29 U3 **Thomas Hill Reservoir** ⊠ Missouri, C USA
25 S5 **Thomaston** Georgia, SE USA 32.53N 84.19W
21 R7 **Thomaston** Maine, NE USA 44.06N 69.10W
27 T12 **Thomaston** Texas, SW USA 28.56N 97.07W
25 O6 **Thomasville** Alabama, S USA 31.54N 87.42W
25 T8 **Thomasville** Georgia, SE USA 30.49N 83.57W
23 S9 **Thomasville** North Carolina, SE USA 35.52N 80.04W
37 N5 **Thomes Creek** ≈ California, W USA
9 W12 **Thompson** Manitoba, C Canada 55.45N 97.54W
31 R4 **Thompson** North Dakota, N USA 47.45N 97.07W
(0) F8 **Thompson** ≈ Alberta/British Columbia, SW Canada
35 O8 **Thompson Falls** Montana, NW USA 47.36N 115.20W
31 Q10 **Thompson, Lake** ◎ South Dakota, N USA
36 M3 **Thompson Peak** ▲ California, W USA 41.00N 123.01W
29 S2 **Thompson River** ≈ Missouri, C USA
193 A22 **Thompson Sound** *sound* South Island, NZ
15 Hh1 **Thomsen** ≈ Banks Island, Northwest Territories, NW Canada
25 V4 **Thomson** Georgia, SE USA 33.28N 82.30W
105 T10 **Thonon-les-Bains** Haute-Savoie, E France 46.22N 6.30E
105 O15 **Thoré** *var.* Thore. ≈ S France
39 P11 **Thoreau** New Mexico, SW USA 35.24N 108.13W
Thorenburg *see* Turda
94 J3 **Thórisvatn** ◎ C Iceland
94 P4 **Thor, Kapp** *headland* S Svalbard 76.25N 25.01E
94 I4 **Thorlákshöfn** Sudhurland, SW Iceland 63.51N 21.24W
Thorn *see* Toruń
27 T10 **Thorndale** Texas, SW USA 30.36N 97.12W
12 H10 **Thorne** Ontario, S Canada 46.38N 79.04W
99 J14 **Thornhill** S Scotland, UK 55.13N 3.46W
27 U8 **Thornton** Texas, SW USA 31.24N 96.34W
Thornton Island *see* Millennium Island
12 H16 **Thorold** Ontario, S Canada 43.07N 79.15W
34 I9 **Thorp** Washington, NW USA 47.03N 120.40W
205 S3 **Thorshavnheiane** *physical region* Antarctica
94 L1 **Thórshöfn** Nordhurland Eystra, NE Iceland 66.09N 15.18W
Thospitis *see* Van Gölü
178 J14 **Thôt Nôt** Cân Thơ, S Vietnam 10.16N 105.31E
104 K8 **Thouars** Deux-Sèvres, W France 46.58N 0.13W
159 X14 **Thoubal** Manipur, NE India 24.40N 94.00E
104 K9 **Thouet** ≈ W France
Thoune *see* Thun
20 H7 **Thousand Islands** *island* Canada/USA
37 S15 **Thousand Oaks** California, W USA 34.10N 118.50W
116 L12 **Thrace** *cultural region* SE Europe
116 J13 **Thracian Sea** *Gk.* Thrakikó Pélagos; *anc.* Thracium Mare. *sea* Greece/Turkey
Thracium Mare/Thrakikó Pélagos *see* Thracian Sea
Thrá Lí, Bá *see* Tralee Bay
35 R11 **Three Forks** Montana, NW USA 45.53N 111.34W
166 M8 **Three Gorges Dam** *dam* Hubei, C China 30.55N 111.00E
9 Q16 **Three Hills** Alberta, SW Canada 51.43N 113.15W
191 N15 **Three Hummock Island** *island* Tasmania, SE Australia
192 H1 **Three Kings Islands** *island group* N NZ
183 P10 **Three Kings Rise** *undersea feature* W Pacific Ocean
79 O18 **Three Points, Cape** *headland* S Ghana 4.43N 2.03W
33 P10 **Three Rivers** Michigan, N USA 41.56N 85.37W
27 S13 **Three Rivers** Texas, SW USA 28.27N 98.10W
85 G24 **Three Sisters** Northern Cape, SW South Africa 31.51S 23.04E
34 H13 **Three Sisters** ▲ Oregon, NW USA 44.08N 121.46W
195 Z16 **Three Sisters Islands** *island group* SE Solomon Islands
Thrissur *see* Trichūr
27 Q6 **Throckmorton** Texas, SW USA 33.10N 99.10W
188 M10 **Throssell, Lake** *salt lake* Western Australia
117 K25 **Thrýptis** ▲ Kríti, Greece, E Mediterranean Sea 35.06N 25.51E
178 Jj14 **Thu Dâu Môt** *var.* Phu Cương. Sông Be, S Vietnam 10.58N 106.40E
178 Jj6 **Thu Do** ✕ (Ha Nôi) Ha Nôi, N Vietnam 21.13N 105.46E
101 G21 **Thuin** Hainaut, S Belgium 50.21N 4.18E
155 Q12 **Thul** Sind, SE Pakistan 28.13N 68.49E
Thule *see* Qaanaaq
85 J18 **Thuli** *var.* Tuli. ≈ S Zimbabwe
Thumrayt *see* Thamarīt
110 D9 **Thun** *Fr.* Thoune. Bern, W Switzerland 46.46N 7.37E
10 C12 **Thunder Bay** Ontario, S Canada 48.27N 89.12W
32 M1 **Thunder Bay** *lake bay* S Canada
33 R6 **Thunder Bay** *lake bay* Michigan, N USA
33 R6 **Thunder Bay River** ≈ Michigan, N USA
29 N11 **Thunderbird, Lake** ⊠ Oklahoma, C USA
30 L8 **Thunder Butte Creek** ≈ South Dakota, N USA
110 E9 **Thuner See** ◎ C Switzerland
178 H16 **Thung Song** *var.* Cha Mai. Nakhon Si Thammarat, SW Thailand 8.10N 99.40E
110 H7 **Thur** ≈ N Switzerland
110 G6 **Thurgau** *Fr.* Thurgovie. ⬖ *canton* NE Switzerland
Thurgovie *see* Thurgau
Thuringe *see* Thüringen
110 J7 **Thüringen** Vorarlberg, W Austria 47.12N 9.48E
103 J17 **Thüringen** *Eng.* Thuringia, *Fr.* Thuringe. ⬖ *state* C Germany
103 J17 **Thüringer Wald** *Eng.* Thuringian Forest. ▲▲ C Germany
Thuringia *see* Thüringen
Thuringian Forest *see* Thüringer Wald
99 D19 **Thurles** *Ir.* Durlas. S Ireland 52.40N 7.49W
23 W2 **Thurmont** Maryland, NE USA 39.36N 77.22W
Thurø *see* Thurø By
97 H24 **Thurø By** *var.* Thurø. Fyn, C Denmark 55.03N 10.43E
12 M12 **Thurso** Québec, SE Canada 45.36N 75.13W
98 J6 **Thurso** N Scotland, UK 58.34N 3.31W
204 I10 **Thurston Island** *island* Antarctica
110 I9 **Thusis** Graubünden, S Switzerland 46.40N 9.27E
117 C15 **Thýamis** *var.* Thiamis. ≈ W Greece
97 E21 **Thyborøn** *var.* Tyborøn. Ringkøbing, W Denmark 56.40N 8.12E
205 U3 **Thyer Glacier** *glacier* Antarctica
117 L20 **Thýmaina** *island* Dodekánisos, Greece, Aegean Sea
85 N15 **Thyolo** *var.* Cholo. Southern, S Malawi 16.03S 35.11E
191 U6 **Tia** New South Wales, SE Australia 31.14S 151.51E
56 H5 **Tía Juana** Zulia, NW Venezuela 10.18N 71.22W
Tiancheng *see* Chongyang
166 J14 **Tiandong** *var.* Pingma. Guangxi Zhuangzu Zizhiqu, S China 23.37N 107.06E
167 O3 **Tianjin** *var.* Tientsin. Tianjin Shi, E China 39.12N 117.06E
Tianjin *see* Tianjin Shi
167 P3 **Tianjin Shi** *var.* Jin, Tianjin, T'ien-ching, Tientsin. ⬖ *municipality* E China
165 S10 **Tianjun** *var.* Xinyuan. Qinghai, C China 37.16N 99.03E
166 J13 **Tianlin** *var.* Leli. Guangxi Zhuangzu Zizhiqu, S China 24.27N 106.03E
Tian Shan *see* Tien Shan
165 W11 **Tianshui** Gansu, C China 34.33N 105.51E
156 I7 **Tianshuihai** Xinjiang Uygur Zizhiqu, W China 35.16N 79.30E
167 S10 **Tiantai** Zhejiang, SE China 29.11N 121.01E
166 J14 **Tianyang** *var.* Tianzhou. Guangxi Zhuangzu Zizhiqu, S China 23.45N 106.54E
Tianzhou *see* Tianyang
165 U9 **Tianzhu** *var.* Huazangsi, Tianzhu Zangzu Zizhixian. Gansu, C China 37.01N 103.04E
Tianzhu Zangzu Zizhixian *see* Tianzhu
203 Q7 **Tiarei** Tahiti, W French Polynesia 17.31S 149.19W
76 J6 **Tiaret** *var.* Tihert. NW Algeria 35.23N 1.18E
79 N17 **Tiassalé** S Ivory Coast 5.54N 4.49W
198 Bb8 **Ti'avea** Upolu, SE Samoa 13.58S 171.30W
Tiba *see* Chiba
62 J11 **Tibagi** *var.* Tibaji. Paraná, S Brazil 24.28S 50.28W
62 J10 **Tibagi, Rio** *var.* Rio Tibají. ≈ S Brazil
Tibaji *see* Tibagi
Tibají, Rio *see* Tibagi, Rio
145 Q9 **Tibal, Wādī** *dry watercourse* S Iraq
56 G9 **Tibaná** Boyacá, C Colombia 5.19N 73.25W
81 F14 **Tibati** Adamaoua, N Cameroon 6.28N 12.37E
78 K15 **Tibé, Pic de** ▲ SE Guinea 8.39N 8.58W
Tiber *see* Tivoli, Italy
Tiber *see* Tevere, Italy
Tiberias *see* Teverya
144 G8 **Tiberias, Lake** *var.* Chinnereth, Sea of Bahr Tabariya, Sea of Galilee, *Ar.* Bahrat Tabariya, *Heb.* Yam Kinneret. ◎ N Israel
69 Q5 **Tibesti** *var.* Tibesti Massif, *Ar.* Tībistī. ▲▲ N Africa
Tibesti Massif *see* Tibesti
Tibetan Autonomous Region *see* Xizang Zizhiqu
Tibet, Plateau of *see* Qingzang Gaoyuan
Tībistī *see* Tibesti
12 K7 **Tiblemont, Lac** ◎ Québec, SE Canada
145 X9 **Ţīb, Nahr aţ** ≈ S Iraq
Tibnī *see* At Tibnī
190 L4 **Tibooburra** New South Wales, SE Australia 29.24S 142.01E
97 L18 **Tibro** Västra Götaland, S Sweden 58.25N 14.10E
42 E5 **Tiburón, Isla** *var.* Isla del Tiburón. *island* NW Mexico
Tiburón, Isla del *see* Tiburón, Isla
25 W14 **Tice** Florida, SE USA 26.40N 81.49W
Tichau *see* Tychy
116 L8 **Ticha, Yazovir** ◎ NE Bulgaria
78 K9 **Tîchît** *var.* Tichitt. Tagant, C Mauritania 18.25N 9.31W
Tichitt *see* Tîchît
110 G11 **Ticino** *Fr./Ger.* Tessin. ⬖ *canton* S Switzerland
108 D8 **Ticino** ≈ Italy/Switzerland
110 H11 **Ticino** *Ger.* Tessin. ≈ SW Switzerland
Ticinum *see* Pavia
43 X12 **Ticul** Yucatán, SE Mexico 20.21N 89.29W
97 K18 **Tidaholm** Västra Götaland, S Sweden 58.12N 13.55E
Tidjikdja *see* Tidjikja
78 J8 **Tidjikja** *var.* Tidjikdja; *prev.* Fort-Cappolani. Tagant, C Mauritania 18.30N 11.24W
Tidore *see* Soasiu
175 Ss7 **Tidore, Pulau** *island* E Indonesia
Tîdra, Ile *see* Et Tîdra
79 N16 **Tiébissou** *var.* Tiebissou. C Ivory Coast 7.10N 5.10W
Tiefa *see* Diaobingshan
110 I9 **Tiefencastel** Graubünden, S Switzerland 46.40N 9.33E
Tiegenhof *see* Nowy Dwór Gdański
T'ieh-ling *see* Tieling
100 K13 **Tiel** Gelderland, C Netherlands 51.54N 5.04E
169 W7 **Tieli** Heilongjiang, NE China 46.57N 128.01E
169 V11 **Tieling** *var.* T'ieh-ling. Liaoning, NE China 42.19N 123.52E
158 L4 **Tielongtan** China/India 35.10N 79.31E
101 D17 **Tielt** *var.* Thielt. West-Vlaanderen, W Belgium 51.00N 3.20E
T'ien-ching *see* Tianjin Shi
101 I18 **Tienen** *var.* Thienen, *Fr.* Tirlemont. Vlaams Brabant, C Belgium 50.48N 4.55E
Tiên Giang, Sông *see* Mekong
153 X9 **Tien Shan** *Chin.* Thian Shan, Tian Shan, T'ien Shan, *Rus.* Tyan'-Shan'. ▲▲ C Asia
Tientsin *see* Tianjin
Tientsin *see* Tianjin Shi
178 K6 **Tiên Yên** Quang Ninh, N Vietnam 21.19N 107.24E
97 O14 **Tierp** Uppsala, C Sweden 60.19N 17.30E
64 H7 **Tierra Amarilla** Atacama, N Chile 27.28S 70.16W
39 R9 **Tierra Amarilla** New Mexico, SW USA 36.42N 106.31W
43 R15 **Tierra Blanca** Veracruz-Llave, E Mexico 18.28N 96.21W
43 O16 **Tierra Colorada** Guerrero, S Mexico 17.10N 99.36W
65 J17 **Tierra Colorada, Bajo de la** *basin* SE Argentina
65 I25 **Tierra del Fuego** *off.* Provincia de la Tierra del Fuego. ⬖ *province* S Argentina
65 J24 **Tierra del Fuego** *island* Argentina/Chile
56 D7 **Tierralta** Córdoba, NW Colombia 8.10N 76.04W
106 K9 **Tiétar** ≈ W Spain
62 L10 **Tietê** São Paulo, S Brazil 23.04S 47.40W
62 J8 **Tietê, Rio** ≈ S Brazil
34 I9 **Tieton** Washington, NW USA 46.41N 120.43W
34 J6 **Tiffany Mountain** ▲ Washington, NW USA 48.40N 119.55W
33 S12 **Tiffin** Ohio, N USA 41.06N 83.10W
33 Q11 **Tiffin River** ≈ Ohio, N USA
Tiflis *see* T'bilisi
25 U7 **Tifton** Georgia, SE USA 31.27N 83.31W
175 Ss11 **Tifu** Pulau Buru, E Indonesia 3.46S 126.36E
197 K6 **Tiga, Île** *island* Îles Loyauté, W New Caledonia
40 L17 **Tigalda Island** *island* Aleutian Islands, Alaska, USA
117 I15 **Tigáni, Akrotírio** *headland* Límnos, E Greece 39.50N 25.03E
175 O1 **Tiga Tarok** Sabah, East Malaysia 6.57N 117.07E
119 O10 **Tighina** *Rus.* Bendery; *prev.* Bender. E Moldova 46.51N 29.27E
127 P10 **Tigil'** Koryakskiy Avtonomnyy Okrug, E Russian Federation 57.43N 158.39E
151 X9 **Tigiretskiy Khrebet** ▲▲ E Kazakhstan
81 F14 **Tignère** Adamaoua, N Cameroon 7.25N 12.49E
11 P14 **Tignish** Prince Edward Island, SE Canada 46.58N 64.03W
Tigranocerta *see* Siirt
82 I11 **Tigray** ⬖ *province* N Ethiopia
43 O11 **Tigre, Cerro del** ▲ C Mexico 23.06N 99.13W
58 F8 **Tigre, Río** ≈ N Peru
145 X10 **Tigris** *Ar.* Dijlah, *Turk.* Dicle. ≈ Iraq/Turkey
78 G9 **Tiguent** Trarza, SW Mauritania 17.15N 16.00W
76 M10 **Tiguentourine** E Algeria 27.59N 9.16E
79 V10 **Tiguidit, Falaise de** *ridge* C Niger
147 N13 **Tihāmah** *var.* Tehama. *plain* Saudi Arabia/Yemen
Tihert *see* Tiaret
Ti-hua/Tihwa *see* Ürümqi
43 Q13 **Tihuatlán** Veracruz-Llave, E Mexico 20.44N 97.30W
42 B1 **Tijuana** Baja California, NW Mexico 32.31N 117.01W
44 E2 **Tikal** Petén, N Guatemala 17.11N 89.36W
160 I9 **Tīkamgarh** *prev.* Tehri. Madhya Pradesh, C India 24.43N 78.49E
164 L7 **Tikanlik** Xinjiang Uygur Zizhiqu, NW China 40.34N 87.37E
79 P12 **Tikaré** N Burkina 13.16N 1.39W
41 O12 **Tikchik Lakes** *lakes* Alaska, USA
203 T9 **Tikehau** *atoll* Îles Tuamotu, C French Polynesia
203 V9 **Tikei** *island* Îles Tuamotu, C French Polynesia
125 B12 **Tikhoretsk** Krasnodarskiy Kray, SW Russian Federation 45.50N 40.07E
128 I13 **Tikhvin** Leningradskaya Oblast', NW Russian Federation 59.37N 33.29E
199 Ll10 **Tiki Basin** *undersea feature* S Pacific Ocean
78 K13 **Tikinsso** ≈ NE Guinea
192 Q8 **Tikitiki** Gisborne, North Island, NZ 37.49S 178.23E
81 D16 **Tiko** Sud-Ouest, SW Cameroon 4.01N 9.19E
145 S6 **Tikrīt** *var.* Tekrit. N Iraq 34.36N 43.42E
128 I8 **Tiksha** Respublika Kareliya, NW Russian Federation 64.07N 32.31E
128 I6 **Tikshozero, Ozero** ◎ NW Russian Federation
126 L7 **Tiksi** Respublika Sakha (Yakutiya), NE Russian Federation 71.40N 128.46E
173 G8 **Tiku** Sumatera, W Indonesia 0.24S 99.55E
44 A6 **Tilapa** San Marcos, SW Guatemala 14.31N 92.11W
44 L13 **Tilarán** Guanacaste, NW Costa Rica 10.28N 84.57W
101 J14 **Tilburg** Noord-Brabant, S Netherlands 51.34N 5.04E
12 D17 **Tilbury** Ontario, S Canada 42.15N 82.25W
190 K4 **Tilcha** South Australia 29.37S 140.52E
Tilcha Creek *see* Callabonna Creek
31 Q14 **Tilden** Nebraska, C USA 42.03N 97.49W
27 R13 **Tilden** Texas, SW USA 28.26N 98.32W
12 H10 **Tilden Lake** Ontario, S Canada 46.35N 79.36W
118 G9 **Tileagd** *Hung.* Mezőtelegd. Bihor, W Romania 47.03N 22.10E
79 Q8 **Tîlemsi, Vallée de** ≈ C Mali
127 Pp8 **Tilichiki** Koryakskiy Avtonomnyy Okrug, E Russian Federation 60.25N 165.55E
Tiligul *see* Tilihul
Tiligul'skiy Liman *see* Tilihul's'kyy Lyman
119 P9 **Tilihul** *Rus.* Tiligul. ≈ SW Ukraine
119 P10 **Tilihul's'kyy Lyman** *Rus.* Tiligul'skiy Liman. ◎ S Ukraine
Tilimsen *see* Tlemcen
Tilio Martius *see* Toulon
79 R11 **Tillabéri** *var.* Tillabéry. Tillabéri, W Niger 14.12N 1.25E
79 R11 **Tillabéri** ⬖ *department* SW Niger
Tillabéry *see* Tillabéri
34 F11 **Tillamook** Oregon, NW USA 45.27N 123.50W
34 E11 **Tillamook Bay** *inlet* Oregon, NW USA
157 Q22 **Tillanchāng Dwīp** *island* Nicobar Islands, India, NE Indian Ocean
97 N15 **Tillberga** Västmanland, C Sweden 59.52N 16.39E
Tillenberg *see* Dyleń
23 S10 **Tillery, Lake** ⊠ North Carolina, SE USA
79 T10 **Tillia** Tahoua, W Niger 16.13N 4.51E
25 N8 **Tillmans Corner** Alabama, S USA 30.35N 88.10W
12 F17 **Tillsonburg** Ontario, S Canada 42.51N 80.41W
117 N22 **Tílos** *island* Dodekánisos, Greece, Aegean Sea
191 N5 **Tilpa** New South Wales, SE Australia 30.56S 144.24E
Tilsit *see* Sovetsk
33 N13 **Tilton** Illinois, N USA 40.06N 87.39W
130 K7 **Tim** Kurskaya Oblast', W Russian Federation 51.39N 37.11E
56 D12 **Timaná** Huila, S Colombia 1.56N 75.57W
Timan Ridge *see* Timanskiy Kryazh
129 Q6 **Timanskiy Kryazh** *Eng.* Timan Ridge. *ridge* NW Russian Federation
193 G20 **Timaru** Canterbury, South Island, NZ 44.22S 171.15E
131 S6 **Timashevo** Samarskaya Oblast', W Russian Federation 53.22N 51.13E
130 K13 **Timashevsk** Krasnodarskiy Kray, SW Russian Federation 45.37N 38.57E
Timbaki/Timbákion *see* Tympáki
24 K10 **Timbalier Bay** *bay* Louisiana, S USA
24 K11 **Timbalier Island** *island* Louisiana, S USA
194 K12 **Timbe** ≈ C Papau New Guinea
78 L10 **Timbedgha** *var.* Timbédra. Hodh ech Chargui, SE Mauritania 16.16N 8.13W
Timbédra *see* Timbedgha
34 G10 **Timber** Oregon, NW USA 45.42N 123.19W
189 O3 **Timber Creek** Northern Territory, N Australia 15.35S 130.21E
30 M8 **Timber Lake** South Dakota, N USA 45.25N 101.01W
56 D12 **Timbío** Cauca, SW Colombia 2.22N 76.41W
56 C12 **Timbiquí** Cauca, SW Colombia 2.41N 77.41W
85 O17 **Timbue, Ponta** *headland* C Mozambique 18.49S 36.22E
Timbuktu *see* Tombouctou
176 Vv10 **Timbuni, Sungai** ≈ Papua, E Indonesia
175 Oo4 **Timbun Mata, Pulau** *island* E Malaysia
79 P8 **Timétrine** *var.* Ti-n-Kâr. *oasis* C Mali 19.18N 0.09W
Timfi *see* Týmfi
Timfristos *see* Tymfristós
79 V9 **Tîmia** Agadez, C Niger 18.07N 8.49E
176 X12 **Timika** Papua, E Indonesia 4.39S 137.15E
76 I9 **Timimoun** C Algeria 29.18N 0.21E
Timiris, Cap *see* Timirist, Râs
78 F8 **Timirist, Râs** *var.* Cap Timiris. *headland* NW Mauritania 19.18N 16.28W
151 O7 **Timiryazevo** Severnyy Kazakhstan, N Kazakhstan 53.45N 66.33E
118 E11 **Timiş** ⬖ *county* SW Romania
12 H9 **Timiskaming, Lake** *Fr.* Lac Témiscamingue. ◎ Ontario/Québec, SE Canada
118 E11 **Timişoara** *Ger.* Temeschwar, Temeswar, *Hung.* Temesvár; *prev.* Temeschburg. Timiş, W Romania 45.46N 21.16E
118 E11 **Timişoara** ✕ Timiş, W Romania 45.50N 21.21E
Timkovichi *see* Tsimkavichy
79 U8 **Ti-m-Meghsoï** ≈ NW Niger
102 K8 **Timmendorfer Strand** Schleswig-Holstein, N Germany 53.59N 10.50E
12 F7 **Timmins** Ontario, S Canada 48.09N 80.00W
23 S12 **Timmonsville** South Carolina, SE USA 34.07N 79.56W
32 K5 **Timms Hill** ▲ Wisconsin, N USA 45.27N 90.12W
176 Vv9 **Timoforo** ≈ Papua, E Indonesia
114 P12 **Timok** ≈ E Serbia and Montenegro (Yugoslavia)
60 N13 **Timon** Maranhão, E Brazil 5.07S 42.52W
175 Rr17 **Timor** *island* East Timor/Indonesia
175 S17 **Timor Sea** *sea* E Indian Ocean
Timor Timur *see* East Timor
Timor Trench *see* Timor Trough
198 G9 **Timor Trough** *var.* Timor Trench. *undersea feature* NE Timor Sea
63 A21 **Timote** Buenos Aires, E Argentina 35.22S 62.13W
56 I6 **Timotes** Mérida, NW Venezuela 8.57N 70.46W
27 X8 **Timpson** Texas, SW USA 31.54N 94.24W
126 Ll13 **Timpton** ≈ NE Russian Federation
95 H17 **Timrå** Västernorrland, C Sweden 62.28N 17.19E
22 J10 **Tims Ford Lake** ⊠ Tennessee, S USA
174 Hh7 **Timun** Pulau Kundur, C Indonesia 0.49N 103.23E
174 H3 **Timur, Banjaran** ▲▲ Peninsular Malaysia
179 R17 **Tinaca Point** *headland* Mindanao, S Philippines 5.35N 125.18E
56 K5 **Tinaco** Cojedes, N Venezuela 9.42N 68.27W
66 Q11 **Tinajo** Lanzarote, Islas Canarias, Spain , NE Atlantic Ocean 29.03N 13.40W
195 W8 **Tinakula** *island* Santa Cruz Islands, E Solomon Islands
56 K5 **Tinaquillo** Cojedes, N Venezuela 9.52N 68.19W
118 F10 **Tinca** *Hung.* Tenke. Bihor, W Romania 46.46N 21.58E
161 J20 **Tīndivanam** Tamil Nādu, SE India 12.15N 79.40E
76 E9 **Tindouf** W Algeria 27.43N 8.09W
76 E9 **Tindouf, Sebkha de** *salt lake* W Algeria
106 J2 **Tineo** Asturias, N Spain 43.19N 6.25W
79 R9 **Ti-n-Essako** Kidal, E Mali 18.30N 2.27E
191 T5 **Tingha** New South Wales, SE Australia 29.56S 151.13E
Tingis *see* Tanger
Tinglett *see* Tinglev
97 F24 **Tinglev** *Ger.* Tinglett. Sønderjylland, SW Denmark 54.57N 9.15E
58 E12 **Tingo María** Huánuco, C Peru 9.19S 75.56W
Tingréla *see* Tengréla
164 K16 **Tingri** *var.* Xêgar. Xizang Zizhiqu, W China 28.40N 87.04E

◆ Country
● Country Capital
◇ Dependent Territory
○ Dependent Territory Capital
⬖ Administrative Region
✕ International Airport
▲ Mountain
▲▲ Mountain Range
Volcano
≈ River
◎ Lake
⊠ Reservoir

TINGSRYD – TORI-SHIMA

97 M21 **Tingsryd** Kronoberg, S Sweden 56.30N 15.00E
97 P19 **Tingstäde** Gotland, SE Sweden 57.45N 18.36E
64 H12 **Tinguiririca, Volcán** ▲ C Chile 34.52S 70.24W
96 F9 **Tingvoll** Møre og Romsdal, S Norway 62.55N 8.13E
194 M9 **Tingwon Island** *island* N PNG
196 K8 **Tinian** *island* S Northern Mariana Islands
Ti-n-Kâr *see* Timétrine
Tinnevelly *see* Tirunelveli
97 G15 **Tinnoset** Telemark, S Norway 59.43N 9.03E
97 F15 **Tinnsjø** ◎ S Norway
Tino *see* Chino
117 J20 **Tínos** Tínos, Kykládes, Greece, Aegean Sea 37.32N 25.10E
117 J20 **Tínos** *anc.* Tenos. *island* Kykládes, Greece, Aegean Sea
159 R14 **Tinpahar** Jhārkhand, NE India 25.00N 87.43E
124 O14 **Tīn, Ra's al** *headland* N Libya 32.36N 23.10E
159 X11 **Tinsukia** Assam, NE India 27.28N 95.19E
78 K10 **Tîntâne** Hodh el Gharbi, S Mauritania 16.25N 10.08W
64 L7 **Tintina** Santiago del Estero, N Argentina 27.03S 62.42W
190 K10 **Tintinara** South Australia 35.54S 140.04E
106 I14 **Tinto** ≈ SW Spain
79 S8 **Ti-n-Zaouâtene** Kidal, NE Mali 19.56N 2.45E
Tiobraid Árann *see* Tipperary
30 K3 **Tioga** North Dakota, N USA 48.24N 102.56W
20 G12 **Tioga** Pennsylvania, NE USA 41.54N 77.07W
27 T5 **Tioga** Texas, SW USA 33.28N 96.55W
37 Q8 **Tioga Pass** *pass* California, W USA 37.53N 119.15W
20 G12 **Tioga River** ≈ New York/Pennsylvania, NE USA
176 Y11 **Tiom** Papua, E Indonesia 3.49S 138.22E
Tioman Island *see* Tioman, Pulau
174 I5 **Tioman, Pulau** *var.* Tioman Island. *island* Peninsular Malaysia
20 C12 **Tionesta** Pennsylvania, NE USA 41.31N 79.30W
20 D12 **Tionesta Creek** ≈ Pennsylvania, NE USA
173 G11 **Tiop** Pulau Pagai Selatan, W Indonesia 3.12S 100.21E
175 Qq12 **Tioro, Selat** *var.* Tiworo. *strait* Sulawesi, C Indonesia
79 O12 **Tiou** NW Burkina 13.42N 2.34W
20 H11 **Tioughnioga River** ≈ New York, NE USA
176 U10 **Tip** Papua, E Indonesia 1.50S 130.04E
76 J5 **Tipasa** *var.* Tipaza. N Algeria 36.34N 2.27E
Tipaza *see* Tipasa
44 J10 **Tipitapa** Managua, W Nicaragua 12.10N 86.04W
33 R13 **Tipp City** Ohio, N USA 39.57N 84.10W
33 O12 **Tippecanoe River** ≈ Indiana, N USA
99 D20 **Tipperary** *Ir.* Tiobraid Árann. S Ireland 52.28N 8.10W
99 D19 **Tipperary** *Ir.* Tiobraid Árann. *cultural region* S Ireland
37 R12 **Tipton** California, W USA 36.02N 119.19W
33 P13 **Tipton** Indiana, N USA 40.19N 86.00W
31 Y14 **Tipton** Iowa, C USA 41.46N 91.07W
29 U5 **Tipton** Missouri, C USA 38.39N 92.46W
38 I10 **Tipton, Mount** ▲ Arizona, SW USA 35.32N 114.11W
22 F8 **Tiptonville** Tennessee, S USA 36.22N 89.28W
10 E12 **Tip Top Mountain** ▲ Ontario, S Canada 48.18N 86.06W
161 G19 **Tiptūr** Karnātaka, W India 13.17N 76.31E
Tiquisate *see* Pueblo Nuevo Tiquisate
60 L13 **Tiracambu, Serra do** ▲▲ E Brazil
Tirana *see* Tiranë
115 K19 **Tirana Rinas** ✈ Durrës, W Albania 41.25N 19.41E
115 L20 **Tiranë** *var.* Tirana. ● (Albania) Tiranë, C Albania 41.19N 19.49E
115 K20 **Tiranë** ◐ *district* W Albania
146 I5 **Tirān, Jazīrat** *island* Egypt/Saudi Arabia
108 F6 **Tirano** Lombardia, N Italy 46.13N 10.10E
190 I2 **Tirari Desert** *desert* South Australia
119 O10 **Tiraspol** *Rus.* Tiraspol'. E Moldova 46.50N 29.34E
192 M8 **Tirau** Waikato, North Island, NZ 37.59S 175.44E
142 C14 **Tire** İzmir, SW Turkey 38.04N 27.45E
143 O11 **Tirebolu** Giresun, N Turkey 41.01N 38.49E
98 F11 **Tiree** *island* W Scotland, UK
Tîrgovişte *see* Târgovişte
Tîrgu *see* Târgu Cărbuneşti
Tîrgu Bujor *see* Târgu Bujor
Tîrgu Frumos *see* Târgu Frumos
Tîrgu Jiu *see* Targu Jui
Tîrgu Lăpuş *see* Târgu Lăpuş
Tîrgu Mures *see* Târgu Mureş
Tîrgu-Neamţ *see* Târgu-Neamţ
Tîrgu Ocna *see* Târgu Ocna
Tîrgu Secuiesc *see* Târgu Secuiesc
155 T3 **Tirich Mīr** ▲ NW Pakistan 36.12N 71.51E
78 J5 **Tiris Zemmour** ◐ *region* N Mauritania
Tirlemont *see* Tienen
131 W5 **Tirlyanskiy** Respublika Bashkortostan, W Russian Federation 54.09N 58.32E
Tîrnava Mare *see* Târnava Mare
Tîrnava Mică *see* Târnava Mică
Tîrnăveni *see* Târnăveni
Tírnavos *see* Týrnavos
Tirnovo *see* Veliko Tŭrnovo
160 J11 **Tirodi** Madhya Pradesh, C India 21.40N 79.43E
110 K8 **Tirol** *off.* Land Tirol, *var.* Tyrol, *It.* Tirolo. ◐ *state* W Austria
Tirolo *see* Tirol
Tirreno, Mare *see* Tyrrhenian Sea
109 B19 **Tirso** ≈ Sardegna, Italy, C Mediterranean Sea
97 H22 **Tirstrup** ✈ (Århus) Århus, C Denmark 56.17N 10.36E
161 I21 **Tiruchchirāppalli** *prev.* Trichinopoly. Tamil Nādu, SE India 10.49N 78.43E
161 H23 **Tirunelveli** *var.* Tinnevelly. Tamil Nādu, SE India 8.45N 77.43E
161 J19 **Tirupati** Andhra Pradesh, E India 13.39N 79.25E
161 I20 **Tiruppattūr** Tamil Nādu, SE India 12.28N 78.31E
161 H21 **Tiruppūr** Tamil Nādu, SW India 11.04N 77.19E
161 I20 **Tiruvannāmalai** Tamil Nādu, SE India 12.13N 79.07E
114 L10 **Tisa** *Ger.* Theiss, *Hung.* Tisza, *Rus.* Tissa, *Ukr.* Tysa. ≈ SE Europe *see also* Tisza
Tischnowitz *see* Tišnov
9 U14 **Tisdale** Saskatchewan, S Canada 52.51N 104.01W
29 O13 **Tishomingo** Oklahoma, C USA 34.14N 96.40W
97 M17 **Tisnaren** ◎ S Sweden
113 F18 **Tišnov** *Ger.* Tischnowitz. Jihomoravský Kraj, SE Czech Republic 49.21N 16.24E
Tissa *see* Tisa/Tisza
76 J6 **Tissemsilt** N Algeria 35.37N 1.48E
159 S12 **Tista** ≈ NE India
114 L8 **Tisza** *Ger.* Theiss, *Rom./Slvn./SCr.* Tisa, *Rus.* Tissa, *Ukr.* Tysa. ≈ SE Europe *see also* Tisa
113 L23 **Tiszaföldvár** Jász-Nagykun-Szolnok, E Hungary 47.00N 20.16E
113 M22 **Tiszafüred** Jász-Nagykun-Szolnok, E Hungary 47.34N 20.45E
113 L23 **Tiszakécske** Bács-Kiskun, C Hungary 46.55N 20.04E
113 M21 **Tiszaújváros** *prev.* Leninváros. Borsod-Abaúj-Zemplén, NE Hungary 47.55N 21.03E
113 N21 **Tiszavasvári** Szabolcs-Szatmár-Bereg, NE Hungary 47.57N 21.24E
Titibu *see* Chichibu
59 I17 **Titicaca, Lake** ◎ Bolivia/Peru
202 H17 **Titikaveka** Rarotonga, S Cook Islands 21.16S 159.45W
160 M13 **Titilāgarh** Orissa, E India 20.18N 83.09E
174 Gg4 **Titiwangsa, Banjaran** ▲▲ Peninsular Malaysia
Titograd *see* Podgorica
Titose *see* Chitose
Titova Mitrovica *see* Kosovska Mitrovica
Titovo Užice *see* Užice
115 M18 **Titov Vrv** ▲ NW FYR Macedonia 41.58N 20.49E
96 F7 **Titran** Sør-Trøndelag, S Norway 63.40N 8.20E
33 Q8 **Tittabawassee River** ≈ Michigan, N USA
118 J13 **Titu** Dâmboviţa, S Romania 44.40N 25.31E
81 M16 **Titule** Orientale, N Dem. Rep. Congo 3.19N 25.23E
25 X11 **Titusville** Florida, SE USA 28.34N 80.48W
20 C12 **Titusville** Pennsylvania, NE USA 41.36N 79.39W
78 G11 **Tivaouane** W Senegal 14.59N 16.50W
115 I17 **Tivat** Montenegro, SW Serbia and Montenegro (Yugoslavia) 42.25N 18.43E
12 E14 **Tiverton** Ontario, S Canada 44.15N 81.31W
99 J23 **Tiverton** SW England, UK 50.54N 3.30W
21 O12 **Tiverton** Rhode Island, NE USA 41.38N 71.10W
109 I15 **Tivoli** *anc.* Tiber. Lazio, C Italy 41.58N 12.45E
27 U13 **Tivoli** Texas, SW USA 28.26N 96.54W
176 W11 **Tiwarra** Papua, E Indonesia 2.54S 133.52E
147 Z8 **Ţīwī** NE Oman 22.43N 59.20E
Tiworo *see* Tioro, Selat
176 Ww12 **Tiyo, Pegunungan** ▲▲ Papua, E Indonesia
43 Y11 **Tizimín** Yucatán, SE Mexico 21.10N 88.09W
76 K5 **Tizi Ouzou** *var.* Tizi-Ouzou. N Algeria 36.44N 4.06E
76 D8 **Tiznit** SW Morocco 29.43N 9.39W
115 I14 **Tjentište** Republika Srpska, SE Bosnia and Herzegovina 43.23N 18.42E
Tjepoe/Tjepu *see* Cepu
100 L7 **Tjeukemeer** ◎ N Netherlands
Tjiamis *see* Ciamis
Tjiandjoer *see* Cianjur
Tjilatjap *see* Cilacap
Tjiledoeg *see* Ciledug
97 F23 **Tjæreborg** Ribe, W Denmark 55.28N 8.34E
97 I18 **Tjörn** *island* S Sweden
94 O3 **Tjuvfjorden** *fjord* S Svalbard
Tkvarcheli *see* Tqvarch'eli
42 L8 **Tlahualillo** Durango, N Mexico 26.06N 103.25W
43 P14 **Tlalnepantla** México, C Mexico 19.37N 99.09W
43 Q13 **Tlapacoyán** Veracruz-Llave, E Mexico 19.57N 97.18W
43 P16 **Tlapa de Comonfort** Guerrero, S Mexico 17.33N 98.33W
42 L13 **Tlaquepaque** Jalisco, C Mexico 20.36N 103.19W
Tlascala *see* Tlaxcala
43 P14 **Tlaxcala** *var.* Tlascala, Tlaxcala de Xicohténcatl. Tlaxcala, C Mexico 19.17N 98.15W
43 P14 **Tlaxcala** ◐ *state* S Mexico
Tlaxcala de Xicohténcatl *see* Tlaxcala
43 P14 **Tlaxco** *var.* Tlaxco de Morelos. Tlaxcala, S Mexico 19.37N 98.07W
Tlaxco de Morelos *see* Tlaxco
43 Q16 **Tlaxiaco** *var.* Santa María Asunción Tlaxiaco. Oaxaca, S Mexico 17.18N 97.42W
76 I6 **Tlemcen** *var.* Tilimsen, Tlemsen. NW Algeria 34.52N 1.21W
Tlemsen *see* Tlemcen
144 L4 **Tlété Ouâte Rharbi, Jebel** ▲ N Syria
118 J7 **Tlumach** Ivano-Frankivs'ka Oblast', W Ukraine 48.53N 25.00E
131 P17 **Tlyarata** Respublika Dagestan, SW Russian Federation 42.10N 46.30E
118 K10 **Toaca, Vârful** *prev.* Vîrful Toaca. ▲ NE Romania 46.58N 25.55E
Toaca, Vîrful *see* Toaca, Vârful
197 C13 **Toak** Ambrym, C Vanuatu 16.21S 168.16E
180 J4 **Toamasina** *var.* Tamatave. Toamasina, E Madagascar 18.10S 49.22E
180 J4 **Toamasina** ◐ *province* E Madagascar
180 J4 **Toamasina** ✈ Toamasina, E Madagascar 18.10S 49.22E
23 X6 **Toano** Virginia, NE USA 37.22N 76.46W
203 U10 **Toau** *atoll* Îles Tuamotu, C French Polynesia
47 T6 **Toa Vaca, Embalse** ▣ C Puerto Rico
64 K13 **Toay** La Pampa, C Argentina 36.43S 64.22W
165 R14 **Toba** Xizang Zizhiqu, W China 31.16N 97.37E
171 Hh16 **Toba** Mie, Honshū, SW Japan 34.28N 136.49E
173 Ff5 **Toba, Danau** ◎ Sumatera, W Indonesia
47 Y16 **Tobago** *island* NE Trinidad and Tobago
155 Q9 **Toba Kākar Range** ▲▲ NW Pakistan
175 T10 **Tobalai, Selat** *strait* Maluku, E Indonesia
175 Q9 **Tobamawu** Sulawesi, N Indonesia 1.16S 121.42E
107 Q12 **Tobarra** Castilla-La Mancha, C Spain 38.36N 1.40W
155 U9 **Toba Tek Singh** Punjab, E Pakistan 30.54N 72.30E
175 T6 **Tobelo** Pulau Halmahera, E Indonesia 1.45N 127.58E
12 E12 **Tobermory** Ontario, S Canada 45.13N 81.39W
98 G10 **Tobermory** W Scotland, UK 56.37N 6.12W
172 Oo5 **Tōbetsu** Hokkaidō, NE Japan 43.12N 141.28E
188 M6 **Tobin Lake** ◎ Western Australia
9 U14 **Tobin Lake** ◎ Saskatchewan, C Canada
37 T4 **Tobin, Mount** ▲ Nevada, W USA 40.25N 117.28W
171 L10 **Tobi-shima** *island* C Japan
174 J11 **Toboali** Pulau Bangka, W Indonesia 2.57S 106.25E
150 M8 **Tobol** *Kaz.* Tobyl. Kostanay, N Kazakhstan 52.42N 62.36E
150 L8 **Tobol** *Kaz.* Tobyl. ≈ Kazakhstan/Russian Federation
125 F11 **Tobol'sk** Tyumenskaya Oblast', C Russian Federation 58.15N 68.12E
Tobruch/Tobruk *see* Ţubruq
129 R3 **Tobseda** Nenetskiy Avtonomnyy Okrug, NW Russian Federation 68.37N 52.24E
Tobyl *see* Tobol
129 Q6 **Tobysh** ≈ NW Russian Federation
56 F10 **Tocaima** Cundinamarca, C Colombia 4.30N 74.37W
61 K16 **Tocantins** *off.* Estado do Tocantins. ◐ *state* C Brazil
61 K15 **Tocantins, Rio** ≈ N Brazil
25 T2 **Toccoa** Georgia, SE USA 34.34N 83.19W
171 K15 **Tochigi** *var.* Totigi. Tochigi, Honshū, S Japan 36.24N 139.42E
171 Kk15 **Tochigi** *off.* Tochigi-ken, *var.* Totigi. ◐ *prefecture* Honshū, S Japan
171 K13 **Tochio** *var.* Totio. Niigata, Honshū, C Japan 37.27N 139.00E
97 I15 **Töcksfors** Värmland, C Sweden 59.30N 11.49E
44 J5 **Tocoa** Colón, N Honduras 15.36N 86.01W
64 H4 **Tocopilla** Antofagasta, N Chile 22.06S 70.08W
64 I4 **Tocorpuri, Cerro de** ▲ Bolivia/Chile 22.25S 67.52W
191 O10 **Tocumwal** New South Wales, SE Australia 35.53S 145.35E
56 K4 **Tocuyo de La Costa** Falcón, NW Venezuela 11.02N 68.27W
158 H13 **Toda Rāisingh** Rājasthān, N India 26.01N 75.34E
108 H13 **Todi** Umbria, C Italy 42.46N 12.25E
110 G9 **Tödi** ▲ NE Switzerland 46.52N 8.53E
176 Uu9 **Todlo** Papua, E Indonesia 0.46S 130.50E
172 N12 **Todoga-saki** *headland* Honshū, C Japan 39.33N 142.02E
61 P17 **Todos os Santos, Baía de** *bay* E Brazil
42 F10 **Todos Santos** Baja California Sur, W Mexico 23.26N 110.14W
42 B2 **Todos Santos, Bahía de** *bay* NW Mexico
Toeban *see* Tuban
Toekang Besi Eilanden *see* Tukangbesi, Kepulauan
Tōen *see* T'aoyüan
193 D25 **Toetoes Bay** *bay* South Island, NZ
9 Q14 **Tofield** Alberta, SW Canada 53.22N 112.39W
8 K17 **Tofino** Vancouver Island, British Columbia, SW Canada 49.04N 125.51W
201 X17 **Tofol** Kosrae, E Micronesia
97 J20 **Tofta** Halland, S Sweden 57.10N 12.19E
97 H15 **Tofte** Buskerud, S Norway 59.31N 10.33E
97 F24 **Toftlund** Sønderjylland, SW Denmark 55.12N 9.04E
200 S13 **Tofua** *island* Ha'apai Group, C Tonga
197 B10 **Toga** *island* Torres Islands, N Vanuatu
171 Kk17 **Tōgane** Chiba, Honshū, S Japan 35.32N 140.22E
82 N13 **Togdheer** *off.* Gobolka Togdheer. ◐ *region* NW Somalia
Toghyzaq *see* Toguzak
171 Ii12 **Togi** Ishikawa, Honshū, SW Japan 37.06N 136.43E
41 N13 **Togiak** Alaska, USA 59.03N 160.31W
175 Qq8 **Togian, Kepulauan** *island group* C Indonesia
79 Q15 **Togo** *off.* Togolese Republic; *prev.* French Togoland. ◆ *republic* W Africa
168 F8 **Tögrög** Govĭ-Altay, SW Mongolia 45.51N 95.04E
168 E7 **Tögrög** Hovd, W Mongolia 47.24N 92.06E
165 N12 **Togton He** *var.* Tuotuo He. ≈ C China
Togton Heyan *see* Tanggulashan
150 L7 **Toguzak** *Kaz.* Toghyzaq. ≈ Kazakhstan/Russian Federation
39 P10 **Tohatchi** New Mexico, SW USA 35.51N 108.45W
203 O7 **Tohiea, Mont** ⛰ Moorea, W French Polynesia 17.33S 149.48W
95 O17 **Tohmajärvi** Itä-Suomi, E Finland 62.12N 30.19E
143 N14 **Tohma Çayı** ≈ C Turkey
95 L16 **Toholampi** Länsi-Suomi, W Finland 63.46N 24.15E
168 M10 **Töhöm** Dornogovĭ, SE Mongolia 44.25N 108.18E
25 X12 **Tohopekaliga, Lake** ◎ Florida, SE USA
171 J17 **Toi** Shizuoka, Honshū, S Japan 34.55N 138.45E
202 B15 **Toi** N Niue 18.57S 169.51W
95 L19 **Toijala** Länsi-Suomi, W Finland 61.09N 23.51E
175 Qq9 **Toima** Sulawesi, N Indonesia 0.48S 122.21E
170 C17 **Toi-misaki** *headland* Kyūshū, SW Japan 31.21N 131.18E
175 Rr17 **Toineke** Timor, S Indonesia 10.06S 124.22E
Toirc, Inis *see* Inishturk
37 U6 **Toiyabe Range** ▲▲ Nevada, W USA
Tojikiston, Jumhurii *see* Tajikistan
153 R12 **Tojikobod** *Rus.* Tadzhikabad. C Tajikistan 39.08N 70.54E
170 F13 **Tōjō** Hiroshima, Honshū, SW Japan 34.54N 133.15E
41 T10 **Tok** Alaska, USA 63.20N 142.59W
172 P5 **Tokachi-dake** ▲ Hokkaidō, NE Japan 43.24N 142.41E
172 Pp7 **Tokachi-gawa** *var.* Tokati Gawa. ≈ Hokkaidō, NE Japan
171 Hh16 **Tōkai** Aichi, Honshū, SW Japan 35.01N 136.51E
113 N21 **Tokaj** Borsod-Abaúj-Zemplén, NE Hungary 48.07N 21.25E
171 Jj13 **Tōkamachi** Niigata, Honshū, C Japan 37.08N 138.46E
193 D25 **Tokanui** Southland, South Island, NZ 46.33S 169.01E
82 I7 **Tokar** *var.* Ţawkar. Red Sea, NE Sudan 18.27N 37.40E
142 L12 **Tokat** Tokat, N Turkey 40.19N 36.34E
142 L12 **Tokat** ◐ *province* N Turkey
Tokati Gawa *see* Tokachi-gawa
169 X15 **Tŏkchŏk-gundo** *island group* NW South Korea
Tōke *see* Taka Atoll
202 J9 **Tokelau** ◇ *NZ overseas territory* W Polynesia
Tőketerebes *see* Trebišov
Tokhtamyshbek *see* Tükhtamish
26 M6 **Tokio** Texas, SW USA 33.09N 102.31W
Tokio *see* Tōkyō
201 W11 **Toki Point** *point* NW Wake Island 19.19N 166.36E
Tokkuztara *see* Gongliu
153 V7 **Tokmak** *Kir.* Tokmok. Chuyskaya Oblast', N Kyrgyzstan 42.49N 75.18E
119 V9 **Tokmak** *var.* Velykyy Tokmak. Zaporiz'ka Oblast', SE Ukraine 47.13N 35.42E
Tokmok *see* Tokmak
192 Q8 **Tokomaru Bay** Gisborne, North Island, NZ 38.10S 178.18E
171 Hh16 **Tokoname** Aichi, Honshū, SW Japan 34.54N 136.49E
172 Qq5 **Tokoro** Hokkaidō, NE Japan 44.06N 144.03E
192 M8 **Tokoroa** Waikato, North Island, NZ 38.14S 175.52E
172 Q6 **Tokoro-gawa** ≈ Hokkaidō, NE Japan
78 K14 **Tokounou** Haute-Guinée, C Guinea 9.43N 9.46W
40 M12 **Toksook Bay** Alaska, USA 60.33N 165.01W
Toksu *see* Xinhe
Toksum *see* Toksun
164 L6 **Toksun** *var.* Toksum. Xinjiang Uygur Zizhiqu, NW China 42.46N 88.37E
153 T8 **Toktogul** Talasskaya Oblast', NW Kyrgyzstan 41.51N 72.56E
153 T9 **Toktogul'skoye Vodokhranilishche** ▣ W Kyrgyzstan
Toktomush *see* Tükhtamish
200 Ss12 **Toku** *island* Vava'u Group, N Tonga
172 Qq14 **Tokunoshima** Kagoshima, Tokuno-shima, SW Japan
172 Q14 **Tokuno-shima** *island* Nansei-shotō, SW Japan
170 Ff15 **Tokushima** *var.* Tokusima. Tokushima, Shikoku, SW Japan 34.04N 134.28E
170 F15 **Tokushima** *off.* Tokushima-ken, *var.* Tokusima. ◐ *prefecture* Shikoku, SW Japan
Tokusima *see* Tokushima
170 E13 **Tokuyama** Yamaguchi, Honshū, SW Japan 34.04N 131.48E
171 Jj16 **Tōkyō** *var.* Tokio. ● (Japan) Tōkyō, Honshū, S Japan 35.40N 139.45E
171 J15 **Tōkyō** *off.* Tōkyō-to. ◐ *capital district* Honshū, S Japan
171 K17 **Tōkyō-wan** *bay* S Japan
151 T12 **Tokyrau** ≈ C Kazakhstan
155 O3 **Tokzār** *Pash.* Tukzār. Sar-e Pol, N Afghanistan 35.47N 66.28E
151 W13 **Tokzhaylau** *prev.* Dzerzhinskoye. Almaty, SE Kazakhstan 45.49N 81.04E
201 U12 **Tol** *atoll* Chuuk Islands, C Micronesia
192 Q9 **Tolaga Bay** Gisborne, North Island, NZ 38.22S 178.17E
180 I7 **Tôlañaro** *prev.* Faradofay, Fort-Dauphin. Toliara, SE Madagascar
168 D6 **Tolbo** Bayan-Ölgiy, W Mongolia 48.22N 90.22E
Tolbukhin *see* Dobrich
62 G11 **Toledo** Paraná, S Brazil 24.45S 53.41W
56 G8 **Toledo** Norte de Santander, N Colombia 7.16N 72.28W
179 Qq13 **Toledo** *off.* Toledo City. Cebu, C Philippines 10.23N 123.39E
107 N9 **Toledo** *anc.* Toletum. Castilla-La Mancha, C Spain 39.52N 4.01W
32 M14 **Toledo** Illinois, N USA 39.16N 88.15W
31 W13 **Toledo** Iowa, C USA 42.00N 92.34W
33 R11 **Toledo** Ohio, N USA 41.39N 83.33W
34 F12 **Toledo** Oregon, NW USA 44.37N 123.56W
34 G9 **Toledo** Washington, NW USA 46.27N 122.49W
44 F3 **Toledo** ◐ *district* S Belize
106 M9 **Toledo** ◐ *province* Castilla-La Mancha, C Spain
27 Y7 **Toledo Bend Reservoir** ▣ Louisiana/Texas, SW USA
106 M10 **Toledo, Montes de** ▲▲ C Spain
108 J12 **Tolentino** Marche, C Italy 43.08N 13.17E
Toletum *see* Toledo
96 H10 **Tolga** Hedmark, S Norway 62.25N 11.00E
164 J3 **Toli** Xinjiang Uygur Zizhiqu, NW China 45.55N 83.33E
180 H7 **Toliara** *var.* Toliary; *prev.* Tuléar. Toliara, SW Madagascar 23.19S 43.40E
180 H7 **Toliara** ◐ *province* SW Madagascar
Toliary *see* Toliara
56 D11 **Tolima** *off.* Departamento del Tolima. ◐ *province* C Colombia
175 Pp7 **Tolitoli** Sulawesi, C Indonesia 1.04N 120.49E
97 K22 **Tollarp** Skåne, S Sweden 55.55N 14.00E
102 N9 **Tollense** ≈ NE Germany
102 N10 **Tollensesee** ◎ NE Germany
38 K13 **Tolleson** Arizona, SW USA 33.25N 112.15W
152 M13 **Tollimarjon** *Rus.* Talimardzhan. Qashqadaryo Viloyati, S Uzbekistan 38.22N 65.31E
Tolmein *see* Tolmin
108 J6 **Tolmezzo** Friuli-Venezia Giulia, NE Italy 46.27N 13.01E
111 S11 **Tolmin** *Ger.* Tolmein, *It.* Tolmino. W Slovenia 46.12N 13.39E
Tolmino *see* Tolmin
113 J25 **Tolna** *Ger.* Tolnau. Tolna, S Hungary 46.25N 18.46E
113 I24 **Tolna** *off.* Tolna Megye. ◐ *county* SW Hungary
Tolnau *see* Tolna
81 I20 **Tolo** Bandundu, W Dem. Rep. Congo 2.57S 18.35E
Tolochin *see* Talachyn
202 D12 **Toloke** Île Futuna, W Wallis and Futuna
32 M13 **Tolono** Illinois, N USA 39.59N 88.16W
107 Q3 **Tolosa** País Vasco, N Spain 43.09N 2.04W
Tolosa *see* Toulouse
175 Qq10 **Tolo, Teluk** *bay* Sulawesi, C Indonesia
41 R9 **Tolovana River** ≈ Alaska, USA
127 Oo10 **Tolstoy, Mys** *headland* E Russian Federation 59.12N 155.04E
65 G15 **Toltén** Araucanía, C Chile 39.13S 73.10W
65 G15 **Toltén, Río** ≈ S Chile
56 E6 **Tolú** Sucre, NW Colombia 9.31N 75.34W
43 O14 **Toluca** *var.* Toluca de Lerdo. México, S Mexico 19.19N 99.40W
Toluca de Lerdo *see* Toluca
43 O14 **Toluca, Nevado de** ⛰ C Mexico 19.05N 99.45W
131 R6 **Tol'yatti** *prev.* Stavropol'. Samarskaya Oblast', W Russian Federation 53.31N 49.27E
126 H14 **Tom'** ≈ S Russian Federation
79 O12 **Toma** NW Burkina 12.46N 2.51W
32 K7 **Tomah** Wisconsin, N USA 43.59N 90.31W
32 L5 **Tomahawk** Wisconsin, N USA 45.27N 89.40W
119 T8 **Tomakivka** Dnipropetrovs'ka Oblast', E Ukraine 47.47N 34.45E
172 O6 **Tomakomai** Hokkaidō, NE Japan 42.38N 141.32E
172 P3 **Tomamae** Hokkaidō, NE Japan 44.18N 141.38E
106 G9 **Tomar** Santarém, W Portugal 39.36N 8.25W
127 O15 **Tomari** Ostrov Sakhalin, Sakhalinskaya Oblast', SE Russian Federation 47.47N 142.09E
117 C16 **Tómaros** ▲ W Greece 39.31N 20.45E
Tomaschow *see* Tomaszów Lubelski, Poland
Tomaschow *see* Tomaszów Mazowiecki, Poland
63 E16 **Tomás Gomensoro** Artigas, N Uruguay 30.28S 57.28W
119 N7 **Tomashpil'** Vinnyts'ka Oblast', C Ukraine 48.32N 28.31E
Tomaszów *see* Tomaszów Mazowiecki
113 P15 **Tomaszów Lubelski** *Ger.* Tomaschow. Lubelskie, E Poland 50.28N 23.22E
Tomaszów Mazowiecka *see* Tomaszów Mazowiecki
112 L13 **Tomaszów Mazowiecki** *var.* Tomaszów Mazowiecka; *prev.* Tomaszów, *Ger.* Tomaschow. Łodzkie, C Poland 51.33N 20.00E
42 J13 **Tomatlán** Jalisco, C Mexico 19.53N 105.18W
170 F12 **Tombara** Shimane, Honshū, SW Japan 35.04N 132.46E
83 F15 **Tombe** Jonglei, S Sudan 5.52N 31.40E
25 N4 **Tombigbee River** ≈ Alabama/Mississippi, S USA
84 A10 **Tomboco** Zaire, NW Angola 6.47S 13.18E
79 O10 **Tombouctou** *Eng.* Timbuktu. Tombouctou, N Mali 16.47N 3.03W
79 N9 **Tombouctou** ◐ *region* W Mali
39 N16 **Tombstone** Arizona, SW USA 31.42N 110.04W
85 A15 **Tombua** *Port.* Porto Alexandre. Namibe, SW Angola 15.49S 11.52E
85 J19 **Tom Burke** Limpopo, NE South Africa 23.07S 28.01E
152 L9 **Tomdibuloq** *Rus.* Tamdybulak. Navoiy Viloyati, N Uzbekistan 41.48N 64.33E
152 L9 **Tomditov-Tog'lari** ▲▲ N Uzbekistan
64 G13 **Tomé** Bío Bío, C Chile 36.39S 72.53W
60 L12 **Tomé-Açu** Pará, NE Brazil 2.25S 48.09W
97 L23 **Tomelilla** Skåne, S Sweden 55.33N 14.00E
107 O10 **Tomelloso** Castilla-La Mancha, C Spain 39.09N 3.01W
12 H10 **Tomiko Lake** ◎ Ontario, S Canada
79 N12 **Tominian** Ségou, C Mali 13.18N 4.39W
175 Pp8 **Tomini, Gulf of** *var.* Teluk Tomini; *prev.* Teluk Gorontalo. *bay* Sulawesi, C Indonesia
Tomini, Teluk *see* Tomini, Gulf of
172 Ll15 **Tomioka** Fukushima, Honshū, C Japan 37.19N 140.57E
172 Jj15 **Tomioka** Gunma, Honshū, S Japan 36.15N 138.51E
115 G14 **Tomislavgrad** Federacija Bosna I Hercegovina, SW Bosnia and Herzegovina 43.43N 17.15E
189 O9 **Tomkinson Ranges** ▲▲ South Australia/Western Australia
126 Ll12 **Tommot** Respublika Sakha (Yakutiya), NE Russian Federation 58.56N 126.24E
175 Rr7 **Tomohon** Sulawesi, N Indonesia 1.19N 124.49E
56 K9 **Tomo, Río** ≈ E Colombia
115 L21 **Tomorrit, Mali i** ▲ S Albania 40.43N 20.12E
9 S17 **Tompkins** Saskatchewan, S Canada 50.03N 108.49W
22 K8 **Tompkinsville** Kentucky, S USA 36.42N 85.41W
175 Pp7 **Tompo** Sulawesi, N Indonesia 0.56N 120.16E
188 I8 **Tom Price** Western Australia 22.48S 117.49E
126 H13 **Tomsk** Tomskaya Oblast', C Russian Federation 56.30N 85.04E
126 Gg12 **Tomskaya Oblast'** ◐ *province* C Russian Federation
20 K16 **Toms River** New Jersey, NE USA 39.56N 74.09W
Tom Steed Lake *see* Tom Steed Reservoir
28 L12 **Tom Steed Reservoir** *var.* Tom Steed Lake. ▣ Oklahoma, C USA
176 Vv10 **Tomu** Papua, E Indonesia 2.07S 133.01E
194 F13 **Tomu** ≈ W PNG
164 H6 **Tomür Feng** *var.* Pobeda Peak, *Rus.* Pik Pobedy. ▲ China/Kyrgyzstan 42.02N 80.07E *see also* Pobedy, Pik
201 N13 **Tomworoahlang** Pohnpei, E Micronesia
43 U17 **Tonalá** Chiapas, SE Mexico 16.03N 93.43W
108 F6 **Tonale, Passo del** *pass* N Italy 46.16N 10.37E
171 Ii13 **Tonami** Toyama, Honshū, SW Japan 36.39N 136.57E
60 C12 **Tonantins** Amazonas, W Brazil 2.58S 67.30W
34 K6 **Tonasket** Washington, NW USA 48.41N 119.27W
57 Y9 **Tonate** *var.* Macouria. N French Guiana 05.00N 52.28W
20 D10 **Tonawanda** New York, NE USA 43.00N 78.51W
175 Rr7 **Tondano** Sulawesi, C Indonesia 1.19N 124.55E
175 Rr7 **Tondano, Danau** ◎ Sulawesi, N Indonesia
106 H7 **Tondela** Viseu, N Portugal 40.31N 8.04W
97 F24 **Tønder** *Ger.* Tondern. Sønderjylland, SW Denmark 54.57N 8.52E
Tondern *see* Tønder
171 K16 **Tone-gawa** ≈ Honshū, S Japan
149 N4 **Tonekābon** *var.* Shahsawar, Tonkābon; *prev.* Shahsavār. Māzandarān, N Iran 36.49N 51.51E
Tonezh *see* Tonyezh
200 S15 **Tonga** *off.* Kingdom of Tonga, *var.* Friendly Islands. ◆ *monarchy* SW Pacific Ocean
183 R9 **Tonga** *island group* SW Pacific Ocean
85 K23 **Tongaat** KwaZulu/Natal, E South Africa 29.31S 31.09E
167 Q13 **Tong'an** *var.* Datong, Tong an. Fujian, SE China 24.43N 118.07E
29 Q4 **Tonganoxie** Kansas, C USA 39.06N 95.05W
41 Y13 **Tongass National Forest** *reserve* Alaska, USA
200 Qq16 **Tongatapu** ✈ Tongatapu, S Tonga 21.10S 175.10W
200 R15 **Tongatapu** *island* Tongatapu Group, S Tonga
200 S14 **Tongatapu Group** *island group* S Tonga
183 S9 **Tonga Trench** *undersea feature* S Pacific Ocean
167 N8 **Tongbai Shan** ▲▲ C China
167 P8 **Tongcheng** Anhui, E China 31.16N 117.00E
166 L6 **Tongchuan** Shaanxi, C China 35.10N 109.03E
166 L12 **Tongdao** *var.* Tongdao Dongzu Zizhixian; *prev.* Shuangjiang. Hunan, S China 26.06N 109.46E
165 T11 **Tongde** *var.* Gabasumdo. Qinghai, C China 35.13N 100.39E
101 K19 **Tongeren** *Fr.* Tongres. Limburg, NE Belgium 50.46N 5.28E
169 Y14 **Tonghae** NE South Korea 37.25N 129.08E
166 G13 **Tonghai** *var.* Xiushan. Yunnan, SW China 24.06N 102.45E
169 X8 **Tonghe** Heilongjiang, NE China 46.00N 128.45E
169 W11 **Tonghua** Jilin, NE China 41.43N 125.56E
194 L8 **Tong Island** *island* N PNG
169 Z6 **Tongjiang** Heilongjiang, NE China 47.39N 132.29E
169 Y13 **Tongjosŏn-man** *prev.* Broughton Bay. *bay* E North Korea
169 V7 **Tongken He** ≈ NE China
178 K7 **Tongking, Gulf of** *Chin.* Beibu Wan, *Vtn.* Vinh Băc Bô. *gulf* China/Vietnam
169 U10 **Tongliao** Nei Mongol Zizhiqu, N China 43.37N 122.15E
167 Q9 **Tongling** Anhui, E China 30.54N 117.51E
167 R9 **Tonglu** Zhejiang, SE China 29.49N 119.37E
197 D14 **Tongoa** *island* Shepherd Islands, S Vanuatu
64 G9 **Tongoy** Coquimbo, C Chile 30.20S 71.28W
166 L11 **Tongren** Guizhou, S China 27.43N 109.10E
165 T11 **Tongren** *var.* Rongwo. Qinghai, C China 35.31N 101.58E
Tongres *see* Tongeren
159 U11 **Tongsa** *var.* Tongsa Dzong. C Bhutan 27.33N 90.30E
Tongsa Dzong *see* Tongsa
Tongshan *see* Xuzhou
Tongshi *see* Wuzhishan
165 P12 **Tongtian He** ≈ C China
98 I6 **Tongue** N Scotland, UK 58.29N 4.24W
46 H3 **Tongue of the Ocean** *strait* C Bahamas
35 X10 **Tongue River** ≈ Montana, NW USA
35 W11 **Tongue River Resevoir** ▣ Montana, NW USA
165 V11 **Tongwei** Gansu, C China 35.09N 105.15E
165 W9 **Tongxin** Ningxia, N China 37.00N 105.41E
169 U9 **Tongyu** *var.* Kaitong. Jilin, NE China 44.49N 123.08E
166 J11 **Tongzi** Guizhou, S China 28.07N 106.49E
42 G5 **Tónichi** Sonora, NW Mexico 28.34N 109.33W
83 D14 **Tonj** Warab, SW Sudan 7.18N 28.40E
158 H13 **Tonk** Rājasthān, N India 26.10N 75.49E
Tonkābon *see* Tonekābon
29 N8 **Tonkawa** Oklahoma, C USA 36.40N 97.18W
178 Ii12 **Tônlé Sap** *Eng.* Great Lake. ◎ W Cambodia
104 L14 **Tonneins** Lot-et-Garonne, SW France 44.21N 0.21E
105 Q7 **Tonnerre** Yonne, C France 47.50N 4.00E
Tonoas *see* Dublon
37 U8 **Tonopah** Nevada, W USA 38.04N 117.13W
170 Ff14 **Tonoshō** Okayama, Shōdo-shima, SW Japan 34.29N 134.10E
45 S17 **Tonosí** Los Santos, S Panama 7.23N 80.25W
97 H16 **Tønsberg** Vestfold, S Norway 59.16N 10.25E
41 T11 **Tonsina** Alaska, USA 61.39N 145.10W
97 D17 **Tonstad** Vest-Agder, S Norway 58.40N 6.42E
200 S14 **Tonumea** *island* Nomuka Group, W Tonga
143 O11 **Tonya** Trabzon, NE Turkey 40.52N 39.16E
121 K20 **Tonyezh** *Rus.* Tonezh. Homyel'skaya Voblasts', SE Belarus 51.49N 27.48E
38 L3 **Tooele** Utah, W USA 40.31N 112.18W
126 Ii15 **Toora-Khem** Respublika Tyva, S Russian Federation 52.25N 96.01E
191 O5 **Toorale East** New South Wales, SE Australia 30.29S 145.25E
85 H25 **Toorberg** ▲ S South Africa 32.02S 24.02E
120 G5 **Tootsi** Pärnumaa, SW Estonia 58.35N 24.46E
191 U3 **Toowoomba** Queensland, E Australia 27.34S 151.54E
29 Q4 **Topeka** *state capital* Kansas, C USA 39.03N 95.40W
113 M18 **Topľa** *Hung.* Toplya. ≈ NE Slovakia
126 H14 **Topki** Kemerovskaya Oblast', S Russian Federation 55.12N 85.40E
Toplicza *see* Topliţa
118 J10 **Topliţa** *Ger.* Töplitz, *Hung.* Maroshévíz; *prev.* Topliţa Română, *Hung.* Oláh-Toplicza, Toplicza. Harghita, C Romania 46.57N 25.22E
Topliţa Română/Töplitz *see* Topliţa
Toplya *see* Topľa
113 I20 **Topoľčany** *Hung.* Nagytapolcsány. Nitriansky Kraj, SW Slovakia 48.33N 18.10E
42 G8 **Topolobampo** Sinaloa, C Mexico 25.37N 109.02W
118 I13 **Topoloveni** Argeş, S Romania 44.49N 25.01E
116 L11 **Topolovgrad** *prev.* Kavakli. Khaskovo, S Bulgaria 42.06N 26.20E
Topolya *see* Bačka Topola
128 I6 **Topozero, Ozero** ◎ NW Russian Federation
34 J10 **Toppenish** Washington, NW USA 46.22N 120.18W
189 P4 **Top Springs Roadhouse** Northern Territory, N Australia 16.37S 131.49E
201 U11 **Tora** *island* Chuuk, C Micronesia
Toraigh *see* Tory Island
201 U11 **Tora Island Pass** *passage* Chuuk Islands, C Micronesia
149 U5 **Torbat-e Ḩeydarīyeh** *var.* Turbat-i-Haidari. Khorāsān, NE Iran 35.18N 59.12E
149 V5 **Torbat-e Jām** *var.* Turbat-i-Jam. Khorāsān, NE Iran 35.16N 60.36E
41 Q11 **Torbert, Mount** ▲ Alaska, USA 61.30N 152.15W
33 P6 **Torch Lake** ◎ Michigan, N USA
Törcsvár *see* Bran
Torda *see* Turda
106 L6 **Tordesillas** Castilla-León, N Spain 41.30N 5.00W
94 K13 **Töre** Norrbotten, N Sweden 65.55N 22.40E
97 L17 **Töreboda** Västra Götaland, S Sweden 58.40N 14.07E
97 J21 **Torekov** Skåne, S Sweden 56.25N 12.39E
94 O3 **Torell Land** *physical region* SW Svalbard
119 Y8 **Torez** Donets'ka Oblast', SE Ukraine 48.02N 38.45E
103 N14 **Torgau** Sachsen, E Germany 51.34N 13.01E
Torgay Üstirti *see* Turgayskaya Stolovaya Strana
Torghay *see* Turgay
97 N22 **Torhamn** Blekinge, S Sweden 56.04N 15.49E
101 C17 **Torhout** West-Vlaanderen, W Belgium 51.04N 3.06E
108 B8 **Torino** *Eng.* Turin. Piemonte, NW Italy 45.03N 7.39E
172 Q13 **Tori-shima** *island* Izu-shotō, SE Japan

◆ Country
● Country Capital
◇ Dependent Territory
○ Dependent Territory Capital
◐ Administrative Region
✈ International Airport
▲ Mountain
▲▲ Mountain Range
⛰ Volcano
≈ River
◎ Lake
▣ Reservoir

Torit – Troppau

83 F16 **Torit** Eastern Equatoria, S Sudan 4.27N 32.31E
195 O11 **Toriu** New Britain, E PNG 4.39S 151.42E
154 M4 **Torkestān, Selseleh-ye Band-e** *var.* Bandi-i Turkistan. ⛰ NW Afghanistan
106 L7 **Tormes** ∽ W Spain
Tornacum *see* Tournai
Torneå *see* Tornio
94 K12 **Torneälven** *var.* Torniojoki, *Fin.* Tornionjoki. ∽ Finland/Sweden
94 I11 **Torneträsk** ◎ N Sweden
11 O4 **Torngat Mountains** ⛰ Newfoundland and Labrador, NE Canada
26 H8 **Tornillo** Texas, SW USA 31.26N 106.06W
94 K13 **Tornio** *Swe.* Torneå. Lappi, NW Finland 65.50N 24.17E
Torniojoki/Tornionjoki *see* Torneälven
63 B23 **Tornquist** Buenos Aires, E Argentina 38.05S 62.13W
106 L6 **Toro** Castilla-León, N Spain 41.31N 5.24W
64 H9 **Toro, Cerro del** ▲ N Chile 29.10S 69.43W
79 R12 **Torodi** Tillabéri, SW Niger 13.05N 1.46E
Törökbecse *see* Novi Bečej
195 S12 **Torokina** Bougainville Island, NE PNG 6.12S 155.04E
113 L23 **Törökszentmiklós** Jász-Nagykun-Szolnok, E Hungary 47.10N 20.25E
44 G7 **Torola, Río** ∽ El Salvador/Honduras
Toronaíos, Kólpos *see* Kassándras, Kólpos
12 H15 **Toronto** Ontario, S Canada 43.42N 79.25W
33 V12 **Toronto** Ohio, N USA 40.27N 80.36W
Toronto *see* Lester B.Pearson
29 P6 **Toronto Lake** ⊞ Kansas, C USA
37 V16 **Toro Peak** ▲ California, W USA 33.31N 116.25W
128 H16 **Toropets** Tverskaya Oblast', W Russian Federation 56.29N 31.37E
83 G18 **Tororo** E Uganda 0.46N 34.12E
142 H16 **Toros Dağları** *Eng.* Taurus Mountains. ⛰ S Turkey
191 N13 **Torquay** Victoria, SE Australia 38.21S 144.18E
99 J24 **Torquay** SW England, UK 50.28N 3.30W
106 M5 **Torquemada** Castilla-León, N Spain 42.02N 4.17W
37 S16 **Torrance** California, W USA 33.49N 118.19W
106 G12 **Torrão** Setúbal, S Portugal 38.18N 8.13W
106 H8 **Torre, Alto da** ▲ C Portugal 40.21N 7.31W
109 K18 **Torre Annunziata** Campania, S Italy 40.45N 14.27E
107 T8 **Torreblanca** País Valenciano, E Spain 40.13N 0.12E
106 L15 **Torrecilla** ▲ S Spain 36.38N 4.54W
107 P4 **Torrecilla en Cameros** La Rioja, N Spain 42.18N 2.33W
107 N13 **Torredelcampo** Andalucía, S Spain 37.45N 3.52W
109 K17 **Torre del Greco** Campania, S Italy 40.46N 14.22E
106 I6 **Torre de Moncorvo** *var.* Moncorvo, Tôrre de Moncorvo. Bragança, N Portugal 41.10N 7.03W
106 J9 **Torrejoncillo** Extremadura, W Spain 39.54N 6.28W
107 O8 **Torrejón de Ardoz** Madrid, C Spain 40.27N 3.28W
107 N7 **Torrelaguna** Madrid, C Spain 40.49N 3.33W
107 N2 **Torrelavega** Cantabria, N Spain 43.21N 4.03W
109 M16 **Torremaggiore** Puglia, SE Italy 41.42N 15.17E
106 M15 **Torremolinos** Andalucía, S Spain 36.37N 4.30W
190 I6 **Torrens, Lake** *salt lake* South Australia
107 S10 **Torrent** *Cas.* Torrente *var.* Torrent de l'Horta. País Valenciano, E Spain 39.27N 0.28W
Torrent de l'Horta/Torrente *see* Torrent
42 L8 **Torreón** Coahuila de Zaragoza, NE Mexico 25.47N 103.21W
107 R13 **Torre Pacheco** Murcia, SE Spain 37.43N 0.57W
108 A8 **Torre Pellice** Piemonte, NE Italy 44.49N 7.12E
107 O13 **Torreperogil** Andalucía, S Spain 38.01N 3.16W
63 J15 **Torres** Rio Grande do Sul, S Brazil 29.19S 49.46W
Torrès, Îles *see* Torres Islands
197 B10 **Torres Islands** *Fr.* Îles Torrès. *island group* N Vanuatu
106 G9 **Torres Novas** Santarém, C Portugal 39.28N 8.31W
189 V1 **Torres Strait** *strait* Australia/PNG
106 F10 **Torres Vedras** Lisboa, C Portugal 39.04N 9.15W
107 S13 **Torrevieja** País Valenciano, E Spain 37.58N 0.40W
194 F9 **Torricelli Mountains** ⛰ NW PNG
98 G8 **Torridon, Loch** *inlet* NW Scotland, UK
108 D9 **Torriglia** Liguria, NW Italy 44.31N 9.08E
106 M9 **Torrijos** Castilla-La Mancha, C Spain 39.58N 4.18W
20 L12 **Torrington** Connecticut, NE USA 41.48N 73.07W
35 Z15 **Torrington** Wyoming, C USA 42.04N 104.10W
Torröjen *see* Torrön
96 F16 **Torrön** *prev.* Torröjen. ◎ C Sweden
107 N15 **Torrox** Andalucía, S Spain 36.45N 3.58W
96 N13 **Torsåker** Gävleborg, C Sweden 60.31N 16.30E
97 N21 **Torsås** Kalmar, S Sweden 56.24N 16.00E
97 J14 **Torsby** Värmland, C Sweden 60.07N 13.00E
97 N16 **Torshälla** Södermanland, C Sweden 59.25N 16.28E
97 B19 **Tórshavn** *Dan.* Thorshavn *Dependent territory capital* Faeroe Islands 62.02N 6.47W
Torshiz *see* Kāshmar
152 I9 **To'rtkok'l** *var.* Türtkül, *Rus.* Turtkul'; *prev.* Petroaleksandrovsk. Qoraqalpog'iston Respublikasi, W Uzbekistan 41.34N 61.00E
47 T9 **Tortola** *island* C British Virgin Islands
108 D9 **Tortona** *anc.* Dertona. Piemonte, NW Italy 44.54N 8.52E
109 L23 **Tortorici** Sicilia, Italy, C Mediterranean Sea 38.01N 14.49E
107 U7 **Tortosa** *anc.* Dertosa. Cataluña, E Spain 40.49N 0.31E
Tortosa *see* Ṭarṭūs
107 U7 **Tortosa, Cap** *headland* E Spain 40.43N 0.52E
46 L8 **Tortue, Île de la** *var.* Tortuga Island. *island* N Haiti
57 Y10 **Tortue, Montagne** ⛰ C French Guiana
Tortuga, Isla *see* La Tortuga, Isla
Tortuga Island *see* Tortue, Île de la
56 C11 **Tortugas, Golfo** *gulf* W Colombia
47 T5 **Tortuguero, Laguna** *lagoon* N Puerto Rico
143 Q12 **Tortum** Erzurum, NE Turkey 40.15N 41.30E
Torugart, Pereval *see* Turugart Shankou
143 O12 **Torul** Gümüşhane, NE Turkey 40.34N 39.18E
112 J10 **Toruń** *Ger.* Thorn. Toruń, Kujawsko-pomorskie, C Poland 53.01N 18.36E
97 K20 **Torup** Halland, S Sweden 56.57N 13.04E
120 I6 **Tõrva** *Ger.* Törwa. Valgamaa, S Estonia 58.00N 25.54E
Törwa *see* Tõrva
98 D13 **Tory Island** *Ir.* Toraigh. *island* NW Ireland
113 N19 **Torysa** *Hung.* Tarca. ∽ NE Slovakia
Torzhok *see* Bran
128 J16 **Torzhok** Tverskaya Oblast', W Russian Federation 57.04N 34.55E
170 Ee15 **Tosa** Kōchi, Shikoku, SW Japan 33.28N 133.25E
170 E16 **Tosa-Shimizu** *var.* Tosasimizu. Kōchi, Shikoku, SW Japan 32.46N 132.55E
Tosasimizu *see* Tosa-Shimizu
170 Ee16 **Tosa-wan** *bay* SW Japan
85 H21 **Tosca** North-West, N South Africa 25.51S 23.56E
108 F12 **Toscana** *Eng.* Tuscany. ◈ *region* C Italy
109 E14 **Toscano, Archipelago** *Eng.* Tuscan Archipelago. *island group* C Italy
108 G10 **Tosco-Emiliano, Appennino** *Eng.* Tuscan-Emilian Mountains. ⛰ C Italy
Tōsei *see* Tungshih
171 J18 **To-shima** *island* Izu-shotō, SE Japan
153 Q9 **Toshkent** *Eng./Rus.* Tashkent. ● (Uzbekistan) Toshkent Viloyati, E Uzbekistan 41.19N 69.17E
153 Q9 **Toshkent** ✕ Toshkent Viloyati, E Uzbekistan 41.13N 69.15E
153 P9 **Toshkent Viloyati** *Rus.* Tashkentskaya Oblast'. ◈ *province* E Uzbekistan
128 H13 **Tosno** Leningradskaya Oblast', NW Russian Federation 59.34N 30.48E
165 Q10 **Toson Hu** ◎ C China
168 H6 **Tosontsengel** Dzavhan, NW Mongolia 48.42N 98.14E
152 I8 **Tosquduq Qumlari** *prev.* Goshquduq Qum, *Rus.* Peski Taskuduk. *desert* W Uzbekistan
107 U4 **Tossal de l'Orri** *var.* Llorri. ▲ NE Spain 42.24N 1.15E
63 A15 **Tostado** Santa Fe, C Argentina 29.14S 61.43W
120 F6 **Tõstamaa** *Ger.* Testama. Pärnumaa, SW Estonia 58.19N 23.58E
102 I10 **Tostedt** Niedersachsen, NW Germany 53.16N 9.42E
142 J11 **Tosya** Kastamonu, N Turkey 41.01N 34.01E
97 F15 **Totak** ◎ S Norway
107 R13 **Totana** Murcia, SE Spain 37.45N 1.30W
96 H13 **Toten** *physical region* S Norway
85 G18 **Toteng** Ngamiland, C Botswana 20.19S 22.57E
104 M3 **Tôtes** Seine-Maritime, N France 49.40N 1.02E
Totigi *see* Tochigi
Totio *see* Tochio
Totis *see* Tata
201 U13 **Totiw** *island* Chuuk, C Micronesia
129 N13 **Tot'ma** *var.* Totma. Vologodskaya Oblast', NW Russian Federation 59.58N 42.42E
Tot'ma *see* Sukhona
57 V9 **Totness** Coronie, N Suriname 5.51N 56.19W
44 C5 **Totonicapán** Totonicapán, W Guatemala 14.54N 91.18W
44 A2 **Totonicapán** *off.* Departamento de Totonicapán. ◈ *department* W Guatemala
63 B18 **Totoras** Santa Fe, C Argentina 32.34S 61.10W
197 K15 **Totoya** *island* S Fiji
191 Q7 **Tottenham** New South Wales, SE Australia 32.16S 147.23E
171 Gg13 **Tottori** Tottori, Honshū, SW Japan 35.28N 134.14E
170 Ff13 **Tottori** *off.* Tottori-ken. ◈ *prefecture* Honshū, SW Japan
78 I6 **Touâjil** Tiris Zemmour, N Mauritania 22.03N 12.39W
78 L15 **Touba** W Ivory Coast 8.16N 7.40W
78 G11 **Touba** W Senegal 14.55N 15.53W
76 E7 **Toubkal, Jbel** ▲ W Morocco 31.00N 7.50W
34 K10 **Touchet** Washington, NW USA 46.03N 118.40W
105 P7 **Toucy** Yonne, C France 47.45N 3.18E
79 O12 **Tougan** W Burkina 13.06N 3.03W
76 L7 **Touggourt** NE Algeria 33.07N 6.04E
79 Q12 **Tougouri** N Burkina 13.22N 0.25W
78 J13 **Tougué** Moyenne-Guinée, NW Guinea 11.28N 11.48W
78 K12 **Toukoto** Kayes, W Mali 13.24N 9.52W
105 S5 **Toul** Meurthe-et-Moselle, NE France 48.40N 5.54E
78 L16 **Toulépleu** *var.* Toulobli. W Ivory Coast 6.37N 8.27W
167 S14 **Touliu** C Taiwan 23.44N 120.27E
13 U3 **Toulnustouc** ∽ Québec, SE Canada
Toulobli *see* Toulépleu
105 T16 **Toulon** *anc.* Telo Martius, Tilio Martius. Var, SE France 43.07N 5.55E
32 K12 **Toulon** Illinois, N USA 41.04N 89.54W
104 M15 **Toulouse** *anc.* Tolosa. Haute-Garonne, S France 43.36N 1.24E
104 M15 **Toulouse** ✕ Haute-Garonne, S France 43.38N 1.19E
79 N16 **Toumodi** C Ivory Coast 6.34N 5.01W
76 G9 **Tounassine, Hamada** *hill range* W Algeria
177 G7 **Toungoo** Pegu, C Myanmar 18.57N 96.25E
104 L8 **Touraine** *cultural region* C France
Tourane *see* Đa Nẵng
105 P1 **Tourcoing** Nord, N France 50.43N 3.10E
106 F2 **Touriñán, Cabo** *headland* NW Spain 43.02N 9.20W
78 J6 **Tourine** Tiris Zemmour, N Mauritania 22.22N 11.49W
104 J3 **Tourlaville** Manche, N France 49.39N 1.34W
101 D19 **Tournai** *var.* Tournay, *Dut.* Doornik; *anc.* Tornacum. Hainaut, SW Belgium 50.36N 3.24E
104 L16 **Tournay** Hautes-Pyrénées, S France 43.10N 0.16E
Tournay *see* Tournai
105 R12 **Tournon** Ardèche, E France 45.04N 4.49E
105 R9 **Tournus** Saône-et-Loire, C France 46.33N 4.53E
61 Q14 **Touros** Rio Grande do Norte, E Brazil 5.10S 35.28W
104 L8 **Tours** *anc.* Caesarodunum, Turoni. Indre-et-Loire, C France 47.22N 0.40E
191 Q17 **Tourville, Cape** *headland* Tasmania, SE Australia 42.09S 148.20E
168 L8 **Töv** ◈ *province* C Mongolia
56 H7 **Tovar** Mérida, NW Venezuela 8.21N 71.45W
130 L5 **Tovarkovskiy** Tul'skaya Oblast', W Russian Federation 53.41N 38.18E
Tovil'-Dora *see* Tavildara
Tövis *see* Teiuş
143 V11 **Tovuz** *Rus.* Tauz. W Azerbaijan 40.58N 45.41E
172 N9 **Towada** Aomori, Honshū, C Japan 40.36N 141.11E
172 N9 **Towada-ko** *var.* Towada Ko. ◎ Honshū, C Japan
192 K3 **Towai** Northland, North Island, NZ 35.29S 174.06E
20 H12 **Towanda** Pennsylvania, NE USA 41.45N 76.25W
31 W4 **Tower** Minnesota, N USA 47.48N 92.16W
175 Pp8 **Towera** Sulawesi, N Indonesia 0.29S 120.01E
Tower Island *see* Genovesa, Isla
188 M13 **Tower Peak** ▲ Western Australia 33.23S 123.27E
37 U11 **Towne Pass** *pass* California, W USA
31 N3 **Towner** North Dakota, N USA 48.20N 100.27W
35 R10 **Townsend** Montana, NW USA 46.19N 111.31W
189 X6 **Townsville** Queensland, NE Australia 19.24S 146.52E
Towoeti Meer *see* Towuti, Danau
175 Q10 **Towori, Teluk** *bay* Sulawesi, C Indonesia
154 K4 **Towraghoudī** Herāt, NW Afghanistan 35.12N 62.19E
23 X3 **Towson** Maryland, NE USA 39.22N 76.33W
175 Q11 **Towuti, Danau** *Dut.* Towoeti Meer. ◎ Sulawesi, C Indonesia
Toxkan He *see* Ak-say
26 K9 **Toyah** Texas, SW USA 31.18N 103.47W
172 Nn6 **Tōya-ko** ◎ Hokkaidō, NE Japan
171 Ii13 **Toyama** Toyama, Honshū, SW Japan 36.41N 137.12E
171 Ii13 **Toyama** *off.* Toyama-ken. ◈ *prefecture* Honshū, SW Japan
171 J13 **Toyama-wan** *bay* W Japan
170 F16 **Tōyo** Ehime, Shikoku, SW Japan 33.57N 133.02E
170 Ee14 **Tōyo** Kōchi, Shikoku, SW Japan 33.28N 134.13E
Toyohara *see* Yuzhno-Sakhalinsk
171 Hh16 **Toyohashi** *var.* Toyohasi. Aichi, Honshū, SW Japan 34.45N 137.22E
Toyohasi *see* Toyohashi
171 I16 **Toyokawa** Aichi, Honshū, SW Japan 34.49N 137.22E
171 Gg13 **Toyooka** Hyōgo, Honshū, SW Japan 35.33N 134.48E
171 Kk12 **Toyosaka** Niigata, Honshū, C Japan 37.54N 139.12E
171 I16 **Toyota** Aichi, Honshū, SW Japan 35.04N 137.09E
172 Pp2 **Toyotomi** Hokkaidō, NE Japan 45.07N 141.45E
170 Dd12 **Toyoura** Yamaguchi, Honshū, SW Japan 34.09N 130.55E
Toytepa *see* To'ytepa
153 Q10 **To'ytepa** *Rus.* Toytepa. Toshkent Viloyati, E Uzbekistan 41.04N 69.22E
76 M6 **Tozeur** *var.* Tawzar. W Tunisia 34.00N 8.09E
41 Q8 **Tozi, Mount** ▲ Alaska, USA 65.45N 151.01W
143 Q9 **Tqvarch'eli** *Rus.* Tkvarcheli. NW Georgia 42.51N 41.42E
Trâblous *see* Tripoli
143 O11 **Trabzon** *Eng.* Trebizond; *anc.* Trapezus. Trabzon, NE Turkey 41.00N 39.43E
143 O11 **Trabzon** *Eng.* Trebizond. ◈ *province* NE Turkey
11 P13 **Tracadie** New Brunswick, SE Canada 47.31N 64.57W
Trachenberg *see* Żmigród
13 O11 **Tracy** Québec, SE Canada 45.59N 73.07W
37 O8 **Tracy** California, W USA 37.43N 121.27W
31 S10 **Tracy** Minnesota, N USA 44.14N 95.37W
22 K10 **Tracy City** Tennessee, S USA 35.15N 85.44W
108 D7 **Tradate** Lombardia, N Italy 45.43N 8.57E
86 F6 **Traena Bank** *undersea feature* E Norwegian Sea
31 W13 **Traer** Iowa, C USA 42.11N 92.28W
106 J16 **Trafalgar, Cabo de** *headland* SW Spain 36.10N 6.03W
Traiectum ad Mosam/ Traiectum Tungorum *see* Maastricht
Tráigh Mhór *see* Tramore
9 O17 **Trail** British Columbia, SW Canada 49.04N 117.46W
60 B11 **Traíra, Serra do** ⛰ NW Brazil
111 V5 **Traisen** Niederösterreich, NE Austria 48.03N 15.37E
111 W4 **Traisen** ∽ NE Austria
111 X4 **Traiskirchen** Niederösterreich, NE Austria 48.01N 16.18E
Trajani Portus *see* Civitavecchia
Trajectum ad Rhenum *see* Utrecht
121 H14 **Trakai** *Ger.* Traken, *Pol.* Troki. Vilnius, SE Lithuania 54.39N 24.58E
Traken *see* Trakai
99 B20 **Tralee** *Ir.* Trá Lí. SW Ireland 52.16N 9.42W
99 A20 **Tralee Bay** *Ir.* Bá Thrá Lí. *bay* SW Ireland
Trá Lí *see* Tralee
Trälleborg *see* Trelleborg
Tralles *see* Aydın
63 J16 **Tramandaí** Rio Grande do Sul, S Brazil 30.01S 50.11W
110 C7 **Tramelan** Bern, W Switzerland 47.13N 7.07E
Trá Mhór *see* Tramore
99 E20 **Tramore** *Ir.* Tráigh Mhór, Trá Mhór. S Ireland 52.10N 7.10W
97 L18 **Tranås** Jönköping, S Sweden 58.03N 15.00E
64 J7 **Trancas** Tucumán, N Argentina 26.10S 65.19W
106 I7 **Trancoso** Guarda, N Portugal 40.46N 7.21W
97 H22 **Tranebjerg** Århus, C Denmark 55.51N 10.36E
97 K19 **Tranemo** Västra Götaland, S Sweden 57.30N 13.19E
178 Gg16 **Trang** Trang, S Thailand 7.33N 99.36E
176 W14 **Trangan, Pulau** *island* Kepulauan Aru, E Indonesia
Trâng Dinh *see* Thất Khê
191 Q7 **Trangie** New South Wales, SE Australia 32.01S 147.58E
96 K12 **Trängslet** Dalarna, C Sweden 61.22N 13.43E
109 N16 **Trani** Puglia, SE Italy 41.16N 16.24E
63 F17 **Tranqueras** Rivera, NE Uruguay 31.13S 55.45W
65 G17 **Tranqui, Isla** *island* S Chile
41 V6 **Trans-Alaska pipeline** *oil pipeline* Alaska, USA
205 Q10 **Transantarctic Mountains** ⛰ Antarctica
Transcarpathian Oblast *see* Zakarpats'ka Oblast'
Transilvania *see* Transylvania
Transilvaniei, Alpi *see* Carpaţii Meridionali
Transjordan *see* Jordan
180 L11 **Transkei Basin** *undersea feature* SW Indian Ocean
119 O10 **Transnistria** *cultural region* E Moldova
127 N17 **Trans-Siberian Railway** *Railroad* Russian Federation
Transsylvanische Alpen/ Transylvanian Alps *see* Carpaţii Meridionali
96 K12 **Transtrand** Dalarna, C Sweden 61.06N 13.19E
118 G10 **Transylvania** *Eng.* Ardeal, Transilvania, *Ger.* Siebenbürgen, *Hung.* Erdély. *cultural region* NW Romania
178 Jj15 **Tra Ôn** Vinh Long, S Vietnam 9.58N 105.58E
109 H23 **Trapani** *anc.* Drepanum. Sicilia, Italy, C Mediterranean Sea 38.02N 12.31E
178 J12 **Trâpeăng Vêng** Kâmpóng Thum, C Cambodia 12.37N 104.58E
Trapezus *see* Trabzon
116 L9 **Trapoklovo** Sliven, C Bulgaria 42.40N 26.36E
191 P13 **Traralgon** Victoria, SE Australia 38.15S 146.35E
78 H9 **Trarza** ◈ *region* SW Mauritania
Trasimenischersee *see* Trasimeno, Lago
108 H12 **Trasimeno, Lago** *Eng.* Lake of Perugia, *Ger.* Trasimenischersee. ◎ C Italy
97 J20 **Träslövsläge** Halland, S Sweden 57.02N 12.18E
Trás-os-Montes *see* Cucumbi
106 I6 **Trás-os-Montes e Alto Douro** *former province* N Portugal
178 I13 **Trat** *var.* Bang Phra. Trat, S Thailand 12.16N 102.30E
Trá Tholl, Inis *see* Inishtrahull
Traù *see* Trogir
111 T4 **Traun** Oberösterreich, N Austria 48.14N 14.13E
111 S5 **Traun** ∽ N Austria
Traun, Lake *see* Traunsee
103 N23 **Traunreut** Bayern, SE Germany 47.58N 12.36E
111 S5 **Traunsee** *var.* Gmundner See, *Eng.* Lake Traun. ◎ N Austria
Trautenau *see* Trutnov
23 P11 **Travelers Rest** South Carolina, SE USA 34.58N 82.26W
190 L8 **Travellers Lake** *seasonal lake* New South Wales, SE Australia
33 P6 **Traverse City** Michigan, N USA 44.45N 85.37W
31 R7 **Traverse, Lake** ◎ Minnesota/South Dakota, N USA
193 I16 **Travers, Mount** ▲ South Island, NZ 42.01S 172.46E
9 P17 **Travers Reservoir** ⊞ Alberta, SW Canada
178 Jj15 **Tra Vinh** *var.* Phu Vinh. Tra Vinh, S Vietnam 9.57N 106.19E
27 S10 **Travis, Lake** ⊞ Texas, SW USA
114 H12 **Travnik** Federacija Bosna I Hercegovina, C Bosnia and Herzegovina 44.14N 17.40E
111 V11 **Trbovlje** *Ger.* Trifail. C Slovenia 46.09N 15.03E
25 V13 **Treasure Island** Florida, SE USA 27.46N 82.46W
Treasure State *see* Montana
195 S14 **Treasury Islands** *island group* NW Solomon Islands
108 D9 **Trebbia** *anc.* Trebia. ∽ NW Italy
102 N8 **Trebel** ∽ NE Germany
105 O16 **Trèbes** Aude, S France 43.12N 2.25E
Trebia *see* Trebbia
113 F18 **Třebíč** *Ger.* Trebitsch. Vysočina, S Czech Republic 49.13N 15.52E
115 I16 **Trebinje** Republika Srpska, S Bosnia and Herzegovina 42.42N 18.19E
Trebišnica *see* Trebišnjica
115 H16 **Trebišnjica** *var.* Trebišnica. ∽ S Bosnia and Herzegovina
113 N20 **Trebišov** *Hung.* Tőketerebes. Košický Kraj, E Slovakia 48.36N 21.44E
Trebitsch *see* Třebíč
Trebizond *see* Trabzon
Trebnitz *see* Trzebnica
111 V12 **Trebnje** SE Slovenia 45.54N 15.01E
113 D19 **Třeboň** *Ger.* Wittingau. Jihočeský Kraj, S Czech Republic 49.00N 14.46E
106 J15 **Trebujena** Andalucía, S Spain 36.52N 6.10W
102 I7 **Treene** ∽ N Germany
Tree Planters State *see* Nebraska
111 S9 **Treffen** Kärnten, S Austria 46.40N 13.51E
Trefynwy *see* Monmouth
104 G5 **Tréguier** Côtes d'Armor, NW France 48.50N 3.12W
63 G18 **Treinta y Tres** Treinta y Tres, E Uruguay 33.12S 54.19W
63 F18 **Treinta y Tres** ◈ *department* E Uruguay
125 E11 **Trëkhgornyy** Chelyabinskaya Oblast', C Russian Federation 54.42N 58.25E
116 F9 **Treklyanska Reka** ∽ W Bulgaria
175 R10 **Treko, Kepulauan** *island group* N Indonesia
104 K8 **Trélazé** Maine-et-Loire, NW France 47.27N 0.28W
65 K17 **Trelew** Chubut, SE Argentina 43.13S 65.15W
97 K23 **Trelleborg** *var.* Trälleborg. Skåne, S Sweden 55.22N 13.10E
115 P15 **Trem** ▲ SE Serbia and Montenegro (Yugoslavia) 43.10N 22.12E
13 N11 **Tremblant, Mont** ▲ Québec, SE Canada 46.13N 74.34W
101 H17 **Tremelo** Vlaams Brabant, C Belgium 50.59N 4.34E
109 M15 **Tremiti, Isole** *island group* SE Italy
32 K12 **Tremont** Illinois, N USA 40.30N 89.31W
38 L1 **Tremonton** Utah, W USA 41.42N 112.09W
107 U4 **Tremp** Cataluña, NE Spain 42.09N 0.53E
32 J7 **Trempealeau** Wisconsin, N USA 44.00N 91.25W
13 P8 **Trenche** ∽ Québec, SE Canada
13 O7 **Trenche, Lac** ◎ Québec, SE Canada
113 I20 **Trenčiansky Kraj** ◈ *region* W Slovakia
113 I19 **Trenčín** *Ger.* Trentschin, *Hung.* Trencsén. Trenčiansky Kraj, W Slovakia 48.54N 18.03E
Trencsén *see* Trenčín
Trengganu *see* Terengganu
63 A21 **Trenque Lauquen** Buenos Aires, E Argentina 36.00S 62.46W
12 J14 **Trent** ∽ Ontario, SE Canada
99 N18 **Trent** ∽ C England, UK
Trent *see* Trento
108 F5 **Trentino-Alto Adige** *prev.* Venezia Tridentina. ◈ *region* N Italy
108 G6 **Trento** *Eng.* Trent, *Ger.* Trient; anc.Tridentum. Trentino-Alto Adige, N Italy 46.04N 11.07E
12 J15 **Trenton** Ontario, SE Canada 44.06N 77.36W
25 V10 **Trenton** Florida, SE USA 29.36N 82.49W
25 R1 **Trenton** Georgia, SE USA 34.52N 85.27W
33 S10 **Trenton** Michigan, N USA 42.08N 83.10W
29 S2 **Trenton** Missouri, C USA 40.04N 93.37W
30 M17 **Trenton** Nebraska, C USA 40.10N 101.00W
20 J15 **Trenton** *state capital* New Jersey, NE USA 40.13N 74.44W
23 W10 **Trenton** North Carolina, SE USA 35.03N 77.20W
22 G9 **Trenton** Tennessee, S USA 35.58N 88.56W
38 L1 **Trenton** Utah, W USA 41.53N 111.57W
Trentschin *see* Trenčín
Treptow an der Rega *see* Trzebiatów
63 C23 **Tres Arroyos** Buenos Aires, E Argentina 38.21S 60.16W
63 J15 **Três Cachoeiras** Rio Grande do Sul, S Brazil 29.21S 49.48W
108 E7 **Trescore Balneario** Lombardia, N Italy 45.43N 9.52E
43 V17 **Tres Cruces, Cerro** ▲ SE Mexico 15.28N 92.27W
59 K18 **Tres Cruces, Cordillera** ⛰ W Bolivia
115 N18 **Treska** ∽ NW FYR Macedonia
115 I14 **Treskavica** ⛰ SE Bosnia and Herzegovina
61 J20 **Três Lagoas** Mato Grosso do Sul, SW Brazil 20.46S 51.43W
42 H12 **Tres Marías, Islas** *island group* C Mexico
61 M19 **Três Marias, Represa** ⊞ SE Brazil
65 F20 **Tres Montes, Península** *headland* S Chile 46.49S 75.29W
107 O3 **Trespaderne** Castilla-León, N Spain 42.46N 3.24W
62 G13 **Três Passos** Rio Grande do Sul, S Brazil 27.28S 53.55W
63 A23 **Tres Picos, Cerro** ▲ E Argentina 38.10S 61.54W
65 G17 **Tres Picos, Cerro** ▲ SW Argentina 42.22S 71.51W
62 I12 **Três Pinheiros** Paraná, S Brazil 25.25S 51.57W
61 M21 **Três Pontas** Minas Gerais, SE Brazil 21.33S 45.18W
Tres Puntas, Cabo *see* Manabique, Punta
62 P9 **Três Rios** Rio de Janeiro, SE Brazil 22.06S 43.15W
Tres Tabernae *see* Saverne
Trestenberg/Trestendorf *see* Tăşnad
43 R15 **Tres Valles** Veracruz-Llave, SE Mexico 18.14N 96.03W
96 H12 **Tretten** Oppland, S Norway 61.19N 10.19E
Treuburg *see* Olecko
103 K21 **Treuchtlingen** Bayern, S Germany 48.57N 10.55E
102 N13 **Treuenbrietzen** Brandenburg, E Germany 52.06N 12.52E
97 F16 **Treungen** Telemark, S Norway 59.00N 8.34E
65 H17 **Trevelín** Chubut, SW Argentina 43.02S 71.27W
Treves/Trèves *see* Trier
108 I13 **Trevi** Umbria, C Italy 42.52N 12.46E
108 E7 **Treviglio** Lombardia, N Italy 45.31N 9.34E
106 J4 **Trevinca, Peña** ▲ NW Spain 42.10N 6.49W
107 P3 **Treviño** Castilla-León, N Spain 42.45N 2.41W
108 I7 **Treviso** *anc.* Tarvisium. Veneto, NE Italy 45.40N 12.15E
99 G24 **Trevose Head** *headland* SW England, UK 50.33N 5.03W
Trg *see* Feldkirchen in Kärnten
191 P17 **Triabunna** Tasmania, SE Australia 42.33S 147.55E
23 W4 **Triangle** Virginia, NE USA 38.30N 77.17W
85 L18 **Triangle** Masvingo, SE Zimbabwe 20.58S 31.28E
117 L23 **Tría Nisiá** *island* Kykládes, Greece, Aegean Sea
Triberg *see* Triberg im Schwarzwald
103 G23 **Triberg im Schwarzwald** *var.* Triberg. Baden-Württemberg, SW Germany 48.07N 8.13E
159 P11 **Tribhuvan** ✕ (Kathmandu) Central, C Nepal
56 C9 **Tribugá, Golfo de** *gulf* W Colombia
189 W4 **Tribulation, Cape** *headland* Queensland, NE Australia 16.14S 145.48E
110 M8 **Tribulaun** ▲ SW Austria 46.59N 11.18E
9 U17 **Tribune** Saskatchewan, S Canada 49.16N 103.50W
28 H5 **Tribune** Kansas, C USA 38.28N 101.45W
109 N18 **Tricarico** Basilicata, S Italy 40.37N 16.09E
109 Q19 **Tricase** Puglia, SE Italy 39.56N 18.21E
Trichinopoly *see* Tiruchchirāppalli
117 D18 **Trichonída, Límni** ◎ C Greece
161 G22 **Trichūr** *var.* Thrissur. Kerala, SW India 10.31N 76.13E
Tricorno *see* Triglav
191 O8 **Trida** New South Wales, SE Australia 33.02S 145.03E
37 S1 **Trident Peak** ▲ Nevada, W USA 41.52N 118.22W
Tridentum/Trient *see* Trento
111 T6 **Trieben** Steiermark, SE Austria 47.29N 14.27E
103 D19 **Trier** *Eng.* Treves, *Fr.* Trèves; *anc.* Augusta Treverorum. Rheinland-Pfalz, SW Germany 49.45N 6.39E
108 K7 **Trieste** *Slvn.* Trst. Friuli-Venezia Giulia, NE Italy 45.39N 13.45E
Trieste, Golfo di/Triest, Golf von *see* Trieste, Gulf of
108 J8 **Trieste, Gulf of** *Cro.* Tršćanski Zaljev, *Ger.* Golf von Triest, *It.* Golfo di Trieste, *Slvn.* Tržaški Zaliv. *gulf* S Europe
111 W4 **Triesting** ∽ W Austria
Trifail *see* Trbovlje
118 L9 **Trifeşti** Iaşi, NE Romania 47.30N 27.31E
111 S10 **Triglav** *It.* Tricorno. ▲ NW Slovenia 46.22N 13.40E
106 I14 **Trigueros** Andalucía, S Spain 37.24N 6.49W
117 E16 **Tríkala** *prev.* Trikkala. Thessalía, C Greece 39.33N 21.46E
117 E17 **Trikeriōtis** ∽ C Greece
Trikkala *see* Tríkala
Trikomo/Tríkomon *see* İskele
99 F17 **Trim** *Ir.* Baile Átha Troim. E Ireland 53.34N 6.46W
110 E7 **Trimbach** Solothurn, NW Switzerland 47.21N 7.49E
111 Q5 **Trimmelkam** Oberösterreich, N Austria 48.02N 12.55E
31 U11 **Trimont** Minnesota, N USA 43.45N 94.42W
Trimontium *see* Plovdiv
Trinacria *see* Sicilia
161 K24 **Trincomalee** *var.* Trinkomali. Eastern Province, NE Sri Lanka 8.34N 81.13E
67 K16 **Trindade, Ilha da** *island* Brazil, W Atlantic Ocean
49 Y9 **Trindade Spur** *undersea feature* SW Atlantic Ocean
113 J17 **Třinec** *Ger.* Trzynietz. Moravskoslezský Kraj, E Czech Republic 49.42N 18.37E
59 M16 **Trinidad** Beni, N Bolivia 14.52S 64.54W
56 H9 **Trinidad** Casanare, E Colombia 5.25N 71.39W
46 E6 **Trinidad** Sancti Spíritus, C Cuba 21.48N 80.00W
39 U8 **Trinidad** Colorado, C USA 37.10N 104.31W
63 E19 **Trinidad** Flores, S Uruguay 33.34S 56.54W
47 Y17 **Trinidad** *island* C Trinidad and Tobago
Trinidad *see* Jose Abad Santos
47 Y16 **Trinidad and Tobago** *off.* Republic of Trinidad and Tobago. ◆ *republic* SE West Indies
65 F22 **Trinidad, Golfo** *gulf* S Chile
63 B24 **Trinidad, Isla** *island* E Argentina
109 N16 **Trinitapoli** Puglia, SE Italy 41.22N 16.06E
57 X10 **Trinité, Montagnes de la** ⛰ C French Guiana
27 W9 **Trinity** Texas, SW USA 30.57N 95.22W
11 U12 **Trinity Bay** *inlet* Newfoundland and Labrador, E Canada
41 P15 **Trinity Islands** *island group* Alaska, USA
37 N2 **Trinity Mountains** ⛰ California, W USA
37 S4 **Trinity Peak** ▲ Nevada, W USA 40.13N 118.43W
37 S5 **Trinity Range** ⛰ Nevada, W USA
37 N2 **Trinity River** ∽ California, W USA
27 V8 **Trinity River** ∽ Texas, SW USA
Trinkomali *see* Trincomalee
181 Y15 **Triolet** NW Mauritius 20.04S 57.31E
109 O20 **Trionto, Capo** *headland* S Italy 39.37N 16.46E
173 Ee4 **Tripa, Krueng** ∽ Sumatera, NW Indonesia
117 J16 **Tripití, Akrotírio** *headland* Ágios Efstrátios, E Greece 39.28N 24.58E
144 G6 **Tripoli** *var.* Tarābulus, Ṭarābulus ash Shām, Trâblous; *anc.* Tripolis. N Lebanon 34.30N 35.42E
31 X12 **Tripoli** Iowa, C USA 42.48N 92.15W
Tripoli *see* Ṭarābulus
117 F20 **Trípoli** *prev.* Trípolis. Pelopónnisos, S Greece 37.31N 22.22E
Tripolis *see* Tripoli, Lebanon
Trípolis *see* Trípoli, Greece
31 Q12 **Tripp** South Dakota, N USA 43.12N 97.57W
159 V15 **Tripura** *var.* Hill Tippera. ◈ *state* NE India
110 K8 **Trisanna** ∽ W Austria
102 H8 **Trischen** *island* NW Germany
67 M24 **Tristan da Cunha** ◇ *dependency of Saint Helena* SE Atlantic Ocean
69 P15 **Tristan da Cunha** *island* SE Atlantic Ocean
67 L18 **Tristan da Cunha Fracture Zone** *tectonic feature* S Atlantic Ocean
178 J14 **Tri Tôn** An Giang, S Vietnam 10.25N 105.01E
178 Ll11 **Triton Island** *island* S Paracel Islands
161 G24 **Trivandrum** *var.* Thiruvanathapuram. Kerala, SW India 8.30N 76.57E
113 H20 **Trnava** *Ger.* Tyrnau, *Hung.* Nagyszombat. Trnavský Kraj, W Slovakia 48.22N 17.36E
113 H20 **Trnavský Kraj** ◈ *region* W Slovakia
Trnovo *see* Veliko Tŭrnovo
Trobriand Island *see* Kiriwina Island
Trobriand Islands *see* Kiriwina Islands
9 Q16 **Trochu** Alberta, SW Canada 51.48N 113.12W
111 U7 **Trofaiach** Steiermark, SE Austria 47.24N 14.56E
95 F14 **Trofors** Troms, N Norway 65.31N 13.19E
115 E14 **Trogir** *It.* Traù. Split-Dalmacija, S Croatia 43.32N 16.13E
114 F13 **Troglav** ▲ Bosnia and Herzegovina/Croatia 44.00N 16.36E
109 M16 **Troia** Puglia, SE Italy 41.21N 15.19E
109 K24 **Troina** Sicilia, Italy, C Mediterranean Sea 37.48N 14.33E
181 O16 **Trois-Bassins** W Réunion 21.04S 55.18E
103 E17 **Troisdorf** Nordrhein-Westfalen, W Germany 50.49N 7.09E
76 H5 **Trois Fourches, Cap des** *headland* NE Morocco 35.27N 2.58W
13 T8 **Trois-Pistoles** Québec, SE Canada 48.07N 69.10W
101 L21 **Trois-Ponts** Liège, E Belgium 50.22N 5.52E
13 P11 **Trois-Rivières** Québec, SE Canada 46.21N 72.34W
57 Y12 **Trois Sauts** S French Guiana 2.15N 52.52W
101 M22 **Troisvierges** Diekirch, N Luxembourg 50.07N 6.00E
125 Ee12 **Troitsk** Chelyabinskaya Oblast', S Russian Federation 54.04N 61.31E
129 T9 **Troitsko-Pechorsk** Respublika Komi, NW Russian Federation 62.39N 56.06E
131 V7 **Troitskoye** Orenburgskaya Oblast', W Russian Federation 52.23N 56.24E
Troki *see* Trakai
96 F9 **Trolla** ▲ S Norway 62.41N 9.47E
97 J18 **Trollhättan** Västra Götaland, S Sweden 58.16N 12.19E
96 G9 **Trollheimen** ⛰ S Norway
96 E9 **Trolltindan** ▲ S Norway 62.30N 7.43E
60 H11 **Trombetas, Rio** ∽ NE Brazil
132 L16 **Tromelin, Île** *island* N Réunion
94 I9 **Troms** ◈ *county* N Norway
94 I9 **Tromsø** *Fin.* Tromssa. Troms, N Norway 69.42N 19.00E
86 F5 **Tromsøflaket** *undersea feature* W Barents Sea
Tromssa *see* Tromsø
96 H10 **Tron** ▲ S Norway 62.12N 10.46E
37 U12 **Trona** California, W USA 35.46N 117.21W
65 G16 **Tronador, Cerro** ▲ S Chile 41.12S 71.51W
96 H8 **Trondheim** *Ger.* Drontheim; *prev.* Nidaros, Trondhjem. Sør-Trøndelag, S Norway 63.25N 10.24E
96 H7 **Trondheimsfjorden** *fjord* S Norway
Trondhjem *see* Trondheim
109 J14 **Tronto** ∽ C Italy
Troodos *see* Ólympos
124 N3 **Troódos** *var.* Troodos Mountains. ⛰ C Cyprus
Troodos Mountains *see* Troódos
98 I13 **Troon** W Scotland, UK 55.32N 4.41W
109 M22 **Tropea** Calabria, SW Italy 38.40N 15.52E
38 L7 **Tropic** Utah, W USA 37.37N 112.04W
66 L10 **Tropic Seamount** *var.* Banc du Tropique. *undersea feature* E Atlantic Ocean 23.49N 20.40W
Tropique, Banc du *see* Tropic Seamount
Tropoja *see* Tropojë
115 L17 **Tropojë** *var.* Tropoja. Kukës, N Albania 42.25N 20.09E
Troppau *see* Opava

◆ Country ● Country Capital ◇ Dependent Territory ○ Dependent Territory Capital ◈ Administrative Region ✕ International Airport ▲ Mountain ⛰ Mountain Range Volcano ∽ River ◎ Lake ⊞ Reservoir

TROSA – TÜRTKÜL

97 O16 **Trosa** Södermanland, C Sweden *58.54N 17.34E*
120 H12 **Troškūnai** Utena, E Lithuania *55.36N 24.55E*
103 G23 **Trossingen** Baden-Württemberg, SW Germany *48.04N 8.37E*
119 T4 **Trostyanets'** *Rus.* Trostyanets. Sums'ka Oblast', NE Ukraine *50.29N 34.58E*
119 N7 **Trostyanets'** *Rus.* Trostyanets. Vinnyts'ka Oblast', C Ukraine *48.35N 29.10E*
118 L11 **Trotuş** ≈ E Romania
46 M8 **Trou-du-Nord** N Haiti *19.34N 71.57W*
27 W7 **Troup** Texas, SW USA *32.08N 95.07W*
15 H8 **Trout** ≈ Northwest Territories, NW Canada
35 N8 **Trout Creek** Montana, NW USA *47.51N 115.40W*
34 H10 **Trout Lake** Washington, NW USA *45.59N 121.33W*
10 B9 **Trout Lake** ◎ Ontario, S Canada
35 T12 **Trout Peak** ▲ Wyoming, C USA *44.36N 109.33W*
104 L4 **Trouville** Calvados, N France *49.21N 0.07E*
99 L22 **Trowbridge** S England, UK *51.19N 2.13W*
25 Q6 **Troy** Alabama, S USA *31.48N 85.58W*
29 Q3 **Troy** Kansas, C USA *39.46N 95.05W*
29 W4 **Troy** Missouri, C USA *38.58N 90.58W*
20 L10 **Troy** New York, NE USA *42.43N 73.37W*
23 S10 **Troy** North Carolina, SE USA *35.21N 79.53W*
33 R13 **Troy** Ohio, N USA *40.02N 84.12W*
27 T9 **Troy** Texas, SW USA *31.12N 97.18W*
116 I9 **Troyan** Lovech, N Bulgaria *42.53N 24.43E*
116 I9 **Troyanski Prokhod** *pass* N Bulgaria *42.48N 24.38E*
151 N6 **Troyebratskiy** Severnyy Kazakhstan, N Kazakhstan *54.21N 66.07E*
105 Q6 **Troyes** *anc.* Augustobona Tricassium. Aube, N France *48.18N 4.04E*
119 X5 **Troyits'ke** Luhans'ka Oblast', E Ukraine *49.55N 38.18E*
37 W7 **Troy Peak** ▲ Nevada, W USA *38.18N 115.27W*
115 G15 **Trpanj** Dubrovnik-Neretva, S Croatia *43.00N 17.18E*
Trščanski Zaljev *see* Trieste, Gulf of
Trst *see* Trieste
115 N14 **Trstenik** Serbia, C Serbia and Montenegro (Yugoslavia) *43.38N 21.01E*
130 I6 **Trubchevsk** Bryanskaya Oblast', W Russian Federation *52.33N 33.45E*
Trubchular *see* Orlyak
39 S10 **Truchas Peak** ▲ New Mexico, SW USA *35.57N 105.38W*
149 P16 **Trucial Coast** *physical region* C UAE
Trucial States *see* United Arab Emirates
37 Q6 **Truckee** California, W USA *39.18N 120.10W*
37 R5 **Truckee River** ≈ Nevada, W USA
131 Q13 **Trudfront** Astrakhanskaya Oblast', SW Russian Federation *45.56N 47.42E*
12 I9 **Truite, Lac à la** ◎ Québec, SE Canada
44 K4 **Trujillo** Colón, NE Honduras *15.59N 85.54W*
58 C12 **Trujillo** La Libertad, NW Peru *8.04S 79.02W*
106 K10 **Trujillo** Extremadura, W Spain *39.28N 5.52W*
56 I6 **Trujillo** Trujillo, NW Venezuela *9.19N 70.37W*
56 I6 **Trujillo** *off.* Estado Trujillo. ◈ *state* W Venezuela
Truk *see* Chuuk
Truk Islands *see* Chuuk Islands
31 U10 **Truman** Minnesota, N USA *43.49N 94.26W*
29 X10 **Trumann** Arkansas, C USA *35.40N 90.30W*
38 J9 **Trumbull, Mount** ▲ Arizona, SW USA *36.22N 113.09W*
116 F9 **Trŭn** Pernik, W Bulgaria *42.51N 22.37E*
191 Q8 **Trundle** New South Wales, SE Australia *32.55S 147.43E*
133 U13 **Trung Phân** *physical region* S Vietnam
Trupcilar *see* Orlyak
11 Q15 **Truro** Nova Scotia, SE Canada *45.20N 63.14W*
99 H25 **Truro** SW England, UK *50.16N 5.03W*
27 P5 **Truscott** Texas, SW USA *33.43N 99.48W*
118 K9 **Truşeşti** Botoşani, NE Romania *47.45N 27.01E*
118 H6 **Truskavets'** L'vivs'ka Oblast', W Ukraine *49.15N 23.30E*
97 H22 **Trustrup** Århus, C Denmark *56.20N 10.46E*
8 M11 **Trutch** British Columbia, W Canada *57.42N 123.00W*
39 Q14 **Truth Or Consequences** New Mexico, SW USA *33.07N 107.15W*
113 F15 **Trutnov** *Ger.* Trautenau. Královéhradecký Kraj, NE Czech Republic *50.34N 15.52E*
105 P13 **Truyère** ≈ C France
116 K9 **Tryavna** Lovech, N Bulgaria *42.52N 25.30E*
30 M14 **Tryon** Nebraska, C USA *41.31N 100.56W*
96 I11 **Trysilelva** ≈ S Norway
114 D10 **Tržac** Federacija Bosna I Hercegovina, NW Bosnia and Herzegovina *44.58N 15.48E*
Tržaški Zaliv *see* Trieste, Gulf of
112 G10 **Trzcianka** *Ger.* Schönlanke. Piła, Wielkopolskie, C Poland *53.01N 16.24E*
112 E7 **Trzebiatów** *Ger.* Treptow an der Rega. Zachodnio-pomorskie, NW Poland *54.04N 15.14E*
113 G14 **Trzebnica** *Ger.* Trebnitz. Dolnośląskie, SW Poland *51.18N 17.03E*
111 T10 **Tržič** *Ger.* Neumarktl. NW Slovenia *46.22N 14.17E*
Trzynietz *see* Třinec
Tsabong *see* Tshabong
168 G7 **Tsagaanchuluut** Dzavhan, C Mongolia *47.06N 96.40E*
169 P7 **Tsagaanders** Dornod, NE Mongolia *48.03N 114.16E*
169 S8 **Tsagaannuur** Dornod, E Mongolia *47.30N 118.45E*
168 G8 **Tsagaan-Olom** Govĭ-Altay, C Mongolia *46.42N 96.30E*
168 J8 **Tsagaan-Ovoo** Övörhangay, C Mongolia *45.57N 101.25E*
168 D5 **Tsagaantüngi** Bayan-Ölgiy, NW Mongolia *49.06N 90.26E*
131 P12 **Tsagan Aman** Respublika Kalmykiya, SW Russian Federation *47.37N 46.43E*
25 V11 **Tsala Apopka Lake** ◎ Florida, SE USA
Tsamkong *see* Zhanjiang
Tsangpo *see* Brahmaputra
168 L9 **Tsant** Dundgovĭ, C Mongolia *46.16N 106.55E*
85 G17 **Tsao** Ngamiland, NW Botswana *20.08S 22.29E*
180 I4 **Tsaratanana** Mahajanga, C Madagascar *16.46S 47.40E*
116 N10 **Tsarevo** *prev.* Michurin. Burgas, E Bulgaria *42.10N 27.51E*
Tsarigrad *see* İstanbul
Tsaritsyn *see* Volgograd
128 G13 **Tsarskoye Selo** *prev.* Pushkin. Leningradskaya Oblast', NW Russian Federation *59.42N 30.24E*
119 T7 **Tsarychanka** Dnipropetrovs'ka Oblast', E Ukraine *48.56N 34.29E*
85 H21 **Tsatsu** Southern, S Botswana *25.21S 24.45E*
83 J20 **Tsavo** Coast, S Kenya *2.58S 38.28E*
85 E21 **Tsawisis** Karas, S Namibia *26.18S 18.07E*
Tschakathurn *see* Čakovec
Tschaslau *see* Čáslav
Tschenstochau *see* Częstochowa
Tschernembl *see* Črnomelj
30 K6 **Tschida, Lake** ▣ North Dakota, N USA
Tschorna *see* Mustvee
85 I17 **Tsebanana** Central, NE Botswana *19.50S 26.29E*
Tsefat *see* Ẕefat
168 G8 **Tseel** Govĭ-Altay, SW Mongolia *45.45N 95.54E*
130 M13 **Tselina** Rostovskaya Oblast', SW Russian Federation *46.31N 41.01E*
Tselinograd *see* Astana
Tselinogradskaya Oblast' *see* Akmola
168 J6 **Tsengel** Hövsgöl, N Mongolia *49.29N 101.09E*
168 E7 **Tsenher** Hovd, W Mongolia *47.07N 92.04E*
Tsentral'nyye Nizmennyye Garagumy *see* Merkezi Garagumy
85 E21 **Tses** Karas, S Namibia *25.54S 18.09E*
Tseshevlya *see* Tsyeshawlya
168 E7 **Tsetsegnuur** Hovd, W Mongolia *46.30N 93.16E*
Tsetsen Khan *see* Öndörhaan
168 J7 **Tsetserleg** Arhangay, C Mongolia *47.28N 101.19E*
79 R16 **Tsévié** S Togo *6.25N 1.13E*
85 G21 **Tshabong** *var.* Tsabong. Kgalagadi, SW Botswana *26.01S 22.24E*
85 G20 **Tshane** Kgalagadi, SW Botswana *24.02S 21.54E*
Tshangalele, Lac *see* Lufira, Lac de Retenue de la
85 H17 **Tshauxaba** Central, C Botswana *19.56S 25.09E*
81 F21 **Tshela** Bas-Congo, W Dem. Rep. Congo *4.55S 13.01E*
81 K22 **Tshibala** Kasai Occidental, S Dem. Rep. Congo *6.53S 22.01E*
81 J22 **Tshikapa** Kasai Occidental, SW Dem. Rep. Congo *6.23S 20.47E*
81 L22 **Tshilenge** Kasai Oriental, S Dem. Rep. Congo *6.16S 23.48E*
81 L24 **Tshimbalanga** Katanga, S Dem. Rep. Congo *9.42S 23.04E*
81 L22 **Tshimbulu** Kasai Occidental, S Dem. Rep. Congo *6.27S 22.54E*
Tshiumbe *see* Chiumbe
81 M21 **Tshofa** Kasai Oriental, C Dem. Rep. Congo *5.13S 25.13E*
81 K18 **Tshuapa** ≈ C Dem. Rep. Congo
Tshwane *see* Pretoria
116 G7 **Tsibritsa** ≈ NW Bulgaria
Tsien Tang *see* Puyang Jiang
116 I12 **Tsigansko Gradishte** ▲ Bulgaria/Greece *41.24N 24.41E*
14 G3 **Tsiigehtchic** *prev.* Arctic Red River. Northwest Territories, NW Canada *67.24N 133.40W*
129 Q7 **Tsil'ma** ≈ NW Russian Federation
121 J17 **Tsimkavichy** *Rus.* Timkovichi. Minskaya Voblasts', C Belarus *53.04N 26.58E*
130 M11 **Tsimlyansk** Rostovskaya Oblast', SW Russian Federation *47.39N 42.05E*
131 N11 **Tsimlyanskoye Vodokhranilishche** *var.* Tsimlyansk Vodoskhovshche, *Eng.* Tsimlyansk Reservoir ▣ SW Russian Federation
Tsimlyansk Reservoir *see* Tsimlyanskoye Vodokhranilishche
Tsimlyansk Vodoskhovshche *see* Tsimlyanskoye Vodokhranilishche
Tsinan *see* Jinan
Tsing Hai *see* Qinghai Hu, China
Tsinghai *see* Qinghai, China
Tsingtao/Tsingtau *see* Qingdao
Tsingyuan *see* Baoding
Tsinkiang *see* Quanzhou
Tsintao *see* Qingdao
85 D17 **Tsintsabis** Otjikoto, N Namibia *18.44S 17.57E*
180 H8 **Tsiombe** *var.* Tsihombe. Toliara, S Madagascar
126 Kk14 **Tsipa** ≈ S Russian Federation
180 H5 **Tsiribihina** ≈ W Madagascar
180 I5 **Tsiroanomandidy** Antananarivo, C Madagascar *18.43S 46.01E*
201 U13 **Tsis** *island* Chuuk, C Micronesia
Tsitsihar *see* Qiqihar
131 Q3 **Tsivil'sk** Chavash Respubliki, W Russian Federation *55.51N 47.30E*
143 T9 **Ts'khinvali** *prev.* Staliniri. C Georgia *42.12N 43.58E*
121 J19 **Tsna** ≈ SW Belarus
128 I15 **Tsna** *var.* Zna. ≈ W Russian Federation
168 K11 **Tsoohor** Ömnögovĭ, S Mongolia *43.15N 104.03E*
171 H16 **Tsu** *var.* Tu. Mie, Honshū, SW Japan *34.40N 136.30E*
171 K13 **Tsubame** *var.* Tubame. Niigata, Honshū, C Japan *37.39N 138.55E*
171 Ii13 **Tsubata** Ishikawa, Honshū, SW Japan *36.33N 136.42E*
172 Q6 **Tsubetsu** Hokkaidō, NE Japan *43.43N 144.01E*
171 Kk16 **Tsuchiura** *var.* Tutiura. Ibaraki, Honshū, S Japan *36.03N 140.09E*
172 N7 **Tsugaru-kaikyō** *strait* N Japan
171 Kk13 **Tsugawa** Niigata, Honshū, C Japan *37.40N 139.26E*
172 Oo5 **Tsukigata** Hokkaidō, NE Japan *43.18N 141.37E*
170 Dd15 **Tsukumi** *var.* Tukumi. Ōita, Kyūshū, SW Japan *33.02N 131.51E*
168 E5 **Tsul-Ulaan** Bayan-Ölgiy, W Mongolia *48.51N 91.13E*
85 D17 **Tsumeb** Otjikoto, N Namibia *19.13S 17.42E*
85 F17 **Tsumkwe** Otjozondjupa, NE Namibia *19.35S 20.26E*
170 Cc16 **Tsuno** Miyazaki, Kyūshū, SW Japan *32.43N 131.32E*
170 D11 **Tsuno-shima** *island* SW Japan
171 H14 **Tsuruga** *var.* Turuga. Fukui, Honshū, SW Japan *35.38N 136.01E*
170 F15 **Tsurugi-san** ▲ Shikoku, SW Japan *33.50N 134.04E*
170 Dd15 **Tsurumi-zaki** *headland* Kyūshū, SW Japan *32.55N 132.03E*
171 L11 **Tsuruoka** *var.* Turuoka. Yamagata, Honshū, C Japan *38.43N 139.48E*
171 Hh15 **Tsushima** *var.* Tusima. Aichi, Honshū, SW Japan *35.10N 136.45E*
170 C10 **Tsushima** *var.* Tsushima-tō, Tusima. *island group* SW Japan
Tsushima-tō *see* Tsushima
170 E12 **Tsuwano** Shimane, Honshū, SW Japan *34.28N 131.43E*
170 Ff13 **Tsuyama** *var.* Tuyama. Okayama, Honshū, SW Japan *35.03N 133.57E*
85 G19 **Tswaane** Ghanzi, W Botswana *22.21S 21.52E*
121 N17 **Tsyakhtsin** *Rus.* Tekhtin. Mahilyowskaya Voblasts', E Belarus *53.52N 29.43E*
121 P19 **Tsyerakhowka** *Rus.* Terekhovka. Homyel'skaya Voblasts', SE Belarus *52.13N 31.24E*
121 I17 **Tsyeshawlya** *Rus.* Cheshevlya, Tseshevlya. Brestskaya Voblasts', SW Belarus *53.13N 25.49E*
Tsyurupinsk *see* Tsyurupyns'k
119 R10 **Tsyurupyns'k** *Rus.* Tsyurupinsk. Khersons'ka Oblast', S Ukraine *46.34N 32.42E*
Tu *see* Tsu
194 H13 **Tua** ≈ C PNG
Tuaim *see* Tuam
192 L6 **Tuakau** Waikato, North Island, NZ *37.16S 174.56E*
99 C17 **Tuam** *Ir.* Tuaim. W Ireland *53.31N 8.49W*
193 K14 **Tuamarina** Marlborough, South Island, NZ *41.27S 174.00E*
Tuamotu, Archipel des *see* Tuamotu, Îles
199 M10 **Tuamotu Fracture Zone** *tectonic feature* E Pacific Ocean
203 W9 **Tuamotu, Îles** *var.* Archipel des Tuamotu, Dangerous Archipelago, Tuamotu Islands. *island group* N French Polynesia
Tuamotu Islands *see* Tuamotu, Îles
183 X10 **Tuamotu Ridge** *undersea feature* C Pacific Ocean
178 Ii5 **Tuân Giao** Lai Châu, N Vietnam *21.34N 103.24E*
179 P8 **Tuao** Luzon, N Philippines *17.42N 121.25E*
202 B15 **Tuapa** NW Niue *18.57S 169.58W*
45 N7 **Tuapi** Región Autónoma Atlántico Norte, NE Nicaragua *14.10N 83.18W*
130 K15 **Tuapse** Krasnodarskiy Kray, SW Russian Federation *44.07N 39.07E*
175 Nn2 **Tuaran** Sabah, East Malaysia *6.12N 116.12E*
106 I6 **Tua, Rio** ≈ N Portugal
198 B7 **Tuasivi** Savai'i, C Samoa *13.37S 172.07W*
193 B24 **Tuatapere** Southland, South Island, NZ *46.09S 167.43E*
38 M9 **Tuba City** Arizona, SW USA *36.08N 111.14W*
144 H11 **Ţūbah, Qaşr aţ** *castle* Ma'ān, C Jordan *31.22N 36.39E*
Tubame *see* Tsubame
174 Ll14 **Tuban** *prev.* Toeban. Jawa, C Indonesia *6.55S 112.01E*
147 O16 **Tuban, Wādī** *dry watercourse* SW Yemen
62 K14 **Tubarão** Santa Catarina, S Brazil *28.29S 49.00W*
100 O10 **Tubbergen** Overijssel, E Netherlands *52.25N 6.46E*
Tubeke *see* Tubize
103 H22 **Tübingen** *var.* Tuebingen. Baden-Württemberg, SW Germany *48.31N 9.04E*
131 W6 **Tubinskiy** Respublika Bashkortostan, W Russian Federation *52.48N 58.18E*
101 G19 **Tubize** *Dut.* Tubeke. Walloon Brabant, C Belgium *50.43N 4.14E*
78 J16 **Tubmanburg** NW Liberia *6.50N 10.53W*
179 Qq15 **Tubod** Mindanao, S Philippines *7.58N 123.46E*
77 T7 **Ţubruq** *Eng.* Tobruk, *It.* Tobruch. NE Libya *32.04N 23.58E*
203 T13 **Tubuai** *island* Îles Australes, SW French Polynesia
Tubuai, Îles/Tubuai Islands *see* Australes, Îles
42 F3 **Tubutama** Sonora, NW Mexico *30.51N 111.31W*
56 K4 **Tucacas** Falcón, N Venezuela *10.46N 68.19W*
61 P16 **Tucano** Bahia, E Brazil *10.52S 38.48W*
59 P19 **Tucavaca, Río** ≈ E Bolivia
112 H8 **Tuchola** Kujawsko-pomorskie, C Poland *53.36N 17.50E*
113 M17 **Tuchów** Małopolskie, SE Poland *49.53N 21.04E*
25 S3 **Tucker** Georgia, SE USA *33.53N 84.10W*
29 W10 **Tuckerman** Arkansas, C USA *35.43N 91.12W*
66 B12 **Tucker's Town** E Bermuda *32.19N 64.42W*
Tuckum *see* Tukums
38 M15 **Tucson** Arizona, SW USA *32.13N 111.00W*
64 J7 **Tucumán** *off.* Provincia de Tucumán. ◈ *province* N Argentina
Tucumán *see* San Miguel de Tucumán
39 V11 **Tucumcari** New Mexico, SW USA *35.10N 103.43W*
60 H13 **Tucunaré** Pará, N Brazil *5.15S 55.49W*
57 Q6 **Tucupita** Delta Amacuro, NE Venezuela *9.01N 62.04W*
60 K13 **Tucuruí, Represa de** ▣ NE Brazil
112 F9 **Tuczno** Zachodnio-pomorskie, NW Poland *53.12N 16.08E*
Tuddo *see* Tudu
107 Q5 **Tudela** *Basq.* Tutera; *anc.* Tutela. Navarra, N Spain *42.04N 1.37W*
106 M6 **Tudela de Duero** Castilla-León, N Spain *41.35N 4.34W*
144 K6 **Tudmur** *var.* Tadmur, Tamar, *Gk.* Palmyra; *Bibl.* Tadmor. Ḩimş, C Syria *34.36N 38.15E*
120 J4 **Tudu** *Ger.* Tuddo. Lääne-Virumaa, NE Estonia *59.12N 26.52E*
Tuebingen *see* Tübingen
126 H16 **Tuekta** Respublika Altay, S Russian Federation *50.51N 85.52E*
106 I5 **Tuela, Rio** ≈ N Portugal
159 X12 **Tuensang** Nāgāland, NE India *26.16N 94.45E*
142 L15 **Tufanbeyli** Adana, C Turkey *38.15N 36.13E*
Tüffer *see* Laško
194 M15 **Tufi** Northern, S PNG *9.04S 149.15E*
199 L3 **Tufts Plain** *undersea feature* N Pacific Ocean
Tugalan *see* Kolkhozobod
69 V14 **Tugela** ≈ SE South Africa
23 P6 **Tug Fork** ≈ S USA
41 P15 **Tugidak Island** *island* Trinity Islands, Alaska, USA
179 P8 **Tuguegarao** Luzon, N Philippines *17.36N 121.42E*
127 N13 **Tugur** Khabarovskiy Kray, SE Russian Federation *53.43N 137.00E*
167 P4 **Tuhai He** ≈ E China
106 G4 **Tui** Galicia, NW Spain *42.02N 8.37W*
79 O13 **Tui** *var.* Grand Balé. ≈ W Burkina
59 J16 **Tuichi, Río** ≈ W Bolivia
66 Q11 **Tuineje** Fuerteventura, Islas Canarias, Spain, NE Atlantic Ocean *28.18N 14.03W*
45 X16 **Tuira, Río** ≈ SE Panama
Tuisarkan *see* Tūysarkān
Tujiabu *see* Yongxiu
131 W5 **Tukan** Respublika Bashkortostan, W Russian Federation *53.58N 57.29E*
175 R13 **Tukangbesi, Kepulauan** *Dut.* Toekang Besi Eilanden. *island group* C Indonesia
153 V13 **Tŭkhtamish** *Rus.* Toktomush, *prev.* Tokhtamyshbek. SE Tajikistan *37.51N 74.41E*
192 O12 **Tukituki** ≈ North Island, NZ
Tu-k'ou *see* Panzhihua
124 N15 **Tūkrah** NE Libya *32.28N 20.36E*
14 G2 **Tuktoyaktuk** Northwest Territories, NW Canada *69.27N 133.00W*
173 Ff6 **Tuktuk** Pulau Samosir, W Indonesia *2.32N 98.43E*
Tukumi *see* Tsukumi
120 E9 **Tukums** *Ger.* Tuckum. Tukums, W Latvia *56.58N 23.12E*
83 G24 **Tukuyu** *prev.* Neu-Langenburg. Mbeya, S Tanzania *9.13S 33.39E*
Tukzār *see* Tokzār
43 O13 **Tula** *var.* Tula de Allende. Hidalgo, C Mexico *20.01N 99.17W*
43 O11 **Tula** Tamaulipas, C Mexico *22.59N 99.43W*
130 K5 **Tula** Tul'skaya Oblast', W Russian Federation *54.10N 37.39E*
Tulach Mhór *see* Tullamore
Tula de Allende *see* Tula
165 N10 **Tulage Ar Gol** ≈ W China
195 X15 **Tulaghi** *var.* Tulagi. Florida Islands, C Solomon Islands *9.04S 160.09E*
Tulagi *see* Tulaghi
43 P13 **Tulancingo** Hidalgo, C Mexico *20.34N 98.24W*
37 R11 **Tulare** California, W USA *36.12N 119.21W*
31 P9 **Tulare** South Dakota, N USA *44.43N 98.29W*
37 Q12 **Tulare Lake Bed** *salt flat* California, W USA
39 S14 **Tularosa** New Mexico, SW USA *33.04N 106.01W*
39 P13 **Tularosa Mountains** ▲▲ New Mexico, SW USA
39 S15 **Tularosa Valley** *basin* New Mexico, SW USA
85 E25 **Tulbagh** Western Cape, SW South Africa *33.16S 19.09E*
58 C5 **Tulcán** Carchi, N Ecuador *0.44N 77.43W*
119 N13 **Tulcea** Tulcea, E Romania *45.11N 28.48E*
119 N13 **Tulcea** ◈ *county* SE Romania
Tul'chin *see* Tul'chyn
119 N7 **Tul'chyn** *Rus.* Tul'chin. Vinnyts'ka Oblast', C Ukraine *48.40N 28.48E*
Tuléar *see* Toliara
37 O1 **Tulelake** California, W USA *41.57N 121.30W*
118 J10 **Tulgheş** *Hung.* Gyergyótölgyes. Harghita, C Romania *46.57N 25.46E*
Tul'govichi *see* Tul'havichy
121 N20 **Tul'havichy** *Rus.* Tul'govichi. Homyel'skaya Voblasts', SE Belarus *51.45N 29.41E*
Tuli *see* Thuli
27 N4 **Tulia** Texas, SW USA *34.32N 101.45W*
15 Gg6 **Tulita** *prev.* Fort Norman, Norman. Northwest Territories, NW Canada *64.55N 125.25W*
22 J10 **Tullahoma** Tennessee, S USA *35.21N 86.12W*
191 N12 **Tullamarine** ✖ (Melbourne) Victoria, SE Australia *37.40S 144.46E*
191 Q7 **Tullamore** New South Wales, SE Australia *32.39S 147.35E*
99 E18 **Tullamore** *Ir.* Tulach Mhór. C Ireland *53.16N 7.30W*
105 N12 **Tulle** *anc.* Tutela. Corrèze, C France *45.16N 1.46E*
111 X3 **Tulln** *var.* Oberhollabrunn. Niederösterreich, NE Austria *48.19N 16.01E*
111 W4 **Tulln** ≈ NE Austria
24 H6 **Tullos** Louisiana, S USA *31.48N 92.19W*
99 F19 **Tullow** *Ir.* An Tullach. SE Ireland *52.48N 6.43W*
189 W5 **Tully** Queensland, NE Australia *18.03S 145.55E*
128 J3 **Tuloma** ≈ NW Russian Federation
116 K10 **Tulovo** Stara Zagora, C Bulgaria *42.34N 25.34E*
29 P9 **Tulsa** Oklahoma, C USA *36.09N 95.59W*
159 N11 **Tulsipur** Mid Western, W Nepal *28.01N 82.22E*
130 K6 **Tul'skaya Oblast'** ◈ *province* W Russian Federation
130 L14 **Tul'skiy** Respublika Adygeya, SW Russian Federation *44.26N 40.12E*
194 K8 **Tulu** Manus Island, N PNG *1.58S 146.50E*
56 D10 **Tuluá** Valle del Cauca, W Colombia *4.01N 76.16W*
118 M12 **Tuluceşti** Galaţi, E Romania *45.35N 28.01E*
41 N12 **Tuluksak** Alaska, USA *61.06N 160.57W*
43 Z12 **Tulum, Ruinas de** *ruins* Quintana Roo, SE Mexico *20.13N 87.24W*
126 Ii15 **Tulun** Irkutskaya Oblast', S Russian Federation *54.28N 100.18E*
174 Ll15 **Tulungagung** *prev.* Toeloengagoeng. Jawa, C Indonesia *8.03S 111.54E*
195 S11 **Tulun Islands** *var.* Kilinailau Islands; *prev.* Carteret Islands. *island group* NE PNG
130 M4 **Tuma** Ryazanskaya Oblast', W Russian Federation *55.09N 40.27E*
56 B12 **Tumaco** Nariño, SW Colombia *1.51N 78.46W*
56 B12 **Tumaco, Bahía de** *bay* SW Colombia
Tuman-gang *see* Tumen
44 L8 **Tuma, Río** ≈ N Nicaragua
97 O16 **Tumba** Stockholm, C Sweden *59.12N 17.49E*
Tumba, Lac *see* Ntomba, Lac
174 M9 **Tumbangsenamang** Borneo, C Indonesia *1.16S 112.21E*
191 Q10 **Tumbarumba** New South Wales, SE Australia *35.47S 148.03E*
58 A8 **Tumbes** Tumbes, NW Peru *3.33S 80.27W*
58 A9 **Tumbes** *off.* Departamento de Tumbes. ◈ *department* NW Peru
21 P5 **Tumbledown Mountain** ▲ Maine, NE USA *45.27N 70.28W*
9 N13 **Tumbler Ridge** British Columbia, W Canada *55.06N 120.51W*
178 I12 **Tumbŏt, Phnum** ▲ W Cambodia *12.23N 102.57E*
190 G9 **Tumby Bay** South Australia *34.22S 136.05E*
169 Y10 **Tumen** Jilin, NE China *42.58N 129.52E*
169 Y11 **Tumen** *Chin.* Tumen Jiang, *Kor.* Tuman-gang, *Rus.* Tumyn'tszyan. ≈ E Asia
Tumen Jiang *see* Tumen
57 Q8 **Tumeremo** Bolívar, E Venezuela *7.19N 61.28W*
161 G19 **Tumkūr** Karnātaka, W India *13.19N 77.06E*
98 I10 **Tummel** ≈ C Scotland, UK
196 B15 **Tumon Bay** *bay* W Guam
79 P14 **Tumu** NW Ghana *10.51N 1.58W*
60 I10 **Tumuc Humac Mountains** *var.* Serra Tumucumaque. ▲▲ N South America
Tumucumaque, Serra *see* Tumuc Humac Mountains
191 Q10 **Tumut** New South Wales, SE Australia *35.19S 148.12E*
Tumyn'tszyan *see* Tumen
Tūn *see* Ferdows
47 U14 **Tunapuna** Trinidad, Trinidad and Tobago *10.38N 61.23W*
62 K11 **Tunas** Paraná, S Brazil *24.57S 49.05W*
Tunbridge Wells *see* Royal Tunbridge Wells
116 L11 **Tunca Nehri** *Bul.* Tundzha. ≈ Bulgaria/Turkey *see also* Tundzha
143 O14 **Tunceli** *var.* Kalan. Tunceli, E Turkey *39.07N 39.34E*
143 O14 **Tunceli** ◈ *province* C Turkey
158 J12 **Tūndla** Uttar Pradesh, N India *27.13N 78.13E*
83 I25 **Tunduru** Ruvuma, S Tanzania *11.07S 37.21E*
116 L10 **Tundzha** *Turk.* Tunca Nehri. ≈ Bulgaria/Turkey *see also* Tunca Nehri
161 H17 **Tungabhadra** ≈ S India
161 F17 **Tungabhadra Reservoir** ▣ S India
203 P2 **Tungaru** *prev.* Gilbert Islands. *island group* W Kiribati
179 Q16 **Tungawan** Mindanao, S Philippines *7.33N 122.22E*
Tungdor *see* Mainling
174 Hh9 **Tungkal** ≈ Sumatera, W Indonesia
T'ung-shan *see* Xuzhou
167 Q16 **Tungsha Tao** *Chin.* Dongsha Qundao, *Eng.* Pratas Island. *island* S Taiwan
167 S13 **Tungshih** *Jap.* Tōsei. N Taiwan *24.13N 120.54E*
14 G7 **Tungsten** Northwest Territories, W Canada *62.00N 128.09W*
Tung-t'ing Hu *see* Dongting Hu
58 A13 **Tungurahua** ◈ *province* C Ecuador
97 F14 **Tunhovdfjorden** ◎ S Norway
24 K2 **Tunica** Mississippi, S USA *34.40N 90.22W*
77 N5 **Tunis** *var.* Tūnis. ● (Tunisia) NE Tunisia *36.52N 10.10E*
77 N5 **Tunis, Golfe de** *Ar.* Khalīj Tūnis. *gulf* NE Tunisia
77 N6 **Tunisia** *off.* Republic of Tunisia, *Ar.* Al Jumhūrīyah at Tūnisīyah, *Fr.* République Tunisienne. ◆ *republic* N Africa
Tūnisīyah, Al Jumhūrīyah at *see* Tunisia
Tūnis, Khalīj *see* Tunis, Golfe de
56 G9 **Tunja** Boyacá, C Colombia *5.33N 73.22W*
95 F14 **Tunnsjøen** *Lapp.* Dåtnejaevrie. ◎ C Norway
41 N12 **Tuntutuliak** Alaska, USA *60.21N 162.40W*
153 U8 **Tunuk** Chuyskaya Oblast', C Kyrgyzstan *42.11N 73.55E*
11 Q6 **Tunungayualok Island** *island* Newfoundland and Labrador, E Canada
64 H11 **Tunuyán** Mendoza, W Argentina *33.28S 69.01W*
207 P14 **Tunu** ◈ *province* E Greenland
64 I11 **Tunuyán, Río** ≈ W Argentina
Tunxi *see* Huangshan
Tuodian *see* Shuangbai
Tuoji *see* Zhongba
37 P9 **Tuolumne River** ≈ California, W USA
Tuong Buong *see* Tương Đương
178 J7 **Tương Đương** *var.* Tuong Buong. Nghê An, N Vietnam *19.14N 104.30E*
166 I13 **Tuoniang Jiang** ≈ S China
Tuotuo He *see* Togton He
Tuotuoheyan *see* Tanggulashan
Tüp *see* Tyup
62 J9 **Tupã** São Paulo, S Brazil *21.57S 50.28W*
203 S10 **Tupai** *var.* Motu Iti. *atoll* Îles Sous le Vent, W French Polynesia
63 G15 **Tupanciretã** Rio Grande do Sul, S Brazil *29.06S 53.48W*
24 M2 **Tupelo** Mississippi, S USA *34.15N 88.42W*
126 L14 **Tupik** Chitinskaya Oblast', S Russian Federation *54.21N 119.56E*
61 K18 **Tupiraçaba** Goiás, S Brazil *14.33S 48.40W*
59 L21 **Tupiza** Potosí, S Bolivia *21.27S 65.45W*
9 N13 **Tupper** British Columbia, W Canada *55.30N 119.59W*
20 J8 **Tupper Lake** ◎ New York, NE USA
152 J10 **Tuproqqal'a** *Rus.* Turpakkla. Xorazm Viloyati, W Uzbekistan *40.52N 62.00E*
64 H11 **Tupungato, Volcán** ▲ W Argentina *33.27S 69.42W*
169 T9 **Tuquan** Nei Mongol Zizhiqu, N China *45.21N 121.36E*
56 C13 **Túquerres** Nariño, SW Colombia *1.06N 77.37W*
159 U13 **Tura** Meghālaya, NE India *25.33N 90.14E*
126 J10 **Tura** Evenkiyskiy Avtonomnyy Okrug, N Russian Federation *64.19N 100.16E*
125 F11 **Tura** ≈ C Russian Federation
146 M10 **Turabah** Makkah, W Saudi Arabia *21.27N 41.40E*
57 O8 **Turagua, Cerro** ▲ C Venezuela *6.59N 64.34W*
192 L12 **Turakina** Manawatu-Wanganui, North Island, NZ *40.03S 175.13E*
193 K15 **Turakirae Head** *headland* North Island, NZ *41.26S 174.54E*
194 G13 **Turama** ≈ S PNG
126 I15 **Turan** Respublika Tyva, S Russian Federation *52.11N 93.40E*
192 M10 **Turangi** Waikato, North Island, NZ *39.01S 175.46E*
152 F11 **Turan Lowland** *var.* Turan Plain, *Kaz.* Turan Oypaty, *Rus.* Turanskaya Nizmennost', *Turk.* Turan Pesligi, *Uzb.* Turon Pasttekisligi. *plain* C Asia
Turan Oypaty/Turan Pesligi/Turan Plain/Turanskaya Nizmennost' *see* Turan Lowland
144 K7 **Ţurāq al 'Ilab** *hill range* S Syria
121 K20 **Turaw** *Rus.* Turov. Homyel'skaya Voblasts', SE Belarus *52.04N 27.41E*
146 L2 **Ţurayf** Al Ḩudūd ash Shamālīyah, NW Saudi Arabia *31.43N 38.39E*
Turba *see* Teruel
56 E5 **Turbaco** Bolívar, N Colombia *10.19N 75.25W*
154 K15 **Turbat** Baluchistān, SW Pakistan *26.02N 62.56E*
Turbat-i-Haidari *see* Torbat-e Ḩeydarīyeh
Turbat-i-Jam *see* Torbat-e Jām
56 D7 **Turbo** Antioquia, NW Colombia *8.06N 76.43W*
Turčianský Svätý Martin *see* Martin
118 H10 **Turda** *Ger.* Thorenburg, *Hung.* Torda. Cluj, NW Romania *46.34N 23.49E*
148 M7 **Ţūreh** Markazī, W Iran
203 X12 **Tureia** *atoll* Îles Tuamotu, SE French Polynesia
112 I12 **Turek** Wielkopolskie, C Poland *52.01N 18.30E*
95 L19 **Turenki** Etelä-Suomi, S Finland *60.55N 24.37E*
Turfan *see* Turpan
151 R8 **Turgay** *Kaz.* Torghay. Akmola, W Kazakhstan *51.43N 72.46E*
151 N10 **Turgay** *Kaz.* Torgay. ≈ C Kazakhstan
150 M8 **Turgayskaya Stolovaya Strana** *Kaz.* Torgay Üstirti. *plateau* Kazakhstan/Russian Federation
Turgel *see* Türi
116 L8 **Tŭrgovishte** *prev.* Eski Dzhumaya. Tŭrgovishte, N Bulgaria *43.15N 26.33E*
116 L8 **Tŭrgovishte** ◈ *province* N Bulgaria
142 C14 **Turgutlu** Manisa, W Turkey *38.30N 27.43E*
142 L12 **Turhal** Tokat, N Turkey *40.23N 36.06E*
120 H4 **Türi** *Ger.* Turgel. Järvamaa, N Estonia *58.49N 25.25E*
107 S9 **Turia** ≈ E Spain
60 M12 **Turiaçu** Maranhão, E Brazil *1.40S 45.22W*
Turin *see* Torino
118 I3 **Turiys'k** Volyns'ka Oblast', NW Ukraine *51.05N 24.31E*
Turja *see* Tur"ya
126 K15 **Turka** Respublika Buryatiya, S Russian Federation *53.02N 108.19E*
118 H6 **Turka** L'vivs'ka Oblast', W Ukraine *49.07N 23.01E*
83 H16 **Turkana, Lake** *var.* Lake Rudolf. ◎ N Kenya
151 P16 **Turkestan** *Kaz.* Türkistan. Yuzhnyy Kazakhstan, S Kazakhstan *43.18N 68.18E*
153 Q12 **Turkestan Range** *Rus.* Turkestanskiy Khrebet. ▲▲ C Asia
Turkestanskiy Khrebet *see* Turkestan Range
113 M23 **Túrkeve** Jász-Nagykun-Szolnok, E Hungary *47.07N 20.48E*
27 O4 **Turkey** Texas, SW USA *34.23N 100.54W*
142 H14 **Turkey** *off.* Republic of Turkey, *Turk.* Türkiye Cumhuriyeti. ◆ *republic* SW Asia
189 N4 **Turkey Creek** Western Australia *16.54S 128.12E*
28 M9 **Turkey Creek** ≈ Oklahoma, C USA
39 T9 **Turkey Mountains** ▲▲ New Mexico, SW USA
31 X11 **Turkey River** ≈ Iowa, C USA
131 N7 **Turki** Saratovskaya Oblast', W Russian Federation *52.00N 43.16E*
124 Nn2 **Turkish Republic of Northern Cyprus** ◇ *disputed territory* Cyprus
Türkistan *see* Turkestan
Turkistan, Bandi-i *see* Torkestān, Selseleh-ye Band-e
Türkiye Cumhuriyeti *see* Turkey
152 K12 **Türkmenabat** *prev. Rus.* Chardzhev, Chardzhou, Chardzhui, Lenin-Turkmenski, *Turkm.* Chärjew. Lebap Welaýaty, E Turkmenistan *39.07N 63.30E*
152 A11 **Türkmen Aylagy** *Rus.* Turkmenskiy Zaliv. *lake gulf* W Turkmenistan
Türkmenbashi *see* Türkmenbaşy
152 A10 **Türkmenbaşy** *Rus.* Turkmenbashi; *prev.* Krasnovodsk. Balkan Welaýaty, W Turkmenistan *40.00N 53.04E*
152 A10 **Türkmenbaşy Aylagy** *prev. Rus.* Krasnovodskiy Zaliv, *Turkm.* Krasnowodsk Aylagy. *lake gulf* W Turkmenistan
152 J14 **Türkmengala** *Rus.* Turkmen-kala; *prev.* Turkmen-Kala. Mary Welaýaty, S Turkmenistan *37.25N 62.19E*
152 G13 **Turkmenistan** *off.* Turkmenistan; *prev.* Turkmenskaya Soviet Socialist Republic. ◆ *republic* C Asia
Turkmen-kala/Turkmen-Kala *see* Türkmengala
Turkmenskaya Soviet Socialist Republic *see* Turkmenistan
Turkmenskiy Zaliv *see* Türkmen Aylagy
142 L16 **Türkoğlu** Kahramanmaraş, S Turkey *37.24N 36.49E*
46 L6 **Turks and Caicos Islands** ◇ *UK dependent territory* N West Indies
66 G10 **Turks and Caicos Islands** *island group* N West Indies
47 N6 **Turks Islands** *island group* SE Turks and Caicos Islands
95 K19 **Turku** *Swe.* Åbo. Länsi-Suomi, W Finland *60.27N 22.16E*
83 H17 **Turkwel** *seasonal river* NW Kenya
29 P9 **Turley** Oklahoma, C USA *36.14N 95.58W*
37 P9 **Turlock** California, W USA *37.29N 120.52W*
120 I12 **Turmantas** Utena, NE Lithuania *55.41N 26.27E*
56 L5 **Turmero** Aragua, N Venezuela *10.14N 66.40W*
Turmberg *see* Wieżyca
192 N13 **Turnagain, Cape** *headland* North Island, NZ *40.30S 176.36E*
Turnau *see* Turnov
44 H2 **Turneffe Islands** *island group* E Belize
20 M11 **Turners Falls** Massachusetts, NE USA *42.36N 72.31W*
9 P16 **Turner Valley** Alberta, SW Canada *50.43N 114.19W*
101 I16 **Turnhout** Antwerpen, N Belgium *51.19N 4.57E*
111 V5 **Turnitz** Niederösterreich, E Austria *47.56N 15.26E*
9 S12 **Turnor Lake** ◎ Saskatchewan, C Canada
113 E15 **Turnov** *Ger.* Turnau. Liberecký Kraj, N Czech Republic *50.36N 15.10E*
Tŭrnovo *see* Veliko Tŭrnovo
118 I15 **Turnu Măgurele** *var.* Turnu-Măgurele. Teleorman, S Romania *43.43N 24.52E*
Turnu Severin *see* Drobeta-Turnu Severin
Turócszentmárton *see* Martin
Turoni *see* Tours
Turon Pasttekisligi *see* Turan Lowland
Turov *see* Turaw
Turpakkla *see* Tuproqqal'a
164 M6 **Turpan** *var.* Turfan. Xinjiang Uygur Zizhiqu, NW China *42.54N 89.06E*
Turpan Depression *see* Turpan Pendi
164 M6 **Turpan Pendi** *Eng.* Turpan Depression. *depression* NW China
164 M5 **Turpan Zhan** Xinjiang Uygur Zizhiqu, W China *43.10N 89.06E*
Turpentine State *see* North Carolina
46 H8 **Turquino, Pico** ▲ E Cuba *19.54N 76.55W*
29 Y10 **Turrell** Arkansas, C USA *35.22N 90.13W*
45 N14 **Turrialba** Cartago, E Costa Rica *9.52N 83.40W*
98 K8 **Turriff** NE Scotland, UK *57.32N 2.28W*
145 V7 **Tursāq** E Iraq *33.27N 45.47E*
Turshiz *see* Kāshmar
Tursunzade *see* Tursunzoda
153 P13 **Tursunzoda** *Rus.* Tursunzade; *prev.* Regar. W Tajikistan *38.30N 68.10E*
168 J4 **Turt** Hövsgöl, N Mongolia *51.30N 100.40E*
Türtkül *see* To'rtko'l

◆ Country ● Country Capital ◇ Dependent Territory ○ Dependent Territory Capital ◈ Administrative Region ✖ International Airport ▲ Mountain ▲▲ Mountain Range Volcano ≈ River ◎ Lake ▣ Reservoir

TURTLE CREEK – 'UNAYZAH

31 O9 **Turtle Creek** South Dakota, N USA
32 K4 **Turtle Flambeau Flowage** Wisconsin, N USA
9 S14 **Turtleford** Saskatchewan, S Canada *53.21N 108.48W*
30 M4 **Turtle Lake** North Dakota, N USA *47.31N 100.53W*
94 K12 **Turtola** Lappi, NW Finland *66.39N 23.55E*
126 Jj10 **Turu** N Russian Federation
Turuga *see* Tsuruga
153 V10 **Turugart Pass** *pass* China/Kyrgyzstan *40.33N 74.04E*
164 E7 **Turugart Shankou** *var.* Pereval Torugart. *pass* China/Kyrgyzstan *40.33N 75.21E*
126 Hh9 **Turukhan** N Russian Federation
126 I9 **Turukhansk** Krasnoyarskiy Kray, N Russian Federation *65.50N 87.48E*
145 N3 **Ţurumbah** *well* NE Syria *36.09N 40.24E*
Turuoka *see* Tsuruoka
150 H14 **Turush** Mangistau, SW Kazakhstan *45.24N 56.02E*
62 K7 **Turvo, Rio** S Brazil
118 J2 **Tur''ya** *Pol.* Turja, *Rus.* Tur'ya. NW Ukraine
25 O4 **Tuscaloosa** Alabama, S USA *33.12N 87.34W*
25 O4 **Tuscaloosa, Lake** Alabama, S USA
Tuscan Archipelago *see* Toscano, Archipelago
Tuscan-Emilian Mountains *see* Tosco-Emiliano, Appennino
Tuscany *see* Toscana
37 V2 **Tuscarora** Nevada, W USA *41.16N 116.13W*
20 F15 **Tuscarora Mountain** *ridge* Pennsylvania, NE USA
32 M14 **Tuscola** Illinois, N USA *39.46N 88.19W*
27 P7 **Tuscola** Texas, SW USA *32.12N 99.48W*
25 O2 **Tuscumbia** Alabama, S USA *34.43N 87.42W*
94 O4 **Tusenøyane** *island group* S Svalbard
150 K13 **Tushchybas, Zaliv** *prev.* Zaliv Paskevicha. *lake gulf* SW Kazakhstan
Tusima *see* Tsushima
176 Z14 **Tusirah** Papua, E Indonesia *6.46S 140.19E*
25 Q5 **Tuskegee** Alabama, S USA *32.25N 85.41W*
96 E8 **Tustna** *island* S Norway
41 R12 **Tustumena Lake** Alaska, USA
112 K13 **Tuszyn** Łodzkie, C Poland *51.36N 19.31E*
143 S13 **Tutak** Ağrı, E Turkey *39.34N 42.48E*
193 C20 **Tutamoe Range** ▲ North Island, NZ
Tutasev *see* Tutayev
128 L15 **Tutayev** *var.* Tutasev. Yaroslavskaya Oblast', W Russian Federation *57.51N 39.29E*
Tutela *see* Tulle, France
Tutela *see* Tudela, Spain
Tutera *see* Tudela
161 H23 **Tuticorin** Tamil Nādu, SE India *8.48N 78.10E*
115 L15 **Tutin** Serbia, S Serbia and Montenegro (Yugoslavia) *43.00N 20.20E*
192 O10 **Tutira** Hawke's Bay, North Island, NZ *39.14S 176.53E*
Tutiura *see* Tsuchiura
126 Ii10 **Tutonchany** Evenkiyskiy Avtonomnyy Okrug, N Russian Federation *64.12N 93.52E*
116 L6 **Tutrakan** Silistra, NE Bulgaria *44.03N 26.38E*
31 N5 **Tuttle** North Dakota, N USA *47.07N 99.58W*
28 M11 **Tuttle** Oklahoma, C USA *35.17N 97.48W*
29 O3 **Tuttle Creek Lake** Kansas, C USA
103 H23 **Tuttlingen** Baden-Württemberg, S Germany *47.58N 8.49E*
175 Ss16 **Tutuala** W East Timor *8.23S 127.12E*
198 Cc9 **Tutuila** *island* W American Samoa
85 I18 **Tutume** Central, E Botswana *20.27S 26.58E*
41 N7 **Tututalak Mountain** ▲ Alaska, USA *67.51N 161.27W*
24 K3 **Tutwiler** Mississippi, S USA *34.00N 90.25W*
168 L8 **Tuul Gol** N Mongolia
95 O16 **Tuupovaara** Itä-Suomi, E Finland *62.30N 30.40E*
Tuva *see* Tyva, Respublika
202 E7 **Tuvalu** *prev.* Ellice Islands. ◆ *commonwealth republic* SW Pacific Ocean
197 L17 **Tuvana-i-colo** *prev.* Tuvana-i-tholo. *island* Lau Group, SE Fiji
197 L18 **Tuvana-i-ra** *island* Lau Group, SE Fiji
Tuvana-i-tholo *see* Tuvana-i-colo
Tuvinskaya ASSR *see* Tyva, Respublika
197 L14 **Tuvuca** *prev.* Tuvutha. *island* Lau Group, E Fiji
Tuvutha *see* Tuvuca
147 P9 **Ţuwayq, Jabal** ▲ C Saudi Arabia
144 H13 **Ţuwayyil ash Shihāq** *desert* S Jordan
9 U16 **Tuxford** Saskatchewan, S Canada *50.33N 105.32W*
178 K13 **Tu Xoay** Đắc Lắc, S Vietnam *12.18N 107.33E*
42 L14 **Tuxpan** Jalisco, C Mexico *19.33N 103.21W*
42 J12 **Tuxpan** Nayarit, C Mexico *21.57N 105.12W*
43 Q12 **Tuxpán** *var.* Tuxpán de Rodríguez Cano. Veracruz-Llave, E Mexico *20.58N 97.22W*
Tuxpán de Rodríguez Cano *see* Tuxpán
43 R15 **Tuxtepec** *var.* San Juan Bautista Tuxtepec. Oaxaca, S Mexico *18.01N 96.05W*
43 U16 **Tuxtla** *var.* Tuxtla Gutiérrez. Chiapas, SE Mexico *16.43N 93.03W*
Tuxtla *see* San Andrés Tuxtla
Tuxtla Gutiérrez *see* Tuxtla
Tuyama *see* Tsuyama
178 Jj5 **Tuyên Quang** Tuyên Quang, N Vietnam *21.48N 105.10E*
178 K14 **Tuy Hoa** Bình Thuân, S Vietnam *11.03N 108.12E*
178 Kk12 **Tuy Hoa** Phu Yên, S Vietnam *13.01N 109.15E*
131 U5 **Tuymazy** Respublika Bashkortostan, W Russian Federation *54.36N 53.40E*
148 L6 **Tūysarkān** *var.* Tuisarkan, Tuyserkān. Hamadān, W Iran *34.31N 48.30E*
Tuyserkān *see* Tūysarkān
151 W16 **Tuyuk** *Kaz.* Tuyyq. Almaty, SE Kazakhstan *43.07N 79.24E*
Tuyyq *see* Tuyuk
142 I14 **Tuz Gölü** C Turkey
129 Q15 **Tuzha** Kirovskaya Oblast', NW Russian Federation *57.37N 48.02E*
115 K17 **Tuzi** Montenegro, SW Serbia and Montenegro (Yugoslavia) *42.22N 19.21E*
145 T5 **Ţūz Khurmātū** N Iraq *34.55N 44.37E*
114 I11 **Tuzla** Federacija Bosna I Hercegovina, NE Bosnia and Herzegovina *44.33N 18.40E*
119 N15 **Tuzla** Constanţa, SE Romania *43.58N 28.38E*
143 T12 **Tuzluca** Iğdır, NE Turkey *40.01N 43.39E*
97 J20 **Tvååker** Halland, S Sweden *57.04N 12.25E*
97 F17 **Tvedestrand** Aust-Agder, S Norway *58.37N 8.55E*
128 J16 **Tver'** *prev.* Kalinin. Tverskaya Oblast', W Russian Federation *56.52N 35.52E*
Tverya *see* Teverya
130 I15 **Tverskaya Oblast'** ◐ *province* W Russian Federation
128 I15 **Tvertsa** W Russian Federation
112 H13 **Twardogóra** *Ger.* Festenberg. Dolnośląskie, SW Poland *51.21N 17.27E*
12 J14 **Tweed** Ontario, SE Canada *44.28N 77.19W*
98 K13 **Tweed** England/Scotland, UK
100 O7 **Tweede-Exloërmond** Drenthe, NE Netherlands *52.55N 6.55E*
191 V3 **Tweed Heads** New South Wales, SE Australia *28.10S 153.32E*
100 M11 **Twello** Gelderland, E Netherlands *52.13N 6.07E*
37 W15 **Twentynine Palms** California, W USA *34.08N 116.03W*
27 P9 **Twin Buttes Reservoir** Texas, SW USA
35 O15 **Twin Falls** Idaho, NW USA *42.33N 114.27W*
41 N13 **Twin Hills** Alaska, USA *59.06N 160.21W*
9 O11 **Twin Lakes** Alberta, W Canada *57.46N 117.30W*
35 O12 **Twin Peaks** ▲ Idaho, NW USA *44.37N 114.24W*
193 I14 **Twins, The** ▲ South Island, NZ *41.14S 172.38E*
31 S5 **Twin Valley** Minnesota, N USA *47.15N 96.15W*
102 G11 **Twistringen** Niedersachsen, NW Germany *52.48N 8.39E*
193 E20 **Twizel** Canterbury, South Island, NZ *44.15S 170.06E*
31 X5 **Two Harbors** Minnesota, N USA *47.01N 91.40W*
9 R14 **Two Hills** Alberta, SW Canada *53.40N 111.43W*
33 N7 **Two Rivers** Wisconsin, N USA *44.10N 87.33W*
118 H8 **Tyachiv** Zakarpats'ka Oblast', W Ukraine *48.02N 23.35E*
Tyan'-Shan' *see* Tien Shan
177 Ff3 **Tyao** Myanmar/India
119 R6 **Tyas'myn** N Ukraine
25 X6 **Tybee Island** Georgia, SE USA *32.00N 80.51W*
Tyborøn *see* Thyborøn
113 J16 **Tychy** *Ger.* Tichau. Śląskie, S Poland *50.12N 19.01E*
113 O16 **Tyczyn** Podkarpackie, SE Poland *49.58N 22.03E*
96 I8 **Tydal** Sør-Trøndelag, S Norway *63.01N 11.36E*
117 H24 **Tyflós** Kríti, Greece, E Mediterranean Sea
23 S3 **Tygart Lake** West Virginia, NE USA
126 M15 **Tygda** Amurskaya Oblast', SE Russian Federation *53.07N 126.12E*
23 Q11 **Tyger River** South Carolina, SE USA
34 I11 **Tygh Valley** Oregon, NW USA *45.15N 121.12W*
96 F12 **Tyin** S Norway
31 S10 **Tyler** Minnesota, N USA *44.16N 96.07W*
27 W7 **Tyler** Texas, SW USA *32.21N 95.18W*
27 W7 **Tyler, Lake** Texas, SW USA
24 K7 **Tylertown** Mississippi, S USA *31.07N 90.08W*
119 P10 **Tylihuls'kyy Lyman** SW Ukraine
Tylos *see* Bahrain
126 Gg12 **Tym** C Russian Federation
117 C15 **Týmfi** *var.* Timfi. ▲ W Greece *39.58N 20.51E*
117 E17 **Tymfristós** *var.* Timfristos. ▲ C Greece *38.57N 21.49E*
127 O14 **Tymovskoye** Ostrov Sakhalin, Sakhalinskaya Oblast', SE Russian Federation *50.36N 142.45E*
117 J25 **Tympáki** *var.* Timbaki; *prev.* Timbákion. Kríti, Greece, E Mediterranean Sea *35.04N 24.46E*
126 Ll14 **Tynda** Amurskaya Oblast', SE Russian Federation *55.09N 124.43E*
31 Q12 **Tyndall** South Dakota, N USA *42.57N 97.52W*
99 L14 **Tyne** N England, UK
99 M14 **Tynemouth** NE England, UK *55.01N 1.24W*
99 L14 **Tyneside** *cultural region* NE England, UK
96 H10 **Tynset** Hedmark, S Norway *61.45N 10.48E*
41 Q12 **Tyonek** Alaska, USA *61.04N 151.08W*
Tyôsi *see* Chōshi
Tyras *see* Dniester, Moldova/Ukraine
Tyras *see* Bilhorod-Dnistrovs'kyy, Ukraine
Tyre *see* Soûr
97 G14 **Tyrifjorden** S Norway
97 K22 **Tyringe** Skåne, S Sweden *56.09N 13.34E*
127 N15 **Tyrma** Khabarovskiy Kray, SE Russian Federation *50.00N 132.04E*
Tyrnau *see* Trnava
117 F15 **Týrnavos** *var.* Tírnavos. Thessalía, C Greece *39.45N 22.18E*
131 N16 **Tyrnyauz** Kabardino-Balkarskaya Respublika, SW Russian Federation *43.19N 42.55E*
Tyrol *see* Tirol
20 E14 **Tyrone** Pennsylvania, NE USA *40.41N 78.12W*
99 E15 **Tyrone** *cultural region* W Northern Ireland, UK
190 M10 **Tyrrell, Lake** *salt lake* Victoria, SE Australia
86 H14 **Tyrrhenian Basin** *undersea feature* Tyrrhenian Sea, C Mediterranean Sea
123 L9 **Tyrrhenian Sea** *It.* Mare Tirreno. *sea* N Mediterranean Sea
96 J12 **Tyrsil** Hedmark, S Norway *61.18N 12.16E*
Tysa *see* Tisa/Tisza
118 J7 **Tysmenytsya** Ivano-Frankivs'ka Oblast', W Ukraine *48.54N 24.50E*
97 C14 **Tysnesøya** *island* S Norway
97 C14 **Tysse** Hordaland, S Norway *60.23N 5.46E*
97 D14 **Tyssedal** Hordaland, S Norway *60.07N 6.36E*
97 O17 **Tystberga** Södermanland, C Sweden *58.51N 17.15E*
120 E12 **Tytuvėnai** Šiauliai, C Lithuania *55.36N 23.14E*
150 D14 **Tyub-Karagan, Mys** *headland* SW Kazakhstan *44.40N 50.19E*
153 V8 **Tyugel'-Say** Narynskaya Oblast', C Kyrgyzstan *41.57N 74.40E*
125 Ff13 **Tyukalinsk** Omskaya Oblast', C Russian Federation *55.56N 72.02E*
131 V7 **Tyul'gan** Orenburgskaya Oblast', W Russian Federation *52.27N 56.08E*
125 F11 **Tyumen'** Tyumenskaya Oblast', C Russian Federation *57.10N 65.28E*
125 Ff10 **Tyumenskaya Oblast'** ◐ *province* C Russian Federation
126 Kk10 **Tyung** NE Russian Federation
153 Y7 **Tyup** *Kir.* Tüp. Issyk-Kul'skaya Oblast', NE Kyrgyzstan *42.43N 78.18E*
126 I16 **Tyva, Respublika** *prev.* Tannu-Tuva, Tuva, Tuvinskaya ASSR. ◐ *autonomous republic* C Russian Federation
119 N7 **Tyvriv** Vinnyts'ka Oblast', C Ukraine *49.01N 28.28E*
99 J21 **Tywi** S Wales, UK
99 I19 **Tywyn** W Wales, UK *52.34N 4.06W*
85 K20 **Tzaneen** Limpopo, NE South Africa *23.49S 30.09E*
Tzekung *see* Zigong
43 X12 **Tzucacab** Yucatán, SE Mexico *20.04N 89.03W*

U

84 B12 **Uaco Cungo** *var.* Waku Kungo, *Port.* Santa Comba. Cuanza Sul, C Angola *11.21S 15.04E*
UAE *see* United Arab Emirates
203 X7 **Ua Huka** *island* Îles Marquises, NE French Polynesia
60 E10 **Uaiacás** Roraima, N Brazil *3.28N 63.13W*
Uamba *see* Wamba
Uanle Uen *see* Wanlaweyn
203 W7 **Ua Pu** *island* Îles Marquises, NE French Polynesia
83 L17 **Uar Garas** *spring/well* SW Somalia *1.19N 41.22E*
60 G12 **Uatumã, Rio** C Brazil
Ua Uíbh Fhailí *see* Offaly
60 C11 **Uaupés, Rio** *var.* Río Vaupés. Brazil/Colombia *see also* Vaupés, Río
151 X9 **Uba** E Kazakhstan
151 N16 **Ubagan** *Kaz.* Obagan. Kazakhstan/Russian Federation
195 N12 **Ubai** New Britain, E PNG *5.38S 150.45E*
81 J15 **Ubangi** *Fr.* Oubangui. C Africa
Ubangi-Shari *see* Central African Republic
118 M3 **Ubarts'** *Ukr.* Ubort'. Belarus/Ukraine *see also* Ubort'
56 F9 **Ubaté** Cundinamarca, C Colombia *5.19N 73.49W*
62 N10 **Ubatuba** São Paulo, S Brazil *23.24S 45.06W*
155 R12 **Ubauro** Sind, SE Pakistan *28.07N 69.43E*
179 Qq14 **Ubay** Bohol, C Philippines *10.02N 124.29E*
105 U14 **Ubaye** SE France
Ubayid, Wadi al *see* Ubayyiḑ, Wādī al
145 N8 **Ubaylah** W Iraq *33.06N 40.13E*
145 O10 **Ubayyiḑ, Wādī al** *var.* Wadi al Ubayid. *dry watercourse* SW Iraq
100 L13 **Ubbergen** Gelderland, E Netherlands *51.49N 5.54E*
170 Dd13 **Ube** Yamaguchi, Honshū, SW Japan *33.56N 131.14E*
107 O13 **Úbeda** Andalucía, S Spain *38.01N 3.22W*
111 V7 **Übelbach** *var.* Markt-Übelbach. Steiermark, SE Austria *47.13N 15.15E*
61 L20 **Uberaba** Minas Gerais, SE Brazil *19.46S 47.57W*
59 Q19 **Uberaba, Laguna** E Bolivia
61 K19 **Uberlândia** Minas Gerais, SE Brazil *18.16S 48.16W*
103 H24 **Überlingen** Baden-Württemberg, S Germany *47.46N 9.10E*
79 U16 **Ubiaja** Edo, S Nigeria *6.39N 6.23E*
106 K3 **Ubiña, Peña** ▲ NW Spain *43.01N 5.58W*
59 H17 **Ubinas, Volcán** S Peru *16.16S 70.49W*
Ubol Rajadhani/Ubol Ratchathani *see* Ubon Ratchathani
178 Ii9 **Ubolratna Reservoir** C Thailand
178 J10 **Ubon Ratchathani** *var.* Muang Ubon, Ubol Rajadhani, Ubol Ratchathani, Udon Ratchathani. Ubon Ratchathani, E Thailand *15.15N 104.49E*
121 L20 **Ubort'** *Bel.* Ubarts'. Belarus/Ukraine *see also* Ubarts'
106 K15 **Ubrique** Andalucía, S Spain *36.42N 5.27W*
Ubsu-Nur, Ozero *see* Uvs Nuur
81 M18 **Ubundu** Orientale, C Dem. Rep. Congo *0.24S 25.30E*
152 J13 **Uçajy** *var.* Üchajy, *Rus.* Uch-Adzhi. Mary Welaýaty, C Turkmenistan *38.06N 62.44E*
143 X11 **Ucar** *Rus.* Udzhary. C Azerbaijan *40.31N 47.40E*
58 G13 **Ucayali** *off.* Departamento de Ucayali. ◐ *department* E Peru
58 F10 **Ucayali, Río** C Peru
Uccle *see* Ukkel
Uch-Adzhi/Üchajy *see* Uçajy
131 X4 **Uchaly** Respublika Bashkortostan, W Russian Federation *54.19N 59.33E*
151 W13 **Ucharal** *Kaz.* Üsharal. Almaty, E Kazakhstan *46.07N 80.55E*
170 C17 **Uchinoura** Kagoshima, Kyūshū, SW Japan *31.16N 131.04E*
172 Nn6 **Uchiura-wan** *bay* NW Pacific Ocean
Uchkuduk *see* Uchquduq
Uchkurghan *see* Uchqo'rg'on
153 S9 **Uchqo'rg'on** *Rus.* Uchkurghan. Namangan Viloyati, E Uzbekistan *41.06N 72.04E*
152 K8 **Uchquduq** *Rus.* Uchkuduk. Navoiy Viloyati, N Uzbekistan *42.12N 63.27E*
Uchsay *see* Uchsoy
152 G6 **Uchsoy** *Rus.* Uchsay. Qoraqalpog'iston Respublikasi, NW Uzbekistan *43.51N 58.51E*
Uchtagan Gumy/Uchtagan, Peski *see* Uçtagan Gumy
126 Mm12 **Uchur** E Russian Federation
102 O10 **Uckermark** *cultural region* E Germany
8 K17 **Ucluelet** Vancouver Island, British Columbia, SW Canada *48.58N 125.28W*
152 D10 **Uçtagan Gumy** *var.* Uchtagan Gumy, *Rus.* Peski Uchtagan. *desert* NW Turkmenistan
126 Ii14 **Uda** S Russian Federation
126 Mm13 **Uda** E Russian Federation
126 K9 **Udachnyy** Respublika Sakha (Yakutiya), NE Russian Federation *66.27N 112.18E*
161 G21 **Udagamandalam** *var.* Udhagamandalam; *prev.* Ootacamund. Tamil Nādu, SW India *11.28N 76.42E*
158 F14 **Udaipur** *prev.* Oodeypore. Rājasthān, N India *24.34N 73.40E*
Udayadhani *see* Uthai Thani
149 N16 **'Udayd, Khawr al** *var.* Khor al Udeid. *inlet* Qatar/Saudi Arabia
114 D11 **Udbina** Lika-Senj, W Croatia *44.33N 15.46E*
97 I18 **Uddevalla** Västra Götaland, S Sweden *58.19N 11.55E*
Uddjaur *see* Uddjaure
94 H13 **Uddjaure** *var.* Uddjaur. N Sweden
Udeid, Khor al *see* 'Udayd, Khawr al
101 K14 **Uden** Noord-Brabant, SE Netherlands *51.40N 5.37E*
Uden *see* Udenhout
101 J14 **Udenhout** *var.* Uden. Noord-Brabant, S Netherlands *51.37N 5.09E*
161 H14 **Udgīr** Mahārāshtra, C India *18.23N 77.06E*
Udhagamandalam *see* Udagamandalam
158 H6 **Udhampur** Jammu and Kashmir, NW India *32.55N 75.07E*
145 X14 **'Udhaybah, 'Uqlat al** *well* S Iraq *29.46N 46.50E*
108 J7 **Udine** *anc.* Utina. Friuli-Venezia Giulia, NE Italy *46.04N 13.10E*
183 T14 **Udintsev Fracture Zone** *tectonic feature* S Pacific Ocean
Udipi *see* Udupi
Udmurtia *see* Udmurtskaya Respublika
131 S2 **Udmurtskaya Respublika** *Eng.* Udmurtia. ◐ *autonomous republic* NW Russian Federation
128 J15 **Udomlya** Tverskaya Oblast', W Russian Federation *57.53N 34.59E*
Udon Ratchathani *see* Ubon Ratchathani
178 Ii9 **Udon Thani** *var.* Ban Mak Khaeng, Udorndhani. Udon Thani, N Thailand *17.25N 102.45E*
Udorndhani *see* Udon Thani
201 U12 **Udot** *atoll* Chuuk Islands, C Micronesia
127 N13 **Udskaya Guba** *bay* E Russian Federation
161 E19 **Udupi** *var.* Udipi. Karnātaka, SW India *13.18N 74.46E*
Udzhary *see* Ucar
175 Q9 **Uebonti, Teluk** *bay* Sulawesi, C Indonesia
102 O9 **Uecker** NE Germany
102 O9 **Ueckermünde** Mecklenburg-Vorpommern, NE Germany *53.43N 14.03E*
171 J14 **Ueda** *var.* Uyeda. Nagano, Honshū, S Japan *36.25N 138.14E*
81 L16 **Uele** *var.* Welle. NE Dem. Rep. Congo
Uele (upper course) *see* Uolo, Río, Equatorial Guinea/Gabon
Uele (upper course) *see* Kibali, Dem. Rep. Congo
127 Q3 **Uelen** Chukotskiy Avtonomnyy Okrug, NE Russian Federation *66.01N 169.52W*
102 J11 **Uelzen** Niedersachsen, N Germany *52.58N 10.34E*
171 H15 **Ueno** Mie, Honshū, SW Japan *34.45N 136.09E*
131 V4 **Ufa** Respublika Bashkortostan, W Russian Federation *54.46N 56.02E*
131 V4 **Ufa** W Russian Federation
Ufra *see* Kenar
85 C18 **Ugab** C Namibia
120 D8 **Ugāle** Ventspils, NW Latvia *57.16N 21.58E*
83 F17 **Uganda** *off.* Republic of Uganda. ◆ *republic* E Africa
144 G4 **Ugarit** *Ar.* Ra's Shamrah. *site of ancient city* Al Lādhiqīyah, NW Syria *35.34N 35.45E*
41 O14 **Ugashik** Alaska, USA *57.30N 157.24W*
109 Q19 **Ugento** Puglia, SE Italy *39.53N 18.09E*
107 O15 **Ugíjar** Andalucía, S Spain *36.58N 3.03W*
105 T11 **Ugine** Savoie, E France *45.45N 6.25E*
126 M14 **Uglegorsk** Amurskaya Oblast', S Russian Federation *51.40N 128.05E*
127 O15 **Uglegorsk** Ostrov Sakhalin, Sakhalinskaya Oblast', SE Russian Federation *49.01N 142.04E*
129 V13 **Ugleural'sk** Permskaya Oblast', NW Russian Federation *58.57N 57.37E*
128 L15 **Uglich** Yaroslavskaya Oblast', W Russian Federation *57.33N 38.23E*
128 I14 **Uglovka** *var.* Okulovka. Novgorodskaya Oblast', W Russian Federation *58.24N 33.15E*
127 Pp5 **Ugol'nyye Kopi** Chukotskiy Avtonomnyy Okrug, NE Russian Federation *64.43N 105.46E*
130 I4 **Ugra** W Russian Federation
153 V9 **Ugyut** Narynskaya Oblast', C Kyrgyzstan *41.22N 74.49E*
113 H19 **Uherské Hradiště** *Ger.* Ungarisch-Hradisch. Zlínský kraj, E Czech Republic *49.04N 17.26E*
113 H19 **Uherský Brod** *Ger.* Ungarisch-Brod. Zlínský kraj, E Czech Republic *49.01N 17.37E*
113 B17 **Úhlava** *Ger.* Angel. W Czech Republic
Uhorshchyna *see* Hungary
33 T13 **Uhrichsville** Ohio, N USA *40.23N 81.21W*
Uhuru Peak *see* Kilimanjaro
98 G8 **Uig** N Scotland, UK *57.35N 6.22W*
84 B10 **Uíge** *Port.* Carmona, Vila Marechal Carmona. Uíge, NW Angola *7.37S 15.02E*
84 B10 **Uíge** ◐ *province* N Angola
200 Ss13 **Uiha** *island* Ha'apai Group, C Tonga
201 U13 **Uijec** *island* Chuuk, C Micronesia
169 X14 **Ŭijŏngbu** *Jap.* Giseifu. NW South Korea *37.42N 127.02E*
150 H10 **Uil** *Kaz.* Oyyl. Aktyubinsk, W Kazakhstan *49.06N 54.41E*
150 H10 **Uil** *Kaz.* Oyyl. W Kazakhstan
38 M3 **Uinta Mountains** ▲ Utah, W USA
85 C18 **Uis** Erongo, NW Namibia *21.15S 14.54E*
85 I25 **Uitenhage** Eastern Cape, S South Africa *33.43S 25.27E*
100 H9 **Uitgeest** Noord-Holland, W Netherlands *52.31N 4.43E*
100 I11 **Uithoorn** Noord-Holland, C Netherlands *52.13N 4.49E*
100 O4 **Uithuizen** Groningen, NE Netherlands *53.24N 6.40E*
100 O4 **Uithuizermeeden** Groningen, NE Netherlands *53.25N 6.43E*
201 R6 **Ujae Atoll** *var.* Wūjae. *atoll* Ralik Chain, W Marshall Islands
Ujain *see* Ujjain
113 I16 **Ujazd** Opolskie, S Poland *50.22N 18.20E*
Új-Becse *see* Novi Bečej
Ujda *see* Oujda
201 N5 **Ujelang Atoll** *var.* Wujlān. *atoll* Ralik Chain, W Marshall Islands
113 N21 **Újfehértó** Szabolcs-Szatmár-Bereg, E Hungary *47.48N 21.41E*
Újgradiska *see* Nova Gradiška
171 H15 **Uji** *var.* Uzi. Kyōto, Honshū, SW Japan *34.52N 135.47E*
170 Aa16 **Uji-guntō** *island* Nansei-shotō, SW Japan
83 E21 **Ujiji** Kigoma, W Tanzania *4.55S 29.39E*
160 G10 **Ujjain** *prev.* Ujain. Madhya Pradesh, C India *23.10N 75.49E*
Újlak *see* Ilok
'Ujmān *see* 'Ajmān
Újmoldova *see* Moldova Nouă
Újszentanna *see* Sântana
Ujungpandang *see* Makassar
Ujung Salang *see* Phuket
Újvidék *see* Novi Sad
160 E11 **Ukāi Reservoir** W India
83 G19 **Ukara Island** *island* N Tanzania
'Ukash, Wādī *see* 'Akāsh, Wādī
83 F19 **Ukerewe Island** *island* N Tanzania
145 S9 **Ukhaydhir** C Iraq *32.28N 43.36E*
159 X13 **Ukhrul** Manipur, NE India *25.07N 94.24E*
129 S9 **Ukhta** Respublika Komi, NW Russian Federation *63.30N 53.47E*
36 L6 **Ukiah** California, W USA *39.07N 123.14W*
34 K12 **Ukiah** Oregon, NW USA *45.06N 118.57W*
101 G18 **Ukkel** *Fr.* Uccle. Brussels, C Belgium *50.47N 4.19E*
120 G13 **Ukmergė** *Pol.* Wiłkomierz. Vilnius, C Lithuania *55.16N 24.46E*
Ukraina *see* Ukraine
118 L6 **Ukraine** *off.* Ukraine, *Rus.* Ukraina, *Ukr.* Ukrayina; *prev.* Ukrainian Soviet Socialist Republic, Ukrainskaya S.S.R. ◆ *republic* SE Europe
Ukrainskay S.S.R/Ukrayina *see* Ukraine
84 B13 **Uku** Cuanza Sul, NW Angola *11.25S 14.18E*
170 Bb12 **Uku-jima** *island* Gotō-rettō, SW Japan
85 F20 **Ukwi** Kgalagadi, SW Botswana *23.41S 20.26E*
120 M13 **Ula** *Rus.* Ulla. Vitsyebskaya Voblasts', N Belarus *55.13N 29.15E*
142 C16 **Ula** Muğla, SW Turkey *37.07N 28.25E*
120 M13 **Ula** *Rus.* Ulla. N Belarus
168 L7 **Ulaanbaatar** *Eng.* Ulan Bator; *prev.* Urga. ● (Mongolia) Töv, C Mongolia *47.54N 106.57E*
169 N8 **Ulaan-Ereg** Hentiy, E Mongolia *46.50N 109.39E*
168 E5 **Ulaangom** Uvs, NW Mongolia *49.56N 92.06E*
168 E7 **Ulaantolgoy** Hovd, W Mongolia *46.39N 92.50E*
168 I8 **Ulaan-Uul** Bayanhongor, C Mongolia *46.03N 100.52E*
169 O10 **Ulaan-Uul** Dornogovĭ, SE Mongolia *44.21N 111.06E*
168 M14 **Ulan** *var.* Otog Qi. Nei Mongol Zizhiqu, N China *39.05N 107.58E*
165 R10 **Ulan** *var.* Xireg; *prev.* Xiligou. Qinghai, C China *36.59N 98.21E*
Ulan Bator *see* Ulaanbaatar
168 L13 **Ulan Buh Shamo** *desert* N China
Ulanhad *see* Chifeng
169 T8 **Ulanhot** Nei Mongol Zizhiqu, N China *46.02N 122.00E*
131 Q14 **Ulan Khol** Respublika Kalmykiya, SW Russian Federation *45.27N 46.48E*
168 M13 **Ulansuhai Nur** N China
126 Jj16 **Ulan-Ude** *prev.* Verkhneudinsk. Respublika Buryatiya, S Russian Federation *51.55N 107.40E*
165 N12 **Ulan Ul Hu** C China
195 Z16 **Ulawa Island** *island* SE Solomon Islands
144 J7 **'Ulayyānīyah, Bi'r al** *var.* Al Hilbeh. *well* S Syria *34.01N 38.06E*
127 Nn13 **Ul'banskiy Zaliv** *strait* E Russian Federation
Ulbo *see* Olib
115 J18 **Ulcinj** Montenegro, SW Serbia and Montenegro (Yugoslavia) *41.56N 19.14E*
169 O7 **Uldz** Hentiy, NE Mongolia *48.47N 112.01E*
Uleåborg *see* Oulu
Uleälv *see* Oulujoki
97 G16 **Ulefoss** Telemark, S Norway *59.16N 9.16E*
Uleträsk *see* Oulujärvi
115 L19 **Ulëz** *var.* Ulëza. Dibër, C Albania *41.42N 19.52E*
Ulëza *see* Ulëz
97 F22 **Ulfborg** Ringkøbing, W Denmark *56.16N 8.21E*
100 N13 **Ulft** Gelderland, E Netherlands *51.52N 6.22E*
168 G7 **Uliastay** *prev.* Jibhalanta. Dzavhan, W Mongolia *47.46N 96.53E*
196 F8 **Ulimang** Babeldaob, N Palau
69 T10 **Ulindi** W Dem. Rep. Congo
196 H14 **Ulithi Atoll** *atoll* Caroline Islands, W Micronesia
114 N10 **Uljma** Serbia, NE Serbia and Montenegro (Yugoslavia) *45.04N 21.08E*
150 L11 **Ul'kayak** *Kaz.* Ölkeyek. C Kazakhstan
151 Q7 **Ul'ken-Karoy, Ozero** N Kazakhstan
Ülkenözen *see* Bol'shoy Uzen'
Ülkenqobda *see* Bol'shaya Khobda
106 G3 **Ulla** NW Spain
Ulla *see* Ula
191 S10 **Ulladulla** New South Wales, SE Australia *35.22S 150.28E*
159 T14 **Ullapara** Rajshahi, W Bangladesh *24.19N 89.34E*
98 H7 **Ullapool** N Scotland, UK *57.54N 5.10W*
97 J20 **Ullared** Halland, S Sweden *57.07N 12.45E*
107 T7 **Ulldecona** Cataluña, NE Spain *40.36N 0.27E*
94 I9 **Ullsfjorden** *fjord* N Norway
99 K15 **Ullswater** NW England, UK
103 I22 **Ulm** Baden-Württemberg, S Germany *48.24N 9.58E*
35 R8 **Ulm** Montana, NW USA *47.27N 111.32W*
191 V5 **Ulmarra** New South Wales, SE Australia *29.37S 153.06E*
118 K13 **Ulmeni** Buzău, C Romania *45.08N 26.43E*
118 K14 **Ulmeni** Călăraşi, S Romania *44.08N 26.43E*
44 L7 **Ulmukhuás** Región Autónoma Atlántico Norte, NE Nicaragua *14.21N 84.34W*
196 C8 **Ulong** *var.* Aulong. *island* Palau Islands, N Palau
85 N14 **Ulonguè** *var.* Ulongwé. Tete, NW Mozambique *14.42S 34.21E*
Ulongwé *see* Ulonguè
97 K19 **Ulricehamn** Västra Götaland, S Sweden *57.57N 13.25E*
100 N5 **Ulrum** Groningen, NE Netherlands *53.24N 6.20E*
169 Z16 **Ulsan** *Jap.* Urusan. SE South Korea *35.33N 129.19E*
96 D10 **Ulsteinvik** Møre og Romsdal, S Norway *62.19N 5.52E*
99 D15 **Ulster** ◐ *province* Northern Ireland, UK/Ireland
175 S5 **Ulu** Pulau Siau, N Indonesia *2.46N 125.22E*
126 Ll12 **Ulu** Respublika Sakha (Yakutiya), NE Russian Federation *60.18N 127.27E*
44 H5 **Ulúa, Río** NW Honduras
142 D12 **Ulubat Gölü** NW Turkey
142 E12 **Uludağ** ▲ NW Turkey *40.08N 29.13E*
164 D7 **Ulugqat** Xinjiang Uygur Zizhiqu, W China *39.45N 74.10E*
142 J16 **Ulukışla** Niğde, S Turkey *37.33N 34.28E*
201 O15 **Ulul** *island* Caroline Islands, C Micronesia
85 L22 **Ulundi** KwaZulu/Natal, E South Africa *28.18S 31.25E*
164 M3 **Ulungur He** NW China
164 K2 **Ulungur Hu** NW China
189 P8 **Uluru** *var.* Ayers Rock. *rocky outcrop* Northern Territory, C Australia *25.20S 130.59E*
Ulveah *see* Lopevi
99 K16 **Ulverston** NW England, UK *54.12N 3.07W*
191 O16 **Ulverstone** Tasmania, SE Australia *41.13S 146.09E*
96 D13 **Ulvik** Hordaland, S Norway *60.34N 6.53E*
95 J18 **Ulvila** Länsi-Suomi, W Finland *61.25N 21.55E*
119 O8 **Ulyanivka** *Rus.* Ul'yanovka. Kirovohrads'ka Oblast', C Ukraine *48.18N 30.15E*
Ul'yanovka *see* Ulyanivka
131 Q5 **Ul'yanovsk** *prev.* Simbirsk. Ul'yanovskaya Oblast', W Russian Federation *54.16N 48.21E*
131 Q5 **Ul'yanovskaya Oblast'** ◐ *province* W Russian Federation
151 S10 **Ul'yanovskiy** Karaganda, C Kazakhstan *50.04N 73.45E*
Ul'yanovskiy Kanal *see* Ul'yanow Kanali
152 M13 **Ul'yanow Kanali** *Rus.* Ul'yanovskiy Kanal. *canal* Turkmenistan/Uzbekistan
Ulyshylanshyq *see* Uly-Zhylanshyk
28 H6 **Ulysses** Kansas, C USA *37.34N 101.21W*
151 O12 **Ulytau, Gory** ▲ C Kazakhstan
126 K14 **Ulyunkhan** Respublika Buryatiya, S Russian Federation *54.48N 111.01E*
151 N11 **Uly-Zhylanshyk** *Kaz.* Ulyshylanshyq. C Kazakhstan
114 A9 **Umag** *It.* Umago. Istra, NW Croatia *45.25N 13.32E*
Umago *see* Umag
201 V13 **Uman** *atoll* Chuuk Islands, C Micronesia
119 O7 **Uman'** *Rus.* Uman. Cherkas'ka Oblast', C Ukraine *48.45N 30.10E*
43 W12 **Umán** Yucatán, SE Mexico *20.51N 89.45W*
Umanak/Umanaq *see* Uummannaq
'Umān, Khalīj *see* Oman, Gulf of
'Umān, Salṭanat *see* Oman
176 Ww12 **Umari** Papua, E Indonesia *4.18S 135.22E*
160 K10 **Umaria** Madhya Pradesh, C India *23.34N 80.49E*
155 R16 **Umar Kot** Sind, SE Pakistan *25.19N 69.45E*
196 B17 **Umatac** SW Guam *13.17N 144.40E*
196 A17 **Umatac Bay** *bay* SW Guam
145 S6 **Umayqah** C Iraq *34.32N 43.45E*
128 J5 **Umba** Murmanskaya Oblast', NW Russian Federation *66.39N 34.24E*
144 I8 **Umbāshī, Khirbat al** *ruins* As Suwaydā', S Syria *33.05N 37.00E*
82 A12 **Umbelasha** W Sudan
108 H12 **Umbertide** Umbria, C Italy *43.16N 12.21E*
63 B17 **Umberto** *var.* Humberto. Santa Fe, C Argentina *30.52S 61.19W*
194 K11 **Umboi Island** *var.* Rooke Island. *island* C PNG
128 J4 **Umbozero, Ozero** NW Russian Federation
108 H13 **Umbria** ◐ *region* C Italy
Umbrian-Machigian Mountains *see* Umbro-Marchigiano, Appennino
108 I12 **Umbro-Marchigiano, Appennino** *Eng.* Umbrian-Machigian Mountains. ▲ C Italy
95 J16 **Umeå** Västerbotten, N Sweden *63.49N 20.15E*
95 H14 **Umeälven** N Sweden
41 Q5 **Umiat** Alaska, USA *69.22N 152.08W*
85 K23 **Umlazi** KwaZulu/Natal, E South Africa *29.58S 30.50E*
145 X10 **Umm al Baqar, Hawr** *var.* Birkat ad Dawaymah. *spring* S Iraq *31.43N 46.50E*
147 U12 **Umm al Ḩayt, Wādī** *var.* Wādī Amilḩayt. *seasonal river* SW Oman
Umm al Qaiwain *see* Umm al Qaywayn
149 R15 **Umm al Qaywayn** *var.* Umm al Qaiwain. Umm al Qaywayn, NE UAE *25.43N 55.54E*
145 Q5 **Umm al Ţūz** C Iraq *34.53N 42.42E*
144 J3 **Umm 'Āmūd** Ḩalab, N Syria *35.57N 37.39E*
147 Y10 **Umm ar Ruşāş** *var.* Umm Ruşayş. W Oman *20.26N 58.48E*
147 X9 **Umms Samīn** *salt flat* C Oman
147 V9 **Umm az Zumūl** *oasis* E Saudi Arabia *22.39N 54.45E*
82 A9 **Umm Buru** Western Darfur, W Sudan *15.01N 23.36E*
82 A12 **Umm Dafag** Southern Darfur, W Sudan *10.28N 23.19E*
Umm Durmān *see* Omdurman
144 F9 **Umm el Fahm** Haifa, N Israel *32.30N 35.06E*
82 F9 **Umm Inderab** Northern Kordofan, C Sudan *15.18N 31.56E*
82 C10 **Umm Keddada** Northern Darfur, W Sudan *13.36N 26.42E*
146 J7 **Umm Lajj** Tabūk, W Saudi Arabia *25.01N 37.19E*
144 L10 **Umm Maḩfur** N Jordan
145 Y13 **Umm Qaşr** SE Iraq *30.01N 47.55E*
Umm Ruşayş *see* Umm ar Ruşāş
82 F11 **Umm Ruwaba** *var.* Umm Ruwāba, Um Ruwāba. Northern Kordofan, C Sudan *12.54N 31.13E*
Umm Ruwābah *see* Umm Ruwaba
149 N16 **Umm Sa'īd** *var.* Musay'īd. S Qatar *24.57N 51.31E*
144 K10 **Umm Ţuways, Wādī** *dry watercourse* N Jordan
40 J17 **Umnak Island** *island* Aleutian Islands, Alaska, USA
34 F13 **Umpqua River** Oregon, NW USA
84 D13 **Umpulo** Bié, C Angola *12.43S 17.42E*
160 I12 **Umred** Mahārāshtra, C India *20.54N 79.19E*
145 Y10 **Umr Sawān, Hawr** S Iraq
Um Ruwāba *see* Umm Ruwaba
85 J24 **Umtata** Eastern Cape, SE South Africa *31.33S 28.47E*
79 V17 **Umuahia** Abia, SW Nigeria *5.30N 7.33E*
62 H10 **Umuarama** Paraná, S Brazil *23.45S 53.19W*
Umvuma *see* Mvuma
85 K18 **Umzingwani** S Zimbabwe
114 D11 **Una** Bosnia and Herzegovina/Croatia
114 E12 **Unac** W Bosnia and Herzegovina
25 T6 **Unadilla** Georgia, SE USA *32.15N 83.44W*
20 I10 **Unadilla River** New York, NE USA
61 L18 **Unaí** Minas Gerais, SE Brazil *16.24S 46.49W*
41 N10 **Unalakleet** Alaska, USA *63.52N 160.47W*
40 K17 **Unalaska Island** *island* Aleutian Islands, Alaska, USA
193 I16 **Una, Mount** ▲ South Island, NZ *42.12S 172.34E*
84 N13 **Unango** Niassa, N Mozambique *12.45S 35.28E*
Unao *see* Unnão
94 L12 **Unari** Lappi, N Finland *67.07N 25.37E*
147 O6 **'Unayzah** *var.* Anaiza. Al Qaşīm, C Saudi Arabia *26.03N 44.00E*

◆ Country ● Country Capital ◇ Dependent Territory ○ Dependent Territory Capital ◐ Administrative Region ✕ International Airport ▲ Mountain ▲ Mountain Range Volcano River Lake Reservoir

'UNAYZAH, JABAL – VALDEMĀRPILS

144 L10 **'Unayzah, Jabal** ▲ Jordan/Saudi Arabia *32.09N 39.10E*
Unci *see* Almería
59 K19 **Uncía** Potosí, C Bolivia *18.30S 66.29W*
39 Q7 **Uncompahgre Peak** ▲ Colorado, C USA *38.04N 107.27W*
39 P6 **Uncompahgre Plateau** *plain* Colorado, C USA
97 L17 **Unden** ◎ S Sweden
30 M4 **Underwood** North Dakota, N USA *47.25N 101.09W*
176 Uu11 **Undur** Pulau Seram, E Indonesia *3.41S 130.38E*
Undur Khan *see* Öndörhaan
194 M11 **Unea Island** *island* C PNG
130 H6 **Unecha** Bryanskaya Oblast', W Russian Federation *52.51N 32.38E*
41 N16 **Unga** Unga Island, Alaska, USA *55.14N 160.34W*
Ungaria *see* Hungary
191 P8 **Ungarie** New South Wales, SE Australia *33.39S 146.54E*
Ungarisch-Brod *see* Uherský Brod
Ungarisches Erzgebirge *see* Slovenské rudohorie
Ungarisch-Hradisch *see* Uherské Hradiště
Ungarn *see* Hungary
10 M4 **Ungava Bay** *bay* Québec, E Canada
10 J2 **Ungava, Péninsule d'** *peninsula* Québec, SE Canada
Ungeny *see* Ungheni
118 M9 **Ungheni** *Rus.* Ungeny. W Moldova *47.13N 27.48E*
Unguja *see* Zanzibar
152 G10 **Üngüz Angyrsyndaky Garagum** *Rus.* Zaungukskiye Garagumy. *desert* N Turkmenistan
152 H11 **Unguz, Solonchakovyye Vpadiny** *salt marsh* C Turkmenistan
Ungvár *see* Uzhhorod
62 I12 **União da Vitória** Paraná, S Brazil *26.13S 51.04W*
113 G17 **Uničov** *Ger.* Mährisch-Neustadt. Olomoucký Kraj, E Czech Republic *49.46N 17.05E*
112 J12 **Uniejów** Łódzkie, C Poland *51.58N 18.46E*
114 A11 **Unije** *island* W Croatia
40 L16 **Unimak Island** *island* Aleutian Islands, Alaska, USA
40 L16 **Unimak Pass** *strait* Aleutian Islands, Alaska, USA
29 W5 **Union** Missouri, C USA *38.27N 91.01W*
34 L12 **Union** Oregon, NW USA *45.12N 117.51W*
23 Q11 **Union** South Carolina, SE USA *34.40N 81.35W*
23 R6 **Union** West Virginia, NE USA *37.33N 80.33W*
64 J12 **Unión** San Luis, C Argentina *35.09S 65.55W*
63 B25 **Unión, Bahía** *bay* E Argentina
33 Q13 **Union City** Indiana, N USA *40.12N 84.50W*
33 Q10 **Union City** Michigan, N USA *42.03N 85.06W*
20 C12 **Union City** Pennsylvania, NE USA *41.54N 79.51W*
22 G8 **Union City** Tennessee, S USA *36.25N 89.01W*
34 G14 **Union Creek** Oregon, NW USA *42.54N 122.26W*
85 G25 **Uniondale** Western Cape, SW South Africa *33.40S 23.07E*
42 K13 **Unión de Tula** Jalisco, SW Mexico *19.58N 104.20W*
32 M9 **Union Grove** Wisconsin, N USA *42.39N 88.03W*
47 Y15 **Union Island** *island* S Saint Vincent and the Grenadines
65 K5 **Union Reefs** *reef* SW Mexico
(0) D7 **Union Seamount** *undersea feature* NE Pacific Ocean *49.34N 132.45W*
25 Q6 **Union Springs** Alabama, S USA *32.08N 85.43W*
22 H6 **Uniontown** Kentucky, S USA *37.46N 87.55W*
20 C16 **Uniontown** Pennsylvania, NE USA *39.54N 79.43W*
29 T1 **Unionville** Missouri, C USA *40.28N 93.00W*
147 V8 **United Arab Emirates** *Ar.* Al Imārāt al 'Arabīyah al Muttaḥidah, *abbrev.* UAE; *prev.* Trucial States. ◆ *federation* SW Asia
United Arab Republic *see* Egypt
99 H14 **United Kingdom** *off.* UK of Great Britain and Northern Ireland, *abbrev.* UK. ◆ *monarchy* NW Europe
United Mexican States *see* Mexico
United Provinces *see* Uttar Pradesh
18 L9 **United States of America** *off.* United States of America, *var.* America, The States, *abbrev.* U.S., USA. ◆ *federal republic*
128 J10 **Unitsa** Respublika Kareliya, NW Russian Federation *62.31N 34.31E*
9 S15 **Unity** Saskatchewan, S Canada *52.27N 109.10W*
Unity State *see* Wahda
107 Q8 **Universales, Montes** ▲ C Spain
29 X4 **University City** Missouri, C USA *38.40N 90.19W*
197 B13 **Unmet** Malekula, C Vanuatu *16.09S 167.16E*
103 F15 **Unna** Nordrhein-Westfalen, W Germany *51.31N 7.40E*
158 L12 **Unnāo** *prev.* Unao. Uttar Pradesh, N India *26.31N 80.30E*
197 D15 **Unpongkor** Erromango, S Vanuatu *18.48S 169.01E*
Unruhstadt *see* Kargowa
98 M1 **Unst** *island* NE Scotland, UK
103 K16 **Unstrut** ~ C Germany
Unterdrauburg *see* Dravograd
Unterlimbach *see* Lendava
103 L23 **Unterschleissheim** Bayern, SE Germany *48.16N 11.34E*
103 H24 **Untersee** ◎ Germany/Switzerland
102 O10 **Unterueckersee** ◎ NE Germany
110 F9 **Unterwalden** ◈ *canton* C Switzerland
57 N12 **Unturán, Sierra de** ▲ Brazil/Venezuela
165 N11 **Unuli Horog** Qinghai, W China *35.10N 91.49E*
142 M11 **Ünye** Ordu, W Turkey *41.07N 37.14E*
Unza *see* Unzha
129 O14 **Unzha** *var.* Unza. ~ NW Russian Federation
81 E17 **Uolo, Río** *var.* Eyo (lower course), Mbini, Uele (upper course), Woleu; *prev.* Benito. ~ Equatorial Guinea/Gabon
57 Q10 **Uonán** Bolívar, SE Venezuela *4.33N 62.10W*
167 T12 **Uotsuri-shima** *island* China/Japan/Taiwan
171 J13 **Uozu** Toyama, Honshū, SW Japan *36.48N 137.23E*
44 L12 **Upala** Alajuela, NW Costa Rica *10.52N 85.00W*
57 P7 **Upata** Bolívar, E Venezuela *8.01N 62.25W*
81 M23 **Upemba, Lac** ◎ SE Dem. Rep. Congo
207 O12 **Upernavik** *var.* Upernivik. Kitaa, C Greenland *73.06N 55.42W*
Upernivik *see* Upernavik
85 F22 **Upington** Northern Cape, W South Africa *28.24S 21.13E*
Uplands *see* Ottawa
198 Bb8 **Upolu** *island* SE Samoa
40 G11 **'Upolu Point** *var.* Upolu Point *headland* Hawai'i, USA, C Pacific Ocean *20.15N 155.51W*
Upper Austria *see* Oberösterreich
Upper Bann *see* Bann
12 M13 **Upper Canada Village** *tourist site* Ontario, SE Canada *44.57N 75.04W*
20 I16 **Upper Darby** Pennsylvania, NE USA *39.57N 75.15W*
30 L2 **Upper Des Lacs Lake** ⊞ North Dakota, N USA
193 L14 **Upper Hutt** Wellington, North Island, NZ *41.08S 174.58E*
31 X11 **Upper Iowa River** ~ Iowa, C USA
34 H15 **Upper Klamath Lake** ◎ Oregon, NW USA
36 M6 **Upper Lake** California, W USA *39.07N 122.53W*
37 Q1 **Upper Lake** ◎ California, W USA
8 K9 **Upper Liard** Yukon Territory, W Canada *60.01N 128.59W*
99 E16 **Upper Lough Erne** ◎ SW Northern Ireland, UK
82 F12 **Upper Nile** ◈ *state* E Sudan
31 T3 **Upper Red Lake** ◎ Minnesota, N USA
33 S12 **Upper Sandusky** Ohio, N USA *40.49N 83.16W*
Upper Volta *see* Burkina
97 O15 **Upplandsväsby** *var.* Upplands Väsby. Stockholm, C Sweden *59.28N 17.49E*
97 O15 **Uppsala** Uppsala, C Sweden *59.52N 17.37E*
97 O14 **Uppsala** ◈ *county* C Sweden
40 J12 **Upright Cape** *headland* Saint Matthew Island, Alaska, USA *60.19N 172.15W*
22 K6 **Upton** Kentucky, S USA *37.25N 85.53W*
35 Y13 **Upton** Wyoming, C USA *44.06N 104.37W*
147 N7 **'Uqlat aş Şuqūr** Al Qaşīm, W Saudi Arabia *25.51N 42.12E*
Uqturpan *see* Wushi
56 C7 **Urabá, Golfo de** *gulf* NW Colombia
Uracas *see* Farallon de Pajaros
Uradar'ya *see* O'radaryo
Urad Qianqi *see* Xishanzui
171 Jj17 **Uraga-suidō** *strait* S Japan
172 Pp7 **Urahoro** Hokkaidō, NE Japan *42.47N 143.41E*
172 Oo8 **Urakawa** Hokkaidō, NE Japan *42.11N 142.42E*
131 X6 **Ural** *Kaz.* Zayyq. ~ Kazakhstan/Russian Federation
191 T6 **Uralla** New South Wales, SE Australia *30.39S 151.30E*
Ural Mountains *see* Ural'skiye Gory
150 F8 **Ural'sk** *Kaz.* Oral. Zapadnyy Kazakhstan, NW Kazakhstan *51.12N 51.17E*
Ural'skaya Oblast' *see* Zapadnyy Kazakhstan
131 W5 **Ural'skiye Gory** *var.* Ural'skiy Khrebet, *Eng.* Ural Mountains. ▲ Kazakhstan/Russian Federation
Ural'skiy Khrebet *see* Ural'skiye Gory
144 I3 **Urām aş Şughrá** Ḩalab, N Syria *36.10N 36.55E*
191 P10 **Urana** New South Wales, SE Australia *35.22S 146.16E*
9 S10 **Uranium City** Saskatchewan, C Canada *59.30N 108.46W*
60 F10 **Uraricoera** Roraima, N Brazil *3.26N 60.54W*
49 S5 **Uraricoera, Rio** ~ N Brazil
Ura-Tyube *see* Üroteppa
171 K16 **Urawa** Saitama, Honshū, S Japan *35.51N 139.37E*
125 F10 **Uray** Khanty-Mansiyskiy Avtonomnyy Okrug, C Russian Federation *60.07N 64.38E*
147 R7 **'Uray'irah** Ash Sharqīyah, E Saudi Arabia *25.59N 48.51E*
32 M13 **Urbana** Illinois, N USA *40.06N 88.12W*
33 R13 **Urbana** Ohio, N USA *40.04N 83.46W*
31 V14 **Urbandale** Iowa, C USA *41.37N 93.42W*
108 I11 **Urbania** Marche, C Italy *43.40N 12.33E*
176 Uu8 **Urbinasopon** Papua, E Indonesia *0.19S 131.12E*
108 I11 **Urbino** Marche, C Italy *43.45N 12.38E*
59 H16 **Urcos** Cusco, S Peru *13.45S 71.37W*
150 D10 **Urda** Zapadnyy Kazakhstan, W Kazakhstan *48.52N 47.31E*
107 N10 **Urda** Castilla-La Mancha, C Spain *39.25N 3.43W*
168 F7 **Urdgol** Hovd, W Mongolia *47.39N 92.46E*
Urdunn *see* Jordan
151 X12 **Urdzhar** *Kaz.* Ürzhar. Vostochnyy Kazakhstan, E Kazakhstan *47.06N 81.37E*
99 L16 **Ure** ~ N England, UK
121 K18 **Urechcha** *Rus.* Urech'ye. Minskaya Voblasts', S Belarus *52.57N 27.54E*
Urech'ye *see* Urechcha
131 P2 **Uren'** Nizhegorodskaya Oblast', W Russian Federation *57.29N 45.47E*
126 H9 **Urengoy** Yamalo-Nenetskiy Avtonomnyy Okrug, N Russian Federation *65.52N 78.42E*
192 K10 **Urenui** Taranaki, North Island, NZ *38.59S 174.25E*
197 B10 **Ureparapara** *island* Banks Islands, N Vanuatu
42 G5 **Ures** Sonora, NW Mexico *29.25N 110.24W*
Urfa *see* Şanlıurfa
Urga *see* Ulaanbaatar
152 H9 **Urganch** *Rus.* Urgench; *prev.* Novo-Urgench. Xorazm Viloyati, W Uzbekistan *41.39N 60.32E*
Urgench *see* Urganch
142 J14 **Ürgüp** Nevşehir, C Turkey *38.39N 34.55E*
153 O12 **Urgut** Samarqand Viloyati, C Uzbekistan *39.25N 67.15E*
164 K3 **Urho** Xinjiang Uygur Zizhiqu, W China *46.04N 84.51E*
158 G5 **Uri** Jammu and Kashmir, NW India *34.04N 74.03E*
110 G9 **Uri** ◈ *canton* C Switzerland
56 F11 **Uribe** Meta, C Colombia *3.01N 74.33W*
56 H4 **Uribia** La Guajira, N Colombia *11.45N 72.19W*
118 G12 **Uricani** *Hung.* Hobicaurikány. Hunedoara, SW Romania *45.18N 23.03E*
59 M21 **Uriondo** Tarija, S Bolivia *21.40S 64.37W*
42 I7 **Urique** Chihuahua, N Mexico *27.16N 107.51W*
42 I7 **Urique, Río** ~ N Mexico
58 E9 **Uritiyacu, Río** ~ N Peru
Uritskiy *see* Sarykol'
100 K8 **Urk** Flevoland, N Netherlands *52.40N 5.34E*
142 B14 **Urla** İzmir, W Turkey *38.19N 26.46E*
118 K13 **Urlaţi** Prahova, SE Romania *44.58N 26.15E*
131 V4 **Urman** Respublika Bashkortostan, W Russian Federation *54.53N 56.52E*
153 P12 **Urmetan** W Tajikistan *39.27N 68.13E*
Urmia *see* Orūmīyeh
Urmia, Lake *see* Orūmīyeh, Daryācheh-ye
Urmiyeh *see* Orūmīyeh
115 N17 **Uroševac** *Alb.* Ferizaj. Serbia, S Serbia and Montenegro (Yugoslavia) *42.23N 21.09E*
153 P11 **Üroteppa** *Rus.* Ura-Tyube. NW Tajikistan *39.54N 68.57E*
56 D8 **Urrao** Antioquia, W Colombia *6.16N 76.10W*
Ursat'yevskaya *see* Xovos
168 I11 **Urt** Ömnögovĭ, S Mongolia *43.16N 101.00E*
131 X7 **Urtazym** Orenburgskaya Oblast', W Russian Federation *52.12N 58.48E*
61 K18 **Uruaçu** Goiás, C Brazil *14.37S 49.06W*
42 M14 **Uruapan** *var.* Uruapan del Progreso. Michoacán de Ocampo, SW Mexico *19.25N 102.04W*
Uruapan del Progreso *see* Uruapan
59 G15 **Urubamba, Cordillera** ▲ C Peru
59 G14 **Urubamba, Río** ~ C Peru
60 G12 **Urucará** Amazonas, N Brazil *2.30S 57.45W*
63 E16 **Uruguaiana** Rio Grande do Sul, S Brazil *29.45S 57.04W*
Uruguai, Rio *see* Uruguay
63 E18 **Uruguay** *off.* Oriental Republic of Uruguay; *prev.* La Banda Oriental. ◆ *republic* E South America
63 E15 **Uruguay** *var.* Rio Uruguai, Río Uruguay. ~ E South America
Uruguay, Río *see* Uruguay
Urumchi *see* Ürümqi
164 L5 **Ürümqi** *var.* Tihwa, Urumchi, Urumqi, Urumtsi, Wu-lu-k'o-mu-shi, Wu-lu-mu-ch'i; *prev.* Ti-hua. *autonomous region capital* Xinjiang Uygur Zizhiqu, NW China *43.52N 87.31E*
Urumtsi *see* Ürümqi
Urundi *see* Burundi
191 V6 **Urunga** New South Wales, SE Australia *30.33S 152.58E*
196 C15 **Uruno Point** *headland* NW Guam *13.37N 144.49E*
127 P15 **Urup, Ostrov** *island* Kuril'skiye Ostrova, SE Russian Federation
147 P11 **'Urūq al Mawārid** *desert* S Saudi Arabia
Urusan *see* Ulsan
131 T5 **Urussu** Respublika Tatarstan, W Russian Federation *54.34N 53.23E*
192 K10 **Uruti** Taranaki, North Island, NZ *38.57S 174.32E*
59 K19 **Uru Uru, Lago** ◎ W Bolivia
57 P9 **Uruyén** Bolívar, SE Venezuela *5.40N 62.25W*
155 O7 **Urūzgān** *var.* Oruzgān, Orūzgān. Urūzgān, C Afghanistan *32.58N 66.39E*
155 N6 **Urūzgān** *Per.* Orūzgān. ◈ *province* C Afghanistan
172 P6 **Uryū-gawa** ~ Hokkaidō, NE Japan
172 P4 **Uryū-ko** ◎ Hokkaidō, NE Japan
131 N8 **Uryupinsk** Volgogradskaya Oblast', SW Russian Federation *50.51N 41.59E*
Ürzhar *see* Urdzhar
129 R16 **Urzhum** Kirovskaya Oblast', NW Russian Federation *57.09N 49.56E*
118 K13 **Urziceni** Ialomiţa, SE Romania *44.43N 26.39E*
U.S./USA *see* United States of America
170 D13 **Usa** Ōita, Kyūshū, SW Japan *33.32N 131.20E*
121 L16 **Usa** *Rus.* Usa. ~ C Belarus
129 T6 **Usa** ~ NW Russian Federation
142 E14 **Uşak** *prev.* Ushak. Uşak, W Turkey *38.42N 29.25E*
142 D14 **Uşak** *var.* Ushak. ◈ *province* W Turkey
85 C19 **Usakos** Erongo, W Namibia *22.01S 15.31E*
83 J21 **Usambara Mountains** ▲ NE Tanzania
83 G23 **Usangu Flats** *wetland* SW Tanzania
67 D24 **Usborne, Mount** ▲ East Falkland, Falkland Islands *51.34S 58.57W*
102 O8 **Usedom** *island* NE Germany
101 M24 **Useldange** Diekirch, C Luxembourg *49.46N 5.58E*
120 L12 **Ushacha** *Rus.* Ushacha. Vitsyebskaya Voblasts', N Belarus *55.31N 28.30E*
Ushachi *see* Ushacha
120 L13 **Ushachy** *Rus.* Ushachi. Vitsyebskaya Voblasts', N Belarus *55.09N 28.37E*
Ushak *see* Uşak
126 I2 **Ushakova, Ostrov** *island* Severnaya Zemlya, N Russian Federation
Ushant *see* Ouessant, Île d'
Üsharal *see* Ucharal
170 Bb14 **Ushibuka** *var.* Usibuka. Kumamoto, Shimo-jima, SW Japan *32.13N 130.01E*
Ushi Point *see* Sabaneta, Puntan
151 V14 **Ushtobe** *Kaz.* Üshtöbe. Almaty, SE Kazakhstan *45.15N 77.58E*
65 I25 **Ushuaia** Tierra del Fuego, S Argentina *54.48S 68.19W*
41 R10 **Usibelli** Alaska, USA *63.54N 148.41W*
Usibuka *see* Ushibuka
194 I12 **Usino** Madang, N PNG *5.40S 145.31E*
129 U6 **Usinsk** Respublika Komi, NW Russian Federation *66.00N 57.37E*
99 K22 **Usk** *Wel.* Wysg. ~ SE Wales, UK
Uskočke Planine/Uskokengebirge *see* Gorjanci/Žumberačko Gorje
Uskoplje *see* Gornji Vakuf
Üsküb *see* Skopje
116 M11 **Üsküpdere** Kırklareli, NW Turkey *41.41N 27.21E*
130 L7 **Usman'** Lipetskaya Oblast', W Russian Federation *52.04N 39.41E*
120 D8 **Usmas Ezers** ◎ NW Latvia
129 U13 **Usol'ye** Permskaya Oblast', NW Russian Federation *59.27N 56.33E*
126 J15 **Usol'ye-Sibirskoye** Irkutskaya Oblast', C Russian Federation *52.48N 103.40E*
43 T16 **Uspanapa, Río** ~ SE Mexico
151 R11 **Uspenskiy** Karaganda, C Kazakhstan *48.45N 72.46E*
105 O11 **Ussel** Corrèze, C France *45.33N 2.18E*
169 Z6 **Ussuri** *var.* Usuri, Wusuri, *Chin.* Wusuli Jiang. ~ China/Russian Federation
127 Nn18 **Ussuriysk** *prev.* Nikol'sk, Nikol'sk-Ussuriyskiy, Voroshilov. Primorskiy Kray, SE Russian Federation *43.48N 131.58E*
142 J10 **Usta Burnu** *headland* N Turkey *41.58N 34.30E*
155 P13 **Usta Muhammad** Baluchistān, SW Pakistan *28.07N 68.00E*
126 K15 **Ust'-Barguzin** Respublika Buryatiya, S Russian Federation *53.28N 109.00E*
127 P12 **Ust'-Bol'sheretsk** Kamchatskaya Oblast', E Russian Federation *52.48N 156.12E*
131 N9 **Ust'-Buzulukskaya** Volgogradskaya Oblast', SW Russian Federation *50.12N 42.06E*
113 C16 **Ústecký Kraj** ◈ *region* NW Czech Republic
110 G7 **Uster** Zürich, NE Switzerland *47.20N 8.40E*
109 J22 **Ustica, Isola d'** *island* S Italy
126 J13 **Ust'-Ilimsk** Irkutskaya Oblast', C Russian Federation *57.57N 102.30E*
113 C15 **Ústí nad Labem** *Ger.* Aussig. Ústecký Kraj, NW Czech Republic *50.40N 14.04E*
113 F17 **Ústí nad Orlicí** *Ger.* Wildenschwert. Pardubický Kraj, E Czech Republic *49.58N 16.24E*
Ustinov *see* Izhevsk
115 J14 **Ustipraĉa** Republika Srpska, SE Bosnia and Herzegovina *43.42N 19.03E*
125 Ff12 **Ust'-Ishim** Omskaya Oblast', C Russian Federation *57.42N 70.58E*
112 G6 **Ustka** *Ger.* Stolpmünde. Pomorskie, N Poland *54.34N 16.50E*
127 Pp10 **Ust'-Kamchatsk** Kamchatskaya Oblast', E Russian Federation *56.13N 162.28E*
151 X9 **Ust'-Kamenogorsk** *Kaz.* Öskemen. Vostochnyy Kazakhstan, E Kazakhstan *49.58N 82.36E*
127 Oo10 **Ust'-Khayryuzovo** Koryakskiy Avtonomnyy Okrug, E Russian Federation *57.07N 156.37E*
126 H16 **Ust'-Koksa** Respublika Altay, S Russian Federation *50.15N 85.45E*
129 S11 **Ust'-Kulom** Respublika Komi, NW Russian Federation *61.42N 53.42E*
126 Jj14 **Ust'-Kut** Irkutskaya Oblast', C Russian Federation *56.49N 105.31E*
126 M7 **Ust'-Kuyga** Respublika Sakha (Yakutiya), NE Russian Federation *69.59N 135.27E*
130 L14 **Ust'-Labinsk** Krasnodarskiy Kray, SW Russian Federation *44.40N 40.46E*
126 Mm11 **Ust'-Maya** Respublika Sakha (Yakutiya), NE Russian Federation *60.27N 134.28E*
127 N9 **Ust'-Nera** Respublika Sakha (Yakutiya), NE Russian Federation *64.28N 143.01E*
126 Ll13 **Ust'-Nyukzha** Amurskaya Oblast', S Russian Federation *56.30N 121.32E*
126 Kk6 **Ust'-Olenëk** Respublika Sakha (Yakutiya), NE Russian Federation *73.03N 119.34E*
127 O10 **Ust'-Omchug** Magadanskaya Oblast', E Russian Federation *61.07N 149.17E*
126 Jj15 **Ust'-Ordynskiy** Ust'-Ordynskiy Buryatskiy Avtonomnyy Okrug, S Russian Federation *52.49N 104.42E*
126 J15 **Ust'-Ordynskiy Buryatskiy Avtonomnyy Okrug** ◈ *autonomous district* S Russian Federation
129 N8 **Ust'-Pinega** Arkhangel'skaya Oblast', NW Russian Federation *64.09N 41.55E*
126 Hh8 **Ust'-Port** Taymyrskiy (Dolgano-Nenetskiy) Avtonomnyy Okrug, N Russian Federation *69.42N 84.25E*
116 L11 **Ustrem** *prev.* Vakav. Yambol, E Bulgaria *42.01N 26.28E*
113 O18 **Ustrzyki Dolne** Podkarpackie, SE Poland *49.26N 22.36E*
Ust'-Sysol'sk *see* Syktyvkar
129 R7 **Ust'-Tsil'ma** Respublika Komi, NW Russian Federation *65.25N 52.09E*
Ust Urt *see* Ustyurt Plateau
129 O11 **Ust'ya** ~ NW Russian Federation
127 P12 **Ust'yevoye** *prev.* Kirovskiy. Kamchatskaya Oblast', E Russian Federation *54.06N 155.48E*
119 R8 **Ustynivka** Kirovohrads'ka Oblast', C Ukraine *47.58N 32.32E*
150 H15 **Ustyurt Plateau** *var.* Ust Urt, *Uzb.* Ustyurt Platosi. *plateau* Kazakhstan/Uzbekistan
Ustyurt Platosi *see* Ustyurt Plateau
128 K14 **Ustyuzhna** Vologodskaya Oblast', NW Russian Federation *58.50N 36.25E*
164 J4 **Usu** Xinjiang Uygur Zizhiqu, NW China *44.27N 84.37E*
175 Q10 **Usu** Sulawesi, C Indonesia *2.34S 120.58E*
170 Dd14 **Usuki** Ōita, Kyūshū, SW Japan *33.07N 131.46E*
44 G8 **Usulután** Usulután, SE El Salvador *13.19N 88.26W*
44 B9 **Usulután** ◈ *department* SE El Salvador
43 W16 **Usumacinta, Río** ~ Guatemala/Mexico
Usumbura *see* Bujumbura
Usuri *see* Ussuri
176 X12 **Uta** Papua, E Indonesia *4.28S 136.03E*
38 K5 **Utah** *off.* State of Utah; also known as Beehive State, Mormon State. ◈ *state* W USA
38 L3 **Utah Lake** ◎ Utah, W USA
Utaidhani *see* Uthai Thani
95 M14 **Utajärvi** Oulu, C Finland *64.45N 26.25E*
Utamboni *see* Mitemele, Río
Utaradit *see* Uttaradit
173 G3 **Utara, Selat** *strait* Peninsular Malaysia
172 P5 **Utashinai** *var.* Utasinai. Hokkaidō, NE Japan *43.32N 142.03E*
Utasinai *see* Utashinai
176 X12 **Uta, Sungai** ~ Papua, E Indonesia
200 Ss12 **'Uta Vava'u** *island* Vava'u Group, N Tonga
39 V9 **Ute Creek** ~ New Mexico, SW USA
120 H12 **Utena** Utena, E Lithuania *55.30N 25.34E*
120 H12 **Utena** ◈ *province* E Lithuania
39 V10 **Ute Reservoir** ⊞ New Mexico, SW USA
178 H10 **Uthai Thani** *var.* Muang Uthai Thani, Udayadhani, Utaidhani. Uthai Thani, W Thailand *15.22N 100.03E*
155 O15 **Uthal** Baluchistān, SW Pakistan *25.53N 66.37E*
20 I10 **Utica** New York, NE USA *43.06N 75.15W*
107 R10 **Utiel** País Valenciano, E Spain *39.33N 1.13W*
9 O13 **Utikuma Lake** ◎ Alberta, W Canada
44 I4 **Utila, Isla de** *island* Islas de la Bahía, N Honduras
Utina *see* Udine
61 O17 **Utinga** Bahia, E Brazil *12.05S 41.07W*
Utirik *see* Utrik Atoll
97 M22 **Utlängan** *island* S Sweden
119 U11 **Utlyuts'kyy Lyman** *bay* S Ukraine
170 Cc14 **Uto** Kumamoto, Kyūshū, SW Japan *32.40N 130.37E*
97 P16 **Utö** Stockholm, C Sweden *58.55N 18.19E*
27 Q12 **Utopia** Texas, SW USA *29.30N 99.31W*
100 J11 **Utrecht** *Lat.* Trajectum ad Rhenum. Utrecht, C Netherlands *52.06N 5.07E*
85 K22 **Utrecht** KwaZulu/Natal, E South Africa *27.34S 30.19E*
100 I11 **Utrecht** ◈ *province* C Netherlands
106 K14 **Utrera** Andalucía, S Spain *37.10N 5.46W*
201 V4 **Utrik Atoll** *var.* Utirik, Utrōk, Utrönk. *atoll* Ratak Chain, N Marshall Islands
Utrōk/Utrönk *see* Utrik Atoll
97 B16 **Utsira** *island* SW Norway
94 L8 **Utsjoki** *var.* Ohcejohka. Lappi, N Finland *69.54N 27.01E*
171 Kk15 **Utsunomiya** *var.* Utunomiya. Tochigi, Honshū, S Japan *36.36N 139.52E*
131 P13 **Utta** Respublika Kalmykiya, SW Russian Federation *46.22N 46.03E*
178 Hh8 **Uttaradit** *var.* Utaradit. Uttaradit, N Thailand *17.37N 100.04E*
158 J9 **Uttaranchal** ◈ *state* N India
158 J8 **Uttarkāshi** Uttaranchal, N India *30.45N 78.19E*
158 K11 **Uttar Pradesh** *prev.* United Provinces, United Provinces of Agra and Oudh. ◈ *state* N India
47 T5 **Utuado** C Puerto Rico *18.16N 66.43W*
164 K3 **Utubulak** Xinjiang Uygur Zizhiqu, W China *46.49N 86.15E*
41 N5 **Utukok River** ~ Alaska, USA
Utunomiya *see* Utsunomiya
195 X9 **Utupua** *island* Santa Cruz Islands, E Solomon Islands
150 G9 **Utva** ~ NW Kazakhstan
201 Y15 **Utwe** Kosrae, E Micronesia
201 X15 **Utwe Harbor** *harbor* Kosrae, E Micronesia
168 J7 **Uubulan** Arhangay, C Mongolia *48.37N 101.58E*
120 G6 **Uulu** Pärnumaa, SW Estonia *58.15N 24.31E*
207 N13 **Uummannaq** *var.* Umanak, Umanaq. Kitaa, C Greenland *70.37N 52.25W*
Uummannarsuaq *see* Nunap Isua
168 E4 **Üüreg Nuur** ◎ NW Mongolia
Uusikaarlepyy *see* Nykarleby
95 J19 **Uusikaupunki** *Swe.* Nystad. Länsi-Suomi, W Finland *60.48N 21.25E*
131 S2 **Uva** Udmurtskaya Respublika, NW Russian Federation *56.41N 52.15E*
115 L14 **Uvac** ~ W Serbia and Montenegro (Yugoslavia)
27 Q12 **Uvalde** Texas, SW USA *29.13N 99.49W*
161 K25 **Uva Province** ◈ *province* SE Sri Lanka
121 O18 **Uvaravichy** *Rus.* Uvarovichi. Homyel'skaya Voblasts', SE Belarus *52.36N 30.43E*
56 J11 **Uvá, Río** ~ E Colombia
Uvarovichi *see* Uvaravichy
131 N7 **Uvarovo** Tambovskaya Oblast', W Russian Federation *51.58N 42.13E*
125 Ff11 **Uvat** Tyumenskaya Oblast', C Russian Federation *59.11N 68.37E*
202 G12 **Uvea, Île** *island* N Wallis and Futuna
83 E21 **Uvinza** Kigoma, W Tanzania *5.04S 30.24E*
81 O20 **Uvira** Sud Kivu, E Dem. Rep. Congo *3.24S 29.04E*
168 E5 **Uvs** ◈ *province* NW Mongolia
168 F5 **Uvs Nuur** *var.* Ozero Ubsu-Nur. ◎ Mongolia/Russian Federation
170 E15 **Uwa** Ehime, Shikoku, SW Japan *33.22N 132.29E*
170 E15 **Uwajima** *var.* Uwazima. Ehime, Shikoku, SW Japan *33.13N 132.32E*
82 B5 **'Uwaynāt, Jabal al** *var.* Jebel Uweinat. ▲ Libya/Sudan *21.51N 25.01E*
Uwazima *see* Uwajima
Uweinat, Jebel *see* 'Uwaynāt, Jabal al
176 Z14 **Uwimmerah, Sungai** ~ Papua, E Indonesia
12 H14 **Uxbridge** Ontario, S Canada *44.07N 79.07W*
Uxellodunum *see* Issoudun
Uxin Qi *see* Dabqig
43 X12 **Uxmal, Ruinas** *ruins* Yucatán, SE Mexico *20.20N 89.46W*
133 Q5 **Uy** ~ Kazakhstan/Russian Federation
150 K15 **Uyaly** Kzylorda, S Kazakhstan *44.22N 61.16E*
126 Mm7 **Uyandina** ~ NE Russian Federation
168 L10 **Üydzen** Ömnögovĭ, S Mongolia *44.08N 106.48E*
Uyeda *see* Ueda
126 Hh3 **Uyedineniya, Ostrov** *island* N Russian Federation
79 V17 **Uyo** Akwa Ibom, S Nigeria *5.00N 7.57E*
168 D8 **Üyönch** Hovd, W Mongolia *46.04N 92.05E*
151 Q15 **Uyuk** Zhambyl, S Kazakhstan *43.46N 70.55E*
147 V13 **'Uyūn** SW Oman *17.12N 53.46E*
59 K20 **Uyuni** Potosí, W Bolivia *20.26S 66.48W*
59 J20 **Uyuni, Salar de** *wetland* SW Bolivia
152 I9 **Uzbekistan** *off.* Republic of Uzbekistan. ◆ *republic* C Asia
164 D8 **Uzbel Shankou** *Rus.* Pereval Kyzyl-Dzhiik. *pass* China/Tajikistan *38.33N 73.46E*
152 B11 **Uzboy** *prev. Rus.* Imeni 26 Bakinskikh Komissarov, *Turkm.* 26 Baku Komissarlary Adyndaky. Balkan Welaýaty, W Turkmenistan *39.24N 54.04E*
121 J17 **Uzda** *Rus.* Uzda. Minskaya Voblasts', C Belarus *53.29N 27.10E*
105 N12 **Uzerche** Corrèze, C France *45.24N 1.35E*
105 R14 **Uzès** Gard, S France *44.00N 4.25E*
153 T10 **Uzgen** *Kir.* Özgön. Oshskaya Oblast', SW Kyrgyzstan *40.42N 73.17E*
119 O3 **Uzh** ~ N Ukraine
Uzhgorod *see* Uzhhorod
118 G7 **Uzhhorod** *Rus.* Uzhgorod; *prev.* Ungvár. Zakarpats'ka Oblast', W Ukraine *48.36N 22.19E*
126 Hh14 **Uzhur** Krasnoyarskiy Kray, S Russian Federation *55.18N 89.36E*
Uzi *see* Uji
114 K13 **Užice** *prev.* Titovo Užice. Serbia, W Serbia and Montenegro (Yugoslavia) *43.52N 19.51E*
Uzin *see* Uzyn
130 L5 **Uzlovaya** Tul'skaya Oblast', W Russian Federation *54.01N 38.15E*
110 H7 **Uznach** Sankt Gallen, NE Switzerland *47.12N 9.00E*
151 U16 **Uzunagach** Almaty, SE Kazakhstan *43.07N 76.19E*
142 B10 **Uzunköprü** Edirne, NW Turkey *41.15N 26.42E*
120 D11 **Užventis** Šiauliai, C Lithuania *55.49N 22.38E*
119 P5 **Uzyn** *Rus.* Uzin. Kyyivs'ka Oblast', N Ukraine *49.52N 30.28E*
151 N7 **Uzynkol'** *prev.* Lenin, Leninskoye. Kostanay, N Kazakhstan *54.04N 65.22E*

V

Vääksy *see* Asikkala
85 H23 **Vaal** ~ C South Africa
95 M14 **Vaala** Oulu, C Finland *64.34N 26.49E*
95 N19 **Vaalimaa** Etelä-Suomi, SE Finland *60.34N 27.49E*
101 M19 **Vaals** Limburg, SE Netherlands *50.46N 6.01E*
95 J16 **Vaasa** *Swe.* Vasa; *prev.* Nikolainkaupunki. Vaasa, W Finland *63.07N 21.39E*
100 L10 **Vaassen** Gelderland, E Netherlands *52.18N 5.58E*
120 G11 **Vabalninkas** Panevėžys, NE Lithuania *55.59N 24.45E*
Vabkent *see* Vobkent
113 J22 **Vác** *Ger.* Waitzen. Pest, N Hungary *47.46N 19.07E*
63 I14 **Vacaria** Rio Grande do Sul, S Brazil *28.30S 50.57W*
37 N7 **Vacaville** California, W USA *38.21N 121.59W*
105 R15 **Vaccarès, Étang de** ◎ SE France
46 L10 **Vache, Île à** *island* SW Haiti
181 Y16 **Vacoas** W Mauritius *20.18S 57.28E*
34 G10 **Vader** Washington, NW USA *46.23N 122.58W*
96 D12 **Vadheim** Sogn og Fjordane, S Norway *61.12N 5.48E*
124 O3 **Vadili** *Gk.* Vatili. C Cyprus *35.09N 33.39E*
160 D11 **Vadodara** *prev.* Baroda. Gujarāt, W India *22.19N 73.13E*
94 M8 **Vadsø** *Fin.* Vesisaari. Finnmark, N Norway *70.07N 29.47E*
97 L17 **Vadstena** Östergötland, S Sweden *58.25N 14.55E*
110 I8 **Vaduz** ● (Liechtenstein) W Liechtenstein *47.07N 9.31E*
Vág *see* Váh
129 N12 **Vaga** ~ NW Russian Federation
96 G11 **Vågåmo** Oppland, S Norway *61.52N 9.06E*
114 D12 **Vaganski Vrh** ▲ W Croatia *44.24N 15.32E*
97 A19 **Vágar** *Dan.* Vågø *Island* Faeroe Islands *62.03N 7.19W*
Vágbeszterce *see* Považská Bystrica
97 L19 **Vaggeryd** Jönköping, S Sweden *57.30N 14.10E*
195 U14 **Vaghena** *var.* Wagina. *island* NW Solomon Islands
97 O16 **Vagnhärad** Södermanland, C Sweden *58.57N 17.31E*
106 G7 **Vagos** Aveiro, N Portugal *40.33N 8.42W*
Vágsellye *see* Sal'a
94 H10 **Vågsfjorden** *fjord* N Norway
96 C10 **Vågsøy** *island* S Norway
Vágújhely *see* Nové Mesto nad Váhom
113 I21 **Váh** *Ger.* Waag, *Hung.* Vág. ~ W Slovakia
95 K16 **Vähäkyrö** Länsi-Suomi, W Finland *63.04N 22.04E*
203 X11 **Vahitahi** *atoll* Îles Tuamotu, E French Polynesia
Vahtjer *see* Gällivare
Vaidei *see* Vulcan
24 L4 **Vaiden** Mississippi, S USA *33.19N 89.42W*
161 J23 **Vaigai** ~ SE India
203 V16 **Vaihu** Easter Island, Chile, E Pacific Ocean *27.10S 109.22W*
120 I6 **Väike Emajõgi** ~ S Estonia
120 I4 **Väike-Maarja** *Ger.* Klein-Marien. Lääne-Virumaa, NE Estonia *59.07N 26.13E*
Väike-Salatsi *see* Mazsalaca
39 R4 **Vail** Colorado, C USA *39.36N 106.20W*
200 Qq15 **Vaina** Tongatapu, S Tonga *21.12S 175.10W*
120 E5 **Väinameri** *prev.* Muhu Väin, *Ger.* Moon-Sund. *sea* E Baltic Sea
95 N18 **Vainikkala** Etelä-Suomi, SE Finland *60.54N 28.18E*
120 D10 **Vaiņode** Liepāja, SW Latvia *56.25N 21.52E*
161 H23 **Vaippār** ~ SE India
203 W11 **Vairaatea** *atoll* Îles Tuamotu, C French Polynesia
203 R8 **Vairao** Tahiti, W French Polynesia *17.48S 149.16W*
105 R14 **Vaison-la-Romaine** Vaucluse, SE France *44.15N 5.04E*
202 G11 **Vaitupu** Île Uvea, E Wallis and Futuna *13.13S 176.09W*
202 F7 **Vaitupu** *atoll* C Tuvalu
Vajdahunyad *see* Hunedoara
Vajdej *see* Vulcan
80 K12 **Vakaga** ◈ *prefecture* NE Central African Republic
116 H10 **Vakarel** Sofiya, W Bulgaria *42.34N 23.43E*
Vakav *see* Ustrem
143 O11 **Vakfıkebir** Trabzon, NE Turkey *41.03N 39.19E*
126 H11 **Vakh** ~ C Russian Federation
Vakhon, Qatorkŭhi *see* Nicholas Range
153 P14 **Vakhsh** SW Tajikistan *37.46N 68.48E*
153 Q12 **Vakhsh** ~ SW Tajikistan
131 P1 **Vakhtan** Nizhegorodskaya Oblast', W Russian Federation *58.00N 46.43E*
96 C13 **Vaksdal** Hordaland, S Norway *60.28N 5.45E*
129 O8 **Vashka** ~ NW Russian Federation
195 O15 **Vakuta Island** *island* Kiriwina Islands, SE PNG
Valachia *see* Wallachia
110 D11 **Valais** *Ger.* Wallis. ◈ *canton* SW Switzerland
115 M21 **Valamarës, Mali i** ▲ SE Albania *40.48N 20.31E*
131 S2 **Valamaz** Udmurtskaya Respublika, NW Russian Federation *57.36N 52.07E*
115 Q19 **Valandovo** SE FYR Macedonia *41.20N 22.33E*
113 I18 **Valašské Meziříčí** *Ger.* Wallachisch-Meseritsch, *Pol.* Wałeckie Międzyrzecze. Zlínský Kraj, E Czech Republic *49.28N 17.57E*
117 I17 **Valáxa** *island* Vóreioi Sporádes, Greece, Aegean Sea
97 K16 **Vålberg** Värmland, C Sweden *59.24N 13.12E*
118 H12 **Vâlcea** *prev.* Vîlcea. ◈ *county* SW Romania
65 J16 **Valcheta** Río Negro, E Argentina *40.42S 66.07W*
13 P12 **Valcourt** Québec, SE Canada *45.28N 72.18W*
Valdai Hills *see* Valdayskaya Vozvyshennost'
106 M3 **Valdavia** ~ N Spain
128 I15 **Valday** Novgorodskaya Oblast', W Russian Federation *57.56N 33.19E*
128 I15 **Valdayskaya Vozvyshennost'** *var.* Valdai Hills. *hill range* W Russian Federation
106 L9 **Valdecañas, Embalse de** ⊞ W Spain
120 E8 **Valdemārpils** *Ger.* Sassmacken. Talsi, NW Latvia *57.23N 22.36E*

◆ Country ● Country Capital ◇ Dependent Territory ○ Dependent Territory Capital ◈ Administrative Region ✈ International Airport ▲ Mountain ▲ Mountain Range Volcano ~ River ◎ Lake ⊞ Reservoir

Valdemarsvik – Venjansjön

97 N18 **Valdemarsvik** Östergötland, S Sweden *58.13N 16.34E*
107 N8 **Valdemoro** Madrid, C Spain *40.12N 3.40W*
107 O11 **Valdepeñas** Castilla-La Mancha, C Spain *38.46N 3.24W*
106 L5 **Valderaduey** ∾ NE Spain
106 L5 **Valderas** Castilla-León, N Spain *42.04N 5.27W*
107 T7 **Valderrobres** *var.* Vall-de-roures. Aragón, NE Spain *40.52N 0.07E*
65 K17 **Valdés, Península** *peninsula* SE Argentina
41 S11 **Valdez** Alaska, USA *61.07N 146.21W*
58 C5 **Valdéz** *var.* Limones. Esmeraldas, NW Ecuador *1.17N 78.56W*
Valdia *see* Weldiya
105 U11 **Val d'Isère** Savoie, E France *45.23N 7.03E*
65 G15 **Valdivia** Los Lagos, C Chile *39.49S 73.12W*
Valdivia Bank *see* Valdivia Seamount
67 P17 **Valdivia Seamount** *var.* Valdivia Bank. *undersea feature* E Atlantic Ocean *26.15S 6.25E*
105 N4 **Val-d'Oise** ◆ *department* N France
12 J8 **Val-d'Or** Québec, SE Canada *48.05N 77.42W*
25 U8 **Valdosta** Georgia, SE USA *30.49N 83.16W*
96 G13 **Valdres** *physical region* S Norway
34 L13 **Vale** Oregon, NW USA *43.58N 117.14W*
118 F9 **Valea lui Mihai** *Hung.* Érmihályfalva. Bihor, NW Romania *47.31N 22.08E*
9 N15 **Valemount** British Columbia, SW Canada *52.46N 119.17W*
61 O17 **Valença** Bahia, E Brazil *13.22S 39.06W*
106 F4 **Valença do Minho** Viana do Castelo, N Portugal *42.01N 8.37W*
61 N14 **Valença do Piauí** Piauí, E Brazil *6.25S 41.46W*
105 N8 **Valençay** Indre, C France *47.10N 1.31E*
105 R13 **Valence** *anc.* Valentia, Valentia Julia, Ventia. Drôme, E France *44.55N 4.54E*
107 S10 **Valencia** País Valenciano, E Spain *39.28N 0.24W*
56 K5 **Valencia** Carabobo, N Venezuela *10.11N 68.02W*
107 R10 **Valencia** *Cat.* València. ◆ *province* País Valenciano, E Spain
107 S10 **Valencia** ✕ Valencia, E Spain
València/Valencia *see* País Valenciano
106 I10 **Valencia de Alcántara** Extremadura, W Spain *39.25N 7.13W*
106 L4 **Valencia de Don Juan** Castilla-León, N Spain *42.16N 5.31W*
107 U9 **Valencia, Golfo de** *var.* Gulf of Valencia. *gulf* E Spain
Valencia, Gulf of *see* Valencia, Golfo de
99 A21 **Valencia Island** *Ir.* Dairbhre. *island* SW Ireland
105 P2 **Valenciennes** Nord, N France *50.21N 3.31E*
118 K13 **Vălenii de Munte** Prahova, SE Romania *45.10N 26.01E*
Valentia *see* Valence, France
Valentia *see* País Valenciano
Valentia Julia *see* Valence
105 T8 **Valentigney** Doubs, E France *47.27N 6.49E*
30 M12 **Valentine** Nebraska, C USA *42.52N 100.31W*
26 J10 **Valentine** Texas, SW USA *30.35N 104.30W*
Valentine State *see* Oregon
108 C8 **Valenza** Piemonte, NW Italy *45.01N 8.37E*
96 I13 **Våler** Hedmark, S Norway *60.39N 11.52E*
56 I6 **Valera** Trujillo, NW Venezuela *9.21N 70.37W*
199 K13 **Valerie Guyot** *undersea feature* S Pacific Ocean *33.00S 164.00W*
Valetta *see* Valletta
120 I7 **Valga** *Ger.* Walk, *Latv.* Valka. Valgamaa, S Estonia *57.48N 26.04E*
120 I7 **Valgamaa** *off.* Valga Maakond. ◆ *province* S Estonia
45 Q15 **Valiente, Península** *peninsula* NW Panama
105 X16 **Valinco, Golfe de** *gulf* Corse, France, C Mediterranean Sea
114 L12 **Valjevo** Serbia, W Serbia and Montenegro (Yugoslavia) *44.16N 19.54E*
Valjok *see* Válljohka
120 I7 **Valka** *Ger.* Walk. Valka, N Latvia *57.48N 26.01E*
Valka *see* Valga
95 L18 **Valkeakoski** Länsi-Suomi, W Finland *61.16N 24.04E*
95 M19 **Valkeala** Etelä-Suomi, S Finland *60.55N 26.49E*
101 L18 **Valkenburg** Limburg, SE Netherlands *50.52N 5.46E*
101 K15 **Valkenswaard** Noord-Brabant, S Netherlands *51.21N 5.28E*
121 G15 **Valkininkai** Alytus, S Lithuania *54.22N 24.51E*
119 U5 **Valky** Kharkivs'ka Oblast', E Ukraine *49.51N 35.40E*
43 Y12 **Valladolid** Yucatán, SE Mexico *20.39N 88.13W*
106 M5 **Valladolid** Castilla-León, NW Spain *41.39N 4.45W*
106 L5 **Valladolid** ◆ *province* Castilla-León, N Spain
105 U15 **Vallauris** Alpes-Maritimes, SE France *43.34N 7.03E*
Vall-de-roures *see* Valderrobres
107 S9 **Vall d'Uxó** País Valenciano, E Spain *39.49N 0.15W*
97 E16 **Valle** Aust-Agder, S Norway *59.13N 7.33E*
107 N2 **Valle** Cantabria, N Spain *43.14N 4.16W*
44 H8 **Valle** ◆ *department* S Honduras
107 N8 **Vallecas** Madrid, C Spain *40.22N 3.37W*
39 Q8 **Vallecito Reservoir** ▣ Colorado, C USA
108 A7 **Valle d'Aosta** ◆ *region* NW Italy
43 O14 **Valle de Bravo** México, S Mexico *19.19N 100.08W*
57 N5 **Valle de Guanape** Anzoátegui, N Venezuela *9.49N 65.34W*
56 M6 **Valle de La Pascua** Guárico, N Venezuela *09.15N 66.00W*
56 B11 **Valle del Cauca** *off.* Departamento del Valle del Cauca. ◆ *province* W Colombia
43 N13 **Valle de Santiago** Guanajuato, C Mexico *20.21N 101.13W*
42 J7 **Valle de Zaragoza** Chihuahua, N Mexico *27.25N 105.50W*
56 G5 **Valledupar** Cesar, N Colombia *10.31N 73.16W*
78 G10 **Vallée de Ferlo** ∾ NW Senegal
59 M19 **Vallegrande** Santa Cruz, C Bolivia *18.30S 64.06W*
43 P8 **Valle Hermoso** Tamaulipas, C Mexico *25.39N 97.49W*
37 N8 **Vallejo** California, W USA *38.07N 122.16W*
64 G8 **Vallenar** Atacama, N Chile *28.35S 70.44W*
97 O15 **Vallentuna** Stockholm, C Sweden *59.31N 18.04E*
123 I112 **Valletta** *prev.* Valetta. ● (Malta) E Malta *35.54N 14.30E*
29 N6 **Valley Center** Kansas, C USA *37.49N 97.22W*
31 Q5 **Valley City** North Dakota, N USA *46.57N 97.58W*
34 I15 **Valley Falls** Oregon, NW USA *42.28N 120.16W*
Valleyfield *see* Salaberry-de-Valleyfield
23 S4 **Valley Head** West Virginia, NE USA *38.33N 80.01W*
27 T8 **Valley Mills** Texas, SW USA *31.36N 97.27W*
77 W10 **Valley of the Kings** *ancient monument* E Egypt *25.41N 32.30E*
31 R11 **Valley Springs** South Dakota, N USA *43.34N 96.28W*
22 K5 **Valley Station** Kentucky, S USA *38.06N 85.52W*
9 O13 **Valleyview** Alberta, W Canada *55.01N 117.16W*
27 T5 **Valley View** Texas, SW USA *33.27N 97.08W*
63 C21 **Vallimanca, Arroyo** ∾ E Argentina
94 L9 **Válljohka** *var.* Valjok Finnmark, N Norway *69.39N 25.52E*
109 M19 **Vallo della Lucania** Campania, S Italy *40.13N 15.15E*
110 B9 **Vallorbe** Vaud, W Switzerland *46.43N 6.21E*
107 V6 **Valls** Cataluña, NE Spain *41.18N 1.15E*
96 N11 **Vallsta** Gävleborg, C Sweden *61.30N 16.25E*
96 N12 **Vallvik** Gävleborg, C Sweden *61.10N 17.15E*
9 T17 **Val Marie** Saskatchewan, S Canada *49.15N 107.43W*
120 H7 **Valmiera** *Est.* Volmari, *Ger.* Wolmar. Valmiera, N Latvia *57.33N 25.26E*
107 N3 **Valnera** ▲ N Spain *43.08N 3.39W*
104 J3 **Valognes** Manche, N France *49.31N 1.28W*
Valona *see* Vlorë
Valona Bay *see* Vlorës, Gjiri i
106 G6 **Valongo** *var.* Valongo de Gaia. Porto, N Portugal *41.10N 8.30W*
Valongo de Gaia *see* Valongo
106 M5 **Valoria la Buena** Castilla-León, N Spain *41.48N 4.33W*
121 J15 **Valozhyn** *Pol.* Wołożyn, *Rus.* Volozhin. Minskaya Voblasts', C Belarus *54.07N 26.31E*
106 I5 **Valpaços** Vila Real, N Portugal *41.36N 7.16W*
25 P8 **Valparaiso** Florida, SE USA *30.30N 86.28W*
33 N11 **Valparaiso** Indiana, N USA *41.28N 87.04W*
64 G11 **Valparaíso** Valparaíso, C Chile *33.04S 71.18W*
42 L11 **Valparaíso** Zacatecas, C Mexico *22.49N 103.28W*
64 G11 **Valparaíso** *off.* Región de Valparaíso. ◆ *region* C Chile
Valpo *see* Valpovo
114 I9 **Valpovo** *Hung.* Valpo. Osijek-Baranja, E Croatia *45.40N 18.25E*
105 R14 **Valréas** Vaucluse, SE France *44.22N 5.00E*
Vals *see* Vals-Platz
160 D12 **Valsād** *prev.* Bulsar. Gujarāt, W India *20.40N 72.55E*
Valsbaai *see* False Bay
176 Uu10 **Valse Pisang, Kepulauan** *island group* E Indonesia
110 H9 **Vals-Platz** *var.* Vals. Graubünden, S Switzerland *46.39N 9.09E*
176 Xx16 **Vals, Tanjung** *headland* Papua, SE Indonesia *8.25S 137.34E*
95 N15 **Valtimo** Itä-Suomi, E Finland *63.39N 28.49E*
117 D17 **Váltou** ▲▲ C Greece
131 O12 **Valuyevka** Rostovskaya Oblast', SW Russian Federation *46.48N 43.49E*
130 K9 **Valuyki** Belgorodskaya Oblast', W Russian Federation *50.11N 38.07E*
38 L2 **Val Verda** Utah, W USA *40.51N 111.53W*
66 N12 **Valverde** Hierro, Islas Canarias, Spain, NE Atlantic Ocean *27.48N 17.55W*
106 I13 **Valverde del Camino** Andalucía, S Spain *37.34N 6.45W*
97 G23 **Vamdrup** Vejle, C Denmark *55.25N 9.18E*
96 L12 **Våmhus** Dalarna, C Sweden *61.07N 14.30E*
95 K18 **Vammala** Länsi-Suomi, W Finland *61.19N 22.55E*
Vámosudvarhely *see* Odorheiu Secuiesc
143 S14 **Van** Van, E Turkey *38.30N 43.22E*
27 V7 **Van** Texas, SW USA *32.31N 95.38W*
143 T14 **Van** ◆ *province* E Turkey
143 T11 **Vanadzor** *prev.* Kirovakan. N Armenia *40.49N 44.28E*
27 U5 **Van Alstyne** Texas, SW USA *33.25N 96.34W*
35 W10 **Vananda** Montana, NW USA *46.22N 106.58W*
118 I11 **Vânători** *Hung.* Héjjasfalva; *prev.* Vînători. Mureș, C Romania *46.13N 24.56E*
203 W12 **Vanavana** *atoll* Îles Tuamotu, SE French Polynesia
Vana-Vändra *see* Vändra
126 J12 **Vanavara** Evenkiyskiy Avtonomnyy Okrug, C Russian Federation *60.19N 102.19E*
13 Q8 **Van Bruyssel** Québec, SE Canada *47.56N 72.08W*
29 R10 **Van Buren** Arkansas, C USA *35.26N 94.21W*
21 S1 **Van Buren** Maine, NE USA *47.07N 67.57W*
29 W7 **Van Buren** Missouri, C USA *37.00N 91.00W*
21 T5 **Vanceboro** Maine, NE USA *45.31N 67.25W*
23 W10 **Vanceboro** North Carolina, SE USA *35.16N 77.06W*
23 O4 **Vanceburg** Kentucky, S USA *38.32N 83.18W*
Vanch *see* Vanj
8 L17 **Vancouver** British Columbia, SW Canada *49.13N 123.06W*
34 G11 **Vancouver** Washington, NW USA *45.38N 122.39W*
8 L17 **Vancouver** ✕ British Columbia, SW Canada *49.03N 123.00W*
8 K16 **Vancouver Island** *island* British Columbia, SW Canada
Vanda *see* Vantaa
176 Xx11 **Van Daalen** ∾ Papua, E Indonesia
32 L15 **Vandalia** Illinois, N USA *38.57N 89.05W*
29 V3 **Vandalia** Missouri, C USA *39.18N 91.29W*
33 R13 **Vandalia** Ohio, N USA *39.53N 84.12W*
27 U13 **Vanderbilt** Texas, SW USA *28.45N 96.37W*
33 Q10 **Vandercook Lake** Michigan, N USA *42.11N 84.23W*
8 L14 **Vanderhoof** British Columbia, SW Canada *53.54N 124.00W*
20 K8 **Vanderwhacker Mountain** ▲ New York, NE USA *43.54N 74.06W*
189 P1 **Van Diemen Gulf** *gulf* Northern Territory, N Australia
Van Diemen's Land *see* Tasmania
120 H5 **Vändra** *Ger.* Fennern; *prev.* Vana-Vändra. Pärnumaa, SW Estonia *58.40N 25.01E*
Vandsburg *see* Więcbork
36 L4 **Van Duzen River** ∾ California, W USA
120 F13 **Vandžiogala** Kaunas, C Lithuania *55.07N 23.55E*
43 N10 **Vanegas** San Luis Potosí, C Mexico *23.53N 100.55W*
Vaner, Lake *see* Vänern
97 K17 **Vänern** *Eng.* Lake Vaner; *prev.* Lake Vener. ◎ S Sweden
97 J18 **Vänersborg** Västra Götaland, S Sweden *58.16N 12.22E*
96 F12 **Vang** Oppland, S Norway *61.07N 8.34E*
180 I7 **Vangaindrano** Fianarantsoa, SE Madagascar *23.21S 47.34E*
143 S14 **Van Gölü** *Eng.* Lake Van; *anc.* Thospitis. *salt lake* E Turkey
195 V15 **Vangunu** *island* New Georgia Islands, NW Solomon Islands
26 J9 **Van Horn** Texas, SW USA *31.03N 104.51W*
195 X9 **Vanikolo** *var.* Vanikoro. *island* Santa Cruz Islands, E Solomon Islands
Vanikoro *see* Vanikolo
194 E9 **Vanimo** Sandaun, NW PNG *2.43S 141.22E*
127 O15 **Vanino** Khabarovskiy Kray, SE Russian Federation *49.10N 140.18E*
161 G19 **Vānīvilāsa Sāgara** ◎ SW India
153 S13 **Vanj** *Rus.* Vanch. S Tajikistan *38.22N 71.27E*
118 G14 **Vânju Mare** *prev.* Vînju Mare. Mehedinți, SW Romania *44.25N 22.52E*
127 P3 **Vankarem** Chukotskiy Avtonomnyy Okrug, NE Russian Federation *67.48N 176.11W*
13 N12 **Vankleek Hill** Ontario, SE Canada *45.32N 74.39W*
Van, Lake *see* Van Gölü
95 I16 **Vännäs** Västerbotten, N Sweden *63.54N 19.43E*
95 I15 **Vännäsby** Västerbotten, N Sweden *63.55N 19.53E*
104 H7 **Vannes** *anc.* Dariorigum. Morbihan, NW France *47.40N 2.45W*
94 I8 **Vannøya** *island* N Norway
105 T12 **Vanoise, Massif de la** ▲▲ E France
176 Xx10 **Van Rees, Pegunungan** ▲▲ Papua, E Indonesia
85 E24 **Vanrhynsdorp** Western Cape, SW South Africa *31.33S 18.42E*
23 P7 **Vansant** Virginia, NE USA *37.13N 82.03W*
96 L13 **Vansbro** Dalarna, C Sweden *60.31N 14.15E*
97 D18 **Vanse** Vest-Agder, S Norway *58.04N 6.40E*
15 M4 **Vansittart Island** *island* Nunavut, NE Canada
95 M20 **Vantaa** *Swe.* Vanda. Etelä-Suomi, S Finland *60.18N 25.01E*
95 L19 **Vantaa** ✕ (Helsinki) Etelä-Suomi, S Finland *60.18N 25.01E*
34 J9 **Vantage** Washington, NW USA *46.55N 119.55W*
197 K14 **Vanua Balavu** *prev.* Vanua Mbalavu. *island* Lau Group, E Fiji
197 C10 **Vanua Lava** *island* Banks Islands, N Vanuatu
197 J12 **Vanua Levu** *island* N Fiji
197 I12 **Vanua Levu Barrier Reef** *reef* C Fiji
Vanua Mbalavu *see* Vanua Balavu
197 B10 **Vanuatu** *off.* Republic of Vanuatu; *prev.* New Hebrides. ◆ *republic* SW Pacific Ocean
183 P8 **Vanuatu** *island group* SW Pacific Ocean
197 K15 **Vanua Vatu** *island* Lau Group, E Fiji
33 Q12 **Van Wert** Ohio, N USA *40.52N 84.34W*
197 K7 **Vao** Province Sud, S New Caledonia *22.40S 167.29E*
Vapincum *see* Gap
119 N7 **Vapnyarka** Vinnyts'ka Oblast', C Ukraine *48.32N 28.44E*
105 T15 **Var** ◆ *department* SE France
105 U14 **Var** ∾ SE France
97 J18 **Vara** Västra Götaland, S Sweden *58.16N 12.57E*
Varadinska Županija *see* Varaždin
120 J10 **Varakļani** Madona, C Latvia *56.36N 26.40E*
108 C7 **Varallo** Piemonte, NE Italy *45.51N 8.16E*
149 O5 **Varāmīn** *var.* Veramin. Tehrān, N Iran *35.19N 51.40E*
159 N14 **Vārānasi** *prev.* Banaras, Benares, *hist.* Kasi. Uttar Pradesh, N India *25.20N 83.00E*
129 T3 **Varandey** Nenetskiy Avtonomnyy Okrug, NW Russian Federation *68.48N 57.54E*
94 M8 **Varangerbotn** Finnmark, N Norway *70.09N 28.28E*
94 M8 **Varangerfjorden** *Lapp.* Várjjatvuotna. *fjord* N Norway
94 M8 **Varangerhalvøya** *Lapp.* Várnjárga. *peninsula* N Norway
Varannó *see* Vranov nad Topľou
109 M15 **Varano, Lago di** ◎ SE Italy
120 J13 **Varapayeva** *Rus.* Voropayevo. Vitsyebskaya Voblasts', NW Belarus *55.09N 27.13E*
Varasd *see* Varaždin
114 E7 **Varaždin** *Ger.* Warasdin, *Hung.* Varasd. Varaždin, N Croatia *46.18N 16.20E*
114 E7 **Varaždin** *off.* Varadinska Županija. ◆ *province* N Croatia
108 C10 **Varazze** Liguria, NW Italy *44.21N 8.35E*
97 J20 **Varberg** Halland, S Sweden *57.06N 12.15E*
Vardak *see* Wardag
115 Q19 **Vardar** *Gk.* Axiós. ∾ FYR Macedonia/Greece *see also* Axiós
97 F23 **Varde** Ribe, W Denmark *55.37N 8.31E*
143 V12 **Vardenis** E Armenia *40.11N 45.43E*
94 N8 **Vardø** *Fin.* Vuoreija. Finnmark, N Norway *70.22N 31.04E*
117 E18 **Vardoúsia** ▲▲ C Greece
Vareia *see* Logroño
102 G10 **Varel** Niedersachsen, NW Germany *53.24N 8.07E*
121 G15 **Varėna** *Pol.* Orany. Alytus, S Lithuania *54.13N 24.35E*
13 O12 **Varennes** Québec, SE Canada *45.42N 73.25W*
105 P10 **Varennes-sur-Allier** Allier, C France *46.17N 3.24E*
114 I12 **Vareš** Federacija Bosna I Hercegovina, E Bosnia and Herzegovina *44.12N 18.19E*
108 D7 **Varese** Lombardia, N Italy *45.49N 8.49E*
118 J12 **Vârful Moldoveanu** *var.* Moldoveanul; *prev.* Vîrful Moldoveanu. ▲ C Romania *45.35N 24.48E*
Varganzi *see* Warganza
97 J18 **Vårgårda** Västra Götaland, S Sweden *58.00N 12.49E*
125 F12 **Vargashi** Kurganskaya Oblast', C Russian Federation *55.22N 65.39E*
97 J18 **Vargön** Västra Götaland, S Sweden *58.21N 12.22E*
97 C17 **Varhaug** Rogaland, S Norway *58.37N 5.39E*
Várjjatvuotna *see* Varangerfjorden
95 N17 **Varkaus** Itä-Suomi, C Finland *62.19N 27.49E*
94 J2 **Varmahlíð** Nordhurland Vestra, N Iceland *65.32N 19.33W*
97 J15 **Värmland** ◆ *county* C Sweden
97 K16 **Värmlandsnäs** *peninsula* S Sweden
116 N8 **Varna** *prev.* Stalin, *anc.* Odessus. Varna, E Bulgaria *43.13N 27.55E*
116 N8 **Varna** ✕ Varna, E Bulgaria *43.16N 27.52E*
116 N8 **Varna** ◆ *province* E Bulgaria
97 L20 **Värnamo** Jönköping, S Sweden *57.10N 14.03E*
116 N8 **Varnenski Zaliv** *prev.* Stalinski Zaliv. *bay* E Bulgaria
116 N8 **Varnensko Ezero** *estuary* E Bulgaria
120 D11 **Varniai** Telšiai, W Lithuania *55.45N 22.22E*
Várnjárga *see* Varangerhalvøya
Varnoús *see* Baba
113 D14 **Varnsdorf** *Ger.* Warnsdorf. Ústecký Kraj, N Czech Republic *50.55N 14.34E*
113 I23 **Várpalota** Veszprém, W Hungary *47.13N 18.07E*
Varshava *see* Warszawa
120 K6 **Värska** Põlvamaa, SE Estonia *57.58N 27.37E*
100 N12 **Varsseveld** Gelderland, E Netherlands *51.55N 6.28E*
117 D19 **Vartholomió** *prev.* Vartholomión. Dytikí Ellás, S Greece *37.52N 21.12E*
Vartholomión *see* Vartholomió
143 Q14 **Varto** Muş, E Turkey *39.10N 41.28E*
97 K18 **Vartofta** Västra Götaland, S Sweden *58.06N 13.40E*
95 O17 **Värtsilä** Itä-Suomi, E Finland *62.10N 30.35E*
Värtsilä *see* Vyartsilya
119 R4 **Varva** Chernihivs'ka Oblast', NE Ukraine *50.31N 32.43E*
61 H18 **Várzea Grande** Mato Grosso, SW Brazil *15.39S 56.07W*
108 D9 **Varzi** Lombardia, N Italy *44.51N 9.13E*
Varzimanor Ayni *see* Ayní
128 K5 **Varzuga** ∾ NW Russian Federation
105 P8 **Varzy** Nièvre, C France *47.22N 3.22E*
113 G23 **Vas** *off.* Vas Megye. ◆ *county* W Hungary
Vasa *see* Vaasa
202 A9 **Vasafua** *island* Funafuti Atoll, C Tuvalu
113 O21 **Vásárosnamény** Szabolcs-Szatmár-Bereg, E Hungary *48.07N 22.19E*
106 H13 **Vascão, Ribeira de** ∾ S Portugal
118 G10 **Vașcău** *Hung.* Vaskoh. Bihor, NE Romania *46.26N 22.30E*
Vascongadas, Provincias *see* País Vasco
Vashess Bay *see* Vaskess Bay
Vāsht *see* Khāsh
Vasilevichi *see* Vasilyevichy
117 G14 **Vasiliká** Kentrikí Makedonía, NE Greece *40.28N 23.07E*
117 C18 **Vasilikí** Lefkáda, Iónioi Nísoi, Greece, C Mediterranean Sea *38.36N 20.37E*
117 K25 **Vasilikí** Kríti, Greece, E Mediterranean Sea *35.04N 25.49E*
121 G16 **Vasilishki** *Pol.* Wasiliszki, *Rus.* Vasilishki. Hrodzyenskaya Voblasts', W Belarus *53.46N 24.51E*
Vasil Kolarov *see* Pamporovo
Vasil'kov *see* Vasyl'kiv
121 N19 **Vasilyevichy** *Rus.* Vasilevichi. Homyel'skaya Voblasts', SE Belarus *52.15N 29.49E*
203 Y3 **Vaskess Bay** *var.* Vashess Bay. *bay* Kiritimati, E Kiribati
Vaskoh *see* Vașcău
Vaskohsziklás *see* Știei
118 M10 **Vaslui** Vaslui, C Romania *46.38N 27.44E*
118 L11 **Vaslui** ◆ *county* NE Romania
33 R8 **Vassar** Michigan, N USA *43.22N 83.34W*
97 E15 **Vassdalsegga** ▲ S Norway *59.47N 7.07E*
62 P9 **Vassouras** Rio de Janeiro, SE Brazil *22.24S 43.38W*
97 N15 **Västerås** Västmanland, C Sweden *59.37N 16.33E*
95 G15 **Västerbotten** ◆ *county* N Sweden
96 K12 **Västerdalälven** ∾ C Sweden
97 O16 **Västerhaninge** Stockholm, C Sweden *59.07N 18.06E*
96 M10 **Västernorrland** ◆ *county* C Sweden
97 N19 **Västervik** Kalmar, S Sweden *57.44N 16.40E*
97 M15 **Västmanand** ◆ *county* C Sweden
109 L15 **Vasto** *anc.* Histonium. Abruzzo, C Italy *42.07N 14.43E*
97 J19 **Västra Götaland** ◆ *county* S Sweden
97 J16 **Västra Silen** ◎ S Sweden
113 G23 **Vasvár** *Ger.* Eisenburg. Vas, W Hungary *47.04N 16.46E*
119 U9 **Vasylivka** Zaporiz'ka Oblast', SE Ukraine *47.26N 35.18E*
119 O5 **Vasyl'kiv** *Rus.* Vasil'kov. Kyyivs'ka Oblast', N Ukraine *50.10N 30.18E*
126 Gg12 **Vasyugan** ∾ C Russian Federation
105 N8 **Vatan** Indre, C France *47.06N 1.49E*
Vaté *see* Efate
109 G15 **Vatican City** *off.* Vatican City State. ◆ *papal state* S Europe
109 M22 **Vaticano, Capo** *headland* S Italy *38.37N 15.49E*
Vatilí *see* Vadili
94 K3 **Vatnajökull** *glacier* SE Iceland
97 P15 **Vätö** Stockholm, C Sweden *59.48N 18.55E*
197 L16 **Vatoa** *island* Lau Group, SE Fiji
180 J5 **Vatomandry** Toamasina, E Madagascar *19.19S 48.58E*
118 J9 **Vatra Dornei** *Ger.* Dorna Watra. Suceava, NE Romania *47.19N 25.21E*
118 J9 **Vatra Moldoviței** Suceava, NE Romania *47.37N 25.36E*
Vatter, Lake *see* Vättern
97 L18 **Vättern** *Eng.* Lake Vatter; *prev.* Lake Vetter. ◎ S Sweden
197 H14 **Vatukoula** Viti Levu, W Fiji *17.33S 105.49E*
197 H15 **Vatulele** *island* SW Fiji
119 P7 **Vatutine** Cherkas'ka Oblast', C Ukraine *49.01N 31.04E*
197 J14 **Vatu Vara** *island* Lau Group, E Fiji
105 R14 **Vaucluse** ◆ *department* SE France
105 S5 **Vaucouleurs** Meuse, NE France *48.37N 5.38E*
110 B9 **Vaud** *Ger.* Waadt. ◆ *canton* SW Switzerland
13 N12 **Vaudreuil** Québec, SE Canada *45.24N 74.01W*
39 T12 **Vaughn** New Mexico, SW USA *34.36N 105.12W*
56 I14 **Vaupés** *off.* Comisaría del Vaupés. ◆ *province* SE Colombia
56 J13 **Vaupés, Río** *var.* Rio Uaupés. ∾ Brazil/Colombia *see also* Uaupés, Rio
105 Q15 **Vauvert** Gard, S France *43.42N 4.16E*
9 R17 **Vauxhall** Alberta, SW Canada *50.04N 112.09W*
101 K23 **Vaux-sur-Sûre** Luxembourg, SE Belgium *49.55N 5.34E*
180 J4 **Vavatenina** Toamasina, E Madagascar *17.25S 49.10E*
200 Ss12 **Vava'u Group** *island group* N Tonga
78 M16 **Vavoua** W Ivory Coast *7.22N 6.28W*
131 S2 **Vavozh** Udmurtskaya Respublika, NW Russian Federation *56.48N 51.53E*
161 K23 **Vavuniya** Northern Province, N Sri Lanka *8.45N 80.30E*
121 G17 **Vawkavysk** *Pol.* Wołkowysk, *Rus.* Volkovysk. Hrodzyenskaya Voblasts', W Belarus *53.10N 24.28E*
121 F17 **Vawkavyskaye Wzvyshsha** *Rus.* Volkovyskiye Vysoty. *hill range* W Belarus
97 P15 **Vaxholm** Stockholm, C Sweden *59.43N 18.57E*
97 L21 **Växjö** *var.* Vexiö. Kronoberg, S Sweden *56.52N 14.49E*
129 T1 **Vaygach, Ostrov** *island* NW Russian Federation
143 V13 **Vayk'** *prev.* Azizbekov. SE Armenia *39.41N 45.28E*
Vazáš *see* Vittangi
129 P8 **Vazhgort** *prev.* Chasovo. Respublika Komi, NW Russian Federation *64.06N 46.44E*
47 V10 **V.C.Bird** ✕ (St John's) Antigua, Antigua and Barbuda *17.07N 61.49W*
97 C16 **Veavågen** Rogaland, S Norway *59.18N 5.13E*
31 Q7 **Veblen** South Dakota, N USA *45.50N 97.17W*
100 N9 **Vecht** *Ger.* Vechte. ∾ Germany/Netherlands *see also* Vechte
102 G12 **Vechta** Niedersachsen, NW Germany *52.44N 8.16E*
102 E12 **Vechte** *Dut.* Vecht. ∾ Germany/Netherlands *see also* Vecht
120 I8 **Vecpiebalga** Cēsis, C Latvia *57.03N 25.47E*
120 G9 **Vecumnieki** Bauska, C Latvia *56.36N 24.30E*
Vedāvati *see* Hagari
97 J20 **Veddige** Halland, S Sweden *57.16N 12.19E*
118 J15 **Vedea** ∾ S Romania
131 P16 **Vedeno** Chechenskaya Respublika, SW Russian Federation *42.57N 46.02E*
197 H14 **Ve Drala Reef** *reef* N Fiji
100 O6 **Veendam** Groningen, NE Netherlands *53.04N 6.52E*
100 K12 **Veenendaal** Utrecht, C Netherlands *52.03N 5.33E*
101 E14 **Veere** Zeeland, SW Netherlands *51.33N 3.40E*
26 M2 **Vega** Texas, SW USA *35.14N 102.25W*
94 E13 **Vega** *island* C Norway
47 T5 **Vega Baja** C Puerto Rico *18.27N 66.23W*
40 D17 **Vega Point** *headland* Kiska Island, Alaska, USA *51.49N 105.19E*
97 F17 **Vegår** ◎ S Norway
101 K14 **Veghel** Noord-Brabant, S Netherlands *51.37N 5.33E*
Veglia *see* Krk
116 E13 **Vegorítis, Límni** ◎ N Greece
9 Q14 **Vegreville** Alberta, SW Canada *53.30N 112.01W*
97 K21 **Veinge** Halland, S Sweden *56.33N 13.04E*
63 B21 **Veinticinco de Mayo** *var.* 25 de Mayo. Buenos Aires, E Argentina *35.27S 60.11W*
65 I14 **Veinticinco de Mayo** La Pampa, C Argentina *37.45S 67.40W*
121 F15 **Veisiejai** Alytus, S Lithuania *54.06N 23.41E*
97 F23 **Vejen** Ribe, W Denmark *55.28N 9.09E*
106 K16 **Vejer de la Frontera** Andalucía, S Spain *36.15N 5.58W*
97 G23 **Vejle** Vejle, C Denmark *55.43N 9.33E*
97 F23 **Vejle** *off.* Vejle Amt. ◆ *county* C Denmark
116 M7 **Vekilski** Shumen, NE Bulgaria *43.33N 27.19E*
56 G3 **Vela, Cabo de la** *headland* NE Colombia *12.13N 72.13W*
Vela Goa *see* Goa
115 F15 **Vela Luka** Dubrovnik-Neretva, S Croatia *42.57N 16.43E*
63 G19 **Velázquez** Rocha, E Uruguay *34.04S 54.16W*
103 E15 **Velbert** Nordrhein-Westfalen, W Germany *51.19N 7.03E*
111 S9 **Velden** Kärnten, S Austria *46.37N 13.59E*
Veldes *see* Bled
101 K15 **Veldhoven** Noord-Brabant, S Netherlands *51.24N 5.24E*
114 C11 **Velebit** ▲▲ C Croatia
116 N11 **Veleka** ∾ SE Bulgaria
111 V10 **Velenje** *Ger.* Wöllan. N Slovenia *46.22N 15.07E*
202 E12 **Vele, Pointe** *headland* Île Futuna, S Wallis and Futuna
115 O18 **Veles** *Turk.* Köprülü. C FYR Macedonia *41.43N 21.49E*
115 M20 **Velešta** SW FYR Macedonia *41.16N 20.37E*
117 F16 **Velestíno** *prev.* Velestínon. Thessalía, C Greece *39.22N 22.43E*
Velestínon *see* Velestíno
Velevshchina *see* Vyelyewshchyna
56 F9 **Vélez** Santander, C Colombia *6.01N 73.37W*
107 Q13 **Vélez Blanco** Andalucía, S Spain *37.43N 2.07W*
106 M17 **Vélez de la Gomera, Peñon de** *island group* S Spain
107 N15 **Vélez-Málaga** Andalucía, S Spain *36.46N 4.06W*
107 Q13 **Vélez Rubio** Andalucía, S Spain *37.39N 2.04W*
Velha Goa *see* Goa
Velho *see* Porto Velho
114 E8 **Velika Gorica** Zagreb, N Croatia *45.43N 16.03E*
114 C9 **Velika Kapela** ▲▲ NW Croatia
Velika Kikinda *see* Kikinda
114 D10 **Velika Kladuša** Federacija Bosna I Hercegovina, NW Bosnia and Herzegovina *45.10N 15.48E*
114 N11 **Velika Morava** *var.* Glavn'a Morava, Morava, *Ger.* Grosse Morava. ∾ C Serbia and Montenegro (Yugoslavia)
114 N12 **Velika Plana** Serbia, C Serbia and Montenegro (Yugoslavia) *44.20N 21.01E*
111 U10 **Velika Raduha** ▲ N Slovenia *46.24N 14.46E*
127 Pp5 **Velikaya** ∾ NE Russian Federation
128 F15 **Velikaya** ∾ W Russian Federation
Velikaya Berestovitsa *see* Vyalikaya Byerastavitsa
Velikaya Lepetikha *see* Velyka Lepetykha
Veliki Bečkerek *see* Zrenjanin
114 P12 **Veliki Krš** *var.* Stol. ▲ E Serbia and Montenegro (Yugoslavia) *44.10N 22.09E*
116 L8 **Veliki Preslav** *prev.* Preslav. Shumen, NE Bulgaria *43.09N 26.46E*
114 B9 **Veliki Risnjak** ▲ NW Croatia *45.30N 14.31E*
111 T13 **Veliki Snežnik** *Ger.* Schneeberg, *It.* Monte Nevoso. ▲ SW Slovenia *45.36N 14.25E*
114 J13 **Veliki Stolac** ▲ E Bosnia and Herzegovina *43.55N 19.15E*
Velikiy Bor *see* Vyaliki Bor
128 G16 **Velikiye Luki** Pskovskaya Oblast', W Russian Federation *56.19N 30.27E*
128 H14 **Velikiy Novgorod** *prev.* Novgorod. Novgorodskaya Oblast', W Russian Federation *58.31N 31.15E*
129 P12 **Velikiy Ustyug** Vologodskaya Oblast', NW Russian Federation *60.46N 46.18E*
114 N11 **Veliko Gradište** Serbia, NE Serbia and Montenegro (Yugoslavia) *44.46N 21.28E*
161 I18 **Velikonda Range** ▲▲ SE India
116 K9 **Veliko Tŭrnovo** *prev.* Tirnovo, Trnovo, Tŭrnovo. Veliko Tŭrnovo, N Bulgaria *43.04N 25.40E*
116 K8 **Veliko Tŭrnovo** ◆ *province* N Bulgaria
Velikovec *see* Völkermarkt
129 R5 **Velikovisochnoye** Nenetskiy Avtonomnyy Okrug, NW Russian Federation *67.13N 52.00E*
78 H12 **Vélingara** C Senegal *15.00N 14.39W*
78 H11 **Vélingara** S Senegal *13.12N 14.04W*
116 H11 **Velingrad** Pazardzhik, C Bulgaria *42.01N 24.00E*
130 H3 **Velizh** Smolenskaya Oblast', W Russian Federation *55.30N 31.06E*
113 F16 **Velká Deštná** *var.* Deštná, Grosskoppe, *Ger.* Deschnaer Koppe. ▲ NE Czech Republic *50.18N 16.25E*
113 F18 **Velké Meziříčí** *Ger.* Grossmeseritsch. Vysočina, C Czech Republic *49.22N 16.01E*
94 N1 **Velkomstpynten** *headland* NW Svalbard *79.51N 11.37E*
113 K21 **Veľký Krtíš** Banskobystrický Kraj, C Slovakia *48.13N 19.21E*
195 T14 **Vella Lavella** *var.* Mbilua. *island* New Georgia Islands, NW Solomon Islands
109 I15 **Velletri** Lazio, C Italy *41.43N 12.43E*
97 K23 **Vellinge** Skåne, S Sweden *55.29N 13.00E*
161 I19 **Vellore** Tamil Nādu, SE India *12.55N 79.09E*
Velobriga *see* Viana do Castelo
117 G21 **Velopoúla** *island* S Greece
100 M12 **Velp** Gelderland, SE Netherlands *52.00N 5.59E*
Velsen *see* Velsen-Noord
100 H9 **Velsen-Noord** *var.* Velsen. Noord-Holland, W Netherlands *52.27N 4.40E*
129 N12 **Vel'sk** *var.* Velsk. Arkhangel'skaya Oblast', NW Russian Federation *61.02N 42.00E*
Velsuna *see* Orvieto
100 K10 **Veluwemeer** *lake channel* C Netherlands
30 M3 **Velva** North Dakota, N USA *48.03N 100.55W*
117 E14 **Velvendós** *var.* Velvendos. Dytikí Makedonía, N Greece *40.15N 22.04E*
119 S5 **Velyka Bahachka** Poltavs'ka Oblast', C Ukraine *49.46N 33.44E*
119 S9 **Velyka Lepetykha** *Rus.* Velikaya Lepetikha. Khersons'ka Oblast', S Ukraine *47.10N 33.55E*
119 O10 **Velyka Mykhaylivka** Odes'ka Oblast', SW Ukraine *47.07N 29.49E*
119 W8 **Velyka Novosilka** Donets'ka Oblast', E Ukraine *47.49N 36.49E*
119 S9 **Velyka Oleksandrivka** Khersons'ka Oblast', S Ukraine *47.17N 33.16E*
119 T4 **Velyka Pysanivka** Sums'ka Oblast', NE Ukraine *50.25N 35.28E*
118 G6 **Velykyy Bereznyy** Zakarpats'ka Oblast', W Ukraine *48.54N 22.27E*
119 W4 **Velykyy Burluk** Kharkivs'ka Oblast', E Ukraine *50.04N 37.25E*
Velykyy Tokmak *see* Tokmak
181 P7 **Vema Fracture Zone** *tectonic feature* W Indian Ocean
67 P18 **Vema Seamount** *undersea feature* SW Indian Ocean *31.37S 8.19E*
95 F17 **Vemdalen** Jämtland, C Sweden *62.26N 13.50E*
97 N19 **Vena** Kalmar, S Sweden *57.31N 16.00E*
43 N11 **Venado** San Luis Potosí, C Mexico *22.54N 101.06W*
64 L11 **Venado Tuerto** Entre Ríos, E Argentina *33.45S 61.55W*
63 A19 **Venado Tuerto** Santa Fe, C Argentina *33.46S 61.57W*
109 K16 **Venafro** Molise, C Italy *41.28N 14.03E*
57 Q9 **Venamo, Cerro** ▲ E Venezuela *5.56N 61.25W*
108 B8 **Venaria** Piemonte, NW Italy *45.09N 7.40E*
105 U15 **Vence** Alpes-Maritimes, SE France *43.45N 7.07E*
106 H5 **Venda Nova** Vila Real, N Portugal *41.40N 7.58W*
106 G11 **Vendas Novas** Évora, S Portugal *38.40N 8.27W*
104 J9 **Vendée** ◆ *department* NW France
105 Q6 **Vendeuvre-sur-Barse** Aube, NE France *48.08N 4.17E*
104 M7 **Vendôme** Loir-et-Cher, C France *47.48N 1.04E*
Venedig *see* Venezia
Vener, Lake *see* Vänern
108 I8 **Veneta, Laguna** *lagoon* NE Italy
Venetia *see* Venezia
41 S7 **Venetie** Alaska, USA *67.00N 146.25W*
108 H8 **Veneto** *var.* Venezia Euganea. ◆ *region* NE Italy
116 M7 **Venets** Shumen, NE Bulgaria *43.33N 26.56E*
130 L5 **Venev** Tul'skaya Oblast', W Russian Federation *54.18N 38.16E*
108 I8 **Venezia** *Eng.* Venice, *Fr.* Venise, *Ger.* Venedig; anc. Venetia. Veneto, NE Italy *45.25N 12.19E*
Venezia Euganea *see* Veneto
Venezia, Golfo di *see* Venice, Gulf of
Venezia Tridentina *see* Trentino-Alto Adige
56 K8 **Venezuela** *off.* Republic of Venezuela; *prev.* Estados Unidos de Venezuela, United States of Venezuela. ◆ *republic* N South America
Venezuela, Cordillera de *see* Costa, Cordillera de la
56 I4 **Venezuela, Golfo de** *Eng.* Gulf of Maracaibo, Gulf of Venezuela. *gulf* NW Venezuela
Venezuela, Gulf of *see* Venezuela, Golfo de
66 F11 **Venezuelan Basin** *undersea feature* E Caribbean Sea
161 D16 **Vengurla** Mahārāshtra, W India *15.55N 73.39E*
41 O15 **Veniaminof, Mount** ▲ Alaska, USA *56.12N 159.24W*
25 V14 **Venice** Florida, SE USA *27.06N 82.27W*
24 L10 **Venice** Louisiana, S USA *29.15N 89.20W*
Venice *see* Venezia
108 J8 **Venice, Gulf of** *It.* Golfo di Venezia, *Slvn.* Beneški Zaliv. *gulf* N Adriatic Sea
Venise *see* Venezia
96 K13 **Venjan** Dalarna, C Sweden *60.58N 13.55E*
96 K13 **Venjansjön** ◎ C Sweden

◆ Country
● Country Capital
◇ Dependent Territory
○ Dependent Territory Capital
◆ Administrative Region
✕ International Airport
▲ Mountain
▲▲ Mountain Range
⚠ Volcano
∾ River
◎ Lake
▣ Reservoir

Venkatagiri – Villa Orestes Pereyra

161 *J18* **Venkatagiri** Andhra Pradesh, E India *14.00N 79.39E*
101 *M15* **Venlo** *prev.* Venloo. Limburg, SE Netherlands *51.22N 6.10E*
Venloo *see* Venlo
97 *E18* **Vennesla** Vest-Agder, S Norway *58.15N 7.58E*
109 *M17* **Venosa** *anc.* Venusia. Basilicata, S Italy *40.57N 15.49E*
Venoste, Alpi *see* Ötztaler Alpen
Venraij *see* Venray
101 *M14* **Venray** *var.* Venraij. Limburg, SE Netherlands *51.31N 5.58E*
120 *C8* **Venta** *Ger.* Windau. ≈ Latvia/Lithuania
Venta Belgarum *see* Winchester
42 *G9* **Ventana, Punta Arena de la** *var.* Punta de la Ventana. *headland* W Mexico *24.03N 109.49W*
Ventana, Punta de la *see* Ventana, Punta Arena de la
63 *B23* **Ventana, Sierra de la** *hill range* E Argentina
Ventia *see* Valence
203 *S11* **Vent, Îles du** *var.* Windward Islands. *island group* Archipel de la Société, W French Polynesia
203 *R10* **Vent, Îles Sous le** *var.* Leeward Islands. *island group* Archipel de la Société, W French Polynesia
108 *B11* **Ventimiglia** Liguria, NW Italy *43.46N 7.37E*
99 *M24* **Ventnor** S England, UK *50.36N 1.10W*
20 *J17* **Ventnor City** New Jersey, NE USA *39.19N 74.27W*
105 *S14* **Ventoux, Mont** ▲ SE France *44.12N 5.21E*
120 *C8* **Ventspils** *Ger.* Windau. Ventspils, NW Latvia *57.22N 21.34E*
56 *M10* **Ventuari, Río** ≈ S Venezuela
37 *R15* **Ventura** California, W USA *34.15N 119.14W*
190 *F8* **Venus Bay** South Australia *33.15S 134.42E*
Venusia *see* Venosa
203 *P7* **Vénus, Pointe** *var.* Pointe Tataaihoa. *headland* Tahiti, W French Polynesia *17.28S 149.28W*
43 *V16* **Venustiano Carranza** Chiapas, SE Mexico *16.24N 92.04W*
43 *N7* **Venustiano Carranza, Presa** ⊠ NE Mexico
63 *B15* **Vera** Santa Fe, C Argentina *29.28S 60.10W*
107 *Q14* **Vera** Andalucía, S Spain *37.15N 1.51W*
65 *K18* **Vera, Bahía** *bay* E Argentina
43 *R14* **Veracruz** *var.* Veracruz Llave. Veracruz-Llave, E Mexico *19.09N 96.09W*
43 *Q13* **Veracruz-Llave** *var.* Veracruz. ⬖ *state* E Mexico
45 *Q16* **Veraguas** *off.* Provincia de Veraguas. ⬖ *province* W Panama
Veramin *see* Varāmīn
160 *B12* **Verāval** Gujarāt, W India *20.54N 70.22E*
108 *C6* **Verbania** Piemonte, NW Italy *45.55N 8.34E*
109 *N20* **Verbicaro** Calabria, SW Italy *39.44N 15.51E*
110 *D11* **Verbier** Valais, SW Switzerland *46.06N 7.14E*
Vercellae *see* Vercelli
108 *C8* **Vercelli** *anc.* Vercellae. Piemonte, NW Italy *45.19N 8.25E*
105 *S13* **Vercors** *physical region* E France
Verdal *see* Verdalsøra
95 *E16* **Verdalsøra** *var.* Verdal. Nord-Trøndelag, C Norway *63.46N 11.27E*
Verde, Cabo *see* Cape Verde
46 *J5* **Verde, Cape** *headland* Long Island, C Bahamas *22.51N 75.50W*
106 *M2* **Verde, Costa** *coastal region* N Spain
Verde Grande, Río/Verde Grande y de Belem, Río *see* Verde, Río
102 *H11* **Verden** Niedersachsen, NW Germany *52.55N 9.13E*
61 *J19* **Verde, Rio** ≈ SE Brazil
59 *P16* **Verde, Río** ≈ Bolivia/Brazil
42 *M12* **Verde, Río** *var.* Río Verde Grande, Río Verde Grande y de Belem. ≈ C Mexico
43 *Q16* **Verde, Río** ≈ SE Mexico
38 *L13* **Verde River** ≈ Arizona, SW USA
Verdhikoúsa/Verdhikoússa *see* Verdikoússa
29 *Q8* **Verdigris River** ≈ Kansas/Oklahoma, C USA
117 *E15* **Verdikoússa** *var.* Verdhikoúsa, Verdhikoússa. Thessalía, C Greece *39.46N 21.58E*
105 *S15* **Verdon** ≈ SE France
13 *O12* **Verdun** Québec, SE Canada *45.27N 73.36W*
105 *S4* **Verdun** *var.* Verdun-sur-Meuse; *anc.* Verodunum. Meuse, NE France *49.09N 5.25E*
Verdun-sur-Meuse *see* Verdun
85 *J21* **Vereeniging** Gauteng, NE South Africa *26.40S 27.55E*
Veremeyki *see* Vyeramyeyki
129 *T14* **Vereshchagino** Permskaya Oblast', NW Russian Federation *58.06N 54.38E*
78 *G14* **Verga, Cap** *headland* W Guinea *10.12N 14.27W*
63 *G18* **Vergara** Treinta y Tres, E Uruguay *32.58S 53.54W*
110 *G11* **Vergeletto** Ticino, S Switzerland *46.13N 8.34E*
20 *L8* **Vergennes** Vermont, NE USA *44.09N 73.13W*
Veria *see* Véroia
106 *I5* **Verín** Galicia, NW Spain *41.55N 7.25W*
Verin T'alin *see* T'alin
120 *K6* **Veriora** Põlvamaa, SE Estonia *57.57N 27.23E*
119 *T7* **Verkhivtseve** Dnipropetrovs'ka Oblast', E Ukraine *48.27N 34.15E*
Verkhnedvinsk *see* Vyerkhnyadzvinsk
126 *Hh11* **Verkhneimbatsk** Krasnoyarskiy Kray, N Russian Federation *63.06N 88.03E*
128 *I3* **Verkhnetulomskiy** Murmanskaya Oblast', NW Russian Federation *68.37N 31.46E*
128 *I3* **Verkhnetulomskoye Vodokhranilishche** ⊠ NW Russian Federation
Verkhneudinsk *see* Ulan-Ude
126 *L11* **Verkhnevilyuysk** Respublika Sakha (Yakutiya), NE Russian Federation *63.44N 119.59E*
131 *W3* **Verkhniye Kigi** Respublika Bashkortostan, W Russian Federation *55.25N 58.40E*
131 *W5* **Verkhniy Avzyan** Respublika Bashkortostan, W Russian Federation *53.31N 57.26E*
131 *Q11* **Verkhniy Baskunchak** Astrakhanskaya Oblast', SW Russian Federation *48.14N 46.43E*
119 *T9* **Verkhniy Rohachyk** Khersons'ka Oblast', S Ukraine *47.16N 34.16E*
126 *Ll12* **Verkhnyaya Amga** Respublika Sakha (Yakutiya), NE Russian Federation *59.34N 127.07E*
129 *V6* **Verkhnyaya Inta** Respublika Komi, NW Russian Federation *65.55N 60.07E*
126 *Ii6* **Verkhnyaya Taymyra** ≈ N Russian Federation
129 *O10* **Verkhnyaya Toyma** Arkhangel'skaya Oblast', NW Russian Federation *62.12N 44.57E*
130 *K6* **Verkhov'ye** Orlovskaya Oblast', W Russian Federation *52.49N 37.20E*
118 *I8* **Verkhovyna** Ivano-Frankivs'ka Oblast', W Ukraine *48.09N 24.48E*
126 *M8* **Verkhoyansk** Respublika Sakha (Yakutiya), NE Russian Federation *67.27N 133.27E*
126 *L8* **Verkhoyanskiy Khrebet** ▲▲ NE Russian Federation
119 *T7* **Verkhn'odniprovs'k** Dnipropetrovs'ka Oblast', E Ukraine *48.40N 34.17E*
103 *G14* **Verl** Nordrhein-Westfalen, NW Germany *51.52N 8.30E*
94 *N1* **Verlegenhuken** *headland* N Svalbard *80.03N 16.15E*
84 *A9* **Vermelha, Ponta** *headland* NW Angola *5.40S 12.09E*
105 *P7* **Vermenton** Yonne, C France *47.40N 3.43E*
9 *R14* **Vermilion** Alberta, SW Canada *53.21N 110.52W*
33 *T11* **Vermilion** Ohio, N USA *41.25N 82.21W*
24 *I10* **Vermilion Bay** *bay* Louisiana, S USA
31 *V4* **Vermilion Lake** ◎ Minnesota, N USA
12 *F9* **Vermilion River** ≈ Ontario, S Canada
32 *L12* **Vermilion River** ≈ Illinois, N USA
31 *R12* **Vermillion** South Dakota, N USA *42.46N 96.55W*
31 *R12* **Vermillion River** ≈ South Dakota, N USA
13 *O9* **Vermillon, Rivière** ≈ Québec, SE Canada
117 *E14* **Vérmio** ▲▲ N Greece
20 *L8* **Vermont** *off.* State of Vermont; also known as The Green Mountain State. ⬖ *state* NE USA
115 *K16* **Vermosh** *var.* Vermoshi. Shkodër, N Albania *42.37N 19.42E*
Vermoshi *see* Vermosh
39 *O3* **Vernal** Utah, W USA *40.27N 109.31W*
12 *G11* **Verner** Ontario, S Canada *46.24N 80.04W*
104 *M5* **Verneuil-sur-Avre** Eure, N France *48.44N 0.55E*
116 *D13* **Vérno** ▲▲ N Greece
9 *N17* **Vernon** British Columbia, SW Canada *50.16N 119.19W*
104 *M4* **Vernon** Eure, N France *49.04N 1.28E*
25 *N3* **Vernon** Alabama, S USA *33.45N 88.06W*
33 *P15* **Vernon** Indiana, N USA *38.58N 85.39W*
27 *Q4* **Vernon** Texas, SW USA *34.10N 99.16W*
34 *G10* **Vernonia** Oregon, NW USA *45.51N 123.11W*
12 *G12* **Vernon, Lake** ◎ Ontario, S Canada
24 *G7* **Vernon Lake** ⊠ Louisiana, S USA
25 *Y13* **Vero Beach** Florida, SE USA *27.38N 80.24W*
Verőcze *see* Virovitica
Verodunum *see* Verdun
117 *E14* **Véroia** *var.* Veria, Vérroia, *Turk.* Karaferiye. Kentrikí Makedonía, N Greece *40.31N 22.14E*
108 *E8* **Verolanuova** Lombardia, N Italy *45.20N 10.06E*
12 *K14* **Verona** Ontario, SE Canada *44.30N 76.42W*
108 *G8* **Verona** Veneto, NE Italy *45.26N 11.00E*
31 *P6* **Verona** North Dakota, N USA *46.19N 98.03W*
32 *L9* **Verona** Wisconsin, N USA *42.59N 89.33W*
63 *E20* **Verónica** Buenos Aires, E Argentina *35.25S 57.16W*
24 *J9* **Verret, Lake** ◎ Louisiana, S USA
Vérroia *see* Véroia
195 *P10* **Verron Range** ▲▲ New Ireland, NE PNG
105 *N5* **Versailles** Yvelines, N France *48.48N 2.07E*
33 *P15* **Versailles** Indiana, N USA *39.04N 85.16W*
22 *M5* **Versailles** Kentucky, S USA *38.03N 84.43W*
29 *U5* **Versailles** Missouri, C USA *38.25N 92.50W*
33 *Q13* **Versailles** Ohio, N USA *40.13N 84.28W*
Versecz *see* Vršac
110 *A10* **Versoix** Genève, SW Switzerland *46.16N 6.10E*
13 *Z6* **Verte, Pointe** *headland* Québec, SE Canada *48.36N 64.10W*
113 *I22* **Vértes** ▲▲ NW Hungary
46 *G6* **Vertientes** Camagüey, C Cuba *21.15N 78.09W*
116 *G13* **Vertískos** ▲▲ N Greece
104 *I8* **Vertou** Loire-Atlantique, NW France *47.10N 1.28W*
Verulamium *see* St Albans
101 *L19* **Verviers** Liège, E Belgium *50.36N 5.52E*
105 *Y14* **Vescovato** Corse, France, C Mediterranean Sea *42.30N 9.27E*
101 *L20* **Vesdre** ≈ E Belgium
119 *U10* **Vesele** *Rus.* Veseloye. Zaporiz'ka Oblast', S Ukraine *47.00N 34.52E*
113 *D18* **Veselí nad Lužnicí** *var.* Weseli an der Lainsitz, *Ger.* Frohenbruck. Jihočeský Kraj, S Czech Republic *49.11N 14.40E*
116 *M9* **Veselinovo** Shumen, E Bulgaria *43.01N 27.02E*
130 *L12* **Veselovskoye Vodokhranilishche** ⊠ SW Russian Federation
Veseloye *see* Vesele
119 *Q9* **Veselynove** Mykolayivs'ka Oblast', S Ukraine *47.21N 31.15E*
Veseya *see* Vyasyeya
130 *M10* **Veshenskaya** Rostovskaya Oblast', SW Russian Federation *49.37N 41.43E*
131 *Q5* **Veshkayma** Ul'yanovskaya Oblast', W Russian Federation *54.04N 47.06E*
Vesisaari *see* Vadsø
Vesontio *see* Besançon
105 *T7* **Vesoul** *anc.* Vesulium, Vesulum. Haute-Saône, E France *47.37N 6.09E*
97 *J20* **Vessigebro** Halland, S Sweden *56.58N 12.40E*
97 *D17* **Vest-Agder** ⬖ *county* S Norway
25 *P4* **Vestavia Hills** Alabama, S USA *33.27N 86.47W*
86 *F6* **Vesterålen** *island* NW Norway
94 *G10* **Vesterålen** *island group* N Norway
89 *V3* **Vestervig** Viborg, NW Denmark *56.46N 8.19E*
94 *H2* **Vestfirdhir** ⬖ *region* NW Iceland
94 *G11* **Vestfjorden** *fjord* C Norway
97 *G16* **Vestfold** ⬖ *county* S Norway
97 *B18* **Vestmanna** *Dan.* Vestmanhavn Faeroe Islands *62.09N 7.11W*
94 *I4* **Vestmannaeyjar** Sudhurland, S Iceland *63.26N 20.13W*
96 *E9* **Vestnes** Møre og Romsdal, S Norway *62.39N 7.00E*
97 *I23* **Vestsjælland** *off.* Vestsjællands Amt. ⬖ *county* E Denmark
94 *H3* **Vesturland** ⬖ *region* W Iceland
94 *G11* **Vestvågøya** *island* C Norway
Vesulium/Vesulum *see* Vesoul
Vesuna *see* Périgueux
109 *K17* **Vesuvio** *Eng.* Vesuvius. ⛰ S Italy *40.48N 14.29E*
Vesuvius *see* Vesuvio
128 *K14* **Ves'yegonsk** Tverskaya Oblast', W Russian Federation *58.40N 37.13E*
113 *I23* **Veszprém** *Ger.* Veszprim. Veszprém, W Hungary *47.06N 17.54E*
113 *H23* **Veszprém** *off.* Veszprém Megye. ⬖ *county* W Hungary
Veszprim *see* Veszprém
Vetka *see* Vyetka
97 *M19* **Vetlanda** Jönköping, S Sweden *57.25N 15.04E*
131 *P1* **Vetluga** Nizhegorodskaya Oblast', W Russian Federation *57.51N 45.45E*
129 *P14* **Vetluga** ≈ NW Russian Federation
129 *O14* **Vetluzhskiy** Kostromskaya Oblast', NW Russian Federation *58.21N 45.25E*
131 *P2* **Vetluzhskiy** Nizhegorodskaya Oblast', W Russian Federation *57.10N 45.07E*
109 *H14* **Vetralla** Lazio, C Italy *42.18N 12.03E*
116 *M9* **Vetren** *prev.* Zhitarovo. Burgas, E Bulgaria *42.38N 27.22E*
116 *M8* **Vetrino** Varna, E Bulgaria *43.19N 27.26E*
Vetrino *see* Vyetryna
126 *Ii6* **Vetrovaya, Gora** ▲ N Russian Federation *73.54N 95.00E*
Vetter, Lake *see* Vättern
108 *J13* **Vettore, Monte** ▲ C Italy *42.49N 13.15E*
101 *A17* **Veurne** *var.* Furnes. West-Vlaanderen, W Belgium *51.04N 2.40E*
33 *Q15* **Vevay** Indiana, N USA *38.45N 85.07W*
110 *C10* **Vevey** *Ger.* Vivis; *anc.* Vibiscum. Vaud, SW Switzerland *46.28N 6.51E*
Vexiö *see* Växjö
105 *S13* **Veynes** Hautes-Alpes, SE France *44.33N 5.51E*
105 *N11* **Vézère** ≈ W France
116 *I9* **Vezhen** ▲ C Bulgaria *42.45N 24.22E*
142 *K11* **Vezirköprü** Samsun, N Turkey *41.09N 35.27E*
59 *J18* **Viacha** La Paz, W Bolivia *16.40S 68.16W*
29 *R10* **Vian** Oklahoma, C USA *35.30N 94.56W*
Viana de Castelo *see* Viana do Castelo
106 *H12* **Viana do Alentejo** Évora, S Portugal *38.20N 8.00W*
106 *I4* **Viana do Bolo** Galicia, NW Spain *42.10N 7.06W*
106 *G5* **Viana do Castelo** *var.* Viana de Castelo; *anc.* Velobriga. Viana do Castelo, NW Portugal *41.40N 8.49W*
106 *G5* **Viana do Castelo** *var.* Viana de Castelo. ⬖ *district* N Portugal
100 *J12* **Vianen** Zuid-Holland, C Netherlands *52.00N 5.06E*
178 *Ii8* **Viangchan** *Eng./Fr.* Vientiane. ● (Laos) C Laos *17.57N 102.38E*
178 *I6* **Viangphoukha** *var.* Vieng Pou Kha. Louang Namtha, N Laos *20.41N 101.03E*
106 *K13* **Viar** ≈ SW Spain
108 *E11* **Viareggio** Toscana, C Italy *43.52N 10.15E*
105 *O14* **Viaur** ≈ S France
Vibiscum *see* Vevey
97 *G21* **Viborg** Viborg, NW Denmark *56.28N 9.25E*
31 *R12* **Viborg** South Dakota, N USA *43.10N 97.04W*
97 *F21* **Viborg** *off.* Viborg Amt. ⬖ *county* NW Denmark
109 *N22* **Vibo Valentia** *prev.* Monteleone di Calabria; *anc.* Hipponium. Calabria, SW Italy *38.40N 16.06E*
107 *W5* **Vic** *var.* Vich; *anc.* Ausa, Vicus Ausonensis. Cataluña, NE Spain *41.55N 2.16E*
104 *K16* **Vic-en-Bigorre** Hautes-Pyrénées, S France *43.22N 0.03E*
42 *K10* **Vicente Guerrero** Durango, C Mexico *23.30N 104.24W*
43 *P10* **Vicente Guerrero, Presa** *var.* Presa de las Adjuntas. ⊠ NE Mexico
Vicentia *see* Vicenza
108 *G8* **Vicenza** *anc.* Vicentia. Veneto, NE Italy *45.31N 11.31E*
Vich *see* Vic
56 *J10* **Vichada** *off.* Comisaría del Vichada. ⬖ *province* E Colombia
56 *K10* **Vichada, Río** ≈ E Colombia
63 *G17* **Vichadero** Rivera, NE Uruguay *31.45S 54.40W*
Vichegda *see* Vychegda
128 *M16* **Vichuga** Ivanovskaya Oblast', W Russian Federation *57.13N 41.51E*
105 *P10* **Vichy** Allier, C France *46.08N 3.26E*
28 *K9* **Vici** Oklahoma, C USA *36.09N 99.18W*
33 *P10* **Vicksburg** Michigan, N USA *42.07N 85.31W*
24 *J5* **Vicksburg** Mississippi, S USA *32.21N 90.52W*
105 *O12* **Vic-sur-Cère** Cantal, C France *45.00N 2.36E*
31 *X14* **Victor** Iowa, C USA *41.45N 92.18W*
61 *I21* **Víctor** Mato Grosso do Sul, SW Brazil *21.39S 53.21W*
190 *I10* **Victor Harbor** South Australia *35.33S 138.37E*
63 *C18* **Victoria** Entre Ríos, E Argentina *32.36S 60.12W*
8 *L17* **Victoria** Vancouver Island, British Columbia, SW Canada *48.25N 123.22W*
47 *R14* **Victoria** NW Grenada *12.11N 61.42W*
44 *H6* **Victoria** Yoro, NW Honduras *15.01N 87.28W*
123 *J16* **Victoria** *var.* Rabat. Gozo, NW Malta *36.02N 14.14E*
118 *I12* **Victoria** *Ger.* Viktoriastadt. Braşov, C Romania *45.43N 24.40E*
180 *H17* **Victoria** ● (Seychelles) Mahé, SW Seychelles *4.37S 28.28E*
27 *U13* **Victoria** Texas, SW USA *28.47N 96.58W*
191 *N12* **Victoria** ⬖ *state* SE Australia
182 *K7* **Victoria** ≈ Western Australia
Victoria *see* Labuan, East Malaysia
Victoria *see* Masvingo, Zimbabwe
Victoria Bank *see* Vitória Seamount
9 *Y15* **Victoria Beach** Manitoba, S Canada *50.40N 96.30W*
Victoria de Durango *see* Durango
Victoria de las Tunas *see* Las Tunas
85 *I16* **Victoria Falls** Matabeleland North, W Zimbabwe *17.55S 25.48E*
85 *I16* **Victoria Falls** ✈ Matabeleland North, W Zimbabwe *18.03S 25.48E*
85 *I16* **Victoria Falls** *waterfall* Zambia/Zimbabwe *18.03S 25.50E*
Victoria Falls *see* Iguaçu, Salto do
65 *F19* **Victoria, Isla** *island* Archipiélago de los Chonos, S Chile
15 *J2* **Victoria Island** *island* Northwest Territories/Nunavut, NW Canada
190 *L8* **Victoria, Lake** ◎ New South Wales, SE Australia
70 *I12* **Victoria, Lake** *var.* Victoria Nyanza. ◎ E Africa
205 *S13* **Victoria Land** *physical region* Antarctica
177 *F5* **Victoria, Mount** ▲ W Myanmar *21.13N 93.53E*
197 *I14* **Victoria, Mount** ▲ Viti Levu, W Fiji *17.37S 178.00E*
194 *K15* **Victoria, Mount** ▲ S PNG *8.51S 147.36E*
83 *F17* **Victoria Nile** *var.* Somerset Nile. ≈ C Uganda
Victoria Nyanza *see* Victoria, Lake
44 *G3* **Victoria Peak** ▲ SE Belize *16.50N 88.38W*
193 *H16* **Victoria Range** ▲▲ South Island, NZ
189 *O3* **Victoria River** ≈ Northern Territory, N Australia
189 *P3* **Victoria River Roadhouse** Northern Territory, N Australia *15.37S 131.07E*
13 *Q11* **Victoriaville** Québec, SE Canada *46.03N 71.55W*
Victoria-Wes *see* Victoria West
85 *G24* **Victoria West** *Afr.* Victoria-Wes. Northern Cape, W South Africa *31.22S 23.06E*
64 *J13* **Victorica** La Pampa, C Argentina *36.14S 65.21W*
205 *T3* **Victor, Mount** ▲ Antarctica *72.49S 33.01E*
37 *U14* **Victorville** California, W USA *34.32N 117.17W*
64 *G9* **Vicuña** Coquimbo, N Chile *30.00S 70.44W*
64 *K11* **Vicuña Mackenna** Córdoba, C Argentina *33.52S 64.25W*
Vicus Ausonensis *see* Vic
Vicus Elbii *see* Viterbo
35 *X7* **Vida** Montana, NW USA *47.52N 105.30W*
25 *V6* **Vidalia** Georgia, SE USA *32.13N 82.24W*
24 *J7* **Vidalia** Louisiana, S USA *31.34N 91.25W*
97 *F22* **Videbæk** Ringkøbing, C Denmark *56.07N 8.37E*
62 *I13* **Videira** Santa Catarina, S Brazil *27.00S 51.08W*
118 *J14* **Videle** Teleorman, S Romania *44.15N 25.27E*
Videm-Krško *see* Krško
Vídeň *see* Wien
106 *H12* **Vidigueira** Beja, S Portugal *38.12N 7.48W*
116 *J9* **Vidima** ≈ N Bulgaria
116 *G7* **Vidin** *anc.* Bononia. Vidin, NW Bulgaria *44.00N 22.50E*
116 *F8* **Vidin** ⬖ *province* NW Bulgaria
160 *H10* **Vidisha** Madhya Pradesh, C India *23.30N 77.49E*
27 *Y10* **Vidor** Texas, SW USA *30.07N 94.01W*
97 *L20* **Vidöstern** ◎ S Sweden
94 *J13* **Vidsel** Norrbotten, N Sweden *65.49N 20.31E*
120 *H9* **Vidzemes Augstiene** ▲▲ C Latvia
120 *J12* **Vidzy** *Rus.* Vidzy. Vitsyebskaya Voblasts', NW Belarus *55.22N 26.37E*
65 *L16* **Viedma** Río Negro, E Argentina *40.50S 62.57W*
65 *H22* **Viedma, Lago** ◎ S Argentina
47 *O11* **Vieille Case** *var.* Itassi. N Dominica *15.36N 61.24W*
106 *M2* **Vieja, Peña** ▲ N Spain *43.09N 4.47W*
42 *E4* **Viejo, Cerro** ▲ NW Mexico *30.16N 112.18W*
58 *B9* **Viejo, Cerro** ▲ N Peru *4.54S 79.24W*
120 *E10* **Viekšniai** Telšiai, NW Lithuania *56.14N 22.33E*
107 *U3* **Vielha** *var.* Viella. Cataluña, NE Spain *42.40N 0.46E*
Viella *see* Vielha
101 *L21* **Vielsalm** Luxembourg, E Belgium *50.16N 5.55E*
Vieng Pou Kha *see* Viangphoukha
25 *T6* **Vienna** Georgia, SE USA *32.05N 83.48W*
32 *L17* **Vienna** Illinois, N USA *37.22N 88.51W*
29 *V5* **Vienna** Missouri, C USA *38.11N 91.57W*
23 *Q3* **Vienna** West Virginia, NE USA *39.19N 81.33W*
Vienna *see* Wien, Austria
Vienna *see* Vienne, France
105 *R11* **Vienne** *anc.* Vienna. Isère, E France *45.31N 4.52E*
104 *L10* **Vienne** ⬖ *department* W France
104 *L9* **Vienne** ≈ W France
Vientiane *see* Viangchan
Vientos, Paso de los *see* Windward Passage
47 *V6* **Vieques** *var.* Isabel Segunda. E Puerto Rico *18.08N 65.27W*
47 *V6* **Vieques, Isla de** *island* E Puerto Rico
47 *V6* **Vieques, Pasaje de** *passage* E Puerto Rico
47 *V5* **Vieques, Sonda de** *sound* E Puerto Rico
Vierdörfer *see* Săcele
95 *M15* **Vieremä** Itä-Suomi, C Finland *63.42N 27.02E*
101 *M14* **Vierlingsbeek** Noord-Brabant, SE Netherlands *51.36N 6.01E*
103 *G20* **Viernheim** Hessen, W Germany *49.31N 8.34E*
103 *D15* **Viersen** Nordrhein-Westfalen, W Germany *51.15N 6.24E*
110 *G8* **Vierwaldstätter See** *Eng.* Lake of Lucerne. ◎ C Switzerland
105 *N8* **Vierzon** Cher, C France *47.13N 2.04E*
42 *L8* **Viesca** Coahuila de Zaragoza, NE Mexico *25.25N 102.45W*
120 *H10* **Viesīte** *Ger.* Eckengraf. Jēkabpils, S Latvia *56.21N 25.30E*
109 *N15* **Vieste** Puglia, SE Italy *41.52N 16.10E*
178 *Jj9* **Vietnam** *off.* Socialist Republic of Vietnam, *Vtn.* Công Hoa Xa Hôi Chu Nghia Việt Nam. ◆ *republic* SE Asia
178 *J5* **Việt Quang** Ha Giang, N Vietnam *22.24N 104.48E*
Vietri *see* Việt Tri
178 *Jj6* **Việt Tri** *var.* Vietri. Vinh Phu, N Vietnam *21.19N 105.25E*
32 *L4* **Vieux Desert, Lac** ◎ Michigan/Wisconsin, N USA
47 *Y13* **Vieux Fort** S Saint Lucia *13.43N 60.57W*
47 *X6* **Vieux-Habitants** Basse Terre, SW Guadeloupe *16.03N 61.45W*
121 *G14* **Vievis** Vilnius, S Lithuania *54.46N 24.51E*
179 *P8* **Vigan** Luzon, N Philippines *17.34N 102.21E*
108 *D8* **Vigevano** Lombardia, N Italy *45.19N 8.51E*
109 *N18* **Viggiano** Basilicata, S Italy *40.21N 15.54E*
60 *L12* **Vigia** Pará, NE Brazil *0.49S 48.07W*
43 *Y12* **Vigía Chico** Quintana Roo, SE Mexico *19.49N 87.31W*
Vigie *see* George F L Charles
104 *K17* **Vignemale** *var.* Pic de Vignemale. ▲ France/Spain *42.48N 0.06W*
Vignemale, Pic de *see* Vignemale
108 *G10* **Vignola** Emilia-Romagna, C Italy *44.28N 11.00E*
106 *G4* **Vigo** Galicia, NW Spain *42.15N 8.43W*
106 *G4* **Vigo, Ría de** *estuary* NW Spain
96 *D9* **Vigra** *island* S Norway
97 *C17* **Vigrestad** Rogaland, S Norway *58.34N 5.42E*
95 *L15* **Vihanti** Oulu, C Finland *64.28N 25.00E*
155 *U10* **Vihāri** Punjab, E Pakistan *30.03N 72.31E*
104 *K8* **Vihiers** Maine-et-Loire, NW France *47.09N 0.37W*
113 *O19* **Vihorlat** ▲ E Slovakia *48.54N 22.09E*
95 *L19* **Vihti** Etelä-Suomi, S Finland *60.25N 24.16E*
Viipuri *see* Vyborg
95 *M16* **Viitasaari** Länsi-Suomi, W Finland *63.05N 25.52E*
120 *K3* **Viivikonna** Ida-Virumaa, NE Estonia *59.19N 27.40E*
161 *K16* **Vijayawāda** *prev.* Bezwada. Andhra Pradesh, SE India *16.34N 80.40E*
Vijosa/Vijosë *see* Aóos, Albania/Greece
Vijosa/Vijosë *see* Vjosës, Lumi i, Albania/Greece
Vik *see* Vikøyri
94 *J4* **Vík** Sudhurland, S Iceland *63.25N 18.58W*
96 *L13* **Vika** Dalarna, C Sweden *60.55N 14.30E*
94 *L12* **Vikajärvi** Lappi, N Finland *66.37N 26.10E*
96 *L13* **Vikarbyn** Dalarna, C Sweden *60.57N 15.00E*
97 *J22* **Viken** Skåne, S Sweden *56.09N 12.36E*
97 *L17* **Viken** ◎ C Sweden
97 *G15* **Vikersund** Buskerud, S Norway *59.58N 9.58E*
126 *J14* **Vikhorevka** Irkutskaya Oblast', S Russian Federation *56.09N 99.09E*
116 *G11* **Vikhren** ▲ SW Bulgaria *41.45N 23.24E*
9 *R15* **Viking** Alberta, SW Canada *53.07N 111.49W*
86 *E7* **Viking Bank** *undersea feature* N North Sea
97 *M14* **Vikmanshyttan** Dalarna, C Sweden *60.19N 15.55E*
96 *D12* **Vikøyri** *var.* Vik. Sogn og Fjordane, S Norway *61.04N 6.34E*
95 *H17* **Viksjö** Västernorrland, C Sweden *62.45N 17.30E*
Viktoriastadt *see* Victoria
Vila *see* Port-Vila
Vila Arriaga *see* Bibala
Vila Artur de Paiva *see* Cubango
Vila Bela da Santissima Trindade *see* Mato Grosso
60 *B12* **Vila Bittencourt** Amazonas, NW Brazil *1.25S 69.24W*
Vila da Ponte *see* Cubango
66 *O2* **Vila da Praia da Vitória** Terceira, Azores, Portugal, NE Atlantic Ocean *38.43N 27.04W*
Vila de Aljustrel *see* Cangamba
Vila de Almoster *see* Chiange
Vila de João Belo *see* Xai-Xai
Vila de Macia *see* Macia
Vila de Manhiça *see* Manhiça
Vila de Manica *see* Manica
Vila de Mocímboa da Praia *see* Mocímboa da Praia
85 *N16* **Vila de Sena** *var.* Sena. Sofala, C Mozambique *17.25S 34.59E*
106 *F14* **Vila do Bispo** Faro, S Portugal *37.04N 8.52W*
106 *G6* **Vila do Conde** Porto, NW Portugal *41.21N 8.45W*
Vila do Maio *see* Maio
66 *P3* **Vila do Porto** Santa Maria, Azores, Portugal, NE Atlantic Ocean *36.57N 25.10W*
85 *K15* **Vila do Zumbo** *prev.* Vila do Zumbu, Zumbo. Tete, NW Mozambique *15.36S 30.30E*
Vila do Zumbu *see* Vila do Zumbo
106 *I6* **Vila Flor** *var.* Vila Flôr. Bragança, N Portugal *41.18N 7.09W*
107 *V6* **Vilafranca del Penedès** *var.* Villafranca del Panadés. Cataluña, NE Spain *41.21N 1.42E*
106 *F10* **Vila Franca de Xira** *var.* Vilafranca de Xira. Lisboa, C Portugal *38.57N 8.58W*
Vila Gago Coutinho *see* Lumbala N'Guimbo
106 *G3* **Vilagarcía de Arousa** *var.* Villagarcía de Arosa. Galicia, NW Spain *42.34N 8.45W*
Vila General Machado *see* Camacupa
Vila Henrique de Carvalho *see* Saurimo
104 *I7* **Vilaine** ≈ NW France
Vila João de Almeida *see* Chibia
120 *K8* **Viļaka** *Ger.* Marienhausen. Balvi, NE Latvia *57.11N 27.42E*
106 *I2* **Vilalba** Galicia, NW Spain *43.16N 7.40W*
Vila Marechal Carmona *see* Uíge
Vila Mariano Machado *see* Ganda
180 *G3* **Vilanandro, Tanjona** *headland* W Madagascar *16.10S 44.27E*
Vilanculos *see* Vilankulo
120 *J10* **Viļāni** Rēzekne, E Latvia *56.33N 26.55E*
85 *N19* **Vilankulo** *var.* Vilanculos. Inhambane, E Mozambique *22.01S 35.19E*
Vila Norton de Matos *see* Balombo
106 *G6* **Vila Nova de Famalicão** *var.* Vila Nova de Famalicao. Braga, N Portugal *41.24N 8.31W*
106 *I6* **Vila Nova de Foz Côa** *var.* Vila Nova de Fozcôa. Guarda, N Portugal *41.04N 7.09W*
106 *F6* **Vila Nova de Gaia** Porto, NW Portugal *41.07N 8.37W*
Vila Nova de Portimão *see* Portimão
107 *V6* **Vilanova i La Geltrú** Cataluña, NE Spain *41.15N 1.42E*
Vila Pereira de Eça *see* N'Giva
106 *H6* **Vila Pouca de Aguiar** Vila Real, N Portugal *41.30N 7.37W*
106 *H6* **Vila Real** *var.* Vila Rial. Vila Real, N Portugal *41.16N 7.45W*
106 *H6* **Vila Real** ⬖ *district* N Portugal
107 *T9* **Vila-real de los Infantes** *var.* Villarreal. País Valenciano, E Spain *39.55N 0.07W*
106 *H14* **Vila Real de Santo António** Faro, S Portugal *37.12N 7.25W*
106 *J7* **Vilar Formoso** Guarda, N Portugal *40.37N 6.49W*
Vila Rial *see* Vila Real
61 *J15* **Vila Rica** Mato Grosso, W Brazil *9.52S 50.44W*
Vila Robert Williams *see* Caála
Vila Salazar *see* N'Dalatando
Vila Serpa Pinto *see* Menongue
Vila Teixeira da Silva *see* Bailundo
Vila Teixeira de Sousa *see* Luau
106 *H9* **Vila Velha de Ródão** Castelo Branco, C Portugal *39.39N 7.40W*
106 *G5* **Vila Verde** Braga, N Portugal *41.39N 8.27W*
106 *H11* **Vila Viçosa** Évora, S Portugal *38.46N 7.25W*
59 *G15* **Vilcabamba, Cordillera de** ▲▲ C Peru
Vîlcea *see* Vâlcea
126 *Hh1* **Vil'cheka, Zemlya** *Eng.* Wilczek Land. *island* Zemlya Frantsa-Iosifa, NW Russian Federation
97 *F22* **Vildbjerg** Ringkøbing, C Denmark *56.12N 8.46E*
Vileyka *see* Vilyeyka
95 *H15* **Vilhelmina** Västerbotten, N Sweden *64.37N 16.40E*
61 *F17* **Vilhena** Rondônia, W Brazil *12.40S 60.07W*
117 *G19* **Vília** Attikí, C Greece *38.09N 23.21E*
Viliya *see* Viliya
121 *I14* **Viliya** *Lith.* Neris, *Rus.* Viliya. ≈ W Belarus
Viliya *see* Neris
120 *H5* **Viljandi** *Ger.* Fellin. Viljandimaa, S Estonia *58.22N 25.34E*
120 *H5* **Viljandimaa** *off.* Viljandi Maakond. ⬖ *province* SW Estonia
121 *E14* **Vilkaviškis** *Pol.* Wyłkowyszki. Marijampolė, SW Lithuania *54.39N 23.03E*
120 *F13* **Vilkija** Kaunas, C Lithuania *55.02N 23.36E*
207 *V9* **Vil'kitskogo, Proliv** *strait* N Russian Federation
Vilkovo *see* Vylkove
59 *L21* **Villa Abecia** Chuquisaca, S Bolivia *21.01S 65.12W*
43 *N5* **Villa Acuña** *var.* Ciudad Acuña. Coahuila de Zaragoza, NE Mexico *29.17N 100.57W*
42 *J4* **Villa Ahumada** Chihuahua, N Mexico *30.37N 106.30W*
47 *O9* **Villa Altagracia** C Dominican Republic *18.37N 70.11W*
58 *L13* **Villa Bella** Beni, N Bolivia *10.21S 65.25W*
106 *J3* **Villablino** Castilla-León, N Spain *42.55N 6.21W*
56 *K6* **Villa Bruzual** Portuguesa, N Venezuela *9.19N 69.06W*
107 *O9* **Villacañas** Castilla-La Mancha, C Spain *39.37N 3.19W*
107 *O12* **Villacarrillo** Andalucía, S Spain *38.07N 3.04W*
106 *M7* **Villacastín** Castilla-León, N Spain *40.46N 4.25W*
Villa Cecilia *see* Ciudad Madero
111 *S9* **Villach** *Slvn.* Beljak. Kärnten, S Austria *46.36N 13.49E*
109 *B20* **Villacidro** Sardegna, Italy, C Mediterranean Sea *39.27N 8.43E*
Villa Concepción *see* Concepción
106 *L4* **Villada** Castilla-León, N Spain *42.15N 4.58W*
42 *M10* **Villa de Cos** Zacatecas, C Mexico *23.20N 102.20W*
56 *L5* **Villa de Cura** *var.* Cura. Aragua, N Venezuela *10.00N 67.30W*
Villa del Nevoso *see* Ilirska Bistrica
Villa del Pilar *see* Pilar
106 *M13* **Villa del Río** Andalucía, S Spain *37.58N 4.16W*
Villa de Méndez *see* Méndez
44 *H6* **Villa de San Antonio** Comayagua, W Honduras *14.24N 87.37W*
107 *N4* **Villadiego** Castilla-León, N Spain *42.31N 4.01W*
107 *T8* **Villafames** País Valenciano, E Spain *40.07N 0.03W*
43 *U16* **Villa Flores** Chiapas, SE Mexico *16.12N 93.16W*
106 *J3* **Villafranca del Bierzo** Castilla-León, N Spain *42.36N 6.49W*
107 *S8* **Villafranca del Cid** País Valenciano, E Spain *40.25N 0.15W*
106 *J11* **Villafranca de los Barros** Extremadura, W Spain *38.34N 6.19W*
107 *N10* **Villafranca de los Caballeros** Castilla-La Mancha, C Spain *39.25N 3.21W*
Villafranca del Panadés *see* Vilafranca del Penedès
108 *F8* **Villafranca di Verona** Veneto, NE Italy *45.22N 10.51E*
109 *J23* **Villafrati** Sicilia, Italy, C Mediterranean Sea *37.53N 13.30E*
Villagarcía de Arosa *see* Vilagarcía de Arousa
43 *O9* **Villagrán** Tamaulipas, C Mexico *24.28N 99.30W*
63 *C17* **Villaguay** Entre Ríos, E Argentina *31.55S 59.01W*
64 *O6* **Villa Hayes** Presidente Hayes, S Paraguay *25.04S 57.25W*
43 *U15* **Villahermosa** *prev.* San Juan Bautista. Tabasco, SE Mexico *17.56N 92.50W*
107 *O11* **Villahermosa** Castilla-La Mancha, C Spain *38.46N 2.52W*
66 *O11* **Villahermoso** Gomera, Islas Canarias, Spain, NE Atlantic Ocean *38.46N 2.52W*
Villa Hidalgo *see* Hidalgo
107 *T12* **Villajoyosa** *Cat.* La Vila Joíosa. País Valenciano, E Spain *38.31N 0.13W*
Villa Juárez *see* Juárez
Villalba *see* Collado Villalba
43 *N8* **Villaldama** Nuevo León, NE Mexico *26.29N 100.27W*
106 *L5* **Villalón de Campos** Castilla-León, N Spain *42.04N 5.03W*
63 *A25* **Villalonga** Buenos Aires, E Argentina *39.55S 62.34W*
106 *L5* **Villalpando** Castilla-León, N Spain *41.51N 5.25W*
42 *K9* **Villa Madero** *var.* Francisco I.Madero. Durango, C Mexico *24.27N 104.11W*
43 *O9* **Villa Mainero** Tamaulipas, C Mexico *24.32N 99.39W*
Villamaña *see* Villamañán
106 *L4* **Villamañán** *var.* Villamaña. Castilla-León, N Spain *42.19N 5.34W*
64 *L10* **Villa María** Córdoba, C Argentina *32.22S 63.15W*
63 *C17* **Villa María Grande** Entre Ríos, E Argentina *31.39S 59.54W*
59 *K21* **Villa Martín** Potosí, SW Bolivia *20.48S 67.36W*
106 *K15* **Villamartin** Andalucía, S Spain *36.50N 5.39W*
64 *J8* **Villa Mazán** La Rioja, NW Argentina *28.43S 66.25W*
Villa Mercedes *see* Mercedes
Villamil *see* Puerto Villamil
Villa Nador *see* Nador
56 *G5* **Villanueva** La Guajira, N Colombia *10.37N 72.58W*
44 *H5* **Villanueva** Cortés, NW Honduras *15.17N 87.58W*
42 *L11* **Villanueva** Zacatecas, C Mexico *22.24N 102.52W*
44 *I9* **Villa Nueva** Chinandega, NW Nicaragua *12.58N 86.46W*
39 *T11* **Villanueva** New Mexico, SW USA *35.18N 105.20W*
106 *M12* **Villanueva de Córdoba** Andalucía, S Spain *38.19N 4.37W*
107 *O12* **Villanueva del Arzobispo** Andalucía, S Spain *38.10N 3.00W*
106 *K11* **Villanueva de la Serena** Extremadura, W Spain *38.58N 5.48W*
106 *L5* **Villanueva del Campo** Castilla-León, N Spain *41.58N 5.25W*
107 *O11* **Villanueva de los Infantes** Castilla-La Mancha, C Spain *38.45N 3.01W*
63 *C14* **Villa Ocampo** Santa Fe, C Argentina *28.28S 59.22W*
42 *J8* **Villa Ocampo** Durango, C Mexico *26.26N 105.28W*
42 *J7* **Villa Orestes Pereyra** Durango, C Mexico *26.30N 105.38W*

344

◆ Country ● Country Capital ◇ Dependent Territory ○ Dependent Territory Capital ⬖ Administrative Region ✈ International Airport ▲ Mountain ▲▲ Mountain Range ⛰ Volcano ≈ River ◎ Lake ⊠ Reservoir

Villarcayo – Vresse-sur-Semois

107 N3 **Villarcayo** Castilla-León, N Spain 42.55N 3.34W
106 L5 **Villardefrades** Castilla-León, N Spain 41.43N 5.15W
107 S9 **Villar del Arzobispo** País Valenciano, E Spain 39.43N 0.49W
107 Q6 **Villaroya de la Sierra** Aragón, NE Spain 41.28N 1.46W
Villarreal see Vila-real de los Infantes
64 P6 **Villarrica** Guairá, SE Paraguay 25.45S 56.28W
65 G15 **Villarrica, Volcán** 🌋 S Chile 39.28S 71.57W
107 P10 **Villarrobledo** Castilla-La Mancha, C Spain 39.16N 2.36W
107 N10 **Villarrubia de los Ojos** Castilla-La Mancha, C Spain 39.13N 3.36W
20 J17 **Villas** New Jersey, NE USA 39.01N 74.54W
107 O3 **Villasana de Mena** Castilla-León, N Spain 43.04N 3.16W
109 M23 **Villa San Giovanni** Calabria, S Italy 38.12N 15.39E
63 D18 **Villa San José** Entre Ríos, E Argentina 32.12S 58.15W
Villa Sanjurjo see Al-Hoceïma
107 P6 **Villasayas** Castilla-León, N Spain 41.19N 2.36W
109 C20 **Villasimius** Sardegna, Italy, C Mediterranean Sea 39.10N 9.30E
43 N6 **Villa Unión** Coahuila de Zaragoza, NE Mexico 28.18N 100.43W
42 K10 **Villa Unión** Durango, C Mexico 23.58N 104.01W
42 J10 **Villa Unión** Sinaloa, C Mexico 23.13N 106.10W
64 K12 **Villa Valeria** Córdoba, C Argentina 34.21S 64.55W
107 N8 **Villaverde** Madrid, C Spain 40.21N 3.43W
56 F10 **Villavicencio** Meta, C Colombia 4.09N 73.37W
106 L2 **Villaviciosa** Asturias, N Spain 43.28N 5.25W
106 L12 **Villaviciosa de Córdoba** Andalucía, S Spain 38.04N 5.00W
59 L22 **Villazón** Potosí, S Bolivia 22.04S 65.34W
12 J8 **Villebon, Lac** ◎ Québec, SE Canada
Ville de Kinshasa see Kinshasa
104 J5 **Villedieu-les-Poêles** Manche, N France 48.51N 1.12W
Villefranche see Villefranche-sur-Saône
105 N16 **Villefranche-de-Lauragais** Haute-Garonne, S France 43.24N 1.42E
105 N14 **Villefranche-de-Rouergue** Aveyron, S France 44.21N 2.01E
105 R10 **Villefranche-sur-Saône** var. Villefranche. Rhône, E France 46.00N 4.40E
12 H9 **Ville-Marie** Québec, SE Canada 47.21N 79.25W
104 M15 **Villemur-sur-Tarn** Haute-Garonne, S France 43.50N 1.32E
107 S11 **Villena** País Valenciano, E Spain 38.39N 0.52W
Villeneuve-d'Agen see Villeneuve-sur-Lot
104 L13 **Villeneuve-sur-Lot** var. Villeneuve-d'Agen; hist. Gajac. Lot-et-Garonne, SW France 44.24N 0.43E
105 P6 **Villeneuve-sur-Yonne** Yonne, C France 48.04N 3.21E
24 H8 **Ville Platte** Louisiana, S USA 30.41N 92.16W
105 R11 **Villeurbanne** Rhône, E France 45.46N 4.54E
103 G23 **Villingen-Schwenningen** Baden-Württemberg, S Germany 48.04N 8.27E
31 T15 **Villisca** Iowa, C USA 40.55N 94.58W
Villmanstrand see Lappeenranta
Vilna see Vilnius
121 H14 **Vilnius** Pol. Wilno, Ger. Wilna; prev. Rus. Vilna. ● (Lithuania) Vilnius, SE Lithuania 54.41N 25.19E
121 H15 **Vilnius** ◈ province SE Lithuania
121 H14 **Vilnius** ✈ Vilnius, SE Lithuania 54.33N 25.17E
119 S7 **Vil'nohirs'k** Dnipropetrovs'ka Oblast', E Ukraine 48.31N 34.01E
119 U8 **Vil'nyans'k** Zaporiz'ka Oblast', SE Ukraine 47.56N 35.22E
95 L17 **Vilppula** Länsi-Suomi, W Finland 62.01N 24.30E
103 M20 **Vils** ≈ SE Germany
120 C5 **Vilsandi Saar** island W Estonia
119 P8 **Vil'shanka** Rus. Olshanka. Kirovohrads'ka Oblast', C Ukraine 48.12N 30.54E
103 O22 **Vilshofen** Bayern, SE Germany 48.36N 13.10E
161 J20 **Viluppuram** Tamil Nādu, SE India 12.54N 79.40E
115 I16 **Vilusi** Montenegro, SW Serbia and Montenegro (Yugoslavia) 42.44N 18.34E
101 G18 **Vilvoorde** Fr. Vilvorde. Vlaams Brabant, C Belgium 50.55N 4.25E
Vilvorde see Vilvoorde
121 J14 **Vilyeyka** Pol. Wilejka, Rus. Vileyka. Minskaya Voblasts', NW Belarus 54.30N 26.54E
126 Kk11 **Vilyuy** ≈ NE Russian Federation
127 P11 **Vilyuchinsk** Kamchatskaya Oblast', E Russian Federation 52.55N 158.28E
126 L10 **Vilyuysk** Respublika Sakha (Yakutiya), NE Russian Federation 63.42N 121.20E
126 K11 **Vilyuyskoye Vodokhranilishche** ▣ NE Russian Federation
106 G2 **Vimianzo** Galicia, NW Spain 43.06N 9.03W
97 M19 **Vimmerby** Kalmar, S Sweden 57.40N 15.49E
104 L5 **Vimoutiers** Orne, N France 48.56N 0.10E
95 L16 **Vimpeli** Länsi-Suomi, W Finland 63.10N 23.49E
81 G14 **Vina** ≈ Cameroon/Chad
64 G11 **Viña del Mar** Valparaíso, C Chile 33.01S 71.34W
21 R8 **Vinalhaven Island** island Maine, NE USA
107 T8 **Vinaròs** País Valenciano, E Spain 40.28N 0.28E
Vinători see Vânători
33 N15 **Vincennes** Indiana, N USA 38.42N 87.30W
205 Y12 **Vincennes Bay** bay Antarctica
27 O7 **Vincent** Texas, SW USA 32.30N 101.10W
97 H24 **Vindeby** Fyn, C Denmark 54.55N 11.09E
95 I15 **Vindeln** Västerbotten, N Sweden 64.10N 19.45E
97 F21 **Vinderup** Ringkøbing, C Denmark 56.28N 8.48E
Vindhya Mountains see Vindhya Range
159 N14 **Vindhya Range** var. Vindhya Mountains. ▲▲ N India
Vindobona see Wien
22 K6 **Vine Grove** Kentucky, S USA 37.48N 85.58W
20 J17 **Vineland** New Jersey, NE USA 39.28N 75.01W
118 E11 **Vinga** Arad, W Romania 46.00N 21.14E
97 M16 **Vingåker** Södermanland, C Sweden 59.01N 15.52E
178 Jj8 **Vinh** Nghê An, N Vietnam 18.42N 105.40E
106 I5 **Vinhais** Bragança, N Portugal 41.50N 7.00W
178 K9 **Vinh Linh** Quang Tri, C Vietnam 17.02N 107.03E
Vinh Loi see Bac Liêu
178 Jj14 **Vinh Long** var. Vinhlong. Vinh Long, S Vietnam 10.15N 105.58E
115 Q18 **Vinica** NE FYR Macedonia 41.53N 22.30E
111 V13 **Vinica** SE Slovenia 45.28N 15.12E
116 G8 **Vinishte** Montana, NW Bulgaria 43.30N 23.04E
29 Q8 **Vinita** Oklahoma, C USA 36.38N 95.09W
Vinju Mare see Vânju Mare
100 I11 **Vinkeveen** Utrecht, C Netherlands 52.13N 4.55E
118 L6 **Vin'kivtsi** Khmel'nyts'ka Oblast', W Ukraine 49.02N 27.13E
114 I10 **Vinkovci** Ger. Winkowitz, Hung. Vinkovcze. Vukovar-Srijem, E Croatia 45.18N 18.45E
Vinkovcze see Vinkovci
Vinnitsa see Vinnytsya
Vinnitskaya Oblast'/Vinnytsya see Vinnyts'ka Oblast'
118 M7 **Vinnyts'ka Oblast'** var. Vinnytsya, Rus. Vinnitskaya Oblast'. ◈ province C Ukraine
119 N6 **Vinnytsya** Rus. Vinnitsa. Vinnyts'ka Oblast', C Ukraine 49.14N 28.30E
119 N6 **Vinnytsya** ✈ Vinnyts'ka Oblast', N Ukraine 49.13N 28.40E
Vinogradov see Vynohradiv
204 L8 **Vinson Massif** ▲ Antarctica 78.45S 85.19W
96 G11 **Vinstra** Oppland, S Norway 61.36N 9.44E
118 K12 **Vintilă Vodă** Buzău, SE Romania 45.28N 26.44E
31 X13 **Vinton** Iowa, C USA 42.10N 92.01W
24 F9 **Vinton** Louisiana, S USA 30.10N 93.37W
161 J17 **Vinukonda** Andhra Pradesh, E India 16.03N 79.41E
Vioara see Ocnele Mari
85 E23 **Vioolsdrif** Northern Cape, SW South Africa 28.50S 17.38E
111 S12 **Vipava** ≈ SW Slovenia
84 M13 **Viphya Mountains** ▲▲ C Malawi
179 Qq11 **Virac** Catanduanes Island, N Philippines 13.39N 124.17E
128 K8 **Virandozero** Respublika Kareliya, NW Russian Federation 63.59N 36.00E
143 P16 **Viranşehir** Şanlıurfa, SE Turkey 37.13N 39.31E
160 D13 **Virār** Mahārāshtra, W India 19.30N 72.48E
9 W16 **Virden** Manitoba, S Canada 49.49N 100.57W
32 K14 **Virden** Illinois, N USA 39.30N 89.46W
Virdois see Virrat
104 J5 **Vire** Calvados, N France 48.49N 0.52W
104 J4 **Vire** ≈ N France
85 A15 **Virei** Namibe, SW Angola 15.43S 12.54E
Virful Moldoveanu see Vârful Moldoveanu
37 R5 **Virgina Peak** ▲ Nevada, W USA 39.46N 119.26W
47 U9 **Virgin Gorda** island C British Virgin Islands
85 I22 **Virginia** Free State, C South Africa 28.04S 26.51E
32 K13 **Virginia** Illinois, N USA 39.57N 90.12W
31 W4 **Virginia** Minnesota, N USA 47.31N 92.32W
23 T6 **Virginia** off. Commonwealth of Virginia; also known as Mother of Presidents, Mother of States, Old Dominion. ◈ state NE USA
23 Y7 **Virginia Beach** Virginia, NE USA 36.51N 75.58W
35 R11 **Virginia City** Montana, NW USA 45.17N 111.54W
37 Q6 **Virginia City** Nevada, W USA 39.19N 119.39W
12 H8 **Virginiatown** Ontario, S Canada 48.09N 79.35W
Virgin Islands see British Virgin Islands
47 T9 **Virgin Islands (US)** var. Virgin Islands of the United States; prev. Danish West Indies. ◇ US unincorporated territory E West Indies
47 T9 **Virgin Passage** passage Puerto Rico/Virgin Islands (US)
37 Y10 **Virgin River** ≈ Nevada/Utah, W USA
Virihaur see Virihaure
94 H12 **Virihaure** var. Virihaur. ◎ N Sweden
178 Jj11 **Virôchey** Rôtânôkiri, NE Cambodia 13.58N 106.49E
95 N19 **Virolahti** Etelä-Suomi, S Finland 60.33N 27.37E
32 J8 **Viroqua** Wisconsin, N USA 43.33N 90.54W
114 G8 **Virovitica** Ger. Virovititz, Hung. Verőcze; prev. Ger. Werowitz. Virovitica-Podravina, NE Croatia 45.49N 17.25E
114 G8 **Virovitica-Podravina** off. Virovitičko-Podravska Županija. ◈ province NE Croatia
Virovitiz see Virovitica
115 J17 **Virpazar** Montenegro, SW Serbia and Montenegro (Yugoslavia) 42.15N 19.06E
95 L17 **Virrat** Swe. Virdois. Länsi-Suomi, SW Finland 62.13N 23.49E
97 M20 **Virserum** Kalmar, S Sweden 57.17N 15.18E
101 K25 **Virton** Luxembourg, SE Belgium 49.34N 5.31E
120 F5 **Virtsu** Ger. Werder. Läänemaa, W Estonia 58.35N 23.32E
58 C12 **Virú** La Libertad, C Peru 8.27S 78.44W
Virudhunagar see Virudunagar
161 H23 **Virudunagar** var. Virudhunagar. Tamil Nādu, SE India 9.34N 77.57E
120 I3 **Viru-Jaagupi** Ger. Sankt-Jakobi. Lääne-Virumaa, NE Estonia 59.13N 26.28E
59 N19 **Viru-Viru** var. Santa Cruz. ✈ (Santa Cruz) Santa Cruz, C Bolivia 17.49S 63.12W
115 E15 **Vis** It. Lissa; anc. Issa. island S Croatia
Vis see Fish
120 I12 **Visaginas** prev. Sniečkus. Utena, E Lithuania 55.36N 26.22E
161 M15 **Visākhapatnam** Andhra Pradesh, SE India 17.45N 83.19E
37 R11 **Visalia** California, W USA 36.19N 119.19W
Vişău see Vişeu
179 Qq12 **Visayan Sea** sea C Philippines
97 P19 **Visby** Ger. Wisby. Gotland, SE Sweden 57.37N 18.19E
207 N9 **Viscount Melville Sound** prev. Melville Sound. sound Northwest Territories/Nunavut, N Canada
101 L19 **Visé** Liège, E Belgium 50.43N 5.42E
114 K13 **Višegrad** Republika Srpska, E Bosnia and Herzegovina 43.46N 19.18E
60 L12 **Viseu** Pará, NE Brazil 1.10S 46.09W
106 H7 **Viseu** prev. Vizeu. Viseu, N Portugal 40.40N 7.55W
106 H7 **Viseu** var. Vizeu. ◈ district N Portugal
118 I8 **Vişeu** Hung. Visó; prev. Vişău. ≈ NW Romania
118 I8 **Vişeu de Sus** var. Vişeul de Sus, Ger. Oberwischau, Hung. Felsővisó. Maramureş, N Romania 47.43N 23.24E
Vişeul de Sus see Vişeu de Sus
129 R10 **Vishera** ≈ NW Russian Federation
97 J19 **Viskafors** Västra Götaland, S Sweden 57.37N 12.49E
97 J20 **Viskan** ≈ S Sweden
97 L21 **Vislanda** Kronoberg, S Sweden 56.46N 14.30E
Vislinskiy Zaliv see Vistula Lagoon
Visó see Vişeu
114 H13 **Visoko** Federacija Bosna I Hercegovina, C Bosnia and Herzegovina 43.58N 18.12E
108 A9 **Viso, Monte** ▲ NW Italy 44.42N 7.04E
110 E10 **Visp** Valais, SW Switzerland 46.18N 7.52E
110 E10 **Vispa** ≈ S Switzerland
97 M21 **Vissefjärda** Kalmar, S Sweden 56.31N 15.34E
102 I11 **Visselhövede** Niedersachsen, NW Germany 52.58N 9.36E
97 G23 **Vissenbjerg** Fyn, C Denmark 55.22N 10.07E
37 U17 **Vista** California, W USA 33.12N 117.14W
60 C11 **Vista Alegre** Amazonas, NW Brazil 1.23N 68.13W
116 J13 **Vistonída, Límni** ◎ NE Greece
94 K12 **Visttasjohka** ≈ N Sweden
Vistula see Wisła
121 A14 **Vistula Lagoon** Ger. Frisches Haff, Pol. Zalew Wiślany, Rus. Vislinskiy Zaliv. lagoon Poland/Russian Federation
116 I8 **Vit** ≈ NW Bulgaria
Vitebsk see Vitsyebsk
Vitebskaya Oblast' see Vitsyebskaya Voblasts'
109 H14 **Viterbo** anc. Vicus Elbii. Lazio, C Italy 42.25N 12.07E
114 H12 **Vitez** Federacija Bosna I Hercegovina, C Bosnia and Herzegovina 44.08N 17.47E
178 J15 **Vi Thanh** Cân Thơ, S Vietnam 9.45N 105.28E
Viti see Fiji
194 K12 **Vitiaz Strait** strait NE PNG
106 J7 **Vitigudino** Castilla-León, N Spain 41.00N 6.26W
197 H15 **Viti Levu** island W Fiji
126 Kk14 **Vitim** ≈ C Russian Federation
126 Kk13 **Vitimskiy** Irkutskaya Oblast', C Russian Federation 58.12N 113.10E
111 V2 **Vitis** Niederösterreich, N Austria 48.45N 15.09E
Vitória see Vitoria-Gasteiz
61 O20 **Vitória** Espírito Santo, SE Brazil 20.19S 40.21W
Vitoria Bank see Vitória Seamount
61 N18 **Vitória da Conquista** Bahia, E Brazil 14.52S 40.52W
107 P3 **Vitoria-Gasteiz** var. Vitoria, Eng. Vittoria. País Vasco, N Spain 42.51N 2.40W
67 J16 **Vitória Seamount** var. Victoria Bank, Vitoria Bank. undersea feature C Atlantic Ocean 18.48S 37.24W
114 F13 **Vitorog** ▲ SW Bosnia and Herzegovina 44.06N 17.03E
104 J6 **Vitré** Ille-et-Vilaine, NW France 48.07N 1.12W
105 R5 **Vitry-le-François** Marne, N France 48.43N 4.36E
116 D13 **Vítsoi** ▲ N Greece 40.39N 21.23E
120 N13 **Vitsyebsk** Rus. Vitebsk. Vitsyebskaya Voblasts', NE Belarus 55.11N 30.10E
120 K13 **Vitsyebskaya Voblasts'** prev. Rus. Vitebskaya Oblast'. ◈ province N Belarus
94 J11 **Vittangi** Lapp. Vazáš. Norrbotten, N Sweden 67.40N 21.39E
105 R8 **Vitteaux** Côte d'Or, C France 47.24N 4.31E
105 S6 **Vittel** Vosges, NE France 48.13N 5.57E
97 N15 **Vittinge** Västmanland, C Sweden 59.52N 17.04E
109 K25 **Vittoria** Sicilia, Italy, C Mediterranean Sea 36.55N 14.30E
Vittoria see Vitoria-Gasteiz
108 I7 **Vittorio Veneto** Veneto, NE Italy 45.58N 12.18E
183 Q9 **Vitu Levu** island W Fiji
199 Jj7 **Vityaz Seamount** undersea feature C Pacific Ocean 13.30N 173.15W
183 Q7 **Vityaz Trench** undersea feature W Pacific Ocean
110 G8 **Vitznau** Luzern, W Switzerland 47.01N 8.28E
106 I1 **Viveiro** Galicia, NW Spain 43.39N 7.34W
107 S9 **Viver** País Valenciano, E Spain 39.55N 0.36W
105 Q13 **Viverais, Monts du** ▲▲ C France
126 Ii10 **Vivi** ≈ N Russian Federation
24 F4 **Vivian** Louisiana, S USA 32.52N 93.59W
31 N10 **Vivian** South Dakota, N USA 43.53N 100.16W
105 R13 **Viviers** Ardèche, E France 44.31N 4.40E
Vivis see Vevey
85 K19 **Vivo** Limpopo, NE South Africa 22.58S 29.13E
104 L10 **Vivonne** Vienne, W France 46.25N 0.15E
197 G14 **Viwa** island Yasawa Group, NW Fiji
Vizakna see Ocna Sibiului
107 O2 **Vizcaya** Basq. Bizkaia. ◈ province País Vasco, N Spain
Vizcaya, Golfo de see Biscay, Bay of
142 C10 **Vize** Kırklareli, NW Turkey 41.33N 27.49E
126 I2 **Vize, Ostrov** island Severnaya Zemlya, N Russian Federation
Vizeu see Viseu
161 M15 **Vizianagaram** var. Vizianagram. Andhra Pradesh, E India 18.07N 83.25E
Vizianagram see Vizianagaram
105 S12 **Vizille** Isère, E France 45.05N 5.46E
129 R11 **Vizinga** Respublika Komi, NW Russian Federation 61.06N 50.09E
118 M13 **Viziru** Brăila, SE Romania 45.00N 27.43E
115 K21 **Vjosës, Lumi i** var. Vijosa, Vijosë, Gk. Aóos. ≈ Albania/Greece see also Aóos
101 H18 **Vlaams Brabant** ◈ province C Belgium
Vlaanderen see Flanders
100 G12 **Vlaardingen** Zuid-Holland, SW Netherlands 51.55N 4.21E
118 F10 **Vlădeasa, Vârful** prev. Virful Vlădeasa. ▲ NW Romania 46.45N 22.46E
Vlădeasa, Virful see Vlădeasa, Vârful
115 P16 **Vladičin Han** Serbia, SE Serbia and Montenegro (Yugoslavia) 42.44N 22.04E
131 O16 **Vladikavkaz** prev. Dzaudzhikau, Ordzhonikidze. Respublika Severnaya Osetiya, SW Russian Federation 42.58N 44.41E
130 M3 **Vladimir** Vladimirskaya Oblast', W Russian Federation 56.09N 40.21E
150 M7 **Vladimirovka** Kostanay, N Kazakhstan 53.28N 64.01E
Vladimirovka see Yuzhno-Sakhalinsk
130 L3 **Vladimirskaya Oblast'** ◈ province W Russian Federation
130 I3 **Vladimirskiy Tupik** Smolenskaya Oblast', W Russian Federation 55.45N 33.25E
Vladimir-Volynskiy see Volodymyr-Volyns'kyy
127 Nn18 **Vladivostok** Primorskiy Kray, SE Russian Federation 43.09N 131.53E
119 U13 **Vladyslavivka** Respublika Krym, S Ukraine 45.09N 35.25E
100 P6 **Vlagtwedde** Groningen, NE Netherlands 53.01N 7.07E
Vlajna see Kukavica
114 J12 **Vlasenica** Republika Srpska, E Bosnia and Herzegovina 44.10N 18.57E
114 G12 **Vlašić** ▲ C Bosnia and Herzegovina 44.18N 17.40E
113 D17 **Vlašim** Ger. Wlaschim. Středočeský Kraj, C Czech Republic 49.42N 14.54E
115 P15 **Vlasotince** Serbia, SE Serbia and Montenegro (Yugoslavia) 42.58N 22.07E
126 Ll7 **Vlasovo** Respublika Sakha (Yakutiya), NE Russian Federation 70.41N 134.49E
100 I11 **Vleuten** Utrecht, C Netherlands 52.07N 5.01E
100 I5 **Vlieland** Fris. Flylân. island Waddeneilanden, N Netherlands
100 I5 **Vliestroom** strait NW Netherlands
101 J14 **Vlijmen** Noord-Brabant, S Netherlands 51.42N 5.13E
101 E15 **Vlissingen** Eng. Flushing, Fr. Flessingue. Zeeland, SW Netherlands 51.25N 3.34E
Vlodava see Włodawa
Vlonë/Vlora see Vlorë
115 K22 **Vlorë** prev. Vlonë, It. Valona, Vlora. Vlorë, SW Albania 40.27N 19.31E
115 K22 **Vlorë** ◈ district SW Albania
115 K22 **Vlorës, Gjiri i** var. Valona Bay. bay SW Albania
Vlotslavsk see Włocławek
113 C16 **Vltava** Ger. Moldau. ≈ W Czech Republic
130 K3 **Vnukovo** ✈ (Moskva) Gorod Moskva, W Russian Federation 55.30N 36.52E
152 L11 **Vobkent** Rus. Vabkent. Buxoro Viloyati, C Uzbekistan 40.01N 64.25E
27 Q9 **Voca** Texas, SW USA 30.58N 99.09W
111 R5 **Vöcklabruck** Oberösterreich, NW Austria 48.01N 13.37E
114 D13 **Vodice** Šibenik-Knin, S Croatia 43.46N 15.46E
128 K10 **Vodlozero, Ozero** ◎ NW Russian Federation
114 A10 **Vodnjan** It. Dignano d'Istria. Istra, NW Croatia 44.57N 13.51E
129 S9 **Vodnyy** Respublika Komi, NW Russian Federation 63.31N 53.21E
97 G20 **Vodskov** Nordjylland, N Denmark 57.07N 10.01E
94 H4 **Vogar** Sudhurland, SW Iceland 63.58N 22.20W
195 N16 **Vogel, Cape** headland SE PNG 9.42S 150.04E
Vogelkop see Doberai, Jazirah
79 X15 **Vogel Peak** prev. Dim lang. ▲ E Nigeria 8.16N 11.44E
103 H17 **Vogelsberg** ▲▲ C Germany
108 D8 **Voghera** Lombardia, N Italy 44.58N 9.01E
114 I13 **Vogošća** Federacija Bosna I Hercegovina, SE Bosnia and Herzegovina 43.55N 18.20E
103 M17 **Vogtland** historical region E Germany
129 V12 **Vogul'skiy Kamen', Gora** ▲ NW Russian Federation 60.10N 58.41E
197 H6 **Voh** Province Nord, C New Caledonia 20.57S 164.41E
Vohémar see Iharaña
180 H8 **Vohimena, Tanjona** Fr. Cap Sainte Marie. headland S Madagascar 25.20S 45.06E
180 J6 **Vohipeno** Fianarantsoa, SE Madagascar 22.21S 47.51E
120 H5 **Võhma** Ger. Wõchma. Viljandimaa, S Estonia 58.37N 25.34E
83 J20 **Voi** Coast, S Kenya 3.22S 38.34E
78 K15 **Voinjama** N Liberia 8.23N 9.48W
105 S12 **Voiron** Isère, E France 45.22N 5.34E
111 V8 **Voitsberg** Steiermark, SE Austria 47.04N 15.09E
97 F24 **Vojens** Ger. Woyens. Sønderjylland, SW Denmark 55.15N 9.19E
114 K9 **Vojvodina** Ger. Wojwodina. Region N Serbia and Montenegro (Yugoslavia)
13 S6 **Volant** ≈ Québec, SE Canada
Volaterrae see Volterra
45 P15 **Volcán** var. Hato del Volcán. Chiriquí, W Panama 8.45N 82.38W
Volchansk see Vovchans'k
Volchya see Vovcha
96 D10 **Volda** Møre og Romsdal, S Norway 62.07N 6.04E
100 J9 **Volendam** Noord-Holland, C Netherlands 52.30N 5.04E
128 L15 **Volga** Yaroslavskaya Oblast', W Russian Federation 57.56N 38.23E
31 R10 **Volga** South Dakota, N USA 44.19N 96.55W
125 Cc11 **Volga** ≈ NW Russian Federation
Volga-Baltic Waterway see Volgo-Baltiyskiy Kanal
Volga Hills/Volga Uplands see Privolzhskaya Vozvyshennost'
128 L13 **Volgo-Baltiyskiy Kanal** Eng. Volga-Baltic Waterway. canal NW Russian Federation
130 M12 **Volgodonsk** Rostovskaya Oblast', SW Russian Federation 47.34N 42.03E
131 O10 **Volgograd** prev. Stalingrad, Tsaritsyn. Volgogradskaya Oblast', SW Russian Federation 48.42N 44.28E
131 N9 **Volgogradskaya Oblast'** ◈ province SW Russian Federation
131 P10 **Volgogradskoye Vodokhranilishche** ▣ SW Russian Federation
103 J19 **Volkach** Bayern, C Germany 49.51N 10.15E
111 U9 **Völkermarkt** Slvn. Velikovec. Kärnten, S Austria 46.39N 14.37E
128 I12 **Volkhov** Leningradskaya Oblast', NW Russian Federation 59.56N 32.19E
103 D20 **Völklingen** Saarland, SW Germany 49.15N 6.51E
Volkovysk see Vawkavysk
Volkovyskiye Vysoty see Vawkavyskaye Wzvyshsha
85 K22 **Volksrust** Mpumalanga, E South Africa 27.18S 29.53E
100 L8 **Vollenhove** Overijssel, N Netherlands 52.40N 5.58E
121 L16 **Volma** Rus. Volma. ≈ C Belarus
Volmari see Valmiera
119 W9 **Volnovakha** Donets'ka Oblast', SE Ukraine 47.36N 37.32E
118 K6 **Volochys'k** Khmel'nyts'ka Oblast', W Ukraine 49.32N 26.14E
119 O6 **Volodarka** Kyyivs'ka Oblast', N Ukraine 49.31N 29.55E
119 W9 **Volodars'ke** Donets'ka Oblast', E Ukraine 47.11N 37.19E
131 R13 **Volodarskiy** Astrakhanskaya Oblast', SW Russian Federation 46.23N 48.39E
Volodarskoye see Saumalkol'
119 N8 **Volodars'k-Volyns'kyy** Zhytomyrs'ka Oblast', N Ukraine 50.37N 28.28E
118 K3 **Volodymerets'** Rivnens'ka Oblast', NW Ukraine 51.24N 25.52E
118 I3 **Volodymyr-Volyns'kyy** Pol. Włodzimierz, Rus. Vladimir-Volynskiy. Volyns'ka Oblast', NW Ukraine 50.51N 24.19E
128 L14 **Vologda** Vologodskaya Oblast', W Russian Federation 59.10N 39.55E
128 L12 **Vologodskaya Oblast'** ◈ province NW Russian Federation
130 K3 **Volokolamsk** Moskovskaya Oblast', W Russian Federation 56.03N 35.57E
130 K9 **Volokonovka** Belgorodskaya Oblast', W Russian Federation 50.30N 37.54E
117 G16 **Vólos** Thessalía, C Greece 39.21N 22.58E
128 M11 **Voloshka** Arkhangel'skaya Oblast', NW Russian Federation 61.19N 40.06E
Vološinovo see Novi Bečej
118 H7 **Volovets'** Zakarpats'ka Oblast', W Ukraine 48.42N 23.12E
116 K7 **Volovo** Ruse, N Bulgaria 43.33N 25.49E
Volozhin see Valozhyn
131 Q7 **Vol'sk** Saratovskaya Oblast', W Russian Federation 52.04N 47.19E
79 Q17 **Volta** ≈ SE Ghana
Volta Blanche see White Volta
79 P16 **Volta, Lake** ▣ SE Ghana
Volta Noire see Black Volta
62 O9 **Volta Redonda** Rio de Janeiro, SE Brazil 22.31S 44.04W
Volta Rouge see Red Volta
108 F12 **Volterra** anc. Volaterrae. Toscana, C Italy 43.25N 10.51E
109 K17 **Volturno** ≈ S Italy
115 I15 **Volujak** ▲ SW Serbia and Montenegro (Yugoslavia)
Volunteer Island see Starbuck Island
67 F24 **Volunteer Point** headland East Falkland, Falkland Islands 51.31S 57.43W
Volunteer State see Tennessee
116 H13 **Vólvi, Límni** ◎ N Greece
Volyn see Volyns'ka Oblast'
118 I3 **Volyns'ka Oblast'** var. Volyn, Rus. Volynskaya Oblast'. ◈ province NW Ukraine
Volynskaya Oblast' see Volyns'ka Oblast'
131 Q3 **Volzhsk** Respublika Mariy El, W Russian Federation 55.53N 48.21E
131 O10 **Volzhskiy** Volgogradskaya Oblast', SW Russian Federation 48.48N 44.40E
180 I7 **Vondrozo** Fianarantsoa, SE Madagascar 22.49S 47.19E
116 K9 **Voneshta Voda** Veliko Tŭrnovo, N Bulgaria 42.55N 25.40E
41 P10 **Von Frank Mountain** ▲ Alaska, USA 63.36N 154.29W
117 C17 **Vónitsa** Dytikí Ellás, W Greece 38.55N 20.52E
120 J6 **Võnnu** Ger. Wendau. Tartumaa, SE Estonia 58.15N 27.04E
100 G12 **Voorburg** Zuid-Holland, W Netherlands 52.04N 4.22E
100 H11 **Voorschoten** Zuid-Holland, W Netherlands 52.07N 4.25E
100 M11 **Voorst** Gelderland, E Netherlands 52.10N 6.10E
100 K11 **Voorthuizen** Gelderland, C Netherlands 52.12N 5.36E
94 L2 **Vopnafjördhur** Austurland, E Iceland 65.45N 14.51W
94 L2 **Vopnafjördhur** bay E Iceland
Vora see Vorë
121 H15 **Voranava** Pol. Werenów, Rus. Voronovo. Hrodzyenskaya Voblasts', W Belarus 54.10N 25.21E
110 I8 **Vorarlberg** off. Land Vorarlberg. ◈ state W Austria
111 X7 **Vorau** Steiermark, E Austria 47.22N 15.55E
100 N11 **Vorden** Gelderland, E Netherlands 52.07N 6.18E
110 H9 **Vorderrhein** ≈ SE Switzerland
94 J2 **Vordhufell** ▲ N Iceland 65.42N 18.45W
97 I24 **Vordingborg** Storstrøm, SE Denmark 55.01N 11.55E
115 K19 **Vorë** var. Vora. Tiranë, W Albania 41.23N 19.37E
117 H17 **Vóreioi Sporádes** var. Vórioi Sporádhes, Eng. Northern Sporades. island group E Greece
117 J17 **Vóreion Aigaíon** Eng. Aegean North. ◈ region SE Greece
117 G18 **Voreiós Evvoïkós Kólpos** gulf E Greece
207 S16 **Voring Plateau** undersea feature N Norwegian Sea
Vórioi Sporádhes see Vóreioi Sporádes
129 W4 **Vorkuta** Respublika Komi, NW Russian Federation 67.27N 64.00E
97 I14 **Vorma** ≈ S Norway
120 E4 **Vormsi** var. Vormsi Saar, Ger. Worms, Swed. Ormsö. island W Estonia
Vormsi Saar see Vormsi
126 Hh12 **Vorogovo** Krasnoyarskiy Kray, C Russian Federation 61.01N 89.25E
131 N7 **Vorona** ≈ W Russian Federation
130 L7 **Voronezh** Voronezhskaya Oblast', W Russian Federation 51.39N 39.13E
130 L7 **Voronezh** ≈ W Russian Federation
130 K8 **Voronezhskaya Oblast'** ◈ province W Russian Federation
Voronovitsya see Voronovytsya
Voronovo see Voranava
119 N6 **Voronovytsya** Rus. Voronovitsa. Vinnyts'ka Oblast', C Ukraine 49.06N 28.49E
126 Hh7 **Vorontsovo** Taymyrskiy (Dolgano-Nenetskiy) Avtonomnyy Okrug, N Russian Federation 71.45N 83.31E
128 K3 **Voron'ya** ≈ NW Russian Federation
Voropayevo see Varapayeva
Voroshilov see Ussuriysk
Voroshilovgrad see Luhans'k, Ukraine
Voroshilovgrad see Luhans'ka Oblast', Ukraine
Voroshilovgradskaya Oblast' see Luhans'ka Oblast'
Voroshilovsk see Stavropol', Russian Federation
Voroshilovsk see Alchevs'k, Ukraine
143 V13 **Vorotan** Az. Bärgușad. ≈ Armenia/Azerbaijan
131 P3 **Vorotynets** Nizhegorodskaya Oblast', W Russian Federation 56.06N 46.06E
119 S3 **Vorozhba** Sums'ka Oblast', NE Ukraine 51.09N 34.16E
119 T5 **Vorskla** ≈ Russian Federation/Ukraine
101 I17 **Vorst** Antwerpen, N Belgium 51.06N 5.01E
85 G21 **Vorstershoop** North-West, N South Africa 25.46S 22.57E
120 H6 **Võrtsjärv** Ger. Wirz-See. ◎ SE Estonia
120 J7 **Võru** Ger. Werro. Võrumaa, SE Estonia 57.51N 27.00E
153 R11 **Vorukh** N Tajikistan 39.51N 70.34E
120 I7 **Võrumaa** off. Võru Maakond. ◈ province SE Estonia
85 G24 **Vosburg** Northern Cape, W South Africa 30.33S 22.49E
153 Q14 **Vose'** Rus. Vose; prev. Aral. SW Tajikistan 37.51N 69.31E
105 S6 **Vosges** ◈ department NE France
105 U6 **Vosges** ▲▲ NE France
130 L4 **Voskresensk** Moskovskaya Oblast', W Russian Federation 55.19N 38.42E
131 P2 **Voskresenskoye** Nizhegorodskaya Oblast', W Russian Federation 57.00N 45.33E
131 V6 **Voskresenskoye** Respublika Bashkortostan, W Russian Federation 53.07N 56.07E
128 K13 **Voskresenskoye** Vologodskaya Oblast', NW Russian Federation 59.25N 37.56E
96 D13 **Voss** Hordaland, S Norway 60.37N 6.25E
96 D13 **Voss** physical region S Norway
101 I16 **Vosselaar** Antwerpen, N Belgium 51.19N 4.55E
96 D13 **Vosso** ≈ S Norway
Vostochno-Kazakhstanskaya Oblast' see Shygys Konyrat
151 T12 **Vostochno-Kounradskiy** Kaz. Shyghys Qongyrat. Zhezkazgan, C Kazakhstan 47.01N 75.05E
127 N4 **Vostochno-Sibirskoye More** Eng. East Siberian Sea. sea Arctic Ocean
151 X10 **Vostochnyy Kazakhstan** off. Vostochno-Kazakhstanskaya Oblast', var. East Kazakhstan, Kaz. Shyghys Qazaqstan Oblysy. ◈ province E Kazakhstan
Vostochnyy Sayan see Eastern Sayans
Vostock Island see Vostok Island
205 U10 **Vostok** Russian research station Antarctica 77.18S 105.32E
203 X5 **Vostok Island** var. Vostock Island; prev. Stavers Island. island Line Islands, SE Kiribati
131 T2 **Votkinsk** Udmurtskaya Respublika, NW Russian Federation 57.04N 54.00E
129 U15 **Votkinskoye Vodokhranilishche** var. Votkinsk Reservoir. ▣ NW Russian Federation
Votkinsk Reservoir see Votkinskoye Vodokhranilishche
62 J7 **Votuporanga** São Paulo, S Brazil 20.25S 49.52W
106 H7 **Vouga, Rio** ≈ N Portugal
117 E14 **Voúrinos** ▲ N Greece
117 G24 **Voúxa, Akrotírio** headland Kríti, Greece, E Mediterranean Sea 35.37N 23.34E
105 R4 **Vouziers** Ardennes, N France 49.24N 4.42E
119 V7 **Vovcha** Rus. Volchya. ≈ E Ukraine
119 V4 **Vovchans'k** Rus. Volchansk. Kharkivs'ka Oblast', E Ukraine 50.19N 36.54E
105 N6 **Voves** Eure-et-Loir, C France 48.18N 1.39E
81 M14 **Vovodo** ≈ S Central African Republic
96 M12 **Voxna** Gävleborg, C Sweden 61.20N 15.34E
96 L11 **Voxnan** ≈ C Sweden
116 F7 **Voynishka Reka** ≈ NW Bulgaria
129 T9 **Voyvozh** Respublika Komi, NW Russian Federation 62.54N 54.52E
128 M12 **Vozhega** Vologodskaya Oblast', NW Russian Federation 60.27N 40.11E
128 L12 **Vozhe, Ozero** ◎ NW Russian Federation
119 Q9 **Voznesens'k** Rus. Voznesensk. Mykolayivs'ka Oblast', S Ukraine 47.33N 31.22E
128 J12 **Voznesen'ye** Leningradskaya Oblast', NW Russian Federation 61.00N 35.24E
150 J14 **Vozrozhdeniya, Ostrov** Uzb. Wozrojdeniye Oroli. island Kazakhstan/Uzbekistan
97 G20 **Vrå** var. Vraa. Nordjylland, N Denmark 57.21N 9.57E
Vraa see Vrå
116 H9 **Vrachesh** Sofiya, NW Bulgaria 42.52N 23.45E
117 C19 **Vrachíonas** ▲ Zákynthos, Iónioi Nísoi, Greece, C Mediterranean Sea 37.49N 20.43E
119 P8 **Vradiyivka** Mykolayivs'ka Oblast', S Ukraine 47.51N 30.37E
115 G14 **Vran** ▲ SW Bosnia and Herzegovina 43.35N 17.30E
118 K12 **Vrancea** ◈ county E Romania
153 T14 **Vrang** SE Tajikistan 37.03N 72.26E
127 Oo2 **Vrangelya, Ostrov** Eng. Wrangel Island. island NE Russian Federation
114 H13 **Vranica** ▲ C Bosnia and Herzegovina 43.57N 17.43E
115 O16 **Vranje** Serbia, SE Serbia and Montenegro (Yugoslavia) 42.33N 21.55E
Vranov see Vranov nad Topl'ou
113 N19 **Vranov nad Topl'ou** var. Vranov, Hung. Varannó. Prešovský Kraj, E Slovakia 48.54N 21.40E
116 H8 **Vratsa** Vratsa, NW Bulgaria 43.13N 23.33E
116 H8 **Vratsa** ◈ province NW Bulgaria
116 F10 **Vrattsa** prev. Mirovo. Kyustendil, W Bulgaria 42.16N 22.39E
114 G11 **Vrbanja** ≈ NW Bosnia and Herzegovina
114 K9 **Vrbas** Serbia, NW Serbia and Montenegro (Yugoslavia) 45.34N 19.39E
114 G13 **Vrbas** ≈ N Bosnia and Herzegovina
114 E8 **Vrbovec** Zagreb, N Croatia 45.53N 16.24E
114 C9 **Vrbovsko** Primorje-Gorski Kotar, NW Croatia 45.22N 15.06E
113 E15 **Vrchlabí** Ger. Hohenelbe. Královéhradecký Kraj, NE Czech Republic 50.37N 15.37E
85 J22 **Vrede** Free State, E South Africa 27.25S 29.10E
102 E13 **Vreden** Nordrhein-Westfalen, NW Germany 52.01N 6.50E
85 E25 **Vredenburg** Western Cape, SW South Africa 32.55S 18.00E
101 I23 **Vresse-sur-Semois** Namur, SE Belgium 49.52N 4.56E

◆ Country ● Country Capital ◇ Dependent Territory ○ Dependent Territory Capital ◈ Administrative Region ✈ International Airport ▲ Mountain ▲▲ Mountain Range 🌋 Volcano ≈ River ◎ Lake ▣ Reservoir
345

Vretstorp – Warm Springs

97 L16 **Vretstorp** Örebro, C Sweden 59.03N 14.51E
115 G15 **Vrgorac** *prev.* Vrhgorac. Split-Dalmacija, SE Croatia 43.10N 17.24E
Vrhgorac *see* Vrgorac
111 T12 **Vrhnika** *Ger.* Oberlaibach. W Slovenia 45.57N 14.18E
161 I21 **Vriddhāchalam** Tamil Nādu, SE India 11.33N 79.18E
100 N6 **Vries** Drenthe, NE Netherlands 53.04N 6.34E
100 O10 **Vriezenveen** Overijssel, E Netherlands 52.25N 6.39E
97 L20 **Vrigstad** Jönköping, S Sweden 57.19N 14.30E
110 H9 **Vrin** Graubünden, S Switzerland 46.40N 9.06E
114 E13 **Vrlika** Split-Dalmacija, S Croatia 43.54N 16.24E
115 M14 **Vrnjačka Banja** Serbia, C Serbia and Montenegro (Yugoslavia) 43.36N 20.55E
Vrondádhes/Vrondados *see* Vrontádos
117 L18 **Vrontádos** *var.* Vrondados; *prev.* Vrondádhes. Chíos, E Greece 38.25N 26.07E
100 N9 **Vroomshoop** Overijssel, E Netherlands 52.28N 6.34E
114 N10 **Vršac** *Ger.* Werschetz, *Hung.* Versecz. Serbia, NE Serbia and Montenegro (Yugoslavia) 45.08N 21.17E
114 M10 **Vršački Kanal** *canal* N Serbia and Montenegro (Yugoslavia)
85 H21 **Vryburg** North-West, N South Africa 26.57S 24.43E
85 K22 **Vryheid** KwaZulu/Natal, E South Africa 27.45S 30.48E
113 I18 **Vsetín** *Ger.* Wsetin. Zlínský Kraj, E Czech Republic 49.21N 17.57E
113 J20 **Vtáčnik** *Hung.* Madaras, Ptacsnik; *prev.* Ptačnik. ▲ W Slovakia 48.38N 18.38E
Vuadil' *see* Wodil
Vuanggava *see* Vuaqava
197 K15 **Vuaqava** *prev.* Vuanggava. *island* Lau Group, SE Fiji
116 I11 **Vŭcha** ⁓ SW Bulgaria
115 N16 **Vučitrn** Serbia, S Serbia and Montenegro (Yugoslavia) 42.49N 21.00E
101 J14 **Vught** Noord-Brabant, S Netherlands 51.37N 5.19E
119 W8 **Vuhledar** Donets'ka Oblast', E Ukraine 47.48N 37.11E
114 J9 **Vuka** ⁓ E Croatia
115 K17 **Vukël** *var.* Vukli. Shkodër, N Albania 42.29N 19.39E
Vukli *see* Vukël
114 J9 **Vukovar** *Hung.* Vukovár. Vukovar-Srijem, E Croatia 45.18N 18.45E
114 I10 **Vukovar-Srijem** *off.* Vukovarsko-Srijemska Županija. ◈ *province* E Croatia
129 U8 **Vuktyl** Respublika Komi, NW Russian Federation 63.49N 57.07E
9 Q17 **Vulcan** Alberta, SW Canada 50.27N 113.12W
118 G12 **Vulcan** *Ger.* Wulkan, *Hung.* Zsilyvajdevulkán; *prev.* Crivadia Vulcanului, Vaidei, *Hung.* Sily-Vajdej, Vajdej. Hunedoara, W Romania 45.22N 23.16E
118 M12 **Vulcănești** *Rus.* Vulkaneshty. S Moldova 45.41N 28.25E
109 L22 **Vulcano, Isola** *island* Isole Eolie, S Italy
116 G7 **Vŭlchedrŭm** Montana, NW Bulgaria 43.42N 23.25E
116 N8 **Vŭlchidol** *prev.* Kurt-Dere. Varna, NE Bulgaria 43.25N 27.33E
Vulkaneshty *see* Vulcănești
127 P11 **Vulkannyy** Kamchatskaya Oblast', E Russian Federation 53.01N 158.26E
38 J13 **Vulture Mountains** ▲ Arizona, SW USA
178 K14 **Vung Tau** *prev. Fr.* Cape Saint Jacques, Cap Saint-Jacques. Ba Ria-Vung Tau, S Vietnam 10.21N 107.04E
197 I15 **Vunisea** Kadavu, SE Fiji 19.04S 178.09E
Vuohčču *see* Vuotso
95 N15 **Vuokatti** Oulu, C Finland 64.08N 28.16E
95 M15 **Vuolijoki** Oulu, C Finland 64.09N 27.00E
Vuolleriebme *see* Vuollerim
94 J13 **Vuollerim** *Lapp.* Vuolleriebme. Norrbotten, N Sweden 66.24N 20.36E
Vuoreija *see* Vardø
94 L10 **Vuotso** *Lapp.* Vuohčču. Lappi, N Finland 68.04N 27.05E
116 J11 **Vŭrbitsa** *prev.* Filevo. Khaskovo, S Bulgaria 42.02N 25.25E
116 J12 **Vŭrbitsa** ⁓ S Bulgaria
131 Q4 **Vurnary** Chavash Respubliki, W Russian Federation 55.30N 46.59E
116 G8 **Vŭrshets** Montana, NW Bulgaria 43.14N 23.20E
121 F17 **Vyalikaya Byerastavitsa** *Pol.* Brzostowica Wielka, *Rus.* Bol'shaya Berëstovitsa; *prev.* Velikaya Berestovitsa. Hrodzyenskaya Voblasts', SW Belarus 53.12N 24.03E
121 N20 **Vyaliki Bor** *Rus.* Velikiy Bor. Homyel'skaya Voblasts', SE Belarus 52.01N 29.54E
121 J18 **Vyaliki Rozhan** *Rus.* Bol'shoy Rozhan. Minskaya Voblasts', S Belarus 52.46N 27.07E
128 H10 **Vyartsilya** *Fin.* Värtsilä. Respublika Kareliya, NW Russian Federation 62.07N 30.43E
121 K17 **Vyasyeya** *Rus.* Veseya. Minskaya Voblasts', C Belarus 53.04N 27.40E
129 R15 **Vyatka** ⁓ NW Russian Federation
Vyatka *see* Kirov
129 S16 **Vyatskiye Polyany** Kirovskaya Oblast', NW Russian Federation 56.15N 51.06E
127 Nn16 **Vyazemskiy** Khabarovskiy Kray, SE Russian Federation 47.28N 134.39E
130 I4 **Vyaz'ma** Smolenskaya Oblast', W Russian Federation 55.09N 34.20E
131 N3 **Vyazniki** Vladimirskaya Oblast', W Russian Federation 56.15N 42.06E
131 O8 **Vyazovka** Volgogradskaya Oblast', SW Russian Federation 50.57N 43.57E
121 J14 **Vyazyn'** *Rus.* Vyazyn'. Minskaya Voblasts', NW Belarus 54.25N 27.10E
128 G11 **Vyborg** *Fin.* Viipuri. Leningradskaya Oblast', NW Russian Federation 60.44N 28.47E
129 P11 **Vychegda** *var.* Vichegda. ⁓ NW Russian Federation
126 Jj16 **Vydrino** Respublika Buryatiya, S Russian Federation 51.22N 104.34E
121 L14 **Vyelyewshchyna** *Rus.* Velevshchina. Vitsyebskaya Voblasts', N Belarus 54.44N 28.33E
121 P16 **Vyeramyeyki** *Rus.* Veremeyki. Mahilyowskaya Voblasts', E Belarus 53.46N 31.18E
120 K11 **Vyerkhnyadzvinsk** *Rus.* Verkhnedvinsk. Vitsyebskaya Voblasts', N Belarus 55.46N 27.55E
121 P18 **Vyetka** *Rus.* Vetka. Homyel'skaya Voblasts', SE Belarus 52.34N 31.13E
120 L12 **Vyetryna** *Rus.* Vetrino. Vitsyebskaya Voblasts', N Belarus 55.24N 28.28E
Vygonovskoye, Ozero *see* Vyhanawskaye, Vozyera
128 J9 **Vygozero, Ozero** ◎ NW Russian Federation
Vyhanashchanskaye Vozyera *see* Vyhanawskaye, Vozyera
121 I18 **Vyhanawskaye, Vozyera** *var.* Vyhanashchanskaye Vozyera, *Rus.* Ozero Vygonovskoye. ◎ SW Belarus
131 N4 **Vyksa** Nizhegorodskaya Oblast', W Russian Federation 55.21N 42.10E
119 O12 **Vylkove** *Rus.* Vilkovo. Odes'ka Oblast', SW Ukraine 45.24N 29.37E
129 R9 **Vym'** ⁓ NW Russian Federation
118 H8 **Vynohradiv** *Cz.* Sevluš, *Hung.* Nagyszöllős, *Rus.* Vinogradov; *prev.* Sevlyush. Zakarpats'ka Oblast', W Ukraine 48.09N 23.01E
128 G13 **Vyritsa** Leningradskaya Oblast', NW Russian Federation 59.25N 30.20E
99 J19 **Vyrnwy** *Wel.* Afon Efyrnwy. ⁓ E Wales, UK
151 X9 **Vysheivanovskiy Belak, Gora** ▲ E Kazakhstan 50.16N 83.46E
119 P4 **Vyshhorod** Kyyivs'ka Oblast', N Ukraine 50.36N 30.28E
128 I15 **Vyshniy Volochek** Tverskaya Oblast', W Russian Federation 57.37N 34.33E
113 G18 **Vyškov** *Ger.* Wischau. Jihomoravský Kraj, SE Czech Republic 49.16N 16.58E
113 E18 **Vysočina** *prev.* Jihlavský Kraj. ◈ *region* C Czech Republic
113 F17 **Vysoké Mýto** *Ger.* Hohenmauth. Pardubický Kraj, C Czech Republic 49.58N 16.08E
119 S9 **Vysokopillya** Khersons'ka Oblast', S Ukraine 47.28N 33.30E
130 K3 **Vysokovsk** Moskovskaya Oblast', W Russian Federation 56.12N 36.42E
128 K12 **Vytegra** Vologodskaya Oblast', NW Russian Federation 60.59N 36.27E
118 J8 **Vyzhnytsya** Chernivets'ka Oblast', W Ukraine 48.14N 25.10E

W

79 O14 **Wa** NW Ghana 10.07N 2.28W
Waadt *see* Vaud
Waag *see* Váh
Waagbistritz *see* Považská Bystrica
Waagneustadtl *see* Nové Mesto nad Váhom
83 M16 **Waajid** Gedo, SW Somalia 3.37N 43.19E
100 L13 **Waal** ⁓ S Netherlands
197 G4 **Waala** Province Nord, W New Caledonia 19.46S 163.41E
101 I14 **Waalwijk** Noord-Brabant, S Netherlands 51.42N 5.04E
101 E16 **Waarschoot** Oost-Vlaanderen, NW Belgium 51.09N 3.35E
194 G12 **Wabag** Enga, W PNG 5.28S 143.40E
13 N7 **Wabano** ⁓ Québec, SE Canada
9 P11 **Wabasca** ⁓ Alberta, SW Canada
33 P12 **Wabash** Indiana, N USA 40.46N 85.48W
31 X9 **Wabasha** Minnesota, N USA 44.22N 92.01W
33 N13 **Wabash River** ⁓ N USA
12 C7 **Wabatongushi Lake** ◎ Ontario, S Canada
83 L15 **Wabē Gestro Wenz** ⁓ SE Ethiopia
12 B9 **Wabos** Ontario, S Canada 46.48N 84.06W
9 W13 **Wabowden** Manitoba, C Canada 54.57N 98.37W
112 J9 **Wąbrzeźno** Kujawsko-pomorskie, N Poland 53.18N 18.55E
194 G14 **Wabuda Island** *island* SW PNG
23 U12 **Waccamaw River** ⁓ South Carolina, SE USA
25 U11 **Waccasassa Bay** *bay* Florida, SE USA
101 F16 **Wachtebeke** Oost-Vlaanderen, NW Belgium 51.10N 3.52E
27 T8 **Waco** Texas, SW USA 31.33N 97.09W
28 M3 **Waconda Lake** *var.* Great Elder Reservoir. ▣ Kansas, C USA
Wadai *see* Ouaddaï
Wad Al-Hajarah *see* Guadalajara
171 Gg13 **Wadayama** Hyōgo, Honshū, SW Japan 35.19N 134.51E
82 D10 **Wad Banda** Western Kordofan, C Sudan 13.07N 27.55E
77 P9 **Waddān** NW Libya 29.10N 16.07E
100 J4 **Waddeneilanden** *Eng.* West Frisian Islands. *island group* N Netherlands
100 J6 **Waddenzee** *var.* Wadden Zee. *sea* SE North Sea
8 L16 **Waddington, Mount** ▲ British Columbia, SW Canada 51.17N 125.16W
100 H12 **Waddinxveen** Zuid-Holland, C Netherlands 52.03N 4.37E
9 U15 **Wadena** Saskatchewan, S Canada 51.57N 103.48W
31 T6 **Wadena** Minnesota, N USA 46.27N 95.07W
110 G7 **Wädenswil** Zürich, N Switzerland 47.13N 8.39E
23 S11 **Wadesboro** North Carolina, SE USA 34.58N 80.04W
161 G16 **Wādi** Karnātaka, C India 17.00N 76.58E
144 G10 **Wādi as Sīr** *var.* Wadi es Sir. Al 'Āşimah, NW Jordan 31.57N 35.49E
Wadi es Sir *see* Wādi as Sīr
82 F5 **Wadi Halfa** *var.* Wādi Ḩalfā'. Northern, N Sudan 21.46N 31.16E
144 G13 **Wādī Mūsā** *var.* Petra. Ma'ān, S Jordan 30.19N 35.28E
25 V4 **Wadley** Georgia, SE USA 32.52N 82.24W
Wad Madanī *see* Wad Medani
82 G10 **Wad Medani** *var.* Wad Madanī. Gezira, C Sudan 14.24N 33.30E
82 F10 **Wad Nimr** White Nile, C Sudan 14.31N 32.10E
172 Q14 **Wadomari** Kagoshima, Okinoerabu-jima, SW Japan 27.25N 128.40E
113 K17 **Wadowice** Małopolskie, S Poland 49.52N 19.30E
37 R5 **Wadsworth** Nevada, W USA 39.39N 119.16W
33 T12 **Wadsworth** Ohio, N USA 41.01N 81.43W
27 T11 **Waelder** Texas, SW USA 29.42N 97.16W
Waereghem *see* Waregem
169 U13 **Wafangdian** *var.* Fuxian, Fu Xian. Liaoning, NE China 39.36N 122.00E
175 S11 **Waflia** Pulau Buru, E Indonesia 3.09S 126.05E
Wagadugu *see* Ouagadougou
100 K12 **Wageningen** Gelderland, SE Netherlands 51.58N 5.40E
57 V9 **Wageningen** Nickerie, NW Suriname 5.43N 56.45W
15 Ll5 **Wager Bay** *inlet* Nunavut, N Canada
176 Y10 **Wageseri** Papua, E Indonesia 1.48S 138.19E
191 P10 **Wagga Wagga** New South Wales, SE Australia 35.10S 147.22E
188 J13 **Wagin** Western Australia 33.16S 117.25E
Wagina *see* Vaghena
110 H8 **Wägitaler See** ◎ SW Switzerland
31 P12 **Wagner** South Dakota, N USA 43.04N 98.17W
29 Q9 **Wagoner** Oklahoma, C USA 35.57N 95.22W
39 U10 **Wagon Mound** New Mexico, SW USA 36.00N 104.42W
34 J14 **Wagontire** Oregon, NW USA 43.15N 119.51W
112 H10 **Wągrowiec** Wielkopolskie, NW Poland 52.49N 17.10E
155 U6 **Wāh** Punjab, NE Pakistan 33.49N 72.43E
176 U10 **Wahai** Pulau Seram, E Indonesia 2.48S 129.28E
175 O7 **Wahau, Sungai** ⁓ Borneo, C Indonesia
Wahaybah, Ramlat Al *see* Wahībah, Ramlat Āl
82 D13 **Wahda** *var.* Unity State. ◈ *state* S Sudan
40 D9 **Wahiawā** *var.* Wahiawa. O'ahu, Hawai'i, USA, C Pacific Ocean 21.30N 158.01W
Wahībah, Ramlat Ahl *see* Wahībah, Ramlat Āl
147 Y9 **Wahībah, Ramlat Āl** *var.* Ramlat Ahl Wahībah, Ramlat Al Wahaybah, *Eng.* Wahibah Sands. *desert* N Oman
Wahibah Sands *see* Wahībah, Ramlat Āl
103 E16 **Wahn** ✈ (Köln) Nordrhein-Westfalen, W Germany 50.51N 7.09E
31 R15 **Wahoo** Nebraska, C USA 41.12N 96.37W
31 R6 **Wahpeton** North Dakota, N USA 46.16N 96.36W
Wahran *see* Oran
38 J6 **Wah Wah Mountains** ▲ Utah, W USA
40 D9 **Waialua** O'ahu, Hawai'i, USA, C Pacific Ocean 21.34N 158.07W
40 D9 **Wai'anae** *var.* Waianae. O'ahu, Hawai'i, USA, C Pacific Ocean 21.26N 158.11W
192 Q8 **Waiapu** ⁓ North Island, NZ
193 I17 **Waiau** Canterbury, South Island, NZ 42.39S 173.03E
193 I17 **Waiau** ⁓ South Island, NZ
193 B23 **Waiau** ⁓ South Island, NZ
103 H21 **Waiblingen** Baden-Württemberg, S Germany 48.49N 9.19E
Waidhofen *see* Waidhofen an der Ybbs, Niederösterreich, Austria
Waidhofen *see* Waidhofen an der Thaya, Niederösterreich, Austria
111 V2 **Waidhofen an der Thaya** *var.* Waidhofen. Niederösterreich, NE Austria 48.49N 15.16E
111 U5 **Waidhofen an der Ybbs** *var.* Waidhofen. Niederösterreich, E Austria 47.57N 14.47E
176 Uu8 **Waigeo, Pulau** *island* Maluku, E Indonesia
192 L5 **Waiheke Island** *island* N NZ
192 M7 **Waihi** Waikato, North Island, NZ 37.24S 175.49E
193 C20 **Waihou** ⁓ North Island, NZ
Waikaboebak *see* Waikabubak
175 P17 **Waikabubak** *prev.* Waikaboebak. Pulau Sumba, C Indonesia 9.40S 119.25E
193 D23 **Waikaia** ⁓ South Island, NZ
193 D23 **Waikaka** Southland, South Island, NZ 45.55S 168.59E
192 L13 **Waikanae** Wellington, North Island, NZ 40.52S 175.04E
192 M7 **Waikare, Lake** ◎ North Island, NZ
192 O9 **Waikaremoana, Lake** ◎ North Island, NZ
193 I17 **Waikari** Canterbury, South Island, NZ 42.50S 172.41E
192 L8 **Waikato** *off.* Waikato Region. ◈ *region* North Island, NZ
192 M8 **Waikato** ⁓ North Island, NZ
190 J9 **Waikerie** South Australia 34.12S 139.57E
193 F23 **Waikouaiti** Otago, South Island, NZ 45.36S 170.39E
40 H11 **Wailea** Hawai'i, USA, C Pacific Ocean 19.53N 155.07W
40 F10 **Wailuku** Maui, Hawai'i, USA, C Pacific Ocean 20.53N 156.30W
193 H18 **Waimakariri** ⁓ South Island, NZ
40 D9 **Waimānalo Beach** *var.* Waimanalo Beach. O'ahu, Hawai'i, USA, C Pacific Ocean 21.20N 157.42W
193 G15 **Waimangaroa** West Coast, South Island, NZ 41.41S 171.49E
193 G21 **Waimate** Canterbury, South Island, NZ 44.44S 171.03E
40 G11 **Waimea** *var.* Kamuela. Hawai'i, USA, C Pacific Ocean 20.01N 155.39W
40 B8 **Waimea** Kaua'i, Hawai'i, USA, C Pacific Ocean 21.57N 159.39W
40 D9 **Waimea** *var.* Maunawai. O'ahu, Hawai'i, USA, C Pacific Ocean 21.38N 158.03W
101 M20 **Waimes** Liège, E Belgium 50.25N 6.10E
160 J11 **Wainganga** *var.* Wain River. ⁓ C India
Waingapoe *see* Waingapu
175 Pp17 **Waingapu** *prev.* Waingapoe. Pulau Sumba, C Indonesia 9.40S 120.16E
57 S7 **Waini** ⁓ N Guyana
57 S7 **Waini Point** *headland* NW Guyana 8.24N 59.48W
Wain River *see* Wainganga
9 R15 **Wainwright** Alberta, SW Canada 52.49N 110.51W
41 O5 **Wainwright** Alaska, USA 70.38N 160.02W
192 K4 **Waiotira** Northland, North Island, NZ 35.56S 174.11E
192 M11 **Waiouru** Manawatu-Wanganui, North Island, NZ 39.27S 175.40E
176 X11 **Waipa** Papua, E Indonesia 3.47S 136.16E
192 L8 **Waipa** ⁓ North Island, NZ
192 P9 **Waipaoa** ⁓ North Island, NZ
193 D25 **Waipapa Point** *headland* South Island, NZ 46.39S 168.51E
193 I18 **Waipara** Canterbury, South Island, NZ 43.03S 172.44E
192 N12 **Waipawa** Hawke's Bay, North Island, NZ 39.57S 176.35E
192 K4 **Waipu** Northland, North Island, NZ 35.58S 174.25E
192 N12 **Waipukurau** Hawke's Bay, North Island, NZ 40.01S 176.34E
176 Vv13 **Wair** Pulau Kai Besar, E Indonesia 5.16S 133.09E
Wairakai *see* Wairakei
192 N9 **Wairakei** *var.* Wairakai. Waikato, North Island, NZ 38.37S 176.05E
193 M14 **Wairarapa, Lake** ◎ North Island, NZ
193 J15 **Wairau** ⁓ South Island, NZ
192 P10 **Wairoa** Hawke's Bay, North Island, NZ 39.03S 105.25E
192 P10 **Wairoa** ⁓ North Island, NZ
192 J4 **Wairoa** ⁓ North Island, NZ
192 N9 **Waitahanui** Waikato, North Island, NZ 38.48S 176.04E
192 M6 **Waitakaruru** Waikato, North Island, NZ 37.14S 175.22E
193 F21 **Waitaki** ⁓ South Island, NZ
192 K10 **Waitara** Taranaki, North Island, NZ 39.01S 174.14E
192 M7 **Waitoa** Waikato, North Island, NZ 37.36S 175.37E
192 L8 **Waitomo Caves** Waikato, North Island, NZ 38.17S 175.06E
192 L11 **Waitotara** Taranaki, North Island, NZ 39.49S 174.43E
192 L11 **Waitotara** ⁓ North Island, NZ
34 L10 **Waitsburg** Washington, NW USA 46.16N 118.09W
Waitzen *see* Vác
192 L6 **Waiuku** Auckland, North Island, NZ 37.15S 174.44E
171 J12 **Wajima** *var.* Wazima. Ishikawa, Honshū, SW Japan 37.21N 136.53E
83 K17 **Wajir** North Eastern, NE Kenya 1.43N 40.04E
83 I14 **Waka** Southern, SW Ethiopia 7.12N 37.19E
81 J17 **Waka** Equateur, NW Dem. Rep. Congo 1.04N 20.11E
12 D9 **Wakami Lake** ◎ Ontario, S Canada
170 G13 **Wakasa** Tottori, Honshū, SW Japan 35.18N 134.25E
171 H13 **Wakasa-wan** *bay* C Japan
193 C22 **Wakatipu, Lake** ◎ South Island, NZ
9 T15 **Wakaw** Saskatchewan, S Canada 52.40N 105.45W
197 I14 **Wakaya** *island* C Fiji
170 Ff15 **Wakayama** Wakayama, Honshū, SW Japan 34.12N 135.09E
170 G16 **Wakayama** *off.* Wakayama-ken. ◈ *prefecture* Honshū, SW Japan
28 K4 **Wa Keeney** Kansas, C USA 39.01N 99.52W
193 I14 **Wakefield** Tasman, South Island, NZ 41.24S 173.03E
99 M17 **Wakefield** N England, UK 53.42N 1.28W
29 O4 **Wakefield** Kansas, C USA 39.12N 97.00W
32 L4 **Wakefield** Michigan, N USA 46.27N 89.55W
23 U9 **Wake Forest** North Carolina, SE USA 35.58N 78.30W
Wakeham Bay *see* Kangiqsujuaq
201 Y11 **Wake Island** ◇ *US unincorporated territory* NW Pacific Ocean
201 Y12 **Wake Island** ✈ NW Pacific Ocean
201 Y12 **Wake Island** *atoll* NW Pacific Ocean
201 X12 **Wake Lagoon** *lagoon* Wake Island, NW Pacific Ocean
177 Ff9 **Wakema** Irrawaddy, SW Myanmar 16.36N 95.10E
Wakhan *see* Khandūd
170 Ff15 **Waki** Tokushima, Shikoku, SW Japan 34.04N 134.10E
172 N8 **Wakinosawa** Aomori, Honshū, C Japan 41.08N 140.47E
172 Pp1 **Wakkanai** Hokkaidō, NE Japan 45.24N 141.39E
85 K22 **Wakkerstroom** Mpumalanga, E South Africa 27.21S 30.10E
12 C10 **Wakomata Lake** ◎ Ontario, S Canada
191 N10 **Wakool** New South Wales, SE Australia 35.30S 144.22E
Wakra *see* Al Wakrah
Waku Kungo *see* Uaco Cungo
195 S12 **Wakunai** Bougainville Island, NE PNG 5.52S 155.13E
Walachei/Walachia *see* Wallachia
175 Pp12 **Walanae, Sungai** ⁓ Sulawesi, C Indonesia
161 K26 **Walawe Ganga** ⁓ S Sri Lanka
113 F15 **Wałbrzych** *Ger.* Waldenburg, Waldenburg in Schlesien. Dolnośląskie, SW Poland 50.44N 16.19E
191 T6 **Walcha** New South Wales, SE Australia 31.01S 151.38E
103 K24 **Walchensee** ◎ SE Germany
101 D14 **Walcheren** *island* SW Netherlands
31 Z14 **Walcott** Iowa, C USA 41.34N 90.46W
35 W16 **Walcott** Wyoming, C USA 41.46N 106.46W
101 G21 **Walcourt** Namur, S Belgium 50.15N 4.26E
112 G9 **Wałcz** *Ger.* Deutsch Krone. Zachodnio-pomorskie, NW Poland 53.16N 16.28E
110 H7 **Wald** Zürich, N Switzerland 47.16N 8.54E
111 U3 **Waldaist** ⁓ N Austria
188 I9 **Waldburg Range** ▲ Western Australia
39 R3 **Walden** Colorado, C USA 40.43N 106.16W
20 K13 **Walden** New York, NE USA 41.35N 74.09W
Waldenburg/Waldenburg in Schlesien *see* Wałbrzych
9 T15 **Waldheim** Saskatchewan, S Canada 52.38N 106.35W
Waldia *see* Weldiya
103 M23 **Waldkraiburg** Bayern, SE Germany 48.10N 12.23E
29 T14 **Waldo** Arkansas, C USA 33.21N 93.18W
25 V9 **Waldo** Florida, SE USA 29.47N 82.07W
21 R7 **Waldoboro** Maine, NE USA 44.06N 69.22W
23 W4 **Waldorf** Maryland, NE USA 38.36N 76.54W
34 F12 **Waldport** Oregon, NW USA 44.25N 124.04W
29 S11 **Waldron** Arkansas, C USA 34.54N 94.05W
205 Y13 **Waldron, Cape** *headland* Antarctica 66.08S 116.00E
103 F24 **Waldshut-Tiengen** Baden-Württemberg, S Germany 47.37N 8.13E
175 Qq9 **Walea, Selat** *strait* Sulawesi, C Indonesia
Wałeckie Międzyrzecze *see* Valašské Meziříčí
110 H8 **Walensee** ◎ NW Switzerland
40 L8 **Wales** Alaska, USA 65.36N 168.02W
99 J20 **Wales** *Wel.* Cymru. *national region* UK
15 Ll3 **Wales Island** *island* Nunavut, NE Canada
79 P14 **Walewale** N Ghana 10.21N 0.48W
101 M24 **Walferdange** Luxembourg, C Luxembourg 49.39N 6.07E
191 Q5 **Walgett** New South Wales, SE Australia 30.02S 148.13E
204 K10 **Walgreen Coast** *physical region* Antarctica
31 Q2 **Walhalla** North Dakota, N USA 48.55N 97.55W
23 O11 **Walhalla** South Carolina, SE USA 34.45N 83.03W
81 O19 **Walikale** Nord Kivu, E Dem. Rep. Congo 1.28S 28.04E
194 G9 **Walis Island** *island* NW PNG
Walk *see* Valga, Estonia
Walk *see* Valka, Latvia
31 U5 **Walker** Minnesota, N USA 47.06N 94.35W
13 V4 **Walker, Lac** ◎ Québec, SE Canada
37 S7 **Walker Lake** ◎ Nevada, W USA
37 R6 **Walker River** ⁓ Nevada, W USA
30 K10 **Wall** South Dakota, N USA 43.58N 102.12W
181 U9 **Wallaby Plateau** *undersea feature* E Indian Ocean
35 N8 **Wallace** Idaho, NW USA 47.28N 115.55W
23 V11 **Wallace** North Carolina, SE USA 34.42N 77.59W
12 D17 **Wallaceburg** Ontario, S Canada 42.36N 82.22W
24 F5 **Wallace Lake** ▣ Louisiana, S USA
9 P13 **Wallace Mountain** ▲ Alberta, W Canada 54.50N 115.57W
118 J14 **Wallachia** *var.* Walachia, *Ger.* Walachei, *Rom.* Valachia. *cultural region* S Romania
Wallachisch-Meseritsch *see* Valašské Meziříčí
191 U4 **Wallangarra** New South Wales, SE Australia 28.56S 151.57E
190 I8 **Wallaroo** South Australia 33.56S 137.38E
34 L10 **Walla Walla** Washington, NW USA 46.03N 118.20W
47 V9 **Wallblake** ✈ (The Valley) C Anguilla 18.12N 63.02W
103 H19 **Walldürn** Baden-Württemberg, SW Germany 49.34N 9.22E
102 F12 **Wallenhorst** Niedersachsen, NW Germany 52.21N 8.01E
Wallenthal *see* Hațeg
111 S4 **Wallern** Oberösterreich, N Austria 48.13N 13.58E
Wallern *see* Wallern im Burgenland
111 Z5 **Wallern im Burgenland** *var.* Wallern. Burgenland, E Austria 47.43N 16.56E
20 M9 **Wallingford** Vermont, NE USA 43.27N 72.56W
27 V11 **Wallis** Texas, SW USA 29.37N 96.04W
Wallis *see* Valais
199 Jj10 **Wallis and Futuna** *Fr.* Territoire de Wallis et Futuna. ◇ *French overseas territory* C Pacific Ocean
110 G7 **Wallisellen** Zürich, N Switzerland 47.25N 8.36E
202 H11 **Wallis, Îles** *island group* N Wallis and Futuna
101 H19 **Wallon Brabant** ◈ *province* C Belgium
33 Q5 **Walloon Lake** ◎ Michigan, N USA
34 K10 **Wallula** Washington, NW USA 46.03N 118.54W
34 K10 **Wallula, Lake** ◎ Washington, NW USA
23 S8 **Walnut Cove** North Carolina, SE USA 36.18N 80.08W
37 N8 **Walnut Creek** California, W USA 37.52N 122.04W
28 K5 **Walnut Creek** ⁓ Kansas, C USA
29 W9 **Walnut Ridge** Arkansas, C USA 36.06N 90.56W
27 S7 **Walnut Springs** Texas, SW USA 32.05N 97.42W
190 L10 **Walpeup** Victoria, SE Australia 35.09S 142.01E
197 L7 **Walpole, Île** *island* SE New Caledonia
41 N13 **Walrus Islands** *island group* Alaska, USA
99 L19 **Walsall** C England, UK 52.34N 1.58W
39 T7 **Walsenburg** Colorado, C USA 37.37N 104.46W
9 S17 **Walsh** Alberta, SW Canada 49.58N 110.03W
39 W7 **Walsh** Colorado, C USA 37.20N 102.17W
102 I11 **Walsrode** Niedersachsen, NW Germany 52.52N 9.36E
Waltenberg *see* Zalău
23 R14 **Walterboro** South Carolina, SE USA 32.54N 80.40W
Walter F. George Lake *see* Walter F. George Reservoir
25 R6 **Walter F. George Reservoir** *var.* Walter F. George Lake. ▣ Alabama/Georgia, SE USA
28 M12 **Walters** Oklahoma, C USA 34.21N 98.18W
103 J16 **Waltershausen** Thüringen, C Germany 50.53N 10.33E
181 N10 **Walters Shoal** *var.* Walters Shoals. *reef* S Madagascar
Walters Shoals *see* Walters Shoal
24 M3 **Walthall** Mississippi, S USA 33.36N 89.16W
22 M4 **Walton** Kentucky, S USA 38.52N 84.36W
20 J11 **Walton** New York, NE USA 42.10N 75.07W
81 O20 **Walungu** Sud Kivu, E Dem. Rep. Congo 2.40S 28.37E
Walvisbaai *see* Walvis Bay
85 C19 **Walvis Bay** *Afr.* Walvisbaai. Erongo, NW Namibia 22.59S 14.33E
85 B19 **Walvis Bay** *bay* NW Namibia
Walvish Ridge *see* Walvis Ridge
67 O17 **Walvis Ridge** *var.* Walvish Ridge. *undersea feature* E Atlantic Ocean
176 Yy15 **Wamal** Papua, E Indonesia 8.00S 139.06E
176 W13 **Wamar, Pulau** *island* Kepulauan Aru, E Indonesia
79 V15 **Wamba** Nassarawa, C Nigeria 8.57N 8.35E
81 O17 **Wamba** Orientale, NE Dem. Rep. Congo 2.10N 27.58E
81 H22 **Wamba** *var.* Uamba. ⁓ Angola/Dem. Rep. Congo
29 P4 **Wamego** Kansas, C USA 39.12N 96.18W
20 I10 **Wampsville** New York, NE USA 43.03N 75.40W
44 K6 **Wampú, Río** ⁓ E Honduras
176 Xx16 **Wan** Papua, E Indonesia 8.15S 138.00E
Wan *see* Anhui
191 N4 **Wanaaring** New South Wales, SE Australia 29.42S 144.07E
193 D21 **Wanaka** Otago, South Island, NZ 44.42S 169.09E
193 D20 **Wanaka, Lake** ◎ South Island, NZ
176 Ww12 **Wanapiri** Papua, E Indonesia 4.21S 135.52E
12 F9 **Wanapitei** ⁓ Ontario, S Canada
12 F10 **Wanapitei Lake** ◎ Ontario, S Canada
20 K14 **Wanaque** New Jersey, NE USA 41.02N 74.17W
176 V9 **Wanau** Papua, E Indonesia 1.20S 132.40E
193 F22 **Wanbrow, Cape** *headland* South Island, NZ 45.07S 170.59E
Wanchuan *see* Zhangjiakou
176 X11 **Wandai** *var.* Komeyo. Papua, E Indonesia 3.35S 136.15E
169 Z8 **Wanda Shan** ▲ NE China
207 R11 **Wandel Sea** *sea* Arctic Ocean
166 D13 **Wanding** *var.* Wandingzhen. Yunnan, SW China 24.12N 98.05E
Wandingzhen *see* Wanding
176 Z14 **Wandip** Papua, E Indonesia 6.08S 140.47E
101 H20 **Wanfercée-Baulet** Hainaut, S Belgium 50.27N 4.37E
192 L12 **Wanganui** Manawatu-Wanganui, North Island, NZ 39.56S 175.02E
192 L11 **Wanganui** ⁓ North Island, NZ
191 P11 **Wangaratta** Victoria, SE Australia 36.22S 146.16E
166 J8 **Wangcang** *var.* Hongjiang; *prev.* Fengjiaba. Sichuan, C China 32.15N 106.16E
Wangda *see* Zogang
103 I24 **Wangen im Allgäu** Baden-Württemberg, S Germany 47.40N 9.49E
Wangerin *see* Węgorzyno
102 F9 **Wangerooge** *island* NW Germany
176 Ww11 **Wanggar** Papua, E Indonesia 3.22S 135.15E
166 J13 **Wangmo** *var.* Fuxing. Guizhou, S China 25.10N 106.07E
Wangolodougou *see* Ouangolodougou
167 S9 **Wangpan Yang** *sea* E China
169 Y10 **Wangqing** Jilin, NE China 43.19N 129.42E
178 I9 **Wang Saphung** Loei, C Thailand 17.18N 101.45E
177 H6 **Wan Hsa-la** Shan State, E Myanmar 20.27N 98.39E
57 W9 **Wanica** ◈ *district* N Suriname
81 M18 **Wanie-Rukula** Orientale, C Dem. Rep. Congo 0.12N 25.31E
Wankie *see* Hwange
Wanki, Río *see* Coco, Río
83 N17 **Wanlaweyn** *var.* Wanle Weyn, *It.* Uanle Uen. Shabeellaha Hoose, SW Somalia 2.36N 44.47E
Wanle Weyn *see* Wanlaweyn
188 I12 **Wanneroo** Western Australia 31.37S 115.43E
166 L17 **Wanning** Hainan, S China 18.55N 110.27E
178 Ii8 **Wanon Niwat** Sakon Nakhon, E Thailand 17.39N 103.45E
161 H16 **Wanparti** Andhra Pradesh, C India 16.19N 78.06E
Wansen *see* Wiązów
166 L11 **Wanshan** Guizhou, S China 27.45N 109.12E
101 M14 **Wanssum** Limburg, SE Netherlands 51.31N 6.04E
192 N12 **Wanstead** Hawke's Bay, North Island, NZ 40.09S 176.31E
Wanxian *see* Wanzhou
196 F16 **Wanyaan** Yap, Micronesia
166 K8 **Wanyuan** Sichuan, C China 32.04N 108.07E
167 O11 **Wanzai** *var.* Kangle. Jiangxi, S China 28.06N 114.27E
101 J20 **Wanze** Liège, E Belgium 50.32N 5.16E
166 K9 **Wanzhou** *var.* Wanxian. Chongqing Shi, C China 30.48N 108.21E
33 R12 **Wapakoneta** Ohio, N USA 40.34N 84.11W
10 D7 **Wapaseese** ⁓ Ontario, C Canada
34 I10 **Wapato** Washington, NW USA 46.27N 120.25W
31 Y15 **Wapello** Iowa, C USA 41.10N 91.13W
194 H12 **Wapenamanda** Enga, W PNG 5.36S 143.51E
9 N13 **Wapiti** ⁓ Alberta/British Columbia, SW Canada
29 X7 **Wappapello Lake** ▣ Missouri, C USA
20 K13 **Wappingers Falls** New York, NE USA 41.36N 73.54W
31 X13 **Wapsipinicon River** ⁓ Iowa, C USA
194 G14 **Wapumba Island** *island* SW PNG
12 L9 **Wapus** ⁓ Québec, SE Canada
166 H7 **Waqên** Sichuan, C China 33.04N 102.41E
23 Q7 **War** West Virginia, NE USA 37.18N 81.39W
82 D13 **Warab** Warab, SW Sudan 8.13N 28.52E
83 D14 **Warab** ◈ *state* SW Sudan
161 J15 **Warangal** Andhra Pradesh, C India 18.00N 79.35E
Waraşdin *see* Varaždin
191 O16 **Waratah** Tasmania, SE Australia 41.28S 145.34E
191 O14 **Waratah Bay** *bay* Victoria, SE Australia
103 H15 **Warburg** Nordrhein-Westfalen, W Germany 51.30N 9.10E
188 M9 **Warburton** Western Australia 26.17S 126.18E
190 I1 **Warburton Creek** *seasonal river* South Australia
101 M20 **Warche** ⁓ E Belgium
155 P5 **Wardag** *var.* Wardak, *Per.* Vardak. ◈ *province* E Afghanistan
Wardak *see* Wardag
34 K9 **Warden** Washington, NW USA 46.58N 119.02W
160 I12 **Wardha** Mahārāshtra, W India 20.40N 78.40E
194 L14 **Ward Hunt, Cape** *headland* S PNG 8.03S 148.15E
195 N16 **Ward Hunt Strait** *strait* S PNG
123 J16 **Wardija, Ras il-** *var.* Wardija Point. *headland* Gozo, NW Malta 36.03N 14.11E
145 P3 **Wardīyah** N Iraq 36.18N 41.45E
193 E19 **Ward, Mount** ▲ South Island, NZ 43.49S 169.54E
176 Ww9 **Wardo** Papua, E Indonesia 0.54S 135.52E
8 L11 **Ware** British Columbia, W Canada 57.25N 125.40W
101 D18 **Waregem** *var.* Waereghem. West-Vlaanderen, W Belgium 50.52N 3.25E
101 J19 **Waremme** Liège, E Belgium 50.40N 5.15E
102 N10 **Waren** Mecklenburg-Vorpommern, NE Germany 53.31N 12.42E
176 X10 **Waren** Papua, E Indonesia 2.13S 136.21E
103 F14 **Warendorf** Nordrhein-Westfalen, W Germany 51.57N 8.00E
23 P12 **Ware Shoals** South Carolina, SE USA 34.24N 82.15W
100 N4 **Warffum** Groningen, NE Netherlands 53.22N 6.34E
83 O15 **Wargalo** Mudug, E Somalia 6.06N 47.40E
152 M12 **Warganza** *Rus.* Varganzi. Qashqadaryo Viloyati, S Uzbekistan 39.18N 66.00E
Wargla *see* Ouargla
194 K14 **Waria** ⁓ S PNG
191 T4 **Warialda** New South Wales, SE Australia 29.34S 150.35E
160 F13 **Wāri Godri** Mahārāshtra, C India 19.28N 75.43E
176 W11 **Warika** Papua, E Indonesia 3.45S 134.16E
176 W13 **Warilau** Pulau Warilau, E Indonesia 5.19S 134.33E
176 Ww13 **Warilau, Pulau** *island* Kepulauan Aru, E Indonesia
178 J10 **Warin Chamrap** Ubon Ratchathani, E Thailand 15.10N 104.51E
27 R11 **Waring** Texas, SW USA 29.56N 98.48W
41 O8 **Waring Mountains** ▲ Alaska, USA
112 M12 **Warka** Mazowieckie, E Poland 51.45N 21.12E
192 L5 **Warkworth** Auckland, North Island, NZ 36.24S 174.39E
176 V8 **Warmandi** Papua, E Indonesia 0.21S 132.38E
85 E22 **Warmbad** Karas, S Namibia 28.28S 18.40E
100 H8 **Warmenhuizen** Noord-Holland, NW Netherlands 52.43N 4.45E
112 L8 **Warmińsko-Mazurskie** ◈ *province* NW Poland
99 L22 **Warminster** S England, UK 51.13N 2.12W
20 I15 **Warminster** Pennsylvania, NE USA 40.11N 75.04W
37 V8 **Warm Springs** Nevada, W USA 38.10N 116.21W
34 H12 **Warm Springs** Oregon, NW USA 44.51N 121.24W

346

◆ Country ● Country Capital ◇ Dependent Territory ○ Dependent Territory Capital ◈ Administrative Region ✈ International Airport ▲ Mountain ▲ Mountain Range ⚠ Volcano ⁓ River ◎ Lake ▣ Reservoir

Warm Springs – West Lafayette

23 S5 **Warm Springs** Virginia, NE USA 38.02N 79.46W
102 M8 **Warnemünde** Mecklenburg-Vorpommern, NE Germany 54.10N 12.03E
29 Q10 **Warner** Oklahoma, C USA 35.29N 95.18W
37 Q2 **Warner Mountains** ▲ California, W USA
25 T5 **Warner Robins** Georgia, SE USA 32.38N 83.38W
59 N18 **Warnes** Santa Cruz, C Bolivia 17.30S 63.07W
102 M9 **Warnow** ≈ NE Germany
Warnsdorf see Varnsdorf
100 M11 **Warnsveld** Gelderland, E Netherlands 52.07N 6.13E
176 Uu10 **Waropen, Teluk** bay Papua, E Indonesia
160 I13 **Warora** Mahārāshtra, C India 20.12N 79.01E
190 L11 **Warracknabeal** Victoria, SE Australia 36.17S 142.26E
191 O13 **Warragul** Victoria, SE Australia 38.10S 145.55E
191 O4 **Warrego River** seasonal river New South Wales/Queensland, E Australia
191 Q6 **Warren** New South Wales, SE Australia 31.41S 147.51E
9 X16 **Warren** Manitoba, S Canada 50.05N 97.33W
29 V14 **Warren** Arkansas, C USA 33.36N 92.03W
33 S10 **Warren** Michigan, N USA 42.28N 83.01W
31 R3 **Warren** Minnesota, N USA 48.12N 96.46W
33 U11 **Warren** Ohio, N USA 41.14N 80.49W
20 D12 **Warren** Pennsylvania, NE USA 41.52N 79.09W
27 X10 **Warren** Texas, SW USA 30.33N 94.24W
99 G16 **Warrenpoint** Ir. An Pointe. SE Northern Ireland, UK 54.07N 6.15W
29 S4 **Warrensburg** Missouri, C USA 38.45N 93.44W
85 H22 **Warrenton** Northern Cape, N South Africa 28.06S 24.49E
25 U4 **Warrenton** Georgia, SE USA 33.24N 82.39W
29 W4 **Warrenton** Missouri, C USA 38.48N 91.08W
23 V8 **Warrenton** North Carolina, SE USA 36.22N 78.09W
23 V4 **Warrenton** Virginia, NE USA 38.42N 77.48W
79 U17 **Warri** Delta, S Nigeria 5.26N 5.34E
99 L18 **Warrington** C England, UK 53.24N 2.37W
25 O9 **Warrington** Florida, SE USA 30.22N 87.16W
25 P3 **Warrior** Alabama, S USA 33.49N 86.49W
190 L13 **Warrnambool** Victoria, SE Australia 38.22S 142.30E
31 T2 **Warroad** Minnesota, N USA 48.55N 95.18W
191 S6 **Warrumbungle Range** ▲ New South Wales, SE Australia
160 J12 **Wārsa** Mahārāshtra, C India 20.42N 79.58E
33 P11 **Warsaw** Indiana, N USA 41.13N 85.52W
22 L4 **Warsaw** Kentucky, S USA 38.45N 84.51W
29 T5 **Warsaw** Missouri, C USA 38.14N 93.22W
20 E10 **Warsaw** New York, NE USA 42.44N 78.06W
23 V10 **Warsaw** North Carolina, SE USA 35.00N 78.05W
23 X5 **Warsaw** Virginia, NE USA 37.57N 76.45W
Warsaw/Warschau see Warszawa
83 N17 **Warshiikh** Shabeellaha Dhexe, C Somalia 2.22N 45.52E
103 G15 **Warstein** Nordrhein-Westfalen, W Germany 51.27N 8.21E
112 M11 **Warszawa** Eng. Warsaw, Ger. Warschau, Rus. Varshava. ● (Poland) Mazowieckie, C Poland 52.15N 21.00E
112 J13 **Warta** Sieradz, C Poland 51.43N 18.37E
112 D11 **Warta** Ger. Warthe. ≈ W Poland
Wartberg see Senec
22 M9 **Wartburg** Tennessee, S USA 36.06N 84.34W
110 J7 **Warth** Vorarlberg, NW Austria 47.16N 10.11E
Warthe see Warta
175 O9 **Waru** Borneo, C Indonesia 1.24S 116.37E
176 Uu11 **Waru** Pulau Seram, E Indonesia 3.24S 130.38E
145 N6 **Wa'r, Wādī al** dry watercourse E Syria
191 U3 **Warwick** Queensland, E Australia 28.12S 152.00E
13 Q11 **Warwick** Québec, SE Canada 45.55N 72.00W
99 M20 **Warwick** C England, UK 52.16N 1.34W
20 K13 **Warwick** New York, NE USA 41.15N 74.21W
31 P4 **Warwick** North Dakota, N USA 47.49N 98.42W
21 O12 **Warwick** Rhode Island, NE USA 41.40N 71.21W
99 L20 **Warwickshire** cultural region C England, UK
12 G14 **Wasaga Beach** Ontario, S Canada 44.30N 80.00W
79 U13 **Wasagu** Kebbi, NW Nigeria 11.25N 5.48E
38 M2 **Wasatch Range** ▲ W USA
37 R12 **Wasco** California, W USA 35.34N 119.20W
31 V10 **Waseca** Minnesota, N USA 44.04N 93.30W
12 H13 **Washago** Ontario, S Canada 44.46N 79.48W
21 S2 **Washburn** Maine, NE USA 46.46N 68.08W
30 M5 **Washburn** North Dakota, N USA 47.15N 101.02W
32 K3 **Washburn** Wisconsin, N USA 46.40N 90.52W
33 S14 **Washburn Hill** hill Ohio, N USA 39.10N 83.25W
160 H13 **Wāshīm** Mahārāshtra, C India 20.06N 77.08E
99 M14 **Washington** NE England, UK 54.54N 1.31W
25 U3 **Washington** Georgia, SE USA 33.44N 82.44W
32 L12 **Washington** Illinois, N USA 40.42N 89.24W
33 N15 **Washington** Indiana, N USA 38.40N 87.10W
31 X15 **Washington** Iowa, C USA 41.18N 91.41W
29 O3 **Washington** Kansas, C USA 39.46N 97.03W
29 W5 **Washington** Missouri, C USA 38.31N 91.01W
23 X9 **Washington** North Carolina, SE USA 35.33N 77.03W
20 B15 **Washington** Pennsylvania, NE USA 40.10N 80.16W
27 V10 **Washington** Texas, SW USA 30.18N 96.08W
38 J8 **Washington** Utah, W USA 37.07N 113.30W
23 V4 **Washington** Virginia, NE USA 38.40N 78.10W
34 I9 **Washington** off. State of Washington; also known as Chinook State, Evergreen State. ◐ state NW USA
Washington see Washington Court House
33 S14 **Washington Court House** var. Washington. Ohio, NE USA 39.31N 83.25W
23 W4 **Washington DC** ● (USA) District of Columbia, NE USA 38.54N 77.02W
33 O5 **Washington Island** island Wisconsin, N USA
Washington Island see Teraina
21 O7 **Washington, Mount** ▲ New Hampshire, NE USA 44.16N 71.18W
28 M11 **Washita River** ≈ Oklahoma/Texas, C USA
99 O18 **Wash, The** inlet E England, UK
34 L9 **Washtucna** Washington, NW USA 46.44N 118.19W
Wasiliszki see Vasilishki
112 P9 **Wasilków** Podlaskie, NE Poland 53.12N 23.15E
41 R11 **Wasilla** Alaska, USA 61.34N 149.26W
57 U9 **Wasjabo** Sipaliwini, NW Suriname 5.09N 57.09W
9 X11 **Waskaiowaka Lake** ◎ Manitoba, C Canada
9 T14 **Waskesiu Lake** Saskatchewan, C Canada 53.55N 106.04W
27 X7 **Waskom** Texas, SW USA 32.28N 94.03W
112 G13 **Wąsosz** Dolnośląskie, SW Poland 51.36N 16.30E
44 M6 **Waspam** var. Waspán. Región Autónoma Atlántico Norte, NE Nicaragua 14.40N 84.04W
Waspán see Waspam
172 P4 **Wassamu** Hokkaidō, NE Japan 44.01N 142.25E
110 G9 **Wassen** Uri, C Switzerland 46.42N 8.34E
100 G11 **Wassenaar** Zuid-Holland, W Netherlands 52.07N 4.24E
101 N24 **Wasserbillig** Grevenmacher, E Luxembourg 49.43N 6.30E
Wasserburg see Wasserburg am Inn
103 M23 **Wasserburg am Inn** var. Wasserburg. Bayern, SE Germany 48.02N 12.12E
103 I17 **Wasserkuppe** ▲ C Germany 50.30N 9.55E
105 R5 **Wassy** Haute-Marne, N France 48.32N 4.54E
175 Pp12 **Watampone** var. Bone. Sulawesi, C Indonesia 4.31S 120.15E
175 Ss11 **Watawa** Pulau Buru, E Indonesia 3.36S 127.13E
Watenstedt-Salzgitter see Salzgitter
20 M13 **Waterbury** Connecticut, NE USA 41.33N 73.01W
23 R11 **Wateree Lake** ⊠ South Carolina, SE USA
23 R12 **Wateree River** ≈ South Carolina, SE USA
99 E20 **Waterford** Ir. Port Láirge. S Ireland 52.15N 7.07W
33 S9 **Waterford** Michigan, N USA 42.42N 83.24W
99 E20 **Waterford** Ir. Port Láirge. cultural region S Ireland
99 E21 **Waterford Harbour** Ir. Cuan Phort Láirge. inlet S Ireland
100 G12 **Wateringen** Zuid-Holland, W Netherlands 52.01N 4.16E
101 G19 **Waterloo** Wallon Brabant, C Belgium 50.43N 4.24E
12 F16 **Waterloo** Ontario, S Canada 43.28N 80.31W
13 P12 **Waterloo** Québec, SE Canada 45.20N 72.28W
32 K16 **Waterloo** Illinois, N USA 38.20N 90.09W
31 X13 **Waterloo** Iowa, C USA 42.31N 92.16W
20 G10 **Waterloo** New York, NE USA 42.54N 76.51W
32 L4 **Watersmeet** Michigan, N USA 46.16N 89.10W
25 V9 **Watertown** Florida, SE USA 30.11N 82.36W
20 I8 **Watertown** New York, NE USA 43.37N 75.55W
31 R9 **Watertown** South Dakota, N USA 44.54N 97.06W
32 M8 **Watertown** Wisconsin, N USA 43.12N 88.44W
24 L3 **Water Valley** Mississippi, S USA 34.09N 89.37W
29 O3 **Waterville** Kansas, C USA 39.41N 96.45W
19 Ss4 **Waterville** Maine, NE USA 44.34N 69.40W
31 V10 **Waterville** Minnesota, N USA 44.13N 93.34W
20 I10 **Waterville** New York, NE USA 42.55N 75.18W
12 E16 **Watford** Ontario, S Canada 42.57N 81.51W
99 N21 **Watford** SE England, UK 51.39N 0.24W
30 K4 **Watford City** North Dakota, N USA 47.48N 103.16W
147 X12 **Wāṭif** S Oman 18.34N 56.31E
20 G11 **Watkins Glen** New York, NE USA 42.22N 76.52W
Watlings Island see San Salvador
176 V13 **Watnil** Pulau Kai Kecil, E Indonesia 5.45S 132.39E
28 M10 **Watonga** Oklahoma, C USA 35.50N 98.24W
9 T16 **Watrous** Saskatchewan, S Canada 51.40N 105.28W
39 T10 **Watrous** New Mexico, SW USA 35.48N 104.58W
81 P16 **Watsa** Orientale, NE Dem. Rep. Congo 3.00N 29.31E
33 N12 **Watseka** Illinois, N USA 40.46N 87.44W
81 J19 **Watsikengo** Equateur, C Dem. Rep. Congo 0.49S 20.34E
190 C5 **Watson** South Australia 30.32S 131.28E
9 U15 **Watson** Saskatchewan, S Canada 52.13N 104.30W
205 O10 **Watson Escarpment** ▲ Antarctica
8 K9 **Watson Lake** Yukon Territory, W Canada 60.04N 128.46W
37 N10 **Watsonville** California, W USA 36.53N 121.43W
178 I8 **Wattay** ✕ (Viangchan) Viangchan, C Laos 18.03N 102.36E
111 N7 **Wattens** Tirol, W Austria 47.18N 11.37E
22 M9 **Watts Bar Lake** ⊠ Tennessee, S USA
110 H7 **Wattwil** Sankt Gallen, NE Switzerland 47.19N 9.04E
176 Uu12 **Watubela, Kepulauan** island group E Indonesia
103 N24 **Watzmann** ▲ SE Germany 47.32N 12.56E
194 J13 **Wau** Morobe, C PNG 7.18S 146.38E
83 D14 **Wau** var. Wāw. Western Bahr el Ghazal, S Sudan 7.43N 28.01E
31 Q8 **Waubay** South Dakota, N USA 45.19N 97.18W
31 Q8 **Waubay Lake** ◎ South Dakota, N USA
191 U7 **Wauchope** New South Wales, SE Australia 31.30S 152.46E
25 W13 **Wauchula** Florida, SE USA 27.33N 81.48W
32 M10 **Wauconda** Illinois, N USA 42.15N 88.08W
190 J7 **Waukaringa** South Australia 32.19S 139.27E
33 N10 **Waukegan** Illinois, N USA 42.21N 87.50W
32 M9 **Waukesha** Wisconsin, N USA 43.01N 88.13W
31 X11 **Waukon** Iowa, C USA 43.16N 91.28W
32 L8 **Waunakee** Wisconsin, N USA 43.13N 89.28W
32 L7 **Waupaca** Wisconsin, N USA 44.22N 89.04W
32 M8 **Waupun** Wisconsin, N USA 43.40N 88.43W
28 M13 **Waurika** Oklahoma, C USA 34.10N 98.00W
28 M12 **Waurika Lake** ⊠ Oklahoma, C USA
32 L6 **Wausau** Wisconsin, N USA 44.58N 89.40W
33 R11 **Wauseon** Ohio, N USA 41.33N 84.08W
32 L7 **Wautoma** Wisconsin, N USA 44.04N 89.16W
32 M9 **Wauwatosa** Wisconsin, N USA 43.03N 88.03W
24 L9 **Waveland** Mississippi, S USA 30.17N 89.22W
99 Q20 **Waveney** ≈ E England, UK
192 L11 **Waverley** Taranaki, North Island, NZ 39.46S 174.37E
31 W12 **Waverly** Iowa, C USA 42.43N 92.28W
29 T4 **Waverly** Missouri, C USA 39.12N 93.31W
31 R15 **Waverly** Nebraska, C USA 40.56N 96.27W
20 G12 **Waverly** New York, NE USA 42.00N 76.33W
22 H8 **Waverly** Tennessee, S USA 36.04N 87.47W
23 W7 **Waverly** Virginia, NE USA 37.02N 77.06W
101 H19 **Wavre** Wallon Brabant, C Belgium 50.43N 4.37E
177 G8 **Waw** Pegu, SW Myanmar 17.25N 96.40E
Wāw see Wau
12 B7 **Wawa** Ontario, S Canada 47.59N 84.43W
79 T14 **Wawa** Niger, W Nigeria 9.52N 4.33E
77 Q11 **Wāw al Kabīr** S Libya 25.21N 16.40E
45 N7 **Wawa, Río** var. Rio Huahua. ≈ NE Nicaragua
194 G13 **Wawoi** ≈ SW PNG
Wawosungu, Teluk see Staring, Teluk
27 T7 **Waxahachie** Texas, SW USA 32.23N 96.51W
164 J9 **Waxxari** Xinjiang Uygur Zizhiqu, NW China 38.43N 87.11E
197 H14 **Waya** island Yasawa Group, NW Fiji
25 V7 **Waycross** Georgia, SE USA 31.12N 82.21W
188 K10 **Way, Lake** ◎ Western Australia
33 P9 **Wayland** Michigan, N USA 42.40N 85.38W
31 R13 **Wayne** Nebraska, C USA 42.13N 97.01W
20 K14 **Wayne** New Jersey, NE USA 40.57N 74.16W
23 P5 **Wayne** West Virginia, NE USA 38.13N 82.26W
25 V4 **Waynesboro** Georgia, SE USA 33.04N 82.01W
24 M7 **Waynesboro** Mississippi, S USA 31.40N 88.39W
22 H10 **Waynesboro** Tennessee, S USA 35.19N 87.45W
23 U5 **Waynesboro** Virginia, NE USA 38.04N 78.53W
20 B16 **Waynesburg** Pennsylvania, NE USA 39.51N 80.10W
29 U6 **Waynesville** Missouri, C USA 37.49N 92.12W
23 O10 **Waynesville** North Carolina, SE USA 35.29N 82.59W
28 L8 **Waynoka** Oklahoma, C USA 36.36N 98.53W
Wazan see Ouazzane
Wazima see Wajima
155 V7 **Wazīrābād** Punjab, NE Pakistan 32.28N 74.04E
Wazzan see Ouazzane
112 I8 **Wda** var. Czarna Woda, Ger. Schwarzwasser. ≈ N Poland
197 K6 **Wé** Province des Îles Loyauté, E New Caledonia 20.55S 167.15E
99 O23 **Weald, The** lowlands SE England, UK
194 E15 **Weam** Western, SW PNG 8.33S 141.10E
99 L15 **Wear** ≈ N England, UK
Wearmouth see Sunderland
28 L10 **Weatherford** Oklahoma, C USA 35.31N 98.42W
27 S6 **Weatherford** Texas, SW USA 32.45N 97.48W
36 M3 **Weaverville** California, W USA 40.42N 122.57W
29 R7 **Webb City** Missouri, C USA 37.07N 94.28W
198 G9 **Weber Basin** undersea feature S Ceram Sea
Webfoot State see Oregon
20 F9 **Webster** New York, NE USA 43.12N 77.25W
31 Q8 **Webster** South Dakota, N USA 45.19N 97.31W
31 V13 **Webster City** Iowa, C USA 42.28N 93.49W
29 X5 **Webster Groves** Missouri, C USA 38.32N 90.20W
23 S4 **Webster Springs** var. Addison. West Virginia, NE USA 38.27N 80.24W
175 T8 **Weda, Teluk** bay Pulau Halmahera, E Indonesia
67 B25 **Weddell Island** var. Isla San Jose. Island W Falkland Islands
67 K22 **Weddell Plain** undersea feature SW Atlantic Ocean
67 K23 **Weddell Sea** sea SW Atlantic Ocean
67 B25 **Weddell Settlement** Weddell Island, W Falkland Islands 52.52S 60.54W
190 M11 **Wedderburn** Victoria, SE Australia 36.26S 143.37E
102 I9 **Wedel** Schleswig-Holstein, N Germany 53.35N 9.42E
94 N3 **Wedel Jarlsberg Land** physical region SW Svalbard
102 I12 **Wedemark** Niedersachsen, NW Germany 52.33N 9.43E
8 M17 **Wedge Mountain** ▲ British Columbia, SW Canada 50.10N 122.43W
25 R4 **Wedowee** Alabama, S USA 33.16N 85.28W
176 Vv13 **Weduar** Pulau Kai Besar, E Indonesia 5.55S 132.51E
176 Vv14 **Weduar, Tanjung** headland Pulau Kai Besar, SE Indonesia 5.58S 132.49E
37 N2 **Weed** California, W USA 41.26N 122.24W
13 Q12 **Weedon Centre** Québec, SE Canada 45.40N 71.28W
20 E13 **Weedville** Pennsylvania, NE USA 41.15N 78.28W
102 F10 **Weener** Niedersachsen, NW Germany 53.09N 7.19E
31 S16 **Weeping Water** Nebraska, C USA 40.52N 96.08W
101 L16 **Weert** Limburg, SE Netherlands 51.15N 5.43E
100 I10 **Weesp** Noord-Holland, C Netherlands 52.18N 5.03E
191 S5 **Wee Waa** New South Wales, SE Australia 30.16S 149.27E
112 N7 **Węgorzewo** Ger. Angerburg. Warmińsko-Mazurskie, NE Poland 54.12N 21.49E
112 E9 **Węgorzyno** Ger. Wangerin. Zachodnio-pomorskie, NW Poland 53.34N 15.35E
112 N11 **Węgrów** Ger. Bingerau. Mazowieckie, E Poland 52.22N 22.00E
100 N5 **Wehe-Den Hoorn** Groningen, NE Netherlands 53.20N 6.29E
100 M12 **Wehl** Gelderland, E Netherlands 51.58N 6.13E
Wehlau see Znamensk
173 E2 **Weh, Pulau** island NW Indonesia
Wei see Weifang
167 P1 **Weichang** prev. Zhuizishan. Hebei, E China 41.55N 117.45E
Weichsel see Wisła
103 M16 **Weida** Thüringen, C Germany 50.46N 12.05E
Weiden see Weiden in der Oberpfalz
103 M19 **Weiden in der Oberpfalz** var. Weiden. Bayern, SE Germany 49.40N 12.10E
167 Q4 **Weifang** var. Wei, Wei-fang; prev. Weihsien. Shandong, E China 36.43N 119.10E
167 S4 **Weihai** Shandong, E China 37.30N 122.04E
166 K6 **Wei He** ≈ C China
Weihsien see Weifang
103 G17 **Weilburg** Hessen, W Germany 50.31N 8.18E
103 K24 **Weilheim in Oberbayern** Bayern, SE Germany 47.50N 11.09E
191 P4 **Weilmoringle** New South Wales, SE Australia 29.13S 146.51E
103 L16 **Weimar** Thüringen, C Germany 50.58N 11.19E
27 U11 **Weimar** Texas, SW USA 29.42N 96.46W
166 L6 **Weinan** Shaanxi, C China 34.30N 109.30E
110 H6 **Weinfelden** Thurgau, NE Switzerland 47.33N 9.09E
103 I24 **Weingarten** Baden-Württemberg, S Germany 47.49N 9.37E
103 G20 **Weinheim** Baden-Württemberg, SW Germany 49.33N 8.40E
166 H11 **Weining** var. Weining Yizu Huizu Miaozu Zizhixian. Guizhou, S China 26.51N 104.16E
Weining Yizu Huizu Miaozu Zizhixian see Weining
189 V2 **Weipa** Queensland, NE Australia 12.43S 142.01E
9 Y11 **Weir River** Manitoba, C Canada 56.44N 94.06W
23 R1 **Weirton** West Virginia, NE USA 40.25N 80.35W
34 M13 **Weiser** Idaho, NW USA 44.15N 116.58W
166 F12 **Weishan** Yunnan, SW China 25.22N 100.19E
167 P6 **Weishan Hu** ◎ E China
103 M15 **Weisse Elster** Eng. White Elster. ≈ Czech Republic/Germany
Weisse Körös/Weisse Kreisch see Crișul Alb
110 L7 **Weissenbach am Lech** Tirol, W Austria 47.27N 10.39E
103 K21 **Weissenburg in Bayern** Bayern, SE Germany 49.02N 10.58E
Weissenburg see Wissembourg, France
Weissenburg see Alba Iulia, Romania
103 M15 **Weissenfels** var. Weißenfels. Sachsen-Anhalt, C Germany 51.12N 11.58E
111 R9 **Weissensee** ◎ S Austria
Weissenstein see Paide
110 E11 **Weisshorn** var. Flüela Wisshorn. ▲ SW Switzerland 46.06N 7.43E
Weisskirchen see Bela Crkva
25 R3 **Weiss Lake** ⊠ Alabama, S USA
103 Q14 **Weisswasser** Lus. Běla Woda. Sachsen, E Germany 51.30N 14.37E
101 M22 **Weiswampach** Diekirch, N Luxembourg 50.07N 6.04E
111 U2 **Weitra** Niederösterreich, N Austria 48.41N 14.54E
167 O4 **Weixian** var. Wei Xian. Hebei, E China 36.58N 115.15E
165 V11 **Weiyuan** Gansu, C China 35.07N 104.12E
Weiyuan see Shuangjiang
166 F14 **Weiyuan Jiang** ≈ SW China
111 W7 **Weiz** Steiermark, SE Austria 47.13N 15.37E
Weizhou see Wenchuan
166 K16 **Weizhou Dao** island S China
112 I6 **Wejherowo** Pomorskie, NW Poland 54.36N 18.12E
29 Q8 **Welch** Oklahoma, C USA 36.52N 95.06W
26 M6 **Welch** Texas, SW USA 32.52N 102.06W
23 Q6 **Welch** West Virginia, NE USA 37.25N 81.34W
47 O14 **Welchman Hall** C Barbados 13.10N 59.34W
82 J11 **Weldiya** var. Waldia, It. Valdia. Amhara, N Ethiopia 11.45N 39.39E
23 W8 **Weldon** North Carolina, SE USA 36.25N 77.36W
27 V9 **Weldon** Texas, SW USA 31.00N 95.33W
101 M19 **Welkenraedt** Liège, E Belgium 50.40N 5.58E
199 L2 **Welker Seamount** undersea feature N Pacific Ocean 55.07N 140.18W
85 I22 **Welkom** Free State, C South Africa 27.58S 26.43E
12 H16 **Welland** Ontario, S Canada 43.58N 79.13W
12 G16 **Welland** ≈ Ontario, S Canada
99 O19 **Welland** ≈ C England, UK
12 H17 **Welland Canal** canal Ontario, S Canada
161 K25 **Wellawaya** Uva Province, SE Sri Lanka 6.43N 81.07E
Welle see Uele
189 T4 **Wellesley Islands** island group Queensland, N Australia
101 J22 **Wellin** Luxembourg, SE Belgium 50.06N 5.05E
99 N20 **Wellingborough** C England, UK 52.19N 0.42W
191 R7 **Wellington** New South Wales, SE Australia 32.34S 148.55E
12 J15 **Wellington** Ontario, SE Canada 43.57N 77.24W
193 L14 **Wellington** ● (NZ) Wellington, North Island, NZ 41.16S 174.46E
85 E26 **Wellington** Western Cape, SW South Africa 33.39S 19.00E
39 T2 **Wellington** Colorado, C USA 40.42N 105.00W
29 N7 **Wellington** Kansas, C USA 37.16N 97.22W
37 R7 **Wellington** Nevada, W USA 38.45N 119.22W
33 T11 **Wellington** Ohio, N USA 41.10N 82.13W
27 P3 **Wellington** Texas, SW USA 34.51N 100.12W
38 M4 **Wellington** Utah, W USA 39.31N 110.45W
193 M14 **Wellington** off. Wellington Region. ◐ region North Island, NZ
193 L14 **Wellington** ✕ Wellington, North Island, NZ 41.19S 174.48E
Wellington see Wellington, Isla
65 F22 **Wellington, Isla** var. Wellington. island S Chile
191 P12 **Wellington, Lake** ◎ Victoria, SE Australia
31 X14 **Wellman** Iowa, C USA 41.27N 91.50W
26 M6 **Wellman** Texas, SW USA 33.03N 102.25W
99 K22 **Wells** SW England, UK 51.13N 2.39W
31 V11 **Wells** Minnesota, N USA 43.45N 93.43W
37 X2 **Wells** Nevada, W USA 41.06N 114.57W
27 W8 **Wells** Texas, SW USA 31.28N 94.54W
20 F12 **Wellsboro** Pennsylvania, NE USA 41.43N 77.39W
23 R1 **Wellsburg** West Virginia, NE USA 40.16N 80.36W
192 K4 **Wellsford** Auckland, North Island, NZ 36.17S 174.30E
188 L9 **Wells, Lake** ◎ Western Australia
189 N4 **Wells, Mount** ▲ Western Australia 17.39S 127.08E
99 P18 **Wells-next-the-Sea** E England, UK 52.58N 0.48E
33 T15 **Wellston** Ohio, N USA 39.07N 82.31W
29 O10 **Wellston** Oklahoma, C USA 35.41N 97.03W
20 E11 **Wellsville** New York, NE USA 42.06N 77.55W
33 V12 **Wellsville** Ohio, N USA 40.36N 80.39W
38 L1 **Wellsville** Utah, W USA 41.38N 111.55W
38 I14 **Wellton** Arizona, SW USA 32.40N 114.09W
111 S4 **Wels** anc. Ovilava. Oberösterreich, N Austria 48.10N 14.01E
101 K15 **Welschap** ✕ (Eindhoven) Noord-Brabant, S Netherlands 51.27N 5.22E
102 P10 **Welse** ≈ NE Germany
24 H9 **Welsh** Louisiana, S USA 30.12N 92.49W
99 K19 **Welshpool** Wel. Y Trallwng. E Wales, UK 52.38N 3.06W
99 O21 **Welwyn Garden City** SE England, UK 51.48N 0.13W
81 K18 **Wema** Equateur, NW Dem. Rep. Congo 0.25S 21.33E
83 G21 **Wembere** ≈ C Tanzania
9 N13 **Wembley** Alberta, W Canada 55.07N 119.12W
10 I9 **Wemindji** prev. Nouveau-Comptoir, Paint Hills. Québec, C Canada 53.00N 78.42W
101 G18 **Wemmel** Vlaams Brabant, C Belgium 50.54N 4.18E
34 J8 **Wenatchee** Washington, NW USA 47.49N 120.48W
166 M17 **Wenchang** Hainan, S China 19.34N 110.46E
167 R11 **Wencheng** var. Daxue. Zhejiang, SE China 27.48N 120.01E
79 P16 **Wenchi** W Ghana 7.45N 2.01W
Wen-chou/Wenchow see Wenzhou
166 H8 **Wenchuan** var. Weizhou. Sichuan, C China 31.29N 103.39E
Wendau see Võnnu
Wenden see Cēsis
167 S4 **Wendeng** Shandong, E China 37.14N 122.06E
83 J14 **Wendo** Southern, S Ethiopia 6.34N 38.28E
38 J2 **Wendover** Utah, W USA 40.41N 114.00W
12 D9 **Wenebegon** ≈ Ontario, S Canada
12 D8 **Wenebegon Lake** ◎ Ontario, S Canada
110 E9 **Wengen** Bern, W Switzerland 46.38N 7.57E
167 O13 **Wengyuan** var. Longxian. Guangdong, S China 24.22N 114.06E
201 P15 **Weno** prev. Moen. Chuuk, C Micronesia
201 V12 **Weno** prev. Moen. atoll Chuuk Islands, C Micronesia
164 N13 **Wenquan** Qinghai, C China 33.16N 91.43E
165 H4 **Wenquan** var. Arixang. Xinjiang Uygur Zizhiqu, NW China 45.00N 81.02E
Wenquan see Yingshan
166 H14 **Wenshan** var. Kaihua. Yunnan, SW China 23.22N 104.21E
164 H6 **Wensu** Xinjiang Uygur Zizhiqu, W China 41.15N 80.10E
190 L8 **Wentworth** New South Wales, SE Australia 34.04S 141.53E
29 W4 **Wentzville** Missouri, C USA 38.48N 90.51W
165 V12 **Wenxian** var. Wen Xian. Gansu, C China 32.57N 104.42E
167 S10 **Wenzhou** var. Wen-chou, Wenchow. Zhejiang, SE China 28.02N 120.36E
36 L4 **Weott** California, W USA 40.19N 123.57W
101 I20 **Wépion** Namur, SE Belgium 50.24N 4.53E
102 O11 **Werbellinsee** ◎ NE Germany
101 L21 **Werbomont** Liège, E Belgium 50.22N 5.43E
85 G20 **Werda** Kgalagadi, S Botswana 25.13S 23.16E
Werder see Virtsu
83 N14 **Werdēr** Somali, E Ethiopia 6.59N 45.20E
Werenów see Voranava
176 V11 **Weri** Papua, E Indonesia 3.10S 132.39E
100 I13 **Werkendam** Noord-Brabant, S Netherlands 51.48N 4.54E
103 M20 **Wernberg-Köblitz** Bayern, SE Germany 49.31N 12.10E
103 J18 **Werneck** Bayern, C Germany 50.00N 10.06E
103 K14 **Wernigerode** Sachsen-Anhalt, C Germany 51.51N 10.48E
Werowitz see Virovitica
103 J16 **Werra** ≈ C Germany
191 N12 **Werribee** Victoria, SE Australia 37.55S 144.39E
191 T6 **Werris Creek** New South Wales, SE Australia 31.22S 150.40E
Werro see Võru
Werschetz see Vršac
103 K23 **Wertach** ≈ S Germany
103 I19 **Wertheim** Baden-Württemberg, SW Germany 49.45N 9.31E
100 J8 **Wervershoof** Noord-Holland, NW Netherlands 52.43N 5.09E
Wervicq see Wervik
101 C18 **Wervik** var. Wervicq, Werwick. West-Vlaanderen, W Belgium 50.46N 3.03E
Werwick see Wervik
103 D14 **Wesel** Nordrhein-Westfalen, W Germany 51.40N 6.37E
Weseli an der Lainsitz see Veselí nad Lužnicí
Wesenberg see Rakvere
102 H12 **Weser** ≈ NW Germany
Wes-Kaap see Western Cape
27 S17 **Weslaco** Texas, SW USA 26.09N 97.59W
12 J13 **Weslemkoon Lake** ◎ Ontario, S Canada
189 R1 **Wessel Islands** island group Northern Territory, N Australia
31 P9 **Wessington** South Dakota, N USA 44.27N 98.40W
31 P10 **Wessington Springs** South Dakota, N USA 44.02N 98.33W
27 T8 **West** Texas, SW USA 31.48N 97.05W
West see Ouest
32 M9 **West Allis** Wisconsin, N USA 43.01N 88.00W
190 E8 **Westall, Point** headland South Australia 32.54S 134.04E
West Antarctica see Lesser Antarctica
12 G11 **West Arm** Ontario, S Canada 46.16N 80.25W
West Azerbaijan see Āzarbāyjān-e Gharbī
144 F10 **West Bank** disputed region SW Asia
9 N17 **Westbank** British Columbia, SW Canada 49.50N 119.37W
12 E11 **West Bay** Manitoulin Island, Ontario, S Canada 45.48N 82.09W
24 L11 **West Bay** bay Louisiana, S USA
32 M8 **West Bend** Wisconsin, N USA 43.25N 88.13W
159 R16 **West Bengal** ◐ state NE India
West Borneo see Kalimantan Barat
31 Y14 **West Branch** Iowa, C USA 41.40N 91.21W
33 R7 **West Branch** Michigan, N USA 44.16N 84.13W
20 F13 **West Branch Susquehanna River** ≈ Pennsylvania, NE USA
99 L20 **West Bromwich** C England, UK 52.28N 1.59W
21 P8 **Westbrook** Maine, NE USA 43.42N 70.21W
31 T10 **Westbrook** Minnesota, N USA 44.02N 95.26W
31 Y15 **West Burlington** Iowa, C USA 40.49N 91.09W
98 L2 **West Burra** island NE Scotland, UK
32 J8 **Westby** Wisconsin, N USA 43.39N 90.52W
46 L6 **West Caicos** island W Turks and Caicos Islands
193 A24 **West Cape** headland South Island, NZ 45.51S 166.26E
182 L4 **West Caroline Basin** undersea feature SW Pacific Ocean
20 I16 **West Chester** Pennsylvania, NE USA 39.56N 75.35W
193 E18 **West Coast** off. West Coast Region. ◐ region South Island, NZ
27 V12 **West Columbia** Texas, SW USA 29.08N 95.39W
31 W10 **West Concord** Minnesota, N USA 44.09N 92.54W
31 V14 **West Des Moines** Iowa, C USA 41.33N 93.42W
39 Q6 **West Elk Peak** ▲ Colorado, C USA 38.43N 107.12W
46 F1 **West End** Grand Bahama Island, N Bahamas 26.36N 78.55W
46 F1 **West End Point** headland Grand Bahama Island, N Bahamas 26.40N 78.58W
100 O7 **Westerbork** Drenthe, NE Netherlands 52.49N 6.36E
100 N3 **Westereems** strait Germany/Netherlands
100 O9 **Westerhaar-Vriezenveensewijk** Overijssel, E Netherlands 52.28N 6.38E
102 G6 **Westerland** Schleswig-Holstein, N Germany 54.54N 8.19E
101 I17 **Westerlo** Antwerpen, N Belgium 51.05N 4.55E
21 N13 **Westerly** Rhode Island, NE USA 41.22N 71.45W
83 G18 **Western** ◐ province W Kenya
159 N11 **Western** ◐ zone C Nepal
194 E14 **Western** ◐ province SW PNG
195 T14 **Western** off. Western Province. ◐ province NW Solomon Islands
85 G15 **Western** ◐ province SW Zambia
188 K8 **Western Australia** ◐ state W Australia
82 A13 **Western Bahr el Ghazal** ◐ state SW Sudan
Western Bug see Bug
85 F25 **Western Cape** off. Western Cape Province, Afr. Wes-Kaap. ◐ province SW South Africa
82 A11 **Western Darfur** ◐ state W Sudan
Western Desert see Sahara el Gharbîya
120 G9 **Western Dvina** Bel. Dzvina, Ger. Düna, Latv. Daugava, Rus. Zapadnaya Dvina. ≈ W Europe
83 D15 **Western Equatoria** ◐ state SW Sudan
161 E16 **Western Ghats** ▲ SW India
194 G12 **Western Highlands** ◐ province C PNG
Western Isles see Outer Hebrides
82 C12 **Western Kordofan** ◐ state C Sudan
23 T3 **Westernport** Maryland, NE USA 39.29N 79.03W
161 J26 **Western Province** ◐ province SW Sri Lanka
76 B10 **Western Sahara** ◇ disputed territory N Africa
Western Samoa see Samoa
Western Sayans see Zapadnyy Sayan
Western Scheldt see Westerschelde
Western Sierra Madre see Madre Occidental, Sierra
101 E15 **Westerschelde** Eng. Western Scheldt; prev. Honte. inlet S North Sea
33 S13 **Westerville** Ohio, N USA 40.07N 82.55W
103 F17 **Westerwald** ▲ W Germany
67 C25 **West Falkland** var. Gran Malvina, Isla Gran Malvina. island W Falkland Islands
31 R5 **West Fargo** North Dakota, N USA 46.49N 96.51W
196 M15 **West Fayu Atoll** atoll Caroline Islands, C Micronesia
20 C11 **Westfield** New York, NE USA 42.18N 79.34W
32 L7 **Westfield** Wisconsin, N USA 43.56N 89.31W
West Flanders see West-Vlaanderen
29 S10 **West Fork** Arkansas, C USA 35.55N 94.11W
31 P16 **West Fork Big Blue River** ≈ Nebraska, C USA
31 U12 **West Fork Des Moines River** ≈ Iowa/Minnesota, C USA
27 S5 **West Fork Trinity River** ≈ Texas, SW USA
32 L16 **West Frankfort** Illinois, N USA 37.54N 88.55W
100 I8 **West-Friesland** physical region NW Netherlands
West Frisian Islands see Waddeneilanden
21 T5 **West Grand Lake** ◎ Maine, NE USA
20 M12 **West Hartford** Connecticut, NE USA 41.44N 72.45W
20 M13 **West Haven** Connecticut, NE USA 41.16N 72.57W
29 X12 **West Helena** Arkansas, C USA 34.33N 90.38W
30 M2 **Westhope** North Dakota, N USA 48.54N 101.01W
205 Y8 **West Ice Shelf** ice shelf Antarctica
49 R2 **West Indies** island group SE North America
West Irian see Papua
West Java see Jawa Barat
38 L3 **West Jordan** Utah, W USA 40.37N 111.55W
West Kalimantan see Kalimantan Barat
101 D14 **Westkapelle** Zeeland, SW Netherlands 51.32N 3.26E
33 O13 **West Lafayette** Indiana, N USA 40.24N 86.54W

◆ Country
● Country Capital
◇ Dependent Territory
○ Dependent Territory Capital
◐ Administrative Region
✕ International Airport
▲ Mountain
▲ Mountain Range
⩓ Volcano
≈ River
◎ Lake
⊠ Reservoir

WEST LAFAYETTE – WINSTON

33 T13 West Lafayette Ohio, N USA 40.16N 81.45W
West Lake see Kagera
31 Y14 West Liberty Iowa, C USA 41.34N 91.15W
23 O5 West Liberty Kentucky, S USA 38.04N 83.22W
Westliche Morava see Zapadna Morava
15 I13 Westlock Alberta, SW Canada 54.12N 113.49W
12 E17 West Lorne Ontario, S Canada 42.36N 81.34W
98 J12 West Lothian cultural region S Scotland, UK
101 H16 Westmalle Antwerpen, N Belgium 51.18N 4.40E
199 H6 West Mariana Basin var. Perece Vela Basin. undersea feature W Pacific Ocean
99 E17 Westmeath Ir. An Iarmhí, Na h-Iarmhidhe. cultural region C Ireland
29 Y11 West Memphis Arkansas, C USA 35.09N 90.11W
23 W2 Westminster Maryland, NE USA 39.34N 77.00W
23 O11 Westminster South Carolina, SE USA 34.39N 83.06W
24 I5 West Monroe Louisiana, S USA 32.31N 92.09W
20 D15 Westmont Pennsylvania, NE USA 40.16N 78.55W
29 O3 Westmoreland Kansas, C USA 39.23N 96.30W
37 W17 Westmorland California, W USA 33.02N 115.37W
194 L11 West New Britain ◈ province E PNG
West New Guinea see Papua
85 K18 West Nicholson Matabeleland South, S Zimbabwe 21.06S 29.23E
31 T14 West Nishnabotna River ~ Iowa, C USA
183 P11 West Norfolk Ridge undersea feature W Pacific Ocean
27 P12 West Nueces River ~ Texas, SW USA
West Nusa Tenggara see Nusa Tenggara Barat
31 T11 West Okoboji Lake ◎ Iowa, C USA
35 R16 Weston Idaho, NW USA 42.01N 119.29W
23 R4 Weston West Virginia, NE USA 39.02N 80.28W
99 J22 Weston-super-Mare SW England, UK 51.21N 2.58W
25 Z14 West Palm Beach Florida, SE USA 26.43N 80.03W
West Papua see Papua
196 E9 West Passage passage Babeldaob, N Palau
25 O9 West Pensacola Florida, SE USA 30.25N 87.16W
29 V8 West Plains Missouri, C USA 36.43N 91.51W
37 P7 West Point California, W USA 38.21N 120.33W
25 R5 West Point Georgia, SE USA 32.52N 85.10W
24 M3 West Point Mississippi, S USA 33.36N 88.39W
31 R14 West Point Nebraska, C USA 41.50N 96.42W
23 X6 West Point Virginia, NE USA 37.31N 76.48W
190 G10 West Point headland South Australia 35.01S 135.58E
67 B24 Westpoint Island Settlement Westpoint Island, NW Falkland Islands 51.21S 60.40W
25 R4 West Point Lake ⊠ Alabama/Georgia, SE USA
99 B16 Westport Ir. Cathair na Mart. W Ireland 53.48N 9.31W
193 G15 Westport West Coast, South Island, NZ 41.46S 171.37E
34 F10 Westport Oregon, NW USA 46.07N 123.22W
34 F9 Westport Washington, NW USA 46.53N 124.06W
33 S15 West Portsmouth Ohio, N USA 38.45N 83.01W
West Punjab see Punjab
9 V14 Westray Manitoba, C Canada 53.30N 101.19W
98 J4 Westray island NE Scotland, UK
12 F9 Westree Ontario, S Canada 47.25N 81.32W
99 L16 West Riding cultural region N England, UK
West River see Xi Jiang
32 J7 West Salem Wisconsin, N USA 43.54N 91.04W
67 H21 West Scotia Ridge undersea feature W Scotia Sea
West Sepik see Sandaun
181 N4 West Sheba Ridge undersea feature W Indian Ocean
West Siberian Plain see Zapadno-Sibirskaya Ravnina
33 S11 West Sister Island island Ohio, N USA
West-Skylge see West-Terschelling
West Sumatra see Sumatera Barat
100 J5 West-Terschelling Fris. West-Skylge. Friesland, N Netherlands 53.22N 5.14E
66 J7 West Thulean Rise undersea feature N Atlantic Ocean
31 X12 West Union Iowa, C USA 42.57N 91.48W
33 R15 West Union Ohio, N USA 38.47N 83.33W
23 R3 West Union West Virginia, NE USA 39.18N 80.46W
33 N13 Westville Illinois, N USA 40.02N 87.38W
23 R3 West Virginia off. State of West Virginia; also known as The Mountain State. ◈ state NE USA
101 A17 West-Vlaanderen Eng. West Flanders. ◈ province W Belgium
37 R7 West Walker River ~ California/Nevada, W USA
37 P4 Westwood California, W USA 40.18N 121.02W
191 P9 West Wyalong New South Wales, SE Australia 33.56S 147.10E
179 N14 West York Island island N Spratly Islands
175 S15 Wetar, Pulau island Kepulauan Damar, E Indonesia
175 Ss16 Wetar, Selat var. Wetar Strait. strait Nusa Tenggara, S Indonesia
Wetar Strait see Wetar, Selat
9 Q15 Wetaskiwin Alberta, SW Canada 52.57N 113.19W
83 K21 Wete Pemba, E Tanzania 5.03S 39.40E
177 G4 Wetlet Sagaing, C Myanmar 22.21N 95.49E
39 T6 Wet Mountains ▲▲ Colorado, C USA
103 E15 Wetter Nordrhein-Westfalen, W Germany 51.22N 7.24E
103 H17 Wetter ~ W Germany
101 F17 Wetteren Oost-Vlaanderen, NW Belgium 51.06N 3.58E
110 F7 Wettingen Aargau, N Switzerland 47.30N 8.14E
29 P11 Wetumka Oklahoma, C USA 35.14N 96.14W
25 Q5 Wetumpka Alabama, S USA 32.32N 86.12W
110 G7 Wetzikon Zürich, N Switzerland 47.19N 8.48E
103 G17 Wetzlar Hessen, W Germany 50.33N 8.30E
101 C18 Wevelgem West-Vlaanderen, W Belgium 50.48N 3.12E
40 M6 Wevok var. Wewuk. Alaska, USA 68.52N 166.05W
25 R9 Wewahitchka Florida, SE USA 30.06N 85.12W
194 G10 Wewak East Sepik, NW PNG 3.32S 143.36E
29 O11 Wewoka Oklahoma, C USA 35.09N 96.29W
Wewuk see Wevok
99 F20 Wexford Ir. Loch Garman. SE Ireland 52.21N 6.31W
99 F20 Wexford Ir. Loch Garman. cultural region SE Ireland
32 L7 Weyauwega Wisconsin, N USA 44.16N 88.54W
9 U17 Weyburn Saskatchewan, S Canada 49.39N 103.51W
Weyer see Weyer Markt
111 U5 Weyer Markt var. Weyer. Oberösterreich, N Austria 47.52N 14.39E
102 H11 Weyhe Niedersachsen, NW Germany 53.00N 8.52E
99 L24 Weymouth S England, UK 50.36N 2.28W
21 P11 Weymouth Massachusetts, NE USA 42.13N 70.56W
101 H18 Wezembeek-Oppem Vlaams Brabant, C Belgium 50.51N 4.28E
100 M9 Wezep Gelderland, E Netherlands 52.28N 6.00E
192 M9 Whakamaru Waikato, North Island, NZ 38.27S 175.48E
192 O8 Whakatane Bay of Plenty, North Island, NZ 37.58S 105.00E
192 O8 Whakatane ~ North Island, NZ
15 L7 Whale Cove Nunavut, C Canada 62.13N 92.10W
98 M2 Whalsay island NE Scotland, UK
192 L11 Whangaehu ~ North Island, NZ
192 M6 Whangamata Waikato, North Island, NZ 37.13S 175.51E
192 Q9 Whangara Gisborne, North Island, NZ 38.34S 178.12E
192 K3 Whangarei Northland, North Island, NZ 35.44S 174.18E
192 K3 Whangaruru Harbour inlet North Island, NZ
27 V12 Wharton Texas, SW USA 29.19N 96.08W
181 U8 Wharton Basin var. West Australian Basin. undersea feature E Indian Ocean
193 E18 Whataroa West Coast, South Island, NZ 43.16S 170.19E
15 Hh7 Wha Ti prev. Lac La Martre. Northwest Territories, W Canada 63.10N 117.12W
192 K6 Whatipu Auckland, North Island, NZ 37.17S 174.44E
35 Y16 Wheatland Wyoming, C USA 42.03N 104.57W
12 D18 Wheatley Ontario, S Canada 42.06N 82.27W
32 M10 Wheaton Illinois, N USA 41.52N 88.06W
31 R7 Wheaton Minnesota, N USA 45.48N 96.30W
39 T4 Wheat Ridge Colorado, C USA 39.44N 105.06W
27 P2 Wheeler Texas, SW USA 35.26N 100.16W
25 O2 Wheeler Lake ⊠ Alabama, S USA
37 Y6 Wheeler Peak ▲ Nevada, W USA 39.00N 114.17W
39 T9 Wheeler Peak ▲ New Mexico, SW USA 36.34N 105.25W
33 S15 Wheelersburg Ohio, N USA 38.43N 82.51W
23 R2 Wheeling West Virginia, NE USA 40.03N 80.43W
99 L16 Whernside ▲ N England, UK 54.13N 2.27W
190 F9 Whidbey, Point headland South Australia 34.36S 135.08E
188 I7 Whim Creek Western Australia 20.51S 117.54E
8 L17 Whistler British Columbia, SW Canada 50.07N 122.57W
23 W8 Whitakers North Carolina, SE USA 36.06N 77.43W
12 H15 Whitby Ontario, S Canada 43.53N 78.54W
99 N15 Whitby N England, UK 54.28N 0.37W
8 G6 White ~ Yukon Territory, W Canada
11 T11 White Bay bay Newfoundland and Labrador, E Canada
22 I8 White Bluff Tennessee, S USA 36.06N 87.13W
30 J6 White Butte ▲ North Dakota, N USA 46.23N 103.18W
21 R5 White Cap Mountain ▲ Maine, NE USA 45.33N 69.15W
24 J9 White Castle Louisiana, S USA 30.10N 91.09W
190 M5 White Cliffs New South Wales, SE Australia 30.52S 143.04E
33 P8 White Cloud Michigan, N USA 43.34N 85.46W
9 P14 Whitecourt Alberta, SW Canada 54.10N 115.37W
27 O2 White Deer Texas, SW USA 35.26N 101.10W
White Elster see Weisse Elster
26 M5 Whiteface Texas, SW USA 33.36N 102.36W
20 K7 Whiteface Mountain ▲ New York, NE USA 44.22N 73.54W
31 W5 Whiteface Reservoir ⊠ Minnesota, N USA
35 O7 Whitefish Montana, NW USA 48.24N 114.20W
33 N9 Whitefish Bay Wisconsin, N USA 43.09N 87.54W
33 Q3 Whitefish Bay lake bay Canada/USA
12 E11 Whitefish Falls Ontario, S Canada 46.06N 81.42W
12 B7 Whitefish Lake ◎ Ontario, S Canada
31 U6 Whitefish Lake ◎ Minnesota, C USA
33 Q3 Whitefish Point headland Michigan, N USA 46.46N 84.57W
33 O4 Whitefish River ~ Michigan, N USA
27 O4 Whiteflat Texas, SW USA 34.06N 100.55W
29 V12 White Hall Arkansas, C USA 34.18N 92.05W
32 K14 White Hall Illinois, N USA 39.26N 90.24W
33 O8 Whitehall Michigan, N USA 43.24N 86.21W
20 L9 Whitehall New York, NE USA 43.33N 73.24W
33 S13 Whitehall Ohio, N USA 39.58N 82.53W
32 J7 Whitehall Wisconsin, N USA 44.22N 91.19W
99 J15 Whitehaven NW England, UK 54.33N 3.34W
8 I8 Whitehorse territory capital Yukon Territory, W Canada 60.40N 135.07W
192 O7 White Island island NE NZ
12 K13 White Lake ◎ Ontario, SE Canada
24 H10 White Lake ◎ Louisiana, S USA
195 N12 Whiteman Range ▲▲ New Britain, E PNG
191 Q15 Whitemark Tasmania, SE Australia 40.10S 148.01E
37 S9 White Mountains ▲▲ California/Nevada, W USA
21 N7 White Mountains ▲▲ Maine/New Hampshire, NE USA
82 F11 White Nile ◈ state C Sudan
69 U7 White Nile var. Bahr el Jebel. ~ S Sudan
83 E14 White Nile Ar. Al Baḥr al Abyaḍ, An Nil al Abyaḍ, Bahr el Jebel. ~ SE Sudan
27 W5 White Oak Creek ~ Texas, SW USA
8 H9 White Pass pass Canada/USA 59.35N 135.05W
34 I9 White Pass pass Washington, NW USA 46.38N 121.23W
23 O9 White Pine Tennessee, S USA 36.06N 83.17W
20 K14 White Plains New York, NE USA 41.01N 73.45W
27 O5 White River ~ Texas, SW USA
30 M11 White River South Dakota, N USA 43.34N 100.45W
29 W12 White River ~ Arkansas, SE USA
39 P3 White River ~ Colorado/Utah, C USA
33 N15 White River ~ Indiana, N USA
33 O8 White River ~ Michigan, N USA
30 K11 White River ~ South Dakota, N USA
20 M8 White River ~ Vermont, NE USA
39 N13 Whiteriver Arizona, SW USA 33.50N 109.57W
27 O5 White River Lake ⊠ Texas, SW USA
34 H11 White Salmon Washington, NW USA 45.43N 121.29W
20 I10 Whitesboro New York, NE USA 43.07N 75.17W
27 T5 Whitesboro Texas, SW USA 33.39N 96.54W
23 O7 Whitesburg Kentucky, S USA 37.16N 82.55W
White Sea see Beloye More
White Sea-Baltic Canal/White Sea Canal see Belomorsko-Baltiyskiy Kanal
65 I25 Whiteside, Canal channel S Chile
35 S10 White Sulphur Springs Montana, NW USA 46.33N 110.54W
23 R6 White Sulphur Springs West Virginia, NE USA 37.48N 80.18W
22 J6 Whitesville Kentucky, S USA 37.40N 86.48W
34 I10 White Swan Washington, NW USA 46.22N 120.46W
23 U12 Whiteville North Carolina, SE USA 34.20N 78.42W
22 F10 Whiteville Tennessee, S USA 35.19N 89.09W
79 Q13 White Volta var. Nakambé, Fr. Volta Blanche. ~ Burkina/Ghana
32 M9 Whitewater Wisconsin, N USA 42.51N 88.43W
39 P14 Whitewater Baldy ▲ New Mexico, SW USA 33.19N 108.38W
25 X17 Whitewater Bay bay Florida, SE USA
33 Q14 Whitewater River ~ Indiana/Ohio, N USA
9 V16 Whitewood Saskatchewan, S Canada 50.19N 102.16W
30 J9 Whitewood South Dakota, N USA 44.27N 103.38W
27 U5 Whitewright Texas, SW USA 33.30N 96.23W
99 I15 Whithorn S Scotland, UK 54.43N 4.26W
192 M6 Whitianga Waikato, North Island, NZ 36.49S 175.42E
21 N11 Whitinsville Massachusetts, NE USA 42.06N 71.40W
22 M8 Whitley City Kentucky, S USA 36.40N 84.28W
23 Q11 Whitmire South Carolina, SE USA 34.30N 81.36W
33 R10 Whitmore Lake Michigan, N USA 42.26N 83.44W
205 N9 Whitmore Mountains ▲▲ Antarctica
12 I12 Whitney Ontario, SE Canada 45.29N 78.11W
27 T8 Whitney Texas, SW USA 31.56N 97.20W
27 S8 Whitney, Lake ⊠ Texas, SW USA
37 S11 Whitney, Mount ▲ California, W USA 37.45N 119.55W
189 Y6 Whitsunday Group island group Queensland, E Australia
27 S6 Whitt Texas, SW USA 32.55N 98.01W
31 U12 Whittemore Iowa, C USA 43.03N 94.25W
41 R12 Whittier Alaska, USA 60.46N 148.40W
37 T15 Whittier California, W USA 33.58N 118.01W
85 I25 Whittlesea Eastern Cape, S South Africa 32.08S 26.51E
22 K10 Whitwell Tennessee, S USA 35.12N 85.31W
15 J9 Wholdaia Lake ◎ Northwest Territories, NW Canada
190 H7 Whyalla South Australia 33.04S 137.34E
Whydah see Ouidah
12 F13 Wiarton Ontario, S Canada 44.44N 81.09W
175 Q11 Wiau Sulawesi, C Indonesia 3.08S 121.22E
113 H15 Wiązów Ger. Wansen. Dolnośląskie, SW Poland 50.49N 17.13E
35 Y8 Wibaux Montana, NW USA 46.57N 104.11W
29 N6 Wichita Kansas, C USA 37.41N 97.20W
27 R5 Wichita Falls Texas, SW USA 33.54N 98.29W
28 L11 Wichita Mountains ▲▲ Oklahoma, C USA
28 R5 Wichita River ~ Texas, SW USA
98 K6 Wick N Scotland, UK 58.25N 3.06W
38 K13 Wickenburg Arizona, SW USA 33.57N 112.41W
26 L8 Wickett Texas, SW USA 31.34N 103.00W
188 I7 Wickham Western Australia 20.40S 117.11E
190 M14 Wickham, Cape headland Tasmania, SE Australia 39.36S 143.55E
22 G7 Wickliffe Kentucky, S USA 37.14N 89.16W
99 G19 Wicklow Ir. Cill Mhantáin. E Ireland 52.58N 6.03W
99 F19 Wicklow Ir. Cill Mhantáin. cultural region E Ireland
99 G19 Wicklow Head Ir. Ceann Chill Mhantáin. headland E Ireland 52.57N 6.00W
99 F18 Wicklow Mountains Ir. Sléibhte Chill Mhantáin. ▲▲ E Ireland
12 H10 Wicksteed Lake ◎ Ontario, S Canada
Wida see Ouidah
67 G15 Wideawake Airfield ✈ (Georgetown) SW Ascension Island
195 P11 Wide Bay bay New Britain, PNG
175 Tt9 Widi, Kepulauan island group E Indonesia
99 K18 Widnes C England, UK 53.22N 2.43W
112 H9 Więcbork Ger. Vandsburg. Kujawsko-pomorskie, C Poland 53.21N 17.31E
103 E17 Wied ~ W Germany
103 F16 Wiehl Nordrhein-Westfalen, W Germany 50.57N 7.33E
113 L17 Wieliczka Małopolskie, S Poland 50.00N 20.02E
112 G12 Wielkopolskie ◈ province C Poland
113 J14 Wieluń Sieradz, C Poland 51.13N 18.33E
111 X4 Wien Eng. Vienna, Hung. Bécs, Slvk. Vídeň, Slvn. Dunaj; anc. Vindobona. ● (Austria) Wien, NE Austria 48.13N 16.22E
111 X4 Wien off. Land Wien, Eng. Vienna. ◈ state NE Austria
111 X5 Wiener Neustadt Niederösterreich, E Austria 47.49N 16.07E
112 G7 Wieprza Ger. Wipper. ~ NW Poland
100 O10 Wierden Overijssel, E Netherlands 52.22N 6.34E
100 I7 Wieringerwerf Noord-Holland, NW Netherlands 52.51N 5.01E
Wieruschow see Wieruszów
113 I14 Wieruszów Ger. Wieruschow. Łódzkie, C Poland 51.18N 18.09E
111 V9 Wies Steiermark, SE Austria 46.40N 15.16E
Wiesbachhorn see Grosses Wiesbachhorn
103 G18 Wiesbaden Hessen, W Germany 50.06N 8.13E
Wieselburg and Ungarisch-Altenburg/Wieselburg-Ungarisch-Altenburg see Mosonmagyaróvár
Wiesenhof see Ostrołęka
103 G20 Wiesloch Baden-Württemberg, SW Germany 49.18N 8.42E
102 F10 Wiesmoor Niedersachsen, NW Germany 53.22N 7.46E
112 I7 Wieżyca Ger. Turmberg. hill Pomorskie, N Poland 54.13N 18.06E
99 L17 Wigan NW England, UK 53.33N 2.37W
39 U3 Wiggins Colorado, C USA 40.11N 104.03W
24 M8 Wiggins Mississippi, S USA 30.50N 89.09W
Wigorna Ceaster see Worcester
99 I14 Wigtown S Scotland, UK 54.52N 4.26W
99 H14 Wigtown cultural region SW Scotland, UK
99 I15 Wigtown Bay bay SW Scotland, UK
100 L13 Wijchen Gelderland, SE Netherlands 51.48N 5.43E
94 N1 Wijdefjorden fjord NW Svalbard
100 M10 Wijhe Overijssel, E Netherlands 52.22N 6.07E
100 J12 Wijk bij Duurstede Utrecht, C Netherlands 51.58N 5.21E
100 J13 Wijk en Aalburg Noord-Brabant, S Netherlands 51.46N 5.06E
101 H16 Wijnegem Antwerpen, N Belgium 51.13N 4.31E
12 E11 Wikwemikong Manitoulin Island, Ontario, S Canada 45.46N 81.43W
110 H7 Wil Sankt Gallen, NE Switzerland 47.28N 9.03E
31 R16 Wilber Nebraska, C USA 40.28N 96.57W
34 K8 Wilbur Washington, NW USA 47.45N 118.42W
29 Q11 Wilburton Oklahoma, C USA 34.55N 95.18W
190 M6 Wilcannia New South Wales, SE Australia 31.34S 143.23E
20 D12 Wilcox Pennsylvania, NE USA 41.34N 78.40W
Wilczek Land see Vil'cheka, Zemlya
111 U6 Wildalpen Steiermark, E Austria 47.40N 14.54E
33 O13 Wildcat Creek ~ Indiana, N USA
110 L9 Wilde Kreuzspitze It. Picco di Croce. ▲ Austria/Italy 46.53N 10.51E
Wildenschwert see Ústí nad Orlicí
100 O6 Wildervank Groningen, NE Netherlands 53.04N 6.52E
102 G11 Wildeshausen Niedersachsen, NW Germany 52.54N 8.26E
110 D10 Wildhorn ▲ SW Switzerland 46.21N 7.22E
9 R17 Wild Horse Alberta, SW Canada 49.00N 110.19W
29 N12 Wildhorse Creek ~ Oklahoma, C USA
30 L14 Wild Horse Hill ▲ Nebraska, C USA 41.52N 101.56W
111 W8 Wildon Steiermark, SE Austria 46.53N 15.29E
26 M2 Wildorado Texas, SW USA 35.12N 102.10W
31 R6 Wild Rice River ~ Minnesota/North Dakota, N USA
Wilejka see Vilyeyka
205 Y9 Wilhelm II Coast physical region Antarctica
205 X9 Wilhelm II Land physical region Antarctica
57 U11 Wilhelmina Gebergte ▲▲ C Suriname
20 B13 Wilhelm, Lake ⊠ Pennsylvania, NE USA
194 I12 Wilhelm, Mount ▲ C PNG 5.51S 147.25E
94 O2 Wilhelmøya island C Svalbard
Wilhelm-Pieck-Stadt see Guben
111 W4 Wilhelmsburg Niederösterreich, E Austria 48.07N 15.36E
102 G10 Wilhelmshaven Niedersachsen, NW Germany 53.31N 8.07E
Wilia/Wilja see Neris
20 H13 Wilkes Barre Pennsylvania, NE USA 41.15N 75.49W
23 R9 Wilkesboro North Carolina, SE USA 36.09N 81.09W
205 W15 Wilkes Coast physical region Antarctica
201 W12 Wilkes Island island N Wake Island
205 X12 Wilkes Land physical region Antarctica
9 S15 Wilkie Saskatchewan, S Canada 52.27N 108.42W
204 I6 Wilkins Ice Shelf ice shelf Antarctica
190 D4 Wilkinson Lakes salt lake South Australia
Wilkomierz see Ukmergė
190 K11 Willalooka South Australia 36.24S 140.20E
34 G11 Willamette River ~ Oregon, NW USA
191 O8 Willandra Billabong Creek seasonal river New South Wales, SE Australia
34 F9 Willapa Bay inlet Washington, NW USA
29 T7 Willard Missouri, C USA 37.18N 93.25W
39 S12 Willard New Mexico, SW USA 34.36N 106.01W
33 S12 Willard Ohio, N USA 41.03N 82.43W
38 L1 Willard Utah, W USA 41.23N 112.01W
195 N11 Willaumez Peninsula headland New Britain, E PNG 5.03S 150.04E
39 N15 Willcox Arizona, SW USA 32.13N 109.49W
39 N16 Willcox Playa salt flat Arizona, SW USA
101 G17 Willebroek Antwerpen, C Belgium 51.04N 4.22E
47 P16 Willemstad ○ (Netherlands Antilles) Curaçao, Netherlands Antilles 12.06N 68.54W
101 G14 Willemstad Noord-Brabant, S Netherlands 51.40N 4.27E
9 S11 William ~ Saskatchewan, C Canada
25 O6 William "Bill" Dannelly Reservoir ⊠ Alabama, S USA
190 G3 William Creek South Australia 28.55S 136.23E
189 T15 William, Mount ▲ South Australia
38 K11 Williams Arizona, SW USA 35.15N 112.11W
31 X14 Williamsburg Iowa, C USA 41.39N 92.00W
22 M8 Williamsburg Kentucky, S USA 36.43N 84.06W
33 R15 Williamsburg Ohio, N USA 39.00N 84.02W
23 X6 Williamsburg Virginia, NE USA 37.16N 76.41W
8 M15 Williams Lake British Columbia, SW Canada 52.07N 122.09W
23 P6 Williamson West Virginia, NE USA 37.40N 82.16W
33 N13 Williamsport Indiana, N USA 40.18N 87.18W
20 G13 Williamsport Pennsylvania, NE USA 41.13N 76.59W
23 W9 Williamston North Carolina, SE USA 35.51N 77.03W
23 P11 Williamston South Carolina, SE USA 34.37N 82.28W
22 M4 Williamstown Kentucky, S USA 38.38N 84.33W
20 L10 Williamstown Massachusetts, NE USA 42.41N 73.11W
20 J16 Willingboro New Jersey, NE USA 40.01N 74.52W
9 Q14 Willingdon Alberta, SW Canada 53.49N 112.08W
27 W10 Willis Texas, SW USA 30.25N 95.28W
110 F8 Willisau Luzern, W Switzerland 47.07N 8.00E
85 F24 Williston Northern Cape, W South Africa 31.19S 20.52E
25 V10 Williston Florida, SE USA 29.23N 82.27W
30 J3 Williston North Dakota, N USA 48.07N 103.37W
23 Q13 Williston South Carolina, SE USA 33.24N 81.25W
8 L12 Williston Lake ⊠ British Columbia, W Canada
36 L5 Willits California, W USA 39.24N 123.22W
31 T8 Willmar Minnesota, N USA 45.07N 95.02W
8 K11 Will, Mount ▲ British Columbia, W Canada 57.31N 128.48W
33 T11 Willoughby Ohio, N USA 41.38N 81.24W
9 U17 Willow Bunch Saskatchewan, S Canada 49.30N 105.40W
34 J11 Willow Creek ~ Oregon, NW USA
41 R11 Willow Lake Alaska, USA 61.44N 150.02W
15 H7 Willowlake ~ Northwest Territories, NW Canada
85 H25 Willowmore Eastern Cape, S South Africa 33.18S 23.30E
32 L5 Willow Reservoir ⊠ Wisconsin, N USA
37 N5 Willows California, W USA 39.28N 122.12W
29 V7 Willow Springs Missouri, C USA 36.59N 91.58W
190 I7 Wilmington South Australia 32.42S 138.08E
23 Y2 Wilmington Delaware, NE USA 39.45N 75.33W
23 V12 Wilmington North Carolina, SE USA 34.13N 77.57W
33 R14 Wilmington Ohio, N USA 39.27N 83.49W
22 M6 Wilmore Kentucky, S USA 37.51N 84.39W
31 R8 Wilmot South Dakota, N USA 45.24N 96.51W
Wilna/Wilno see Vilnius
103 G16 Wilnsdorf Nordrhein-Westfalen, W Germany 50.49N 8.06E
101 G16 Wilrijk Antwerpen, N Belgium 51.10N 4.24E
102 I10 Wilseder Berg hill NW Germany 53.10N 9.56E
69 Z12 Wilshaw Ridge undersea feature W Indian Ocean
23 V9 Wilson North Carolina, SE USA 35.42N 77.54W
27 N5 Wilson Texas, SW USA 33.21N 101.44W
190 A7 Wilson Bluff headland South Australia/Western Australia 31.41S 129.01E
37 Y7 Wilson Creek Range ▲▲ Nevada, W USA
25 O1 Wilson Lake ⊠ Alabama, S USA
28 M4 Wilson Lake ⊠ Kansas, SE USA
39 P7 Wilson, Mount ▲ Colorado, C USA 37.50N 107.59W
191 P13 Wilsons Promontory peninsula Victoria, SE Australia
31 Y14 Wilton Iowa, C USA 41.35N 91.01W
21 P7 Wilton Maine, NE USA 44.35N 70.15W
30 M5 Wilton North Dakota, N USA 47.09N 100.46W
99 L22 Wiltshire cultural region S England, UK
101 M23 Wiltz Diekirch, NW Luxembourg 49.58N 5.55E
188 K9 Wiluna Western Australia 26.34S 120.14E
101 M23 Wilwerwiltz Diekirch, NE Luxembourg 49.59N 6.00E
31 P5 Wimbledon North Dakota, N USA 47.08N 98.25W
44 K7 Wina var. Güina. Jinotega, N Nicaragua 13.58N 85.14W
33 O12 Winamac Indiana, N USA 41.03N 86.37W
83 G19 Winam Gulf var. Kavirondo Gulf. gulf SW Kenya
85 I22 Winburg Free State, C South Africa 28.31S 27.01E
21 N10 Winchendon Massachusetts, NE USA 42.41N 72.01W
12 M13 Winchester Ontario, SE Canada 45.07N 75.19W
99 M23 Winchester hist. Wintanceaster, Lat. Venta Belgarum. S England, UK 51.04N 1.19W
34 M10 Winchester Idaho, NW USA 46.13N 116.35W
32 J14 Winchester Illinois, N USA 39.37N 90.28W
33 Q13 Winchester Indiana, N USA 40.09N 84.58W
22 M5 Winchester Kentucky, S USA 37.59N 84.10W
20 M10 Winchester New Hampshire, NE USA 42.46N 72.21W
22 K10 Winchester Tennessee, S USA 35.11N 86.06W
23 V3 Winchester Virginia, NE USA 39.11N 78.09W
101 L22 Wincrange Diekirch, NW Luxembourg 50.03N 5.55E
8 I5 Wind ~ Yukon Territory, NW Canada
191 S8 Windamere, Lake ◎ New South Wales, SE Australia
Windau see Ventspils, Latvia
Windau see Venta, Latvia/Lithuania
20 D15 Windber Pennsylvania, NE USA 40.12N 78.47W
25 T3 Winder Georgia, SE USA 33.59N 83.43W
99 K15 Windermere NW England, UK 54.24N 2.54W
12 C7 Windermere Lake ◎ Ontario, S Canada
33 U11 Windham Ohio, N USA 41.14N 81.03W
85 D19 Windhoek Ger. Windhuk. ● (Namibia) Khomas, C Namibia 22.34S 17.06E
85 D20 Windhoek ✈ Khomas, C Namibia 22.31S 17.04E
Windhuk see Windhoek
13 O8 Windigo Québec, SE Canada 47.45N 73.19W
13 O8 Windigo ~ Québec, SE Canada
Windischfeistritz see Slovenska Bistrica
111 T6 Windischgarsten Oberösterreich, W Austria 47.42N 14.21E
Windischgraz see Slovenj Gradec
39 T16 Wind Mountain ▲ New Mexico, SW USA 32.01N 105.35W
31 T10 Windom Minnesota, N USA 43.52N 95.07W
39 Q7 Windom Peak ▲ Colorado, C USA 37.37N 107.35W
189 U9 Windorah Queensland, C Australia 25.25S 142.40E
39 O10 Window Rock Arizona, SW USA 35.40N 109.03W
33 N9 Wind Point headland Wisconsin, N USA 42.46N 87.46W
35 U14 Wind River ~ Wyoming, C USA
11 P15 Windsor Nova Scotia, SE Canada 44.58N 64.13W
12 C17 Windsor Ontario, S Canada 42.18N 83.00W
13 Q12 Windsor Québec, SE Canada 45.34N 72.00W
99 N22 Windsor S England, UK 51.29N 0.39W
39 T3 Windsor Colorado, C USA 40.28N 104.54W
20 M12 Windsor Connecticut, NE USA 41.51N 72.38W
29 T5 Windsor Missouri, C USA 38.31N 93.31W
23 X9 Windsor North Carolina, SE USA 36.00N 76.57W
20 M12 Windsor Locks Connecticut, NE USA 41.55N 72.37W
27 R5 Windthorst Texas, SW USA 33.34N 98.26W
47 Z14 Windward Islands island group E West Indies
Windward Islands see Vent, Îles du, Archipel de la Société, French Polynesia
Windward Islands see Barlavento, Ilhas de, Cape Verde
46 K8 Windward Passage Sp. Paso de los Vientos. channel Cuba/Haiti
57 T9 Wineperu C Guyana 6.10N 58.34W
25 O3 Winfield Alabama, S USA 33.55N 87.49W
31 Y15 Winfield Iowa, C USA 41.07N 91.26W
29 O7 Winfield Kansas, C USA 37.14N 97.00W
27 W6 Winfield Texas, SW USA 33.10N 95.06W
23 Q4 Winfield West Virginia, NE USA 38.30N 81.54W
31 N5 Wing North Dakota, N USA 47.06N 100.16W
191 U7 Wingham New South Wales, SE Australia 31.52S 152.24E
10 G16 Wingham Ontario, S Canada 43.54N 81.19W
35 T8 Winifred Montana, NW USA 47.33N 109.26W
10 E8 Winisk ~ Ontario, S Canada
10 E9 Winisk Lake ◎ Ontario, C Canada
26 L8 Wink Texas, SW USA 31.45N 103.09W
38 M14 Winkelman Arizona, SW USA 32.59N 110.46W
9 X17 Winkler Manitoba, S Canada 49.12N 97.55W
111 Q9 Winklern Tirol, W Austria 46.54N 12.54E
Winkowitz see Vinkovci
34 G9 Winlock Washington, NW USA 46.29N 122.56W
79 P17 Winneba SE Ghana 5.22N 0.37W
31 U11 Winnebago Minnesota, N USA 43.46N 94.10W
31 R13 Winnebago Nebraska, C USA 42.14N 96.28W
32 M7 Winnebago, Lake ◎ Wisconsin, N USA
32 M7 Winneconne Wisconsin, N USA 44.07N 88.44W
37 T3 Winnemucca Nevada, W USA 40.58N 117.43W
37 R4 Winnemucca Lake ◎ Nevada, W USA
103 H21 Winnenden Baden-Württemberg, SW Germany 48.52N 9.22E
31 N11 Winner South Dakota, N USA 43.22N 99.51W
35 U9 Winnett Montana, NW USA 47.00N 108.18W
12 I9 Winneway Québec, SE Canada 47.35N 78.33W
24 H6 Winnfield Louisiana, S USA 31.55N 92.38W
31 U4 Winnibigoshish, Lake ◎ Minnesota, N USA
27 X11 Winnie Texas, SW USA 29.49N 94.22W
9 Y16 Winnipeg Manitoba, S Canada 49.52N 97.10W
9 X16 Winnipeg ✈ Manitoba, S Canada 49.56N 97.16W
(0) J8 Winnipeg ~ Manitoba, S Canada
9 X16 Winnipeg Beach Manitoba, S Canada 50.25N 96.59W
9 W14 Winnipeg, Lake ◎ Manitoba, C Canada
9 W15 Winnipegosis Manitoba, S Canada 51.36N 99.59W
9 W15 Winnipegosis, Lake ◎ Manitoba, C Canada
21 O8 Winnipesaukee, Lake ◎ New Hampshire, NE USA
24 I6 Winnsboro Louisiana, S USA 32.09N 91.43W
23 R12 Winnsboro South Carolina, SE USA 34.22N 81.05W
27 W6 Winnsboro Texas, SW USA 33.01N 95.16W
31 X10 Winona Minnesota, N USA 44.03N 91.37W
24 L4 Winona Mississippi, S USA 33.30N 89.42W
29 W7 Winona Missouri, C USA 37.00N 91.19W
27 W7 Winona Texas, SW USA 32.29N 95.10W
20 M7 Winooski River ~ Vermont, NE USA
100 P6 Winschoten Groningen, NE Netherlands 53.09N 7.03E
102 J10 Winsen Niedersachsen, N Germany 53.22N 10.13E
38 M11 Winslow Arizona, SW USA 35.01N 110.42W
21 Q7 Winslow Maine, NE USA 44.33N 69.35W
20 M12 Winsted Connecticut, NE USA 41.55N 73.03W
34 F14 Winston Oregon, NW USA 43.07N 123.24W

◆ Country ● Country Capital ◇ Dependent Territory ○ Dependent Territory Capital ◈ Administrative Region ✈ International Airport ▲ Mountain ▲▲ Mountain Range Volcano ~ River ◎ Lake ⊠ Reservoir

WINSTON SALEM – XO'JAYLI

23 S9 Winston Salem North Carolina, SE USA 36.06N 80.14W
100 N5 Winsum Groningen, NE Netherlands 53.19N 5.37E
Wintanceaster see Winchester
25 W11 Winter Garden Florida, SE USA 28.34N 81.35W
8 J16 Winter Harbour Vancouver Island, British Columbia, SW Canada 50.28N 128.03W
25 W12 Winter Haven Florida, SE USA 28.01N 81.43W
25 X11 Winter Park Florida, SE USA 28.36N 81.20W
27 P8 Winters Texas, SW USA 31.57N 99.57W
31 U15 Winterset Iowa, C USA 41.19N 94.00W
100 O12 Winterswijk Gelderland, E Netherlands 51.58N 6.43E
110 G6 Winterthur Zürich, NE Switzerland 47.30N 8.43E
31 U9 Winthrop Minnesota, N USA 44.32N 94.22W
34 J7 Winthrop Washington, NW USA 48.28N 120.13W
189 V7 Winton Queensland, E Australia 22.22S 143.04E
193 C24 Winton Southland, South Island, NZ 46.08S 168.19E
23 X8 Winton North Carolina, SE USA 36.22N 76.56W
103 K15 Wipper ≈ C Germany
103 K14 Wipper ≈ C Germany
Wipper see Wieprza
176 Vv9 Wiriagar, Sungai ≈ Papua, E Indonesia
190 G6 Wirraminna South Australia 31.10S 136.13E
190 F4 Wirrida South Australia 29.34S 134.33E
190 F7 Wirrulla South Australia 32.27S 134.33E
Wirsitz see Wyrzysk
Wirz-See see Võrtsjärv
99 O19 Wisbech E England, UK 52.39N 0.08E
Wisby see Visby
21 Q8 Wiscasset Maine, NE USA 44.01N 69.40W
Wischau see Vyškov
32 J5 Wisconsin off. State of Wisconsin; also known as The Badger State. ◆ state N USA
32 L8 Wisconsin Dells Wisconsin, N USA 43.37N 89.43W
32 L8 Wisconsin, Lake ⊠ Wisconsin, N USA
32 L7 Wisconsin Rapids Wisconsin, N USA 44.24N 89.49W
32 L7 Wisconsin River ≈ Wisconsin, N USA
35 P11 Wisdom Montana, NW USA 45.36N 113.27W
23 P7 Wise Virginia, NE USA 36.58N 82.34W
41 Q7 Wiseman Alaska, USA 67.24N 150.06W
98 J12 Wishaw W Scotland, UK 55.46N 3.55W
31 O6 Wishek North Dakota, N USA 46.12N 99.33W
34 I11 Wishram Washington, NW USA 45.40N 120.53W
113 J17 Wisła Śląskie, S Poland 49.39N 18.49E
112 K11 Wisła Eng. Vistula, Ger. Weichsel. ≈ C Poland
Wiślany, Zalew see Vistula Lagoon
113 M16 Wisłoka ≈ SE Poland
102 L9 Wismar Mecklenburg-Vorpommern, N Germany 53.54N 11.28E
31 R14 Wisner Nebraska, C USA 41.59N 96.54W
105 V4 Wissembourg var. Weissenburg. Bas-Rhin, NE France 49.03N 7.57E
32 J6 Wissota, Lake ⊠ Wisconsin, N USA
99 O18 Witham ≈ E England, UK
99 O17 Withernsea E England, UK 53.45N 0.00W
39 Q13 Withington, Mount ▲ New Mexico, SW USA 33.52N 107.29W
25 U8 Withlacoochee River ≈ Florida/Georgia, SE USA
112 H11 Witkowo Wielkopolskie, C Poland 52.27N 17.49E
99 M21 Witney S England, UK 51.47N 1.30W
103 E15 Witten Nordrhein-Westfalen, W Germany 51.25N 7.19E
103 N14 Wittenberg Sachsen-Anhalt, E Germany 51.52N 12.39E
32 L6 Wittenberg Wisconsin, N USA 44.53N 89.20W
102 L11 Wittenberge Brandenburg, N Germany 52.58N 11.45E
105 U7 Wittenheim Haut-Rhin, NE France 47.49N 7.19E
188 I7 Wittenoom Western Australia 22.17S 118.22E
Wittingau see Třeboň
102 K12 Wittingen Niedersachsen, C Germany 52.42N 10.43E
103 E18 Wittlich Rheinland-Pfalz, SW Germany 49.59N 6.54E
102 F9 Wittmund Niedersachsen, NW Germany 53.34N 7.46E
102 M10 Wittstock Brandenburg, NE Germany 53.09N 12.28E
194 M11 Witu Islands island group E PNG
112 O7 Wiżajny Podlaskie, NE Poland 54.21N 22.51E
57 W10 W.J. van Blommesteinmeer ⊠ E Suriname
112 L11 Wkra Ger. Soldau. ≈ C Poland
112 I6 Władysławowo Pomorskie, N Poland 54.48N 18.25E
Wlaschim see Vlašim
113 E14 Wleń Ger. Lähn. Dolnośląskie, SW Poland 51.00N 15.39E
112 J11 Włocławek Ger./Rus. Vlotslavsk. Kujawsko-pomorskie, C Poland 52.39N 19.02E
112 P13 Włodawa Rus. Vlodava. Lubelskie, SE Poland 51.33N 23.31E
Włodzimierz see Volodymyr-Volyns'kyy
113 K15 Włoszczowa Świętokrzyskie, C Poland 50.51N 19.58E
85 C19 Wlotzkasbaken Erongo, W Namibia 22.25S 14.30E
13 R12 Woburn Québec, SE Canada 45.22N 70.52W
21 O11 Woburn Massachusetts, NE USA 42.28N 71.09W
Wocheiner Feistritz see Bohinjska Bistrica
Wöchma see Võhma
153 S11 Wodil var. Vuadil'. Farg'ona Viloyati, E Uzbekistan 40.10N 71.43E
189 V14 Wodonga Victoria, SE Australia 36.10S 146.55E
113 I17 Wodzisław Śląski Ger. Loslau. Śląskie, S Poland 49.59N 18.27E
100 I11 Woerden Zuid-Holland, C Netherlands 52.06N 4.54E
100 I8 Wognum Noord-Holland, NW Netherlands 52.40N 5.01E
Wohlau see Wołów
110 F7 Wohlen Aargau, NW Switzerland 47.21N 8.16E
205 R2 Wohlthat Mountains ▲▲ Antarctica
176 W9 Woinui, Selat strait Papua, E Indonesia
194 K15 Woitape Central, S PNG 8.35S 147.15E
Wojerecy see Hoyerswerda
Wōjjā see Wotje Atoll
Wojwodina see Vojvodina
176 W13 Wokam, Pulau island Kepulauan Aru, E Indonesia
99 N22 Woking SE England, UK 51.19N 0.34W
Woldenberg Neumark see Dobiegniew
196 K15 Woleai Atoll atoll Caroline Islands, W Micronesia
Woleu see Uolo, Río
81 E17 Woleu-Ntem off. Province du Woleu-Ntem, var. Le Woleu-Ntem. ◆ province W Gabon
34 F15 Wolf Creek Oregon, NW USA 42.40N 123.22W
28 K9 Wolf Creek ≈ Oklahoma/Texas, SW USA
39 R7 Wolf Creek Pass pass Colorado, C USA 37.28N 106.48W
21 O9 Wolfeboro New Hampshire, NE USA 43.34N 71.10W
27 U5 Wolfe City Texas, SW USA 33.22N 96.04W
12 L15 Wolfe Island island Ontario, SE Canada
103 M14 Wolfen Sachsen-Anhalt, E Germany 51.40N 12.16E
102 J13 Wolfenbüttel Niedersachsen, C Germany 52.10N 10.31E
111 T4 Wolfern Oberösterreich, N Austria 48.06N 14.16E
111 Q6 Wolfgangsee var. Abersee, St Wolfgangsee. ◎ N Austria
41 P9 Wolf Mountain ▲ Alaska, USA 65.20N 154.08W
35 X7 Wolf Point Montana, NW USA 48.04N 105.40W
24 L8 Wolf River ≈ Mississippi, S USA
32 M7 Wolf River ≈ Wisconsin, N USA
111 U9 Wolfsberg Kärnten, SE Austria 46.49N 14.49E
102 K12 Wolfsburg Niedersachsen, N Germany 52.25N 10.46E
59 B17 Wolf, Volcán ⛰ Galapagos Islands, Ecuador, E Pacific Ocean 0.01N 91.22W
102 O8 Wolgast Mecklenburg-Vorpommern, NE Germany 54.03N 13.47E
110 F8 Wolhusen Luzern, W Switzerland 47.04N 8.06E
112 D8 Wolin Ger. Wollin. Zachodnio-pomorskie, NW Poland 53.52N 14.34E
111 Y3 Wolkersdorf Niederösterreich, NE Austria 48.24N 16.31E
Wołkowysk see Vawkavysk
Wöllan see Velenje
15 I2 Wollaston, Cape headland Victoria Island, Northwest Territories, NW Canada 71.00N 118.21W
65 J25 Wollaston, Isla island S Chile
9 U11 Wollaston Lake Saskatchewan, C Canada 58.04N 103.37W
9 T10 Wollaston Lake ◎ Saskatchewan, C Canada
15 I3 Wollaston Peninsula peninsula Victoria Island, Northwest Territories/Nunavut, NW Canada
Wollin see Wolin
191 S9 Wollongong New South Wales, SE Australia 34.25S 150.52E
Wolmar see Valmiera
102 L13 Wolmirstedt Sachsen-Anhalt, C Germany 52.15N 11.37E
112 M11 Wołomin Mazowieckie, C Poland 52.21N 21.15E
112 G3 Wołów Ger. Wohlau. Dolnośląskie, SW Poland 51.21N 16.39E
Wołożyn see Valozhyn
12 G11 Wolseley Bay Ontario, S Canada 46.05N 80.16W
31 P10 Wolsey South Dakota, N USA 44.22N 98.28W
112 F12 Wolsztyn Wielkopolskie, W Poland 52.06N 16.06E
100 M7 Wolvega Fris. Wolvegea. Friesland, N Netherlands 52.53N 6.00E
Wolvegea see Wolvega
99 K19 Wolverhampton C England, UK 52.36N 2.07W
Wolverine State see Michigan
101 G18 Wolvertem Vlaams Brabant, C Belgium 50.55N 4.19E
101 H16 Wommelgem Antwerpen, N Belgium 51.12N 4.31E
176 W11 Wondiwoi, Pegunungan ▲▲ Papua, E Indonesia
194 J13 Wonenara var. Wonerara. Eastern Highlands, C PNG 6.46S 145.54E
Wonerara see Wonenara
Wongalara Lake see Wongalarroo Lake
191 N6 Wongalarroo Lake var. Wongalara Lake. seasonal lake New South Wales, SE Australia
169 Y15 Wŏnju Jap. Genshū. N South Korea 37.21N 127.57E
8 M12 Wonowon British Columbia, W Canada 56.46N 121.54W
169 X13 Wŏnsan SE North Korea 39.11N 127.21E
191 O13 Wonthaggi Victoria, SE Australia 38.37S 145.37E
25 N2 Woodall Mountain ▲ Mississippi, S USA 34.47N 88.14W
25 W7 Woodbine Georgia, SE USA 30.58N 81.43W
31 S14 Woodbine Iowa, C USA 41.44N 95.42W
20 J17 Woodbine New Jersey, NE USA 39.12N 74.47W
23 W4 Woodbridge Virginia, NE USA 38.39N 77.14W
191 V4 Woodburn New South Wales, SE Australia 29.07S 153.23E
34 G11 Woodburn Oregon, NW USA 45.08N 122.51W
22 K9 Woodbury Tennessee, S USA 35.49N 86.04W
191 V5 Wooded Bluff headland New South Wales, SE Australia 29.24S 153.22E
191 V3 Woodenbong New South Wales, SE Australia 28.24S 152.39E
37 R11 Woodlake California, W USA 36.24N 119.06W
37 N7 Woodland California, W USA 38.39N 121.46W
21 T5 Woodland Maine, NE USA 45.10N 67.25W
34 G10 Woodland Washington, NW USA 45.54N 122.44W
39 T5 Woodland Park Colorado, C USA 38.59N 105.03W
195 P15 Woodlark Island var. Murua Island. island SE PNG
Woodle Island see Kuria
9 T17 Wood Mountain ▲▲ Saskatchewan, S Canada
32 K15 Wood River Illinois, N USA 38.51N 90.06W
31 P16 Wood River Nebraska, C USA 40.48N 98.33W
41 R9 Wood River ≈ Alaska, USA
41 O13 Wood River Lakes lakes Alaska, USA
190 C1 Woodroffe, Mount ▲ South Australia 26.19S 131.42E
23 P11 Woodruff South Carolina, SE USA 34.44N 82.02W
32 K4 Woodruff Wisconsin, N USA 45.55N 89.41W
27 T14 Woodsboro Texas, SW USA 28.14N 97.19W
33 U13 Woodsfield Ohio, N USA 39.45N 81.07W
189 P4 Woods, Lake ◎ Northern Territory, N Australia
9 Z16 Woods, Lake of the Fr. Lac des Bois. ◎ Canada/USA
27 Q6 Woodson Texas, SW USA 33.00N 99.01W
11 N14 Woodstock New Brunswick, SE Canada 46.10N 67.37W
12 F16 Woodstock Ontario, S Canada 43.07N 80.46W
32 M10 Woodstock Illinois, N USA 42.18N 88.27W
20 M9 Woodstock Vermont, NE USA 43.37N 72.33W
23 U4 Woodstock Virginia, NE USA 38.51N 78.28W
21 N8 Woodsville New Hampshire, NE USA 44.07N 72.01W
192 M12 Woodville Manawatu-Wanganui, North Island, NZ 40.21S 175.58E
24 J7 Woodville Mississippi, S USA 31.06N 91.18W
27 X9 Woodville Texas, SW USA 30.46N 94.25W
28 K9 Woodward Oklahoma, C USA 36.25N 99.23W
31 O5 Woodworth North Dakota, N USA 47.06N 99.19W
176 Y12 Woogi Papua, E Indonesia 3.59S 138.45E
176 Ww9 Wool Papua, E Indonesia 1.38S 135.34E
191 V5 Woolgoolga New South Wales, E Australia 30.04S 153.09E
190 H6 Woomera South Australia 31.12S 136.52E
21 O12 Woonsocket Rhode Island, NE USA 41.58N 71.27W
31 P10 Woonsocket South Dakota, N USA 44.03N 98.16W
33 T12 Wooster Ohio, N USA 40.48N 81.56W
82 L12 Woqooyi Galbeed off. Gobolka Woqooyi Galbeed. ◆ region NW Somalia
110 E8 Worb Bern, C Switzerland 46.54N 7.36E
85 F26 Worcester Western Cape, SW South Africa 33.41S 19.22E
99 L20 Worcester hist. Wigorna Ceaster. W England, UK 52.10N 2.13W
21 N11 Worcester Massachusetts, NE USA 42.17N 71.48W
99 L20 Worcestershire cultural region C England, UK
34 H16 Worden Oregon, NW USA 42.04N 121.50W
111 O6 Wörgl Tirol, W Austria 47.28N 12.04E
176 Ww14 Workai, Pulau island Kepulauan Aru, E Indonesia
99 J15 Workington NW England, UK 54.39N 3.33W
100 K7 Workum Friesland, N Netherlands 52.58N 5.25E
35 V13 Worland Wyoming, C USA 44.01N 107.57W
Wormatia see Worms
101 N25 Wormeldange Grevenmacher, E Luxembourg 49.37N 6.25E
100 I9 Wormer Noord-Holland, C Netherlands 52.30N 4.49E
103 G19 Worms anc. Augusta Vangionum, Borbetomagus, Wormatia. Rheinland-Pfalz, SW Germany 49.37N 8.22E
Worms see Vormsi
103 K21 Wörnitz ≈ S Germany
103 G21 Wörth am Rhein Rheinland-Pfalz, SW Germany 49.04N 8.16E
27 U8 Wortham Texas, SW USA 31.47N 96.27W
111 S9 Wörther See ◎ S Austria
99 O23 Worthing SE England, UK 50.48N 0.22W
31 S11 Worthington Minnesota, N USA 43.37N 95.36W
33 S13 Worthington Ohio, N USA 40.05N 83.01W
37 W8 Worthington Peak ▲ Nevada, W USA 37.57N 115.32W
176 Y12 Wosi Papua, E Indonesia 3.55S 138.54E
176 W11 Wosimi Papua, E Indonesia 2.44S 134.34E
201 R5 Wotho Atoll var. Wōtto. atoll Ralik Chain, W Marshall Islands
201 V5 Wotje Atoll var. Wōjjā. atoll Ratak Chain, E Marshall Islands
Wotoe see Wotu
Wottawa see Otava
Wōtto see Wotho Atoll
175 Pp10 Wotu prev. Wotoe. Sulawesi, C Indonesia 2.34S 120.46E
100 K11 Woudenberg Utrecht, C Netherlands 52.04N 5.25E
100 I13 Woudrichem Noord-Brabant, S Netherlands 51.49N 5.00E
45 N8 Wounta var. Huaunta. Región Autónoma Atlántico Norte, NE Nicaragua 13.33N 83.31W
175 R12 Wowoni, Pulau island C Indonesia
175 Qq12 Wowoni, Selat strait Sulawesi, C Indonesia
83 J17 Woyamdero Plain plain E Kenya
Woyens see Vojens
Wozrojdeniye Oroli see Vozrozhdeniya, Ostrov
Wrangel Island see Vrangelya, Ostrov
41 Y13 Wrangell Wrangell Island, Alaska, USA 56.28N 132.22W
40 C15 Wrangell, Cape headland Attu Island, Alaska, USA 52.55N 172.28E
41 S11 Wrangell, Mount ▲ Alaska, USA 62.00N 144.01W
41 T11 Wrangell Mountains ▲▲ Alaska, USA
207 S7 Wrangel Plain undersea feature Arctic Ocean
98 H6 Wrath, Cape headland N Scotland, UK 58.37N 5.01W
39 W3 Wray Colorado, C USA 40.01N 102.12W
46 K13 Wreck Point headland C Jamaica 17.50N 76.55W
85 C23 Wreck Point headland W South Africa 28.52S 16.17E
25 V4 Wrens Georgia, SE USA 33.12N 82.23W
99 K18 Wrexham NE Wales, UK 53.03N 3.00W
29 R13 Wright City Oklahoma, C USA 34.03N 95.00W
204 J12 Wright Island island Antarctica
11 N9 Wright, Mont ▲ Québec, E Canada 52.36N 67.40W
27 X5 Wright Patman Lake ⊠ Texas, SW USA
38 M16 Wrightson, Mount ▲ Arizona, SW USA 31.42N 110.51W
25 U5 Wrightsville Georgia, SE USA 32.43N 82.43W
23 W12 Wrightsville Beach North Carolina, SE USA 34.12N 77.48W
37 T15 Wrightwood California, W USA 34.21N 117.37W
15 Gg7 Wrigley Northwest Territories, W Canada 63.16N 123.39W
113 G14 Wrocław Eng./Ger. Breslau. Dolnośląskie, SW Poland 51.06N 17.01E
112 F10 Wronki Ger. Fronicken. Wielkopolskie, NW Poland 52.42N 16.21E
112 H11 Września Wielkopolskie, C Poland 52.19N 17.33E
112 F12 Wschowa Lubuskie, W Poland 51.48N 16.18E
Wsetin see Vsetín
167 O5 Wu'an Hebei, E China 36.45N 114.12E
188 I12 Wubin Western Australia 30.05S 116.43E
169 W9 Wuchang Heilongjiang, NE China 44.55N 127.13E
Wuchang see Wuhan
Wu-chou/Wuchow see Wuzhou
166 M16 Wuchuan var. Meilu. Guangdong, S China 21.30N 110.40E
166 K10 Wuchuan var. Duru, Gelaozu Miaozu Zizhixian. Guizhou, S China 28.40N 108.04E
169 O13 Wuchuan Nei Mongol Zizhiqu, N China 41.04N 111.28E
169 V6 Wudalianchi Heilongjiang, NE China 48.40N 126.06E
169 V6 Wudalianchi prev. Dedu, Qingshan. Heilongjiang, NE China 48.30N 126.17E
165 O11 Wudaoliang Qinghai, C China 35.16N 93.03E
147 Q13 Wuday'ah spring/well S Saudi Arabia 17.03N 47.06E
79 V13 Wudil Kano, N Nigeria 11.46N 8.49E
166 G12 Wuding var. Jincheng. Yunnan, SW China 25.31N 102.24E
190 G8 Wudinna South Australia 33.06S 135.30E
163 P10 Wudu Gansu, C China 33.22N 105.01E
166 L9 Wufeng Hubei, C China 30.09N 110.31E
167 O11 Wugong Shan ▲▲ S China
163 P7 Wuhai var. Haibowan. Nei Mongol Zizhiqu, N China 39.40N 106.48E
167 O9 Wuhan var. Han-kou, Han-k'ou, Hanyang, Wuchang, Wu-han; prev. Hankow. Hubei, C China 30.34N 114.19E
167 Q7 Wuhe Anhui, E China 33.10N 117.50E
Wuhsi/Wu-hsi see Wuxi
Wuhsien see Suzhou
167 Q8 Wuhu var. Wu-na-mu. Anhui, E China 31.22N 118.25E
Wujae see Ujae Atoll
166 K11 Wu Jiang ≈ C China
Wujlān see Ujelang Atoll
79 W15 Wukari Taraba, E Nigeria 7.51N 9.49E
166 H11 Wulian Feng ▲▲ SW China
166 F13 Wuliang Shan ▲▲ SW China
176 U15 Wuliaru, Pulau island Kepulauan Tanimbar, E Indonesia
166 K11 Wuling Shan ▲▲ S China
111 Y5 Wulka ≈ E Austria
Wulkan see Vulcan
111 T3 Wullowitz Oberösterreich, N Austria 48.37N 14.27E
Wu-lu-k'o-mu-shi/Wu-lu-mu-ch'i see Ürümqi
81 D14 Wum Nord-Ouest, NE Cameroon 6.24N 10.04E
166 H12 Wumeng Shan ▲▲ SW China
166 K14 Wuming Guangxi Zhuangzu Zizhiqu, S China 22.55N 108.16E
102 I10 Wümme ≈ NW Germany
Wu-na-mu see Wuhu
176 Y11 Wunen Papua, E Indonesia 3.40S 138.31E
10 D9 Wunnummin Lake ◎ Ontario, C Canada
82 D13 Wun Rog Warab, S Sudan 09.00N 28.20E
103 M18 Wunsiedel Bayern, E Germany 50.02N 12.00E
102 I12 Wunstorf Niedersachsen, NW Germany 52.25N 9.25E
177 G3 Wuntho Sagaing, N Myanmar 23.52N 95.43E
103 F15 Wupper ≈ W Germany
103 E15 Wuppertal prev. Barmen-Elberfeld. Nordrhein-Westfalen, W Germany 51.16N 7.12E
166 K5 Wuqi Shaanxi, C China 36.55N 108.13E
167 P4 Wuqiao var. Sangyuan. Hebei, E China 37.40N 116.21E
103 L23 Würm ≈ SE Germany
79 T12 Wurno Sokoto, NW Nigeria 13.15N 5.24E
103 I19 Würzburg Bayern, SW Germany 49.48N 9.55E
103 N15 Wurzen Sachsen, E Germany 51.21N 12.48E
166 L9 Wu Shan ▲▲ C China
164 G7 Wushi var. Uqturpan. Xinjiang Uygur Zizhiqu, NW China 41.07N 79.09E
Wusih see Wuxi
67 N18 Wüst Seamount undersea feature S Atlantic Ocean 32.00S 0.06E
Wusuli Jiang/Wusuri see Ussuri
167 N3 Wutai Shan var. Beitai Ding. ▲ C China 39.00N 114.00E
166 H10 Wutongqiao Sichuan, C China 29.24N 103.54E
165 P6 Wutongwozi Quan spring NW China 42.30N 95.21E
194 E9 Wutung Sandaun, NW PNG 2.39S 141.01E
101 H15 Wuustwezel Antwerpen, N Belgium 51.24N 4.34E
194 G8 Wuvulu Island island NW PNG
165 U9 Wuwei var. Liangzhou. Gansu, C China 38.02N 102.30E
167 R8 Wuxi var. Wuhsi, Wu-hsi, Wusih. Jiangsu, E China 31.34N 120.19E
Wuxing see Huzhou
166 L14 Wuxuan Guangxi Zhuangzu Zizhiqu, S China 23.40N 109.41E
Wuyang see Zhenyuan
166 K11 Wuyang He ≈ S China
169 X6 Wuyiling Heilongjiang, NE China 48.36N 129.24E
163 T12 Wuyi Shan ▲▲ SE China
167 Q11 Wuyishan prev. Chong'an. Fujian, SE China 27.48N 118.03E
168 M13 Wuyuan Nei Mongol Zizhiqu, N China 41.04N 108.15E
166 L17 Wuzhishan prev. Tongshi. Hainan, S China 18.37N 109.34E
166 L17 Wuzhi Shan ▲ S China 18.52N 109.36E
165 W8 Wuzhong Ningxia, N China 37.58N 106.09E
166 M14 Wuzhou var. Wu-chou, Wuchow. Guangxi Zhuangzu Zizhiqu, S China 23.30N 111.19E
20 H12 Wyalusing Pennsylvania, NE USA 41.40N 76.13W
190 M10 Wycheproof Victoria, SE Australia 36.06S 143.13E
99 K21 Wye Wel. Gwy. ≈ England/Wales, UK
Wyłkowyszki see Vilkaviškis
99 P19 Wymondham E England, UK 52.29N 1.10E
31 R17 Wymore Nebraska, C USA 40.07N 96.39W
190 E5 Wynbring South Australia 30.34S 133.27E
189 N3 Wyndham Western Australia 15.28S 128.07E
31 R6 Wyndmere North Dakota, N USA 46.16N 97.07W
29 X11 Wynne Arkansas, C USA 35.13N 90.47W
29 N12 Wynnewood Oklahoma, C USA 34.39N 97.09W
191 O15 Wynyard Tasmania, SE Australia 40.57S 145.33E
9 U15 Wynyard Saskatchewan, S Canada 51.46N 104.10W
35 V11 Wyola Montana, NW USA 45.07N 107.23W
190 A4 Wyola Lake salt lake South Australia
33 P9 Wyoming Michigan, N USA 42.54N 85.42W
35 V14 Wyoming off. State of Wyoming; also known as The Equality State. ◆ state C USA
35 S15 Wyoming Range ▲▲ Wyoming, C USA
191 T8 Wyong New South Wales, SE Australia 33.18S 151.27E
112 G9 Wyrzysk Ger. Wirsitz. Wielkopolskie, C Poland 53.09N 17.15E
Wysg see Usk
112 O10 Wysokie Mazowieckie Łomża, E Poland 52.54N 22.34E
112 M11 Wyszków Ger. Probstberg. Mazowieckie, C Poland 52.36N 21.27E
112 L11 Wyszogród Mazowieckie, C Poland 52.24N 20.14E
23 R7 Wytheville Virginia, NE USA 36.57N 81.05W

X

82 Q12 Xaafuun It. Hafun. Bari, NE Somalia 10.25N 51.17E
82 Q12 Xaafuun, Raas var. Ras Hafun. headland NE Somalia 10.36N 51.09E
Xàbia see Jávea
44 C4 Xaclbal, Río var. Xalbal. ≈ Guatemala/Mexico
143 Y10 Xaçmaz Rus. Khachmas. N Azerbaijan 41.26N 48.46E
82 O12 Xadeed var. Haded. physical region N Somalia
165 O14 Xagquka Xizang Zizhiqu, W China 31.46N 92.46E
178 I6 Xai var. Muang Xay, Muong Sai. Oudômxai, N Laos 20.41N 102.00E
164 F10 Xaidulla Xinjiang Uygur Zizhiqu, W China 36.27N 77.46E
178 I7 Xaignabouli prev. Muang Xaignabouri, Fr. Sayaboury. Xaignabouli, N Laos 19.16N 101.43E
178 J7 Xai Lai Leng, Phou ▲ Laos/Vietnam 19.13N 104.09E
164 L15 Xainza Xizang Zizhiqu, W China 30.54N 88.36E
164 L16 Xaitongmoin Xizang Zizhiqu, W China 29.27N 88.13E
85 M20 Xai-Xai prev. João Belo, Vila de João Bel. Gaza, S Mozambique 25.00S 33.37E
Xalbal see Xaclbal, Río
82 P13 Xalin Nugaal, N Somalia 9.16N 49.00E
152 H7 Xalqobod Rus. Khalkabad. Qoraqalpog'iston Respublikasi, W Uzbekistan 42.42N 59.46E
178 J6 Xam Nua var. Sam Neua. Houaphan, N Laos 20.24N 104.03E
84 D11 Xá-Muteba Port. Cinco de Outubro. Lunda Norte, NE Angola 9.31S 17.46E
Xangda see Nangqên
85 C16 Xangongo Port. Rocadas. Cunene, SW Angola 16.41S 14.58E
143 W12 Xankändi Rus. Khankendi; prev. Stepanakert. SW Azerbaijan 39.50N 46.44E
143 V11 Xanlar Rus. Khanlar. NW Azerbaijan 40.37N 46.18E
116 J13 Xánthi Anatolikí Makedonía kai Thráki, NE Greece 41.09N 24.54E
62 H13 Xanxerê Santa Catarina, S Brazil 26.52S 52.25W
83 O15 Xarardheere Mudug, E Somalia 4.45N 47.54E
143 Z11 Xärä Zirä Adası Rus. Ostrov Bulla. island E Azerbaijan
168 K13 Xar Burd prev. Bayan Nuru. Nei Mongol Zizhiqu, N China 40.09N 104.48E
169 T11 Xar Moron ≈ NE China
Xarra see Xarrë
115 L23 Xarrë var. Xarra. Vlorë, S Albania 39.45N 20.01E
84 D12 Xassengue Lunda Sul, NW Angola 10.28S 18.32E
107 S11 Xátiva var. Jativa; anc. Setabis. País Valenciano, E Spain 39.00N 0.32W
Xauen see Chefchaouen
62 K10 Xavantes, Represa de var. Represa de Chavantes. ⊠ S Brazil
164 I7 Xayar Xinjiang Uygur Zizhiqu, W China 41.16N 82.52E
Xäzär Dänizi see Caspian Sea
178 Jj9 Xé Bangfai ≈ C Laos
178 Jj10 Xé Banghiang var. Bang Hieng. ≈ S Laos
Xégar see Tingri
33 R14 Xenia Ohio, N USA 39.40N 83.55W
Xeres see Jeréz de la Frontera
117 E15 Xeriás ≈ C Greece
117 G17 Xeró ▲ Évvoia, C Greece 38.52N 23.18E
85 H18 Xhumo Central, C Botswana 21.13S 24.37E
167 N15 Xiachuan Dao island S China
Xiacun see Rushan
Xiaguan see Dali
165 U11 Xiahe var. Labrang. Gansu, C China 35.12N 102.28E
167 Q13 Xiamen var. Hsia-men; prev. Amoy. Fujian, SE China 24.28N 118.04E
166 L6 Xi'an var. Changan, Sian, Signan, Siking, Singan, Xian. Shaanxi, C China 34.16N 108.54E
166 L10 Xianfeng var. Gaoleshan. Hubei, C China 29.39N 109.07E
Xiang see Hunan
167 N7 Xiangcheng Henan, C China 33.52N 113.29E
166 F10 Xiangcheng var. Sampê, Tib. Qagcheng. Sichuan, C China 28.52N 99.45E
166 M8 Xiangfan var. Xiangyang. Hubei, C China 32.07N 112.00E
167 N10 Xiang Jiang ≈ S China
Xiangkhoang see Pèk
178 Ii7 Xiangkhoang, Plateau de var. Plain of Jars. plateau N Laos
167 N11 Xiangtan var. Hsiang-t'an, Siangtan. Hunan, S China 27.52N 112.54E
167 N11 Xiangxiang Hunan, S China 27.50N 112.31E
Xiangyang see Xiangfan
167 S10 Xianju Zhejiang, SE China 28.53N 120.41E
Xianshui see Dawu
166 F8 Xianshui He ≈ C China
167 N9 Xiantao var. Mianyang. Hubei, C China 30.19N 113.31E
167 R10 Xianxia Ling ▲▲ SE China
166 K6 Xianyang Shaanxi, C China 34.23N 118.40E
164 L5 Xiaocaohu Xinjiang Uygur Zizhiqu, W China 43.45N 90.07E
167 O9 Xiaogan Hubei, C China 30.55N 113.54E
Xiaogang see Dongxiang
169 W6 Xiao Hinggan Ling Eng. Lesser Khingan Range. ▲▲ NE China
166 M6 Xiao Shan ▲▲ C China
166 M12 Xiao Shui ≈ S China
Xiaoxi see Pinghe
167 P6 Xiaoxian var. Longcheng, Xiao Xian. Anhui, E China 34.12N 116.55E
166 G11 Xichang Sichuan, C China 27.52N 102.16E
43 P11 Xicoténcatl Tamaulipas, C Mexico 22.59N 98.54W
Xieng Khouang see Pèk
Xieng Ngeun see Muong Xiang Ngeun
166 J11 Xifeng var. Yongjing. Guizhou, S China 27.15N 106.44E
Xifeng see Qingyang
Xigang see Helan
164 L16 Xigazê var. Jih-k'a-tse, Shigatse, Xigaze. Xizang Zizhiqu, W China 29.18N 88.49E
165 W11 Xihe var. Hanyuan. Gansu, C China 34.00N 105.24E
166 I8 Xi He ≈ C China
Xihuachi see Heshui
165 W10 Xiji Ningxia, N China 36.02N 105.33E
166 M14 Xi Jiang var. Hsi Chiang, Eng. West River. ≈ S China
165 Q7 Xijian Quan spring NW China 40.52N 96.31E
166 K15 Xijin Shuiku ⊠ S China
Xilagani see Xylaganí
Xiligou see Ulan
166 I13 Xilin var. Bada. Guangxi Zhuangzu Zizhiqu, S China 24.30N 105.00E
169 Q10 Xilinhot var. Silinhot. Nei Mongol Zizhiqu, N China 43.58N 116.06E
Xilinji see Mohe
Xilokastro see Xylókastro
Xin see Xinjiang Uygur Zizhiqu
167 R10 Xin'anjiang Shuiku ⊠ SE China
Xin'anzhen see Xinyi
Xin Barag Youqi see Altan Emel
Xin Barag Zuoqi see Amgalang
169 W12 Xinbin var. Xinbin Manzu Zizhixian. Liaoning, NE China 41.39N 125.04E
Xinbin Manzu Zizhixian see Xinbin
167 O7 Xincai Henan, C China 32.46N 114.54E
Xincheng see Zhaojue
Xindu see Luhuo
167 O13 Xinfeng var. Jiading. Jiangxi, S China 25.30N 114.52E
167 O14 Xinfengjiang Shuiku ⊠ S China
Xingba see Lhünzê
169 T13 Xingcheng Liaoning, NE China 40.38N 120.47E
84 E11 Xinge Lunda Norte, NE Angola 9.44S 19.10E
167 P12 Xingguo var. Lianjiang. Jiangxi, S China 26.25N 115.22E
165 S11 Xinghai var. Ziketan. Qinghai, C China 35.12N 102.28E
167 R7 Xinghua Jiangsu, E China 32.54N 119.48E
Xingi Hu see Khanka, Lake
167 P13 Xingning Guangdong, S China 24.13N 115.38E
166 I13 Xingren Guizhou, S China 25.25N 105.07E
167 O4 Xingtai Hebei, E China 37.07N 114.28E
61 J14 Xingu, Rio ≈ C Brazil
165 P6 Xingxingxia Xinjiang Uygur Zizhiqu, NW China 41.48N 95.01E
166 I13 Xingyi Guizhou, S China 25.04N 104.51E
164 I6 Xinhe var. Toksu. Xinjiang Uygur Zizhiqu, NW China 41.34N 82.30E
169 Q10 Xin Hot var. Abag Qi. Nei Mongol Zizhiqu, N China 43.58N 114.59E
Xinhua see Funing
169 T12 Xinhui var. Aohan Qi. Nei Mongol Zizhiqu, N China 42.12N 119.57E
165 T10 Xining var. Hsining, Hsi-ning, Sining. province capital Qinghai, C China 36.37N 101.46E
167 O4 Xinji prev. Shulu. Hebei, E China 37.55N 115.14E
167 P10 Xinjian Jiangxi, S China 28.42N 115.43E
Xinjiang see Xinjiang Uygur Zizhiqu
168 D8 Xinjiang Uygur Zizhiqu var. Sinkiang, Sinkiang Uighur Autonomous Region, Xin, Xinjiang. ◆ autonomous region NW China
166 H9 Xinjin var. Meixing, Tib. Zainlha. Sichuan, C China 30.24N 103.48E
Xinjin see Pulandian
Xinjing see Jingxi
169 U12 Xinmin Liaoning, NE China 41.58N 122.51E
166 M12 Xinning var. Jinshi. Hunan, S China 26.34N 110.57E
Xinpu see Lianyungang
Xinshan see Anyuan
167 P5 Xintai Shandong, E China 35.54N 117.44E
Xinwen see Suncun
Xin Xian see Xinzhou
167 N6 Xinxiang Henan, C China 35.13N 113.48E
167 O8 Xinyang var. Hsin-yang, Sinyang. Henan, C China 32.09N 114.04E
167 Q6 Xinyi var. Xin'anzhen. Jiangsu, E China 34.25N 118.19E
167 Q6 Xinyi He ≈ E China
167 O11 Xinyu Jiangxi, S China 27.51N 115.00E
164 I5 Xinyuan var. Künes. Xinjiang Uygur Zizhiqu, NW China 43.25N 83.12E
Xinyuan see Tianjun
167 N3 Xinzhou var. Xin Xian. Shanxi, C China 38.24N 112.43E
Xinzhou see Longlin
106 H4 Xinzo de Limia Galicia, NW Spain 42.04N 7.45W
Xions see Książ Wielkopolski
167 O7 Xiping Henan, C China 33.22N 114.00E
Xiping see Songyang
165 T11 Xiqing Shan ▲▲ C China
61 N16 Xique-Xique Bahia, E Brazil 10.46S 42.43W
Xireg see Ulan
117 E14 Xirovoúni ▲ N Greece 40.31N 21.58E
168 M13 Xishanzui var. Urad Qianqi. Nei Mongol Zizhiqu, N China 40.43N 108.41E
166 J11 Xishui Guizhou, S China 28.24N 106.09E
Xi Ujimqin Qi see Bayan Ul
166 K11 Xiushan var. Zhonghe. Chongqing Shi, C China 28.23N 108.52E
Xiushan see Tonghai
167 O10 Xiu Shui ≈ S China
152 H9 Xiva var. Khiwa, Rus. Khiva. Xorazm Viloyati, W Uzbekistan 41.22N 60.21E
164 J16 Xixabangma Feng ▲ W China 28.25N 85.47E
166 M7 Xixia Henan, C China 33.19N 111.25E
Xixón see Gijón
Xixona see Jijona
Xizang see Xizang Zizhiqu
Xizang Gaoyuan see Qingzang Gaoyuan
166 E9 Xizang Zizhiqu var. Thibet, Tibetan Autonomous Region, Xizang, Eng. Tibet. ◆ autonomous region W China
169 U14 Xizhong Dao island N China
Xoi see Qüxü
152 H8 Xo'jayli Rus. Khodzheyli. Qoraqalpog'iston Respublikasi, W Uzbekistan 42.23N 59.27E

◆ Country ● Country Capital ◇ Dependent Territory ○ Dependent Territory Capital ◆ Administrative Region ✈ International Airport ▲ Mountain ▲▲ Mountain Range ⛰ Volcano ≈ River ◎ Lake ⊠ Reservoir

Xolotlán see Managua, Lago de
152 I9 **Xonqa** var. Khonqa, Rus. Khanka. Xorazm Viloyati, W Uzbekistan 41.31N 60.39E
152 H9 **Xorazm Viloyati** Rus. Khorezmskaya Oblast'. ◐ province W Uzbekistan
165 N9 **Xorkol** Xinjiang Uygur Zizhiqu, NW China 38.45N 91.07E
153 P11 **Xovos** var. Ursat'yevskaya, Rus. Khavast. Sirdaryo Viloyati, E Uzbekistan 40.14N 68.46E
43 X14 **Xpujil** Quintana Roo, E Mexico 18.30N 89.24W
167 Q8 **Xuancheng** var. Xuanzhou. Anhui, E China 30.59N 118.43E
178 Jj9 **Xuân Đuc** Quang Binh, C Vietnam 17.19N 106.38E
166 L9 **Xuan'en** var. Zhushan. Hubei, C China 30.03N 109.26E
166 K8 **Xuanhan** Sichuan, C China 31.25N 107.41E
167 O2 **Xuanhua** Hebei, E China 40.37N 115.04E
167 P4 **Xuanhui He** ≈ E China
Xuanzhou see Xuancheng
167 N7 **Xuchang** Henan, C China 34.03N 113.48E
143 X10 **Xudat** Rus. Khudat. NE Azerbaijan 41.37N 48.39E
83 M16 **Xuddur** var. Hudur, It. Oddur. Bakool, SW Somalia 4.06N 43.47E
82 O13 **Xudun** Nugaal, N Somalia 9.12N 47.34E
166 L11 **Xuefeng Shan** ⛰ S China
Xulun Hobot Qagan see Qagan Nur
44 F2 **Xunantunich** ruins Cayo, W Belize 17.06N 89.10W
169 W6 **Xun He** ≈ NE China
166 L7 **Xun He** ≈ C China
166 L14 **Xun Jiang** ≈ S China
169 W5 **Xunke** var. Qike. Heilongjiang, NE China 49.36N 128.25E
167 P13 **Xunwu** var. Changning. Jiangxi, S China 24.58N 115.37E
167 O3 **Xushui** Hebei, E China 39.01N 115.37E
166 L16 **Xuwen** Guangdong, S China 20.20N 110.09E
166 I11 **Xuyong** var. Yongning. Sichuan, C China 28.16N 105.21E
167 P6 **Xuzhou** var. Hsu-chou, Suchow, Tongshan; prev. T'ung-shan. Jiangsu, E China 34.16N 117.09E
116 K13 **Xylaganí** var. Xilaganí. Anatolikí Makedonía kai Thráki, NE Greece 40.58N 25.27E
117 F19 **Xylókastro** var. Xilokastro. Pelopónnisos, S Greece 38.04N 22.36E

Y

166 H9 **Ya'an** var. Yaan. Sichuan, C China 30.00N 102.57E
190 L10 **Yaapeet** Victoria, SE Australia 35.48S 142.03E
81 D15 **Yabassi** Littoral, W Cameroon 4.30N 9.58E
83 J15 **Yabēlo** Oromo, C Ethiopia 4.53N 38.00E
172 Pp5 **Yabetsu-gawa** var. Yūbetsu-gawa. ≈ Hokkaidō, NE Japan
116 H9 **Yablanitsa** Lovech Oblast, W Bulgaria 43.02N 24.04E
45 N7 **Yablis** Región Autónoma Atlántico Norte, NE Nicaragua 14.02N 83.44W
126 Kk16 **Yablonovyy Khrebet** ⛰ S Russian Federation
168 J14 **Yabrai Shan** ⛰ NE China
47 U6 **Yabucoa** E Puerto Rico 18.03N 65.52W
197 K14 **Yacata** island Lau Group, E Fiji
166 J11 **Yachi He** ≈ S China
34 H10 **Yacolt** Washington, NW USA 45.49N 122.22W
56 M10 **Yacuaray** Amazonas, S Venezuela 4.12N 66.30W
59 M22 **Yacuiba** Tarija, S Bolivia 22.03S 63.40W
59 K16 **Yacuma, Río** ≈ C Bolivia
161 H16 **Yādgīr** Karnātaka, C India 16.46N 77.09E
23 R8 **Yadkin River** ≈ North Carolina, SE USA
23 R9 **Yadkinville** North Carolina, SE USA 36.07N 80.39W
131 P3 **Yadrin** Chavash Respubliki, W Russian Federation 55.55N 46.10E
197 I13 **Yadua** prev. Yandua. island NW Fiji
172 Oo17 **Yaeyama-shotō** var. Yaegama-shotō. island group SW Japan
77 O8 **Yafran** NW Libya 32.04N 12.31E
197 L15 **Yagasa Cluster** island group Lau Group, E Fiji
172 Oo3 **Yagashiri-tō** island NE Japan
67 H21 **Yaghan Basin** undersea feature SE Pacific Ocean
127 Nn9 **Yagodnoye** Magadanskaya Oblast', E Russian Federation 62.37N 149.18E
Yagotin see Yahotyn
80 G12 **Yagoua** Extrême-Nord, NE Cameroon 10.22N 15.13E
165 Q11 **Yagradagzê Shan** ▲ C China 35.06N 95.41E
Yaguachi see Yaguachi Nuevo
58 B7 **Yaguachi Nuevo** var. Yaguachi. Guayas, W Ecuador 2.06S 79.43W
Yaguarón, Río see Jaguarão, Rio
171 I16 **Yahagi-gawa** ≈ Honshū, SW Japan
119 Q11 **Yahorlyts'kyy Lyman** bay S Ukraine
119 Q5 **Yahotyn** Rus. Yagotin. Kyyivs'ka Oblast', N Ukraine 50.15N 31.48E
42 L12 **Yahualica** Jalisco, SW Mexico 21.12N 102.52W
81 L17 **Yahuma** Orientale, N Dem. Rep. Congo 1.12N 23.00E
142 K15 **Yahyalı** Kayseri, C Turkey 38.07N 35.22E
178 Gg15 **Yai, Khao** ▲ SW Thailand 8.45N 99.32E
171 Kk15 **Yaita** Tochigi, Honshū, S Japan 36.47N 139.54E
171 Ii17 **Yaizu** Shizuoka, Honshū, S Japan 34.52N 138.19E
166 G9 **Yajiang** var. Hekou, Tib. Nyagquka. Sichuan, C China 30.05N 100.57E
121 O14 **Yakawlyevichi** Rus. Yakovlevichi. Vitsyebskaya Voblasts', NE Belarus 54.21N 30.29E
169 S6 **Yakeshi** Nei Mongol Zizhiqu, N China 49.16N 120.42E
34 I9 **Yakima** Washington, NW USA 46.36N 120.30W
34 J10 **Yakima River** ≈ Washington, NW USA
116 G7 **Yakimovo** Montana, NW Bulgaria 43.39N 23.21E
Yakkabag see Yakkabog'
153 N12 **Yakkabog'** Rus. Yakkabag. Qashqadaryo Viloyati, S Uzbekistan 38.57N 66.35E
154 L12 **Yakmach** Baluchistān, SW Pakistan 28.48N 63.48E
79 O12 **Yako** W Burkina 12.58N 2.15W
41 W13 **Yakobi Island** island Alexander Archipelago, Alaska, USA
81 K16 **Yakoma** Equateur, N Dem. Rep. Congo 4.04N 22.22E
116 H11 **Yakoruda** Blagoevgrad, SW Bulgaria 42.01N 23.40E
Yakovlevichi see Yakawlyevichi
131 T2 **Yakshur-Bod'ya** Udmurtskaya Respublika, NW Russian Federation 57.10N 53.10E
172 N6 **Yakumo** Hokkaidō, NE Japan 42.18N 140.15E
170 B17 **Yaku-shima** island Nansei-shotō, SW Japan
41 V12 **Yakutat** Alaska, USA 59.33N 139.43W
41 U12 **Yakutat Bay** inlet Alaska, USA
Yakutia/Yakutiya/Yakutiya, Respublika see Sakha (Yakutiya), Respublika
126 M11 **Yakutsk** Respublika Sakha (Yakutiya), NE Russian Federation 62.10N 129.49E
178 Hh17 **Yala** Yala, SW Thailand 6.31N 101.19E
190 D6 **Yalata** South Australia 31.30S 131.53E
33 S9 **Yale** Michigan, N USA 43.07N 82.45W
188 I11 **Yalgoo** Western Australia 28.23S 116.43E
116 O12 **Yalıköy** İstanbul, NW Turkey 41.29N 28.19E
81 L14 **Yalinga** Haute-Kotto, C Central African Republic 6.47N 23.09E
121 M17 **Yalizava** Rus. Yelizovo. Mahilyowskaya Voblasts', E Belarus 53.24N 29.01E
46 L13 **Yallahs Hill** ▲ E Jamaica 17.53N 76.31W
24 L3 **Yalobusha River** ≈ Mississippi, S USA
81 H15 **Yaloké** Ombella-Mpoko, W Central African Republic 5.15N 17.12E
166 E7 **Yalong Jiang** ≈ C China
142 E11 **Yalova** Yalova, NW Turkey 40.40N 29.16E
142 E11 **Yalova** ◐ province NW Turkey
Yaloveny see Ialoveni
Yalpug see Ialpug
Yalpug, Ozero see Yalpuh, Ozero
119 N12 **Yalpuh, Ozero** Rus. Ozero Yalpug. ◎ SW Ukraine
119 T14 **Yalta** Respublika Krym, S Ukraine 44.30N 34.09E
169 W12 **Yalu** Chin. Yalu Jiang, Jap. Oryokko, Kor. Amnok-kang. ≈ China/North Korea
Yalu Jiang see Yalu
125 F12 **Yalutorovsk** Tyumenskaya Oblast', C Russian Federation 56.36N 66.09E
142 F14 **Yalvaç** İsparta, SW Turkey 38.16N 31.09E
172 N12 **Yamada** Iwate, Honshū, C Japan 39.27N 141.56E
170 Cc14 **Yamaga** Kumamoto, Kyūshū, SW Japan 33.01N 130.42E
171 L12 **Yamagata** Yamagata, Honshū, C Japan 38.15N 140.19E
171 Ll12 **Yamagata** off. Yamagata-ken. ◐ prefecture Honshū, C Japan
170 Bb16 **Yamagawa** Kagoshima, Kyūshū, SW Japan 31.12N 130.37E
170 Dd12 **Yamaguchi** var. Yamaguti. Yamaguchi, Honshū, SW Japan 34.10N 131.26E
170 Dd12 **Yamaguchi** off. Yamaguchi-ken, var. Yamaguti. ◐ prefecture Honshū, SW Japan
Yamaguti see Yamaguchi
129 X5 **Yamalo-Nenetskiy Avtonomnyy Okrug** ◐ autonomous district N Russian Federation
126 Gg6 **Yamal, Poluostrov** peninsula N Russian Federation
171 J16 **Yamanashi** off. Yamanashi-ken, var. Yamanasi. ◐ prefecture Honshū, S Japan
Yamanasi see Yamanashi
Yamanīyah, Al Jumhūrīyah al see Yemen
131 W5 **Yamantau** ▲ W Russian Federation 53.11N 57.30E
126 K16 **Yamarovka** Chitinskaya Oblast', S Russian Federation 50.36N 110.25E
Yamasaki see Yamazaki
13 P12 **Yamaska** ≈ Québec, SE Canada
171 Jj17 **Yamato** Kanagawa, Honshū, S Japan 35.30N 139.25E
199 Gg4 **Yamato Ridge** undersea feature S Sea of Japan
170 G14 **Yamazaki** var. Yamasaki. Hyōgo, Honshū, SW Japan 35.00N 134.31E
191 V5 **Yamba** New South Wales, SE Australia 29.28S 153.22E
83 D16 **Yambio** var. Yambiyo. Western Equatoria, S Sudan 4.34N 28.21E
Yambiyo see Yambio
116 L10 **Yambol** Turk. Yanboli. Yambol, E Bulgaria 42.28N 26.30E
116 M11 **Yambol** ◐ province E Bulgaria
81 M17 **Yambuya** Orientale, N Dem. Rep. Congo 1.22N 24.21E
176 Uu15 **Yamdena, Pulau** prev. Jamdena. island Kepulauan Tanimbar, E Indonesia
170 Cc13 **Yame** Fukuoka, Kyūshū, SW Japan 33.12N 130.31E
177 G6 **Yamethin** Mandalay, C Myanmar 20.25N 96.08E
194 G11 **Yaminbot** East Sepik, NW PNG 4.30S 143.44E
171 L15 **Yamizo-san** ▲ Honshū, C Japan 36.56N 140.14E
189 U9 **Yamma Yamma, Lake** ◎ Queensland, C Australia
78 M16 **Yamoussoukro** ● (Ivory Coast) C Ivory Coast 6.51N 5.21W
39 P3 **Yampa River** ≈ Colorado, C USA
119 S2 **Yampil'** Sums'ka Oblast', NE Ukraine 51.57N 33.49E
118 M8 **Yampil'** Vinnyts'ka Oblast', C Ukraine 48.15N 28.18E
127 Oo10 **Yamsk** Magadanskaya Oblast', E Russian Federation 59.33N 154.04E
158 J8 **Yamuna** prev. Jumna. ≈ N India
158 I9 **Yamunānagar** Haryāna, N India 30.07N 77.16E
Yamundá see Nhamundá, Rio
151 U8 **Yamyshevo** Pavlodar, NE Kazakhstan 51.49N 77.28E
165 N16 **Yamzho Yumco** ◎ W China
126 Ll6 **Yana** ≈ NE Russian Federation
195 P15 **Yanaba Island** island SE PNG
170 C13 **Yanagawa** Fukuoka, Kyūshū, SW Japan 33.08N 130.23E
170 E13 **Yanai** Yamaguchi, Honshū, SW Japan 33.56N 132.05E
161 L16 **Yanam** var. Yanaon. Pondicherry, E India 16.45N 82.16E
166 L5 **Yan'an** var. Yanan. Shaanxi, C China 36.34N 109.26E
Yanaon see Yanam
131 U3 **Yanaul** Respublika Bashkortostan, W Russian Federation 56.15N 54.57E
120 O12 **Yanavichy** Rus. Yanovichi. Vitsyebskaya Voblasts', NE Belarus 55.16N 30.42E
Yanboli see Yambol
146 K8 **Yanbu' al Baḩr** Al Madīnah, W Saudi Arabia 24.06N 38.03E
23 T8 **Yanceyville** North Carolina, SE USA 36.24N 79.20W
167 R7 **Yancheng** Jiangsu, E China 33.27N 120.10E
165 W8 **Yanchi** Ningxia, N China 37.49N 107.24E
166 L5 **Yanchuan** Shaanxi, C China 36.54N 110.04E
191 O10 **Yanco Creek** seasonal river New South Wales, SE Australia
191 O6 **Yanda Creek** seasonal river New South Wales, SE Australia
190 K4 **Yandama Creek** seasonal river New South Wales/South Australia
167 S11 **Yandang Shan** ⛰ SE China
197 G5 **Yandé, Île** island Îles Belep, W New Caledonia
Yandua see Yadua
165 O6 **Yandun** Xinjiang Uygur Zizhiqu, W China 42.24N 94.07E
78 L13 **Yanfolila** Sikasso, SW Mali 11.08N 8.12W
81 M18 **Yangambi** Orientale, N Dem. Rep. Congo 0.46N 24.24E
164 M15 **Yangbajain** Xizang Zizhiqu, W China 30.04N 90.34E
Yangchow see Yangzhou
166 M15 **Yangchun** Guangdong, S China 22.16N 111.49E
167 N2 **Yanggao** Shanxi, C China 40.24N 113.51E
Yanggeta see Yaqeta
Yangiabad see Yangiobod
Yangibazar see Dzhany-Bazar, Kyrgyzstan
Yangi-Bazar see Kofarnihon, Tajikistan
Yangiklshak see Yangiqishloq
152 M13 **Yangi-Nishon** Rus. Yang-Nishan. Qashqadaryo Viloyati, S Uzbekistan 38.37N 65.39E
153 Q9 **Yangiobod** Rus. Yangiabad. Toshkent Viloyati, E Uzbekistan 41.10N 70.10E
153 O10 **Yangiqishloq** Rus. Yangiklshak. Jizzax Viloyati, C Uzbekistan 40.27N 67.06E
153 P11 **Yangiyer** Sirdaryo Viloyati, E Uzbekistan 40.19N 68.48E
153 P9 **Yangiyo'l** Rus. Yangiyul'. Toshkent Viloyati, E Uzbekistan 41.12N 69.05E
166 M15 **Yangjiang** Guangdong, S China 21.52N 111.55E
Yangku see Taiyuan
Yang-Nishan see Yangi-Nishon
177 G9 **Yangon** Eng. Rangoon. ● (Myanmar) Yangon, S Myanmar 16.49N 96.10E
177 G8 **Yangon** Eng. Rangoon. ◐ division SW Myanmar
166 K17 **Yangpu Gang** harbour Hainan, S China
167 N4 **Yangquan** Shanxi, C China 37.52N 113.28E
167 N13 **Yangshan** Guangdong, S China 24.32N 112.36E
178 Kk13 **Yang Sin, Chu** ▲ S Vietnam 12.23N 108.25E
Yangtze see Chang Jiang/Jinsha Jiang
Yangtze Kiang see Chang Jiang
167 R7 **Yangzhou** var. Yangchow. Jiangsu, E China 32.22N 119.22E
166 L5 **Yan He** ≈ C China
169 Y10 **Yanji** Jilin, NE China 42.53N 129.31E
Yanji see Longjing
Yanjing see Yanyuan
31 Q12 **Yankton** South Dakota, N USA 42.52N 97.24W
167 O12 **Yanling** prev. Lingxian, Ling Xian. Hunan, S China 26.32N 113.48E
Yannina see Ioánnina
126 M6 **Yano-Indigirskaya Nizmennost'** plain NE Russian Federation
Yanovichi see Yanavichy
161 K24 **Yan Oya** ≈ N Sri Lanka
164 K6 **Yanqi** var. Yanqi Huizu Zizhixian. Xinjiang Uygur Zizhiqu, NW China 42.04N 86.32E
Yanqi Huizu Zizhixian see Yanqi
167 Q10 **Yanshan** var. Hekou. Jiangxi, S China 28.17N 117.47E
166 H14 **Yanshan** var. Jiangna. Yunnan, SW China 23.36N 104.20E
167 P2 **Yan Shan** ⛰ E China
169 X8 **Yanshou** Heilongjiang, NE China 45.27N 128.19E
126 Ll6 **Yanskiy Zaliv** bay N Russian Federation
191 O4 **Yantabulla** New South Wales, SE Australia 29.22S 145.00E
167 R4 **Yantai** var. Yan-t'ai; prev. Chefoo, Chih-fu. Shandong, E China 37.30N 121.22E
120 A13 **Yantarnyy** Ger. Palmnicken. Kaliningradskaya Oblast', W Russian Federation 54.53N 19.59E
116 J9 **Yantra** Gabrovo, N Bulgaria 42.58N 25.19E
116 K9 **Yantra** ≈ N Bulgaria
166 G11 **Yanyuan** var. Yanjing. Sichuan, C China 27.30N 101.22E
167 P5 **Yanzhou** Shandong, E China 35.34N 116.52E
81 E16 **Yaoundé** var. Yaunde. ● (Cameroon) Centre, S Cameroon 3.51N 11.31E
196 I14 **Yap** ◐ state W Micronesia
196 F16 **Yap** island Caroline Islands, W Micronesia
59 M18 **Yapacani, Rio** ≈ C Bolivia
176 Ww12 **Yapa Kopra** Papua, E Indonesia 4.18S 135.05E
Yapan see Yapen, Selat
Yapanskoye More see East Sea/Japan, Sea of
79 P15 **Yapei** N Ghana 9.10N 1.08W
10 M10 **Yapeitso, Mont** ▲ Québec, E Canada 52.18N 70.24W
176 X10 **Yapen, Pulau** prev. Japen. island E Indonesia
176 X9 **Yapen, Selat** var. Yapan. strait Papua, E Indonesia
63 E15 **Yapeyú** Corrientes, NE Argentina 29.28S 56.49W
142 I11 **Yapraklı** Çankın, N Turkey 40.45N 33.46E
182 M3 **Yap Trench** var. Yap Trough. undersea feature SE Philippine Sea
Yap Trough see Yap Trench
Yapurá see Caquetá, Río, Brazil/Colombia
Yapurá see Japurá, Rio, Brazil/Colombia
176 U11 **Yaputih** Pulau Seram, E Indonesia 3.16S 129.29E
197 I13 **Yaqaga** island N Fiji
197 H13 **Yaqeta** prev. Yanggeta. island Yasawa Group, NW Fiji
42 G6 **Yaqui** Sonora, NW Mexico 27.21N 109.59W
34 E12 **Yaquina Bay** bay Oregon, NW USA
42 G6 **Yaqui, Río** ≈ NW Mexico
176 Y14 **Yar** channel Papua, E Indonesia
56 K5 **Yaracuy** off. Estado Yaracuy. ◐ state NW Venezuela
Yaradzhi see Yarajy
152 E13 **Yarajy** Rus. Yaradzhi. Ahal Welaýaty, C Turkmenistan 38.12N 57.40E
129 Q15 **Yaransk** Kirovskaya Oblast', NW Russian Federation 57.18N 47.52E
142 F17 **Yardımcı Burnu** headland SW Turkey 36.10N 30.25E
99 Q19 **Yare** ≈ E England, UK
129 S9 **Yarega** Respublika Komi, NW Russian Federation 63.27N 53.28E
118 I7 **Yaremcha** Ivano-Frankivs'ka Oblast', W Ukraine 48.27N 24.34E
201 Q9 **Yaren** SW Nauru 0.33S 166.54E
129 Q10 **Yarensk** Arkhangel'skaya Oblast', NW Russian Federation 62.09N 49.03E
161 F16 **Yargatti** Karnātaka, W India 16.07N 75.11E
171 Ii14 **Yariga-take** ▲ Honshū, S Japan 36.20N 137.38E
147 O15 **Yarīm** W Yemen 14.15N 44.22E
56 F14 **Yarí, Río** ≈ SW Colombia
56 K5 **Yaritagua** Yaracuy, N Venezuela 10.04N 69.07W
Yarkand see Yarkant He
Yarkant see Shache
164 E9 **Yarkant He** var. Yarkand. ≈ NW China
155 U3 **Yarkhūn** ≈ NW Pakistan
Yarlung Zangbo Jiang see Brahmaputra
118 L6 **Yarmolyntsi** Khmel'nyts'ka Oblast', W Ukraine 49.13N 26.53E
11 O16 **Yarmouth** Nova Scotia, SE Canada 43.53N 66.08W
Yarmouth see Great Yarmouth
Yaroslav see Jarosław
128 L15 **Yaroslavl'** Yaroslavskaya Oblast', W Russian Federation 57.38N 39.52E
128 K14 **Yaroslavskaya Oblast'** ◐ province W Russian Federation
126 Kk12 **Yaroslavskiy** Respublika Sakha (Yakutiya), NE Russian Federation 60.10N 114.12E
191 P13 **Yarram** Victoria, SE Australia 38.36S 146.40E
191 O11 **Yarrawonga** Victoria, SE Australia 36.04S 145.58E
190 L4 **Yarriarraburra Swamp** wetland New South Wales, SE Australia
126 Gg8 **Yar-Sale** Yamalo-Nenetskiy Avtonomnyy Okrug, N Russian Federation 66.52N 70.42E
126 I12 **Yartsevo** Krasnoyarskiy Kray, C Russian Federation 60.15N 90.09E
130 I4 **Yartsevo** Smolenskaya Oblast', W Russian Federation 55.03N 32.46E
56 E8 **Yarumal** Antioquia, NW Colombia 6.58N 75.25W
197 H13 **Yasawa** island Yasawa Group, NW Fiji
197 G13 **Yasawa Group** island group NW Fiji
79 V12 **Yashi** Katsina, N Nigeria 12.21N 7.56E
79 S14 **Yashikera** Kwara, W Nigeria 9.40N 3.19E
153 T14 **Yashilkŭl** Rus. Ozero Yashil'kul'. ◎ SE Tajikistan
Yashil'kul', Ozero see Yashilkŭl
171 Ll11 **Yashima** Akita, Honshū, C Japan 39.10N 140.10E
170 Dd14 **Ya-shima** island SW Japan
170 E14 **Yashiro-jima** island SW Japan
131 P13 **Yashkul'** Respublika Kalmykiya, SW Russian Federation 46.09N 45.22E
152 F13 **Yashlyk** Ahal Welaýaty, C Turkmenistan 37.46N 58.51E
Yasinovataya see Yasynuvata
116 N10 **Yasna Polyana** Burgas, SE Bulgaria 42.18N 27.35E
126 M14 **Yasnyy** Amurskaya Oblast', SE Russian Federation 53.03N 127.52E
178 J10 **Yasothon** Yasothon, E Thailand 15.46N 104.12E
191 R10 **Yass** New South Wales, SE Australia 34.52S 148.55E
Yassy see Iaşi
170 Ff12 **Yasugi** Shimane, Honshū, SW Japan 35.25N 133.14E
149 N10 **Yāsūj** var. Yesuj; prev. Tal-e Khosravī. Kohgīlūyeh va Būyer Aḩmad, C Iran 30.40N 51.34E
142 M11 **Yasun Burnu** headland N Turkey 41.07N 37.40E
119 X8 **Yasynuvata** Rus. Yasinovataya. Donets'ka Oblast', SE Ukraine 48.04N 37.56E
142 C15 **Yatağan** Muğla, SW Turkey 37.22N 28.07E
171 M9 **Yatate-tōge** pass Honshū, C Japan 40.25N 140.36E
197 J7 **Yaté** Province Sud, S New Caledonia 22.10S 166.56E
29 P6 **Yates Center** Kansas, C USA 37.52N 95.43W
193 B21 **Yates Point** headland South Island, NZ 44.30S 167.49E
15 Kk7 **Yathkyed Lake** ◎ Nunavut, NE Canada
176 U15 **Yatoke** Pulau Babar, E Indonesia 7.51S 129.49E
81 M18 **Yatolema** Orientale, N Dem. Rep. Congo 0.25N 24.34E
171 J15 **Yatsuga-take** ▲ Honshū, S Japan 35.58N 138.22E
170 C14 **Yatsushiro** var. Yatusiro. Kumamoto, Kyūshū, SW Japan 32.30N 130.34E
170 C15 **Yatsushiro-kai** bay SW Japan
144 F11 **Yatta** var. Yuta. S West Bank 31.29N 35.10E
83 J20 **Yatta Plateau** plateau SE Kenya
Yatusiro see Yatsushiro
59 F17 **Yauca, Río** ≈ SW Peru
47 S6 **Yauco** W Puerto Rico 18.02N 66.51W
176 Xx9 **Yauke** Papua, E Indonesia 1.34S 137.56E
Yaunde see Yaoundé
Yavan see Yovon
Yavarí see Javari, Rio
58 G9 **Yavari Mirim, Río** ≈ NE Peru
42 G7 **Yavaros** Sonora, NW Mexico 26.40N 109.32W
160 I13 **Yavatmāl** Mahārāshtra, C India 20.22N 78.10E
56 M9 **Yaví, Cerro** ▲ C Venezuela 5.43N 65.51W
45 W16 **Yaviza** Darién, SE Panama 8.09N 77.40W
144 F10 **Yavne** Central, W Israel 31.52N 34.45E
118 H5 **Yavoriv** Pol. Jaworów, Rus. Yavorov. L'vivs'ka Oblast', NW Ukraine 49.57N 23.21E
Yavorov see Yavoriv
170 E15 **Yawatahama** Ehime, Shikoku, SW Japan 33.27N 132.24E
Ya Xian see Sanya
142 L17 **Yayladaği** Hatay, S Turkey 35.55N 36.03E
129 V13 **Yayva** Permskaya Oblast', NW Russian Federation 59.19N 57.15E
129 V12 **Yayva** ≈ NW Russian Federation
149 Q9 **Yazd** var. Yezd. Yazd, C Iran 31.55N 54.22E
149 Q8 **Yazd** off. Ostān-e Yazd, var. Yezd. ◐ province C Iran
Yazgulemskiy Khrebet see Yazgulom, Qatorkŭhi
153 S13 **Yazgulom, Qatorkŭhi** Rus. Yazgulemskiy Khrebet. ⛰ S Tajikistan
24 K5 **Yazoo City** Mississippi, S USA 32.51N 90.24W
24 K5 **Yazoo River** ≈ Mississippi, S USA
131 Q5 **Yazykovo** Ul'yanovskaya Oblast', W Russian Federation 54.19N 47.22E
111 U4 **Ybbs** Niederösterreich, NE Austria 48.10N 15.03E
111 U4 **Ybbs** ≈ C Austria
97 G22 **Yding Skovhøj** hill C Denmark 55.58N 9.45E
117 G20 **Ýdra** var. Ídhra, Idra. Ýdra, S Greece 37.20N 23.27E
117 G21 **Ýdra** var. Ídhra. island S Greece
117 G20 **Ýdras, Kólpos** strait S Greece
178 Gg10 **Ye** Mon State, S Myanmar 15.15N 97.49E
191 O12 **Yea** Victoria, SE Australia 37.15S 145.27E
Yebaishou see Jianping
80 I5 **Yebbi-Bou** Borkou-Ennedi-Tibesti, N Chad 21.12N 17.55E
164 F9 **Yecheng** var. Kargilik. Xinjiang Uygur Zizhiqu, NW China 37.54N 77.25E
107 R11 **Yecla** Murcia, SE Spain 38.36N 1.07W
42 H6 **Yécora** Sonora, NW Mexico 28.20N 108.55W
Yedintsy see Edineţ
128 J13 **Yefimovskiy** Leningradskaya Oblast', NW Russian Federation 59.32N 34.34E
176 Uu9 **Yeflio** Papua, E Indonesia 1.01S 131.17E
130 K6 **Yefremov** Tul'skaya Oblast', W Russian Federation 53.09N 38.02E
Yêgainnyin see Henan
143 U12 **Yeghegis** Rus. Yekhegis. ≈ C Armenia
151 T10 **Yegindybulak** Kaz. Egindibulaq. Karaganda, C Kazakhstan 49.45N 75.45E
130 L4 **Yegor'yevsk** Moskovskaya Oblast', W Russian Federation 55.29N 39.03E
Yehuda, Haré see Judaean Hills
83 E15 **Yei** ≈ S Sudan
167 P8 **Yeji** var. Yejiaji. Anhui, E China 31.52N 115.58E
Yejiaji see Yeji
125 Ee11 **Yekaterinburg** prev. Sverdlovsk. Sverdlovskaya Oblast', C Russian Federation 56.52N 60.34E
Yekaterinodar see Krasnodar
Yekaterinoslav see Dnipropetrovs'k
126 Mm15 **Yekaterinoslavka** Amurskaya Oblast', SE Russian Federation 50.23N 129.03E
131 O7 **Yekaterinovka** Saratovskaya Oblast', W Russian Federation 52.01N 44.11E
78 K16 **Yekepa** NE Liberia 7.34N 8.31W
131 T3 **Yelabuga** Respublika Tatarstan, W Russian Federation 55.46N 52.07E
Yela Island see Rossel Island
131 O8 **Yelan'** Volgogradskaya Oblast', SW Russian Federation 51.00N 43.40E
119 Q9 **Yelanets'** Rus. Yelanets. Mykolayivs'ka Oblast', S Ukraine 47.40N 31.51E
125 G13 **Yelanka** Novosibirskaya Oblast', C Russian Federation 55.38N 75.23E
130 L7 **Yelets** Lipetskaya Oblast', W Russian Federation 52.37N 38.29E
129 W4 **Yeletskiy** Respublika Komi, NW Russian Federation 67.03N 64.05E
78 J11 **Yélimané** Kayes, W Mali 15.06N 10.43W
Yelisavetpol see Gäncä
Yelizavetgrad see Kirovohrad
127 O13 **Yelizavety, Mys** headland SE Russian Federation 54.20N 142.39E
127 Pp11 **Yelizovo** Kamchatskaya Oblast', E Russian Federation 53.12N 158.18E
Yelizovo see Yalizava
131 S5 **Yelkhovka** Samarskaya Oblast', W Russian Federation 53.51N 50.16E
98 M1 **Yell** island NE Scotland, UK
161 E17 **Yellāpur** Karnātaka, W India 15.06N 74.50E
9 U17 **Yellow Grass** Saskatchewan, S Canada 49.51N 104.09W
Yellowhammer State see Alabama
9 O15 **Yellowhead Pass** pass Alberta/British Columbia, SW Canada 52.54N 118.44W
15 Hh8 **Yellowknife** territory capital Northwest Territories, W Canada 62.30N 114.28W
15 I7 **Yellowknife** ≈ Northwest Territories, NW Canada
194 F10 **Yellow River** ≈ NW PNG
25 P8 **Yellow River** ≈ Alabama/Florida, S USA
32 I4 **Yellow River** ≈ Wisconsin, N USA
32 J6 **Yellow River** ≈ Wisconsin, N USA
32 K7 **Yellow River** ≈ Wisconsin, N USA
Yellow River see Huang He
163 V8 **Yellow Sea** Chin. Huang Hai, Kor. Hwang-Hae. sea E Asia
35 S13 **Yellowstone Lake** ◎ Wyoming, C USA
35 T13 **Yellowstone National Park** national park Wyoming, NW USA
35 Y8 **Yellowstone River** ≈ Montana/Wyoming, NW USA
98 L1 **Yell Sound** strait N Scotland, UK
29 U9 **Yellville** Arkansas, C USA 36.13N 92.40W
126 Hh11 **Yeloguy** ≈ C Russian Federation
Yëloten see Ýolöten
121 M20 **Yel'sk** Rus. Yel'sk. Homyel'skaya Voblasts', SE Belarus 51.49N 29.09E
79 T13 **Yelwa** Kebbi, W Nigeria 10.52N 4.46E
125 Ee12 **Yemanzhelinsk** Chelyabinskaya Oblast', C Russian Federation 54.43N 61.08E
23 R15 **Yemassee** South Carolina, SE USA 32.41N 80.51W
147 O15 **Yemen** off. Republic of Yemen, Ar. Al Jumhūrīyah al Yamanīyah, Al Yaman. ◆ republic SW Asia
118 M4 **Yemil'chyne** Zhytomyrs'ka Oblast', N Ukraine 50.51N 27.49E
128 M10 **Yemtsa** Arkhangel'skaya Oblast', NW Russian Federation 63.04N 40.18E
128 M10 **Yemtsa** ≈ NW Russian Federation
129 R10 **Yemva** prev. Zheleznodorozhnyy. Respublika Komi, NW Russian 62.38N 50.58E
79 U17 **Yenagoa** Bayelsa, S Nigeria 4.58N 6.16E
119 X7 **Yenakiyeve** Rus. Yenakiyevo; prev. Ordzhonikidze, Rykovo. Donets'ka Oblast', E Ukraine 48.13N 38.13E
Yenakiyevo see Yenakiyeve
177 Ff6 **Yenangyaung** Magwe, W Myanmar 20.28N 94.54E
178 Jj5 **Yên Bai** Yên Bai, N Vietnam 21.43N 104.54E
191 P9 **Yenda** New South Wales, SE Australia 34.16S 146.15E
176 W10 **Yende** Papua, E Indonesia 2.19S 134.34E
79 Q14 **Yendi** NE Ghana 9.23N 0.02W
Yêndum see Zhag'yab
164 E8 **Yengisar** Xinjiang Uygur Zizhiqu, NW China 38.50N 76.10E
124 O3 **Yeniboğaziçi** var. Ayios Seryios, Gk. Ágios Sérgios. E Cyprus 35.10N 33.53E
124 Oo2 **Yenierenköy** var. Yialousa, Gk. Agialoúsa. NE Cyprus 35.32N 34.12E
Yenipazar see Novi Pazar
142 E12 **Yenişehir** Bursa, NW Turkey 40.16N 29.37E
Yenisei Bay see Yeniseyskiy Zaliv
126 Hh8 **Yenisey** ≈ Mongolia/Russian Federation
126 I13 **Yeniseysk** Krasnoyarskiy Kray, C Russian Federation 58.23N 92.06E
207 W10 **Yeniseyskiy Zaliv** var. Yenisei Bay. bay N Russian Federation
131 Q12 **Yenotayevka** Astrakhanskaya Oblast', SW Russian Federation 47.16N 47.01E
128 L4 **Yenozero, Ozero** ◎ NW Russian Federation
Yenping see Nanping
41 Q11 **Yentna River** ≈ Alaska, USA
188 M10 **Yeo, Lake** salt lake Western Australia
191 R7 **Yeoval** New South Wales, SE Australia 32.45S 148.39E
99 K23 **Yeovil** SW England, UK 50.57N 2.39W
42 H6 **Yepachic** Chihuahua, N Mexico 28.27N 108.25W
189 Y8 **Yeppoon** Queensland, E Australia 23.04S 150.42E
130 M5 **Yerakhtur** Ryazanskaya Oblast', W Russian Federation 54.45N 41.09E
Yeraliyev see Kuryk
152 F12 **Yerbent** Ahal Welaýaty, C Turkmenistan 39.19N 58.34E
126 Jj12 **Yerbogachen** Irkutskaya Oblast', C Russian Federation 61.07N 108.03E
143 T12 **Yerevan** Eng. Erivan. ● (Armenia) C Armenia 40.12N 44.31E
143 U12 **Yerevan** ✈ C Armenia 40.07N 44.34E
151 R9 **Yereymentau** var. Jermentau, Yermentau, Kaz. Ereymentaū. Akmola, C Kazakhstan 51.37N 73.10E
131 O12 **Yergeni** hill range SW Russian Federation
Yeriho see Jericho
37 R6 **Yerington** Nevada, W USA 38.58N 119.10W
142 J13 **Yerköy** Yozgat, C Turkey 39.39N 34.28E
116 L13 **Yerlisu** Edirne, NW Turkey 40.45N 26.38E
Yermak see Aksu
151 R9 **Yermenytau** Kaz. Ereymentaū, Jermentau. Akmola, C Kazakhstan 51.37N 73.10E
151 R9 **Yermenytau, Gory** ⛰ C Kazakhstan
129 R5 **Yermitsa** Respublika Komi, NW Russian Federation 66.57N 52.15E
37 V14 **Yermo** California, W USA 34.54N 116.49W
126 Ll14 **Yerofey Pavlovich** Amurskaya Oblast', SE Russian Federation 53.58N 121.49E
101 F15 **Yerseke** Zeeland, SW Netherlands 51.30N 4.03E
131 Q8 **Yershov** Saratovskaya Oblast', W Russian Federation 51.18N 48.16E
129 P9 **Yërtom** Respublika Komi, NW Russian Federation 63.27N 47.52E
58 D13 **Yerupaja, Nevado** ▲ C Peru 10.23S 76.58W
Yerushalayim see Jerusalem
107 R4 **Yesa, Embalse de** ▣ NE Spain
150 F9 **Yesensay** Zapadnyy Kazakhstan, NW Kazakhstan 49.58N 51.19E
151 V15 **Yesik** Kaz. Esik; prev. Issyk. Almaty, SE Kazakhstan 43.23N 77.31E
151 O8 **Yesil'** Kaz. Esil. Akmola, C Kazakhstan 51.58N 66.22E
142 K15 **Yeşilhisar** Kayseri, C Turkey 38.22N 35.07E
142 L11 **Yeşilırmak** anc. Iris. ≈ N Turkey
39 U12 **Yeso** New Mexico, SW USA 34.25N 104.36W
Yeso see Hokkaidō
131 N15 **Yessentuki** Stavropol'skiy Kray, SW Russian Federation 44.06N 42.51E
126 J9 **Yessey** Evenkiyskiy Avtonomnyy Okrug, N Russian Federation 68.18N 101.49E
107 P12 **Yeste** Castilla-La Mancha, C Spain 38.21N 2.18W
Yesuj see Yāsūj
191 T4 **Yetman** New South Wales, SE Australia 28.56S 150.47E
78 L4 **Yetti** physical region N Mauritania
177 G4 **Ye-u** Sagaing, C Myanmar 22.49N 95.25E
104 H9 **Yeu, Île d'** island NW France
Yevlakh see Yevlax
143 W11 **Yevlax** Rus. Yevlakh. C Azerbaijan 40.36N 47.09E
119 S13 **Yevpatoriya** Respublika Krym, S Ukraine 45.12N 33.22E
125 B17 **Yevreyskaya Avtonomnaya Oblast'** Eng. Jewish Autonomous Oblast. ◐ autonomous province SE Russian Federation
130 K12 **Yeya** ≈ SW Russian Federation
164 I10 **Yeyik** Xinjiang Uygur Zizhiqu, W China 36.43N 83.13E
130 K12 **Yeysk** Krasnodarskiy Kray, SW Russian Federation 46.41N 38.15E
Yezd see Yazd
Yezerishche see Yezyaryshcha
Yezhou see Jianshi
Yezo see Hokkaidō
120 N11 **Yezyaryshcha** Rus. Yezerishche. Vitsyebskaya Voblasts', NE Belarus 55.49N 29.58E
Yialí see Gyalí
Yialousa see Yenierenköy
169 V7 **Yi'an** Heilongjiang, NE China 47.52N 125.13E
Yiannitsá see Giannitsá
166 I10 **Yibin** Sichuan, C China 28.47N 104.36E
164 K13 **Yibug Caka** ◎ W China
166 M9 **Yichang** Hubei, C China 30.37N 111.02E
166 L5 **Yichuan** Shaanxi, C China 36.05N 110.02E
163 W3 **Yichun** Heilongjiang, NE China 47.40N 129.10E
169 X6 **Yichun** var. I-ch'un. Heilongjiang, NE China 47.39N 128.54E
167 O11 **Yichun** Jiangxi, S China 27.45N 114.22E
166 M9 **Yidu** prev. Zhicheng. Hubei, C China 30.21N 111.27E
Yidu see Qingzhou
196 C15 **Yigo** NE Guam 13.33N 144.52E
167 Q5 **Yi He** ≈ E China
169 X8 **Yilan** Heilongjiang, NE China 46.18N 129.36E
142 C9 **Yıldız Dağları** ⛰ NW Turkey
142 L13 **Yıldızeli** Sivas, N Turkey 39.52N 36.37E
169 U4 **Yilehuli Shan** ⛰ NE China
169 S7 **Yimin He** ≈ NE China
165 W8 **Yinchuan** var. Yinch'uan, Yin-ch'uan, Yinchwan. Ningxia, N China 38.30N 106.19E
Yinchwan see Yinchuan
Yindu He see Indus
167 N14 **Yingde** Guangdong, S China 24.08N 113.21E
167 O7 **Ying He** ≈ C China
169 U13 **Yingkou** var. Ying-k'ou, Yingkow; prev. Newchwang, Niuchwang. Liaoning, NE China 40.38N 122.17E
Yingkow see Yingkou
167 P9 **Yingshan** var. Wenquan. Hubei, C China 30.45N 115.41E

◆ Country
● Country Capital
◇ Dependent Territory
○ Dependent Territory Capital
◐ Administrative Region
✈ International Airport
▲ Mountain
⛰ Mountain Range
⩘ Volcano
≈ River
◎ Lake
▣ Reservoir

YINGSHAN – ZAPATA, PENÍNSULA DE

Yingshan see Guangshui
167 Q10 Yingtan Jiangxi, C China 28.17N 117.03E
Yin-hsien see Ningbo
164 H5 Yining var. I-ning, Uigh. Gulja, Kuldja. Xinjiang Uygur Zizhiqu, NW China 43.53N 81.18E
166 K11 Yinjiang var. Yinjiang Tujiazu Miaozu Zizhixian. Guizhou, S China 28.22N 108.07E
Yinjiang Tujiazu Miaozu Zizhixian see Yinjiang
177 Ff4 Yinmabin Sagaing, C Myanmar 22.04N 94.57E
169 N13 Yin Shan ▲ N China
Yin-tu Ho see Indus
165 P15 Yi'ong Zangbo ∽ W China
Yioúra see Gyáros
83 J14 Yirga 'Alem It. Irgalem. Southern, S Ethiopia 6.43N 38.24E
63 E19 Yí, Río ∽ C Uruguay
83 E14 Yirol El Buhayrat, S Sudan 6.34N 30.33E
169 S8 Yirshi var. Yirxie. Nei Mongol Zizhiqu, N China 47.16N 119.51E
Yirxie see Yirshi
167 Q5 Yishui Shandong, E China 35.49N 118.39E
Yisrael/Yisra'el see Israel
Yíthion see Gýtheio
Yitiaoshan see Jingtai
169 W10 Yitong var. Yitong Manzu Zizhixian. Jilin, NE China 43.22N 125.19E
Yitong Manzu Zizhixian see Yitong
165 P5 Yiwu var. Aratürük. Xinjiang Uygur Zizhiqu, NW China 43.16N 94.38E
169 U12 Yiwulü Shan ▲ N China
169 T12 Yixian var. Yizhou. Liaoning, NE China 41.29N 121.21E
167 N10 Yiyang Hunan, S China 28.39N 112.19E
167 Q10 Yiyang Jiangxi, S China 28.23N 117.24E
167 N13 Yizhang Hunan, S China 25.24N 112.55E
Yizhou see Yixian
95 K19 Yläne Länsi-Suomi, W Finland 60.50N 22.25E
95 L14 Yli-Ii Oulu, C Finland 65.21N 25.55E
95 L14 Ylikiiminki Oulu, C Finland 65.00N 26.10E
94 N13 Yli-Kitka ◎ NE Finland
95 K17 Ylistaro Länsi-Suomi, W Finland 62.58N 22.30E
94 K13 Ylitornio Lappi, NW Finland 66.16N 23.39E
95 L15 Ylivieska Oulu, W Finland 64.04N 24.30E
95 L18 Ylöjärvi Länsi-Suomi, W Finland 61.31N 23.37E
97 N17 Yngaren ◎ C Sweden
27 T12 Yoakum Texas, SW USA 29.17N 97.09W
79 X13 Yobe ◐ state NE Nigeria
172 Nn4 Yobetsu-dake ▲ Hokkaidō, NE Japan 43.15N 140.27E
176 Xx10 Yobi Papua, E Indonesia 1.42S 138.09E
82 L11 Yoboki C Djibouti 11.30N 42.04E
170 C12 Yobuko Saga, Kyūshū, SW Japan 33.31N 129.50E
24 M4 Yockanookany River ∽ Mississippi, S USA
24 L2 Yocona River ∽ Mississippi, S USA
176 Yy15 Yodom Papua, E Indonesia 7.12S 139.24E
174 Kk15 Yogyakarta prev. Djokjakarta, Jogjakarta, Jokyakarta. Jawa, C Indonesia 7.48S 110.24E
174 Kk16 Yogyakarta off. Daerah Istimewa Yogyakarta, var. Djokjakarta, Jogjakarta, Jokyakarta. ◐ autonomous district S Indonesia
172 O5 Yoichi Hokkaidō, NE Japan 43.11N 140.45E
44 G6 Yojoa, Lago de ◎ NW Honduras
81 G16 Yokadouma Est, SE Cameroon 3.25N 15.06E
171 H15 Yōkaichi var. Yôkaiti. Shiga, Honshū, SW Japan 35.07N 136.10E
Yôkaiti see Yōkaichi
171 H15 Yokkaichi var. Yokkaiti. Mie, Honshū, SW Japan 34.58N 136.36E
Yokkaiti see Yokkaichi
81 E15 Yoko Centre, C Cameroon 5.28N 12.19E
172 Qq12 Yokoate-jima island Nansei-shotō, SW Japan
172 N9 Yokohama Aomori, Honshū, C Japan 41.04N 141.14E
171 Jj16 Yokohama Kanagawa, Honshū, S Japan 35.26N 139.37E
171 Jj17 Yokosuka Kanagawa, Honshū, S Japan 35.15N 139.39E
170 F12 Yokota Shimane, Honshū, SW Japan 35.10N 133.03E
171 M11 Yokote Akita, Honshū, C Japan 39.19N 140.33E
172 Nn7 Yokotsu-dake ▲ Hokkaidō, NE Japan 41.54N 140.48E
79 Y14 Yola Adamawa, E Nigeria 9.07N 12.24E
81 L19 Yolombo Equateur, C Dem. Rep. Congo 1.36S 23.13E
152 J14 Yǒlöten Rus. Yëloten, prev. Iolotan'. Mary Welaýaty, S Turkmenistan 37.15N 62.18E
176 W10 Yomber Papua, E Indonesia 2.04S 134.22E
172 T16 Yome-jima island Ogasawara-shotō, SE Japan
78 K16 Yomou Guinée-Forestière, SE Guinea 7.30N 9.13W
176 Y15 Yomuka Papua, E Indonesia 7.25S 138.36E
196 C16 Yona E Guam 13.24N 144.46E
170 Ff12 Yonago Tottori, Honshū, SW Japan 35.30N 134.15E
172 O17 Yonaguni Okinawa, SW Japan 24.29N 123.00E
172 Nn16 Yonaguni-jima island Nansei-shotō, SW Japan
172 Pp14 Yonaha-dake ▲ Okinawa, SW Japan 26.43N 128.13E
169 X14 Yonan SW North Korea 37.50N 126.15E
171 L13 Yonezawa Yamagata, Honshū, C Japan 37.54N 140.06E
167 Q12 Yong'an var. Yongan. Fujian, SE China 25.58N 117.25E
Yong'an see Fengjie
165 T9 Yongchang Gansu, N China 38.15N 101.55E
167 P7 Yongcheng Henan, C China 33.55N 116.21E
169 Z15 Yǒngch'ŏn Jap. Eisen. SE South Korea 35.56N 128.55E
166 J10 Yongchuan Chongqing Shi, C China 29.27N 105.56E
165 U10 Yongdeng Gansu, C China 35.58N 103.27E
Yongding see Yongren
133 W9 Yongding He ∽ E China
167 P11 Yongfeng var. Enjiang. Jiangxi, S China 27.19N 115.22E
164 L5 Yongfengqu Xinjiang Uygur Zizhiqu, W China 43.28N 87.09E
166 L13 Yongfu Guangxi Zhuangzu Zizhiqu, S China 24.57N 109.59E
169 X13 Yǒnghǔng E North Korea 39.30N 127.13E
165 U10 Yongjing Gansu, C China 36.00N 103.30E
Yongjing see Xifeng
169 Y15 Yǒngju Jap. Eishū. C South Korea 36.48N 128.37E
Yongning see Xuyong
166 E12 Yongping Yunnan, SW China 25.30N 99.28E
166 G12 Yongren var. Yongding. Yunnan, SW China 26.11N 101.49E
166 L10 Yongshun var. Lingxi. Hunan, S China 29.01N 109.48E
167 P10 Yongxiu var. Tujiabu. Jiangxi, S China 29.08N 115.47E
166 M12 Yongzhou Hunan, S China 26.12N 111.36E
20 K14 Yonkers New York, NE USA 40.56N 73.51W
105 Q7 Yonne ◐ department C France
105 P6 Yonne ∽ C France
56 H9 Yopal var. El Yopal. Casanare, C Colombia 5.19N 72.19W
164 E8 Yopurga var. Yukuriawat. Xinjiang Uygur Zizhiqu, NW China 39.13N 76.44E
153 S11 Yordan var. Iordan, Rus. Jardan. Farg'ona Viloyati, E Uzbekistan 39.58N 71.43E
188 J12 York Western Australia 31.55S 116.52E
99 M16 York anc. Eboracum, Eburacum. N England, UK 53.58N 1.04W
25 N5 York Alabama, S USA 32.29N 88.18W
31 Q15 York Nebraska, C USA 40.52N 97.35W
20 G16 York Pennsylvania, NE USA 39.55N 76.42W
23 R11 York South Carolina, SE USA 34.59N 81.14W
12 J13 York ∽ Ontario, SE Canada
13 X6 York ∽ Québec, SE Canada
189 V1 York, Cape headland Queensland, NE Australia 10.40S 142.36E
190 I9 Yorke Peninsula peninsula South Australia
190 I9 Yorketown South Australia 35.01S 137.38E
21 P9 York Harbor Maine, NE USA 43.10N 70.37W
23 X6 York River ∽ Virginia, NE USA
99 M16 Yorkshire cultural region N England, UK
99 L16 Yorkshire Dales physical region N England, UK
9 V16 Yorkton Saskatchewan, S Canada 51.12N 102.28W
27 T12 Yorktown Texas, SW USA 28.58N 97.30W
23 X6 Yorktown Virginia, NE USA 37.13N 76.29W
32 M11 Yorkville Illinois, N USA 41.38N 88.27W
44 I5 Yoro Yoro, C Honduras 15.06N 87.09W
44 H5 Yoro ◐ department N Honduras
172 Pp14 Yoron-jima island Nansei-shotō, SW Japan
79 N13 Yorosso Sikasso, S Mali 12.18N 4.44W
37 R8 Yosemite National Park national park California, W USA
170 Ff14 Yoshii-gawa ∽ Honshū, SW Japan
170 Ff15 Yoshino-gawa var. Yosino Gawa. ∽ Shikoku, SW Japan
131 Q3 Yoshkar-Ola Respublika Mariy El, W Russian Federation 56.37N 47.53E
Yosino Gawa see Yoshino-gawa
Yösönbulag see Altay
176 Y15 Yos Sudarso, Pulau var. Pulau Dolak, Pulau Kolepom; prev. Jos Sudarso. island E Indonesia
176 Z10 Yos Sudarso, Teluk bay Papua, E Indonesia
169 Y17 Yǒsu Jap. Reisui. S South Korea 34.45N 127.48E
172 Nn5 Yotei-zan ▲ Hokkaidō, NE Japan 42.50N 140.46E
99 D21 Youghal Ir. Eochaill. S Ireland 51.57N 7.49W
99 D21 Youghal Bay Ir. Cuan Eochaille. inlet S Ireland
20 C15 Youghiogheny River ∽ Pennsylvania, NE USA
166 K14 You Jiang ∽ S China
191 Q9 Young New South Wales, SE Australia 34.19S 148.19E
9 T15 Young Saskatchewan, S Canada 51.44N 105.44W
63 E18 Young Río Negro, W Uruguay 32.43S 57.36W
190 G5 Younghusband, Lake salt lake South Australia
190 J10 Younghusband Peninsula peninsula South Australia
192 Q10 Young Nicks Head headland North Island, NZ 39.38S 105.03E
193 D20 Young Range ▲ South Island, NZ
203 Q15 Young's Rock island Pitcairn Island, Pitcairn Islands
9 R16 Youngstown Alberta, SW Canada 51.31N 111.12W
33 V12 Youngstown Ohio, N USA 41.06N 80.39W
165 N9 Youshashan Qinghai, C China 38.12N 90.58E
Youth, Isle of see Juventud, Isla de la
79 N11 Youvarou Mopti, C Mali 15.19N 4.15W
166 K10 Youyang var. Zhongduo. Chongqing Shi, C China 28.48N 108.48E
169 Y7 Youyi Heilongjiang, NE China 46.51N 131.54E
153 P13 Yovon Rus. Yavan. SW Tajikistan 38.19N 69.02E
142 J13 Yozgat Yozgat, C Turkey 39.49N 34.48E
142 K13 Yozgat ◐ province C Turkey
64 O6 Ypacaraí var. Ypacarai. Central, S Paraguay 25.22S 57.16W
Ypacaray see Ypacaraí
64 P5 Ypané, Río ∽ C Paraguay
Ypres see Ieper
116 I13 Ypsário var. Ipsario. ▲ Thásos, E Greece 40.43N 24.39E
33 R10 Ypsilanti Michigan, N USA 42.12N 83.36W
36 M1 Yreka California, W USA 41.43N 122.38W
Yrendagüé see General Eugenio A. Garay
195 N8 Ysabel Channel channel N PNG
12 K8 Yser, Lac ◎ Québec, SE Canada
153 Y8 Yshtyk Issyk-Kul'skaya Oblast', E Kyrgyzstan 41.34N 78.21E
Yssel see IJssel
105 Q12 Yssingeaux Haute-Loire, C France 45.09N 4.07E
97 K23 Ystad Skåne, S Sweden 55.25N 13.51E
Ysyk-Köl see Balykchy, Kyrgyzstan
Ysyk-Köl see Issyk-Kul', Ozero, Kyrgyzstan
Ysyk-Köl Oblasty see Issyk-Kul'skaya Oblast'
98 L8 Ythan ∽ NE Scotland, UK
Y Trallwng see Welshpool
96 C13 Ytre Arna Hordaland, S Norway 60.28N 5.25E
96 B12 Ytre Sula island S Norway
95 G17 Ytterhogdal Jämtland, C Sweden 62.10N 14.55E
126 M10 Ytyk-Kyuyel' Respublika Sakha (Yakutiya), NE Russian Federation 62.22N 133.37E
Yu see Henan
Yuan Jiang see Red River
167 S13 Yüanlin Jap. Inrin. C Taiwan 23.57N 120.33E
167 N3 Yuanping Shanxi, C China 38.26N 112.42E
Yuanquan see Anxi
Yuanshan see Lianping
167 O11 Yuan Shui ∽ S China
170 G16 Yuasa Wakayama, Honshū, SW Japan 34.00N 135.08E
194 H10 Yuat ∽ N PNG
37 O6 Yuba City California, W USA 39.07N 121.40W
172 Oo6 Yūbari Hokkaidō, NE Japan 43.09N 141.00E
172 P6 Yūbari-sanchi ▲ Hokkaidō, NE Japan
37 O6 Yuba River ∽ California, W USA
82 H13 Yubdo Oromo, C Ethiopia 9.05N 35.28E
172 Q5 Yūbetsu Hokkaidō, NE Japan 44.13N 143.34E
Yūbetsu-gawa see Yabetsu-gawa
130 L3 Yubileynyy Moskovskaya Oblast', W Russian Federation 55.56N 37.47E
43 X12 Yucatán ◐ state SE Mexico
49 O3 Yucatan Basin var. Yucatan Deep. undersea feature N Caribbean Sea
Yucatán, Canal de see Yucatan Channel
43 Y10 Yucatan Channel Sp. Canal de Yucatán. channel Cuba/Mexico
Yucatan Deep see Yucatan Basin
Yucatan Peninsula see Yucatán, Península de
43 X13 Yucatán, Península de Eng. Yucatan Peninsula. peninsula Guatemala/Mexico
38 I11 Yucca Arizona, SW USA 34.49N 114.06W
37 V15 Yucca Valley California, W USA 34.06N 116.30W
167 P4 Yucheng Shandong, E China 37.01N 116.37E
Yuci see Jinzhong
133 X5 Yudoma ∽ E Russian Federation
167 P12 Yudu var. Gongjiang. Jiangxi, C China 26.02N 115.24E
Yue see Guangdong
Yuecheng see Yuexi
166 M12 Yuecheng Ling ▲ S China
Yuegaitan see Qumarlêb
189 P7 Yuendumu Northern Territory, N Australia 22.19S 131.51E
166 H10 Yuexi var. Yuecheng. Sichuan, C China 28.50N 102.36E
167 N10 Yueyang Hunan, S China 29.24N 113.08E
129 U14 Yug Permskaya Oblast', NW Russian Federation 57.49N 56.08E
129 P13 Yug ∽ NW Russian Federation
127 N11 Yugorenok Respublika Sakha (Yakutiya), NE Russian Federation 59.46N 137.36E
125 F10 Yugorsk Khanty-Mansiyskiy Avtonomnyy Okrug, C Russian Federation 61.17N 63.25E
125 G6 Yugorskiy Poluostrov peninsula NW Russian Federation
Yugoslavia see Serbia and Montenegro (Yugoslavia)
152 K14 Yugo-Vostochnyye Garagumy prev. Yugo-Vostochnyye Karakumy. desert E Turkmenistan
Yugo-Vostochnyye Karakumy see Yugo-Vostochnyye Garagumy
Yuhu see Eryuan
167 S10 Yuhuan Dao island SE China
166 L14 Yu Jiang ∽ S China
Yujin see Qianwei
127 Nn7 Yukagirskoye Ploskogor'ye plateau NE Russian Federation
120 L11 Yukhavichy Rus. Yukhovichi. Vitsyebskaya Voblasts', N Belarus 56.02N 28.39E
130 J4 Yukhnov Kaluzhskaya Oblast', W Russian Federation 54.43N 35.15E
Yukhovichi see Yukhavichy
81 J20 Yuki var. Yuki Kengunda. Bandundu, W Dem. Rep. Congo 3.52S 19.32E
Yuki Kengunda see Yuki
28 M10 Yukon Oklahoma, C USA 35.30N 97.45W
(0) F4 Yukon ∽ Canada/USA
Yukon see Yukon Territory
41 S7 Yukon Flats salt flat Alaska, USA
14 F5 Yukon Territory var. Yukon, Fr. Territoire du Yukon. ◐ territory NW Canada
143 T16 Yüksekova Hakkâri, SE Turkey 37.34N 44.16E
126 Jj11 Yukta Evenkiyskiy Avtonomnyy Okrug, C Russian Federation 63.16N 106.04E
170 Dd13 Yukuhashi var. Yukuhasi. Fukuoka, Kyūshū, SW Japan 33.41N 131.00E
Yukuhasi see Yukuhashi
Yukuriawat see Yopurga
129 O9 Yula ∽ NW Russian Federation
189 P8 Yulara Northern Territory, N Australia 25.15S 130.57E
131 W6 Yuldybayevo Respublika Bashkortostan, W Russian Federation 52.22N 57.55E
25 W8 Yulee Florida, SE USA 30.37N 81.36W
164 K7 Yuli var. Lopnur. Xinjiang Uygur Zizhiqu, NW China 41.24N 86.12E
167 T14 Yüli C Taiwan 23.23N 121.18E
166 L15 Yulin Guangxi Zhuangzu Zizhiqu, S China 22.37N 110.07E
166 L4 Yulin Shaanxi, C China 38.22N 109.47E
167 T14 Yüli Shan ▲ E Taiwan 23.22N 121.13E
166 F11 Yulong Xueshan ▲ SW China 27.09N 100.10E
38 H14 Yuma Arizona, SW USA 32.40N 114.38W
39 W3 Yuma Colorado, C USA 40.07N 102.43W
56 K5 Yumare Yaracuy, N Venezuela 10.37N 68.40W
65 G14 Yumbel Bío Bío, C Chile 37.07S 72.33W
81 N19 Yumbi Maniema, E Dem. Rep. Congo 1.13S 26.13E
165 R8 Yumen var. Laojunmiao, Yümen. Gansu, N China 39.49N 97.46E
165 Q7 Yumenzhen Gansu, N China 40.15N 97.03E
164 J3 Yumin Xinjiang Uygur Zizhiqu, NW China 46.14N 82.52E
Yun see Yunnan
142 G14 Yunak Konya, W Turkey 38.49N 31.42E
47 O8 Yuna, Río ∽ E Dominican Republic
40 I17 Yunaska Island island Aleutian Islands, Alaska, USA
166 M6 Yuncheng Shanxi, C China 35.07N 110.45E
167 N14 Yunfu Guangdong, S China 22.56N 112.02E
59 L18 Yungas physical region E Bolivia
Yungki see Jilin
Yung-ning see Nanning
166 I12 Yungui Gaoyuan plateau SW China
Yunjinghong see Jinghong
166 M15 Yunkai Dashan ▲ S China
Yunki see Jilin
166 E11 Yun Ling ▲ SW China
167 N9 Yunmeng Hubei, C China 30.59N 113.44E
163 N14 Yunnan var. Yun, Yunnan Sheng, Yünnan, Yun-nan. ◐ province SW China
Yunnan see Kunming
Yunnan Sheng see Yunnan
170 Cc15 Yunomae Kumamoto, Kyūshū, SW Japan 32.16N 131.00E
167 N8 Yun Shui ∽ C China
190 J7 Yunta South Australia 32.37S 139.33E
167 Q14 Yunxiao Fujian, SE China 23.56N 117.16E
166 K9 Yunyang Sichuan, C China 31.03N 109.43E
200 Nn10 Yupanqui Basin undersea feature E Pacific Ocean
Yuping see Libo, Guizhou, China
Yuping see Pingbian, Yunnan, China
Yuratishki see Yuratsishki
121 I15 Yuratsishki Pol. Juraciszki, Rus. Yuratishki. Hrodzyenskaya Voblasts', W Belarus 54.01N 25.55E
Yurev see Tartu
126 H14 Yurga Kemerovskaya Oblast', S Russian Federation 55.42N 84.59E
58 E10 Yurimaguas Loreto, N Peru 5.54S 76.07W
131 P3 Yurino Respublika Mariy El, W Russian Federation 56.19N 46.15E
43 N13 Yuriria Guanajuato, C Mexico 20.12N 101.09W
129 T13 Yurla Komi-Permyatskiy Avtonomnyy Okrug, NW Russian Federation 59.18N 54.19E
Yurua, Río see Juruá, Río
116 M13 Yürük Tekirdağ, NW Turkey 40.58N 27.09E
164 G10 Yurungkax He ∽ W China
129 Q14 Yur'ya var. Jarja. Kirovskaya Oblast', NW Russian Federation 59.01N 49.22E
Yur'yev see Tartu
129 N16 Yur'yevets Ivanovskaya Oblast', W Russian Federation 57.19N 43.01E
130 M3 Yur'yev-Pol'skiy Vladimirskaya Oblast', W Russian Federation 56.28N 39.39E
119 V7 Yur"yivka Dnipropetrovs'ka Oblast', E Ukraine 48.45N 36.01E
126 K6 Yuryung-Khaya Respublika Sakha (Yakutiya), NE Russian Federation 72.45N 113.32E
44 I7 Yuscarán El Paraíso, S Honduras 13.58N 86.48W
167 P12 Yu Shan ▲ S China
165 R13 Yushu var. Gyêgu. Qinghai, C China 33.03N 97.00E
131 P12 Yusta Respublika Kalmykiya, SW Russian Federation 47.06N 46.16E
128 I10 Yustozero Respublika Kareliya, NW Russian Federation 62.44N 33.31E
143 Q11 Yusufeli Artvin, NE Turkey 40.49N 41.31E
170 E15 Yusuhara Kōchi, Shikoku, SW Japan 33.22N 132.52E
129 T14 Yus'va Permskaya Oblast', NW Russian Federation 58.48N 54.59E
Yuta see Yatta
167 P2 Yutian Hebei, E China 39.52N 117.43E
164 H10 Yutian var. Keriya. Xinjiang Uygur Zizhiqu, NW China 36.49N 81.31E
64 K5 Yuto Jujuy, NW Argentina 23.35S 64.28W
64 P7 Yuty Caazapá, S Paraguay 26.28S 56.11W
166 G13 Yuxi Yunnan, SW China 24.22N 102.28E
167 O2 Yuxian prev. Yu Xian. Hebei, E China 39.50N 114.33E
171 M11 Yuzawa Akita, Honshū, C Japan 39.11N 140.29E
129 N16 Yuzha Ivanovskaya Oblast', W Russian Federation 56.34N 42.00E
Yuzhno-Alichurskiy Khrebet see Alichuri Janubí, Qatorkŭhi
Yuzhno-Kazakhstanskaya Oblast' see Yuzhnyy Kazakhstan
127 Oo15 Yuzhno-Sakhalinsk Jap. Toyohara; prev. Vladimirovka. Ostrov Sakhalin, Sakhalinskaya Oblast', SE Russian Federation 46.58N 142.45E
131 P14 Yuzhno-Sukhokumsk Respublika Dagestan, SW Russian Federation 44.43N 45.32E
125 Ee12 Yuzhnoural'sk Chelyabinskaya Oblast', C Russian Federation 54.28N 61.13E
126 I13 Yuzhno-Yeniseyskiy Krasnoyarskiy Kray, C Russian Federation 58.40N 94.49E
151 Z10 Yuzhnyy Altay, Khrebet ▲ E Kazakhstan
Yuzhnyy Bug see Pivdennyy Buh
151 O15 Yuzhnyy Kazakhstan off. Yuzhno-Kazakhstanskaya Oblast', Eng. South Kazakhstan, Kaz. Ongtüstik Qazaqstan Oblysy; prev. Chimkentskaya Oblast'. ◐ province S Kazakhstan
127 Oo10 Yuzhnyy, Mys headland E Russian Federation 57.44N 156.49E
131 W6 Yuzhnyy Ural var. Southern Urals. ▲ W Russian Federation
165 V10 Yuzhong Gansu, C China 35.52N 104.09E
Yuzhou see Chongqing
105 N5 Yvelines ◐ department N France
110 B9 Yverdon var. Yverdon-les-Bains, Ger. Iferten; anc. Eborodunum. Vaud, W Switzerland 46.46N 6.37E
Yverdon-les-Bains see Yverdon
104 M3 Yvetot Seine-Maritime, N France 49.37N 0.48E
152 H8 Ýylanly Rus. Il'yaly. Daşoguz Welaýaty, N Turkmenistan 41.56N 59.42E

Z

153 T12 Zaalayskiy Khrebet Taj. Qatorkŭhi Pasi Oloy. ▲ Kyrgyzstan/Tajikistan
Zaamin see Zomin
Zaandam see Zaanstad
100 I10 Zaanstad prev. Zaandam. Noord-Holland, C Netherlands 52.27N 4.49E
Zabadani see Az Zabdānī
121 L18 Zabalatstsye Rus. Zabolot'ye. Homyel'skaya Voblasts', SE Belarus 52.38N 28.35E
114 L9 Žabalj Ger. Josefsdorf, Hung. Zsablya; prev. Józseffalva;. Serbia, N Serbia and Montenegro (Yugoslavia) 45.22N 20.01E
Zāb aş Şaghīr, Nahraz see Little Zab
126 L16 Zabaykal'sk Chitinskaya Oblast', S Russian Federation 49.37N 117.19E
Zāb-e Kūchek, Rūdkhāneh-ye see Little Zab
Zabeln see Sabile
Zabéré see Zabré
Zabern see Saverne
147 N16 Zabīd W Yemen 14.00N 43.00E
147 O16 Zabīd, Wādī dry watercourse SW Yemen
Zabinka see Zhabinka
Ząbkowice see Ząbkowice Śląskie
113 G15 Ząbkowice Śląskie var. Ząbkowice, Ger. Frankenstein, Frankenstein in Schlesien. Dolnośląskie, SW Poland 50.34N 16.48E
112 P10 Zabłudów Podlaskie, NE Poland 53.00N 23.21E
114 D8 Zabok Krapina-Zagorje, N Croatia 46.00N 15.48E
149 W9 Zābol var. Shahr-i-Zabul, Zabul; prev. Nasratabad. Sīstān va Balūchestān, E Iran 31.00N 61.32E
Zābol see Zābul
149 W13 Zāboli Sīstān va Balūchestān, SE Iran 27.09N 61.31E
Zabolot'ye see Zabalatstsye
79 Q13 Zabré var. Zabéré. S Burkina 11.13N 0.34W
113 G17 Zábřeh Ger. Hohenstadt. Olomoucký Kraj, E Czech Republic 49.52N 16.52E
113 J16 Zabrze Ger. Hindenburg, Hindenburg in Oberschlesien. Śląskie, S Poland 50.19N 18.52E
155 O7 Zābul Per. Zābol. ◐ province SE Afghanistan
Zabul see Zābol
44 E6 Zacapa Zacapa, E Guatemala 14.59N 89.32W
44 A3 Zacapa off. Departamento de Zacapa. ◐ department E Guatemala
42 M14 Zacapú Michoacán de Ocampo, SW Mexico 19.49N 101.52W
43 V14 Zacatal Campeche, SE Mexico 18.37N 91.52W
42 M11 Zacatecas Zacatecas, C Mexico 22.45N 102.33W
42 L10 Zacatecas ◐ state C Mexico
44 F8 Zacatecoluca La Paz, S El Salvador 13.28N 88.51W
43 P15 Zacatepec Morelos, S Mexico 18.40N 99.11W
43 Q13 Zacatlán Puebla, S Mexico 19.54N 97.59W
150 F8 Zachagansk Zapadnyy Kazakhstan, NW Kazakhstan 51.04N 51.13E
117 D20 Zacháro var. Zaharo, Zakháro. Dytikí Ellás, S Greece 37.28N 21.40E
24 J8 Zachary Louisiana, S USA 30.39N 91.09W
119 U6 Zachepylivka Kharkivs'ka Oblast', E Ukraine 49.13N 35.15E
Zachist'ye see Zachystsye
112 E9 Zachodnio-pomorskie ◐ province NW Poland
121 L14 Zachystsye Rus. Zachist'ye. Minskaya Voblasts', NW Belarus 54.24N 28.45E
42 L13 Zacoalco var. Zacoalco de Torres. Jalisco, SW Mexico 20.12N 103.31W
Zacoalco de Torres see Zacoalco
43 P13 Zacualtipán Hidalgo, C Mexico 20.39N 98.42W
114 C12 Zadar It. Zara; anc. Iader. Zadar, W Croatia 44.06N 15.14E
114 C12 Zadar off. Zadarsko-Kninska Županija prev. Zadar-Knin. ◐ province SW Croatia
Zadar-Knin see Zadar
177 G14 Zadetkyi Kyun var. St. Matthew's Island. island Mergui Archipelago, S Myanmar
69 Q9 Zadié var. Djadié. ∽ NE Gabon
165 Q13 Zadoi var. Qapugtang. Qinghai, C China 32.56N 95.21E
130 L7 Zadonsk Lipetskaya Oblast', W Russian Federation 52.25N 38.55E
77 X8 Za'farâna E Egypt 29.06N 32.34E
155 W7 Zafarwāl Punjab, E Pakistan 32.19N 74.52E
124 P1 Zafer Burnu var. Cape Andreas, Cape Apostolas Andreas, Gk. Akrotiri Apostólou Andréa. headland NE Cyprus 35.42N 34.34E
109 J23 Zafferano, Capo headland Sicilia, Italy, C Mediterranean Sea 38.06N 13.31E
116 M7 Zafirovo Silistra, NE Bulgaria 44.00N 26.51E
117 L23 Zaforá island Kykládes, Greece, Aegean Sea
106 J12 Zafra Extremadura, W Spain 38.25N 6.27W
112 E13 Żagań var. Zagań, Żegań, Ger. Sagan. Lubuskie, W Poland 51.37N 15.18E
120 F12 Žagarė Pol. Żagory. Šiauliai, N Lithuania 56.22N 23.16E
77 W7 Zagazig var. Az Zaqāzīq. N Egypt 30.35N 31.31E
76 M5 Zaghouan var. Zaghwān. NE Tunisia 36.26N 10.05E
Zaghwān see Zaghouan
117 G16 Zagorá Thessalía, C Greece 39.27N 23.06E
Zagorod'ye see Zaharoddzye
Zagory see Žagarė
Zágráb see Zagreb
114 E8 Zagreb Ger. Agram, Hung. Zágráb. ● (Croatia) Zagreb, N Croatia 45.48N 15.57E
114 E8 Zagreb prev. Grad Zagreb. ◐ province NC Croatia
148 L7 Zāgros, Kūhhā-ye Eng. Zagros Mountains. ▲ W Iran
Zagros Mountains see Zāgros, Kūhhā-ye
114 O12 Žagubica Serbia, E Serbia and Montenegro (Yugoslavia) 44.13N 21.47E
Zagunao see Lixian
113 L22 Zagyva ∽ N Hungary
Zaharo see Zacháro
121 G19 Zaharoddzye Rus. Zagorod'ye. physical region SW Belarus
149 W11 Zāhedān var. Zahidan; prev. Duzdab. Sīstān va Balūchestān, SE Iran 29.31N 60.51E
Zahidan see Zāhedān
Zahlah see Zahlé
144 H7 Zahlé var. Zaḩlah. C Lebanon 33.51N 35.54E
152 J14 Zähmet Rus. Zakhmet. Mary Welaýaty, C Turkmenistan 37.48N 62.33E
113 O20 Záhony Szabolcs-Szatmár-Bereg, NE Hungary 48.26N 22.10E
147 N13 Zahrān 'Asīr, S Saudi Arabia 17.47N 43.27E
145 R12 Zahrat al Baṭn hill range S Iraq
123 I12 Zahrez Chergui var. Zahrez Chergüi. marsh N Algeria
Zainlha see Xinjin
131 S4 Zainsk Respublika Tatarstan, W Russian Federation 55.12N 52.01E
84 A10 Zaire prev. Congo. ◐ province NW Angola
Zaire see Congo (Democratic Republic of)
Zaire see Congo (river)
114 P13 Zaječar Serbia, E Serbia and Montenegro (Yugoslavia) 43.54N 22.16E
85 L18 Zaka Masvingo, E Zimbabwe 20.19S 31.27E
126 J16 Zakamensk Respublika Buryatiya, S Russian Federation 50.18N 102.57E
118 G7 Zakarpats'ka Oblast' Eng. Transcarpathian Oblast, Rus. Zakarpatskaya Oblast'. ◐ province W Ukraine
Zakarpatskaya Oblast' see Zakarpats'ka Oblast'
Zakataly see Zaqatala
Zakháro see Zacháro
Zakhidnyy Buh/Zakhodni Buh see Bug
Zakhmet see Zähmet
145 Q1 Zākhō var. Zākhū. N Iraq 37.09N 42.40E
Zākhū see Zākhō
Zákinthos see Zákynthos
113 L18 Zakopane Małopolskie, S Poland 49.17N 19.57E
80 J12 Zakouma Salamat, S Chad 10.47N 19.51E
117 L25 Zákros Kríti, Greece, E Mediterranean Sea 35.06N 26.12E
117 C19 Zákynthos var. Zákinthos. Zákynthos, W Greece 37.46N 20.54E
117 C20 Zákynthos var. Zákinthos, It. Zante. island Iónioi Nísoi, Greece, C Mediterranean Sea
117 C19 Zakýnthou, Porthmós strait SW Greece
113 G24 Zala off. Zala Megye. ◐ county W Hungary
113 G24 Zala ∽ W Hungary
144 M4 Zalābiyah Dayr az Zawr, C Syria 35.39N 39.51E
113 G24 Zalaegerszeg Zala, W Hungary 46.51N 16.49E
106 K11 Zalamea de la Serena Extremadura, W Spain 38.38N 5.37W
106 J13 Zalamea la Real Andalucía, S Spain 37.40N 6.40W
169 U7 Zalantun var. Butha Qi. Nei Mongol Zizhiqu, N China 47.57N 122.43E
126 J15 Zalari Irkutskaya Oblast', S Russian Federation 53.31N 102.10E
113 G23 Zalaszentgrót Zala, SW Hungary 46.57N 17.04E
Zalatna see Zlatna
118 G9 Zalău Ger. Waltenberg, Hung. Zilah; prev. Ger. Zillenmarkt. Sălaj, NW Romania 47.10N 23.03E
111 V10 Žalec Ger. Sachsenfeld. C Slovenia 46.15N 15.08E
119 S9 Zalenodol's'k Dnipropetrovs'ka Oblast', E Ukraine 47.31N 33.56E
112 K8 Zalewo Ger. Saalfeld. Warmińsko-Mazurskie, NE Poland 53.54N 19.39E
147 N9 Ẓalim Makkah, W Saudi Arabia 22.46N 42.12E
82 A11 Zalingei var. Zalinje. Western Darfur, W Sudan 12.51N 23.28E
Zalinje see Zalingei
118 K7 Zalishchyky Ternopil's'ka Oblast', W Ukraine 48.40N 25.43E
Zallah see Zillah
100 J13 Zaltbommel Gelderland, C Netherlands 51.49N 5.15E
128 H15 Zaluch'ye Novgorodskaya Oblast', NW Russian Federation 57.40N 31.45E
Zamak see Zamakh
147 Q14 Zamakh var. Zamak. N Yemen 16.25N 47.35E
142 K15 Zamantı Irmağı ∽ C Turkey
Zambesi/Zambeze see Zambezi
85 G14 Zambezi North Western, W Zambia 13.33S 23.08E
85 K15 Zambezi var. Zambesi, Port. Zambeze. ∽ S Africa
85 O15 Zambézia off. Província da Zambézia. ◐ province C Mozambique
85 I14 Zambia off. Republic of Zambia; prev. Northern Rhodesia. ◆ republic S Africa
179 Q16 Zamboanga off. Zamboanga City. Mindanao, S Philippines 6.56N 122.03E
56 E5 Zambrano Bolívar, N Colombia 9.45N 74.49W
112 N10 Zambrów Łomża, E Poland 52.59N 22.14E
85 L14 Zambué Tete, NW Mozambique 15.03S 30.49E
79 T13 Zamfara ∽ NW Nigeria
Zamkog see Zamtang
58 C9 Zamora Zamora Chinchipe, S Ecuador 4.05S 78.58W
106 K6 Zamora Castilla-León, NW Spain 41.30N 5.45W
106 K5 Zamora ◐ province Castilla-León, NW Spain
Zamora see Barinas
58 A13 Zamora Chinchipe ◐ province S Ecuador
42 M13 Zamora de Hidalgo Michoacán de Ocampo, SW Mexico 20.00N 102.18W
113 P15 Zamość Rus. Zamoste. Lubelskie, E Poland 50.43N 23.16E
Zamoste see Zamość
166 G7 Zamtang var. Zamkog; prev. Gamba. Sichuan, C China 32.19N 100.55E
77 O8 Zamzam, Wādī dry watercourse NW Libya
81 F20 Zanaga La Lékoumou, S Congo 2.49S 13.52E
43 T16 Zanatepec Oaxaca, SE Mexico 16.28N 94.24W
107 P9 Záncara ∽ C Spain
Zancle see Messina
164 G14 Zanda Xizang Zizhiqu, W China 31.28N 79.49E
100 H10 Zandvoort Noord-Holland, W Netherlands 52.22N 4.31E
41 P8 Zane Hills hill range Alaska, USA
33 T13 Zanesville Ohio, N USA 39.55N 82.01W
Zanga see Hrazdan
148 L4 Zanjān var. Zenjan, Zinjan. Zanjān, NW Iran 36.40N 48.30E
148 L4 Zanjān off. Ostān-e Zanjān, var. Zenjan, Zinjan. ◐ province NW Iran
Zante see Zákynthos
83 J22 Zanzibar Zanzibar, E Tanzania 6.10S 39.12E
83 J22 Zanzibar ◐ region E Tanzania
83 J22 Zanzibar Swa. Unguja. island E Tanzania
83 J22 Zanzibar Channel channel E Tanzania
171 Ll13 Zaō-san ▲ Honshū, C Japan 38.06N 140.27E
167 N8 Zaoyang Hubei, C China 32.11N 112.42E
126 I14 Zaozernyy Krasnoyarskiy Kray, S Russian Federation 55.53N 94.37E
128 J2 Zaozërsk Murmanskaya Oblast', NW Russian Federation 69.25N 32.25E
167 Q6 Zaozhuang Shandong, E China 34.52N 117.37E
30 L4 Zap North Dakota, N USA 47.18N 101.55W
114 L13 Zapadna Morava Ger. Westliche Morava. ∽ C Serbia and Montenegro (Yugoslavia)
128 H16 Zapadnaya Dvina Tverskaya Oblast', W Russian Federation 56.16N 32.03E
Zapadnaya Dvina see Western Dvina
126 H10 Zapadno-Sibirskaya Ravnina Eng. West Siberian Plain. plain C Russian Federation
Zapadnyy Bug see Bug
150 E9 Zapadnyy Kazakhstan off. Zapadno-Kazakhstanskaya Oblast', Eng. West Kazakhstan, Kaz. Batys Qazaqstan Oblysy; prev. Ural'skaya Oblast'. ◐ province NW Kazakhstan
126 Hh15 Zapadnyy Sayan Eng. Western Sayans. ▲ S Russian Federation
65 H15 Zapala Neuquén, W Argentina 38.54S 70.06W
64 I4 Zapaleri, Cerro var. Cerro Sapaleri. ▲ N Chile 22.51S 67.10W
27 Q16 Zapata Texas, SW USA 26.54N 99.16W
46 D5 Zapata, Península de peninsula W Cuba

◆ Country ● Country Capital ◇ Dependent Territory ○ Dependent Territory Capital ◐ Administrative Region ✕ International Airport ▲ Mountain ▲ Mountain Range ▲ Volcano ∽ River ◎ Lake ⊠ Reservoir

63 G19 **Zapicán** Lavalleja, S Uruguay 33.31S 54.55W
67 J19 **Zapiola Ridge** *undersea feature* SW Atlantic Ocean
67 L19 **Zapiola Seamount** *undersea feature* S Atlantic Ocean 38.15S 26.15W
128 I2 **Zapolyarnyy** Murmanskaya Oblast', NW Russian Federation 69.24N 30.53E
119 U8 **Zaporizhzhya** *Rus.* Zaporozh'ye; *prev.* Aleksandrovsk. Zaporiz'ka Oblast', SE Ukraine 47.46N 35.12E
Zaporizhzhya *see* Zaporiz'ka Oblast'
119 U9 **Zaporiz'ka Oblast'** *var.* Zaporizhzhya, *Rus.* Zaporozhskaya Oblast'. ◈ *province* SE Ukraine
Zaporozhskaya Oblast' *see* Zaporiz'ka Oblast'
Zaporozh'ye *see* Zaporizhzhya
42 L14 **Zapotiltic** Jalisco, SW Mexico 19.35N 103.25W
164 G13 **Zapug** Xizang Zizhiqu, W China
143 V10 **Zaqatala** *Rus.* Zakataly. NW Azerbaijan 41.38N 46.37E
165 P13 **Zaqên** Qinghai, W China 33.22N 94.31E
165 Q13 **Za Qu** ∿ C China
142 M13 **Zara** Sivas, C Turkey 39.55N 37.43E
Zara *see* Zadar
Zarafshan *see* Zarafshon
153 P12 **Zarafshon** *Rus.* Zeravshan. W Tajikistan 39.12N 68.36E
152 L9 **Zarafshon** *Rus.* Zarafshan. Navoiy Viloyati, N Uzbekistan 41.33N 64.09E
Zarafshon *see* Zeravshan
153 O12 **Zarafshon, Qatorkŭhi** *Rus.* Zeravshanskiy Khrebet, *Uzb.* Zarafshon Tizmasi. ⛰ Tajikistan/Uzbekistan
Zarafshon Tizmasi *see* Zarafshon, Qatorkŭhi
56 E7 **Zaragoza** Antioquia, N Colombia 7.30N 74.52W
42 I5 **Zaragoza** Chihuahua, N Mexico 29.36N 107.41W
43 N6 **Zaragoza** Coahuila de Zaragoza, NE Mexico 28.30N 100.52W
43 O10 **Zaragoza** Nuevo León, NE Mexico 23.59N 99.49W
107 R5 **Zaragoza** *Eng.* Saragossa; *anc.* Caesaraugusta, Salduba. Aragón, NE Spain 41.39N 0.54W
107 R6 **Zaragoza** ◈ *province* Aragón, NE Spain
107 R5 **Zaragoza** ✈ Aragón, NE Spain 41.37N 0.52W
149 S10 **Zarand** Kermān, C Iran 30.49N 56.34E
154 J9 **Zaranj** Nīmrūz, SW Afghanistan 30.59N 61.54E
120 I11 **Zarasai** Utena, E Lithuania 55.44N 26.17E
64 N12 **Zárate** *prev.* General José F.Uriburu. Buenos Aires, E Argentina 34.06S 59.03W
107 Q2 **Zarautz** *var.* Zarauz. País Vasco, N Spain 43.16N 2.10W
Zarauz *see* Zarautz
Zaravecchia *see* Biograd na Moru
Zarāyīn *see* Zarēn
130 L4 **Zaraysk** Moskovskaya Oblast', W Russian Federation 54.48N 38.54E
57 N6 **Zaraza** Guárico, N Venezuela 9.21N 65.19W
Zarbdar *see* Zarbdor
153 P11 **Zarbdor** *Rus.* Zarbdar. Jizzax Viloyati, C Uzbekistan 40.04N 68.10E
148 M8 **Zard Kūh** ▲ SW Iran 32.19N 50.03E
128 I5 **Zarechensk** Murmanskaya Oblast', NW Russian Federation 66.39N 31.27E
131 P6 **Zarechnyy** Penzenskaya Oblast', W Russian Federation 53.12N 45.12E
155 Q7 **Zareh Sharan** Paktīkā, E Afghanistan 33.07N 68.46E
41 Y14 **Zarembo Island** *island* Alexander Archipelago, Alaska, USA
145 V4 **Zarēn** *var.* Zarāyīn. E Iraq 35.16N 45.43E
155 Q7 **Zarghūn Shahr** *var.* Katawaz. Paktīkā, SE Afghanistan 32.40N 68.19E
79 V13 **Zaria** Kaduna, C Nigeria 11.06N 7.42E
118 K2 **Zarichne** Rivnens'ka Oblast', NW Ukraine 51.49N 26.09E
126 H14 **Zarinsk** Altayskiy Kray, S Russian Federation 53.34N 85.22E
118 J12 **Zărnești** *Hung.* Zernest. Brașov, C Romania 45.34N 25.18E
117 J25 **Zarós** Kríti, Greece, E Mediterranean Sea 35.07N 24.54E
102 O9 **Zarow** ∿ NE Germany
Zarqa/Zarqā', Muḥāfaẓat az *see* Az Zarqā'
113 G20 **Záruby** ▲ W Slovakia 48.30N 17.24E
58 B8 **Zaruma** El Oro, SW Ecuador 3.41S 79.32W
112 E13 **Żary** *Ger.* Sorau, Sorau in der Niederlausitz. Lubuskie, W Poland 51.43N 15.09E
56 D10 **Zarzal** Valle del Cauca, W Colombia 4.22N 76.03W
44 I7 **Zarzalar, Cerro** ▲ S Honduras 14.15N 86.49W
158 I5 **Zāskār** ∿ NE India
158 I5 **Zāskār Range** ⛰ NE India
121 K15 **Zaslawye** Minskaya Voblasts', C Belarus 54.01N 27.16E
118 K7 **Zastavna** Chernivets'ka Oblast', W Ukraine 48.30N 25.51E
113 B16 **Žatec** *Ger.* Saaz. Ústecký Kraj, NW Czech Republic 50.19N 13.32E
Zaumgarten *see* Chrzanów
152 **Zaungukskiye Garagumy** *see* Üngüz Angyrsyndaky Garagum
27 X9 **Zavalla** Texas, SW USA 31.09N 94.25W
101 H18 **Zaventem** Vlaams Brabant, C Belgium 50.52N 4.28E
101 H18 **Zaventem** ✈ (Brussel/Bruxelles) Vlaams Brabant, C Belgium 50.55N 4.28E
Zavertse *see* Zawiercie
116 L7 **Zavet** Razgrad, NE Bulgaria 43.46N 26.40E
131 O12 **Zavetnoye** Rostovskaya Oblast', SW Russian Federation 47.10N 43.54E
162 M3 **Zavhan Gol** ∿ W Mongolia
114 H12 **Zavidovići** Federacija Bosna I Hercegovina, N Bosnia and Herzegovina 44.26N 18.07E
126 Mm16 **Zavitinsk** Amurskaya Oblast', SE Russian Federation 50.23N 128.57E
125 F12 **Zavodoukovsk** Tyumenskaya Oblast', C Russian Federation 56.27N 66.37E
Zawia *see* Az Zāwiyah
113 K15 **Zawiercie** *Rus.* Zavertse. Śląskie, S Poland 50.28N 19.24E
77 P11 **Zawīlah** *var.* Zuwaylah, *It.* Zueila. C Libya 26.10N 15.07E
144 I4 **Zāwīyah, Jabal az** ⛰ NW Syria
111 Y3 **Zaya** ∿ NE Austria
177 G8 **Zayatkyi** Pegu, C Myanmar 17.48N 96.27E
151 Y11 **Zaysan** Vostochnyy Kazakhstan, E Kazakhstan 47.28N 84.48E
Zaysan Köl *see* Zaysan, Ozero
151 Y11 **Zaysan, Ozero** *Kaz.* Zaysan Köl. ◎ E Kazakhstan
165 R16 **Zayü** *var.* Gyigang. Xizang Zizhiqu, W China 28.36N 97.25E
Zayyq *see* Ural
46 F6 **Zaza** ∿ C Cuba
118 K5 **Zbarazh** Ternopil's'ka Oblast', W Ukraine 49.40N 25.47E
118 J5 **Zboriv** Ternopil's'ka Oblast', W Ukraine 49.40N 25.07E
113 F18 **Zbraslav** Jihomoravský Kraj, SE Czech Republic 49.13N 16.19E
118 K6 **Zbruch** ∿ W Ukraine
Žďár *see* Žďár nad Sázavou
113 F17 **Žďár nad Sázavou** *Ger.* Saar in Mähren; *prev.* Žďár. Vysočina, C Czech Republic 49.34N 15.55E
118 K4 **Zdolbuniv** *Pol.* Zdolbunów, *Rus.* Zdolbunov. Rivnens'ka Oblast', NW Ukraine 50.33N 26.15E
Zdolbunov/Zdolbunów *see* Zdolbuniv
112 J13 **Zduńska Wola** Sieradz, C Poland 51.37N 18.57E
119 O4 **Zdvizh** ∿ N Ukraine
Zdzięciół *see* Dzyatlava
113 I16 **Zdzieszowice** *Ger.* Odertal. Opolskie, S Poland 50.24N 18.06E
Zealand *see* Sjælland
196 K6 **Zealandia Bank** *undersea feature* C Pacific Ocean
65 H20 **Zeballos, Monte** ▲ S Argentina 47.04S 71.32W
85 K20 **Zebediela** Limpopo, NE South Africa 24.16S 29.21E
115 L18 **Zebë, Mal** *var.* Mali i Zebës. ▲ NE Albania 41.57N 20.16E
Zebës, Mali i *see* Zebë, Mal
23 V9 **Zebulon** North Carolina, SE USA 35.49N 78.19W
114 K8 **Žednik** *Hung.* Bácsjózseffalva. Serbia, N Serbia and Montenegro (Yugoslavia) 45.58N 19.40E
101 C15 **Zeebrugge** West-Vlaanderen, NW Belgium 51.19N 3.13E
191 N16 **Zeehan** Tasmania, SE Australia 41.54S 145.19E
101 L14 **Zeeland** Noord-Brabant, SE Netherlands 51.42N 5.40E
31 N7 **Zeeland** North Dakota, N USA 45.57N 99.49W
101 E14 **Zeeland** ◈ *province* SW Netherlands
85 I21 **Zeerust** North-West, N South Africa 25.33S 26.04E
100 K10 **Zeewolde** Flevoland, C Netherlands 52.19N 5.31E
144 G8 **Ẕefat** *var.* Safed, Tsefat, *Ar.* Safad. Northern, N Israel 32.57N 35.27E
Żegań *see* Żagań
Zehden *see* Cedynia
102 O11 **Zehdenick** Brandenburg, NE Germany 52.58N 13.19E
Zē-i Bādīnān *see* Great Zab
Zeiden *see* Codlea
152 M14 **Zeidskoye Vodokhranilishche** ▣ E Turkmenistan
Zē-i Kōya *see* Little Zab
189 P7 **Zeil, Mount** ▲ Northern Territory, C Australia 23.31S 132.41E
100 J12 **Zeist** Utrecht, C Netherlands 52.04N 5.15E
103 M16 **Zeitz** Sachsen-Anhalt, E Germany 51.03N 12.07E
165 T11 **Zêkog** *var.* Sonag. Qinghai, C China 35.03N 101.30E
Zelaya Norte *see* Atlántico Norte, Región Autónoma
Zelaya Sur *see* Atlántico Sur, Región Autónoma
101 F17 **Zele** Oost-Vlaanderen, NW Belgium 51.04N 4.01E
112 N12 **Żelechów** Lubelskie, E Poland 51.49N 21.57E
115 H14 **Zelena Glava** ▲ SE Bosnia and Herzegovina 43.32N 17.55E
115 I14 **Zelengora** ⛰ S Bosnia and Herzegovina
128 I5 **Zelenoborskiy** Murmanskaya Oblast', NW Russian Federation 66.52N 32.25E
131 R3 **Zelenodol'sk** Respublika Tatarstan, W Russian Federation 55.52N 48.49E
126 I13 **Zelenogorsk** Krasnoyarskiy Kray, C Russian Federation 56.08N 94.29E
128 G12 **Zelenogorsk** *Fin.* Terijoki. Leningradskaya Oblast', NW Russian Federation 60.08N 30.06E
130 K3 **Zelenograd** Moskovskaya Oblast', W Russian Federation 56.02N 37.08E
120 B13 **Zelenogradsk** *Ger.* Cranz, Kranz. Kaliningradskaya Oblast', W Russian Federation 54.57N 20.30E
131 O15 **Zelenokumsk** Stavropol'skiy Kray, SW Russian Federation 44.22N 43.48E
172 Rr7 **Zelënyy, Ostrov** *var.* Shibotsu-jima. *island* NE Russian Federation
Železna Kapela *see* Eisenkappel
Železna Vrata *see* Demir Kapija
114 L11 **Železniki** Serbia, N Serbia and Montenegro (Yugoslavia) 44.45N 20.23E
100 N12 **Zelhem** Gelderland, E Netherlands 52.00N 6.21E
115 N18 **Želino** NW FYR Macedonia 42.00N 21.06E
115 M14 **Željin** ⛰ C Serbia and Montenegro (Yugoslavia)
103 K17 **Zella-Mehlis** Thüringen, C Germany 50.40N 10.40E
111 P7 **Zell am See** *var.* Zell-am-See. Salzburg, S Austria 47.19N 12.48E
111 N7 **Zell am Ziller** Tirol, W Austria 47.13N 11.52E
Zelle *see* Celle
111 W2 **Zellerndorf** Niederösterreich, NE Austria 48.40N 15.57E
111 U7 **Zeltweg** Steiermark, S Austria 47.10N 14.43E
121 G17 **Zel'va** *Pol.* Zelwa. Hrodzyenskaya Voblasts', W Belarus 53.09N 24.49E
120 H13 **Želva** Vilnius, C Lithuania 55.13N 25.07E
Zelwa *see* Zel'va
101 E16 **Zelzate** *var.* Selzaete. Oost-Vlaanderen, NW Belgium 51.12N 3.49E
120 E11 **Žemaičių Aukštumas** *physical region* W Lithuania
120 C12 **Žemaičių Naumiestis** Klaipėda, SW Lithuania 55.22N 21.39E
Zembin *see* Zyembin
131 N6 **Zemetchino** Penzenskaya Oblast', W Russian Federation 53.31N 42.35E
81 M15 **Zémio** Haut-Mbomou, E Central African Republic 5.04N 25.07E
43 R16 **Zempoaltepec, Cerro** ▲ SE Mexico 17.04N 95.54W
101 G17 **Zemst** Vlaams Brabant, C Belgium 50.59N 4.28E
114 L11 **Zemun** Serbia, N Serbia and Montenegro (Yugoslavia) 44.51N 20.24E
Zendajan *see* Zendeh Jan
154 J5 **Zendeh Jan** *var.* Zendajan, Zindajān. Herāt, NW Afghanistan 34.55N 61.53E
Zengg *see* Senj
114 H12 **Zenica** Federacija Bosna I Hercegovina, C Bosnia and Herzegovina 44.12N 17.52E
Zenjan *see* Zanjān
Zen'kov *see* Zin'kiv
Zenshū *see* Chŏnju
Zenta *see* Senta
170 Ff14 **Zentsūji** *var.* Zentûzi. Kagawa, Shikoku, SW Japan 34.13N 133.45E
Zentûzi *see* Zentsūji
84 B11 **Zenza do Itombe** Cuanza Norte, NW Angola 9.22S 14.10E
114 H12 **Žepče** Federacija Bosna I Hercegovina, N Bosnia and Herzegovina 44.26N 18.00E
25 W12 **Zephyrhills** Florida, SE USA 28.13N 82.10W
199 J10 **Zephyr Reef** *reef* Pacific Ocean
164 F9 **Zepu** *var.* Poskam. Xinjiang Uygur Zizhiqu, NW China 38.10N 77.18E
153 Q12 **Zeravshan** *Taj./Uzb.* Zarafshon. ∿ Tajikistan/Uzbekistan
Zeravshan *see* Zarafshon
Zeravshanskiy Khrebet *see* Zarafshon, Qatorkŭhi
103 M14 **Zerbst** Sachsen-Anhalt, E Germany 51.57N 12.05E
151 P8 **Zerenda** Akmola, N Kazakhstan 52.55N 69.09E
112 H12 **Żerków** Wielkopolskie, C Poland 52.03N 17.33E
110 E11 **Zermatt** Valais, SW Switzerland 46.00N 7.44E
Zernest *see* Zărnești
110 J9 **Zernez** Graubünden, SE Switzerland 46.42N 10.06E
130 L12 **Zernograd** Rostovskaya Oblast', SW Russian Federation 46.52N 40.13E
Zestafoni *see* Zestap'oni
143 S9 **Zestap'oni** *Rus.* Zestafoni. C Georgia 42.09N 43.00E
100 H12 **Zestienhoven** ✈ (Rotterdam) Zuid-Holland, SW Netherlands 51.57N 4.30E
115 J16 **Zeta** ∿ SW Serbia and Montenegro (Yugoslavia)
15 J2 **Zeta Lake** ◎ Victoria Island, Nunavut, N Canada
100 L12 **Zetten** Gelderland, SE Netherlands 51.55N 5.43E
103 M17 **Zeulenroda** Thüringen, C Germany 50.40N 11.58E
102 H10 **Zeven** Niedersachsen, NW Germany 53.17N 9.16E
100 M12 **Zevenaar** Gelderland, SE Netherlands 51.55N 6.04E
101 H14 **Zevenbergen** Noord-Brabant, S Netherlands 51.39N 4.36E
126 M14 **Zeya** Amurskaya Oblast', SE Russian Federation 53.51N 126.53E
133 X6 **Zeya** ∿ SE Russian Federation
Zeya Reservoir *see* Zeyskoye Vodokhranilishche
149 T11 **Zeynalābād** Kermān, C Iran 29.55N 57.28E
126 M14 **Zeyskoye Vodokhranilishche** *Eng.* Zeya Reservoir. ▣ SE Russian Federation
106 H8 **Zêzere, Rio** ∿ C Portugal
Zgerzh *see* Zgierz
144 H6 **Zgharta** N Lebanon 34.24N 35.54E
112 K12 **Zgierz** *Ger.* Neuhof, *Rus.* Zgerzh. Łódź, C Poland 51.55N 19.19E
113 E14 **Zgorzelec** *Ger.* Görlitz. Dolnośląskie, SW Poland 51.10N 15.00E
164 I15 **Zhabdün** Xizang Zizhiqu, W China 29.37N 84.11E
121 F19 **Zhabinka** *Pol.* Żabinka, *Rus.* Zhabinka. Brestskaya Voblasts', SW Belarus 52.12N 24.01E
Zhaggo *see* Luhuo
165 R15 **Zhag'yab** *var.* Yêndum. Xizang Zizhiqu, W China 30.42N 97.33E
150 L9 **Zhailma** *Kaz.* Zhayylma. Kostanay, N Kazakhstan 51.34N 61.39E
151 V16 **Zhalanash** Almaty, SE Kazakhstan 43.07N 78.40E
Zhalashash *see* Dzhalagash
151 S7 **Zhalauly, Ozero** ◎ NE Kazakhstan
150 E9 **Zhalpatkal** *prev.* Furmanovo. Zapadnyy Kazakhstan, W Kazakhstan 49.40N 49.27E
121 G16 **Zhaludok** *Rus.* Zheludok. Hrodzyenskaya Voblasts', W Belarus 53.36N 24.58E
Zhaman-Akkol', Ozero *see* Akkol', Ozero
Zhambyl *see* Taraz
151 Q14 **Zhambyl** *off.* Zhambylskaya Oblast', *Kaz.* Zhambyl Oblysy; *prev.* Dzhambulskaya Oblast'. ◈ *province* S Kazakhstan
Zhambyl Oblysy/ Zhambylskaya Oblast' *see* Zhambyl
Zhamo *see* Bomi
151 S12 **Zhamshy** ∿ C Kazakhstan
150 M15 **Zhanadar'ya** Kzylorda, S Kazakhstan 44.41N 64.39E
151 O15 **Zhanakorgan** *Kaz.* Zhangaqorghan. Kzylorda, S Kazakhstan 43.57N 67.14E
165 N16 **Zhanang** *var.* Chatang. Xizang Zizhiqu, W China 29.15N 91.19E
151 T12 **Zhanaortalyk** Karaganda, C Kazakhstan 47.31N 75.42E
150 F15 **Zhanaozen** *Kaz.* Zhangaözen, *prev.* Novyy Uzen'. Mangistau, W Kazakhstan 43.21N 52.50E
151 Q16 **Zhanatas** Zhambyl, S Kazakhstan 43.33N 69.40E
Zhangaözen *see* Zhanaozen
Zhangaqazaly *see* Ayteke Bi
Zhangaqorghan *see* Zhanakorgan
167 O2 **Zhangbei** Hebei, E China 41.13N 114.43E
Zhangdian *see* Zibo
Zhanggu *see* Danba
169 X9 **Zhangguangcai Ling** ⛰ NE China
151 W10 **Zhangiztobe** Vostochnyy Kazakhstan, E Kazakhstan 49.16N 81.16E
165 W11 **Zhangjiachuan** Gansu, N China 34.55N 106.25E
166 L10 **Zhangjiajie** *var.* Dayong. Hunan, S China 29.10N 110.22E
167 O2 **Zhangjiakou** *var.* Changkiakow, Zhang-chia-k'ou, *Eng.* Kalgan; *prev.* Wanchuan. Hebei, E China 40.48N 114.51E
167 Q13 **Zhangping** Fujian, SE China 25.21N 117.29E
167 Q13 **Zhangpu** *var.* Sui'an. Fujian, SE China 24.07N 117.36E
169 U11 **Zhangwu** Liaoning, NE China 42.21N 122.32E
165 S8 **Zhangye** *var.* Ganzhou. Gansu, N China 38.59N 100.27E
167 Q13 **Zhangzhou** Fujian, SE China 24.31N 117.40E
169 W6 **Zhan He** ∿ NE China
Zhanibek/Zhänibek *see* Dzhanibek
166 L16 **Zhanjiang** *var.* Chanchiang, Chan-chiang, *Cant.* Tsamkong, *Fr.* Fort-Bayard. Guangdong, S China 21.10N 110.19E
Zhansügirov *see* Dzhansugurov
169 V8 **Zhaodong** Heilongjiang, NE China 46.03N 125.58E
Zhaoge *see* Qixian
166 H11 **Zhaojue** *var.* Xincheng. Sichuan, C China 28.03N 102.50E
167 N14 **Zhaoqing** Guangdong, S China 23.07N 112.26E
Zhaoren *see* Changwu
164 H5 **Zhaosu** *var.* Mongolküre. Xinjiang Uygur Zizhiqu, NW China 43.09N 81.07E
166 H11 **Zhaotong** Yunnan, SW China 27.17N 103.42E
169 V9 **Zhaoyuan** Heilongjiang, NE China 45.30N 125.04E
169 V9 **Zhaozhou** Heilongjiang, NE China 45.40N 125.16E
151 X13 **Zharbulak** Vostochnyy Kazakhstan, E Kazakhstan 46.05N 82.06E
164 J15 **Zhari Namco** ◎ W China
150 I12 **Zharkamys** *Kaz.* Zharqamys. Aktyubinsk, W Kazakhstan 47.58N 56.33E
151 W15 **Zharkent** *prev.* Panfilov. Almaty, SE Kazakhstan 44.10N 80.01E
128 H17 **Zharkovskiy** Tverskaya Oblast', W Russian Federation 55.51N 32.19E
151 W11 **Zharma** Vostochnyy Kazakhstan, E Kazakhstan 48.48N 80.55E
150 F14 **Zharmysh** Mangistau, SW Kazakhstan 44.12N 52.27E
Zharqamys *see* Zharkamys
120 L13 **Zhary** *Rus.* Zhary. Vitsyebskaya Voblasts', N Belarus 55.04N 28.40E
Zhaslyk *see* Jasliq
126 Ll11 **Zhatay** Respublika Sakha (Yakutiya), NE Russian Federation 62.07N 129.42E
164 J14 **Zhaxi Co** ◎ W China
Zhayylma *see* Zhailma
Zhdanov *see* Beyläqan, Azerbaijan
Zhdanov *see* Mariupol', Ukraine
Zhe *see* Zhejiang
167 R10 **Zhejiang** *var.* Che-chiang, Chekiang, Zhe, Zhejiang Sheng. ◈ *province* SE China
Zhejiang Sheng *see* Zhejiang
151 S7 **Zhelezinka** Pavlodar, N Kazakhstan 53.35N 75.16E
121 C14 **Zheleznodorozhnyy** *Ger.* Gerdauen. Kaliningradskaya Oblast', W Russian Federation 54.21N 21.17E
126 J13 **Zheleznodorozhnyy** Irkutskaya Oblast', C Russian Federation 57.54N 102.40E
Zheleznodorozhnyy *see* Yemva
130 J7 **Zheleznogorsk** Kurskaya Oblast', W Russian Federation 52.22N 35.21E
126 Jj14 **Zheleznogorsk-Ilimskiy** Irkutskaya Oblast', S Russian Federation 56.38N 103.53E
131 N15 **Zheleznovodsk** Stavropol'skiy Kray, SW Russian Federation 44.12N 43.01E
Zhëltyye Vody *see* Zhovti Vody
Zheludok *see* Zhaludok
Zhem *see* Emba
166 K7 **Zhenba** Shaanxi, C China 32.42N 107.55E
166 I13 **Zhenfeng** Guizhou, S China 25.27N 105.38E
Zhengjiatun *see* Shuangliao
165 X10 **Zhengning** Gansu, N China 35.28N 108.21E
Zhengxiangbai Qi *see* Qagan Nur
167 N6 **Zhengzhou** *var.* Ch'eng-chou, Chengchow; *prev.* Chenghsien. Henan, C China 34.45N 113.37E
167 R8 **Zhenjiang** *var.* Chenkiang. Jiangsu, E China 32.12N 119.30E
126 I13 **Zheleznogorsk** Krasnoyarskiy Kray, C Russian Federation 56.20N 93.36E
169 U9 **Zhenlai** Jilin, NE China 45.52N 123.11E
166 I11 **Zhenxiong** Yunnan, SW China 27.31N 104.52E
166 K11 **Zhenyuan** *var.* Wuyang. Guizhou, S China 27.07N 108.33E
167 R11 **Zherong** *var.* Shuangcheng. Fujian, SE China 27.16N 119.54E
151 U15 **Zhetigen** *prev.* Nikolayevka. Almaty, SE Kazakhstan 43.39N 77.10E
Zhetiqara *see* Zhitikara
150 F15 **Zhetybay** Mangistau, SW Kazakhstan 43.30N 52.09E
151 P17 **Zhetysay** *var.* Dzhetysay. Yuzhnyy Kazakhstan 40.45N 68.18E
166 M11 **Zhexi Shuiku** ▣ C China
151 O12 **Zhezdy** Karaganda, C Kazakhstan 48.06N 67.01E
151 O12 **Zhezkazgan** *Kaz.* Zhezqazghan; *prev.* Dzhezkazgan. Karaganda, C Kazakhstan 47.48N 67.43E
Zhezqazghan *see* Zhezkazgan
Zhicheng *see* Yidu
Zhidachov *see* Zhydachiv
165 Q12 **Zhidoi** *var.* Gyaijêpozhanggê. Qinghai, C China 33.55N 95.39E
126 Jj15 **Zhigalovo** Irkutskaya Oblast', S Russian Federation 54.47N 105.00E
126 L9 **Zhigansk** Respublika Sakha (Yakutiya), NE Russian Federation 66.45N 123.20E
131 R6 **Zhigulevsk** Samarskaya Oblast', W Russian Federation 53.24N 49.30E
120 D13 **Zhilino** *Ger.* Schillen. Kaliningradskaya Oblast', W Russian Federation 54.55N 21.54E
Zhiloy, Ostrov *see* Çiloy Adası
131 O8 **Zhirnovsk** Volgogradskaya Oblast', SW Russian Federation 51.01N 44.49E
Zhitarovo *see* Vetren
150 L8 **Zhitikara** *Kaz.* Zhetiqara, *prev.* Dzhetygara. Kostanay, NW Kazakhstan 52.10N 61.12E
Zhitkovichi *see* Zhytkavichy
131 P10 **Zhitkur** Volgogradskaya Oblast', SW Russian Federation 49.00N 46.16E
Zhitomir *see* Zhytomyr
Zhitomirskaya Oblast' *see* Zhytomyrs'ka Oblast'
130 J5 **Zhizdra** Kaluzhskaya Oblast', W Russian Federation 53.38N 34.39E
121 N18 **Zhlobin** Homyel'skaya Voblasts', SE Belarus 52.52N 30.01E
Zhmerinka *see* Zhmerynka
118 M7 **Zhmerynka** *Rus.* Zhmerinka. Vinnyts'ka Oblast', C Ukraine 49.01N 28.01E
155 R9 **Zhob** *var.* Fort Sandeman. Baluchistān, SW Pakistan 31.22N 69.25E
155 R8 **Zhob** ∿ C Pakistan
Zhodino *see* Zhodzina
121 L15 **Zhodzina** *Rus.* Zhodino. Minskaya Voblasts', C Belarus 54.05N 28.19E
126 Mm3 **Zhokhova, Ostrov** *island* Novosibirskiye Ostrova, NE Russian Federation
Zholkev/Zholkva *see* Zhovkva
Zholsaly *see* Dzhusaly
Zhondor *see* Jondor
164 I15 **Zhongba** *var.* Tuoji. Xizang Zizhiqu, W China 29.45N 83.59E
166 F11 **Zhongdian** Yunnan, SW China 27.48N 99.40E
Zhongduo *see* Youyang
Zhonghe *see* Xiushan
Zhonghua Renmin Gongheguo *see* China
165 V9 **Zhongning** Ningxia, N China 37.25N 105.40E
Zhongping *see* Huize
167 N15 **Zhongshan** Guangdong, S China 22.30N 113.19E
205 X7 **Zhongshan** *Chinese research station* Antarctica 69.23S 76.34E
166 M6 **Zhongtiao Shan** ⛰ C China
165 V9 **Zhongwei** Ningxia, N China 37.31N 105.10E
166 K9 **Zhongxian** *var.* Zhong Xian, Zhongzhou. Chongqing Shi, C China 30.16N 108.03E
167 N9 **Zhongxiang** Hubei, C China 31.12N 112.35E
Zhongzhou *see* Zhongxian
167 O7 **Zhoukou** *var.* Zhoukouzhen. Henan, C China 33.37N 114.34E
Zhoukouzhen *see* Zhoukou
167 S9 **Zhoushan** Zhejiang, S China
167 S9 **Zhoushan Qundao** *Eng.* Zhoushan Islands. *island group* SE China
118 I5 **Zhovkva** *Pol.* Żółkiew, *Rus.* Zholkev, Zholkva; *prev.* Nesterov. L'vivs'ka Oblast', NW Ukraine 50.03N 24.00E
119 S7 **Zhovti Vody** *Rus.* Zhëltyye Vody. Dnipropetrovs'ka Oblast', E Ukraine 48.24N 33.30E
119 Q10 **Zhovtneve** *Rus.* Zhovtnevoye. Mykolayivs'ka Oblast', S Ukraine 46.50N 32.00E
Zhovtnevoye *see* Zhovtneve
116 K9 **Zhrebchevo, Yazovir** ▣ C Bulgaria
169 V13 **Zhuanghe** Liaoning, NE China 39.43N 122.57E
165 W11 **Zhuanglang** *var.* Shuiluocheng. Gansu, C China 35.06N 106.21E
151 P15 **Zhuantobe** *Kaz.* Zhūantöbe. Yuzhnyy Kazakhstan, S Kazakhstan 44.45N 68.50E
167 Q5 **Zhucheng** Shandong, E China 35.58N 119.24E
165 V12 **Zhugqu** Gansu, C China 33.51N 104.14E
167 N15 **Zhuhai** Guangdong, S China 22.16N 113.30E
Zhuizishan *see* Weichang
Zhuji *see* Shangqiu
130 I5 **Zhukovka** Bryanskaya Oblast', W Russian Federation 53.33N 33.48E
167 N7 **Zhumadian** Henan, C China 32.58N 114.03E
167 O3 **Zhuozhou** *prev.* Zhuo Xian. Hebei, E China 39.22N 115.40E
168 L14 **Zhuozi Shan** ▲ N China 39.28N 106.58E
Zhuravichi *see* Zhuravichy
121 O17 **Zhuravichy** *Rus.* Zhuravichi. Homyel'skaya Voblasts', SE Belarus 53.15N 30.29E
151 Q8 **Zhuravlevka** Akmola, N Kazakhstan 51.56N 69.56E
119 Q4 **Zhurivka** Kyyivs'ka Oblast', N Ukraine 50.28N 31.48E
150 J11 **Zhuryn** Aktyubinsk, W Kazakhstan 49.13N 57.36E
151 T15 **Zhusandala, Step'** *grassland* SE Kazakhstan
166 L8 **Zhushan** Hubei, C China 32.11N 110.05E
Zhushan *see* Xuan'en
Zhuyang *see* Dazhu
167 N11 **Zhuzhou** Hunan, S China 27.52N 112.52E
118 I6 **Zhydachiv** *Pol.* Żydaczów, *Rus.* Zhidachov. L'vivs'ka Oblast', NW Ukraine 49.22N 24.09E
150 G9 **Zhympity** *Kaz.* Zhympīty, *prev.* Dzhambeyty. Zapadnyy Kazakhstan, W Kazakhstan 50.16N 52.34E
121 K19 **Zhytkavichy** *Rus.* Zhitkovichi. Homyel'skaya Voblasts', SE Belarus 52.13N 27.52E
119 N4 **Zhytomyr** *Rus.* Zhitomir. Zhytomyrs'ka Oblast', NW Ukraine 50.17N 28.39E
Zhytomyr *see* Zhytomyrs'ka Oblast'
118 M4 **Zhytomyrs'ka Oblast'** *var.* Zhytomyr, *Rus.* Zhitomirskaya Oblast'. ◈ *province* N Ukraine
159 U15 **Zia** ✈ (Dhaka) Dhaka, C Bangladesh
113 J20 **Žiar nad Hronom** *var.* Sväty Kríž nad Hronom, *Ger.* Heiligenkreuz, *Hung.* Garamszentkereszt. Banskobystrický Kraj, C Slovakia 48.36N 18.52E
167 Q4 **Zibo** *var.* Zhangdian. Shandong, E China 36.51N 118.01E
166 L4 **Zichang** *prev.* Wayaobu. Shaanxi, C China 37.08N 109.40E
Zichenau *see* Ciechanów
113 G15 **Ziębice** *Ger.* Münsterberg in Schlesien. Dolnośląskie, SW Poland 50.37N 17.01E
Ziebingen *see* Cybinka
Ziegenhais *see* Głuchołazy
112 E12 **Zielona Góra** *Ger.* Grünberg, Grünberg in Schlesien, Grüneberg. Lubuskie, W Poland 51.55N 15.30E
101 F14 **Zierikzee** Zeeland, SW Netherlands 51.39N 3.55E
166 I10 **Zigong** *var.* Tzekung. Sichuan, C China 29.19N 104.48E
78 G12 **Ziguinchor** SW Senegal 12.33N 16.19W
43 N16 **Zihuatanejo** Guerrero, S Mexico 17.39N 101.33W
Ziketan *see* Xinghai
Zilah *see* Zalău
131 W7 **Zilair** Respublika Bashkortostan, W Russian Federation 52.12N 57.15E
142 L12 **Zile** Tokat, N Turkey 40.18N 35.52E
113 J18 **Žilina** *Ger.* Sillein, *Hung.* Zsolna. Žilinský Kraj, N Slovakia 49.13N 18.43E
113 J19 **Žilinský Kraj** ◈ *region* N Slovakia
77 Q9 **Zillah** *var.* Zallah. C Libya 28.30N 17.33E
Zillenmarkt *see* Zalău
111 N7 **Ziller** ∿ W Austria
Zillertal Alps *see* Zillertaler Alpen
111 N8 **Zillertaler Alpen** *Eng.* Zillertal Alps, *It.* Alpi Aurine. ⛰ Austria/Italy
120 K10 **Zilupe** *Ger.* Rosenhof. Ludza, E Latvia 56.10N 28.06E
126 J15 **Zima** Irkutskaya Oblast', S Russian Federation 53.57N 101.57E
43 O13 **Zimapán** Hidalgo, C Mexico 20.42N 99.23W
85 I16 **Zimba** Southern, S Zambia 17.16S 26.10E
85 J17 **Zimbabwe** *off.* Republic of Zimbabwe; *prev.* Rhodesia. ◆ *republic* S Africa
118 H10 **Zimbor** *Hung.* Magyarzsombor. Sălaj, NW Romania 47.00N 23.16E
Zimmerbude *see* Svetlyy
118 J15 **Zimnicea** Teleorman, S Romania 43.39N 25.21E
116 L9 **Zimnitsa** Yambol, E Bulgaria 42.34N 26.37E
131 N12 **Zimovniki** Rostovskaya Oblast', SW Russian Federation 47.07N 42.28E
Zindajān *see* Zendeh Jan
79 V12 **Zinder** Zinder, S Niger 13.46N 9.01E
79 W11 **Zinder** ◈ *department* S Niger
79 P12 **Ziniaré** C Burkina 12.35N 1.21W
Zinjan *see* Zanjān
147 P16 **Zinjibār** SW Yemen 13.07N 45.22E
119 T4 **Zin'kiv** *var.* Zen'kov. Poltavs'ka Oblast', NE Ukraine 50.11N 34.21E
Zinov'yevsk *see* Kirovohrad
Zintenhof *see* Sindi
33 N10 **Zion** Illinois, N USA 42.27N 87.49W
56 F10 **Zipaquirá** Cundinamarca, C Colombia 5.03N 74.01W
Zipser Neudorf *see* Spišská Nová Ves
113 H23 **Zirc** Veszprém, W Hungary 47.16N 17.52E
115 D14 **Žirje** *It.* Zuri. *island* S Croatia
Zirknitz *see* Cerknica
110 M7 **Zirl** Tirol, W Austria 47.16N 11.16E
103 K20 **Zirndorf** Bayern, SE Germany 49.27N 10.57E
166 M11 **Zi Shui** ∿ C China
111 Y3 **Zistersdorf** Niederösterreich, NE Austria 48.31N 16.45E
43 O14 **Zitácuaro** Michoacán de Ocampo, SW Mexico 19.28N 100.21W
Zito *see* Lhorong
103 Q16 **Zittau** Sachsen, E Germany 50.53N 14.48E
114 I12 **Živinice** Federacija Bosna I Hercegovina, E Bosnia and Herzegovina 44.26N 18.39E
Ziwa Magharibi *see* Kagera
83 J14 **Ziway Hāyk'** ◎ C Ethiopia
167 N12 **Zixing** Hunan, S China 26.01N 113.25E
131 W7 **Ziyanchurino** Orenburgskaya Oblast', W Russian Federation 51.36N 56.58E
166 K8 **Ziyang** Shaanxi, C China 32.33N 108.27E
113 I20 **Zlaté Moravce** *Hung.* Aranyosmarót. Nitriansky Kraj, SW Slovakia 48.22N 18.22E
114 K13 **Zlatibor** ⛰ W Serbia and Montenegro (Yugoslavia)
116 L9 **Zlati Voyvoda** Sliven, E Bulgaria 42.36N 26.13E
118 G11 **Zlatna** *Ger.* Kleinschlatten, *Hung.* Zalatna; *prev. Ger.* Goldmarkt. Alba, C Romania 46.07N 23.10E
116 I8 **Zlatna Panega** Lovech, N Bulgaria 43.07N 24.09E
116 N8 **Zlatni Pyasŭtsi** Dobrich, NE Bulgaria 43.19N 28.03E
125 E11 **Zlatoust** Chelyabinskaya Oblast', C Russian Federation 55.12N 59.33E
113 M19 **Zlatý Stôl** *Ger.* Goldener Tisch, *Hung.* Aranyosasztal. ▲ C Slovakia 48.45N 20.39E
115 P18 **Zletovo** NE FYR Macedonia 42.00N 22.14E
113 H18 **Zlín** *prev.* Gottwaldov. Zlínský Kraj, SE Czech Republic 49.13N 17.40E
113 H19 **Zlinský Kraj** ◈ *region* E Czech Republic
77 O7 **Zlīṭan** W Libya 32.28N 14.34E
112 F9 **Złocieniec** *Ger.* Falkenburg in Pommern. Zachodnio-pomorskie, NW Poland 53.31N 16.01E
112 J13 **Złoczew** Sieradz, S Poland 51.24N 18.36E
Złoczów *see* Zolochiv
113 F14 **Złotoryja** *Ger.* Goldberg. Dolnośląskie, W Poland 51.07N 15.57E
112 G9 **Złotów** Wielkopolskie, NW Poland 53.22N 17.01E
126 Gg15 **Zmeinogorsk** Altayskiy Kray, S Russian Federation 51.07N 82.16E
112 G13 **Żmigród** *Ger.* Trachenberg. Dolnośląskie, SW Poland 51.31N 16.55E
130 J6 **Zmiyevka** Orlovskaya Oblast', W Russian Federation 52.39N 36.20E
119 V5 **Zmiyiv** Kharkivs'ka Oblast', E Ukraine 49.40N 36.22E
Zna *see* Tsna
Znaim *see* Znojmo
130 M7 **Znamenka** Tambovskaya Oblast', W Russian Federation 52.24N 42.28E
Znamenka *see* Znam"yanka
121 C14 **Znamens** Astrakhanskaya Oblast', SW Russian Federation 54.37N 21.13E
131 P10 **Znamensk** *Ger.* Wehlau. Kaliningradskaya Oblast', W Russian Federation 48.33N 46.18E
125 Ff12 **Znamenskoye** Omskaya Oblast', C Russian Federation 57.09N 73.40E
119 R7 **Znam"yanka** *Rus.* Znamenka. Kirovohrads'ka Oblast', C Ukraine 48.41N 32.39E
112 H10 **Żnin** Kujawsko-pomorskie, C Poland 52.50N 17.40E
113 F19 **Znojmo** *Ger.* Znaim. Jihomoravský Kraj, S Czech Republic 48.52N 16.04E
81 N16 **Zobia** Orientale, N Dem. Rep. Congo 2.57N 25.55E
85 N15 **Zóbuè** Tete, NW Mozambique 15.28S 34.25E
100 G12 **Zoetermeer** Zuid-Holland, W Netherlands 52.04N 4.30E
110 E7 **Zofingen** Aargau, N Switzerland 47.16N 7.56E
165 R15 **Zogang** *var.* Wangda. Xizang Zizhiqu, W China 29.41N 97.54E
108 E7 **Zogno** Lombardia, N Italy 45.49N 9.42E
148 M10 **Zohreh, Rūd-e** ∿ SW Iran
166 H7 **Zoigê** *var.* Dagcagoin. Sichuan, C China 33.44N 102.57E
Zółkiew *see* Zhovkva
110 D8 **Zollikofen** Bern, W Switzerland 47.01N 7.28E
Zolochev *see* Zolochiv
119 U4 **Zolochiv** *Rus.* Zolochev. Kharkivs'ka Oblast', E Ukraine 50.16N 35.58E
118 J5 **Zolochiv** *Pol.* Złoczów, *Rus.* Zolochev. L'vivs'ka Oblast', W Ukraine 49.48N 24.51E
119 X7 **Zolote** *Rus.* Zolotoye. Luhans'ka Oblast', E Ukraine 48.42N 38.33E
119 Q6 **Zolotonosha** Cherkas'ka Oblast', C Ukraine 49.39N 32.04E
Zolotoye *see* Zolote
Zólyom *see* Zvolen
85 N15 **Zomba** Southern, S Malawi 15.22S 35.22E
Zombor *see* Sombor
101 D17 **Zomergem** Oost-Vlaanderen, NW Belgium 51.07N 3.31E
153 P11 **Zomin** *Rus.* Zaamin. Jizzax Viloyati, C Uzbekistan 39.56N 68.16E
81 I15 **Zongo** Equateur, N Dem. Rep. Congo 4.17N 18.42E
142 G10 **Zonguldak** Zonguldak, NW Turkey 41.25N 31.46E
142 H10 **Zonguldak** ◈ *province* NW Turkey
101 K17 **Zonhoven** Limburg, NE Belgium 50.58N 5.22E
148 J2 **Zonūz** Āẕarbāyjān-e Khāvarī, NW Iran 38.31N 45.54E
105 Y16 **Zonza** Corse, France, C Mediterranean Sea 41.49N 9.13E
Zoppot *see* Sopot
Zorgho *see* Zorgo
79 Q13 **Zorgo** *var.* Zorgho. C Burkina 12.15N 0.37W
106 K10 **Zorita** Extremadura, W Spain 39.18N 5.42W
153 U14 **Zorkŭl** *Rus.* Ozero Zorkul'. ◎ SE Tajikistan
Zorkul', Ozero *see* Zorkŭl
58 A8 **Zorritos** Tumbes, N Peru 3.40S 80.36W
113 J16 **Żory** *var.* Zory, *Ger.* Sohrau. Śląskie, S Poland 50.03N 18.41E
78 K15 **Zorzor** N Liberia 7.46N 9.28W
101 E18 **Zottegem** Oost-Vlaanderen, NW Belgium 50.52N 3.49E
79 R15 **Zou** ∿ S Benin
80 H6 **Zouar** Borkou-Ennedi-Tibesti, N Chad 20.24N 16.28E
78 J6 **Zouérat** *var.* Zouérate, Zouîrât. Tiris Zemmour, N Mauritania 22.44N 12.29W

◆ Country
● Country Capital
◇ Dependent Territory
○ Dependent Territory Capital
◈ Administrative Region
✈ International Airport
▲ Mountain
⛰ Mountain Range
Volcano
∿ River
◎ Lake
▣ Reservoir

PICTURE CREDITS

DORLING KINDERSLEY *would like to express their thanks to the following individuals, companies and institutions for their help in preparing this Atlas.*

Earth Resources Mapping Ltd., *Egham, Surrey*
Brian Groombridge, World Conservation Monitoring Centre, *Cambridge*
The British Library, *London*
British Library of Political and Economic Science, *London*
The British Museum, *London*
The City Business Library, *London*
King's College, *London*
National Meteorological Library and Archive, *Bracknell, Berkshire*
The Printed Word, *London*
The Royal Geographical Society, *London*
University of London Library
Paul Beardmore
Philip Boyes
Hayley Crockford
Alistair Dougal
Nick Drake
Reg Grant
Louise Keane
Zoe Livesley
Laura Porter
Jeff Eidenshink
Chris Hornby
Rachelle Smith
Ray Pinchard
Robert Meisner
Fiona Strawbridge
Wim Jenkins

T = top, B = bottom, A=above, L = left, R = right, C = centre

Every effort has been made to trace the copyright holders and we apologize in advance for any unintentional omissions. We would be pleased to insert the appropriate acknowledgement in any subsequent edition of this publication.

Adams Picture Library: 88CLA; **G Andrews:** 194CR; **Ardea London Ltd:** K Ghana 156C; M Iljima 140TC; R Waller 154TR; **Aspect Picture Library:** P Carmichael 137CRB, 166TR; G Tompkinson 202TRB; **Axiom:** C Bradley 154CA, 165CA; J Holmes xivCRA, xxivBCR, xxviiCRB, 156TCR, 172BC, 172TL, J Morris 77TL, 77CRB, J Spaull 134BL; **Bridgeman Art Library, London / New York:** Collection of the Earl of Pembroke, Wilton House xxBC; **The J. Allan Cash Photolibrary:** xlBR, xliiCLA, xlivCL, 8BC, 62CL, 71CLB, 72CL, 74CLB, 77BR, 78BC, 89BL, 111BR, 144BCL, 147TL, 160CR, 186BR, 189TR; **Bruce Coleman Ltd:** 88BC, 100CL, 102TC; S Alden 198BR; Atlantide xxviTCR, 144BR; E Bjurstrom 147BR; S Bond 98CRB; T Buchholz xvCL, 96TR, 130TCL; J Burton xxiiiC; J Cancalosi 189TRB; B J Coates xxvBL, 198BC; B Coleman 65TL; B & C Colhoun 2TR, 38CB; A Compost xxiiiCBR; Dr S Coyne 47TL; G Cubitt xviTCL, 173BCL, 186TR, 192TR; P Davey xxviiCLB, 123BL; N Devore 201CBL; S J Doylee xxiiCRR; H Flygare xviiCRA; M P L Fogden 17CB; Jeff Foott Productions xxiiiCRB, 9CRA; M Freeman 93BRA; P van Gaalen 88TR; G Gualco 146C; B Henderson 200CR; Dr C Henneghien 71C; HPH Photography, H Van den Berg 71CR; C Hughes 71BCL; C James xxxixTC; J Johnson 41CR, 207TR; J Jurka 93CA; S C Kaufman 30C; S J Krasemann 35TR; H Lange 8TRB, 70CA; C Lockwood 34BC; L C Marigo xxiiBC, xxviiCLA, 51CRA, 61BR; M McCoy 195TR; D Meredith 3CR; J Murray xvCR, 187BR; Orion Press 172TR; Orion Services & Trading Co. Inc. 171TR; C Ott 18BL; Dr E Pott 14C, 42CL, 89C, 95TL, 204CLB; F Prenzel 197C, 200CB; M Read 44BR, 45CRB; H Reinhard xxiiCR, xxviiTR, 204BR; L Lee Rue III 157BCL; J Shaw xixTL; K N Swenson 204BC; P Terry 117CR; N Tomalin 56BCL; P Ward 80TC; S Widstrand 59TR; K Wothe 93C, 181TCL; J T Wright 131BR; **Colorific:** Black Star / L Mulvehil 162CL; Black Star / R Rogers 59BR; Black Star / J Rupp 167BCR; Camera Tres / C. Meyer 61BRA; R Caputo / Matrix 80CL; J. Hill 119CLB; M Koene 57TR; G Satterley xliiCLAR; M Yamashita 162BL, 179CA; **Comstock:** 110CRB; **D Cousens:** 153 CRA; **Sue Cunningham Photographic:** 53CR; **James Davis Travel Photography:** xxxviTCB, xxxviTR, xxxviCL, xxxiii CRA; 11CA, 21BC, 51TLB, 58BCR, 59CLA, 63BCL, 95BC, 96TC, 104TR, 122CB, 164BC, 187CRA, 203BR; **G Dunnet:** 128CA; **Environmental Picture Library:** Chris Westwood 130C; **Eye Ubiquitous:** xCA; Marcus Stone xxxiii tr; L. Fordyce 10CLA; L Johnstone 6CRA, 30BLA, 32CB; S. Miller xxiCA; M Southern 75BLA; **Chris Fairclough Colour Library:** xliBR; **Ffotograff:** C Aithie 137CL, N. Tapsell 164CL; **Geoscience Features:** xviBCR, xviBR, 104CL, 110BC, 127BR; Solar Film 66TC; **Robert Harding Picture Library:** xviiTC, xxivCR, xxxC, xxxvTC, Gavin Heller xxxiii cl; 2TLB, 3CA, 13CRB, 13CR, 39BC, 40CRA, 52BL, 97BR, 101CR, 116CR, 126BL, 138CLA, 148CB, 149TL, 153TR, 162TR, 173CA, 177BR; P G. Adam 11TCB; D Atchison-Jones 72BLA; J Bayne 74BCL; B Schuster 82CR; C Bowman 52BR, 55CA, 64CL, 72CRL; C Campbell xxiBC; G Corrigan 165CRB, 167CRB; P Craven xxxvBL; R Cundy 71BR; Delu 81BC; A Durand 113BR; Financial Times 148BR; R Frerck 53BL; T Gervis 3BCL, 7CR; I Griffiths xxxCL, 79TL; T Hall 177CRA; D Harney 148CA; S Harris xliiiBCL; G Hellier xvCRB, 135BL; F Jackson 143BCR; Jacobs xxxviiTL; P Koch 145TR; F Joseph Land 125TR; Y Marcoux 16BR; S Massif xvBC; A Mills 90CLB; L Murray 116TR; R Rainford xlivBL; G Renner 76CB, 204C; C Rennie 50CL, 118BR; R Richardson 120CL; P Van Riel 50BR; E Rooney 128TR; Sassoon xxivCL, 154CLB; P Scholey 184TR; M Short 143TL; E Simanor xxviiCR; V Southwell 145CR; J Strachan 44TR, 113BL, 136BCR; C Tokeley 140CLA; A C Waltham 167C; T Waltham xviiBL, xxiiCLLL, 144CRB; Westlight 39CR; N Wheeler 145BL; A Williams xxxviiiBR, xlTR; A Woolfitt 97BRA; **Paul Harris:** 126TR, 174TC; **Hutchison Library:** 6BL, 140BCL; P. Collomb 143CR; C. Dodwell 139TR; S Errington 72BCL; P. Hellyer 148BC; J. Horner xxxiTC; R. Ian Lloyd 134CRA; N. Durrell McKenna xxviBCR; J.Nowell 135CLB, 149TC; A Zvoznikov xxiiCL; **Image Bank:** 89BR; J Banagan 202BCA; A Becker xxivBCL; P Hendrie 174BC; M Isy-Schwart 200C, 203CL; M Khansa 124BR; K Forest 169TR; Lomeo xxivTCR; T Madison 177CR; C Molyneux xxiiCRRR; K Mori 200TC; C Navajas xviiiTR; Ocean Images Inc. 198CLB; J van Os xviiTCR; S Proehl 6CL; T Rakke xixTC, 66CL; M Reitz 206CA; M Romanelli 177BL; G A Rossi 157BCR, 184BLA; B Roussel 111TL; S Satushek xviiBCR; Stock Photos / J M Spielman xxivTRL; **Images Colour Library:** xxiiCLL, xxxixTR, xliCR, xliiiBL, 3BR, 21BR, 39TL, 46TL, 64TC, 93BR, 104CLB, 105CR, 156CL, 171CL, 172TRB, 188CA; **Impact Photos:** J & G Andrews 194BL; C. Bluntzer 162BR; Cosmos / G. Buthaud 67BC; S Franklin 130BL; A. le Garsmeur 137CRA; A Indge xxviiTC; C Jones xxxiCB, 72BL; V. Nemirousky 143BR; J Nicholl 78TCR; C. Penn 197BR; G Sweeney xviiBR, 206CB, 206TR; **JVZ Picture Library:** T Nilson 135TC; **Frank Lane Picture Agency:** xxiTCR, xxiiiBL, 95TR; A Christiansen 60CRA; J Holmes xivBL; S. McCutcheon 3C; Silvestris 181TCR; D Smith xxiiBCL; W Wisniewsli 126TL, 205BR; **Leeds Castle Foundation:** xxxviiBC; **Magnum:** Abbas 85CR, 142CA; S Franklin 134CRB; D Hurn 4BCL; P. Jones-Griffiths 203BL; H Kubota xviBCL, 162CLB; F Maver xviBL; S McCurry 75CL, 141BCR; G. Rodger 76TR; C Steele Perkins 74BL; **Mountain Camera / John Cleare:** 159TR; C Monteath 159CR; **Nature Photographers:** E.A. Janes 114CL; **Natural Science Photos:** M Andera 112C; **Network Photographers Ltd.:** C Sappa / Rapho 121BL; **N.H.P.A.:** N. J. Dennis xxiiiCL; D Heuchlin xxiiiCLA; Jane Gifford xxxiii bl; S Krasemann 13BL, 27BR, 40TC; K Schafer 51CB; R Tidman 166CLB; D Tomlinson 151CR; M Wendler 50TR; **Nottingham Trent University:** T Waltham xivCL, xvBR; **Novosti:** 150BLA; **Oxford Scientific Films:** D Allan xxiiTR; H R Bardarson xviiiBC; D Bown xxiiiCBLL; M Brown 146BL; M Colbeck 153CAR; W Faidley 3TL; L Gould xxiiiTRB; D Guravich xxiiiTR; P Hammerschmidy / Okapia 89CLA; M Hill 59TL, 205TR; C Menteath 140TR; J Netherton 2CRB; S Osolinski 84CA; R Packwood 74CA; M Pitts 187TC; N Rosing xxiiiCBL, 9TR, 207BR; D Simonson 59C; Survival Anglia / C Catton 143TR; R Toms xxiiiBR; K Wothe xxiBL, xviiCLA; **Panos Pictures:** B Aris 141C; P Barker xxivBR; T Bolstao 159BR; N Cooper 84CB, 159TC; J-L Dugast 177CB, 178BC; J Hartley 75CA, 92CL; J Holmes 155BC; J Morris 78CLB; M Rose 152TR; D Sansoni 161CL; C Stowers 169TL; **Edward Parker:** 51TL, 51CLB; **Pictor International:** xivBR, xvBRA, xixTCL, xxCL, 3CLA, 19BR, 22TR, 22CRB, 25BCA, 25CL, 28CB, 29BC, 32CA, 35TRB, 36BC, 36BR, 36CR, 40CB, 40CL, 45CL, 65BR, 67TC, 84CL, 85CLB, 101BR, 109CLA, 177TCR, 178BR, 179CR, 188CLB, 193TL; **Pictures Colour Library:** xxiBCL, xxiiBR, xxviBCL, 6BR, 13TR, 14TC, 17TR, 21TL, 22BL, 26C, 26CLA, 29TR, 34TRB, 38BC, 43CA, 45CRA, 70BL, 92TCB, 96BL, 101BL, 108CA, 109CLB, 109CR, 109BR, 119BL, 170BC, 171BR, 198CL; **Planet Earth Pictures:** 200BL; D Barrett 154CB, 192CA; R Coomber 17BL; G Douwma 180BR; E Edmonds 181BR; HC Heap 124TR; J Lythgoe 206BL; A Mounter 137BCR, 180CR; M Potts 6CA; P Scoones xxTR; J Walencik 112TR; J Waters 55BCL; **Popperfoto:** Reuters / J Drake xxxiiCLA; **Rex Features:** 170CR; Antelope xxxiiCLB; M Friedel xxiCR; I McIlgorm xxxCBR; J Shelley xxxCR; Sipa Press xxxCR; Sipa Press / Alix xxxCBL; Sipa Press / Chamussy 184BL; **Russia & Republics Photolibrary:** M Wadlow 120CR, 121CL, 128BC, 128CL, 129TL, 129BR, 130TCR; **Science Photo Library:** CNES, 1990 Distribution Spot Image 137BL; Earth Satellite Corporation xixTRB, xxxiCR, 51BCL; F Gohier xiCR; J Heseltine xviTCB; K Kent xvBLA; P Menzell xvBL; N.A.S.A. xBC; D Parker xivBC; University of Cambridge Collection Air Pictures 89CLB; RJ Wainscoat / P Arnold, Inc. xiBC; D Weintraub xiBL; **South American Pictures:** 59BL, 64TR; R Francis 54BL; Guyana Space Centre 52TR; T Morrison 51CRB, 51BL, 52CR, 54TR, 56TR, 62BL, 63C; **Southampton Oceanography:** xviiiBL; **Sovofoto / Eastfoto:** xxxiiCBR; **Spectrum Colour Library:** 52BC, 166BC; J King 151BR; **Frank Spooner Pictures / Gamma:** 28CRB; E. Baitel xxxiiBC; Bernstein xxxiCL; Contrast 114CR; Diard / Photo News 115CL; Liaison / C. Hires xxxiiTCB; Liaison / Nickelsberg xxxiiTR; Liaison / Vogel 140BL; Marleen 115TL; Novosti 118CA; P. Piel xxxCA; N Quidu 135CL; H Stucke 196CLB, 202CA; Torrengo / Figaro 80BR; A Zamur 115BL; **Still Pictures:** C Caldicott 79TC; A Crump 201CL; M & C Denis-Huot xxiiBL, 80CR, 83BL; M Edwards xxiCRL, 55BL, 66CR, 71BLA, 161BR; J Frebet 55CLB; H Giradet 55TC; M Gunther 123BC; E Parker 54CL; R Seitre 137CA, 138BL, 138TL; **Tony Stone Images:** xxviTR, 4CA, 7BL, 7CL, 11CRB, 41BR, 60C, 99BC, 103BR, 108TR, 111CL, 111CRB, 141BR, 170CLB, 171C,188CB, 189BR, 196BC, 198TR; G Allison 20TR, 33CRB, 195CRB; D Armand 12TCB; D Austen 188TR, 194CL, 195CL; J Beatty 76CL; O Benn xxviBR; K Biggs xxiTL; R Bradbury 46BR; R A Butcher xxviTL; J Callahan xxviiCRA; P Chesley 193BCL, 196C; W Clay 32BL, 33CRA; J Cornish 98BL, 109TL; C Condina 43CB; T Craddock xxivTR; P Degginger 38CLB; Demetrio 5BR; N DeVore xxivBC; A Diesendruck 62BR; S Egan 89CRA, 98BR; R Elliot xxiiBCR; S Elmore 21C; R Frerck 122TR; J Garrett 75CR; S Grandadam 12BR; R Grosskopf 30BL; D Hanson 106BC; C Harvey 71TL; G Hellier 112BL, 172CR; S Huber 105CRB; D Hughs xxxiBR; A Husmo 93TR; G Irvine 33BC; J Jangoux 60CL; G Johnson 138CLB; D Johnston xviiTR; A Kehr 115C; R Koskas xviTR; J Lamb 98CRA; J Lawrence 77CRA; L Lefkowitz 7CA; M Lewis 47CLA; S Mayman 57BR; Murray & Associates 47CR; G Norways 106CA; N Parfitt xxviiCL, 70TCR, 83TL; R Passmore 123TR; N Press xviBCA; E Pritchard 90CA, 92CLR; T Raymond 23BL, 31TR; L Resnick 76BR; M Rogers 82BR; A Sacks 30TCB; C Saule 92CR; S Schulhof xxivTC; P Seaward 36CL; M Segal 34BL; V Shenai 158CL; R Sherman 28CL; H Sitton 142CR; R Smith xxvBLA, 58C; S Studd 110CLA; H Strand 51BR, 65TR; P Tweedie 185CR; L Ulrich 19BL; M Vines 19TC; A B Wadham 62CR; J Warden 65CLB; R Wells 25CRA, 199BL; G Yeowell 36BL; **Telegraph Colour Library:** 63CRB, 63TCR, 163TL; R Antrobus xxxixBR; J Sims 28BR; **Topham Picturepoint:** xxxiCBL, 137BCL, 139CR, 168BR, 174TR, 176BC; 184BL; **Travel Ink:** A Cowin 90TR; **Trip:** 146BR, 150CA, 161CRA; B Ashe 165TR; D Cole 202BCL, 202CR; D Davis 91BL; I Deineko xxxiTR; J Dennis 24BL; Dinodia 160CL; Eye Ubiquitous / L Fordyce 2CLB; A Gasson 155CR; W Jacobs 45TL, 56BL, 185BC, 186CLA, 193BCR, 197BL; P Kingsbury 114C; K Knight 185BR; V Kolpakov 153BL; T Noorits 89TL, 121BR, 152CL; R Power 43TR; N Ray 176CA; C Rennie 118CLB; V Sidoropolev 151TR; E Smith 191BC, 191TL; **Woodfin Camp & Associates:** 94BLR; **World Pictures:** xvCRA, xviiCRA, 16CRB, 24CL, 25BC, 26BL, 37BL, 42TR, 53TR, 73BR, 82TCR, 84TR, 85BL, 88BCR, 98TC, 100BL, 102CR, 103CR, 105BC, 107TC, 123CB, 124BL, 163BL, 167BCL, 168CLB, 180CLB, 180BC, 187BL, 190CB, 191C, 192CL, 193CR; **Zefa Picture Library:** xviBLR, xviiBCL, xviiiCL, 3CL, 11BC, 12TC, 17CA, 23TL, 24CRB, 27BL, 34TCR, 38BCR, 61BCL, 67TCL, 71CLA, 81TL, 83BR, 89CRB, 94C, 100C, 101TL, 102BL, 109TR, 120CRB, 122BL, 126CB, 128CLA, 170CA, 191TR; Anatol 115BR; Barone 116BL; Brandenburg 5C; A J Brown 46TR; H J Clauss 57CLB; Damm 73BC; Evert 94BL; W Felger 3BL; J Fields 201CRA; R Frerck 4BL; G Heil 58BR; K Heibig 117BR; Heilman 30BC; Hunter 8C; Kitchen 8TR, 14CL, 14BL, 16TR; Dr H Kramarz 7BLA, 127CRA; Mehlio 161BL; J F Raga 26TR; Rossenbach 107BR, 122CA; Streichan 91TL; T Stewart 11TR, 21CR; Sunak 56BR, 168TR; D H Teuffen 97TL; B Zaunders 42BC. **Additional Photography:** Geoff Dann; Rob Reichenfeld; H Taylor; Jerry Young.

◆ COUNTRY ● COUNTRY CAPITAL ◇ DEPENDENT TERRITORY ○ DEPENDENT TERRITORY CAPITAL ◐ ADMINISTRATIVE REGION ✈ INTERNATIONAL AIRPORT ▲ MOUNTAIN ▲▲ MOUNTAIN RANGE VOLCANO ≈ RIVER ⊛ LAKE ⊠ RESERVOIR

Abyssal plain A broad plain found in the depths of the ocean, more than 10,000 ft (3,000 m) below sea level.

Air mass A huge, homogeneous mass of air, within which horizontal patterns of temperature and humidity are consistent. Air masses are separated by fronts.

Alluvial fan Large fan-shaped deposit of fine sediments deposited by a river as it emerges from a narrow, mountain valley onto a broad, open plain.

Alluvium Material deposited by rivers. Nowadays usually only applied to finer particles of silt and clay.

Anticline A geological fold that forms an arch shape, curving upward in the rock strata.

Aquifer A body of rock that can absorb water. .

Arête A thin, jagged mountain ridge that divides two adjacent cirques, found in regions where glaciation has occurred.

Artesian well A naturally occurring source of underground water, stored in an aquifer.

Atoll A ring-shaped island or coral reef often enclosing a lagoon of sea water.

Badlands A landscape that has been heavily eroded and dissected by rain-water, and which has little or no vegetation.

Back slope The gentler windward slope of a sand dune or gentler slope of a cuesta.

Bajos An alluvial fan deposited by a river at the base of mountains and hills that encircle desert areas.

Bar, coastal An offshore strip of sand or shingle, either above or below the water. Usually parallel to the shore but sometimes crescent-shaped or at an oblique angle.

Barchan A crescent-shaped sand dune, formed where wind direction is very consistent. The horns of the crescent point downwind and where there is enough sand the barchan is mobile.

Base level The level below which flowing water cannot erode the land.

Basement rock A mass of ancient rock often of PreCambrian age, covered by a layer of more recent sedimentary rocks. Commonly associated with shield areas.

Bedrock Solid, consolidated and relatively unweathered rock, found on the surface of the land or just below a layer of soil or weathered rock.

Bluff The steep bank of a meander, formed by the erosive action of a river.

Breccia A type of rock composed of sharp fragments, cemented by a fine-grained material such as clay.

Butte An isolated, flat-topped hill with steep or vertical sides, buttes are the eroded remnants of a former land surface.

Calcite Hexagonal crystals of calcium carbonate.

Caldera A huge volcanic vent, often containing a number of smaller vents, and sometimes a crater lake.

Carbonation Process whereby rocks are broken down by carbonic acid. Carbon dioxide in the air dissolves in rainwater, forming carbonic acid.

Castle kopje Hill or rock outcrop, especially in southern Africa, where steep sides, and a summit composed of blocks, give a castle-like appearance.

Cataracts A series of stepped waterfalls created as a river flows over a band of hard, resistant rock.

Chernozem A fertile soil, also known as "black earth" consisting of a layer of dark topsoil, rich in decaying vegetation, overlying a lighter chalky layer.

Confluence The point at which two rivers meet.

Continental drift The theory that the continents of today are fragments of one or more prehistoric supercontinents that have moved across the Earth's surface, creating ocean basins.

Continental shelf An area of the continental crust, below sea level, which slopes gently.

Continental slope A steep slope running from the edge of the continental shelf to the ocean floor.

Core The center of the Earth, consisting of a dense mass of iron and nickel.

Coulées A US / Canadian term for a ravine formed by river erosion.

Craton A large block of the Earth's crust which has remained stable for a long period of geological time. It is made up of ancient shield rocks.

Cretaceous A period of geological time beginning about 145 million years ago and lasting until c. 65 million years ago.

Crevasse A deep crack in a glacier.

Crust The hard, thin outer shell of the Earth. It floats on the mantle, which is softer and more dense.

Crystalline rock Rocks formed when molten magma crystallizes (igneous rocks) or when heat or pressure cause re-crystallization (metamorphic rocks).

Cuesta A hill which rises into a steep slope on one side but has a gentler gradient on its other slope.

Delta Low-lying, fan-shaped area at a river mouth, formed by the deposition of successive layers of sediment.

Denudation The combined effect of weathering, erosion, and mass movement, which, over long periods, exposes underlying rocks.

Deposition The laying down of material that has accumulated: after being eroded and then transported by wind, ice, or water; as organic remains, such as coal and coral; as the result of evaporation and chemical precipitation.

Depression 1 In climatic terms it is a large low pressure system; 2 a complex fold, producing a large valley, which incorporates both a syncline and an anticline.

Detritus Piles of rock deposited by an erosive agent such as a river or glacier.

Distributary A minor branch of a river, which does not rejoin the main stream, common at deltas.

Divide A US term describing the area of high ground separating two drainage basins.

Donga A steep-sided gully, resulting from erosion by a river or by floods.

Drainage basin The area drained by a single river system, its boundary is marked by a watershed or divide.

Drumlin A long, streamlined hillock composed of material deposited by a glacier. They often occur in groups known as swarms.

Earthflow The rapid movement of soil and other loose surface material down a slope, when saturated by water.

Ephemeral A nonpermanent feature, often used in connection with seasonal rivers or lakes in dry areas.

Epicenter The point on the Earth's surface directly above the underground origin or focus of an earthquake.

Erg An extensive area of sand dunes, particularly in the Sahara Desert.

Erosion The processes which wear away the surface of the land. Glaciers, wind, rivers, waves, and currents all carry debris that causes erosion.

Escarpment A steep slope at the margin of a level, upland surface. In a landscape created by folding, escarpments (or scarps) frequently lie behind a more gentle backward slope.

Esker A narrow, winding ridge of sand and gravel deposited by streams of water flowing beneath or at the edge of a glacier.

Erratic A rock transported by a glacier and deposited some distance from its place of origin.

Eustacy A world-wide fall or rise in ocean levels.

Exfoliation A kind of weathering whereby scalelike flakes of rock are peeled or broken off by the development of salt crystals in water within the rocks.

Extrusive rock Igneous rock formed when molten material (magma) pours forth at the Earth's surface and cools rapidly. It usually has a glassy texture.

Fault A fracture or crack in rock, where strains (tectonic movement) have caused blocks to move, vertically or laterally, relative to each other.

Ferrel cell A component in the global pattern of air circulation, which rises in the colder latitudes (60° N and S) and descends in warmer latitudes (30° N and S).

Fissure A deep crack in a rock or a glacier.

Fjord A deep, narrow inlet, created when the sea inundates the U-shaped valley created by a glacier.

Flash flood A sudden, short-lived rise in the water level of a river or stream, or surge of water down a dry river channel, or wadi, caused by heavy rainfall.

Floodplain The broad, flat part of a river valley, adjacent to the river itself, formed by sediment deposited during flooding.

Fold A bend in the rock strata of the Earth's crust, resulting from compression.

Frost shattering A form of weathering where water freezes in cracks, causing expansion. As temperatures fluctuate and the ice melts and refreezes, it eventually causes the rocks to shatter.

Geosyncline A concave fold (syncline) or large depression in the Earth's crust, extending hundreds of miles.

Geothermal energy Heat derived from hot rocks within the Earth's crust and resulting in hot springs, steam, or hot rocks at the surface.

Geyser A jet of steam and hot water that intermittently erupts from vents in the ground in areas that are, or were, volcanic.

Glaciation The growth of glaciers and ice sheets, and their impact on the landscape.

Glacier A body of ice moving downslope under the influence of gravity and consisting of compacted and frozen snow.

Glacio-eustacy A worldwide change in the level of the oceans, caused when the formation of ice sheets takes up water or when their melting returns water to the ocean.

Glaciofluvial To do with glacial meltwater, the landforms it creates and its processes; erosion, transportation, and deposition.

Glacis A gentle slope or pediment.

Gondwanaland The supercontinent thought to have existed over 200 million years ago in the southern hemisphere.

Graben A block of rock let down between two parallel faults. Where the graben occurs within a valley, the structure is known as a rift valley.

Grease ice Slicks of ice that form in Antarctic seas, when ice crystals are bonded together by wind and wave action.

Groundwater Water that has seeped into the pores, cavities, and cracks of rocks or into soil and water held in an aquifer.

Gully A deep, narrow channel eroded in the landscape by ephemeral streams.

Guyot A small, flat-topped submarine mountain, formed as a result of subsidence which occurs during sea-floor spreading.

Hadley cell A large-scale component in the global pattern of air circulation. Warm air rises over the Equator and blows at high altitude toward the poles, sinking in subtropical regions (30° N and 30° S) and creating high pressure. The air then flows at the surface toward the Equator in the form of trade winds.

Hamada An Arabic word for a plateau of bare rock in a desert.

Hanging valley A tributary valley that ends suddenly, high above the bed of the main valley.

Headwards The action of a river eroding back upstream, as opposed to the normal process of downstream erosion. Headwards erosion is often associated with gullying.

Hoodos Pinnacles of rock that have been worn away by weathering in semiarid regions.

Horst A block of the Earth's crust that has been left upstanding by the sinking of adjoining blocks along fault lines.

Hot spot A region of the Earth's crust where high thermal activity occurs, often leading to volcanic eruptions.

Hydrolysis The chemical breakdown of rocks in reaction with water, forming new compounds.

Ice Age A period in the Earth's history when surface temperatures in the temperate latitudes were much lower and ice sheets expanded considerably. There have been ice ages from Pre-Cambrian times onward.

Ice cap A permanent dome of ice in highland areas.

Ice floe A large, flat mass of ice floating free on the ocean surface. It is usually formed after the breakup of winter ice by heavy storms.

Ice sheet A continuous, very thick layer of ice and snow. The term is usually used of ice masses which are continental in extent.

Ice shelf A floating mass of ice attached to the edge of a coast. The seaward edge is usually a sheer cliff up to 100 ft (30 m) high.

Ice wedge Massive blocks of ice up to 6.5 ft (2 m) wide at the top and extending 32 ft (10 m) deep.

Iceberg A large mass of ice in a lake or a sea, which has broken off from a floating ice sheet (an ice shelf) or from a glacier.

Igneous rock Rock formed when molten material, magma, from the hot, lower layers of the Earth's crust, cools, solidifies, and crystallizes, either within the Earth's crust (intrusive) or on the surface (extrusive).

Inselberg An isolated, steep-sided hill, rising from a low plain in semiarid and savannah landscapes.

Interglacial A period of global climate, between two ice ages, when temperatures rise and ice sheets and glaciers retreat.

Intraplate volcano A volcano that lies in the center of one of the Earth's tectonic plates, rather than, as is more common, at its edge.

Intrusion (intrusive igneous rock) Rock formed when molten material, magma, penetrates existing rocks below the Earth's surface before cooling and solidifying.

Isostasy The state of equilibrium that the Earth's crust maintains as its lighter and heavier parts float on the denser underlying mantle.

Isthmus A narrow strip of land connecting two larger landmasses or islands.

Joint A crack in a rock, formed where blocks of rock have not shifted relative to each other, as is the case with a fault. Joints are created by folding; by shrinkage in igneous rock as it cools or sedimentary rock as it dries out; and by the release of pressure in a rock mass when overlying materials are removed by erosion.

Kame A mound of stratified sand and gravel with steep sides, deposited in a crevasse by meltwater running over a glacier. When the ice retreats, this forms an undulating terrain of hummocks.

Karst A barren limestone landscape created by carbonic acid in streams and rainwater, in areas where limestone is close to the surface.

Kettle hole A round hollow formed in a glacial deposit by a detached block of glacial ice, which later melted. They can fill with water to form kettle-lakes.

Lagoon A shallow stretch of coastal salt-water behind a partial barrier such as a sandbank or coral reef. Also used to describe the water encircled by an atoll.

Laterite A hard red deposit left by chemical weathering in tropical conditions, and consisting mainly of oxides of iron and aluminum.

Latitude The angular distance from the Equator, to a given point on the Earth's surface. Imaginary lines of latitude running parallel to the Equator encircle the Earth, and are measured in degrees north or south of the Equator. The Equator is 0°, the poles 90° South and North respectively. Also called parallels.

Laurasia In the theory of continental drift, the northern part of the great supercontinent of Pangaea. Laurasia is said to consist of N America, Greenland and all of Eurasia north of the Indian subcontinent.

Lava The molten rock, magma, which erupts onto the Earth's surface through a volcano, or through a fault or crack in the Earth's crust.

Leaching The process whereby water dissolves minerals and moves them down through layers of soil or rock.

Levée A raised bank alongside the channel of a river. Levées are either human-made or formed in times of flood when the river overflows its channel, slows and deposits much of its sediment load.

Lithosphere The rigid, upper layer of the Earth, comprising the crust and the upper part of the mantle..

Loess Fertile, fine-grained, yellow deposits of unstratified silts and sands.

Longitude A division of the Earth which pinpoints how far east or west a given place is from the Prime Meridian (0°) which runs through the Royal Observatory at Greenwich, England (UK). Imaginary lines of longitude are drawn around the world from pole to pole. The world is divided into 360 degrees.

Longshore drift The movement of sand and silt along the coast, carried by waves hitting the beach at an angle.

Magma Undground, molten rock, which is very hot and highly charged with gas. It is generated at great pressure, at depths 10 miles (16 km) or more below the Earth's surface.

Mantle The layer of the Earth between the crust and the core. it is about 1,800 miles (2,900 km) thick.

Massif A single very large mountain or an area of mountains with uniform characteristics and clearly-defined boundaries.

Meltwater Water resulting from the melting of a glacier or ice sheet.

Mesa A broad, flat-topped hill, characteristic of arid regions.

Metamorphic rocks Rocks that have been altered from their original form, in terms of texture, composition, and structure by intense heat, pressure, or by the introduction of new chemical substances – or a combination of more than one of these.

Milankovitch hypothesis A theory suggesting that there are a series of cycles that slightly alter the Earth's position when rotating about the Sun.

Mistral A strong, dry, cold northerly or north-westerly wind, which blows from the Massif Central of France to the Mediterranean Sea.

Mohorovičić discontinuity (Moho) The structural divide at the margin between the Earth's crust and the mantle. On average it is 20 miles (35 km) below the continents and 6 miles (10 km) below the oceans.

Monsoon A wind that changes direction biannually. The change is caused by the reversal of pressure over landmasses and the adjacent oceans. Because the inflowing moist winds bring rain, the term monsoon is also used to refer to the rains themselves.

Moraine Debris, transported and deposited by a glacier or ice sheet in unstratified, mixed, piles of rock, boulders, pebbles, and clay.

Mountain-building The formation of fold mountains by tectonic activity. Also known as orogeny, mountain-building often occurs on the margin where two tectonic plates collide.

Nappe A mass of rocks that has been overfolded by repeated thrust faulting.

Oasis A fertile area in the midst of a desert, usually watered by an underground aquifer.

Oceanic ridge A mid-ocean ridge formed, according to the theory of plate tectonics, when plates drift apart and hot magma pours through to form new oceanic crust.

Onion-skin weathering The weathering away or exfoliation of a rock or outcrop by the peeling off of surface layers.

Outwash plain Glaciofluvial material (typically clay, sand, and gravel) carried beyond an ice sheet by meltwater streams, forming a broad, flat deposit.

Oxbow lake A crescent-shaped lake formed on a river floodplain when a river erodes the outside bend of a meander, making the neck of the meander narrower until the river cuts across the neck. The meander is cut off and is dammed off with sediment, creating an oxbow lake.

Oxidation A form of chemical weathering where oxygen dissolved in water reacts with minerals in rocks – particularly iron to form oxides.

Pack ice Ice masses more than 10 ft (3 m) thick that form on the sea surface and are not attached to a landmass.

Pancake ice Thin discs of ice, up to 8 ft (2.4 m) wide which form when slicks of grease ice are tossed together by winds and stormy seas.

Pangaea In the theory of continental drift, Pangaea is the original great land mass which, about 190 million years ago, began to split into Gondwanaland in the south and Laurasia in the north, separated by the Tethys Sea.

Pediment A gently-sloping ramp of bedrock below a steeper slope, often found at mountain edges in desert areas, but also in other climatic zones. Pediments may include depositional elements such as alluvial fans.

Periglacial Regions on the edges of ice sheets or glaciers or, more commonly, cold regions experiencing intense frost action, permafrost or both.

Permafrost Permanently frozen ground, typical of Arctic regions.

Permeable rocks Rocks through which water can seep, because they are either porous or cracked.

Phreatic eruption A volcanic eruption which occurs when lava combines with groundwater, superheating the water and causing a sudden emission of steam at the surface.

Pingo A dome of earth with a core of ice, found in tundra regions. Pingos are formed either when groundwater freezes and expands, pushing up the land surface, or when trapped, freezing water in a lake expands and pushes up lake sediments to form the pingo dome.

Placer A belt of mineral-bearing rock strata lying at or close to the Earth's surface, from which minerals can be easily extracted.

Plate, plate tectonics The study of tectonic plates, that helps to explain continental drift, mountain formation and volcanic activity. The movement of tectonic plates may be explained by the currents of rock rising and falling from within the Earth's mantle, as it heats up and then cools. The boundaries of the plates are known as plate margins and most mountains, earthquakes, and volcanoes occur at these margins. Constructive margins are moving apart; destructive margins are crunching together and conservative margins are sliding past one another.

Pleistocene A period of geological time spanning from about 5.2 million years ago to 1.6 million years ago.

Plutonic rock Igneous rocks found deep below the surface. They are coarse-grained because they cooled and solidified slowly.

Polje A long, broad depression found in karst (limestone) regions.

Polygonal patterning Typical ground patterning, found in areas where the soil is subject to severe frost action, often in periglacial regions.

Porosity A measure of how much water can be held within a rock or a soil.

PreCambrian The earliest period of geological time dating from over 570 million years ago.

Precipitation The fall of moisture from the atmosphere onto the surface of the Earth, whether as dew, hail, rain, sleet, or snow.

Pyramidal peak A steep, isolated mountain summit, formed when the back walls of three or more cirques are cut back and move toward each other. The cliffs around such a horned peak, or horn, are divided by sharp arêtes.

Pyroclasts Fragments of rock ejected during volcanic eruptions.

Quaternary The current period of geological time, which started about 1.6 million years ago.

Reg A large area of stony desert, where tightly-packed gravel lies on top of clayey sand. A reg is formed where the wind blows away the finer sand.

Resistance The capacity of a rock to resist denudation, by processes such as weathering and erosion.

Ria A flooded V-shaped river valley or estuary, flooded by a rise in sea level (eustacy) or sinking land. It is shorter than a fjord and gets deeper as it meets the sea.

Rift valley A long, narrow depression in the Earth's crust, formed by the sinking of rocks between two faults.

Roche moutonée A rock found in a glaciated valley. The side facing the flow of the glacier has been smoothed and rounded, while the other side has been left more rugged because the glacier, as it flows over it, has plucked out frozen fragments and carried them away.

Runoff Water draining from a land surface by flowing across it.

Sabkha The floor of an isolated depression that occurs in an arid environment – usually covered by salt deposits and devoid of vegetation.

Salt plug A rounded hill produced by the upward doming of rock strata caused by the movement of salt or other evaporite deposits under intense pressure.

Sastrugi Ice ridges formed by wind action. They lie parallel to the direction of the wind.

Scree Piles of rock fragments beneath a cliff or rock face, caused by mechanical weathering, especially frost shattering, where the expansion and contraction of freezing and thawing water within the rock, gradually breaks it up.

Sea-floor spreading The process whereby tectonic plates move apart, allowing hot magma to erupt and solidify.

Seamount An isolated, submarine mountain or hill, probably of volcanic origin.

Sediment Grains of rock transported and deposited by rivers, sea, ice, or wind.

Sedimentary rocks Rocks formed from the debris of preexisting rocks or of organic material. They are found in many environments on the ocean floor, on beaches, rivers, and deserts.

Seif A sand dune which lies parallel to the direction of the prevailing wind. Seifs form steep-sided ridges, sometimes extending for miles.

Selva A region of wet forest found in the Amazon Basin.

Shale (marine shale) A compacted sedimentary rock, with fine-grained particles. Marine shale is formed on the seabed. Fuel such as oil may be extracted from it.

Sheetwash Water that runs downhill in thin sheets without forming channels. It can cause sheet erosion.

Sheet erosion The washing away of soil by a thin film or sheet of water, known as sheetwash.

Shield A vast stable block of the Earth's crust, which has experienced little or no mountain-building.

Sinkhole A circular depression in a limestone region. They are formed by the collapse of an underground cave system or the chemical weathering of the limestone.

Slip face The steep leeward side of a sand dune or slope. Opposite side to a back slope.

Soil creep The very gradual downslope movement of rock debris and soil, under the influence of gravity. This is a type of mass movement.

Solifluction A kind of soil creep, where water in the surface layer has saturated the soil and rock debris which slips slowly downhill. It often happens where frozen top-layer deposits thaw, leaving frozen layers below them.

Spit A thin linear deposit of sand or shingle extending from the sea shore.

Stack A tall, isolated pillar of rock near a coastline, created as wave action erodes away the adjacent rock.

Strike-slip fault Occurs where plates move sideways past each other and blocks of rocks move horizontally in relation to each other, not up or down as in normal faults.

Subduction zone A region where two tectonic plates collide, forcing one beneath the other.

Submarine fan Deposits of silt and alluvium, carried by large rivers forming great fan-shaped deposits on the ocean floor.

Supercontinent A large continent that breaks up to form smaller continents or that forms when smaller continents merge.

Syncline A basin-shaped downfold in rock strata, created when the strata are compressed, for example where tectonic plates collide.

Tableland A highland area with a flat or gently undulating surface.

Tectonic plates Plates, or tectonic plates, are the rigid slabs which form the Earth's outer shell, the lithosphere. Eight big plates and several smaller ones have been identified.

Thermokarst Subsidence created by the thawing of ground ice in periglacial areas, creating depressions.

Till Unstratified glacial deposits or drift left by a glacier or ice sheet. Includes mixtures of clay, sand, gravel, and boulders.

Topography The typical shape and features of a given area such as land height and terrain.

Tombolo A large sand spit which attaches part of the mainland to an island.

Transform fault In plate tectonics, a fault of continental scale, occurring where two plates slide past each other, staying close together for example, the San Andreas Fault. The jerky, uneven movement creates earthquakes but does not destroy or add to the Earth's crust

Trench (oceanic trench) A long, deep trough in the ocean floor, formed, according to the theory of plate tectonics, when two plates collide and one dives under the other, creating a subduction zone.

Tropic of Cancer A line of latitude or imaginary circle round the Earth, lying at 23° 28' N.

Tropic of Capricorn A line of latitude or imaginary circle round the Earth, lying at 23° 28' S.

U-shaped valley A river valley that has been deepened and widened by a glacier. They are characteristically flat-bottomed and steep-sided and generally much deeper than river valleys.

V-shaped valley A typical valley eroded by a river in its upper course.

Wadi The dry bed left by a torrent of water. Also classified as a ephemeral stream, found in arid and semiarid regions, which are subject to sudden and often severe flash flooding.

Watershed The dividing line between one drainage basin an area where all streams flow into a single river system – and another. In the US, watershed also means the whole drainage basin of a single river system its catchment area.

Waterspout A rotating column of water in the form of cloud, mist, and spray which form on open water. Often has the appearance of a small tornado.

Weathering The decay and breakup of rocks at or near the Earth's surface, caused by water, wind, heat, or ice, organic material, or the atmosphere. Physical weathering includes the effects of frost and temperature changes. Biological weathering includes the efects of paint roots, burrowing animals and the acids produced by animals, especially as they decay after death. Carbonation and hydrolysis are among many kinds of chemical weathering.

NORTH AMERICA

CANADA
PAGES 8–16

UNITED STATES OF AMERICA
PAGES 17–41

MEXICO
PAGES 42–43

BELIZE
PAGES 44–45

COSTA RICA
PAGES 44–45

EL SALVADOR
PAGES 44–45

GUATEMALA
PAGES 44–45

HONDURAS
PAGES 44–45

SOUTH AMERICA

GRENADA
PAGES 46–47

HAITI
PAGES 46–47

JAMAICA
PAGES 46–47

ST KITTS & NEVIS
PAGES 46–47

ST LUCIA
PAGES 46–47

ST VINCENT & THE GRENADINES
PAGES 46–47

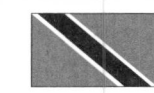
TRINIDAD & TOBAGO
PAGES 46–47

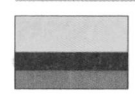
COLOMBIA
PAGES 56–57

AFRICA

URUGUAY
PAGES 62–63

CHILE
PAGES 64–65

PARAGUAY
PAGES 64–65

ALGERIA
PAGES 76–77

EGYPT
PAGES 76–77

LIBYA
PAGES 76–77

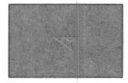
MOROCCO
PAGES 76–77

TUNISIA
PAGES 76–77

LIBERIA
PAGES 78–79

MALI
PAGES 78–79

MAURITANIA
PAGES 78–79

NIGER
PAGES 78–79

NIGERIA
PAGES 78–79

SENEGAL
PAGES 78–79

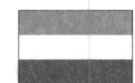
SIERRA LEONE
PAGES 78–79

TOGO
PAGES 78–79

BURUNDI
PAGES 82–83

DJIBOUTI
PAGES 82–83

ERITREA
PAGES 82–83

ETHIOPIA
PAGES 82–83

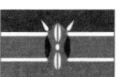
KENYA
PAGES 82–83

RWANDA
PAGES 82–83

SOMALIA
PAGES 82–83

SUDAN
PAGES 82–83

EUROPE

SOUTH AFRICA
PAGES 84–85

SWAZILAND
PAGES 84–85

ZAMBIA
PAGES 84–85

ZIMBABWE
PAGES 84–85

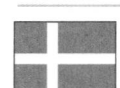
DENMARK
PAGES 94–97

FINLAND
PAGES 94–95

ICELAND
PAGES 94–95

NORWAY
PAGES 94–97

MONACO
PAGES 104–105

ANDORRA
PAGES 106–107

PORTUGAL
PAGES 106–107

SPAIN
PAGES 106–107

ITALY
PAGES 108–109

SAN MARINO
PAGES 108–109

VATICAN CITY
PAGES 108–109

AUSTRIA
PAGES 110–111

BOSNIA & HERZEGOVINA
PAGES 114–115

CROATIA
PAGES 114–115

MACEDONIA
PAGES 114–115

**SERBIA & MONTENEGRO
(YUGOSLAVIA)**
PAGES 114–115

BULGARIA
PAGES 116–117

GREECE
PAGES 116–117

MOLDOVA
PAGES 118–119

ROMANIA
PAGES 118–119

ASIA

ARMENIA
PAGES 142–143

AZERBAIJAN
PAGES 142–143

GEORGIA
PAGES 142–143

TURKEY
PAGES 142–143/116–117

IRAQ
PAGES 144–145

ISRAEL
PAGES 144–145

JORDAN
PAGES 144–145

LEBANON
PAGES 144–145

IRAN
PAGES 148–149

KAZAKHSTAN
PAGES 150–151

KYRGYZSTAN
PAGES 152–153

TAJIKISTAN
PAGES 152–153

TURKMENISTAN
PAGES 152–153

UZBEKISTAN
PAGES 152–153

AFGHANISTAN
PAGES 154–155

PAKISTAN
PAGES 154–157

TAIWAN
PAGES 166–167

JAPAN
PAGES 170–172

MYANMAR
PAGES 173–176

CAMBODIA
PAGES 173–176

LAOS
PAGES 173–176

PHILIPPINES
PAGES 173–176

THAILAND
PAGES 177–179

VIETNAM
PAGES 177–179

AUSTRALASIA & OCEANIA

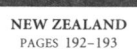
MAURITIUS
PAGES 180–181

SEYCHELLES
PAGES 180–181

AUSTRALIA
PAGES 188–191

NEW ZEALAND
PAGES 192–193

PAPUA NEW GUINEA
PAGES 194–195

FIJI
PAGES 194–195

SOLOMON ISLANDS
PAGES 196/201

VANUATU
PAGES 196/201